AUTHORS' NAMES

This edition of AUTHORS' NAMES was prepared by the
R.R. Bowker Company's Department of Bibliography
Product Research and Development and Technical Development
Departments in collaboration with its Publications Systems
Departments.

Senior staff of the Department of Bibliography working on this
project includes:
Gertrude Jennings, Manager, Product Research and Development,
Debra K. Brown, Manager, Technical Development Department,
Scott D. MacFarland, Project Manager, Technical
Development Department,
Keith L. Schiffman, Assistant Librarian, Technical
Development Department.

Senior Staff of the Systems Group includes:
Michael B. Howell, Business Systems Manager.

Andrew H. Uszak, Vice-President and Publisher,
Data Services Division.

"AUTHORS' NAMES"

An Authoritative Listing of Personal and Corporate Names

R.R. BOWKER COMPANY

New York & London

Published by the R.R. Bowker Company (a Xerox Publishing Company)
1180 Avenue of the Americas, New York, N.Y. 10036
Copyright© 1981 by Xerox Corporation
International Standard Book Number: 0-8352-1095-2
International Standard Serial Number: 0000-0639
Printed and bound in the United States of America

PREFACE

The R.R. Bowker Company, publishers of *Books in Print, Weekly Record*, the *American Book Publishing Record* and the *American Book Publishing Record Cumulatives 1876-1949* and *1950-1977,* is pleased to publish *Authors' Names: An Authoritative Listing of Personal and Corporate Names*.

Authors' Names presents a standard version based on Library of Congress cataloging of some 90,000 personal and corporate names found in 140,000 *Books in Print 1980-1981* entries. In addition to its many other uses *Authors' Names* functions as a standard name index to *Books in Print*. A standard listing of authors' names appearing in *Books in Print* has been needed since the publication of the first edition in that *Books in Print* information comes from publishers and often from more than one publisher for any author and is, therefore, inconsistent.

The standard name of an author has always been essential in acquisition or cataloging functions and other bibliographic functions, but recent developments in the library community and their cumulative affects on the libraries' services and functions make it essential to have authoritative lists of authors' names. To name a few of these changes: The new AACR2 cataloging rules, the closing of the Library of Congress card catalog, automated ordering, cataloging and circulation systems in libraries, MAchine Readable Cataloging (MARC) and on-going planning of a national bibliographic network.

Countless seminars, meetings and papers have been conducted and written in the late seventies regarding authority control in automated bibliographic databases. A primary component of bibliographic control is the creation of authority files. The recognized central agency of dissemination of authority data in the bibliographic community is the Library of Congress (LC). LC's printed and microfiche lists of Library of Congress *Subject Headings, Name Headings with References* and *Name Authorities* (COM edition) are principle sources of subject and name authorities. However, these tools do not provide access to the actual bibliographic entry. *Authors' Names* is the only reference work which does.

The publication *Authors' Names* is the direct result of a survey of some 1500 public, college and university librarians over three years. These librarians expressed overwhelmingly, 92.5%, that "the use of the Library of Congress established form for an author's name would be useful to their library's needs" and confirmed the design and format of this service.

METHODOLOGY

Authors' Names was produced from information stored on magnetic tape, edited by computer programs and set in type by computer controlled photocomposition.

Authors' Names is the result of a computer comparison or match of the *Books in Print* database, some 543,000 entries, and the *American Book Publishing Record* database of 1.63 million cataloged entries. The match algorithm between the two databases was a comparison of the author and title elements based on 1) the author's last name only (personal names) and 2) the title. The title was matched with all articles, conjunctions, prepositions and numerics having been dropped. The authoritative linkage for the corporate entries was editorially prepared using the *Name Headings with References* and *Name Authorities* (COM edition).

This first edition of *Authors' Names* indexes only the authority names and variant *Books in Print* personal names which resulted from this machine-method, some 140,000 *Books in Print* entries and all *Books in Print* corporate names which could be found in the *American Book Publishing Record* 1950-1977, 1978, 1979, and 1980 databases. The result of these two methods is an authority heading file of some 86,500 personal names and 3,500 corporate names which are linked to the *Books in Print* entries.

BOOK ARRANGEMENT

Authors' Names is an alphabetic arrangement with the primary entry containing the authoritative form of an author's name, birth and death date(s), variant form of name as it appears on the *Books in Print* database, author's function, if other than primary, as entered in the *Books in Print* database, title(s) and publisher/distributor also from the *Books in Print* database. Additionally, cross-references are provided for all variant forms directing the user to the authority form.

Authors' Names is an on-going project with a primary purpose aimed at producing authority files for all entries in the *Books in Print* database based on the comprehensiveness of the *American Book Publishing Record* database now totalling some 1.63 million cataloged entries. A new edition is planned for 1982 completing research for the remaining names in the *Books in Print* database not represented in this first edition.

As a result of the computer-processing which created *Authors' Names*, a direct link now exists between the cataloged entries of the *American Book Publishing Record* database and the *Books in Print* database entries to facilitate the implementation of the authority file in Bowker's on-line usage.

Authors' Names is the conception of Gertrude Jennings, Manager, Product Research and Development. Debra K. Brown, Manager, Technical Development, is responsible for the system design, production and technical liaison with the Publications Systems Group and direction of computer processing.

A special thanks is extended to Scott MacFarland, Project Manager, and Keith Schiffman, Assistant Librarian, for their contributions in the preparation of this first edition.

Gertrude Jennings
Manager, Product Research and Development
Data Services Division

Debra K. Brown
Manager,
Technical Development
Data Services Division

HOW TO USE
AUTHORS' NAMES

GENERAL EDITORIAL POLICY

In keeping with the intended focus of the first edition of *Authors' Names,* criteria for inclusion is based on the machine-matching of both personal author's name and title elements between the *Books in Print* database and the *American Book Publishing Record* database. Corporate names are included based on editorial comparison of *Books in Print* corporate-styled names to the cataloged corporate entries found in the *American Book Publishing Record Cumulative* 1950-1977, 1978, 1979 and 1980 databases.

The names of publishers and distributors are abbreviated. A key to these abbreviations, with the addresses of the publishing or distributing firms whose titles are listed in *Authors' Names* will be found in the "Key to Publishers' and Distributors' Abbreviations" index. The full name, ISBN prefix, editorial address, telephone number, ordering address (if different from the editorial address), and imprints follow the abbreviation.

For example:

Bowker, (Bowker, R.R., Co., 0 8352)
A Xerox Publishing Co., 1180 Ave. of
the Americas, New York, NY 10036
Tel 212-764-5100; Orders To: P.O. Box
1807, Ann Arbor, MI 48106

MAIN INDEX

Entries are arranged alphabetically by author name with personal and corporate names interfiled.

M', Mc and Mac are filed strictly alphabetically. For example:

Mac Liammoir, Michael, 1899-
Macadam, David L., 1910-
M'Bengue, Mamadou Seyni
McAdam, Robert Everett, 1920-

Entries include the following information, when available: Full authority form of personal or corporate name, author's birth and death dates, variant form of name(s) as indexed in *Books in Print,* title, subtitle and publisher or distributor abbreviations as indexed in *Books in Print.* Cross-references are indexed for variant forms of names to the authority form when applicable. See the sample entry for details.

SAMPLE ENTRY

Abramson, David I. *see* Abramson, David Irwin
Author variant cross-reference   Authority form reference

Abramson, David Irwin, 1905-
Author   Authority name   date

xAbramson, David I.
Author variant form

ed. Circulation in the Extremities. Acad Pr.
Author function   Title   Publisher/Distributor abbreviation

Circulatory Diseases of the Limbs: A Primer. Grune
Title   Subtitle

Vascular Disorders of the Extremities. Har-Row.

NAMES INDEX

AACP. *see* American Association of Colleges of Pharmacy.

AACP Section of Librarians. *see* American Association of Colleges of Pharmacy. Section of Librarians. Committee on Standards.

AAG Consulting Panel, 1974. *see* Association of American Geographers.

AAG Consulting Services Panel. *see* Association of American Geographers.

AAHPER Convention, Seattle, 1977. *see* American Alliance for Health, Physical Education and Recreation.

AAHPER National Convention, Milwaukee. *see* American Alliance for Health, Physical Education and Recreation.

Aaker, David A.
  xAaker, David A.
    Advertising Management. P-H.

Aal, Katharyn M. *see* Aal, Katharyn Machan.

Aal, Katharyn Machan, 1953-
  xAal, Katharyn M.
    ed. Rapunzel, Rapunzel: Poetry, Prose & Photographs by Women on the Subject of Hair. McBooks Pr.

Aandahl, Andrew R. *see* Aandahl, Andrew Russell.

Aandahl, Andrew Russell, 1912-
  xAandahl, Andrew R.
    Soil Teaching Aid. U of Nebr Pr.

AAOS. *see* American Academy of Orthopaedic Surgeons.

Aardema, Verna.
  xAardema, Verna.
    Ji-Nongo-Nongo Means Riddles. Schol Bk Serv.

Aaron, Benjamin.
  xAaron, Benjamin.
    Legal Status of Employee Benefit Rights Under Private Pension Plans. Irwin.
    ed. Public-Sector Bargaining. BNA.

Aaron, Chester.
  xAaron, Chester.
    An American Ghost. HarBraceJ.
    Catch Calico!. Dutton.
    Spill. Atheneum.

Aaron, Daniel, 1912-
  xAaron, Daniel.

Men of Good Hope: A Story of American Progressives. Oxford U Pr.

Aaron, Henry J.
  xAaron, Henry J.
    Politics & the Professors: The Great Society in Perspective. Brookings.
    Who Pays the Property Tax?: A New View. Brookings.

Aaron, James E.
  xAaron, James E.
    First Aid Emergency Care: Prevention & Protection of Injuries. Macmillan.

Aaron, R. I. *see* Aaron, Richard Ithamar.

Aaron, Richard Ithamar, 1901-
  xAaron, R. I.
    Our Knowledge of Universals. Haskell.

Aaronovitch, Sam.
  xAaronovitch, Sam.
    The Ruling Class: A Study of British Finance Capital. Greenwood.

Aarons, Edward S.
  xAarons, Edward S.
    The Art Studio Murders. Manor Bks.
    Assignment - Manchurian Doll. Fawcett.
    Assignment--Amazon Queen. Fawcett.
    Assignment--Ankara. Fawcett.
    Assignment--Ceylon. Fawcett.
    Assignment--Unicorn. Fawcett.
    Assignment--Zoraya. Fawcett.
    Death Is My Shadow. Manor Bks.

Aarons, Edward S. *see* Aarons, Edward Sidney.

Aarons, Edward Sidney, 1916-
  xAarons, Edward S.
    Assignment--Budapest. Fawcett.
    Assignment--Quayle Question. Fawcett.

Aarons, Will B.
  xAarons, Will B.
    Assignment--Sheba. Fawcett.
    Assignment--Tiger Devil. Fawcett.

Aaronson, David E.
  xAaronson, David E.
    Maryland Criminal Jury Instructions & Commentary. Michie.

Aaronson, Doris.
  xAaronson, Doris.

    ed. Developmental Psycholinguistics & Communication Disorders. NY Acad Sci.
    ed. Psycholinguistic Research: Implications & Applications. Halsted Pr.

Aaronson, Sheldon, 1922-
  xAaronson, Sheldon.
    Experimental Microbial Ecology. Acad Pr.

Aas, Kjell, 1924-
  xAas, Kjell.
    The Bronchial Provocation Test. C C Thomas.

AASA. *see* American Association of School Administrators.

Aaseng, Nathan.
  xAaseng, Nathan.
    photos by Basketball's High Flyers. Lerner Pubns.
    photos by Football's Fierce Defenses. Lerner Pubns.
    Little Giants of Pro Sports. Lerner Pubns.

Aaseng, Rolf. *see* Aaseng, Rolf E.

Aaseng, Rolf E.
  xAaseng, Rolf.
    God Is Great, God Is Good: Devotions for Families. Augsburg.

Abailard, Pierre.
  xAbailard, Pierre.
    Abailard's Ethics. Richwood Pub.

Abarbanel, Jay S.
  xAbarbanel, Jay S.
    Co-Operative Farmer & Welfare State: Economic Change in an Israeli Moshav. Humanities.

Abba, R. *see* Abba, Raymond.

Abba, Raymond.
  xAbba, R.
    Nature & Authority of the Bible. Attic Pr.

Abbas, K. A. *see* Abbas, Khwaja Ahmad.

Abbas, Khwaja Ahmad.
  xAbbas, K. A.
    I Am Not an Island: An Experiment in Autobiography. South Asia Bks.

Abbas, Mekki.
  xAbbas, Mekki.

Sudan Question: The Dispute Over the
Anglo-Egyptian Condominium, 1884-1951.
Russell.

Abbate, Fred J.
xAbbate, Fred J.
A Preface to the Philosophy of State.
Wadsworth Pub.

Abbazia, Patrick.
xAbbazia, Patrick.
Nathanael Greene, Commander of the
American Continental Army in the South.
SamHar Pr.

Abbe, Derek Van. *see* Van Abbe, Derek.

Abbe, Dorothy.
xAbbe, Dorothy.
The Dwiggins Marionettes: A Complete
Experimental Theatre in Miniature. Plays.

Abbe, George, 1911-
xAbbe, George.
Funeral. The Smith.

Abbey, Barbara, 1903-
xAbbey, Barbara.
The Complete Book of Knitting. Viking Pr.

Abbey, Charles J. *see* Abbey, Charles John.

Abbey, Charles John, 1833-
xAbbey, Charles J.
English Church & Its Bishops, 1700-1800.
AMS Pr.
The English Church & Its Bishops: 1700-1800.
Scholarly.

Abbey, Edward.
xAbbey, Edward.
Cactus Country. Time-Life.
Cactus Country. Silver.
Desert Solitaire: A Season in the Wilderness.
Ballantine.
Fire on the Mountain. U of NM Pr.
The Monkey Wrench Gang. Avon.
The Monkey Wrench Gang. Lippincott.

Abbey, Harlan C.
xAbbey, Harlan C.
Horses & Horse Shows. A S Barnes.

Abbey, Lloyd. *see* Abbey, Lloyd Robert.

Abbey, Lloyd Robert, 1943-
xAbbey, Lloyd.
Destroyer & Preserver: Shelley's Poetic
Skepticism. U of Nebr Pr.

Abbey, Merrill R.
xAbbey, Merrill R.
Communication in Pulpit & Parish.
Westminster.

Abbo, Fred E., 1924-
xAbbo, Fred E.
Steps to a Longer Life. Anderson World.

Abbot, Abiel, 1773-1828
xAbbot, Abiel.
Letters Written in the Interior of Cuba. Arno.

Abbot, Charles G. *see* Abbot, Charles Greeley.

Abbot, Charles Greeley.
xAbbot, Charles G.
Adventures in the World of Science. Pub Aff
Pr.

Abbot, Francis E. *see* Abbot, Francis Ellingwood.

Abbot, Francis Ellingwood, 1836-1903
xAbbot, Francis E.
Scientific Theism. AMS Pr.

Abbot, W. W. *see* Abbot, William W.

Abbot, William W., 1922-
xAbbot, W. W.
The Colonial Origins of the United States,
1607-1763. Wiley.

Abbott, Claude C. *see* Abbott, Claude Colleer.

Abbott, Claude Colleer, 1889-
xAbbott, Claude C.

Boswell. Arden Lib.
Boswell. Darby Bks.
Boswell. Folcroft.
Boswell. Porter.
Early Mediaeval French Lyrics. Folcroft.
Life & Letters of George Darley, Poet & Critic.
Oxford U Pr.

Abbott, David W.
xAbbott, David W.
ed. Political Parties. Rand.

Abbott, Edith, 1876-1957
xAbbott, Edith.
Public Assistance: American Principles &
Policies. Russell.
ed. Some American Pioneers in Social Welfare:
Select Documents with Editorial Notes.
Russell.

Abbott, Edwin A. *see* Abbott, Edwin Abbott.

Abbott, Edwin Abbott, 1838-1926
xAbbott, Edwin A.
Flatland: A Romance of Many Dimensions.
B&N.
Flatland: A Romance of Many Dimensions.
Dover.
Flatland: A Romance of Many Dimensions.
Gannon.
Flatland: A Romance of Many Dimensions.
Har-Row.

Abbott, Evelyn, 1843-1901
xAbbott, Evelyn.
Pericles & the Golden Age of Athens. Cooper
Sq.
Pericles & the Golden Age of Athens. Gordon
Pr.

Abbott, Frank F. *see* Abbott, Frank Frost.

Abbott, Frank Frost, 1860-1924
xAbbott, Frank F.
The Common People of Ancient Rome: Studies
of Roman Life & Literature. Biblo.
Municipal Administration in the Roman
Empire. Russell.
Society & Politics in Ancient Rome: Essays &
Sketches. Biblo.

Abbott, George C.
xAbbott, George C.
International Indebtedness & the Developing
Countries. M E Sharpe.

Abbott, Grace, 1878-1939
xAbbott, Grace.
The Immigrant & the Community. Ozer.

Abbott, Isabella A. *see* Abbott, Isabella Aiona.

Abbott, Isabella Aiona.
xAbbott, Isabella A.
Marine Algae of California. Stanford U Pr.

Abbott, J. *see* Abbott, Joan.

Abbott, J. C. *see* Abbott, John Cave.

Abbott, Jacob, 1803-1879
xAbbott, Jacob.
The Franconia Stories. Garland Pub.

Abbott, Janet S. *see* Abbott, Janet Stearn.

Abbott, Janet Stearn.
xAbbott, Janet S.
The Whole Thing. P-H.

Abbott, Jerry L., 1938-
xAbbott, Jerry L.
Auxiliary Teacher Program: A Complete
Manual & Guide. P-H.

Abbott, Joan.
xAbbott, J.
Student Life in a Class Society. Pergamon.

Abbott, John Cave.
xAbbott, J. C.
Agricultural Marketing Boards: Their
Establishment & Operation. Unipub.

Abbott, John S. *see* Abbott, John Stevens Cabot.

Abbott, John Stevens Cabot, 1805-1877
xAbbott, John S.

South & North: Or, Impressions Received
During a Trip to Cuba & the South. Negro U
Pr.

Abbott, Kenneth M. *see* Abbott, Kenneth Morgan.

Abbott, Kenneth Morgan, 1906-
xAbbott, Kenneth M.
Index Verborum in Ciceronis Rhetorica:
Necnon Incerti Auctoris Libros Ad
Herrenium. U of Ill Pr.

Abbott, Lawrence, 1902-
xAbbott, Lawrence.
The Listener's Book on Harmony. AMS Pr.
Quality & Competition: An Essay in Economic
Theory. Greenwood.

Abbott, Lyman, 1835-1922
xAbbott, Lyman.
Christianity & Social Problems. Johnson Repr.
The Evolution of Christianity. Johnson Repr.
The Evolution of Christianity. Scholarly.

Abbott, Philip.
xAbbott, Philip.
Furious Fancies: American Political Thought in
the Post-Liberal Era. Greenwood.

Abbott, R. Tucker. *see* Abbott, Robert Tucker.

Abbott, Richard H.
xAbbott, Richard H.
Cobbler in Congress: The Life of Henry
Wilson, 1812-1875. U Pr of Ky.

Abbott, Robert Tucker, 1919-
xAbbott, R. Tucker.
American Seashells. Van Nos Reinhold.
How to Know the American Marine Shells.
NAL.

Abbott, Rona.
xAbbott, Rona.
Dining in Houston. Peanut Butter.

Abbott, Shirley.
xAbbott, Shirley.
The Art of Food. Oxmoor Hse.

Abbott, Sidney.
xAbbott, Sidney.
Sappho Was a Right-on Woman: A Liberated
View of Lesbianism. Stein & Day.

Abbott, Simon.
xAbbott, Simon.
The Prevention of Racial Discrimination in
Britain. Oxford U Pr.

Abbott, Susan.
xAbbott, Susan.
ed. Predicting Sociocultural Change. U of Ga
Pr.

Abbott, Susan Emma Woodruff.
xAbbott, Susan W.
Families of Early Milford, Connecticut.
Genealog Pub.

Abbott, Susan W. *see* Abbott, Susan Emma Woodruff.

Abbott, Wilbur C. *see* Abbott, Wilbur Cortez.

Abbott, Wilbur Cortez, 1869-1947
xAbbott, Wilbur C.
Conflicts with Oblivion. Kennikat.

Abbs, Peter.
xAbbs, Peter.
Proposal for a New College. Heinemann Ed.

Abby Aldrich Rockefeller Folk Art Museum. *see* Abby
Aldrich Rockefeller Folk Art Collection,
Williamsburg, Virginia.

**Abby Aldrich Rockefeller Folk Art Collection,
Williamsburg, Virginia.**
xAbby Aldrich Rockefeller Folk Art Museum.
Christmas Decorations from Williamsburg's
Folk Art Collection. Williamsburg.

Abcarian, Gilbert.
xAbcarian, Gilbert.
Society in Conflict: An Introduction to Social
Science. Har-Row.

Abcarian, Richard.
xAbcarian, Richard.

ed. Literature: The Human Experience. St Martin.

Words in Flight: An Introduction to Poetry. Wadsworth Pub.

Abcarius, Michel F. *see* Abcarius, Michel Fred.

Abcarius, Michel Fred, 1884-
xAbcarius, Michel F.
Palestine Through the Fog of Propaganda. Hyperion Conn.

Abdel-Massih, Ernest T.
xAbdel-Massih, Ernest T.
Advanced Moroccan Arabic. Ctr for NE & North African Stud.

Abdel-Monem, Mahmoud M.
xAbdel-Monem, Mahmoud M.
Essentials of Drug Product Quality: Concepts & Methodology. Mosby.

Abdi, Ali Issa.
xAbdi, Ali Issa.
Commercial Banks & Economic Development: The Experience of Eastern Africa. Praeger.

Abduhu, G. R. *see* Abduhu, G. Rasool.

Abduhu, G. Rasool, 1921-
xAbduhu, G. R.
Educational Ideas of Maulana Abul Kalam Azad. Verry.

Abdul, Raoul.
xAbdul, Raoul.
ed. Famous Black Entertainers of Today. Dodd.

Abdul-Rauf, Muhammad, 1917-
xAbdul-Rauf, Muhammed.
Marriage in Islam: A Manual. Exposition.

Abdul-Rauf, Muhammed. *see* Abdul-Rauf, Muhammad.

Abdullah, Achmed, 1881-1945
xAbdullah, Achmed.
Alien Souls. Arno.
Dreamers of Empire. Arno.
Honourable Gentleman, & Others. Arno.
Swinging Caravan. Arno.

Abdushelishvili, M. G. *see* Abdushelishvili, Malkhaz Grigorevich.

Abdushelishvili, Malkhaz Grigorevich.
xAbdushelishvili, M. G.
Contributions to the Physical Anthropology of Central Asia & the Caucasus. AMS Pr.

Abdy, Edward S. *see* Abdy, Edward Strutt.

Abdy, Edward Strutt, 1791-1846
xAbdy, Edward S.
Journal of a Residence & Tour in the United States of North America, from April, 1833, to October, 1834. Negro U Pr.

Abe, K Ob O, 1924-
xAbe, Kobo.
Secret Rendezvous. Knopf.
The Secret Rendezvous. Putnam.

Abe, Kobo. *see* Abe, K Ob O.

Abeel, Erica.
xAbeel, Erica.
Only When I Laugh. Ballantine.
Only When I Laugh. Morrow.

Abel, Andrew B., 1952-
xAbel, Andrew B.
Investment & the Value of Capital. Garland Pub.

Abel, Annie H. *see* Abel, Annie Heloise.

Abel, Annie Heloise, 1873-
xAbel, Annie H.
The American Indian As Participant in the Civil War. Johnson Repr.
The American Indian Under Reconstruction. Johnson Repr.
History of Events Resulting in Indian Consolidation West of the Mississippi. AMS Pr.

Abel, Ernest L., 1943-
xAbel, Ernest L.

Ancient Views on the Origins of Life. Fairleigh Dickinson.
Compiled by A Comprehensive Guide to the Cannabis Literature. Greenwood.
Drugs & Behavior: A Primer in Neuropsychopharmacology. Krieger.
Drugs & Behavior: A Primer in Neuropsychopharmacology. Wiley.

Abel, Francis. *see* Abel, Francis L.

Abel, Francis L.
xAbel, Francis.
Cardiovascular Function: Principles & Applications. Little.

Abel, Peter, 1932-
xAbel, Peter.
Programming Assembler Language. Reston.

Abel, Reuben, 1911-
xAbel, Reuben.
Pragmatic Humanism of F. C. S. Schiller. AMS Pr.

Abeles, Frederick B.
xAbeles, Frederick B.
Ethylene in Plant Biology, 1973. Acad Pr.

Abeles, Kim V. *see* Abeles, Kim Victoria.

Abeles, Kim Victoria, 1952-
xAbeles, Kim V.
Crafts, Cookery & Country Living. Van Nos Reinhold.

Abell, D. *see* Abell, Derek F.

Abell, Derek F., 1938-
xAbell, D.
Defining the Business: The Starting Point of Strategic Planning. P-H.
xAbell, Derek F.
Strategic Market Planning: Problems & Analytical Approaches. P-H.

Abell, G. O. *see* Abell, George Ogden.

Abell, George Ogden, 1927-
xAbell, G. O.
Exploration of the Universe. HR&W.

Abell, Richard G. *see* Abell, Richard Gurley.

Abell, Richard Gurley.
xAbell, Richard G.
Own Your Own Life. Berkley Pub.
Own Your Own Life. McKay.

Abella, Alex.
xAbella, Alex.
The Total Banana. HarBraceJ.

Abella, Irving M., 1940-
xAbella, Irving M.
Nationalism, Communism & Canadian Labour: The CIO, the Communist Party, & the Canadian Congress of Labour, 1935-56. U of Toronto Pr.

Abeloff, Martin D.
xAbeloff, Martin D.
ed. Complications of Cancer: Diagnosis & Management. Johns Hopkins.

Abels. *see* Abels, Alexander.

Abels, Alexander.
xAbels.
Painting: Materials & Methods. G&D.

Abels, Harriette S. *see* Abels, Harriette Sheffer.

Abels, Harriette Sheffer.
xAbels, Harriette S.
Call Me Clown. Childrens.
The Creature of Saxony Woods. Childrens.
A Forgotten World. Crestwood Hse.
Meteor from the Moon. Crestwood Hse.
Mystery on Mars. Crestwood Hse.
Planet of Ice. Crestwood Hse.
The Silent Invaders. Crestwood Hse.
Unwanted Visitors. Crestwood Hse.

Abelsett, Bob, 1943-
xAbelsett, Bob.
Coaching Basketball's Combination Defenses. P-H.

Abelson, Harold.
xAbelson, Harold.

Calculus of Elementary Functions. HarBraceJ.

Abelson, Peter.
xAbelson, Peter.
Cost Benefit Analysis & Environmental Problems. Lexington Bks.

Abelson, Philip H.
xAbelson, Philip H.
Energy for Tomorrow. U of Wash Pr.

Abelson, Raziel.
xAbelson, Raziel.
Ethics for Modern Life. St Martin.
Persons: A Study in Philosophical Psychology. St Martin.

Aberbach, Joel D.
xAberbach, Joel D.
Race in the City: Political Trust & Public Policy in the New Urban System. Little.

Abercrombie, Barbara.
xAbercrombie, Barbara.
Amanda & Heather & Company. Dandelion Pr.
Good Riddance. Har-Row.
Good Riddance. Playboy Pbks.
The Other Side of a Poem. Har-Row.

Abercrombie, Lascelles, 1881-1938
xAbercrombie, Lascelles.
Idea of Great Poetry. Arno.
The Idea of Great Poetry. R West.
The Idea of Great Poetry. Scholarly.
Interludes & Poems. Core Collection.
Principles of Literary Criticism. Greenwood.
Revaluations: Studies in Biography. Haskell.
Theory of Poetry. Biblo.
The Theory of Poetry. Scholarly.

Abercrombie, M. *see* Abercrombie, Michael.

Abercrombie, M. L. *see* Abercrombie, Minnie Louie Johnson.

Abercrombie, Michael.
xAbercrombie, M.
The Penguin Dictionary of Biology. Viking Pr.

Abercrombie, Minnie Louie Johnson.
xAbercrombie, M. L.
The Anatomy of Judgement: An Investigation into the Processes of Perception & Reasoning. Humanities.

Abercrombie, Nigel.
xAbercrombie, Nigel.
Artists & Their Public. Unipub.

Aberle, David F. *see* Aberle, David Friend.

Aberle, David Friend.
xAberle, David F.
Chahar & Dagor Mongol Bureaucratic Administration: 1912-45. HRAFP.

Abernathy, David.
xAbernathy, David M.
Ideas, Inventions & Patents: An Introduction to Patent Information. Pioneer Ga.

Abernathy, David M. *see* Abernathy, David.

Abernathy, Elton.
xAbernathy, Elton.
Directing Speech Activities. University Pr.

Abernathy, M. Glenn. *see* Abernathy, Mabra Glenn.

Abernathy, Mabra Glenn, 1921-
xAbernathy, M. Glenn.
Civil Liberties Under the Constitution. Har-Row.

Abernathy, William J.
xAbernathy, William J.
The Productivity Dilemma: Roadblock to Innovation in the Automobile Industry. Johns Hopkins.

Abernethy, David S.
xAbernethy, David S.
Regulating Hospital Costs: The Development of Public Policy. Health Admin Pr.

Abernethy, E. M. *see* Abernethy, Ethel Mae.

Abernethy, Ethel Mae.
xAbernethy, E. M.
Relationships Between Mental & Physical Growth. Kraus Repr.

Abernethy, Francis E. *see* Abernethy, Francis Edward.

Abernethy, Francis Edward.
  xAbernethy, Francis E.
    Observations & Reflections on Texas Folklore.
      Encino Pr.
    ed. Some Still Do: Essays on Texas Customs.
      Encino Pr.
    ed. Tales from the Big Thicket. U of Tex Pr.
Abernethy, Thomas P. *see* Abernethy, Thomas Perkins.
Abernethy, Thomas Perkins, 1890-
  xAbernethy, Thomas P.
    The Burr Conspiracy. Peter Smith.
    From Frontier to Plantation in Tennessee: A
      Study in Frontier Democracy. Greenwood.
    South in the New Nation, 1789-1819. La State
      U Pr.
Abers, Ernest S.
  xAbers, Ernest S.
    Matter in Motion: The Spirit & Evolution of
      Physics. Allyn.
Abersold, John. *see* Abersold, John Russell.
Abersold, John Russell.
  xAbersold, John.
    Cases in Labor Relations: An Arbitration
      Experience. P-H.
Abert, James G. *see* Abert, James Goodear.
Abert, James Goodear.
  xAbert, James G.
    Economic Policy & Planning in the
      Netherlands, 1950-1965. Yale U Pr.
Aberth, Oliver.
  xAberth, Oliver.
    Computable Analysis. McGraw.
Abhyankar, S. *see* Abhyankar, Shreeram Shankar.
Abhyankar, S. S. *see* Abhyankar, Shreeram Shankar.
Abhyankar, Shreeram Shankar.
  xAbhyankar, S.
    Ramification Theoretic Methods in Algebraic
      Geometry. Princeton U Pr.
  xAbhyankar, S. S.
    ed. Geometric Theory of Algebraic Space
      Curves. Springer-Verlag.
Abi-Saab, Georges.
  xAbi-Saab, Georges.
    The United Nations Operation in the Congo,
      1960-1964. Oxford U Pr.
Abian, Alexander, 1925-
  xAbian, Alexander.
    Boolean Rings. Branden.
    Linear Associative Algebras. Pergamon.
Abidin, Richard R.
  xAbidin, Richard R.
    Parent Education & Intervention Handbook. C
      C Thomas.
Abidjan, Ivory Coast. Universite.
  xUniversity of Abidjan.
    Vocabulaire Essential de l'Enseignement
      Primaire. Clearwater Pub.
Abilene Christian College.
  xAbilene Christian College Lectureship.
    Crowning Fifty Years. Bibl Res Pr.
Abilene Christian College Lectureship. *see* Abilene
  Christian College.
Abimbola, 'Wande.
  xAbimbola, Wande.
    Ifa: An Exposition of Ifa Literary Corpus.
      Oxford U Pr.
Abimbola, Wande. *see* Abimbola, 'Wande.
Abingdon Abbey. *see* Abingdon Abbey, England.
Abingdon Abbey, England.
  xAbingdon Abbey.
    Accounts of the Obedientiars of Abingdon
      Abbey. Johnson Repr.
Abir, Mondechai. *see* Abir, Mordechai.
Abir, Mordechai.
  xAbir, Mondechai.
    Oil, Power & Politics: Conflict in Arabia, the
      Red Sea & the Gulf. Biblio Dist.
Abisch, Roz.
  xAbisch, Roz.

    Do You Know What Time It Is. P-H.
    Let's Find Out About Butterflies. Watts.
    The Munchy, Crunchy, Healthy Kid's Snack
      Book. Walker & Co.
    Textiles. Watts.
Abish, Walter.
  xAbish, Walter.
    Alphabetical Africa. New Directions.
    In the Future Perfect. New Directions.
Able, Augustus. *see* Able, Augustus Henry.
Able, Augustus H. *see* Able, Augustus Henry.
Able, Augustus Henry, 1900-
  xAble, Augustus.
    George Meredith & Thomas Love Peacock: A
      Study in Literary Influence. Folcroft.
  xAble, Augustus H.
    George Meredith & Thomas Love Peacock: A
      Study in Literary Influence. Phaeton.
Abler, Ronald.
  xAbler, Ronald.
    Spatial Organization: The Geographer's View
      of the World. P-H.
    The Twin Cities of St. Paul & Minneapolis.
      Ballinger Pub.
Abodaher, David J.
  xAbodaher, David J.
    Compacts, Subs & Minis: Be Your Own
      Mechanic. Messner.
    The Speedmakers: Great Race Drivers.
      Messner.
Abood, Edward F.
  xAbood, Edward F.
    Underground Man. Chandler & Sharp.
Abouchar, Alan.
  xAbouchar, Alan.
    ed. The Socialist Price Mechanism. Duke.
    Soviet Planning & Spatial Efficiency: The
      Prewar Cement Industry. Ind U Pr.
Abouleish, Ezzat.
  xAbouleish, Ezzat.
    Pain Control in Obstetrics. Lippincott.
Abragam, A.
  xAbragam, A.
    Principles of Nuclear Magnetism. Oxford U Pr.
Abraham. *see* Abraham, Henry Julian.
Abraham, Ashley P. *see* Abraham, Ashley Perry.
Abraham, Ashley Perry, 1876-1951
  xAbraham, Ashley P.
    Some Portraits of the Lake Poets & Their
      Homes. Arden Lib.
    Some Portraits of the Lake Poets, & Their
      Homes. Folcroft.
Abraham, Claude. *see* Abraham, Claude Kurt.
Abraham, Claude K. *see* Abraham, Claude Kurt.
Abraham, Claude Kurt, 1931-
  xAbraham, Claude.
    Tristan L'Hermite. Twayne.
  xAbraham, Claude K.
    Enfin Malherbe: The Influence of Malherbe on
      French Lyric Prosody, 1605-1674. U Pr of
      Ky.
    Strangers: The Tragic World of Tristan
      l'Hermite. U Presses Fla.
Abraham, F. *see* Abraham, Farid F.
Abraham, Farid F.
  xAbraham, F.
    ed. An Introduction to Computer Simulation in
      Applied Science. Plenum Pub.
  xAbraham, Farid F.
    Homogeneous Nucleation Theory: The
      Pretransition Theory of Vapor Condensation.
      Acad Pr.
Abraham, G. *see* Abraham, Gerald Ernest Heal.
Abraham, George.
  xAbraham, George.

    Green Thumb Book of Fruit & Vegetable
      Gardening. P-H.
    Green Thumb Garden Handbook. P-H.
    Raise Vegetables Without a Garden.
      Countryside Bks.
Abraham, Gerald. *see* Abraham, Gerald Ernest Heal.
Abraham, Gerald E. *see* Abraham, Gerald Ernest Heal.
Abraham, Gerald Ernest Heal, 1904-
  xAbraham, G.
    Nietzsche. Gordon Pr.
    Nietzsche. Haskell.
  xAbraham, Gerald.
    The Concise Oxford History of Music. Oxford
      U Pr.
    Hundred Years of Music. Biblio Dist.
    ed. The Music of Sibelius. Da Capo.
    ed. The Music of Tchaikovsky. Norton.
  xAbraham, Gerald E.
    Beethoven's Second-Period Quartets. Scholarly.
    On Russian Music: Critical & Historical
      Studies of Glinka's Operas. Johnson Repr.
Abraham, Henry J. *see* Abraham, Henry Julian.
Abraham, Henry Julian, 1921-
  xAbraham.
    The Judiciary: The Supreme Court in the
      Governmental Process. Allyn.
  xAbraham, Henry J.
    Freedom & the Court: Civil Rights & Liberties
      in the United States. Oxford U Pr.
Abraham, Herbert J. *see* Abraham, Herbert John.
Abraham, Herbert John, 1904-
  xAbraham, Herbert J.
    World Problems in the Classroom: A Teachers
      Guide to Some United Nations Tasks.
      Unipub.
Abraham, Karl.
  xAbraham, Karl.
    Clinical Papers & Essays on Psycho-Analysis.
      Brunner-Mazel.
Abraham, M. Francis.
  xAbraham, M. Francis.
    Perspectives of Modernization: Toward a
      General Theory of Third World
      Development. U Pr of Amer.
Abraham, R. J. *see* Abraham, Raymond John.
Abraham, Ralph.
  xAbraham, Ralph.
    Foundations of Mechanics: A Mathematical
      Exposition of Classical Mechanics with an
      Introduction to the Qualitative Theory of
      Dynamical Systems & Applications to the
      Three-Body Problem. Benjamin-Cummings.
Abraham, Raymond John, 1933-
  xAbraham, R. J.
    Analysis of High Resolution NMR Spectra.
      Elsevier.
Abraham, Roberta, 1931-
  xAbraham, Roberta G.
    Structure & Meaning. Newbury Hse.
Abraham, Roberta G. *see* Abraham, Roberta.
Abraham, Samuel V.
  xAbraham, Samuel V.
    Real Estate Dictionary & Reference Guide.
      Career Pub.
Abraham, Sidney.
  xAbraham, Sidney.
    Preliminary Findings of the First Health &
      Nutrition Examination Survey, U.S.,
      Nineteen Seventy-One to Nineteen
      Seventy-Two, Dietary Intake & Biochemical
      Findings. Natl Ctr Health Stats.
Abraham, Willard.
  xAbraham, Willard.
    Guide for the Study of Exceptional Children.
      Porter Sargent.
Abrahams, G. *see* Abrahams, Gerald.
Abrahams, Gerald, 1907-
  xAbrahams, G.

A History of the Maghrib. Cambridge U Pr.
Aby, Carroll. *see* Aby, Carroll D.
Aby, Carroll D.
  xAby, Carroll.
    Financial Management Classics. Goodyear.
  xAby, Carroll D.
    ed. Investment Classics. Goodyear.
Academy of Management.
  xAcademy of Management, 40th Annual Meeting,
    1980.
    Proceedings. Acad of Mgmt.
Academy of Management, 40th Annual Meeting, 1980.
  see Academy of Management.
Academy of Motion Picture Arts & Sciences. *see*
  Academy of Motion Picture Arts and Sciences.
Academy of Motion Picture Arts and Sciences.
  xAcademy of Motion Picture Arts & Sciences.
    Annual Index to Motion Picture Credits, 1979.
    Greenwood.
Academy of Natural Sciences of Philadelphia.
  xAcademy of Natural Sciences, Philadelphia.
    Catalog of the Library of the Academy of
    Natural Sciences of Philadelphia. G K Hall.
Academy of Natural Sciences, Philadelphia. *see* Academy
  of Natural Sciences of Philadelphia.
Academy of Political Science. *see* Academy of Political
  Science, New York.
Academy of Political Science, New York.
  xAcademy of Political Science.
    Municipal Income Taxes: Proceedings. Peter
    Smith.
    The Soviet Union Since Khrushchev: New
    Trends & Old Problems. Kraus Repr.
Academy of Religion and Mental Health. Academy
Symposium.
  xAcademy Of Religion And Mental Health.
    Psychological Testing for Ministerial Selection:
    Proceedings of the Seventh Academy
    Symposium. Fordham.
Accounting Symposium, Ohio State University, 1968.
  xAccounting Symposium, Ohio State Univ, 1968.
    Behavioral Aspects of Accounting Data for
    Performance Evaluation. Ohio St U Admin
    Sci.
Accounting Symposium, Ohio State University, 1972.
  xAccounting Symposium, Ohio State Univ., 1972.
    Behavioral Experiments in Accounting: Papers,
    Critiques, Discussion, & Commentary. Ohio
    St U Admin Sci.
Ace, Stroker.
  xAce, Stroker.
    Stand on It. Little.
Acerrano, Anthony J.
  xAcerrano, Anthony J.
    The Outdoorsman's Emergency Manual.
    Winchester Pr.
    The Practical Hunter's Handbook. Winchester
    Pr.
Ache, Hans J.
  xAche, Hans J.
    ed. Positronium & Muonium Chemistry. Am
    Chemical.
Achebe, Chinua.
  xAchebe, Chinua.
    Arrow of God. Doubleday.
    How the Leopard Got His Claws. Okpaku
    Communications.
    No Longer at Ease. Astor-Honor.
    No Longer at Ease. Fawcett.
    Things Fall Apart. Astor-Honor.
    Things Fall Apart. Fawcett.
Achelis, Elisabeth, 1880-
  xAchelis, Elisabeth.
    World Calendar: Addresses & Occasional
    Papers Chronologically Arranged on the
    Progress of Calendar Reform Since 1930.
    Gale.
Achen, Sven T. *see* Achen, Sven Tito.
Achen, Sven Tito.
  xAchen, Sven T.

Symbols Around Us. Van Nos Reinhold.
Achenbach, Thomas M., 1940-
  xAchenbach, Thomas M.
    Developmental Psychopathology. Wiley.
Achenbaum, W. Andrew.
  xAchenbaum, W. Andrew.
    Old Age in the New Land: The American
    Experience Since 1790. Johns Hopkins.

Acheson, Dean. *see* Acheson, Dean Gooderham.

Acheson, Dean Gooderham.

  xAcheson, Dean.
    Pattern of Responsibility. Kelley.
    Struggle for a Free Europe. Norton.
    This Vast External Realm. Norton.

Acheson, Patricia C.
  xAcheson, Patricia C.
    Our Federal Government: How It Works: An
    Introduction to the United States
    Government. Dodd.
Achilles, Paul S. *see* Achilles, Paul Strong.
Achilles, Paul Strong.
  xAchilles, Paul S.
    ed. Psychology at Work. Arno.
Achinstein, Asher, 1900-
  xAchinstein, Asher.
    Buying Power of Labor & Post-War Cycles.
    AMS Pr.
Achinstein, Peter.
  xAchinstein, Peter.
    Concepts of Science: A Philosophical Analysis.
    Johns Hopkins.
Achtemeier, Paul J.
  xAchtemeier, Paul J.
    Mark. Fortress.
    The Old Testament Roots of Our Faith.
    Fortress.
ACI Committee 116. *see* American Concrete Institute
  Committee 116.
ACI Committee 209. *see* American Concrete Institute
  Committee 209.
ACI Committee 224. *see* American Concrete Institute
  Committee 224.
ACI Committee 311. *see* American Concrete Institute
  Committee 311.
ACI Committee 315. *see* American Concrete Institute
  Committee 315.
ACI Committee 318. *see* American Concrete Institute
  Committee 318.
ACI Committee 340. *see* American Concrete Institute
  Committee 340.
Acker, D. *see* Acker, Duane.
Acker, Duane.
  xAcker, D.
    Animal Science & Industry. P-H.
Acker, H. *see* Acker, Helmut.
Acker, Helmut.
  xAcker, H.
    ed. Chemoreception in the Carotid Body.
    Springer-Verlag.
Acker, William R. *see* Acker, William Reynolds Beal.
Acker, William Reynolds Beal, 1907-
  xAcker, William R.
    tr. Some Tang & Pre-Tang Texts on Chinese
    Painting. Hyperion Conn.
Ackerknecht, Erwin H. *see* Ackerknecht, Erwin Heinz.
Ackerknecht, Erwin Heinz.
  xAckerknecht, Erwin H.
    Medicine & Ethnology: Selected Essays. Intl
    Pubns Serv.
    Medicine at the Paris Hospital, 1794-1848.
    Johns Hopkins.
Ackerley, J. R. *see* Ackerley, Joe Randolph.
Ackerley, Joe Randolph, 1896-
  xAckerley, J. R.

My Dog Tulip. Fleet.
My Father & Myself. HarBraceJ.
Ackerman, Bruce A.
  xAckerman, Bruce A.
    ed. Economic Foundations of Property Law.
    Little.
    Private Property & the Constitution. Yale U Pr.
    The Uncertain Search for Environmental
    Quality. Free Pr.
Ackerman, C. W. *see* Ackerman, Carl William.
Ackerman, Carl William, 1890-
  xAckerman, C. W.
    George Eastman. Kelley.
Ackerman, Diane.
  xAckerman, Diane.
    Twilight of the Tenderfoot: A Western
    Memoir. Morrow.
Ackerman, Dorothy.
  xAckerman, Dorothy.
    A Quaker Looks at Yoga. Pendle Hill.
Ackerman, Eugene.
  xAckerman, Eugene.
    Biophysical Science. P-H.
    Mathematical Models in the Health Sciences:
    A Computer-Aided Approach. U of Minn Pr.
Ackerman, J. Mark, 1939-
  xAckerman, J. Mark.
    Operant Conditioning Techniques for the
    Classroom Teacher. Scott F.
Ackerman, James S.
  xAckerman, James S.
    Palladio. Penguin.
Ackerman, Lauren V. *see* Ackerman, Lauren Vedder.
Ackerman, Lauren Vedder.
  xAckerman, Lauren V.
    Surgical Pathology. Mosby.
Ackerman, Marian.
  xAckerman, Marian.
    Saints & Sinners. Pan-Am Publishing Co.
Ackerman, Nathan W. *see* Ackerman, Nathan Ward.
Ackerman, Nathan Ward, 1908-
  xAckerman, Nathan W.
    ed. Family Process. Basic.
    Psychodynamics of Family Life: Diagnosis &
    Treatment of Family Relationships. Basic.
Ackerman, Phyllis, 1893-
  xAckerman, Phyllis.
    Tapestry, the Mirror of Civilization. AMS Pr.
Ackerman, Robert W. *see* Ackerman, Robert William.
Ackerman, Robert William, 1910-
  xAckerman, Robert W.
    Index of the Arthurian Names in Middle
    English. AMS Pr.
Ackerman, Walter. *see* Ackerman, Walter I.
Ackerman, Walter I.
  xAckerman, Walter.
    Out of Our People's Past: Sources for the
    Study of Jewish History. United Syn Bk.
Ackermann, Jean M. *see* Ackermann, Jean Marie.
Ackermann, Jean Marie.
  xAckermann, Jean M.
    ed. Films of a Changing World: A Critical
    International Guide. Soc Intl Dev.
Acklan, William H. *see* Acklan, William Hayes.
Acklan, William Hayes.
  xAcklan, William H.
    Sterope: The Veiled Pleiad. Arno.
Ackland, Donald.
  xAckland, Donald.
    ed. Los Angeles: The Complete Guide to
    Living, Going Out & Touring. Mayflower
    Bks.
Ackland, Valentine.
  xAckland, Valentine.
    The Nature of the Moment. New Directions.
Ackley, P. O. *see* Ackley, Parker O.
Ackley, Parker O.
  xAckley, P. O.
    Home Gun Care & Repair. Stackpole.
Ackoff, R. L. *see* Ackoff, Russell Lincoln.

Ackoff, Russell L. *see* Ackoff, Russell Lincoln.
Ackoff, Russell Lincoln, 1919-
  xAckoff, R. L.
    Concept of Corporate Planning. Wiley.
  xAckoff, Russell L.
    Design of Social Research. U of Chicago Pr.
    ed. Designing a National Scientific &
      Technological Communication System. U of
      Pa Pr.
    On Purposeful Systems. Beresford Bk Serv.
Ackroyd, Peter R.
  xAckroyd, Peter R.
    Exile & Restoration: A Study of Hebrew
      Thought of the Sixth Century B. C.
      Westminster.
Ackworth, Robert. *see* Ackworth, Robert C.
Ackworth, Robert C.
  xAckworth, Robert.
    The Takers. Ballantine.
    The Takers. Bobbs.
Acland, James H.
  xAcland, James H.
    Medieval Structure: The Gothic Vault. U of
      Toronto Pr.
Acland, Robert D.
  xAcland, Robert D.
    Microsurgery Practice Manual. Mosby.
ACS Committee on Chemistry & Public Affairs. *see*
  American Chemical Society. Committee on Chemistry
  and Public Affairs.
ACS Committee On Chemistry And Public Affairs. *see*
  American Chemical Society. Committee on Chemistry
  and Public Affairs.
Action Center.
  xTheAction Center.
    Food on Campus. Rodale Pr Inc.
Acton, E. *see* Acton, Edward.
Acton, Edward.
  xActon, E.
    Alexander Herzen & the Role of the
      Intellectual Revolutionary. Cambridge U Pr.
Acton, F. S. *see* Acton, Forman S.
Acton, Forman S.
  xActon, F. S.
    Analysis of Straight-Line Data. Peter Smith.
Acton, H. B. *see* Acton, Harry Burrows.
Acton, Harold. *see* Acton, Harold Mario Mitchell.
Acton, Harold Mario Mitchell.
  xActon, Harold.
    Modern Chinese Poetry. Krishna Pr.
    The Pazzi Conspiracy: The Plot Against the
      Medici. Thames Hudson.
Acton, Harry Burrows, 1908-
  xActon, H. B.
    The Illusion of the Epoch: Marxism-Leninism
      As a Philosophical Creed. Routledge &
      Kegan.
Acton, Henry.
  xActon, Henry.
    Religious Opinions & Example of Milton,
      Locke, & Newton. AMS Pr.
Acton, John E. *see* Acton, John Emerich Edward
  Dalberg Acton.
Acton, John Emerich Edward Dalberg Acton.
  xActon, John E.
    History of Freedom, & Other Essays. Arno.
    Lectures on the French Revolution. AMS Pr.
    Lord Acton & His Circle. B Franklin.
    Lord Acton & His Circle. R West.
  xActon, Lord.
    Lectures on the French Revolution. Gordon Pr.
Acton, Lord. *see* Acton, John Emerich Edward Dalberg
  Acton.
Acworth, A. W. *see* Acworth, Angus Whiteford.
Acworth, Angus Whiteford.
  xAcworth, A. W.
    Buildings of Architectural or Historic Interest
      in the British West Indies. Johnson Repr.
Acworth, Bernard.
  xAcworth, Bernard.

    Swift. Folcroft.
Acworth, William M. *see* Acworth, William Mitchell.
Acworth, William Mitchell.
  xAcworth, William M.
    The Elements of Railway Economics. Hyperion
      Conn.
Aczel, J.
  xAczel, J.
    Measures of Information & Their
      Characterizations. Acad Pr.
    On Applications & Theory of Functional
      Equations. Acad Pr.
Ad Hoc Committee on the Report of the Joint
  Commission on the Mental Health of Children.
  xGAP Ad Hoc Committee.
    Crisis in Child Mental Health: Critical
      Assessment. Adv Psychiatry.
A.D. Little, Inc. *see* Little (Arthur D.) Inc.
Adachi, Barbara, 1924-
  xAdachi, Barbara.
    The Voices & Hands of Bunraku. Kodansha.
Adair, Casey.
  xAdair, Casey.
    Word Is Out: Stories of Some of Our Lives.
      New Glide.
Adair, E. R. *see* Adair, Edward Robert.
Adair, Edward Robert, 1888-1965
  xAdair, E. R.
    Sources for the History of the Council in the
      Sixteenth & Seventeenth Centuries. Kennikat.
Adair, Ian.
  xAdair, Ian.
    Complete Guide to Conjuring. A S Barnes.
    The Complete Party Planner. A S Barnes.
Adair, John.
  xAdair, John.
    Navajo & Pueblo Silversmiths. U of Okla Pr.
Adair, John. *see* Adair, John Eric.
Adair, John Eric, 1934-
  xAdair, John.
    The Pilgrim's Way: Shrines & Saints in Britain
      & Ireland. Thames Hudson.
Adair, Margaret W. *see* Adair, Margaret Weeks.
Adair, Margaret Weeks.
  xAdair, Margaret W.
    Folk Puppet Plays for the Social Studies. John
      Day.
Adam, Adela M. *see* Adam, Adela Marion Kensington.
Adam, Adela Marion Kensington.
  xAdam, Adela M.
    Plato, Moral & Political Ideals. Folcroft.
Adam, Antoine.
  xAdam, Antoine.
    The Art of Paul Verlaine. NYU Pr.
Adam, Everett E.
  xAdam, Everett E.
    Production & Operations Management:
      Concepts, Models & Behavior. P-H.
Adam, G. *see* Adam, G. Stuart.
Adam, G. Stuart.
  xAdam, G.
    Journalism, Communication & the Law. P-H.
Adam, Helen, 1909-
  xAdam, Helen.
    Ghosts & Grinning Shadows. Hanging Loose.
Adam, Heribert.
  xAdam, Heribert.
    Ethnic Power Mobilized: Can South Africa
      Change?. Yale U Pr.
Adam, Ian.
  xAdam, Ian.
    ed. This Particular Web: Essays on
      Middlemarch. U of Toronto Pr.
Adam, Isabel.
  xAdam, Isabel.
    Witch Hunt: A True Story. St Martin.
Adam, James, 1860-1907
  xAdam, James.

    Religious Teachers of Greece. Arno.
    The Religious Teachers of Greece. Kelley.
Adam, Karl, 1876-
  xAdam, Karl.
    One & Holy. Greenwood.
    The Spirit of Catholicism. Doubleday.
Adam, Michael.
  xAdam, Michael.
    Womankind: A Celebration. Har-Row.
    Womankind: A Celebration. Har-Row.
Adam, Ruth.
  xAdam, Ruth.
    What Shaw Really Said. Schocken.
Adam, Ruth C.
  xAdam, Ruth C.
    Living with Mysterious Epilepsy: My 48-Year
      Victory Over Fear. Exposition.
Adamic, Louis, 1899-1951
  xAdamic, Louis.
    Eagle & the Roots. Greenwood.
Adamovich, Shirley G. *see* Adamovich, Shirley Gray.
Adamovich, Shirley Gray.
  xAdamovich, Shirley G.
    ed. Reader in Library Technology. IHS-PDS.
Adams. *see* Adams, James Frederick.
Adams, A. *see* Adams, Arthur E.
Adams, A. E. *see* Adams, Arthur E.
Adams, A. K.
  xAdams, A. K.
    ed. Home Book of Humorous Quotations.
      Dodd.
Adams, Adrienne.
  xAdams, Adrienne.
    illus. The Christmas Party. Scribner.
    illus. The Easter Egg Artists. Scribner.
Adams, Alice. *see* Adams, Alice Boyd.
Adams, Alice Boyd, 1926-
  xAdams, Alice.
    Listening to Billie. Knopf.
Adams, Alice D. *see* Adams, Alice Dana.
Adams, Alice Dana, 1864-
  xAdams, Alice D.
    The Neglected Period of Anti-Slavery in
      America 1808-1831. Corner Hse.
    Neglected Period of Anti-Slavery in America,
      1808-1831. Peter Smith.
Adams, Andy, 1859-1935
  xAdams, Andy.
    Cattle Brands: A Collection of Western
      Campfire Stories. Arno.
Adams, Ann. *see* Adams, Anne H.
Adams, Anne H.
  xAdams, Ann.
    Reading for Survival in Today's Society.
      Goodyear.
Adams, Ansel. *see* Adams, Ansel Easton.
Adams, Ansel Easton, 1902-
  xAdams, Ansel.
    Ansel Adams. NYGS.
    The Camera. NYGS.
    Natural Light Photography. NYGS.
    The Portfolios of Ansel Adams. NYGS.
Adams, Arthur B. *see* Adams, Arthur Barto.
Adams, Arthur Barto, 1887-
  xAdams, Arthur B.
    Marketing Perishable Farm Products. AMS Pr.
Adams, Arthur E.
  xAdams, A.
    Stalin & His Times. HR&W.
  xAdams, A. E.
    Men Versus Systems: Agriculture in the U. S.
      S. R., Poland, & Czechoslovakia. Free Pr.
Adams, Arvil V.
  xAdams, Arvil V.
    The Lingering Crisis of Youth Unemployment.
      Upjohn Inst.
Adams, B. *see* Adams, Brian C.
Adams, Bill. *see* Adams, William D.
Adams, Brian. *see* Adams, Brian C.

Adams, Brian C.
xAdams, B.
Medical Implications of Karate Blows.
Wehman.
xAdams, Brian.
Medical Implications of Karate Blows. A S
Barnes.
Adams, Brooks, 1848-1927
xAdams, Brooks.
Law of Civilization & Decay: An Essay on
History. Arno.
Adams, Bruce.
xAdams, Bruce.
Promise & Performance: Carter Builds a New
Administration. Lexington Bks.
Adams, C. K. *see* Adams, Charles K.
Adams, Charles C. *see* Adams, Charles Christopher.
Adams, Charles Christopher, 1873-1955
xAdams, Charles C.
Guide to the Study of Animal Ecology. Arno.
Adams, Charles D. *see* Adams, Charles Darwin.
Adams, Charles Darwin, 1856-
xAdams, Charles D.
Demosthenes & His Influence. Cooper Sq.
Adams, Charles F. *see* Adams, Charles Francis.
Adams, Charles Follen, 1842-1918
xAdams, Charles F.
Dialect Ballads. Scholarly.
Adams, Charles Francis.
xAdams, Charles F.
Life of John Adams. Haskell.
Life of John Adams. Scholarly.
Adams, Charles J.
xAdams, Charles J.
ed. A Reader's Guide to the Great Religions.
Free Pr.
Adams, Charles K.
xAdams, C. K.
Build-It Book of Optoelectronic Projects. TAB
Bks.
Adams, Charles M. *see* Adams, Charles Marshall.
Adams, Charles Marshall, 1907-
xAdams, Charles M.
Randall Jarrell: A Bibliography. Folcroft.
Adams, Chuck.
xAdams, Chuck.
The Complete Book of Bowhunting.
Winchester Pr.
The Digest Book of Duck & Goose Hunting.
Follett.
Adams, D. M. *see* Adams, David Michael.
Adams, D. P. *see* Adams, David Philip.
Adams, Daniel J.
xAdams, Daniel J.
Thomas Merton's Shared Contemplation: A
Protestant Perspective. Cistercian Pubns.
Adams, David Michael, 1933-
xAdams, D. M.
Inorganic Solids: An Introduction to Concepts
in Solid State Structural Chemistry. Wiley.
Adams, David Philip, 1929-
xAdams, D. P.
Tudors & Stuarts. Dufour.
Adams, Donald R.
xAdams, Donald R.
Finance & Enterprise in Early America: A
Study of Stephen Girard's Bank, 1812-1831.
U of Pa Pr.
Adams, Doris Sutcliffe.
xAdams, Doris Sutcliffe.
Power of Darkness. Nordon Pubns.
Adams, Douglas P. *see* Adams, Douglas Payne.
Adams, Douglas Payne, 1909-
xAdams, Douglas P.
Nomography: Theory & Application. Shoe
String.
Adams, E. *see* Adams, Ernest Wilcox.
Adams, E. B. *see* Adams, Edward Barry.
Adams, E. M. *see* Adams, Elie Maynard.

Adams, Edward Barry.
xAdams, E. B.
A Companion to Clinical Medicine in the
Tropics & Subtropics. Oxford U Pr.
Adams, Edward L.
xAdams, Edward L.
Career Advancement Guide. McGraw.
Adams, Eleanor N. *see* Adams, Eleanor Nathalie.
Adams, Eleanor Nathalie.
xAdams, Eleanor N.
Old English Scholarship in England from
1556-1800. Shoe String.
Adams, Elie M. *see* Adams, Elie Maynard.
Adams, Elie Maynard, 1919-
xAdams, E. M.
The Idea of America: A Reassessment of the
American Experiment. Ballinger Pub.
xAdams, Elie M.
Ethical Naturalism & the Modern World-View.
Greenwood.
Adams, Ephraim D. *see* Adams, Ephraim Douglass.
Adams, Ephraim Douglass, 1865-1930
xAdams, Ephraim D.
British Interests & Activities in Texas,
1838-1846. Peter Smith.
Power of Ideals in American History. AMS Pr.
Adams, Ernest Wilcox, 1926-
xAdams, E.
The Logic of Conditionals: An Application of
Probability to Deductive Logic. Kluwer
Boston.
Adams, Eugene T. *see* Adams, Eugene Taylor.
Adams, Eugene Taylor.
xAdams, Eugene T.
American Idea. Arno.
Adams, Eugenia.
xAdams, Eugenia.
Assault on Eden. Eerdmans.
Adams, Evelyn C. *see* Adams, Evelyn Crady.
Adams, Evelyn Crady, 1884-
xAdams, Evelyn C.
American Indian Education: Government
Schools & Economic Progress. Arno.
Adams, F. C. *see* Adams, Francis Colburn.
Adams, F. Gerard. *see* Adams, Francis Gerard.
Adams, Fay (Greene), Mrs, 1903-
xAdams, Fay G.
The Initiation of an Activity Program into a
Public School. AMS Pr.
Adams, Fay G. *see* Adams, Fay (Greene).
Adams, Florence.
xAdams, Florence.
Catch a Sunbeam: A Book of Solar Study &
Experiments. HarBraceJ.
Make Your Own Baby Furniture. M Evans.
Mushy Eggs. Putnam.
Adams, Francis.
xAdams, Francis.
Free School System of the United States. Arno.
Adams, Francis Colburn.
xAdams, F. C.
Uncle Tom at Home: A Review of the
Reviewers & Repudiators of Uncle Tom's
Cabin by Mrs. Stowe. Arno.
Adams, Francis Gerard.
xAdams, F. Gerard.
Econometric Modeling of World Commodity
Policy. Lexington Bks.
Econometric Models of World Agricultural
Commodity Markets: Cocoa, Coffee, Tea,
Wool, Cotton, Sugar, Wheat, Rice. Ballinger
Pub.
Adams, Frank.
xAdams, Frank.
Unearthing Seeds of Fire: The Idea of
Highlander. Blair.
Adams, Frank C.
xAdams, Frank C.

College & University Student Work Programs:
Implications & Implementations. S Ill U Pr.
Adams, Frederick U. *see* Adams, Frederick Upham.
Adams, Frederick Upham, 1859-1921
xAdams, Frederick U.
Conquest of the Tropics: The Story of the
Creative Enterprises Conducted by the
United Fruit Company. Arno.
Adams, G. B. *see* Adams, George Burton.
Adams, George, 1936-
xAdams, George.
How to Photograph a Woman. Avon.
Adams, George. *see* Adams, George Fowler.
Adams, George B. *see* Adams, George Burton.
Adams, George Burton, 1851-1925
xAdams, G. B.
History of England from the Norman Conquest
to the Death of John, 1066-1216. Kraus
Repr.
xAdams, George B.
History of England from the Norman Conquest
to the Death of John. AMS Pr.
History of England from the Norman Conquest
to the Death of John, 1066-1216.
Greenwood.
Adams, George Fowler.
xAdams, George.
Essentials of Geriatric Medicine. Oxford U Pr.
Adams, Grace. *see* Adams, Grace Kinckle.
Adams, Grace Kinckle, 1900-
xAdams, Grace.
Workers on Relief. Arno.
Adams, H. E. *see* Adams, Henry E.
Adams, Harland B.
xAdams, Harland B.
Guide to Legal Gambling. T Y Crowell.
Adams, Harry Baker, 1924-
xAdams, Harry Baker.
Priorities & People. Bethany Pr.
Adams, Hazard, 1926-
xAdams, Hazard.
The Academic Tribes. Liveright.
Critical Theory Since Plato. HarBraceJ.
Adams, Henry.
xAdams, Henry.
The Degradation of the Democratic Dogma.
Peter Smith.
Democracy: An American Novel. Scholarly.
ed. Documents Relating to New England
Federalism, 1800-1815. B Franklin.
The Education of Henry Adams. HM.
Education of Henry Adams. HM.
The Education of Henry Adams. Larlin Corp.
Historical Essays. Adler.
The Life of George Cabot Lodge. Schol
Facsimiles.
Adams, Henry C. *see* Adams, Henry Carter.
Adams, Henry Carter, 1851-1921
xAdams, Henry C.
Public Debts: An Essay in the Science of
Finance. Arno.
Taxation in the United States 1789-1816. AMS
Pr.
Taxation in the United States: 1789-1816. B
Franklin.
Taxation in the United States: 1789-1816.
Johnson Repr.
Two Essays: Relation of the State to Industrial
Action & Economics & Jurisprudence.
Kelley.
Adams, Henry E.
xAdams, H. E.
Psychology of Adjustment. Wiley.
xAdams, Henry E.
Advances in Experimental Clinical Psychology.
Pergamon.
Adams, Henry H. *see* Adams, Henry Hitch.
Adams, Henry Hitch.
xAdams, Henry H.

ed. Dramatic Essays of the Neoclassic Age. Arno.

Adams, Herbert B. *see* Adams, Herbert Baxter.

Adams, Herbert Baxter, 1850-1901
  xAdams, Herbert B.
    The Church & Popular Education. AMS Pr.
    The Church & Popular Education. Johnson Repr.
    Columbus & His Discovery of America. AMS Pr.
    Columbus & His Discovery of America. Johnson Repr.
    Historical Scholarship in the United States, 1876-1901: As Revealed in the Correspondence of Herbert B. Adams. AMS Pr.
    Maryland's Influence Upon Land Cessions to the United States: With Minor Papers on George Washington's Interest in Western Lands, the Potomac Company & a National University. Johnson Repr.
    Notes on the Literature of Charities. AMS Pr.
    Notes on the Literature of Charities. Johnson Repr.
    Public Educational Work in Baltimore. AMS Pr.
    Public Educational Work in Baltimore. Johnson Repr.

Adams, Herbert F. *see* Adams, Herbert F. R.

Adams, Herbert F. R.
  xAdams, Herbert F.
    SI Metric Units: An Introduction. McGraw.

Adams, Hugh.
  xAdams, Hugh.
    Modern Painting. Mayflower Bks.

Adams, J. *see* Adams, John Crawford.

Adams, J. D. *see* Adams, James Donald.

Adams, J. Donald. *see* Adams, James Donald.

Adams, J. T. *see* Adams, Jeannette T.

Adams, Jack *see* Adams, Jack A.

Adams, Jack A.
  xAdams, Jack.
    Learning & Memory: An Introduction. Dorsey.
  xAdams, Jack A.
    Human Memory. McGraw.
    Learning & Memory: An Introduction. Dorsey.

Adams, James. *see* Adams, James R.

Adams, James Donald, 1891-1968
  xAdams, J. D.
    Literary Frontiers. Kraus Repr.
  xAdams, J. Donald.
    Copey of Harvard: A Biography of Charles Townsend Copeland. Greenwood.

Adams, James Frederick, 1927-
  xAdams.
    Understanding Adolescence: Current Developments in Adolescent Psychology. Allyn.

Adams, James L.
  xAdams, James L.
    Conceptual Blockbusting: A Guide to Better Ideas. Norton.

Adams, James R.
  xAdams, James.
    Autopsy. Year Bk Med.

Adams, James T. *see* Adams, James Truslow.

Adams, James Truslow, 1878-1949
  xAdams, James T.
    The Adams Family. Darby Bks.
    The Adams Family. Greenwood.
    The Adams Family. NAL.
    History of New England. Scholarly.
    Provincial Society: 1690-1763. New Viewpoints.

Adams, Jan S.
  xAdams, Jan S.
    Citizen Inspectors in the Soviet Union: The Peoples Control Committee. Praeger.

Adams, Jane.
  xAdams, Jane.
    Sex & the Single Parent. Coward.

Adams, Jane L.
  xAdams, Jane L.
    An Education Curriculum for the Moderately, Severely & Profoundly Mentally Handicapped Pupil. C C Thomas.

Adams, Jay E.
  xAdams, Jay E.
    Christian Counselor's Casebook. Baker Bk.
    Christian Counselor's Casebook. Presby & Reformed.

Adams, Jeannette T.
  xAdams, J. T.
    The Complete Home Electrical Wiring Handbook. Arco.
  xAdams, Jeannette T.
    Home Appliances: Selection, Use & Repair. Arco.

Adams, John.
  xAdams, John.
    The Adams-Jefferson Letters: The Complete Correspondence Between Thomas Jefferson & Abigail & John Adams. U of NC Pr.
    ed. The Contemporary International Economy: A Reader. St Martin.
    Teach Your Child Soccer. Transatlantic.

Adams, John A., 1951-
  xAdams, John A.
    We Are the Aggies: The Texas A&M University Association of Former Students. Tex A&M Univ Pr.

Adams, John Crawford.
  xAdams, J.
    Arthritis & Back Pain. Univ Park.

Adams, John F. *see* Adams, John Frank.

Adams, John Festus, 1930-
  xAdams, John F.
    Two Plus Two Equals Minus Seven. Macmillan.

Adams, John Frank
  xAdams, John F.
    Algebraic Topology: A Student's Guide. Cambridge U Pr.

Adams, John M. *see* Adams, John Milton.

Adams, John Milton, 1905-
  xAdams, John M.
    Multiple Sclerosis--Scars of Childhood: New Horizons & Hope. C C Thomas.

Adams, John P., 1923-
  xAdams, John P.
    At the Heart of the Whirlwind. Har-Row.

Adams, John Q. *see* Adams, John Quincy.

Adams, John Quincy, Pres. U.S., 1767-1848
  xAdams, John Q.
    Argument of John Quincy Adams Before the Supreme Court of the United States in the Case of the United States Vs. Cinque & Others, Africans, Captured in the Schooner Amistad. Arno.
    Argument of John Quincy Adams, Before the Supreme Court of the United States. Negro U Pr.
    Memoirs of John Quincy Adams, Comprising Portions of His Diary from 1795 to 1848. Arno.

Adams, John R., 1900-
  xAdams, John R.
    Edward Everett Hale. Twayne.

Adams, Joseph Q. *see* Adams, Joseph Quincy.

Adams, Joseph Quincy, 1881-1946
  xAdams, Joseph Q.
    Conventual Buildings of Blackfriars, London, & the Playhouses Constructed Therein. AMS Pr.

Adams, Kramer. *see* Adams, Kramer A.

Adams, Kramer A.
  xAdams, Kramer.
    Logging Railroads of the West. Superior Pub.

Adams, Lane.
  xAdams, Lane.
    How Come It's Taking Me So Long to Get Better?. Tyndale.

Adams, Laura.
  xAdams, Laura.
    Existential Battles: The Growth of Norman Mailer. Ohio U Pr.
    Norman Mailer: A Comprehensive Bibliography. Scarecrow.

Adams, Laurie.
  xAdams, Laurie.
    Art on Trial: From Whistler to Rothko. Walker & Co.

Adams, Leon D. *see* Adams, Leon David.

Adams, Leon David, 1905-
  xAdams, Leon D.
    Leon D Adams' Commonsense Book of Wine. HM.

Adams, Leonard P. *see* Adams, Leonard Palmer.

Adams, Leonard Palmer, 1906-
  xAdams, Leonard P.
    Agricultural Depression & Farm Relief in England, 1813-1852. Kelley.
    Public Employment Service in Transition, 1933-1968: Evolution of a Placement Service into a Manpower Agency. NY Sch Indus Rel.

Adams, Linda.
  xAdams, Linda.
    Effectiveness Training for Women (E. T. W.). Wyden.

Adams, Louis J. *see* Adams, Louis Jerold.

Adams, Louis Jerold, 1939-
  xAdams, Louis J.
    Theory, Law, & Policy of Contemporary Japanese Treaties. Oceana.

Adams, Lovincy J. *see* Adams, Lovincy Joseph.

Adams, Lovincy Joseph.
  xAdams, Lovincy J.
    Analytic Geometry & Calculus. Oxford U Pr.

Adams, Maurianne.
  xAdams, Maurianne.
    Autobiography. Bobbs.

Adams, Michael C. *see* Adams, Michael C. C.

Adams, Michael C. C., 1945-
  xAdams, Michael C.
    Our Masters the Rebels: A Speculation on Union Military Failure in the East, 1861-1865. Harvard U Pr.

Adams, Morley.
  xAdams, Morley.
    Omar's Interpreter: A New Life of Edward Fitzgerald. Folcroft.

Adams, Neal.
  xAdams, Neal.
    Well Control Problems & Solutions. Pennwell Pub.

Adams, Nehemiah, 1806-1878
  xAdams, Nehemiah.
    South-Side View of Slavery: Or Three Months at the South, 1854. Negro U Pr.

Adams, Nicholson B. *see* Adams, Nicholson Barney.

Adams, Nicholson Barney.
  xAdams, Nicholson B.
    Spanish for Today. HR&W.
    Spanish Literature: A Brief Survey. Littlefield.

Adams, Norman.
  xAdams, Norman.
    Drawing Animals. Watson-Guptill.

Adams, Oscar F. *see* Adams, Oscar Fay.

Adams, Oscar Fay, 1855-1919
  xAdams, Oscar F.

A Brief Handbook of American Authors.
  Longwood Pr.
A Brief Handbook of American Authors. R
  West.
Dictionary of American Authors. Gale.
A Dictionary of American Authors. Gordon
  Pr.
A Dictionary of American Authors. Longwood
  Pr.
The Story of Jane Austen's Life. Arden Lib.
The Story of Jane Austen's Life. Folcroft.
Adams, Paul L., 1924-
  xAdams, Paul L.
  A Primer of Child Psychotherapy. Little.
Adams, Percy G.
  xAdams, Percy G.
  Graces of Harmony: Alliteration, Assonance, &
    Consonance in Eighteenth-Century British
    Poetry. U of Ga Pr.
Adams, R. J. see Adams, Ralph James Q.
Adams, Ralph James Q., 1943-
  xAdams, R. J.
  Arms & the Wizard: Lloyd George & the
    Ministry of Munitions, 1915-1916. Tex A&M
    Univ Pr.
Adams, Ramon F. see Adams, Ramon Frederick.
Adams, Ramon Frederick, 1889-
  xAdams, Ramon F.
  Come An' Get It: The Story of the Old
    Cowboy Cook. U of Okla Pr.
Adams, Ramona S. see Adams, Ramona Shepherd.
Adams, Ramona Shepherd.
  xAdams, Ramona S.
  Letting Go: Uncomplicating Your Life.
    Macmillan.
Adams, Raymond D. see Adams, Raymond Delacy.
Adams, Raymond Delacy.
  xAdams, Raymond D.
  Principles of Neurology. McGraw.
Adams, Richard.
  xAdams, Richard.
  The Plague Dogs. Fawcett.
  The Plague Dogs. Knopf.
Adams, Richard. see Adams, Richard George.
Adams, Richard E. see Adams, Richard E. W.
Adams, Richard E. W.
  xAdams, Richard E.
  Prehistoric Mesoamerica. Little.
  xAdams, Richard W.
  ed. The Origins of Maya Civilization. U of NM
    Pr.
Adams, Richard George.
  xAdams, Richard.
  The Girl in a Swing. Knopf.
  Nature Through the Seasons. Penguin.
  Nature Through the Seasons. S&S.
  The Tyger Voyage. Knopf.
Adams, Richard N.
  xAdams, Richard N.
  Cultural Surveys of Panama, Nicaragua,
    Guatemala, El Salvador, Honduras. Blaine
    Ethridge.
Adams, Richard N. see Adams, Richard Newbold.
Adams, Richard Newbold, 1924-
  xAdams, Richard N.
  Crucifixion by Power: Essays on Guatemalan
    National Social Structure, 1944-1966. U of
    Tex Pr.
  Energy & Structure: A Theory of Social Power.
    U of Tex Pr.
Adams, Richard W. see Adams, Richard E. W.
Adams, Robert.
  xAdams, Robert.
  Castaways in Time. Donning Co.
  The Coming of the Horseclans. Pinnacle Bks.
  Dry Lands: Man & Plants. St Martin.
  Swords of the Horseclans. Pinnacle Bks.
Adams, Robert. see Adams, Robert Hickman.
Adams, Robert H. see Adams, Robert Hickman.

Adams, Robert Hickman, 1937-
  xAdams, Robert.
  The Architecture & Art of Early Hispanic
    Colorado. Colo Assoc.
  xAdams, Robert H.
  White Churches of the Plains: Examples from
    Colorado. Colo Assoc.
Adams, Robert M. see Adams, Robert Martin.
Adams, Robert Martin, 1915-
  xAdams, Robert.
  The Lost Museum: Glimpses of Vanished
    Originals. Viking Pr.
  xAdams, Robert M.
  After Joyce: Studies in Fiction After Ulysses.
    Oxford U Pr.
  Bad Mouth: Fugitive Papers on the Dark Side.
    U of Cal Pr.
  Nil: Episodes in the Literary Conquest of Void
    During the Nineteenth Century. Oxford U
    Pr.
Adams, Robert W. see Adams, Robert Wynne.
Adams, Robert Wynne, 1939-
  xAdams, Robert W.
  Adding Solar Heat to Your Home. TAB Bks.
Adams, Roger.
  xAdams, Roger.
  Laboratory Experiments in Organic Chemistry.
    Macmillan.
Adams, Ronald C.
  xAdams, Ronald C.
  ed. Games, Sports & Exercises for the
    Physically Handicapped. Lea & Febiger.
Adams, Ruth. see Adams, Ruth (Holland).
Adams, Ruth (Holland), 1904-
  xAdams, Ruth.
  One Little Candle. Macoy Pub.
Adams, Sam.
  xAdams, Sam.
  Teaching Mathematics: With Emphasis on the
    Diagnostic Approach. Har-Row.
Adams, Samuel H. see Adams, Samuel Hopkins.
Adams, Samuel Hopkins, 1871-1958
  xAdams, Samuel H.
  Average Jones. Arno.
  Our Square & the People in It. Arno.
Adams, Sexton.
  xAdams, Sexton.
  Corporate Promotables. Gulf Pub.
Adams, Sherman, 1899-
  xAdams, Sherman.
  Firsthand Report: The Story of the Eisenhower
    Administration. Greenwood.
Adams, Spencer L. see Adams, Spencer Lionel.
Adams, Spencer Lionel, 1870-
  xAdams, Spencer L.
  The Long House of the Iroquois. AMS Pr.
Adams, T. F. M. see Adams, Thomas Francis Morton.
Adams, Thomas, 1871-1940
  xAdams, Thomas.
  The Design of Residential Areas: Basic
    Considerations, Principles & Methods. Arno.
Adams, Thomas F. see Adams, Thomas Francis.
Adams, Thomas Francis, 1927-
  xAdams, Thomas F.
  Introduction to the Administration of Criminal
    Justice: An Overview of the Justice System &
    Its Components. P-H.
Adams, Thomas Francis Morton.
  xAdams, T. F. M.
  A Financial History of the New Japan.
    Kodansha.
  World of Japanese Business. Kodansha.
Adams, Thomas M. see Adams, Thomas Mcconnell.
Adams, Thomas Mcconnell, 1913-
  xAdams, Thomas M.
  The Master Guide to Electronic Circuits. TAB
    Bks.
Adams, Thomas W.
  xAdams, Thomas W.

Cyprus Between East & West. Johns Hopkins.
Adams, Virginia.
  xAdams, Virginia.
  Crime. Time-Life.
Adams, Vyvyan, 1900-1951
  xAdams, Vyvyon.
  Men in Our Time. Arno.
Adams, Vyvyon. see Adams, Vyvyan.
Adams, W. see Adams, William J.
Adams, W. Claude. see Adams, W Claudo.
Adams, W. J. see Adams, William J.
Adams, W. Royce.
  xAdams, W. Royce.
  Developing Reading Versatility. HR&W.
  How to Read the Sciences. Scott F.
  Prep: For Better Reading. HR&W.
  Reading Beyond Words. HR&W.
  Think, Read, React, Plan, Write, Rewrite.
    HR&W.
Adams, W Claudo, 1873-
  xAdams, W. Claude.
  History of Dentistry in Oregon. Binford.
Adams, Walter, 1922 (aug. 27)-
  xAdams, Walter.
  Structure of American Industry. Macmillan.
Adams, William, 1936-
  xAdams, William.
  ed. Afro-American Authors. HM.
  ed. Television Network News: Issues in
    Content Research. SPIA-GWU.
Adams, William D.
  xAdams, Bill.
  Shrubs & Vines for Southern Landscapes.
    Pacesetter Pr.
  Vegetable Growing for Southern Gardens.
    Pacesetter Pr.
Adams, William D. see Adams, William Davenport.
Adams, William Davenport, 1851-1904
  xAdams, William D.
  A Book of Burlesque: Sketches of English
    Stage Travestie & Parody. Folcroft.
  A Book of Burlesque: Sketches of English
    Stage Travestie & Parody. R West.
  Dictionary of English Literature Being a
    Comprehensive Guide to English Authors &
    Their Works. R West.
Adams, William E. see Adams, William Edwin.
Adams, William Edwin, 1832-
  xAdams, William E.
  Memoirs of a Social Atom. Kelley.
Adams, William J.
  xAdams, W.
  Fundamentals of Mathematics for Business,
    Social, & Life Sciences. P-H.
  xAdams, W. J.
  Calculus for Business & Social Science. Wiley.
  xAdams, William J.
  The Life & Times of the Central Limit
    Theorem. Kaedmon.
Adams, William W.
  xAdams, W.
  Introduction to Number Theory. P-H.
Adamson, Arthur. see Adamson, Arthur W.
Adamson, Arthur W.
  xAdamson, Arthur.
  A Textbook of Physical Chemistry. Acad Pr.
  xAdamson, Arthur W.
  Concepts of Inorganic Photochemistry. Wiley.
  Understanding Physical Chemistry. Benjamin
    Cummings.
Adamson, Douglas.
  xAdamson, Douglas.
  Charles Bear & the Mystery of the Forest. D
    Adamson.
  illus. Charles Bear & the Mystery of the Forest.
    HM.
Adamson, Joy.
  xAdamson, Joy.

Born Free: A Lioness of Two Worlds.
Pantheon.
Forever Free. HarBraceJ.
The Searching Spirit: Joy Adamson's
Autobiography. HarBraceJ.
Adamson, Robert, 1852-1902
xAdamson, Robert.
The Development of Modern Philosophy.
Arno.
Adamthwaite, Anthony.
xAdamthwaite, Anthony P.
France & the Coming of the Second World
War. Biblio Dist.
Adamthwaite, Anthony P. see Adamthwaite, Anthony.
Adas, Michael, 1943-
xAdas, Michael.
Prophets of Rebellion: Millenarian Protest
Movements Against the European Colonial
Order. U of NC Pr.
Adburgham, Alison.
xAdburgham, Alison.
Shopping in Style: London from the
Restoration to Edwardian Elegance. Thames
Hudson.
Adby, P. R.
xAdby, P. R.
Applied Circuit Theory: Matrix & Computer
Methods. Halsted Pr.
Adcock, Fleur.
xAdcock, Fleur.
The Inner Harbour. Oxford U Pr.
Adcock, Frank E. see Adcock, Frank Ezra.
Adcock, Frank Ezra, 1886-
xAdcock, Frank E.
Caesar As Man of Letters. R West.
The Greek & Macedonian Art of War. U of
Cal Pr
Adcock, Larry.
xAdcock, Larry.
CB Angel. Popular Lib.
Adcock, Mabel.
xAdcock, Mabel.
Creative Activities. Warner Pr.
Addams, Charles, 1912-
xAddams, Charles.
Monster Rally. S&S.
xAddams, Chas.
Chas Addams' Favorite Haunts. S&S.
Addams, Chas. see Addams, Charles.
Addams, Jane, 1860-1935
xAddams, Jane.
My Friend, Julia Lathrop. Arno.
Addington, Jack. see Addington, Jack Ensign.
Addington, Jack E. see Addington, Jack Ensign.
Addington, Jack Ensign.
xAddington, Jack.
The Perfect Power Within You. De Vorss.
xAddington, Jack E.
All About Goals & How to Achieve Them. De
Vorss.
Psychogenesis: Everything Begins in the Mind.
Dodd.
Addington, Robert M. see Addington, Robert Milford.
Addington, Robert Milford, 1867-
xAddington, Robert M.
History of Scott County, Virginia. Regional.
Addis, Laird.
xAddis, Laird.
The Logic of Society: A Philosophical Study. U
of Minn Pr.
Addison, Gwen.
xAddison, Gwen.
Storm Over Fox Hill. PB.
Addison, James T. see Addison, James Thayer.
Addison, James Thayer, 1887-
xAddison, James T.

The Christian Approach to the Moslem. AMS
Pr.
Addison, John.
xAddison, John.
Ancient Africa. John Day.
Addison, John. see Addison, John T.
Addison, John T.
xAddison, John.
The Market for Labor: An Analytical
Treatment. Goodyear.
Addison, Joseph.
xAddison, Joseph.
Miscellaneous Works of Joseph Addison.
Scholarly.
Addison, Medora C.
xAddison, Medora C.
Dreams & a Sword. AMS Pr.
Addison, William. see Addison, William Wilkinson.
Addison, William Wilkinson, Sir, 1905-
xAddison, William.
Understanding English Surnames. David &
Charles.
Addy, George M.
xAddy, George M.
Enlightenment in the University of Salamanca.
Duke.
Addy, John.
xAddy, John.
The Textile Revolution. Longman.
Addy, Sidney O. see Addy, Sidney Oldall.
Addy, Sidney Oldall, 1848-1933
xAddy, Sidney O.
Church & Manor: A Study in English
Economic History. Kelley.
Folk Tales & Superstitions. Rowman.
Ade, George, 1866-1944
xAde, George.
Bang! Bang!: A Collection of Stories Intended
to Recall Memories of the Nickel Library
Days When Boys Were Superhuman &
Murder a Fine Art. Arno.
In Pastures New. Irvington.
One Afternoon with Mark Twain. Folcroft.
The Permanent Ade: The Living Writings of
George Ade. Hyperion Conn.
Adedeji, Adebayo.
xAdedeji, Adebayo.
Nigerian Federal Finance: Its Development,
Problems & Prospects. Holmes & Meier.
Adegoke, Olu S. see Adegoke, Oluwafayisola S.
Adegoke, Oluwafayisola S.
xAdegoke, Olu S.
Stratigraphy & Paleontology of the Marine
Neogene Formations of the Coalinga Region,
California. U of Cal Pr.
Adell, Judith.
xAdell, Judith.
Compiled by A Guide to Non-Sexist Children's
Books. Academy Chi Ltd.
Adelman, Irma.
xAdelman, Irma.
ed. Practical Approaches to Development
Planning: Korea's Second Five-Year Plan.
Johns Hopkins.
Society, Politics, & Economic Development: A
Quantitative Approach. Johns Hopkins.
Theories of Economic Growth & Development.
Stanford U Pr.
ed. The Theory & Design of Economic
Development. Johns Hopkins.
Adelman, Irving.
xAdelman, Irving.
The Contemporary Novel: A Checklist of
Critical Literature on the British & American
Novel Since 1945. Scarecrow.
Adelman, Janet.
xAdelman, Janet.

The Common Liar: An Essay on 'Antony &
Cleopatra'. Yale U Pr.
Adelman, Jonathan R.
xAdelman, Jonathan R.
The Revolutionary Armies: The Historical
Development of the Soviet & the Chinese
People's Liberation Armies. Greenwood.
Adelman, M. A. see Adelman, Morris Albert.
Adelman, Morris Albert.
xAdelman, M. A.
The World Petroleum Market. Johns Hopkins.
Adelmann, Howard B. see Adelmann, Howard Bernhardt.
Adelmann, Howard Bernhardt.
xAdelmann, Howard B.
Marcello Malpighi & the Evolution of
Embryology. Cornell U Pr.
Adelson, Lester, 1914-
xAdelson, Lester.
The Pathology of Homicide: A Vade Mecum
for Pathologist, Prosecutor & Defense
Counsel. C C Thomas.
Adelstein, Michael E.
xAdelstein, Michael E.
Contemporary Business Writing. Random.
The Reading Commitment. HarBraceJ.
ed. Women's Liberation. St Martin.
The Writing Commitment. HarBraceJ.
Aden, John M.
xAden, John M.
ed. Critical Opinions of John Dryden: A
Dictionary. Vanderbilt U Pr.
Pope's Once & Future Kings: Satire & Politics
in the Early Career. U of Tenn Pr.
Something Like Horace: Studies in the Art &
Allusion of Pope's Horatian Satires.
Vanderbilt U Pr.
Adeney, Walter F. see Adeney, Walter Frederic.
Adeney, Walter Frederic, 1849-1920
xAdeney, Walter F.
The Greek & Eastern Churches. Kelley.
Ader, Emile B. see Ader, Emile Bertrand.
Ader, Emile Bertrand, 1921-
xAder, Emile B.
Communism: Classic & Contemporary. Barron.
Ader, Paul. see Ader, Paul Fassett.
Ader, Paul Fassett, 1918-
xAder, Paul.
How to Make a Million at the Track. Contemp
Bks.
Ades, Hawley.
xAdes, Hawley.
Choral Arranging. Shawnee Pr.
Adesanya, M. O.
xAdesanya, M. O.
Business Law in Nigeria. Holmes & Meier.
Adey, Margaret.
xAdey, Margaret.
Galeria Hispanica. McGraw.
Adian, S. I.
xAdian, S. I.
The Burnside Problem & Identities in Groups.
Springer-Verlag.
Adickes, Erich, 1866-1928
xAdickes, Erich.
German Kantian Bibliography. B Franklin.
Adie, Donald W.
xAdie, Donald W.
Marinas: A Working Guide to Their
Development and Design. CBI Pub.
Marinas: A Working Guide to Their
Development & Design. Nichols Pub.
Adie, R. see Adie, Robert F.
Adie, Robert F.
xAdie, R.
Latin America: The Politics of Immobility.
P-H.
Adjali, Mia, 1939-
xAdjali, Mia.

Of Life & Hope: Toward Effective Witness in
Human Rights. Friend Pr.

Adkins, Bill.
xAdkins, Bill.
Prison at Obregon. Popular Lib.

Adkins, Jan.
xAdkins, Jan.
The Art & Ingenuity of the Woodstove.
Everest Hse.
The Craft of Sail. Walker & Co.
illus. Letterbox: The Art & History of Letters.
Walker & Co.
Moving Heavy Things. HM.
illus. Wooden Ship. HM.

Adler. *see* Adler, Mortimer Jerome.

Adler, Alfred.
xAdler, Alfred.
ed. Co-Operation Between the Sexes: Writings
on Women, Love & Marriage Sexuality, & Its
Disorders. Doubleday.
Education of Children. Regnery-Gateway.
Education of the Individual. Greenwood.
Individual Psychology of Alfred Adler: A
Systematic Presentation in Selections from
His Writings. Basic.
Individual Psychology of Alfred Adler: A
Systematic Presentation in Selections from
His Writings. Har-Row.
Superiority & Social Interest: A Collection of
Later Writings. Northwestern U Pr.
Superiority & Social Interest: A Collection of
Later Writings. Norton.

Adler, Bill.
xAdler, Bill.
Hip Kids' Letters from Camp. NAL.
Letters from Camp. Manor Bks.
The Second Time Is Better. Playboy Pbks.
Woody Allen: Clown Prince of American
Humor. Pinnacle Bks.

Adler, C. S. *see* Adler, Carole S.

Adler, Carole S.
xAdler, C. S.
In Our House Scott Is My Brother. Macmillan.
The Magic of the Glits. Macmillan.
The Silver Coach. Coward.

Adler, Cy A.
xAdler, Cy A.
Ecological Fantasies. Dell.

Adler, Cyrus, 1863-1940
xAdler, Cyrus.
I Have Considered the Days. United Syn Bk.

Adler, David. *see* Adler, David A.

Adler, David A.
xAdler, David.
Cam Jansen & the Mystery of the Stolen
Diamonds. Viking Pr.
xAdler, David A.
Passover Fun Book: Puzzles, Riddles, Magic &
More. Hebrew Pub.
You Think It's Fun to Be a Clown. Doubleday.

Adler, Dorothy R.
xAdler, Dorothy R.
British Investment in American Railways
1834-1898. U Pr of Va.

Adler, Elkan N. *see* Adler, Elkan Nathan.

Adler, Elkan Nathan, 1861-1946
xAdler, Elkan N.
About Hebrew Manuscripts. Hermon.

Adler, Freda.
xAdler, Freda.
The Criminology of Deviant Women. HM.

Adler, Gerald.
xAdler, Gerald.
Confrontation in Psychotherapy. Aronson.

Adler, Gerhard, 1904-
xAdler, Gerhard.
Studies in Analytical Psychology. C G Jung
Foun.
Studies in Analytical Psychology. Greenwood.

Adler, I. *see* Adler, Isidore.

Adler, Irene.
xAdler, Irene.
Peter Frampton. Music Sales.

Adler, Irving.
xAdler, Irving.
Adler Book of Puzzles & Riddles: Or, Sam
Loyd Up-To-Date. John Day.
Atomic Energy. John Day.
Calendar. John Day.
The Changing Tools of Science: From
Yardstick to Synchrotron. John Day.
Dust. John Day.
The Earth's Crust. John Day.
Energy. John Day.
The Environment. John Day.
Hot & Cold. John Day.
Houses. John Day.
How Life Began. John Day.
The Impossible in Mathematics. NCTM.
The Stars: Decoding Their Messages. T Y
Crowell.
Story of Light. Harvey.
Sun & Its Family. John Day.

Adler, Isidore.
xAdler, I.
Geochemical Exploration of the Moon & the
Planets. Springer-Verlag.

Adler, Jacob H. *see* Adler, Jacob Henry.

Adler, Jacob Henry, 1926-
xAdler, Jacob H.
Reach of Art: A Study in the Prosody of Pope.
U Presses Fla.

Adler, Joan.
xAdler, Joan.
The Retirement Book: A Complete
Early-Planning Guide to Finances, New
Activities, & Where to Live. Morrow.

Adler, K. *see* Adler, Kurt.

Adler, Kraig.
xAdler, Kraig.
Intro. by Early Herpetological Studies &
Surveys in the Eastern United States:
Original Anthology. Arno.

Adler, Kurt, 1907-
xAdler, K.
The Art of Accompanying & Coaching. Da
Capo.

Adler, Larry, 1939-
xAdler, Larry.
Famous Horses in America. McKay.
The Texas Rangers. McKay.

Adler, Lenore L. *see* Adler, Leonore Loeb.

Adler, Leonore Loeb.
xAdler, Lenore L.
This Is the Dachshund. TFH Pubns.

Adler, M. W. *see* Adler, Martin W.

Adler, Margot.
xAdler, Margot.
Drawing Down the Moon: Witches, Druids,
Goddess-Worshippers & Other Pagans in
America Today. Beacon Pr.
Drawing Down the Moon: Witches, Druids,
Goddess-Worshippers, & Other Pagans in
America Today. Viking Pr.

Adler, Martin W.
xAdler, M. W.
ed. Factors Affecting the Action of Narcotics.
Raven.

Adler, Morris.
xAdler, Morris.
The World of the Talmud. Schocken.

Adler, Mortimer J. *see* Adler, Mortimer Jerome.

Adler, Mortimer Jerome, 1902-
xAdler.
How to Read a Book. S&S.
xAdler, Mortimer J.

Art & Prudence. Arno.
The Great Treasury of Western Thought: A
Compendium of Important Statements &
Comments on Man & His Institutions by the
Great Thinkers in Western History. Bowker.
How to Read a Book. S&S.

Adler, Norman T.
xAdler, Norman T.
ed. Mating Reflexes. Mss Info.

Adler, Peggy.
xAdler, Peggy.
illus. Geography Puzzles. Watts.

Adler, R. L. *see* Adler, Roy L.

Adler, Renata.
xAdler, Renata.
Speedboat. Popular Lib.
Speedboat. Random.

Adler, Richard.
xAdler, Richard.
All in the Family: A Critical Appraisal.
Praeger.
xAdler, Richard P.
The Effects of Television Advertising on
Children: Review & Recommendations.
Lexington Bks.

Adler, Richard P. *see* Adler, Richard.

Adler, Roy L.
xAdler, R. L.
Topological Entropy & Equivalence of
Dynamical Systems. Am Math.

Adler, Samuel, 1928-
xAdler, Samuel.
Sight Singing: Pitch, Interval, Rhythm. Norton.

Adler, Sol, 1925-
xAdler, Sol.
The Non-Verbal Child: An Introduction to
Pediatric Language Pathology. C C Thomas.
Poverty Children & Their Language:
Implications for Teaching & Treating. Grune.

Adler, Stephen.
xAdler, Stephen.
International Migration & Dependence.
Renouf.

Adler, Warren.
xAdler, Warren.
Blood Ties. PB.
Blood Ties. Putnam.
The Henderson Equation. PB.

Adoff, Arnold.
xAdoff, Arnold.
Eats: Poems. Lothrop.
ed. I Am the Darker Brother: An Anthology of
Modern Poems by Negro Americans.
Macmillan.
I am the running girl. Har-Row.
ed. My Black Me: A Beginning Book of Black
Poetry. Dutton.
Tornado! Poems. Delacorte.
Where Wild Willie. Har-Row.

Adolfson, John.
xAdolfson, John A.
Perception & Performance Underwater.
Krieger.

Adolfson, John A. *see* Adolfson, John.

Adolph, E. F. *see* Adolph, Edward Frederick.

Adolph, Edward Frederick, 1895-
xAdolph, E. F.
Origins of Physiological Regulations. Acad Pr.

Adorjan, Carol. *see* Adorjan, Carol Madden.

Adorjan, Carol M. *see* Adorjan, Carol Madden.

Adorjan, Carol Madden.
xAdorjan, Carol.
Cat Sitter Mystery. Schol Bk Serv.
Jonathan Bloom's Room. O'Hara.
xAdorjan, Carol M.
Someone I Know. Random.

Adorno, T. W. *see* Adorno, Theodor W.

Adorno, Theodor W., 1903-
xAdorno, T. W.

Optical Methods of Radio-Frequency
Spectroscopy. Halsted Pr.
Agard, Walter R. *see* Agard, Walter Raymond.
Agard, Walter Raymond, 1894-
xAgard, Walter R.
The Greek Mind. Krieger.
AGARD-NATO. *see* North Atlantic Treaty
Organization. Advisory Group for Aerospace Research
and Development. Combustion and Propulsion Panel.
Agard-Nato Specialists' Meeting, Marseille, 1964.
xAGARD-NATO.
Fluid Dynamic Aspects of Space Flight.
Gordon.
Agarwal, M. K.
xAgarwal, M. K.
ed. Antihormones. Elsevier.
Agarwal, N. R. *see* Agarwal, Radha Raman.
Agarwal, Radha Raman, 1911-
xAgarwal, N. R.
Soil Fertility in India. Asia.
Agarwala, Amar N. *see* Agarwala, Amar Narain.
Agarwala, Amar Narain, 1917-
xAgarwala, Amar N.
Education for Business in a Developing
Society. Mich St U Busn.
Agassi, Joseph.
xAgassi, Joseph.
Faraday As a Natural Philosopher. U of
Chicago Pr.
Agassi, Judith B.
xAgassi, Judity B.
Women on the Job: The Attitudes of Women
to Their Work. Lexington Bks.
Agassi, Judity B. *see* Agassi, Judith B.
Agassiz, Louis, 1807-1873
xAgassiz, Louis.
Contributions to the Natural History of the
United States of America. Scholarly.
A Journey in Brazil. Scholarly.
Agate, James. *see* Agate, James Evershed.
Agate, James Evershed, 1877-1947
xAgate, James.
Around Cinemas. Arno.
At Half-Past Eight: Essays on the Theatre
1921-1922. Arno.
More First Nights. Arno.
Rachel. Arno.
These Were Actors: Extracts from a
Newspaper Cutting Book, 1811-1833. Arno.
Those Were the Nights. Arno.
Agate, John. *see* Agate, John Norman.
Agate, John Norman.
xAgate, John.
Taking Care of Old People at Home. Allen
Unwin.
Agawa, Hiroyuki, 1920-
xAgawa, Hiroyuki.
The Reluctant Admiral: Yamamoto & the
Imperial Navy. Kodansha.
Agee, Doris.
xAgee, Doris.
Edgar Cayce on E.S.P.. Warner Bks.
Agee, James, 1909-1955
xAgee, James.
Collected Poems of James Agee. Yale U Pr.
The Collected Short Prose of James Agee.
Larlin Corp.
Death in the Family. AMSCO Sch.
Death in the Family. Bantam.
Letters of James Agee to Father Flye. Larlin
Corp.
Agee, M. *see* Agee, Marvin H.
Agee, Marvin H.
xAgee, M.
Quantitative Analysis for Management
Decisions. P-H.
Agee, Philip.
xAgee, Philip.

Dirty Work: The CIA in Western Europe. Lyle
Stuart.
Inside the Company: CIA Diary. Bantam.
Inside the Company: CIA Diary. S&S.
Agee, Rucker.
xAgee, Rucker.
Twenty Alabama Books. E A Seemann.
Agee, Vicki L.
xAgee, Vicki L.
Treatment of the Violent Incorrigible
Adolescent. Lexington Bks.
Agee, Warren K. *see* Agee, Warren Kendall.
Agee, Warren Kendall.
xAgee, Warren K.
Introduction to Mass Communications.
Har-Row.
ed. Press & the Public Interest. Pub Aff Pr.
Agee, William C.
xAgee, William C.
Raymond Duchamp-Villon. Walker & Co.
Agehananda Bharati, Swami, 1923-
xAgehananda Bharati.
The Tantric Tradition. Greenwood.
Ageloff, Roy.
xAgeloff, Roy.
Applied Basic Programming. Wadsworth Pub.
Fundamentals of Fortran for Management.
Wadsworth Pub.
Aggarwal, J. K. *see* Aggarwal, Jagdishkumar Keshoram.
Aggarwal, Jagdish K. *see* Aggarwal, Jagdishkumar
Keshoram.
Aggarwal, Jagdishkumar Keshoram.
xAggarwal, J. K.
ed. Computer Methods in Image Analysis. Inst
Electrical.
ed. Computer Methods in Image Analysis.
Wiley.
xAggarwal, Jagdish K.
Notes on Nonlinear Systems. Van Nos
Reinhold.
Aggarwal, Raj.
xAggarwal, Raj.
Management Science: Cases & Applications.
Holden-Day.
Aggeler, Geoffrey, 1939-
xAggeler, Geoffrey.
Anthony Burgess: The Artist As Novelist. U of
Ala Pr.
Agger, Eugene E. *see* Agger, Eugene Ewald.
Agger, Eugene Ewald, 1879-1966
xAgger, Eugene E.
Budget in the American Commonwealths.
AMS Pr.
Agger, L. T. *see* Agger, Lee Thomas.
Agger, Lee Thomas, 1903-
xAgger, L. T.
Introduction to Electricity. Oxford U Pr.
Aggertt, Otis J.
xAggertt, Otis J.
Communicative Reading. Macmillan.
Aghassi, M. *see* Aghassi, Marjorie Ewing.
Aghassi, Marjorie Ewing.
xAghassi, M.
Getting Good Grades: How to Succeed in
College. P-H.
Agid, Susan R.
xAgid, Susan R.
Fair Employment Litigation: Proving &
Defending a Title VII Case. PLI.
Aginsky, Ethel G. *see* Aginsky, Ethel Gertrude.
Aginsky, Ethel Gertrude, 1910-
xAginsky, Ethel G.
A Grammar of the Mende Language. Kraus
Repr.
Agirre, Julen.
xAgirre, Julen.
Operation Ogro: The Execution of Admiral
Luis Carrero Blanco. Times Bks.
Agle, Nan H. *see* Agle, Nan Hayden.

Agle, Nan Hayden.
xAgle, Nan H.
Maple Street. HM.
Princess Mary of Maryland. Gale.
Susan's Magic. HM.
Aglietta, Michel.
xAglietta, Michel.
A Theory of Capitalist Regulation: The U. S.
Experience. Schocken.
Agnello, Virginia L.
xAgnello, Virginia L.
Workbook for Voice Improvement. Interstate.
Agnew, Daniel, 1809-1902
xAgnew, Daniel.
History of the Region of Pennsylvania North of
the Ohio & West of the Allegheny River.
Arno.
Agnew, James B.
xAgnew, James B.
Eggnog Riot: The Christmas Mutiny at West
Point. Presidio Pr.
Agnew, Jeanne, 1917-
xAgnew, Jeanne.
Explorations in Number Theory. Brooks-Cole.
Agnew, Peter L. *see* Agnew, Peter Lawrence.
Agnew, Peter Lawrence.
xAgnew, Peter L.
Clerical Office Practice. SW Pub.
Full-Keyboard Adding-Listing Machine Course.
SW Pub.
Agnew, Spiro. *see* Agnew, Spiro T.
Agnew, Spiro T., 1918-
xAgnew, Spiro.
The Canfield Decision. Berkley Pub.
xAgnew, Spiro T.
Go Quietly . . . or Else. Morrow.
Agnew, Vijay, 1946-
xAgnew, Vijay.
Elite Women in Indian Politics. Advent Bk.
Agnihotri, S. N.
xAgnihotri, S. N.
Sanskrit Without Tears. Himalayan Intl Inst.
Agnihotri, V. K.
xAgnihotri, V. K.
India & Other Poems. InterCulture.
Agnon, S. Y. *see* Agnon, Samuel Joseph.
Agnon, Samuel Joseph, 1888-
xAgnon, S. Y.
A Guest for the Night. Schocken.
xAgnon, Shmuel Y.
Twenty-One Stories. Schocken.
Agnon, Shmuel Y. *see* Agnon, Samuel Joseph.
Agonito, Rosemary.
xAgonito, Rosemary.
ed. History of Ideas on Woman: A Source
Book. Putnam.
Agor, Weston H.
xAgor, Weston H.
Chilean Senate: Internal Distribution of
Influence. U of Tex Pr.
Agostinelli, Maria E. *see* Agostinelli, Maria Enrica.
Agostinelli, Maria Enrica.
xAgostinelli, Maria E.
On Wings of Love: The United Nations
Declaration of the Rights of the Child.
Philomel.
Agoston, G. A. *see* Agoston, George A.
Agoston, George A., 1920-
xAgoston, G. A.
Color Theory & Its Application in Art &
Design. Springer-Verlag.
Agoston, Max K.
xAgoston, Max K.
Algebraic Topology: A First Course. Dekker.
Agran, Larry.
xAgran, Larry.
Cancer Connection: And What We Can Do
About It. HM.
Agranoff, B. W. *see* Agranoff, Bernard W.

Agranoff, Bernard W.
xAgranoff, B. W.
 ed. Advances in Neurochemistry. Plenum Pub.
Agras, Stewart. *see* Agras, W. Stewart.
Agras, W. Stewart.
xAgras, Stewart.
 ed. Behavior Modification: Principles &
 Clinical Applications. Little.
xAgras, W. Stewart.
 Behavior Therapy: Toward an Applied Clinical
 Science. W H Freeman.
Agrawal, R. C.
xAgrawal, R. C.
 Operations Research Methods for Agricultural
 Decisions. Iowa St U Pr.
Agress, Clarence. *see* Agress, Clarence M.
Agress, Clarence M.
xAgress, Clarence.
 Energetics. G&D.
Agrest, M. M. *see* Agrest, Matest Mandeleevich.
Agrest, Matest Mandeleevich.
xAgrest, M. M.
 Theory of Incomplete Cylindrical Functions &
 Their Applications. Springer-Verlag.
Agribusiness Council. *see* Conference on Science and
 Agribusiness in the Seventies, London, 1974.
Agricultural Production Team.
xAgricultural Production Team.
 Report on India's Food Crisis & Steps to Meet
 It. Arno.
Agricultural Research Service of the U. S. Department of
 Agriculture. *see* United States. Agricultural Research
 Service.
Agriculture & Renewable Resources Board, National
 Research Council. *see* National Research Council.
 Board on Agriculture and Renewable Resources.
Agrimson, J. Elmo.
xAgrimson, J. Elmo.
 ed. Gifts of the Spirit & the Body of Christ:
 Perspectives on the Charismatic Movement.
 Augsburg.
Agrios, George N., 1936-
xAgrios, George N.
 Plant Pathology. Acad Pr.
Agudo, Philomena, 1925-
xAgudo, Philomena.
 Affirming the Human & the Holy. Affirmation.
Aguiar, Neuma.
xAguiar, Neuma.
 ed. The Structure of Brazilian Development.
 Transaction Bks.
Aguiar, Walter R.
xAguiar, Walter R.
 Maya Land in Color. Hastings.
Aguilar, Luis. *see* Aguilar, Luis E.
Aguilar, Luis E.
xAguilar, Luis.
 Marxism in Latin America. Phila Bk Co.
xAguilar, Luis E.
 Intro. by & ed. Marxism in Latin America.
 Temple U Pr.
Aguilar, Rodolfo J.
xAguilar, Rodolfo J.
 Systems Analysis & Design in Engineering,
 Architecture, Construction, & Planning. P-H.
Aguilera, Donna C.
xAguilera, Donna C.
 Review of Psychiatric Nursing. Mosby.
Aguilera, Robert. *see* Aguilera, Roberto.
Aguilera, Roberto.
xAguilera, Robert.
 Naturally Fractured Reservoirs. Pennwell Pub.
Aguirre, Adalberto.
xAguirre, Adalberto.
 An Experimental Sociolinguistic Study of
 Chicano Bilingualism. R & E Res Assoc.
Agulla, Juan C. *see* Agulla, Juan Carlos.
Agulla, Juan Carlos.
xAgulla, Juan C.

 Eclipse of an Aristocracy: An Investigation of
 the Ruling Elites of the City of Cordoba. U
 of Ala Pr.
Aguolu, Christian. *see* Aguolu, Christian Chukwunedu.
Aguolu, Christian Chukwunedu, 1940-
xAguolu, Christian.
 Nigerian Civil War, 1967-1970: An Annotated
 Bibliography. G K Hall.
Agus, Jacob B. *see* Agus, Jacob Bernard.
Agus, Jacob Bernard, 1911-
xAgus, Jacob B.
 The Evolution of Jewish Thought. Arno.
 High Priest of Rebirth: The Life, Times &
 Thought of Abraham Isaac Kuk. Bloch.
Agwani, M. S. *see* Agwani, Mohammed Shafi.
Agwani, Mohammed Shafi.
xAgwani, M. S.
 Communism in the Arab East. Asia.
Aharoni, Yair.
xAharoni, Yair.
 Markets, Planning & Development: The Private
 & Public Sectors in Economic Development.
 Ballinger Pub.
Ahearn, Daniel S.
xAhearn, Daniel S.
 Federal Reserve Policy Reappraised,
 1951-1959. Columbia U Pr.
Ahearn, Harry J.
xAhearn, Harry J.
 Ghetto Fire Fighter. Vantage.
Ahern, Dee Dee.
xAhern, Dee Dee.
 The Economics of Being a Woman. Macmillan.
Ahern, Emily M.
xAhern, Emily M.
 Cult of the Dead in a Chinese Village. Stanford
 U Pr.
Ahern, John F.
xAhern, John F.
 Ideas: A Handbook for Elementary Social
 Studies. Har-Row.
Ahern, William. *see* Ahern, William R.
Ahern, William R.
xAhern, William.
 Oil & the Outer Coastal Shelf: The Georges
 Bank Case. Ballinger Pub.
Aherne, Brian.
xAherne, Brian.
 A Dreadful Man. S&S.
Ahl, Frederick M.
xAhl, Frederick M.
 Lucan: An Introduction. Cornell U Pr.

Ahlberg, J. Harold.

xAhlberg, J. Harold.
 Theory of Splines & Their Applications. Acad
 Pr.

Ahlberg, Janet.

xAhlberg, Janet.
 illus. Burglar Bill. Penguin.
 illus. Burglar Bill. Greenwillow.
 illus. Cops & Robbers. Greenwillow.
 Each Peach Pear Plum: An I-Spy Story. Viking
 Pr.
 jt. auth. The Little Worm Book. Viking Pr.
 The Old Joke Book. Penguin.
 The Old Joke Book. Viking Pr.
Ahlbrandt, Roger S.
xAhlbrandt, Roger S.
 Neighborhood Revitalization: Theory &
 Practice. Lexington Bks.

Ahlstrand, Alan.
xAhlstrand, Alan.

 Capri Service Repair Handbook All Models,
 1970-1976. Clymer Pubns.
 Datsun Service-Repair Handbook L521, Pl521,
 Pl620 Pickups, 1968-1977. Clymer Pubns.
 Triumph Service-Repair Handbook: TR 7
 Series, 1975-1977. Clymer Pubns.
Ahlstrom, S. E. *see* Ahlstrom, Sydney E.
Ahlstrom, Sydney E.
xAhlstrom, S. E.
 Religious History of the American People.
 Doubleday.
 A Religious History of the American People.
 Yale U Pr.
xAhlstrom, Sydney E.
 ed. Theology in America: The Major Protestant
 Voices from Puritanism to Neo-Orthodoxy.
 Bobbs.
Ahlum, Carol.
xAhlum, Carol.
 ed. High School Feminist Studies. Feminist Pr.
Ahluwalia, H. P. *see* Ahluwalia, H. P. S.
Ahluwalia, H. P. S.
xAhluwalia, H. P.
 Higher Than Everest: Memoirs of a
 Mountaineer. Intl Bk Dist.
Ahmad, Feroz.
xAhmad, Feroz.
 The Turkish Experiment in Democracy: 1950
 to 1975. Westview.
Ahmad, Imtiaz, 1940-
xAhmad, Imtiaz.
 ed. Caste & Social Stratification Among
 Muslims. South Asia Bks.
Ahmad, Jaleel.
xAhmad, Jaleel.
 Import Substitution, Trade & Development. Jai
 Pr.
Ahmad, Qazi. *see* Ahmad, Qazi Shakil.
Ahmad, Qazi Shakil, 1932-
xAhmad, Qazi.
 Indian Cities: Characteristics & Correlates. U
 Chicago Dept Geog.
Ahmad, Saghir, 1936-1971
xAhmad, Saghir.
 Class & Power in a Punjabi Village. Monthly
 Rev.
Ahmad, Yusaf J. *see* Ahmad, Yusuf J.
Ahmad, Yusuf J.
xAhmad, Yusuf J.
 Absorptive Capacity of the Egyptian Economy:
 An Examination of Problems & Prospects.
 OECD.
Ahmadjian, Vernon.
xAhmadjian, Vernon.
 Flowering Plants of Massachusetts. U of Mass
 Pr.
 ed. The Lichens. Acad Pr.
Ahmann, J. Stanley.
xAhmann, J. Stanley.
 Measuring & Evaluating Educational
 Achievement. Allyn.
xAhmann, Stanley.
 How Much Are Our Young People Learning?:
 The Story of the National Assessment. Phi
 Delta Kappa.
Ahmann, Stanley. *see* Ahmann, J. Stanley.
Ahmed. *see* Ahmed, Paul I.
Ahmed, Mukhtar.
xAhmed, Mukhtar.
 Coloring of Plastics: Theory & Practice. Van
 Nos Reinhold.
Ahmed, N. *see* Ahmed, Nasir.
Ahmed, Nasir.
xAhmed, N.
 Orthogonal Transforms for Digital Signal
 Processing. Springer-Verlag.
Ahmed, Paul I.
xAhmed.

ed. Toward a New Definition of Health:
Psychosocial Dimensions. Plenum Pub.
Ahmed, S. Basheer.
xAhmed, S. Basheer.
Nuclear Fuel & Energy Policy. Lexington Bks.
Ahn, Michael.
xAhn, Michael.
Industrial Bibliography. Urban Land.
Ahnebrink, Lars.
xAhnebrink, Lars.
The Influence of Emile Zola on Frank Norris.
Arden Lib.
The Influence of Emile Zola on Frank Norris.
Folcroft.
Ahnefeld, F. W. *see* Ahnefeld, Friedrich Wilhelm.
Ahnefeld, Friedrich Wilhelm.
xAhnefeld, F. W.
ed. Parenteral Nutrition. Springer-Verlag.
Aho, Alfred. *see* Aho, Alfred V.
Aho, Alfred V.
xAho, Alfred.
The Design & Analysis of Computer
Algorithms. A-W.
xAho, Alfred V.
Principles of Compiler Design. A-W.
Theory of Parsing, Translation, & Compiling.
P-H.
Aho, James A. *see* Aho, James Alfred.
Aho, James Alfred, 1942-
xAho, James A.
German Realpolitik & American Sociology: An
Inquiry into the Sources & the Political
Significance of the Sociology of Conflict.
Bucknell U Pr.
Aho, Jennifer J.
xAho, Jennifer J.
jt. auth. Learning About Sex: A Guide for
Children & Their Parents. HR&W.
Ahokas, Jaakko, 1923-
xAhokas, Jaakko.
A History of Finnish Literature. Mouton.
Ahrendt, Kenneth M.
xAhrendt, Kenneth M.
Community College Reading Programs. Intl
Reading.
Ahrens, Michael.
xAhrens, Michael.
Activities for Intellectually Handicapped
Children. Intl Pubns Serv.
Ahsen, Akhter.
xAhsen, Akhter.
Eidetic Parents Test & Analysis. Brandon Hse.
Ahuja, Savitri.
xAhuja, Savitri.
Savitri's Way to Perfect Fitness Through Hatha
Yoga. S&S.
AIA Journal.
xAIA Journal.
New American Architecture. McGraw.
Aichele, Douglas B.
xAichele, Douglas B.
Readings in Secondary School Mathematics.
Prindle.
Aichinger, Ilse.
xAichinger, Ilse.
Bound Man, & Other Stories. Arno.
Aichinger, Peter, 1933-
xAichinger, Peter.
The American Soldier in Fiction,1880-1963: A
History of Attitudes Toward Warfare & the
Military Establishment. Iowa St U Pr.
Earle Birney. Twayne.
Aidala, Joseph B.
xAidala, Joseph B.
Transients in Electric Circuits. P-H.
Aiello, J. R. *see* Aiello, John R.
Aiello, John R.
xAiello, J. R.

ed. Residential Crowding & Design. Plenum
Pub.
Aigner, D. J. *see* Aigner, Dennis J.
Aigner, Dennis J.
xAigner, D. J.
ed. Latent Variables in Socio-Economic
Models. Elsevier.
xAigner, Dennis J.
Principles of Statistical Decision Making.
Macmillan.
Aigner, M. *see* Aigner, Martin.
Aigner, Martin, 1942-
xAigner, M.
Combinatorial Theory. Springer-Verlag.
Aihara, Cornellia.
xAihara, Cornellia.
The Calendar Cookbook. G Ohsawa.
Aihe, D. O.
xAihe, D. O.
Cases & Materials on Constitutional Law in
Nigeria. Oxford U Pr.
Aikat, Amulyachandra.
xAikat, Amulyachandra.
On the Poetry of Matthew Arnold, Robert
Browning & Rabindranath Tagore. Arden
Lib.
On the Poetry of Matthew Arnold, Robert
Browning & Rabindranath Tagore. Folcroft.
Aikawa, Jerry K. *see* Aikawa, Jerry Kazuo.
Aikawa, Jerry Kazuo.
xAikawa, Jerry K.
Computerizing a Clinical Laboratory. C C
Thomas.
Relationship of Magnesium to Disease in
Domestic Animals & in Humans. C C
Thomas.
Aiken, Conrad. *see* Aiken, Conrad Potter.
Aiken, Conrad P. *see* Aiken, Conrad Potter.
Aiken, Conrad Potter, 1889-
xAiken, Conrad.
Gehenna. Folcroft.
Gehenna. Porter.
Turns & Movies & Other Tales in Verse.
Arden Lib.
Turns & Movies & Other Tales in Verse.
Folcroft.
xAiken, Conrad P.
Collected Poems. Oxford U Pr.
Ushant: An Essay. Oxford U Pr.
Aiken, Eula.
xAiken, Eula.
The Different Student. Davis Co.
Aiken, Henry D. *see* Aiken, Henry David.
Aiken, Henry David, 1912-
xAiken, Henry D.
Reason & Conduct: New Bearings in Moral
Philosophy. Greenwood.
Aiken, Irene.
xAiken, Irene.
Daddy, Come Home. Victor Bks.
Aiken, Joan.
xAiken, Joan.
Arabel's Raven. Doubleday.
Castle Barebane. Viking Pr.
Cluster of Separate Sparks. Doubleday.
A Cluster of Separate Sparks. PB.
The Crystal Crow. PB.
Dark Interval. PB.
Died on a Rainy Sunday. HR&W.
The Faithless Lollybird. Doubleday.
The Five-Minute Marriage. Warner Bks.
Go Saddle the Sea. Doubleday.
Last Movement. Doubleday.
Last Movement. G K Hall.
The Last Movement. Warner Bks.
The Silence of Herondale. PB.
Aiken, Joyce.
xAiken, Joyce.

The Portable Needlepoint Boutique. Taplinger.
The Total Tote Bag Book: Designer Totes to
Craft & Carry. Taplinger.
Aiken, Lewis R., 1931-
xAiken, Lewis R.
Later Life. Saunders.
Psychological Testing & Assessment. Allyn.
Aiken, Riley.
xAiken, Riley.
Mexican Folktales from the Borderland. SMU
Press.
Aiken, William.
xAiken, William.
ed. Whose Child?: Children's Rights, Parental
Authority, & State Power. Littlefield.
ed. Whose Child?: Children's Rights, Parental
Authority, & State Power. Rowman.
World Hunger & Moral Obligation. P-H.
Aikens, C. Melvin.
xAikens, C. Melvin.
Hogup Cave. AMS Pr.
Hogup Cave. U of Utah Pr.
Aikin, J. *see* Aikin, John.
Aikin, John, 1747-1822
xAikin, J.
A Description of the Country from Thirty to
Forty Miles Round Manchester 1795. David
& Charles.
Description of the Country from Thirty to
Forty Miles Round Manchester. Kelley.
Aikman, Lonnelle.
xAikman, Lonnelle.
Nature's Healing Arts: From Folk Medicine to
Modern Drugs. Natl Geog.
Ainger, Alfred, 1837-1904
xAinger, Alfred.
Charles Lamb. AMS Pr.
Charles Lamb. Arden Lib.
Charles Lamb. R West.
Charles Lamb. Scholarly.
Crabbe. Darby Bks.
Crabbe. Gale.
Crabbe. R West.
Lectures & Essays. AMS Pr.
Ainscow, Mel.
xAinscow, Mel.
Preventing Classroom Failure: An Objectives
Approach. Wiley.
Ainslie, Alan C.
xAinslie, Alan C.
Practical Electronic Project Building. Hayden.
Ainslie, Tom.
xAinslie, Tom.
Ainslie's Complete Guide to Thoroughbred
Racing. S&S.
Ainslie's Complete Guide to Thoroughbred
Racing. Trident.
Ainslie's Complete Hoyle. S&S.
Ainslie's Encyclopedia of Thoroughbred
Handicapping. Morrow.
Compleat Horseplayer. Trident.
How to Gamble in a Casino: The Most Fun at
the Least Risk. Morrow.
Ainsworth, Barbara A.
xAinsworth, Barbara A.
Education Through Travel. Nelson-Hall.
Ainsworth, Geoffrey C. *see* Ainsworth, Geoffrey Clough.
Ainsworth, Geoffrey Clough.
xAinsworth, Geoffrey C.
ed. Fungi: An Advanced Treatise. Acad Pr.
Ainsworth, Ralph M., 1901-
xAinsworth, Ralph M.
Basic Principles of Successful Commodity
Futures Speculation. Inst Econ Finan.
Ainsworth, Ruth.
xAinsworth, Ruth.
Talking Rock. Andre Deutsch.
Ainsworth, Stanley.
xAinsworth, Stanley.

Steady-State Enzyme Kinetics. Univ Park.
Ainsworth, Stanley. *see* Ainsworth, Stanley Humphreys.
Ainsworth, Stanley Humphreys, 1913-
   xAinsworth, Stanley.
      Galloping Sounds. Expression.
      Stuttering: What It Is & What to Do About It.
       Cliffs.
Ainsworth, Thomas H.
   xAinsworth, Thomas H.
      Quality Assurance in Long Term Care. Aspen
       Systems.
Ainsworth, William H. *see* Ainsworth, William Harrison.
Ainsworth, William Harrison, 1805-1882
   xAinsworth, William H.
      Auriol: Or, the Elixir of Life. Arno.
Ainsztein, Reuben.
   xAinsztein, Reuben.
      Warsaw Ghetto Revolt. Schocken.
AIP & American Academy of Arts & Sciences Joint
   Conference, Brookline, Mass., 1967 & 1969. *see*
   Exploratory Conference on the History of Nuclear
   Physics, 1st, 2nd, Brookline, Mass., 1967, 1969.
AIP Conference. *see* International Conference on High
   Energy Collisions, 5th, Stony Brook, N.Y., 1973.
AIP Conference, Corning, N.Y., 1971. *see* Thermal
   Expansion Symposium, Corning, N.Y., 1971.
AIP Conference, Philadelphia 1974. *see* International
   Conference on Neutrino Physics and Astrophysics,
   4th, Downington, Pa, 1974.
AIP Conference, Princeton, 1970. *see* Symposium on
   Feedback and Dynamic Control of Plasmas, Princeton,
   N.J., 1970.
AIP Conference, Univ. of British Columbia, Vancouver,
   1972. *see* International Cyclotron Conference, 6th,
   Vancouver, B.C.1972.
AIP Conference, Univ. of California at Irvine, Dec.,
   1971 *see* Conference on Particle Physics, University
   of California, Irvine, 1971.
AIP Conference, Univ. of Rochester, 1971. *see* Rochester
   Conference on Superconductivity in D- and F-Band
   Metals, 1976.
AIP Conference, Yorktown Heights. *see* International
   Conference on Tetrahedrally Bonded Amorphous
   Semiconductors, Yorktown Heights, N.Y., 1974.
AIP International Conf., Williamsburg, 1976. *see*
   International Conference on Structure and Excitations
   of Amorphous Solids, Williamsburg, Va., 1976.
Air Conditioning & Refrigeration Institute. *see*
   Air-Conditioning and Refrigeration Institute.
Airasian, Peter W.
   xAirasian, Peter W.
      Minimal Competency Testing. Educ Tech
       Pubns.
Air-Conditioning and Refrigeration Institute.
   xAir Conditioning & Refrigeration Institute.
      Refrigeration & Air Conditioning. P-H.
Aird, Catherine, Pseud.
   xAird, Catherine.
      Parting Breath. Doubleday.
Airola, P. *see* Airola, Paavo O.
Airola, Paavo O.
   xAirola, P.
      There Is a Cure for Arthritis. P-H.
Aisenberg, Alan C. *see* Aisenberg, Alan Clifford.
Aisenberg, Alan Clifford, 1926-
   xAisenberg, Alan C.
      Glycolysis & Respiration of Tumors. Acad Pr.
Aissen, Judith, 1948-
   xAissen, Judith.
      The Syntax of Causative Constructions.
       Garland Pub.
Aistrop, Jack. *see* Aistrop, Jack Bentley.
Aistrop, Jack Bentley, 1916-
   xAistrop, Jack.
      Enjoying Pets. Vanguard.
Aitchison, J. *see* Aitchison, John.
Aitchison, Jean.
   xAitchison, Jean.

The Articulate Mammal: An Introduction to
   Psycholinguistics. McGraw.
The Articulate Mammal: An Introduction to
   Psycholinguistics. Universe.
Aitchison, John.
   xAitchison, J.
      Statistical Prediction Analysis. Cambridge U
       Pr.
   xAitchison, John.
      Choice Against Chance: An Introduction to
       Statistical Decision Theory. A-W.
Aitken, Amy.
   xAitken, Amy.
      illus. Ruby!. Bradbury Pr.
Aitken, George A. *see* Aitken, George Atherton.
Aitken, George Atherton, 1860-1917
   xAitken, George A.
      Life of Richard Steele. Greenwood.
      Life of Richard Steele. Haskell.
      The Life of Richard Steele. R West.
Aitken, Hannah.
   xAitken, Hannah.
      ed. A Forgotten Heritage: Original Folk Tales
       of Lowland Scotland. Rowman.
Aitken, Thomas, 1910-
   xAitken, Thomas.
      The Multinational Man: The Role of the
       Manager Abroad. Halsted Pr.
Aitken-Swan, Jean.
   xAitken-Swan, Jean.
      Fertility Control & the Medical Profession.
       Biblio Dist.
Aiton, Arthur S. *see* Aiton, Arthur Scott.
Aiton, Arthur Scott, 1894-1955
   xAiton, Arthur S.
      Antonio De Mendoza, First Viceroy of New
       Spain. Russell.
Ajami, Riad A.
   xAjami, Riad A.
      Arab Response to Multinationals. Praeger.
Ajar, Emile.
   xAjar, Emile.
      Madame Rosa. Berkley Pub.
Ajaya, Swami, 1940-
   xAjaya, Swami.
      ed. Foundations of Eastern & Western
       Psychology. Himalayan Intl Inst.
Ajaya, Swami. *see* Ajaya.
Ajayi, J. F. *see* Ajayi, J. F. Ade.
Ajayi, J. F. Ade.
   xAjayi, J. F.
      ed. History of West Africa. Columbia U Pr.
Ajdukiewicz, K. *see* Ajdukiewicz, Kazimierz.
Ajdukiewicz, Kazimierz.
   xAjdukiewicz, K.
      Problems & Theories of Philosophy. Cambridge
       U Pr.
Ajilvsgi, Geyata, 1933-
   xAjilvsgi, Geyata.
      Wild Flowers of the Big Thicket, East Texas, &
       Western Louisiana. Tex A&M Univ Pr.
Akademia Nauk USSR. *see* Akademiia Nauk Sssr.
Akademiia Nauk SSSR.
   xAkademia Nauk USSR.
      Pacific: Russian Scientific Investigations.
       Greenwood.
   xAkademiia Nauk SSSR.
      Sovetsko-Kitaiskie Otnosheniia, Nineteen
       Seventeen to Nineteen Fifty-Seven: Sbornik
       Dokumentov. AMS Pr.
Akademiia Nauk SSSR. Matematicheskii Institut.
   xSteklov Institute of Mathematics, No. 112.
      Collection of Articles, I: Proceedings. Am
       Math.
Akcasu, Ziya.
   xAkcasu, Ziya.
      Mathematical Methods in Nuclear Reactor
       Dynamics. Acad Pr.
Akehurst, Michael. *see* Akehurst, Michael Barton.

Akehurst, Michael Barton.
   xAkehurst, Michael.
      A Modern Introduction to International Law.
       Allen Unwin.
Akers, Alan B. *see* Akers, Alan Burt.
Akers, Alan Burt.
   xAkers, Alan B.

      The Captive Scorpio. DAW Bks.

      Prince of Scorpio. DAW Bks.
      The Suns of Scorpio. DAW Bks.

      Swordships of Scorpio. DAW Bks.

Akers, Herbert. *see* Akers, Herbert W.
Akers, Herbert W.
   xAkers, Herbert.
      Modern Mailroom Management. McGraw.
Akers, Ronald L.
   xAkers, Ronald L.
      Deviant Behavior: A Social Learning
       Approach. Wadsworth Pub.
      Law & Control in Society. P-H.
Akert, K. *see* Akert, Konrad.
Akert, Konrad.
   xAkert, K.
      ed. Mechanisms of Synaptic Transmission.
       Elsevier.
Akhavi, Shahrough, 1940-
   xAkhavi, Shahrough.
      Religion & Politics in Contemporary Iran:
       Clergy-State Relations in the Pahlavi Period.
       State U NY Pr.
Akhiezer, A. I. *see* Akhiezer, Aleksandr Il'Ich.
Akhiezer, Aleksandr Il'Ich, 1911-
   xAkhiezer, A. I.
      Collective Oscillations in a Plasma. Pergamon.
Akhiezer, N. I. *see* Akhiezer, Naum Il'Ich.
Akhiezer, Naum Il'Ich, 1901-
   xAkhiezer, N. I.
      Theory of Approximation. Ungar.
Akhmanova, O. *see* Akhmanova, Olga Sergeevna.
Akhmanova, O. S.
   xAkhmanova, O. S.
      Exact Methods in Linguistic Research. U of
       Cal Pr.
Akhmanova, Olga Sergeevna.
   xAkhmanova, O.
      Optimization of Natural Communication
       Systems. Mouton.
Akhmatova, Anna. *see* Akhmatova, Anna Andreevna.
Akhmatova, Anna Andreevna.
   xAkhmatova, Anna.
      Way of All Earth. Ohio U Pr.
      Way of All the Earth. Ohio U Pr.
Akhrem, A. A. *see* Akhrem, Afanasii Andreevich.
Akhrem, Afanasii Andreevich.
   xAkhrem, A. A.
      Total Steroid Synthesis. Plenum Pub.
Aki, Keiiti.
   xAki, Keiiti.
      Quantitative Seismology: Theory & Methods.
       W H Freeman.
Akin, E. *see* Akin, Ethan.
Akin, Ethan, 1946-
   xAkin, E.
      The Geometry of Population Genetics.
       Springer-Verlag.
Akin, Richard H.
   xAkin, Richard H.
      The Private Investigator's Basic Manual. C C
       Thomas.
Akin, Ronald E.
   xAkin, Ronald E.
      ed. The Book of Festivals in the Midwest, 1980
       & 1981. Icarus.
Akins. *see* Akins, W. R.
Akins, W. R.
   xAkins.

The Crossing. Braziller.
Albert, Arthur. *see* Albert, Arthur E.
Albert, Arthur E.
  xAlbert, Arthur.
    Regression & the Moore-Penrose
      Pseudo-Inverse. Acad Pr.
Albert, Burton.
  xAlbert, Burton.
    Codes for Kids. A Whitman.
    More Codes for Kids. A Whitman.
    Sharks & Whales. Platt.
Albert, Daniel M.
  xAlbert, Daniel M.
    ed. Foundations of Ophthalmic Pathology.
      ACC.
Albert, Herman W.
  xAlbert, Herman W.
    Odyssey of a Desert Prospector. U of Okla Pr.
Albert, Kenneth J., 1943-
  xAlbert, Kenneth J.
    Handbook of Business Problem Solving.
      McGraw.
    How to Be Your Own Management
      Consultant. McGraw.
    How to Pick the Right Small Business
      Opportunity: The Key to Success in Your
      Own Business. McGraw.
Albert, Martin L.
  xAlbert, Martin L.
    The Bilingual Brain: Neuropsychological &
      Neurolinguistic Aspects of Bilingualism. Acad
      Pr.
Albert, Marvin H.
  xAlbert, Marvin H.
    The Dark Goddess. Doubleday.
Alberti, Leon B. *see* Alberti, Leone Battista.
Alberti, Leone B. *see* Alberti, Leone Battista.
Alberti, Leone Battista.
  xAlberti, Leon B.
    On Painting. Yale U Pr.
  xAlberti, Leone B.
    On Painting. Greenwood.
Alberti, R. E. *see* Alberti, Robert E.
Alberti, Robert E.
  xAlberti, R. E.
    Stand up, Speak Out, Talk Back!. PB.
  xAlberti, Robert E.
    ed. Assertiveness: Innovations, Applications,
      Issues. Impact Pubs Cal.
Albertson, Dean, 1920-
  xAlbertson, Dean.
    ed. Eisenhower As President. Hill & Wang.
Albertson, Ralph, 1866-1951
  xAlbertson, Ralph.
    A Survey of Mutualistic Communities in
      America. AMS Pr.
Alberty, Robert A.
  xAlberty, Robert A.
    Physical Chemistry. Wiley.
Albin, Peter. *see* Albin, Peter S.
Albin, Peter S.
  xAlbin, Peter.
    The Analysis of Complex Socio-Economic
      Systems. Lexington Bks.
    Progress Without Poverty: Socially Responsible
      Economic Growth. Basic.
Albini, Joseph L.
  xAlbini, Joseph L.
    American Mafia: Genesis of a Legend.
      Irvington.
Albinski, Henry S. *see* Albinski, Henry Stephen.
Albinski, Henry Stephen.
  xAlbinski, Henry S.
    Australian Policies & Attitudes Toward China.
      Princeton U Pr.
    Canadian & Australian Politics in Comparative
      Perspective. Oxford U Pr.
    Politics & Foreign Policy in Australia: The
      Impact of Vietnam & Conscription. Duke.
Albion, Robert G. *see* Albion, Robert Greenhalgh.

Albion, Robert Greenhalgh, 1896-
  xAlbion, Robert G.
    Introduction to Military History. AMS Pr.
Albran, Kehlog.
  xAlbran, Kehlog.
    The Profit. Price Stern.
Albrecht, Bob L. *see* Albrecht, Robert L.
Albrecht, Gary L.
  xAlbrecht, Gary L.
    Health, Illness, & Medicine: A Reader in
      Medical Sociology. Rand.
    ed. The Sociology of Physical Disability &
      Rehabilitation. U of Pittsburgh Pr.
Albrecht, Gene H. *see* Albrecht, Gene Harrison.
Albrecht, Gene Harrison.
  xAlbrecht, Gene H.
    The Craniofacial Morphology of the Sulawesi
      Macaques: Multivariate Analysis As a Tool in
      Systematics. S Karger.
Albrecht, K. *see* Albrecht, Karl G.
Albrecht, Karl. *see* Albrecht, Karl G.
Albrecht, Karl G.
  xAlbrecht, K.
    Brainpower: Learn to Improve Your Thinking
      Skills. P-H.
  xAlbrecht, Karl.
    Stress & the Manager: Making It Work for
      You. P-H.
    Successful Management by Objectives: An
      Action Manual. P-H.
Albrecht, Lillie (Vanderveer).
  xAlbrecht, Lillie V.
    Spinning Wheel Secret. Hastings.
    Susanna's Candlestick. Hastings.
Albrecht, Lillie V. *see* Albrecht, Lillie (Vanderveer).
Albrecht, R. L. *see* Albrecht, Robert L.
Albrecht, Robert C.
  xAlbrecht, Robert C.
    ed. World of Short Fiction. Free Pr.
Albrecht, Robert L.
  xAlbrecht, Bob L.
    Atari Basic. Wiley.
  xAlbrecht, R. L.
    Basic for Home Computers. Wiley.
Albrecht, Ulrich, 1941-
  xAlbrecht, Ulrich.
    A Short Research Guide to Arms & Armed
      Forces. Facts on File.
Albrecht, W. *see* Albrecht, William P.
Albrecht, W. P. *see* Albrecht, William Price.
Albrecht, William P.
  xAlbrecht, W.
    Macroeconomic Principles. P-H.
  xAlbrecht, William P.
    Economics. P-H.
    Microeconomic Principles. P-H.
Albrecht, William Price, 1907-
  xAlbrecht, W. P.
    The Sublime Pleasures of Tragedy: A Study of
      Critical Theory from Dennis to Keats.
      Regents Pr Ks.
Albrecht-Carrie, Rene, 1904-
  xAlbrecht-Carrie, Rene.
    ed. Concert of Europe. Walker & Co.
    France, Europe & the Two World Wars.
      Greenwood.
Albright, David E.
  xAlbright, David E.
    Communism & Political Systems in Western
      Europe. Westview.
    ed. Communism in Africa. Ind U Pr.
Albright, Gifford H.
  xAlbright, Gifford H.
    ed. Planning Atomic Shelters: Guidebook for
      Architects & Engineers. Pa St U Pr.
Albright, Hardie, 1903-
  xAlbright, Hardie.
    Stage Direction in Transition. Dickenson.
Albright, Horace M. *see* Albright, Horace Marden.

Albright, Horace Marden.
  xAlbright, Horace M.
    Oh, Ranger!. Scholars Ref Lib.
Albright, James.
  xAlbright, James A.
    ed. The Scientific Basis of Orthopaedics. ACC.
Albright, James A. *see* Albright, James.
Albright, Lyle F. *see* Albright, Lyle Frederick.
Albright, Rod. *see* Albright, Rodney.
Albright, William F. *see* Albright, William Foxwell.
Albright-Knox Art Gallery.
  xAlbright-Knox Art Gallery.
    Painting & Sculpture from Antiquity to
      Nineteen Forty-Two. Buffalo Acad.
    Thirty Seventh Western New York Exhibition.
      Buffalo Acad.
Albright, Lyle Frederick.
  xAlbright, Lyle F.
    ed. Industrial & Laboratory Alkylations. Am
      Chemical.
    Processes for Major Addition-Type Plastics &
      Their Monomers. Krieger.
    Processes for Major Addition-Type Plastics &
      Their Monomers. McGraw.
Albright, Rodney.
  xAlbright, Rod.
    Walks in the Great Smokies. East Woods.
Albright, William Foxwell, 1891-
  xAlbright, William F.
    Archaeology of Palestine. Peter Smith.
Albury, Paul.
  xAlbury, Paul.
    The Story of the Bahamas. St Martin.
Albus, James S. *see* Albus, James Sacra.
Albus, James Sacra.
  xAlbus, James S.
    Peoples' Capitalism: The Economics of the
      Robot Revolution. New World Bks.
Alcaly, Roger. *see* Alcaly, Roger E.
Alcaly, Roger E.
  xAlcaly, Roger.
    The Fiscal Crisis of American Cities: Essays on
      the Political Economy of Urban America
      with Special Reference to New York.
      Random.
Alcaraz, Ramon.
  xAlcaraz, Ramon.
    The Other Side: Or Notes for the History of
      the War Between Mexico & the United
      States. Scholarly.
Alchourron, C. E. *see* Alchourron, Carlos E.
Alchourron, Carlos E.
  xAlchourron, C. E.
    Normative Systems. Springer-Verlag.
Alcock, Antony. *see* Alcock, Antony Evelyn.
Alcock, Antony E. *see* Alcock, Antony Evelyn.
Alcock, Antony Evelyn.
  xAlcock, Antony.
    History of the International Labor
      Organization. Octagon.
  xAlcock, Antony E.
    ed. The Future of Cultural Minorities. St
      Martin.
Alcock, L. *see* Alcock, Leslie.
Alcock, Leslie.
  xAlcock, L.
    Arthur's Britain: History & Archaeology AD
      367-634. St Martin.
Alcock, Randal H. *see* Alcock, Randal Hibbert.
Alcock, Randal Hibbert, 1833-1885
  xAlcock, Randal H.
    Botanical Names for English Readers. Gale.
Alcock, Rutherford, Sir, 1809-1897
  xAlcock, Rutherford.
    Capital of the Tycoon: A Narrative of a Three
      Years' Residence in Japan. Greenwood.
Alcorn, John, 1923-
  xAlcorn, John.

The Nature Novel from Hardy to Lawrence.
Columbia U Pr.

Alcosser, Edward.
xAlcosser, Edward.
How to Build a Working Digital Computer.
Hayden.

Alcosser, Murray, 1937-
xAlcosser, Murray.
Sweets. Abrams.

Alcott, A. Bronson.
xAlcott, A. Bronson.
Concord Days. Saifer.

Alcott, A. Bronson. *see* Alcott, Amos Bronson.

Alcott, Amos B. *see* Alcott, Amos Bronson.

Alcott, Amos Bronson, 1799-1888
xAlcott, A. Bronson.
Sonnets & Canzonets. Norwood Edns.
Sonnets & Canzonets. Saifer.
xAlcott, Amos B.
Ralph Waldo Emerson: An Estimate of His
Character & Genius, in Prose & Verse.
Haskell.
Sonnets & Canzonets. AMS Pr.

Alcott, L. M. *see* Alcott, Louisa May.

Alcott, Louisa M. *see* Alcott, Louisa May.

Alcott, Louisa May, 1832-1888
xAlcott, L. M.
Little Women. Western Pub.
xAlcott, Louisa M.
Diana & Persis. Arno.
Eight Cousins. Western Pub.
Eight Cousins. G&D.
Eight Cousins. Little.
Flower Fables. Scholarly.
Flower Fables. Core Collection.
Garland for Girls. G&D.
Little Women. Biblio Dist.
Little Women. Dutton.
Little Women. Gordon Pr.
Little Women. Hippocrene Bks.
Little Women. Macmillan.
Little Women. Saphrograph.
Little Women. G&D.
Little Women. G&D.
Little Women. Penguin.
Little Women. Philomel.
Little Women. Raintree Child.
Little Women. Schol Bk Serv.
Little Women. Airmont.
Little Women. Macmillan.
Little Women. Little.
Louisa May Alcott: Her Life Letters &
Journals. R West.
An Old-Fashioned Thanksgiving. Lippincott.
Under the Lilacs. Little.
Work: A Story of Experience. Scholarly.
xAlcott, Louisa May.
Work: A Story of Experience. Arno.

Alcott, William A. *see* Alcott, William Andrus.

Alcott, William Andrus, 1798-1859
xAlcott, William A.
Confessions of a School Master. Arno.

Alcouffe, Daniel.
xAlcouffe, Daniel.
Restorer's Handbook of Furniture. Van Nos
Reinhold.

Ald, Roy.
xAld, Roy.
Side Dish Cookbook. S&S.

Alda, Frances.
xAlda, Frances.
Men, Women & Tenors. AMS Pr.
Men, Women & Tenors. Arno.

Aldag, Ramon J.
xAldag, Ramon J.
Task Design & Employee Motivation. Scott F.

Aldan, Daisy.
xAldan, Daisy.

Between High Tides: Poems. Folder Edns.
Love Poems of Daisy Aldan. Barlenmir.

Aldcroft, Derek H. *see* Aldcroft, Derek Howard.

Aldcroft, Derek Howard.
xAldcroft, Derek H.
Studies in British Transport History,
1870-1970. David & Charles.

Alden, Douglas W. *see* Alden, Douglas William.

Alden, Douglas William, 1912-
xAlden, Douglas W.
Marcel Proust & His French Critics. Russell.

Alden, Edmund K.
xAlden, Edmund K.
The World's Representative Assemblies of
to-Day: A Study in Comparative Legislation.
AMS Pr.

Alden, J. *see* Alden, Jeremy.

Alden, Jay.
xAlden, Jay.
Backward Chaining: Teaching Task
Performance. Educ Tech Pubns.

Alden, Jeremy.
xAlden, J.
Regional Planning: A Comprehensive View.
Halsted Pr.

Alden, John. *see* Alden, John Richard.

Alden, John R. *see* Alden, John Richard.

Alden, John Richard, 1908-
xAlden, John.
The First South. Peter Smith.
xAlden, John R.
First South. La State U Pr.
History of the American Revolution. Knopf.
South in the Revolution, 1763-1789. La State
U Pr.
The South in the Revolution, 1763-1819. La
State U Pr.

Alden, Raymond M. *see* Alden, Raymond Macdonald.

Alden, Raymond Macdonald, 1873-1924
xAlden, Raymond M.
Alfred Tennyson, How to Know Him. Folcroft.

Alder, Henry L.
xAlder, Henry L.
Introduction to Probability & Statistics. W H
Freeman.

Alder, Kurt.
xAlder, Kurt.
ed. Coulomb Excitation: A Collection of
Reprints. Acad Pr.

Alderfer, Clayton. *see* Alderfer, Clayton P.

Alderfer, Clayton P.
xAlderfer, Clayton.
Learning from Changing: Organizational
Diagnosis & Development. Sage.
xAlderfer, Clayton P.
Existence, Relatedness & Growth: Human
Needs in Organizational Settings. Free Pr.

Alderfer, Helen.
xAlderfer, Helen.
ed. Farthing in Her Hand: Stewardship for
Women. Herald Pr.

Alderman, Clifford L. *see* Alderman, Clifford Lindsey.

Alderman, Clifford Lindsey.
xAlderman, Clifford L.
Annie Oakley & the World of Her Time.
Macmillan.
Colonists for Sale: The Story of Indentured
Servants in America. Macmillan.
The Colony of Connecticut. Watts.
The Dark Eagle: The Story of Benedict Arnold.
Macmillan.
Devil's Shadow: The Story of Witchcraft in
Massachusetts. Messner.
Rhode Island Colony. Macmillan.
Story of the Thirteen Colonies. Random.
Symbols of Magic: Amulets & Talismans.
Messner.

Alderman, Harold.
xAlderman, Harold G.

Nietzsche's Gift. Ohio U Pr.

Alderman, Harold G. *see* Alderman, Harold.

Alderman, Joy.
xAlderman, Joy.
Renewed in Strength. Judson.

Alderman, Michael H.
xAlderman, Michael H.
ed. Hypertension: The Nurse's Role in
Ambulatory Care. Springer Pub.

Alderman, Paul R., Jr
xAlderman, Paul R.
God's Spotlight on Tomorrow: Seven Sevens
Concerning the Return of Christ. Loizeaux.

Alderman, R. B. *see* Alderman, Richard B.

Alderman, Richard B.
xAlderman, R. B.
Psychological Behavior in Sport. HR&W.

Alderman, Rosalie G. *see* Alderman, Rosalie Givens.

Alderman, Rosalie Givens.
xAlderman, Rosalie G.
Take Heart. Broadman.

Alderson, Frederick.
xAlderson, Frederick.
Inland Resorts & Spas of Britain. David &
Charles.

Alderson, George.
xAlderson, George.
How You Can Influence Congress: The
Complete Handbook for the Citizen Lobbyist.
Dutton.

Alderson, Michael.
xAlderson, Michael.
An Introduction to Epidemiology. PSG Pub.

Alderson, Wroe.
xAlderson, Wroe.
Marketing Behavior & Executive Action. Arno.

Alding, Peter.
xAlding, Peter.
Murder Is Suspected. Walker & Co.
Ransom Town. Walker & Co.

Aldington, Richard, 1892-1962
xAldington, Richard.
Balls, & Another Book for Suppression..
Folcroft.
D. H. Lawrence. Arden Lib.
D. H. Lawrence: A Complete List of His
Works, Together with a Critical Appreciation.
Folcroft.
D. H. Lawrence: An Indiscretion. Folcroft.
D. H. Lawrence: Portrait of a Genius But--.
Macmillan.
Death of a Hero: A Novel. Scholarly.
Fifty Romance Lyric Poems. Folcroft.
Last Straws. Folcroft.
Literary Studies & Reviews. Arno.
A Passionate Prodigality: Letters to Alan Bird
from Richard Aldington, 1949-1962. NY Pub
Lib.

Aldis, Dorothy. *see* Aldis, Dorothy (Keeley).

Aldis, Dorothy (Keeley).
xAldis, Dorothy.
Nothing Is Impossible: The Story of Beatrix
Potter. Atheneum.

Aldis, Harry G. *see* Aldis, Harry Gidney.

Aldis, Harry Gidney, 1863-1919
xAldis, Harry G.
List of Books Printed in Scotland Before 1700:
Including Those Printed Furth of the Realm
for Scottish Booksellers, with Brief Notes on
the Printers & Stationers. B Franklin.

Aldiss, Brian.
xAldiss, Brian.
Galaxies Like Grains of Sand. NAL.
xAldiss, Brian W.
Galaxies Like Grains of Sand. Gregg.

Aldiss, Brian. *see* Aldiss, Brian Wilson.

Aldiss, Brian W. *see* Aldiss, Brian Wilson.

Aldiss, Brian Wilson, 1925-
xAldiss, Brian.

Enemies of the System: A Tale of Homo
Uniformis. Har-Row.
Long Afternoon of Earth. NAL.
A Rude Awakening. Charter Bks.
Starswarm. NAL.
Who Can Replace a Man?. NAL.
xAldiss, Brian W.
Cryptozoic. Avon.
Frankenstein Unbound. Random.
Hothouse. Gregg.
A Rude Awakening. Random.
Starswarm. Gregg.
Aldous, Allan.
xAldous, Allan.
Bushfire. Abelard.
Aldous, Joan.
xAldous, Joan.
Family Careers: Developmental Change in
Families. Wiley.
Aldred, Cyril.
xAldred, Cyril.
Egypt to the End of the Old Kingdom.
McGraw.
Tutankhamun's Egypt. Scribner.
Aldred, Guy. *see* Aldred, Guy Alfred.
Aldred, Guy Alfred, 1886-1963
xAldred, Guy.
Bakunin. Haskell.
Aldrich, Arthur.
xAldrich, Arthur.
Flowers & Flowering Plants. Watts.
Aldrich, Bess S. *see* Aldrich, Bess Streeter.
Aldrich, Bess Streeter, 1881-1954
xAldrich, Bess S.
The Drum Goes Dead. Amereon Ltd.
A Song of Years. Amereon Ltd.
A White Bird Flying. Amereon Ltd.
Aldrich, Charles R. *see* Aldrich, Charles Roberts
Aldrich, Charles Roberts, 1877-1933
xAldrich, Charles R.
Primitive Mind & Modern Civilization. AMS
Pr.
The Primitive Mind & Modern Civilization.
Greenwood.
Aldrich, Ella V. *see* Aldrich, Ella Virginia.
Aldrich, Ella Virginia, 1902-
xAldrich, Ella V.
Using Books & Libraries. P-H.
Aldrich, Howard.
xAldrich, Howard.
Organizations & Environments. P-H.
Aldrich, Joe.
xAldrich, Joe.
Secrets to Inner Beauty. Vision Hse.
Aldrich, Peggy.
xAldrich, Peggy.
My First. Nordon Pubns.
Aldrich, Putnam.
xAldrich, Putnam.
Ornamentation in J. S. Bach's Organ Works.
Da Capo.
Aldrich, Richard S. *see* Aldrich, Richard Stoddard.
Aldrich, Richard Stoddard.
xAldrich, Richard S.
Gertrude Lawrence As Mrs. A: An Intimate
Biography of the Great Star. Greenwood.
Aldrich, Samuel R.
xAldrich, Samuel R.
Modern Corn Production. Thomson Pub CA.
Aldrich, Terry M. *see* Aldrich, Terry Mark.
Aldrich, Terry Mark.
xAldrich, Terry M.
Rates of Return on Investment in Technical
Education in the Ante-Bellum American
Economy. Arno.
Aldrich, Thomas B. *see* Aldrich, Thomas Bailey.
Aldrich, Thomas Bailey, 1836-1907
xAldrich, Thomas B.

Marjorie Daw & Other Stories. Arno.
Marjorie Daw & Other Stories. Somerset Pub.
Ponkapog Papers. Arno.
The Stillwater Tragedy. Irvington.
Aldridge. *see* Aldridge, Bill G.
Aldridge, Alan. *see* Aldridge, Alan E.
Aldridge, Alan E.
xAldridge, Alan.
Power, Authority & Restrictive Practices: A
Sociological Essay on Industrial Relations.
Biblio Dist.
Aldridge, Alfred O. *see* Aldridge, Alfred Owen.
Aldridge, Alfred Owen, 1915-
xAldridge, Alfred O.
Franklin & His French Contemporaries.
Greenwood.
xAldridge, Alfred Owen.
Franklin & his French Contemporaries. NYU
Pr.
Aldridge, Bill G.
xAldridge.
Mathematics for Physical Science. Merrill.
Aldridge, James.
xAldridge, James.
The Marvelous Mongolian. Little.
One Last Glimpse. Little.
Aldridge, Josephine H. *see* Aldridge, Josephine Haskell.
Aldridge, Josephine Haskell.
xAldridge, Josephine H.
Penny & a Periwinkle. Parnassus.
Aldridge, Melanie.
xAldridge, Melanie.
Paula's Feeling Angry. Childs World.
Aldridge, Meryl.
xAldridge, Meryl.
British New Towns: A Programme Without a
Policy. Routledge & Kegan.
Aldridge, Sarah
xAldridge, Sarah.
All True Lovers. Naiad Pr.
Cytherea's Breath. Naiad Pr.
The Latecomer. Naiad Pr.
Tottie: The Tale of the Sixties. Naiad Pr.
Aldwinckle, Russell. *see* Aldwinckle, Russell Foster.
Aldwinckle, Russell Foster.
xAldwinckle, Russell.
More Than Man: A Study in Christology.
Eerdmans.
Aleamoni, Laurence M.
xAleamoni, Lawrence A.
Methods of Implementing College Placement &
Exemption Programs. College Bd.
Aleamoni, Lawrence A. *see* Aleamoni, Laurence M.
Aledort, L. M. *see* Aledort, Louis M.
Aledort, Louis M.
xAledort, L. M.
Outpatient Medicine. Raven.
Aleksander, Igor.
xAleksander, Igor.
Automata Theory: An Engineering Approach.
Crane-Russak Co.
Alekseev, V. P. *see* Alekseev, Valerii Pavlovich.
Alekseev, Valerii Pavlovich.
xAlekseev, V. P.
Contributions to the Archaeology of Armenia.
AMS Pr.
Alemasov, V. E. *see* Alemasov, Viacheslav Evgenevich.
Alemasov, Viacheslav Evgenevich.
xAlemasov, V. E.
Thermodynamic & Thermophysical Properties
of Combustion Products, Vol. 3: Oxygen &
Air Based Propellants. Intl Schol Bk Serv.
Alessandra, Anthony J.
xAlessandra, Anthony J.
Non-Manipulative Selling. Courseware.
Alessandro, Robert D. *see* D'Alessandro, Robert.
Alessi, Vincie.
xAlessi, Vincie.

Evangelism in Your Church School. Judson.
Alexander, Alfred.
xAlexander, Alfred.
ed. Stories of Sicily. Merrimack Bk Serv.
ed. Stories of Sicily. Schocken.
Alexander, Anne.
xAlexander, Anne.
Connie. Atheneum.
Trouble on Treat Street. Atheneum.
Alexander, Archibald, 1772-1851
xAlexander, Archibald.
Evidences of the Authenticity, Inspiration, &
Canonical Authority of the Holy Scriptures.
Arno.
History of Colonization of the Western Coast
of Africa. Arno.
History of Colonization on the Western Coast
of Africa. Negro U Pr.
Alexander, Arthur F. *see* Alexander, Arthur Francis
O'Donel.
Alexander, Arthur Francis O'Donel.
xAlexander, Arthur F.
The Planet Saturn: A History of Observation,
Theory & Discovery. Dover.
Alexander, C. P. *see* Alexander, Charles Paul.
Alexander, Carter, 1881-1965
xAlexander, Carter.
Some Present Aspects of the Work of
Teacher's Voluntary Association in the
United States. AMS Pr.
Alexander, Charles C.
xAlexander, Charles C.
Holding the Line: The Eisenhower Era
1952-1961. Ind U Pr.
Alexander, Charles Paul, 1889-
xAlexander, C. P.
The Crane Flies of California. U of Cal Pr.
Alexander, Christopher.
xAlexander, Christopher.
The Oregon Experiment. Oxford U Pr.
A Pattern Language: Towns, Buildings,
Construction. Oxford U Pr.
xAlexander, Christopher W.
Notes on the Synthesis of Form. Harvard U Pr.
Alexander, Christopher W. *see* Alexander, Christopher.
Alexander, Conel Hugh O'Donel.
xAlexander, Hugh.
The Penguin Book of Chess Positions. Penguin.
Alexander, Dale. *see* Alexander, Dan Dale.
Alexander, Dan Dale.
xAlexander, Dale.
Arthritis & Common Sense. Witkower.
Alexander, David.
xAlexander, David.
Eerdmans' Handbook to the Bible. Eerdmans.
Alexander, David J.
xAlexander, David J.
A Public Policy Analysis of Bilingual
Education in California. R & E Res Assoc.
Alexander, David M.
xAlexander, David M.
The Chocolate Spy. Coward.
The Chocolate Spy. Playboy Pbks.
Alexander, De Alva S. *see* Alexander, De Alva
Stanwood.
Alexander, De Alva Stanwood, 1846-1925
xAlexander, De Alva S.
History & Procedure of the House of
Representatives. B Franklin.
Alexander, Edward.
xAlexander, Edward.
Matthew Arnold & John Stuart Mill. Columbia
U Pr.
Matthew Arnold, John Ruskin, & the Modern
Temper. Ohio St U Pr.
The Resonance of Dust: Essays on Holocaust
Literature & Jewish Fate. Ohio St U Pr.
Alexander, Frank, 1943-
xAlexander, Frank.

I'm in Love with a Mannequin. Kokono.
Alexander, Franz. *see* Alexander, Franz Gabriel.
Alexander, Franz Gabriel, 1891-1964
  xAlexander, Franz.
    Fundamentals of Psychoanalysis. Norton.
    ed. Impact of Freudian Psychiatry. U of
      Chicago Pr.
    Psychoanalytic Therapy: Principles &
      Application. U of Nebr Pr.
Alexander, George J.
  xAlexander, George J.
    Commercial Torts. A Smith Co..
    Honesty & Competition: False Advertising,
      Law, & Policy Under FTC Administration.
      Syracuse U Pr.
Alexander, Gerard L.
  xAlexander, Gerard L.
    Guide to Atlases - World, Regional, National,
      Thematic: An International Listing of Atlases
      Published Since 1950. Scarecrow.
Alexander, Gordon, 1901-
  xAlexander, Gordon.
    General Zoology. Har-Row.
Alexander, Guy B.
  xAlexander, Guy B.
    Chromatography: An Adventure in Graduate
      School. Am Chemical.
Alexander, Harley Burr, 1873-1939
  xAlexander, Hartley B.
    North American Mythology. Cooper Sq.
Alexander, Harold H.
  xAlexander, Harold H.
    Design: Criteria for Decisions. Macmillan.
Alexander, Hartley B. *see* Alexander, Hartley Burr.
Alexander, Hartley Burr, 1873-1939
  xAlexander, Hartley B.
    Nature & Human Nature: Essays Metaphysical
      & Historical. AMS Pr.
    World's Rim: Great Mysteries of the North
      American Indians. U of Nebr Pr.
Alexander, Herbert. *see* Alexander, Herbert E.
Alexander, Herbert E.
  xAlexander, Herbert.
    Financing Politics: Money, Elections and
      Political Reform. Congr Quarterly.
  xAlexander, Herbert E.
    Campaign Money: Reform & Reality in the
      States. Free Pr.
    Money in Politics. Pub Aff Pr.
    Political Finance. Sage.
Alexander, Holmes. *see* Alexander, Holmes Moss.
Alexander, Holmes M. *see* Alexander, Holmes Moss.
Alexander, Holmes Moss, 1906-
  xAlexander, Holmes.
    How to Read the Federalist. Western Islands.
    Pen & Politics: The Autobiography of a
      Working Writer. McClain.
  xAlexander, Holmes M.
    American Talleyrand: The Career &
      Contemporaries of Martin Van Buren.
      Russell.
Alexander, Horace. *see* Alexander, Horace Gundry.
Alexander, Horace Gundry, 1889-
  xAlexander, Horace.
    Gandhi Remembered. Pendle Hill.
Alexander, Hugh. *see* Alexander, Conel Hugh O'Donel.
Alexander, Ian. *see* Alexander, Ian C.
Alexander, Ian C.
  xAlexander, Ian.
    Office Location & Public Policy. Longman.
Alexander, J. Estill.
  xAlexander, J. Estill.
    Attitudes & Reading. Intl Reading.
    Teaching Reading. Little.
Alexander, J. H. *see* Alexander, John H.
Alexander, J. J. G. *see* Alexander, Jonathan James
  Graham.
Alexander, J. P. *see* Alexander, John Paul.
Alexander, J. Wesley.
  xAlexander, J. Wesley.

Fundamentals of Clinical Immunology.
  Saunders.
Alexander, Jason.
  xAlexander, Jason.
    Philosophy for Investors. Sitnalta Pr.
Alexander, Jean, 1926-
  xAlexander, Jean.
    Affidavits of Genius: Edgar Allan Poe & the
      French Critics, 1847-1924. Kennikat.
Alexander, Joan.
  xAlexander, Joan.
    One Sunny Day. Berkley Pub.
Alexander, John H., D.phil
  xAlexander, J. H.
    Two Studies in Romantic Reviewing:
      Edinburgh Reviewers & the English
      Tradition. Humanities.
Alexander, John K.
  xAlexander, John K.
    Render Them Submissive: Responses to
      Poverty in Philadelphia, 1760-1800. U of
      Mass Pr.
Alexander, John Paul.
  xAlexander, J. P.
    Odd Order Group Actions & Witt
      Classification of Innerproducts.
      Springer-Verlag.
Alexander, John T.
  xAlexander, John T.
    The Bubonic Plague in Early Modern Russia:
      Public Health & Urban Disaster. Johns
      Hopkins.
Alexander, John W. *see* Alexander, John Wesley.
Alexander, John Wesley, 1918-
  xAlexander, John W.
    Economic Geography. P-H.
Alexander, Jonathan James Graham.
  xAlexander, J. J. G.
    The Decorated Letter. Braziller.
Alexander, Joseph A. *see* Alexander, Joseph Addison.
Alexander, Joseph Addison, 1809-1860
  xAlexander, Joseph A.
    Commentary on the Prophecies of Isaiah.
      Zondervan.
Alexander, Karen.
  xAlexander, Karen.
    Palaces of Desire. Ballantine.
Alexander, Kern.
  xAlexander, Kern.
    College & University Law. Michie.
    ed. Educational Need in the Public Economy.
      U Presses Fla.
    School Law. West Pub.
Alexander, L. G.
  xAlexander, L. G.
    Take a Stand: Discussion Topics for
      Intermediate Adult Students. Longman.
    Talk It Over: Discussion Topics for
      Intermediate Students. Longman.
Alexander, Laurence A.
  xAlexander, Laurence A.
    ed. Financing Downtown Action: A Practical
      Guide to Private & Public Funding Sources.
      Downtown Res.
Alexander, Leroy E. *see* Alexander, Leroy Elbert.
Alexander, Leroy Elbert, 1910-
  xAlexander, Leroy E.
    X-Ray Diffraction Methods in Polymer
      Science. Krieger.
Alexander, Lewis M.
  xAlexander, Lewis M.
    The Northeastern United States. Van Nos
      Reinhold.
Alexander, Lloyd.
  xAlexander, Lloyd.

Book of Three. HR&W.
The Book of Three. Dell.
Castle of Llyr. Dell.
Castle of Llyr. HR&W.
The Castle of Llyr. Dell.
The Cat Who Wished to Be a Man. Dutton.
Coll & His White Pig. HR&W.
First Two Lives of Lukas-Kasha. Dutton.
Taran Wanderer. Dell.
Taran Wanderer. HR&W.
Taran Wanderer. Dell.
Alexander, Martha. *see* Alexander, Martha G.
Alexander, Martha G.
  xAlexander, Martha.
    illus. And My Mean Old Mother Will Be
      Sorry, Blackboard Bear. Dial.
    illus. And My Mean Old Mother Will Be
      Sorry, Blackboard Bear. Dial.
    illus. I'll Be the Horse If You'll Play with Me.
      Dial.
    illus. I'll Protect You from the Jungle Beasts.
      Dial.
    illus. Maybe a Monster. Dial.
    illus. No Ducks in Our Bathtub. Dial.
    illus. Nobody Asked Me If I Wanted a Baby
      Sister. Dial.
    illus. Nobody Asked Me If I Wanted a Baby
      Sister. Dial.
    illus. Out, Out, Out. Dial.
    illus. We're in Big Trouble, Blackboard Bear.
      Dial.
Alexander, Marthann.
  xAlexander, Marthann.
    Simple Weaving. Taplinger.
Alexander, Martin, 1930-
  xAlexander, Martin.
    Introduction to Soil Microbiology. Wiley.
Alexander, Mary. *see* Alexander, Mary Merkel.
Alexander, Mary J. *see* Alexander, Mary Jean.
Alexander, Mary Jean.
  xAlexander, Mary J.
    Designing Interior Environment. HarBraceJ.
    Designing Your Own Room. Watts.
    Handbook of Decorative Design & Ornament.
      L Amiel Pub.
  xAlexander, Mary Jean.
    Decorating Made Simple. Doubleday.
Alexander, Mary M. *see* Alexander, Mary Merkel.
Alexander, Mary Merkel.
  xAlexander, Mary.
    jt. auth. Pediatric Physical Diagnosis for
      Nurses. McGraw.
  xAlexander, Mary M.
    Pediatric History Taking & Physical Diagnosis
      for Nurses. McGraw.
Alexander, Michael. *see* Alexander, Michael J.
Alexander, Michael J.
  xAlexander, Michael.
    The Poetic Achievement of Ezra Pound. U of
      Cal Pr.
Alexander, Noy.
  xAlexander, Noy.
    Let's Make Candy. C E Tuttle.
Alexander, Pat, 1937-
  xAlexander, Patricia.
    ed. Eerdman's Family Encyclopedia of the
      Bible. Eerdmans.
Alexander, Patricia. *see* Alexander, Pat.
Alexander, Patrick, 1926-
  xAlexander, Patrick.
    Death of a Thin-Skinned Animal. BJ Pub
      Group.
    Show Me a Hero. Viking Pr.
Alexander, Patsy R.
  xAlexander, Patsy R.
    Textile Products: Selection, Use & Care. HM.
Alexander, Paul J. *see* Alexander, Paul Julius.
Alexander, Paul Julius, 1910-
  xAlexander, Paul J.

The Oracle of Baalbek: The Tiburtine Sibyl in
   Greek Dress. Dumbarton Oaks.
The Patriarch Nicephorus of Constantinople:
   Ecclesiastical Policy & Image Worship in the
   Byzantine Empire. AMS Pr.
Alexander, Peter, 1893-
   xAlexander, Peter.
      Shakespeare's Life & Art. Greenwood.
      Shakespeare's Life & Art. NYU Pr.
Alexander, R. Mcneill.
   xAlexander, R. McNeill.
      The Chordates. Cambridge U Pr.
      The Invertebrates. Cambridge U Pr.
      ed. Mechanics & Energetics of Animal
         Locomotion. Methuen Inc.
Alexander, Richard D.
   xAlexander, Richard D.
      Darwinism & Human Affairs. U of Wash Pr.
Alexander, Robert J. *see* Alexander, Robert Jackson.
Alexander, Robert Jackson.
   xAlexander, Robert J.
      Arturo Alessandri: A Biography. Univ
         Microfilms.
      Communism in Latin America. Rutgers U Pr.
      Peron Era. Russell.
      Trotskyism in Latin America. Hoover Inst Pr.
Alexander, Robert L., 1920-
   xAlexander, Robert L.
      The Architecture of Maximilian Godefroy.
         Johns Hopkins.
Alexander, Robert S. *see* Alexander, Robert Spence.
Alexander, Robert Spence, 1917-
   xAlexander, Robert S.
      Case Studies in Medical Physiology. Little.
Alexander, Roy, 1925-
   xAlexander, Roy.
      Mehdi: Nothing Is Impossible. Farnswth Pub.
Alexander, Samuel, 1859-1938
   xAlexander, Samuel
      Art & Instinct. Folcroft.
      Locke. Kennikat.
Alexander, Shana.
   xAlexander, Shana.
      Anyone's Daughter. Bantam.
      Anyone's Daughter. Viking Pr.
      Talking Woman. Delacorte.
Alexander, Sue.
   xAlexander, Sue.
      Marc the Magnificent. Pantheon.
      Peacocks Are Very Special. Doubleday.
      Seymour the Prince. Pantheon.
Alexander, Taylor. *see* Alexander, Taylor Richard.
Alexander, Taylor Richard.
   xAlexander, Taylor.
      Botany. Western Pub.
Alexander, Theron, 1913-
   xAlexander, Theron.
      Human Development in an Urban Age. P-H.
Alexander, Thomas B. *see* Alexander, Thomas Benjamin.
Alexander, Thomas Benjamin.
   xAlexander, Thomas B.
      Anatomy of the Confederate Congress: A
         Study of the Influences of Member
         Characteristics on Legislative Voting
         Behavior, 1861-1865. Vanderbilt U Pr.
      Political Reconstruction in Tennessee. Russell.
      Thomas A. R. Nelson of East Tennessee. U of
         Tenn Pr.
Alexander, Thomas G.
   xAlexander, Thomas G.
      A Clash of Interests: Interior Department &
         Mountain West 1863-96. Brigham.
Alexander, Thomas W.
   xAlexander, Tom.
      Project Apollo: Man to the Moon. Har-Row.
Alexander, Tom. *see* Alexander, Thomas W.
Alexander, Truman H. *see* Alexander, Truman Hudson.
Alexander, Truman Hudson, 1891-
   xAlexander, Truman H.

Loot. Arno.
Alexander, Uhlman S. *see* Alexander, Uhlman Seymour.
Alexander, Uhlman Seymour, 1894-
   xAlexander, Uhlman S.
      Special Legislation Affecting Public Schools.
         AMS Pr.
Alexander, William, 1826-1894
   xAlexander, William.
      Notes & Sketches Illustrative of Northern
         Rural Life in the Eighteenth Century.
         Folcroft.
Alexander, Yonah.
   xAlexander, Yonah.
      ed. Control of Terrorism: International
         Documents. Crane-Russak Co.
      ed. Political Terrorism & Business: The Threat
         & the Response. Praeger.
Alexandersson, Gunnar.
   xAlexandersson, Gunnar.
      Geography of Manufacturing. P-H.
Alexandre, Arsene, 1859-
   xAlexandre, Arsene.
      Intro. by Decorative Art of Leon Bakst. Arno.
Alexandre, Pierre.
   xAlexandre, Pierre.
      ed. French Perspectives in African Studies: A
         Collection of Translated Essays. Oxford U Pr.
Alexandrian, Sarane.
   xAlexandrian, Sarane.
      Surrealist Art. Oxford U Pr.
Alexandrides, C. G.
   xAlexandrides, C. G.
      Export Marketing Management. Praeger.
Alexandrova, Vera, pseud
   xAlexandrova, Vera.
      History of Soviet Literature. Greenwood.
Alexandrowicz, Charles H. *see* Alexandrowicz, Charles
   Henry.
Alexandrowicz, Charles Henry.
   xAlexandrowicz, Charles H.
      Law of Global Communications. Columbia U
         Pr.
Alexenberg, M. *see* Alexenberg, Melvin L.
Alexenberg, Melvin L.
   xAlexenberg, M.
      Light & Sight. P-H.
   xAlexenberg, Melvin L.
      Sound Science. P-H.
Alexopoulos, Constantine J. *see* Alexopoulos, Constantine
   John.
Alexopoulos, Constantine John.
   xAlexopoulos, Constantine J.
      Algae & Fungi. Macmillan.
      Introductory Mycology. Wiley.
Alfange, Dean, 1897-
   xAlfange, Dean.
      Supreme Court & the National Will. Kennikat.
Alfassy, Leo.
   xAlfassy, Leo.
      ed. Baroque & Folk Tunes for Recorder. Music
         Sales.
Alfieri, Dino, 1886-
   xAlfieri, Dino.
      Dictators Face to Face. Greenwood.
Alfieri, Vittorio.
   xAlfieri, Vittorio.
      The Prince & Letters. U of Toronto Pr.
Alfoldi, Andras, 1895-
   xAlfoldi, Andras.
      A Conflict of Ideas in the Late Roman Empire:
         The Clash Between the Senate & Valentinian
         I. Greenwood.
      A Conflict of Ideas in the Late Roman Empire:
         The Clash Between the Senate & Valentinian
         I. Hyperion Conn.
Alfoldy, Geza.
   xAlfoldy, Geza.
      Noricum. Routledge & Kegan.
Alfonsi, Ferdinando.
   xAlfonsi, Ferdinando P.

An Annotated Bibliography of Moravia
   Criticism in Italy & the English-Speaking
   World. Garland Pub.
Alfonsi, Ferdinando P. *see* Alfonsi, Ferdinando.
Alfonso, Oscar M.
   xAlfonso, Oscar M.
      Theodore Roosevelt & the Philippines,
         1897-1909. Oriole Edns.
Alford, Delton L.
   xAlford, Delton L.
      Music in the Pentecostal Church. Pathway Pr.
Alford, Lady M. *see* Alford, Marianne Margaret
   Compton Cust.
Alford, M. *see* Alford, Marianne Margaret Compton
   Cust.
**Alford, Marianne Margaret Compton Cust, Vicountess,
1817-1888**
   xAlford, Lady M.
      Needlework As Art. Charles River Bks.
   xAlford, M.
      Needlework As Art. Beekman Pubs.
Alford, Robert R.
   xAlford, Robert R.
      Party & Society: The Anglo-American
         Democracies. Greenwood.
Alford, Terry W.
   xAlford, Terry W.
      Facility Planning, Design, & Construction of
         Rural Health Centers. Ballinger Pub.
Alford, Violet.
   xAlford, Violet.
      The Hobby Horse & Other Animal Masks.
         Rowman.
      Introduction to English Folklore. Arden Lib.
      Introduction to English Folklore. Folcroft.
      Sword Dance & Drama. Dufour.
Alfred, J. Tyrone. *see* Alfred, Joseph Tyrone.
Alfred, Joseph Tyrone.
   xAlfred, J. Tyrone.
      Medical Handbook for the Layman. Alfred.
Alfred, Richard L.
   xAlfred, Richard L.
      A Conceptual Framework for Institutional
         Research in Community Colleges. College
         Bd.
Alfsen, E. M. *see* Alfsen, Erik Magnus.
Alfsen, Erik M. *see* Alfsen, Erik Magnus.
Alfsen, Erik Magnus, 1930-
   xAlfsen, E. M.
      Compact Convex Sets & Boundary Integrals.
         Springer-Verlag.
   xAlfsen, Erik M.
      Non-Commutative Spectral Theory for Affine
         Function Spaces on Convex Sets. Am Math.
Alfven, H. *see* Alfven, Hannes.
Alfven, Hannes, 1908-
   xAlfven, H.
      Structure & Evolutionary History of the Solar
         System. Kluwer Boston.
   xAlfven, Hannes.
      Atom, Man, & the Universe: The Long Chain
         of Complications. W H Freeman.
      Living on the Third Planet. W H Freeman.
      On the Origin of the Solar System.
         Greenwood.
Algarin, Miguel.
   xAlgarin, Miguel.
      On Call. Arte Publico.
Algeo, John.
   xAlgeo, John.
      Exercises in Contemporary English. HarBraceJ.
      On Defining the Proper Name. U Presses Fla.
Alger, Horatio, 1832-1899
   xAlger, Horatio.

Cast Upon the Breakers. Popular Lib.
Digging for Gold: A Story of California.
Macmillan.
Digging the Gold: A Story of California.
Amereon Ltd.
Ragged Dick & Mark the Match Boy.
Macmillan.
Alger, Philip L. see Alger, Philip Langdon.
Alger, Philip Langdon.
xAlger, Philip L.
Mathematics for Science & Engineering.
McGraw.
Alger, R. A. see Alger, Russell Alexander.
Alger, Russell A. see Alger, Russell Alexander.
Alger, Russell Alexander, 1836-1907
xAlger, R. A.
The Spanish-American War. Gordon Pr.
xAlger, Russell A.
Spanish-American War. Arno.
Alger, William R. see Alger, William Rounseville.
Alger, William Rounseville.
xAlger, William R.
Destiny of the Soul: Critical History of the
Doctrine of a Future Life. Greenwood.
Algren, Nelson, 1909-
xAlgren, Nelson.
The Neon Wilderness. Peter Smith.
A Walk on the Wild Side. Greenwood.
A Walk on the Wild Side. Penguin.
Alhadeff, David A.
xAlhadeff, David A.
Competition & Controls in Banking: A Study
of the Regulation of Bank Competition in
Italy, France & England. U of Cal Pr.
Alhashim, Dhia D.
xAlhashim, Dhia D.
Accounting for Multinational Enterprises.
Bobbs.
Ali, Abdullah Yusuf, 1872-1952
xAli, Abdullah Yusuf.
A Cultural History of India During the British
Period. AMS Pr.
Ali, Ameer.
xAli, Syed A.
The Spirit of Islam: A History of the Evolution
& Ideals of Islam with a Life of the Prophet.
Humanities.
Ali, Syed A. see Ali, Ameer.
Ali, Tariq.
xAli, Tariq.
Trotsky for Beginners. Pantheon.
Aliano, Richard A.
xAliano, Richard A.
American Defense Policy from Eisenhower to
Kennedy: The Politics of Changing Military
Requirements, 1957-1961. Ohio U Pr.
The Crime of World Power: Politics Without
Government in the International System.
Putnam.
Aliber, Robert Z.
xAliber, Robert Z.
The International Money Game. Basic.
National Monetary Policies & the International
Financial System. U of Chicago Pr.
Aliboni, Roberto.
xAliboni, Roberto.
ed. Arab Industrialization & Economic
Integration. St Martin.
Alico, Stella H.
xAlico, Stella H.
Benjamin Franklin - Martin Luther King Jr..
Pendulum Pr.
Elvis Presley - The Beatles. Pendulum Pr.
Aligarh, India. Muslim University.
xAligarh Muslim University.
ed. Changing Concept of the Universe. Asia.
ed. Messages of Freedom. Asia.
ed. Readings in Democracy. Asia.
xAlighar Muslim University.

Significant Writings on Life & Man. Asia.
Aligarh Muslim University. see Aligarh, India. Muslim
University.
Alighar Muslim University. see Aligarh, India. Muslim
University.
Alihan, Milla.
xAlihan, Milla.
Corporate Etiquette. NAL.
Alikonis, Justin J.
xAlikonis, Justin J.
Candy Technology. AVI.
Alinsky, Saul. see Alinsky, Saul David.
Alinsky, Saul David, 1909-
xAlinsky, Saul.
Reveille for Radicals. Random.
Aliotta, Antonio, 1881-1964
xAliotta, Antonio.
The Idealistic Reaction Against Science. Arno.
Aliprantis, Charalambos D.
xAliprantis, Charalambos D.
Locally Solid Riesz Spaces. Acad Pr.
Alireza, Marianne.
xAlireza, Marianne.
At the Drop of a Veil. HM.
Alisky, Marvin.
xAlisky, Marvin.
Historical Dictionary of Peru. Scarecrow.
Alison, Archibald, Sir, Bart, 1792-1867
xAlison, Archibald.
History of Europe from the Commencement of
the French Revolution to the Restoration of
the Bourbons. AMS Pr.
Alissi, Albert S.
xAlissi, Albert S.
Boys in Little Italy: A Comparison of Their
Individual Value Orientations, Family
Patterns, & Peer Group Associations. R & E
Res Assoc.
ed. Perspectives on Social Group Work
Practice: A Book of Readings. Free Pr.
Alitto, Guy.
xAlitto, Guy S.
The Last Confucian: Liang Shu-Ming & the
Chinese Dilemma of Modernity. U of Cal Pr.
Alitto, Guy S. see Alitto, Guy.
Alkema, Chester J. see Alkema, Chester Jay.
Alkema, Chester Jay.
xAlkema, Chester J.
Alkema's Complete Guide to Creative Art for
Young People. Sterling.
Crafting with Nature's Materials. Sterling.
Masks. Sterling.
Monster Masks. Sterling.
Puppet-Making. Sterling.
Starting with Papier Mache. Sterling.
Alker, Hayward R.
xAlker, Howard R.
Mathematical Approaches to Politics. Elsevier.
Alker, Howard R. see Alker, Hayward R.
Alkin, E. G. M.
xAlkin, Glyn.
TV Sound Operations. Focal Pr.
Alkin, Glyn. see Alkin, E. G. M.
Alkin, Marvin C.
xAlkin, Marvin C.
Using Evaluations: Does Evaluation Make a
Difference. Sage.
Alkon, Paul K. see Alkon, Paul Kent.
Alkon, Paul Kent.
xAlkon, Paul K.
Defoe & Fictional Time. U of Ga Pr.
All India Sociological Conference. see All-India
Sociological Conference.
All-India Sociological Conference.
xAll India Sociological Conference.
Sociology, Social Research, & Social Problems
in India. Greenwood.
Allaback, Steven.
xAllaback, Steven.

Alexander Solzhenitsyn. Taplinger.
Allaby, M. see Allaby, Michael.
Allaby, Michael.
xAllaby, M.
World Food Resources: Actual & Potential.
Burgess-Intl Ideas.
xAllaby, Michael.
A Dictionary of the Environment. Van Nos
Reinhold.
Allain, Louis J. see Allain, Louis John Joseph.
Allain, Louis John Joseph.
xAllain, Louis J.
Capital Investment Models of the Oil & Gas
Industry: A Systems Approach. Arno.
Allain, Violet A. see Allain, Violet Anselmini.
Allain, Violet Anselmini.
xAllain, Violet A.
Futuristics & Education. Phi Delta Kappa.
Allamand, Pascale.
xAllamand, Pascale.
The Animals Who Changed Their Colors.
Lothrop.
illus. The Camel Who Left the Zoo. Scribner.
Cocoa Beans & Daisies: How Swiss Chocolate
Is Made. Warne.
illus. The Little Goat in the Mountains. Warne.
Allamong, Betty D.
xAllamong, Betty D.
Energy for Life: Photosynthesis & Respiration.
Wiley.
Allan, David.
xAllan, David.
An Illustrated Guide to Common Rocks &
Their Minerals. Naturegraph.
Allan, Mabel E. see Allan, Mabel Esther.
Allan, Mabel Esther.
xAllan, Mabel E.
Bridge of Friendship. Dodd.
Catrin in Wales. Vanguard.
The Flash Children. Dodd.
A Lovely Tomorrow. Dodd.
The Night Wind. Atheneum.
Allan, Mea.
xAllan, Mea.
Darwin & His Flowers: The Key to Natural
Selection. Taplinger.
Plants That Changed Our Gardens. David &
Charles.
Allan, Mowbray, 1934-
xAllan, Mowbray.
T. S. Eliot's Impersonal Theory of Poetry.
Bucknell U Pr.
Allan, Stella.
xAllan, Stella.
An Inside Job. Avon.
An Inside Job. Scribner.
A Mortal Affair. Scribner.
Allan, William, 1904-
xAllan, William.
The African Husbandman. Greenwood.
Alland, Alexander, 1931-
xAlland, Alexander.
Adaptation in Cultural Evolution: An
Approach to Medical Anthropology.
Columbia U Pr.
Human Diversity. Columbia U Pr.
The Human Imperative. Columbia U Pr.
To Be Human: An Introduction to
Anthropology. Wiley.
When the Spider Danced: Notes from an
African Village. Doubleday.
Alland, Guy.
xAlland, Guy.
The Auto Repair Primer. Little.
Allanson, B. R. see Allanson, Brian R.
Allanson, Brian R.
xAllanson, B. R.
ed. Lake Sibaya. Kluwer Boston.
Allard, Harry.
xAllard, Harry.

Bumps in the Night. Doubleday.
Crash Helmet. P-H.
I Will Not Go to Market Today. Dial.
May I Stay?. P-H.
The Stupids Have a Ball. HM.
The Stupids Step Out. HM.
Allard, Lucile E. *see* Allard, Lucile Edna.
Allard, Lucile Edna, 1889-
  xAllard, Lucile E.
    A Study of the Leisure Activities of Certain
      Elementary School Teachers of Long Island.
      AMS Pr.
Allard, R. J.
  xAllard, R. J.
    An Approach to Econometrics. Krieger.
Allard, Robert W. *see* Allard, Robert Wayne.
Allard, Robert Wayne, 1919-
  xAllard, Robert W.
    Principles of Plant Breeding. Wiley.
Allardyce, Paula.
  xAllardyce, Paula.
    The Rogue's Lady. Playboy Pbks.
Allbut, R. *see* Allbut, Robert.
Allbut, Robert.
  xAllbut, R.
    Rambles in Dickens' Land. Haskell.
  xAllbut, Robert.
    Rambles in Dicken's Land. R West.
Allchin, Bridget.
  xAllchin, Bridget.
    ed. The Prehistory & Palaeogeography of the
      Great Indian Desert. Acad Pr.
Allcorn, Seth.
  xAllcorn, Seth.
    Internal Auditing for Hospitals. Aspen Systems.
Allcott, John V.
  xAllcott, John V.
    Colonial Homes in North Carolina. NC
      Archives.
Allday, Elizabeth.
  xAllday, Elizabeth.
    Stefan Zweig: A Critical Biography. O'Hara.
Alldis, James. *see* Alldis, Jim.
Alldis, Jim.
  xAlldis, James.
    Animals As Friends: A Head Keeper
      Remembers London Zoo. Taplinger.
Alldridge, J. C. *see* Alldridge, James C.
Alldridge, James C.
  xAlldridge, J. C.
    Ilse Aichinger. Dufour.
Alldritt, Keith.
  xAlldritt, Keith.
    Eliot's Four Quartets: Poetry As Chamber
      Music. Biblio Dist.
    The Good Pit Man. St Martin.
Allegre, C. J. *see* Allegre, Claude J.
Allegre, Claude J.
  xAllegre, C. J.
    Introduction to Geochemistry. Kluwer Boston.
Allegro, J. M. *see* Allegro, John Marco.
Allegro, John Marco, 1923-
  xAllegro, J. M.
    Dead Sea Scrolls. Penguin.
Allen. *see* Allen, George Herbert.
Allen, A. *see* Allen, Leslie.
Allen, Alex B.
  xAllen, Alex B.
    Danger on Broken Arrow Trail. A Whitman.
    Fifth Down. A Whitman.
    No Place for Baseball. A Whitman.
Allen, Anita.
  xAllen, Anita.
    The False Face of Death. Doubleday.
Allen, Anne S., 1923-
  xAllen, Anne S.
    Introduction to Health Professions. Mosby.
Allen, B. M.
  xAllen, B. M.

Soldering & Welding. Sterling.
Allen, Bruce T.
  xAllen, Bruce T.
    Market for Electrical Generating Equipment.
      Mich St U Busn.
Allen, C. W. *see* Allen, Clabon Walter.
Allen, Catherine. *see* Allen, Catherine B.
Allen, Catherine B.
  xAllen, Catherine.
    The New Lottie Moon Story. Broadman.
Allen, Charles, 1827-1913
  xAllen, Charles.
    Notes of the Bacon-Shakespeare Question.
      Gordon Pr.
    Notes on the Bacon-Shakespeare Question.
      AMS Pr.
    ed. Plain Tales from the Raj: Images of British
      India in the Twentieth Century. St Martin.
    Tales from the Dark Continent. St Martin.
Allen, Charles L. *see* Allen, Charles Livingstone.
Allen, Charles Livingstone, 1913-
  xAllen, Charles L.
    All Things Are Possible Through Prayer. Pillar
      Bks.
    All Things Are Possible Through Prayer.
      Revell.
    Charles L. Allen Treasury. Revell.
    Christmas. Revell.
    Life More Abundant. Pillar Bks.
    Life of Christ. Revell.
    Perfect Peace. Revell.
    Touch of the Master's Hand: Christ's Miracles
      for Today. Revell.
    When You Graduate. Revell.
    When You Lose a Loved One. Revell.
Allen, Clabon Walter.
  xAllen, C. W.
    Astrophysical Quantities. Humanities.
Allen, Clifford, 1902-
  xAllen, Clifford.
    The Sexual Perversions & Abnormalities: A
      Study in the Psychology of Paraphilia.
      Greenwood.
Allen, Clifton J., 1901-
  xAllen, Clifton J.
    Life Is Worth Your Best. Broadman.
Allen, Clinton M. *see* Allen, Clinton Mcclarty.
Allen, Clinton Mcclarty, 1878-
  xAllen, Clinton M.
    Some Effects Produced in an Individual by
      Knowledge of His Own Intellectual Level.
      AMS Pr.
Allen, Devere, 1891-1955
  xAllen, Devere.
    ed. Adventurous Americans. Arno.
    Fight for Peace. Garland Pub.
    The Fight for Peace. Ozer.
    ed. Pacifism in the Modern World. Ozer.
Allen, Dick. *see* Allen, Richard Stanley.
Allen, Don C. *see* Allen, Don Cameron.
Allen, Don Cameron, 1904-
  xAllen, Don C.
    The Harmonious Vision: Studies in Milton's
      Poetry. Octagon.
    The Legend of Noah: Renaissance Rationalism
      in Art, Science & Letters. U of Ill Pr.
  xAllen, Don Cameron.
    ed. A Celebration of Poets. Johns Hopkins.
    The Harmonious Vision: Studies in Miltons
      Poetry. Johns Hopkins.
Allen, Don L.
  xAllen, Don L.
    Periodontics for the Dental Hygienist. Lea &
      Febiger.
Allen, Donald R. *see* Allen, Donald Roy.
Allen, Donald Roy, 1937-
  xAllen, Donald R.
    French Views of America in the 1930's.
      Garland Pub.
Allen, Durward L. *see* Allen, Durward Leon.

Allen, Durward Leon, 1910-
  xAllen, Durward L.
    Our Wildlife Legacy. T Y Crowell.
    Our Wildlife Legacy. T Y Crowell.
  xAllen, Durwood.
    Wolves of Minong: Their Vital Role in a Wild
      Community. HM.
Allen, Durwood. *see* Allen, Durward Leon.
Allen, Dwight W. *see* Allen, Dwight William.
Allen, Dwight William.
  xAllen, Dwight W.
    ed. The Teacher's Handbook. Scott F.
Allen, E. L. *see* Allen, Edgar Leonard.
Allen, E. W. *see* Allen, Edward W.
Allen, Earl R. *see* Allen, R. Earl.
Allen, Edgar L. *see* Allen, Edgar Leonard.
Allen, Edgar Leonard.
  xAllen, E. L.
    Freedom in God: A Guide to the Thought of
      Nicholas Berdyaev. Arden Lib.
    Freedom in God: A Guide to the Thought of
      Nicholas Berdyaev. Folcroft.
    From Plato to Nietzsche. Fawcett.
  xAllen, Edgar L.
    Existentialism from Within. Greenwood.
Allen, Edward, 1938-
  xAllen, Edward.
    How Buildings Work: The Natural Order of
      Architecture. Oxford U Pr.
    Stone Shelters. MIT Pr.
Allen, Edward B.
  xAllen, Edward B.
    Early American Wall Paintings, 1710-1850. Da
      Capo.
  xAllen, Edward D.
    Early American Wall Paintings. Century Hse.
Allen, Edward D. *see* Allen, Edward B.
Allen, Edward David.
  xAllen, Edward D.
    Classroom Techniques: Foreign Languages &
      English As a Second Language. HarBraceJ.
    Modern Language Classroom Techniques: A
      Handbook. HarBraceJ.
Allen, Edward F. *see* Allen, Edward Frank.
Allen, Edward Frank.
  xAllen, Edward F.
    How to Write & Speak Effective English.
      Fawcett.
Allen, Edward H.
  xAllen, Edward H.
    Handbook of Energy Policy for Local
      Governments. Lexington Bks.
Allen, Edward S. *see* Allen, Edward Switzer.
Allen, Edward Switzer, 1887-
  xAllen, Edward S.
    Freedom in Iowa: The Role of the Iowa Civil
      Liberties Union. Iowa St U Pr.
Allen, Edward W.
  xAllen, E. W.
    Essentials of Ophthalmic Optics. Oxford U Pr.
Allen, Eliot D.
  xAllen, Eliot D.
    Student Writer's Guide. Everett-Edwards.
Allen, Everett S.
  xAllen, Everett S.
    Children of the Light: The Rise & Fall of New
      Bedford Whaling & the Death of the Arctic
      Fleet. Little.
Allen, Everett T.
  xAllen, Everett T.
    Pension Planning: Pensions, Profit Sharing &
      Other Deferred Compensation Plans. Irwin.
Allen, Francis A.
  xAllen, Francis A.
    Borderland of Criminal Justice: Essays in Law
      & Criminology. U of Chicago Pr.
    Crimes of Politics: Political Dimensions of
      Criminal Justice. Harvard U Pr.
    Law, Intellect, & Education. U of Mich Pr.
Allen, Frank C. *see* Allen, Frank Charles.

Allen, Frank Charles.
　xAllen, Frank C.
　　A Critical Edition of Robert Browning's
　　"Bishop Blougram's Apology". Humanities.
Allen, Frank Kenyon.
　xAllen, Frank Kenyon.
　　Golfer's Bible. Doubleday.
Allen, Frederick H. see Allen, Frederick Harold.
Allen, Frederick Harold, 1890-
　xAllen, Frederick H.
　　Psychotherapy with Children. U of Nebr Pr.
Allen, Frederick L. see Allen, Frederick Lewis.
Allen, Frederick Lewis, 1890-1954
　xAllen, Frederick L.
　　Only Yesterday. Har-Row.
Allen, G. C. see Allen, George Cyril.
Allen, G. E. see Allen, Garland E.
Allen, G. Freeman. see Allen, Geoffrey Freeman.
Allen, Gardner W. see Allen, Gardner Weld.
Allen, Gardner Weld, 1856-1944
　xAllen, Gardner W.
　　Naval History of the American Revolution.
　　Corner Hse.
　　Our Naval War with France. Shoe String.
Allen, Garland E.
　xAllen, G. E.
　　Life & Science in the Twentieth Century.
　　Cambridge U Pr.
Allen, Gary.
　xAllen, Gary.
　　Communist Revolution in the Streets. Western
　　Islands.
　　None Dare Call It Conspiracy. Concord Pr.
Allen, Gay W. see Allen, Gay Wilson.
Allen, Gay Wilson, 1903-
　xAllen, Gay W.
　　American Prosody. Octagon.
　　Aspects of Walt Whitman. Arden Lib.
　　Aspects of Walt Whitman. Folcroft.
　　ed. Literary Criticism: Pope to Croce. Wayne
　　St U Pr.
　　Twenty-Five Years of Walt Whitman
　　Bibliography, 1918-1942. Folcroft.
　xAllen, Gay Wilson.
　　Carl Sandburg. U of Minn Pr.
　　A Reader's Guide to Walt Whitman. Octagon.
　　The Solitary Singer: A Critical Biography of
　　Walt Whitman. NYU Pr.
Allen, Geoffrey Freeman.
　xAllen, G. Freeman.
　　Fastest Trains in the World. Scribner.
Allen, George. see Allen, George Herbert.
Allen, George Cyril, 1900-
　xAllen, G. C.
　　British Industry & Economic Policy. Holmes &
　　Meier.
　　Japan's Economic Policy. Holmes & Meier.
Allen, George Herbert, 1923-
　xAllen.
　　Pass Defense Drills. A-W.
　xAllen, George.
　　George Allen's New Handbook of Football
　　Drills. P-H.
Allen, George N.
　xAllen, George N.
　　RI. P-H.
Allen, George R. see Allen, George Richard.
Allen, George Richard, 1934-
　xAllen, George R.
　　The Graduate Students' Guide to Theses &
　　Dissertations: A Practical Manual for Writing
　　& Research. Jossey-Bass.
Allen, Gerald D., 1924-
　xAllen, Gerald D.
　　ed. Dental Analgesia. PSG Pub.
　　Dental Anesthesia & Analgesia. Williams &
　　Wilkins.
Allen, Gertrude E.
　xAllen, Gertrude E.

Everyday Insects. HM.
　　Everyday Turtles, Toads, & Their Kin. HM.
　　Everyday Wildflowers. HM.
Allen, Grant, 1848-1899
　xAllen, Grant.
　　The British Barbarians. Arno.
　　The British Barbarians. Garland Pub.
Allen, H. C. see Allen, Harry Cranbrook.
Allen, H. G. see Allen, Howard G.
Allen, Harold B. see Allen, Harold Byron.
Allen, Harold Byron, 1902-
　xAllen, Harold B.
　　Linguistic Atlas of the Upper Midwest. U of
　　Minn Pr.
　　Compiled by Linguistics & English Linguistics.
　　AHM Pub.
　　A Survey of the Teaching of English to
　　Non-English Speakers in the United States.
　　Arno.
Allen, Harold C.
　xAllen, Harold C.
　　Great Black Americans. Pendulum Pr.
Allen, Harry Cranbrook.
　xAllen, H. C.
　　Anglo-American Predicament: British
　　Commonwealth & United States & European
　　Unity. St Martin.
　　ed. Contrast and Connection: Bicentennial
　　Essays in Anglo-American History. Ohio U
　　Pr.
Allen, Harry E.
　xAllen, Harry E.
　　ed. Reform in Corrections: Problems & Issues.
　　Praeger.
Allen, Harvey. see Allen, Hervey.
Allen, Henry E. see Allen, Henry Elisha.
Allen, Henry Elisha.
　xAllen, Henry E.
　　Turkish Transformation: A Study in Social &
　　Religious Development. Greenwood.
Allen, Herman R.
　xAllen, Herman R.
　　Open Door to Learning: The Land-Grant
　　System Enters Its Second Century. U of Ill
　　Pr.
Allen, Hervey, 1889-1949
　xAllen, Harvey.
　　Du Bose Heyward: A Critical & Biographical
　　Sketch. Arden Lib.
　　Du Bose Heyward: Critical & Biographical
　　Sketch. Folcroft.
　xAllen, Hervey.
　　Anthony Adverse. HR&W.
Allen, Howard G.
　xAllen, H. G.
　　Analysis & Design of Structural Sandwich
　　Panels. Pergamon.
　　Background to Buckling. McGraw.
Allen, Hugh, 1882-
　xAllen, Hugh.
　　The House of Goodyear: A Story of Rubber &
　　of Modern Business. Arno.
Allen, J. P. see Allen, John Patrick Brierley.
Allen, J. W. see Allen, John William.
Allen, James, 1864-1912
　xAllen, James.
　　As a Man Thinketh. Collins Pubs.
　　As a Man Thinketh. De Vorss.
　　As a Man Thinketh. G&D.
　　As a Man Thinketh. Miller Bks.
　　As a Man Thinketh. Peter Pauper.
　　As a Man Thinketh. Revell.
　　Learn to Play Tennis. Rand.
Allen, James. see Allen, James E.
Allen, James A. see Allen, James Albert.
Allen, James Albert.
　xAllen, James A.
　　Studies in Innovation in the Steel & Chemical
　　Industries. Kelley.
Allen, James E. see Allen, James Edward.

Allen, James Edward.
　xAllen, James E.
　　Managing Teenage Pregnancy: Access to
　　Abortion, Contraception & Sex Education.
　　Praeger.
Allen, James Egert, 1896-
　xAllen, James Egert.
　　The Negro in New York. Exposition.
Allen, James L. see Allen, James Lane.
Allen, James Lane.
　xAllen, James L.
　　The Choir Invisible. AMS Pr.
　　The Choir Invisible. Folcroft.
　　Choir Invisible. Scholarly.
　　The Reign of Law: A Tale of the Kentucky
　　Hemp Fields. Arno.
Allen, James R.
　xAllen, James.
　　Guide to Psychiatry: A Handbook on
　　Psychiatry for Health Professionals. Med
　　Exam.
Allen, James T. see Allen, James Turney.
Allen, James Turney, 1873-
　xAllen, James T.
　　First Year of Greek. Macmillan.
Allen, Jana.
　xAllen, Jana.
　　Innards & Other Variety Meats. One Hund
　　One Prods.
Allen, Janet.
　xAllen, Janet.
　　Exciting Things to Do with Color. Lippincott.
Allen, Jean.
　xAllen, Jean.
　　Build a Better - & Slimmer - You. Arlington
　　Hse.
Allen, Jerry, 1911-
　xAllen, Jerry.
　　The Adventures of Mark Twain. Peter Smith.
Allen, Joan M., 1938-
　xAllen, Joan M.
　　Candles & Carnival Lights: The Catholic
　　Sensibility of F. Scott Fitzgerald. NYU Pr.
Allen, Joe. see Allen, Joseph.
Allen, Joel A. see Allen, Joel Asaph.
Allen, Joel Asaph, 1838-1921
　xAllen, Joel A.
　　History of the North American Pinnipeds: A
　　Monograph of the Walruses, Sea-Lions,
　　Sea-Bears & Seals of North America. Arno.
Allen, John.
　xAllen, John.
　　Assault with a Deadly Weapon: The
　　Autobiography of a Street Criminal.
　　McGraw.
　xAllen, John C.
　　Inquiry into the Rise & Growth of the Royal
　　Prerogative in England. B Franklin.
Allen, John. see Allen, John Piers.
Allen, John A. see Allen, John Alexander.
Allen, John Alexander.
　xAllen, John A.
　　Lean Divider. Golden Quill.
Allen, John C. see Allen, John.
Allen, John E. see Allen, John Edward.
Allen, John Edward.
　xAllen, John E.
　　ed. Practical Points in Pediatrics. Med Exam.
Allen, John Houghton.
　xAllen, John Houghton.
　　Southwest. U of NM Pr.
Allen, John L. see Allen, John Logan.
Allen, John Logan, 1941-
　xAllen, John L.
　　Passage Through the Garden: Lewis & Clark &
　　the Image of the American Northwest. U of
　　Ill Pr.
Allen, John Patrick Brierley.
　xAllen, J. P.

ed. The Edinburgh Course in Applied
Linguistics. Oxford U Pr.
Allen, John Piers, 1912-
xAllen, John.
Masters of British Drama. Citadel Pr.
Masters of European Drama. Citadel Pr.
Allen, John W.
xAllen, John W.
Legends & Lore of Southern Illinois. Univ
Graphics.
Allen, John William, 1865-
xAllen, J. W.
A History of Political Thought in the Sixteenth
Century. Rowman.
Allen, Jon. *see* Allen, Jon L.
Allen, Jon L.
xAllen, Jon.
Aviation & Space Museums of America. Arco.
xAllen, Jon L.
Stamp Collector's Guide to Europe. Arco.
Allen, Joseph.
xAllen, Joe.
Effective Business Communication: A Practical
Guide. Goodyear.
Allen, Joseph. *see* Allen, Robert Joseph.
Allen, Judson B. *see* Allen, Judson Boyce.
Allen, Judson Boyce, 1932-
xAllen, Judson B.
Friar As Critic: Literary Attitudes in the Later
Middle Ages. Vanderbilt U Pr.
Allen, Judy.
xAllen, Judy.
Exciting Things to Do with Nature Materials.
Lippincott.
Allen, Kenneth W.
xAllen, Kenneth W.
Organization & Administration of the Learning
Resources Center in the Community College.
Shoe String.
Allen, L. *see* Allen, Leslie
Allen, Laura J. *see* Allen, Laura Jean.
Allen, Laura Jean.
xAllen, Laura J.
illus. Ottie & the Star. Har-Row.
Allen, Leslie.
xAllen, A.
Optical Resonance & Two-Level Atoms. Wiley.
xAllen, L.
Essentials of Lasers. Pergamon.
Allen, Linda.
xAllen, Linda.
Lionel & the Spy Next Door. Morrow.
Mr. Simkin's Grandma. Morrow.
Allen, Loring.
xAllen, Loring.
OPEC Oil. Oelgeschlager.
Venezuelan Economic Development: A
Politico-Economic Analysis. Jai Pr.
Allen, Louis L, 1925-
xAllen, Louis L.
Starting & Succeeding in Your Own Small
Business. G&D.
Allen, M. L.
xAllen, M. L.
Murder in the Language Lab. Newbury Hse.
Allen, Marcus. *see* Allen, Mark.
Allen, Margaret.
xAllen, Margaret.
Guides to Creative Motion Musicianship.
Dorrance.
Allen, Margaret V. *see* Allen, Margaret Vanderhaar.
Allen, Margaret Vanderhaar.
xAllen, Margaret V.
The Achievement of Margaret Fuller. Pa St U
Pr.
Allen, Marjorie. *see* Allen, Marjorie N.
Allen, Marjorie N.
xAllen, Marjorie.
Farley, Are You for Real?. Coward.
xAllen, Marjorie N.

Farley, Are You for Real?. Schol Bk Serv.
Allen, Mark, 1946-
xAllen, Marcus.
Tantra for the West: A Guide to Personal
Freedom. Whatever Pub.
Allen, Martha. *see* Allen, Martha Dickson.
Allen, Martha Dickson.
xAllen, Martha.
Meet the Monkeys. P-H.
Allen, Mary, 1939-
xAllen, Mary.
The Necessary Blankness: Women in Major
American Fiction of the Sixties. U of Ill Pr.
Allen, Maury, 1932-
xAllen, Maury.
Damn Yankee: The Billy Martin Story. Times
Bks.
Where Have You Gone, Joe DiMaggio?: The
Story of America's Last Hero. NAL.
You Could Look It up: The Life of Casey
Stengel. Times Bks.
Allen, Michael. *see* Allen, Michael Derek.
Allen, Michael Derek, 1939-
xAllen, Michael.
Spence & the Holiday Murders. Walker & Co.
Spence at the Blue Bazaar. Walker & Co.
Allen, Nancy, 1950-
xAllen, Nancy.
Film Study Collections: A Guide to Their
Development & Use. Ungar.
Allen, Ned B. *see* Allen, Ned Bliss.
Allen, Ned Bliss, 1899-
xAllen, Ned B.
Sources of John Dryden's Comedies. Gordian.
The Sources of John Dryden's Comedies. R
West.
Allen, Oliver. *see* Allen, Oliver E.
Allen, Oliver E.
xAllen, Oliver.
Pruning & Grafting. Time-Life.
The Windjammers. Time-Life.
xAllen, Oliver E.
Pruning & Grafting. Silver.
Shade Gardens. Silver.
Shade Gardens. Time-Life.
The Windjammers. Silver.
Winter Gardens. Time-Life.
Allen, P. W. *see* Allen, Peter William.
Allen, Pamela.
xAllen, Pamela.
Mr. Archimedes' Bath. Morrow.
Mr Archimedes' Bath. Lothrop.
Allen, Paul, 1775-1826
xAllen, Paul.
The Life of Charles Brockden Brown. Schol
Facsimiles.
Allen, Peter William.
xAllen, P. W.
Natural Rubber & the Synthetics. Halsted Pr.
Allen, R. *see* Allen, Robert W.
Allen, R. E. *see* Allen, Reginald E.
Allen, R. Earl.
xAllen, Earl R.
Prayers That Changed History. Broadman.
xAllen, R. Earl.
Jesus Loves Me. Broadman.
Allen, R. G. D. *see* Allen, Roy George Douglas.
Allen, R. H. *see* Allen, Rutillus Harrison.
Allen, Reginald E., 1931-
xAllen, R. E.
Intro. by Socrates & Legal Obligation. U of
Minn Pr.
xAllen, Reginald E.
ed. Studies in Plato's Metaphysics. Humanities.
Allen, Rex W. *see* Allen, Rex Whitaker.
Allen, Rex Whitaker.
xAllen, Rex W.
Hospital Planning Handbook. Wiley.
Allen, Richard. *see* Allen, Richard Sanders.

Allen, Richard C., 1926-
xAllen, Richard C.
ed. Mental Health in America: The Years of
Crisis. Marquis.
ed. Readings in Law and Psychiatry. Johns
Hopkins.
Allen, Richard Hugh Sedley, Sir, 1903-
xAllen, Richard.
Imperialism & Nationalism in the Fertile
Crescent: Sources & Prospects of the
Arab-Israeli Conflict. Oxford U Pr.
Allen, Richard K., 1931-
xAllen, Richard K.
Organizational Management Through
Communication. Har-Row.
Allen, Richard S. *see* Allen, Richard Sanders.
Allen, Richard Sanders, 1917-
xAllen, Richard.
Rails in the North Woods. North Country.
xAllen, Richard S.
Covered Bridges of the Northeast. Greene.
Allen, Richard Stanley.
xAllen, Dick.
Looking Ahead: The Vision of Science Fiction.
HarBraceJ.
Allen, Robert, 1946-
xAllen, Robert.
Valhalla at the Ok. SBD.
Allen, Robert D.
xAllen, Robert D.
Psychotheatrics: The New Art of Self
Transformation. Garland Pub.
Allen, Robert F. *see* Allen, Robert Francis.
Allen, Robert Francis.
xAllen, Robert F.
Beat the System!: A Way to Create More
Human Environments. McGraw.
Allen, Robert Joseph, 1911-
xAllen, Joseph.
Story of Superstition Mountain & the Lost
Dutchman Gold Mine. PB.
Allen, Robert L. *see* Allen, Robert Loring.
Allen, Robert Loring.
xAllen, Robert L.
Soviet Economic Warfare. Pub Aff Pr.
Allen, Robert M.
xAllen, Robert M.
Intellectual Evaluation of the Mentally
Retarded Child: A Handbook. Western
Psych.
Psychosocial & Educational Aspects &
Problems of Mental Retardation. C C
Thomas.
Allen, Robert S. *see* Allen, Robert Sharon.
Allen, Robert Sharon, 1900-
xAllen, Robert S.
ed. Our Fair City. Arno.
Allen, Robert W.
xAllen, R.
Industrial Hygiene. P-H.
Allen, Ron R. *see* Allen, Ronald Royce.
Allen, Ronald R. *see* Allen, Ronald Royce.
Allen, Ronald Royce.
xAllen, Ron R.
Speech Communication in the Secondary
School. Allyn.
xAllen, Ronald R.
The Pragmatics of Public Communication.
Merrill.
Allen, Roy.
xAllen, Roy.
Major Airports of the World. Scribner.
Allen, Roy F., 1937-
xAllen, Roy F.
German Expressionist Poetry. Twayne.
Allen, Roy G. *see* Allen, Roy George Douglas.
Allen, Roy George Douglas, Sir.
xAllen, R. G. D.

27

Index Numbers in Theory & Practice. Aldine Pub.
 xAllen, Roy G.
  Mathematical Analysis for Economists. St Martin.
Allen, Rupert C.
 xAllen, Rupert C.
  Psyche & Symbol in the Theater of Federico Garcia Lorca: Perlimplin, Yerma, Blood Wedding. U of Tex Pr.
  The Symbolic World of Federico Garcia Lorca. Lib Soc Sci.
Allen, Rutillus Harrison, 1907-
 xAllen, R. H.
  Part-Time Farming in the Southeast. Da Capo.
Allen, Sarah S.
 xAllen, Sarah S.
  Ginger Hill. Blair.

Allen, Scottie.

 xAllen, Scottie.
  jt. auth. Living in Washington: A Moving Experience. Crown.

Allen, Steve, 1921-
 xAllen, Steve.
  Meeting of Minds. Crown.
Allen, T. Harrell. *see* Allen, Thomas Harrell.
Allen, Ted.
 xAllen, Ted.
  The World of Cats in Color. Arco.
Allen, Terence.
 xAllen, Terence.
  Particle Size Measurement. Methuen Inc.

Allen, Thomas B.
 xAllen, Thomas B.
  Vanishing Wildlife of North America. Natl Geog.
Allen, Thomas B. *see* Allen, Thomas Benton.
Allen, Thomas Benton.
 xAllen, Thomas B.
  A Short Life. Berkley Pub.
Allen, Thomas Harrell.
 xAllen, T. Harrell.
  The Bottom Line: Communicating in the Organization. Nelson-Hall.
Allen, Vernon L., 1933-
 xAllen, Vernon L.
  ed. Children As Teachers: Theory & Research on Tutoring. Acad Pr.
Allen, Virginia F. *see* Allen, Virginia French.
Allen, Virginia French.
 xAllen, Virginia F.
  English As a Second Language: A Comprehensive Bibliography. Arno.
Allen, W. Gore. *see* Allen, Walter Gore.
Allen, Walter, 1840-1907
 xAllen, Walter.
  Governor Chamberlain's Administration in South Carolina: A Chapter of Reconstruction in the Southern States. Negro U Pr.
Allen, Walter. *see* Allen, Walter Ernest.
Allen, Walter E. *see* Allen, Walter Ernest.
Allen, Walter Ernest, 1911-
 xAllen, Walter.
  Reading a Novel. Folcroft.
  Reading a Novel. Humanities.
 xAllen, Walter E.
  Arnold Bennett. AMS Pr.
  Reading a Novel. Arden Lib.
Allen, Walter Gore, 1910-
 xAllen, W. Gore.
  Renaissance in the North. Arno.
Allen, William. *see* Allen, William H.
Allen, William A.
 xAllen, William A.

Learning to Live Without Cigarettes. Doubleday.
Allen, William G.
 xAllen, William G.
  American Prejudice Against Color. Arno.
Allen, William H, 1924-
 xAllen, William.
  Halfmoons & Dwarf Parrots. TFH Pubns.
Allen, William O. *see* Allen, William Osborne Bird.
Allen, William Osborne Bird.
 xAllen, William O.
  Two Hundred Years: The History of the Society for Promoting Christian Knowledge, 1698-1898. B Franklin.
Allen, William S. *see* Allen, William Sheridan.
Allen, William Sheridan.
 xAllen.
  The Nazi Seizure of Power: The Experience of a Single German Town, 1930-1935. Watts.
 xAllen, William S.
  Nazi Seizure of Power: The Experience of a Single German Town, 1930-1935. New Viewpoints.
Allen, Woody.
 xAllen, Woody.
  Getting Even. Random.
  Getting Even. Random.
Allenbright, J. P.
 xAllenbright, J. P.
  The Ten-Dollar Wildcat. Arlington Hse.
Allendoerfer, Carl B. *see* Allendoerfer, Carl Barnett.
Allendoerfer, Carl Barnett.
 xAllendoerfer, Carl B.
  Fundamentals of Freshman Mathematics. McGraw.
  Principles of Mathematics. McGraw.
Allendorf, Katherine.
 xAllendorf, Katherine.
  Applique. Lerner Pubns.
Allentuck, Marcia. *see* Allentuck, Marcia Epstein.
Allentuck, Marcia Epstein, 1928-
 xAllentuck, Marcia.
  ed. Achievement of Isaac Bashevis Singer. S Ill U Pr.
Aller, Lawrence H. *see* Aller, Lawrence Hugh.
Aller, Lawrence Hugh.
 xAller, Lawrence H.
  Atoms, Stars, & Nebulae. Harvard U Pr.
Alley, Gloria. *see* Alley, Gloria I.
Alley, Gloria I.
 xAlley, Gloria.
  This Very Madness. Golden Quill.
Alley, Reuben E.
 xAlley, Reuben E.
  History of the University of Richmond: 1830-1971. U Pr of Va.
Alley, Robert.
 xAlley, Robert.
  The Front. PB.
Alley, Sam.
 xAlley, Sam.
  ed. Paraprofessionals in Mental Health: Theory & Practice. Human Sci Pr.
Alleyne, Reginald H.
 xAlleyne, Reginald H.
  Collective Bargaining in Public Employment. BNA.
Allford, Dorothy.
 xAllford, Dorothy.
  Instant Creation-Not Evolution. Stein & Day.
Allhoff, Fred.
 xAllhoff, Fred.
  Lightning in the Night. P-H.
Allibone, S. Austin. *see* Allibone, Samuel Austin.
Allibone, Samuel. *see* Allibone, Samuel Austin.
Allibone, Samuel Austin, 1816-1889
 xAllibone, S. Austin.

Critical Dictionary of English Literature & British & American Authors. Gale.
Critical Dictionary of English Literature & British & American Authors. R West.
 xAllibone, Samuel.
  Critical Dictionary of English Literature & British & American Authors. Gordon Pr.
Allies, Jabez, 1787-1856
 xAllies, Jabez.
  On the Ancient British, Roman & Saxon Antiquities & Folk-Lore of Worcestershire. Arno.
Alliger, G. *see* Alliger, Glen.
Alliger, Glen.
 xAlliger, G.
  ed. Vulcanization of Elastomers: Principles & Practice of Vulcanization of Commercial Rubbers. Krieger.
Allin, Cephas D. *see* Allin, Cephas Daniel.
Allin, Cephas Daniel.
 xAllin, Cephas D.
  Annexation, Preferential Trade & Reciprocity: An Outline of the Canadian Annexation Movement of 1849-50, with Special Reference to the Questions of Preferential Trade and Reciprocity. Greenwood.
Alling, Charles C.
 xAlling, Charles C.
  ed. Facial Pain. Lea & Febiger.
Allinger, Norman L.
 xAllinger, Norman L.
  Organic Chemistry. Worth.
Allingham, Helen. *see* Allingham, Helen (Paterson).
Allingham, Helen (Paterson).
 xAllingham, Helen.
  ed. Letters to William Allingham. AMS Pr.
Allingham, Margery. *see* Allingham, Margery Louise.
Allingham, Margery Louise, 1904-1966
 xAllingham, Margery.
  Crime at Black Dudley. Penguin.
  Death of a Ghost. Am Repr-Rivercity Pr.
  Death of a Ghost. Manor Bks.
  Sweet Danger. Penguin.
Allingham, William, 1824-1889
 xAllingham, William.
  Fifty Modern Poems. AMS Pr.
  Laurence Bloomfield in Ireland: A Modern Poem. AMS Pr.
  Robin Redbreast, & Other Verses. Core Collection.
  Songs, Ballads, & Stories. AMS Pr.
Allington, Richard. *see* Allington, Richard L.
Allington, Richard L.
 xAllington, Richard.
  Learning Through Reading in the Content Areas. Heath.
 xAllington, Richard L.
  Hearing. Raintree Pubs.
  Looking. Raintree Pubs.
  Opposites. Raintree Pubs.
  Shapes & Sizes. Raintree Pubs.
  Smelling. Raintree Pubs.
  Tasting. Raintree Pubs.
  Touching. Raintree Pubs.
Allinson, E. P. *see* Allinson, Edward Pease.
Allinson, Edward P. *see* Allinson, Edward Pease.
Allinson, Edward Pease.
 xAllinson, E. P.
  The City Government of Philadelphia. Johnson Repr.
 xAllinson, Edward P.
  The City Government of Philadelphia. AMS Pr.
Allinson, Francis G. *see* Allinson, Francis Greenleaf.
Allinson, Francis Greenleaf, 1856-
 xAllinson, Francis G.
  Lucian, Satirist & Artist. Cooper Sq.
Allinson, Gary D.
 xAllinson, Gary D.

Suburban Tokyo: A Comparative Study in Politics & Social Change. U of Cal Pr.

Allio, Robert J.
xAllio, Robert J.
Corporate Planning: Techniques & Applications. Am Mgmt.

Allis, Oswald T. *see* Allis, Oswald Thompson.

Allis, Oswald Thompson, 1880-
xAllis, Oswald T.
God Spake by Moses: An Exposition of the Pentateuch. Baker Bk.

Allis, Sarah.
xAllis, Sarah.
Nightwind. Fawcett.

Allison, A. C. *see* Allison, Anthony.

Allison, Alexander W. *see* Allison, Alexander Ward.

Allison, Alexander Ward.
xAllison, Alexander W.
Masterpieces of the Drama. Macmillan.
ed. Norton Anthology of Poetry. Norton.

Allison, Alida.
xAllison, Alida.
The Toddler's Potty Book. SC Prodns.

Allison, Anthony, 1925-
xAllison, A. C.
ed. Structure & Function of Plasma Proteins. Plenum Pub.

Allison, C. FitzSimons. *see* Allison, Christopher Fitz Simmons.

Allison, Christopher Fitz Simmons, 1927-
xAllison, C. FitzSimons.
Fear, Love, & Worship. Seabury.

Allison, Graham. *see* Allison, Graham T.

Allison, Graham T.
xAllison, Graham.
Remaking Foreign Policy: The Organizational Connection. Basic.

Allison, John M. *see* Allison, John Maudgridge Snowden.

Allison, John Maudgridge Snowden, 1880-1911
xAllison, John M.
Thiers & the French Monarchy. Shoe String.

Allison, K. W.
xAllison, K. W.
Liverworts of New Zealand. Intl Pubns Serv.

Allison, Lincoln.
xAllison, Lincoln.
Environmental Planning: A Political & Philosophical Analysis. Rowman.

Allison, Linda.
xAllison, Linda.
Rags: Making a Little Something Out of Almost Nothing. Crown.
illus. The Reasons for Seasons: The Great Cosmic Megagalactic Trip Without Moving from Your Chair. Little.
illus. The Sierra Club Summer Book. Sierra.

Allison, R. Bruce.
xAllison, R. Bruce.
Democrats in Exile 1968-1972: Political Confessions of a New England Liberal. Wisconsin Bks.

Allison, Ralph.
xAllison, Ralph.
Minds in Many Pieces: The Making of a Very Special Doctor. Rawson Wade.

Allison, Thomas, 1869-
xAllison, Thomas.
English Religious Life in the Eighth Century As Illustrated by Contemporary Letters. AMS Pr.

Alliss, Peter.
xAlliss, Peter.
Easier Golf. A S Barnes.

Allman, Eileen J. *see* Allman, Eileen Jorge.

Allman, Eileen Jorge, 1940-
xAllman, Eileen J.
Player King & Adversary: Two Faces of Play in Shakespeare. La State U Pr.

Allman, George J. *see* Allman, George Johnston.

Allman, George Johnston, 1824-1904
xAllman, George J.
Greek Geometry from Thales to Euclid. Arno.

Allman, James, 1943-
xAllman, James.
ed. Women's Status & Fertility in the Muslim World. Praeger.

Allman, Joe.
xAllman, Joe.
Creative Politics. Goodyear.

Allman, John, 1935-
xAllman, John.
Walking Four Ways in the Wind. Princeton U Pr.

Allman, Lawrence R.
xAllman, Lawrence R.
ed. Readings in Abnormal Psychology: Contemporary Perspectives 1976-1977. Har-Row.
ed. Readings in Adult Psychology: Contemporary Perspectives. Har-Row.

Allman, Ruth. *see* Allman, Ruth Cooper.

Allman, Ruth Cooper.
xAllman, Ruth.
Canaan Valley & the Black Bear. McClain.

Allmendinger, David.
xAllmendinger, David.
ed. The American People in the Antebellum North. Pendulum Pr.

Allmendinger, Susan.
xAllmendinger, Susan.
The American People in the Industrial City. Pendulum Pr.

Allon, Natalie.
xAllon, Natalie.
Urban Life Styles. Wm C Brown.

Allphin, Willard.
xAllphin, Willard.
Primer of Lamps & Lighting. A-W.

Allport, Gordon W. *see* Allport, Gordon Willard.

Allport, Gordon Willard, 1897-1967
xAllport, Gordon W.
The Nature of Prejudice. A-W.

Allport, J. A.
xAllport, J. A.
Economics. Cambridge U Pr.

Allred, Dorald M.
xAllred, Dorald M.
Living Things: An Introduction to Natural History. Brigham.

Allred, G. Hugh.
xAllred, G. Hugh.
How to Strengthen Your Marriage and Family. Brigham.
xAllred, Hugh.
How to Make a Good Mission Great. Deseret Bk.

Allred, Gordon. *see* Allred, Gordon T.

Allred, Gordon T.
xAllred, Gordon.
Lonesome Coyote. Lantern.
Old Crackfoot. Astor-Honor.
xAllred, Gordon T.
God the Father. Deseret Bk.

Allred, Hugh. *see* Allred, G. Hugh.

Allred, Mary.
xAllred, Mary.
The Move to a New House. Broadman.

Allsburg, Chris Van. *see* Van Allsburg, Chris.

Allsen, Philip E.
xAllsen, Philip E.
Conditioning & Physical Fitness: Current Answers to Relevant Questions. Wm C Brown.
Fitness for Life: An Individualized Approach. Wm C Brown.

Allshouse, Mary.
xAllshouse, Mary.

They Named Me Christopher Noel. Grossmont Pr.

Allston, Washington, 1779-1843
xAllston, Washington.
Lectures on Art - Poems. Da Capo.

Allswang, John M.
xAllswang, John M.
A House for All Peoples: Ethnic Politics in Chicago, 1890-1936. U Pr of Ky.
The New Deal & American Politics: A Study in Political Change. Wiley.

Allton, David.
xAllton, David.
Valuing Outdoor Recreation Benefits: An Annotated Bibliography. Vance Biblios.

Allum, P. A.
xAllum, P. A.
Politics & Society in Post-War Naples, 1945-1970. Cambridge U Pr.

Allvine. *see* Allvine, Glendon.

Allvine, Fred C.
xAllvine, Fred C.
Competition, Ltd.: The Marketing of Gasoline. Ind U Pr.
Highway Robbery: An Analysis of the Gasoline Crisis. Ind U Pr.

Allvine, Glendon.
xAllvine.
The Greatest Fox of Them All. Lyle Stuart.

Allworth, Edward.
xAllworth, Edward.
Central Asian Publishing & the Rise of Nationalism: An Essay & a List of Publications in the New York Public Library. NY Pub Lib.
ed. Nationality Group Survival in Multi-Ethnic States: Shifting Support Patterns in the Soviet Baltic Region. Praeger.
ed. The Nationality Question in Soviet Central Asia. Irvington.
ed. Soviet Nationality Problems. Columbia U Pr.

Allyn, John.
xAllyn, John.
Forty-Seven Ronin Story. C E Tuttle.

Alman, David.
xAlman, David.
World Full of Strangers. AMS Pr.

Almand, Joan.
xAlmand, Joan.
Establishing Values. Pathway Pr.

Almeda, Frank.
xAlmeda, Frank.
Systematics of the Genus Monochaetum (Melastomataceae) in Mexico & Central America. U of Cal Pr.

Almedingen, E. M. *see* Almedingen, Martha Edith.

Almedingen, Martha Edith, 1898-
xAlmedingen, E. M.
Anna. FS&G.
Candle at Dusk. FS&G.

Almeida, Jose.
xAlmeida, Jose.
Descubrir y Crear. Har-Row.

Almgren, Frederick J. *see* Almgren, Frederick J. Jr.

Almgren, Frederick J. , Jr.
xAlmgren, Frederick J.
Plateau's Problem: An Invitation to Varifold Geometry. Benjamin-Cummings.

Almon, Bert, 1943-
xAlmon, Bert.
Poems for the Nuclear Family. San Marcos.

Almon, Clopper.
xAlmon, Clopper.
Matrix Methods in Economics. A-W.

Almon, John, 1737-1805
xAlmon, John.

ed. A Collection of Papers Relative to the
Dispute Between Great Britain & America,
1764-1775. Da Capo.
Memoirs of a Late Eminent Bookseller. Kelley.
Almond, Gabriel A. *see* Almond, Gabriel Abraham.
Almond, Gabriel Abraham.
xAlmond, Gabriel A.
The Civic Culture: Political Attitudes &
Democracy in Five Nations. Little.
Civic Culture: Political Attitudes & Democracy
in Five Nations. Princeton U Pr.
ed. Comparative Politics Today: A World
View. Little.
ed. Politics of the Developing Areas. Princeton
U Pr.
Almond, Joseph P.
xAlmond, Joseph P.
Plumbers' Handbook. Audel.
Almquist, Elizabeth. *see* Almquist, Elizabeth M.
Almquist, Elizabeth M.
xAlmquist, Elizabeth.
Sociology: Women, Men & Society. West Pub.
xAlmquist, Elizabeth M.
Minorities, Gender & Work. Lexington Bks.
Almy, Amy B. *see* Almy, Amy Bruner.
Almy, Amy Bruner.
xAlmy, Amy B.
At Christmas Time the World Grows Young.
Arno.
Almy, Gerald, 1951-
xAlmy, Gerald.
Tying & Fishing Terrestrials. Stackpole.
Almy, Millie C. *see* Almy, Millie Corinne.
Almy, Millie Corinne, 1915-
xAlmy, Millie C.
Children's Experiences Prior to First Grade &
Success in Beginning Reading. AMS Pr.
Alo, R. A. *see* Alo, Richard A.
Alo, Richard A.
xAlo, R. A.
Normal Topological Spaces. Cambridge U Pr.
Alofsin, Dorothy, 1898-
xAlofsin, Dorothy.
America's Triumph: Stories of American
Jewish Heroes. Arno.
Aloisi, Ralph M. *see* Aloisi, Ralph Michael.
Aloisi, Ralph Michael, 1945-
xAloisi, Ralph M.
Principles of Immunodiagnostics. Mosby.
Alonso, Ose Rizal Y. *see* Rizal Y Alonso, Jose.
Alonso, William.
xAlonso, William.
Location & Land Use: Toward a General
Theory of Land Rent. Harvard U Pr.
Alotta, Robert I.
xAlotta, Robert I.
Old Names & New Places. Westminster.
Street Names of Philadelphia. Temple U Pr.
Alper, T. *see* Alper, Tikvah.
Alper, Tikvah, 1909-
xAlper, T.
Cellular Radiobiology. Cambridge U Pr.
Alpern, Andrew.
xAlpern, Andrew.
Apartments for the Affluent: A Historical
Survey of Buildings in New York. McGraw.
Alpern, Henry, 1895-
xAlpern, Henry.
March of Philosophy. Kennikat.
Alpers, Antony, 1919-
xAlpers, Antony.
The Life of Katherine Mansfield. Viking Pr.
Alpers, Bernard J. *see* Alpers, Bernard Jacob.
Alpers, Bernard Jacob.
xAlpers, Bernard J.
Essentials of the Neurological Examination.
Davis Co.
Alpert, Augusta, 1898-
xAlpert, Augusta.

The Solving of Problem-Situations by Preschool
Children. AMS Pr.
Alpert, George, 1922-
xAlpert, George.
The Queens. Da Capo.
Alpert, Hollis.
xAlpert, Hollis.
How to Play Double Bogey Golf. Times Bks.
Alpert, Leo M.
xAlpert, Leo M.
Florida Automobile Accident Law. Michie.
Alpert, M. E.
xAlpert, M. E.
Chemical & Radionuclide Food Contamination.
Mss Info.
Alpert, Martin A.
xAlpert, Martin A.
Cardiac Arrhythmias: A Bedside Guide to
Diagnosis & Treatment. Year Bk Med.
Alpert, Norman. *see* Alpert, Norman R.
Alpert, Norman R.
xAlpert, Norman.
Cardiac Hypertrophy. Acad Pr.
Alpert, Paul.
xAlpert, Paul.
Partnership or Confrontation?: Poor Lands &
Rich. Free Pr.
Alpert, Stephen P.
xAlpert, Stephen P.
Amusement Tokens of the United States &
Canada. Mead Co.
Alphen, Corry Van. *see* Van Alphen, Corry.
Alpiner, Jerome G., 1932-
xAlpiner, Jerome G.
Handbook of Adult Rehabilitative Audiology.
Williams & Wilkins.
Speech & Hearing Disorders in Children. HM.
Alsberg, Carl L. *see* Alsberg, Carl Lucas.
Alsberg, Carl Lucas, 1877-1940
xAlsberg, Carl L.
Combination in the American Bread-Baking
Industry: With Some Observations on the
Mergers of 1924-25. Arno.
Alschuler, Alfred S., 1939-
xAlschuler, Alfred S.
School Discipline: A Socially Literate Solution.
McGraw.
Alsever, Robert N.
xAlsever, Robert N.
Handbook of Endocrine Tests in Adults &
Children. Year Bk Med.
Alsop, Em B. *see* Alsop, Em Bowles.
Alsop, Em Bowles.
xAlsop, Em B.
ed. Greatness of Woodrow Wilson 1856-1956.
Kennikat.
Alsop, Stewart, 1914-
xAlsop, Stewart.
Stay of Execution: A Sort of Memoir.
Lippincott.
Alston, Eugenia.
xAlston, Eugenia.
Growing up Chimpanzee. T Y Crowell.
Alston, Patrick L.
xAlston, Patrick L.
Education & the State in Tsarist Russia.
Stanford U Pr.
Alstyne, Dorothy Van. *see* Van Alstyne, Dorothy.
Alsup, Fisher, 1877-1952
xAlsup, Fisher.
The Lost Crucifix of Our Lady of Guadalupe.
Shoal Creek Pub.
Alt, Arthur T. *see* Alt, Arthur Tilo.
Alt, Arthur Tilo, 1931-
xAlt, Arthur T.
Theodor Storm. Twayne.
Alt, Ruth R. *see* Alt, Ruth Ruggles.
Alt, Ruth Ruggles.
xAlt, Ruth R.

Steps to Composition: A Pre-Composition
Workbook for Students of English As a
Second Language. Georgetown U Pr.
Alta.
xAlta.
Letters to Women. Shameless Hussy.
Altamira y Crevea, Rafael, 1866-1951
xAltamira Y Crevea, Rafael.
History of Spanish Civilization. AMS Pr.
Altankov, Nikolay G.
xAltankov, Nikolay G.
The Bulgarian-Americans. Ragusan Pr.
Altbach, Edith H. *see* Altbach, Edith Hoshino.
Altbach, Edith Hoshino.
xAltbach, Edith H.
ed. From Feminism to Liberation. Schenkman.
Altbach, Philip G.
xAltbach, Philip G.
Comparative Higher Education Abroad:
Bibliography & Analysis. Interbk Inc.
ed. Comparative Higher Education Abroad:
Bibliography & Analysis. Praeger.
Higher Education in Developing Nations: A
Selected Bibliography. Interbk Inc.
The Student Internationals. Scarecrow.
ed. Students Protest. Am Acad Pol Soc Sci.
Altenbernd, Lynn.
xAltenbernd, Lynn.
Exploring Literature: Fiction, Poetry, Drama &
Criticism. Macmillan.
Alter, Judy.
xAlter, Judy.
After Pa Was Shot. Morrow.
Alter, Robert.
xAlter, Robert.
Defenses of the Imagination: Jewish Writers &
Modern Historical Crisis. Jewish Pubn.
ed. Modern Hebrew Literature. Behrman.
Partial Magic: The Novel As Self-Conscious
Genre. U of Cal Pr.
Alter, Stephen.
xAlter, Stephen.
Neglected Lives. FS&G.
Alterman, Hyman.
xAlterman, Hyman.
Counting People: The Census in History.
HarBraceJ.
Alternatives (Corporation).
xAlternatives Staff.
Alternate Catalogue. Alternatives.
Alternate Celebrations Catalogue. Alternatives.
Alternatives Staff. *see* Alternatives (Corporation).
Altfest, Lewis J.
xAltfest, Lewis J.
Introduction to Business. B&N.
Altgeld, John P. *see* Altgeld, John Peter.
Altgeld, John Peter, 1847-1902
xAltgeld, John P.
Live Questions. Gordon Pr.
Altgelt. *see* Altgelt, Klaus H.
Altgelt, Klaus H.
xAltgelt.
Chromatography in Petroleum Analysis.
Dekker.
Alth, Max.
xAlth, Max.
All About Bikes & Bicycling. Dutton.
All About Locks & Locksmithing. Dutton.
Do-It-Yourself Plumbing. Har-Row.
Do-It-Yourself Roofing & Siding. Dutton.
Homeowner's Quick-Repair & Emergency
Guide. Har-Row.
How to Farm Your Backyard the Mulch
Organic Way. McGraw.
Masonry & Concrete Work. Har-Row.
Motorcycles & Motorcycling. Watts.
The Stain Removal Handbook. Dutton.
Althaus, Paul, 1888-1966
xAlthaus, Paul.

The Ethics of Martin Luther. Fortress.
Fact & Faith in the Kerygma of Today.
   Greenwood.
Theology of Martin Luther. Fortress.
Althauser, R. P. *see* Althauser, Robert P.
Althauser, Robert P.
   xAlthauser, R. P.
   The Unequal Elites. Krieger.
Altheide, D. L. *see* Altheide, David L.
Altheide, David L.
   xAltheide, D. L.
   Creating Reality: How TV News Distorts
      Events. Sage.
   xAltheide, David L.
   Media Logic. Sage.
Althoen, Steven C.
   xAlthoen, Steven C.
   Finite Mathematics. Norton.
   Matrix Methods in Finite Mathematics: An
      Introduction with Applications to Business &
      Industry. Norton.
Altholz. *see* Altholz, Gertrude S.
Altholz, Gertrude S.
   xAltholz.
   Type Right!: A Complete Program for Business
      Typewriting. Pitman Learning.
Altholz, Josef L. *see* Altholz, Josef Lewis.
Altholz, Josef Lewis, 1933-
   xAltholz, Josef L.
   Churches in the Nineteenth Century. Bobbs.
Althouse, Andrew. *see* Althouse, Andrew Daniel.
Althouse, Andrew Daniel.
   xAlthouse, Andrew.
   Modern Refrigeration & Air Conditioning.
      Goodheart.
Althouse, Lavonne.
   xAlthouse, LaVonne.
   When Jew & Christian Meet. Friend Pr.
Althusser, Louis.
   xAlthusser, Louis.
   Lenin & Philosophy & Other Essays. Monthly
      Rev.
   Reading Capital. Schocken.
Altick, R. D. *see* Altick, Richard Daniel.
Altick, Richard D. *see* Altick, Richard Daniel.
Altick, Richard Daniel, 1915-
   xAltick, R. D.
   Preface to Critical Reading. HR&W.
   xAltick, Richard D.
   Art of Literary Research. Norton.
   Browning's Roman Murder Story: A Reading
      of the Ring & the Book. U of Chicago Pr.
   The Cowden Clarkes. Greenwood.
   English Common Reader: A Social History of
      the Mass Reading Public, 1800-1900. U of
      Chicago Pr.
   ed. Guide to Doctoral Dissertations in
      Victorian Literature, 1886-1958. Greenwood.
   Selective Bibliography for the Study of English
      & American Literature. Macmillan.
   The Shows of London. Harvard U Pr.
Altieri, Charles, 1942-
   xAltieri, Charles.
   Enlarging the Temple: New Directions in
      American Poetry During the 1960's. Bucknell
      U Pr.
   xAltieri, Charles F.
   Modern Poetry. AHM Pub.
Altieri, Charles F. *see* Altieri, Charles.
Altland, Millard, 1910-
   xAltland, Millard.
   The Pennsylvania Citizen. Penns Valley.
Altman. *see* Altman, Mary Ann.
Altman, Frances.
   xAltman, Frances.
   Reggie, the Goat. Denison.
Altman, H. B.
   xAltman, H. B.

A Guide to Collecting & Selling Netsuke. Pilot
   Bks.
Altman, Ida.
   xAltman, Ida.
   ed. Provinces of Early Mexico: Variants of
      Spanish American Regional Evolution. UCLA
      Lat Am Ctr.
Altman, Irwin.
   xAltman, Irwin.
   Culture & Environment. Brooks-Cole.
   ed. Human Behavior & Environment: Advances
      in Theory & Research. Plenum Pub.
Altman, J. C. *see* Altman, Jon C.
Altman, Joel B.
   xAltman, Joel B.
   The Tudor Play of Mind: Rhetorical Inquiry &
      the Development of Elizabethan Drama. U of
      Cal Pr.
Altman, Jon C.
   xAltman, J. C.
   The Economic Status of Australian Aborigines.
      Cambridge U Pr.
Altman, Joseph, 1925-
   xAltman, Joseph.
   Organic Foundations of Animal Behavior.
      Irvington.
Altman, Larry, 1928-
   xAltman, Larry.
   The Call of the Cricket. Celestial Arts.
Altman, Leon L., 1911-
   xAltman, Leon L.
   The Dream in Psychoanalysis. Intl Univs Pr.
Altman, Mary Ann.
   xAltman.
   How to Manage Your Law Office. Bender.
Altman, Michael L.
   xAltman, Michael L.
   Standards Relating to Juvenile Records &
      Information Systems. Ballinger Pub.
Altman, Millys.
   xAltman, Millys N.
   Racing in Her Blood. Lippincott.
Altman, Millys N. *see* Altman, Millys.
Altman, Philip L.
   xAltman, Philip L.
   ed. Cell Biology. FASEB.
Altman, S. P. *see* Altman, Samuel Ap.
Altman, Samuel P.
   xAltman, S. P.
   Orbital Hodograph Analysis. Am Astronaut.
Altman, Sig.
   xAltman, Sig.
   Comic Image of the Jew: Explorations of a Pop
      Culture Phenomenon. Fairleigh Dickinson.
Altman, Steven.
   xAltman, Steven.
   Readings in Organizational Behavior. HR&W.
Altmann, Simon L., 1924-
   xAltmann, Simon L.
   Induced Representations in Crystals &
      Molecules: Point, Space & Nonrigid Molecule
      Groups. Acad Pr.
Altmann, Stuart A.
   xAltmann, Stuart A.
   Baboon Ecology: African Field Research. U of
      Chicago Pr.
Altmeyer, Arthur J. *see* Altmeyer, Arthur Joseph.
Altmeyer, Arthur Joseph.
   xAltmeyer, Arthur J.
   Formative Years of Social Security. U of Wis
      Pr.
Altrocchi, John.
   xAltrocchi, John.
   Abnormal Behavior. HarBraceJ.
Altschul, Michael.
   xAltschul, Michael.
   A Baronial Family in Medieval England: The
      Clares, 1217-1314. AMS Pr.
Altschul, Siri V. *see* Altschul, Siri Von Reis.

Altschul, Siri Von Reis.
   xAltschul, Siri V.
   Drugs & Foods from Little Known Plants:
      Notes in Harvard University Herbaria.
      Harvard U Pr.
Altschule, Mark D. *see* Altschule, Mark David.
Altschule, Mark David.
   xAltschule, Mark D.
   ed. Frontiers of Pineal Physiology. MIT Pr.
   Nutritional Factors in General Medicine:
      Effects of Stress & Distorted Diets. C C
      Thomas.
   Origins of Concepts in Human Behavior: Social
      & Cultural Factors. Krieger.
Altshuler, Alan A., 1936-
   xAltshuler, Alan A.
   ed. Politics of the Federal Bureaucracy.
      Har-Row.
   The Urban Transportation System: Politics &
      Policy Innovation. MIT Pr.
Aluko, Olajide.
   xAluko, Olajide.
   ed. Ghana & Nigeria 1957-1970: A Study in
      Inter-African Discord. B&N.
Alvarez, A. *see* Alvarez, Alfred.
Alvarez, Alfred.
   xAlvarez, A.
   Hunt. S&S.
   Stewards of Excellence: Studies in Modern
      English & American Poets. Gordian.
Alvarez, E. C. *see* Alvarez, E. Charles.
Alvarez, E. Charles.
   xAlvarez, E. C.
   Fundamental Circuit Analysis. SRA.
Alvarez, Joseph. *see* Alvarez, Joseph A.
Alvarez, Joseph A.
   xAlvarez, Joseph.
   Politics in America. Creative Ed.
   xAlvarez, Joseph A.
   From Reconstruction to Revolution: The
      Blacks' Struggle for Equality. Atheneum.
Alvarez, Rodolfo.
   xAlvarez, Rodolfo.
   Discrimination in Organizations: Using Social
      Indicators to Manage Social Change.
      Jossey-Bass.
Alvarez, Russell R. De. *see* De Alvarez, Russell R.
Alvarez, Walter C. *see* Alvarez, Walter Clement.
Alvarez, Walter Clement, 1884-
   xAlvarez, Walter C.
   Alvarez on Alvarez. Strawberry Hill.
   Nerves in Collision. BJ Pub Group.
Alverson, Charles. *see* Alverson, Charles E.
Alverson, Charles E.
   xAlverson, Charles.
   Not Sleeping, Just Dead. Playboy Pbks.
Alves, Ron. *see* Alves, Ronald.
Alves, Ronald.
   xAlves, Ron.
   Living with Energy. Viking Pr.
Alvey, Edward.
   xAlvey, Edward.
   History of Mary Washington College,
      1908-1972. U Pr of Va.
Alvin, Juliette.
   xAlvin, Juliette.
   Music for the Handicapped Child. Oxford U
      Pr.
   Music Therapy. Basic.
   Music Therapy for the Autistic Child. Oxford
      U Pr.
Alwin, Robert. *see* Alwin, Robert H.
Alwin, Robert H.
   xAlwin, Robert.
   Algebra Programmed. P-H.
   xAlwin, Robert H.
   Algebra Programmed. P-H.
Alworth, William L., 1939-
   xAlworth, William L.

Stereochemistry & Its Application in
Biochemistry: The Relation Between
Substrate Symmetry & Biological
Stereospecificity. Wiley.

Aly, H. H.
xAly, H. H.
Lectures on Particles & Fields. Gordon.

Aly, Lucile F. *see* Aly, Lucile Folse.

Aly, Lucile Folse, 1913-
xAly, Lucile F.
John G. Neihardt: A Critical Biography.
Humanities.

Alyea, Paul E. *see* Alyea, Paul Edgar.

Alyea, Paul Edgar.
xAlyea, Paul E.
Fairhope, 1894-1954: The Story of a Single Tax
Colony. AMS Pr.

Alyeshmerni, Mansoor.
xAlyeshmerni, Mansoor.
Working with Aspects of Language. HarBraceJ.

Alzaga, Florinda, 1930-
xAlzaga, Florinda.
Las Ansias De Infinito En la Avellaneda.
Ediciones.

Alzona, Encarnacion, 1895-
xAlzona, Encarnacion.
Some French Contemporary Opinions of the
Russian Revolution of 1905. AMS Pr.

Amacher, Peter.
xAmacher, Peter.
Freud's Neurological Education & Its Influence
on Psychoanalytic Theory. Intl Univs Pr.

Amacher, Richard E.
xAmacher, Richard E.
American Political Writers: 1588-1800.
Twayne.
Edward Albee. Twayne.

Amacher, Ryan C.
xAmacher, Ryan C.
ed. The Economic Approach to Public Policy:
Selected Readings. Cornell U Pr.

Amado, Jorge, 1912-
xAmado, Jorge.
Gabriela, Clove & Cinnamon. Avon.
Gabriela, Clove & Cinnamon. Knopf.
Home Is the Sailor. Avon.
The Violent Land. Avon.
Violent Land. Knopf.

Amaducci, L. *see* Amaducci, Luigi.

Amaducci, Luigi.
xAmaducci, L.
ed. Aging of the Brain & Dementia. Raven.

Amann, Dick.
xAmann, Dick.
Forgotten Women of Computer History. Prog
Studies.

Amann, Peter, 1927-
xAmann, Peter H.
Revolution & Mass Democracy: The Paris Club
Movement of 1848. Princeton U Pr.

Amann, Peter H. *see* Amann, Peter.

Amanuddin, Syed.
xAmanuddin, Syed.
The Age of Female Eunuchs. Poetry Eastwest.

Amary, Issam B.
xAmary, Issam B.
Creative Recreation for the Mentally Retarded.
C C Thomas.
Effective Meal Planning & Food Preparation
for the Mentally Retarded-Developmentally
Disabled: Comprehensive & Innovative
Teaching Methods. C C Thomas.
The Rights of the Mentally Retarded -
Developmentally Disabled to Treatment &
Education. C C Thomas.

Amateur Swimming Association.
xAmateur Swimming Association.
The Teaching of Swimming. British Bk Ctr.

Amato, Antony.
xAmato, Antony.

Affair. Ballantine.
Affair. Putnam.

Amazing Life Games. *see* Amazing Life Games
Company.

Amazing Life Games Company.
xAmazing Life Games.
Good Cents. HM.
Good Cents. HM.

Amberley, John R. *see* Amberley, John Russell.

Amberley, John Russell, Viscount, 1842-1876
xAmberley, John R.
An Analysis of Religious Belief. Arno.
An Analysis of Religious Belief. Gordon Pr.

Ambers, Henry J.
xAmbers, Henry J.
The Dirigible & the Future. Edelweiss Pr.

Ambirajan, S.
xAmbirajan, S.
Classical Political Economy & British Policy in
India. Cambridge U Pr.
Taxation of Corporate Income in India. Asia.

Ambler, Eric.
xAmbler, Eric.
Cause for Alarm. Am Repr-Rivercity Pr.
Cause for Alarm. Ballantine.
A Coffin for Dimitrios. Am Repr-Rivercity Pr.
A Coffin for Dimitrios. Ballantine.
A Coffin for Dimitrios. Pubs Inc.
Journey into Fear. Ballantine.
The Light of Day. Am Repr-Rivercity Pr.
The Light of Day. Ballantine.
The Siege of the Villa Lipp. Ballantine.
The Siege of the Villa Lipp. G K Hall.
The Siege of the Villa Lipp. Random.

Ambler, John S. *see* Ambler, John Steward.

Ambler, John Steward.
xAmbler, John S.
French Army in Politics, 1945-1962. Ohio St U
Pr.

Ambrecht, Biliana C. *see* Ambrecht, Biliana C. S.

Ambrecht, Biliana C. S.
xAmbrecht, Biliana C.
Politicizing the Poor: The Legacy of the War
on Poverty in a Mexican American
Community. Praeger.

Ambron, Sueann R. *see* Ambron, Sueann Robinson.

Ambron, Sueann Robinson.
xAmbron, Sueann R.
Child Development. HR&W.
Lifespan Human Development. HR&W.

Ambrose. *see* Ambrose, Edmund Jack.

Ambrose, E. J. *see* Ambrose, Edmund Jack.

Ambrose, Edmund Jack.
xAmbrose.
Cell Biology. Univ Park.
xAmbrose, E. J.
Cell Biology. A-W.

Ambrose, Harrison. *see* Ambrose, Harrison W.

Ambrose, Harrison W.
xAmbrose, Harrison.
Handbook of Biological Investigation. Hunter
NC.

Ambrose, James. *see* Ambrose, James E.

Ambrose, James E.
xAmbrose, James.
Simplified Design of Building Structures.
Wiley.

Ambrose, Stephen E.
xAmbrose, Stephen E.
Rise to Globalism: American Foreign Policy,
1938-1980. Penguin.

Ambrose, William G.
xAmbrose, William G.
College Algebra. Macmillan.
College Algebra & Trigonometry. Macmillan.

Ambrose-Grillet, Jeane.
xAmbrose-Grillet, Jeane.
Glossary of Transformational Grammar.
Newbury Hse.

Ambrose-Grillet, Jeanne. *see* Ambrose-Grillet, Jeane.

Ambrosius, St.
xAmbrosius.
Opera. Johnson Repr.

Ambrus, Victor G.
xAmbrus, Victor G.
illus. Mishka. Warne.

Amedeo, Douglas.
xAmedeo, Douglas.
Introduction to Scientific Reasoning in
Geography. Wiley.

Ameiss, A. *see* Ameiss, Albert P.

Ameiss, Albert P.
xAmeiss, A.
Accountant's Desk Handbook. P-H.

Amelinckx, S. *see* Amelinckx, Severin.

Amelinckx, Severin.
xAmelinckx, S.
Diffraction & Imaging Techniques in Material
Science. Elsevier.
The Direct Observation of Dislocations. Acad
Pr.

Amen, Carol.
xAmen, Carol.
Hyacinths to Feed the Soul. Southern Pub.
Love Is the Motive. Southern Pub.
Teetering on the Tightrope. Southern Pub.

Amend, Victor E. *see* Amend, Victor Earl.

Amend, Victor Earl.
xAmend, Victor E.
Readings from Left to Right. Free Pr.

Amendola, J. *see* Amendola, Joseph.

Amendola, Joseph.
xAmendola, J.
Ice Carving Made Easy. Corner.
xAmendola, Joseph.
Baker's Manual for Quantity Baking & Pastry
Making. Hayden.
Ice Carving Made Easy. Radio City.
Practical Cooking & Baking for Schools &
Institutions. Hayden.

Amenta, Peter S. *see* Amenta, Peter Sebastian.

Amenta, Peter Sebastian, 1927-
xAmenta, Peter S.
ed. Histology. Med Exam.

Amerian Society of Civil Engineers. *see* American
Society of Civil Engineers.

America, Richard F.
xAmerica, Richard F.
Developing the Afro-American Economy:
Building on Strength. Lexington Bks.

American Abstract Artist.
xAmerican Abstract Artists.
ed. World of Abstract Art. Wittenborn.

American Abstract Artists. *see* American Abstract Artist.

American Academy of Arts and Letters.
xAmerican Academy Of Arts And Letters.
Academy Papers. Arno.
Commemorative Tributes of the Academy,
1905-1941. Arno.
Four Addresses in Commemoration of the
Twentieth Anniversary of the Founding of
the Academy: Academy Publ., No. 54. Arno.

American Academy of Arts and Sciences, Boston.
xAmerican Academy of Arts and Sciences, Boston.
Science & the Modern Mind: A Symposium.
Arno.

American Academy of Orthopaedic Surgeons.
xAAOS
AAOS Instructional Course Lectures. Mosby.
Symposium on Reconstructive Surgery of the
Knee. Mosby.
xAmerican Academy of Orthopaedic Surgeons.

Atlas of Limb Prosthetics: Surgical &
Prosthetic Principles. Mosby.

Atlas of Orthotics: Biomechanical Principals &
Applications. Mosby.

Symposium on Microsurgery: Practical Use in
Orthopaedics. Mosby.

Symposium on Myelomeningocele. Mosby.

Symposium on Tendon Surgery in the Hand.
Mosby.

Symposium on the Athlete's Knee: Surgical
Repair & Reconstruction. Mosby.

xAmerican Academy of Orthopedic Surgeons.
Joint Motion: Method of Measuring &
Recording. Churchill.

xTheAmerican Academy of Orthopaedic Surgery.
Selective Bibliography of Orthopaedic Surgery.
Mosby.

American Academy of Orthopedic Surgeons. *see*
American Academy of Orthopaedic Surgeons.

American Academy of Pediatrics.
xAmerican Academy Of Pediatrics.
Child Health Services & Pediatric Education:
Report of the Committee for the Study of
Child Health Services. Arno.
jt. auth. Growing Pains. AMA.

American Academy of Podiatric Sports Medicine.
xMembers of the American Academy of Podiatric
Sports Medicine.
Sports Medicine Nineteen Eighty: A Review
by the Members of the American Academy
of Podiatric Sports Medicine. Futura Pub.

American Academy of Political & Social Science. *see*
American Academy of Political and Social Science,
Philadelphia.

**American Academy of Political and Social Science,
Philadelphia.**
xAmerican Academy of Political & Social Science.
American Indians & American Life. Kraus
Repr.
American Negro. Kraus Repr.
America's Race Problems. Haskell.
Annals of the American Academy of Political
& Social Science. Arno.
ed. City Bosses & Political Machines. Arno.
Design for International Relations Research:
Scope, Theory, Methods & Relevance. Am
Acad Pol Soc Sci.
Education for Urban Administration. Am Acad
Pol Soc Sci.
Eightieth Anniversary Index, Jan. 1966-Nov.
1970. Am Acad Pol Soc Sci.
Harmonizing Technological Developments &
Social Policy in America. Am Acad Pol Soc
Sci.
Instruction in Diplomacy: The Liberal Arts
Approach. Am Acad Pol Soc Sci.
Integration of the Social Sciences Through
Policy Analysis. Am Acad Pol Soc Sci.
International Studies: Present Status & Future.
Am Acad Pol Soc Sci.
Language & Area Studies Review. Am Acad
Pol Soc Sci.
The Police & the Crime Problem. AMS Pr.
Present Day Immigration with Special
Reference to the Japanese. R & E Res Assoc.
Prisons in Transformation: Proceedings.
Greenwood.
Public Service Professional Associations & the
Public Interest. Am Acad Pol Soc Sci.
xAmerican Academy Of Political And Social
Science.
America's Race Problems. Negro U Pr.
Negro's Progress in Fifty Years. Negro U Pr.
Reform in Administration of Justice. AMS Pr.

American Adventures Association.
xAmerican Adventures Association.

International Adventure Travelguide, 1979.
Random.
Nineteen Hundred Eighty Worldwide
Adventure Travelguide. Random.

**American Alliance for Health, Physical Education and
Recreation.**
xAAHPER Convention, Seattle, 1977.
Abstracts of Research Papers. AAHPER.
xAAHPER National Convention, Milwaukee.
Abstracts of Research Papers. AAHPER.
xAmerican Alliance for Health, Physical
Education, & Recreation.
Abstracts of Research Papers, 1971. AAHPER.
Abstracts of Research Papers, 1972. AAHPER.
Abstracts of Research Papers, 1973. AAHPER.
Abstracts of Research Papers, 1975. AAHPER.
Administration of Athletics in Colleges &
Universities. AAHPER.
Annotated Bibliography on Perceptual-Motor
Development. AAHPER.
Annotated Research, Bibliography in Physical
Education Recreation & Psychomotor
Function of Mentally Retarded Persons.
AAHPER.
Annual Safety Education Review, 1972.
AAHPER.
Archery Selected Articles, 1971. AAHPER.
Athletics in Education. AAHPER.
Basketball Guide 1978-79. AAHPER.
Basketball Rules 1978-79. AAHPER.
Basketball Selected Articles. AAHPER.
Bibliography of Research Involving Female
Subjects. AAHPER.
Certification of High School Coaches.
AAHPER.
Children's Dance. AAHPER.
College Physical Education: The General
Program. AAHPER.
Completed Research in Health, Physical
Education, & Recreation. AAHPER.
Crowd Control for High School Athletics.
AAHPER.
Dance Facilities. AAHPER.
Directory of Professional Preparation Programs
in Recreation, Parks & Related Area.
AAHPER.
Drugs & the Coach. AAHPER.
Essentials of a Quality Elementary School
Physical Education Program. AAHPER.
Evaluating the High School Athletic Program.
AAHPER.
Evaluation Instruments in Health Education.
AAHPER.
Field Hockey Guide 1978-80. AAHPER.
Field Hockey-Lacrosse Selected Articles.
AAHPER.
Flag Football-Speedball Guide 1978-80.
AAHPER.
Focus on Dance: Dance Therapy. AAHPER.
Foundations & Practices in Perceptual-Motor
Learning. AAHPER.
Gymnastics Guide 1978-80. AAHPER.
Gymnastics Selected Articles, 1971. AAHPER.
Health Education 1975. AAHPER.
Healthful School Environment. AAHPER.
Intramural Portfolio. AAHPER.
Introduction to School Nursing Curriculum.
AAHPER.
Kinesiology, Four. AAHPER.
Kinesiology, Three. AAHPER.
Knowledge & Understanding in Physical
Education. AAHPER.
League Constitution & by-Laws for Girl's
Interscholastic Sports - a Suggested Guide.
AAHPER.
Learning About Alcohol: A Resource Book for
Teachers. AAHPER.
Leisure Today: Selected Readings. AAHPER.
Materials on the Creative Arts: For Persons
with Handicapping Conditions. AAHPER.

Mental Health & School Health Services.
AAHPER.
Movement Activities for Places & Spaces.
AAHPER.
NAGWS Research Reports. AAHPER.
Nutrition for Athletes: A Handbook for
Coaches. AAHPER.
Outdoor Education. AAHPER.
Physical Education & Recreation for the
Visually Handicapped. AAHPER.
Physical Education Around the World:
Monograph No. 2-6. AAHPER.
Physical Education for High School Students.
AAHPER.
Planning & Financing School-Community
Recreation. AAHPER.
Practical Guide for Teaching the Mentally
Retarded to Swim. AAHPER.
Preparing Teachers for a Changing Society.
AAHPER.
Preparing the Elementary Specialist. AAHPER.
Professional Preparation in Aquatics Education:
Curriculum Guidelines. AAHPER.
Professional Preparation in Dance, Physical
Education, Recreation Education, Safety
Education, & School Health Education.
AAHPER.
Professional Preparation in Physical Education
& Coaching. AAHPER.
Professional Preparation in Safety Education &
School Health Education. AAHPER.
Professional Preparation of the Elementary
School Physical Education Teacher.
AAHPER.
Professional Standards for Aquatics Education.
AAHPER.
Proficiency Testing in Physical Education.
AAHPER.
Programmed Instruction in Health & Physical
Education. AAHPER.
Recreation & Physical Activity for the
Mentally Retarded. AAHPER.
Research in Dance. AAHPER.
Resource Book for Drug Abuse Education.
AAHPER.
Resource Guide in Sex Education for the
Mentally Retarded. AAHPER.
Riding Selected Articles. AAHPER.
Safety in Aquatic Activities. AAHPER.
Safety in Individual & Dual Sports. AAHPER.
Selected Problems in Sports Safety. AAHPER.
Special Olympics Instructional Manual: From
Beginners to Champions. AAHPER.
Sports Safety. AAHPER.
State Requirements in Physical Education for
Teachers & Students. AAHPER.
Suggested School Health Policies. AAHPER.
Swimnastics Is Fun. AAHPER.
Teacher's Handbook on Venereal Disease
Education. AAHPER.
Teaching Safety in the Elementary School.
AAHPER.
Tennis Group Instruction. AAHPER.
Utilization of Disadvantaged Workers in Public
Park & Recreation Services. AAHPER.
Volleyball Guide 1978-79. AAHPER.
Volleyball Rules 1978-79. AAHPER.
Volleyball Scorebook: Official. AAHPER.
What Recreation Research Says to the
Recreation Practitioner. AAHPER.
What Research Tells the Coach About
Baseball. AAHPER.
What Research Tells the Coach About
Distance Running. AAHPER.
What Research Tells the Coach About
Football. AAHPER.
What Research Tells the Coach About
Swimming. AAHPER.
Women's Athletics: Coping with Controversy.
AAHPER.

American Anti-Slave Society. *see* American Anti-Slavery
Society.

American Anti-Slavery Society - Philadelphia -1853. *see*
American Anti-Slavery Society.

American Antiquarian Society. *see* American Antiquarian
Society, Worcester, Mass.

American Antiquarian Society, Worcester, Mass.
xAmerican Antiquarian Society.
Catalogue of the Manuscript Collections of the
American Antiquarian Society. G K Hall.
Transactions & Collections. Johnson Repr.

American Anti-Slavery Society.
xAmerican Anti-Slave Society.
Slavery & the Internal Slave Trade in the U. S.
Scholarly.
xAmerican Anti-Slavery Society.
American Anti-Slavery Reporter. Negro U Pr.
Anti-Slavery Examiner. Negro U Pr.
Anti-Slavery History of the John Brown Year.
Negro U Pr.
Anti-Slavery History of the John Brown Year:
Being the Twenty-Seventh Report of the
American Anti-Slavery Society. Arno.
Anti-Slavery Record. Negro U Pr.
Anti-Slavery Tracts. Negro U Pr.
Legion of Liberty & Force of Truth, Containing
the Thoughts, Words, & Deeds of Some
Prominent Apostles, Champions, & Martyrs.
Arno.
Proceedings of the American Anti-Slavery
Society at Its Third Decade. Arno.
Proceedings of the American Anti-Slavery
Society at Its Third Decade. Negro U Pr.
xAmerican Anti-Slavery Society - Philadelphia
-1853.
Proceedings of the American Anti-Slavery
Society at Its Second Decade. Negro U Pr.

American Arbitration Association.
xAmerican Arbitration Association.
Dictionary of Arbitration & Its Terms. Oceana.
New Strategies for Peaceful Resolution of
International Business Disputes. Oceana.

American Artist.
xAmerican Artist Magazine Staff.
Twenty Figure Painters & How They Work.
Watson-Guptill.
xAmerican Artist Staff.
ed. American Artist: Norman Rockwell.
Crown.
ed. American Artist: Portrait of America.
Crown.

American Artist Magazine Staff. *see* American Artist.
American Artist Staff. *see* American Artist.

American Artists Congress.
xAmerican Artists' Congress.
Graphic Works of the American '30s. Da
Capo.

American Artists' Congress. *see* American Artists
Congress.

American Assembly.
xAmerican Assembly.
Arms Control. Arno.
Economic Security for Americans. Arno.
Outer Space: Prospects for Man and Society.
Arno.
Secretary of State. Arno.
United States & Africa. Arno.
The United States & the Middle East. Arno.
U. S. Monetary Policy. Arno.

American Association for Gifted Children.
xAmerican Association for Gifted Children.
The Gifted Child. Greenwood.
On Being Gifted. Walker & Co.

**American Association for Health, Physical Education
and Recreation.**
xAmerican Association for Health, Physical
Education & Recreation.
Memories Beyond Bloomers. AAHPER.
Professional Preparation Directory for

Elementary School Physical Education.
AAHPER.

American Association for State & Local History. *see*
American Association for State and Local History.

American Association for State and Local History.

xAmerican Association for State & Local History.

Directory of Historical Societies & Agencies in
the United States & Canada. AASLH.

One Hundred One Ideas from History News.
AASLH.

American Association for the Advancement of Science.
xAmerican Association for the Advancement of
Science.
Industrial Science, Present & Future. Arno.
The Proceedings of the Conference on National
Energy Policy. AAAS.

American Association for the Advancement of Science,
Dallas, December, 1968. *see* Symposium on the
Global Effects of Environmental Pollution, Dallas,
1968.

American Association of Agricultural College Editors.
xAmerican Association of Agricultural College
Editors.
Communications Handbook. Interstate.

American Association of Colleges of Pharmacy.
xAACP.
AACP Roster of Teachers in Schools of
Pharmacy: Annual. Am Assn Coll Pharm.
Doctoral Roster. Am Assn Coll Pharm.
Shall I Study Pharmacy?. Am Assn Coll
Pharm.

**American Association of Colleges of Pharmacy. Section
of Librarians. Committee on Standards.**
xAACP Section of Librarians.
Standards & Planning Guide for Pharmacy
Library Service, 1975. Am Assn Coll Pharm.

American Association of Community & Junior Colleges.
see American Association of Community and Junior
Colleges.

**American Association of Community and Junior
Colleges.**
xAmerican Association of Community & Junior
Colleges.
Community, Junior, & Technical College
Directory: 1976. Am Assn Comm Jr Coll.

American Association of Hospital Consultants.
xAmerican Association Of Hospital Consultants.
Functional Planning of General Hospitals.
McGraw.

American Association of Museums.
xAmerican Association of Museums.
A Statistical Survey of Museums in the United
States & Canada. Arno.

American Association of School Administrators.
xAASA.
New Forms for Community Education. Am
Assn Sch Admin.
xAmerican Association Of School Administrators.
Administrator's Handbook on Educational
Accountability. Am Assn Sch Admin.
American Elementary & Secondary Schools
Abroad. Am Assn Sch Admin.
Christopher Jencks in Perspective. Am Assn
Sch Admin.
Developing Vocational Education Programs in
the Schools. Am Assn Sch Admin.
Educational Planning. Am Assn Sch Admin.
Impact of Racial Issues on Educational
Administration. Am Assn Sch Admin.
Open Space Schools. Am Assn Sch Admin.
Sex Equality in Educational Administration.
Am Assn Sch Admin.

American Association of School Librarians.
xAmerican Association of School Librarians.

Certification Model for Professional School
Media Personnel. ALA.

**American Association of Veterinary Laboratory
Diagnosticians. Committee on Salmonellosis and
Arizonosis.**
xCommittee on Salmonellosis & Arizonosis of the
American Assn. of Vet. Lab Diagnosticians.
ed. Culture Methods for the Detection of
Animal Salmonellosis & Arizonosis. Iowa St
U Pr.

American Astronautical Society.
xAmerican Astronautical Society.
Lunar Flight Problems. Am Astronaut.
Post Apollo Space Exploration. Am Astronaut.
xSecond Zero Gravity Symposium-Los
Angeles-1963.
Physical & Biological Phenomena in a
Weightless State. Am Astronaut.

American Bar Association, Committee on International
Labor Law Section of Labor Relations Law. *see*
American Bar Association. International Labor Law
Committee.

**American Bar Association. International Labor Law
Committee.**
xAmerican Bar Association, Committee on
International Labor Law Section of Labor
Relations Law.
The Labor Relations Law of Canada. BNA.

American Bible Society.
xAmerican Bible Society.
Good News for Modern Man: The New
Testament in Today's English Version. PB.
The Psalms for Modern Man: In Today's
English Version. PB.
ed. Scriptures of the World; a Compilation of
1,603 Languages in Which at Least One
Book of the Bible Has Been Published.
United Bible.
Today's English Version of the New Testament
& Psalms. Macmillan.

American Bookseller's Association. *see* American
Booksellers Association.

American Booksellers Assn. *see* American Booksellers
Association.

American Booksellers Association.
xAmerican Bookseller's Association.
ed. A Manual on Bookselling: How to Open &
Run Your Own Bookstore. Crown.
xAmerican Booksellers Assn.
A Manual on Bookselling: How to Open &
Run Your Own Bookstore. Crown.

American Bureau of Metal Statistics.
xAmerican Bureau of Metal Statistics Staff.
ABMS Non-Ferrous Metal Data Publication.
Am Bur Metal.
ed. & Compiled by ABMS Non-Ferrous Metal
Data Publication: 1974 Yearbook. Am Bur
Metal.
ed. ABMS Non-Ferrous Metal Data
Publication: 1976 Year Book. Am Bur Metal.
ed. Fifty-Second Annual Yearbook. Am Bur
Metal.
Non-Ferrous Metal Data Yearbook, 1978. Am
Bur Metal.
Non-Ferrous Motal Data Yearbook, 1979. Am
Bur Metal.
Compiled by Year Book of the American
Bureau of Metal Statistics. Am Bur Metal.

American Camping Association.
xAmerican Camping Association.
Camp Standards with Interpretations for the
Accreditation of Organized Camps. Am
Camping.
Guide to a Counselor-in-Training Program. Am
Camping.
Parents' Guide to Accredited Camps: 1979.
Am Camping.

American Cancer Society. Ohio Division.
xAmerican Cancer Society, Ohio Division, Inc.

Ohio Celebrity Cookbook. Wimmer Bks.

American Catholic Philosophical Association.
xAmerican Catholic Philosophical Association.
Ethics & Other Knowledge: Proceedings.
Johnson Repr.
Natural Law & International Relations.
Johnson Repr.
Philosophy & the Experimental Sciences:
Proceedings. Johnson Repr.
Role of the Christian Philosopher, Proceedings.
Johnson Repr.

American Ceramic Society.
xAmerican Ceramic Society.
Cements Research Progress 1975. Am Ceramic.

American Chamber of Commerce in Japan.
xAmerican Chamber of Commerce in Japan.
ACCJ Directory of Members. A M Newman.

Japanese Court Decisions in Patent
Infringement Cases. A M Newman.

Japanese Court Decisions in Trademarks &
Unfair Competition Cases. A M Newman.

Living in Japan. A M Newman.

Manual of Employment Practices in Japan. A
M Newman.

**American Chemical Society. Committee on Chemistry
and Public Affairs.**
xACS Committee on Chemistry & Public Affairs.
Chemistry & the Food System. Am Chemical.
xACS Committee On Chemistry And Public
Affairs.
Cleaning Our Environment: The Chemical
Basis for Action. Am Chemical.

American Civil Liberties Union.
xAmerican Civil Liberties Union.
ACLU 1976 Policy Guide. Lexington Bks.

American College of Emergency Physicians.
xAmerican College of Emergency Physicians.
Emergency Department Organization &
Management. Mosby.

American College of Sports Medicine.
xAmerican College of Sports Medicine.
ed. The Encyclopedia of Sport Sciences &
Medicine. Macmillan.
ed. Guidelines for Graded Exercise: Testing &
Exercise Prescription. Lea & Febiger.
xPapers Presented Before the College of Sports
Medicine.
Exercise & Aging: The Scientific Basis. Enslow
Pubs.

American College of Surgeons.
xAmerican College of Surgeons.
Early Care of the Injured Patient. Saunders.
xTheAmerican College of Surgeons.
Surgical Nutrition. Saunders.

**American College of Surgeons. Committee on Pre and
Postoperative Care.**
xAmerican College of Surgeons Committee on Pre
& Postoperative Care.
Manual of Preoperative & Postoperative Care.
Saunders.
xCommittee on Pre & Postoperative Care
American College of Surgeons.
Manual of Surgical Intensive Care. Saunders.

American Colonization Society.
xAmerican Colonization Society.
Annual Reports: First to Ninety First, Ninety
Third. Negro U Pr.

American Concrete Institute Committee 116.
xACI Committee 116.
Cement & Concrete Terminology. ACI.

American Concrete Institute Committee 209.
xACI Committee 209.

Shrinkage & Creep in Concrete. ACI.

American Concrete Institute Committee 224.
xACI Committee 224.
Causes, Mechanism, & Control of Cracking in
Concrete. ACI.

American Concrete Institute Committee 311.
xACI Committee 311.
ACI Manual of Concrete Inspection. ACI.

American Concrete Institute Committee 315.
xACI Committee 315.
Manual of Standard Practice for Detailing
Reinforced Concrete Structures: ACI 315-74.
ACI.

American Concrete Institute Committee 318.
xACI Committee 318.
Building Code Requirements for Reinforced
Concrete: ACI 318-63 ANSI A89.1-1964.
ACI.
Building Code Requirements for Reinforced
Concrete: ACI 318-77 ANSI a89.1-1972.
ACI.
Building Code Requirements for Reinforced
Concrete SI Metric Edition: ACI 318-71.
ACI.
Commentary on Building Code Requirements
for Reinforced Concrete: ACI 318-77. ACI.
Supplement to ACI 318-71 & Commentary,
1975. ACI.

American Concrete Institute Committee 340.
xACI Committee 340.
Design Handbook in Accordance with the
Strength Design Method of ACI 318-71.
ACI.

American Correctional Association.
xAmerican Correctional Association.
Correctional Classification & Treatment.
Anderson Pub Co.

**American Council of Learned Societies Devoted to
Humanistic Studies.**
xAmerican Council Of Learned Societies.
ed. Dictionary of American Biography.
Scribner.
Dictionary of Scientific Biography. Scribner.

**American Council of Learned Societies Devoted to
Humanistic Studies. Committee on Linguistic and
National Stocks in the Population of the United
States.**
xAmerican Council of Learned Societies,
Committee on Linguistics & National Stocks.
Surnames in the United States Census of 1790.
Genealog Pub.

American Council on Education.
xAmerican Council on Education.
General Education: Explorations in Evaluation;
the Final Report. Greenwood.
Youth & the Future: Ageneral Report of the
American Youth Commission. Greenwood.
xAmerican Council on Education, Oct. 1974.
Formulating Policy for Postsecondary
Education: The Search for Alternatives,
Proceedings. ACE.

**American Council on Education. Committee on
Education and Social Security.**
xAmerican Council on Education, Committee on
Education & Social Security.
People & Process in Social Security.
Greenwood.

**American Council on Education. Committee on Religion
and Education.**
xAmerican Council on Education Committee of
Religion & Education.
Function of the Public Schools in Dealing with
Religion. ACE.

American Council on Education, Oct. 1974. see
American Council on Education.

American Craft Council. see American Crafts Council.

American Crafts Council.
xAmerican Craft Council.

Clay: A Bibliography. Am Craft.
Enamel: A Bibliography. Am Craft.
Glass: A Bibliography. Am Craft.
Metal: A Bibliography. Am Craft.
Photographing Crafts. Am Craft.
Pricing & Promotion: A Guide for
Craftspeople. Am Craft.
Wood: A Bibliography. Am Craft.
xAmerican Crafts Council.
Compiled by Contemporary Crafts Market
Place: 1977-1978. Bowker.
Crafts Business Bookshelf: An Annotated
Bibliography for Craftsmen & Retailers. Am
Craft.
Fiber: A Bibliography. Am Craft.

American Dental Association.
xAmerican Dental Association.
Chairside Instructor. Am Dental.
So Many Things to See. Am Dental.
Tooth Survival Book. Am Dental.
Update in Clinical Dentistry, 1978. Am Dental.

American Dental Association - Bureau of Library &
Indexing Service. see American Dental Association.
Bureau of Library and Indexing Service.

**American Dental Association. Council on Dental
Therapeutics.**
xAmerican Dental Association-Council on Dental
Therapeutics.
Accepted Dental Therapeutics. Am Dental.

**American Dental Association. Bureau of Library and
Indexing Service.**
xAmerican Dental Association - Bureau of Library
& Indexing Service.
Index to Dental Literature. Am Dental.

American Dental Association-Council on Dental
Therapeutics. see American Dental Association.
Council on Dental Therapeutics.

American Diabetes Association.
xTheAmerican Diabetes Association.
The American Diabetes Association, American
Dietetic Association Family Cookbook. P-H.

American Dietetic Association.
xAmerican Dietetic Association.
Handbook of Clinical Dietetics. Yale U Pr.
xAmerican Dietetic Association Members.
Your Future As a Dietician. Arco.
xMembers of the American Dietetic Assoc.
Your Future As a Dietian. Rosen Pr.
Your Future As a Dietitian. Rosen Pr.

American Dietetic Association Members. see American
Dietetic Association.

American Economic Association.
xAmerican Economic Association.
Index of Economic Articles. Irwin.
Readings in Business Cycle Theory. AMS Pr.
ed. Readings in the Social Control of Industry.
Arno.
Readings in the Theory of Income Distribution.
AMS Pr.
xAmerican Economic Association Committee.
Compiled by Readings in Business Cycle
Theory. AMS Pr.
Compiled by Readings in the Theory of
Income Distribution. AMS Pr.

American Economic Association Committee. see
American Economic Association.

American Engineering Council.
xFederated American Engineering Societies.
Waste in Industry. Hive Pub.

**American Enterprise Institute for Public Policy
Research.**
xU. S. Congress, 92nd.
Consumer Product Safety Bills. Am Enterprise.
Review-1970 Session of the Congress & Index
of AEI, Publications. Am Enterprise.

American Ethnological Society.
xAmerican Ethnological Society.

American Indian Intellectuals: 1976
Proceedings. West Pub.
Forms of Play of Native North Americans:
Proceedings. West Pub.
Material Culture: Styles, Organization &
Dynamics of Technology. West Pub.
The New Ethnicity, Perspectives from
Ethnology: Proceedings. West Pub.
Publications of the American Ethnological
Society. AMS Pr.
xAmerican Ethnological Society, 1974.
American Anthropology, the Early Years:
Proceedings. West Pub.
American Ethnological Society, 1974. *see* American
Ethnological Society.
American Fabrics.
xAmerican Fabrics Magazine.
ed. Encyclopedia of Textiles. P-H.
Encyclopedia of Textiles. Textile Bk.
American Fabrics Magazine. *see* American Fabrics.
American Federation of Arts.
xAmerican Federation of Arts.
Cultural Resources of Boston. October.
New Chinese Landscape. October.
Thirty-Third Biennial Exhibition of Art,
Venice, 1966. October.
American Federation of Labor.
xAmerican Federation of Labor.
Reports of the Proceedings of the Annual
Conventions of the American Federation of
Labor. AMS Pr.

American Film Institute.
xAmerican Film Institute.

ed. American Film Heritage. Acropolis.

Guide to College Courses in Film & Television.
Acropolis.
American Forestry Association.
xAmerican Forestry Association.
Trees Every Boy & Girl Should Know. Am
Forestry.
American Foundation.
xAmerican Foundation.
Medical Research: A Midcentury Survey.
Greenwood.
American Foundation for the Blind (New York). *see*
American Foundation for the Blind, Inc., New York.
American Foundation for the Blind, Inc., New York.
xAmerican Foundation for the Blind (New York).
Dictionary Catalog of the M. C. Migel
Memorial Library. G K Hall.
American Foundrymen's Society.
xAmerican Foundrymen's Society.
Basic Metallurgy: Principles of Physical
Metallurgy for Ferrous Castings. A-W.
Basic Metallurgy: Principles of Production
Metallurgy for Ferrous Castings. A-W.
Basic Principles of Risering. A-W.
American Friends Service Committee. *see* Friends,
Society Of. American Friends Service Committee.
American Gas Association.
xAmerican Gas Association.
Gas Engineers Handbook. Indus Pr.
American Genealogical Research Institute.
xAmerican Genealogical Research Institute Staff.
How to Trace Your Family Tree. Doubleday.
American Geographical Society. *see* American
Geographical Society of New York.
American Geographical Society - Map Department, New
York. *see* American Geographical Society of New
York. Map Department.
American Geographical Society Map Department (New
York). *see* American Geographical Society of New
York. Map Department.
American Geographical Society of New York.
xAmerican Geographical Society.
New England's Prospect: 1933. AMS Pr.
xAmerican Geographical Society of New York.

Oriental Explorations & Studies. AMS Pr.
Pioneer Settlement. Arno.
**American Geographical Society of New York. Map
Department.**
xAmerican Geographical Society - Map
Department, New York.
Index to Maps in Books & Periodicals. G K
Hall.
xAmerican Geographical Society Map Department
(New York).
Index to Maps in Books & Periodicals, Second
Suppl. G K Hall.
xAmerican Geographical Society-Map
Department-New York.
Index to Maps in Books & Periodicals, First
Supplement. G K Hall.
American Geographical Society-Map Department-New
York. *see* American Geographical Society of New
York. Map Department.
American Geological Institute.
xAmerican Geological Institute.
Deep Sea Drilling Project, Legs 1-25. Am
Geol.
Deep Sea Drilling Project, Legs 26-44. Am
Geol.
Deep Sea Drilling Project, Legs 45-62. Am
Geol.
Dictionary of Geological Terms. Doubleday.
Directory of Geoscience Departments: 1976-77
Edition. Am Geol.
Directory of Geoscience Departments:
1978-1979. Am Geol.
Directory of Geoscience Departments:
1979-1980. Am Geol.
Directory of the Geologic Division, U. S.
Geological Survey. Am Geol.
Geokhimiya Translations Nineteen Sixty-Nine:
A Supplement to Geochemistry International.
Am Geol.
Geokhimiya Translations 1964: A Supplement
to Geochemistry International, Vol. 1. Am
Geol.
Geokhimiya Translations 1965: A Supplement
to Geochemistry International, Vol. 2. Am
Geol.
Geokhimiya Translations 1966: A Supplement
to Geochemistry International, Vol. 3. Am
Geol.
Geokhimiya Translations 1967: A Supplement
to Geochemistry International, Vol. 4. Am
Geol.
Geokhimiya Translations 1968: A Supplement
to Geochemistry International. Am Geol.
Geological Data Sheets. Am Geol.
Geology: Science & Profession. Am Geol.
American Girl.
xAmerican Girl Magazine Staff.
American Girl Book of Horse Stories. Random.
American Girl Book of Teen-Age Questions.
Random.
American Girl Cookbook. Random.
American Girl Magazine Staff. *see* American Girl.
American Heart Association.
xAmerican Heart Association.
The American Heart Association Cookbook.
McKay.
The Heart Book. Dutton.
American Heritage.
xAmerican Heritage.
ed. The American Heritage Cookbook. Am
Heritage.
Concise Heritage Dictionary. HM.
Great Historic Places. S&S.
Historical Houses of America. S&S.
Natural Wonders of America. S&S.
The Word Book. HM.
xAmerican Heritage Editors.

ed. American Album. Ballantine.
The American Heritage Pictorial History of the
Presidents of the United States. Am Heritage.
ed. American Heritage School Dictionary. HM.
Great Historic Places: An American Heritage
Guide. Am Heritage.
Great Historic Places: An American Heritage
Guide. S&S.
Historic Houses of America Open to the
Public: An American Heritage Guide. S&S.
Natural Wonders of America: An American
Heritage Guide. Am Heritage.
Natural Wonders of America: An American
Heritage Guide. S&S.
American Heritage Editors. *see* American Heritage.
American Historical Assn. *see* American Historical
Association.
American Historical Association.
xAmerican Historical Assn.
War As a Social Institution: The Historian's
Perspective. AMS Pr.
American Hospital Assn. *see* American Hospital
Association.
American Hospital Association.
xAmerican Hospital Assn.
Digest of Hospital Cost Containment Projects.
Am Hospital.
xAmerican Hospital Association.
Alcoholism - Whose Responsibility?:
Coordinator's Guide. Am Hospital.
Alcoholism - Whose Responsibility?:
Participant's Manual. Am Hospital.
Alcoholism - Whose Responsibility?: Subgroup
Leader's Guide. Am Hospital.
American Hospital Association Guide to the
Health Care Field.: Annual Ed.. Am
Hospital.
Auxiliary Gift & Coffee Shop Management.
Am Hospital.
Auxiliary: New Concepts, New Directions. Am
Hospital.
Basic Personnel Policies & Programs for a
Health Care Institution: Guidelines for
Development. Am Hospital.
Budgeting Procedures for Hospitals. Am
Hospital.
Capital Financing for Hospitals. Am Hospital.
Catalog of the Library of the American
Hospital Association, Asa S. Bacon Memorial
Chicago. G K Hall.
Comparative Statistics on Health Facilities &
Population: Metropolitan & Nonmetropolitan
Areas.. Am Hospital.
Cost Finding & Rate Setting for Hospitals. Am
Hospital.
Cumulative Index of Hospital Literature:
1965-1969. Am Hospital.
Delivery of Health Care in Rural America. Am
Hospital.
Developing Policies & Procedures for
Long-Term Care Institutions. Am Hospital.
Diet & Menu Guide for Hospitals. Am
Hospital.
Directory of Architects for Health Facilities:
1979 Edition. Am Hospital.
Directory of Multihospital Systems. Am
Hospital.
Directory of Shared Services Organizations for
Health Care Institutions. Am Hospital.
Educational Programs in the Health Field. Am
Hospital.
Essentials of Social Work Programs in
Hospitals. Am Hospital.
The Extended Care Unit in a General Hospital:
A Guide to Planning, Organization, &
Management. Am Hospital.
Financial Aid Programs in Support of Health
Occupations: A Guide for Auxiliaries. Am
Hospital.
Financial Relationships Between Hospitals &

Comprehensive Health Care Delivery Organizations. Am Hospital.

Fire Safety Training in Health Care Institutions. Am Hospital.

Food Service Manual for Health Care Institutions. Am Hospital.

A Guide for Hospital Participation in an Emergency Medical Communications System. Am Hospital.

The Hospital Admitting Department. Am Hospital.

Hospital Cost Containment Through Operations Management. Am Hospital.

Hospital Design Checklist. Am Hospital.

Hospital Engineering Handbook. Am Hospital.

Hospital Housekeeping Handbook. Am Hospital.

Hospital Literature Index: 1979. Am Hospital.

Hospital Medical Records: Guidelines for Their Use & the Release of Medical Information. Am Hospital.

Hospital Statistics: Data from the American Hospital Association 1977 Annual Survey. Am Hospital.

The Hospital Trustee Reader: Selections from Trustee Magazine. Am Hospital.

Housekeeping Manual for Health Care Facilities. Am Hospital.

ICD-Nine-CM Coding Handbook for Entry-Level Coders. Am Hospital.

Implementing Patient Education in the Hospital. Am Hospital.

Improving Work Methods in Small Hospitals. Am Hospital.

Internal Control & Internal Auditing for Hospitals. Am Hospital.

Internal Control, Internal Auditing, & Operations Auditing for Hospitals. Am Hospital.

Interpreters' Services & the Role of Health Care Volunteers. Am Hospital.

The Management of Hospital Employee Productivity: An Introductory Handbook. Am Hospital.

Managerial Cost Accounting for Hospitals. Am Hospital.

Manual on Hospital Chaplaincy. Am Hospital.

Media Handbook: A Guide to Selecting, Producing & Using Media for Patient Education Programs. Am Hospital.

Medical Records Departments in Hospitals: Guide to Organization. Am Hospital.

Medical Staff Cost Containment: Digest of Hospital Projects & Selected Bibliography. Am Hospital.

Multihospital Arrangements: Public Policy Implications. Am Hospital.

A Portfolio of Architecture for Health. Am Hospital.

Practical Approaches to Effective Functioning of the Department of Nursing Service: A Guide for Administrators of Nursing Service. Am Hospital.

Principles of Disaster Preparedness for Hospitals. Am Hospital.

Psychiatric Services in Institutional Settings: Selected Conference Papers. Am Hospital.

Readings in Disaster Preparedness for Hospitals. Am Hospital.

Readings in Health Education. Am Hospital.

Readings in Hospital Central Service. Am Hospital.

Readings in Materials Management. Am Hospital.

Rehabilitation Services in Hospitals & Related Facilities: A Guide to Planning, Organization, & Management. Am Hospital.

Reshaping Ambulatory Care Programs: Report & Recommendations of a Conference on Ambulatory Care. Am Hospital.

Safety Guide for Health Care Institutions. Am Hospital.

Selected Community Hospital Indicators: 1977 Data. Am Hospital.

Selection & Employment of Management Consultants for Health Care. Am Hospital.

Sharing Responsibility for Patient Safety. Am Hospital.

Survey of Charges in Community Hospitals As of January 1, 1975. Am Hospital.

Technology Evaluation & Acquisition Methods (TEAM) for Hospitals. Am Hospital.

Volunteer in Long-Term Care. Am Hospital.

The Volunteer Services Department in a Health Care Institution. Am Hospital.

Who Cares About an Alcoholism Program in the General Hospital?. Am Hospital.

Winds of Change: Report of a Conference on Activity Programs in Long-Term Care Institutions. Am Hospital.

American Hospital Association. American Society for Hospital Food Service Administration.

xAmerican Society for Hospital Food Service Administrators.

Determination Allocation of Food Service Costs. Am Hospital.

American Hospital Association. Society of Patient Representatives.

xSociety of Patient Representatives of the American Hospital Association.

The Patient Representative's Participation in Risk Management. Am Hospital.

American Insect Control Delegation.

xCommittee on Scholarly Communication with the People's Republic of China (CSCPRC).

Insect Control in the People's Republic of China: A Trip Report of the American Insect Control Delegation. Natl Acad Pr.

American Institute of Architects.

xAmerican Institute of Architects.

AIA Energy Notebook. Am Inst Arch.

AIA Metric Building & Construction Guide. Wiley.

Compensation Guidelines for Architectural & Engineering Services. Am Inst Arch.

Comprehensive Architectural Services: General Principles & Practice. McGraw.

Creative Control of Building Costs. McGraw.

Design Review Boards: A Guide for Communities. Am Inst Arch.

Manual of Built-up Roof Systems. McGraw.

New Towns in America: The Design & Development Process. Wiley.

Uniform Construction Index: A System of Formats for Specifications, Data Filing, Cost Analysis & Project Filing. Am Inst Arch.

xThe American Institute of Architects.

Architects Handbook of Professional Practice. Am Inst Arch.

Glossary of Construction Industry Terms. Am Inst Arch.

American Institute of Biological Science.

xAmerican Institute Of Biological Sciences.

Directory of Bioscience Departments in the United States & Canada. Van Nos Reinhold.

American Institute of Certified Public Accountants.

xAmerican Institute Of Certified Public Accountants.

Accountants' Index: 26th Supplement, 1977. Am Inst CPA.

Accountants International Studies. Am Inst CPA.

Accounting for Depreciable Assets. Am Inst CPA.

Accounting Trends & Techniques in Published Corporate Annual Reports. Am Inst CPA.

Behavior of Major Statistical Estimators in Sampling Accounting Populations. Am Inst CPA.

Illustrations of Departures from the Auditor's Standard Report. Am Inst CPA.

Illustrations of Interperiod Tax Allocation. Am Inst CPA.

Illustrations of Reporting Accounting Changes. Am Inst CPA.

Illustrations of Reporting the Results of Operations. Am Inst CPA.

Illustrations of the Disclosure of Related Party Transactions. Am Inst CPA.

Illustrations of the Statement of Changes in Financial Position. Am Inst CPA.

Illustrations of the Summary of Operations & Related Management Discussion & Analysis. Am Inst CPA.

Management of an Accounting Practice Handbook. Am Inst CPA.

Management Services Technical Studies. Am Inst CPA.

Tax Practice Management. Am Inst CPA.

Tax Research Techniques. Am Inst CPA.

American Institute of Chemical Engineers.

xAmerican Institute Of Chemical Engineers.

Twenty-Five Years of Chemical Engineering Progress. Arno.

American Institute of Decorators.

xAmerican Institute of Decorators.

Interior Design & Decoration: A Bibliography. NY Pub Lib.

American Institute of Physics.

xAmerican Institute of Physics.

American Institute of Physics Handbook. McGraw.

Analytical Balance. McGraw.

Automobile Collisions. McGraw.

Automobile Ignition Systems. McGraw.

The Binoculars. McGraw.

Cathode Ray Tube. McGraw.

The Cloud Chamber. McGraw.

The Electric Fan. McGraw.

The Fluorescent Lamp. McGraw.

The Guitar. McGraw.

Hydraulic Devices. McGraw.

The Incandescent Lamp. McGraw.

The Loudspeaker. McGraw.

The Multimeter. McGraw.

Photodetectors. McGraw.

Physics of Technology Project Ser.. McGraw.

The Pile Driver. McGraw.

The Power Transistor. McGraw.

The Pressure Cooker. McGraw.

The Salenoid. McGraw.

The Slide Projector. McGraw.

The Spectrophotometer. McGraw.

The Strobascope. McGraw.

The Toaster. McGraw.

The Torque Wrench. McGraw.

American Institute of Real Estate Appraisers.

xAmerican Institute Of Real Estate Appraisers.

Appraisal Journal Bibliography, 1932-1969. Am Inst Real Estate Appraisers.

The Appraisal of Real Estate. Am Inst Real Estate Appraisers.

ed. Condemnation Appraisal Practice, Vol. 2. Am Inst Real Estate Appraisers.

ed. Readings in Real Estate Investment Analysis. Ballinger Pub.

Readings in Real Property Valuation Principles. Ballinger Pub.

Readings in the Income Approach to Real Property Valuation. Ballinger Pub.

ed. Real Estate Appraisal Bibliography. Am Inst Real Estate Appraisers.

Study Guide Course 1-B: Capitalization Theory & Techniques. Am Inst Real Estate Appraisers.

American Institute of Timber Construction.

xAmerican Institute of Timber Construction.

Timber Construction Manual. Wiley.

American Jewish Archives, Cincinnati. *see* Hebrew Union College-Jewish Institute of Religion. American Jewish Archives.

American Jewish Committee.

xAmerican Jewish Committee.

The Jews in Nazi Germany. Fertig.

American Jewish Historical Society.

xPapers Presented at the Conference, Convened by the American Jewish Historical Society & the Theodor Herzl Foundation in New York City, December 26-27, 1955.

Early History of Zionism in America: Proceedings. Arno.

American Kennel Club.

xAmerican Kennel Club.

The Complete Dog Book: The Official Publication of the American Kennel Club. Howell Bk.

American Legion. National Americanism Commission.

xAmerican Legion. National Americanism Commission.

Isms: A Review of Alien Isms, Revolutionary Communism, & Their Active Sympathizers in the United States. Arno.

American Library Association.

xAmerican Library Association.

A. L. A. Glossary of Library Terms: With a Selection of Terms in Related Fields. ALA.

A. L. A. Portrait Index. B Franklin.

Books for Children, Preschool Through Junior High School 1969-1970: As Selected & Reviewed by The Booklist, September 1969 - August 1970. ALA.

Books for Children 1960-1965: As Selected & Reviewed by the Booklist & Subscription Books Bulletin, September 1960-August 1965. ALA.

Books for Children 1965-1966: As Selected & Reviewed by the Booklist & Subscription Books Bulletin, September 1965-August 1966. ALA.

Books for Children, 1966-1967: As Selected & Reviewed by the Booklist & Subscription Books Bulletin, September 1966-August 1967. ALA.

Books for Children 1967-1968: As Selected & Reviewed by the Booklist & Subscription Books Bulletin, September 1967-August 1968. ALA.

Catalog Card Reproduction: Report on a Study Conducted by George Fry & Associates. ALA.

Circulation Policies of Academic Libraries. ALA.

Freedom of Inquiry: Supporting the Library Bill of Rights. ALA.

An Index to General Literature: The ALA Index. Arno.

Librarian's Copyright Kit. ALA.

Library Furniture & Equipment: Proceedings of a Three - Day Institute, June 14-16, 1962. ALA.

Minimum Standards for Public Library Systems, 1966. ALA.

New Copyright Law: Questions Teachers & Librarians Ask. ALA.

Protecting the Library & Its Resources: A Guide to Physical Protection & Insurance. ALA.

Storytelling. ALA.

Task Analysis Survey Instrument. ALA.

American Library Association - Children's Services Division. *see* American Library Association. Children's Services Division.

American Library Association - Library Technology Project. *see* American Library Association. Library Technology Project.

American Library Association - Reference and Subscription Books Reviews Committee. *see* American Library Association. Reference and Subscription Books Review Committee.

American Library Association - Resources & Technical Services Division. *see* American Library Association. Resources and Technical Services Division.

American Library Association - Young Adult Services Division. *see* American Library Association. Young Adult Services Division.

American Library Association. Ad Hoc Reference Books Review Committee.

xCommittee of RSD, ALA.

Reference Books for Small & Medium Sized Libraries. ALA.

American Library Association. Bookdealer-Library Relations Committee.

xAmerican Library Association. Bookdealer-Library Relations Committee.

Guidelines for Handling Library Orders for Microforms. ALA.

American Library Association. Buildings for College and University Libraries Committee.

xAmerican Library Association, Library Administration Division, Buildings & Equipment Section, Buildings for College & University Libraries Committee.

Running Out of Space: What Are the Alternatives. ALA.

American Library Association. Children's Services Division.

xAmerican Library Association - Children's Services Division.

Notable Children's Books, 1940-1970. ALA.

American Library Association. Committee on Outreach Programs for Young Adults (Ad Hoc).

xYASD Committee.

ed. Look, Listen, Explain. ALA.

American Library Association. Library Service to the Disadvantaged Child Committee.

xCommittee of the Children's Services Division.

I Read, You Read, We Read, I See, You See, We See, I Hear, You Hear, We Hear, I Learn, You Learn, We Learn. ALA.

American Library Association. Library Technology Project.

xAmerican Library Association - Library Technology Project.

Development of Performance Standards for Library Binding, Phase 1: Report of the Survey Team, April 1961. ALA.

American Library Association, Library Administration Division, Buildings & Equipment Section, Buildings for College & University Libraries Committee. *see* American Library Association. Buildings for College and University Libraries Committee.

American Library Association. Office for Intellectual Freedom.

xAmerican Library Association-Office for Intellectual Freedom.

Intellectual Freedom Manual. ALA.

American Library Association. Reference and Subscription Books Review Committee.

xAmerican Library Association - Reference and Subscription Books Reviews Committee.

Reference & Subscription Books Reviews 1968-1970. ALA.

xAmerican Library Association, Reference & Subscription Books Review Committee.

Reference & Subscription Book Reviews: 1976-1977. ALA.

Reference & Subscription Books Review 1972-1974. ALA.

Reference & Subscription Books Reviews, 1970-72. ALA.

Reference Books for Small & Medium-Sized Libraries. ALA.

American Library Association. Resources and Technical Services Division.

xAmerican Library Association - Resources & Technical Services Division.

International Subscription Agents. ALA.

American Library Association. Young Adult Services Division.

xAmerican Library Association - Young Adult Services Division.

Doors to More Mature Reading: Detailed Notes on Adult Books for Use with Young People. ALA.

American Library Association. Young Adult Services Division. Research Committee.

xCommittee of the Young Adult Services Division, ALA.

Media & the Young Adult: A Selected Bibliography 1950-1972. ALA.

American Library Association. Young Adult Services Division. Services Statement Development Committee.

xAmerican Library Association, Young Adult Services Division, Services Statement Development Committee.

Directions for Library Service to Young Adults. ALA.

American Library Association-Office for Intellectual Freedom. *see* American Library Association. Office for Intellectual Freedom.

American Machine and Foundry Company.
    xAmerican Machines & Foundry Co.
      Acoustic Study Program. Paladin Ent.
American Machines & Foundry Co. *see* American
    Machine and Foundry Company.
American Machinist.
    xDidactic Systems Staff.
      Planning for Growth. Didactic Syst.
American Management Association.
    xAmerican Management Association.
      New Products - New Profits. Am Mgmt.
American Map Co Inc. *see* American Map Company,
    Inc., New York.
American Map Company. *see* American Map Company,
    Inc., New York.
American Map Company, Inc., New York.
    xAmerican Map Co Inc.
      Business Control Atlas of the United States &
        Canada: 1979 Edition. Am Map.
      General World Atlas. Am Map.
      General World Atlas, No. 9550. Am Map.
    xAmerican Map Company.
      Atlas Mundial, No. 9555. Am Map.
      Commercial Atlas. Am Map.
      Executive Sales Control Atlas. Am Map.
      Master Sales Control Atlas. Am Map.
      Scholastic World Atlas: No. 9552. Am Map.
      Students Indexed World Atlas. Am Map.
      Students Indexed World Atlas: No. 9551. Am
        Map.
American Mathematical Monthly. *see* American
    Mathematical Society.
American Mathematical Society.
    xAmerican Mathematical Monthly.
      To Lester R. Ford, on His Seventieth Birthday:
        Supplement to the American Mathematical
        Monthly October 1957. Math Assn.
    xAmerican Mathematical Society.
      Norbert Wiener, 1894-1964. Am Math.
    xAmerican Mathematical Society Special Session,
      San Francisco, Jan, 1974.
      A Crash Course on Kleinian Groups:
        Proceedings. Springer-Verlag.
American Mathematical Society Special Session, San
    Francisco, Jan, 1974. *see* American Mathematical
    Society.
American Medical Association.
    xAmerican Medical Association.
      AMA Drug Evaluations. PSG Pub.
      The AMA Handbook of First Aid &
        Emergency Care. Random.
      American Medical Directory. PSG Pub.
      Computer Assisted Medical Practice: AMA's
        Role. AMA.
      Digest of Official Actions: 1959-1968. AMA.
      Directory of Health Sciences Libraries, 1973.
        AMA
      Distribution of Physicians, Hospitals, &
        Hospital Beds in the U. S., 1970. AMA.
      Foreign Medical Graduates in the U. S., 1970..
        AMA.
      Fundamentals of Athletic Training. AMA.
      Growing Pains. AMA.
      Guides to the Evaluation of Permanent
        Impairment. AMA.
      Human Sexuality. AMA.
      Medicolegal Forms with Legal Analysis. AMA.
      Mental Retardation: A Handbook for the
        Primary Physician. AMA.
      Psychoactive Drugs. AMA.
      Standard Nomenclature of Diseases &
        Operations. McGraw.
      Stylebook-Editorial Manual. PSG Pub.
American Medical Association. Judicial Council.
    xAmerican Medical Association Judicial Council.
      Opinion & Report of the Judicial Council:
        1977. AMA.
American Meteorological Society.
    xAmerican Meteorological Society - Boston.

      Cumulated Bibliography & Index to
        Meteorological & Geoastrophysical Abstracts:
        1950-1969. G K Hall.
American Meteorological Society - Boston. *see* American
    Meteorological Society.
American Mothers Committee.
    xAmerican Mothers Committee, Bicentennial
      Project 1974-1976.
      Compiled by Mothers of Achievement in
        American History: 1776-1976. C E Tuttle.
American Mothers Committee, Bicentennial Project
    1974-1976. *see* American Mothers Committee.
American Museum of Natural History.
    xAmerican Museum of Natural History.
      ed. Research Catalog of the Library of the
        American Museum of Natural History:
        Authors. G K Hall.
American National Red Cross. *see* Red Cross. United
    States. American National Red Cross.
American National Standards Institute.
    xAmerican National Standards Institute, Standards
      Committee Z39 on Library Work,
      Documentation & Related Publishing Practices.
      American National Standard for Bibliographic
        Informatiion Interchange on Magnetic Tape.
        ANSI.
      American National Standard Title Leaves of a
        Book. ANSI.
**American National Standards Institute. Subcommittee
Eight on Proof Corrections.**
    xAmerican National Standards Institute, Standards
      Committee Z39 on Library Work,
      Documentation & Related Publishing Practices.
      American National Standard Proof Corrections,
        Z39.22. ANSI.
**American National Standards Institute. Subcommittee
Seventeen on Standard Book Numbering.**
    xAmerican National Standards Institute, Standards
      Committee Z39 on Library Work,
      Documentation & Related Publishing Practices.
      American National Standard for Book
        Numbering, Z39.21. ANSI.
American Negro Academy. *see* American Negro
    Academy, Washington, D.C.
American Negro Academy, Washington, D.C.
    xAmerican Negro Academy.
      American Negro Academy Occasional Papers
        Nos. 1-22. Arno.
American Neurological Assoc. *see* American
    Neurological Association.
American Neurological Association.
    xAmerican Neurological Assoc.
      Transactions: 1978. Springer Pub.
    xAmerican Numismatic Association.
      Official A.N.A. Grading Guide. Western Pub.
American Numismatic Association. *see* American
    Neurological Association.
American Numismatic Society.
    xAmerican Numismatic Society.
      A Survey of Numismatic Research, 1966-71.
        Am Numismatic.
American Numismatic Society. Library.
    xAmerican Numismatic Society Library.
      Dictionary & Auction Catalogues of the
        Library of the American Numismatic Society,
        New York, 7 Vols. G K Hall.
American Personnel & Guidance Assn. *see* American
    Personnel and Guidance Association.
American Personnel and Guidance Association.
    xAmerican Personnel & Guidance Assn.
      How to Visit Colleges. Am Personnel.
American Pharmaceutical Association.
    xAmerican Pharmaceutical Association.
      The National Formulary: 1975. Mack Pub.
American Philosophical Society.
    xAmerican Philosophical Society.

      Aspects of American Liberty. Am Philos.
      Catalogue of Instruments & Models. Am
        Philos.
      Catalogue of Portraits & Other Works of Art.
        Am Philos.
      Early Transactions. Am Philos.
      Year Book. Am Philos.
American Physical Therapy Association (Founded 1921).
    xAmerican Physical Therapy Association.
      Physical Therapy Administration &
        Management. Williams & Wilkins.
American Physiological Society. *see* American
    Physiological Society (Founded 1887).
American Physiological Society (Founded 1887).
    xAmerican Physiological Society.
      Disturbances in Body Fluid Osmolality.
        Williams & Wilkins.
      Handbook of Physiology, Section 3:
        Respiration. Williams & Wilkins.
      Handbook of Physiology, Section 4: Adaptation
        to the Environment. Williams & Wilkins.
      Handbook of Physiology, Section 5: Adipose
        Tissue. Williams & Wilkins.
      Handbook of Physiology, Section 6: The
        Alimentary Canal. Williams & Wilkins.
      The Nervous System, Section 1: Celluar
        Biology of Neurons. Williams & Wilkins.
      Pulmonary Edema. Williams & Wilkins.
      Reactions to Environmental Agents. Williams
        & Wilkins.
**American Phytopathological Society. Source Book
Committee.**
    xAmerican Phytopathological Society - Sourcebook
      Committee.
      Sourcebook of Laboratory Exercises in Plant
        Pathology. W H Freeman.
American Plywood Association.
    xAmerican Plywood Association
      The Plywood Planbook. H P Bks.
American Political Science Association.
    xAmerican Political Science Association.
      Research Support for Political Scientists. Am
        Political.
      Toward a More Responsible Two-Party System:
        A Report. Johnson Repr.
**American Political Science Association. Committee on
Public Information.**
    xAmerican Political Science Association, &
      Committee on American Legislatures.
      American State Legislatures. Greenwood.
American Psychiatric Assn. *see* American Psychiatric
    Association.
American Psychiatric Assn., Committee on Public
    Information. *see* American Psychiatric Association.
    Committee on Public Information.
American Psychiatric Association.
    xAmerican Psychiatric Assn.
      ed. A Psychiatric Glossary. Little.
    xAmerican Psychiatric Association.
      Behavior Therapy in Psychiatry. Aronson.
      Electroconvulsive Therapy. Am Psychiatric.
**American Psychiatric Association. Ad Hoc Committee
on the Chronic Mental Patient.**
    xAmerican Psychiatric Association Ad Hoc
      Committee on the Chronic Mental Patient.
      The Chronic Mental Patient: Problems,
        Solutions, & Recommendations for a Public
        Policy. Am Psychiatric.
**American Psychiatric Association. Committee on
Nomenclature and Statistics.**
    xAmerican Psychiatric Association, Committee on
      Nomenclature & Statistics.
      Diagnostic & Statistical Manual of Mental
        Disorders. Am Psychiatric.
**American Psychiatric Association. Committee on Public
Information.**
    xAmerican Psychiatric Assn., Committee on Public
      Information.

A Psychiatric Glossary, 4th Ed.. Basic.
American Psychiatric Association. Peer Review Committee.
   xPeer Review Committee of the American Psychiatric Assn.
      ed. Manual of Psychiatric Peer Review. Am Psychiatric.
American Psychiatric Association. Task Force on Psychohistory.
   xAmerican Psychiatric Association's Task Force on Psychohistory.
      ed. The Psychiatrist As Psychohistorian. Am Psychiatric.
American Psychiatric Association. Task Force on Religion and Psychiatry.
   xAmerican Psychiatric Association's Task Force on Religion & Psychiatry.
      ed. Psychiatrists' Viewpoints on & Their Services to Religious Institutions & the Ministry. Am Psychiatric.
American Psychiatric Association's Task Force on Psychohistory. *see* American Psychiatric Association. Task Force on Psychohistory.
American Psychological Association.
   xAmerican Psychological Association.
   Careers in Psychology. Am Psychol.
   Ethical Principles in the Conduct of Research with Human Participants. Am Psychol.
   Graduate Study in Psychology: Nineteen Eighty to Nineteen Eighty-One. Am Psychol.
   Publication Manual of the American Psychological Association. Am Psychol.
   Standards for Educational & Psychological Tests. Am Psychol.
American Psychopathological Association.
   xAmerican Psychopathological Association.
   Neurobiological Aspects of Psychopathology: Proceedings. Grune.
   Psychopathology of Adolescence: Proceedings. Grune.
   Psychopathology of Mental Development: Proceedings. Grune.
   Social Psychiatry: Proceedings. Grune.
   Trends of Mental Disease. Arno.
American Public Health Association.
   xAmerican Public Health Association.
   Standard Methods for the Examination of Dairy Products. Am Pub Health.
American Public Works Association.
   xAmerican Public Works Association.
   History of Public Works in the United States, 1776-1976. Am Public Works.
American Pure and Applied Mathematics Delegation.
   xCommittee on Scholarly Communications with the Peoples Republic of China National Research Council.
   Pure & Applied Mathematics in the Peoples Republic of China. Natl Tech Info.
American Radio Relay League.
   xAmerican Radio Relay League.
   The ARRL Antenna Anthology. Am Radio.
   ARRL Antenna Book. Am Radio.
   A Course in Radio Fundamentals. Am Radio.
   FM & Repeaters for the Radio Amateur. Am Radio.
   Hints & Kinks. Am Radio.
   Radio Amateur's Handbook: 1979 Edition. Am Radio.
   Radio Amateur's License Manual. Am Radio.
   The Radio Amateur's V. H. F. Manual. Am Radio.
   Radio Frequency Interference. Am Radio.
   Single Sideband for the Radio Amateur. Am Radio.
   Solid State Basics. Am Radio.
   Understanding Amateur Radio. Am Radio.
American Red Cross. *see* Red Cross. United States. American National Red Cross.
American Scandinavian Foundation. *see* American-Scandinavian Foundation, New York.

American-Scandinavian Foundation, New York.
   xAmerican Scandinavian Foundation.
   Index Nordicus: A Cumulative Index to English-Language Periodicals on Scandinavian Studies. G K Hall.
American School Band Directors Association. *see* American School Band Directors' Association.
American School Band Directors' Association.
   xAmerican School Band Directors Association.
      ed. The ASBDA Curriculum Guide: Reference Book for School Band Directors. Volkwein Bros.
American School of Classical Studies at Athens.
   xAmerican School of Classical Studies at Athens.
   Catalogue of the Gennadius Library, American School of Classical Studies at Athens. G K Hall.
American School of Needlework.
   xAmerican School of Needlework.
   The Great Granny Crochet Book. P-H.
American Society for Engineering Education.
   xAmerican Society for Engineering Education.
   Papers on Scientific Management. Hive Pub.
American Society for Hospital Engineering.
   xAmerican Society for Hospital Engineering.
   Arrhythmia Monitoring Systems. Am Hospital.
   Hospital Engineering Handbook. Am Hospital.
   Mass Spectrometer Respiratory Monitoring Systems. Am Hospital.
American Society for Hospital Food Service Administrators. *see* American Hospital Association. American Society for Hospital Food Service Administration.
American Society for Legal History.
   xAmerican Society for Legal History.
   Essays in Jurisprudence in Honor of Roscoe Pound. Greenwood.
American Society for Training & Development. *see* American Society for Training and Development.
American Society for Training and Development.
   xAmerican Society for Training & Development.
   Training & Development Handbook. McGraw.
   Training & Development Handbook: A Guide to Human Resource Development. McGraw.
American Society of Adlerian Psychology.
   xAmerican Society of Adlerian Psychology.
      ed. Alfred Adler: His Influence on Psychology Today. Noyes.
American Society of African Culture.
   xAmerican Society of African Culture.
   Pan-Africanism Reconsidered. Greenwood.
American Society of Anesthesiologists.
   xAmerican Society of Anesthesiologists.
   ASA Refresher Courses in Anesthesiology. Lippincott.
   Regional Refresher Courses in Anesthesiology. Lippincott.
American Society of Appraisers.
   xAmerican Society of Appraisers.
   The Bibliography of Appraisal Literature. Am Soc Appraisers.
American Society of Civil Engineering. *see* American Society of Civil Engineers.
American Society of Civil Engineers.
   xAmerian Society of Civil Engineers.
      Compiled by Legal, Institutional, & Social Aspects of Irrigation & Drainage & Water Resources Planning & Management. Am Soc Civil Eng.
   xAmerican Society of Civil Engineering.
      Compiled by Readings in Cost Engineering. Am Soc Civil Eng.
      Compiled by Sedimentation Engineering. Am Soc Civil Eng.
   xAmerican Society of Civil Engineers.
      Compiled By Acid Rain. Am Soc Civil Eng.
      Compiled By Agricultural & Urban Considerations in Irrigation & Drainage. Am Soc Civil Eng.

Compiled By Air Resource Management Primer. Am Soc Civil Eng.
Compiled By Air Supported Structures. Am Soc Civil Eng.
Compiled By American Wooden Bridges. Am Soc Civil Eng.
Compiled By Analysis & Design in Geotechnical Engineering. Am Soc Civil Eng.
Compiled By Applied Techniques for Cold Environments. Am Soc Civil Eng.
Appropriate Technology in Water Supply & Waste Disposal: Proceedings. Am Soc Civil Eng.
Compiled By ASCE-ICE-CSCE: Joint Conference on Predicting & Designing for Natural & Man Made Hazards, 1978. Am Soc Civil Eng.
Compiled By Assessment of Resources & Needs in Highway Technology Education. Am Soc Civil Eng.
Compiled By Award Winning ASCE Papers in Geotechnical Engineering. Am Soc Civil Eng.
Compiled By Bibliography of Bolted & Riveted Joints. Am Soc Civil Eng.
Compiled By Bicycle-Pedestrian Planning & Design. Am Soc Civil Eng.
Compiled By A Biographical Dictionary of American Civil Engineers. Am Soc Civil Eng.
Compiled By City Planning Bibliography. Am Soc Civil Eng.
Compiled By Civil & Environmental Aspects of Energy Complexes: Proceedings. Am Soc Civil Eng.
Compiled By Civil Engineering Classics: Outstanding Papers of Thomas R. Camp. Am Soc Civil Eng.
Compiled By Civil Engineering Education. Am Soc Civil Eng.
Compiled By Civil Engineering Education: Engineering Practice & Nations Needs. Am Soc Civil Eng.
Compiled By Civil Engineering in the Oceans III. Am Soc Civil Eng.
Compiled By Civil Engineering Software Center. Am Soc Civil Eng.
Compiled By Civil Engineer's Role in Productivity in the Construction Industry: Proceedings. Am Soc Civil Eng.
Compiled By Clean Water for Our Future Environment. Am Soc Civil Eng.
Compiled By Coastal Sediments: Proceedings. Am Soc Civil Eng.
Compiled By Coastal Structures. Am Soc Civil Eng.
Compiled By Coastal Zone: Proceedings. Am Soc Civil Eng.
Compiled By Combined Sewer Seperation Using Pressure Sewers. Am Soc Civil Eng.
Compiled By Composite or Mixed Steel: Concrete Construction for Buildings. Am Soc Civil Eng.
Compiled By Computing in Civil Engineering: Proceedings. Am Soc Civil Eng.
Compiled By Conservation & Utilization of Water & Energy Resources. Am Soc Civil Eng.
Compiled By Construction Cost Control. Am Soc Civil Eng.
Compiled By Consulting Engineering: A Guide to the Engagement of Engineering Services. Am Soc Civil Eng.
Compiled By Consumptive Use of Water. Am Soc Civil Eng.
Compiled By Contribution of Irrigation & Drainage to World Food Supply. Am Soc Civil Eng.
Compiled By Current Geotechnical Practice in Mine Waste Disposal. Am Soc Civil Eng.
Compiled By Current Research on Tall Buildings. Am Soc Civil Eng.

Compiled By Design & Construction of Steel Chimney Liners. Am Soc Civil Eng.

Compiled By A Design Guide & Commentary on Wood Structures. Am Soc Civil Eng.

Compiled By Design of Foundations to Control Settlements. Am Soc Civil Eng.

Compiled By Dredging & Its Environmental Effects. Am Soc Civil Eng.

Compiled By Dynamic Planning for Environmental Quality in the Eighties. Am Soc Civil Eng.

Compiled By Economical Construction of Concrete Dams. Am Soc Civil Eng.

Compiled By The Economics of High-Rise Apartment Buildings of Alternate Design Configuration. Am Soc Civil Eng.

Compiled by Electric Power & the Civil Engineer: Proceedings. Am Soc Civil Eng.

Compiled By Electric Power Today. Am Soc Civil Eng.

Compiled By Engineering & Contracting Procedure for Foundations. Am Soc Civil Eng.

Compiled By Engineering Ethics: Proceedings. Am Soc Civil Eng.

Compiled by Engineering Mechanics Specialty Conference, 3rd. Am Soc Civil Eng.

Compiled By Environmental Aspects of Irrigation & Drainage: Proceedings. Am Soc Civil Eng.

Compiled By Environmental Impact: Proceedings. Am Soc Civil Eng.

Compiled By Environmental Impacts of International Civil Engineering Projects & Practices: Proceedings. Am Soc Civil Eng.

Compiled By Ethics, Professionalism, & Maintaining Competence: Proceedings. Am Soc Civil Eng.

Compiled By Evaluation & Prediction of Subsidence: Proceedings. Am Soc Civil Eng.

Compiled By Evaluation of Dam Safety: Proceedings. Am Soc Civil Eng.

Compiled By Fatigue Life of Prestressed Concrete Beams: Reinforced Concrete Remote Control. Am Soc Civil Eng.

Compiled By Field Test Sections Save Cost in Tunnel Support. Am Soc Civil Eng.

Compiled By Financing & Charges for Wastewater Systems. Am Soc Civil Eng.

Compiled By Foundations for Dams: Proceedings. Am Soc Civil Eng.

Compiled By Ground Water Management. Am Soc Civil Eng.

Compiled By Guide for Collection, Analysis, & Use of Urban Stormwater Data: Proceedings. Am Soc Civil Eng.

Compiled By Guide for the Design of Steel Transmission Towers. Am Soc Civil Eng.

Compiled By Guide to Investigation of Structural Failures. Am Soc Civil Eng.

Compiled by Hydraulic Engineering & the Environment. Am Soc Civil Eng.

Compiled by Hydraulics in the Coastal Zone. Am Soc Civil Eng.

Compiled by Implementing Highway Safety Improvements. Am Soc Civil Eng.

Compiled by In Situ Measurement of Soil Properties. Am Soc Civil Eng.

Compiled by Inspection, Maintenance & Rehabilitation of Old Dams. Am Soc Civil Eng.

Compiled by Interdisciplinary Analysis of Water Resource Systems. Am Soc Civil Eng.

Compiled by International Air Transport Conference. Am Soc Civil Eng.

Compiled by International Seminar on Probabilistic & Extreme Load Design of Nuclear Plant Facilities. Am Soc Civil Eng.

Compiled by International Symposium on Stratified Flow. Am Soc Civil Eng.

Compiled by Irrigation & Drainage in an Age of Competition for Resources. Am Soc Civil Eng.

Compiled by Irrigation & Drainage in the Nineteen Eighties. Am Soc Civil Eng.

Compiled by Is Water Quality Enhancement Feasible. Am Soc Civil Eng.

Compiled by Land Application of Residual Materials. Am Soc Civil Eng.

Compiled by Lateral Stresses in the Ground & Design of Earth Retaining Structures. Am Soc Civil Eng.

Compiled by Lessons from Dam Incidents. Am Soc Civil Eng.

Compiled by Lifeline Earthquake Engineering. Am Soc Civil Eng.

Compiled by A List of Translations of Foreign Literature on Hydraulics. Am Soc Civil Eng.

Compiled by Man-Transportation Interface. Am Soc Civil Eng.

Compiled by Management of Engineering of Control Systems for Water Pipelines. Am Soc Civil Eng.

Compiled by Mathematical Model of Aggregate Plant Production. Am Soc Civil Eng.

Compiled by Metal Bridges. Am Soc Civil Eng.

Compiled by Methods of Structural Analysis. Am Soc Civil Eng.

Compiled by Modeling Seventy-Five. Am Soc Civil Eng.

Compiled by Modes of Transportation. Am Soc Civil Eng.

Compiled by National Conference on Construction Contracts. Am Soc Civil Eng.

Compiled by National Conference on Environmental Engineering. Am Soc Civil Eng.

Compiled by National Specialty Conference on Disinfection. Am Soc Civil Eng.

Compiled by Need for National Policy for the Use of Underground Space. Am Soc Civil Eng.

Compiled by New Approaches to Urban Transportation Needs. Am Soc Civil Eng.

Compiled by New Horizons in Rock Mechanics. Am Soc Civil Eng.

Compiled by Nineteen Seventy-Nine Conference on Environmental Engineering. Am Soc Civil Eng.

Compiled by Nineteen Seventy-Nine International Air Transportation Conference. Am Soc Civil Eng.

Compiled by Numerical Methods in Geomechanics. Am Soc Civil Eng.

Compiled by Ocean Wave Measure & Analysis. Am Soc Civil Eng.

Compiled by Operation & Maintenance of Irrigation & Drainage Systems. Am Soc Civil Eng.

Compiled by An Overview of the Alaska Highway Gas Pipeline. Am Soc Civil Eng.

Compiled by Passenger Psychological Dynamics. Am Soc Civil Eng.

Compiled by Performance of Earth & Earth-Supported Structures. Am Soc Civil Eng.

Compiled by Pipeline Design for Hydrocarbon Gases & Liquids. Am Soc Civil Eng.

Compiled by Pipeline Design for Water & Wastewater. Am Soc Civil Eng.

Compiled by Pipeline in Adverse Environments. Am Soc Civil Eng.

Compiled by Pipelines in the Oceans. Am Soc Civil Eng.

Compiled by Placement & Improvement of Soils. Am Soc Civil Eng.

Compiled by Planning, Design & Implementation of Bicycle & Pedestrian Facilities. Am Soc Civil Eng.

Compiled by Planning, Engineering, &

Constructing the Super Projects. Am Soc Civil Eng.

Compiled by Plastic Design in Steel-A Guide & Commentary. Am Soc Civil Eng.

Compiled by Port Structure Costs. Am Soc Civil Eng.

Compiled by Ports Seventy-Seven. Am Soc Civil Eng.

Compiled by Practical Highway Esthetics. Am Soc Civil Eng.

Compiled by Probabalistic Mechanics & Structural Reliability. Am Soc Civil Eng.

Compiled by Prospects for Metropolitan Water Management. Am Soc Civil Eng.

Compiled by Public Works & Society. Am Soc Civil Eng.

Compiled by Pumped Storage. Am Soc Civil Eng.

Compiled by Quality System in Construction. Am Soc Civil Eng.

Compiled by Recreation Planning & Development. Am Soc Civil Eng.

Compiled by Reevaluating Spillway Adequacy of Existing Dams. Am Soc Civil Eng.

Compiled by Reinforced Concrete Floor Slabs-Research & Design. Am Soc Civil Eng.

Compiled by Repair & Strengthening of Old Steel Truss Bridges. Am Soc Civil Eng.

Compiled by Report on Highway & Bridge Surveys. Am Soc Civil Eng.

Compiled by Report on Pipeline Location. Am Soc Civil Eng.

Compiled by Report on Small Craft Harbors. Am Soc Civil Eng.

Compiled by Research Conference on Shear Strength of Cohesive Soils. Am Soc Civil Eng.

Compiled by Research Directions in Computer Control of Urban Traffic Systems. Am Soc Civil Eng.

Compiled by Residential Erosion & Sediment Control. Am Soc Civil Eng.

Compiled by Residential Storm Water Management. Am Soc Civil Eng.

Compiled by Residential Streets. Am Soc Civil Eng.

Residential Streets: Objective Principles & Design Considerations. Urban Land.

Compiled by Rivers Seventy-Six. Am Soc Civil Eng.

Compiled by Rock Engineering for Foundations & Slopes. Am Soc Civil Eng.

Compiled by Safety & Reliability of Metal Structures. Am Soc Civil Eng.

Compiled by Safety of Small Dams. Am Soc Civil Eng.

Compiled by Second International Waterbone Transportation Conference. Am Soc Civil Eng.

Compiled by Selected Abstracts on Structural Applications of Plastics. Am Soc Civil Eng.

Compiled by Site Characterization & Exploration. Am Soc Civil Eng.

Compiled By Soil Improvement: History, Capability & Outlook. Am Soc Civil Eng.

Compiled by Solid Waste Research & Development Needs for Emerging Coal Technologies. Am Soc Civil Eng.

Compiled by Source Book on Environmental & Safety Considerations for Planning & Design of LNG Marine Terminals. Am Soc Civil Eng.

Compiled by Stability & Performance of Slopes & Embankments. Am Soc Civil Eng.

Compiled by Stability of Rock Slopes. Am Soc Civil Eng.

Compiled by Stability of Structures Under Static & Dynamic Loads. Am Soc Civil Eng.

Compiled by Structural Design of Nuclear Plant Facilities. Am Soc Civil Eng.

Compiled by Structural Failures-Modes,
Causes, Responsibilities. Am Soc Civil Eng.
Compiled by Structural-Induced Response to
Explosion-Induced Motions. Am Soc Civil
Eng.
Compiled by Structural Plastics-Properites &
Possibilities. Am Soc Civil Eng.
Compiled by A Study of Damage to
Residential Structures from Blast Vibrations.
Am Soc Civil Eng.
Compiled by Subsurface Exploration for
Underground Excavation & Heavy
Construction. Am Soc Civil Eng.
Compiled by Subsurface Investigation for
Design & Construction for Foundations of
Buildings. Am Soc Civil Eng.
Compiled by Survey of Current Structural
Research. Am Soc Civil Eng.
Compiled by Symposium on Earth
Reinforcement. Am Soc Civil Eng.
Compiled by Symposium on Rearation
Research. Am Soc Civil Eng.
Compiled by Technical Procedure for City
Surveys. Am Soc Civil Eng.
Compiled by Technology & Decisions in
Airport Access. Am Soc Civil Eng.
Compiled by Terzaghi Lectures. Am Soc Civil
Eng.
Compiled by Timber Piles & Construction
Timbers. Am Soc Civil Eng.
Compiled by Transportation & Energy. Am
Soc Civil Eng.
Compiled by Transportation Facilities
Workshop. Am Soc Civil Eng.
Compiled by Underground Rock Chambers.
Am Soc Civil Eng.
Compiled by Urban Planning Guide. Am Soc
Civil Eng.
Compiled by Urban Runoff-Quantity &
Quality. Am Soc Civil Eng.
Compiled by Urban Transportation Efficiency.
Am Soc Civil Eng.
Compiled by Urban Transportation Innovation.
Am Soc Civil Eng.
Compiled by Use of Shotcrete for Underground
Structural Support. Am Soc Civil Eng.
Compiled by The Use of Underground Space to
Achieve National Goals. Am Soc Civil Eng.
Compiled by Verification of Mathematical &
Physical Models in Hydraulic Engineering.
Am Soc Civil Eng.
Compiled by Wastewater Treatment Plant
Design. Am Soc Civil Eng.
Compiled by Water & Metropolitan Man. Am
Soc Civil Eng.
Compiled by Water & Wastewater Control
Engineering: Glossary. Am Soc Civil Eng.
Compiled by Water Conservation-Needs &
Implementing Strategies. Am Soc Civil Eng.
Compiled by Water for the Southwest:
Historical Survey & Guide to Historic Sites.
Am Soc Civil Eng.
Compiled by Water Management for Irrigation
& Drainage. Am Soc Civil Eng.
Compiled by Water Problems of Urbanizing
Areas. Am Soc Civil Eng.
Compiled by Water Systems Nineteen
Seventy-Nine. Am Soc Civil Eng.
Compiled by Water Treatment Plant Design.
Am Soc Civil Eng.
Compiled by Watershed Management. Am Soc
Civil Eng.

**American Society of Civil Engineers. Engineering
Mechanics Division.**
xAmerican Society of Civil Engineers, Conference,
North Carolina State Univ., May 1977.
Advances in Civil Engineering Through
Engineering Mechanics: Proceedings. Am Soc
Civil Eng.

American Society of Composers, Authors and Publishers.
xAmerican Society of Composers, Authors &
Publishers.
ed. ASCAP Symphonic Catalog 1977. Bowker.
Copyright Law Symposium. Columbia U Pr.
Copyright Law Symposium, No. Twenty-One:
Proceedings. Columbia U Pr.
American Society of Hospital Attorneys.
xAmerican Society of Hospital Attorneys.
Federal Regulation: Hospital Attorney's Desk
Reference. Am Hospital.
American Society of Hospital Pharmacists.
xAmerican Society of Hospital Pharmacists.
Clinical Pharmacy Sourcebook: Key Articles
from the American Journal of Hospital
Pharmacy. PSG Pub.
Multi-Source Drug Products. Am Soc Hosp
Pharm.
Sourcebook on Clinical Pharmacy. PSG Pub.
ed. Sourcebook on Unit Dose Drug
Distribution Systems. Am Soc Hosp Pharm.
ed. Unit Dose Products. Am Soc Hosp Pharm.
American Society of International Law.
xAmerican Society Of International Law.
International Law in the Twentieth Century.
Irvington.
American Society of Journalists & Authors. *see* Society
of Magazine Writers.
American Society of Mechanical Engineers.
xAmerican Society of Mechanical Engineers.
ASME Handbook: Engineering Tables.
McGraw.
ASME Handbook: Metals Engineering-Design.
McGraw.
ASME Handbook: Metals Engineering:
Processes. McGraw.
ASME Handbook: Metals Properties. McGraw.
Report on Diesel & Gas Engine Power Costs,
1974. ASME.
xBiomechanics Symposium, 1973.
AMD: Proceedings. ASME.
xBiomechanics Symposium, 1977.
Proceedings: Amd Vol. 23. ASME.
American Society of Planning Officials.
xAmerican Society of Planning Officials.
Planned Unit Development Ordinances. Urban
Land.
American Society of Tool & Manufacturing Engineers.
see American Society of Tool and Manufacturing
Engineers.
American Society of Tool and Manufacturing Engineers.
xAmerican Society of Tool & Manufacturing
Engineers.
Fundamentals of Tool Design. P-H.
xAmerican Society Of Tool And Manufacturing
Engineers.
A S T M E Die Design Handbook. McGraw.
Handbook of Fixture Design. McGraw.
Manufacturing Planning & Estimating
Handbook. McGraw.
American Sociological Association.
xAmerican Sociological Association.
Experiences in Inquiry: HSGP & SRSS. Allyn.
xAmerican Sociological Society.
The Family. Arno.
Social Problems - Social Processes: Selected
Papers from the Proceedings of the American
Sociological Society, 1932. Arno.
American Sociological Society. *see* American Sociological
Association.
American Theatre Planning Board.
xTheAmerican Theatre Planning Board.
Theatre Check List: A Guide to the Planning
& Construction of Proscenium & Open Stage
Theatres. Columbia U Pr.
American Thoracic Society.
xAmerican Thoracic Society.
The Health Effects of Air Pollution. Am Lung Assn.

American Tract Society.
xAmerican Tract Society.
The American Tract Society Documents,
Eighteen Twenty Four to Nineteen Twenty
Five. Arno.
American Tract Society: Homes & Hospitals.
Milford Hse.
Enormity of the Slave-Trade. Arno.
American Trade Union Delegation to the Soviet Union.
xAmerican Trade Union Delegation to the Soviet
Union.
Soviet Russia in the Second Decade. Arno.
American Unitarian Association.
xAmerican Unitarian Association.
From Servitude to Service. Arno.
American Universities Field Service Staff. *see* American
Universities Field Staff.
American Universities Field Staff.
xAmerican Universities Field Service Staff.
Population: Perspective, 1971. Freeman C.
Population: Perspective, 1972. Freeman C.
Population: Perspective, 1973. Freeman C.
xAmerican Universities Field Staff.
City & Nation in the Developing World: AUFS
Readings. Am U Field.
Developing World: AUFS Readings. Am U
Field.
A Select Bibliography: Asia, Africa, Eastern
Europe, Latin America. Am U Field.
American Vacuum Society. Education Committee.
xAmerican Vacuum Society Education Comm.
ed. Experimental Vacuum Science &
Technology. Dekker.
American Water Works Association.
xAmerican Water Works Association.
American National Standard for Gray-Iron &
Ductile-Iron Fitting, 3 in. Through 48 in., for
Water & Other Liquids: C10-A21, 10-77. Am
Water Wks Assn.
American National Standard for Thickness
Design of Cast-Iron Pipe: C101-A21,1-67.
Am Water Wks Assn.
American National Standard for Vertical
Turbine Pumps - Line Shaft & Submersible
Types: E101-77. Am Water Wks Assn.
Annual Conference: Proceedings: 1975. Am
Water Wks Assn.
Annual Conference: Proceedings: 1976. Am
Water Wks Assn.
Annual Conference: Proceedings: 1977. Am
Water Wks Assn.
Annual Conference: Proceedings: 1978. Am
Water Wks Assn.
Annual Conference Proceedings, 1980. Am
Water Wks Assn.
Automation & Instrumentation - M2. Am
Water Wks Assn.
AWWA Distribution System Symposium
Nineteen Eighty: Proceedings: 1980. Am
Water Wks Assn.
AWWA Standard for Deep Wells: A100-66.
Am Water Wks Assn.
AWWA Standard for the Selection of
Asbestos-Cement Transmission & Feeder
Main Pipe, Sizes 18 in. Through 42 in.:
C403-78. Am Water Wks Assn.
AWWA Standard for Welded Steel Elevated
Tanks, Standpipes, & Reservoirs for Water
Storage: D-100-73. Am Water Wks Assn.
Basic Water Treatment Operator's Practices -
M18. Am Water Wks Assn.
Community Relations Newsletter Collection,
May 1975-April 1977. Am Water Wks Assn.
Computer-Based Automation in Water
Systems. Am Water Wks Assn.
Concrete Pressure Pipe-M9: AWWA Manuals.
Am Water Wks Assn.
Controlling Corrosion Within Water Systems.
Am Water Wks Assn.

Specification for Carbon Steel Filler Metals for Gas Shielded Arc Welding: AWS A5.18. Am Welding.
xAWS A5 Committee on Filler Metal.
Specification for Carbon Steel Electrodes for Flux Cored Arc Welding: AWS A5.20-79. Am Welding.
xAWS Committee on Filler Metal.
Specification for Bare Low Alloy Steel Electrodes for Submerged Arc Welding: A5.23-76. Am Welding.
Specification for Corrosion-Resisting Chromium & Chromium-Nickel Steel Covered Welding Electrodes: AWS A5.4-78. Am Welding.
xAWS Committee on Filler Metals.
Specification for Carbon Steel Covered Arc Welding Electrodes: AWS A51.-78. Am Welding.

American Welding Society. Committee on Machinery and Equipment.
xAWS Committee on Machinery & Equipment.
Specification for Welding Earthmoving & Construction Equipment: D14.3-77. Am Welding.
Standard for Classification & Application of Welded Joints for Machinery & Equipment. Am Welding.

American Welding Society. Committee on Qualification.
xAWS Committee on Qualification.
Welding Procedure & Performance Qualification: B3.0-77. Am Welding.

American Welding Society. Committee on Thermal Spraying.
xAmerican Welding Society Committee on Thermal Spraying.
Nineteen-Year Corrosion Tests of Flame-Sprayed Coated Steels, C2.14-74. Am Welding.

American Welding Society. Structural Welding Committee.
xAWS Structural Welding Committee.
Structural Welding Code--Steel: AWS D1.1-79. Am Welding.
Structural Welding Code: AWS D1-1-75. Am Welding.

American Welding Society. Technical Dept.
xAmerican Welding Society, Technical Department.
Welding Zinc-Coated Steels: D19.0-72. Am Welding.
Amerine, M. A. see Amerine, Maynard Andrew.
Amerine, Maynard Andrew.
xAmerine, M. A.
Methods for Analysis of Musts & Wines. Wiley.
Technology of Wine Making. AVI.
Ameringer, Charles D., 1926-
xAmeringer, Charles D.
Don Pepe: A Political Biography of Jose Figueres of Costa Rica. U of NM Pr.
Ameringer, Oscar, 1870-1943
xAmeringer, Oscar.
If You Don't Weaken: The Autobiography of Oscar Ameringer. Greenwood.
Amerman, Lockhart.
xAmerman, Lockhart.
Cape Cod Casket. HarBraceJ.
Amery, Colin.
xAmery, Colin.
The Rape of Britain. Merrimack Bk Serv.
Ames, Angela T. see Ames, Angela Taylor.
Ames, Angela Taylor.
xAmes, Angela T.
Eve. PB.
Ames, Bernice, 1915-
xAmes, Bernice.
In Syllables of Stars. Golden Quill.
Ames, Blanche. see Ames, Blanche Ames.
Ames, Blanche Ames.
xAmes, Blanche.

Drawings of Florida Orchids. E M Coleman Ent.
Ames, David W.
xAmes, David W.
Glossary of Hausa Music & Its Social Contexts. Northwestern U Pr.
Ames, Francis.
xAmes, Francis.
That Callahan Spunk!. Ace Bks.
Ames, Francis. see Ames, Francis H.
Ames, Francis H.
xAmes, Francis.
Callahan Goes South. G K Hall.
xAmes, Francis H.
Callahan Goes South. Doubleday.
Ames, Gerald.
xAmes, Gerald.
Earth's Story. Creative Ed.
Ames, Jessie (Daniel), 1883-
xAmes, Jessie D.
Changing Character of Lynching: Review of Lynching 1931-1941, with a Discussion of Recent Developments in This Field. AMS Pr.
Ames, Jessie D. see Ames, Jessie (Daniel).
Ames, Joseph S. see Ames, Joseph Sweetman.
Ames, Joseph Sweetman.
xAmes, Joseph S.
Theoretical Mechanics: An Introduction to Mathematical Physics. Gannon.
Ames, Louise B. see Ames, Louise Bates.
Ames, Louise Bates.
xAmes, Louise B.
Don't Push Your Preschooler. Har-Row.
The Gesell Institute's Child from One to Six: Evaluating the Behavior of the Pre-School Child. Har-Row.
Stop School Failure. Har-Row.
Ames, Mary, 1831-1903
xAmes, Mary.
From a New England Woman's Diary in Dixie in 1865. Negro U Pr.
Ames, Mildred.
xAmes, Mildred.
Nicky & the Joyous Noise. Scribner.
The Wonderful Box. Dutton.
Ames, Oakes, 1874-
xAmes, Oakes.
Orchids in Retrospect: A Collection of Essays on the Orchidaceae. E M Coleman Ent.
Ames, Russell, 1912-
xAmes, Russell.
Citizen Thomas More & His Utopia. Russell.
Ames, Van M. see Ames, Van Meter.
Ames, Van Meter, 1898-
xAmes, Van M.
Aesthetics of the Novel. Gordian.
Introduction to Beauty. Arno.
Proust & Santayana: The Aesthetic Way of Life. Russell.
Ames, W. F. see Ames, William F.
Ames, William.
xAmes, William.
Technometry. U of Pa Pr.
Ames, William F.
xAmes, W. F.
ed. Nonlinear Partial Differential Equations: A Symposium on Methods of Solution. Acad Pr.
ed. Nonlinear Partial Differential Equations in Engineering. Acad Pr.
xAmes, William F.
ed. Nonlinear Ordinary Differential Equations in Transport Processes. Acad Pr.
Ames, Winthrop.
xAmes, Winthrop.
What Shall We Name the Baby?. PB.
ed. What Shall We Name the Baby. S&S.
AMETEK. see Ametek Inc.
Ametek Inc.
xAMETEK.

Solar Energy Handbook: Theory & Application. Chilton.
Amichai, Yehuda.
xAmichai, Yehuda.
Songs of Jerusalem & Myself. Har-Row.
Amici, R. see Amici, Raffaele.
Amici, Raffaele.
xAmici, R.
Cerebellar Tumors: Clinical Analysis & Physiopathologic Correlations. S Karger.
Amidon, Eva V.
xAmidon, Eva V.
Easy Quillery: Projects with Paper Coils & Scrolls. Morrow.
Amiel, Henri Frederic, 1821-1881
xAmiel, Henri-F.
Jean Jacques Rousseau. R West.
xAmiel, Henri-Frederic.
Jean Jacques Rousseau. Folcroft.
Amiel, Henri-F. see Amiel, Henri Frederic.
Amiel, Henri-Frederic. see Amiel, Henri Frederic.
Amiel, J. J. see Amiel, Joseph.
Amiel, Joseph.
xAmiel, J. J.
Hawks. Popular Lib.
Hawks. Putnam.
Amin, Galal. see Amin, Galal A.
Amin, Galal A., 1935-
xAmin, Galal.
Food Supply & Economic Development with Special Reference to Egypt. Biblio Dist.
xAmin, Galal A.
Food Supply & Economic Development with Special Reference to Egypt. Kelley.
Amin, Samir.
xAmin, Samir.
Accumulation on a World Scale: A Critique of the Theory of Underdevelopment. Monthly Rev.
Class & Nation, Historically & in the Current Crisis. Monthly Rev.
Imperialism & Unequal Development. Monthly Rev.
The Law of Value & Historical Materialism. Monthly Rev.
Neo-Colonialism in West Africa. Monthly Rev.
Aminoff, Michael J. see Aminoff, Michael Jeffrey.
Aminoff, Michael Jeffrey.
xAminoff, Michael J.
Electromyography in Clinical Practice. A-W.
Amir, Menachem, 1930-
xAmir, Menachem.
Patterns in Forcible Rape. U of Chicago Pr.
Amir, Ziv. see Amir, Ziva.
Amir, Ziva, 1930-
xAmir, Ziv.
Arabesque: Decorative Needlework from the Holy Land. Van Nos Reinhold.
Amirsadeghi, Hossein.
xAmirsadeghi, Hossein.
ed. Twentieth Century Iran. Holmes & Meier.
Amis, Edward S. see Amis, Edward Stephen.
Amis, Edward Stephen.
xAmis, Edward S.
Solvent Effects on Chemical Phenomena. Acad Pr.
Amis, Kingsley.
xAmis, Kingsley.

Fields of Applied Psychology. McGraw.
Individual Differences. Wiley.
Psychological Testing. Macmillan.

Anastasi, Thomas E.
xAnastasi, Thomas E.
Communicating for Results.
Benjamin-Cummings.

Anastasio, Dina.
xAnastasio, Dina.
A Question of Time. Dutton.

Anastasiow, Nicholas. see Anastasiow, Nicholas J.

Anastasiow, Nicholas J.
xAnastasiow, Nicholas.
Oral Language: Expression of Thought. Intl
Reading.

Anatoli, A., 1929-
xAnatoli, A.
Babi Yar: A Document in the Form of a
Novel. Bentley.

Anchor, Robert.
xAnchor, Robert.
The Enlightenment Tradition. U of Cal Pr.
Germany Confronts Modernization: German
Culture & Society, 1790-1890. Heath.

Ancona, George.
xAncona, George.
And What Do You Do?: A Book About People
& Their Work. Dutton.
I Feel: A Picture Book of Emotions. Dutton.
photos by It's a Baby!. Dutton.
illus. Monsters on Wheels. Dutton.

Andacht, Sandra.
xAndacht, Sandra.
Satsuma: An Illustrated Guide.
Wallace-Homestead.

Andelin, Helen. see Andelin, Helen B.

Andelin, Helen B.
xAndelin, Helen.
Fascinating Womanhood. Bantam.
xAndelin, Helen B.
The Fascinating Girl. Pacific Santa Barbara.
Fascinating Womanhood. Pacific Santa Barbara.

Andemicael, Berhanykun.
xAndemicael, Berhanykun.
The OAU & the UN: Relations Between the
Organization of African Unity & the United
Nations. Holmes & Meier.

Anderberg, Michael R.
xAnderberg, Michael R.
Cluster Analysis for Applications. Acad Pr.

Anderegg, Michael. see Anderegg, Michael A.

Anderegg, Michael A.
xAnderegg, Michael.
William Wyler. Twayne.

Anders, Gerhard.
xAnders, Gerhard.
ed. The Economics of Mineral Extraction.
Praeger.

Anders, Leslie.
xAnders, Leslie.
The Twenty-First Missouri: From Home Guard
to Union Regiment. Greenwood.

Anders, Mary E. see Anders, Mary Edna.

Anders, Mary Edna.
xAnders, Mary E.
Libraries & Library Services in the Southeast:
A Report of the Southeastern States
Cooperative Library Survey, 1972-1974. U of
Ala Pr.

Anders, Nedda (Casson).
xAnders, Nedda C.
Applique Old & New, Including Patchwork &
Embroidery. Dover.
Applique Old & New, Including Patchwork &
Embroidery. Peter Smith.

Anders, Nedda C. see Anders, Nedda (Casson).

Anders, Rebecca.
xAnders, Rebecca.

Camping Out. Lerner Pubns.
Clover the Calf. Carolrhoda Bks.
Dolly the Donkey. Carolrhoda Bks.
Lorito the Parrot. Carolrhoda Bks.
Whiskers the Rabbit. Carolrhoda Bks.

Anders-Richards, Donald.
xAnders-Richards, Donald.
The Drama of the Psalms. Judson.

Andersch, E. G. see Andersch, Elizabeth G.

Andersch, Elizabeth G.
xAndersch, E. G.
Communication in Everyday Use. HR&W.

Andersdatter, Karla M. see Andersdatter, Karla
Margaret.

Andersdatter, Karla Margaret.
xAndersdatter, Karla M.
I Don't Know Whether to Laugh or Cry Cause
I Lost the Map to Where I Was Going.
Second Coming.

Andersen, A. C. see Andersen, Allen C.

Andersen, Allen C.
xAndersen, A. C.
ed. Dogs & Other Large Mammals in Aging
Research. Mss Info.

Andersen, Arlow W. see Andersen, Arlow William.

Andersen, Arlow William.
xAndersen, Arlow W.
The Immigrant Takes His Stand: The
Norwegian-American Press & Public Affairs,
1847-1872. Greenwood.
The Norwegian-Americans. Twayne.

Andersen, Carl M.
xAndersen, Carl M.
Classroom Activities for Modifying
Misbehavior in Children. Ctr Appl Res.

Andersen, Clifton R. see Andersen, R. Clifton.

Andersen, Hans C. see Andersen, Hans Christian.

Andersen, Hans Christian.
xAndersen, Hans C.
Andersen's Fairy Tales. Macmillan.
Andersen's Fairy Tales. G&D.
Fir Tree. Har-Row.
Hans Andersen's Fairy Tales. Biblio Dist.
Hans Andersen's Fairy Tales. Oxford U Pr.
Hans Christian Andersen's Fairy Tales.
Airmont.
Little Match Girl. HM.
Little Mermaid. Vanous.
The Princess & the Pea. HM.
The Steadfast Tin Soldier. HM.
Steadfast Tin Soldier. Scribner.
Ugly Duckling. Scribner.
Ugly Duckling. Troll Assocs.
xAndersen, Hans Christian.
The Complete Fairy Tales & Stories.
Doubleday.
Hans Andersen's Fairy Tales. Schocken.
Hans Andersen's Fairy Tales. Schocken.

Andersen, Hans H. see Andersen, Hans Henrik.

Andersen, Hans Henrik.
xAndersen, Hans H.
ed. Hydrogen Stopping Powers & Ranges in
All Elements. Pergamon.

Andersen, Hans O.
xAndersen, Hans O.
Toward More Effective Science Instruction in
Secondary Education. Macmillan.

Andersen, Ian.
xAndersen, Ian.
Turning the Tables on Las Vegas. Random.
Turning the Tables on Las Vegas. Vanguard.

Andersen, Isabelle, 1911-
xAndersen, Isabelle.
Gentle Asylum: Life at a Mental Hospital.
Continuum.

Andersen, Johannes C. see Andersen, Johannes Carl.

Andersen, Johannes Carl, 1873-1962
xAndersen, Johannes C.

Maori Life in Ao-tea. AMS Pr.
Maori Music, with Its Polynesian Background.
AMS Pr.
Maori String Figures. AMS Pr.

Andersen, Kenneth. see Andersen, Kenneth E.

Andersen, Kenneth E.
xAndersen, Kenneth.
Persuasion: Theory & Practice. Allyn.

Andersen, Linda.
xAndersen, Linda.
Classroom Activities for Helping Perceptually
Handicapped Children. Ctr Appl Res.

Andersen, Martin P.
xAndersen, Martin P.
Speaker & His Audience: Dynamic
Interpersonal Communication. Har-Row.

Andersen, N. R. see Andersen, Neil R.

Andersen, Neil R.
xAndersen, N. R.
ed. The Fate of Fossil Fuel CO_2 in the Oceans.
Plenum Pub.
xAndersen, Neil R.
ed. Oceanic Sound Scattering Prediction.
Plenum Pub.

Andersen, Poul Gerhard.
xAndersen, Poul-Gerhard.
Organ Building & Design. Allen Unwin.

Andersen, Poul-Gerhard. see Andersen, Poul Gerhard.

Andersen, R. Clifton.
xAndersen, Clifton R.
ed. Marketing Insights: Selected Readings.
Austin Pr.

Andersen, Richard, 1946-
xAndersen, Richard.
Muckaluck. Delacorte.
Straight Cut Ditch. Ashley Bks.
William Goldman. Twayne.

Andersen, Ronald.
xAndersen, Ronald.
Decade of Health Services: Social Survey
Trends in Use & Expenditure. U of Chicago
Pr.
Total Survey Error: Applications to Improve
Health Surveys. Jossey-Bass.
Two Decades of Health Services: Social Survey
Trends in Use & Expenditure. Ballinger Pub.

Andersen, Tryggve, 1866-1920
xAndersen, Tryggve.
In the Days of the Councillor. Am
Scandinavian.

Andersland, Orlando B.
xAndersland, Orlando B.
ed. Geotechnical Engineering for Cold Regions.
McGraw.

Anderson. see Anderson, James E.

Anderson, A. E. see Anderson, Augustus Emmett.

Anderson, A. J. see Anderson, Arthur James.

Anderson, A. L. see Anderson, Ardis Leroy.

Anderson, Alan D.
xAnderson, Alan D.
The Origin & Resolution of an Urban Crisis:
Baltimore,1890-1930. Johns Hopkins.

Anderson, Alan R. see Anderson, Alan Ross.

Anderson, Alan Ross.
xAnderson, Alan R.
Entailment: The Logic of Relevance &
Necessity. Princeton U Pr.
ed. The Logical Enterprise. Yale U Pr.

Anderson, Alexander W. see Anderson, Alexander
Walter.

Anderson, Alexander Walter, 1901-
xAnderson, Alexander W.
How We Got Our Flowers. Peter Smith.

Anderson, Alexandra.
xAnderson, Alexandra.
Anderson & Archer's Soho: The Essential
Guide to Art & Life in Lower Manhattan.
S&S.

Anderson, Anders H.
xAnderson, Anders H.

The Cactus Wren. U of Ariz Pr.
Anderson, Andy, 1927-
 xAnderson, Andy.
  Fasting Changed My Life. Broadman.
  Where Action Is. Broadman.
Anderson, Annelise G. *see* Anderson, Annelise Graebner.
Anderson, Annelise Graebner.
 xAnderson, Annelise G.
  The Business of Organized Crime: A Cosa
   Nostra Family. Hoover Inst Pr.
Anderson, Ardis Leroy, 1924-
 xAnderson, A. L.
  The Way. Northwest Pub.
Anderson, Arthur James, 1863-
 xAnderson, A. J.
  The Artistic Side of Photography in Theory &
   Practice. Arno.
  Problems in Intellectual Freedom &
   Censorship. Bowker.
Anderson, Arthur L. *see* Anderson, Arthur Leroy.
Anderson, Arthur Leroy, 1932-
 xAnderson, Arthur L.
  Divided We Stand: Institutional Religion As a
   Reflection of Pluralism & Integration in
   America. Kendall-Hunt.
Anderson, Arvid C.
 xAnderson, Arvid C.
  Masters of Music. Arno.
Anderson, Augustus Emmett.
 xAnderson, A. E.
  Pathology of Disruptive Pulmonary
   Emphysema. C C Thomas.
Anderson, B. *see* Anderson, Barbara G.
Anderson, B. Robert.
 xAnderson, B. Robert.
  Professional Selling. P-H.
Anderson, B. W.
 xAnderson, B. W.
  Gemstones for Everyman. Van Nos Reinhold.
Anderson, B. W. *see* Anderson, Basil William.
Anderson, Barbara. *see* Anderson, Barbara G.
Anderson, Barbara G.
 xAnderson, B.
  Emergency Childbirth Handbook. Van Nos
   Reinhold.
 xAnderson, Barbara.
  Obstetrics for the Nurse. Delmar.
Anderson, Barry F.
 xAnderson, Barry F.
  The Complete Thinker: A Handbook of
   Techniques for Creative & Critical Problem
   Solving. P-H.
Anderson, Basil W. *see* Anderson, Basil William.
Anderson, Basil William, 1901-
 xAnderson, B. W.
  Gem Testing. Butterworths.
 xAnderson, Basil W.
  Gem Testing. Emerson.
Anderson, Benjamin M. *see* Anderson, Benjamin
 Mcalester.
Anderson, Benjamin McAlester, 1886-1949
 xAnderson, Benjamin M.
  Social Value: A Study in Economic Theory
   Critical & Constructive. Kelley.
Anderson, Bern.
 xAnderson, Bern.
  By Sea & by River: The Naval History of the
   Civil War. Greenwood.
Anderson, Bernhard W.
 xAnderson, Bernhard W.
  The Living Word of the Bible. Westminster.
  Out of the Depths: The Psalms Speak for Us
   Today. Westminster.
  Understanding the Old Testament. P-H.
Anderson, Bernice G.
 xAnderson, Bernice G.
  Trickster Tales from Prairie Lodgefires.
   Abingdon.
Anderson, Bob, 1945-
 xAnderson, Bob.

Stretching. Shelter Pubns.
Anderson, Bob. *see* Anderson, Robert.
Anderson, Bobby D.
 xAnderson, Bobby D.
  The Law & the Teacher in Mississippi: A
   Guide for Teachers, Administrators, &
   Potential Teachers. U Pr of Miss.
Anderson, Brad.
 xAnderson, Brad.
  The Marmaduke Treasury. Andrews &
   McMeel.
Anderson, Brian. *see* Anderson, Brian D. O.
Anderson, Brian D. O.
 xAnderson, Brian.
  Optimal Filtering. P-H.
Anderson, Bruce. *see* Anderson, Bruce N.
Anderson, Bruce N.
 xAnderson, Bruce.
  The Solar Home Book: Heating, Cooling, &
   Designing with the Sun. Brick Hse Pub.
Anderson, C. L. *see* Anderson, Carl Leonard.
Anderson, C. W. *see* Anderson, Clarence William.
Anderson, Carl L. *see* Anderson, Carl Leonard.
Anderson, Carl Leonard, 1901-
 xAnderson, C. L.
  Community Health. Mosby.
  School Health Practice. Mosby.
 xAnderson, Carl L.
  School Health Practice. Mosby.
Anderson, Carl R.
 xAnderson, Carl R.
  Readings in Management: An Organizational
   Perspective. Little.
Anderson, Charles D. *see* Anderson, Charles Dixon.
Anderson, Charles Dixon, 1941-
 xAnderson, Charles D.
  ed. Outlaws of the Old West. Mankind Pub.
Anderson, Charles H., 1938-
 xAnderson, Charles H.
  Toward a New Sociology. Dorsey.
Anderson, Charles R. *see* Anderson, Charles Roberts.
Anderson, Charles Robert, 1943-
 xAnderson, Charles R.
  The Grunts. Presidio Pr.
Anderson, Charles Roberts, 1902-
 xAnderson, Charles R.
  Person, Place & Thing in Henry James's
   Novels. Duke.
Anderson, Charles S.
 xAnderson, Charles S.
  Augsburg Historical Atlas of Christianity in the
   Middle Ages & Reformation. Augsburg.
Anderson, Chester.
 xAnderson, Chester.
  The Butterfly Kid. Gregg.
  The Butterfly Kid. PB.
Anderson, Chester G.
 xAnderson, Chester G.
  ed. Growing Up in Minnesota: Ten Writers
   Remember Their Childhoods. U of Minn Pr.
  Word Index to James Joyce's Stephen Hero.
   Arden Lib.
Anderson, Clarence W. *see* Anderson, Clarence William.
Anderson, Clarence William, 1891-
 xAnderson, C. W.
  illus. Afraid to Ride. Schol Bk Serv.
  Complete Book of Horses & Horsemanship.
   Macmillan.
  Lonesome Little Colt. Macmillan.
 xAnderson, Clarence W.
  Afraid to Ride. Macmillan.
  illus. Crooked Colt. Macmillan.
  Lonesome Little Colt. Macmillan.
  illus. Outlaw. Macmillan.
  illus. Pony for Linda. Macmillan.
  illus. Pony for Three. Macmillan.
  illus. Twenty Gallant Horses. Macmillan.
Anderson, Colena. *see* Anderson, Colena M.
Anderson, Colena M.
 xAnderson, Colena.

Joy Beyond Grief. Zondervan.
 xAnderson, Colena M.
  Don't Put on Your Slippers Yet. Zondervan.
  Friendship's Bright Shinings. Zondervan.
Anderson, D. A. *see* Anderson, David A.
Anderson, D. R. *see* Anderson, Daniel R.
Anderson, Daniel R.
 xAnderson, D. R.
  Instructional Programming for the Handicapped
   Student. C C Thomas.
 xFairchild Market Research Division.
  Women's Sportswear, Seperates, Jeans &
   Active Wear. Fairchild.
Anderson, Dave.
 xAnderson, Dave.
  Great Pass Receivers of the NFL. Random.
  Sports of Our Times. Random.
  The Yankees: The Four Fabulous Eras of
   Baseball's Most Famous Team. Random.
Anderson, David. *see* Anderson, David J.
Anderson, David A.
 xAnderson, D. A.
  All the Trees & Woody Plants of the Bible.
   Word Bks.
 xAnderson, David.
  Forestry Curriculum Guide. Interstate.
Anderson, David B. *see* Anderson, David D.
Anderson, David D.
 xAnderson, David B.
  Woodrow Wilson. G K Hall.
  Woodrow Wilson. Twayne.
 xAnderson, David D.
  Abraham Lincoln. Twayne.
  Louis Bromfield. Coll & U Pr.
Anderson, David J.
 xAnderson, David.
  Homeopathic Remedies for Physicians, Laymen
   & Therapists. Himalayan Intl Inst.
Anderson, David L.
 xAnderson, David L.
  Compiled by Symbolism: A Bibliography of
   Symbolism as an International &
   Multi-Disciplinary Movement. NYU Pr.
Anderson, David Ray.
 xAnderson.
  An Introduction to Management Science:
   Quantitative Approaches to Decision Making.
   West Pub.
 xAnderson, David.
  Essentials of Management Science:
   Applications to Decision Making. West Pub.
  Linear Programming for Decision Making: An
   Applications Approach. West Pub.
Anderson, Dean Albert, 1905-
 xAnderson.
  Introduction to Microbiology. Mosby.
Anderson, Donald L.
 xAnderson, Donald L.
  Information Analysis in Management
   Accounting. Wiley.
Anderson, Doris. *see* Anderson, Doris (Jones).
Anderson, Doris (Jones), 1918-
 xAnderson, Doris.
  Encyclopedia of Games. Zondervan.
Anderson, Douglas, 1902-
 xAnderson, Douglas.
  All About Cribbage. G K Hall.
  All About Cribbage. Winchester Pr.
  The One Real Poem Is Life. Braziller.
 xAnderson, G. Douglas.
  All About Cribbage. Winchester Pr.
Anderson, Earl W. *see* Anderson, Earl William.
Anderson, Earl William, 1897-
 xAnderson, Earl W.
  The Teacher's Contract & Other Legal Phases
   of Teacher Status. AMS Pr.
Anderson, Edgar, 1897-
 xAnderson, Edgar.

Plants, Man & Life. U of Cal Pr.
Anderson, Edwin P., 1895-
    xAnderson, Edwin P.
        Home Appliance Servicing. Audel.
Anderson, Einar, 1909-
    xAnderson, Einar.
        Inside Story of Mormonism. Kregel.
Anderson, Elizabeth M. *see* Anderson, Elizabeth Marian.
Anderson, Elizabeth Marian.
    xAnderson, Elizabeth M.
        Disabled Schoolchild: A Study of Integration in
            Primary Schools. Methuen Inc.
Anderson, Elliott.
    xAnderson, Elliott.
        ed. The Little Magazine in America: A
            Modern, Documentary History. Pushcart Pr.
Anderson, Eloise. *see* Anderson, Eloise A.
Anderson, Eloise A.
    xAnderson, Eloise.
        Carlos Goes to School. Warne.
Anderson, Elwood G.
    xAnderson, Elwood G.
        Therapy for Young Stutterers: The Kopp
            Method. Wayne St U Pr.
Anderson, Eric.
    xAnderson, Eric.
        Performance Rallying. TAB Bks.
Anderson, Eric. *see* Anderson, Eric G.
Anderson, Eric G.
    xAnderson, Eric.
        Plane Safety & Survival. Aero.
Anderson, Evelyn.
    xAnderson, Evelyn M.
        Good Morning, Lord: Devotions for the
            Mature Years. Baker Bk.
Anderson, Evelyn M. *see* Anderson, Evelyn McCullough.
Anderson, Evelyn McCullough.
    xAnderson, Evelyn M.
        Only a Woman. Baker Bk.
Anderson, Farris, 1938-
    xAnderson, Farris.
        Alfonso Sastre. Irvington.
Anderson, Frances E.
    xAnderson, Frances E.
        Christopher Smart. Twayne.
Anderson, Frances E. *see* Anderson, Frances Elisabeth.
Anderson, Frances Elisabeth, 1941-
    xAnderson, Frances E.
        Art for All the Children: A Creative
            Sourcebook for the Impaired Child. C C
            Thomas.
Anderson, Frank J., 1912-
    xAnderson, Frank J.
        An Illustrated Treasury of Cultivated Flowers.
            Abbeville Pr.
        An Illustrated Treasury of Orchids. Abbeville
            Pr.
        Private Presswork: A Bibliographic Approach
            to Printing As an Avocation. A S Barnes.
        Submarines, Diving, & the Underwater World:
            A Bibliography. Shoe String.
Anderson, Frank R. *see* Anderson, Frank Russell.
Anderson, Frank Russell, 1923-
    xAnderson, Frank R.
        Quality Controlled Investing: Or How to Avoid
            the Pick & Pray Method. Wiley.
Anderson, Frederick. *see* Anderson, Frederick R.
Anderson, Frederick R.
    xAnderson, Frederick.
        NEPA in the Courts: A Legal Analysis of the
            National Environmental Policy Act. Johns
            Hopkins.
    xAnderson, Frederick R.
        Environmental Improvement Through
            Economic Incentives. Johns Hopkins.
Anderson, G. A. *see* Anderson, Gerald A.
Anderson, G. Douglas. *see* Anderson, Douglas.
Anderson, G. L. *see* Anderson, George Lincoln.
Anderson, G. W. *see* Anderson, George Wishart.
Anderson, Gary. *see* Anderson, Gary L.

Anderson, Gary L., 1939-
    xAnderson, Gary.
        Marksmanship. S&S.
        Marksmanship. S&S.
Anderson, Gene.
    xAnderson, Gene.
        Coring & Core Analysis Handbook. Pennwell
            Pub.
Anderson, George B.
    xAnderson, George B.
        Physical Fitness Digest. Follett.
Anderson, George L. *see* Anderson, George Lincoln.
Anderson, George Lincoln, 1920-
    xAnderson, G. L.
        ed. Masterpieces of the Orient. Norton.
    xAnderson, George L.
        ed. Masterpieces of the Orient. Norton.
Anderson, George Wishart.
    xAnderson, G. W.
        Tradition & Interpretation. Oxford U Pr.
Anderson, Gerald A., 1950-
    xAnderson, G. A.
        Surgery with Coefficients. Springer-Verlag.
Anderson, Gerald H.
    xAnderson, Gerald H.
        ed. Studies in Philippine Church History.
            Cornell U Pr.
Anderson, Gordon J.
    xAnderson, Gordon J.
        How to Compete Successfully in Real Estate
            Investing: A Guide to Exploring &
            Understanding the Factors That Affect
            Values. Exposition.
Anderson, Henry P.
    xAnderson, Henry P.
        The Bracero Program in California: With
            Particular Reference to Health Status,
            Attitudes, & Practices. Arno.
Anderson Hospital. *see* Anderson Hospital and Tumor
    Institute, Houston, Texas.
Anderson, Howard J.
    xAnderson, Howard J.
        Primer of Equal Employment Opportunity.
            BNA.
**Anderson Hospital and Tumor Institute, Houston,
Texas.**
    xAnderson Hospital.
        Cancer Chemotherapy: Fundamental Concepts
            & Recent Advances. Year Bk Med.
        Cancer Patient Care at M. D. Anderson
            Hospital & Tumor Institute. Year Bk Med.
        Current Concepts in the Management of
            Primary Bone & Soft Tissue Tumors. Year Bk
            Med.
        Leukemia-Lymphoma. Year Bk Med.
        Neoplasms of the Skin & Malignant Melanoma.
            Year Bk Med.
        Radiologic & Other Biophysical Methods in
            Tumor Diagnosis. Year Bk Med.
Anderson, Irvine H., 1928-
    xAnderson, Irvine H.
        The Standard-Vacuum Oil Company & United
            States East Asian Policy, 1933-1941.
            Princeton U Pr.
Anderson, J. A. *see* Anderson, John Alvin.
Anderson, J. C. *see* Anderson, J. R.
Anderson, J. D. *see* Anderson, James Drummond.
Anderson, J. E. *see* Anderson, John E.
Anderson, J. G. *see* Anderson, John Graham Comrie.
Anderson, J. J.
    xAnderson, J. J.
        ed. Cleanness. B&N.
Anderson, J. K. *see* Anderson, John Kinloch.
Anderson, J. N. *see* Anderson, James Norman
    Dalrymple.
Anderson, J. R.
    xAnderson, J. C.

    ed. Chemisorption & Reactions on Metallic
        Films. Acad Pr.
Anderson, Jack, 1935-
    xAnderson, Jack.
        Dance. Newsweek.
        Toward the Liberation of the Left Hand. U of
            Pittsburgh Pr.
Anderson, Jack A.
    xAnderson, Jack A.
        Change & Innovation in Education. Mss Info.
Anderson, James, Book Annotator.
    xAnderson, James.
        British Novels of the Twentieth Century.
            Arden Lib.
        British Novels of the Twentieth Century.
            Folcroft.
Anderson, James *see* Anderson, James Francis.
Anderson, James Drummond, 1852-1920
    xAnderson, J. D.
        Manual of the Bengali Language. Ungar.
Anderson, James E.
    xAnderson.
        Public Policy & Politics in America. Duxbury
            Pr.
    xAnderson, James E.
        ed. Economic Regulatory Policies. Lexington
            Bks.
        ed. Economic Regulatory Policies. S Ill U Pr.
        Public Policy-Making. HR&W.
        Public Policy-Making. Krieger.
        Texas Politics: An Introduction. Har-Row.
Anderson, James Francis, 1910-
    xAnderson, James
        Natural Theology: The Metaphysics of God.
            Glencoe.
Anderson, James L.
    xAnderson, James L.
        Principles of Relativity Physics. Acad Pr.
Anderson, James M.
    xAnderson, James M.
        Readings in Romance Linguistics. Mouton.
Anderson, James M. *see* Anderson, James Maxwell.
Anderson, James Maxwell.
    xAnderson, James M.
        Historical Romance Morphology. Univ
            Microfilms.
        Structural Aspects of Language Change.
            Longman.
Anderson, James Norman Dalrymple, Sir.
    xAnderson, J. N.
        The World's Religions. Eerdmans.
    xAnderson, Norman.
        Law Reform in the Muslim World. Humanities.
        The Mystery of the Incarnation. Inter-Varsity.
Anderson, Jane, 1944-
    xAnderson, Jane.
        Inn Perspective: A Guide to New England
            Country Inns. Har-Row.
Anderson, Jean, 1929-
    xAnderson, Jean.
        The Grass Roots Cookbook. Times Bks.
        Jean Anderson's Processor Cooking. Morrow.
Anderson, Jennifer, 1942-
    xAnderson, Jennifer.
        Cave Exploring. Follett.
        The Thinking Woman's Beauty Book. Avon.
Anderson, Joan W. *see* Anderson, Joan Wester.
Anderson, Joan Wester.
    xAnderson, Joan W.
        Love, Lollipops & Laundry. Our Sunday
            Visitor.
Anderson, Joanne. *see* Anderson, Joanne Manning.
Anderson, Joanne Manning, 1942-
    xAnderson, Joanne.
        For the People: A Consumer Action
            Handbook. A-W.
Anderson, John.
    xAnderson, John.

Public Media Manual for Museums. Tex Assn
Mus.
Anderson, John. *see* Anderson, John Richard Lane.
Anderson, John Alvin.
    xAnderson, J. A.
      jt. auth. Crying for a Vision: Rosebud Sioux
        Trilogy 1886-1976. Morgan.
Anderson, John D. *see* Anderson, John David.
Anderson, John David.
    xAnderson, John D.
      Introduction to Flight: Its Engineering &
        History. McGraw.
Anderson, John E., 1940-
    xAnderson, J. E.
      Organization & Financing of Self-Help
        Education in Kenya. Unipub.
Anderson, John Graham Comrie.
    xAnderson, J. G.
      The Structure of the British Isles. Pergamon.
      The Structure of Western Europe. Pergamon.
Anderson, John Kinloch.
    xAnderson, J. K.
      Ancient Greek Horsemanship. U of Cal Pr.
Anderson, John L. *see* Anderson, John Lonzo.
Anderson, John Lonzo.
    xAnderson, John L.
      Night of the Silent Drums. Popular Lib.
    xAnderson, Lonzo.
      The Halloween Party. Scribner.
Anderson, John P. *see* Anderson, John Peyton.
Anderson, John Peyton, 1905-
    xAnderson, John P.
      A Study of the Relationships Between Certain
        Aspects of Parental Behavior & Attitudes &
        the Behavior of Junior High School Pupils.
        AMS Pr.
Anderson, John Q.
    xAnderson, John Q.
      The Liberating Gods: Emerson on Poets &
        Poetry. U of Miami Pr.
Anderson, John R. *see* Anderson, John Robert.
Anderson, John Richard Lane, 1911-
    xAnderson, John.
      Festival. St Martin.
Anderson, John Robert.
    xAnderson, John R.
      Human Associative Memory: A Brief Edition.
        L Erlbaum Assocs.
Anderson, John Warwick, 1940-
    xAnderson.
      Sulphur in Biology. Univ Park.
Anderson, Jon.
    xAnderson, Jon.
      Death & Friends. U of Pittsburgh Pr.
      In Sepia. U of Pittsburgh Pr.
      Looking for Jonathan. U of Pittsburgh Pr.
Anderson, Jonathan.
    xAnderson, Jonathan.
      Thesis & Assignment Writing. Wiley.
Anderson, Joseph Chapman.
    xAnderson, J. C.
      Materials Science. Halsted Pr.
Anderson, Joy. *see* Anderson, Joy (Coonrad).
Anderson, Joy (Coonrad).
    xAnderson, Joy.
      Pai-Pai Pig. HarBraceJ.
Anderson, Judith H.
    xAnderson, Judith H.
      The Growth of a Personal Voice: Piers
        Plowman & "the Faerie Queene". Yale U Pr.
Anderson, Kay.
    xAnderson, Kay.
      I & Thou in the Here & Now. Word Bks.
Anderson, Kenneth N.
    xAnderson, Kenneth N.
      The Newsweek Encyclopedia of Family Health.
        Newsweek.
Anderson, Kent.
    xAnderson, Kent.

      ed. Television Fraud: The History &
        Implications of the Quiz Show Scandals.
        Greenwood.
Anderson, L. L. *see* Anderson, Larry Lavon.
Anderson, L. O. *see* Anderson, Leroy Oscar.
Anderson, Larry L. *see* Anderson, Larry Lavon.
Anderson, Larry Lavon.
    xAnderson, L. L.
      ed. Fuels from Waste. Acad Pr.
    xAnderson, Larry L.
      Synthetic Fuels from Coal: Overview &
        Assessment. Wiley.
Anderson, Lavere.
    xAnderson, LaVere.
      Abe Lincoln & the River Robbers. Garrard.
      Story of Johnny Appleseed. Garrard.
Anderson, Lawrence L. *see* Anderson, Lawrence Leslie.
Anderson, Lawrence Leslie, 1894-
    xAnderson, Lawrence L.
      Art of the Silversmith in Mexico: 1519-1936.
        Hacker.
Anderson, Lee F.
    xAnderson, Lee F.
      Legislative Roll-Call Analysis. Northwestern U
        Pr.
Anderson, Leone C. *see* Anderson, Leone Castell.
Anderson, Leone Castell.
    xAnderson, Leone C.
      It's O.K. to Cry. Childs World.
Anderson, LeRoy O. *see* Anderson, Leroy Oscar.
Anderson, Leroy Oscar, 1905-
    xAnderson, L. O.
      How to Build a Wood-Frame House. Dover.
      How to Build a Wood-Frame House. Gannon.
      Wood Decks: Construction & Maintenance.
        Sterling.
      Wood Houses for Country Living. Sterling.
    xAnderson, LeRoy O.
      Handbook of Home Remodeling &
        Improvement. Van Nos Reinhold.
Anderson, Lewis F. *see* Anderson, Lewis Flint.
Anderson, Lewis Flint, 1866-1932
    xAnderson, Lewis F.
      The Anglo-Saxon Scop. Folcroft.
Anderson, Linda. *see* Anderson, Linda M.
Anderson, Linda M.
    xAnderson, Linda.
      Libraries for Small Museums. Mus Anthro Mo.
Anderson, Lois L., 1923-
    xAnderson.
      Group Arts & Crafts Projects for the
        Elementary School. P-H.
Anderson, Lonzo. *see* Anderson, John Lonzo.
Anderson, Lorraine.
    xAnderson, Lorraine.
      Leathercraft. Lerner Pubns.
Anderson, Luther A.
    xAnderson, Luther A.
      Hunting the Woodlands for Small & Big Game.
        A S Barnes.
Anderson, Lynn, 1936-
    xAnderson, Lynn.
      Steps to Life. Bibl Res Pr.
Anderson, M. *see* Anderson, Malcolm.
Anderson, M. E. *see* Anderson, Maurice Edward.
Anderson, M. S. *see* Anderson, Matthew Smith.
Anderson, Madelyn K. *see* Anderson, Madelyn Klein.
Anderson, Madelyn Klein.
    xAnderson, Madelyn K.
      Iceberg Alley. Messner.
Anderson, Malcolm.
    xAnderson, M.
      Government in France: An Introduction to the
        Executive Power. Pergamon.
Anderson, Margaret. *see* Anderson, Margaret Jean.
Anderson, Margaret J.
    xAnderson, Margaret J.
      The Christian Writer's Handbook. Har-Row.
      Exploring the Insect World. McGraw.
Anderson, Margaret J. *see* Anderson, Margaret Jean.

Anderson, Margaret Jean, 1931-
    xAnderson, Margaret.
      In the Keep of Time. Knopf.
      In the Keep of Time. Schol Bk Serv.
    xAnderson, Margaret J.
      Exploring City Trees & the Need for Urban
        Forests. McGraw.
      In the Circle of Time. Knopf.
Anderson, Marian S.
    xAnderson, Marian S.
      ed. Weekend Projects for the Radio Amateur.
        Am Radio.
Anderson, Marilyn, 1937-
    xAnderson, Marilyn.
      Guatemalan Textiles Today. Watson-Guptill.
Anderson, Mark, 1951-
    xAnderson, Mark.
      The Broken Boat. SBD.
Anderson, Martin.
    xAnderson, Martin.
      ed. Conscription: A Select & Annotated
        Bibliography. Hoover Inst Pr.
Anderson, Mary.
    xAnderson, Mary.
      A Comparative Study of the English-Speaking
        & Spanish-Speaking Beginners in the Public
        Schools. R & E Res Assoc.
      F.T.C. & Company. Atheneum.
      I'm Nobody! Who Are You?. Atheneum.
      Matilda's Masterpiece. Atheneum.
      Step on a Crack. Atheneum.
Anderson, Matthew Smith.
    xAnderson, M. S.
      The Ascendancy of Europe: Aspects of
        European History 1815-1914. Longman.
      Europe in the Eighteenth Century 1713-1783.
        Longman.
      ed. Great Powers & the Near East. St Martin.
Anderson, Maurice Edward.
    xAnderson, M. E.
      Questions & Answers on Refrigeration.
        Hayden.
Anderson, Michael.
    xAnderson, Michael.
      Family Structure in Nineteenth Century
        Lancashire. Cambridge U Pr.
Anderson, Mildred.
    xAnderson, Mildred.
      Papier Mache Crafts. Sterling.
Anderson, Montgomery D. *see* Anderson, Montgomery
Drummond.
Anderson, Montgomery Drummond.
    xAnderson, Montgomery D.
      Fluctuations in General Business. Chris Mass.
Anderson, Nels, 1889-
    xAnderson, Nels.
      Desert Saints: The Mormon Frontier in Utah.
        U of Chicago Pr.
      The Hobo: The Sociology of the Homeless
        Man. U of Chicago Pr.
      Men on the Move. Da Capo.
      Our Industrial Urban Civilization. Asia.
Anderson, Norma J., 1932-
    xAnderson, Norma J.
      Pediatric Nursing: A Self Study Guide. Mosby.
Anderson, Norman. *see* Anderson, James Norman
Dalrymple.
Anderson, O. J.
    xAnderson, O. J.
      Outline of Business Law. Littlefield.
Anderson, O. Roger, 1937-
    xAnderson, O. Roger.
      The Experience of Science: A New Perspective
        for Laboratory Teaching. Tchrs Coll.
      Teaching Modern Ideas of Biology. Tchrs Coll.
Anderson, Odin W. *see* Anderson, Odin Waldemar.
Anderson, Odin Waldemar, 1914-
    xAnderson, Odin W.

The Uneasy Equilibrium: Private & Public
Financing of Health Services in the United
States, 1875-1965. Coll & U Pr.

Anderson, Olive.
xAnderson, Olive.
Liberal State at War: English Politics &
Economics During the Crimean War. St
Martin.
xAnderson, Olive M.
Seeker at Cassandra Marsh. Christian Herald.

Anderson, Olive M. *see* Anderson, Olive.

Anderson, P. C. *see* Anderson, Pauline Carter.

Anderson, P. D. *see* Anderson, Patrick Donald.

Anderson, P. W. *see* Anderson, Philip W.

Anderson, Patrick Donald.
xAnderson, P. D.
In Its Own Image: The Cinematic Vision of
Hollywood. Arno.

Anderson, Paul, 1926-
xAnderson, Poul.
Brain Wave. Ballantine.

Anderson, Paul. *see* Anderson, Poul.

Anderson, Paul D.
xAnderson, Paul D.
Clinical Anatomy & Physiology for Allied
Health Sciences. Saunders.

Anderson, Paul E. *see* Anderson, Paul Edward.

Anderson, Paul Edward, 1925-
xAnderson, Paul E.
Tax Factors in Real Estate Operations. P-H.

Anderson, Paul L. *see* Anderson, Paul Lewis.

Anderson, Paul Lewis, 1880-1956
xAnderson, Paul L.
The Fine Art of Photography. Arno.

Anderson, Paul M., 1926-
xAnderson, Paul M.
Analysis of Faulted Power Systems. Iowa St U
Pr.

Anderson, Paul S.
xAnderson, Paul S.
Language Skills in Elementary Education.
Macmillan.

Anderson, Pauline Carter.
xAnderson, P. C.
The Dental Assistant. Delmar.

Anderson, Pauline R. *see* Anderson, Pauline Safford
(Relyea).

Anderson, Pauline Safford (Relyea).
xAnderson, Pauline R.
Background of Anti-English Feeling in
Germany, 1890-1902. Octagon.

Anderson, Peggy.
xAnderson, Peggy.
Nurse. Berkley Pub.
Nurse. St Martin.

Anderson, Penny S.
xAnderson, Penny S.
The Operation. Childs World.
A Pretty Good Team. Childs World.

Anderson, Perry.
xAnderson, Perry.
Lineages of the Absolutist State. Schocken.
Passages from Antiquity to Feudalism.
Schocken.

Anderson, Philip A.
xAnderson, Philip A.
Church Meetings That Matter. Pilgrim NY.

Anderson, Philip W., 1923-
xAnderson, P. W.
Concepts in Solids: Lectures on the Theory of
Solids. Benjamin-Cummings.

Anderson, Poul, 1926-
xAnderson, Paul.
The Broken Sword. Ballantine.
Day of Their Return. NAL.
Vault of the Ages. Berkley Pub.
xAnderson, Poul.

Agent of the Terran Empire. Ace Bks.
Agent of the Terran Empire. Gregg.
The Avatar. Berkley Pub.
The Avatar. Putnam.
The Byworlder. Gregg.
A Circus of Hells. Gregg.
Dancer from Atlantis. NAL.
The Demon of Scattery. Ace Bks.
The Earth Book of Stormgate. Berkley Pub.
The Earth Book of Stormgate. Putnam.
Ensign Flandry. Gregg.
Fire Time. Ballantine.
Homeward & Beyond. Berkley Pub.
The Horn of Time. Gregg.
Infinite Voyage: Man's Future in Space.
Macmillan.
The Long Way Home. Gregg.
The Merman's Children. Berkley Pub.
The Night Face & Other Stories. Gregg.
Operation Chaos. Berkley Pub.
Orbit Unlimited. Gregg.
People of the Wind. Gregg.
People of the Wind. NAL.
The Queen of Air & Darkness. Gregg.
The Star Fox. Berkley Pub.
Star Prince Charlie. Berkley Pub.
Tales of the Flying Mountains. Macmillan.
Tau Zero. Berkley Pub.
The Trouble Twisters. Berkley Pub.
Two Worlds. Gregg.
Vault of the Ages. Gregg.
The Worlds of Poul Anderson. Ace Bks.

Anderson, Poul. *see* Anderson, Paul.

Anderson, R. *see* Anderson, Ruth I.

Anderson, R. D. *see* Anderson, Robert David.

Anderson, R. J. *see* Anderson, Robert James.

Anderson, R. L.
xAnderson, R. L.
The Abominable Spaceman. Hobby Horse.

Anderson, Randall C.
xAnderson, Randall C.
Current Trends in Secondary School Social
Studies. Prof Educ Pubn.

Anderson, Rasmus Bjorn, 1846-1936
xAnderson, Rasmuus B.
Norse Mythology: The Religion of Our
Forefathers, Containing All the Myths of the
Eddas, Systematized & Interpreted. Scholarly.

Anderson, Rasmuus B. *see* Anderson, Rasmus Bjorn.

Anderson, Richard C. *see* Anderson, Richard Chase.

Anderson, Richard Chase.
xAnderson, Richard C.
Educational Psychology: The Science of
Instruction & Learning. Har-Row.

Anderson, Richard L., 1944-
xAnderson, Richard L.
Art in Primitive Societies. P-H.

Anderson, Rob. *see* Anderson, Robert Orlie.

Anderson, Robert, 1805-1871
xAnderson, Bob.
Gospel Music Encyclopedia. Sterling.
xAnderson, Robert.
Artillery Officer in the Mexican War,
1846-1847: Letters of Robert Anderson.
Arno.
The Cultural Context: An Introduction to
Cultural Anthropology. Burgess.
Forgotten Truths. Kregel.
The Silence of God. Kregel.
Types in Hebrews. Kregel.

Anderson, Robert. *see* Anderson, Robert Arthur.

Anderson, Robert A.
xAnderson, Robert A.
Stress Power: How to Turn Tension into
Energy. Human Sci Pr.

Anderson, Robert Arthur.
xAnderson, Robert.
Lexicon of Literary Terms. Monarch Pr.

Anderson, Robert B. *see* Anderson, Robert Bernard.

Anderson, Robert Bernard, 1915-
xAnderson, Robert B.
ed. Experimental Methods in Catalytic
Research. Acad Pr.

Anderson, Robert David.
xAnderson, R. D.
Education in France 1848-1870. Oxford U Pr.
France, 1870-1914: Politics & Society.
Routledge & Kegan.

Anderson, Robert E. *see* Anderson, Robert Earle.

Anderson, Robert Earle, 1881-
xAnderson, Robert E.
The Merchant Marine & World Frontiers.
Greenwood.

Anderson, Robert Edward.
xAnderson, Robert E.
The Story of Extinct Civilizations of the East.
R West.

Anderson, Robert F. *see* Anderson, Robert Fendel.

Anderson, Robert Fendel.
xAnderson, Robert F.
Hume's First Principles. U of Nebr Pr.

Anderson, Robert James.
xAnderson, R. J.
Clinical Use of Drugs in Renal Failure. C C
Thomas.

Anderson, Robert M.
xAnderson, R.
Individualizing Educational Materials for
Special Children in the Mainstream. Univ
Park.

Anderson, Robert M. *see* Anderson, Robert Meredith.

Anderson, Robert Mapes.
xAnderson, Robert M.
Vision of the Disinherited: The Making of
American Pentecostalism. Oxford U Pr.

Anderson, Robert Meredith.
xAnderson, Robert M.
ed. Educating the Severely & Profoundly
Retarded. Univ Park.
Instructional Resources for Teachers of the
Culturally Disadvantaged & Exceptional. C C
Thomas.

Anderson, Robert Morris, 1939-
xAnderson, Robert M.
Divided Loyalties: Whistle-Blowing at Bart.
Purdue Univ Bks.

Anderson, Robert Orlie, 1945-
xAnderson, Rob.
Students As Real People: Interpersonal
Communication & Education. Hayden.

Anderson, Robert P., 1924-
xAnderson, Robert P.
Child with Learning Disabilities & Guidance.
HM.

Anderson, Robert R. *see* Anderson, Robert Roland.

Anderson, Robert Roland, 1927-
xAnderson, Robert R.
Spanish American Modernism: A Selected
Bibliography. U of Ariz Pr.

Anderson, Robert W. *see* Anderson, Robert William.

Anderson, Robert William, 1926-
xAnderson, Robert W.
Party Politics in Puerto Rico. Stanford U Pr.

Anderson, Robert Woodruff, 1917-
xAnderson, Robert.
Getting up & Going Home. S&S.

Anderson, Robin, 1913-
xAnderson, Robin.
St. Pius V - A Brief Account of His Life,
Times, Virtues & Miracles. TAN Bks Pubs.

Anderson, Rodney D., 1938-
xAnderson, Rodney D.
Outcasts in Their Own Land: Mexican
Industrial Workers 1906-1911. N Ill U Pr.

Anderson, Roger F. *see* Anderson, Roger Fabian.

Anderson, Roger Fabian.
xAnderson, Roger F.
Forest & Shade Tree Entomology. Wiley.

Anderson, Ronald A. *see* Anderson, Ronald Aberdeen.

Anderson, Ronald Aberdeen.
  xAnderson.
    Business Law Principles & Cases. SW Pub.
  xAnderson, Ronald A.
    Business Law, Principles & Cases. SW Pub.
    Government & Business. SW Pub.
Anderson, Roy A. *see* Anderson, Roy Allan.
Anderson, Roy Allan.
  xAnderson, Roy A.
    Secrets of the Spirit World. Pacific Pr Pub
      Assn.
Anderson, Ruth I.
  xAnderson, Ruth I.
    The Administrative Secretary. McGraw.
  xAnderson, Ruth I.
    Word Finder. Pitman Learning.
Anderson, Ruth M. *see* Anderson, Ruth Matilda.
Anderson, Ruth Matilda.
  xAnderson, Ruth M.
    Costumes Painted by Sorolla in His Provinces
      of Spain. Hispanic Soc.
Anderson, Scarvia B.
  xAnderson, Scarvia B.
    The Profession & Practice of Program
      Evaluation. Jossey-Bass.
Anderson, Sherwood, 1876-1941
  xAnderson, Sherwood.
    Alice & the Lost Novel. Arden Lib.
    Alice & the Lost Novel. Folcroft.
    Alice & the Lost Novel. Porter.
    Buck Fever Papers. U Pr of Va.
    Nearer the Grass Roots. Arden Lib.
    Nearer the Grass Roots. Folcroft.
    No Swank. Appel.
    Perhaps Women. Appel.
    Puzzled America. Appel.
Anderson, Stanford.
  xAnderson, Stanford
    On Streets. MIT Pr.
Anderson, Stanley F.
  xAnderson, Stanley F.
    Art of Making Beer. Dutton.
    Art of Making Wine. Dutton.
Anderson, Stephen R.
  xAnderson, Stephen R.
    The Organization of Phonology. Acad Pr.
Anderson, Susanne.
  xAnderson, Susanne.
    Song of the Earth Spirit. Friends Earth.
Anderson, Sydney, 1927-
  xAnderson, Sydney.
    Lives of Animals. Creative Ed.
Anderson, T.
  xAnderson, T.
    ed. Computing Systems Reliability. Cambridge
      U Pr.
Anderson, Terry L. *see* Anderson, Terry Lee.
Anderson, Terry Lee, 1946-
  xAnderson, Terry L.
    The Economic Growth of Seventeenth Century
      New England: A Measurement of Regional
      Income. Arno.
Anderson, Theodore W. *see* Anderson, Theodore Wilbur.
Anderson, Theodore Wilbur.
  xAnderson, Theodore W.
    Introduction to Multivariate Statistical
      Analysis. Wiley.
Anderson, Thomas C., 1935-
  xAnderson, Thomas C.
    The Foundation & Structure of Sartrean Ethics.
      Regents Pr KS.
Anderson, Thomas J. *see* Anderson, Thomas Johnston.
Anderson, Thomas Johnston.
  xAnderson, Thomas J.
    Word Processing. Am Mgmt.
Anderson, Thomas P., 1934-
  xAnderson, Thomas P.

    Matanza: El Salvador's Communist Revolt of
      1932. U of Nebr Pr.
Anderson, Tom, 1910-
  xAnderson, Tom.
    Silence Is Not Golden - It's Yellow. Western
      Islands.
Anderson, Troyer S. *see* Anderson, Troyer Steele.
Anderson, Troyer Steele, 1900-1948
  xAnderson, Troyer S.
    The Command of the Howe Brothers During
      the American Revolution. Octagon.
Anderson, V. V. *see* Anderson, Victor Vance.
Anderson, Vernon F.
  xAnderson, Vernon F.
    In the Arena: The Care & Feeding of
      American Politics. Har-Row.
Anderson, Victor Vance, 1878-1960
  xAnderson, V. V.
    Psychiatry in Industry. Arno.
Anderson, Virgil A. *see* Anderson, Virgil Antris.
Anderson, Virgil Antris.
  xAnderson, Virgil A.
    Improving the Child's Speech. Oxford U Pr.
Anderson, W. A. *see* Anderson, William Arnold Douglas.
Anderson, W. A. D. *see* Anderson, William Arnold
  Douglas.
Anderson, W. Ferguson. *see* Anderson, William
  Ferguson.
Anderson, W. H. *see* Anderson, William Henry Locke.
Anderson, W. Thomas.
  xAnderson, W. Thomas.
    Multidimensional Marketing: Managerial,
      Societal & Philosophical. Austin Pr.
Anderson, Walt, 1933-
  xAnderson, Walt.
    Open Secrets: A Western Guide to Tibetan
      Buddhism. Penguin.
    Open Secrets: A Western Guide to Tibetan
      Buddhism. Viking Pr.
    Politics & the New Humanism. Goodyear.
  xAnderson, Walter.
    A Place of Power: The American Episode in
      Human Evolution. Goodyear.
Anderson, Walter. *see* Anderson, Walt.
Anderson, Warren D.
  xAnderson, Warren D.
    Matthew Arnold & the Classical Tradition. U
      of Mich Pr.
Anderson, Wilbert L. *see* Anderson, Wilbert Lee.
Anderson, Wilbert Lee, 1857-1915
  xAnderson, Wilbert L.
    The Country Town: A Study of Rural
      Evolution. Arno.
Anderson, William.
  xAnderson, William.
    Dante the Maker. Routledge & Kegan.
    The Nation & the States, Rivals or Partners?.
      Greenwood.
Anderson, William. *see* Anderson, William Angor.
Anderson, William Angor, 1937-
  xAnderson, William.
    In His Light: A Path into Catholic Belief. Wm
      C Brown.
Anderson, William Arnold Douglas.
  xAnderson, W. A.
    Synopsis of Pathology. Mosby.
  xAnderson, W. A. D.
    Pathology. Mosby.
    Synopsis of Pathology. Mosby.
Anderson, William Ferguson.
  xAnderson, W. Ferguson.
    ed. Geriatric Medicine. Acad Pr.
Anderson, William G.
  xAnderson.
    Analysis of Teaching Physical Education.
      Mosby.
Anderson, William Henry Locke, 1933-
  xAnderson, W. H.

    National Income Theory & Its Price Theoretic
      Foundations. McGraw.
Anderssen, R. S.
  xAnderssen, R. S.
    ed. The Complexity of Computational Problem
      Solving. U of Queensland Pr.
Andersson, Hans.
  xAndersson, Hans.
    Strindberg's Master Olof & Shakespeare.
      Folcroft.
Andersson, Johan G. *see* Andersson, Johan Gunnar.
Andersson, Johan Gunnar, 1874-1960
  xAndersson, Johan G.
    Children of the Yellow Earth: Studies in
      Prehistoric China. Gordon Pr.
Andersson, Theodore, 1903-
  xAndersson, Theodore.
    Carlos Maria Ocantos, Argentine Novelist: A
      Study of Indigenous French & Spanish
      Elements in His Work. AMS Pr.
    Resource Guide to Bilingual Education: A
      Selective Bibliography of Recent Publications.
      NELP.
Andersson, Theodore M. *see* Andersson, Theodore
  Murdock.
Andersson, Theodore Murdock, 1934-
  xAndersson, Theodore M.
    Early Epic Scenery: Homer, Virgil, & the
      Medieval Legacy. Cornell U Pr.
Andes, Eugene.
  xAndes, Eugene.
    Far Beyond the Fringe: Three Dimensional
      Knotting Techniques Using Macrame &
      Nautical Ropework. Van Nos Reinhold.
Andoh, Elizabeth.
  xAndoh, Elizabeth.
    At Home with Japanese Cooking. Knopf.
Andolfi, Maurizio.
  xAndolfi, Maurizio.
    Family Therapy: An Interactional Approach.
      Plenum Pub.
Andorka, Rudolf.
  xAndorka, Rudolf.
    Determinants of Fertility in Advanced
      Societies. Free Pr.
Andors, Stephen, 1938-
  xAndors, Stephen.
    China's Industrial Revolution: Politics,
      Planning, & Management--1949 to the
      Present. Pantheon.
    ed. Workers & Workplaces in Revolutionary
      China. M E Sharpe.
Andracki, Stanislaw.
  xAndracki, Stanislaw.
    Immigration of Orientals into Canada with
      Special Reference to Chinese. Arno.
Andrade, E. N. *see* Andrade, Edward Neville Da Costa.
Andrade, Edward Neville Da Costa, 1887-
  xAndrade, E. N.
    An Approach to Modern Physics. Peter Smith.
    Isaac Newton. Folcroft.
    Isaac Newton. Sharon Hill.
Andrade, Manuel C. *see* Andrade, Manuel Correia De
  Oliveira.
Andrade, Manuel C. de. *see* Andrade, Manuel C.
Andrade, Manuel Correia De Oliveira.
  xAndrade, Manuel C.
    The Land & People of Northeast Brazil. U of
      NM Pr.
Andrade, Manuel J. *see* Andrade, Manuel Jose.
Andrade, Manuel Jose, 1885-1941
  xAndrade, Manuel J.
    Quileute Texts. AMS Pr.
Andras, L. T. *see* Andras, Laszlo T.
Andras, Laszlo T.
  xAndras, L. T.
    How to Say It in Hungarian: An
      English-Hungarian Phrase-Book with Lists of
      Words. Heinman.
Andrassy, Stella. *see* Andrassy, Stella Kuylenstierna.

Fifty New Devotional Programs. Baker Bk.
Andrews, F. Emerson. *see* Andrews, Frank Emerson.
Andrews, F. T.
  xAndrews, F. T.
    Building Mechanical Systems. Krieger.
Andrews, Fannie F. *see* Andrews, Fannie Fern Phillips.
Andrews, Fannie Fern Phillips, 1867-1950
  xAndrews, Fannie F.
    The Holy Land Under Mandate. Hyperion
    Conn.
Andrews, Frank Emerson, 1902-
  xAndrews, F. Emerson.
    Foundation Watcher. Franklin & Marsh.
    ed. Legal Instruments of Foundations. Russell
    Sage.
    Nobody Comes to Dinner. Little.
Andrews, Frank M.
  xAndrews, Frank M.
    A Guide for Selecting Statistical Techniques
    for Analyzing Social Science Data. U of
    Mich Soc Res.
    Multiple Classification Analysis: A Report on a
    Computer Program for Multiple Regression
    Using Categorical Predictors. U of Mich Soc
    Res.
    Multivariate Nominal Scale Analysis: A Report
    on a New Analysis Technique & a Computer
    Program. U of Mich Soc Res.
Andrews, George.
  xAndrews, George.
    ed. The Coca Leaf & Cocaine Papers.
    HarBraceJ.
Andrews, George E., 1938-
  xAndrews, George E.
    On the General Rogers-Ramanujan Theorem.
    Am Math.
Andrews, Hank.
  xAndrews, Hank.
    How to Fish for Smallmouth Bass. Contemp
    Bks.
Andrews, Harry C.
  xAndrews, Harry C.
    Introduction to Mathematical Techniques in
    Pattern Recognition. Wiley.
Andrews, Helen H. *see* Andrews, Helen Holmes.
Andrews, Helen Holmes.
  xAndrews, Helen H.
    Food Preparation. McGraw.
Andrews, Henry N. *see* Andrews, Henry Nathaniel.
Andrews, Henry Nathaniel, 1910-
  xAndrews, Henry N.
    The Fossil Hunters: In Search of Ancient
    Plants. Cornell U Pr.
    Studies in Paleobotany. Wiley.
Andrews, Herbert K. *see* Andrews, Herbert Kennedy.
Andrews, Herbert Kennedy.
  xAndrews, Herbert K.
    The Technique of Byrd's Vocal Polyphony.
    Greenwood.
Andrews, Howard L. *see* Andrews, Howard Lucius.
Andrews, Howard Lucius, 1906-
  xAndrews, Howard L.
    Radiation Biophysics. P-H.
Andrews, I. *see* Andrews, Ian.
Andrews, Ian.
  xAndrews, I.
    Pompeii. Cambridge U Pr.
  xAndrews, Ian.
    Boudicca's Revolt. Cambridge U Pr.
    Pompeii. Lerner Pubns.
Andrews, J. Cutler, 1908-
  xAndrews, J. Cutler.
    South Reports the Civil War. Princeton U Pr.
Andrews, J. D.
  xAndrews, J. D.
    ed. Early Childhood Education: It's an Art?
    It's a Science?. Natl Assn Child Ed.
Andrews, J. H. *see* Andrews, John Harwood.
Andrews, J. Richard. *see* Andrews, James Richard.

Andrews, J. S.
  xAndrews, J. S.
    Cargo for a King. Dutton.
Andrews, James R. *see* Andrews, James Robertson.
Andrews, James Richard, 1924-
  xAndrews, J. Richard.
    Introduction to Classical Nahuatl. U of Tex Pr.
Andrews, James Robertson, 1936-
  xAndrews, James R.
    ed. A Choice of Worlds: The Practice &
    Criticism of Public Discourse. Har-Row.
Andrews, John, 1939-
  xAndrews, John.
    Birds. Transatlantic.
Andrews, John Harwood, 1927-
  xAndrews, J. H.
    A Paper Landscape: The Ordnance Survey in
    Nineteenth-Century Ireland. Oxford U Pr.
Andrews, John Robert.
  xAndrews, Robert J.
    The Radiobiology of Human Cancer
    Radiotherapy. Univ Park.
Andrews, John W. *see* Andrews, John Williams.
Andrews, John Williams, 1898-
  xAndrews, John W.
    Prelude to Icaros. Branden.
    Triptych for the Atomic Age. Branden.
Andrews, Joseph L.
  xAndrews, Joseph L.
    ed. The Law in the United States of America:
    A Selective Bibliographical Guide. NYU Pr.
Andrews, K. R. *see* Andrews, Kenneth R.
Andrews, Kenneth R.
  xAndrews, K. R.
    The Spanish Caribbean: Trade & Plunder,
    1530-1630. Yale U Pr.
Andrews, Kenneth R. *see* Andrews, Kenneth Richmond.
Andrews, Kenneth Richmond, 1916-
  xAndrews, Kenneth R.
    Nook Farm: Mark Twain's Hartford Circle. U
    of Wash Pr.
Andrews, Linton.
  xAndrews, Linton.
    Lords & Laborers of the Press: Men Who
    Fashioned the Modern British Newspaper. S
    Ill U Pr.
Andrews, Lorrin, 1795-1868
  xAndrews, Lorrin.
    Grammar of the Hawaiian Language. AMS Pr.
Andrews, Malcolm.
  xAndrews, Malcolm.
    Dickens on England & the English. B&N.
Andrews, Michael.
  xAndrews, Michael.
    The Life That Lives on Man. Taplinger.
Andrews, Miriam.
  xAndrews, Miriam.
    Fifty Poems. Branden.
Andrews, Peter.
  xAndrews, Peter.
    ed. Christmas in Germany. World
    Bk-Childcraft.
Andrews, Ralph W. *see* Andrews, Ralph Warren.
Andrews, Ralph Warren, 1897-
  xAndrews, Ralph W.
    Heroes of the Western Woods. Superior Pub.
    This Was Logging. Superior Pub.
Andrews, Richard N. *see* Andrews, Richard N. L.
Andrews, Richard N. L.
  xAndrews, Richard N.
    Environmental Policy & Administrative
    Change: Implementation of the National
    Environmental Policy Act. Lexington Bks.
Andrews, Robert J. *see* Andrews, John Robert.
Andrews, Roy C. *see* Andrews, Roy Chapman.
Andrews, Roy Chapman, 1884-1960
  xAndrews, Roy C.

All About Whales. Random.
    In the Days of the Dinosaurs. Random.
Andrews, Ruth.
  xAndrews, Ruth.
    ed. How to Know American Folk Art: Eleven
    Experts Discuss Many Aspects of the Field.
    Dutton.
Andrews, Stanley, 1894-
  xAndrews, Stanley.
    Agriculture & the Common Market. Iowa St U
    Pr.
Andrews, Terry.
  xAndrews, Terry.
    The Story of Harold. Avon.
Andrews, V. C.
  xAndrews, V. C.
    Flowers in the Attic. PB.
    Flowers in the Attic. S&S.
Andrews, Valerie.
  xAndrews, Valerie.
    The Psychic Power of Running: How the Body
    Can Illuminate the Mysteries of the Mind.
    Rawson Wade.
Andrews, Victor L.
  xAndrews, Victor L.
    Financial Management: Cases & Readings.
    Irwin.
Andrews, W. *see* Andrews, William A.
Andrews, W. H. Horner.
  xAndrews.
    Liver. Univ Park.
Andrews, Wayne.
  xAndrews, Wayne.
    Architecture, Ambition, & Americans: A Social
    History of American Architecture. Free Pr.
    Architecture in Chicago & Mid-America: A
    Photographic History. Har Row.
    Architecture in New York: A Photographic
    History. Har-Row.
    Pride of the South: A Social History of
    Southern Architecture. Atheneum.
Andrews, William, 1848-1908
  xAndrews, William.
    Bygone Punishments. Patterson Smith.
Andrews, William A., 1930-
  xAndrews, W.
    Guide to the Study of Environmental Pollution.
    P-H.
    Guide to the Study of Freshwater Ecology.
    P-H.
    Guide to the Study of Soil Ecology. P-H.
    Guide to the Study of Terrestrial Ecology. P-H.
Andrews, William D., 1931-
  xAndrews, William D.
    Basic Federal Income Taxation. Little.
Andrews, William G. *see* Andrews, William George.
Andrews, William George, 1930-
  xAndrews, William G.
    ed. American National Political Institutions:
    Some Key Readings. Van Nos Reinhold.
    ed. Constitutions & Constitutionalism. Van Nos
    Reinhold.
Andreyev, Olga C. *see* Andreyev, Olga Chernov.
Andreyev, Olga Chernov.
  xAndreyev, Olga C.
    Cold Spring in Russia. Ardis Pubs.
Andreyev, Vladimir, Pseud.
  xAndreyev, Vladimir.
    Gamailis & Other Tales from Stalin's Russia.
    Greenwood.
Andric, Ivo, 1892-1975
  xAndric, Ivo.
    The Bridge of the Drina. U of Chicago Pr.
    The Bridge on the Drina. Allen Unwin.
    Devil's Yard. Greenwood.
Andrisani, Paul J.
  xAndrisani, Paul J.

Work Attitudes & Labor Market Experience:
Evidence from the National Longitudinal
Surveys. Praeger.

Andrist, Ralph K.
xAndrist, Ralph K.
California Gold Rush. Am Heritage.

Andronov, A. A. *see* Andronov, Aleksandr
Aleksandrovich.

Andronov, Aleksandr Aleksandrovich, 1901-1952
xAndronov, A. A.
Qualitative Theory of Second-Order Dynamic
Systems. Halsted Pr.
xAndronov, Alexander.
Theory of Oscillators. Pergamon.

Andronov, Alexander. *see* Andronov, Aleksandr
Aleksandrovich.

Andros, Dee G.
xAndros, Dee G.
Power T Football. P-H.

Andrulis, Richard S.
xAndrulis, Richard S.
Adult Assessment: A Source Book of Tests &
Measures of Human Behavior. C C Thomas.

Andrus, Hyrum L. *see* Andrus, Hyrum Leslie.

Andrus, Hyrum Leslie, 1924-
xAndrus, Hyrum L.
Joseph Smith & World Government. Hawkes
Pub Inc.

Andrus, Lisa F. *see* Andrus, Lisa Fellows.

Andrus, Lisa Fellows.
xAndrus, Lisa F.
Measure & Design in American Painting,
1760-1860. Garland Pub.

Andry, Andrew C.
xAndry, Andrew C.
How Babies Are Made. Time-Life.

Andry, Carl F. *see* Andry, Carl Franklin.

Andry, Carl Franklin.
xAndry, Carl F.
Paul & the Early Christians. Prinit Pr.
Problems in Early Christianity. Prinit Pr.

Andrzejewski, Jerzy.
xAndrzejewski, Jerzy.
Ashes & Diamonds. Penguin.
The Inquisitors. Greenwood.

Anell, Lars.
xAnell, Lars.
The Developing Countries & the World
Economic Order. St Martin.

Anesaki, Masaharu, 1873-1949
xAnesaki, Masaharu.
Art, Life & Nature in Japan. Greenwood.
xAnesaki, Masharu.
Nichiren: The Buddhist Prophet. Peter Smith.

Anesaki, Masharu. *see* Anesaki, Masaharu.

Anfinsen, C. B.
xAnfinsen, C. B.
ed. Current Research in Oncology. Acad Pr.

Anfinsen, C. B. *see* Anfinsen, Christian B.

Anfinsen, Christian B.
xAnfinsen, C. B.
ed. Aspects of Protein Biosynthesis. Acad Pr.
ed. Current Topics in Biochemistry. Acad Pr.

Angebert, Jean Michel.
xAngebert, Jean-Michel.
The Occult & the Third Reich: The Mystical
Origins of Nazism & the Search for the Holy
Grail. McGraw.

Angebert, Jean-Michel. *see* Angebert, Jean Michel.

Angel, J. Lawrence. *see* Angel, John Lawrence.

Angel, John Lawrence.
xAngel, J. Lawrence.
The People of Lerna: Analysis of a Prehistoric
Aegean Population. Smithsonian.

Angel, Juvenal L. *see* Angel, Juvenal Londono.

Angel, Juvenal Londono, 1907-
xAngel, Juvenal L.

Directory of International Agencies. Monarch
Pr.
Directory of Professional & Occupational
Licensing in the United States. Monarch Pr.
Looking for Employment in Foreign Countries
Reference Handbook. World Trade.

Angel, Marie.
xAngel, Marie.
The Art of Calligraphy: A Practical Guide.
Scribner.

Angel, Martin V. *see* Angel, Martin Vivian.

Angel, Martin Vivian.
xAngel, Martin V.
Animals of the Oceans: The Ecology of Marine
Life. Two Continents.

Angel, Myron.
xAngel, Myron.
ed. History of Nevada. Arno.

Angel, Robert.
xAngel, Robert.
The Day of Reckoning. Mojave Bks.

Angeli, Helen (Rossetti).
xAngeli, Helen R.
Pre-Raphaelite Twilight: The Story of Charles
Augustus Howell. Scholarly.

Angeli, Helen R. *see* Angeli, Helen (Rossetti).

Angelini, Anthony.
xAngelini, Anthony.
International Lending, Risk & the Euromarkets.
Halsted Pr.

Angell, C. Roy. *see* Angell, Charles Roy.

Angell, Charles Roy.
xAngell, C. Roy.
God's Gold Mines. Broadman.
Price Tags of Life. Broadman.

Angell, Ellen.
xAngell, Ellen.
The Layman's Handbook of Interior Design.
Exposition.

Angell, George.
xAngell, George.
Winning in the Commodities Market: A
Money-Making Guide to Commodity Futures
Trading. Doubleday.

Angell, James B. *see* Angell, James Burrill.

Angell, James Burrill, 1829-1916
xAngell, James B.
The Reminiscences of James Burrill Angell.
Arno.

Angell, James R. *see* Angell, James Rowland.

Angell, James Rowland, 1869-1949
xAngell, James R.
Psychology. Darby Bks.

Angell, Judie.
xAngell, Judie.
In Summertime, It's Tuffy. Dell.
In Summertime It's Tuffy. Bradbury Pr.
Ronnie & Rosey. Dell.
Ronnie & Rosey. Bradbury Pr.
Secret Selves. Bradbury Pr.

Angell, Madeline.
xAngell, Madeline.
America's Best-Loved Wild Animals. Bobbs.

Angell, Norman, Sir, 1874-1967
xAngell, Norman.
Fruits of Victory: A Sequel to "The Great
Illusion". Garland Pub.
Great Illusion: A Study of the Relation of
Military Power in Nations to Their Economic
& Social Advantage. Garland Pub.
The Great Illusion, 1933. Arno.

Angell, Richard B.
xAngell, Richard B.
Reasoning & Logic. Irvington.

Angell, Robert C. *see* Angell, Robert Cooley.

Angell, Robert Cooley, 1899-
xAngell, Robert C.

The Family Encounters the Depression. Peter
Smith.
The Integration of American Society: A Study
of Groups & Institutions. Russell.
The Quest for World Order. U of Mich Pr.

Angell, Roger.
xAngell, Roger.
A Day in the Life of Roger Angell. Penguin.
The Summer Game. Popular Lib.

Angell, Tony.
xAngell, Tony.
Owls. Hancock Hse.
Owls. U of Wash Pr.
Ravens, Crows, Magpies, & Jays. U of Wash
Pr.

Angelo, E. James. *see* Angelo, Ernest James.

Angelo, Ernest James.
xAngelo, E. James.
Electronics: BJT's, FET's & Microcircuits.
Krieger.

Angelo, Henry, 1756-1835
xAngelo, Henry.
Reminiscences of Henry Angelo. Arno.

Angelo, Valenti, 1897-
xAngelo, Valenti.
Golden Gate. Arno.

Angeloglou, M. *see* Angeloglou, Maggie.

Angeloglou, Maggie.
xAngeloglou, M.
All About Herbs. Charles River Bks.

Angelopoulos, Angelos. *see* Angelopoulos, Angelos
Theodorou.

Angelopoulos, Angelos Theodorou, 1904-
xAngelopoulos, Angelos.
The Third World & the Rich Countries:
Prospects for the Year 2000. Irvington.

Angelou, Maya.
xAngelou, Maya.
And Still I Rise. Random.
Gather Together in My Name. Random.
Gather Together in My Name. Bantam.
I Know Why the Caged Bird Sings. Random.
I Know Why the Caged Bird Sings. Bantam.
Oh Pray My Wings Are Gonna Fit Me Well.
Bantam.
Oh Pray My Wings Are Gonna Fit Me Well.
Random.

Angelucci, Enzo.
xAngelucci, Enzo.
The Automobile: From Steam to Gasoline.
McGraw.
World Aircraft - 1918-1935. Rand.

Anger, Kenneth.
xAnger, Kenneth.
Hollywood Babylon. Dell.
Hollywood Babylon. S&S.

Angerbauer. *see* Angerbauer, George J.

Angerbauer, George J., 1918-
xAngerbauer.
Principles of DC & AC Circuits. Duxbury Pr.

Angier, Bradford.
xAngier, Bradford.

Ask for Love & They Give You Rice Pudding.
HM.
Color Field Guide to Common Wild Edibles.
Stackpole.
Field Guide to Edible Wild Plants. Stackpole.
Field Guide to Medicinal Wild Plants.
Stackpole.
Food from the Woods Cooking. Macmillan.
Home in Your Pack: A Modern Handbook of
Back Packing. Macmillan.
How to Live in the Woods on Pennies a Day.
Stackpole.
How to Stay Alive in the Woods. Macmillan.
Introduction to Canoeing. Stackpole.
The Master Backwoodsman. Fawcett.
The Master Backwoodsman. Stackpole.
One Acre & Security: How to Live off the
Earth Without Ruining It. Random.
Wilderness Neighbors. Stein & Day.
Angier, Bradford. see Angier, Vena.
Angier, Vena.
xAngier, Bradford.
At Home in the Woods: Living the Life of
Thoreau Today. Macmillan.
At Home in the Woods: Living the Life of
Thoreau Today. Sheridan.
Angiolillo, Paul F. see Angiolillo, Paul Francis Mathew.
Angiolillo, Paul Francis Mathew, 1917-
xAngiolillo, Paul F.
A Criminal As Hero: Angelo Duca. Regents Pr
KS.
Angione, Genevieve.
xAngione, Genevieve.
All Dolls Are Collectible. Crown
Anglade, Joseph, 1868-1930
xAnglade, Joseph.
Histoire Sommaire De la Litterature
Meridionale Au Moyen Age. AMS Pr.
Angle, John.
xAngle, John.
Language Maintenance, Language Shift, &
Occupational Achievement in the United
States. R & E Res Assoc.
Angle, Paul M. see Angle, Paul McClelland.
Angle, Paul McClelland, 1900-
xAngle, Paul M.
On a Variety of Subjects. Chicago Hist.
**Anglesey, George Charles Henry Victor Paget, 7th
Marquis Of, 1922-**
xAnglesey, Marquess of.
A History of British Cavalry 1816-1919. Shoe
String.
Anglesey, Marquess of. see Anglesey, George Charles
Henry Victor Paget, 7th Marquis Of.
Anglin, Douglas G. see Anglin, Douglas George.
Anglin, Douglas George.
xAnglin, Douglas G.
ed. Conflict & Change in Southern Africa:
Papers from a Scandinavian-Canadian
Conference. U Pr of Amer.
Zambia's Foreign Policy: Studies in Diplomacy
& Dependence. Westview.
Anglin, Jeremy M.
xAnglin, Jeremy M.
Growth of Word Meaning. MIT Pr.
Word, Object, & Conceptual Development.
Norton.
Anglund, Joan W. see Anglund, Joan Walsh.
Anglund, Joan Walsh.
xAnglund, Joan W.
illus. A Child's Book of Old Nursery Rhymes.
Atheneum.
illus. Christmas Is a Time of Giving.
HarBraceJ.
illus. Cowboy & His Friend. HarBraceJ.
Cowboy & His Friend. HarBraceJ.
illus. Love Is a Special Way of Feeling.
HarBraceJ.
Angoff, Allan.
xAngoff, Allan.

ed. Public Relations for Libraries: Essays in
Communications Techniques. Greenwood.
Angoff, Charles, 1902-
xAngoff, Charles.
Memory of Autumn. A S Barnes.
The Sun at Noon. A S Barnes.
Toward the Horizon. A S Barnes.
When I Was a Boy in Boston. Arno.
Angold, M. J. see Angold, Michael.
Angold, Michael.
xAngold, M. J.
A Byzantine Government in Exile:
Government & Society Under the Laskarids
of Nicaea 1204-1261. Oxford U Pr.
Angrist, Shirley S.
xAngrist, Shirley S.
Careers & Contingencies: How College Women
Juggle with Gender. Kennikat.
Angrist, Stanley W.
xAngrist, Stanley W.
Closing the Loop: The Story of Feedback. T Y
Crowell.
Other Worlds, Other Beings. T Y Crowell.
Angrosino, Michael V.
xAngrosino, Michael V.
ed. Do Applied Anthropologists Apply
Anthropology?. U of Ga Pr.
Angus, Douglas.
xAngus, Douglas.
ed. Contemporary American Short Stories.
Fawcett.
ed. Great Modern European Short Stories.
Fawcett.
Angus, Fay.
xAngus, Fay.
Catalyst. Tyndale.
The White Pagoda. Tyndale.
Angus, H. T. see Angus, Harold T.
Angus, Harold T.
xAngus, H. T.
Cast Iron: Physical & Engineering Properties.
Butterworths.
Angus, Henry F. see Angus, Henry Forbes.
Angus, Henry Forbes.
xAngus, Henry F.
ed. British Columbia & the United States: The
North Pacific Slope from Fur Trade to
Aviation. Russell.
Angus, Ian.
xAngus, Ian.
Fell's Guide to Coins & Money Tokens of the
World. Fell.
Angus, Sylvia.
xAngus, Sylvia.
Dead to Rites Penguin.
Dead to Rites. G K Hall.
Anikouchine, W. see Anikouchine, William A.
Anikouchine, William A.
xAnikouchine, W.
World Ocean: An Introduction to
Oceanography. P-H.
Anisman, H. see Anisman, Hymie.
Anisman, Hymie.
xAnisman, H.
ed. Psychopharmacology of Aversively
Motivated Behavior. Plenum Pub.
Ankeney, Jeanelle, 1930-
xAnkeney, Jeanelle.
Any Child Can Swim. Contemp Bks.
Anker, Carol T. see Anker, Carol Teig.
Anker, Carol Teig.
xAnker, Carol T.
Teaching Exceptional Children: A Special
Career. Messner.
Ankli, Robert E. see Ankli, Robert Eugene.
Ankli, Robert Eugene.
xAnkli, Robert E.

Gross Farm Revenue in Pre-Civil War Illinois.
Arno.
Anna, Timothy E., 1944-
xAnna, Timothy E.
The Fall of the Royal Government in Mexico
City. U of Nebr Pr.
The Fall of the Royal Government in Peru. U
of Nebr Pr.
Annan, Noel G. see Annan, Noel Gilroy.
Annan, Noel Gilroy, 1916-
xAnnan, Noel G.
Leslie Stephen, His Thought & Character in
Relation to His Time. AMS Pr.
Annarino, Anthony A.
xAnnarino, Anthony A.
Curriculum Theory & Design in Physical
Education. Mosby.
Developmental Conditioning for Women &
Men. Mosby.
Annas, George J.
xAnnas, George J.
Informed Consent to Human Experimentation:
The Subject's Dilemma. Ballinger Pub.
Annenberg, Maurice, 1907-
xAnnenberg, Maurice.
Type Foundries of America & Their Catalogs.
M Annenberg.
Annett, Cora.
xAnnett, Cora.
Dog Who Thought He Was a Boy. HM.
How the Witch Got Alf. Watts.
Annis, Linda F. see Annis, Linda Ferrill.
Annis, Linda Ferrill, 1943-
xAnnis, Linda F.
The Child Before Birth. Cornell U Pr.
Annino, Joseph S.
xAnnino, Joseph S.
Clinical Chemistry: Principles & Procedures.
Little.
Annixter, Jane.
xAnnixter, Jane.
Brown Rats, Black Rats. P-H.
Buffalo Chief. Holiday.
Monkeys & Apes. Watts.
White Shell Horse. Holiday.
Annixter, Paul.
xAnnixter, Paul.
Swiftwater. Schol Bk Serv.
Anno, J. N. see Anno, James N.
Anno, James N.
xAnno, J. N.
Mechanics of Liquid Jets. Lexington Bks.
Anno, Mitsumasa, 1926-
xAnno, Mitsumasa.
illus. Anno's Alphabet: An Adventure in
Imagination. T Y Crowell.
Anno's Animals. Philomel.
illus. Anno's Counting Book. T Y Crowell.
illus. Anno's Italy. Philomel.
Anno's Journey. Philomel.
illus. Topsy-Turvies: Pictures to Stretch the
Imagination. Weatherhill.
Annual Meeting of the Deutsche Gesellschaft Fuer
Neurochirurgie, Heidelberg, May 1-3, 1975. see
Deutsche Gesellschaft Fuer Neurochirurgie.
Annual Research Conference, 13th, UCLA, 1970. see
Research Conference in Industrial Relations, 13th,
University of California, los Angeles, 1970.
Annual Research Conference, 14th, UCLA, 1972. see
Research Conference in Industrial Relations, 14th,
University of California, los Angeles, 1971.
Annual Research Conference, 8th, UCLA, 1965. see
California. University. University at los Angeles.
Institute of Industrial Relations.
Annual West Coast Cancer Symposium, 10th, San
Francisco, Calif., September 1974. see San Francisco
Cancer Symposium, 10th, 1974.
Anobile, Richard J.
xAnobile, Richard J.

The Wiz Scrapbook. Berkley Pub.
Anobile, Ulla.
xAnobile, Ulla.
Beyond Open Marriage. A & W Pubs.
Anolik, Alexander.
xAnolik, Alexander.
The Law & the Travel Industry. Alchemy Bks.
Anosike, Benji O.
xAnosike, Benji O.
How to Do Your Own Divorce Without a
Lawyer. Do-It-Yourself Pubns.
Anouilh, Jean.
xAnouilh, Jean.
Leocadia. Irvington.
Ansbacher, Max G.
xAnsbacher, Max G.
The New Options Market. Walker & Co.
Anschel, Eugene.
xAnschel, Eugene.
ed. American Appraisals of Soviet Russia:
1917-1977. Scarecrow.
The American Image of Russia, 1775-1917.
Ungar.
Anscombe, G. E. *see* Anscombe, Gertrude Elizabeth
Margaret.
Anscombe, Gertrude Elizabeth Margaret.
xAnscombe, G. E.
Intention. Cornell U Pr.
Anscombe, Isabelle.
xAnscombe, Isabelle.
Arts & Crafts in Britain & America. Rizzoli
Intl.
Ansel, Howard C., 1933-
xAnsel, Howard C.
Introduction to Pharmaceutical Dosage Forms.
Lea & Febiger.
Ansel, Walter.
xAnsel, Walter.
Hitler & the Middle Sea. Duke.
Ansel, Willits D. *see* Ansel, Willits Dyer.
Ansel, Willits Dyer.
xAnsel, Willits D.
The Whaleboat: A Study of Design,
Construction & Use. Mystic Seaport.
Ansell, Jack.
xAnsell, Jack.
Dynasty of Air. Arbor Hse.
Ansell, Mary.
xAnsell, Mary.
Dogs & Men. Arno.
Ansfield, Fred J., 1910-
xAnsfield, Fred J.
Chemotherapy of Malignant Neoplasms. C C
Thomas.
Anshen, Melvin.
xAnshen, Melvin.
Corporate Strategies for Social Performance.
Macmillan.
Anshen, Ruth N. *see* Anshen, Ruth Nanda.
Anshen, Ruth Nanda.
xAnshen, Ruth N.
ed. Our Emergent Civilization. Arno.
Ansley, Norman.
xAnsley, Norman.
ed. Legal Admissibility of the Polygraph. C C
Thomas.
Ansley, Robert E.
xAnsley, Robert E.
Discrimination in Housing. CPL Biblios.
Ansoff, H. Igor.
xAnsoff, H. Igor.
Corporate Strategy: An Analytic Approach to
Business Policy for Growth & Expansion.
McGraw.
Strategic Management. Halsted Pr.
xAnsoff, Igor.
ed. From Strategic Planning to Strategic
Management. Wiley.
Ansoff, Igor. *see* Ansoff, H. Igor.

Anson, Barbara.
xAnson, Barbara.
Golem. Nordon Pubns.
Anson, Barry J. *see* Anson, Barry Joseph.
Anson, Barry Joseph.
xAnson, Barry J.
Surgical Anatomy. Saunders.
Anson, Elva.
xAnson, Elva.
The Compleat Family Book. Moody.
Anson, Jay, 1921-
xAnson, Jay.
The Amityville Horror. Bantam.
The Amityville Horror. G K Hall.
Anson, Mike.
xAnson, Mike.
Customizing Your Pickup. TAB Bks.
Anson, William R. *see* Anson, William Reynell.
Anson, William Reynell, Sir, Bart, 1843-1914
xAnson, William R.
The Law & Custom of the Constitution.
Johnson Repr.
Anstey, Roger.
xAnstey, Roger.
The Atlantic Slave Trade & British Abolition,
1760-1810. Humanities.
Antek, Samuel.
xAntek, Samuel.
This Was Toscanini. Vanguard.
Antelman, M. S. *see* Antelman, Marvin S.
Antelman, Marvin S.
xAntelman, M. S.
The Analytical Encyclopedia of Thermoplastic
Materials. Heyden.
Analytical Encyclopedia of Thermoplastic
Materials. Sadtler Res.
Anthes, Richard A.
xAnthes, Richard A.
The Atmosphere. Merrill.
Anthoine, Robert.
xAnthoine, Robert.
ed. Tax Incentives for Private Investment in
Developing Countries: Published Under the
Auspices of the Tax Committee of the
Section of Business Law of the International
Bar Association. Kluwer Boston.
Anthologia Graeca. Selections.
xAnthologia Graeca Selections.
Poems from the Greek Anthology, in English
Paraphrase. Greenwood.
Anthony, Catherine P. *see* Anthony, Catherine Parker.
Anthony, Catherine Parker.
xAnthony, Catherine P.
Basic Concepts in Anatomy & Physiology: A
Programmed Presentation. Mosby.
Structure & Function of the Body. Mosby.
Textbook of Anatomy & Physiology. Mosby.
Anthony, E. James. *see* Anthony, Elwyn James.
Anthony, Edgar W. *see* Anthony, Edgar Waterman.
Anthony, Edgar Waterman, 1890-1947
xAnthony, Edgar W.
Early Florentine Architecture & Decoration.
Hacker.
History of Mosaics. Hacker.
Anthony, Elwyn James.
xAnthony, E. James.
ed. Explorations in Child Psychiatry. Plenum
Pub.
Anthony, Evelyn.
xAnthony, Evelyn.
The Return. Coward.
The Return. NAL.
The Silver Falcon. Coward.
Silver Falcon. NAL.
Anthony, Gene.
xAnthony, Gene.
The Summer of Love. Celestial Arts.
Anthony, Geraldine, 1919-
xAnthony, Geraldine.

Stage Voices: Twelve Canadian Playwrights
Talk About Their Lives & Work. Doubleday.
Anthony, Gloria M.
xAnthony, Gloria M.
Echoes in a Shell. Orovan Bks.
Anthony, James R.
xAnthony, James R.
French Baroque Music: From Beaujoyeulx to
Rameau. Norton.
Anthony, John D. *see* Anthony, John Duke.
Anthony, John Duke.
xAnthony, John D.
Historical & Cultural Dictionary of the
Sultanate of Oman & the Emirates of Eastern
Arabia. Scarecrow.
Anthony, Katharine. *see* Anthony, Katharine Susan.
Anthony, Katharine S. *see* Anthony, Katharine Susan.
Anthony, Katharine Susan, 1877-1965
xAnthony, Katharine.
Catherine the Great. Greenwood.
xAnthony, Katharine S.
Louisa May Alcott. Greenwood.
Anthony, Ole.
xAnthony, Ole.
Cross Fire. Logos.
Anthony, P. D. *see* Anthony, Peter.
Anthony, Peter.
xAnthony, P. D.
The Ideology of Work. Methuen Inc.
Anthony, Piers.
xAnthony, Piers.
Chaining the Lady. Avon.
Ox. Avon.
A Spell for Chameleon. Ballantine.
Split Infinity. Ballantine.
Anthony, R. N. *see* Anthony, Robert Newton.
Anthony, Robert N. *see* Anthony, Robert Newton.
Anthony, Robert Newton, 1916-
xAnthony, R. N.
Essentials of Accounting. A-W.
xAnthony, Robert N.
Accounting for the Cost of Interest. Lexington
Bks.
Accounting Principles. Irwin.
Fundamentals of Management Accounting.
Irwin.
Planning and Control Systems: A Framework
for Analysis. Harvard Busn.
Anthony, Susan B. *see* Anthony, Susan Brownell.
Anthony, Susan Brownell, 1820-1906
xAnthony, Susan B.
An Account of the Proceedings on the Trial of
Susan B. Anthony on the Charge of Illegal
Voting at the Presidential Election in Nov.
1872. Arno.
The Ghost in My Life. Chosen Bks Pub.
Anthony, William P.
xAnthony, William P.
Participative Management. A-W.
Anti-Sabbath Convention, Boston.
xAnti-Sabbath Convention, Melodeon, Boston.
Proceedings. Kennikat.
Anti-Sabbath Convention, Melodeon, Boston. *see*
Anti-Sabbath Convention, Boston.
Anticaglia, Elizabeth, 1939-
xAnticaglia, Elizabeth.
A Housewife's Guide to Women's Liberation.
Nelson-Hall.
Antico, John.
xAntico, John.
Insight Through Fiction: Dealing Effectively
with the Short Story. Benjamin-Cummings.
Antieau, Chester J. *see* Antieau, Chester James.
Antieau, Chester James.
xAntieau, Chester J.
Modern Constitutional Law. Lawyers Co-Op.
The Antioch Review.
xAntioch Review.

Antioch Review Anthology. Arno.
Antin, David.
xAntin, David.
Talking. Kulchur Foun.
Talking at the Boundaries. New Directions.
Antin, Mary, 1881-1949
xAntin, Mary.
The Promised Land. Arno.
The Promised Land. Dynamic Learn Corp.
Antique Airplane Association.
xAntique Airplane Association.
Classic Airplanes of the Thirties - Aircraft of
the Roaring Twenties. Arno.
Antiques.
xAntiques Magazine.
ed. Living with Antiques: A Treasury of
Private Homes in America. Dutton.
Antiques Magazine. *see* Antiques.
Antoine, Andre, 1858-1943
xAntoine, Andre.
Memories of the Theatre-Libre. U of Miami Pr.
Anton, Ferdinand.
xAnton, Ferdinand.
Art of the Maya. Thames Hudson.
Anton, Hector R.
xAnton, Hector R.
Contemporary Issues in Cost & Managerial
Accounting: A Discipline in Transition. HM.
Anton, Howard.
xAnton, Howard.
Applied Finite Mathematics. Acad Pr.
Anton, John P. *see* Anton, John Peter.
Anton, John Peter, 1920-
xAnton, John P.
ed. Naturalism & Historical Understanding:
Essays on the Philosophy of John Herman
Randall, Jr. State U NY Pr.
Anton, Rita.
xAnton, Rita.
The Far off Hills. Doubleday.
Anton, Thomas. *see* Anton, Thomas Julius.
Anton, Thomas J. *see* Anton, Thomas Julius.
Anton, Thomas Julius.
xAnton, Thomas.
Occupational Safety & Health Management.
McGraw.
xAnton, Thomas J.
Administered Politics: Elite Political Culture in
Sweden. Kluwer Boston.
Antonacci, Robert J. *see* Antonacci, Robert Joseph.
Antonacci, Robert Joseph.
xAntonacci, Robert J.
Football for Young Champions. McGraw.
Antonaccio, Michael J.
xAntonaccio, Michael J.
ed. Cardiovascular Pharmacology. Raven.
Antonelli, P. L. *see* Antonelli, Peter L.
Antonelli, Peter L.
xAntonelli, P. L.
Concordance-Homotopy Groups of Geometric
Automorphism Groups. Springer-Verlag.
Antoniades, Harry N.
xAntoniades, Harry N.
ed. Hormones in Human Blood: Detection &
Assay. Harvard U Pr.
Antoniak, Helen.
xAntoniak, Helen.
Alone: Emotional, Legal & Financial Help for
the Widowed or Divorced Woman. Les
Femmes Pub.
Antonini, Gustavo A.
xAntonini, Gustavo A.
Population & Energy: A Systems Analysis of
Resource Utilization in the Dominican
Republic. U Presses Fla.
Antonioni, Michelangelo.
xAntonioni, Michelangelo.
L'Avventura: A Film. Grove.
Antoniou, Andreas, 1938-
xAntoniou, Andreas.

Digital Filters: Analysis & Design. McGraw.
Antonopulos, Barbara, 1947-
xAntonopulos, Barbara.
The Abominable Snowman. Raintree Pubs.
Antonovskii. *see* Antonovskii, Mikhail Iakovlevich.
Antonovskii, Mikhail Iakovlevich.
xAntonovskii.
Topological Semifields & Their Applications to
General Topology. Am Math.
Antony, Judith.
xAntony, Judith.
Where Time Becomes Space. Franciscan
Herald.
Antoun, Richard T.
xAntoun, Richard T.
Arab Village: A Social Structural Study of a
Transjordanian Peasant Community. Ind U
Pr.
Antreassian, Jack. *see* Antreassian, Jack Arthur.
Antreassian, Jack Arthur, 1920-
xAntreassian, Jack.
The Confessions of Kitchoonie. Ashod Pr.
Antrim, Earl.
xAntrim, Earl.
Civil War Prisons & Their Covers. Collectors.
Anttila, Raimo.
xAnttila, Raimo A.
An Introduction to Historical & Comparative
Linguistics. Macmillan.
Anttila, Raimo A. *see* Anttila, Raimo.
Antwerp, William C. Van. *see* Van Antwerp, William C.
Anuchin, V. A.
xAnuchin, V. A.
Theoretical Problems of Geography. Ohio St U
Pr.
Anwar, Chairil.
xAnwar, Chairil.
Complete Poetry & Prose of Chairil Anwar.
State U NY Pr.
Anweiler, Oskar.
xAnweiler, Oskar.
The Soviets: The Russian Workers, Peasants, &
Soldiers Councils, 1905-1921. Pantheon.
Anyan, Walter R.
xAnyan, Walter R.
Adolescent Medicine in Primary Care. Wiley.
Aoki, Harro. *see* Aoki, Haruo.
Aoki, Haruo.
xAoki, Harro.
Nez Perce Grammar. U of Cal Pr.
xAoki, Haruo.
Nez Perce Texts. U of Cal Pr.
Aoki, M. *see* Aoki, Masanao.
Aoki, Masanao.
xAoki, M.
Optimal Control & System Theory in Dynamic
Economic Analysis. Elsevier.
xAoki, Masanao.
ed. New Trends in Dynamic System Theory &
Economics. Acad Pr.
Ap Evans, Humphrey, 1922-
xAp Evans, Humphrey.
Falconry. Arco.
Apel, Willi, 1893-
xApel, Willi.
Gregorian Chant. Ind U Pr.
History of Keyboard Music to 1700. Ind U Pr.
Apelt, Otto, b. 1845
xApelt, Otto.
Platonische Aufsatze. Arno.
Apes, William, b. 1798
xApes, William.
Indian Nullification of the Unconstitutional
Laws of Massachusetts, Relative to the
Marshpee Tribe: Or, the Pretended Riot
Explained. E M Coleman Ent.
Apfel, Necia H.
xApfel, Necia H.

Architecture of the Universe.
Benjamin-Cummings.
Apha Bioavailability Project.
xBioavailability of Drug Products Project.
Intro. by The Bioavailability of Drug Products.
Am Pharm Assn.
Apicella, Anthony J.
xApicella, Anthony J.
Simplicity in Music Appreciation. P-H.
Apilado, Vincent P.
xApilado, Vincent P.
Cases in Financial Management. West Pub.
Personal Financial Management. West Pub.
Aplin, Richard D. *see* Aplin, Richard David.
Aplin, Richard David.
xAplin, Richard D.
Capital Investment Analysis: Using Discounted
Cash Flows. Grid Pub.
Aponte, Barbara B. *see* Aponte, Barbara Bockus.
Aponte, Barbara Bockus.
xAponte, Barbara B.
Alfonso Reyes & Spain: His Dialogue with
Unamuno, Valle-Inclan, Ortega y Gasset,
Jimenez & Gomez De la Serna. U of Tex Pr.
Apostol, Robert Z.
xApostol, Robert Z.
ed. Human Values in a Secular World.
Humanities.
Apostol, Tom M.
xApostol, Tom M.
Introduction to Analytic Number Theory.
Springer-Verlag.
Mathematical Analysis: A Modern Approach
to Advanced Calculus. A-W.
Apostolon, Billy.
xApostolon, Billy.
Preaching of the Cross. Baker Bk.
Special Days & Occasions. Baker Bk.
Appadorai, A. *see* Appadorai, Angadipuram.
Appadorai, Angadipuram, 1902-
xAppadorai, A.
ed. Documents on Political Thought in Modern
India. Oxford U Pr.
ed. Status of Women in South Asia. Zenger
Pub.
Appel, Benjamin, 1907-
xAppel, Benjamin.
The People Talk. Johnson Repr.
Appel, Georg.
xAppel, Georgius.
De Romanorum Precationibus. Arno.
Appel, Georgius. *see* Appel, Georg.
Appel, Gerald.
xAppel, Gerald.
Double Your Money Every Three Years.
Arlington Hse.
Double Your Money Every Three Years.
Windsor.
Appel, Karel.
xAppel, Karel.
Karel Appel: Works on Paper. Abbeville Pr.
Appel, Marsha C.
xAppel, Marsha C.
Illustration Index. Scarecrow.
Appel, Robert, 1951-
xAppel, Robert.
The Used Car Believer's Handbook: A
Complete Guide for the Subsequent Owner.
Van Nos Reinhold.
Appel, Theodore, 1823-1907
xAppel, Theodore.
Life & Work of John Williamson Nevin. Arno.
Appelbaum, Richard P.
xAppelbaum, Richard P.

The Effects of Urban Growth: A Population
Impact Analysis. Praeger.
Size, Growth, & U. S. Cities. Praeger.
Theories of Social Change. Rand.

Applegate, Ray D.
xApplegate, Ray D.
ed. Trolleys & Streetcars on American Picture
Postcards. Dover.

Appell, Madeleine.
xAppell, Madeleine.
One-Stitch Stitchery. Sterling.

Appell, Paul. *see* Appell, Paul Emile.

Appell, Paul Emile.
xAppell , Paul.
Theorie Des Fonctions Algebriques. Chelsea
Pub.

Appenzeller, Herb.
xAppenzeller, Herb.
Athletics & the Law. Michie.
Physical Education & the Law. Michie.

Apperson, George L. *see* Apperson, George Latimer.

Apperson, George Latimer, 1857-1937
xApperson, George L.
English Proverbs & Proverbial Phrases: A
Historical Dictionary. Gale.

Appignanesi, Richard.
xAppignanesi, Richard.
Freud for Beginners. Pantheon.
Lenin for Beginners. Pantheon.

Applbaum, Ronald. *see* Applbaum, Ronald L.

Applbaum, Ronald L.
xApplbaum, Ronald.
The Process of Group Communication. SRA.

Apple, David F.
xApple, David F.
Medicine for Sport. Year Bk Med.

Apple, J. Lawrence. *see* Apple, Jay Lawrence.

Apple, James M. *see* Apple, James MacGregor.

Apple, James MacGregor, 1915-
xApple, James M.
Material Handling Systems Design. Wiley.

Apple, Jay Lawrence.
xApple, J. Lawrence.
ed. Integrated Pest Management. Plenum Pub.

Apple, Max.
xApple, Max.
The Oranging of America & Other Stories.
Viking Pr.

Apple, Michael W.
xApple, Michael W.
Educational Evaluation: Analysis &
Responsibility. McCutchan.
Ideology & Curriculum. Routledge & Kegan.

Apple, Nick P.
xApple, Nick P.
The Air Force Museum. Crown.

Applebaum, Edmond L.
xApplebaum, Edward L.
ed. Reader in Technical Services. IHS-PDS.

Applebaum, Edward L. *see* Applebaum, Edmond L.

Applebaum, William.
xApplebaum, William.
Guide to Store Location Research: With
Emphasis on Super Markets. A-W.
Store Location Strategy Cases. A-W.

Applebee, Arthur N.
xApplebee, Arthur N.
The Child's Concept of Story: Ages Two to
Seventeen. U of Chicago Pr.
A Survey of Teaching Conditions in English,
1977. NCTE.

Appleby, Andrew B.
xAppleby, Andrew B.
Famine in Tudor & Stuart England. Stanford U
Pr.

Appleby, Joyce O. *see* Appleby, Joyce Oldham.

Appleby, Joyce Oldham.
xAppleby, Joyce O.

Economic Thought & Ideology in
Seventeenth-Century England. Princeton U
Pr.

Appleby, Paul H. *see* Appleby, Paul Henson.

Appleby, Paul Henson, 1891-1963
xAppleby, Paul H.
Morality & Administration in Democratic
Government. Greenwood.
Public Administration for a Welfare State.
Asia.

Applegarth, Albert C. *see* Applegarth, Albert Clayton.

Applegarth, Albert Clayton.
xApplegarth, Albert C.
Quakers in Pennsylvania. AMS Pr.
Quakers in Pennsylvania. Johnson Repr.

Applegate, Dorothy.
xApplegate, Dorothy.
Mission a - Go - Go. Apple-Gems.

Applegate, Frank G. *see* Applegate, Frank Guy.

Applegate, Frank Guy, 1882-1931
xApplegate, Frank G.
Indian Stories from the Pueblos. Rio Grande.

Applegate, Howard G.
xApplegate, Howard G.
Environmental Problems of the Borderlands.
Tex Western.

Applegate, Kay.
xApplegate, Kay.
The Breakfast Book. Lightning Tree.

Applegate, Mauree.
xApplegate, Mauree.
Easy in English: An Imaginative Approach to
the Teaching of the Language Arts. Har-Row.

Applegate, Richard. *see* Applegate, Richard B.

Applegate, Richard B.
xApplegate, Richard.
Atishwin: The Dream Helper in South-Central
California. Ballena Pr.

Appleman, Philip, 1926-
xAppleman, Philip.
ed. Darwin. Norton.
ed. Darwin. Norton.
Summer Love & Surf: Poems. Vanderbilt U Pr.

Appleton, Arthur.
xAppleton, Arthur.
Mary Ann Cotton: Her Story & Trial.
Transatlantic.

Appleton, George, Abp.
xAppleton, George.
Daily Prayer & Praise. Westminster.

Appleton, Jane.
xAppleton, Jane.
How Not to Split up. Berkley Pub.
How Not to Split up. Doubleday.

Appleton, Jay.
xAppleton, Jay H.
The Experience of Landscape. Wiley.

Appleton, Jay H. *see* Appleton, Jay.

Appleton, Jon H.
xAppleton, Jon H.
ed. The Development & Practice of Electronic
Music. P-H.

Appleton, Leroy. *see* Appleton, Leroy H.

Appleton, Leroy H.
xAppleton, Leroy.
American Indian Design & Decoration. Dover.
xAppleton, Leroy H.
American Indian Design & Decoration. Peter
Smith.

Appleton, Lilla E. *see* Appleton, Lilla Estelle.

Appleton, Lilla Estelle, 1858-1937
xAppleton, Lilla E.
A Comparative Study of the Play Activities of
Adult Savages & Civilized Children. Arno.

Appleton, Marion B. *see* Appleton, Marion Brymner.

Appleton, Marion Brymner.
xAppleton, Marion B.

ed. Index of Pacific Northwest Portraits. U of
Wash Pr.

Appleton, William S.
xAppleton, William S.
Practical Clinical Psychopharmacology.
Williams & Wilkins.

Applewhite, Cynthia.
xApplewhite, Cynthia.
Sundays. Avon.

Applewhite, Karen M. *see* Applewhite, Karen Miller.

Applewhite, Karen Miller.
xApplewhite, Karen M.
On the Road to Nowhere: A History of Greer,
Arizona, 1879-1979. Applewhite.

Applewhite, Philip.
xApplewhite, Philip.
Understanding Biology. HR&W.

Appley, Dee G.
xAppley, Dee G.
T-Groups & Therapy Groups in a Changing
Society. Jossey-Bass.

Appley, M. H. *see* Appley, Mortimer H.

Appley, Mortimer H.
xAppley, M. H.
Adaptation-Level Theory: A Symposium. Acad
Pr.

Appleyard, Donald.
xAppleyard, Donald.
ed. Conservation of European Cities. MIT Pr.
Planning a Pluralist City: Conflicting Realities
in Ciudad Guayana. MIT Pr.

Apps, Jerold W.
xApps, Jerold W.
Barns of Wisconsin. Tamarack Pr.
How to Improve Adult Education in Your
Church. Augsburg.
Ideas for Better Church Meetings. Augsburg.
Problems in Continuing Education. McGraw.
Toward a Working Philosophy of Adult
Education. Syracuse U Cont Ed.

Aproberts, Ruth.
xApRoberts, Ruth.
The Moral Trollope. Ohio U Pr.

Apsimon, John.
xApsimon, John.
The Total Synthesis of Natural Products.
Wiley.
xApSimon, John W.
ed. The Total Synthesis of Natural Products.
Wiley.

ApSimon, John W. *see* Apsimon, John.

Apsler, Alfred.
xApsler, Alfred.
From Witch Doctor to Biofeedback: The Story
of Healing by Suggestion. Messner.
An Introduction to Social Science. Random.
Sie Kamen aus Deutschen Landen. Irvington.

Apte, V. S. *see* Apte, Vaman Shivram.

Apte, Vaman Shivram.
xApte, V. S.
Student's English-Sanskrit Dictionary. Colton
Bk.
The Student's English-Sanskrit Dictionary.
Orient Bk Dist.
Student's English-Sanskrit Dictionary. Verry.

Apter, David. *see* Apter, David E.

Apter, David E.
xApter, David.
Politics of Modernization. U of Chicago Pr.

Apter, David E. *see* Apter, David Ernest.

Apter, David Ernest, 1924-
xApter, David E.
Choice & the Politics of Allocation: A
Developmental Theory. Yale U Pr.
An Introduction to Political Analysis.
Winthrop.
ed. Multinational Corporation & Social
Change.. Praeger.

Apter, Michael J.
xApter, Michael J.

The Computer in Psychology. Wiley.

Apter, S., 1907-
xApter, Samson.
tr. The Preisingers: A Novel. A S Barnes.

Apter, Samson. *see* Apter, S.

Aptheker, Herbert, 1915-
xAptheker, Herbert.
American Foreign Policy & the Cold War. Kraus Repr.
American Negro Slave Revolts. Intl Pub Co.
Czechoslovakia & Counter-Revolution: Why the Socialist Countries Intervened. New Outlook.
ed. A Documentary History of the Negro People in the United States: 1910-1932. Citadel Pr.
ed. Nat Turner's Slave Rebellion: Together with the Full Text of the So-Called "Confessions" of Nat Turner Made in Prison in 1831. Humanities.
Nature of Democracy, Freedom & Revolution. Intl Pub Co.
The Truth About Hungary. Kraus Repr.

Apthorp, W. F. *see* Apthorp, William Foster.

Apthorp, William F. *see* Apthorp, William Foster.

Apthorp, William Foster, 1848-1913
xApthorp, W. F.
The Opera, Past & Present. Gordon Pr.
xApthorp, William F.
Musicians & Music-Lovers & Other Essays. Longwood Pr.
Musicians & Music-Lovers & Other Essays. R West.
Opera, Past & Present. Arno.
The Opera Past & Present. Longwood Pr.

Aquila, Richard E., 1944-
xAquila, Richard E.
Intentionality: A Study of Mental Acts. Pa St U Pr.

Aquinas, Thomas. *see* Thomas Aquinas.

Aquino, John.
xAquino, John T.
Artists As Teachers. Phi Delta Kappa.

Aquino, John T. *see* Aquino, John.

Arab World & Iran Business Guides. *see* Arab World and Iran Business Guides, Inc.

Arab World and Iran Business Guides, Inc.
xArab World & Iran Business Guides.
The Arab World & Iran in Trade with the USA, UK, EEC, Comecon, Japan & the Third World: 1978. Guides Multinatl Busn.
Corporate & Personal Taxation in the Arab World: 1978. Guides Multinatl Busn.
Economic Development Projects in the Arab World & Iran: 1978. Guides Multinatl Busn.
Foreign Investment Regulations & Labour Employment Conditions in the Arab World. Guides Multinatl Busn
Nineteen Seventy-Nine Businessman's Guide to the Arab World & Iran: 1979. Guides Multinatl Busn.
Oil Pricing, the Oil Weapon & the Arms Race in the Middle East. Guides Multinatl Busn.

Arac, Jonathan, 1945-
xArac, Jonathan.
Commissioned Spirits: The Shaping of Social Motion in Dickens, Carlyle, Melville, & Hawthorne. Rutgers U Pr.

Arad, Ruth W.
xArad, Ruth W.
Sharing Global Resources. McGraw.

Arago, Dominique Francois Jean, 1786-1853
xArago, M.
Historical Eloge of James Watt. Arno.

Arago, M. *see* Arago, Dominique Francois Jean.

Aragon, Ray J. De. *see* De Aragon, Ray J.

Aragones, Sergio.
xAragones, Sergio.
In Mad We Trust. Warner Bks.

Arakawa, H. *see* Arakawa, Hidetoshi.

Arakawa, Hidetoshi, 1907-
xArakawa, H.
ed. Climates of Northern & Eastern Asia. Elsevier.

Arakeri, H. R. *see* Arakeri, Hanumappa Ramappa.

Arakeri, Hanumappa Ramappa, 1919-
xArakeri, H. R.
Soil Management in India. Asia.

Araki, Chiyo.
xAraki, Chiyo.
Origami in the Classroom. C E Tuttle.

Araki, James T.
xAraki, James T.
The Ballad-Drama of Medieval Japan. C E Tuttle.

Araldo, Josephine, 1897-
xAraldo, Josephine.
Cooking with Josephine. Strawberry Hill.
Sounds from Josephine's Kitchen. Strawberry Hill.

Aram, John D., 1942-
xAram, John D.
Dilemmas of Administrative Behavior. P-H.

Aranda, Francisco. *see* Aranda, J. Francisco.

Aranda, J. Francisco, 1926-
xAranda, Francisco.
Luis Bunuel: A Critical Biography. Da Capo.

Arangis, Louise. *see* Arangis, Louise M.

Arangis, Louise M.
xArangis, Louise.
The Red, White & Blue Art Ideas Handbook: Patriotic Themes for the Elementary Grades. P-H.

Arango, E. Ramon. *see* Arango, Ergasto Ramon.

Arango, Ergasto Ramon.
xArango, E. Ramon.
The Spanish Political System: Franco's Legacy. Westview.

Aranha, Jose P. *see* Aranha, Jose Pereira Da Graca.

Aranha, Jose Pereira Da Graca, 1868-1931
xAranha, Jose P.
Canaan. Gordon Pr.

Arata, Esther S. *see* Arata, Esther Spring.

Arata, Esther Spring.
xArata, Esther S.
More Black American Playwrights: A Bibliography. Scarecrow.

Arato, Andrew.
xArato, Andrew.
The Young Lukacs & the Origins of Western Marxism. Continuum.

Arber, Edward, 1836-1912
xArber, Edward.
ed. English Scholar's Library of Old & Modern Works. AMS Pr.

Arberry, Arthur J. *see* Arberry, Arthur John.

Arberry, Arthur John, 1905-
xArberry, Arthur J.
Arabic Poetry: A Primer for Students. Cambridge U Pr.

Arbib, Michael A.
xArbib, Michael A.
ed. Arrows, Structures & Functors: The Categorical Imperative. Acad Pr.

Arbib, Robert S.
xArbib, Robert S.
Lord's Woods. Norton.

Arbital, Samuel L.
xArbital, Samuel L.
Cities & Metropolitan Areas. Creative Ed.

Arbogast, Karen K. *see* Arbogast, Karen Kramer.

Arbogast, Karen Kramer.
xArbogast, Karen K.
Exchange Lists & Diet Patterns. Van Nos Reinhold.

Arbona, Guillermo.
xArbona, Guillermo.
Regionalization of Health Services: The Puerto Rican Experience. Oxford U Pr.

Arbore, Lily.
xArbore, Lily.
Princess & the Unicorn. Carolrhoda Bks.

Arbuckle, Dugald S. *see* Arbuckle, Dugald Sinclair.

Arbuckle, Dugald Sinclair, 1912-
xArbuckle, Dugald S.
Counseling & Psychotherapy: An Existential-Humanistic View. Allyn.

Arbuckle, W. S. *see* Arbuckle, Wendell Sherwood.

Arbuckle, Wendell S. *see* Arbuckle, Wendell Sherwood.

Arbuckle, Wendell Sherwood, 1911-
xArbuckle, W. S.
Ice Cream Service Handbook. AVI.
xArbuckle, Wendell S.
Ice Cream. AVI.

Arbuthnot, Archibald.
xArbuthnot, Archibald.
Memoirs of the Remarkable Life & Surprizing Adventures of Miss Jenny Cameron: Philamours & Philamena; or, Genuine Memoirs of a Late Affecting Transaction, 1746. Garland Pub.

Arbuthnot, May H. *see* Arbuthnot, May Hill.

Arbuthnot, May Hill.
xArbuthnot, May H.
Compiled by The Arbuthnot Anthology of Children's Literature. Lothrop.

Arc Books, Inc., New York.
xArc Editorial Board.
One Thousand Ideas for Term Papers in Economics. Arc Bks.
One Thousand Ideas for Term Papers in Sociology. Arc Bks.
One Thousand Ideas for Term Papers in Sociology. Arco.

Arc Editorial Board. *see* Arc Books, Inc., New York.

Arce, Hector.
xArce, Hector.
Gary Cooper an Intimate Biography. Morrow.
Groucho. Putnam.
The Secret Life of Tyrone Power. Morrow.

Arce De Vazquez, Margot.
xArce de Vazquez, Margot.
Gabriela Mistral: The Poet & Her Work. NYU Pr.

Arceneaux, Thelma H. *see* Arceneaux, Thelma Hoffmann Tyler.

Arceneaux, Thelma Hoffmann Tyler.
xArceneaux, Thelma H.
They Emerged from the Shade. T H Arceneaux.

Archbold, William A. *see* Archbold, William Arthur Jobson.

Archbold, William Arthur Jobson, 1865-1947
xArchbold, William A.
ed. Twentieth-Century Essays & Addresses. Arno.

Archer, Christon I., 1940-
xArcher, Christon I.
The Army in Bourbon Mexico, 1760-1810. U of NM Pr.

Archer, Dane.
xArcher, Dane.
How to Expand Your S. I. Q. (Social Intelligence Quotient). M Evans.

Archer, Gleason L. *see* Archer, Gleason Leonard.

Archer, Gleason Leonard, 1916-
xArcher, Gleason L.
A Survey of Old Testament Introduction. Moody.

Archer, Jeffrey, 1940-
xArcher, Jeffrey.
Kane & Abel. S&S.

Archer, John, 1923-
xArcher, John.
The Archer Method of Winning at 21. Contemp Bks.

Archer, John C. *see* Archer, John Clark.

Archer, John Clark, 1881-1957
xArcher, John C.
Sikhs in Relation to Hindus, Moslems,
Christians & Ahmadiyyas: A Study in
Comparative Religion. Russell.
Archer, John F., 1946-
xArcher, John F.
Susohn: A Personal Journey. Atavistic Pr.
Archer, Jules.
xArcher, Jules.
China in the Twentieth Century. Macmillan.
Famous Young Rebels. Messner.
Hunger on Planet Earth. T Y Crowell.
Legacy of the Desert: Understanding the
Arabs. Little.
Superspies: The Secret Side of Government.
Delacorte.
You Can't Do That to Me: Famous Fights for
Human Rights. Macmillan.
Archer, Katherine B.
xArcher, Kathy.
Perfect Needlepoint Projects from Start to
Finish. St Martin.
Archer, Kathy. *see* Archer, Katherine B.
Archer, Margaret.
xArcher, Margaret.
Glass Candlesticks. Collector Bks.
Archer, R. K. *see* Archer, Richard Kendray.
Archer, Richard Kendray.
xArcher, R. K.
ed. Comparative Clinical Haematology.
Lippincott.
Archer, Sellers G. *see* Archer, Sellers Gambrell.
Archer, Sellers Gambrell, 1908-
xArcher, Sellers G.
Soil Conservation. U of Okla Pr.
Archer, Thomas A. *see* Archer, Thomas Andrew.
Archer, Thomas Andrew.
xArcher, Thomas A.
The Crusade of Richard I, 1189-92. AMS Pr.
Archer, W. G. *see* Archer, William George.
Archer, W. Harry. *see* Archer, William Harry.
Archer, William, 1856-1924
xArcher, William.
Real Conversations. Folcroft.
Archer, William George, 1907-
xArcher, W. G.
Indian Paintings from the Punjab Hills: A
Survey & History of Pahari Miniature
Painting. Biblio Dist.
Archer, William Harry.
xArcher, W. Harry.
Oral & Maxillofacial Surgery. Saunders.
Archibald, G. C. *see* Archibald, George Christopher.
Archibald, George Christopher.
xArchibald, G. C.
An Introduction to Mathematical Economics:
Methods & Applications. Har-Row.
Archibald, Joe. *see* Archibald, Joseph.
Archibald, Joseph, 1898-
xArchibald, Joe.
Backcourt Commando. Macrae.
Centerfield Rival. Macrae.
Fast Break Fury. Macrae.
Long Pass. Macrae.
Payoff Pitch. Macrae.
Powerback. Macrae.
Pro Coach. Macrae.
Right Field Rookie. Macrae.
Right Field Runt. Macrae.
Southpaw Speed. Macrae.
Two Time Rookie. Macrae.
Archibald, Raymond Clare.
xArchibald, Raymond C.
Outline of the History of Mathematics.
Johnson Repr.
Archibald, Raymond C. *see* Archibald, Raymond Clare.
Architectural Record.
xArchitectural Record.

Great American Architect Series for the
Architectural Record. Da Capo.
xArchitectural Record Editors.
Affordable Houses Designed by Architects.
McGraw.
Apartments, Townhouses & Condominiums.
McGraw.
Campus Planning & Design. McGraw.
Great Houses for View Sites, Beach Sites,
Wood Sites, Meadows Sites, Small Sites,
Sloping Sites, Steep Sites, Flat Sites.
McGraw.
Hospitals, Clinics, & Health Centers. McGraw.
Houses Architects Design for Themselves.
McGraw.
Houses of the West. McGraw.
Interior Spaces Designed by Architects.
McGraw.
Office Building Design. McGraw.
Record Houses of 1971. McGraw.
Recycling Buildings: Renovations,
Remodelings, & Reuses. McGraw.
Techniques of Successful Practice for
Architectural Engineering. McGraw.
xArchitectural Record Magazine.
Architecture 1970-1980: A Decade of Change.
McGraw.
Energy-Efficient Buildings. McGraw.
Record Houses of 1980. McGraw.
A Treasury of Contemporary Houses. McGraw.
Architectural Record Editors. *see* Architectural Record.
Architectural Record Magazine. *see* Architectural
Record.
Arciniegas, German, 1900-
xArciniegas, German.
Germans in the Conquest of America: A
Sixteenth Century Venture. Hafner.
Arco Editiorial Board. *see* Arco Publishing Company.
Arco Editorial Board. *see* Arco Publishing Company.
Arco Publishing Company.
xArco Editiorial Board.
Practice for Air Force Placement Tests. Arco.
xArco Editorial Board.

Able Seaman-Deckhand-Scowman. Arco.
Accountant-Auditor. Arco.
Administrative Assistant. Arco.
Advanced Placement & College Board
Achievement in Physics. Arco.
Advanced Placement & College Level
Examinations in Biology. Arco.
Advanced Placement & College Level
Examinations in Chemistry. Arco.
Advanced Placement, College Level
Examination & College Board Achievement
Tests in European History. Arco.
American Foreign Service Officer. Arco.
American History & Social Studies
Achievement Test. Arco.
Apprentice-Mechanical Trades. Arco.
Attorney-Assistant Trainee. Arco.
Auto Mechanic, Auto Serviceman. Arco.
Aviation Weather. Arco.
Bank Examiner: Trainee & Assistant. Arco.
Battalion & Deputy Chief, F. D. Arco.
Beginning Office Worker. Arco.
Beverage Control Investigator. Arco.
Bookkeeper-Account Clerk. Arco.
Bridge & Tunnel Officer--Special Officer. Arco.
Building Custodian. Arco.
Bus Maintainer - Bus Mechanic. Arco.
Bus Operator: Conductor. Arco.
Buyer, Assistant Buyer, Purchase Inspector.
Arco.
California High School Proficiency
Examination. Arco.
Captain, Police Department. Arco.
Carpenter. Arco.
Case Worker. Arco.
ed. Cashier, Housing Teller. Arco.
CBAT College Board Achievement Test in
English Composition. Arco.
CDP-CCP-CLEP Data Processing
Examinations. Arco.
Chemist-Assistant Chemist. Arco.
City Planner. Arco.
Civil Service Handbook. Arco.
Clerk-Steno Transcriber. Arco.
College Level Examinations in Mathematics:
Algebra, Algebra-Trigonometry,
Trigonometry. Arco.
College Office Assistant. Arco.
Construction Foreman - Supervisor - Inspector.
Arco.
Correction Captain - Deputy Warden. Arco.
Court Officer. Arco.
Dental Admission Test. Arco.
Early Childhood Education: Teaching Area
Exam for the National Teacher Examination.
Arco.
Education: Advanced Test for the G.R.E..
Arco.
Education in the Elementary School: Teaching
Area Exam for the National Teacher
Examination. Arco.
Elevator Operator. Arco.
English Language & Literature: Teaching Area
Exam for the National Teacher Examination.
Arco.
Federal Aviation Regulations. Arco.
ed. Fire Administration & Technology. Arco.
Fireman, F. D.. Arco.
Food Service Supervisor, School Lunch
Manager. Arco.
Foreman. Arco.
Foreman of Auto Mechanics. Arco.
Gardener--Assistant Gardener. Arco.
General Entrance Series. Arco.
General Test Practice for One Hundred & One
U. S. Jobs. Arco.
Graduate Management Admission Test. Arco.
Graduate Record Examination Aptitude Test.
Arco.
History: Advanced Test for the G.R.E.. Arco.

Hospital Attendant. Arco.
Hospital Care Investigator Trainee: Social Case
    Worker 1. Arco.
Hospital Clerk. Arco.
Housing Assistant. Arco.
Housing Caretaker. Arco.
Housing Inspector. Arco.
Housing Manager--Assistant Housing Manager.
    Arco.
Housing Patrolman. Arco.
How to Win Success in the Mail Order
    Business. Arco.
Investigator-Inspector. Arco.
Junior Administrator Development
    Examination: JADE. Arco.
Laboratory Aide. Arco.
Laborer: Federal, State & City Jobs. Arco.
Laundry Worker. Arco.
Law & Court Stenographer. Arco.
Librarian. Arco.
Lieutenant, F. D.. Arco.
Lieutenant, P. D.. Arco.
Literature: Advanced Test for the G. R. E..
    Arco.
Machinist - Machinist's Helper. Arco.
Machinist--Machinist's Helper. Arco.
Maintainer's Helper, Group A & C: Transit
    Electrical Helper. Arco.
Maintenance Man. Arco.
Management & Administration Quizzer. Arco.
Mathematics, Simplified & Self Taught. Arco.
Mathematics: Teaching Area Exam for the
    National Teacher Exam. Arco.
Mechanical Apprentice (Maintainer's Helper
    B). Arco.
Mechanical Engineer: Junior, Assistant &
    Senior Grades. Arco.
Messenger. Arco.
Mortuary Caretaker. Arco.
Motor Vehicle License Examiner. Arco.
Motorman: Subways. Arco.
National Teacher Examination. Arco.
Notary Public. Arco.
Nurse. Arco.
Office Assistant: GS Two-Four. Arco.
Office Machines Operator. Arco.
Oil Burner Installer. Arco.
Painter. Arco.
Parking Enforcement Agent. Arco.
Patrol Inspector. Arco.
Personnel Examiner - Junior Personnel
    Examiner. Arco.
Plumber: Plumber's Helper. Arco.
Police Officer: Patrolman, P. D.. Arco.
Police Science Advancement. Arco.
Policewoman. Arco.
Post Office Clerk-Carrier. Arco.
Post Office Motor Vehicle Operator. Arco.
Postal Inspector. Arco.
Postal Promotion Foreman - Supervisor. Arco.
Postal Service Officer. Arco.
Practice for the Armed Forces Tests. Arco.
Principal Clerk-Stenographer. Arco.
Probation & Parole Officer. Arco.
Professional Careers Tests. Arco.
Professional Trainee - Administrative Aide.
    Arco.
Public Health Sanitarian. Arco.
Railroad Clerk. Arco.
Railroad Porter. Arco.
Resident Building Superintendent. Arco.
Sanitation Foreman: Foreman & Asst.
    Foreman. Arco.
Sanitation Man. Arco.
Scholastic Aptitude Tests. Arco.
School Crossing Guard. Arco.
Science Review for Medical College Admission
    Test. Arco.
Senior Clerical Series. Arco.
Senior Clerk-Stenographer. Arco.

Staff Attendant. Arco.
State Trooper. Arco.
Stationary Engineer & Fireman. Arco.
Statistician, Statistical Clerk. Arco.
Stenographer-Typist: Practical Preparation.
    Arco.
Stenographer-Typist: U. S. Government
    Positions. Arco.
Storekeeper-Stockman, Senior Storekeeper.
    Arco.
Structural Apprentice: Maintainer's Helper,
    Group D. Arco.
Structural Design: Reinforced Concrete, Wood
    & Steel Structures. Arco.
Supervising Clerk-Stenographer. Arco.
Supervision Course: Civil Service & Business.
    Arco.
Surface Line Dispatcher. Arco.
Tabulating Machine Operator, I. B. M. Arco.
Telephone Operator. Arco.
Test of Standard Written English (TSWE).
    Arco.
Towerman: Municipal Subway System. Arco.
Trackman: Municipal Subway System. Arco.
Train Dispatcher. Arco.
Transit Sergeant-Lieutenant. Arco.
    ed. Treasury Enforcement Agent. Arco.
Welder. Arco.

Arcocha, Juan, 1927-
    xArcocha, Juan.
        Candle in the Wind. Lyle Stuart.
Arcos, Joseph C.
    xArcos, Joseph C.
        Chemical Induction of Cancer. Acad Pr.
Arctic Institute of North America.
    xArctic Institute of North America (Montreal,
    Canada).
        Catalogue of the Library of the Arctic Institute
        of North America, Third Supplement. G K
        Hall.
    xArctic Institute of North America, Montreal.
        Catalogue of the Library of the Arctic Institute
        of North America, First Supplement. G K
        Hall.
    xArctic Institute of North America-Montreal.
        Catalogue of the Library of the Artic Institute
        of North America, Second Supplement. G K
        Hall.
Arctic Institute of North America (Montreal, Canada).
    see Arctic Institute of North America.
Arctic Institute of North America, Montreal. see Arctic
    Institute of North America.
Arctic Institute of North America-Montreal. see Arctic
    Institute of North America.
Ard, Ben N.
    xArd, Ben N.
        ed. Handbook of Marriage Counseling. Sci &
        Behavior.
Ardell, Donald. see Ardell, Donald B.
Ardell, Donald B.
    xArdell, Donald.
        ed. Author's Guide to Journals in the Health
        Field. Haworth Pr.
Ardener, Shirley.
    xArdener, Shirley.
        ed. Defining Females: The Nature of Women
        in Society. Halsted Pr.
        ed. Perceiving Women. Halsted Pr.
Ardies, Tom.
    xArdies, Tom.
        Palm Springs. Berkley Pub.
        Palm Springs. Doubleday.
Ardiff, Martha.
    xArdiff, Martha B.
        Great Ideas. Newbury Hse.
Ardiff, Martha B. see Ardiff, Martha.
Arditti, Joseph.
    xArditti, Joseph.

        ed. Orchid Biology: Reviews & Perspectives.
        Cornell U Pr.
Arditti, Rita.
    xArditti, Rita.
        ed. Science & Liberation. South End Pr.
Ardman. see Ardman, Perri.
Ardman, Perri.
    xArdman.
        The Woman's Day Book of Fund Raising. St
        Martin.
Ardoin, John.
    xArdoin, John.
        The Callas Legacy. Scribner.
Ardon, Michael, 1928-
    xArdon, Michael.
        Oxygen: Elementary Forms & Hydrogen
        Peroxide. Benjamin-Cummings.
Ardrey, Robert.
    xArdrey, Robert.
        The Hunting Hypothesis: A Personal
        Conclusion Concerning the Evolutionary
        Nature of Man. Atheneum.
Areeda, Philip.
    xAreeda, Phillip.
        Antitrust Analysis: Problems, Text, Cases.
        Little.
Areeda, Phillip. see Areeda, Philip.
Areen, Judith. see Areen, Judith C.
Areen, Judith C.
    xAreen, Judith.
        Standards Relating to Youth Service Agencies.
        Ballinger Pub.
Arellano, Michael. see Arellano, Mick.
Arellano, Mick.
    xArellano, Michael.
        Teach Yourself to Swim...Despite Your Fear of
        Water. Dutton.
Arena, Jay M.
    xArena, Jay M.
        Child Safety Is No Accident: A Parents'
        Handbook of Emergencies. Duke.
Arena, John. see Arena, John I.
Arena, John I.
    xArena, John.
        How to Write an IEP. Acad Therapy.
Arenas, Reinaldo, 1943-
    xArenas, Reinaldo.
        Hallucinations: Being an Account of the Life &
        Adventures of Friar Servando Teresa De
        Mier. Ultramarine Pub.
Arends, Richard.
    xArends, Richard I.
        Systems Change Strategies in Educational
        Settings. Human Sci Pr.
Arends, Richard I. see Arends, Richard
Arendt, Hannah.
    xArendt, Hannah.
        Eichmann in Jerusalem: A Report of the
        Banality of Evil. Penguin.
        Human Condition. U of Chicago Pr.
        Men in Dark Times. HarBraceJ.
        Men in Dark Times. HarBraceJ.
        On Revolution. Penguin.
        On Violence. HarBraceJ.
        Rahel Varnhagen: The Life of a Jewish
        Woman. HarBraceJ.
        Intro. by Rahel Varnhagen: The Life of a
        Jewish Woman. HarBraceJ.
Arendzen, J. P. see Arendzen, John Peter.
Arendzen, John Peter.
    xArendzen, J. P.
        Purgatory & Heaven. TAN Bks Pubs.
Arens, Richard, 1921-
    xArens, Richard.
        ed. Genocide in Paraguay. Temple U Pr.
        Insanity Defense. Philos Lib.
Arens, W., 1940-
    xArens, W.

The Man-Eating Myth: Anthropology &
Anthropophagy. Oxford U Pr.
Arensberg, Conrad M. *see* Arensberg, Conrad Maynadier.
Arensberg, Conrad Maynadier.
xArensberg, Conrad M.
Culture & Community. Peter Smith.
Arent, Emma, 1881-
xArent, Emma.
The Relation of the State of Private Education
in Norway: A Study of the Historical
Development of State Regulations Governing
the Various Types of Private Education in
Norway. AMS Pr.
Aresvik, Oddvar, 1915-
xAresvik, Oddvar.
The Agricultural Development of Jordan.
Praeger.
The Agricultural Development of Turkey.
Praeger.
Arfken, George. *see* Arfken, George Brown.
Arfken, George Brown, 1922-
xArfken, George.
Mathematical Methods for Physicists. Acad Pr.
Argabright, Loren.
xArgabright, Loren.
Fourier Analysis of Unbounded Measures on
Locally Compact Abelian Groups. Am Math.
Argan, Giulio. *see* Argan, Giulio Carlo.
Argan, Giulio Carlo.
xArgan, Giulio.
The Renaissance City. Braziller.
Argea, Angelo.
xArgea, Angelo.
The Bear & I: The Story of the World's Most
Famous Caddie. Atheneum.
Argelander, Hermann.
xArgelander, Hermann.
The Initial Interview in Psychotherapy. Human
Sci Pr.
Argenti, Nicholas.
xArgenti, Nicholas.
The Postage Stamps of New Brunswick Nova
Scotia. Quarterman.
Argenzio, Victor.
xArgenzio, Victor.
Crystal Clear: The Story of Diamonds. McKay.
Argersinger, Peter H.
xArgersinger, Peter H.
Populism & Politics: William Alfred Peffer &
the People's Party. U Pr of Ky.
Argo, Ellen.
xArgo, Ellen.
The Crystal Star. Putnam.
Argoff, Allen.
xArgoff, Allen.
The Social Studies Student Investigates Money.
Rosen Pr.
Arguedas, Jose M. *see* Arguedas, Jose Maria.
Arguedas, Jose Maria.
xArguedas, Jose M.
Deep Rivers. U of Tex Pr.
Arguelles, Miriam.
xArguelles, Miriam.
The Feminine: Spacious As the Sky. Shambhala
Pubns.
Arguilla, Manuel E. *see* Arguilla, Manuel Estabillo.
Arguilla, Manuel Estabillo, 1911-
xArguilla, Manuel E.
How My Brother Leon Brought Home a Wife
& Other Stories. Greenwood.
Argyle, M. *see* Argyle, Michael.
Argyle, Michael.
xArgyle, M.
Gaze & Mutual Gaze. Cambridge U Pr.
xArgyle, Michael.
The Psychology of Interpersonal Behaviour.
Gannon.
Argyris, C. *see* Argyris, Chris.
Argyris, Chris, 1923-
xArgyris, C.

The Applicability of Organizational Sociology.
Cambridge U Pr.
xArgyris, Chris.
Integrating the Individual & the Organization.
Wiley.
Organization of a Bank: Study of the Nature of
Organization & the Fusion Process. Arno.
Organizational Learning: A Theory of Action
Perspective. A-W.
Theory in Practice: Increasing Professional
Effectiveness. Jossey-Bass.
Arhin, Kwame.
xArhin, Kwame.
West African Traders in Ghana in the
Nineteenth & Twentieth Centuries. Longman.
Arian, Alan.
xArian, Alan.
The Choosing People: Voting Behavior in
Israel. UPBS.
Arias, Harmodio, Pres. Panama, 1886-
xArias, Harmodio.
Panama Canal: A Study in International Law &
Diplomacy. Arno.
Arica Institute.
xArica Institute.
Psychocalisthenics. S&S.
Aricha, Amos.
xAricha, Amos.
Phoenix. NAL.
Phoenix. NAL.
Ariens, E. J. *see* Ariens, Everhardous Jacobus.
Ariens, Everhardous Jacobus.
xAriens, E. J.
ed. Drug Design. Acad Pr.
Aries, Philippe.
xAries, Philippe.
Centuries of Childhood: A Social History of
Family Life. Random.
Aries, R. S. *see* Aries, Robert Sancier.
Aries, Robert Sancier.
xAries, R. S.
Chemical Engineering Cost Estimation.
McGraw.
Arieti, Silvano.
xArieti, Silvano.
Creativity: The Magic Synthesis. Basic.
On Schizophrenia, Phobias, Depression,
Psychotherapy & the Farther Shores of
Psychiatry: Selected Papers of Silvano Arieti.
Brunner-Mazel.
Understanding & Helping the Schizophrenic: A
Guide for Family & Friends. Basic.
Arifov, U. A. *see* Arifov, Ubai Arifovich.
Arifov, Ubai Arifovich.
xArifov, U. A.
Interaction of Atomic Particles with a Solid
Surface. Plenum Pub.
Arijon, Daniel.
xArijon, Daniel.
Grammar of the Film Language. Focal Pr.
Arin, M. K. *see* Arin, Michael Kenneth.
Arin, Michael Kenneth.
xArin, M. K.
Successful Wedding Photography. Amphoto.
Arinc Research Corporation.
xArinc Research Corporation.
Reliability Engineering. P-H.
Ariosto, Lodovico.
xAriosto, Ludovico.
Orlando Furioso. Oxford U Pr.
Ariosto, Ludovico. *see* Ariosto, Lodovico.
Ariste, Paul, 1905-
xAriste, Paul.
Grammar of the Votic Language. Res Ctr Lang
Semiotic.
Aristophanes.
xAristophanes.

The Acharnians of Aristophanes. Arno.
Clouds. NAL.
Clouds. Oxford U Pr.
Ecclesiazusae. Oxford U Pr.
**Aristotelian Society for the Systematic Study of
Philosophy, London.**
xAristotelian Society For The Systematic Study Of
Philosophy.
Knowledge & Foreknowledge: Proceedings,
Supplementary Vol. 16. Johnson Repr.
Knowledge, Experience & Realism:
Proceedings, Supplementary Vol. 9. Johnson
Repr.
Life & Finite Individuality: Proceedings,
Supplementary Vol. 1. Johnson Repr.
Logic & Reality: Proceedings, Supplmentary
Vol. 20. Johnson Repr.
Logical Positivism & Ethics: Proceedings,
Supplementary Vol. 22. Johnson Repr.
Men & Machines: Proceedings, Supplmentary
Vol. 26. Johnson Repr.
Mind, Matter & Purpose: Proceedings,
Supplementary Vol. 8. Johnson Repr.
Mind, Objectivity & Fact: Proceedings,
Supplementary Vol. 7. Johnson Repr.
Modern Tendencies in Philosophy:
Proceedings, Supplementary Vol. 13. Johnson
Repr.
Phenomenology: Proceedings, Supplementary
Vol. 11. Johnson Repr.
Philosophy & Metaphysics: Proceedings,
Supplementary Vol. 5. Johnson Repr.
Politics, Psychology & Art: Proceedings,
Supplementary Vol. 23. Johnson Repr.
Problems in Psychotherapy & Jurisprudence:
Proceedings, Supplementary Vol. 29. Johnson
Repr.
Problems of Science & Philosophy:
Proceedings, Supplementary Vol. 2. Johnson
Repr.
Proceedings, New Series: Vols. 1-61,
1900-1961. Johnson Repr.
Proceedings, Old Series: Vols. 1-3, 1887-1896.
Johnson Repr.
Psychical Research, Ethics & Logic:
Proceedings, Supplementary Vol. 24. Johnson
Repr.
Relativity, Logic & Mysticism: Proceedings,
Supplementary Vol. 3. Johnson Repr.
Science History & Theology: Proceedings.
Johnson Repr.
What Can Philosophy Determine: Proceedings.
Johnson Repr.
Ariyan. *see* Ariyan, Stephan.
Ariyan, Stephan.
xAriyan.
The Hand Book. Williams & Wilkins.
Ariyoshi, Sawako, 1931-
xAriyoshi, Sawako.
The Doctor's Wife. Kodansha.
Arizona. University. Library.
xUniversity Library, the University of Arizona.
ed. The Arizona Index: A Subject Index to
Periodical Articles About the State. G K
Hall.
Arjani, K. A.
xArjani, K. A.
Structured Programming Flowcharts. Collegium
Bk Pubs.
Arkava, Morton L.
xArkava, Morton L.
Psychological Tests & Social Work Practice:
An Introductory Guide. C C Thomas.
Arkes, Hadley.
xArkes, Hadley.
Bureaucracy, the Marshall Plan, & the National
Interest. Princeton U Pr.
Arkes, Hal R.
xArkes, Hal R.

Psychological Theories of Motivation.
  Brooks-Cole.
Arkham, Candace. see Arkham, Candice.
Arkham, Candice.
  xArkham, Candace.
    Splendors of the Heart. Dell.
Arkin, Alan.
  xArkin, Alan.
    The Lemming Condition. Bantam.
    The Lemming Condition. Har-Row.
Arkin, Arthur M.
  xArkin, Arthur M.
    ed. The Mind in Sleep: Psychology &
      Psychophysiology. Halsted Pr.
Arkin, Marcus.
  xArkin, Marcus.
    Aspects of Jewish Economic History. Jewish
      Pubn.
Arkoff. see Arkoff, Abe.
Arkoff, Abe.
  xArkoff.
    Psychology & Personal Growth. Allyn.
  xArkoff, Abe.
    Adjustment & Mental Health. McGraw.
Arlen, Michael, 1895-1956
  xArlen, Michael.
    Ghost Stories. Arno.
Arlen, Michael J.
  xArlen, Michael J.
    Exiles. Ballantine.
    Exiles. FS&G.
    Exiles - Passage to Ararat. FS&G.
    Passage to Ararat. FS&G.
    Thirty Seconds. FS&G.
Arlow, Jacob A.
  xArlow, Jacob A.
    Legacy of Sigmund Freud. Intl Univs Pr.

Arman, David.

  xArman, David.

    Historical Staffordshire: Illustrated Checklist.

    Arman Ent.
Armanino, Dominic C.
  xArmanino, Dominic C.
    Dominoes: Popular Games, Rules & Strategy.
      Sterling.
Armbruster, C. H. see Armbruster, Carl Hubert.
Armbruster, Carl Hubert, 1874-
  xArmbruster, C. H.
    Dongolese Nubian: A Grammar. Cambridge U
      Pr.
Armbruster, David A. see Armbruster, David Alvin.
Armbruster, David Alvin.
  xArmbruster, David A.
    Sports & Recreational Activities for Men &
      Women. Mosby.
    Swimming & Diving. Mosby.
Armbruster, Maxim. see Armbruster, Maxim Ethan.
Armbruster, Maxim E. see Armbruster, Maxim Ethan.
Armbruster, Maxim Ethan, 1902-
  xArmbruster, Maxim.
    The Presidents of the United States & Their
      Administrations from Washington to the
      Present. Horizon.
  xArmbruster, Maxim E.
    The Presidents of the United States & Their
      Administrations from Washington to Ford.
      Horizon.
Armbruster, Wally.
  xArmbruster, Wally.
    illus. A Bag of Noodles. Concordia.
Armed Forces - NRC Committee On Vision. see Armed
  Forces-National Research Council Vision Committee.
**Armed Forces-National Research Council Vision
  Committee.**
    xArmed Forces - NRC Committee On Vision.

Recent Developments in Vision Research. Natl
  Acad Pr.
Armendariz, Efraim P.
  xArmendariz, Efraim P.
    Elementary Number Theory. Macmillan.
Armengol, Joseph.
  xArmengol, Joseph.
    ed. English-Spanish Guide for Medical
      Personnel. Med Exam.
Armenini, Giovanni B. see Armenini, Giovanni Battista.
Armenini, Giovanni Battista.
  xArmenini, Giovanni B.
    On the True Precepts of the Art of Painting. B
      Franklin.
Armento, Richard. see Armento, Richard F.
Armento, Richard F.
  xArmento, Richard.
    Automotive Cooling System Training &
      Reference Manual. Reston.
Armer, Michael.
  xArmer, Michael.
    African Social Psychology: Review &
      Annotated Bibliography. Holmes & Meier.
Armerding, Hudson T.
  xArmerding, Hudson T.
    Leadership. Tyndale.
Armes, Ethel. see Armes, Ethel Marie.
Armes, Ethel Marie.
  xArmes, Ethel.
    The Story of Coal & Iron in Alabama. Arno.
Armes, Roy.
  xArmes, Roy.
    The Ambiguous Image: Narrative Style in
      Modern European Cinema. Ind U Pr.
    Film & Reality: An Historical Survey. Peter
      Smith.
Armey, Richard K., 1940-
  xArmey, Richard K.
    Price-Theory: A Policy-Welfare Approach.
      P-H.
Armfield, W. A.
  xArmfield, W. A.
    Investment in Subsidized Housing:
      Opportunities & Risks. Pilot Bks.
Armin, Robert, fl. 1610
  xArmin, Robert.
    The Collected Works of Robert Armin.
      Johnson Repr.
Armistead, J. M.
  xArmistead, J. M.
    Nathaniel Lee. Twayne.
Armitage, Merle, 1893-
  xArmitage, Merle.
    Dance Memoranda. Arno.
    ed. Martha Graham: The Early Years. Da
      Capo.
Armitage, Richard.
  xArmitage, Richard.
    Fundamentals of Spanish Grammar. HM.
Armond, Dale De. see De Armond, Dale.
Armond, R. N. De. see De Armond, R. N.
Armore, Sidney J., 1914-
  xArmore, Sidney J.
    Introduction to Statistical Analysis & Inference
      for Psychology & Education. Wiley.
    Statistics: A Conceptual Approach. Merrill.
Armour, Richard. see Armour, Richard Willard.
Armour, Richard Willard, 1906-
  xArmour, Richard.

The Academic Bestiary. Morrow.
Armour's Almanac: Around the Year in 365
  Days. McGraw.
Armoury of Light Verse. Branden.
Going Around in Academic Circles: A Low
  View of Higher Education. McGraw.
Going Like Sixty: A Lighthearted Look at the
  Later Years. McGraw.
Going Like Sixty: A Lighthearted Look at the
  Later Years. McGraw.
Golf Is a Four-Letter Word: The Intimate
  Confessions of a Hooked Slicer. McGraw.
Out of My Mind. McGraw.
The Strange Dreams of Rover Jones. McGraw.
Strange Monsters of the Sea. McGraw.
Writing Light Verse & Prose Humor. Writer.
Armour, Robert. see Armour, Robert A.
Armour, Robert A.
  xArmour, Robert.
    Fritz Lang. Twayne.
Arms, George. see Arms, George Warren.
Arms, George Warren, 1912-
  xArms, George.
    The Fields Were Green: A New View of
      Bryant, Whittier, Holmes, Lowell &
      Longfellow, with a Selection of Their Poems.
      Stanford U Pr.
Arms, Karen.
  xArms, Karen.
    Biology. HR&W.
Arms, W. Y.
  xArms, W. Y.
    A Practical Approach to Computing. Wiley.
Armsby, Leonora (Wood).
  xArmsby, Leonora W.
    Musicians Talk. Arno.
Armsby, Leonora W. see Armsby, Leonora (Wood).
Armson, K A.
  xArmson, K. A.
    Forest Soils: Properties & Processes. U of
      Toronto Pr.
Armstrong, A. H. see Armstrong, Arthur Hilary.
Armstrong, April Oursler, 1926-
  xArmstrong, April Oursler.
    Cry Babel: The Nightmare of Aphasia & a
      Courageous Woman's Struggle to Rebuild
      Her Life. Doubleday.
Armstrong, Arthur Hilary.
  xArmstrong, A. H.
    Cambridge History of Later Greek & Early
      Medieval Philosophy. Cambridge U Pr.
Armstrong, Ben.
  xArmstrong, Ben.
    The Electric Church. Nelson.
Armstrong, Cecil F. see Armstrong, Cecil Ferard.
Armstrong, Cecil Ferard.
  xArmstrong, Cecil F.
    A Century of Great Actors 1750-1850.
      Norwood Edns.
Armstrong, Charlotte.
  xArmstrong, Charlotte.
    A Little Less Than Kind. Berkley Pub.
Armstrong, Constance H.
  xArmstrong, Constance H.
    Senior Adult Camping. Am Camping.
Armstrong, Daniel.
  xArmstrong, Daniel.
    ed. Roman Jakobson: Echoes of His
      Scholarship. Humanities.
Armstrong, David G.
  xArmstrong, David G.
    Instructional Skills Handbook. Educ Tech
      Pubns.
    Social Studies in Secondary Education.
      Macmillan.
Armstrong, Edward C. see Armstrong, Edward Cooke.
Armstrong, Edward Cooke, 1871-
  xArmstrong, Edward C.

Authorship of the Vengement Alixandre & of
the Venjance Alixandre. Kraus Repr.
Armstrong, Evelyn S. *see* Armstrong, Evelyn Stewart.
Armstrong, Evelyn Stewart.
xArmstrong, Evelyn S.
Valdoro's Mistress. PB.
Armstrong, Fiona. *see* Armstrong, Fiona Ann.
Armstrong, Fiona Ann.
xArmstrong, Fiona.
Getting Ready for the World of Work.
McGraw.
A Realistic Job Search. McGraw.
Realizing What's Available in the World of
Work. McGraw.
Armstrong, Frank B. *see* Armstrong, Frank Bradley.
Armstrong, Frank Bradley.
xArmstrong, Frank B.
Biochemistry. Oxford U Pr.
Armstrong, Garner T. *see* Armstrong, Garner Ted.
Armstrong, Garner Ted.
xArmstrong, Garner T.
The Real Jesus. Avon.
Armstrong, George D. *see* Armstrong, George Dodd.
Armstrong, George Dodd, 1813-1899
xArmstrong, George D.
Christian Doctrine of Slavery. Negro U Pr.
Armstrong, H. C. *see* Armstrong, Harold Courtenay.
Armstrong, Harold Courtenay, 1891-1943
xArmstrong, H. C.
Grey Wolf: Mustafa Kemal: An Intimate Study
of a Dictator. Arno.
Armstrong, J. D. *see* Armstrong, James David.
Armstrong, J. Scott. *see* Armstrong, Jon Scott.
Armstrong, James, 1924-
xArmstrong, James.
The Nation Yet to Be: Christian Mission & the
New Patriotism. Friend Pr.
Armstrong, James David, 1945-
xArmstrong, J. D.
Revolutionary Diplomacy: Chinese Foreign
Policy & the United Front Doctrine. U of Cal
Pr.
Armstrong, John, 1709-1779
xArmstrong, John.
The Art of Preserving Health: A Poem. Arno.
Armstrong, John A. *see* Armstrong, John Alexander.
Armstrong, John Alexander, 1922-
xArmstrong, John A.
The European Administrative Elite. Princeton
U Pr.
Armstrong, John H.
xArmstrong, John A.
The Model Railroad Track Plan Book. TAB
Bks.
Armstrong, John M. *see* Armstrong, John Morrison.
Armstrong, John Morrison.
xArmstrong, John M.
Coastal Waters: A Management Analysis. Ann
Arbor Science.
Armstrong, Jon Scott, 1937-
xArmstrong, J. Scott.
Long Range Forecasting: From Crystal Ball to
Computer. Ronald Pr.
Long-Range Forecasting: From Crystal Ball to
Computer. Wiley.
Armstrong, L. *see* Armstrong, Lloyd.
Armstrong, Lilian.
xArmstrong, Lilian.
The Paintings & Drawings of Marco Zoppo.
Garland Pub.
Armstrong, Lloyd, 1940-
xArmstrong, L.
Theory of the Hyperfine Structure of Free
Atoms. Krieger.
Armstrong, Louise.
xArmstrong, Louise.

Arthur Gets What He Spills. HarBraceJ.
How to Turn Up into Down into Up: A
Child's Guide to Inflation, Depression, &
Economic Recovery. HarBraceJ.
How to Turn War into Peace: A Child's Guide
to Conflict Resolution. HarBraceJ.
Saving the Big-Deal Baby. Dutton.
Armstrong, M. *see* Armstrong, Mary Frances (Morgan).

Armstrong, Mark A. *see* Armstrong, Mark Anthony.
Armstrong, Mark Anthony.
xArmstrong, Mark A.
Basic Topology. McGraw.
Armstrong, Martin D. *see* Armstrong, Martin
Donisthorpe.
Armstrong, Martin Donisthorpe, 1882-
xArmstrong, M.
George Borrow. Haskell.
xArmstrong, Martin D.
Puppet Show. Arno.
Armstrong, Mary F. *see* Armstrong, Mary Frances
(Morgan).
Armstrong, Mary Frances (Morgan).
xArmstrong, M.
Hampton & Its Students. Arno.
xArmstrong, Mary F.
Hampton & Its Students. AMS Pr.
Armstrong, Michael.
xArmstrong, Michael.
Principles & Practice of Salary Administration.
Intl Pubns Serv.
Armstrong, Moses K. *see* Armstrong, Moses Kimball.
Armstrong, Moses Kimball, 1832-1906
xArmstrong, Moses K.
Early Empire Builders of the Great West.
Arno.
Armstrong, Muriel.
xArmstrong, M.
The Canadian Economy & Its Problems. P-H.
Armstrong, O. K.
xArmstrong, O. K.
Baptists Who Shaped a Nation. Broadman.

Armstrong, O. K. *see* Armstrong, Orland Kay.

Armstrong, O. V. *see* Armstrong, Oscar Vance.

Armstrong, Orland Kay.

xArmstrong, O. K.
The Baptists in America. Doubleday.

Armstrong, Oscar Vance, 1876-
xArmstrong, O. V.
Compiled by Comfort for Those Who Mourn.
Abingdon.
ed. Prayer Poems. Arno.
Armstrong, Patricia M. *see* Armstrong, Patricia Mees.
Armstrong, Patricia Mees.
xArmstrong, Patricia M.
Good Causes & Warm Corners. Windy Row.
Armstrong, Philip B. *see* Armstrong, Philip Brownell M.
D.
Armstrong, Philip Brownell M. D., 1898-
xArmstrong, Philip B.
Stages in the Development of Ictalurus
Nebulosus. Syracuse U Pr.
Armstrong, Richard S. *see* Armstrong, Richard Stoll.
Armstrong, Richard Stoll, 1924-
xArmstrong, Richard S.
Service Evangelism. Westminster.
Armstrong, Robert, 1938-
xArmstrong, Robert.

The Centers. Creative Ed.
The Coaches. Creative Ed.
Dave Cowens. Creative Ed.
The Forwards. Creative Ed.
George McGinnis. Creative Ed.
The Guards. Creative Ed.
Rick Barry. Creative Ed.
Armstrong, Robert C. *see* Armstrong, Robert Cornell.
Armstrong, Robert Cornell.
xArmstrong, Robert C.
Light from the East: Studies in Japanese
Confucianism. Krishna Pr.
Armstrong, Robert P. *see* Armstrong, Robert Plant.
Armstrong, Robert Plant.
xArmstrong, Robert P.
The Affecting Presence: An Essay in
Humanistic Anthropology. U of Ill Pr.
Armstrong, T. R. *see* Armstrong, Terry R.
Armstrong, Terence. *see* Armstrong, Terence E.
Armstrong, Terence E.
xArmstrong, Terence.
The Circumpolar North: A Political &
Economic Geography. Halsted Pr.
Armstrong, Terry R.
xArmstrong, T. R.
Power & Authority in Law Enforcement. C C
Thomas.
Armstrong, Thomas H.
xArmstrong, Thomas H.
Dental Hygiene Examination Review. Arco.
Armstrong, Virginia I. *see* Armstrong, Virginia Irving.
Armstrong, Virginia Irving.
xArmstrong, Virginia I.
ed. I Have Spoken: American History Through
the Voices of the Indians. Swallow.
Armstrong, Walter, Sir, 1850-1918
xArmstrong, Walter.
Lawrence. AMS Pr.
Armstrong, William. *see* Armstrong, William Howard.
Armstrong, William E.
xArmstrong, William E.
Purser's Handbook. Cornell Maritime.
Armstrong, William H.
xArmstrong, William H.
Organs for America: The Life & Work of
David Tannenberg. U of Pa Pr.
Armstrong, William H. *see* Armstrong, William Howard.
Armstrong, William Howard, 1914-
xArmstrong, William.
The Tale of Tawny & Dingo. Har-Row.
xArmstrong, William H.
Barefoot in the Grass: The Story of Grandma
Moses. Doubleday.
My Animals. Doubleday.
Sounder. Har-Row.
Sounder. Har-Row.
Sounder. Har-Row.
Sour Land. Har-Row.
Sour Land. Har-Row.
Study Tips: How to Study Effectively & Get
Better Grades. Barron.
Armstrong, William M.
xArmstrong, William M.
E. L. Godkin: A Biography. State U NY Pr.
Armstrong, William N.
xArmstrong, William N.
Around the World with a King. C E Tuttle.
Armstrong, Zella.
xArmstrong, Zella.
Notable Southern Families. Genealog Pub.
Notable Southern Families. Gordon Pr.
Notable Southern Families. Reprint.
Some Tennessee Heroes of the Revolution.
Genealog Pub.
Twenty-Four Hundred Tennessee Pensioners:
Revolution & War of 1812. Genealog Pub.
Army Times Editors. *see* Army Times, Washington, D.C.
Army Times, Washington, D.C.
xArmy Times Editors.

American Heroes of the Asian Wars. Dodd.

Arn, E. A., 1928-
  xArn, E. A.
    Group Technology: An Integrated Planning &
    Implementation Concept for Small &
    Medium Batch Production. Springer-Verlag.

Arnason, H. H. see Arnason, H. Harvard.

Arnason, H. Harvard.
  xArnason, H. H.
    History of Modern Art: Painting, Sculpture, &
    Architecture. Abrams.

Arnberger, Leslie P. see Arnberger, Leslie Preston.

Arnberger, Leslie Preston, 1924-
  xArnberger, Leslie P.
    Flowers of the Southwest Mountains. SW Pks
    Mnmts.

Arndt, Heinz W. see Arndt, Heinz Wolfgang.

Arndt, Heinz Wolfgang.
  xArndt, Heinz W.
    The Australian Trading Banks. Intl Schol Bk
    Serv.

Arndt, Karl J. see Arndt, Karl John Richard.

Arndt, Karl J. R. see Arndt, Karl John Richard.

Arndt, Karl John Richard.
  xArndt, Karl J.
    George Rapp's Successors & Material Heirs:
    1847-1916. Fairleigh Dickinson.
  xArndt, Karl J. R.
    George Rapp's Harmony Society: 1785-1847.
    Fairleigh Dickinson.

Arndt, Richard. see Arndt, Rick.

Arndt, Rick, 1956-
  xArndt, Richard.
    Safe at Home. Concordia.

Arner, Douglas G. see Arner, Douglas Gene.

Arner, Douglas Gene, 1926-
  xArner, Douglas G.
    Perception, Reason, & Knowledge: An
    Introduction to Epistemology. Scott F.

Arneson, Ben A. see Arneson, Ben Albert.

Arneson, Ben Albert, 1883-1958
  xArneson, Ben A.
    The Democratic Monarchies of Scandinavia.
    Greenwood.

Arneson, Donald.
  xArneson, Donald.
    Arnie, Knight of the Day. Bookmaker.

Arnett, Alex M. see Arnett, Alex Mathews.

Arnett, Alex Mathews, 1888-
  xArnett, Alex M.
    Claude Kitchin & the Wilson War Policies.
    Russell.
    Populist Movement in Georgia: A View of the
    Agrarian Crusade in the Light of Solid-South
    Politics. AMS Pr.

Arnett, Caroline.
  xArnett, Caroline.
    Clarissa. Fawcett.
    Melinda. Fawcett.
    Theodora. Fawcett.

Arnett, Carroll, 1927-
  xArnett, Carroll.
    Come. SBD.
    Earlier. SBD.

Arnett, Edward M. see Arnett, Edward McC.

Arnett, Edward McC.
  xArnett, Edward M.
    ed. Computer Based Chemical Information.
    Dekker.

Arnett, Ethel S. see Arnett, Ethel Stephens.

Arnett, Ethel Stephens.
  xArnett, Ethel S.
    Mrs. James Madison: The Incomparable
    Dolley. Straughan.

Arnett, Willard E. see Arnett, Willard Eugene.

Arnett, Willard Eugene, 1921-
  xArnett, Willard E.

Religion & Judgment: An Essay on the Method
  & Meaning of Religion. Irvington.

Arnheim, Daniel D.
  xArnheim, Daniel D.
    The Clumsy Child: A Program of Motor
    Therapy. Mosby.
    Dance Injuries: Their Prevention & Care.
    Mosby.

Arnheim, M. T. see Arnheim, M. T. W.

Arnheim, M. T. W.
  xArnheim, M. T.
    Aristocracy in Greek Society. Thames Hudson.

Arnheim, Rudolf.
  xArnheim, Rudolf.
    Entropy & Art: An Essay on Disorder &
    Order. U of Cal Pr.
    Film as Art. U of Cal Pr.

Arno, Peter.
  xArno, Peter.
    Peter Arno. Dodd.

Arno, Stephen F.
  xArno, Stephen F.
    Northwest Trees. Mountaineers.

Arnold. see Arnold, Arnold.

Arnold, Alvin L.
  xArnold, Alvin L.
    The Arnold Encyclopedia of Real Estate.
    Warren.

Arnold, Armin.
  xArnold, Armin.
    Friedrich Durrenmatt. Ungar.

Arnold, Arnold.
  xArnold, Arnold.
    World Book of Children's Games. Fawcett.
  xArnold, Arnold.
    The Crowell Book of Arts & Crafts for
    Children. T Y Crowell.
    World Book of Children's Games. T Y
    Crowell.

Arnold, Benjamin W. see Arnold, Benjamin William.

Arnold, Benjamin William, 1870-
  xArnold, Benjamin W.
    History of the Tobacco Industry in Virginia
    from 1860 to 1894. AMS Pr.
    History of the Tobacco Industry in Virginia
    from 1860 to 1894. Johnson Repr.

Arnold, Bruce.
  xArnold, Bruce.
    A Singer at the Wedding. David & Charles.

Arnold, C. R. see Arnold, Christopher R.

Arnold, Caroline.
  xArnold, Caroline.
    Five Nests. Dutton.

Arnold, Charlotte. see Arnold, Charlotte E.

Arnold, Charlotte E.
  xArnold, Charlotte.
    Group Readings for the Church. Baker Bk.

Arnold, Christopher R.
  xArnold, C. R.
    Applied Photography. Focal Pr.

Arnold, Corliss R. see Arnold, Corliss Richard.

Arnold, Corliss Richard.
  xArnold, Corliss R.
    Organ Literature: A Comprehensive Survey.
    Scarecrow.

Arnold, D. M. see Arnold, David M.

Arnold, David.
  xArnold, David.
    Chain of Letters. Trike.

Arnold, David M.
  xArnold, D. M.
    ed. Abelian Group Theory: Proceedings of the
    2nd New Mexico State University
    Bicentennial Conference on Abelian Group,
    Held at Las Cruces, New Mexico, Dec. 9-12
    1976. Springer-Verlag.

Arnold, Dennis M.
  xArnold, Dennis M.

The Needlepoint Pattern Book. Morrow.

Arnold, Eberhard, 1883-1935
  xArnold, Eberhard.
    Children's Education in Community: The Basis
    of Bruderhof Education. Plough.
    Inner Land: A Guide into the Heart & Soul of
    the Bible. Plough.
    Living Churches: The Essence of Their Life -
    Love to Christ & Love to the Brothers.
    Plough.

Arnold, Edmund C.
  xArnold, Edmund C.
    Modern Newspaper Design. Har-Row.

Arnold, Elliott, 1912-
  xArnold, Elliott.
    Blood Brother. U of Nebr Pr.
    The Spirit of Cochise. Scribner.

Arnold, Emmett. see Arnold, Emmett L.

Arnold, Emmett L.
  xArnold, Emmett.
    Gold-Camp Drifter: 1906-1910. U of Nev Pr.

Arnold, Emmy.
  xArnold, Emmy.
    ed. Inner Words for Every Day of the Year.
    Plough.
    Torches Together: The Beginning & Early
    Years of the Bruderhof Communities. Plough.

Arnold, Francena H. see Arnold, Francena Harriet.

Arnold, Francena Harriet, 1888-
  xArnold, Francena H.
    Brother Beloved. Moody.
    Deepening Stream. Zondervan.
    Straight Down a Crooked Lane. Moody.

Arnold, Frederick, 1833-1891
  xArnold, Frederick.
    Turning Points in Life. Arno.

Arnold, G. see Arnold, Guy.

Arnold, G. W.
  xArnold, G. W.
    Ethology of Free Ranging Domestic Animals.
    Elsevier.

Arnold, Genevieve.
  xArnold, Genevieve.
    Sound Ladder Game. Expression.

Arnold, Grant, 1904-
  xArnold, Grant.
    Creative Lithography & How to Do It. Dover.
    Creative Lithography & How to Do It. Peter
    Smith.

Arnold, Guy.
  xArnold, G.
    Economic Co-operation in the Commonwealth.
    Pergamon.
  xArnold, Guy.
    Aid in Africa. Nichols Pub.
    Modern Nigeria. Longman.
    Strategic Highways of Africa. St Martin.

Arnold, H. J. see Arnold, Harry John Philip.

Arnold, Harry John Philip, 1932-
  xArnold, H. J.
    William Henry Fox Talbot: Pioneer of
    Photography & Man of Science. Merrimack
    Bk Serv.

Arnold Harvey Associates.
  xArnold Harvey Associates.
    Anatomy of an Art Auction. A Harvey.

Arnold, Heini, 1913-
  xArnold, Heini.
    In the Image of God: Marriage & Chastity in
    Christian Life. Plough.

Arnold, Henry F.
  xArnold, Henry F.
    Trees in Urban Design. Van Nos Reinhold.

Arnold, Henry H. see Arnold, Henry Harley.

Arnold, Henry Harley, 1886-1950
  xArnold, Henry H.
    Global Mission. Arno.

Arnold, Horace L. see Arnold, Horace Lucien.

Arnold, Horace Lucien.
  xArnold, Horace L.

Ford Methods & the Ford Shops. Arno.
Arnold, Isaac N. see Arnold, Isaac Newton.
Arnold, Isaac Newton, 1815-1884
  xArnold, Isaac N.
    The Life of Benedict Arnold. Arno.
Arnold, J. Barto.
  xArnold, J. Barto.
    The Nautical Archeology of Padre Island: The
      Spanish Shipwrecks of 1554. Acad Pr.
Arnold, James.
  xArnold, James.
    All Drawn by Horses. David & Charles.
    Farm Waggons & Carts. David & Charles.
Arnold, James T.
  xArnold, James T.
    Simplified Digital Automation with
      Microprocessors. Acad Pr.
Arnold, June, 1926-
  xArnold, June.
    Applesauce. Daughters.
    The Cook & the Carpenter. Daughters.
Arnold, Lionel K. see Arnold, Lionel Kenneth.
Arnold, Lionel Kenneth, 1895-
  xArnold, Lionel K.
    Introduction to Plastics. Iowa St U Pr.
Arnold, Matthew, 1822-1888
  xArnold, Matthew.
    God & the Bible: A Review of Objections to
      Literature & Dogma. AMS Pr.
    God & the Bible: A Review of Objections to
      Literature & Dogma. R West.
    Letters of Matthew Arnold to Arthur Hugh
      Clough. Oxford U Pr.
    Letters of Matthew Arnold to Arthur Hugh
      Clough. Russell.
    Literature & Dogma: An Essay Towards a
      Better Apprehension of the Bible. AMS Pr.
    On Translating Homer. AMS Pr.
    The Works of Matthew Arnold. AMS Pr.
    Works of Matthew Arnold. Scholarly.
Arnold, Ned.
  xArnold, Ned.
    The Great Science Magic Show. Watts.
Arnold, Norman R.
  xArnold, Norman R.
    Occlusal Treatment: Preventive & Corrective
      Occlusal Adjustment. Lea & Febiger.
Arnold, O. Carroll. see Arnold, Otto Carroll.
Arnold, Oren.
  xArnold, Oren.
    A Boundless Privilege. Madrona Pr.
    Marvels of the U. S. Mint. Abelard.
    ed. More Steeple Stories. Kregel.
    Steeple Stories of Saints & Sinners. Kregel.
    Story of Cattle Ranching. Harvey.
    What's in a Name: Famous Brand Names.
      Messner.
Arnold, Otto Carroll.
  xArnold, O. Carroll.
    Religious Freedom on Trial. Judson.
Arnold, Peter, 1943-
  xArnold, Peter.
    How to Protect Your Child Against Crime.
      Follett.
Arnold, Richard, 1912-
  xArnold, Richard.
    Clay Pigeon Shooting. Intl Pubns Serv.
Arnold, Robert E.
  xArnold, Robert E.
    Poisonous Plants. Terra Pub.
    Poisonous Plants. Two Continents.
    What to Do About Bites & Stings of Venomous
      Animals. Macmillan.
    What to Do About Bites & Stings of Venomous
      Animals. Macmillan.
Arnold, Robert R.
  xArnold, Robert R.
    Modern Data Processing. Wiley.
Arnold, Sir Thomas Walker, 1864-1930
  xArnold, Thomas W.

Painting in Islam: A Study of the Place of
      Pictorial Art in Muslim Culture. Dover.
Arnold, Stanley. see Arnold, Stanley Norman.
Arnold, Stanley Norman, 1915-
  xArnold, Stanley.
    I Ran Against Jimmy Carter. Manor Bks.
Arnold, T. W. see Arnold, Thomas Walker.
Arnold, Thomas W. see Arnold, Thomas Walker.
Arnold, Thomas Walker.
  xArnold, T. W.
    The Legacy of Islam. Gordon Pr.
  xArnold, Thomas W.
    The Preaching of Islam: A History of
      Propagation of the Muslim Faith. AMS Pr.
Arnold, Thurman W. see Arnold, Thurman Wesley.
Arnold, Thurman Wesley, 1891-1969
  xArnold, Thurman W.
    The Bottlenecks of Business. Da Capo.
    Folklore of Capitalism. Elliots Bks.
    The Folklore of Capitalism. Greenwood.
Arnold, V. I. see Arnold, Vladimir Igorevich.
Arnold, Vladimir Igorevich.
  xArnold, V. I.
    Ordinary Differential Equations. MIT Pr.
Arnold, William E.
  xArnold, William E.
    Communicating Through Behavior. West Pub.
Arnold, William H. see Arnold, William Harkness.
Arnold, William Harkness.
  xArnold, William H.
    French Diction for Singers & Speakers. AMS
      Pr.
Arnold, William V., 1941-
  xArnold, William V.
    Divorce: Prevention or Survival. Westminster.
    When Your Parents Divorce. Westminster.
Arnold, Zach M. see Arnold, Zach Mclendon.
Arnold, Zach McLendon, 1921-
  xArnold, Zach M.
    Observations on the Biology of Protozoan
      Gromia Oviformis Dujardin. U of Cal Pr.
Arnold-Forster, Mark.
  xArnold-Forster, Mark.
    The World at War. Stein & Day.
Arnon, Isaac. see Arnon, Itzhak.
Arnon, Itzhak, 1909-
  xArnon, Isaac.
    Organisation & Administration of Agricultural
      Research. Intl Ideas.
Arnosky, Jim.
  xArnosky, Jim.
    illus. Nathaniel. A-W.
    Outdoors on Foot. Coward.
Arnot, William, 1808-1875
  xArnot, William.
    Studies in Acts: The Church in the House.
      Kregel.
Arnott, Kathleen.
  xArnott, Kathleen.
    Spiders, Crabs, & Creepy Crawlers: Two
      African Folktales. Garrard.
Arnott, Peter D.
  xArnott, Peter D.
    Greek Scenic Conventions in the Fifth Century
      B.C.. Greenwood.
Arnould, Arthur, 1833-1895
  xArnould, Arthur.
    Histoire populaire et parlementaire de la
      Commune de Paris. AMS Pr.
Arnov, Boris.
  xArnov, Boris.
    Water: Experiments to Understand It. Lothrop.
    Water: Experiments to Understand It. Morrow.
Arnow, E. Earle. see Arnow, Leslie Earle.
Arnow, Harriette. see Arnow, Harriette Louisa Simpson.
Arnow, Harriette Louisa Simpson, 1908-
  xArnow, Harriette.
    Hunter's Horn. Avon.
  xArnow, Harriette Simpson.

Old Burnside. U Pr of Ky.
Arnow, Harriette Simpson. see Arnow, Harriette Louisa
  Simpson.
Arnow, L. Earle. see Arnow, Leslie Earle.
Arnow, Leslie Earle, 1909-
  xArnow, E. Earle.
    Food Power: A Doctor's Guide to
      Commonsense Nutrition. Nelson-Hall.
  xArnow, L. Earle.
    Introduction to Physiological & Pathological
      Chemistry. Mosby.
Arnspiger, Varney C. see Arnspiger, Varney Clyde.
Arnspiger, Varney Clyde, 1896-
  xArnspiger, Varney C.
    Measuring the Effectiveness of Sound Pictures
      As Teaching Aids. AMS Pr.
Arnstein, Helene S.
  xArnstein, Helene S.
    Brothers & Sisters - Sisters & Brothers. Dutton.
    Getting Along with Your Grown-up Children.
      M Evans.
Arnstein, William E.
  xArnstein, William E.
    Direct Costing. Am Mgmt.
Arntson, Herbert E, 1911-
  xArntson, Herbert E.
    Caravan to Oregon. Binford.
Aron, Milton.
  xAron, Milton.
    Ideas & Ideals of the Hassidim. Citadel Pr.
Aron, R. see Aron, Raymond.
Aron, Raymond, 1905-
  xAron, R.
    The Imperial Republic: The United States &
      the World 1945-1973. P-H.
  xAron, Raymond.
    German Sociology. Arno.
    German Sociology. Greenwood.
    On War. Norton.
    The Opium of the Intellectuals. Greenwood.
    Opium of the Intellectuals. Norton.
    Politics & History: Selected Essays. Free Pr.
Aronin, Ben.
  xAronin, Ben.
    The Secret of the Sabbath Fish. Jewish Pubn.
Aronin, Jeffrey E. see Aronin, Jeffrey Ellis.
Aronin, Jeffrey Ellis, 1927-
  xAronin, Jeffrey E.
    Climate & Architecture. AMS Pr.
Aronoff, Craig. see Aronoff, Craig E.
Aronoff, Craig E.
  xAronoff, Craig.
    Business & the Media. Goodyear.
Aronoff, M. J. see Aronoff, Myron Joel.
Aronoff, Myron Joel.
  xAronoff, M. J.
    Power & Ritual in the Israel Labor Party: A
      Study in Political Anthropology. Humanities.
Aronofsky, J. S. see Aronofsky, Julius S.
Aronofsky, Julius S.
  xAronofsky, J. S.
    ed. Energy Policy. Elsevier.
Aronowitz, Stanley.
  xAronowitz, Stanley.
    Food, Shelter & the American Dream.
      Continuum.
Arons, Arnold. see Arons, Arnold B.
Arons, Arnold B.
  xArons, Arnold.
    The Various Language: An Inquiry Approach
      to the Physical Sciences. Oxford U Pr.
Arons, Harry.
  xArons, Harry.
    Hypnosis in Criminal Investigation. Borden.
Aronsohn, Alan J. see Aronsohn, Alan J. B.
Aronsohn, Alan J. B.
  xAronsohn, Alan J.
    Partnership Income Taxes. PLI.
Aronson, Alex, 1912-
  xAronson, Alex.

Music & the Novel: A Study in Twentieth
Century Fiction. Rowman.
Aronson, Charles N., 1913-
xAronson, Charles N.
Free Enterprise. C N Aronson.
In the Labor Pool. C N Aronson.
Mud & Dust. C N Aronson.
Regimen for Weight Control in Retired
Couples & Others Who Want to Control
Weight Happily. C N Aronson.
Aronson, Dan R.
xAronson, Dan R.
The City Is Our Farm: Seven Migrant Ijebu
Yoruba Families. Schenkman.
Aronson, Elliot.
xAronson, Elliot.
ed. Readings About the Social Animal. W H
Freeman.
The Social Animal. Viking Pr.
The Social Animal. W H Freeman.
Aronson, Harvey.
xAronson, Harvey.
Establishment of Innocence. Berkley Pub.
Aronson, J. Hugo. *see* Aronson, John Hugo.
Aronson, James.
xAronson, James.
The Press & the Cold War. Beacon Pr.
Aronson, John Hugo.
xAronson, J. Hugo.
Galloping Swede. Mountain Pr.
Aronson, Jonathan D. *see* Aronson, Jonathan David.
Aronson, Jonathan David.
xAronson, Jonathan D.
ed. Debt & the Less Developed Countries.
Westview.
Aronson, Joseph, 1898-
xAronson, Joseph.
Encyclopedia of Furniture. Crown.
Aronson, Robert L. *see* Aronson, Robert Louis.
Aronson, Robert Louis.
xAronson, Robert L.
ed. The Localization of Federal Manpower
Planning. NY Sch Indus Rel.
Aronson, Sara P.
xAronson, Sara P.
Communicable Disease Nursing. Med Exam.
Arora, Shirley L. *see* Arora, Shirley Lease.
Arora, Shirley Lease.
xArora, Shirley L.
Proverbial Comparisons in Ricardo Palma's
Tradiciones Peruanas. U of Cal Pr.
Arpan, Jeffrey S.
xArpan, Jeffrey S.
ed. Directory of Foreign Manufacturers in the
United States. Ga St U Busn Pub.
Arpel, Adrien.
xArpel, Adrien.
How to Look Ten Years Younger. Rawson
Wade.
Arpin, Gary Q.
xArpin, Gary Q.
Master of the Baffled House: The Dream Songs
of John Berryman. Rook Pr.
Arrabal, Fernando.
xArrabal, Fernando.
And They Put Handcuffs on the Flowers.
Grove.
Architect & the Emperor of Assyria. Grove.
Arreola, Juan J. *see* Arreola, Juan Jose.
Arreola, Juan Jose.
xArreola, Juan J.
Confabulario & Other Inventions. U of Tex Pr.
Arrick, Fran.
xArrick, Fran.
Steffie Can't Come Out to Play. Bradbury Pr.
Tunnel Vision. Bradbury Pr.
Arridge, R. G. *see* Arridge, R. G. C.
Arridge, R. G. C.
xArridge, R. G.

Mechanics of Polymers. Oxford U Pr.
Arrighi, Mel.
xArrighi, Mel.
The Death Collection. Popular Lib.
Delphine. Atheneum.
Delphine. NAL.
On Tour. Atheneum.
Turkish White. BJ Pub Group.
Turkish White. HarBraceJ.
Arrigoni-Martelli, Edoardo, 1930-3
xArrigoni-Martelli, Edoardo.
Inflammation & Antiinflammatories. Halsted
Pr.
Arrington, L. R. *see* Arrington, Lewis R.
Arrington, Leonard J.
xArrington, Leonard J.
A Dependent Commonwealth: Utah's
Economy from Statehood to the Great
Depression. Brigham.
Federally-Financed Industrial Plants
Constructed in Utah During World War Two.
Utah St U Pr.
Great Basin Kingdom: An Economic History of
the Latter-Day Saints, 1830-1900. U of Nebr
Pr.
The Mormon Experience: A History of the
Latter-Day Saints. Knopf.
The Mormon Experience: A History of the
Latter-Day Saints. Random.
Arrington, Lewis R.
xArrington, L. R.
Domestic Rabbit Biology & Production. U
Presses Fla.
Arrom, Jose. *see* Arrom, Jose Juan.
Arrom, Jose J. *see* Arrom, Jose Juan.
Arrom, Jose Juan, 1910-
xArrom, Jose.
Hispanoamerica: Panorama Contemporaneo De
Su Cultura. Har-Row.
xArrom, Jose J.
Historia De la Literatura Dramatica Cubana.
AMS Pr.
Arrow, Kenneth. *see* Arrow, Kenneth Joseph.
Arrow, Kenneth J. *see* Arrow, Kenneth Joseph.
Arrow, Kenneth Joseph.
xArrow, Kenneth.
ed. Applied Research for Social Policy: The
United States & the Federal Republic of
Germany Compared. Abt Assoc.
xArrow, Kenneth J.
The Limits of Organization. Norton.
Public Investment, the Rate of Return, &
Optimal Fiscal Policy. Johns Hopkins.
Arrow Pub. Staff. *see* Arrow Publishing Co., Newton
Upper Falls, Mass.
Arrow Publishing Co., Newton Upper Falls, Mass.
xArrow Pub. Staff.
ed. Arrow Street Guide of Atlanta. Arrow Pub.
ed. Arrow Street Guide of Baltimore. Arrow
Pub.
ed. Arrow Street Guide of Berkshire County.
Arrow Pub..
ed. Arrow Street Guide of Boston. Arrow Pub.
ed. Arrow Street Guide of Cincinnati. Arrow
Pub.
ed. Arrow Street Guide of Cleveland. Arrow
Pub.
ed. Arrow Street Guide of Greater Hartford.
Arrow Pub.
ed. Arrow Street Guide of Lowell, Lawrence &
Haverhill. Arrow Pub.
ed. Arrow Street Guide of Syracuse. Arrow
Pub.
ed. Arrow Street Guide of the North Shore.
Arrow Pub.
ed. Zip Code Directory. Arrow Pub.
Arrowood, Charles F. *see* Arrowood, Charles Flinn.
Arrowood, Charles Flinn.
xArrowood, Charles F.

ed. Thomas Jefferson & Education in a
Republic. AMS Pr.
ed. Thomas Jefferson & Education in a
Republic. Scholarly.
Arrowsmith, Nancy.
xArrowsmith, Nancy.
A Field Guide to the Little People. PB.
Arroyo, Stephen.
xArroyo, Stephen.
Astrology, Karma & Transformation: The Inner
Dimensions of the Birthchart. CRCS Pubns
WA.
Relationships & Life Cycles: Modern
Dimensions of Astrology. CRCS Pubns WA.
Arsdell, Paul M. Van. *see* Van Arsdell, Paul M.
Arsenault, J. E.
xArsenault, J. E.
ed. Reliability & Maintainability of Electronic
Systems. Computer Sci.
Arshinov, P. *see* Arshinov, Petr Andreevich.
Arshinov, Petr Andreevich, 1887-
xArshinov, P.
History of the Makhnovist Movement
(1918-1921). Black & Red.
Art Directors Club. *see* Art Directors Club of New York.
Art Directors Club of N. Y. *see* Art Directors Club of
New York.
Art Directors Club of New York.
xArt Directors Club.
The Fifty-First Annual of Advertising, Editorial
& Television Art & Design. Watson-Guptill.
xArt Directors Club of N. Y.
The Fifty-Second Annual of Advertising,
Editorial & Television Art & Design with the
13th Annual Copy Awards. Watson-Guptill.
xArt Directors Club of New York.
The Fifty-Fifth Annual of Advertising,
Editorial & Television Art & Design.
Watson-Guptill.
The Fifty-Ninth Art Directors Annual. ADC
NY.
Art Directors Club, 3rd Communications Conference,
New York. *see* Visual Communications Conference,
3rd, New York, 1958.
Art Directors Club, 4th Communications Conference,
New York. *see* Visual Communications Conference,
4th, New York, 1959.
Art Gallery of Ontario.
xArt Gallery of Ontario.
Exposure. Morrow.
Art Institute of Chicago. *see* Chicago Art Institute.
Art Institute of Chicago, Ryerson Library. *see* Chicago
Art Institute. Ryerson Library.
The Art Journal.
xArt-Journal.
Crystal Palace Exhibition Illustrated Catalogue.
London, 1851. Dover.
Art Research Libraries of Ohio.
xArt Research Libraries of Ohio.
Union List of Periodicals & Serials in Ohio Art
Research Libraries. Ohio St U Lib.
Art-Journal. *see* The Art Journal.
Artandi, Susan.
xArtandi, Susan B.
An Introduction to Computers in Information
Science. Scarecrow.
Artandi, Susan B. *see* Artandi, Susan.
Artel, Linda. *see* Artel, Linda J.
Artel, Linda J.
xArtel, Linda.
Positive Images: A Guide to 400 Non-Sexist
Films for Young People. Booklegger Pr.
Artemiadis, Nicolas. *see* Artemiadis, Nicolas K.
Artemiadis, Nicolas K.
xArtemiadis, Nicolas.
Real Analysis. S Ill U Pr.
Arter, Jared M. *see* Arter, Jared Maurice.
Arter, Jared Maurice.
xArter, Jared M.

Echoes from a Pioneer Life. Arno.
Arthey, V. D.
    xArthey, V. D.
        Quality of Horticultural Products. Halsted Pr.
Arthos, John, 1908-
    xArthos, John.
        The Art of Shakespeare. Folcroft.
        Pref. by Dante, Michelangelo, & Milton.
            Greenwood.
        On the Poetry of Spenser & the Form of
            Romances. Arno.
        Shakespeare's Use of Dream & Vision.
            Rowman.
Arthur, Bradford.
    xArthur, Bradford.
        Teaching English to Speakers of English.
            HarBraceJ.
Arthur, Burt.
    xArthur, Burt.
        The Drifter. Manor Bks.
        Gunsmoke in Nevada. Manor Bks.
        Gunsmoke in Paradise. Belmont-Tower.
        Outlaw Fury. Nordon Pubns.
        Return of the Texan. Nordon Pubns.
        Trouble at Moon Pass. Belmont-Tower.
Arthur, Catherine.
    xArthur, Catherine.
        My Sister's Silent World. Childrens.
Arthur D. Little Inc. *see* Little (Arthur D.) Inc.
Arthur, Elizabeth, 1953-
    xArthur, Elizabeth.
        Island Sojourn. Har-Row.
Arthur, Eric. *see* Arthur, Eric Ross.
Arthur, Eric Ross.
    xArthur, Eric.
        The Barn: A Vanishing Landmark in North
            America. A & W Pubs.
        The Barn: A Vanishing Landmark in North
            America. NYGS.
Arthur, Henry B.
    xArthur, Henry B.
        Commodity Futures As a Business
            Management Tool. Harvard Busn.
Arthur, Mildred. *see* Arthur, Mildred H.
Arthur, Mildred H.
    xArthur, Mildred.
        Holidays of Legend: From New Years to
            Christmas. Harvey.
    xArthur, Mildred H.
        God, Why Am I So Miserable?. Concordia.
Arthur, Robert.
    xArthur, Robert.
        Alfred Hitchcock & the Three Investigators in
            the Mystery of the Green Ghost. Random.
        Ghosts & More Ghosts. Random.
        ed. Spies & More Spies. Random.
Arthur, Ruth. *see* Arthur, Ruth M.
Arthur, Ruth M.
    xArthur, Ruth.
        A Candle in Her Room. Atheneum.
    xArthur, Ruth M.
        Miss Ghost. Atheneum.
        On the Wasteland. Atheneum.
Arthur, Timothy S. *see* Arthur, Timothy Shay.
Arthur, Timothy Shay, 1809-1885
    xArthur, Timothy S.
        The Hand but Not the Heart. Irvington.
        Sowing the Wind & Other Stories. Arno.
        Sunshine at Home & Other Stories. Arno.
Arthur, William J.
    xArthur, William J.
        A Financial Planning Model for Private
            Colleges: A Research Report. U Pr of Va.
Arthurs, A. M.
    xArthurs, A. M.
        Calculus of Variations. Routledge & Kegan.
        Probability Theory. Routledge & Kegan.
Artin, M. *see* Artin, Michael.
Artin, Michael.
    xArtin, M.

Etale Homotopy. Springer-Verlag.
Artinian, Artine, 1907-
    xArtinian, Artine.
        Maupassant Criticism in France, 1880-1940.
            Russell.
Artley, Bob.
    xArtley, Bob.
        Memories of a Former Kid. Iowa St U Pr.
Arts Council of Great Britain.
    xArts Council Of Great Britain.
        Pictorial History of Shakespearean Production
            in England, 1576-1946. Arno.
Artsimovich, L. A. *see* Artsimovich, Lev Andreevich.
Artsimovich, Lev Andreevich.
    xArtsimovich, L. A.
        ed. Controlled Thermonuclear Reactions.
            Gordon.
Artwick, B. *see* Artwick, Bruce A.
Artwick, Bruce A.
    xArtwick, B.
        Microcomputer Interfacing. P-H.
Artz, Curtis P. *see* Artz, Curtis Price.
Artz, Curtis Price.
    xArtz, Curtis P.
        Brief Textbook of Surgery. Saunders.
        Burns-A Team Approach. Saunders.
Artz, Frederick B. *see* Artz, Frederick Binkerd.
Artz, Frederick Binkerd, 1894-
    xArtz, Frederick B.
        France Under the Bourbon Restoration,
            1814-1830. Russell.
        From the Renaissance to Romanticism: Trends
            in Style in Art, Literature, & Music
            1300-1830. U of Chicago Pr.
        Reaction & Revolution: 1814-1832. Har-Row.
Artzy, Rafael.
    xArtzy, Rafael.
        Linear Geometry. A-W.
Aruego, Jose.
    xAruego, Jose.
        Look What I Can Do. Scribner.
        We Hide, You Seek. Greenwillow.
Arundel, Honor.
    xArundel, Honor.
        A Family Failing. Elsevier-Nelson.
        The Longest Weekend. G&D.
Arundel, Jocelyn.
    xArundel, Jocelyn.
        Lions & Tigers. Natl Wildlife.
Arundell, Dennis. *see* Arundell, Dennis Drew.
Arundell, Dennis D. *see* Arundell, Dennis Drew.
Arundell, Dennis Drew.
    xArundell, Dennis.
        The Critic at the Opera: Contemporary
            Comments on Opera in London Over Three
            Centuries. Da Capo.
        The Story of Sadler's Wells, 1683-1977.
            Rowman.
    xArundell, Dennis D.
        Story of Sadler's Wells, 1683-1964. Theatre
            Arts.
Arvey, Richard D.
    xArvey, Richard D.
        Fairness in Selecting Employees. A-W.
Arvin, Evelyn F. *see* Arvin, Evelyn Ferguson.
Arvin, Evelyn Ferguson.
    xArvin, Evelyn F.
        Ante-Bellum Homes of Lunenburg. Va Bk.
Arvin, Newton, 1900-1963
    xArvin, Newton.
        Whitman. Russell.
Arvon, Henri, 1914-
    xArvon, Henri.
        Marxist Esthetics. Cornell U Pr.
Arvonen, Helen.
    xArvonen, Helen.
        The Summer of Evil. Ace Bks.
Arwas, Victor.
    xArwas, Victor.

Art Deco. Abrams.
        Art Deco. St Martin.
Arx, William S. Von. *see* Von Arx, William S.
Ary, Donald.
    xAry, Donald.
        Introduction to Research in Education.
            HR&W.
Arya, Atam P. *see* Arya, Atam Parkash.
Arya, Atam Parkash.
    xArya, Atam P.
        Introductory College Physics. Macmillan.
Arya, J. C. *see* Arya, Jagdish C.
Arya, Jagdish C.
    xArya, J. C.
        Mathematics for the Biological Sciences. P-H.
Arya, Suresh C.
    xArya, Suresh C.
        Design of Structures & Foundations for
            Vibrating Machines. Gulf Pub.
Arya, Usharbudh.
    xArya, Usharbudh.
        God. Himalayan Intl Inst.
        Meditation & the Art of Dying. Himalayan Intl
            Inst.
Arzans De Orsua y Vela, Bartolome, 1676-1736
    xArzans de Orsua y Vela, Bartolome.
        Tales of Potosi. Brown U Pr.
Arzelies, H. *see* Arzelies, Henri.
Arzelies, Henri, 1913-
    xArzelies, H.
        Relativistic Point Dynamics. Pergamon.
Asai, Toshinobu, 1902-
    xAsai, Toshinobu.
        Acetic Acid Bacteria: Classification &
            Biochemical Activities. Univ Park.
Asakawa, Kanichi, 1873-1948
    xAsakawa, Kanichi.
        tr. & ed. The Documents of Iriki, Illustrative of
            the Development of the Feudal Institutions of
            Japan. Greenwood.
Asamani, J. O., 1934-
    xAsamani, J. O.
        Index Africanus. Hoover Inst Pr.
Asante, Molefi K.
    xAsante, Molefi K.
        ed. Handbook of Intercultural Communication.
            Sage.
Asante, S. K. *see* Asante, S. K. B.
Asante, S. K. B.
    xAsante, S. K.
        Pan African Protest: West Africa & the
            Italo-Ethiopian Crisis, 1934-41. Longman.
Asantewa, Doris.
    xAsantewa, Doris.
        Two Make a Team. Pambili Bks.
Asbestos Textile Institute.
    xAsbestos Textile Institute.
        Handbook of Asbestos Textiles. Textile Bk.
Asbury, Arthur K.
    xAsbury, Arthur K.
        Pathology of Peripheral Nerve. Saunders.
Asbury, Herbert, 1891-1963
    xAsbury, Herbert.
        Great Illusion: An Informal History of
            Prohibition. Greenwood.
        Suckers Progress: An Informal History of
            Gambling in America from the Colonies to
            Canfield. Patterson Smith.
Asch, Berta.
    xAsch, Berta.
        Farmers on Relief & Rehabilitation. Da Capo.
Asch, Frank.
    xAsch, Frank.

illus. Country Pie. Greenwillow.
illus. Monkey Face. Schol Bk Serv.
illus. Moon Bear. Scribner.
illus. Popcorn. Parents.
illus. Rebecka. Har-Row.
Running with Rachel. Dial.
illus. Starbaby. Scribner.
Asch, Peter.
xAsch, Peter.
Economic Theory & the Antitrust Dilemma.
Wiley.
Asch, Shalom.
xAsch, Sholem.
Children of Abraham: The Short Stories of
Sholem Asch. Arno.
In the Beginning: Stories from the Bible.
Schocken.
In the Beginning: Stories from the Bible.
Schocken.
Tales of My People. Arno.
Asch, Sholem. *see* Asch, Shalom.
Aschaffenburg, Gustav, 1866-
xAschaffenburg, Gustav.
Crime & Its Repression. Patterson Smith.
Ascham, Anthony. *see* Ascham, Antony.
Ascham, Antony, d. 1650
xAscham, Anthony.
Of the Confusions & Revolutions of
Governments. Schol Facsimiles.
Aschenbrenner, J. *see* Aschenbrenner, Joyce.
Aschenbrenner, Joyce.
xAschenbrenner, J.
Lifelines: Black Families in Chicago. HR&W.
Aschenbrenner, Karl.
xAschenbrenner, Karl.
The Concepts of Criticism. Kluwer Boston.
Ascher, Abraham, 1928-
xAscher, Abraham.
Pavel Axelrod & the Development of
Menshevism. Harvard U Pr.
Ascher, William.
xAscher, William.
Forecasting: An Appraisal for Policy Makers &
Planners. Johns Hopkins.
Aschmann, Homer, 1920-
xAschmann, Homer.
Central Desert of Baja California: Demography
& Ecology. Manessier.
Asdell, S. A. *see* Asdell, Sydney Arthur.
Asdell, Sydney Arthur, 1897-
xAsdell, S. A.
Patterns of Mammalian Reproduction.
Comstock.
Asen, Robert.
xAsen, Robert.
How to Make Money Selling Stock Options.
P-H.
Asfour, Edmund Y.
xAsfour, Edmund Y.
Syria: Development & Monetary Policy.
Harvard U Pr.
Ash, Anthony L. *see* Ash, Anthony Lee.
Ash, Anthony Lee.
xAsh, Anthony L.
The Gospel According to Luke. Sweet.
Psalms. Sweet.
The Word of Faith. Bibl Res Pr.
Ash, Brian.
xAsh, Brian.
Faces of the Future: The Lessons of Science
Fiction. Taplinger.
Ash, Cay Van. *see* Van Ash, Cay.
Ash, Fenton.
xAsh, Fenton.
A Trip to Mars. Arno.
Ash, J. Marshall.
xAsh, Marshall J.
ed. Studies in Harmonic Analysis. Math Assn.
Ash, John, 1724?-1779
xAsh, John.

Grammatical Institutes. Schol Facsimiles.
Ash, Marshall J. *see* Ash, J. Marshall.
Ash, Milton.
xAsh, Milton.
Optimal Shutdown Control of Nuclear
Reactors. Acad Pr.
xAsh, Milton S.
Nuclear Reactor Kinetics. McGraw.
Ash, Milton S. *see* Ash, Milton.
Ash, R. B. *see* Ash, Robert B.
Ash, Robert B.
xAsh, R. B.
Information Theory. Wiley.
xAsh, Robert B.
Complex Variables. Acad Pr.
Real Analysis & Probability. Acad Pr.
Ash, William, 1917-
xAsh, William.
Morals & Politics: The Ethics of Revolution.
Routledge & Kegan.
Ashberry, Anne.
xAshberry, Anne.
Miniature Gardens. David & Charles.
Ashbery, John.
xAshbery, John.
As We Know. Penguin.
As We Know. Viking Pr.
The Double Dream of Spring. Ecco Pr.
Houseboat Days. Penguin.
Houseboat Days. Viking Pr.
Some Trees. Corinth Bks.
Some Trees. Ecco Pr.
Ashbrook, Frank G. *see* Ashbrook, Frank Getz.
Ashbrook, Frank Getz, 1892-
xAshbrook, Frank G.
Butchering, Processing & Preservation of Meat.
Van Nos Reinhold.
Ashbrook, James B.
xAshbrook, James B.
Christianity for Pious Skeptics. Abingdon.
Ashby, Cliff.
xAshby, Cliff.
The Dogs of Dewsbury. Persea Bks.
Ashby, Eric, Sir, 1904-
xAshby, Eric.
Adapting Universities to a Technological
Society. Jossey-Bass.
Portrait of Haldane at Work on Education.
Shoe String.
The Structure of Higher Education: A World
View. Interbk Inc.
Ashby, G. F. *see* Ashby, Gerald Francis.
Ashby, Gerald Francis.
xAshby, G. F.
Pre-School Theories & Strategies. Intl Schol Bk
Serv.
Ashby, Maurice.
xAshby, Maurice.
Introduction to Plant Ecology. St Martin.
Ashby, Thomas, 1874-1931
xAshby, Thomas.
The Roman Campagna in Classical Times.
Greenwood.
Ashby, W. Ross. *see* Ashby, William Ross.
Ashby, William J.
xAshby, William J.
Clitic Inflection in French: An Historical
Perspective. Humanities.
Ashby, William Ross.
xAshby, W. Ross.
Introduction to Cybernetics. Methuen Inc.
Ashcraft, Norman.
xAshcraft, Norman.
Colonialism & Underdevelopment: Processes of
Political Economic Change in British
Honduras. Tchrs Coll.
People Space: The Making & Breaking of
Human Boundaries. Doubleday.
Ashcroft, John D.
xAshcroft, John D.

College Law for Business. SW Pub.
Ashcroft, Neil W.
xAshcroft, Neil W.
Solid State Physics. HR&W.
Ashcroft, S. J.
xAshcroft, S. J.
Thermochemistry of Transition Metal
Complexes. Acad Pr.
Ashdown, Charles H. *see* Ashdown, Charles Henry.
Ashdown, Charles Henry.
xAshdown, Charles H.
British & Continental Arms & Armour. Dover.
British & Continental Arms & Armour. Peter
Smith.
Ashdown, Dulcie M.
xAshdown, Dulcie M.
Princess of Wales. Scribner.
Ashdown, John.
xAshdown, John.
The Buildings of Oxford. Holmes & Meier.
Ashdown, Margaret, 1892-
xAshdown, Margaret.
English & Norse Documents Relating to the
Reign of Ethelred the Unready. Russell.
Ashdown-Sharp, Patricia, 1941-
xAshdown-Sharp, Patricia.
A Guide to Pregnancy & Parenthood for
Women on Their Own. Random.
Ashe, Arthur.
xAshe, Arthur.
Getting Started in Tennis. Atheneum.
Ashe, Geoffrey.
xAshe, Geoffrey.
Gandhi. Stein & Day.
The Quest for Arthur's Britain. Academy Chi
Ltd.
Ashe, Jim.
xAshe, Jim.
Handbook of IC Circuit Projects. TAB Bks.
Ashe, Rosalind.
xAshe, Rosalind.
The Hurricane Wake. HR&W.
The Hurricane Wake. Warner Bks.
Ashe, Samuel A. *see* Ashe, Samuel A'Court.
Ashe, Samuel A'Court, 1840-1938
xAshe, Samuel A.
History of North Carolina. Reprint.
Asheim, Lester. *see* Asheim, Lester Eugene.
Asheim, Lester Eugene, 1914-
xAsheim, Lester.
ed. Forum on the Public Library Inquiry.
Greenwood.
Asher, C. *see* Asher, Cecile.
Asher, Cecile.
xAsher, C.
Postural Variations in Childhood. Butterworths.
Asher, Don.
xAsher, Don.
Blood Summer. Berkley Pub.
Blood Summer. Putnam.
Asher, Herbert. *see* Asher, Herbert B.
Asher, Herbert B.
xAsher, Herbert.
Presidential Elections & American Politics.
Voters, Candidates, & Campaigns Since 1952.
Dorsey.
xAsher, Herbert B.
Causal Modeling. Sage.
Presidential Elections & American Politics:
Voters, Candidates & Campaigns Since 1952.
Dow Jones-Irwin.
Asher, J. William. *see* Asher, John William.
Asher, Jeremiah, b. 1812
xAsher, Jeremiah.
Incidents in the Life of the Rev. J. Asher.
Arno.
Asher, John William, 1927-
xAsher, J. William.

Educational Research & Evaluation Methods.
Little.

Asher, Maxine.
xAsher, Maxine K.
Ancient Energy: Key to the Universe.
Har-Row.
Asher, Maxine K. *see* Asher, Maxine.
Asher, Sandra F. *see* Asher, Sandy Fenichel.
Asher, Sandy Fenichel.
xAsher, Sandra F.
Summer Begins. Elsevier-Nelson.
Asher, Spring.
xAsher, Spring.
The Money Making Book for Kids. Wanderer
Bks.
Ashford, Alison. *see* Ashford, Alison E.
Ashford, Alison E.
xAshford, Alison.
Rex, Abyssinian & Turkish Cats. Arco.
Ashford, Ann.
xAshford, Ann.
If I Found a Wistful Unicorn. Peachtree Pubs.
Ashford, Douglas. *see* Ashford, Douglas Elliott.
Ashford, Douglas Elliott.
xAshford, Douglas.
Ideology & Participation. Sage.
Ashford, Nicholas A.
xAshford, Nicholas A.
Crisis in the Workplace: Occupational Disease
& Injury - (a Report to the Ford
Foundation). MIT Pr.
Ashford, Norman.
xAshford, Norman.
Airport Engineering. Wiley.
Ashford, Theodore H. *see* Ashford, Theodore H. A.
Ashford, Theodore H. A.
xAshford, Theodore H.
A Programmed Introduction to the
Fundamentals of Music. Wm C Brown.
Ashkar, F. *see* Ashkar, Fuad S.
Ashkar, Fuad S.
xAshkar, F.
ed. Practical Nuclear Medicine. Krieger.
Ashkenasi, Abraham.
xAshkenasi, Abraham.
Modern German Nationalism. Halsted Pr.
Ashlee, Ted, 1914-
xAshlee, Ted.
Gabby, Ernie & Me: A Vancouver Boyhood.
Intl Schol Bk Serv.
Ashley, Bernard.
xAshley, Bernard.
All My Men. S G Phillips.
Ashley, Brian.
xAshley, Brian.
Law & Order. Soccer.
Ashley, Carlos. *see* Ashley, Carlos C.
Ashley, Carlos C.
xAshley, Carlos.
That Spotted Sow & Other Texas Hill Country
Ballads. Shoal Creek Pub.
Ashley, George, 1930-
xAshley, George.
The Punctured Thumb: Cactus & Other
Succulents. One Hund One Prods.
Ashley, Howard J.
xAshley, Howard J.
Accurate Perspective Simplified. Abak Pr.
Ashley, John. *see* Ashley, John P.
Ashley, John P.
xAshley, John.
Principles of Intermediate Algebra. Glencoe.
Ashley, Maurice. *see* Ashley, Maurice Percy.
Ashley, Maurice Percy.
xAshley, Maurice.
General Monck. Rowman.
A History of Europe: 1648-1815. P-H.
Ashley, Michael.
xAshley, Mike.

Souls in Metal: An Anthology of Robot
Futures. BJ Pub Group.
Who's Who in Horror & Fantasy Fiction.
Taplinger.
Ashley, Mike. *see* Ashley, Michael.
Ashley, R. *see* Ashley, Ruth.
Ashley, Richard.
xAshley, Richard.
Dictionary of Nutrition. PB.
Ashley, Rosalind M. *see* Ashley, Rosalind Minor.
Ashley, Rosalind Minor.
xAshley, Rosalind M.
Activities for Motivating & Teaching Bright
Children. P-H.
Simplified Teaching Techniques & Materials for
Flexible Group Instruction. P-H.
Successful Techniques for Teaching Elementary
Language Arts. P-H.
Ashley, Ruth.
xAshley, R.
Background Math for a Computer World.
Wiley.
xAshley, Ruth.
ANS Cobol. Wiley.
Background Math for a Computer World.
Wiley.
Dental Anatomy & Terminology. Wiley.
Human Anatomy. Wiley.
Ashley, Steven.
xAshley, Steven.
Stalking Blind. Dial.
Ashley, William J. *see* Ashley, William James.
Ashley, William James, Sir, 1860-1927
xAshley, William J.
Tariff Problem. Kelley.
Ashline, Nelson F.
xAshline, Nelson F.
ed. Education, Inequality & National Policy.
Lexington Bks.
Ashlock, Patrick.
xAshlock, Patrick.
Educational Therapy Materials from the
Ashlock Learning Center. C C Thomas.
Teaching Reading to Individuals with Learning
Difficulties. C C Thomas.
Ashlock, Robert B.
xAshlock, Robert B.
Teaching Elementary School Mathematics
Through Motor Learning. C C Thomas.
Ashman, Chuck.
xAshman, Chuck.
The Gospel According to Billy. Lyle Stuart.
Ashmarin, Nikolai Ivanovich.
xAshmarin, Nikolaj I.
Thesaurus Linguae Tschuvaschorum. Res Ctr
Lang Semiotic.
Ashmarin, Nikolaj I. *see* Ashmarin, Nikolai Ivanovich.
Ashmead-Bartlett, Ellis, 1881-1931
xAshmead-Bartlett, Ellis.
Passing of the Shereefian Empire. Negro U Pr.
Ashmole, Bernard, 1894-
xAshmole, Bernard.
Architect & Sculptor in Classical Greece. NYU
Pr.
Ashmole, Elias, 1617-1692
xAshmole, Elias.
Institution, Laws & Ceremonies of the Most
Noble Order of the Garter. Genealog Pub.
Ashmore, Owen.
xAshmore, Owen.
Industrial Archaeology of Lancashire. Kelley.
Ashmun, Jehudi, 1794-1828
xAshmun, Jehudi.
Memoir of the Life & Character of the Rev.
Samuel Bacon. Arno.
Ashton, Dore.
xAshton, Dore.

The New York School: A Cultural Reckoning.
Penguin.
Ashton, Dudley.
xAshton, Dudley.
Administration of Physical Education for
Women. Wiley.
Ashton, H. *see* Ashton, Harry.
Ashton, Harry, 1882-1952
xAshton, H.
A Preface to Moliere. Folcroft.
Ashton, J. *see* Ashton, John.
Ashton, John, b. 1834
xAshton, J.
The Devil in Britain & America. Gordon Pr.
xAshton, John.
Century of Ballads. Gale.
ed. Chap-Books of the Eighteenth Century.
Arno.
ed. Chapbooks of the Eighteenth Century.
Kelley.
The Devil in Britain & America. Borgo Pr.
Devil in Britain & America. Gale.
Devil in Britain & America. Newcastle Pub.
Eighteenth Century Waifs. Arno.
Eighteenth Century Waifs. Gale.
History of English Lotteries. Gale.
History of Gambling in England. B Franklin.
History of Gambling in England. Gale.
History of Gambling in England. Patterson
Smith.
Humour, Wit & Satire of the Seventeenth
Century. B Franklin.
Humour, Wit & Satire of the Seventeenth
Century. Gale.
ed. Real Sailor-Songs. Arno.
Ashton, John W. *see* Ashton, John William.
Ashton, John William, 1900-
xAshton, John W.
ed. Types of English Drama. Somerset Pub.
Ashton, Rick J.
xAshton, Rick J.
Genealogy Beginner's Manual. Newberry.
Ashton, Sherley.
xAshton, Shirley.
How to Retire Successfully. Sterling.
Ashton, Shirley. *see* Ashton, Sherley.
Ashton, Thomas L.
xAshton, Thomas L.
ed. Byron's Hebrew Melodies. U of Tex Pr.
Ashton, Thomas S. *see* Ashton, Thomas Southcliffe.
Ashton, Thomas Southcliffe.
xAshton, Thomas S.
Coal Industry of the Eighteenth Century.
Kelley.
Industrial Revolution: 1760-1830. Oxford U Pr.
Ashton, Violet.
xAshton, Violet.
Love's Triumphant Heart. Fawcett.
Ashton, Winifred.
xAshton, Winifred.
Legend. Greenwood.
Regiment of Women. Greenwood.
Ashton-Warner, Sylvia.
xAshton-Warner, Sylvia.
I Passed This Way. Knopf.
Teacher. Bantam.
Ashwood, Thomas. *see* Ashwood, Thomas M.
Ashwood, Thomas M.
xAshwood, Thomas.
This Is Your Captain Speaking: A Handbook
for Air Travelers. Stein & Day.
Ashworth, J. M.
xAshworth, J. M.
Cell Differentiation. Methuen Inc.
Ashworth, Kenneth H.
xAshworth, Kenneth H.
American Higher Education in Decline. Tex
A&M Univ Pr.
Ashworth, M. F. *see* Ashworth, Michael Raymond
Frederick.

Ashworth, Michael Raymond Frederick.
  xAshworth, M. F.
    Analytical Methods for Organic Cyano Groups.
    Pergamon.
Ashworth, P. D.
  xAshworth, P. D.
    Social Interaction & Consciousness. Wiley.
Ashworth, Wilfred.
  xAshworth, Wilfred.
    Special Librarianship. K G Saur.
Asian-African Legal Consultative Committee Secretariat.
  see Asian African Legal Consultative Committee.
  Secretariat.
Asian African Legal Consultative Committee.
  Secretariat.
    xAsian-African Legal Consultative Committee
    Secretariat.
      ed. Constitutions of Asian Countries. Intl
      Pubns Serv.
Asian Cultural Centre for Unesco.
  xUNESCO-Asian Cultural Center.
    Stories from Asia Today. Weatherhill.
Asian Development Bank.
  xAsian Development Bank.
    Asian Agricultural Survey..U of Wash Pr.
    Rural Asia: Challenge & Opportunity. Praeger.
Asian-Pacific Congress of Cardiology - 4th. *see* Asian
  Pacific Congress of Cardiology, 4th, Jerusalem and
  Tel-Aviv, 1968.
Asian Pacific Congress of Cardiology, 4th, Jerusalem
  and Tel-Aviv, 1968.
  xAsian-Pacific Congress of Cardiology - 4th.
    Cardiology. Current Topics & Progress. Acad
    Pr.
    Proceedings. Acad Pr.

Asiatic Exclusion League.
  xAsiatic Exclusion League, 1907-1913.
    Proceedings. Arno.
Asiatic Exclusion League, 1907-1913. *see* Asiatic
  Exclusion League.
Asiedu, E. S. *see* Asiedu, Edward Seth.
Asiedu, Edward Seth.
  xAsiedu, E. S.
    ed. Public Administration in English-Speaking
    West Africa: An Annotated Bibliography. G
    K Hall.
Asihene, E. V.
  xAsihene, Emmanuel V.
    Understanding the Traditional Art of Ghana.
    Fairleigh Dickinson.
Asihene, Emmanuel V. *see* Asihene, E. V.
Asimakopulos, A., 1930-
  xAsimakopulos, A.
    An Introduction to Economic Theory:
    Microeconomics. Oxford U Pr.
Asimov. *see* Asimov, Isaac.
Asimov, I. *see* Asimov, Isaac.
Asimov, Isaac, 1920-
  xAsimov.
    Asimov's Guide to Shakespeare. Bonanza.
  xAsimov, I.
    Intro. by Moon. Abelard.
  xAsimov, Isaac.

Alpha Centauri, the Nearest Star. Lothrop.
Animals of the Bible. Doubleday.
Asimov on Astronomy. Doubleday.
Asimov on Chemistry. Doubleday.
Asimov on Numbers. Doubleday.
Asimov on Numbers. PB.
Asimov on Physics. Avon.
Asimov on Physics. Doubleday.
Asimov's Biographical Encyclopedia of Science
  & Technology: The Lives & Achievements of
  1195 Great Scientists from Ancient Times to
  the Present Chronologically Arranged.
  Doubleday.
Asimov's Guide to Science. Basic.
Asimov's Mysteries. Doubleday.
Asimov's Mysteries. Fawcett.
Asimov's Sherlockian Limericks. Mysterious
  Pr.
Building Blocks of the Universe. Abelard.
Caves of Steel. Fawcett.
Clock We Live On. Abelard.
The Collapsing Universe. PB.
Comets & Meteors. Follett.
Constantinople: The Forgotten Empire. HM.
Dark Ages. HM.
Double Planet. Abelard.
Earth: Our Crowded Spaceship. Fawcett.
Earth: Our Crowded Spaceship. John Day.
Easy Introduction to the Slide Rule. HM.
Eyes on the Universe: A History of the
  Telescope. HM.
Familiar Poems, Annotated. Doubleday.
Fantastic Voyage. Bantam.
Fantastic Voyage. HM.
ed. Fifty Short Science Fiction Tales.
  Macmillan.
Foundation. Avon.
Foundation. Doubleday.
Foundation & Empire. Avon.
Foundation & Empire. Doubleday.
Galaxies. Follett.
Genetic Code. NAL.
The Gods Themselves. Doubleday.
The Gods Themselves. Fawcett.
illus. The Golden Door: The United States
  from 1865 to 1918. HM.
Great Ideas of Science. HM.
How Did We Find Out About Antarctica?.
  Walker & Co.
How Did We Find Out About Atoms. Walker
  & Co.
How Did We Find Out About Black Holes?.
  Walker & Co.
How Did We Find Out About Comets?.
  Walker & Co.
How Did We Find Out About Dinosaurs.
  Walker & Co..
How Did We Find Out About Earthquakes.
  Walker & Co.
How Did We Find Out About Electricity?.
  Walker & Co.
How Did We Find Out About Germs. Walker
  & Co.
How Did We Find Out About Nuclear Power?.
  Walker & Co.
How Did We Find Out About Our Human
  Roots?. Walker & Co.
How Did We Find Out About Vitamins?.
  Walker & Co.
How Did We Find Out the Earth Is Round?.
  Walker & Co.
In Joy Still Felt: The Autobiography of Isaac
  Asimov, 1954-1978. Doubleday.
In Memory Yet Green: The Autobiography of
  Isaac Asimov 1920-1954. Doubleday.
ed. Isaac Asimov Presents the Great Science
  Fiction Stories. Daw Bks.
Lecherous Limericks. Walker & Co.
Left Hand of the Electron. Dell.
The Left Hand of the Electron. Doubleday.

Life & Energy. Avon.
Life & Time. Avon.
Life & Time. Doubleday.
Lucky Starr & the Rings of Saturn. Fawcett.
Mars, the Red Planet. Lothrop.
Moon. Follett.
More Lecherous Limericks. Walker & Co.
More Tales of the Black Widowers. Doubleday.
More Tales of the Black Widowers. Fawcett.
More Words of Science. HM.
Murder at the ABA. Doubleday.
Murder at the ABA. Fawcett.
Near East: 10,000 Years of History. HM.
Noble Gases. Basic.
Of Matters Great & Small. Ace Bks.
Only a Trillion. Ace Bks.
Pebble in the Sky. Fawcett.
The Planet That Wasn't. Avon.
The Planet That Wasn't. Doubleday.
Quick & Easy Math. HM.
The Road to Infinity. Doubleday.
Saturn & Beyond. Lothrop.
A Short History of Chemistry. Greenwood.
The Sun. Follett.
Tales of the Black Widowers. Fawcett.
Twentieth Century Discovery. Ace Bks.
Where Do We Go from Here?. Fawcett.
A Whiff of Death. Fawcett.
Words from the Exodus. HM.
Words from the Myths. NAL.
Words from the Myths. HM.
Words on the Map. HM.
  xAsimov, Issac.
    Our World in Space. NYGS.
    The Solar System. Follett.
Asimov, Issac. *see* Asimov, Isaac.
Asinger, F. *see* Asinger, Friedrich.
Asinger, Friedrich.
  xAsinger, F.
    Mono-Olefins: Chemistry & Technology.
    Pergamon.
Asinof, Eliot, 1919-
  xAsinof, Eliot.
    Bleeding Between the Lines. HR&W.
    Eight Men Out: The Black Sox & the 1919
    World Series. HR&W.
    The Fox Is Crazy Too. Morrow.
Asis Workshop on Computer Composition, Washington,
  D.C., 1970.
  xASIS Workshop on Computer Composition.
    Proceedings. Am Soc Info Sci.
Askari, Hossein.
  xAskari, Hossein.
    Agricultural Supply Response: A Survey of the
    Econometric Evidence. Praeger.
    Oil, OECD, & the Third World: A Vicious
    Triangle?. U of Tex Pr.
Askenasy, Hans, 1930-
  xAskenasy, Hans.
    Are We All Nazis?. Lyle Stuart.
Askew, R. R. *see* Askew, Richard Robinson.
Askew, Richard Robinson.
  xAskew, R. R.
    Parasitic Insects. Elsevier.
Askin, A. Bradley.
  xAskin, A. Bradley.
    Econometric Dimensions of Energy Demand &
    Supply. Lexington Bks.
    ed. How Energy Affects the Economy.
    Lexington Bks.
Askwith, George R. *see* Askwith, George Ranken
  Askwith.
Askwith, George Ranken Askwith, Baron, 1861-1942
  xAskwith, George R.
    Industrial Problems & Disputes. Arno.
Asmussen, Patricia D.
  xAsmussen, Patricia D.

Simplified Recipes for Day Care Centers. CBI
Pub.

Asopa, D. N.
xAsopa, D. N.
Political System of West Germany: A Study in
Party Politics & Parliamentary Process. Intl
Pubns Serv.

Aspaturian, Vernon V.
xAspaturian, Vernon V.
Soviet Union in the World Communist System.
Hoover Inst Pr.

**Aspen Systems Corporation. Center for Compliance
Information.**
xCenter for Compliance Information.
Noise Control in the Workplace. Aspen
Systems.
xTheCenter for Compliance Information.
The Energy Sourcebook. Aspen Systems.

Aspin, Isabel S. *see* Aspin, Isabel Stewart Todt.

Aspin, Isabel Stewart Todt.
xAspin, Isabel S.
ed. Anglo-Norman Political Songs. Johnson
Repr.

Aspinall, Arthur, 1901-
xAspinall, Arthur.
Lord Brougham & the Whig Party. Shoe String.

Aspinall, D.
xAspinall, David.
ed. Introduction to Microprocessors. Acad Pr.

Aspinall, David. *see* Aspinall, D.

Aspland, Clifford W.
xAspland, Clifford W.
ed. A Medieval French Reader. Oxford U Pr.

Asplund, Uno.
xAsplund, Uno.
Chaplin's Films. A S Barnes.

Asprey, Robert B.
xAsprey, Robert B.
The First Battle of the Marne. Greenwood.

Asprin, Robert.
xAsprin, Robert.
Another Fine Myth. Donning Co.
The Bug Wars. Dell.
The Bug Wars. St Martin.
The Cold Cash War. Dell.
The Cold Cash War. St Martin.
Myth Conceptions. Donning Co.

Asquith, Annunziata.
xAsquith, Annunziata.
Marie Antoinette. Taplinger.

Asquith, Cynthia. *see* Asquith, Cynthia Mary Evelyn
(Charteris).

Asquith, Cynthia M. *see* Asquith, Cynthia Mary Evelyn
(Charteris).

**Asquith, Cynthia Mary Evelyn (Charteris), Lady,
1887-1960**
xAsquith, Cynthia.
Married to Tolstoy. Dufour.
Portrait of Barrie. Greenwood.
Portrait of Barrie. R West.
xAsquith, Cynthia M.
Married to Tolstoy. Greenwood.

Asquith, George. *see* Asquith, George B.

Asquith, George B.
xAsquith, George.
Log Analysis by Microcomputer. Pennwell Pub.

Asquith, Glenn H.
xAsquith, Glenn H.
Church Officers at Work. Judson.
Footprints in the Sand. Judson.
Living Creatively As an Older Adult. Herald
Pr.
Preaching According to Plan. Judson.

Asquith, Peter.
xAsquith, Peter.
Immunology of the Gastrointestinal Tract.
Churchill.

Asquith, R. S. *see* Asquith, Raymond Smith.

Asquith, Raymond Smith, 1925-
xAsquith, R. S.

ed. Chemistry of Natural Protein Fibers.
Plenum Pub.

Assaf, Karen.
xAssaf, Karen.
Handbook of Mathematical Calculations: For
Science Students & Researchers. Iowa St U
Pr.

Assagioli, Roberto, 1888-
xAssagioli, Roberto.
Act of Will. Penguin.

Assali, Nicholas S.
xAssali, Nicholas S.
A Doctor's Life. HarBraceJ.

Assefi, Touraj, 1941-
xAssefi, Touraj.
Stochastic Processes & Estimation Theory with
Applications. Wiley.

Asselin, E. Donald.
xAsselin, E. Donald.
Scandinavian Cookbook. Univ Microfilms.

Asselineau, Jean.
xAsselineau, Jean.
The Bacterial Lipids. Intl Pubns Serv.

Asselineau, Roger.
xAsselineau, Roger.
ed. The Literary Reputation of Hemingway in
Europe. NYU Pr.

Assembly of Life Sciences, National Research Council.
see National Research Council. Committee on
Orthodontic Conditions.

Assembly on University Goals & Governance. *see*
Assembly on University Goals and Governance.

Assembly on University Goals and Governance.
xAssembly on University Goals & Governance.
The Students Themselves. Schenkman.

Assenheim, Harry M. *see* Assenheim, Harry Michael.

Assenheim, Harry Michael.
xAssenheim, Harry M.
Introduction to Electron Spin Resonance.
Plenum Pub.

Assimakopoulos, Pat.
xAssimakopoulos, Pat.
Both Feet in the Water. Christian Herald.

Assistant Masters Association. *see* Assistant Masters'
Association.

Assistant Masters' Association.
xAssistant Masters Association.
Teaching of Mathematics in Secondary
Schools. Cambridge U Pr.

Assmann, Hugo, 1933-
xAssmann, Hugo.
A Theology for a Nomad Church. Orbis Bks.

Assn. of Commonwealth Universities. *see* The
Association of Commonwealth Universities.

Associated Councils of the Arts.
xAssociated Councils of the Arts.
The Visual Artist & the Law. Praeger.

Associated Press.
xAssociated Press.
The Associated Press Stylebook. Lorenz Pr.
One Hundred One Select Dream Houses.
Hammond Inc.
The World in Nineteen Seventy-Five: History
As We Lived It. Watts.
The World in Nineteen-Seventy Seven. Watts.
The World in Nineteen Seventy-Six: History
As We Lived It. Watts.
The World in 1971: History As We Lived It.
Watts.

Association for Asian Studies.
xAssociation For Asian Studies.
Cumulative Bibliography of Asian Studies,
1941-1965, Author Bibliography. G K Hall.
Cumulative Bibliography of Asian Studies,
1941-1965, Subject Bibliography. G K Hall.

Association for Childhood Education International.
xAssociation for Childhood Education
International.

And Everywhere, Children!. Greenwillow.
Sung Under the Silver Umbrella. Macmillan.
Told Under the Blue Umbrella. Macmillan.
Told Under the Christmas Tree. Macmillan.
Told Under the Green Umbrella. Macmillan.
Told Under the Magic Umbrella. Macmillan.
Told Under the Stars & Stripes. Macmillan.
Toward Self-Discipline: Guide for Parents &
Teachers. ACEI.

**Association for Counselor Education and Supervision.
Experimental Design Committee.**
xExperimental Designs Committee of the
Association for Counselor Education and
Supervision.
Research Guidelines for High School
Counselors. College Bd.

**Association for Educational Communications and
Technology.**
xAssociation for Educational Communications &
Technology & Association of Media Producers.
Copyright & Educational Media: A Guide to
Fair Use & Permissions Procedures. Assn Ed
Comm Tech.

**Association for Educational Communications and
Technology. Task Force on Definition and
Terminology.**
xAssociation for Educational Communications &
Technology. Task Force on Definition &
Terminology.
The Definition of Educational Technology.
Assn Ed Comm Tech.
Educational Technology: A Glossary of Terms.
Assn Ed Comm Tech.

**Association for Latin American Studies. Midwest
Council.**
xMidwest Council Association For Latin America -
1967.
Human Resources in Latin America, an
International Focus: Proceedings. Ind U Busn
Res.

**Association for Programmed Learning and Education
Technology.**
xAssociation for Programmed Learning &
Educational Technology.
Aspects of Educational Technology X:
Individualized Learning: Proceedings. Nichols
Pub.
Aspects of Educational Technology XII:
Educational Technology in a Changing
World. Nichols Pub.

Association for Recorded Sound Collections.
xAssociation For Recorded Sound Collections.
Preliminary Directory of Sound Recordings
Collections in the United States & Canada.
NY Pub Lib.

Association for Research & Enlightenment, Inc. Virginia
Beach, Va. Study Groups. *see* Association for
Research and Enlightenment, Virginia Beach, Va.

**Association for Research and Enlightenment, Virginia
Beach, Va.**
xAssociation for Research & Enlightenment, Inc.
Virginia Beach, Va. Study Groups.
ed. Search for God. ARE Pr.

**Association for Research in Nervous and Mental
Disease.**
xAssociation For Research In Nervous And
Mental Disease.

Biology of the Major Psychoses: A
Comparative Analysis. Raven.
Brain Dysfunction in Metabolic Disorders.
Raven.
The Circulation of the Brain & Spinal Cord.
Hafner.
Disorders of Communication: Proceedings.
Hafner.
Effect of Pharmacologic Agents on the
Nervous System: Proceedings. Hafner.
Hypothalamus & Central Levels of Autonomic
Function: Proceedings. Hafner.
Neuromuscular Disorders: Proceedings. Hafner.
Association for Science Education.
xAssociation For Science Education.
Science Masters' Book, Ser. 2 Pt. 2: Chemistry
& Biology. Transatlantic.
Science Masters' Book, Ser. 3, Pt. 4:
Experiments for Modern Schools.
Transatlantic.
Science Masters' Book, Ser. 4, Pt. 3: Biology.
Transatlantic.
Teaching of Science in Secondary Schools.
Transatlantic.
Teaching Science at the Secondary Stage.
Transatlantic.
Association for Supervision & Curriculum Development.
see Association for Supervision and Curriculum
Development.
**Association for Supervision and Curriculum
Development.**
xAssociation for Supervision & Curriculum
Development.
Changing Curriculum: Mathematics. Assn
Supervision.
xAssociation For Supervision And Curriculum
Development.
Discipline for Today's Children & Youth. Assn
Supervision.
Evaluation As Feedback & Guide. Assn
Supervision.
Freeing Capacity to Learn. Assn Supervision.
Humanities & the Curriculum. Assn
Supervision.
Improving Educational Assessment & an
Inventory of Measures of Affective Behavior.
Assn Supervision.
International Dimension of Education. Assn
Supervision.
Interpreting Language Arts Research for the
Teacher. Assn Supervision.
Learning & Mental Health in the School. Assn
Supervision.
Life Skills in School & Society. Assn
Supervision.
Linguistics & the Classroom Teacher. Assn
Supervision.
Supervision: Emerging Profession. Assn
Supervision.
Supervision: Perspectives & Propositions. Assn
Supervision.
**Association for Supervision and Curriculum
Development. Yearbook Committee.**
xHenderson, George.
Education for Peace: Focus on Mankind. Assn
Supervision.
Association for the Improvement of the Conditions of the
Poor. *see* Baltimore Association for the Improvement
of the Condition of the Poor.
Association of American Colleges.
xAssociation of American Colleges.
Reflections on the Role of Liberal Education.
ACE.
**Association of American Colleges. Commission on
International Understanding.**
xAssociation Of American Colleges Commission
On International Understanding.

Non-Western Studies in the Liberal Arts
College. ACE.
Association of American Geographers.
xAAG Consulting Panel, 1974.
Self-Study Data Forms. Assn Am Geographers.
xAAG Consulting Services Panel.
Suggestions for Self-Evaluation of Geography
Programs. Assn Am Geographers.
Association Of American Law School. *see* Association of
American Law Schools.
Association of American Law Schools.
xAssociation Of American Law School.
Law Books Recommended for Libraries.
Rothman.
xAssociation of American Law Schools.
Selected Essays in Anglo-American Legal
History 1907-09. Oceana.
Association of American University Presses.
xAssociation of American University Presses.
ed. One Book-Five Ways: The Publishing
Procedures of Five University Presses. W
Kaufmann.
Association of Clinical Scientists.
xAssociation Of Clinical Scientists.
Measurements of Exocrine & Endocrine
Functions of the Pancreas: With a Section on
Fibrocystic Disease. Lippincott.
Association of College & Research Libraries. *see*
Association of College and Research Libraries.
Association of College and Research Libraries.
xAssociation of College & Research Libraries.
Books for College Libraries. ALA.
Association of Commonwealth Universities. *see* The
Association of Commonwealth Universities.
The Association of Commonwealth Universities.
xAssn. of Commonwealth Universities.
ed. Awards for Commonwealth University
Staff, 1978-80. Intl Pubns Serv.
xAssociation of Commonwealth Universities.
The Compendium of University Entrance
Requirements: For First Degree Courses in
the United Kingdom 1980-81. Intl Pubns
Serv.
xAssociation of Commonwealth Universities.
Schedule of Postgraduate Courses in United
Kingdom Universities, 1979-1980. Intl Pubns
Serv.
Scholarships Guide for Commonwealth
Postgraduate Students, 1980-82. Intl Pubns
Serv.
xBritish Council & the Assn. of Commonwealth
Universities.
Higher Education in the United Kingdom
1978-80. Longman.
Association of Hospital & Institutional Libraries. *see*
Association of Hospital and Institution Libraries.
Association of Hospital and Institution Libraries.
xAssociation of Hospital & Institutional Libraries.
Standards for Library Services in Health Care
Institutions. ALA.
Association of Operative Millers.
xAssociation of Operative Millers.
Cereal Miller's Handbook. AG Pr.
Technical Bulletins: 1944-1974. AG Pr.
Technical Bulletins: 1944-1975. AG Pr.
Association of Pacific Coast Geographers.
xAssociation of Pacific Coast Geographers.
Yearbook of the Association of Pacific Coast
Geographers: 1935-1978. Oreg St U Pr.
Association of Specialized & Cooperative Library
Agencies. *see* Association of Specialized and
Cooperative Library Agencies.
**Association of Specialized and Cooperative Library
Agencies.**
xAssociation of Specialized & Cooperative Library
Agencies.

Standards of Service for the Library of
Congress Network of Libraries for the Blind
& Physically Handicapped. ALA.
Association of Teachers of Mathematics.
xAssociation Of Teachers Of Mathematics.
Mathematical Reflections. Cambridge U Pr.
Notes on Mathematics for Children. Cambridge
U Pr.
**Association of Teachers of Social Studies in the City of
New York.**
xAssociation of Teachers of Social Studies in the
City of New York.
A Handbook for the Teaching of Social
Studies. Allyn.
Association of the Bar of the City of New York.
xAssociation Of The Bar Of The City Of N.Y.
Benjamin N. Cardozo Memorial Lectures.
Bender.
Mental Illness & Due Process: Report &
Recommendations on Admissions to Mental
Hospitals Under New York Law. Cornell U
Pr.
Opinions of the Committees on Professional
Ethics of the Association of the Bar of the
City of New York & the New York County
Lawyer's Association. Columbia U Pr.
ed. Professional Responsibility of the Lawyer:
The Murky Divide Between Right and
Wrong. Oceana.
xTheAssociation of the Bar of the City of New
York.
Report of the Special Committee on the
Federal Loyalty Security Program. Da Capo.
**Association of the Bar of the City of New York.
Committee on the Medical Expert Testimony Project.**
xSpecial Committee, New York City Bar
Association.
Mental Illness, Due Process & the Criminal
Defendant. Fordham.
Astaire, Fred.
xAstaire, Fred.
Steps in Time. Da Capo.
Astarita, G. *see* Astarita, Giovanni.
Astarita, Giovanni.
xAstarita, G.
Principles of Non-Newtonian Fluid Mechanics.
McGraw.
Asten, K. J.
xAsten, Kenneth J.
Data Communications for Business Information
Systems. Macmillan.
Asten, Kenneth J. *see* Asten, K. J.
Aster, Sidney, 1942-
xAster, Sidney.
Anthony Eden. St Martin.
Astin, A. E.
xAstin, Alan E.
Cato the Censor. Oxford U Pr.
Astin, Alan E. *see* Astin, A. E.
Astin, Alexander W.
xAstin, Alexander W.
Academic Gamesmanship: Student-Oriented
Change in Higher Education. Praeger.
College Environment. ACE.
Maximizing Leadership Effectiveness: Impact
of Administrative Style on Faculty &
Students. Jossey-Bass.
Astiz, Carlos A. *see* Astiz, Carlos Alberto.
Astiz, Carlos Alberto.
xAstiz, Carlos A.
ed. Latin American International Politics:
Ambitions, Capabilities & the National
Interests of Mexico, Brazil & Argentina. U of
Notre Dame Pr.
Aston, Athina.
xAston, Athina.
How to Play with Your Baby. Fountain Pub Co
NY.
Aston, Margaret.
xAston, Margaret.

The Fifteenth Century: The Prospect of
  Europe. HarBraceJ.
The Fifteenth Century: The Prospect of
  Europe. Norton.
Aston, W. G. see Aston, William George.
Aston, William George, 1841-1911
  xAston, W. G.
    History of Japanese Literature. C E Tuttle.
    History of Japanese Literature. Johnson Repr.
    A History of Japanese Literature. Krishna Pr.
Astro, Richard.
  xAstro, Richard.
    Edward F. Ricketts. Boise St Univ.
Astroff, Milton T.
  xAstroff, Milton T.
    Convention Sales & Services. Wm C Brown.
Astrom, K. J. see Astrom, Karl Johan.
Astrom, Karl Johan, 1934-
  xAstrom, K. J.
    Introduction to Stochastic Control Theory.
      Acad Pr.
Astrop, John.
  xAstrop, John.
    illus. The Jumbo Book of Board Games.
      Elsevier-Nelson.
Astrup, Christian.
  xAstrup, Christian.
    The Chronic Schizophrenias. Universitet.
Asturias, Miguel A. see Asturias, Miguel Angel.
Asturias, Miguel Angel.
  xAsturias, Miguel A.
    Strong Wind. Dell.
Astwood, Edwin B.
  xAstwood, Edwin B.
    ed. Clinical Endocrinology. Grune.
Aswad, Barbara C.
  xAswad, Barbara C.
    Arabic Speaking Communities in American
      Cities. Ctr Migration.
Aswell, James R., 1911-
  xAswell, James R.
    ed. Native American Humor. Arno.
Atal, Yogesh.
  xAtal, Yogesh.
    Local Communities & National Politics: A
      Study in Communication Links & Political
      Involvement. Intl Pubns Serv.
    Local Communities & National Politics: A
      Study in Communication Links & Political
      Involvement. Verry.
Atassi, M. Z.
  xAtassi, M. Z.
    ed. Immunochemistry of Proteins. Plenum Pub.
Ataya, Chafic.
  xAtaya, Chafic.
    The Earth Woman. Libra.
Atchison, Thomas J.
  xAtchison, Thomas J.
    Management Today: Managing Work in
      Organizations. HarBraceJ.
Atchity, John Kenneth.
  xAtchity, Kenneth J.
    Homer's Iliad: The Shield of Memory. S Ill U
      Pr.
Atchity, Kenneth J. see Atchity, John Kenneth.
Atchley, Robert C.
  xAtchley, Robert C.
    Social Forces in Later Life: An Introduction to
      Social Gerontology. Wadsworth Pub.
Athans, Greg.
  xAthans, Greg.
    Ski Free. Dutton.
Athay, R. G. see Athay, R. Grant.
Athay, R. Grant.
  xAthay, R. G.
    The Solar Chromosphere & Corona: Quiet Sun.
      Kluwer Boston.
Athearn, James L.
  xAthearn, James L.

General Insurance Agency Management. Irwin.
Athearn, Robert G.
  xAthearn, Robert G.
    The Coloradans. U of NM Pr.
    The Denver & Rio Grande Western Railroad:
      Rebel of the Rockies. U of Nebr Pr.
    In Search of Canaan: Black Migration to
      Kansas, 1879-80. Regents Pr KS.
    Thomas Francis Meagher: An Irish
      Revolutionary in America. Arno.
Athenagoras.
  xAthenagoras.
    Legatio & De Resurrectione. Oxford U Pr.
Atherton, D. P.
  xAtherton, D. P.
    Nonlinear Control Engineering. Van Nos
      Reinhold.
Atherton, Gertrude. see Atherton, Gertrude Franklin
  (Horn).
Atherton, Gertrude F. see Atherton, Gertrude Franklin
  (Horn).
Atherton, Gertrude Franklin (Horn), 1857-1948
  xAtherton, Gertrude.
    California: An Intimate History. Arno.
    California: An Intimate History. Norwood
      Edns.
    The Californians. Folcroft.
  xAtherton, Gertrude F.
    The Californians. Irvington.
    Can Women Be Gentlemen?. Arno.
    Patience Sparhawk. Irvington.
    Rezanov. Irvington.
Atherton, Henry V.
  xAtherton, Henry V.
    Chemistry & Testing of Dairy Products. AVI.
Atherton, J. S. see Atherton, James S.
Atherton, James S.
  xAtherton, J. S.
    The Books at the Wake: A Study of Literary
      Allusions in James Joyce's "Finnegans
      Wake". Appel.
  xAtherton, James S.
    The Books at the Wake: A Study of Literary
      Allusions in James Joyce's "Finnegans
      Wake". S Ill U Pr.
Atherton, John. see Atherton, John C.
Atherton, John C., 1900-1952
  xAtherton, John.
    The Fly & the Fish. Freshet Pr.
Atherton, Lewis. see Atherton, Lewis Eldon.
Atherton, Lewis E. see Atherton, Lewis Eldon.
Atherton, Lewis Eldon.
  xAtherton, Lewis.
    Cattle Kings. Ind U Pr.
    The Cattle Kings. U of Nebr Pr.
  xAtherton, Lewis E.
    Frontier Merchant in Mid-America. U of Mo
      Pr.
    Southern Country Store, 1800-1860.
      Greenwood.
Atherton, Pauline.
  xAtherton, Pauline.
    Librarians & Online Services. Knowledge
      Indus.
Atherton, Wallace N.
  xAtherton, Wallace N.
    Theory of Union Bargaining Goals. Princeton
      U Pr.
Athey, I. J. see Athey, Irene J.
Athey, Irene J.
  xAthey, I. J.
    Educational Implications of Piaget's Theory.
      Wiley.
Athey, Margaret.
  xAthey, Margaret.
    A Galaxy of Games for the Music Class. P-H.
Athletes in Action. see Athletes in Action (Basketball
  Team).
Athletes in Action (Basketball Team).
  xAthletes in Action.

One Way to Play Basketball. Beta Bk.
Athreya, Balu H.
  xAthreya, Balu H.
    Clinical Methods in Pediatric Diagnosis. Van
      Nos Reinhold.
Athreya, K. B. see Athreya, Krishna B.
Athreya, Krishna B.
  xAthreya, K. B.
    Branching Processes. Springer-Verlag.
Atiya, Aziz S. see Atiya, Aziz Suryal.
Atiya, Aziz Suryal, 1898-
  xAtiya, Aziz S.
    The Crusade: Historiography & Bibliography.
      Greenwood.
    Crusade in the Later Middle Ages. Kraus Repr.
    The Crusade of Nicopolis. AMS Pr.
Atiyah, Edward. see Atiyah, Edward Selim.
Atiyah, Edward Selim, 1903-
  xAtiyah, Edward.
    The Arabs. Intl Bk Ctr.
Atiyah, Michael F. see Atiyah, Michael Francis.
Atiyah, Michael Francis.
  xAtiyah, Michael F.
    Introduction to Commutative Algebra. A-W.
Atkeson, Ray.
  xAtkeson, Ray.
    photos by The Oregon Coast. Graphic Arts
      Ctr.
    photos by Oregon II. Graphic Arts Ctr.
    Portrait of Oregon. Graphic Arts Ctr.
Atkin, Edith. see Atkin, Edith Lesser.
Atkin, Edith Lesser.
  xAtkin, Edith.
    Part-Time Father. Vanguard.
Atkin, John Michael.
  xAtkin, John Michael.
    British Overseas Investment: 1918-1931. Arno.
Atkin, Mary G. see Atkin, Mary Gage.
Atkin, Mary Gage.
  xAtkin, Mary G.
    Paul Cuffe & the African Promised Land.
      Elsevier-Nelson.
Atkin, N. B. see Atkin, Niels Bentzen.
Atkin, Niels Bentzen.
  xAtkin, N. B.
    Cytogenetic Aspects of Malignant
      Transformation. S Karger.
Atkin, William W. see Atkin, William Wilson.
Atkin, William Wilson.
  xAtkin, William W.
    Architectural Presentation Techniques. Van
      Nos Reinhold.
Atkins. see Atkins, Harold N.
Atkins, B. see Atkins, Burton M.
Atkins, Burton M.
  xAtkins, B.
    ed. Prisons, Protest & Politics. P-H.
Atkins, Frederick C. see Atkins, Frederick Charles.
Atkins, Frederick Charles, 1912-
  xAtkins, Frederick C.
    Mushroom Growing To-Day. Macmillan.
Atkins, G. Pope, 1934-
  xAtkins, G. Pope.
    Latin America in the International Political
      System. Free Pr.
Atkins, Harold N.
  xAtkins:
    Highway Materials, Soils & Concretes. Reston.
Atkins, J. W. see Atkins, John William Hey.
Atkins, John. see Atkins, John Alfred.
Atkins, John Alfred, 1916-
  xAtkins, John.
    Graham Greene. Arden Lib.
    Graham Greene. Humanities.
    Graham Greene. R West.
Atkins, John W. see Atkins, John William Hey.
Atkins, John William Hey, 1874-
  xAtkins, J. W.

Literary Criticism in Antiquity: A Sketch of Its
Development. Arden Lib.
xAtkins, John W.
English Literary Criticism: The Medieval
Phase. Peter Smith.
Atkins, Kenneth R. see Atkins, Kenneth Robert.
Atkins, Kenneth Robert.
xAtkins, Kenneth R.
Essentials of Physical Science. Wiley.
Atkins, M. H.
xAtkins, M. H.
Economics of Pollution Control in the
Non-Ferrous Metals Industry. Pergamon.
Pollution Control Costs in Industry: An
Economic Study. Pergamon.
Atkins, Michael D.
xAtkins, Michael D.
Introduction to Insect Behavior. Macmillan.
Atkins, P. W. see Atkins, Peter William.
Atkins, Peter William.
xAtkins, P. W.
Quanta: A Handbook of Concepts. Oxford U
Pr.
Atkins, Robert.
xAtkins, Robert.
Specialty Board Review: Psychiatry. Arco.
Atkins, Ruth.
xAtkins, Ruth.
The Government of the Australian Capital
Territory. U of Queensland Pr.
Atkins, Ruth E. see Atkins, Ruth Ellen.
Atkins, Ruth Ellen, 1885-
xAtkins, Ruth E.
The Measurement of the Intelligence of Young
Children by an Object-Fitting Test.
Greenwood.
Atkins, Susan.
xAtkins, Susan.
Child of Satan, Child of God. Bantam.
Child of Satan, Child of God. Logos.
Atkins, Thomas R., 1939-
xAtkins, Thomas R.
Frederick Wiseman. Monarch Pr.
Graphic Violence on the Screen. Monarch Pr.
Atkinson, A. B. see Atkinson, Anthony Barnes.
Atkinson, Anthony B. see Atkinson, Anthony Barnes.
Atkinson, Anthony Barnes.
xAtkinson, A. B.
Distribution of Personal Wealth in Britain.
Cambridge U Pr.
The Economics of Inequality. Oxford U Pr.
ed. Personal Distribution of Incomes. Allen
Unwin.
Poverty in Britain & the Reform of Social
Security. Cambridge U Pr.
xAtkinson, Anthony B.
ed. The Personal Distribution of Incomes.
Westview.
Atkinson, Betty J.
xAtkinson, Betty J.
The Medical Assistant: Clinical Practice.
Delmar.
Atkinson, Brooks. see Atkinson, Justin Brooks.
Atkinson, Christopher T. see Atkinson, Christopher
Thomas.
Atkinson, Christopher Thomas.
xAtkinson, Christopher T.
A History of Germany, 1715-1815.
Greenwood.
Atkinson, David, 1932-
xAtkinson, David.
Menu French. Pergamon.
Atkinson, Donald R.
xAtkinson, Donald R.
Counseling American Minorities: A
Cross-Cultural Perspective. Wm C Brown.
Atkinson, F. V.
xAtkinson, F. V.

Discrete & Continuous Boundary Problems.
Acad Pr.
Atkinson, Gary.
xAtkinson, Gary M.
A Moral Evaluation of Contraception &
Sterilization: A Dialogical Study. Pope John
Ctr.
Atkinson, Gary M. see Atkinson, Gary.
Atkinson, Geoffroy, 1892-1960
xAtkinson, Geoffroy.
Extraordinary Voyage in French Literature
Before 1700. AMS Pr.
Atkinson, I. see Atkinson, Ian.
Atkinson, Ian, 1936-
xAtkinson, I.
The Viking Ships. Cambridge U Pr.
xAtkinson, Ian.
The Viking Ships. Lerner Pubns.
Atkinson, J. Brooks. see Atkinson, Justin Brooks.
Atkinson, J. Maxwell. see Atkinson, John Maxwell.
Atkinson, J. W. see Atkinson, John William.
Atkinson, James, 1794-1834
xAtkinson, James.
An Account of the State of Agriculture &
Grazing in New South Wales. Intl Schol Bk
Serv.
Atkinson, Jennifer M. see Atkinson, Jennifer McCabe.
Atkinson, Jennifer McCabe, 1937-
xAtkinson, Jennifer M.
Eugene O'Neill: A Descriptive Bibliography. U
of Pittsburgh Pr.
Atkinson, John Maxwell.
xAtkinson, J. Maxwell.
Discovering Suicide: Studies in the Social
Organization of Sudden Death. U of
Pittsburgh Pr.
Atkinson, John W. see Atkinson, John William.
Atkinson, John William, 1923-
xAtkinson, J. W.
ed. Theory of Achievement Motivation.
Krieger.
xAtkinson, John W.
Introduction to Motivation. D Van Nostrand.
Atkinson, Julia, 1915-
xAtkinson, Julia.
Eleven Out of Twelve: A Bibliography.
Independence Unltd.
Atkinson, Justin Brooks, 1894-
xAtkinson, Brooks.
Broadway. Macmillan.
New England's White Mountains: At Home in
the Wild. NYGS.
xAtkinson, J. Brooks.
Broadway Scrapbook. Greenwood.
Atkinson, Kendall E.
xAtkinson, Kendall E.
An Introduction to Numerical Analysis. Wiley.
A Survey of Numerical Methods for the
Solution of Fredholm Integral Equations of
the Second Kind. Soc Indus-Appl Math.
Atkinson, Leslie D.
xAtkinson, Leslie D.
Nursing Process: What It Is & How It Is Used.
Macmillan.
Atkinson, Linda.
xAtkinson, Linda.
Alternatives to College. Watts.
Psychic Stories Strange but True. Watts.
Atkinson, R. C. see Atkinson, Raymond Cumings.
Atkinson, Raymond C. see Atkinson, Raymond Cumings.
Atkinson, Raymond Cumings, 1895-
xAtkinson, R. C.
The Federal Role in Unemployment
Compensation Administration: A Report
Prepared for the Committee on Social
Security. Arno.
xAtkinson, Raymond C.

Public Employment Service in the United
States. Arno.
Atkinson, Richard C.
xAtkinson, Richard C.
ed. Studies in Mathematical Psychology.
Stanford U Pr.
Atkinson, Ron.
xAtkinson, Ron.
Looking for My Name. Bookstore Pr.
Atkinson, Sallyanne, 1942-
xAtkinson, Sallyanne.
Around Brisbane: Including Gold Coast,
Sunshine Coast & Toowoomba. U of
Queensland Pr.
Atkinson, Thomas W. see Atkinson, Thomas Witlam.
Atkinson, Thomas Witlam, 1799-1861
xAtkinson, Thomas W.
Oriental & Western Siberia: A Narrative of
Seven Years' Explorations & Adventures in
Siberia, Mongolia, the Kirghissteppes,
Chinese Tartary & Part of Central Asia.
Arno.
Atkyns, Robert.
xAtkyns, Robert.
Ancient & Present State of Glostershire.
Rowman.
Atlanta Historical Society.
xAtlanta Historical Society.
Thirty-Two Picture Postcards of Old Atlanta.
Dover.
Atlanta University.
xAtlanta University.
Atlanta University Publications. Arno.
Atlantic Council. see Atlantic Council of the United
States.
Atlantic Council of the United States.
xAtlantic Council.
Nuclear Fuels Policy: Report of the Atlantic
Council's Nuclear Fuels Policy Working
Group. Lexington Bks.
xAtlantic Council of the United States.
GATT Plus-A Proposal for Trade Reform:
With the Text of the General Agreement.
Praeger.
Nuclear Fuels Policy: Report of the Atlantic
Council's Nuclear Fuels Policy Working
Group. Westview.
Atlas Corporation.
xAtlas Corporation.
ed. Proceedings of the Workshop on Economic
& Operational Requirements & Status of
Large Scale Wind Systems. Solar Energy
Info.
Atlas, James.
xAtlas, James.
Delmore Schwartz: The Life of an American
Poet. Avon.
Delmore Schwartz: The Life of an American
Poet. FS&G.
Atta, Winfred Van. see Van Atta, Winfred.
Attaway, William.
xAttaway, William.
Let Me Breathe Thunder. Chatham Bkseller.
Atteberry, Pat H. see Atteberry, Pat Herman.
Atteberry, Pat Herman, 1909-
xAtteberry, Pat H.
Power Mechanics. Goodheart.
Atteberry, William.
xAtteberry, William.
Modern Real Estate Finance. Grid Pub.
xAtteberry, William L.
Real Estate Law. Grid Pub.
Atteberry, William L. see Atteberry, William.
Attenberger, Walburga.
xAttenberger, Walburga.
The Little Man in Winter. Random.
Attenborough, Bessie M.
xAttenborough, Bessie M.

Craft of Tatting. Branford.
Atterbury, Paul.
    xAtterbury, Paul.
        ed. Antiques: An Encyclopedia of the
        Decorative Arts. Mayflower Bks.
Atthill, William L. *see* Atthill, William Lombe.
Atthill, William Lombe, 1807-1884
    xAtthill, William L.
        ed. Documents Relating to the Foundation &
        Antiquities of the Collegiate Church of
        Middleham, County of York. Johnson Repr.
Attia, Rafik. *see* Attia, Rafik R.
Attia, Rafik R.
    xAttia, Rafik.
        ed. Practical Anesthetic Pharmacology. ACC.
Attinger, E. O. *see* Attinger, Ernst O.
Attinger, Ernst O.
    xAttinger, E. O.
        Global Systems Dynamics. Halsted Pr.
Attitude Research Conference.
    xAttitude Research Conference, October, 1974,
        San Francisco.
        Attitude Research at Bay: Proceedings. Am
        Mktg.
Attitude Research Conference, October, 1974, San
    Francisco. *see* Attitude Research Conference.
Attoe, Wayne.
    xAttoe, Wayne.
        Architecture & Critical Imagination. Wiley.
Attwater, Donald, 1892-
    xAttwater, Donald.
        Penguin Dictionary of Saints. Penguin.
Attwood, Stanley B. *see* Attwood, Stanley Bearce.
Attwood, Stanley Bearce.
    xAttwood, Stanley B.
        Length & Breadth of Maine. U Maine Orono.
Atwan, Robert.
    xAtwan, Robert.
        American Mass Media: Industries & Issues.
        Random.
Atwater, Constance.
    xAtwater, Constance.
        Tap Dancing: Techniques, Routines,
        Terminology. C E Tuttle.
Atwater, Elton, 1912-
    xAtwater, Elton.
        American Regulation of Arms Exports.
        Johnson Repr.
Atwater, H. A. *see* Atwater, Harry Albert.
Atwater, Harry Albert, 1921-
    xAtwater, H. A.
        Introduction to General Relativity. Pergamon.
Atwater, James D., 1928-
    xAtwater, James D.
        Time Bomb. G K Hall.
        Time Bomb. Penguin.
Atwater, Mary M. *see* Atwater, Mary Meigs.
Atwater, Mary Meigs, 1878-
    xAtwater, Mary M.
        Byways in Handweaving. Macmillan.
Atwater, Maxine.
    xAtwater, Maxine.
        The Natural Foods Cookbook. Nitty Gritty.
Atwater, Montgomery. *see* Atwater, Montgomery Meigs.
Atwater, Montgomery Meigs.
    xAtwater, Montgomery.
        Avalanche Hunters. Macrae.
Atwell, Lee, 1941-
    xAtwell, Lee.
        G. W. Pabst. Twayne.
Atwood, Ann.
    xAtwood, Ann.
        illus. Little Circle. Scribner.
Atwood, E. Bagby. *see* Atwood, Elmer Bagby.
Atwood, Elmer Bagby, 1906-
    xAtwood, E. Bagby.
        The Regional Vocabulary of Texas. U of Tex
        Pr.
Atwood, Evangeline.
    xAtwood, Evangeline.

Frontier Politics: Alaska's James Wickersham.
        Binford.
Atwood, Jerry W.
    xAtwood, Jerry W.
        The Systems Analyst: How to Design
        Computer-Based Systems. Hayden.
Atwood, Margaret. *see* Atwood, Margaret Eleanor.
Atwood, Margaret Eleanor, 1939-
    xAtwood, Margaret.
        Life Before Man. S&S.
        Power Politics. U of Toronto Pr.
        Surfacing. Popular Lib.
        Surfacing. S&S.
Atwood, Mary A. *see* Atwood, Mary Anne South.
Atwood, Mary Anne. *see* Atwood, Mary Anne South.
Atwood, Mary Anne South, 1817-1910
    xAtwood, Mary A.
        A Suggestive Inquiry into the Hermetic
        Mystery. Arno.
    xAtwood, Mary Anne.
        A Suggestive Inquiry into the Hermetic
        Mystery. Yoga.
Atyeo, Henry C. *see* Atyeo, Henry Clay.
Atyeo, Henry Clay, 1905-
    xAtyeo, Henry C.
        The Excursion As a Teaching Technique. AMS
        Pr.
Aubert, Charles, 1851-
    xAubert, Charles.
        Art of Pantomime. Arno.
Aubert, Marcel, 1884-1962
    xAubert, Marcel.
        French Sculpture at the Beginning of the
        Gothic Period, 1140-1225. Hacker.
Aubert, Roger.
    xAubert, Roger.
        Prophets in the Church. Paulist Pr.
Aubignac, Francois H. *see* Aubignac, Francois Hedelin.
Aubignac, Francois Hedelin, Abbe D', 1604-1676
    xAubignac, Francois H.
        The Whole Art of the Stage. Arno.
Aubin, Jean-Pierre.
    xAubin, Jean-Pierre.
        Applied Abstract Analysis. Wiley.
        Applied Functional Analysis. Wiley.
        Approximation of Elliptic Boundary-Value
        Problems. Krieger.
Auboyer, Jeannine.
    xAuboyer, Jeannine.
        Oriental Art: A Handbook of Styles & Forms.
        Rizzoli Intl.
Aubrey, Frank.
    xAubrey, Frank.
        A Queen of Atlantis: Romance of the
        Caribbean Sea. Arno.
Aubrey, Henry G.
    xAubrey, Henry G.
        Coexistence: Economic Challenge & Response.
        Greenwood.
Aubrey, John, 1626-1697
    xAubrey, John.
        Natural History of Wiltshire. Kelley.
Aubrey, Philip.
    xAubrey, Philip.
        The Defeat of James Stuart's Armada, 1692.
        Rowman.
Aubry, Arthur S.
    xAubry, Arthur S.
        Criminal Interrogation. C C Thomas.
Aubry, Pierre.
    xAubry, Pierre.
        Trouveres & Troubadours: A Popular Treatise.
        Cooper Sq.
Aucamp, A. J. *see* Aucamp, Anna Jacoba.
Aucamp, Anna Jacoba, 1892-
    xAucamp, A. J.
        Bilingual Education & Nationalism with Special
        Reference to South Africa. Arno.
Auchincloss, Louis.
    xAuchincloss, Louis.

The Country Cousin. Ballantine.
        The Country Cousin. HM.
        The Dark Lady. Ballantine.
        The Dark Lady. HM.
        The House of the Prophet. HM.
        I Come As a Thief. HM.
        Law for the Lion. Queens Hse.
        Life, Law, & Letters: Essays & Sketches. HM.
        The Partners. HM.
        The Partners. Warner Bks.
        Persons of Consequence: Queen Victoria & Her
        Circle. Random.
        Pursuit of the Prodigal. Avon.
        Reading Henry James. U of Minn Pr.
        The Rector of Justin. HM.
        Reflections of a Jacobite. Kelley.
        Sybil. Greenwood.
        Writer's Capital. HM.
        A Writer's Capital. U of Minn Pr.
Auden. *see* Auden, Wystan Hugh.
Auden, W. H. *see* Auden, Wystan Hugh.
Auden, Wystan H. *see* Auden, Wystan Hugh.
Auden, Wystan Hugh, 1907-
    xAuden.
        Selected Poems. Merrimack Bk Serv.
    xAuden, W. H.
        Certain World: A Commonplace Book. Viking
        Pr.
        Collected Shorter Poems: 1927 to 1957.
        Random.
        Collected Shorter Poems 1927-1957. Random.
        The Double Man. Greenwood.
        The English Auden: Poems, Essays & Dramatic
        Writings. Random.
        Forewords & Afterwords. Random.
        Forewords & Afterwords. Random.
        Homage to Clio. Random.
        Journey to a War. Octagon.
        Letters from Iceland. Random.
        ed. The Oxford Book of Light Verse. Oxford U
        Pr.
        ed. Portable Greek Reader. Penguin.
        Selected Poems. Random.
        Thank You, Fog: Last Poems. Random.
    xAuden, Wystan H.
        The Orators: An English Study. Scholarly.
Audette, Larry.
    xAudette, Larry.
        Bjorn Borg. Music Sales.
Audit Bureau of Circulations.
    xAudit Bureau of Circulations.
        Scientific Space Selection. Arno.
Audouze, Jean.
    xAudouze, Jean.
        An Introduction to Nuclear Astrophysics: The
        Formation & Evolution of Matter in the
        Universe. Kluwer Boston.
Audretsch, H. *see* Audretsch, H. A. H.
Audretsch, H. A. H.
    xAudretsch, H.
        Supervision in European Community Law:
        Observance by the Member States of Their
        Treaty Obligations - a Treatise on
        International & Supranational Supervision.
        Elsevier.
Audubon, John J. *see* Audubon, John James.
Audubon, John James, 1785-1851
    xAudubon, John J.
        The Art of Audubon: The Complete Birds &
        Mammals. Times Bks.
        Audubon & His Journals. Arno.
        Audubon & His Journals. Peter Smith.
        The Quadrupeds of North America. Arno.
    xAudubon, Maria.
        ed. Audubon & His Journals. Peter Smith.
    xAudubon, Maria R.
        ed. Audubon & His Journals. Arno.
Audubon, Maria. *see* Audubon, John James.
Audubon, Maria R. *see* Audubon, John James.
Audubon Society. *see* National Audubon Society.

Audy, Robert.
   xAudy, Robert.
      Tap Dancing: How to Teach Yourself to Tap.
      Random.
Auer, J. Jeffery. *see* Auer, John Jeffery.
Auer, James E.
   xAuer, James E.
      The Postwar Rearmament of Japanese
        Maritime Forces 1945-1971. Irvington.
Auer, John J. *see* Auer, John Jeffery.
Auer, John Jeffery, 1913-
   xAuer, J. Jeffery.
      ed. On Teaching Speech in Elementary &
        Junior High Schools. Ind U Pr.
   xAuer, John J.
      An Introduction to Research in Speech.
        Greenwood.
Auer, Leopold, 1845-1930
   xAuer, Leopold.
      Violin Masterworks & Their Interpretation.
        Hyperion Conn.
      Violin Playing As I Teach It. Dover.
      Violin Playing As I Teach It. Greenwood.
Auerbach, Aline B. *see* Auerbach, Aline Sophie
   (Buchman).
Auerbach, Aline Sophie (Buchman).
   xAuerbach, Aline B.
      Parents Learn Through Discussion: Principles
        & Practices of Parent Group Education.
        Krieger.
Auerbach, Erich, 1892-1957
   xAuerbach, Erich.
      Literary Language & Its Public in Late Latin
        Antiquity & in the Middle Ages. Princeton U
        Pr.
Auerbach, Jerold S.
   xAuerbach, Jerold S.
      Unequal Justice: Lawyers & Social Change in
        Modern America. Oxford U Pr.
Auerbach, Nina, 1943
   xAuerbach, Nina.
      Communities of Women: An Idea in Fiction.
        Harvard U Pr.
Auerbach, Stevanne.
   xAuerbach, Stevanne.
      Confronting the Child Care Crisis. Beacon Pr.
Auf der Heide, Ralph.
   xAuf Der Heide, Ralph.
      The Illustrated Wine Making Book. Doubleday.
Aufmann, Richard N.
   xAufmann, Richard N.
      Arithmetic: An Applied Approach. HM.
Aufricht, Hans, 1902-
   xAufricht, Hans.
      ed. Central Banking Legislation: A Collection
        of Central Bank, Monetary & Banking Laws,
        Europe. Intl Monetary.
Augarde, Steve.
   xAugarde, Steve.
      Barnaby Shrew Goes to Sea. Andre Deutsch.
Augelli, John P.
   xAugelli, John P.
      Caribbean Lands. Fideler.
Auger, C. P. *see* Auger, Charles Peter.
Auger, Charles Peter.
   xAuger, C. P.
      Use of Reports in Literature. Butterworths.
Aughey, John H. *see* Aughey, John Hill.
Aughey, John Hill, 1828-1911
   xAughey, John H.
      Tupelo. Arno.
Augsburger, David N. *see* Augsburger, David W.
Augsburger, David W.
   xAugsburger, David N.
      Anger & Assertiveness in Pastoral Care.
        Fortress.
Augsburger, Myron. *see* Augsburger, Myron S.
Augsburger, Myron S.
   xAugsburger, Myron.

      Faithful Unto Death: Fifteen Young People
        Who Were Not Afraid to Die for Their
        Faith. Word Bks.
   xAugsburger, Myron S.
      Broken Chalice. Herald Pr.
      Quench Not the Spirit. Herald Pr.
      Quench Not the Spirit. Keats.
Augustine. *see* Augustine, Robert L.
Augustine, Robert L., 1932-
   xAugustine.
      Carbon-Carbon Bond Formation. Dekker.
Augustinos, Gerasimos.
   xAugustinos, Gerasimos.
      Consciousness & History: Nationalist Critics of
        Greek Society, 1897-1914. East Eur
        Quarterly.
Augustinus, Aurelius.
   xAugustinus, Aurelius.
      Liber Qvi Appellatvr Specvlvm et Liber De
        Divinis Scriptvris. Johnson Repr.
Augustithis, S. S.
   xAugustithis, S. S.
      Atlas of the Textural Patterns of Basalts &
        Their Genetic Significance. Elsevier.
      Atlas of the Textural Patterns of Basic &
        Ultrabasic Rocks & Their Genetic
        Significance. De Gruyter.
Aukee, Waino E.
   xAukee, Waino E.
      ed. Inside the Management Team. Interstate.
Aukema, Susan.
   xAukema, Susan.
      The Curity Baby Book: A Commonsense Guide
        to Baby Care. Dorison Hse.
Aukerman, Robert C., 1910-
   xAukerman, Robert C.
      Approaches to Beginning Reading. Wiley.
      Reading in the Secondary School Classroom.
        McGraw.
      ed. Some Persistent Questions on Beginning
        Reading. Intl Reading.
Aulard, Alphonse. *see* Aulard, Francois Victor Alphonse.
Aulard, Francois Victor Alphonse, 1849-1928
   xAulard, Alphonse.
      Christianity & the French Revolution. Fertig.
Auld, B. *see* Auld, Bertram Alexander.
Auld, Bertram Alexander, 1922-
   xAuld, B.
      Acoustic Fields & Waves in Solids. Wiley.
Auld, Margaret E.
   xAuld, Margaret E.
      The Challenge of Nursing: A Book of
        Readings. Mosby.
Auld, William M. *see* Auld, William Muir.
Auld, William Muir, 1884-1941
   xAuld, William M.
      Christmas Traditions. Gale.
      Christmas Traditions. Gordon Pr.
Aulen, Gustaf E. *see* Aulen, Gustaf Emanuel Hildebrand.
Aulen, Gustaf Emanuel Hildebrand, Bp, 1879-
   xAulen, Gustaf E.
      Reformation & Catholicity. Greenwood.
Auletta, Ken.
   xAuletta, Ken.
      The Streets Were Paved with Gold. Random.
Aulls, Mark W., 1942-
   xAulls, Mark W.
      Developmental & Remedial Reading in the
        Middle Grades. Allyn.
Aulnoy, Marie C. *see* Aulnoy, Marie Catherine (Jumelle
   De Berneville).
**Aulnoy, Marie Catherine (Jumelle De Berneville),
   Comtesse D', d. 1705**
   xAulnoy, Marie C.
      The Prince of Carency. Garland Pub.
Ault, Frederick K.
   xAult, Frederick K.
      Chemistry: A Conceptual Introduction. Scott F.
Ault, Leonard. *see* Ault, Leonard A.

Ault, Leonard A.
   xAult, Leonard.
      ed. Federal R&D & Scientific Innovation. Am
        Chemical.
Ault, Phil. *see* Ault, Phillip H.
Ault, Phillip H., 1914-
   xAult, Phil.
      These Are the Great Lakes. Dodd.
      Wonders of the Mosquito World. Dodd.
Ault, Ruth L.
   xAult, Ruth L.
      Children's Cognitive Development: Piaget's
        Theory & the Process Approach. Oxford U
        Pr.
Ault, Warren O. *see* Ault, Warren Ortman.
Ault, Warren Ortman, 1887-
   xAult, Warren O.
      Open-Field Husbandry & the Village
        Community: A Study of Agrarian By-Laws in
        Medieval England. Am Philos.
Aultman, Donald S.
   xAultman, Donald S.
      Guiding Youth. Pathway Pr.
Aumann, Francis R. *see* Aumann, Francis Robert.
Aumann, Francis Robert, 1901-
   xAumann, Francis R.
      Changing American Legal System: Some
        Selected Phases. Da Capo.
Aumann, R. J. *see* Aumann, Robert J.
Aumann, Robert J.
   xAumann, R. J.
      Values of Non-Atomic Games. Princeton U Pr.
Aumont, Jean-Pierre.
   xAumont, Jean-Pierre.
      Sun & Shadow. Norton.
Aune, Bruce, 1933-
   xAune, Bruce.
      Kant's Theory of Morals. Princeton U Pr.
Aurand, Harold W
   xAurand, Harold W.
      From the Molly Maguires to the United Mine
        Workers: The Social Ecology of an Industrial
        Union, 1869-97. Temple U Pr.
Aurand, Leonard W. *see* Aurand, Leonard William.
Aurand, Leonard William.
   xAurand, Leonard W.
      Food Chemistry. AVI.
Aurandt, Paul.
   xAurandt, Paul.
      More of Paul Harvey's the Rest of the Story.
        Morrow.
Aurandt, Paul. *see* Aurandt, Paul Harvey.
Aurandt, Paul Harvey, 1918-
   xAurandt, Paul.
      Paul Harvey's the Rest of the Story. Bantam.
      Paul Harvey's the Rest of the Story.
        Doubleday
Aurelia, Joseph C.
   xAurelia, Joseph C.
      Aphasia Therapy Manual. Interstate.
Auricchio, Father John. *see* Auricchio, John.
Auricchio, John.
   xAuricchio, Father John.
      Future of Theology. Alba.
Aurousseau, Marcel.
   xAurousseau, Marcel.
      The Rendering of Geographical Names.
        Greenwood.
Ausband, John R.
   xAusband, John R.
      ed. Ear, Nose and Throat Disorders: A
        Practitioners Guide. Med Exam.
Auser, Cortland P. *see* Auser, Courtland P.
Auser, Courtland P., 1919-
   xAuser, Cortland P.
      Nathaniel P. Willis. Coll & U Pr.
Ausland, John C.
   xAusland, John C.
      Norway, Oil & Foreign Policy. Westview.
Auslander. *see* Auslander, David M.

Auslander, David M.
xAuslander.
Introducing Systems & Control. McGraw.
Auslander, L.
xAuslander, Louis.
Flat Lorentz 3-Manifolds. Am Math.
Auslander, L. see Auslander, Louis.
Auslander, Louis.
xAuslander, L.
Lecture Notes on Nil-Theta Functions. Am Math.
xAuslander, Louis.
Mathematics Through Statistics. Krieger.
Auslander, Louis. see Auslander, L.
Auslander, M. Arthur. see Auslander, Maurice Arthur.
Auslander, Maurice Arthur, 1923-
xAuslander, M. Arthur.
Protecting & Profiting from Your Business Ideas. Pilot Bks.
Auspices of the International Union Against Cancer. see International Union Against Cancer.
Austen, Jane, 1775-1817
xAusten, Jane.
Emma. Aurora Pubs.
Emma. Beekman Pubs.
Emma. Buccaneer Bks.
Emma. Dutton.
Emma. HM.
Emma. Merrimack Bk Serv.
Emma. NAL.
Emma. Norton.
Emma. Oxford U Pr.
Emma. Penguin.
Emma. Airmont.
Northanger Abbey. Beekman Pubs.
Northanger Abbey. Dutton.
Northanger Abbey. Heinemann Ed.
Northanger Abbey. Merrimack Bk Serv.
Northanger Abbey. NAL.
Northanger Abbey. Oxford U Pr.
Northanger Abbey. Penguin.
Plan of a Novel According to Hints from Various Quarters. Folcroft.
Pride & Prejudice. Beekman Pubs.
Pride & Prejudice. Buccaneer Bks.
Pride & Prejudice. Dell.
Pride & Prejudice. Dutton.
Pride & Prejudice. Dutton.
Pride & Prejudice. G K Hall.
Pride & Prejudice. Heinemann Ed.
Pride & Prejudice. Merrimack Bk Serv.
Pride & Prejudice. NAL.
Pride & Prejudice. Norton.
Pride & Prejudice. Oxford U Pr.
Pride & Prejudice. PB.
Pride & Prejudice. Penguin.
Pride & Prejudice. Pendulum Pr.
Pride & Prejudice. AMSCO Sch.
Pride & Prejudice. HM.
Pride & Prejudice. Macmillan.
Pride & Prejudice. PB.
Pride & Prejudice. Airmont.
Austen-Leigh, Mary A. see Austen-Leigh, Mary Augusta.
Austen-Leigh, Mary Augusta.
xAusten-Leigh, Mary A.
Personal Aspects of Jane Austen. Arden Lib.
Personal Aspects of Jane Austen. Folcroft.
Auster, Rolf.
xAuster, Rolf.
Depreciation Desk Book. Inst Busn Plan.
Austerman, Miriam, 1923-
xAusterman, Miriam.
Animals: Unique Moments. Theorex.
Austgen, Robert J.
xAustgen, Robert J.
Natural Motivation in the Pauline Epistles. U of Notre Dame Pr.
Austin. see Austin, Bill R.
Austin, A. see Austin, Alfred.

Austin, Alfred, 1835-1913
xAustin, A.
The Autobiography of Alfred Austin, Poet Laureate. Kraus Repr.
xAustin, Alfred.
Autobiography of Alfred Austin, Poet Laureate, 1835-1910. AMS Pr.
Bridling of Pegasus: Prose Papers on Poetry. Arno.
Austin, Allan E.
xAustin, Allan E.
Roy Fuller. Twayne.
Austin, Anne L., 1891-
xAustin, Anne L.
The Woolsey Sisters of New York: A Family's Involvement in the Civil War & a New Profession. Am Philos.
Austin Association for the Education of Young Children.
xAustin Association for the Education of Young Children.
The Idea Box. Natl Assn Child Ed.
Austin, Bertram. see Austin, Bertram Herbert.
Austin, Bertram Herbert.
xAustin, Bertram.
The Secret of High Wages. Arno.
Austin, Bill R.
xAustin.
What Would Jesus Do. Broadman.
Austin, C. R. see Austin, Colin Russell.
Austin, Charles J.
xAustin, Charles J.
Information Systems for Hospital Administration. Health Admin Pr.
The Politics of National Health Insurance: An Interdisciplinary Research Study. Trinity U Pr.
Austin, Colin Russell.
xAustin, C. R.
ed. Germ Cells & Fertilization. Cambridge U Pr.
ed. Hormones in Reproduction. Cambridge U Pr.
ed. Mechanisms of Hormone Action. Cambridge U Pr.
Austin, Dennis.
xAustin, Dennis.
ed. Politicians & Soldiers in Ghana, 1966-1972. Biblio Dist.
Politics in Africa. U Pr of New Eng.
Austin, Douglas V.
xAustin, Douglas V.
Corporations in Conflict ... the Tender Offer. Masterco Pr.
Proxy Contests & Corporate Reform. U Mich Busn Div Res.
Austin, E. V., 1932-
xAustin, E. V.
A House by the Side of the Road. Iris Pr.
Austin, Frederick B. see Austin, Frederick Britten.
Austin, Frederick Britten, 1885-1941
xAustin, Frederick B.
When Mankind Was Young. Arno.
Austin, Gabriel.
xAustin, Gabriel.
Library of Jean Grolier: A Preliminary Catalogue. Grolier Club.
Austin, Gene.
xAustin.
Homeowner's Handy Do-It Manual. TAB Bks.
Austin, George, 1916-
xAustin, George.
Spinal Cord: Basic Aspects & Surgical Considerations. C C Thomas.
Austin, George L. see Austin, George Lowell.
Austin, George Lowell, 1849-1893
xAustin, George L.
Life & Times of Wendell Phillips. Metro Bks.
The Life of Franz Schubert. AMS Pr.
Austin, Gilbert.
xAustin, Gilbert.

Chironomia: Or, a Treatise on Rhetorical Delivery. S Ill U Pr.
Austin, Glenn.
xAustin, Glenn.
ed. The Parents' Guide to Child Raising. P-H.
Parents' Medical Manual. P-H.
Austin, Granville.
xAustin, Granville.
The Indian Constitution: Cornerstone of a Nation. Oxford U Pr.
Austin, Jacqueline.
xAustin, Jacqueline.
Technical Mathematics. HR&W.
Austin, James C.
xAustin, James C.
American Humor in France: Two Centuries of French Criticism of the Comic Spirit in American Literature. Iowa St U Pr.
Artemus Ward. Coll & U Pr.
Fields of the Atlantic Monthly: Letters to an Editor, 1861-1870. Huntington Lib.
Austin, James E.
xAustin, James E.
Nutrition Intervention in the United States: Cases & Concepts. Ballinger Pub.
Austin, John O. see Austin, John Osborne.
Austin, John Osborne.
xAustin, John O.
Genealogical Dictionary of Rhode Island: Comprising Three Generations of Settlers Who Came Before 1690 with Many Families Carried to the Fourth Generation. Genealog Pub.
One Hundred & Sixty Allied Families. Genealog Pub.
Austin, L. Allan.
xAustin, L. Allan.
Zero-Base Budgeting: A Decision Package Manual. Am Mgmt.
Austin, M. M.
xAustin, M. M.
Economic & Social History of Ancient Greece: An Introduction. U of Cal Pr.
Austin, Marilyn.
xAustin, Marilyn.
Holly Hathaway, Physical Therapist. Btoureg.
Austin, Mary. see Austin, Mary Hunter.
Austin, Mary Hunter, 1868-1934
xAustin, Mary.
Experiences Facing Death. Arno.
The Flock. Gannon.
Austin, Michael J.
xAustin, Michael J.
Delivering Human Services: An Introductory Programmed Text. Har-Row.
Management Simulations for Mental Health & Human Services Administration. Haworth Pr.
Professionals & Paraprofessionals. Human Sci Pr.
Austin, Mildred C. see Austin, Mildred Chandler.
Austin, Mildred Chandler, 1926-
xAustin, Mildred C.
Woman's Divine Destiny. Deseret Bk.
Austin, Norman.
xAustin, Norman.
Archery at the Dark of the Moon: Poetic Problems in Homer's Odyssey. U of Cal Pr.
Austin, O. L. see Austin, Oliver Luther.
Austin, Oliver L. see Austin, Oliver Luther.
Austin, Oliver Luther, 1903-
xAustin, O. L.
ed. Antarctic Bird Studies. Am Geophysical.
xAustin, Oliver L.
Families of Birds. Western Pub.
Austin, Reginald P. see Austin, Reginald Percy.
Austin, Reginald Percy.
xAustin, Reginald P.

The Stoichedon Style in Greek Inscriptions. Arno.

Austin, Richard.
xAustin, Richard.
Natalia Makarova, Ballerina. Dance Horiz.

Austin, Robert.
xAustin, Robert.
Bamboo. Weatherhill.

Austin, Virginia.
xAustin, Virginia.
Learning Fundamental Concepts of Music: An Activities Approach. Kendall-Hunt.

Austin, William G.
xAustin, William G.
The Social Psychology of Intergroup Relations. Brooks-Cole.

Austin, William H.
xAustin, William H.
The Relevance of Natural Science to Theology. B&N.

Austin, William M. *see* Austin, William Mandeville.

Austin, William Mandeville.
xAustin, William M.
ed. Papers in Linguistics in Honor of Leon Dostert. Mouton.

Austing, G. Ronald.
xAusting, G. Ronald.
World of the Great Horned Owl. Lippincott.

Australia Bureau of Census & Statistics. *see* Australia. Bureau of Census and Statistics.

Australia. Bureau of Census and Statistics.
xAustralia Bureau of Census & Statistics.
The Mathematical Theory of Population, of Its Character & Fluctuations, & of the Factors Which Influence Them. Arno.

Australian Academy of the Humanities.
xAustralian Academy of the Humanities, 1977.
Art, Science & Imagination. Intl Schol Bk Serv. Proceedings. Intl Schol Bk Serv.
Research on Western European Languages & Literatures in Australia Since 1958. Intl Schol Bk Serv.

Australian Conference on Combinatorial Mathematics, 2nd, University of Melbourne, 1973.
xAustralian Conference on Combinatorial Mathematics.
Proceedings. Springer-Verlag.

Australian Conference on Combinatorial Mathematics, 3rd, University of Queensland, 1974.
xAustralian Conference, 3rd, Queensland, 1974.
Combinatorial Mathematics Three: Proceedings. Springer-Verlag.

Australian Conference, 3rd, Queensland, 1974. *see* Australian Conference on Combinatorial Mathematics, 3rd, University of Queensland, 1974.

Australian Institute of International Affairs.
xAustralian Institute Of International Affairs.
Australia & the Pacific. Arno.

Australian Institute of Political Science.
xAustralian Institute of Political Science.
Industrial Australia, 1975-2000. Intl Pubns Serv.

Australian Museum. *see* Australian Museum, Sydney.

Australian Museum, Sydney.
xAustralian Museum.
Indonesia Today. Reed.

Australian National University. *see* Australian National University, Canberra.

Australian National University, Canberra.
xAustralian National University.
People & Places in a Landscape: Canberra Companions. Bks Australia.

Australian Union of Students.
xAustralian Union of Students.
The Budget Traveler's Asia: 1979-80. Dutton.

Austrian, Geoffrey.
xAustrian, Geoffrey.
Truth About Drugs. Doubleday.

Ausubel, David P. *see* Ausubel, David Paul.

Ausubel, David Paul.
xAusubel, David P.
Ego Psychology & Mental Disorder: A Developmental Approach to Psychopathology. Grune.
Psychology of Meaningful Verbal Learning: An Introduction to School Learning. Grune.
Theory & Problems of Adolescent Development. Grune.
Theory & Problems of Child Development. Grune.
What Every Well-Informed Person Should Know About Drug Addiction. Nelson-Hall.

Ausubel, Herman.
xAusubel, Herman.
Historians & Their Craft: A Study of the Presidential Addresses of the American Historical Association, 1884-1945. Russell.
In Hard Times: Reformers Among the Late Victorians. Greenwood.

The Auto Car.
xAutocar Editors.
MG Sports Cars. St Martin.

Autocar Editors. *see* The Auto Car.

Automobile Association.
xAutomobile Association of England.
Book of British Towns. Norton.
Book of the Car. Norton.
Folklore, Myths & Legends of Britain. Norton.
Hand-Picked Tours of Britain. Norton.
Illustrated Guide to Britain. Norton.
New Book of the Road. Norton.
New Road Book of Europe. Norton.
ed. Treasures of Britain. Norton.

Automobile Association, Auckland, New Zealand.
xAutomobile Associations of New Zealand.
AA Road Atlas of New Zealand. Intl Pubns Serv.

Automobile Association of England. *see* Automobile Association.

Automobile Associations of New Zealand. *see* Automobile Association, Auckland, New Zealand.

Automobile Club D'Italia.
xAutomobile Club of Italy.
ed. World Car Catalogue, 1971. Herald Bks.
Compiled by World Cars, 1972. Herald Bks.
ed. World Cars 1973. Herald Bks.
ed. World Cars 1974. Herald Bks.
ed. World Cars, 1975. Herald Bks.
ed. World Cars 1978. Herald Bks.
ed. World Cars 1979. Herald Bks.

Automobile Club of Italy. *see* Automobile Club D'Italia.

Autrum, H. *see* Autrum, Hansjochem.

Autrum, Hansjochem.
xAutrum, H.
ed. Comparative Physiology & Evolution of Vision in Invertebrates: A: Invertebrate Photoreceptors. Springer-Verlag.

Autry, Gene.
xAutry, Gene.
Back in the Saddle Again. Doubleday.

Auty, Susan G.
xAuty, Susan G.
The Comic Spirit of Eighteenth Century Novels. Kennikat.

Auvil, Daniel L.
xAuvil, Daniel L.
Intermediate Algebra. A-W.

Avakian, Arra S.
xAvakian, Arra S.
The Armenians in America. Lerner Pubns.

Avant, D. A., 1885-
xAvant, D. A.
Like a Straight Pine Tree: Stories of Reconstruction Days in Alabama & Florida 1855-1971. L'Avant Studios.

Avary, Myrta (Lockett).
xAvary, Myrta L.
Dixie After the War: An Exposition of Social Conditions Existing in the South, During the 12 Years Succeeding the Fall of Richmond. Da Capo.

Avary, Myrta L. *see* Avary, Myrta (Lockett).

Avebury, John L. *see* Avebury, John Lubbock.

Avebury, John Lubbock, Baron, 1834-1913
xAvebury, John L.
Origin of Civilisation & the Primitive Condition of Man. Arno.

Aved, Thomas G.
xAved, Thomas G.
Toomas, the Little Armenian Boy: Childhood Reminiscence of Turkish-Armenia. Pioneer Pub Co.

Avedon, Elliott M.
xAvedon, Elliott M.
Therapeutic Recreation Service: An Applied Behavioral Science Approach. P-H.

Avedon, Richard.
xAvedon, Richard.
Avedon Photographs: 1947-1977. FS&G.
Portraits. FS&G.

Aveling, Edward B. *see* Aveling, Edward Bibbins.

Aveling, Edward Bibbins.
xAveling, Edward B.
Working Class Movement in America. Arno.

Aveling, Harry.
xAveling, Harry.
ed. The Development of Indonesian Society. St Martin.
A Thematic History of Indonesian Poetry, 1920-1974. Cellar.

Aveling, James H. *see* Aveling, James Hobson.

Aveling, James Hobson, 1828-1892
xAveling, James H.
English Midwives. Their History & Prospects. AMS Pr.

Aven, Del.
xAven, Del.
God Has Special Places. Broadman.

Aveni, Anthony F.
xAveni, Anthony F.
ed. Archaeoastronomy in Pre-Columbian America. U of Tex Pr.
ed. Native American Astronomy. U of Tex Pr.

Avent, Sue, 1950-
xAvent, Sue.
Spells, Chants, & Potions. Raintree Pubs.

Averbakh, Iurii Lvovich.
xAverbakh, Yuri.
Queen V. Rook Minor Piece Endings. David & Charles.

Averbakh, Yuri. *see* Averbakh, Iurii Lvovich.

Averch, Harvey. *see* Averch, Harvey A.

Averch, Harvey A.
xAverch, Harvey.
Matrix of Policy in the Philippines. Princeton U Pr.

Averill, Esther. *see* Averill, Esther Holden.

Averill, Esther Holden.
xAverill, Esther.
Captains of the City Streets: A Story of the Cat Club. Har-Row.
Captains of the City Streets: A Story of the Cat Club. Har-Row.
Cartier Sails the St. Lawrence. Har-Row.
illus. Fire Cat. Har-Row.
Hotel Cat. Har-Row.

Averill, James H., 1947-
xAverill, James H.
Wordsworth & the Poetry of Human Suffering. Cornell U Pr.

Averitt, Max W. *see* Averitt, Max Wade.

Averitt, Max Wade.
xAveritt, Max W.
Boatwatch. Scribner.

Avers, Charlotte J.
xAvers, Charlotte J.

Evolution. Har-Row.

Avery, Arthur C.
xAvery, Arthur C.
A Modern Guide to Foodservice Equipment. CBI Pub.

Avery, C. Louise. *see* Avery, Clara Louise.

Avery, Charles.
xAvery, Charles.
Florentine Renaissance Sculpture. Har-Row.

Avery, Clara Louise, 1891-
xAvery, C. Louise.
Early American Silver. Russell.

Avery, Curtis E.
xAvery, Curtis E.
Love & Marriage: A Guide for Young People. HarBraceJ.

Avery, David D.
xAvery, David D.
Experimental Methodology in Psychology. Brooks-Cole.

Avery, Gordon B.
xAvery, Gordon B.
ed. Neonatology: Pathophysiology & Management of the Newborn. Lippincott.

Avery, Graeme S.
xAvery, Graeme S.
ed. Drug Treatment: Principles & Practice of Clinical Pharmacology & Therapeutics. ADIS Pr.

Avery, J.
xAvery, J.
ed. Membrane Structure and Mechanisms of Biological Energy Transduction. Plenum Pub.

Avery, Mary W. *see* Avery, Mary Williamson.

Avery, Mary Williamson, 1907-
xAvery, Mary W.
Government of Washington State. U of Wash Pr.

Avery, Robert S. *see* Avery, Robert Sterling.

Avery, Robert Sterling, 1917-
xAvery, Robert S.
Experiment in Management: Personnel Decentralization in the Tennessee Valley Authority. U of Tenn Pr.

Avery, T. E. *see* Avery, Thomas Eugene.

Avery, Thomas Eugene.
xAvery, T. E.
Natural Resources Measurements. McGraw.

Avi-Yonah, Michael, 1904-
xAvi-Yonah, Michael.
ed. The Encyclopedia of Archaeological Excavations in the Holy Land. P-H.

Avicenna.
xAvicenna.
Avicenna on Theology. Hyperion Conn.

Avignone, F. T., 1933-
xAvignone, Frank T.
A Modern Nuclear Laboratory Course. U of SC Pr.

Avignone, Frank T. *see* Avignone, F. T.

Avila, Fernando B. de. *see* Avila, Fernando Bastos De.

Avila, Fernando Bastos De.
xAvila, Fernando B. de.
Economic Impacts of Immigration: The Brazilian Immigration Problem. Greenwood.

Avina, Rose H. *see* Avina, Rose Hollenbaugh.

Avina, Rose Hollenbaugh.
xAvina, Rose H.
Spanish & Mexican Land Grants in California. Arno.
Spanish & Mexican Land Grants in California. R & E Res Assoc.

Avineri, Shlomo.
xAvineri, Shlomo.
ed. Marx's Socialism. Lieber-Atherton.

Avins, Alfred.
xAvins, Alfred.
Penalties for Misconduct on the Job. Oceana.

Avio, K. L. *see* Avio, Kenneth L.

Avio, Kenneth L.
xAvio, K. L.
Property Crime in Canada: An Econometric Study. U of Toronto Pr.

Avitzur, Betzalel, 1925-
xAvitzur, Betzalel.
Metal Forming: Processes & Analysis. Krieger.

Avner, Sidney H.
xAvner, Sidney H.
Introduction to Physical Metallurgy. McGraw.

Avnet, I. Duke, 1908-
xAvnet, I. Duke.
How to Prove Damages in Wrongful Personal Injury & Death Cases. P-H.

Avrett, E. H.
xAvrett, Eugene.
ed. Frontiers of Astrophysics. Harvard U Pr.

Avrett, Eugene. *see* Avrett, E. H.

Avrich, Paul.
xAvrich, Paul.
An American Anarchist: The Life of Voltairine De Cleyre. Princeton U Pr.
ed. The Anarchists in the Russian Revolution. Cornell U Pr.
The Modern School Movement: Anarchism & Education in the United States. Princeton U Pr.

Avriel, M., 1939-
xAvriel, Mordecai.
ed. Advances in Geometric Programming. Plenum Pub.

Avriel, Mordecai. *see* Avriel, M.

Avrutis, Raymond.
xAvrutis, Raymond.
How to Collect Unemployment Benefits. Schocken.

Avtorkhanov, Abdurakham. *see* Avtorkhanov, Abdurakhman.

Avtorkhanov, Abdurakhman, 1908-
xAvtorkhanov, Abdurakham.
The Reign of Stalin. Hyperion Conn.

Awad, Elias M.
xAwad, Elias M.
Automatic Data Processing: Principles & Procedures. P-H.
Business Data Processing. P-H.
Introduction to Computers in Business. P-H.

Awh, Robert Y.
xAwh, Robert Y.
Exercises in Microeconomics. Wiley.

Awolalu, J. Omosade.
xAwolalu, Joseph O.
Yoruba Beliefs & Sacrificial Rites. Longman.

Awolalu, Joseph O. *see* Awolalu, J. Omosade.

Awoonor, Kofi, 1935-
xAwoonor, Kofi.
The Breast of the Earth: A Survey of the History, Culture & Literature of Africa South of the Sahara. NOK Pubs.

AWS A2 Committee on Definitions & Symbols. *see* American Welding Society. Committee on Definitions and Symbols.

AWS A5 Committee on Filler Metal. *see* American Welding Society. Committee on Filler Metal.

AWS Committee on Definitions, Symbols & Metric Practice. *see* American Welding Society. Committee on Definitions, Symbols, and Metric Practice.

AWS Committee on Filler Metal. *see* American Welding Society. Committee on Filler Metal.

AWS Committee on Filler Metals. *see* American Welding Society. Committee on Filler Metal.

AWS Committee on Machinery & Equipment. *see* American Welding Society. Committee on Machinery and Equipment.

AWS Committee on Qualification. *see* American Welding Society. Committee on Qualification.

AWS C5 Committee on Arc Welding & Arc Cutting. *see* American Welding Society. Arc Welding and Arc Cutting Committee.

AWS Structural Welding Committee. *see* American Welding Society. Structural Welding Committee.

AWS-SAE Joint Committee on Automotive Welding.
xAWS-SAE Joint Committee on Automotive Welding.
Standard for Automotive Resistance Spot Welding Electrodes. Am Welding.

Axelbank, Albert.
xAxelbank, Albert.
The China Challenge. Watts.

Axelrad, Allan M.
xAxelrad, Allan M.
History & Utopia: A Study of the World View of James Fenimore Cooper. Norwood Edns.

Axelrod, C. Warren.
xAxelrod, C. Warren.
Computer Effectiveness: Bridging the Management-Technology Gap. Info Resources.

Axelrod, Charles D. *see* Axelrod, Charles David.

Axelrod, Charles David.
xAxelrod, Charles D.
Studies in Intellectual Breakthrough: Freud, Simmel, & Buber. U of Mass Pr.

Axelrod, Herbert. *see* Axelrod, Herbert R.

Axelrod, Herbert R.
xAxelrod, Herbert.
Tropical Fish in Your Home. Sterling.
xAxelrod, Herbert R.
Axelrod's Tropical Fish Book. Arco.
Tropical Fish in Your Home. Har-Row.

Axelrod, Robert. *see* Axelrod, Robert M.

Axelrod, Robert M.
xAxelrod, Robert.
The Structure of Decision: The Cognitive Maps of Political Elites. Princeton U Pr.

Axford, Lavonne B.
xAxford, Lavonne B.
An Index to the Poems of Ogden Nash. Scarecrow.

Axford, Roger W.
xAxford, Roger W.
Spanish-Speaking Heroes. Pendell Pub.

Axinn, June.
xAxinn, June.
Social Welfare: A History of the American Response to Need. Har-Row.

Axler, Bruce H.
xAxler, Bruce H.
Breakfast Cookery. Bobbs.
Building Care for Hospitality Operations. Bobbs.
Buying & Using Convenience Foods. Bobbs.
Foodservice: A Managerial Approach. Heath.
Increasing Lodging Revenues & Restaurant Checks. Bobbs.
Practical Wine Knowledge. Bobbs.
Security for Hotels, Motels, & Restaurants. Bobbs.
Tableservice Techniques. Bobbs.

Axley, Jim.
xAxley, Jim.
Oranges & Sweet Red Wines. Lightning Tree.

Axline, Virginia M. *see* Axline, Virginia Mae.

Axline, Virginia Mae, 1911-
xAxline, Virginia M.
Play Therapy. Ballantine.

Axline, W. Andrew.
xAxline, W. Andrew.
European Community Law & Organizational Development. Oceana.

Axman, Steve, 1947-
xAxman, Steve.
Attacking Modern Defenses with Multiple-Formation Veer Offense. P-H.

Axtell, James. *see* Axtell, James L.

Axtell, James L.
xAxtell, James.

ed. The Native American People of the East.
Pendulum Pr.
Axthelm, Pete. *see* Axthelm, Peter M.
Axthelm, Peter M.
xAxthelm, Pete.
The Kid. Viking Pr.
Axton, Richard.
xAxton, Richard.
European Drama of the Early Middle Ages. U
of Pittsburgh Pr.
Axum, Donna.
xAxum, Donna.
The Outer You...the Inner You. Word Bks.
Ayal, Ora.
xAyal, Ora.
tr. Ugbu. Har-Row.
Ayala, F. *see* Ayala, Francisco Jose.
Ayala, Francisco. *see* Ayala, Francisco Jose.
Ayala, Francisco J. *see* Ayala, Francisco Jose.
Ayala, Francisco Jose.
xAyala, F.
Modern Genetics. A-W.
xAyala, Francisco.
Modern Genetics. Benjamin-Cummings.
xAyala, Francisco J.
Evolving: The Theory & Processes of Organic
Evolution. Benjamin-Cummings.
Ayalon, David.
xAyalon, David.
Gunpowder & Firearms in the Mamluk
Kingdom: A Challenge to Mediaeval Society.
Biblio Dist.
Ayandele, E. A. *see* Ayandele, Emmanuel Ayankanmi.
Ayandele, Emmanuel Ayankanmi.
xAyandele, E. A.
African Historical Studies. Biblio Dist.
Holy Johnson, Pioneer of African Nationalism:
1836-1917. Biblio Dist.
Nigerian Historical Studies. Biblio Dist.
Ayd, Frank J.
xAyd, Frank J.
ed. Medical, Moral & Legal Issues in Mental
Health Care. Krieger.
Aydelotte, William O. *see* Aydelotte, William Osgood.
Aydelotte, William Osgood.
xAydelotte, William O.
ed. The Dimensions of Quantitative Research
in History. Princeton U Pr.
History of Parliamentary Behavior. Princeton U
Pr.
Quantification in History. A-W.
Ayella, Robert J.
xAyella, Robert J.
Radiologic Management of the Massively
Traumatized Patient. Williams & Wilkins.
Ayeni, Bola, 1945-
xAyeni, Bola.
Concepts & Techniques in Urban Analysis. St
Martin.
Ayensu, Edward S.
xAyensu, Edward S.
Endangered & Threatened Plants of the United
States. Smithsonian.
Medicinal Plants of West Africa. Ref Pubns.
Ayer, A. J. *see* Ayer, Alfred Jules.
Ayer, Adelaide M. *see* Ayer, Adelaide May.
Ayer, Adelaide May, 1881-
xAyer, Adelaide M.
Some Difficulties in Elementary School
History. AMS Pr.
Ayer, Alfred J. *see* Ayer, Alfred Jules.
Ayer, Alfred Jules, Sir, 1910-
xAyer, A. J.
Hume. Hill & Wang.
Part of My Life: The Memoirs of a
Philosopher. HarBraceJ.
xAyer, Alfred J.

ed. Logical Positivism. Free Pr.
Logical Positivism. Greenwood.
Origins of Pragmatism: Studies in the
Philosophy of Charles Sanders Peirce &
William James. Freeman C.
Philosophical Essays. Greenwood.
Probability & Evidence. Columbia U Pr.
Problem of Knowledge. Penguin.
Ayer, James C. *see* Ayer, James Cook.
Ayer, James Cook, 1818-1878
xAyer, James C.
Some of the Usages & Abuses in the
Management of Our Manufacturing
Corporations. B Franklin.
Ayer, William A.
xAyer, William A.
ed. Psychology & Dentistry: Selected Readings.
C C Thomas.
Ayers, Donald M.
xAyers, Donald M.
English Words from Latin & Greek Elements.
U of Ariz Pr.
Ayers, Gwendoline M.
xAyers, Gwendoline M.
England's First State Hospitals & the
Metropolitan Asylums Board 1867-1930. U
of Cal Pr.
Ayers, Robert H. *see* Ayers, Robert Hyman.
Ayers, Robert Hyman.
xAyers, Robert H.
ed. Religious Language & Knowledge. U of Ga
Pr.
Ayers, Ronald.
xAyers, Ronald.
Case of the Deadly Triangle. Holloway.
Ayers, Rose.
xAyers, Rose.
The Street Sparrows. Ballantine
The Street Sparrows. Coward.
Ayers, William, 1922-
xAyers, William.
Chang Chih-Tung & Educational Reform in
China. Harvard U Pr.
Ayisi, Eric O.
xAyisi, Eric O.
An Introduction to the Study of African
Culture. Heinemann Ed.
Aylesworth, Thomas G.
xAylesworth, Thomas G.
Cars, Boats, Trains & Planes of Today &
Tomorrow. Walker & Co.
Geological Disasters: Earthquakes &
Volcanoes. Watts.
Monsters from the Movies. Bantam.
Monsters from the Movies. Lippincott.
Palmistry. Watts.
The Story of Witches. McGraw.
This Vital Air, This Vital Water: Man's
Environmental Crisis. Rand.
Understanding Body Talk. Watts.
Vampires & Other Ghosts. A-W.
Aylett, B. J.
xAylett, B. J.
Organometallic Compounds. Methuen Inc.
Ayling, Ronald.
xAyling, Ronald.
Sean O'Casey: A Bibliography. U of Wash Pr.
Ayling, Stanley. *see* Ayling, Stanley Edward.
Ayling, Stanley Edward.
xAyling, Stanley.
John Wesley. Abingdon.
John Wesley. Abingdon.
Ayllon, Candido.
xAyllon, Candido.
Spanish Composition Through Literature. P-H.
Ayllon, Teodoro.
xAyllon, Teodoro.

Correctional Rehabilitation & Management: A
Psychological Approach. Wiley.
Aylmer, G. E.
xAylmer, G. E.
ed. A History of York Minster. Oxford U Pr.
ed. The Levellers in the English Revolution.
Cornell U Pr.
Struggle for the Constitution, 1603-1689:
England in the Seventeenth Century.
Humanities.
Aynsley, R. M.
xAynsley, R. M.
Architectural Aerodynamics. Burgess-Intl Ideas.
Ayoob, Massad F.
xAyoob, Massad F.
Fundamentals of Modern Police Impact
Weapons. C C Thomas.
Ayoob, Mohadded. *see* Ayoob, Mohammed.
Ayoob, Mohammed, 1942-
xAyoob, Mohadded.
Conflict & Intervention in the Third World. St
Martin.
Ayre, Leslie.
xAyre, Leslie.
The Gilbert & Sullivan Companion. NAL.
Ayre, P. C. I.
xAyre, Peter.
ed. Finance in Developing Countries. Biblio
Dist.
Ayre, Peter. *see* Ayre, P. C. I.
Ayres. *see* Ayres, Stephen M.
Ayres, C. E. *see* Ayres, Clarence Edwin.
Ayres, Clarence Edwin, 1891-
xAyres, C. E.
Toward a Reasonable Society: The Values of
Industrial Civilization. U of Tex Pr.
Ayres, Edward.
xAyres, Edward.
What's Good for GM. Aurora Pubs.
Ayres, J. A. *see* Ayres, John Augustus.
Ayres, John Augustus.
xAyres, J. A.
ed. Decontamination of Nuclear Reactors &
Equipment. Wiley.
Ayres, John C. *see* Ayres, John Clifton.
Ayres, John Clifton.
xAyres, John C.
Microbiology of Foods. W H Freeman.
Ayres, Leonard P. *see* Ayres, Leonard Porter.
Ayres, Leonard Porter.
xAyres, Leonard P.
Cleveland School Survey: Summary Volume.
Arno.
Turning Points in Business Cycles. Kelley.
Ayres, Michael.
xAyres, Michael.
Over the Sticks: The Sport of National Hunt
Racing. Assoc Univ Prs.
Ayres, Quincy C. *see* Ayres, Quincy Claude.
Ayres, Quincy Claude, 1891-
xAyres, Quincy C.
Soil Erosion & Its Control. Arno.
Ayres, Robert U.
xAyres, Robert U.
Uncertain Futures: Challenges for
Decision-Makers. Wiley.
Ayres, Stephen M.
xAyres.
Care of the Critically Ill. ACC.
Ayscough, Florence. *see* Ayscough, Florence (Wheelock).
Ayscough, Florence (Wheelock).
xAyscough, Florence.
tr. Fir-Flower Tablets. Hyperion Conn.
Ayyildiz, Judy.
xAyyildiz, Judy.
Smuggled Seeds. Gusto Pr.
Azad, Abul K. *see* Azad, Abul Kalaam.
Azad, Abul Kalaam.
xAzad, Abul K.

Tarjuman Al-Qur'an. Asia.
Azar, J. J. *see* Azar, Jamal J.
Azar, Jamal J.
    xAzar, J. J.
        Matrix Structural Analysis. Pergamon.
Azarnoff, Daniel L.
    xAzarnoff, Daniel L.
        Steroid Therapy. Saunders.
Azarnoff, Pat.
    xAzarnoff, Pat.
        A Pediatric Play Program: Developing a
        Therapeutic Play Program for Children in
        Medical Settings. C C Thomas.
Azaroff, Leonid V.
    xAzaroff, Leonid V.
        Introduction to Solids. Krieger.
        Powder Method in X-Ray Crystallography.
        McGraw.
Azarya, Victor.
    xAzarya, Victor.
        Aristocrats Facing Change: The Fulbe in
        Guinea, Nigeria, & Cameroon. U of Chicago
        Pr.
Azerrad, Jacob, 1936-
    xAzerrad, Jacob.
        Anyone Can Have a Happy Child: The Simple
        Secret of Positive Parenting. M Evans.
Azevedo, Aluisio. *see* Azevedo, Aluizio.
Azevedo, Aluizio, 1857-1913
    xAzevedo, Aluisio.
        A Brazilian Tenement. Fertig.
    xAzevedo, Aluizio.
        A Brazilian Tenement. Gordon Pr.
Azevedo, Fernando De, 1894-
    xAzevedo, Fernando De.
        Brazilian Culture: An Introduction to the Study
        of Culture in Brazil. Hafner.
Azevedo, Mario J.
    xAzevedo, Mario J.
        The Returning Hunter. InterCulture.
Azevedo, Milton M. *see* Azevedo, Milton Mariano.
Azevedo, Milton Mariano, 1942-
    xAzevedo, Milton M.
        Passive Sentences in English & Portuguese.
        Georgetown U Pr.
Azhary, M. S. El. *see* El Azhary, M. S.
Azikiwe, Nnamdi, 1904-
    xAzikiwe, Nnamdi.
        Liberia in World Politics. Negro U Pr.
        Renascent Africa. Biblio Dist.
        Renascent Africa. Humanities.
        Renascent Africa. Negro U Pr.
Aziz, Khalid.
    xAziz, Khalid.
        Step by Step Guide to Indian Cooking.
        Transatlantic.
Aziz, Sartaj.
    xAziz, Sartaj.
        ed. Hunger, Politics & Markets: The Real
        Issues in the Food Crisis. NYU Pr.
Azrael, Jeremy R., 1935-
    xAzrael, Jeremy R.
        ed. Soviet Nationality Policies & Practices.
        Praeger.
Azuela, M. *see* Azuela, Mariano.
Azuela, Mariano.
    xAzuela, M.
        ed. Los De Abajo: Novela De la Revolucion
        Mexicana. P-H.
    xAzuela, Mariano.
        Two Novels of Mexico: The Flies & The
        Bosses. U of Cal Pr.
Azumi, Koya, 1930-
    xAzumi, Koya.
        Higher Education & Business Recruitment in
        Japan. Tchrs Coll.
Azzam, Abd-Al-Rahman. *see* Azzam, Abdel Rahman.
Azzam, Abdel Rahman, 1893-
    xAzzam, Abd-Al-Rahman.

Eternal Message of Muhammad. Devin.
B'nai B'rith Vocational Service 1967 Professional Staff
    Conference. *see* B'Nai B'Rith Vocational Service.
Ba, Sylvia W. *see* Ba, Sylvia Washington.
Ba, Sylvia Washington, 1937-
    xBa, Sylvia W.
        The Concept of Negritude in the Poetry of
        Leopold Sedar Senghor. Princeton U Pr.
Baack, Lawrence J.
    xBaack, Lawrence J.
        Christian Bernstorff & Prussia: Diplomacy &
        Reform Conservatism, 1818-1832. Rutgers U
        Pr.
Baali, Fuad.
    xBaali, Fuad.
        Relation of the People to the Land in Southern
        Iraq. U Presses Fla.
Baar, H. S.
    xBaar, H. S.
        Disorders of Blood & Blood-Forming Organs in
        Childhood. Hafner.
Baar, James, 1929-
    xBaar, James A.
        Great Free Enterprise Gambit. HM.
Baar, James A. *see* Baar, James.
Baars, Conrad. *see* Baars, Conrad W.
Baars, Conrad W.
    xBaars, Conrad.
        The Homosexual's Search for Happiness.
        Franciscan Herald.
    xBaars, Conrad W.
        Born Only Once: The Miracle of Affirmation.
        Franciscan Herald.
        Feeling & Healing Your Emotions. Logos.
        How to Treat & Prevent the Crisis in the
        Priesthood. Franciscan Herald.
Baase, Sara.
    xBaase, Sara.
        Computer Algorithms: Introduction to Design
        & Analysis. A-W.
Baatz, Charles A. *see* Baatz, Charles Albert.
Baatz, Charles Albert.
    xBaatz, Charles A.
        ed. Philosophy of Education: A Guide to
        Information Sources. Gale.
Babb, Hugh W. *see* Babb, Hugh Webster.
Babb, Hugh Webster.
    xBabb, Hugh W.
        Business Law: Uniform Commercial Code
        Edition. Har-Row.
        Soviet Legal Philosophy. Johnson Repr.
Babb, Lawrence.
    xBabb, Lawrence.
        Moral Cosmos of Paradise Lost. Mich St U Pr.
Babb, Lawrence A.
    xBabb, Lawrence A.
        The Divine Hierarchy: Popular Hinduism in
        Central India. Columbia U Pr.
Babb, Warren.
    xBabb, Warren.
        ed. Hucbald, Guido & John on Music: Three
        Medieval Treatises. Yale U Pr.
Babbage, C. *see* Babbage, Charles.
Babbage, Charles, 1792-1871
    xBabbage, C.
        Passages from the Life of a Philosopher.
        Dawson Pub.
    xBabbage, Charles.
        Comparative View of the Various Institutions
        for the Assurance of Lives. Kelley.
        On the Economy of Machinery &
        Manufactures. Kelley.
        Passages from the Life of a Philosopher.
        Kelley.
Babbidge, Homer D.
    xBabbidge, Homer D.
        The Federal Interest in Higher Education.
        Greenwood.
Babbie, Earl R.
    xBabbie, Earl R.

Practice of Social Research. Wadsworth Pub.
Babbitt, Al.
    xBabbitt, Al.
        When Will the Mob Rule?. Chris Mass.
Babbitt, Diane H.
    xBabbitt, Diane H.
        Gymnastic Apparatus Exercises for Girls.
        Wiley.
Babbitt, Irving, 1865-1933
    xBabbitt, Irving.
        Democracy & Leadership. Liberty Fund.
        Rousseau & Romanticism. AMS Pr.
        Rousseau & Romanticism. U of Tex Pr.
Babbitt, Natalie.
    xBabbitt, Natalie.
        illus. Goody Hall. FS&G.
        illus. Something. FS&G.
        The Something. Dell.
        Tuck Everlasting. Bantam.
        Tuck Everlasting. FS&G.
Babbitt, Samuel. *see* Babbitt, Samuel F.
Babbitt, Samuel F.
    xBabbitt, Samuel.
        Forty-Ninth Magician. Pantheon.
Babcock, C. L. *see* Babcock, Clarence Lloyd.
Babcock, Clarence Lloyd, 1904-
    xBabcock, C. L.
        Silicate Glass Technology Methods. Wiley.
Babcock, Dennis.
    xBabcock, Dennis.
        Careers in the Theater. Lerner Pubns.
Babcock, Dorothy E. *see* Babcock, Dorothy Ellen.
Babcock, Dorothy Ellen.
    xBabcock, Dorothy E.
        Introduction to Growth, Development &
        Family Life. Davis Co.
Babcock, George D. *see* Babcock, George De Albert.
Babcock, George De Albert.
    xBabcock, George D.
        The Taylor System in Franklin Management.
        Hive Pub.
Babcock, Harold. *see* Babcock, Harold Lester.
Babcock, Harold L. *see* Babcock, Harold Lester.
Babcock, Harold Lester, 1886-1953
    xBabcock, Harold.
        Turtles of the North-Eastern United States.
        Peter Smith.
    xBabcock, Harold L.
        Turtles of the Northeastern United States.
        Dover.
Babcock, Leland.
    xBabcock, Leland S.
        German & Germany in Review. Van Nos
        Reinhold.
Babcock, Leland S. *see* Babcock, Leland.
Babcock, Maltbie D. *see* Babcock, Maltbie Davenport.
Babcock, Maltbie Davenport, 1858-1901
    xBabcock, Maltbie D.
        Letters from Egypt & Palestine. Arno.
Babcock, Robert H.
    xBabcock, Robert H.
        Gompers in Canada: A Study in American
        Continentalism Before the First World War.
        U of Toronto Pr.
Babcock, William H. *see* Babcock, William Henry.
Babcock, William Henry, 1849-1922
    xBabcock, William H.
        Legendary Islands of the Atlantic: Study in
        Medieval Geography. Arno.
Babcock, Winifred.
    xBabcock, Winifred.
        The Palestinian Mystery Play. Dodd.
Babcoke, Carl. *see* Babcoke, Carl H.
Babcoke, Carl H.
    xBabcoke, Carl.
        RCA Color TV Service Manual. TAB Bks.
        RCA Monochrome TV Service Manual. TAB
        Bks.
Babe, R. E. *see* Babe, Robert E.

Babe, Robert E.
  xBabe, R. E.
    Cable Television & Telecommunications in
      Canada: An Economic Analysis. Mich St U
      Busn.
Babin, David E.
  xBabin, David E.
    Celebration of Life: Our Changing Liturgy.
      Morehouse.
Babin, Lawrence J. *see* Babin, Lawrence James.
Babin, Lawrence James.
  xBabin, Lawrence J.
    Cecilia of Rome. Pyquag.
Babin, Maria T. *see* Babin, Maria Teresa.
Babin, Maria Teresa, 1910-
  xBabin, Maria T.
    Estudios Lorquianos. U of PR Pr.
Babinger, Franz. *see* Babinger, Franz Carl Heinrich.
Babinger, Franz Carl Heinrich, 1891-1967
  xBabinger, Franz.
    Mehmed the Conqueror & His Time. Princeton
      U Pr.
Babington, Caroline H. *see* Babington, Caroline Hastings.
Babington, Caroline Hastings, 1919-
  xBabington, Caroline H.
    Cooking Creatively for Your Diabetic Child.
      Doubleday.
Babinski, Hubert F., 1936-
  xBabinski, Hubert F.
    The Mazeppa Legend in European
      Romanticism. Columbia U Pr.
Babister, A. W.
  xBabister, A. W.
    Aircraft Dynamic Stability & Response.
      Pergamon.
Babkin, Boris P. *see* Babkin, Boris Petrovich.
Babkin, Boris Petrovich, 1877-1950
  xBabkin, Boris P.
    Pavlov: A Biography. U of Chicago Pr.
Bablet, Denis.
  xBablet, Denis
    Edward Gordon Craig. Theatre Arts.
Babris, Peter J.
  xBabris, Peter J.
    Silent Churches: Persecution of Religions in
      Soviet Dominated Areas. Res Publs.
Babson, Marian.
  xBabson, Marian.
    Murder, Murder, Little Star. Walker & Co.
  xBabson, Marion.
    Lord Mayor of Death. Walker & Co.
Babson, Marion. *see* Babson, Marian.
Babson, Roger W. *see* Babson, Roger Ward.
Babson, Roger Ward, 1875-1967
  xBabson, Roger W.
    The Folly of Instalment Buying. Arno.
Babunakis, Michael.
  xBabunakis, Michael.
    Budgets: An Analytical & Procedural
      Handbook for Government & Non-Profit
      Organizations. Greenwood.
Bacall, Lauren, 1924-
  xBacall, Lauren.
    Lauren Bacall by Myself. Ballantine.
    Lauren Bacall by Myself. Knopf.
Bacchus, Habeeb, 1928-
  xBacchus, Habeeb.
    Essentials of Gynecologic & Obstetric
      Endocrinology. Univ Park.
    Rational Management of Diabetes. Univ Park.
Bacchus, William I., 1940-
  xBacchus, William I.
    Foreign Policy & the Bureaucratic Process: The
      State Department's Country Director System.
      Princeton U Pr.
Bacchylides.
  xBacchylides.
    Complete Poems. Greenwood.
Bach, Alice.
  xBach, Alice.

    A Father Every Few Years. Dell.
    A Father Every Few Years. Har-Row.
    Grouchy Uncle Otto. Dell.
    Grouchy Uncle Otto. Har-Row.
    The Meat in the Sandwich. Har-Row.
    The Most Delicious Camping Trip Ever. Dell.
    The Most Delicious Camping Trip Ever.
      Har-Row.
    They'll Never Make a Movie Starring Me.
      Dell.
    They'll Never Make a Movie Starring Me.
      Har-Row.
    Warren Weasel's Worse Than Measles.
      Har-Row.
Bach, Bert C.
  xBach, Bert C.
    Drama for Composition. Scott F.
    ed. The Liberating Form: A
      Handbook-Anthology of English & American
      Poetry. Har-Row.
Bach, Emmon. *see* Bach, Emmon W.
Bach, Emmon W., 1929-
  xBach, Emmon.
    Syntactic Theory. HR&W.
Bach, Fritz H.
  xBach, Fritz H.
    ed. Clinical Immunobiology. Acad Pr.
Bach, G. L. *see* Bach, George Leland.
Bach, George. *see* Bach, George Robert.
Bach, George L. *see* Bach, George Leland.
Bach, George Leland.
  xBach, G. L.
    Economics: An Introduction to Analysis &
      Policy. P-H.
  xBach, George L
    Economics: An Introduction to Analysis &
      Policy. P-H.
    Macroeconomics: Analysis & Applications.
      P-H.
Bach, George R. *see* Bach, George Robert.
Bach, George Robert.
  xBach, George.
    Stop! You're Driving Me Crazy. Berkley Pub.
  xBach, George R.
    Pairing. Avon.
    Stop! You're Driving Me Crazy. Putnam.
Bach, Jean Francois.
  xBach, Jean-Francois.
    ed. Immunology. Wiley.
Bach, Jean-Francois. *see* Bach, Jean Francois.
Bach, Kent.
  xBach, Kent.
    Linguistic Communication & Speech Acts. MIT
      Pr.
Bach, Lester.
  xBach, Lester.
    Take Time for Sunsets. Franciscan Herald.
Bach, Marcus, 1906-
  xBach, Marcus.
    The World of Serendipity. De Vorss.
Bach, Michael K. *see* Bach, Michael Klaus.
Bach, Michael Klaus, 1931-
  xBach, Michael K.
    ed. Immediate Hypersensitivity: Modern
      Concepts & Developments. Dekker.
Bach, R. *see* Bach, Richard.
Bach, Richard.
  xBach, R.
    Jonathan Livingston Seagull. Watts.
  xBach, Richard.

    A Gift of Wings. Delacorte.
    Gift of Wings. Dell.
    Illusions: The Adventures of a Reluctant
      Messiah. Delacorte.
    Illusions: The Adventures of a Reluctant
      Messiah. Dell.
    Jonathan Livingston Seagull. Avon.
    Jonathan Livingston Seagull. Macmillan.
    Stranger to the Ground. Har-Row.
    There's No Such Place As Far Away.
      Delacorte.
Bach, Wilfred. *see* Bach, Wilfrid.
Bach, Wilfrid.
  xBach, Wilfred.
    Handbook of Air Quality in the United States.
      U Pr of Hawaii.
  xBach, Wilfrid.
    Atmospheric Pollution. McGraw.
Bacharach, A. L. *see* Bacharach, Alfred Louis.
Bacharach, Alfred Louis.
  xBacharach, A. L.
    ed. The Musical Companion. HarBraceJ.
Bacharach, Bert.
  xBacharach, Bert.
    How to Do Almost Everything. Popular Lib.
    How to Do Almost Everything. S&S.
Bacharach, Jere L., 1938-
  xBacharach, Jere L.
    A Near East Studies Handbook. U of Wash Pr.
Bacharach, Michael.
  xBacharach, Michael.
    Economics & the Theory of Games. Westview.
Bache, William B.
  xBache, William B.
    Measure for Measure As Dialectical Art.
      Purdue.
Bachelard, Gaston, 1884-1962
  xBachelard, Gaston.
    On Poetic Imagination & Reverie: Selections
      from the Works of Gaston Bachelard. Bobbs.
    Psychoanalysis of Fire. Beacon Pr.
Bachelder, Joseph E.
  xBachelder, Joseph E.
    ed. Employee Stock Ownership Plans. PLI.
Bachelder, Louise.
  xBachelder, Louise.
    ed. The Gift of Music. Peter Pauper.
Bacheller, Irving, 1859-1950
  xBacheller, Irving.
    Eben Holden: A Tale of the North Country.
      Scholarly.
Bacher, Robert F. *see* Bacher, Robert Fox.
Bacher, Robert Fox.
  xBacher, Robert F.
    ed. Atomic Energy States, As Derived from the
      Analyses of Optical Spectra. Greenwood.
Bachert, Russel E.
  xBachert, Russel E.
    Hundreds of Ideas for Outdoor Education.
      Interstate.
    Outdoor Education Equipment: Plans for
      Easy-to-Make Items. Interstate.
  xBachert, Russell E.
    Eco-Sketch: Ideas for Environmental
      Education. Am Camping.
Bachert, Russell E. *see* Bachert, Russel E.
Bachhofer, Ludwig, 1894-
  xBachhofer, Ludwig.
    Early Indian Sculpture. Hacker.
Bachhuber, Andrew H.
  xBachhuber, Andrew H.
    Introduction to Logic. P-H.
Bachhuber, Thomas D.
  xBachhuber, Thomas D.
    Directions: A Guide to Career Planning. HM.
Bachman, Christian G., 1931-
  xBachman, Christian G.

Laser Radar Systems & Techniques. Artech
Hse.
Bachman, George.
xBachman, George.
Functional Analysis. Acad Pr.
Bachman, Jerald C. *see* Bachman, Jerald G.
Bachman, Jerald G.
xBachman, Jerald C.
The All-Volunteer Force: A Study of Ideology
in the Military. U of Mich Pr.
Bachmann, Alberto. *see* Bachmann, Alberto Abraham.
Bachmann, Alberto Abraham, 1875-
xBachmann, Alberto.
An Encyclopedia of the Violin. Da Capo.
Bachner, John P. *see* Bachner, John Phillip.
Bachner, John Phillip.
xBachner, John P.
Public Relations for Nursing Homes. C C
Thomas.
Bachrach, Ann W.
xBachrach, Ann W.
Developmental Therapy for Young Children
with Autistic Characteristics. Univ Park.
Bachrach, Arthur J.
xBachrach, Arthur J.
Psychological Research: An Introduction.
Random.
Bachrach, Bernard S., 1939-
xBachrach, Bernard S.
Early Medieval Jewish Policy in Western
Europe. U of Minn Pr.

Bachrach, Peter.

xBachrach, Peter.
Power & Poverty: Theory & Practice. Oxford
U Pr.

The Theory of Democratic Elitism: A Critique.
U Pr of Amer.

Bachrach, Uriel.
xBachrach, Uriel.
Function of Naturally Occuring Polyamines.
Acad Pr.

Bacigalupo, Leonard.
xBacigalupo, Leonard.
The Franciscans & Italian Immigration in
America. Exposition.
Bacik, James J., 1936-
xBacik, James J.
Apologetics & the Eclipse of Mystery::
Mystagogy According to Karl Rahner. U of
Notre Dame Pr.
Baciu, Stefan.
xBaciu, Stefan.
Compiled by Antologia de la Poesia
Latinoamericana, 1950-1970. State U NY Pr.
Back, Joe.
xBack, Joe.
Horses, Hitches & Rocky Trails. Johnson Colo.
Backer, John H., 1902-
xBacker, John H.
The Decision to Divide Germany: American
Foreign Policy in Transition. Duke.
Backer, Morton.
xBacker, Morton.
Financial Reporting for Security Investment &
Credit Decisions. Natl Assn Accts.
Backer, S. *see* Backer, Stanley.
Backer, Stanley, 1920-
xBacker, S.
Textile Fabric Flammability. MIT Pr.
Backhurst, J. R.
xBackhurst, J. R.
Process Plant Design. Elsevier.
Backman, Jules, 1910-
xBackman, Jules.

Advertising & Competition. NYU Pr.
Changing Marketing Strategies in a New
Economy. Bobbs.
The Economics of the Electrical Machinery
Industry. NYU Pr.
ed. Multinational Corporations, Trade & the
Dollar in the Seventies. NYU Pr.
Backscheider, Paula.
xBackscheider, Paula R.
ed. Probability, Time & Space in
Eighteenth-Century Literature. AMS Pr.
Backscheider, Paula R. *see* Backscheider, Paula.
Backstrom, Charles H. *see* Backstrom, Charles Herbert.
Backstrom, Charles Herbert.
xBackstrom, Charles H.
Survey Research. Northwestern U Pr.
Survey Research. Wiley.
Backus, Charles E., 1937-
xBackus, Charles E.
ed. Solar Cells. Inst Electrical.
Solar Cells. Wiley.
Backus, Isaac.
xBackus, Isaac.
The Diary of Isaac Backus. Brown U Pr.
Backus, John.
xBackus, John.
Acoustical Foundations of Music. Norton.
Backus, Sharron.
xBackus, Sharron.
Inside Softball for Women. Contemp Bks.
Bacon. *see* Bacon, Dennis Henry.
Bacon, Dennis Henry.
xBacon.
Mechanical Technology. Butterworths.
Bacon, Edmund N.
xBacon, Edmund N.
Design of Cities. Penguin.
Bacon, Ernst, 1898-
xBacon, Ernst.
Notes on the Piano. Syracuse U Pr.
Notes on the Piano. U of Wash Pr.
Words on Music. Greenwood.
Bacon, Francis.
xBacon, Francis.
The Advancement of Learning. Humanities.
The Advancement of Learning. Rowman.
Bacon's Essays. Arno.
History of the Reign of King Henry the
Seventh. Bobbs.
Reading on the Statute of Uses. Garland Pub.
Works. Adler.
Works, 1857-74. Scholarly.
Bacon, Helen H.
xBacon, Helen H.
Barbarians in Greek Tragedy. Elliots Bks.
Bacon, James, 1914-
xBacon, James.
Hollywood Is a Four Letter Town. Avon.
Bacon, Josephine D. *see* Bacon, Josephine Dodge
(Daskam).
Bacon, Josephine Dodge (Daskam), 1876-1961
xBacon, Josephine D.
Imp & the Angel. Arno.
In the Border Country. Arno.
Bacon, Leonard, 1802-1881
xBacon, Leonard.
The Genesis of the New England Churches.
Arno.
Bacon, Martha. *see* Bacon, Martha Sherman.
Bacon, Martha Sherman.
xBacon, Martha.
Sophia Scrooby Preserved. Little.
Bacon, P. *see* Bacon, Phillip.
Bacon, Phillip.
xBacon, P.
Regions Around the World. A-W.
Bacon, Richard M.
xBacon, Richard M.

The Art & Craft of Wall Stenciling. T Y
Crowell.
The Forgotten Art of Growing, Gardening &
Cooking with Herbs. Yankee Bks.
The Forgotten Arts: Yesterday's Techniques
Adapted to Today's Materials. Yankee Bks.
Bacon, Robert. *see* Bacon, Robert William.
Bacon, Robert L.
xBacon, Robert L.
Secrets of Professional Turf Betting. Landau.
Bacon, Robert William.
xBacon, Robert.
Britain's Economic Problem: Too Few
Producers. St Martin.
Bacon, Wallace A., 1914-
xBacon, Wallace A.
The Art of Interpretation. HR&W.
Bacote, Samuel W. *see* Bacote, Samuel William.
Bacote, Samuel William.
xBacote, Samuel W.
Who's Who Among the Colored Baptists of the
United States. Arno.
Bacq, Z. M. *see* Bacq, Zenon M.
Bacq, Zenon M.
xBacq, Z. M.
Chemical Transmission of Nerve Impulses: A
Historical Sketch. Pergamon.
ed. Fundamentals of Biochemical
Pharmacology. Pergamon.
Sulfur Containing Radio-Protective Agents.
Pergamon.
Bacry, Henri.
xBacry, Henri.
Lectures on Group Theory & Particle Theory.
Gordon.
Baczynsky, Mark.
xBaczynsky, Mark.
Photocrafts Book of Guides. Embee Pr.
Badash, Lawrence.
xBadash, Lawrence.
Radioactivity in America: Growth & Decay of
a Science. Johns Hopkins.
Badawy, Alexander.
xBadawy, Alexander.
Architecture in Ancient Egypt & Near East.
MIT Pr.
Coptic Art & Archaeology: The Art of the
Christian Egyptians from the Late Antique to
the Middle Ages. MIT Pr.
The Tomb of Nyhetep-Ptah at Giza & the
Tomb of 'Ankhm' Ahor at Saqqara. U of Cal
Pr.
Badcock, C. R.
xBadcock, C. R.
Levi-Strauss: Structuralism & Sociological
Theory. Holmes & Meier.
Baddeley, Alan D., 1934-
xBaddeley, Alan D.
The Psychology of Memory. Basic.
Bade, William F. *see* Bade, William Frederic.
Bade, William Frederic, 1871-1936
xBade, William F.
Life & Letters of John Muir. AMS Pr.
Badea, Florin.
xBadea, Florin.
Reaction Mechanisms in Organic Chemistry.
Intl Schol Bk Serv.
Baden-Powell, Baden H. *see* Baden-Powell, Baden Henry.
Baden-Powell, Baden Henry, 1841-1901
xBaden-Powell, Baden H.
The Origin & Growth of Village Communities
in India. Johnson Repr.
Badenoch, Alec W. *see* Badenoch, Alec William.
Badenoch, Alec William.
xBadenoch, Alec W.
Manual of Urology. Year Bk Med.
Badgley, Anne V.
xBadgley, Anne V.
The Rembrandt Decisions. Dodd.
Badgley, F. I. *see* Badgley, Franklin Isley.

Badgley, Franklin Isley.
  xBadgley, F. I.
    Profiles of Wind, Temperature, & Humidity
      Over the Arabian Sea. U Pr of Hawaii.
Badham, Paul.
  xBadham, Paul.
    Christian Beliefs About Life After Death.
      B&N.
Badian, E.
  xBadian, E.
    Studies in Greek & Roman History. Biblio
      Dist.
Badmaieff, Alexis.
  xBadmaieff, Alexis.
    How to Build Speaker Enclosures. Sams.
Badner, Mino.
  xBadner, Mino.
    A Possible Focus of Andean Artistic Influence
      in Mesoamerica. Dumbarton Oaks.
Badrig, Robert H.
  xBadrig, Robert H.
    Florenz Ziegfeld, Twentieth Century Showman.
      SamHar Pr.
Bady, Donald B.
  xBady, Donald B.
    Colt Automatic Pistols. Borden.
Badzinski, S. see Badzinski, Stanley.
Badzinski, Stanley.
  xBadzinski, S.
    Carpentry in Commercial Construction. P-H.
    Carpentry in Residential Construction. P-H.
  xBadzinski, Stanley.
    Carpentry in Residential Construction. P-H.
    Home Construction & Estimating. P-H.
    House Construction: A Guide to Buying,
      Building, & Evaluating. P-H.
Baechler, Jean.
  xBaechler, Jean.
    The Origins of Capitalism. St Martin.
    Revolution. Har-Row
Baeckler, Virginia.
  xBaeckler, Virginia Van W.
    PR for Pennies: Low-Cost Library Public
      Relations. Sources.
Baeckler, Virginia Van W. see Baeckler, Virginia.
Baeder, John.
  xBaeder, John.
    Diners. Abrams.
Baehr, Patricia G. see Baehr, Patricia Goehner.
Baehr, Patricia Goehner.
  xBaehr, Patricia G.
    The Way to Windra. Warne.
Baelz, Peter.
  xBaelz, Peter.
    Ethics & Belief. Seabury.
Baelz, Peter R.
  xBaelz, Peter R.
    Prayer & Providence: A Background Study.
      Allenson.
Baen, James.
  xBaen, Jim.
    ed. Destinies. Ace Bks.
Baen, Jim. see Baen, James.
Baer, Charles J.
  xBaer, Charles J.
    Electrical & Electronics Drawing. McGraw.
    Electrical & Electronics Drawing. McGraw.
Baer, D. Richard.
  xBaer, D. Richard.
    Film Buff's Bible of Motion Pictures
      (1915-1972). Hollywd Film Arch.
    ed. The Film Buff's Checklist of Motion
      Pictures (1912-1979). Hollywd Film Arch.
Baer, Edith.
  xBaer, Edith.
    Wonder of Hands. Schol Bk Serv.
    Words Are Like Faces. Pantheon.
Baer, Eleanora A.
  xBaer, Eleanora A.

Titles in Series: A Handbook for Librarians &
    Students. Scarecrow.
Baer, Eric.
  xBaer, Eric.
    Engineering Design for Plastics. Krieger.
Baer, Gabriel.
  xBaer, Gabriel.
    Population & Society in the Arab East.
      Greenwood.
Baer, George M.
  xBaer, George M.
    ed. The Natural History of Rabies. Acad Pr.
Baer, Hans P.
  xBaer, Hans P.
    Physiological & Regulatory Functions of
      Adenosine & Adenine Nucleotides. Raven.
Baer, Harold.
  xBaer, Harold.
    How to Prepare & Negotiate Cases for
      Settlement. Law-Arts.
Baer, Herbert R.
  xBaer, Herbert R.
    Admiralty Law of the Supreme Court. Michie.
Baer, J. A. see Baer, J. Arthur.
Baer, J. Arthur.
  xBaer, J. A.
    Dining In-St. Louis. Peanut Butter.
Baer, Judith A.
  xBaer, Judith A.
    The Chains of Protection: The Judicial
      Response to Women's Labor Legislation.
      Greenwood.
Baer, Klaus.
  xBaer, Klaus.
    Rank & Title in the Old Kingdom: The
      Structure of the Egyptian Administration in
      the Fifth & Sixth Dynasties. U of Chicago Pr.
Baer, Louis S. see Baer, Louis Shattuck.
Baer, Louis Shattuck, 1914-
  xBaer, Louis S.
    Let the Patient Decide: A Doctor's Advice to
      Older Persons. Westminster.
Baer, Max F. see Baer, Max Frank.
Baer, Max Frank.
  xBaer, Max F.
    Occupational Information: The Dynamics of Its
      Nature & Use. SRA.
Baer, Melvin J.
  xBaer, Melvyn J.
    Growth & Maturation: An Introduction to
      Physical Development. Howard Doyle.
Baer, Melvyn J. see Baer, Melvin J.
Baer, W. S. see Baer, Walter S.
Baer, Walter E.
  xBaer, Walter E.
    The Operating Manager's Labor Relations
      Guidebook. Kendall Hunt.
Baer, Walter S.
  xBaer, W. S.
    Cable Television: Franchising Considerations.
      Crane-Russak Co.
Baer, Werner, 1931-
  xBaer, Werner.
    Development of the Brazilian Steel Industry.
      Vanderbilt U Pr.
    Industrialization & Economic Development in
      Brazil. Yale U Pr.
Baer, William P.
  xBaer, William P.
    The Aphasic Patient: A Program for Auditory
      Comprehension & Language Training,
      Clinician's Edition. C C Thomas.
Baerlein, Henry. see Baerlein, Henry Philip Bernard.
Baerlein, Henry Philip Bernard, 1875-1960
  xBaerlein, Henry.
    March of the Seventy Thousand. Arno.
Baerresen, Donald W.
  xBaerresen, Donald W.

Latin American Trade Patterns. Greenwood.
Baerwald, Hans H.
  xBaerwald, Hans H.
    The Purge of Japanese Leaders Under the
      Occupation. Greenwood.
Baes, Charles F.
  xBaes, Charles F.
    The Hydrolysis of Cations. Wiley.
Baeza, R. see Baeza, Ricardo.
Baeza, Ricardo, 1942-
  xBaeza, R.
    Quadratic Forms Over Semilocal Rings.
      Springer-Verlag.
Bagai, Leona B.
  xBagai, Leona B.
    East Indians & Pakistanis in America. Lerner
      Pubns.
Bagby, Daniel G.
  xBagby, Daniel G.
    Understanding Anger in the Church.
      Broadman.
Bagby, Joseph R.
  xBagby, Joseph R.
    Real Estate Financing Desk Book. Inst Busn
      Plan.
Bagdikian, Ben H.
  xBagdikian, Ben H.
    Caged: Eight Prisoners & Their Keepers.
      Har-Row.
    Information Machines: Their Impact on Men &
      the Media. Har-Row.
Bage, Robert, 1728-1801
  xBage, Robert.
    Barham Downs. Garland Pub.
    The Fair Syrian. Garland Pub.
    James Wallace. Garland Pub.
    Man As He Is. Garland Pub.
    Mount Henneth. Garland Pub.
Bagehot. see Bagehot, Walter.
Bagehot, Walter, 1826-1877
  xBagehot.
    Estimations in Criticism. Folcroft.
  xBagehot, Walter.
    Economic Studies. Kelley.
    Economic Studies. Scholarly.
    The English Constitution. Garland Pub.
    English Constitution. Oxford U Pr.
    The English Constitution. Cornell U Pr.
    Estimates of Some Englishmen & Scotchmen.
      Folcroft.
    Estimations in Criticism. Arden Lib.
    Lombard Street. Arno.
    Lombard Street: A Description of the Money
      Market. Hyperion Conn.
    Practical Plan for Assimilating the English &
      American Money, As a Step Towards a
      Universal Money. Greenwood.
Bager, Bertel, 1890-
  xBager, Bertel.
    Nature As Designer: A Botanical Art Study.
      Van Nos Reinhold.
Bagg, Alan.
  xBagg, Alan.
    Fifty Short Climbs in the Midwest. Contemp
      Bks.
  xBagg, Alan R.
    Back-Country Ski Camping. Contemp Bks.
Bagg, Alan R. see Bagg, Alan.
Bagg, Elma W.
  xBagg, Elma W.
    Cooking Without a Grain of Salt. Bantam.
    Cooking Without a Grain of Salt. Doubleday.
Bagg, Richard.
  xBagg, Richard.
    Intro. by & ed. Grading Coins: A Collection of
      Readings. Essex Pubns.
Baggelaar, Kristin.
  xBaggelaar, Kristin.

Folk Music: More Than a Song. T Y Crowell.
Baginski, Frank.
    xBaginski, Frank.
        Splitsville. Dutton.
Bagley, Christopher.
    xBagley, Christopher.
        ed. Race, Education & Identity. St Martin.
Bagley, Desmond, 1923-
    xBagley, Desmond.
        The Enemy. Doubleday.
        The Enemy. Fawcett.
        Flyaway. Doubleday.
Bagley, James R., 1946-
    xBagley, James R.
        The Star & Other Poems. Golden Quill.
Bagley, John J., 1908-
    xBagley, John J.
        History of Lancashire. Dufour.
Bagnall, Nicholas.
    xBagnall, Nicholas.
        ed. Parent Power: A Dictionary Guide to Your
            Child's Education & Schooling. Routledge &
            Kegan.
Bagnall, Oscar.
    xBagnall, Oscar.
        Origin & Properties of the Human Aura.
            Weiser.
Bagnall, Roger S.
    xBagnall, Roger S.
        Regnal Formulas in Byzantine Egypt. Scholars
            Pr Ca.
Bagnasco, Erminio.
    xBagnasco, Erminio.
        Submarines of World War Two. Naval Inst Pr.
Bagnasco, John J.
    xBagnasco, John J.
        Plants for the Home. Nature Life.
Bagnel, Joan.
    xBagnel, Joan.
        Gone the Rainbow, Gone the Dove. PB.
        Gone the Rainbow, Gone the Dove. Trident.
Bagnold, Enid.
    xBagnold, Enid.
        Loved & Envied. Greenwood.
        National Velvet. Archway.
        National Velvet. Morrow.
Bagshaw, Joseph C. see Bagshaw, Joseph Charles.
Bagshaw, Joseph Charles.
    xBagshaw, Joseph C.
        ed. Biochemistry of Artemia Development.
            Univ Microfilms.
Baguley, David.
    xBaguley, David.
        Fecondite D'Emile Zola: Roman a These,
            Evangile, Mythe. U of Toronto Pr.
Bagus, Paul.
    xBagus, Paul.
        ed. Topics in Surface Chemistry. Plenum Pub.
Bahadur, Dinesh.
    xBahadur, Dinesh.
        Come Fight a Kite. Harvey.
Bahl, Roy. see Bahl, Roy W.
Bahl, Roy W.
    xBahl, Roy.
        ed. The Fiscal Outlook for Cities: Implications
            of a National Urban Policy. Syracuse U Pr.
    xBahl, Roy W.
        Fiscal Centralization & Tax Burdens: State and
            Regional Finance of City Services. Ballinger
            Pub.
        ed. Public Employment & State & Local
            Government Finance. Ballinger Pub.
Bahlke, George W., 1934-
    xBahlke, George W.
        The Later Auden: From "New Year Letter" to
            About the House. Rutgers U Pr.
Bahm, Archie J.
    xBahm, Archie J.

ed. Directory of American Philosophers
    1980-81. Philos Document.
ed. Directory of American Philosophers 2,
    1964-65. Bahm.
ed. Directory of American Philosophers 4,
    1968-69. Bahm.
ed. Directory of American Philosophers 5,
    1970-71. Bahm.
        Ethics As a Behavioral Science. C C Thomas.
        The Philosopher's World Model. Greenwood.
        World's Living Religions. S Ill U Pr.
Bahme, Charles W. see Bahme, Charles William.
Bahme, Charles William, 1914-
    xBahme, Charles W.
        Fire Officer's Guide to Disaster Control. Natl
            Fire Prot.
        Fire Officer's Guide to Emergency Action.
            Natl Fire Prot.
        Fire Service & the Law. Natl Fire Prot.
Bahn, Gilbert S.
    xBahn, Gilbert S.
        ed. Reaction Rate Compilation for the H-O-N
            System. Gordon.
Bahnick, Karen R.
    xBahnick, Karen R.
        The Determination of Stages in the Historical
            Development of the Germanic Languages by
            Morphological Criteria: An Evaluation.
            Mouton.
Bahr, Alice.
    xBahr, Alice H.
        Book Theft & Library Security Systems,
            1978-79. Knowledge Indus.
        Book Theft & Library Security Systems: 1980
            to 1981. Knowledge Indus.
Bahr, Alice H. see Bahr, Alice.
Bahr, Alice Harrison.
    xBahr, Alice H.
        Automated Library Circulation Systems,
            1979-1980. Knowledge Indus.
Bahr, Ehrhard.
    xBahr, Ehrhard.
        Georg Lukacs. Ungar.
Bahr, Howard M.
    xBahr, Howard M.
        American Ethnicity. Heath.
Bahr, Jerome.
    xBahr, Jerome.
        Five Novellas. Trempealeau.
Bahr, Robert.
    xBahr, Robert.
        The Great Blizzard. Dandelion Pr.
Bahti, Mark.
    xBahti, Mark.
        Collecting Southwestern Native American
            Jewelry. McKay.
Bahti, Tom.
    xBahti, Tom.
        Southwestern Indian Ceremonials. K C Pubns.
        Southwestern Indian Tribes. K C Pubns.
Baiardi, John C.
    xBaiardi, John C.
        ed. Aquatic Sciences. NY Acad Sci.
Baier, Kurt.
    xBaier, Kurt.
        Moral Point of View: A Rational Basis of
            Ethics. Cornell U Pr.
        Moral Point of View: A Rational Basis of
            Ethics. Random.
Baierlein, Ralph.
    xBaierlein, Ralph.
        Atoms & Information Theory: An Introduction
            to Statistical Mechanics. W H Freeman.
Baig, M. R. see Baig, M. R. A.
Baig, M. R. A., 1905-
    xBaig, M. R.
        Muslim Dilemma in India. Intl Bk Dist.
Baig, Tara A. see Baig, Tara Ali.
Baig, Tara Ali.
    xBaig, Tara A.

India's Woman Power. Verry.
Baigell, Matthew.
    xBaigell, Matthew.
        Dictionary of American Art. Har-Row.
Bailar, J. C. see Bailar, John Christian.
Bailar, John Christian.
    xBailar, J. C.
        ed. Comprehensive Inorganic Chemistry.
            Pergamon.
Bailard, Thomas E.
    xBailard, Thomas E.
        Personal Money Management. SRA.
Bailes, N. J.
    xBailes, N. J.
        ed. Layman's Guide to Virginia Law. Michie.
Bailey, Adrian.
    xBailey, Adrian.
        The Book of Color Photography. Knopf.
Bailey, Albert E. see Bailey, Albert Edward.
Bailey, Albert Edward, 1871-1951
    xBailey, Albert E.
        Notes on the Literary Aspects of Tennyson's
            Princess. Folcroft.
Bailey, Albina.
    xBailey, Albina.
        Dressing Dolls in Nineteenth Century
            Fashions. Wallace-Homestead.
Bailey, Alfred G. see Bailey, Alfred Goldsworthy.
Bailey, Alfred Goldsworthy.
    xBailey, Alfred G.
        The Conflict of European & Eastern Algonkian
            Cultures, 1504-1700: A Study in Canadian
            Civilization. U of Toronto Pr.
Bailey, Alfred M. see Bailey, Alfred Marshall.
Bailey, Alfred Marshall.
    xBailey, Alfred M.
        Subantarctic Campbell Island. Denver Mus
            Natl Hist.
Bailey, Anthony.
    xBailey, Anthony.
        Acts of Union: Reports on Ireland, 1973-79.
            Random.
        Rembrandt's House. HM.
Bailey, Barry, 1926-
    xBailey, Barry.
        Living with Your Feelings. Abingdon.
Bailey, Bernadine. see Bailey, Bernadine Freeman.
Bailey, Bernadine Freeman, 1901-
    xBailey, Bernadine.
        Wonders of the World of Bears. Dodd.
Bailey, C. A. see Bailey, Colin Alfred.
Bailey, Carolyn S. see Bailey, Carolyn Sherwin.
Bailey, Carolyn Sherwin.
    xBailey, Carolyn S.
        For the Children's Hour. Gale.
        The Little Rabbit Who Wanted Red Wings.
            Platt.
        ed. Plays for the Children's Hour: An
            American Childhood Presentation. Core
            Collection.
        Stories for Every Holiday. Gale.
Bailey, Charles James Nice.
    xBailey, Charles-James N.
        Variation & Linguistic Theory. Ctr Appl Ling.
Bailey, Charles R.
    xBailey, Charles R.
        French Secondary Education, 1763-1790: The
            Secularization of Ex-Jesuit Colleges. Am
            Philos.
Bailey, Charles-James N. see Bailey, Charles James Nice.
Bailey, Colin Alfred, 1931-
    xBailey, C. A.
        Advanced Cryogenics. Plenum Pub.
Bailey, Conner.
    xBailey, Conner.

Broker, Mediator, Patron, & Kinsman: An
Historical Analysis of Key Leadership Roles
in a Rural Malaysian District. Ohio U Ctr
Intl.

Bailey, Covert.
xBailey, Covert.
Fit or Fat. HM.

Bailey, Cyril, 1871-
xBailey, Cyril.
ed. Legacy of Rome. Oxford U Pr.

Bailey, D. Sherwin. *see* Bailey, Derrick Sherwin.

Bailey, Daniel E. *see* Bailey, Daniel Edgar.

Bailey, Daniel Edgar, 1930-
xBailey, Daniel E.
ed. Computer Science in Social & Behavioral
Science Education. Educ Tech Pubns.

Bailey, David S.
xBailey, David S.
Therapeutic Approaches to the Care of the
Mentally Ill. Davis Co.

Bailey, De Witt.
xBailey, De Witt.
English Gunmakers: The Birmingham &
Provincial Gun Trade in the 18th & 19th
Century. Arco.

Bailey, Derrick Sherwin, 1910-
xBailey, D. Sherwin.
Homosexuality & the Western Christian
Tradition. Shoe String.

Bailey, Earl L., 1924-
xBailey, Earl L.
Marketing-Cost Ratios of U. S. Manufacturers:
A Technical Analysis. Conference Bd.
ed. Pricing Practices & Strategies. Conference
Bd.

Bailey, Edward P.
xBailey, Edward P.
The Practical Writer: Paragraph to Theme.
HR&W

Bailey, Elmer J. *see* Bailey, Elmer James.

Bailey, Elmer James.
xBailey, Elmer J.
Religious Thought in the Greater American
Poets. Arno.

Bailey, F. G. *see* Bailey, Frederick George.

Bailey, F. Lee. *see* Bailey, Francis Lee.

Bailey, Foster.
xBailey, Foster.
Changing Esoteric Values. Lucis.

Bailey, Francis Lee.
xBailey, F. Lee.
The Defense Never Rests. NAL.
The Defense Never Rests. U Mich Busn Div
Res.
For the Defense. NAL.
Fundamentals of Criminal Advocacy. Lawyers
Co-Op.
Secrets. Bantam.
Secrets. Stein & Day.
Successful Techniques for Criminal Trials.
Lawyers Co-Op.

Bailey, Frank E. *see* Bailey, Frank Edgar.

Bailey, Frank Edgar, 1904-
xBailey, Frank E.
British Policy & the Turkish Reform
Movement: A Study in Anglo-Turkish
Relations, 1826-1853. Fertig.

Bailey, Frederic W. *see* Bailey, Frederic William.

Bailey, Frederic William, d. 1918
xBailey, Frederic W.
Early Connecticut Marriages As Found on
Ancient Church Records Prior to 1800.
Genealog Pub.

Bailey, Frederick George.
xBailey, F. G.

ed. Gifts & Poison: The Politics of Reputation.
Schocken.
Politics & Social Change: Orissa in 1959. U of
Cal Pr.
Stratagems & Spoils: A Social Anthropology of
Politics. Biblio Dist.
Stratagems & Spoils: A Social Anthropology of
Politics. Schocken.

Bailey, Gerald E. *see* Bailey, Gerald Earl.

Bailey, Gerald Earl.
xBailey, Gerald E.
Sword of Poyana. Berkley Pub.
Sword of the Nurlingas. Berkley Pub.

Bailey, Gertrude Blackwell.
xBailey, Gertrude Blackwell.
If Words Could Set Us Free. Exposition.

Bailey, Gilbert E.
xBailey, Gilbert E.
California's Disappearing Coast: A Legislative
Challenge. Inst Gov Stud Berk.

Bailey, Helen M. *see* Bailey, Helen Miller.

Bailey, Helen Miller.
xBailey, Helen M.
Fifteen Famous Latin Americans. P-H.
Latin America: The Development of Its
Civilization. P-H.

Bailey, Henry J., 1916-
xBailey, Henry J.
Brady on Bank Checks. Warren.

Bailey, Herbert. *see* Bailey, Herbert Smith.

Bailey, Herbert S. *see* Bailey, Herbert Smith.

Bailey, Herbert Smith.
xBailey, Herbert.
The Art & Science of Book Publishing. U of
Tex Pr.
xBailey, Herbert S.
Art & Science of Book Publishing. Har-Row.

Bailey, Hugh C.
xBailey, Hugh C.
Liberalism in the New South: Southern Social
Reformers & the Progressive Movement. U of
Miami Pr.

Bailey, J. O. *see* Bailey, James Osler.

Bailey, J. W. *see* Bailey, Jackson William.

Bailey, Jack, 1898-
xBailey, Jack.
The British Co-Operative Movement.
Greenwood.

Bailey, Jack S.
xBailey, Jack S.
Let Not Your Heart Be Troubled: Answers to
the Problems of Human Suffering. Horizon
Utah.

Bailey, Jackson William.
xBailey, J. W.
Veterinary Handbook for Cattlemen. Springer
Pub.

Bailey, James. *see* Bailey, James Edward.

Bailey, James Edward, 1942-
xBailey, James.
Energy Systems: An Analysis for Engineers &
Policy Makers. Dekker.

Bailey, James Osler, 1903-
xBailey, J. O.
Thomas Hardy & the Cosmic Mind: A New
Reading of "the Dynasts". Greenwood.

Bailey, Janice.
xBailey, Janice.
Those Meddling Women. Judson.

Bailey, Jill.
xBailey, Jill.
Living Together. Mayflower Bks.
The Quest for Food. Mayflower Bks.

Bailey, John. *see* Bailey, John Cann.

Bailey, John C. *see* Bailey, John Cann.

Bailey, John Cann, 1864-1931
xBailey, John.
Dr. Johnson & His Circle. R West.
xBailey, John C.

Continuity of Letters. Arno.
Dr. Johnson & His Circle. Folcroft.
English Elegies. Arden Lib.
English Elegies. Folcroft.

Bailey, John Swartwout, 1907-
xBailey, John.
Intent on Laughter. Times Bks.

Bailey, John W., 1934-
xBailey, John W.
Pacifying the Plains: General Alfred Terry &
the Decline of the Sioux, 1866-1890.
Greenwood.

Bailey, Joseph A. *see* Bailey, Joseph Alexander.

Bailey, Joseph Alexander, 1935-
xBailey, Joseph A.
Disproportionate Short Stature: Diagnosis &
Management. Saunders.

Bailey, June T.
xBailey, June T.
Decision Making in Nursing: Tools for Change.
Mosby.

Bailey, Kenneth K. *see* Bailey, Kenneth Kyle.

Bailey, Kenneth Kyle, 1923-
xBailey, Kenneth K.
Southern White Protestantism in the Twentieth
Century. Peter Smith.

Bailey, Larry P.
xBailey, Larry P.
Contemporary Auditing. Har-Row.

Bailey, Leo L.
xBailey, Leo L.
A Step-by-Step Guide to Landscaping &
Gardening. Exposition.

Bailey, Liberty H. *see* Bailey, Liberty Hyde.

Bailey, Liberty Hyde.
xBailey, Liberty H.
Hortus Third: A Concise Dictionary of Plants
Cultivated in the United States & Canada.
Macmillan.
How Plants Get Their Names. Dover.
How Plants Get Their Names. Gale.
How Plants Get Their Names. Peter Smith.

Bailey, Lloyd R., 1936-
xBailey, Lloyd R.
Biblical Perspectives on Death. Fortress.

Bailey, Mark W.
xBailey, Mark W.
Electricity. Raintree Child.

Bailey, Martha J.
xBailey, Martha J.
The Special Librarian As a Supervisor or
Middle Manager. SLA.

Bailey, Ney.
xBailey, Ney.
Faith Is Not a Feeling. Campus Crusade.

Bailey, Norman. *see* Bailey, Norman A.

Bailey, Norman A.
xBailey, Norman.
Operational Conflict Analysis. Pub Aff Pr.

Bailey, Norman T. *see* Bailey, Norman T. J.

Bailey, Norman T. J.
xBailey, Norman T.
Mathematics, Statistics & Systems for Health.
Wiley.

Bailey, Patrick.
xBailey, Patrick.
Teaching Geography. David & Charles.

Bailey, Paul. *see* Bailey, Paul Dayton.

Bailey, Paul B.
xBailey, Paul B.
Nonlinear Two Point Boundary Value
Problems. Acad Pr.

Bailey, Paul C. *see* Bailey, Paul Clinton.

Bailey, Paul Clinton.
xBailey, Paul C.
Introduction to Modern Biology. Har-Row.

Bailey, Paul Dayton, 1906-
xBailey, Paul.

Hawaii's Royal Prime Minister: The Life &
Times of Walter Murray Gibson. Hastings.
Holy Smoke: A Dissertation on the Utah War.
Westernlore.

Bailey, Pearl.
xBailey, Pearl.
Duey's Tale. HarBraceJ.
Hurry up, America, & Spit. HarBraceJ.
Raw Pearl. HarBraceJ.
The Raw Pearl. PB.
Talking to Myself. HarBraceJ.
Talking to Myself. PB.

Bailey, Philip.
xBailey, Phillip.
They Can Make Music. Oxford U Pr.

Bailey, Philip S.
xBailey, Philip S.
Organic Chemistry: A Brief Survey of Concepts
& Applications. Allyn.
Bailey, Phillip. *see* Bailey, Philip.
Bailey, R. A. *see* Bailey, Ronald Albert.

Bailey, Raymond.
xBailey, Raymond.
Thomas Merton on Mysticism. Doubleday.

Bailey, Raymond C.
xBailey, Raymond C.
Popular Influence Upon Public Policy:
Petitioning in Eighteenth-Century Virginia.
Greenwood.

Bailey, Richard.
xBailey, Richard.
Africa's Industrial Future. Westview.
Energy: The Rude Awakening. Energy Educ.

Bailey, Richard M.
xBailey, Richard M.
Clinical Laboratories & the Practice of
Medicine: An Economic Perspective.
McCutchan.

Bailey, Richard W.
xBailey, Richard W.
An Annotated Bibliography of Statistical
Stylistics. Mich Slavic Pubns.
English Stylistics: A Bibliography. MIT Pr.
Varieties of Present-Day English. Macmillan.

Bailey, Robert.
xBailey, Robert.
Radicals in Urban Politics: The Alinsky
Approach. U of Chicago Pr.
Bailey, Robert. *see* Bailey, Robert W.
Bailey, Robert L. *see* Bailey, Robert Leo.

Bailey, Robert Lee.
xBailey, Robert L.
An Examination of Prime Time Network
Television Special Programs: 1948-1966.
Arno.

Bailey, Robert Leo, 1927-
xBailey, Robert L.
Disciplined Creativity for Engineers. Ann
Arbor Science.
Solar-Electrics Research & Development. Ann
Arbor Science.

Bailey, Robert W.
xBailey, Robert.
Coping with Stress in the Minister's Home.
Broadman.
xBailey, Robert W.
God's Questions & Answers: Contemporary
Studies in Malachi. Seabury.
Ministering to the Grieving. Zondervan.
Bailey, Robert W. *see* Bailey, Robert Wayne.

Bailey, Robert Wayne.
xBailey, Robert W.
Pref. by The Cervical Spine. Lea & Febiger.

Bailey, Roger B.
xBailey, Roger B.
Guide to Chinese Poetry & Drama. G K Hall.

Bailey, Ronald Albert, 1933-
xBailey, R. A.
Chemistry of the Environment. Acad Pr.
Bailey, Stephen. *see* Bailey, Stephen Kemp.

Bailey, Stephen K. *see* Bailey, Stephen Kemp.

Bailey, Stephen Kemp.
xBailey, Stephen.
The Purposes of Education. Phi Delta Kappa.
xBailey, Stephen K.
Congress in the Seventies. St Martin.
Congress Makes a Law: The Story Behind the
Employment Act of 1946. Greenwood.
Education Interest Groups in the Nation's
Capital. ACE.
Bailey, Sydney D. *see* Bailey, Sydney Dawson.

Bailey, Sydney Dawson.
xBailey, Sydney D.
British Parliamentary Democracy. Greenwood.
The General Assembly of the United Nations:
A Study of Procedure & Practice.
Greenwood.
ed. Political Parties & the Party System in
Britain: A Symposium. Hyperion Conn.
The Procedure of the UN Security Council.
Oxford U Pr.
Prohibitions & Restraints in War. Oxford U Pr.
Bailey, T. A. *see* Bailey, Thomas Andrew.

Bailey, Temple.
xBailey, Temple.
Radiant Tree, & Other Stories. Arno.
Bailey, Thomas A. *see* Bailey, Thomas Andrew.

Bailey, Thomas Andrew, 1902-
xBailey, T. A.
Woodrow Wilson & the Great Betrayal. Peter
Smith.
xBailey, Thomas A.
The American Pageant: A History of the
Republic. Heath.
A Diplomatic History of the American People.
P-H.
Hitler Vs. Roosevelt: The Undeclared Naval
War. Free Pr.
The Marshall Plan Summer: An Eyewitness
Report on Europe & the Russians in 1947.
Hoover Inst Pr.
Presidential Greatness: The Image & the Man
from George Washington to the Present.
Irvington.
Woodrow Wilson & the Great Betrayal. Times
Bks.
Woodrow Wilson & the Lost Peace. Peter
Smith.
Woodrow Wilson & the Lost Peace. Times Bks.
xBailey, Thoms A.
Probing America's Past: A Critical
Examination of Major Myths &
Misconceptions. Heath.
Bailey, Thoms A. *see* Bailey, Thomas Andrew.

Bailey, Trevor.
xBailey, Trevor.
History of Cricket. Allen Unwin.

Bailie, R. C.
xBailie, Richard C.
Energy Conversion Engineering. A-W.
Bailie, Richard C. *see* Bailie, R. C.

Bailie, William.
xBailie, William.
Josiah Warren, the First American Anarchist:
A Sociological Study. AMS Pr.
Bailkey, Nels. *see* Bailkey, Nels M.

Bailkey, Nels M.
xBailkey, Nels.
ed. Readings in Ancient History: From
Gilgamesh to Diocletian. Heath.
Baillie, A. H. *see* Baillie, Archibald Hannah.

Baillie, Archibald Hannah.
xBaillie, A. H.
Developments in Steroid Histochemistry. Acad
Pr.

Baillie, John, 1886-1960
xBaillie, John.

Diary of Private Prayer. Scribner.
The Idea of Revelation in Recent Thought.
Columbia U Pr.

Baillie, Sheila.
xBaillie, Sheila.
Graphics for Interior Space. U of Nebr Pr.
Bailor, Edwin M. *see* Bailor, Edwin Maurice.

Bailor, Edwin Maurice, 1890-
xBailor, Edwin M.
Content & Form in Tests of Intelligence. AMS
Pr.
Baily, P. J. *see* Baily, Peter J. H.

Baily, Peter J. H.
xBaily, P. J.
Purchasing & Supply Management. Methuen
Inc.

Bailyn, Bernard.
xBailyn, Bernard.
Education in the Forming of American Society:
Needs & Opportunities for Study. U of NC
Pr.
The Great Republic: A History of the
American People. Heath.
The Great Republic: A History of the
American People. Little.
Ideological Origins of the American
Revolution. Harvard U Pr.
The Ordeal of Thomas Hutchinson. Harvard U
Pr.
Origins of American Politics. Knopf.
Origins of American Politics. Random.

Bain, Alexander, 1818-1903
xBain, Alexander.
Practical Essays. Arno.

Bain, Carl E.
xBain, Carl E.
ed. The Norton Introduction to Literature.
Norton.
Bain, Chester A. *see* Bain, Chester Arthur.

Bain, Chester Arthur, 1912-
xBain, Chester A.
The Far East. Littlefield.

Bain, David.
xBain, David.
Actors & Audience: A Study of Asides &
Related Conventions in Greek Drama.
Oxford U Pr.
Bain, Foster H. *see* Bain, Harry Foster.
Bain, G. S. *see* Bain, George Sayers.
Bain, George S. *see* Bain, George Sayers.

Bain, George Sayers.
xBain, G. S.
A Bibliography of British Industrial Relations.
Cambridge U Pr.
xBain, George S.
Growth of White-Collar Unionism. Oxford U
Pr.

Bain, Harry Foster.
xBain, Foster H.
Ores & Industry in South America. Arno.
Bain, Kenneth R. *see* Bain, Kenneth Ray.

Bain, Kenneth Ray, 1942-
xBain, Kenneth R.
The March to Zion: United States Policy & the
Founding of Israel. Tex A&M Univ Pr.
Bain, Mary A. *see* Bain, Mary Albertus.

Bain, Mary Albertus, 1911-
xBain, Mary A.
Ancient Landmarks: A Social & Economic
History of the Victoria District, Western
Australia, 1839-1894. Intl Schol Bk Serv.

Bain, Mildred.
xBain, Mildred.
ed. From Freedom to Freedom: African Roots
in American Soil. Purnell Ref Bks.
ed. From Freedom to Freedom: African Roots
in American Soil. Random.
Bain, R. Nisbet. *see* Bain, Robert Nisbet.

Bain, Richard C.
xBain, Richard C.

ed. Functional Morphology of the Heart. S
    Karger.
Bak, Janos. *see* Bak, Janos M.
Bak, Janos M.
    xBak, Janos.
        ed. The German Peasant War of 1525. Biblio
            Dist.
Bakal, Carl, 1918-
    xBakal, Carl.
        Charity U. S. A.: An Investigation into the
            Hidden World of the Multi-Billion Dollar
            Charity Industry. Times Bks.
Bakal, Donald A.
    xBakal, Donald A.
        Psychology & Medicine: Psychobiological
            Dimensions of Health & Illness. Springer
            Pub.
Bakalis, Michael J.
    xBakalis, Michael J.
        A Strategy for Excellence: Reaching for New
            Standards in Education. Shoe String.
Bakamis, William A.
    xBakamis, William A.
        Improving Instruction in Industrial Arts.
            Glencoe.
Bakan, David.
    xBakan, David.
        And They Took Themselves Wives: The
            Emergence of Patriarchy in Western Society.
            Har-Row.
        Disease, Pain & Sacrifice: Toward a Psychology
            of Suffering. Beacon Pr.
        On Method: Toward a Reconstruction of
            Psychological Investigation. Jossey-Bass.
        Sigmund Freud & the Jewish Mystical
            Tradition. Beacon Pr.
Bakeless, Katherine. *see* Bakeless, Katherine (Little).
Bakeless, Katherine (Little).
    xBakeless, Katherine.
        Confederate Spy Stories. Lippincott.
Bakely, Donald C.
    xBakely, Donald C.
        If...a Big Word with the Poor. Faith & Life.
Baken, Lenore.
    xBaken, Lenore.
        How to Camp Europe by Train. Ariel Pubns.
Baker. *see* Baker, David E. U.
Baker, A. A.
    xBaker, A. A.
        Border War. Bouregy.
        Rebel Guns. Bouregy.
        Vengeance Rides West. Bouregy.
Baker, Adelaide N.
    xBaker, Adelaide N.
        Return to Arcady. Lawrence Hill.
Baker, Alan R. *see* Baker, Alan R. H.
Baker, Alan R. H.
    xBaker, Alan R.
        ed. Progress in Historical Geography. Halsted
            Pr.
Baker, Albert E. *see* Baker, Albert Edward.
Baker, Albert Edward, 1884-
    xBaker, Albert E.
        Prophets for a Day of Judgment. Arno.
Baker, Alton W. *see* Baker, Alton Wesley.
Baker, Alton Wesley.
    xBaker, Alton W.
        Ratios of Staff to Line Employees & Stages of
            Differentiation of Staff Functions. Ohio St U
            Admin Sci.
Baker, Arthur.
    xBaker, Arthur.
        Calligraphic Alphabets. Dover.
        Calligraphic Alphabets. Peter Smith.
        Calligraphy. Dover.
        Calligraphy. Peter Smith.
        The House Is Sitting. Greenwood.
Baker, Arthur D.
    xBaker, Arthur D.

Organic Chemistry: Problems & Solutions.
    Allyn.
Baker, Augusta.
    xBaker, Augusta.
        Storytelling: Art & Technique. Bowker.
Baker, B. H. *see* Baker, Brian Howard.
Baker, B. R. *see* Baker, Bernard Randall.
Baker, Barton. *see* Baker, Henry Barton.
Baker, Bernard Randall, 1915-
    xBaker, B. R.
        Design of Active-Site Directed Irreversible
            Enzyme Inhibitors: The Organic Chemistry of
            the Enzymic Active-Site. Krieger.
Baker, Bernard S.
    xBaker, Bernard S.
        ed. Hydrocarbon Fuel Cell Technology: A
            Symposium. Acad Pr.
Baker, Betty.
    xBaker, Betty.
        All-by-Herself. Greenwillow.
        All-by-Herself. Morrow.
        And One Was a Wooden Indian. Macmillan.
        Do Not Annoy the Indians. Macmillan.
        Dupper. Greenwillow.
        Latki & the Lightning Lizard. Macmillan.
        No Help at All. Greenwillow.
        Partners. Greenwillow.
        Spirit Is Willing. Macmillan.
        A Stranger & Afraid. Macmillan.
Baker, Betty S. *see* Baker, Betty Sue.
Baker, Betty Sue.
    xBaker, Betty S.
        A Study of Social Status, Personality
            Characteristics, & Motor Ability of Mentally
            Handicapped Girls. R & E Res Assoc.
Baker, Bill.
    xBaker, Bill.
        How to Beat the Energy Crisis & Still Live in
            Style. Putnam.
Baker, Bill R.
    xBaker, Bill R.
        Catch the Vision: The Life of Henry L.
            Whitfield of Mississippi. U Pr of Miss.
Baker, Bobby. *see* Baker, Robert Gene.
Baker, Brian Howard.
    xBaker, B. H.
        Geology of the Eastern Rift System of Africa.
            Geol Soc.
Baker, C. *see* Baker, Charlotte.
Baker, C. C. *see* Baker, Cyril Clarence Thomas.
Baker, C. J. *see* Baker, Christopher John.
Baker, C. L. *see* Baker, Carl Lee.
Baker, C. Richard.
    xBaker, C. Richard.
        Accounting, Finance, & Taxation: A Basic
            Guide for Small Business. CBI Pub.
Baker, Carl Lee, 1939-
    xBaker, C. L.
        Introduction to Generative-Transformational
            Syntax. P-H.
Baker, Charles L. *see* Baker, Charles Laurence.
Baker, Charles Laurence, 1887-
    xBaker, Charles L.
        Geologic Reconnaissance in the Eastern
            Cordillera of Mexico. Geol Soc.
Baker, Charlotte, 1910-
    xBaker, C.
        Cockleburr Quarters. P-H.
    xBaker, Charlotte.
        Cockleburr Quarters. Avon.
Baker, Christopher John, 1948-
    xBaker, C. J.
        The Politics of South India, 1920-1937.
            Cambridge U Pr.
Baker, Cozy, 1927-
    xBaker, Cozy.
        A Cozy Getaway. Acropolis.
Baker, Cyril Clarence Thomas, 1907-
    xBaker, C. C.

Introduction to Calculus. Arc Bks.
Introduction to Mathematics. Arc Bks.
Baker, Daisy, 1894-
    xBaker, Daisy.
        More Travels in a Donkey Trap. Intl Schol Bk
            Serv.
Baker, Daniel, 1949-
    xBaker, Daniel.
        Projects in Optical Properties of the
            Atmosphere, Upper Atmospheric Turbulence
            & Structure, Ionospheric Reflection
            Properties, Plasma Physics, Data Reduction
            & Perspective Drawing. Mgmt Info Serv.
Baker, David, 1944-
    xBaker, David.
        The Larousse Guide to Astronomy. Larousse.
Baker, David E. U.
    xBaker.
        Changing Political Leadership in an Indian
            Province: The Central Provinces & Berar
            1919-1939. Oxford U Pr.
Baker, Denys Val. *see* Val Baker, Denys.
Baker, Donna.
    xBaker, Donna.
        I Want to Be a Librarian. Childrens.
        I Want to Be a Pilot. Childrens.
        I Want to Be a Police Officer. Childrens.
Baker, E. H.
    xBaker, E. H.
        Structural Analysis of Shells. Krieger.
Baker, Elizabeth, 1944-
    xBaker, Elizabeth.
        Love Around the House. Victor Bks.
Baker, Elizabeth. *see* Baker, Elizabeth (Faulkner).
Baker, Elizabeth (Faulkner), 1885-
    xBaker, Elizabeth.
        Protective Labor Legislation, with Special
            Reference to Women in the State of New
            York. AMS Pr.
Baker, Elizabeth (Gillette).
    xBaker, Elizabeth.
        Tammy Camps in the Rocky Mountains. HM.
Baker, Elsworth. *see* Baker, Elsworth F.
Baker, Elsworth F.
    xBaker, Elsworth.
        Man in the Trap. Macmillan.
    xBaker, Elsworth F.
        Man in the Trap. Macmillan.
Baker, Eric W.
    xBaker, Eric W.
        Faith of a Methodist. Abingdon.
Baker, Ernest A. *see* Baker, Ernest Albert.
Baker, Ernest Albert, 1869-1941
    xBaker, Ernest A.
        Guide to Historical Fiction. Argosy.
        Guide to Historical Fiction. B Franklin.
Baker, Eugene. *see* Baker, Eugene H.
Baker, Eugene H.
    xBaker, Eugene.
        I Want to Be a Basketball Player. Childrens.
        I Want to Be a Draftsman. Childrens.
        I Want to Be a Football Player. Childrens.
        I Want to Be a Gymnast. Childrens.
        I Want to Be a Hockey Player. Childrens.
        I Want to Be a Postal Clerk. Childrens.
        I Want to Be a Service Station Attendant.
            Childrens.
        I Want to Be a Soccer Player. Childrens.
        I Want to Be a Swimmer. Childrens.
        I Want to Be a Tennis Player. Childrens.
        I Want to Be a Waitress. Childrens.
        I Want to Be a Weatherman. Childrens.
        In the Detective's Lab. Childrens.
        In the Detective's Lab. Childs World.
Baker, Eva L.
    xBaker, Eva L.
        ed. Educational Testing & Evaluation: Design,
            Analysis, & Policy. Sage.
Baker, F. J. *see* Baker, Francis Joseph.

Baker, Fay.
   xBaker, Fay.
     My Darling Darling Doctors. Braziller.
Baker, Francis Joseph.
   xBaker, F. J.
     Introduction to Medical Laboratory
      Technology. Butterworths.
Baker, Frank B.
   xBaker, Frank B.
     Computer Managed Instruction: Theory &
      Practice. Educ Tech Pubns.
Baker, George A., 1932-
   xBaker, George A.
     Essentials of Pade Approximants. Acad Pr.
     ed. Pade Approximant in Theoretical Physics.
      Acad Pr.
Baker, George P. *see* Baker, George Pierce.
Baker, George Philip, 1879-1951
   xBaker, George P.
     Constantine the Great & the Christian
      Revolution. Rowman.
Baker, George Pierce, 1866-1935
   xBaker, George P.
     Development of Shakespeare As a Dramatist.
      AMS Pr.
     Dramatic Technique. Da Capo.
     Dramatic Technique. Greenwood.
     Dramatic Technique. R West.
     Formation of the New England Railroad
      Systems: A Study of Railroad Combination in
      the Nineteenth Century. Greenwood.
     Modern American Plays. Arno.
Baker, Glen E.
   xBaker, Glenn E.
     Wood Technology. Bobbs.
Baker, Glenn E. *see* Baker, Glen E.
Baker, Gordon E.
   xBaker, Gordon E.
     Reapportionment Revolution: Representation,
      Political Power & the Supreme Court. Phila
      Bk Co.
     Rural Versus Urban Political Power: The
      Nature & Consequences of Unbalanced
      Representation. Greenwood.
Baker, Henry Barton, 1845-1906
   xBaker, Barton.
     History of the London Stage & Its Famous
      Players 1576-1903. Arno.
Baker, Herbert, Sir, 1862-1946
   xBaker, Herbert.
     Cecil Rhodes. Arno.
Baker, Herbert G.
   xBaker, Herbert G.
     Plants & Civilization. Wadsworth Pub.
Baker, Herschel. *see* Baker, Herschel Clay.
Baker, Herschel C. *see* Baker, Herschel Clay.
Baker, Herschel Clay.
   xBaker, Herschel.
     ed. Four Essays on Romance. Harvard U Pr.
     ed. Later Renaissance in England: Nondramatic
      Verse & Prose, 1600-1660. HM.
   xBaker, Herschel C.
     Hyder Edward Rollins: A Bibliography.
      Harvard U Pr.
Baker, Houston A.
   xBaker, Houston A.
     The Journey Back: Issues in Black Literature &
      Criticism. U of Chicago Pr.
     Long Black Song: Essays in Black American
      Literature & Culture. U Pr of Va.
Baker, Howard, 1905-
   xBaker, Howard.
     Ode to the Sea & Other Poems. Swallow.
     Persephone's Cave: Cultural Accumulations of
      the Early Greeks. U of Ga Pr.
Baker, Hugh. *see* Baker, Hugh D. R.
Baker, Hugh D. R.
   xBaker, Hugh.
     Chinese Family & Kinship. Columbia U Pr.
   xBaker, Hugh R.

     Chinese Family & Kinship. Columbia U Pr.
Baker, Hugh R. *see* Baker, Hugh D. R.
Baker, J. K. *see* Baker, James K.
Baker, James C. *see* Baker, James Calvin.
Baker, James Calvin.
   xBaker, James C.
     American Banks Abroad: Edge Act Companies
      & Multinational Banking. Praeger.
Baker, James K.
   xBaker, J. K.
     Approved Practices in Swine Production.
      Interstate.
Baker, James T. *see* Baker, James Thomas.
Baker, James Thomas.
   xBaker, James T.
     Faith for a Dark Saturday. Judson.
     A Southern Baptist in the White House.
      Westminster.
Baker, Jean H.
   xBaker, Jean H.
     Ambivalent Americans: The Know-Nothing
      Party in Maryland. Johns Hopkins.
     The Politics of Continuity: Maryland Political
      Parties from 1858 to 1870. Johns Hopkins.
Baker, Jeffrey J. *see* Baker, Jeffrey J. W.
Baker, Jeffrey J. W.
   xBaker, Jeffrey J.
     Course in Biology. A-W.
     Hypothesis, Prediction, & Implication in
      Biology. A-W.
   xBaker, Jeffrey W.
     Matter, Energy & Life: An Introduction for
      Biology Students. A-W.
Baker, Jeffrey W. *see* Baker, Jeffrey J. W.
Baker, Jennifer.
   xBaker, Jennifer.
     The Horse Show. Allen Unwin.
Baker, Jerry.
   nBaker, Jerry.
     I Never Met a House Plant I Didn't Like. PB.
     I Never Met a House Plant I Didn't Like.
      S&S.
Baker, Jim.
   xBaker, Jim.
     How to Be a Kid Again. Ohio Hist Soc.
     O. J. Simpson's Most Memorable Games.
      Putnam.
Baker, John.
   xBaker, John.
     English Stained Glass of the Medieval Period.
      Thames Hudson.
     The Neighbourhood Advice Centre: A
      Community Project in Camden. Routledge &
      Kegan.
Baker, John A. *see* Baker, John Alec.
Baker, John Alec.
   xBaker, John A.
     Peregrine. Har-Row.
Baker, John M. *see* Baker, John Milnes.
Baker, John Milnes, 1932-
   xBaker, John M.
     illus. How to Build a House with an Architect.
      Lippincott.
Baker, Josephine.
   xBaker, Josephine.
     Josephine. Har-Row.
Baker, K. *see* Baker, Katherine Read.
Baker, Katherine Read.
   xBaker, K.
     Understanding & Guiding Young Children.
      P-H.
Baker, Keith.
   xBaker, Keith.
     Comprehensive Services to Rural Poor
      Families: An Evaluation of the Arizona Job
      College Program. Praeger.
Baker, Kenneth R., 1943-
   xBaker, Kenneth R.

     Introduction to Sequencing & Scheduling.
      Wiley.
Baker, Laura N. *see* Baker, Laura Nelson.
Baker, Laura Nelson, 1911-
   xBaker, Laura N.
     Go Away, Ruthie. Knopf.
     Somebody, Somewhere. Knopf.
Baker, Leonard.
   xBaker, Leonard.
     Days of Sorrow & Pain: Leo Baeck & the
      Berlin Jews. Macmillan.
     Days of Sorrow & Pain: Leo Baeck & the
      Berlin Jews. Oxford U Pr.
Baker, Leslie A.
   xBaker, Leslie A.
     The Art Teacher's Resource Book. Reston.
Baker, Lillian.
   xBaker, Lillian.
     The Collector's Encyclopedia of Hatpins &
      Hatpin Holders. Collector Bks.
Baker, Lucinda, 1916-
   xBaker, Lucinda.
     Memoirs of the First Baroness. Putnam.
Baker, Margaret, 1928-
   xBaker, Margaret.
     Gardener's Magic & Folklore. Universe.
   xBaker, Margret.
     Folklore of the Sea. David & Charles.
Baker, Margret. *see* Baker, Margaret.
Baker, Marilyn.
   xBaker, Marilyn.
     Exclusive!: The Inside Story of Patricia Hearst
      & the SLA. Macmillan.
Baker, Michael.
   xBaker, Michael.
     The Rise of the Victorian Actor. Rowman.
Baker, Michael J. *see* Baker, Michael John.
Baker, Michael John.
   xBaker, Michael J.
     Marketing in Adversity. Holmes & Meier.
     Marketing New Industrial Products. Holmes &
      Meier.
Baker, Muriel. *see* Baker, Muriel L.
Baker, Muriel L.
   xBaker, Muriel.
     ed. Scribner Book of Embroidery Designs.
      Scribner.
   xBaker, Muriel L.
     Handbook of American Crewel Embroidery. C
      E Tuttle.
     Stumpwork: The Art of Raised Embroidery.
      Scribner.
Baker, Nancy C.
   xBaker, Nancy C.
     Babyselling: The Scandal of Black-Market
      Adoption. Vanguard.
Baker, Oleda.
   xBaker, Oleda.
     How to Create the Illusion of a More Perfect
      Figure. P-H.
Baker, P. *see* Baker, Paul R.
Baker, P. Randall. *see* Baker, Randall.
Baker, Pat A., 1931-
   xBaker, Pat A.
     In This Moment. Abingdon.
Baker, Paul R.
   xBaker, P.
     Atomic Bomb: The Great Decision. HR&W.
   xBaker, Paul R.
     Richard Morris Hunt. MIT Pr.
Baker, R. Robin. *see* Baker, Reginald Robin.
Baker, R. Robinson. *see* Baker, Ralph Robinson.
Baker, Ralph.
   xBaker, Ralph.
     ed. Evaluating Alternative Law-Enforcement
      Policies. Lexington Bks.
Baker, Ralph Robinson, 1928-
   xBaker, R. Robinson.

ed. Current Trends in the Management of
Breast Cancer. Johns Hopkins.
Baker, Randall.
xBaker, P. Randall.
King Husain & the Kingdom of Hejaz.
Oleander Pr.
Baker, Ray P. *see* Baker, Ray Palmer.
Baker, Ray Palmer, 1883-
xBaker, Ray P.
History of English-Canadian Literature to the
Confederation: Its Relation to the Literature
of Great Britain & the U. S.. Russell.
Baker, Raymond W. *see* Baker, Raymond William.
Baker, Raymond William, 1942-
xBaker, Raymond W.
Egypt's Uncertain Revolution Under Nasser &
Sadat. Harvard U Pr.
Baker, Reginald Robin, 1944-
xBaker, R. Robin.
The Evolutionary Ecology of Animal
Migration. Holmes & Meier.
Baker, Robert A. *see* Baker, Robert Andrew.
Baker, Robert Andrew.
xBaker, Robert A.
The Southern Baptist Convention & Its People.
Broadman.
Summary of Christian History. Broadman.
Baker, Robert F. *see* Baker, Robert Fulton.
Baker, Robert Fulton.
xBaker, Robert F.
Handbook of Highway Engineering. Van Nos
Reinhold.
Public Policy Development: Linking the
Technical & Political Processes. Wiley.
Baker, Robert Gene.
xBaker, Bobby.
Wheeling & Dealing: Confessions of a Capitol
Hill Operator. Norton.
Baker, Robert J.
xBaker, Robert J.
God Healed Me. Herald Pr.
God Healed Me. Keats.
Baker, Robert K., 1948-
xBaker, Robert K.
Introduction to Library Research in French
Literature. Westview.
Baker, Robert L. *see* Baker, Robert Lesis.
Baker, Robert Lesis, 1922-
xBaker, Robert L.
English Customs Service, 1307-1343: A Study
of Medieval Administration. Am Philos.
Baker, Roger D. *see* Baker, Roger Denio.
Baker, Roger Denio, 1902-
xBaker, Roger D.
Human Infection with Fungi, Actinomycetes &
Algae. Springer-Verlag.
Baker, Ronald L.
xBaker, Ronald L.
Folklore in the Writings of Rowland E.
Robinson. Bowling Green Univ..
Indiana Place Names. Ind U Pr.
Baker, Roscoe.
xBaker, Roscoe.
The American Legion & American Foreign
Policy. Greenwood.
Baker, Ross K.
xBaker, Ross K.
Friend & Foe in the U. S. Senate. Free Pr.
Baker, S. *see* Baker, Sheridan Warner.
Baker, S. Josephine. *see* Baker, Sara Josephine.
Baker, Samuel W. *see* Baker, Samuel White.
Baker, Samuel White, Sir, 1821-1893
xBaker, Samuel W.
In the Heart of Africa. Negro U Pr.
Baker, Sara Josephine, 1873-1945
xBaker, S. Josephine.
Fighting for Life. Arno.
Fighting for Life. Krieger.
Baker, Scott.
xBaker, Scott.

Nightchild. Putnam.
Baker, Sheridan. *see* Baker, Sheridan Warner.
Baker, Sheridan Warner, 1918-
xBaker, S.
The Practical Stylist. Har-Row.
xBaker, Sheridan.
The Complete Stylist & Handbook. Har-Row.
On the Sentence. Har-Row.
The Practical Stylist. Har-Row.
Baker, Stanley L.
xBaker, Stanley L.
The Railroadiana Collector's Price Guide.
Dutton.
Baker, Stephen, 1924-
xBaker, Stephen.
Games Dogs Play. McGraw.
How to Live with a Neurotic Dog. P-H.
How to Live with a Neurotic Dog. PB.
The Systematic Approach to Advertising
Creativity. McGraw.
Baker, T. Lindsay.
xBaker, T. Lindsay.
The First Polish Americans: Silesian
Settlements in Texas. Tex A&M Univ Pr.
Baker, Timothy. *see* Baker, Timothy D.
Baker, Timothy D.
xBaker, Timothy.
Assessment of Health Status & Needs. Springer
Pub.
Baker, Wilfred E.
xBaker, Wilfred E.
Explosions in Air. U of Tex Pr.
Baker, Will, 1944-
xBaker, Will.
Chip. HarBraceJ.
Baker, William D.
xBaker, William D.
Reading Skills. P-H.
Baker, William E. *see* Baker, William Edwin.
Baker, William Edwin, 1935-
xBaker, William E.
Syntax in English Poetry, 1870-1930. U of Cal
Pr.
Baker, William H. *see* Baker, William Henry.
Baker, William Henry, 1937-
xBaker, William H.
ed. Diagnosis & Treatment of Carotid Artery
Disease: With Special Emphasis on
Noninvasive Diagnosis & Surgical Technique.
Futura Pub.
Baker, William P. *see* Baker, William Pearson.
Baker, William Pearson.
xBaker, William P.
The English Village. Greenwood.
Baker, Yvonne. *see* Baker, Yvonne G.
Baker, Yvonne G.
xBaker, Yvonne.
From God's Natural Storehouse: Practical
Alternatives to Cooking with Junk. Cook.
Bakerman, Theodore.
xBakerman, Theodore.
Anthracite Coal: A Study in Advanced
Industrial Decline. Arno.
Bakewell, Charles. *see* Bakewell, Charles Montague.
Bakewell, Charles Montague, 1867-1957
xBakewell, Charles.
Source Book in Ancient Philosophy. Gordian.
Bakewell, P. J. *see* Bakewell, Peter John.
Bakewell, Paul, 1889-
xBakewell, Paul.
Inflation in the United States. Caxton.
Bakewell, Peter John.
xBakewell, P. J.
Silver Mining & Society in Colonial Mexico,
Zacatecas, 1546-1700. Cambridge U Pr.
Bakewell, Robert, 1768-1843
xBakewell, Robert.
An Introduction to Geology. Arno.
Bakhtin, M. *see* Bakhtin, Mikhail Mikhailovich.

Bakhtin, Mikhail Mikhailovich.
xBakhtin, M.
Rabelais & His World. MIT Pr.
Bakish, David.
xBakish, David.
Richard Wright. Ungar.
Bakke, E. Wight. *see* Bakke, Edward Wight.
Bakke, Edward Wight.
xBakke, E. Wight.
Campus Challenge: Student Activism in
Perspective. Shoe String.
Citizens Without Work: A Study of the Effects
of Unemployment Upon the Workers' Social
Relations & Practices. Shoe String.
Revolutionary Democracy: Challenge & Testing
in Japan. Shoe String.
Bakken, Henry H. *see* Bakken, Henry Harrison.
Bakken, Henry Harrison.
xBakken, Henry H.
ed. Futures Trading in Livestock: Origins and
Concepts. Mimir.
Bakker, Cornelis. *see* Bakker, Cornelis B.
Bakker, Cornelis B.
xBakker, Cornelis.
No Trespassing!: Explorations in Human
Territoriality. Chandler & Sharp.
Baklanoff, Eric N.
xBaklanoff, Eric N.
The Economic Transformation of Spain &
Portugal. Praeger.
ed. Mediterranean Europe & the Common
Market: Studies of Economic Growth &
Integration. U of Ala Pr.
Bako, Elemer.
xBako, Elemer.
Guide to Hungarian Studies. Hoover Inst Pr.
Bakos, Jack D.
xBakos, Jack D.
Structural Analysis for Engineering
Technology. Merrill.
Bakst, James.
xBakst, James.
A History of Russian-Soviet Music.
Greenwood.
Bakunin, M. A. *see* Bakunin, Mikhail Aleksandrovich.
Bakunin, Mikhail Aleksandrovich, 1814-1876
xBakunin, M. A.
Bakunin's Writings. Kraus Repr.
Balaban, John, 1943-
xBalaban, John.
After Our War. U of Pittsburgh Pr.
ed. Ca Dao Vietnam: Bilingual Anthology of
Vietnamese Folk Poetry. Unicorn Pr.
Balabkins, Nicholas.
xBalabkins, Nicholas.
Germany Under Direct Controls: Economic
Aspects of Industrial Disarmament,
1945-1948. Rutgers U Pr.
Balachandran, M.
xBalachandran, M.
ed. A Guide to Trade & Securities Statistics.
Pierian.
Balachandran, S. *see* Balachandran, Sarojini.
Balachandran, Sarojini.
xBalachandran, S.
ed. Reference Book Review Index: 1973-1975.
Pierian.
xBalachandran, Sarojini.
ed. New Product Planning. Gale.
Balakian, Anna. *see* Balakian, Anna Elizabeth.
Balakian, Anna Elizabeth, 1915-
xBalakian, Anna.
Literary Origins of Surrealism: A New
Mysticism in French Poetry. NYU Pr.
Balakian, Nona.
xBalakian, Nona.

The Creative Present: Notes on Contemporary
   American Fiction. Gordian.
   Critical Encounters: Literary Views & Reviews
   1953-1977. Bobbs.
Balakrishnan, A. V.
   xBalakrishnan, A. V.
   Applied Functional Analysis. Springer-Verlag.
Balakrishnan, T. R.
   xBalakrishnan, T. R.
   Fertility & Family Planning in a Canadian
   Metropolis. McGill-Queens U Pr.
Balan, Jorge.
   xBalan, Jorge.
   Men in a Developing Society: Geographic &
   Social Mobility in Monterrey, Mexico. U of
   Tex Pr.
Balanchine, George.
   xBalanchine, George.
   Balanchine's Complete Stories of the Great
   Ballets. Doubleday.
Balas, Robert.
   xBalas, Robert S.
   Qu'est-Ce Qui Se Passe?:
   Conversation--Revision De Grammaire.
   Rand.
Balas, Robert S. see Balas, Robert.
Balasuriya, Tissa.
   xBalasuriya, Tissa.
   The Eucharist & Human Liberation. Orbis Bks.
Balazs, E. A. see Balazs, Endre A.
Balazs, Endre A.
   xBalazs, E. A.
   ed. Chemistry & Molecular Biology of the
   Intercellular Matrix. Acad Pr.
Balazs, Mary.
   xBalazs, Mary W.
   ed. Touching This Earth: Poems by Women.
   Dawn Valley.
Balazs, Mary W. see Balazs, Mary.
Balbes, Raymond.
   xBalbes, Raymond.
   Distributive Lattices. U of Mo Pr.
Balch, Emily. see Balch, Emily Tapscott Clark.
Balch, Emily G. see Balch, Emily Greene.
Balch, Emily Greene, 1867-1961
   xBalch, Emily G.
   Occupied Haiti. Negro U Pr.
   ed. Occupied Haiti: Being the Report of a
   Committee of Six Disinterested Americans
   Representing Organizations Exclusively
   American. Garland Pub.
   Our Slavic Fellow Citizens. Arno.
Balch, Emily Tapscott Clark, 1893-1953
   xBalch, Emily.
   Innocence Abroad. Greenwood.
Balch, Glenn.
   xBalch, Glenn.
   Horse of Two Colors. T Y Crowell.
Balch, Thomas, 1821-1877
   xBalch, Thomas.
   The French in America During the War of
   Independence of the United States. Irvington.
Balch, Thomas W. see Balch, Thomas Willing.
Balch, Thomas Willing, 1866-1927
   xBalch, Thomas W.
   Alabama Arbitration. Arno.
Balck, William, 1859-1924
   xBalck, William.
   Tactics. Greenwood.
Balcom, Mary G. see Balcom, Mary Gilmore.
Balcom, Mary Gilmore.
   xBalcom, Mary G.
   The Catholic Church in Alaska. Balcom.
Balcomb, Mary. see Balcomb, Mary N.
Balcomb, Mary N.
   xBalcomb, Mary.
   Nicolai Fechin. Northland.
Balcon, Michael, Sir, 1896-
   xBalcon, Michael.

   Twenty Years of British Film: 1925-1945.
   Arno.
Bald, Marjory A. see Bald, Marjory Amelia.
Bald, Marjory Amelia.
   xBald, Marjory A.
   Women-Writers of the Nineteenth Century.
   Russell.
Bald, Robert C. see Bald, Robert Cecil.
Bald, Robert Cecil, 1901-
   xBald, Robert C.
   Donne's Influence in English Literature. Peter
   Smith.
   Literary Friendships in the Age of
   Wordsworth: An Anthology. Scholarly.
Baldassare, Mark.
   xBaldassare, Mark.
   Residential Crowding in Urban America. U of
   Cal Pr.
Balder, A. P. see Balder, Alton Parker.
Balder, Alton Parker.
   xBalder, A. P.
   Sport Diving: The Complete Manual for Skin &
   Scuba Divers. Macmillan.
Balderson, Margaret.
   xBalderson, Margaret.
   When Jays Fly to Barbmo. Gregg.
Balderston, Katharine C. see Balderston, Katharine
Canby.
Balderston, Katharine Canby, 1895-
   xBalderston, Katharine C.
   A Census of the Manuscripts of Oliver
   Goldsmith. Arden Lib.
   xBalderston, Katherine C.
   A Census of the Manuscripts of Oliver
   Goldsmith. Folcroft.
Balderston, Katherine C. see Balderston, Katharine
Canby.
Balderston, Marion.
   xBalderston, Marion.
   Pref. by & ed. The Lost War: Letters from
   British Officers During the American
   Revolution. Horizon.
Baldessarini, Ross J., 1937-
   xBaldessarini, Ross J.
   Chemotherapy in Psychiatry. Harvard U Pr.
Baldi, Philip.
   xBaldi, Philip.
   ed. Readings in Historical Phonology: Chapters
   in the Theory of Sound Change. Pa St U Pr.
Baldock, Cora V. see Baldock, Cora Vellekoop.
Baldock, Cora Vellekoop.
   xBaldock, Cora V.
   Sociology in Australia & New Zealand: Theory
   & Methods. Greenwood.
Baldock, Peter.
   xBaldock, Peter.
   Community Work & Social Work. Routledge &
   Kegan.
Baldridge, J. V. see Baldridge, J. Victor.
Baldridge, J. Victor.
   xBaldridge, J. V.
   Power & Conflict in the University: Research
   in the Sociology of Complex Organizations.
   Wiley.
Baldry, H. C.
   xBaldry, H. C.
   Ancient Greek Literature in Its Living Context.
   McGraw.
   The Greek Tragic Theatre. Norton.
Baldus, David C.
   xBaldus, David C.
   Statistical Proof of Discrimination. McGraw.
Baldwin, A. L. see Baldwin, Alfred Lee.
Baldwin, Alexinia Y.
   xBaldwin, Alexinia Y.
   ed. Educational Planning for the Gifted:
   Overcoming Cultural, Geographic, &
   Socioeconomic Barriers. Coun Exc Child.
Baldwin, Alfred L. see Baldwin, Alfred Lee.

Baldwin, Alfred Lee, 1914-
   xBaldwin, A. L.
   Theories of Child Development. Wiley.
   xBaldwin, Alfred L.
   Theories of Child Development. Wiley.
Baldwin, Allen J.
   xBaldwin, Allen J.
   A Programmed Review of Engineering
   Fundamentals. Van Nos Reinhold.
Baldwin, Anne N. see Baldwin, Anne Norris.
Baldwin, Anne Norris.
   xBaldwin, Anne N.
   A Little Time. Viking Pr.
   Sunflowers for Tina. Schol Bk Serv.
Baldwin, Bird T. see Baldwin, Bird Thomas.
Baldwin, Bird Thomas.
   xBaldwin, Bird T.
   Farm Children: Investigation of Rural Child
   Life in Selected Areas of Iowa. Arno.
Baldwin, Charles C. see Baldwin, Charles Crittenton.
Baldwin, Charles Crittenton, 1888-
   xBaldwin, Charles C.
   Men Who Make Our Novels. Arno.
   Men Who Make Our Novels. R West.
   Stanford White. Da Capo.
Baldwin, Charles S. see Baldwin, Charles Sears.
Baldwin, Charles Sears, 1867-1935
   xBaldwin, Charles S.
   Introduction to English Medieval Literature.
   Folcroft.
Baldwin, Christina.
   xBaldwin, Christina.
   One to One: Self-Understanding Through
   Journal Writing. M Evans.
Baldwin, Clare C. see Baldwin, Clare Charles.
Baldwin, Clare Charles, 1904-
   xBaldwin, Clare C.
   Organization & Administration of
   Substitute-Teaching Service in City School
   Systems. AMS Pr.
Baldwin, Clifford T. see Baldwin, Clifford Thomas.
Baldwin, Clifford Thomas.
   xBaldwin, Clifford T.
   Fundamentals of Electrical Measurements.
   Ungar.
Baldwin, E. see Baldwin, Ernest.
Baldwin, Elaine.
   xBaldwin, E.
   Differentiation & Co-Operation in an Israeli
   Veteran Moshav. Humanities.
Baldwin, Ernest.
   xBaldwin, E.
   An Introduction to Comparative Biochemistry.
   Cambridge U Pr.
Baldwin, Ernest. see Baldwin, Ernest Hubert Francis.
Baldwin, Ernest Hubert Francis.
   xBaldwin, Ernest.
   Nature of Biochemistry. Cambridge U Pr.
Baldwin, Ewart M. see Baldwin, Ewart Merlin.
Baldwin, Ewart Merlin, 1915-
   xBaldwin, Ewart M.
   Geology of Oregon. Kendall-Hunt.
Baldwin, Faith.
   xBaldwin, Faith.
   Alimony. Amereon Ltd.
Baldwin, George B. see Baldwin, George Benedict.
Baldwin, George Benedict.
   xBaldwin, George B.
   Planning & Development in Iran. Johns
   Hopkins.
Baldwin, George C. see Baldwin, George Curriden.
Baldwin, George Curriden, 1917-
   xBaldwin, George C.
   An Introduction to Nonlinear Optics. Plenum
   Pub.
   An Introduction to Nonlinear Optics. Plenum
   Pub.
Baldwin, Gordon C. see Baldwin, Gordon Cortis.
Baldwin, Gordon Cortis, 1908-
   xBaldwin, Gordon C.

The Apache Indians: Raiders of the Southwest.
Schol Bk Serv.
Baldwin, Henry, 1780-1844
xBaldwin, Henry.
A General View of the Origin & Nature of the
Constitution & Government of the United
States. Da Capo.
Baldwin, J. *see* Baldwin, James Tennant.
Baldwin, James.
xBaldwin, J.
Story of Roland. Scribner.
Story of Siegfried. Scribner.
xBaldwin, James.
Another Country. Dial.
Fire Next Time. Dell.
Fire Next Time. Dial.
Fire Next Time. Watts.
Go Tell It on the Mountain. Dell.
Go Tell It on the Mountain. Dial.
Going to Meet the Man. Dell.
Going to Meet the Man. Dial.
Horse Fair. Core Collection.
If Beale Street Could Talk. Dial.
If Beale Street Could Talk. NAL.
Just Above My Head. Dell.
Just Above My Head. Dial.
No Name in the Street. Dell.
No Name in the Street. Dial.
The Story of Siegfried. R West.
Thirty More Famous Stories Retold. Core
Collection.
Baldwin, James M. *see* Baldwin, James Mark.
Baldwin, James Mark, 1861-1934
xBaldwin, James M.
Thought & Things: A Study of the
Development & Meaning of Thought or
Genetic Logic. AMS Pr.
Thought & Things: Study of the Development
& Meaning of Thought or Genetic Logic.
Arno.
Baldwin, James Tennant.
xBaldwin, J.
ed. Soft Tech. Penguin.
Baldwin, Leland D. *see* Baldwin, Leland Dewitt.
Baldwin, Leland Dewitt, 1897-
xBaldwin, Leland D.
Survey of American History. Van Nos
Reinhold.
Baldwin, Marshall W. *see* Baldwin, Marshall Whithed.
Baldwin, Marshall Whithed, 1903-
xBaldwin, Marshall W.
ed. Christianity Through the Thirteenth
Century. Walker & Co.
Raymond III of Tripolis & the the Fall of
Jerusalem: 1140-1187. AMS Pr.
Baldwin, Neil.
xBaldwin, Neil.
ed. The Manuscripts & Letters of William
Carlos Williams in the Poetry Collection of
the Lockwood Memorial Library, State
University of New York at Buffalo. G K
Hall.
Baldwin, Nick.
xBaldwin, Nick.
Farm Tractors. Warne.
Baldwin, Pamela L.
xBaldwin, Pamela L.
Onshore Planning for Offshore Oil: Lessons
from Scotland. Conservation Foun.
Baldwin, R. L. *see* Baldwin, Ransom Leland.
Baldwin, Ralph B. *see* Baldwin, Ralph Balknap.
Baldwin, Ralph Balknap, 1912-
xBaldwin, Ralph B.
Measure of the Moon. U of Chicago Pr.
Baldwin, Ransom Leland.
xBaldwin, R. L.

ed. Animals, Feed, Food & People: An
Analysis of the Role of Animals in Food
Production. Westview.
Baldwin, Robert E.
xBaldwin, Robert E.
Nontariff Distortions of International Trade.
Brookings.
Baldwin, Roger E.
xBaldwin, Roger E.
Genetics. Wiley.
Baldwin, Sidney, 1922-
xBaldwin, Sidney.
Poverty & Politics: The Rise & Decline of the
Farm Security Administration. U of NC Pr.
Baldwin, Stanley. *see* Baldwin, Stanley Baldwin, 1st Earl.
Baldwin, Stanley Baldwin, 1st Earl, 1867-1947
xBaldwin, Stanley.
On England, & Other Addresses. Arno.
Baldwin, Summerfield, 1896-1955
xBaldwin, Summerfield.
Business in the Middle Ages. Cooper Sq.
Baldwin, Thomas W. *see* Baldwin, Thomas Whitfield.
Baldwin, Thomas Whitfield, 1890-
xBaldwin, Thomas W.
On the Compositional Genetics of The
Comedy of Errors. U of Ill Pr.
Organization & Personnel of the Shakespearean
Company. Russell.
Baldwin, William L. *see* Baldwin, William Lee.
Baldwin, William Lee.
xBaldwin, William L.
Antitrust & the Changing Corporation. Duke.
Structure of the Defense Market, 1955-1964.
Duke.
Baldyga, D. G. *see* Baldyga, Daniel G.
Baldyga, Daniel G.
xBaldyga, D. G.
How to Settle Your Own Insurance Claim.
Macmillan.
Balek, J.
xBalek, Jaroslav.
Hydrology & Water Resources in Tropical
Africa. Elsevier.
Balek, Jaroslav. *see* Balek, J.
Bales, Charles F., 1897-
xBales, Charles F.
Twice a Boy. Sycamore Pr.
Bales, R. F. *see* Bales, Robert Freed.
Bales, Robert F. *see* Bales, Robert Freed.
Bales, Robert Freed, 1916-
xBales, R. F.
Personality & Interpersonal Behavior. HR&W.
xBales, Robert F.
Symlog: A System for the Multiple Level
Observation of Groups. Free Pr.
Balestrino, Philip.
xBalestrino, Philip.
Hot As an Ice Cube. T Y Crowell.
Baley, James A.
xBaley, James A.
Illustrated Guide to Developing Athletic
Strength, Power, & Agility. P-H.
Baley, John. *see* Baley, John D.
Baley, John D.
xBaley, John.
Algebra: A First Course. Wadsworth Pub.
Balfour, Campbell.
xBalfour, Campbell.
Incomes Policy & the Public Sector. Routledge
& Kegan.
ed. Participation in Industry. Rowman.
Balfour, Graham, Sir, 1859-1929
xBalfour, Graham.
Life of Robert Louis Stevenson. R West.
Life of Robert Louis Stevenson. Scholarly.
Balian, Lorna.
xBalian, Lorna.

illus. The Aminal. Abingdon.
Bah! Humbug?. Abingdon.
Humbug Rabbit. Abingdon.
Leprechauns Never Lie. Abingdon.
Sometimes It's Turkey, Sometimes It's
Feathers. Abingdon.
illus. The Sweet Touch. Abingdon.
illus. A Sweetheart for Valentine. Abingdon.
Balint, John A.
xBalint, John A.
Gastrointestinal Bleeding: Diagnosis &
Management. Wiley.
Balint, Michael.
xBalint, Michael.
The Basic Fault: Therapeutic Aspects of
Regression. Brunner-Mazel.
Problems of Human Pleasure & Behavior.
Liveright.
Balio, Tino.
xBalio, Tino.
ed. The American Film Industry. U of Wis Pr.
Balizet, Carol.
xBalizet, Carol.
The Seven Last Years. Bantam.
Balkin, Richard.
xBalkin, Richard.
A Writer's Guide to Book Publishing. Dutton.
Ball, Adrian.
xBall, Adrian.
The Last Day of the Old World. Greenwood.
Ball, Brian.
xBall, Brian.
Space Guardians. Amereon Ltd.
Ball, Brian. *see* Ball, Brian N.
Ball, Brian N.
xBall, Brian.
Death of a Low Handicap Man. Walker & Co.
Montenegrin Gold. Walker & Co.
Ball, Charles.
xBall, Charles.
Fifty Years in Chains: Or, the Life of an
American Slave. Arno.
Fifty Years in Chains: Or the Life of an
American Slave. Scholarly.
Ball, Charles F. *see* Ball, Charles Ferguson.
Ball, Charles Ferguson.
xBall, Charles F.
Life & Journeys of Paul. Moody.
Ball, Clyde L.
xBall, Clyde L.
The General Assembly of North Carolina: A
Handbook for Legislators. U of NC Inst Gov.
Ball, Derek.
xBall, Derek S.
An Introduction to Real Analysis. Pergamon.
Ball, Derek S. *see* Ball, Derek.
Ball, Don.
xBall, Don.
Railroads: An American Journey. NYGS.
Ball, Edith L.
xBall, Edith L.
Leisure Services Preparation: A Competency
Based Approach. P-H.
Ball, Frances.
xBall, Frances.
The Development of Reading Skills: A Book of
Resources for Teachers. Biblio Dist.
Ball, Francis E. *see* Ball, Francis Elrington.
Ball, Francis Elrington, d. 1928
xBall, Francis E.
Swift's Verse: An Essay. Octagon.
Ball, Howard, 1937-
xBall, Howard.
Constitutional Powers: Cases on the Separation
of Powers & Federalism. West Pub.
Courts & Politics: The Federal Judicial System.
P-H.
No Pledge of Privacy: The Watergate Tapes
Litigation, 1973-1974. Kennikat.
Ball, J. Dyer. *see* Ball, James Dyer.

Ball, James D. *see* Ball, James Dyer.
Ball, James Dyer, 1847-1919
  xBall, J. Dyer.
    Things Chinese: Or Notes Connected with
      China. Gale.
  xBall, James D.
    Things Chinese: Or Notes Connected with
      China. Krishna Pr.
Ball, John. *see* Ball, John Dudley.
Ball, John A., 1935-
  xBall, John A.
    Algorithms for RPN Calculators. Wiley.
Ball, John Dudley, 1911-
  xBall, John.
    ed. Cop Cade. Doubleday.
    In the Heat of the Night. Har-Row.
    Miss One Thousand Spring Blossoms. Avon.
    ed. The Mystery Story. Penguin.
    The Mystery Story. Pubs Inc.
Ball, John E.
  xBall, John E.
    Carpenters & Builders Library. Audel.
    Exterior & Interior Trim. Delmar.
    Exterior & Interior Trim. Van Nos Reinhold.
    Practical Problems in Mathematics for Masons.
      Delmar.
Ball, John W.
  xBall, John W.
    Casting & Fishing the Artificial Fly. Caxton.
Ball, Joseph. *see* Ball, Joseph A.
Ball, Joseph A., 1947-
  xBall, Joseph.
    Factorization & Model Theory for Contraction
      Operators with Unitary Part. Am Math.
Ball, Joyce.
  xBall, Joyce.
    ed. Foreign Statistical Documents: A
      Bibliography of General, International Trade,
      & Agricultural Statistics, Including Holdings
      of the Stanford University Libraries. Hoover
      Inst Pr.
Ball, Katherine M., 1859-
  xBall, Katherine M.
    Decorative Motives of Oriental Art. Hacker.
Ball, M. Margaret. *see* Ball, Mary Margaret.
Ball, Marion J.
  xBall, Marion J.
    ed. How to Select a Computerized Hospital
      Information System. S Karger.
Ball, Mary Margaret, 1909-
  xBall, M. Margaret.
    NATO & the European Union Movement.
      Greenwood.
    Open Commonwealth. Duke.
Ball, Robert R.
  xBall, Robert R.
    The I Feel Formula. Word Bks.
Ball, Robert S. *see* Ball, Robert Stawell.
Ball, Robert Stawell, Sir, 1840-1913
  xBall, Robert S.
    Great Astronomers. Arno.
    Great Astronomers. Folcroft.
    Great Astronomers. Ridgeway Bks.
Ball, Terence.
  xBall, Terence.
    ed. Political Theory & Praxis: New
      Perspectives. U of Minn Pr.
Ball, Victoria K. *see* Ball, Victoria Kloss.
Ball, Victoria Kloss.
  xBall, Victoria K.
    Architecture & Interior Design: A Basic
      History Through the Seventeenth Century.
      Wiley.
    Architecture & Interior Design: Europe &
      America from the Colonial Era to Today.
      Wiley.
Ball, W. Rouse. *see* Ball, Walter William Rouse.
Ball, W. W. *see* Ball, Walter William Rouse.
Ball, Walter W. *see* Ball, Walter William Rouse.

Ball, Walter William Rouse, 1850-1925
  xBall, W. Rouse.
    Mathematical Recreations & Essays.
      Macmillan.
  xBall, W. W.
    Fun with String Figures. Gannon.
    Fun with String Figures. Dover.
  xBall, Walter W.
    Mathematical Recreations & Essays. U of
      Toronto Pr.
Ball, William M. *see* Ball, William Macmahon.
Ball, William Macmahon, 1901-
  xBall, William M.
    Nationalism & Communism in East Asia. AMS
      Pr.
Ball, Zachary, Pseud.
  xBall, Zachary.
    Bristle Face. Holiday.
    Bristle Face. Schol Bk Serv.
    North to Abilene. Holiday.
Balla, Ignatius. *see* Balla, Ignazia.
Balla, Ignazia.
  xBalla, Ignatius.
    Our Continuing Yes. Dghtrs St Paul.
Ballabh, R. *see* Ballabh, Ram.
Ballabh, Ram, 1918-
  xBallabh, R.
    Hydrodynamic Superposability. Asia.
Ballagh, J. C. *see* Ballagh, James Curtis.
Ballagh, James C. *see* Ballagh, James Curtis.
Ballagh, James Curtis.
  xBallagh, J. C.
    White Servitude in the Colony of Virginia: A
      Study of the System of Indentured Labor in
      the American Colonies. Johnson Repr.
  xBallagh, James C.
    White Servitude in the Colony of Virginia: A
      Study of the System of Indentured Labor in
      the American Colonies. AMS Pr.
Ballantine, Richard.
  xBallantine, Richard.
    Richard's Bicycle Book, 1975. Ballantine.
Ballantyne, R. M. *see* Ballantyne, Robert Michael.
Ballantyne, Robert. *see* Ballantyne, Robert Michael.
Ballantyne, Robert Michael, 1825-1894
  xBallantyne, R. M.
    The Coral Island. Biblio Dist.
  xBallantyne, Robert.
    The Coral Island. Garland Pub.
Ballard, Bill.
  xBallard, Bill.
    The Illustrated Guide to Platform Tennis. Van
      Nos Reinhold.
Ballard, Ernesta D. *see* Ballard, Ernesta Drinker.
Ballard, Ernesta Drinker.
  xBallard, Ernesta D.
    Garden in Your House. Har-Row.
Ballard, G. A. *see* Ballard, George Alexander.
Ballard, George A. *see* Ballard, George Alexander.
Ballard, George Alexander, 1862-1948
  xBallard, G. A.
    The Influence of the Sea on the Political
      History of Japan. Biblio Dist.
  xBallard, George A.
    The Influence of the Sea on the Political
      History of Japan. Greenwood.
Ballard, J. G., 1930-
  xBallard, J. G.
    Concrete Island. FS&G.
    Crash. FS&G.
    Crystal World. Avon.
    High-Rise. HR&W.
    High Rise. Popular Lib.
Ballard, Mignon F. *see* Ballard, Mignon Franklin.
Ballard, Mignon Franklin.
  xBallard, Mignon F.
    Aunt Matilda's Ghost. Aurora Pubs.
Ballard, R. E. *see* Ballard, Roy E.
Ballard, Roy E.
  xBallard, R. E.

    Photoelectron Spectroscopy & Molecular
      Orbital Theory. Halsted Pr.
Ballard, Todhunter. *see* Ballard, Willis Todhunter.
Ballard, Willis Todhunter, 1903-
  xBallard, Todhunter.
    Home to Texas. Dell.
Ballast, Daniel L.
  xBallast, Daniel L.
    Guidance Program Development. C C Thomas.
Ballbach, Nathan A. *see* Ballbach, Nathan Anthony.
Ballbach, Nathan Anthony, 1905-1974
  xBallbach, Nathan A.
    The Gooseneck Tidings. Northlands MI.
Ballem, John B. *see* Ballem, John Bishop.
Ballem, John Bishop.
  xBallem, John B.
    Oil & Gas Lease in Canada. U of Toronto Pr.
Ballenger, John J. *see* Ballenger, John Jacob.
Ballenger, John Jacob, 1914-
  xBallenger, John J.
    ed. Diseases of the Nose, Throat & Ear. Lea &
      Febiger.
Ballenger, Marcus.
  xBallenger, Marcus.
    Primary School Potpourri. ACEI.
Ballentine, J. Gregory.
  xBallentine, J. Gregory.
    Equity, Efficiency & the U. S. Corporation
      Income Tax. Am Enterprise.
Ballentine, Martha. *see* Ballentine, Rudolph M.
Ballentine, Rudolph M., Mrs
  xBallentine, Martha.
    Himalayan Mountain Cookery. Himalayan Intl
      Inst.
Ballesteros, Octavio A., 1936-
  xBallesteros, Octavio A.
    Behind Jail Bars. Philos Lib.
    The Effectiveness of Public School Education
      for Mexican-American Students As Perceived
      by Principals of Elementary Schools of
      Predominantly Mexican-American
      Enrollment. R & E Res Assocs.
Ballew, Hunter.
  xBallew, Hunter.
    Teaching Children Mathematics. Merrill.
Ballhatchet, Kenneth.
  xBallhatchet, Kenneth.
    Race, Sex & Class Under the Raj: Imperial
      Attitudes & Policies & Their Critics,
      1793-1905. St Martin.
Ballhausen, C. J. *see* Ballhausen, Carl Johan.
Ballhausen, Carl Johan, 1926-
  xBallhausen, C. J.
    Molecular Electronic Structures of Transition
      Metal Complexes. McGraw.
Balliett, G. *see* Balliett, Gene.
Balliett, Gene.
  xBalliett, G.
    Getting Started in Private Practice. Med
      Economics.
Balliett, Whitney.
  xBalliett, Whitney.
    American Singers. Oxford U Pr.
    Dinosaurs in the Morning: 41 Pieces on Jazz.
      Greenwood.
    Improvising: Sixteen Jazz Musicians & Their
      Art. Oxford U Pr.
Ballinger, Bill S. *see* Ballinger, William Sanborn.
Ballinger, Harry R. *see* Ballinger, Harry Russell.
Ballinger, Harry Russell, 1892-
  xBallinger, Harry R.
    Painting Landscapes. Watson-Guptill.
Ballinger, Raymond A., 1907-
  xBallinger, Raymond A.
    Art & Reproduction: Graphic Reproduction
      Techniques. Van Nos Reinhold.
Ballinger, William Sanborn, 1912-
  xBallinger, Bill S.

Lost City of Stone: The Story of Nan Madol, the "Atlantis" of the Pacific. S&S.

Ballou, Adin.
xBallou, Adin.
History of the Hopedale Community, from Its Inception to Its Virtual Submergence in the Hopedale Parish. AMS Pr.

Ballou, Maturin M. *see* Ballou, Maturin Murray.

Ballou, Maturin Murray, 1820-1895
xBallou, Maturin M.
Notable Thoughts About Women: A Literary Mosaic. Gale.

Ballowe, James.
xBallowe, James.
The Coal Miners. Spoon Riv Poetry.

Balls, Edward K.
xBalls, Edward K.
Early Uses of California Plants. U of Cal Pr.

Balme, Joshua R. *see* Balme, Joshua Rhodes.

Balme, Joshua Rhodes.
xBalme, Joshua R.
American States, Churches, & Slavery. Negro U Pr.

Balme, M. G.
xBalme, M. G.
Intellegenda: Comprehension Exercises in Latin Prose & Verse. Oxford U Pr.

Balmer. *see* Balmer, Edwin.

Balmer, Edwin.
xBalmer.
When Worlds Collide. Warner Bks.
xBalmer, Edwin.
When Worlds Collide. Arden Lib.
When Worlds Collide. Warner Bks.

Balmer, William T. *see* Balmer, William Turnbull.

Balmer, William Turnbull.
xBalmer, William T.
History of the Akan Peoples of the Gold Coast. Negro U Pr.

Balnaves, John.
xBalnaves, John.
Australian Libraries. Shoe String.

Balog, Paul.
xBalog, Paul.
Umayyad, Abbasid & Tulunid Glass Weights & Vessel Stamps. Am Numismatic.

Balogh, Thomas, Baron Balogh, 1905-
xBalogh, Thomas.
The Economics of Poverty. M E Sharpe.
Fact & Fancy in International Economic Relations: An Essay on International Monetary Reform. Pergamon.

Baloh, Robert W.
xBaloh, Robert W.
ed. Clinical Neurophysiology of the Vestibular System. Davis Co.

Baloian, James C., 1945-
xBaloian, James C.
The Ararat Papers. Ararat Pr.

Balows, Albert.
xBalows, Albert.
Clinical Microbiology: How to Start & When to Stop. C C Thomas.

Balsdon, J. P. *see* Balsdon, John Percy Vyvian Dacre.

Balsdon, John Percy Vyvian Dacre, 1901-
xBalsdon, J. P.
Romans & Aliens. U of NC Pr.

Balshofer, Fred J.
xBalshofer, Fred J.
One Reel a Week. U of Cal Pr.

Balsiger, Dave.
xBalsiger, David W.
In Search of Noah's Ark. Schick Sunn.
The Lincoln Conspiracy. Schick Sunn.
Southern California Amusement Attractions. Mini Guide Bks.

Balsiger, David W. *see* Balsiger, Dave.

Balson, Diane.
xBalson, Diane.

Nothing but the Best. HarBraceJ.

Balston, Thomas.
xBalston, Thomas.
James Whatman, Father & Son. Garland Pub.
William Balston, Paper Maker, 1759-1849. Garland Pub.

Baltake, Joe.
xBaltake, Joe.
The Films of Jack Lemmon. Citadel Pr.

Baltaxe, Christiane A. *see* Baltaxe, Christiane A. M.

Baltaxe, Christiane A. M.
xBaltaxe, Christiane A.
Foundations of Distinctive Feature Theory. Univ Park.

Baltaxe, Harold A.
xBaltaxe, Harold A.
Coronary Angiography. C C Thomas.

Baltay, Charles.
xBaltay, Charles.
ed. Experimental Meson Spectroscopy. Columbia U Pr.

Baltermants, Dmitri. *see* Baltermants, Dmitrii Nikolaevich.

Baltermants, Dmitrii Nikolaevich.
xBaltermants, Dmitri.
Nikolai Lives in Moscow. Hastings.

Baltes, H. P. *see* Baltes, Heinrich P.

Baltes, Heinrich P.
xBaltes, H. P.
ed. Inverse Source Problems in Optics. Springer-Verlag.

Baltes, Paul. *see* Baltes, Paul B.

Baltes, Paul B.
xBaltes, Paul.
Life-Span Developmental Psychology: Introduction to Research Methods. Brooks-Cole.

Baltimore Association for the Improvement of the Condition of the Poor.
xAssociation for the Improvement of the Conditions of the Poor.
Housing Conditions in Baltimore: Report of a Special Committee of the Assoc. for the Improvement of the Condition of the Poor and the Charity Organization Society. Arno.

Baltimore Conference, 1975. *see* International Workshop on Human Gene Mapping, 3rd, Baltimore, 1975.

Baltzell, E. Digby. *see* Baltzell, Edward Digby.

Baltzell, Edward Digby, 1915-
xBaltzell, E. Digby.
Philadelphia Gentlemen: The Making of a National Upper Class. Times Bks.
Puritan Boston & Quaker Philadelphia. Free Pr.

Baltzer, Friedrich, 1884-
xBaltzer, Fritz.
Theodor Boveri: The Life & Work of a Great Biologist, 1862-1915. U of Cal Pr.

Baltzer, Fritz. *see* Baltzer, Friedrich.

Balyuzi, H. M.
xBalyuzi, H. M.
The Bab: The Herald of the Day of Days. Baha'i.
Muhammad & the Course of Islam. Baha'i.

Balzac, Honore De, 1799-1850
xBalzac, Honore De.
History of the Thirteen. Penguin.
Lost Illusions. Penguin.
Old Goriot. Dutton.
Old Goriot. Penguin.

Balzano, Michael P.
xBalzano, Michael P.
Reorganizing the Federal Bureaucracy: The Rhetoric & the Reality. Am Enterprise.

Balzer, Richard.
xBalzer, Richard.
Clockwork: Life in & Outside an American Factory. Doubleday.

Balzhiser, R. E. *see* Balzhiser, Richard E.

Balzhiser, Richard E.
xBalzhiser, R. E.

Engineering Thermodynamics. P-H.

Bambara, Toni C. *see* Bambara, Toni Cade.

Bambara, Toni Cade.
xBambara, Toni C.
Gorilla, My Love. Random.
The Salt Eaters. Random.

Bamberger, Bernard. *see* Bamberger, Bernard Jacob.

Bamberger, Bernard J. *see* Bamberger, Bernard Jacob.

Bamberger, Bernard Jacob, 1904-
xBamberger, Bernard.
Proselytism in the Talmudic Period. Ktav.
xBamberger, Bernard J.
Story of Judaism. Schocken.
Story of Judaism. UAHC.

Bamberger, Jeanne S. *see* Bamberger, Jeanne Shapiro.

Bamberger, Jeanne Shapiro.
xBamberger, Jeanne S.
The Art of Listening: Developing Musical Perception. Har-Row.

Bamborough, Philip.
xBamborough, Philip.
Antique Oriental Rugs & Carpets. Sterling.

Bambrick, Susan.
xBambrick, Susan.
Australian Minerals & Energy Policy. Bks Australia.

Bame, Louise.
xBame, Louise.
Pants Fit for Your Figure: Point-by-Point Pattern Adjustment. Vista CA.

Bamesberger, Velda C. *see* Bamesberger, Velda Christena.

Bamesberger, Velda Christena, 1896-
xBamesberger, Velda C.
An Appraisal of a Social Studies Course, in Terms of Its Effect Upon the Achievement, Activities & Interests of Pupils. AMS Pr.

Bamford, C. H.
xBamford, C. H.
ed. Comprehensive Chemical Kinetics. Elsevier.
Synthetic Polypeptides: Preparation, Structure, & Properties. Acad Pr.

Bamford, Joan.
xBamford, Joan.
Collecting Antiques for the Future. Intl Ideas.

Bamford, Paul W. *see* Bamford, Paul Walden.

Bamford, Paul Walden, 1921-
xBamford, Paul W.
Fighting Ships & Prisons: The Mediterranean Galleys of France in the Age of Louis XIV. U of Minn Pr.
Forests & French Sea Power, 1660-1789. U of Toronto Pr.

Bamman, H. A. *see* Bamman, Henry A.

Bamman, Henry A.
xBamman, H. A.
Free to Read: A Guide to Effective Reading. Benjamin-Cummings.
xBamman, Henry A.
How to Study Successfully. Pacific Bks.

Ban, Joseph D.
xBan, Joseph D.
Education for Change. Judson.

Ban, Thomas A.
xBan, Thomas A.
Psychopharmacology. Krieger.
Psychopharmacology of Thiothixene. Raven.

Banas, Josef.
xBanas, Josef.
The Scapegoats: The Exodus of the Remnants of Polish Jewry. Holmes & Meier.

Banathy, Bela H.
xBanathy, Bela H.
A Design for Foreign Language Curriculum. Heath.

Banchek, Linda.
xBanchek, Linda.
Snake In, Snake Out. T Y Crowell.

Bancroft, Caroline.
xBancroft, Caroline.

Silver Queen: The Fabulous Story of Baby Doe
Tabor. Johnson Colo.

Bancroft, Edward, 1744-1821
xBancroft, Edward.
The History of Charles Wentworth, Esq., 1770.
Garland Pub.

Bancroft, Frederic, 1860-1945
xBancroft, Frederic.
Calhoun & the South Carolina Nullification
Movement. Peter Smith.

Bancroft, George.
xBancroft, George.
History of the United States of America from
the Discovery of the Continent. U of Chicago
Pr.

Bancroft, Griffing.
xBancroft, Griffing.
Vanishing Wings: A Tale of Three Birds of
Prey. Watts.

Bancroft, Henrietta.
xBancroft, Henrietta.
Animals in Winter. T Y Crowell.
Down Come the Leaves. T Y Crowell.

Bancroft, John D.
xBancroft, John D.
Histopathological Stains & Their Diagnostic
Uses. Churchill.
ed. Theory and Practice of Histological
Techniques. Churchill.

Band, Arnold J.
xBand, Arnold J.
Nostalgia and Nightmare: A Study in the
Fiction of S. Y. Agnon. U of Cal Pr.

Bandara, H. H.
xBandara, H. H.
Cultural Policy in Sri Lanka. Unipub.

Bandel, Eugene, 1835-1889
xBandel, Eugene.
Frontier Life in the Army: 1854-1861.
Porcupine Pr.

Bandelier, Adolph Francis Alphonse.
xBandelier, Adolphe F.
Indians of the Rio Grande Valley. Cooper Sq.
xBandelier, Francis A.
Indians of the Rio Grande Valley. AMS Pr.
Bandelier, Adolphe F. see Bandelier, Adolph Francis
Alphonse.
Bandelier, Francis A. see Bandelier, Adolph Francis
Alphonse.

Bandello, Matteo, 1485-1561
xBandello, Matteo.
Certain Tragical Discourses of Bandello. AMS
Pr.

Bander, Edward J.
xBander, Edward J.
Change of Name & Law of Names. Oceana.
Medical Legal Dictionary. Oceana.
ed. Turmoil on the Campus. Wilson.

Bander, Peter.
xBander, Peter.
The Prophecies of St. Malachy. TAN Bks
Pubs.

Bander, Robert G.
xBander, Robert G.
From Sentence to Paragraph: A Writing
Workbook in English As a Second Language.
HR&W.
Bandholtz, Harry H. see Bandholtz, Harry Hill.

Bandholtz, Harry Hill.
xBandholtz, Harry H.
Undiplomatic Diary. AMS Pr.

Bandler, Richard.
xBandler, Richard.
Frogs into Princes: Neuro Linguistic
Programming. Real People.
Patterns of Hypnotic Techniques of Milton H.
Erickson, M. D.. Meta Pubns.

Bandman, Bertram.
xBandman, Bertram.

Place of Reason in Education. Ohio St U Pr.
Bandmann, H. J. see Bandmann, Hans-Jurgen.

Bandmann, Hans-Jurgen.
xBandmann, H. J.
Patch Testing. Springer-Verlag.

Bandura, Albert, 1925-
xBandura, Albert.
Principles of Behavior Modification. HR&W.
ed. Psychological Modeling: Conflicting
Theories. Lieber-Atherton.

Bandy, Orville L.
xBandy, Orville L.
ed. Radiometric Dating & Paleontologic
Zonation. Geol Soc.

Bane, Bernard M.
xBane, Bernard M.
Is President John F. Kennedy Alive...and
Well?. BMB Pub Co.

Banel, Joseph.
xBanel, Joseph.
Lee Wong, Boy Detective. Garrard.

Banerjea, Pramathanath.
xBanerjea, Pramathanath.
Public Administration in Ancient India. Intl
Pubns Serv.
Banerjee, K. S. see Banerjee, Kali S.

Banerjee, Kali S.
xBanerjee, K. S.
Cost of Living Index Numbers: Practice,
Precision, & Theory. Dekker.
Banerjee, Nikunja V. see Banerjee, Nikunja Vihari.

Banerjee, Nikunja Vihari.
xBanerjee, Nikunja V.
The Spirit of Indian Philosophy. Humanities.

Banerjee, Srikumar.
xBanerjee, Srikumar.
Critical Theories & Poetic Practice in the
Lyrical Ballads. Arden Lib.
Banerji, Sures C. see Banerji, Sures Chandra.

Banerji, Sures Chandra, 1917-
xBanerji, Sures C.
Aspects of Ancient Indian Life from Sanskrit
Sources. Verry.

Banes, Daniel.
xBanes, Daniel.
The Provocative Merchant of Venice. Malcolm
Hse.
Shakespeare, Shylock & Kabbalah. Malcolm
Hse.

Banes, Sally.
xBanes, Sally.
Terpsichore in Sneakers: Post-Modern Dance.
HM.

Banet, Anthony G.
xBanet, Anthony G.
ed. Creative Psychotherapy: A Source Book.
Univ Assocs.

Banfield, Edward C.
xBanfield, Edward C.
American Foreign Aid Doctrines. Am
Enterprise.
The City & the Revolutionary Tradition. Am
Enterprise.
City Politics. Harvard U Pr.
City Politics. Random.

Bang, Betsy.
xBang, Betsy.
The Cucumber Stem. Greenwillow.
Tuntuni, the Tailor Bird. Greenwillow.

Bang, Garrett.
xBang, Garrett.
illus. & tr. Men from the Village Deep in the
Mountains, & Other Japanese Folk Tales.
Macmillan.

Bang, Molly.
xBang, Molly.

illus. The Goblins Giggle & Other Stories.
Scribner.
The Grey Lady & the Strawberry Snatcher.
Schol Bk Serv.
Bang-Yen Chen, . see Chen, Bang-Yen.

Bangert, William V.
xBangert, William V.
A History of the Society of Jesus. Inst Jesuit.

Bangerter, Lowell A., 1941-
xBangerter, Lowell A.
Hugo Von Hofmannsthal. Ungar.
Banghart, Frank W. see Banghart, Frank William.

Banghart, Frank William.
xBanghart, Frank W.
Educational Planning. Macmillan.
Bangs, John K. see Bangs, John Kendrick.

Bangs, John Kendrick, 1862-1922
xBangs, John K.
Ghosts I Have Met, & Some Others. Borgo Pr.
Ghosts I Have Met & Some Others. Mss Info.
Ghosts I Have Met & Some Others. Somerset
Pub.
House-Boat on the Styx. AMS Pr.
A Houseboat on the Styx. Queens Hse.
A Houseboat on the Styx. Scholarly.
Little Book of Christmas. Arno.
Over the Plum Pudding. Arno.
Over the Plum-Pudding. Folcroft.
ed. Potted Fiction: Being a Series of Extracts
from the World's Best Sellers, Put up in Thin
Slices for Hurried Consumers. Arno.
Bangs, Robert B. see Bangs, Robert Babbitt.

Bangs, Robert Babbitt, 1914-
xBangs, Robert B.
Financing Economic Development: Fiscal
Policy for Emerging Countries. U of Chicago
Pr.
Banham, Rayner. see Banham, Reyner.

Banham, Reyner.
xBanham, Rayner.
Theory & Design in the First Machine Age.
MIT Pr.
xBanham, Reyner.
The Age of the Masters: A Personal View of
Modern Architecture. Har-Row.
Los Angeles: The Architecture of Four
Ecologies. Har-Row.

Banim, John, 1798-1842
xBanim, John.
The Boyne Water: A Tale. AMS Pr.
The Denounced. Garland Pub.
Banis, V. J. see Banis, Victor J.

Banis, Victor J.
xBanis, V. J.
The Earth & All It Holds. St Martin.
This Splendid Earth. Fawcett.
This Splendid Earth. St Martin.

Banish, Roslyn, 1942-
xBanish, Roslyn.
City Families: Chicago & London. Pantheon.

Banister, Judith.
xBanister, Judith.
Late Georgian & Regency Silver. Transatlantic.

Banister, Manly.
xBanister, Manly.
Conquest of Earth. Assoc Bk.
Banister, Margaret. see Banister, Margaret S.

Banister, Margaret S.
xBanister, Margaret.
Burn Then, Little Lamp. Popular Lib.
Bank, Alice. see Bank, Alisa Vladimirovna.

Bank, Alisa Vladimirovna.
xBank, Alice.
Intro. by Byzantine Art in the Collections of
Soviet Museums. Abrams.
Bank, Dena C. see Bank, Dena Citron.

Bank, Dena Citron.
xBank, Dena C.

How Things Get Done: The Nitty-Gritty of
Parliamentary Procedure. U of SC Pr.
Bank, Mirra.
xBank, Mirra.
Anonymous Was a Woman. St Martin.
Banker, G. see Banker, Gilbert S.
Banker, Gilbert S.
xBanker, G.
Modern Pharmaceutics. Dekker.
Banker, John C.
xBanker, John C.
Personal Finances for Ministers. Westminster.
Banki, L. see Banki, Laszlo.
Banki, Laszlo.
xBanki, L.
Bioassay of Pesticides in the Laboratory:
Research & Quality Control. Intl Pubns Serv.
Bankowski, Zenon.
xBankowski, Zenon.
Images of Law. Routledge & Kegan.
Banks, Arthur.
xBanks, Arthur.
A World Atlas of Military History: Up to
1485. Hippocrene Bks.
A World Atlas of Military History: 1861-1945.
Hippocrene Bks.
Banks, Barbara.
xBanks, Barbara.
Dragonseeds. St Martin.
Banks, C. Tillery.
xBanks, C. Tillery.
Hello to Me with Love: Poems of Self
Discovery. Morrow.
Banks, Carolyn.
xBanks, Carolyn.
The Darkroom. Viking Pr.
Mr. Right. Viking Pr.
Mr. Right. Warner Bks.
Banks, Charles E. see Banks, Charles Edward.
Banks, Charles Edward, 1854-1931
xBanks, Charles E.
The Planters of the Commonwealth: A Study
of the Emigrants & Emigration in Colonial
Times. Genealog Pub.
Topographical Dictionary of 2885 English
Emigrants to New England, 1620-1650.
Genealog Pub.
Banks, D. C. see Banks, David Charles.
Banks, David Charles.
xBanks, D. C.
ABC of Medical Treatment. Churchill.
Banks, Enoch M. see Banks, Enoch Marvin.
Banks, Enoch Marvin, 1877-
xBanks, Enoch M.
Economics of Land Tenure in Georgia. AMS
Pr.
Banks, F. R. see Banks, Francis Richard.
Banks, Ferdinand E.
xBanks, Ferdinand E.
The Economics of Natural Resources. Plenum
Pub.
The International Economy: A Modern
Approach. Lexington Bks.
Banks, Francis Richard.
xBanks, F. R.
The Penguin Guide to London. Penguin.
Banks, J. A. see Banks, Joseph Ambrose.
Banks, James. see Banks, James A.
Banks, James A.
xBanks, James.
Multiethnic Education: Practices & Promises.
Phi Delta Kappa.
xBanks, James A.

March Toward Freedom: A History of Black
Americans. Pitman Learning.
ed. Teaching Social Studies to Culturally
Different Children. A-W.
Teaching Strategies for Ethnic Studies. Allyn.
Teaching Strategies for the Social Studies:
Inquiry, Valuing & Decision-Making. A-W.
Banks, Joseph Ambrose.
xBanks, J. A.
The Sociology of Social Movements.
Humanities.
Banks, Louis A. see Banks, Louis Albert.
Banks, Louis Albert, 1855-1933
xBanks, Louis A.
Immortal Hymns & Their Story. Longwood Pr.
Banks, Lynne R. see Banks, Lynne Reid.
Banks, Lynne Reid.
xBanks, Lynne R.
Backward Shadow. S&S.
Dark Quartet: The Story of the Brontes.
Delacorte.
My Darling Villain. Har-Row.
xBanks, Lynne Reid.
The Farthest-Away Mountain. Doubleday.
Banks, Michael. see Banks, Mike.
Banks, Mike, 1922-
xBanks, Michael.
Greenland. Rowman.
Banks, Olive.
xBanks, Olive.
The Sociology of Education. Schocken.
Banks, Peter A.
xBanks, Peter A.
Pancreatitis. Plenum Pub.
Banks, Peter M.
xBanks, Peter M.
Introduction to Computer Science. Wiley.
Banks, R. C. see Banks, Richard C.
Banks, R. E. see Banks, Ronald Eric.
Banks, Richard C.
xBanks, R. C.
Introductory Problems in Spectroscopy. A-W.
xBanks, Richard C.
Introductory Problems in Spectroscopy.
Benjamin-Cummings.
Banks, Ronald Eric.
xBanks, R. E.
Organofluorine Chemicals & Their Industrial
Applications. Halsted Pr.
Banks, Ronald F.
xBanks, Ronald F.
A History of Maine: A Collection of Readings
on the History of Maine 1600-1976.
Kendall-Hunt.
Banks, Russell, 1940-
xBanks, Russell.
The Book of Jamaica. HM.
Banks, Sam W. see Banks, Samuel Wallace.
Banks, Samuel Wallace.
xBanks, Sam W.
Atlas of Surgical Exposures of the Extremities.
Saunders.
Banks, Stuart.
xBanks, Stuart.
The Complete Handbook of Poultry Keeping.
Van Nos Reinhold.
Banks, William J.
xBanks, William J.
Histology & Comparative Organology: A
Text-Atlas. Krieger.
Bankson, N. see Bankson, Nicholas W.
Bankson, Nicholas W.
xBankson, N.
Bankson Language Screening Test. Univ Park.
Bankwitz, Philip C. see Bankwitz, Philip Charles Farwell.
Bankwitz, Philip Charles Farwell.
xBankwitz, Philip C.

Maxime Weygand & Civil-Military Relations in
Modern France. Harvard U Pr.
Bannan, John F.
xBannan, John F.
Law, Morality & Vietnam: The Peace Militants
& the Courts. Ind U Pr.
Bannasch, P. see Bannasch, Peter.
Bannasch, Peter.
xBannasch, P.
Cytoplasm of Hepatocytes During
Carcinogenesis: Electron & Lightmicroscopial
Investigations of the
Nitrosomorphiline-Intoxicated Rat Liver.
Springer-Verlag.
Bannatyne, Alexander.
xBannatyne, Alexander.
How Your Children Can Learn to Live a
Rewarding Life: Behavior Modification for
Parents & Teachers. C C Thomas.
Banner, Angela.
xBanner, Angela.
Ant & Bee Time. Watts.
Banner, David K.
xBanner, David K.
The Politics of Social Program Evaluation.
Ballinger Pub.
Banner, Hubert S. see Banner, Hubert Stewart.
Banner, Hubert Stewart, 1891-
xBanner, Hubert S.
Calamities of the World. Gale.
Bannerman, Glenn. see Bannerman, Glenn Q.
Bannerman, Glenn Q.
xBannerman, Glenn.
Guide for Recreation Leaders. John Knox.
Bannerman, Helen. see Bannerman, Helen Brodie Cowan
(Watson).
**Bannerman, Helen Brodie Cowan (Watson), 1862 or
3-1946**
xBannerman, Helen.
Story of Little Black Sambo. Lippincott.
Banning, Margaret C. see Banning, Margaret Culkin.
Banning, Margaret Culkin, 1891-
xBanning, Margaret C.
Echo Answers. Manor Bks.
Such Interesting People. G K Hall.
Such Interesting People. Har-Row.
Banning, Robert, 1947-
xBanning, Robert.
Zero Down: How to Buy a Closely Held
Company Without Using Any of Your Own
Money. Tiburon.
Bannister, Anthony.
xBannister, Anthony.
Namibia: Africa's Harsh Paradise. Quality Bks
IL.
Bannister, Constance.
xBannister, Constance.
Organization Baby. S&S.
Bannister, Don.
xBannister, Don.
Sam Chard. Knopf.
Bannister, Peter.
xBannister, Peter.
Introduction to Physiological Plant Ecology.
Halsted Pr.
Bannister, Robert C.
xBannister, Robert C.
American Values in Transition: A Reader.
HarBraceJ.
Social Darwinism: Science & Myth in
Anglo-American Social Thought. Temple U
Pr.
Bannock, Graham.
xBannock, Graham.
Penguin Dictionary of Economics. Penguin.
Bannon, Edward.
xBannon, Edward.
Operational Amplifiers: Theory & Servicing.
Reston.
Bannon, John F. see Bannon, John Francis.

Bannon, John Francis.
xBannon, John F.
Latin America. Glencoe.
The Spanish Borderlands Frontier,1513-1821.
U of NM Pr.
Bannon, Joseph J.
xBannon, Joseph J.
Problem Solving in Recreation & Parks. P-H.
Bannon, Laura.
xBannon, Laura.
Who Walks the Attic. A Whitman.
Bannon, Lois.
xBannon, Lois.
Handbook of Audubon Prints. Pelican.
Bansal, Raj K.
xBansal, Raj K.
Nomenclature of Organic Compounds.
McGraw.
Banta, Martha.
xBanta, Martha.
Discovery & Response: Drama, Fiction &
Poetry with an Appendix on Writing &
Reading. Macmillan.
Failure & Success in America: A Literary
Debate. Princeton U Pr.
Bantock, G. H. see Bantock, Geoffrey Herman.
Bantock, Gavin, 1939-
xBantock, Gavin.
Anhaga. SBD.
Bantock, Geoffrey Herman, 1914-
xBantock, G. H.
Education, Culture, & the Emotions. Ind U Pr.
T. S. Eliot & Education. Phila Bk Co.
Banton, Michael. see Banton, Michael P.
Banton, Michael P.
xBanton, Michael.
The Idea of Race. Westview.
xBanton, Michael P.
White & Coloured: The Behavior of the British
People Towards Coloured Immigrants.
Greenwood.
Banus, B. S. see Banus, Barbara Sharpe.
Banus, Barbara. see Banus, Barbara Sharpe.
Banus, Barbara Sharpe.
xBanus, B. S.
The Developmental Therapist. C B Slack.
xBanus, Barbara.
The Developmental Therapist. C B Slack.
Banus, Tudor.
xBanus, Tudor.
The Muppet Show Book. Abrams.
Banville, Thomas G.
xBanville, Thomas G.
How to Listen-How to Be Heard. Nelson-Hall.
Banwart, George J.
xBanwart, George J.
Basic Food Microbiology. AVI.
Bany, Mary A.
xBany, Mary A.
Educational Social Psychology. Macmillan.
Baptista, Luis F. see Baptista, Luis Felipe.
Baptista, Luis Felipe.
xBaptista, Luis F.
Song Dialects & Demes in Sedentary
Populations of the White-Crowned Sparrow
(Zonotrichia Leucophrys Nuttali) U of Cal
Pr.
Baptiste, H. Prentice.
xBaptiste, H. Prentice.
Developing the Multicultural Process in
Classroom Instruction: Competencies for
Teachers. U Pr of Amer.
Bar Hebraeus, 1226-1286
xBar Hebraeus.
The Laughable Stories. AMS Pr.
Bar, Lois E. Le. see Le Bar, Lois E.
Bar-Hillel, Y. see Bar-Hillel, Yehoshua.
Bar-Hillel, Yehoshua.
xBar-Hillel, Y.

ed. Pragmatics of Natural Languages. Kluwer
Boston.
Bar-Zohar, Michael.
xBar-Zohar, Michael.
The Deadly Document. Delacorte.
Barach, Arnold. see Barach, Arnold B.
Barach, Arnold B.
xBarach, Arnold.
Famous American Trademarks. Pub Aff Pr.
Barach, Jeffrey. see Barach, Jeffrey A.
Barach, Jeffrey A., 1934-
xBarach, Jeffrey.
The Individual, Business & Society. P-H.
Baradat, Leon P., 1940-
xBaradat, Leon P.
Political Ideologies: Their Origins & Impact.
P-H.
Baraheni, Reza, 1935-
xBaraheni, Reza.
tr. God's Shadow: Prison Poems. Ind U Pr.
Baraka, Amiri. see Baraka, Imamu Amiri.
Baraka, Imamu Amiri, 1934-
xBaraka, Amiri.
Selected Poetry of Amiri Baraka-Leroi Jones.
Morrow.
Barakat, Halim. see Barakat, Halim Isber.
Barakat, Halim Isber.
xBarakat, Halim.
Lebanon in Strife: Student Preludes to the Civil
War. U of Tex Pr.
Baral, David P.
xBaral, David P.
Achievement Levels Among Foreign-Born &
Native-Born Mexican American Students. R
& E Res Assoc.
Baral, Jaya K. see Baral, Jaya Krishna.
Baral, Jaya Krishna.
xBaral, Jaya K.
The Pentagon & the Making of US Foreign
Policy: A Case Study of Vietnam 1960-1968.
Humanities.
Baram, Michael S.
xBaram, Michael S.
Environmental Law & the Siting of Facilities:
Issues in Land Use & Coastal Zone
Management.. Ballinger Pub.
Baran, Paul A.
xBaran, Paul A.
Longer View: Essays Toward a Critique of
Political Economy. Monthly Rev.
Baranson, Jack.
xBaranson, Jack.
Automotive Industries in Developing
Countries. Johns Hopkins.
Manufacturing Problems in India: The
Cummins Diesel Experience. Syracuse U Pr.
Barante, Amable G. see Barante, Amable Guillaume
Prosper Brugiere.
**Barante, Amable Guillaume Prosper Brugiere, Baron
De, 1782-1866**
xBarante, Amable G.
Histoire de la Convention Nationale. AMS Pr.
Histoire du directoire de la Republique
francaise. AMS Pr.
Barash, Samuel T., 1921-
xBarash, Samuel T.
How to Reduce Your Real Estate Taxes. Arco.
Barbach, Lonnie G. see Barbach, Lonnie Garfield.
Barbach, Lonnie Garfield, 1946-
xBarbach, Lonnie G.
For Yourself: The Fulfillment of Female
Sexuality. Doubleday.
Women Discover Orgasm: A Therapist's Guide
to a New Treatment Approach. Free Pr.
Barbalace, Roberta C. see Barbalace, Roberta Crowell.
Barbalace, Roberta Crowell.
xBarbalace, Roberta C.

An Introduction to Light Horse Management.
Burgess.
Barban, Arnold M.
xBarban, Arnold M.
Advertising Media Sourcebook & Workbook.
Grid Pub.
Essentials of Media Planning: A Marketing
Viewpoint. Crain Bks.
Barbara, Dominick A.
xBarbara, Dominick A.
Art of Listening. C C Thomas.
How to Make People Listen to You. C C
Thomas.
Loving & Making Love: A Psychiatrist's Guide
to Happiness & Pleasure. NAL.
Barbara, Dominick A. see Barbara, Dominick A. M. D.
Barbara, Dominick A. M. D.
xBarbara, Dominick A.
Questions & Answers on Stuttering. C C
Thomas.
Barbaresi, Sara M.
xBarbaresi, Sara M.
How to Raise & Train a Boxer. TFH Pubns.
How to Raise & Train a Collie. TFH Pubns.
How to Raise & Train a German Shepherd.
TFH Pubns.
Barbary, James.
xBarbary, James.
Puritan & Cavalier: The English Civil War.
Elsevier-Nelson.
Barbasso, Salvatore.
xBarbasso, Salvatore.
Precalculus: A Functional Approach with
Applications. HarBraceJ.
Barbe, D. F. see Barbe, David F.
Barbe, David F.
xBarbe, D. F.
ed. Charge-Coupled Devices. Springer-Verlag.
Barbe, W. B. see Barbe, Walter Burke.
Barbe, Walter. see Barbe, Walter Burke.
Barbe, Walter B. see Barbe, Walter Burke.
Barbe, Walter Burke.
xBarbe, W. B.
ed. Psychology & Education of the Gifted.
Halsted Pr.
xBarbe, Walter.
Personalized Reading Instruction: New
Techniques That Increase Reading Skill and
Comprehension. P-H.
xBarbe, Walter B.
ed. Psychology & Education of the Gifted.
Irvington.
Teaching Reading: Selected Materials. Oxford
U Pr.
Barbe-Marbois, Francois.
xBarbe-Marbois, Francois.
The History of Louisiana, Particularly of the
Cession of That Colony to the United States
of America. La State U Pr.
Our Revolutionary Forefathers: The Letters of
Francois, Marquis De Barbe-Marbois During
His Residence in the United States As
Secretary of the French Legation 1779-1785.
Arno.
Barbeau, Andre.
xBarbeau, Andre.
ed. Choline & Lecithin in Brain Disorders.
Raven.
ed. Taurine & Neurological Disorders. Raven.
Barbeau, Clayton C.
xBarbeau, Clayton D.
Creative Marriage: The Middle Years. Seabury.
Barbeau, Clayton D. see Barbeau, Clayton C.
Barbedette, Hippolyte, 1827-1901
xBarbedette, Hippolyte.
Stephen Heller: His Life & Works. Info Coord.
Barber, A. see Barber, Alfred W.
Barber, Alfred W., 1906-
xBarber, A.

Practical Guide to Digital Integrated Circuits.
P-H.
xBarber, Alfred W.
Experimenter's Guide to Solid State
Electronics Projects. P-H.
Barber, Benjamin R., 1939-
xBarber, Benjamin R.
Death of Communal Liberty: The History of
Freedom in a Swiss Mountain Canton.
Princeton U Pr.
Barber, Bernard.
xBarber, Bernard.
European Social Class: Stability & Change.
Greenwood.
Informed Consent in Medical Therapy &
Research. Rutgers U Pr.
ed. Medical Ethics & Social Change. Am Acad
Pol Soc Sci.
Science & the Social Order. Greenwood.
Barber, C. L. *see* Barber, Charles Laurence.
Barber, Charles Laurence.
xBarber, C. L.
Idea of Honour in the English Drama
1591-1700. Folcroft.
Barber, Cyril J.
xBarber, Cyril J.
Nehemiah & the Dynamics of Effective
Leadership. Loizeaux.
Barber, E. J. W., 1940-
xBarber, W. J.
Archaeological Decipherment: A Handbook.
Princeton U Pr.
Barber, Edwin A. *see* Barber, Edwin Atlee.
Barber, Edwin Atlee, 1851-1916
xBarber, Edwin A.
Marks of American Potters. Ars Ceramica.
Tulip Ware of the Pennsylvania-German
Potters: An Historical Sketch of the Art of
Slip Decoration in the United States. Peter
Smith.
Barber, Geoffrey, 1904-
xBarber, Geoffrey.
Country Doctor. Rowman.
Barber, Godfrey L. *see* Barber, Godfrey Louis.
Barber, Godfrey Louis.
xBarber, Godfrey L.
The Historian Ephorus. AMS Pr.
Barber, H. R. *see* Barber, Hugh R. K.
Barber, Hugh R. *see* Barber, Hugh R. K.
Barber, Hugh R. K., 1918-
xBarber, H. R.
Immunobiology for the Clinician. Wiley.
xBarber, Hugh R.
Quick Reference to OB-Gyn Procedures.
Lippincott.
Surgical Disease in Pregnancy. Saunders.
Barber, J. *see* Barber, James.
Barber, J. W. *see* Barber, John Wilfrid.
Barber, James.
xBarber, J.
ed. The Intact Chloroplast. Elsevier.
ed. Photosynthesis in Relation to Model
Systems. Elsevier.
ed. Primary Processes of Photosynthesis.
Elsevier.
Barber, James. *see* Barber, James P.
Barber, James D. *see* Barber, James David.
Barber, James David.
xBarber, James D.
ed. Choosing the President. Am Assembly.
ed. Choosing the President. P-H.
The Lawmakers: Recruitment & Adaptation to
Legislative Life. Greenwood.
The Presidential Character: Predicting
Performance in the White House. P-H.
The Pulse of Politics: The Rhythm of
Presidential Elections in the Twentieth
Century. Norton.
Barber, James P.
xBarber, James.

South Africa's Foreign Policy, 1945-1970.
Oxford U Pr.
Barber, Janet.
xBarber, Janet.
My Learn to Sew Book. Western Pub.
Barber, Janet M. *see* Barber, Janet Miller.
Barber, Janet Miller.
xBarber, Janet M.
Adult & Child Care: A Client Approach to
Nursing. Mosby.
Handbook of Emergency Pharmacology.
Mosby.
Mosby's Manual of Emergency Care: Practices
& Procedures. Mosby.
Barber, John W. *see* Barber, John Warner.
Barber, John Warner.
xBarber, John W.
Early Woodcut Views of New York & New
Jersey: 304 Illustrations from the "Historical
Collection". Peter Smith.
History of the Amistad Captives. Arno.
Barber, John Wilfrid.
xBarber, J. W.
ed. Industrial Training Handbook. A S Barnes.
Barber, Lester E., 1938-
xBarber, Lester E.
Misogonus. Garland Pub.
Barber, Lucie W.
xBarber, Lucie W.
Celebrating the Second Year of Life: A
Parent's Guide for a Happy Child. Religious
Educ.
Barber, Lynn.
xBarber, Lynn.
How to Improve Your Man in Bed. PB.
Barber, M. N. *see* Barber, Michael N.
Barber, Michael N.
xBarber, M. N.
Random & Restricted Walks: Theory &
Applications. Gordon.
Barber, Noel.
xBarber, Noel.
The Fall of Shanghai. Coward.
The Sultans. S&S.
Barber, Olive.
xBarber, Olive.
Meet Me in Juneau. Binford.
Barber, Richard. *see* Barber, Richard W.
Barber, Richard J.
xBarber, Richard J.
Politics of Research. Pub Aff Pr.
Barber, Richard W.
xBarber, Richard.
A Companion to World Mythology. Delacorte.
Edward Prince of Wales & Aquitaine: A
Biography of the Black Prince. Scribner.
The Figure of Arthur. Rowman.
The Reign of Chivalry. St Martin.
Barber, Sotirios. *see* Barber, Sotirios A.
Barber, Sotirios A.
xBarber, Sotirios.
Introduction to Problem Solving in Political
Science. Merrill.
xBarber, Sotirios A.
The Constitution & the Delegation of
Congressional Power. U of Chicago Pr.
Barber, T. X. *see* Barber, Theodore Xenophon.
Barber, Theodore X. *see* Barber, Theodore Xenophon.
Barber, Theodore Xenophon.
xBarber, T. X.
Hypnosis, Imagination & Human Potentialities.
Pergamon.
xBarber, Theodore X.
Hypnosis, Imagination & Human Potentialities.
Pergamon.
Pitfalls in Human Research: Ten Pivotal Points.
Pergamon.
Barber, Thomas G. *see* Barber, Thomas Gerrard.
Barber, Thomas Gerrard, 1875-1952
xBarber, Thomas G.

Byron & Where He Is Buried. Folcroft.
Barber, Thomas H.
xBarber, Thomas H.
Where We Are At. Arno.
Barber, W. J. *see* Barber, E. J. W.
Barber, William J.
xBarber, William J.
The History of Economic Thought. Penguin.
Barbereux-Parry, M. *see* Barbereux-Parry, Mame.
Barbereux-Parry, Mame, 1868-
xBarbereux-Parry, M.
Vocal Resonance: Its Source & Command.
Chris Mass.
Barbery, Willard S. *see* Barbery, Willard Sanders.
Barbery, Willard Sanders.
xBarbery, Willard S.
Story of the Life of Robert Sayers Sheffey: A
Courier of the Long Trail-God's Gentlemen.
Scholarly.
Barbey, K. *see* Barbey, Klaus.
Barbey, Klaus.
xBarbey, K.
Abstract Analytic Function Theory & Hardy
Algebras. Springer-Verlag.
Barbier, George.
xBarbier, George.
The Illustrations of George Barbier in Full
Color. Dover.
Barbier, M. *see* Barbier, Michel.
Barbier, Michel, 1928-
xBarbier, M.
Introduction to Chemical Ecology. Longman.
Barbieri, Louis. *see* Barbieri, Louis A.
Barbieri, Louis A.
xBarbieri, Louis.
First & Second Peter. Moody.
Barbosa, Jorge F. *see* Barbosa, Jorge Fairbanks.
Barbosa, Jorge Fairbanks.
xBarbosa, Jorge F.
Surgical Treatment of Head & Neck Tumors.
Grune.
Barbotin, Edmond.
xBarbotin, Edmond.
Faith for Today. Orbis Bks.
The Humanity of God. Orbis Bks.
The Humanity of Man. Orbis Bks.
Barbour, Alan G.
xBarbour, Alan G.
Humphrey Bogart. Brown Bk.
Barbour, Arthur. *see* Barbour, Arthur J.
Barbour, Arthur J., 1926-
xBarbour, Arthur.
Painting the Seasons in Watercolor.
Watson-Guptill.
xBarbour, Arthur J.
Painting Buildings in Watercolor.
Watson-Guptill.
Painting the Seasons in Watercolor.
Watson-Guptill.
Barbour, Beverly, 1927-
xBarbour, Beverly.
The Complete Food Preservation Book: How
to Can, Freeze, Preserve, Pickle, & Cure
Edibles. McKay.
Barbour, Brian M., 1943-
xBarbour, Brian M.
ed. American Transcendentalism: An
Anthology of Criticism. U of Notre Dame Pr.
ed. Benjamin Franklin: A Collection of Critical
Essays. P-H.
Barbour, David M. *see* Barbour, David Miller.
Barbour, David Miller, Sir, 1841-
xBarbour, David M.
Theory of Bimetallism & the Effects of the
Partial Demonetisation of Silver on England
& India. Greenwood.
Barbour, Harriet Buxton.
xBarbour, Harriot B.
Story of Music. Summy.
Barbour, Harriot B. *see* Barbour, Harriet Buxton.

Barbour, Hugh.
    xBarbour, Hugh.
        Margaret Fell Speaking. Pendle Hill.
Barbour, J. Murray. *see* Barbour, James Murray.
Barbour, James Murray, 1897-
    xBarbour, J. Murray.
        Trumpets, Horns & Music. Mich St U Pr.
    xBarbour, James Murray.
        Tuning & Temperament: A Historical Survey.
        Da Capo.
Barbour, John A. *see* Barbour, John Andrews.
Barbour, John Andrews, 1928-
    xBarbour, John A.
        In the Wake of the Whale. Macmillan.
Barbour, Lucius B. *see* Barbour, Lucius Barnes.
Barbour, Lucius Barnes, 1878-1934
    xBarbour, Lucius B.
        Families of Early Hartford, Connecticut.
        Genealog Pub.
Barbour, R. *see* Barbour, Robert.
Barbour, Robert, 1916-
    xBarbour, R.
        Glassblowing for Laboratory Technicians.
        Pergamon.
Barbour, Roger W. *see* Barbour, Roger William.
Barbour, Roger William.
    xBarbour, Roger W.
        Bats of America. U Pr of Ky.
Barbour, Ruth P.
    xBarbour, Ruth P.
        Cruise of the Snap Dragon. Blair.
Barbour, Violet, 1884-
    xBarbour, Violet.
        Capitalism in Amsterdam in the Seventeenth
        Century. AMS Pr.
Barbree, Jay.
    xBarbree, Jay.
        The Hydra Pit. Ashley Bks.
Barbrook, Alec.
    xBarbrook, Alec T.
        God Save the Commonwealth: An Electoral
        History of Massachusetts. U of Mass Pr.
Barbrook, Alec T. *see* Barbrook, Alec.
Barbu, Zevedei.
    xBarbu, Zevedei.
        Problems of Historical Psychology. Greenwood.
        Society, Culture & Personality: An
        Introduction to Social Science. Schocken.
Barcham, William L.
    xBarcham, William L.
        The Imaginary View Scenes of Antonio
        Canaletto. Garland Pub.
Barchas, Jack D.
    xBarchas, Jack D.
        ed. Psychopharmacology: From Theory to
        Practice. Oxford U Pr.
Barck, Oscar T. *see* Barck, Oscar Theodore.
Barck, Oscar Theodore.
    xBarck, Oscar T.
        Colonial America. Macmillan.
Barclay, Alexander, Of Jamaica.
    xBarclay, Alexander.
        Practical View of the Present State of Slavery
        in the West Indies. Arno.
Barclay, George W.
    xBarclay, George W.
        Colonial Development & Population in Taiwan.
        Kennikat.
Barclay, Glen. *see* Barclay, Glen St. John.
Barclay, Glen St. John, 1930-
    xBarclay, Glen.
        Struggle for a Continent: The Diplomatic
        History of South America, 1917-1945. NYU
        Pr.
Barclay, Irene.
    xBarclay, Irene.
        People Need Roots: The Story of the St.
        Pancras Housing Association. Intl Pubns
        Serv.
Barclay, James R. *see* Barclay, James Ralph.

Barclay, James Ralph, 1926-
    xBarclay, James R.
        Controversial Issues in Testing. HM.
        Counseling & Philosophy: A Theoretical
        Exposition. HM.
        Foundations of Counseling Strategies. Krieger.
Barclay, William.
    xBarclay, William.
        All-Sufficient Christ: Studies in Paul's Letter to
        the Colossians. Westminster.
        And He Had Compassion. Judson.
        And Jesus Said: A Handbook on the Parables
        of Jesus. Westminster.
        By What Authority. Judson.
        Ethics in a Permissive Society. Har-Row.
        Fishers of Men. Westminster.
        God's Young Church. Westminster.
        Great Themes of the New Testament.
        Westminster.
        In the Hands of God. Collins Pubs.
        Introduction to John & the Acts of the
        Apostles. Westminster.
        A Life of Christ. Har-Row.
        The Life of Jesus for Everyman. Har-Row.
        The Lord Is My Shepherd: Expositions of
        Selected Psalms. Westminster.
        Many Witnesses, One Lord. Baker Bk.
        Marching Orders: Daily Readings for Younger
        People. Westminster.
        Men & Affairs. Westminster.
        Prayers for Help & Healing. Har-Row.
        Prayers for Young People. Collins Pubs.
        The Promise of the Spirit. Westminster.
        ed. Racial Conflict, Discrimination, & Power:
        Historical & Contemporary Studies. AMS Pr.
        Turning to God: A Study of Conversion in the
        Book of Acts & Today. Baker Bk.
Barclay, William. *see* Barclay, William, Lecturer in the
University of Glasgow.
Barclay, William, Lecturer in the University of Glasgow.
    xBarclay, William.
        The Master's Men. Abingdon.
        Master's Men. Pillar Bks.
Barcroft, Joseph, Sir, 1872-1947
    xBarcroft, Joseph.
        The Brain & Its Environment. Kennikat.
Barcus, F. Earle. *see* Barcus, Francis Earle.
Barcus, Francis Earle.
    xBarcus, F. Earle.
        Children's Television: An Analysis of
        Programming & Advertising. Praeger.
Bard. *see* Bard, Allan J.
Bard, A. *see* Bard, Allan J.
Bard, Allan J.
    xBard.
        Encyclopedia of the Electrochemistry of the
        Elements. Dekker.
    xBard, A.
        ed. Encyclopedia of Electrochemistry of the
        Elements. Dekker.
    xBard, Allen.
        ed. Encyclopedia of Electrochemistry of the
        Elements. Dekker.
    xBard, Allen J.
        ed. Encyclopedia of Electrochemistry of the
        Elements. Dekker.
Bard, Allen. *see* Bard, Allan J.
Bard, Allen J. *see* Bard, Allan J.
Bard, Erwin W. *see* Bard, Erwin Wilkie.
Bard, Erwin Wilkie, 1903-
    xBard, Erwin W.
        Port of New York Authority. AMS Pr.
Bard, Morton.
    xBard, Morton.
        The Crime Victim's Book. Basic.
Bard, Yonathan.
    xBard, Yonathan.
        Nonlinear Parameter Estimation. Acad Pr.
Bardach, Eugene.
    xBardach, Eugene.

        The California Coastal Plan: A Critique. Inst
        Contemporary.
Bardakjian, Kevork B.
    xBardakjian, Kevork B.
        Textbook of Modern Western Armenian.
        Caravan Bks.
Bardeche, Maurice.
    xBardeche, Maurice.
        History of Motion Pictures. Arno.
Barden, John G. *see* Barden, John Glenn.
Barden, John Glenn, 1900-
    xBarden, John G.
        A Suggested Program of Teacher Training for
        Mission Schools Among the Batetela. AMS
        Pr.
Barden, Leonard.
    xBarden, Leonard.
        Introduction to Chess Moves & Tactics Simply
        Explained. Dover.
        Modern Chess Miniatures. Dover.
Barden, R. G. *see* Barden, Ronald G.
Barden, Ronald G.
    xBarden, R. G.
        Sound Pollution. U of Queensland Pr.
Barden, William. *see* Barden, William T.
Barden, William T.
    xBarden, William.
        Guidebook to Small Computers. Bobbs.
        How to Buy & Use Minicomputers &
        Microcomputers. Sams.
        How to Program Microcomputers. Sams.
        Microcomputers for Business Applications.
        Sams.
Bardens, Dennis.
    xBardens, Dennis.
        Ghosts & Hauntings. Taplinger.
Barder, R. E. *see* Barder, Richard Charles Remilly.
Barder, Richard Charles Remilly, 1937-
    xBarder, R. E.
        Spinning for Pike. David & Charles.
Bardin, John F. *see* Bardin, John Franklin.
Bardin, John Franklin.
    xBardin, John F.
        Purloining Tiny. Har-Row.
Bardis, Panos D. *see* Bardis, Panos Demetrios.
Bardis, Panos Demetrios.
    xBardis, Panos D.
        The Future of the Greek Language in the
        United States. R & E Res Assoc.
Bardolph, Richard, 1915-
    xBardolph, Richard.
        The Negro Vanguard. Negro U Pr.
Bardos, C. *see* Bardos, Claude.
Bardos, Claude.
    xBardos, C.
        ed. Bifurcation & Nonlinear Eigenvalue
        Problems: Proceedings. Springer-Verlag.
Bardwick, Judith. *see* Bardwick, Judith M.
Bardwick, Judith M., 1933-
    xBardwick, Judith.
        In Transition: How Feminism, Sexual
        Liberation, & the Search for Self-Fulfillment
        Have Altered America. HR&W.
    xBardwick, Judith M.
        Feminine Personality & Conflict. Brooks-Cole.
        Psychology of Women: A Study of Biocultural
        Conflicts. Har-Row.
        Readings on the Psychology of Women.
        Har-Row.
Bare, Colleen S. *see* Bare, Colleen Stanley.
Bare, Colleen Stanley.
    xBare, Colleen S.
        The Durable Desert Tortoise. Dodd.
Bare, Janet E.
    xBare, Janet E.
        Wildflowers & Weeds of Kansas. Regents Pr
        KS.
Bare, William K.
    xBare, William K.

Fundamentals of Fire Prevention. Wiley.
Barea, Arturo, 1897-1957
xBarea, Arturo.
Lorca: The Poet & His People. Cooper Sq.
Barefoot, J. Kirk.
xBarefoot, J. Kirk.
Employee Theft Investigation. Butterworths.
Undercover Investigation. C C Thomas.
Barenblatt. see Barenblatt, G. I.
Barenblatt, G. I.
xBarenblatt.
ed. Similarity, Self-Similarity & Intermediate
Asymptotics. Plenum Pub.
Barenboim, Grigorii Matveevich.
xBarenboim, Grigory M.
Luminescence of Biopolymers & Cells. Plenum
Pub.
Barenboim, Grigory M. see Barenboim, Grigorii
Matveevich.
Bares, Richard.
xBares, Richard.
Analysis of Beam Grids & Orthotropic Plates
by the Guyon-Massonnet-Bares Method.
Ungar.
Barfield, Owen, 1898-
xBarfield, Owen.
History, Guilt, & Habit. Columbia U Pr.
Barford, Carol.
xBarford, Carol.
Let Me Hear the Music. HM.
Bargar, B. D.
xBargar, Bradley D.
Lord Dartmouth & the American Revolution.
U of SC Pr.
Bargar, Bradley D. see Bargar, B. D.
Bargate, Verity.
xBargate, Verity.
No Mama No. Har-Row.
Bargen, Richard, 1946-
xBargen, Richard.
The Vegetarian's Self-Defense Manual. Theos
Pub Hse.
Barger, Harold.
xBarger, Harold.
American Agriculture, 1899-1939: A Study of
Output, Employment & Productivity. AMS
Pr.
American Agriculture, 1899-1939: A Study of
Output, Employment, & Productivity. Arno.
Barger, Vernon D.
xBarger, Vernon D.
Classical Mechanics: A Modern Perspective.
McGraw.
Barghoorn, Frederick C. see Barghoorn, Frederick
Charles.
Barghoorn, Frederick Charles, 1911-
xBarghoorn, Frederick C.
Detente & the Democratic Movement in the
USSR. Free Pr.
Soviet Foreign Propaganda. Princeton U Pr.
Soviet Russian Nationalism. Greenwood.
Barham, Jerry N.
xBarham, Jerry N.
Mechanical Kinesiology. Mosby.
Structural Kinesiology. Macmillan.
Barich, Bill.
xBarich, Bill.
Laughing in the Hills. Viking Pr.
Barigozzi, Claudio.
xBarigozzi, Claudio.
ed. Origin & Natural History of Cell Lines:
Proceedings of a Conference Held at
Accademia Nazionale dei Lincei, Rome,
1977. A R Liss.
Barin, I. see Barin, Ihsan.
Barin, Ihsan.
xBarin, I.

Thermochemical Properties of Inorganic
Substances. Springer-Verlag.
Baring, Maurice, 1874-1945
xBaring, Maurice.
The Collected Poems of Maurice Baring. AMS
Pr.
Diminutive Dramas. Core Collection.
Diminutive Dramas. R West.
Half a Minute's Silence & Other Stories. Arno.
An Outline of Russian Literature. Greenwood.
An Outline of Russian Literature. R West.
Punch & Judy & Other Essays. Arno.
Baring-Gould, S. see Baring-Gould, Sabine.
Baring-Gould, Sabine, 1834-1924
xBaring-Gould, S.
Curious Myths of the Middle Ages. Gordon Pr.
Family Names & Their Story. Gordon Pr.
Legends of the Patriarchs & Prophets & Other
Old Testament Characters. Folcroft.
An Old English Home & Its Dependencies.
Gordon Pr.
xBaring-Gould, Sabine.
Book of Werewolves: Being an Account of
Terrible Superstition. Gale.
Cliff Castles & Cave Dwellings of Europe.
Gale.
Curious Myths of the Middle Ages. Oxford U
Pr.
Curious Myths of the Middle Ages. Scholarly.
Family Names & Their Story. Gale.
Family Names & Their Story. Genealog Pub.
Old Country Life. Gale.
Old English Home & Its Dependencies. Gale.
Strange Survivals, Some Chapters in the
History of Man. Gale.
Baringer, William. see Baringer, William Eldon.
Baringer, William Eldon, 1909-
xBaringer, William.
Lincoln's Rise to Power. Scholarly.
Barish, Louis.
xBarish, Louis.
Varieties of Jewish Belief. Jonathan David.
Barish, Norman N.
xBarish, Norman N.
Economic Analysis for Engineering &
Managerial Decision Making. McGraw.
Baritz, Loren, 1928-
xBaritz, Loren.
ed. American Left: Radical Political Thought in
the Twentieth Century. Basic.
City on a Hill: A History of Ideas & Myths in
America. Greenwood.
Bark, Dennis L.
xBark, Dennis L.
Agreement on Berlin: A Study of the 1970-72
Quadripartite Negotiations. Am Enterprise.
Bark, L. S.
xBark, L. S.
Thermometric Titrimetry. Pergamon.
Bark, Willaim Carroll, 1908-
xBark, William C.
Origins of the Medieval World. Stanford U Pr.
Bark, William C. see Bark, Willaim Carroll.
Barkai, Haim, 1925-
xBarkai, Haim.
Growth Patterns of the Kibbutz Economy.
Elsevier.
Barkalow, Frederick S. see Barkalow, Frederick Schenck.
Barkalow, Frederick Schenck.
xBarkalow, Frederick S.
The World of the Gray Squirrel. Lippincott.
Barkan, Joel D.
xBarkan, Joel D.
Politics & Public Policy in Kenya & Tanzania.
Praeger.
Barkan, Leonard.
xBarkan, Leonard.
Nature's Work of Art: The Human Body As
Image of the World. Yale U Pr.
Barkas, J. L. see Barkas, Janet L.

Barkas, Janet L.
xBarkas, J. L.
The Help Book. Scribner.
Barkdull, Tom, 1912-
xBarkdull, Tom.
Lonesome Walls: An Odyssey Through Ghost
Towns of the Old West. Exposition.
Barkenbus, Jack N.
xBarkenbus, Jack N.
Deep Seabed Resources: Politics & Technology.
Free Pr.
Barker, A. J.
xBarker, A. J.
Japanese Army Handbook. Hippocrene Bks.
Panzers at War. Intl Pubns Serv.
Panzers at War. Scribner.
Barker, Alan.
xBarker, Alan.
Civil War in America. Doubleday.
Barker, Albert, 1900-
xBarker, Albert.
From Settlement to City. Messner.
Barker, Anthony J.
xBarker, Anthony J.
The African Link: British Attitudes to the
Negro in the Era of the Atlantic Slave Trade,
1550-1807. Biblio Dist.
Barker, Arthur E. see Barker, Arthur Edward.
Barker, Arthur Edward, 1911-
xBarker, Arthur E.
Compiled by The Seventeenth Century: Bacon
Through Marvell. AHM Pub.
Barker, Brian. see Barker, Brian, O. B. E.
Barker, Brian, O. B. E.
xBarker, Brian.
The Symbols of Sovereignty. Rowman.
Barker, C. Edward. see Barker, Charles Edward.
Barker, Charles Edward, 1908-
xBarker, C. Edward.
Psychology's Impact on the Christian Faith.
Transatlantic.
Barker, D. J. see Barker, David James Purslove.
Barker, David James Purslove.
xBarker, D. J.
Practical Epidemiology. Churchill.
Barker, Elisabeth.
xBarker, Elisabeth.
Churchill & Eden at War. St Martin.
Barker, Ernest, Sir, 1874-1960
xBarker, Ernest.
Britain & the British People. Greenwood.
Character of England. Greenwood.
Church, State & Study: Essays. Greenwood.
Citizen's Choice. Arno.
The Crusades. Arno.
Development of Public Services in Western
Europe, 1660-1930. Shoe String.
Ideas & Ideals of the British Empire.
Greenwood.
National Character & the Factors in Its
Formation. Hyperion Conn.
Oliver Cromwell & the English People. Arno.
Political Thought of Plato & Aristotle. Dover.
Political Thought of Plato & Aristotle. Peter
Smith.
Political Thought of Plato & Aristotle. Russell.
Barker, Eugene C. see Barker, Eugene Campbell.
Barker, Eugene Campbell, 1874-1956
xBarker, Eugene C.
Life of Stephen F. Austin, Founder of Texas,
1793-1836: A Chapter in the Westward
Movement of the Anglo-American People.
Tex St Hist Assn.
Barker, F. see Barker, Fred.
Barker, Forrest L.
xBarker, Forrest L.
Mathematics for Electronics.
Benjamin-Cummings.
Barker, Francis, 1952-
xBarker, Francis.

Solzhenitsyn: Politics & Form. B&N.
Barker, Fred, 1928-
  xBarker, F.
  ed. Trondhjemites, Dacites, & Related Rocks.
    Elsevier.
Barker, George, 1913-
  xBarker, George.
  Villa Stellar. Merrimack Bk Serv.
Barker, Gerard A.
  xBarker, Gerard A.
  Twice-Told Tales: An Anthology of Short
    Fiction. HM.
Barker, Gray.
  xBarker, Gray.
  Silver Bridge. Saucerian.
Barker, John.
  xBarker, John C.
  Strange Contrarieties: Pascal in England
    During the Age of Reason. McGill-Queens U
    Pr.
Barker, John C. *see* Barker, John.
Barker, John W.
  xBarker, John W.
  Manuel Ii Palaeologus, 1391-1425: A Study in
    Late Byzantine Statesmanship. Rutgers U Pr.
Barker, Joseph.
  xBarker, Joseph.
  Fourth at Junction. St Martin.
Barker, June.
  xBarker, June.
  Decorative Braiding & Weaving. Branford.
Barker, Kenneth. *see* Barker, Kenneth R.
Barker, Kenneth R.
  xBarker, Kenneth.
  Laboratory Manual of Comparative Anatomy.
    McGraw.
Barker, Larry L. *see* Barker, Larry Lee.
Barker, Larry Lee, 1941-
  xBarker, Larry L.
  Communication. P-H
  Communication Vibrations. P-H.
  Groups in Process: An Introduction to Small
    Group Communication. P-H.
  ed. Speech Communication Behavior:
    Perspectives & Principles. P-H.
Barker, Lucious J. *see* Barker, Lucius Jefferson.
Barker, Lucius. *see* Barker, Lucius Jefferson.
Barker, Lucius Jefferson.
  xBarker, Lucious J.
  Black Americans & the Political System.
    Winthrop.
  xBarker, Lucius.
  Black Americans & the Political System.
    Winthrop.
Barker, Nancy N. *see* Barker, Nancy Nichols.
Barker, Nancy Nichols.
  xBarker, Nancy N.
  Distaff Diplomacy: The Empress Eugenie &
    the Foreign Policy of the Second Empire. U
    of Tex Pr.
  ed. French Legation in Texas. Tex St Hist
    Assn.
Barker, Nicholas P.
  xBarker, Nicholas P.
  Purpose & Function in Prose. Phila Bk Co.
Barker, Nicolas.
  xBarker, Nicolas.
  The Oxford University Press & the Spread of
    Learning: An Illustrated History, 1478-1978.
    Oxford U Pr.
  xBarker, Nicolas J.
  Stanley Morison. Harvard U Pr.
Barker, Nicolas J. *see* Barker, Nicolas.
Barker, P. *see* Barker, Philip.
Barker, Philip.
  xBarker, P.
  Wargaming. Charles River Bks.
Barker, Philip. *see* Barker, Philip Alan.
Barker, Philip Alan.
  xBarker, Philip.

Basic Child Psychiatry. Aronson.
Barker, Ralph, 1917-
  xBarker, Ralph.
  The Last Blue Mountain. Mountaineers.
  Not Here, but in Another Place. St Martin.
Barker, Raymond C. *see* Barker, Raymond Charles.
Barker, Raymond Charles.
  xBarker, Raymond C.
  The Power of Decision. Dodd.
Barker, Richard H. *see* Barker, Richard Hindry.
Barker, Richard Hindry, 1902-1968
  xBarker, Richard H.
  Thomas Middleton. Greenwood.
Barker, Robert.
  xBarker, Robert.
  Love Forty. Lippincott.
  Organic Chemistry of Biological Compounds.
    P-H.
Barker, Rodney.
  xBarker, Rodney.
  Political Ideas in Modern Britain. Methuen Inc.
Barker, Roger. *see* Barker, Roger Garlock.
Barker, Roger G. *see* Barker, Roger Garlock.
Barker, Roger Garlock.
  xBarker, Roger.
  Frustration & Regression: An Experiment with
    Young Children. Arno.
  xBarker, Roger G.
  Ecological Psychology: Concepts & Methods
    for Studying the Environment of Human
    Behavior. Stanford U Pr.
Barker, S. F. *see* Barker, Stephen Francis.
Barker, Shirley.
  xBarker, Shirley.
  Dark Hills Under. AMS Pr.
Barker, Stephen. *see* Barker, Stephen Francis.
Barker, Stephen F. *see* Barker, Stephen Francis.
Barker, Stephen Francis.
  xBarker, S. F.
  Induction & Hypothesis: A Study of the Logic
    of Confirmation. Cornell U Pr.
  xBarker, Stephen.
  Elements of Logic. McGraw.
  xBarker, Stephen F.
  Elements of Logic. McGraw.
Barker, Wiley F.
  xBarker, Wiley F.
  Peripheral Arterial Disease. Saunders.
Barker, Will.
  xBarker, Will.
  Familiar Animals of America. Har-Row.
  Familiar Reptiles & Amphibians of America.
    Har-Row.
Barker, William P. *see* Barker, William Pierson.
Barker, William Pierson.
  xBarker, William P.
  Everyone in the Bible. Revell.
Barkhouse, Bob.
  xBarkhouse, Bob.
  Engine Repair: Head Assembly & Valve Gear.
    McKnight.
Barkin, Carol.
  xBarkin, Carol.
  The Complete Babysitter's Handbook.
    Wanderer Bks.
  Slapdash Decorating. Lothrop.
  Slapdash Decorating. Wanderer Bks.
Barkin, David.
  xBarkin, David.
  Regional Economic Development: The River
    Basin Approach in Mexico. Cambridge U Pr.
Barkin, Solomon, 1907-
  xBarkin, Solomon.
  ed. Worker Militancy & Its Consequences,
    1965-75: New Directions in Western
    Industrial Relations. Praeger.
Barkins, Evelyn. *see* Barkins, Evelyn (Werner).
Barkins, Evelyn (Werner), 1918-
  xBarkins, Evelyn.

A Grandparent's Garden of Verses. Fell.
  Love Poems of a Marriage. Fell.
Barkley, Deanne.
  xBarkley, Deanne.
  Freeway. Macmillan.
  Freeway. Popular Lib.
Barkley, Katherine Traver.
  xBarkley, Katherine Traver.
  The Ambulance: The Story of Emergency
    Transportation of Sick & Wounded Through
    the Centuries. Exposition.
Barkley, Paul W.
  xBarkley, Paul W.
  Economics: The Way We Choose. HarBraceJ.
  An Introduction to Macroeconomics.
    HarBraceJ.
  An Introduction to Microeconomics.
    HarBraceJ.
Barkman, Alma.
  xBarkman, Alma.
  Sunny-Side up. Moody.
Barkun, Michael.
  xBarkun, Michael.
  Disaster & the Millennium. Yale U Pr.
  ed. Law & the Social System. Lieber-Atherton.
Barling, Tom.
  xBarling, Tom.
  The Olympic Sleeper. Fawcett.
Barlough, J. Ernest, 1953-
  xBarlough, J. Ernest.
  The Archaicon: A Collection of Unusual
    Archaic English. Scarecrow.
Barlow, Brent A., 1941-
  xBarlow, Brent A.
  Understanding Death. Deseret Bk.
Barlow, David, M.R.C.P.
  xBarlow, David.
  Sexually Transmitted Diseases: The Facts.
    Oxford U Pr.
Barlow, Frank.
  xBarlow, Frank.
  Edward the Confessor. U of Cal Pr.
  The Feudal Kingdom of England: 1042-1216.
    Longman.
Barlow, George, 1948-
  xBarlow, George.
  Gabriel. Broadside.
  The Genius of Dickens. Folcroft.
  The Genius of Dickens. Haskell.
  The Genius of Dickens. R West.
Barlow, Harold.
  xBarlow, Harold.
  Compiled by Dictionary of Musical Themes.
    Crown.
Barlow, Hugh D.
  xBarlow, Hugh D.
  Introduction to Criminology. Little.
Barlow, Ima C. *see* Barlow, Ima Christina.
Barlow, Ima Christina.
  xBarlow, Ima C.
  Agadir Crisis. Shoe String.
Barlow, Iola.
  xBarlow, Iola.
  Dolls in National Costume. Branford.
Barlow, Jane, 1860-1917
  xBarlow, Jane.
  Creel of Irish Stories. Arno.
  Strangers at Lisconnel: A Second Series of
    Irish Idylls. Arno.
Barlow, Jeffrey G.
  xBarlow, Jeffrey G.
  Sun Yat-Sen & the French, 1900-1908. IEAS
    Ctr Chinese Stud.
Barlow, Melvin L.
  xBarlow, Melvin L.
  History of Industrial Education in the United
    States. Bennett Co.
Barlow, Richard B. *see* Barlow, Richard Burgess.
Barlow, Richard Burgess, 1927-
  xBarlow, Richard B.

History & Prospects of the Social Sciences.
Revisionist Pr.
History & Social Intelligence. Revisionist Pr.
History of Historical Writing. Dover.
A History of the Penal, Reformatory, &
Correctional Institutions of the State of New
Jersey: Analytical & Documentary. Arno.
In Quest of Truth & Justice: De-Bunking the
War Guilt Myth. Arno.
In Quest of Truth & Justice: Debunking the
War Guilt Myth. R Myles.
Pearl Harbor After a Quarter of a Century.
Arno.
Revisionism: A Key to Peace. Revisionist Pr.
Society in Transition. Greenwood.
Sociology Before Comte. Revisionist Pr.
Story of Punishment: A Record of Man's
Inhumanity to Man. Patterson Smith.
The Twilight of Christianity. Revisionist Pr.
Barnes, Hazel E. see Barnes, Hazel Estella.
Barnes, Hazel Estella.
xBarnes, Hazel E.
An Existentialist Ethics. U of Chicago Pr.
Humanistic Existentialism: The Literature of
Possibility. U of Nebr Pr.
The Meddling Gods: Four Essays on Classical
Themes. U of Nebr Pr.
Barnes, Homer F. see Barnes, Homer Francis.
Barnes, Homer Francis, 1895-
xBarnes, Homer F.
Charles Fenno Hoffman. AMS Pr.
Barnes, Hubert Lloyd.
xBarnes, H. L.
ed. Geochemistry of Hydrothermal Ore
Deposits. Wiley.
Barnes, Jack.
xBarnes, Jack
Prospects for Socialism in America. Path Pr
NY.
Barnes, John, 1935-
xBarnes, John.
Evita--First Lady: A Biography of Eva Peron.
Grove.
Evita--First Lady: A Biography of Eva Peron.
Grove.
How to Have More Money. Morrow.
More Money for Your Retirement. Har-Row.
More Money for Your Retirement. Har-Row.
Barnes, Julian.
xBarnes, Julian.
Metroland. St Martin.
Barnes, K. R.
xBarnes, K. R.
Optical Transfer Function. Elsevier.
Barnes, Margaret A. see Barnes, Margaret Anne.
Barnes, Margaret Anne.
xBarnes, Margaret A.
Murder in Coweta County. PB.
Barnes, Margaret C. see Barnes, Margaret Campbell.
Barnes, Margaret Campbell, 1891-
xBarnes, Margaret C.
Tudor Rose. Macrae.
Barnes, Mary.
xBarnes, Mary.
Mary Barnes: Two Accounts of a Journey
Through Madness. Ballantine.
Mary Barnes: Two Accounts of Journey
Through Madness. Ballantine.
Barnes, Maude. see Barnes, Maude (Fiero).
Barnes, Maude (Fiero), 1871-
xBarnes, Maude.
Renaissance Vistas. Arno.
Barnes, Mildred. see Barnes, Mildred J.
Barnes, Mildred J.
xBarnes, Mildred.
Girl's Basketball. Sterling.
xBarnes, Mildred J.

Field Hockey: The Coach & the Player. Allyn.
Women's Basketball. Allyn.
Barnes, Myra Edwards.
xBarnes, Myra J.
Linguistics & Languages in Science
Fiction-Fantasy. Arno.
Barnes, Myra J. see Barnes, Myra Edwards.
Barnes, Patricia.
xBarnes, Patricia.
The Children of Theatre Street. Penguin.
Barnes, Peter, 1931-
xBarnes, Peter.
Laughter. Heinemann Ed.
Barnes, R. see Barnes, Ronald.
Barnes, R. A. see Barnes, Robert A.
Barnes, Ralph M. see Barnes, Ralph Mosser.
Barnes, Ralph Mosser, 1900-
xBarnes, Ralph M.
Industrial Engineering & Management
Problems & Policies. Hive Pub.
Work Sampling. Krieger.
Barnes, Ramon M.
xBarnes, Ramon M.
ed. Applications of Inductively Coupled
Plasmas to Emission Spectroscopy. Franklin
Inst Pr.
Barnes, Robert. see Barnes, Robert William.
Barnes, Robert A.
xBarnes, R. A.
Fundamentals of Music: A Program for
Self-Instruction. McGraw.
Barnes, Robert William.
xBarnes, Robert.
Marriages & Deaths from Baltimore
Newspapers, 1796-1816. Genealog Pub.
Maryland Marriages: 1634-1777. Genealog
Pub.
Maryland Marriages: 1778-1800. Genealog
Pub.
Barnes, Ron. see Barnes, Ronald E.
Barnes, Ronald.
xBarnes, R.
Get Your Tenses Right. Cambridge U Pr.
Barnes, Ronald E.
xBarnes, Ron.
Learning Systems for the Future. Phi Delta
Kappa.
Barnes, Samuel H. see Barnes, Samuel Henry.
Barnes, Samuel Henry.
xBarnes, Samuel H.
Political Action: Mass Participation in Five
Western Democracies. Sage.
Barnes, Thomas. see Barnes, Thomas G.
Barnes, Thomas G.
xBarnes, Thomas.
Origin & Destiny of the Earth's Magnetic
Field. CLP Pubs.
xBarnes, Thomas G.
List & Index to the Proceedings in Star
Chamber for the Reign of James I
(1603-1625) in the Public Record Office,
London: Class STAC8. Am Bar Foun.
Barnes, Thomas G. see Barnes, Thomas Garden.
Barnes, Thomas Garden.
xBarnes, Thomas G.
ed. Renaissance, Reformation, & Absolutism:
1400-1660. Little.
Barnes, William C. see Barnes, William Croft.
Barnes, William Croft, 1858-1936
xBarnes, William C.
Western Grazing Grounds & Forest Ranges.
Arno.
Barnes, William H. see Barnes, William Horatio.
Barnes, William Horatio.
xBarnes, William H.
History of the Thirty-Ninth Congress of the
United States. Negro U Pr.
Barness, Richard.
xBarness, Richard.

Graystone College. Lerner Pubns.
Listen to Me!. Lerner Pubns.
Barnet, Richard J.
xBarnet, Richard J.
Economy of Death. Atheneum.
Global Reach: The Power of the Multinational
Corporations. S&S.
ed. Security in Disarmament. Princeton U Pr.
Barnet, Sylvan.
xBarnet, Sylvan.
A Dictionary of Literary, Dramatic, &
Cinematic Terms. Little.
Nine Modern Classics: An Anthology of Short
Novels. Little.
A Short Guide to Writing About Literature.
Little.
Types of Drama: Plays & Essays. Little.
Barnett, Correlli.
xBarnett, Correlli.
The Collapse of British Power. Morrow.
The Great War. Putnam.
The Swordbearers: Supreme Command in the
First World War. Ind U Pr.
Barnett, David.
xBarnett, David.
Stevenson Study, Treasure Island. Folcroft.
Barnett, Dick.
xBarnett, Dick.
Inside Basketball. Contemp Bks.
Barnett, Eugene H.
xBarnett, Eugene H.
Programming Time-Shared Computers in
BASIC. Wiley.
Barnett, Franklin.
xBarnett, Franklin.
Dictionary of Prehistoric Indian Artifacts of
the American Southwest. Northland.
Barnett, Gene A. see Barnett, Gene Austin.
Barnett, Gene Austin.
xBarnett, Gene A.
Denis Johnston. Twayne.
Barnett, George E. see Barnett, George Ernest.
Barnett, George Ernest, 1873-1938
xBarnett, George E.
Chapters on Machinery & Labor. S Ill U Pr.
Mediation, Investigation & Arbitration in
Industrial Disputes. Arno.
Barnett, George L. see Barnett, George Leonard.
Barnett, George Leonard.
xBarnett, George L.
Charles Lamb. Twayne.
Charles Lamb: The Evolution of Elia. Haskell.
Barnett, Harold J.
xBarnett, Harold J.
Atomic Energy in the United States Economy:
A Consideration of Certain Industrial,
Regional, & Economic Development Aspects.
Arno.
Barnett, Homer. see Barnett, Homer Garner.
Barnett, Homer G. see Barnett, Homer Garner.
Barnett, Homer Garner, 1906-
xBarnett, Homer.
Indian Shakers: A Messianic Cult of the Pacific
Northwest. S Ill U Pr.
xBarnett, Homer G.
The Coast Salish of British Columbia.
Greenwood.
Barnett, Horace L. see Barnett, Horace Leslie.
Barnett, Horace Leslie.
xBarnett, Horace L.
Illustrated Genera of Imperfect Fungi. Burgess.
Barnett, James, 1920-
xBarnett, James.
Backfire Is Hostile. St Martin.
Head of the Force. St Martin.
Barnett, James H. see Barnett, James Harwood.
Barnett, James Harwood, 1906-
xBarnett, James H.

The American Christmas: A Study in National
Culture. Arno.

Barnett, Joe R.
   xBarnett, Joe R.
      The People Who Tested God. Sweet.
Barnett, Lincoln. *see* Barnett, Lincoln Kinnear.
Barnett, Lincoln Kinnear.
   xBarnett, Lincoln.
      The Ancient Adirondacks. Time-Life.
      The Ancient Adirondacks. Silver.
Barnett, Lionel. *see* Barnett, Lionel David.
Barnett, Lionel D. *see* Barnett, Lionel David.
Barnett, Lionel David, 1871-1960
   xBarnett, Lionel.
      Greek Drama. Folcroft.
   xBarnett, Lionel D.
      The Greek Drama. Arden Lib.
Barnett, Lloyd G.
   xBarnett, Lloyd G.
      The Constitutional Law of Jamaica. Oxford U
      Pr.
Barnett, Louise K.
   xBarnett, Louise K.
      Ignoble Savage: American Literary Racism,
      1790-1890. Greenwood.
Barnett, M. R. *see* Barnett, Marguerite Ross.
Barnett, M. T. *see* Barnett, Marva T.
Barnett, Marguerite R. *see* Barnett, Marguerite Ross.
Barnett, Marguerite Ross.
   xBarnett, M. R.
      The Politics of Cultural Nationalism in South
      India. Princeton U Pr.
   xBarnett, Marguerite R.
      ed. Public Policy for the Black Community:
      Strategies & Perspectives. Alfred Pub.
Barnett, Marva T.
   xBarnett, M. T.
      Effective Communication for Public Safety
      Personnel. Delmar.
Barnett, Naomi.
   xBarnett, Naomi.
      I Know a Dentist. Putnam.
Barnett, R. A. *see* Barnett, Raymond A.
Barnett, Randy E.
   xBarnett, Randy E.
      ed. Assessing the Criminal: Restitution,
      Retribution & the Legal Process. Ballinger
      Pub.
Barnett, Raymond. *see* Barnett, Raymond A.
Barnett, Raymond A.
   xBarnett, R. A.
      Vectors. Krieger.
   xBarnett, Raymond.
      Analytic Trigonometry with Applications.
      Wadsworth Pub.
   xBarnett, Raymond A.
      College Algebra. McGraw.
      College Algebra with Trigonometry. McGraw.
      Intermediate Algebra: Structure & Use.
      McGraw.
Barnett, Richard C., 1932-
   xBarnett, Richard C.
      Place, Profit, & Power: A Study of the Servants
      of William Cecil, Elizabethan Statesman. U of
      NC Pr.
Barnett, Roy N., 1914-
   xBarnett, Roy N.
      Clinical Laboratory Statistics. Little.
Barnett, S.
   xBarnett, Stephen.
      Introduction to Mathematical Control Theory.
      Oxford U Pr.
Barnett, S. A. *see* Barnett, Samuel Anthony.
Barnett, Samuel A. *see* Barnett, Samuel Augustus.
Barnett, Samuel Anthony.
   xBarnett, S. A.
      The Rat: A Study in Behavior. U of Chicago
      Pr.
Barnett, Samuel Augustus.
   xBarnett, Samuel A.

Practicable Socialism: Essays on Social Reform.
Arno.
Barnett, Stephen. *see* Barnett, S.
Barnett, Steve, 1946-
   xBarnett, Steve.
      Cross-Country Downhill & Other Nordic
      Mountain Skiing Techniques. Pacific Search.
Barnett, Ursula A.
   xBarnett, Ursula A.
      Ezekiel Mphahlele. Twayne.
Barnett, Vic.
   xBarnett, Vic.
      Outliers in Statistical Data. Wiley.
Barnette. *see* Barnette, Warren Leslie.
Barnette, Warren Leslie, 1910-
   xBarnette.
      Readings in Psychological Tests &
      Measurements. Oxford U Pr.
Barney, Kenneth D.
   xBarney, Kenneth D.
      A Faith to Live by. Gospel Pub.
      If You Love Me.... Gospel Pub.
      It Began in an Upper Room. Gospel Pub.
      Preparing for the Storm. Gospel Pub.
Barney, Natalie C. *see* Barney, Natalie Clifford.
Barney, Natalie Clifford.
   xBarney, Natalie C.
      Aventures De L'esprit. Arno.
Barney, Stephen. *see* Barney, Stephen A.
Barney, Stephen A.
   xBarney, Stephen.
      ed. Chaucer's "Troilus": Essays in Criticism.
      Shoe String.
   xBarney, Stephen A.
      Allegories of History, Allegories of Love. Shoe
      String.
      Word-Hoard: An Introduction to Old English
      Vocabulary. Yale U Pr.
Barnhart, Clarence L. *see* Barnhart, Clarence Lewis.
Barnhart, Clarence Lewis.
   xBarnhart, Clarence L.
      ed. The Barnhart Dictionary of New English
      Since 1963. Har-Row.
      ed. The World Book Dictionary. World
      Bk-Childcraft.
Barnhart, J. D. *see* Barnhart, John Donald.
Barnhart, J. E. *see* Barnhart, Joe E.
Barnhart, Joe E., 1931-
   xBarnhart, J. E.
      Religion & the Challenge of Philosophy.
      Littlefield.
Barnhart, John D. *see* Barnhart, John Donald.
Barnhart, John Donald, 1895-
   xBarnhart, J. D.
      Valley of Democracy: The Frontier Versus the
      Plantation in the Ohio Valley, 1775-1818.
      Kraus Repr.
   xBarnhart, John D.
      Valley of Democracy: The Frontier Versus the
      Plantation in the Ohio Valley, 1775-1818. U
      of Nebr Pr.
Barnhart, Peter.
   xBarnhart, Peter.
      The Wounded Duck. Scribner.
Barnhart, Sara A.
   xBarnhart, Sarah A.
      Introduction to Interpersonal Communication.
      Har-Row.
Barnhart, Sarah A. *see* Barnhart, Sara A.
Barnhouse, Donald G. *see* Barnhouse, Donald Grey.
Barnhouse, Donald Grey, 1895-1960
   xBarnhouse, Donald G.
      Bible Truth Illustrated. Keats.
Barnicoat, John, 1924-
   xBarnicoat, John.
      A Concise History of Posters. Oxford U Pr.
      A Concise History of Posters: 1870-1970.
      Abrams.
Barnoon, Shlomo.
   xBarnoon, Shlomo.

Measuring the Effectiveness of Medical
Decisions: An Operations Research
Approach. C C Thomas.
Barnoski, Michael K., 1940-
   xBarnoski, Michael K.
      ed. An Introduction to Integrated Optics.
      Plenum Pub.
Barnouw, Erik, 1908-
   xBarnouw, Erik.
      Documentary: A History of the Non-Fiction
      Film. Oxford U Pr.
      Documentary: A History of the Non-Fiction
      Film. Oxford U Pr.
      Indian Film. Oxford U Pr.
      Tube of Plenty: The Evolution of American
      Television. Oxford U Pr.
      Tube of Plenty: The Evolution of American
      Television. Oxford U Pr.
Barnouw, Victor.
   xBarnouw, Victor.
      Anthropology: A General Introduction. Dorsey.
      Culture & Personality. Dorsey.
Barns, Cass G. *see* Barns, Cass Grove.
Barns, Cass Grove, 1848-
   xBarns, Cass G.
      Sod House. U of Nebr Pr.
Barnstone, Aliki.
   xBarnstone, Aliki.
      ed. A Book of Women Poets from Antiquity to
      Now. Schocken.
      Real Tin Flower: Poems About the World at
      Nine. Macmillan.
Barnstone, Willis.
   xBarnstone, Willis.
      Day in the Country. Har-Row.
      tr. Greek Lyric Poetry. Schocken.
Barnum, Phineas T. *see* Barnum, Phineas Taylor.
Barnum, Phineas Taylor, 1810-1891
   xBarnum, Phineas T.
      Humbugs of the World. Gale.
      Struggles & Triumphs. Arno.
Baro, Gene.
   xBaro, Gene.
      Graphicstudio U. S. F.: An Experiment in Art
      & Education. Bklyn Mus.
      Twenty-First National Print Exhibition. Bklyn
      Mus.
Barofsky, Ivan.
   xBarofsky, Ivan.
      ed. Medication Compliance: A Behavioral
      Management Approach. C B Slack.
Barolini, Helen, 1925-
   xBarolini, Helen.
      Umbertina. Bantam.
      Umbertina. Seaview Bks.
Barolsky, Paul, 1941-
   xBarolsky, Paul.
      Infinite Jest: Wit & Humor in Italian
      Renaissance Art. U of Mo Pr.
Baron. *see* Baron, Harold.
Baron, Dona, 1943-
   xBaron, Dona.
      ed. The National Purpose Reconsidered.
      Columbia U Pr.
Baron, George.
   xBaron, George.
      The Government & Management of Schools.
      Humanities.
Baron, Hans, 1900-
   xBaron, Hans.
      Crisis of the Early Italian Renaissance: Civic
      Humanism & Republican Liberty in an Age
      of Classicism & Tyranny. Princeton U Pr.
      Humanistic & Political Literature in Florence &
      Venice at the Beginning of the Quattrocento:
      Studies in Criticism & Chronology. Russell.
Baron, Harold.
   xBaron.

Clerical Record Keeping Course I. SW Pub.
Clerical Record Keeping Course II. SW Pub.

Baron, Harry, 1919-
xBaron, Harry.
Card Tricks for Beginners. Emerson.

Baron, Herman, 1941-
xBaron, Herman.
Author Index to Esquire 1933-1973.
Scarecrow.

Baron, Howard C.
xBaron, Howard C.
Varicose Veins: A Commonsense Approach to
Their Management. Morrow.
Varicose Veins: A Commonsense Approach to
Their Management. Morrow.

Baron, Jennette M. see Baron, Salo Wittmayer.

Baron, Mary.
xBaron, Mary.
Letters for the New England Dead. Godine.

Baron, Nancy.
xBaron, Nancy.
illus. Getting Started in Calligraphy. Sterling.

Baron, R. A. see Baron, Robert A.

Baron, Robert. see Baron, Robert A.

Baron, Robert A.
xBaron, R. A.
Human Aggression. Plenum Pub.
xBaron, Robert.
Psychology: Understanding Behavior. HR&W.
Psychology: Understanding Behavior. HR&W.
xBaron, Robert A.
Exploring Social Psychology. Allyn.

Baron, Robert J.
xBaron, Robert J.
Data Structures & Their Implementation. Van
Nos Reinhold.

Baron, Salo W. see Baron, Salo Wittmayer.

Baron, Salo Wittmayer.
xBaron, Jennette M.
Palestinian Messengers in America: 1849-79: A
Record of Four Journeys. Arno.
xBaron, Salo W.
Economic History of the Jews. Schocken.
Modern Nationalism & Religion. Arno.
Steeled by Adversity: Essays & Addresses on
American Jewish Life. Jewish Pubn.

Baron, W. M. see Baron, William Michael Muir.

Baron, William Michael Muir.
xBaron, W. M.
Organization in Plants. Halsted Pr.

Baroni, Daniele.
xBaroni, Daniele.
The Furniture of Gerrit Thomas Rietveld.
Barron.

Barr, A. see Barr, Andrew M.

Barr, Amelia. see Barr, Amelia Edith Huddleston.

Barr, Amelia E. see Barr, Amelia Edith Huddleston.

Barr, Amelia Edith Huddleston, 1831-1919
xBarr, Amelia.
Remember the Alamo. Gregg.
Remember the Alamo. Lighthouse Pr NY.
xBarr, Amelia E.
Remember the Alamo. Sharon Hill.

Barr, Andrew M.
xBarr, A.
Master Guide to High-Income Real Estate
Selling. P-H.

Barr, Charles.
xBarr, Charles.
Ealing Studios. Overlook Pr.
Laurel & Hardy. U of Cal Pr.

Barr, David F.
xBarr, David F.
Auditory Perceptual Disorders. C C Thomas.
This Very Day. Herald Pr.

Barr, Doris W. see Barr, Doris Wilson.

Barr, Doris Wilson, 1923-
xBarr, Doris W.

Communication of Business, Professional &
Technical Students. Wadsworth Pub.

Barr, Elisabeth.
xBarr, Elisabeth.
Castle Heritage. Playboy Pbks.
The Sea Treasure. Doubleday.
xBarr, Elizabeth.
The Storm Witch. Popular Lib.

Barr, Elizabeth. see Barr, Elisabeth.

Barr, George.
xBarr, George.
Entertaining with Number Tricks. McGraw.

Barr, James.
xBarr, James.
Fundamentalism. Westminster.

Barr, Jene.
xBarr, Jene.
Good Morning, Teacher. A Whitman.
This Is My Country. A Whitman.

Barr, John H.
xBarr, John H.
Dental Radiology: Pertinent Basic Concepts &
Their Applications in Clinical Practice.
Saunders.

Barr, M. see Barr, Michael.

Barr, Margaret S. see Barr, Margaret Scolari.

Barr, Margaret Scolari.
xBarr, Margaret S.
Medardo Rosso. Arno.

Barr, Michael.
xBarr, M.
Exact Categories & Categories of Sheaves.
Springer-Verlag.

Barr, Pat
xBarr, Pat.
Simla: A Hill Station in British India. Scribner.

Barr, Randolph R.
xBarr, Randolph R.
Automobile Electrical System. Chilton.

Barr, Robert.
xBarr, Robert.
The Dark Island. Bobbs.
In a Steamer Chair, & Other Shipboard Stories.
Arno.
The Measure of the Rule. U of Toronto Pr.

Barr, Robert D.
xBarr, Robert D.
The Nature of the Social Studies. ETC Pubns.

Barr, Stephen.
xBarr, Stephen.
Experiments in Topology. T Y Crowell.

Barr, Stringfellow, 1897-
xBarr, Stringfellow.
Mazzini: Portrait of an Exile. Octagon.

Barr, W. Montfort. see Barr, William Monfort.

Barr, William Monfort.
xBarr, W. Montfort.
Innovative Financing of Public School
Facilities. Interstate.

Barracato, John.
xBarracato, John.
Arson!. Avon.
Arson!. Norton.

Barraclough, E. M. see Barraclough, E. M. C.

Barraclough, E. M. C.
xBarraclough, E. M.
Flags of the World. Warne.

Barraclough, Geoffrey, 1908-
xBarraclough, Geoffrey.

The Crucible of Europe: The Ninth & Tenth
Centuries in European History. U of Cal Pr.
Factors in German History. Greenwood.
An Introduction to Contemporary History.
Gannon.
Introduction to Contemporary History.
Penguin.
Main Trends in History. Holmes & Meier.
tr. Mediaeval Germany, 911-1250: Essays by
German Historians. AMS Pr.

Barraga, Natalie.
xBarraga, Natalie.
Increased Visual Behavior in Low Vision
Children. Am Foun Blind.

Barrante, James R., 1938-
xBarrante, James R.
Applied Mathematics for Physical Chemistry.
P-H.

Barratt, G. R. V.
xBarratt, Glynn.
The Rebel on the Bridge: A Life of the
Decembrist Baron Andrey Rozen (1800-84).
Ohio U Pr.

Barratt, Glynn. see Barratt, G. R. V.

Barratt, John.
xBarratt, John.
ed. Accelerated Development in Southern
Africa. St Martin.
ed. Strategy for Development. St Martin.

Barratt, Marcia.
xBarratt, Marcia.
Foundations for Movement. Wm C Brown.

Barrault, Jean L. see Barrault, Jean Louis.

Barrault, Jean Louis.
xBarrault, Jean L.
Reflections on the Theatre. Hyperion Conn.
xBarrault, Jean-Louis.
Rabelais: A Dramatic Game in Two Parts
Taken from the Five Books of Francois
Rabelais. Hill & Wang.

Barrault, Jean-Louis. see Barrault, Jean Louis.

Barre, Mary E.
xBarre, Mary E.
College Information & Guidance. HM.

Barre, W. L.
xBarre, W. L.
Life & Public Services of Millard Fillmore. B
Franklin.

Barre, Weston La. see La Barre, Weston.

Barreau, Jean C. see Barreau, Jean Claude.

Barreau, Jean Claude.
xBarreau, Jean C.
Religious Impulse. Paulist Pr.

Barreda, Pedro. see Barreda, Pedro, 1k933-.

Barreda, Pedro, 1k933-.
xBarreda, Pedro.
The Black Protagonist in the Cuban Novel. U
of Mass Pr.

Barrell, G. R. see Barrell, Geoffrey Richard.

Barrell, Geoffrey Richard.
xBarrell, G. R.
Teachers & the Law. Methuen Inc.

Barrell, John.
xBarrell, John.
Idea of Landscape & the Sense of Place,
1730-1840: An Approach to the Poetry of
John Clare. Cambridge U Pr.

Barrera, Mario.
xBarrera, Mario.
Race & Class in the Southwest: A Theory of
Racial Inequality. U of Notre Dame Pr.

Barret, Richard C. see Barret, Richard Carter.

Barret, Richard Carter.
xBarret, Richard C.
How to Identify Bennington Pottery. Greene.

Barrett. see Barrett, Richard H.

Barrett, A. J.
xBarrett, A. J.

ed. Proteinases in Mammalian Cells & Tissues. Elsevier.

Barrett, Albert M. *see* Barrett, Albert Michael.

Barrett, Albert Michael.
  xBarrett, Albert M.
    People Under Pressure. Coll & U Pr.
    When Thinking Begins: Lessons Learned from Helping Preaverage Intelligence Individuals. C C Thomas.

Barrett, Bob.
  xBarrett, Bob.
    Pembrook vs the West. Doubleday.

Barrett, C. *see* Barrett, Craig R.

Barrett, C. K. *see* Barrett, Charles Kingsley.

Barrett, C. S. *see* Barrett, Charles Sanborn.

Barrett, Charles D., 1933-
  xBarrett, Charles D.
    Understanding the Christian Faith. P-H.

Barrett, Charles Kingsley.
  xBarrett, C. K.
    The Gospel of John & Judaism. Fortress.
    Reading Through Romans. Fortress.

Barrett, Charles Sanborn.
  xBarrett, C. S.
    Structure of Metals: Crystallographic Methods, Principles & Data. Pergamon.

Barrett, Clifford.
  xBarrett, Clifford.
    ed. Contemporary Idealism in America. Russell.

Barrett, Craig R.
  xBarrett, C.
    The Principles of Engineering Materials. P-H.

Barrett, Diana.
  xBarrett, Diana.
    Multihospital Systems: The Process of Development. Oelgeschlager.

Barrett, Don C. *see* Barrett, Don Carlos.

Barrett, Don Carlos.
  xBarrett, Don C.
    The Greenbacks & the Resumption of Specie Payments. Peter Smith.

Barrett, Douglas. *see* Barrett, Douglas E.

Barrett, Douglas E.
  xBarrett, Douglas.
    Indian Painting. Rizzoli Intl.

Barrett, E. C. *see* Barrett, Eric Charles.

Barrett, Eric Charles.
  xBarrett, E. C.
    Climatology from Satellites. Methuen Inc.
    Introduction to Environmental Remote Sensing. Methuen Inc.

Barrett, Ethel.
  xBarrett, Ethel.
    As told to Barrett: A Street Cop Who Cared. Revell.
    If I Had a Wish. Regal.
    I'm No Hero. Regal.
    People Who Couldn't Be Stopped. Regal.
    The Strangest Thing Happened.... Regal.
    There I Stood in All My Splendor. Regal.
    Which Way to Nineveh. Regal.

Barrett, Harold.
  xBarrett, Harold.
    Practical Uses of Speech Communication. HR&W.

Barrett, James T., 1927-
  xBarrett, James T.
    Basic Immunology & Its Medical Application. Mosby.
    Textbook of Immunology: An Introduction to Immunochemistry & Immunobiology. Mosby.

Barrett, Jean. *see* Barrett, Jean A.

Barrett, Jean A.
  xBarrett, Jean.
    Archery. Goodyear.
  xBarrett, Jean A.
    Archery. Goodyear.

Barrett, John. *see* Barrett, John M.

Barrett, John G. *see* Barrett, John Gilchrist.

Barrett, John Gilchrist.
  xBarrett, John G.
    Civil War in North Carolina. U of NC Pr.
    North Carolina As a Civil War Battleground, 1861-1865. NC Archives.

Barrett, John M.
  xBarrett, John.
    Daniel Discovers Daniel. Human Sci Pr.
    The Day the Toys Came to Silver Dollar City. Silver Dollar.
    Oscar, the Selfish Octopus. Human Sci Pr.
    Zeke Hatfield & a Ghost Named Rocky. Silver Dollar.
  xBarrett, John M.
    No Time for Me. Human Sci Pr.

Barrett, John W.
  xBarrett, John W.
    ed. Regional Silviculture of the United States. Wiley.

Barrett, Judi. *see* Barrett, Judith.

Barrett, Judith.
  xBarrett, Judi.
    I Hate to Go to Bed. Schol Bk Serv.
    I Hate to Take a Bath. Schol Bk Serv.
  xBarrett, Judith.
    Animals Should Definitely Not Wear Clothing. Atheneum.
    Animals Should Definitely Not Wear Clothing. Atheneum.
    An Apple a Day. Atheneum.
    Cloudy with a Chance of Meatballs. Atheneum.

Barrett, Lawrence, 1838-1891
  xBarrett, Lawrence.
    Charlotte Cushman, a Lecture. B Franklin.
    Edwin Forrest. Arno.
    Edwin Forrest. Scholarly.

Barrett, Leonard E.
  xBarrett, Leonard E.
    The Rastafarians: Sounds of Cultural Dissonance. Beacon Pr.

Barrett, Marvin.
  xBarrett, Marvin.
    Meet Thomas Jefferson. Random.

Barrett, Maurice.
  xBarrett, Maurice.
    Art Education: A Strategy for Course Design. Heinemann Ed.

Barrett, Maye.
  xBarrett, Maye.
    The Crystal Palace. Berkley Pub.

Barrett, Michael, 1924-
  xBarrett, Michael.
    Last Flowers. FS&G.

Barrett, Nancy S. *see* Barrett, Nancy Smith.

Barrett, Nancy Smith.
  xBarrett, Nancy S.
    The Theory of Macroeconomic Policy. P-H.
    The Theory of Microeconomic Policy. Heath.

Barrett, Richard H.
  xBarrett.
    Oral Myofunctional Disorders. Mosby.

Barrett, S. A. *see* Barrett, Samuel Alfred.

Barrett, Samuel A. *see* Barrett, Samuel Alfred.

Barrett, Samuel Alfred, 1879-1965
  xBarrett, S. A.
    Pomo Indian Basketry. Rio Grande.
  xBarrett, Samuel A.
    Ancient Aztalan. Greenwood.
    The Dream Dance of the Chippewa & Menominee Indians of Northern Wisconsin. AMS Pr.
    Material Aspects of Pomo Culture. AMS Pr.

Barrett, Susan E.
  xBarrett, Susan E.
    Ms Noah Touches Earth. Artichoke.

Barrett, W. H. *see* Barrett, Walter Henry.

Barrett, Walter Henry.
  xBarrett, W. H.

East Anglian Folklore & Other Tales. Routledge & Kegan.

Barrett, Ward J.
  xBarrett, Ward J.
    Sugar Hacienda of the Marqueses Del Valle. U of Minn Pr.

Barrett, Wayne.
  xBarrett, Wayne.
    Prince Edward Island. Oxford U Pr.

Barrett, William, 1913-
  xBarrett, William.
    The Illusion of Technique: A Search for Meaning in a Technological Civilization. Doubleday.
    The Illusion of Technique: A Search for Meaning in a Technological Civilization. Doubleday.

Barrett, William. *see* Barrett, William Edmund.

Barrett, William A. *see* Barrett, William Alexander.

Barrett, William Alexander, 1836-1891
  xBarrett, William A.
    English Glee & Madrigal Writers. Longwood Pr.

Barrett, William E.
  xBarrett, William.
    The Left Hand of God. Queens Hse.
  xBarrett, William E.
    The Left Hand of God. Doubleday.

Barrett, William Edmund.
  xBarrett, William.
    The Edge of Things. Queens Hse.

Barricelli, Gian P. *see* Barricelli, Jean Pierre.

Barricelli, Jean Pierre.
  xBarricelli, Gian P.
    Alessandro Manzoni. Twayne.

Barrick, Augusta I.
  xBarrick, Augusta I.
    The Power of Effective Speech. Coll & U Pr.

Barrie, J. M. *see* Barrie, James Matthew.

Barrie, James. *see* Barrie, James Matthew.

Barrie, James M. *see* Barrie, James Matthew.

Barrie, James Matthew, Sir, Bart, 1860-1937
  xBarrie, J. M.
    The Little Minister. Harmony & Co.
  xBarrie, James.
    Little Minister. Airmont.
  xBarrie, James M.
    Auld Licht Manse, - Other Sketches. Arno.
    Holiday in Bed, & Other Sketches: With a Short Biographical Sketch of the Author. Arno.
    Margaret Ogilvy. Scholarly.

Barrier, N. Gerald.
  xBarrier, N. Gerald.
    Banned: Controversial Literature & Political Control in British India, 1907-1947. U of Mo Pr.

Barrier, N. Gerald. *see* Barrier, Norman Gerald.

Barrier, Norman Gerald.
  xBarrier, N. Gerald.
    Punjab History in Printed British Documents: A Bibliographic Guide to Parliamentary Papers & Select, Nonserial Publications, 1843-1947. U of Mo Pr.

Barrilleaux, Doris.
  xBarrilleaux, Doris.
    Inside Weight Training for Women. Contemp Bks.

Barringer, Bugs.
  xBarringer, Bugs.
    Rocky Mount: A Pictorial History. Donning Co.

Barringer, Leslie.
  xBarringer, Leslie.
    Gerfalcon. Borgo Pr.

Barrington, E. J. *see* Barrington, Ernest James William.

Barrington, Ernest J. *see* Barrington, Ernest James William.

Barrington, Ernest James William.
  xBarrington, E. J.

Environmental Biology. Halsted Pr.
An Introduction to General & Comparative
Endocrinology. Oxford U Pr.
xBarrington, Ernest J.
Hormones & Evolution. Krieger.

Barrington, George, 1929-
xBarrington, George.
God Will Not Let Me Go. Herald Hse.

Barrios, Alfred A.
xBarrios, Alfred A.
Towards Greater Freedom & Happiness.
Self-Prog Control.

Barris, Alex.
xBarris, Alex.
Hollywood According to Hollywood. A S
Barnes.
Hollywood's Other Men. A S Barnes.
Hollywood's Other Women. A S Barnes.

Barris, George.
xBarris, George.
Cars of the Stars. Jonathan David.
Famous Custom & Show Cars. Dutton.

Barro, R. J. see Barro, Robert J.

Barro, Robert J.
xBarro, R. J.
Money, Employment & Inflation. Cambridge U
Pr.

Barrol, Grady.
xBarrol, Grady.
The Little Book of Anagrams. Harvey.

Barroll, Clare.
xBarroll, Clare.
A Strange Place for Murder. Scribner.

Barroll, J. Leeds. see Barroll, John Leeds.

Barroll, John Leeds, 1928-
xBarroll, J. Leeds.
Artificial Persons: The Formation of Character
in the Tragedies of Shakespeare. U of SC Pr.

Barron, Ann F. see Barron, Ann Forman.

Barron, Ann Forman.
xBarron, Ann F.
Banner Bold & Beautiful. Fawcett.

Barron, Clarence W. see Barron, Clarence Walker.

Barron, Clarence Walker, 1855-1928
xBarron, Clarence W.
More They Told Barron. Arno.

Barron, Frank. see Barron, Frank X.

Barron, Frank X., 1922-
xBarron, Frank.
LSD, Man & Society. Greenwood.
xBarron, Frank X.
Artists in the Making. Acad Pr.

Barron, Gayle.
xBarron, Gayle.
The Beauty of Running. HarBraceJ.

Barron, Gloria J.
xBarron, Gloria J.
Leadership in Crisis: FDR & the Path to
Intervention. Kennikat.

Barron, Howard H.
xBarron, Howard H.
Orson Hyde: Missionary, Apostle, Colonizer.
Horizon Utah.

Barron, Jerome A.
xBarron, Jerome A.
Freedom of the Press for Whom?: The Right of
Access to Mass Media. Ind U Pr.
Handbook of Free Speech & Free Press. Little.

Barron, Linda.
xBarron, Linda.
Mathematics Experiences for the Early
Childhood Years. Merrill.

Barron, Paul.
xBarron, Paul.
Federal Regulation of Real Estate: The Real
Estate Settlement Procedures Act. Warren.

Barros, James.
xBarros, James.

Office Without Power: Secretary-General Sir
Eric Drummond 1919-1933. Oxford U Pr.

Barrow, Andrew.
xBarrow, Andrew.
Gossip: A History of High Society, 1920-1970.
Coward.

Barrow, Bennet H. see Barrow, Bennet Hilliard.

Barrow, Bennet Hilliard.
xBarrow, Bennet H.
Plantation Life in the Florida Parishes of
Louisiana 1836-1846, As Reflected in the
Diary of Bennet H. Barrow. AMS Pr.

Barrow, Georgia.
xBarrow, Georgia.
Aging, Ageism, & Society. West Pub.

Barrow, Gordon M.
xBarrow, Gordon M.
Introduction to Chemistry. Wadsworth Pub.
Introduction to Molecular Spectroscopy.
McGraw.
Structure of Molecules: An Introduction to
Molecular Spectroscopy.
Benjamin-Cummings.

Barrow, Graeme.
xBarrow, Graeme T.
Canberra's Embassies. Bks Australia.

Barrow, Graeme T. see Barrow, Graeme.

Barrow, Harold M. see Barrow, Harold Marion.

Barrow, Harold Marion.
xBarrow, Harold M.
A Practical Approach to Measurement in
Physical Education. Lea & Febiger.

Barrow, Leo L.
xBarrow, Leo L.
Negation in Baroja: A Key to His Novelistic
Creativity. U of Ariz Pr.

Barrow, Reginald H. see Barrow, Reginald Haynes.

Barrow, Reginald Haynes, 1893-
xBarrow, Reginald H.
Plutarch & His Times. AMS Pr.

Barrow, Robin.
xBarrow, Robin.
Common Sense & the Curriculum. Allen
Unwin.
Common Sense & the Curriculum. Shoe String.
Happiness & Schooling. St Martin.
Moral Philosophy for Education. Allen Unwin.
Moral Philosophy for Education. Shoe String.
Plato & Education. Routledge & Kegan.
Plato, Utilitarianism & Education. Routledge &
Kegan.
Radical Education: A Critique of Freeschooling
& Deschooling. Halsted Pr.

Barrow, Sarah F. see Barrow, Sarah Field.

Barrow, Sarah Field.
xBarrow, Sarah F.
Medieval Society Romances. Folcroft.
The Medieval Society Romances. Octagon.

Barrow, Terence.
xBarrow, Terence.
Maori Art of New Zealand. Reed.

Barrow, Terence. see Barrow, Tui Terence.

Barrow, Tui Terence.
xBarrow, Terence.
Incredible Hawaii. C E Tuttle.

Barrowman, J. A.
xBarrowman, J. A.
Physiology of the Gastro-Intestinal Lymphatic
System. Cambridge U Pr.

Barrows, Marjorie.
xBarrows, Marjorie.
ed. One Hundred Best Poems for Boys & Girls.
Core Collection.
One Thousand Beautiful Things. Dutton.

Barrows, Walter.
xBarrows, Walter.

Grassroots Politics in an African State:
Integration & Development in Sierra Leone.
Holmes & Meier.

Barrows, William, 1815-1891
xBarrows, William.
The Indian's Side of the Indian Question.
Arno.

Barrus, Clara, 1864-1931
xBarrus, Clara.
Life & Letters of John Burroughs. Russell.
Our Friend, John Burroughs. Haskell.
Our Friend, John Burroughs. R West.

Barry, Arthur L.
xBarry, Arthur L.
The Antimicrobic Susceptibility Test: Principles
& Practices. Lea & Febiger.

Barry, B. see Barry, Brian M.

Barry, Brian. see Barry, Brian M.

Barry, Brian M.
xBarry, B.
Sociologists, Economists & Democracy.
Macmillan.
xBarry, Brian.
The Liberal Theory of Justice: A Critical
Examination of the Principal Doctrines in -
A Theory of Justice by John Rawls. Oxford
U Pr.
Sociologists, Economists & Democracy. U of
Chicago Pr.

Barry, David S. see Barry, David Sheldon.

Barry, David Sheldon, 1859-1936
xBarry, David S.
Forty Years in Washington. Beekman Pubs.

Barry, Donald D.
xBarry, Donald D.
Contemporary Soviet Politics: An Introduction.
P-H.

Barry, Florence V. see Barry, Florence Valentine.

Barry, Florence Valentine.
xBarry, Florence V.
A Century of Children's Books. Gale.
A Century of Children's Books. Gordon Pr.

Barry, Iris, 1895-
xBarry, Iris.
Let's Go to the Movies. Arno.

Barry, Jackson G.
xBarry, Jackson G.
Dramatic Structure: The Shaping of
Experience. U of Cal Pr.

Barry, James P.
xBarry, James P.
The Great Lakes. Watts.
The Louisiana Purchase, April 1803: Thomas
Jefferson Doubles the Area of the United
States. Watts.

Barry, Jan.
xBarry, Jan.
Demilitarized Zones: Veterans After Vietnam.
East River Anthol.

Barry, John M., 1944-
xBarry, John M.
The Natural Vegetation of South Carolina. U of
SC Pr.

Barry, Joseph. see Barry, Joseph Amber.

Barry, Joseph Amber, 1917-
xBarry, Joseph.
France. Macmillan.
The Infamous Woman: The Life of George
Sand. Doubleday.

Barry, Kathleen.
xBarry, Kathleen.
Female Sexual Slavery. P-H.

Barry, M. Martin. see Barry, Mary Martin.

Barry, Mary J.
xBarry, Mary J.
A History of Mining on the Kenai Peninsula.
Alaska Northwest.

Barry, Mary Martin, Sister, 1903-
xBarry, M. Martin.

An Analysis of the Prosodic Structure of
  Selected Poems of T. S. Eliot. Intl Schol Bk
  Serv.
Barry, Patrick.
  xBarry, Patrick.
    The Theory & Practice of the International
      Trade of the United States & England, & of
      the Trade of the United States & Canada.
      Garland Pub.
Barry, Peter J.
  xBarry, Peter J.
    jt. auth. Financial Management in Agriculture.
      Interstate.
Barry, R. G. *see* Barry, Roger Graham.
Barry, Roger D.
  xBarry, Roger D.
    Organic Chemistry. Bobbs.
Barry, Roger Graham.
  xBarry, R. G.
    Atmosphere, Weather & Climate. Methuen Inc.
Barry, Scott.
  xBarry, Scott.
    illus. The Kingdom of Wolves. Putnam.
Barry, Sheila A. *see* Barry, Sheila Anne.
Barry, Sheila Anne.
  xBarry, Sheila A.
    Super-Colossal Book of Puzzles, Tricks &
      Games. Sterling.
Barry, Thomas E.
  xBarry, Thomas E.
    ed. Marketing & the Black Consumer: An
      Annotated Bibliography. Am Mktg.
Barry, Vincent. *see* Barry, Vincent E.
Barry, Vincent E.
  xBarry, Vincent.
    Moral Issues in Business. Wadsworth Pub.
    The Practical Logic. HR&W.
Barry, William F. *see* Barry, William Francis.
Barry, William Francis, 1849-1930
  xBarry, William F.
    The Two Standards. Garland Pub.
Barrymore, John, 1882-1942
  xBarrymore, John.
    Confessions of an Actor. Arno.
Barsacq, Leon, 1906-1969
  xBarsacq, Leon.
    Caligari's Cabinet & Other Grand Illusions: A
      History of Film Design. NAL.
Barsali, G.
  xBarsali, G.
    Looking at Pisa. Intl Pubns Serv.
Barsam, Richard M. *see* Barsam, Richard Meran.
Barsam, Richard Meran.
  xBarsam, Richard M.
    In the Dark: A Primer for the Movies. Viking
      Pr.
    ed. Nonfiction Film: Theory & Criticism.
      Dutton.
Barsch, Ray H.
  xBarsch, Ray H.
    Parent of the Handicapped Child: The Study of
      Child-rearing Practices. C C Thomas.
Barsewisch, B. von. *see* Barsewisch, Bernhard Von.
Barsewisch, Bernhard Von, 1935-
  xBarsewisch, B. von.
    Perinatal Retinal Haemorrhages: Morphology,
      Aetiology & Significanace. Springer-Verlag.
Barsh, Russel L. *see* Barsh, Russel Lawrence.
Barsh, Russel Lawrence.
  xBarsh, Russel L.
    The Road: Indian Tribes & Political Liberty. U
      of Cal Pr.
Barshay, Jacob.
  xBarshay, Jacob.
    Topics in Ring Theory. Benjamin-Cummings.
Barsis, Max, 1894- -
  xBarsis, Max.

The Common Man Through the Centuries: A
  Book of Costume Drawings. Ungar.
Barsness, John.
  xBarsness, John.
    Hunting the Great Plains. Mountain Pr.
Barson, J. G. *see* Barson, John.
Barson, John.
  xBarson, J. G.
    Textuellement. HR&W.
Bart, Benjamin F.
  xBart, Benjamin F.
    Flaubert. Syracuse U Pr.
Bart, Pauline.
  xBart, Pauline B.
    The Student Sociologist's Handbook. Scott F.
Bart, Pauline B. *see* Bart, Pauline.
Bart, Peter.
  xBart, Peter.
    Destinies. S&S.
Barta, Ginevera.
  xBarta, Ginevera.
    Metric Cooking for Beginners. Enslow Pubs.
Bartas, Sieur Du. *see* Du Bartas, Sieur.
Bartee, Thomas.
  xBartee, Thomas C.
    Introduction to Computer Science. McGraw.
Bartee, Thomas. *see* Bartee, Thomas C.
Bartee, Thomas C.
  xBartee, Thomas.
    Digital Computer Fundamentals. McGraw.
  xBartee, Thomas C.
    Digital Computer Fundamentals. McGraw.
Bartee, Thomas C. *see* Bartee, Thomas.
Bartel, C. R. *see* Bartel, Carl R.
Bartel, Carl R.
  xBartel, C. R.
    Instructional Analysis & Materials
      Development. Am Technical.
Bartel, Floyd. *see* Bartel, Floyd G.
Bartel, Floyd G.
  xBartel, Floyd.
    A New Look at Church Growth. Faith & Life.
Bartell, Ernest, 1932-
  xBartell, Ernest.
    Costs & Benefits of Catholic Elementary &
      Secondary Schools. U of Notre Dame Pr.
Bartels, Robert, 1913-
  xBartels, Robert.
    The History of Marketing Thought. Grid Pub.
    Marketing Theory & Metatheory. Am Mktg.
    Swimming Fundamentals. Merrill.
Barten, Harvey H., 1933-
  xBarten, Harvey H.
    Brief Therapies. Human Sci Pr.
    ed. Children & Their Parents in Brief Therapy.
      Human Sci Pr.
Bartenev, G. M. *see* Bartenev, Georgii Mikhailovich.
Bartenev, Georgii Mikhailovich.
  xBartenev, G. M.
    ed. Relaxation Phenomena in Polymers.
      Halsted Pr.
Barth, Alan.
  xBarth, Alan.
    Government by Investigation. Kelley.
    The Price of Liberty. Da Capo.
Barth, E. M.
  xBarth, E. M.
    The Logic of the Articles in Traditional
      Philosophy: A Contribution to the Study of
      Conceptual Structures. Kluwer Boston.
Barth, Edna.
  xBarth, Edna.
    I'm Nobody, Who Are You: The Story of
      Emily Dickinson. HM.
    Lilies, Rabbits, & Painted Eggs: The Story of
      the Easter Symbols. HM.
    Turkeys, Pilgrims, & Indian Corn: The Story of
      the Thanksgiving Symbols. HM.
Barth, Gunther. *see* Barth, Gunther Paul.

Barth, Gunther Paul.
  xBarth, Gunther.
    Instant Cities: Urbanization & the Rise of San
      Francisco & Denver. Oxford U Pr.
Barth, Hans, 1904-1965
  xBarth, Hans.
    Truth & Ideology. U of Cal Pr.
Barth, J. Robert.
  xBarth, J. Robert.
    Coleridge & Christian Doctrine. Harvard U Pr.
Barth, John.
  xBarth, John.
    Chimera. Fawcett.
    Chimera. Random.
Barth, Joseph, 1906-
  xBarth, Joseph.
    Art of Staying Sane. Arno.
Barth, Karl.
  xBarth, Karl.
    Deliverance to the Captives. Greenwood.
    Deliverance to the Captives. Har-Row.
    Evangelical Theology: An Introduction.
      Eerdmans.
    Final Testimonies. Eerdmans.
    Humanity of God. John Knox.
    Protestant Theology in the Nineteenth
      Century: Its Background & History. Judson.
    The Resurrection of the Dead. Arno.
Barth, Peter S.
  xBarth, Peter S.
    Workers' Compensation & Work-Related
      Illnesses & Diseases. MIT Pr.
Barth, Roland S.
  xBarth, Roland S.
    Open Education & the American School.
      Agathon.
Barthe, Joe De. *see* De Barthe, Joe.
Barthel, J. *see* Barthel, Josef.
Barthel, Josef.
  xBarthel, J.
    Thermometric Titrations. Wiley.
Barthelme, Donald.
  xBarthelme, Donald.
    Amateurs. FS&G.
    Amateurs. PB.
    City Life. FS&G.
    City Life. PB.
    The Dead Father. FS&G.
    The Dead Father. PB.
    Great Days. PB.
    Guilty Pleasures. Dell.
    Guilty Pleasures. FS&G.
Barthelmess, Harriet M. *see* Barthelmess, Harriet May.
Barthelmess, Harriet May, 1892-
  xBarthelmess, Harriet M.
    The Validity of Intelligence Test Elements.
      AMS Pr.
Barthes, Roland.
  xBarthes, Roland.
    The Eiffel Tower & Other Mythologies. Hill &
      Wang.
    Image-Music-Text. Hill & Wang.
    A Lover's Discourse: Fragments. Hill & Wang.
    New Critical Essays. Hill & Wang.
    On Racine. Octagon.
Barthol, Robert G.
  xBarthol, Robert G.
    Protect Yourself: A Self Defense Guide for
      Women-from Prevention to Counterattack.
      P-H.
Barthold, Walter.
  xBarthold, Walter.
    Attorney's Guide to Effective Discovery
      Techniques. P-H.
Bartholomeusz, Dennis.
  xBartholomeusz, Dennis.
    Macbeth & the Players. Cambridge U Pr.
Bartholomew, D. J. *see* Bartholomew, David J.
Bartholomew, David J.
  xBartholomew, D. J.

Stochastic Models for Social Processes. Wiley.
xBartholomew, David J.
Statistical Techniques for Manpower Planning.
Wiley.
Bartholomew, Paul C. see Bartholomew, Paul Charles.
Bartholomew, Paul Charles, 1907-
xBartholomew, Paul C.
Indiana Third Congressional District: A
Political History. U of Notre Dame Pr.
Public Administration. Littlefield.
Summaries of the Leading Cases on the
Constitution. Littlefield.
Bartholomew, Ralph L.
xBartholomew, Ralph L.
Gopher Hole Treasure Hunt. Victor Bks.
Bartholomew, Wilmer T. see Bartholomew, Wilmer
Tillett.
Bartholomew, Wilmer Tillett, 1902-
xBartholomew, Wilmer T.
Acoustics of Music. Greenwood.
Bartke, Wolfgang.
xBartke, Wolfgang.
Oil in the People's Republic of China: Industry
Structure, Production, Exports.
McGill-Queens U Pr.
Bartky, Walter, 1901-
xBartky, Walter.
Highlights of Astronomy. U of Chicago Pr.
Bartle, Graham.
xBartle, Graham.
Music in Australian Schools. Verry.
Bartlett, Alice. see Bartlett, Alice (Hunt).
Bartlett, Alice (Hunt), 1870-1949
xBartlett, Alice.
The Anthology of Cities. Century Bookbindery.
Bartlett, Bruce R., 1951-
xBartlett, Bruce R.
Cover-Up: The Politics of Pearl Harbor,
1941-1946. Arlington Hse.
Bartlett, C. J. see Bartlett, Christopher John.
Bartlett, Christopher John.
xBartlett, C. J.
Castlereagh. Humanities.
A History of Postwar Britain, 1945-74.
Longman.
Bartlett, David.
xBartlett, David.
Adam's New Friend & Other Stories from the
Bible. Judson.
Bartlett, David L. see Bartlett, David Lyon.
Bartlett, David Lyon, 1941-
xBartlett, David L.
Fact & Faith. Judson.
Bartlett, E. G. see Bartlett, Eric George.
Bartlett, Elizabeth.
xBartlett, Elizabeth.
Address in Time. Dufour.
Bartlett, Eric George.
xBartlett, E. G.
Basic Karate. Merrimack Bk Serv.
Bartlett, F. C. see Bartlett, Frederic Charles.
Bartlett, Frederic C. see Bartlett, Frederic Charles.
Bartlett, Frederic Charles, Sir, 1887-
xBartlett, F. C.
Political Propaganda. Octagon.
xBartlett, Frederic C.
Psychology & Primitive Culture. Greenwood.
Remembering: A Study in Experimental &
Social Psychology. Cambridge U Pr.
Bartlett, Gene E.
xBartlett, Gene E.
The Authentic Pastor. Judson.
Bartlett, Harriett M. see Bartlett, Harriett Moulton.
Bartlett, Harriett Moulton.
xBartlett, Harriett M.

Common Base of Social Work Practice. Natl
Assn Soc Wkrs.
Social Work Practice in the Health Field. Natl
Assn Soc Wkrs.
Bartlett, Harry R.
xBartlett, Harry R.
Guide to Teaching Percussion. Wm C Brown.
Bartlett, Irving H.
xBartlett, Irving H.
American Mind in the Mid-nineteenth
Century. AHM Pub.
Daniel Webster. Norton.
Bartlett, James H. see Bartlett, James Holley.
Bartlett, James Holley, 1904-
xBartlett, James H.
Classical & Modern Mechanics. U of Ala Pr.
Bartlett, James R. see Bartlett, James Ronald.
Bartlett, James Ronald, 1934-
xBartlett, James R.
A Word Index to Rainer Maria Rilke's
German Lyric Poetry. Univ Microfilms.
Bartlett, Jean A. see Bartlett, Jean Anne.
Bartlett, Jean Anne.
xBartlett, Jean A.
Angelica. Popular Lib.
Valago Crest. Popular Lib.
xBartlett, Jean Anne.
Theodosia. Popular Lib.
Bartlett, Jen.
xBartlett, Jen.
The Flight of the Snowgeese. Stein & Day.
Bartlett, Jerry F.
xBartlett, Jerry F.
Getting Started in Alabama Real Estate.
Kendall-Hunt.
Bartlett, Jonathan, 1931-
xBartlett, Jonathan.
ed. The First Amendment in a Free Society.
Wilson.
ed. The Ocean Environment. Wilson.
The Peasant Gourmet. McGraw.
Bartlett, Josiah.
xBartlett, Josiah.
The Papers of Josiah Bartlett. U Pr of New
Eng.
Bartlett, Kim.
xBartlett, Kim.
The Finest Kind: The Fisherman of Gloucester.
Norton.
The Finest Kind: The Fishermen of Gloucester.
Avon.
Bartlett, Lee, 1950-
xBartlett, Lee.
ed. Benchmark & Blaze: The Emergence of
William Everson. Scarecrow.
Karl Shapiro: A Descriptive Bibliography.
Garland Pub.
Bartlett, Margaret F. see Bartlett, Margaret Farrington.
Bartlett, Margaret Farrington.
xBartlett, Margaret F.
Clean Brook. T Y Crowell.
Where Does All the Rain Go?. Coward.
Where the Brook Begins. T Y Crowell.
Who Will Answer the Owl?. Coward.
Bartlett, Paul D.
xBartlett, Paul D.
Nonclassical Ions: Reprints & Commentary.
Benjamin-Cummings.
Bartlett, R. E. see Bartlett, Ronald Ernest.
Bartlett, Randall, 1945-
xBartlett, Randall.
Economic Foundations of Political Power. Free
Pr.
Bartlett, Richard. see Bartlett, Richard A.
Bartlett, Richard A.
xBartlett, Richard.
Freedom's Trail. HM.
xBartlett, Richard A.

Great Surveys of the American West. U of
Okla Pr.
Nature's Yellowstone. U of NM Pr.
Bartlett, Robert M. see Bartlett, Robert Merrill.
Bartlett, Robert Merrill, 1898-
xBartlett, Robert M.
They Dared to Live. Arno.
They Did Something About It. Arno.
They Work for Tomorrow. Arno.
Bartlett, Roland W. see Bartlett, Roland Willey.
Bartlett, Roland Willey, 1900-
xBartlett, Roland W.
Success of Modern Private Enterprise.
Interstate.
Bartlett, Ronald E. see Bartlett, Ronald Ernest.
Bartlett, Ronald Ernest, 1920-
xBartlett, R. E.
ed. Developments in Sewerage. Burgess-Intl
Ideas.
Surface Water Sewerage. Halsted Pr.
xBartlett, Ronald E.
Pumping Stations for Water & Sewage. Halsted
Pr.
Bartlett, Ruhl J. see Bartlett, Ruhl Jacob.
Bartlett, Ruhl Jacob, 1897-
xBartlett, Ruhl J.
Policy & Power: Two Centuries of American
Foreign Relations. Greenwood.
Bartlett, Samuel C. see Bartlett, Samuel Colcord.
Bartlett, Samuel Colcord.
xBartlett, Samuel C.
Historical Sketches of the Missions of the
American Board. Arno.
Bartlett, Vernon, 1894-
xBartlett, Vernon.
Central Italy. Hastings.
Topsy-Turvy. Arno.
Bartlett, Virginia.
xBartlett, Virginia K.
Pickles & Pretzels: Pennsylvania's World of
Food. U of Pittsburgh Pr.
Bartlett, Virginia K. see Bartlett, Virginia.
Bartlett, William I. see Bartlett, William Irving.
Bartlett, William Irving.
xBartlett, William I.
Jones Very, Emerson's Brave Saint.
Greenwood.
Bartley, Ernest R., 1918-
xBartley, Ernest R.
The Tidelands Oil Controversy. Arno.
Bartley, Numan V.
xBartley, Numan V.
From Thurmond to Wallace: Political
Tendencies in Georgia 1948-1968. Johns
Hopkins.
Southern Elections: County & Precinct Data,
1950-1972. La State U Pr.
Southern Politics & the Second Reconstruction.
Johns Hopkins.
Bartley, Russell H.
xBartley, Russell H.
Latin America in Basic Historical Collections:
A Working Guide. Hoover Inst Pr.
ed. Soviet Historians on Latin America: Recent
Scholarly Contributions. U of Wis Pr.
Bartley, S. Howard. see Bartley, Samuel Howard.
Bartley, Samuel Howard.
xBartley, S. Howard.
Introduction to Perception. Har-Row.
Bartok, Bela.
xBartok, Bela.
Hungarian Folk Music. AMS Pr.
Hungarian Folk Music. Hyperion Conn.
Turkish Folk Music from Asia Minor.
Princeton U Pr.
Bartol, Curt R., 1940-
xBartol, Curt R.
Criminal Behavior: A Psychosocial Approach.
P-H.
Bartol'D, Vasilii V. see Bartol'D, Vasilii Vladimirovich.

Bartol'D, Vasilii Vladimirovich, 1869-1930
xBartol'D, Vasilii V.
Turkestan Down to the Mongol Invasion.
Porcupine Pr.
Bartoli, Jennifer.
xBartoli, Jennifer.
In a Meadow, Two Hares Hide. A Whitman.
Bartollas, Clemens.
xBartollas, Clemens.
Correctional Administration: Theory &
Practice. McGraw.
Bartolomei De la Cruz, Hector G.
xBartolomei De La Cruz, Hector G.
Protection Against Anti-Union Discrimination.
Intl Labour Office.
Barton, A. D. see Barton, Allan D.
Barton, A. F. see Barton, Allan F. M.
Barton, Allan D.
xBarton, A. D.
Anatomy of Accounting. U of Queensland Pr.
Barton, Allan F. M.
xBarton, A. F.
Resource Recovery & Recycling. Wiley.
Barton, Allen H, 1924-
xBarton, Allen H.
Organizational Measurement & Its Bearing on
the Study of College Environments. College
Bd.
Barton, Benjamin S. see Barton, Benjamin Smith.
Barton, Benjamin Smith, 1766-1815
xBarton, Benjamin S.
Notes on the Animals of North America, 1793.
Arno.
Barton, Bruce W. see Barton, Bruce Walter.
Barton, Bruce Walter, 1935-
xBarton, Bruce W.
The Tree at the Center of the World: The
Story of the California Missions.
Ross-Erikson.
Barton, Byron.
xBarton, Byron.
Buzz, Buzz, Buzz. Penguin.
illus. Buzz, Buzz, Buzz. Macmillan.
illus. Wheels. T Y Crowell.
illus. Where's Al. HM.
Barton, Clara, 1821-1912
xBarton, Clara.
Story of the Red Cross. Airmont.
Barton, David K. see Barton, David Knox.
Barton, David Knox, 1927-
xBarton, David K.
Radar System Analysis. Artech Hse.
ed. Radars. Artech Hse.
Barton, Elizabeth W.
xBarton, Elizabeth W.
The Compleat Blueberry Cookbook. Phoenix
Pub.
Barton, G.
xBarton, G.
Introduction to Advanced Field Theory.
Krieger.
Barton, George A. see Barton, George Aaron.
Barton, George Aaron, 1859-1942
xBarton, George A.
Religions of the World. Greenwood.
Barton, H. Arnold. see Barton, Hildor Arnold.
Barton, Hildor Arnold, 1929-
xBarton, H. Arnold.
ed. Letters from the Promised Land: Swedes in
America, 1840-1914. U of Minn Pr.
The Search for Ancestors: A
Swedish-American Family Saga. S Ill U Pr.
Barton, Jim T. see Barton, Jim Tom.
Barton, Jim Tom, 1910-
xBarton, Jim T.
Eighter from Decatur: Growing up in North
Texas. Tex A&M Univ Pr.
Barton, Josef. see Barton, Josef J.
Barton, Josef J.
xBarton, Josef.

Peasants & Strangers: Italians, Rumanians, &
Slovaks in an American City, 1890-1950.
Harvard U Pr.
xBarton, Josef J.
Compiled by Brief Ethnic Bibliography: An
Annotated Guide to the Ethnic Experience in
the U. S.. Langdon Assocs.
Barton, Karel.
xBarton, Karel.
Protection Against Atmospheric Corrosion:
Theories & Methods. Wiley.
Barton, Lucy, 1891-
xBarton, Lucy.
Appreciating Costume. Baker's Plays.
Historic Costume for the Stage. Baker's Plays.
Barton, Margaret, 1897-
xBarton, Margaret.
Garrick. Greenwood.
Barton, Peggy, 1931-
xBarton, Peggy.
John the Baptist. Deseret Bk.
Barton, Peggy Ann.
xBarton, Peggy Ann.
Step-by-Step Sugar Artistry. Exposition.
Barton, Robert, 1942-
xBarton, Robert.
Atlas of the Sea. T Y Crowell.
The Oceans. Facts on File.
Barton, Roger, 1903-
xBarton, Roger.
Handbook of Advertising Management.
McGraw.
Barton, Roy F. see Barton, Roy Franklin.
Barton, Roy Franklin, 1883-1947
xBarton, Roy F.
The Half-Way Sun: Life Among the
Headhunters of the Philippines. AMS Pr.
Ifugao Law. U of Cal Pr.
Philippine Pagans: The Autobiographies of
Three Ifugaos. AMS Pr.
Barton, Walter E.
xBarton, Walter E.
ed. Law & the Mental Health Professions:
Friction at the Interface. Intl Univs Pr.
Barton, William A. see Barton, William Alexander.
Barton, William Alexander, 1890-
xBarton, William A.
Outlining As a Study Procedure. AMS Pr.
Barton, William E. see Barton, William Eleazar.
Barton, William Eleazar, 1861-1930
xBarton, William E.
Abraham Lincoln & Walt Whitman. Kennikat.
Bartos, Otomar. see Bartos, Otomar J.
Bartos, Otomar J.
xBartos, Otomar.
The Process & Outcome of Negotiations.
Columbia U Pr.
xBartos, Otomar J.
Simple Models of Group Behavior. Columbia U
Pr.
Bartow, Gene.
xBartow, Gene.
Winning Basketball. Forum Pr MO.
Bartram, Alan.
xBartram, Alan.
Street Name Lettering in the British Isles.
Watson-Guptill.
Tombstone Lettering in the British Isles.
Watson-Guptill.
Bartram, George, 1931-
xBartram, George.
Fair Game. Macmillan.
Bartrum, Royal J.
xBartrum, Royal J.
Case Studies in Ultrasound. Saunders.
Bartsch, Hans Jochen.
xBartsch, Hans-Jochen.
Handbook of Mathematical Formulas. Acad Pr.
Bartsch, Hans-Jochen. see Bartsch, Hans Jochen.

Bartsch, Karl.
xBartsch, Karl.
Skills in Life-Career Planning. Brooks-Cole.
Bartz, Albert E.
xBartz, Albert E.
Descriptive Statistics for Education & the
Behavioral Sciences. Burgess.
Bartz, Patricia M. see Bartz, Patricia Mcbride.
Bartz, Patricia Mcbride, 1921-
xBartz, Patricia M.
South Korea. Oxford U Pr.
Baru, A. V. see Baru, Alla Vladimirovna.
Baru, Alla Vladimirovna.
xBaru, A. V.
The Brain & Hearing: Hearing Disturbances
Associated with Local Brain Lesions. Plenum
Pub.
Barua, Birinchi K. see Barua, Birinchi Kumar.
Barua, Birinchi Kumar.
xBarua, Birinchi K.
History of Assamese Literature. Verry.
Baruch, Dorothy. see Baruch, Dorothy (Walter).
Baruch, Dorothy (Walter), 1899-
xBaruch, Dorothy.
One Little Boy. Dell.
Baruk, Henri.
xBaruk, Henri.
Patients Are People Like Us: The Experiences
of Half a Century in Neuropsychiatry.
Morrow.
Barut, A. O. see Barut, Asim Orhan.
Barut, Asim Orhan, 1926-
xBarut, A. O.
ed. Foundations of Radiation Theory &
Quantum Electrodynamics. Plenum Pub.
Baruth, Leroy G.
xBaruth, Leroy G.
A Single Parent's Survival Guide: How to
Raise the Children. Kendall-Hunt.
Barwell, Eve.
xBarwell, Eve.
Disguises You Can Make. Lothrop.
Barwell, F. T. see Barwell, Frederick Thomas.
Barwell, Frederick Thomas.
xBarwell, F. T.
Automation & Control in Transport. Pergamon.
Barwise, J. see Barwise, Jon.
Barwise, Jon.
xBarwise, J.
ed. Handbook of Mathematical Logic. Elsevier.
Bary, Constantine W.
xBary, Constantine W.
Operational Economics of Electric Utilities.
Columbia U Pr.
Bary, William T. De. see De Bary, William T.
Barzanti, Sergio.
xBarzanti, Sergio.
Underdeveloped Areas Within the Common
Market. Princeton U Pr.
Barzman, Sol.
xBarzman, Sol.
Credit in Early America. NACM.
Everyday Credit Checking: A Practical Guide.
T Y Crowell.
Barzun, Jacques, 1907-
xBarzun, Jacques.

Classic, Romantic & Modern. U of Chicago Pr.
Clio & the Doctors: Psycho-History,
    Quanto-History, & History. U of Chicago Pr.
The Energies of Art: Studies of Authors Classic
    & Modern. Greenwood.
The House of Intellect. Greenwood.
The House of Intellect. U of Chicago Pr.
Of Human Freedom. Greenwood.
On Writing, Editing, & Publishing: Essays
    Explicative & Hortatory. U of Chicago Pr.
Race: A Study in Superstition. AMS Pr.
Simple & Direct: A Rhetoric for Writers.
    Har-Row.
Simple & Direct: A Rhetoric for Writers.
    Har-Row.

Basagni, Fabio.
    xBasagni, Fabio.
        ed. Monetary Relations & World Development.
        Praeger.
Basch, Michael.
    xBasch, Michael F.
        Doing Psychotherapy. Basic.
Basch, Michael F. see Basch, Michael.
Basch, Samuel. see Basch, Samuel Siegfried Karl.
Basch, Samuel Siegfried Karl, Ritter Von, 1837-1905
    xBasch, Samuel.
        Memories of Mexico: History of the Last Ten
        Months of the Empire. Trinity U Pr.
Basche, James R., 1926-
    xBasche, James R.
        Evolving Corporate Policy & Organization for
        East-West Trade. Conference Bd.
        Experience with Foreign Production Work
        Forces. Conference Bd.
        Foreign Production Costs: A Survey of Recent
        Trends & Their Effects on Business Policy.
        Conference Bd.
Bascom, Willard.
    xBascom, Willard.
        Waves & Beaches: The Dynamics of the Ocean
        Surface. Doubleday.
Bascom, William. see Bascom, William Russell.
Bascom, William R. see Bascom, William Russell.
Bascom, William Russell.
    xBascom, William.
        Ifa Divination: Communication Between Gods
        & Men in West Africa. Ind U Pr.
    xBascom, William R.
        ed. Continuity & Change in African Cultures.
        U of Chicago Pr.
Basedow, Herbert, 1881-1933
    xBasedow, Herbert.
        The Australian Aboriginal. AMS Pr.
Baselt, Randall C.
    xBaselt, Randall C.
        Analytical Procedures for Therapeutic Drug
        Monitoring & Emergency Toxicology.
        Biomed Pubns.
Baserga, Renato.
    xBaserga, Renato.
        ed. Cell Cycle & Cancer. Dekker.
        ed. Multiplication & Division in Mammalian
        Cells. Dekker.
Basford, Kathleen.
    xBasford, Kathleen.
        The Green Man. Rowman.
Basgoz, Ilhan. see Basgoz, M. Ilhan.
Basgoz, M. Ilhan.
    xBasgoz, Ilhan.
        Educational Problems in Turkey, 1920-1940.
        Res Ctr Lang Semiotic.
        Turkish Folklore Reader. Res Ctr Lang
        Semiotic.
Bash, Ewald.
    xBash, Ewald.
        Legends from the Future. Friend Pr.
Bash, Frank N.
    xBash, Frank N.
        Astronomy. Har-Row.
Bash, H. H. see Bash, Harry H.

Bash, Harry H.
    xBash, H. H.
        Sociology, Race & Ethnicity: A Critique of
        American Ideological Infusions Upon
        Sociological Theory. Gordon.
Bash, James H.
    xBash, James H.
        Effective Teaching in the Desegregated School.
        Phi Delta Kappa.
Basham, A. L.
    xBasham, A. L.
        ed. A Cultural History of India. Oxford U Pr.
Basham, A. L. see Basham, Arthur Llewellyn.
Basham, Arthur Llewellyn.
    xBasham, A. L.
        Wonder That Was India: A Survey of the
        History & Culture of the Indian
        Sub-Continent Before the Coming of the
        Muslims. Taplinger.
Basham, Donald J.
    xBasham, Donald J.
        Traffic Accident Management. C C Thomas.
Bashaw, W. L.
    xBashaw, W. L.
        Mathematics for Statistics. Wiley.
Bashkin, S. see Bashkin, Stanley.
Bashkin, Stanley.
    xBashkin, S.
        Atomic Energy Levels & Grotrian Diagrams.
        Elsevier.
Bashline, L. James.
    xBashline, L. James.
        ed. The Eastern Trail. Freshet Pr.
        Night Fishing for Trout. Freshet Pr.
Basi, Santokh, 1933-
    xBasi, Santokh.
        Semiconductor Pulse & Switching Circuits.
        Wiley.
Basil, Douglas C. see Basil, Douglas Constantine.
Basil, Douglas Constantine, 1923-
    xBasil, Douglas C.
        Leadership Skills for Executive Action. Am
        Mgmt.
Basinger, Jeanine.
    xBasinger, Jeanine.
        Anthony Mann. Twayne.
Baskervill, William M. see Baskervill, William Malone.
Baskervill, William Malone, 1850-1899
    xBaskervill, William M.
        Southern Writers: Biographical & Critical
        Studies. Gordian.
Baskerville, Barnet.
    xBaskerville, Barnet.
        The People's Voice: The Orator in American
        Society. U Pr of Ky.
Baskerville, Rosetta G. see Baskerville, Rosetta Gage
    (Harvey).
**Baskerville, Rosetta Gage (Harvey), Mrs. George
    Baskerville.**
    xBaskerville, Rosetta G.
        Flame Tree & Other Folklore Stories from
        Uganda. Negro U Pr.
Baskett, Edward. see Baskett, Edward Eugene.
Baskett, Edward Eugene.
    xBaskett, Edward.
        Entrapped. Lawrence Hill.
Baskett, William D. see Baskett, William Denny.
Baskett, William Denny.
    xBaskett, William D.
        Parts of the Body in the Later Germanic
        Dialects. AMS Pr.
Baskette, Floyd K.
    xBaskette, Floyd K.
        Art of Editing. Macmillan.
Baskin, Alex.
    xBaskin, Alex.
        ed. The American Civil Liberties Union Papers:
        A Guide to the Records of the A.C.L.U.
        Cases 1912-1946. Archives Soc Hist.
Baskin, Barbara H. see Baskin, Barbara Holland.

Baskin, Barbara Holland.
    xBaskin, Barbara H.
        Notes from a Different Drummer: A Guide to
        Juvenile Fiction Portraying the Handicapped.
        Bowker.
Baskin, Joseph R.
    xBaskin, Joseph R.
        Why I Believe in Jesus Christ. Broadman.
Baskin, Leonard, 1922-
    xBaskin, Leonard.
        Figures of Dead Men. U of Mass Pr.
        jt. auth. Hosie's Alphabet. Viking Pr.
        jt. auth. Hosie's Aviary. Viking Pr.
Baskin, Wade.
    xBaskin, Wade.
        ed. Classics in Chinese Philosophy. Philos Lib.
        Dictionary of Black Culture. Philos Lib.
        Dictionary of Satanism. Citadel Pr.
        The Sorcerer's Handbook. Citadel Pr.
Baskir, Lawrence M.
    xBaskir, Lawrence M.
        Chance & Circumstance: The Draft, the War,
        & the Vietnam Generation. Knopf.
Basler, Lucille.
    xBasler, Lucille.
        A Tour of Old Ste. Genevieve. Patrice Pr.
Basler, Roy P. see Basler, Roy Prentice.
Basler, Roy Prentice, 1906-
    xBasler, Roy P.
        The Muse & the Librarian. Greenwood.
Basmajian. see Basmajian, John V.
Basmajian, John V., 1921-
    xBasmajian.
        Biofeedback: Principles & Practice for
        Clinicians. Williams & Wilkins.
    xBasmajian, John V.
        Primary Anatomy. Williams & Wilkins.
        Surface Anatomy: An Instruction Manual.
        Williams & Wilkins.
        Therapeutic Exercise. Williams & Wilkins.
Bason, Cecilia H. see Bason, Cecilia Hatrick.
Bason, Cecilia Hatrick, 1887-
    xBason, Cecilia H.
        Study of the Homeland & Civilization in the
        Elementary Schools of Germany. AMS Pr.
Bason, Lillian.
    xBason, Lillian.
        Those Foolish Molboes!. Coward.
Basov, N. G. see Basov, Nikolai Gennadievich.
Basov, Nikolai Gennadievich, 1922-
    xBasov, N. G.
        ed. Coherent Cooperative Phenomena. Plenum
        Pub.
        ed. Cosmic Rays in the Stratosphere & in Near
        Space. Plenum Pub.
        ed. Exciton & Domain Luminescence of
        Semiconductors. Plenum Pub.
        ed. High-Power Lasers & Laser Plasmas.
        Plenum Pub.
        ed. Microwave Studies of Exciton
        Condensation in Germanium. Plenum Pub.
        ed. Problems in the General Theory of
        Relativity & the Theory of Group
        Representations. Plenum Pub.
        ed. Pulse Gas Discharge Atomic & Molecular
        Lasers. Plenum Pub.
        ed. Pulsed Neutron Research. Plenum Pub.
        ed. Radio, Submillimeter, & X-Ray Telescopes.
        Plenum Pub.
        ed. Superconductivity. Plenum Pub.
        ed. Synchrotron Radiation. Plenum Pub.
        ed. Theoretical Problems in Spectroscopy &
        Gas Dynamics of Lasers. Plenum Pub.
Basquette, Lina.
    xBasquette, Lina.
        How to Raise & Train a Great Dane. TFH
        Pubns.
Bass. see Bass, Bernard M.
Bass, Bernard M.
    xBass.

People, Work & Organizations: An
  Introduction to Industrial & Organizational
  Psychology. Allyn.
xBass, Bernard M.
  Assessment of Managers: An International
    Comparison. Free Pr.
  Leadership, Psychology, & Organizational
    Behavior. Greenwood.
  Organizational Psychology. Allyn.
Bass, Clarence B.
xBass, Clarence B.
  Backgrounds to Dispensationalism: Its
    Historical Genesis and Ecclesiastical
    Implications. Baker Bk.
Bass, Ellen.
xBass, Ellen.
  I'm Not Your Laughing Daughter. U of Mass
    Pr.
Bass, George F. see Bass, George Fletcher.
Bass, George Fletcher.
xBass, George F.
  Archaeology Beneath the Sea. Har-Row.
Bass, Howard. see Bass, Howard L.
Bass, Howard L.
xBass, Howard.
  Divorce Law: The Complete Practical Guide.
    P-H.
xBass, Howard L.
  Divorce or Marriage: A Legal Guide. P-H.
Bass, Hyman.
xBass, Hyman.
  Introduction to Some Methods of Algebraic
    K-Theory. Am Math.
Bass, Lee W.
xBass, Lee W.
  The Style & Management of a Pediatric
    Practice. U of Pittsburgh Pr.
Bass, Mary Ann.
xBass, Mary Ann.
  Community Nutrition & Individual Food
    Behavior. Burgess.
Bass, R. see Bass, Reiner.
Bass, Reiner, 1930-
xBass, R.
  Nuclear Reactions with Heavy Ions.
    Springer-Verlag.
Bassan, Fernande.
xBassan, Fernande.
  An Annotated Bibliography of French
    Language & Literature. Garland Pub.
Bassan, M. see Bassan, Maurice.
Bassan, Maurice.
xBassan, M.
  ed. Stephen Crane: A Collection of Critical
    Essays. P-H.
Bassani, Giorgio.
xBassani, Giorgio.
  Five Stories of Ferrara. HarBraceJ.
Bassett, Fletcher S.
xBassett, Fletcher S.
  The Folk-Lore Manual. Folcroft.
  Legends & Superstitions of the Sea & of
    Sailors, in All Lands & at All Times. Gale.
Bassett, G. W. see Bassett, George William.
Bassett, George William.
xBassett, G. W.
  Individual Differences: Guidelines for
    Educational Practice. Allen Unwin.
Bassett, John S. see Bassett, John Spencer.
Bassett, John Spencer, 1867-1928
xBassett, John S.

Anti-Slavery Leaders of North Carolina. AMS
  Pr.
Anti-Slavery Leaders of North Carolina.
  Johnson Repr.
Anti-Slavery Leaders of North Carolina.
  Reprint.
The Constitutional Beginnings of North
  Carolina: 1662-1729. Johnson Repr.
Expansion and Reform 1889-1926. Kennikat.
Federalist System, 1789-1801. Greenwood.
Life of Andrew Jackson. Shoe String.
  ed. Southern Plantation Overseer As Revealed
    in His Letters. Greenwood.
Bassett, Margaret. see Bassett, Margaret Byrd.
Bassett, Margaret Byrd, 1902-
xBassett, Margaret.
  Abraham & Mary Todd Lincoln. Wheelwright.
Bassett, Reginald, 1901-
xBassett, Reginald G.
  Democracy & Foreign Policy: Case History of
    the Sino-Japanese Dispute 1931-33. Biblio
    Dist.
Bassett, Reginald G. see Bassett, Reginald.
Bassett, Richard.
xBassett, Richard.
  ed. The Open Eye in Learning: The Role of
    Art in General Education. MIT Pr.
Bassett, Ronald E.
xBassett, Ronald E.
  Communication & Instruction. Har-Row.
Bassett, S. Denton.
xBassett, S. Denton.
  Public Religious Services in the Hospital. C C
    Thomas.
Bassett, T. Robert, 1908-
xBassett, T. Robert.
  Education for the Individual: A Humanistic
    Introduction. Har-Row.
Bassett, William W.
xBassett, William W.
  ed. Celibacy in the Church. Seabury.
Bassham, Ben L.
xBassham, Ben L.
  The Theatrical Photographs of Napoleon
    Sarony. Kent St U Pr.
Bassin, Milton. see Bassin, Milton G.
Bassin, Milton G.
xBassin, Milton.
  Statics & Strength of Materials. McGraw.
xBassin, Milton G.
  Statics & Strength of Materials. McGraw.
Bassindale, Bob, 1923-
xBassindale, Bob.
  How Speakers Make People Laugh. P-H.
Bassiouni, M. Cherif, 1936-
xBassiouni, M. Cherif.
  Citizen's Arrest: The Law of Arrest, Search &
    Seizure for Private Citizens & Private Police.
    C C Thomas.
  The Criminal Justice System of the USSR. C C
    Thomas.
  ed. Law of Dissent & Riots. C C Thomas.
  Substantive Criminal Law. C C Thomas.
Bassler, Richard A.
xBassler, Richard A.
  Applications of Computer Systems. College
    Readings.
  Introduction to Computer Systems. College
    Readings.
Bassler, Thomas J.
xBassler, Thomas J.
  The Whole Life Diet: An Integrated Program
    of Nutrition & Exercise for a Lifestyle of
    Total Health. M Evans.
Basso, Aldo P.
xBasso, Aldo P.
  Coins, Medals & Tokens of the Philippines.
    Shirjieh Pubs.
Basso, K. H. see Basso, Keith H.
Basso, Keith. see Basso, Keith H.

Basso, Keith H.
xBasso, K. H.
  The Cibecue Apache. HR&W.
xBasso, Keith.
  ed. Meaning in Anthropology. U of NM Pr.
xBasso, Keith H.
  ed. Apachean Culture History & Ethnology. U
    of Ariz Pr.
Bassoff, Bruce, 1941-
xBassoff, Bruce.
  Toward Loving: The Poetics of the Novel &
    the Practice of Henry Green. U of SC Pr.
Basson, Philip W.
xBasson, Philip W.
  Fossil Flora of the Drywood Formation of
    Southwestern Missouri. U of Mo Pr.
Bassow, H.
xBassow, H.
  Construction & Use of Atomic & Molecular
    Models. Pergamon.
Bassow, H. see Bassow, Herbert.
Bassow, Herbert.
xBassow, H.
  Air Pollution Chemistry: An Experimenter's
    Sourcebook. Hayden.
Bassuk, Ellen L.
xBassuk, Ellen L.
  The Practitioner's Guide to Psychoactive
    Drugs. Plenum Pub.
Bastable, Patrick K.
xBastable, Patrick K.
  Logic: Depth Grammar of Rationality, a
    Textbook on the Science & History of Logic.
    Humanities.
Basten, Fred E.
xBasten, Fred E.
  Glorious Technicolor: The Movies' Magic
    Rainbow. A S Barnes.
Baster, A. S. see Baster, Albert Stephen James.
Baster, Albert Stephen James, 1904-1957
xBaster, A. S.
  The Imperial Banks. Arno.
Baster, Nancy.
xBaster, Nancy.
  ed. Measuring Development: The Role &
    Adequacy of Development Indicators. Biblio
    Dist.
Bastiat, Frederic.
xBastiat, Frederic.
  Law. Foun Econ Ed.
Bastide, Roger, 1898-
xBastide, Roger.
  Applied Anthropology. Har-Row.
Bastien, James W.
xBastien, James W.
  How to Teach Piano Successfully. Kjos.
  A Parent's Guide to Piano Lessons. Kjos.
Bastin, E. W. see Bastin, Ted.
Bastin, Ted.
xBastin, E. W.
  ed. Quantum Theory & Beyond: Essays &
    Discussions Arising from a Colloquium.
    Cambridge U Pr.
Bastron, R. Dennis.
xBastron, R. Dennis.
  Anesthesia & the Kidney. Grune.
Basu, Aparna.
xBasu, Aparna.
  The Growth of Education & Political
    Development in India 1898-1920. Oxford U
    Pr.
Basu, Nitish K.
xBasu, Nitish K.
  Literature & Criticism. Folcroft.
Basu, T. K. see Basu, Tapan Kumer.
Basu, Tapan Kumer.
xBasu, T. K.
  Clinical Implications of Drug Use. CRC Pr.
Bataille, Georges, 1897-1962
xBataille, Georges.

Death & Sensuality: A Study of Eroticism &
the Taboo. Arno.
Literature & Evil. Humanities.
Literature & Evil. Urizen Bks.
Story of the Eye. Urizen Bks.

Bataille, Gretchen M.
xBataille, Gretchen M.
ed. The Worlds Between Two Rivers:
Perspectives on American Indians in Iowa.
Iowa St U Pr.

Batalden, Paul B.
xBatalden, Paul B.
Quality Assurance in Ambulatory Care. Aspen
Systems.

Batchelder, Samuel, 1784-1879
xBatchelder, Samuel.
Introduction & Early Progress of the Cotton
Manufacture in the United States. Kelley.

Batcheller, John.
xBatcheller, John M.
Music in Early Childhood. Ctr Appl Res.

Batcheller, John M. *see* Batcheller, John.

Batchelor, Bruce G.
xBatchelor, Bruce G.
Practical Approach to Pattern Classification.
Plenum Pub.

Batchelor, George K. *see* Batchelor, George Keith.

Batchelor, George Keith.
xBatchelor, George K.
Introduction to Fluid Dynamics. Cambridge U
Pr.

Batchelor, Vivien.
xBatchelor, Vivien.
Observer's Book of Show Jumping & Eventing.
Scribner.

Bate, Lucy.
xBate, Lucy.
Little Rabbit's Loose Tooth. Crown.
Little Rabbit's Loose Tooth. Schol Bk Serv.

Bate, Marjorie. *see* Bate, Marjorie Dunlap.

Bate, Marjorie D. *see* Bate, Marjorie Dunlap.

Bate, Marjorie Dunlap.
xBate, Marjorie.
Legal Office Procedures. McGraw.
xBate, Marjorie D.
Legal Office Procedures. McGraw.

Bate, R. R. *see* Bate, Roger R.

Bate, Roger R.
xBate, R. R.
Fundamentals of Astrodynamics. Peter Smith.
xBate, Roger R.
Fundamentals of Astrodynamics. Dover.

Bate, W. Jackson. *see* Bate, Walter Jackson.

Bate, Walter J. *see* Bate, Walter Jackson.

Bate, Walter Jackson, 1918-
xBate, W. Jackson.
Burden of the Past & the English Poet.
Harvard U Pr.
The Burden of the Past & the English Poet.
Norton.
xBate, Walter J.
The Achievement of Samuel Johnson. U of
Chicago Pr.
Criticism: The Major Texts. HarBraceJ.
Negative Capability: The Intuitive Approach in
Keats. AMS Pr.

Bate, Weston. *see* Bate, Weston Arthur.

Bate, Weston Arthur.
xBate, Weston.
The Lucky City: The First Generation at
Ballarat 1851-1901. Intl Schol Bk Serv.

Bateman, Alan M. *see* Bateman, Alan Mara.

Bateman, Alan Mara.
xBateman, Alan M.
Formation of Mineral Deposits. Wiley.

Bateman, Barbara D.
xBateman, Barbara D.

ed. Reading Performance & How to Achieve It.
Spec Child.

Bateman, D. L.
xBateman, D. L.
Hot Melt Adhesives. Noyes.

Bateman, Edward A. *see* Bateman, Edward Allen.

Bateman, Edward Allen, 1895-
xBateman, Edward A.
Development of the County-Unit School
District in Utah: A Study in Adaptability.
AMS Pr.

Bateman, Hugh E.
xBateman, Hugh E.
A Clinical Approach to Speech Anatomy &
Physiology. C C Thomas.

Bateman, James A.
xBateman, James A.
Animal Traps & Trapping. Stackpole.

Bateman, John.
xBateman, John.
ed. Great Landowners of Great Britain &
Ireland. Kelley.

Bateman, Peter. *see* Bateman, Peter L. G.

Bateman, Peter L. G.
xBateman, Peter.
Household Pests: A Guide to the Identification
& Control of Insect, Rodent Damp &
Fungoid Problems in the Home. Sterling.

Bateman, Py.
xBateman, Py.
Fear into Anger: A Manual of Self-Defense for
Women. Nelson-Hall.

Bateman, Robert L. *see* Bateman, Robert Lake.

Bateman, Robert Lake.
xBateman, Robert L.
ed. Chemical Marketing: The Challenges of the
Seventies. Am Chemical.

Bates, Alan, 1929
xBates, Alan.
Compiled by Directory of Stage Coach Services
1836. Kelley.

Bates, Alan P.
xBates, Alan P.
Sociology: Understanding Social Behavior. HM.

Bates, Albert D.
xBates, Albert D.
Retailing & Its Environment. D Van Nostrand.

Bates, Arlo, 1850-1918
xBates, Arlo.
In the Bundle of Time. Arno.
The Pagans. Irvington.
The Puritans. Irvington.

Bates, Barbara.
xBates, Barbara.
A Guide to Physical Examination. Lippincott.

Bates, Betty, 1921-
xBates, Betty.
Bugs in Your Ears. PB.
Bugs in Your Ears. Archway.
Bugs in Your Ears. Holiday.
Love Is Like Peanuts. Holiday.
My Mom, the Money Nut. Holiday.

Bates, Billy P. *see* Bates, Billy Prior.

Bates, Billy Prior.
xBates, Billy P.
Typewriting Identification (I.S.Q.T.):
Identification System for Questioned
Typewriting. C C Thomas.

Bates, Charles F.
xBates, Charles F.
Central Information File: Conversion and
Implementation. Bankers.

Bates, David R. *see* Bates, David Robert.

Bates, David Robert, 1916-
xBates, David R.
ed. Atomic & Molecular Processes. Acad Pr.

Bates, Donald L.
xBates, Donald L.

Strategy & Policy: Analysis, Formulation, &
Implementation. Wm C Brown.

Bates, Elizabeth.
xBates, Elizabeth.
The Emergence of Symbols: Cognition &
Communication in Infancy. Acad Pr.

Bates, Erica. *see* Bates, Erica Margaret.

Bates, Erica M. *see* Bates, Erica Margaret.

Bates, Erica Margaret.
xBates, Erica.
Models of Madness. U of Queensland Pr.
xBates, Erica M.
Mental Disorder or Madness: Alternative
Theories. U of Queensland Pr.

Bates, Ernest. *see* Bates, Ernest Sutherland.

Bates, Ernest S. *see* Bates, Ernest Stuart.

Bates, Ernest Stuart, 1876-
xBates, Ernest S.
Touring in 1600: Study in the Development of
Travel As a Means of Education. B Franklin.

Bates, Ernest Sutherland, 1879-1939
xBates, Ernest.
This Land of Liberty. Da Capo.
xBates, Ernest S.
Study of Shelley's Drama-The Cenci. Folcroft.

Bates, Esther W. *see* Bates, Esther Willard.

Bates, Esther Willard, 1884-
xBates, Esther W.
Edwin Arlington Robinson & His Manuscripts.
Folcroft.

Bates, F. L. *see* Bates, Frederick L.

Bates, Frank G. *see* Bates, Frank Greene.

Bates, Frank Greene, 1868-
xBates, Frank G.
Rhode Island & the Formation of the Union.
AMS Pr

Bates, Frederick L.
xBates, F. L.
The Structure of Social Systems. Halsted Pr.

Bates, Grace E. *see* Bates, Grace Elizabeth.

Bates, Grace Elizabeth, ,1914-
xBates, Grace E.
Probability. A-W.

Bates, Herbert E. *see* Bates, Herbert Ernest.

Bates, Herbert Ernest, 1905-1974
xBates, Herbert E.
Edward Garnett. Folcroft.
Oh to Be in England. FS&G.

Bates, Joseph D., 1903-
xBates, Joseph D.
Atlantic Salmon Flies & Fishing. Stackpole.
How to Find Fish & Make Them Strike.
Har-Row.

Bates, Katharine L. *see* Bates, Katherine Lee.

Bates, Katherine Lee, 1859-1929
xBates, Katharine L.
ed. Ballad Book. Arno.

Bates, Marston, 1906-
xBates, Marston.
Gluttons & Libertines: Human Problems of
Being Natural. Random.

Bates, R. C. *see* Bates, Richard C.

Bates, Richard C.
xBates, R. C.
The Fine Art of Understanding Patients. Med
Economics.
The Fine Art of Understanding Patients. Van
Nos Reinhold.

Bates, Robert H.
xBates, Robert H.
Agricultural Development in Africa: Issues of
Public Policy. Praeger.
Patterns of Uneven Development: Causes &
Consequences in Zambia. U of Denver Intl.

Bates, Robert L. *see* Bates, Robert Latimer.

Bates, Robert Latimer, 1912-
xBates, Robert L.

Geology of the Industrial Rocks & Minerals.
Dover.
Geology of the Industrial Rocks & Minerals.
Peter Smith.
Bates, Roger G. see Bates, Roger Gordon.
Bates, Roger Gordon, 1912-
xBates, Roger G.
Determination of pH: Theory & Practice.
Wiley.
Bates, Sanford, 1884-
xBates, Sanford.
Prisons & Beyond. Arno.
Bates, Steven L.
xBates, Steven L.
Concordance to the Poems of Ben Jonson.
Ohio U Pr.
Bates, William N. see Bates, William-Nickerson.
Bates, William Nickerson, 1867-1949
xBates, William N.
Sophocles, Poet & Dramatist. Russell.
Bateson. see Bateson, William.
Bateson, Charles.
xBateson, Charles.
Gold Fleet for California: Forty-Niners from
Australia & New Zealand. Mich St U Pr.
Bateson, F. W. see Bateson, Frederick Wilse.
Bateson, Frederick W. see Bateson, Frederick Wilse.
Bateson, Frederick Wilse, 1901-
xBateson, F. W.
A Guide to English & American Literature.
Gordian.
A Guide to English & American Literature.
Longman.
xBateson, Frederick W.
English Poetry: A Critical Introduction.
Greenwood.
Bateson, Gregory.
xBateson, Gregory.
Mind & Nature: A Necessary Unity. Dutton.
Bateson, Mary, 1865-1906
xBateson, Mary.
Mediaeval England, 1066-1350. Arno.
Mediaeval England 1066-1350. R West.
Bateson, Robert.
xBateson, Robert.
Introduction to Control System Technology.
Merrill.
Bateson, William, 1861-1926
xBateson.
Problems of Genetics. Yale U Pr.
Batey, Richard. see Batey, Richard A.
Batey, Richard A., 1933-
xBatey, Richard.
Letter of Paul to the Romans. Sweet.
xBatey, Richard A.
Thank God, I'M O.K.: The Gospel According
to T.A.. Abingdon.
Bath, Markus.
xBath, Markus.
Introduction to Seismology. Birkhauser.
Bath, Virginia C. see Bath, Virginia Churchill.
Bath, Virginia Churchill.
xBath, Virginia C.
Lace. Penguin.
Batham, M. J.
xBatham, M. J.
Guide to Travel Agency Accounting. Merton
Hse.

Bathe, Greville.

xBathe, Greville.

Oliver Evans: A Chronicle of Early American
Engineering. Arno.

Batherman, Muriel.
xBatherman, Muriel.

Animals Live Here. Greenwillow.
Some Things You Should Know About My
Dog. P-H.
Bathgate, M. A.
xBathgate, M. A.
The Structure of Rural Supply to the Honiara
Market in the Solomon Islands. Bks
Australia.
Batho, Edith C. see Batho, Edith Clara.
Batho, Edith Clara, 1895-
xBatho, Edith C.
Ettrick Shepherd. Greenwood.
Bathory, Peter D. see Bathory, Peter Dennis.
Bathory, Peter Dennis.
xBathory, Peter D.
ed. Leadership in America: Consensus,
Corruption, & Charisma. Longman.
Bathurst, Bill.
xBathurst, Bill.
How to Continue. New Glide.
Batiffol, Louis, 1865-1946
xBatiffol, Louis.
Century of the Renaissance. AMS Pr.
Batliwalla, Minoo R.
xBatliwalla, Minoo R.
Investment Decision: Capital Budgeting with
the Aid of the Discounted Cash Flow
Technique. Asia.
Batra, Lekh R.
xBatra, Lekh R.
ed. Insect-Fungus Symbiosis: Nutrition,
Mutualism & Commensalism. Allanheld &
Schram.
ed. Insect-Fungus Symbiosis: Nutrition,
Mutualism & Commensalism. Halsted Pr.
Batra, R. N. see Batra, Raveendra N.
Batra, Raveendra N.
xBatra, R. N.
The Pure Theory of International Trade Under
Uncertainty. Halsted Pr.
Batsakis, John G.
xBatsakis, John G.
Pathology of the Salivary Glands. Am Soc
Clinical.
Tumors of the Head & Neck: Clinical &
Pathological Considerations. Williams &
Wilkins.
Batschelet, E. see Batschelet, Edward.
Batschelet, Edward.
xBatschelet, E.
Introduction to Mathematics for Life Scientists.
Springer-Verlag.
Batson, Benjamin A.
xBatson, Benjamin A.
ed. Siam's Political Future: Documents from
the End of the Absolute Monarchy. Cornell
SE Asia.
Batson, Larry.
xBatson, Larry.
Evel Knievel. Creative Ed.
Batson, Trenton W.
xBatson, Trenton W.
ed. The Deaf Experience: An Anthology of
Literature by & about the Deaf.
Merriam-Eddy.
Batson, Wade T.
xBatson, Wade T.
Genera of the Eastern Plants. Wiley.
Battan, Louis J.
xBattan, Louis J.
Cloud Physics & Cloud Seeding. Greenwood.
Fundamentals of Meteorology. P-H.
**Battelle Memorial Institute, Columbus, Ohio. Pacific
Northwest Laboratory, Richland, Wash.**
xPacific Northwest Laboratory.
Export Potential for Photovoltaic Systems.
Solar Energy Info.
Batten, Charles.
xBatten, Charles L.

Pleasurable Instruction: Form & Convention in
Eighteenth-Century Travel Literature. U of
Cal Pr.
Batten, Charles L. see Batten, Charles.
Batten, H. Mortimer. see Batten, Harry Mortimer.
Batten, Harry Mortimer, 1888-1958
xBatten, H. Mortimer.
Tales of Wild Bird Life. Transatlantic.
Batten, J. D. see Batten, Joe D.
Batten, J. W. see Batten, James W.
Batten, Jack.
xBatten, Jack.
The Complete Jogger. BJ Pub Group.
The Complete Jogger. HarBraceJ.
Batten, James W.
xBatten, J. W.
Soils, Their Nature, Classes, Distribution, Uses,
& Care. U of Ala Pr.
Batten, Joe D.
xBatten, J. D.
Developing a Tough-Minded Climate for
Results. Am Mgmt.
Tough-Minded Management. Am Mgmt.
Batten, Thomas R. see Batten, Thomas Reginald.
Batten, Thomas Reginald.
xBatten, Thomas R.
Communities & Their Development: An
Introductory Study with Special Reference to
the Tropics. Greenwood.
Communities & Their Development: An
Introductory Study with Special Reference to
the Tropics. Oxford U Pr.
Battenberg, Terry D., 1946-
xBattenberg, Terry D.
Complete Book of Basketball Post Play. P-H.
Battenfield, Jackie.
xBattenfield, Jackie.
Ikat Technique. Van Nos Reinhold.
Battenhouse, Henry Martin, 1885-
xBattenhouse, Henry W.
English Romantic Writers. Barron.
Battenhouse, Henry W. see Battenhouse, Henry Martin.
Battenhouse, Roy W. see Battenhouse, Roy Wesley.
Battenhouse, Roy Wesley, 1912-
xBattenhouse, Roy W.
ed. A Companion to the Study of St.
Augustine. Baker Bk.
Batterberry, Ariane R. see Batterberry, Ariane Ruskin.
Batterberry, Ariane Ruskin.
xBatterberry, Ariane R.
The Pantheon Story of Art for Young People.
Pantheon.
Batterberry, Michael.
xBatterberry, Michael.
Art of the Early Renaissance. McGraw.
Art of the Middle Ages. McGraw.
Mirror, Mirror: A Social History of Fashion.
HR&W.
Primitive Art. McGraw.
Batterham, T. J., 1933-1972
xBatterHam, T. J.
NMR Spectra of Simple Heterocycles. Krieger.
Battersby, James L.
xBattersby, James L.
Rational Praise & Natural Lamentation:
Johnson, Lycidas, & Principles of Criticism.
Fairleigh Dickinson.
Battersby, Martin.
xBattersby, Martin.
Decorative Thirties. Walker & Co.
Decorative Twenties. Walker & Co.
Battestin, Martin C.
xBattestin, Martin C.
Moral Basis of Fielding's Art: A Study of
Joseph Andrews. Columbia U Pr.
The Providence of Wit: Aspects of Form in
Augustan Literature & the Arts. Oxford U
Pr.
Battey, Thomas C.
xBattey, Thomas C.

The Holocaust in Historical Perspective. U of
  Wash Pr.
The Jewish Emergence from Powerlessness. U
  of Toronto Pr.
They Chose Life: Jewish Resistance in the
  Holocaust. Am Jewish Comm.
Baugh, A. see Baugh, Albert Croll.
Baugh, Albert C. see Baugh, Albert Croll.
Baugh, Albert Croll, 1891-
  xBaugh, A.
    ed. Literary History of England. P-H.
  xBaugh, Albert C.
    ed. Chaucer. AHM Pub.
    History of the English Language. P-H.
Baugh, Daniel A.
  xBaugh, Daniel A.
    ed. Aristocratic Government & Society in
      Eighteenth-Century England: The
      Foundations of Stability. New Viewpoints.
    British Naval Administration in the Age of
      Walpole. Princeton U Pr.
Baugh, Edward.
  xBaugh, Edward.
    ed. Critics on Caribbean Literature: Readings in
      Literary Criticism. St Martin.
Baugh, James R.
  xBaugh, James R.
    Solution Training: Overcoming Blocks in
      Problem Solving. Pelican.
Baughan, Peter E.
  xBaughan, Peter E.
    Railways of Wharfedale. Kelley.
Baughen, Michael. see Baughen, Michael A.
Baughen, Michael A.
  xBaughen, Michael.
    The Moses Principle: Leadership & the Venture
      of Faith. Shaw Pubs.
Baugher, Jacob I. see Baugher, Jacob Ira.
Baugher, Jacob Ira, 1889-1949
  xBaugher, Jacob I.
    Organization & Administration of
      Practice-Teaching in Privately Endowed
      Colleges of Liberal Arts. AMS Pr.
Baughman, Ernest W. see Baughman, Ernest Warren.
Baughman, Ernest Warren, 1916-
  xBaughman, Ernest W.
    Type & Motif-Index of the Folktales of
      England & North America. Mouton.
Baughman, James P.
  xBaughman, James P.
    Charles Morgan & the Development of
      Southern Transportation. Vanderbilt U Pr.
    Environmental Analysis for Management.
      Irwin.
Baughman, M. see Baughman, Millard Dale.
Baughman, Martin L.
  xBaughman, Martin L.
    Electric Power in the United States: Models &
      Policy Analysis. MIT Pr.
Baughman, Millard Dale, 1919-
  xBaughman, M.
    Administration & Supervision of the Modern
      Secondary School. P-H.
Baughn, William H. see Baughn, William Hubert.
Baughn, William Hubert.
  xBaughn, William H.
    ed. The Banker's Handbook. Dow Jones-Irwin.
Bauland, Peter.
  xBauland, Peter.
    Hooded Eagle: Modern German Drama on the
      New York Stage. Syracuse U Pr.
Baum, Alan. see Baum, John Alan.
Baum, Andrew.
  xBaum, Andrew.
    Architecture & Social Behavior: Psychological
      Studies of Social Density. Halsted Pr.
    ed. Human Response to Crowding. Halsted Pr.
Baum, Andrew. see Baum, Andrew E.
Baum, Andrew E.
  xBaum, Andrew.

The Income Approach to Property Valuation.
  Routledge & Kegan.
Baum, Arline.
  xBaum, Arline.
    One Bright Monday Morning. Random.
Baum, Betty.
  xBaum, Betty.
    Patricia Crosses Town. Knopf.
Baum, Daniel J. see Baum, Daniel Jay.
Baum, Daniel Jay.
  xBaum, Daniel J.
    Toward a Free Housing Market. U of Miami
      Pr.
Baum, Edward.
  xBaum, Edward.
    Chief Executives in Black Africa & Southeast
      Asia: A Descriptive Analysis of Social
      Background Characteristics. Ohio U Ctr Intl.
    Compiled by A Comprehensive Periodical
      Bibliography of Nigeria: 1960-1970. Ohio U
      Ctr Intl.
Baum, Frederic S.
  xBaum, Frederic S.
    Law of Self-Defense. Oceana.
Baum, Gerald L.
  xBaum, Gerald L.
    ed. Textbook of Pulmonary Diseases. Little.
Baum, Gilbert.
  xBaum, Gilbert.
    Fundamentals of Medical Ultrasonography.
      Putnam.
Baum, Gregory, 1923-
  xBaum, Gregory.
    ed. Religion & Alienation: A Theological
      Reading of Sociology. Paulist Pr.
    The Social Imperative. Paulist Pr.
    Truth Beyond Relativism: Karl Mannheim's
      Sociology of Knowledge. Marquette.
Baum, John Alan.
  xBaum, Alan.
    Montesquieu & Social Theory. Pergamon.
Baum, L. Frank. see Baum, Lyman Frank.
Baum, Lloyd.
  xBaum, Lloyd.
    Operative Dentistry for the General
      Practitioner: Some Useful Applications of
      Pins & Other Materials. C C Thomas.
Baum, Lyman Frank.
  xBaum, L. Frank.
    American Fairy Tales. Dover.
    Dorothy & the Wizard in Oz. Ballantine.
    The Life & Adventures of Santa Claus. Dover.
    The Life & Adventures of Santa Claus. Peter
      Smith.
    The Life & Adventures of Santa Claus.
      Exposition.
    Ozma of Oz. Ballantine.
    The Patchwork Girl of Oz. Ballantine.
    Patchwork Girl of Oz. Contemp Bks.
    Surprising Adventures of the Magical Monarch
      of Mo & His People. Dover.
Baum, Paull F. see Baum, Paull Franklin.
Baum, Paull Franklin, 1886-
  xBaum, Paull F.
    Principles of English Versification. Shoe String.
Baum, R. see Baum, Robert.
Baum, Richard, 1940-
  xBaum, Richard.
    ed. China's Four Modernizations: The New
      Technological Revolution. Westview.
    Prelude to Revolution: Mao, the Party, & the
      Peasant Question, 1962-66. Columbia U Pr.
Baum, Robert, 1941-
  xBaum, R.
    Logic. HR&W.
  xBaum, Robert.
    Logic. HR&W.
  xBaum, Robert J.
    Ethical Arguments for Analysis. HR&W.
Baum, Robert J. see Baum, Robert.

Baum, Stephen J.
  xBaum, Stephen J.
    A Practical Guide to Flexible Working Hours.
      Intl Pubns Serv.
Baum, Stuart J.
  xBaum, Stuart J.
    Introduction to Organic & Biological
      Chemistry. Macmillan.
Baum, Thomas.
  xBaum, Thomas.
    Hugo the Hippo. HarBraceJ.
Baum, Vicki.
  xBaum, Vicki.
    Grand Hotel. Am Repr-Rivercity Pr.
    Theme for Ballet. Popular Lib.
Baum, Willa K.
  xBaum, Willa K.
    Oral History for the Local Historical Society.
      AASLH.
Bauman, Edward W.
  xBauman, Edward W.
    Life & Teaching of Jesus. Westminster.
Bauman, John W.
  xBauman, John W.
    Renal Function: Physiological & Medical
      Aspects. Mosby.
Bauman, Karl E.
  xBauman, Karl E.
    Research Methods for Community Health &
      Welfare: An Introduction. Oxford U Pr.
Bauman, Richard.
  xBauman, Richard.
    For the Reputation of Truth: Politics, Religion,
      & Conflict Among the Pennsylvania Quakers,
      1750-1800. Johns Hopkins.
Bauman, W. Scott, 1930-
  xBauman, W. Scott.
    Estimating the Present Value of Common
      Stocks by the Variable Rate Method. U Mich
      Busn Div Res.
Bauman, Zygmunt.
  xBauman, Zygmunt.
    Culture As Praxis. Routledge & Kegan.
    Socialism: The Active Utopia. Allen Unwin.
    Socialism: The Active Utopia. Holmes &
      Meier.
    Towards a Critical Sociology: An Essay on
      Commonsense & Emancipation. Routledge &
      Kegan.
Baumann, Arthur. see Baumann, Arthur Anthony.
Baumann, Arthur A. see Baumann, Arthur Anthony.
Baumann, Arthur Anthony, 1856-1936
  xBaumann, Arthur.
    The Last Victorians. Norwood Edns.
  xBaumann, Arthur A.
    Last Victorians. Arno.
Baumann, Charles H., 1924-
  xBaumann, Charles H.
    The Influence of Angus Snead MacDonald &
      the Snead Bookstack on Library Architecture.
      Scarecrow.
Baumann, Duane. see Baumann, Duane D.
Baumann, Duane D.
  xBaumann, Duane.
    Water Resources for Our Cities. Assn Am
      Geographers.
  xBaumann, Duane D.
    ed. Planning for Water Reuse. Maaroufa Pr.
    ed. Planning for Water Reuse. Methuen Inc.
Baumann, Elwood. see Baumann, Elwood D.
Baumann, Elwood D.
  xBaumann, Elwood.
    The Loch Ness Monster. Watts.
  xBaumann, Elwood D.
    The Devil's Triangle. Watts.
    Monsters of North America. Watts.
    They Came from Space. Watts.
    Vampires. Watts.
Baumann, Hans.
  xBaumann, Hans.

Caves of the Great Hunters. Pantheon.
In the Land of Ur: The Discovery of Ancient
Mesopotamia. Pantheon.
illus. Lion Gate & Labyrinth. Pantheon.

Baumann, J. Daniel.
xBaumann, J. Daniel.
An Introduction to Contemporary Preaching.
Baker Bk.

Baumann, Judy, 1944-
xBaumann, Judy.
ed. Community Human Service Centers: Three
Successful Experiments. Social Matrix.

Baumann, Ludwig.
xBaumann, Ludwig.
Introduction to Ore Deposits. Halsted Pr.

Baumann, Michael L.
xBaumann, Michael L.
B. Traven: An Introduction. U of NM Pr.

Baumback, Clifford M. *see* Baumback, Clifford Mason.

Baumback, Clifford Mason.
xBaumback, Clifford M.
How to Organize & Operate a Small Business.
P-H.

Baumer, Franklin L. *see* Baumer, Franklin le Van.

Baumer, Franklin le Van.
xBaumer, Franklin L.
Early Tudor Theory of Kingship. Russell.

Baumer, Franz, 1925-
xBaumer, Franz.
Franz Kafka. Ungar.

Baumer, Rachel. *see* Baumer, Rachel Van M.

Baumer, Rachel Van M., 1928-
xBaumer, Rachel.
ed. Aspects of Bengali History & Society. U Pr
of Hawaii.

Baumer, William H. *see* Baumer, William Henry.

Baumer, William Henry.
xBaumer, William H.
Politics Is Your Business. Dial.

Baumgaertner, John H.
xBaumgaertner, John H.
Meet the Twelve. Augsburg.

Baumgardt, John P. *see* Baumgardt, John Philip.

Baumgardt, John Philip.
xBaumgardt, John P.
How to Prune Almost Everything. Morrow.
The Practical Vegetable Gardener. Music Sales.

Baumgarten, Paul. *see* Baumgarten, Paul A.

Baumgarten, Paul A.
xBaumgarten, Paul.
Producing, Financing, & Distributing Film.
Drama Bk.
xBaumgarten, Paul A.
Legal & Business Problems of Financing
Motion Pictures, 1979. PLI.

Baumgarten, Reuben L.
xBaumgarten, Reuben L.
Organic Chemistry: A Brief Survey. Wiley.

Baumgartner, J. S. *see* Baumgartner, John Stanley.

Baumgartner, John Stanley.
xBaumgartner, J. S.
Systems Management. BNA.

Baumgartner, Ted. *see* Baumgartner, Ted A.

Baumgartner, Ted A.
xBaumgartner, Ted.
Measurement for Evaluation in Physical
Education. HM.

Baumhover, Lorin A.
xBaumhover, Lorin S.
ed. Handbook of American Aging Programs.
Greenwood.

Baumhover, Lorin S. *see* Baumhover, Lorin A.

Bauml, Betty J.
xBauml, Betty J.
A Dictionary of Gestures. Scarecrow.

Baumol, William J.
xBaumol, William J.

Economics, Environmental Policy & the
Quality of Life. P-H.
Economics of Academic Libraries. ACE.
Stock Market & Economic Efficiency.
Fordham.

Baumont, Maurice.
xBaumont, Maurice.
The Origins of the Second World War. Yale U
Pr.

Baumwoll, Dennis.
xBaumwoll, Dennis.
Advanced Reading & Writing: Exercises in
English As a Second Language. HR&W.

Baur, Robert C.
xBaur, Robert C.
Gardens in Glass Containers. Hearthside.

Baus, Herbert M., 1914-
xBaus, Herbert M.
The Experts Crossword Puzzle Dictionary.
Doubleday.

Bausert, John.
xBausert, John.
Complete Book of Wicker & Cane Furniture
Making. Sterling.

Bauske, Robert J., 1921-
xBauske, Robert J.
Home Horticulture. West Pub.

Bautier, Robert Henri.
xBautier, Robert-Henri.
The Economic Development of Medieval
Europe. HarBraceJ.

Bautier, Robert-Henri. *see* Bautier, Robert Henri.

Bauwens, Eleanor.
xBauwens, Eleanor E.
ed. The Anthropology of Health. Mosby.

Bauwens, Eleanor E. *see* Bauwens, Eleanor.

Bavelas, Janet. *see* Bavelas, Janet Beavin.

Bavelas, Janet Beavin, 1940-
xBavelas, Janet.
Personality: Current Theory & Research.
Brooks-Cole.

Baver, Leonard D. *see* Baver, Leonard David.

Baver, Leonard David.
xBaver, Leonard D.
Soil Physics. Wiley.

Bavinck, Herman, 1854-1921
xBavinck, Herman.
Doctrine of God. Baker Bk.
The Doctrine of God. Banner of Truth.

Bavousett, Glenn. *see* Bavousett, Glenn B.

Bavousett, Glenn B.
xBavousett, Glenn.
World War II Aircraft in Combat. Arco.

Bawden, Liz-Anne.
xBawden, Liz-Anne.
ed. Oxford Companion to Film. Oxford U Pr.

Bawden, Nina, 1925-
xBawden, Nina.
Carrie's War. G K Hall.
Carrie's War. Penguin.
Carrie's War. Penguin.
Carrie's War. Lippincott.
Devil by the Sea. Avon.
Devil by the Sea. Lippincott.
A Little Love, a Little Learning. Queens Hse.
The Peppermint Pig. Penguin.
The Peppermint Pig. Lippincott.
The Robbers. Lothrop.
Under the Skin. Queens Hse.

Bax, Arnold E. *see* Bax, Arnold Edward Trevor.

Bax, Arnold Edward Trevor, Sir, 1883-1953
xBax, Arnold E.
Farewell My Youth. Greenwood.

Bax, Clifford, 1886-
xBax, Clifford.
Pretty Witty Nell: An Account of Nell Gwyn
& Her Environment. Arno.

Bax, E. Belfort. *see* Bax, Ernest Belfort.

Bax, Ernest B. *see* Bax, Ernest Belfort.

Bax, Ernest Belfort, 1854-1926
xBax, E. Belfort.
Reminiscences & Reflexions of a Mid & Late
Victorian. Kelley.
xBax, Ernest B.
Outlooks from the New Standpoint. Arno.
Peasants War in Germany, 1525-1526. Russell.

Bax, Martin.
xBax, Martin.
The Hospital Ship. New Directions.

Baxandall, Michael.
xBaxandall, Michael.
Painting & Experience in Fifteenth Century
Italy: A Primer in the Social History of
Pictorial Style. Oxford U Pr.
Painting & Experience in Fifteenth Century
Italy: A Primer in the Social History of
Pictorial Style. Oxford U Pr.

Baxel, Eleanor. *see* Baxel, Eleanor Adams.

Baxel, Eleanor Adams.
xBaxel, Eleanor.
A Guide for Solo Travel Abroad. Berkshire
Traveller.

Baxt, George.
xBaxt, George.
The Neon Graveyard. St Martin.
A Queer Kind of Death. St Martin.

Baxter, Bertram.
xBaxter, Bertram.
Stone Blocks & Iron Rails. David & Charles.

Baxter, Caroline, 1956-
xBaxter, Caroline.
The Stolen Telesm. Lippincott.

Baxter, Charles.
xBaxter, Charles.
Chameleon. SBD.
The South Dakota Guidebook. SBD.

Baxter, Ian F. *see* Baxter, Ian F. G.

Baxter, Ian F. G.
xBaxter, Ian F.
Marital Property. Lawyers Co-Op.

Baxter, J. D. *see* Baxter, John D.

Baxter, J. Sidlow. *see* Baxter, James Sidlow.

Baxter, James P. *see* Baxter, James Phinney.

Baxter, James Phinney, 1831-1921
xBaxter, James P.
The Greatest of Literary Problems: The
Authorship of the Shakespeare Works. AMS
Pr.
Introduction of the Ironclad Warship. Shoe
String.

Baxter, James Sidlow.
xBaxter, J. Sidlow.
Rethinking Our Priorities: The Church, Its
Pastor & People. Zondervan.

Baxter, John, 1939-
xBaxter, John.
The Bidders. Berkley Pub.
The Bidders. Lippincott.
The Hermes Fall. Ballantine.
The Hermes Fall. S&S.
The Hollywood Exiles. Taplinger.

Baxter, John D.
xBaxter, J. D.
ed. Glucocorticoid Hormone Action.
Springer-Verlag.

Baxter, Lorna.
xBaxter, Lorna.
The Eggchild. Dutton.

Baxter, Lucy E. *see* Baxter, Lucy E. Barnes.

Baxter, Lucy E. Barnes, 1837-1902
xBaxter, Lucy E.
The Cathedral Builders: The Story of a Great
Masonic Guild. Longwood Pr.
Life of William Barnes, Poet & Philologist.
Scholarly.
Sculpture, Renaissance & Modern. Longwood
Pr.

Baxter, Maurice G. *see* Baxter, Maurice Glen.

Baxter, Maurice Glen, 1920-
  xBaxter, Maurice G.
    Daniel Webster & the Supreme Court. U of
      Mass Pr.
Baxter, P. T. *see* Baxter, Paul Trevor William.
Baxter, Paul Trevor William.
  xBaxter, P. T.
    ed. Age, Generation & Time: Some Features of
      East African Age Organizations. St Martin.
Baxter, R. *see* Baxter, Richard Stephen.
Baxter, Richard, 1615-1691
  xBaxter, Richard.
    The Reformed Pastor. Banner of Truth.
Baxter, Richard Stephen.
  xBaxter, R.
    Population Forecasting & Uncertainty at the
      National & Local Scale. Pergamon.
Baxter, Robert. *see* Baxter, Robert G.
Baxter, Robert G.
  xBaxter, Robert.
    Baxter's Britrail Guide. Rail Europe.
Baxter, William F., 1929-
  xBaxter, William F.
    People or Penguins: The Case for Optimal
      Pollution. Columbia U Pr.
    Retail Banking in the Electronic Age: The Law
      & Economics of Electronic Funds Transfer.
      Allanheld.
Baxter, William T. *see* Baxter, William Threipland.
Baxter, William Threipland, 1906-
  xBaxter, William T.
    House of Hancock: Business in Boston,
      1724-1775. Russell.
Bay, Christian, 1921-
  xBay, Christian.
    The Structure of Freedom. Stanford U Pr.
Bay, Howard.
  xBay, Howard.
    Stage Design. Drama Bk.
Bay, Kenneth E., 1920-
  xBay, Kenneth E.
    ed. The American Fly Tyer's Handbook.
      Winchester Pr.
    How to Tie Freshwater Flies. Winchester Pr.
Bayard, Charles J. *see* Bayard, Charles Judah.
Bayard, Charles Judah.
  xBayard, Charles J.
    The Development of the Public Land Policy,
      1783-1820, with Special Reference to
      Indiana. Arno.
Bayard, James A. *see* Bayard, James Asheton.
Bayard, James Asheton.
  xBayard, James A.
    Papers of James A. Bayard. Da Capo.
Bayer, Constance P. *see* Bayer, Constance Pole.
Bayer, Constance Pole, 1908-
  xBayer, Constance P.
    And in the New World. Bayer.
Bayer, Leona M. *see* Bayer, Leona Mayer.
Bayer, Leona Mayer.
  xBayer, Leona M.
    Children with Congenital Intracardiac Defects:
      A Pictorial Atlas of Individual Somatic &
      Neuropsychologic Development Before &
      After Open Heart Surgery. C C Thomas.
    Growth Diagnosis: Selected Methods for
      Interpreting & Predicting Physical
      Development from One Year to Maturity. U
      of Chicago Pr.
Bayer, R. *see* Bayer, Rudolf.
Bayer, Rudolf.
  xBayer, R.
    ed. Operating Systems: An Advanced Course.
      Springer-Verlag.
Bayer Symposium, 5th - Proteinase Conference, 2nd,
  Cologne, Germany, 1973. *see* International Research
  Conference of Proteinase Inhibitors, 2nd, Grosse
  Ledder, 1973.
Bayer, William. *see* Bayer, William S.

Bayer, William S.
  xBayer, William.
    The Great Movies. G&D.
  xBayer, William S.
    Breaking Through Selling Out Dropping Dead.
      Dell.
Bayerschmidt, Carl F. *see* Bayerschmidt, Carl Frank.
Bayerschmidt, Carl Frank.
  xBayerschmidt, Carl F.
    tr. Njal's Saga. Am Scandinavian.
    ed. Njal's Saga. Greenwood.
    tr. Njal's Saga. Irvington.
Bayitch, S. A.
  xBayitch, Stojan A.
    ed. Latin America & the Caribbean: A
      Bibliographical Guide to Works in English.
      Oceana.
Bayitch, Stojan A. *see* Bayitch, S. A.
Bayles, Michael D.
  xBayles, Michael D.
    ed. Ethics & Population. Schenkman.
Bayles, William D. *see* Bayles, William David.
Bayles, William David, 1908-
  xBayles, William D.
    Caesars in Goose Step. Kennikat.
Bayless, Raymond.
  xBayless, Raymond.
    Animal Ghosts. Univ Bks.
    Enigma of the Poltergeist. P-H.
Bayley, Barrington. *see* Bayley, Barrington J.
Bayley, Barrington J.
  xBayley, Barrington.
    Star Winds. DAW Bks.
  xBayley, Barrington J.
    Soul of the Robot. Condor Pub Co.
Bayley, David H.
  xBayley, David H.
    Forces of Order: Police Behavior in Japan &
      the United States. U of Cal Pr.
Bayley, J. *see* Bayley, John.
Bayley, John, 1925-
  xBayley, J.
    An Essay on Hardy. Cambridge U Pr.
Bayley, Nancy, 1899-
  xBayley, Nancy.
    Development of Motor Abilities During the
      First Three Years. Kraus Repr.
Bayley, Nicola.
  xBayley, Nicola.
    illus. Nicola Bayley's Book of Nursery
      Rhymes. Knopf.
    illus. One Old Oxford Ox. Atheneum.
Baylis, John.
  xBaylis, John.
    ed. British Defence Policy in a Changing
      World. Biblio Dist.
    Contemporary Strategy: Theories & Policies.
      Holmes & Meier.
Bayliss, Leonard E. *see* Bayliss, Leonard Ernest.
Bayliss, Leonard Ernest, 1900-1964
  xBayliss, Leonard E.
    Living Control Systems. W H Freeman.
Bayliss, William B. *see* Bayliss, William Bradford.
Bayliss, William Bradford, 1906-
  xBayliss, William B.
    An Evaluation of a Plan for Character
      Education Involving the Use of a Pledge, an
      Award & a Sponsor. AMS Pr.
Baylor, Byrd.
  xBaylor, Byrd.
    Coyote Cry. Lothrop.
    The Desert Is Theirs. Scribner.
    Guess Who My Favorite Person Is. Scribner.
    If You Are a Hunter of Fossils. Scribner.
    The Other Way to Listen. Scribner.
    Sometimes I Dance Mountains. Scribner.
    They Put on Masks. Scribner.
    When Clay Sings. Scribner.
Baylor, Robert.
  xBaylor, Robert.

    People & Ideas: A Rhetoric Reader. McGraw.
Bayly, Brian.
  xBayly, Brian.
    Introduction to Petrology. P-H.
Bayly, C. A. *see* Bayly, Christopher Alan.
Bayly, Christopher Alan.
  xBayly, C. A.
    The Local Roots of Indian Politics: Allahabad
      1880-1920. Oxford U Pr.
Bayly, Joseph. *see* Bayly, Joseph T.
Bayly, Joseph T.
  xBayly, Joseph.
    I Love to Tell the Story. Cook.
    Psalms of My Life. Tyndale.
Baym, Gordon.
  xBaym, Gordon.
    Lectures on Quantum Mechanics.
      Benjamin-Cummings.
Baym, Max I. *see* Baym, Max Isaac.
Baym, Max Isaac.
  xBaym, Max I.
    A History of Literary Aesthetics in America.
      Ungar.
Bayne, David C. *see* Bayne, David Cowan.
Bayne, David Cowan.
  xBayne, David C.
    Conscience, Obligation & the Law: The Moral
      Binding Power of the Civil Law. Loyola.
Bayne, E. A.
  xBayne, E. A.
    Four Ways of Politics: State & Nation in Italy,
      Somalia, Israel, Iran. Am U Field.
Baynes, Helton G. *see* Baynes, Helton Godwin.
Baynes, Helton Godwin, 1882-1943
  xBaynes, Helton G.
    Germany Possessed. AMS Pr.
Baynes, Ken.
  xBaynes, Ken.
    Art in Society. Overlook Pr.
Baynes, Norman H. *see* Baynes, Norman Hepburn.
Baynes, Norman Hepburn, 1877-1961
  xBaynes, Norman H.
    The Byzantine Empire. AMS Pr.
    Byzantine Studies & Other Essays. Greenwood.
    Constantine the Great & the Christian Church.
      Gordon Pr.
    Constantine the Great & the Christian Church.
      Haskell.
Baynton-Power, Henry, 1890-
  xBaynton-Power, Henry.
    How to Compose Music: A Simple Guide for
      the Amateur to the Composition of Melodies
      & to Their Effective Harmonization.
      Greenwood.
Bayon, Damian. *see* Bayon, Damian Carlos.
Bayon, Damian Carlos.
  xBayon, Damian.
    The Changing Shape of Latin American
      Architecture: Conversations with Ten
      Leading Architects. Wiley.
Bayor, Ronald H.
  xBayor, Ronald H.
    Neighbors in Conflict: The Irish, Germans,
      Jews, & Italians of New York City,
      1929-1941. Johns Hopkins.
Bayrd, Edwin.
  xBayrd, Edwin.
    The Thin Game. Newsweek.
Bays, Daniel H.
  xBays, Daniel H.
    China Enters the Twentieth Century: Chang
      Chih-Tung & the Issues of a New Age,
      1895-1909. U of Mich Pr.
Bazan, Emilia Pardo. *see* Pardo Bazan, Emilia.
Bazant, J. *see* Bazant, Jan.
Bazant, Jan.
  xBazant, J.

A Concise History of Mexico from Hidalgo to
   Cardenas 1805-1940. Cambridge U Pr.
Bazaraa, M. S.
   xBazaraa, M. S.
      Foundations of Optimization. Springer-Verlag.
   xBazaraa, Mokhtar S.
      Linear Programming & Network Flows. Wiley.
      Nonlinear Programming: Theory & Algorithms.
         Wiley.
Bazaraa, Mokhtar S. *see* Bazaraa, M. S.
Bazeley, E. T. *see* Bazeley, Elsie Theodora.
Bazeley, Elsie Theodora.
   xBazeley, E. T.
      Homer Lane & the Little Commonwealth.
         Schocken.
Bazelon, David T., 1923-
   xBazelon, David T.
      The Paper Economy. Greenwood.
Bazik, Martha. *see* Bazik, Martha S.
Bazik, Martha S.
   xBazik, Martha.
      The Life & Works of Luis Carlos Lopez. U of
         NC Pr.
Bazin, Andre, 1918-1958
   xBazin, Andre.
      Orson Welles: A Critical View. Har-Row.
BBC. *see* British Broadcasting Corporation.
BCC Staff. *see* Business Communications Co.
Bea, Augustin, Cardinal, 1881-1968
   xBea, Augustin.
      Church & Mankind. Franciscan Herald.
      Word of God & Mankind. Franciscan Herald.
Beach, Belle.
   xBeach, Belle.
      Riding & Driving for Women. North River.
Beach, Dale S.
   xBeach, Dale S.
      Managing People at Work: Readings in
         Personnel. Macmillan.
Beach, Don M.
   xBeach, Don M.
      Reaching Teenagers: Learning Centers for the
         Secondary Classroom. Goodyear.
Beach, Edward L. *see* Beach, Edward Lattimer.
Beach, Edward Lattimer, 1918-
   xBeach, Edward L.
      Run Silent, Run Deep. HR&W.
Beach, Frank A. *see* Beach, Frank Ambrose.
Beach, Frank Ambrose.
   xBeach, Frank A.
      Human Sexuality in Four Perspectives. Johns
         Hopkins.
Beach, Fred F. *see* Beach, Fred Francis.
Beach, Fred Francis, 1905-
   xBeach, Fred F.
      The Custody of School Funds: An Appraisal of
         Systems of School Fund Custody with
         Particular Reference to New York State.
         AMS Pr.
Beach, Joseph W. *see* Beach, Joseph Warren.
Beach, Joseph Warren, 1880-1957
   xBeach, Joseph W.
      Comic Spirit in George Meredith: An
         Interpretation. Russell.
      The Concept of Nature in Nineteenth Century
         English Poetry. Russell.
      Outlook for American Prose. Arno.
      Outlook for American Prose. Greenwood.
      Outlook for American Prose. Kennikat.
Beach, Mark.
   xBeach, Mark.
      Words for the Wise: A Field Guide to
         Academic Terms. Coast to Coast.
Beach, Mary, 1919-
   xBeach, Mary.
      A Two-Fisted Banana: Electric & Gothic.
         Cherry Valley.
Beach, Rex E. *see* Beach, Rex Ellingwood.
Beach, Rex Ellingwood, 1877-1949
   xBeach, Rex E.

   Pardners. Arno.
Beach, Richard.
   xBeach, Richard.
      Ecological Planning Resources: A Selected
         Annotated Bibliography. Vance Biblios.
Beach, Scott, 1931-
   xBeach, Scott.
      Musicdotes. Ten Speed Pr.
Beach, Seth C. *see* Beach, Seth Curtis.
Beach, Seth Curtis.
   xBeach, Seth C.
      Daughters of the Puritans: A Group of Brief
         Biographies. Arno.
Beach, Sylvia.
   xBeach, Sylvia.
      Shakespeare & Company. U of Nebr Pr.
Beach, Waldo.
   xBeach, Waldo.
      ed. Christian Ethics-Sources of the Living
         Tradition. Wiley.
      Christian Life. John Knox.
      The Wheel & the Cross: A Christian Response
         to the Technological Revolution. John Knox.
Beach, Walter E. *see* Beach, Walter Edwards.
Beach, Walter Edwards.
   xBeach, Walter E.
      British International Gold Movements &
         Banking Policy, 1881-1913. Greenwood.
Beacham, Daniel W. *see* Beacham, Daniel Winston.
Beacham, Daniel Winston.
   xBeacham, Daniel W.
      Synopsis of Gynecology. Mosby.
Beacham, Hans.
   xBeacham, Hans.
      Architecture of Mexico: Yesterday & Today.
         Architectural.
      Architecture of Mexico: Yesterday & Today.
         Hastings
Beachley, Norman H.
   xBeachley, Norman H.
      Introduction to Dynamic System Analysis.
         Har-Row.
Beaconsfield, B. D. *see* Beaconsfield, Benjamin Disraeli,
   1st Earl Of.
Beaconsfield, Benjamin Disraeli, 1st Earl Of, 1804-1881
   xBeaconsfield, B. D.
      Home Letters. Kraus Repr.
Beadle, George W. *see* Beadle, George Wells.
Beadle, George Wells, 1903-
   xBeadle, George W.
      Genetics & Modern Biology. Am Philos.
Beadle, Leigh. *see* Beadle, Leigh P.
Beadle, Leigh P.
   xBeadle, Leigh.
      The New Brew It Yourself. FS&G.
Beadle, Muriel.
   xBeadle, Muriel.
      The Cat: History, Biology & Behavior. S&S.
      These Ruins Are Inhabited. U of Chicago Pr.
      Where Has All the Ivy Gone: A Memoir of
         University Life with a New Epilogue. U of
         Chicago Pr.
Beagle, Peter. *see* Beagle, Peter S.
Beagle, Peter S.
   xBeagle, Peter.
      Last Unicorn. Ballantine.
   xBeagle, Peter S.
      I See by My Outfit. Ballantine.
Beaglehole, Ernest, 1906-
   xBeaglehole, Ernest.
      Notes on Hopi Economic Life. AMS Pr.
Beaglehole, J. C. *see* Beaglehole, John Cawte.
Beaglehole, John Cawte.
   xBeaglehole, J. C.
      The Life of Captain James Cook. Stanford U
         Pr.
Beagley, H. A.
   xBeagley, H. A.

      ed. Auditory Investigation: The Scientific &
         Technological Basis. Oxford U Pr.
Beahrs, Virginia O. *see* Beahrs, Virginia Oakley.
Beahrs, Virginia Oakley, 1911-
   xBeahrs, Virginia O.
      The Fire & the Glory: Lafayette & America's
         Fight for Freedom. Westminster.
Beakley, George C.
   xBeakley, George C.
      Careers in Engineering & Technology.
         Macmillan.
      Engineering: An Introduction to a Creative
         Profession. Macmillan.
      Introduction to Engineering Graphics.
         Macmillan.
Beal, Edwin F. *see* Beal, Edwin Fletcher.
Beal, Edwin Fletcher.
   xBeal, Edwin F.
      Practice of Collective Bargaining. Irwin.
Beal, Fred E. *see* Beal, Fred Erwin.
Beal, Fred Erwin, 1896-1954
   xBeal, Fred E.
      Proletarian Journey: New England, Gastonia,
         Moscow. Arno.
Beal, George M.
   xBeal, George M.
      Leadership & Dynamic Group Action. Iowa St
         U Pr.
      ed. Sociological Perspectives of Domestic
         Development. Iowa St U Pr.
Beal, J. D. *see* Beal, John David.
Beal, John David.
   xBeal, J. D.
      Cine Craft. Focal Pr.
Beal, John M.
   xBeal, John M.
      Diagnosis of Acute Abdominal Disease. Lea &
         Febiger.
      Intensive & Recovery Room Care. Macmillan.
Beal, Merrill D., 1898-
   xBeal, Merrill D.
      Grand Canyon: The Story Behind the Scenery.
         K C Pubns.
Beal, Samuel, 1825-1889
   xBeal, Samuel.
      Buddhism in China. Krishna Pr.
Beale, Howard K. *see* Beale, Howard Kennedy.
Beale, Howard Kennedy, 1899-1959
   xBeale, Howard K.
      Charles A. Beard: An Appraisal. Octagon.
      Critical Year: A Study of Andrew Johnson &
         Reconstruction. Ungar.
      History of Freedom of Teaching in American
         Schools. Octagon.
      Theodore Roosevelt & the Rise of America to
         World Power. Macmillan.
Beale, Jack G.
   xBeale, Jack G.
      The Manager & the Environment: General
         Theory & Practice of Environmental
         Management. Pergamon.
Beale, Robert C. *see* Beale, Robert Cecil.
Beale, Robert Cecil.
   xBeale, Robert C.
      The Development of the Short Story in the
         South. Folcroft.
Beale, Walter H. *see* Beale, Walter M.
Beale, Walter M.
   xBeale, Walter H.
      Old & Middle English Poetry: A Guide to
         Information Sources. Gale.
Bealer, Alex W.
   xBealer, Alex W.
      The Art of Blacksmithing. T Y Crowell.
      Old Ways of Working Wood. Barre.
      Old Ways of Working Wood. Potter.
Beall, Chandler B. *see* Beall, Chandler Baker.
Beall, Chandler Baker, 1901-
   xBeall, Chandler B.

Chateaubriand et le Tasse. Johnson Repr.

Beall, Elizabeth, 1896-
xBeall, Elizabeth.
The Relation of Various Anthropometric
Measurements of Selected College Women to
Success in Certain Physical Activities. AMS
Pr.

Beall, James. *see* Beall, James Lee.

Beall, James L. *see* Beall, James Lee.

Beall, James Lee.
xBeall, James.
Laying the Foundation. Logos.
xBeall, James L.
How to Achieve Security, Confidence, &
Peace. Logos.
Strong in the Spirit. Revell.

Beall, John.
xBeall, John.
Toward a Faculty Self-Appraisal System. Ga St
U Busn Pub.

Beals. *see* Beals, Carleton.

Beals, Carleton, 1893-
xBeals.
Nomads & Empire Builders: Native Peoples &
Cultures of South America. Citadel Pr.
xBeals, Carleton.
Banana Gold. Arno.
Colonial Rhode Island. Elsevier-Nelson.
Crime of Cuba. Arno.
Porfirio Diaz, Dictator of Mexico. Greenwood.
Story of Huey P. Long. Greenwood.

Beals, Ralph L. *see* Beals, Ralph Leon.

Beals, Ralph Leon, 1901-
xBeals, Ralph L.
The Aboriginal Culture of the Cahita Indians.
AMS Pr.
The Ethnology of the Western Mixe. Cooper
Sq.
Introduction to Anthropology. Macmillan.
The Peasant Marketing System of Oaxaca,
Mexico. U of Cal Pr.

Beals, Richard, 1938-
xBeals, Richard.
Topics in Operator Theory. U of Chicago Pr.

Beam, Jacob, 1908-
xBeam, Jacob D.
Multiple Exposure: An American
Ambassador's Unique Perspective on
East-West Issues. Norton.

Beam, Jacob D. *see* Beam, Jacob.

Beaman, Joyce P. *see* Beaman, Joyce Proctor.

Beaman, Joyce Proctor.
xBeaman, Joyce P.
Broken Acres. Blair.

Beams, Floyd A.
xBeams, Floyd A.
Advanced Accounting. P-H.

Bean, A. R. *see* Bean, Arthur Robert.

Bean, Arthur Robert.
xBean, A. R.
Lighting Fittings, Performance & Design.
Pergamon.

Bean, Frank D.
xBean, Frank D.
ed. Demography of Racial & Ethnic Groups.
Acad Pr.

Bean, Joseph. *see* Bean, Joseph J.

Bean, Joseph J.
xBean, Joseph.
Decentralizing Hospital Management: A
Manual for Supervisors. A-W.
xBean, Joseph J.
Understanding Hospital Labor Relations: An
Orientation for Supervisors. A-W.

Bean, Judy A.
xBean, Judy A.

Distribution & Properties of Variance
Estimators for Complex Multistage
Probability Samples. Natl Ctr Health Stats.

Bean, Lee L.
xBean, Lee L.
Population & Family Planning Manpower &
Training. Population Coun.

Bean, Louis H. *see* Bean, Louis Hyman.

Bean, Louis Hyman, 1896-
xBean, Louis H.
Compiled by Graphic Method of Curvilinear
Correlation. Kelley.
How to Predict Elections. Greenwood.

Bean, Lowell J. *see* Bean, Lowell John.

Bean, Lowell John.
xBean, Lowell J.
Mukat's People: The Cahuilla Indians of
Southern California. U of Cal Pr.
ed. Native Californians: A Theoretical
Retrospective. Ballena Pr.

Bean, Philip.
xBean, Philip.
Rehabilitation & Deviance. Routledge &
Kegan.

Bean, Walton.
xBean, Walton.
Boss Ruef's San Francisco: The Story of the
Union Labor Party, Big Business, & the Graft
Prosecution. U of Cal Pr.
California: An Interpretive History. McGraw.

Beaney, Jan.
xBeaney, Jan.
Buildings, in Picture, Collage & Design. Barron.

Beaney, William M. *see* Beaney, William Merritt.

Beaney, William Merritt, 1918-
xBeaney, William M.
The Right to Counsel in American Courts.
Greenwood.

Bear. *see* Bear, Firman Edward.

Bear, David.
xBear, David.
Keeping Time. St Martin.

Bear, Firman Edward, 1884-
xBear.
Soils in Relation to Crop Growth. Krieger.

Bear, Fred.
xBear, Fred.
The Archer's Bible. Doubleday.

Bear, H. S. *see* Bear, Herbert Stanley.

Bear, Herbert Stanley.
xBear, H. S.
Algebra & Elementary Functions. Burgess.
Algebra & Elementary Functions. Page-Ficklin.
Algebra for College Students. Page-Ficklin.
College Algebra. Burgess.
Lectures on Gleason Parts. Springer-Verlag.

Bear, Jacob.
xBear, Jacob.
Hydraulics of Ground Water. McGraw.

Beard, Annie E. *see* Beard, Annie E. S.

Beard, Annie E. S., d. 1930
xBeard, Annie E.
Our Foreign-Born Citizens. T Y Crowell.

Beard, Charles. *see* Beard, Charles Austin.

Beard, Charles A. *see* Beard, Charles Austin.

Beard, Charles Austin, 1874-1948
xBeard, Charles.
The Industrial Revolution. Gordon Pr.
xBeard, Charles A.

ed. America Faces the Future. Arno.
American Foreign Policy in the Making,
1932-1940: A Study in Responsibilities. Shoe
String.
ed. Century of Progress. Arno.
Contemporary American History 1877-1913.
Kennikat.
Devil Theory of War: An Inquiry into the
Nature of History & the Possibility of
Keeping Out of War. Greenwood.
Documents on the State-Wide Initiative,
Referendum & Recall. Da Capo.
Economic Basis of Politics. Arno.
Economic Interpretation of the Constitution of
the United States. Free Pr.
The Idea of National Interest: An Analytical
Study in American Foreign Policy.
Greenwood.
Industrial Revolution. Greenwood.
Office of Justice of the Peace in England in Its
Origin & Development. AMS Pr.
Office of the Justice of the Peace in England in
Its Origin and Development. B Franklin.
The Open Door at Home: A Trial Philosophy
of National Interest. Greenwood.
President Roosevelt & the Coming of the War,
1941: A Study in Appearances & Realities.
Shoe String.
The Presidents in American History. Messner.
ed. Whither Mankind: A Panorama of Modern
Civilization. Arno.

Beard, Charles R. *see* Beard, Charles Relly.

Beard, Charles Relly, 1891-1958
xBeard, Charles R.
Lucks & Talismans: A Chapter of Popular
Superstition. Arno.
Lucks & Talismans: A Chapter of Popular
Superstition. Gale.

Beard, Crowell, 1912-
xBeard, Crowell.
Ptosis. Mosby.

Beard, Donald.
xBeard, Donald.
Dakota Love Story. Ashley Bks.

Beard, Edmund.
xBeard, Edmund.
Congressional Ethics: The View from the
House. Brookings.
Developing the ICBM: A Study in Bureaucratic
Politics. Columbia U Pr.

Beard, G. M. *see* Beard, George Miller.

Beard, Geoffrey. *see* Beard, Geoffrey W.

Beard, Geoffrey W.
xBeard, Geoffrey.
The Work of Robert Adam. Arco.

Beard, George Miller.
xBeard, G. M.
Practical Treatise on Nervous Exhaustion
(Neurasthenia): Its Symptoms, Nature,
Sequences, Treatment. Kraus Repr.

Beard, James. *see* Beard, James Andrews.

Beard, James Andrews, 1903-
xBeard, James.
Hors D'oeuvre & Canapes. Morrow.
How to Eat & Drink Your Way Through a
French or Italian Menu. Atheneum.
How to Eat Better for Less Money. PB.

Beard, James B.
xBeard, James B.
ed. Turfgrass Bibliography from 1672-1972.
Mich St U Pr.

Beard, Mary. *see* Beard, Mary (Ritter).

Beard, Mary (Ritter), 1876-1958
xBeard, Mary.
Force of Women in Japanese History. Pub Aff
Pr.
xBeard, Mary R.

ed. America Through Women's Eyes.
Greenwood.
Mary Ritter Beard: A Sourcebook. Schocken.
On Understanding Women. Greenwood.
On Understanding Women. R West.
Beard, Mary R. *see* Beard, Mary (Ritter).
Beard, Michael.
xBeard, Michael.
Duet. A Wofsy Fine Arts.
Beard, Robert S. *see* Beard, Robert Stanley.
Beard, Robert Stanley.
xBeard, Robert S.
Patterns in Space. Creative Pubns.
Beard, Ruth M. *see* Beard, Ruth Mary.
Beard, Ruth Mary.
xBeard, Ruth M.
Outline of Piaget's Developmental Psychology
for Students & Teachers. Basic.
An Outline of Piaget's Developmental
Psychology for Students & Teachers. NAL.
Beard, Thomas R.
xBeard, Thomas R.
ed. Louisiana Economy. La State U Pr.
Beard, Timothy F. *see* Beard, Timothy Field.
Beard, Timothy Field.
xBeard, Timothy F.
How to Find Your Family Roots. McGraw.
Bearden, H. Joe. *see* Bearden, Henry Joe.
Bearden, Henry Joe.
xBearden, H. Joe.
Applied Animal Reproduction. Reston.
Beardon, A. F.
xBeardon, A. F.
Complex Analysis: The Argument Principle in
Analysis & Topology. Wiley.
Beardslee, William A.
xBeardslee, William A.
Human Achievement & Divine Vocation in the
Message of Paul. Allenson.
Literary Criticism of the New Testament.
Fortress.
Beardsley, Aubrey. *see* Beardsley, Aubrey Vincent.
Beardsley, Aubrey Vincent.
xBeardsley, Aubrey.
Collected Drawings of Aubrey Beardsley.
Crown.
The Later Work of Aubrey Beardsley. Da
Capo.
Later Work of Aubrey Beardsley. Peter Smith.
Later Work of Aubrey Beardsley. Dover.
Under the Hill. Paddington.
Beardsley, Charles.
xBeardsley, Charles.
The Eyes of Love. Popular Lib.
Beardsley, Grace M. *see* Beardsley, Grace Maynard
Hadley.
Beardsley, Grace Maynard Hadley, 1896-
xBeardsley, Grace M.
Negro in Greek & Roman Civilization. Russell.
Beardsley, Lou.
xBeardsley, Lou.
The Fulfilled Woman. Harvest Hse.
Beardsley, Monroe. *see* Beardsley, Monroe C.
Beardsley, Monroe C.
xBeardsley, Monroe.
Practical Logic. P-H.
xBeardsley, Monroe C.
Aesthetics from Classical Greece to the
Present: A Short History. U of Ala Pr.
Aesthetics: Problems in the Philosophy of
Criticism. HarBraceJ.
Thinking Straight: Principles of Reasoning for
Readers & Writers. P-H.
Beardsley, Theodore S., 1936-
xBeardsley, Theodore S.
Hispano-Classical Translations Printed Between
1482 & 1699. Hispanic Soc.
Beardsmore, R. W.
xBeardsmore, R. W.

Moral Reasoning. Schocken.
Beardwood, Roger, 1932-
xBeardwood, Roger.
The Winner's Share: A Novel About Power,
Jealousy, & Suspicion. Doubleday.
Beare, J. I. *see* Beare, John Isaac.
Beare, John Isaac, d. 1918
xBeare, J. I.
Greek Theories of Elementary Cognition from
Alcmaeon to Aristotle. Irvington.
Bearman, Jane.
xBearman, Jane.
illus. David. Jonathan David.
Bearns, Robert J. *see* Bearns, Robert James.
Bearns, Robert James.
xBearns, Robert J.
The Awakening Electromagnetic Spectrum.
Awakening Prods.
Bearse, Austin.
xBearse, Austin.
Reminiscences of Fugitive Slave Law Days in
Boston. Arno.
Bearse, Ray.
xBearse, Ray.
The Canoe Camper's Handbook. Winchester
Pr.
Beasley, M. Robert.
xBeasley, M. Robert.
Fell's Guide to Buying, Building & Financing a
Home. Fell.
Beasley, Maurine H. *see* Beasley, Maurine Hoffman.
Beasley, Maurine Hoffman.
xBeasley, Maurine H.
Voices of Change: Southern Pulitzer Winners.
U Pr of Amer.
Beasley, W. Conger. *see* Beasley, William Conger.
Beasley, W. G.
xBeasley, W. G.
ed. Modern Japan: Aspects of History,
Literature & Society.. U of Cal Pr.
Beasley, W. G. *see* Beasley, William G.
Beasley, William Conger.
xBeasley, W. Conger.
Over DeSoto's Bones. Ahsahta Pr.
Beasley, William G.
xBeasley, W. G.
The Meiji Restoration. Stanford U Pr.
The Modern History of Japan. HR&W.
Beasley-Murray, G. R. *see* Beasley-Murray, George
Raymond.
Beasley-Murray, George Raymond, 1916-
xBeasley-Murray, G. R.
Baptism in the New Testament. Eerdmans.
Beaton, A. E. *see* Beaton, Albert E.
Beaton, Albert E.
xBeaton, A. E.
Changes in the Verbal Abilities of High School
Seniors, College Entrants, & SAT Candidates
Between 1960 & 1972. College Bd.
Beaton, W. R. *see* Beaton, William R.
Beaton, William R.
xBeaton, W. R.
Real Estate Investment. P-H.
xBeaton, William R.
Real Estate. Goodyear.
Real Estate Finance. P-H.
Beatson, Robert, 1742-1818
xBeatson, Robert.
Naval & Military Memoirs of Great Britain,
from 1727-1783. Irvington.
Beattie, Ann.
xBeattie, Ann.
Chilly Scenes of Winter. Popular Lib.
Distortions. Popular Lib.
Beattie, James, 1735-1803
xBeattie, James.
Theory of Language. AMS Pr.
Beattie, John.
xBeattie, John.

Spirit Mediumship & Society in Africa. Holmes
& Meier.
Beattie, William, 1793-1875
xBeattie, William.
Life & Letters of Thomas Campbell. AMS Pr.
Beatty, Alice.
xBeatty, Alice.
The Hook Book. Stackpole.
Beatty, Donald R.
xBeatty, Donald R.
History of the Legal Status of the American
Indian with Particular Reference to
California: Thesis. R & E Res Assoc.
Beatty, Eleanor.
xBeatty, Eleanor.
jt. auth. Center in on Music: Individualized
Learning Centers in the Elementary
Classroom. Mark Foster Mus.
Beatty, Jackson.
xBeatty, Jackson.
Introduction to Physiological Psychology:
Information Processing in the Nervous
System. Brooks-Cole.
Beatty, James W. *see* Beatty, James Wayne.
Beatty, James Wayne.
xBeatty, James W.
Reaction Kinetics. U Pr of Amer.
Beatty, Jerome.
xBeatty, Jerome.
Maria Looney & the Cosmic Circus. Avon.
Matthew Looney & the Space Pirates. A-W.
Matthew Looney & the Space Pirates. Avon.
Beatty, John. *see* Beatty, John Louis.
Beatty, John Louis.
xBeatty, John.
At the Seven Stars. Macmillan.
Campion Towers. Macmillan.
Master Rosalind. Morrow.
Pirate Royal. Macmillan.
Who Comes to King's Mountain?. Morrow.
Beatty, Kenneth J. *see* Beatty, Kenneth James.
Beatty, Kenneth James.
xBeatty, Kenneth J.
Human Leopards: Account of the Trials of
Human Leopards Before the Special
Commisson Court. AMS Pr.
Beatty, Patricia.
xBeatty, Patricia.
The Bad Bell of San Salvador. Morrow.
By Crumbs, It's Mine. Morrow.
Hail Columbia. Morrow.
How Many Miles to Sundown. Morrow.
I Want My Sunday, Stranger. Morrow.
Lacy Makes a Match. Morrow.
A Long Way to Whiskey Creek. Morrow.
Me, California Perkins. Morrow.
The Queen's Own Grove. Morrow.
Something to Shout About. Morrow.
The Staffordshire Terror. Morrow.
That's One Ornery Orphan. Morrow.
Beatty, Richard C. *see* Beatty, Richmond Croom.
Beatty, Richmond Croom, 1905-1961
xBeatty, Richard C.
Lord Macaulay, Victorian Liberal. Shoe String.
Beaty, David.
xBeaty, David.
Excellency. Morrow.
The White Sea-Bird. Morrow.
Beaty, Frederick L., 1926-
xBeaty, Frederick L.
Light from Heaven: Love in British Romantic
Literature. N Ill U Pr.
Beaucamp, Evode.
xBeaucamp, Evode.
Prophetic Intervention in the History of Man.
Alba.
Beauchamp, Edward R., 1933-
xBeauchamp, Edward R.

Learning to Be Japanese: Selected Readings on
Japanese Society & Education. Shoe String.
Beauchamp, George A., 1912-
xBeauchamp, George A.
Curriculum Theory. Kagg Pr.
Beauchamp, Thom. *see* Beauchamp, Tom L.
Beauchamp, Tom L.
xBeauchamp, Thom.
Ethical Issues in Death & Dying. P-H.
xBeauchamp, Tom L.
Contemporary Issues in Bioethics. Dickenson.
ed. Ethical Theory & Business. P-H.
Ethics & Public Policy. P-H.
Principles of Biomedical Ethics. Oxford U Pr.
Beauchamp, William.
xBeauchamp, William.
The Style of Nerval's Aurelia. Mouton.
Beauchamp, William M. *see* Beauchamp, William Martin.
Beauchamp, William Martin, 1830-1925
xBeauchamp, William M.
Aboriginal Chipped Stone Implements of New
York. AMS Pr.
Aboriginal Occupation of New York. AMS Pr.
Aboriginal Use of Wood in New York. AMS
Pr.
Horn & Bone Implements of the New York
Indians. AMS Pr.
Moravian Journals Relating to Central New
York. AMS Pr.
Beauchet, Ludovic, 1855-1914
xBeauchet, Ludovic.
Histoire Du Droit Prive De la Republique
Athenienne. Arno.
Beaudreau, D. E. *see* Beaudreau, David E.
Beaudreau, David E.
xBeaudreau, D. E.
Atlas of Fixed Partial Prosthesis. C C Thomas.
Beaudry, Antoinette.
xBeaudry, Antoinette.
Tropic of Desire. Pinnacle Bks.
Beaufre, Andre.
xBeaufre, Andre.
Strategy for Tomorrow. Crane-Russak Co.
Beaujeu-Garnier, J. *see* Beaujeu-Garnier, Jacqueline.
Beaujeu-Garnier, Jacqueline.
xBeaujeu-Garnier, J.
Geography of Population. Longman.
Beaulac, Willard L. *see* Beaulac, Willard Leon.
Beaulac, Willard Leon, 1899-
xBeaulac, Willard L.
Diplomat Looks at Aid to Latin America. S Ill
U Pr.
Beaumarchais. *see* Beaumarchais, Pierre Augustin Caron
De.
Beaumarchais, Pierre Augustin Caron De.
xBeaumarchais.
The Barber of Seville & The Marriage of
Figaro. Penguin.
Beaumont, C. W. *see* Beaumont, Cyril William.
Beaumont, Charles A. *see* Beaumont, Charles Allen.
Beaumont, Charles Allen.
xBeaumont, Charles A.
Swift's Classical Rhetoric. U of Ga Pr.
Beaumont, Cyril W. *see* Beaumont, Cyril William.
Beaumont, Cyril William, 1891-
xBeaumont, C. W.
Vaslav Nijinsky. Haskell.
xBeaumont, Cyril W.
History of Harlequin. Arno.
A Manual of the Theory & Practice of
Classical Theatrical Dancing (Methode
Cecchetti). Dover.
A Manual of the Theory & Practice of
Classical Theatrical Dancing (Methode
Cecchetti). Peter Smith.
Beaumont, Francis.
xBeaumont, Francis.

The Works of Francis Beaumont & John
Fletcher. AMS Pr.
Beaurline, Lester A.
xBeaurline, Lester A.
Jonson & Elizabethan Comedy: Essays in
Dramatic Rhetoric. Huntington Lib.
Beausay, William J.
xBeausay, William J.
ed. Outlines & Readings in Educational Tests
& Measurements. Mss Info.
Beaver, Bonnie V. *see* Beaver, Bonnie V. G.
Beaver, Bonnie V. G., 1944-
xBeaver, Bonnie V.
Your Horse's Health: A Handbook for Owners
& Trainers. A S Barnes.
Beaver, Bruce.
xBeaver, Bruce.
As It Was. U of Queensland Pr.
Beaver, Ninette.
xBeaver, Ninette.
jt. auth. Caril. Lippincott.
Beaver, Patrick.
xBeaver, Patrick.
A History of Lighthouses. Citadel Pr.
Beaver, Philip, 1766-1813
xBeaver, Philip.
African Memoranda: Relative Attempt to
Establish a British Settlement on the Island
of Bulama, on the Western Coast of Africa in
the Year 1792. Negro U Pr.
Beaver, R. Pierce. *see* Beaver, Robert Pierce.
Beaver, Robert Pierce, 1906-
xBeaver, R. Pierce.
Ecumenical Beginnings in Protestant World
Mission: A History of Comity. Allenson.
ed. The Native American Christian
Community: A Directory of Indian, Aleut, &
Eskimo Churches. MARCC.
Beaverbrook, W. M. *see* Beaverbrook, William Maxwell
Aitken.
**Beaverbrook, William Maxwell Aitken, Baron,
1879-1964**
xBeaverbrook, W. M.
Politicians & the War, 1914-1916. Shoe String.
Beavers, W. Robert, 1929-
xBeavers, W. Robert.
Psychotherapy & Growth: A Family Systems
Perspective. Brunner-Mazel.
Beazer, William F.
xBeazer, William F.
The Commercial Future of Hong Kong.
Praeger.
Beazley, George G., 1914-
xBeazley, George G.
The Christian Church (Disciples of Christ): An
Interpretative Examination in the Cultural
Text. Bethany Pr.
Beazley, J. D. *see* Beazley, John Davidson.
Beazley, John Davidson, 1885-
xBeazley, J. D.
The Development of Attic Black-Figure. U of
Cal Pr.
Beazley, Ronald I. *see* Beazley, Ronald Inglis.
Beazley, Ronald Inglis.
xBeazley, Ronald I.
Predicting the Success of Alternative
Government Incentive Programs: A Case
Analysis of Small Woodland Owner Behavior.
S Ill U Pr.
Bebarta, Prafulla C.
xBebarta, Prafulla C.
Family Type & Fertility in India. Chris Mass.
Bebbington, Jim.
xBebbington, Jim.
The Young Player's Guide to Soccer. David &
Charles.
Bebel, August, 1840-1913
xBebel, August.

Nicht Stehendes Heer, Sondern Volkswehr.
Garland Pub.
Bebey, Francis.
xBebey, Francis.
The Ashanti Doll. Lawrence Hill.
Beccaria, Cesare B. *see* Beccaria, Cesare Bonesana.
Beccaria, Cesare Bonesana, Marchese Di, 1738-1794
xBeccaria, Cesare B.
Discourse on Public Economy & Commerce. B
Franklin.
Becher. *see* Becher, Paul.
Becher, Paul.
xBecher.
Emulsions Latices & Dispersions. Dekker.
Becher, Tony.
xBecher, Tony.
ed. Accountability in Education. Humanities.
Becher, William D., 1929-
xBecher, William D.
Logical Design Using Integrated Circuits.
Hayden.
Bechet, Sidney.
xBechet, Sidney.
Treat It Gentle: An Autobiography. Da Capo.
Bechhoefer, Bernard G.
xBechhoefer, Bernhard G.
Postwar Negotiations for Arms Control.
Greenwood.
Bechhoefer, Bernhard G. *see* Bechhoefer, Bernard G.
Bechko, P. A.
xBechko, P. A.
Gunman's Justice. Manor Bks.
Hawke's Indians. Doubleday.
Bechtle, Thomas C.
xBechtle, Thomas C.
Dissertations in Philosophy Accepted in
American Universities, 1861-1975. Garland
Pub.
Bechtold, Peter K.
xBechtold, Peter K.
Politics in the Sudan: Parliamentary & Military
Rule in an Emerging African Nation.
Praeger.
Beck, Aaron T.
xBeck, Aaron T.
Cognitive Therapy & Emotional Disorders. Intl
Univs Pr.
Cognitive Therapy & the Emotional Disorders.
NAL.
The Prediction of Suicide. Charles.
Beck, Anatole.
xBeck, Anatole.
Excursions into Mathematics. Worth.
Beck, Ann, 1903-
xBeck, Ann.
History of the British Medical Administration
of East Africa, 1900-1950. Harvard U Pr.
Beck, Arthur C.
xBeck, Arthur C.
A Practical Approach to Organization
Development Through MBO: Selected
Readings. A-W.
Beck, Barbara. *see* Beck, Barbara L.
Beck, Barbara L.
xBeck, Barbara.
First Book of the Ancient Maya. Watts.
First Book of the Aztecs. Watts.
Beck, Carl.
xBeck, Carl.
Contempt of Congress: A Study of the
Prosecutions Initiated by the Committee on
un-American Activities, 1945-1957. Da Capo.
ed. Political Science Thesaurus. Am Political.
Beck, Charles B.
xBeck, Charles B.
ed. Origin & Early Evolution of Angiosperms.
Columbia U Pr.
Beck, David, 1939-
xBeck, David.

Ski Touring in California. Pika Pr.
Beck, Doris M. *see* Beck, Doris May.
Beck, Doris May.
  xBeck, Doris M.
    Custom Tailoring for Homemakers. Bennett
      Co.
Beck, Dorothy F. *see* Beck, Dorothy Fahs.
Beck, Dorothy Fahs.
  xBeck, Dorothy F.
    Progress on Family Problems: A Nationwide
      Study of Clients' & Counselors' Views on
      Family Agency Services. Family Serv.
Beck, Earl R. *see* Beck, Earl Ray.
Beck, Earl Ray, 1916-
  xBeck, Earl R.
    On Teaching History in Colleges &
      Universities. U Presses Fla.
    A Time of Triumph & of Sorrow: Spanish
      Politics During the Reign of Alfonso Xii,
      Eighteen Seventy-Four to Eighteen
      Eighty-Five. S Ill U Pr.
Beck, Henry C. *see* Beck, Henry Charlton.
Beck, Henry Charlton, 1902-
  xBeck, Henry C.
    Forgotten Towns of Southern New Jersey.
      Rutgers U Pr.
    More Forgotten Towns of Southern New
      Jersey. Rutgers U Pr.
    Tales & Towns of Northern New Jersey.
      Rutgers U Pr.
Beck, Henry J.
  xBeck, Henry J.
    Computerized Accounting. Merrill.
Beck, Horace. *see* Beck, Horace C.
Beck, Horace C.
  xBeck, Horace.
    Classification & Nomenclature of Beads &
      Pendants. Shumway.
Beck, Hubert. *see* Beck, Hubert F.
Beck, Hubert F.
  xBeck, Hubert.
    Fantasies for Fantastic Christians. Concordia.
Beck, J. Walter.
  xBeck, J. Walter.
    Medical Parasitology. Mosby.
Beck, Jacob.
  xBeck, Jacob.
    Surface Color Perception. Cornell U Pr.
Beck, James.
  xBeck, James.
    Leonardo's Rules of Painting: An
      Unconventional Approach to Modern Art.
      Viking Pr.
Beck, James M. *see* Beck, James Montgomery.
Beck, James Montgomery, 1861-1936
  xBeck, James M.
    May It Please the Court. Arden Lib.
    May It Please the Court. Arno.
Beck, James V.
  xBeck, James V.
    Parameter Estimation in Engineering &
      Science. Wiley.
Beck, Jane C., 1941-
  xBeck, Jane C.
    To Windward of the Land: The Occult World
      of Alexander Charles. Ind U Pr.
Beck, Julian.
  xBeck, Julian.
    The Life of the Theatre: The Relation of the
      Artist to the Struggle of the People. City
      Lights.
Beck, Leslie J. *see* Beck, Leslie John.
Beck, Leslie John.
  xBeck, Leslie J.
    The Metaphysics of Descartes: A Study of the
      Meditations. Greenwood.
Beck, Lewis C. *see* Beck, Lewis Caleb.
Beck, Lewis Caleb, 1798-1853
  xBeck, Lewis C.

A Gazetteer of the States of Illinois &
  Missouri. Arno.
Beck, Lewis W. *see* Beck, Lewis White.
Beck, Lewis White.
  xBeck, Lewis W.
    The Actor & the Spectator. Yale U Pr.
    Commentary on Kant's Critique of Practical
      Reason. U of Chicago Pr.
    Early German Philosophy: Kant & His
      Predecessors. Harvard U Pr.
Beck, M. S. *see* Beck, M. Susan.
Beck, M. Susan.
  xBeck, M. S.
    Baby Talk: How Your Child Learns to Speak.
      NAL.
Beck, R. *see* Beck, Rasmus.
Beck, Rasmus.
  xBeck, R.
    Table of Laser Lines in Gases & Vapors.
      Springer-Verlag.
Beck, Robert. *see* Beck, Robert Ernest.
Beck, Robert E. *see* Beck, Robert Ernest.
Beck, Robert Ernest, 1924-
  xBeck, Robert.
    Experiencing Biography. Hayden.
  xBeck, Robert E.
    ed. Literature of the Supernatural.
      McDougal-Littell.
    ed. Literature of the Supernatural. Lothrop.
Beck, Robert H. *see* Beck, Robert Holmes.
Beck, Robert Holmes.
  xBeck, Robert H.
    Changing Structure of Europe: Economic,
      Social, & Political Trends. U of Minn Pr.
Beck, Robert N. *see* Beck, Robert Nelson.
Beck, Robert Nelson, 1924-
  xBeck, Robert N.
    Handbook in Social Philosophy. Macmillan.
Beck, Ronald D.
  xBeck, Ronald D.
    Plastic Product Design. Van Nos Reinhold.
Beck, Simone.
  xBeck, Simone.
    New Menus from Simca's Cuisine. HarBraceJ.
    Simca's Cuisine. Knopf.
    Simca's Cuisine. Random.
Beck, Stanley. *see* Beck, Stanley D.
Beck, Stanley D.
  xBeck, Stanley.
    Insect Photoperiodism. Acad Pr.
  xBeck, Stanley D.
    Insect Photoperiodism. Acad Pr.
Beck, Thomas. *see* Beck, Thomas D.
Beck, Thomas D.
  xBeck, Thomas.
    French Legislators 1800-1834: A Study in
      Quantitative History. U of Cal Pr.
Beck, Thomasina.
  xBeck, Thomasina.
    Embroidered Gardens. Viking Pr.
Beck, Toni.
  xBeck, Toni.
    Fashion Your Figure: The Ten-Minutes-A-Day
      Program for Fitness. HM.
Beck, Warren.
  xBeck, Warren.
    Imagination & Four Other One-Act Plays for
      Boys & Girls. Core Collection.
Beck, Warren A.
  xBeck, Warren A.
    Historical Atlas of California. U of Okla Pr.
    Historical Atlas of New Mexico. U of Okla Pr.
    Understanding American History Through
      Fiction. McGraw.
Beck, William S. *see* Beck, William Samson.
Beck, William Samson, 1923-
  xBeck, William S.

Human Design: Molecular, Cellular &
  Systematic Physiology. HarBraceJ.
Becke, Louis, 1855-1913
  xBecke, Louis.
    By Reef & Palm. Arno.
    Pacific Tales. Arno.
    Under Tropic Skies. Arno.
Beckenbach, Edwin F.
  xBeckenbach, Edwin F.
    Modern College Algebra & Trigonometry.
      Wadsworth Pub.
Beckenstein, Alan.
  xBeckenstein, Alan.
    Performance Measurement of the Petroleum
      Industry: Functional Profitability &
      Alternatives. Lexington Bks.
Beckenstein, E. *see* Beckenstein, Edward.
Beckenstein, Edward.
  xBeckenstein, E.
    Topological Algebras. Elsevier.
Becker, A. C.
  xBecker, A. C.
    The Complete Book of Fishing. A S Barnes.
Becker, Alida, 1948-
  xBecker, Alida.
    ed. The Tolkien Scrapbook. Running Pr.
Becker, Arthur H.
  xBecker, Arthur H.
    Guilt: Curse or Blessing. Augsburg.
Becker, Bruce.
  xBecker, Bruce.
    Backgammon for Blood. Avon.
Becker, C. H. *see* Becker, Carl Heinrich.
Becker, Carl Heinrich, 1876-1933
  xBecker, C. H.
    Christianity & Islam. B Franklin.
Becker, Carl L. *see* Becker, Carl Lotus.
Becker, Carl Lotus, 1873-
  xBecker, Carl L.
    Cornell University: Founders & the Founding.
      Cornell U Pr.
    Detachment & the Writing of History: Essays
      & Letters of Carl L. Becker. Greenwood.
    How New Will the Better World Be?: A
      Discussion of Post-War Reconstruction.
      Arno.
Becker, Carol A.
  xBecker, Carol A.
    Community Information Service: A Directory
      of Public Library Involvement. U of Md Lib
      Serv.
Becker, Charles H., 1923-
  xBecker, Charles H.
    Plant Manager's Handbook. P-H.
Becker, Edwin D.
  xBecker, Edwin D.
    High Resolution NMR: Theory & Chemical
      Applications. Acad Pr.
Becker, Edwin L.
  xBecker, Edwin L.
    Responding to God's Call. Bethany Pr.
Becker, Elle F. *see* Becker, Elle Friedman.
Becker, Elle Friedman.
  xBecker, Elle F.
    Female Sexuality Following Spinal Cord Injury.
      Cheever Pub.
Becker, Ernest.
  xBecker, Ernest.
    Angel in Armor: A Post-Freudian Perspective
      on the Nature of Man. Free Pr.
    The Denial of Death. Free Pr.
    The Lost Science of Man. Braziller.
    The Revolution in Psychiatry: The New
      Understanding of Man. Free Pr.
Becker, Ernest I.
  xBecker, Ernest I.
    Organometallic Reactions. Krieger.
Becker, Ernst, 1929-
  xBecker, Ernst.

Gas Dynamics. Acad Pr.
Becker, Franklin D.
xBecker, Franklin D.
Housing Messages. DH&R.
Becker, Gary S. *see* Becker, Gary Stanley.
Becker, Gary Stanley, 1930-
xBecker, Gary S.
The Economic Approach to Human Behavior.
U of Chicago Pr.
Economic Theory. Knopf.
Economics of Discrimination. U of Chicago Pr.
Human Capital: A Theoretical & Empirical
Analysis, with Special Reference to
Education. U of Chicago Pr.
Becker, George J. *see* Becker, George Joseph.
Becker, George Joseph.
xBecker, George J.
ed. Documents of Modern Literary Realism.
Princeton U Pr.
Realism in Modern Literature. Ungar.
Becker, H. A. *see* Becker, Henry A.
Becker, Harold K.
xBecker, Harold K.
Police of America: A Personal View,
Introduction & Commentary. C C Thomas.
Becker, Henry A.
xBecker, H. A.
Dimensionless Parameters: Theory &
Methodology. Halsted Pr.
Becker, Howard S. *see* Becker, Howard Saul.
Becker, Howard Saul, 1928-
xBecker, Howard S.
Boys in White: Student Culture in Medical
School. Irvington.
ed. Boys in White: Student Culture in Medical
School. Transaction Bks.
ed. Campus Power Struggle. Transaction Bks.
Outsiders: Studies in the Sociology of
Deviance. Free Pr.
Sociological Work: Method & Substance.
Transaction Bks.
Becker, J. *see* Becker, Joachim.
Becker, James.
xBecker, James.
Education for a Global Society. Phi Delta
Kappa.
Becker, Joachim, 1931-
xBecker, J.
Formation of the Old Testament. Franciscan
Herald.
xBecker, Joachim.
Messianic Expectation in the Old Testament.
Fortress.
Becker, Joseph. *see* Becker, Joseph M.
Becker, Joseph M.
xBecker, Joseph.
Experience Rating in Unemployment
Insurance: An Experiment in Competitive
Socialism. Johns Hopkins.
xBecker, Joseph M.
ed. Guaranteed Income for the Unemployed:
The Story of S U B. Johns Hopkins.
In Aid of the Unemployed. Greenwood.
Becker, Julie.
xBecker, Julie.
Animals of the Fields & Meadows. EMC.
Animals of the Ponds & Streams. EMC.
Animals of the Woods & Forests. EMC.
Becker, Jurek, 1937-
xBecker, Jurek.
Sleepless Days. HarBraceJ.
Becker, Lucille F. *see* Becker, Lucille Frackman.
Becker, Lucille Frackman.
xBecker, Lucille F.
Georges Simenon. Twayne.
Louis Aragon. Irvington.
Becker, Mary L. *see* Becker, Mary Lamb.
Becker, Mary Lamb.
xBecker, Mary L.

The Mitten Book. Two Continents.
Becker, Peter, 1921-
xBecker, Peter.
Inland Tribes of Southern Africa. Beekman
Pubs.
Becker, Peter W.
xBecker, Peter W.
Design of Systems & Circuits for Maximum
Reliability or Maximum Production Yield.
McGraw.
Becker, R. *see* Becker, Richard.
Becker, Ralph. *see* Becker, Ralph Sherman.
Becker, Ralph S. *see* Becker, Ralph Sherman.
Becker, Ralph Sherman.
xBecker, Ralph.
General Chemistry. HM.
xBecker, Ralph S.
General Chemistry. HM.
Becker, Raymond B. *see* Becker, Raymond Brown.
Becker, Raymond Brown, 1892-
xBecker, Raymond B.
Dairy Cattle Breeds: Origin & Development. U
Presses Fla.
Becker, Richard.
xBecker, R.
Theory of Heat. Springer-Verlag.
Becker, Russell J.
xBecker, Russell J.
When Marriage Ends. Fortress.
Becker, Selwyn W. *see* Becker, Selwyn William.
Becker, Selwyn William.
xBecker, Selwyn W.
The Efficient Organization. Elsevier.
Becker, Stephen.
xBecker, Stephen.
The Chinese Bandit. Berkley Pub.
The Chinese Bandit. Random.
Becker, Stephen. *see* Becker, Stephen D.
Becker, Stephen D., 1927-
xBecker, Stephen.
The Last Mandarin. Berkley Pub.
The Last Mandarin. Random.
When the War Is Over. Random.
Becker, Theodore L. *see* Becker, Theodore Lewis.
Becker, Theodore Lewis.
xBecker, Theodore L.
ed. The Impact of Supreme Court Decisions:
Empirical Studies. Oxford U Pr.
ed. Political Trials. Bobbs.
Becker, Walter E.
xBecker, Walter E.
ed. Reaction Injection Molding. Van Nos
Reinhold.
Becker-Donner, Etta, 1911-
xBecker-Donner, Etta.
Hinterland Liberia. AMS Pr.
Beckett, A. H. *see* Beckett, Arnold Heyworth.
Beckett, Arnold Heyworth.
xBeckett, A. H.
Practical Pharmaceutical Chemistry.
Humanities.
Beckett, Derrick.
xBeckett, Derrick.
Limit State Design of Reinforced Concrete
Structures. Halsted Pr.
Beckett, Hilary.
xBeckett, Hilary.
Street Fair Summer. Dodd.
Beckett, J. C. *see* Beckett, James Camlin.
Beckett, James Camlin, 1912-
xBeckett, J. C.
The Anglo-Irish Tradition. Cornell U Pr.
Beckett, Jennifer.
xBeckett, Jennifer.
The Trap. Popular Lib.
Beckett, Paul L. *see* Beckett, Paul Louis.
Beckett, Paul Louis, 1913-
xBeckett, Paul L.

From Wilderness to Enabling Act: The
Evolution of a State of Washington. Wash St
U Pr.
Beckett, Peter G. *see* Beckett, Peter G. S.
Beckett, Peter G. S.
xBeckett, Peter G.
Adolescents Out of Step: Their Treatment in a
Psychiatric Hospital. Wayne St U Pr.
Beckett, Samuel, 1906-
xBeckett, Samuel.
Collected Poems in English & French. Grove.
Collected Poems in English & French. Grove.
tr. First Love & Other Shorts. Grove.
tr. First Love & Other Shorts. Grove.
Fizzles. Grove.
Fizzles. Grove.
I Can't Go On, I'll Go On: A Selection from
Samuel Beckett's Work. Grove.
The Lost Ones. Grove.
The Lost Ones. Grove.
More Pricks Than Kicks. Grove.
More Pricks Than Kicks. Grove.
Murphy. French & Eur.
Murphy. Grove.
Murphy. Grove.
Proust. Grove.
Proust. Grove.
Stories & Texts for Nothing. Grove.
Stories & Texts for Nothing. Grove.
Beckett, W. H.
xBeckett, W. H.
Akokoaso, a Survey of a Gold Coast Village.
AMS Pr.
Beckey, H. D. *see* Beckey, Hans Dieter.
Beckey, Hans Dieter.
xBeckey, H. D.
Principles of Field Ionization & Field
Desorption Mass Spectrometry. Pergamon.
Beckford, Grania.
xBeckford, Grania.
Touch the Fire. Berkley Pub.
Touch the Fire. St Martin.
Beckford, James A.
xBeckford, James A.
The Trumpet of Prophecy: A Sociological
Study of Jehovah's Witnesses. Halsted Pr.
Beckhard, R. *see* Beckhard, Richard.
Beckhard, Richard.
xBeckhard, R.
Organizational Transitions: Managing Complex
Change. A-W.
Beckinsale, Monica.
xBeckinsale, Monica.
Southern Europe: A Systematic Geographical
Study. Holmes & Meier.
Beckman, Delores.
xBeckman, Delores.
My Own Private Sky. Dutton.
Beckman, Erik.
xBeckman, Erik.
The Criminal Justice Dictionary. Pierian.
Beckman, Gail M. *see* Beckman, Gail Mcknight.
Beckman, Gail Mcknight.
xBeckman, Gail. M.
Law for Business & Management. McGraw.
Beckman, Gunnel.
xBeckman, Gunnel.
Girl Without a Name. HarBraceJ.
That Early Spring. Viking Pr.
xBeckman, Gunnell.
Admission to the Feast. Dell.
Beckman, Gunnell. *see* Beckman, Gunnel.
Beckman, Per, 1913-
xBeckman, Per.
illus. Looking for Lucas. D White.
Beckman, Thea.
xBeckman, Thea.
Crusade in Jeans. Scribner.
Beckman, Theodore N.
xBeckman, Theodore N.

The Chain Store Problem: A Critical Analysis.
Arno.
Marketing. Wiley.

Beckmann, David M.
xBeckmann, David M.
Eden Revival: Spiritual Churches in Ghana.
Concordia.

Beckmann, Martin J.
xBeckmann, Martin J.
Dynamic Programming of Economic Decisions.
Springer-Verlag.

Beckmann, Petr.
xBeckmann, Petr.
Orthogonal Polynomials for Engineers &
Physicists. Golem.
The Structure of Language: A New Approach.
Golem.

Beckmann, Uwe.
xBeckmann, Uwe.
Sky Diving. Sterling.

Becknell, Eileen. see Becknell, Eileen Pearlman.

Becknell, Eileen Pearlman.
xBecknell, Eileen.
System of Nursing Practice: A Clinical Nursing
Assessment Tool. Davis Co.

Beckner, Steven K.
xBeckner, Steven K.
The Hard Money Book: An Insider's Guide to
Successful Investment in Currency, Gold,
Silver & Precious Stones. Capitalist Reporter.
The Hard Money Book: An Insider's Guide to
Successful Investment in Currency, Gold,
Silver & Precious Stones. Dutton.

Beckson, Karl. see Beckson, Karl E.

Beckson, Karl E.
xBeckson, Karl.
Literary Terms: A Dictionary. FS&G.

Beckwith, B. K. see Beckwith, Brainerd Kellogg.

Beckwith, Brainerd Kellogg, 1903-
xBeckwith, B. K.
The Longden Legend. A S Barnes.

Beckwith, Burnham Putnam.
xBeckwith, Burnham Putnam.
The Case for Liberal Socialism. Exposition.
Government by Experts: The Next Stage in
Political Evolution. Exposition.
Liberal Socialism: The Pure Welfare Economics
of a Liberal Socialist Economy. Exposition.

Beckwith, Hiram W. see Beckwith, Hiram Williams.

Beckwith, Hiram Williams, 1833-1903
xBeckwith, Hiram W.
The Illinois & Indiana Indians. Arno.

Beckwith, Howard B.
xBeckwith, Howard B.
Calculus for Business & Life. Wadsworth Pub.

Beckwith, John, 1918-
xBeckwith, John.
Early Christian & Byzantine Art. Penguin.
Early Christian & Byzantine Art. Viking Pr.
Early Medieval Art. Oxford U Pr.

Beckwith, John A.
xBeckwith, John A.
ed. Contemporary American Biography. Arno.
Gem Minerals of Idaho. Caxton.

Beckwith, Lillian.
xBeckwith, Lillian.
The Hills Is Lonely. Merrimack Bk Serv.

Beckwith, Thomas G.
xBeckwith, Thomas G.
Mechanical Measurements. A-W.

Bedau, Hugo A. see Bedau, Hugo Adam.

Bedau, Hugo Adam.
xBedau, Hugo A.

ed. Capital Punishment in the United States.
AMS Pr.
ed. Civil Disobedience: Theory & Practice.
Pegasus.
The Courts, the Constitution, & Capital
Punishment. Lexington Bks.
ed. Death Penalty in America: An Anthology.
Aldine Pub.

Beddoes, Thomas L. see Beddoes, Thomas Lovell.

Beddoes, Thomas Lovell, 1803-1849
xBeddoes, Thomas L.
The Letters of Thomas Lovell Beddoes. Arno.
The Works of Thomas Lovell Beddoes.
Scholarly.

Bedell, William. see Bedell, William D.

Bedell, William D.
xBedell, William.
True Relation of the Life & Death of the Right
Reverend Father in God William Bedell,
Lord Bishop of Kilmore in Ireland. Johnson
Repr.

Bedenbaugh, John H.
xBedenbaugh, John H.
Introductory Chemistry. Allyn.

Beder, Harold W.
xBeder, Harold W.
Development, Demonstration, &
Dissemination: Case Studies of Selected
Special Projects in Adult Basic Education.
Syracuse U Cont Ed.

Beder, O. E. see Beder, Oscar Edward.

Beder, Oscar Edward.
xBeder, O. E.
Fundamentals for Maxillofacial Prosthetics. C
C Thomas.

Bedford. see Bedford, Norton M.

Bedford, Arthur, 1668-1745
xBedford, Arthur.
The Evil & Danger of Stage Plays. Garland
Pub.

Bedford, Bruce L., 1942-
xBedford, Bruce L.
Challenge Underground. Zephyrus Pr.

Bedford, Burnice D. see Bedford, Burnice Doyle.

Bedford, Burnice Doyle.
xBedford, Burnice D.
Principles of Inverter Circuits. Wiley.

Bedford, Emmett G.
xBedford, Emmett G.
ed. Concordance to the Poems of Alexander
Pope. Gale.

Bedford, F. W. see Bedford, Frederick Warren.

Bedford, Frances.
xBedford, Frances.
Twentieth-Century Harpsichord Music: A
Classified Catalog. Eur-Am Music.

Bedford, Frederick Warren.
xBedford, F. W.
Vector Calculus. McGraw.

Bedford, Henry F.
xBedford, Henry F.
The Americans: A Brief History. HarBraceJ.

Bedford, Jessie.
xBedford, Jessie.
English Children in the Olden Time. Folcroft.

Bedford, M. A. see Bedford, Michael Alison.

Bedford, Michael Alison.
xBedford, M. A.
Color Atlas of Ocular Tumors. Year Bk Med.

Bedford, Mitchell.
xBedford, Mitchell.
Existentialism & Creativity. Philos Lib.

Bedford, Norton M.
xBedford.
Income Determination Theory: An Accounting
Framework. A-W.
xBedford, Norton M.

Advanced Accounting: An Organizational
Approach. Wiley.

Bedford, Randolph, 1868-1941
xBedford, Randolph.
Naught to Thirty-Three. Intl Schol Bk Serv.

Bedford, Richard C.
xBedford, Richard C.
English Experienced: Teaching Foreign
Students by Staging Communication. Wayne
St U Pr.

Bedford, Sybille.
xBedford, Sybille.
A Legacy. Ecco Pr.

Bedger, Jean E.
xBedger, Jean E.
Teenage Pregnancy: Research Related to
Clients & Services. C C Thomas.

Bedi, Ajit S. see Bedi, Ajit Singh.

Bedi, Ajit Singh, 1921-
xBedi, Ajit S.
Freedom of Expression & Security: A
Comparative Study of the Function of the
Supreme Courts of the United States of
American & India. Asia.

Bedichek, Roy, 1878-1959
xBedichek, Roy.
Adventures with a Texas Naturalist. U of Tex
Pr.

Bedient, Calvin.
xBedient, Calvin.
Eight Contemporary Poets: Charles Tomlinson,
Donald Davie, R. S. Thomas, Philip Larkin,
Ted Hughes, Thomas Kinsella, Stevie Smith,
W. S. Graham. Oxford U Pr.

Bedini, Silvio A.
xBedini, Silvio A.
Thinkers & Tinkers: Early American Men of
Science. Scribner.

Bedjaoui, Mohammed.
xBedjaoui, Mohammed.
Towards a New International Economic Order.
Holmes & Meier.

Bednarz, Robert S., 1946-
xBednarz, Robert S.
The Effect of Air Pollution on Property Value
in Chicago. U Chicago Dept Geog.

Bedoukian, Kerop, 1907-
xBedoukian, Kerop.
Some of Us Survived: The Story of an
Armenian Boy. FS&G.

Bedrossian, E. Howard.
xBedrossian, E. Howard.
Surgical & Nonsurgical Management of
Strabismus. C C Thomas.

Bedunnah, Gary P.
xBeDunnah, Gary P.
A History of the Chinese in Nevada,
1855-1904. R & E Res Assoc.

Bedwell, C.
xBedwell, C.
ed. Developments in Electronics for Offshore
Fields. Burgess-Intl Ideas.

Bee, Robert L.
xBee, Robert L.
Patterns & Processes: An Introduction to
Anthropological Strategies for the Study of
Sociocultural Change. Free Pr.

Beebe, Ann.
xBeebe, Ann.
Easy Cooking, Simple Recipes for Beginning
Cooks. Morrow.

Beebe, Frank L. see Beebe, Frank Lyman.

Beebe, Frank Lyman.
xBeebe, Frank L.
jt. ed. & ed. North American Falconry &
Hunting Hawks. North Am Fal Hunt.

Beebe, Gilbert W. see Beebe, Gilbert Wheeler.

Beebe, Gilbert Wheeler, 1912-
xBeebe, Gilbert W.

Contraception & Fertility in the Southern
  Appalachians. Arno.
Beebe, Hugh G.
  xBeebe, Hugh G.
    Complications in Vascular Surgery. Lippincott.
Beebe, Lucius. *see* Beebe, Lucius Morris.
Beebe, Lucius Morris.
  xBeebe, Lucius.
    Narrow Gauge in the Rockies. Howell-North.
Beebe-Center, John G. *see* Beebe-Center, John Gilbert.
Beebe-Center, John Gilbert, 1897-1958
  xBeebe-Center, John G.
    Psychology of Pleasantness & Unpleasantness.
    Russell.
Beeby, Clarence E. *see* Beeby, Clarence Edward.
Beeby, Clarence Edward, 1902-
  xBeeby, Clarence E.
    Quality of Education in Developing Countries.
    Harvard U Pr.
Beech, G. *see* Beech, Graham.
Beech, Graham.
  xBeech, G.
    ed. Computer Assisted Learning in Science
    Education. Pergamon.
Beech, H. R.
  xBeech, H. R.
    Obsessional States. Methuen Inc.
Beech, Mervyn W. *see* Beech, Mervyn Worcester
Howard.
Beech, Mervyn Worcester Howard.
  xBeech, Mervyn W.
    Suk: Their Language & Folklore. Negro U Pr.
Beecham, Thomas, Sir, Bart, 1879-1961
  xBeecham, Thomas.
    Frederick Delius. Vienna Hse.
Beechel, Edith E. *see* Beechel, Edith Emma.
Beechel, Edith Emma, 1881-
  xBeechel, Edith E.
    A Citizenship Program for Elementary Schools.
    AMS Pr.
Beecher, Catharine. *see* Beecher, Catherine Esther.
Beecher, Catherine Esther, 1800-1878
  xBeecher, Catharine.
    Letters to the People on Health & Happiness.
    Arno.
Beecher, Charles E. *see* Beecher, Charles Emerson.
Beecher, Charles Emerson, 1856-1904
  xBeecher, Charles E.
    Studies in Evolution. Arno.
Beecher, Henry K. *see* Beecher, Henry Knowles.
Beecher, Henry Knowles.
  xBeecher, Henry K.
    Medicine at Harvard: The First Three Hundred
    Years. U Pr of New Eng.
Beecher, Henry W. *see* Beecher, Henry Ward.
Beecher, Henry Ward.
  xBeecher, Henry W.
    Lectures & Orations. AMS Pr.
    Star Papers: Or, Experiences of Art & Nature.
    Arno.
Beecher, Willis J. *see* Beecher, Willis Judson.
Beecher, Willis Judson, 1838-1912
  xBeecher, Willis J.
    Prophets & the Promise. Baker Bk.
Beeching, Cyril L. *see* Beeching, Cyril Leslie.
Beeching, Cyril Leslie.
  xBeeching, Cyril L.
    Dictionary of Eponyms. K G Saur.
Beeching, H. C. *see* Beeching, Henry Charles.
Beeching, Henry C. *see* Beeching, Henry Charles.
Beeching, Henry Charles, 1859-1919
  xBeeching, H. C.
    Character of Shakespeare. Folcroft.
  xBeeching, Henry C.
    The Character of Shakespeare. R West.
Beeching, Jack.
  xBeeching, Jack.

The Chinese Opium Wars. HarBraceJ.
The Chinese Opium Wars. HarBraceJ.
Beecroft, Glynis.
  xBeecroft, Glynis.
    Carving Techniques. Watson-Guptill.
    Casting Techniques for Sculpture. David &
    Charles.
Beede, Gretchen.
  xBeede, Gretchen.
    Simple Sewing. Lerner Pubns.
Beedle, Lynn S.
  xBeedle, Lynn S.
    Plastic Design of Steel Frames. Wiley.
Beegle, Charles W.
  xBeegle, Charles W.
    ed. Observational Methods in the Classroom.
    Assn Supervision.
Beehler, Paul J.
  xBeehler, Paul J.
    Contemporary Cash Management: Principles,
    Practices, Perspectives. Ronald Pr.
Beehler, Rodger, 1938-
  xBeehler, Rodger.
    Moral Life. Rowman.
Beek, Gus W. Van. *see* Van Beek, Gus W.
Beekman, Daniel.
  xBeekman, Daniel.
    The Mechanical Baby: A Popular History of
    the Theory & Practice of Child Raising.
    NAL.
Beeks, Graydon.
  xBeeks, Graydon.
    Hosea Globe & the Fantastical Peg-Legged
    Chu. Atheneum.
Beeler, Janet.
  xBeeler, Janet.
    Dowry: Poems. U of Mo Pr.
Beeler, M. Fancher. *see* Beeler, M. G. Fancher.
Beeler, M. G. Fancher.
  xBeeler, M. Fancher.
    Measuring the Quality of Library Service: A
    Handbook. Scarecrow.
Beeler, Nelson F. *see* Beeler, Nelson Frederick.
Beeler, Nelson Frederick.
  xBeeler, Nelson F.
    Experiments in Optical Illusion. T Y Crowell.
    Experiments with a Microscope. T Y Crowell.
    Experiments with Light. T Y Crowell.
Beeler, Samuel. *see* Beeler, Samuel C.
Beeler, Samuel C.
  xBeeler, Samuel.
    Understanding Your Car. McKnight.
Beeley, Arthur. *see* Beeley, Arthur Lawton.
Beeley, Arthur Lawton, 1890_-
  xBeeley, Arthur.
    Bail System in Chicago. U of Chicago Pr.
Beeman, D. L. *see* Beeman, Donald.
Beeman, Donald.
  xBeeman, D. L.
    ed. Industrial Power Systems Handbook.
    McGraw.
Beeman, Richard R.
  xBeeman, Richard R.
    The Old Dominion & the New Nation,
    1788-1801. U Pr of Ky.
Beenstock, Michael, 1946-
  xBeenstock, Michael.
    The Foreign Exchanges: Theory, Modelling &
    Policy. St Martin.
Beer, A. C. *see* Beer, Albert C.
Beer, Alan E.
  xBeer, Alan E.
    The Immunobiology of Mammalian
    Reproduction. P-H.
Beer, Albert C.
  xBeer, A. C.
    Galvanomagnetic Effects in Semiconductors.
    Acad Pr.
Beer, Barrett L.
  xBeer, Barrett L.

Northumberland: The Political Career of John
  Dudley, Earl of Warwick & Duke of
  Northumberland. Kent St U Pr.
Beer, Ethel S.
  xBeer, Ethel S.
    Working Mothers & the Day Nursery. Verry.
Beer, Francis A.
  xBeer, Francis A.
    Integration & Disintegration in NATO:
    Processes of Alliance Cohesion & Prospects
    for Atlantic Community. Ohio St U Pr.
Beer, Gretel.
  xBeer, Gretel.
    Austrian Cooking & Baking. Dover.
Beer, John. *see* Beer, John B.
Beer, John B.
  xBeer, John.
    Wordsworth in Time. Merrimack Bk Serv.
  xBeer, John B.
    Coleridge the Visionary. Greenwood.
Beer, Lawrence W. *see* Beer, Lawrence Ward.
Beer, Lawrence Ward, 1932-
  xBeer, Lawrence W.
    ed. Constitutionalism in Asia: Asian Views of
    the American Influence. U of Cal Pr.
Beer, Lisl.
  xBeer, Lisl.
    This My Island. Branden.
Beer, Max, 1864-
  xBeer, Max.
    A History of British Socialism. Arno.
Beer, Michael, 1926-
  xBeer, Michael.
    The Many Arts of Sales Management. Chilton.
Beer, Patricia.
  xBeer, Patricia.
    Reader, I Married Him: A Study of the
    Women Characters of Jane Austen, Charlotte
    Bronte, Elizabeth Gaskell & George Eliot.
    B&N.
    Reader, I Married Him: A Study of the
    Women Characters of Jane Austen, Charlotte
    Bronte, Elizabeth Gaskell & George Eliot.
    Har-Row.
Beer, Rudiger R. *see* Beer, Rudiger Robert.
Beer, Rudiger Robert.
  xBeer, Rudiger R.
    Unicorn: Myth & Reality. Van Nos Reinhold.
Beer, Samuel H. *see* Beer, Samuel Hutchison.
Beer, Samuel Hutchison.
  xBeer, Samuel H.
    British Political System. Random.
    City of Reason. Greenwood.
Beer, Stafford.
  xBeer, Stafford.
    Decision & Control: The Meaning of
    Operational Research & Management
    Cybernetics. Wiley.
    Designing Freedom. Wiley.
    The Heart of Enterprise. Wiley.
Beer, Thomas, 1889-1940
  xBeer, Thomas.
    The Mauve Decade: American Life at the End
    of the Nineteenth Century. Octagon.
Beer, Tom.
  xBeer, Tom.
    Atmospheric Waves. Halsted Pr.
Beerbohm, Max, Sir, 1872-1956
  xBeerbohm, Max.
    Around Theatres. Greenwood.
    Around Theatres. Taplinger.
    Last Theatres. Taplinger.
    Observations. Haskell.
    Observations. R West.
    Seven Men & Two Others. Oxford U Pr.
Beere, Carole A., 1944-
  xBeere, Carole A.

Women & Women's Issues: A Handbook of
Tests & Measures. Jossey Bass.
Beermann, W.
xBeermann, W.
ed. Developmental Studies on Giant
Chromosomes. Springer-Verlag.
Beers, Burton F.
xBeers, Burton F.
Vain Endeavor: Robert Lansing's Attempts to
End the American-Japanese Rivalry. Duke.
Beers, F. W. *see* Beers, Frederick W.
Beers, Frederick W.
xBeers, F. W.
Atlas of the City of Worcester, Worcester
County, Massachusetts. C E Tuttle.
Atlas of Windham County, Vermont. Greene.
Atlas of Worcester County, Massachusetts. C E
Tuttle.
Beers, Gil, 1928-
xBeers, Gilbert.
The Children's Illustrated Bible Dictionary.
Nelson.
Beers, Gilbert. *see* Beers, Gil.
Beers, Gilbert V. *see* Beers, Victor Gilbert.
Beers, Henry A. *see* Beers, Henry Augustin.
Beers, Henry Augustin, 1847-1926
xBeers, Henry A.
Connecticut Wits, & Other Essays. AMS Pr.
The Connecticut Wits & Other Essays. Elliots
Bks.
The Connecticut Wits & Other Essays. R West.
A History of English Romanticism in the
Eighteenth Century. Arden Lib.
History of English Romanticism in the
Eighteenth Century. Dover.
History of English Romanticism in the
Eighteenth Century. Gordian.
History of English Romanticism in the
Eighteenth Century. R West.
Nathaniel Parker Willis. AMS Pr.
Nathaniel Parker Willis. Folcroft.
Nathaniel Parker Willis. Scholarly.
Beers, Henry P. *see* Beers, Henry Putney.
Beers, Henry Putney, 1907-
xBeers, Henry P.
The French & British in the Old Northwest: A
Bibliographical Guide to the Archive &
Manuscript Sources. Wayne St U Pr.
Spanish & Mexican Records of the American
Southwest: A Bibliographical Guide to
Archive & Manuscript Sources. U of Ariz Pr.
Beers, Roland F.
xBeers, Roland F.
ed. Mechanisms of Pain & Analgesic
Compounds. Raven.
Beers, V. Gilbert. *see* Beers, Victor Gilbert.
Beers, Victor Gilbert.
xBeers, Gilbert V.
Around the World with My Red Balloon.
Moody.
xBeers, V. Gilbert.
A Gaggle of Green Geese. Moody.
Honeyphants & Elebees. Moody.
The House in the Hole in the Side of the Tree.
Moody.
Over Buttonwood Bridge. Moody.
Under the Tagalong Tree. Moody.
Beery, Donald.
xBeery, Donald.
Call of the Mountains. McClain.
Beery, John R. *see* Beery, John Replogle.
Beery, John Replogle, 1909-
xBeery, John R.
Current Conceptions of Democracy. AMS Pr.
Beesley, Michael.
xBeesley, Michael.
Corporate Social Responsibility: A
Reassessment. Biblio Dist.
Beesly, Edward S. *see* Beesly, Edward Spencer.

Beesly, Edward Spencer, 1831-1915
xBeesly, Edward S.
Queen Elizabeth. Arno.
Queen Elizabeth. Folcroft.
Beeson, Kenneth. *see* Beeson, Kenneth C.
Beeson, Kenneth C.
xBeeson, Kenneth.
The Soil Factor in Nutrition: Animal &
Human. Dekker.
Beeson, Margaret. *see* Beeson, Margaret E.
Beeson, Margaret E.
xBeeson, Margaret.
Hispanic Writers in French Journals: An
Annotated Bibliography. Society Sp &
Sp-Am.
Beet, E. A. *see* Beet, Ernest Agar.
Beet, Ernest Agar.
xBeet, E. A.
Mathematical Astronomy for Amateurs.
Norton.
Beeton, Douglas R. *see* Beeton, Douglas Ridley.
Beeton, Douglas Ridley.
xBeeton, Douglas R.
A Dictionary of English Usage in Southern
Africa. Oxford U Pr.
Beeton, I. M. *see* Beeton, Isabella Mary (Mayson).
Beeton, Isabella Mary (Mayson).
xBeeton, I. M.
Hot & Cold Sweets. Soccer.
Beets, M. G. *see* Beets, Muus Gerrit Jan.
Beets, Muus Gerrit Jan.
xBeets, M. G.
ed. Structure-Activity Relationships in Human
Chemoreception. Burgess-Intl Ideas.
Beevers, L. *see* Beevers, Leonard.
Beevers, Leonard.
xBeevers, L.
Nitrogen Metabolism in Plants. Univ Park.
Beezley, P. C.
xBeezley, P. C.
They Have Sown the Wind. Munson Bks.
Begay, Keats.
xBegay, Laura A.
ed. Navajos & World War II. Navajo Coll Pr.
Begay, Laura A. *see* Begay, Keats.
Begemann, H. *see* Begemann, Herbert.
Begemann, Herbert.
xBegemann, H.
Atlas of Clinical Haematology. Springer-Verlag.
Begg, Paul.
xBegg, Paul.
Into Thin Air: People Who Disappear. David &
Charles.
Beggs, Donald L.
xBeggs, Donald L.
Measurement & Evaluation in the Schools.
HM.
Begin, Menachem. *see* Begin, Menahem.
Begin, Menahem, 1913-
xBegin, Menachem.
The Revolt. Nash Pub.
White Nights: The Story of a Prisoner in
Russia. Har-Row.
Begle, Edward G. *see* Begle, Edward Griffith.
Begle, Edward Griffith, 1914-
xBegle, Edward G.
The Mathematics of the Elementary School.
McGraw.
Begley, Edward R.
xBegley, Edward R.
Guide to Refractory & Glass Reactions. CBI
Pub.
Begley, Eve.
xBegley, Eve.
Of Scottish Ways. Har-Row.
xBegley, Evelyn M.
Of Scottish Ways. Dillon.
Begley, Evelyn M. *see* Begley, Eve.
Begley, Kathleen A.
xBegley, Kathleen A.

Deadline. Dell.
Deadline. Putnam.
Begnal, Michael H.
xBegnal, Michael H.
ed. A Conceptual Guide to Finnegans Wake.
Pa St U Pr.
Narrator & Character in "Finnegans Wake".
Bucknell U Pr.
Begner, Edith.
xBegner, Edith.
Accident of Birth. Avon.
Begner, Edith. *see* Begner, Edith P.
Begner, Edith P.
xBegner, Edith.
Son & Heir. Avon.
Bego, Mark.
xBego, Mark.
Barry Manilow. G&D.
Behague, Gerard.
xBehague, Gerard.
Music in Latin America: an Introduction. P-H.
Behan, P. O. *see* Behan, Peter O.
Behan, Peter O.
xBehan, P. O.
Clinical Neuroimmunology. Saunders.
Behari, Bepin.
xBehari, Bepin.
Economic Growth & Technological Change in
India. Intl Bk Dist.
Behbehani, Abbas M.
xBehbehani, Abbas M.
Human Viral, Bedsonial & Rickettsial Diseases:
A Diagnostic Handbook for Physicians. C C
Thomas.
Behee, John R. *see* Behee, John Richard.
Behee, John Richard.
xBehee, John R.
Hail to the Victors. J & J Bks.
Beheim, Martin.
xBeheim, Martin.
Chess with the Masters. Arc Bks.
Behling, Orlando.
xBehling, Orlando.
Organizational Behavior: Theory, Research &
Application. Allyn.
Behlmer, Rudy.
xBehlmer, Rudy.
Hollywood's Hollywood: The Movies About
the Movies. Citadel Pr.
Behm, Ernst G. *see* Behm, Ernst Gustav.
Behm, Ernst Gustav, 1892-
xBehm, Ernst G.
ed. Papacy Evaluated. Northwest Pub.
Behm, Marc.
xBehm, Marc.
The Eye of the Beholder. Dial.
The Queen of the Night. Avon.
Behn, Aphra. *see* Behn, Aphra (Amis).
Behn, Aphra (Amis).
xBehn, Aphra.
Oroonoko & Other Prose Narratives. Arno.
Behn, Harry.
xBehn, Harry.
tr. More Cricket Songs: Japanese Haiku.
HarBraceJ.
Two Uncles of Pablo. HarBraceJ.
Behnke, Albert R. *see* Behnke, Albert Richard.
Behnke, Albert Richard.
xBehnke, Albert R.
Evaluation & Regulation of Body Build &
Composition. P-H.
Behnke, Frances L.
xBehnke, Frances L.
The Natural History of Termites. Scribner.
Behnke, John.
xBehnke, John.
Stories of Jesus. Paulist Pr.
Behnke, John A.
xBehnke, John A.

ed. Challenging Biological Problems: Directions
Toward Their Solution. Oxford U Pr.

Behnke, Roy H., 1947-
xBehnke, Roy H.
The Herders of Cyrenaica: Ecology, Economy,
& Kinship Among the Bedouin of Eastern
Libya. U of Ill Pr.

Behnken, Eloise M., 1947-
xBehnken, Eloise M.
Thomas Carlyle: Calvinist Without the
Theology. U of Mo Pr.

Behnken, John W. *see* Behnken, John William.

Behnken, John William, 1884-
xBehnken, John W.
This I Recall. Concordia.

Behr, Edward, 1926-
xBehr, Edward.
The Algerian Problem. Greenwood.

Behr, Marcia W. *see* Behr, Marcia Ward.

Behr, Marcia Ward.
xBehr, Marcia W.
Drama Integrates Basic Skills: Lesson Plans for
the Learning Disabled. C C Thomas.

Behr, Marlyn J. *see* Behr, Merlyn J.

Behr, Merlyn J.
xBehr, Marlyn J.
Fundamentals of Elementary Mathematics
Geometry. Acad Pr.

Behrangi, Samad.
xBehrangi, Samad.
The Little Black Fish & Other Modern Persian
Stories. Three Continents.

Behrend, Arthur.
xBehrend, Arthur.
As from Kemmel Hill: An Adjutant in France
& Flanders, 1917 & 1918. Greenwood.

Behrend, William, 1861-1940
xBehrend, William.
Ludwig Van Beethoven's Pianoforte Sonatas.
AMS Pr.

Behrendt, Douglas M.
xBehrendt, Douglas M.
Patient Care in Cardiac Surgery. Little.

Behrendt, Leo, 1889-
xBehrendt, Leo.
Ethical Teaching of Hugo of Trimberg. AMS
Pr.

Behrens, C. B. *see* Behrens, Catherine Betty Abigail.

Behrens, C. E. *see* Behrens, Charles Frederick.

Behrens, Catherine Betty Abigail.
xBehrens, C. B.
The Ancien Regime. HarBraceJ.

Behrens, Charles Frederick.
xBehrens, C. E.
Atomic Medicine. Krieger.

Behrens, Helen K. *see* Behrens, Helen Kindler.

Behrens, Helen Kindler, 1922-
xBehrens, Helen K.
Diplomatic Dining. Times Bks.

Behrens, June.
xBehrens, June.
Can You Walk the Plank?. Childrens.
Canal Boats West. Childrens.
Colonial Farm. Childrens.
Death Valley. Childrens.
How I Feel. Childrens.
Lighthouse Family. Childrens.
Looking at Beasties. Childrens.
Looking at Children. Childrens.
Looking at Horses. Childrens.
True Book of Metric Measurement. Childrens.
Twisters. Childrens.

Behrens, Robert H., 1931-
xBehrens, Robert H.
Commercial Problem Loans: How to Identify,
Supervise & Collect the Problem Loan.
Bankers.

Behrensmeyer, Anna K.
xBehrensmeyer, Anna K.

ed. Fossils in the Making: Vertebrate
Taphonomy & Paleoecology. U of Chicago
Pr.

Behrman, Daniel.
xBehrman, Daniel.
Solar Energy: The Awakening Science. Little.

Behrman, Howard T. *see* Behrman, Howard Taft.

Behrman, Howard Taft.
xBehrman, Howard T.
Common Skin Diseases: Diagnosis &
Treatment. Grune.

Behrman, Jack N.
xBehrman, Jack N.
Industry Ties with Science & Technology
Policies in Developing Countries.
Oelgeschlager.
Overseas R & D Activities of Transnational
Companies. Oelgeschlager.
Regional Integration & the Trade of Latin
America. Comm Econ Dev.
Science & Technology for Development:
Corporate & Government Policies &
Practices. Oelgeschlager.

Behrman, Lucy. *see* Behrman, Lucy C.

Behrman, Lucy C.
xBehrman, Lucy.
Muslim Brotherhoods & Politics in Senegal.
Harvard U Pr.

Behrman, S. J. *see* Behrman, Samuel J.

Behrman, Samuel J.
xBehrman, S. J.
ed. Progress in Infertility. Little.

Behrmann, Polly.
xBehrmann, Polly.
Activities for Developing Visual Perception.
Acad Therapy.

Beichman, Arnold.
xBeichman, Arnold.
Nine Lies About America. Open Court.

Beidelman, William.
xBeidelman, William.
Story of the Pennsylvania Germans: Embracing
an Account of Their Origin, Their History,
Their Dialect. Gale.

Beidler, Peter G.
xBeidler, Peter G.
The American Indian in Short Fiction: An
Annotated Bibliography. Scarecrow.
Fig Tree John: An Indian in Fact & Fiction. U
of Ariz Pr.

Beier, Ernst G. *see* Beier, Ernst Gunter.

Beier, Ernst Gunter.
xBeier, Ernst G.
People-Reading: How We Control Others, How
They Control Us. Stein & Day.
People-Reading: How We Control Others, How
They Control Us. Warner Bks.
Silent Language of Psychotherapy: Social
Reinforcement of Unconscious Processes.
Aldine Pub.

Beier, Ulli.
xBeier, Ulli.
The Stolen Images. Cambridge U Pr.
ed. Words of Paradise: Poetry of Papua-New
Guinea. Unicorn Pr.

Beightler, C. *see* Beightler, Charles S.

Beightler, Charles S.
xBeightler, C.
jt. auth. Foundations of Optimization. P-H.
xBeightler, Charles S.
Applied Geometric Programming. Wiley.
Foundations of Optimization. P-H.

Beighton, Peter.
xBeighton, Peter.
Inherited Disorders of the Skeleton. Churchill.

Beigie, Carl E.
xBeigie, Carl E.
Inflation Is a Social Malady. Natl Planning.

Beijer, Agne.
xBeijer, Agne.

Court Theatres of Drottningholm & Gripsholm.
Arno.

Beik, Paul H. *see* Beik, Paul Harold.

Beik, Paul Harold, 1915-
xBeik, Paul H.
French Revolution. Walker & Co.

Beilby, M. H. *see* Beilby, Michael Harry.

Beilby, Michael Harry.
xBeilby, M. H.
Economics & Operational Research. Acad Pr.

Beilenson, Laurence W., 1899-
xBeilenson, Lawrence W.
Power Through Subversion. Pub Aff Pr.

Beilenson, Lawrence W. *see* Beilenson, Laurence W.

Beiler, Edna.
xBeiler, Edna.
Mattie Mae. Herald Pr.

Beilke, Marlan, 1940-
xBeilke, Marlan.
Shining Clarity: God & Man in the Works of
Robinson Jeffers. Quintessence.

Beilner, H.
xBeilner, H.
ed. Measuring, Modelling & Evaluating
Computer Systems: Proceedings of the Third
International Workshop on Modelling &
Performance Evaluation of Computer
Systems, Bonn. Elsevier.

Beim, George.
xBeim, George.
Principles of Modern Soccer. HM.

Beim, Jerrold.
xBeim, Jerrold.
Country School. Morrow.
Thin Ice. Morrow.

Beim, Lorraine. *see* Beim, Lorraine (Levey).

Beim, Lorraine (Levey), 1909-
xBeim, Lorraine.
Triumph Clear. HarBraceJ.
Two Is a Team. HarBraceJ.
Two Is a Team. HarBraceJ.

Beirne, Charles J. *see* Beirne, Charles Joseph.

Beirne, Charles Joseph.
xBeirne, Charles J.
The Problem of Americanization in the
Catholic Schools of Puerto Rico. U of PR Pr.

Beiser, Arthur.
xBeiser, Arthur.
Concepts of Modern Physics. McGraw.
The Earth. Silver.
Introduction to Earth Science. McGraw.
Modern Technical Physics.
Benjamin-Cummings.
The Proper Yacht. Intl Marine.
Proper Yacht. Macmillan.

Beisner, Monika.
xBeisner, Monika.
Fantastic Toys. Follett.

Beitler, Ethel J. *see* Beitler, Ethel Jane.

Beitler, Ethel Jane.
xBeitler, Ethel J.
Creating from Remnants: Stitchery with
Imperfect Fabrics. Sterling.
Design for You. Wiley.

Beitz, Charles R.
xBeitz, Charles R.
Political Theory & International Relations.
Princeton U Pr.

Beitz, Les. *see* Beitz, Lester V.

Beitz, Lester V.
xBeitz, Les.
Overlooked Treasures. A S Barnes.

Beitzinger, Alfons J.
xBeitzinger, Alfons J.
Edward G. Ryan: Lion of the Law. State Hist
Soc Wis.

Bejerot, Nils.
xBejerot, Nils.

Addiction & Society. C C Thomas.

Bekefi, George.
    xBekefi, George.
        Principles of Laser Plasmas. Wiley.

Beken, Frank.
    xBeken, Frank.
        The Glory of Sail. Dodd.

Beker, J. Christiaan. *see* Beker, Johan Christiaan.

Beker, Johan Christiaan, 1924-
    xBeker, J. Christiaan.
        Paul the Apostle: The Triumph of God in Life
        & Thought. Fortress.

Bekker, M. G. *see* Bekker, Mieczyslaw Gregory.

Bekker, Mieczyslaw Gregory.
    xBekker, M. G.
        Off-The-Road Locomotion: Research &
        Development in Terramechanics. U of Mich
        Pr.

Bekker, Paul, 1882-1937
    xBekker, Paul.
        Story of Music: An Historical Sketch of the
        Changes in Musical Form. AMS Pr.

Bekker, W. G. *see* Bekker, Willem Gerard.

Bekker, Willem Gerard.
    xBekker, W. G.
        Historical & Critical Review of Samuel Butlers'
        Literary Works. Haskell.

Bel Geddes, Joan.
    xBel Geddes, Joan.
        How to Parent Alone: A Guide for Single
        Parents. Continuum.

Belafonte, Dennis.
    xBelafonte, Dennis.
        The Films of Tyrone Power. Citadel Pr.

Belanger, Jerome. *see* Belanger, Jerome D.

Belanger, Jerome D.
    xBelanger, Jerome.
        The Homesteader's Handbook to Raising Small
        Livestock. Rodale Pr Inc.
        Raising the Homestead Hog. Rodale Pr Inc.
    xBelanger, Jerome D.
        The Homesteader's Handbook to Raising Small
        Livestock. Rodale Pr Inc.
    xBelanger, Jerry.
        Raising Milk Goats the Modern Way. Garden
        Way Pub.

Belanger, Jerry. *see* Belanger, Jerome D.

Belanger, Merlyn.
    xBelanger, Merlyn.
        On Religious Maturity. Philos Lib.

Belasco, David, 1853-1931
    xBelasco, David.
        Theatre Through Its Stage Door. Arno.

Belasco, J. A. *see* Belasco, James A.

Belasco, James A.
    xBelasco, J. A.
        Assessment of Change in Training & Therapy.
        McGraw.

Belasco, Warren J. *see* Belasco, Warren James.

Belasco, Warren James.
    xBelasco, Warren J.
        Americans on the Road: From Autocamp to
        Motel. MIT Pr.

Belcher, David W.
    xBelcher, David W.
        Compensation Administration. P-H.

Belcher, E. H. *see* Belcher, Ernest Hugh.

Belcher, Ernest Hugh.
    xBelcher, E. H.
        ed. Radioisotopes in Medical Diagnosis.
        Butterworths.

Belcher, R. *see* Belcher, Ronald.

Belcher, Richard. *see* Belcher, Richard P.

Belcher, Richard P., 1934-
    xBelcher, Richard.
        Layman's Guide to the Inerrancy Debate.
        Moody.

Belcher, Ronald.
    xBelcher, R.

        ed. Instrumental Organic Elemental Analysis.
        Acad Pr.

Belcher, Wyatt W. *see* Belcher, Wyatt Winton.

Belcher, Wyatt Winton, 1907-
    xBelcher, Wyatt W.
        Economic Rivalry Between St. Louis &
        Chicago, 1850-1880. AMS Pr.

Belden, Jack, 1910-
    xBelden, Jack.
        China Shakes the World. Monthly Rev.
        Still Time to Die. Da Capo.

Belden, Mary M. *see* Belden, Mary Megie.

Belden, Mary Megie, 1879-
    xBelden, Mary M.
        Dramatic Work of Samuel Foote. Shoe String.

Belderson, R. H.
    xBelderson, R. H.
        Sonographs of the Sea Floor: A Picture Atlas.
        Elsevier.

Belew, Richard. *see* Belew, Richard C.

Belew, Richard C., 1928-
    xBelew, Richard.
        How to Negotiate a Business Loan. Van Nos
        Reinhold.

Belfer, Nancy.
    xBelfer, Nancy.
        Designing in Stitching & Applique. Davis
        Mass.
        Designing in Stitching & Applique. P-H.

Belford. *see* Belford, James N.

Belford, James N.
    xBelford.
        Mauser Self Loading Pistol. Borden.

Belfrage, Cedric, 1904-
    xBelfrage, Cedric.
        Promised Land. Garland Pub.

Belgion, Montgomery, 1892-
    xBelgion, Montgomery.
        Human Parrot, & Other Essays. Arno.

Belgium. Parlement. Bibliotheque.
    xBelgium. Parliament. Library.
        Catalogue systematique de la Bibliotheque de la
        Chambre des representants. B Franklin.

Belgium. Parliament. Library. *see* Belgium. Parlement.
Bibliotheque.

Belgrad, Muzej Nikole Tesle.
    xTesla Museum.
        Nikola Tesla: Colorado Diary. Vanous.
        Nikola Tesla: Tribute. Vanous.

Belgrave, Charles. *see* Belgrave, Charles Dalrymple.

Belgrave, Charles Dalrymple, Sir, 1894-
    xBelgrave, Charles.
        The Pirate Coast. Intl Bk Ctr.

Beliaev, Aleksandr Romanovich, 1884-1942
    xBeliaev, Alexander.
        Professor Dowell's Head. Macmillan.

Beliaev, Alexander. *see* Beliaev, Aleksandr Romanovich.

Belinfante, F. J. *see* Belinfante, Frederik Jozef.

Belinfante, Frederik Jozef.
    xBelinfante, F. J.
        Survey of Hidden Variables Theories.
        Pergamon.

Beling, Willard A.
    xBeling, Willard A.
        Developing Nations: A Quest for a Model. Van
        Nos Reinhold.
        ed. King Faisal & the Modernisation of Saudi
        Arabia. Westview.

Belinkoff, Stanton.
    xBelinkoff, Stanton.
        Introduction to Respiratory Care. Little.

Belitt, Ben, 1911-
    xBelitt, Ben.

Adam's Dream: A Preface to Translation.
    Grove.
Adam's Dream: A Preface to Translation.
    Grove.
The Double Witness: Poems, 1970-1976.
    Princeton U Pr.
The Enemy Joy: New & Selected Poems. U of
    Chicago Pr.

Belk, Fred R. *see* Belk, Fred Richard.

Belk, Fred Richard, 1937-
    xBelk, Fred R.
        The Great Trek of the Russian Mennonites to
        Central Asia, 1880-1884. Herald Pr.

Belkin, Gary S.
    xBelkin, Gary S.
        Counseling: Directions in Theory & Practice.
        Kendall-Hunt.
        Educational Psychology: An Introduction. Wm
        C Brown.
        An Introduction to Counseling. Wm C Brown.
        Perspectives in Educational Psychology. Wm C
        Brown.
        Practical Counseling in the Schools. Wm C
        Brown.

Belkin, Samuel.
    xBelkin, Samuel.
        In His Image: The Jewish Philosophy of Man
        As Expressed in Rabbinic Tradition.
        Greenwood.

Belkind, Allen.
    xBelkind, Allen.
        ed. Dos Passos, the Critics & the Writer's
        Intention. S Ill U Pr.

Belknap, George N. *see* Belknap, George Nicholas.

Belknap, George Nicholas, 1905-
    xBelknap, George N.
        Oregon Imprints 1845-1870. U of Oreg Bks.

Belknap, Jeremy, 1744-1798
    xBelknap, Jeremy.
        History of New Hampshire. Arno.
        The History of New Hampshire. Johnson Repr.

Belknap, Michael R. *see* Belknap, Michal R.

Belknap, Michal R.
    xBelknap, Michael R.
        Cold War Political Justice: The Smith Act, the
        Communist Party, & American Civil
        Liberties. Greenwood.

Belknap, Waldron P. *see* Belknap, Waldron Phoenix.

Belknap, Waldron Phoenix, 1899- 1949
    xBelknap, Waldron P.
        De Peyster Genealogy. Harvard U Pr.

Bell. *see* Bell, Mary L.

Bell & Howell Audio-Visual Products Division. *see* Bell
and Howell Company. Audio-Visual Products
Division.

Bell, A. *see* Bell, Alan.

Bell, Alan.
    xBell, A.
        ed. Syllables & Segments. Elsevier.

Bell, Alan P.
    xBell, Alan P.
        Homosexualities: A Study of Diversity Among
        Men & Women. S&S.

Bell, Alexander G. *see* Bell, Alexander Graham.

Bell, Alexander Graham, 1847-1922
    xBell, Alexander G.
        Memoir Upon the Formation of a Deaf Variety
        of the Human Race. Alexander Graham.

**Bell and Howell Company. Audio-Visual Products
Division.**
    xBell & Howell Audio-Visual Products Division.
        Master It! with the Language Master. Pitman
        Learning.

Bell, Aubrey F. *see* Bell, Aubrey Fitz Gerald.

Bell, Aubrey Fitz Gerald, 1882-1950
    xBell, Aubrey F.
        Portuguese Literature. Oxford U Pr.

Bell, Bill D.
    xBell, Bill D.

Contemporary Social Gerontology: Significant
   Developments in the Field of Aging. C C
   Thomas.
Bell, Bob, 1925-
   xBell, Bob.
      Hunting the Long Tailed Bird. Freshet Pr.
Bell, C. see Bell, Clive.
Bell, C. F. see Bell, Colin Frank.
Bell, Charles. see Bell, Charles Alfred.
Bell, Charles Alfred, Sir, 1870-1945
   xBell, Charles.
      Grammar of Colloquial Tibetan. Dover.
      Grammar of Colloquial Tibetan. Peter Smith.
Bell, Charles G.
   xBell, Charles G.
      The Half Gods. Ultramarine Pub.
Bell, Clive, 1881-1964
   xBell, C.
      Proust. Gordon Pr.
   xBell, Clive.
      Civilization & Old Friends. U of Chicago Pr.
      Proust. Arden Lib.
      Proust. Folcroft.
      Since Cezanne. Arno.
Bell, Colin.
   xBell, Colin.
      Community Studies: An Introduction to the
         Sociology of the Local Community. Allen
         Unwin.
      ed. Doing Sociological Research. Free Pr.
      ed. Inside the Whale: Ten Personal Accounts
         of Social Research. Pergamon.
Bell, Colin E.
   xBell, Colin E.
      Quantitative Methods for Administration.
         Irwin.
Bell, Colin F. see Bell, Colin Frank.
Bell, Colin Frank.
   xBell, C. F.
      Syntheses & Physical Studies of Inorganic
         Compounds. Pergamon.
   xBell, Colin F.
      Principles & Applications of Metal Chelation.
         Oxford U Pr.
Bell, Coral.
   xBell, Coral.
      The Diplomacy of Detente: The Kissinger Era.
         St Martin.
Bell, Coral. see Bell, Coral Mary.
Bell, Coral Mary.
   xBell, Coral.
      Negotiation from Strength: A Study in the
         Politics of Power. Greenwood.
Bell, Daniel.
   xBell, Daniel.
      Coming of Post-Industrial Society: A Venture
         in Social Forecasting. Basic.
      The Cultural Contradictions of Capitalism.
         Basic.
      Marxian Socialism in the United States.
         Princeton U Pr.
Bell, David, 1930-
   xBell, David A.
      Fundamentals of Electronic Devices. Reston.
Bell, David. see Bell, David A.
Bell, David A., 1930-
   xBell, David.
      Fundamentals of Electric Circuits. Reston.
   xBell, David A.
      Solid State Pulse Circuits. Reston.
Bell, David A. see Bell, David.
Bell, David V. see Bell, David V. J.
Bell, David V. J.
   xBell, David V.
      Power, Influence & Authority: An Essay in
         Political Linguistics. Oxford U Pr.
Bell, Derrick. see Bell, Derrick A.
Bell, Derrick A.
   xBell, Derrick.

Race, Racism, & American Law. Little.
Bell, E. A. see Bell, Ernst Arthur.
Bell, Eric T. see Bell, Eric Temple.
Bell, Eric Temple, 1883-1960
   xBell, Eric T.
      Numerology. Hyperion Conn.
Bell, Ernst Arthur.
   xBell, E. A.
      ed. Secondary Plant Products. Springer-Verlag.
Bell, Evelyn.
   xBell, Evelyn.
      Industry & Resources. Heinemann Ed.
Bell, Frederick H.
   xBell, Frederick H.
      Teaching and Learning Mathematics (in
         Secondary Schools). LKA Inc.
Bell, Frederick W.
   xBell, Frederick W.
      Food from the Sea: The Economics & Politics
         of Ocean Fisheries. Westview.
Bell, George. see Bell, George I.
Bell, George I.
   xBell, George.
      ed. Theoretical Immunology. Dekker.
   xBell, George I.
      Nuclear Reactor Theory. Krieger.
Bell, George K. see Bell, George Kennedy Allen.
**Bell, George Kennedy Allen, Bp. of Chichester,
1883-1958**
   xBell, George K.
      The Kingship of Christ: The Story of the World
         Council of Churches. Greenwood.
Bell, Gertrude.
   xBell, Gertrude.
      First Crop. Independence Pr.
      Where Runs the River. Independence Pr.
Bell, Gertrude L. see Bell, Gertrude Lowthian.
Bell, Gertrude Lowthian, 1868-1926
   xBell, Gertrude L.
      Syria: The Desert & the Sown. Arno.
Bell, Gordon. see Bell, Gordon B.
Bell, Gordon B.
   xBell, Gordon.
      The Golden Troubador. McGraw.
Bell, Gwen, 1934-
   xBell, Gwen.
      ed. Strategies for Human Settlements: Habitat
         & Environment. U Pr of Hawaii.
Bell, H. C. see Bell, Herbert Clifford.
Bell, H. I. see Bell, Harold Idris.
Bell, H. Idris. see Bell, Harold Idris.
Bell, Harold Idris, Sir, 1879-
   xBell, H. I.
      Cults & Creeds in Graeco-Roman Egypt. Ares.
   xBell, H. Idris.
      Literature & Life: Addresses to the English
         Association. Kennikat.
      Literature & Life: Addresses to the English
         Association. R West.
Bell, Harry. see Bell, Harry H.
Bell, Harry H.
   xBell, Harry.
      Teacher Centers and Inservice Education. Phi
         Delta Kappa.
Bell, Henry H. see Bell, Henry Hesketh Joudou.
Bell, Henry Hesketh Joudou, Sir, 1864-1952
   xBell, Henry H.
      Obeah: Witchcraft in the West Indies. Negro U
         Pr.
Bell, Herbert Clifford.
   xBell, H. C.
      Guide to British West Indian Archive
         Materials, in London & in the Islands, for the
         History of the United States. Kraus Repr.
Bell, Herbert Clifford Francis, 1881-1966
   xBell, H. C.
      Woodrow Wilson & the People. Shoe String.
Bell, Hershel M., 1906-
   xBell, Hershel M.

Rangeland Management for Livestock
   Production. U of Okla Pr.
Bell, Howard H. see Bell, Howard Holman.
Bell, Howard Holman, 1913-
   xBell, Howard H.
      Survey of the Negro Convention Movement.
         Arno.
Bell, Inge P. see Bell, Inge Powell.
Bell, Inge Powell.
   xBell, Inge P.
      CORE & the Strategy of Nonviolence. Phila
         Bk Co.
Bell, Irene W. see Bell, Irene Wood.
Bell, Irene Wood.
   xBell, Irene W.
      Basic Media Skills Through Games. Libs Unl.
Bell, J. Bowyer, 1931-
   xBell, J. Bowyer.
      Assassin!. St Martin.
      On Revolt: Strategies of National Liberation.
         Harvard U Pr.
Bell, James C. see Bell, James Christy.
Bell, James Christy, 1889-
   xBell, James C.
      Opening a Highway to the Pacific, 1838-1846.
         AMS Pr.
Bell, John F. see Bell, John Fred.
Bell, John Fred, 1898-
   xBell, John F.
      A History of Economic Thought. Krieger.
Bell, John L. see Bell, John Lane.
Bell, John Lane.
   xBell, John L.
      Boolean-Valued Models & Independence Proofs
         in Set Theory. Oxford U Pr.
Bell, Joseph N. see Bell, Joseph Norment.
Bell, Joseph Norment.
   xBell, Joseph N.
      Love Theory in Later Hanbalite Islam. State U
         NY Pr.
Bell, Josephine, 1897-
   xBell, Josephine.
      Stroke of Death. Walker & Co.
      Treachery in Type. Walker & Co.
Bell, Ken.
   xBell, Ken.
      Not in Vain. U of Toronto Pr.
Bell, Landon C. see Bell, Landon Covington.
Bell, Landon Covington, 1880-1960
   xBell, Landon C.
      Poe & Chivers. Folcroft.
Bell, Leland V.
   xBell, Leland V.
      In Hitler's Shadow: The Anatomy of American
         Nazism. Kennikat.
Bell, Margaret E. see Bell, Margaret Elizabeth.
Bell, Margaret Elizabeth, 1898-
   xBell, Margaret E.
      Love Is Forever. Morrow.
Bell, Marion L.
   xBell, Marion L.
      Crusade in the City: Revivalism in
         Nineteenth-Century Philadelphia. Bucknell U
         Pr.
Bell, Martin.
   xBell, Martin.
      Nenshu & the Tiger: Parables of Life & Death.
         Seabury.
Bell, Martin L.
   xBell, Martin L.
      Marketing: Concepts & Strategy. HM.
Bell, Mary L.
   xBell.
      Speed Typing. SW Pub.
Bell, Max S.
   xBell, Max S.

Algebraic & Arithmetic Structures: A Concrete
Approach for Elementary School Teachers.
Free Pr.

Bell, Millicent.
xBell, Millicent.
Edith Wharton & Henry James: The Story of
Their Friendship. Braziller.
Marquand: An American Life. Little.

Bell, Norman T.
xBell, Norman T.
Developing Audio-Visual Instructional Modules
for Vocational & Technical Training. Educ
Tech Pubns.

Bell, Norman W.
xBell, Norman W.
ed. Modern Introduction to the Family. Free
Pr.

Bell, O. O.
xBell, O. O.
Goaling up. Everest Pub.

Bell, Oliver.
xBell, Oliver.
ed. America's Changing Population. Wilson.

Bell, Paul A.
xBell, Paul A.
Environmental Psychology. Saunders.

Bell, Philip W.
xBell, Philip W.
Economic Theory: An Integrated Text with
Special Reference to Tropical Africa & Other
Developing Areas. Oxford U Pr.

Bell, Quentin.
xBell, Quentin.
On Human Finery. Schocken.

Bell, R. C. see Bell, Robert Charles.
Bell, R. L.
xBell, R. L.
Negative Electron Affinity Devices. Oxford U
Pr.

Bell, R. P. see Bell, Ronald Percy.
Bell, Reginald, 1894-
xBell, Reginald.
Public School Education of Second-Generation
Japanese in California. Arno.

Bell, Richard O.
xBell, Richard O.
Auditions & Scenes from Shakespeare. Armado
& Moth.

Bell, Richard Q.
xBell, Richard Q.
Child Effects on Adults. Halsted Pr.
Child Effects on Adults. U of Nebr Pr.

Bell, Robert. see Bell, Robert E.
Bell, Robert C. see Bell, Robert Charles.
Bell, Robert Charles, 1917-
xBell, R. C.
Board & Table Games from Many
Civilizations. Dover.
xBell, Robert C.
The Boardgame Book. Knapp Pr.

Bell, Robert E.
xBell, Robert.
Patterns of Education in the British Isles. Allen
Unwin.

Bell, Robert E. see Bell, Robert Eugene.
Bell, Robert Eugene, 1914-
xBell, Robert E.
Oklahoma Archaeology: An Annotated
Bibliography. U of Okla Pr.

Bell, Robert P.
xBell, Robert P.
Typewriting Office Practice for Colleges. SW
Pub.

Bell, Robert R.
xBell, Robert R.
Marriage & Family Interaction. Dorsey.

Bell, Robert W. see Bell, Robert Wayne.
Bell, Robert Wayne.
xBell, Robert W.

ed. Maternal Influences & Early Behavior.
Spectrum Pub.

Bell, Ronald Percy.
xBell, R. P.
The Proton in Chemistry. Cornell U Pr.

Bell, Roseann P.
xBell, Roseann P.
Sturdy Black Bridges: Visions of Black Women
in Literature. Doubleday.

Bell, Rudolf. see Bell, Rudolph M.
Bell, Rudolph M.
xBell, Rudolf.
Party & Faction in American Politics: The
House of Representatives, 1789-1801.
Greenwood.
xBell, Rudolph M.
Fate & Honor, Family & Village: Demographic
& Cultural Change in Rural Italy Since
Eighteen Hundred. U of Chicago Pr.

Bell, S. Peter.
xBell, S. Peter.
Dissertations on British History, 1815-1914:
An Index to British & American Theses.
Scarecrow.

Bell, Sadie.
xBell, Sadie.
Church, the State, & Education in Virginia.
Arno.

Bell, Sallie L. see Bell, Sallie Lee.
Bell, Sallie Lee.
xBell, Sallie L.
The Barrier. Zondervan.
Light from the Hill. Zondervan.
The Long Search. Zondervan.

Bell, Stephen, 1864-
xBell, Stephen.
Rebel, Priest & Prophet: A Biography of Dr.
Edward McGlynn. Hyperion Conn.

Bell, Terrel H. see Bell, Terrel Howard.
Bell, Terrel Howard, 1921-
xBell, Terrel H.
Performance Accountability System for School
Administrators. P-H.

Bell, Thomas, 1903-1961.
xBell, Thomas.
Out of This Furnace. U of Pittsburgh Pr.

Bell, Trevor.
xBell, Trevor.
Industrial Decentralisation in South Africa.
Oxford U Pr.

Bell, Walter G. see Bell, Walter George.
Bell, Walter George, 1867-1942.
xBell, Walter G.
Great Fire of London in 1666. Greenwood.
The Great Plague in London in 1665. AMS Pr.

Bell, Welden E.
xBell, Welden E.
Orofacial Pains: Differential Diagnosis. Year
Bk Med.

Bell, Wendell.
xBell, Wendell.
Decisions of Nationhood: Political & Social
Development in the British Caribbean. U of
Denver Intl.

Bell, Whitfield J. see Bell, Whitfield Jenks.
Bell, Whitfield Jenks.
xBell, Whitfield J.
The Colonial Physician & Other Essays. N
Watson.

Bell, Winthrop P. see Bell, Winthrop Pickard.
Bell, Winthrop Pickard.
xBell, Winthrop P.
Foreign Protestants & the Settlement of Nova
Scotia: The History of a Piece of Arrested
British Policy in the Eighteenth Century. U
of Toronto Pr.

Bellace, Janice R.
xBellace, Janice R.

The Landrum-Griffin Act: Twenty Years of
Federal Protection of Union Members'
Rights. Indus Res Unit-Wharton.

Bellack, Alan S.
xBellack, Alan S.
Introduction to Clinical Psychology. Oxford U
Pr.

Bellack, Arno A.
xBellack, Arno A.
ed. Theory & Research in Teaching. Tchrs
Coll.

Bellagio Conference. see Conference on Regional
Economic Development, 1st, Bellagio, Italy, 1960.
Bellairs, Angus. see Bellairs, Angus D'A.
Bellairs, Angus D'A.
xBellairs, Angus.
Life of Reptiles. Universe.

Bellairs, John.
xBellairs, John.
The House with a Clock in Its Walls. Dell.
The House with a Clock in Its Walls. Dial.
The Letter, the Witch & the Ring. Dell.
The Letter, the Witch, & the Ring. Dial.

Bellairs, Ruth.
xBellairs, Ruth.
Developmental Processes in Higher
Vertebrates. U of Miami Pr.

Bellak, Leopold, 1916-
xBellak, Leopold.
ed. A Concise Handbook of Community
Psychiatry & Community Mental Health.
Grune.
ed. Disorders of the Schizophrenic Syndrome.
Basic.
Ego Functions in Schizophrenics, Neurotics, &
Normals: A Systematic Study of Conceptual,
Diagnostic, & Therapeutic Aspects. Wiley.
Overload: The New Human Condition. Human
Sci Pr.

Bellamann, Katherine J. see Bellamann, Katherine Jones.
Bellamann, Katherine Jones.
xBellamann, Katherine J.
Two Sides of a Poem. AMS Pr.

Bellamy, A. J. see Bellamy, Anthony J.
Bellamy, Anthony J.
xBellamy, A. J.
Introduction to Conservation of Orbital
Symmetry: A Programmed Text. Longman.

Bellamy, Charles. see Bellamy, Charles Joseph.
Bellamy, Charles Joseph, 1852-1910
xBellamy, Charles.
Experiment in Marriage. Schol Facsimiles.

Bellamy, Edward, 1850-1898
xBellamy, Edward.
Looking Backward. Am Repr-Rivercity Pr.
Looking Backward. Hendricks House.
Looking Backward. NAL.
Looking Backward. AMSCO Sch.
Looking Backward 2000-1887. Harvard U Pr.
Looking Backward: 2000-1887. HM.
Religion of Solidarity. Folcroft.
Talks on Nationalism. Arno.

Bellamy, G. Thomas.
xBellamy, T.
Vocational Rehabilitation of Severely
Handicapped Persons. Univ Park.

Bellamy, J. G.
xBellamy, J. G.
Law of Treason in England in the Later Middle
Ages. Cambridge U Pr.
xBellamy, John.
The Tudor Law of Treason: An Introduction. U
of Toronto Pr.

Bellamy, John. see Bellamy, J. G.
Bellamy, Joyce M.
xBellamy, Joyce M.
ed. Dictionary of Labour Biography. Kelley.

Bellamy, l J.
xBellamy, L. J.

The Infrared Spectra of Complex Molecules.
  Methuen Inc.
Bellamy, R. see Bellamy, Robert Lowe.
Bellamy, R. L. see Bellamy, Robert Lowe.
Bellamy, Ralph, 1904-
  xBellamy, Ralph.
    When the Smoke Hit the Fan. Doubleday.
Bellamy, Robert L. see Bellamy, Robert Lowe.
Bellamy, Robert Lowe.
  xBellamy, R.
    Byron the Man. Gordon Pr.
  xBellamy, R. L.
    Byron, the Man. Arden Lib.
  xBellamy, Robert L.
    Byron the Man. Folcroft.
Bellamy, T. see Bellamy, G. Thomas.
Bellamy, Virginia W. see Bellamy, Virginia Woods.
Bellamy, Virginia Woods.
  xBellamy, Virginia W.
    And the Evening & the Morning. Wheelwright.
Bellanca, James A., 1937-
  xBellanca, James A.
    Values & the Search for Self. NEA.
Bellante, Donald.
  xBellante, Donald.
    Labor Economics: Choice in Labor Markets.
      McGraw.
Bellanti, Joseph A., 1934-
  xBellanti, Joseph A.
    Immunology II. Saunders.
Bellany, Ian.
  xBellany, Ian.
    Australia in the Nuclear Age: National
      Defence & National Development. Intl Schol
      Bk Serv.
Bellarmino, Roberto F. see Bellarmino, Roberto
  Francesco Romolo.
**Bellarmino, Roberto Francesco Romolo, Saint,
  1542-1621**
  xBellarmino, Roberto F.
    De Laicis: Or, the Treatise on Civil
      Government. Hyperion Conn.
Bellasis, Edward, 1852-1922
  xBellasis, Edward.
    Cherubini: Memorials Illustrative of His Life &
      Work. Da Capo.
Belle, R. see Belle, Rene.
Belle, Rene.
  xBelle, R.
    Promenades en France. HR&W.
Bellegarde, Ida.
  xBellegarde, Ida R.
    Haiku Reflections. Bell Ent.
    Idylls of the Seasons. Bell Ent.
Bellegarde, Ida R. see Bellegarde, Ida.
Bellenger, Danny.
  xBellenger, Danny N.
    Qualitative Research in Marketing. Am Mktg.
Bellenger, Danny N.
  xBellenger, Danny N.
    Marketing Research: A Management
      Information Approach. Irwin.
Bellenger, Danny N. see Bellenger, Danny.
Belleni-Morante, A. see Belleni-Morante, Aldo.
Belleni-Morante, Aldo.
  xBelleni-Morante, A.
    Applied Semigroups & Evolution Equations.
      Oxford U Pr.
Beller, Anne S. see Beller, Anne Scott.
Beller, Anne Scott.
  xBeller, Anne S.
    Fat & Thin: A Natural History of Obesity.
      FS&G.
    Fat & Thin: A Natural History of Obesity.
      McGraw.
Bellet, Samuel, 1899-
  xBellet, Samuel.

Clinical Disorders of the Heart Beat. Lea &
  Febiger.
Bellevue Art Museum. see Bellevue Art Museum,
  Bellevue Wash.
Bellevue Art Museum, Bellevue Wash.
  xBellevue Art Museum.
    Glen Alps Retrospective: The Collagraph Idea,
      Nineteen Fifty Six to Nineteen Eighty. U of
      Wash Pr.
Bellew, Frank.
  xBellew, Frank.
    The Art of Amusing. Arno.
Bellg, Albert, 1953-
  xBellg, Albert.
    Tactical Soccer for Players & Coaches. A S
      Barnes.
Belli, Melvin M, 1907-
  xBelli, Melvin M.
    Modern Damages. Bobbs.
Bellinger, Alfred R. see Bellinger, Alfred Raymond.
Bellinger, Alfred Raymond, 1893-
  xBellinger, Alfred R.
    Spires & Poplars. AMS Pr.
Bellingrath, George C. see Bellingrath, George Council.
Bellingrath, George Council, 1897-
  xBellingrath, George C.
    Qualities Associated with Leadership in the
      Extra-Curricular Activities of the High
      School. AMS Pr.
Bellis, Herbert F.
  xBellis, Herbert F.
    Architectural Drafting. McGraw.
Bellis, Paul.
  xBellis, Paul.
    Marxism & the USSR: The Theory of
      Proletarian Dictatorship & the Marxist
      Analysis of Soviet Society. Humanities.
Bellisimo, Lou.
  xBellisimo, Lou.
    The Bowler's Manual. P-H.
Belliveau, Fred.
  xBelliveau, Fred.
    Understanding Human Sexual Inadequacy.
      Bantam.
Bellman, Beryl L. see Bellman, Beryl Larry.
Bellman, Beryl Larry.
  xBellman, Beryl L.
    A Paradigm for Looking: Cross-Cultural
      Research with Visual Media. Ablex Pub.
Bellman, Richard. see Bellman, Richard Ernest.
Bellman, Richard E. see Bellman, Richard Ernest.
Bellman, Richard Ernest, 1920-
  xBellman, Richard.
    An Introduction to Artificial Intelligence: Can
      Computers Think?. Boyd & Fraser.
    An Introduction to Invariant Imbedding. Wiley.
    Modern Elementary Differential Equations.
      A-W.
  xBellman, Richard E.
    Adaptive Control Processes: A Guided Tour.
      Princeton U Pr.
    Applied Dynamic Programming. Princeton U
      Pr.
    Differential-Difference Equations. Acad Pr.
Bellman, Samuel I. see Bellman, Samuel Irving.
Bellman, Samuel Irving, 1926-
  xBellman, Samuel I.
    Marjorie Kinnan Rawlings. Twayne.
Bello, Ignacio.
  xBello, Ignacio.
    Contemporary Basic Mathematical Skills.
      Har-Row.
Bello, Nino Lo. see Lo Bello, Nino.
Belloc, Hilaire. see Belloc, Hilaire Joseph Hilaire Pierre
  Belloc.
Belloc, Hilaire Joseph Hilaire Pierre Belloc, 1870-1953
  xBelloc, Hilaire.

Bad Child's Book of Beasts. Peter Smith.
Characters of the Reformation. Arno.
The Crisis of Civilization. Greenwood.
Danton: A Study. AMS Pr.
The French Revolution. Arden Lib.
Great Heresies. Arno.
The Green Overcoat. Greenwood.
Hills & the Sea. Greenwood.
How the Reformation Happened. Peter Smith.
Marie Antoinette. Arno.
Matilda Who Told Lies & Was Burned to
  Death. Dial.
On Anything. Arno.
On Everything. Arno.
On Nothing & Kindred Subjects. Arno.
On Something. Arno.
On the Place of Gilbert Chesterton in English
  Letters. Patmos Pr.
The Path to Rome. Allen Unwin.
Places. Arno.
Richelieu: A Study. Arden Lib.
This & That, & the Other. Arno.
Bellone, Enrico.
  xBellone, Enrico.
    The World on Paper: Studies on the Second
      Scientific Revolution. MIT Pr.
Belloni, Frank P.
  xBelloni, Frank P.
    ed. Faction Politics: Political Parties &
      Factionalism in Comparative Perspective.
      ABC-Clio.
Bellony-Rewald, Alice.
  xBellony-Rewald, Alice.
    The Lost World of the Impressionists. NYGS.
Bellos, David.
  xBellos, David.
    Balzac Criticism in France, 1850-1900: The
      Making of a Reputation. Oxford U Pr.
Bellow, Saul.
  xBellow, Saul.
    Dangling Man. NAL.
    Dangling Man. Vanguard.
    ed. Great Jewish Short Stories. Dell.
    Humboldt's Gift. Avon.
    Humboldt's Gift. Viking Pr.
    The Portable Saul Bellow. Penguin.
    The Portable Saul Bellow. Viking Pr.
Bellows, John G. see Bellows, John Goldfreed.
Bellows, John Goldfreed, 1903-
  xBellows, John G.
    ed. Cataract & Abnormalities of the Lens.
      Grune.
Belluco, Umberto.
  xBelluco, Umberto.
    Organometallic & Coordination Chemistry of
      Platinum. Acad Pr.
Bellush, Bernard, 1917-
  xBellush, Bernard.
    The Failure of the NRA. Norton.
    Franklin D. Roosevelt As Governor of New
      York. AMS Pr.
Bellwood, Peter. see Bellwood, Peter S.
Bellwood, Peter S.
  xBellwood, Peter.
    Man's Conquest of the Pacific: The Prehistory
      of Southeast Asia & Oceania. Oxford U Pr.
    The Polynesians: Prehistory of an Island
      People. Thames Hudson.
Belman, H. S. see Belman, Harry S.
Belman, Harry S.
  xBelman, H. S.
    My Career Guidebook. Glencoe.
Belmont, David E., 1937-
  xBelmont, David E.
    Approaching Greek. Univ Microfilms.
Belmont, Nicole.
  xBelmont, Nicole.

Arnold Van Gennep: The Creator of French
    Ethnography. U of Chicago Pr.
Belmont, Perry, 1850-1947
    xBelmont, Perry.
        Return to Secret Party Funds. Arno.
Belmonte, Thomas, 1946-
    xBelmonte, Thomas.
        The Broken Fountain. Columbia U Pr.
Belnap, Nuel D.
    xBelnap, Nuel D.
        The Logic of Questions & Answers. Yale U Pr.
Beloff, M. see Beloff, Max.
Beloff, Max, 1913-
    xBeloff, M.
        Thomas Jefferson & American Democracy.
            Verry.
    xBeloff, Max.
        American Federal Government. Oxford U Pr.
        Foreign Policy & the Democratic Process.
            Greenwood.
        Foreign Policy & the Democratic Process.
            Johns Hopkins.
        Future of British Foreign Policy. Taplinger.
        The Government of the United Kingdom:
            Political Authority in a Changing Society.
            Norton.
        The Great Powers: Essays in Twentieth
            Century Politics. Greenwood.
        Public Order & Popular Disturbances:
            1660-1714. Biblio Dist.
        Soviet Policy in the Far East, 1944-1951.
            Arno.
        Thomas Jefferson & American Democracy.
            Macmillan.
Beloff, Michael, 1942-
    xBeloff, Michael.
        The Plateglass Universities Fairleigh
            Dickinson.
Belohlavek, John M.
    xBelohlavek, John M.
        George Mifflin Dallas: Jacksonian Patrician. Pa
            St U Pr.
Belotserkovskii, Sergei M. see Belotserkovskii, Sergei
    Mikhailovich.
Belotserkovskii, Sergei Mikhailovich.
    xBelotserkovskii, Sergei M.
        Theory of Thin Wings in Subsonic Flow.
            Plenum Pub.
Belove, Charles.
    xBelove, Charles.
        Systems & Circuits for Electrical Engineering
            Technology. McGraw.
Belpre, Pura.
    xBelpre, Pura.
        Ote: A Puerto Rican Folk Tale. Pantheon.
        The Rainbow-Colored Horse. Warne.
Belshaw, Cyril S.
    xBelshaw, Cyril S.
        Changing Melanesia: Social Economics of
            Culture Contact. Greenwood.
        The Sorcerer's Apprentice: An Anthropology
            of Public Policy. Pergamon.
        Under the Ivi Tree: Society & Economic
            Growth in Rural Fiji. U of Cal Pr.
Belsley, David A.
    xBelsley, David A.
        Regression Diagnostics: Identifying Influential
            Data & Sources of Collinearity. Wiley.
Belson, William A.
    xBelson, William A.
        Television Violence & the Adolescent Boy.
            Lexington Bks.
Belsterling, C. A. see Belsterling, Charles A.
Belsterling, Charles A.
    xBelsterling, C. A.
        Fluidic Systems Design. Krieger.
Belt, Elmer, 1893-
    xBelt, Elmer.

Leonardo the Anatomist. Greenwood.
Belt, Guy Chester, d. 1969
    xBelt, Guy Chester.
        Love's Answer from Eternity. Exposition.
Belt, T. Edwin. see Belt, Thomas Edwin.
Belt, Thomas Edwin, 1913-
    xBelt, T. Edwin.
        Plants Unsafe for Winemaking. British Bk Ctr.
Belth, Joseph M.
    xBelth, Joseph M.
        Life Insurance: A Consumer's Handbook. Ind
            U Pr.
Belth, Marc.
    xBelth, Marc.
        The Process of Thinking. Longman.
Belth, Nathan C.
    xBelth, Nathan C.
        A Promise to Keep: A Narrative of the
            American Encounter with Anti-Semitism.
            Times Bks.
Belting, Natalia. see Belting, Natalia Maree.
Belting, Natalia Maree.
    xBelting, Natalia.
        Our Fathers Had Powerful Songs. Dutton.
        Whirlwind Is a Ghost Dancing. Dutton.
Belting, Paul E. see Belting, Paul Everett.
Belting, Paul Everett, 1886-
    xBelting, Paul E.
        Development of the Free Public High School in
            Illinois to 1860. Arno.
Belton, Howard C.
    xBelton, Howard C.
        Under Eleven Governors. Binford.
Beltrametti, Franco.
    xBeltrametti, Franco.
        ed. An Alleghany Star Route Anthology. SBD.
Beltrami, E. J. see Beltrami, Edward J.
Beltrami, Edward J.
    xBeltrami, E. J.
        Algorithmic Approach to Nonlinear Analysis &
            Optimization. Acad Pr.
Beltsville Symposia in Agricultural Research. see
    Beltsville Symposium in Agricultural Research.
Beltsville Symposium in Agricultural Research.
    xBeltsville Symposia in Agricultural Research.
        Biosystematics in Agriculture. Halsted Pr.
Beltz, George F. see Beltz, George Frederick.
Beltz, George Frederick, 1777-1841
    xBeltz, George F.
        Memorials of the Most Noble Order of the
            Garter from Its Foundation to the Present
            Time. AMS Pr.
Belves, Pierre.
    xBelves, Pierre.
        Enjoying the World of Art. Lion.
Belytschko, T.
    xBelytschko, Ted.
        ed. Finite Element Analysis of Transient
            Nonlinear Structural Behavior: AMD, Vol.
            14. ASME.
Belytschko, Ted. see Belytschko, T.
Belz, Carl.
    xBelz, Carl.
        The Story of Rock. Har-Row.
        The Story of Rock. Oxford U Pr
Belz, Herman.
    xBelz, Herman.
        Reconstructing the Union: Theory & Policy
            During the Civil War. Greenwood.
Belzer. see Belzer, Jack.
Belzer, Jack.
    xBelzer.
        Encyclopedia of Computer Science &
            Technology. Dekker.
    xBelzer, Jack.
        ed. Encyclopedia of Computer Science &
            Technology. Dekker.
Bem, Robyn.
    xBem, Robyn.

Everyone's Guide to Home Composting. Van
    Nos Reinhold.
Bemelmans, Ludwig, 1898-1962
    xBemelmans, Ludwig.
        illus. Parsley. Har-Row.
        Parsley. Har-Row.
Bemis, E. W. see Bemis, Edward Webster.
Bemis, Edward W. see Bemis, Edward Webster.
Bemis, Edward Webster, 1860-1930
    xBemis, E. W.
        Cooperation in New England. Johnson Repr.
        Cooperation in the Middle States. Johnson
            Repr.
    xBemis, Edward W.
        Cooperation in New England. AMS Pr.
        Cooperation in New England. Arno.
        Cooperation in the Middle States. AMS Pr.
Bemis, Samuel F. see Bemis, Samuel Flagg.
Bemis, Samuel Flagg, 1891-
    xBemis, Samuel F.
        Diplomacy of the American Revolution. Ind U
            Pr.
        Diplomacy of the American Revolution. Peter
            Smith.
        The Hussey-Cumberland Mission & American
            Independence: An Essay in the Diplomacy of
            the American Revolution. Peter Smith.
Bemis, Virginia.
    xBemis, Virginia.
        Energy Guide: A Directory of Information
            Resources. Garland Pub.
Bemiss, Elijah.
    xBemiss, Elijah.
        The Dyer's Companion. Dover.
        The Dyer's Companion. Peter Smith.
Bemont, Charles, 1848-1939
    xBemont, Charles.
        Simon De Montfort, Earl of Leicester,
            1208-1265. Greenwood.
Bemporad, Jules.
    xBemporad, Jules R.
        Child Development in Normality &
            Psychopathology. Brunner-Mazel.
Bemporad, Jules R. see Bemporad, Jules.
Ben-Amos, D. see Ben-Amos, Dan.
Ben-Amos, Dan.
    xBen-Amos, D.
        ed. Folklore: Performance & Communication.
            Mouton.
    xBen-Amos, Dan.
        Sweet Words: Storytelling Events in Benin. Inst
            Study Human.
Ben-Asher, Naomi.
    xBen-Asher, Naomi.
        ed. Junior Jewish Encyclopedia. Shengold.
Ben-Meir, Alon, 1937-
    xBen-Meir, Alon.
        Israel: The Challenge of the Fourth Decade.
            Cyrco Pr.
        Israel: The Challenge of the Fourth Decade.
            Irvington.
Benabo, Brian.
    xBenabo, Brian.
        Moonlight Kingdom. St Martin.
Benacerraf. see Benacerraf, Baruj.
Benacerraf, Baruj, 1920-
    xBenacerraf.
        Immunogenetics & Immunodeficiency. Univ
            Park.
    xBenacerraf, Baruj.
        Textbook of Immunology. Williams & Wilkins.
Benade, A. H. see Benade, Arthur H.
Benade, Arthur H.
    xBenade, A. H.
        Fundamentals of Musical Acoustics. Oxford U
            Pr.
    xBenade, Arthur H.

135

Horns, Strings & Harmony. Doubleday.
Horns, Strings, & Harmony. Greenwood.
Benarde, Anita.
xBenarde, Anita.
illus. Games from Many Lands. Lion.
The Pumpkin Smasher. Walker & Co.
Benarde, Melvin. *see* Benarde, Melvin A.
Benarde, Melvin A.
xBenarde, Melvin.
Our Precarious Habitat. Norton.
xBenarde, Melvin A.
ed. Disinfection. Dekker.
Benario, Herbert W.
xBenario, Herbert W.
An Introduction to Tacitus. U of Ga Pr.
Benary-Isbert, Margot.
xBenary-Isbert, Margot.
Ark. HarBraceJ.
The Ark. HarBraceJ.
Long Way Home. HarBraceJ.
Under a Changing Moon. HarBraceJ.
Benasutti, Marion.
xBenasutti, Marion.
No Steady Job for Papa. Vanguard.
Benbow, Audrey M.
xBenbow, Audrey M.
How to Raise & Train a Scottish Deerhound.
TFH Pubns.
Bence, Richard, 1943-
xBence, Richard.
Handbook of Clinical Endodontics. Mosby.
Bench, Johnny.
xBench, Johnny.
Catch You Later: The Autobiography of
Johnny Bench. Har-Row.
Benchimol, Alberto.
xBenchimol, Alberto.
Non-Invasive Diagnostic Techniques in
Cardiology. Williams & Wilkins.
Vectorcardiography. Krieger.
Benchley, Nathaniel.
xBenchley, Nathaniel.
The Deep Dives of Stanley Whale. Har-Row.
Flying Lesson of Gerald Pelican. Har-Row.
George the Drummer Boy. Har-Row.
Ghost Named Fred. Har-Row.
A Ghost Named Fred. Har-Row.
Gone & Back. Har-Row.
Kilroy & the Gull. Har-Row.
Kilroy & the Gull. Har-Row.
Only Earth & Sky Last Forever. Har-Row.
Only Earth & Sky Last Forever. Har-Row.
Oscar Otter. Har-Row.
Oscar Otter. Har-Row.
Portrait of a Scoundrel. Doubleday.
Portrait of a Scoundrel. G K Hall.
Portrait of a Scoundrel. G K Hall.
Running Owl the Hunter. Har-Row.
Strange Disappearance of Arthur Cluck.
Har-Row.
The Strange Disappearance of Arthur Cluck.
Har-Row.
Sweet Anarchy. Doubleday.
Benchley, Peter.
xBenchley, Peter.
The Deep. Bantam.
The Deep. Doubleday.
The Deep. G K Hall.
The Island. Bantam.
The Island. Doubleday.
Benda, Harry J. *see* Benda, Harry Jindrich.
Benda, Harry Jindrich.
xBenda, Harry J.
The Crescent & the Rising Sun: Indonesian
Islam Under the Japanese Occupation
1942-1945. Mouton.
Bendann, E. *see* Bendann, Effie.
Bendann, Effie.
xBendann, E.

Death Customs: An Analytical Study of Burial
Rites. Dawson Pub.
Death Customs: An Analytical Study of Burial
Rites. Gordon Pr.
xBendann, Effie.
Death Customs: An Analytical Study of Burial
Rites. Gale.
Bendat, Julius S.
xBendat, Julius S.
Principles & Applications of Random Noise
Theory. Krieger.
Random Data: Analysis & Measurement
Procedures. Wiley.
Bendau, Clifford P., 1950-
xBendau, Clifford P.
Still Worlds Collide: Philip Wylie & the End of
the American Dream. Borgo Pr.
Bendavid, Avrom.
xBendavid, Avrom.
Regional Economic Analysis for Practitioners:
An Introduction to Common Descriptive
Methods. Praeger.
Bender, A. E. *see* Bender, Arnold E.
Bender, Arnold. *see* Bender, Arnold E.
Bender, Arnold E.
xBender, A. E.
Dictionary of Nutrition & Food Technology.
Chem Pub.
xBender, Arnold.
Food Processing & Nutrition. Acad Pr.
Pocket Encyclopedia of Calories & Nutrition.
S&S.
xBender, Arnold E.
Dictionary of Nutrition & Food Technology.
Butterworths.
xBender, Arnold F.
The Facts of Food. Oxford U Pr.
Bender, Arnold F. *see* Bender, Arnold E.
Bender, Averam B. *see* Bender, Averam Burton.
Bender, Averam Burton, 1891-
xBender, Averam B.
The March of Empire: Frontier Defense in the
Southwest, 1848-1860. Greenwood.
Bender, Carl M.
xBender, Carl M.
Advanced Mathematical Methods for Scientists
& Engineers. McGraw.
Bender, David A.
xBender, David A.
Amino Acid Metabolism. Wiley.
Bender, David L.
xBender, David L.
ed. Liberals & Conservatives: A Debate on the
Welfare State. Greenhaven.
Bender, Edward A., 1942-
xBender, Edward A.
An Introduction to Mathematical Modeling.
Wiley.
Bender, Filmore. *see* Bender, Filmore Edmund.
Bender, Filmore Edmund.
xBender, Filmore.
Systems Analysis for the Food Industry. AVI.
Bender, Gerald J.
xBender, Gerald J.
Angola Under the Portuguese: The Myth & the
Reality. U of Cal Pr.
Bender, Harold S. *see* Bender, Harold Stauffer.
Bender, Harold Stauffer, 1897-1962
xBender, Harold S.
Anabaptists & Religious Liberty in the
Sixteenth Century. Fortress.
Bender, Henry E., 1937-
xBender, Henry E.
Uintah Railway: The Gilsonite Route.
Howell-North.
Bender, James F. *see* Bender, James Frederick.
Bender, James Frederick, 1905-
xBender, James F.

How to Sell Well: The Art & Science of
Professional Salesmanship. McGraw.
How to Talk Well. McGraw.
Bender, John B.
xBender, John B.
Spenser and Literary Pictorialism. Princeton U
Pr.
Bender, Leonard F.
xBender, Leonard F.
Prostheses & Rehabilitation After Arm
Amputation. C C Thomas.
Bender, Lucy E. *see* Bender, Lucy Ellen.
Bender, Lucy Ellen.
xBender, Lucy E.
Outside World. Herald Pr.
Bender, Lynn D. *see* Bender, Lynn Darrell.
Bender, Lynn Darrell.
xBender, Lynn D.
The Politics of Hostility: Castro's Revolution &
United States Policy. Inter Am U Pr.
Bender, Michael.
xBender, Michael.
Disadvantaged Preschool Children: A Source
Book for Teachers. P H Brookes.
Bender, Morris B.
xBender, Morris B.
ed. Approach to Diagnosis in Modern
Neurology. Grune.
Bender, Peter, 1923-
xBender, Peter.
East Europe in Search of Security. Johns
Hopkins.
Bender, Thomas.
xBender, Thomas.
Community & Social Change in America.
Rutgers U Pr.
Bender, Todd K.
xBender, Todd K.
A Concordance to Conrad's Heart of
Darkness. Garland Pub.
Concordance to Conrad's Secret Agent.
Garland Pub.
Gerard Manley Hopkins: The Classical
Background and Critical Reception of His
Work. Johns Hopkins.
Bender, Urie A.
xBender, Urie A.
Hurt in the Heart. Herald Pr.
Soldiers of Compassion. Herald Pr.
Bendick, J. *see* Bendick, Jeanne.
Bendick, Jeanne.
xBendick, J.
Ecology. Watts.
xBendick, Jeanne.
The Consumer's Catalog of Economy &
Ecology. McGraw.
Exploring an Ocean Tide Pool. Garrard.
The First Book of Airplanes. Watts.
illus. First Book of Automobiles. Watts.
illus. First Book of Space Travel. Watts.
illus. How to Make a Cloud. Enslow Pubs.
illus. Human Senses. Watts.
illus. Living Things. Watts.
Mathematics Illustrated Dictionary: Facts,
Figures & People, Including the New Math.
McGraw.
illus. Measuring. Watts.
The Mystery of Man-Made Men: Will They
Replace Us?. McGraw.
illus. Observation. Watts.
illus. Putting the Sun to Work. Garrard.
Solids, Liquids & Gases. Watts.
Bendinelli, Cesare.
xBendinelli, Cesare.
The Entire Art of Trumpet Playing. Brass Pr.
Bendiner, Elmer.
xBendiner, Elmer.

The Fall of Fortresses: A Personal Account of
the Most Daring & Deadly American Air
Battles of World War II. Putnam.

Bendiner, Robert.
xBendiner, Robert.
Politics of Schools: A Crisis in
Self-Government. Har-Row.

Bending, C. W.
xBending, C. W.
Communication & the Schools. Pergamon.

Benditt, Theodore M.
xBenditt, Theodore M.
Law As Rule & Principle: Problems of Legal
Philosophy. Stanford U Pr.

Bendix, G.
xBendix, G.
Press Point Therapy. Avon.

Bendix, Reinhard.
xBendix, Reinhard.
Kings or People: Power & the Mandate to
Rule. U of Cal Pr.
Max Weber: An Intellectual Portrait. U of Cal
Pr.
Nation-Building & Citizenship: Studies of Our
Changing Social Order. U of Cal Pr.
Work & Authority in Industry: Ideologies of
Management in the Course of
Industrialization. U of Cal Pr.

Bendixen, H. H.
xBendixen, H. H.
Respiratory Care. Mosby.
Bendz, Ernst. see Bendz, Ernst Paulus.
Bendz, Ernst P. see Bendz, Ernst Paulus.

Bendz, Ernst Paulus, 1880-
xBendz, Ernst.
Influence of Pater & Matthew Arnold in the
Prose Writings of Oscar Wilde. Folcroft.
xBendz, Ernst P.
Joseph Conrad: An Appreciation. Folcroft.

Benecke, Gerhard.
xBenecke, Gerhard.
Germany in the Thirty Years War. St Martin.

Benedetta, Mary.
xBenedetta, Mary.
The Street Markets of London. Arno.
Benedetti, Robert. see Benedetti, Robert L.

Benedetti, Robert L.
xBenedetti, Robert.
The Actor at Work. P-H.
xBenedetti, Robert L.
Actor at Work. P-H.

Benedict, Howard M.
xBenedict, Howard M.
Calculator Techniques for Real Estate. Realtors
Natl.

Benedict, Lynn.
xBenedict, Lynn.
Whisper of Heather. PB.

Benedict, Madeline, 1895-
xBenedict, Madeline.
That Bridge Again. Golden Quill.
Benedict, Michael L. see Benedict, Michael Les.

Benedict, Michael Les.
xBenedict, Michael L.
A Compromise of Principle: Congressional
Republicans & Reconstruction 1863-1869.
Norton.
The Impeachment & Trial of Andrew Johnson.
Norton.

Benedict, Rex, 1920-
xBenedict, Rex.

The Ballad of Cactus Jack. Pantheon.
Good Luck Arizona Man. Pantheon.
Last Stand at Goodbye Gulch. Pantheon.

Benedict, Robert P.
xBenedict, Robert P.
Fundamentals of Temperature, Pressure, &
Flow Measurements. Wiley.
Handbook of Generalized Gas Dynamics. IFI
Plenum.
Benedict, Ruth. see Benedict, Ruth Fulton.
Benedict, Ruth F. see Benedict, Ruth Fulton.

Benedict, Ruth Fulton, 1887-1948
xBenedict, Ruth.
An Anthropologist at Work: Writings of Ruth
Benedict. Greenwood.
Tales of the Cochiti Indians. Gordon Pr.
Tales of the Cochiti Indians. Scholarly.
xBenedict, Ruth F.
Concept of the Guardian Spirit in North
America. Kraus Repr.
Benedictis, Daniel J. De. see DeBenedictis, Daniel J.

Benedictus, David.
xBenedictus, David.
The Rabbi's Wife. Fawcett.
The Rabbi's Wife. M Evans.

Benedikt, Michael.
xBenedikt, Michael.
Night Cries. Columbia U Pr.

Benefield, June.
xBenefield, June.
Laughing to Keep from Crying. Gulf Pub.
Beneke, E. S. see Beneke, Everett Smith.

Beneke, Everett Smith.
xBeneke, E. S.
Medical Mycology Manual. Burgess.

Beneke, Raymond R.
xBeneke, Raymond R.
Linear Programming Applications to
Agriculture. Iowa St U Pr.

Benell, Julie.
xBenell, Julie.
Let's Eat at Home. Shoal Creek Pub.
Benes, V. E. see Benes, Vaclav E.
Benes, Vaclav. see Benes, Vaclav E.

Benes, Vaclav E.
xBenes, V. E.
Mathematical Theory of Connecting Networks
& Telephone Traffic. Acad Pr.
xBenes, Vaclav.
General Stochastic Processes in the Theory of
Queues. A-W.

Benet, George.
xBenet, George.
A Place in Colusa. Miles & Weir.

Benet, Laura.
xBenet, Laura.
Famous New England Authors. Dodd.
When William Rose, Stephen Vincent & I
Were Young. Dodd.
Benet, Mary K. see Benet, Mary Kathleen.

Benet, Mary Kathleen.
xBenet, Mary K.
The Politics of Adoption. Free Pr.
Benet, Stephen V. see Benet, Stephen Vincent.

Benet, Stephen Vincent, 1898-1943
xBenet, Stephen V.
Devil & Daniel Webster. HR&W.
Spanish Bayonet. Scholarly.

Benet, Sula, 1903-
xBenet, Sula.
Song, Dance, & Customs of Peasant Poland.
AMS Pr.
Benet, W. R. see Benet, William Rose.
Benet, William R. see Benet, William Rose.

Benet, William Rose, 1886-1950
xBenet, W. R.
Stephen Vincent Benet. Porter.
xBenet, William R.

First Person Singular. Scholarly.
The Prose & Poetry of Elinor Wylie. Arden
Lib.
Prose & Poetry of Elinor Wylie. Folcroft.
ed. Reader's Encyclopedia. T Y Crowell.
Stephen Vincent Benet. Folcroft.
Benevolo, Leonard. see Benevolo, Leonardo.

Benevolo, Leonardo.
xBenevolo, Leonard.
Architecture of the Renaissance. Westview.
xBenevolo, Leonardo.
Origins of Modern Town Planning. MIT Pr.
Benezet, Louis T. see Benezet, Louis Tomlinson.

Benezet, Louis Tomlinson, 1915-
xBenezet, Louis T.
General Education in the Progressive College.
Arno.

Benfey, Theodor, 1809-1881
xBenfey, Theodore.
Geschichte der Sprachwissenschaft und
Orientalischen Philologie in Deutschland Seit
Dem Anfange Des Neunzehnten
Jahrhunderts. Johnson Repr.
Benfey, Theodore. see Benfey, Theodor.

Benfield, Warren.
xBenfield, Warren A.
The Art of Double Bass Playing. Summy.
Benfield, Warren A. see Benfield, Warren.

Benford, Gregory.
xBenford, Gregory.
If the Stars Are Gods. Berkley Pub.
If the Stars Are Gods. Berkley Pub.
Shiva Descending. Avon.
The Stars in Shroud. Berkley Pub.

Benge, Ken.
xBenge, Ken.
The Art of Juggling. Anderson World.
Benge, Ronald. see Benge, Ronald C.

Benge, Ronald C.
xBenge, Ronald.
Libraries & Cultural Change. Shoe String.

Bengelsdorf, Winnie.
xBengelsdorf, Winnie.
Ethnic Studies in Higher Education. Arno.

Bengis, Ingrid.
xBengis, Ingrid.
I Have Come Here to Be Alone. NAL.
I Have Come Here to Be Alone. S&S.

Bengtson, Hermann, 1909-
xBengtson, Hermann.
Introduction to Ancient History. U of Cal Pr.

Bengtson, Phil.
xBengtson, Phil.
Packer Dynasty. Doubleday.

Bengtsson, Gerda.
xBengtsson, Gerda.
Flower Designs in Cross Stitch. Van Nos
Reinhold.

Bengtsson, Hans.
xBengtsson, Hans.
Orienteering for Sport & Pleasure. Greene.
Benham, Allen R. see Benham, Allen Rogers.

Benham, Allen Rogers, 1879-
xBenham, Allen R.
English Literature from Widsith to the Death
of Chaucer: A Source Book. Arno.
Benhase, Carl. see Benhase, Carl K.

Benhase, Carl K.
xBenhase, Carl.
Ohio High School Football. P-H.

Benice, Daniel D.
xBenice, Daniel D.
Arithmetic & Algebra. P-H.
Introduction to Computers & Data Processing.
P-H.
Mathematics: Ideas & Applications. Acad Pr.
Modern Business Data Processing. P-H.
Precalculus Algebra & Trigonometry. P-H.

Benitez, Fernando, 1911-
xBenitez, Fernando.

Century After Cortes. U of Chicago Pr.
In the Magic Land of Peyote. U of Tex Pr.
In the Magic Land of Peyote. Warner Bks.
Benitez, Frank.
  xBenitez, Frank.
    Practical Spanish for the Health Professions.
    Pioneer Pub Co.
Benitez, Mario A.
  xBenitez, Mario A.
    The Education of the Mexican American: A
    Selected Bibliography. Natl Clearinghse
    Bilingual Ed.
Benjamin, Asher, 1773-1845
  xBenjamin, Asher.
    American Builder's Companion: Or, a System
    of Architecture, Particularly Adapted to the
    Present Style of Building. Dover.
    The American Builder's Companion: Or, a
    System of Architecture Particularly Adapted
    to the Present Style of Building. Scholarly.
    The Practical House Carpenter: Being a
    Complete Development of the Grecian
    Orders of Architecture. Scholarly.
Benjamin, Ben E., 1944-
  xBenjamin, Ben E.
    Sports Without Pain. Summit Bks.
Benjamin, Bernard, 1910-
  xBenjamin, Bernard.
    Demographic Analysis. Allen Unwin.
Benjamin, Bruce.
  xBenjamin, Bruce.
    Atlas of Paediatric Endoscopy: Upper
    Respiratory Tract & Oesophagus. Oxford U
    Pr.
Benjamin, C. see Benjamin, Carol Lea.
Benjamin, Carol L. see Benjamin, Carol Lea.
Benjamin, Carol Lea.
  xBenjamin, C.
    Running Basics. P-H.
  xBenjamin, Carol L.
    illus. Dog Training for Kids. Wanderer Bks.
    Dog Training for Kids. Howell Bk.
Benjamin, Claude, Pseud.
  xBenjamin, Claude.
    Medical Itch. Astor-Honor.
Benjamin, David.
  xBenjamin, David.
    The Idol. Berkley Pub.
    The Idol. Putnam.
Benjamin, Gerald.
  xBenjamin, Gerald.
    Race Relations & the New York City
    Commission on Human Rights. Cornell U Pr.
Benjamin, Jules R.
  xBenjamin, Jules R.
    A Student's Guide to History. St Martin.
Benjamin, Lewis S. see Benjamin, Lewis Saul.
Benjamin, Lewis Saul.
  xBenjamin, Lewis S.
    ed. Great German Short Stories. Arno.
    South Sea Bubble. B Franklin.
Benjamin, Park, 1849-1922
  xBenjamin, Park.
    A History of Electricity. Arno.
Benjamin, Roger. see Benjamin, Roger W.
Benjamin, Roger W.
  xBenjamin, Roger.
    The Limits of Politics: Collective Goods &
    Political Change in Postindustrial Societies. U
    of Chicago Pr.
Benjamin, S. G. see Benjamin, Samuel Greene Wheeler.
Benjamin, Samuel G. see Benjamin, Samuel Greene
  Wheeler.
Benjamin, Samuel Greene Wheeler, 1837-1914
  xBenjamin, S. G.
    Art in America: A Critical & Historical Sketch.
    Garland Pub.
  xBenjamin, Samuel G.

Persia. Arno.
Benjamin, Thomas.
  xBenjamin, Thomas E.
    Techniques & Materials of Tonal Music: With
    an Introduction to Twentieth Century
    Techniques. HM.
Benjamin, Thomas E. see Benjamin, Thomas.
Benjamin, Walter, 1892-1940
  xBenjamin, Walter.
    Illuminations. Schocken.
Benjamin, William P., 1935-
  xBenjamin, William P.
    Plastic Tooling: Techniques & Applications.
    McGraw.
Benjaminson, Peter.
  xBenjaminson, Peter.
    The Story of Motown. Grove.
Benke, William, 1927-
  xBenke, William.
    All About Land Investment. McGraw.
Benkert, Joseph W.
  xBenkert, Joseph W.
    Introduction to Aviation Science. P-H.
Benn, Alfred W. see Benn, Alfred William.
Benn, Alfred William, 1843-1915
  xBenn, Alfred W.
    Early Greek Philosophy. Kennikat.
Benn, M. B. see Benn, Maurice B.
Benn, Maurice B., 1914-
  xBenn, M. B.
    The Drama of Revolt: A Critical Study of
    Georg Buchner. Cambridge U Pr.
Benn, S. I. see Benn, Stanley I.
Benn, Stanley I.
  xBenn, S. I.
    ed. Rationality & the Social Sciences:
    Contributions to the Philosophy &
    Methodology of the Social Sciences.
    Routledge & Kegan.
Bennassar, Bartolome.
  xBennassar, Bartolome.
    The Spanish Character: Attitudes & Mentalities
    from the Sixteenth to the Nineteenth
    Century. U of Cal Pr.
Benne, Kenneth D. see Benne, Kenneth Dean.
Benne, Kenneth Dean, 1908-
  xBenne, Kenneth D.
    Conception of Authority: An Introductory
    Study. Russell.
    Education for Tragedy: Essays in Disenchanted
    Hope for Modern Man. U Pr of Ky.
Benner, George.
  xBenner, George.
    Footprints: A Humanistic View of Science
    Education. Interstate.
Benner, Judith A. see Benner, Judith Ann.
Benner, Judith Ann.
  xBenner, Judith A.
    Lone Star Rebel. Blair.
Benner, Patricia.
  xBenner, Patricia.
    The New Nurse's Work Entry: A Troubled
    Sponsorship. Tiresias Pr.
Bennet, Harold L.
  xBennet, Harold L.
    Glimpse at Wall Street & Its Markets:
    Descriptions of Important Railroad &
    Industrial Properties. Greenwood.
Bennett. see Bennett, Corwin.
Bennett, A. E. see Bennett, Albert Edward.
Bennett, A. Wayne. see Bennett, Archie Wayne.
Bennett, Addison C.
  xBennett, Addison C.
    Improving Management Performance in Health
    Care Institutions: A Total Systems Approach.
    Am Hospital.
Bennett, Alan, 1934-
  xBennett, Alan.

The Old Country. Merrimack Bk Serv.
Bennett, Albert Edward.
  xBennett, A. E.
    ed. Recent Advances in Community Medicine.
    Churchill.
Bennett, Annette, 1889-
  xBennett, Annette.
    A Comparative Study of Subnormal Children in
    Elementary Grades. AMS Pr.
Bennett, Archie Wayne, 1937-
  xBennett, A. Wayne.
    Introduction to Computer Simulation. West
    Pub.
Bennett, Arnold. see Bennett, Arnold Enoch.
Bennett, Arnold Enoch, 1867-1931
  xBennett, Arnold.
    Compiled by The Arnold Bennett Calendar.
    Arno.
    The Author's Craft. Arno.
    Books & Persons: Being Comments on a Past
    Epoch, 1908-1911. Greenwood.
    The Bright Island. Arno.
    Buried Alive. Arno.
    Clayhanger. Arno.
    Denry the Audacious. Arno.
    Frank Swinnerton: Personal Sketches :
    Together with Notes and Comments on the
    Novels of Frank Swinnerton. Folcroft.
    The Grand Babylon Hotel. Arno.
    The Grim Smile of the Five Towns. Arno.
    Hilda Lessways. Arno.
    Honeymoon: A Comedy in Three Acts.
    Scholarly.
    How to Live on 24 Hours a Day. Arno.
    How to Make the Best of Life. Arno.
    The Human Machine. Arno.
    Imperial Palace. Arno.
    Journal of Arnold Bennett. Arno.
    Journal of Things New & Old. Arno.
    Lilian. Arno.
    Married Life. Arno.
    The Matador of the Five Towns & Other
    Stories. Arno.
    Matador of the Five Towns & Other Stories.
    Scholarly.
    The Night Visitor & Other Stories. Arno.
    Old Wives' Tale. Academy Chi Ltd.
    The Old Wives' Tale. Arno.
    The Pretty Lady. Arno.
    Pretty Lady. Scholarly.
    The Price of Love. Arno.
    Tales of the Five Towns. Arno.
    These Twain. Arno.
    The Truth About an Author. Arno.
Bennett, Barbara.
  xBennett, Barbara.
    The Beggar's Virtue. St Martin.
Bennett, Benjamin, 1939-
  xBennett, Benjamin.
    Modern Drama & German Classicism:
    Renaissance from Lessing to Brecht. Cornell
    U Pr.
Bennett, Bob, 1936-
  xBennett, Robert.
    Raising Rabbits the Modern Way. Garden Way
    Pub.
Bennett, Brian C. see Bennett, Brian Carey.
Bennett, Brian Carey.
  xBennett, Brian C.
    Sutivan: A Dalmatian Village in Social &
    Economic Transition. R & E Res Assoc.
    Sutivan: A Dalmatian Village in Social &
    Economic Transition. Ragusan Pr.
Bennett, Bruce L. see Bennett, Bruce Lanyon.
Bennett, Bruce Lanyon.
  xBennett, Bruce L.
    Comparative Physical Education & Sport. Lea
    & Febiger.
Bennett, C. Richard. see Bennett, Charles Richard.
Bennett, Carl A. see Bennett, Carl Allen.

Bennett, Carl Allen.
xBennett, Carl A.
ed. Evaluation & Experiment: Some Critical
Issues in Assessing Social Programs (Based
Upon a Symposium). Acad Pr.
Bennett, Charles E. *see* Bennett, Charles Edwin.
Bennett, Charles Edwin, 1858-1921
xBennett, Charles E.
Critique of Some Recent Subjunctive Theories.
Johnson Repr.
Bennett, Charles Richard, 1938-
xBennett, C. Richard.
Conscious Sedation in Dental Practice. Mosby.
Bennett, Chester C. *see* Bennett, Chester Clarke.
Bennett, Chester Clarke, 1906-
xBennett, Chester C.
An Inquiry into the Genesis of Poor Reading.
AMS Pr.
Bennett, Corwin.
xBennett.
Spaces for People: Human Factors in Design.
P-H.
Bennett, D. R. *see* Bennett, Donald Raymond.
Bennett, David. *see* Bennett, David C.
Bennett, David C.
xBennett, David.
Spatial & Temporal Uses of English
Prepositions: An Essay in Stratificational
Semantics. Longman.
Bennett, Dennis. *see* Bennett, Dennis J.
Bennett, Dennis J.
xBennett, Dennis.
Trinity of Man. Logos.
Bennett, Dink.
xBennett, Dink.
Living Reflections. Standard Pub.
Bennett, Donald Raymond, 1926-
xBennett, D. R.
ed. Atlas of Electroencephalography in Coma
& Cerebral Death: EEG at the Bedside or in
the Intensive Care Unit. Raven.
Bennett, Dorothea.
xBennett, Dorothea.
The Maynard Hayes Affair. Coward.
Bennett, Dudley.
xBennett, Dudley.
TA & the Manager. Am Mgmt.
Bennett, Dwight.
xBennett, Dwight.
Legend in the Dust. Manor Bks.
The Texans. Doubleday.
The Texans. Pinnacle Bks.
Bennett, E. J. *see* Bennett, Edward John.
Bennett, E. W. *see* Bennett, Ernest Walter.
Bennett, Earl. *see* Bennett, Earl Dean.
Bennett, Earl Dean.
xBennett, Earl.
Business Policy: Case Problems of the General
Manager. Merrill.
Bennett, Edna.
xBennett, Edna.
Nature Photography Simplified. Amphoto.
Bennett, Edna M. *see* Bennett, Edna Mae.
Bennett, Edna Mae.
xBennett, Edna M.
Turquoise Jewelry of the Indians of the
Southwest. Turquoise Bks.
Bennett, Edward John, 1928-
xBennett, E. J.
Fluids for Anesthesia & Surgery in the
Newborn & Infant. C C Thomas.
Bennett, Edward W.
xBennett, Edward W.
German Rearmament & the West, 1932-1933.
Princeton U Pr.
Bennett, Emerson, 1822-1905
xBennett, Emerson.

Forest Rose: A Tale of the Frontier. Ohio U
Pr.
The Prairie Flower. Irvington.
Bennett, Ernest N. *see* Bennett, Ernest Nathaniel.
Bennett, Ernest Nathaniel, Sir, 1868-1947
xBennett, Ernest N.
Apparitions & Haunted Houses: A Survey of
Evidence. Gale.
Bennett, Ernest Walter.
xBennett, E. W.
Structural Concrete Elements. Methuen Inc.
Bennett, F. Lawrence.
xBennett, F. Lawrence.
Critical Path Precedence Networks: A
Handbook on Activity-on-Node Networking
for the Construction Industry. Van Nos
Reinhold.
Bennett, Frederick.
xBennett, Frederick.
Cataloguing in Practice: The Organisation of
Book Acquisition in Libraries. Shoe String.
Bennett, G. V. *see* Bennett, Gareth Vaughan.
Bennett, Gareth Vaughan.
xBennett, G. V.
The Tory Crisis in Church & State 1688-1730:
The Career of Francis Atterbury, Bishop of
Rochester. Oxford U Pr.
Bennett, George, 1912-
xBennett, George.
In His Healing Steps. Judson.
When the Mental Patient Comes Home.
Westminster.
Bennett, George N.
xBennett, George N.
The Realism of William Dean Howells,
1889-1920. Vanderbilt U Pr.
Bennett, Gordon. *see* Bennett, Gordon A.
Bennett, Gordon A.
xBennett, Gordon.
ed. China's Finance & Trade: A Policy Reader.
M E Sharpe.
Huadong: The Story of a Chinese People's
Commune. Westview.
Bennett, Gordon C.
xBennett, Gordon C.
From Nineveh to Now: Three Dramatic
Fantasies Based on the Old Testament.
Bethany Pr.
Readers Theatre Comes to Church. John Knox.
Bennett, H. *see* Bennett, Harry.
Bennett, H. S. *see* Bennett, Henry Stanley.
Bennett, Hal Z. *see* Bennett, Harold.
Bennett, Hank.
xBennett, Hank.
The Complete Shortwave Listener's Handbook.
Tab Bks.
Bennett, Harold, 1936-
xBennett, Hal Z.
Sewing for the Outdoors. Potter.
Bennett, Harold C.
xBennett, Harold C.
God's Awesome Challenge. Broadman.
Bennett, Harry, 1895-
xBennett, H.
Practical Emulsions. Chem Pub.
xBennett, Harry.
ed. Concise Chemical & Technical Dictionary.
Chem Pub.
Bennett, Henry S. *see* Bennett, Henry Stanley.
Bennett, Henry Stanley, 1889-
xBennett, H. S.
England from Chaucer to Caxton. Folcroft.
xBennett, Henry S.
ed. England from Chaucer to Caxton. Arno.
England from Chaucer to Caxton. R West.
Bennett, Howard F.
xBennett, Howard F.
Precision Power: The First Half Century of
Bodine Electric Company. Arno.
Bennett, Hugh H. *see* Bennett, Hugh Hammond.

Bennett, Hugh Hammond, 1881-1960
xBennett, Hugh H.
Soil Conservation. Arno.
Bennett, Iva.
xBennett, Iva.
The Prudent Diet. D White.
Bennett, J. *see* Bennett, Jonathan Francis.
Bennett, James C.
xBennett, James C.
Drug Abuse & What We Can Do About It. C
C Thomas.
Bennett, James D.
xBennett, James D.
Frederick Jackson Turner. Twayne.
Bennett, James G. *see* Bennett, James Gordon.
Bennett, James Gordon, 1911-
xBennett, James G.
Command-Train Your Dog: Foolproof
Obedience Techniques for Home & Show.
P-H.
Bennett, Jay.
xBennett, Jay.
The Killing Tree. Avon.
The Killing Tree. Watts.
The Pigeon. Methuen Inc.
Bennett, Jesse Lee, 1885-1931
xBennett, Jesse Lee.
The Diffusion of Science. Arno.
Bennett, Joan. *see* Bennett, Joan Frankau.
Bennett, Joan Frankau.
xBennett, Joan.
George Eliot: Her Mind & Her Art. Cambridge
U Pr.
Bennett, John, 1938-
xBennett, John.
The Night of the Great Butcher. December Pr.
Bennett, John. *see* Bennett, John V.
Bennett, John B. *see* Bennett, John Boyce.
Bennett, John Boyce, 1911-
xBennett, John B.
Rational Thinking: A Study in Basic Logic.
Nelson-Hall.
Bennett, John C. *see* Bennett, John Coleman.
Bennett, John Coleman, 1902-
xBennett, John C.
Christian Values & Economic Life. Arno.
Moral Tensions in International Affairs. Coun
Rel & Intl.
The Radical Imperative: From Theology to
Social Ethics. Westminster.
Bennett, John Frederic.
xBennett, John.
Struck Leviathan: Poems on Moby Dick. U of
Mo Pr.
Bennett, John M.
xBennett, John M.
Found Objects. SBD.
Bennett, John P., 1931-
xBennett, John P.
Chemical Contraception. Columbia U Pr.
Bennett, John R. *see* Bennett, John Reginald.
Bennett, John Reginald.
xBennett, John R.
A Catalogue of Vocal Recordings from the
English Catalogues of the Gramophone
Company, 1898-1899; The Gramophone
Company Limited, 1899-1900; The
Gramophone & Typewriter Company
Limited, 1901-1907; ; the Gramophone
Company Limited, 1907-1925. Greenwood.
Bennett, John V.
xBennett, John.
Hospital Infections. Little.
Bennett, John W. *see* Bennett, John William.
Bennett, John William, 1915-
xBennett, John W.

Hutterian Brethren: The Agricultural Economy
& Social Organization of a Communal
People. Stanford U Pr.
Northern Plainsmen: Adaptive Strategy &
Agrarian Life. AHM Pub.
Bennett, Jonathan. *see* Bennett, Jonathan Francis.
Bennett, Jonathan Francis.
xBennett, J.
Linguistic Behaviour. Cambridge U Pr.
xBennett, Jonathan.
Rationality: An Essay Towards an Analysis.
Humanities.
Bennett, Josephine W. *see* Bennett, Josephine Waters.
Bennett, Josephine Waters.
xBennett, Josephine W.
Evolution of the Faerie Queene. B Franklin.
Evolution of the Faerie Queene. Somerset Pub.
Measure for Measure As Royal Entertainment.
Columbia U Pr.
Bennett, Judith.
xBennett, Judith.
Sex Signs. St Martin.
Bennett, Kenneth A.
xBennett, Kenneth A.
Fundamentals of Biological Anthropology. Wm
C Brown.
The Indians of Point of Pines, Arizona: A
Comparative Study of Their Physical
Characteristics. U of Ariz Pr.
Bennett, Lawrence A.
xBennett, Lawrence A.
Counseling in Correctional Environments.
Human Sci Pr.
Bennett, Lerone, 1928-
xBennett, Lerone.
The Challenge of Blackness. Johnson Chi.
Bennett, M. V. *see* Bennett, Michael Vander Laan.
Bennett, Margaret, fl. 1967-
xBennett, Margaret.
Cross-Country Skiing for the Fun of It. Dodd.
Peripatetic Diabetic. Dutton.
Bennett, Marilyn. *see* Bennett, Merilyn Brottman.
Bennett, Merilyn Brottman.
xBennett, Marilyn.
How We Talk: The Story of Speech. Lerner
Pubns.
Bennett, Meryl.
xBennett, Meryl.
House Renovator's Primer. Sterling.
The Renovator's Primer. Sterling.
Bennett, Michael Vander Laan, 1931-
xBennett, M. V.
ed. Synaptic Transmission & Neuronal
Interaction. Raven.
Bennett, Miriam F.
xBennett, Miriam F.
Living Clocks in the Animal World. C C
Thomas.
Bennett, Neville.
xBennett, Neville.
Teaching Styles & Pupil Progress. Harvard U
Pr.
Bennett, Noel.
xBennett, Noel.
Working with the Wool: How to Weave a
Navajo Rug. Northland.
Bennett, Norman R.
xBennett, Norman R.
Studies in East African History. Holmes &
Meier.
Bennett, Norman R. *see* Bennett, Norman Robert.
Bennett, Norman Robert, 1932-
xBennett, Norman R.
A History of the Arab State of Zanzibar.
Methuen Inc.
ed. Leadership in Eastern Africa: Six Political
Biographies. Holmes & Meier.
Bennett, Paul. *see* Bennett, Paul L.
Bennett, Paul L.
xBennett, Paul.

Living Things. Orchard.
Bennett, R. J. *see* Bennett, Robert John.
Bennett, Richard.
xBennett, Richard.
History of Corn Milling. B Franklin.
Bennett, Robert. *see* Bennett, Bob.
Bennett, Robert A.
xBennett, Robert A.
The Bible for Today's Church. Seabury.
Bennett, Robert John.
xBennett, R. J.
Environmental Systems: Philosophy, Analysis,
& Control. Princeton U Pr.
Bennett, Robert L., 1925-
xBennett, Robert L.
Careers Through Cooperative Work
Experience. Wiley.
Bennett, Russell H.
xBennett, Russell H.
The Compleat Rancher. Denison.
Bennett, Ruth.
xBennett, Ruth.
ed. Aging, Isolation & Resocialization. Van
Nos Reinhold.
Bennett, Susan.
xBennett, Susan.
illus. The Underground Cats. Macmillan.
Bennett, Thomas L.
xBennett, Thomas L.
Brain & Behavior. Brooks-Cole.
Bennett, W. A. *see* Bennett, William Arthur.
Bennett, W. Lance.
xBennett, W. Lance.
Public Opinion in American Politics.
HarBraceJ.
Bennett, W. R. *see* Bennett, William Ralph.
Bennett, Walter H. *see* Bennett, Walter Hartwell.
Bennett, Walter Hartwell, 1907-
xBennett, Walter H.
American Theories of Federalism. U of Ala Pr.
ed. Letters from the Federal Farmer to the
Republican. U of Ala Pr.
Bennett, Wendell C. *see* Bennett, Wendell Clark.
Bennett, Wendell Clark.
xBennett, Wendell C.
The Tarahumara; an Indian Tribe of Northern
Mexico. Rio Grande.
Bennett, William Arthur.
xBennett, W. A.
Aspects of Language & Language Teaching.
Cambridge U Pr.
Bennett, William R. *see* Bennett, William Ralph.
Bennett, William Ralph.
xBennett, W. R.
Introduction to Computer Applications for
Non-Science Students (BASIC). P-H.
xBennett, William R.
Data Transmission. McGraw.
Introduction to Signal Transmission. McGraw.
Bennett-Sandler, G.
xBennett-Sandler, Georgette.
Law Enforcement & Criminal Justice: An
Introduction. HM.
Bennett-Sandler, Georgette. *see* Bennett-Sandler, G.
Bennetts, Pamela.
xBennetts, Pamela.
Don Pedro's Captain. St Martin.
Bennigsen, Alexandre.
xBennigsen, Alexandre A.
Muslim National Communism in the Soviet
Union: A Revolutionary Strategy for the
Colonial World. U of Chicago Pr.
Bennigsen, Alexandre A. *see* Bennigsen, Alexandre.
Bennington, Ed.
xBennington, Ed.
Surplus Dollars. E Bennington.
Bennington, J. *see* Bennington, James L.
Bennington, James L.
xBennington, J.

Financial Operation & Management Concepts
in Nuclear Medicine. Univ Park.
xBennington, James L.
ed. Financial Management of the Clinical
Laboratory. Univ Park.
Bennis, W. G. *see* Bennis, Warren G.
Bennis, Warren. *see* Bennis, Warren G.
Bennis, Warren G.
xBennis, W. G.
ed. Planning of Change. HR&W.
xBennis, Warren.
Essays in Interpersonal Dynamics. Dorsey.
The Leaning Ivory Tower. Jossey-Bass.
The Unconscious Conspiracy: Why Leaders
Can't Lead. Am Mgmt.
xBennis, Warren G.
ed. American Bureaucracy. Transaction Bks.
Organization Development: Its Nature, Origins
& Prospects. A-W.
Bennitt, Mark.
xBennitt, Mark.
ed. History of the Louisiana Purchase
Exposition. Arno.
Benns, F. Lee. *see* Benns, Frank Lee.
Benns, Frank Lee, 1889-
xBenns, F. Lee.
American Struggle for the British West India
Carrying-Trade 1815-1830. Kelley.
Benois, Alexandre, 1870-1960
xBenois, Alexandre.
Reminiscences of the Russian Ballet. Da Capo.
Benoist, Jean Marie.
xBenoist, Jean-Marie.
The Structural Revolution. St Martin.
Benoist, Jean-Marie. *see* Benoist, Jean Marie.
Benoit, Emile.
xBenoit, Emile.
ed. Disarmament & the Economy. Greenwood.
Benoit, Jehane. *see* Benoit, Jehane Patenaude.
Benoit, Jehane Patenaude, 1904-
xBenoit, Jehane.
Enjoying the Art of Canadian Cooking.
Pagurian.
Benoit-Levy, Jean. *see* Benoit-Levy, Jean Albert.
Benoit-Levy, Jean Albert, 1888-1959
xBenoit-Levy, Jean.
Art of the Motion Picture. Arno.
Benowicz, Robert J.
xBenowicz, Robert J.
Non-Prescription Drugs & Their Side Effects.
G&D.
Vitamins & You. G&D.
Benrey, Ronald.
xBenrey, Ronald.
How to Get the Most Out of Your Low-Cost
Electronic Calculator. Hayden.
xBenrey, Ronald M.
CB Accessories You Can Build. Hayden.
Benrey, Ronald M. *see* Benrey, Ronald.
Bens, A. *see* Bens, Allis Rice.
Bens, Allis Rice, 1924-
xBens, A.
Active English: Pronunciation & Speech. P-H.
Bensinger, Charles.
xBensinger, Charles.
The Home Video Handbook. Video-Info.
The Video Guide. Video-Info.
Bensman, Joseph.
xBensman, Joseph.
Between Public & Private: The Lost Boundaries
of the Self. Free Pr.
Benson, A. *see* Benson, Thomas W.
Benson, A. *see* Benson, Adolph Burnett.
Benson, Adolph Burnett.
xBenson, A.
Swedes in America, 1638-1938. Haskell.
Benson, Arthur C. *see* Benson, Arthur Christopher.
Benson, Arthur Christopher, 1862-1925
xBenson, Arthur C.

Alfred Tennyson. Greenwood.
At Large. Arno.
Edward Fitzgerald. Greenwood.
Edward Fitzgerald. R West.
Edward Fitzgerald. Scholarly.
From a College Window. Scholarly.
Benson, Ben, 1911-
xBenson, Ben.
Critical Path Methods in Building
Construction. P-H.
Benson, Bob.
xBenson, Bob.
Come Share the Being. Impact Tenn.
Something's Going on Here. Impact Tenn.
Benson, Carl. *see* Benson, Carl Frederick.
Benson, Carl Frederick.
xBenson, Carl.
The Idea of Tragedy. Scott F.
Benson, Carol E.
xBenson, Carol E.
The Algal Flora of Huntington Canyon Utah,
U. S. A.. Intl Schol Bk Serv.
Benson, Charles S. *see* Benson, Charles Scott.
Benson, Charles Scott.
xBenson, Charles S.
The Economics of Public Education. HM.
Implementing the Learning Society: New
Strategies for Financing Social Objectives.
Jossey-Bass.
Benson, Christopher.
xBenson, Christopher.
Careers in Agriculture. Lerner Pubns.
Careers in Animal Care. Lerner Pubns.
Careers in Auto Sales & Service. Lerner Pubns.
Careers in Conservation. Lerner Pubns.
Careers in Education. Lerner Pubns.
Careers with the City. Lerner Pubns.
Benson, Dennis C.
xBenson, Dennis C.
Making Tracks: Meditations Along the Jogging
Trail. Abingdon.
Benson, Denzel E.
xBenson, Denzel E.
ed. Readings in Deviant Behavior. Mss Info.
Benson, E. F.
xBenson, E. F.
Raven's Brood. Popular Lib.
Benson, E. F. *see* Benson, Edward Frederic.
Benson, Edward F. *see* Benson, Edward Frederic.
Benson, Edward Frederic, 1867-1940
xBenson, E. F.
Charlotte Bronte. Arno.
Charlotte Bronte. Folcroft.
Dodo. T Y Crowell.
xBenson, Edward F.
Charlotte Bronte. Arno.
Benson, Elizabeth P.
xBenson, Elizabeth P.
ed. The Cult of the Feline: A Conference in
Pre-Columbian Iconography, October 31 &
November 1, 1970. Dumbarton Oaks.
ed. Death & the Afterlife in Pre-Columbian
America: A Conference at Dumbarton Oaks,
October 27, 1973. Dumbarton Oaks.
ed. Maya World. T Y Crowell.
An Olmec Figure at Dumbarton Oaks.
Dumbarton Oaks.
Benson, Ellen.
xBenson, Ellen.
Philip's Little Sister. Childrens.
Benson, Ezra T. *see* Benson, Ezra Taft.
Benson, Ezra Taft.
xBenson, Ezra T.
Cross Fire: The Eight Years with Eisenhower.
Greenwood.
This Nation Shall Endure. Deseret Bk.
Benson, F. A. *see* Benson, Frank Atkinson.
Benson, Frank Atkinson.
xBenson, F. A.

Problems in Electronics with Solutions.
Methuen Inc.
Benson, George, 1924-
xBenson, George A.
What to Do When You're Depressed: A
Christian Psychoanalyst Helps You
Understand & Overcome Your Depression.
Augsburg.
Benson, George A. *see* Benson, George.
Benson, George C. *see* Benson, George Charles Sumner.
Benson, George Charles Sumner, 1908-
xBenson, George C.
The Politics of Urbanism: The New Federalism.
Barron.
Benson, Hazel B.
xBenson, Hazel B.
Behavior Modification & the Child: An
Annotated Bibliography. Greenwood.
Benson, Henry C. *see* Benson, Henry Clark.
Benson, Henry Clark, b. 1815
xBenson, Henry C.
Life Among the Choctaw Indians & Sketches
of the Southwest. Johnson Repr.
Benson, Herbert.
xBenson, Herbert.
The Relaxation Response. Avon.
The Relaxation Response. G K Hall.
The Relaxation Response. Morrow.
Benson, J. L. *see* Benson, Jack Leonard.
Benson, Jack Leonard.
xBenson, J. L.
Bamboula at Kourion: The Necropolis & the
Finds, Excavated by J. F. Daniel. U of Pa Pr.
Benson, Jeanette.
xBenson, Jeanette.
Becoming Family. St Mary's.
Benson, John.
xBenson, John.
British Coalminers in the Nineteenth Century:
A Social History. Humanities.
Benson, John L.
xBenson, John L.
Who Is the Antichrist?. Reg Baptist.
Benson, Kenneth R.
xBenson, Kenneth R.
Creative Crafts for Children. P-H.
Benson, L. *see* Benson, Lou.
Benson, Larry D. *see* Benson, Larry Dean.
Benson, Larry Dean.
xBenson, Larry D.
ed. The Learned & the Lewed: Studies in
Chaucer & Medieval Literature. Harvard U
Pr.
Benson, Lee.
xBenson, Lee.
Concept of Jacksonian Democracy: New York
As a Test Case. Princeton U Pr.
Pref. by Turner & Beard: American Historical
Writing Reconsidered. Greenwood.
Benson, Leslie.
xBenson, Leslie.
Proletarians & Parties: Five Essays in Social
Class. Methuen Inc.
Benson, Lou, 1922-
xBenson, L.
Images, Heroes & Self Perceptions: The
Struggle for Identity from Maskwearing to
Authenticity. P-H.
Benson, Lyman. *see* Benson, Lyman David.
Benson, Lyman David, 1909-
xBenson, Lyman.
The Cacti of Arizona. U of Ariz Pr.
The Native Cacti of California. Stanford U Pr.
Plant Classification. Heath.
Benson, Mary.
xBenson, Mary.
At the Still Point. Gambit.
Benson, Morton.
xBenson, Morton.

English - SerboCroatian Dictionary. U of Pa
Pr.
Benson, Oliver E. *see* Benson, Oliver Earl.
Benson, Oliver Earl, 1911-
xBenson, Oliver E.
Political Science Laboratory. Merrill.
Benson, Ragnar.
xBenson, Ragnar.
Survival Poaching. Paladin Ent.
Benson, Ralph C. *see* Benson, Ralph Criswell.
Benson, Ralph Criswell, 1911-
xBenson, Ralph C.
ed. Current Obstetric & Gynecologic Diagnosis
& Treatment. Lange.
Benson, Robert H. *see* Benson, Robert Hugh.
Benson, Robert Hugh, 1871-1914
xBenson, Robert H.
Lord of the World. Arno.
The Necromancers. Arno.
Benson, Rolf.
xBenson, Rolf.
Skydiving. Lerner Pubns.
Benson, Rowland S.
xBenson, Rowland S.
Advanced Engineering Thermodynamics.
Pergamon.
Benson, Sidney W. *see* Benson, Sidney William.
Benson, Sidney William, 1918-
xBenson, Sidney W.
Chemical Calculations: An Introduction to the
Use of Mathematics in Chemistry. Wiley.
Foundations of Chemical Kinetics. Krieger.
Foundations of Chemical Kinetics. McGraw.
Thermochemical Kinetics: Methods for the
Estimation of Thermochemical Data & Rate
Parameters. Wiley.
Benson, Stella, 1892-1933
xBenson, Stella.
The Far-Away Bride. Greenwood.
Benson, Thomas W.
xBenson.
An Orientation to Nonverbal Communication.
SRA.
xBenson, Thomas W.
ed. Readings in Classical Rhetoric. Ind U Pr.
Benson, Vladimir, 1919-
xBenson, Vladimir.
The Failure of the American Dream & the
Moral Responsibility of the United States for
the Crisis in the Middle East & for the
Collapse of the World Order. Inst Econ Pol.
Bensoussan, A. *see* Bensoussan, Alain.
Bensoussan, Alain.
xBensoussan, A.
Asymptotic Analysis for Periodic Structures.
Elsevier.
Benstock, Shari.
xBenstock, Shari.
Who's He When He's at Home: A James
Joyce Directory. U of Ill Pr.
Benston, George J.
xBenston, George J.
The Anti-Redlining Rules: An Analysis of the
Federal Home Loan Bank Board's Proposed
Non Discrimination Requirements. Law &
Econ U Miami.
Contemporary Cost Accounting & Control.
CBI Pub.
Contemporary Cost Accounting & Control.
Dickenson.
Benston, Margaret L. *see* Benston, Margaret Lowe.
Benston, Margaret Lowe.
xBenston, Margaret L.
Quantitative Chemistry. Van Nos Reinhold.
Bent, A. C. *see* Bent, Arthur Cleveland.
Bent, A. J. Van Der. *see* Van Der Bent, A. J.
Bent, Arthur C. *see* Bent, Arthur Cleveland.
Bent, Arthur Cleveland, 1866-1954
xBent, A. C.

Berdahl, Robert Oliver.
  xBerdahl, Robert O.
    British Universities & the State. Arno.
Berdiaev, Nicolas. *see* Berdiaev, Nikolai Aleksandrovich.
Berdiaev, Nikolai. *see* Berdiaev, Nikolai Aleksandrovich.
Berdiaev, Nikolai A. *see* Berdiaev, Nikolai
  Aleksandrovich.
Berdiaev, Nikolai Aleksandrovich, 1874-1948
  xBerdiaev, Nicolas.
    Leontiev. Academic Intl.
  xBerdiaev, Nikolai.
    The Destiny of Man. Hyperion Conn.
    Solitude & Society. Greenwood.
  xBerdiaev, Nikolai A.
    Leontiev. Arden Lib.
    The Russian Idea. Greenwood.
Berdjis, Charles C., 1908-
  xBerdjis, Charles C.
    Pathology of Irradiation. Krieger.
    What Should We Know About Health
      Hazards?. Vantage.
Berdt, Dennys De. *see* De Berdt, Dennys.
Bere, May, 1893-
  xBere, May.
    A Comparative Study of the Mental Capacity
      of Children of Foreign Parentage. AMS Pr.
Bereday, George Z. *see* Bereday, George Z. F.
Bereday, George Z. F.
  xBereday, George Z.
    ed. The Politics of Soviet Education.
      Greenwood.
    ed. Public Education in America: A New
      Interpretation of Purpose & Practice.
      Greenwood.
Bereiter, Carl.
  xBereiter, Carl.
    Teaching Disadvantaged Children in the
      Preschool. P-H.
Berelson, Bernard, 1912-
  xBerelson, Bernard.
    Graduate Education in the United States.
      McGraw.
    The Great Debate on Population Policy: An
      Instructive Entertainment. Population Coun.
    The Library's Public: A Report of the Public
      Library Inquiry. Greenwood.
    Population Policy in Developed Countries.
      McGraw.
Berenbaum, Esai.
  xBerenbaum, Esai.
    Municipal Public Safety: A Guide for the
      Implementation of Consolidated Police-Fire
      Services. C C Thomas.
Berenbaum, Michael, 1945-
  xBerenbaum, Michael.
    The Vision of the Void: Theological Reflections
      on the Works of Elie Wiesel. Columbia U Pr.
Berenbeim, Ronald.
  xBerenbeim, Ronald.
    Nonunion Complaint Systems: A Corporate
      Appraisal. Conference Bd.
Berenblum, I. *see* Berenblum, Isaac.
Berenblum, Isaac, 1903-
  xBerenblum, I.
    Cancer Research Today. Pergamon.
Berends, Polly. *see* Berends, Polly Berrien.
Berends, Polly B. *see* Berends, Polly Berrien.
Berends, Polly Berrien.
  xBerends, Polly.
    The Case of the Elevator Duck. Dell.
  xBerends, Polly B.
    The Case of the Elevator Duck. Random.
    Ladybug & Dog & the Night Walk. Random.
Berendt, Joachim Ernst.
  xBerendt, Joachim-Ernst.
    Jazz: A Photo History. Schirmer Bks.
Berendt, Joachim-Ernst. *see* Berendt, Joachim Ernst.
Berenson, Bernard. *see* Berenson, Bernhard.
Berenson, Bernhard, 1865-
  xBerenson, Bernard.

    Studies in Medieval Painting. Da Capo.
  xBerenson, Bernhard.
    Aesthetics & History. Somerset Pub.
    Drawings of the Florentine Painters.
      Greenwood.
Berenson, M. *see* Berenson, Mark L.
Berenson, Mark L.
  xBerenson, M.
    Basic Business Statistics: Concepts &
      Applications. P-H.
Berenstain, Michael.
  xBerenstain, Michael.
    The Armor Book. McKay.
Berenstain, Stan. *see* Berenstain, Stanley.
Berenstain, Stanley.
  xBerenstain, Stan.
    The Berenstain Bears' Christmas Tree.
      Random.
    Papa's Pizza: A Berenstain Bear Sniffy Book.
      Random.
  xBerenstain, Stanley.
    Old Hat, New Hat. Random.
Berenstein, C. A. *see* Berenstein, Carlos A.
Berenstein, Carlos A.
  xBerenstein, C. A.
    Analytically Uniform Spaces & Their
      Applications to Convolution Equations.
      Springer-Verlag.
Bereny, Justin A.
  xBereny, Justin A.
    Survey of the Emerging Solar Energy Industry.
      Solar Energy Info.
Beres, Louis R. *see* Beres, Louis Rene.
Beres, Louis Rene.
  xBeres, Louis R.
    Constructing Alternative World Futures:
      Reordering the Planet. Schenkman.
    ed. Planning Alternative World Futures:
      Values, Methods, & Models. Praeger.
Beresford, Elizabeth.
  xBeresford, Elizabeth.
    Curious Magic. Elsevier-Nelson.
    Echoes of Love. Dell.
Beresford, H. Richard, 1930-
  xBeresford, H. Richard.
    Legal Aspects of Neurologic Practice. Davis
      Co.
Beresford, J. D. *see* Beresford, John Davys.
Beresford, John, 1888-1940
  xBeresford, John.
    Storm & Peace. Arno.
Beresford, John D. *see* Beresford, John Davys.
Beresford, John Davys, 1873-1947
  xBeresford, J. D.
    H. G. Wells. Haskell.
    The Hampdenshire Wonder. Arno.
    The Hampdenshire Wonder. Garland Pub.
  xBeresford, John D.
    Nineteen Impressions. Arno.
Beresford, M. W. *see* Beresford, Maurice Warwick.
Beresford, Margaret.
  xBeresford, Margaret.
    How to Make Puppets & Teach Puppetry.
      Taplinger.
Beresford, Maurice W. *see* Beresford, Maurice Warwick.
Beresford, Maurice Warwick.
  xBeresford, M. W.
    Medieval England: An Aerial Survey.
      Cambridge U Pr.
  xBeresford, Maurice W.
    English Medieval Boroughs: A Handlist.
      Rowman.
Beresford, Michael.
  xBeresford, Michael.
    Complete Russian Course for Scientists. Oxford
      U Pr.
Beresiner, Yasha.
  xBeresiner, Yasha.

    A Collector's Guide to Paper Money. Stein &
      Day.
Berezanskii, Iurii Makarovich.
  xBerezanskii, Ju. M.
    Nine Papers on Functional Analysis. Am Math.
Berezanskii, Ju. M. *see* Berezanskii, Iurii Makarovich.
Berezhnoi, A. I. *see* Berezhnoi, Anatolii Ivanovich.
Berezhnoi, Anatolii Ivanovich.
  xBerezhnoi, A. I.
    Glass-Ceramics & Photo-Sitalls. Plenum Pub.
Berezkin, V. G. *see* Berezkin, Viktor Grigorevich.
Berezkin, Viktor G. *see* Berezkin, Viktor Grigorevich.
Berezkin, Viktor Grigorevich.
  xBerezkin, V. G.
    Gas-Chromatographic Analysis of Trace
      Impurities. Plenum Pub.
  xBerezkin, Viktor G.
    Analytical Reaction Gas Chromatography.
      Plenum Pub.
    Gas Chromatography of Polymers. Elsevier.
Berfenstam, Ragnar.
  xBerfenstam, Ragnar.
    Early Child Care in Sweden. Gordon.
Berg, Annemarie.
  xBerg, Annemarie.
    Great State Seals of the United States. Dodd.
Berg, Barbara. *see* Berg, Barbara J.
Berg, Barbara J.
  xBerg, Barbara.
    The Remembered Gate: Origins of American
      Feminism - the Woman & the City
      1800-1860. Oxford U Pr.
  xBerg, Barbara J.
    The Remembered Gate: Origins of American
      Feminism - the Woman & the City,
      1800-1860. Oxford U Pr.
Berg, Dave.
  xBerg, Dave.
    Dave Berg's Mad Trash. Warner Bks.
Berg, Francie M.
  xBerg, Francie M.
    North Dakota: Land of Changing Seasons.
      Flying Diamond Bks.
Berg, Frederick S.
  xBerg, Frederick S.
    Educational Audiology: Hearing & Speech
      Management. Grune.
Berg, Gary. *see* Berg, Gary A.
Berg, Gary A., 1944-
  xBerg, Gary.
    Using Calculators for Business Problems. SRA.
Berg, Gerald, 1928-
  xBerg, Gerald.
    ed. Indicators of Viruses in Water & Food.
      Ann Arbor Science.
Berg, I. *see* Berg, Ivar E.
Berg, Irwin A. *see* Berg, Irwin August.
Berg, Irwin August, 1913-
  xBerg, Irwin A.
    ed. Response Set in Personality Assessment.
      Irvington.
Berg, Ivar E.
  xBerg, I.
    Industrial Sociology. P-H.
Berg, Kare.
  xBerg, Kare.
    ed. Genetic Damage in Man Caused by
      Environmental Agents. Acad Pr.
Berg, L. D. Thomas.
  xBerg, Thomas.
    Aim for a Job in Welding. Rosen Pr.
Berg, Lasse.
  xBerg, Lasse.
    Face to Face: Fascism & Revolution in India.
      Ramparts.
Berg, Leila.
  xBerg, Leila.
    Reading & Loving. Routledge & Kegan.
Berg, Patricia Jane.
  xBerg, Patty.

Inside Golf for Women. Contemp Bks.
Berg, Patty. *see* Berg, Patricia Jane.
Berg, Rick, 1951-
xBerg, Rick.
The Art & Adventure of Traveling Cheaply.
And-or Pr.
Berg, Sandra B. *see* Berg, Sandra Beth.
Berg, Sandra Beth.
xBerg, Sandra B.
The Book of Esther: Motifs, Themes &
Structure. Scholars Pr Ca.
Berg, Thomas. *see* Berg, L. D. Thomas.
Berg, William.
xBerg, William.
Early Virgil. Humanities.
Bergan, John R.
xBergan, John R.
Psychology & Education: A Science for
Instruction. Wiley.
Bergaust, Erik.
xBergaust, Erik.
Colonizing Space. Putnam.
Berge, Claude.
xBerge, Claude.
Principles of Combinatorics. Acad Pr.
Bergelson, David, 1884-1952
xBergelson, David.
tr. When All Is Said & Done. Ohio U Pr.
Bergen, C. M. *see* Bergen, Catharine Mary.
Bergen, Catharine Mary, 1912-
xBergen, C. M.
Some Sources of Childrens Science
Information: An Investigation of Sources of
Information & Attitudes Toward Such
Sources As Used or Expressed by Children.
AMS Pr.
Bergen, Polly.
xBergen, Polly.
I'd Love to, but What'll I Wear?. Wideview
Bks.
Bergendoff, Conrad. *see* Bergendoff, Conrad John
Immanuel.
Bergendoff, Conrad John Immanuel, 1895-
xBergendoff, Conrad.
Augustana - A Profession of Faith: A History
of Augustana College, 1860-1935. Augustana
Coll.
Bergengren, Ralph W. *see* Bergengren, Ralph Wilhelm.
Bergengren, Ralph Wilhelm, 1871-
xBergengren, Ralph W.
Perfect Gentleman. Arno.
Berger. *see* Berger, Marie Streng.
Berger & Associated Cost Consultants, Inc. *see* Berger
Associates, Inc., Salt Lake City.
Berger, A. J.
xBerger, A. J.
Lady Luck's Companion: How to Play. How to
Enjoy. How to Bet. How to Win.. Har-Row.
Berger, Adolf.
xBerger, Adolf.
Encyclopedic Dictionary of Roman Law. Am
Philos.
Berger, Alan S.
xBerger, Alan S.
The City: Urban Communities & Their
Problems. Wm C Brown.
Berger, Alexander.
xBerger, Alexander.
ed. PreTest Family Practice Assessment
Program. McGraw-Pretest.
Berger, Arthur. *see* Berger, Arthur Victor.
Berger, Arthur A. *see* Berger, Arthur Asa.
Berger, Arthur Asa.
xBerger, Arthur A.
ed. Film in Society. Transaction Bks.
Berger, Arthur S.
xBerger, Arthur.
Liberation of the Person. Philos Lib.
Berger, Arthur Victor, 1912-
xBerger, Arthur.

Aaron Copland. Greenwood.
Berger Associates, Inc., Salt Lake City.
xBerger & Associated Cost Consultants, Inc.
Compiled By Design Cost File, Nineteen
Seventy-Eight. Van Nos Reinhold.

Berger, Brian.
xBerger, Brian.
Beautiful Chicago. Beautiful Am.
Beautiful Oklahoma. Beautiful Am.
Beautiful Wyoming. Beautiful Am.
Berger, Charles, 1943-
xBerger, Charles.
Image Tibet. Artisan Pr.
Berger, Charles J.
xBerger, Charles J.
How to Raise & Train an Alaskan Malamute.
TFH Pubns.
Berger, David L., 1929-
xBerger, David L.
Industrial Security. Butterworths.
Berger, Fred R., 1937-
xBerger, Fred R.
Freedom of Expression. Wadsworth Pub.
Berger, Gene.
xBerger, Gene.
Bowling for Everyone. St Martin.
Berger, Gilda.
xBerger.
The Gifted & Talented. Watts.
xBerger, Gilda.
The Coral Reef: What Lives There. Coward.
Home Economics Careers. Watts.
Learning Disabilities & Handicaps. Watts.
Physical Disabilities. Watts.
Berger, Gordon M. *see* Berger, Gordon Mark, 1942.
Berger, Gordon Mark, 1942.
xBerger, Gordon M.
Parties Out of Power in Japan, 1931-1941.
Princeton U Pr.
Berger, H. Jean. *see* Berger, Harriet Jean.
Berger, Harriet Jean.
xBerger, H. Jean.
Program Activities for Camps. Burgess.
Berger, J. *see* Berger, Joseph.
Berger, Jason.
xBerger, Jason.
London in Your Pocket. G&D.
Paris in Your Pocket. G&D.
Spain in Your Pocket. G&D.

Berger, John.

xBerger, John.
About Looking. Pantheon.
The Success & Failure of Picasso. Pantheon.

Berger, Joseph.

xBerger, J.
Status Characteristics & Social Interaction: An
Expectation-States Approach. Elsevier.
xBerger, Joseph.
Types of Formalization in Small-Group
Research. Greenwood.
Berger, Karol, 1947-
xBerger, Karol.
Theories of Chromatic & Enharmonic Music in
Late Sixteenth Century Italy. Univ
Microfilms.
Berger, Laurence B.
xBerger, Laurence B.
Measuring Hospital Inflation: A Composite
Index for the Measurement & Determination
of Hospital Costs in the Commonwealth of
Massachusetts. Lexington Bks.
Berger, Marie S. *see* Berger, Marie Streng.
Berger, Marie Streng, 1929-
xBerger.

Management for Nurses: A Multidisciplinary
Approach. Mosby.
xBerger, Marie S.
ed. Management for Nurses: A
Multidisciplinary Approach. Mosby.
Berger, Mark, 1946-
xBerger, Mark.
Taking the Fifth: The Supreme Court & the
Privilege Against Self-Incrimination.
Lexington Bks.
Berger, Max, 1914-
xBerger, Max.
The British Traveller in America, 1836-1860.
Peter Smith.
Berger, Melvin.
xBerger, Melvin.
Animal Hospital. John Day.
Building Construction. Watts.
Cancer Lab. John Day.
Computers. Coward.
Consumer Protection Labs. John Day.
Energy from the Sun. T Y Crowell.
FBI. Watts.
The Flute Book. Lothrop.
Medical Center Lab. John Day.
Oceanography Lab. John Day.
Planets, Stars & Galaxies. Putnam.
Pollution Lab. John Day.
Printing Plant. Watts.
Quasars, Pulsars & Black Holes in Space.
Putnam.
South Pole Station. John Day.
The Stereo-Hi Fi Handbook. Lothrop.
The Story of Folk Music. S G Phillips.
The Supernatural: From ESP to UFO's. John
Day.
The Trumpet Book. Lothrop.
The World of Dance. S G Phillips.
Berger, Michael.
xBerger, Michael.
Firearms in American History. Watts.
xBerger, Michael L.
The Devil Wagon in God's Country: The
Automobile & Social Change in Rural
America Eighteen Hundred & Ninety-Three
to Nineteen Twenty-Nine. Shoe String.
The Public Education System. Watts.
Berger, Michael L. *see* Berger, Michael.
Berger, Milton M. *see* Berger, Milton Miles.
Berger, Milton Miles.
xBerger, Milton M.
Working with People Called Patients.
Brunner-Mazel.
Berger, Morroe.
xBerger, Morroe.
Freedom & Control in Modern Society.
Octagon.
Real & Imagined Worlds: The Novel & Social
Science. Harvard U Pr.
Berger, Peter. *see* Berger, Peter L.
Berger, Peter L.
xBerger, Peter.
Against the World for the World: The Hartford
Appeal & the Future of American Religion.
Seabury.
Protocol of a Damnation: A Novel. Seabury.
xBerger, Peter L.

Facing up to Modernity: Excursions in Society,
Politics, Religion. Basic.
The Heretical Imperative: Contemporary
Possibilities of Religious Affirmation.
Doubleday.
The Heretical Imperative: Contemporary
Possibilities of Religious Affirmation.
Doubleday.
Homeless Mind: Modernization &
Consciousness. Irvington.
Homeless Mind: Modernization &
Consciousness. Random.
Berger, Phil.
xBerger, Phil.
The Boys of Indy. Corwin.
The Boys of Indy. Pinnacle Bks.
More Championship Teams of the NFL.
Random.
Berger, Ralph.
xBerger, Ralph.
Psyclosis: The Circularity of Experience. W H
Freeman.
Berger, Raoul, 1901-
xBerger, Raoul.
Executive Privilege: A Constitutional Myth.
Harvard U Pr.
Government by Judiciary: The Transformation
of the Fourteenth Amendment. Harvard U
Pr.
Berger, Robert, 1938-
xBerger, Robert.
Undecidability of the Domino Problem. Am
Math.
Berger, Robert J.
xBerger, Robert J.
Experiment in a Juvenile Court: Study of a
Program of Volunteers Working with Juvenile
Probationers. U of Mich Soc Res.
Berger, Suzanne.
xBerger, Suzanne.
French Political System. Random.
Berger, Suzanne E, 1944-
xBerger, Suzanne E.
These Rooms. Penmaen Pr.
Berger, Terry.
xBerger, Terry.
How Does It Feel When Your Parents Get
Divorced?. Messner.
I Have Feelings. Human Sci Pr.
I Have Feelings Too. Human Sci Pr.
Special Friends. Messner.
Stepchild. Messner.
Berger, Thomas.
xBerger, Thomas.
Crazy in Berlin. Ballantine.
Little Big Man. Delacorte.
Little Big Man. Fawcett.
Reinhart in Love. Ballantine.
Who Is Teddy Villanova?. Dell.
Berger, Thomas L.
xBerger, Thomas L.
ed. An Index of Characters in English Printed
Drama to the Restoration. IHS-PDS.
Bergeron, David M. see Bergeron, David Moore.
Bergeron, David Moore.
xBergeron, David M.
English Civic Pageantry, 1558-1642. U of SC
Pr.
Bergeron, Eugene, 1900-
xBergeron, Eugene.
How to Clean Sea Shells. Great Outdoors.
Bergersen, Betty S.
xBergersen, Betty S.
Review of Pharmacology in Nursing. Mosby.
Bergerson, Frederic A.
xBergerson, Frederic A.

The Army Gets an Air Force: The Tactics of
Insurgent Bureaucratic Politics. Johns
Hopkins.
Bergerud, Marly.
xBergerud, Marly.
Word Processing: Concepts & Careers. Wiley.
Berges, Ruth.
xBerges, Ruth.
The Collector's Cabinet. A S Barnes.
Bergeson, J. B. see Bergeson, John B.
Bergeson, John B.
xBergeson, J. B.
Learning Activities for Disadvantaged
Children: Selected Readings. Macmillan.
Bergethon, Bjornar.
xBergethon, Bjornar.
Musical Growth in the Elementary School.
HR&W.
Bergevin, Patrick R.
xBergevin, Patrick R.
Guide to Therapeutic Oncology. Williams &
Wilkins.
Bergevin, Paul. see Bergevin, Paul Emile.
Bergevin, Paul Emile.
xBergevin, Paul.
Participation Training for Adult Education.
Bethany Pr.
Bergfield, Philip B.
xBergfield, Philip B.
California Real Estate Law. Irwin.
Principles of Real Estate Law. McGraw.
Bergh, A. A.
xBergh, Arpad A.
Light-Emitting Diodes. Oxford U Pr.
Bergh, Arpad A. see Bergh, A. A.
Bergh, Kit.
xBergh, Kit.
Northern Pike Fishing: The Angler's Complete
Handbook. Dillon.
Berghahn, Marion, 1941-
xBerghahn, Marion.
Images of Africa in Black American Literature.
Rowman.
Berghahn, V. R. see Berghahn, Volker Rolf.
Berghahn, Volker Rolf.
xBerghahn, V. R.
Germany & the Approach of War in 1914. St
Martin.
Berghe, Pierre L. Van Den. see Van Den Berghe, Pierre
L.
Berghe, Pierre Van Den. see Van Den Berghe, Pierre L.
Bergin, Thomas G. see Bergin, Thomas Goddard.
Bergin, Thomas Goddard, 1904-
xBergin, Thomas G.
Dante. Greenwood.
Giovanni Verga. Greenwood.
Bergler, E. see Bergler, Edmund.
Bergler, Edmund, 1899-
xBergler, E.
Principles of Self-Damage. Thieme-Stratton.
xBergler, Edmund.
Laughter & the Sense of Humor.
Thieme-Stratton.
Money & Emotional Conflicts. Intl Univs Pr.
Parents Not Guilty of Their Children's
Neuroses. Liveright.
Psychology of Gambling. Intl Univs Pr.
The Superego - Unconscious Conscience.
Grune.
Bergling, J. M. see Bergling, John Mauritz.
Bergling, John Mauritz, 1866-1933
xBergling, J. M.
Art Alphabets & Lettering. Gem City Coll.
Berglund, J. F. see Berglund, John F.
Berglund, John F.
xBerglund, J. F.

A Compact Right Topological Semigroups &
Generalizations of Almost Periodicity.
Springer-Verlag.
Compact Semitopological Semigroups &
Weakly Almost Periodic Functions.
Springer-Verlag.
Bergman, Abraham B.
xBergman, Abraham B.
Sudden Unexpected Death in Infants. Mss
Info.
Bergman, Edward F.
xBergman, Edward F.
A Geography of the New York Metropolitan
Region. Kendall Hunt.
Bergman, Gosta M. see Bergman, Gosta Mauritz.
Bergman, Gosta Mauritz, 1905-1975
xBergman, Gosta M.
Lighting in the Theatre. Rowman.
Bergman, Hannah E., 1925-
xBergman, Hannah E.
Luis Quinones de Benavente. Twayne.
Bergman, Jerry.
xBergman, Jerry.
Teaching About the Creation-Evolution
Controversy. Phi Delta Kappa.
Bergman, Jules.
xBergman, Jules.
Anyone Can Fly. Doubleday.
Bergman, Madeleine, 1944-
xBergman, Madeleine.
Hieronymus Bosch & Alchemy: A Study on
the St. Anthony Triptych. Humanities.
Bergman, P. H. see Bergman, Peter M.
Bergman, Paul, 1943-
xBergman, Paul B.
Trial Advocacy in a Nutshell. West Pub.
Bergman, Paul B. see Bergman, Paul.
Bergman, Peter M.
xBergman, P. H.
Concise Dictionary of Twenty-Six Languages in
Simultaneous Translation. NAL.
xBergman, Peter M.
Compiled by The Basic English-Chinese,
Chinese-English Dictionary. NAL.
The Negro in the Continental Congress.
Humanities.
Bergman, Ray, 1891-1966
xBergman, Ray.
Trout. Knopf.
Bergman, Ronald A. see Bergman, Ronald Arly.
Bergman, Ronald Arly.
xBergman, Ronald A.
Atlas of Microscopic Anatomy: A Companion
to Histology & Neuroanatomy. Saunders.
Bergman, Samuel.
xBergman, Samuel.
Introduction to Computers & Computer
Programming. A-W.
Bergmann, Frithjof.
xBergmann, Frithjof.
On Being Free. U of Notre Dame Pr.
Bergmann, Gustav. see Bergmann, Gustav_.
Bergmann, Gustav_, 1906
xBergmann, Gustav.
Meaning & Existence. U of Wis Pr.
Realism: A Critique of Brentano & Meinong. U
of Wis Pr.
Bergmann, Hellmuth.
xBergmann, Hellmuth.
Guide to the Economic Evaluation of Irrigation
Projects. OECD.
Bergmann, Leola Marjorie (Nelson), 1912-
xBergmann, Leola N.
Music Master of the Middle West: The Story
of F. Melius Christiansen & the St. Olaf
Choir. Da Capo.
Bergmann, Leola N. see Bergmann, Leola Marjorie
(Nelson).
Bergmann, Martin S.
xBergmann, Martin S.

ed. The Evolution of Psychoanalytic
Technique. Basic.
Bergmann, Merrie.
xBergmann, Merrie.
The Logic Book. Random.
xBergmann, Merriee.
The Logic Book. Knopf.
Bergmann, Merriee. *see* Bergmann, Merrie.
Bergmann, Peter G. *see* Bergmann, Peter Gabriel.
Bergmann, Peter Gabriel.
xBergmann, Peter G.
Riddle of Gravitation. Scribner.
Bergmann, Thesi.
xBergmann, Thesi.
Children in the Hospital. Intl Univs Pr.
Bergmeyer, H. U. *see* Bergmeyer, Hans Ulrich.
Bergmeyer, Hans Ulrich.
xBergmeyer, H. U.
Principles of Enzymatic Analysis. Verlag
Chemie.
Bergon, Frank.
xBergon, Frank.
Stephen Crane's Artistry. Columbia U Pr.
Bergonzi, Bernard.
xBergonzi, Bernard.
Gerard Manley Hopkins. Macmillan.
H. G. Wells: A Collection of Critical Essays.
P-H.
Reading the Thirties: Texts & Contexts. U of
Pittsburgh Pr.
T. S. Eliot. Macmillan.
T. S. Eliot. Macmillan.
The Turn of a Century: Essays on Victorian &
Modern English Literature. Humanities.
Bergquist, Patricia R.
xBergquist, Patricia R.
Sponges. U of Cal Pr.
Bergreen, Laurence.
xBergreen, Laurence
Look Now Pay Later: The Rise of Network
Broadcasting. Doubleday.
Bergsma, Daniel.
xBergsma, Daniel.
ed. Limb Malformations. March of Dimes.
ed. Medical Genetics Today. Johns Hopkins.
ed. Medical Genetics Today. March of Dimes.
ed. Natural History of Specific Birth Defects.
March of Dimes.
Bergsma, Lily C. *see* Bergsma, Lily Chu.
Bergsma, Lily Chu.
xBergsma, Lily C.
A Cross-Cultural Study of Conformity in
Americans & Chinese. R & E Res Assoc.
Bergson, Abram, 1914-
xBergson, Abram.
Planning & Productivity Under Soviet
Socialism. Columbia U Pr.
Soviet National Income & Product in 1937.
Greenwood.
Bergson, Henri. *see* Bergson, Henri Louis.
Bergson, Henri L. *see* Bergson, Henri Louis.
Bergson, Henri Louis, 1859-1941
xBergson, Henri.
The Two Sources of Morality & Religion.
Greenwood.
The Two Sources of Morality & Religion. U of
Notre Dame Pr.
xBergson, Henri L.
Creative Evolution. Greenwood.
Creative Evolution. R West.
Creative Mind. Greenwood.
Bergstein, Eleanor.
xBergstein, Eleanor.
Advancing Paul Newman. Popular Lib.
Bergsten, A. C. Fred. *see* Bergsten, C. Fred.
Bergsten, Bebe.
xBergsten, Bebe.
The Great Dane & the Great Northern Film
Company. Locare.
Bergsten, C. F. *see* Bergsten, C. Fred.

Bergsten, C. Fred.
xBergsten, A. C. Fred.
ed. World Politics & International Economics.
Brookings.
xBergsten, C. F.
Approaches to Greater Flexibility of Exchange
Rates: The Burgenstock Papers. Princeton U
Pr.
The International Economic Policy of the
United States: Selected Papers of C. Fred
Bergsten, 1977-1979. Lexington Bks.
xBergsten, C. Fred.
American Multinationals & American Interests.
Brookings.
xBergsten, Fred C.
The Dilemmas of the Dollar: The Economics &
Politics of the United States International
Monetary Policy. NYU Pr.
Bergsten, Fred C. *see* Bergsten, C. Fred.
Bergstrom, Corinne.
xBergstrom, Corinne.
Losing Your Best Friend. Human Sci Pr.
Bergstrom, Louise.
xBergstrom, Louise.
Dangerous Paradise. Bouregy.
The House of the Evening Star. Bouregy.
Strange Legacy. Bouregy.
Bergstrom, Theo.
xBergstrom, Theo.
Stonehenge. Two Continents.
Beringause, Arthur F., 1919-
xBeringause, Arthur F.
Brooks Adams: A Biography. Octagon.
Beringer, Richard E., 1933-
xBeringer, Richard E.
Historical Analysis: Contemporary Approaches
to Clio's Craft. Wiley.
Berk, Fred, 1911-
xBerk, Fred.
Chasidic Dance. UAHC.
Berk, James L.
xBerk, James L.
Handbook of Critical Care. Little.
Berk, Juliene.
xBerk, Juliene.
The Down Comforter. St Martin.
Berk, Phyllis L.
xBerk, Phyllis L.
Duke's Command. Lantern.
Berk, Richard A.
xBerk, Richard A.
Labor & Leisure at Home: Content &
Organization of the Household Day. Sage.
Prison Reform & State Elites. Ballinger Pub.
Berk, Robert N.
xBerk, Robert N.
Radiology of the Gallbladder & Bile Ducts.
Saunders.
Radiology of the Ileocecal Area. Saunders.
Berk, William R., 1946-
xBerk, William R.
ed. Chinese Healing Arts: Internal Kung-Fu.
Peace Pr.
Berkanovic, Emil.
xBerkanovic, Emil.
Perceptions of Medical Care: The Impact of
Prepayment. Lexington Bks.
Berke, Jacqueline.
xBerke, Jacqueline.
Twenty Questions for the Writer: A Rhetoric
with Readings. HarBraceJ.
Berke, Sally, 1950-
xBerke, Sally.
Monster at Loch Ness. Raintree Pubs.
When T V Began: The First TV Shows. Silver.
Berkebile, Don H. *see* Berkebile, Donald H.
Berkebile, Donald H.
xBerkebile, Don H.

ed. American Carriages, Sleighs, Sulkies &
Carts: 168 Illustrations from Victorian
Sources. Peter Smith.
Carriage Terminology: An Historical
Dictionary. Shumway.
Carriage Terminology: An Historical
Dictionary. Smithsonian.
**Berkeley Actuarial Research Conference on Credibility,
University of California, 1974.**
xBerkeley Actuarial Research Conference, Sept.
1974.
Credibility - Theory & Applications:
Proceedings, Theory & Applications. Acad
Pr.
Berkeley, George, Bp. of Cloyne, 1685-1753
xBerkeley, George.
Three Dialogues Between Hylas & Philonous.
Bobbs.
Three Dialogues Between Hylas & Philonous.
Hackett Pub.
Three Dialogues Between Hylas & Philonous.
Open Court.
Berkeley, George F. *see* Berkeley, George Fitz-Hardinge.
Berkeley, George Fitz-Hardinge, 1870-
xBerkeley, George F.
Campaign of Adowa & the Rise of Menelik.
Negro U Pr.
Berkeley, Henry R. *see* Berkeley, Henry Robinson.
Berkeley, Henry Robinson, 1840-1918
xBerkeley, Henry R.
Four Years in the Confederate Artillery: The
Diary of Private Henry Robinson Berkeley. U
Pr of Va.
Berkeley Holistic Health Center.
xBerkeley Holistic Health Center.
Holistic Health Handbook. And-or Pr.
Berkeley, Humphry, 1926-
xBerkeley, Humphry.
The Myth That Will Not Die: The Formation
of the National Government 1931. Biblio
Dist.
Berkey, Barry. *see* Berkey, Barry R.
Berkey, Barry R.
xBerkey, Barry.
Robbers, Bones & Mean Dogs. A-W.
xBerkey, Barry R.
Halfway Through the Tunnel. Philos Lib.
Berkhof, Hendrik. *see* Berkhof, Hendrikus.
Berkhof, Hendrikus.
xBerkhof, Hendrik.
Christ & the Powers. Herald Pr.
xBerkhof, Hendrikus.
Doctrine of the Holy Spirit. John Knox.
Berkhof, Louis.
xBerkhof, Louis.
History of Christian Doctrines. Baker Bk.
The History of Christian Doctrines. Banner of
Truth.
Berkhofer, Robert F.
xBerkhofer, Robert F.
The White Man's Indian: Images of the
American Indian from Columbus to the
Present. Knopf.
The White Man's Indian: Images of the
American Indian from Columbus to the
Present. Random.
Berki, R. N.
xBerki, Robert.
Socialism. St Martin.
Berki, Robert. *see* Berki, R. N.
Berki, Sylvester E.
xBerki, Sylvester E.
Hospital Economics. Lexington Bks.
Berkin, Carol.
xBerkin, Carol.
Women of America: A History. HM.
xBerkin, Carol R.
ed. Women, War & Revolution. Holmes &
Meier.
Berkin, Carol R. *see* Berkin, Carol.

Berkley, George. *see* Berkley, George E.
Berkley, George E.
 xBerkley, George.
  Cancer: How to Prevent It, & How to Help
   Your Doctor Fight It. P-H.
 xBerkley, George E.
  The Craft of Public Administration. Allyn.
Berkman, Alexander, 1870-1936
 xBerkman, Alexander.
  Prison Memoirs of an Anarchist. Frontier Press
   Calif.
  Prison Memoirs of an Anarchist. Schocken.
Berkman, Harold. *see* Berkman, Harold W.
Berkman, Harold W.
 xBerkman, Harold.
  Consumer Behavior: Concepts & Strategies.
   Dickenson.
  Contemporary Perspectives in International
   Business. Rand.
Berkman, Joyce. *see* Berkman, Joyce Avrech.
Berkman, Joyce Avrech.
 xBerkman, Joyce.
  Olive Schreiner: Feminism on the Frontier.
   Eden Women.
Berkman, Ronald.
 xBerkman, Ronald.
  Opening the Gates: The Rise of the Prisoners
   Movement. Lexington Bks.
Berkman, Ted.
 xBerkman, Ted.
  Cast a Giant Shadow: The Story of Mickey
   Marcus, a Soldier for All Humanity. Jewish
   Pubn.
Berko, Roy M.
 xBerko, Roy M.
  Communicating: A Social & Career Focus.
   HM.
  This Business of Communicating. Wm C
   Brown.
Berkoff, N. A.
 xBerkoff, N. A.
  English Grammar & Structure. Arc Bks.
Berkouwer, G. C. *see* Berkouwer, Gerrit Cornelis.
Berkouwer, Gerrit Cornelis, 1903-
 xBerkouwer, G. C.
  The Church. Eerdmans.
Berkovits, Eliezer, 1908-
 xBerkovits, Eliezer.
  Crisis & Faith. Hebrew Pub.
  Faith After the Holocaust. Ktav.
Berkovitz, L. D. *see* Berkovitz, Leonard David.
Berkovitz, Leonard David, 1924-
 xBerkovitz, L. D.
  Optimal Control Theory. Springer-Verlag.
Berkow, Ira.
 xBerkow, Ira.
  Maxwell Street: Survival in a Bazaar.
   Doubleday.
Berkowitz, David S. *see* Berkowitz, David Sandler.
Berkowitz, David Sandler, 1913-
 xBerkowitz, David S.
  In Remembrance of Creation: Evolution of Art
   & Scholarship in the Medieval & Renaissance
   Bible. U Pr of New Eng.
Berkowitz, Freda P. *see* Berkowitz, Freda Pastor.
Berkowitz, Freda Pastor.
 xBerkowitz, Freda P.
  Popular Titles & Subtitles of Musical
   Compositions. Scarecrow.
Berkowitz, Gerald M.
 xBerkowitz, Gerald M.
  David Garrick: A Reference Guide. G K Hall.
Berkowitz, Leonard, 1926-
 xBerkowitz, Leonard.
  Development of Motives & Values in the
   Child. Basic.
  A Survey of Social Psychology. HR&W.
Berkowitz, Mona.
 xBerkowitz, Mona.

  How to Raise & Train an Old English
   Sheepdog. TFH Pubns.
Berkowitz, Monroe, 1919-
 xBerkowitz, Monroe.
  An Evaluation of Policy-Related Rehabilitation
   Research. Praeger.
  Public Policy Toward Disability. Praeger.
Berkowitz, Morton I.
 xBerkowitz, Morton I.
  A Primer on School Mental Health
   Consultation. C C Thomas.
Berkowitz, N. *see* Berkowitz, Norbert.
Berkowitz, Norbert, 1923-
 xBerkowitz, N.
  An Introduction to Coal Technology. Acad Pr.
Berkowitz, Pearl H.
 xBerkowitz, Pearl H.
  The Disturbed Child: Recognition &
   Psychoeducational Therapy in the Classroom.
   NYU Pr.
Berkowitz, Sol.
 xBerkowitz, Sol.
  Improvisation Through Keyboard Harmony.
   P-H.
Berkson, Isaac B. *see* Berkson, Isaac Baer.
Berkson, Isaac Baer, 1891-
 xBerkson, Isaac B.
  The Ideal & the Community: A Philosophy of
   Education. Greenwood.
  Theories of Americanization: A Critical Study.
   Arno.
Berkson, Larry C. *see* Berkson, Larry Charles.
Berkson, Larry Charles.
 xBerkson, Larry C.
  The Concept of Cruel & Unusual Punishment.
   Lexington Bks.
Berland, Marshall.
 xBerland, Marshall.
  Cooking Without a Kitchen. A & W Pubs.
Berland, Theodore, 1929-
 xBerland, Theodore.
  Fight for Quiet. P-H.
  Living with Your Bronchitis & Emphysema. St
   Martin.
  Living with Your Eye Operation. G K Hall.
  Living with Your Eye Operation. St Martin.
  Living with Your Ulcer. St Martin.
Berlandier, Jean L. *see* Berlandier, Luis.
Berlandier, Luis.
 xBerlandier, Jean L.
  The Indians of Texas in 1830. Smithsonian.
Berlant, Jeffrey L.
 xBerlant, Jeffrey L.
  Profession & Monopoly: A Study of Medicine
   in the United States & Great Britain. U of
   Cal Pr.
Berlau, A. Joseph. *see* Berlau, Abraham Joseph.
Berlau, Abraham Joseph.
 xBerlau, A. Joseph.
  German Social Democratic Party, 1914-1921.
   Octagon.
Berle, Adolf A. *see* Berle, Adolf Augustus.
Berle, Adolf Augustus.
 xBerle, Adolf A.
  Modern Corporation & Private Property.
   HarBraceJ.
  Power. HarBraceJ.
  Power Without Property: A New Development
   in American Political Economy. HarBraceJ.
Berleth, Richard.
 xBerleth, Richard.
  The Twilight Lords: An Irish Chronicle. Knopf.
Berlin, Brent.
 xBerlin, Brent.
  Principles of Tzeltal Plant Classification: An
   Introduction to the Botanical Ethnography of
   a Mayan Speaking People of Highland
   Chiapas. Acad Pr.
Berlin, Charles, 1936-
 xBerlin, Charles.

  Index to Festschriften in Jewish Studies. Ktav.
Berlin, Edward.
 xBerlin, Edward.
  Perspective on Power: A Study of the
   Regulation & Pricing of Electric Power.
   Ballinger Pub.
Berlin, Helene.
 xBerlin, Helene.
  ed. Real Estate Advertising Ideas. Realtors
   Natl.
Berlin, Howard M.
 xBerlin, Howard M.
  The Design of Active Filters with Experiments.
   E & L Instru.
  Design of Active Filters, with Experiments.
   Sams.
  The Design of Operational Amplifier Circuits,
   with Experiments. E & L Instru.
  Design of Phase-Locked Loop Circuits, with
   Experiments. Sams.
  Guide to CMOS Basics, Circuits, &
   Experiments. Sams.
Berlin, I. N. *see* Berlin, Irving Norman.
Berlin, Irving Norman.
 xBerlin, I. N.
  ed. Learning & Its Disorders. Sci & Behavior.
Berlin, Isaiah.
 xBerlin, Isaiah.
  Against the Current: Essays in the History of
   Ideas. Viking Pr.
  ed. Age of Enlightenment: The Eighteenth
   Century Philosophers. NAL.
  Concepts & Categories: Philosophical Essays.
   Penguin.
  Four Essays on Liberty. Oxford U Pr.
  Four Essays on Liberty. Oxford U Pr.
  Russian Thinkers. Penguin.
  Russian Thinkers. Viking Pr.
Berlin, Nathaniel. *see* Berlin, Nathaniel I.
Berlin, Nathaniel I.
 xBerlin, Nathaniel.
  ed. Polycythemia. Grune.
Berlin, Normand.
 xBerlin, Normand.
  Thomas Sackville. Twayne.
Berlin, Richard. *see* Berlin, Richard D.
Berlin, Richard D.
 xBerlin, Richard.
  ed. Molecular Basis of Biological Degradative
   Processes. Acad Pr.
Berlin, Sven.
 xBerlin, Sven.
  Amergin: An Enigma of the Forest. David &
   Charles.
Berlin, William S.
 xBerlin, William S.
  On the Edge of Politics: The Roots of Jewish
   Political Thought in America. Greenwood.
Berliner, Don.
 xBerliner, Don.
  Airplane Racing. Lerner Pubns.
  Home-Built Airplanes. Lerner Pubns.
  Yesterday's Airplanes. Lerner Pubns.
Berliner, Joseph S.
 xBerliner, Joseph S.
  Innovation Decision in Soviet Industry. MIT
   Pr.
Berliner, Lawrence J.
 xBerliner, Lawrence J.
  ed. Spin Labeling: Theory & Applications.
   Acad Pr.
Berliner, Ross.
 xBerliner, Ross.
  Manhood Ceremony. NAL.
  The Manhood Ceremony. S&S.
Berling, Judith A.
 xBerling, Judith A.

The Syncretic Religion of Lin Chao-En.
Columbia U Pr.

Berlinghoff, William P.
xBerlinghoff, William P.
A Mathematical Panorama: Topics for the
Liberal Arts. Heath.

Berlinski, David. *see* Berlinski, David J.

Berlinski, David J.
xBerlinski, David.
On Systems Analysis: An Essay Concerning
the Limitations of Some Mathematical
Methods in the Social, Political, & Biological
Sciences. MIT Pr.

Berlitz, Charles. *see* Berlitz, Charles Frambach.

Berlitz, Charles Frambach, 1913-
xBerlitz, Charles.
French Step by Step. Everest Hse.
German Step by Step. Everest Hse.
Italian Step by Step. Everest Hse.
Spanish Step by Step. Everest Hse.

Berlitz Editors. *see* Berlitz School of Languages of
America, Inc.

Berlitz School of Languages of America, Inc.
xBerlitz Editors.
Danish-English, English-Danish Pocket
Dictionary. Macmillan.
Danish for Travellers. Macmillan.
Dutch-English, English-Dutch Pocket
Dictionary. Macmillan.
Dutch for Travellers. Macmillan.
English (British) for Italian Travellers.
Macmillan.
English (British) for Spanish Travellers.
Macmillan.
English for Danish Travellers. Macmillan.
English for Dutch Travellers. Macmillan.
English for Finnish Travellers. Macmillan.
English for Norwegian Travellers. Macmillan.
English for Swedish Travellers. Macmillan.
English (North American) for French
Travellers. Macmillan.
English (North American) for German
Travellers. Macmillan.
English (North American) for Italian
Travellers. Macmillan.
English (North American) for Spanish
Travellers. Macmillan.
European Phrase Book. Macmillan.
Finnish-English, English-Finnish Pocket
Dictionary. Macmillan.
Finnish for Travellers. Macmillan.
French-English, English-French Pocket
Dictionary. Macmillan.
German-English, English-German Pocket
Dictionary. Macmillan.
Italian English, English-Italian Pocket
Dictionary. Macmillan.
Italian for Travellers. Macmillan.
Latin American Spanish for Travellers.
Macmillan.
Norwegian-English, English-Norwegian Pocket
Dictionary. Macmillan.
Polish for Travellers. Macmillan.
Serbo-Croatian for Travellers. Macmillan.
Spanish-Danish, Danish-Spanish Pocket
Dictionary. Macmillan.
Spanish-Dutch, Dutch-Spanish Pocket
Dictionary. Macmillan.
Swahili for Travellers. Macmillan.
Swedish-English, English-Swedish Pocket
Dictionary. Macmillan.
Turkish for Travellers. Macmillan.
xBerlitz Schools Of Languages.

Berlitz Sin Maestro Ingles or, English for the
Spanish-Speaking People. G&D.
Self-Teacher: French. G&D.
Self-Teacher: German. G&D.
Self-Teacher: Hebrew. G&D.
Self-Teacher: Italian. G&D.
Self-Teacher: Portuguese. G&D.
Self-Teacher: Russian. G&D.
Self-Teacher: Spanish. G&D.

Berlitz Schools Of Languages. *see* Berlitz School of
Languages of America, Inc.

Berlman, I. *see* Berlman, Isadore B.

Berlman, Isadore B.
xBerlman, I.
Energy Transfer Parameters of Aromatic
Compounds. Acad Pr.
xBerlman, Isadore B.
Handbook of Fluorescence Spectra of Aromatic
Molecules. Acad Pr.

Berlye, M. K. *see* Berlye, Milton K.

Berlye, Milton K.
xBerlye, M. K.
Encyclopedia of Working with Glass. Oceana.
xBerlye, Milton K.
How to Sell Your Artwork: A Complete Guide
for Commercial & Fine Artists. P-H.

Berlyn, Graeme P.
xBerlyn, Graeme P.
Botanical Microtechnique & Cytochemistry.
Iowa St U Pr.

Berlyne, D. E.
xBerlyne, D. E.
Conflict, Arousal, & Curiosity. McGraw.
Structure & Direction in Thinking. Krieger.

Berman. *see* Berman, Steve.

Berman, Alan J.
xBerman, Alan J.
Basic Business Communication: Writing Your
Way to a Successful Career. Pella Pub.

Berman, Alvin L.
xBerman, Alvin L.
Brain Stem of the Cat: A Cytoarchitectonic
Atlas with Stereotaxic Coordinates. U of Wis
Pr.

Berman, Arthur I.
xBerman, Arthur I.
Space Flight. Doubleday.

Berman, Bruce D.
xBerman, Bruce D.
Encyclopedia of American Shipwrecks.
Mariners Boston.

Berman, Claire.
xBerman, Claire.
Great City for Kids: A Parent's Guide to a
Child's New York. Bobbs.
Making It As a Stepparent: New Roles-New
Rules. Doubleday.

Berman, Connie.
xBerman, Connie.
Leif Garrett. G&D.

Berman, Daniel S.
xBerman, Daniel S.
How to Reap Profits in Local Real Estate
Syndicates. P-H.
Tax Saving Opportunities in Real Estate Deals.
P-H.

Berman, David R.
xBerman, David R.
American Government, Politics &
Policymaking. Palisades Pubs.

Berman, Edgar.
xBerman, Edgar.
Hubert: The Triumph & Tragedy of the
Humphrey I Knew. Putnam.
The Politician Primeval: From the Amoeba to
the White House. Macmillan.
The Solid Gold Stethoscope. Ballantine.

Berman, Gerald.
xBerman, Gerald.

Introduction to Combinatorics. Acad Pr.

Berman, Greta.
xBerman, Greta.
The Lost Years: Mural Painting in New York
City Under the Works Progress
Administration's Federal Art Project
1935-1943. Garland Pub.

Berman, Hannah.
xBerman, Hannah.
Melutovna: A Novel. Arno.

Berman, Harold B. *see* Berman, Harold Joseph.

Berman, Harold Joseph.
xBerman, Harold B.
Disarmament Inspection Under Soviet Law.
Oceana.

Berman, Howard J.
xBerman, Howard J.
ed. Economics in Health Care. Aspen Systems.
The Financial Management of Hospitals.
Health Admin Pr.

Berman, Jeffrey, 1945-
xBerman, Jeffrey.
Joseph Conrad: Writing As Rescue. Hippocrene
Bks.

Berman, Larry.
xBerman, Larry.
The Office of Management & Budget & the
Presidency: 1921-1979. Princeton U Pr.

Berman, Louis.
xBerman, Louis.
Exploring the Cosmos. Little.

Berman, Louise M.
xBerman, Louise M.
From Thinking to Behaving. Tchrs Coll.
Supervision, Staff Development & Leadership.
Merrill.

Berman, Marshall, 1940-
xBerman, Marshall.
Politics of Authenticity: Radical Individualism
& the Emergence of Modern Society.
Atheneum.

Berman, Michelle.
xBerman, Michelle.
I Can Make It on My Own: Functional
Reading Ideas & Activities for Daily Survival.
Goodyear.

Berman, Norman.
xBerman, Norman.
Art from Clutter. Rosen Pr.

Berman, Peter I.
xBerman, Peter I.
Inflation & the Money Supply in the United
States, 1956-1977. Lexington Bks.

Berman, Phil.
xBerman, Phillip L.
Winning in Catamarans. Wind Pub.

Berman, Phillip L. *see* Berman, Phil.

Berman, R. *see* Berman, Robert.

Berman, R. J.
xBerman, R. J.
Browning's Duke. Rosen Pr.

Berman, Robert.
xBerman, R.
Thermal Conduction in Solids. Oxford U Pr.

Berman, Robert P., 1950-
xBerman, Robert P.
Soviet Air Power in Transition. Brookings.

Berman, Ronald.
xBerman, Ronald.
Reader's Guide to Shakespeare's Plays: A
Discursive Bibliography. Scott F.
xBerman, Ronald S.
Intellect & Education in a Revolutionary
Society. Am Enterprise.

Berman, Ronald S. *see* Berman, Ronald.

Berman, Sanford. *see* Berman, Sanford I.

Berman, Sanford I.
xBerman, Sanford.

Understanding & Being Understood. Intl Gen
　　Semantics.
Berman, Shelley.
　　xBerman, Shelley.
　　　A Hotel Is a Place. Price Stern.
Berman, Steve.
　　xBerman.
　　　Relationships. Dutton.
Berman, Susan.
　　xBerman, Susan.
　　　Driver, Give a Soldier a Lift. Berkley Pub.
　　　Underground Guide to the College of Your
　　　　Choice. NAL.
Berman, William.
　　xBerman, William.
　　　How to Dissect: Exploring with Probe &
　　　　Scalpel. Arco.
Berman, William C., 1932-
　　xBerman, William C.
　　　Politics of Civil Rights in the Truman
　　　　Administration. Ohio St U Pr.
Bermant, Gordon.
　　xBermant, Gordon.
　　　Primate Utilization & Conservation. Krieger.
Bermel, Albert.
　　xBermel, Albert.
　　　Artaud's Theatre of Cruelty. Taplinger.
　　　Contradictory Characters: An Interpretation of
　　　　the Modern Theatre. Dutton.
Bermont, Hubert. *see* Bermont, Hubert Ingram.
Bermont, Hubert Ingram.
　　xBermont, Hubert.
　　　How to Become a Successful Consultant in
　　　　Your Own Field. Bermont Bks.
Bermosk, Loretta S. *see* Bermosk, Loretta Sue.
Bermosk, Loretta Sue.
　　xBermosk, Loretta S.
　　　Women's Health & Human Wholeness. ACC.
Bermudez, Andrea B., 1941-
　　xBermudez, Andrea B.
　　　Influence of the Institution of Free Learning on
　　　　Spanish Education. Ediciones.
Bernabe, Emma.
　　xBernabe, Emma.
　　　Ilokano Lessons. U Pr of Hawaii.
Bernabei, Alfio.
　　xBernabei, Alfio.
　　　Avventura. EMC.
Bernacchi, Richard L.
　　xBernacchi, Richard L.
　　　Data Processing Contracts & the Law. Little.
Bernal, Ignacio.
　　xBernal, Ignacio.
　　　The Iconography of Middle American
　　　　Sculpture. Metro Mus Art.
　　　The Olmec World. U of Cal Pr.
Bernal, Ivan.
　　xBernal, Ivan.
　　　Symmetry: A Stereoscopic Guide for Chemists.
　　　　W H Freeman.
Bernanos, George. *see* Bernanos, Georges.
Bernanos, Georges, 1888-1948
　　xBernanos, George.
　　　Diary of a Country Priest. Macmillan.
　　xBernanos, Georges.
　　　The Diary of a Country Priest. Doubleday.
　　　Last Essays. Greenwood.
Bernanos, Michel.
　　xBernanos, Michel.
　　　The Other Side of the Mountain. Larlin Corp.
Bernard, Art, 1910-
　　xBernard, Art.
　　　Dog Days. Caxton.
Bernard, Bruce.
　　xBernard, Bruce.
　　　Photodiscovery: Masterworks of Photography
　　　　1840-1940. Abrams.
Bernard, Christine.
　　xBernard, Christine.

Retold by A Host of Ghosts. Lippincott.
Bernard, Claude, 1813-1878
　　xBernard, Claude.
　　　Lectures on the Phenomena of Life Common
　　　　to Animals & Plants. C C Thomas.
Bernard, Dan.
　　xBernard, Dan.
　　　ed. Charging for Computer Services: Principles
　　　　& Guidelines. Petrocelli.
Bernard, Etienne A.
　　xBernard, Etienne A.
　　　Compendium of Lecture Notes for Training
　　　　Personnel in the Applications of Meteorology
　　　　to Economic & Social Development. Unipub.
Bernard, George, 1939-
　　xBernard, George.
　　　Inside the National Enquirer: Confessions of an
　　　　Undercover Reporter. Ashley Bks.
Bernard, H. W. *see* Bernard, Harold Wright.
Bernard, Harold W.
　　xBernard, Harold W.
　　　Weather Watch: How to Make the Most of
　　　　America's Changing Weather. Walker & Co.
Bernard, Harold W. *see* Bernard, Harold Wright.
Bernard, Harold Wright.
　　xBernard, H. W.
　　　Psychology of Learning & Teaching. McGraw.
　　xBernard, Harold W.
　　　The Dynamics of Personal Adjustment. Allyn.
　　　Dynamics of Personal Adjustment. Holbrook.
　　　Human Development in Western Culture.
　　　　Allyn.
　　　Principles of Guidance. Har-Row.
Bernard, Henri.
　　xBernard, Henri.
　　　Matteo Ricci's Scientific Contribution to
　　　　China. Hyperion Conn.
Bernard, Jessie. *see* Bernard, Jessie Shirley.
Bernard, Jessie Shirley, 1903-
　　xBernard, Jessie.
　　　Academic Women. NAL.
　　　The Future of Motherhood. Dial.
　　　The Future of Motherhood. Penguin.
　　　Remarriage: A Study of Marriage. Russell.
　　　The Sociology of Community. Scott F.
Bernard, Jules E. *see* Bernard, Jules Eugene.
Bernard, Jules Eugene, 1913-
　　xBernard, Jules E.
　　　Prosody of the Tudor Interlude. Shoe String.
Bernard, Matt.
　　xBernard, Matt.
　　　Mario Lanza. Manor Bks.
Bernard, Mountague, 1820-1882
　　xBernard, Mountague.
　　　Historical Account of the Neutrality of Great
　　　　Britain During the American Civil War. B
　　　　Franklin.
Bernard, Nora.
　　xBernard, Nora.
　　　Hollywood's Irish Rose. Avon.
Bernard, Paul P.
　　xBernard, Paul P.
　　　The Limits of Enlightenment: Joseph II & the
　　　　Law. U of Ill Pr.
Bernard, Richard, 1948-
　　xBernard, Richard M.
　　　The Poles in Oklahoma. U of Okla Pr.
Bernard, Richard M. *see* Bernard, Richard.
Bernard, Theos, 1908-
　　xBernard, Theos.
　　　Hindu Philosophy. Greenwood.
Bernardo, Aldo S. *see* Bernardo, Also S.
Bernardo, Also S.
　　xBernardo, Aldo S.
　　　Francesco Petrarca, Citizen of the World. State
　　　　U NY Pr.
Bernardo, Robert M.
　　xBernardo, Robert M.

Theory of Moral Incentives in Cuba. U of Ala
　　Pr.
Bernardoni, Gus.
　　xBernardoni, Gus.
　　　Golf God's Way. Creation Hse.
Bernatzik, Hugo A. *see* Bernatzik, Hugo Adolf.
Bernatzik, Hugo Adolf, 1897-1953
　　xBernatzik, Hugo A.
　　　Akha & Miao: Problems of Applied
　　　　Ethnography in Farther India. HRAFP.
Bernatzky, A. *see* Bernatzky, Aloys.
Bernatzky, Aloys.
　　xBernatzky, A.
　　　Tree Ecology & Preservation. Elsevier.
Bernays, Anne.
　　xBernays, Anne.
　　　The First to Know. Popular Lib.
　　　Growing Up Rich. Little.
Bernays, Edward L., 1891-
　　xBernays, Edward L.
　　　Your Future in a Public Relations Career.
　　　　Rosen Pr.
Bernays, Jakob, 1824-1881
　　xBernays, Jakob.
　　　Joseph Justus Scaliger. B Franklin.
Bernd, Clifford A.
　　xBernd, Clifford A.
　　　Theodor Storm's Craft of Fiction: The Torment
　　　　of a Narrator. AMS Pr.
Berndt, Alan F.
　　xBerndt, Alan F.
　　　Dental Fluoride Chemistry. C C Thomas.
Berndt, R. M. *see* Berndt, Ronald Murray.
Berndt, Ronald M. *see* Berndt, Ronald Murray.
Berndt, Ronald Murray.
　　xBerndt, R. M.
　　　ed. Aborigines & Change: Australia in the 70's.
　　　　Humanities.
　　xBerndt, Ronald M.
　　　Love Songs of Arnhem Land. U of Chicago Pr.
　　　ed. Politics in New Guinea: Traditional & in
　　　　the Context of Change, Some
　　　　Anthropological Perspectives. U of Wash Pr.
Berndtson, Arthur, 1913-
　　xBerndtson, Arthur.
　　　Art Expression & Beauty. Krieger.
Berne, Bruce J.
　　xBerne, Bruce J.
　　　Dynamic Light Scattering: With Applications
　　　　to Chemistry, Biology & Physics. Wiley.
Berne, Eric.
　　xBerne, Eric.
　　　Layman's Guide to Psychiatry &
　　　　Psychoanalysis. Ballantine.
　　　The Structure & Dynamics of Organizations &
　　　　Groups. Ballantine.
Berne, N.Y. Bicentennial Commission.
　　xTown of Berne Bicentennial Commission.
　　　Our Heritage. Hope Farm.
Berne, Robert M.
　　xBerne, Robert M.
　　　Cardiovascular Physiology. Mosby.
Berne, Stanley, 1923-
　　xBerne, Stanley.
　　　Future Language. Am Canadian.
　　　Future Language. Horizon.
Bernen, Robert.
　　xBernen, Robert.
　　　Tales from the Blue Stacks. Scribner.
Berner, Elsa R.
　　xBerner, Elsa R.
　　　Integrating Library Instruction with Classroom
　　　　Teaching at Plainview Junior High School.
　　　　ALA.
Berner, Jeff.
　　xBerner, Jeff.
　　　The Holography Book. Avon.
　　　The Holography Book. Delacorte.
Berner, R. A. *see* Berner, Robert A.

Berner, R. Thomas.
xBerner, R. Thomas.
Language Skills for Journalists. HM.
Berner, Richard O. *see* Berner, Richard Olin.
Berner, Richard Olin.
xBerner, Richard O.
Constraints on the Regulatory Process: A Case
Study of Regulation of Cable Television.
Ballinger Pub.
Berner, Robert A., 1935-
xBerner, R. A.
Principles of Chemical Sedimentology.
McGraw.
Berner, Wolfgang.
xBerner, Wolfgang.
The Soviet Union 1973: Domestic Policy,
Economics, Foreign Policy. Holmes & Meier.
The Soviet Union 1974-75: Domestic Policy,
Economics, Foreign Policy. Holmes & Meier.
The Soviet Union 1975-76: Domestic Policy,
Economics, Foreign Policy. Holmes & Meier.
Berners, Juliana.
xBerners, Juliana.
A Treatise on Fishing with a Hook. North
River.
Berney, Arthur L.
xBerney, Arthur L.
Legal Problems of the Poor: Cases & Materials.
Little.
Berney, Donald W.
xBerney, Donald W.
American Government for Law Enforcement
Training. Nelson-Hall.
Berney, Saffold.
xBerney, Saffold.
Handbook of Alabama: A Complete Index to
the State, with Map. Reprint.
Bernhard, C. G. *see* Bernhard, Carl Gustaf.
Bernhard, Carl Gustaf.
xBernhard, C. G.
Developmental Neurology. Elsevier.
Bernhard, Edgar, 1898-
xBernhard, Edgar.
Speakers on the Spot: A Treasury of Anecdotes
for Coping with Sticky Situations. P-H.
Bernhard, Thomas.
xBernhard, Thomas.
Correction. Knopf.
Bernhard, Virginia, 1937-
xBernhard, Virginia.
Elites, Masses, & Modernization in Latin
America, 1850-1930. U of Tex Pr.
Bernhardsen, Christian. *see* Bernhardsen, Einar Christian
Rosenvinge.
Bernhardsen, Einar Christian Rosenvinge, 1923-
xBernhardsen, Christian.
Fight in the Mountains. HarBraceJ.
Bernhardt, Arthur D.
xBernhardt, Arthur D.
Building Tomorrow: The Mobile-Manufactured
Housing Industry. MIT Pr.
Bernhardt, Ernest C.
xBernhardt, Ernest C.
ed. Processing of Thermoplastic Materials.
Krieger.
Bernhardt, Joshua, 1893-
xBernhardt, Joshua.
The Alaskan Engineering Commission: Its
History, Activities & Organization. AMS Pr.
The Division of Conciliation: Its History,
Activities & Organization. AMS Pr.
The Railroad Labor Board: Its History,
Activities & Organization. AMS Pr.
The Tariff Commission: Its History, Activities
& Organization. AMS Pr.
Bernhardt, Sarah, 1844-1923
xBernhardt, Sarah.

Art of the Theatre. Arno.
Art of the Theatre. Scholarly.
Bernheim, Gotthardt D. *see* Bernheim, Gotthardt
Dellmann.
Bernheim, Gotthardt Dellmann, 1827-1916
xBernheim, Gotthardt D.
History of the German Settlements & of the
Lutheran Church in North & South Carolina.
Regional.
History of the German Settlements & of the
Lutheran Church in North & South Carolina.
Reprint.
Bernheim, Kayla F.
xBernheim, Kayla F.
Schizophrenia: Symptoms, Causes, Treatments.
Norton.
Bernheim, M. *see* Bernheim, Marc.
Bernheim, Marc.
xBernheim, M.
jt. auth. Growing Up in Old New England.
Macmillan.
xBernheim, Marc.
African Success Story: The Ivory Coast.
HarBraceJ.
jt. auth. The Drums Speak: The Story of Kofi,
a Boy of West Africa. HarBraceJ.
Growing Up in Old New England. Macmillan.
In Africa. Atheneum.
Bernheimer, Alan W. *see* Bernheimer, Alan Weyl.
Bernheimer, Alan Weyl, 1913-
xBernheimer, Alan W.
Mechanisms in Bacterial Toxinology. Wiley.
Bernice P. Bishop Museum - Honolulu. *see* Bernice P.
Bishop Museum, Honolulu.
Bernice P. Bishop Museum, Honolulu.
xBernice P. Bishop Museum - Honolulu.
Dictionary Catalog of the Library of the
Bernice P. Bishop Museum. G K Hall.
xBernice Pauahi Bishop Museum, Honolulu.
Museum of Polynesian Ethnology & Natural
History: Honolulu Bulletins, Nos. 1-12,
14-223. Kraus Repr.
Bernice Pauahi Bishop Museum, Honolulu. *see* Bernice P.
Bishop Museum, Honolulu.
Bernick, E. Lee. *see* Bernick, Emil Lee.
Bernick, Emil Lee.
xBernick, E. Lee.
Legislative Voting Patterns & Partisan
Cohesion in a One-Party Dominant
Legislature. Univ OK Gov Res.
Bernier, Charles L.
xBernier, Charles L.
Cogent Communication: Overcoming Reading
Overload. Greenwood.
Bernier, Paul, 1937-
xBernier, Paul.
ed. Bread from Heaven. Paulist Pr.
Bernikow, Louise, 1940-
xBernikow, Louise.
Abel. Trident.
ed. The World Split Open: Four Centuries of
Women Poets in England & America,
1552-1950. Random.
Berninger, Louis, 1929-
xBerninger, Louis M.
Profitable Garden Center Management. Reston.
Berninger, Louis M. *see* Berninger, Louis.
Berninghausen, David K.
xBerninghausen, David K.
The Flight from Reason: Essays on Intellectual
Freedom in the Academy,the Press, & the
Library. ALA.
Berns, Walter. *see* Berns, Walter Fred.
Berns, Walter Fred, 1919-
xBerns, Walter.

The First Amendment & the Future of
American Democracy. Basic.
For Capital Punishment: Crime & the Morality
of the Death Penalty. Basic.
Freedom, Virtue & the First Amendment.
Greenwood.
Bernsohn, Joseph.
xBernsohn, Joseph.
ed. Lipid Storage Diseases: Enzymatic Defects
& Clinical Implications. Acad Pr.
Bernstein, Abraham. *see* Bernstein, Abraham Alexander.
Bernstein, Abraham Alexander, 1906-
xBernstein, Abraham.
Teaching English in High School. Phila Bk Co.
Bernstein, Al.
xBernstein, Al.
Boxing for Beginners. Contemp Bks.
Bernstein, Ann. *see* Bernstein, Anne C.
Bernstein, Anne. *see* Bernstein, Anne C.
Bernstein, Anne C., 1944-
xBernstein, Ann.
Flight of the Stork. Dell.
xBernstein, Anne.
The Flight of the Stork. Delacorte.
Bernstein, Barton J.
xBernstein, Barton J.
ed. The Atomic Bomb: The Critical Issues.
Little.
ed. Politics & Policies of the Truman
Administration. New Viewpoints.
ed. Towards a New Past: Dissenting Essays in
American History. Random.
Bernstein, Burton.
xBernstein, Burton.
Look, Ma, I Am Kool & Other Casuals. P-H.
Sinai: The Great & Terrible Wilderness. Viking
Pr.
Bernstein, Carl.
xBernstein, Carl.
All the President's Men. S&S.
All the President's Men. Warner Bks.
Bernstein, Carol L., 1933-
xBernstein, Carol L.
Precarious Enchantment: A Reading of
Meredith's Poetry. Intl Schol Bk Serv.
Bernstein, Douglas A.
xBernstein, Douglas A.
Introduction to Clinical Psychology. McGraw.
Progressive Relaxation Training: A Manual for
the Helping Professions. Res Press.
Bernstein, E. *see* Bernstein, Eduard.
Bernstein, Eduard, 1850-1932
xBernstein, E.
Pref. by Ferdinand Lassalle As a Social
Reformer. Scholarly.
xBernstein, Eduard.
Cromwell & Communism: Socialism &
Democracy in the Great English Revolution.
Biblio Dist.
Ferdinand Lassalle As a Social Reformer.
Greenwood.
xBernstein, Edward.
Ferdinand Lassalle As a Social Reformer.
Scholarly.
Bernstein, Edward. *see* Bernstein, Eduard.
Bernstein, Gary.
xBernstein, Gary.
Burning Cold. Crown.
Bernstein, Harry, 1909-
xBernstein, Harry.
Origins of Inter-American Interest, 1700-1812.
Russell.
Bernstein, Irving, 1916-
xBernstein, Irving.
Arbitration of Wages. U of Cal Pr.
The Lean Years: A History of the American
Worker 1920-1933. HM.
Bernstein, James D.
xBernstein, James D.

Rural Health Centers in the United States.
Ballinger Pub.
Bernstein, Jeremy, 1924-
xBernstein, Jeremy.
Ascent: Of the Invention of Mountain
Climbing & Its Practice. U of Nebr Pr.
Einstein. Penguin.
Experiencing Science. Basic.
Bernstein, Jerrold G., 1941-
xBernstein, Jerrold G.
ed. Clinical Psychopharmacology. PSG Pub.
Bernstein, Joanne. *see* Bernstein, Joanne E.
Bernstein, Joanne E.
xBernstein, Joanne.
Fiddle with a Riddle: Write Your Own Riddles.
Dutton.
Loss & How to Cope with It. HM.
xBernstein, Joanne E.
Compiled by Books to Help Children Cope
with Separation & Loss. Bowker.
When People Die. Dutton.
Bernstein, John.
xBernstein, John.
Pacifism & Rebellion in the Writings of
Herman Melville. Folcroft.
Bernstein, Julian L. *see* Bernstein, Julian Lawrence.
Bernstein, Julian Lawrence.
xBernstein, Julian L.
Audio Systems. Krieger.
Bernstein, Leonard, 1918-
xBernstein, Leonard.
The Unanswered Question: Six Talks at
Harvard. Harvard U Pr.
Bernstein, Margery.
xBernstein, Margery.
Coyote Goes Hunting for Fire: A California
Indian Myth. Scribner.
The First Morning: An African Myth. Scribner.
Bernstein, Martin.
xBernstein, Martin.
Introduction to Music. P-H.
Bernstein, Marver H.
xBernstein, Marver H.
Politics of Israel: The First Decade of
Statehood. Greenwood.
Regulating Business by Independent
Commission. Greenwood.
Bernstein, Penny.
xBernstein, Penny L.
Eight Theoretical Approaches in
Dance-Movement Therapy. Kendall-Hunt.
Bernstein, Penny L. *see* Bernstein, Penny.
Bernstein, Peter L.
xBernstein, Peter L.
A Primer on Money, Banking & Gold.
Random.
Bernstein, Philip S. *see* Bernstein, Philip Sidney.
Bernstein, Philip Sidney, 1901-
xBernstein, Philip S.
What the Jews Believe. Greenwood.
Bernstein, Richard J.
xBernstein, Richard J.
Praxis & Action: Contemporary Philosophies of
Human Activity. U of Pa Pr.
The Restructuring of Social & Political Theory.
HarBraceJ.
The Restructuring of Social & Political Theory.
U of Pa Pr.
Bernstein, Robert A. *see* Bernstein, Robert Alan.
Bernstein, Robert Alan.
xBernstein, Robert A.
An Introduction to Political Science Methods.
P-H.
Bernstein, Samuel, 1898-
xBernstein, Samuel.
First International in America. Kelley.
Bernstein, Samuel J.
xBernstein, Samuel J.

ed. Computers in Public Administration: An
International Perspective. Pergamon.
Public Administration: Organizations, People,
& Public Policy. Har-Row.
Bernstein, Seymour.
xBernstein, Seymour.
ed. Chemical & Biological Aspects of Steroid
Conjugation. Springer-Verlag.
Bernstein, Susan.
xBernstein, Susan.
ed. Dog Digest. Follett.
Bernstein, Theodore M. *see* Bernstein, Theodore
Menline.
Bernstein, Theodore Menline, 1904-
xBernstein, Theodore M.
Careful Writer: A Modern Guide to English
Usage. Atheneum.
Do's, Don'ts, & Maybes of English Usage.
Times Bks.
Berofsky, Bernard.
xBerofsky, Bernard.
Determinism. Princeton U Pr.
ed. Free Will & Determinism. Har-Row.
Berolzheimer, Fritz, 1869-1920
xBerolzheimer, Fritz.
World's Legal Philosophies. Kelley.
Berra, Betty.
xBerra, Betty.
The Sophomores. Branden.
Berrall, Julia. *see* Berrall, Julia S.
Berrall, Julia S.
xBerrall, Julia.
The Garden: An Illustrated History. Penguin.
xBerrall, Julia S.
The Garden: An Illustrated History. Viking Pr.
Berreman, Gerald D. *see* Berreman, Gerald Duane.
Berreman, Gerald Duane, 1930-
xBerreman, Gerald D.
Hindus of the Himalayas: Ethnography &
Change. U of Cal Pr.
Berrens, L. *see* Berrens, Lubertus.
Berrens, Lubertus.
xBerrens, L.
The Chemistry of Atopic Allergens. S Karger.
Berrett, Lamar C.
xBerrett, LaMar C.
Discovering the World of the Bible. Nelson.
Berridge, Robert I.
xBerridge, Robert I.
The Community Education Handbook. Pendell
Pub.
Berridge, William A. *see* Berridge, William Arthur.
Berridge, William Arthur.
xBerridge, William A.
Purchasing Power of the Consumer: A
Statistical Index. Arno.
Berrien, F. Kenneth. *see* Berrien, Frederick Kenneth.
Berrien, Frederick Kenneth.
xBerrien, F. Kenneth.
General & Social Systems. Rutgers U Pr.
Berrier, H. H.
xBerrier, Harry H.
Animal Sanitation & Disease Prevention.
Kendall-Hunt.
Berrier, Harry H. *see* Berrier, H. H.
Berrigan, Daniel.
xBerrigan, Daniel.
Geography of Faith: Conversations Between
Daniel Berrigan, When Underground &
Robert Coles. Beacon Pr.
Prison Poems. Unicorn Pr.
The Raft Is Not the Shore: Conversations
Toward a Buddhist-Christian Awareness.
Beacon Pr.
Uncommon Prayer: A Book of Psalms.
Seabury.
Berrigan, Philip.
xBerrigan, Philip.

Punishment for Peace. Macmillan.
Berrigan, Ted.
xBerrigan, Ted.
So Going Around Cities: New & Selected
Poems, 1958-1979. Blue Wind.
Berrill, Jacquelyn.
xBerrill, Jacquelyn.
Wonders of Animal Nurseries. Dodd.
illus. Wonders of How Animals Learn. Dodd.
Wonders of the World of Wolves. Dodd.
Berrill, N. J. *see* Berrill, Norman John.
Berrill, Norman J. *see* Berrill, Norman John.
Berrill, Norman John.
xBerrill, N. J.
Development. McGraw.
Journey into Wonder. Sharon Hill.
Life of Sea Islands. McGraw.
xBerrill, Norman J.
Growth, Development, & Pattern. W H
Freeman.
Berrington, Hugh.
xBerrington, Hugh B.
Backbench Opinion in the House of Commons,
1945-1955. Pergamon.
Berrington, Hugh B. *see* Berrington, Hugh.
Berrios-Ortiz, A. *see* Berrios-Ortiz, Angel.
Berrios-Ortiz, Angel.
xBerrios-Ortiz, A.
Skeletal Musculature in Larval Phases of the
Beetle Epicauta Segmenta, (Coleoptera,
Meloidae). Kluwer Boston.
Berrisford, Judith. *see* Berrisford, Judith Mary.
Berrisford, Judith Mary, 1921-
xBerrisford, Judith.
Backyards & Tiny Gardens. Merrimack Bk
Serv.
The Weekend Garden. Merrimack Bk Serv.
Berrow, Norman.
xBerrow, Norman.
The Ghost House. St Martin.
Berrurier, Diane O. le. *see* Le Berrurier, Diane O.
Berry, Adrian.
xBerry, Adrian.
The Next Ten Thousand Years: A Vision of
Man's Future in the Universe. Dutton.
The Next Ten Thousand Years: A Vision of
Man's Future in the Universe. NAL.
Berry, Albert. *see* Berry, R. Albert.
Berry, Ana M.
xBerry, Ana M.
Animals in Art. Gale.
Berry, Barbara. *see* Berry, Barbara J.
Berry, Barbara J.
xBerry, Barbara.
The Thoroughbreds. Bobbs.
xBerry, Barbara J.
The Standardbreds. A S Barnes.
Berry, Bill.
xBerry, Bill.
Water-Skiing. Transatlantic.
Berry, Boyd M.
xBerry, Boyd M.
Process of Speech: Puritan Religious Writing &
Paradise Lost. Johns Hopkins.
Berry, Brewton.
xBerry, Brewton.
Almost White. Macmillan.
Race & Ethnic Relations. HM.
Berry, Brian J. *see* Berry, Brian Joe Lobley.
Berry, Brian J. L. *see* Berry, Brian Joe Lobley.
Berry, Brian Joe Lobley.
xBerry, Brian J.
ed. The Nature of Change in Geographical
Ideas. N Ill U Pr.
The Open Housing Question: Race & Housing
in Chicago 1966-1976. Ballinger Pub.
Theories of Urban Location. Assn Am
Geographers.
xBerry, Brian J. L.

Geography of Economic Systems. P-H.

Berry, Burton Y. see Berry, Burton Yost.

Berry, Burton Yost.
  xBerry, Burton Y.
    Out of the Past: The Istanbul Grand Bazaar. Arco.

Berry, Calvin W.
  xBerry, Calvin W.
    Arrest, Search, & Seizure. Michie.
    Criminal Practice in Municipal & County Courts. Michie.

Berry, Charles H. see Berry, Charles Harris.

Berry, Charles Harris, 1930-
  xBerry, Charles H.
    Corporate Growth & Diversification. Princeton U Pr.

Berry, Dorothea M.
  xBerry, Dorothea M.
    A Guide to Writing Research Papers. McGraw.

Berry, George R. see Berry, George Ricker.

Berry, George Ricker.
  xBerry, George R.
    A Dictionary of New Testament Greek Synonyms. Zondervan.

Berry, Gerald L, 1915-
  xBerry, Gerald L.
    Religions of the World. Har-Row.

Berry, H. Margaret.
  xBerry, Margaret.
    Introduction to Systemic Linguistics. St Martin.

Berry, Henry.
  xBerry, Henry.
    Boston Red Sox. Macmillan.

Berry, Herbert.
  xBerry, Herbert.
    ed. The First Public Playhouse: The Theatre in Shoreditch, 1576-1598. McGill-Queens U Pr.

Berry, I. William.
  xBerry, William I.
    Where to Ski: A Guide to Skiing in the U. S. A.. NAL.

Berry, J. W.
  xBerry, J. W.
    Applied Cross Cultural Psychology. Humanities.

Berry, J. W. see Berry, John Widdup.

Berry, James, 1852-1913
  xBerry, James.
    My Experiences As an Executioner. Gale.

Berry, Jo.
  xBerry, Jo.
    Growing, Sharing, Serving. Cook.

Berry, John Widdup, 1939-
  xBerry, J. W.
    Human Ecology & Cognitive Style: Comparative Studies in Cultural & Psychological Adaptation. Halsted Pr.

Berry, Juliet.
  xBerry, Juliet.
    Social Work with Children. Routledge & Kegan.

Berry, Leonard.
  xBerry, Leonard.
    ed. Making the Most of the Least: Alternative Development for Poor Nations. Holmes & Meier.

Berry, Leonard L.
  xBerry, Leonard L.
    Marketing for the Bank Executive. Van Nos Reinhold.

Berry, M. see Berry, Michael V.

Berry, Margaret. see Berry, H. Margaret.

Berry, Mary C. see Berry, Mary Clay.

Berry, Mary Clay.
  xBerry, Mary C.
    Alaska Pipeline: The Politics of Oil & Native Land Claims. Ind U Pr.

Berry, Michael V.
  xBerry, M.

Principles of Cosmology and Gravitation. Cambridge U Pr.

Berry, Mildred F. see Berry, Mildred Freburg.

Berry, Mildred Freburg.
  xBerry, Mildred F.
    Speech Disorders: Principles & Practices of Therapy. P-H.
    Teaching Linguistically Handicapped Children. P-H.

Berry, Paul, 1935-
  xBerry, Paul.
    The Essential Self: An Introduction to Literature. McGraw.

Berry, R. see Berry, Ralph.

Berry, R. Albert.
  xBerry, Albert.
    Income Distribution in Colombia. Yale U Pr.
  xBerry, R. Albert.
    ed. Politics of Compromise: Coalition Government in Colombia. Transaction Bks.

Berry, R. Stephen.
  xBerry, R. Stephen.
    Physical Chemistry. Wiley.

Berry, Ralph, 1931-
  xBerry, R.
    How to Write a Research Paper. Pergamon.

Berry, Ralph E.
  xBerry, Ralph E.
    The Economic Cost of Alcohol Abuse. Free Pr.

Berry, Robert W.
  xBerry, Robert W.
    Thin Film Technology. Krieger.

Berry, Romeyn.
  xBerry, Romeyn.
    Stoneposts in the Sunset. Century Hse.

Berry, Sara S.
  xBerry, Sara S.
    Cocoa, Custom, & Socio-Economic Change in Rural Western Nigeria. Oxford U Pr.

Berry, Thomas E. see Berry, Thomas Elliott.

Berry, Thomas Elliott.
  xBerry, Thomas E.
    The Craft of Writing. McGraw.
    Journalism in America: An Introduction to the News Media. Hastings.

Berry, W. B. see Berry, William B. N.

Berry, Wallace.
  xBerry, Wallace.
    Eighteenth Century Imitative Counterpoint: Music for Analysis. P-H.
    Form in Music: An Examination of Traditional Techniques of Musical Structure & Their Application in Historical & Contemporary Styles. P-H.

Berry, Wendell, 1934-
  xBerry, Wendell.
    A Continuous Harmony: Essays Cultural & Agricultural. HarBraceJ.
    The Country of Marriage. HarBraceJ.
    The Memory of Old Jack. HarBraceJ.
    The Memory of Old Jack. HarBraceJ.

Berry, William B. see Berry, William B. N.

Berry, William B. N.
  xBerry, W. B.
    Silurian & Devonian Graptolites of Central Nevada. U of Cal Pr.
  xBerry, William B.
    Growth of a Prehistoric Time Scale, Based on Organic Evolution. W H Freeman.

Berry, William I. see Berry, I. William.

Berry, William L.
  xBerry, William L.
    Management Decision Sciences: Cases & Readings. Irwin.

Berryman, Charles, 1939-
  xBerryman, Charles.

From Wilderness to Wasteland: The Trial of the Puritan God in the American Imagination. Kennikat.

Berryman, John, 1914-
  xBerryman, John.
    Dream Songs. FS&G.
    Love & Fame. FS&G.
    Stephen Crane. Octagon.

Bers, Lipman.
  xBers, Lipman.
    Calculus. HR&W.

Bersani, Leo.
  xBersani, Leo.
    Balzac to Beckett: Center & Circumference in French Fiction. Oxford U Pr.
    A Future for Astyanax: Character & Desire in Literature. Little.

Berscheid, Ellen.
  xBerscheid, Ellen.
    Interpersonal Attraction. A-W.

Bershady, H. see Bershady, Harold J.

Bershady, Harold J.
  xBershady, H.
    Ideology & Social Knowledge. Halsted Pr.

Bersohn, M. see Bersohn, Malcolm.

Bersohn, Malcolm.
  xBersohn, M.
    Introduction to Electron Paramagnetic Resonance. Benjamin-Cummings.

Berson, Dvera.
  xBerson, Dvera.
    Pain-Free Arthritis. G K Hall.
    Pain-Free Arthritis. S&S.

Berson, Harold.
  xBerson, Harold.
    Balarin's Goat. Crown.
    Charles & Claudine. Macmillan.
    Joseph & the Snake. Macmillan.
    illus. A Moose Is Not a Mouse. Crown.

Berssenbrugge, Mei-Mei, 1947-
  xBerssenbrugge, Mei-Mei.
    Random Possession. Reed & Cannon.

Berston, Hyman M. see Berston, Hyman Maxwell.

Berston, Hyman Maxwell.
  xBerston, Hyman M.
    California Real Estate Practice. Irwin.
    California Real Estate Principles. Irwin.
    Collegiate Business Mathematics. Irwin.

Bertaux, Felix.
  xBertaux, Felix.
    A Panorama of German Literature from 1871-1931. Cooper Sq.

Bertcher, Harvey J.
  xBertcher, Harvey J.
    Creating Groups. Sage.

Berte, John B.
  xBerte, John B.
    Pulmonary Emergencies. Lippincott.

Bertele, Umberto.
  xBertele, Umberto.
    Nonserial Dynamic Programming. Acad Pr.

Bertherat, Therese.
  xBertherat, Therese.
    The Body Has Its Reasons: Anti-Exercises & Self-Awareness. Pantheon.

Berthoff, Ann E.
  xBerthoff, Ann E.
    Forming-Thinking-Writing: The Composing Imagination. Hayden.

Berthoff, Warner.
  xBerthoff, Warner.
    Edmund Wilson. U of Minn Pr.
    Example of Melville. Norton.
  xBerthoff, Werner.
    A Literature Without Qualities: American Writing Since 1945. U of Cal Pr.

Berthoff, Werner. see Berthoff, Warner.

Berthold, Arthur B. see Berthold, Arthur Benedict.

Berthold, Arthur Benedict, 1905-
  xBerthold, Arthur B.

American Colonial Printing As Determined by Contemporary Cultural Forces. B Franklin.

Berthold, Margot, 1922-
xBerthold, Margot.
A History of World Theater. Ungar.

Berthoud, Jacques. *see* Berthoud, Jacques A.

Berthoud, Jacques A., 1935-
xBerthoud, Jacques.
Joseph Conrad: The Major Phase. Cambridge U Pr.

Berthouex, P. Mac.
xBerthouex, P. Mac.
Strategy of Pollution Control. Wiley.

Berthrong, Donald J.
xBerthrong, Donald J.
Southern Cheyennes. U of Okla Pr.

Berti, Luciano.
xBerti, Luciano.
Raphael. Norton.

Bertillon, Alphonse, 1853-1914
xBertillon, Alphonse.
Alphonse Bertillon's Instructions for Taking Descriptions for the Identification of Criminals, & Others by Means of Anthropometric Indications. AMS Pr.

Bertin, Eugene P., 1921-
xBertin, Eugene P.
Principles & Practice of X-Ray Spectrometric Analysis. Plenum Pub.

Bertin, John J.
xBertin, John J.
Aerodynamics for Engineers. P-H.

Bertocci, Peter A. *see* Bertocci, Peter Anthony.

Bertocci, Peter Anthony.
xBertocci, Peter A.
Religion As Creative Insecurity. Greenwood.

Bertol, Roland.
xBertol, Roland.
Charles Drew. T Y Crowell.

Bertolet, Mary M.
xBertolet, Mary M.
ed. Hospital Liability: Law & Tactics. PLI.

Bertolotti, Antonino, 1836-1893
xBertolotti, Antonino.
Artisti Bolognesi, Ferraresi Ed Alcuni Altri Del Gia Stato Pontificio in Roma Nei Secoli Quin Dici, Sei Dici, Dicitasette. B Franklin.
Artisti Lombardi a Roma Nei Secoli XV, XVI & XVII: Studi e Ricerche Archivi Romani. B Franklin.

Berton, Peter. *see* Berton, Peter Alexander Menquez.

Berton, Peter Alexander Menquez, 1922-
xBerton, Peter.
Soviet Works on China: A Bibliography of Non-Periodical Literature, 1946-1955. U of S Cal Pr.
Soviet Works on Southeast Asia: A Bibliography of Non-Periodical Literature 1946-1965. U of S Cal Pr.

Berton, Pierre, 1920-
xBerton, Pierre.
The Dionne Years: A Thirties Melodrama. Norton.
Drifting Home. Knopf.

Bertram, Brian, 1944-
xBertram, Brian.
A Pride of Lions. Scribner.

Bertram, James M.
xBertram, James M.
First Act in China: The Story of the Sian Mutiny. Da Capo.
First Act in China: The Story of the Sian Mutiny. Hyperion Conn.

Bertrand, Ian. *see* Bertrand, Ina Winneford.

Bertrand, Ina Winneford, 1939-
xBertrand, Ian.
Film Censorship in Australia. U of Queensland Pr.

Bertrand, Marc.
xBertrand, Marc.

L'Oeuvre de Jean Prevost. U of Cal Pr.

Bertsch, Gary K.
xBertsch, Gary K.
ed. Comparative Communism: The Soviet, Chinese, & Yugoslav Models. W H Freeman.

Bertsekas, Dimitri P.
xBertsekas, Dimitri P.
Dynamic Programming & Stochastic Control. Acad Pr.
Stochastic Optimal Control: The Discrete Time Case. Acad Pr.

Berven, Ken.
xBerven, Ken.
I Love Being Married to a Grandma. Nelson.

Berwanger, Eugene H.
xBerwanger, Eugene H.
As They Saw Slavery. Krieger.
The Frontier Against Slavery: Western Anti-Negro Prejudice & the Slavery Extension Controversy. U of Ill Pr.

Berwick, Donald M.
xBerwick, Donald M.
Cholesterol, Children, & Heart Disease: An Analysis of Alternatives. Oxford U Pr.

Berwick, W. E. *see* Berwick, William Edward Hodgson.

Berwick, William Edward Hodgson, 1888-
xBerwick, W. E.
Integral Bases. Hafner.

Berzins, Alfreds, 1899-
xBerzins, Alfreds.
Two Faces of Co-Existence. Speller.

Berzon, Betty.
xBerzon, Betty.
ed. Positively Gay. Celestial Arts.

Berzon, Judith R., 1945-
xBerzon, Judith R.
Neither White nor Black: The Mulatto Character in American Fiction. NYU Pr.

Bes, J.
xBes, J.
Chartering & Shipping Terms. Heinman.

Besancon, Robert M. *see* Besancon, Robert Martin.

Besancon, Robert Martin.
xBesancon, Robert M.
ed. Encyclopedia of Physics. Van Nos Reinhold.

Besant, Walter, Sir, 1836-1901
xBesant, Walter.
Autobiography of Sir Walter Besant. R West.
Autobiography of Sir Walter Besant. Scholarly.
The Rebel Queen. Arno.
Studies in Early French Poetry. Arno.

Beschloss, Michael R.
xBeschloss, Michael R.
Kennedy & Roosevelt: The Uneasy Alliance. Norton.

Beschner. *see* Beschner, George M.

Beschner, George M.
xBeschner.
ed. Youth Drug Abuse: Problems, Issues, & Treatment. Lexington Bks.

Besedovskii, Grigorii Z. *see* Besedovskii, Grigorii Zinovevich.

Besedovskii, Grigorii Zinovevich.
xBesedovskii, Grigorii Z.
Revelations of a Soviet Diplomat. Hyperion-Conn.

Beseler, D. v. *see* Beseler, Dora Hedwig Von.

Beseler, Dora Hedwig Von.
xBeseler, D. v.
ed. Law Dictionary: Technical Dictionary of Anglo-American Legal Terminology, German-English. De Gruyter.

Besford, Pat.
xBesford, Pat.
Compiled by Encyclopaedia of Swimming. St Martin.

Besier, Rudolf.
xBesier, Rudolf.

The Barretts of Wimpole Street. Little.

Besov, Oleg V. *see* Besov, Oleg Vladimirovich.

Besov, Oleg Vladimirovich.
xBesov, Oleg V.
Integral Representations of Functions & Imbedding Theorems. Halsted Pr.

Bespaloff, Alexis.
xBespaloff, Alexis.
Alexis Bespaloff's Guide to Inexpensive Wines. S&S.

Bess, David.
xBess, H. David.
Marine Transportation. Interstate.

Bess, Fred H.
xBess, Fred H.
ed. Childhood Deafness: Causation, Assessment & Management. Grune.

Bess, H. David. *see* Bess, David.

Bessant, B. *see* Bessant, Bob.

Bessant, Bob.
xBessant, B.
Teachers in Conflict. Intl Schol Bk Serv.

Besser, Gretchen R.
xBesser, Gretchen R.
Nathalie Sarraute. Twayne.

Besserman, Lawrence L., 1945-
xBesserman, Lawrence L.
The Legend of Job in the Middle Ages. Harvard U Pr.

Besset, Maurice.
xBesset, Maurice.
Art of the Twentieth Century. Universe.

Bessie, Alvah. *see* Bessie, Alvah Cecil.

Bessie, Alvah Cecil, 1904-
xBessie, Alvah.
Spain Again. Chandler & Sharp.

Bessinger, J. B. *see* Bessinger, Jess B.

Bessinger, Jess B.
xBessinger, J. B.
ed. A Concordance to the "Anglo-Saxon Poetic Records". Cornell U Pr.

Bessis, M. *see* Bessis, Marcel.

Bessis, Marcel, 1919-
xBessis, M.
Corpuscles: Atlas of Red Blood Cell Shapes. Springer-Verlag.
Living Blood Cells & Their Ultrastructure. Springer-Verlag.

Bessom, Malcolm E.
xBessom, Malcolm E.
Supervising the Successful School Music Program. P-H.

Best, Alan C. *see* Best, Alan C. G.

Best, Alan C. G.
xBest, Alan C.
An African Survey. Wiley.

Best, David.
xBest, David.
Philosophy & Human Movement. Allen Unwin.

Best, Elsdon, 1856-1931
xBest, Elsdon.
Fishing Methods & Devices of the Maori. AMS Pr.
The Maori. AMS Pr.
Maori Religion & Mythology. AMS Pr.

Best, Ernest.
xBest, Ernest.
From Text to Sermon: Responsible Use of the New Testament in Preaching. John Knox.

Best, F. *see* Best, Fred.

Best, Fred.
xBest, F.
ed. Future of Work. P-H.
xBest, Fred.
Flexible Life Scheduling: Breaking the Education-Work-Retirement Lockstep. Praeger.

Best, Gary A., 1939-
xBest, Gary A.

Individuals with Physical Disabilities: An
Introduction for Educators. Mosby.
Best, Gary D. *see* Best, Gary Dean.
Best, Gary Dean.
xBest, Gary D.
The Politics of American Individualism:
Herbert Hoover in Transition, 1918-1921.
Greenwood.
Best, Gerald M.
xBest, Gerald M.
The Ulster & Delaware: Railroad Through the
Catskills. Golden West.
Best, Judith.
xBest, Judith.
The Case Against Direct Election of the
President: A Defense of the Electoral
College. Cornell U Pr.
Best, Kenneth Y.
xBest, Kenneth Y.
Cultural Policy in Liberia. Unipub.
Best, Mary A. *see* Best, Mary Agnes.
Best, Mary Agnes, d. 1942
xBest, Mary A.
Rebel Saints. Arno.
Rebel Saints. Century Bookbindery.
Best, Michael H.
xBest, Michael H.
The Politicized Economy. Heath.
Best, Thomas W.
xBest, Thomas W.
Humanist Ulrich Von Hutten: A Reappraisal of
His Humor. U of NC Pr.
Bester, Alfred.
xBester, Alfred.
Computer Connection. Berkley Pub.
The Computer Connection. Berkley Pub.
The Demolished Man. Garland Pub.
The Demolished Man. PB.
Golem. S&S.
The Stars My Destination. Baronet.
The Stars My Destination. Berkley Pub.
The Stars My Destination. Gregg.
xBester, Alred.
Demolished Man. NAL.
Bester, Alred. *see* Bester, Alfred.
Besterfield, Dale H.
xBesterfield, Dale H.
Quality Control: A Practical Approach. P-H.
Besterman, Theodore.
xBesterman, Theodore.
A World Bibliography of African
Bibliographies. Rowman.
A World Bibliography of Oriental
Bibliographies. Rowman.
Bestic, Alan.
xBestic, Alan.
Praise the Lord & Pass the Contribution.
Taplinger.
Bestor, Dorothy K., 1913-
xBestor, Dorothy K.
Aside from Teaching English, What in the
World Can You Do?. U of Wash Pr.
Betancourt, Romulo, Pres. Venezuela, 1908-
xBetancourt, Romulo.
Venezuela's Oil. Allen Unwin.
Betcherman, Barbara.
xBetcherman, Barbara.
Suspicions. Putnam.
Beteille, Andre.
xBeteille, Andre.
Caste, Class & Power: Changing Patterns of
Stratification in a Tanjore Village. U of Cal
Pr.
Inequality Among Men. Biblio Dist.
Betenson, Lula P. *see* Betenson, Lula Parker.
Betenson, Lula Parker.
xBetenson, Lula P.
Butch Cassidy, My Brother. Brigham.
Butch Cassidy, My Brother. Penguin.
Beth, E. W. *see* Beth, Evert Willem.

Beth, Evert Willem.
xBeth, E. W.
Mathematical Epistemology & Psychology.
Gordon.
Beth, Loren P.
xBeth, Loren P.
Development of the American Constitution,
1877-1917. Har-Row.
Bethancourt, Ernesto T. *see* Bethancourt, T. Ernesto.
Bethancourt, T. Ernesto.
xBethancourt, Ernesto T.
Dr. Doom Superstar. Bantam.
xBethancourt, T. Ernesto.
The Dog Days of Arthur Cane. Holiday.
Instruments of Darkness. Holiday.
The Mortal Instruments. Holiday.
Mortal Instruments. Bantam.
Nightmare Town. Holiday.
Tune in Yesterday. Holiday.
Bethe, Hans A. *see* Bethe, Hans Albrecht.
Bethe, Hans Albrecht.
xBethe, Hans A.
Quantum Mechanics of One- & Two-Electron
Atoms. Plenum Pub.
Bethea, Doris C.
xBethea, Doris C.
Introductory Maternity Nursing. Lippincott.
Bethel, Dell.
xBethel, Dell.
Coaching Winning Baseball. Contemp Bks.
The Complete Book of Baseball Instruction.
Contemp Bks.
Inside Baseball: Tips & Techniques for Coaches
& Players. Contemp Bks.
Bethel, May.
xBethel, May.
Healing Power of Natural Foods. Wilshire.
Bethell, Jean.
xBethell, Jean.
Bathtime. HR&W.
How to Care for Your Dog. Schol Bk Serv.
How to Care for Your Dog. Schol Bk Serv.
Bethell, Nicholas. *see* Bethell, Nicholas William.
Bethell, Nicholas William, Baron Bethell, 1938-
xBethell, Nicholas.
The Palestine Triangle: The Struggle for the
Holy Land 1935-48. Putnam.
Bethell, S. L. *see* Bethell, Samuel Leslie.
Bethell, Samuel L. *see* Bethell, Samuel Leslie.
Bethell, Samuel Leslie.
xBethell, S. L.
The Literary Outlook. Arden Lib.
xBethell, Samuel L.
Literary Outlook. Folcroft.
Bethell, Tom.
xBethell, Tom.
George Lewis: A Jazzman from New Orleans.
U of Cal Pr.
Bethge, K. *see* Bethge, Klaus.
Bethge, Klaus, 1931-
xBethge, K.
ed. Experimental Methods in Heavy Ion
Physics. Springer-Verlag.
Bethune, George W. *see* Bethune, George Washington.
Bethune, George Washington, 1805-1862
xBethune, George W.
British Female Poets: With Biographical &
Critical Notices. Arno.
Bethune, J. *see* Bethune, James D.
Bethune, James D., 1941-
xBethune, J.
Essentials of Drafting. P-H.
Betjeman, John.
xBetjeman, John.

ed. English, Scottish & Welsh Landscape,
1700-C. 1860. Granger Bk.
London's Historic Railway Stations.
Transatlantic.
A Nip in the Air. Norton.
Bett, Henry, 1876-1953
xBett, Henry.
Nicholas of Cusa. Richwood Pub.
Some Secrets of Style. Kennikat.
Studies in Literature. Kennikat.
Studies in Literature. R West.
Bett, K. E.
xBett, K. E.
Thermodynamics for Chemical Engineers. MIT
Pr.
Bettelheim, Bruno.
xBettelheim, Bruno.
Children of the Dream. Avon.
Dialogues with Mothers. Avon.
Dialogues with Mothers. Free Pr.
A Home for the Heart. Knopf.
Informed Heart: Autonomy in a Mass Age.
Free Pr.
Surviving & Other Essays. Knopf.
Surviving & Other Essays. Random.
Truants from Life: The Rehabilitation of
Emotionally Disturbed Children. Free Pr.
The Uses of Enchantment: The Meaning &
Importance of Fairy Tales. Knopf.
The Uses of Enchantment: The Meaning &
Importance of Fairy Tales. Random.
Bettelheim, Charles.
xBettelheim, Charles.
Cultural Revolution & Industrial Organization
in China: Changes in Management & the
Division of Labor. Monthly Rev.
Economic Calculation & Forms of Property.
Monthly Rev.
Bettelheim, R. *see* Bettelheim, Ruth.
Bettelheim, Ruth.
xBettelheim, R.
Early Schooling in Asia. McGraw.
Betten, Neil.
xBetten, Neil.
Catholic Activism & the Industrial Worker. U
Presses Fla.
Bettenson, Henry. *see* Bettenson, Henry Scowcroft.
Bettenson, Henry Scowcroft.
xBettenson, Henry.
tr. & ed. The Later Christian Fathers: A
Selection from the Writings of the Fathers
from St. Cyril of Jerusalem to St. Leo the
Great. Oxford U Pr.
Better Business Bureau. *see* Better Business Bureau of
Western New York, Inc.
Better Business Bureau of Western New York, Inc.
xBetter Business Bureau.
Consumer's Buying Guide: How to Get Your
Money's Worth. B&N.
xTheBetter Business Bureau.
The Better Business Bureau Guide to Wise
Buying. Paddington.
Better Business Bureau Wise Buying Guide.
Facts on File.
Better Homes & Garden Books. *see* Better Homes and
Gardens.
Better Homes & Gardens. *see* Better Homes and
Gardens.
Better Homes & Gardens Bks. *see* Better Homes and
Gardens.
Better Homes & Gardens Book Editors. *see* Better
Homes and Gardens.
Better Homes & Gardens Books. *see* Better Homes and
Gardens.
Better Homes & Gardens Books Editors. *see* Better
Homes and Gardens.
Better Homes & Gardens Editors. *see* Better Homes and
Gardens.
Better Homes and Gardens.
xBetter Homes & Garden Books.

ed. Better Homes & Gardens All-Time Favorite Barbecue Recipes. Meredith Corp.

xBetter Homes & Gardens.

ed. After Work Cook Book. Meredith Corp.

ed. Better Homes & Gardens New Baby Book. Bantam.

xBetter Homes & Gardens Bks.

ed. Better Homes & Gardens Crockery Cooker Cook Book. Meredith Corp.

ed. Better Homes & Gardens Home Style Cooking. Meredith Corp.

ed. Better Homes & Gardens Microwave Cook Book. Meredith Corp.

xBetter Homes & Gardens Book Editors.

Better Homes & Gardens All-Time Favorite Beef Recipes. Meredith Corp.

Better Homes & Gardens All-Time Favorite Casserole Recipes. Meredith Corp.

Better Homes & Gardens Gourmet Recipes Made Easy. Meredith Corp.

xBetter Homes & Gardens Books.

ed. Better Homes & Gardens All-Time Favorite Hamburger & Ground Meats Recipes. Meredith Corp.

ed. Better Homes & Gardens Blender Cook Book. BH&G.

ed. Better Homes & Gardens Calorie Counter's Cook Book. BH&G.

ed. Better Homes & Gardens Chicken & Turkey Cook Book. Meredith Corp.

ed. Better Homes & Gardens Complete Guide to Home Repair, Maintenance & Improvement. Meredith Corp.

ed. Better Homes & Gardens Cooking for Two. BH&G.

ed. Better Homes & Gardens Creative Crafts & Stitchery. Meredith Corp.

ed. Better Homes & Gardens Crepes Cook Book. Meredith Corp.

ed. Better Homes & Gardens Crocheting & Knitting. Meredith Corp.

ed. Better Homes & Gardens Favorite Houseplants. Meredith Corp.

ed. Better Homes & Gardens Fondue & Tabletop Cooking. BH&G.

ed. Better Homes & Gardens Gifts from Your Kitchen. Meredith Corp.

ed. Better Homes & Gardens Heritage Cook Book. BH&G.

ed. Better Homes & Gardens House Plants. BH&G.

ed. Better Homes & Gardens Low-Cost Cooking. Meredith Corp.

ed. Better Homes & Gardens Meat Cook Book. BH&G.

ed. Better Homes & Gardens Story Book. BH&G.

xBetter Homes & Gardens Books Editors.

Better Homes & Gardens After-40 Health & Medical Guide. Meredith Corp.

Better Homes & Gardens All-Time Favorite Bread Recipes. Meredith Corp.

Better Homes & Gardens All-Time Favorite Cake & Cookie Recipes. Meredith Corp.

Better Homes & Gardens All-Time Favorite Fish & Seafood Recipes. Meredith Corp.

ed. Better Homes & Gardens All-Time Favorite Salad Recipes. Meredith Corp.

ed. Better Homes & Gardens All-Time Favorite Pie. Meredith Corp.

Better Homes & Gardens All-Time Favorite Vegetable Recipes. Meredith Corp.

ed. Better Homes & Gardens Annuals You Can Grow. Meredith Corp.

ed. Better Homes & Gardens Applique. Meredith Corp.

Better Homes & Gardens Bath & Bedroom Projects You Can Build. Meredith Corp.

Better Homes & Gardens Calorie-Trimmed Recipes. Meredith Corp.

Better Homes & Gardens Complete Guide to Gardening. Meredith Corp.

ed. Better Homes & Gardens Complete Step-by-Step Cook Book. Meredith Corp.

ed. Better Homes & Gardens Container Plants You Can Grow. Meredith Corp.

ed. Better Homes & Gardens Easiest Plants You Can Grow. Meredith Corp.

Better Homes & Gardens Eat & Stay Slim. Meredith Corp.

ed. Better Homes & Gardens Embroidery. Meredith Corp.

ed. Better Homes & Gardens Energy Saving Projects You Can Build. Meredith Corp.

ed. Better Homes & Gardens Favorite American Wines & How to Enjoy Them. Meredith Corp.

ed. Better Homes & Gardens Fix It Fast Cook Book. Meredith Corp.

ed. Better Homes & Gardens Food Processor Cook Book. Meredith Corp.

Better Homes & Gardens Italian Cook Book. Meredith Corp.

ed. Better Homes & Gardens Meals for One or Two. Meredith Corp.

Better Homes & Gardens More from Your Microwave. Meredith Corp.

ed. Better Homes & Gardens Needlepoint. Meredith Corp.

ed. Better Homes & Gardens New Baby Book. Meredith Corp.

ed. Better Homes & Gardens New Cookbook. Bantam.

ed. Better Homes & Gardens New Junior Cook Book. Meredith Corp.

Better Homes & Gardens Outdoor Projects You Can Build. Meredith Corp.

Better Homes & Gardens Patchwork & Quilting. Meredith Corp.

ed. Better Homes & Gardens Perennials You Can Grow. Meredith Corp.

Better Homes & Gardens Pork, Sausage & Ham Cook Book. Meredith Corp.

ed. Better Homes & Gardens Roses You Can Grow. Meredith Corp.

ed. Better Homes & Gardens Rug Making. Meredith Corp.

ed. Better Homes & Gardens Soups & Stews Cook Book. Meredith Corp.

Better Homes & Gardens Step-by-Step Basic Wiring. Meredith Corp.

ed. Better Homes & Gardens Storage Projects You Can Build. Meredith Corp.

Better Homes & Gardens Treasury of Christmas Crafts & Foods. Meredith Corp.

ed. Better Homes & Gardens Vegetables & Herbs You Can Grow. Meredith Corp.

xBetter Homes & Gardens Editors.

Better Homes & Gardens All-Time Favorite Barbecue Recipes. Bantam.

Better Homes & Gardens All-Time Favorite Fruit Recipes. Meredith Corp.

ed. Better Homes & Gardens Baby Book. Bantam.

Better Homes & Gardens Deck & Patio Projects You Can Build. Meredith Corp.

ed. Better Homes & Gardens Decorating Book. Meredith Corp.

ed. Better Homes & Gardens Family Medical Guide. Meredith Corp.

Better Homes & Gardens Family Room Projects You Can Build. Meredith Corp.

Better Homes & Gardens Furniture Projects You Can Build. Meredith Corp.

Better Homes & Gardens Handyman Book. Bantam.

The Better Homes & Gardens Home Canning Cookbook. Bantam.

ed. Better Homes & Gardens Homemade Cookies Cook Book. Meredith Corp.

Better Homes & Gardens Kitchen Projects You Can Build. Meredith Corp.

Better Homes & Gardens Mexican Cook Book. Meredith Corp.

ed. Better Homes & Gardens Oriental Cook Book. Meredith Corp.

Better Homes & Gardens Woodworking Projects You Can Build. Meredith Corp.

Betteridge, Harold T.

xBetteridge, Harold T.

Cassell's German Dictionary: German-English English-German. Macmillan.

Betters, Paul V. *see* Betters, Paul Vernon.

Betters, Paul Vernon, 1906-1956

xBetters, Paul V.

The Bureau of Home Economics: Its History, Activities & Organization. AMS Pr.

Federal Services to Municipal Governments. Arno.

The Personnel Classification Board: Its History, Activities & Organization. AMS Pr.

Bettersworth, John K. *see* Bettersworth, John Knox.

Bettersworth, John Knox, 1909-

xBettersworth, John K.

Confederate Mississippi: The People & Policies of a Cotton State in Wartime. Porcupine Pr.

People's University: A History of Mississippi State University. U Pr of Miss.

Bettey, J. H.

xBettey, J. H.

Church & Community: The Parish Church in English Life. B&N.

Dorset. David & Charles.

Bettger, Frank.

xBettger, Frank.

How I Raised Myself from Failure to Success in Selling. Cornerstone.

How I Raised Myself from Failure to Success in Selling. P-H.

Betti, Claudia W.

xBetti, Claudia W.

Drawing: A Contemporary Approach. HR&W.

Bettinghaus, Erwin P. *see* Bettinghaus, Erwin Paul.

Bettinghaus, Erwin Paul, 1930-

xBettinghaus, Erwin P.

The Nature of Proof. Bobbs.

Bettman, James R.

xBettman, James R.

Information Processing Theory of Consumer Choice. A-W.

Bettmann, Otto.

xBettmann, Otto L.

Good Old Days - They Were Terrible!. Random.

Bettmann, Otto L. *see* Bettmann, Otto.

Bettoni, Efrem.

xBettoni, Efrem.

Duns Scotus: The Basic Principles of His
Philosophy. Greenwood.
Betts, C. Wyllys. see Betts, Charles Wyllys.
Betts, Charles Wyllys, 1845-1887
xBetts, C. Wyllys.
American Colonial History Illustrated by
Contemporary Medals (1894). Quarterman.
Betts, Donni.
xBetts, Donni.
Growing Together. Celestial Arts.
Betts, Douglas A.
xBetts, Douglas A.
Chess: An Annotated Bibliography of Works
Published in the English Language,
1850-1968. G K Hall.
Betts, Edward. see Betts, Edward H.
Betts, Edward H., 1920-
xBetts, Edward.
Master Class in Watercolor. Watson-Guptill.
Betts, Edwin M. see Betts, Edwin Morris.
Betts, Edwin Morris.
xBetts, Edwin M.
Thomas Jefferson's Flower Garden at
Monticello. U Pr of Va.
Betts, George, 1944-
xBetts, George.
Farewells Are Only Beginnings. Celestial Arts.
My Gift to You. Celestial Arts.
Betts, J. see Betts, John Arthur.
Betts, Jerry W., 1936-
xBetts, Jerry W.
Football Fundamentals for Kids & Parents. A S
Barnes.
Betts, John Arthur.
xBetts, J.
Signal Processing, Modulation & Noise.
Elsevier.
Betts, John R. see Betts, John Rickards.
Betts, John Rickards, 1917-1971
xBetts, John R.
America's Sporting Heritage: 1850-1950. A-W.
Betts, Raymond F.
xBetts, Raymond F.
Assimilation & Association in French Colonial
Theory 1890-1914. AMS Pr.
Europe in Retrospect: A Brief History of the
Past Two Hundred Years. Heath.
The False Dawn: European Imperialism in the
Nineteenth Century. U of Minn Pr.
ed. Ideology of Blackness. Heath.
Betts, Reginald R. see Betts, Reginald Robert.
Betts, Reginald Robert, 1903-1961
xBetts, Reginald R.
ed. Central & South East Europe, 1945-1948.
Greenwood.
Betts, Richard K., 1947-
xBetts, Richard K.
Soldiers, Statesmen, & Cold War Crises.
Harvard U Pr.
Betts, Robert B.
xBetts, Robert B.
Along the Ramparts of the Tetons: The Saga of
Jackson Hole, Wyoming. Colo Assoc.
Betts, Roland. see Betts, Roland W.
Betts, Roland W.
xBetts, Roland.
Acting Out: Coping with Big City Schools.
Little.
Betzner, Jean, 1888-
xBetzner, Jean.
Content & Form of Original Compositions
Dictated by Children from Five to Eight
Years of Age. AMS Pr.
Beuchat, L. R. see Beuchat, Larry R.
Beuchat, Larry R.
xBeuchat, L. R.
Food & Beverage Mycology. AVI.
Beucler, Andre, 1898-
xBeucler, Andre.

Last of the Bohemians: Twenty Years with
Leon-Paul Fargue. Greenwood.
Beuf, Ann H., 1938-
xBeuf, Ann H.
Biting off the Bracelet: A Study of Children in
Hospitals. U of Pa Pr.
Beutel, Frederick K. see Beutel, Frederick Keating.
Beutel, Frederick Keating, 1897-
xBeutel, Frederick K.
Bank Officer's Handbook of Commercial
Banking Law. Warren.
Democracy of the Scientific Method in Law &
Policy Making. U of PR Pr.
The Operation of the Bad Check Laws of
Puerto Rico. U of PR Pr.
Beutelspacher, H.
xBeutelspacher, H.
Atlas of Electron Microscopy of Clay Minerals
& Their Admixtures. Elsevier.
Beutner, E. H. see Beutner, Ernst H.
Beutner, Ernst H.
xBeutner, E. H.
Immunopathology of the Skin. Wiley.
Bevan, Clifford.
xBevan, Clifford.
The Tuba Family. Scribner.
Bevan, David, 1943-
xBevan, David.
Charles-Ferdinand Ramuz. Twayne.
Bevan, E. Dean.
xBevan, E. Dean.
ed. Concordance to the Plays & Prefaces of
Bernard Shaw. Gale.
Bevan, Edwyn. see Bevan, Edwyn Robert.
Bevan, Edwyn R. see Bevan, Edwyn Robert.
Bevan, Edwyn Robert, 1870-1943
xBevan, Edwyn.
Stoics & Sceptics. Arno.
xBevan, Edwyn R.
Holy Images: An Inquiry into Idolatry &
Image-Worship in Ancient Paganism & in
Christianity. AMS Pr.
ed. Later Greek Religion. AMS Pr.
Symbolism & Belief. Folcroft.
Bevan, James. see Bevan, James Stuart.
Bevan, James Stuart.
xBevan, James.
The Simon & Schuster Handbook of Anatomy
& Physiology. S&S.
Bevan, John. see Bevan, John Michael.
Bevan, John Michael.
xBevan, John.
Introduction to Statistics. Philos Lib.
Bevan, Ruth A.
xBevan, Ruth A.
Marx & Burke: A Revisionist View. Open
Court.
Bevans, Jerry T.
xBevans, Jerry T.
ed. Thermophysics: Applications to Thermal
Design of Spacecraft. Acad Pr.
Bevelander, Gerrit, 1905-
xBevelander, Gerrit.
Atlas of Oral Histology & Embryology. Lea &
Febiger.
Essentials of Histology. Mosby.
Outline of Histology. Mosby.
Bevenot, Maurice.
xBevenot, Maurice.
The Tradition of Manuscripts: A Study in the
Transmission of St. Cyprian's Treatises.
Greenwood.
Bevensee, R. M.
xBevensee, Robert M.
Handbook of Conical Antennas & Scatterers.
Gordon.
Bevensee, Robert M. see Bevensee, R. M.
Bever, James A.
xBever, James A.

Coming of Age in America: VERCAP, a Guide
for High School Students. Natl Assn
Principals.
Beveridge, Agnes.
xBeveridge, Agnes.
Expressive Language Remediation for the
Older Elementary Child. Interstate.
Beveridge, Andrew A.
xBeveridge, Andrew A.
African Businessmen and Development in
Zambia. Princeton U Pr.
Beveridge, Elizabeth, 1905-
xBeveridge, Elizabeth.
Choosing & Using Home Equipment. Iowa St
U Pr.
Beveridge, Gordon S. G.
xBeveridge, S. G.
Optimization Theory & Practice. McGraw.
Beveridge, S. G. see Beveridge, Gordon S. G.
Beveridge, W. I. see Beveridge, William Ian Beardmore.
Beveridge, W. I. B. see Beveridge, William Ian
Beardmore.
Beveridge, William H. see Beveridge, William Henry
Beveridge.
Beveridge, William Henry Beveridge, Baron, 1879-1963
xBeveridge, William H.
Causes & Cures of Unemployment. AMS Pr.
Causes & Cures of Unemployment.
Greenwood.
ed. The Evidence for Voluntary Action, Being
Memoranda by Organisations & Individuals
& Other Materials Relevant to Voluntary
Action. Greenwood.
Unemployment: A Problem of Industry. AMS
Pr.
Beveridge, William I. see Beveridge, William Ian
Beardmore.
Beveridge, William Ian Beardmore.
xBeveridge, W. I.
Art of Scientific Investigation. Norton.
xBeveridge, W. I. B.
Frontiers in Comparative Medicine. U of Minn
Pr.
xBeveridge, William I.
Art of Scientific Investigation. Random.
Beverly Hills Bar Association.
xBeverly Hills Bar Association. Barristers
Committee for the Arts.
The Actor's Manual: A Practical Legal Guide.
Dutton.
The Musician's Manual: A Practical Career
Guide. Dutton.
Beverly Hills Bar Association. Barristers Committee for
the Arts. see Beverly Hills Bar Association.
Bevier, Michael J.
xBevier, Michael J.
Politics Backstage: Inside the California
Legislature. Temple U Pr.
Bevington, David. see Bevington, David M.
Bevington, David M.
xBevington, David.
Medieval Drama. HM.
xBevington, David M.
Tudor Drama & Politics: A Critical Approach
to Topical Meaning. Harvard U Pr.
Bevington, Philip R., 1933-
xBevington, Philip R.
Data Reduction & Error Analysis for the
Physical Sciences. McGraw.
Bevlin, Marjorie. see Bevlin, Marjorie Elliott.
Bevlin, Marjorie Elliott.
xBevlin, Marjorie.
Design Through Discovery. HR&W.
Bewick, Michael W. see Bewick, Michael W. M.
Bewick, Michael W. M.
xBewick, Michael W.
ed. Handbook of Organic Waste Conversion.
Van Nos Reinhold.
Bewley, L. V. see Bewley, Loyal Vivian.

Bhattacharya, Rabindra Nath.
  xBhattacharya, R. N.
    Normal Approximation & Asymptotic
    Expansions. Wiley.
Bhattacharya, Sachchidananda.
  xBhattacharya, Sachchidananda.
    A Dictionary of Indian History. Greenwood.
Bhattacharya, Srinibas, 1921-
  xBhattacharya, Srinibas.
    New Perspectives in Mental Retardation.
    Verry.
Bhattacharyya, Arunodoy.
  xBhattacharyya, Arunodoy.
    The Sonnet & the Major English Romantic
    Poets. South Asia Bks.
Bhattacharyya, Narendra N. *see* Bhattacharyya, Narendra
  Nath.
Bhattacharyya, Narendra Nath.
  xBhattacharyya, Narendra N.
    Ancient Indian Rituals & Their Social
    Contents. Rowman.
Bhoothalingam, M. *see* Bhoothalingam, Mathuram.
Bhoothalingam, Mathuram.
  xBhoothalingam, M.
    Story of Rama. Asia.
Bhutani, V. C., 1940-
  xBhutani, V. C.
    The Apotheosis of Imperialism: Indian Land
    Economy Under Curzon. Verry.
Bial, Morrison D. *see* Bial, Morrison David.
Bial, Morrison David, 1917-
  xBial, Morrison D.
    Liberal Judaism at Home: The Practices of
    Modern Reform Judaism. UAHC.
    Your Jewish Child. UAHC.
Biale, David, 1949-
  xBiale, David.
    Gershom Scholem: Kabbalah &
    Counter-History. Harvard U Pr.
Bialer, S. *see* Bialer, Seweryn.
Bialer, Seweryn.
  xBialer, S.
    ed. Sources of Contemporary Radicalism.
    Westview.
Bianchi, Bruno.
  xBianchi, Bruno.
    The Rules of Sailing Races. Dodd.
Bianco, Lucien.
  xBianco, Lucien.
    Origins of the Chinese Revolution, 1915-1949.
    Stanford U Pr.
Bianco, Margery W. *see* Bianco, Margery Williams.
Bianco, Margery Williams.
  xBianco, Margery W.
    The Hurdy-Gurdy Man. Gregg.
Bianco, Pamela, 1906-
  xBianco, Pamela.
    Valentine Party. Lippincott.
Biancolli, Louis. *see* Biancolli, Louis Leopold.
Biancolli, Louis L. *see* Biancolli, Louis Leopold.
Biancolli, Louis Leopold.
  xBiancolli, Louis.
    ed. The Opera Reader. Greenwood.
  xBiancolli, Louis L.
    ed. Analytical Concert Guide. Greenwood.
Biasin, Gian-Paolo.
  xBiasin, Gian-Paolo.
    Literary Diseases: Theme & Metaphor in the
    Italian Novel. U of Tex Pr.
Bibb, Benjamin O.
  xBibb, Benjamin O.
    Amazing Secrets of Psychic Healing. P-H.
Bibb, Clifford. *see* Bibb, Thomas Clifford.
Bibb, Porter.
  xBibb, Porter.
    The CB Bible. Doubleday.
Bibb, Thomas Clifford.
  xBibb, Clifford.

    The Humanities: A Cross-Cultural Approach.
    Kendall-Hunt.
Bibbero, Robert J.
  xBibbero, Robert J.
    Systems Approach to Air Pollution Control.
    Wiley.
Bibby, Cyril. *see* Bibby, Harold Cyril.
Bibby, Harold Cyril.
  xBibby, Cyril.
    The Art of the Limerick. Shoe String.
Bibby, John.
  xBibby, John.
    Prediction & Improved Estimation in Linear
    Models. Wiley.
Bibby, Violet.
  xBibby, Violet.
    Many Waters Cannot Quench Love. Morrow.
Biberman, L. M. *see* Biberman, Lucien M.
Biberman, Lucien M.
  xBiberman, L. M.
    ed. Perception of Displayed Information.
    Plenum Pub.
Bibliographic Society of Northern Illinois. *see*
  Bibliographical Society of Northern Illinois.
Bibliographical Society of Northern Illinois.
  xBibliographic Society of Northern Illinois.
    Index to Reviews of Bibliographical
    Publications, Nineteen Seventy-Seven. G K
    Hall.
Bibliotheque Imperiale Publique De St. Petersbourg. *see*
  Leningrad. Publichnaia Biblioteka.
Bibliotheque Nationale. *see* Paris. Bibliotheque Nationale.
Bibliotheque Nationale. Departement des Imprimes,
  Paris. *see* Paris. Bibliotheque Nationale.
Bibliotheque Nationale, Paris. *see* Paris. Bibliotheque
  Nationale.
Bibo, Istvan.
  xBibo, Istvan.
    The Paralysis of International Institutions &
    the Remedies: A Study of
    Self-Determination, Concord Among the
    Major Powers & Political Arbitration. Halsted
    Pr.
    The Paralysis of International Institutions &
    the Remedies: A Study of
    Self-Determination, Concord Among the
    Major Powers, & Political Arbitration.
    Krieger.
Bibring, Grete L.
  xBibring, Grete L.
    Lectures in Medical Psychology: An
    Introduction to the Care of Patients. Intl
    Univs Pr.
    ed. The Teaching of Dynamic Psychiatry: A
    Reappraisal of the Goals & Techniques in the
    Teaching of Psychoanalytic Psychiatry. Intl
    Univs Pr.
Bicanic, R. *see* Bicanic, Rudolf.
Bicanic, Rudolf.
  xBicanic, R.
    Economic Policy in Socialist Yugoslavia.
    Cambridge U Pr.
Bicha, Karel D.
  xBicha, Karel D.
    The Czechs in Oklahoma. U of Okla Pr.
Bichowsky, F. Russell. *see* Bichowsky, Francis Russell.
Bichowsky, Francis Russell, 1889-1951
  xBichowsky, F. Russell.
    Industrial Research. Arno.
Bick, T. A. *see* Bick, Theodore A.
Bick, Theodore A., 1930-
  xBick, T. A.
    Introduction to Abstract Mathematics. Acad
    Pr.
Bickel, Alexander M.
  xBickel, Alexander M.

    The Least Dangerous Branch: The Supreme
    Court at the Bar of Politics. Bobbs.
    The Least Dangerous Branch: The Supreme
    Court at the Bar of Politics. Irvington.
    The Morality of Consent. Yale U Pr.
    Politics & the Warren Court. Da Capo.
    The Supreme Court & the Idea of Progress.
    Yale U Pr.
Bickel, H. *see* Bickel, Horst.
Bickel, Horst.
  xBickel, H.
    ed. Neonatal Screening for Inborn Errors of
    Metabolism. Springer-Verlag.
Bickel, P. J. *see* Bickel, Peter J.
Bickel, Peter J.
  xBickel, P. J.
    Mathematical Statistics: Basic Ideas & Selected
    Topics. Holden-Day.
Bickelhaupt, David L. *see* Bickelhaupt, David Lynn.
Bickelhaupt, David Lynn.
  xBickelhaupt, David L.
    General Insurance. Irwin.
Bickerman, E. J. *see* Bickerman, Elias Joseph.
Bickerman, Elias, 1897-
  xBickerman, Elias.
    From Ezra to the Last of the Maccabees:
    Foundations of Post-Biblical Judaism.
    Schocken.
Bickerman, Elias. *see* Bickerman, Elias Joseph.
Bickerman, Elias Joseph.
  xBickerman, E. J.
    Chronology of the Ancient World. Cornell U
    Pr.
  xBickerman, Elias.
    The Ancient History of Western Civilization.
    Har-Row.
Bickerstaffe-Drew, Francis B. *see* Bickerstaffe-Drew,
  Francis Browning Drew.
**Bickerstaffe-Drew, Francis Browning Drew, Count,
  1858-1928**
  xBickerstaffe-Drew, Francis B.
    Discourses & Essays. Arno.
Bickersteth, G. L. *see* Bickersteth, Geoffrey Langdale.
Bickersteth, Geoffrey L. *see* Bickersteth, Geoffrey
  Langdale.
Bickersteth, Geoffrey Langdale, 1884-
  xBickersteth, G. L.
    Golden World of King Lear. Porter.
  xBickersteth, Geoffrey L.
    The Golden World of "King Lear". Norwood
    Edns.
Bickerton, Derek.
  xBickerton, Derek.
    King of the Sea. Random.
Bicket, Zenas J.
  xBicket, Zenas J.
    The Effective Pastor. Gospel Pub.
Bickford, Elwood D.
  xBickford, Elwood D.
    Lighting for Plant Growth. Kent St U Pr.
Bickham, Jack. *see* Bickham, Jack M.
Bickham, Jack M.
  xBickham, Jack.
    The Regensburg Legacy. Doubleday.
    Twister. PB.
    The Winemakers. PB.
  xBickham, Jack M.
    Baker's Hawk. Doubleday.
    Dinah, Blow Your Horn. Doubleday.
    Excalibur Disaster. Doubleday.
    The Excalibur Disaster. Playboy Pbks.
Bickley, Francis. *see* Bickley, Francis Lawrence.
Bickley, Francis L. *see* Bickley, Francis Lawrence.
Bickley, Francis Lawrence, 1885-
  xBickley, Francis.
    Life of Matthew Prior. Folcroft.
  xBickley, Francis L.
    An English Letter Book. Folcroft.
Bickley, Harmon C.
  xBickley, Harmon C.

Practical Concepts in Human Disease. Williams & Wilkins.

Bicks, Alexander, 1901-
xBicks, Alexander.
Contracts for the Sale of Realty. PLI.

Bicksler, James L.
xBicksler, James L.
ed. Capital Market Equilibrium & Efficiency: Implications for Accounting, Finance, & Portfolio Decision Making. Lexington Bks.

Bicycling.
xBicycling Magazine.
ed. Bicycle Commuting. Rodale Pr Inc.
ed. The Most Frequently Asked Questions About Bicycling. Rodale Pr Inc.

Bicycling Magazine. see Bicycling.

Biczok, I. see Biczok, Imre.

Biczok, Imre.
xBiczok, I.
Concrete Corrosion & Concrete Protection. Adler.

Bidart, Frank, 1939-
xBidart, Frank.
Golden State. Braziller.

Biddiss, Michael D. see Biddiss, Michael Denis.

Biddiss, Michael Denis.
xBiddiss, Michael D.
The Age of the Masses: Ideas & Society in Europe Since 1870. Humanities.
ed. Images of Race. Holmes & Meier.

Biddle, Arthur W.
xBiddle, Arthur W.
ed. The Literature of Vermont: A Sampler. U Pr of New Eng.

Biddle, B. J. see Biddle, Bruce Jesse.

Biddle, Bruce Jesse.
xBiddle, B. J.
Role Theory: Concepts & Research. Krieger.

Biddle, Edward.
xBiddle, Edward.
Life & Works of Thomas Sully. Da Capo.

Biddle, Francis. see Biddle, Francis Beverley.

Biddle, Francis Beverley, 1886-1968
xBiddle, Francis.
In Brief Authority. Greenwood.

Biddle, Gordon.
xBiddle, Gordon.
British Railway Station. David & Charles.

Biddle, Nicholas.
xBiddle, Nicholas.
Correspondence of Nicholas Biddle Dealing with National Affairs, 1807-1844. Canner.

Biddle, Perry H., 1932-
xBiddle, Perry H.
Abingdon Funeral Manual. Abingdon.
Abingdon Marriage Manual. Abingdon.

Biddle, William W. see Biddle, William Wishart.

Biddle, William Wishart, 1900-
xBiddle, William W.
Propaganda & Education. AMS Pr.

Biddulph, Michael W.
xBiddulph, Michael W.
The Golf Shot. Norton.

Bidermann, Jacob. see Bidermann, Jakob.

Bidermann, Jakob, 1577 or 8-1639
xBidermann, Jacob.
Cenodoxus. U of Tex Pr.

Bidlack, Russell E. see Bidlack, Russell Eugene.

Bidlack, Russell Eugene, 1920-
xBidlack, Russell E.
The ALA Accreditation Process, 1973-1976: A Survey of Library Schools Whose Programs Were Evaluated Under the 1972 Standards for Accreditation. ALA.

Bidney, David, 1908-
xBidney, David.
ed. Concept of Freedom in Anthropology. Mouton.
Theoretical Anthropology. Columbia U Pr.

Bidwell, Charles. see Bidwell, Charles Everett.

Bidwell, Charles Everett.
xBidwell, Charles.
Issues in Macroanalysis. Ballinger Pub.

Bidwell, James K.
xBidwell, James K.
ed. Readings in the History of Mathematics Education. NCTM.

Bidwell, Percy W. see Bidwell, Percy Wells.

Bidwell, Percy W. see Bidwell, Percy Wells.

Bidwell, Percy Wells.
xBidwell, Percy.
History of Agriculture in the Northern United States 1620-1860. Kelley.
xBidwell, Percy W.
History of Agriculture in the Northern United States: 1620-1860. Peter Smith.
Raw Materials: A Study of American Policy. Greenwood.

Bidwell, R. G. see Bidwell, Roger Crafton Shelford.

Bidwell, Roger Crafton Shelford, 1927-
xBidwell, R. G.
Plant Physiology. Macmillan.

Bieber, Margarete, 1879-
xBieber, Margarete.
Ancient Copies: Contributions to the History of Greek & Roman Art. NYU Pr.

Bieber, Ralph P. see Bieber, Ralph Paul.

Bieber, Ralph Paul, 1894-
xBieber, Ralph P.
ed. Southern Trails to California in 1849. Porcupine Pr.
ed. Southwest Historical Series. Porcupine Pr.

Biedenharn, C. see Biedenharn, L. C.

Biedenharn, L. C.
xBiedenharn, C.
ed. Quantum Theory of Angular Momentum: A Collection of Reprints & Original Papers. Acad Pr.

Biederman, Kenneth R.
xBiederman, Kenneth R.
Taxation & Regulation of the Savings & Loan Industry. Lexington Bks.

Biegeleisen, J. I. see Biegeleisen, Jacob Israel.

Biegeleisen, Jacob Israel, 1910-
xBiegeleisen, J. I.
Antique Alphabets. Signs of Times.
Design & Print Your Own Posters. Watson-Guptill.
Silk Screen Techniques. Dover.
Silk Screen Techniques. Peter Smith.

Biehler, Robert F. see Biehler, Robert Frederick.

Biehler, Robert Frederick, 1927-
xBiehler, Robert F.
Child Development: An Introduction. HM.
Psychology Applied to Teaching. HM.

Bielawski, Joseph G.
xBielawski, Joseph G.
ed. Guide to Educational Technology: Elementary Education. Technomic.

Bieler, H. G. see Bieler, Henry G.

Bieler, Henry G.
xBieler, H. G.
Food Is Your Best Medicine. Random.
xBieler, Henry G.
Food Is Your Best Medicine. Random.

Bielschowsky, Albert.
xBielschowsky, Albert.
Life of Goethe. AMS Pr.
Life of Goethe. Haskell.

Biemond, A. see Biemond, Arie.

Biemond, Arie, 1902-
xBiemond, A.
ed. Brain Diseases. Elsevier.

Bien, David D.
xBien, David D.
The Calas Affair: Persecution, Toleration, & Heresy in Eighteenth-Century Toulouse. Greenwood.

Bien, Peter.
xBien, Peter.

Demotic Greek. U Pr of New Eng.

Bienek, Horst, 1930-
xBienek, Horst.
The Cell. Unicorn Pr.

Bienen, Henry.
xBienen, Henry.
Armies & Parties in Africa. Holmes & Meier.
Tanzania: Party Transformation & Economic Development. Princeton U Pr.

Bienenfeld, Florence.
xBienenfeld, Florence.
My Mom & Dad Are Getting a Divorce. EMC.

Biennial Conference, Dundee, Great Britain, June 28-July 1, 1977. see Dundee Biennial Conference on Numerical Analysis.

Biennial Seminar of the Canadian Mathematical Congress, 14th Univ. of Western Ontario, August 1973. see Canadian Mathematical Congress.

Biennial World Congress of the International College of Surgeons, 20th, Athens, 23-27 May 1976. see International College of Surgeons. Congress.

Bienstock, Gregory.
xBienstock, Gregory.
Struggle for the Pacific. Kennikat.

Bienz, D. R., 1926-
xBienz, D. R.
The Why & How of Home Horticulture. W H Freeman.

Bierce. see Bierce, Ambrose.

Bierce, Ambrose, 1842-1914?
xBierce.
Devil's Dictionary. Peter Pauper.
xBierce, Ambrose.
Can Such Things Be?. Am Repr-Rivercity Pr.
Can Such Things Be?. Citadel Pr.
Collected Works. Gordon Pr.
The Devil's Dictionary. Am Repr-Rivercity Pr.
The Devil's Dictionary. Dover.
The Devil's Dictionary. Gannon.
Devil's Dictionary. Hill & Wang.
The Devil's Dictionary. Peter Smith.
The Devil's Dictionary. Stemmer Hse.
Fantastic Fables. Am Repr-Rivercity Pr.
Fantastic Fables. Dover.
Fantastic Fables. Gannon.
Ghost & Horror Stories. Peter Smith.
Stories & Fables of Ambrose Bierce. Stemmer Hse.

Bierhorst, John.
xBierhorst, John.
illus. A Cry from the Earth: Music of the North American Indians. Schol Bk Serv.
ed. In the Trail of the Wind: American Indian Poems & Ritual Orations. FS&G.

Bieri, Arthur P. see Bieri, Arthur Peter.

Bieri, Arthur Peter.
xBieri, Arthur P.
Action Games. Pitman Learning.

Bieri, S. see Bieri, Stephan.

Bieri, Stephan.
xBieri, S.
Fiscal Federalism in Switzerland. Bks Australia.

Bierley, Paul E.
xBierley, Paul E.
Office Fun!. Integrity.

Bierman, C. Warren. see Bierman, Charles Warren.

Bierman, Charles Warren.
xBierman, C. Warren.
ed. Allergic Diseases of Infancy, Childhood & Adolescence. Saunders.

Bierman, Elenore C.
xBierman, Elenore C.
There's an Iguana in My Plumbing. Ashley Bks.

Bierman, Gerald J.
xBierman, Gerald J.

Factorization Methods for Discrete Sequential
Estimation. Acad Pr.
Bierman, Harold.
xBierman, Harold.
The Capital Budgeting Decision: Economic
Analysis of Investment Projects. Macmillan.
Decision Making & Planning for the Corporate
Treasurer. Ronald Pr.
An Introduction to Managerial Finance.
Norton.
Bierman, Howard, 1925-
xBierman, Howard.
How to Plan & Install Electronic Burglar
Alarms. Hayden.
Bierman, Sheldon L.
xBierman, Sheldon L.
Geothermal Energy in the Western United
States: Innovation Versus Monopoly. Praeger.
Biermann, June.
xBiermann, June.
The Diabetic's Sports & Exercise Book: How
to Play Your Way to Better Health.
Lippincott.
The Woman's Holistic Headache Relief Book.
St Martin.
Biersdorf, John E., 1930-
xBiersdorf, John E.
ed. Creating an Intentional Ministry. Abingdon.
Bierstedt, Robert, 1913-
xBierstedt, Robert.
Power & Progress: Essays on Sociological
Theory. McGraw.
Biesanz, John. see Biesanz, John Berry.
Biesanz, John B. see Biesanz, John Berry.
Biesanz, John Berry.
xBiesanz, John.
Introduction to Sociology. P-H.
xBiesanz, John B.
Costa Rican Life. Greenwood.
Biese, Alfred, 1856-1930
xBiese, Alfred.
The Development of the Feeling for Nature in
the Middle Ages and Modern Times. B
Franklin.
Biestek, Felix P. see Biestek, Felix Paul.
Biestek, Felix Paul, 1912-
xBiestek, Felix P.
The Casework Relationship. Loyola.
Client Self-Determination in Social Work: A
Fifty Year History. Loyola.
Biever, Bruce F. see Biever, Bruce Francis.
Biever, Bruce Francis.
xBiever, Bruce F.
Religion, Culture & Values: A Cross-Cultural
Analysis of Motivational Factors in Native
Irish & American Irish Catholicism. Arno.
Bifulco, John. see Bifulco, John M.
Bifulco, John M.
xBifulco, John.
How to Estimate Construction Costs of
Electrical Power Substations. Van Nos
Reinhold.
Bigart, Robert.
xBigart, Robert.
ed. Environmental Pollution in Montana.
Mountain Pr.
Bigelow, Erastus B. see Bigelow, Erastus Brigham.
Bigelow, Erastus Brigham, 1814-1879
xBigelow, Erastus B.
The Tariff Policy of England & of the United
States Contrasted. Garland Pub.
Bigelow, Gordon E.
xBigelow, Gordon E.
Frontier Eden: The Literary Career of Marjorie
Kinnan Rawlings. U Presses Fla.
Rhetoric & American Poetry of the Early
National Period. U Presses Fla.
Bigelow, Howard E. see Bigelow, Howard Elson.
Bigelow, Howard Elson, 1923-
xBigelow, Howard E.

The Mushroom Pocket Field Guide.
Macmillan.
Mushroom Pocket Field Guide. Macmillan.
Bigelow, Marybelle S.
xBigelow, Marybelle S.
Fashion in History: Western Dress, Prehistoric
to Present. Burgess.
Bigelow, Melville M. see Bigelow, Melville Madison.
Bigelow, Melville Madison.
xBigelow, Melville M.
Centralization & the Law: Scientific Legal
Education, an Illustration. Rothman.
Bigge, L. Morris. see Bigge, Morris L.
Bigge, Morris L.
xBigge, L. Morris.
Psychological Foundations of Education: An
Introduction to Human Motivation,
Development, & Learning. Har-Row.
xBigge, Morris L.
Learning Theories for Teachers. Har-Row.
Biggers, Earl D. see Biggers, Earl Derr.
Biggers, Earl Derr, 1884-1933
xBiggers, Earl D.
Charlie Chan Carries on. Buccaneer Bks..
Biggle, Lloyd, 1923-
xBiggle, Lloyd.
A Galaxy of Strangers. Doubleday.
The Whirligig of Time. Doubleday.
Biggs, Charles L.
xBiggs, Charles L.
Managing the Systems Development Process.
P-H.
Biggs, Don.
xBiggs, Don.
Pressure Cooker. Norton.
Survival Afloat. McKay.
Biggs, Donald C.
xBiggs, Donald C.
Conquer & Colonize: Stevenson's Regiment &
California. Presidio Pr.
Biggs, J. B. see Biggs, John Burville.
Biggs, John, 1895-
xBiggs, John.
The Guilty Mind: Psychiatry & the Law of
Homicide. Johns Hopkins.
Biggs, John Burville.
xBiggs, J. B.
Information & Human Learning. Scott F.
Biggs, John M. see Biggs, John Melvin.
Biggs, John Melvin.
xBiggs, John M.
Introduction to Structural Dynamics. McGraw.
Biggs, N. L. see Biggs, Norman.
Biggs, Norman.
xBiggs, N. L.
Permutation Groups & Combinatorial
Structures. Cambridge U Pr.
Biggs, Robert D.
xBiggs, Robert D.
Inscriptions from Tell Abu Salabikh. U of
Chicago Pr.
Biggs, W. D. see Biggs, William Derrick.
Biggs, William Derrick.
xBiggs, W. D.
The Mechanical Behaviour of Engineering
Materials. Pergamon.
Bigland, E. see Bigland, Eileen.
Bigland, Eileen.
xBigland, E.
Mary Shelley. R West.
xBigland, Eileen.
In the Steps of George Borrow. Dynamic Learn
Corp.
Bigler, Robert M.
xBigler, Robert M.
The Politics of German Protestantism: The
Rise of the Protestant Church Elite in
Prussia, 1815-1848. U of Cal Pr.
Bigley, Nancy J.
xBigley, Nancy J.

Immunologic Fundamentals. Year Bk Med.
Bigman, David.
xBigman, David.
ed. The Functioning of Floating Exchange
Rates: Theory, Evidence & Policy
Implications. Ballinger Pub.
Bignell, Merle.
xBignell, Merle.
The Fruit of the Country: A History of the
Shire of Gnowangerup Western Australia.
Intl Schol Bk Serv.
Bigner, Jerry J.
xBigner, Jerry J.
Parent-Child Relations: An Introduction to
Parenting. Macmillan.
Bigo, Pierre.
xBigo, Pierre.
The Church & Third World Revolution. Orbis
Bks.
Bigsby, C. W. see Bigsby, C. W. E.
Bigsby, C. W. E.
xBigsby, C. W.
The Second Black Renaissance: Essays in Black
Literature. Greenwood.
Bigwood, E. J. see Bigwood, Edouard Jean.
Bigwood, Edouard Jean.
xBigwood, E. J.
ed. Protein & Amino Acid Functions.
Pergamon.
Bihalji-Merin, Oto.
xBihalji-Merin, Oto.
Intro. by Art Treasures of Yugoslavia. Abrams.
Bihari. see Bihari, Otto.
Bihari, Otto.
xBihari.
The Constitutional Models of Socialist State
Organization. Heyden.
xBihari, Otto.
The Constitutional Models of Socialist State
Organization. Intl Pubns Serv.
Bijou. see Bijou, Sidney William.
Bijou, Sidney William, 1908-
xBijou.
Child Development: The Basic Stage of Early
Childhood. P-H.
Bikai, P. M. see Bikai, Patricia Maynor.
Bikai, Patricia Maynor.
xBikai, P. M.
The Pottery of Tyre. Intl Schol Bk Serv.
Bikales, Norbert M.
xBikales, Norbert M.
ed. Adhesion & Bonding. Wiley.
ed. Extrusion & Other Plastics Operations.
Wiley.
ed. Mechanical Properties of Polymers. Wiley.
Bikerman, J. J. see Bikerman, Jacob Joseph.
Bikerman, Jacob Joseph, 1898-
xBikerman, J. J.
Foams. Springer-Verlag.
Bikkie, James A., 1929-
xBikkie, James A.
Careers in Marketing. McGraw.
Biklen, Sari K. see Biklen, Sari Knopp.
Biklen, Sari Knopp.
xBiklen, Sari K.
Women & Educational Leadership. Lexington
Bks.
Biko, Stephen.
xBiko, Steve.
Black Consciousness in South Africa. Random.
Biko, Steve. see Biko, Stephen.
Bila, Dennis, 1941-
xBila, Dennis.
Core Mathematics. Worth.
Mathematics for Health Occupations.
Winthrop.
Mathematics for Technical Occupations.
Winthrop.
Bilan, R. P.
xBilan, R. P.

The Literary Criticism of F. R. Leavis.
Cambridge U Pr.
Bilateral U.S.-Japan Seminar in Hydrology, 1st, University of Hawaii, 1971.
xBilateral U.S.-Japan Seminar in Hydrology, 1st, Honolulu, Jan. 11-17, 1971.
Systems Approach to Hydrology: Proceedings. WRP.
Bilbrough, A.
xBilbrough, A.
Developing Patterns in Physical Education. Intl Pubns Serv.
Bilenkin, Dmitri. *see* Bilenkin, Dmitrii Aleksandrovich.
Bilenkin, Dmitrii Aleksandrovich.
xBilenkin, Dmitri.
The Uncertainty Principle. Macmillan.
The Uncertainty Principle. Macmillan.
Biles, Roy E. *see* Biles, Roy Edwin.
Biles, Roy Edwin.
xBiles, Roy E.
Complete Illustrated Book of Garden Magic. Doubleday.
Biles, William E.
xBiles, William E.
Optimization & Industrial Experimentation. Wiley.
Bilinsky, Yaroslav.
xBilinsky, Yaroslav.
Changes in the Central Committee, Communist Party of the Soviet Union, 1961-66. U of Denver Intl.
Bilio, Beth De. *see* De Bilio, Beth.
Bill, A. H. *see* Bill, Alfred Hoyt.
Bill, Alfred H. *see* Bill, Alfred Hoyt.
Bill, Alfred Hoyt.
xBill, A. H.
A House Called Morven: Its Role in American History. Princeton U Pr.
xBill, Alfred H.
Rehearsal for Conflict: The War with Mexico, 1846-1848. Cooper Sq.
Bill, Erastus, 1826-1905
xBill, Erastus D.
Citizen: An American Boy's Early Manhood Aboard a Sag Harbor Whale-Ship Chasing Delirium & Death Around the World, 1843-1849. O W Frost.
Bill, Erastus D. *see* Bill, Erastus.
Bill, James A.
xBill, James A.
Politics in the Middle East. Little.
Billcliffe, Roger.
xBillcliffe, Roger.
Charles Rennie Mackintosh: The Complete Furniture, Furniture Drawings, & Interior Designs. Taplinger.
Biller, Henry B.
xBiller, Henry B.
Father, Child & Sex Role: Paternal Determinants in Personality Development. Lexington Bks.
Billet, R. *see* Billet, Reinhard.
Billet, Reinhard.
xBillet, R.
Distillation Engineering. Chem Pub.
Billett, Roy O. *see* Billett, Roy Oren.
Billett, Roy Oren, 1891-
xBillett, Roy O.
Improving the Secondary-School Curriculum: A Guide to Effective Curriculum Planning. Lieber-Atherton.
Billias, G. A. *see* Billias, George Athan.
Billias, George A. *see* Billias, George Athan.
Billias, George Athan.
xBillias, G. A.
American History: Retrospect & Prospect. Free Pr.
xBillias, George A.

The American Revolution: How Revolutionary Was It?. HR&W.
ed. George Washington's Generals. Greenwood.
The Massachusetts Land Bankers of 1740. U Maine Orono.
Billiet, W. E. *see* Billiet, Walter E.
Billiet, Walter E.
xBilliet, W. E.
Automotive Electrical Systems. Am Technical.
xBilliet, Walter E.
Automotive Suspensions, Steering, Alignment & Brakes. Am Technical.
Billig, Otto.
xBillig, Otto.
The Painted Message. Halsted Pr.
Billings, Charles E.
xBillings, Charles E.
Racism & Prejudice. Hayden.
Billings, John S. *see* Billings, John Shaw.
Billings, John Shaw, 1838-1913
xBillings, John S.
History & Literature of Surgery. Argosy.
Billings, Marland P. *see* Billings, Marland Pratt.
Billings, Marland Pratt, 1902-
xBillings, Marland P.
Structural Geology. P-H.
Billings, Peggy.
xBillings, Peggy.
Paradox & Promise in Human Rights. Friend Pr.
Billings, William R.
xBillings, William R.
Some Details of Water-Works Construction. Noyes.
Billingsley, Ed. *see* Billingsley, Edmond.
Billingsley, Edmond.
xBillingsley, Ed.
Career Planning & Job Hunting for Today's Student: The Non-Job Interview. Goodyear.
Billingsley, P. *see* Billingsley, Patrick.
Billingsley, Patrick.
xBillingsley, P.
Convergence of Probability Measures. Wiley.
xBillingsley, Patrick.
Ergodic Theory & Information. Krieger.
Probability & Measure. Wiley.
Billington, D. P. *see* Billington, David P.
Billington, David P.
xBillington, D. P.
Thin Shell Concrete Structures. McGraw.
Billington, Elizabeth T.
xBillington, Elizabeth T.
Adventure with Flowers. Warne.
Part-Time Boy. Warne.
Understanding Ecology. Warne.
Billington, James H.
xBillington, James H.
Icon & the Axe: An Interpretive History of Russian Culture. Random.
Billington, Monroe L. *see* Billington, Monroe Lee.
Billington, Monroe Lee.
xBillington, Monroe L.
The Political South in the Twentieth Century. Scribner.
xBillington, Montoe L.
South: A Central Theme?. Peter Smith.
Billington, Montoe L. *see* Billington, Monroe Lee.
Billington, Rachel.
xBillington, Rachel.
A Woman's Age. Summit Bks.
Billington, Ray A. *see* Billington, Ray Allen.
Billington, Ray Allen, 1903-
xBillington, Ray A.

ed. The Frontier Thesis: Valid Interpretation of American History?. Krieger.
Genesis of the Frontier Thesis: A Study in Historical Creativity. Huntington Lib.
The Origins of Nativism in the United States, 1800-1844. Arno.
Billinton, Roy.
xBillinton, Roy.
Power-System Reliability Calculations. MIT Pr.
Billmeyer, F. W. *see* Billmeyer, Fred W.
Billmeyer, Fred W.
xBillmeyer, F. W.
Principles of Color Technology. Wiley.
xBillmeyer, Fred W.
Entering Industry: A Guide for Young Professionals. Wiley.
Principles of Color Technology. Wiley.
Textbook of Polymer Science. Wiley.
Billmeyer, Pat.
xBillmeyer, Pat.
The Encyclopedia of Wild Game Cleaning & Cooking. ABC Pub.
Bills, Garland D.
xBills, Garland D.
Introduction to Spoken Bolivian Quechua. U of Tex Pr.
Bills, Robert E.
xBills, Robert E.
A System for Assessing Affectivity. U of Ala Pr.
Billson, Charles J. *see* Billson, Charles James.
Billson, Charles James.
xBillson, Charles J.
Popular Poetry of the Finns. AMS Pr.
Billy Graham Center.
xBilly Graham Center.
ed. An Evangelical Agenda: Nineteen Eighty-Four & Beyond. William Carey Lib.
Bilmanis, Alfred. *see* Bilmanis, Alfreds.
Bilmanis, Alfreds, 1887-1948
xBilmanis, Alfred.
History of Latvia. Greenwood.
Bilokur, Borys.
xBilokur, Borys.
A Concordance to the Russian Poetry of Fedor I. Tiutchev. Brown U Pr.
Biloon, F. *see* Biloon, Frank.
Biloon, Frank, 1920-
xBiloon, F.
Medical Equipment Service Manual: Theory & Maintenance Procedures. P-H.
Bilsborrow, Richard E.
xBilsborrow, Richard E.
Population in Development Planning: Background & Bibliography. Carolina Pop Ctr.
Bilski, Audrey.
xBilski, Audrey.
Problems of Your Child's Vital Years. Intl Schol Bk Serv.
Bilsky, Lester J., 1935-
xBilsky, Lester J.
ed. Historical Ecology: Essays on Environment & Social Change. Kennikat.
Bilz, H. *see* Bilz, Heinz.
Bilz, Heinz.
xBilz, H.
Phonon Dispersion Relations in Insulators. Springer-Verlag.
Bimba, Anthony.
xBimba, Anthony.
History of the American Working Class. Greenwood.
Bimler, Rich. *see* Bimler, Richard.
Bimler, Richard.
xBimler, Rich.
Pray, Praise & Hooray. Concordia.
Bin-Nun, Aaron.
xBin-Nun, Aaron.

The Language of Faith. Shengold.
Binchy, D. A. *see* Binchy, Daniel A.
Binchy, Daniel A., 1899-
    xBinchy, D. A.
        Church & State in Fascist Italy. Oxford U Pr.
Binder, George A.
    xBinder, George A.
        Computed Tomography of the Brain in Axial,
        Coronal, & Sagittal Planes. Little.
Binder, K. *see* Binder, Kurt.
Binder, Kurt.
    xBinder, K.
        ed. Monte Carlo Methods in Statistical Physics.
        Springer-Verlag.
Binder, Leonard.
    xBinder, Leonard.
        ed. Crises & Sequences in Political
        Development. Princeton U Pr.
        Ideological Revolution in the Middle East.
        Krieger.
        In a Moment of Enthusiasm: Political Power &
        the Second Stratum in Egypt. U of Chicago
        Pr.
        The Study of the Middle East: Research &
        Scholarship in the Humanities & Social
        Sciences. Wiley.
Binder, Raymond C. *see* Binder, Raymond Charles.
Binder, Raymond Charles.
    xBinder, Raymond C.
        Fluid Mechanics. P-H.
Bindoff, S. T. *see* Bindoff, Stanley Thomas.
Bindoff, Stanley Thomas, 1908-
    xBindoff, S. T.
        Tudor England. Gannon.
Bindra, Dalbir.
    xBindra, Dalbir.
        A Theory of Intelligent Behavior. Wiley.
Bindra, Jasjit S.
    xBindra, Jasjit S.
        Creativity in Organic Synthesis. Acad Pr.
        Prostaglandin Synthesis. Acad Pr.
Bines, Harvey E.
    xBines, Harvey E.
        Law of Investment Management. Warren.
Binford, Charles M.
    xBinford, Charles M.
        Loss Control in the OSHA Era. McGraw.
Bing, Gordon.
    xBing, Gordon.
        Corporate Divestment. Gulf Pub.
Bing, Jon.
    xBing, Jon.
        Legal Decisions & Information Systems.
        Universitet.
Bing, Stephen. *see* Bing, Stephen R.
Bing, Stephen R.
    xBing, Stephen.
        Standards Relating to Monitoring. Ballinger
        Pub.
Bingham, Alfred M. *see* Bingham, Alfred Mitchell.
Bingham, Alfred Mitchell.
    xBingham, Alfred M.
        ed. Challenge to the New Deal. Arno.
Bingham, Alma.
    xBingham, Alma I.
        Improving Children's Facility in Problem
        Solving. Tchrs Coll.
Bingham, Alma I. *see* Bingham, Alma.
Bingham, Caroline, 1938-
    xBingham, Caroline.
        The Stewart Kingdom of Scotland. St Martin.
Bingham, Earl G.
    xBingham, Earl G.
        Pocketbook for Writers: A Guide to Writing &
        Revision. Wadsworth Pub.
Bingham, Edwin R.
    xBingham, Edwin R.

        ed. Northwest Perspectives: Essays on the
        Culture of the Pacific Northwest. U of Wash
        Pr.
Bingham, Joan.
    xBingham, Joan.
        The Energy Crunch Cookbook. Chilton.
Bingham, John E.
    xBingham, John E.
        Planning for Data Communications. Halsted Pr.
Bingham, June, 1919-
    xBingham, June.
        Courage to Change: An Introduction to the
        Life & Thought of Reinhold Niebuhr. Kelley.
Bingham, Millicent (Todd), 1880-
    xBingham, Millicent T.
        Ancestors' Brocades: The Literary Discovery
        of Emily Dickinson: The Editing &
        Publication of Her Letters & Poems. Dover.
Bingham, Millicent T. *see* Bingham, Millicent (Todd).
Bingham, Nelson Eldred, 1901-
    xBingham, Nelson G.
        Teaching Nutrition in Biology Classes: An
        Experimental Investigation of High School
        Biology Pupils in Their Study of the Relation
        of Food to Physical Well-Being. AMS Pr.
Bingham, Nelson G. *see* Bingham, Nelson Eldred.
Bingham, Richard D.
    xBingham, Richard D.
        The Adoption of Innovation by Local
        Government. Lexington Bks.
        The Politics of Raising State & Local Revenue.
        Praeger.
        Public Housing & Urban Renewal: An Analysis
        of Federal-Local Relations. Praeger.
Bingham, Robert E.
    xBingham, Robert E.
        Traps to Avoid in Good Administration.
        Broadman.
Bingham, William C., 1923-
    xBingham, William C.
        The Counselor & Youth Employment. HM.
Bining, Arthur C. *see* Bining, Arthur Cecil.
Bining, Arthur Cecil, 1893-1957
    xBining, Arthur C.
        British Regulation of the Colonial Iron
        Industry. Kelley.
        Pennsylvania Iron Manufacture in the
        Eighteenth Century. Kelley.
        Pennsylvania Iron Manufacture in the
        Eighteenth Century. Pa Hist & Mus.
Binion, Alice.
    xBinion, Alice.
        Antonio & Francesco Guardi: Their Life &
        Milieu: With a Catalogue of Their Figure
        Drawings. Garland Pub.
Binion, R. *see* Binion, Rudolph.
Binion, Rudolph.
    xBinion, R.
        Hitler Among the Germans. Elsevier.
    xBinion, Rudolph.
        Defeated Leaders: The Political Fate of
        Caillaux, Jouvenel & Tardieu. Greenwood.
        Frau Lou: Nietzsche's Wayward Disciple.
        Princeton U Pr.
Binion, T. *see* Binion, W. T.
Binion, W. T., 1932-
    xBinion, T.
        High School Marching Band. P-H.
Binkin, Martin.
    xBinkin, Martin.
        Where Does the Marine Corps Go from Here?.
        Brookings.
        Youth or Experience?: Manning the Modern
        Military. Brookings.
Binkley, Clark.
    xBinkley, Clark S.
        Interceptor Sewers & Urban Sprawl. Lexington
        Bks.
Binkley, Clark S. *see* Binkley, Clark.
Binkley, Luther J. *see* Binkley, Luther John.

Binkley, Luther John, 1925-
    xBinkley, Luther J.
        Conflict of Ideals: Changing Values in Western
        Society. Van Nos Reinhold.
Binkley, Robert C.
    xBinkley, Robert C.
        Realism & Nationalism: 1852-1871. Har-Row.
Binkley, Wilfred E. *see* Binkley, Wilfred Ellsworth.
Binkley, Wilfred Ellsworth, 1883-
    xBinkley, Wilfred E.
        The Powers of the President: Problems of
        American Democracy. Russell.
Binney, Edwin.
    xBinney, Edwin.
        Turkish Miniature Paintings & Manuscripts
        from the Collection of Edwin Binney, Third.
        Metro Mus Art.
Binnick, Robert I.
    xBinnick, Robert I.
        Modern Mongolian: A Transformational
        Syntax. U of Toronto Pr.
Binnie-Clark, Georgina.
    xBinnie-Clark, Georgina.
        Wheat & Woman. U of Toronto Pr.
Binns, Henry B. *see* Binns, Henry Bryan.
Binns, Henry Bryan, 1873-
    xBinns, Henry B.
        Life of Walt Whitman. Haskell.
Binns, J. W.
    xBinns, J. W.
        ed. Latin Literature of the Fourth Century.
        Routledge & Kegan.
        ed. The Latin Poetry of English Poets.
        Routledge & Kegan.
        ed. Ovid. Routledge & Kegan.
Binstock, Robert H.
    xBinstock, Robert H.
        The Handbook of Aging & the Social Sciences.
        Van Nos Reinhold.
Binswanger, Hans P.
    xBinswanger, Hans P.
        Induced Innovation: Technology, Institutions &
        Development. Johns Hopkins.
Binyon, Laurence.
    xBinyon, Laurence.
        Persian Miniature Painting: Including a Critical
        & Descriptive Catalogue of the Miniatures
        Exhibited at Burlington House, January
        Through March, 1931. Dover.
        Tradition & Reaction in Modern Poetry.
        Folcroft.
Binzen, Bill.
    xBinzen, Bill.
        Alfred Goes Flying. Doubleday.
        First Day in School. Doubleday.
Binzen, Peter.
    xBinzen, Peter.
        Whitetown, U. S. A. Random.
Bioavailability of Drug Products Project. *see* Apha
    Bioavailability Project.
Biobaku, S. O. *see* Biobaku, Saburi Oladeni.
Biobaku, Saburi Oladeni.
    xBiobaku, S. O.
        ed. Sources of Yoruba History. Oxford U Pr.
Biochemical Society, London. Symposium.
    xBiochemical Society Symposium, 27th.
        Metabolic Roles of Citrate: Proceedings. Acad
        Pr.
    xBiochemical Society Symposium, 28th.
        Porphyrins & Related Compounds:
        Proceedings. Acad Pr.
    xBiochemical Society Symposium, 29th.
        Natural Substances Formed Biologically from
        Mevalonic Acid: Proceedings. Acad Pr.
    xBiochemical Society Symposium, 30th.
        British Biochemistry: Past & Present. Acad Pr.
    xBiochemical Society Symposium, 31st.

Chemical Reactivity & Biological Role of
Functional Groups in Enzymes: Proceedings.
Acad Pr.
xBiochemical Society Symposium, 32nd.
Biochemistry of Steroid Hormone Action:
Proceedings. Acad Pr.
xBiochemical Society Symposium, 33rd.
Plasma Lipoproteins: Proceedings. Acad Pr.
xBiochemical Society Symposium, 34th.
Biological Hydroxylation Mechanisms:
Proceedings. Acad Pr.
xBiochemical Society Symposium, 35th.
Current Trends in the Biochemistry of Lipids:
Proceedings. Acad Pr.
Biochemical Society Symposium, 27th. see Biochemical
Society, London. Symposium.
Biochemical Society Symposium, 28th. see Biochemical
Society, London. Symposium.
Biochemical Society Symposium, 29th. see Biochemical
Society, London. Symposium.
Biochemical Society Symposium, 30th. see Biochemical
Society, London. Symposium.
Biochemical Society Symposium, 31st. see Biochemical
Society, London. Symposium.
Biochemical Society Symposium, 32nd. see Biochemical
Society, London. Symposium.
Biochemical Society Symposium, 33rd. see Biochemical
Society, London. Symposium.
Biochemical Society Symposium, 34th. see Biochemical
Society, London. Symposium.
Biochemical Society Symposium, 35th. see Biochemical
Society, London. Symposium.
Biological Laboratory, Imperial Household. see
Seibutsugaku Fokenkyujo, Tokyo.
Biological Science Curriculum Study. see Biological
Sciences Curriculum Study.
Biological Sciences Curriculum Study.
xBiological Science Curriculum Study.
Biological Science: Interaction of Experiments
& Ideas (BSCS Second Course). P-H.
xBiological Sciences Curriculum Study.
Biological Science: Patterns & Processes.
HR&W.
Biology Teacher's Handbook. Wiley.
Energy & Society: Investigations in Decision
Making. Hubbard Sci.
Research Problems in Biology. Oxford U Pr.
Biology And Agriculture Division. see National Academy
of Sciences, Washington, D.C.
Biology Colloquium, Oregon State University.
xBiology Colloquium, 22nd, Oregon State
University, 1961.
Physiology of Reproduction: Proceedings. Oreg
St U Pr.
Biology Colloquium, 22nd, Oregon State University,
1961. see Biology Colloquium, Oregon State
University.
**Biology Colloquium, 32nd, Oregon State University,
1971.**
xBiology Colloquium, 32nd, Oregon State
University, 1971.
The Biology of Behavior: Proceedings. Oreg St
U Pr.
Biology Colloquium, 33rd, Oregon St. U., 1972. see
Oregon. State University, Corvallis.
Biology Colloquium, 37th, Oregon State University, 1976.
see Oregon. State University, Corvallis.
Biomechanics Symposium, 1973. see American Society of
Mechanical Engineers.
Biomechanics Symposium, 1977. see American Society of
Mechanical Engineers.
Biondo, Vincent J.
xBiondo, Vincent J.
ed. English Is a Happy Thing: A Book of
Readings. Mss Info.
Biorklund, Elis, 1889-
xBiorklund, Elis.

International Atomic Policy During a Decade:
An Historical-Political Investigation into the
Problems of Atomic Weapons During the
Period 1945-55. Greenwood.
Birbaumer, Niels.
xBirbaumer, Niels.
ed. Biofeedback & Self-Regulation. Halsted Pr.
Birch, A. see Birch, Alexander A.
Birch, A. H. see Birch, Anthony Harold.
Birch, Alexander A.
xBirch, A.
Anesthesia for the Uninterested. Univ Park.
Birch, Anthony H. see Birch, Anthony Harold.
Birch, Anthony Harold.
xBirch, A. H.
The British System of Government. Allen
Unwin.
xBirch, Anthony H.
British System of Government. Allen Unwin.
Birch, Bruce C.
xBirch, Bruce C.
The Predicament of the Prosperous.
Westminster.
Birch, Cyril.
xBirch, Cyril.
Intro. by & ed. Studies in Chinese Literary
Genres. U of Cal Pr.
Birch, David L.
xBirch, David L.
Economic Future of City & Suburb. Comm
Econ Dev.
Birch, G. G. see Birch, Gordon Gerard.
Birch, G. R. see Birch, Geof R.
Birch, Geof R.
xBirch, G. R.
Backpacking Equipment: Making It & Using It.
Sterling.
Birch, Gordon G. see Birch, Gordon Gerard.
Birch, Gordon Gerard.
xBirch, G. G.
ed. Sugar: Science & Technology. Burgess-Intl
Ideas.
xBirch, Gordon G.
Food Science. Pergamon.
Birch, Herbert G. see Birch, Herbert George.
Birch, Herbert George, 1918-1973
xBirch, Herbert G.
Mental Subnormality in the Community: A
Clinical & Epidemiologic Study. Krieger.
Birch, T. W. see Birch, Thomas William.
Birch, Thomas.
xBirch, Thomas.
Court & Times of James the First. AMS Pr.
Birch, Thomas William.
xBirch, T. W.
Maps: Topographical & Statistical. Oxford U
Pr.
Birchenall, Joan.
xBirchenall, Joan.
Care of the Older Adult. Lippincott.
xBirchenall, Joan M.
Introduction to Health Careers. Lippincott.
Birchenall, Joan M. see Birchenall, Joan.
Birchfield, John C.
xBirchfield, John C.
Contemporary Quantity Recipe File. CBI Pub.
Bird, A. J. see Bird, Alfred John.
Bird, Alan F.
xBird, Alan F.
Structure of Nematodes. Acad Pr.
Bird, Alfred John, 1909-1976
xBird, A. J.
History on the Ground: An Inventory of
Unrecorded Material Relating to the
Mid-Anglo-Welsh Borderland, with
Introductory Chapters. Verry.
Bird, Brian.
xBird, Brian.

Talking with Patients. Lippincott.
Bird, Caroline.
xBird, Caroline.
Enterprising Women. NAL.
The Two-Paycheck Marriage: How Women at
Work Are Changing Life in America. Rawson
Wade.
Bird, G. J. see Bird, Gordon Joseph Alexander.
Bird, George L. see Bird, George Lloyd.
Bird, George Lloyd.
xBird, George L.
ed. Press & Society: A Book of Readings.
Greenwood.
Bird, Gordon Joseph Alexander.
xBird, G. J.
Radar Precision & Resolution. Halsted Pr.
Radar Precision & Resolution. Krieger.
Bird, John.
xBird, John.
Percy Grainger. Merrimack Bk Serv.
Bird, John M.
xBird, John M.
Lower, Middle & Upper Cambrian Faunas in
the Taconic Sequence of Eastern New York:
Stratigraphic & Biostratigraphic Significance.
Geol Soc.
Bird, Joseph W.
xBird, Joseph W.
Freedom of Sexual Love. Doubleday.
Marriage Is for Grownups. Doubleday.
Bird, Patricia.
xBird, Patricia.
Staged for Death. Bouregy.
Bird, R. M. see Bird, Richard Miller.
Bird, Richard. see Bird, Richard Miller.
Bird, Richard M. see Bird, Richard Miller.
Bird, Richard Miller.
xBird, R. M.
Residential Property Tax Relief in Ontario. U
of Toronto Pr.
xBird, Richard.
ed. Readings on Taxation in Developing
Countries. Johns Hopkins.
xBird, Richard M.
Taxing Agricultural Land in Developing
Countries. Harvard U Pr.
Birdsall, Steve.
xBirdsall, Steve.
Log of the Liberators: An Illustrated History of
the B-24. Doubleday.
Birdsell, Joseph B. see Birdsell, Joseph Benjamin.
Birdsell, Joseph Benjamin, 1908-
xBirdsell, Joseph B.
Human Evolution: An Introduction to the New
Physical Anthropology. Rand.
Birdseye, Clarence.
xBirdseye, Clarence.
Growing Woodland Plants. Dover.
Growing Woodland Plants. Peter Smith.
Birdsong, Robert E.
xBirdsong, Robert E.
The Revelations of Hermes: An Exposition of
Adamic Christianity. Sirius Bks.
Sensory Awareness & Psychic Manifestation.
Sirius Bks.
Birk, Dorothy D. see Birk, Dorothy Daniels.
Birk, Dorothy Daniels.
xBirk, Dorothy D.
The World Came to St. Louis: A Visit to the
1904 World's Fair. Bethany Pr.
Birk, Newman P. see Birk, Newman Peter.
Birk, Newman Peter.
xBirk, Newman P.
A Handbook of Grammar, Rhetoric, Mechanics
& Usage. Odyssey Pr.
The Odyssey Reader: Ideas & Style. Odyssey
Pr.
Understanding & Using English. Odyssey Pr.
Birkbeck, Morris, 1764-1825
xBirkbeck, Morris.

Letters from Illinois. Da Capo.
Birkeland, Peter W.
    xBirkeland, Peter W.
        Pedology, Weathering & Geomorphological
        Research. Oxford U Pr.
Birkenhager, W. H.
    xBirkenhager, W. H.
        Control Mechanisms in Essential Hypertension.
        Elsevier.
Birkenhead, Frederick Dwin Smith, 1st Earl Of,
    1872-1930
    xBirkenhead, Frederick E.
        Last Essays. Arno.
        Law, Life & Letters. Arno.
        Turning Points in History. Arno.
Birkenhead, Frederick E. *see* Birkenhead, Frederick Dwin
    Smith, 1st Earl Of.
Birkenshaw, Lois.
    xBirkenshaw, Lois.
        Music for Fun, Music for Learning. HR&W.
Birket-Smith, Kaj, 1893-
    xBirket-Smith, Kaj.
        Ethnographical Collections from the Northwest
        Passage. AMS Pr.
        Geographical Notes on the Barren Grounds.
        AMS Pr.
        Paths of Culture: A General Ethnology. U of
        Wis Pr.
Birkhead, Edith.
    xBirkhead, Edith.
        Christina Rossetti & Her Poetry. AMS Pr.
        Christina Rossetti & Her Poetry. Arden Lib.
        Tale of Terror: A Study of the Gothic
        Romance. Russell.
Birkhimer, William E. *see* Birkhimer, William Edward.
Birkhimer, William Edward, 1848-1914
    xBirkhimer, William E.
        Historical Sketch of the Organization,
        Administration, Materiel & Tactics of the
        Artillery. Greenwood.
Birkhoff, G. *see* Birkhoff, Garrett.
Birkhoff, Garrett, 1911-
    xBirkhoff, G.
        Modern Applied Algebra. McGraw.
    xBirkhoff, Garrett.
        Hydrodynamics: A Study in Logic, Fact, &
        Similitude. Greenwood.
        Ordinary Differential Equations. Wiley.
        A Source Book in Classical Analysis. Harvard
        U Pr.
    xBirkhoff, Garrett D.
        Dynamical Systems. Am Math.

Birkhoff, George D. *see* Birkhoff, George David.

Birkhoff, George David, 1884-1944
    xBirkhoff, George D.
        Collected Mathematical Papers. Dover.
Birkos, Alexander S.
    xBirkos, Alexander S.
        African & Black American Studies. Libs Unl.
        East European and Soviet Economic Affairs: A
        Bibliography (1965-1973). Libs Unl.
        Historiography, Method, History Teaching: A
        Bibliography of Books & Articles in English,
        1965-1973. Shoe String.
        Soviet Cinema: Directors & Films. Shoe String.
Birks, J. B. *see* Birks, John Betteley.
Birks, J. S.
    xBirks, J. S.
        Across the Savannas to Mecca: The Overland
        Pilgrimage Route from West Africa. Biblio
        Dist.
Birks, John Betteley.
    xBirks, J. B.
        ed. Organic Molecular Photophysics. Wiley.
Birks, L. S.
    xBirks, L. S.
        Electron Probe Microanalysis. Krieger.
Birks, Tony.
    xBirks, Tony.

Art of the Modern Potter. Van Nos Reinhold.
Birla Institute of Scientific Research. Economic
    Research Division.
    xBirla Institute of Scientific Research.
        Defence Production & Development. Verry.
        Fiscal Policy & Economic Growth: India.
        Verry.
        India Two Thousand One. Verry.
        Structural Transformation & Economic
        Development. Humanities.
Birla, L. N.
    xBirla, L. N.
        Folk Tales from Rajasthan. Asia.
Birley, Derek.
    xBirley, Derek.
        Planning & Education. Routledge & Kegan.
Birley, Robert, Sir, 1903-
    xBirley, Robert.
        Sunk Without Trace: Some Forgotten
        Masterpieces Reconsidered. Greenwood.
Birman, Joan S., 1927-
    xBirman, Joan S.
        Braids, Links & Mapping Class Groups.
        Princeton U Pr.
Birman, Joseph H. *see* Birman, Joseph Harold.
Birman, Joseph Harold, 1924-
    xBirman, Joseph H.
        Glacial Geology Across the Crest of the Sierra
        Nevada, California. Geol Soc.
Birmingham City Museums. *see* Birmingham Museums
    and Art Gallery.
Birmingham, Jacqueline. *see* Birmingham, Jacqueline
    Joseph.
Birmingham, Jacqueline Joseph.
    xBirmingham, Jacqueline.
        The Problem-Oriented Record: A Self-Learning
        Module. McGraw.
Birmingham Museums and Art Gallery.
    xBirmingham City Museums.
        Pre-Raphaelite Drawings by Dante Gabriel
        Rossetti. U of Chicago Pr.
Birmingham, Stephen.
    xBirmingham, Stephen.
        Jacqueline Bouvier Kennedy Onassis. PB.
        Life at the Dakota: New York's Most Unusual
        Address. Random.
Birn, Raymond.
    xBirn, Raymond.
        Crisis, Absolutism, Revolution: Europe,
        1648-1789,1791. HR&W.
Birnbach, Martin.
    xBirnbach, Martin.
        Neo-Freudian Social Philosophy. Stanford U
        Pr.
Birnbaum. *see* Birnbaum, Martin L.
Birnbaum, Henry.
    xBirnbaum, Henry.
        Limits & Trials. NYU Pr.
Birnbaum, Howard.
    xBirnbaum, Howard.
        The Cost of Catastrophic Illness. Lexington
        Bks.
Birnbaum, Karl E., 1924-
    xBirnbaum, Karl E.
        Peace Moves & U-Boat Warfare: A Study of
        Imperial Germany's Policy Towards the
        United States, April 18, 1916 - January 9,
        1917. Shoe String.
Birnbaum, Martin L.
    xBirnbaum.
        Content for Training in Project ENABLE.
        Jewish Bd Family.
Birnbaum, Milton, 1919-
    xBirnbaum, Milton.
        Aldous Huxley's Quest for Values. U of Tenn
        Pr.
Birnbaum, Norman.
    xBirnbaum, Norman.

Crisis of Industrial Society. Oxford U Pr.
    Toward a Critical Sociology. Oxford U Pr.
Birnbaum, Philip.
    xBirnbaum, Philip.
        Fluent Hebrew. Hebrew Pub.
Birnbaum, Ruth F.
    xBirnbaum, Ruth F.
        The Prometheus Trilogy. Coronado Pr.
Birnbaum, Stephen.
    xBirnbaum, Stephen.
        The Caribbean, Bermuda, & the Bahamas,
        1980. HM.
Birnberg, Thomas B.
    xBirnberg, Thomas B.
        Colonial Development: An Econometric Study.
        Yale U Pr.
Birney, A. A. *see* Birney, Arthur A.
Birney, Arthur A., 1927-
    xBirney, A. A.
        Noon Sight Navigation: Simplified Celestial.
        Cornell Maritime.
Birney, James G. *see* Birney, James Gillespie.
Birney, James Gillespie, 1792-1857
    xBirney, James G.
        American Churches, the Bulwarks of American
        Slavery. Arno.
        Letters: 1831-1857. Peter Smith.
Birnholz, Jason C.
    xBirnholz, Jason C.
        Clinical Diagnostic Pearls. Med Exam.
Birnie, G. D.
    xBirnie, G. D.
        Subnuclear Components: Preparation &
        Fractionation. Butterworths.
Biro, Lajos.
    xBiro, Lajos.
        The Private Life of Henry VIII. Garland Pub.
Birot, Pierre.
    xBirot, Pierre.
        The Cycle of Erosion in Different Climates. U
        of Cal Pr.
Birrell, Augustine, 1850-1933
    xBirrell, Augustine.
        Andrew Marvell. Arno.
        Andrew Marvell. Folcroft.
        Life of Charlotte Bronte. AMS Pr.
        Life of Charlotte Bronte. Folcroft.
        More Obiter Dicta. Arno.
Birrell, Gordon, 1942-
    xBirrell, Gordon.
        The Boundless Present: Space & Time in the
        Literary Fairy Tales of Novalis & Tieck. U of
        NC Pr.
Birrell, Verla. *see* Birrell, Verla Leone.
Birrell, Verla Leone, 1903-
    xBirrell, Verla.
        The Textile Arts: A Handbook of Weaving,
        Braiding, Printing, & Other Textile
        Techniques. Schocken.
Birren, Faber, 1900-
    xBirren, Faber.
        Color & Human Response. Van Nos Reinhold.
        Color in Your World. Macmillan.
        Color Perception in Art. Van Nos Reinhold.
        Creative Color. Van Nos Reinhold.
        Principles of Color: A Review of Past
        Traditions & Modern Theories. Van Nos
        Reinhold.
Birren, James E.
    xBirren, James E.
        ed. Handbook of Mental Health & Aging. P-H.
        Psychology of Aging. P-H.
Birss, R. R. *see* Birss, Robert R.
Birss, Robert R.
    xBirss, R. R.
        Symmetry & Magnetism. Elsevier.
Birstein, Ann.
    xBirstein, Ann.
        American Children. Doubleday.
Birt, D. *see* Birt, David.

Birt, David.
xBirt, D.
Games & Simulations in History. Longman.
Birtchnell, J.
xBirtchnell, J.
Effects of Early Parent Death. Mss Info.
Birth Defects Conference.
xBirth Defects Conference, Kansas City, Mo., May 1975.
Growth Problems & Clinical Advances: Proceedings. A R Liss.
xBirth Defects Conference, 1975, Kansas City, Missouri.
Cytogentics, Environment, & Malformation Syndromes: Proceedings. A R Liss.
xBirth Defects Conference-1975, Kansas City, Missouri.
Cancer & Genetics: Proceedings. A R Liss.
xBirth Defects Converence, 1978, San Francisco.
Risk, Communication, & Decision Making in Genetic Counseling: Proceedings, Annual Review of Birth Defects, 1978. A R Liss.
Birth Defects Conference, Kansas City, Mo., May 1975. see Birth Defects Conference.
Birth Defects Conference, 1975, Kansas City, Missouri. see Birth Defects Conference.
Birth Defects Conference-1975, Kansas City, Missouri. see Birth Defects Conference.
Birth Defects Converence, 1978, San Francisco. see Birth Defects Conference.
Bisagno. see Bisagno, John R.
Bisagno, John. see Bisagno, John R.
Bisagno, John R.
xBisagno.
The Word of the Lord. Broadman.
xBisagno, John.
Power of Positive Praying. Zondervan.
xBisagno, John R.
How to Build an Evangelistic Church. Broadman.
Power of Positive Living. Broadman.
Bisanz, Rudolf. see Bisanz, Rudolf M.
Bisanz, Rudolf M.
xBisanz, Rudolf.
The Rene Von Schleinitz Collection of the Milwaukee Art Center: Major Schools of German Nineteenth-Century Popular Painting. U of Wis Pr.
xBisanz, Rudolf M.
German Romanticism & Philipp Otto Runge: A Study in Nineteenth-Century Art Theory & Iconography. N Ill U Pr.
Bisch, Louis E. see Bisch, Louis Edward.
Bisch, Louis Edward, 1885-
xBisch, Louis E.
ed. Cure Your Nerves Yourself. Fawcett.
Bischel, Jon E.
xBischel, Jon E.
ed. Income Tax Treaties. PLI.
Taxation of Patents, Trademarks, Copyrights & Know-How. Warren.
Bischof, Ledford J.
xBischof, Ledford J.
Adult Psychology. Har-Row.
Bischoff. see Bischoff, James L.
Bischoff, David.
xBischoff, David.
ed. Quest. Raintree Pubs.
ed. Strange Encounters. Raintree Pubs.
xBischoff, David F.
Tin Woodman. Doubleday.
Bischoff, David F. see Bischoff, David.
Bischoff, Henry.
xBischoff, Henry.
From Pioneer Settlement to Suburb: A History of Mahwah, New Jersey, 1700-1976. A S Barnes.
Bischoff, James L.
xBischoff.

ed. Marine Geology & Oceanography of the Pacific Manganese Nodule Province. Plenum Pub.
Bish, Robert L.
xBish, Robert L.
Coastal Resource Use: Decisions on Puget Sound. U of Wash Pr.
Understanding Urban Government: Metropolitan Reform Reconsidered. Am Enterprise.
Bish, Tommy. see Bish, Tommy L.
Bish, Tommy L.
xBish, Tommy.
Home Gunsmithing Digest. Follett.
Bisheff, Steve.
xBisheff, Steve.
Los Angeles Rams. Macmillan.
Bisher, Furman.
xBisher, Furman.
Strange But True Baseball Stories. Random.
Bishirjian, Richard. see Bishirjian, Richard J.
Bishirjian, Richard J.
xBishirjian, Richard.
ed. A Public Philosophy Reader. Arlington Hse.
Bishop, Adele.
xBishop, Adele.
The Art of Decorative Stenciling. Penguin.
The Art of Decorative Stenciling. Viking Pr.
Bishop, Albert B. see Bishop, Albert Bentley.
Bishop, Albert Bentley, 1929-
xBishop, Albert B.
Introduction to Discrete-Linear Controls: Theory & Applications. Acad Pr.
Bishop, Ann.
xBishop, Ann.
Chicken Riddle. A Whitman.
Noah Riddle?. A Whitman.
Oh, Riddlesticks!. A Whitman.
Riddle Ages. A Whitman.
Riddle-Iculous Rid-Alphabet Book. A Whitman.
Riddle Red Riddle Book. A Whitman.
Bishop, Bob, 1949-
xBishop, Bob.
The Running Saga of Walter Stack. Celestial Arts.
Bishop, Charles E.
xBishop, Charles E.
Farm Labor in the United States. Columbia U Pr.
Bishop, Claire H. see Bishop, Claire Huchet.
Bishop, Claire Huchet.
xBishop, Claire H.
Twenty & Ten. Penguin.
Twenty & Ten. Viking Pr.
Bishop, Cortlandt F. see Bishop, Cortlandt Field.
Bishop, Cortlandt Field, 1870-1935
xBishop, Cortlandt F.
History of Elections in the American Colonies. AMS Pr.
History of Elections in the American Colonies. B Franklin.
Bishop, Curtis. see Bishop, Curtis Kent.
Bishop, Curtis Kent, 1912-
xBishop, Curtis.
Little League Little Brother. Lippincott.
Little League Stepson. Lippincott.
Little League Victory. Lippincott.
Lonesome End. Lippincott.
Bishop, D. H. see Bishop, Donald H.
Bishop, David M.
xBishop, David M.
Group Theory & Chemistry. Oxford U Pr.
Bishop, Denis.
xBishop, Denis.
Railways & War Since 1917. Hippocrene Bks.
xBishop, Dennis.
Vehicles at War. A S Barnes.
Bishop, Dennis. see Bishop, Denis.

Bishop, Donald G. see Bishop, Donald Gordon.
Bishop, Donald Gordon.
xBishop, Donald G.
The Administration of British Foreign Relations. Greenwood.
Bishop, Donald H.
xBishop, D. H.
Pref. by & ed. Indian Thought: An Introduction. Halsted Pr.
Bishop, Douglas D.
xBishop, Douglas D.
Working in Plant Science. McGraw.
Bishop, E. see Bishop, Edmund.
Bishop, Edmund, 1920-
xBishop, E.
Indicators. Pergamon.
Bishop, Elizabeth, 1911-
xBishop, Elizabeth.
The Complete Poems. FS&G.
Bishop, Ferman.
xBishop, Ferman.
Allen Tate. Coll & U Pr.
Henry Adams. G K Hall.
Henry Adams. Twayne.
Bishop, Ian.
xBishop, Ian.
Pearl in Its Setting: A Critical Study of the Structure & Meaning of the Middle English Poem. Biblio Dist.
Bishop, Isabella L. see Bishop, Isabella Lucy (Bird).
Bishop, Isabella Lucy (Bird), 1831-1904
xBishop, Isabella L.
The Aspects of Religion in the United States of America. Arno.
Bishop, Jim.
xBishop, Jim.
The Day Christ Was Born. Har-Row.
Bishop, Joel P. see Bishop, Joel Prentiss.
Bishop, Joel Prentiss, 1814-1905
xBishop, Joel P.
Commentaries on the Criminal Law. AMS Pr.
Bishop, John, 1908-
xBishop, John.
A Word in Season. Abingdon.
Bishop, John. see Bishop, John Peale.
Bishop, John L. see Bishop, John Lyman.
Bishop, John Lyman.
xBishop, John L.
Colloquial Short Story in China: A Study of the San-Yen Collections. Harvard U Pr.
ed. Studies in Chinese Literature. Harvard U Pr.
Bishop, John P. see Bishop, John Peale.
Bishop, John Peale, 1892-1944
xBishop, John.
Undertaker's Garland. Folcroft.
xBishop, John P.
The Undertaker's Garland. Haskell.
xBishop, John Peale.
The Collected Essays of John Peale Bishop. Octagon.
The Collected Poems of John Peale Bishop. Octagon.
Bishop, Jonathan.
xBishop, Jonathan.
Something Else. Braziller.
Bishop, Joseph. see Bishop, Joseph P.
Bishop, Joseph B. see Bishop, Joseph Bucklin.
Bishop, Joseph Bucklin, 1847-1928
xBishop, Joseph B.
Notes & Anecdotes of Many Years. Arno.
Bishop, Joseph P.
xBishop, Joseph.
The Eye of the Storm. Chosen Bks Pub.
xBishop, Joseph P.
New Beginnings. Chosen Bks Pub.
Bishop, Lee.
xBishop, Lee.

Gunblaze. Nordon Pubns.

Bishop, Michael.
xBishop, Michael.
Catacomb Years. Berkley Pub.
Catacomb Years. Putnam.
A Little Knowledge. Berkley Pub.
A Little Knowledge. Berkley Pub.
Stolen Faces. Dell.
Stolen Faces. Har-Row.

Bishop, Mike.
xBishop, Mike.
Arctic Cat: Snowmobile Service-Repair, 1974-1977. Clymer Pubns.
Chevrolet & GMC--4-Wheel Drive Maintenance: Blazer, Jimmy, Pickups & Suburbans, 1967-1977. Clymer Pubns.
CZ Service-Repair Handbook: Single Exhaust Models-Through 1978. Clymer Pubns.
Ford Tune-up & Maintenance: Vans & Pickups, 1969-1978. Clymer Pubns.
Polaris Snowmobile Service-Repair: 1973-1977. Clymer Pubns.
Suzuki Gs750 Fours, 1977-1979: Service, Repair, Performance. Clymer Pubns.
Yamaha SR500 Singles: 1977-1979 Service-Repair-Performance. Clymer Pubns.

Bishop, Morris, 1893-
xBishop, Morris.
ed. Classical Storybook. Cornell U Pr.
Pascal, the Life of Genius. Greenwood.
Bishop, R. E. see Bishop, Richard Evelyn Donohue.

Bishop, Richard B.
xBishop, Richard B.
Practical Polymerization for Polystyrene. CBI Pub.

Bishop, Richard Evelyn Donohue.
xBishop, R. E.
The Mechanics of Vibration. Cambridge U Pr.
Vibration. Cambridge U Pr.
Bishop, Robert. see Bishop, Robert Charles.

Bishop, Robert Charles.
xBishop, Robert.
Folk Painters of America. Dutton.
How to Know American Antique Furniture. Dutton.
The World of Antiques, Art & Architecture in Victorian America. Dutton.

Bishop, Ron.
xBishop, Ron.
Rebuilding the Famous Ford Flathead. TAB Bks.

Bishop, Sharon.
xBishop, Sharon.
Philosophy & Women. Wadsworth Pub.

Bishop, Sheila.
xBishop, Sheila.
Lucasta. Fawcett.
The Rules of Marriage. Fawcett.
A Speaking Likeness. Fawcett.

Bishop, Vaughn F.
xBishop, Vaughn F.
Comparing Nations: The Developed & the Developing Worlds. Heath.

Bishop, Walter W.
xBishop, Walter W.
ed. Background to Evolution in Africa. U of Chicago Pr.
Bishop, William W. see Bishop, William Warner.

Bishop, William Warner, 1871-1955
xBishop, William W.
Backs of Books, & Other Essays in Librarianship. Arno.
Checklist of American Copies of Short-Title Catalogue Books. Greenwood.
Bispham, David. see Bispham, David Scull.

Bispham, David Scull, 1857-1921
xBispham, David.
A Quaker Singer's Recollections. Arno.

Bisplinghoff, Raymond L.
xBisplinghoff, Raymond L.

Principles of Aeroelasticity. Dover.
Bissell, Claude T. see Bissell, Claude Thomas.

Bissell, Claude Thomas, 1916-
xBissell, Claude T.
Halfway up Parnassus: A Personal Account of the University of Toronto, 1932-1971. U of Toronto Pr.
Strength of the University: A Selection from the Addresses of Claude T. Bissell. U of Toronto Pr.

Bissell, Elaine.
xBissell, Elaine.
Women Who Wait. M Evans.
Women Who Wait. Popular Lib.
Bissell, Frederick O. see Bissell, Frederick Olds.

Bissell, Frederick Olds, 1902-
xBissell, Frederick O.
Fielding's Theory of the Novel. Cooper Sq.

Bisseret, Noelle.
xBisseret, Noelle.
Education, Class Language & Ideology. Routledge & Kegan.
Bisson, T. N. see Bisson, Thomas N.
Bisson, Thomas A. see Bisson, Thomas Arthur.

Bisson, Thomas Arthur, 1900-
xBisson, Thomas A.
America's Far Eastern Policy. AMS Pr.

Bisson, Thomas N.
xBisson, T. N.
Assemblies & Representation in Languedoc in the Thirteenth Century. Princeton U Pr.
xBisson, Thomas N.
Conservation of Coinage: Monetary Exploitation & Its Restraint in France, Catalonia, & Aragon C.1000-1225 A.D.. Oxford U Pr.

Bissonnier, Henri, 1911-
xBissonnier, Henri.
The Pedagogy of Resurrection: The Christian Formation of the Handicapped. Paulist Pr.

Bisswanger, Hans.
xBisswanger, Hans.
ed. Multifunctional Proteins. Wiley.

Bistner, Stephen I.
xBistner, Stephen I.
Atlas of Veterinary Ophthalmic Surgery. Saunders.
Biswas, Anil K. see Biswas, Anil Kumar.

Biswas, Anil Kumar.
xBiswas, Anil K.
Principles of Steel Making. Asia.
xBiswas, Asit K.
Extractive Metallurgy of Copper. Pergamon.

Biswas, Asit K.
xBiswas, Asit K.
ed. Systems Approach to Water Management. McGraw.
Biswas, Asit K. see Biswas, Anil Kumar.

Biswas, Margaret R.
xBiswas, Margaret R.
ed. Food, Climate & Man. Wiley.
Biswas, N. N. see Biswas, Nripendra Nath.

Biswas, Nripendra Nath, 1928-
xBiswas, N. N.
Principles of Telegraphy. Asia.
xBiswas, Nripendra U.
Introduction to Logic & Switching Theory. Gordon.
Biswas, Nripendra U. see Biswas, Nripendra Nath.

Bisztray, George, 1938-
xBisztray, George.
Marxist Models of Literary Realism. Columbia U Pr.

Bithell, Jethro, 1878-
xBithell, Jethro.
Life & Writings of Maurice Maeterlinck. Kennikat.

Bittar, E. Edward.
xBittar, E. Edward.

ed. Membrane Structure & Function. Wiley.

Bittel, Lester R.
xBittel, Lester R.
Encyclopedia of Professional Management. McGraw.
Improving Supervisory Performance. McGraw.
The Nine Master Keys of Management. McGraw.
Bitter. see Bitter, Gary G.

Bitter, Gary G.
xBitter.
Activities Handbook for Teaching with the Hand Held Calculator. Allyn.
xBitter, Gary G.
Exploring with Metrics. Messner.
Exploring with Pocket Calculators. Messner.
One Step at a Time. EMC.
Bittermann, Henry J. see Bittermann, Henry John.

Bittermann, Henry John.
xBittermann, Henry J.
The Refunding of International Debt. Duke.

Bitters, Stan.
xBitters, Stan.
Environmental Ceramics. Van Nos Reinhold.

Bittiger, H.
xBittiger, H.
ed. Concanavalin A As a Tool. Wiley.
Bittinger, Desmond. see Bittinger, Desmond Wright.

Bittinger, Desmond Wright, 1905-
xBittinger, Desmond.
The Song of the Drums: African Life & Love Under the Monkey Bread Tree. Vantage.
Bittinger, Lucy F. see Bittinger, Lucy Forney.

Bittinger, Lucy Forney, 1859-1907
xBittinger, Lucy F.
Germans in Colonial Times. Russell.

Bittinger, Marvin L.
xBittinger, Marvin L.
Calculus: A Modeling Approach. A-W.
The Consumer Survival Book. Barron.

Bittker, Boris I.
xBittker, Boris I.
Federal Income Taxation of Corporations & Shareholders. Warren.

Bittlinger, Arnold, 1928-
xBittlinger, Arnold.
Gifts & Ministries. Eerdmans.

Bittman, Sam.
xBittman, Sam.
Expectant Fathers. Dutton.

Bittner, Egon.
xBittner, Egon.
Standards Relating to Police Handling of Juvenile Problems. Ballinger Pub.
Bittner, J. see Bittner, John R.

Bittner, John R., 1943-
xBittner, J.
Broadcasting: An Introduction. P-H.
xBittner, John R.
Radio Journalism. P-H.

Bittner, Vernon J.
xBittner, Vernon J.
You Can Help with Your Healing: A Guide for Recovering Wholeness in Body, Mind, & Spirit. Augsburg.

Bitton, Davis, 1930-
xBitton, Davis.
French Nobility in Crisis, 1560-1640. Stanford U Pr.
Guide to Mormon Diaries & Autobiographies. Brigham.
Bivins, Frank J. see Bivins, Frank Jarris.

Bivins, Frank Jarris, 1872-
xBivins, Frank J.
The Farmer's Political Economy. Arno.

Bivins, John.
xBivins, John.
The Moravian Potters in North Carolina. U of NC Pr.
Bixler, Julius S. see Bixler, Julius Seelye.

Bixler, Julius Seelye, 1894-
  xBixler, Julius S.
    Conversations with an Unrepentant Liberal.
      Kennikat.
    A Faith That Fulfills. Greenwood.
Bixler, Norma.
  xBixler, Norma.
    Burmese Journey. Kent St U Pr.
Bizien, Yves.
  xBizien, Yves.
    Population & Economic Development. Praeger.
Bizzarro, Salvatore.
  xBizzarro, Salvatore.
    Historical Dictionary of Chile. Scarecrow.
    Pablo Neruda: All Poets the Poet. Scarecrow.
Bjerhammar, A. *see* Bjerhammar, Arne.
Bjerhammar, Arne, 1917-
  xBjerhammar, A.
    Theory of Errors & Generalized Matrix
      Inverses. Elsevier.
Bjorge, James R.
  xBjorge, James R.
    Lord of the Mountain: Messages for Lent &
      Easter. Augsburg.
Bjorgum, Kenneth.
  xBjorgum, Kenneth.
    The Betrayed. Doubleday.
Bjork, Robert M. *see* Bjork, Robert Marshall.
Bjork, Robert Marshall.
  xBjork, Robert M.
    Alternatives to Growth: Education for a Stable
      Society. Phi Delta Kappa.
Bjorken, James D.
  xBjorken, James D.
    Relativistic Quantum Mechanics. McGraw.
Bjorklund, Lorence. *see* Bjorklund, Lorence F.
Bjorklund, Lorence F.
  xBjorklund, Lorence.
    illus. Faces of the Frontier. Dodd.
  xBjorklund, Lorence F.
    Faces of the Frontier. Dodd.
Bjorkman, David.
  xBjorkman, David.
    Write, Publish, & Sell It Yourself!: The
      Complete How-to Guide. Citizens Law.
Bjorkman, Edwin. *see* Bjorkman, Edwin August.
Bjorkman, Edwin August, 1866-1951
  xBjorkman, Edwin.
    Gates of Life. Scholarly.
    The Soul of a Child. Scholarly.
Bjorn, L. O. *see* Bjorn, Lars Olof.
Bjorn, Lars Olof, 1936-
  xBjorn, L. O.
    Light & Life. Crane-Russak Co.
Bjorn, Thyra F. *see* Bjorn, Thyra Ferre.
Bjorn, Thyra Ferre.
  xBjorn, Thyra F.
    Dear Papa. Revell.
    The Golden Acre. Revell.
    The Home Has a Heart. Revell.
    Papa's Daughter. Revell.
    Papa's Wife. Bantam.
    Papa's Wife. Revell.
  xBjorn, Thyre F.
    Dear Papa. Pillar Bks.
Bjorn, Thyre F. *see* Bjorn, Thyra Ferre.
Blaauw, G. A.
  xBlaauw, Gerritt A.
    Digital System Implementation. P-H.
Blaauw, Gerritt A. *see* Blaauw, G. A.
Blache, Stephen E.
  xBlache, Stephen E.
    ed. The Acquisition of Distinctive Features.
      Univ Park.
Blachly, Paul H., 1929-
  xBlachly, Paul H.

Seduction: A Conceptual Model in Drug
  Dependencies & Other Contagious Ills. C C
  Thomas.
Blachut, T. J.
  xBlachut, T. J.
    Urban Surveying & Mapping. Springer-Verlag.
Black. *see* Black, Irma (Simonton).
Black, Algernon D. *see* Black, Algernon David.
Black, Algernon David, 1900-
  xBlack, Algernon D.
    The People & the Police. Greenwood.
Black, Allen. *see* Black, Andrew Allen.
Black, Anderson. *see* Black, J. Anderson.
Black, Andrew Allen, 1937-
  xBlack, Allen.
    Modern Belly T Football. P-H.
Black, Bertram J.
  xBlack, Bertram J.
    Principles of Industrial Therapy for the
      Mentally Ill. Grune.
Black, C. A. *see* Black, Charles Allen.
Black, C. E. *see* Black, Cyril Edwin.
Black, Charles Allen.
  xBlack, C. A.
    Soil-Plant Relationships. Wiley.
Black, Charles L. *see* Black, Charles Lund.
Black, Charles Lund, 1915-
  xBlack, Charles L.
    The People & the Court: Judicial Review in a
      Democracy. Greenwood.
    Structure & Relationship in Constitutional Law.
      La State U Pr.
Black, Colette.
  xBlack, Colette.
    Art of Parisian Cooking. Macmillan.
    Low-Calorie Cookbook. Macmillan.
Black, Cyril E. *see* Black, Cyril Edwin.
Black, Cyril Edwin.
  xBlack, C. E.
    Twentieth Century Europe: A History. Knopf.
  xBlack, Cyril E.
    ed. Communism & Revolution: The Strategic
      Uses of Political Violence. Princeton U Pr.
    ed. Comparative Modernization: A Reader.
      Free Pr.
    The Dynamics of Modernization: A Study in
      Comparative History. Har-Row.
Black, Duncan.
  xBlack, Duncan.
    Incidence of Income Taxes. Biblio Dist.
    Incidence of Income Taxes. Kelley.
    Theory of Committees & Elections. Cambridge
      U Pr.
Black, Earl, 1942-
  xBlack, Earl.
    Southern Governors & Civil Rights: Racial
      Segregation As a Campaign Issue in the
      Second Reconstruction. Harvard U Pr.
Black, Edwin.
  xBlack, Edwin.
    Rhetorical Criticism: A Study in Method. U of
      Wis Pr.
Black, Edwin R.
  xBlack, Edwin R.
    Divided Loyalties: Canadian Concepts of
      Federalism. McGill-Queens U Pr.
Black, Elinor G.
  xBlack, Elinor G.
    From Adam's Rib to Women's Lib & Other
      Ventures. Exposition.
Black, Esther B. *see* Black, Esther Boulton.
Black, Esther Boulton.
  xBlack, Esther B.
    Rancho Cucamonga & Dona Merced. San
      Bernardino.
Black, Eugene C. *see* Black, Eugene Charlton.
Black, Eugene Charlton.
  xBlack, Eugene C.

The Association: British Extraparliamentary
  Political Organization, 1769-1793. Harvard U
  Pr.
Black, F. O. *see* Black, Franklin O.
Black, Franklin O., 1937-
  xBlack, F. O.
    Congenital Deafness: A New Approach to
      Early Detection of Deafness Through a High
      Risk Register. Colo Assoc.
Black, George, 1920-
  xBlack, George.
    Sales Engineering: An Emerging Profession.
      Gulf Pub.
Black, George F. *see* Black, George Fraser.
Black, George Fraser, 1866-1948
  xBlack, George F.
    ed. Calendar of Cases of Witchcraft in
      Scotland, 1510-1727. Arno.
    ed. Calendar of Cases of Witchcraft in
      Scotland, 1510-1727. NY Pub Lib.
    A Gypsy Bibliography. Folcroft.
    Gypsy Bibliography. Gale.
    Surnames of Scotland: Their Origin, Meaning
      & History. NY Pub Lib.
Black, George W.
  xBlack, George W.
    American Science & Technology: A
      Bicentennial Bibliography. S Ill U Pr.
Black, Hallie.
  xBlack, Hallie.
    Dirt Cheap: Evolution of Renewable Resource
      Management. Morrow.
Black, Harold.
  xBlack, Harold.
    Manual of Horsemanship: Instructions from
      Mexico's Renowned Escuela Ecuestre. Dodd.
Black, Harry G.
  xBlack, Harry G.
    The Lost Dutchman Mine: A Short Story of a
      Tall Tale. Branden.
Black, Helen C.
  xBlack, Helen C.
    Notable Women Authors of the Day. R West.
Black, Henry C. *see* Black, Henry Campbell.
Black, Henry Campbell, 1860-1927
  xBlack, Henry C.
    The Relation of the Executive Power to
      Legislation. Arno.
Black, Homer A.
  xBlack, Homer A.
    ed. The Managerial & Cost Accountant's
      Handbook. Dow Jones-Irwin.
Black, Homer A. *see* Black, Homer Augustus.
Black, Homer Augustus.
  xBlack, Homer A.
    Accounting in Business Decisions: Theory,
      Method, & Use. P-H.
Black, Hugh C.
  xBlack, Hugh C.
    The Great Educators: Readings for Leaders in
      Education. Nelson-Hall.
Black, Hugo L. *see* Black, Hugo Lafayette.
Black, Hugo Lafayette, 1886-1971
  xBlack, Hugo L.
    Constitutional Faith. Knopf.
Black, Ian S. *see* Black, Ian Stuart.
Black, Ian Stuart, 1915-
  xBlack, Ian S.
    Journey to a Safe Place. St Martin.
Black, Irma (Simonton).
  xBlack.
    Little Old Man Who Could Not Read. Schol
      Bk Serv.
  xBlack, Irma S.
    Little Old Man Who Cooked & Cleaned. A
      Whitman.
    Little Old Man Who Could Not Read. A
      Whitman.
Black, Irma S. *see* Black, Irma (Simonton).

Black, J. Anderson.
  xBlack, Anderson.
    A History of Fashion. Morrow.
    The Story of Jewelry. Morrow.
  xBlack, J. Anderson.
    A History of Fashion. Morrow.
Black, J. L. see Black, Joseph Laurence.
Black, J. M. see Black, James Menzies.
Black, J. W. see Black, James William.
Black, James M. see Black, James Menzies.
Black, James Menzies.
  xBlack, J. M.
    How to Get Results from Interviewing: A
      Practical Guide for Operating Management.
      McGraw.
  xBlack, James M.
    Front-Line Management: A Guide to Effective
      Supervisory Action. McGraw.
    Positive Discipline. Am Mgmt.
Black, James W. see Black, James William.
Black, James William, 1866-1934
  xBlack, J. W.
    Maryland's Attitude in the Struggle for
      Canada. Johnson Repr.
  xBlack, James W.
    Maryland's Attitude in the Struggle for
      Canada. AMS Pr.
Black, John, 1931-
  xBlack, John.
    The Economics of Modern Britain: An
      Introduction to Macroeconomics. Biblio Dist.
Black, John B. see Black, John Bennett.
Black, John Bennett, 1883-1964
  xBlack, John B.
    The Art of History: A Study of Four Great
      Historians of the Eighteenth Century.
      Gordon Pr.
Black, John D. see Black, John Donald.
Black, John Donald, 1883-1960
  xBlack, John D.
    Parity, Parity, Parity. Da Capo.
Black, Jonathan.
  xBlack, Jonathan.
    The House on the Hill. Berkley Pub.
    Oil. Bantam.
    Streisand. Nordon Pubns.
Black, Joseph Laurence, 1937-
  xBlack, J. L.
    Citizens for the Fatherland: Education,
      Educators, & Pedagogical Ideals in
      Eighteenth Century Russia. East Eur
      Quarterly.
Black, Ladbroke Lionel Day, 1877-
  xBlack, Landbroke.
    Some Queer People. Folcroft.
Black, Landbroke. see Black, Ladbroke Lionel Day.
Black, Laura.
  xBlack, Laura.
    Glendraco. St Martin.
    Glendraco. Warner Bks.
    Ravenburn. St Martin.
    Ravenburn. Warner Bks.
    Wild Cat. St Martin.
Black, Lionel.
  xBlack, Lionel.
    Death by Hoax. Avon.
Black, Maggie.
  xBlack, Maggie.
    Home-Made Butter, Cheese & Yoghurt.
      Charles River Bks.
    Home-Made Butter, Cheese & Yoghurt. Intl
      Pubns Serv.
Black, Martha E.
  xBlack, Martha E.
    Speech Therapy in the Public Schools. Bobbs.
Black, Martin M.
  xBlack, Martin M.

  ed. Developments in Biomedical Engineering.
    Crane-Russak Co.
Black, Max, 1909-
  xBlack, Max.
    Caveats & Critiques: Philosophical Essays in
      Language, Logic, & Art. Cornell U Pr.
    Companion to Wittgenstein's Tractatus. Cornell
      U Pr.
  ed. Importance of Language. Cornell U Pr.
    Margins of Precision: Essays in Logic &
      Language. Cornell U Pr.
    Problems of Analysis: Philosophical Essays.
      Greenwood.
  ed. The Social Theories of Talcott Parsons: A
      Critical Examination. S Ill U Pr.
Black, Peter E.
  xBlack, Peter E.
  ed. Readings in Environmental Impact. Mss
    Info.
  ed. Readings in Soil & Water Conservation.
    Mss Info.
  ed. Working with NEPA: Environmental
    Impact Analysis for the Resource Manager.
    Mss Info.
Black, R. Collison. see Black, R. D. Collison.
Black, R. D. Collison.
  xBlack, R. Collison.
  ed. The Marginal Revolution in Economics:
    Interpretation & Evaluation. Duke.
Black, Robert C., 1914-
  xBlack, Robert C.
    Railroads of the Confederacy. U of NC Pr.
Black, Stanley W.
  xBlack, Stanley W.
    Floating Exchange Rates & National Economic
      Policy. Yale U Pr.
Black, Susan.
  xBlack, Susan.
    Crash in the Wilderness. Raintree Pubs.
Black, W. Wayne, 1935-
  xBlack, W. Wayne.
    An Introduction to On-Line Computers.
      Gordon.
Black, William, 1841-1898
  xBlack, William.
    Goldsmith. AMS Pr.
    Goldsmith. Folcroft.
Black, William G. see Black, William George.
Black, William George, 1857-1932
  xBlack, William G.
    Folk-Medicine: A Chapter in the History of
      Culture. B Franklin.
Blackall, Eric A. see Blackall, Eric Albert.
Blackall, Eric Albert.
  xBlackall, Eric A.
    Goethe & the Novel. Cornell U Pr.
Blackborow, J.
  xBlackborow, J. R.
    Metal Vapour Synthesis in Organometallic
      Chemistry. Springer-Verlag.
Blackborow, J. R. see Blackborow, J.
Blackburn, Alexander.
  xBlackburn, Alexander.
    The Cold War of Kitty Pentecost: A Novel.
      Swallow.
    The Myth of Picaro: Continuity &
      Transformation of the Picaresque Novel,
      1554-1954. U of NC Pr.
Blackburn, Charles.
  xBlackburn, Charles.
    The Pillow Book. Vanguard.
Blackburn, Graham, 1940-
  xBlackburn, Graham.

    Illustrated Basic Carpentry. Little.
    The Illustrated Encyclopedia of Ships, Boats,
      Vessels & Other Water-Borne Craft.
      Overlook Pr.
    An Illustrated Encyclopedia of Woodworking
      Handtools Instruments & Devices. S&S.
    An Illustrated Encyclopedia of Woodworking,
      Handtools, Instruments & Devices. S&S.
    Illustrated Furniture Making. S&S.
    Illustrated Housebuilding. Overlook Pr.
    Illustrated Interior Carpentry. Bobbs.
    Illustrated Interior Carpentry. Overlook Pr.
    The Parts of a House. Marek.
Blackburn, H. P.
  xBlackburn, H. P.
    Hell Fire Ranch. Nordon Pubns.
Blackburn, Jack.
  xBlackburn, Jack.
    Understanding Unions in the Public Sector. U
      Cal LA Indus Rel.
Blackburn, Jack E.
  xBlackburn, Jack E.
    One at a Time All at Once: The Creative
      Teacher's Guide to Individualized Instruction
      Without Anarchy. Goodyear.
Blackburn, Laurence H., 1897-
  xBlackburn, Laurence H.
    God Wants You to Be Well. Morehouse.
Blackburn, Lois H.
  xBlackburn, Lois H.
    A Handbook for Planning & Conducting
      Tennis Tournaments. USTA.
Blackburn, Norma D. see Blackburn, Norma Davis.
Blackburn, Norma Davis.
  xBlackburn, Norma D.
    Legal Secretaryship. P-H.
  xBlackburn, Norma Davis.
    Secretaryship. Goodyear.
Blackburn, Robin.
  xBlackburn, Robin.
  ed. Revolution & Class Struggle: A Reader in
    Marxist Politics. Humanities.
Blackburn, Roderic H.
  xBlackburn, Roderic H.
    Cherry Hill: The History & Collections of a
      Van Rensselaer Family. Pub Ctr Cult Res.
Blackburn, S. see Blackburn, Simon.
Blackburn, Simon.
  xBlackburn, S.
    Reason & Prediction. Cambridge U Pr.
Blackburn, Stanley.
  xBlackburn, S.
  ed. Amino Acid Determination: Methods &
    Techniques. Dekker.
Blackburn, Thomas, 1916-
  xBlackburn, Thomas.
    The Price of an Eye. Greenwood.
Blackburn, Thomas C.
  xBlackburn, Thomas C.
  ed. December's Child: A Book of Chumash
    Oral Narratives. U of Cal Pr.
Blackburn, Thomas Wakefield.
  xBlackburn, Tom.
    Navajo Canyon. Dell.
  xBlackburn, Tom W.
    Buckskin Man. Dell.

    Ranchero. Dell.

Blackburn, Tom. see Blackburn, Thomas Wakefield.

Blackburn, Tom W. see Blackburn, Thomas Wakefield

Blackburn, William M. see Blackburn, William Maxwell.
Blackburn, William Maxwell, 1899-
  xBlackburn, William M.
  ed. Under Twenty-Five: Duke Narrative &
    Verse, 1945-1962. Duke.
    Under Twenty Five: Duke Narrative Verse
      1945-1962. Duke.
Blacker, Carmen.
  xBlacker, Carmen.

ed. Ancient Cosmologies. Rowman.
The Catalpa Bow: A Study of Shamanistic
Practices in Japan. Rowman.
Blacker, Charles P. *see* Blacker, Charles Paton.
Blacker, Charles Paton, 1895-
xBlacker, Charles P.
Eugenics: Galton & After. Hyperion Conn.
Blackey, Robert.
xBlackey, Robert.
Revolution & the Revolutionary Ideal.
Schenkman.
Blackford, Jason C.
xBlackford, Jason C.
Ohio Corporation Law & Practice: Including
Ohio & Federal Securities Law & Regulation.
Banks-Baldwin.
Blackford, Mansel G., 1944-
xBlackford, Mansel G.
The Politics of Business in California,
1890-1920. Ohio St U Pr.
Blackhall, David S. *see* Blackhall, David Scott.
Blackhall, David Scott, 1910-
xBlackhall, David S.
This House Had Windows. Astor-Honor.
Blackham, H. J. *see* Blackham, Harold John.
Blackham, Harold John, 1903-
xBlackham, H. J.
Humanism. Intl Pubns Serv.
Objections to Humanism. Greenwood.
Blackhurst, W. E.
xBlackhurst, W. E.
Afterglow: A Collection of Short Stories &
Poems. McClain.
Of Men & a Mighty Mountain. McClain.
Blackie, C. *see* Blackie, Christina.
Blackie, Christina.
xBlackie, C.
Geographical Etymology: A Dictionary of
Place-Names Giving Their Derivations. Gale.
Blackie, John S. *see* Blackie, John Stuart.
Blackie, John Stuart, 1809-1895
xBlackie, John S.
Life of Robert Burns. Arden Lib.
Life of Robert Burns. R West.
Blacking, John.
xBlacking, John.
ed. The Anthropology of the Body. Acad Pr.
How Musical Is Man?. U of Wash Pr.
Blackith, R. E.
xBlackith, R. E.
Multivariate Morphometrics. Acad Pr.
Blackledge, Ethel.
xBlackledge, Ethel.
An Hour Is Forever. Avon.
Blacklock, Les.
xBlacklock, Les.
The High West. Penguin.
Blackman, Derek.
xBlackman, Derek.
Operant Conditioning: An Experimental
Analysis of Behaviour. Methuen Inc.
Blackman, Edwin C. *see* Blackman, Edwin Cyril.
Blackman, Edwin Cyril.
xBlackman, Edwin C.
Marcion & His Influence. AMS Pr.
Blackman, John L.
xBlackman, John L.
Presidential Seizure in Labor Disputes. Harvard
U Pr.
Blackman, L. C. *see* Blackman, Lionel Cyril Francis.
Blackman, Lionel Cyril Francis.
xBlackman, L. C.
Modern Aspects of Graphite Technology. Acad
Pr.
Blackman, R. B. *see* Blackman, Ralph Beebe.
Blackman, Ralph Beebe, 1904-
xBlackman, R. B.

Linear Data Smoothing & Prediction in Theory
& Practice. A-W.
Measurement of Power Spectra from the Point
of View of Communications Engineering.
Dover.
Blackman, Winifred S. *see* Blackman, Winifred Susan.
Blackman, Winifred Susan.
xBlackman, Winifred S.
Fellahin of Upper Egypt: Their Religious,
Social & Industrial Life. Biblio Dist.
Blackmar, F. *see* Blackmar, Frank Wilson.
Blackmar, F. W. *see* Blackmar, Frank Wilson.
Blackmar, Frank W. *see* Blackmar, Frank Wilson.
Blackmar, Frank Wilson, 1854-1931
xBlackmar, F.
Spanish Colonization in the Southwest. Gordon
Pr.
xBlackmar, F. W.
Spanish Colonization in the Southwest.
Johnson Repr.
xBlackmar, Frank W.
The Life of Charles Robinson: The First State
Governor of Kansas. Arno.
Spanish Colonization in the Southwest. AMS
Pr.
Spanish Institutions of the Southwest. AMS Pr.
Spanish Institutions of the Southwest. Rio
Grande.
Blackmore, R. D. *see* Blackmore, Richard Doddridge.
Blackmore, Richard D. *see* Blackmore, Richard
Doddridge.
Blackmore, Richard Doddridge, 1825-1900
xBlackmore, R. D.
Lorna Doone. Biblio Dist.
xBlackmore, Richard D.
Lorna Doone. Airmont.
Blackmore, Simon A. *see* Blackmore, Simon Augustine.
Blackmore, Simon Augustine, 1848-1926
xBlackmore, Simon A.
The Riddles of Hamlet & the Newest Answers.
Folcroft.
Blackmur, R. P. *see* Blackmur, Richard P.
Blackmur, Richard P., 1904-1965
xBlackmur, R. P.
The Lion & the Honeycomb: Essays in
Solicitude & Critique. Greenwood.
Blackorby, C. *see* Blackorby, Charles.
Blackorby, Charles.
xBlackorby, C.
Duality, Separability & Functional Structure:
Theory & Economic Applications. Elsevier.
Blacksell, Mark, 1942-
xBlacksell, Mark.
Post-War Europe: A Political Geography.
Westview.
Blackstock, Charity.
xBlackstock, Charity.
A House Possessed. Queens Hse.
Blackstock, Nelson.
xBlackstock, Nelson.
Cointelpro: The FBI's Secret War on Political
Freedom. Monad Pr.
Blackstock, Paul W.
xBlackstock, Paul W.
Intelligence, Espionage, Counterespionage &
Covert Operations: A Guide to Information
Sources. Gale.
Blackstone, Bernard, 1911-
xBlackstone, Bernard.
Byron: A Survey. Longman.
The Consecrated Urn: An Interpretation of
Keats in Terms of Growth & Form.
Greenwood.
Blackstone, Harry.
xBlackstone, Harry.
There's One Born Every Minute. BJ Pub
Group.
Blackstone, Orin.
xBlackstone, Orin.

Index to Jazz: Jazz Recordings, 1917-1944.
Greenwood.
Blackstone, Tessa, 1942-
xBlackstone, Tessa.
Education & Day Care for Young Children in
Need: The American Experience. Intl Pubns
Serv.
Blackstone, William.
xBlackstone, William.
Ehrlich's Blackstone. Greenwood.
Blackstone, William T.
xBlackstone, William T.
Political Philosophy: An Introduction.
Har-Row.
Blackwelder, Richard E. *see* Blackwelder, Richard Eliot.
Blackwelder, Richard Eliot, 1909-
xBlackwelder, Richard E.
Classification of the Animal Kingdom. S Ill U
Pr.
Guide to the Taxonomic Literature of
Vertebrates. Iowa St U Pr.
Blackwell, A. S. *see* Blackwell, Alice Stone.
Blackwell, Alice S. *see* Blackwell, Alice Stone.
Blackwell, Alice Stone, 1857-1950
xBlackwell, A. S.
Lucy Stone, Pioneer of Woman's Rights. Kraus
Repr.
xBlackwell, Alice S.
tr. Some Spanish-American Poets. Biblo.
tr. Some Spanish-American Poets. Greenwood.
Blackwell, David.
xBlackwell, David A.
Theory of Games & Statistical Decisions.
Dover.
Blackwell, David A. *see* Blackwell, David.
Blackwell, Gene, 1932-
xBlackwell, Gene.
The Private Investigator. Butterworths.
Blackwell, Leslie, 1885-
xBlackwell, Leslie.
African Occasions: Reminiscences of Thirty
Years of Bar, Bench, & Politics in South
Africa. Negro U Pr.
Blackwell, Marian. *see* Blackwell, Marian Willard.
Blackwell, Marian Willard.
xBlackwell, Marian.
Care of the Mentally Retarded. Little.
Blackwell, Richard J., 1929-
xBlackwell, Richard J.
Discovery in the Physical Sciences. U of Notre
Dame Pr.
Blackwell, Robert B.
xBlackwell, Robert B.
ed. Learning Disabilities Handbook for
Teachers. C C Thomas.
Blackwell, Thomas E. *see* Blackwell, Thomas Edward.
Blackwell, Thomas Edward.
xBlackwell, Thomas E.
ed. College Law Digest, 1935-1970. Rothman.
Blackwell, William. *see* Blackwell, William L.
Blackwell, William L.
xBlackwell, William.
Working Partners Working Parents. Broadman.
xBlackwell, William L.
Industrialization of Russia: An Historical
Perspective. AHM Pub.
Blackwood, Algernon, 1869-1951
xBlackwood, Algernon.
The Centaur. Arno.
Lost Valley, & Other Stories. Arno.
Pan's Garden: A Volume of Nature Stories.
Arno.
Strange Stories. Arno.
Blackwood, Andrew W. *see* Blackwood, Andrew
Watterson.
Blackwood, Andrew Watterson, 1882-
xBlackwood, Andrew W.

Planning a Year's Pulpit Work. Baker Bk.
Preaching from the Bible. Baker Bk.
When God Came Down. Baker Bk.
Blackwood, Caroline.
xBlackwood, Caroline.
Great Granny Webster. Scribner.
Great Granny Webster. G K Hall.
The Stepdaughter. Scribner.
Blackwood, Easley, 1903-
xBlackwood, Easley.
Play of the Hand with Blackwood. Corwin.
Blackwood, James R. see Blackwood, James Russell.
Blackwood, James Russell.
xBlackwood, James R.
House on College Avenue: The Comptons at
Wooster, 1891-1913. MIT Pr.
Blackwood, Oswald H. see Blackwood, Oswald Hance.
Blackwood, Oswald Hance.
xBlackwood, Oswald H.
General Physics. Wiley.
Bladen, Ashby.
xBladen, Ashby.
How to Cope with Developing Financial Crisis.
McGraw.
How to Cope with the Developing Financial
Crisis. McGraw.
Bladen, V. W. see Bladen, Vincent Wheeler.
Bladen, Vincent Wheeler.
xBladen, V. W.
From Adam Smith to Maynard Keynes: The
Heritage of Political Economy. U of Toronto
Pr.
Blades, Ann.
xBlades, Ann.
A Boy of Tache. Tundra Bks.
Mary of Mile 18. Tundra Bks.
Blades, James.
xBlades, James.
Orchestral Percussion Technique. Oxford U Pr.
Percussion Instruments & Their History.
Merrimack Bk Serv.
Blades, Joseph D. see Blades, Joseph Dalton.
Blades, Joseph Dalton.
xBlades, Joseph D.
A Comparative Study of Selected American
Film Critics, 1958-1974. Arno.
Blades, William, 1824-1890
xBlades, William.
Books in Chains & Other Bibliographical
Papers. Gale.
Blagowidow, George.
xBlagowidow, George.
Last Train from Berlin. Hippocrene Bks.
Blahove, Marcos.
xBlahove, Marcos.
Painting Children in Oil. Watson-Guptill.
Blaiklock, D. A. see Blaiklock, David A.
Blaiklock, David A.
xBlaiklock, D. A.
ed. Living Is Now. Baker Bk.
Blaiklock, E. M.
xBlaiklock, E. M.
Commentary on the New Testament. Revell.
Blain, Daniel.
xBlain, Daniel.
ed. The History of American Psychiatry: A
Teaching & Research Guide. Am Psychiatric.
Blaine, Marge.
xBlaine, Marge.
Dvora's Journey. HR&W.
Blaine, Martha R. see Blaine, Martha Royce.
Blaine, Martha Royce, 1923-
xBlaine, Martha R.
The Ioway Indians. U of Okla Pr.
Blaine, Thomas R., 1895-
xBlaine, Tom R.
The Easy, Natural Way to Reduce. Keats.
Nutrition & Your Heart. Keats.
Prevent That Heart Attack. Citadel Pr.
Blaine, Tom R. see Blaine, Thomas R.

Blaine, William L.
xBlaine, William L.
Practical Guide for the Unmarried Couple.
Two Continents.
Blainey, Geoffrey.
xBlainey, Geoffrey.
The Causes of War. Free Pr.
The Peaks of Lyell. Intl Schol Bk Serv.
The Rush That Never Ended: A History of
Australian Mining. Intl Schol Bk Serv.
Triumph of the Nomads: A History of
Aboriginal Australia. Overlook Pr.
Blair. see Blair, Roger D.
Blair, Anne D. see Blair, Anne Denton.
Blair, Anne Denton.
xBlair, Anne D.
Where's Rachel?: Another Adventure of
Arthur, the White House Mouse. Acropolis.
Blair, Arthur W. see Blair, Arthur Witt.
Blair, Arthur Witt.
xBlair, Arthur W.
Growth & Development of the Preadolescent.
Irvington.
Blair, Caroline G. see Blair, Caroline Grant.
Blair, Caroline Grant.
xBlair, Caroline G.
Prayers for Mothers. Judson.
Blair, Carvel H. see Blair, Carvel Hall.
Blair, Carvel Hall.
xBlair, Carvel H.
A Guide to Fishing Boats & Their Gear.
Cornell Maritime.
Blair, Clay, 1925-
xBlair, Clay.
Silent Victory: The U. S. Submarine War
Against Japan. Lippincott.
Survive!. Berkley Pub.
Blair, Dike.
xBlair, Dike.
Books & Bedlam. Vermont Bks.
Blair, Dorothy.
xBlair, Dorothy.
A History of Glass in Japan. Corning.
A History of Glass in Japan. Kodansha.
A History of Glass in Japan. U Pr of Va.
Blair, Ed.
xBlair, Ed.
Odyssey of Terror. Broadman.
Blair, Edward P. see Blair, Edward Payson.
Blair, Edward Payson, 1910-
xBlair, Edward P.
Abingdon Bible Handbook. Abingdon.
Blair, Eulalia. see Blair, Eulalia C.
Blair, Eulalia C.
xBlair, Eulalia.
Breakfast & Brunch Dishes for Food Service
Menu Planning. CBI Pub.
xBlair, Eulalia C.
Casseroles & Vegetables for Foodservice Menu
Planning. CBI Pub.
Meat & Poultry Entrees for Foodservice Menu
Planning. CBI Pub.
xBlair, Eulilia C.
Fish & Seafood Dishes for Foodservice Menu
Planning. CBI Pub.
Blair, Eulilia C. see Blair, Eulalia C.
Blair, Frank.
xBlair, Frank.
Let's Be Frank About It. Doubleday.
Blair, George S.
xBlair, George S.
Government at the Grass-Roots. Palisades Pub.
Blair, Glenn M. see Blair, Glenn Myers.
Blair, Glenn Myers.
xBlair, Glenn M.
Educational Psychology. Macmillan.
Blair, Hugh, 1718-1800
xBlair, Hugh.

Lectures on Rhetoric & Belles Lettres. R West.
Lectures on Rhetoric & Belles Lettres.
Ridgeway Bks.
Lectures on Rhetoric & Belles Lettres. S Ill U
Pr.
Blair, J. Allen.
xBlair, J. Allen.
Living Eternally: Devotional Study in the
Gospel of John. Loizeaux.
Blair, Joan.
xBlair, Joan.
Return from the River Kwai. S&S.
Blair, John.
xBlair, John.
The Illustrated Discography of Surf Music:
1959-1965. J Bee Prods.
Blair, John. see Blair, John Malcolm.
Blair, John G.
xBlair, John G.
The Confidence Man in Modern Fiction: A
Rogue's Gallery of Six Portraits. B&N.
Blair, John M. see Blair, John Malcolm.
Blair, John Malcolm, 1914-
xBlair, John.
The Control of Oil. Random.
xBlair, John M.
The Control of Oil. Pantheon.
Blair, Karen. see Blair, Karen J.
Blair, Karen J.
xBlair, Karen.
The Club Woman As Feminist: True
Womanhood Redefined, 1868 to 1914.
Holmes & Meier.
Blair, Lawrence.
xBlair, Lawrence.
Rhythms of Vision: The Changing Patterns of
Belief. Schocken.
Blair, Louis H.
xBlair, Louis H.
Drug Program Assessment: A Community
Guide. Drug Abuse.
Blair, Margot C. see Blair, Margot Carter.
Blair, Margot Carter.
xBlair, Margot C.
Banners & Flags: How to Sew a Celebration.
HarBraceJ.
Blair, P. H. see Blair, Peter Hunter.
Blair, Peter H. see Blair, Peter Hunter.
Blair, Peter Hunter.
xBlair, P. H.
An Introduction to Anglo-Saxon England.
Cambridge U Pr.
xBlair, Peter H.
World of Bede. St Martin.
Blair, Robert, 1921-
xBlair, Robert.
Tales of the Superstitions: Origins of the Lost
Dutchman Legend. AZ Hist Foun.
Blair, Roger D.
xBlair.
Regulating the Professions: A Public-Policy
Symposium. Lexington Bks.
Blair, Thomas L. see Blair, Thomas Lucien Vincent.
Blair, Thomas Lucien Vincent.
xBlair, Thomas L.
Retreat to the Ghetto: The End of a Dream?.
Hill & Wang.
Blair, W. Frank, 1912-
xBlair, W. Frank.
ed. Evolution in the Genus "Bufo". U of Tex
Pr.
Blair, Walter, 1900-
xBlair, Walter.

American Literature: A Brief History. Scott F.
Approaches to Poetry. Irvington.
Mark Twain & Huck Finn: 1855-1873. U of
   Cal Pr.
Native American Humor. Har-Row.
Native American Humor: 1800-1900. Arden
   Lib.

Blais, Madeleine.
   xBlais, Madeleine.
   They Say You Can't Have a Baby: The
      Dilemma of Infertility. Norton.
Blais, Modeleine. *see* Blais, Madeleine.
Blaisdell, Donald C. *see* Blaisdell, Donald Christy.
Blaisdell, Donald Christy, 1899-
   xBlaisdell, Donald C.
   Government & Agriculture: Growth of Federal
      Farm Aid. Da Capo.
Blaisdell, F. William. *see* Blaisdell, Frank William.
Blaisdell, Frank William.
   xBlaisdell, F. William.
   Respiratory Distress Syndrome of Shock &
      Trauma: Post-Traumatic Respiratory Failure.
      Saunders.
Blaisdell, Gus.
   xBlaisdell, Gus.
   Dented Fenders: Poems. SBD.
Blaise, Clark.
   xBlaise, Clark.
   Days & Nights in Calcutta. Doubleday.
   Lunar Attractions. Doubleday.
Blake, Alexander.
   xBlake, Alexander.
   Design of Curved Members for Machines.
      Krieger.
Blake, Alma C. *see* Blake, Alma Carwile.
Blake, Alma Carwile, 1909-
   xBlake, Alma C.
   Of Life & Love & Things. McClain.
Blake, B. J. *see* Blake, Barry J.
Blake, Barry J.
   xBlake, B. J.
   Case Marking in Australian Languages.
      Humanities.
Blake, Claire. *see* Blake, Claire L.
Blake, Claire L.
   xBlake, Claire.
   Greenhouse Gardening for Fun. Morrow.
Blake, Clarence N.
   xBlake, Clarence N.
   Quiz Book on Black America. HM.
Blake, Fay M., 1920-
   xBlake, Fay M.
   The Strike in the American Novel. Scarecrow.
Blake, Gary.
   xBlake, Gary.
   The Status Book. Doubleday.
Blake, George C. *see* Blake, George Gascoigne.
Blake, George Gascoigne, 1885-
   xBlake, George C.
   History of Radio Telegraphy & Telephony.
      Arno.
Blake, Henry. *see* Blake, Henry N.
Blake, Henry N.
   xBlake, Henry.
   Talking with Horses. Bantam.
Blake, Ian F.
   xBlake, Ian F.
   An Introduction to Algebraic & Combinatorial
      Coding Theory. Acad Pr.
   Introduction to Applied Probability. Wiley.
   The Mathematical Theory of Coding. Acad Pr.
Blake, Irving H. *see* Blake, Irving Hill.
Blake, Irving Hill, 1888-1968
   xBlake, Irving H.
   A Comparison of the Animal Communities of
      Coniferous & Deciduous Forests. Johnson
      Repr.
Blake, James N. *see* Blake, James Neal.
Blake, James Neal.
   xBlake, James N.

Monty Monkey-Shines with Speech Sounds. C
   C Thomas.
Speech Education Activities for Children. C C
   Thomas.
Speech, Language & Learning Disorders:
   Education & Therapy. C C Thomas.
Word Clowns & Sentence Circuses. C C
   Thomas.
Blake, Jennifer.
   xBlake, Jennifer.
   Love's Wild Desire. Popular Lib.
Blake, Jim.
   xBlake, Jim.
   The Great Perpetual Learning Machine: A
      Stupendous Collection of Ideas, Games,
      Experiments, Activities, & Recommendations
      for Further Exploration--with Tons of
      Illustrations. Little.
Blake, John B. *see* Blake, John Ballard.
Blake, John Ballard.
   xBlake, John B.
   ed. Medical Reference Works, 1679-1966: A
      Selected Bibliography. Med Lib Assn.
   Public Health in the Town of Boston,
      1630-1822. Harvard U Pr.
Blake, Kathleen.
   xBlake, Kathleen.
   Play, Games, & Sport: The Literary Works of
      Lewis Carroll. Cornell U Pr.
Blake, Kathryn A.
   xBlake, Kathryn A.
   College Reading Skills. P-H.
Blake, M. B. *see* Blake, Mabelle Babcock.
Blake, Mabelle Babcock, 1880-
   xBlake, M. B.
   Education of the Modern Girl. Arno.
Blake, Mindy.
   xBlake, Mindy.
   The Golf Swing of the Future. Norton.
   The Golf Swing of the Future. PB.
Blake, Neil F. *see* Blake, Neil Ffrench.
Blake, Neil Ffrench.
   xBlake, Neil F.
   The World of Show Jumping. Printed Horse.
Blake, Nicholas.
   xBlake, Nicholas.
   The Beast Must Die. Har-Row.
   The Sad Variety. Har-Row.
   Thou Shell of Death. Har-Row.
   The Whisper in the Gloom. Har-Row.
Blake, O. William.
   xBlake, O. William.
   Lead-up Games to Team Sports. P-H.
Blake, Olive.
   xBlake, Olive.
   Mystery of the Lost Letter. Troll Assocs.
Blake, Patricia.
   xBlake, Patricia.
   ed. Dissonant Voices in Soviet Literature.
      Greenwood.
Blake, Peter, 1920-
   xBlake, Peter.
   Form Follows Fiasco: Why Modern
      Architecture Hasn't Worked. Little.
   The Master Builders: Le Corbusier, Mies Van
      der Rohe, Frank Lloyd Wright. Norton.
Blake, Quentin.
   xBlake, Quentin.
   jt. auth. The Improbable Book of Records.
      Atheneum.
Blake, Reed H.
   xBlake, Reed H.
   A Taxonomy of Concepts in Communication.
      Hastings.
Blake, Richard. *see* Blake, Richard T.
Blake, Richard T.
   xBlake, Richard.

Water Treatment for HVAC & Potable Water
   Systems. McGraw.
Blake, Robert, Baron of Braydeston, 1916-
   xBlake, Robert.
   A History of Rhodesia. Knopf.
Blake, Robert R. *see* Blake, Robert Rogers.
Blake, Robert Rogers.
   xBlake, Robert R.
   Building a Dynamic Corporation Through Grid
      Organization Development. A-W.
   Corporate Excellence Through Grid
      Organization Development. Gulf Pub.
   Diary of an OD Man. Gulf Pub.
   The Social Worker Grid. C C Thomas.
Blake, Roland P. *see* Blake, Roland Patton.
Blake, Roland Patton.
   xBlake, Roland P.
   Industrial Safety. P-H.
Blake, Wendon.
   xBlake, Wendon.
   Acrylic Painting. Watson-Guptill.
   The Acrylic Painting Book. Watson-Guptill.
   Acrylic Watercolor Painting. Watson-Guptill.
   Complete Guide to Acrylic Painting.
      Watson-Guptill.
   Creative Color: A Practical Guide for Oil
      Painters. Watson-Guptill.
   Landscapes in Oil. Watson-Guptill.
   Landscapes in Watercolor. Watson-Guptill.
   Oil Painting. Watson-Guptill.
   The Oil Painting Book. Watson-Guptill.
   Seascapes in Acrylic. Watson-Guptill.
   Watercolor Painting. Watson-Guptill.
Blake, William.
   xBlake, William.
   Book of Thel: A Facsimile & a Critical Text.
      Brown U Pr.
   The Book of Thel: A Facsimile & a Critical
      Text. NY Pub Lib.
   The Book of Urizen. Shambhala Pubns.
   The Book of Urizen. U of Miami Pr.
   Drawings of William Blake: 92 Pencil Studies.
      Peter Smith.
   Letters from William Blake to Thomas Butts.
      Folcroft.
   The Marriage of Heaven & Hell. Oxford U Pr.
   The Marriage of Heaven & Hell. Oxford U Pr.
   The Marriage of Heaven & Hell. U of Miami
      Pr.
   Portable Blake. Penguin.
   The Portable Blake. Viking Pr.
   Songs of Innocence. Dover.
   Works of William Blake, Poetic, Symbolic, &
      Critical. AMS Pr.
Blakeborough, Richard, d. 1918
   xBlakeborough, Richard.
   Legends of Highwaymen & Others. Gale.
Blakebrough, Ken.
   xBlakebrough, Ken.
   Fireball Outfit: The 457th Bombardment Group
      in the Skies Over Europe. Aero.
Blakeley, Walter R.
   xBlakeley, Walter R.
   Calculus for Engineering Technology. Wiley.
Blakelock, John H.
   xBlakelock, John H.
   Automatic Control of Aircraft & Missiles.
      Wiley.
Blakely, James.
   xBlakely, James.
   The Science of Animal Husbandry. Reston.
Blakely, Robert J.
   xBlakely, Robert J.
   To Serve the Public Interest: Educational
      Broadcasting in the United States. Syracuse
      U Pr.
Blakemore, Colin.
   xBlakemore, Colin.

Mechanics of the Mind. Cambridge U Pr.
Blakemore, Harold.
  xBlakemore, Harold.
    British Nitrates & Chilean Politics, 1886-1896:
      Balmaceda & North. Humanities.
Blaker, Alfred A., 1928-
  xBlaker, Alfred A.
    Field Photography: Beginning & Advanced
      Techniques. W H Freeman.
    Photography: Art & Technique. W H Freeman.
Blaker, J. W. see Blaker, J. Warren.
Blaker, J. Warren.
  xBlaker, J. W.
    Geometric Optics: The Matrix Theory. Dekker.
Blaker, Richard, 1893-1940
  xBlaker, Richard.
    The Needle-Watcher: The Will Adams Story,
      British Samurai. C E Tuttle.
Blakeslee, Albert F. see Blakeslee, Albert Francis.
Blakeslee, Albert Francis.
  xBlakeslee, Albert F.
    Northeastern Trees in Winter. Peter Smith.
Blakeslee, Leroy L.
  xBlakeslee, LeRoy L.
    World Food Production, Demand, & Trade.
      Iowa St U Pr.
Blakeslee, Richard.
  xBlakeslee, Richard.
    Dental Technology: Theory & Practice. Mosby.
Blakeslee, Thomas R., 1937-
  xBlakeslee, Thomas R.
    Digital Design with Standard MSI & LSI:
      Design Techniques for the Microcomputer
      Age. Wiley.
Blakey, George. see Blakey, George G.
Blakey, George G., 1934-
  xBlakey, George.
    ed. The Gambler's Companion. Paddington.
Blakey, Robert, 1795-1878
  xBlakey, Robert.
    The History of Political Literature from the
      Earliest Times. Irvington.
Blakey, Scot. see Blakey, Scott.
Blakey, Scott.
  xBlakey, Scot.
    Prisoner at War: The Survival of Commander
      Richard A. Stratton. Penguin.
Blakiston, Georgiana.
  xBlakiston, Georgiana.
    Lord William Russell & His Wife - 1815-1846.
      Scholarly Res Inc.
Blalock, H. see Blalock, Hubert M.
Blalock, H. M. see Blalock, Hubert M.
Blalock, Hubert M.
  xBlalock, H.
    Theory Construction: From Verbal to
      Mathematical Formulations. P-H.
  xBlalock, H. M.
    ed. Causal Models in the Social Sciences.
      Aldine Pub.
    ed. Measurement in the Social Sciences:
      Theories & Strategies. Aldine Pub.
  xBlalock, Hubert M.
    Causal Inferences in Nonexperimental
      Research. Norton.
    Causal Inferences in Nonexperimental
      Research. U of NC Pr.
    Intergroup Processes: A Micro-Macro
      Perspective. Free Pr.
    Social Statistics. McGraw.
Blalock, Joyce.
  xBlalock, Joyce.
    Civil Liability of Law Enforcement Officers. C
      C Thomas.
Blamires, Harry.
  xBlamires, Harry.
    The Christian Mind. Servant.
Blan, L. B. see Blan, Louis Benjamin.
Blan, Louis Benjamin, 1881-
  xBlan, L. B.

Special Study of the Incidence of Retardation.
    AMS Pr.
Blanc, Charles, 1813-1882
  xBlanc, Charles.
    Art in Ornament & Dress. Gale.
Blanc, Louis, 1811-1882
  xBlanc, Louis.
    History of Ten Years, 1830-1840. Kelley.
Blanc, Robert P.
  xBlanc, Robert P.
    ed. Computer Networking. Inst Electrical.
    ed. Computer Networking. Wiley.
Blanc-Lapierre, Andre.
  xBlanc-LaPierre, Andre.
    Theory of Random Functions. Gordon.
Blanch, Robert J.
  xBlanch, Robert J.
    ed. Style & Symbolism in Piers Plowman: A
      Modern Critical Anthology. U of Tenn Pr.
Blanchard, Benjamin S.
  xBlanchard, Benjamin S.
    Engineering Organization & Management. P-H.
    Logistics Engineering & Management. P-H.
Blanchard, C. see Blanchard, Converse H.
Blanchard, Converse H.
  xBlanchard, C.
    Introduction to Modern Physics. P-H.
Blanchard, Frederic T. see Blanchard, Frederic Thomas.
Blanchard, Frederic Thomas, 1878-
  xBlanchard, Frederic T.
    Fielding the Novelist: A Study in Historical
      Criticism. Russell.
Blanchard, Howard L. see Blanchard, Howard Lawrence.
Blanchard, Howard Lawrence.
  xBlanchard, Howard L.
    Organization & Administration of Pupil
      Personnel Services. C C Thomas.
Blanchard, Johathan. see Blanchard, Jonathan.
Blanchard, Jonathan.
  xBlanchard, Johathan.
    Debate on Slavery. Scholarly.
  xBlanchard, Jonathan.
    Debate on Slavery. Negro U Pr.
Blanchard, Kendall, 1942-
  xBlanchard, Kendall.
    The Economics of Sainthood: Religious Change
      Among the Rimrock Navajos. Fairleigh
      Dickinson.
Blanchard, Majorie P. see Blanchard, Marjorie P.
Blanchard, Marjorie. see Blanchard, Marjorie P.
Blanchard, Marjorie P.
  xBlanchard, Majorie P.
    The Vegetarian Menu Cookbook. Watts.
  xBlanchard, Marjorie.
    Backyard Harvest. Bobbs.
    The Home Gardener's Cookbook. Garden Way
      Pub.
  xBlanchard, Marjorie P.
    The Outdoor Cookbook. Watts.
Blanchard, Paula.
  xBlanchard, Paula.
    Margaret Fuller: From Transcendentalism to
      Revolution. Dell.
Blanchard, Robert O.
  xBlanchard, Robert O.
    ed. Congress & the News Media. Hastings.
Blanchard, Tim.
  xBlanchard, Tim.
    A Practical Guide to Finding Your Spiritual
      Gifts. Tyndale.
Blanche, R. see Blanche, Robert.
Blanche, Robert.
  xBlanche, R.
    Axiomatics. Routledge & Kegan.
Blanck, Gertrude.
  xBlanck, Gertrude.
    Ego Psychology II: Psychoanalytic
      Developmental Psychology. Columbia U Pr.
Blanck, Rubin.
  xBlanck, Rubin.

Marriage & Personal Development. Columbia
    U Pr.
Blanco. see Blanco, Ralph F.
Blanco, Ralph F.
  xBlanco.
    Case Studies in Clinical & School Psychology.
      C C Thomas.
  xBlanco, Ralph F.
    Prescriptions for Children with Learning &
      Adjustment Problems. C C Thomas.
Bland, Alexander.
  xBland, Alexander.
    Fonteyn & Nureyev: The Story of a
      Partnership. Times Bks.
Bland, Brian F.
  xBland, Brian F.
    Crop Production: Cereals & Legumes. Acad Pr.
Bland, Carole J.
  xBland, Carole J.
    Faculty Development Through Workshops. C
      C Thomas.
Bland, D. R. see Bland, David Russel.
Bland, David Russel.
  xBland, D. R.
    Solutions of Laplace's Equation. Routledge &
      Kegan.
Bland, Hamilton.
  xBland, Hamilton.
    Competitive Swimming. Sterling.
Bland, John. see Bland, John Hardesty.
Bland, John H. see Bland, John Hardesty.
Bland, John Hardesty, 1917-
  xBland, John.
    Forests of Lilliput: The Realm of Mosses &
      Lichens. P-H.
  xBland, John H.
    Arthritis: Medical Treatment & Home Care.
      Macmillan.
Bland, John O. see Bland, John Otway Percy.
Bland, John Otway Percy, 1863-1945
  xBland, John O.
    Li Hung-Chang. Arno.
Bland, Randall W. see Bland, Randall Walton.
Bland, Randall Walton.
  xBland, Randall W.
    Private Pressure on Public Law: Legal Career
      of Justice Thurgood Marshall. Kennikat.
    Private Pressure on Public Law: The Legal
      Career of Justice Thurgood Marshall.
      Kennikat.
Bland, Roger G.
  xBland, Roger G.
    How to Know the Insects. Wm C Brown.
Blanda, George.
  xBlanda, George.
    Over Forty: Feeling Great & Looking Good!.
      S&S.
Blandford, Linda.
  xBlandford, Linda.
    Super Wealth: The Secret Lives of the Oil
      Sheikhs. Morrow.
Blandford, Percy. see Blandford, Percy W.
Blandford, Percy W.
  xBlandford, Percy.
    How to Make Early American & Colonial
      Furniture. TAB Bks.
    The Woodworker's Bible. TAB Bks.
    Woodworking with Scraps. TAB Bks.
  xBlandford, Percy W.
    Country Craft Tools. Gale.
    Country Craft Tools. T Y Crowell.
    Old Farm Tools & Machinery: An Illustrated
      History. Gale.
    Practical Knots & Ropework. TAB Bks.
Blandin, I. M. see Blandin, Isabella Margaret Elizabeth
  John.
Blandin, Isabella Margaret Elizabeth John.
  xBlandin, I. M.

History of Higher Education of Women in the
South Prior to 1860. Zenger Pub.

Blandino, Giovanni.
xBlandino, Giovanni.
Theories on the Nature of Life. Philos Lib.

Blandy, John. see Blandy, John P.

Blandy, John P., 1927-
xBlandy, John.
Lecture Notes on Urology. Lippincott.

Blandy, Thomas.
xBlandy, Thomas.
All Through the House: A Guide to Home
Weatherization. McGraw.

Blane, Linda.
xBlane, Linda.
Development of Psycho-Motor Competence:
Selected Readings. Mss Info.

Blane, William N. see Blane, William Newnham.

Blane, William Newnham, 1800-1825
xBlane, William N.
Excursion Through the United States & Canada
During the Years 1822-1823. Negro U Pr.

Blank, Leland T.
xBlank, Leland T.
Statistical Procedures for Engineering,
Management & Science. McGraw.

Blank, Leonard.
xBlank, Leonard.
Age of Shrinks. Ewing Pubns.
Psychology for Everyday Living. Mayflower
Bks.

Blank, Marion.
xBlank, Marion.
Preschool Language Assessment Instrument:
Language of Learning in Practice. Grune.
Teaching Learning in the Preschool: A
Dialogue Approach. Merrill.
xBlank, Marion S.
Compiled by Working with People: A Selected
Social Casework Bibliography. Family Serv.

Blank, Marion S. see Blank, Marion.

Blank, R. see Blank, Robert H.

Blank, Robert H.
xBlank, R.
Political Parties: An Introduction. P-H.

Blankenbaker, E. Keith.
xBlankenbaker, E. Keith.
Modern Plumbing. Goodheart.

Blankenhorn, Heber.
xBlankenhorn, Heber.
The Strike for Union. Arno.

Blankenship, A. B. see Blankenship, Albert Breneman.

Blankenship, Albert Breneman, 1914-
xBlankenship, A. B.
Professional Telephone Surveys. McGraw.

Blankenship, Albert S. see Blankenship, Albert Silvanus.

Blankenship, Albert Silvanus, 1880-
xBlankenship, Albert S.
The Accessibility of Rural Schoolhouses in
Texas. AMS Pr.

Blankenship, Jane.
xBlankenship, Jane.
ed. Rhetoric & Communication: Studies in the
University of Illinois Tradition. U of Ill Pr.

Blankenship, Martha L. see Blankenship, Martha Lee.

Blankenship, Martha Lee.
xBlankenship, Martha L.
Home Economics Education. HM.

Blankenship, Ralph L., 1937-
xBlankenship, Ralph L.
ed. Colleagues in Organization: The Social
Construction of Professional Work. Krieger.

Blankenship, Russell.
xBlankenship, Russell.
American Literature As an Expression of the
National Mind. Cooper Sq.

Blankenship, Samuel M.
xBlankenship, Samuel M.

A Backpacking Guide to the Southern
Mountains. Mockingbird Bks.

Blankenship, William D.
xBlankenship, William D.
The Programmed Man. Manor Bks.

Blankfort, Michael, 1907-
xBlankfort, Michael.
Take the A Train. Dutton.

Blanksten, George I.
xBlanksten, George I.
Peron's Argentina. U of Chicago Pr.

Blanning, T. C. see Blanning, T. C. W.

Blanning, T. C. W.
xBlanning, T. C.
Reform & Revolution in Mainz, 1743-1803.
Cambridge U Pr.

Blanpain, Jan.
xBlanpain, Jan.
Community Health Investment: Health Services
Research in Belgium, France, Federal
German Republic & the Netherlands. Oxford
U Pr.

Blanpain, Roger.
xBlanpain, Roger.
The O E C D Guidelines for Multinational
Enterprises & Labour Relations: 1976-1979
Experience & Review. Kluwer Boston.
Public Employee Unionism in Belgium. U of
Mich Inst Labor.

Blanqui, Jerome Adolphe, 1798-1854
xBlanqui, Jerome-Adolphe.
History of Political Economy in Europe.
Gordon Pr.
History of Political Economy in Europe.
Kelley.

Blanqui, Jerome-Adolphe. see Blanqui, Jerome Adolphe.

Blanshard, Audrey.
xBlanshard, Audrey.
Lucetta. Fawcett.
The Shy Young Denbury. Fawcett.

Blanshard, B. see Blanshard, Frances Margaret
(Bradshaw).

Blanshard, Brand, 1892-
xBlanshard, Brand.
ed. Education in the Age of Science. Arno.
On Philosophical Style. Greenwood.
Reason & Analysis. Open Court.
Reason & Belief. Yale U Pr.
Reason & Goodness. Humanities.
The Uses of a Liberal Education, & Other
Talks to Students. Open Court.

Blanshard, Frances. see Blanshard, Frances Margaret
(Bradshaw).

Blanshard, Frances M. see Blanshard, Frances Margaret
(Bradshaw).

Blanshard, Frances Margaret (Bradshaw), 1895-1966
xBlanshard, B.
Pref. by Frank Aydelotte of Swarthmore.
Columbia U Pr.
xBlanshard, Frances.
Frank Aydelotte of Swarthmore. Columbia U
Pr.
xBlanshard, Frances M.
Retreat from Likeness in the Theory of
Painting. Arno.

Blanshard, Paul, 1892-
xBlanshard, Paul.
ed. Classics of Free Thought. Prometheus Bks.
Communism, Democracy, & Catholic Power.
Greenwood.
Personal & Controversial: An Autobiography.
Beacon Pr.
Some of My Best Friends Are Christians. Open
Court.

Blanton, Richard E.
xBlanton, Richard E.
ed. Monte Alban: Settlement Patterns at the
Ancient Zapotec Capital. Acad Pr.

Blanton, William.
xBlanton, William E.

ed. Measuring Reading Performance. Intl
Reading.

Blanton, William E. see Blanton, William.

Blanton, Wyndham. see Blanton, Wyndham Bolling.

Blanton, Wyndham B. see Blanton, Wyndham Bolling.

Blanton, Wyndham Bolling, 1890-1960
xBlanton, Wyndham.
Medicine in Virginia in the Seventeenth
Century. Arno.
xBlanton, Wyndham B.
Medicine in Virginia in the Seventeenth
Century. Reprint.

Blaquiere, A. see Blaquiere, Austin.

Blaquiere, Austin.
xBlaquiere, A.
Quantitative & Qualitative Games. Acad Pr.
xBlaquiere, Austin.
Nonlinear System Analysis. Acad Pr.

Blascoer, Frances.
xBlascoer, Frances.
Colored School Children in New York. Negro
U Pr.

Blase, Melvin G.
xBlase, Melvin G.
ed. Institutions in Agricultural Development.
Iowa St U Pr.

Blashfield, Jean F.
xBlashfield, Jean F.
Apartment Greenery: Growing Plants in
Unpromising Places. Little.
The Healthy House Plant: A Guide to the
Prevention, Detection, & Cure of Pests &
Diseases. Little.

Blashford-Snell, J. N.
xBlashford-Snell, John.
ed. Expeditions: The Experts' Way. Merrimack
Bk Serv.

Blashford-Snell, John. see Blashford-Snell, J. N.

Blasi, Anthony J.
xBlasi, Anthony J.
Segregationist Violence & Civil Rights
Movements in Tuscaloosa. U Pr of Amer.
Toward an Interpretive Sociology. U Pr of
Amer.

Blasier, Cole.
xBlasier, Cole.
ed. Cuba in the World. U of Pittsburgh Pr.
The Hovering Giant: U. S. Responses to
Revolutionary Change in Latin America. U of
Pittsburgh Pr.

Blasis, Celeste De. see De Blasis, Celeste.

Blass, Thomas.
xBlass, Thomas.
Contemporary Social Psychology:
Representative Readings. Peacock Pubs.
ed. Personality Variables in Social Behavior.
Halsted Pr.

Blassingame, John W., 1940-
xBlassingame, John W.
The Slave Community: Plantation Life in the
Ante-Bellum South. Oxford U Pr.

Blassingame, Wyatt.
xBlassingame, Wyatt.

His Kingdom for a Horse. Arno.
How Davy Crockett Got a Bearskin Coat.
    Garrard.
The Incas & the Spanish Conquest. Messner.
Joseph Stalin & Communist Russia. Garrard.
The Little Killers: Fleas, Lice & Mosquitoes.
    Putnam.
Paul Bunyan Fights the Monster Plants.
    Garrard.
Pecos Bill & the Wonderful Clothesline Snake.
    Garrard.
Pecos Bill Catches a Hidebehind. Garrard.
Pecos Bill Rides a Tornado. Garrard.
Story of the Boy Scouts. Garrard.
Story of the United States Flag. Garrard.
Wonders of Alligators & Crocodiles. Dodd.
Wonders of Alligators & Crocodiles. Schol Bk
    Serv.
Wonders of Crows. Dodd.
Wonders of Frogs & Toads. Dodd.
Wonders of Raccoons. Dodd.
Wonders of the Turtle World. Dodd.

Blatch, Mervyn.
    xBlatch, Mervyn.
    Parish Churches of England in Colour.
        Transatlantic.

Blatt, Burton.
    xBlatt, Burton.
    The Family Papers: A Return to Purgatory.
        Longman.

Blatt, Frank J.
    xBlatt, J.
    Thermoelectric Power of Metals. Plenum Pub.
Blatt, J. see Blatt, Frank J.
Blatt, John M. see Blatt, John Markus.

Blatt, John Markus.
    xBlatt, J.
    Theoretical Nuclear Physics. Springer-Verlag.
    xBlatt, John M.
    Theory of Superconductivity. Acad Pr.

Blattberg, Robert C., 1942-
    xBlattberg, Robert C.
    ed. The Economy in Transition. NYU Pr.
Blatter, Alfred. see Blatter, Alfred W.

Blatter, Alfred W.
    xBlatter, Alfred.
    Instrumentation Orchestration. Longman.
Blatter, Joerg. see Blatter, Jorg.

Blatter, Jorg.
    xBlatter, Joerg.
    Grothendieck Spaces in Approximation Theory.
        Am Math.
Blatty, William P. see Blatty, William Peter.

Blatty, William Peter.
    xBlatty, William P.
    The Exorcist. Bantam.
    Exorcist. Har-Row.
    I'll Tell Them I Remember You. Norton.
    The Ninth Configuration. Bantam.
    The Ninth Configuration. Har-Row.

Blatz, Hanson.
    xBlatz, Hanson.
    Introduction to Radiological Health. McGraw.
Blatz, William E. see Blatz, William Emet.

Blatz, William Emet, 1895-1964
    xBlatz, William E.
    Collected Studies on the Dionne Quintuplets
        Arno.
Blau, Joseph L. see Blau, Joseph Leon.

Blau, Joseph Leon, 1909-
    xBlau, Joseph L.
    Men & Movements in American Philosophy.
        Greenwood.
    ed. Social Theories of Jacksonian Democracy,
        1825-1850: Representative Writings of the
        Period, 1825-1850. Bobbs.
    The Story of Jewish Philosophy. Ktav.
Blau, Joshua. see Blau, Yehoshua.
Blau, K. see Blau, Karl Hermann Friedrich.

Blau, Karl Hermann Friedrich.
    xBlau, K.
    ed. Handbook of Derivatives for
        Chromatography. Heyden.
Blau, Melinda. see Blau, Melinda E.

Blau, Melinda E.
    xBlau, Melinda.
    First Over the Oceans. Silver.
Blau, Peter M. see Blau, Peter Michael.

Blau, Peter Michael.
    xBlau, Peter M.
    The American Occupational Structure. Free Pr.
    ed. Approaches to the Study of Social
        Structure. Free Pr.
    Bureaucracy in Modern Society. Random.
    Exchange & Power in Social Life. Wiley.
    Inequality & Heterogeneity: A Primitive
        Theory of Social Structure. Free Pr.
    On the Nature of Organizations. Wiley.

Blau, Yehoshua.
    xBlau, Joshua.
    A Grammar of Biblical Hebrew. Intl Pubns
        Serv.

Blauch, Lloyd E., 1889-
    xBlauch, Lloyd E.
    Federal Cooperation in Agricultural Extension
        Work, Vocational Education, & Vocational
        Rehabilitation. Arno.

Blaufarb, Douglas S.
    xBlaufarb, Douglas S.
    The Counterinsurgency Era: U. S. Doctrine &
        Performance 1950 to Present. Free Pr.
Blaug, M. see Blaug, Mark.

Blaug, Mark.
    xBlaug, M.
    Economic Theory in Retrospect. Cambridge U
        Pr.
    Economics of Education: A Selected
        Annotated Bibliography. Pergamon
    xBlaug, Mark.
    ed. The Economics of the Arts. Westview.

Blauner, Robert.
    xBlauner, Robert.
    Alienation & Freedom: The Factory Worker &
        His Industry. U of Chicago Pr.
    Racial Oppression in America. Har-Row.
Blaustein, A. see Blaustein, Ancel U.

Blaustein, Albert P.
    xBlaustein, Albert P.
    ed. Constitutions of Dependencies & Special
        Sovereignties. Oceana.
    Independence Documents of the World.
        Oceana.
    ed. Manual on Foreign Legal Periodicals &
        Their Index. Oceana.
Blaustein, Ancel. see Blaustein, Ancel U.

Blaustein, Ancel U.
    xBlaustein, A.
    ed. Pathology of the Female Genital Tract.
        Springer-Verlag.
    xBlaustein, Ancel.
    Interpretation of Biopsy of Endometrium.
        Raven.
Blavatsky, Helena P. see Blavatsky, Helene Petrovna
Hahn-Hahn.
Blavatsky, Helene P. see Blavatsky, Helene Petrovna
Hahn-Hahn.

Blavatsky, Helene Petrovna Hahn-Hahn, 1831-1891
    xBlavatsky, Helena P.
    Dynamics of the Psychic World: Comments by
        H. P. Blavatsky on Magic, Mediumship,
        Psychism, & the Powers of the Spirit. Theos
        Pub Hse.
    Studies in Occultism. Theos U Pr.
    xBlavatsky, Helene P.
    Theosophical Glossary. Gale.

Blaze, Wayne.
    xBlaze, Wayne.

Guide to Alternative Colleges & Universities.
    Garrett Pk.

Blazer, Don, 1939-
    xBlazer, Don.
    Horses Don't Care About Women's Lib. Joyce
        Pr.
    Natural Western Riding. HM.

Blazevic, Donna J.
    xBlazevic, Donna J.
    ed. Principles of Biochemical Tests in
        Diagnostic Microbiology. Wiley.

Blazier, Kenneth D.
    xBlazier, Kenneth D.
    Building an Effective Church School: Guide for
        the Superintendent & Board of Christian
        Education. Judson.
    A Growing Church School. Judson.

Blazynski, George, 1914-
    xBlazynski, George.
    Flashpoint Poland. Pergamon.

Bleakley, Robert.
    xBleakley, Robert.
    Intro. by African Masks. St Martin.
Bleakney, Thomas. see Bleakney, Thomas P.

Bleakney, Thomas P.
    xBleakney, Thomas.
    Retirement Systems for Public Employees.
        Irwin.
Bleaney, M. see Bleaney, M. F.

Bleaney, M. F.
    xBleaney, M.
    Underconsumption Theories: A History &
        Critical Analysis. Beekman Pubs.
Bleasdale, J. K. see Bleasdale, J. K. A.

Bleasdale, J. K. A.
    xBleasdale, J. K.
    Plant Physiology in Relation to Horticulture.
        AVI

Blechman, Barry M.
    xBlechman, Barry M.
    Guide to Far Eastern Navies. Naval Inst Pr.
    xBlechman, Barry M. C.
    Force Without War: U. S. Armed Forces As a
        Political Instrument.. Brookings.
    xBlechman, Barry M. G.
    The Soviet Military Buildup & U.S. Defense
        Spending. Brookings.
Blechman, Barry M. C. see Blechman, Barry M.
Blechman, Barry M. G. see Blechman, Barry M.
Bleck, Eugene E. see Bleck, Eugene Edmund.

Bleck, Eugene Edmund.
    xBleck, Eugene E.
    Atlas of Plaster Cast Techniques. Year Bk
        Med.
    Orthopaedic Management of Cerebral Palsy.
        Saunders.
Bledsoe, Samuel T. see Bledsoe, Samuel Thomas.

Bledsoe, Samuel Thomas, 1868-1939
    xBledsoe, Samuel T.
    Indian Land Laws. Arno.

Bledsoe, Terry.
    xBledsoe, Terry.
    Line Drive. Raintree Pubs.
Bledsoe, Wayne. see Bledsoe, Wayne M.

Bledsoe, Wayne M.
    xBledsoe, Wayne.
    The Advent of Civilization. Heath.
Bleecker, Ann E. see Bleecker, Ann Eliza Schuyler.

Bleecker, Ann Eliza Schuyler, 1752-1783
    xBleecker, Ann E.
    Posthumous Works. Irvington.

Bleed, Peter.
    xBleed, Peter.
    Archaeology of Petaga Point: The Preceramic
        Component. Minn Hist.

Bleeker, Sonia.
    xBleeker, Sonia.

The Ashanti of Ghana. Morrow.
The Pueblo Indians: Farmers of the Rio
    Grande. Morrow.
Blegen, Carl W. *see* Blegen, Carl William.
Blegen, Carl William, 1887-
    xBlegen, Carl W.
    The North Cemetery. Am Sch Athens.
Blegen, Theodore C. *see* Blegen, Theodore Christian.
Blegen, Theodore Christian, 1891-
    xBlegen, Theodore C.
    Grass Roots History. Kennikat.
    Norwegian Migration to America, 1825-1860.
        Arno.
    Norwegian Migration to America, 1825-60.
        Haskell.
Blegvad, Erik.
    xBlegvad, Erik.
    illus. Burnie's Hill: A Traditional Rhyme.
        Atheneum.
Blegvad, Lenore.
    xBlegvad, Lenore.
    Great Hamster Hunt. HarBraceJ.
    Moon-Watch Summer. HarBraceJ.
Bleiberg, Aaron H.
    xBleiberg, Aaron H.
    Parents Guide to Cleft Palate Habilitation: The
        Team Approach. Exposition.
Bleich, D. J. *see* Bleich, J. David.
Bleich, David.
    xBleich, David.
    Readings & Feelings: An Introduction to
        Subjective Criticism. NCTE.
    Subjective Criticism. Johns Hopkins.
Bleich, J. David.
    xBleich, D. J.
    Contemporary Halakhic Problems. Ktav.
Bleier, Inge J.
    xBleier, Inge J.
    Bedside Maternity Nursing. Saunders.
Bleier, Rocky.
    xBleier, Rocky.
    Fighting Back. Stein & Day.
    Fighting Back. Warner Bks.
Bleifeld, Maurice.
    xBleifeld, Maurice.
    Modern Biology in Review. Barron.
Bleikasten, Andre.
    xBleikasten, Andre.
    Faulkner's As I Lay Dying. Ind U Pr.
Bleiler, E. F. *see* Bleiler, Everett Franklin.
Bleiler, Everett. *see* Bleiler, Everett Franklin.
Bleiler, Everett Franklin, 1920-
    xBleiler, E. F.
    ed. Eight Dime Novels. Peter Smith.
    Marmaduke Multiply's Merry Method of
        Making Minor Mathematicians. Dover.
    ed. Three Victorian Detective Novels. Dover.
    xBleiler, Everett.
    ed. A Treasury of Victorian Detective Stories.
        Scribner.
Bleistein, Norman.
    xBleistein, Norman.
    Asymptotic Expansions of Integrals. Irvington.
Bleiweiss, Robert M.
    xBleiweiss, Robert M.
    ed. Marching to Freedom: The Life of Martin
        Luther King Jr. NAL.
Blenkinsopp, J. *see* Blenkinsopp, Joseph.
Blenkinsopp, Joseph, 1927-
    xBlenkinsopp, J.
    Gibeon & Israel: The Role of Gibeon & the
        Gibeonites in the Political and Religious
        History of Early Israel. Cambridge U Pr.
    xBlenkinsopp, Joseph.
    Prophecy & Canon: A Contribution to the
        Study of Jewish Origins. U of Notre Dame
        Pr.
Blenman, Jonathan.
    xBlenman, Jonathan.

Remarks on Several Acts of Parliament
    Relating More Especially to the Colonies
    Abroad. Arno.
Blenner-Hassett, Roland, 1909-
    xBlenner-Hassett, Roland.
    Study of the Place-Names in Lawman's Brut.
        AMS Pr.
Blennerhassett, Charlotte J. *see* Blennerhassett, Charlotte
    Julia (Von Leyden).
**Blennerhassett, Charlotte Julia (Von Leyden), Lady,
1843-1917**
    xBlennerhassett, Charlotte J.
    Sidelights. Arno.
Blesh, Rudi.
    xBlesh, Rudi.
    They All Played Ragtime. Music Sales.
Blesser, William B., 1924-
    xBlesser, William B.
    Systems Approach to Bio-Medicine. McGraw.
    A Systems Approach to Biomedicine. Krieger.
Blessing, Patrick. *see* Blessing, Patrick J.
Blessing, Patrick J.
    xBlessing, Patrick.
    The British & Irish in Oklahoma. U of Okla Pr.
Blessing, Richard A. *see* Blessing, Richard Allen.
Blessing, Richard Allen.
    xBlessing, Richard A.
    Theodore Roethke's Dynamic Vision. Ind U
        Pr.
Blessington, Francis C., 1942-
    xBlessington, Francis C.
    Paradise Lost & the Classical Epic. Routledge
        & Kegan.
Blessington, John P.
    xBlessington, John P.
    Let My Children Work. Doubleday.
Blessington, Marguerite P. *see* Blessington, Marguerite
    Power Farmer Gardiner.
**Blessington, Marguerite Power Farmer Gardiner,
Countess Of, 1789-1849**
    xBlessington, Marguerite P.
    The Works of Lady Blessington. AMS Pr.
Blessman, Lyle. *see* Blessman, Lyle L.
Blessman, Lyle L., 1936-
    xBlessman, Lyle.
    The Blessman Approach. Farnswth Pub.
Bleuler, Eugen, 1857-1939
    xBleuler, Eugen.
    Textbook of Psychiatry. Arno.
    xBleuler, Eugene.
    Autistic Undisciplined Thinking in Medicine &
        How to Overcome It. Hafner.
Bleuler, Eugene. *see* Bleuler, Eugen.
Bleuler, K. *see* Bleuler, Konrad.
Bleuler, Konrad.
    xBleuler, K.
    ed. Differential Geometrical Methods in
        Mathematical Physics. Springer-Verlag.
Blevin, Margo.
    xBlevin, Margo.
    The Low Blood Sugar Cookbook. Doubleday.
Blevins, Dorothy. *see* Blevins, Dorothy R.
Blevins, Dorothy R.
    xBlevins, Dorothy.
    The Diabetic & Nursing Care. McGraw.
Blevins, Robert D.
    xBlevins, Robert D.
    Flow-Induced Vibration. Van Nos Reinhold.
    Formulas for Natural Frequency & Mode
        Shape. Van Nos Reinhold.
Blewitt, Mary.
    xBlewitt, Mary.
    Celestial Navigation for Yachtsmen. Beekman
        Pubs.
    Celestial Navigation for Yachtsmen. De Graff.
    Navigation for Yachtsmen. Beekman Pubs.
Bley, Helmut.
    xBley, Helmut.

South-West Africa Under German Rule,
    1894-1914. Northwestern U Pr.
Bleyer, Willard G. *see* Bleyer, Willard Grosvenor.
Bleyer, Willard Grosvenor, 1873-1935
    xBleyer, Willard G.
    Newspaper Writing & Editing. Scholarly.
Blickenstaff, Robert T.
    xBlickenstaff, Robert T.
    Total Synthesis of Steroids. Acad Pr.
Blickle, Katrinka.
    xBlickle, Katrinka.
    Heart of the Harbor. Doubleday.
Blicksilver, Edith.
    xBlicksilver, Edith.
    The Ethnic American Woman: Problems,
        Protests, Lifestyle. Kendall-Hunt.
Blij, Harm J. De. *see* De Blij, Harm J.
Blinchikoff, Herman J.
    xBlinchikoff, Herman J.
    Filtering in the Time & Frequency Domains.
        Wiley.
Blind, M. *see* Blind, Mathilde.
Blind, Mathilde, 1841-1896
    xBlind, M.
    George Eliot. Gordon Pr.
    xBlind, Mathilde.
    George Eliot. Haskell.
Blinder, Alan S.
    xBlinder, Alan S.
    The Economics of Public Finance. Brookings.
    Toward an Economic Theory of Income
        Distribution. MIT Pr.
Blinder, Martin.
    xBlinder, Martin.
    Psychiatry in the Everyday Practice of Law.
        Lawyers Co-Op.
Blinder, S. M., 1932-
    xBlinder, S. M.
    Foundations of Quantum Dynamics. Acad Pr.
Blinderman, Abraham, 1916-
    xBlinderman, Abraham.
    American Writers on Education After 1865.
        Twayne.
Blinderman, Rita, 1940-
    xBlinderman, Rita.
    Pizza: Theme & Variations. Greene.
Blinkhorn, M. *see* Blinkhorn, Martin.
Blinkhorn, Martin, 1941-
    xBlinkhorn, M.
    Carlism & Crisis in Spain: 1931-1939.
        Cambridge U Pr.
Blinkov, S. M. *see* Blinkov, Samuil Mikhailovich.
Blinkov, Samuil Mikhailovich.
    xBlinkov, S. M.
    Brain Displacements & Deformations. Plenum
        Pub.
Blish, James.
    xBlish, James.
    And All the Stars a Stage. Avon.
    A Case of Conscience. Ballantine.
    Torrent of Faces. Ace Bks.
Blishen, Edward, 1920-
    xBlishen, Edward.
    ed. Encyclopedia of Education. Philos Lib.
    ed. Junior Pears Encyclopaedia. Merrimack Bk
        Serv.
    ed. Oxford Book of Poetry for Children. Watts.
Bliss, Alan J. *see* Bliss, Alan Joseph.
Bliss, Alan Joseph.
    xBliss, Alan J.
    An Introduction to Old English Metre.
        Folcroft.
Bliss, Anne.
    xBliss, Anne.
    Weeds: A Guide for Dyers & Herbalists.
        Juniper Hse.
Bliss, B. P. *see* Bliss, Brian Peter.
Bliss, Brian Peter.
    xBliss, B. P.

Aims & Motives in Clinical Medicine: A
Practical Approach to Medical Ethics.
Beekman Pubs.
Aims & Motives in Clinical Medicine: A
Practical Approach to Medical Ethics. State
Mutual Bk.

Bliss, Dennis C.
xBliss, Dennis C.
The Effects of the Juvenile Justice System on
Self-Concept. R & E Res Assoc.

Bliss, Edwin C.
xBliss, Edwin C.
Getting Things Done: The ABC's of Time
Management. Scribner.
Bliss, William R. *see* Bliss, William Root.

Bliss, William Root, 1825-1906
xBliss, William R.
Side Glimpses from the Colonial Meeting
House. Gale.

Blit, Lucjan.
xBlit, Lucjan.
Origins of Polish Socialism: The History &
Ideas of the First Polish Socialist Party,
1878-1886. Cambridge U Pr.

Blitch, John D.
xBlitch, John D.
How to Become a Civilian & Succeed in Your
New Career. CS Pubns.
Blitsten, Dorothy R. *see* Blitsten, Dorothy Rubovits.

Blitsten, Dorothy Rubovits, 1907-
xBlitsten, Dorothy R.
Human Social Development: Psychobiological
Roots & Social Consequences. Coll & U Pr.

Blitz, Marcia.
xBlitz, Marcia.
Donald Duck. Crown.

Blitzer, Charles.
xBlitzer, Charles.
Immortal Commonwealth: The Political
Thought of James Harrington. Shoe String.

Bliven, Bruce, 1916-
xBliven, Bruce.
Book Traveller. Dodd.
The Finishing Touch. Dodd.
Men Who Make the Future. Arno.
The Men Who Make the Future. Folcroft.
ed. What the Informed Citizen Needs to Know.
Arno.

Blixt, Raymond.
xBlixt, Raymond.
The Nature of Prejudice. St Marys.

Bloch, Barbara.
xBloch, Barbara.
Meat Board Meat Book. McGraw.

Bloch, Bernard.
xBloch, Bernard.
Plastics Materials in Surgery. C C Thomas.

Bloch, Carolyn.
xBloch, Carolyn C.
Federal Energy Information Sources & Data
Bases. Noyes.
Bloch, Carolyn C. *see* Bloch, Carolyn.

Bloch, Ernest.
xBloch, Ernest.
Impending Changes for Securities Markets:
What Role for the Exchanges?. Jai Pr.
Bloch, Herbert. *see* Bloch, Herbert Aaron.
Bloch, Herbert A. *see* Bloch, Herbert Aaron.

Bloch, Herbert Aaron, 1904-1965
xBloch, Herbert.
Gang: A Study in Adolescent Behavior. Philos
Lib.
xBloch, Herbert A.
Concept of Our Changing Loyalties: An
Introductory Study into the Nature of the
Social Individual. AMS Pr.
The Gang: A Study in Adolescent Behavior.
Greenwood.

Bloch, Iwan, 1872-1922
xBloch, Iwan.

Odoratus Sexualis: A Scientific & Literary
Study of Sexual Scents & Erotic Perfumes.
AMS Pr.

Bloch, Kurt.
xBloch, Kurt.
German Interests & Policies in the Far East.
AMS Pr.
Bloch, Marc. *see* Bloch, Marc Leopold Benjamin.

Bloch, Marc Leopold Benjamin, 1886-1944
xBloch, Marc.
French Rural History: An Essay on Its Basic
Characteristics. U of Cal Pr.
Ile-De-France: The Country Around Paris.
Cornell U Pr.
Strange Defeat: A Statement of Evidence
Written in 1940. Norton.
Strange Defeat: A Statement of Evidence
Written in 1940. Octagon.
Bloch, Marie H. *see* Bloch, Marie Halun.

Bloch, Marie Halun.
xBloch, Marie H.
Aunt America. Atheneum.
Displaced Person. Lothrop.

Bloch, Max.
xBloch, Max.
Lecture Notes for American Pension Fund
Actuaries. Johnson Higgins.

Bloch, Norman J.
xBloch, Norman J.
Linear Algebra. McGraw.

Bloch, R. Howard.
xBloch, R. Howard.
Medieval French Literature & Law. U of Cal
Pr.

Bloch, Robert, 1917-
xBloch, Robert.
Cold Chills. Doubleday.
Cold Chills. Nordon Pubns.
Out of the Mouths of Graves. Mysterious Pr.

Bloch, Sidney.
xBloch, Sidney.
ed. An Introduction to the Psychotherapies.
Oxford U Pr.

Bloch-Hoell, Nils.
xBloch-Hoell, Nils.
The Pentecostal Movement: Its Origin,
Development & Distinctive Character.
Universitet.

Blocher, Donald H.
xBlocher, Donald H.
Developmental Counseling. Ronald Pr.
Blochman, Lawrence G. *see* Blochman, Lawrence
Goldtree.

Blochman, Lawrence Goldtree, 1900-
xBlochman, Lawrence G.
Understanding Your Body. Macmillan.
Block, Adrienne F. *see* Block, Adrienne Fried.

Block, Adrienne Fried.
xBlock, Adrienne F.
ed. Women in American Music: A
Bibliography of Music & Literature.
Greenwood.
Block, Anita R. *see* Block, Anita Rowe.

Block, Anita Rowe.
xBlock, Anita R.
Love Is a Four Letter Word. Arno.

Block, Eric.
xBlock, Eric.
ed. Reactions of Organosulfur Compounds.
Acad Pr.

Block, Fred L.
xBlock, Fred L.
The Origins of International Economic
Disorder: A Study of United States
International Monetary Policy from World
War Two to the Present. U of Cal Pr.
Block, Haskell. *see* Block, Haskell M.

Block, Haskell M.
xBlock, Haskell.

ed. Masters of Modern Drama. Random.
xBlock, Haskell M.
Naturalistic Triptych: The Fictive & the Real
in Zola, Mann & Dreiser. Phila Bk Co.

Block, Irvin.
xBlock, Irvin.
The Lives of Pearl Buck: A Tale of China &
America. T Y Crowell.

Block, J. Bradford, 1933-
xBlock, J. Bradford.
The Signs & Symptoms of Chemical Exposure.
C C Thomas.
Block, J. L. *see* Block, Jean Libman.

Block, Jack.
xBlock, Jack.
Challenge of Response Sets: Unconfounding
Meaning, Acquiescence, & Social Desirability
in the M. M. P. I. Irvington.
Lives Through Time. Bancroft Bks.
Understanding Historical Research: A Search
for Truth. Research Pubns.

Block, James H.
xBlock, James H.
Mastery Learning & Classroom Instruction.
Macmillan.

Block, Jean F.
xBlock, Jean F.
Hyde Park Houses: An Informal History,
1856-1910. U of Chicago Pr.

Block, Jean Libman.
xBlock, J. L.
Back in Circulation. Macmillan.

Block, Joel D.
xBlock, Joel D.
To Marry Again. G&D.

Block, John H.
xBlock, John H.
Inorganic Medicinal & Pharmaceutical
Chemistry. Lea & Febiger.

Block, Lawrence.
xBlock, Lawrence.
Burglar in the Closet. Random.
The Burglar Who Liked to Quote Kipling.
Random.
Burglars Can't Be Choosers. BJ Pub Group.
Burglars Can't Be Choosers. Random.
Me Tanner, You Jane. Macmillan.
Block, Ned. *see* Block, Ned Joel.

Block, Ned Joel, 1942-
xBlock, Ned.
ed. Readings in the Philosophy of Psychology.
Harvard U Pr.
Block, Rudolph E. *see* Block, Rudolph Edgar.

Block, Rudolph Edgar, 1870-1940
xBlock, Rudolph E.
Children of Men. Arno.
Block, Seymour S. *see* Block, Seymour Stanton.

Block, Seymour Stanton.
xBlock, Seymour S.
ed. Disinfection, Sterilization, & Preservation.
Lea & Febiger.

Block, Stanley B.
xBlock, Stanley B
Foundations of Financial Management. Irwin.
Problems in Basic Business Finance. Har-Row.
Block, Thomas. *see* Block, Thomas H.

Block, Thomas H.
xBlock, Thomas.
Mayday. Marek.
Blocker, Gene. *see* Blocker, H. Gene.

Blocker, H. Gene.
xBlocker, Gene.
Introduction to Philosophy. D Van Nostrand.
xBlocker, H. Gene.
Philosophy of Art. Scribner.

Blocker, Jack S.
xBlocker, Jack S.

ed. Alcohol, Reform & Society: The Liquor
Issue in Social Context. Greenwood.
Retreat from Reform: The Prohibition
Movement in the United States, 1890-1913.
Greenwood.

Blockhaus, Arthur P., 1924-
xBlockhaus, Arthur P.
Grievance Arbitration Case Studies. CBI Pub.

Blodget, Samuel, 1757-1814
xBlodget, Samuel.
Economica: A Statistical Manual for the
United States of America. Kelley.

Blodgett, Ralph. *see* Blodgett, Ralph H.

Blodgett, Ralph H., 1940-
xBlodgett, Ralph.
Rapture!: Is It for Real?. Pacific Pr Pub Assn.

Blodgett, Richard. *see* Blodgett, Richard E.

Blodgett, Richard E.
xBlodgett, Richard.
New York Times Book of Money. Times Bks.
xBlodgett, Richard E.
The New York Times Book of Money. Times
Bks.

Bloem, Diane. *see* Bloem, Diane Brummel.

Bloem, Diane B. *see* Bloem, Diane Brummel.

Bloem, Diane Brummel.
xBloem, Diane.
Challenging Bible Crossword Puzzles.
Zondervan.
xBloem, Diane B.
Challenging Bible Crossword Puzzles.
Zondervan.

Blofeld, John. *see* Blofeld, John Eaton Calthorpe.

Blofeld, John Eaton Calthorpe, 1913-
xBlofeld, John.
Gateway to Wisdom: Taoist & Buddhist
Contemplative & Healing Yogas Adapted for
Western Students of the Way. Shambhala
Pubns.
Tantric Mysticism of Tibet: A Practical Guide.
Dutton.
Taoism: The Road to Immortality. Shambhala
Pubns.
The Wheel of Life: The Autobiography of a
Western Buddhist. Shambhala Pubns.

Blois, John T.
xBlois, John T.
Gazetteer of the State of Michigan. Arno.

Blok, Petrus J. *see* Blok, Petrus Johannes.

Blok, Petrus Johannes, 1855-1929
xBlok, Petrus J.
History of the People of the Netherlands. AMS
Pr.
The Life of Admiral De Ruyter. Greenwood.

Blokhintsev, D. I.
xBlokhintsev, D. I.
Quantum Mechanics. Gordon.
Quantum Mechanics. Kluwer Boston.

Blom, Dorothea. *see* Blom, Dorothea Johnson.

Blom, Dorothea Johnson, 1911-
xBlom, Dorothea.
Art Responds to the Bible. Pendle Hill.

Blom, Edward C. *see* Blom, Edward Charles.

Blom, Edward Charles, 1891-
xBlom, Edward C.
Radio & Electric Power Supply Equipment for
Schools. AMS Pr.

Blom, Eric.
xBlom, Eric.

Compiled by Everyman's Dictionary of Music.
St Martin.
Everyman's Dictionary of Music. NAL.
A General Index to Modern Musical Literature
in the English Language: Including
Periodicals for the Years 1915-1926. Da
Capo.
The Limitations of Music: A Study in
Aesthetics. Arno.
The Limitations of Music: A Study of
Aesthetics. Scholarly.
Stepchildren of Music. Arno.

Blom-Cooper, Louis. *see* Blom-Cooper, Louis Jacques.

Blom-Cooper, Louis Jacques.
xBlom-Cooper, Louis.
ed. Progress in Penal Reform. Oxford U Pr.

Blomback, Birger.
xBlomback, Birger.
ed. Plasma Proteins. Wiley.

Blomberg, Thomas G.
xBlomberg, Thomas G.
Social Control & the Proliferation of Juvenile
Court Services. R & E Res Assoc.

Blomfield, Reginald T. *see* Blomfield, Reginald Theodore.

Blomfield, Reginald Theodore, Sir, 1856-1942
xBlomfield, Reginald T.
Formal Garden in England. AMS Pr.

Blond, Anne G.
xBlond, Anne G.
Spectrum of Visual Arts for Young Children.
Double M Pr.

Blond, Anthony.
xBlond, Anthony.
Family Business. Har-Row.
Family Business. Popular Lib.

Blonde, Allan.
xBlonde, Allan.
The Complete Guide to Researching & Writing
the English Term Paper. Scholium Intl.

Blondel, Jean, 1929-
xBlondel, Jean.
Comparative Legislatures. P-H.
Government of France. Har-Row.
Thinking Politically. Westview.

Blondis, Marion N.
xBlondis, Marion N.
Nonverbal Communication with Patients: Back
to the Human Touch. Wiley.

Blood, Bob. *see* Blood, Robert O.

Blood, Charles L.
xBlood, Charles L.
The Goat in the Rug. Schol Bk Serv.

Blood, D. C. *see* Blood, Douglas Charles.

Blood, Don F.
xBlood, Donald F.
Educational Measurement & Evaluation.
Har-Row.

Blood, Donald F. *see* Blood, Don F.

Blood, Douglas Charles.
xBlood, D. C.
Veterinary Medicine: A Textbook of the
Diseases of Cattle, Sheep, Pigs & Horses. Lea
& Febiger.

Blood Horse. *see* Thoroughbred Owners and Breeders
Association.

Blood, Robert O.
xBlood, Bob.
Marriage. Free Pr.
xBlood, Robert O.
Husbands & Wives: The Dynamics of Married
Living. Free Pr.
Husbands & Wives: The Dynamics of Married
Living. Greenwood.

Blood-Horse. *see* Thoroughbred Owners and Breeders
Association.

Blood-Horse-Thoroughbred Owners & Breeders Assn. *see*
Thoroughbred Owners and Breeders Association.

Bloodstein, Oliver.
xBloodstein, Oliver.

Speech Pathology: An Introduction. HM.

Bloodworth, Dennis.
xBloodworth, Dennis.
Any Number Can Play. FS&G.
The Chinese Looking Glass. FS&G.
An Eye for the Dragon: Southeast Asia
Observed, 1954-1970. FS&G.

Bloodworth, Jessie A. *see* Bloodworth, Jessie Athen.

Bloodworth, Jessie Athen.
xBloodworth, Jessie A.
Personal Side. Arno.

Bloom, A. *see* Bloom, Arnold.

Bloom, A. L. *see* Bloom, Arthur Leroy.

Bloom, Alan.
xBloom, Alan.
Perennials for Your Garden. Scribner.

Bloom, Anthony.
xBloom, Anthony.
Courage to Pray. Paulist Pr.
God & Man. Paulist Pr.

Bloom, Arnold.
xBloom, A.
ed. Whittington Postgraduate Medicine.
Butterworths.

Bloom, Arnold L.
xBloom, Arnold L.
Gas Lasers. Krieger.

Bloom, Arthur L. *see* Bloom, Arthur Leroy.

Bloom, Arthur Leroy, 1928-
xBloom, A. L.
Surface of the Earth. P-H.
xBloom, Arthur L.
Geomorphology: A Systematic Analysis of Late
Cenozoic Landforms. P-H.

Bloom, Benjamin S. *see* Bloom, Benjamin Samuel.

Bloom, Benjamin Samuel, 1913-
xBloom, Benjamin S.
Human Characteristics & School Learning.
McGraw.

Bloom, Bernard L.
xBloom, Bernard L.
Changing Patterns of Psychiatric Care. Human
Sci Pr.
Community Mental Health: A General
Introduction. Brooks-Cole.

Bloom, D. M. *see* Bloom, David M.

Bloom, David M., 1936-
xBloom, D. M.
Linear Algebra & Geometry. Cambridge U Pr.

Bloom, Edward A. *see* Bloom, Edward Alan.

Bloom, Edward Alan.
xBloom, Edward A.

Joseph Addison's Sociable Animal: In the
Market Place, On the Hustings, In the Pulpit.
Brown U Pr.

Satire's Persuasive Voice. Cornell U Pr.

ed. The Variety of Fiction: A Critical
Anthology. Odyssey Pr.

ed. The Variety of Poetry: An Anthology.
Odyssey Pr.

Bloom, George F.
xBloom, George F.
Appraising the Single Family Residence. Am
Inst Real Estate Appraisers.
Appraising the Single Family Residence.
Ballinger Pub.

Bloom, Gordon F. *see* Bloom, Gordon Falk.

Bloom, Gordon Falk.
xBloom, Gordon F.
Economics of Labor Relations. Irwin.

Bloom, H. J. *see* Bloom, Harris Julian Gaster.

Bloom, Harold.
xBloom, Harold.

The Anxiety of Influence: A Theory of Poetry. Oxford U Pr.
Anxiety of Influence: A Theory of Poetry. Oxford U Pr.
Deconstruction & Criticism. Continuum.
Figures of Capable Imagination. Continuum.
The Flight to Lucifer: A Gnostic Fantasy. FS&G.
The Flight to Lucifer: A Gnostic Fantasy. Random.
A Map of Misreading. Oxford U Pr.
Bloom, Harris Julian Gaster, 1923-
  xBloom, H. J.
    ed. Cancer in Children: Clinical Management. Springer-Verlag.
Bloom, Herbert I. *see* Bloom, Herbert Ivan.
Bloom, Herbert Ivan, 1899-
  xBloom, Herbert I.
    Economic Activities of the Jews of Amsterdam in the Seventeenth & Eighteenth Centuries. Kennikat.
Bloom, J. Harvey. *see* Bloom, James Harvey.
Bloom, James H. *see* Bloom, James Harvey.
Bloom, James Harvey, 1860-
  xBloom, J. Harvey.
    Folk Lore, Old Customs & Superstitions in Shakespeare Land. Gale.
    Folklore, Old Customs & Superstitions in Shakespeare Land. Norwood Edns.
  xBloom, James H.
    Folk Lore, Old Customs & Superstitions in Shakespeare Land. Folcroft.
Bloom, Lois.
  xBloom, Lois.
    One Word at a Time: The Use of Single Word Utterances Before Syntax. Mouton.
    ed. Readings in Language Development. Wiley.
Bloom, Lynda.
  xBloom, Lynda.
    Fitting & Showing the Halter Horse. Arco.
Bloom, Paul N.
  xBloom, Paul N.
    Advertising, Competition & Public Policy: A Simulation Study. Ballinger Pub.
Bloom, Robert, 1930-
  xBloom, Robert.
    Anatomies of Egotism: A Reading of the Last Novels of H. G. Wells. U of Nebr Pr.
Bloom, Samuel W. *see* Bloom, Samuel William.
Bloom, Samuel William, 1921-
  xBloom, Samuel W.
    Doctor & His Patient: A Sociological Interpretation. Free Pr.
    Power & Dissent in the Medical School. Free Pr.
Bloom, William.
  xBloom, William.
    A Textbook of Histology. Saunders.
Bloomberg, Edward, 1937-
  xBloomberg, Edward.
    Student Violence. Pub Aff Pr.
Bloomberg, Marty.
  xBloomberg, Marty.
    An Introduction to Classification & Number Building in Dewey. Libs Unl.
    Introduction to Public Services for Library Technicians. Libs Unl.
Bloome, Enid.
  xBloome, Enid.
    Dogs Don't Belong on Beds. Doubleday.
Bloomenthal, Harold. *see* Bloomenthal, Harold S.
Bloomenthal, Harold S.
  xBloomenthal, Harold.
    Securities & Federal Corporate Law. Boardman.
Bloomer, Carolyn M.
  xBloomer, Carolyn M.

Principles of Visual Perception. Van Nos Reinhold.
Bloomfield, Arthur E. *see* Bloomfield, Arthur Edward.
Bloomfield, Arthur Edward, 1895-
  xBloomfield, Arthur E.
    How to Recognize the Antichrist. Bethany Fell.
    Where Is the Ark of the Covenant?. Bethany Fell.
Bloomfield, Arthur I. *see* Bloomfield, Arthur Irving.
Bloomfield, Arthur Irving.
  xBloomfield, Arthur I.
    Monetary Policy Under the International Gold Standard. Arno.
Bloomfield, Derek, 1940-
  xBloomfield, Derek.
    From Arithmetic to Algebra. Reston.
Bloomfield, Gerald. *see* Bloomfield, Gerald T.
Bloomfield, Gerald T.
  xBloomfield, Gerald.
    The World Automotive Industry. David & Charles.
Bloomfield, Jon.
  xBloomfield, Jonathan.
    The Passive Revolution: Politics & the Czechoslovak Working Class 1945-48. St Martin.
Bloomfield, Jonathan. *see* Bloomfield, Jon.
Bloomfield, Leonard.
  xBloomfield, Leonard.
    Leonard Bloomfield Anthology. Ind U Pr.
    Menomini Texts. AMS Pr.
    Plains Cree Texts. AMS Pr.
Bloomfield, Lincoln P. *see* Bloomfield, Lincoln Palmer.
Bloomfield, Lincoln Palmer.
  xBloomfield, Lincoln P.
    In Search of American Foreign Policy: The Humane Use of Power. Oxford U Pr.
    The Power to Keep Peace, Today & in a World Without War. World Without War.
    U. N. & Vietnam. Carnegie Endow.
Bloomfield, Morton W. *see* Bloomfield, Morton Wilfred.
Bloomfield, Morton Wilfred.
  xBloomfield, Morton W.
    Linguistic Introduction to the History of English. Greenwood.
Bloomfield, Paul, 1898-
  xBloomfield, Paul.
    Imaginary Worlds: Or, the Evolution of Utopia. Gordon Pr.
Bloomfield, Peter, 1946-
  xBloomfield, Peter.
    Fourier Analysis of Time Series: An Introduction. Wiley.
Bloomfield, Robert, 1766-1823
  xBloomfield, Robert.
    Collected Poems, 1800-1822. Schol Facsimiles.
Bloomfield, Valerie.
  xBloomfield, Valerie.
    Commonwealth Elections, 1945-1970: A Bibliography. Greenwood.
Bloomgarden, Barry. *see* Bloomgarden, Barry H.
Bloomgarden, Barry H.
  xBloomgarden, Barry.
    Your Future in Insurance Careers. Rosen Pr.
Bloomingdale, Teresa, 1930-
  xBloomingdale, Teresa.
    I Should Have Seen It Coming When the Rabbit Died. Doubleday.
  xBloomingdale, Tergsa.
    I Should Have Seen It Coming When the Rabbit Died. Bantam.
Bloomingdale, Tergsa. *see* Bloomingdale, Teresa.
Bloomstein, Morris J.
  xBloomstein, Morris J.
    Consumer's Guide to Fighting Back. Dodd.
Bloor, Colin M.
  xBloor, Colin M.

Cardiac Pathology. Lippincott.
The Pulmonary & Bronchial Circulations in Congenital Heart Disease. Plenum Pub.
Bloor, R. H. *see* Bloor, Robert Henry Underwood.
Bloor, Robert Henry Underwood.
  xBloor, R. H.
    English Novel from Chaucer to Galsworthy. Folcroft.
Bloss, F. D. *see* Bloss, Fred Donald.
Bloss, Fred Donald, 1920-
  xBloss, F. D.
    Crystallography & Crystal Chemistry. HR&W.
Bloss, Margaret V. *see* Bloss, Margaret Varner.
Bloss, Margaret Varner.
  xBloss, Margaret V.
    Badminton. Wm C Brown.
Blossom, Aline.
  xBlossom, Aline.
    My Beloved. M Jones.
Blotner, Joseph L. *see* Blotner, Joseph Leo.
Blotner, Joseph Leo, 1923-
  xBlotner, Joseph L.
    The Political Novel. Greenwood.
Blouet, Brian W.
  xBlouet, Brian W.
    ed. Images of the Plains: The Role of Human Nature in Settlement. U of Nebr Pr.
Blough, Dorris.
  xBlough, Dorris.
    The Brass Ring. Brethren.
Blough, Glenn O. *see* Blough, Glenn Orlando.
Blough, Glenn Orlando.
  xBlough, Glenn O.
    Discovering Cycles. McGraw.
    Elementary School Science & How to Teach It. HR&W.
Blouin, Lenora P.
  xBlouin, Lenora P.
    May Sarton: A Bibliography. Scarecrow.
Blount, Ben G.
  xBlount, Ben G.
    ed. Sociocultural Dimensions of Language Change. Acad Pr.
Blount, Edward. *see* Blount, Edward Charles.
Blount, Edward Charles, Sir, 1809-
  xBlount, Edward.
    Memoirs of Sir Edward Blount.. Arno.
Blount, James H. *see* Blount, James Henderson.
Blount, James Henderson, 1869-1918
  xBlount, James H.
    American Occupation of the Philippines 1898-1912. Oriole Edns.
Blount, Paul G. *see* Blount, Paul Groves.
Blount, Paul Groves.
  xBlount, Paul G.
    George Sand & the Victorian World. U of Ga Pr.
Blount, Raymond.
  xBlount, Raymond N.
    Housekeeping Procedures for the Small Hospital. C C Thomas.
Blount, Raymond N. *see* Blount, Raymond.
Blount, Roy.
  xBlount, Roy.
    About Three Bricks Shy of a Load: A Highly Irregular Lowdown on the Year the Pittsburgh Steelers Were Super but Missed the Bowl. Little.
Blount, W. P. *see* Blount, Walter Putnam.
Blount, Walter Putnam.
  xBlount, W. P.
    Fractures in Children. Krieger.
    Milwaukee Brace. Williams & Wilkins.
Blue, Frederick J.
  xBlue, Frederick J.
    The Free Soilers: Third Party Politics, 1848-54. U of Ill Pr.
Blue, Rose.
  xBlue, Rose.

Cold Rain on the Water. McGraw.
Grandma Didn't Wave Back. Dell.
Grandma Didn't Wave Back. Watts.
Nikki 108. Watts.
The Preacher's Kid. Watts.
Quiet Place. Watts.
Wishful Lying. Human Sci Pr.

Bluebond-Langner, Myra, 1948-
xBluebond-Langner, Myra.
The Private Worlds of Dying Children.
Princeton U Pr.

Bluem, A. William.
xBluem, A. William.
ed. Religious Television Programs: A Study in
Relevance. Hastings.

Bluestone, Barry.
xBluestone, Barry.
Low Wages & the Working Poor. U of Mich
Inst Labor.

Bluestone, Max.
xBluestone, Max.
From Story to Stage: The Dramatic Adaptation
of Prose Fiction in the Period of Shakespeare
& His Contemporaries. Mouton.

Bluestone, Morton D.
xBluestone, Morton D.
Accounting: A Self-Instruction Guide to
Procedures & Theory. Macmillan.
How to Program Computers in COBOL.
Macmillan.

Bluestone, Rodney.
xBluestone, Rodney.
ed. Rheumatology. HM Prof Med Div.

Bluh, Bonnie. *see* Bluh, Bonnie Charles.

Bluh, Bonnie Charles.
xBluh, Bonnie.
The Old Speak Out. Horizon.

Bluhm, William T. *see* Bluhm, William Theodore.

Bluhm, William Theodore, 1923-
xBluhm, William T.
Building an Austrian Nation: The Political
Integration of a Western State. Yale U Pr.
Theories of the Political System: Classics of
Political Thought & Modern Political
Analysis. P-H.

Blum, Albert. *see* Blum, Albert A.

Blum, Albert A.
xBlum, Albert.
White Collar Workers. Phila Bk Co.
xBlum, Albert A.
A History of the American Labor Movement.
Am Hist Assn.

Blum, Andre, 1881-
xBlum, Andre.
The Origin & Early History of Engraving in
France. Hacker.

Blum, David, 1935-
xBlum, David.
Casals & the Art of Interpretation. Holmes &
Meier.
Casals & the Art of Interpretation. U of Cal Pr.

Blum, E. K. *see* Blum, Edward K.

Blum, Edward K.
xBlum, E. K.
ed. Mathematical Studies of Information
Processing: Proceedings, International
Conference, Kyoto, Japan, August 23-26,
1978. Springer-Verlag.

Blum, Eleanor.
xBlum, Eleanor.
Basic Books in the Mass Media: An
Annotated, Selected Booklist Covering
General Communications, Book Publishing,
Broadcasting, Film, Editorial Journalism, &
Advertising. U of Ill Pr.

Blum, Eva M. *see* Blum, Eva Maria.

Blum, Eva Maria.
xBlum, Eva M.

Alcoholism: Modern Psychological Approaches
to Treatment. Jossey-Bass.

Blum, Gerald S., 1922-
xBlum, Gerald S.
Psychoanalytic Theories of Personality.
McGraw.
Psychodynamics: The Science of Unconscious
Mental Forces. Brooks-Cole.

Blum, Henrik L.
xBlum, Henrik L.
Planning for Health: Development &
Application of Social Change Theory. Human
Sci Pr.

Blum, Jeffrey. *see* Blum, Jeffrey M.

Blum, Jeffrey M., 1949-
xBlum, Jeffrey.
Pseudoscience & Mental Ability: The Origins
& Fallacies of the IQ Controversy. Monthly
Rev.

Blum, Jerome, 1913-
xBlum, Jerome.
The End of the Old Order in Rural Europe.
Princeton U Pr.

Blum, John M. *see* Blum, John Morton.

Blum, John Morton, 1921-
xBlum, John M.
The National Experience: A History of the
United States. HarBraceJ.
V Was for Victory: Politics & American
Culture During World War II. HarBraceJ.

Blum, Joseph J., 1934-
xBlum, Joseph J.
Introduction to Analog Computation.
HarBraceJ.

Blum, Leon.
xBlum, Leon.
For All Mankind. Peter Smith.
Marriage. AMS Pr.

Blum, Milton L., 1912-
xBlum, Milton L.
Psychology & Consumer Affairs. Har-Row.

Blum, Murray S. *see* Blum, Murray Sheldon.

Blum, Murray Sheldon.
xBlum, Murray S.
ed. Sexual Selection & Reproductive
Competition in Insects. Acad Pr.

Blum, Richard H.
xBlum, Richard H.
Deceivers & Deceived: Observations on
Confidence Men & Their Victims, Informants
& Their Quarry, Political & Industrial Spies
& Ordinary Citizens. C C Thomas.
Drug Education: Results & Recommendations.
Lexington Bks.
Horatio Alger's Children: The Role of the
Family in the Origin & Prevention of Drug
Risk. Jossey-Bass.
Utopiates: The Use & Users of LSD-25.
Beresford Bk Serv.

Blum, Stella.
xBlum, Stella.
Ackermann's Costume Plates: Women's
Fashions in England, 1818-1828. Dover.

Blum, Virgil C.
xBlum, Virgil C.
Freedom of Choice in Education. Greenwood.

Blum, Walter J.
xBlum, Walter J.
The Uneasy Case for Progressive Taxation. U
of Chicago Pr.

Bluman, G. W.
xBluman, G. W.
Similarity Methods for Differential Equations.
Springer-Verlag.

Blumberg, Abraham S.
xBlumberg, Abraham S.
Criminal Justice. New Viewpoints.

Blumberg, Albert. *see* Blumberg, Albert Emanuel.

Blumberg, Albert Emanuel.
xBlumberg, Albert.

Logic: A First Course. Knopf.

Blumberg, Arnold, 1925-
xBlumberg, Arnold.
The Diplomacy of the Mexican Empire,
1863-1867. Am Philos.

Blumberg, Arthur, 1923-
xBlumberg, Arthur.
Supervisors & Teachers: A Private Cold War.
McCutchan.

Blumberg, Dorothy R. *see* Blumberg, Dorothy Rose.

Blumberg, Dorothy Rose.
xBlumberg, Dorothy R.
Florence Kelley: The Making of a Social
Pioneer. Kelley.

Blumberg, Harris M.
xBlumberg, Harris M.
A Program of Sequential Language
Development: A Theoretical & Practical
Guide for Remediation of Language, Reading
& Learning Disorders. C C Thomas.

Blumberg, Melvin.
xBlumberg, Melvin.
Job Switching in Autonomous Groups: A
Descriptive & Exploratory Study in an
Underground Coal Mine. R & E Res Assoc.

Blumberg, Paul.
xBlumberg, Paul.
The Impact of Social Class: A Book of
Readings. Har-Row.
Industrial Democracy: The Sociology of
Participation. Schocken.

Blumberg, Phillip I., 1919-
xBlumberg, Phillip I.
The Megacorporation in American Society:
The Scope of Corporate Power. P-H.

Blumberg, Rhoda.
xBlumberg, Rhoda.
Backyard Bestiary. Coward.
Famine. Watts.
Fire Fighters. Watts.
First Ladies. Watts.
Sharks. Avon.
Sharks. Watts.
The Truth About Dragons. Schol Bk Serv.
UFO. Watts.
Witches. Watts.

Blumberg, Robert S.
xBlumberg, Robert S.
The Fine Wines of California. Doubleday.

Blume, Eli.
xBlume, Eli.
Workbook in French Three Years. AMSCO
Sch.

Blume, Helmut, 1920-
xBlume, Helmut.
The Caribbean Islands. Longman.

Blume, Judy.
xBlume, Judy.
Are You There God? Its Me Margaret. Dell.
Forever. Bradbury Pr.
Forever. PB.
Freckle Juice. Dell.
Freckle Juice. Schol Bk Serv.
Iggies House. Dell.
Otherwise Known As Sheila the Great. Dell.
Starring Sally J. Freedman As Herself. Dell.
Starring Sally J. Freedman As Herself.
Bradbury Pr.

Blume, Stuart S., 1942-
xBlume, Stuart S.
Toward a Political Sociology of Science. Free
Pr.

Blumenberg, Richard M.
xBlumenberg, Richard M.
Critical Focus: An Introduction to Film.
Wadsworth Pub.

Blumenfeld, Hans.
xBlumenfeld, Hans.

Modern Metropolis: Its Origins, Growth,
Characteristics, & Planning, Selected Essays.
MIT Pr.

Blumenfeld, Milton J.
xBlumenfeld, Milton J.
photos by Careers in Photography. Lerner
Pubns.

Blumenfeld, Samuel L.
xBlumenfeld, Samuel L.
How to Tutor. Mott Media.
The Retreat from Motherhood. Arlington Hse.

Blumenfeld, Warren S.
xBlumenfeld, Warren S.
Development & Evaluation of Job Performance
Criteria: A Procedural Guide. Ga St U Busn
Pub.

Blumenfrucht, Israel.
xBlumenfrucht, Israel.
Tax Questions & Answers: A Tax Review
Handbook for CPA Candidates, Tax
Practitioners, Students & Taxpayers. P-H.

Blumenson, John J. *see* Blumenson, John J. G.

Blumenson, John J. G., 1942-
xBlumenson, John J.
Identifying American Architecture: A Pictorial
Guide to Styles & Terms, 1600-1945.
AASLH.

Blumenson, Martin.
xBlumenson, Martin.
Liberation. Silver.
Liberation. Time-Life.

Blumenthal, Arthur. *see* Blumenthal, Arthur L.

Blumenthal, Arthur L.
xBlumenthal, Arthur.
Process of Cognition. P-H.

Blumenthal, Friedrich.
xBlumenthal, Friedrich.
Lord Byron's Mystery "Cain" & Its Relation to
Milton's "Paradise Lost" & Gesner's "Death
of Abel". Folcroft.

Blumenthal, Gerda.
xBlumenthal, Gerda.
Andre Malraux: The Conquest of Dread.
Greenwood.

Blumenthal, H. T. *see* Blumenthal, Herman T.

Blumenthal, Herman T.
xBlumenthal, H. T.
ed. The Regulatory Role of the Nervous
System in Aging. S Karger.

Blumenthal, Joseph, 1897-
xBlumenthal, Joseph.
The Printed Book in America. Godine.

Blumenthal, Joseph C.
xBlumenthal, Joseph C.
English 2200: A Programed Course in
Grammar & Usage. HarBraceJ.
English 2600: A Programed Course in
Grammar & Usage. HarBraceJ.
English 3200: A Programed Course in
Grammar & Usage. HarBraceJ.

Blumenthal, L. Roy.
xBlumenthal, L. Roy.
The Practice of Public Relations. Macmillan.

Blumenthal, Lassor A.
xBlumenthal, Lassor A.
Great Sales by Today's Great Salesmen.
Macmillan.
The Hand Book: All Kinds of Jokes, Tricks &
Games to Do with Your Hands. Doubleday.

Blumenthal, Leonard M. *see* Blumenthal, Leonard
Mascot.

Blumenthal, Leonard Mascot.
xBlumenthal, Leonard M.
Studies in Geometry. W H Freeman.
Theory & Applications of Distance Geometry.
Chelsea Pub.

Blumenthal, Monica D.
xBlumenthal, Monica D.

More About Justifying Violence:
Methodological Studies of Attitudes &
Behavior. U of Mich Soc Res.

Blumenthal, Robert M. *see* Blumenthal, Robert
McCallum.

Blumenthal, Robert McCallum.
xBlumenthal, Robert M.
Markov Processes & Potential Theory. Acad
Pr.

Blumenthal, W. B. *see* Blumenthal, Warren B.

Blumenthal, Walter H. *see* Blumenthal, Walter Hart.

Blumenthal, Walter Hart, 1883-1969
xBlumenthal, Walter H.
Brides from Bridewell: Female Felons Sent to
Colonial America. Greenwood.

Blumenthal, Warren B.
xBlumenthal, W. B.
The Chemical Behavior of Zirconium. Krieger.

Blumer, Herbert, 1900-
xBlumer, Herbert.
Symbolic Interactionism: Perspective &
Method. P-H.

Blumhagen, Kathleen O. *see* Blumhagen, Kathleen
O'Connor.

Blumhagen, Kathleen O'Connor.
xBlumhagen, Kathleen O.
ed. Women's Studies: An Interdisciplinary
Collection. Greenwood.

Blumhardt, Christoph, 1842-1919
xBlumhardt, Christoph.
Evening Prayers for Every Day in the Year.
Plough.

Blumler, J. C. *see* Blumler, Jay G.

Blumler, Jay G.
xBlumler, J. C.
The Uses of Mass Communications: Current
Perspectives on Gratifications Research. Sage.

Blumner, Hugo, 1844-1919
xBlumner, Hugo.
Home Life of the Ancient Greeks. Cooper Sq.

Blumstein, James F.
xBlumstein, James F.
ed. Growing Metropolis: Aspects of
Development in Nashville. Vanderbilt U Pr.

Blunck, Jurgen.
xBlunck, Jurgen.
Mars & Its Satellites: A Detailed Commentary
on the Nomenclature. Exposition.

Blundell, Mary. *see* Blundell, Mary E. (Sweetman).

Blundell, Mary E. (Sweetman), d. 1930
xBlundell, Mary.
Pastorals of Dorset. Arno.

Blunden, Edmund. *see* Blunden, Edmund Charles.

Blunden, Edmund C. *see* Blunden, Edmund Charles.

Blunden, Edmund Charles, 1896-
xBlunden, Edmund.
Edward Gibbon & His Age. Arden Lib.
Nature in English Literature. Folcroft.
Nature in English Literature. Kennikat.
Sons of Light: A Series of Lectures on English
Writers. Folcroft.
Thomas Hardy. St Martin.
xBlunden, Edmund C.
Edward Gibbon & His Age. Folcroft.
On the Poems of Henry Vaughan:
Characteristics & Intimations. Russell.

Blunden, John. *see* Blunden, John Russell.

Blunden, John Russell.
xBlunden, John.
Fundamentals of Human Geography: A
Reader. Har-Row.
ed. Fundamentals of Human Geography: A
Reader. Har-Row.

Blunden, Maria.
xBlunden, Maria.
Impressionists & Impressionism. Rizzoli Intl.

Blunt. *see* Blunt, Anthony.

Blunt, Anthony, Sir, 1907-
xBlunt.

The Drawings of Poussin. Yale U Pr.
xBlunt, Anthony.
Art & Architecture in France: 1500-1700.
Penguin.
The Art of William Blake. Har-Row.
Artistic Theory in Italy, 1450-1600. Oxford U
Pr.
Borromini. Harvard U Pr.
xBlunt, Anthony F.
Art of William Blake. Columbia U Pr.

Blunt, Anthony F. *see* Blunt, Anthony.

Blunt, Hugh F. *see* Blunt, Hugh Francis.

Blunt, Hugh Francis, 1877-
xBlunt, Hugh F.
Great Penitents. Arno.

Blunt, Jerry.
xBlunt, Jerry.
Composite Art of Acting. Macmillan.
More Stage Dialects. Har-Row.

Blunt, John H. *see* Blunt, John Henry.

Blunt, John Henry, 1823-1884
xBlunt, John H.
Dictionary of Sects, Heresies, Ecclesiastical
Parties & Schools of Religious Thought. Gale.

Blunt, Michael J.
xBlunt, Michael J.
Multiple Choice Questions in Anatomy &
Neurobiology for Undergraduates.
Butterworths.

Bluntschli, J. K. *see* Bluntschli, Johann Kaspar.

Bluntschli, Johann K. *see* Bluntschli, Johann Kaspar.

Bluntschli, Johann Kaspar, 1808-1881
xBluntschli, J. K.
The Theory of the State. Arden Lib.
xBluntschli, Johann K.
Theory of the State. Arno.

Bluske, Margaret K. *see* Bluske, Margaret Keidel.

Bluske, Margaret Keidel.
xBluske, Margaret K.
Das Erste Jahr. Har-Row.

Blustin, Lewis.
xBlustin, Lewis.
How to Subcontract Your House:
Building-Remodeling. TAB Bks.

Bly, Robert.
xBly, Robert.
Leaping Poetry: An Idea with Poems &
Translations. Beacon Pr.
ed. News of the Universe: Poems of Twofold
Consciousness. Sierra.
This Tree Will Be Here for a Thousand Years.
Har-Row.
This Tree Will Be Here for a Thousand Years.
Har-Row.

Blyth, Conrad. *see* Blyth, Conrad Alexander.

Blyth, Conrad Alexander.
xBlyth, Conrad.
Inflation in New Zealand. Allen Unwin.

Blyth, John W. *see* Blyth, John William.

Blyth, John William, 1909-
xBlyth, John W.
Whitehead's Theory of Knowledge. Kraus
Repr.

Blyth, Myrna.
xBlyth, Myrna.
For Better & for Worse. Fawcett.

Blyth, R. H. *see* Blyth, Reginald Horace.

Blyth, Reginald Horace.
xBlyth, R. H.
History of Haiku. Heian Intl.

Blythe, Leonora.
xBlythe, Leonora.
Felicia. Fawcett.

Blythe, Peter.
xBlythe, Peter.
Hypnotism: Its Power & Practice. Taplinger.

Blythe, Ronald, 1922-
xBlythe, Ronald.

Akenfield: Portrait of an English Village.
  Pantheon.
Blyton, Enid.
  xBlyton, Enid.
    Five Fall into Adventure. Atheneum.
    Five on the Track of a Spook Train.
      Atheneum.
Blyton, Gifford.
  xBlyton, Gifford.
    Speaking Out: Two Centuries of Kentucky
      Orators. Hunter NC.
B'Nai B'Rith Vocational Service.
  xB'nai B'rith Vocational Service 1967 Professional
    Staff Conference.
    Proceedings. B'nai B'rith Car.
BNA Editorial Staff. *see* Bureau of National Affairs,
  Washington, D.C.
BNA Editorial Staff of Construction Labor Report. *see*
  Bureau of National Affairs, Washington, D.C.
BNA Editorial Staff of Labor Relations Reporter. *see*
  Bureau of National Affairs, Washington, D.C.
Bna Editorial Staff of the Criminal Law Reporter. *see*
  Bureau of National Affairs, Washington, D.C.
Bo, Walter J.
  xBo, Walter J.
    Basic Atlas of Cross-Sectional Anatomy.
      Saunders.
Boa, Elizabeth.
  xBoa, Elizabeth.
    Critical Strategies: German Fiction in the
      Twentieth Century. McGill-Queens U Pr.
Boa, Kenneth.
  xBoa, Kenneth.
    Cults, World Religions, & You. Victor Bks.
    God I Don't Understand. Victor Bks.
Boadella, David.
  xBoadella, David.
    ed. In the Wake of Reich. Ashley Bks.
Boaden, James, 1762-1839
  xBoaden, James.
    An Inquiry into the Authenticity of Various
      Pictures & Prints Which, from the Decease of
      the Poet to Our Own Times Have Been
      Offered to the Public As Portraits of
      Shakespeare. AMS Pr.
    Memoirs of the Life of John Philip Kemble.
      Arno.
Boak, Denis.
  xBoak, Denis.
    Andre Malraux. Oxford U Pr.
Boakes, R. A.
  xBoakes, R. A.
    Inhibition & Learning. Acad Pr.
Boal, Augusto.
  xBoal, Augusto.
    The Theater of the Oppressed. Urizen Bks.
Boalt, Gunnar.
  xBoalt, Gunnar.
    European Orders of Chivalry. S Ill U Pr.
    Sociology of Research. S Ill U Pr.
Boar, B. H., 1947-
  xBoar, B. H.
    Abend Debugging for Cobol Programmers.
      Wiley.
Board of Aldermen. *see* New York (City). Board of
  Aldermen.
Board Of Education Of The City Of New York. *see* New
  York (City). Board of Education.
Board of Governers, Federal Reserve System. *see* United
  States. Board of Governors of the Federal Reserve
  System.
Board of Music Trade of the United States of America.
  xBoard of Music Trade of the USA.
    Complete Catalogue of Sheet Music & Musical
      Works. Da Capo.
Board of Music Trade of the USA. *see* Board of Music
  Trade of the United States of America.
Board of Publication of the Reorganized Church of Jesus
  Christ of Latter Day Saints. *see* The Reader'S Digest.

Board of Regents of IIA. *see* Institute of Internal
  Auditors.
Board on Agriculture & Renewable Resources. *see*
  National Research Council. Board on Agriculture and
  Renewable Resources.
Board on Agriculture and Renewable Resources, National
  Research Council. *see* National Research Council.
  Board on Agriculture and Renewable Resources.
Board on Energy Studies. *see* National Research Council.
  Committee on Energy and the Environment.
  Implications of Environmental Regulations for Energy
  Production and Consumption.
Board on Mineral & Energy Resources. *see* National
  Research Council. Board on Mineral and Energy
  Sources.
Board on Toxicology & Environmental Health Hazards.
  see National Research Council. Board on Toxicology
  and Environmental Health Hazards.
Board, R. G.
  xBoard, R. G.
    ed. Some Methods for Microbiological Assay.
      Acad Pr.
Boardman, A. D.
  xBoardman, Allan D.
    Symmetry & Its Applications in Science.
      Halsted Pr.
Boardman, Allan D. *see* Boardman, A. D.
Boardman, Charles W. *see* Boardman, Charles Willis.
Boardman, Charles Willis, 1885-1959
  xBoardman, Charles W.
    Professional Tests As Measures of Teaching
      Efficiency in High School. AMS Pr.
Boardman, Eugene P. *see* Boardman, Eugene Powers.
Boardman, Eugene Powers.
  xBoardman, Eugene P.
    Christian Influence Upon the Ideology of the
      Taiping Rebellion, 1851-1864. Octagon.
Boardman, Fon. *see* Boardman, Fon Wyman.
Boardman, Fon Wyman.
  xBoardman, Fon.
    Tyrants & Conquerors. Walck.
Boardman, Gwen R. *see* Boardman, Gwenn R.
Boardman, Gwenn R.
  xBoardman, Gwen R.
    Graham Greene: The Aesthetics of
      Exploration. U Presses Fla.
  xBoardman, Gwenn R.
    Living in Singapore. Elsevier-Nelson.
Boardman, J. M. *see* Boardman, John M.
Boardman, James.
  xBoardman, James.
    America, & the Americans. Arno.
Boardman, John, 1927-
  xBoardman, John.
    Archaic Greek Gems: Schools & Artists in the
      Sixth & Early Fifth Centuries. Northwestern
      U Pr.
    Athenian Black Figure Vases. Oxford U Pr.
    Athenian Red Figure Vases: The Archaic
      Period, a Handbook. Oxford U Pr.
    Engraved Gems: The Ionides Collection.
      Northwestern U Pr.
    Greek Art. Oxford U Pr.
Boardman, John M.
  xBoardman, J. M.
    Homotopy Invariant Algebraic Structures on
      Topological Spaces. Springer-Verlag.
Boardman, Philip.
  xBoardman, Philip.
    The Worlds of Patrick Geddes: Biologist, Town
      Planner, Re-Educator, Peace-Warrior.
      Routledge & Kegan.
Boas, Franz, 1858-1942
  xBoas, Franz.

Central Eskimo. U of Nebr Pr.
Contributions to the Ethnology of the
  Kwakiutl. AMS Pr.
The Decorative Art of the Indians of the North
  Pacific Coast. AMS Pr.
Facial Paintings of the Indians of Northern
  British Columbia. AMS Pr.
Geographical Names of the Kwakiutl Indians.
  AMS Pr.
Materials for the Study of Inheritance in Man.
  AMS Pr.
Primitive Art. Dover.
Primitive Art. Peter Smith.
Race & Democratic Society. Biblo.
Race & Democratic Society. J J Augustin.
Race, Language & Culture. Free Pr.
Religion of the Kwakiutl Indians. AMS Pr.
Boas, Franziska.
  xBoas, Franziska.
    The Function of Dance in Human Society.
      Dance Horiz.
Boas, Frederich S. *see* Boas, Frederick Samuel.
Boas, Frederick. *see* Boas, Frederick Samuel.
Boas, Frederick S. *see* Boas, Frederick Samuel.
Boas, Frederick Samuel, 1862-1957
  xBoas, Frederich S.
    Thomas Heywood. Phaeton.
  xBoas, Frederick.
    ed. Songs & Lyrics from the English Masques
      & Light Operas. Scholarly.
  xBoas, Frederick S.
    American Scenes, Tudor to Georgian, in the
      English Literary Mirror. Folcroft.
    ed. Five Pre-Shakespearean Comedies. Oxford
      U Pr.
    An Introduction to Eighteenth Century Drama,
      1700-1780. Greenwood.
    Queen Elizabeth in Drama & Related Studies.
      Arno.
    Queen Elizabeth in Drama & Related Studies.
      Scholarly.
    ed. Songs & Lyrics from the English Masques
      & Light Operas. Greenwood.
    Thomas Heywood. Folcroft.
    Thomas Heywood. Somerset Pub.
Boas, George, 1891-
  xBoas, George.
    Challenge of Science. U of Wash Pr.
    Critical Analysis of the Philosophy of Emile
      Meyerson. Arno.
    Critical Analysis of the Philosophy of Emile
      Meyerson. Greenwood.
    History of Ideas: An Introduction. Scribner.
    Limits of Reason. Greenwood.
    Primer for Critics. Greenwood.
    Primer for Critics. Phaeton.
    Rationalism in Greek Philosophy. Johns
      Hopkins.
Boas, Guy, 1896-
  xBoas, Guy.
    Modern English Prose. Century Bookbindery.
Boas, Louise S. *see* Boas, Louise Schutz.
Boas, Louise Schutz.
  xBoas, Louise S.
    Harriet Shelley: Five Long Years. Greenwood.
Boas, Maurits I. *see* Boas, Maurits Ignatius.
Boas, Maurits Ignatius, 1892-
  xBoas, Maurits I.
    Preludes. Fell.
Boas, R. P. *see* Boas, Ralph Philip.
Boas, Ralph P. *see* Boas, Ralph Philip.
Boas, Ralph Philip.
  xBoas, R. P.
    Integrability Theorems for Trigonometric
      Transforms. Springer-Verlag.
  xBoas, Ralph P.
    Entire Functions. Acad Pr.
    A Primer of Real Functions. Math Assn.
Boas, Ralph Philip Jr.
  xBoas, R. P.

Polynomial Expansions of Analytic Functions. Springer-Verlag.
Boase, Alan M. *see* Boase, Alan Martin.
Boase, Alan Martin.
xBoase, Alan M.
Fortunes of Montaigne: A History of the Essays in France, 1580-1669. Octagon.
Boase, Paul H.
xBoase, Paul H.
The Rhetoric of Christian Socialism. Peter Smith.
Boase, Roger.
xBoase, Roger.
The Origin & Meaning of Courtly Love: A Critical Study of European Scholarship. Rowman.
Boase, T. S. *see* Boase, Thomas Sherrer Ross.
Boase, Thomas Sherrer Ross, 1898-1974
xBoase, T. S.
ed. Cilician Kingdom of Armenia. St Martin.
Boase, Wendy.
xBoase, Wendy.
Early China. Watts.
The Folklore of Hampshire & the Isle of Wight. Rowman.
The Sky's the Limit: Women Pioneers in Aviation. Macmillan.
Boasson, C. *see* Boasson, Charles.
Boasson, Charles.
xBoasson, C.
Approaches to the Study of International Relations. Humanities.
Boateng, E. A.
xBoateng, E. A.
Geography of Ghana. Cambridge U Pr.
Boatman, Russel. *see* Boatman, Russell.
Boatman, Russell.
xBoatman, Russel.
What the Bible Says About the End Time. College Pr Pub.
Boatright, M. C. *see* Boatright, Mody Coggin.
Boatright, Mody C. *see* Boatright, Mody Coggin.
Boatright, Mody Coggin.
xBoatright, M. C.
Folk Laughter on the American Frontier. Peter Smith.
xBoatright, Mody C.
ed. Backwoods to Border. SMU Press.
ed. From Hell to Breakfast. SMU Press.
Boaz, Martha. *see* Boaz, Martha Terosse.
Boaz, Martha Terosse, 1913-
xBoaz, Martha.
ed. Current Concepts in Library Management. Libs Unl.
Bobath, Berta.
xBobath, Berta.
Abnormal Postural Reflex Activity Caused by Brain Lesions. Heinman.
Abnormal Postural Reflex Activity Caused by Brain Lesions. Intl Ideas.
Bobbitt. *see* Bobbitt, Arch N.
Bobbitt, Arch N., 1895-
xBobbitt.
Indiana Appellate Practice & Procedure. Michie.
Bobbitt, H. R. *see* Bobbitt, H. Randolph.
Bobbitt, H. Randolph, 1938-
xBobbitt, H. R.
Organizational Behavior: Understanding & Prediction. P-H.
Bobbitt, James M.
xBobbitt, James M.
Introduction to Chromatography. Van Nos Reinhold.
Bober, G. F. *see* Bober, Gerald F.
Bober, Gerald F., 1940-
xBober, G. F.
Protection & the Law. McGraw.
Bober, William.
xBober, William.

Fluid Mechanics. Wiley.
Bober, Wolffgang Von. *see* Von Bober, Wolffgang.
Bobgan, Martin.
xBobgan, Martin.
The Psychological Way-the Spiritual Way. Bethany Fell.
Bobik, Joseph, 1927-
xBobik, Joseph.
ed. Nature of Philosophical Inquiry. U of Notre Dame Pr.
Bobillier, P. A.
xBobillier, P. A.
Simulation with Gpss & Gpssv. P-H.
Bobinski, George S. *see* Bobinski, George Sylvan.
Bobinski, George Sylvan.
xBobinski, George S.
Carnegie Libraries: Their History & Impact on American Public Library Developments. ALA.
Bobker, Lee. *see* Bobker, Lee R.
Bobker, Lee R.
xBobker, Lee.
Elements of Film. HarBraceJ.
xBobker, Lee R.
Elements of Film. HarBraceJ.
The Unicorn Group. Morrow.
Bobrow, David B. *see* Bobrow, Davis B.
Bobrow, Davis B.
xBobrow, David B.
Understanding Foreign Policy Decisions: The Chinese Case. Free Pr.
Boccaccio, Giovanni, 1313-1375
xBoccaccio, Giovanni.
Decameron. AMS Pr.
Decameron. Dutton.
The Decameron. Norton.
The Decameron. Penguin.
Earliest Lives of Dante. R West.
Earliest Lives of Dante. Russell.
Genealogie. Garland Pub.
Bocchino, Anthony J.
xBocchino, Anthony J.
North Carolina Trial Evidence Manual. Michie.
Bocci, Jeri.
xBocci, Jeri.
Detective Thumb & Sergeant Print & the Mysterious Black Tunnel. Omni Pubs.
Bochenski, Innocentius M., 1902-
xBochenski, Innocenty M.
History of Formal Logic. Chelsea Pub.
Bochenski, Innocenty M. *see* Bochenski, Innocentius M.
Bochkov, A. E. *see* Bochkov, Aleksei Feodosevich.
Bochkov, Aleksei Feodosevich.
xBochkov, A. E.
Chemistry of the O-Glycosidic Bond: Formation & Cleavage. Pergamon.
Bochmann, G. V. *see* Bochmann, Gregor V.
Bochmann, Gregor V., 1941-
xBochmann, G. V.
Architecture of Distributed Computer Systems. Springer-Verlag.
Bochner, Felix.
xBochner, Felix.
Handbook of Clinical Pharmacology. Little.
Bochroch, Albert R.
xBochroch, Albert R.
American Automobile Racing: An Illustrated History. Viking Pr.
Bociurkiw, B. R. *see* Bociurkiw, Bohdan R.
Bociurkiw, Bohdan R.
xBociurkiw, B. R.
ed. Religion & Atheism in the U.S.S.R. & Eastern Europe. U of Toronto Pr.
Bock, Betty, 1915-
xBock, Betty.
Line of Business Reporting: Problems in the Formulation of a Data Program. Conference Bd.
Bock, Darrell. *see* Bock, Richard Darrell.

Bock, P. G.
xBock, P. G.
Internal Migration Policy & New Towns: The Mexican Experience. U of Ill Pr.
Bock, Paul, 1922-
xBock, Paul.
In Search of a Responsible World Society: The Social Teachings of the World Council of Churches. Westminster.
Bock, Philip K.
xBock, Philip K.
Continuities in Psychological Anthropology: A Historical Introduction. W H Freeman.
Bock, Richard.
xBock, Richard.
Camper Cookery. Lorenz Pr.
The Galley Guide to Fine Food. Lorenz Pr.
Bock, Richard Darrell, 1927-
xBock, Darrell.
Multivariate Statistical Methods in Behavioral Research. McGraw.
Bockar, Joyce A.
xBockar, Joyce A.
The Last Best Diet Book. Stein & Day.
Bockl, George.
xBockl, George.
How Real Estate Fortunes Are Made. P-H.
Bockle, Franz.
xBockle, Franz.
ed. The Death Penalty & Torture. Seabury.
ed. Understanding the Signs of the Times. Paulist Pr.
Bockris, J. *see* Bockris, John O'M.
Bockris, J. O'M. *see* Bockris, John O'M.
Bockris, John O'M.
xBockris, J.
An Introduction to Electrochemical Science. Crane Russak Co.
An Introduction to Electrochemical Science. Springer Verlag.
xBockris, J. O'M.
ed. Environmental Chemistry. Plenum Pub.
Fundamental Aspects of Electrocrystallization. Plenum Pub.
A Workbook of Electrochemistry. Plenum Pub.
xBockris, John O'M.
Modern Electrochemistry: An Introduction to an Interdisciplinary Area. Plenum Pub.
Bockus, H. William.
xBockus, H. William.
Advertising Graphics. Macmillan.
Bockus, Henry L. *see* Bockus, Henry Leroy.
Bockus, Henry Leroy, 1894-
xBockus, Henry L.
ed. Gastroenterology. Saunders.
Bocock, Robert.
xBocock, Robert.
Freud & Modern Society: An Outline & Analysis of Freud's Sociology. Holmes & Meier.
Bocuse, Paul, 1926-
xBocuse, Paul.
Paul Bocuse's French Cooking. Pantheon.
Bodard, Lucien.
xBodard, Lucien.
The French Consul. Knopf.
Bodde, Derk, 1909-
xBodde, Derk.
China's Cultural Tradition: What & Whither. HR&W.
Peking Diary: A Year of Revolution. Octagon.
Boddewyn, J. J. *see* Boddewyn, Jean J.
Boddewyn, Jean J.
xBoddewyn, J. J.
Comparison Advertising: A Worldwide Study. Hastings.
Boddie, John B. *see* Boddie, John Bennett.
Boddie, John Bennett, 1880-
xBoddie, John B.

Colonial Surry. Genealog Pub.
Historical Southern Families. Genealog Pub.
Southside Virginia Families. Genealog Pub.
Boddy, Frederick A.
xBoddy, Frederick A.
Ground Cover & Other Ways to Weed-Free
Gardens. David & Charles.
Boddy, John.
xBoddy, John.
Brain Systems & Psychological Concepts.
Wiley.
Bode, Boyd H. *see* Bode, Boyd Henry.
Bode, Boyd Henry, 1873-1953
xBode, Boyd H.
How We Learn. Greenwood.
Progressive Education at the Crossroads. Arno.
Bode, Carl, 1911-
xBode, Carl.
American Lyceum: Town Meeting of the Mind.
S Ill U Pr.
Half-World of American Culture: A
Miscellany. S Ill U Pr.
Mencken. S Ill U Pr.
Bode, Elroy, 1931-
xBode, Elroy.
Alone in the World Looking. Tex Western.
Home & Other Moments. Tex Western.
To Be Alive. Tex Western.
Bode, Hans, 1905-
xBode, Hans.
Lead Acid Batteries. Wiley.
Bode, Hans H. *see* Bode, Hans Henning.
Bode, Hans Henning.
xBode, Hans H.
ed. Parenteral Nutrition in Infancy &
Childhood. Plenum Pub.
Bode, Wilhelm. *see* Bode, Wilhelm Von.
Bode, Wilhelm Von.
xBode, Wilhelm.
Florentine Sculptors of the Renaissance.
Hacker.
Bodecker, N. M.
xBodecker, N. M.
The Mushroom Center Disaster. Atheneum.
The Mushroom Center Disaster. Atheneum.
illus. A Person from Britain & Other
Limericks. Atheneum.
Bodelsen, Anders, 1937-
xBodelsen, Anders.
Operation Cobra. Elsevier-Nelson.
Think of a Number. BJ Pub Group.
Boden, Margaret. *see* Boden, Margaret A.
Boden, Margaret A.
xBoden, Margaret.
Artificial Intelligence & Natural Man. Basic.
xBoden, Margaret A.
Jean Piaget. Penguin.
Jean Piaget. Viking Pr.
Bodenheim, Maxwell, 1893-1954
xBodenheim, Maxwell.
Replenishing Jessica. AMS Pr.
Bodger, Lorraine.
xBodger, Lorraine.
Crafts for All Seasons. Universe.
Paper Dreams. Universe.
Bodi, Jack.
xBodi, Jack.
A Gardener's Book of Needlepoint. S&S.
Bodie, Idella.
xBodie, Idella.
Ghost in the Capitol. Sandlapper Store.
Bodie, Scott.
xBodie, Scott.
Confessions of a Fish Doctor. Workman Pub.
Bodin, Harry S. *see* Bodin, Harry Sabbath.
Bodin, Harry Sabbath.
xBodin, Harry S.
ed. Civil Litigation & Trial Techniques. PLI.
Bodine, A. Aubrey, 1907-
xBodine, A. Aubrey.

Chesapeake Bay & Tidewater. Bodine.
Bodkin, Cora.
xBodkin, Cora.
Crafts for Your Leisure Years. HM.
Bodkin, Maud.
xBodkin, Maud.
Archetypal Patterns in Poetry: Psychological
Studies of Imagination. AMS Pr.
Archetypal Patterns in Poetry: Psychological
Studies of Imagination. Arden Lib.
Archetypal Patterns in Poetry: Psychological
Studies of Imagination. Oxford U Pr.
Quest for Salvation in an Ancient & a Modern
Play. Folcroft.
Bodle, David W., 1904-
xBodle, David W.
Characterization of the Electrical Environment.
U of Toronto Pr.
Bodle, Yvonne. *see* Bodle, Yvonne Gallegos.
Bodle, Yvonne Gallegos.
xBodle, Yvonne.
Retail Selling. McGraw.
Bodmer, W. F. *see* Bodmer, Walter F.
Bodmer, Walter F.
xBodmer, W. F.
Genetics, Evolution, & Man. W H Freeman.
Bodnar. *see* Bodnar, George H.
Bodnar, George H.
xBodnar.
Accounting Information Systems. Allyn.
Bodnar, John. *see* Bodnar, John E.
Bodnar, John E., 1944-
xBodnar, John.
Immigration & Industrialization: Ethnicity in
an American Mill Town, 1870-1940. U of
Pittsburg Pr.
xBodnar, John E.
Intro. by & ed. The Ethnic Experience in
Pennsylvania. Bucknell U Pr.
Bodner, Henry, 1910-
xBodner, Henry.
Diagnostic & Therapeutic Aids in Urology. C
C Thomas.
Bodo, John R.
xBodo, John R.
A Gallery of New Testament Rogues: From
Herod to Satan. Westminster.
Bodo, Peter.
xBodo, Peter.
Inside Tennis: A Season on the Pro Tour.
Delacorte.
Pele's New World. Norton.
Bodsworth, Fred, 1918-
xBodsworth, Fred.
The Last of the Curlews. Dell.
Bodurtha, Frank T.
xBodurtha, Frank T.
Industrial Explosion Prevention & Protection.
McGraw.
Bodwell, C. E.
xBodwell, C. E.
Evaluation of Proteins for Humans. AVI.
Boecker, Alexander.
xBoecker, Alexander.
Probable Italian Source of Shakespeare's Julius
Caesar. AMS Pr.
Boegehold, Betty.
xBoegehold, Betty.
What the Wind Told. Schol Bk Serv.
What the Wind Told. Schol Bk Serv.
Boegehold, Betty. *see* Boegehold, Betty Virginia Doyle.
Boegehold, Betty Virginia Doyle.
xBoegehold, Betty.
Hurray for Pippa!. Knopf.
Pippa Pops Out!. Knopf.
Boehm, Ann E.
xBoehm, Ann E.
The Classroom Observer: Guide to Developing
Observation Skills. Tchrs Coll.
Boehm, B. W. *see* Boehm, Barry W.

Boehm, Barry W.
xBoehm, B. W.
Characteristics of Software Quality. Elsevier.
Boehm, William D.
xBoehm, William D.
Glacier Bay. Alaska Northwest.
Boehner, P. *see* Boehner, Philotheus.
Boehner, Philotheus, Father.
xBoehner, P.
Medieval Logic: An Outline of Its
Development from 1250 to c. 1400. State
Mutual Bk.
Boeke, Julius H. *see* Boeke, Julius Herman.
Boeke, Julius Herman, 1884-
xBoeke, Julius H.
Economics & Economic Policy of Dual
Societies, As Exemplified by Indonesia. AMS
Pr.
Boeker, M. *see* Boeker, Mary (Draper).
Boeker, Mary (Draper), 1905-
xBoeker, M.
Status of the Beginning Calculus Students in
Pre-Calculus College Mathematics: Study
Carried Out with Students in Brooklyn
College & City College of New York. AMS
Pr.
Boelen, Bernard J. *see* Boelen, Bernard Jacque Marie.
Boelen, Bernard Jacque Marie, 1916-
xBoelen, Bernard J.
Personal Maturity: The Existential Dimension.
Continuum.
Boer, Charles, 1939-
xBoer, Charles.
Charles Olson in Connecticut. Swallow.
Odes. Swallow.
Boer, Harry R.
xBoer, Harry R.
Above the Battle: The Bible & Its Critics.
Eerdmans.
Pentecost & Missions. Eerdmans.
Boer, John J. De. *see* De Boer, John J.
Boericke. *see* Boericke, Art.
Boericke, Art.
xBoericke.
The Craftsman Builder. S&S.
Boers, Hendrikus.
xBoers, Hendrikus.
What Is New Testament Theology?: The Rise
of Criticism & the Problem of a Theology of
the New Testament. Fortress.
Boesch, Donald F.
xBoesch, Donald F.
Oil Spills & the Marine Environment. Ballinger
Pub.
Boeschen, John.
xBoeschen, John.
How to Make Money Freelancing: A Guide to
Writing & Selling Nonfiction Articles.
Wordworks.
Successful Playhouses. Structures Pub.
Boesen, Victor.
xBoesen, Victor.
Doing Something About the Weather. Putnam.
Boesing, Martha.
xBoesing, Martha.
Journeys Along the Matrix: Three Plays.
Vanilla.
Boetger, Gary.
xBoetger, Gary.
In Search of Balance. Libra.
Boethius, Axel.
xBoethius, Axel.
Etruscan & Early Roman Architecture.
Penguin.
Etruscan & Early Roman Architecture. Viking
Pr.
Boettcher, Robert. *see* Boettcher, Robert B.
Boettcher, Robert B.
xBoettcher, Robert.

Gifts of Deceit: Sun Myung Moon, Tongsun Park & the Korean Scandal. HR&W.

Boettiger, John R.
xBoettiger, John R.
A Love in Shadow. Norton.

Boff, Leonardo.
xBoff, Leonardo.
Liberating Grace. Orbis Bks.

Bogan, Louise, 1897-1970
xBogan, Louise.
What the Woman Lived: Selected Letters of Louise Bogan 1920-1970. HarBraceJ.

Bogard, Travis.
xBogard, Travis.
Contour in Time: The Plays of Eugene O'Neill. Oxford U Pr.

Bogarde, Dirk, 1921-
xBogarde, Dirk.
A Gentle Occupation. Knopf.
Snakes & Ladders. HR&W.

Bogardus, Edgar.
xBogardus, Edgar.
Various Jangling Keys. AMS Pr.

Bogardus, Emory S. see Bogardus, Emory Stephen.

Bogardus, Emory Stephen, 1882-
xBogardus, Emory S.
The Development of Social Thought. Greenwood.
Fundamentals of Social Psychology. Arno.
Immigration & Race Attitudes. Ozer.

Bogardus, James, 1800-1874
xBogardus, James.
Origins of Cast Iron Architecture in America. Da Capo.

Bogardus, Mary.
xBogardus, Mary.
Crisis in the Catskills. Hope Farm.

Bogart, Leo.
xBogart, Leo.
Age of Television: A Study of Viewing Habits & the Impact of Television on American Life. Ungar.

Bogdan, R. J. see Bogdan, Radu J.

Bogdan, Radu J.
xBogdan, R. J.
ed. Local Induction. Kluwer Boston.

Bogdan, Robert.
xBogdan, Robert.
An Introduction to Qualitative Research Methods: A Phenomenological Approach to the Social Sciences. Wiley.
Participant Observation in Organizational Settings. Syracuse U Pr.

Bogdanor, Vernon, 1943-
xBogdanor, Vernon.
Devolution. Oxford U Pr.

Boggess, Bill.
xBoggess, Bill.
American Brilliant Cut Glass. Crown.

Boggess, Louise.
xBoggess, Louise.
How to Write Short Stories that Sell. Writers Digest.

Boggs, Dane R.
xBoggs, Dane R.
White Cell Manual. Davis Co.

Boggs, Donald L.
xBoggs, Donald L.
Live Animal Carcass Evaluation & Selection Manual. Kendall-Hunt.

Boggs, James.
xBoggs, James.
American Revolution: Pages from a Negro Worker's Notebook. Monthly Rev.
Racism & the Class Struggle: Further Pages from a Black Worker's Notebook. Monthly Rev.
Revolution & Evolution in the Twentieth Century. Monthly Rev.

Boggs, R. S. see Boggs, Ralph Steele.

Boggs, Ralph Steele.
xBoggs, R. S.
Everyday Spanish Idioms. Regents Pub.

Boggs, Winthrop S. see Boggs, Winthrop Smillie.

Boggs, Winthrop Smillie.
xBoggs, Winthrop S.
Postage Stamps & Postal History of Newfoundland. Quarterman.

Bogin, Meg.
xBogin, Meg.
The Women Troubadours. Norton.
The Women Troubadours. Paddington.

Bogle, Michael.
xBogle, Michael.
Textile Dyes, Finishes & Auxiliaries. Garland Pub.

Bognar, J. see Bognar, Janos.

Bognar, Janos.
xBognar, J.
Indefinite Inner Product Spaces. Springer-Verlag.

Bogner, Norman, 1935-
xBogner, Norman.
Arena. Delacorte.
Arena. Dell.

Bogner, R. E.
xBogner, R. E.
ed. Introduction to Digital Filtering. Wiley.

Bogoch, A. see Bogoch, Abraham.

Bogoch, Abraham, 1922-
xBogoch, A.
Gastroenterology. McGraw.

Bogoliubov, N. N. see Bogoliubov, Nikolai Nikolaevich.

Bogoliubov, Nikolai Nikolaevich.
xBogoliubov, N. N.
Introduction to the Theory of Quantized Fields. Wiley.
ed. Theory of Superconductivity. Gordon.

Bogoraz, Vladimir G. see Bogoraz, Vladimir Germanovich.

Bogoraz, Vladimir Germanovich, 1865-1936
xBogoraz, Vladimir G.
The Chukchee. AMS Pr.
Chukchee. Johnson Repr.
Chukchee Mythology. AMS Pr.

Bograd, Larry.
xBograd, Larry.
Egon. Macmillan.
Felix in the Attic. Harvey.

Bogue, Allan G.
xBogue, Allan G.
Money at Interest: The Farm Mortgage on the Middle Border. Russell.
Money at Interest: The Farm Mortgage on the Middle Border. U of Nebr Pr.

Bogue, Donald J. see Bogue, Donald Joseph.

Bogue, Donald Joseph.
xBogue, Donald J.
Economic Areas of the United States. Free Pr.
Structure of the Metropolitan Community: A Study of Dominance & Subdominance. Russell.

Bogue, Lucile Maxfield, 1911-
xBogue, Lucille M.
Typhoon, Typhoon: An Illustrated Haiku Sequence. C E Tuttle.

Bogue, Lucille M. see Bogue, Lucile Maxfield.

Bogue, Margaret B. see Bogue, Margaret Beattie.

Bogue, Margaret Beattie, 1924-
xBogue, Margaret B.
Patterns from the Sod. Arno.

Boguslavskii, Leonid I. see Boguslavskii, Leonid Isaakovich.

Boguslavskii, Leonid Isaakovich.
xBoguslavskii, Leonid I.
Organic Semiconductors & Biopolymers. Plenum Pub.

Boguslaw, Robert.
xBoguslaw, Robert.

Prologue to Sociology. Goodyear.

Boguslawski, Dorothy B. see Boguslawski, Dorothy Beers.

Boguslawski, Dorothy Beers.
xBoguslawski, Dorothy B.
Guide for Establishing & Operating Day Care Centers for Young Children. Child Welfare.

Bohannan, Paul.
xBohannan, Paul.
Africa & Africans. Natural Hist.
ed. African Homicide & Suicide. Atheneum.
ed. Law & Warfare: Studies in the Anthropology of Conflict. U of Tex Pr.

Bohart, R. M. see Bohart, Richard Mitchell.

Bohart, Richard Mitchell.
xBohart, R. M.
A Revision of the Genus Zethus Fabricius in the Western Hemisphere (Hymenoptera: Eumenidae). U of Cal Pr.
Sphecid Wasps of the World: A Generic Revision. U of Cal Pr.

Bohigian, Haig E. see Bohigian, Haig Edward.

Bohigian, Haig Edward.
xBohigian, Haig E.
The Foundations & Mathematical Models of Operations Research with Extensions to the Criminal Justice System. Gazette Pr.

Bohinski, Robert C.
xBohinski, Robert C.
Modern Concepts in Biochemistry. Allyn.

Bohl, Marilyn.
xBohl, Marilyn.
Flowcharting Techniques. SRA.
A Guide for Programmers. P-H.
Information Processing. SRA.

Bohle, Bruce.
xBohle, Bruce W.
ed. Human Life: Controversies & Concerns. Wilson.

Bohle, Bruce W. see Bohle, Bruce.

Bohlmann, F.
xBohlmann, F.
Naturally Occurring Acetylenes. Acad Pr.

Bohm, A. see Bohm, Arno.

Bohm, Arno, 1936-
xBohm, A.
Quantum Mechanics. Springer-Verlag.

Bohm, David.
xBohm, David.
Fragmentation & Wholeness: An Inquiry into the Function of Language & Thought. Humanities.
Quantum Theory. P-H.

Bohm, Ewald. see Bohm, Ewald Bernhard.

Bohm, Ewald Bernhard, 1903-
xBohm, Ewald.
Textbook in Rorschach Test Diagnosis for Psychologists, Physicians & Teachers. Grune.

Bohme, Frederick G.
xBohme, Frederick G.
A History of the Italians in New Mexico. Arno.

Bohme, H. see Bohme, Horst.

Bohme, Horst.
xBohme, H.
ed. Iminium Salts in Organic Chemistry. Wiley.

Bohn, Dave.
xBohn, Dave.
House of Three Turkeys: Anasazi Redoubt. Capra Pr.
Rambles Through an Alaskan Wild: Katmai & the Valley of the Smokes. Capra Pr.

Bohn, Hinrich. see Bohn, Hinrich L.

Bohn, Hinrich L.
xBohn, Hinrich.
Soil Chemistry. Wiley.

Bohn, Raymond J.
xBohn, Raymond J.
Learning About Time. Richards Pub.

Bohn, Thomas W.
xBohn, Thomas W.

Light & Shadows: A History of Motion
Pictures. Alfred Pub.

Bohne, Harald.
xBohne, Harold.
Publishing: The Creative Business. U of
Toronto Pr.
Bohne, Harold. *see* Bohne, Harald.
Bohr, Niels. *see* Bohr, Niels Henrik David.
Bohr, Niels Henrik David, 1885-
xBohr, Niels.
Atomic Theory & the Description of Nature.
AMS Pr.
Bohrer, Walt.
xBohrer, Walt.
Tales Up. Aero.
This Is Your Captain Speaking. Aero.
Bohrod, Aaron.
xBohrod, Aaron.
Decade of Still Life. U of Wis Pr.
Pottery Sketchbook. U of Wis Pr.
Bohrs, Mary Ann.
xBohrs, Mary Ann.
Getting Ready for Christmas. Judson.
Boice, James M. *see* Boice, James Montgomery.
Boice, James Montgomery, 1938-
xBoice, James M.
Awakening to God. Inter-Varsity.
Can You Run Away from God?. Victor Bks.
God the Redeemer. Inter-Varsity.
The Gospel of John: An Expositional
Commentary. Zondervan.
The Sovereign God. Inter-Varsity.
Boies, Henry M. *see* Boies, Henry Martyn.
Boies, Henry Martyn, 1837-1903
xBoies, Henry M.
Prisoners & Paupers: A Study of the Abnormal
Increase of Criminals & the Public Burden of
Pauperism in the United States; the Causes &
Remedies. Arno.
Boikess, Robert S.
xBoikess, Robert S.
Chemical Principles. Har-Row.
Boillot, Michael. *see* Boillot, Michel H.
Boillot, Michel. *see* Boillot, Michel H.
Boillot, Michel H.
xBoillot, Michael.
Understanding Fortran. West Pub.
xBoillot, Michel.
Basic. West Pub.
xBoillot, Michel H.
Essentials of Flowcharting. Wm C Brown.
Understanding WATFIV. West Pub.
Bois, W. E. Du. *see* Du Bois, W. E.
Bois, William E. Du. *see* Du Bois, William E.
Boisen, Anton T. *see* Boisen, Anton Theophilus.
Boisen, Anton Theophilus, 1876-
xBoisen, Anton T.
Religion in Crisis & Custom: A Sociological &
Psychological Study. Greenwood.
Boissard, Janine.
xBoissard, Janine.
A Matter of Feeling. Little.
Boissevain, Jeremy.
xBoissevain, Jeremy.
A Village in Malta. HR&W.
Boissier, Gaston, 1823-1908
xBoissier, Gaston.
Cicero & His Friends: A Study of Roman
Society in the Time of Caesar. Cooper Sq.
Boissier, J. R.
xBoissier, J. R.
jt. ed. & ed. Differential Psychopharmacology
on Anxiolytics & Sedatives. S Karger.
Bojarski, Richard.
xBojarski, Richard.
The Films of Boris Karloff. Citadel Pr.
Bojrab, M. Joseph.
xBojrab, M. Joseph.

ed. Current Techniques in Small Animal
Surgery. Lea & Febiger.
Bok, Bart J. *see* Bok, Bart Jan.
Bok, Bart Jan.
xBok, Bart J.
Objections to Astrology. Prometheus Bks.
Bok, Sissela.
xBok, Sissela.
Lying: Moral Choice in Public & Private Life.
Random.
Bol, L. J. *see* Bol, Laurens Johannes.
Bol, Laurens Johannes, 1898-
xBol, L. J.
Adriaen Coorte: A Unique Late Seventeenth
Century Dutch Still-Life Painter. Humanities.
Boland, Bridget.
xBoland, Bridget.
Gardener's Magic & Other Old Wives Lore.
FS&G.
Bolander, D. O. *see* Bolander, Donald O.
Bolander, Donald O.
xBolander, D. O.
The Instant Quotation Dictionary. Watts.
xBolander, Donald O.
Instant Quotation Dictionary. Career Inst.
Bolander, Karen.
xBolander, Karen.
Assessing Personality Through Tree Drawings.
Basic.
Bolc, L. *see* Bolc, Leonard.
Bolc, Leonard, 1934-
xBolc, L.
ed. Natural Language Communication with
Computers. Springer-Verlag.
Bold, Alan. *see* Bold, Alan Norman.
Bold, Alan Norman, 1943-
xBold, Alan.
The Ballad. Methuen Inc.
George Mackay Brown. B&N.
Bold, Harold C. *see* Bold, Harold Charles.
Bold, Harold Charles.
xBold, Harold C.
Morphology of Plants & Fungi. Har-Row.
The Plant Kingdom. P-H.
Bolden, John H.
xBolden, John H.
Developing a Competency-Based Instructional
Supervisory System: A School Management
Development Program. Exposition.
Bolden, Theodore E. *see* Bolden, Theodore Edward.
Bolden, Theodore Edward.
xBolden, Theodore E.
Dental Hygiene Examination Review Book.
Med Exam.
Bolding, Amy.
xBolding, Amy.
Fingertip Devotions. Baker Bk.
Installation Services for All Groups. Broadman.
Bolduc, Jean B. *see* Bolduc, Jean Baptiste Zacharie.
Bolduc, Jean Baptiste Zacharie.
xBolduc, Jean B.
Mission of the Columbia. Ye Galleon.
Boler, John F. *see* Boler, John Francis.
Boler, John Francis.
xBoler, John F.
Charles Peirce & Scholastic Realism: A Study
of Peirce's Relation to John Duns Scotus. U
of Wash Pr.
Boles, Donald E. *see* Boles, Donald Edward.
Boles, Donald Edward, 1926-
xBoles, Donald E.
Two Swords: Commentaries & Cases in
Religion & Education. Iowa St U Pr.
Boles, Harold W.
xBoles, Harold W.

Introduction to Educational Leadership.
Har-Row.
Intro. by Multidisciplinary Readings in
Educational Leadership. Mss Info.
Boles, Janet K., 1944-
xBoles, Janet K.
The Politics of the Equal Rights Amendment:
Conflict & the Decision Process. Longman.
Boles, John B.
xBoles, John B.
Religion in Antebellum Kentucky. U Pr of Ky.
Boles, Paul D. *see* Boles, Paul Darcy.
Boles, Paul Darcy, 1916-
xBoles, Paul D.
Glory Day. Dell.
Glory Day. Random.
Boley, Jack. *see* Boley, Jack W.
Boley, Jack W.
xBoley, Jack.
A Guide to Effective Industrial Safety. Gulf
Pub.
Bolgar, R. R.
xBolgar, R. R.
The Classical Heritage & Its Beneficiaries.
Cambridge U Pr.
Bolhuis, John L.
xBolhuis, John L.
The Financial Ingredient in Food Service
Management. Heath.
Bolian. *see* Bolian, Polly.
Bolian, Polly.
xBolian.
Growing Up Slim. McGraw.
xBolian, Polly.
Symbols: The Language of Communication.
Watts.
Bolich, Gregory G.
xBolich, Gregory G.
Karl Barth & Evangelicalism. Inter-Varsity.
Bolingbroke, Henry, Saint-John, 1st Viscount, 1678-1751
xBolingbroke, Henry S.
Works of Lord Bolingbroke. Kelley.
Bolingbroke, Henry S. *see* Bolingbroke, Henry.
Bolinger, Dwight. *see* Bolinger, Dwight le Merton.
Bolinger, Dwight le Merton, 1907-
xBolinger, Dwight.
Aspects of Language. HarBraceJ.
Intensive Spanish. Folcroft.
Meaning & Form. Longman.
That's That. Mouton.
Bolino. *see* Bolino, August Constantino.
Bolino, August Constantino, 1922-
xBolino.
Development of the American Economy.
Merrill.
Bolitho, H. *see* Bolitho, Harold.
Bolitho, Harold.
xBolitho, H.
Meiji Japan. Cambridge U Pr.
xBolitho, Harold.
Meiji Japan. Lerner Pubns.
Bolker, Ethan D.
xBolker, Ethan D.
First Year Calculus. A-W.
Bolker, Henry. *see* Bolker, Henry I.
Bolker, Henry I.
xBolker, Henry.
Natural & Synthetic Polymers: An
Introduction. Dekker.
Bolkosky, Sidney M.
xBolkosky, Sidney M.
The Distorted Image: German Jewish
Perceptions of Germans & Germany,
1918-1935. Elsevier.
Boll, C. R. *see* Boll, Carl R.
Boll, Carl R.
xBoll, C. R.
Executive Jobs Unlimited. Macmillan.
Boll, Heinrich, 1917-
xBoll, Heinrich.

And Never Said a Word. McGraw.
And Never Said a Word. McGraw.
The Bread of Those Early Years. McGraw.
Children Are Civilians Too. McGraw.
End of a Mission. McGraw.
Group Portrait with Lady. Avon.
Group Portrait with Lady. McGraw.
Bollan, William, d. 1776
  xBollan, William.
    The Freedom of Speech & Writing Upon
      Public Affairs Considered. Da Capo.
Bolland, John.
  xBolland, John.
    Hampstead Psychoanalytic Index: A Study of
      the Psychoanalytic Case Material of a
      Two-Year-Old Boy. Intl Univs Pr.
Bolland, O. Nigel.
  xBolland, O. Nigel.
    The Formation of a Colonial Society: Belize,
      from Conquest to Crown Colony. Johns
      Hopkins.
Bolle, Kees W.
  xBolle, Kees W.
    Freedom of Man in Myth. Vanderbilt U Pr.
Bollen, J. D. see Bollen, John David.
Bollen, John David.
  xBollen, J. D.
    Protestantism & Social Reform in New South
      Wales 1890-1910. Intl Schol Bk Serv.
Bollens, John C. see Bollens, John Constantinus.
Bollens, John Constantinus, 1920-
  xBollens, John C.
    Appointed Executive Local Government: The
      California Experience. Greenwood.
    ed. Exploring the Metropolitan Community. U
      of Cal Pr.
    Special District Governments in the United
      States. Greenwood.
Boller, Francois.
  xBoller, Francois.
    ed. Auditory Comprehension: Clinical &
      Experimental Studies with the Token Test.
      Acad Pr.
Boller, Paul F.
  xBoller, Paul F.
    George Washington & Religion. SMU Press.
    Quotemanship: The Use & Abuse of
      Quotations for Polemical & Other Purposes.
      SMU Press.
Bolles, Albert S. see Bolles, Albert Sidney.
Bolles, Albert Sidney, 1846-1939
  xBolles, Albert S.
    Bank Officers: Their Authority, Duty &
      Liability. Greenwood.
Bolles, Robert. see Bolles, Robert C.
Bolles, Robert C.
  xBolles, Robert.
    Learning Theory. HR&W.
  xBolles, Robert C.
    Theory of Motivation. Har-Row.
Bollier, John A., 1927-
  xBollier, John A.
    The Literature of Theology: A Guide for
      Students & Pastors. Westminster.
Bollinger, Donald E., 1930-
  xBollinger, Donald E.
    Band Directors Complete Handbook. P-H.
Bollinger, Edward T. see Bollinger, Edward Taylor.
Bollinger, Edward Taylor.
  xBollinger, Edward T.
    Rails That Climb: A Narrative History of the
      Moffat Road. CO RR Mus.
Bollinger, G. A.
  xBollinger, G. A.
    Blast Vibration Analysis. S Ill U Pr.
Bollinger, L. L. see Bollinger, Lynn Louis.
Bollinger, Lynn Louis.
  xBollinger, L. L.

Personal Aircraft Business at Airports.
  Pergamon.
Bollinger, Rick L.
  xBollinger, Rick L.
    Communication Management of the Geriatric
      Patient. Interstate.
Bollobas, B. see Bollobas, Bela.
Bollobas, Bela.
  xBollobas, B.
    Graph Theory: An Introductory Course.
      Springer-Verlag.
Bollom, C. see Bollom, Chris.
Bollom, Chris.
  xBollom, C.
    Attitudes & Second Homes in Rural Wales.
      Verry.
Bolloten, Burnett, 1909-
  xBolloten, Burnett.
    The Spanish Revolution: The Left & the
      Struggle for Power During the Civil War. U
      of NC Pr.
Bolmeier, Edward C. see Bolmeier, Edward Claude.
Bolmeier, Edward Claude, 1898-
  xBolmeier, Edward C.
    Legality of Student Disciplinary Practices.
      Michie.
Bologh, Roslyn W. see Bologh, Roslyn Wallach.
Bologh, Roslyn Wallach.
  xBologh, Roslyn W.
    Dialectical Phenomenology: Marx's Method.
      Routledge & Kegan.
Bolognese, Don.
  xBolognese, Don.
    illus. Drawing Horses & Foals. Watts.
Bolognese, Ronald J.
  xBolognese, Ronald J.
    Perinatal Medicine: Clinical Management of
      the High Risk Fetus & Neonate. Williams &
      Wilkins.
Bolooki, Hooshang, 1937-
  xBolooki, Hooshang.
    ed. Clinical Application of Intra-Aortic Balloon
      Pump. Futura Pub.
Bolotin, David, 1944-
  xBolotin, David.
    Plato's Dialogue on Friendship: An
      Interpretation of the "Lysis," with a New
      Translation. Cornell U Pr.
Bolotin, Norm.
  xBolotin, Norm.
    Klondike Lost: A Decade of Photographs by
      Kinsey & Kinsey. Alaska Northwest.
Bolshakoff, Serge.
  xBolshakoff, Sergius.
    In Search of True Wisdom: Visits to Eastern
      Spiritual Fathers. Doubleday.
Bolshakoff, Sergius. see Bolshakoff, Serge.
Bolt, Bruce A., 1930-
  xBolt, Bruce A.
    Earthquakes: A Primer. W H Freeman.
    Intro. by Earthquakes & Volcanoes: Readings
      from Scientific American. W H Freeman.
Bolt, David. see Bolt, David Langstone.
Bolt, David Langstone, 1927-
  xBolt, David.
    Adam. Shaw Pubs.
Bolt, Gordon J.
  xBolt, Gordon J.
    Communicating with EEC Markets. Intl Pubns
      Serv.
Bolte, Charles G. see Bolte, Charles Guy.
Bolte, Charles Guy, 1920-
  xBolte, Charles G.
    Libraries & the Arts & Humanities. Gaylord
      Prof Pubns.
Boltho, Andrea.
  xBoltho, Andrea.

Foreign Trade Criteria in Socialist Economies.
  Cambridge U Pr.
Boltin, Lee.
  xBoltin, Lee.
    Closed on Account of Death, Not Sam.
      Ballantine.
Bolton, Brian. see Bolton, Brian F.
Bolton, Brian F.
  xBolton, Brian.
    ed. Handbook of Measurement & Evaluation in
      Rehabilitation. Univ Park.
    Introduction to Rehabilitation Research. C C
      Thomas.
    ed. Rehabilitation Counseling: Theory &
      Practice. Univ Park.
Bolton, Carole.
  xBolton, Carole.
    Little Girl Lost. Elsevier-Nelson.
    The Stage Is Set. Morrow.
Bolton, Charles K. see Bolton, Charles Knowles.
Bolton, Charles Knowles, 1867-1950
  xBolton, Charles K.
    The Founders: Portraits of Persons Born
      Abroad Who Came to the Colonies in North
      America Before the Year 1701. Genealog
      Pub.
    The Real Founders of New England: Stories of
      Their Life Along the Coast 1602-1628.
      Genealog Pub.
Bolton, Dale L., 1927-
  xBolton, Dale L.
    Evaluating Administrative Personnel in School
      Systems. Tchrs Coll.
Bolton, Derek.
  xBolton, Derek.
    An Approach to Wittgensteins' Philosophy.
      Humanities.
Bolton, Douglas.
  xBolton, Douglas.
    Garden or Wilderness. Schenkman.
Bolton, Eileen. see Bolton, Eileen M.
Bolton, Eileen M.
  xBolton, Eileen.
    Lichens for Vegetable Dyeing. Robin & Russ.
Bolton, Ethel (Stanwood).
  xBolton, Ethel S.
    American Samplers. Peter Smith.
    Immigrants to New England, 1700-1775.
      Genealog Pub.
Bolton, Ethel S. see Bolton, Ethel (Stanwood).
Bolton, Evelyn.
  xBolton, Evelyn.
    Dream Dancer. Creative Ed.
    Ride When You're Ready. Creative Ed.
Bolton, Frank G.
  xBolton, Frank G.
    The Pregnant Adolescent: Problems of
      Premature Parenthood. Sage.
Bolton, G. C. see Bolton, Geoffrey Curgenven.
Bolton, Gary R.
  xBolton, Gary R.
    Handbook of Canine Electrocardiography.
      Saunders.
Bolton, Geoffrey Curgenven.
  xBolton, G. C.
    The Passing of the Irish Act of Union: A Study
      in Parliamentary Politics. Oxford U Pr.
Bolton, Herbert E. see Bolton, Herbert Eugene.
Bolton, Herbert Eugene, 1870-
  xBolton, Herbert E.
    Guide to Materials for the History of the
      United States in the Principal Archives of
      Mexico. Kraus Repr.
    Padre on Horseback. Loyola.
    ed. Spanish Exploration in the Southwest,
      1542-1706. B&N.
Bolton, Neil.
  xBolton, Neil.
    The Psychology of Thinking. Methuen Inc.
Bolton, Reginald P. see Bolton, Reginald Pelham.

Bolton, Reginald Pelham, 1856-1942
xBolton, Reginald P.
Indian Life of Long Ago in the City of New
York. Kennikat.
Bolton, Robert, 1814-1877
xBolton, Robert.
A Guide to New Rochelle & Its Vicinity:
Pelham, West Chester, West Farms,
Morrisania, Fordham, Yonkers, East Chester,
White Plains, Mamaroneck & Rye. Harbor
Hill Bks.
xBolton, Robert H.
People Skills: How to Assert Yourself, Listen
to Others & Resolve Conflicts. P-H.
Bolton, Robert H. see Bolton, Robert.
Bolton, Sarah K. see Bolton, Sarah Knowles.
Bolton, Sarah Knowles, 1841-1916
xBolton, Sarah K.
Ralph Waldo Emerson. Folcroft.
Bolton, Theodore, 1889-
xBolton, Theodore.
Early American Portrait Draughtsmen in
Crayons. Da Capo.
Boltz, C. L. see Boltz, Cecil Leonard.
Boltz, Carol. see Boltz, Carol J.
Boltz, Carol J.
xBoltz, Carol.
Language & Reality: A Rhetoric & Reader.
Alfred Pub.
Boltz, Cecil Leonard, 1900-
xBoltz, C. L.
Crown to Mend: A Letter on Poetry. R West.
Boltz, David F. see Boltz, David Ferdinand.
Boltz, David Ferdinand.
xBoltz, David F.
ed. Colorimetric Determination of Nonmetals.
Wiley.
Boltzmann, Ludwig, 1844-1906
xBoltzmann, Ludwig.
Theoretical Physics & Philosophical Problems:
Selected Writings. Kluwer Boston.
Bolwell, Robert George Whitney, 1891-
xBolwell, Robert W.
Life & Works of John Heywood. AMS Pr.
Bolwell, Robert W. see Bolwell, Robert George Whitney.
Bolz, Roger W. see Bolz, Roger William.
Bolz, Roger William.
xBolz, Roger W.
Production Processes: The Productivity
Handbook. Conquest.
Understanding Automation: Elements for
Managers. Conquest.
Bolza, Oskar, 1857-1942
xBolza, Oskar.
Lectures on the Calculus of Variations. Chelsea
Pub.
Bombaugh, Charles C. see Bombaugh, Charles Carroll.
Bombaugh, Charles Carroll, 1828-1906
xBombaugh, Charles C.
Gleanings for the Curious from the Harvest
Fields of Literature: A Melange of Excerpta.
Gale.
Bombeck, Erma.
xBombeck, Erma.

At Wit's End. Doubleday.
At Wit's End. Fawcett.
The Grass Is Always Greener Over the Septic
Tank. Fawcett.
The Grass Is Always Greener Over the Septic
Tank. G K Hall.
The Grass Is Always Greener Over the Septic
Tank. McGraw.
I Lost Everything in the Post-Natal
Depression. Doubleday.
I Lost Everything in the Post-Natal
Depression. Fawcett.
If Life Is a Bowl of Cherries - What Am I
Doing in the Pits?. G K Hall.
If Life Is a Bowl of Cherries, What Am I
Doing in the Pits?. Fawcett.
If Life Is a Bowl of Cherries, What Am I
Doing in the Pits. McGraw.
Bombelles, Joseph T.
xBombelles, Joseph T.
Economic Development of Communist
Yugoslavia, 1947-1964. Hoover Inst Pr.
Bomers, G. B. see Bomers, G. B. J.
Bomers, G. B. J.
xBomers, G. B.
Multinational Corporations & Industrial
Relations: A Comparative Study of West
Germany & the Netherlands. Humanities.
Bompas, Cecil H. see Bompas, Cecil Henry.
Bompas, Cecil Henry.
xBompas, Cecil H.
Folklore of the Santal Parganas. Arno.
Bompas, George C.
xBompas, George C.
The Problem of the Shakespeare Plays.
Folcroft.
Bomse, Marguerite D., 1916-
xBomse, Marguerite D.
Practical Spanish Dictionary & Phrasebook.
Pergamon.
Practical Spanish for Medical & Hospital
Personnel. Pergamon.
Practical Spanish for School Personnel,
Firemen, Policemen & Community Agencies.
Pergamon.
Practical Spanish Grammar. Pergamon.
Bonanno, Margaret W. see Bonanno, Margaret Wander.
Bonanno, Margaret Wander.
xBonanno, Margaret W.
A Certain Slant of Light. Seaview Bks.
Ember Days. Seaview Bks.
Bonansea, Bernardino M.
xBonansea, Bernardino M.
God & Atheism: A Philosophical Approach to
the Problem of God. Intl Schol Bk Serv.
Bonaparte, Marie, Princess, 1882-
xBonaparte, Marie.
Female Sexuality. Intl Univs Pr.
Bonar, Andrew A. see Bonar, Andrew Alexander.
Bonar, Andrew Alexander, 1810-1892
xBonar, Andrew A.
Christ & His Church in the Book of Psalms.
Kregel.
A Commentary on the Book of Leviticus.
Baker Bk.
Bonar, Ann.
xBonar, Ann.
Shrubs for All Seasons. Transatlantic.
Bonar, D. D.
xBonar, D. D.
On Annular Functions. Adler.
Bonar, Horatius, 1808-1889
xBonar, Horatius.
Thoughts on Genesis. Kregel.
Bonar, James, 1852-1941
xBonar, James.

Tables Turned. Kelley.
Theories of Population from Raleigh to Arthur
Young. Biblio Dist.
Theories of Population from Raleigh to Arthur
Young. Kelley.
Bonavia, David.
xBonavia, David.
Peking. Time-Life.
Bonavia, Ferruccio, 1877- 1950
xBonavia, Ferruccio.
ed. Musicians on Music. Hyperion Conn.
Bonavia, Michael. see Bonavia, Michael Robert.
Bonavia, Michael Robert.
xBonavia, Michael.
Birth of British Rail. Allen Unwin.
Bonazza, Blaze O. see Bonazza, Blaze Odell.
Bonazza, Blaze Odell.
xBonazza, Blaze O.
ed. Studies in Fiction. Har-Row.
Bonbright, James C. see Bonbright, James Cummings.
Bonbright, James Cummings, 1891-
xBonbright, James C.
Principles of Public Utility Rates. Columbia U
Pr.
Public Utilities & the National Power Policies.
Da Capo.
Bond, Ann S. see Bond, Ann Sharpless.
Bond, Ann Sharpless.
xBond, Ann S.
Saturdays in the City. HM.
Bond, Beverley W. see Bond, Beverley Waugh.
Bond, Beverley Waugh, 1881-
xBond, Beverley W.
The Monroe Mission to France, 1794-1796.
AMS Pr.
Bond, Bob.
xBond, Bob.
The Handbook of Sailing. Knopf.
Bond, Christopher.
xBond, Christopher.
Citizens Band & Monitor Radio Handbook.
RBX Res.
Bond, Donald F. see Bond, Donald Frederic.
Bond, Donald Frederic, 1898-
xBond, Donald F.
Compiled by Age of Dryden. AHM Pub.
Bond, Elias A. see Bond, Elias Austin.
Bond, Elias Austin, 1873-
xBond, Elias A.
The Professional Treatment of the Subject
Matter of Arithmetic for Teacher-Training
Institutions. AMS Pr.
Bond, Evelyn.
xBond, Evelyn.
The Clouded Mirror. Manor Bks.
House of Shadows. Manor Bks.
Bond, Frederic D. see Bond, Frederic Drew.
Bond, Frederic Drew, 1876-
xBond, Frederic D.
Stock Movements & Speculation. Arno.
Bond, George. see Bond, George C.
Bond, George C.
xBond, George.
ed. African Christianity: Patterns of Religious
Continuity. Acad Pr.
xBond, George C.
The Politics of Change in a Zambian
Community. U of Chicago Pr.
Bond, Gladys B. see Bond, Gladys Baker.
Bond, Gladys Baker.
xBond, Gladys B.
Album of Cats. Rand.
Bond, Gordon C.
xBond, Gordon C.
The Grand Expedition: The British Invasion of
Holland in 1809. U of Ga Pr.
Bond, Guy L. see Bond, Guy Loraine.
Bond, Guy Loraine, 1904-
xBond, Guy L.

The Auditory & Speech Characteristics of Poor
Readers. AMS Pr.
Bond, Harold, 1939-
xBond, Harold.
The Way It Happens to You. Ararat Pr.
Bond, Harold L.
xBond, Harold L.
The Literary Art of Edward Gibbon.
Greenwood.
Bond, Harold Lewis.
xBond, Harold Lewis.
An Encyclopedia of Antiques. Gale.
Bond, Horace M. see Bond, Horace Mann.
Bond, Horace Mann, 1904-
xBond, Horace M.
Education of the Negro in the American Social
Order. Octagon.
Negro Education in Alabama: A Study in
Cotton & Steel. Atheneum.
Bond, J. Mark. see Bond, Mark J.
Bond, John. see Bond, John L.
Bond, John L.
xBond, John.
ed. Friends Search for Wholeness. Friends
United.
Bond, Jules. see Bond, Jules Jerome.
Bond, Jules Jerome.
xBond, Jules.
The Outdoor Cookbook. PB.
Bond, Mark J.
xBond, J. Mark.
Half a Treasure. Nordon Pubns.
Bond, Mary W. see Bond, Mary Wickham.
Bond, Mary Wickham.
xBond, Mary W.
Far Afield in the Caribbean: Migratory Flights
of a Naturalist's Wife. Livingston.
Bond, Michael.
xBond, Michael.
Fun & Games with Paddington. Collins Pubs.
More About Paddington. Dell.
More About Paddington. HM.
Paddington Abroad. HM.
Paddington Abroad. Dell.
Paddington at the Circus. Random.
Paddington at the Seaside. Random.
Paddington at the Tower. Random.
Paddington at Work. Dell.
Paddington at Work. HM.
Paddington Bear. Random.
Paddington Goes to Town. HM.
Paddington Goes to Town. Dell.
Paddington on Top. Dell.
Paddington on Top. HM.
Paddington Takes the Air. HM.
Paddington Takes to the Air. Dell.
Paddington Takes to T.V.. Dell.
Paddington Takes to TV. HM.
Paddington's Garden. Random.
Paddington's Lucky Day. Random.
The Tales of Olga Da Polga. Macmillan.
Bond, Michael R.
xBond, Michael R.
Pain - Its Nature, Analysis, & Treatment.
Churchill.
Bond, Nancy.
xBond, Nancy.
Country of Broken Stone. Atheneum.
A String in the Harp. Atheneum.
Bond, Nelson S. see Bond, Nelson Slade.
Bond, Nelson Slade, 1908-
xBond, Nelson S.
Thirty-First of February. Arno.
Bond, Richard W. see Bond, Richard Warwick.
Bond, Richard Warwick.
xBond, Richard W.
ed. Early Plays from the Italian. Arno.
Bond, Richmond P. see Bond, Richmond Pugh.
Bond, Richmond Pugh, 1899-
xBond, Richmond P.

Queen Anne's American Kings. Octagon.
Bond, Robert D., 1946-
xBond, Robert D.
ed. Contemporary Venezuela & Its Role in
International Affairs. NYU Pr.
Bond, Robert J.
xBond, Robert J.
California Real Estate Finance. Wiley.
California Real Estate Practice. Goodyear.
Getting Started in California Real Estate.
Kendall-Hunt.
Bond, W. L. see Bond, Walter Lysander.
Bond, Walter Lysander, 1903-
xBond, W. L.
Crystal Technology. Wiley.
Bondanella, Peter. see Bondanella, Peter E.
Bondanella, Peter E., 1943-
xBondanella, Peter.
ed. Federico Fellini: Essays in Criticism.
Oxford U Pr.
xBondanella, Peter E.
ed. Federico Fellini: Essays in Criticism.
Oxford U Pr.
Francesco Guicciardini. Twayne.
Bondi, H. see Bondi, Hermann.
Bondi, Hermann.
xBondi, H.
Assumption & Myth in Physical Theory.
Cambridge U Pr.
Bondi, Joseph.
xBondi, Joseph.
Developing Middle Schools: A Guidebook. Mss
Info.
Developing Middle Schools: A Guidebook.
Whitehall Co..
Bone, Christopher.
xBone, Christopher.
The Disinherited Children: A Study of the
New Left & the Generation Gap. Halsted Pr.
Bone, H. see Bone, Hugh Alvin.
Bone, Hugh A. see Bone, Hugh Alvin.
Bone, Hugh Alvin, 1909-
xBone, H.
Politics & Voters. McGraw.
xBone, Hugh A.
Party Committees & National Politics. U of
Wash Pr.
Politics & Voters. McGraw.
Bone, J. F. see Bone, Jesse Franklin.
Bone, Jesse F. see Bone, Jesse Franklin.
Bone, Jesse Franklin, 1916-
xBone, J. F.
Confederation Matador. Donning Co.
xBone, Jesse F.
Animal Anatomy & Physiology. Reston.
Bone, Philip J. see Bone, Philip James.
Bone, Philip James.
xBone, Philip J.
The Guitar & Mandolin: Biographies of
Celebrated Players & Composers. Scholarly.
Bone, Robert. see Bone, Robert W.
Bone, Robert C.
xBone, Robert C.
American Government. B&N.
Dynamics of the Western New Guinea (Irian
Barat) Problem. Cornell Mod Indo.
Bone, Robert W.
xBone, Robert.
Maverick Guide to Hawaii. Pelican.
xBone, Robert W.
Maverick Guide to Australia. Pelican.
Bone, Woutrina A. see Bone, Woutrina Agatha.
Bone, Woutrina Agatha.
xBone, Woutrina A.
Children's Stories & How to Tell Them. Gale.
Bonell, Harold C.
xBonell, Harold C.
Sparks for the Kindling. Judson.
Bonello, Frank J.
xBonello, Frank J.

ed. Alternative Directions in Economic Policy.
U of Notre Dame Pr.
Bonenko, Allen. see Bonenko, Allen
Bonenko, Allen
xBonenko, Allen.
Pacific Salmon Fishing. A S Barnes.
Boner, C. J. see Boner, Charles J.
Boner, Charles J.
xBoner, C. J.
Manufacture & Application of Lubricating
Greases. Krieger.
Boner, Harold A.
xBoner, Harold A.
Hungry Generations: The Nineteenth-Century
Case Against Malthusianism. Russell.
Boner, Marian, 1909-
xBoner, Marian.
A Reference Guide to Texas Law & Legal
History: Sources & Documentation. U of Tex
Pr.
Bonewit, Kathy.
xBonewit, Kathy.
Clinical Procedures for Medical Assistants.
Saunders.
Boney, C. D. see Boney, Cecil De Witt.
Boney, Cecil De Witt, 1902-
xBoney, C. D.
Study of Library Reading in the Primary
Grades. AMS Pr.
Boney, William J. see Boney, William Jerry.
Boney, William Jerry.
xBoney, William J.
ed. Baptists & Ecumenism. Judson.
Bonfante, Larissa.
xBonfante, Larissa.
Etruscan Dress. Johns Hopkins.
Bonfiglioli, Kyril.
xBonfiglioli, Kyril.
All the Tea in China. Pantheon.
Bongard, M. see Bongard, Mikhail Moiseevich.
Bongard, Mikhail Moiseevich.
xBongard, M.
Pattern Recognition. Hayden.
Bonge, John W.
xBonge, John W.
Concepts for Corporate Strategy: Readings in
Business Policy. Macmillan.
Bonger, Willem A. see Bonger, Willem Adriaan.
Bonger, Willem Adriaan, 1876-1940
xBonger, Willem A.
Race & Crime. Patterson Smith.
xBonger, William A.
Criminality & Economic Conditions. Agathon.
Bonger, William A. see Bonger, Willem Adriaan.
Bongiovanni, Gail.
xBongiovanni, Gail.
Medical Spanish. McGraw.
Bonham. see Bonham, Frank.
Bonham, Aubrey R., 1902
xBonham, Aubrey R.
Coaching the Flexible Man-to-Man Defense.
P-H.
Bonham, Barbara.
xBonham, Barbara.
Passion's Price. Playboy Pbks.
Bonham, Betty, 1926-
xBonham, Betty.
Open the Door to the Bible. Bethany Fell.
Bonham, Frank.
xBonham.
The Rascals from Haskell's Gym. Schol Bk
Serv.
xBonham, Frank.

Chief. Dutton.
Cool Cat. Dell.
Cool Cat. Dutton.
Defiance Mountain. Berkley Pub.
Devilhorn. Dutton.
A Dream of Ghosts. Dutton.
Durango Street. Dell.
Durango Street. Dutton.
The Forever Formula. Dutton.
The Friends of the Loony Lake Monster.
Dutton.
The Golden Bees of Tulami. Dell.
Golden Bees of Tulami. Dutton.
The Loud, Resounding Sea. T Y Crowell.
Night Raid. Berkley Pub.
The Nitty Gritty. Dell.
Nitty Gritty. Dutton.
The Rascals from Haskell's Gym. Dutton.
Vagabundos. Dutton.
Bonham, Marilyn.
xBonham, Marilyn.
Laughter & Tears of Children. Macmillan.
Bonham, Milledge L. see Bonham, Milledge Louis.
Bonham, Milledge Louis, 1880-1941
xBonham, Milledge L.
British Consuls in the Confederacy. AMS Pr.
Bonhoeffer, Dietrich, 1906-1945
xBonhoeffer, Dietrich.
Cost of Discipleship. Macmillan.
Ethics. Macmillan.
Letters & Papers from Prison. Macmillan.
Life Together. Har-Row.
Psalms: The Prayer Book of the Bible.
Augsburg.
Boni, Margaret. see Boni, Margaret Bradford.
Boni, Margaret Bradford, 1893-
xBoni, Margaret.
Fireside Book of Folk Songs. S&S.
Bonic, Robert. see Bonic, Robert A.
Bonic, Robert A.
xBonic, Robert.
Freshman Calculus. Heath.
xBonic, Robert A.
Linear Functional Analysis. Gordon.
Bonica, John J.
xBonica, John J.
ed. Pain. Raven.
Bonin, Gerhardt Von, 1890-
xBonin, Gerhardt Von.
The Evolution of the Human Brain. U of
Chicago Pr.
Bonin, Jane F.
xBonin, Jane F.
Prize-Winning American Drama: A
Bibliographical & Descriptive Guide.
Scarecrow.
Boning, Richard A.
xBoning, Richard A.
The Cardiff Giant. Dexter & Westbrook.
Horror Overhead. Dexter & Westbrook.
Joshua James. Dexter & Westbrook.
The Long Search. Dexter & Westbrook.
Soldier Girl. Dexter & Westbrook.
Bonington, Chris. see Bonington, Christian.
Bonington, Christian.
xBonington, Chris.
Annapurna South Face. McGraw.
Everest -- the Hard Way. Random.
The Ultimate Challenge: The Hardest Way up
the Highest Mountain in the World. Stein &
Day.
Bonjean, C. M. see Bonjean, Charles M.
Bonjean, Charles M.
xBonjean, C. M.
Community Politics: A Behavioral Approach.
Free Pr.
Bonjour, Adrien.
xBonjour, Adrien.
The Structure of Julius Caesar. Folcroft.
Bonk, Wallace J. see Bonk, Wallace John.

Bonk, Wallace John.
xBonk, Wallace J.
Building Library Collections. Scarecrow.
Bonne, Alfred, 1899-1959
xBonne, Alfred.
Studies in Economic Development: With
Special Reference to Conditions in the
Underdeveloped Areas of Western Asia and
India. Greenwood.
Bonnefoy, Yves.
xBonnefoy, Yves.
On the Motion & Immobility of Douve. Ohio
U Pr.
Bonnell, Peter.
xBonnell, Peter.
Conversation in French: Points of Departure. D
Van Nostrand.
Conversation in French: Points of Departure.
Van Nos Reinhold.
Conversation in German: Points of Departure.
D Van Nostrand.
Conversation in German: Points of Departure.
Van Nos Reinhold.
Bonner, Anthony.
xBonner, Anthony.
tr. & ed. Songs of the Troubadours. Schocken.
Bonner, Clint.
xBonner, Clint.
Hymn Is Born. Broadman.
Bonner, G. A. see Bonner, George Alan.
Bonner, George Alan.
xBonner, G. A.
British Transport Law by Road & Rail. David
& Charles.
Bonner, James. see Bonner, James Frederick.
Bonner, James C. see Bonner, James Calvin.
Bonner, James Calvin, 1904-
xBonner, James C.
Georgia's Last Frontier: The Development of
Carroll County. U of Ga Pr.
ed. Studies in Georgia History & Government.
Reprint.
Bonner, James Frederick.
xBonner, James.
ed. Plant Biochemistry. Acad Pr.
Bonner, John T. see Bonner, John Tyler.
Bonner, John Tyler.
xBonner, John T.
Cells & Societies. Atheneum.
Cells & Societies. Princeton U Pr.
The Evolution of Culture in Animals. Princeton
U Pr.
On Development: The Biology of Form.
Harvard U Pr.
Bonner, Mary G. see Bonner, Mary Graham.
Bonner, Mary Graham, 1890-
xBonner, Mary G.
Wonders Around the Sun. Lantern.
Bonner, Robert J. see Bonner, Robert Johnson.
Bonner, Robert Johnson.
xBonner, Robert J.
The Administration of Justice from Homer to
Aristotle. AMS Pr.
Administration of Justice from Homer to
Aristotle. Greenwood.
Aspects of Athenian Democracy. Russell.
Lawyers & Litigants in Ancient Athens: The
Genesis of the Legal Profession. Arno.
Bonner, Willard Hallam.
xBonner, William H.
De Quincey at Work. Folcroft.
Bonner, William H. see Bonner, Willard Hallam.
Bonners, Susan.
xBonners, Susan.
Panda. Delacorte.
Bonney, Orin H. see Bonney, Orrin H.
Bonney, Orrin H.
xBonney, Orin H.

Guide to the Wyoming Mountains &
Wilderness Areas. Swallow.
Bonney, T. G. see Bonney, Thomas George.
Bonney, Thomas George, 1833-1923
xBonney, T. G.
Abbeys & Churches of England & Wales.
Longwood Pr.
Bonnie, Fred.
xBonnie, Fred.
Growing Plants in Containers. Oxmoor Hse.
House Plants. Oxmoor Hse.
Bonnie, Richard J.
xBonnie, Richard J.
The Marihuana Conviction: A History of
Marihuana Prohibition in the United States.
U Pr of Va.
Bonnifield, Mathew Paul, 1937-
xBonnifield, Paul.
The Dust Bowl: Men, Dirt, & Depression. U of
NM Pr.
Bonnifield, Paul. see Bonnifield, Mathew Paul.
Bono, Edward De. see De Bono, Edward.
Bono, Philip.
xBono, Philip.
Frontiers of Space. Macmillan.
Bonola, Roberto, 1874-1911
xBonola, Roberto.
Non-Euclidean Geometry: A Critical &
Historical Study of Its Development.
Gannon.
Bonoma, Thomas V.
xBonoma, Thomas V.
ed. Organizational Buying Behavior. Am Mktg.
Bononcini, Antonio M. see Bononcini, Antonio Maria.
Bononcini, Antonio Maria.
xBononcini, Antonio M.
Griselda. Garland Pub.
Bonow, Raysa R. see Bonow, Raysa Rose.
Bonow, Raysa Rose.
xBonow, Raysa R.
How to Be a Thin Person. Random.
Bonsal, Philip W. see Bonsal, Philip Wilson.
Bonsal, Philip Wilson, 1903-
xBonsal, Philip W.
Cuba, Castro, & the United States. U of
Pittsburgh Pr.
Bonsal, Stephen, 1865-1951
xBonsal, Stephen.
Suitors & Suppliants: The Little Nations at
Versailles. Kennikat.
Bonsall, Crosby. see Bonsall, Crosby Newell.
Bonsall, Crosby N. see Bonsall, Crosby Newell.
Bonsall, Crosby Newell.
xBonsall, Crosby.
illus. The Case of the Cat's Meow. Har-Row.
The Case of the Hungry Stranger. Har-Row.
The Goodbye Summer. Archway.
Goodbye Summer. Greenwillow.
illus. Who's Afraid of the Dark?. Har-Row.
xBonsall, Crosby N.
And I Mean It, Stanley. Har-Row.
illus. Case of the Cat's Meow. Har-Row.
illus. Case of the Hungry Stranger. Har-Row.
What Spot. Har-Row.
Bonser, Frederick G. see Bonser, Frederick Gordon.
Bonser, Frederick Gordon, 1875-1931
xBonser, Frederick G.
The Reasoning Ability of Children in the
Fourth, Fifth, & Sixth School Grades. AMS
Pr.
Bonser, Wilfred. see Bonser, Wilfrid.
Bonser, Wilfrid, 1887-1972
xBonser, Wilfred.
A Prehistoric Bibliography. Biblio Dist.
xBonser, Wilfrid.
Anglo-Saxon & Celtic Bibliography 450-1078.
Folcroft.
Bonsignore, John J.
xBonsignore, John J.

Before the Law: An Introduction to the Legal
Process. HM.
Bonta, I. *see* Bonta, I. L.
Bonta, I. L.
xBonta, I.
ed. Connective Tissue Changes in Rheumatoid
Arthritis & the Use of Penicillamine.
Birkhauser.
Bonta, Juan. *see* Bonta, Juan Pablo.
Bonta, Juan Pablo.
xBonta, Juan.
Architecture & Its Interpretation: A Study of
Expressive Systems in Architecture. Rizzoli
Intl.
Bonta, Marcia, 1940-
xBonta, Marcia.
The Escape to the Mountain: A Family's
Adventures in the Wilderness. A S Barnes.
Bontecou, Eleanor.
xBontecou, Eleanor.
The Federal Loyalty-Security Program.
Greenwood.
Bontemps, Arna. *see* Bontemps, Arna Wendell.
Bontemps, Arna W. *see* Bontemps, Arna Wendell.
Bontemps, Arna Wendell, 1902-
xBontemps, Arna.
Famous Negro Athletes. Dodd.
ed. Great Slave Narratives. Beacon Pr.
xBontemps, Arna W.
God Sends Sunday. AMS Pr.
Bontly, Thomas J.
xBontly, Thomas J.
Celestial Chess. Har-Row.
Bonville, W. J.
xBonville, W. J.
Footnotes to a Fairytale: A Study in the
Nature of Expression in the Arts. Green.
Bonwick, Colin.
xBonwick, Colin
English Radicals & the American Revolution.
U of NC Pr.
Bonwick, James, 1817-1906
xBonwick, James.
The Lost Tasmanian Race. Johnson Repr.
Bony, Jean.
xBony, Jean.
The English Decorated Style: Gothic
Architecture Transformed 1250-1350. Cornell
U Pr.
Boocock, Sarane S. *see* Boocock, Sarane Spence.
Boocock, Sarane Spence.
xBoocock, Sarane S.
Simulation Games in Learning. Sage.
Sociology of Education: An Introduction. HM.
Boodberg, Peter A. *see* Boodberg, Peter Alexis.
Boodberg, Peter Alexis.
xBoodberg, Peter A.
Selected Works of Peter A. Boodberg. U of Cal
Pr.
Boody, Bertha M. *see* Boody, Bertha May.
Boody, Bertha May, 1877-
xBoody, Bertha M.
Psychological Study of Immigrant Children at
Ellis Island. Arno.
A Psychological Study of Immigrant Children
at Ellis Island. R & E Res Assoc.
Boogher, William F. *see* Boogher, William Fletcher.
Boogher, William Fletcher.
xBoogher, William F.
Gleanings of Virginia History: An Historical &
Genealogical Collection, Largely from
Original Sources. Genealog Pub.
Booher, Dianna D. *see* Booher, Dianna Daniels.
Booher, Dianna Daniels.
xBooher, Dianna D.
Coping-When Your Family Falls Apart.
Messner.
The Faces of Death. Broadman.
Booher, L. J.
xBooher, L. J.

Surface Irrigation. Unipub.
Book, Stephen A.
xBook, Stephen A.
Essentials of Statistics. McGraw.
Book, Susan W.
xBook, Susan W. .
The Chinese in Butte County, California,
1860-1920. R & E Res Assoc.
Bookbinder, Albert I. A.
xBookbinder, Albert I. A.
Security Options Strategy. Prog Pr.
Bookbinder, David.
xBookbinder, David.
What Folk Music Is All About. Messner.
Bookbinder, Robert.
xBookbinder, Robert.
The Films of Bing Crosby. Citadel Pr.
Bookchin, Murray.
xBookchin, Murray.
The Spanish Anarchists: The Heroic Years,
1868-1936. Free Life.
Booker, Christopher.
xBooker, Christopher.
Neophiliacs. Gambit.
Booker, P. J. *see* Booker, Peter Jeffrey.
Booker, Peter Jeffrey.
xBooker, P. J.
Project Apollo: The Way to the Moon.
Elsevier.
Bookstein, F. L. *see* Bookstein, Fred L.
Bookstein, Fred L., 1947-
xBookstein, F. L.
The Measurement of Biological Shape & Shape
Change. Springer-Verlag.
Bookwalter, John. *see* Bookwalter, John Wesley.
Bookwalter, John Wesley, 1837-1915
xBookwalter, John.
Siberia & Central Asia. Longwood Pr.
Boolootian, Richard A.
xBoolootian, Richard A.
College Zoology. Macmillan.
Zoology: An Introduction to the Study of
Animals. Macmillan.
Boolos, G. S. *see* Boolos, George.
Boolos, George.
xBoolos, G. S.
Computability & Logic. Cambridge U Pr.
Boom, Corrie Ten. *see* Ten Boom, Corrie.
Boon, Louis P. *see* Boon, Louis Paul.
Boon, Louis Paul.
xBoon, Louis P.
Chapel Road. Hippocrene Bks.
Boone, Clinton C. *see* Boone, Clinton Caldwell.
Boone, Clinton Caldwell.
xBoone, Clinton C.
Liberia As I Know It. Negro U Pr.
Boone, Donna C., 1932-
xBoone, Donna C.
Comprehensive Management of Hemophilia.
Davis Co.
Boone, Gladys, 1895-
xBoone, Gladys.
Women's Trade Union Leagues in Great
Britain & United States of America. AMS Pr.
Boone, L. V. *see* Boone, Lester V.
Boone, Lester V.
xBoone, L. V.
Producing Farm Crops. Interstate.
Boone, Louis E.
xBoone, Louis E.
Contemporary Marketing. Dryden Pr.
Foundations of Marketing. Dryden Pr.
Marketing Strategy: A Marketing Decision
Game. Merrill.
Boone, Shirley.
xBoone, Shirley.

The Honeymoon Is Over. Creation Hse.
The Honeymoon Is Over. Nelson.
One Woman's Liberation. Nelson.
Boone, William T., 1944-
xBoone, William T.
Better Gymnastics: How to Spot the Performer.
Anderson World.
Boonin, Joseph M.
xBoonin, Joseph M.
An Index to the Solo Songs of Robert Franz.
Eur-Am Music.
Boor, C. De. *see* De Boor, C.
Boor, John, 1930-1974
xBoor, John.
Ziegler-Natta Catalysts & Polymerizations.
Acad Pr.
Boorer, Wendy.
xBoorer, Wendy.
Dogs: Selection, Care, Training. Bantam.
Boorman, John T.
xBoorman, John T.
Money Supply, Money Demand &
Macroeconomic Models. AHM Pub.
Boorman, Scott A.
xBoorman, Scott A.
Protracted Game: A Wei-Ch'i Interpretation of
Maoist Revolutionary Strategy. Oxford U Pr.
Protracted Game: A Wei-Ch'i Interpretation of
Maoist Revolutionary Strategy. Oxford U Pr.
Boorstein, Edward, 1915-
xBoorstein, Edward.
Allende's Chile: An Inside View. Intl Pub Co.
Boorstin, Daniel. *see* Boorstin, Daniel Joseph.
Boorstin, Daniel J. *see* Boorstin, Daniel Joseph.
Boorstin, Daniel Joseph, 1914-
xBoorstin, Daniel.
The Exploring Spirit: America & the World,
Then & Now. Random.
xBoorstin, Daniel J.
America & the Image of Europe: Reflections
on American Thought. Peter Smith.
ed. American Primer. NAL.
ed. An American Primer. U of Chicago Pr.
The Americans: The Colonial Experience.
Random.
The Americans: The Democratic Experience.
Random.
The Americans: The Democratic Experience.
Random.
Decline of Radicalism: Reflections of America
Today. Random.
Democracy & Its Discontents: Reflections on
Everyday America. Random.
Democracy & Its Discontents: Reflections on
Everyday America. Random.
The Exploring Spirit: America & the World,
Then & Now. Random.
Genius of American Politics. U of Chicago Pr.
Image: A Guide to Pseudo-Events in America.
Atheneum.
Lost World of Thomas Jefferson. Peter Smith.
Boorstin, Paul.
xBoorstin, Paul.
The Accursed. NAL.
Savage. Marek.
Boorstin, Sharon.
xBoorstin, Sharon.
Keep on Rollin': The Complete Guide to
Roller Skating in America. Warner Bks.
Booth, Alice L. *see* Booth, Alice Lynn.
Booth, Alice Lynn.
xBooth, Alice L.
Careers in Politics for the New Woman. Watts.
Booth, Charles.
xBooth, Charles.
Charles Booth on the City: Physical Pattern &
Social Structure. U of Chicago Pr.
Booth, Edwin.
xBooth, Edwin.

Ambush at Adams Crossing. Bouregy.
Boot Heel Range. Assoc Bk.
The Colt-Packin' Parson. Bouregy.
Crossfire. Ace Bks.
Booth, Eugene.
xBooth, Eugene.
At the Beach. Raintree Child.
At the Circus. Raintree Child.
At the Fair. Raintree Child.
At the Zoo. Raintree Child.
In the Air. Raintree Child.
In the City. Raintree Child.
In the Garden. Raintree Child.
In the Jungle. Raintree Child.
In the Park. Raintree Child.
On the Farm. Raintree Child.
Under the Ground. Raintree Child.
Under the Ocean. Raintree Child.
Booth, George.
xBooth, George.
ed. Animals Animals Animals. Har-Row.
Rehearsal's off!. Avon.
Rehearsal's Off. Dodd.
Think Good Thoughts About a Pussycat. Avon.
Think Good Thoughts About a Pussycat.
Dodd.
Booth, George C.
xBooth, George C.
The Food & Drink of Mexico. Dover.
The Food & Drink of Mexico. Peter Smith.
Booth, Grayce M., 1931-
xBooth, Grayce M.
Functional Analysis of Information Processing:
A Structured Approach for Simplifying
Systems Design. Wiley.
Booth, K. M. see Booth, Kenneth McIvor.
Booth, Ken.
xBooth, Ken.
ed. American Thinking About Peace & War:
New Essays on American Thought &
Attitudes. B&N.
Strategy & Ethnocentrism. Holmes & Meier.
Booth, Kenneth McIvor.
xBooth, K. M.
Dictionary of Refrigeration & Air
Conditioning. Burgess-Intl Ideas.
Booth, Martin.
xBooth, Martin.
Brevities. SBD.
Booth, Norman.
xBooth, Norman.
Industrial Gases. Pergamon.
Booth, Philip. see Booth, Philip E.
Booth, Philip E.
xBooth, Philip.
Available Light. Viking Pr.
Booth, Taylor L.
xBooth, Taylor L.
Computing Fundamentals & Applications.
Wiley.
Booth, W. D.
xBooth, William D.
Selling Commercial & Industrial Construction
Projects. Van Nos Reinhold.
Booth, Wayne C.
xBooth, Wayne C.
Critical Understanding: The Powers & Limits
of Pluralism. U of Chicago Pr.
Modern Dogma & the Rhetoric of Assent. U of
Chicago Pr.
Modern Dogma & the Rhetoric of Assent. U of
Notre Dame Pr.
Rhetoric of Fiction. U of Chicago Pr.
A Rhetoric of Irony. U of Chicago Pr.
Booth, William, 1829-1912
xBooth, William.
In Darkest England & the Way Out. Mss Info.
In Darkest England & the Way Out. Patterson
Smith.
Booth, William D. see Booth, W. D.

Boothe, Viva B. see Boothe, Viva Belle.
Boothe, Viva Belle, 1893-
xBoothe, Viva B.
The Political Party As a Social Process. Arno.
Booty, John E.
xBooty, John E.
The Church in History. Seabury,
Booz, Gretchen.
xBooz, Gretchen.
Kendra. Herald Hse.
Bopp, William J.
xBopp, William J.
Principles of American Law Enforcement &
Criminal Justice. C C Thomas.
Borack, Barbara.
xBorack, Barbara.
Gooney. Har-Row.
Grandpa. Har-Row.
Borah, William E. see Borah, William Edgar.
Borah, William Edgar, 1865-1940
xBorah, William E.
American Problems: A Selection of Speeches &
Prophecies. AMS Pr.
American Problems: A Selection of Speeches &
Prophecies. Scholarly.
Borawska, M. Albertine.
xBorawska, M. Albertine.
How to Have Fun Making a Rug. Creative Ed.
Borch, Karl H. see Borch, Karl Henrik.
Borch, Karl Henrik.
xBorch, Karl H.
Economics of Uncertainty. Princeton U Pr.
Borchard, Edwin M. see Borchard, Edwin Montefiore.
Borchard, Edwin Montefiore.
xBorchard, Edwin M.
Convicting the Innocent: Errors of Criminal
Justice. Da Capo.
Borchardt, D. H. see Borchardt, Dietrich Hans.
Borchardt, Dietrich Hans, 1916-
xBorchardt, D. H.
Australian Bibliography: A Guide to Printed
Sources of Information. Pergamon.
How to Find Out in Philosophy & Psychology.
Pergamon.
Borcherding, Thomas E.
xBorcherding, Thomas E.
ed. Budgets & Bureaucrats: The Sources of
Government Growth. Duke.
Borchert, Donald M.
xBorchert, Donald M.
ed. Being Human in a Technological Age. Ohio
U Pr.
Borchert, Gerald L.
xBorchert, Gerald L.
Dynamics of Evangelism. Word Bks.
Bordeaux, Henry, 1870-1963
xBordeaux, Henry.
Georges Guynemer, Knight of the Air. Arno.
Borden, Emanuel.
xBorden, Emanuel.
ed. Hand in Art. Borden.
Borden, G. see Borden, George A.
Borden, George A.
xBorden, G.
Human Communication: The Process of
Relating. Benjamin-Cummings.
Borden, Gloria J.
xBorden, Gloria J.
Speech Science Primer: Physiology, Acoustics
& Perception of Speech. Williams & Wilkins.
Borden, Morton.
xBorden, Morton.
ed. The American Tory. P-H.
Federalism of James A. Bayard. AMS Pr.
Parties & Politics in the Early Republic,
1789-1815. AHM Pub.
Speculations on American History. Heath.
Borden, Neil H. see Borden, Neil Hopper.
Borden, Neil Hopper, 1931-
xBorden, Neil H.

Acceptance of New Food Products by
Supermarkets. Fairchild.
Advertising in Our Economy. Arno.
Advertising in Our Economy. R West.
The Economic Effects of Advertising. Arno.
Borden, Weston T., 1943-
xBorden, Weston T.
Modern Molecular Orbital Theory for Organic
Chemists. P-H.
Border, Barbara. see Border, Barbara A.
Border, Barbara A.
xBorder, Barbara.
Food Safety & Sanitation. McGraw.
Bordes, Francois.
xBordes, Francois.
Tale of Two Caves. Har-Row.
Bordicks, Katherine J.
xBordicks, Katherine J.
Patterns of Shock: Implications for Nursing
Care. Macmillan.
Bordley, James.
xBordley, James.
Two Centuries of American Medicine:
1776-1976. Saunders.
Bordman, Gerald. see Bordman, Gerald Martin.
Bordman, Gerald Martin.
xBordman, Gerald.
Jerome Kern: His Life & Music. Oxford U Pr.
Bordwell, David.
xBordwell, David.
Film Art: An Introduction. A-W.
Filmguide to La Passion De Jeanne D'Arc. Ind
U Pr.
Boreham, Paul.
xBoreham, Paul.
ed. The Professions in Australia: A Critical
Appraisal. U of Queensland Pr.
Borek, C. see Borek, Carmia.
Borek, Carmia.
xBorek, C.
ed. Aging, Cancer & Cell Membranes.
Thieme-Stratton.
Borek, Ernest, 1911-
xBorek, Ernest.
Atoms Within Us. Columbia U Pr.
Code of Life. Columbia U Pr.
Borella, Anne.
xBorella, Anne.
The Home Canning Handbook: A Guide to
Preserving Food at Home. Benjamin Co.
Boren, James. see Boren, James H.
Boren, James H.
xBoren, James.
When in Doubt, Mumble: A Bureaucrat's
Handbook. Van Nos Reinhold.
Borenius, Tancred.
xBorenius, Tancred.
English Medieval Painting. Hacker.
Borenstein, Emily.
xBorenstein, Emily.
Cancer Queen. Barlenmir.
Borer, J. R.
xBorer, J. R.
Design & Control of Chemical Process
Systems. McGraw.
Borg, Dorothy.
xBorg, Dorothy.
ed. Uncertain Years: Chinese-American
Relations, 1947-1950. Columbia U Pr.
Borg, S. F. see Borg, Sidney F.
Borg, Sidney F.
xBorg, S. F.
Fundamentals of Engineering Elasticity.
Krieger.
Borg, Walter R.
xBorg, Walter R.
Educational Research: An Introduction.
Longman.
Borgaonkar, Digamber S.
xBorgaonkar, Digamber S.

Chromosomal Variation in Man: A Catalog of Chromosomal Variants & Anomalies. A R Liss.

Borgatta, Edgar F.
xBorgatta, Edgar F.
ed. Aggregate Data: Analysis & Interpretation. Sage.
ed. Sociological Methodology 1970. Jossey-Bass.

Borgen, C. Winston.
xBorgen, Winston.
Learning Experiences in Retailing: Text & Cases. Goodyear.
Borgen, Winston. *see* Borgen, C. Winston.
Borger, R. *see* Borger, Robert.

Borger, Robert.
xBorger, R.
ed. Explanation in the Behavioural Sciences. Cambridge U Pr.
Borgerhoff, Elbert B. *see* Borgerhoff, Elbert Benton Op'T Eynde.

Borgerhoff, Elbert Benton Op'T Eynde, 1908-1968
xBorgerhoff, Elbert B.
Freedom of French Classicism. Russell.
Borgerhoff, Joseph L. *see* Borgerhoff, Joseph Leopold.

Borgerhoff, Joseph Leopold, 1870-
xBorgerhoff, Joseph L.
ed. Nineteenth Century French Plays. Irvington.
Borgert, U. H. *see* Borgert, Udo H. G.

Borgert, Udo H. G.
xBorgert, U. H.
German Reference Grammar. Intl Schol Bk Serv.
Borges, Jorge L. *see* Borges, Jorge Luis.

Borges, Jorge Luis.
xBorges, Jorge L.
Borges on Writing. Dutton.
Dreamtigers. U of Tex Pr.
In Praise of Darkness. Dutton.
An Introduction to American Literature. Schocken.
Introduction to American Literature. U Pr of Ky.
An Introduction to English Literature. U Pr of Ky.

Borgese, Elisabeth (Mann).
xBorgese, Elizabeth M.
Pacem in Maribus. Dodd.
Borgese, Elizabeth M. *see* Borgese, Elisabeth (Mann).
Borgese, Giuseppe A. *see* Borgese, Giuseppe Antonio.

Borgese, Giuseppe Antonio, 1882-1952
xBorgese, Giuseppe A.
Goliath: The March of Fascism. AMS Pr.
xBorgese, Guiseppe A.
Goliath: The March of Fascism. Hyperion Conn.
Borgese, Guiseppe A. *see* Borgese, Giuseppe Antonio.
Borgeson, Frithiof C. *see* Borgeson, Frithiof Carl.

Borgeson, Frithiof Carl, 1899-
xBorgeson, Frithiof C.
The Administration of Elementary & Secondary Education in Sweden. AMS Pr.

Borghese, Anita.
xBorghese, Anita
The Down to Earth Cookbook. Scribner.
The Great Year-Round Turkey Cookbook. Stein & Day.
Borgman, Albert S. *see* Borgman, Albert Stephens.

Borgman, Albert Stephens, 1890-1954
xBorgman, Albert S.
Thomas Shadwell: His Life & Comedies. Arno.

Borgman, Harry.
xBorgman, Harry.
Art & Illustration Techniques. Watson-Guptill.
Drawing in Ink. Watson-Guptill.

Borgman, Robert D.
xBorgman, Robert D.

Social Conflict & Mental Health Services. C C Thomas.

Borgnis, Mervin E.
xBorgnis, Mervin E.
We Had a Shore Fast Line. Exposition.

Borgstrom, Georg, 1912-
xBorgstrom, Georg.
Hungry Planet: The Modern World at the Edge of Famine. Macmillan.

Borhek, James T.
xBorhek, James T.
A Sociology of Belief. Krieger.
Sociology of Belief. Wiley.

Borhek, Mary V., 1922-
xBorhek, Mary V.
My Son Eric. Pilgrim NY.

Borich, Gary D.
xBorich, Gary D.
Appraisal of Teaching: Concepts & Process. A-W.
Evaluating Classroom Instruction: A Source-Book of Instruments. A-W.
ed. Evaluating Educational Programs & Products. Educ Tech Pubns.

Borick, Paul M., 1924-
xBorick, Paul M.
ed. Chemical Sterilization. Acad Pr.
Bories, J. *see* Bories, Jacques.

Bories, Jacques.
xBories, J.
ed. The Diagnostic Limitations of Computerised Axial Tomography. Springer-Verlag.
Borisenko, A. I. *see* Borisenko, Aleksandr Ivanovich.

Borisenko, Aleksandr Ivanovich.
xBorisenko, A. I.
Vector & Tensor Analysis with Applications. Dover.
Borisov, O. B. *see* Borisov, Oleg Borisovich.

Borisov, Oleg Borisovich.
xBorisov, O. B.
Soviet-Chinese Relations, 1945-1970. Ind U Pr.
Borisov, S. N. *see* Borisov, Sergei Nikolaevich.

Borisov, Sergei Nikolaevich.
xBorisov, S. N.
Organosilicon Heteropolymers & Heterocompounds. Plenum Pub.
Boritt, Gabor S. *see* Boritt, S. Gabor.

Boritt, S. Gabor, 1940-
xBoritt, Gabor S.
Lincoln & the Economics of the American Dream. Memphis St Univ.

Borja, Corinne.
xBorja, Corinne.
jt. auth. Making Chinese Paper Cuts. A Whitman.
Bork, Albert W. *see* Bork, Albert William.

Bork, Albert William.
xBork, Albert W.
Historical Dictionary of Ecuador. Scarecrow.

Bork, Paul F., 1924-
xBork, Paul F.
The World of Moses. Southern Pub.

Bork, Robert H.
xBork, Robert H.
The Antitrust Paradox: A Policy at War with Itself. Basic.

Borkenau, Franz, 1900-1957
xBorkenau, Franz.
Pareto. Hyperion Conn.
World Communism: A History of the Communist International. U of Mich Pr.

Borkin, Joseph.
xBorkin, Joseph.
The Crime & Punishment of I. G. Farben. Free Pr.
The Crime & Punishment of I. G. Farben. PB.

Borkin, Sheldon A.
xBorkin, Sheldon A.

Data Models: A Semantic Approach for Database Systems. MIT Pr.

Borko, Harold.
xBorko, Harold.
Indexing Concepts & Methods. Acad Pr.
Targets for Research in Library Education. ALA.
Borland, Hal. *see* Borland, Hal Glen.
Borland, Hal G. *see* Borland, Hal Glen.

Borland, Hal Glen.
xBorland, Hal.
The Golden Circle: A Book of Months. T Y Crowell.
Hal Borland's Book of Days. Knopf.
The History of Wildlife in America. Natl Wildlife.
How to Write & Sell Non-Fiction. Greenwood.
When the Legends Die. Bantam.
xBorland, Hal G.
When the Legends Die. Lippincott.

Borland, Harriet.
xBorland, Harriet.
Soviet Literary Theory & Practice During the First Five-Year Plan, 1928-1932. Greenwood.

Borland, James A., 1944-
xBorland, James A.
Christ in the Old Testament. Moody.

Bormann, Ernest G.
xBormann, Ernest G.
Discussion & Group Methods: Theory & Practice. Har-Row.
Effective Committees & Groups in the Church. Augsburg.
Effective Small Group Communication. Burgess.
Bormann, F. H. *see* Bormann, F. Herbert.

Bormann, F. Herbert.
xBormann, F. H.
Pattern & Process in a Forested Ecosystem: Disturbance, Development & the Steady State Based on the Hubbard Brook Ecosystem Study. Springer-Verlag.
Borms, J. *see* Borms, Jan.

Borms, Jan.
xBorms, J.
ed. Pediatric Work Physiology. S Karger.

Born, Joachim.
xBorn, Joachim.
Folded-Plate (Hipped-Plate) Structures: Their Theory & Analysis. Ungar.
Born, M. *see* Born, Max.

Born, Max.
xBorn, M.
Principles of Optics: Electromagnetic Theory of Propagation Interference & Diffraction of Light. Pergamon.
xBorn, Max.
Problems of Atomic Dynamics. MIT Pr.
Restless Universe. Dover.

Born, Wina.
xBorn, Wina.
Famous Dishes of the World. Macmillan.

Born, Wolfgang, 1893-
xBorn, Wolfgang.
American Landscape Painting: An Interpretation. Greenwood.
Still-Life Painting in America. Hacker.

Borneman, Ernest, 1915-
xBorneman, Ernest.
ed. The Psychoanalysis of Money. Urizen Bks.
Borneman, Henry S. *see* Borneman, Henry Stauffer.

Borneman, Henry Stauffer, 1870-1955
xBorneman, Henry S.
Pennsylvania German Illuminated Manuscripts: A Classification of Fraktur-Schriften & an Inquiry into Their History & Art. Peter Smith.
Borneman, Walter. *see* Borneman, Walter R.

Borneman, Walter R.
xBorneman, Walter.

Climbing Guide to Colorado's Fourteeners.
Pruett.
Bornheimer, Deane G.
xBornheimer, Deane G.
Faculty in Higher Education. Interstate.
Borns, Steven.
xBorns, Steven.
People of Plains, Ga.. McGraw.
Bornstein. *see* Bornstein, Ruth.
Bornstein, Jerry.
xBornstein, Jerry.
What Is Genetics?. Messner.
Bornstein, Marc H.
xBornstein, Marc H.
ed. Comparative Methods in Psychology. L
Erlbaum Assocs.
ed. Psychological Development from Infancy:
Image to Intention. Halsted Pr.
Bornstein, Morris, 1927-
xBornstein, Morris.
ed. Comparative Economic Systems: Models &
Cases. Irwin.
ed. Economic Planning, East & West. Ballinger
Pub.
Bornstein, Ruth.
xBornstein.
Little Gorilla. Schol Bk Serv.
xBornstein, Ruth.
illus. Annabelle. T Y Crowell.
illus. I'll Draw a Meadow. Har-Row.
illus. Little Gorilla. HM.
illus. Of Course a Goat. Har-Row.
xBornstein, Ruth L.
I'll Draw a Meadow. Har-Row.
Bornstein, Ruth L. *see* Bornstein, Ruth.
Boros, James M.
xBoros, James M.
How to Get a Fast Start in Today's Job
Market. P-H.
Boros, Julius, 1920-
xBoros, Julius.
Swing Easy, Hit Hard. Cornerstone.
Boros, Ladislaus.
xBoros, Ladislaus.
Angels & Men. Seabury.
Being a Christian Today. Crossroad NY.
Christian Prayer. Seabury.
The Closeness of God. Seabury.
Pain & Providence. Seabury.
Borovits, Israel.
xBorovits, Israel.
Computer Systems Performance Evaluation:
Criteria, Measurement, Techniques, & Costs.
Lexington Bks.
Borovkov, A. A. *see* Borovkov, Aleksandr Alekseevich.
Borovkov, Aleksandr Alekseevich.
xBorovkov, A. A.
Stochastic Processes in Queueing Theory.
Springer-Verlag.
Borow, Henry.
xBorow, Henry.
Career Guidance for a New Age. HM.
Borowik, Ann, 1930-
xBorowik, Ann.
Lions Three, Christians Nothing. Manor Bks.
Borowitz, Eugene. *see* Borowitz, Eugene B.
Borowitz, Eugene B.
xBorowitz, Eugene.
Understanding Judaism. UAHC.
xBorowitz, Eugene B.
Choosing a Sex Ethic: A Jewish Inquiry.
Schocken.
Borrego, Eva R.
xBorrego, Eva R.
Teaching English As a Foreign Language to
Children: First Three Grades. R & E Res
Assoc.
Borrego, John.
xBorrego, John.

Space Grid Structures: Skeletal Frameworks &
Stressed Skin Systems. MIT Pr.
Borrell, Clive.
xBorrell, Clive.
Crime in Britain Today. Routledge & Kegan.
Borrello, Alfred.
xBorrello, Alfred.
E. M. Forster Dictionary. Scarecrow.
An E. M. Forster Glossary. Scarecrow.
Gabriel Fielding. Twayne.
Borren, Charles V. *see* Borren, Charles Van Den.
Borren, Charles Van Den.
xBorren, Charles V.
Sources of Keyboard Music in England.
Greenwood.
Sources of Keyboard Music in England.
Scholarly.
Borrie, W. D. *see* Borrie, Wilfrid David.
Borrie, Wilfrid David.
xBorrie, W. D.
Population, Environment, & Society. Oxford U
Pr.
Borroff, Edith, 1925-
xBorroff, Edith.
Music in Europe & the United States: A
History. P-H.
Music in Perspective. HarBraceJ.
The Music of the Baroque. Da Capo.
Borroff, Marie.
xBorroff, Marie.
Language & the Poet: Verbal Artistry in Frost,
Stevens, & Moore. U of Chicago Pr.
Borror, Donald J. *see* Borror, Donald Joyce.
Borror, Donald Joyce, 1907-
xBorror, Donald J.
Common Bird Songs. Dover.
Field Guide to the Insects of America North of
Mexico. HM.
Borrow, George. *see* Borrow, George Henry.
Borrow, George H. *see* Borrow, George Henry.
Borrow, George Henry, 1803-1881
xBorrow, George.
Celtic Bards, Chiefs & Kings. Norwood Edns.
xBorrow, George H.
Celtic Bards, Chiefs, & Kings. Folcroft.
Borrowman, Merle L.
xBorrowman, Merle L.
The Liberal & Technical in Teacher Education:
A Historical Survey of American Thought.
Greenwood.
ed. Teacher Education in America: A
Documentary History. Tchrs Coll.
Borsch, Frederick. *see* Borsch, Frederick Houk.
Borsch, Frederick H. *see* Borsch, Frederick Houk.
Borsch, Frederick Houk.
xBorsch, Frederick.
Introducing the Lessons of the Church Year: A
Guide for Lay Readers & Congregations.
Seabury.
xBorsch, Frederick H.
Christian & Gnostic Son of Man. Allenson.
Son of Man in Myth & History. Westminster.
Borsenik, Frank D.
xBorsenik, Frank D.
The Management of Maintenance &
Engineering Systems in Hospitality
Industries. Wiley.
Borsodi, Ralph, 1888-
xBorsodi, Ralph.
The Distribution Age: A Study of the
Economy of Modern Distribution. Arno.
This Ugly Civilization. Porcupine Pr.
Borssuck, B.
xBorssuck, B.
Picture Your Dog in Needlework. Arco.
Star of David Needlepoint Book. Arco.
Borsuk, Karol.
xBorsuk, Karol.

Theory of Retracts. Intl Pubns Serv.
Borten, Helen.
xBorten, Helen.
illus. Do You Move As I Do. Abelard.
illus. Halloween. T Y Crowell.
Borthwick, Bruce.
xBorthwick, Bruce M.
Comparative Politics of the Middle East: An
Introduction. P-H.
Borthwick, Bruce M. *see* Borthwick, Bruce.
Bortner, Morton.
xBortner, Morton.
ed. Evaluation & Education of Children with
Brain Damage. C C Thomas.
Borts, George H.
xBorts, George H.
Economic Growth in a Free Market. Columbia
U Pr.
Bortstein, Larry.
xBortstein, Larry.
After Olympic Glory: The Lives of Ten
Outstanding Medalists. Warne.
Boruch, Robert F.
xBoruch, Robert F.
Assuring the Confidentiality of Social Research
Data. U of Pa Pr.
Borus, Michael E.
xBorus, Michael E.
Measuring the Impact of Employment Related
Social Programs: A Primer on the Evaluation
of Employment & Training, Vocational
Education, Vocational Rehabilitation, Other
Job Oriented Programs. Upjohn Inst.
Measuring the Impact of Manpower Programs:
A Primer. U of Mich Inst Labor.
Boruvka, O. *see* Boruvka, Otakar.
Boruvka, Otakar.
xBoruvka, O.
Foundations of the Theory of Groupoids &
Groups. Birkhauser.
Bos, A. P.
xBos, A. P.
On the Elements: Aristotle's Early Cosmology.
Humanities.
Bos, Beverley J. *see* Bos, Beverly J.
Bos, Beverly J.
xBos, Beverley J.
Don't Move the Muffin Tins: A Hands-off
Guide to Art for the Young Child. Burton
Gallery.
Bos, Charles Du. *see* Du Bos, Charles.
Bos, H. C. *see* Bos, Hendricus Cornelius.
Bos, Hendricus Cornelius, 1926-
xBos, H. C.
Private Foreign Investment in Developing
Countries: A Quantitative Study on the
Evaluation of Its Macro-Economic Impact.
Kluwer Boston.
Spatial Dispersion of Economic Activity.
Gordon.
Bosanquet, Bernard, 1848-1923
xBosanquet, Bernard.
Croce's Aesthetic. Gordon Pr.
What Religion Is. Greenwood.
Bosanquet, T. *see* Bosanquet, Theodora.
Bosanquet, Theodora.
xBosanquet, T.
Paul Valery. Gordon Pr.
Paul Valery. Haskell.
Paul Valery. R West.
Bosch, David J. *see* Bosch, David Jacobus.
Bosch, David Jacobus.
xBosch, David J.
A Spirituality of the Road. Herald Pr.
Witness to the World: The Christian Mission in
Theological Perspective. John Knox.
Bosch, L. *see* Bosch, Leendert.
Bosch, Leendert.
xBosch, L.

ed. The Mechanism of Protein Synthesis & Its
  Regulation. Elsevier.
Bosco, F. J. *see* Bosco, Frederick J.
Bosco, Frederick J.
  xBosco, F. J.
  Incontro Con l'Italiano: Primo Corso. Wiley.
Bose, Amalendu.
  xBose, Amalendu.
  The Early Victorian Verse-Novel. Arden Lib.
  The Early Victorian Verse-Novel. Folcroft.
Bose, Buddhadeva.
  xBose, Buddladeva.
  Rain Through the Night. InterCulture.
Bose, Buddladeva. *see* Bose, Buddhadeva.
Bose, Keith. *see* Bose, Keith W.
Bose, Keith W.
  xBose, Keith.
  Aviation Electronics. Sams.
Bose, Nirmal Kumar.
  xBose, Nirmal Kumar.
  Culture & Society in India. Asia.
Bose, Sudhindra, 1883-
  xBose, Sudhindra.
  Fifteen Years in America. Arno.
Bose, Tarun C. *see* Bose, Tarun Chandra.
Bose, Tarun Chandra.
  xBose, Tarun C.
  The Superpowers & the Middle East. Asia.
Boserup, Ester.
  xBoserup, Ester.
  Conditions of Agricultural Growth: The
    Economics of Agrarian Change Under
    Population Pressurcs. Aldine Pub.
Boshear, Walton C.
  xBoshear, Walton C.
  Understanding People: Models & Concepts.
    Univ Assocs.
Boshell, Buris R. 1926.
  xBoshell, Buris R.
  Diabetic at Work & Play. C C Thomas.
Bosk, Charles L.
  xBosk, Charles L.
  Forgive & Remember: Managing Medical
    Failure. U of Chicago Pr.
Bosker, A.
  xBosker, A.
  Literary Criticism in the Age of Johnson.
    Folcroft.
  xBosker, Aisso.
  Literary Criticism in the Age of Johnson.
    Gordian.
Bosker, Aisso. *see* Bosker, A.
Boskin, Joseph.
  xBoskin, Joseph.
  Oppenheimer Affair: A Political Play in Three
    Acts. Glencoe.
  ed. Seasons of Rebellion: Protest & Radicalism
    in Recent America. U Pr of Amer.
Boskoff, Alvin.
  xBoskoff, Alvin.
  Sociology of Urban Regions. P-H.
Bosler, Raymond T.
  xBosler, Raymond T.
  What They Ask About Marriage. Ave Maria.
Bosley, Jo Ann.
  xBosley, Jo Ann.
  Strangest Summer. Blair.
Bosley, Richard.
  xBosley, Richard.
  Aspects of Aristotle's Logic. Humanities.
Boslooper, Thomas.
  xBoslooper, Thomas.
  The Femininity Game. Stein & Day.
Bosmajian, Haig. *see* Bosmajian, Haig A.
Bosmajian, Haig A.
  xBosmajian, Haig.

ed. Obscenity & Freedom of Expression. B
  Franklin.
The Rhetoric of Nonverbal Communication:
  Readings. Scott F.
xBosmajian, Haig A.
  ed. Dissent, Symbolic Behavior & Rhetorical
    Strategies. Greenwood.
  Rhetoric of the Civil Rights Movement. Phila
    Bk Co.
Bosmajian, Hamida.
  xBosmajian, Hamida.
  Metaphors of Evil: Contemporary German
    Literature & the Shadow of Nazism. U of
    Iowa Pr.
Bosniak, M. A. *see* Bosniak, Morton A.
Bosniak, Morton A.
  xBosniak, M. A.
  The Adrenal, Retroperitoneum & the Lower
    Urinary Tract. Year Bk Med.
Bosquet, Michel.
  xBosquet, Michel.
  Capitalism in Crisis & Everyday Life.
    Humanities.
Boss, Richard W.
  xBoss, Richard W.
  The Library Manager's Guide to Automation.
    Knowledge Indus.
Boss, Valentin.
  xBoss, Valentine.
  Newton & Russia: The Early Influence,
    1698-1796. Harvard U Pr.
Boss, Valentine. *see* Boss, Valentin.
Bossard, James. *see* Bossard, James Herbert Siward.
Bossard, James H. *see* Bossard, James Herbert Siward.
Bossard, James Herbert Siward.
  xBossard, James.
  Girl That You Marry. Macrae.
  xBossard, James H.
  Family Situations: An Introduction to the
    Study of Child Behavior. Greenwood.
  Parent & Child: Studies in Family Behavior. U
    of Pa Pr.
Bosselman, Fred P.
  xBosselman, Fred P.
  In the Wake of the Tourist: Managing Special
    Places in Eight Countries. Conservation
    Foun.
Bossone, Richard M.
  xBossone, Richard M.
  English Proficiency: Developing Your Reading
    & Writing Power. McGraw.
  Handbook of Basic English Skills. Wiley.
Bosstick, Maurice.
  xBosstick, Maurice.
  Patterns in the Sand: An Exploration in
    Mathematics. Glencoe.
Bossuet, Jacques Benigne, Bp. of Meaux, 1627-1704
  xBossuet, Jacques-Benigne.
  Discourse on Universal History. U of Chicago
    Pr.
Bossuet, Jacques-Benigne. *see* Bossuet, Jacques Benigne.
Bostock, C. J.
  xBostock, C. J.
  The Eukaryotic Chromosome. Elsevier.
Bostock, E. H. *see* Bostock, Edward Henry.
Bostock, Edward Henry, 1858-
  xBostock, E. H.
  Menageries, Circuses & Theatres. Arno.
Bostock, William.
  xBostock, William.
  I, Cleopatra. Warner Bks.
Boston Athenaeum.
  xBoston Athenaeum.
  Index of Obituaries in Boston Newspapers,
    1704-1800. G K Hall.
Boston. Children's Hospital Medical Center.
  xBoston Children's Medical Center.

Child Health Encyclopedia. Dell.
Pregnancy, Birth & the Newborn Baby.
  Delacorte.
xChildren's Hospital Medical Center, the Health
  Education Department, Boston, Mass.
  Manual of Pediatric Therapeutics. Little.
  Your Child & Ileal Conduit Surgery: A
    Guidebook for Parents. C C Thomas.
Boston Children's Medical Center. *see* Boston.
  Children's Hospital Medical Center.
Boston. City Council.
  xBoston City Council.
  Memorial of Crispus Attucks, Samuel
    Maverick, James Caldwell, Samuel Gray &
    Patrick Carr, from the City of Boston. Arno.
Boston, L. M. *see* Boston, Lucy Maria.
Boston, Lucy M. *see* Boston, Lucy Maria.
Boston, Lucy Maria, 1892-
  xBoston, L. M.
  The Children of Green Knowe. HarBraceJ.
  An Enemy at Green Knowe. HarBraceJ.
  The Fossil Snake. Atheneum.
  The Guardians of the House. Atheneum.
  Nothing Said. HarBraceJ.
  The Stones of Green Knowe. Atheneum.
  A Stranger at Green Knowe. HarBraceJ.
  xBoston, Lucy M.
  Children of Green Knowe. HarBraceJ.
  Memory in a House. Macmillan.
  Stranger at Green Knowe. HarBraceJ.
  Strongholds. HarBraceJ.
Boston Medical Commission. *see* Boston. Medical
  Commission to Investigate the Sanitary Condition of
  the City.
**Boston. Medical Commission to Investigate the Sanitary
  Condition of the City.**
  xBoston Medical Commission.
  The Sanitary Condition of Boston: The Report
    of a Medical Commission. Arno.
Boston Medical Library.
  xHarvard Medical Library.
  Author-Title Catalogue of the Francis A.
    Countway Library of Medicine for Imprints
    Through 1959. G K Hall.
Boston. Museum of Fine Arts.
  xBoston Museum of Fine Arts.
  Bulletin of the Boston Museum of Fine Arts,
    1903-1942. Arno.
  xDepartment of Classical Art.
  Art of Ancient Cyprus. Mus Fine Arts Boston.
**Boston. Museum of Fine Arts. Department of American
  Decorative Arts and Sculpture.**
  xDepartment of American Decorative Arts &
    Sculpture, Museum of Fine Arts, Boston.
  Paul Revere's Boston: Seventeen Thirty-Five to
    Eighteen Eighteen. Mus Fine Arts Boston.
Boston. Public Library.
  xBoston Public Library.

Ecclesiastes Speaks to Us Today. John Knox.

Bottorff, William K., 1931-
 xBottorff, William K.
 Thomas Jefferson. G K Hall.
 Thomas Jefferson. Twayne.
Bottrall, Margaret. *see* Bottrall, Margaret (Smith).
Bottrall, Margaret (Smith).
 xBottrall, Margaret.
 George Herbert. Folcroft.
Botume, Elizabeth H. *see* Botume, Elizabeth Hyde.
Botume, Elizabeth Hyde.
 xBotume, Elizabeth H.
 First Days Amongst the Contrabands. Arno.
Botvinnik, M. M. *see* Botvinnik, Mikhail Moiseevich.
Botvinnik, Mikhael M. *see* Botvinnik, Mikhail
 Moiseevich.
Botvinnik, Mikhail Moiseevich, 1911-
 xBotvinnik, M. M.
 Computers, Chess & Long-Range Planning.
 Springer-Verlag.
 xBotvinnik, Mikhael M.
 Anatoly Karpov: His Road to the World
 Championship. Pergamon.
Botwinick, Jack.
 xBotwinick, Jack.
 Aging & Behavior: A Comprehensive
 Integration of Research Findings. Springer
 Pub.
 Memory, Related Functions & Age. C C
 Thomas.
Botzow, Hermann S. *see* Botzow, Hermann S. D.
Botzow, Hermann S. D.
 xBotzow, Hermann S.
 Auto Fleet Management. Wiley.
Boublik. *see* Boublik, Tomas.
Boublik, Tomas.
 xBoublik.
 Statistical Thermodynamics of Simple Liquids
 & Their Mixtures. Elsevier.
Bouc, Alain.
 xBouc, Alain.
 Mao Tse-Tung: A Guide to His Thought. St
 Martin.
Bouchard, Robert. *see* Bouchard, Robert H.
Bouchard, Robert H.
 xBouchard, Robert.
 Let's Play the Recorder. Branden.
Bouche-Leclercq, Auguste, 1842-1923
 xBouche-Leclercq, Auguste.
 Histoire De la Divination Dans L'antiquite.
 Arno.
Boucher, Bernard.
 xBoucher, Bernard.
 The Megawind Cancellation. Atheneum.
Boucher, Carl O.
 xBoucher, Carl O.
 ed. Current Clinical Dental Terminology: A
 Glossary of Accepted Terms in All
 Disciplines of Dentistry. Mosby.
 Prosthodontic Treatment for Edentulous
 Patients. Mosby.
Boucher, John G.
 xBoucher, John G.
 Contrastes. Allyn.
Boucher, Louis J., 1922-
 xBoucher, Louis J.
 A Comprehensive Review of Dentistry.
 Saunders.
Boucher, Paul E. *see* Boucher, Paul Edward.
Boucher, Paul Edward, 1893-
 xBoucher, Paul E.
 Fundamentals of Photography. Morgan.
Bouchet, Ph.
 xBouchet, Philippe.
 Seashells of Western Europe. Am
 Malacologists.
Bouchet, Philippe. *see* Bouchet, Ph.
Bouchier, David.
 xBouchier, David.

Idealism & Revolution: New Ideologies of
 Liberation in Britain & the United States. St
 Martin.
Boucicault, Dion, 1820-1890
 xBoucicault, Dion.
 The Octoroon. Irvington.
Boucot, A. J. *see* Boucot, Arthur James.
Boucot, Arthur J. *see* Boucot, Arthur James.
Boucot, Arthur James.
 xBoucot, A. J.
 Evolution & Extinction Rate Controls. Elsevier.
 ed. Geology of the Arisaig Area, Antigonish
 County, Nova Scotia. Geol Soc.
 xBoucot, Arthur J.
 Early Devonian Brachiopod Zoogeography.
 Geol Soc.
Boudin, Louis B. *see* Boudin, Louis Boudianoff.
Boudin, Louis Boudianoff, 1874-1952
 xBoudin, Louis B.
 Government by Judiciary. Russell.
 Socialism & War. Garland Pub.
Boudinot, Elias, 1740-1821
 xBoudinot, Elias.
 Star in the West: A Humble Attempt to
 Discover the Long Lost Ten Tribes of Israel.
 Arno.
Boudon, Raymond.
 xBoudon, Raymond.
 Education, Opportunity & Social Inequality:
 Changing Prospects in Western Society.
 Wiley.
 Mathematical Structures of Social Mobility.
 Elsevier.
Boudreau, Amy.
 xBoudreau, Amy.
 Story of the Acadians. Pelican.
Boudreau, E. *see* Boudreau, Eugene H.
Boudreau, Eugene. *see* Boudreau, Eugene H.
Boudreau, Eugene H.
 xBoudreau, E.
 Buying Country Land. Macmillan.
 xBoudreau, Eugene.
 Buying Country Land. Macmillan.
Boudreaux, E. A. *see* Boudreaux, Edward A.
Boudreaux, Edward A.
 xBoudreaux, E. A.
 Theory & Applications of Molecular
 Paramagnetism. Wiley.
Boudreaux, H. Bruce, 1914-
 xBoudreaux, H. Bruce.
 Arthropod Phylogeny with Special Reference
 to Insects. Wiley.
Bougainville, Louis A. De. *see* Bougainville, Louis
 Antoine De.
Bougainville, Louis Antoine De.
 xBougainville, Louis A. De.
 Adventure in the Wilderness: The American
 Journals of Louis Antoine De Bougainville
 1756-1760. U of Okla Pr.
Bough, Max E.
 xBough, Max E.
 ed. The American Intermediate School: A
 Book of Readings. Interstate.
Boughey, Arthur S.
 xBoughey, Arthur S.
 Ecology of Populations. Macmillan.
 Readings in Man, the Environment, & Human
 Ecology. Macmillan.
Boughey, Howard.
 xBoughey, Howard.
 Insights of Sociology: An Introduction. Allyn.
Boughner. *see* Boughner, Howard.
Boughner, Daniel C. *see* Boughner, Daniel Cliness.
Boughner, Daniel Cliness, 1909-
 xBoughner, Daniel C.
 The Devil's Disciple: Ben Jonson's Debt to
 Machiavelli. Greenwood.
Boughner, Howard.
 xBoughner.

Posters. G&D.
Boughton, James M.
 xBoughton, James M.
 Monetary Policy & the Federal Funds Market.
 Duke.
 The Principles of Monetary Economics. Irwin.
Boughton, Rutland, 1878-1960
 xBoughton, Rutland.
 The Reality of Music. Arno.
Boughton, Terence.
 xBoughton, Terrence.
 Story of the British Light Aeroplane.
 Transatlantic.
Boughton, Terrence. *see* Boughton, Terence.
Bouissac, Paul.
 xBouissac, Paul.
 Circus & Culture: A Semiotic Approach. Ind U
 Pr.
Boulby, Mark.
 xBoulby, Mark.
 Uwe Johnson. Ungar.
Boulden, James B.
 xBoulden, James B.
 Computer-Assisted Planning Systems:
 Management Concept, Application &
 Implementation. McGraw.
Boulder Conference on High Energy Physics, 1969.
 xBoulder Conference On High Energy Physics.
 Proceedings. Colo Assoc.
Boulding, K. E. *see* Boulding, Kenneth Ewart.
Boulding, Kenneth E. *see* Boulding, Kenneth Ewart.
Boulding, Kenneth Ewart.
 xBoulding, K. E.
 Economics As a Science. McGraw.
 xBoulding, Kenneth E.
 Ecodynamics: A New Theory of Societal
 Evolution. Sage.
 Economics of Peace. Arno.
 Economics of Pollution. NYU Pr.
 From Abundance to Scarcity: Implications for
 the American Tradition. Ohio St U Pr.
 The Image: Knowledge in Life & Society. U of
 Mich Pr.
 The Impact of the Social Sciences. Rutgers U
 Pr.
 ed. Peace & the War Industry. Transaction
 Bks.
Boulenger, George A. *see* Boulenger, George Albert.
Boulenger, George Albert, 1858-1937
 xBoulenger, George A.
 The Tailless Batrachians of Europe. Arno.
Boulestin, X. Marcel. *see* Boulestin, Xavier Marcel.
Boulestin, Xavier Marcel.
 xBoulestin, X. Marcel.
 Boulestin's Round-the-Year Cookbook. Dover.
Boulez, Pierre, 1925-
 xBoulez, Pierre.
 Boulez on Music Today. Merrimack Bk Serv.
Boulger, Demetrius C. *see* Boulger, Demetrius Charles
 De Kavanagh.
Boulger, Demetrius Charles De Kavanagh, 1853-1928
 xBoulger, Demetrius C.
 History of China. Arno.
 The History of China. Krishna Pr.
Boullata, Issa. *see* Boullata, Issa J.
Boullata, Issa J., 1929-
 xBoullata, Issa.
 ed. Modern Arab Poets, 1950-1975. Three
 Continents.
Boulle, Pierre, 1912-
 xBoulle, Pierre.

Bridge Over the River Kwai. Vanguard.
Bridge Over the River Kwai. Bantam.
Desperate Games. Vanguard.
Ears of the Jungle. Vanguard.
Executioner. Vanguard.
Garden on the Moon. Vanguard.
The Good Leviathan. Vanguard.
The Marvelous Palace & Other Stories.
   Vanguard.
Not the Glory. Manor Bks.
Not the Glory. Vanguard.
Planet of the Apes. Vanguard.
Planet of the Apes. NAL.

Boulting, William.
  xBoulting, William.
    Tasso & His Times. Haskell.
    Tasso & His Times. R West.
Boulton, Alfredo.
  xBoulton, Alfredo.
    Pissarro in Venezuela. Interbk Inc.
Boulton, Jane.
  xBoulton, Jane.
    Opal. Macmillan.
Boulton, Marjorie.
  xBoulton, Marjorie.
    The Anatomy of Drama. Routledge & Kegan.
    Anatomy of the Novel. Routledge & Kegan.
Boulton, W. H. see Boulton, William Henry.
Boulton, William Henry, 1869-
  xBoulton, W. H.
    Pageant of Transport Through the Ages. Arno.
    The Pageant of Transport Through the Ages.
      Gordon Pr.
Boulware, Lemuel R., 1895-
  xBoulware, Lemuel R.
    Truth About Boulwarism: Trying to Do Right
      Voluntarily. BNA.
Bouma, J. L.
  xBouma, J. L.
    The Avenging Gun. Belmont-Tower.
    Border Vengeance. Nordon Pubns.
    Burning Valley. Nordon Pubns.
    Longrider. Nordon Pubns.
Bouma, Jim.
  xBouma, Jim.
    The Delaware-Style Wing-T for High School
      Football. P-H.
Bouma, Mary L. see Bouma, Mary Lagrand.
Bouma, Mary La Grand. see Bouma, Mary Lagrand.
Bouma, Mary Lagrand.
  xBouma, Mary L.
    Intro. by The Creative Homemaker. Bethany
      Fell.
  xBouma, Mary La Grand.
    Divorce in the Parsonage. Bethany Fell.
Boumans, Paul W. see Boumans, Paul Willy Joseph
  Maria.
Boumans, Paul Willy Joseph Maria.
  xBoumans, Paul W.
    Theory of Spectrochemical Excitation. Plenum
      Pub.
Bounds, E. M. see Bounds, Edward M.
Bounds, Edward M.
  xBounds, E. M.
    The Necessity of Prayer. Baker Bk.
Boundy, Suzanne S. see Boundy, Suzanne Styers.
Boundy, Suzanne Styers.
  xBoundy, Suzanne S.
    ed. Current Concepts in Dental Hygiene.
      Mosby.
Bouquet, A. C. see Bouquet, Alan Coates.
Bouquet, Alan C. see Bouquet, Alan Coates.
Bouquet, Alan Coates, 1884-
  xBouquet, A. C.
    Everyday Life in New Testament Times.
      Scribner.
  xBouquet, Alan C.

The Christian Faith & Non-Christian Religions.
  Greenwood.
Bourcard, Gustave.
  xBourcard, Gustave.
    Felix Buhot Catalogue Descriptif De Son
      Oeuvre Grave. Martin Gordon.
Bourdieu, P. see Bourdieu, Pierre.
Bourdieu, Pierre.
  xBourdieu, P.
    Outline of a Theory of Practice. Cambridge U
      Pr.
Bourdon, Clinton C.
  xBourdon, Clinton C.
    Union & Open-Shop Construction:
      Compensation, Work Practices, & Labor
      Markets. Lexington Bks.
Bourdon, David.
  xBourdon, David.
    Calder: Mobilist, Ringmaster, Innovator.
      Macmillan.
Bourgeois, Andre. see Bourgeois, Andre M. G.
Bourgeois, Andre M. G., 1902-
  xBourgeois, Andre.
    Studies in French Literature. Rice Univ.
Bourgeois, E. see Bourgeois, Emile.
Bourgeois, Emile, 1857-1934
  xBourgeois, E.
    History of Modern France, 1815-1913.
      Octagon.
Bourgeois, Jacques, 1910-
  xBourgeois, Jacques.
    Animating Films Without a Camera. Sterling.
Bourget, Paul C. see Bourget, Paul Charles Joseph.
Bourget, Paul Charles Joseph, 1852-1935
  xBourget, Paul C.
    Monica & Other Stories. Arno.
Bourgin, Georges, 1879-1958
  xBourgin, Georges.
    Histoire De La Commune. AMS Pr.
Bourgoin, J. see Bourgoin, Jules.
Bourgoin, Jules, 1838-
  xBourgoin, J.
    Arabic Geometrical Pattern & Design. Dover.
    Arabic Geometrical Pattern & Design. Peter
      Smith.
Bourguignon, Erika, 1924-
  xBourguignon, Erika.
    Possession. Chandler & Sharp.
    Psychological Anthropology: An Introduction
      to Human Nature & Cultural Differences.
      HR&W.
    ed. Religion, Altered States of Consciousness,
      & Social Change. Ohio St U Pr.
    ed. A World of Women: Anthropological
      Studies of Women in the Societies of the
      World. Praeger.
Bourguignon, Henry J.
  xBourguignon, Henry J.
    The First Federal Court: The Federal Appellate
      Prize Court of the American Revolution,
      1775-1787. Am Philos.
Bourinot, J. G. see Bourinot, John George.
Bourinot, John G. see Bourinot, John George.
Bourinot, John George, Sir, 1837-1902
  xBourinot, J. G.
    Federal Government in Canada. Johnson Repr.
    Local Government in Canada: A Historical
      Study. Johnson Repr.
  xBourinot, John G.
    Federal Government in Canada. AMS Pr.
    Local Government in Canada: An Historical
      Study. AMS Pr.
Bourjaily, Vance. see Bourjaily, Vance Nye.
Bourjaily, Vance Nye.
  xBourjaily, Vance.
    Hound of Earth. Dial.
Bourke, John G. see Bourke, John Gregory.
Bourke, John Gregory, 1846-1896
  xBourke, John G.

On the Border with Crook. Greenwood.
On the Border with Crook. U of Nebr Pr.
Bourke-White, Margaret, 1905-1971
  xBourke-White, Margaret.
    Eyes on Russia. AMS Pr.
Bourne, Eulalia.
  xBourne, Eulalia.
    Nine Months Is a Year-At Baboquivari School.
      U of Ariz Pr.
    Ranch Schoolteacher. U of Ariz Pr.
Bourne, Frank C. see Bourne, Frank Card.
Bourne, Frank Card, 1914-
  xBourne, Frank C.
    History of the Romans. Heath.
Bourne, G. H. see Bourne, Geoffrey Howard.
Bourne, Geoffrey H. see Bourne, Geoffrey Howard.
Bourne, Geoffrey Howard, 1909-
  xBourne, G. H.
    ed. Human & Veterinary Nutrition. S Karger.
    ed. Human & Veterinary Nutrition,
      Biochemical Aspects of Nutrients. S Karger.
  xBourne, Geoffrey H.
    In Vivo Techniques in Histology. Krieger.
    ed. Some Aspects of Human & Veterinary
      Nutrition. S Karger.
    ed. Some Special Aspects of Nutrition. S
      Karger.
    The Structure & Function of Muscle. Acad Pr.
  xBourne, H. C.
    ed. Some Aspects of Human Nutrition. S
      Karger.
Bourne, Gordon. see Bourne, Gordon Lionel.
Bourne, Gordon Lionel.
  xBourne, Gordon.
    Pregnancy. Har-Row.
Bourne, H. C. see Bourne, Geoffrey Howard.
Bourne, Henry R. see Bourne, Henry Richard Fox.
Bourne, Henry Richard Fox, 1837-1909
  xBourne, Henry R.
    English Newspapers: Chapters in the History of
      Journalism. Russell.
Bourne, Kenneth.
  xBourne, Kenneth.
    Britain & the Balance of Power in North
      America, 1815-1908. U of Cal Pr.
Bourne, Larry S.
  xBourne, Larry S.
    ed. Systems of Cities: Readings on Structure
      Growth & Policy. Oxford U Pr.
    ed. Urban Housing Markets: Recent Directions
      in Research & Policy. U of Toronto Pr.
Bourne, Lyle E. see Bourne, Lyle Eugene.
Bourne, Lyle Eugene.
  xBourne, Lyle E.
    Cognitive Processes. P-H.
    Psychology: Its Principles & Meanings.
      HR&W.
    Psychology of Thinking. P-H.
Bourne, Miriam A. see Bourne, Miriam Anne.
Bourne, Miriam Anne.
  xBourne, Miriam A.
    Patsy Jefferson's Diary. Coward.
    Raccoons Are for Loving. Random.
    White House Children. Random.
Bourne, Peter   see Bourne, Peter G.
Bourne, Peter G.
  xBourne, Peter
    ed. Acute Drug Abuse Emergencies: A
      Treatment Manual. Acad Pr.
Bourne, Richard B.
  xBourne, Richard B.
    Artificial Insemination. Mss Info.
Bourne, William O. see Bourne, William Oland.
Bourne, William Oland.
  xBourne, William O.
    History of the Public School Society of the
      City of New York. Arno.
Bournonville, August. see Bournonville, Auguste.
Bournonville, Auguste, 1805-1879
  xBournonville, August.

My Theatre Life. Columbia U Pr.
Bouscaren, Anthony. *see* Bouscaren, Anthony Trawick.
Bouscaren, Anthony J. *see* Bouscaren, Anthony Trawick.
Bouscaren, Anthony T. *see* Bouscaren, Anthony Trawick.
Bouscaren, Anthony Trawick.
   xBouscaren, Anthony.
      Tshombe. Guild Bks.
   xBouscaren, Anthony J.
      Imperial Communism. Greenwood.
   xBouscaren, Anthony T.
      The Security Aspects of Immigration Work.
        Marquette.
      Textbook on Communism. Glencoe.
Bousfield, A. K. *see* Bousfield, Aldridge Knight.
Bousfield, Aldridge Knight.
   xBousfield, A. K.
      Homotopy Limits, Completions &
        Localizations. Springer-Verlag.
Bousquet, Georges H. *see* Bousquet, Georges Henri.
Bousquet, Georges Henri.
   xBousquet, Georges H.
      A French View of the Netherlands Indies.
        AMS Pr.
Boussard, Jacques.
   xBoussard, Jacques.
      Civilization of Charlemagne. McGraw.
Boustead, I.
   xBoustead, I.
      Handbook of Industrial Energy Analysis.
        Halsted Pr.
Boutell, Charles.
   xBoutell, Charles.
      Boutell's Heraldry. Warne.
Bouten, J. *see* Bouten, Jacob.
Bouten, Jacob.
   xBouten, J.
      Mary Wollstonecraft & the Beginnings of
        Female Emancipation in France & England.
        Gordon Pr.
   xBouten, Jacob.
      Mary Wollstonecraft & the Beginnings of
        Female Emancipation in France & England.
        Porcupine Pr.
Boutin, Otto. *see* Boutin, Otto J.
Boutin, Otto J.
   xBoutin, Otto.
      Otto's Night Watch. North Am Pub Co.
Bouton, Josephine.
   xBouton, Josephine.
      ed. Favorite Poems for the Children's Hour.
        Platt.
Boutroux, Emile.
   xBoutroux, Emile.
      Historical Studies in Philosophy. Kennikat.
Boutwell, George S. *see* Boutwell, George Sewall.
Boutwell, George Sewall, 1818-1905
   xBoutwell, George S.
      Reminiscences of Sixty Years in Public Affairs.
        Greenwood.
Bouvard, Marguerite.
   xBouvard, Marguerite.
      The Intentional Community Movement:
        Building a New Moral World. Kennikat.
Bouve, Pauline C. *see* Bouve, Pauline Carrington (Rust).
Bouve, Pauline Carrington (Rust).
   xBouve, Pauline C.
      Their Shadows Before: A Story of the
        Southampton Insurrection. Arno.
Bouwer, Herman.
   xBouwer, Herman.
      Groundwater Hydrology. McGraw.
Bouwsma, Ward D.
   xBouwsma, Ward D.
      Geometry for Teachers. Macmillan.
Bouwsma, William J. *see* Bouwsma, William James.
Bouwsma, William James, 1923-
   xBouwsma, William J.

The Culture of Renaissance Humanism. Am
    Hist Assn.
    Venice & the Defense of Republican Liberty:
      Renaissance Values in the Age of the
      Counter Reformation. U of Cal Pr.
Bouyer, L. *see* Bouyer, Louis.
Bouyer, Louis, 1913-
   xBouyer, L.
      Decomposition of Catholicism. Franciscan
        Herald.
   xBouyer, Louis.
      Liturgy & Architecture. U of Notre Dame Pr.
Bova, Ben.
   xBova, Ben.
      Colony. PB.
Bova, Ben. *see* Bova, Benjamin.
Bova, Benjamin.
   xBova, Ben.
      ed. Analog Science Fact Reader. St Martin.
      As on a Darkling Plain. Dell.
      ed. The Best of Analog. Baronet.
      End of Exile. Dutton.
      Exiled from Earth. Dutton.
      Flight of Exiles. Dutton.
      Maxwell's Demons. Baronet.
      Multiple Man. Ballantine.
      Notes to a Science Fiction Writer. Scribner.
      The Starcrossed. BJ Pub Group.
      Workshops in Space. Dutton.
Bovbjerg, Dana.
   xBovbjerg, Dana.
      The Joy of Cheesecake. Barron.
Bove, Paul A., 1949-
   xBove, Paul A.
      Destructive Poetics: Heidegger & Modern
        American Poetry. Columbia U Pr.
Bovey, Frank A. *see* Bovey, Frank Alden.
Bovey, Frank Alden, 1918-
   xBovey, Frank A.
      High Resolution NMR of Macromolecules.
        Acad Pr.
      NMR Data Tables for Organic Compounds.
        Wiley.
Bovill, E. W.
   xBovill, Edward W.
      Golden Trade of the Moors. Oxford U Pr.
Bovill, Edward W. *see* Bovill, E. W.
Bovin, Murray.
   xBovin, Murray.
      Silversmithing & Art Metal for Schools,
        Tradesmen, Craftsmen. Bovin.
Bowden, Aberdeen O. *see* Bowden, Aberdeen Orlando.
Bowden, Aberdeen Orlando, 1881-1946
   xBowden, Aberdeen O.
      Consumers Uses of Arithmetic: An
        Investigation to Determine the Actual Uses
        Made of Arithmetic in Adult Social Life.
        AMS Pr.
Bowden, Charles. *see* Bowden, Charles L.
Bowden, Charles L.
   xBowden, Charles.
      Psychopharmacology for Primary Care
        Physicians. Williams & Wilkins.
Bowden, David K.
   xBowden, David K.
      The Execution of Isaac Hayne. Sandlapper
        Store.
Bowden, Douglas M.
   xBowden, Douglas M.
      Aging in Nonhuman Primates. Van Nos
        Reinhold.
Bowden, Edwin T.
   xBowden, Edwin T.
      Themes of Henry James: A System of
        Observation Through the Visual Arts. Shoe
        String.
Bowden, Henry W. *see* Bowden, Henry Warner.
Bowden, Henry Warner.
   xBowden, Henry W.

Dictionary of American Religious Biography.
    Greenwood.
Bowden, J. J., 1927-
   xBowden, J. J.
      Spanish & Mexican Land Grants in the
        Chihuahuan Acquisition. Tex Western.
      Surveying the Texas & Pacific Land Grant
        West of the Pecos River. Tex Western.
Bowden, James, b. 1811
   xBowden, James.
      The History of the Society of Friends in
        America. Arno.
      The History of the Society of Friends in
        America. Scholarly.
Bowden, Joan. *see* Bowden, Joan Chase.
Bowden, Joan C. *see* Bowden, Joan Chase.
Bowden, Joan Chase.
   xBowden, Joan.
      Why the Tides Ebb & Flow. HM.
   xBowden, Joan C.
      The Bean Boy. Macmillan.
      Strong John. Macmillan.
Bowden, Leonard W.
   xBowden, Leonard W.
      Diffusion of the Decision to Irrigate:
        Simulation of the Spread of a New Resource
        Management Practice in the Colorado
        Northern High Plains. U Chicago Dept Geog.
Bowden, Muriel. *see* Bowden, Muriel Amanda.
Bowden, Muriel Amanda.
   xBowden, Muriel.
      A Reader's Guide to Geoffrey Chaucer.
        Octagon.
Bowden, Peter J, 1925-
   xBowden, Peter J.
      Wool Trade in Tudor & Stuart England. Biblio
        Dist.
Bowden, Robert.
   xBowden, Robert.
      Get That Picture. Amphoto.
Bowden, Robert D. *see* Bowden, Robert Douglas.
Bowden, Robert Douglas, 1889-
   xBowden, Robert D.
      In Defense of Tomorrow. Arno.
Bowden, Tom.
   xBowden, Tom.
      The Breakdown of Public Security: The Case of
        Ireland 1916-1921 & Palestine 1936-1939.
        Sage.
Bowden, Witt, 1886-
   xBowden, Witt.
      The Industrial History of the United States.
        Arden Lib.
      Industrial History of the United States. B
        Franklin.
      Industrial History of the United States. Kelley.
Bowder, Diana.
   xBowder, Diana.
      The Age of Constantine & Julian. B&N.

Bowditch, Nathaniel, 1773-1838
   xBowditch, Nathaniel.
      Bowditch's Coastal Navigation. Arco.

Bowditch, Nathaniel I. *see* Bowditch, Nathaniel Ingersoll.

Bowditch, Nathaniel Ingersoll, 1805-1861
   xBowditch, Nathaniel I.
      A History of the Massachusetts General
        Hospital to August 5, 1851. Arno.

Bowditch, Vincent Y. *see* Bowditch, Vincent Yardley.

Bowditch, Vincent Yardley, 1852-1929
   xBowditch, Vincent Y.
      Life & Correspondence of Henry Ingersoll
        Bowditch. Arno.

Bowdler, G. W.
   xBowdler, G. W.

Measurements in High-Voltage Test Circuits.
  Pergamon.
Bowe, William J. *see* Bowe, William Joseph.
Bowe, William Joseph, 1906-
  xBowe, William J.
  Estate Planning & Taxation. Irwin.
Bowen. *see* Bowen, B. A.
Bowen, Angela. *see* Bowen, Angela J. M.
Bowen, Angela J. M., 1932-
  xBowen, Angela.
  The Diabetic Gourmet. B&N.
  The Diabetic Gourmet. Har-Row.
Bowen, Anna M. *see* Bowen, Anna Maude.
Bowen, Anna Maude, d. 1900
  xBowen, Anna M.
  The Sources & Text of Richard Wagner's
    Opera "Die Meistersinger Von Nuernberg".
    AMS Pr.
Bowen, B. A.
  xBowen.
  The Logical Design of Multiple Microprocessor
    Systems. P-H.
Bowen, Barbara C.
  xBowen, Barbara C.
  Age of Bluff: Paradox & Ambiguity in Rabelais
    & Montaigne. U of Ill Pr.
Bowen, Catherine (Drinker), 1897-
  xBowen, Catherine D.
  The Lion & the Throne: The Life & Times of
    Sir Edward Coke. Little.
Bowen, Catherine D. *see* Bowen, Catherine (Drinker).
Bowen, E. J. *see* Bowen, Edmund John.
Bowen, Edmund John, 1898-
  xBowen, E. J.
  ed. Luminescence in Chemistry. Van Nos
    Reinhold.
Bowen, Elizabeth, 1899-1973
  xBowen, Elizabeth.
  Bowen's Court. Ecco Pr.
  The Death of the Heart. Avon.
  Death of the Heart. Knopf.
  The Death of the Heart. Random.
  Eva Trout or Changing Scenes. Avon.
  Good Tiger. Knopf.
  The Hotel. Avon.
  The Hotel. Greenwood.
  The House in Paris. Avon.
  The Last September. Avon.
  The Little Girls. Avon.
  A World of Love. Avon.
Bowen, Ezra.
  xBowen, Ezra.
  The High Sierra. Time-Life.
  The High Sierra. Silver.
  Hypothesis of Population Growth. AMS Pr.
Bowen, Frank M.
  xBowen, Frank M.
  Limiting State Spending: The Legislature or the
    Electorate. Inst Gov Stud Berk.
Bowen, Godfrey.
  xBowen, Godfrey.
  Wool Away: The Art & Technique of Shearing.
    Van Nos Reinhold.
Bowen, Howard. *see* Bowen, Howard Rothmann.
Bowen, Howard R. *see* Bowen, Howard Rothmann.
Bowen, Howard Rothmann, 1908-
  xBowen, Howard.
  Toward Social Economy. S Ill U Pr.
  xBowen, Howard R.
  The Business Enterprise As a Subject for
    Research. Kraus Repr.
Bowen, Ian, 1908-
  xBowen, Ian.
  Economics & Demography. Allen Unwin.
Bowen, Irene.
  xBowen, Irene.
  Suddenly - a Witch. Lippincott.
Bowen, James, 1928-
  xBowen, James.

A History of Western Education. St Martin.
  Soviet Education: Anton Makarenko & the
    Years of Experiment. U of Wis Pr.
Bowen, James K.
  xBowen, James K.
  ed. American Short Fiction: Readings &
    Criticism. Bobbs.
Bowen, John. *see* Bowen, John Langford.
Bowen, John Langford, 1916-
  xBowen, John.
  ed. Scale Model Warships. Mayflower Bks.
Bowen, K. C. *see* Bowen, Kenneth Crewdson.
Bowen, Kenneth Crewdson.
  xBowen, K. C.
  Research Games: An Approach to the Study of
    Decision Processes. Halsted Pr.
Bowen, Kernochan.
  xBowen, Kernochan.
  Four-Harness Weaving. Watson-Guptill.
Bowen, Leslie.
  xBowen, Leslie.
  The Art & Craft of Growing Orchids. Putnam.
Bowen, Marjorie, Pseud.
  xBowen, Marjorie.
  ed. Some Famous Love Letters. Folcroft.
  Sundry Great Gentlemen: Some Essays in
    Historical Biography. Arno.
Bowen, Mary E. *see* Bowen, Mary Elizabeth.
Bowen, Mary Elizabeth.
  xBowen, Mary E.
  ed. Writing About Science. Oxford U Pr.
Bowen, Michael.
  xBowen, Michael.
  Journey to Nepal. City Lights.
Bowen, R. B. *see* Bowen, Robert.
Bowen, Robert.
  xBowen, R. B.
  Ground Water. Burgess-Intl Ideas.
  xBowen, Robert.
  Geothermal Resources. Halsted Pr.
  Ground Water. Halsted Pr.
Bowen, Robert. *see* Bowen, Robert Napier Clive.
Bowen, Robert A. *see* Bowen, Robert Adger.
Bowen, Robert Adger.
  xBowen, Robert A.
  When Sweet Birds Sing. Foun Hist Rest.
Bowen, Robert Napier Clive.
  xBowen, Robert.
  Grouting in Engineering Practice. Halsted Pr.
Bowen, Robert S. *see* Bowen, Robert Sidney.
Bowen, Robert Sidney, 1900-
  xBowen, Robert S.
  Born to Fly. Abelard.
  Hot Rod Showdown. Abelard.
  Infield Flash. Lothrop.
  Lightning Southpaw. Lothrop.
Bowen, Roger.
  xBowen, Roger.
  Inga. Normandie.
Bowen, Thomas J.
  xBowen, Thomas J.
  Central Africa: Adventures & Missionary
    Labors in Several Countries in the Interior of
    Africa, from 1849-1856. Negro U Pr.
Bowen, W. G. *see* Bowen, William G.
Bowen, William G.
  xBowen, W. G.
  Economics of Labor Force Participation.
    Princeton U Pr.
Bowen, Zack. *see* Bowen, Zack R.
Bowen, Zack R.
  xBowen, Zack.
  Mary Lavin. Bucknell U Pr.
  Padraic Colum: A Biographical-Critical
    Introduction. S Ill U Pr.
Bower, Donald. *see* Bower, Donald E.
Bower, Donald E.
  xBower, Donald.

Fred Rosenstock: A Legend in Books & Art.
  Northland.
Bower, E. M. *see* Bower, Eli Michael.
Bower, Eli M. *see* Bower, Eli Michael.
Bower, Eli Michael.
  xBower, E. M.
  Early Identification of Emotionally
    Handicapped Children in School. C C
    Thomas.
  xBower, Eli M.
  Early Identification of Emotionally
    Handicapped Children in School. C C
    Thomas.
  ed. Orthopsychiatry & Education. Wayne St U
    Pr.
Bower, Fay L. *see* Bower, Fay Louise.
Bower, Fay Louise.
  xBower, Fay L.
  Fundamentals of Nursing Practice: Concepts,
    Roles & Functions. Mosby.
  Nutrition in Nursing. Wiley.
  The Process of Planning Nursing Care: A
    Model for Practice. Mosby.
Bower, James B.
  xBower, James B.
  Hospital Income Flow: A Study of the Effects
    of Source of Payment on Hospital Income.
    Mimir.
  Income Tax Procedure. SW Pub.
Bower, Joseph L.
  xBower, Joseph L.
  Public Management: Text & Cases. Irwin.
Bower, Robert T.
  xBower, Robert T.
  Ethics in Social Research: Protecting the
    Interests of Human Subjects. Praeger.
Bower, Sharon. *see* Bower, Sharon Anthony.
Bower, Sharon Anthony.
  xBower, Sharon.
  jt. auth. Asserting Yourself: A Practical Guide
    for Positive Change. A-W.
Bower, T. G. *see* Bower, T. G. R.
Bower, T. G. R., 1941-
  xBower, T. G.
  Human Development. W H Freeman.
  The Perceptual World of the Child. Harvard U
    Pr.
  A Primer of Infant Development. W H
    Freeman.
  xBower, T. G. R.
  Development in Infancy. W H Freeman.
Bower. William C. *see* Bower, William Clayton.
Bower, William Clayton.
  xBower, William C.
  ed. Church at Work in the Modern World.
    Arno.
  Living Bible. Arno.
Bowerman. *see* Bowerman, Jack W.
Bowerman, Jack W., 1938-
  xBowerman.
  Radiology & Injury in Sport. ACC.
Bowerman, Melissa.
  xBowerman, Melissa.
  Early Syntactic Development: A Cross
    Linguistic Study with Special Reference to
    Finnish. Cambridge U Pr.
Bowerman, William J.
  xBowerman, William J.
  Coaching Track & Field. HM.
Bowers, C. A.
  xBowers, C. A.
  The Progressive Educator & the Depression:
    The Radical Years. Peter Smith.
  Progressive Educator & the Depression: The
    Radical Years. Phila Bk Co.
Bowers, Claude. *see* Bowers, Claude Gernade.

Bowers, Claude Gernade, 1879-1958
  xBowers, Claude.
     Party Battles of the Jackson Period. Octagon.
Bowers, David. see Bowers, David G.
Bowers, David F. see Bowers, David Frederick.
Bowers, David Frederick.
  xBowers, David F.
     ed. Foreign Influences in American Life:
       Essays & Critical Bibliographies. Princeton U
       Pr.
Bowers, David G.
  xBowers, David.
     Systems of Organization: Management of the
       Human Resource. U of Mich Pr.
  xBowers, David G.
     Survey-Guided Development I: Data-Based
       Organizational Change. Univ Assocs.
Bowers, Edgar.
  xBowers, Edgar.
     The Form of Loss. AMS Pr.
     Living Together: New & Selected Poems.
       Godine.
Bowers, Faubion, 1917-
  xBowers, Faubion.
     Dance in India. AMS Pr.
Bowers, Fredson. see Bowers, Fredson Thayer.
Bowers, Fredson T. see Bowers, Fredson Thayer.
Bowers, Fredson Thayer.
  xBowers, Fredson.
     Textual & Literary Criticism. Cambridge U Pr.
  xBowers, Fredson T.
     Principles of Bibliographical Description.
       Russell.
Bowers, Hazel.
  xBowers, Hazel.
     Cricket Voices. Golden Quill.
Bowers, John W. see Bowers, John Waite.
Bowers, John Waite.
  xBowers, John W.
     The Rhetoric of Agitation & Control. A-W.
Bowers, John Z.
  xBowers, John Z.
     ed. Medicine & Society in China. J Macy
       Foun.
     ed. Opportunities for Philanthropy - 1976:
       Report of an International Conference. J
       Macy Foun.
Bowers, Kenneth. see Bowers, Kenneth S.
Bowers, Kenneth S.
  xBowers, Kenneth.
     Hypnosis for the Seriously Curious. Aronson.
Bowers, Malcolm B.
  xBowers, Malcolm B.
     Retreat from Sanity: The Structure of
       Emerging Psychosis. Human Sci Pr.
Bowers, Margaretta. see Bowers, Margaretta K.
Bowers, Margaretta K.
  xBowers, Margaretta.
     Counseling the Dying. Aronson.
Bowers, Melvyn K.
  xBowers, Melvyn K.
     Library Instruction in the Elementary School.
       Scarecrow.
Bowers, Michael. see Bowers, Michael T.
Bowers, Michael T.
  xBowers, Michael.
     ed. Gas Phase Ion Chemistry. Acad Pr.
Bowers, Mildred.
  xBowers, Mildred.
     Twist O' Smoke. AMS Pr.
Bowers, Nathan A. see Bowers, Nathan Abbott.
Bowers, Nathan Abbott, 1886-
  xBowers, Nathan A.
     Cone-Bearing Trees of the Pacific Coast.
       Pacific Bks.
Bowers, Pete. see Bowers, Peter M.
Bowers, Peter. see Bowers, Peter M.
Bowers, Peter M.
  xBowers, Pete.

Modern Soaring Guide. TAB Bks.
  xBowers, Peter.
     Guide to Homebuilts. TAB Bks.
  xBowers, Peter M.
     Aircraft Photo Album. Aviation.
     A Complete Guide to Aviation Photography.
       TAB Bks.
Bowers, Q. David.
  xBowers, Q. David.
     Encyclopedia of Automatic Musical
       Instruments. Vestal.
Bowers, Raymond.
  xBowers, Raymond.
     ed. Communications for a Mobile Society: An
       Assessment of New Technology. Sage.
Bowers, William L.
  xBowers, William L.
     The Country Life Movement in America.
       Kennikat.
Bowersox, Donald J.
  xBowersox, Donald J.
     Dynamic Simulation of Physical Distribution
       . Systems. Mich St U Busn.
Bowes, Frederick P. see Bowes, Frederick Patten.
Bowes, Frederick Patten, 1902-
  xBowes, Frederick P.
     The Culture of Early Charleston. Greenwood.
Bowes, Pratima.
  xBowes, Pratima.
     The Hindu Religious Tradition: A Philosophical
       Approach. Routledge & Kegan.
Bowett, D. see Bowett, D. W.
Bowett, D. W.
  xBowett, D.
     The Legal Regime of Islands in International
       Law. Sijthoff & Noordhoff.
  xBowett, Derek.
     The Legal Regime of Islands in International
       Law. Oceana.
Bowett, Derek. see Bowett, D. W.
Bowie, Donald.
  xBowie, Donald.
     Station Identification: Confessions of a Video
       Kid. M Evans.
Bowie, M. see Bowie, Malcolm.
Bowie, Malcolm.
  xBowie, M.
     Mallarme & the Art of Being Difficult.
       Cambridge U Pr.
Bowie, Norman E.
  xBowie, Norman E.
     The Individual & the Political Order: An
       Introduction to Social & Political Philosophy.
       P-H.
Bowie, Theodore. see Bowie, Theodore Robert.
Bowie, Theodore Robert.
  xBowie, Theodore.
     ed. Carrey Drawings of the Parthenon
       Sculptures. Ind U Pr.
     The Drawings of Hokusai. Greenwood.
Bowker, Albert. see Bowker, Albert Hosmer.
Bowker, Albert Hosmer.
  xBowker, Albert.
     Engineering Statistics. P-H.
Bowker, Gordon.
  xBowker, Gordon.
     ed. Race & Ethnic Relations: Sociological
       Readings. Holmes & Meier.
Bowker, John.
  xBowker, John.
     Problems of Suffering in the Religions of the
       World. Cambridge U Pr.
Bowker, John. see Bowker, John Westerdale.
Bowker, John Westerdale.
  xBowker, John.
     The Religious Imagination & the Sense of God.
       Oxford U Pr.
Bowker, Lee H. see Bowker, Lee Harrington.
Bowker, Lee Harrington.
  xBowker, Lee H.

Drug Use Among American Women, Old &
     Young: Sexual Oppression & Other Themes.
     R & E Res Assoc.
     Drug Use at a Small Liberal Arts College. R &
     E Res Assoc.
     Prisoner Subcultures. Lexington Bks.
     Prisons & Prisoners: A Bibliographic Guide. R
     & E Res Assoc.
Bowlby, John.
  xBowlby, John.
     The Making & Breaking of Affectional Bonds.
       Methuen Inc.
Bowle, John.
  xBowle, John.
     Charles I: A Biography. Little.
     Hobbes & His Critics: A Study in Seventeenth
       Century Constitutionalism. Biblio Dist.
Bowler, Arthur, 1930-
  xBowler, R. Arthur.
     Logistics & the Failure of the British Army in
       America, 1775-1783. Princeton U Pr.
Bowler, M. G.
  xBowler, M. G.
     Gravitation & Relativity. Pergamon.
Bowler, R. Arthur. see Bowler, Arthur.
Bowles, Charles, 1901-
  xBowles, Chester.
     Africa's Challenge to America. Negro U Pr.
Bowles, Chester, 1901-
  xBowles, Chester.
     Ideas, People & Peace. Greenwood.
     Promises to Keep: My Years in Public Life
       1941-1969. Har-Row.
Bowles, Chester see Bowles, Charles
Bowles, Edward A. see Bowles, Edward Augustus.
Bowles, Edward Augustus.
  xBowles, Edward A.
     My Garden in Spring. Theophrastus.
Bowles, Ella (Shannon), 1886-
  xBowles, Ella S.
     About Antiques. Gale.
     Homespun Handicrafts. Arno.
Bowles, Ella S. see Bowles, Ella (Shannon).
Bowles, Frank H. see Bowles, Frank Hamilton.
Bowles, Frank Hamilton.
  xBowles, Frank H.
     How to Get into College. Dutton.
Bowles, Gordon T. see Bowles, Gordon Townsend.
Bowles, Gordon Townsend.
  xBowles, Gordon T.
     The People of Asia. Scribner.
Bowles, John B.
  xBowles, John B.
     Distribution & Biogeography of Mammals of
       Iowa. Tex Tech Pr.
Bowles, Joseph E.
  xBowles, Joseph E.
     Physical & Geotechnical Properties of Soils.
       McGraw.
     Structural Steel Design. McGraw.
Bowles, Paul. see Bowles, Paul Frederic.
Bowles, Paul Frederic, 1911-
  xBowles, Paul.
     Hundred Camels in the Courtyard. City Lights.
     Things Gone & Things Still Here. Black
       Sparrow.
Bowles, Roger A.
  xBowles, Roger A.
     Macroeconomic Planning. Allen Unwin.
Bowles, Samuel.
  xBowles, Samuel.
     Planning Educational Systems for Economic
       Growth. Harvard U Pr.
Bowles, Stephen E., 1943-
  xBowles, Stephen E.
     ed. Index to Critical Film Reviews in British &
       American Film Periodicals. B Franklin.
Bowley, Arthur L. see Bowley, Arthur Lyon.
Bowley, Arthur Lyon.
  xBowley, Arthur L.

F. Y. Edgeworth's Contributions to
   Mathematical Statistics. Kelley.
   Some Economic Consequences of the Great
   War. Hyperion Conn.
Bowley, Marian, 1911-
   xBowley, Marian.
   Nassau Senior & Classical Economics.
      Octagon.
Bowlin, Oswald D. *see* Bowlin, Oswald Doniece.
Bowlin, Oswald Doniece.
   xBowlin, Oswald D.
   Guide to Financial Analysis. McGraw.
Bowlin, William R. *see* Bowlin, William Ray.
Bowlin, William Ray, 1881-
   xBowlin, William R.
   ed. A Book of Treasured Poems. Arno.
Bowling, Evelyn B. *see* Bowling, Evelyn Burge.
Bowling, Evelyn Burge, 1931-
   xBowling, Evelyn B.
   Voice Power. Stackpole.
Bowling, G. A. *see* Bowling, George Augustus.
Bowling, George Augustus, 1902-
   xBowling, G. A.
   A History of Ayrshire Cattle in the United
      States. McClain.
Bowly, Devereux, 1942-
   xBowly, Devereux.
   The Poorhouse: Subsidized Housing in Chicago,
      1895-1976. S Ill U Pr.
Bowman. *see* Bowman, Arthur G.
Bowman, Arthur G.
   xBowman.
   California Real Estate Principles. Goodyear.
   xBowman, Arthur G.
   California Real Estate Principles. Goodyear.
   Real Estate Law in California. P-H.
Bowman, Claude C. *see* Bowman, Claude Charleton.
Bowman, Claude Charleton, 1908-
   xBowman, Claude C.
   The College Professor in America: An Analysis
      of Articles Published in the General
      Magazines, 1890-1938. Arno.
Bowman, Frank, 1891-
   xBowman, Frank.
   Introduction to Bessel Functions. Dover.
Bowman, George E. *see* Bowman, George Ernest.
Bowman, George Ernest.
   xBowman, George E.
   The Mayflower Reader: A Selection of Articles
      from the Mayflower Descendant. Genealog
      Pub.
Bowman, George M., 1920-
   xBowman, George M.
   Clock Wise. Revell.
Bowman, George W.
   xBowman, George W.
   Talks for Children. Baker Bk.
Bowman, Gerald.
   xBowman, Gerald.
   Let's Look at Ships. A Whitman.
Bowman, Hank W. *see* Bowman, Hank Wieand.
Bowman, Hank Wieand.
   xBowman, Hank W.
   Famous Guns from the Smithsonian Collection.
      Arco.
   Famous Old Cars. Arco.
Bowman, Harold M. *see* Bowman, Harold Martin.
Bowman, Harold Martin, 1876-1949
   xBowman, Harold M.
   Administration of Iowa: A Study in
      Centralization. AMS Pr.
Bowman, Henry A. *see* Bowman, Henry Adelbert.
Bowman, Henry Adelbert, 1903-
   xBowman, Henry A.
   Marriage for Moderns. McGraw.
   Marriage for Moderns. Norwood Edns.
   Modern Marriage. McGraw.
Bowman, Isa.
   xBowman, Isa.

Lewis Carroll As I Knew Him. Dover.
Bowman, Isaiah, 1878-1950
   xBowman, Isaiah.
   Desert Trails of Atacama. AMS Pr.
   Desert Trails of Atacama. Norwood Edns.
   Design for Scholarship. Arno.
   xBowman, Isiah.
   Desert Trails of Atacama. Arden Lib.
Bowman, Isiah. *see* Bowman, Isaiah.
Bowman, J. C. *see* Bowman, John Christopher.
Bowman, James C. *see* Bowman, James Cloyd.
Bowman, James Cloyd.
   xBowman, James C.
   Tales from a Finnish Tupa. A Whitman.
Bowman, Joel P.
   xBowman, Joel P.
   Effective Business Correspondence. Har-Row.
Bowman, John, 1916-
   xBowman, John.
   The Fourth Gospel & the Jews: A Study of R.
      Akiba, Esther, & the Gospel of John.
      Pickwick.
Bowman, John Christopher.
   xBowman, J. C.
   ed. The Future of Beef Production in the
      European Community. Kluwer Boston.
Bowman, John W. *see* Bowman, John Wick.
Bowman, John Wick, 1894-
   xBowman, John W.
   Which Jesus?. Westminster.
Bowman, Larry G.
   xBowman, Larry G.
   Captive Americans: Prisoners During the
      American Revolution. Ohio U Pr.
Bowman, Larry W.
   xBowman, Larry W.
   Politics in Rhodesia: White Power in an
      African State. Harvard U Pr.
Bowman, Leonard.
   xBowman, Leonard.
   The Importance of Being Sick: A Christian
      Reflection. McGrath.
Bowman, Locke E.
   xBowman, Locke E.
   Straight Talk About Teaching in Today's
      Church. Westminster.
   Teaching Today: The Church's First Ministry.
      Westminster.
Bowman, Lynn.
   xBowman, Lynn.
   Los Angeles: Epic of a City. Howell-North.
Bowman, M. J. *see* Bowman, Malcolm J.
Bowman, Malcolm J.
   xBowman, M. J.
   ed. Oceanic Fronts in Coastal Processes:
      Proceedings of a Workshop Held at the
      Marine Science Research Center, May 25-27,
      1977. Springer-Verlag.
Bowman, W. *see* Bowman, William J.
Bowman, Ward S. *see* Bowman, Ward Simon.
Bowman, Ward Simon, 1911-
   xBowman, Ward S.
   Patent & Antitrust Law: A Legal & Economic
      Appraisal. U of Chicago Pr.
Bowman, William D. *see* Bowman, William Dodgson.
Bowman, William Dodgson.
   xBowman, William D.
   Story of Surnames. Gale.
Bowman, William J.
   xBowman, W.
   Graphic Communication. Wiley.
Bowne, Borden P. *see* Bowne, Borden Parker.
Bowne, Borden Parker, 1847-1910
   xBowne, Borden P.
   The Immanence of God. AMS Pr.
   Metaphysics.... AMS Pr.
   The Principles of Ethics. AMS Pr.
Bowne, Ford.
   xBowne, Ford.

Drygulchers. Manor Bks.
Bowra, C. M. *see* Bowra, Cecil Maurice.
Bowra, Cecil M. *see* Bowra, Cecil Maurice.
Bowra, Cecil Maurice, Sir, 1898-1971
   xBowra, C. M.
   Classical Greece. Time-Life.
   Classical Greece. Silver.
   Edith Sitwell. Haskell.
   Periclean Athens. Dial.
   xBowra, Cecil M.
   Early Greek Elegists. Cooper Sq.
   Edith Sitwell. Folcroft.
   Greek Experience. NAL.
   In General & Particular. Arno.
   Inspiration & Poetry. Arno.
   Inspiration & Poetry. Folcroft.
   Simplicity of Racine. Folcroft.
   xBowra, Maurice.
   The Simplicity of Racine. Arden Lib.
Bowra, Maurice. *see* Bowra, Cecil Maurice.
Bowring, Dave.
   xBowring, Dave.
   How to Fish Streams. Winchester Pr.
   How to Hunt. Winchester Pr.
Bowring, Mary.
   xBowring, Mary.
   The Animals Come First. S&S.
Bowron, P.
   xBowron, P.
   Active Filters for Communication &
      Instrumentation. McGraw.
Bowry, T. R.
   xBowry, T. R.
   Immunology Simplified. Oxford U Pr.
Bowser, Eileen.
   xBowser, Eileen.
   ed. Film Notes. Museum Mod Art.
Bowser, Frederick P.
   xBowser, Frederick P.
   The African Slave in Colonial Peru, 1524-1650.
      Stanford U Pr.
Bowskill. *see* Bowskill, Derek.
Bowskill, Derek.
   xBowskill.
   Acting: An Introduction. P-H.
   xBowskill, Derek.
   All About Cinema. Transatlantic.
Bowyer, Chaz.
   xBowyer, Chaz.
   Guns in the Sky: The Air Gunners of World
      War Two. Scribner.
   Sunderland at War. Intl Pubns Serv.
Bowyer, Jack.
   xBowyer, Jack.
   History of Building. Beekman Pubs.
   History of Building. Renouf.
Bowyer, John. *see* Bowyer, John Wilson.
Bowyer, John W. *see* Bowyer, John Wilson.
Bowyer, John Wilson, 1901-
   xBowyer, John.
   Celebrated Mrs. Centlivre. SBD.
   xBowyer, John W.
   Celebrated Mrs. Centlivre. Greenwood.
Bowyer, Mathew J.
   xBowyer, Mathew J.
   Collecting Americana. A S Barnes.
Box, Doris.
   xBox, Doris.
   The Church Kitchen. Broadman.
Box, George E. *see* Box, George E. P.
Box, George E. P.
   xBox, George E.
   Evolutionary Operation: A Statistical Method
      for Process Improvement. Wiley.
Box, Pelham H. *see* Box, Pelham Horton.
Box, Pelham Horton, 1898-1937
   xBox, Pelham H.
   Origins of the Paraguayan War. Russell.
Boxer, A. H.
   xBoxer, A. H.

ed. Aspects of the Australian Economy. Intl
    Schol Bk Serv.
Boxer, Baruch.
    xBoxer, Baruch.
        Ocean Shipping in the Evolution of Hong
            Kong. U Chicago Dept Geog.
Boxer, C. R. *see* Boxer, Charles Ralph.
Boxer, Charles Ralph, 1904-
    xBoxer, C. R.
        The Christian Century in Japan: 1549-1650. U
            of Cal Pr.
        The Church Militant & Iberian Expansion:
            1440-1770. Johns Hopkins.
        The Dutch in Brazil, 1624-1654. Shoe String.
Boxerman, David.
    xBoxerman, David.
        Alpha Brain Waves. Celestial Arts.
Boy Scouts of America.
    xBoy Scouts Of America.
        American Business. BSA.
        American Heritage. BSA.
        Animal Science. BSA.
        Archery. BSA.
        Architecture. BSA.
        Art. BSA.
        Astronomy. BSA.
        Athletics. BSA.
        Atomic Energy. BSA.
        Aviation. BSA.
        Basketry. BSA.
        Bear Cub Scout Book. BSA.
        Beekeeping. BSA.
        Bird Study. BSA.
        Bookbinding. BSA.
        Botany. BSA.
        Boy Scout Fieldbook. Workman Pub.
        Boy Scout Handbook. S&S.
        Camping. BSA.
        Camping Skill Book. BSA.
        Canoeing. BSA.
        Citizenship in the Community. BSA.
        Citizenship in the Nation. BSA.
        Citizenship in the World. BSA.
        Citizenship Skill Book. BSA.
        Coin Collecting. BSA.
        Communications. BSA.
        Community Living Skill Book. BSA.
        Computers. BSA.
        Consumer Buying. BSA.
        Cooking. BSA.
        Cooking Skill Book. BSA.
        Crafts for Cub Scouts. BSA.
        Cub Scout Activities. BSA.
        Cub Scout Family Book. BSA.
        Cub Scout Fun Book. BSA.
        Cub Scout Magic. BSA.
        Cub Scout Songbook. BSA.
        Cubmaster's Packbook. BSA.
        Cycling. BSA.
        Den Chief's Denbook. BSA.
        Den Leader's Book. BSA.
        Dentistry. BSA.
        Dog Care. BSA.
        Drafting. BSA.
        Ecology Workshop. BSA.
        Electricity. BSA.
        Electronics. BSA.
        Emergency Preparedness. BSA.
        Engineering. BSA.
        Environmental Science. BSA.
        Exploring Emergency Service. BSA.
        Exploring Reference Book. BSA.
        Family Living Skill Book. BSA.
        Farm Mechanics. BSA.
        Fieldbook. BSA.
        Fingerprinting. BSA.
        Firemanship. BSA.
        First Aid. BSA.
        First Aid Skill Book. BSA.
        Fish & Wildlife Management. BSA.

        Fishing. BSA.
        Food Systems. BSA.
        Forestry. BSA.
        Games for Cub Scouts. BSA.
        Gardening. BSA.
        Genealogy. BSA.
        General Science. BSA.
        Geology. BSA.
        Group Meeting Sparklers. BSA.
        Handbook for Skippers. BSA.
        Hiking. BSA.
        Home Repairs. BSA.
        Horsemanship. BSA.
        Indian Lore. BSA.
        Insect Life. BSA.
        Journalism. BSA.
        Knots & How to Tie Them. BSA.
        Landscape Architecture. BSA.
        Law. BSA.
        Leadership Corps. BSA.
        Leatherwork. BSA.
        Lifesaving. BSA.
        Machinery. BSA.
        Mammals. BSA.
        Masonry. BSA.
        Metals Engineering. BSA.
        Metalwork. BSA.
        Model Design & Building. BSA.
        Motorboating. BSA.
        Music & Bugling. BSA.
        Nature. BSA.
        Oceanography. BSA.
        Orienteering. BSA.
        Painting. BSA.
        Patrol & Troop Activities. BSA.
        Patrol & Troop Leadership. BSA.
        Personal Fitness. BSA.
        Personal Management. BSA.
        Pets. BSA.
        Photography. BSA.
        Physical Fitness Skill Book. BSA.
        Pigeon Raising. BSA.
        Pioneering. BSA.
        Plant Science. BSA.
        Plumbing. BSA.
        Pottery. BSA.
        Printing. BSA.
        Public Health. BSA.
        Public Speaking. BSA.
        Pulp & Paper. BSA.
        Rabbit Raising. BSA.
        Radio. BSA.
        Railroading. BSA.
        Reptile Study. BSA.
        Rifle & Shotgun Shooting. BSA.
        Rowing. BSA.
        Safe Boating. BSA.
        Safety. BSA.
        Salesmanship. BSA.
        Scholarship. BSA.
        Scout Songbook. BSA.
        Scouting for the Deaf. BSA.
        Scouting for the Physically Handicapped. BSA.
        Scouting for the Visually Handicapped. BSA.
        Scoutmaster's Handbook. BSA.
        Sculpture. BSA.
        Sea Explorer Advanced Seamanship
            Instructor's Guide. BSA.
        Sea Exploring Manual. BSA.
        Signaling. BSA.
        Skating. BSA.
        Skiing. BSA.
        Skits & Puppets. BSA.
        Small-Boat Sailing. BSA.
        Soil & Water Conservation. BSA.
        Space Exploration. BSA.
        Sports. BSA.
        Stamp Collecting. BSA.
        Surveying. BSA.
        Swimming. BSA.

        Textile. BSA.
        Theater. BSA.
        Traffic Safety. BSA.
        Truck Transportation. BSA.
        Veterinary Science. BSA.
        Water Skiing. BSA.
        Weather. BSA.
        Webelos Den Activities. BSA.
        Webelos Den Leader's Book. BSA.
        Webelos Scout Book. BSA.
        Wilderness Survival. BSA.
        Wolf Cub Scout Book. BSA.
        Wood Carving. BSA.
        Woodwork. BSA.
        Your Flag. BSA.
    xBoy Socuts of America.
        Chemistry. BSA.
    xBoys Scouts Of America.
        Communications Skill Book. BSA.
        Reading. BSA.
        Scouting for the Mentally Retarded. BSA.
Boy Scouts of America. Exploring Division.
    xBoy Scouts of America, Exploring Division.
        Exploring Techniques: Exploring for the
            Handicapped. BSA.
Boy Socuts of America. *see* Boy Scouts of America.
Boy's Life Magazine Editors. *see* Boy'S Life.
Boyan, A. Stephen, 1938-
    xBoyan, A. Stephen.
        ed. Constitutional Aspects of Watergate:
            Documents & Materials. Oceana.
Boyar, Jane.
    xBoyar, Jane.
        World Class. Popular Lib.
        World Class. Random.
Boyars, Carl.
    xBoyars, Carl.
        ed. Propellants Manufacture, Hazards, &
            Testing. Am Chemical.
Boyarsky, Saul.
    xBoyarsky, Saul.
        Care of the Patient with Neurogenic Bladder.
            Little.
Boyce, Byrl N.
    xBoyce, Byrl N.
        ed. Real Estate Appraisal Terminology.
            Ballinger Pub.
Boyce, Chris.
    xBoyce, Chris.
        Catchworld. Fawcett.
Boyce, George A. *see* Boyce, George Arthur.
Boyce, George Arthur.
    xBoyce, George A.
        ed. Some People Are Indians. Vanguard.
Boyce, Jefferson. *see* Boyce, Jefferson C.
Boyce, Jefferson C.
    xBoyce, Jefferson.
        Microprocessor & Microcomputer Basics. P-H.
    xBoyce, Jefferson C.
        Digital Computer Fundamentals. P-H.
    xBoyce, Jefferson D.
        Digital Logic & Switching Circuits: Operation
            & Analysis. P-H.
Boyce, Jefferson D. *see* Boyce, Jefferson C.
Boyce, John C. *see* Boyce, John G.
Boyce, John G.
    xBoyce, John C.
        Mathematics for Technical & Vocational
            Schools. Wiley.
Boyce, Mary.
    xBoyce, Mary.
        A Persian Stronghold of Zoroastrianism.
            Oxford U Pr.
Boyce, P. J. *see* Boyce, Peter.
Boyce, Peter.
    xBoyce, P. J.
        Foreign Affairs for New States: Some
            Questions of Credentials. St Martin.
Boyce, Ronald R.
    xBoyce, Ronald R.

ed. Regional Development & the Wabash
Basin. U of Ill Pr.

Boyce, Timothy J.
xBoyce, Timothy J.
Fair Representation, the NLRB, & the Courts.
Indus Res Unit-Wharton.

Boyce, Tommy.
xBoyce, Tommy.
How to Write a Hit Song & Sell It. Wilshire.

Boyce, William D.
xBoyce, William D.
Moral Reasoning: A
Psychological-Philosophical Integration. U of
Nebr Pr.

Boyce, William F. *see* Boyce, William Francis.

Boyce, William Francis, 1916-
xBoyce, William F.
Hi-Fi Stereo Handbook. Sams.

Boycott, J. A.
xBoycott, J. A.
Natural History of Infectious Disease. St
Martin.

Boyd, A. F. *see* Boyd, Alexander F.

Boyd, A. J. *see* Boyd, William Alexander Jennyns.

Boyd, Alexander F.
xBoyd, A. F.
Aspects of the Russian Novel. Rowman.

Boyd, Anne.
xBoyd, Anne.
Life in a Fifteenth Century Monastery. Lerner
Pubns.

Boyd, Bradford B.
xBoyd, Bradford B.
Management-Minded Supervision: A Self-Study
Training Program. McGraw.

Boyd, Carl.
xBoyd, Carl.
The Extraordinary Envoy: General Hiroshi
Oshima & Diplomacy in the Third Reich
1934-1939. U Pr of Amer.

Boyd, Carolyn P., 1944-
xBoyd, Carolyn P.
Praetorian Politics in Liberal Spain. U of NC
Pr.

Boyd, Doug.
xBoyd, Doug.
Swami. Random.

Boyd, E. *see* Boyd, Ernest Augustus.

Boyd, Eldon M.
xBoyd, Eldon M.
Respiratory Tract Fluid. C C Thomas.

Boyd, Elizabeth N. *see* Boyd, Elizabeth Nicely.

Boyd, Elizabeth Nicely, 1899-
xBoyd, Elizabeth N.
A Diagnostic Study of Student's Difficulties in
General Mathematics in First Year College
Work. AMS Pr.

Boyd, Ernest. *see* Boyd, Ernest Augustus.

Boyd, Ernest A. *see* Boyd, Ernest Augustus.

Boyd, Ernest Augustus, 1887-1946
xBoyd, E.
H. L. Mencken. Haskell.
xBoyd, Ernest.
H. L. Mencken. Folcroft.
Studies from Ten Literatures. Kennikat.
xBoyd, Ernest A.
Appreciations & Depreciations: Irish Literary
Studies. Arno.
Literary Blasphemies. Greenwood.
Studies from Ten Literatures. Arno.
Studies from Ten Literatures. Johnson Repr.

Boyd, Fannie L. *see* Boyd, Fannie Lee.

Boyd, Fannie Lee.
xBoyd, Fannie L.
Handbook of Consumer Education: A Guide
for Teaching Process & Content. Allyn.

Boyd, Gertrude A.
xBoyd, Gertrude A.

Linguistics in the Elementary School. Peacock
Pubs.

Boyd, Harper W.
xBoyd, Harper W.
Marketing Management. HarBraceJ.

Boyd, Harry.
xBoyd, Harry.
A Creative Approach to Controlling
Photography. Heidelberg Pubs.

Boyd, Jack.
xBoyd, Jack.
Teaching Choral Sight Reading. P-H.

Boyd, James, 1891-
xBoyd, James.
Goethe's Knowledge of English Literature.
Haskell.
Goethe's Knowledge of English Literature. R
West.

Boyd, James S.
xBoyd, James S.
Practical Farm Buildings: A Text & Handbook.
Interstate.

Boyd, John, 1935-
xBoyd, John.
Community Education & Urban Schools.
Longman.

Boyd, John R.
xBoyd, John R.
Alice Blows a Fuse: Fifty Strip Stories in
American English. P-H.

Boyd, Julian P. *see* Boyd, Julian Parks.

Boyd, Julian Parks, 1903-
xBoyd, Julian P.
Anglo-American Union: Joseph Galloway's
Plans to Preserve the British Empire,
1774-1788. Octagon.

Boyd, L. M.
xBoyd, L. M.
Boyd's Book of Odd Facts. NAL.
Boyd's Book of Odd Facts. Sterling.

Boyd, Lawrence H.
xBoyd, Lawrence H.
Contextual Analysis: Concepts & Statistical
Techniques. Wadsworth Pub.

Boyd, Lester C.
xBoyd, Lester C.
Atlantic Surf Fishing: Maine to Maryland.
Stone Wall Pr.

Boyd, Lizzie.
xBoyd, Lizzie.
ed. British Cookery: A Complete Guide to
Culinary Practice in England, Scotland,
Ireland & Wales. Overlook Pr.

Boyd, Malcolm, 1923-
xBoyd, Malcolm.
Am I Running with You, God?. G K Hall.
Human Like Me, Jesus. BJ Pub Group.

Boyd, Margaret A. *see* Boyd, Margaret Ann.

Boyd, Margaret Ann.
xBoyd, Margaret A.
Directory of Shop-by-Mail Bargain Sources.
Pilot Bks.
Where-to-Sell-It Directory. Pilot Bks.

Boyd, Melba J. *see* Boyd, Melba Joyce.

Boyd, Melba Joyce.
xBoyd, Melba J.
Cat Eyes & Dead Wood. Fallen Angel.

Boyd, Minnie C. *see* Boyd, Minnie Clare.

Boyd, Minnie Clare, 1898-
xBoyd, Minnie C.
Alabama in the Fifties: A Social Study. AMS
Pr.

Boyd, Neil. *see* Boyd, Niel.

Boyd, Niel.
xBoyd, Niel.
Bless Me, Father. Popular Lib.
Bless Me, Father. St Martin.

Boyd, R. L. *see* Boyd, R. L. F.

Boyd, R. L. F.
xBoyd, R. L.

Space Physics: The Study of Plasmas in Space.
Oxford U Pr.

Boyd, Robin.
xBoyd, Robin.
Puzzle of Architecture. Intl Schol Bk Serv.

Boyd, Shylah.
xBoyd, Shylah.
American Made. Fawcett.
American Made. FS&G.

Boyd, Steven R.
xBoyd, Steven R.
The Politics of Opposition: Antifederalists &
the Acceptance of the Constitution. Kraus
Intl.

Boyd, Theo E.
xBoyd, Theo E.
Poetic Reflections from the Dust. Herald Hse.

Boyd, Thomas A. *see* Boyd, Thomas Alvin.

Boyd, Thomas Alvin, 1888-
xBoyd, Thomas A.
Professional Amateur: The Biography of
Charles Franklin Kettering. Arno.

Boyd, Thomas H. *see* Boyd, Thomas Hulings Stockton.

Boyd, Thomas Hulings Stockton.
xBoyd, Thomas H.
History of Montgomery County, Maryland,
from Its Earliest Settlement in 1650-1879.
Regional.

Boyd, Waldo T.
xBoyd, Waldo T.
The World of Energy Storage. Putnam.

Boyd, William, 1874-
xBoyd, William.
Educational Theory of Jean Jacques Rousseau.
Russell.
The History of Western Education. B&N.
The History of Western Education. Norwood
Edns.

Boyd, William Alexander Jennyns, 1842-1928
xBoyd, A. J.
Old Colonials. Intl Schol Bk Serv.

Boyd, William C. *see* Boyd, William Clouser.

Boyd, William Clouser.
xBoyd, William C.
Races & People. Abelard.

Boyd, William K. *see* Boyd, William Kenneth.

Boyd, William Kenneth, 1879-1938
xBoyd, William K.
Some Eighteenth Century Tracts Concerning
North Carolina. Reprint.

Boyd-Bowman, Peter.
xBoyd-Bowman, Peter.
From Latin to Romance in Sound Charts.
Georgetown U Pr.

Boydston, Jo Ann.
xBoydston, Jo Ann.
ed. Checklist of Writings About John Dewey,
1887-1977. S Ill U Pr.

Boyen, J. L. *see* Boyen, John L.

Boyen, John L., 1911-
xBoyen, J. L.
Practical Heat Recovery. Wiley.

Boyer. *see* Boyer, Richard G.

Boyer, Brian. *see* Boyer, Brian D.

Boyer, Brian D.
xBoyer, Brian.
Prince of Thieves: Memoirs of the World's
Greatest Forger. Dial.

Boyer, Bruce H. *see* Boyer, Bruce Hatton.

Boyer, Bruce Hatton, 1946-
xBoyer, Bruce H.
The Solstice Cipher. Lippincott.

Boyer, Calvin J., 1939-
xBoyer, Calvin J.
The Doctoral Dissertation As an Information
Source: A Study of Scientific Information
Flow. Scarecrow.

Boyer, Carl B. *see* Boyer, Carl Benjamin.

Boyer, Carl Benjamin, 1906-
xBoyer, Carl B.

Introduction to the Short Story. Hayden.
Sounds & Silences: Poems for Performing.
    Hayden.

Boynton, Sandra.
    xBoynton, Sandra.
    Gopher Baroque, & Other Beastly Conceits.
        Dutton.
    Hester in the Wild. Har-Row.
    illus. Hester in the Wild. Har-Row.
    Hippos Go Berserk. Little.
    illus. If at First.... Little.
Boys Scouts Of America. *see* Boy Scouts of America.
Boys' Clubs of America.
    xBoys' Clubs of America.
    Alcohol Abuse Prevention: A Comprehensive
        Guide for Youth Organization. Boys Clubs.
Boy'S Life.
    xBoy's Life Magazine Editors.
    ed. Best Jokes from Boys' Life. Putnam.
    xBoys' Life Magazine Editors.
    Boys' Life Book of Outer Space Stories.
        Random.
    Boys' Life Book of World War Two Stories.
        Random.
Boys' Life Magazine Editors. *see* Boy'S Life.
Boytinck, Paul. *see* Boytinck, Paul W.
Boytinck, Paul W.
    xBoytinck, Paul.
    C. P. Snow: A Reference Guide. G K Hall.
Bozak, Richard E.
    xBozak, Richard E.
    Solving Organic Chemistry Problems. Merrill.
Bozarth-Campbell, Alla, 1947-
    xBozarth-Campbell, Alla.
    Womanpriest: A Personal Odyssey. Wisdom
        House.
Bozeman, Adda B. *see* Bozeman, Adda Bruemmer.
Bozeman, Adda Bruemmer, 1908-
    xBozeman, Adda B.
    Future of Law in a Multicultural World.
        Princeton U Pr.
Bozeman, Barry.
    xBozeman, Barry.
    Public Management & Policy Analysis. St
        Martin.
Bozeman, Theodore D. *see* Bozeman, Theodore Dwight.
Bozeman, Theodore Dwight, 1942-
    xBozeman, Theodore D.
    Protestants in an Age of Science: Baconian
        Ideal & Antebellum American Religious
        Thought. U of NC Pr.
Braaten, Carl E., 1929-
    xBraaten, Carl E.
    The Flaming Center: A Theology of the
        Christian Mission. Fortress.
Brabazon, Francis.
    xBrabazon, Francis.
    The Word at World's End. Meher Baba Info.
Brabb, George. *see* Brabb, George Jacob.
Brabb, George Jacob, 1925-
    xBrabb, George.
    Computers & Information Systems in Business.
        HM.
Brabec, Barbara.
    xBrabec, Barbara.
    Creative Cash: How to Sell Your Crafts,
        Needlework, Designs, & Know-How.
        Countryside Bks.
Brace, Beverly W. *see* Brace, Beverly Waltmire.
Brace, Beverly Waltmire, 1924-
    xBrace, Beverly W.
    Humboldt Years: 1930-39. B W Brace.
Brace, C. L. *see* Brace, C. Loring.
Brace, C. Loring.
    xBrace, C. L.
    Atlas of Human Evolution. HR&W.
Brace, G. *see* Brace, Geoffrey.
Brace, Geoffrey.
    xBrace, G.

Listen! Music & Nature. Cambridge U Pr.
Brace, Gerald W. *see* Brace, Gerald Warner.
Brace, Gerald Warner, 1901-
    xBrace, Gerald W.
    Days That Were. Norton.
    The Stuff of Fiction. Norton.
Brace, Richard M. *see* Brace, Richard Munthe.
Brace, Richard Munthe, 1915-
    xBrace, Richard M.
    Bordeaux & the Gironde, 1789-1794. Russell.
Bracegirdle, Brian.
    xBracegirdle, Brian.
    The Archaeology of the Industrial Revolution.
        Fairleigh Dickinson.
    An Atlas of Chordate Structure. Heinemann
        Ed.
    Thomas Telford. David & Charles.
Bracewell, R. *see* Bracewell, Ronald Newbold.
Bracewell, Ronald N. *see* Bracewell, Ronald Newbold.
Bracewell, Ronald Newbold, 1921-
    xBracewell, R.
    The Fourier Transform & Its Applications.
        McGraw.
    xBracewell, Ronald N.
    The Galactic Club: Intelligent Life in Outer
        Space. Norton.
    The Galactic Club: Intelligent Life in Outer
        Space. SF Bk Co.
Bracey, H. E.
    xBracey, Howard E.
    In Retirement: Pensioners in Great Britain &
        the United States. La State U Pr.
    Neighbours: Subdivision Life in England & the
        United States. La State U Pr.
Bracey, Howard E. *see* Bracey, H. E.
Bracey, Robert, 1870-
    xBracey, Robert.
    Eighteenth Century Studies & Other Papers.
        Folcroft.
Brachet, J. *see* Brachet, Jean.
Brachet, Jean.
    xBrachet, J.
    Introduction to Molecular Embryology.
        Springer-Verlag.
    xBrachet, Jean.
    Chemical Embryology. Hafner.
Bracht, Neil F.
    xBracht, Neil F.
    Social Work in Health Care: A Guide to
        Professional Practice. Haworth Pr.
Bracken, Joseph A.
    xBracken, Joseph A.
    What Are They Saying About the Trinity?.
        Paulist Pr.
Bracken, Peg.
    xBracken, Peg.
    The I Hate to Cook Almanack: A Book of
        Days. HarBraceJ.
Brackenridge, Celia.
    xBrackenridge, Celia.
    Women's Lacrosse. Barron.
Brackenridge, Hugh H. *see* Brackenridge, Hugh Henry.
Brackenridge, Hugh Henry.
    xBrackenridge, Hugh H.
    Father Bombo's Pilgrimage to Mecca, 1770.
        Princeton Lib.
Brackenridge, R. Douglas.
    xBrackenridge, R. Douglas.
    Iglesia Presbiteriana: A History of
        Presbyterians & Mexican Americans in the
        Southwest. Trinity U Pr.
Brackett, Jeffrey R. *see* Brackett, Jeffrey Richardson.
Brackett, Jeffrey Richardson, 1860-1949
    xBrackett, Jeffrey R.
    The Negro in Maryland: A Study of the
        Institution of Slavery. AMS Pr.
    Negro in Maryland: A Study of the Institution
        of Slavery. Negro U Pr.
Brackett, Leigh.
    xBrackett, Leigh.

The Coming of the Terrans. Ace Bks.
The Long Tomorrow. Ballantine.
The Sword of Rhiannon. Ace Bks.
Sword of Rhiannon. Gregg.
Brackman, Arnold. *see* Brackman, Arnold C.
Brackman, Arnold C.
    xBrackman, Arnold.
    The Search for the Gold of Tutankhamen. Van
        Nos Reinhold.
    xBrackman, Arnold C.
    A Delicate Arrangement: Untold Story of the
        Darwinian Conspiracy. Times Bks.
    Indonesian Communism: A History.
        Greenwood.
    The Search for the Gold of Tutankhamen. PB.
Brada, Josef C.
    xBrada, Josef C.
    Pref. by East-West Trade: Theory & Evidence.
        Intl Development.
Bradac, G. B.
    xBradac, G. B.
    Angiography in Cerebro-Arterial Occlusive
        Diseases: Including Computer Tomography &
        Radionuclide Methods. Springer-Verlag.
Bradbrook, Muriel C. *see* Bradbrook, Muriel Clara.
Bradbrook, Muriel Clara.
    xBradbrook, Muriel C.
    The Growth & Structure of Elizabethan
        Comedy. Cambridge U Pr.
    Growth & Structure of Elizabethan Comedy.
        Humanities.
    Themes & Conventions of Elizabethan
        Tragedy. Cambridge U Pr.
Bradburn, Norman M.
    xBradburn, Norman M.
    Racial Integration in American Neighborhoods:
        A Comparative Study. NORC.
    Structure of Psychological Well-Being. NORC.
Bradbury, Bianca.
    xBradbury, Bianca.
    Boy on the Run. HM.
    I'm Vinny, I'm Me. HM.
    In Her Father's Footsteps. HM.
    Mixed-up Summer. HM.
    Mutt. HM.
    Mutt. HM.
    Those Traver Kids. HM.
    Two on an Island. HM.
    Where's Jim Now. HM.
Bradbury, Dorothy E. *see* Bradbury, Dorothy Edith.
Bradbury, Dorothy Edith.
    xBradbury, Dorothy E.
    Some Principles of Good Writing & the Library
        Search. Natl Assn Soc Wkrs.
Bradbury, Farel.
    xBradbury, Farel.
    Hydraulic Systems & Maintenance.
        Transatlantic.
Bradbury, J. Platt. *see* Bradbury, John Platt.
Bradbury, John Platt.
    xBradbury, J. Platt.
    Diatom Stratigraphy & Human Settlement in
        Minnesota. Geol Soc.
Bradbury, Malcolm.
    xBradbury, Malcolm.
    ed. The Contemporary English Novel. Holmes
        & Meier.
Bradbury, Michael.
    xBradbury, Michael.
    The Concept of a Blood-Brain Barrier. Wiley.
Bradbury, Ray, 1920-
    xBradbury, Ray.

Golden Apples of the Sun. Greenwood.
Golden Apples of the Sun. Bantam.
The Halloween Tree. Knopf.
The Halloween Tree. Bantam.
Illustrated Man. Doubleday.
Illustrated Man. Bantam.
Long After Midnight. Bantam.
Long After Midnight. Knopf.
Mars & the Mind of Man. Har-Row.
The Martian Chronicles. Doubleday.
The Martian Chronicles. Doubleday.
Martian Chronicles. Bantam.
A Medicine for Melancholy. Bantam.
R Is for Rocket. Doubleday.
R Is for Rocket. Bantam.
Switch on the Night. Pantheon.
Where Robot Mice & Robot Men Run Round
in Robot Towns. Knopf.
Bradbury, Ted C. see Bradbury, Ted Clay.
Bradbury, Ted Clay, 1932-
xBradbury, Ted C.
Theoretical Mechanics. Krieger.
Bradbury, Wilbur.
xBradbury, Wilbur.
The Adult Years. Silver.
Bradbury, William C. see Bradbury, William Chapman.
Bradbury, William Chapman.
xBradbury, William C.
Mass Behavior in Battle & Captivity: The
Communist Soldier in the Korean War. U of
Chicago Pr.
Bradby, David.
xBradby, David.
People's Theatre. Rowman.
Bradby, G. F. see Bradby, Godfrey Fox.
Bradby, Godfrey F. see Bradby, Godfrey Fox.
Bradby, Godfrey Fox, 1863-1947
xBradby, G. F.
About Shakespeare & His Plays. Haskell.
About Shakespeare & His Plays. Norwood
Edns.
xBradby, Godfrey F.
About English Poetry. Folcroft.
About English Poetry. R West.
Brontes, & Other Essays. Arno.
Braddick, Henderson B., 1920-
xBraddick, Henderson B.
Germany, Czechoslovakia, & the "Grand
Alliance" in the May Crisis, 1938. U of
Denver Intl.
Braddock, Ellsworth C.
xBraddock, Ellsworth C.
Memories of North Carver Village. Channing
Bks.
Braddon, Russell.
xBraddon, Russell.
All the Queen's Men: The Household Cavalry
& the Brigade of Guards. Hippocrene Bks.
The Thirteenth Trick. Norton.
Braddy, Haldeen, 1908-
xBraddy, Haldeen.
Chaucer & the French Poet Graunson.
Kennikat.
Hamlet's Wounded Name. Humanities.
The Paradox of Pancho Villa. Tex Western.
Bradeen, Donald W. see Bradeen, Donald William.
Bradeen, Donald William, 1918-1973
xBradeen, Donald W.
Inscriptions: The Funerary Monuments. Am
Sch Athens.
Studies in Fifth-Century Attic Epigraphy. U of
Okla Pr.
Braden, C. S. see Braden, Charles Samuel.
Braden, Charles S. see Braden, Charles Samuel.
Braden, Charles Samuel, 1887-
xBraden, C. S.
Religious Aspects of the Conquest of Mexico.
Gordon Pr.
xBraden, Charles S.

Christian Science Today: Power, Policy,
Practice. SMU Press.
Religious Aspects of the Conquest of Mexico.
AMS Pr.
Braden, Gordon, 1947-
xBraden, Gordon.
The Classics & English Renaissance Poetry:
Three Case Studies. Yale U Pr.
Braden, Spruille, 1953-
xBraden, Spruille.
Graphic Standards of Solar Energy. CBI Pub.
Successful Solar Energy Solutions. Van Nos
Reinhold.
Braden, Su.
xBraden, Su.
Artists & People. Routledge & Kegan.
Braden, Waldo W. see Braden, Waldo Warder.
Braden, Waldo Warder, 1911-
xBraden, Waldo W.
ed. Oratory in the New South. La State U Pr.
Bradfield, Maitland.
xBradfield, Richard M.
Natural History of Associations: A Study in
the Meaning of Community. Intl Univs Pr.
Bradfield, Richard M. see Bradfield, Maitland.
Bradford, Barbara. see Bradford, Barbara Taylor.
Bradford, Barbara T. see Bradford, Barbara Taylor.
Bradford, Barbara Taylor, 1933-
xBradford, Barbara.
How to Solve Your Decorating Problems. S&S.
xBradford, Barbara T.
Making Space Grow. S&S.
A Woman of Substance. Avon.
xBradford, Barbara Taylor.
A Woman of Substance. Doubleday.
Bradford, Gamaliel, 1863-1932
xBradford, Gamaliel.
Daughters of Eve. Kennikat.
Portraits & Personalities. Arno.
Portraits of Women. Arno.
A Prophet of Joy. Arno.
Quick & the Dead. Kennikat.
Soul of Samuel Pepys. Kennikat.
Soul of Samuel Pepys. R West.
Bradford, J. Allyn.
xBradford, J. Allyn.
Transactional Awareness: Now I've Got You
in Business. A-W.
Bradford, Larry J.
xBradford, Larry J.
ed. Hearing & Hearing Impairment. Grune.
Bradford, Leland P. see Bradford, Leland Powers.
Bradford, Leland Powers, 1905-
xBradford, Leland P.
ed. Group Development. Univ Assocs.
ed. T-Group Theory & Laboratory Method:
Innovation in Re-Education. Wiley.
Bradford, Robert, 1916-
xBradford, Robert.
Mathematics for Carpenters. Delmar.
Bradford, Samuel C. see Bradford, Samuel Clement.
Bradford, Samuel Clement, 1878-1948
xBradford, Samuel C.
Documentation. Pub Aff Pr.
Bradford, Sax. see Bradford, Saxton E.
Bradford, Saxton E., 1907-
xBradford, Sax.
Spain in the World. Van Nos Reinhold.
Bradford, William, 1588-1657
xBradford, William.
History of Plymouth Plantation, 1620-1647.
Russell.
Brading, D. A.
xBrading, D. A.
Haciendas & Ranchos in the Mexican Bajio
Leon 1700-1860. Cambridge U Pr.
Bradlee, Ben.
xBradlee, Ben.

The Ambush Murders: The True Account of
the Killing of Two California Policemen.
Dodd.
Bradlee, Benjamin.
xBradlee, Benjamin C.
Conversations with Kennedy. Norton.
Bradlee, Benjamin C. see Bradlee, Benjamin.
Bradley, A. C. see Bradley, Andrew Cecil.
Bradley, A. G. see Bradley, Arthur Granville.
Bradley, Alfred.
xBradley, Alfred.
Paddington on Stage. Dell.
Paddington on Stage. HM.
Bradley, Amos D. see Bradley, Amos Day.
Bradley, Amos Day, 1905-
xBradley, Amos D.
A Geometry of Repeating Design & Geometry
of Design for High Schools. AMS Pr.
Bradley, Andrew C. see Bradley, Andrew Cecil.
Bradley, Andrew Cecil, 1851-1935
xBradley, A. C.
The Reaction Against Tennyson. Gordon Pr.
xBradley, Andrew C.
Coriolanus. Folcroft.
English Poetry & German Philosophy in the
Age of Wordsworth. Folcroft.
The Reaction Against Tennyson. Arden Lib.
Bradley, Anthony, 1942-
xBradley, Anthony.
William Butler Yeats. Ungar.
Bradley, Ardyth.
xBradley, Ardyth.
Inside the Bones Is Flesh. SBD.
Bradley, Arthur Granville, 1850-1943
xBradley, A. G.
Fight with France for North America. Arno.
Bradley, Bill. see Bradley, William Warren.
Bradley, Buff.
xBradley, Buff.
Endings: A Book About Death. A-W.
Bradley, C. J. see Bradley, Christopher John.
Bradley, Carol J. see Bradley, Carol June.
Bradley, Carol June.
xBradley, Carol J.
ed. Reader in Music Librarianship. IHS-PDS.
Bradley, Carolyn G. see Bradley, Carolyn Gertrude.
Bradley, Carolyn Gertrude.
xBradley, Carolyn G.
Western World Costume: An Outline History.
P-H.
Bradley, Christopher John.
xBradley, C. J.
The Mathematical Theory of Symmetry in
Solids: Representation Theory for Point
Groups & Space Groups. Oxford U Pr.
Bradley, D. C.
xBradley, D. C.
Metal Alkoxides. Acad Pr.
Bradley, David, 1950-
xBradley, David.
South Street. NAL.
Bradley, David G.
xBradley, David G.
Guide to the World's Religions. P-H.
Bradley, Donald M.
xBradley, Matt.
Matt Bradley's Arkansas. Rose Pub.
Bradley, Edward, 1827-1889
xBradley, Edward.
The White Wife, with Other Stories
Supernatural, Romantic, & Legendary.
Folcroft.
Bradley, Edward S. see Bradley, Edward Sculley.
Bradley, Edward Sculley, 1897-
xBradley, Edward S.

America's Horses & Ponies. HM.
illus. America's Horses & Ponies. HM.
illus. Doodlebug. HM.
Brady, J. M.
xBrady, J. M.
The Theory of Computer Science: A
Programming Approach. Methuen Inc.
Brady, James, 1928-
xBrady, James.
Nielsen's Children. Berkley Pub.
Nielsen's Children. Putnam.
Brady, James E.
xBrady, James E.
General Chemistry: Principles & Structure.
Wiley.
Brady, John, 1934-
xBrady.
Biological Clocks. Univ Park.
Brady, John P. *see* Brady, John Paul.
Brady, John Paul.
xBrady, John P.
Classics of American Psychiatry (1810-1934).
Green.
ed. Controversy in Psychiatry. Saunders.
Brady, Leo.
xBrady, Leo.
The Love Tap. Popular Lib.
Brady, M. Michael.
xBrady, Michael.
Cross-Country Ski Gear. Mountaineers.
Brady, M. Rosalie. *see* Brady, Mary Rosalie.
Brady, Mari.
xBrady, Mari.
Please Remember Me. Doubleday.
Please Remember Me. PB.
Please Remember Me. Archway.
Brady, Mary Rosalie, Sister, 1911-
xBrady, M. Rosalie.
Thought & Style in the Works of Leon Bloy.
AMS Pr.
Brady, Maureen.
xBrady, Maureen.
Give Me Your Good Ear. Spinsters Ink.
Brady, Michael. *see* Brady, M. Michael.
Brady, Nicholas.
xBrady, Nicholas.
Bad Guy. Belmont-Tower.
The Homecoming. Belmont-Tower.
Inside Job. Nordon Pubns.
Brady, Nyle C.
xBrady, Nyle C.
The Nature & Properties of Soils. Macmillan.
Brady, Robert A. *see* Brady, Robert Alexander.
Brady, Robert Alexander, 1901-
xBrady, Robert A.
Business As a System of Power. Arno.
Spirit & Structure of German Fascism. Citadel
Pr.
The Spirit & Structure of German Fascism.
Dynamic Learn Corp.
The Spirit & Structure of German Fascism.
Fertig.
Brady, Sheila.
xBrady, Shiela.
Memoirs of an Ex-Porno Queen. PB.
Brady, Shiela. *see* Brady, Sheila.
Brady, Terence.
xBrady, Terence.
The Fight Against Slavery. Norton.
Braeman, John.
xBraeman, John.
ed. Twentieth-Century American Foreign
Policy. Ohio St U Pr.
Braeman, Shirley. *see* Braeman, Shirley W.
Braeman, Shirley W.
xBraeman, Shirley.
Fold, Tie, Dip & Dye. Lerner Pubns.
Braemer, Alice.
xBraemer, Alice.

Cultism to Charisma: My Seven Years with
Jeane Dixon. Exposition.
Braestrup, Peter.
xBraestrup, Peter.
Big Story: How the American Press &
Television Reported & Interpreted the Crises
of Tet 1968 in Vietnam & Washington.
Westview.
Braga, Joseph.
xBraga, Joseph.
Children & Adults: Activities for Growing
Together. P-H.
Braga, Laurie.
xBraga, Laurie.
Learning & Growing: A Guide to Child
Development. P-H.
Bragaw, Louis K.
xBragaw, Louis K.
The Challenge of Deepwater Terminals.
Lexington Bks.
Bragdon, Claude. *see* Bragdon, Claude Fayette.
Bragdon, Claude Fayette, 1866-1946
xBragdon, Claude.
The Arch Lectures: Eighteen Discourses on a
Great Variety of Subjects. Core Collection.
Architecture & Democracy. Gordon Pr.
Bragdon, Clifford R.
xBragdon, Clifford R.
ed. Noise Pollution: A Guide to Information
Sources. Gale.
Brager, George A.
xBrager, George A.
ed. Community Action Against Poverty:
Readings from the Mobilization Experience.
Coll & U Pr.
Bragg, Bette.
xBragg, Bette J.
Bragg About Your House. Branden.
Bragg, Bette J. *see* Bragg, Bette.
Bragg, Emma W.
xBragg, Emma W.
Background Factors: A Study of Work
Motivation Attitudes of Urban & Rural
Apparel Workers in Tennessee. Univ
Microfilms.
The Prediction of Job Behavior from Attitudes
of Work Motivation & Demographic
Characteristics Among Apparel Workers: A
Summary. Univ Microfilms.
A Profile of Work Motivation Attitudes of
Apparel Workers. Univ Microfilms.
The Relationship Between Work Motivation
Attitudes & Demographic Characteristics
Among Apparel Workers: A Summary. Univ
Microfilms.
Bragg, Gordon M., 1939-
xBragg, Gordon M.
Principles of Experimentation & Measurement.
P-H.
Bragg, Paul C. *see* Bragg, Paul Chappuis.
Bragg, Paul Chappuis.
xBragg, Paul C.
Building Powerful Nerve Force. Health Sci.
Golden Keys to Internal Physical Fitness.
Health Sci.
How to Keep the Heart Healthy Fit. Health
Sci.
Bragin, Joan.
xBragin, Joan.
The Weekend Connoisseur: The Antique
Collector's Guide to the Best in Antiquing,
Dining, Regional Museums & Just Plain
Lovely Things to Do When Touring.
Doubleday.
Bragstad, Paul.
xBragstad, Paul.
The Family of Runners. Paddington.
Braham, Randolph L.
xBraham, Randolph L.

The Hungarian Labor Service System,
1939-1945. East Eur Quarterly.
Braham, Raymond L.
xBraham, Raymond L.
Textbook of Pediatric Dentistry. Williams &
Wilkins.
Braibanti, Ralph J. *see* Braibanti, Ralph J. D.
Braibanti, Ralph J. D.
xBraibanti, Ralph J.
ed. Asian Bureaucratic Systems Emergent from
the British Imperial Tradition. Duke.
Braider, Donald, 1923-
xBraider, Donald.
The Life, History & Magic of the Horse. G&D.
Braidwood, Robert J. *see* Braidwood, Robert John.
Braidwood, Robert John, 1907-
xBraidwood, Robert J.
Prehistoric Men. Scott F.
Brain. *see* Brain, Joseph D.
Brain, Joseph D.
xBrain.
Respiratory Defense Mechanisms. Dekker.
Brain, Peter J.
xBrain, Peter J.
Population, Immigration & the Australian
Economy. Biblio Dist.
Brain, Robert.
xBrain, Robert.
Bangwa Kinship & Marriage. Cambridge U Pr.
Friends & Lovers. Basic.
Friends & Lovers. PB.
Brainard, Joe, 1942-
xBrainard, Joe.
I Remember. Full Court NY.
Brainard, John B.
xBrainard, John B.
Control of Migraine. Norton.
Braine, John.
xBraine, John.
J. B. Priestley. B&N.
Life at the Top. Methuen Inc.
Room at the Top. Methuen Inc.
Waiting for Sheila. Methuen Inc.
Brainerd, Charles J.
xBrainerd, Charles J.
The Origins of the Number Concept. Praeger.
Brainerd, George W. *see* Brainerd, George Walton.
Brainerd, George Walton, 1909-
xBrainerd, George W.
The Maya Civilization. AMS Pr.
The Maya Civilization. Southwest Mus.
Brainerd, John W., 1918-
xBrainerd, John W.
Working with Nature: A Practical Guide.
Oxford U Pr.
Brainerd, Walter S.
xBrainerd, Walter S.
Introduction to Computer Programming.
Har-Row.
Theory of Computation. Wiley.
Brainina, K. Z. *see* Brainina, Khena Zalmanovna.
Brainina, Khena Zalmanovna.
xBrainina, K. Z.
Stripping Voltammetry in Chemical Analysis.
Halsted Pr.
Braithwaite, Henry W. *see* Braithwaite, Henry Warwick.
Braithwaite, Henry Warwick, 1896-1971
xBraithwaite, Henry W.
The Conductor's Art. Greenwood.
Braithwaite, John, 1700?-1768?
xBraithwaite, John.
History of the Revolutions in the Empire of
Morocco, Upon the Death of the Late
Emperor, Muley Ishmael. Arno.
Inequality, Crime & Public Policy. Routledge &
Kegan.
Braithwaite, Lee F.
xBraithwaite, Lee F.

Graptolites from the Lower Ordovician
Pogonip Group of Western Utah. Geol Soc.
Braithwaite, William T. *see* Braithwaite, William Thomas.
Braithwaite, William Thomas.
xBraithwaite, William T.
Who Judges the Judges?: A Study of
Procedures for Removal & Retirement. Am
Bar Foun.
Brake, J. R. *see* Brake, John R.
Brake, John R.
xBrake, J. R.
ed. Farm & Personal Finance. Interstate.
Brake, Mike.
xBrake, Mike.
The Sociology of Youth Culture & Youth
Subcultures. Routledge & Kegan.
Braker, Ulrich, 1735-1798
xBraker, Ulrich.
A Few Words About William Shakespeare's
Plays. Ungar.
Braly, Malcolm, 1925-
xBraly, Malcolm.
On the Yard. Penguin.
xBraly, Malcom.
Felony Tank. PB.
Braly, Malcom. *see* Braly, Malcolm.
Bram, Elizabeth.
xBram, Elizabeth.
illus. A Dinosaur Is Too Big. Greenwillow.
illus. I Don't Want to Go to School.
Greenwillow.
One Day I Closed My Eyes & the World
Disappeared. Dial.
illus. There Is Someone Standing on My Head.
Dial.
illus. Woodruff & the Clocks. Dial.
Brambell Symposium.
xBrambell Symposium 2nd, Wales, July 1978.
Protein Transmission Through Living
Membranes: Proceedings. Elsevier.
Brambell Symposium 2nd, Wales, July 1978. *see*
Brambell Symposium.
Bramble, Forbes, 1939-
xBramble, Forbes.
Regent Square. PB.
Bramblett, Claud A.
xBramblett, Claud A.
Patterns of Primate Behavior. Mayfield Pub.
Brame, Edward G. *see* Brame, Edward Grant.
Brame, Edward Grant, 1927-
xBrame, Edward G.
ed. Applications of Polymer Spectroscopy.
Acad Pr.
Brame, Michael K., 1944-
xBrame, Michael K.
Base Generated Syntax. Noit Amrofer.
ed. Contributions to Generative Phonology. U
of Tex Pr.
Brameld, Theodore B. *see* Brameld, Theodore Burghard
Hurt.
Brameld, Theodore Burghard Hurt, 1904-
xBrameld, Theodore B.
Ends & Means in Education: A Midcentury
Appraisal. Greenwood.
Bramhall, John, Abp. of Armagh, 1594-1663
xBramhall, John.
Castigations of Mr. Hobbes. Garland Pub.
Bramley, G. A. *see* Bramley, Gerald.
Bramley, Gerald.
xBramley, G. A.
History of Library Education. Shoe String.
xBramley, Gerald.
World Trends in Library Education. Shoe
String.
Bramly, Serge, 1949-
xBramly, Serge.

Macumba: The Teachings of Maria-Jose,
Mother of the Gods. Avon.
Macumba: The Teachings of Maria Jose,
Mother of the Gods. St Martin.
Brammer, Lawrence M.
xBrammer, Lawrence M.
The Helping Relationship: Process & Skills.
P-H.
Brams, Steven J.
xBrams, Steven J.
Biblical Games: Strategic Analysis of Stories in
the Old Testament. MIT Pr.
Game Theory & Politics. Free Pr.
Paradoxes in Politics: An Introduction to the
Nonobvious in Political Science. Free Pr.
The Presidential Election Game. Yale U Pr.
Brams, William A. *see* Brams, William Alexander.
Brams, William Alexander, 1890-
xBrams, William A.
Living with Your High Blood Pressure. Arco.
Bramscher, Cynthia S., 1948-
xBramscher, Cynthia S.
Treasury of Musical Motivators for the
Elementary Classroom. P-H.
Bramsted, Ernest. *see* Bramsted, Ernest Kohn.
Bramsted, Ernest Kohn.
xBramsted, Ernest.
Aristocracy & the Middle-Classes in Germany:
Social Types in German Literature,
1830-1900. U of Chicago Pr.
Bramstedt, Wayne G.
xBramstedt, Wayne G.
Intro. by North American Indians in Towns &
Cities: A Bibliography. Vance Biblios.
Branam, George C. *see* Branam, George Curtis.
Branam, George Curtis, 1923-
xBranam, George C.
Eighteenth-Century Adaptations of
Shakespearean Tragedy. Folcroft.
Eighteenth-Century Adaptations of
Shakespearean Tragedy. Norwood Edns.
Branan, Carl.
xBranan, Carl.
The Fractionator Analysis Pocket Handbook.
Gulf Pub.
xBranan, Carl R.
Process Engineer's Pocket Handbook. Gulf
Pub.
Branan, Carl R. *see* Branan, Carl.
Brancato, Robin. *see* Brancato, Robin F.
Brancato, Robin F.
xBrancato, Robin.
Blinded by the Light. Knopf.
Something Left to Lose. Bantam.
Something Left to Lose. Knopf.
xBrancato, Robin F.
Blinded by the Light. Bantam.
Come Alive at 505. Knopf.
Don't Sit Under the Apple Tree. Bantam.
Don't Sit Under the Apple Tree. Knopf.
Brancazio, Peter J.
xBrancazio, Peter J.
The Nature of Physics. Macmillan.
Branch, Alan E.
xBranch, Alan E.
Elements of Export Practice. Methuen Inc.
Branch, Ben, 1943-
xBranch, Ben.
Fundamentals of Investing. Wiley.
Branch, E. Douglas. *see* Branch, Edward Douglas.
Branch, Edward Douglas, 1905-1954
xBranch, E. Douglas.
Hunting of the Buffalo. U of Nebr Pr.
Branch, Melville C. *see* Branch, Melville Campbell.
Branch, Melville Campbell, 1913-
xBranch, Melville C.
Planning Urban Environment. DH&R.
Branchaw, Bernadine P.
xBranchaw, Bernadine P.

English Made Easy. McGraw.
Brand, Carl F. *see* Brand, Carl Fremont.
Brand, Carl Fremont.
xBrand, Carl F.
The British Labour Party: A Short History.
Hoover Inst Pr.
Brand, Eugene, 1931-
xBrand, Eugene L.
Baptism: A Pastoral Perspective. Augsburg.
Brand, Eugene L. *see* Brand, Eugene.
Brand, Gerd.
xBrand, Gerd.
The Essential Wittgenstein. Basic.
Brand, J.
xBrand, Jack.
Local Government Reform in England,
1888-1974. Shoe String.
Brand, Jack, 1934-
xBrand, Jack.
The National Movement in Scotland.
Routledge & Kegan.
Brand, Jack. *see* Brand, J.
Brand, Jeanne L.
xBrand, Jeanne L.
Doctors & the State: The British Medical
Profession and Government Action in Public
Health, 1870-1912. Johns Hopkins.
Brand, John.
xBrand, John.
Observations on the Popular Antiquities of
Great Britain: Chiefly Illustrating the Origin
of Our Vulgar & Provincial Customs,
Ceremonies & Superstitions. Gale.
Brand, Max.
xBrand, Max.
Border Guns. Warner Bks.
Cheyenne Gold. Warner Bks.
Danger Trail. Amereon Ltd.
Danger Trail. PB.
Dead or Alive. Amereon Ltd.
Golden Lightning. Warner Bks.
Hunted Riders. PB.
Pleasant Jim. PB.
Pleasant Jim. Warner Bks.
Silvertip's Search. PB.
Twenty Notches. Ace Bks.
Brand, Myles.
xBrand, Myles.
ed. The Nature of Causation. U of Ill Pr.
Brand, Norman.
xBrand, Norman.
Legal Writing: The Strategy of Persuasion. St
Martin.
Brand, Oscar.
xBrand, Oscar.
The Ballad Mongers: Rise of the Modern Folk
Song. Greenwood.
When I First Came to This Land. Putnam.
Brand, P. *see* Brand, Patrick C.
Brand, Patrick C.
xBrand, P.
Breast Cancer: Psycho-Social Aspects of Early
Detection & Treatment. Univ Park.
Brand, Paul. *see* Brand, Paul Wilson.
Brand, Paul Wilson.
xBrand, Paul.
Fearfully & Wonderfully Made. Zondervan.
Brand, R. E. *see* Brand, Ronald E.
Brand, Richard W.
xBrand, Richard W.
Anatomy of Orofacial Structures. Mosby.
Brand, Ronald E.
xBrand, R. E.
Falsework & Access Scaffolds in Tubular Steel.
McGraw.
Brand, Sandra.
xBrand, Sandra.
I Dared to Live. Shengold.
Brand, Stewart.
xBrand, Stewart.

ed. Space Colonies. Penguin.
Brand, W. *see* Brand, Willem.
Brand, Willem.
  xBrand, W.
      The Struggle for a Higher Standard of Living:
         The Problem of the Underdeveloped
         Countries. Mouton.
Brandal, W. *see* Brandal, Willy.
Brandal, Willy, 1942-
  xBrandal, W.
      Commutative Rings Whose Finitely Generated
         Modules Decompose. Springer-Verlag.
Brandauer, Frederick P.
  xBrandauer, Frederick P.
      Tung Yueh. Twayne.
Brandeis, Louis D. *see* Brandeis, Louis Dembitz.
Brandeis, Louis Dembitz, 1856-1941
  xBrandeis, Louis D.
      Other People's Money & How the Bankers
         Use It. Kelley.
      Other People's Money & How the Bankers
         Use It. Norwood Edns.
Brandeis University - Poses Institute of Fine Arts. *see*
  Brandeis University, Waltham, Mass. Poses Institute
  of Fine Arts.
**Brandeis University, Waltham, Mass. Poses Institute of
Fine Arts.**
  xBrandeis University - Poses Institute of Fine Arts.
      ed. Art Criticism in the Sixties. October.
Brandejs, Jan F.
  xBrandejs, Jan F.
      Physician's Primer on Computers: Private
         Practice. Lexington Bks.
Brandel, Marc, 1919-
  xBrandel, Marc.
      Lizard's Tail. S&S.
      Survivor. S&S.
Brandel-Syrier, Mia.
  xBrandel-Syrier, Mia.
      Reeftown Elite: Social Mobility in a Black
         African Community on the Johannesburg
         Reef. Holmes & Meier.
Brandell, Gunnar.
  xBrandell, Gunnar.
      Strindberg in Inferno. Harvard U Pr.
Branden, Nathaniel.
  xBranden, Nathaniel.
      The Disowned Self. Bantam.
Branden, Victoria.
  xBranden, Victoria.
      Mrs. Job. Har-Row.
Brandenberg, Franz.
  xBrandenberg, Franz.
      Everyone Ready?. Greenwillow.
      Fresh Cider & Pie. Macmillan.
      I Once Knew a Man. Macmillan.
      I Wish I Was Sick Too!. Penguin.
      I Wish I Was Sick, Too. Greenwillow.
      It's Not My Fault. Greenwillow.
      Nice New Neighbors. Greenwillow.
      No School Today. Schol Bk Serv.
      No School Today!. Macmillan.
Brander, George C.
  xBrander, George C.
      The Control of Disease. Lea & Febiger.
Brandes, Joseph.
  xBrandes, Joseph.
      Immigrants to Freedom: Jewish Communities
         in Rural New Jersey Since 1882. U of Pa Pr.
Brandes, Norman S.
  xBrandes, Norman S.
      Group Therapy for the Adolescent. Aronson.
Brandes, Paul D. *see* Brandes, Paul Dickerson.
Brandes, Paul Dickerson.
  xBrandes, Paul D.
      Dialect Clash in America: Issues & Answers.
        Scarecrow.
Brandes, Stanley. *see* Brandes, Stanley H.
Brandes, Stanley H.
  xBrandes, Stanley.

Metaphors of Masculinity: Sex & Status in
    Andalusian Folklore. U of Pa Pr.
Brandhorst, Carl T.
  xBrandhorst, Carl T.
      Tale of Whitefoot. S&S.
Brandis, Royall.
  xBrandis, Royall.
      ed. Current Economic Problems: A Book of
        Readings. Irwin.
Brandner, Gary.
  xBrandner, Gary.
      The Howling. Fawcett.
Brando, Anna K. *see* Brando, Anna Kashfi.
Brando, Anna Kashfi.
  xBrando, Anna K.
      Brando for Breakfast. Berkley Pub.
Brandon, Beatrice.
  xBrandon, Beatrice.
      The Cliffs of Night. NAL.
Brandon, Dick H.
  xBrandon, Dick H.
      Data Processing Management: Methods &
        Standards. Macmillan Info.
      Data Processing Organization & Manpower
        Planning. Van Nos Reinhold.
      Project Control Standards. Krieger.
      Project Control Standards. Van Nos Reinhold.
Brandon, Dorothy. *see* Brandon, Dorothy (Barrett).
Brandon, Dorothy (Barrett).
  xBrandon, Dorothy.
      Max Schling Book of Indoor Gardening.
        Astor-Honor.
Brandon, Henry, 1916-
  xBrandon, Henry.
      Anatomy of Error: The Inside Story of the
        Asian War on the Potomac, 1954-1969.
        Gambit.
Brandon, James R.
  xBrandon, James R.
      Brandon's Guide to Theater in Asia. U Pr of
        Hawaii.
      ed. On Thrones of Gold: Three Javanese
        Shadow Plays. Harvard U Pr.
      Studies in Kabuki: Its Acting, Music, &
        Historical Context. U Pr of Hawaii.
Brandon, Joe. *see* Brandon, Joseph.
Brandon, Joseph.
  xBrandon, Joe.
      Paradise in Flames. PB.
Brandon, William.
  xBrandon, William.
      The Men & the Mountain: Fremont's Fourth
        Expedition. Greenwood.
Brandon-Cox, Hugh.
  xBrandon-Cox, Hugh.
      Summer of a Million Wings: Arctic Quest for
        the Sea-Eagle. Taplinger.
Brandreth, Gyles. *see* Brandreth, Gyles Daubeney.
Brandreth, Gyles Daubeney.
  xBrandreth, Gyles.
      The Biggest Tongue-Twister Book in the
        World. Sterling.
      Games for Rains, Planes, & Trains. Greene.
      Home Entertainment for All the Family.
        Greene.
      A Joke-a-Day Book. Sterling.
      The Last Word. Sterling.
      Pranks, Tricks & Practical Jokes. Sterling.
      This Is Your Body. Sterling.
Brandrup, J.
  xBrandrup, Johannes.
      ed. Polymer Handbook. Wiley.
Brandrup, Johannes. *see* Brandrup, J.
Brandsberg, George.
  xBrandsberg, George.
      Two Sides in N F O's Battle. Iowa St U Pr.
Brandstatter, A. F. *see* Brandstatter, Arthur F.
Brandstatter, Arthur F.
  xBrandstatter, A. F.

Fundamentals of Law Enforcement. Glencoe.
Brandstatter, Herman. *see* Brandstatter, Hermann.
Brandstatter, Hermann.
  xBrandstatter, Herman.
      ed. Dynamics of Group Decisions. Sage.
Brandt, Catharine.
  xBrandt, Catharine.
      Flowers for the Living. Augsburg.
      Forgotten People. Moody.
      Praise God for This New Day: Second
        Thoughts for Busy Women. Augsburg.
Brandt, Conrad.
  xBrandt, Conrad.
      Stalin's Failure in China, 1924-1927. Norton.
Brandt, Henry. *see* Brandt, Henry R.
Brandt, Henry R.
  xBrandt, Henry.
      I Want Happiness Now!. Zondervan.
      I Want My Marriage to Be Better. Zondervan.
Brandt, Jane L. *see* Brandt, Jane Lewis.
Brandt, Jane Lewis.
  xBrandt, Jane L.
      La Chingada. McGraw.
      La Chingada. PB.
Brandt, Johanna, 1876-
  xBrandt, Johanna.
      The Grape Cure. Lust.
Brandt, John C.
  xBrandt, John C.
      New Horizons in Astronomy. W H Freeman.
Brandt, Lawrence R.
  xBrandt, Lawrence R.
      ed. Relevant Geography. Mss Info.
Brandt, Leonore, 1911-
  xBrandt, Leonore.
      Raccoon Family Pets. TFH Pubns.
Brandt, Leslie. *see* Brandt, Leslie F.
Brandt, Leslie F.
  xBrandt, Leslie.
      Growing Together: Prayers for Married People.
        Augsburg.
  xBrandt, Leslie F.
      Book of Christian Prayer. Augsburg.
      Great God, Here I Am. Concordia.
      Prophets Now. Concordia.
Brandt, Patricia.
  xBrandt, Patricia.
      ed. Oregon Biography Index. Oreg St U Pr.
Brandt, Richard B.
  xBrandt, Richard B.
      A Theory of the Good & the Right. Oxford U
        Pr.
Brandt, Robert L.
  xBrandt, Robert L.
      One Way. Gospel Pub.
Brandt, Ronald S.
  xBrandt, Ronald S.
      ed. Partners: Parents & Schools. Assn
        Supervision.
Brandt, Sue R.
  xBrandt, Sue R.
      How to Improve Your Written English. Watts.
Brandt, William J.
  xBrandt, William J.
      The Rhetoric of Argumentation. Irvington.
Brandt, Willy, 1913-
  xBrandt, Willy.
      People & Politics: The Years 1960-1975. Little.
Branford, Jean, 1931-
  xBranford, Jean.
      A Dictionary of South African English. Oxford
        U Pr.
Branford, Kester A. *see* Branford, Kester Adrian.
Branford, Kester Adrian, 1950-
  xBranford, Kester A.
      A Study of Jean-Jacques Bernard's Theatre De
        L'inexprime. Romance.
Branigan, Keith.
  xBranigan, Keith.

Aegean Metalwork in the Early & Middle
  Bronze Age. Oxford U Pr.
Atlas of Ancient Civilizations. T Y Crowell.
Branin, M. Lelyn. see Branin, Manlif Lelyn.
Branin, Manlif Lelyn, 1901-
  xBranin, M. Lelyn.
    The Early Potters & Potteries of Maine.
      Columbia U Pr.
    The Early Potters & Potteries of Maine. Maine
      St Mus.
Brann, Donald. see Brann, Donald R.
Brann, Donald R.
  xBrann, Donald.
    How to Build Colonial Furniture. Easi-Bild.
  xBrann, Donald R.
    Carpeting Simplified. Easi-Bild.
    Concrete Work Simplified. Easi-Bild.
    Electrical Repairs Simplified. Easi-Bild.
    How to Build a Dormer. Easi-Bild.
    How to Build a Patio, Porch, & Sundeck.
      Easi-Bild.
    How to Build a Stable & a Red Barn Tool
      House. Easi-Bild.
    How to Build a Two Car Garage. Easi-Bild.
    How to Build a Vacation or Retirement House.
      Easi-Bild.
    How to Build an Addition. Easi-Bild.
    How to Build Bars. Easi-Bild.
    How to Build Dollhouses & Furniture.
      Easi-Bild.
    How to Build Greenhouses-Sun Houses.
      Easi-Bild.
    How to Build Kitchen Cabinets, Room
      Dividers & Cabinet Furniture. Easi-Bild.
    How to Build Outdoor Furniture. Easi-Bild.
    How to Build Patios & Sundecks. Easi-Bild.
    How to Build Pet Housing. Easi-Bild.
    How to Build Storage Units. Easi-Bild.
    How to Build Workbenches. Easi-Bild.
    How to Construct Built in & Sectional
      Bookcases.. Easi-Bild.
    How to Create Room at the Top. Easi-Bild.
    How to Lay Ceramic Tile. Easi-Bild.
    How to Modernize a Basement. Easi-Bild.
    How to Modernize a Kitchen. Easi-Bild.
    How to Modernize an Attic. Easi-Bild.
    How to Transform a Garage into Living Space.
      Easi-Bild.
    Plumbing Repairs Simplified. Easi-Bild.
    Roofing Simplified. Easi-Bild.
Brann, Eva T. see Brann, Eva T. H.
Brann, Eva T. H.
  xBrann, Eva T.
    Paradoxes of Education in a Republic. U of
      Chicago Pr.
Brann, William C. see Brann, William Cowper.
Brann, William Cowper, 1855-1898
  xBrann, William C.
    Brann's "Scrap Book". Irvington.
Brannan, John.
  xBrannan, John.
    ed. Official Letters of the Military & Naval
      Officers of the United States, During the War
      with Great Britain in the Years 1812, 13, 14,
      & 15: With Some Additional Letters &
      Documents Elucidating the History of That
      Period. Arno.
Brannen, William H.
  xBrannen, William H.
    ed. Small Business Marketing: A Selected &
      Annotated Bibliography. Am Mktg.
    Successful Marketing for Your Small Business.
      P-H.
Branner, Robert.
  xBranner, Robert.
    ed. Chartres Cathedral. Norton.
    Gothic Architecture. Braziller.
    Painted Medallions in the Sainte-Chapelle in
      Paris. Am Philos.
Brannon, Selden. see Brannon, Selden W.

Brannon, Selden W.
  xBrannon, Selden.
    Historic Hampshire: A Symposium of
      Hampshire County & Its People, Past &
      Present. McClain.
Branquart, P. see Branquart, Paul.
Branquart, Paul, 1937-
  xBranquart, P.
    An Optimized Translation Process & Its
      Application to ALGOL 68. Springer-Verlag.
Branscum, Robbie.
  xBranscum, Robbie.
    For Love of Jody. Lothrop.
    Johnny May. Doubleday.
    Johnny May. Avon.
    The Saving of P.S.. Doubleday.
    The Saving of P.S.. Dell.
    Toby & Johnny Joe. Doubleday.
    The Ugliest Boy. Lothrop.
Bransden, B. H., 1926-
  xBransden, B. H.
    Atomic Collision Theory. Benjamin-Cummings.
    The Fundamental Particles. Van Nos Reinhold.
Bransford, John.
  xBransford, John D.
    Human Cognition: Learning, Understanding &
      Remembering. Wadsworth Pub.
Bransford, John D. see Bransford, John.
Bransford, Kent.
  xBransford, Kent.
    Biology Review for the New MCAT. Monarch
      Pr.
    The No-Nonsense Guide to Get You into
      Medical School. Monarch Pr.
    The No-Nonsense Guide to Get You into
      Medical School. Sovereign Bks.
Branson, Branley A.
  xBranson, Branley A.
    Fishes of the Red River Drainage, Eastern
      Kentucky. U Pr of Ky.
Branson, Gary D.
  xBranson, Gary D.
    Home Maintenance & Repair: Walls, Ceilings,
      & Floors. Audel.
Branson, Karen.
  xBranson, Karen.
    The Potato Eaters. Putnam.
Branson, Margaret. see Branson, Margaret Stimmann.
Branson, Margaret Stimmann.
  xBranson, Margaret.
    Civics for Today. HM.
Branson, Mary K. see Branson, Mary Kinney.
Branson, Mary Kinney.
  xBranson, Mary K.
    Who Am I, Anyway?. Broadman.
Branson, O. T. see Branson, Oscar T.
Branson, Oscar T.
  xBranson, O. T.
    Fetishes & Carvings of the Southwest. Treasure
      Chest.
    Indian Jewelry Making. Treasure Chest.
  xBranson, Oscar T.
    Fetishes & Carvings of the Southwest. Van Nos
      Reinhold.
    Indian Jewelry Making. Van Nos Reinhold.
    Indian Jewelry Making. Wallace-Homestead.
Branson, William H.
  xBranson, William H.
    Macroeconomic Theory & Policy. Har-Row.
Brant, Billy G.
  xBrant, Billy G.
    The College Radio Handbook. TAB Bks.
Brantingham, Patricia L.
  xBrantingham, Patricia L.
    ed. Courts & Diversion: Policy & Operations
      Studies. Sage.
Brantingham, Paul J.
  xBrantingham, Paul J.

Structure, Law, & Power: Essays in the
  Sociology of Law. Sage.
Brantl, George.
  xBrantl, George.
    Catholicism. Braziller.
Brantley, Richard E.
  xBrantley, Richard E.
    Wordsworth's "Natural Methodism". Yale U
      Pr.
Branton, D. see Branton, Daniel.
Branton, Daniel.
  xBranton, D.
    Membrane Structure. Springer-Verlag.
Braque, Georges, 1882-1963
  xBraque, Georges.
    Illustrated Notebooks, 1917-1955. Dover.
    Illustrated Notebooks, 1917-1955. Peter Smith.
Braroe, Niels W. see Braroe, Niels Winther.
Braroe, Niels Winther.
  xBraroe, Niels W.
    Indian & White: Self-Image & Interaction in a
      Canadian Plains Community. Stanford U Pr.
Brasch, Ila W. see Brasch, Ila Wales.
Brasch, Ila Wales.
  xBrasch, Ila W.
    A Comprehensive Annotated Bibliography of
      American Black English. La State U Pr.
  xBrasch, Walter M.
    jt. auth. A Comprehensive Annotated
      Bibliography of American Black English. La
      State U Pr.
Brasch, Walter M.
  xBrasch, Walter M.
    The Plain Truth About VD. Brasch & Brasch.
Brasch, Walter M. see Brasch, Ila Wales.
Brase, Charles. see Brase, Charles Henry.
Brase, Charles Henry.
  xBrase, Charles.
    Understandable Statistics: Concepts &
      Methods. Heath.
Brashear, Richard E.
  xBrashear, Richard E.
    Chronic Obstructive Lung Disease: Clinical
      Treatment & Management. Mosby.
Brashear, William R.
  xBrashear, William R.
    The Gorgon's Head: A Study in Tragedy &
      Despair. U of Ga Pr.
Brasher, Nell.
  xBrasher, Nell.
    Daddy Poured the Coffee. Pelican.
Brasher, Thomas L.
  xBrasher, Thomas L.
    Whitman As Editor of the Brooklyn Daily
      Eagle. Wayne St U Pr.
Brashers, H. C.
  xBrashers, H. C.
    Other Side of Love: Two Novellas. Swallow.
Brashler, William.
  xBrashler, William.
    Josh Gibson: A Life in the Negro Leagues.
      Har-Row.
Brasol, Boris. see Brasol, Boris Leo.
Brasol, Boris Leo, 1885-
  xBrasol, Boris.
    Oscar Wilde: The Man, the Artist, the Martyr.
      Octagon.
Brass, Paul R.
  xBrass, Paul R.
    Factional Politics in an Indian State: The
      Congress Party in Uttar Pradesh. U of Cal Pr.
    ed. Radical Politics in South Asia. MIT Pr.
Brasseaux, J. Herman.
  xBrasseaux, J. Herman.
    Readings in Auditing. SW Pub.
Brathwaite, Edward.
  xBrathwaite, Edward.
    Other Exiles. Oxford U Pr.
Bratt, John, b. 1842
  xBratt, John.

Trails of Yesterday. U of Nebr Pr.
Bratton, Fred G. *see* Bratton, Fred Gladstone.
Bratton, Fred Gladstone.
xBratton, Fred G.
The Legacy of the Liberal Spirit: Men &
Movements in the Making of Modern
Thought. Peter Smith.
Bratton, Karl H., 1906-
xBratton, Karl H.
Tales from Once Upon a Time. Chris Mass.
Braude, Abraham I.
xBraude, Abraham I.
Antimicrobial Drug Therapy. Saunders.
Braude, Jacob M. *see* Braude, Jacob Morton.
Braude, Jacob Morton, 1896-
xBraude, Jacob M.
Complete Speaker's & Toastmaster's Library.
P-H.
Braude, Michael.
xBraude, Michael.
Bruce Learns About Life Insurance. Denison.
Braude, Stephen E., 1945-
xBraude, Stephen E.
ESP & Psychokinesis: A Philosophical
Examination. Temple U Pr.
Braudel, Fernand.
xBraudel, Fernand.
Capitalism & Material Life, 1400-1800.
Har-Row.
Capitalism & Material Life, 1400-1800.
Har-Row.
The Mediterranean & the Mediterranean World
in the Age of Philip II. Har-Row.
Braudy, Leo.
xBraudy, Leo.
ed. Great Film Directors: A Critical
Anthology. Oxford U Pr.
ed. Norman Mailer: A Collection of Critical
Essays. P-H.
World in a Frame: What We See in Films.
Doubleday.
Brauer, F. *see* Brauer, Fred.
Brauer, Fred.
xBrauer, F.
Ordinary Differential Equations: A First
Course. Benjamin-Cummings.
Brauer, Gerald C. *see* Brauer, Jerald C.
Brauer, Jerald C.
xBrauer, Gerald C.
ed. Reinterpretation in American Church
History. U of Chicago Pr.
xBrauer, Jerald C.
ed. Images of Religion in America. Fortress.
ed. Impact of the Church Upon Its Culture:
Reappraisals of the History of Christianity. U
of Chicago Pr.
Protestantism in America: A Narrative History.
Westminster.
Brault, Gerard J.
xBrault, Gerard J.
Eight Thirteenth-Century Rolls of Arms in
French & Anglo-Norman Blazon. Pa St U Pr.
Braun, Aurel.
xBraun, Aurel.
Romanian Policy Since 1965. The Political &
Military Limits of Autonomy. Praeger.
Braun, C. *see* Braun, Carl.
Braun, Carl.
xBraun, C.
An Experience Based Approach to Language &
Reading. Univ Park.
Braun, Carl F.
xBraun, Carl F.
Letter Writing in Action. Braun.
Objective Accounting: A Problem of
Communication. Braun.
Braun, D. Duane.
xBraun, D. Duane.

Toward a Theory of Popular Culture: The
Sociology & History of American Music &
Dance 1920-1968. Ann Arbor Pubs.
Braun, E. L. *see* Braun, Emma Lucy.
Braun, Emma Lucy, 1889-
xBraun, E. L.
Deciduous Forests of Eastern North America.
Hafner.
Braun, Eric.
xBraun, Eric.
Deborah Kerr. St Martin.
Braun, Ernest.
xBraun, Ernest.
Living Water. Crown.
Braun, Eunice, 1918-
xBraun, Eunice.
From Strength to Strength: The First Half
Century of the Formative Age of the Baha'i
Faith. Baha'i.
Braun, Herbert, 1903-
xBraun, Herbert.
Jesus of Nazareth: The Man & His Time.
Fortress.
Braun, Hugo. *see* Braun, Hugo E.
Braun, Hugo E.
xBraun, Hugo.
The Language of Real Estate in Michigan.
Follett.
Language of Real Estate in Michigan. Real
Estate Ed Co.
Braun, Jon. *see* Braun, Jon E.
Braun, Jon E.
xBraun, Jon.
Whatever Happened to Hell?. Nelson.
Braun, Loren. *see* Braun, Loren Lyle.
Braun, Loren Lyle.
xBraun, Loren.
Essentials of Organic & Biochemistry. Merrill.
Introduction to Organic & Biochemistry.
Merrill.
Braun, Mathew. *see* Braun, Matthew.
Braun, Matthew.
xBraun, Mathew.
El Paso. PB.
xBraun, Matthew.
Noble Outlaw. Popular Lib.
Braun, Mercedes.
xBraun, Mercedes.
The New Complete Basset Hound. Howell Bk.
Braun, Robert J. *see* Braun, Robert James.
Braun, Robert James, 1946-
xBraun, Robert J.
Dentist's Manual of Emergency Medical
Treatment. Reston.
Braun, Samuel J.
xBraun, Samuel J.
Are You Ready to Mainstream: Helping
Preschoolers with Learning & Behavior
Problems. Merrill.
Braun, Sidney. *see* Braun, Sidney David.
Braun, Sidney D. *see* Braun, Sidney David.
Braun, Sidney David, 1912-
xBraun, Sidney.
ed. Dictionary of French Literature. Philos Lib.
xBraun, Sidney D.
ed. Dictionary of French Literature.
Greenwood.
Braun, T. *see* Braun, Tibor.
Braun, Thomas.
xBraun, Thomas.
Franco Harris. Creative Ed.
The Hitters. Creative Ed.
Meet the Hitters. Creative Ed.
Sonny & Cher. Creative Ed.
Braun, Tibor.
xBraun, T.
ed. Extraction Chromatography. Elsevier.
Braun, Werner, 1914-
xBraun, Werner.

Bacterial Genetics. Saunders.
Braun, Wernher Von. *see* Von Braun, Wernher.
Braun, William E.
xBraun, William E.
HLA & Disease: A Comprehensive Review.
CRC Pr.
Braund, Kathryn.
xBraund, Kathryn.
The Uncommon Dog Breeds. Arco.
Braungart, Richard G., 1935-
xBraungart, Richard G.
Society & Politics: Readings in Political
Sociology. P-H.
Brauns, Robert. *see* Brauns, Robert A. W.
Brauns, Robert A. W.
xBrauns, Robert.
Bankers Desk Reference. Warren.
Braunthal, Alfred.
xBraunthal, Alfred.
Salvation & the Perfect Society: The Eternal
Quest. U of Mass Pr.
Braunthal, Gerard, 1923-
xBraunthal, Gerard.
The Federation of German Industry in Politics.
Cornell U Pr.
Socialist Labor & Politics in Weimar Germany:
The General Federation of German Trade
Unions. Shoe String.
Brautigan, Richard.
xBrautigan, Richard.
Confederate General from Big Sur. Ballantine.
A Confederate General from Big Sur.
Delacorte.
A Confederate General from Big Sur. Dell.
In Watermelon Sugar. Dell.
In Watermelon Sugar. Dell.
Braverman, J. *see* Braverman, Jerome D.
Braverman, Jerome D.
xBraverman, J.
Probability, Logic & Management Decisions.
McGraw.
xBraverman, Jerome D.
Fundamentals of Business Statistics. Acad Pr.
Statistics for Business & Economics. Wiley.
Braverman, Jordan.
xBraverman, Jordan.
Crisis in Health Care. Acropolis.
Braverman, Libbie (Levin), 1900-
xBraverman, Libbie L.
Children of the Emek. Bloch.
Braverman, Libbie L. *see* Braverman, Libbie (Levin).
Braverman, Miriam.
xBraverman, Miriam.
Youth, Society & the Public Library. ALA.
Bravery, H. E.
xBravery, H. E.
Home Brewing Without Failures. Arc Bks.
Successful Winemaking at Home. Arc Bks.
Bravo, F. *see* Bravo, Francisco.
Bravo, Francisco, 1934-
xBravo, F.
Intro. by Christ in the Thought of Teilhard De
Chardin. U of Notre Dame Pr.
xBravo, Francisco.
Christ in the Thought of Teilhard De Chardin.
U of Notre Dame Pr.
Brawley, Benjamin. *see* Brawley, Benjamin Griffith.
Brawley, Benjamin G. *see* Brawley, Benjamin Griffith.
Brawley, Benjamin Griffith, 1882-1939
xBrawley, Benjamin.
Early Negro American Writers: Selections with
Biographical & Critical Introductions. Peter
Smith.
xBrawley, Benjamin G.
Negro in Literature & Art in the United States.
AMS Pr.
Brawley, Ernest.
xBrawley, Ernest.

The Rap. Atheneum.
Selena. Atheneum.
Selena. NAL.
Braxton, Bernard.
　xBraxton, Bernard.
　　Women, Sex, & Race: A Realistic View of
　　　Sexism & Racism. Verta Pr.
Bray, Bonita.
　xBray, Bonita.
　　Afghans: Traditional & Modern. Crown.
Bray, Douglas H.
　xBray, Douglas H.
　　Polynesian & Pakeha in New Zealand
　　　Education. Intl Pubns Serv.
Bray, Douglas W. *see* Bray, Douglas Weston.
Bray, Douglas Weston.
　xBray, Douglas W.
　　Formative Years in Business: A Long Term
　　　AT&T Study of Managerial Lives. Krieger.
Bray, Frank S. *see* Bray, Frank Sewell.
Bray, Frank Sewell.
　xBray, Frank S.
　　The Accounting Mission. Scholars Bk.
Bray, Gerald L. *see* Bray, Gerald Lewis.
Bray, Gerald Lewis.
　xBray, Gerald L.
　　Holiness & the Will of God: Perspectives on
　　　the Theology of Tertullian. John Knox.
Bray, K. H. *see* Bray, Kenneth Hugh Madley.
Bray, Kenneth Hugh Madley.
　xBray, K. H.
　　Matrix Analysis of Structures. Intl Schol Bk
　　　Serv.
Bray, Olin H.
　xBray, Olin H.
　　Data-Base Computers. Lexington Bks.
Bray, R. J.
　xBray, R. J.
　　Sunspots. Dover.
Braybrooke, David.
　xBraybrooke, David.
　　A Strategy of Decision: Policy Evaluation As a
　　　Social Process. Free Pr.
Braybrooke, Neville, 1923-
　xBraybrooke, Neville.
　　ed. T. S. Eliot: A Symposium for His
　　　Seventieth Birthday. Arno.
Braybrooke, P. *see* Braybrooke, Patrick.
Braybrooke, Partick. *see* Braybrooke, Patrick.
Braybrooke, Patrick, 1894-
　xBraybrooke, P.
　　Some Catholic Novelists: Their Art & Outlook.
　　　Gordon Pr.
　xBraybrooke, Partick.
　　Some Goddesses of the Pen. R West.
　xBraybrooke, Patrick.
　　The Amazing Mr. Noel Coward. Folcroft.
　　Genius of Bernard Shaw. Folcroft.
　　Oscar Wilde: A Study. Folcroft.
　　Peeps at the Mighty. Arno.
　　Some Goddesses of the Pen. Arno.
　　Some Victorian & Georgian Catholics: Their
　　　Art & Outlook. R West.
　　Subtlety of George Bernard Shaw. Folcroft.
Brayer, Herbert O. *see* Brayer, Herbert Oliver.
Brayer, Herbert Oliver.
　xBrayer, Herbert O.
　　Pueblo Indian Land Grants of the "Rio Abajo",
　　　New Mexico. Arno.
Brayer, K. *see* Brayer, Kenneth.
Brayer, Kenneth, 1941-
　xBrayer, K.
　　Data Communications Via Fading Channels.
　　　Wiley.
Brazelton, T. Berry, 1918-
　xBrazelton, T. Berry.
　　Doctor & Child. Delacorte.
　　Doctor & Child. Dell.
Brazier, M. A. *see* Brazier, Mary Agnes Burniston.
Brazier, Mary A. *see* Brazier, Mary Agnes Burniston.

Brazier, Mary Agnes Burniston.
　xBrazier, M. A.
　　ed. Growth & Development of the Brain:
　　　Nutritional, Genetic, & Environmental
　　　Factors. Raven.
　xBrazier, Mary A.
　　ed. Architectonics of the Cerebral Cortex.
　　　Raven.
　　Brain Dysfunction in Infantile Febrile
　　　Convulsions. Raven.
**Brazil. Commissao De Linhas Telegraphicas Estrategicas
De Matto-Grosso Ao Amazonas.**
　xBrazil. Commissao de Linhas Telegraphicas
　　Estrategicas de Matto-Grosso ao Amazonas.
　　Lectures Delivered by Colonel Candido
　　　Mariano da Silva Rondon on the 5th, 7th, &
　　　9th of Oct, 1915. Greenwood.
Brazil, K. L.
　xBrazil, K. L.
　　Can We Preach Philosophy. Philos Lib.
Brazziel, William F.
　xBrazziel, William F.
　　Quality Education for All Americans: An
　　　Assessment of Gains of Black Americans
　　　with Proposals for Program Development in
　　　American Schools & Colleges for the Next
　　　Quarter Century. Howard U Pr.
Bready, John W. *see* Bready, John Wesley.
Bready, John Wesley, 1887-1953
　xBready, John W.
　　England, Before & After Wesley: The
　　　Evangelical Revival & Social Reform. Russell.
Break, George F.
　xBreak, George F.
　　Federal Lending & Economic Stability.
　　　Greenwood.
　　Taxation: Myths & Realities. A-W.
Breakefield, X. O. *see* Breakefield, Xandra O.
Breakefield, Xandra O.
　xBreakefield, X. O.
　　ed. Neurogenetics: Genetic Approaches to the
　　　Nervous System. Elsevier.
Brealey, Richard. *see* Brealey, Richard A.
Brealey, Richard A.
　xBrealey, Richard.
　　Principles of Corporate Finance. McGraw.
　xBrealey, Richard A.
　　Introduction to Risk & Return from Common
　　　Stocks. MIT Pr.
Brean, Herbert.
　xBrean, Herbert.
　　How to Stop Smoking. PB.
　　How to Stop Smoking. Vanguard.
Brearley, Arthur.
　xBrearley, Arthur.
　　The Control of Staff-Related Overhead. Verry.
Brearley, C. Paul.
　xBrearley, C. Paul.
　　Social Work, Ageing & Society. Routledge &
　　　Kegan.
Brearley, H. C. *see* Brearley, Harrington Cooper.
Brearley, Harrington Cooper, 1893-1960
　xBrearley, H. C.
　　Homicide in the United States. Patterson
　　　Smith.
Brearley, Molly.
　xBrearley, Molly.
　　Guide to Reading Piaget. Schocken.
Breasted, James H. *see* Breasted, James Henry.
Breasted, James Henry, 1865-1935
　xBreasted, James H.
　　The Dawn of Conscience. Scribner.
　　Development of Religion & Thought in
　　　Ancient Egypt. U of Pa Pr.
Breazile, James E.
　xBreazile, James E.
　　ed. Textbook of Veterinary Physiology. Lea &
　　　Febiger.
Brebbia, C. A.
　xBrebbia, C. A.

The Boundary Element Method for Engineers.
　Halsted Pr.
　ed. Mathematical Models for Environmental
　　Problems: Proceedings of the University of
　　Southampton, England, 8-12 September,
　　1975. Halsted Pr.
Brebner, John B. *see* Brebner, John Bartlet.
Brebner, John Bartlet, 1895-1957
　xBrebner, John B.
　　North Atlantic Triangle: The Interplay of
　　　Canada, the United States, & Great Britain.
　　　Russell.
Brecher. *see* Brecher, Ruth.
Brecher, Irving.
　xBrecher, Irving.
　　Foreign Aid & Industrial Development in
　　　Pakistan. Cambridge U Pr.
Brecher, Jeremy.
　xBrecher, Jeremy.
　　Strike!. South End Pr.
Brecher, Kenneth.
　xBrecher, Kenneth.
　　ed. Astronomy of the Ancients. MIT Pr.
Brecher, Michael.
　xBrecher, Michael.
　　Decisions in Israel's Foreign Policy. Yale U Pr.
　　The Foreign Policy System of Israel: Setting,
　　　Images, Process. Yale U Pr.
　　Nehru's Mantle: The Politics of Succession in
　　　India. Greenwood.
Brecher, Ruth.
　xBrecher.
　　The Rays: A History of Radiology in the
　　　United States & Canada. Krieger.
　xBrecher, Ruth.
　　ed. Analysis of Human Sexual Response. NAL.
Brecher, Steven L., 1945-
　xBrecher, Steven L.
　　Beating the Races with a Computer. Software
　　　Supply.
Brechna, H.
　xBrechna, H.
　　Superconducting Magnet Systems.
　　　Springer-Verlag.
Brecht, Arnold.
　xBrecht, Arnold.
　　Intro. by The Art & Technique of
　　　Administration in German Ministries.
　　　Greenwood.
　　Federalism & Regionalism in Germany: The
　　　Division of Prussia. Russell.
　　Political Theory: The Foundations of
　　　Twentieth-Century Political Thought.
　　　Princeton U Pr.
Brecht, Bertolt.
　xBrecht, Bertolt.
　　Caucasian Chalk Circle. Grove.
　　Collected Plays. Random.
　　Galileo. Grove.
　　Good Woman of Setzuan. Grove.
Brecht, Stefan, 1924-
　xBrecht, Stefan.
　　Poems. City Lights.
Breckenridge, Adam C. *see* Breckenridge, Adam Carlyle.
Breckenridge, Adam Carlyle, 1916-
　xBreckenridge, Adam C.
　　Congress Against the Court. U of Nebr Pr.
　　Executive Privilege: Presidential Control Over
　　　Information. U of Nebr Pr.
　　Right to Privacy. U of Nebr Pr.
Breckenridge, James F.
　xBreckenridge, James F.
　　The Theological Self-Understanding of the
　　　Catholic Charismatic Movement. U Pr of
　　　Amer.
Breckinridge, Sophonisba P. *see* Breckinridge, Sophonisba
　Preston.
Breckinridge, Sophonisba Preston.
　xBreckinridge, Sophonisba P.

Delinquent Child & the Home. Arno.
Legal Tender: A Study in English & American
  Monetary History. Greenwood.
Breckler, Rosemary, 1920-
  xBreckler, Rosemary.
    Where Are the Twins?. Westminster.
Brecknock, Albert.
  xBrecknock, Albert.
    Byron: A Study of the Poet in the Light of
      New Discoveries. Haskell.
Breckon, Bill. *see* Breckon, William.
Breckon, William.
  xBreckon, Bill.
    Accident Action: The Essential Family Guide
      to Home Safety & First Aid. Viking Pr.
Bredahl, A. Carl. *see* Bredahl, Axel Carl.
Bredahl, Axel Carl, 1940-
  xBredahl, A. Carl.
    Melville's Angles of Vision. U Presses Fla.
Bredesen, Harald.
  xBredesen, Harald.
    Need a Miracle?. Revell.
Bredon, Glen E.
  xBredon, Glen E.
    Introduction to Compact Transformation
      Groups. Acad Pr.
Bredon, J. *see* Bredon, Juliet.
Bredon, Juliet.
  xBredon, J.
    The Moon Year: A Record of Chinese Customs
      & Festivals. Chinese Materials.
Bredow, Miriam.
  xBredow, Miriam.
    Medical Office Procedures. McGraw.
Bredsdorff, Jan.
  xBredsdorff, Jan.
    To China & Back. Pantheon.
Bredvold, L. I. *see* Bredvold, Louis Ignatius.
Bredvold, Louis Ignatius, 1888-
  xBredvold, L. I.
    ed. Eighteenth Century Poetry & Prose. Wiley.
Bree, G. *see* Bree, Germaine.
Bree, Germaine.
  xBree, G.
    Twentieth Century French Drama. Macmillan.
  xBree, Germaine.
    World of Marcel Proust. HM.
Breed, Alice G. *see* Breed, Alice Gerster.
Breed, Alice Gerster.
  xBreed, Alice G.
    The Change in Social Welfare from
      Deregulation: The Case of the Natural Gas
      Industry. Arno.
Breed, D. R. *see* Breed, David Riddle.
Breed, David R. *see* Breed, David Riddle.
Breed, David Riddle, 1848-1931
  xBreed, D. R.
    The History & Use of Hymns & Hymn Tunes.
      Gordon Pr.
  xBreed, David R.
    The History & Use of Hymns & Hymn Tunes.
      AMS Pr.
Breed, Paul F. *see* Breed, Paul Francis.
Breed, Paul Francis.
  xBreed, Paul F.
    Dramatic Criticism Index: Bibliography of
      Commentaries on Playwrights from Ibsen to
      the Avant-Garde. Gale.
Breeden, James O.
  xBreeden, James O.
    Joseph Jones, M.D.: Scientist of the Old South.
      U Pr of Ky.
Breeden, Stanley.
  xBreeden, Stanley.
    Life of the Kangaroo. Taplinger.
Breem, Wallace.
  xBreem, Wallace.
    The Leopard & the Cliff. St Martin.
Breen, George E. *see* Breen, George Edward.

Breen, George Edward, 1911-
  xBreen, George E.
    Do-It-Yourself Marketing Research. McGraw.
Breen, Matthew P. *see* Breen, Matthew Patrick.
Breen, Matthew Patrick.
  xBreen, Matthew P.
    Thirty Years of New York Politics, up to Date.
      Arno.
Breese, Gerald W. *see* Breese, Gerald William.
Breese, Gerald William.
  xBreese, Gerald W.
    Approach to Urban Planning. Greenwood.
Breffny, Brian de. *see* De Breffny, Brian.
Breger, Louis.
  xBreger, Louis.
    The Effect of Stress on Dreams. Intl Univs Pr.
Bregman, Marcia S., 1941-
  xBregman, Marcia S.
    Assisting the Health Team: An Introduction for
      the Nurse Assistant. Mosby.
Bregy, Katherine M. *see* Bregy, Katherine Marie
  Cornelia.
Bregy, Katherine Marie Cornelia, 1888-1967
  xBregy, Katherine M.
    From Dante to Jeanne D'Arc: Adventures in
      Medieval Life & Letters. Greenwood.
Brehm, Shirley. *see* Brehm, Shirley A.
Brehm, Shirley A., 1926-
  xBrehm, Shirley.
    A Teacher's Handbook for Study Outside the
      Classroom. Merrill.
Brehman, Thomas R., 1945-
  xBrehman, Thomas R.
    Environmental Demonstrations, Experiments &
      Projects for the Secondary School. P-H.
Breig, Alf, 1910-
  xBreig, Alf.
    Adverse Mechanical Tension of the Central
      Nervous System: An Analysis of Cause &
      Effect. Wiley.
Breihan, Carl W., 1915-
  xBreihan, Carl W.
    The Day Jesse James Was Killed. NAL.
    Great Gunfighters of the West. NAL.
Breiman, Leo.
  xBreiman, Leo.
    Probability. A-W.
    Probability & Stochastic Processes, with a View
      Toward Applications. HM.
Breimyer, Harold F.
  xBreimyer, Harold F.
    Economics of the Product Markets of
      Agriculture. Iowa St U Pr.
Breinburg, Petronella.
  xBreinburg, Petronella.
    Doctor Shawn. T Y Crowell.
    Sally-Ann in the Snow. Merrimack Bk Serv.
Breisach, Ernest A. *see* Breisach, Ernst.
Breisach, Ernst.
  xBreisach, Ernest A.
    Renaissance Europe: 1300-1517. Macmillan.
  xBreisach, Ernst.
    Caterina Sforza: A Renaissance Virago. U of
      Chicago Pr.
    Introduction to Modern Existentialism. Grove.
Breit, Marquita, 1942-
  xBreit, Marquita.
    Thomas Merton: A Bibliography. Scarecrow.
Breiter, Herta S.
  xBreiter, Herta S.
    Fuel & Energy. Raintree Child.
    Pollution. Raintree Child.
Breitmaier, E.
  xBreitmaier, E.
    Atlas of Carbon-13 NMR Data. Heyden.
    ed. Atlas of Carbon-13, NMR Data. IFI
      Plenum.
Breitman, George.
  xBreitman, George.

The Assassination of Malcolm X. Path Pr NY.
The Last Year of Malcolm X: The Evolution of
  a Revolutionary. Path Pr NY.
Breitner, I. E. *see* Breitner, I. Emery.
Breitner, I. Emery.
  xBreitner, I. E.
    The Life of the Victim: A Psychodrama in
      Three Phases. Imibooks Pubns.
Breivik, Patricia S. *see* Breivik, Patricia Senn.
Breivik, Patricia Senn.
  xBreivik, Patricia S.
    Funding Alternatives for Libraries. ALA.
    Open Admissions & the Academic Library.
      ALA.
Brejcha, M. F. *see* Brejcha, Mathias F.
Brejcha, Mathias F.
  xBrejcha, M. F.
    Automotive Chassis & Accessory Circuits. P-H.
Brekke, Milo.
  xBrekke, Milo L.
    Ten Faces of Ministry: Perspectives on Pastoral
      & Congregational Effectiveness Based on
      Survey of 5000 Lutherans. Augsburg.
Brekke, Milo L. *see* Brekke, Milo.
Breland, Osmond P. *see* Breland, Osmond Philip.
Breland, Osmond Philip, 1910-
  xBreland, Osmond P.
    Animal Life & Lore. Har-Row.
Brelot, M. *see* Brelot, Marcel.
Brelot, Marcel.
  xBrelot, M.
    On Topologies & Boundaries in Potential
      Theory. Springer-Verlag.
Breman, Jan.
  xBreman, Jan.
    Patronage & Exploitation: Changing Agrarian
      Relations in South Gujarat, India. U of Cal
      Pr.
Bremer, Cornelius D. *see* Bremer, Cornelius Daniel.
Bremer, Cornelius Daniel, 1896-
  xBremer, Cornelius D.
    American Bank Failures. AMS Pr.
Bremer, Francis J.
  xBremer, Francis J.
    The Puritan Experiment: New England Society
      from Bradford to Edwards. St Martin.
Bremer, Fredrika, 1801-1865
  xBremer, Fredrika.
    The Homes of the New World: Impressions of
      America. Johnson Repr.
    Homes of the New World: Impressions of
      America. Negro U Pr.
Bremer, Stuart A.
  xBremer, Stuart A.
    Simulated Worlds: A Computer Model of
      National Decision-Making. Princeton U Pr.
Bremner, Robert H. *see* Bremner, Robert Hamlett.
Bremner, Robert Hamlett, 1917-
  xBremner, Robert H.
    Compiled by American Social History Since
      1860. AHM Pub.
    ed. Children & Youth in America: A
      Documentary History. Harvard U Pr.
    From the Depths: The Discovery of Poverty in
      the United States. NYU Pr.
Bremond, Henri, 1865-1933
  xBremond, Henri.
    Prayer & Poetry: Contribution to Poetical
      Theory. Folcroft.
Brems, Hans.
  xBrems, Hans.
    Inflation, Interest, & Growth: A Synthesis.
      Lexington Bks.
    Output, Employment, Capital, & Growth: A
      Quantitative Analysis. Greenwood.
    Quantitative Economic Theory: A Synthetic
      Approach. Krieger.
Bremser, Wayne G.
  xBremser, Wayne G.

Quality Control Systems in Accounting: A
  Guide to Implementation. Aspen Systems.
Brena, Steven. *see* Brena, Steven F.
Brena, Steven F.
  xBrena, Steven.
    Pain & Religion: A Psychophysiological Study.
    C C Thomas.
Brenan, Gerald.
  xBrenan, Gerald.
    The Face of Spain. Octagon.
    South from Granada. Cambridge U Pr.
    South from Granada. Octagon.
Brenchley, David L.
  xBrenchley, David L.
    ed. Industrial Source Sampling. Ann Arbor
    Science.
Brendel, Alfred.
  xBrendel, Alfred.
    Musical Thoughts & Afterthoughts. Princeton
    U Pr.
Brendel, Otto, 1901-1973
  xBrendel, Otto J.
    Etruscan Art. Penguin.
    Etruscan Art. Viking Pr.
Brendel, Otto J. *see* Brendel, Otto.
Brendle, T. R. *see* Brendle, Thomas Royce.
Brendle, Thomas Royce.
  xBrendle, T. R.
    Folk Medicine of the Pennsylvania Germans:
    The Non-Occult Cures. Kelley.
Brendon, John A. *see* Brendon, John Adams.
Brendon, John Adams, 1884-
  xBrendon, John A.
    The Age of Chaucer. AMS Pr.
Brendon, Piers.
  xBrendon, Piers.
    Eminent Edwardians. HM.
Breneman, David W.
  xBreneman, David W.
    ed. Public Policy & Private Higher Education.
    Brookings.
Breneman, J. C.
  xBreneman, James C.
    Basics of Food Allergy. C C Thomas.
Breneman, James C. *see* Breneman, J. C.
Breneman, John W. *see* Breneman, John William.
Breneman, John William.
  xBreneman, John W.
    Strength of Materials. McGraw.
Brenes, E. *see* Brenes, Edin.
Brenes, Edin.
  xBrenes, E.
    Learning Spanish the Modern Way. McGraw.
Brengelmann, J. C. *see* Brengelmann, Johannes C.
Brengelmann, Johannes C.
  xBrengelmann, J. C.
    ed. Progress in Behaviour Therapy.
    Springer-Verlag.
Brengle, Richard L.
  xBrengle, Richard L.
    ed. Arthur, King of Britain: History, Romance,
    Chronicle & Criticism. P-H.
Brennan, Alice.
  xBrennan, Alice.
    Castle Mirage. Nordon Pubns.
    Devil Take All. Popular Lib.
Brennan, J. H.
  xBrennan, J. H.
    Getting What You Want. Stein & Day.
  xBrennan, Jan.
    Dream of Destiny. Doubleday.
    The Greythorn Woman. Doubleday.
Brennan, J. M.
  xBrennan, John M.
    The Open Texture of Moral Concepts. B&N.
Brennan, Jan. *see* Brennan, J. H.
Brennan, Jim.
  xBrennan, Jim.

Public Relations Can Be Fun & Easy Especially
  for Nursing Home People. Futura Pub.
Brennan, Joe. *see* Brennan, Joseph.
Brennan, John. *see* Brennan, John A.
Brennan, John A., 1928-
  xBrennan, John.
    Silver & the First New Deal. U of Nev Pr.
Brennan, John M. *see* Brennan, J. M.
Brennan, Joseph.
  xBrennan, Joe.
    Hot Rod Thunder. Doubleday.
  xBrennan, Joseph.
    Social Conditions in Industrial Rhode Island
    1820-1860. Porcupine Pr.
Brennan, Joseph G. *see* Brennan, Joseph Gerard.
Brennan, Joseph Gerard, 1910-
  xBrennan, Joseph G.
    Ethics & Morals. Har-Row.
    Handbook of Logic. Har-Row.
Brennan, Joseph P. *see* Brennan, Joseph Payne.
Brennan, Joseph Payne, 1918-
  xBrennan, Joseph P.
    Stories of Darkness & Dread. Arkham.
Brennan, Louis A.
  xBrennan, Louis A.
    American Dawn: A New Model of American
    Prehistory. Macmillan.
Brennan, M. *see* Brennan, Michael Joseph.
Brennan, Michael J. *see* Brennan, Michael Joseph.
Brennan, Michael Joseph.
  xBrennan, M.
    Theory of Economic Statics. P-H.
  xBrennan, Michael J.
    ed. Patterns of Market Behavior: Essays in
    Honor of Philip Taft. Brown U Pr.
Brennan, Neil. *see* Brennan, Neil Francis.
Brennan, Neil Francis, 1923-
  xBrennan, Neil.
    Anthony Powell. Twayne.
Brennan, Peter.
  xBrennan, Peter.
    Sudden Death. BJ Pub Group.
Brennan, Richard D. *see* Brennan, Richard O.
Brennan, Richard O.
  xBrennan, Richard D.
    Dr. Brennan's Diet Menus. Harvest Hse.
Brennan'S Restaurant. *see* Brennan'S Restaurant, New
  Orleans.
Brennan'S Restaurant, New Orleans.
  xBrennan'S Restaurant.
    Brennan's New Orleans Cookbook. Crager.
Brennecke, E. *see* Brennecke, Ernest.
Brennecke, Ernest, 1896-1969
  xBrennecke, E.
    The Life of Thomas Hardy. Haskell.
  xBrennecke, Ernest.
    Thomas Hardy's Universe: A Study of a Poet's
    Mind. Haskell.
Brennecke, John H.
  xBrennecke, John H.
    Psychology & Human Experience. Glencoe.
    Significance: The Struggle We Share: Book of
    Readings. Glencoe.
    Struggle for Significance. Glencoe.
  xBrennecke, John J.
    Psychology & Human Experience. Glencoe.
Brennecke, John J. *see* Brennecke, John H.
Brenneman, Helen G. *see* Brenneman, Helen Good.
Brenneman, Helen Good.
  xBrenneman, Helen G.
    House by the Side of the Road. Herald Pr.
    Learning to Cope. Herald Pr.
Brenner, Anita, 1905-
  xBrenner, Anita.
    Idols Behind Altars. Biblo.
    Influence of Technique on the Decorative Style
    in the Domestic Pottery of Culhuacan. AMS
    Pr.
Brenner, Barbara.
  xBrenner, Barbara.

Amy's Doll. Knopf.
Baltimore Orioles. Har-Row.
Cunningham's Rooster. Schol Bk Serv.
Faces. Dutton.
Five Pennies. Knopf.
Lizard Tails & Cactus Spines. Har-Row.
On the Frontier with Mr. Audubon. Coward.
The Prince & the Pink Blanket. Schol Bk Serv.
Brenner, Barry M.
  xBrenner, Barry M.
    ed. Acid Base & Potassium Homeostasis.
    Churchill.
    ed. Hormonal Function & the Kidney.
    Churchill.
    ed. Sodium & Water Homeostasis. Churchill.
Brenner, Benjamin, 1898-
  xBrenner, Benjamin.
    Effect of Immediate & Delayed Praise & Blame
    Upon Learning & Recall. AMS Pr.
Brenner, Charles, 1913-
  xBrenner, Charles.
    Psychoanalytic Technique & Psychic Conflict.
    Intl Univs Pr.
Brenner, Egon.
  xBrenner, Egon.
    Analysis of Electric Circuits. McGraw.
Brenner, Michael J.
  xBrenner, Michael J.
    The Politics of International Monetary Reform:
    The Exchange Crisis. Ballinger Pub.
Brenner, Reeve R. *see* Brenner, Reeve Robert.
Brenner, Reeve Robert.
  xBrenner, Reeve R.
    The Faith & Doubt of Holocaust Survivors.
    Free Pr.
Brenner, Saul.
  xBrenner, Saul.
    ed. American Judicial Behavior. Mss Info.
Brenner, Vladimir. *see* Brenner, Wladimir.
Brenner, Wladimir, 1895-
  xBrenner, Vladimir.
    Count Witte: Scenes from His Life and Times,
    1902-1915. Exposition.
Brenner, Y. S.
  xBrenner, Y. S.
    Looking into the Seeds of Time: Social
    Mechanisms in Economic Development.
    Humanities.
Brenni, Vito J. *see* Brenni, Vito Joseph.
Brenni, Vito Joseph, 1923-
  xBrenni, Vito J.
    Edith Wharton: A Bibliography. McClain.
Brent, Allen.
  xBrent, Allen.
    Philosophical Foundations for the Curriculum.
    Allen Unwin.
Brent, Charles H. *see* Brent, Charles Henry.
Brent, Charles Henry, Bp, 1862-1929
  xBrent, Charles H.
    Inspiration of Responsibility, & Other Papers.
    Arno.

Brent, Eva.
  xBrent, Eva.

    Nature in Needlepoint. S&S.

    Oriental Designs in Needlepoint. S&S.

Brent, Joanna.
  xBrent, Joanna.
    A Few Days in Weasel Creek. Seaview Bks.

Brent, Madeleine.
  xBrent, Madeleine.

The Capricorn Stone. Doubleday.
Moonraker's Bride. Doubleday.
Moonraker's Bride. Fawcett.
Stranger at Wildings. Doubleday.
Stranger at Wildings. G K Hall.
xBrent, Madeline.
The Capricorn Stone. G K Hall.
Brent, Madeline. see Brent, Madeleine.
Brent, Patricia. see Brent, Patricia Jenkins.
Brent, Patricia Jenkins.
xBrent, Patricia.
Haircutting. Watts.
Brent, R. Spencer.
xBrent, R. Spencer.
Pattern Play Tennis. Doubleday.
Brentano, Franz. see Brentano, Franz Clemens.
Brentano, Franz C. see Brentano, Franz Clemens.
Brentano, Franz Clemens.
xBrentano, Franz.
Aristotle & His World View. U of Cal Pr.
On the Several Senses of Being in Aristotle. U of Cal Pr.
The Origin of Our Knowledge of Right & Wrong. Humanities.
The Psychology of Aristotle: In Particular His Doctrine of the Active Intellect with an Appendix Concerning the Activity of Aristotle's God. U of Cal Pr.
xBrentano, Franz C.
True & the Evident. Humanities.
Brenton, Myron.
xBrenton, Myron.
Friendship. Stein & Day.
How to Survive Your Child's Rebellious Teens: New Solutions for Troubled Parents. Lippincott.
The Runaways: Children, Husbands, Wives, & Parents. Little.
The Runaways: Children, Husbands, Wives, & Parents. Penguin.
Brereton, Austin, 1862-1922
xBrereton, Austin.
Life of Henry Irving. Arno.
Brereton, Geoffrey.
xBrereton, Geoffrey.
Principles of Tragedy: A Rational Examination of the Tragic Concept in Life & Literature. U of Miami Pr.
Brereton, J. M. see Brereton, John Maurice.
Brereton, John C.
xBrereton, John C.
A Plan for Writing. HR&W.
Brereton, John Maurice.
xBrereton, J. M.
The Horse in War. Arco.
Breslauer, George W.
xBreslauer, George W.
Five Images of the Soviet Future: A Critical Review & Synthesis. U of Cal Intl St.
Breslauer, S. Daniel.
xBreslauer, S. Daniel.
The Chrysalis of Religion: A Guide to the Jewishness of Buber's I & Thou. Abingdon.
Bresler, B. see Bresler, Boris.
Bresler, Boris.
xBresler, B.
Design of Steel Structures. Wiley.
xBresler, Boris.
Reinforced Concrete Engineering. Wiley.
Bresler, David E.
xBresler, David E.
Freedom from Pain. S&S.
Bresler, J. see Bresler, Jack Barry.
Bresler, Jack Barry, 1923-
xBresler, J.
ed. Genetics & Society. A-W.
Breslin, Frederick. see Breslin, Frederick D.
Breslin, Frederick D., 1920-
xBreslin, Frederick.

The Adolescent & Learning. Collegium Bk Pubs.
Breslin, Judson.
xBreslin, Judson.
Distributed Processing Systems: End of the Mainframe Era?. Am Mgmt.
Breslin, Thomas A.
xBreslin, Thomas A.
China, American Catholicism, & the Missionary. Pa St U Pr.
Bresnan, Joan.
xBresnan, Joan W.
Theory of Complementation in English Syntax. Garland Pub.
Bresnan, Joan W. see Bresnan, Joan.
Bresnick, Edward.
xBresnick, Edward.
Functional Dynamics of the Cell. Acad Pr.
Bress, Helene.
xBress, Helene.
The Craft of Macrame. Scribner.
Inkle Weaving. Scribner.
Bressan, A. see Bressan, Aldo.
Bressan, Aldo.
xBressan, A.
Relativistic Theories of Materials. Springer-Verlag.
Bressie, Wes. see Bressie, Wesley.
Bressie, Wesley.
xBressie, Wes.
Relic Trails to Treasure: The Americana Price Guide. Old Time.
Bresson, Mary A. see Bresson, Mary Alfred.
Bresson, Mary Alfred.
xBresson, Mary A.
Contemporary Iowa Opinions Regarding the Influence of Croatians in Waterloo & Vicinity, 1907-1949. R & E Res Assoc.
Contemporary Iowa Opinions Regarding the Influence of Croatians in Waterloo & Vicinity, 1907-1949. Ragusan Pr.
Bresson, Robert.
xBresson, Robert.
Notes on Cinematography. Urizen Bks.
Brest, Paul.
xBrest, Paul.
Processes of Constitutional Decisionmaking: Cases & Materials. Little.
Breternitz, David A.
xBreternitz, David A.
Compiled by Prehistoric Ceramics of the Mesa Verde Region. Mus Northern Ariz.
Breth, Robert D.
xBreth, Robert D.
Dynamic Management Communications. A-W.
Brethower, Dale M.
xBrethower, Dale M.
Programmed Learning: A Practicum. Ann Arbor Pubs.
Bretnor, Reginald.
xBretnor, Reginald.
ed. The Craft of Science Fiction: A Symposium on Writing Science Fiction & Science Fantasy. Har-Row.
Breton, Albert.
xBreton, Albert.
The Economic Constitution of Federal States. U of Toronto Pr.
The Economic Theory of Representative Government. Beresford Bk Serv.
Breton, Andre, 1896-1966
xBreton, Andre.
Surrealism & Painting. Har-Row.
Breton, Anna L. Le. see Le Breton, Anna L.
Breton, Nicholas, 1545?-1626?
xBreton, Nicholas.
Works in Verse & Prose of Nicholas Breton. AMS Pr.
Breton, Preston P. Le. see Le Breton, Preston P.

Bretscher, Paul G.
xBretscher, Paul G.
Cain, Come Home!. Clayton Pub Hse.
Bretsznajder, S. see Bretsznajder, Stanisaw.
Bretsznajder, Stanisaw, 1907-1967
xBretsznajder, S.
Prediction of Transport and Other Physical Properties of Fluids. Pergamon.
Brett, Bill, 1922-
xBrett, Bill.
The Stolen Steers: A Tale of the Big Thicket. Tex A&M Univ Pr.
There Ain't No Such Animal & Other East Texas Tales. Tex A&M Univ Pr.
Brett, George. see Brett, George Sidney.
Brett, George S. see Brett, George Sidney.
Brett, George Sidney.
xBrett, George.
Psychology, Ancient & Modern. Cooper Sq.
xBrett, George S.
Brett's History of Psychology. MIT Pr.
Brett, Gerard.
xBrett, Gerard.
Dinner Is Served: A Study in Manners. Shoe String.
Brett, James, 1927-
xBrett, James.
Looking into Houses. Watson-Guptill.
Brett, M.
xBrett, M.
The English Church Under Henry I. Oxford U Pr.
Brett, Michael, 1921-
xBrett, Michael.
Diamond Kill. Berkley Pub.
Brett, Simon.
xBrett, Simon.
An Amateur Corpse. Berkley Pub.
An Amateur Corpse. Scribner.
Brett, William F.
xBrett, William F.
Contemporary College Mathematics. West Pub.
Brett-James, Anthony. see Brett-James, Antony.
Brett-James, Antony, 1920-
xBrett-James, Anthony.
The Triple Stream: Four Centuries of English, French & German Literature 1531-1930. Folcroft.
Bretton, Henry L., 1916-
xBretton, Henry L.
Power & Politics in Africa. Beresford Bk Serv.
The Power of Money. State U NY Pr.
Bretz, Mary L. see Bretz, Mary Lee.
Bretz, Mary Lee.
xBretz, Mary L.
Concha Espina. Twayne.
Bretz, Rudolf.
xBretz, Rudy.
Taxonomy of Communication Media. Educ Tech Pubns.
Bretz, Rudy. see Bretz, Rudolf.
Breuer, Melvin A.
xBreuer, Melvin A.
Diagnosis & Reliable Design of Digital Systems. Computer Sci.
ed. Digital System Design Automation: Languages, Simulation & Data Base. Computer Sci.
Breuer, R. A. see Breuer, Reinhard A.
Breuer, Reinhard A., 1946-
xBreuer, R. A.
Gravitational Perturbation Theory & Synchrotron Radiation. Springer-Verlag.
Breuil, Henri, 1877-1961
xBreuil, Henri.
Beyond the Bounds of History: Scenes from the Old Stone Age. AMS Pr.
Breul, Frank R.
xBreul, Frank R.

ed. Compassion & Responsibility: Readings in
the History of Social Welfare Policy in the
United States. U of Chicago Pr.

Breunig, Leroy C., 1915-
xBreunig, LeRoy C.
Guillaume Apollinaire. Columbia U Pr.

Brew, Margaret W.
xBrew, Margaret W.
The Burtons of Dunroe. Garland Pub.

Brewer, Clifton H. *see* Brewer, Clifton Hartwell.

Brewer, Clifton Hartwell, 1876-1947
xBrewer, Clifton H.
History of Religious Education in the Episcopal
Church to 1835. Arno.

Brewer, D. S. *see* Brewer, Derek Stanley.

Brewer, David. *see* Brewer, David Josiah.

Brewer, David J. *see* Brewer, David Josiah.

Brewer, David Josiah.
xBrewer, David.
ed. The World's Best Orations. Scholarly.
xBrewer, David J.
ed. World's Best Orations. Scarecrow.

Brewer, Derek. *see* Brewer, Derek Stanley.

Brewer, Derek Stanley.
xBrewer, D. S.
Chaucer in His Time. Longman.
xBrewer, Derek.
Chaucer in His Time. Greenwood.

Brewer, Elisabeth.
xBrewer, Elisabeth.
tr. From Cuchulainn to Gawain: Sources &
Analogues of Sir Gawain & the Green
Knight. Rowman.

Brewer, G. J. *see* Brewer, George J.

Brewer, Gail S. *see* Brewer, Gail Sforza.

Brewer, Gail Sforza.
xBrewer, Gail S.
What Every Pregnant Woman Should Know:
The Truth About Diets & Drugs in
Pregnancy. Penguin.

Brewer, Garry D.
xBrewer, Gary D.
Politicians, Bureaucrats & the Consultant: A
Critique of Urban Problem Solving. Basic.

Brewer, Gary D. *see* Brewer, Garry D.

Brewer, George D.
xBrewer, George D.
The Fighting Editor; or, Warren & the Appeal.
Beekman Pubs.

Brewer, George J., 1930-
xBrewer, G. J.
Introduction to Isozyme Techniques. Acad Pr.

Brewer, J. Gordon. *see* Brewer, James Gordon.

Brewer, J. M. *see* Brewer, John Michael.

Brewer, J. Mason. *see* Brewer, John Mason.

Brewer, J. W. *see* Brewer, Jesse Wayne.

Brewer, Jack A.
xBrewer, Jack A.
Fellowships from A to Z. Broadman.

Brewer, James Gordon.
xBrewer, J. Gordon.
The Literature of Geography: A Guide to Its
Organisation & Use. Shoe String.

Brewer, James H.
xBrewer, James H.
Confederate Negro: Virginia's Craftsmen &
Military Laborers, 1861-1865. Duke.

Brewer, Jesse Wayne.
xBrewer, J. W.
ed. Readings in Insect-Plant Disease
Relationships. Mss Info.

Brewer, Jo.
xBrewer, Jo.
Butterflies. Abrams.

Brewer, John Mason, 1896-
xBrewer, J. Mason.
ed. American Negro Folklore. Times Bks.

Brewer, John Michael.
xBrewer, J. M.

Experimental Techniques in Biochemistry. P-H.

Brewer, John T.
xBrewer, John T.
Deutsche Perspektiven. Heath.

Brewer, L. *see* Brewer, Luther Albertus.

Brewer, Luther A. *see* Brewer, Luther Albertus.

Brewer, Luther Albertus.
xBrewer, L.
Leigh Hunt & Charles Dickens: The Skimpole
Caricature. Haskell.
xBrewer, Luther A.
Leaves from a Leigh Hunt Note-Book.
Folcroft.
Leigh Hunt & Charles Dickens: The Skimpole
Caricature. Folcroft.
Some Lamb & Browning Letters to Leigh
Hunt. Folcroft.

Brewer, Mary.
xBrewer, Mary.
Which Is Biggest?. Childs World.

Brewer, R. *see* Brewer, Roy.

Brewer, Roy.
xBrewer, R.
Fabric & Mineral Analysis of Soils. Krieger.

Brewer, Thomas L., 1941-
xBrewer, Thomas L.
American Foreign Policy: A Contemporary
Introduction. P-H.

Brewer, Waldo L. *see* Brewer, Waldo Lyle.

Brewer, Waldo Lyle, 1913-
xBrewer, Waldo L.
Factors Affecting Student Achievement &
Change in a Physical Science Survey Course.
AMS Pr.

Brewer, Willis.
xBrewer, Willis.
Alabama: Her History, Resources, War Record,
& Public Men, from 1540 to 1872. Reprint.

Brewer, Wilmon, 1895-
xBrewer, Wilmon.
Adventures in Verse. M Jones.
Life of Maurice Parker. M Jones.

Brewington, Marion V. *see* Brewington, Marion Vernon.

Brewington, Marion Vernon, 1902-
xBrewington, Marion V.
Chesapeake Bay Log Canoes & Bugeyes.
Cornell Maritime.

Brewster, Beverly J.
xBrewster, Beverly J.
American Overseas Library Technical
Assistance, 1940-1970. Scarecrow.

Brewster, David, Sir, 1781-1868
xBrewster, David.
The Stereoscope, Its History, Theory &
Construction. Morgan.

Brewster, Dorothy.
xBrewster, Dorothy.
Modern Fiction. Arno.
Virginia Woolf's London. Greenwood.

Brewster, John W.
xBrewster, John W.
Index to Book Reviews in Historical
Periodicals, 1973. Scarecrow.

Brewster, Kingman, 1919-
xBrewster, Kingman.
Antitrust & American Business Abroad. Arno.

Brewster, Letitia.
xBrewster, Letitia.
The Changing American Diet. Ctr Sci Public.

Brewster, Paul G.
xBrewster, Paul G.
ed. Children's Games & Rhymes. Arno.

Brewster, R. *see* Brewster, Ray Quincy.

Brewster, Ray O. *see* Brewster, Ray Quincy.

Brewster, Ray Quincy.
xBrewster, R.
Organic Chemistry. P-H.
xBrewster, Ray O.

Brief Course in Experimental Organic
Chemistry. D Van Nostrand.

Brewton, Sara. *see* Brewton, Sara Westbrook.

Brewton, Sara Westbrook.
xBrewton, Sara.
ed. Laughable Limericks. T Y Crowell.
Of Quarks, Quasars & Other Quirks: Quizzical
Poems for the Supersonic Age. T Y Crowell.

Brey, Catherine F.
xBrey, Catherine F.
The Complete Bloodhound. Howell Bk.

Breyer, Donald E.
xBreyer, Donald E.
Design of Wood Structures. McGraw.

Breyer, Ralph F. *see* Breyer, Ralph Frederick.

Breyer, Ralph Frederick, 1897-
xBreyer, Ralph F.
The Marketing Institution. Arno.
Quantitative Systemic Analysis & Control.
Arno.

Breyer, Siegfried.
xBreyer, Siegfried.
Guide to the Soviet Navy. Naval Inst Pr.

Breyer, Stephen G.
xBreyer, Stephen G.
Energy Regulation by the Federal Power
Commission. Brookings.

Breyfogle, Ethel.
xBreyfogle, Ethel.
Creating a Learning Environment: A Learning
Center Handbook. Goodyear.

Brezhnev, Leonid. *see* Brezhnev, Leonid Ilich.

Brezhnev, Leonid Ilich, 1906-
xBrezhnev, Leonid.
Peace, Detente, & Soviet-American Relations:
A Collection of Public Statements by Leonid
Brezhnev. HarBraceJ.

Brian, Breffny De. *see* De Breffny, Brian.

Brian, Denis.
xBrian, Denis.
Tallulah, Darling: A Biography of Tallulah
Bankhead. Macmillan.

Brian, M. V. *see* Brian, Michael Vaughan.

Brian, Michael Vaughan.
xBrian, M. V.
ed. Production Ecology of Ants & Termites.
Cambridge U Pr.

Brian, P. L. *see* Brian, P. L. Thibaut.

Brian, P. L. Thibaut, 1930-
xBrian, P. L.
Staged Cascades in Chemical Processing. P-H.

Briar, Katharine H.
xBriar, Katharine H.
The Effect of Long-Term Unemployment on
Workers & Their Families. R & E Res Assoc.

Briar, Scott.
xBriar, Scott.
Problems & Issues in Social Casework.
Columbia U Pr.

Briazack, Norman J.
xBriazack, Norman J.
The UFO Guidebook. Citadel Pr.

Brice, William C. *see* Brice, William Charles.

Brice, William Charles.
xBrice, William C.
ed. The Environmental History of the Near &
Middle East Since the Last Ice Age. Acad
Pr.

Brichant, Colette.
xBrichant, Collette.
ed. French for the Humanities. P-H.
French Grammar: The Key to Reading. P-H.

Brichant, Collette. *see* Brichant, Colette.

Brichta, A. *see* Brichta, A. M.

Brichta, A. M.
xBrichta, A.
From Project to Production. Pergamon.

Brickbauer, Elwood A.
xBrickbauer, Elwood A.

Approved Practices in Crop Production.
Interstate.
Brickell, John, 1710?-1745
xBrickell, John.
Natural History of North Carolina. Johnson
NC.
The Natural History of North Carolina.
Johnson Repr.
Bricker, Clark E.
xBricker, Clark E.
Foundations of Chemistry: A Laboratory
Manual. HarBraceJ.
Bricklin, Alice G.
xBricklin, Alice G.
Motherlove: Natural Mothering, Birth to Three
Years. Running Pr.
Bricklin, Mark.
xBricklin, Mark.
The Practical Encyclopedia of Natural Healing.
Rodale Pr Inc.
Brickman, William. see Brickman, William W.
Brickman, William W.
xBrickman, William.
ed. Automation, Education, & Human Values.
Peter Smith.
Brickner, Richard P.
xBrickner, Richard P.
Bringing Down the House. Belmont Tower.
Bridaham, Lester B. see Bridaham, Lester Burbank.
Bridaham, Lester Burbank.
xBridaham, Lester B.
Gargoyles, Chimeres, & the Grotesque in
French Gothic Sculpture. Da Capo.
Bridbury, A. R.
xBridbury, A. R.
England & the Salt Trade in the Later Middle
Ages. Greenwood.
Bride's Magazine Editors. see The Bride'S Magazine.
Bridenbaugh, Carl.
xBridenbaugh, Carl.
Cities in Revolt: Urban Life in America,
1743-1776. Oxford U Pr.
Cities in the Wilderness: The First Century of
Urban Life in America, 1625-1742. Oxford U
Pr.
Colonial Craftsman. U of Chicago Pr.
Silas Downer - Forgotten Patriot: His Life &
Writings. Ri Pubns Soc.
The Bride'S Magazine.
xBride's Magazine.
ed. The Bride's Wedding Planner. Popular Lib.
xBride's Magazine Editors.
Bride's Book of Etiquette. G&D.
Questions & Answers About Love & Sex. St
Martin.
Bridge, Carl J.
xBridge, Carl J.
Alcoholism & Driving. C C Thomas.
Bridge, F. R.
xBridge, F. R.
From Sadowa to Sarajevo: The Foreign Policy
of Austria-Hungary 1866-1914. Routledge &
Kegan.
Bridge, Frederick, Sir, 1844-1924
xBridge, Frederick.
The Old Cryes of London. AMS Pr.
Old Cryes of London. Longwood Pr.
Bridge, Horatio, 1806-1893
xBridge, Horatio.
Personal Recollections of Nathaniel
Hawthorne. Haskell.
Personal Recollections of Nathaniel
Hawthorne. R West.
Bridge, James H. see Bridge, James Howard.
Bridge, James Howard, 1858-1939
xBridge, James H.
Uncle Sam at Home. Arno.
Bridge, R. Gary.
xBridge, R. Gary.

The Determinants of Educational Outcomes:
Impact of Families, Peers, Teachers &
Schools. Ballinger Pub.
Bridge, Raymond.
xBridge, Raymond.
America's Backpacking Book. Scribner.
Bike Touring: The Sierra Club Guide to
Outings on Wheels. Sierra.
The Camper's Guide to Alaska, the Yukon, &
Northern British Columbia. Scribner.
Climbing: A Guide to Mountaineering.
Scribner.
The Complete Canoeist's Guide. Scribner.
The Complete Snow Camper's Guide. Scribner.
Tourguide to the Rocky Mountain Wilderness.
Pruett.
Bridge, Ruth.
xBridge, Ruth E.
Challenge of Change: Three Centuries of
Enfield, Connecticut History. Phoenix Pub.
Bridge, Ruth E. see Bridge, Ruth.
Bridgeman, Harriet.
xBridgeman, Harriet.
ed. Needlework: An Illustrated History.
Paddington.
Society Scandals. David & Charles.
Bridgers, Sue E. see Bridgers, Sue Ellen.
Bridgers, Sue Ellen.
xBridgers, Sue E.
Home Before Dark. Knopf.
Home Before Dark. Bantam.
Bridges, E. M. see Bridges, Edwin Michael.
Bridges, Edwin Michael.
xBridges, E. M.
World Soils. Cambridge U Pr.
Bridges, G. Wilson. see Bridges, George Wilson.
Bridges, George W. see Bridges, George Wilson.
Bridges, George Wilson.
xBridges, G. Wilson.
Annals of Jamaica. Biblio Dist
xBridges, George W.
Annals of Jamaica. Negro U Pr.
Bridges, Horace J. see Bridges, Horace James.
Bridges, Horace James.
xBridges, Horace J.
ed. Aspects of Ethical Religion: Essays in
Honor of Felix Adler on the Fiftieth
Anniversary of His Founding of the Ethical
Movement. Arno.
Taking the Name of Science in Vain. Arno.
Bridges, J. W. see Bridges, James Wilfred.
Bridges, James Wilfred.
xBridges, J. W.
ed. Progress in Drug Metabolism. Wiley.
Bridges, Jerry.
xBridges, Jerry.
The Pursuit of Holiness. NavPress.
Bridges, John H. see Bridges, John Henry.
Bridges, John Henry, 1832-1906
xBridges, John H.
The Life & Work of Roger Bacon: An
Introduction to the Opus Majus. Richwood
Pub.
Bridges, P. K. see Bridges, Paul Kenneth.
Bridges, Paul Kenneth.
xBridges, P. K.
Psychiatric Emergencies: Diagnosis &
Management. C C Thomas.
Bridges, Robert S. see Bridges, Robert Seymour.
Bridges, Robert Seymour, 1844-1930
xBridges, Robert S.
The Shorter Poems of Robert Bridges.
Hyperion Conn.
Bridges, Thomas C. see Bridges, Thomas Charles.
Bridges, Thomas Charles.
xBridges, Thomas C.
Master Minds of Modern Science. Arno.
More Heroes of Modern Adventure. Arno.
Bridges, William, 1901-
xBridges, William.

Gathering of Animals: An Unconventional
History of the New York Zoological Society.
Har-Row.
Lion Island. Morrow.
Bridgman, Elizabeth. see Bridgman, Elizabeth P.
Bridgman, Elizabeth P.
xBridgman, Elizabeth.
How to Travel with Grownups. T Y Crowell.
Bridgman, George B. see Bridgman, George Brant.
Bridgman, George Brant, 1864-1943
xBridgman, George B.
Bridgman's Life Drawing. Dover.
The Human Machine: The Anatomical
Structure & Mechanism of the Human Body.
Dover.
The Human Machine: The Anatomical
Structure & Mechanism of the Human Body.
Peter Smith.
Bridgman, Jon.
xBridgman, Jon.
German Africa: A Select Annotated
Bibliography. Hoover Inst Pr.
German Africa: A Select Annotated
Bibliography. Intl Pubns Serv.
Bridgman, P. W. see Bridgman, Percy Williams.
Bridgman, Percy W. see Bridgman, Percy Williams.
Bridgman, Percy Williams, 1882-
xBridgman, P. W.
The Nature of Thermodynamics. Peter Smith.
xBridgman, Percy W.
Dimensional Analysis. AMS Pr.
The Logic of Modern Physics. Arno.
Reflections of a Physicist. Arno.
Bridgman, Richard.
xBridgman, Richard.
Gertrude Stein in Pieces. Oxford U Pr.
Bridgwater, A. V.
xBridgwater, A. V.
Waste Recycling & Pollution Control
Handbook. Van Nos Reinhold.
Bridston, Keith R.
xBridston, Keith R.
ed. Casebook on Church & Society. Abingdon.
Bridwell, Norman.
xBridwell, Norman.
illus. Clifford the Big Red Dog. Schol Bk Serv.
illus. Clifford's Halloween. Schol Bk Serv.
Brief, Richard P., 1933-
xBrief, Richard P.
Nineteenth Century Capital Accounting &
Business Investment. Arno.
Briefs, Henry W.
xBriefs, Henry W.
Pricing Power & Administrative Inflation:
Concepts Facts & Policy Implications. Am
Enterprise.
Brieger, Gert H.
xBrieger, Gert H.
ed. Medical America in the Nineteenth
Century: Readings from the Literature. Johns
Hopkins.
Brieger, Peter. see Brieger, Peter H.
Brieger, Peter H.
xBrieger, Peter.
Illuminated Manuscripts of the Divine
Comedy. Princeton U Pr.
Brieland, Donald.
xBrieland, Donald.
Contemporary Social Work: An Introduction to
Social Work & Social Welfare. McGraw.
Brier, Bob.
xBrier, Bob.
Intro. by Precognition & the Philosophy of
Science: An Essay on Backward Causation.
Humanities.
Brierley, Alec. see Brierley, Alec Geoffrey.
Brierley, Alec Geoffrey.
xBrierley, Alec.

An Illustrated History of the Kelly Gang. Intl
Schol Bk Serv.
Brierley, John. *see* Brierley, John Keith.
Brierley, John Keith, 1927-
xBrierley, John.
The Growing Brain: Childhood's Crucial Years.
Humanities.
Brierly, James L. *see* Brierly, James Leslie.
Brierly, James Leslie, 1881-1955
xBrierly, James L.
Law of Nations: An Introduction to the
International Law of Peace. Oxford U Pr.
Briffault, Robert, 1876-1948
xBriffault, Robert.
Reasons for Anger. Arno.
Sin & Sex. AMS Pr.
Sin & Sex. Haskell.
Briggaman, Joan. *see* Briggaman, Joan S.
Briggaman, Joan S.
xBriggaman, Joan.
Practical Problems in Mathematics for Office
Workers. Delmar.
Briggs. *see* Briggs, David John.
Briggs, Andrew J.
xBriggs, Andrew J.
Warehouse Operations Planning &
Management. Krieger.
Briggs, Anne K.
xBriggs, Anne K.
Case Simulations in Psychosocial Occupational
Therapy. Davis Co.
Briggs, Asa.
xBriggs, Asa.
Chartist Studies. St Martin.
Iron Bridge to Crystal Palace: Impact & Images
of the Industrial Revolution. Thames Hudson.
Briggs, Charles L., 1953-
xBriggs, Charles L.
The Wood Carvers of Cordova, New Mexico:
Social Dimensions of an Artistic "Revival". U
of Tenn Pr.
Briggs, D. E. *see* Briggs, Dennis Edward.
Briggs, David John.
xBriggs.
Soils. Butterworths.
Briggs, Dennie.
xBriggs, Dennie.
In Place of Prison. Intl Pubns Serv.
Briggs, Dennis Edward.
xBriggs, D. E.
Barley. Methuen Inc.
Briggs, Hilton M. *see* Briggs, Hilton Marshall.
Briggs, Hilton Marshall, 1913-
xBriggs, Hilton M.
Modern Breeds of Livestock. Macmillan.
Briggs, John, 1916-
xBriggs, John.
The Collector's Beethoven. Greenwood.
Briggs, John C.
xBriggs, John C.
Marine Zoogeography. McGraw.
Briggs, K. M. *see* Briggs, Katharine Mary.
Briggs, Katharine. *see* Briggs, Katharine Mary.
Briggs, Katharine M. *see* Briggs, Katharine Mary.
Briggs, Katharine Mary.
xBriggs, K. M.
Kate Crackernuts. Greenwillow.
xBriggs, Katharine.
Abbey Lubbers, Banshees & Boggarts: An
Illustrated Encyclopedia of Fairies. Pantheon.
An Encyclopedia of Fairies: Hobgoblins,
Brownies, Bogies, & Other Supernatural
Creatures. Pantheon.
The Vanishing People: Fairy Lore & Legends.
Pantheon.
xBriggs, Katharine M.
Personnel of Fairyland: A Short Account of the
Fairy People of Great Britain for Those Who
Tell Stories to Children. Gale.
xBriggs, Katherine M.

ed. Folktales of England. U of Chicago Pr.
Pale Hecates Team: Examination of the Beliefs
on Witchcraft and Magic Among
Shakespeare's Contemporaries & His
Immediate Succesors. Arno.
Briggs, Katherine M. *see* Briggs, Katharine Mary.
Briggs, L. Vernon. *see* Briggs, Lloyd Vernon.
Briggs, Lawrence P. *see* Briggs, Lawrence Palmer.
Briggs, Lawrence Palmer.
xBriggs, Lawrence P.
Ancient Khmer Empire. Am Philos.
Briggs, le Baron Russell, 1835-1934
xBriggs, Russell.
Men, Women & Colleges. Arno.
Briggs, Leslie J.
xBriggs, Leslie J.
Instructional Design: Principles & Applications.
Educ Tech Pubns.
Briggs, Lloyd V. *see* Briggs, Lloyd Vernon.
Briggs, Lloyd Vernon, 1863-1941
xBriggs, L. Vernon.
History of the Psychopathic Hospital, Boston,
Massachusetts. Arno.
xBriggs, Lloyd V.
Two Years' Service on the Reorganized State
Board of Insanity in Massachusetts, August,
1914 to August, 1916. Arno.
A Victory for Progress in Mental Medicine.
Arno.
Briggs, Martin S. *see* Briggs, Martin Shaw.
Briggs, Martin Shaw, 1882-
xBriggs, Martin S.
The Architect in History. Da Capo.
Baroque Architecture. Da Capo.
Muhammadan Architecture in Egypt &
Palestine. Da Capo.
Briggs, Mitchell P. *see* Briggs, Mitchell Pirie.
Briggs, Mitchell Pirie.
xBriggs, Mitchell P.
George D. Herron & the European Settlement.
AMS Pr.
Briggs, Nancy E.
xBriggs, Nancy E.
Children's Literature Through Storytelling &
Drama. Wm C Brown.
Briggs, Peter.
xBriggs, Peter.
Men in the Sea. S&S.
Briggs, Philip J.
xBriggs, Philip J.
ed. Politics in America: Readings &
Documents. Mss Info.
Briggs, Raymond.
xBriggs, Raymond.
illus. Father Christmas. Coward.
Father Christmas. Penguin.
Fungus the Bogeyman. Random.
Briggs (Wm.) and Co.
xBriggs, Wm. & Co.
Designs & Patterns for Embroiderers &
Craftsmen: 512 Motifs from the Wm. Briggs
& Co. "Album of Transfer Patterns". Peter
Smith.
Briggs, Russell. *see* Briggs, le Baron Russell.
Briggs, Wm. & Co. *see* Briggs (Wm.) and Co.
Briggum, Sue M.
xBriggum, Sue M.
A Concordance to Conrad's Almayer's Folly.
Garland Pub.
Brigham, Albert P. *see* Brigham, Albert Perry.
Brigham, Albert Perry, 1855-1932
xBrigham, Albert P.

ed. Geographic Influences in American
History. B Franklin.
Geographic Influences in American History.
Gordon Pr.
Geographic Influences in American History.
Kennikat.
Geographic Influences in American History.
Norwood Edns.
Brigham, Amariah, 1798-1849
xBrigham, Amariah.
An Inquiry Concerning the Diseases &
Functions of the Brain, the Spinal Cord the
Nerves. Arno.
Observations on the Influence of Religion
Upon the Health & Physical Welfare of
Mankind. Arno.
Observations on the Influence of Religion
Upon the Health & Physical Welfare of
Mankind, 1835: Remarks on the Influence of
Mental Cultivation & Mental Excitement
Upon Health. Schol Facsimiles.
Brigham, Clarence S. *see* Brigham, Clarence Saunders.
Brigham, Clarence Saunders, 1877-1963
xBrigham, Clarence S.
History & Bibliography of American
Newspapers, 1690-1820. Greenwood.
Journals & Journeymen: A Contribution to the
History of Early American Newspapers.
Greenwood.
Brigham, E. F. *see* Brigham, Eugene F.
Brigham, E. Oran, 1940-
xBrigham, E. Oran.
Fast Fourier Transform. P-H.
Brigham, Eugene. *see* Brigham, Eugene F.
Brigham, Eugene F., 1930-
xBrigham, E. F.
Decisions in Financial Management: Cases.
HR&W.
xBrigham, Eugene.
Liberalized Depreciation & the Cost of Capital.
Mich St U Busn.
xBrigham, Eugene F.
Fundamentals of Financial Management.
Dryden Pr.
Issues in Managerial Finance. Dryden Pr.
Brigham, Grace.
xBrigham, Grace R.
The Serial Number Book for U. S. Cars:
1900-1975. Motorbooks Intl.
Brigham, Grace R. *see* Brigham, Grace.
Brigham, John, 1945-
xBrigham, John.
Constitutional Language: An Interpretation of
Judicial Decision. Greenwood.
Brigham, John C. *see* Brigham, John Carl.
Brigham, John Carl.
xBrigham, John C.
Contemporary Issues in Social Psychology.
Brooks-Cole.
Brigham Young University College of Humanities. *see*
Brigham Young University, Provo, Utah.
Brigham Young University Microbiology Faculty. *see*
Brigham Young University, Provo, Utah.
Brigham Young University, Provo, Utah.
xBrigham Young University College of Humanities.
The Need Beyond Reason & Other Essays.
Brigham.
xBrigham Young University Microbiology Faculty.
Introductory Laboratory Manual of
Microbiology for Health Related Professions.
Burgess.
Bright, Deborah.
xBright, Deborah.
Creative Relaxation: Turning Your Stress into
Positive Energy. HarBraceJ.
Bright, Elizabeth.
xBright, Elizabeth.
Reap the Wild Harvest. PB.
Bright, Elizabeth S.
xBright, Elizabeth S.

A Word Geography of California & Nevada. U
of Cal Pr.
Bright, Greg.
xBright, Greg.
The Great Maze Book: Extraordinary Puzzles
for Extraordinary People. Pantheon.
The Hole Maze Book. Pantheon.
Bright, James F. see Bright, James Franck.
Bright, James Franck, 1832-1920
xBright, James F.
Maria Theresa. Arno.
Bright, James L.
xBright, James L.
Outdoor Recreation Projects. Structures Pub.
Bright, James R. see Bright, James Rieser.
Bright, James Rieser.
xBright, James R.
Automation & Management. Pergamon.
Bright, John.
xBright, John.
The Authority of the Old Testament. Baker Bk.
Covenant & Promise: The Prophetic
Understanding of the Future in Pre-Exilic
Israel. Westminster.
A History of Israel. Westminster.
Bright, Robert, 1902-
xBright, Robert.
Friendly Bear. Doubleday.
illus. Georgie & the Buried Treasure.
Doubleday.
Georgie & the Magician. Doubleday.
Georgie & the Noisy Ghost. Doubleday.
Georgie Goes West. Doubleday.
Georgie's Christmas Carol. Doubleday.
The Life & Death of Little Jo. U of NM Pr.
Me & the Bears. Doubleday.
Bright, William, 1928-
xBright, William.
ed. Coyote Stories. Univ Microfilms.
Brightbill, Charles K. see Brightbill, Charles Kestner.
Brightbill, Charles Kestner, 1910-1966
xBrightbill, Charles K.
Challenge of Leisure. P-H.
Brightfield, Myron F. see Brightfield, Myron Franklin.
Brightfield, Myron Franklin, 1897-1964
xBrightfield, Myron F.
Theodore Hook & His Novels. Scholarly.
Brightfield, Rick.
xBrightfield, Rick.
Outer Space Mazes. Har-Row.
Brightman, Alan.
xBrightman, Alan.
Like Me. Little.
Brightman, Edgar S. see Brightman, Edgar Sheffield.
Brightman, Edgar Sheffield, 1884-1953
xBrightman, Edgar S.
Personality & Religion. AMS Pr.
The Spiritual Life. AMS Pr.
Brightman, Robert.
xBrightman, Robert.
The Home Owner Handbook of Carpentry &
Woodworking. Crown.
Brighton, C. A.
xBrighton, C. A.
Styrene Polymers: Technology &
Environmental Aspects. Burgess-Intl Ideas.
Brighton, Howard.
xBrighton, Howard.
Utilizing Teacher Aides in Differentiated
Staffing. Pendell Pub.
Brigner, Willard L.
xBrigner, Willard L.
Who Love & Make a Lie. Branden.
Brijbhushan, Jamila.
xBrijbhushan, Jamila.
The World of Indian Miniatures. Kodansha.
Brilhart, John K.
xBrilhart, John K.
Effective Group Discussion. Wm C Brown.
Brill, A. A. see Brill, Abraham Arden.

Brill, Abraham Arden, 1874-1948
xBrill, A. A.
Fundamental Conceptions of Psychoanalysis.
Arno.
Brill, Albert, 1891-
xBrill, Albert.
Fundamental Fundamentals. Philos Lib.
Brill, Charles.
xBrill, Charles.
Indian & Free: A Contemporary Portrait of
Life on a Chippewa Reservation. U of Minn
Pr.
Brill, Edith, 1899-
xBrill, Edith.
Old Cotswold. Kelley.
Brilliant, Alan.
xBrilliant, Alan.
Journeyman. Unicorn Pr.
Brilliant, Richard.
xBrilliant, Richard.
Arts of the Ancient Greeks. McGraw.
Brillinger, Peter C.
xBrillinger, Peter C.
Introduction to Data Structures &
Non-Numeric Computation. P-H.
Brillouin, Leon, 1889-
xBrillouin, Leon.
Relativity Reexamined. Acad Pr.
Briloff, Abraham J.
xBriloff, Abraham J.
More Debits Than Credits: The Burnt
Investor's Guide to Financial Statements.
Har-Row.
Unaccountable Accounting. Har-Row.
Brim, Orville G. see Brim, Orville Gilbert.
Brim, Orville Gilbert, 1923-
xBrim, Orville G.
ed. Dying Patient. Russell Sage.
The Dying Patient. Transaction Bks.
Personality & Decision Processes: Studies in
the Social Psychology of Thinking. Stanford
U Pr.
Socialization After Childhood: Two Essays.
Krieger.
xBrim, Q. G.
Socialization After Childhood: Two Essays.
Wiley.
Brim, Q. G. see Brim, Orville Gilbert.
Brimblecombe, R. W. see Brimblecombe, Roger William.
Brimblecombe, Roger William.
xBrimblecombe, R. W.
Drug Actions on Cholinergic Systems. Univ
Park.
Brimer, A. see Brimer, Alan.
Brimer, Alan.
xBrimer, A.
Sources of Difference in School Achievement.
Humanities.
Brimer, John. see Brimer, John Burton.
Brimer, John B. see Brimer, John Burton.
Brimer, John Burton.
xBrimer, John.
Growing Herbs in Pots. S&S.
Growing Herbs in Pots. S&S.
xBrimer, John B.
Homeowner's Complete Outdoor Building
Book. Har-Row.
Brimmer, Andrew F.
xBrimmer, Andrew F.
Capital Shortage: Real or Imagined?. U Mich
Busn Div Res.
Brin, Ruth. see Brin, Ruth Firestone.
Brin, Ruth F. see Brin, Ruth Firestone.
Brin, Ruth Firestone.
xBrin, Ruth.
Butterflies Are Beautiful. Lerner Pubns.
xBrin, Ruth F.

A Rag of Love. Emmett.
The Story of Esther. Lerner Pubns.
Brinckloe, Julie.
xBrinckloe, Julie.
Gordon Goes Camping. Doubleday.
Gordon's House. Doubleday.
The Spider Web. Doubleday.
Brinckman, E. see Brinckman, Eric.
Brinckman, Eric.
xBrinckman, E.
Unconventional Imaging Processes. Focal Pr.
Brindle, Reginald S. see Brindle, Reginald Smith.
Brindle, Reginald Smith, 1917-
xBrindle, Reginald S.
Contemporary Percussion. Oxford U Pr.
Brindley, Louise.
xBrindley, Louise.
They Must Have Seen Me Coming. St Martin.
Brindze, Ruth, 1903-
xBrindze, Ruth.
Charting the Oceans. Vanguard.
Look How Many People Wear Glasses: The
Magic of Lenses. Atheneum.
Not to Be Broadcast: The Truth About the
Radio. Da Capo.
Bringgold, Diane.
xBringgold, Diane.
Life Instead. Word Bks.
Bringhurst, Bruce.
xBringhurst, Bruce.
Antitrust & Oil Monopoly: The Standard Oil
Cases, 1890-1911. Greenwood.
Bringle, Mary.
xBringle, Mary.
Fortunes. Putnam.
Brings, Allen.
xBrings, Allen.
A New Approach to Keyboard Harmony.
Norton.
Bringuier, Jean Claude.
xBringuier, Jean-Claude.
Conversations with Jean Piaget. U of Chicago
Pr.
Bringuier, Jean-Claude. see Bringuier, Jean Claude.
Brininstool, E. A. see Brininstool, Earl Alonzo.
Brininstool, Earl Alonzo, 1870-1957
xBrininstool, E. A.
Fighting Red Cloud's Warriors: True Tales of
Indian Days When the West Was Young.
Cooper Sq.
A Trooper with Custer & Other Historic
Incidents of the Battle of the Little Big Horn.
Cooper Sq.
Brink, Andre. see Brink, Andre Philippus.
Brink, Andre Philippus, 1935-
xBrink, Andre.
A Dry White Season. Morrow.
Brink, Carol R. see Brink, Carol Ryrie.
Brink, Carol Ryrie.
xBrink, Carol R.
The Bad Times of Irma Baumlein. Macmillan.
The Bad Times of Irma Baumlein. Macmillan.
Caddie Woodlawn. Macmillan.
Louly. Macmillan.
Two Are Better Than One. Macmillan.
Brink, Terry L.
xBrink, Terry L.
Geriatric Psychotherapy. Human Sci Pr.
Brink, Victor Z. see Brink, Victor Zinn.
Brink, Victor Zinn.
xBrink, Victor Z.
Modern Internal Auditing: An Operational
Approach. Ronald Pr.
Brink, William P.
xBrink, William P.
Manual of Christian Reformed Church
Government. Bd of Pubns CRC.
Brinker, R. see Brinker, Ray A.
Brinker, Ray A.
xBrinker, R.

Radiology Special Procedure Room. Univ Park.
Brinkerhoff, John S. *see* Brinkerhoff, John Scott.
Brinkerhoff, John Scott, 1944-
xBrinkerhoff, John S.
All in Time. Golden Quill.
Brinkman, George L. *see* Brinkman, George Loris.
Brinkman, George Loris.
xBrinkman, George L.
ed. Development of Rural America. Regents Pr
KS.
Brinkman, Grover, 1903-
xBrinkman, Grover.
Night of the Blood Moon. Independence Pr.
Brinkman, J. A.
xBrinkman, J. A.
A Catalogue of Cuneiform Sources Pertaining
to Specific Monarchs of the Kassite Dynasty.
Oriental Inst.
Brinkmann, H. W. *see* Brinkmann, Heinrich W.
Brinkmann, Heinrich W.
xBrinkmann, H. W.
Linear Algebra & Analytic Geometry. A-W.
Brinkworth, B. J. *see* Brinkworth, Brian Joseph.
Brinkworth, Brian Joseph.
xBrinkworth, B. J.
An Introduction to Experimentation. Elsevier.
Solar Energy for Man. Halsted Pr.
Brinley, Francis, 1800-1889
xBrinley, Francis.
Life of William T. Porter. Arno.
Brinnin, John M. *see* Brinnin, John Malcolm.
Brinnin, John Malcolm, 1916-
xBrinnin, John M.
Sorrows of Cold Stone: Poems, 1940-1950.
Greenwood.
Brinser, Ayers.
xBrinser, Ayers.
Respectability of Mr. Bernard Shaw. Folcroft.
ed. The Respectability of Mr. Bernard Shaw.
Haskell.
Brintnall, D. E. *see* Brintnall, Douglas E.
Brintnall, Douglas E., 1946-
xBrintnall, D. E.
Revolt Against the Dead: The Modernization
of a Mayan Community in the Highlands of
Guatemala. Gordon.
Brinton, Clarence Crane, 1898-1968
xBrinton, Crane.
Civilization in the West. P-H.
Ideas & Men: The Story of Western Thought.
P-H.
Brinton, Crane. *see* Brinton, Clarence Crane.
Brinton, Daniel G. *see* Brinton, Daniel Garrison.
Brinton, Daniel Garrison, 1837-1899
xBrinton, Daniel G.
The American Race: A Linguistic Classification
& Ethnographic Description of the Native
Tribes of North & South America. Johnson
Repr.
ed. The Maya Chronicles. AMS Pr.
The Myths of the New World: A Treatise on
the Symbolism & Mythology of the Red Race
in America. Gale.
Myths of the New World: A Treatise on the
Symbolism & Mythology of the Red Race of
America. Greenwood.
Myths of the New World: A Treatise on the
Symbolism & Mythology of the Red Race of
America. Haskell.
Myths of the New World: A Treatise on the
Symbolism & Mythology of the Red Race of
America. Longwood Pr.
Religions of Primitive Peoples. Negro U Pr.
Brinton, Howard. *see* Brinton, Howard Haines.
Brinton, Howard H. *see* Brinton, Howard Haines.
Brinton, Howard Haines, 1884-
xBrinton, Howard.

Ethical Mysticism in the Society of Friends.
Pendle Hill.
Light & Life in the Fourth Gospel. Pendle Hill.
xBrinton, Howard H.
Guide to Quaker Practice. Pendle Hill.
Religion of George Fox: As Revealed in His
Epistles. Pendle Hill.
Brinton, J. W. *see* Brinton, Job Wells.
Brinton, Job Wells, 1883-
xBrinton, J. W.
Wheat & Politics. Arno.
Brion, John M.
xBrion, John M.
Corporate Marketing Planning. Wiley.
Brion, Marcel, 1895-
xBrion, Marcel.
Pompeii & Herculaneum: The Glory & the
Grief. Merrimack Bk Serv.
Brisbane. *see* Brisbane, Holly E.
Brisbane, Albert, 1809-1890
xBrisbane, Albert.
Association: Or, a Concise Exposition of the
Practical Part of Fourier's Social Science.
AMS Pr.
Brisbane, Holly E.
xBrisbane.
Developing Child. Bennett Co.
xBrisbane, Holly E.
Developing Child. Bennett Co.
Brisco, Norris A. *see* Brisco, Norris Arthur.
Brisco, Norris Arthur, 1875-1944
xBrisco, Norris A.
Economic Policy of Robert Walpole. AMS Pr.
Brisco, Patty.
xBrisco, Patty.
House of Candles. Manor Bks.
Raging Rapids. Creative Ed.
Briscoe. *see* Briscoe, Dennis R.
Briscoe, Catherine.
xBriscoe, Catherine.
ed. Community Work: Learning & Supervision.
Allen Unwin.
Briscoe, D. Stuart.
xBriscoe, D. Stuart.
Living Dangerously. Zondervan.
What Works When Life Doesn't. Victor Bks.
Briscoe, Dennis R.
xBriscoe.
Experiences in Public Administration. Duxbury
Pr.
Briscoe, Jill.
xBriscoe, Jill.
Hush, Hush. Zondervan.
Prime Rib & Apple. Zondervan.
There's a Snake in My Garden. Zondervan.
Brislin, Richard W.
xBrislin, Richard W.
Cross-Cultural Orientation Programs. Halsted
Pr.
Cross-Cultural Orientation Programs. Krieger.
Brisman, S. *see* Brisman, Shimeon.
Brisman, Shimeon.
xBrisman, S.
A History & Guide to Judaic Bibliography.
Ktav.
Brissaud, J. B. *see* Brissaud, Jean Baptiste.
Brissaud, Jean B. *see* Brissaud, Jean Baptiste.
Brissaud, Jean Baptiste, 1854-1904
xBrissaud, J. B.
History of French Private Law. Rothman.
xBrissaud, Jean B.
History of French Private Law. Kelley.
Brissenden. *see* Brissenden, Alan.
Brissenden, Alan.
xBrissenden.
Shakespeare & the Dance. Humanities.
Brissett, Dennis.
xBrissett, Dennis.

Life As Theater: A Dramaturgical Sourcebook.
Aldine Pub.
Brister, C. W.
xBrister, C. W.
The Promise of Counseling. Har-Row.
Take Care. Broadman.
Bristol, Roger P. *see* Bristol, Roger Pattrell.
Bristol, Roger Pattrell.
xBristol, Roger P.
Supplement to Charles Evans' American
Bibliography. U Pr of Va.
Briston, J. H. *see* Briston, John Herbert.
Briston, John Herbert.
xBriston, J. H.
Packaging Management. Beekman Pubs.
Bristow, Alec.
xBristow, Alec.
The Easy Garden. T Y Crowell.
Bristow, Allen P.
xBristow, Allen P.
Field Interrogation. C C Thomas.
Bristow, Edward J.
xBristow, Edward J.
Vice & Vigilance: Purity Movements in Britain
Since 1700. Rowman.
Bristow, Gwen, 1903-
xBristow, Gwen.
Celia Garth. Popular Lib.
Celia Garth. T Y Crowell.
Deep Summer. PB.
Deep Summer. T Y Crowell.
Bristow, Robert.
xBristow, Robert.
Aches & Pains: How the Older Person Can
Find Relief Using Heat, Massages, &
Exercise. Pantheon.
Bristow, Thelma.
xBristow, Thelma.
Comparative Education Through the Literature:
A Bibliographic Guide. Shoe String.
Bristowe, William S. *see* Bristowe, William Syer.
Bristowe, William Syer.
xBristowe, William S.
Louis & the King of Siam. Thai-Am Pubs.
Britan, Gerald M.
xBritan, Gerald M.
ed. Hierarchy & Society: Anthropological
Perspectives on Bureaucracy. Inst Study
Human.
Brite, Robert L.
xBrite, Robert L.
Business Statistics. A-W.
British Amateur Weight Lifters Association.
xBritish Amateur Weight Lifters Association.
Weight Lifting. British Bk Ctr.
British Association for the Advancement of Science.
xBritish Association For The Advancement Of
Science.
Conflicts in Policy Objects. Kelley.
March of Science: A First Quinquennial
Review 1931-1935. Arno.
British Association for the Advancement of Science.
Committee on Local Industries.
xBritish Association For The Advancement Of
Science - Committee On Local Industries.
Resources, Products & Industrial History of
Birmingham & the Midland Hardware
Districts. Kelley.
British Association for the Advancement of Science.
Section F (Economics).
xBritish Association for the Advancement of
Science (Section F Economics).
Economics & Technical Change. Kelley.
Public Sector Economics. Kelley.
British Broadcasting Corporation.
xBBC.
Dictionary of Radio & Television Terms.
Heyden.
xBritish Broadcasting Corporation.

B B C Hymn Book. Oxford U Pr.

BBC Handbook 1979: Incorporating the
Annual Reports & Accounts, 1977-78. Intl
Pubns Serv.

City of Florence. Intl Pubns Serv.

British Ceramic Research Association.

xCeramists' Conference, First, Oct. 1963.

Silicate Analysis. British Bk Ctr.

British Columbia. Provincial Archives.

xProvincial Archives of British Columbia, Victoria.

Dictionary Catalogue of the Library of the
Provincial Archives of British Columbia. G K
Hall.

British Council. *see* Great Britain. British Council.

British Council & the Assn. of Commonwealth
Universities. *see* The Association of Commonwealth
Universities.

British Ecological Society.

xBritish Ecological Society Symposium, 8th.

Animal Population in Relation to Their Food
Resources. Lippincott.

The Measurements of Environmental Factors
in Terrestrial Ecology. Lippincott.

xBritish Ecological Society, 12th.

Mathematical Models In Ecology: Proceedings.
Lippincott.

xBritish Ecological Society, 9th Symposium.

Ecological Aspects of the Mineral Nutrition of
Plants: Proceedings. Lippincott.

British Ecological Society Symposium, 8th. *see* British
Ecological Society.

British Ecological Society, 12th. *see* British Ecological
Society.

British Ecological Society, 9th Symposium. *see* British
Ecological Society.

British Film Institute, London.

xBritish Film Institute, London.

Catalogue of the Book Library of the British
Film Institute. G K Hall.

British Foreign Office. *see* Great Britain. Foreign Office.

British Geotechnical Society. *see* Symposium on Field
Instruments, London, 1973.

British Government Public Record Office. *see* Great
Britain. Public Record Office.

British Interplanetary Society.

xBritish Interplanetary Society.

Handbook of Astronautics. Dufour.

British Leyland (Austin Morris) Limited.

xBritish Leyland Motors.

Complete Official Austin-Healey 100-Six &
3000, 1956-1968. Bentley.

The Complete Official Jaguar 'E': Comprising
the Official Driver's Handbook, Workshop
Manual, Special Tuning Manual. Bentley.

The Complete Official MG Midget 1500,
Model Years 1975-1979, Comprising the
Official Driver's Handbook & Workshop
Manual. Bentley.

The Complete Official MGB Model Years
1962-1974: Comprising the Official Driver's
Handbook, Workshop Manual, Special
Tuning Manual. Bentley.

Complete Official Sprite-Midget 948 & 1098cc:
Comprising the Official Driver's Handbook,
Workshop Manual, Special Tuning Manual.
Bentley.

Complete Official Triumph GT6, GT6 Plus
&GT6 Mk 3 1967-1973: Official Driver's
Handbooks & Official Workshop Manual.
Bentley.

The Complete Official Triumph Spitfire MK
III, MK IV & 1500, Model Years 1968-1974:
Comprising the Official Driver's Handbook &
Workshop Manual. Bentley.

The Complete Official Triumph Spitfire, Model
Years 1975-1980, Comprising the Official
Driver's Handbook & Workshop Manual.
Bentley.

Complete Official Triumph TR 7, 1975-1978:
Comprising the Official Driver's Handbook &
Repair Operation Manual. Bentley.

The Complete Official Triumph TR2 & TR3:
Comprising the Official Driver's Instruction
Book & Service Instruction Manual, Model
Years 1953-1961. Bentley.

Complete Official Triumph TR4 & TR4A
1961-1968: Official Driver's Handbook,
Workshop Manual, Competition Preparation
Manual. Bentley.

The Complete Official 1275 cc Sprite-Midget
1967-1974: Comprising the Official Driver's
Handbook, Workshop Manual, Emission
Control Supplement. Bentley.

British Leyland Motors. *see* British Leyland (Austin
Morris) Limited.

British Museum.

xBritish Museum.

Catalogue of the Books, Manuscripts, Maps &
Drawings in the British Museum. Lubrecht &
Cramer.

Human Biology-an Exhibition of Ourselves.
Cambridge U Pr.

Rhodesian Man & Associated Remains. AMS
Pr.

xBritish Museum. Department of Egyptian &
Assyrian Antiquities.

Babylonian Boundary-Stones & Memorial
Tablets in the British Museum. AMS Pr.

xBritish Museum. Dept. of Egyptian & Assyrian
Antiquities.

Annals of the Kings of Assyria. AMS Pr.

xBritish Museum Staff.

The British Museum Yearbook 1, 1975: The
Classical Tradition. FS&G.

xTheBritish Museum.

The Vikings. Morrow.

British Museum (Natural History).

xBritish Museum, Natural History.

Dinosaurs & Their Living Relatives. Cambridge
U Pr.

Life Before Birth. Cambridge U Pr.

xBritish Museum-Natural History.

Nature at Work. Cambridge U Pr.

British Museum. Department of Egyptian & Assyrian
Antiquities. *see* British Museum.

British Museum. Dept. of Egyptian & Assyrian
Antiquities. *see* British Museum.

British Museum, Natural History. *see* British Museum
(Natural History).

British Museum Staff. *see* British Museum.

British Museum-Natural History. *see* British Museum
(Natural History).

British Occupational Hygiene Society.

xBritish Occupational Hygiene Society.

Hygiene Standards of Chrysotile Asbestos
Dust. Pergamon.

Inhaled Particles III: Proceedings. State Mutual
Bk.

British Schools Council. *see* Great Britain. Schools
Council.

British Shippers' Council.

xBritish Shippers' Council.

Shipping Two Thousand: The Evolution of
Maritime Trade in the Next 10 to 25 Years:
an International Conference Held U Nder the
Auspices of the British Shippers' Council,
London Hilton-June 19th & 20th, 1979.
Biblio Dist.

British Society of Audiology.

xBritish Society of Audiology, 1st Conference,
Univ. of Dundee, July 1971.

Disorders of the Auditory Function:
Proceedings. Acad Pr.

British Society of Audiology, 1st Conference, Univ. of
Dundee, July 1971. *see* British Society of Audiology.

British Sulphur Corporation, Ltd.

xTheBritish Sulphur Corp. Ltd.

World Directory of Fertilizer Manufacturers.
Intl Pubns Serv.

British Tourist Authority.

xBritish Tourist Authority.

Britain Hotels & Restaurants 1978. Intl Pubns
Serv.

Hotels & Restaurants in Britian, 1976-77.
British Bk Ctr.

Britt, Albert, 1874-1969

xBritt, Albert.

Great Biographers. Arno.

Britt, Sam.

xBritt, Samuel S.

The Reality of Teaching. Kendall-Hunt.

Britt, Samuel S. *see* Britt, Sam.

Britt, Steuart Henderson, 1907-

xBritt, Stewart H.

Psychological Principles of Marketing &
Consumer Behavior. Lexington Bks.

Britt, Stewart H. *see* Britt, Steuart Henderson.

Brittain, Bill.

xBrittain, Bill.

All the Money in the World. Har-Row.

Brittain, Fred. *see* Brittain, Frederick.

Brittain, Frederick.

xBrittain, Fred.

Medieval Latin & Romance Lyric to A. D.
1300. Kraus Repr.

Brittain, James E., 1931-

xBrittain, James E.

ed. Turning Points in American Electrical
History. Inst Electrical.

ed. Turning Points in American Electrical
History. Wiley.

Brittain, Joan T., 1928-

xBrittain, Joan T.

Laurence Stallings. Twayne.

Brittain, John A.

xBrittain, John A.

Inheritance & the Inequality of Material
Wealth. Brookings.

The Inheritance of Economic Status.
Brookings.

The Payroll Tax for Social Security. Brookings.

Brittain, Vera. *see* Brittain, Vera Mary.

Brittain, Vera Mary.

xBrittain, Vera.

Valiant Pilgrim: The Story of John Bunyan &
Puritan England. R West.

Brittain, W. Lambert.

xBrittain, W. Lambert.

Creativity, Art, & the Young Child. Macmillan.
Brittan, Arthur.
  xBrittan, Arthur.
    Meanings & Situations. Routledge & Kegan.
    The Privatised World. Routledge & Kegan.
Brittan, Samuel.
  xBrittan, Samuel.
    Capitalism & the Permissive Society.
    Humanities.
    The Economic Consequences of Democracy.
    Holmes & Meier.
Brittan, Samuel. *see* Tyrrell, R. Emmett.
Britten, Emma H. *see* Britten, Emma Hardinge.
Britten, Emma Hardinge, d. 1899
  xBritten, Emma H.
    Nineteenth Century Miracles: Or, Spirits &
    Their Work in Every Country of the Earth.
    Arno.
Britten, Jessie D.
  xBritten, Jessie D.
    Practical Notes on Nursing Procedures.
    Churchill.
Brittin, Norman A.
  xBrittin, Norman A.
    Edna St. Vincent Millay. Coll & U Pr.
    Edna St. Vincent Millay. Twayne.
    Thomas Middleton. Twayne.
Britting, Kenneth R.
  xBritting, Kenneth R.
    Inertial Navigation Systems Analysis. Wiley.
Britton, Anna.
  xBritton, Anna.
    Fike's Point. Coward.
Britton, Edward C.
  xBritton, Edward C.
    Growing from Infancy to Adulthood: A
    Summary of the Changing Characteristics of
    Children & Youth. Irvington.
Britton, Jack R. *see* Britton, Jack Rolf.
Britton, Jack Rolf.
  xBritton, Jack R.
    Topics in Contemporary Mathematics.
    Har-Row.
Britton, Nathaniel L. *see* Britton, Nathaniel Lord.
Britton, Nathaniel Lord.
  xBritton, Nathaniel L.
    Cactaceae: Descriptions & Illustrations of
    Plants of the Cactus Family. Dover.
Brivic, Sheldon R., 1943-
  xBrivic, Sheldon R.
    Joyce Between Freud & Jung. Kennikat.
Brizova, Joza.
  xBrizova, Joza.
    Czechoslovak Cookbook. Crown.
Brizzi, Mary T.
  xBrizzi, Mary T.
    Reader's Guide to Philip Jose Farmer.
    Starmont Hse.
Bro, Harmon H. *see* Bro, Harmon Hartzell.
Bro, Harmon Hartzell, 1919-
  xBro, Harmon H.
    Edgar Cayce on Dreams. Warner Bks.
    Edgar Cayce on Religion & Psychic
    Experience. Warner Bks.
Broad, C. D. *see* Broad, Charlie Dunbar.
Broad, C. Lewis. *see* Broad, Lewis.
Broad, Charles D. *see* Broad, Charlie Dunbar.
Broad, Charlie Dunbar, 1887-1971
  xBroad, C. D.
    Examination of McTaggart's Philosophy.
    Octagon.
    Perception, Physics & Reality: An Enquiry into
    the Information That Physical Science Can
    Supply About the Real. Russell.
  xBroad, Charles D.
    Ethics & the History of Philosophy: Selected
    Essays. Hyperion Conn.
Broad, Lewis.
  xBroad, C. Lewis.

Dictionary to the Plays & Novels of Bernard
    Shaw: With Bibliography of His Works & of
    the Literature Concerning Him with the
    Record of the Principle Shawian Play
    Production. Scholarly.
Broadbent, D. E. *see* Broadbent, Donald Eric.
Broadbent, Donald Eric.
  xBroadbent, D. E.
    Decision & Stress. Acad Pr.
    In Defence of Empirical Psychology. Methuen
    Inc.
Broadbent, Geoffrey.
  xBroadbent, Geoffrey.
    Design in Architecture: Architecture & the
    Human Sciences. Wiley.
    Signs, Symbols & Architecture. Wiley.
Broadbent, R. J.
  xBroadbent, R. J.
    History of Pantomime. Arno.
Broadbent, T. A. *see* Broadbent, Thomas Andrew.
Broadbent, Thomas Andrew.
  xBroadbent, T. A.
    Planning & Profit in the Urban Economy.
    Methuen Inc.
Broadbent, W. W., 1919-
  xBroadbent, W. W.
    How to Be Loved. Warner Bks.
Broadbridge, Seymour. *see* Broadbridge, Seymour A.
Broadbridge, Seymour A.
  xBroadbridge, Seymour.
    Industrial Dualism in Japan: A Problem of
    Economic Growth & Structural Change.
    Biblio Dist.
Broadfoot, Barry.
  xBroadfoot, Barry.
    The City of Vancouver. U of Wash Pr.
Broadhouse, John.
  xBroadhouse, John.
    Musical Acoustics: Or the Phenomena of
    Sound As Connected with Music. Scholarly.
Broadhurst, R. J. *see* Broadhurst, Ronald J. C.
Broadhurst, Ronald J. C.
  xBroadhurst, R. J.
    A History of the Ayyubid Sultans of Egypt.
    Twayne.
Broadribb, Violet.
  xBroadribb, Violet.
    Foundations of Pediatric Nursing. Lippincott.
    Maternal-Child Nursing.. Lippincott.
Broadston, James A.
  xBroadston, James A.
    Control of Surface Quality. Surf-Chek.
Broadus, John A. *see* Broadus, John Albert.
Broadus, John Albert.
  xBroadus, John A.
    On the Preparation & Delivery of Sermons.
    Har-Row.
Broadwell, Martin M.
  xBroadwell, Martin M.
    The Lecture Method of Instruction. Educ Tech
    Pubns.
    New Supervisor. A-W.
    Supervising Today: A Guide for Positive
    Leadership. CBI Pub.
Broat, I. G.
  xBroat, I. G.
    The Master Mechanic. Atheneum.
Broccoletti, Peter P. *see* Broccoletti, Peter Paul Lusardi.
Broccoletti, Peter Paul Lusardi.
  xBroccoletti, Peter P.
    The Notre Dame Weight-Training Program for
    Baseball, Hockey, Wrestling, & Your Body.
    Icarus.
    The Notre Dame Weight Training Program for
    Football. Icarus.
Broce, Gerald.
  xBroce, Gerald.
    History of Anthropology. Burgess.
Broce, Thomas E., 1935-
  xBroce, Thomas E.

Directory of Oklahoma Foundations. U of Okla
    Pr.
    Fund Raising: The Guide to Raising Money
    from Private Sources. U of Okla Pr.
Brochmann, Elizabeth.
  xBrochmann, Elizabeth.
    What's the Matter Girl?. Har-Row.
Brock, Bernard L.
  xBrock, Bernard L.
    Public Policy Decision-Making: Systems
    Analysis & Comparative Advantages Debate.
    Har-Row.
Brock, Betty.
  xBrock, Betty.
    No Flying in the House. Har-Row.
Brock, Clifton.
  xBrock, Clifton.
    The Literature of Political Science: A Guide
    for Students, Librarians & Teachers. Bowker.
Brock, Earl E., 1890-
  xBrock, Earl E.
    Devotional Interpretation of Familiar Hymns.
    Arno.
Brock, Edwin.
  xBrock, Edwin.
    Paroxisms: A Guide to the Isms. New
    Directions.
    The Portraits & the Poses. New Directions.
    The River & the Train. New Directions.
Brock, Greg.
  xBrock, Greg.
    ed. How High School Runners Train. Tafnews.
Brock, H. I. *see* Brock, Henry Irving.
Brock, Henry Irving, 1876-1961
  xBrock, H. I.
    ed. Little Book of Limericks. Arno.
Brock, Horace R.
  xBrock, Horace R.
    Accounting, Principles & Applications.
    McGraw.
Brock, J. H. *see* Brock, James Harry Ernest.
Brock, James H. *see* Brock, James Harry Ernest.
Brock, James Harry Ernest.
  xBrock, J. H.
    Dramatic Purpose of Hamlet. Folcroft.
    Iago & Some Shakespearean Villains. Folcroft.
  xBrock, James H.
    Dramatic Purpose of Hamlet. AMS Pr.
    Iago & Some Shakespearean Villains. AMS Pr.
Brock, Jim.
  xBrock, Jim.
    The Devils' Coach. Cook.
Brock, Luther A.
  xBrock, Luther A.
    How to Build Goodwill Through Credit
    Correspondence. NACM.
    Intro. by How to Communicate by Letter &
    Memo. McGraw.
Brock, Michael.
  xBrock, Michael.
    The Great Reform Act. Humanities.
Brock, Peter, 1920-
  xBrock, Peter.
    Pacifism in Europe to 1914. Princeton U Pr.
    Pacifism in the United States: From the
    Colonial Era to the First World War.
    Princeton U Pr.
Brock, Ray, 1928-
  xBrock, Ray.
    If You're Ready, Here's the Car. Dial.
Brock, Stanley E.
  xBrock, Stanley E.
    Leemo: A True Story of a Man's Friendship
    with a Mountain Lion. Taplinger.
Brock, Stuart.
  xBrock, Stuart.
    Double-Cross Ranch. Bouregy.
Brock, Th. D. *see* Brock, Thomas D.
Brock, Thomas D.
  xBrock, Th. D.

Thermophilic Microorganisms & Life at High
Temperatures. Springer-Verlag.
xBrock, Thomas D.
Biology of Microorganisms. P-H.
Brock, W. H. see Brock, William Hodson.
Brock, W. R. see Brock, William Ranulf.
Brock, William. see Brock, William Ranulf.
Brock, William Hodson.
xBrock, W. H.
ed. H. E. Armstrong & the Teaching of Science
1880-1930. Cambridge U Pr.
Brock, William R. see Brock, William Ranulf.
Brock, William Ranulf.
xBrock, W. R.
Character of American History. Gannon.
Character of American History. St Martin.
xBrock, William.
Parties & Political Conscience: American
Dilemmas, 1840-1850. Kraus Intl.
xBrock, William R.
Conflict & Transformation: The United States,
1844-1877. Penguin.
Lord Liverpool & Liberal Toryism: 1820-27.
Biblio Dist.
Lord Liverpool & Liberal Toryism 1820-1827.
Shoe String.
Brockerhoff, H.
xBrockerhoff, Hans.
Lipolytic Enzymes. Acad Pr.
Brockerhoff, Hans. see Brockerhoff, H.
Brockett, Oscar G. see Brockett, Oscar Gross.
Brockett, Oscar Gross.
xBrockett, Oscar G.
The Essential Theatre. HR&W.
Plays for the Theatre: An Anthology of World
Drama. HR&W.
The Theatre: An Introduction. HR&W.
Brockhurst, Robert J.
xBrockhurst, Robert J.
ed. Controversy in Ophthalmology, Saunders
Brockie, William, 1811-1890
xBrockie, William.
Legends & Superstitions of the County of
Durham. Folcroft.
Brockington, Colin Fraser, 1903-
xBrockington, Fraser.
World Health. Churchill.
Brockington, Fraser. see Brockington, Colin Fraser.
Brocklehurst, J. C. see Brocklehurst, John C.
Brocklehurst, John C.
xBrocklehurst, J. C.
ed. Geriatric Care in Advanced Societies. Univ
Park.
ed. Textbook of Geriatric Medicine &
Gerontology. Churchill.
Brockman, Norbert.
xBrockman, Norbert C.
ed. Contemporary Religion & Social
Responsibility. Alba.
Brockman, Norbert C. see Brockman, Norbert.
Brockway, Fenner, Baron Brockway, 1888-
xBrockway, Fenner.
The Colonial Revolution. St Martin.
Brockway, Lucile.
xBrockway, Lucile H.
Science & Colonial Expansion: The Role of the
British Royal Botanic Gardens. Acad Pr.
Brockway, Lucile H. see Brockway, Lucile.
Brockway, Maureen.
xBrockway, Maureen.
Clay Projects. Lerner Pubns.
Brockway, Zebulon R. see Brockway, Zebulon Reed.
Brockway, Zebulon Reed, 1872-1920
xBrockway, Zebulon R.
Fifty Years of Prison Service: An
Autobiography. Patterson Smith.
Brocquy, Sybil Le. see Le Brocquy, Sybil.
Brod, Max, 1884-
xBrod, Max.

Franz Kafka: A Biography. Schocken.
Paganism - Christianity - Judaism: A
Confession of Faith. U of Ala Pr.
Broda, Paul, 1939-
xBroda, Paul.
Plasmids. W H Freeman.
Brodatz, Phil.
xBrodatz, Phil.
Textures: A Photographic Album for Artists &
Designers. Dover.
Textures: A Photographic Album for Artists &
Designers. Peter Smith.
Wood & Wood Grains: A Photographic Album
for Artists and Designers. Dover.
Wood & Wood Grains: A Photographic Album
for Artists & Designers. Peter Smith.
Brodbeck, May.
xBrodbeck, May.
Readings in the Philosophy of the Social
Sciences. Macmillan.
Broder, David S.
xBroder, David S.
The Party's Over: The Failure of Politics in
America. Har-Row.
Broder, L. E. see Broder, Lawrence E.
Broder, Lawrence E.
xBroder, L. E.
Meningeal Leukemia. Plenum Pub.
Broder, Nathan.
xBroder, Nathan.
The Collector's Bach. Greenwood.
Broder, Patricia J. see Broder, Patricia Janis.
Broder, Patricia Janis.
xBroder, Patricia J.
Bronzes of the American West. Abrams.
Hopi Painting: The World of the Hopis.
Dutton.
Broderick, Carlfred. see Broderick, Carlfred
Bartholomew.
Broderick, Carlfred B. see Broderick, Carlfred
Bartholomew.
Broderick, Carlfred Bartholomew.
xBroderick, Carlfred.
Couples: How to Confront Problems &
Maintain Loving Relationships. S&S.
xBroderick, Carlfred B.
Marriage & the Family. P-H.
Broderick, Dorothy. see Broderick, Dorothy M.
Broderick, Dorothy M.
xBroderick, Dorothy.
Image of the Black in Children's Fiction.
Bowker.
xBroderick, Dorothy M.
Introduction to Children's Work in Public
Libraries. Wilson.
Broderick, J. P. see Broderick, John P.
Broderick, John P.
xBroderick, J. P.
Modern English Linguistics: A Structural &
Transformational Grammar. Har-Row.
Broderick, Robert. see Broderick, Robert C.
Broderick, Robert C., 1913-
xBroderick, Robert.
The Catholic Encyclopedia. Nelson.
Brodeur, Arthur G. see Brodeur, Arthur Gilchrist.
Brodeur, Arthur Gilchrist, 1888-
xBrodeur, Arthur G.
Arthur Dux Bellorum. Folcroft.
Riddle of the Runes. Folcroft.
Brodie, Bernard.
xBrodie, Bernard.
From Crossbow to H-Bomb. Ind U Pr.
Strategy in the Missile Age. Princeton U Pr.
Brodie, Deborah.
xBrodie, Deborah.
ed. Stories My Grandfather Should Have Told
Me. Hebrew Pub.
Brodie, Fawn M. see Brodie, Fawn Mckay.
Brodie, Fawn Mckay, 1915-
xBrodie, Fawn M.

Devil Drives: A Life of Sir Richard Burton.
Norton.
Thaddeus Stevens, Scourge of the South. Peter
Smith.
Thomas Jefferson: An Intimate History.
Norton.
Brodie, Iain.
xBrodie, Iain.
Ferrets & Ferreting. Sterling.
Brodie, John.
xBrodie, John.
Open Field. HM.
Brodin. see Brodin, Pierre.
Brodin, Dorothy. see Brodin, Dorothy R.
Brodin, Dorothy R.
xBrodin, Dorothy.
Marcel Ayme. Columbia U Pr.
Brodin, Pierre.
xBrodin.
Presences contemporaines: Auteurs Francais du
XXe Siecle. French & Eur.
Brodine, Karen.
xBrodine, Karen.
Illegal Assembly. Hanging Loose.
Brodine, Virginia.
xBrodine, Virginia.
Radioactive Contamination. HarBraceJ.
Brodinsky, Ben. see Brodinsky, Benjamin Paul.
Brodinsky, Benjamin Paul, 1910-
xBrodinsky, Ben.
How a School Board Operates. Phi Delta
Kappa.
Brodkin, S. see Brodkin, Sylvia Z.
Brodkin, Sylvia Z.
xBrodkin, S.
On the Air: A Collection of Radio & TV Plays.
Scribner.
Brodrick, Alan H. see Brodrick, Alan Houghton.
Brodrick, Alan Houghton.
xBrodrick, Alan H.
Casual Change. Greenwood.
Little China: The Annamese Lands. AMS Pr.
Mirage of Africa. Greenwood.
Mirage of Africa. Negro U Pr.
Brodrick, G. C. see Brodrick, George Charles.
Brodrick, George C. see Brodrick, George Charles.
Brodrick, George Charles.
xBrodrick, G. C.
History of England from Addington's
Administration to the Close of William
Fourth's Reign, 1801-1837. Kraus Repr.
xBrodrick, George C.
History of England from Addington's
Administration to the Close of William
Fourth's Reign. AMS Pr.
History of England from Addington's
Administration to the Close of William
Fourth's Reign 1801-1837. Greenwood.
Brodrick, James, 1891-
xBrodrick, James.
Origin of the Jesuits. Greenwood.
Procession of Saints. Arno.
Brodshaug, Melvin, 1900-
xBrodshaug, Melvin.
Buildings & Equipment for Home Economics
in Secondary Schools. AMS Pr.
Brodsky, Alyn.
xBrodsky, Alyn.
Imperial Charade: A Biography of Emperor
Napoleon III & Empress Eugenie. Bobbs.
Brodsky, Beverley. see Brodsky, Beverly.
Brodsky, Beverly.
xBrodsky, Beverley.
Secret Places. Lippincott.
Brodsky, M. H. see Brodsky, Marc Herbert.
Brodsky, Marc Herbert, 1938-
xBrodsky, M. H.

ed. Amorphous Semiconductors.
Springer-Verlag.
Brody, Alan, 1937-
xBrody, Alan.
Coming to. Berkley Pub.
English Mummers & Their Plays: Traces of
Ancient Mystery. U of Pa Pr.
Brody, Alvan.
xBrody, Alvan.
The Legal Rights of Nonsmokers. Avon.
Brody, David.
xBrody, David.
ed. The American Labor Movement. Har-Row.
Steelworkers in America: The Nonunion Era.
Har-Row.
Steelworkers in America: The Nonunion Era.
Russell.
Brody, Elaine.
xBrody, Elaine.
The German Lied & Its Poetry. NYU Pr.
The Music Guide to Austria & Germany.
Dodd.
The Music Guide to Great Britain. Dodd.
Brody, Erness B. *see* Brody, Erness Bright.
Brody, Erness Bright.
xBrody, Erness B.
ed. Intelligence: Nature, Determinants, &
Consequences. Acad Pr.
Brody, Eugene B.
xBrody, Eugene B.
The Lost Ones: Social Forces & Mental Illness
in Rio de Janeiro. Intl Univs Pr.
Minority Group Adolescents in the United
States. Krieger.
Brody, Eugene D.
xBrody, Eugene D.
Odds on Investing: Survival & Success in the
New Stock Market. Wiley.
Brody, Harvey.
xBrody, Harvey.
The Book of Low Fire Ceramics. HR&W.
Brody, Howard.
xBrody, Howard.
Ethical Decisions in Medicine. Little.
Placebos & the Philosophy of Medicine:
Clinical, Conceptual, & Ethical Issues. U of
Chicago Pr.
Brody, Hugh.
xBrody, Hugh.
The People's Land: Eskimos & Whites in the
Eastern Arctic. Penguin.
Brody, Jean.
xBrody, Jean.
The Twenty Year Phenomenon. S&S.
Brody, Mitchell.
xBrody, Mitchell D.
Get Some Respect!. HR&W.
Brody, Mitchell D. *see* Brody, Mitchell.
Brody, Saul N. *see* Brody, Saul Nathaniel.
Brody, Saul Nathaniel.
xBrody, Saul N.
The Disease of the Soul: Leprosy in Medieval
Literature. Cornell U Pr.
Brody, Sylvia.
xBrody, Sylvia.
Anxiety & Ego Formation in Infancy. Intl
Univs Pr.
Brody, T. A.
xBrody, T. A.
Tables of Transformation Brackets for Nuclear
Shell-Model Calculations. Gordon.
Broe, Mary L. *see* Broe, Mary Lynn.
Broe, Mary Lynn.
xBroe, Mary L.
Protean Poetic: The Poetry of Sylvia Plath. U
of Mo Pr.
Broeg, Bob. *see* Broeg, Robert M.
Broeg, Robert. *see* Broeg, Robert M.
Broeg, Robert M.
xBroeg, Bob.

Ol' Mizzou: A Story of Missouri Football.
Strode.
xBroeg, Robert.
The Pilot Light & the Gas House Gang.
Bethany Pr.
Broehl, Wayne G.
xBroehl, Wayne G.
Trucks, Trouble & Triumph: The Norwalk
Truck Line Company. Arno.
Broek, C. M. *see* Broek, Jan Otto Marius.
Broek, Jacobus ten. *see* Ten Broek, Jacobus.
Broek, Jan Otto Marius.
xBroek, C. M.
A Geography of Mankind. McGraw.
Broekel, Ray.
xBroekel, Ray.
The Moustache Pickpocket. Carolrhoda Bks.
Now You See It: Easy Magic for Beginners.
Schol Bk Serv.
Now You See It: Easy Magic for Beginners.
Little.
Broekema, Andrew J.
xBroekema, Andrew J.
The Music Listener. Wm C Brown.
Broekhuizen, Richard. *see* Broekhuizen, Richard J.
Broekhuizen, Richard J.
xBroekhuizen, Richard.
Graphic Communications. McKnight.
Broekman, Marcel, 1922-
xBroekman, Marcel.
The Complete Encyclopedia of Practical
Palmistry. P-H.
Broer, Lawrence. *see* Broer, Lawrence R.
Broer, Lawrence R.
xBroer, Lawrence.
The First Time: Initial Sexual Experiences in
Fiction. Bobbs.
Broertjes, C.
xBroertjes, C.
The Application of Mutation Breeding
Methods in the Improvement of Vegetatively
Propagated Crops. Elsevier.
Brogan, D. W. *see* Brogan, Denis William.
Brogan, Denis W. *see* Brogan, Denis William.
Brogan, Denis William, Sir, 1900-1974
xBrogan, D. W.
American Character. Peter Smith.
xBrogan, Denis W.
America in the Modern World. Greenwood.
Brogan, John A.
xBrogan, John A.
Clear Technical Writing. McGraw.
Brogan, William L.
xBrogan, William L.
Modern Control Theory. Quantum Pubs.
Broger, Achim.
xBroger, Achim.
Bruno. Morrow.
Bruno Takes a Trip. Morrow.
Good Morning, Whale. Macmillan.
Little Harry. Morrow.
Outrageous Kasimir. Morrow.
Broholm, Richard R.
xBroholm, Richard R.
Strategic Planning for Church Organizations.
Judson.
Broido, Lucy.
xBroido, Lucy.
French Opera Posters, 1868 - 1930. Dover.
Brokering, Herbert. *see* Brokering, Herbert F.
Brokering, Herbert F.
xBrokering, Herbert.
In a Promise. Augsburg.
xBrokering, Herbert F.
Surprise Me, Jesus. Augsburg.
Brokhin, Yuri, 1934-
xBrokhin, Yuri.

tr. Hustling on Gorky Street: Sex & Crime in
Russia Today. Dial.
Brolin, Brent C.
xBrolin, Brent C.
Architecture in Context: Fitting New Buildings
with Old. Van Nos Reinhold.
Brolin, Donn E.
xBrolin, Donn E.
Career Education for Handicapped Children &
Youth. Merrill.
ed. Life Centered Career Education: A
Competency Based Approach. Coun Exc
Child.
Bromage, Arthur W. *see* Bromage, Arthur Watson.
Bromage, Arthur Watson, 1904-
xBromage, Arthur W.
Councilmen at Work. Wahr.
Introduction to Municipal Government &
Administration. Irvington.
ed. Political Representation in Metropolitan
Agencies. Greenwood.
Bromage, Mary C. *see* Bromage, Mary Cogan.
Bromage, Mary Cogan.
xBromage, Mary C.
Cases in Written Communication II. U Mich
Busn Div Res.
Churchill & Ireland. U of Notre Dame Pr.
De Valera & the March of a Nation.
Greenwood.
Writing Audit Reports. McGraw.
Bromberg, Murray.
xBromberg, Murray.
Words with a Flair. Barron.
Bromberg, Robert S.
xBromberg, Robert S.
Tax Planning for Hospitals & Health Care
Organizations. Warren.
Brombert, Victor. *see* Brombert, Victor H.
Brombert, Victor H.
xBrombert, Victor.
The Intellectual Hero: Studies in the French
Novel 1880-1955. U of Chicago Pr.
xBrombert, Victor H.
ed. Stendhal: A Collection of Critical Essays.
P-H.
Brome, Richard.
xBrome, Richard.
Antipodes. U of Nebr Pr.
Brome, Vincent, 1910-
xBrome, Vincent.
The Ambassador & the Spy. Crown.
Aneurin Bevan: A Biography. Wellington.
H. G. Wells: A Biography. Arno.
H. G. Wells, a Biography. Greenwood.
H. G. Wells: A Biography. R West.
Bromfield, Louis, 1896-1956
xBromfield, Louis.
The Farm. Amereon Ltd.
The Farm. Avon.
Mrs. Parkington. Amereon Ltd.
Mrs. Parkington. Manor Bks.
Night in Bombay. Amereon Ltd.
The Rains Came. Amereon Ltd.
The Rains Came. Manor Bks.
Bromhead, P. A. *see* Bromhead, Peter.
Bromhead, Peter.
xBromhead, P. A.
The House of Lords & Contemporary Politics:
1911-1957. Greenwood.
Private Members' Bills in the British
Parliament. Greenwood.
xBromhead, Peter.
Britain's Developing Constitution. St Martin.
Bromiley, Geoffrey W. *see* Bromiley, Geoffrey William.
Bromiley, Geoffrey William.
xBromiley, Geoffrey W.

Children of Promise: The Case for Baptizing Infants. Eerdmans.
Historical Theology: An Introduction. Eerdmans.
ed. International Standard Bible Encyclopedia. Eerdmans.
Bromley, D. Allan. *see* Bromley, David Allan.
Bromley, D. B. *see* Bromley, Dennis Basil.
Bromley, David Allan.
xBromley, D. Allan.
ed. Facets of Physics. Acad Pr.
Bromley, David G.
xBromley, David G.
Moonies in America: Cult, Church & Crusade. Sage.
Bromley, Dennis Basil, 1924-
xBromley, D. B.
Psychology of Human Ageing. Penguin.
Bromley, Dudley.
xBromley, Dudley.
Bad Moon. Childrens.
Bromley, R. J.
xBromley, Ray.
ed. Casual Work & Poverty in Third World Cities. Wiley.
Bromley, Ray. *see* Bromley, R. J.
Brommer, Gerald F.
xBrommer, Gerald F.
The Art of Collage. Davis Mass.
Relief Printmaking. Davis Mass.
Bromwich, Rachel.
xBromwich, Rachel.
tr. Trioedd Ynys Prydein: The Welsh Triads. Verry.
Bromwich, T. J. *see* Bromwich, Thomas John I'Anson.
Bromwich, Thomas John I'Anson, 1875-1929
xBromwich, T. J.
Quadratic Forms & Their Classification by Means of Invariant Factors. Hafner.
Brondfield, Jerry, 1913-
xBrondfield, Jerry
Great Moments in American Sports. Random.
Brondoli, Michael.
xBrondoli, Michael.
The Love Letter Hack. Paycock Pr.
Broneer, Oscar. *see* Broneer, Oscar Theodore.
Broneer, Oscar Theodore, 1894-
xBroneer, Oscar.
The South Stoa & Its Roman Successors. Am Sch Athens.
Bronfenbrenner, Martin, 1914-
xBronfenbrenner, Martin.
Academic Encounter: The American University in Japan & Korea. Free Pr.
Income Distribution Theory. Aldine Pub.
Macroeconomic Alternatives. AHM Pub.
Bronfenbrenner, Urie, 1917-
xBronfenbrenner, Urie.
The Ecology of Human Development: Experiments by Nature & Design. Harvard U Pr.
Two Worlds of Childhood: U. S. & U. S. S.R. Russell Sage.
Bronin, Andrew.
xBronin, Andrew.
Gus & Buster Work Things Out. Dell.
Gus & Buster Work Things Out. Coward.
I Know a Football Player. Putnam.
Remember the Maine. Viking Pr.
Bronk, J. Ramsey.
xBronk, J. Ramsey.
Chemical Biology: An Introduction to Biochemistry. Macmillan.
Bronk, William.
xBronk, William.
Light & Dark. SBD.
The Meantime. SBD.
That Tantalus. SBD.
Bronner, Edwin, 1926-
xBronner, Edwin.

The Encyclopedia of the American Theatre. A S Barnes.
Bronner, Edwin B., 1920-
xBronner, Edwin B.
Quakerism & Christianity. Pendle Hill.
Bronowski, J. *see* Bronowski, Jacob.
Bronowski, Jacob, 1908-
xBronowski, J.
The Common Sense of Science. Harvard U Pr.
Identity of Man. Natural Hist.
xBronowski, Jacob.
The Ascent of Man. Little.
On Being an Intellectual. Smith Coll.
The Origins of Knowledge & Imagination. Yale U Pr.
Bronson, B. H. *see* Bronson, Bertrand Harris.
Bronson, Bertrand H. *see* Bronson, Bertrand Harris.
Bronson, Bertrand Harris, 1902-
xBronson, B. H.
In Search of Chaucer. U of Toronto Pr.
Studies in the Comic. AMS Pr.
xBronson, Bertrand H.
The Ballad as Song. U of Cal Pr.
Facets of the Enlightenment: Studies in English Literature & Its Contexts. U of Cal Pr.
Five Studies in Literature. Core Collection.
Five Studies in Literature. Folcroft.
Johnson Agonistes & Other Essays. U of Cal Pr.
Studies in the Comic. Folcroft.
Bronson, Edgar B. *see* Bronson, Edgar Beecher.
Bronson, Edgar Beecher.
xBronson, Edgar B.
Reminiscences of a Ranchman. U of Ncbr Pr.
Bronson, Walter C. *see* Bronson, Walter Cochrane.
Bronson, Walter Cochrane, 1862-1928
xBronson, Walter C.
History of Brown University, 1764-1914. Arno.
Bronson, Wilfrid S. *see* Bronson, Wilfrid Swancourt.
Bronson, Wilfrid Swancourt, 1894-
xBronson, Wilfrid S.
illus. Cats. HarBraceJ.
Bronte, Anne, 1820-1849
xBronte, Anne.
The Tenant of Wildfell Hall. Academy Chi Ltd.
The Tenant of Wildfell Hall. Merrimack Bk Serv.
Tenant of Wildfell Hall. Oxford U Pr.
The Tenant of Wildfell Hall. Penguin.
The Tenant of Wildfell Hall. Woodbridge Pr.
Bronte, Charlotte.
xBronte, Charlotte.
Jane Eyre. Beekman Pubs.
Jane Eyre. Dutton.
Jane Eyre. Merrimack Bk Serv.
Jane Eyre. Modern Lib.
Jane Eyre. NYU Pr.
Jane Eyre. Oxford U Pr.
Jane Eyre. PB.
Jane Eyre. Penguin.
Jane Eyre. NAL.
Jane Eyre. Pendulum Pr.
Jane Eyre. Raintree Pubs.
Jane Eyre. Raintree Child.
Jane Eyre. AMSCO Sch.
Jane Eyre. Airmont.
Jane Eyre. Dodd.
Jane Eyre. Macmillan.
Jane Eyre. Norton.
Professor. Dutton.
The Secret & Lily Hart: Two Tales. U of Mo Pr.
Villette. Dutton.
Villette. Merrimack Bk Serv.
Villette. Oxford U Pr.
Villette. Penguin.
Villette. Univ Microfilms.
Bronte, Emily. *see* Bronte, Emily Jane.
Bronte, Emily J. *see* Bronte, Emily Jane.

Bronte, Emily Jane, 1818-1848
xBronte, Emily.
Five Essays Written in French. Folcroft.
Peculiar Music. Macmillan.
xBronte, Emily J.
Five Essays Written in French. Arden Lib.
Bronte, Louisa.
xBronte, Louisa.
Casino Greystone. Ballantine.
Freedom Trail to Greystone. Ballantine.
Greystone Heritage. Ballantine.
Greystone Tavern. Ballantine.
Moonlight at Greystone. Ballantine.
The Vallette Heritage. BJ Pub Group.
The Van Rhyne Heritage. BJ Pub Group.
Bronte Society. *see* Bronte Society. Museum and Library, Haworth.
Bronte Society. Museum and Library, Haworth.
xBronte Society.
Catalogue of the Museum & the Library of the Bronte Society. B Franklin.
Brontman, Lazar K. *see* Brontman, Lazar Konstantinovich.
Brontman, Lazar Konstantinovich.
xBrontman, Lazar K.
On the Top of the World: The Soviet Expedition to the North Pole, 1937. Greenwood.
Brook, C. G. *see* Brook, Charles Groves Darville.
Brook, Charles Groves Darville.
xBrook, C. G.
Practical Paediatric Endocrinology. Grune.
Brook, Donald.
xBrook, Donald.
Composer's Gallery: Biographical Sketches of Contemporary Composers. Arno.
Masters of the Keyboard. Arno.
Masters of the Keyboard. Greenwood.
Pageant of English Actors. Arno.
The Pageant of English Actors. Norwood Edns.
Pageant of English Actors. R West.
Brook, G. L. *see* Brook, George Leslie.
Brook, George L. *see* Brook, George Leslie.
Brook, George Leslie.
xBrook, G. L.
English Sound Changes. Folcroft.
A History of the English Language. Westview.
xBrook, George L.
History of the English Language. Norton.
Brook, Judy, 1926-
xBrook, Judy.
illus. Noah's Ark. Watts.
Brook, Michael.
xBrook, Michael.
Compiled by Reference Guide to Minnesota History: A Subject Bibliography of Books, Pamphlets & Articles in English. Minn Hist.
Brook-Shepherd, Gordon, 1918-
xBrook-Shepherd, Gordon.
Anschluss: The Rape of Austria. Greenwood.
Dollfuss. Greenwood.
Brooke, Avery.
xBrooke, Avery.
As Never Before. Seabury.
Doorway to Meditation. Seabury.
Plain Prayers for a Complicated World. Readers Digest Pr.
Brooke, Bryan N.
xBrooke, Bryan N.
Understanding Cancer. HR&W.
Brooke, Christopher. *see* Brooke, Christopher Nugent Lawrence.
Brooke, Christopher Nugent Lawrence.
xBrooke, Christopher.
The Monastic World. Merrimack Bk Serv.
Structure of Medieval Society. McGraw.
The Twelfth Century Renaissance. HarBraceJ.
Brooke, Dinah.
xBrooke, Dinah.

The County Road. Irvington.
Meadow-Grass: Tales of New England Life. Arno.
Meadow-Grass: Tales of New England Life. Mss Info.
Vanishing Points. Arno.
Brown, Andrew W. see Brown, Andrew Wilson.
Brown, Andrew Wilson, 1890-
xBrown, Andrew W.
The Unevenness of the Abilities of Dull & of Bright Children. AMS Pr.
Brown, Anita D.
xBrown, Anita D.
The Colonial Heritage Cookbook. The Little Brown House.
Brown, Anne E. see Brown, Anne Ensign.
Brown, Anne Ensign.
xBrown, Anne E.
Wonders of Sea Horses. Dodd.
Brown, Annice H. see Brown, Annice Harris.
Brown, Annice Harris, 1897-
xBrown, Annice H.
Thank You, Lord, for Little Things. John Knox.
Brown, Antony.
xBrown, A.
Great Ideas in Communications. Pergamon.
xBrown, Antony.
Great Ideas in Communications. D White. Lloyd's of London. Stein & Day.
Brown, Archibald Haworth.
xBrown, Archie.
ed. Political Culture & Political Change in Communist States. Holmes & Meier.
Brown, Archie. see Brown, Archibald Haworth.
Brown, Arthur C. see Brown, Arthur Charles Lewis.
Brown, Arthur Charles Lewis, 1869-1946
xBrown, Arthur C.
Origin of the Grail Legend. Russell
Brown, Arthur W, 1917-
xBrown, Arthur W.
Always Young for Liberty: Biography of William Ellery Channing. Syracuse U Pr.
Margaret Fuller. Coll & U Pr.
Brown, Ashley.
xBrown, Ashley.
ed. The Achievement of Wallace Stevens. Gordian.
Comedy. Merrill.
Brown, Barbara A., 1946-
xBrown, Barbara A.
Women's Rights & the Law: The Impact of the ERA on State Laws. Praeger.
Brown, Barry S.
xBrown, Barry S.
ed. Addicts & Aftercare: Community Integration of the Former Drug User. Sage.
Brown, Beatrice C. see Brown, Beatrice Curtis.
Brown, Beatrice Curtis.
xBrown, Beatrice C.
Anthony Trollope. R West.
Jonathan Bing. Lothrop.
Jonathan Bing. Dell.
Brown, Benjamin H. see Brown, Benjamin Houston.
Brown, Benjamin Houston, 1915-
xBrown, Benjamin H.
Tariff Reform Movement in Great Britain, 1881-1895. AMS Pr.
Brown, Bernard E. see Brown, Bernard Edward.
Brown, Bernard Edward, 1925-
xBrown, Bernard E.
American Conservatives: The Political Thought of Francis Lieber & John W. Burgess. AMS Pr.
Brown, Bernice.
xBrown, Bernice.
Men of Earth. Arno.
Brown, Beth.
xBrown, Beth.

House Without a Home. Lion.
Brown, Beverly S. see Brown, Beverly Swerdlow.
Brown, Beverly Swerdlow.
xBrown, Beverly S.
The Myth Adventures of Kraken the Sea Monster. Brasch & Brasch.
Brown, Blanche R.
xBrown, Blanche R.
Anticlassicism in Greek Sculpture of the Fourth Century B.C.. NYU Pr.
Brown, Bob.
xBrown, Bob.
How to Fool Your Friends. Western Pub.
Brown, Bonnie.
xBrown, Bonnie.
Sunbeam Portable Electric Cookery. Benjamin Co.
Brown, Brendan, 1951-
xBrown, Brendan.
The Dollar-Mark Axis: On Currency Power. St Martin.
Brown, Burnell R.
xBrown, Burnell R.
Outpatient Anesthesia. Davis Co.
Brown, C. see Brown, Charlene J.
Brown, C. H.
xBrown, C. H.
Structural Materials in Animals. Halsted Pr.
Brown, C. P.
xBrown, C. P.
Primary Commodity Control. Oxford U Pr.
Brown, C. V. see Brown, Charles Victor.
Brown, Calvin S. see Brown, Calvin Smith.
Brown, Calvin Smith, 1909-
xBrown, Calvin S.
A Glossary of Faulkner's South. Yale U Pr.
Music & Literature: A Comparison of the Arts. U of Ga Pr.
Brown, Carter.
xBrown, Carter.
Negative in Blue. NAL.
Brown, Cassie.
xBrown, Cassie.
Standing into Danger: A Dramatic Story of Shipwreck & Rescue. Doubleday.
Brown, Charlene J.

xBrown, C.
The Media & the People. Krieger.

xBrown, Charlene J.
The Media & the People. HR&W.

Brown, Charles A. see Brown, Charles Armitage.
Brown, Charles Armitage.
xBrown, Charles A.
Life of John Keats. Folcroft.
Brown, Charles B. see Brown, Charles Brookden.
Brown, Charles Brookden.
xBrown, Charles B.
Edgar Huntly: Or, Memoirs of a Sleepwalker. AMS Pr.
Brown, Charles H. see Brown, Charles Henry.
Brown, Charles Henry, 1910-
xBrown, Charles H.
Agents of Manifest Destiny: The Lives & Times of the Filibusters. U of NC Pr.
Brown, Charles R. see Brown, Charles Reynolds.
Brown, Charles Reynolds, 1862-1950
xBrown, Charles R.
They Were Giants. Arno.
Brown, Charles Victor.
xBrown, C. V.
Public Sector Economics. Biblio Dist.
Brown, Charles W. see Brown, Charles Walter.
Brown, Charles Walter, 1866-1934
xBrown, Charles W.
ed. Comic Recitations & Readings. Arno.
Brown, Charles William, 1930-
xBrown, Charles W.

Hybridization Among the Subspecies of the Plethodontid Salamander Ensatina Eschscholtzi. U of Cal Pr.
Brown, Cheryl L.
xBrown, Cheryl L.
ed. Feminist Criticism: Essays on Theory, Poetry & Prose. Scarecrow.
Brown, Christy, 1932-
xBrown, Christy.
Of Snails & Skylarks. Stein & Day.
Brown, Claude, 1937-
xBrown, Claude.
Children of Ham. Stein & Day.
Brown, Clement.
xBrown, Clement.
Questions & Answers on Hi-Fi. Hayden.
Questions & Answers on Transistors. Hayden.
Brown, Clifton F., 1943-
xBrown, Clifton F.
Compiled by Ethiopian Perspectives: A Bibliographical Guide to the History of Ethiopia. Greenwood.
Brown, Cora. see Brown, Cora Lovisa (Brackett).
Brown, Cora Lovisa (Brackett).
xBrown, Cora.
The South American Cookbook: Including Central America, Mexico, & the West Indies. Peter Smith.
Brown, Courtney C., 1904-
xBrown, Courtney C.
Beyond the Bottom Line. Free Pr.
Brown, Curtis M. see Brown, Curtis Maitland.
Brown, Curtis Maitland.
xBrown, Curtis M.
Boundary Control & Legal Principles. Wiley.
Evidence & Procedures for Boundary Location. Wiley.
Brown, D. Clayton. see Brown, Duart Clayton.
Brown, D, E,
xBrown, D. E.
Principles of Social Structure: Southeast Asia. Westview.
Brown, D. M. see Brown, Donald Mackenzie.
Brown, D. S. W. see Brown, David Alexander.
Brown, Dale.
xBrown, Dale.
Cooking of Scandinavia. Time-Life.
Cooking of Scandinavia. Silver.
World of Velazquez. Time-Life.
World of Velazquez. Silver.
Brown, Dale. see Brown, Dale W.
Brown, Dale W., 1926-
xBrown, Dale.
Understanding Pietism. Eerdmans.
Brown, Daniel P. see Brown, Daniel Patrick.
Brown, Daniel Patrick.
xBrown, Daniel P.
The Tragedy of Libby & Andersonville Prison Camps. Golden West Hist.
Woodrow Wilson & the Treaty of Versailles: The German Leftist Press Response. Golden West Hist.
Brown, David, 1786-1875
xBrown, David.
The Planter. Irvington.
Brown, David. see Brown, David D.
Brown, David Alexander.
xBrown, D. S. W.
The Geological Evolution of Australia & New Zealand. Pergamon.
Brown, David D.
xBrown, David.
Walter Scott & the Historical Imagination. Routledge & Kegan.
Brown, David G.
xBrown, David G.
Leadership Vitality: A Workbook for Academic Administrators. ACE.
Brown, Deaver.
xBrown, Deaver.

The Entrepreneur's Guide. Macmillan.
Brown, Dee.
  xBrown, Dee.
    Fighting Indians of the West. Ballantine.
Brown, Dee. *see* Brown, Dee Alexander.
Brown, Dee Alexander.
  xBrown, Dee.
    Bury My Heart at Wounded Knee: An Indian
      History of the American West. HR&W.
    Bury My Heart at Wounded Knee: An Indian
      History of the American West. Bantam.
Brown, Deena.
  xBrown, Deena.
    ed. American Yoga. Grove.
Brown, Delmer M. *see* Brown, Delmer Myers.
Brown, Delmer Myers, 1909-
  xBrown, Delmer M.
    Nationalism in Japan: An Introductory
      Historical Analysis. Russell.
Brown, Delwin.
  xBrown, Delwin.
    Process Philosophy & Christian Thought.
      Bobbs.
    Process Philosophy & Christian Thought.
      Irvington.
Brown, Demetra (Vaka).
  xBrown, Demetra V.
    tr. Modern Greek Stories. AMS Pr.
Brown, Demetra V. *see* Brown, Demetra (Vaka).
Brown, Deming Bronson, 1919-
  xBrown, Deming O.
    Soviet Attitudes Toward American Writing.
      Princeton U Pr.
Brown, Deming O. *see* Brown, Deming Bronson.
Brown, Dennis A.
  xBrown, Dennis A.
    A Practical Guide to Preparing a Federal
      Estate Tax Return. Lawyers & Judges.
Brown, Diana.
  xBrown, Diana.
    The Emerald Necklace. St Martin.
Brown, Diana L.
  xBrown, Diana L.
    Developmental Handicaps in Babies & Young
      Children: A Guide for Parents. C C Thomas.
Brown, Dick, 1941-
  xBrown, Dick.
    Hot Air Ballooning. TAB Bks.
Brown, Donald F. *see* Brown, Donald Fowler.
Brown, Donald Fowler, 1909-
  xBrown, Donald F.
    The Catholic Naturalism of Pardo Bazan. U of
      NC Pr.
Brown, Donald Mackenzie, 1908-
  xBrown, D. M.
    Nationalist Movement: Indian Political
      Thought from Ranade to Bhave. Peter Smith.
Brown, Donald R., 1946-
  xBrown, Donald R.
    Neurosciences for Allied Health Therapies.
      Mosby.
Brown, Dorothy H. *see* Brown, Dorothy Hanson.
Brown, Dorothy Hanson.
  xBrown, Dorothy H.
    God & the Tree & Me. Upper Room.
Brown, Dorris D., 1911-
  xBrown, Dorris D.
    Agricultural Development in India's Districts.
      Harvard U Pr.
Brown, Douglas, 1921-
  xBrown, Douglas.
    Thomas Hardy. Greenwood.
Brown, Douglas (Summers).
  xBrown, Douglas S.
    Catawba Indians: The People of the River. U of
      SC Pr.
    A City Without Cobwebs: A History of Rock
      Hill, South Carolina. Reprint.
Brown, Douglas S. *see* Brown, Douglas (Summers).
Brown, Douglas V. *see* Brown, Douglass Vincent.

Brown, Douglass Vincent, 1904-
  xBrown, Douglas V.
    The Economics of the Recovery Program. Da
      Capo.
Brown, Duane.
  xBrown, Duane.
    Students' Vocational Choices: A Review &
      Critique. HM.
Brown, Duart Clayton, 1941-
  xBrown, D. Clayton.
    Electricity for Rural America: The Fight for
      the REA. Greenwood.
Brown, E. Francis. *see* Brown, Ernest Francis.
Brown, E. Richard.
  xBrown, E. Richard.
    Rockefeller Medicine Men: Medicine &
      Capitalism in America. U of Cal Pr.
Brown, Earl L. *see* Brown, Earl Louis.
Brown, Earl Louis.
  xBrown, Earl L.
    Negro & the War. AMS Pr.
Brown, Edward E. *see* Brown, Edward Espe.
Brown, Edward Espe.
  xBrown, Edward E.
    Tassajara Bread Book. Shambhala Pubns.
    Tassajara Cooking. Shambhala Pubns.
Brown, Edward J. *see* Brown, Edward James.
Brown, Edward James, 1909-
  xBrown, Edward J.
    Proletarian Episode in Russian Literature,
      1928-1932. Octagon.
    Stankevich & His Moscow Circle, 1830-1840.
      Stanford U Pr.
Brown, Edwin. *see* Brown, Edwin G.
Brown, Edwin G.
  xBrown, Edwin.
    ed. Neonatal Necrotizing Enterocolitis. Grune.
Brown, Eleanor. *see* Brown, Eleanor Gertrude.
Brown, Eleanor F. *see* Brown, Eleanor Frances.
Brown, Eleanor Frances, 1908-
  xBrown, Eleanor F.
    Cutting Library Costs: Increasing Productivity
      & Raising Revenues. Scarecrow.
    Library Service to the Disadvantaged.
      Scarecrow.
    Modern Branch Libraries & Libraries in
      Systems. Scarecrow.
Brown, Eleanor G. *see* Brown, Eleanor Gertrude.
Brown, Eleanor Gertrude, 1888-1964
  xBrown, Eleanor.
    Milton's Blindness. Octagon.
  xBrown, Eleanor G.
    Milton's Blindness. Folcroft.
Brown, Elijah, 1867-
  xBrown, Elijah.
    The Real America. Arno.
Brown, Elmer B. *see* Brown, Elmer Burrell.
Brown, Elmer Burrell, 1926-
  xBrown, Elmer B.
    ed. Proteins of Iron Metabolism. Grune.
Brown, Elsa, 1930-
  xBrown, Elsa.
    Creative Quilting. Watson-Guptill.
Brown, Ernest F. *see* Brown, Ernest Francis.
Brown, Ernest Francis, 1903-
  xBrown, E. Francis.
    Joseph Hawley: Colonial Radical. AMS Pr.
  xBrown, Ernest F.
    Raymond of the Times. Greenwood.
Brown, Esther L. *see* Brown, Esther Lucile.
Brown, Esther Lucile.
  xBrown, Esther L.
    Lawyers & the Promotion of Justice. Irvington.
    Social Work As a Profession. Arno.
Brown, Evan L.
  xBrown, Evan L.
    Perception & the Senses. Oxford U Pr.
Brown, Everett S. *see* Brown, Everett Somerville.
Brown, Everett Somerville, 1886-1964
  xBrown, Everett S.

Constitutional History of the Louisiana
    Purchase, 1803-1812. Kelley.
Ratification of the Twenty-First Amendment to
    the Constitution of the United States. Da
    Capo.
Brown, F. Lee. *see* Brown, Franklin Lee.
Brown, F. Martin. *see* Brown, Frederick Martin.
Brown, Ford K. *see* Brown, Ford Keeler.
Brown, Ford Keeler.
  xBrown, Ford K.
    The Life of William Godwin. Folcroft.
Brown, Frances A.
  xBrown, Frances A.
    Forkner Shorthand Dictionary. Forkner.
Brown, Francis J. *see* Brown, Francis James.
Brown, Francis James, 1894-1959
  xBrown, Francis J.
    Educational Sociology. Greenwood.
Brown, Franklin Lee.
  xBrown, F. Lee.
    Cars, Cans, & Dumps: Solutions for Rural
      Residuals. Johns Hopkins.
Brown, Frederick, 1860-
  xBrown, Frederick.
    From Tientsin to Peking with the Allied
      Forces. Arno.
Brown, Frederick G. *see* Brown, Frederick Gramm.
Brown, Frederick Gramm.
  xBrown, Frederick G.
    Principles of Educational & Psychological
      Testing. HR&W.
Brown, Frederick Martin.
  xBrown, F. Martin.
    Earth Science. Scott F.
Brown, G. E. *see* Brown, George Eric.
Brown, G. S. *see* Brown, George Ingham.
Brown, G. Wayne.
  xBrown, G. Wayne.
    Applied Mechanics. P-H.
Brown, Gary D. *see* Brown, Gary Deward.
Brown, Gary Deward.
  xBrown, Gary D.
    System-360 Job-Control Language. Wiley.
    System-370 Job Control Language. Wiley.
Brown, Gary E.
  xBrown, Gary E.
    How to Improve Your Grades & Live Happily
      Ever After: A Brief Guide to Academic
      Survival. Libra.
Brown, George, 1935-
  xBrown, George.
    Lecturing & Explaining. Methuen Inc.
Brown, George D. *see* Brown, George Dobbin.
Brown, George Dobbin, 1874-1958
  xBrown, George D.
    Syllabification & Accent in the Paradise Lost.
      AMS Pr.
Brown, George Douglas, 1869-1902
  xBrown, George D.
    House with the Green Shutters. Scholarly.
Brown, George E.
  xBrown, George E.
    The Pruning of Trees, Shrubs & Conifers.
      Merrimack Bk Serv.
Brown, George Eric.
  xBrown, G. E.
    George Bernard Shaw. Arco.
Brown, George I. *see* Brown, George Isaac.
Brown, George Ingham.
  xBrown, G. S.
    Introduction to Inorganic Chemistry. Longman.
Brown, George Isaac.
  xBrown, George I.

Getting It All Together: Confluent Education. Phi Delta Kappa.
Human Teaching for Human Learning: An Introduction to Confluent Education. Penguin.
Brown, George R. *see* Brown, George Rothwell.
Brown, George Rothwell.
xBrown, George R.
The Leadership of Congress. Arno.
Brown, George W. *see* Brown, George Williams.
Brown, George Washington, 1820-1915
xBrown, George W.
Reminiscences of Gov. R. J. Walker: With the True Story of the Rescue of Kansas from Slavery. Arno.
Reminiscences of Gov. R. J. Walker: With the True Story of the Rescue of Kansas from Slavery. Negro U Pr.
Brown, George Williams.
xBrown, George W.
ed. Canada. Arno.
Canada in the Making. Greenwood.
Brown, Glenn, 1854-1932
xBrown, Glenn.
History of the United States Capitol. Da Capo.
Brown, Glenn H.
xBrown, Glenn H.
ed. Advances in Liquid Crystals. Acad Pr.
Brown, Godfrey N.
xBrown, Godfrey N.
Conflict & Harmony in Education in Tropical Africa. Fairleigh Dickinson.
Brown, H. *see* Brown, Huntington.
Brown, H. C. *see* Brown, Herbert Charles.
Brown, H. Douglas, 1941-
xBrown, H. Douglas.
Principles of Language Learning & Teaching. P-H.
Brown, H. Glenn. *see* Brown, Harry Glenn.
Brown, H. Rap, 1943-
xBrown, H. Rap.
Die Nigger Die. Dial.
Brown, Harold, 1934-
xBrown, Harold.
Crystallographic Groups of Four-Dimensional Space. Wiley.
Brown, Harold I., 1940-
xBrown, Harold I.
Perception, Theory & Commitment: A New Philosophy of Science. U of Chicago Pr.
Perception, Theory and Commitment: The New Philosophy of Science. Precedent Pub.
Brown, Harry A. *see* Brown, Harry Alvin.
Brown, Harry Alvin, 1897-1949
xBrown, Harry A.
Certain Basic Teacher-Education Policies & Their Development & Significance in a Selected State. AMS Pr.
Brown, Harry D. *see* Brown, Harry Darrow.
Brown, Harry Darrow, 1925-
xBrown, Harry D.
Chemistry of the Cell Interface. Acad Pr.
Brown, Harry G. *see* Brown, Harry Gunnison.
Brown, Harry Glenn.
xBrown, H. Glenn.
Directory of Printing, Publishing, Bookselling & Allied Trades in Rhode Island to 1865. NY Pub Lib.
Brown, Harry Gunnison, 1880-
xBrown, Harry G.
The Economics of Taxation. U of Chicago Pr.
Brown, Harry M. *see* Brown, Harry Matthew.
Brown, Harry Matthew.
xBrown, Harry M.
Business Writing & Communication: Strategies & Applications. Van Nos Reinhold.
How to Write: A Practical Rhetoric. HR&W.
Brown, Hazel E.
xBrown, Hazel E.

Grant Wood & Marvin Cone: Artists of an Era. Iowa St U Pr.
Brown, Helen (White).
xBrown, Helen W.
Index of Marriage Licenses, Prince George's County, Maryland 1777-1886. Genealog Pub.
Brown, Helen W. *see* Brown, Helen (White).
Brown, Henry, 1920-
xBrown, Henry.
ed. Protein Nutrition. C C Thomas.
Brown, Henry C. *see* Brown, Henry Collins.
Brown, Henry Collins, 1862-1961
xBrown, Henry C.
In the Golden Nineties. Arno.
Brown, Herbert C. *see* Brown, Herbert Charles.
Brown, Herbert Charles, 1912-
xBrown, H. C.
ed. The Nonclassical Ion Problem. Plenum Pub.
xBrown, Herbert C.
Boranes in Organic Chemistry. Cornell U Pr.
Organic Syntheses Via Boranes. Wiley.
Brown, Himan.
xBrown, Himan.
ed. Strange Tales from CBS Radio Mystery Theater. Popular Lib.
Brown, Homer E., 1909-
xBrown, Homer E.
Solution of Large Networks by Matrix Methods. Wiley.
Brown, Howard M. *see* Brown, Howard Mayer.
Brown, Howard Mayer.
xBrown, Howard M.
Instrumental Music Printed Before 1600: A Bibliography. Harvard U Pr.
Music in the Renaissance. P-H.
Musical Iconography: A Manual for Cataloguing Musical Subjects in Western Art Before 1800. Harvard U Pr.
Brown, Hugh, 1933-
xBrown, Hugh.
Brain & Behavior: A Textbook of Physiological Psychology. Oxford U Pr.
Brown, Hugh A. *see* Brown, Hugh Auchincloss.
Brown, Hugh Auchincloss, 1878-
xBrown, Hugh A.
Cataclysms of the Earth. Freedeeds Assocs.
Cataclysms of the Earth. Multimedia.
Brown, Huntington.
xBrown, H.
Rabelais in English Literature. Gordon Pr.
xBrown, Huntington.
Rabelais in English Literature. Biblio Dist.
Rabelais in English Literature. Octagon.
Brown, Ina (Ladd), 1902-
xBrown, Ina L.
Homespun. Golden Quill.
Brown, Ina C. *see* Brown, Ina Corinne.
Brown, Ina Corinne, 1896-
xBrown, Ina C.
Understanding Other Cultures. P-H.
Brown, Ina L. *see* Brown, Ina (Ladd).
Brown, Ina Ladd.
xBrown, Ina L.
Leaves on the Wind. Golden Quill.
Brown, Ira L.
xBrown, Ira L.
Georgia Colony. Macmillan.
Brown, Irving H. *see* Brown, Irving Henry.
Brown, Irving Henry, 1888-1940
xBrown, Irving H.
Leconte De Lisle: A Study of the Man & His Poetry. AMS Pr.
Brown, Ivor. *see* Brown, Ivor Carnegie.
Brown, Ivor Carnegie, 1891-
xBrown, Ivor.
H. G. Wells. Folcroft.
H. G. Wells. Haskell.
Brown, Ivor J. *see* Brown, Ivor John Carnegie.

Brown, Ivor John Carnegie, 1891-
xBrown, Ivor.
Chosen Words. Greenwood.
First Player: The Origin of Drama. Folcroft.
No Idle Words, and Having the Last Word. Greenwood.
Words in Our Time. Greenwood.
Words in Season. Greenwood.
Words on the Level. Transatlantic.
xBrown, Ivor J.
Shaw in His Time. Greenwood.
This Shakespeare Industry: Amazing Monument. Greenwood.
Brown, J. Douglas. *see* Brown, James Douglas.
Brown, J. H. *see* Brown, Jack Harold Upton.
Brown, J. H. U. *see* Brown, J. Harold Upton.
Brown, J. Harold Upton.
xBrown, J. H. U.
ed. Engineering Principles in Physiology. Acad Pr.
Brown, Jack Harold Upton, 1918-
xBrown, J. H.
Integration & Coordination of Metabolic Processes: A Systems Approach to Endocrinology. Van Nos Reinhold.
xBrown, J. H. U.
The Politics of Health Care. Ballinger Pub.
Brown, James.
xBrown, James.
The Art of Politics: Electoral Strategies & Campaign Management. Alfred Pub.
Brown, James D. *see* Brown, James Duff.
Brown, James Douglas, 1898-
xBrown, J. Douglas.
The Human Nature of Organizations. Am Mgmt.
Brown, James Duff.
xBrown, James D.
British Musical Biography: A Dictionary of Musical Artists, Authors & Composers, Born in Britain & Its Colonies. Da Capo.
Brown, James I.
xBrown, James I.
Guide to Effective Reading. Heath.
Brown, James I. *see* Brown, James Isaac.
Brown, James Isaac, 1908-
xBrown, James I.
Efficient Reading. Heath.
Reading Power. Heath.
Brown, James K.
xBrown, James K.
Planning & the Corporate Planning Director. Conference Bd.
This Business of Issues: Coping with the Company's Environments. Conference Bd.
Brown, James R. *see* Brown, James Russell.
Brown, James Russell.
xBrown, James R.
Religion, Society, & the Homosexual. Mss Info.
Brown, Janet, 1952-
xBrown, Janet.
Feminist Drama: Definition & Critical Analysis. Scarecrow.
Brown, Jason W.
xBrown, Jason W.
Aphasia, Apraxia & Agnosia: Clinical & Theoretical Aspects. C C Thomas.
Brown, Jeannette A.
xBrown, Jeannette A.
Organizing & Evaluating Elementary School Guidance Services: What, Why, & How. Brooks-Cole.
Brown, Jerald, 1940-
xBrown, Jerald R.
Instant (Freeze Dried Computer Programming in) BASIC. Intl Schol Bk Serv.
Brown, Jerald R. *see* Brown, Jerald.
Brown, Jerram. *see* Brown, Jerram L.
Brown, Jerram L.
xBrown, Jerram.

The Evolution of Behavior. Norton.
Brown, Jim, 1933-
xBrown, Jim.
The Case for the Cruising Trimaran. Intl
Marine.
Brown, Joan W. see Brown, Joan Winmill.
Brown, Joan Winmill.
xBrown, Joan W.
Every Knee Shall Bow. Revell.
No Longer Alone. Revell.
Brown, Joe D. see Brown, Joe David.
Brown, Joe David.
xBrown, Joe D.
Stars in My Crown. NAL.
Brown, John, 1810-1882
xBrown, John.
Arthur H. Hallam. Folcroft.
The English Puritans. Arden Lib.
The English Puritans. Folcroft.
The History of the English Bible. Folcroft.
Provisional Constitution & Ordinances for the
People of the United States. M&S Pr.
Worship Celebrations for Youth. Judson.
Brown, John A., 1898-
xBrown, John A.
Computers & Automation. Arco.
Brown, John A. see Brown, John Arthur.
Brown, John Arthur.
xBrown, John A.
How a Computer System Works. Arco.
Brown, John C. see Brown, John Crosby.
Brown, John Crombie, d. 1879?
xBrown, John C.
Ethics of George Eliot's Works. Kennikat.
The Ethics of George Eliot's Works. R West.
Brown, John Crosby, 1838-1909
xBrown, John C.
A Hundred Years of Merchant Banking. Arno.
Brown, John G. see Brown, John Gracen.
Brown, John Gracen.
xBrown, John G.
Variation in Verse. Branden.
Brown, John M. see Brown, John Macmillan.
Brown, John Macmillan, 1846-1935
xBrown, John M.
Maori & Polynesian, Their Origin, History &
Culture. AMS Pr.
Peoples & Problems of the Pacific. AMS Pr.
The Riddle of the Pacific. AMS Pr.
Brown, John Mason, 1900-
xBrown, John M.
As They Appear. Greenwood.
Letters from Greenroom Ghosts. Arno.
Still Seeing Things. Greenwood.
Brown, John R. see Brown, John Russell.
Brown, John Russell.
xBrown, John R.
Theatre Language: A Study of Arden, Osborne,
Pinter & Wesker. Taplinger.
Brown, Jonathan.
xBrown, Jonathan.
Images & Ideas in Seventeenth-Century
Spanish Painting. Princeton U Pr.
Brown, Jonathan M.
xBrown, Jonathan M.
Modern Challenges to Halakhah. Whitehall Co.
Brown, Joseph E., 1929-
xBrown, Joseph E.
The Mormon Trek West. Doubleday.
Oil Spills: Danger in the Sea. Dodd.
Brown, Josephine C. see Brown, Josephine Chapin.
Brown, Josephine Chapin.
xBrown, Josephine C.
Public Relief, 1929-1939. Octagon.
Brown, Judith. see Brown, Judith Gwyn.
Brown, Judith G. see Brown, Judith Gwyn.
Brown, Judith Gwyn.
xBrown, Judith.
illus. Muffin. Abelard.
xBrown, Judith G.

Alphabet Dreams. P-H.
Brown, Judith M.
xBrown, Judith M.
Gandhi's Rise to Power: Indian Politics
1915-1922. Cambridge U Pr.
Brown, Judith R.
xBrown, Judith R.
Back to the Beanstalk: Enchantment & Reality
for Couples. Psych & Consul Assocs.
Brown, Karl.
xBrown, Karl.
Adventures with D. W. Griffith. Da Capo.
Brown, Kenneth E., 1904-
xBrown, Kenneth E.
General Mathematics in American Colleges.
AMS Pr.
Brown, Kenneth S.
xBrown, Kenneth S.
Quantitative Methods for Managerial
Decisions. A-W.
Brown, Kenny L.
xBrown, Kenny L.
The Italians in Oklahoma. U of Okla Pr.
Brown, Kent L. see Brown, Kent Louis.
Brown, Kent Louis, 1916-
xBrown, Kent L.
Medical Problems & the Law. C C Thomas.
Brown, L. Carl. see Brown, Leon Carl.
Brown, L. David.
xBrown, L. David.
Take Care: A Guide for Responsible Living.
Augsburg.
Brown, L. M. see Brown, Leslie Melville.
Brown, Lavonn D.
xBrown, Lavorn D.
ed. Salvation in Our Time. Broadman.
Brown, Lavorn D. see Brown, Lavonn D.
Brown, Lawrence K. see Brown, Lawrence Kronseld.
Brown, Lawrence Kronseld, 1917-
xBrown, Lawrence K.
A Thesaurus of Spanish Idioms & Everyday
Language. Ungar.
Brown, Leland.
xBrown, Leland.
Communicating Facts & Ideas in Business.
P-H.
Effective Business Report Writing. P-H.
Brown, Leon Carl, 1928-
xBrown, L. Carl.
ed. From Madina to Metropolis: Heritage &
Change in the Near Eastern City. Darwin Pr.
ed. Psychological Dimensions of Near Eastern
Studies. Darwin Pr.
The Tunisia of Ahmad Bey: 1837-1855.
Princeton U Pr.
Brown, Les, 1928-
xBrown, Les.
Keeping Your Eye on Television. Pilgrim NY.
Brown, Leslie Melville, 1914-
xBrown, L. M.
Aims of Education. Tchrs Coll.
Brown, Lester. see Brown, Lester Russell.
Brown, Lester R. see Brown, Lester Russell.
Brown, Lester Russell.
xBrown, Lester.
Running on Empty: The Future of the
Automobile in an Oil-Short World. Norton.
xBrown, Lester R.

By Bread Alone. Pergamon.
The Future of the Automobile in an Oil-Short
World. Worldwatch Inst.
The Global Economic Prospect: New Sources
of Economic Stress. Worldwatch Inst.
In the Human Interest: A Strategy to Stabilize
World Population. Norton.
In the Human Interest: A Strategy to Stabilize
World Population. Pergamon.
The Politics & Responsibility of the North
American Breadbasket. Worldwatch Inst.
Resource Trends & Population Policy: A Time
for Reassessment. Worldwatch Inst.
Twenty-Two Dimensions of the Population
Problem. Worldwatch Inst.
World Population Trends: Signs of Hope, Signs
of Stress. Worldwatch Inst.
World Without Borders. Random.
The Worldwide Loss of Cropland. Worldwatch
Inst.
Brown, Lloyd. see Brown, Lloyd Arnold.
Brown, Lloyd A. see Brown, Lloyd Arnold.
Brown, Lloyd Arnold.
xBrown, Lloyd.
The Story of Maps. Dover.
xBrown, Lloyd A.
Map Making: The Art That Became a Science.
Little.
Brown, Lloyd L. see Brown, Lloyd Louis.
Brown, Lloyd Louis, 1913-
xBrown, Lloyd L.
Paul Robeson Rediscovered. Am Inst Marxist.
Brown, Lorin W.
xBrown, Lorin W.
Hispano Folklife of New Mexico: The Lorin
W. Brown Federal Writers' Project
Manuscripts. U of NM Pr.
Brown, Louis M. see Brown, Louis Morris.
Brown, Louis Morris, 1909-
xBrown, Louis M.
Preventive Law. Greenwood.
Brown, Louise C.
xBrown, Louise C.
Elephant Seals. Dodd.
Giraffes. Dodd.
Brown, Louise F. see Brown, Louise Fargo.
Brown, Louise Fargo.
xBrown, Louise F.
Men & Centuries of European Civilization.
Arno.
Brown, Louise K., 1897-
xBrown, Louise K.
A Revolutionary Town. Phoenix Pub.
Brown, Lucy G. see Brown, Lucy Gregor.
Brown, Lucy Gregor.
xBrown, Lucy G.
Core Media Collection for Elementary Schools.
Bowker.
Core Media Collection for Secondary Schools.
Bowker.
Brown, Marc. see Brown, Marc Tolon.
Brown, Marc Tolon.
xBrown, Marc.
illus. The Cloud Over Clarence. Dutton.
Lenny & Lola. Dutton.
Moose & Goose. Dutton.
One Two Three: An Animal Counting Book.
Little.
Brown, Marcia.
xBrown, Marcia.
Listen to a Shape. Watts.
Brown, Margaret. see Brown, Margaret Wise.
Brown, Margaret W. see Brown, Margaret Wise.
Brown, Margaret Wise, 1910-1952
xBrown, Margaret.
Wheel on the Chimney. Lippincott.
xBrown, Margaret W.

Introduction to Business: An Integrated
  Approach. Glencoe.
Revolutionary Politics in Massachusetts: The
  Boston Committee of Correspondence & the
  Towns, 1772-1774. Harvard U Pr.
Revolutionary Politics in Massachusetts: The
  Boston Committee of Correspondence & the
  Towns, 1772-1774. Norton.
Brown, Richard E.
  xBrown, Richard E.
  ed. The Effectiveness of Legislative Program
    Review. Transaction Bks.
Brown, Richard Harvey.
  xBrown, R. H.
  ed. Structure, Consciousness, & History.
    Cambridge U Pr.
Brown, Richard M. *see* Brown, Richard Maxwell.
Brown, Richard Maxwell.
  xBrown, Richard M.
  Strain of Violence: Historical Studies of
    American Violence & Vigilantism. Oxford U
    Pr.
  Strain of Violence: Historical Studies of
    American Violence & Vigilantism. Oxford U
    Pr.
Brown, Rita M. *see* Brown, Rita Mae.
Brown, Rita Mae.
  xBrown, Rita M.
  A Plain Brown Rapper. Diana Pr.
  xBrown, Rita Mae.
  Songs to a Handsome Woman. Diana Pr.
Brown, Robert D. *see* Brown, Robert Dean.
Brown, Robert Dean.
  xBrown, Robert D.
  Industrial Education Facilities: A Handbook for
    Organization & Management. Allyn.
Brown, Robert F.
  xBrown.
  jt. auth. Applied Finite Mathematics.
    Wadsworth Pub.
  xBrown, Robert F.
  The Later Philosophy of Schelling: The
    Influence of Boehme on the Works of
    1809-1815. Bucknell U Pr.
  The Lefschetz Fixed Point Theorem. Scott F.
  Mathematics Applied to Business & the Social
    Sciences. Wadsworth Pub.
Brown, Robert H. *see* Brown, Robert Henry.
Brown, Robert Hanbury.
  xBrown, R. Hanbury.
  The Intensity Interferometer: Its Application to
    Astronomy. Halsted Pr.
Brown, Robert Henry.
  xBrown, Robert H.
  Farm Electrification. McGraw.
Brown, Robert K. *see* Brown, Robert Kevin.
Brown, Robert Kevin.
  xBrown, Robert K.
  Corporate Real Estate: Executive Strategies for
    Profit Making. Dow Jones-Irwin.
  Essentials of Real Estate. P-H.
Brown, Robert L. *see* Brown, Robert Louis.
Brown, Robert Leaman, 1921-
  xBrown, Robert L.
  Colorado Ghost Towns, Past & Present.
    Caxton.
  Ghost Towns of the Colorado Rockies. Caxton.
Brown, Robert Louis.
  xBrown, Robert L.
  Cooperative Education. Am Assn Comm Jr
    Coll.
Brown, Robert M. *see* Brown, Robert Musser.
Brown, Robert McAfee, 1920-
  xBrown, Robert M.

Pseudonyms of God. Westminster.
Religion & Violence: A Primer for White
  Americans. Westminster.
Significance of the Church. Westminster.
Theology in a New Key: Responding to
  Liberation Themes. Westminster.
Brown, Robert Michael.
  xBrown.
  CB Radio Operator's Guide. TAB Bks.
  xBrown, Robert M.
  How to Read Electronic Circuit Diagrams.
    TAB Bks.
Brown, Robert Musser.
  xBrown, Robert M.
  Brother, Which Drummer. HarBraceJ.
Brown, Robert W. *see* Brown, Robert Wade.
Brown, Robert Wade.
  xBrown, Robert W.
  Residential Foundations: Design, Behavior &
    Repair. Van Nos Reinhold.
Brown, Robin.
  xBrown, Robin.
  The Lure of the Dolphin. Avon.
Brown, Roger. *see* Brown, Roger William.
Brown, Roger Glenn.
  xBrown, Roger Glenn.
  Fashoda Reconsidered: The Impact of
    Domestic Politics on French Policy in Africa,
    1893-1898. Johns Hopkins.
Brown, Roger J. *see* Brown, Roger James Evan.
Brown, Roger James Evan, 1931-
  xBrown, Roger J.
  Permafrost in Canada: Its Influence on
    Northern Development. U of Toronto Pr.
Brown, Roger William, 1925-
  xBrown, Roger.
  A First Language: The Early Stages. Harvard U
    Pr.
  ed. Psycholinguistics: Selected Papers. Free Pr.
  Psychology. Little.
  Words & Things. Free Pr.
Brown, Rollo W. *see* Brown, Rollo Walter.
Brown, Rollo Walter, 1880-1956
  xBrown, Rollo W.
  Creative Spirit: An Inquiry into American Life.
    Kennikat.
  The Creative Spirit: An Inquiry into American
    Life. R West.
  Lonely Americans. Arno.
Brown, Ronald, 1900-
  xBrown, Ronald.
  The Practical Manager's Guide to Excellence
    in Management. Am Mgmt.
Brown, Ronald C., 1945-
  xBrown, Ronald C.
  Hard-Rock Miners: The Intermountain West,
    1860-1920. Tex A&M Univ Pr.
Brown, Ronald Gordon Sclater.
  xBrown, R. G.
  The Administrative Process in Britain.
    Methuen Inc.
Brown, Rosellen.
  xBrown, Rosellen.
  The Autobiography of My Mother. Doubleday.
  Some Deaths in the Delta & Other Poems. U
    of Mass Pr.
  Street Games. Doubleday.
Brown, Ross. *see* Brown, Ross D.
Brown, Ross D.
  xBrown, Ross.
  ed. Hydrolysis of Cellulose: Mechanisms of
    Enzymatic & Acid Catalysis. Am Chemical.
Brown, Ross E.
  xBrown, Ross E.
  Ultrasonography: Basic Principles & Clinical
    Applications. Green.
Brown, Roy.
  xBrown, Roy.

The Cage. HM.
Day of the Pigeons. Macmillan.
Find Debbie!. HM.
Flight of Sparrows. Macmillan.
No Through Road. HM.
The Swing of the Gate. HM.
Brown, Roy E. *see* Brown, Roy Edward.
Brown, Roy Edward, 1931-
  xBrown, Roy E.
  Starving Children: The Tyranny of Hunger.
    Springer Pub.
Brown, Roy I.
  xBrown, Roy I.
  Psychology & Education of Slow Learners.
    Routledge & Kegan.
Brown, Roy M. *see* Brown, Roy Melton.
Brown, Roy Melton.
  xBrown, Roy M.
  Public Poor Relief in North Carolina. Arno.
Brown, S. F. *see* Brown, Stanley S.
Brown, S. Helen.
  xBrown, S. Helen.
  How to Save Money Building Your Own
    Home. Sterling.
Brown, Sanborn C. *see* Brown, Sanborn Conner.
Brown, Sanborn Conner, 1913-
  xBrown, Sanborn C.
  Benjamin Thompson, Count Rumford. MIT Pr.
  Count Rumford, Physicist Extraordinary.
    Greenwood.
  Electron Molecule Scattering. Wiley.
Brown, Sara L.
  xBrown, Sara L.
  ed. Parents on the Team. U of Mich Pr.
Brown, Scott S. *see* Brown, Scott Shorey.
Brown, Scott Shorey, 1951-
  xBrown, Scott S.
  Bounds on Transfer Principles for Algebraically
    Closed & Complete Discretely Valued Fields.
    Am Math.
Brown, Sheldon S., 1937-
  xBrown, Sheldon S.
  Remade in America: A Grand Tour of Europe,
    Asia, Within the U. S. A.. Old Time.
  Your Career in Court Administration. Arco.
Brown, Stanley.
  xBrown, Stanley.
  Men from Under the Sky: The Arrival of
    Westerners in Fiji. C E Tuttle.
Brown, Stanley C.
  xBrown, Stanley C.
  God's Plan for Marriage. Westminster.
Brown, Stanley S.
  xBrown, S. F.
  ed. Chemical Diagnosis & Disease. Elsevier.
Brown, Sterling. *see* Brown, Sterling Allen.
Brown, Sterling A. *see* Brown, Sterling Allen.
Brown, Sterling Allen, 1901-
  xBrown, Sterling.
  ed. Negro Caravan. Arno.
  xBrown, Sterling A.
  The Last Ride of Wild Bill & Eleven Narrative
    Poems. Broadside.
Brown, Stuart. *see* Brown, Stuart C.
Brown, Stuart C.
  xBrown, Stuart.
  ed. Reason & Religion. Cornell U Pr.
Brown, Stuart E.
  xBrown, Stuart E.
  The Guns of Harpers Ferry. Va Bk.
Brown, Stuart G. *see* Brown, Stuart Gerry.
Brown, Stuart Gerry, 1912-
  xBrown, Stuart G.

Browne, Henry Joseph, 1919-
xBrowne, Henry J.
The Catholic Church & the Knights of Labor.
Arno.
Browne, John R. see Browne, John Ross.
Browne, John Ross, 1821-1875
xBrowne, John R.
Adventures in the Apache Country: A Tour
Through Arizona & Sonora, with Notes on
the Silver Regions of Nevada. Arno.
Browne, Junius H. see Browne, Junius Henri.
Browne, Junius Henri, 1833-1902
xBrowne, Junius H.
Four Years in Secessia. Arno.
Browne, Martha (Griffith), d. 1906
xBrowne, Martha G.
Autobiography of a Female Slave. Negro U Pr.
Browne, Martha G. see Browne, Martha (Griffith).
Browne, Patrick, 1720?-1790
xBrowne, Patrick.
Civil & Natural History of Jamaica. Arno.
Browne, Peter, Bp. of Cork and Ross, d. 1735
xBrowne, Peter.
Procedure, Extent & Limits of the Human
Understanding.. Garland Pub.
Browne, Ray B. see Browne, Ray Broadus.
Browne, Ray Broadus.
xBrowne, Ray B.
ed. Lincoln-Lore: Lincoln in the Popular Mind.
Bowling Green Univ.
ed. Popular Culture & Curricula. Bowling
Green Univ.
Browne, William H. see Browne, William Hand.
Browne, William Hand, 1828-1912
xBrowne, William H.
Maryland, the History of a Palatinate. AMS Pr.
Browne, William P. see Browne, William Paul.
Browne, William Paul, 1945-
xBrowne, William P.
Politics, Programs, & Bureaucrats. Kennikat.
Brownell, Baker, 1887-1965
xBrownell, Baker.
College & the Community: A Critical Study of
Higher Education. Greenwood.
Brownell, Blaine A.
xBrownell, Blaine A.
ed. Bosses & Reformers: Urban Politics in
America, 1880-1920. HM.
ed. The City in Southern History: The Growth
of Urban Civilization in the South. Kennikat.
Brownell, Emery A.
xBrownell, Emery A.
Legal Aid in the United States: A Study of the
Availability of Lawyers Services for Persons
Unable to Pay Fees. Greenwood.
Brownell, John A. see Brownell, John Arnold.
Brownell, John Arnold, 1924-
xBrownell, John A.
A Directory of Selected Resources for the
Study of English in Japan. U Pr of Hawaii.
Brownell, W. C. see Brownell, William Crary.
Brownell, W. E. see Brownell, Wayne E.
Brownell, Wayne E.
xBrownell, W. E.
Structural Clay Products. Springer-Verlag.
Brownell, William C. see Brownell, William Crary.
Brownell, William Crary, 1851-1928
xBrownell, W. C.
The Genius of Style. Folcroft.
xBrownell, William C.
Genius of Style. Kennikat.
Browner, John. see Browner, John P.
Browner, John P.
xBrowner, John.
Death of a Punk. PB.
Browning, B. L. see Browning, Bertie Lee.
Browning, Bertie Lee, 1902-
xBrowning, B. L.

Analysis of Paper. Dekker.
ed. Chemistry of Wood. Krieger.
Browning, Charles H. see Browning, Charles Henry.
Browning, Charles Henry.
xBrowning, Charles H.
Some Colonial Dames of Royal Descent:
Pedigrees Showing Lineal Descent from
Kings of Some Members of the National
Society of the Colonial Dames of America, &
of the Order of the Crown. Genealog Pub.
Browning, Christopher R.
xBrowning, Christopher R.
The Final Solution & the German Foreign
Office. Holmes & Meier.
Browning, Don S.
xBrowning, Don S.
The Moral Context of Pastoral Care.
Westminster.
Browning, Edgar K.
xBrowning, Edgar K.
Public Finance & the Price System. Macmillan.
Browning, Elizabeth. see Browning, Elizabeth Barrett.
Browning, Elizabeth B. see Browning, Elizabeth Barrett.
Browning, Elizabeth Barrett, 1806-1861
xBrowning, Elizabeth.
Twenty-Two Unpublished Letters of Elizabeth
Barrett Browning & Robert Browning
Addressed to Henrietta & Arabella
Moulton-Barrett. Folcroft.
Twenty Two Unpublished Letters of Elizabeth
Barrett Browning & Robert Browning.
Haskell.
xBrowning, Elizabeth B.
Aurora Leigh. Academy Chi Ltd.
Casa Guidi Windows. Browning Inst.
Complete Works of Elizabeth Barrett
Browning. AMS Pr.
Sonnets from the Portuguese. Crown.
Sonnets from the Portuguese. Har-Row.
Sonnets from the Portuguese. Peter Pauper.
Sonnets from the Portuguese. Peter Pauper.
Browning, Iain.
xBrowning, Iain.
Palmyra. Noyes.
Browning, Norma L. see Browning, Norma Lee.
Browning, Norma Lee.
xBrowning, Norma L.
He Saw a Hummingbird. Dutton.
He Saw a Hummingbird. G K Hall.
Omarr: Astrology & the Man. NAL.
Browning, Oscar, 1837-1923
xBrowning, Oscar.
Life of George Eliot. Folcroft.
Browning, Philip L.
xBrowning, Philip L.
Rehabilitation & the Retarded Offender. C C
Thomas.
Browning, Preston M.
xBrowning, Preston M.
Flannery O'Connor. S Ill U Pr.
Browning, Robert, 1914-
xBrowning, Robert.
Byzantium & Bulgaria: A Comparative Study
Across the Early Medieval Frontier. U of Cal
Pr.
The Emperor Julian. U of Cal Pr.
Men & Women. Oxford U Pr.
Pauline. Folcroft.
Browning, Robert M. see Browning, Robert Marcellus.
Browning, Robert Marcellus, 1911-
xBrowning, Robert M.
German Baroque Poetry, 1618-1723. Pa St U
Pr.
Brownlee, Ann T. see Brownlee, Ann Templeton.
Brownlee, Ann Templeton, 1944-
xBrownlee, Ann T.
Community, Culture & Care: A Cross-Cultural
Guide for Health Workers. Mosby.
Brownlee, Harriet.
xBrownlee, Harriet.

The Low-Carbohydrate Gourmet: A Cookbook
for Hungry Dieters. Morrow.
Brownlee, Kenneth A. see Brownlee, Kenneth Alexander.
Brownlee, Kenneth Alexander, 1918-
xBrownlee, Kenneth A.
Statistical Theory & Methodology in Science &
Engineering. Wiley.
Brownlee, Richard S.
xBrownlee, Richard S.
Gray Ghosts of the Confederacy: Guerrilla
Warfare in the West, 1861-65. La State U Pr.
Brownlee, W. see Brownlee, Walter.
Brownlee, W. D. see Brownlee, Walter D.
Brownlee, W. Elliot, 1941-
xBrownlee, W. Elliot.
Dynamics of Ascent: A History of the
American Economy. Knopf.
Progressivism & Economic Growth: The
Wisconsin Income Tax, 1911-1929. Kennikat.
Brownlee, Walter.
xBrownlee, W.
The First Ships Round the World. Cambridge
U Pr.
Brownlee, Walter D.
xBrownlee, W. D.
The First Ships Around the World. Lerner
Pubns.
Brownlie, Ian.
xBrownlie, Ian.
Principles of Public International Law. Oxford
U Pr.
Brownlow, Donald G. see Brownlow, Donald Grey.
Brownlow, Donald Grey.
xBrownlow, Donald G.
Checkmate at Ruweisat: Auchinleck's Finest
Hour. Chris Mass.
Panzer Baron: The Military Exploits of General
Hasso Von Manteuffel. Chris Mass.
Brownlow, F. W. see Brownlow, Frank Walsh.
Brownlow, Frank Walsh, 1934-
xBrownlow, F. W.
Two Shakespearean Sequences: Henry VI to
Richard II & Pericles to Timon of Athens. U
of Pittsburgh Pr.
Brownlow, Kevin.
xBrownlow, Kevin.
The Parade's Gone by. U of Cal Pr.
Brownlow, William G. see Brownlow, William
Gannaway.
Brownlow, William Gannaway, 1805-1877
xBrownlow, William G.
A Political Register, Setting Forth the
Principles of the Whig & Locofoco Parties in
the United States, with the Life & Public
Services of Henry Clay. Reprint.
Brownlow, William R. see Brownlow, William Robert
Bernard.
Brownlow, William Robert Bernard, Bp, 1830-1901
xBrownlow, William R.
Lectures on Slavery & Serfdom in Europe.
Negro U Pr.
Brownrigg, Ronald.
xBrownrigg, Ronald.
The Twelve Apostles. Macmillan.
Brownstein, Samuel. see Brownstein, Samuel C.
Brownstein, Samuel C.
xBrownstein, Samuel.
Vocabulary Builder. Barron.
Brownstone, David M.
xBrownstone, David M.
Island of Hope, Island of Tears. Rawson Wade.
The VNR Dictionary of Business & Finance.
Van Nos Reinhold.
Where to Find Business Information: A
Worldwide Guide for Everyone Who Needs
the Answers to Business Questions. Wiley.
Brownville, Charles Gordon, 1898-
xBrownville, Gordon.
Symbols of the Holy Spirit. Tyndale.
Brownville, Gordon. see Brownville, Charles Gordon.

Brox, Norbert, 1935-
  xBrox, Norbert.
    Understanding the Message of Paul. U of
    Notre Dame Pr.
Broy, Anthony.
  xBroy, Anthony.
    Managing Your Money: How to Make the
    Most of Your Income & Have a Financially
    Secure Future. Watts.
Broyard, Anatole.
  xBroyard, Anatole.
    Men, Women & Other Anticlimaxes. Methuen
    Inc.
Broyelle, Claudie.
  xBroyelle, Claudie.
    Women's Liberation in China. Humanities.
Broyles, Frank. see Broyles, J. Frank.
Broyles, J. Frank.
  xBroyles, Frank.
    Hog Wild: The Autobiography of Frank
    Broyles. Memphis St Univ.
  xBroyles, J. Frank.
    Administration of Athletic Programs: A
    Managerial Approach. P-H.
Broze, Matt C.
  xBroze, Matt C.
    Freestyle Skiing. Arco.
Brubacher, John S. see Brubacher, John Seiler.
Brubacher, John Seiler.
  xBrubacher, John S.
    Higher Education in Transition: A History of
    American Colleges & Universities,
    1636-1976. Har-Row.
    On the Philosophy of Higher Education.
    Jossey-Bass.
Brubaker, Dale. see Brubaker, Dale L.
Brubaker, Dale L.
  xBrubaker, Dale.
    Who's Teaching? Who's Learning?: Active
    Learning in Elementary Schools. Goodyear.
  xBrubaker, Dale L.
    Creative Leadership in Elementary Schools.
    Kendall-Hunt.
Brubaker, Sterling.
  xBrubaker, Sterling.
    In Command of Tomorrow: Resource and
    Environmental Strategies for Americans.
    Johns Hopkins.
Bruccoli, Matthew. see Bruccoli, Matthew Joseph.
Bruccoli, Matthew J. see Bruccoli, Matthew Joseph.
Bruccoli, Matthew Joseph, 1931-
  xBruccoli, Matthew.
    Scott & Ernest: The Authority of Failure & the
    Authority of Success. S Ill U Pr.
  xBruccoli, Matthew J.
    Apparatus for F. Scott Fitzgerald's the Great
    Gatsby: Under the Red, White & Blue. U of
    SC Pr.
    ed. The Chief Glory of Every People: Essays
    on Classic American Writers. S Ill U Pr.
    F. Scott Fitzgerald: A Descriptive Bibliography.
    U of Pittsburgh Pr.
    ed. James Gould Cozzens: New Acquist of
    True Experience. S Ill U Pr.
    The O'Hara Concern: A Biography of John
    O'Hara. Random.
    ed. Pages: The World of Books, Writers &
    Writing. Gale.
    Profile of F. Scott Fitzgerald. Merrill.
    Raymond Chandler: A Checklist. Kent St U Pr.
    Raymond Chandler: A Descriptive
    Bibliography. U of Pittsburgh Pr.
    Supplement to F. Scott Fitzgerald: A
    Descriptive Bibliography. U of Pittsburgh Pr.
Bruce, Andasia K. see Bruce, Andasia Kimbrough.
Bruce, Andasia Kimbrough, 1868-
  xBruce, Andasia K.
    Uncle Tom's Cabin of To-Day. Arno.
Bruce, Charles, Sir, 1836-1920
  xBruce, Charles.

    The Broad Stone of Empire: Problems of
    Crown Colony Administration. Arno.
Bruce, Curt.
  xBruce, Curt.
    The Great Houses of New Orleans. Knopf.
    The Great Houses of San Francisco. Knopf.
Bruce, Dickson D., 1946-
  xBruce, Dickson D.
    And They All Sang Hallelujah: Plain-Folk
    Camp-Meeting Religion, 1800-1845. U of
    Tenn Pr.
    Violence & Culture in the Antebellum South. U
    of Tex Pr.
Bruce, Donald. see Bruce, Donald James Williams.
Bruce, Donald James Williams, 1930-
  xBruce, Donald.
    Topics of Restoration Comedy. St Martin.
Bruce, Erroll.
  xBruce, Erroll.
    Deep Sea Sailing. McKay.
Bruce, F. F. see Bruce, Frederick Fyvie.
Bruce, Frederick Fyvie, 1910-
  xBruce, F. F.
    The Defence of the Gospel in the New
    Testament. Eerdmans.
Bruce, Gustav M. see Bruce, Gustav Marius.
Bruce, Gustav Marius, 1879-1963
  xBruce, Gustav M.
    Luther As an Educator. Greenwood.
Bruce, Hal.
  xBruce, Hal.
    How to Grow Wildflowers & Wild Shrubs &
    Trees in Your Own Garden. Knopf.
Bruce, Harry J. see Bruce, Harry James.
Bruce, Harry James, 1931-
  xBruce, Harry J.
    Distribution & Transportation Handbook. CBI
    Pub.
Bruce, Herbert A. see Bruce, Herbert Alexander.
Bruce, Herbert Alexander, 1868-
  xBruce, Herbert A.
    Our Heritage, & Other Addresses. Arno.
Bruce, John C. see Bruce, John Collingwood.
Bruce, John Collingwood.
  xBruce, John C.
    Northumbrian Minstrelsy: A Collection of the
    Ballads, Melodies, & Small-Pipe Tunes of
    Northumbria. Gale.
Bruce, Jon W., 1944-
  xBruce, Jon W.
    Real Estate Finance in a Nutshell. West Pub.
Bruce, Joseph P. see Bruce, Joseph Percy.
Bruce, Joseph Percy, 1861-
  xBruce, Joseph P.
    Chu Hsi & His Masters: An Introduction to
    Chu Hsi & the Sung School of Chinese
    Philosophy. Krishna Pr.
Bruce, Lennart.
  xBruce, Lennart.
    Subpoemas. Panjandrum.
Bruce, Philip A. see Bruce, Philip Alexander.
Bruce, Philip Alexander, 1856-1933
  xBruce, Philip A.
    The Plantation Negro As a Freeman:
    Observations on His Character, Condition &
    Prospects in Virginia. Metro Bks.
Bruce, Richard L. see Bruce, Richard Loren.
Bruce, Richard Loren, 1938-
  xBruce, Richard L.
    Fundamentals of Physiological Psychology.
    HR&W.
Bruce, Robert, 1951-
  xBruce, Robert.
    Software Debugging for Microcomputers.
    Reston.
Bruce, Robert V.
  xBruce, Robert V.
    Lincoln & the Tools of War. Greenwood.
Bruce, V. see Bruce, Violet Rose.

Bruce, Violet Rose.
  xBruce, V.
    Awakening the Slower Mind. Pergamon.
Bruce-Briggs, B.
  xBruce-Briggs, B.
    The Politics of Planning: A Review & Critique
    of Centralized Economic Planning. Inst
    Contemporary.
Bruce-Gardyne, Jock.
  xBruce-Gardyne, Jock.
    The Power Game: An Examination of
    Decision-Making in Government. Shoe
    String.
Bruce's Son & Co. see Bruce's Son and Company, New
  York.
Bruce's Son & Company. see Bruce's Son and Company,
  New York.
Brucer. see Brucer, Marshall.
Brucer, Marshall.
  xBrucer.
    ed. The Heritage of Nuclear Medicine. Soc
    Nuclear Med.
Bruce's Son and Company, New York.
  xBruce's Son & Co.
    Victorian Frames, Borders & Cuts from the
    1882 Type Catalog of George Bruce's Son &
    Co.. Peter Smith.
  xBruce's Son & Company.
    Victorian Frames, Borders & Cuts. Dover.
Bruch, Charles D.
  xBruch, Charles D.
    Mechanics for Technology. Wiley.
    Strength of Materials for Technology. Wiley.
Bruch, Hilde, 1904-
  xBruch, Hilde.
    The Golden Cage: The Enigma of Anorexia
    Nervosa. Harvard U Pr.
    Learning Psychotherapy: Rationale & Ground
    Rules. Harvard U Pr.
Bruchac, Joseph.
  xBruchac, Joseph.
    Turkey Brother & Other Tales: Iroquois Folk
    Stories. Crossing Pr.
Bruchey, Stuart. see Bruchey, Stuart Weems.
Bruchey, Stuart W. see Bruchey, Stuart Weems.
Bruchey, Stuart Weems.
  xBruchey, Stuart.
    Growth of the Modern American Economy.
    Har-Row.
  xBruchey, Stuart W.
    Robert Oliver, Merchant of Baltimore,
    1783-1819. Arno.
Bruck, Maria.
  xBruck, Maria.
    ed. Parish Celebrations. Paulist Pr.
    ed. Parish Ministry Resources. Paulist Pr.
Bruck, R. H. see Bruck, Richard Hubert.
Bruck, Richard Hubert.
  xBruck, R. H.
    Survey of Binary Systems. Springer-Verlag.
Bruck, Stephen D.
  xBruck, Stephen D.
    Properties of Biomaterials in the Physiological
    Environment. CRC Pr.
Bruck-Kan, Roberta.
  xBruck-Kan, Roberta.
    Introduction to Human Anatomy. Har-Row.
Bruckberger, R. L. see Bruckberger, Raymond Leopold.
Bruckberger, Raymond Leopold, 1907-
  xBruckberger, R. L.
    God & Politics. O'Hara.
Brucker, Gene. see Brucker, Gene A.
Brucker, Gene A.
  xBrucker, Gene.
    People & the Communities in the Western
    World. Dorsey.
  xBrucker, Gene A.

Renaissance Florence. Krieger.
Renaissance Florence. Wiley.
Brucker, Roger W.
  xBrucker, Roger W.
    The Longest Cave. Knopf.
Bruckl, Renate.
  xBruckl, Renate.
    Structural & Thematic Analysis of George
      Meredith's Novel "Diana of the Crossways".
      Humanities.
Bruckner, A. M. see Bruckner, Andrew M.
Bruckner, Andrew M.
  xBruckner, A. M.
    Differentiation of Real Functions.
      Springer-Verlag.
Bruckner, Dwight.
  xBruckner, Dwight.
    Hot Lead. Belmont-Tower.
Brue, Stanley L.
  xBrue, Stanley L.
    Economic Scenes: Theory in Today's World.
      P-H.
Brueggemann, H. P.
  xBrueggemann, H. P.
    Conic Mirrors. Focal Pr.
Brueggemann, Walter.
  xBrueggemann, Walter.
    In Man We Trust: The Neglected Side of
      Biblical Faith. John Knox.
    Living Toward a Vision: Biblical Reflections on
      Shalom. Pilgrim NY.
    The Prophetic Imagination. Fortress.
Bruemmer, Fred.
  xBruemmer, Fred.
    The Life of the Harp Seal. Times Bks.
Brues, Alice M. see Brues, Alice Mossie.
Brues, Alice Mossie, 1913-
  xBrues, Alice M.
    People & Races. Macmillan.
Brues, Charles T. see Brues, Charles Thomas.
Brues, Charles Thomas, 1879-1955
  xBrues, Charles T.
    Insects, Food & Ecology. Dover.
    Insects' Food & Ecology. Peter Smith.
Bruffee, Kenneth A.
  xBruffee, Kenneth A.
    A Short Course in Writing: Practical Rhetoric
      for Composition Courses, Writing Workshops
      & Tutor Training Programs. Winthrop.
Bruford, Walter H. see Bruford, Walter Horace.
Bruford, Walter Horace, 1894-
  xBruford, Walter H.
    Theatre, Drama, & Audience in Goethe's
      Germany. Greenwood.
Bruggen, Theodore Van. see Van Bruggen, Theodore.
Brugger, Bill.
  xBrugger, Bill.
    ed. China Since the Gang of Four. St Martin.
    ed. China: The Impact of the Cultural
      Revolution. B&N.
Bruguera, Miquel.
  xBruguera, Miquel.
    Atlas of Laparoscopy & Biopsy of the Liver.
      Saunders.
Bruins, Paul F.
  xBruins, Paul F.
    ed. Packaging with Plastics. Gordon.
    ed. Polyurethane Technology. Wiley.
Brumback, Carl, 1917-
  xBrumback, Carl.
    Holy Land Hymns. Logos.
    A Sound from Heaven. Gospel Pub.
Brumbaugh. see Brumbaugh, Martin Grove.
Brumbaugh, J. Frank.
  xBrumbaugh, J. Frank.
    Mail Order....Starting up, Making It Pay.
      Chilton.
Brumbaugh, Judy.
  xBrumbaugh, Judy.

His & Hers Tailoring: A Self-Instructional
    Guide. Anna Pub.
Brumbaugh, Martin G. see Brumbaugh, Martin Grove.
Brumbaugh, Martin Grove, 1862-1930
  xBrumbaugh.
    History of the German Baptist Brethren in
      Europe & America. Church History.
  xBrumbaugh, Martin G.
    A History of the German Baptist Brethren in
      Europe & America. AMS Pr.
Brumbaugh, Robert S. see Brumbaugh, Robert Sherrick.
Brumbaugh, Robert Sherrick, 1918-
  xBrumbaugh, Robert S.
    Ancient Greek Gadgets & Machines.
      Greenwood.
    Plato for the Modern Age. Greenwood.
    Plato's Mathematical Imagination: The
      Mathematical Passages in the Dialogues &
      Their Interpretation. Kraus Repr.
Brumbaugh, Sara B. see Brumbaugh, Sara Barbara.
Brumbaugh, Sara Barbara, 1883-
  xBrumbaugh, Sara B.
    Democratic Experience & Education in the
      National League of Women Voters. AMS Pr.
Brumblay, Ray U.
  xBrumblay, Ray U.
    A First Course in Quantitative Analysis. A-W.
    Qualitative Analysis. Har-Row.
    Quantitative Analysis. Har-Row.
Brumfit, Christopher.
  xBrumfit, Christopher.
    Problems & Principles in English Teaching.
      Pergamon.
Brumgardt, John R.
  xBrumgardt, John R.
    People of the Magic Waters: The Cahuilla
      Indians of Palm Springs. ETC Pubns.
Brumm, Ursula.
  xBrumm, Ursula.
    American Thought & Religious Typology.
      Rutgers U Pr.
Brun, Ellen.
  xBrun, Ellen.
    Socialist Korea: A Case Study in the Strategy
      of Economic Development. Monthly Rev.
Brun, Henry J.
  xBrun, Henry J.
    Social Studies Student Investigates the Retreat
      from Imperialism. Rosen Pr.
Brun, Viggo, 1943-
  xBrun, Viggo.
    Sug, the Trickster Who Fooled the Monk: A
      Northern Thai Tale with Vocabulary.
      Humanities.
Bruna, Dick.
  xBruna, Dick.
    Another Story to Tell. Methuen Inc.
    illus. The Egg. Methuen Inc.
    I Can Dress Myself. Methuen Inc.
    I Can Read Difficult Words. Methuen Inc.
Brundage, Burr C. see Brundage, Burr Cartwright.
Brundage, Burr Cartwright, 1912-
  xBrundage, Burr C.
    The Fifth Sun: Aztec Gods, Aztec World. U of
      Tex Pr.
    A Rain of Darts: The Mexica Aztecs. U of Tex
      Pr.
    Two Earths, Two Heavens: An Essay
      Contrasting the Aztecs & the Incas. U of
      NM Pr.
Brundage, Dorothy J., 1930-
  xBrundage, Dorothy J.
    Nursing Management of Renal Problems.
      Mosby.
Brundage, James A.
  xBrundage, James A.
    ed. Medieval Canon Law & the Crusader. U of
      Wis Pr.
    Richard Lion Heart. Scribner.
Brundidge, Harry. see Brundidge, Harry T.

Brundidge, Harry T.
  xBrundidge, Harry.
    Twinkle Twinkle Movie Star. Garland Pub.
Brundin, Robert E.
  xBrundin, Robert E.
    Price Guide to Books on Canada & the
      Canadian Arctic. Univ Microfilms.
Bruneau, T. C. see Bruneau, Thomas C.
Bruneau, Thomas C.
  xBruneau, T. C.
    The Political Transformation of the Brazilian
      Catholic Church. Cambridge U Pr.
Bruner, Edward M.
  xBruner, Edward M.
    ed. Art, Ritual & Society in Indonesia. Ohio U
      Ctr Intl.
Bruner, Jerome. see Bruner, Jerome Seymour.
Bruner, Jerome S. see Bruner, Jerome Seymour.
Bruner, Jerome Seymour.
  xBruner, Jerome.
    Toward a Theory of Instruction. Norton.
  xBruner, Jerome S.
    ed. Human Growth & Development: The
      Wolfson College Lectures, 1976. Oxford U
      Pr.
    On Knowing: Essays for the Left Hand.
      Harvard U Pr.
    Process of Education. Harvard U Pr.
    A Study of Thinking. Krieger.
    Study of Thinking. Wiley.
    Toward a Theory of Instruction. Harvard U Pr.
Brunetiere, F. see Brunetiere, Ferdinand.
Brunetiere, Ferdinand, 1849-1906
  xBrunetiere, F.
    Honore De Balzac. Gordon Pr.
Brunetti, Mendor.
  xBrunetti, Mendor.
    Read, Write, Speak French. Bantam.
Brunhouse, Robert L. see Brunhouse, Robert Levere.
Brunhouse, Robert Levere, 1908-
  xBrunhouse, Robert L.
    The Counter-Revolution in Pennsylvania:
      1776-1790. Pa Hist & Mus.
    Frans Blom, Maya Explorer. U of NM Pr.
    In Search of the Maya: The First
      Archaeologists. U of NM Pr.
    Pursuit of the Ancient Maya: Some
      Archaeologists of Yesterday. U of NM Pr.
    Sylvanus G. Morley & the World of the
      Ancient Mayas. U of Okla Pr.
Bruni, James V.
  xBruni, James V.
    Experiencing Geometry. Wadsworth Pub.
Bruning, James L.
  xBruning, James L.
    Computational Handbook of Statistics. Scott F.
Brunk, H. D.
  xBrunk, H. D.
    Introduction to Mathematical Statistics. Wiley.
Brunk, Jason W., 1923-
  xBrunk, Jason W.
    Child & Adolescent Development. Wiley.
Brunner, Christopher J.
  xBrunner, Christopher J.
    A Syntax of Western Middle Iranian. Caravan
      Bks.
Brunner, Edmund D. see Brunner, Edmund De
  Schweinitz.
Brunner, Edmund De Schweinitz, 1889-
  xBrunner, Edmund D.
    Working with Rural Youth. Arno.
Brunner, Heinrich, 1945-
  xBrunner, Heinrich.
    Cuban Sugar Policy from 1963 to 1970. U of
      Pittsburgh Pr.
Brunner, Heinrich E. see Brunner, Heinrich Emil.
Brunner, Heinrich Emil, 1889-1966
  xBrunner, Heinrich E.

Eternal Hope. Greenwood.

Brunner, John.
xBrunner, John.
Born Under Mars. Ace Bks.
The Productions of Time. DAW Bks.
Quicksand. DAW Bks.
Stand on Zanzibar. Ballantine.
Stand on Zanzibar. Bentley.
Total Eclipse. DAW Bks.
The Whole Man. Ballantine.

Brunner, Joseph F.
xBrunner, Joseph F.
Participating in Secondary Reading: A Practical
Approach. P-H.

Brunner, K. see Brunner, Karl.

Brunner, Karl.
xBrunner, K.
ed. The Problem of Inflation. Elsevier.
ed. Public Policies in Open Economies.
Elsevier.
xBrunner, Karl.
ed. Institutions, Policies & Economic
Performance. Elsevier.
An Outline of Middle English Grammar.
Folcroft.

Brunner, Lillian S. see Brunner, Lillian Sholtis.

Brunner, Lillian Sholtis.
xBrunner, Lillian S.
The Lippincott Manual of Nursing Practice.
Lippincott.
Textbook of Medical-Surgical Nursing.
Lippincott.

Brunner, Marguerite. see Brunner, Marguerite Ashworth.

Brunner, Marguerite A. see Brunner, Marguerite
Ashworth.

Brunner, Marguerite Ashworth.
xBrunner, Marguerite.
Gold Mine of Money-Making Ideas. Lorenz Pr.
xBrunner, Marguerite A.
Antiques for Amateurs on a Shoestring Budget.
A & W Pubs.
Pass It on: How to Make Your Own Family
Keepsakes. Sovereign Bks.

Brunner, Nancy A., 1939-
xBrunner, Nancy A.
Orthopedic Nursing: A Programmed Approach.
Mosby.

Brunner, S. see Brunner, Sam.

Brunner, Sam.
xBrunner, S.
ed. Radiology in Oto-Rhino-Laryngology. S
Karger.

Brunner, William F.
xBrunner, William F.
Practical Vacuum Techniques. Krieger.

Brunnert, H. S. see Brunnert, Ippolit Semenovich.

Brunnert, Ippolit Semenovich.
xBrunnert, H. S.
Present Day Political Organization of China.
Chinese Materials.

Brunnstrom. see Brunnstrom, Signe.

Brunnstrom, Signe.
xBrunnstrom.
Clinical Kinesiology. Davis Co.

Bruno, Carole. see Bruno, Carole A.

Bruno, Carole A.
xBruno, Carole.
Paralegal's Litigation Handbook. Inst Busn
Plan.

Bruno, Frank J. see Bruno, Frank Joe.

Bruno, Frank Joe, 1930-
xBruno, Frank J.
Human Adjustment & Personal Growth: Seven
Pathways. Wiley.
Think Yourself Thin: How Psychology Can
Help You Lose Weight. B&N.

Bruno, Giordano, 1548-1600
xBruno, Giordano.

Cause, Principle & Unity: Five Dialogues.
Greenwood.

Bruno, James E.
xBruno, James E.
Educational Policy Analysis: A Quantitative
Approach. Crane-Russak Co.

Bruno, Vincent J.
xBruno, Vincent J.
ed. The Parthenon. Norton.

Brunor, Martin A.
xBrunor, Martin A.
Arts & Crafts of the Austral Islands: A Special
Exhibition, 17 December 1968 to 30 April
1969. Peabody Mus Salem.

Bruns, Roger.
xBruns, Roger.
ed. Am I Not a Man & a Brother: The
Antislavery Crusade of Revolutionary
America, 1688-1788. Chelsea Hse.

Bruns, W. J. see Bruns, William J.

Bruns, William J.
xBruns, W. J.
Introduction to Accounting: Economic
Measurement for Decisions. A-W.

Brunschwig, Henri, 1904-
xBrunschwig, Henri.
Enlightenment & Romanticism in
Eighteenth-Century Prussia. U of Chicago Pr.

Brunschwig, L. see Brunschwig, Lily.

Brunschwig, Lily, 1906-
xBrunschwig, L.
Study of Some Personality Aspects of Deaf
Children. AMS Pr.

Brunskill, R. W.
xBrunskill, R. W.
Illustrated Handbook of Vernacular
Architecture. Merrimack Bk Serv.
xBrunskill, Ronald.
English Brickwork. Rowman.

Brunskill, Ronald. see Brunskill, R. W.

Brunson, Joel G.
xBrunson, Joel G.
Concepts of Disease: A Textbook of Human
Pathology. Macmillan.

Brunson, Nancy. see Brunson, Nancy M. Harkins.

Brunson, Nancy M. Harkins.
xBrunson, Nancy.
Grieve Not for Wrightsie. Logos.

Brunstein, Karl. see Brunstein, Karl A.

Brunstein, Karl A.
xBrunstein, Karl.
Beyond the Four Dimensions: Reconciling
Physics, Parapsychology & UFO's. Walker &
Co.

Brunswik, Egon, 1903-
xBrunswik, Egon.
The Conceptual Framework of Psychology. U
of Chicago Pr.

Brunt, H. L. Van. see Van Brunt, H. L.

Brunt, Henry Van. see Van Brunt, Henry.

Brunt, LeRoy Van. see Van Brunt, LeRoy.

Brunton, Douglas.
xBrunton, Douglas.
Members of the Long Parliament. Shoe String.

Bruntz, George G.
xBruntz, George G.
Allied Propaganda & the Collapse of the
German Empire in 1918. Arno.

Brunvand, Jan H. see Brunvand, Jan Harold.

Brunvand, Jan Harold.
xBrunvand, Jan H.
Guide for Collectors of Folklore in Utah. U of
Utah Pr.
Readings in American Folklore. Norton.

Brus, Wlodzimierz. see Brus, Wodzimierz.

Brus, Wodzimierz.
xBrus, Wlodzimierz.

The Economics & Politics of Socialism:
Collected Essays. Routledge & Kegan.
The Market in a Socialist Economy. Routledge
& Kegan.

Brusaw, Charles T.
xBrusaw, Charles T.
The Business Writer's Handbook. St Martin.

Bruschi, Arnaldo.
xBruschi, Arnaldo.
Bramante. Thames Hudson.

Bruschi, Arnoldo. see Bruschi, Arnaldo.

Brush, Don O. see Brush, Don Orr.

Brush, Don Orr.
xBrush, Don O.
Buckling of Bars, Plates, Shells. McGraw.

Brush, F. Robert.
xBrush, F. Robert.
ed. Aversive Conditioning & Learning. Acad
Pr.

Brushwood, John S. see Brushwood, John Stubbs.

Brushwood, John Stubbs, 1920-
xBrushwood, John S.
The Spanish American Novel: A
Twentieth-Century Survey. U of Tex Pr.

Brusilov, Aleksei Alekseevich, 1853-1926
xBrusilov, Aleksei A.
Soldiers Note-Book, 1914-1918. Greenwood.

Brusilov, Aleksei A. see Brusilov, Aleksei Alekseevich.

Brusius, Ron.
xBrusius, Ron.
Family Evening Activity Devotions. Concordia.

Bruss, Elizabeth W.
xBruss, Elizabeth W.
Autobiographical Acts: The Changing Situation
of a Literary Genre. Johns Hopkins.

Bruss, Paul, 1943-
xBruss, Paul.
Conrad's Early Sea Fiction: The Novelist As
Navigator. Bucknell U Pr.

Brussard, Peter F.
xBrussard, Peter F.
ed. Ecological Genetics: The Interface.
Springer-Verlag.

Brustein, Robert. see Brustein, Robert Sanford.

Brustein, Robert Sanford, 1927-
xBrustein, Robert.
The Theatre of Revolt: An Approach to the
Modern Drama. Little.
Third Theatre. S&S.

Bruton, Eric.
xBruton, Eric.
The Longcase Clock. Beekman Pubs.
The Longcase Clock. Scribner.

Bruton, Len T.
xBruton, Len T.
RC-Active Networks: Theory & Design. P-H.

Brutten, Milton.
xBrutten, Milton.
Something's Wrong with My Child: A Parents'
Book About Children with Learning
Disabilities. HarBraceJ.

Brutus, Dennis, 1924-
xBrutus, Dennis.
Strains. Troubadour Texas.

Bruun, Bertel.
xBruun, Bertel.
The Larousse Guide to Birds of Britain &
Europe. Larousse.

Bruun, Geoffrey, 1898-
xBruun, Geoffrey.
Clemenceau. Shoe String.

Bruun, Kettil.
xBruun, Kettil.
Drinking Habits Among Northern Youth: A
Cross-National Study in the Scandinavian
Capitals. Rutgers Ctr Alcohol.
The Gentlemen's Club: International Control
of Drugs & Alcohol. U of Chicago Pr.

Bruun, Per.
xBruun, Per.

An Introduction to Immunohematology. Saunders.

Bryant, Paul T.
  xBryant, Paul T.
    H. L. Davis. Twayne.

Bryant, Rosalie.
  xBryant, Rosalie.
    Complete Elementary Physical Education Guide. P-H.

Bryant, Sara C. *see* Bryant, Sara Cone.

Bryant, Sara Cone, 1873-
  xBryant, Sara C.
    How to Tell Stories to Children. Gale.
    How to Tell Stories to Children. Gordon Pr.
    How to Tell Stories to Children. Norwood Edns.

Bryant, Steven. *see* Bryant, Steven Jerome.

Bryant, Steven Jerome.
  xBryant, Steven.
    Precalculus Mathematics: Algebra & Trigonometry. Goodyear.

Bryant, Traphes.
  xBryant, Traphes L.
    Dog Days at the White House: The Outrageous Memoirs of the Presidential Kennel-Keeper Truman to Nixon. Macmillan.

Bryant, Traphes L. *see* Bryant, Traphes.

Bryant, Will.
  xBryant, Will.
    Blue Russell. Fawcett.
    Blue Russell. Random.

Bryant, William C. *see* Bryant, William Cullen.

Bryant, William Cullen, 1794-1878
  xBryant, William C.
    ed. The Library of Poetry & Song. Arden Lib.
    The Library of Poetry & Song. Century Bookbindery.
    ed. Tales of Glauber-Spa. Mss Info.

Bryce, Felicia.
  xBryce, Felicia.
    Government Nurse. Bouregy.
    Portia in Distress. Bouregy.

Bryce, Glendon E.
  xBryce, Glendon E.
    A Legacy of Wisdom: The Egyptian Contribution to the Wisdom of Israel. Bucknell U Pr.

Bryce, Herrington J.
  xBryce, Herrington J.
    Planning Smaller Cities. Lexington Bks.
    ed. Revitalizing Cities. Lexington Bks.

Bryce, James. *see* Bryce, James Bryce.
Bryce, James B. *see* Bryce, James Bryce.

Bryce, James Bryce, Viscount, 1838-1922
  xBryce, James.
    The Holy Roman Empire. Arden Lib.
    The Holy Roman Empire. Norwood Edns.
    South America: Observations & Impressions. Da Capo.
    South America: Observations & Impressions. Norwood Edns.
  xBryce, James B.
    The Holy Roman Empire. AMS Pr.
    Impressions of South Africa. Negro U Pr.
    Predictions of Hamilton & De Tocqueville. AMS Pr.
    The Predictions of Hamilton & De Tocqueville. Johnson Repr.
    Studies in Contemporary Biography. Arno.
    Studies in History & Jurisprudence. Arno.

Bryce, M. Charles. *see* Bryce, Mary Charles.

Bryce, Mary Charles.
  xBryce, M. Charles.
    Come Let Us Eat: Preparing for First Communion. Seabury.

Bryde, John F.
  xBryde, John F.
    Modern Indian Psychology. Dakota Pr.

Bryden, J. M. *see* Bryden, John M.

Bryden, John.
  xBryden, John.
    Agrarian Change in the Scottish Highlands: The Role of the Highlands & Islands Development Board in the Agricultural Economy of the Crofting Counties. Biblio Dist.

Bryden, John M.
  xBryden, J. M.
    Tourism & Development: A Case Study of the Commonwealth Caribbean. Cambridge U Pr.

Bryden, Kenneth.
  xBryden, Kenneth.
    Old Age Pensions & Policy Making in Canada. McGill-Queens U Pr.

Brydson, J. A.
  xBrydson, John A.
    Plastics Materials. Krieger.

Brydson, John A. *see* Brydson, J. A.

Brye, David L., 1938-
  xBrye, David L.
    Wisconsin Voting Patterns in the Twentieth Century, 1900 to 1950. Garland Pub.

Bryer, Jackson. *see* Bryer, Jackson R.

Bryer, Jackson R.
  xBryer, Jackson.
    ed. F. Scott Fitzgerald: The Critical Reception. B Franklin.
    Hamlin Garland & the Critics: An Annotated Bibliography. Whitston Pub.

Bryher. *see* Bryher, Winifred.

Bryher, Winifred, 1894-
  xBryher.
    Coin of Carthage. HarBraceJ.

Bryk, Felix, 1882-
  xBryk, Felix.
    Circumcision in Man & Woman: Its History, Psychology & Ethnology. AMS Pr.
    Dark Rapture: The Sex Life of the African Negro. AMS Pr.

Brykczynski, Terry.
  xBrykczynski, Terry.
    Caged. Crown.

Brylawski, E. Fulton.
  xBrylawski, E. Fulton.
    ed. Legislative History of the 1909 Copyright Act. Rothman.

Brym, Robert J., 1951-
  xBrym, Robert J.
    Intellectuals & Politics. Allen Unwin.

Brymer, Robert A.
  xBrymer, Robert A.
    Introduction to Hotel & Restaurant Management: A Book of Readings. Kendall-Hunt.

Brynner, Irena.
  xBrynner, Irena.
    Jewelry As an Art Form. Van Nos Reinhold.
    Modern Jewelry: Design & Technique. Van Nos Reinhold.

Bryson, Conrey.
  xBryson, Conrey.
    Down Went McGinty: El Paso in the Wonderful Nineties. Tex Western.

Bryson, Harold T.
  xBryson, Harold T.
    Portraits of God. Broadman.

Bryson, Jeff B.
  xBryson, Jeff B.
    ed. Dual-Career Couples. Human Sci Pr.

Bryson, Judy.
  xBryson, Judy.
    ed. Baptist Dishes Worth Blessing. Pelican.

Bryson, R. A. *see* Bryson, Reid A.

Bryson, Reid A.
  xBryson, R. A.
    ed. Climates of North America. Elsevier.
  xBryson, Reid A.

Climates of Hunger: Mankind & the World's Changing Weather. U of Wis Pr.

Bryson, Thomas A., 1931-
  xBryson, Thomas A.
    American Diplomatic Relations with the Middle East, 1784-1975: A Survey. Scarecrow.
    United States-Middle East Diplomatic Relations 1784-1978: An Annotated Bibliography. Scarecrow.

Bryson, William H. *see* Bryson, William Hamilton.

Bryson, William Hamilton, 1941-
  xBryson, William H.
    Census of Law Books in Colonial Virginia. U Pr of Va.
    A Dictionary of Sigla & Abbreviations to & in Law Books Before 1607. U Pr of Va.
    Discovery in Virginia. Michie.

Brzezinski, Zbigniew. *see* Brzezinski, Zbigniew K.

Brzezinski, Zbigniew K., 1928-
  xBrzezinski, Zbigniew.
    ed. Africa & the Communist World. Hoover Inst Pr.
    ed. Africa & the Communist World. Stanford U Pr.
  xBrzezinski, Zbigniew K.
    Ideology & Power in Soviet Politics. Greenwood.

Brzozowski, J. A.
  xBrzozowski, J. A.
    Digital Networks. P-H.

Buache, Freddy.
  xBuache, Freddy.
    The Cinema of Luis Bunuel. A S Barnes.

Buban, Peter.
  xBuban, Peter.
    Understanding Electricity & Electronics. McGraw.

Bube, Richard H., 1927-
  xBube, Richard H.
    Photoconductivity of Solids. Krieger.

Bubel, Nancy.
  xBubel, Nancy W.
    Vegetables Money Can't Buy But You Can Grow. Godine.

Bubel, Nancy W. *see* Bubel, Nancy.

Buber, Martin, 1878-1965
  xBuber, Martin.
    Eclipse of God: Studies in the Relation Between Religion & Philosophy. Greenwood.
    Eclipse of God: Studies in the Relation Between Religion & Philosophy. Humanities.
    For the Sake of Heaven. Greenwood.
    For the Sake of Heaven: A Chronicle. Atheneum.
    Good & Evil: Two Interpretations. Scribner.
    I & Thou. Scribner.
    The Legend of the Baal-Shem. Schocken.
    On Judaism. Schocken.
    On the Bible: Eighteen Studies. Schocken.
    The Origin & Meaning of Hasidism. Horizon.

Bucchieri, Theresa F.
  xBucchieri, Theresa F.
    Feasting with Nonna Serafina. A S Barnes.

Bucco, Martin.
  xBucco, Martin.
    An American Tragedy Notes. Cliffs.
    E. W. Howe. Boise St Univ.

Buchan, Alastair.
  xBuchan, Alastair.
    Europe's Futures Europe's Choices: Models of Western Europe in the 1970's. Columbia U Pr.
    Spare Chancellor: The Life of Walter Bagehot. Mich St U Pr.

Buchan, David. *see* Buchan, David D.

Buchan, David D.
  xBuchan, David.

Animals Without Backbones: An Introduction
to the Invertebrates. U of Chicago Pr.
Buchsbaum, Walter H.
xBuchsbaum, Walter H.
Buchsbaum's Complete Handbook of Practical
Electronic Reference Data. P-H.
Buchwald, Art.
xBuchwald, Art.
The Buchwald Stops Here. Berkley Pub.
The Buchwald Stops Here. Putnam.
Down the Seine & up the Potomac with Art
Buchwald. Fawcett.
Down the Seine & up the Potomac with Art
Buchwald. Putnam.
I Never Danced at the White House. Fawcett.
Buchwald, Emilie.
xBuchwald, Emilie.
Gildaen: The Heroic Adventures of a Most
Unusual Rabbit. HarBraceJ.
Buchwald, Henry.
xBuchwald, Henry.
Surgical Treatment of Hyperlipidemia. Am
Heart.
Buck, Albert H. *see* Buck, Albert Henry.
Buck, Albert Henry, 1842-1922
xBuck, Albert H.
The Growth of Medicine from the Earliest
Times to About 1800. AMS Pr.
Buck, Anne.
xBuck, Anne.
Dress in Eighteenth Century England. Holmes
& Meier.
Buck, C. H. *see* Buck, Christoper Hearn.
Buck, Carl D. *see* Buck, Carl Darling.
Buck, Carl Darling, 1866-
xBuck, Carl D.
Dictionary of Selected Synonyms in the
Principal Indo-European Languages. U of
Chicago Pr.
Buck, Carlton C.
xBuck, Carlton C.
Communion Thoughts & Prayers. Bethany Pr.
Buck, Christoper Hearn.
xBuck, C. H.
Problems of Product Design & Development.
Pergamon.
Buck, Edith.
xBuck, Edith.
Patches. Victor Bks.
Buck, Harry M. *see* Buck, Harry Merwyn.
Buck, Harry Merwyn.
xBuck, Harry M.
ed. Structural Approaches to South India
Studies. Anima Bks.
Buck, James H. *see* Buck, James Harold.
Buck, James Harold.
xBuck, James H.
The Modern Japanese Military System. Sage.
Buck, Lucien A.
xBuck, Lucien A.
Autonomy Psychotherapy: Authoritarian
Control Versus Individual Choice. Chris
Mass.
Psychological Research & Human Values. Chris
Mass.
Buck, Margaret W. *see* Buck, Margaret Waring.
Buck, Margaret Waring.
xBuck, Margaret W.
illus. Where They Go in Winter. Abingdon.
Buck, Norman S. *see* Buck, Norman Sydney.
Buck, Norman Sydney, 1892-
xBuck, Norman S.
Development of the Organisation of
Anglo-American Trade, 1800-1850. Shoe
String.
Buck, P. *see* Buck, Peter.
Buck, Pearl. *see* Buck, Pearl (Sydenstricker).
Buck, Pearl (Sydenstricker), 1892-
xBuck, Pearl.

The Good Earth. Intl Bk Ctr.
A House Divided. PB.
The Long Love. PB.
Pavilion of Women. PB.
Peony. PB.
xBuck, Pearl S.
American Unity & Asia. Arno.
Child Who Never Grew. John Day.
Chinese Story Teller. John Day.
Death in the Castle. PB.
Dragon Seed. PB.
The Exile. PB.
Good Earth. T Y Crowell.
Good Earth. Watts.
The Good Earth. PB.
Letter from Peking. PB.
Mrs. Starling's Problem. John Day.
Pearl S. Buck's Oriental Cookbook. S&S.
The Story Bible. Tyndale.
Buck, Pearl S.
xBuck, Pearl S.
Command the Morning. PB.
The Fighting Angel. PB.
Buck, Pearl S. *see* Buck, Pearl (Sydenstricker).
Buck, Pearl Sydenstricker, 1892-1973
xBuck, Pearl S.
The Lovers & Other Stories. T Y Crowell.
ed. Pearl S. Buck's Book of Christmas. S&S.
The Rainbow. PB.
The Woman Who Was Changed & Other
Stories. T Y Crowell.
Buck, Peggy S.
xBuck, Peggy S.
I'm Divorced - Are You Listening Lord?.
Judson.
Buck, Percy C. *see* Buck, Percy Carter.
Buck, Percy Carter, Sir, 1871-1947
xBuck, Percy C.
Psychology for Musicians. Oxford U Pr.
Buck, Peter, 1943-
xBuck, P.
American Science & Modern China,
1876-1936. Cambridge U Pr.
Buck, Peter H. *see* Buck, Peter Henry.
Buck, Peter Henry, Sir, 1880-1951
xBuck, Peter H.
Anthropology & Religion. Shoe String.
The Material Culture of the Cook Islands
(Aitutaki). AMS Pr.
Buck, Philip W. *see* Buck, Philip Wallenstein.
Buck, Philip Wallenstein, 1900-
xBuck, Philip W.
Amateurs & Professionals in British Politics,
1918 to 1959. U of Chicago Pr.
ed. Control of Foreign Relations in Modern
Nations. Norton.
Politics of Mercantilism. Octagon.
Buck, Philo M. *see* Buck, Philo Melvin.
Buck, Philo Melvin, 1877-1950
xBuck, Philo M.
Directions in Contemporary Literature. Core
Collection.
Buck, R. C. *see* Buck, Robert Creighton.
Buck, R. Creighton. *see* Buck, Robert Creighton.
Buck, Robert Creighton, 1920-
xBuck, R. C.
ed. Studies in Modern Analysis. Math Assn.
xBuck, R. Creighton.
Advanced Calculus. McGraw.
An Introduction to Differential Equations. HM.
Buck, Solon J. *see* Buck, Solon Justus.
Buck, Solon Justus, 1884-1962
xBuck, Solon J.
Granger Movement: A Study of Agricultural
Organization & Its Political, Economic, &
Social Manifestations, 1870-1880. U of Nebr
Pr.
Buck, Stratton, 1906-
xBuck, Stratton.

Gustave Flaubert. Twayne.
Buckalew, M. W.
xBuckalew, M. W.
Learning to Control Stress. Rosen Pr.
Bucke, Richard M. *see* Bucke, Richard Maurice.
Bucke, Richard Maurice, 1837-1902
xBucke, Richard M.
Manuscripts, Autograph Letters, First Editions
& Portraits of Walter Whitman. Folcroft.
Richard Maurice Bucke, Medical Mystic:
Letters of Dr. Bucke to Walt Whitman &
Friends. Wayne St U Pr.
Buckett, M.
xBuckett, M.
Introduction to Livestock Husbandry.
Pergamon.
Buckholdt, David R.
xBuckholdt, David R.
Caretakers: Treating Emotionally Disturbed
Children. Sage.
Buckingham, A. D. *see* Buckingham, Amyand David.
Buckingham, Amyand David.
xBuckingham, A. D.
Organic Liquids: Structure, Dynamics &
Chemical Properties. Wiley.
Buckingham, Hugh W.
xBuckingham, Hugh W.
Neologistic Jargon Aphasia. Humanities.
Neologistic Jargon Aphasia. Swets North Am.
Buckingham, Jamie.
xBuckingham, Jamie.
Coping with Criticism. Logos.
Buckingham, Joseph T. *see* Buckingham, Joseph Tinker.
Buckingham, Joseph Tinker, 1779-1861
xBuckingham, Joseph T.
Personal Memoirs & Recollections of Editorial
Life. Arno.
Buckingham, Nancy.
xBuckingham, Nancy.
Vienna Summer. St Martin.
Buckingham, William B.
xBuckingham, William B.
Primer of Clinical Diagnosis. Har-Row.
Buckland, Charles E. *see* Buckland, Charles Edward.
Buckland, Charles Edward, 1847-1941
xBuckland, Charles E.
Dictionary of Indian Biography. Gale.
Dictionary of Indian Biography. Greenwood.
Dictionary of Indian Biography. Haskell.
Buckland, Raymond.
xBuckland, Raymond.
Anatomy of the Occult. Weiser.
xBuckland, Raymond B.
Practical Candle Burning. Llewellyn Pubns.
Buckland, Raymond B. *see* Buckland, Raymond.
Buckland, W. W. *see* Buckland, William Warwick.
Buckland, William Warwick, 1859-1946
xBuckland, W. W.
Some Reflections on Jurisprudence. Shoe
String.
Buckle, Henry T. *see* Buckle, Henry Thomas.
Buckle, Henry Thomas, 1821-1862
xBuckle, Henry T.
History of Civilization in England. Scholarly.
On Scotland - the Scotch Intellect. U of
Chicago Pr.
On Scotland & the Scotch Intellect. U of
Chicago Pr.
Buckle, Suzann R. *see* Buckle, Suzann R. Thomas.
Buckle, Suzann R. Thomas.
xBuckle, Suzann R.
Bargaining for Justice: Case Disposition &
Reform in the Criminal Courts. Praeger.
Buckler, Beatrice.
xBuckler, Beatrice.
Living with a Mentally Retarded Child: A
Primer for Parents. Dutton.
Buckler, William E. *see* Buckler, William Earl.
Buckler, William Earl, 1924-
xBuckler, William E.

ed. Prose of the Victorian Period. HM.
Buckley, A. R.
xBuckley, A. R.
Canadian Garden Perennials. Hancock Hse.
Garden Perennials. Hancock Hse.
Buckley, Alan D.
xBuckley, Alan D.
International Terrorism: Current Research &
Future Directions. Avery Pub.
Buckley, Helen E. *see* Buckley, Helen Elizabeth.
Buckley, Helen Elizabeth.
xBuckley, Helen E.
Grandmother & I. Lothrop.
Little Boy & the Birthdays. Lothrop.
The Little Pig in the Cupboard. Lothrop.
Wonderful Little Boy. Lothrop.
Buckley, Jerome H. *see* Buckley, Jerome Hamilton.
Buckley, Jerome Hamilton.
xBuckley, Jerome H.
Triumph of Time: A Study of the Victorian
Concepts of Time, History, Progress &
Decadence. Harvard U Pr.
ed. The Worlds of Victorian Fiction. Harvard
U Pr.
Buckley, John W.
xBuckley, John W.
Accounting: An Information Systems
Approach. CBI Pub.
Accounting: An Information Systems
Approach. Dickenson.
Executives Digest of Financial Research-1975.
Finan Exec.
Income Tax Allocation: An Inquiry into
Problems of Methodology & Estimation.
Finan Exec.
Buckley, Marie.
xBuckley, Marie.
Breaking into Prison: A Citizen Guide to
Volunteer Action. Beacon Pr.
Buckley, Page S.
xBuckley, Page S.
Techniques of Process Control. Krieger.
Buckley, Peter.
xBuckley, Peter.
Eat It Raw. Dodd.
Buckley, Rober N. *see* Buckley, Roger Norman.
Buckley, Roger Norman, 1937-
xBuckley, Rober N.
Slaves in Red Coats: The British West India
Regiments, 1795-1815. Yale U Pr.
Buckley, Thomas E., 1939-
xBuckley, Thomas E.
Church & State in Revolutionary Virginia,
1776-1787. U Pr of Va.
Buckley, William F. *see* Buckley, William Frank.
Buckley, William Frank, 1925-
xBuckley, William F.
God & Man at Yale: The Superstitions of
"Academic Freedom". Regnery-Gateway.
A Hymnal: The Controversial Arts. Putnam.
Stained Glass. Doubleday.
Stained Glass. Warner Bks.
Who's on First. Doubleday.
Bucklin, Louis P.
xBucklin, Louis P.
Productivity in Marketing. Am Mktg.
Buckman, Peter.
xBuckman, Peter.
Let's Dance: Social, Ballroom & Folk Dancing.
Paddington.
Let's Dance: Social, Ballroom & Folk Dancing.
Penguin.
The Rothschild Conversion. McGraw.
Buckmaster, Henrietta, Pseud.
xBuckmaster, Henrietta.

Flight to Freedom: The Story of the
Underground Railroad. T Y Crowell.
Freedom Bound. Macmillan.
Freedom Bound. Macmillan.
Women Who Shaped History. Macmillan.
Women Who Shaped History. Macmillan.
Bucknall, Barbara J.
xBucknall, Barbara J.
Religion of Art in Proust. U of Ill Pr.
**Bucknell-Susquehanna Colloquium on Myth in
Literature, 1974.**
xColloquium on Myth in Literature, Bucknell &
Susquehanna Universities, Mar. 21-2, 1974.
The Binding of Proteus, Perspectives on Myth
& the Literary Process: Proceedings. Bucknell
U Pr.
Buckner, Kathryn C. *see* Buckner, Kathryn Current.
Buckner, Kathryn Current, 1926-
xBuckner, Kathryn C.
Littleton's Contribution to the Theory of
Accountancy. Ga St U Busn Pub.
Buckner, Ken.
xBuckner, Ken.
Available Light. Petersen Pub.
Buckner, L. M. *see* Buckner, Leroy M.
Buckner, Leroy M.
xBuckner, L. M.
Customer Services. McGraw.
xBuckner, Leroy M.
Customer Services. McGraw.
Bucknill, John C. *see* Bucknill, John Charles.
Bucknill, John Charles, Sir, 1817-1897
xBucknill, John C.
Medical Knowledge of Shakespeare. AMS Pr.
Medical Knowledge of Shakespeare. R West.
Notes on Asylums for the Insane in America.
Arno.
Psychology of Shakespeare. AMS Pr.
Buckton, La Verne, 1896-
xBuckton, La Verne.
College & University Bands, Their
Organization & Administration. AMS Pr.
Buckwalter, Len.
xBuckwalter, Len.
CB Radio Construction Projects. Sams.
The Homeowner's Handbook of Power Tools.
T Y Crowell.
Bucky, Steven F.
xBucky, Steven F.
The Impact of Alcoholism. Hazelden.
Budak, Aram.
xBudak, Aram.
Circuit Theory Fundamentals & Applications.
P-H.
Buday, George. *see* Buday, Gyorgy.
Buday, Gyorgy, 1907-
xBuday, George.
The History of the Christmas Card. Gale.
Budbill, David.
xBudbill, David.
Christmas Tree Farm. Macmillan.
Budd, Edward C.
xBudd, Edward C.
ed. Inequality & Poverty. Norton.
Budd, Lillian.
xBudd, Lillian.
April Harvest. Avon.
Budd, Richard W.
xBudd, Richard W.
Beyond Media: New Approaches to Mass
Communication. Hayden.
Interdisciplinary Approaches to Human
Communication. Hayden.
Budd, Susan.
xBudd, Susan.
Varieties of Unbelief: Atheists & Agnostics in
English Society 1850-1960. Holmes & Meier.
Budde, James F.
xBudde, James F.

Measuring Performance in Human Service
Systems: Planning, Organization & Control.
Am Mgmt.
Budden, F. J.
xBudden, F. J.
Fascination of Groups. Cambridge U Pr.
Budden, K. G.
xBudden, K. G.
Lectures on Magnetoionic Theory. Gordon.
Budenz, Jozsef, 1836-1892
xBudenz, Jozsef.
Comparative Dictionary of the Finno-Ugric
Elements in the Hungarian Vocabulary. Res
Ctr Lang Semiotic.
Buder, Stanley.
xBuder, Stanley.
Pullman: An Experiment in Industrial Order &
Community Planning, 1880-1930. Oxford U
Pr.
Budevsky, O.
xBudevsky, Omortag.
Foundations of Chemical Analysis. Halsted Pr.
Budevsky, Omortag. *see* Budevsky, O.
Budge, E. A. *see* Budge, Ernest Alfred Thompson Wallis.
Budge, E. Wallis. *see* Budge, Ernest Alfred Thompson
Wallis.
Budge, Ernest A. *see* Budge, Ernest Alfred Thompson
Wallis.
Budge, Ernest Alfred Thompson Wallis, Sir, 1857-1934
xBudge, E. A.
Gods of the Egyptians: Or Studies in Egyptian
Mythology. Peter Smith.
The Gods of the Egyptians: Studies in
Egyptian Mythology. Dover.
Mummy. Biblo.
The Mummy. Macmillan.
xBudge, E. Wallis.
Babylonian Life & History. Cooper Sq.
Osiris & the Egyptian Resurrection. Dover.
Osiris & the Egyptian Resurrection. Peter
Smith.
xBudge, Ernest A.
Babylonian Life & History. AMS Pr.
ed. Coptic Apocrypha in the Dialect of Upper
Egypt. AMS Pr.
ed. Coptic Biblical Texts in the Dialect of
Upper Egypt. AMS Pr.
ed. Coptic Homilies in the Dialect of Upper
Egypt. AMS Pr.
Budig, Gene A.
xBudig, Gene A.
ed. Perceptions in Public Higher Education. U
of Nebr Pr.
Budker, Paul.
xBudker, Paul.
Life of Sharks. Columbia U Pr.
Budlong, Ware.
xBudlong, Ware.
Experimenting with Seeds & Plants. Putnam.
Budney, Blossom.
xBudney, Blossom.
After Dark. Lothrop.
Budnick, Frank S.
xBudnick, Frank S.
Applied Mathematics for Business, Economics,
& the Social Sciences. McGraw.
Principles of Operations Research for
Management. Irwin.
Budnick, J. I.
xBudnick, J. I.
Dynamical Aspects of Critical Phenomena.
Gordon.
Budreckis, Algirdas. *see* Budreckis, Algirdas Martin.
Budreckis, Algirdas Martin.
xBudreckis, Algirdas.
ed. The Lithuanians in America: A Chronology
& Fact Book. Oceana.
Budrys, Algis.
xBudrys, Algis.

Blood & Burning. Berkley Pub.
The Falling Torch. BJ Pub Group.
Some Will Not Die. Donning Co.
Budson, Richard D.
  xBudson, Richard D.
    The Psychiatric Halfway House: A Handbook
      of Theory & Practice. U of Pittsburgh Pr.
Budyko, M. I. *see* Budyko, Mikhail Ivanovich.
Budyko, Mikhail Ivanovich.
  xBudyko, M. I.
    Climate & Life. Acad Pr.
Budzik, Richard S.
  xBudzik, Richard S.
    Precision Sheet Metal Mathematics. Bobbs.
    Precision Sheet Metal Shop Practice. Bobbs.
Bueche, F.
  xBueche, Frederick.
    Principles of Physics. McGraw.
Bueche, Frederick, 1923-
  xBueche, Frederick.
    Introduction to Physics for Scientists &
      Engineers. McGraw.
  xBueche, Frederick J.
    Introduction to Physics for Scientists &
      Engineers. McGraw.
Bueche, Frederick. *see* Bueche, F.
Bueche, Frederick J. *see* Bueche, Frederick.
Buechner, Frederick, 1926-
  xBuechner, Frederick.
    The Alphabet of Grace. Seabury.
    The Book of Bebb. Atheneum.
    Peculiar Treasures: A Biblical Who's Who.
      Har-Row.
Buehler, Calvin A. *see* Buehler, Calvin Adam.
Buehler, Calvin Adam.
  xBuehler, Calvin A.
    Survey of Organic Syntheses. Wiley.
Buehler, Ezra C. *see* Buehler, Ezra Christian.
Buehler, Ezra Christian.
  xBuchler, Ezra C.
    Building the Contest Oration. Wilson.
Buehr, Walter.
  xBuehr, Walter.
    illus. Automobiles, Past & Present. Morrow.
    illus. First Book of Machines. Watts.
    illus. Meat, from Ranch to Table. Morrow.
    illus. Storm Warning: The Story of Hurricanes
      & Tornadoes. Morrow.
Buehrig, Edward H. *see* Buehrig, Edward Henry.
Buehrig, Edward Henry, 1910-
  xBuehrig, Edward H.
    Woodrow Wilson & the Balance of Power.
      Peter Smith.
Buel, J. W.
  xBuel, J. W.
    Life of Wild Bill Hickok. Nordon Pubns.
Buel, Richard.
  xBuel, Richard.
    Securing the Revolution: Ideology & American
      Politics, 1789-1815. Cornell U Pr.
    Securing the Revolution: Ideology in American
      Politics 1789-1815. Cornell U Pr.
Bueler, William M.
  xBueler, William M.
    Chinese Sayings. C E Tuttle.
    U. S. China Policy & the Problem of Taiwan.
      Greenwood.
Buell, Erwin C.
  xBuell, Erwin C.
    The Grass Roots: Readings in State & Local
      Government. Scott F.
Buell, Frederick, 1942-
  xBuell, Frederick.
    Full Summer. Columbia U Pr.
    Theseus & Other Poems. SBD.
Buell, Lawrence.
  xBuell, Lawrence.
    Design of Literature. Pendulum Pr.
Buell, Thomas B.
  xBuell, Thomas B.

Master of Sea Power: A Biography of Fleet
    Admiral Ernest J. King. Little.
Buelow, George J.
  xBuelow, George J.
    Thorough Bass Accompaniment According to
      Johann David Heinichen. U of Cal Pr.
Bueltmann, A. J.
  xBueltmann, A. J.
    Take the High Road. Concordia.
Buenker, John D.
  xBuenker, John D.
    Immigration & Ethnicity: A Guide to
      Information Sources. Gale.
    Progressivism. Schenkman.
Bueno, Dorothy Del. *see* Del Bueno, Dorothy J.
Buergenthal, Thomas.
  xBuergenthal, Thomas.
    ed. Human Rights, International Law & the
      Helsinki Accord. Allanheld.
Buerger, A. A.
  xBuerger, Alfred A.
    Approaches to the Validation of Manipulation
      Therapy. C C Thomas.
Buerger, Alfred A. *see* Buerger, A. A.
Buerger, M. J. *see* Buerger, Martin Julian.
Buerger, Martin J. *see* Buerger, Martin Julian.
Buerger, Martin Julian, 1903-
  xBuerger, M. J.
    Contemporary Crystallography. McGraw.
  xBuerger, Martin J.
    Crystal-Structure Analysis. Krieger.
    Introduction to Crystal Geometry. Krieger.
Buerki, F. A.
  xBuerki, Frederick A.
    Stagecraft for Nonprofessionals. U of Wis Pr.
Buerki, Frederick A. *see* Buerki, F. A.
Buess, Lynn M.
  xBuess, Lynn M.
    The Tarot & Transformation. De Voros.
Buettner-Janusch, John, 1924-
  xBuettner-Janusch, John.
    ed. Evolutionary & Genetic Biology of
      Primates. Acad Pr.
    Origins of Man: Physical Anthropology. Wiley.
Buffa, Elwood S. *see* Buffa, Elwood Spencer.
Buffa, Elwood Spencer, 1923-
  xBuffa, Elwood S.
    Modern Production-Operations Management.
      Wiley.
    Operations Management: The Management of
      Productive Systems. Wiley.
    Production-Inventory Systems: Planning &
      Control. Irwin.
Buffalo Fine Arts Academy.
  xBuffalo Fine Arts Academy.
    Aristide Maillol. Greenwood.
Buffalo Symposium on Modernist Interpretation of
Ancient Logic, 1972.
  xBuffalo Symposium on Modernist Interpretation
    of Ancient Logic, 21&22 April, 1972.
    Ancient Logic & Its Modern Interpretations:
      Proceedings. Kluwer Boston.
Buffie, Edward G.
  xBuffie, Edward G.
    ed. Curriculum Development in Nongraded
      Schools: Bold New Venture. Ind U Pr.
Buffum, Imbrie, 1915-
  xBuffum, Imbrie.
    Agrippa d'Aubigne's "Les Tragiques": A Study
      of the Baroque Style in Poetry. AMS Pr.
Bufithis, Philip H.
  xBufithis, Philip H.
    Norman Mailer. Ungar.
Bufkin, E. C.
  xBufkin, E. C.
    P. H. Newby. Twayne.
Bugbee, Audrey S. *see* Bugbee, Audrey Steiner.
Bugbee, Audrey Steiner.
  xBugbee, Audrey S.

How to Dry Flowers the Easy Way. G K Hall.
Bugbee, James M. *see* Bugbee, James McKellar.
Bugbee, James McKellar, 1837-1913
  xBugbee, James M.
    The City Government of Boston. AMS Pr.
    The City Government of Boston. Johnson
      Repr.
Bugelski, B. R. *see* Bugelski, Bergen Richard.
Bugelski, Bergen Richard.
  xBugelski, B. R.
    Principles of Learning & Memory. Praeger.
    The Psychology of Learning Applied to
      Teaching. Bobbs.
    Some Practical Laws of Learning. Phi Delta
      Kappa.
Bugen, Larry A.
  xBugen, Larry A.
    Death & Dying: Theory, Research & Practice.
      Wm C Brown.
Bugental, James F. *see* Bugental, James F. T.
Bugental, James F. T.
  xBugental, James F.
    Psychotherapy & Process: The Fundamentals of
      an Existential-Humanistic Approach. A-W.
Buggey, J. *see* Buggey, Joanne.
Buggey, Joanne.
  xBuggey, J.
    The Energy Crisis: What Are Our Choices?.
      P-H.
Buglass, Leslie J.
  xBuglass, Leslie J.
    Marine Insurance Claims: American Law &
      Practice. Cornell Maritime.
Bugliarello, G. *see* Bugliarello, George.
Bugliarello, George.
  xBugliarello, G.
    ed. Computer Systems & Water Resources.
      Elsevier.
  xBugliarello, George.
    The Impact of Noise Pollution: A
      Socio-Technological Introduction. Pergamon.
Buhite, Russell D.
  xBuhite, Russell D.
    Nelson T. Johnson & American Policy Toward
      China 1925-1941. Mich St U Pr.
    Patrick J. Hurley & American Foreign Policy.
      Cornell U Pr.
Buhl, Harold R.
  xBuhl, Harold R.
    Creative Engineering Design. Iowa St U Pr.
Buhler, Charlotte. *see* Buhler, Charlotte Malachowski.
Buhler, Charlotte M. *see* Buhler, Charlotte Malachowski.
Buhler, Charlotte Malachowski, 1893-
  xBuhler, Charlotte.
    Childhood Problems & the Teacher.
      Greenwood.
    The First Year of Life. Arno.
    The First Year of Life. Greenwood.
    Introduction to Humanistic Psychology.
      Brooks-Cole.
  xBuhler, Charlotte M.
    The Child & His Family. Greenwood.
Buhler, Curt F. *see* Buhler, Curt Ferdinand.
Buhler, Curt Ferdinand.
  xBuhler, Curt F.
    Standards of Bibliographical Description.
      Greenwood.
Buhler, J. P. *see* Buhler, Joe P.
Buhler, Joe P., 1950-
  xBuhler, J. P.
    Icosahedral Galois Representations.
      Springer-Verlag.
Buhlmann, Walbert.
  xBuhlmann, Walbet.
    Courage, Church!: Essays in Ecclesial
      Spirituality. Orbis Bks.
Buhlmann, Walbet. *see* Buhlmann, Walbert.
Building Research Establishment.
  xBuilding Research Establishment.

Building Construction. Longman.
Building Defects & Maintenance. Longman.
Building Materials. Longman.
ed. Concrete. Longman.
ed. Fibre Reinforced Materials. Longman.
Services & Environmental Engineering.
Longman.
The Strength Properties of Timber. Herman
Pub.
Buitenhuis, Peter.
xBuitenhuis, Peter.
Grasping Imagination: The American Writings
of Henry James. U of Toronto Pr.
Buiter, C. T. *see* Buiter, Cornelis Tekke.
Buiter, Cornelis Tekke.
xBuiter, C. T.
Endoscopy of the Upper Airways. Elsevier.
Buiter, Willem H., 1949-
xBuiter, Willem H.
Temporary Equilibrium & Long-Run
Equilibrium. Garland Pub.
Bukalski, Peter. *see* Bukalski, Peter J.
Bukalski, Peter J.
xBukalski, Peter.
Compiled by Film Research: A Critical
Bibliography with Annotations & Essay. G K
Hall.
Buker, George E., 1923-
xBuker, George E.
Swamp Sailors: Riverine Warfare in the
Everglades. U Presses Fla.
Bukhari, Emir.
xBukhari, Emir Salah.
Napoleon's Cavalry. Presidio Pr.
Bukhari, Emir Salah. *see* Bukhari, Emir.
Bukharin, Nicolai. *see* Bukharin, Nikolai Ivanovich.
Bukharin, Nikolai. *see* Bukharin, Nikolai Ivanovich.
Bukharin, Nikolai I. *see* Bukharin, Nikolai Ivanovich.
Bukharin, Nikolai Ivanovich.
xBukharin, Nicolai.
Imperialism & World Economy. Fertig.
xBukharin, Nikolai.
ABC of Communism. U of Mich Pr.
Imperialism & World Economy. Monthly Rev.
xBukharin, Nikolai I.
Economic Theory of the Leisure Class. AMS
Pr.
Economic Theory of the Leisure Class.
Greenwood.
Economic Theory of the Leisure Class. Kelley.
Economic Theory of the Leisure Class.
Monthly Rev.
Marxism & Modern Thought. Hyperion Conn.
The Politics & Economics of the Transition
Period. Routledge & Kegan.
Bukowski, Charles.
xBukowski, Charles.
Burning in Water, Drowning in Flame. Black
Sparrow.
Factotum. Black Sparrow.
Love Is a Dog from Hell: Poems 1974-1977.
Black Sparrow.
Notes of a Dirty Old Man. City Lights.
Play the Piano Drunk Like a Percussion
Instrument Until the Fingers Begin to Bleed a
Bit. Black Sparrow.
Shakespeare Never Did This. City Lights.
Women. Black Sparrow.
Buksbazen, Lydia. *see* Buksbazen, Lydia (Sitenhof).
Buksbazen, Lydia (Sitenhof), 1908-
xBuksbazen, Lydia.
They Looked for a City. Chr Lit.
Bukstein, Edward J.
xBukstein, Edward J.
Introduction to Biomedical Electronics. Sams.
Practice Problems in Number Systems, Logic,
& Boolean Algebra. Sams.
Bulatkin, Eleanor W. *see* Bulatkin, Eleanor Webster.
Bulatkin, Eleanor Webster.
xBulatkin, Eleanor W.

Structural Arithmetic Metaphor in the Oxford
"Roland.". Ohio St U Pr.
Bulbulian, Arthur H., 1900-
xBulbulian, Arthur H.
Facial Prosthetics. C C Thomas.
Buley, R. Carlyle. *see* Buley, Roscoe Carlyle.
Buley, Roscoe Carlyle.
xBuley, R. Carlyle.
American Life Convention 1906-1952: A Study
in the History of Life Insurance. Irvington.
Bulfinch, Thomas, 1796-1867
xBulfinch, Thomas.
The Age of Chivalry. Gordon Pr.
Age of Chivalry. Airmont.
Age of Fable. Dutton.
Age of Fable. Airmont.
Bulfinch's Mythology. Dell.
Bulfinch's Mythology. T Y Crowell.
Bulgakov, M. *see* Bulgakov, Mikhail Afanasevich.
Bulgakov, Mikhail. *see* Bulgakov, Mikhail Afanasevich.
Bulgakov, Mikhail Afanasevich, 1891-1940
xBulgakov, M.
Master & Margarita. NAL.
xBulgakov, Mikhail.
Flight: A Play in Eight Dreams & Four Acts.
Grove.
Master & Margarita. Grove.
The White Guard. McGraw.
Bulgakov, Valentin. *see* Bulgakov, Valentin Fedorovich.
Bulgakov, Valentin Fedorovich, 1886-
xBulgakov, Valentin.
Last Year of Leo Tolstoy. Dial.
Bulgarian Academy of Sciences. *see* Bulgarska Akademiia
Na Naukite, Sofia.
Bulgarska Akademiia Na Naukite, Sofia.
xBulgarian Academy of Sciences.
ed. Nikola D. Obrechkoff: Opera. Birkhauser.
Bulger, Ruth E. *see* Bulger, Ruth Ellen.
Bulger, Ruth Ellen.
xBulger, Ruth E.
The Functioning Cytoplasm. Plenum Pub.
Bulka, Reuven P.
xBulka, Reuven P.
ed. Mystics & Medics: A Comparison of
Mystical & Psychotherapeutic Encounters.
Human Sci Pr.
Bull, Alan T.
xBull, Alan T.
ed. Companion to Microbiology: Selected
Topics for Further Study. Longman.
Bull, Clarence S. *see* Bull, Clarence Sinclair.
Bull, Clarence Sinclair.
xBull, Clarence S.
The Faces of Hollywood. A S Barnes.
Bull, Deborah.
xBull, Deborah.
Up the Nile: A Photographic Excursion, Egypt
1839-1898. Potter.
Bull, Hedley.
xBull, Hedley.
The Anarchical Society: A Study of Order in
World Politics. Columbia U Pr.
Bull, Henry B. *see* Bull, Henry Bolivar.
Bull, Henry Bolivar, 1905-
xBull, Henry B.
Introduction to Physical Biochemistry. Davis
Co.
Bull, Nina.
xBull, Nina.
The Attitude Theory of Emotion. Johnson
Repr.
Bull, Storm.
xBull, Storm.
Index to Biographies of Contemporary
Composers. Scarecrow.
Bull, William E. *see* Bull, William Emerson.
Bull, William Emerson, 1909-
xBull, William E.

Spanish for Communication. HM.
Spanish for Teachers: Applied Linguistics.
Wiley.
Bulla, Clyde R. *see* Bulla, Clyde Robert.
Bulla, Clyde Robert.
xBulla, Clyde R.
Conquista!. T Y Crowell.
Daniel's Duck. Har-Row.
Dexter. T Y Crowell.
Down the Mississippi. T Y Crowell.
Down the Mississippi. Schol Bk Serv.
Ghost of Windy Hill. T Y Crowell.
Ghost of Windy Hill. Schol Bk Serv.
Indian Hill. T Y Crowell.
Johnny Hong of Chinatown. T Y Crowell.
Jonah & the Great Fish. T Y Crowell.
Keep Running, Allen!. T Y Crowell.
Lincoln's Birthday. T Y Crowell.
Marco Moonlight. Dell.
Marco Moonlight. T Y Crowell.
More Stories of Favorite Operas. T Y Crowell.
Open the Door & See All the People. T Y
Crowell.
The Poppy Seeds. T Y Crowell.
Sugar Pear Tree. T Y Crowell.
Surprise for a Cowboy. T Y Crowell.
Valentine Cat. T Y Crowell.
White Bird. T Y Crowell.
White Sails to China. T Y Crowell.
Bullard, Arthur, 1879-1929
xBullard, Arthur.
Comrade Yetta. Irvington.
Bullard, Brian.
xBullard, Brian.
I Can Dance. Putnam.
Bullard, E. J. *see* Bullard, Edgar John.
Bullard, E. John. *see* Bullard, Edgar John.
Bullard, Edgar John, 1942-
xBullard, E. J.
Degas. McGraw.
xBullard, E. John.
Mary Cassatt Oils & Pastels. Watson-Guptill.
Bullard, Ernie.
xBullard, Ernie.
Triple Jump Encyclopedia. Athletic.
Bullard, Frederic Lauriston, 1866-1952
xBullard, Frederick L.
Famous War Correspondents. Beekman Pubs.
Bullard, Frederick L. *see* Bullard, Frederic Lauriston.
Bullard, John R.
xBullard, John R.
Audiovisual Fundamentals: Basic Equipment
Operation & Simple Materials Production.
Wm C Brown.
Bullard, Oral, 1922-
xBullard, Oral.
Crisis on the Columbia. Touchstone Pr Ore.
Bullard, Scott R.
xBullard, Scott R.
Who's Who in Sherlock Holmes. Taplinger.
Bullard, William R. *see* Bullard, William Rotch.
Bullard, William Rotch, 1926-
xBullard, William R.
ed. Monographs & Papers in Maya
Archaeology. Peabody Harvard.
Bullen, Arthur H. *see* Bullen, Arthur Henry.
Bullen, Arthur Henry.
xBullen, Arthur H.
ed. Collection of Old English Plays. Arno.
Elizabethans. Core Collection.
Bullen, Frank T. *see* Bullen, Frank Thomas.
Bullen, Frank Thomas, 1857-1915
xBullen, Frank T.

The Cruise of the Cachalot. Leetes Isl.
The Cruise of the Cachalot. Ridgeway Bks.
Deep-Sea Plunderings. Arno.
Idylls of the Sea. Arno.
The Men of the Merchant Service. E M
Coleman Ent.

Bullen, Roger.
xBullen, Roger.
Palmerston, Guizot & the Collapse of the
Entente Cordiale. Humanities.

Buller, Walter L. see Buller, Walter Lawry.

Buller, Walter Lawry.
xBuller, Walter L.
Buller's Birds of New Zealand: A History of
the Birds of New Zealand. U Pr of Hawaii.

Bullett, Gerald. see Bullett, Gerald William.

Bullett, Gerald W. see Bullett, Gerald William.

Bullett, Gerald William, 1894-
xBullett, Gerald.
ed. Silver Poets of the Sixteenth Century.
Dutton.
ed. Silver Poets of the Sixteenth Century.
Folcroft.
The Story of English Literature. Folcroft.
xBullett, Gerald W.
Street of the Eye, & Nine Other Tales. Arno.

Bulliet, Richard. see Bulliet, Richard W.

Bulliet, Richard W.
xBulliet, Richard.
The Tomb of the Twelfth Imam. Har-Row.
xBulliet, Richard W.
The Camel & the Wheel. Harvard U Pr.
The Patricians of Nishapur: A Study in
Medieval Islamic Social History. Harvard U
Pr.

Bullis, Jerald, 1944-
xBullis, Jerald.
Taking up the Serpent. SBD.

Bullitt, Orville H.
xBullitt, Orville H.
Phoenicia & Carthage: A Thousand Years to
Oblivion. Dorrance.

Bullmer, Kenneth.
xBullmer, Kenneth.
The Art of Empathy: A Manual for Improving
Accuracy of Interpersonal Perception. Human
Sci Pr.

Bulloch, William, 1868-1941
xBulloch, William.
The History of Bacteriology. Dover.

Bullock, Alan. see Bullock, Alan Louis Charles.

Bullock, Alan Louis Charles, Sir.
xBullock, Alan.
Hitler, a Study in Tyranny. Har-Row.
Hitler, a Study in Tyranny. Har-Row.
Hitler, a Study in Tyranny. Har-Row.

Bullock, Charles J. see Bullock, Charles Jesse.

Bullock, Charles Jesse, 1869-1941
xBullock, Charles J.
Economic Essays. Arno.

Bullock, Charles S.
xBullock, Charles S.
Racial Equality in America: In Search of an
Unfulfilled Goal. Goodyear.

Bullock, Donald H.
xBullock, Donald H.
Programmed Instruction. Educ Tech Pubns.

Bullock, Frederick W. see Bullock, Frederick William
Bagshawe.

Bullock, Frederick William Bagshawe.
xBullock, Frederick W.
A History of Training for the Ministry of the
Church of England in England & Wales from
598 to 1799. Allenson.

Bullock, Henry A. see Bullock, Henry Allen.

Bullock, Henry Allen.
xBullock, Henry A.

History of Negro Education in the South:
From 1619 to the Present. Harvard U Pr.

Bullock, Hugh.
xBullock, Hugh.
Story of Investment Companies. Columbia U
Pr.

Bullock, James. see Bullock, James R.

Bullock, James R., 1910-
xBullock, James.
Whatever Became of Salvation?. John Knox.

Bullock, Lyndal M.
xBullock, Lyndal M.
ed. Educational Aspects of Behavioral
Problems in Children & Youth. Mss Info.

Bullock, Ralph W.
xBullock, Ralph W.
In Spite of Handicaps: Brief Biographical
Sketches with Discussion Outlines of
Outstanding Negroes Now Living Who Are
Achieving Distinction in Various Lines of
Endeavor. Arno.

Bullock, Theodore H. see Bullock, Theodore Holmes.

Bullock, Theodore Holmes.
xBullock, Theodore H.
Introduction to Nervous Systems. W H
Freeman.
Structure & Function in the Nervous Systems
of Invertebrates. W H Freeman.

Bullock-Davies, Constance.
xBullock-Davies, Constance.
English Pronunciation from the Fifteenth to the
Eighteenth Century: A Handbook to the
Study of Historical Grammar. Greenwood.

Bullough. see Bullough, Bonnie.

Bullough, Bonnie.
xBullough.
The Law & the Expanding Nursing Role. ACC.
Poverty, Ethnic Identity & Health Care. ACC
xBullough, Bonnie.
ed. Expanding Horizons for Nurses. Springer
Pub.
ed. The Management of Common Human
Miseries: A Text for Primary Health Care
Practitioners. Springer Pub.
xBullough, Vern.
The Care of the Sick: The Emergence of
Modern Nursing. N Watson.

Bullough, Robert V.
xBullough, Robert V.
Creating Instructional Materials. Merrill.

Bullough, Vern. see Bullough, Vern L.

Bullough, Vern L.
xBullough, Vern.
ed. The Frontiers of Sex Research. Prometheus
Bks.
Sin, Sickness, & Sanity: A History of Sexual
Attitudes. Garland Pub.
Sin, Sickness & Sanity: A History of Sexual
Attitudes. NAL.
xBullough, Vern L.
An Annotated Bibliography of Homosexuality.
Garland Pub.
Prostitution: An Illustrated Social History.
Crown.
Sexual Variance in Society & History. U of
Chicago Pr.
The Subordinate Sex: A History of Attitudes
Toward Women. U of Ill Pr.

Bullough, William A., 1933-
xBullough, William A.
Cities & Schools in the Gilded Age: The
Evolution of an Urban Institution. Kennikat.

Bullough, William S. see Bullough, William Sydney.

Bullough, William Sydney, 1914-
xBullough, William S.
Evolution of Differentiation. Acad Pr.

Bulman, Joan.
xBulman, Joan.

Strindberg & Shakespeare: Shakespeare's
Influence on Strindberg's Historical Drama.
Haskell.

Bulmer, Glenn S.
xBulmer, Glenn S.
Introduction to Medical Mycology. Year Bk
Med.

Bulmer, M G.
xBulmer, M. G.
Principles of Statistics. Dover.

Bulmer, Martin.
xBulmer, Martin.
ed. Censuses, Surveys & Privacy. Holmes &
Meier.
Social Research & Royal Commissions. Allen
Unwin.

Bulow, Bernhard H. see Bulow, Bernhard Heinrich
Martin Karl.

**Bulow, Bernhard Heinrich Martin Karl, Furst Von,
1849-1929**
xBulow, Bernhard H.
Imperial Germany. Greenwood.

Bumagin, Victoria E.
xBumagin, Victoria E.
Aging Is a Family Affair. T Y Crowell.

Bumpass, Larry L.
xBumpass, Larry L.
Later Years of Childbearing. Princeton U Pr.

Bumpus, Jerry.
xBumpus, Jerry.
Things in Place. Fiction Coll.

Bumsted, J. M.
xBumsted, J. M.
ed. Documentary Problems in Canadian
History. Dorsey.

Bunce, Arthur C. see Bunce, Arthur Cyril.

Bunce, Arthur Cyril, 1901-1953
xBunce, Arthur C.
Economic Nationalism & the Farmer.
Greenwood.

Bunce, Donald F. see Bunce, Donald F. M.

Bunce, Donald F. M.
xBunce, Donald F.
Atlas of Arterial Histology. Green.

Bunce, James E.
xBunce, James E.
ed. Long Island As America: A Documentary
History. Kennikat.

Buncel, E.
xBuncel, E.
Tritium in Organic Chemistry. Elsevier.

Bunch, Clarence.
xBunch, Clarence.
ed. Art Education: A Guide to Information
Sources. Gale.

Bunch, Wilton H.
xBunch, Wilton H.
Modern Management of Myelomeningocele.
Green.
Principles of Orthotic Treatment. Mosby.

Bunche, Ralph J. see Bunche, Ralph Johnson.

Bunche, Ralph Johnson, 1904-1971
xBunche, Ralph J.
The Political Status of the Negro in the Age of
FDR. U of Chicago Pr.

Bundy, A. see Bundy, A. R.

Bundy, A. R.
xBundy, A.
ed. Artificial Intelligence: An Introductory
Course. Elsevier.

Bundy, Colin.
xBundy, Colin.
The Rise & Fall of South African Peasantry. U
of Cal Pr.

Bundy, Mcgeorge.
xBundy, McGeorge.
Strength of Government. Harvard U Pr.

Bundy, Murray W. see Bundy, Murray Wright.

Bundy, Murray Wright.
xBundy, Murray W.

Theory of Imagination in Classical &
Mediaeval Thought. Folcroft.
Bundy, Robert.
xBundy, Robert.
ed. Images of the Future: The Twenty-First
Century & Beyond. Prometheus Bks.
Bundy, William P., 1917-
xBundy, William P.
ed. Two Hundred Years of American Foreign
Policy. NYU Pr.
Bunge, M. *see* Bunge, Mario Augusto.
Bunge, M. A. *see* Bunge, Mario Augusto.
Bunge, Mario. *see* Bunge, Mario Augusto.
Bunge, Mario Augusto.
xBunge, M.
Foundations of Physics. Springer-Verlag.
xBunge, M. A.
ed. Rutherford & Physics at the Turn of the
Century. N Watson.
xBunge, Mario.
Causality & Modern Science. Dover.
The Mind-Body Problem: A Psychobiological
Approach. Pergamon.
Bunger, Robert L. *see* Bunger, Robert Louis.
Bunger, Robert Louis.
xBunger, Robert L.
Islamization Among the Upper Pokomo.
Maxwell Schl Citizen.
Buni, Andrew.
xBuni, Andrew.
Negro in Virginia Politics, 1902-1965. U Pr of
Va.
Bunim, Miriam (Schild), 1912-
xBunim, Miriam S.
Space in Medieval Painting & the Forerunners
of Perspective. AMS Pr.
Bunim, Miriam S. *see* Bunim, Miriam (Schild).
Bunin, Ivan. *see* Bunin, Ivan Alekseevich.
Bunin, Ivan A. *see* Bunin, Ivan Alekseevich.
Bunin, Ivan Alekseevich, 1870-1953
xBunin, Ivan.
Fifteen Tales. Core Collection.
xBunin, Ivan A.
Dark Avenues & Other Stories. Hyperion
Conn.
Grammar of Love. Hyperion Conn.
Memories & Portraits. Greenwood.
Bunin, Patricia A. *see* Bunin, Patricia Ann.
Bunin, Patricia Ann.
xBunin, Patricia A.
Do You Think We Could Have Made It &
Other Love Poems for the Separated &
Divorced. Newaves Pub.
Bunker, Barbara. *see* Bunker, Barbara Benedict.
Bunker, Barbara Benedict.
xBunker, Barbara.
Student's Guide to Conducting Social Science
Research. Human Sci Pr.
Bunkley, Allison W. *see* Bunkley, Allison Williams.
Bunkley, Allison Williams.
xBunkley, Allison W.
Life of Sarmiento. Greenwood.
Bunn, Alfred, 1796?-1860
xBunn, Alfred.
Old England & New England, in a Series of
Views Taken on the Spot. Arno.
Bunn, H. Franklin. *see* Bunn, Howard Franklin.
Bunn, Howard Franklin.
xBunn, H. Franklin.
Human Hemoglobins. Saunders.
Bunn, John W. *see* Bunn, John William.
Bunn, John William, 1898-
xBunn, John W.
Art of Officiating Sports. P-H.
Bunn, Matthew, b. 1772?
xBunn, Matthew.
Journal of the Adventures of Matthew Bunn.
Newberry.
Bunn, Ronald F.
xBunn, Ronald F.

German Politics & the Spiegel Affair: A Case
Study of the Bonn System. La State U Pr.
Bunn, Verne A.
xBunn, Verne A.
Buying & Selling a Small Business. Arno.
Bunnag, Jane.
xBunnag, Jane.
Buddhist Monk, Buddhist Layman: A Study of
Urban Monastic Organisation in Central
Thailand. Cambridge U Pr.
Bunnell, David.
xBunnell, David.
Personal Computing: A Beginner's Guide.
Dutton.
Bunnelle, Hasse.
xBunnelle, Hasse.
Cooking for Camp & Trail. Sierra.
Bunner, Henry C. *see* Bunner, Henry Cuyler.
Bunner, Henry Cuyler, 1855-1896
xBunner, Henry C.
More "Short Sixes". Mss Info.
Bunnett, Kay.
xBunnett, Kay.
Ikebana Collection: Studies in Sogetsu Ikebana.
Van Nos Reinhold.
Bunselmeyer, Robert E., 1939-
xBunselmeyer, Robert E.
The Cost of the War 1914-1919: British
Economic War Aims and the Origins of
Reparation. Shoe String.
Bunt, Lucas N. H. *see* Bunt, Lucas Nicolaas Hendrik.
Bunt, Lucas Nicolaas Hendrik.
xBunt, Lucas N. H.
Historical Roots of Elementary Mathematics.
P-H.
Buntain, D N.
xBuntain, D. N.
The Holy Ghost & Fire. Gospel Pub.
Bunting, Bainbridge.
xBunting, Bainbridge.
Early Architecture in New Mexico. U of NM
Pr.
Houses of Boston's Back Bay: An Architectural
History 1840-1917. Harvard U Pr.
Bunting, Basil.
xBunting, Basil.
Collected Poems. Oxford U Pr.
Bunyan, John, 1628-1688
xBunyan, John.
Holy Life: The Beauty of Christianity. Reiner.
Work of Jesus Christ As an Advocate. Reiner.
Bunyan, John A.
xBunyan, John A.
Practical Video: The Manager's Guide to
Applications. Knowledge Indus.
Bunyan, Tony.
xBunyan, Tony.
The Political Police in Britain. St Martin.
Bunyard, Edward A. *see* Bunyard, Edward Ashdown.
Bunyard, Edward Ashdown.
xBunyard, Edward A.
Old Garden Roses. E M Coleman Ent.
Bunye, Maria V. *see* Bunye, Maria Victoria R.
Bunye, Maria Victoria R.
xBunye, Maria V.
Cebuano for Beginners. U Pr of Hawaii.
Bunzel, John A. *see* Bunzel, John H.
Bunzel, John H., 1924-
xBunzel, John A.
The American Small Businessman. Arno.
xBunzel, John H.
Anti-Politics in America: Reflections on the
Anti-Political Temper & Its Distortions of the
Democratic Process. Greenwood.
Bunzel, Ruth L. *see* Bunzel, Ruth Leah.
Bunzel, Ruth Leah, 1898-
xBunzel, Ruth L.

Pueblo Potter: A Study of Creative Imagination
in Primitive Art. AMS Pr.
The Pueblo Potter: A Study of Creative
Imagination in Primitive Art. Dover.
The Pueblo Potter: A Study of Creative
Imagination in Primitive Art. Peter Smith.
Buol, S. W.
xBuol, S. W.
Soil Genesis & Classification. Iowa St U Pr.
Buoncristiano, S.
xBuoncristiano, S.
A Geometric Approach to Homology Theory.
Cambridge U Pr.
Bupp, Irvin C.
xBupp, Irvin C.
Light Water: How the Nuclear Dream
Dissolved. Basic.
Burack, A. S. *see* Burack, Abraham Saul.
Burack, Abraham Saul, 1908-
xBurack, A. S.
ed. How to Write & Sell Fillers, Light Verse &
Short Humor. Writer.
Popular Plays for Classroom Reading. Plays.
Burack, Elmer H.
xBurack, Elmer H.
The Manager's Guide to Change. CBI Pub.
The Manager's Guide to Change. Lifetime
Learn.
Personnel Management: A Human Resource
Systems Approach. West Pub.
Personnel Management: Cases & Exercises.
West Pub.
Burago, Iurii Dmitrievich.
xBurago, Yu D.
ed. Potential Theory & Function Theory for
Irregular Regions. Plenum Pub.
Burago, Yu D. *see* Burago, Iurii Dmitrievich.
Burak, John.
xBurak, John.
There Goes My Aching Back. Exposition.
Buranelli, Vincent.
xBuranelli, Vincent.
Edgar Allan Poe. Coll & U Pr.
Edgar Allan Poe. Twayne.
Gold: An Illustrated History. Hammond Inc.
Josiah Royce. Coll & U Pr.
Burati, Robert.
xBurati, Robert.
Hong Kong. Kodansha.
Burawoy, Michael.
xBurawoy, Michael.
Manufacturing Consent: Changes in the Labor
Process Under Monopoly Capitalism. U of
Chicago Pr.
Burbank, Garin.
xBurbank, Garin.
When Farmers Voted Red: The Gospel of
Socialism in the Oklahoma Countryside,
1910-1924. Greenwood.
Burbank, Rex. *see* Burbank, Rex J.
Burbank, Rex J.
xBurbank, Rex.
Literature of the American Renaissance.
Merrill.
Thornton Wilder. Coll & U Pr.
xBurbank, Rex J.
Thornton Wilder. Twayne.
Burberry, Peter.
xBurberry, Peter.
Building for Energy Conservation. Halsted Pr.
Burbidge, Cile. *see* Burbidge, Cile Bellefleur.
Burbidge, Cile Bellefleur.
xBurbidge, Cile.
Cake Decorating for Any Occasion. Chilton.
Burbidge, Geoffrey. *see* Burbidge, Geoffrey R.
Burbidge, Geoffrey R.
xBurbidge, Geoffrey.
Quasi-Stellar Objects. W H Freeman.
Burbidge, Nancy T.
xBurbidge, Nancy T.

Plant Taxonomic Literature in Australian
Libraries. Intl Schol Bk Serv.
Burbidge, P. G. *see* Burbidge, Peter George.
Burbidge, Peter George.
xBurbidge, P. G.
Prelims & End-Pages. Cambridge U Pr.
Burby, Raymond J., 1916-
xBurby, Raymond J.
Communicating with People: The Supervisor's
Introduction to Verbal Communication &
Decision-Making. A-W.
ed. Energy & Housing: Consumer & Builder
Perspectives. Oelgeschlager.
Burcaw, G. Ellis.
xBurcaw, G. Ellis.
Introduction to Museum Work. AASLH.
Burch, Betty B. *see* Burch, Betty Brand.
Burch, Betty Brand.
xBurch, Betty B.
ed. Dictatorship & Totalitarianism: Selected
Readings. Van Nos Reinhold.
Burch, George B. *see* Burch, George Bosworth.
Burch, George Bosworth, 1902-
xBurch, George B.
Alternative Goals in Religion: Love, Freedom,
Truth. McGill-Queens U Pr.
Early Medieval Philosophy. Arno.
Burch, George E. *see* Burch, George Edward.
Burch, George Edward, 1910-
xBurch, George E.
A Primer of Cardiology. Lea & Febiger.
A Primer of Venous Pressure. C C Thomas.
Burch, John G.
xBurch, John G.
Computer Control & Audit: A Total Systems
Approach. Wiley.
Burch, Mary Lou, 1914-
xBurch, Mary Lou.
Making Leaf Rubbings. Greene.
Burch, Monte.
xBurch, Monte.
Building & Equipping the Garden & Small
Farm Workshop. Garden Way Pub.
Gun Care & Repair. Winchester Pr.
Shotgunner's Guide. Winchester Pr.
Burch, Noel.
xBurch, Noel.
To the Distant Observer: Form & Meaning in
Japanese Cinema. U of Cal Pr.
Burch, Pat.
xBurch, Pat.
Early Losses. Daughters.
Burch, Robert.
xBurch, Robert.
D. J.'s Worst Enemy. Viking Pr.
Doodle & the Go-Cart. Viking Pr.
Hunting Trip. Scribner.
Hut School & the War Time Home-Front
Heroes. Dell.
Hut School & the Wartime Home-Front
Heroes. Viking Pr.
Ida Early Comes Over the Mountain. Viking
Pr.
The Jolly Witch. Dutton.
Two That Were Tough. Viking Pr.
The Whitman Kick. Dutton.
Burch, Virginia M.
xBurch, Virginia M.
How to Raise & Train a Saluki. TFH Pubns.
Burch, William R., 1933-
xBurch, William R.
ed. Readings in Ecology, Energy & Human
Society: Contemporary Perspectives.
Har-Row.
Burchard, Florence.
xBurchard, Florence.
Someone Had to Hold the Lantern. Southern
Pub.
Burchard, John. *see* Burchard, John Ely.

Burchard, John Ely.
xBurchard, John.
The Architecture of America: A Social &
Cultural History. Little.
Burchard, Marshall.
xBurchard, Marshall.
Auto Racing Highlights. Garrard.
Burchard, Peter.
xBurchard, Peter.
illus. Chinwe. Putnam.
Burchardt, Bill.
xBurchardt, Bill.
Buck. Doubleday.
Medicine Man. Doubleday.
Burchell, Robert W.
xBurchell, Robert W.
Future Land Use: Energy, Environmental, and
Legal Constraints. Ctr Urban Pol Res.
Burchell, S. C.
xBurchell, Samuel C.
Age of Progress. Time-Life.
Burchell, Samuel C. *see* Burchell, S. C.
Burchett, Harold E. *see* Burchett, Harold Ewing.
Burchett, Harold Ewing.
xBurchett, Harold E.
People Helping People. Moody.
Burchette, Dorothy.
xBurchette, Dorothy.
More Needlework Blocking & Finishing.
Scribner.
Burchfield, Joe D.
xBurchfield, Joe D.
Lord Kelvin & the Age of the Earth. N
Watson.
Burckhardt, Rudy.
xBurckhardt, Rudy.
Mobile Homes. Z Pr.
Burckhardt, Sigurd, 1916-1966
xBurckhardt, Sigurd.
The Drama of Language: Essays on Goethe &
Kleist. Johns Hopkins.
Burckhardt, T. *see* Burckhardt, Titus.
Burckhardt, Titus.
xBurckhardt, T.
An Introduction to Sufi Doctrine. Orientalia.
Burden, Charles.
xBurden, Charles.
ed. Business in Literature. Longman.
Burden, E. E. *see* Burden, Ernest E.
Burden, Ernest. *see* Burden, Ernest E.
Burden, Ernest E., 1934-
xBurden, E. E.
Architectural Delineation: A Photographic
Approach to Presentation. McGraw.
xBurden, Ernest.
ed. Living Barns: How to Find & Restore a
Barn of Your Own. NYGS.
Burden, George.
xBurden, George.
Understanding Epilepsy. Beekman Pubs.
Burden, J. *see* Burden, James Walter.
Burden, J. W. *see* Burden, James Walter.
Burden, James Walter, 1940-
xBurden, J.
Graphic Reproduction Photography. Hastings.
xBurden, J. W.
Graphic Reproduction Photography. Focal Pr.
Burden, Jean.
xBurden, Jean.
Journey Toward Poetry. October.
Burden, William A. M. *see* Burden, William Armistead
Moale.
Burden, William Armistead Moale, 1906-
xBurden, William A. M.
The Struggle for Airways in Latin America.
Arno.
Burder, John.
xBurder, John.

Work of the Industrial Film Maker. Focal Pr.
Work of the Industrial Film Maker. Hastings.
Burdett, Charles, b. 1815
xBurdett, Charles.
Chances & Changes. Arno.
Burdett, Osbert, 1885-1936
xBurdett, Osbert.
The Brownings. Scholarly.
Critical Essays. Arno.
The Two Carlyles. Arden Lib.
The Two Carlyles. Arno.
The Two Carlyles. Darby Bks.
The Two Carlyles. Folcroft.
Two Carlyles. Haskell.
Burdette, Walter J.
xBurdette, Walter J.
Planning & Analysis of Clinical Studies. C C
Thomas.
Burdic, William S.
xBurdic, William S.
Radar Signal Analysis. P-H.
Burdick, Charles. *see* Burdick, Charles Burton.
Burdick, Charles Burton, 1927-
xBurdick, Charles.
The Frustrated Raider: The Story of the
German Cruiser Cormoran in World War I. S
Ill U Pr.
Burdick, Eugene.
xBurdick, Eugene.
ed. American Voting Behavior. Greenwood.
Fail Safe. Dell.
Fail-Safe. McGraw.
Burdick, Jacques.
xBurdick, Jacques.
Theater. Newsweek.
Bureau of Applied Social Research, Columbia University.
see Columbia University. Bureau of Applied Social
Research.
Bureau of Business Research. *see* University of
Nebraska-Lincoln. Bureau of Business Research.
Bureau of Municipal Research, Philadelphia.
xPhiladelphia Bureau of Municipal Research.
Law Administration & Negro-White Relations
in Philadelphia. Greenwood.
Bureau of National Affairs, Washington, D.C.
xBNA Editorial Staff.
Civil Rights Act of Nineteen Sixty-Four. BNA.
ed. Consumer Product Safety Act. BNA.
ed. Equal Employment Opportunity Act of
1972. BNA.
Federal-State Regulation of Welfare Funds.
BNA.
Grievance Guide. BNA.
Highlights of the New Pension Reform Law.
BNA.
xBNA Editorial Staff of Construction Labor
Report.
Construction Craft Jurisdiction Agreements
1979. BNA.
xBNA Editorial Staff of Labor Relations Reporter.
Labor Relations Yearbook--1979. BNA.
Labor Relations Yearbook 1976. BNA.
Labor Relations Yearbook 1977. BNA.
Labor Relations Yearbook 1978. BNA.
xBna Editorial Staff of the Criminal Law Reporter.
ed. The Criminal Law Revolution & Its
Aftermath: 1960-1977. BNA.
xConstruction Labor Reporter Editorial Staff.
ed. Construction Labor Report's 1974-1975
Wage Rate Guide. BNA.
Bureau of Naval Personnel. *see* United States. Bureau of
Naval Personnel.
Bureau of Railway Economics. *see* Bureau of Railway
Economics, Washington, D.C.
Bureau of Railway Economics, Washington, D.C.
xBureau of Railway Economics.
A List of References to Literature: Relating to
the Union Pacific System. Crofton Pub.
Bureau of Social Science Research. *see* Bureau of Social
Science Research, Washington, D.C.

Bureau of Social Science Research, Washington, D.C.
  xBureau of Social Science Research.
    International Communication & Political
    Opinion. Greenwood.
Bureau of Statistics, U.S. Dept. of Labor. *see* United
  States. Department of Labor.
Bureau Of The Census. *see* United States. Bureau of the
  Census.
Bureau of the Census, U.S. Department of Commerce.
  see United States. Bureau of the Census.
Buren, Martin Van. *see* Van Buren, Martin.
Buren, Paul M. Van. *see* Van Buren, Paul M.
Burfoot, J. C. *see* Burfoot, Jack C.
Burfoot, Jack C.
  xBurfoot, J. C.
    Polar Dielectrics & Their Applications. U of
    Cal Pr.
Burford, E. J.
  xBurford, E. J.
    The Orrible Synne: A Look at London Lechery
    from Roman to Cromwellian Times.
    Humanities.
Burford, Lolah.
  xBurford, Lolah.
    Seacage: A Romance for Another Time, in
    Three Voices. Macmillan.
Burford, Roger L.
  xBurford, Roger L.
    A Projections Model for Small Area
    Economies. Ga St U Busn Pub.
Burg, B. R. *see* Burg, Barry Richard.
Burg, Barry Richard, 1938-
  xBurg, B. R.
    Richard Mather of Dorchester. U Pr of Ky.
Burg, David.
  xBurg, David.
    Solzhenitsyn. Stein & Day.
Burg, David F.
  xBurg, David F.
    Chicago's White City of 1893. U Pr of Ky.
Burgdorf, Robert L., 1948-
  xBurgdorf, Robert L.
    ed. The Legal Rights of Handicapped Persons:
    Cases, Materials, & Text. P H Brookes.
Burger, Angela S. *see* Burger, Angela Sutherland.
Burger, Angela Sutherland.
  xBurger, Angela S.
    Opposition in a Dominant-Party System: A
    Study of the Jan Sangh, the Praja Socialist &
    Socialist Parties in Uttar Pradesh, India. U of
    Cal Pr.
Burger, Carl.
  xBurger, Carl.
    All About Fish. Random.
Burger, Chester.
  xBurger, Chester.
    Survival in the Executive Jungle. Macmillan.
    Survival in the Executive Jungle. Macmillan.
Burger, George V. *see* Burger, George Vanderkarr.
Burger, George Vanderkarr, 1927-
  xBurger, George V.
    Practical Wildlife Management. Winchester Pr.
Burger, Gottfried A. *see* Burger, Gottfried August.
Burger, Gottfried August.
  xBurger, Gottfried A.
    Lenore. Folcroft.
Burger, John R.
  xBurger, John R.
    Children of the Wild. Messner.
Burger, K. *see* Burger, Kalman.
Burger, Kalman.
  xBurger, K.
    Organic Reagents in Metal Analysis.
    Pergamon.
Burger, N. H. *see* Burger, Ninki Hart.
Burger, Ninki H. *see* Burger, Ninki Hart.
Burger, Ninki Hart.
  xBurger, N. H.
    Executive's Wife. Macmillan.
  xBurger, Ninki H.

Executive's Wife. Macmillan.
Burger, Robert. *see* Burger, Robert E.
Burger, Robert E.
  xBurger, Robert.
    The Jug Wine Book. Stein & Day.
  xBurger, Robert E.
    The Chess of Bobby Fischer. McGraw.
Burger, Ronna, 1947-
  xBurger, Ronna.
    Plato's "Phaedrus": A Defense of a Philosophic
    Art of Writing. U of Ala Pr.
Burgers, J. M. *see* Burgers, Johannes Martinus.
Burgers, Johannes Martinus, 1895-
  xBurgers, J. M.
    Flow Equations for Composite Gases. Acad Pr.
Burgess, A. *see* Burgess, Audrey.
Burgess, Andrew J.
  xBurgess, Andrew J.
    Passion, Knowing How, & Understanding: An
    Essay on the Concept of Faith. Scholars Pr
    Ca.
Burgess, Ann Wolbert.
  xBurgess, Ann W.
    Psychiatric Nursing in the Hospital & the
    Community. P-H.
    Rape: Victims of Crisis. R J Brady.
Burgess, Anthony, 1917-
  xBurgess, Anthony.
    Abba Abba. Little.
    The Doctor Is Sick. Norton.
    Ernest Hemingway & His World. Scribner.
    Honey for the Bears. Norton.
    A Long Trip to Tea Time. Stonehill Pub.
    Napoleon Symphony. Norton.
    Right to an Answer. Norton.
    The Right to an Answer. Norton.
Burgess, Audrey.
  xBurgess, A.
    Nurse's Guide to Fluid & Electrolyte Balance.
    McGraw.
  xBurgess, Audrey.
    The Nurse's Guide to Fluid & Electrolyte
    Balance. McGraw.
Burgess, Chester F. *see* Burgess, Chester Francis.
Burgess, Chester Francis.
  xBurgess, Chester F.
    The Fellowship of the Craft: Conrad on Ships
    & Seamen & the Sea. Kennikat.
Burgess, E. T.
  xBurgess, E. T.
    Other Women of the Bible. Baptist Pub Hse.
Burgess, Ernest W. *see* Burgess, Ernest Watson.
Burgess, Ernest Watson.
  xBurgess, Ernest W.
    ed. Contributions to Urban Sociology. U of
    Chicago Pr.
    The Family: From Traditional to
    Companionship. D Van Nostrand.
Burgess, Gelett, 1866-1951
  xBurgess, Gelett.
    illus. More Goops & How Not to Be Them: A
    Manual of Manners for Impolite Infants.
    Dover.
Burgess, John.
  xBurgess, John.
    Metal Ions in Solution. Halsted Pr.
Burgess, John H.
  xBurgess, John H.
    Christian Pagan: A Naturalistic Survey of
    Christian History. Mimir.
    System Design Approaches to Public Services.
    Fairleigh Dickinson.
Burgess, John S. *see* Burgess, John Stewart.
Burgess, John Stewart, 1883-1949
  xBurgess, John S.

Guilds of Peking. AMS Pr.
    The Guilds of Peking. Chinese Materials.
Burgess, John W. *see* Burgess, John William.
Burgess, John William, 1844-1931
  xBurgess, John W.
    Civil War & the Constitution 1859-1865.
    Kennikat.
Burgess, Joseph, 1929-
  xBurgess, Joseph A.
    ed. The Role of the Augsburg Confession:
    Catholic & Lutheran Views. Fortress.
Burgess, Joseph A. *see* Burgess, Joseph.
Burgess, M. Elaine. *see* Burgess, Margaret Elaine.
Burgess, Margaret Elaine.
  xBurgess, M. Elaine.
    Negro Leadership in a Southern City. Coll & U
    Pr.
Burgess, Patricia.
  xBurgess, Patricia.
    Erica's School on the Hill: A Child's Journey
    in Moral Growth. Winston Pr.
Burgess, Philip M.
  xBurgess, Philip M.
    International & Comparative Politics: A
    Handbook. Allyn.
Burgess, R. E. *see* Burgess, Ronald Eric.
Burgess, Robert F. *see* Burgess, Robert Forrest.
Burgess, Robert Forrest.
  xBurgess, Robert F.
    The Cave Divers. Dodd.
    Exploring a Coral Reef. Macmillan.
Burgess, Robert H.
  xBurgess, Robert H.
    Chesapeake Circle. Cornell Maritime.
    This Was Chesapeake Bay. Cornell Maritime.
  xBurgess, Robert H. G.
    Steamboats Out of Baltimore. Cornell
    Maritime.
Burgess, Robert H. G. *see* Burgess, Robert H.
Burgess, Ronald Eric, 1917
  xBurgess, R. E.
    ed. Fluctuation Phenomena in Solids. Acad Pr.
Burgess, Thomas, 1880-1955
  xBurgess, Thomas.
    Greeks in America. R & E Res Assoc.
Burgess, Thornton W. *see* Burgess, Thornton Waldo.
Burgess, Thornton Waldo, 1874-
  xBurgess, Thornton W.
    Adventures of Old Man Coyote. G&D.
    Adventures of Sammy Jay. G&D.
Burgess Wise, David.
  xBurgess Wise, David.
    The Motor Car: An Illustrated International
    History. Putnam.
Burgess-Kohn, Jane.
  xBurgess-Kohn, Jane.
    Straight Talk About Love & Sex for Teenagers.
    Beacon Pr.
Burggraaff, Winfield J.
  xBurggraaff, Winfield J.
    The Venezuelan Armed Forces in Politics,
    1935-1959. U of Mo Pr.
Burghardt, Andrew F. *see* Burghardt, Andrew Frank.
Burghardt, Andrew Frank, 1924-
  xBurghardt, Andrew F.
    Borderland: A Historical & Geographical Study
    of Burgenland, Austria. U of Wis Pr.
Burghardt, Erich.
  xBurghardt, Erich.
    Early Histological Diagnosis of Cervical
    Cancer. Saunders.
Burghardt, Walter J.
  xBurghardt, Walter J.
    Tell the Next Generation: Homilies & Near
    Homilies. Paulist Pr.
Burghes, D. N. *see* Burghes, David N.
Burghes, David N.
  xBurghes, D. N.

Mathematical Models in the Social,
Management & Life Sciences. Halsted Pr.
Burgi, Richard.
xBurgi, Richard T.
History of the Russian Hexameter. Shoe String.
Burgi, Richard T. see Burgi, Richard.
Burgin, John C. see Burgin, John Carroll.
Burgin, John Carroll.
xBurgin, John C.
Teaching Singing. Scarecrow.
Burgin, Miron, 1900-1957
xBurgin, Miron.
Economic Aspects of Argentine Federalism,
1820-1852. Russell.
Burgner, Robert L. see Burgner, Robert Louis.
Burgner, Robert Louis, 1919-
xBurgner, Robert L.
ed. Further Studies of Alaska Sockeye Salmon.
U of Wash Pr.
Burgo, Joseph.
xBurgo, Joseph.
The Lights of Barbrin. PB.
Burgoon, M. see Burgoon, Michael.
Burgoon, Michael.
xBurgoon, M.
Human Communication. HR&W.
Burgoyne, Edward E.
xBurgoyne, Edward E.
A Short Course in Organic Chemistry.
McGraw.
Burickson, Sherwin.
xBurickson, Sherwin.
ed. Concise Dictionary of Contemporary
History. Philos Lib.
Buridan, Jean.
xBuridan, John.
Sophisms on Meaning & Truth. Irvington.
Buridan, John. see Buridan, Jean.
Burington, Richard S. see Burington, Richard Stevens.
Burington, Richard Stevens, 1901-
xBurington, Richard S.
Handbook of Mathematical Tables & Formulas.
McGraw.
Burk, Bruce.
xBurk, Bruce.
Game Bird Carving. Winchester Pr.
Burk, C. A. see Burk, Creighton A.
Burk, Creighton A.
xBurk, C. A.
ed. The Geology of Continental Margins.
Springer-Verlag.
Geology of the Alaska Peninsula: Island Arc &
Continental Margin. Geol Soc.
xBurk, Creighton A.
ed. Impact of the Geosciences on Critical
Energy Resources. Westview.
Burk, Janet L.
xBurk, Janet L.
Environmental Concerns: A Bibliography of
U.S. Government Publications, 1971-1973.
New Issues MI.
Burk, Mary S. see Burk, Mary Sydney.
Burk, Mary Sydney.
xBurk, Mary S.
Doctor of the Hills. Bouregy.
Burkart, A. J. see Burkart, Arthur John.
Burkart, Arthur John.
xBurkart, A. J.
Tourism: Past, Present & Future. Intl Pubns
Serv.
Burke, Arvid J. see Burke, Arvid James.
Burke, Arvid James.
xBurke, Arvid J.
Documentation in Education. Tchrs Coll.
Burke, Bernard. see Burke, John Bernard.
Burke, Catherine G.
xBurke, Catherine G.

Innovation & Public Policy: The Case of
Personal Rapid Transit. Lexington Bks.
Burke, Charles.
xBurke, Charles.
ed. Loneliness. St Marys.
Burke, Charles C.
xBurke, Charles C.
Woodworking for Cave Dwellers. TAB Bks.
Burke, Cornelius G.
xBurke, Cornelius G.
The Collector's Haydn. Greenwood.
Burke, Edmund, 1729?-1797
xBurke, Edmund.
Account of the European Settlements in
America. AMS Pr.
Account of the European Settlements in
America. Arno.
Edmund Burke on Government, Politics, &
Society. Intl Pubns Serv.
Letters, Speeches & Tracts on Irish Affairs.
AMS Pr.
Prelude to Protectorate in Morocco:
Precolonial Protest & Resistance, 1860-1912.
U of Chicago Pr.
Burke, Edmund. see Burke, Edmund H.
Burke, Edmund H.
xBurke, Edmund.
Archery. Arc Bks.
xBurke, Edmund H.
Archery Handbook. Arco.
Field & Target Archery. Arco.
History of Archery. Greenwood.
Burke, Fred G.
xBurke, Fred G.
Local Government & Politics in Uganda.
Syracuse U Pr.
Burke, Helen.
xBurke, Helen Newbury.
Foods from the Founding Fathers: Recipes
from Five Colonial Seaports. Exposition.
Burke, Helen Newbury. see Burke, Helen.
Burke, J. F., 1915-
xBurke, J. F.
Kelly Among the Nightingales. Dutton.
Burke, Jack D.
xBurke, Jack D.
Essentials of Histology. Barron.
Burke, James, 1936-
xBurke, James.
Connections. Little.
Burke, James W. see Burke, James Wakefield.
Burke, James Wakefield.
xBurke, James W.
Sunbelt. Fawcett.
Burke, Jim.
xBurke, Jim.
The World of Jimmy Connors. Nordon Pubns.
Burke, John, 1928-
xBurke, John.
Bible Sharing: How to Grow in the Mystery of
Christ. Alba.
Chivalry, Slavery & Young America. Arno.
The Devil's Footsteps. Popular Lib.
Gospel Power: Toward the Revitalization of
Preaching. Alba.
Burke, John. see Burke, John T.
Burke, John Bernard, Sir, 1814-1892
xBurke, Bernard.
A Genealogical History of the Dormant,
Abeyant, Forfeited, & Extinct Peerages of the
British Empire. Genealog Pub.
Burke, John D., 1917-
xBurke, John D.
Advertising in the Marketplace. McGraw.
Burke, John Frederick, 1922-
xBurke, John.
Life in the Castle in Medieval England.
Rowman.
Burke, John G.
xBurke, John.

Origins of the Science of Crystals. U of Cal Pr.
xBurke, John G.
Intro. by Technology & Change. Boyd &
Fraser.
Burke, John G. see Burke, John Gordon.
Burke, John Gordon.
xBurke, John G.
Guide to Ecology Information & Organizations.
Wilson.
The Monthly Catalog of United States
Government Publications: An Introduction to
Its Use. Shoe String.
Burke, John T.
xBurke, John.
Local Government Budgeting: Financial
Planning & Operational Control. MSU-Inst
Comm Devel.
Burke, Kenneth, 1897-
xBurke, Kenneth.
Collected Poems, 1915-1967. U of Cal Pr.
Counter Statement. Hermes.
Counter-Statement. U of Cal Pr.
Dramatism & Development. Clark U Pr.
A Grammar of Motives. U of Cal Pr.
A Rhetoric of Motives. U of Cal Pr.
The Rhetoric of Religion: Studies in Logology.
U of Cal Pr.
Burke, Louis.
xBurke, Louis.
Colposcopy in Clinical Practice. Davis Co.
Burke, Owen.
xBurke, Owen.
The Figurehead. Coward.
The Figurehead. Fawcett.
Burke, P. G.
xBurke, P. G.
Potential Scattering in Atomic Physics. Plenum
Pub.
Burke, Patrick. see Burke, Thomas Patrick.
Burke, Peter.
xBurke, Peter.
Culture & Society in Renaissance Italy,
1420-1540. Scribner.
Popular Culture in Early Modern Europe.
Har-Row.
Popular Culture in Early Modern Europe.
NYU Pr.
ed. Renaissance Sense of the Past. St Martin.
Burke, Roy.
xBurke, Roy.
Collective Decision Making in Water Resource
Planning. Lexington Bks.
Burke, Shirley R.
xBurke, Shirley R.
The Composition & Function of Body Fluids.
Mosby.
Burke, Theta.
xBurke, Theta.
Sounds of Yourself. Delafield Pr.
Burke, Thomas, 1887-1945
xBurke, Thomas.
Limehouse Nights. Arno.
Limehouse Nights. Horizon.
Night-Pieces: Eighteen Tales. Arno.
Tea-Shop in Limehouse. Arno.
Burke, Thomas Patrick, 1934-
xBurke, Patrick.
The Fragile Universe: An Essay in the
Philosophy of Religions. B&N.
Burke, W. Warner. see Burke, Wyatt Warner.
Burke, William.
xBurke, William.
Additional Reasons for Our Immediately
Emancipating Spanish America. AMS Pr.
Burke, William J. see Burke, William Jeremiah.
Burke, William Jeremiah, 1902-
xBurke, William J.
Literature of Slang. Gale.
Burke, William M. see Burke, William Maxwell.

Burke, William Maxwell, 1870-
   xBurke, William M.
      History & Functions of Central Labor Unions.
      AMS Pr.
Burke, Wyatt Warner, 1935-
   xBurke, W. Warner.
      Current Issues & Strategies in Organization
      Development. Human Sci Pr.
Burken, Judith L.
   xBurken, Judith L.
      Introduction to Reporting. Wm C Brown.
Burkert, Walter, 1931-
   xBurkert, Walter.
      Lore & Science in Ancient Pythagoreanism.
      Harvard U Pr.
      Structure & History in Greek Mythology &
      Ritual. U of Cal Pr.
Burkett, Eva M. see Burkett, Eva Mae.
Burkett, Eva Mae.
   xBurkett, Eva M.
      American Dictionaries of the English Language
      Before 1861. Scarecrow.
Burkett, Molly.
   xBurkett, Molly.
      Foxes Three. Lippincott.
Burkey, Richard M.
   xBurkey, Richard M.
      Ethnic & Racial Groups: The Dynamics of
      Dominance. Benjamin-Cummings.
Burkhard, Arthur.
   xBurkhard, Arthur.
      Matthias Grunewald: Personality &
      Accomplishment. Hacker.
Burkhard, Marianne.
   xBurkhard, Marianne.
      Conrad Ferdinand Meyer. Twayne.
Burkhart, Charles.
   xBurkhart, Charles.
      Anthology for Musical Analysis. HR&W.
Burkhead, Jesse.
   xBurkhead, Jesse.
      Input & Output in Large-City High Schools.
      Syracuse U Pr.
      Public Expenditure. Aldine Pub.
Burkill, J C.
   xBurkill, John C.
      Lebesgue Integral. Cambridge U Pr.
Burkill, John C. see Burkill, John Charles.
Burkill, John Charles, 1900-
   xBurkill, John C.
      First Course in Mathematical Analysis.
      Cambridge U Pr.
Burkill, T. A. see Burkill, T. Alec.
Burkill, T. Alec.
   xBurkill, T. A.
      Evolution of Christian Thought. Cornell U Pr.
Burkitt, Ann.
   xBurkitt, Ann.
      Life Begins at Forty: How to Make Sure You
      Enjoy Middle Age. Merrimack Bk Serv.
Burkitt, B. see Burkitt, Prian.
Burkitt, Francis C. see Burkitt, Francis Crawford.
Burkitt, Francis Crawford, 1864-1935
   xBurkitt, Francis C.
      Church & Gnosis: A Study of Christian
      Thought & Speculation in the Second
      Century. AMS Pr.
Burkitt, M. C. see Burkitt, Miles Crawford.
Burkitt, Miles Crawford, 1890-
   xBurkitt, M. C.
      Our Early Ancestors: An Introductory Study of
      Mesolithic, Neolithic, & Copper Age Cultures
      in Europe & Adjacent Regions. Arno.
Burkitt, Prian.
   xBurkitt, B.
      Trade Unions & the Economy. Holmes &
      Meier.
Burklin, C. R., 1921-
   xBurklin, Ray.

      Process Plant Designer's Pocket Handbook of
      Codes & Standards. Gulf Pub.
Burklin, Ray. see Burklin, C. R.
Burkowsky, Mitchell. see Burkowsky, Mitchell R.
Burkowsky, Mitchell R., 1931-
   xBurkowsky, Mitchell.
      Teaching American Pronunciation to Foreign
      Students. Green.
Burks, Arthur W. see Burks, Arthur Walter.
Burks, Arthur Walter, 1915-
   xBurks, Arthur W.
      Chance, Cause, Reason: An Inquiry into the
      Nature of Scientific Evidence. U of Chicago
      Pr.
Burks, B. D. see Burks, Barnard De Witt.
Burks, Barnard De Witt, 1909-
   xBurks, B. D.
      The Mayflies, or Ephemeroptera, of Illinois.
      Entomological Repr.
Burks, Don M.
   xBurks, Don M.
      ed. Rhetoric, Philosophy, & Literature: An
      Exploration. Purdue.
Burks, Herbert M.
   xBurks, Herbert M.
      Theories of Counseling. McGraw.
Burks, Jayne.
   xBurks, Jayne.
      Temperament Styles in Adult Interaction:
      Applications in Psychotherapy. Brunner
      Mazel.
Burks, R. V. see Burks, Richard Voyles.
Burks, Richard V. see Burks, Richard Voyles.
Burks, Richard Voyles, 1913-
   xBurks, R. V.
      East European History: An Ethnic Approach.
      Am Hist Assn.
      ed. The Future of Communism in Europe.
      Wayne St U Pr.
   xBurks, Richard V.
      The Dynamics of Communism in Eastern
      Europe. Greenwood.
Burl. see Burl, Aubrey.
Burl, Aubrey.
   xBurl.
      Prehistoric Avebury. Yale U Pr.
      The Stone Circles of the British Isles. Yale U
      Pr.
   xBurl, Aubrey.
      Rings of Stone: The Prehistoric Stone Circles
      of Britain & Ireland. Ticknor & Fields.
   xBurl, Audrey.
      The Stone Circles of the British Isles. Yale U
      Pr.
Burl, Audrey. see Burl, Aubrey.
Burlamaqui, Jean J. see Burlamaqui, Jean Jacques.
Burlamaqui, Jean Jacques, 1694-1748
   xBurlamaqui, Jean J.
      The Principles of Natural & Politic Law. Arno.
Burland, C. A. see Burland, Cottie Arthur.
Burland, Cottie A. see Burland, Cottie Arthur.
Burland, Cottie Arthur, 1905-
   xBurland, C. A.
      Echoes of Magic: A Study of Seasonal
      Festivals Through the Ages. Rowman.
   xBurland, Cottie A.
      Adventuring in Archaeology. Warne.
Burleigh, Anne H. see Burleigh, Anne Husted.
Burleigh, Anne Husted.
   xBurleigh, Anne H.
      ed. Education in a Free Society. Liberty Fund.
Burleigh, Thomas D. see Burleigh, Thomas Dearborn.
Burleigh, Thomas Dearborn, 1895-
   xBurleigh, Thomas D.
      Georgia Birds. U of Okla Pr.
Burlend, Rebecca.
   xBurlend, Rebecca.
      A True Picture of Emigration. Citadel Pr.
Burleson, Donald R.
   xBurleson, Donald R.

      Elementary Statistics. Winthrop.
      Topics in Precalculus Mathematics. P-H.
Burley, D. M. see Burley, David Michael.
Burley, David Michael.
   xBurley, D. M.
      Studies in Optimization. Halsted Pr.
Burley, W. J. see Burley, William John.
Burley, William John.
   xBurley, W. J.
      Wycliffe & the Scapegoat. Doubleday.
Burling, Robbins.
   xBurling, Robbins.
      Hill Farms & Padi Fields: Life in Mainland
      Southeast Asia. P-H.
      The Passage of Power: Studies in Political
      Succession. Acad Pr.
      Proto Lolo-Burmese. Res Ctr Lang Semiotic.
Burlingame, Burl.
   xBurlingame, Burl.
      Da Kine Sound: Conversations with People
      Who Create Hawaiian Music. Pr Pacifica.
Burlingame, Dwight.
   xBurlingame, Dwight F.
      The College Learning Resource Center. Libs
      Unl.
Burlingame, Dwight F. see Burlingame, Dwight.
Burlingame, Roger. see Burlingame, Roger William Roger
   Burlingame.
Burlingame, Roger William Roger Burlingame.
   xBurlingame, Roger.
      March of the Iron Men: A Social History of
      Union Through Invention. Arno.
Burlingham, Dorothy.
   xBurlingham, Dorothy.
      Psychoanalytic Studies of the Sighted & the
      Blind. Intl Univs Pr.
Burlingham, Russell, 1923-
   xBurlingham, Russell.
      Forrest Reid: A Portrait & a Study. Folcroft.
Burma, John H.
   xBurma, John H.
      Spanish-Speaking Groups in the United States.
      Blaine Ethridge.
Burman, Ben L. see Burman, Ben Lucien.
Burman, Ben Lucien.
   xBurman, Ben L.
      High Treason at Catfish Bend. Penguin.
      High Treason at Catfish Bend. Vanguard.
      High Water at Catfish Bend. Penguin.
      High Water at Catfish Bend. Taplinger.
      Look Down That Winding River: An Informal
      Profile of the Mississippi. Taplinger.
      The Owl Hoots Twice at Catfish Bend.
      Penguin.
      Sign of the Praying Tiger. Taplinger.
Burman, Bina R. see Burman, Bina Roy.
Burman, Bina Roy, 1929-
   xBurman, Bina R.
      Religion & Politics in Tibet. Advent Bk.
      Religion & Politics in Tibet. Biblio Dist.
Burman, Ian D.
   xBurman, Ian D.
      Lobbying at the Illinois Constitutional
      Convention. U of Ill Pr.
Burman, P. J. see Burman, Peter J.
Burman, Peter J.
   xBurman, P. J.
      Precedence Networks for Project Planning &
      Control. Blitz Pub Co.
Burman, Sandra.
   xBurman, Sandra.
      ed. Accidents in the Home. Biblio Dist.
      Chiefdom Politics & Alien Law. Holmes &
      Meier.
      ed. Fit Work for Women. St Martin.
Burmeister, Edwin.
   xBurmeister, Edwin.
      Mathematical Theories of Economic Growth.
      Macmillan.
Burmeister, Eva E. see Burmeister, Eva Elizabeth.

Burmeister, Eva Elizabeth.
xBurmeister, Eva E.
Forty Five in the Family: The Story of a Home
for Children. Greenwood.
Professional Houseparent. Columbia U Pr.
Burmeister, Magdalene, 1902-
xBurmeister, Magdalene.
Against the Shifting Sands. Golden Quill.
Burn, Barbara B.
xBurn, Barbara B.
ed. Higher Education Reform: Implications for
Foreign Students. Inst Intl Educ.
Burn, R. P.
xBurn, R. P.
Deductive Transformation Geometry.
Cambridge U Pr.
Burn, William L. see Burn, William Laurence.
Burn, William Laurence.
xBurn, William L.
The British West Indies. Greenwood.
Burnam, Tom.
xBurnam, Tom.
The Dictionary of Misinformation. Ballantine.
More Misinformation. T Y Crowell.
Burne, Alfred H. see Burne, Alfred Higgins.
Burne, Alfred Higgins, 1886-
xBurne, Alfred H.
The Crecy War: A Military History of the
Hundred Years War from 1337 to the Peace
of Bretigny, 1360. Greenwood.
Burne, Kevin G.
xBurne, Kevin G.
Functional English for Writers. Scott F.
Burne-Jones, Georgiana. see Burne-Jones, Georgiana
(Macdonald).
Burne-Jones, Georgiana (Macdonald), Lady, 1840-1920
xBurne-Jones, Georgiana.
Memorials of Edward Burne-Jones. Arno.
Memorials of Edward Burne-Jones. R West
xBurne-Jones, Georgiana M.
Memorials of Edward Burne-Jones. Arno.
Burne-Jones, Georgiana M. see Burne-Jones, Georgiana
(Macdonald).
Burner, David, 1937-
xBurner, David.
ed. Diversity of Modern America: Essays in
History Since World War One. Irvington.
The Politics of Provincialism: The Democratic
Party in Transition, 1918-1932. Norton.
Burness, Tad, 1933-
xBurness, Tad.
American Car Spotter's Guide 1920-1939.
Motorbooks Intl.
American Car Spotter's Guide 1940-1965.
Motorbooks Intl.
American Truck Spotter's Guide 1920-1970.
Motorbooks Intl.
Imported Car Spotter's Guide. Motorbooks
Intl.
Burnet, F. Macfarlane. see Burnet, Frank Macfarlane.
Burnet, Frank M. see Burnet, Frank Macfarlane.
Burnet, Frank Macfarlane, Sir, 1899-
xBurnet, F. Macfarlane.
Natural History of Infectious Disease.
Cambridge U Pr.
xBurnet, Frank M.
Integrity of the Body: A Discussion of Modern
Immunological Ideas. Harvard U Pr.
Burnet, Jacob, 1770-1853
xBurnet, Jacob.
Notes on the Early Settlement of the
North-Western Territory. Arno.
Burnet, Jean.
xBurnet, Jean.
Next-Year Country: A Study of Rural Social
Organization in Alberta. U of Toronto Pr.
Burnett, Anne P. see Burnett, Anne Pippin.
Burnett, Anne Pippin, 1925-
xBurnett, Anne P.

Catastrophe Survived: Euripides' Plays of
Mixed Reversal. Oxford U Pr.
Burnett, Bernice.
xBurnett, Bernice.
The First Book of Holidays. Watts.
Burnett, Constance (Buel).
xBurnett, Constance B.
Captain John Ericsson: Father of the Monitor.
Vanguard.
Five for Freedom: Lucretia Mott, Elizabeth
Cady Stanton, Lucy Stone, Susan B.
Anthony, Carrie Chapman Catt. Greenwood.
Burnett, Constance B. see Burnett, Constance (Buel).
Burnett, Edmund C. see Burnett, Edmund Cody.
Burnett, Edmund Cody, 1864-1949
xBurnett, Edmund C.
The Continental Congress. Greenwood.
Burnett, Frances. see Burnett, Frances (Hodgson).
Burnett, Frances (Hodgson), 1849-1924
xBurnett, Frances.
A Little Princess. Harmony & Co.
xBurnett, Frances H.
Little Princess. G&D.
Little Princess. Lippincott.
A Little Princess. Dell.
Burnett, Frances H. see Burnett, Frances (Hodgson).
Burnett, George W. see Burnett, George Wesley.
Burnett, George Wesley.
xBurnett, George W.
Pathogenic Microbiology. Mosby.
Burnett, Hallie. see Burnett, Hallie Southgate.
Burnett, Hallie Southgate.
xBurnett, Hallie.
Fiction Writer's Handbook. Har-Row.
Fiction Writer's Handbook. Har-Row.
Burnett, Jacquetta H.
xBurnett, Jacquetta H.
Anthropology & Education: An Annotated
Bibliographic Guide. HRAFP.
Burnett, John, fl. 1966-
xBurnett, John.
ed. The Annals of Labour: Autobiographies of
British Working Class People, 1820-1920. Ind
U Pr.
Burnett, Joseph D.
xBurnett, Joseph D.
Capital Funds Campaign Manual for Churches.
Judson.
Burnett, Joseph W.
xBurnett, Joseph W.
Clinical Dermatology for Students &
Practitioners. Yorke Med.
Burnett, Ruth.
xBurnett, Ruth.
Dr. Galen's Dilemma. Bouregy.
Burney, Charles, 1726-1814
xBurney, Charles.
An Account of the Musical Performances in
Westminster Abbey. Da Capo.
Burney, Eugenia.
xBurney, Eugenia.
Colonial North Carolina. Elsevier-Nelson.
Colonial South Carolina. Elsevier-Nelson.
Burnford, Sheila.
xBurnford, Sheila.
Bel Ria. Little.
Bel Ria. Bantam.
Burnham, Donald C.
xBurnham, Donald C.
Productivity Improvement. Columbia U Pr.
Burnham, Jack, 1931-
xBurnham, Jack.
Great Western Salt Works: Essays on the
Meaning of Post-Formalist Art. Braziller.
Structure of Art. Braziller.
Burnham, James, 1905-
xBurnham, James.
Coming Defeat of Communism. Greenwood.
Burnham, Jeremy.
xBurnham, Jeremy.

Children of the Stones. Scribner.
Burnham, John C. see Burnham, John Chynoweth.
Burnham, John Chynoweth, 1929-
xBurnham, John C.
Psychoanalysis & American Medicine,
1894-1918: Medicine, Science, & Culture.
Intl Univs Pr.
Burnham, Robert.
xBurnham, Robert.
Burnham's Celestial Handbook: An Observer's
Guide to the Universe Beyond the Solar
System. Dover.
Burnham, Robert E. see Burnham, Robert Edward.
Burnham, Robert Edward.
xBurnham, Robert E.
Who Are the Finns?: A Study in Prehistory.
AMS Pr.
Burnham, Sophy.
xBurnham, Sophy.
Buccaneer. Warne.
The Dogwalker. Warne.
Burnham, W. Dean. see Burnham, Walter Dean.
Burnham, Walter D. see Burnham, Walter Dean.
Burnham, Walter Dean.
xBurnham, W. Dean.
Presidential Ballots, 1836-1892. Arno.
xBurnham, Walter D.
ed. American Politics & Public Policy. MIT Pr.
Critical Elections & the Mainsprings of
American Politics. Norton.
Burnham, William H. see Burnham, William Henry.
Burnham, William Henry, 1855-1941
xBurnham, William H.
Great Teachers & Mental Health: A Study of
Seven Educational Hygienists. Arno.
Burningham, John.
xBurningham, John.
The Baby. T Y Crowell.
illus. Come Away from the Water, Shirley. T Y
Crowell.
illus. The Cupboard. T Y Crowell.
illus. The Dog. T Y Crowell.
illus. The Friend. T Y Crowell.
The Rabbit. T Y Crowell.
illus. Time to Get Out of the Bath, Shirley. T
Y Crowell.
illus. Would You Rather.... T Y Crowell.
Burnley, J. D.
xBurnley, J. D.
Chaucer's Language & the Philosophers'
Tradition. Rowman.
Burnley, James, 1842-1919
xBurnley, James.
History of Wool & Wool-Combing. Kelley.
Burns, A. E. see Burns, Arthur Edward.
Burns, A. R. see Burns, Arthur Robert.
Burns, Alan C. see Burns, Alan Cuthbert.
Burns, Alan Cuthbert, Sir, 1887-
xBurns, Alan C.
History of the British West Indies. Gordon Pr.
Burns, Arthur. see Burns, Arthur Edward.
Burns, Arthur Edward.
xBurns, A. E.
Government Spending & Economic Expansion.
Da Capo.
xBurns, Arthur.
Federal Work, Security, & Relief Programs. Da
Capo.
Burns, Arthur F. see Burns, Arthur Frank.
Burns, Arthur Frank, 1904-
xBurns, Arthur F.
The Frontiers of Economic Knowledge: Essays.
Arno.
Measuring Business Cycles. Natl Bur Econ
Res.
Reflections of an Economic Policy Maker:
Speeches & Congressional Statements,
1969-1978. Am Enterprise.
Burns, Arthur R. see Burns, Arthur Robert.

Burns, Arthur Robert, 1895-
xBurns, A. R.
    Money & Monetary Policy in Early Times.
        Gordon Pr.
xBurns, Arthur R.
    Money & Monetary Policy in Early Times.
        Kelley.
Burns, C. see Burns, Cecil Delisle.
Burns, C. Delisle. see Burns, Cecil Delisle.
Burns, Cecil Delisle, 1879-1942
xBurns, C.
    Greek Ideals: A Study in Social Life. Gordon
        Pr.
xBurns, C. Delisle.
    Greek Ideals: A Study of Social Life. Quality
        Lib.
Burns, Creighton.
xBurns, Creighton L.
    Tait Case. Intl Schol Bk Serv.
Burns, Creighton L. see Burns, Creighton.
Burns, E. Bradford.
xBurns, E. Bradford.
    History of Brazil. Columbia U Pr.
    Latin America: A Concise Interpretive History.
        P-H.
Burns, Edward, 1943-
xBurns, Edward.
    The Development, Use & Abuse of Educational
        Tests. C C Thomas.
Burns, Edward M. see Burns, Edward McNall.
Burns, Edward McNall, 1897-
xBurns, Edward M.
    The American Idea of Mission: Concepts of
        National Purpose & Destiny. Greenwood.
Burns, Eugene.
xBurns, Eugene.
    Last King of Paradise. Arno.
Burns, Eveline M. see Burns, Eveline Mabel Richardson.
Burns, Eveline Mabel Richardson, 1900-
xBurns, Eveline M.
    Social Welfare in the 1980's & Beyond. Inst
        Gov Stud Berk.
Burns, G. P. see Burns, George Plumer.
Burns, George, 1896-
xBurns, George.
    The Third Time Around: Confessions of a
        Happy Hoofer. Putnam.
Burns, George Plumer.
xBurns, G. P.
    The Handbook of Vermont Trees. C E Tuttle.
Burns, George W., 1913-
xBurns, George W.
    Plant Kingdom. Macmillan.
Burns, Gerald.
xBurns, Gerald.
    Introduction to Space Groups for Solid State
        Scientists. Acad Pr.
    Toward a Phenomenology of Written Art.
        Treacle.
Burns, Helen. see Burns, Helen M.
Burns, Helen M.
xBurns, Helen.
    The American Banking Community & New
        Deal Banking Reforms: 1933-1935.
        Greenwood.
Burns, J. A. see Burns, James Aloysius.
Burns, J. T.
xBurns, J. T.
    Framing Pictures. Scribner.
Burns, James Aloysius, 1867-1940
xBurns, J. A.
    Growth & Development of the Catholic School
        System in the United States. Arno.
    The Principles, Origin & Establishment of the
        Catholic School System in the United States.
        Arno.
Burns, James J. see Burns, James Joseph.
Burns, James Joseph, 1910-
xBurns, James J.

The Colonial Agents of New England.
    Porcupine Pr.
Burns, James M. see Burns, James MacGregor.
Burns, James MacGregor.
xBurns, James M.
    Congress on Trial: The Legislative Process &
        the Administrative State. Gordian.
    Edward Kennedy & the Camelot Legacy.
        Norton.
    Leadership. Har-Row.
    Leadership. Har-Row.
Burns, Jim, 1926-
xBurns, Jim.
    Connections: Ways to Discover & Realize
        Community Potentials. McGraw.
Burns, John F. see Burns, John Francis.
Burns, John Francis, 1895-
xBurns, John F.
    Controversies Between Royal Governors &
        Their Assemblies in the Northern American
        Colonies. Russell.
Burns, John H. see Burns, John Hagerty.
Burns, John Hagerty.
xBurns, John H.
    What You Should Know About Reducing
        Credit Losses. Oceana.
Burns, Joseph A.
xBurns, Joseph A.
    ed. Planetary Satellites. U of Ariz Pr.
Burns, Kenneth R.
xBurns, Kenneth R.
    Health Assessment in Clinical Practice. P-H.
Burns, Lawrence D.
xBurns, Lawrence D.
    Transportation, Temporal & Spatial
        Components of Accessibility. Lexington Bks.
Burns, M. A. see Burns, Mary Ann T.
Burns, Marilyn.
xBurns, Marilyn.
    The Book of Think: Or How to Solve a
        Problem Twice Your Size. Little.
    Good for Me!: All About Food in 32 Bites.
        Little.
    This Book Is About Time. Little.
Burns, Mary Ann T.
xBurns, M. A.
    Lingua Latina: Liber Alter. Glencoe.
    Lingua Latina: Liber Primus. Glencoe.
Burns, Norman, 1905-
xBurns, Norman.
    The Tariff of Syria, 1919 to 1932. AMS Pr.
Burns, Norman T.
xBurns, Norman T.
    Christian Mortalism from Tyndale to Milton.
        Harvard U Pr.
Burns, Paul C. see Burns, Paul Clay.
Burns, Paul Callan.
xBurns, Paul C.
    The Portrait Painter's Problem Book.
        Watson-Guptill.
Burns, Paul Clay.
xBurns, Paul C.
    The Language Arts in Childhood Education.
        Rand.
    Reading Activities for Today's Elementary
        Schools. Rand.
    Teaching Reading in Today's Elementary
        Schools. Rand.
Burns, R. G. see Burns, Roger George.
Burns, Rex.
xBurns, Rex.

The Alvarez Journal. Har-Row.
Angle of Attack. Berkley Pub.
Angle of Attack. Har-Row.
The Farnsworth Score. Berkley Pub.
The Farnsworth Score. Har-Row.
Speak for the Dead. Berkley Pub.
Speak for the Dead. Har-Row.
Success in America: The Yeoman Dream & the
    Industrial Revolution. U of Mass Pr.
Burns, Richard D. see Burns, Richard Dean.
Burns, Richard Dean.
xBurns, Richard D.
    ed. Continuing Dialogue: Men & Issues in
        Early American History. Pacific Bks.
    ed. Diplomats in Crisis: United
        States-Chinese-Japanese Relations,
        1919-1941. ABC-Clio.
Burns, Richard W.
xBurns, Richard W.
    ed. Competency-Based Education: An
        Introduction. Educ Tech Pubns.
    ed. Curriculum Design in a Changing Society.
        Educ Tech Pubns.
Burns, Robert.
xBurns, Robert.
    Letters of Robert Burns. Scholarly.
Burns, Robert E. see Burns, Robert Elliott.
Burns, Robert Elliott.
xBurns, Robert E.
    I Am a Fugitive from a Georgia Chain Gang.
        Gale.
Burns, Robert F.
xBurns, Robert F.
    Citizens Band Radio Service Manual. TAB Bks.
Burns, Robert I. see Burns, Robert Ignatius.
Burns, Robert Ignatius.
xBurns, Robert I.
    Medieval Colonialism: Postcrusade Exploitation
        of Islamic Valencia. Princeton U Pr.
Burns, Robert M. see Burns, Robert Martin.
Burns, Robert Martin.
xBurns, Robert M.
    Protective Coatings for Metals. Am Chemical.
Burns, Robert O. see Burns, Robert Obed.
Burns, Robert Obed, 1910-
xBurns, Robert O.
    Innovation: The Management Connection.
        Lexington Bks.
Burns, Roger George.
xBurns, R. G.
    ed. Soil Enzymes. Acad Pr.
Burns, Scott.
xBurns, Scott.
    The Household Economy: Its Shape, Origins, &
        Future. Beacon Pr.
Burns, Sheila L.
xBurns, Shelia L.
    Allergies & You. Messner.
Burns, Shelia L. see Burns, Sheila L.
Burns, T. see Burns, Thomas Junior.
Burns, T. R. see Burns, Tom.
Burns, Thomas J. see Burns, Thomas Junior.
Burns, Thomas Junior.
xBurns, T.
    The Accounting Sampler. McGraw.
xBurns, Thomas J.
    ed. Accounting in Transition: Oral Histories of
        Recent U. S. Experience. Ohio St U Admin
        Sci.
Burns, Tom.
xBurns, T. R.
    ed. Power & Control: Social Structures & Their
        Transformation. Sage.
xBurns, Tom R.
    ed. Work & Power: The Liberation of Work &
        the Control of Political Power. Sage.
Burns, Tom R. see Burns, Tom.
Burns, Wayne, 1918-
xBurns, Wayne.

Charles Reade: A Study in Victorian
Authorship. Cyrco Pr.
Charles Reade: A Study in Victorian
Authorship. Irvington.
Burnside, C. D. *see* Burnside, Clifford Donald.
Burnside, Clifford Donald.
xBurnside, C. D.
Mapping from Aerial Photographs. Halsted Pr.
Burnside, Irene, 1923-
xBurnside, Irene M.
Psychosocial Nursing Care of the Aged.
McGraw.
Burnside, Irene M. *see* Burnside, Irene.
Burnstock, G. *see* Burnstock, Geoffrey.
Burnstock, Geoffrey.
xBurnstock, G.
Adrenergic Neurons: Their Organization,
Function & Development in the Peripheral
Nervous System. Methuen Inc.
Buros, Oscar K. *see* Buros, Oscar Krisen.
Buros, Oscar Krisen.
xBuros, Oscar K.
ed. English Tests & Reviews: A Monograph
Consisting of the English Sections of the
Seven Mental Measurements Yearbooks
(1938-72) & Tests in Print II (1974). U of
Nebr Pr..
ed. Foreign Language Tests & Reviews: A
Monograph Consisting of the Foreign
Language Sections of the Seven Mental
Measurements Yearbooks (1938-72) & Tests
in Print II (1974). U of Nebr Pr..
ed. Intelligence Tests & Reviews: A
Monograph Consisting of the Intelligence
Sections of the Seven Mental Measurements
Yearbooks (1938-1972) & Tests in Print II
(1974). U of Nebr Pr..
ed. Mathematics Tests & Reviews: A
Monograph Consisting of the Mathematics
Sections of the Seven Mental Measurements
Yearbooks (1938-1972) & Tests in Print II
(1974). U of Nebr Pr..
ed. Social Studies Tests & Reviews: A
Monograph Consisting of the Social Studies
Sections of the Seven Mental Measurements
Yearbooks (1938-72) & Tests in Print II
(1974). U of Nebr Pr..
Burow, Daniel R.
xBurow, Daniel R.
I Meet God Through the Strangest People: 110
Devotions for the 9 to 13 Generation.
Concordia.
Burpee, Lawrence J. *see* Burpee, Lawrence Johnstone.
Burpee, Lawrence Johnstone, 1873-1946
xBurpee, Lawrence J.
Discovery of Canada. Arno.
Burr. *see* Burr, Irving Wingate.
Burr, Anna R. *see* Burr, Anna Robeson (Brown).
Burr, Anna Robeson (Brown), 1873-1941
xBurr, Anna R.
The Autobiography: A Critical & Comparative
Study. Folcroft.
Burr, David, 1934-
xBurr, David.
Persecution of Peter Olivi. Am Philos.
Burr, Gillian.
xBurr, Gillian.
ed. More Ways to a Man's Heart. Biblio Dist.
Burr, Gray.
xBurr, Gray.
Choice of Attitudes. Columbia U Pr.
Burr, Irving. *see* Burr, Irving Wingate.
Burr, Irving W. *see* Burr, Irving Wingate.
Burr, Irving Wingate, 1908-
xBurr.
Elementary Statistical Quality Control. Dekker.
xBurr, Irving.
Statistical Quality Control Methods. Dekker.
xBurr, Irving W.

Applied Statistical Methods. Acad Pr.
Burr, Jeanne.
xBurr, Jeanne.
Sex Roles: Rights & Values in Conflict. Facts
on File.
Burr, John R. *see* Burr, John Roy.
Burr, John Roy.
xBurr, John R.
Philosophy & Contemporary Issues. Macmillan.
Burr, Lonnie.
xBurr, Lonnie.
Two for the Show: Great Comedy Teams.
Messner.
Burr, Nelson R. *see* Burr, Nelson Rollin.
Burr, Nelson Rollin, 1904-
xBurr, Nelson R.
Compiled by Religion in American Life. AHM
Pub.
Burr, Robert N.
xBurr, Robert N.
By Reason or Force: Chile & the Balancing of
Power in South America, 1830-1905. U of
Cal Pr.
Our Troubled Hemisphere: Perspectives on
United States-Latin American Relations.
Brookings.
Burr, Wesley R., 1936-
xBurr, Wesley R.
ed. Contemporary Theories About the Family.
Free Pr.
Burra, Peter. *see* Burra, Peter James Salkeld.
Burra, Peter James Salkeld, 1909-
xBurra, Peter.
Wordsworth. Folcroft.
Wordsworth. Haskell.
Burrage, Alfred M. *see* Burrage, Alfred McLelland.
Burrage, Alfred McLelland.
xBurrage, Alfred M.
Someone in the Room. Arno.
Burrell, Arthur, 1859 or 60-
xBurrell, Arthur.
A Guide to Story Telling. Arden Lib.
Guide to Story Telling. Gale.
A Guide to Story Telling. R West.
Burrell, David.
xBurrell, David.
Analogy & Philosophical Language. Yale U Pr.
Burrell, David B.
xBurrell, David B.
Aquinas: God & Action. U of Notre Dame Pr.
ed. Evangelization in the American Context. U
of Notre Dame Pr.
Exercises in Religious Understanding. U of
Notre Dame Pr.
Burrell, Martin, 1858-1938
xBurrell, Martin.
Crumbs Are Also Bread. Arno.
Burrell, O. K. *see* Burrell, Orin Kay.
Burrell, Orin Kay, 1899-1964
xBurrell, O. K.
Gold in the Woodpile: An Informal History of
Banking in Oregon. U of Oreg Bks.
Burrell, R. Michael. *see* Burrell, Robert Michael.
Burrell, Robert.
xBurrell, Robert.
Experimental Immunology. Burgess.
Burrell, Robert Michael.
xBurrell, R. Michael.
Politics, Oil, & the Western Mediterranean.
Sage.
Burrell, William P. *see* Burrell, William Patrick.
Burrell, William Patrick, 1865-
xBurrell, William P.
Twenty-Five Years History of the Grand
Fountain of the United Order of True
Reformers, 1881-1905. Negro U Pr.
Burrello, Leonard C.
xBurrello, Leonard C.

Leadership & Change in Special Education.
P-H.
Burri, C. *see* Burri, Caius.
Burri, Caius.
xBurri, C.
ed. The Caval Catheter. Springer-Verlag.
Burridge, Kenelm.
xBurridge, Kenelm.
Someone, No One: An Essay on Individuality.
Princeton U Pr.
Tangu Traditions: A Study of the Way of Life,
Mythology & Developing Experience of a
New Guinea People. Oxford U Pr.
Burridge, T. D. *see* Burridge, Trevor D.
Burridge, Trevor D.
xBurridge, T. D.
British Labour & Hitler's War. Transatlantic.
Burrin, Frank K. *see* Burrin, Frank Kleiser.
Burrin, Frank Kleiser, 1920-
xBurrin, Frank K.
Edward Charles Elliott, Educator. Purdue.
Burrington, Gillian. *see* Burrington, Gillian A.
Burrington, Gillian A.
xBurrington, Gillian.
How to Find Out About Statistics. Pergamon.
Burris-Meyer, Harold.
xBurris-Meyer, Harold.
Sound in the Theatre. Theatre Arts.
Theatres & Auditoriums. Krieger.
Burriss, Eli E. *see* Burriss, Eli Edward.
Burriss, Eli Edward.
xBurriss, Eli E.
Latin & Greek in Current Use. P-H.
Taboo, Magic, Spirits: A Study of Primitive
Elements in Roman Religion. Greenwood.
Burron, Arnold.
xBurron, Arnold.
Using Reading to Teach Subject Matter:
Fundamentals for Content Teachers. Merrill.
Burros, Marian. *see* Burros, Marian Fox.
Burros, Marian Fox.
xBurros, Marian.
Freeze with Ease. Macmillan.
Burroughs, Alan, 1897-1965
xBurroughs, Alan.
Art Criticism from a Laboratory. Greenwood.
Limners & Likenesses: Three Centuries of
American Painting. Russell.
Burroughs Corporation.
xBurroughs Corporation.
Digital Computer Principles. McGraw.
Burroughs, Edgar R. *see* Burroughs, Edgar Rice.
Burroughs, Edgar Rice.
xBurroughs, Edgar R.

Apache Devil. Ballantine.
Apache Devil. Buccaneer Bks.
At the Earth's Core. Ace Bks.
Back to the Stone Age. Ace Bks.
The Bandit of Hell's Bend. Charter Bks.
The Bandit of Hell's Bend. Gregg.
Cave Girl. Ace Bks.
The Cave Girl. Canaveral.
The Deputy Sheriff of Comanche County.
   Gregg.
Gods of Mars. Canaveral.
I Am a Barbarian. Ace Bks.
The Monster Men. Ace Bks.
Monster Men. Canaveral.
The Moon Maid. Ace Bks.
The Mucker. Ace Bks.
Pellucidar. Ace Bks.
The People That Time Forgot. Ace Bks.
Pirates of Venus. Canaveral.
The Rider. Ace Bks.
Swords of Mars. Ballantine.
Tarzan & the Ant Men. Ballantine.
Tarzan & the Golden Lion. Ballantine.
Tarzan & the Lost Empire. Ballantine.
Tarzan & the Madman. Canaveral.
Tarzan & the Tarzan Twins. Canaveral.
Tarzan of the Apes. Buccaneer Bks.
Tarzan the Invincible. Ballantine.
Tarzan the Terrible. Ballantine.
Tarzan the Untamed. Ballantine.
xBurroughs, Edgar Rice.
   Apache Devil. Gregg.
Burroughs, J. see Burroughs, John.
Burroughs, John, 1837-1921
xBurroughs, J.
   Intro. by Whitman: A Study. Scholarly.
xBurroughs, John.
   Literary Values, & Other Papers. Arno.
   ed. Songs of Nature. Arno.
   Songs of Nature. Folcroft.
   Whitman: A Study. Scholarly.
Burroughs, Polly.
xBurroughs, Polly.
   Exploring Martha's Vineyard. Chatham Pr.
   Guide to Martha's Vineyard. Globe Pequot.
Burroughs, Raymond D. see Burroughs, Raymond
   Darwin.
Burroughs, Raymond Darwin.
xBurroughs, Raymond D.
   ed. Natural History of the Lewis & Clark
      Expedition. Mich St U Pr.
Burroughs, William S., 1914-
xBurroughs, William S.
   Port of Saints. Blue Wind.
   Soft Machine. Grove.
Burrow, Gerard N.
xBurrow, Gerard N.
   Medical Complications During Pregnancy.
      Saunders.
   ed. Neonatal Thyroid Screening. Raven.
Burrow, J. A. see Burrow, John Anthony.
Burrow, John. see Burrow, John Anthony.
Burrow, John Anthony.
xBurrow, J. A.
   A Reading of Sir Gawain & the Green Knight.
      Routledge & Kegan.
xBurrow, John.
   English Verse 1300-1500. Longman.
Burrow, Martha G.
xBurrow, Martha G.
   Developing Women Managers: What Needs to
      Be Done?. Am Mgmt.
Burrow, Thomas.
xBurrow, Thomas.
   The Problem of Shwa in Sanskrit. Oxford U Pr.
Burrows, Benjamin.
xBurrows, Benjamin.
   Respiratory Insufficiency. Year Bk Med.
Burrows, Bernard.
xBurrows, Bernard.

ed. Federal Solutions to European Issues. St
   Martin.
Burrows, David J.
xBurrows, David J.
   Private Dealings; Modern American Writers in
      Search of Integrity. Inscape Corp.
Burrows, E. G. see Burrows, Edwin Gladding.
Burrows, Edwin Gladding, 1917-
xBurrows, E. G.
   The Crossings: Poems. Humble Hills.
Burrows, George M. see Burrows, George Man.
Burrows, George Man, 1771-1846
xBurrows, George M.
   Commentaries on the Causes, Forms,
      Symptoms & Treatment, Moral & Medical, of
      Insanity. Arno.
Burrows, Hal D., 1921-
xBurrows, Hal D.
   The Value Mandate of Emotional Nature. H D
      Burrows.
Burrows, John, 1919-
xBurrows, L. J.
   The Middle School: High Road or Dead End.
      Biblio Dist.
Burrows, L. J. see Burrows, John.
Burrows, Millar, 1889-
xBurrows, Millar.
   Burrows on the Dead Sea Scrolls. Baker Bk.
   Diligently Compared: The Revised Standard
      Version & the King James Version of the Old
      Testament. Allenson.
Burrows, Thomas D.
xBurrows, Thomas D.
   Television Production: Disciplines &
      Techniques. Wm C Brown.
Burrows, William, 1908-
xBurrows, William.
   Textbook of Microbiology. Saunders.
Burrup, Percy E., 1910-
xBurrup, Percy E.
   Teacher & the Public School System. Har-Row.
Burrus, Thomas L.
xBurrus, Thomas L.
   Earth in Crisis: An Introduction to the Earth
      Sciences. Mosby.
Bursell. see Bursell, E.
Bursell, E.
xBursell.
   Introduction to Insect Physiology. Acad Pr.
Bursk, Christopher.
xBursk, Christopher.
   Standing Watch. HM.
Bursk, Edward C. see Bursk, Edward Collins.
Bursk, Edward Collins.
xBursk, Edward C.
   Advanced Cases in Marketing Management.
      P-H.
   ed. Cases in Marketing Management. P-H.
Bursnall, W. see Bursnall, William J.
Bursnall, William J.
xBursnall, W.
   ed. Planning Challenges of the 70's in the
      Public Domain. Am Astronaut.
Burstall, Sara A. see Burstall, Sara Annie.
Burstall, Sara Annie, 1859-1939
xBurstall, Sara A.
   Education of Girls in the United States. Arno.
Burstein, Chaya. see Burstein, Chaya M.
Burstein, Chaya M.
xBurstein, Chaya.
   illus. Rifka Bangs the Teakettle. HarBraceJ.
   Rifka Grows up. Hebrew Pub.
xBurstein, Chaya M.
   illus. A First Jewish Holiday Cookbook.
      Hebrew Pub.
Burstein, Harvey.
xBurstein, Harvey.
   Hotel Security Management. Praeger.
Burstein, Herman, 1918-
xBurstein, Herman.

Questions & Answers About Tape Recording.
   TAB Bks.
Burstein, Milton B.
xBurstein, Milton B.
   What You Should Know About Acquisitions &
      Mergers. Oceana.
   What You Should Know About Selling &
      Salesmanship. Oceana.
Burstein, Stanley M. see Burstein, Stanley Mayer.
Burstein, Stanley Mayer.
xBurstein, Stanley M.
   Outpost of Hellenism: The Emergence of
      Heraclea on the Black Sea. U of Cal Pr.
Burstyn, Joan N.
xBurstyn, Joan N.
   Song Cycle. Woods Hole.
Burt, Bruce C.
xBurt, Bruce C.
   Compiled by Calculators: Readings from the
      Arithmetic Teacher & the Mathematics
      Teacher. NCTM.
Burt, Cyril. see Burt, Cyril Lodowic.
Burt, Cyril L. see Burt, Cyril Lodowic.
Burt, Cyril Lodowic.
xBurt, Cyril.
   The Subnormal Mind. Oxford U Pr.
xBurt, Cyril L.
   ed. How the Mind Works. Arno.
Burt, D. R. see Burt, D. R. R.
Burt, D. R. R.
xBurt, D. R.
   Platyhelminthes & Parasitism: An Introduction
      to Parasitology. Elsevier.
Burt, E. A. see Burt, Edward Angus.
Burt, Edward Angus, 1859-1939
xBurt, E. A.
   Thelephoraceae of North America. Hafner.
Burt, F. Allen. see Burt, Frank Allen.
Burt, Frank Allen, 1885-
xBurt, F. Allen.
   Story of Mount Washington. U Pr of New Eng.
Burt, Jesse. see Burt, Jesse Clifton.
Burt, Jesse Clifton.
xBurt, Jesse.
   Indians of the Southeast - Then & Now.
      Abingdon.
Burt, Marina K.
xBurt, Marina K.
   From Deep to Surface Structure: An
      Introduction to Transformational Syntax.
      Har-Row.
Burt, Maxwell S. see Burt, Maxwell Struthers.
Burt, Maxwell Struthers, 1882-1954
xBurt, Maxwell S.
   Delectable Mountains. Scholarly.
   Other Side. Arno.
Burt, Nathaniel, 1913-
xBurt, Nathaniel.
   The Perennial Philadelphians: The Anatomy of
      an American Aristocracy. Arno.
Burt, Olive (Woolley), 1894-
xBurt, Olive W.
   Ghost Towns of the West. Messner.
   Horse in America. John Day.
   I Am an American. John Day.
   Mary McLeod Bethune: Girl Devoted to Her
      People. Bobbs.
   Negroes in the Early West. Messner.
   Old America Comes Alive: Our Restored
      Villages from Colonial Williamsburg to
      Dodge City. John Day.
   Rescued! America's Endangered Wildlife on
      the Comeback Trail. Messner.
Burt, Olive W. see Burt, Olive (Woolley).
Burt, Robert.
xBurt, Robert A.

Standards Relating to Abuse & Neglect.
    Ballinger Pub.
Taking Care of Strangers: The Rule of Law in
    Doctor-Patient Relations. Free Pr.
Burt, Robert A. *see* Burt, Robert.
Burt, William H. *see* Burt, William Henry.
Burt, William Henry, 1903-
    xBurt, William H.
    ed. Antarctic Pinnipedia. Am Geophysical.
Burtis, C. E. *see* Burtis, C. Edward.
Burtis, C. Edward.
    xBurtis, C. E.
    The Fountain of Youth. Arc Bks.
Burton, Alexis L., 1922-
    xBurton, Alexis L.
    ed. Cinematographic Techniques in Biology &
        Medicine. Acad Pr.
Burton, Alice E. *see* Burton, Elizabeth.
Burton, Anthony.
    xBurton, Anthony.
    Green Bag Travellers: Britain's First Tourists.
        Transatlantic.
    Josiah Wedgwood. Stein & Day.
Burton, Arthur, 1914-
    xBurton, Arthur.
    Modern Humanistic Psychotherapy.
        Jossey-Bass.
    ed. Operational Theories of Personality.
        Brunner-Mazel.
Burton, D. *see* Burton, Dee.
Burton, D. M. *see* Burton, David M.
Burton, David M.
    xBurton, D. M.
    Abstract & Linear Algebra. A-W.
    First Course in Rings & Ideals. A-W.
    Introduction to Modern Abstract Algebra.
        A-W.
Burton, Dee.
    xBurton, D.
    Joy of Quitting: How to Help Young People
        Stop Smoking. Macmillan.
    xBurton, Dee.
    The Joy of Quitting: How to Help Young
        People Stop Smoking. Macmillan.
Burton, Dwight L.
    xBurton, Dwight L.
    Teaching English Today. HM.
Burton, E. Milby.
    xBurton, E. Milby.
    Charleston Furniture, 1700-1825. U of SC Pr.
    Siege of Charleston, 1861-1865. U of SC Pr.
Burton, Elizabeth, 1908-
    xBurton, Alice E.
    Miss Carter & the Ifrit. Arno.
    xBurton, Elizabeth.
    The Pageant of Early Tudor England. Scribner.
    Pageant of Early Victorian England. Scribner.
    Pageant of Elizabethan England. Scribner.
Burton, Elsie C. *see* Burton, Elsie Carter.
Burton, Elsie Carter.
    xBurton, Elsie C.
    Physical Activities for the Developing Child. C
        C Thomas.
Burton, Frank.
    xBurton, Frank.
    The Politics of Legitimacy: Struggles in a
        Belfast Community. Routledge & Kegan.
Burton, Gabrielle.
    xBurton, Gabrielle.
    I'm Running Away from Home, but I'm Not
        Allowed to Cross the Street: A Primer on
        Women's Liberation. Know Inc.
Burton, George G.
    xBurton, George G.
    ed. Respiratory Care: A Guide to Clinical
        Practice. Lippincott.
Burton, Gwendolyn R.
    xBurton, Gwendolyn R.

Microbiology for the Health Sciences.
    Lippincott.
Burton, H. K. *see* Burton, Henrietta (Kolshorn).
Burton, Harry E. *see* Burton, Harry Edwin.
Burton, Harry Edwin, 1868-1945
    xBurton, Harry E.
    Discovery of the Ancient World. Arno.
Burton, Henrietta (Kolshorn), 1893-
    xBurton, H. K.
    The Re-Establishment of the Indians in Their
        Pueblo Life Through the Revival of Their
        Traditional Crafts. Kraus Repr.
    xBurton, Henrietta K.
    The Re-Establishment of the Indians in Their
        Pueblo Life Through the Revival of Their
        Traditional Crafts: A Study in Home
        Extension Education. AMS Pr.
Burton, Henrietta K. *see* Burton, Henrietta (Kolshorn).
Burton, Hester.
    xBurton, Hester.
    Riders of the Storm. T Y Crowell.
Burton, Ian.
    xBurton, Ian.
    The Environment As Hazard. Oxford U Pr.
    ed. Readings in Resource Management &
        Conservation. U of Chicago Pr.
Burton, J. D. *see* Burton, James Dennis.
Burton, J. L. *see* Burton, John Lloyd.
Burton, J. M. *see* Burton, John Marvin.
Burton, James Dennis.
    xBurton, J. D.
    ed. Estuarine Chemistry. Acad Pr.
Burton, Jerome.
    xBurton, Jerome.
    The Fatherhood Formula. Major Bks.
Burton, Jimalee.
    xBurton, Jimalee.
    Indian Heritage, Indian Pride: Stories That
        Touched My Life. U of Okla Pr.
Burton, John, 1745 or 6-1806
    xBurton, John.
    Lectures on Female Education & Manners.
        Hacker.
    The Oxford Book of Insects. Oxford U Pr.
Burton, John. *see* Burton, John Wear.
Burton, John H. *see* Burton, John Hill.
Burton, John Hill, 1809-1881
    xBurton, John H.
    Life & Correspondence of David Hume. B
        Franklin.
    Life & Correspondence of David Hume. Intl
        Pubns Serv.
    Narratives from Criminal Trials in Scotland.
        AMS Pr.
Burton, John Lloyd.
    xBurton, J. L.
    Aids to Medicine for Nurses. Churchill.
    Aids to Postgraduate Medicine. Churchill.
    Aids to Undergraduate Medicine. Churchill.
    Essentials of Dermatology. Churchill.
Burton, John Marvin, 1890-1918
    xBurton, J. M.
    Honore De Balzac & His Figures of Speech.
        Kraus Repr.
Burton, John W. *see* Burton, John Wear.
Burton, John Wear, 1915-
    xBurton, John.
    Deviance, Terrorism & War: The Process of
        Solving Unsolved Social & Political Problems.
        St Martin.
    xBurton, John W.
    Systems, States, Diplomacy & Rules.
        Cambridge U Pr.
    World Society. Cambridge U Pr.
Burton, June. *see* Burton, June K.
Burton, June K.
    xBurton, June.

Napoleon & Clio: Historical Writing, Teaching,
    & Thinking During the First Empire.
    Carolina Acad Pr.
Burton, Katherine (Kurz), 1890-
    xBurton, Katherine K.
    In No Strange Land. Arno.
Burton, Katherine K. *see* Burton, Katherine (Kurz).
Burton, Lindy.
    xBurton, Lindy.
    ed. Care of the Child Facing Death. Routledge
        & Kegan.
    The Family Life of Sick Children: A Study of
        Families Coping with Chronic Childhood
        Disease. Routledge & Kegan.
Burton, Malcolm S.
    xBurton, Malcolm S.
    Applied Metallurgy for Engineers. McGraw.
Burton, Marilee R. *see* Burton, Marilee Robin.
Burton, Marilee Robin.
    xBurton, Marilee R.
    The Elephant's Nest: Four Wordless Stories.
        Har-Row.
Burton, Maurice.
    xBurton, Maurice.
    Deserts. Transatlantic.
    The Family of Animals. Arco.
    Just Like an Animal. Scribner.
    The Life of Insects. Silver.
Burton, Nelson.
    xBurton, Nelson.
    Bowling. Atheneum.
Burton, Philip, 1904-
    xBurton, Philip.
    Early Doors: My Life & the Theatre. Dial.
    The Green Isle. Dial.
Burton, Philip E.
    xBurton, Philip E.
    ed. A Dictionary of Microcomputing. Garland
        Pub.
Burton, Philip W. *see* Burton, Philip Ward.
Burton, Philip Ward, 1910-
    xBurton, Philip W.
    Advertising Copywriting. Grid Pub.
    Advertising Fundamentals. Grid Pub.
Burton, Rebecca.
    xBurton, Rebecca.
    By Love Divided. Nordon Pubns.
Burton, Richard, 1861-1940
    xBurton, Richard.
    Literary Likings. Arno.
    Little Essays in Literature & Life. Arno.
Burton, Richard F. *see* Burton, Richard Francis.
Burton, Richard Francis.
    xBurton, Richard F.
    Nile Basin. Da Capo.
    The Sotadic Zone. Longwood Pr.
    Two Trips to Gorilla Land & the Cataracts of
        the Congo. Johnson Repr.
Burton, Robert, 1577-1640
    xBurton, Robert.
    Anatomy of Melancholy. AMS Pr.
    The Anatomy of Melancholy. Rowman.
    Anatomy of Melancholy. Ungar.
    Animal Senses. Taplinger.
    The Carnivores of Europe. David & Charles.
    The Life & Death of Whales. Universe.
    Ponds: Their Wildlife & Upkeep. David &
        Charles.
    Seals. McGraw.
Burton, Samuel H. *see* Burton, Samuel Holroyd.
Burton, Samuel Holroyd.
    xBurton, Samuel H.
    The Criticism of Poetry. Folcroft.
Burton, Theodore M.
    xBurton, Theodore M.
    God's Greatest Gift. Deseret Bk.
Burton, Thomas L.
    xBurton, Thomas L.
    Experiments in Recreation Research. Rowman.
Burton, Virginia L. *see* Burton, Virginia Lee.

Burton, Virginia Lee, 1909-
  xBurton, Virginia L.
    illus. Life Story. HM.
    Little House. HM.
    Maybelle, the Cable Car. HM.
Burton, Warren, 1800-1866
  xBurton, Warren.
    District School As It Was. Arno.
    The District School As It Was. F E Peters.
Burton, William, 1863-
  xBurton, William.
    A History & Description of English Porcelain.
      Charles River Bks.
Burton, William. see Burton, William Lester.
Burton, William L. see Burton, William Lester.
Burton, William Lester.
  xBurton, William.
    Descriptive Bibliography of Civil War
      Manuscripts in Illinois. Ill St Hist Soc.
  xBurton, William L.
    ed. Descriptive Bibliography of Civil War
      Manuscripts in Illinois. Northwestern U Pr.
Burton, Wilma.
  xBurton, Wilma.
    Without a Man in the House. Good News.
Burton-Bradley, B. G.
  xBurton-Bradley, B. G.
    Stone Age Crisis: A Psychiatric Appraisal.
      Vanderbilt U Pr.
Burtt, Everett. see Burtt, Everett Johnson.
Burtt, Everett Johnson.
  xBurtt, Everett.
    Labor in the American Economy. St Martin.
Burtt, F.
  xBurtt, F.
    Locomotives of the London, Brighton & South
      Coast Railway, 1839-1903. Intl Pubns Serv.
Burtt, George, 1914-
  xBurtt, George.
    The Barter Way to Beat Inflation. Everest Hse.
    Psychographics in Personal Growth. Vector
      Counsel.
    Stop Crying at Your Own Movies: How to
      Solve Personal Problems & Open Your Life
      to Its Full Potential Using the Vector
      Method. Nelson-Hall.
    Vector Handbook. Vector Counsel.
Burtt, Harold E. see Burtt, Harold Ernest.
Burtt, Harold Ernest, 1890-
  xBurtt, Harold E.
    Principles of Employment Psychology.
      Greenwood.
Bury, J. P. T. see Bury, John Patrick Tuer.
Bury, John P. see Bury, John Patrick Tuer.
Bury, John Patrick Tuer.
  xBury, J. P. T.
    France 1814-1940. A S Barnes.
  xBury, John P.
    Gambetta - the National Defence: A
      Republican Dictatorship in France.
      Greenwood.
Bury, Karl V., 1935-
  xBury, Karl V.
    Statistical Models in Applied Science. Wiley.
Buryn, Ed.
  xBuryn, Ed.
    Vagabonding in Europe & North Africa.
      Bookworks.
    Vagabonding in Europe & North Africa.
      Random.
Busacker, Robert G.
  xBusacker, Robert G.
    Finite Graphs & Networks: An Introduction
      with Applications. McGraw.
Busby, F. M.
  xBusby, F. M.

All These Earths. Berkley Pub.
    The Long View: The Final Volume in the Saga
      of Rissa. Berkley Pub.
Buscaglia, Leo F.
  xBuscaglia, Leo F.
    Love. C B Slack.
Busch, Briton C. see Busch, Briton Cooper.
Busch, Briton Cooper.
  xBusch, Briton C.
    Britain & the Persian Gulf, 1894-1914. U of
      Cal Pr.
    Mudros to Lausanne: Britain's Frontier in West
      Asia, 1918-1923. State U NY Pr.
Busch, Daryle H. see Busch, Daryle Hadley.
Busch, Daryle Hadley.
  xBusch, Daryle H.
    Chemistry. Allyn.
Busch, Francis X. see Busch, Francis Xavier.
Busch, Francis Xavier, 1879-
  xBusch, Francis X.
    Law & Tactics in Jury Trials. Michie.
    Prisoners at the Bar: An Account of the Trials
      of the William Haywood Case, the
      Sacco-Vanzetti Case, the Loeb-Leopold Case,
      the Bruno Hauptmann Case. Arno.
Busch, Frederick, 1941-
  xBusch, Frederick.
    Domestic Particulars: A Family Chronicle.
      New Directions.
    The Mutual Friend. Har-Row.
    Rounds. FS&G.
Busch, Fritz, 1890-1951
  xBusch, Fritz.
    Pages from a Musician's Life. Greenwood.
    Pages from a Musician's Life. Scholarly.
Busch, H. see Busch, Harald.
Busch, Harald.
  xBusch, H.
    Pre-Romanesque Art. Macmillan.
Busch, Harris.
  xBusch, Harris.
    Histones & Other Nuclear Proteins. Acad Pr.
Busch, Niven.
  xBusch, Niven.
    Duel in the Sun. PB.
Busch, Phyllis. see Busch, Phyllis S.
Busch, Phyllis S.
  xBusch, Phyllis.
    Cactus in the Desert. T Y Crowell.
  xBusch, Phyllis S.
    Living Things That Poison, Itch, & Sting.
      Walker & Co.
Busch, Wilhelm.
  xBusch, Wilhelm.
    Bushel of Merrythoughts. Dover.
Buschor, E. see Buschor, Ernst.
Buschor, Ernst, 1886-1961
  xBuschor, E.
    Greek Vase Painting. Longwood Pr.
  xBuschor, Ernst.
    Greek Vase Painting. Ares.
    Greek Vase-Painting. Hacker.
    On the Meaning of Greek Statues. U of Mass
      Pr.
Busemann, Herbert, 1905-
  xBusemann, Herbert.
    Geometry of Geodesics. Acad Pr.
    Projective Geometry & Projective Metrics.
      Acad Pr.
Busenbark, Robert.
  xBusenbark, Robert.
    Guide to Mynahs. TFH Pubns.
Busev, A. I.
  xBusev, A. I.
    Analytical Chemistry of Molybdenum. Halsted
      Pr.
Busey, James L.
  xBusey, James L.

Latin America: Political Institutions &
      Processes. Phila Bk Co.
Bush, Barbara.
  xBush, Barbara.
    I Can't Stand Cindy, Lord. Zondervan.
Bush, Bernard J.
  xBush, Bernard J.
    Living in His Love: Essays on Prayer &
      Christian Living. Affirmation.
Bush, Chilton R. see Bush, Chilton Rowlette.
Bush, Chilton Rowlette, 1896-
  xBush, Chilton R.
    Editorial Thinking & Writing: A Textbook with
      Exercises. Greenwood.
    Editorial Thinking & Writing: A Textbook with
      Exercises. Scholarly.
Bush, Christopher, 1885-
  xBush, Christopher.
    Case of the Deadly Diamonds. Macmillan.
Bush, Clifford L.
  xBush, Clifford L.
    Strategies for Reading in the Elementary
      School. Macmillan.
Bush, Douglas, 1896-
  xBush, Douglas.
    Engaged & Disengaged. Harvard U Pr.
    Pagan Myth & Christian Tradition in English
      Poetry. Am Philos.
    Prefaces to Renaissance Literature. Harvard U
      Pr.
    Prefaces to Renaissance Literature. Norton.
    Renaissance & English Humanism. U of
      Toronto Pr.
Bush, Grace. see Bush, Grace A.
Bush, Grace A.
  xBush, Grace.
    The Mathematics of Business. SRA.
Bush, I. E. see Bush, Ian Elcock.
Bush, Ian Elcock.
  xBush, I. E.
    The Chromatography of Steroids. Pergamon.
Bush, Jim.
  xBush, Jim.
    Inside Track. Contemp Bks.
Bush, John C., 1938-
  xBush, John C.
    Disaster Response: A Handbook for Church
      Action. Herald Pr.
Bush, John S.
  xBush, John W.
    Venetia Redeemed: Franco-Italian Relations,
      1864-1866. Syracuse U Pr.
Bush, John W. see Bush, John S.
Bush, Loren S.
  xBush, Loren S.
    Introduction to Fire Science. Glencoe.
Bush, M. L.
  xBush, M. L.
    The Government Policy of Protector Somerset.
      McGill-Queens U Pr.
Bush, M L.
  xBush, M. L.
    Renaissance, Reformation & the Outer World,
      1450-1660. Humanities.
Bush, Sargent.
  xBush, Sargent.
    The Writings of Thomas Hooker: Spiritual
      Adventure in Two Worlds. U of Wis Pr.
Bush, Vannevar, 1890-
  xBush, Vannevar.
    Endless Horizons. Arno.
Bush, Virginia.
  xBush, Virginia.
    The Colossal Sculpture of the Cinquecento.
      Garland Pub.
Bush, Wilma J. see Bush, Wilma Jo.
Bush, Wilma Jo.
  xBush, Wilma J.

Aids to Psycholinguistic Teaching. Merrill.

Bush-Brown, Albert.
xBush-Brown, Albert.
Louis Sullivan. Braziller.

Bush-Brown, James.
xBush-Brown, James.
America's Garden Book. Scribner.

Bushee, Frederick A. *see* Bushee, Frederick Alexander.
Bushee, Frederick Alexander, 1872-
xBushee, Frederick A.
Ethnic Factors in the Population of Boston.
Arno.
Bushell, Raymond.
xBushell, Raymond.
Introduction to Netsuke. C E Tuttle.
Bushkin, Frederic L.
xBushkin, Frederic L.
Postgastrectomy Syndromes. Saunders.
Bushman, John C. *see* Bushman, John Conrad.
Bushman, John Conrad.
xBushman, John C.
ed. Read & Write. Har-Row.
Bushman, Richard L.
xBushman, Richard L.
ed. The Great Awakening: Documents on the
Revival of Religion, 1740-1745. Norton.
ed. The Great Awakening: Documents on the
Revival of Religion, 1740-1745. U of NC Pr.
Bushnell, Catharine.
xBushnell, Catharine.
Raggedy Ann & Andy in the Tunnel of Lost
Toys. Bobbs.
Bushnell, D. D. *see* Bushnell, Donald D.
Bushnell, David, 1923-
xBushnell, David.
Eduardo Santos & the Good Neighbor,
1938-1942. U Presses Fla.
Bushnell, Donald D.
xBushnell, D. D.
Computer in American Education. Krieger.
Bushnell, Horace, 1802-1876
xBushnell, Horace.
Nature & the Supernatural As Together
Constituting the One System of God. AMS
Pr.
Women's Suffrage: The Reform Against
Nature. Zenger Pub.
Bushnell, Howard.
xBushnell, Howard.
Maria Malibran: A Biography of the Singer. Pa
St U Pr.
Bushnell, John. *see* Bushnell, John Alden.
Bushnell, John Alden, 1933-
xBushnell, John.
Australian Company Mergers 1946-1959. Intl
Schol Bk Serv.
Bushnell, Paul P. *see* Bushnell, Paul Palmer.
Bushnell, Paul Palmer, 1900-
xBushnell, Paul P.
An Analytical Contrast of Oral with Written
English. AMS Pr.
Bushong, Stewart. *see* Bushong, Stewart C.
Bushong, Stewart C.
xBushong, Stewart.
Radiologic Science for Technologists: Physics,
Biology & Protection. Mosby.
xBushong, Stewart C.
Radiologic Science for Technologists: Physics,
Biology & Protection. Mosby.
Busi, Frederick.
xBusi, Frederick.
The Transformations of Godot. U Pr of Ky.
Business Communications. *see* Business Communications
Co.
Business Communications Co.
xBCC Staff.

jt. auth. From Recession to Recovery:
Proceedings. BCC.
xBusiness Communications.
ed. Analytical Instrumentation: Growth
Markets. BCC.
ed. Biomass: How? What? Where?. BCC.
ed. Distributed Processing. BCC.
ed. Energy Conservation & Home
Improvements. BCC.
ed. Fermentation Products: Processes & New
Developments. BCC.
ed. Industrial Coatings: New Trends, Markets.
BCC.
ed. Inks & Printing Chemicals: New
Developments. BCC.
ed. Low Energy & Radiation Cures. BCC.
ed. New Consumer Product Electronics:
Growth Trends. BCC.
ed. New Directions in Robots for
Manufacturing. BCC.
ed. New Markets for Small Business
Computers. BCC.
ed. Polishes & Waxes: Shifts & Changes. BCC.
ed. Roadway Maintenance. BCC.
ed. Word Processing Markets, Where? Why?,
G-050. BCC.
xBusiness Communications Co.
Advanced Metal Working Technologies,
GB-052. BCC.
ed. Bulk Vitamins & Their Major Markets.
BCC.
Convenience Foods & Microwave, GA-044:
Directions. BCC.
ed. Foods Under Glass, GA-046. BCC.
ed. Home Do-It Yourself Market. BCC.
ed. Materials Competition in Residential
Construction, GB-056. BCC.
ed. New Trends in Food Retailing, GA-045.
BCC.
ed. Retail Fast Foods, GA-038: Business
Opportunities. BCC.
ed. Special Beverage Study. BCC.
ed. Specialty Agricultural Chemicals, GA-035r.
BCC.
ed. Water Purification Processes, GB-053: A
Technical Market Analysis. BCC.
xBusiness Communications Co. Food Conference,
New York City, March 19, 1975.
What Can Business Do to Help Solve the
World Food Problem?: Proceedings. BCC.
xBusiness Communications Co., Inc.
The Changing Gas Industry: Good &
Bad-E-019. BCC.
xBusiness Communications Staff.
Alternate Energy Sources, E-007: A Study.
BCC.
Electric Power from the Wind: The Ways of
the Future, E-026. BCC.
Energy Conservation & Home Improvement,
E-024. BCC.
Future for Coal As Fuel & Chemical, E-004.
BCC.
Business Communications Co. Food Conference, New
York City, March 19, 1975. *see* Business
Communications Co.
Business Communications Co., Inc. *see* Business
Communications Co.
Business Communications Staff. *see* Business
Communications Co.
**Business Management Clinic for Loggers, Spokane,
Washington, 1977.**
xBusiness Management Clinic for Loggers,
Spokane, Washington, April 1977.
Business Management for Loggers:
Proceedings. Miller Freeman.
Business Systems Research Group. *see* Business Systems
Research Group, Chicago, Ill.
Business Systems Research Group, Chicago, Ill.
xBusiness Systems Research Group.

Small Business Computer Evaluation Program.
Busn Systems Res.
Business Taxation Symposium. *see* Symposium on
Business Taxation, Wayne State University, 1964.
Business Week. *see* The Business Week (New York).
The Business Week (New York).
xBusiness Week.
The Decline of U. S. Power: & What We Can
Do About It. HM.
xBusiness Week Staff.
Business Week Diary & Business Travel
Planner, 1977. McGraw.
Business Week Staff. *see* The Business Week (New
York).
Buske, Dorothea.
xBuske, Dorothea.
The Last Romantic. St Martin.
Buskirk, Richard. *see* Buskirk, Richard Hobart.
Buskirk, Richard H. *see* Buskirk, Richard Hobart.
Buskirk, Richard Hobart, 1927-
xBuskirk, Richard.
Cases & Readings in Marketing. Par Inc.
Retailing. McGraw.
xBuskirk, Richard H.
Handbook of Managerial Tactics. CBI Pub.
Modern Management & Machiavelli. CBI Pub.
Busnar, Gene.
xBusnar, Gene.
It's Rock 'n' Roll. Messner.
Busoni, Ferruccio. *see* Busoni, Ferruccio Benvenuto.
Busoni, Ferruccio B. *see* Busoni, Ferruccio Benvenuto.
Busoni, Ferruccio Benvenuto, 1866-1924
xBusoni, Ferruccio.
Letters to His Wife. Da Capo.
xBusoni, Ferruccio B.
The Essence of Music & Other Papers.
Hyperion Conn.
Buss, A. R. *see* Buss, Allan R.
Buss, Allan R.
xBuss, A. R.
Individual Differences: Traits & Factors.
Halsted Pr.
xBuss, Allan R.
A Dialectical Psychology. Halsted Pr.
ed. Psychology in Social Context. Halsted Pr.
Buss, Arnold H. *see* Buss, Arnold Herbert.
Buss, Arnold Herbert, 1924-
xBuss, Arnold H.
Self-Consciousness & Social Anxiety. W H
Freeman.
ed. Theories of Schizophrenia. Lieber-Atherton.
Buss, Claude A. *see* Buss, Claude Albert.
Buss, Claude Albert.
xBuss, Claude A.
The People's Republic of China. Van Nos
Reinhold.
Buss, William G.
xBuss, William G.
Standards Relating to Schools and Education.
Ballinger Pub.
Bussagli, Mario.
xBussagli, Mario.
Central Asian Painting. Rizzoli Intl.
jt. auth. Oriental Architecture. Abrams.
Bussard, Paul. *see* Bussard, Paul C.
Bussard, Paul C., 1904-
xBussard, Paul.
Life & Death in the Philippines. Vantage.
Bussard, R W.
xBussard, R. W.
Fundamentals of Nuclear Flight. McGraw.
Busse, Ewald W.
xBusse, Ewald W.
ed. Handbook of Geriatric Psychiatry. Van Nos
Reinhold.
Busse, John.
xBusse, John.
Mrs. Montagu, Queen of the Blues. Folcroft.
Busse, Thomas V.
xBusse, Thomas V.

Activities in Child & Adolescent Development.
Har-Row.
Bussell, F. W. see Bussell, Frederick William.
Bussell, Frederick William, 1862-1944
xBussell, F. W.
Religious Thought & Heresy in the Middle
Ages. Kennikat.
Bussey, Lynn E., 1920-
xBussey, Lynn E.
The Economic Analysis of Industrial Projects.
P-H.
Bussing, Irvin, 1898-
xBussing, Irvin.
Public Utility Regulation & the So-Called
Sliding Scale: A Study of the Sliding Scale
As a Means of Encouraging & Rewarding
Efficiency in the Management of Regulated
Monopolies. AMS Pr.
Bussink, Tine.
xBussink, Tine.
ed. Sourcebook on Population 1970-1976.
Population Ref.
Bustin, Edouard.
xBustin, Edouard.
Lunda Under Belgian Rule: The Politics of
Ethnicity. Harvard U Pr.
Busvine, J. R. see Busvine, James Ronald.
Busvine, James Ronald.
xBusvine, J. R.
Insects, Hygiene & History. Humanities.
Buswell, James O. see Buswell, James Oliver.
Buswell, James Oliver, 1895-
xBuswell, James O.
Systematic Theology of the Christian Religion.
Zondervan.
Butcher, Alice M. see Butcher, Alice Mary (Brandreth).
Butcher, Alice Mary (Brandreth), Lady.
xButcher, Alice M.
Memories of George Meredith. R West.
Butcher, Devereux.
xButcher, Devereux.
Exploring Our National Parks & Monuments.
Gambit.
Butcher, Earl O. see Butcher, Earl Orlo.
Butcher, Earl Orlo.
xButcher, Earl O.
Concepts of Neuroanatomy. Hafner.
Butcher, H. H. see Butcher, Harold John.
Butcher, Harold John.
xButcher, H. H.
ed. Contemporary Problems in Higher
Education: An Account of Research.
Crane-Russak Co.
Butcher, James N. see Butcher, James Neal.
Butcher, James Neal, 1933-
xButcher, James N.
Abnormal Psychology. Brooks-Cole.
A Handbook of Cross-National MMPI
Research. U of Minn Pr.
Butcher, Larry L.
xButcher, Larry L.
ed. Cholinergic-Monoaminergic Interactions in
the Brain. Acad Pr.
Butcher, Lee.
xButcher, Lee.
The Condominium Book: A Guide to Getting
the Most for Your Money. Dow Jones-Irwin.
Butcher, S. H. see Butcher, Samuel Henry.
Butcher, Samuel H. see Butcher, Samuel Henry.
Butcher, Samuel Henry, 1850-1910
xButcher, S. H.
Some Aspects of the Greek Genius. R West.
xButcher, Samuel H.
Some Aspects of the Greek Genius. Kennikat.
Butchvarov, Panayot. see Butchvarov, Panayot Krustev.
Butchvarov, Panayot Krustev.
xButchvarov, Panayot.

Being Qua Being: A Theory of Identity,
Existence & Predication. Ind U Pr.
Buteau, June D.
xButeau, June D.
Nonprint Materials on Communication: An
Annotated Directory of Select Films,
Videotapes, Videocassettes, Simulations &
Games. Scarecrow.
Butkov, E. see Butkov, Eugene.
Butkov, Eugene.
xButkov, E.
Mathematical Physics. A-W.
Butland, G. J. see Butland, Gilbert J.
Butland, Gilbert J.
xButland, G. J.
Latin America: A Regional Geography. Halsted
Pr.
Butler, A. see Butler, Alban.
Butler, Alan. see Butler, Alan J.
Butler, Alan J., 1912-
xButler, Alan.
The Law Enforcement Process. Alfred Pub.
Butler, Alban.
xButler, A.
Lives of the Saints. Chr Classics.
Butler, Albert.
xButler, Albert.
Mariposa Gold. Bouregy.
Butler, Alfred J. see Butler, Alfred Joshua.
Butler, Alfred Joshua, 1850-1936
xButler, Alfred J.
The Arab Conquest of Egypt & the Last Thirty
Years of the Roman Dominion. AMS Pr.
The Arab Conquest of Egypt & the Last Thirty
Years of the Roman Dominion. Oxford U Pr.
Butler, Anne.
xButler, Anne.
The Arco Encyclopedia of Embroidery
Stitches. Arco.
Butler, Annie L. see Butler, Annie Louise.
Butler, Annie Louise.
xButler, Annie L.
Play As Development. Merrill.
Butler, Beverly.
xButler, Beverly.
Captive Thunder. Dodd.
Light a Single Candle. Archway.
Light a Single Candle. PB.
My Sister's Keeper. Dodd.
Butler, Bill.
xButler, Bill.
Dictionary of the Tarot. Schocken.
Butler, Charles, d. 1647
xButler, Charles.
Principles of Musik, in Singing & Setting. Da
Capo.
The Principles of Musik, in Singing & Setting.
Walter J Johnson.
Butler, David. see Butler, David E.
Butler, David E.
xButler, David.
ed. Referendums: A Comparative Study of
Practice & Theory. Am Enterprise.
xButler, David E.
British General Election of 1955. Biblio Dist.
British General Election of 1959. Biblio Dist.
British General Election of 1966. St Martin.
British General Election of 1970. St Martin.
Butler, David F.
xButler, David F.
Simplified Furniture Design & Construction. A
S Barnes.
Butler, David J. see Butler, David Jonathan.
Butler, David Jonathan.
xButler, David J.
Cat's Whiskers on Saturday. Carolrhoda Bks.
Butler, Dorothy, 1925-
xButler, Dorothy.
Cushla & Her Books. Horn Bk.
Butler, E. M. see Butler, Eliza Marian.

Butler, Edgar W.
xButler, Edgar W.
Traditional Marriage & Emerging Alternatives.
Har-Row.
Butler, Eliza M. see Butler, Eliza Marian.
Butler, Eliza Marian, 1885-
xButler, E. M.
The Fortunes of Faust. Cambridge U Pr.
Goethe & Byron. Folcroft.
The Myth of the Magus. Cambridge U Pr.
xButler, Eliza M.
The Fortunes of Faust. Hyperion Conn.
The Myth of the Magus. Hyperion Conn.
Rainer Maria Rilke. Octagon.
Butler, Eugenia.
xButler, Eugenia.
An Auto-Instructional Text in Correct Writing.
Heath.
Butler, F. Coit.
xButler, F. Coit.
Instructional Systems Development for
Vocational & Technical Training. Educ Tech
Pubns.
Butler, Francelia. see Butler, Francelia (McWilliams).
Butler, Francelia (McWilliams), 1913-
xButler, Francelia.
Strange Critical Fortunes of Shakespeare's
Timon of Athens. Iowa St U Pr.
Butler, Francine.
xButler, Francine.
Biofeedback: A Survey of the Literature. IFI
Plenum.
Butler, G. see Butler, George.
Butler, G. C. see Butler, Gordon Cecil.
Butler, G. D. see Butler, George Daniel.
Butler, George.
xButler, G.
Corrosion & Its Prevention in Waters. Krieger.
Butler, George Daniel.
xButler, G. D.
Introduction to Community Recreation.
McGraw.
Butler, Gordon Cecil, 1913-
xButler, G. C.
ed. Principles of Ecotoxicology. Wiley.
Butler, Grant C.
xButler, Grant C.
Bali to Bahrein. Devin.
Butler, Gwendoline.
xButler, Gwendoline.
The Red Staircase. Coward.
Butler, H. E. see Butler, Harold Edgeworth.
Butler, Hal.
xButler, Hall.
Inferno!: Fourteen Fiery Tragedies of Our
Time. Contemp Bks.
Butler, Hall. see Butler, Hal.
Butler, Harold E. see Butler, Harold Edgeworth.
Butler, Harold Edgeworth, 1878-
xButler, H. E.
Post-Augustan Poetry from Seneca to Juvenal.
Century Bookbindery.
xButler, Harold E.
Post-Augustan Poetry from Seneca to Juvenal.
Arno.
Butler, Ivan.
xButler, Ivan.
Choosing a Play for Your Amateur Group.
Taplinger.
The Cinema of Roman Polanski. A S Barnes.
Horror in the Cinema. A S Barnes.
Religion in the Cinema. A S Barnes.
Butler, J. A. see Butler, John Alfred Valentine.
Butler, J. Donald. see Butler, James Donald.
Butler, J. R. see Butler, James Ramsay Montagu.
Butler, James Donald, 1908-
xButler, J. Donald.

Four Philosophies & Their Practice in
Education & Religion. Har-Row.
Butler, James H.
xButler, James H.
Theatre & Drama of Greece and Rome.
Har-Row.
Butler, James N. *see* Butler, James Newton.
Butler, James Newton.
xButler, James N.
Problems for Introductory University
Chemistry: With Complete Solutions. A-W.
Butler, James R. M. *see* Butler, James Ramsay Montagu.
Butler, James Ramsay Montagu, 1889-
xButler, J. R.
Passing of the Great Reform Bill. Kelley.
xButler, James R. M.
Passing of the Great Reform Bill. Biblio Dist.
Butler, Jeffrey.
xButler, Jeffrey.
ed. Boston University Papers in African
History. Holmes & Meier.
Butler, Joan.
xButler, Joan.
Ballet for Boys & Girls. P-H.
Butler, John. *see* Butler, Jon.
Butler, John Alfred Valentine, 1899-
xButler, J. A.
Modern Biology & Its Human Implications.
Crane-Russak Co.
Butler, John R.
xButler, John.
Family Doctors & Public Policy: A Study of
Manpower Distribution. Routledge & Kegan.
Butler, Jon.
xButler, John.
Power, Authority, & the Origins of American
Denominational Order: The English Churches
in the Delaware Valley, 1680-1730. Am
Philos.
Butler, Joseph T.
xButler, Joseph T.
Van Cortlandt Manor. Sleepy Hollow.
Butler, Josephine E. *see* Butler, Josephine Elizabeth
Grey.
Butler, Josephine Elizabeth Grey, 1828-1906
xButler, Josephine E.
Personal Reminiscences of a Great Crusade.
Hyperion Conn.
Butler, Joyce.
xButler, Joyce K.
Pages from a Journal. Mercer Hse.
Butler, Joyce K. *see* Butler, Joyce.
Butler, Kathleen T. *see* Butler, Kathleen Theresa Blake.
Butler, Kathleen Theresa Blake, 1883-1950
xButler, Kathleen T.
History of French Literature. Russell.
Butler, L. J. *see* Butler, Lance St. John.
Butler, L. R. *see* Butler, L. R. P.
Butler, L. R. P.
xButler, L. R.
ed. The Analysis of Biological Materials:
Proceedings of a Conference Held in
Pretoria, South Africa, October 1977.
Pergamon.
Butler, Lance St. John.
xButler, L. J.
Thomas Hardy. Cambridge U Pr.
Butler, Marie.
xButler, Marie.
Ron's Story: A Legacy of Love. Good News.
Butler, Marilyn.
xButler, Marilyn.
Maria Edgeworth: A Literary Biography.
Oxford U Pr.
Peacock Displayed: A Satirist in His Context.
Routledge & Kegan.
Butler, Matilda.
xButler, Matilda.

Women & the Mass Media: Sourcebook for
Research & Action. Human Sci Pr.
Butler, Nicholas M. *see* Butler, Nicholas Murray.
Butler, Nicholas Murray, 1862-1947
xButler, Nicholas M.
ed. Education in the United States. Johnson
Repr.
The Effect of the War of 1812 Upon the
Consolidation of the Union. Johnson Repr.
Meaning of Education: Contributions to a
Philosophy of Education. Arno.
True & False Democracy. Arno.
Butler, Octavia. *see* Butler, Octavia E.
Butler, Octavia E.
xButler, Octavia.
Survivor. NAL.
xButler, Octavia E.
Kindred. Doubleday.
Patternmaster. Avon.
Patternmaster. Doubleday.
Butler, Orton C.
xButler, Orton C.
An Introductory Soils Laboratory Handbook.
Exposition.
Butler, Phyllis. *see* Butler, Phyllis Filiberti.
Butler, Phyllis F. *see* Butler, Phyllis Filiberti.
Butler, Phyllis Filiberti.
xButler, Phyllis.
Everywoman's Guide to Political Awareness.
Les Femmes Pub.
xButler, Phyllis F.
The Valley of Santa Clara: Historic Buildings
1792-1920. Jr League San Jose.
Butler, Pierce, 1873-
xButler, Pierce.
Materials for the Life of Shakespeare. AMS Pr.
Butler, Richard, 1925-
xButler, Richard.
Lift off at Satan. St Martin.
xButler, Richard O.
Religious Vocation: An Unnecessary Mystery.
Greenwood.
Butler, Richard O. *see* Butler, Richard.
Butler, Rick.
xButler, Rick.
The Trudeau Decade. Doubleday.
Butler, Robert N.
xButler, Robert N.
Aging & Mental Health: Positive Psychosocial
Approaches. Mosby.
Butler, Ruth (Lapham).
xButler, Ruth L.
ed. Guide to the Hispanic American Historical
Review, 1918-1945. Kraus Repr.
Butler, Ruth L. *see* Butler, Ruth (Lapham).
Butler, Samuel, 1835-1902
xButler, Samuel.
Authoress of the Odyssey. U of Chicago Pr.
Butler, Vera M. *see* Butler, Vera Minnie.
Butler, Vera Minnie.
xButler, Vera M.
Education As Revealed by New England
Newspapers Prior to 1850. Arno.
Butler, W. E. *see* Butler, William Elliott.
Butler, William, 1929-
xButler, William.
Butterfly Revolution. Ballantine.
Butler, William Elliott.
xButler, W. E.
The Soviet Legal System: Selected
Contemporary Legislation & Documents.
Oceana.
Butler, William F. *see* Butler, William Francis Thomas.
Butler, William Francis Thomas, 1869-1930
xButler, William F.
Lombard Communes: A History of the
Republics of North Italy. Greenwood.
Lombard Communes: A History of the
Republics of North Italy. Haskell.
Butlin, R. A. *see* Butlin, Robin A.

Butlin, Robin A.
xButlin, R. A.
ed. The Development of the Irish Town.
Rowman.
Butrick, Richard.
xButrick, Richard.
Deduction & Analysis. U Pr of Amer.
Butscher, Edward.
xButscher, Edward.
Adelaide Crapsey. Twayne.
Butt, John.
xButt, John.
Industrial Archaeology in the British Isles.
B&N.
Writers & Politics in Modern Spain. Holmes &
Meier.
Butt, John. *see* Butt, John Everett.
Butt, John E. *see* Butt, John Everett.
Butt, John Everett.
xButt, John.
The Mid-Eighteenth Century. Oxford U Pr.
Pope's Poetical Manuscripts. Folcroft.
xButt, John E.
The Augustan Age. Greenwood.
Buttaci, Sal St. John.
xButtaci, Salvatore S.
ed. Reflections of the Inward Silence. New
Worlds.
ed. Visions of the Enchanted Spirit. New
Worlds.
ed. Whispers of the Unchained Heart. New
Worlds.
Buttaci, Salvatore S. *see* Buttaci, Sal St. John.
Buttel, Frederick H.
xButtel, Frederick H.
ed. The Rural Sociology of the Advanced
Societies: Critical Perspectives. Allanheld.
Butterfield, Herbert, 1900-
xButterfield, Herbert.
Christianity & History. Scribner.
Herbert Butterfield: Writings on Christianity &
History. Oxford U Pr.
The Peace Tactics of Napoleon, 1806-1808.
Octagon.
Butterfield, Jim.
xButterfield, Jim.
The First Book of KIM. Hayden.
Butterfield, S. M. *see* Butterfield, Sherri M.
Butterfield, Sherri M.
xButterfield, S. M.
The Wonderful World of Soccer. Goodyear.
The Wonderful World of Soccer. G&D.
Butterfield, William H. *see* Butterfield, William Henry.
Butterfield, William Henry, 1910-
xButterfield, William H.
Letters That Build Bank Business. Interstate.
Butterick, George F.
xButterick, George F.
A Guide to the Maximus Poems of Charles
Olson. U of Cal Pr.
Reading Genesis by the Light of a Comet.
Ziesing Bros.
Butters, J. Keith. *see* Butters, John Keith.
Butters, John Keith.
xButters, J. Keith.
Case Problems in Finance. Irwin.
Butterweck, Joseph S. *see* Butterweck, Joseph Seibert.
Butterweck, Joseph Seibert, 1891-
xButterweck, Joseph S.
The Problem of Teaching High School Pupils
How to Study. AMS Pr.
Butterworth, Bill. *see* Butterworth, William Richard.
Butterworth, Byron E.
xButterworth, Byron E.
Strategies for Short-Term Testing for
Mutagens-Carcinogens. CRC Pr.
Butterworth, Charles C., 1894-1957
xButterworth, Charles C.

Literary Lineage of the King James Bible, 1340-1611. Octagon.

Butterworth, Douglas, 1930-
  xButterworth, Douglas S.
    The People of Buena Ventura: Relocation of Slum Dwellers in Post-Revolutionary Cuba. U of Ill Pr.

Butterworth, Douglas S. see Butterworth, Douglas.

Butterworth, E. see Butterworth, Eric.

Butterworth, Eric.
  xButterworth, E.
    Social Welfare in Modern Britain. Watts.
  xButterworth, Eric.
    Discover the Power Within You. Har-Row.
    In the Flow of Life. Har-Row.
    Life Is for Loving. Har-Row.

Butterworth, Hezekiah.
  xButterworth, Hezekiah.
    Story of the Hymns & Tunes. Scholarly.

Butterworth, Oliver.
  xButterworth, Oliver.
    The Narrow Passage. Little.
    The Trouble with Jenny's Ear. Little.

Butterworth, W. E. see Butterworth, William E.

Butterworth, William. see Butterworth, William E.

Butterworth, William E.
  xButterworth, W. E.
    Leroy & the Old Man. Schol Bk Serv.
    Under the Influence. Schol Bk Serv.
    Wheel of a Fast Car. G&D.
  xButterworth, William.
    Next Stop, Earth. Walker & Co.

Butterworth, William Richard, 1942-
  xButterworth, Bill.
    Materials Handling in Farm Production: A Guide to the Control of Handling Costs on the Farm. Halsted Pr.

Buttimer, Anne.
  xButtimer, Anne.
    Society & Milieu in the French Geographic Tradition. Assn Am Geographers.
    Values in Geography. Assn Am Geographers.

Button, K. J. see Button, Kenneth John.

Button, Kenneth. see Button, Kenneth John.

Button, Kenneth John.
  xButton, K. J.
    The Economics of Urban Freight Transport. Holmes & Meier.
  xButton, Kenneth.
    Case Studies in Regional Economics. Heinemann Ed.

Buttrey, D. N. see Buttrey, Douglas Norton.

Buttrey, Douglas Norton, 1918-
  xButtrey, D. N.
    ed. Plastics in Furniture. Intl Ideas.

Buttrey, Theodore V.
  xButtrey, Theodore V.
    ed. Coinage of the Americas. Am Numismatic.
    Coinage of the Americas. Interbk Inc.

Buttrick, George A.
  xButtrick, George A.
    The Parables of Jesus. Baker Bk.

Butts, Allison.
  xButts, Allison.
    ed. Silver, Economics, Metallurgy, & Use. Krieger.

Butts, Carrol M.
  xButts, Carrol M.
    How to Arrange & Rehearse Football Band Shows. P-H.

Butts, David P.
  xButts, David P.
    Children & Science: The Process of Teaching & Learning. P-H.
    Teaching Science in the Elementary School. Free Pr.

Butts, Robert F. see Butts, Robert Freeman.

Butts, Robert Freeman, 1910-
  xButts, Robert F.

American Education in International Development. Arno.

Butwell, Richard. see Butwell, Richard A.

Butwell, Richard A.
  xButwell, Richard.
    U Nu of Burma. Stanford U Pr.

Butzer, Karl. see Butzer, Karl W.

Butzer, Karl W.
  xButzer, Karl.
    Environment & Archeology: An Ecological Approach to Prehistory. Aldine Pub.
  xButzer, Karl W.
    Desert & River in Nubia: Geomorphology & Prehistoric Environments at the Aswan Reservoir. U of Wis Pr.
    Dimensions of Human Geography: Essays on Some Familiar & Neglected Themes. U Chicago Dept Geog.
    Geomorphology from the Earth. Har-Row.

Butzer, Paul L. see Butzer, Paul Leo.

Butzer, Paul Leo.
  xButzer, Paul L.
    Fourier Analysis & Approximation. Acad Pr.

Buultjens, Ralph.
  xBuultjens, Ralph.
    The Decline of Democracy: Essays on an Endangered Political Species. Orbis Bks.

Buxbaum, David C.
  xBuxbaum, David C.
    ed. Chinese Family Law & Social Change in Historical & Comparative Perspective. U of Wash Pr.

Buxbaum, Robert.
  xBuxbaum, Robert C.
    Sports for Life: Fitness Training, Injury Prevention & Nutrition. Beacon Pr.

Buxbaum, Robert C. see Buxbaum, Robert.

Buxton, Charles R. see Buxton, Charles Roden.

Buxton, Charles Roden.
  xBuxton, Charles R.
    ed. Towards a Lasting Settlement. Garland Pub.

Buxton, Claude E.
  xBuxton, Claude E.
    Adolescents in School. Yale U Pr.

Buxton, Graham.
  xBuxton, Graham.
    Effective Marketing Logistics: The Analysis Planning & Control of Distribution Operations. Holmes & Meier.

Buxton, H. J. see Buxton, Harry John Wilmot.

Buxton, Harry John Wilmot.
  xBuxton, H. J.
    German, Flemish & Dutch Painting. Longwood Pr.

Buxton, I. L. see Buxton, Ian Lyon.

Buxton, Ian Lyon.
  xBuxton, I. L.
    Cargo Access Equipment for Merchant Ships. Gulf Pub.

Buxton, Jean. see Buxton, Jean Carlile.

Buxton, Jean Carlile, 1921-
  xBuxton, Jean.
    Religion & Healing in Mandari. Oxford U Pr.

Buxton, John, 1912-
  xBuxton, John.
    The Grecian Taste: The Literature in the Age of Neo-Classicism 1740-1820. B&N.

Buxton, L. H. see Buxton, Leonard Halford Dudley.

Buxton, Leonard Halford Dudley.
  xBuxton, L. H.
    Primitive Labour. Kennikat.

Buxton, N. K.
  xBuxton, N. K.
    British Employment Statistics: A Guide to Sources & Methods. Biblio Dist.

Buyukmihci, Hope S. see Buyukmihci, Hope Sawyer.

Buyukmihci, Hope Sawyer.
  xBuyukmihci, Hope S.

Unexpected Treasure. M Evans.

Buzzell, R. D. see Buzzell, Robert Dow.

Buzzell, Robert Dow.
  xBuzzell, R. D.
    Marketing Research & Information Systems: Text & Cases. McGraw.

Byars. see Byars, Lloyd L.

Byars, Betsy. see Byars, Betsy Cromer.

Byars, Betsy C. see Byars, Betsy Cromer.

Byars, Betsy Cromer.
  xByars, Betsy.
    After the Goat Man. Avon.
    The Cartoonist. Dell.
    Good-Bye, Chicken Little. Har-Row.
    The Night Swimmers. Delacorte.
    Rama, the Gypsy Cat. Avon.
    The Summer of the Swans. Avon.
    Trouble River. Avon.
    The TV Kid. Schol Bk Serv.
  xByars, Betsy C.
    After the Goat Man. Viking Pr.
    The Cartoonist. Viking Pr.
    Go & Hush the Baby. Viking Pr.
    Summer of the Swans. Viking Pr.
    Trouble River. Viking Pr.
    The TV Kid. Viking Pr.

Byars, Lloyd L.
  xByars.
    Readings & Cases in Personnel Management. Dryden Pr.

Byars, Robert S.
  xByars, Robert S.
    ed. Quantitative Social Science Research on Latin America. U of Ill Pr.

Byatt, A. S. see Byatt, Antonia Susan (Drabble).

Byatt, Antonia Susan (Drabble), 1936-
  xByatt, A. S.
    Wordsworth & Coleridge in Their Time. Crane-Russak Co.

Bybee, Rodger W.
  xBybee, Rodger W.
    Personalizing Science Teaching. Natl Sci Tchrs.

Bycer, Bernard B.
  xBycer, Bernard B.
    Flowcharting: Programming, Software Design & Computer Problem Solving. Wiley.

Bychowski, Gustav, 1895-
  xBychowski, Gustav.
    Evil in Man: Anatomy of Hate & Violence. Grune.

Byde, Alan, 1928-
  xByde, Alan.
    Canoe Building in Glass-Reinforced Plastic. Transatlantic.

Byers, David M.
  xByers, David M.
    Evangelists to the Poor: A Catholic Ministry in Appalachia. Glenmary Res Ctr.
    Readings for Town & Country Church Workers: An Annotated Bibliography. Glenmary Res Ctr.

Byers, Horace R. see Byers, Horace Robert.

Byers, Horace Robert, 1906-
  xByers, Horace R.
    General Meteorology. McGraw.

Byers, Stephen.
  xByers, Stephen.
    Touchdown. Raintree Pubs.

Byers, Tracy.
  xByers, Tracy.
    Martha Berry, the Sunday Lady of Possum Trot. Gale.

Byers, William N. see Byers, William Newton.

Byers, William Newton.
  xByers, William N.
    Hand Book to the Gold Fields of Nebraska & Kansas. Arno.

Byfield, Barbara N. see Byfield, Barbara Ninde.

Byfield, Barbara Ninde.
  xByfield, Barbara N.

A Parcel of Their Fortunes. Doubleday.
Bygrave, Mike.
  xBygrave, Mike.
    Rock. Watts.
Byington, Cyrus, 1793-1868
  xByington, Cyrus.
    A Dictionary of the Choctaw Language.
      Scholarly.
Byington, Margaret. *see* Byington, Margaret Frances.
Byington, Margaret F. *see* Byington, Margaret Frances.
Byington, Margaret Frances, 1877-1952
  xByington, Margaret.
    Homestead: The Households of a Milltown. U
      Ctr Intl St.
  xByington, Margaret F.
    Homestead: The Households of a Mill Town.
      Arno.
Bykerk, Cornelius.
  xBykerk, Cornelius.
    Simplified Multiple Offense for Winning
      Basketball. P-H.
Bylander, E. G.
  xBylander, E. G.
    Electronic Displays. McGraw.
    Materials for Semiconductor Functions.
      Hayden.
Bylinsky, Gene.
  xBylinsky, Gene.
    Mood Control. Scribner.
Byng, Edward J. *see* Byng, Edward John.
Byng, Edward John, 1894-
  xByng, Edward J.
    The World of the Arabs. Arno.
Bynner, Witter, 1881-1968
  xBynner, Witter.
    Journey with Genius: Recollections &
      Reflections Concerning D. H. Lawrence.
      Octagon.
  xBynner, Wytter.
    Prose Pieces. FS&G.
Bynner, Wytter. *see* Bynner, Witter.
Byram, H. M. *see* Byram, Harold Moore.
Byram, Harold M. *see* Byram, Harold Moore.
Byram, Harold Moore, 1902-
  xByram, H. M.
    Some Problems in the Provision of Professional
      Education for College Teachers. AMS Pr.
  xByram, Harold M.
    Guidance in Agricultural Education. Interstate.
Byrd, D. H. *see* Byrd, David Harold.
Byrd, David Harold, 1900-
  xByrd, D. H.
    I'm an Endangered Species: The
      Autobiography of a Free Enterpriser.
      Pacesetter Pr.
Byrd, Don, 1944-
  xByrd, Don.
    Charles Olson's Maximus. U of Ill Pr.
Byrd, Elizabeth.
  xByrd, Elizabeth.
    The Famished Land. Avon.
Byrd, Max.
  xByrd, Max.
    Daniel Defoe: A Collection of Critical Essays.
      P-H.
    London Transformed: Images of the City in the
      Eighteenth Century. Yale U Pr.
Byrd, O. *see* Byrd, Oliver Erasmus.
Byrd, Oliver Erasmus.
  xByrd, O.
    Medical Readings on Drug Abuse. A-W.
Byrd, P. F. *see* Byrd, Paul F.
Byrd, Paul F.
  xByrd, P. F.
    Handbook of Elliptic Integrals for Engineers &
      Scientists. Springer-Verlag.
Byrd, Richard E.
  xByrd, Richard E.
    A Guide to Personal Risk Taking. Am Mgmt.
Byrd, Richard E. *see* Byrd, Richard Evelyn.

Byrd, Richard Evelyn, 1888-1957
  xByrd, Richard E.
    Discovery: The Story of the Second Byrd
      Antarctic Expedition. Arno.
    Discovery: The Story of the Second Byrd
      Antarctic Expedition. Gale.
Byrd, Thomas L.
  xByrd, Thomas L.
    The Early Poetry of W. B. Yeats: The Poetic
      Quest. Kennikat.
Byrd, William.
  xByrd, William.
    Histories of the Dividing Line Betwixt Virginia
      & North Carolina. Peter Smith.
Byrde, Penelope.
  xByrde, Penelope.
    The Male Image: Men's Fashion in Britain
      1300-1970. Humanities.
Byres, T. J.
  xByres, T. J.
    ed. Foreign Resources & Economic
      Development: Symposium on the Report of
      the Pearson Commission. Biblio Dist.
Byrn, Edward W. *see* Byrn, Edward Wright.
Byrn, Edward Wright, 1849-1921
  xByrn, Edward W.
    Progress of Invention in the Nineteenth
      Century. Russell.
Byrne, David.
  xByrne, David.
    The Poverty of Education: A Study in the
      Politics of Opportunity. Rowman.
Byrne, Donn.
  xByrne, Donn.
    Messer Marco Polo. Bentley.
  xByrne, Donn B.
    Stories Without Women & a Few with Women.
      Arno.
Byrne, Donn. *see* Byrne, Donn Erwin.
Byrne, Donn B. *see* Byrne, Donn.
Byrne, Donn E. *see* Byrne, Donn Erwin.
Byrne, Donn Erwin.
  xByrne, Donn.
    An Introduction to Personality. P-H.
  xByrne, Donn E.
    The Attraction Paradigm. Acad Pr.
Byrne, Eileen M.
  xByrne, Eileen M.
    Women & Education. Methuen Inc.
Byrne, H. W. *see* Byrne, Herbert W.
Byrne, Herbert W., 1917-
  xByrne, H. W.
    Improving Church Education. Religious Educ.
Byrne, James. *see* Byrne, James E.
Byrne, James E.
  xByrne, James.
    Living in the Spirit: A Handbook on Catholic
      Charismatic Christianity. Paulist Pr.
Byrne, Lee, 1876-
  xByrne, Lee.
    Check List Materials for Public School Building
      Specifications, Covering the General
      Specifications. AMS Pr.
Byrne, R. F.
  xByrne, R. F.
    ed. Studies in Budgeting. Elsevier.
Byrne, Ralph.
  xByrne, Ralph.
    Out of the Mist. Branden.
Byrne, Richard H. *see* Byrne, Richard Hill.
Byrne, Richard Hill.
  xByrne, Richard H.
    Guidance: A Behavioral Approach. P-H.
Byrne, Robert, 1930-
  xByrne, Robert.

Byrne's Standard Book of Pool & Billiards.
    HarBraceJ.
    Memories of a Non-Jewish Childhood. Lyle
      Stuart.
    Strengthening School-Community Relations.
      Natl Assn Principals.
Byrne, Vincent.
  xByrne, Vincent.
    Miracles & Other Poems. Devin.
Byrnes, James F. *see* Byrnes, James Francis.
Byrnes, James Francis, 1879-1972
  xByrnes, James F.
    Speaking Frankly. Greenwood.
Byrnes, Robert F. *see* Byrnes, Robert Francis.
Byrnes, Robert Francis.
  xByrnes, Robert F.
    Soviet-American Academic Exchanges,
      1958-1975. Ind U Pr.
Byrns, John H.
  xByrns, John H.
    Europe's Hidden Flea Markets & Budget
      Antique Shops. Hastings.
Byron, Christopher.
  xByron, Christopher.
    Foreign Matter. Doubleday.
Byron, D. *see* Byron, David.
Byron, David.
  xByron, D.
    The Firearms Price Guide. Crown.
  xByron, David.
    The Firearms Price Guide. Crown.
Byron, F. W. *see* Byron, Frederick W.
Byron, Frederick W.
  xByron, F. W.
    Mathematics of Classical & Quantum Physics.
      A-W.
Byron, George G. *see* Byron, George Gordon Noel
  Byron.
Byron, George Gordon Noel Byron.
  xByron, George G.
    Byron. Folcroft.
    Byron & Greece. Folcroft.
    Fugitive Pieces. Folcroft.
    Fugitive Pieces. Haskell.
    The Ravenna Journal. Folcroft.
    Works. Octagon.
  xByron, Goerge G.
    Life Letters & Journals of Lord Byron.
      Scholarly.
  xByron, Noel.
    jt. auth. The Ravenna Journal. Folcroft.
Byron, Gilbert.
  xByron, Gilbert.
    Chesapeake Duke. Cornell Maritime.
Byron, Goerge G. *see* Byron, George Gordon Noel
  Byron.
Byron, May. *see* Byron, May Clarissa Gillington.
Byron, May C. *see* Byron, May Clarissa Gillington.
Byron, May Clarissa Gillington, d. 1936
  xByron, May.
    A Day with Nathaniel Hawthorne. Folcroft.
    A Day with Samuel Taylor Coleridge. Folcroft.
  xByron, May C.
    A Day with Nathaniel Hawthorne. Norwood
      Edns.
Byron, Noel. *see* Byron, George Gordon Noel Byron.
Byron, Stuart.
  xByron, Stuart.
    ed. The National Society of Film Critics on
      Movie Comedy. Penguin.
Byron, William J.
  xByron, William J.
    Toward Stewardship: An Interim Ethic of
      Poverty, Power & Pollution. Paulist Pr.
Bytheriver, Marylee.
  xBytheriver, Marylee.
    A Short Dictionary of Astrology. Har-Row.
Bywater, Ingram, 1840-1914
  xBywater, Ingram.

Contributions to the Textual Criticism of
Aristotle's Nicomachean Ethics. Arno.

Bywater, William G., 1940-
xBywater, William G.
Clive Bell's Eye. Wayne St U Pr.

C O S P A R, 11th Plenary Meeting, Tokyo, 1968. *see*
International Council of Scientific Unions. Committee
on Space Research, 11th Plenary Meeting, Tokyo,
1968.

C O S P A R, 12th Meeting, Prague, 1969. *see*
International Council of Scientific Unions. Committee
on Space Research, 12th Plenary Meeting, Prague,
1969.

C. S. Hammond & Co. *see* Hammond (C. S.) and
Company, Inc.

Cabaniss, Allen. *see* Cabaniss, James Allen.

Cabaniss, James Allen, 1911-
xCabaniss, Allen.
Liturgy & Literature: Selected Essays. U of Ala
Pr.

Cabanne, Pierre.
xCabanne, Pierre.
The Brothers Duchamp: Jacques Villon,
Raymond Duchamp-Villon, Marcel
Duchamp. NYGS.

Cabannes, Henri.
xCabannes, Henri.
Theoretical Magneto Fluid-Dynamics. Acad Pr.

Cabbell, Paul.
xCabbell, Paul.
God Bless Our Second Mortgage. Fed Legal
Pubns.

Cabeen, Richard M. *see* Cabeen, Richard McP.

Cabeen, Richard McP.
xCabeen, Richard M.
Standard Handbook of Stamp Collecting. T Y
Crowell.

Cabell, James B. *see* Cabell, James Branch.

Cabell, James Branch, 1879-1958
xCabell, James B.
Chivalry. Arno.
Domnei: A Comedy of Woman - Worship.
Scholarly.
The High Place: A Comedy of
Disenchantment. Dover.
Quiet, Please. U Presses Fla.

Cabell, Randolph W.
xCabell, Randolph W.
Problems in Basic Operations Research
Methods for Management. Krieger.

Cable, George W. *see* Cable, George Washington.

Cable, George Washington, 1844-1925
xCable, George W.
Bylow Hill. AMS Pr.
Bylow Hill. Scholarly.
The Cavalier. Norwood Edns.
Dr. Sevier. Mss Info.
Old Creole Days. Arno.
Old Creole Days. Mss Info.
Strange True Stories of Louisiana. Arno.
Strong Hearts. Arno.
Strong Hearts. Mss Info.

Cable, John R. *see* Cable, John Ray.

Cable, John Ray, 1891-
xCable, John R.
Bank of the State of Missouri. AMS Pr.

Cable, Paul.
xCable, Paul.
Bob Dylan: His Unreleased Recordings.
Schirmer Bks.

Cabot, Isabel.
xCabot, Isabel.
Come Summer, Come Love. Bouregy.

Cabot, James E. *see* Cabot, James Elliot.

Cabot, James Elliot, 1821-1903
xCabot, James E.
Memoir of Ralph Waldo Emerson. AMS Pr.

Cabot, Richard C. *see* Cabot, Richard Clarke.

Cabot, Richard Clarke, 1868-1939
xCabot, Richard C.

Social Work: Essays on the Meeting-Ground of
Doctor & Social Worker. Arno.
Social Work: Essays on the Meeting-Ground of
Doctor & Social Worker. Norwood Edns.

Cabot, Thomas D. *see* Cabot, Thomas Dudley.

Cabot, Thomas Dudley, 1897-
xCabot, Thomas D.
Beggar on Horseback: The Autobiography of
Thomas D. Cabot. Godine.

Cabral, Amilcar.
xCabral, Amilcar.
Revolution in Guinea: Selected Texts. Monthly
Rev.
Unity & Struggle: Speeches & Writings.
Monthly Rev.

Cabrera, Y. Arturo. *see* Cabrera, Ysidro Arturo.

Cabrera, Ysidro Arturo.
xCabrera, Y. Arturo.
Community College Conflict: Chicano Under
Fire. Sierra Pubns CO.

Caceres, C. A. *see* Caceres, Cesar A.

Caceres, Cesar A.
xCaceres, C. A.
ed. The Practice of Clinical Engineering. Acad
Pr.

Cada, Lawrence.
xCada, Lawrence.
Shaping the Coming Age of Religious Life.
Seabury.

Cadbury, Edward.
xCadbury, Edward.
Experiments in Industrial Organization. Arno.

Caddell, Robert M.
xCaddell, Robert M.
Deformation & Fracture of Solids. P-H.

Caddy, Eileen.
xCaddy, Eileen.
The Spirit of Findhorn. Har-Row.

Cade, C. Maxwell. *see* Cade, Cecil Maxwell.

Cade, Cecil Maxwell.
xCade, C. Maxwell.
Other Worlds Than Ours. Taplinger.

Cadell, Elizabeth.
xCadell, Elizabeth.
The Cuckoo in Spring. Queens Hse.
The Friendly Air. Morrow.
Game in Diamonds. Morrow.
The Marrying Kind. G K Hall.
The Marrying Kind. Morrow.
Parson's House. G K Hall.
The Past Tense of Love. Zebra.
Return Match. Morrow.
Return Match. G K Hall.
The Round Dozen. G K Hall.
The Round Dozen. Morrow.

Cadieux, Charles L.
xCadieux, Charles L.
Goose Hunting. Stone Wall Pr.

Cadiou, Yves.
xCadiou, Yves.
Modern Firearms. Morrow.

Caditz, J. *see* Caditz, Judith.

Caditz, Judith.
xCaditz, J.
White Liberals in Transition. Halsted Pr.

Cadkin, Alan V.
xCadkin, Alan V.
Clinical Atlas of Gray Scale Ultrasonography
in Obstetrics. C C Thomas.

Cadle, Richard D.
xCadle, Richard D.
The Measurement of Airborne Particles. Wiley.

Cadmus, Bradford.
xCadmus, Bradford.
Operational Auditing Handbook. Inst Inter
Aud.

Cadogan, George.
xCadogan, George.

Cadogan's Crimea. Atheneum.

Cadogan, Gerald.
xCadogan, Gerald.
Palaces of Minoan Crete. Methuen Inc.

Cadoret. *see* Cadoret, Remi J.

Cadoret, Remi J.
xCadoret.
Psychiatry in Primary Care. Mosby.

Cadow, Harry W.
xCadow, Harry W.
Punched-Card Data Processing. SRA.

Cadwallader, S. *see* Cadwallader, Sharon.

Cadwallader, Sharon.
xCadwallader, S.
Whole Earth Cook Book. Bantam.
xCadwallader, Sharon.
Cooking Adventures for Kids. HM.
Whole Earth Cookbook. HM.
Whole Earth Cookbook 2. HM.

Cadwell, James H. *see* Cadwell, James Henry.

Cadwell, James Henry.
xCadwell, James H.
Topics in Recreational Mathematics.
Cambridge U Pr.

Cady. *see* Cady, Lee D.

Cady, Edwin H. *see* Cady, Edwin Harrison.

Cady, Edwin Harrison.
xCady, Edwin H.
Gentleman in America: A Literary Study in
American Culture. Greenwood.
Stephen Crane. Coll & U Pr.
Stephen Crane. Twayne.
Stephen Crane. Twayne.

Cady, Jack, 1932-
xCady, Jack.
The Burning & Other Stories. U of Iowa Pr.

Cady, John F.
xCady, John F.
Restricted Advertising & Competition: The
Case of Retail Drugs. Am Enterprise.

Cady, John F. *see* Cady, John Frank.

Cady, John Frank, 1901-
xCady, John F.
Foreign Intervention in the Rio De La Plata
1838-50: A Study of French, British, &
American Policy in Relation to the Dictator
Juan Manuel Rosas. AMS Pr.
History of Modern Burma. Cornell U Pr.
Southeast Asia: Its Historical Development.
McGraw.

Cady, Lee D., 1927-
xCady.
Computer Techniques in Cardiology. Dekker.

Cady, Wallace M. *see* Cady, Wallace Martin.

Cady, Wallace Martin, 1912-
xCady, Wallace M.
Regional Tectonic Synthesis of Northwestern
New England & Adjacent Quebec. Geol Soc.

Cadzow, James A.
xCadzow, James A.
Discrete Time & Computer Control Systems.
P-H.

Caemmerer, H. Paul. *see* Caemmerer, Hans Paul.

Caemmerer, Hans Paul, 1884-1962
xCaemmerer, H. Paul.
Life of Pierre Charles l'Enfant. Da Capo.

Caen, Herb. *see* Caen, Herbert Eugene.

Caen, Herbert Eugene.
xCaen, Herb.
The Cable Car & the Dragon. Doubleday.
One Man's San Francisco. Comstock Edns.

Caffin, Charles H. *see* Caffin, Charles Henry.

Caffin, Charles Henry, 1854-1918
xCaffin, Charles H.
The Story of American Painting: The Evolution
of Painting in America from Colonial Times
to the Present. Johnson Repr.
Story of Spanish Painting. AMS Pr.

Caffrey, Dorothy C. *see* Caffrey, Dorothy Cruikshank.

Caffrey, Dorothy Cruikshank.
  xCaffrey, Dorothy C.
    Songs for Autumn Singing. Douglas-West.
Caffrey, Kate.
  xCaffrey, Kate.
    The Mayflower. Stein & Day.
Cagan, Carl.
  xCagan, Carl.
    Data Management Systems. Wiley.
Cagan, Phillip.
  xCagan, Phillip.
    The Channels of Monetary Effects on Interest
      Rates. Natl Bur Econ Res.
    Determinants & Effects of Changes in the
      Stock of Money, 1875-1960. Natl Bur Econ
      Res.
    The Hydra-Headed Monster: The Problem of
      Inflation in the United States. Am Enterprise.
Cage, John.
  xCage, John.
    Silence: Lectures & Writings. Columbia U Pr.
Cagle, Malcolm W.
  xCagle, Malcolm W.
    Naval Aviation Guide. Naval Inst Pr.
Cagnone, Nanni.
  xCagnone, Nanni.
    What's Hecuba to Him or He to Hecuba?.
      Oolp Pr.
Cahagnet, Louis A. see Cahagnet, Louis Alphonse.
Cahagnet, Louis Alphonse, 1809-1885
  xCahagnet, Louis A.
    The Celestial Telegraph: Or,Secrets of the Life
      to Come Revealed Through Magnetism....
      Arno.
Cahalan, Don.
  xCahalan, Don.
    Problem Drinking Among American Men. Coll
      & U Pr.
    Problem Drinking Among American Men.
      Rutgers Ctr Alcohol.
Cahall, Raymond D. see Cahall, Raymond Du Bois.
Cahall, Raymond Du Bois, 1884-
  xCahall, Raymond D.
    Sovereign Council of New France: A Study in
      Canadian Constitutional History. AMS Pr.
Cahan, Abraham, 1860-1951
  xCahan, Abraham.
    Education of Abraham Cahan. Jewish Pubn.
    The White Terror & the Red: A Novel of
      Revolutionary Russia. Arno.
Cahill, James. see Cahill, James Francis.
Cahill, James Francis.
  xCahill, James.
    The Art of Southern Sung China. Arno.
    Hills Beyond a River: Chinese Painting of the
      Yuan Dynasty, 1279-1368. Weatherhill.
    Parting at the Shore: Chinese Painting of the
      Early & Middle Ming Dynasty, 1368-1580.
      Weatherhill.
Cahill, Kevin. see Cahill, Kevin M.
Cahill, Kevin M.
  xCahill, Kevin.
    Medical Advice for the Traveler. Popular Lib.
Cahill, Susan.
  xCahill, Susan.
    Earth Angels. Popular Lib.
    A Literary Guide to Ireland. Scribner.
Cahn. see Cahn, Walter.
Cahn, Ann F. see Cahn, Ann Foote.
Cahn, Ann Foote.
  xCahn, Ann F.
    ed. Women in the U. S. Labor Force. Praeger.
Cahn, Edmond. see Cahn, Edmond Nathaniel.
Cahn, Edmond N. see Cahn, Edmond Nathaniel.
Cahn, Edmond Nathaniel.
  xCahn, Edmond.
    ed. Supreme Court & Supreme Law. S&S.
  xCahn, Edmond N.

Confronting Injustice: The Edmond Cahn
      Reader. Arno.
    The Predicament of Democratic Man.
      Greenwood.
    ed. Supreme Court & Supreme Law.
      Greenwood.
Cahn, Frances, 1907-
  xCahn, Frances.
    Federal Employees in War & Peace: Selection,
      Placement, & Removal. Greenwood.
Cahn, Rhoda.
  xCahn, Rhoda.
    No Time for School, No Time for Play: The
      Story of Child Labor in America. Messner.
Cahn, Sammy.
  xCahn, Sammy.
    I Should Care: The Sammy Cahn Story. Arbor
      Hse.
Cahn, Steven M.
  xCahn, Steven M.
    ed. Classics of Western Philosophy. Hackett
      Pub.
    Education & the Democratic Ideal.
      Nelson-Hall.
    Fate, Logic & Time. Yale U Pr.
Cahn, Walter.
  xCahn.
    Romanesque Sculpture in American
      Collections. B Franklin.
  xCahn, Walter.
    Masterpieces: Chapters on the History of an
      Idea. Princeton U Pr.
Cahoon, Herbert.
  xCahoon, Herbert.
    American Literary Autographs from
      Washington Irving to Henry James. Pierpont
      Morgan.
Cahoon, Owen W, 1937
  xCahoon, Owen W.
    A Teacher's Guide to Cognitive Tasks for
      Preschool. Brigham.
Caianiello, E. R. see Caianiello, Eduardo R.
Caianiello, Eduardo R., 1921-
  xCaianiello, E. R.
    Combinatorics & Renormalization in Quantum
      Field Theory. Benjamin-Cummings.
Caicedo, Dorothy.
  xCaicedo, Dorothy M.
    These Are the Lists of My Despairs. Philos
      Lib.
Caicedo, Dorothy M. see Caicedo, Dorothy.
Caiden, Gerald E.
  xCaiden, Gerald E.
    Public Employment Compulsory Arbitration in
      Australia. U of Mich Inst Labor.
Caiden, Naomi.
  xCaiden, Naomi.
    Planning & Budgeting in Poor Countries.
      Transaction Bks.
    Planning & Budgeting in Poor Countries.
      Wiley.
Caidin, Martin, 1927-
  xCaidin, Martin.
    Fork-Tailed Devil: P-38. Ballantine.
    Operation Nuke. Arbor Hse.
    The Saga of Iron Annie. Doubleday.
Caiger, George.
  xCaiger, George.
    ed. Australian Way of Life. Arno.
Cailleux, Andre, 1907-
  xCailleux, Andre.
    Anatomy of the Earth. McGraw.
Cailliet, Emile, 1894-
  xCailliet, Emile.
    Clue to Pascal. Kennikat.
Cailliet, Rene.
  xCailliet, Rene.

Foot & Ankle Pain. Davis Co.
    Low Back Pain Syndrome. Davis Co.
    Neck & Arm Pain. Davis Co.
Caillois, Roger, 1913-
  xCaillois, Roger.
    Man & the Sacred. Greenwood.
    Man, Play, & Games. Free Pr.
    Man, Play, & Games. Schocken.
Cain, Albert C.
  xCain, Albert C.
    ed. Survivors of Suicide. C C Thomas.
Cain, Andrew W.
  xCain, Andrew W.
    History of Lumpkin County for the First
      Hundred Years, 1832-1932. Reprint.
Cain, Errol Le. see Le Cain, Errol.
Cain, James M. see Cain, James Mallahan.
Cain, James Mallahan, 1892-1977
  xCain, James M.
    The Butterfly. Random.
    Love's Lovely Counterfeit. Random.
    The Postman Always Rings Twice. Random.
Cain, Marvin R.
  xCain, Marvin R.
    Lincoln's Attorney General: Edward Bates of
      Missouri. U of Mo Pr.
Cain, Mary. see Cain, Mary (Clough).
Cain, Mary (Clough), 1892-
  xCain, Mary.
    The Historical Development of State Normal
      Schools for White Teachers in Maryland.
      AMS Pr.
Cain, Maureen E. see Cain, Maureen Elizabeth.
Cain, Maureen Elizabeth.
  xCain, Maureen E.
    Society & the Policeman's Role. Routledge &
      Kegan.
Cain, Michael S. see Cain, Michael Scott.
Cain, Michael Scott.
  xCain, Michael S.
    Co-Op Publishing Handbook. Dustbooks.
Cain, Mike.
  xCain, Mike.
    Autos of Interest. M Cain.
Cain, Paul.
  xCain, Paul.
    Fast One. Popular Lib.
    Fast One: A Novel. S Ill U Pr.
Cain, Sandra E.
  xCain, Sandra G.
    Sciencing: An Involvement Approach to
      Elementary Science Methods. Merrill.
Cain, Sandra G. see Cain, Sandra E.
Cain, Stanley A. see Cain, Stanley Adair.
Cain, Stanley Adair, 1902-
  xCain, Stanley A.
    Foundations of Plant Geography. Hafner.
Caine, Jeffrey, 1944-
  xCaine, Jeffrey.
    The Cold Room. Knopf.
    Heathcliff. Fawcett.
    Heathcliff. G K Hall.
    Heathcliff. Knopf.
Caine, Mitchell.
  xCaine, Mitchell.
    Creole Surgeon. Fawcett.
    Worship the Wind. Fawcett.
Caird, Edward, 1835-1908
  xCaird, Edward.
    Evolution of Theology in the Greek
      Philosophers. Kraus Repr.
Caird, F. I. see Caird, Francis Irvine.
Caird, Francis Irvine.
  xCaird, F. I.
    Assessment of the Elderly Patient. Lippincott.
Caird, James. see Caird, James, Sir.
Caird, James, Sir, 1816-1892
  xCaird, James.

English Agriculture in 1850-51. Biblio Dist.
Caird, Janet.
xCaird, Janet.
The Umbrella-Maker's Daughter. St Martin.
Caird, John, 1820-1898
xCaird, John.
Spinoza. Arno.
Spinoza. R West.
Cairncross, Alec. *see* Cairncross, Alexander Kirkland.
Cairncross, Alex. *see* Cairncross, Alexander Kirkland.
Cairncross, Alexander Kirkland.
xCairncross, Alec.
ed. Britain's Economic Prospects Reconsidered.
State U NY Pr.
xCairncross, Alex.
Inflation, Growth & International Finance.
State U NY Pr.
Cairncross, Andrew S. *see* Cairncross, Andrew Scott.
Cairncross, Andrew Scott.
xCairncross, Andrew S.
Problem of Hamlet: A Solution. Folcroft.
Cairnes, John E. *see* Cairnes, John Elliott.
Cairnes, John Elliott, 1823-1875
xCairnes, John E.
Examination into the Principles of Currency
Involved in the Bank Charter Act of 1844.
Kelley.
Some Leading Principles of Political Economy
Newly Expounded. Kelley.
Cairns. *see* Cairns, Dorion.
Cairns, Dorion, 1901-1973
xCairns.
Guide for Translating Husserl. Kluwer Boston.
Cairns, Huntington, 1904-
xCairns, Huntington.
Law & the Social Sciences. Kelley.
Law & the Social Sciences. Rothman.
Legal Philosophy from Plato to Hegel.
Greenwood.
Theory of Legal Science. Kelley.
Theory of Legal Science. Rothman.
Cairns, John, 1923-
xCairns, John.
ed. Aquatic Microbial Communities. Garland
Pub.
Cancer: Science & Society. W H Freeman.
The Recovery Process in Damaged
Ecosystems. Ann Arbor Science.
ed. The Structure & Function of Fresh-Water
Microbial Communities. U Pr of Va.
Cairns, John C. *see* Cairns, John Campbell.
Cairns, John Campbell, 1924-
xCairns, John C.
ed. Contemporary France: Illusion, Conflict &
Regeneration. New Viewpoints.
Cairns, Robert B., 1933-
xCairns, Robert B.
ed. The Analysis of Social Interactions:
Methods, Issues & Illustrations. Halsted Pr.
Social Development: The Origins & Plasticity
of Interchanges. W H Freeman.
Cairns, S. S. *see* Cairns, Stewart Scott.
Cairns, Stewart Scott.
xCairns, S. S.
ed. Differential & Combinatorial Topology: A
Symposium in Honor of Marston Morse.
Princeton U Pr.
Cairns, T. *see* Cairns, Trevor.
Cairns, Trevor.
xCairns, T.
The Old Regime and the Revolution.
Cambridge U Pr.
Power for the People. Cambridge U Pr.
xCairns, Trevor.

Barbarians, Christians & Muslims. Cambridge
U Pr.
ed. Barbarians, Christians, & Muslims. Lerner
Pubns.
ed. Europe & the World. Lerner Pubns.
Europe Finds the World. Cambridge U Pr.
Men Become Civilized. Cambridge U Pr.
The Old Regime & the Revolution. Lerner
Pubns.
ed. People Become Civilized. Lerner Pubns.
Power for the People. Lerner Pubns.
Cairns, William B., 1867-1932
xCairns, William B.
History of American Literature. Johnson Repr.
**Cairo International Workshop on Applications of
Science and Technology for Desert Development,
1978.**
xCairo International Workshop on Applications of
Science & Technology for Desert Development
September 9-15, 1978.
Proceedings. Harwood Academic.
Cajal, Santiago Ramon Y. *see* Ramon Y Cajal, Santiago.
Cajori, Florian, 1859-1930
xCajori, Florian.
A History of Mathematics. Chelsea Pub.
Cake, Patrick.
xCake, Patrick.
The Pro-Am Murders. Proteus Calif.
Calabrese, Edward J., 1946-
xCalabrese, Edward J.
Nutrition & Environmental Health: The
Influence of Nutritional Status on Pollutant
Toxicity & Carcinogenicity: Minerals &
Macronutrients. Wiley.
Pollutants & High Risk Groups: The Biological
Basis of Increased Human Susceptibility to
Environmental & Occupational Pollutants.
Wiley.
Calabresi, Guido, 1932-
xCalabresi, Guido.
Costs of Accidents: Legal & Economic
Analysis. Yale U Pr.
Calabro, S. R.
xCalabro, S. R.
Reliability Principles & Practices. McGraw.
Calas, Nicholas. *see* Calas, Nicolas.
Calas, Nicolas.
xCalas, Nicholas.
Icons & Images of the Sixties. Dutton.
Calasibetta, Charlotte M. *see* Calasibetta, Charlotte
Mankey.
Calasibetta, Charlotte Mankey.
xCalasibetta, Charlotte M.
Fairchild's Dictionary of Fashion. Fairchild.
Calavan, Michael M.
xCalavan, Michael M.
Decisions Against Nature: An Anthropological
Study of Agriculture in Northern Thailand.
Cellar.
Calcote, Lee R.
xCalcote, Lee R.
Analysis of Laminated Composite Structures.
Van Nos Reinhold.
Calde, Mark A., 1945-
xCalde, Mark A.
Conquest. St Martin.
Caldecott, Moyra.
xCaldecott, Moyra.
Shadow on the Stones. Hill & Wang.
Shadow on the Stones. Popular Lib.
The Tall Stones. Popular Lib.
Calder, Alexander, 1898-
xCalder, Alexander.
Animal Sketching. Dover.
Calder: An Autobiography with Pictures.
Pantheon.
Calder, Daniel C. *see* Calder, Daniel Gillmore.
Calder, Daniel Gillmore.
xCalder, Daniel C.

ed. Old English Poetry: Essays on Style. U of
Cal Pr.
Calder, G. *see* Calder, Granville.
Calder, Granville.
xCalder, G.
The Principles & Techniques of Engineering
Estimating. Pergamon.
Calder, Jenni.
xCalder, Jenni.
Chronicles of Conscience: A Study of George
Orwell & Arthur Koestler. U of Pittsburgh
Pr.
There Must Be a Lone Ranger: The American
West in Film & in Reality. Taplinger.
The Victorian & Edwardian Home from Old
Photographs. David & Charles.
Calder, K. J. *see* Calder, Kenneth J.
Calder, Kenneth J.
xCalder, K. J.
Britain & the Origins of the New Europe,
1914-1918. Cambridge U Pr.
Calder, Louisa.
xCalder, Louisa.
Louisa Calder's Creative Crochet. Penguin.
Louisa Calder's Creative Crochet. Viking Pr.
Calder, Nigel.
xCalder, Nigel.
Einstein's Universe. Penguin.
Einstein's Universe. Viking Pr.
Spaceships of the Mind. Penguin.
Spaceships of the Mind. Viking Pr.
Calder, Robert.
xCalder, Robert.
The Dogs. Delacorte.
Calder-Marshall, Arthur, 1908-
xCalder-Marshall, Arthur.
The Grand Century of the Lady: 1720-1820.
Gordon-Cremonesi.
The Two Duchesses. Har-Row.
Calderon, George, 1868-1915
xCalderon, George.
Eight One-Act Plays. Core Collection.
Calderon, W. Frank. *see* Calderon, William Frank.
Calderon, William Frank, 1865-1943
xCalderon, W. Frank.
Animal Painting & Anatomy. Dover.
Animal Painting & Anatomy. Peter Smith.
Calderone, Mary S. *see* Calderone, Mary Steichen.
Calderone, Mary Steichen.
xCalderone, Mary S.
The Family Book About Sexuality. Har-Row.
Calderwood, Henry, 1830-1897
xCalderwood, Henry.
David Hume. Folcroft.
David Hume. R West.
Calderwood, James L.
xCalderwood, James L.
Metadrama in Shakespeare's Henriad: Richard
II to Henry V. U of Cal Pr.
Caldicott, C. E. *see* Caldicott, C. E. J.
Caldicott, C. E. J.
xCaldicott, C. E.
Marcel Pagnol. Twayne.
Caldwell. *see* Caldwell, Esther.
Caldwell, Celeste.
xCaldwell, Celeste.
Thirteen Towers. Belmont-Tower.
Caldwell, Charles, 1772-1853
xCaldwell, Charles.
Autobiography of Charles Caldwell, M. D. Da
Capo.
Caldwell, Elisie (Noble).
xCaldwell, Elsie N.
Last Witness for Robert Louis Stevenson. U of
Okla Pr.
Caldwell, Elsie N. *see* Caldwell, Elisie (Noble).
Caldwell, Erskin. *see* Caldwell, Erskine.
Caldwell, Erskine.
xCaldwell, Erskin.

Close to Home. NAL.
xCaldwell, Erskine.
North of the Danube. Da Capo.
Caldwell, Esther.
xCaldwell.
Geriatrics: A Study of Maturity. Delmar.
xCaldwell, Esther.
Foundation for Medical Communication. Reston.
Caldwell, Francis E.
xCaldwell, Francis E.
Pacific Troller: Life on the Northwest Fishing Grounds. Alaska Northwest.
Caldwell, Inga G. *see* Caldwell, Inga Gilson.
Caldwell, Inga Gilson.
xCaldwell, Inga G.
Giants in My Valley. Douglas-West.
Caldwell, J. Alexander, 1943-
xCaldwell, J. Alexander.
American Economic Aid to Thailand. Lexington Bks.
Caldwell, John, 1938-
xCaldwell, John.
Medieval Music. Ind U Pr.
Caldwell, John. *see* Caldwell, John H.
Caldwell, John C. *see* Caldwell, John Charles.
Caldwell, John Charles.
xCaldwell, John C.
ed. Population Growth & Socioeconomic Change in West Africa. Columbia U Pr.
Caldwell, John Cope, 1913-
xCaldwell, John C.
Let's Visit Brazil. John Day.
Let's Visit China Today. John Day.
Let's Visit Colombia. John Day.
Let's Visit Japan. John Day.
Let's Visit Malaysia. John Day.
Let's Visit Peru. John Day.
Let's Visit Turkey. John Day.
South of Tokyo. R West.
Caldwell, John H., 1928-
xCaldwell, John.
Caldwell on Competitive Cross-Country Skiing. Greene.
Caldwell, Lawrence. *see* Caldwell, Lawrence T.
Caldwell, Lawrence T.
xCaldwell, Lawrence.
Soviet-American Relations in the 1980's: Super-Power Politics & East-West Trade. McGraw.
Caldwell, Louis O.
xCaldwell, Louis O.
Another Tassel Is Moved: Guidelines for College Graduates. Baker Bk.
When Partners Become Parents. Baker Bk.
Caldwell, Lynton K. *see* Caldwell, Lynton Keith.
Caldwell, Lynton Keith.
xCaldwell, Lynton K.
Citizens & the Environment: Case Studies in Popular Action. Ind U Pr.
In Defense of Earth: International Protection of the Biosphere. Ind U Pr.
Caldwell, Malcolm.
xCaldwell, Malcolm.
Cambodia in the Southeast Asian War. Monthly Rev.
Caldwell, Marge.
xCaldwell, Marge.
The Radiant You. Broadman.
Caldwell, Nancy L. *see* Caldwell, Nancy Lee.
Caldwell, Nancy Lee.
xCaldwell, Nancy L.
A History of Brooke County. McClain.
Caldwell, Norman W. *see* Caldwell, Norman Ward.
Caldwell, Norman Ward, 1905-1958
xCaldwell, Norman W.
The French in the Mississippi Valley: 1740-1750. Porcupine Pr.
Caldwell, Robert C. *see* Caldwell, Robert Craig.

Caldwell, Robert Craig.
xCaldwell, Robert C.
A Textbook of Preventive Dentistry. Saunders.
Caldwell, Robert G. *see* Caldwell, Robert Graham.
Caldwell, Robert Graham, 1904-
xCaldwell, Robert G.
Criminology. Wiley.
Foundations of Law Enforcement & Criminal Justice. Bobbs.
Caldwell, Taylor. *see* Caldwell, Taylor Pseud. of Marcus Reback and Janet Taylor (Caldwell) Reback.
Caldwell, Taylor Pseud. of Marcus Reback and Janet Taylor (Caldwell) Reback.
xCaldwell, Taylor.
Grandmother & the Priests. Fawcett.
Late Clara Beame. Fawcett.
A Prologue to Love. Bantam.
A Prologue to Love. Doubleday.
Caldwell, W. E. *see* Caldwell, Wallace Everett.
Caldwell, Wallace Everett, 1890-
xCaldwell, W. E.
Ancient World. HR&W.
Caldwell, William E. *see* Caldwell, William Elmer.
Caldwell, William Elmer, 1903-
xCaldwell, William E.
Family Safari. Binford.
Caldwell, William L., 1929-
xCaldwell, William L.
Cancer of the Urinary Bladder: With Emphasis on Treatment by Irradiation. Green.
Calef, Wesley. *see* Calef, Wesley Carr.
Calef, Wesley Carr.
xCalef, Wesley.
Private Grazing & Public Lands. Arno.
Calero, Henry H.
xCalero, Henry H.
Winning the Negotiation. Dutton.
Caley, George.
xCaley, George.
Reflections on the Colony of New South Wales. Verry.
Calfee, R. *see* Calfee, Robert C.
Calfee, Robert C.
xCalfee, R.
Human Experimental Psychology. HR&W.
Calhoon, Richard P. *see* Calhoon, Richard Percival.
Calhoon, Richard Percival, 1909-
xCalhoon, Richard P.
Personnel Management & Supervision. P-H.
Calhoon, Robert M. *see* Calhoon, Robert McCluer.
Calhoon, Robert McCluer.
xCalhoon, Robert M.
The Loyalists in Revolutionary America 1760-1781. HarBraceJ.
Revolutionary America: An Interpretive Overview. HarBraceJ.
Calhoun, Blue.
xCalhoun, Blue.
The Pastoral Vision of William Morris: The Earthly Paradise. U of Ga Pr.
Calhoun, Calfrey C.
xCalhoun, Calfrey C.
Managing the Learning Process in Business Education. Wadsworth Pub.
Calhoun, Craig J.
xCalhoun, Craig J.
ed. The Anthropological Study of Education. Beresford Bk Serv.
Calhoun, Daniel H. *see* Calhoun, Daniel Hovey.
Calhoun, Daniel Hovey.
xCalhoun, Daniel H.
The Intelligence of a People. Princeton U Pr.
Professional Lives in America: Structure & Aspiration, 1750-1850. Harvard U Pr.
Calhoun, Don.
xCalhoun, Don.
Dando Shaft. Stein & Day.
Calhoun, G. M. *see* Calhoun, George Miller.
Calhoun, George M. *see* Calhoun, George Miller.

Calhoun, George Miller, 1886-1942
xCalhoun, G. M.
A Working Bibliography of Greek Law. Humanities.
xCalhoun, George M.
Athenian Clubs in Politics & Litigation. B Franklin.
Business Life of Ancient Athens. Cooper Sq.
The Growth of Criminal Law in Ancient Greece. Greenwood.
Calhoun, Jack.
xCalhoun, Jack.
Somewhere the Sun Is Shining. Grossmont Pr.
Calhoun, James F.
xCalhoun, James F.
Psychology of Adjustment & Human Relationships. Random.
Calhoun, Karen S.
xCalhoun, Karen S.
Innovative Treatment Methods in Psychopathology. Krieger.
Calhoun, Lawrence G.
xCalhoun, Lawrence G.
Dealing with Crisis: A Guide to Critical Life Problems. P-H.
Calhoun, Mary, 1915-
xCalhoun, Mary.
Adventures with Children: Exploring Ways of Learning & Teaching in the Church School. Abingdon.
Camels Are Meaner Than Mules. Garrard.
Cross-Country Cat. Morrow.
Depend on Katie John. Har-Row.
Depend on Katie John. Har-Row.
Euphonia & the Flood. Schol Bk Serv.
The Flower Mother. Morrow.
Honestly, Katie John. Har-Row.
Honestly, Katie John. Har-Row.
Horse Comes First. Atheneum.
The House of Thirty Cats. Archway.
The Last Two Elves in Denmark. Morrow.
Medicine Show: Conning People & Making Them Like It. Har-Row.
Ownself. Har-Row.
Ownself. Har-Row.
The Witch Who Lost Her Shadow. Har-Row.
Calhoun, Robert.
xCalhoun, Robert.
The Power Profane. Fawcett.
Calian, C. Samuel. *see* Calian, Carnegie Samuel.
Calian, Carnegie Samuel.
xCalian, C. Samuel.
The Gospel According to The Wall Street Journal. John Knox.
Califano, Joseph. *see* Califano, Joseph A.
Califano, Joseph A., 1931-
xCalifano, Joseph.
Presidential Nation. Norton.
xCalifano, Joseph A.
Student Revolution: A Global Confrontation. Norton.
California.
xState of California.
Health Aspects of Wastewater Recharge: A State-of-the-Art Review. Water Info.
California. Department of Education.
xCalifornia State Department of Education.
Pancom: Developmental Instruction in Manual Communication. Joyce Media.
California. Department of Justice.
xCalifornia Dept. of Justice.
Law in the School: A Guide for California Teachers, Parents & Students. Patterson Smith.
California Dept. of Justice. *see* California. Department of Justice.
California Legislature. *see* California. Legislature. Assembly.
California. Legislature. Assembly.
xCalifornia Legislature.

Memorial of the Six Chinese Companies. R & E Res Assoc.

California. Legislature. Senate.
xCalifornia State Senate.
Chinese Immigration: Its Social, Moral & Political Effect. Ozer.

California State Department of Education. *see* California. Department of Education.

California State Senate. *see* California. Legislature. Senate.

California. University.
xUniversity of California.
The Bancroft Library, University of California, Berkeley: Catalog of Printed Books, Third Supplement. G K Hall.
Publications in Economics. Johnson Repr.
Publications in Education. Johnson Repr.
Publications in Geography. Johnson Repr.
Publications in International Relations. Johnson Repr.
Publications in Mathematical & Physical Sciences. Johnson Repr.
Publications in Philosophy. Johnson Repr.
University of California Union Catalog of Monographs Cataloged by the Nine Campuses from 1963 Through 1967. UCDLA.

California University - Committee On International Relations. *see* California. University. Committee on International Relations.

California University - Department Of English. *see* California. University. Department of English.

California. University, Berkeley.
xUniversity Of California - Berkeley.
Bancroft Library, Catalog of Printed Books. G K Hall.
Bancroft Library, Index to Printed Maps. G K Hall.
Dictionary Catalog of the Giannini Foundation of Agricultural Economics Library. G K Hall.
Dictionary Catalog of the Water Resources Center Archives. G K Hall.
Dictionary Catalog of the Water Resources Center Archives, Third Supplement. G K Hall.
xUniversity of California, Berkeley.
Dictionary Catalog of the Water Resources Center Archives, Fourth Suppl. G K Hall.

California. University, Berkeley. Library.
xUniversity of California, Berkeley, Library.
Guide to Special Collections. Scarecrow.

California. University. Committee on International Relations.
xCalifornia University - Committee On International Relations.
Problems of War & Peace in the Society of Nations. Arno.
United States Among the Nations. Arno.
xCalifornia University Committee on International Relations.
Problems of Hemispheric Defense. Arno.
The Southwest Pacific & the War. Greenwood.

California. University. Department of English.
xCalifornia University - Department Of English.
Essays in Criticism: First Series.. Arno.
Essays in Criticism, Second Series. Arno.
xCalifornia. University. Dept. of English.
Essays & Studies. Folcroft.

California. University. Dept. of English. *see* California. University. Department of English.

California. University. Heller Committee for Research in Social Economics.
xUniversity Of California Heller Committee For Research In Social Economics.
Cost of Living Studies. Johnson Repr.

California. University. Institute of Governmental Studies Library.
xUniversity of California, Berkeley, Institute of Governmental Studies Library.

Subject Catalog of the Institute of Governmental Studies Library. G K Hall.

California. University. Library.
xCalifornia University Library.
Spain & Spanish America in the Libraries of the University of California. B Franklin.

California. University. Philosophical Union.
xUniversity Of California Philosophical Union - 1932.
Causality: Lectures. Johnson Repr.
Civilization: Lectures. Johnson Repr.
Essays in Metaphysics: Lectures. Johnson Repr.
Issues & Tendencies in Contemporary Philosophy: Lectures. Johnson Repr.
Meaning & Interpretation: Lectures. Johnson Repr.
Nature of Ideas: Lectures. Johnson Repr.
Nature of Mind: Lectures. Johnson Repr.
Possibility: Lectures. Johnson Repr.
Problem of Substance: Lectures. Johnson Repr.
Problem of the Individual: Lectures. Johnson Repr.
Problem of Time: Lectures. Johnson Repr.
Problem of Truth: Lectures. Johnson Repr.
Reason: Lectures. Johnson Repr.
Studies in the Nature of Facts: Lectures. Johnson Repr.
Studies in the Nature of Truth: Lectures. Johnson Repr.
Studies in the Problems of Norms: Lectures. Johnson Repr.
Studies in the Problems of Relations: Lectures. Johnson Repr.

California. University, San Diego.
xUniversity of California - San Diego.
Catalogs of the Scripps Institution of Oceanography Library, First Supplement to Pt. 1, Author-Title Catalog. G K Hall.

California. University. University at Los Angeles. Institute of Industrial Relations.
xAnnual Research Conference, 8th, UCLA, 1965.
Research Conference on Labor Relations: Proceedings. U Cal LA Indus Rel.

California. University. University at Los Angeles. Moot Court Honors Program.
xUCLA Moot Court Honors Program.
Handbook of Appellate Advocacy. West Pub.

California. University. University at Los Angeles. School of Law.
xLos Angeles Copyright Society.
ed. Copyright & Related Topics: A Choice of Articles. U of Cal Pr.

California. University. University at Los Angeles. William Andrews Clark Memorial Library.
xWilliam Andrews Clark Memorial Library-Los Angeles.
Dictionary Catalog of William Andrews Clark Memorial Library. G K Hall.

California. University. Water Resources Centre.
xWater Resources Center, University at Berkeley, Calif.
Dictionary Catalog of the Water Resources Center: Sixth Supplement. G K Hall.

California. Wine Advisory Board.
xCalifornia Winemakers.
Adventures in Wine Cookery. Wine Appreciation.
xWine Adsisory Bloard.
Gourmet Wine Cooking the Easy Way. Wine Appreciation.
xWine Advisory Board.
Adventures in Wine Cookery by California Winemakers. Piper.
Easy Recipes of California Winemakers. Piper.
Favorite Recipes of California Winemakers. Piper.
Gourmet Wine Cooking the Easy Way. Piper.
xWine Advisory Boards.

Epicurean Recipes of California Winemakers. Piper.

California Winemakers. *see* California. Wine Advisory Board.

Calin, Harold.
xCalin, Harold.
Attack in the Forest. Nordon Pubns.
White Forest Battle. Nordon Pubns.

Calinescu, Matei.
xCalinescu, Matei.
Faces of Modernity: Avant-Garde, Decadence, Kitsch. Ind U Pr.

Calingaert, Peter.
xCalingaert, Peter.
Assemblers, Compilers, & Program Translation. Computer Sci.

Calisch, Rus.
xCalisch, Rus.
Paumalu: A Story of Modern Hawaii. Paumalu Pr.

Calisher, Hortense.
xCalisher, Hortense.
Collected Stories of Hortense Calisher. Arbor Hse.
Eagle Eye. Arbor Hse.
On Keeping Women. Arbor Hse.
On Keeping Women. Berkley Pub.
Standard Dreaming. Arbor Hse.

Calisse, Carlo, 1859-1945
xCalisse, Carlo.
History of Italian Law. Kelley.
History of Italian Law. Rothman.

Caliver, Ambrose, 1894-1962
xCaliver, Ambrose.
Background Study of Negro College Students. Negro U Pr.
Education of Negro Teachers. Negro U Pr.
A Personnel Study of Negro College Students: A Study of the Relations Between Certain Background Factors of Negro College Students & Their Subsequent Careers in College. AMS Pr.
Personnel Study of Negro College Students: A Study of the Relations Between Certain Background Factors of Negro College Studens & Their Subsequent Careers in College. Negro U Pr.

Calkin, Ruth. *see* Calkin, Ruth Harms.

Calkin, Ruth H. *see* Calkin, Ruth Harms.

Calkin, Ruth Harms.
xCalkin, Ruth.
Lord, I Keep Running Back to You. Tyndale.
Two Shall Be One. Cook.
xCalkin, Ruth H.
Lord, You Love to Say Yes. Cook.

Calkins, Earnest E. *see* Calkins, Earnest Elmo.

Calkins, Earnest Elmo, 1868-1964
xCalkins, Earnest E.
They Broke the Prairie: Being Some Account of the Settlement of the Upper Mississippi Valley by Religious & Educational Pioneers, Told in Terms of One City, Galesburg, & of One College, Knox. Greenwood.

Calkins, Erling, 1917-
xCalkins, Erling.
Adventure at Beaver Falls. Southern Pub.

Calkins, Fay.
xCalkins, Fay.
The CIO & the Democratic Party. U of Chicago Pr.

Calkins, Frank, 1932-
xCalkins, Frank.
The Tan-Faced Children. Doubleday.

Calkins, Franklin W. *see* Calkins, Franklin Welles.

Calkins, Franklin Welles, 1857-1928
xCalkins, Franklin W.
Cougar-Tamer & Other Stories of Adventure. Arno.

Calkins, Robert G.
xCalkins, Robert G.

Distribution of Labor: The Illuminators of the
Hours of Catherine of Cleves & Their
Workshop. Am Philos.
Monuments of Medieval Art. Dutton.
Calladine, C. R.
xCalladine, G. R.
Engineering Plasticity. Pergamon.
Calladine, Carol. see Calladine, Carole.
Calladine, Carole.
xCalladine, Carol.
Raising Siblings. Delacorte.
Calladine, G. R. see Calladine, C. R.
Callaghan, Barry.
xCallaghan, Barry.
Van Nostrand Reinhold Manual of
Film-Making. Van Nos Reinhold.
Callaghan, Morley, 1903-
xCallaghan, Morley.
Fine & Private Place. Popular Lib.
Native Argosy. Arno.
That Summer in Paris: Memories of Tangled
Friendships with Hemingway, Fitzgerald &
Some Others. Penguin.
Callahan, Betsy N. see Callahan, Betsy Nicholson.
Callahan, Betsy Nicholson.
xCallahan, Betsy N.
Separation & Divorce. Family Serv.
Callahan, Carolyn M.
xCallahan, Carolyn M.
Developing Creativity in the Gifted &
Talented. Coun Exc Child.
Callahan, Charles C.
xCallahan, Charles C.
Adverse Possession. Ohio St U Pr.
Callahan, Daniel. see Callahan, Daniel J.
Callahan, Daniel J.
xCallahan, Daniel.
Ethics & Population Limitation. Population
Coun.
Callahan, Dorothy. see Callahan, Dorothy M.
Callahan, Dorothy M.
xCallahan, Dorothy.
Under Christophers Hat. Scribner.
Callahan, Ed.
xCallahan, Ed.
Charcoal Cookbook. Nitty Gritty.
Fondue Cookbook. Nitty Gritty.
Callahan, James M. see Callahan, James Morton.
Callahan, James Morton, 1864-1956
xCallahan, James M.
American Foreign Policy in Canadian
Relations. Cooper Sq.
American Foreign Policy in Mexican Relations.
Cooper Sq.
American Relations in the Pacific & the Far
East, 1784-1900. AMS Pr.
Diplomatic History of the Southern
Confederacy. Greenwood.
Diplomatic History of the Southern
Confederacy. Ungar.
Callahan, John F.
xCallahan, John F.
The Illusions of a Nation: Myth & History in
the Novels of F. Scott Fitzgerald. U of Ill Pr.
Callahan, John F. see Callahan, John Francis.
Callahan, John Francis, 1912-
xCallahan, John F.
Four Views of Time in Ancient Philosophy.
Greenwood.
Callahan, Joseph F.
xCallahan, Joseph F.
Innovations & Issues in Education: Planning
for Competence. Macmillan.
Teaching in the Secondary School: Planning for
Competence. Macmillan.
Callahan, Kevin.
xCallahan, Kevin.
Early American Furniture. Sterling.
Callahan, Nelson J.
xCallahan, Nelson J.

Case for Due Process in the Church: Father
Eugene O'Callaghan, American Pioneer of
Dissent. Alba.
Callahan, P. J. see Callahan, Parnell Joseph Terence.
Callahan, Parnell J. see Callahan, Parnell Joseph Terence.
Callahan, Parnell Joseph Terence.
xCallahan, P. J.
Law of Separation & Divorce. Oceana.
xCallahan, Parnell J.
Real Estate Law for the Homeowner & Broker.
Oceana.
Callahan, Philip S., 1923-
xCallahan, Philip S.
Birds & How They Function. Holiday.
The Evolution of Insects. Holiday.
Tuning in to Nature: Solar Energy, Infrared
Radiation & the Insect Communication
System. Devin.
Callahan, Raymond.
xCallahan, Raymond.
The East India Company & Army Reform,
1783-1798. Harvard U Pr.
Callahan, Sterling G. see Callahan, Sterling Grundy.
Callahan, Sterling Grundy.
xCallahan, Sterling G.
Successful Teaching in Secondary Schools: A
Guide for Student & In-Service Teachers.
Scott F.
Callahan, W. J. see Callahan, William James.
Callahan, William E.
xCallahan, William E.
The Continuing Quest: Introductory Readings
in Philosophy. Kendall-Hunt.
Callahan, William J. see Callahan, William James.
Callahan, William James.
xCallahan, W. J.
Church & Society in Catholic Europe of the
Eighteenth Century. Cambridge U Pr.
xCallahan, William J.
Honor, Commerce & Industry in
Eighteenth-Century Spain. Kelley.
Callan, Edward, 1917-
xCallan, Edward.
Alan Paton. Twayne.
Callas, Evangelia.
xCallas, Evangelia.
My Daughter Maria Callas. Arno.
Callaway, Archibald.
xCallaway, Archibald.
Educational Planning & Unemployed Youth.
Unipub.
Callaway, Bob.
xCallaway, Bob.
Platform Tennis. Lippincott.
Callaway, Enoch.
xCallaway, Enoch.
Brain Electrical Potentials & Individual
Psychological Differences. Grune.
ed. Event-Related Brain Potentials in Man.
Acad Pr.
Callaway, Frank.
xCallaway, Frank.
ed. Australian Composition in the Twentieth
Century. Oxford U Pr.
Callaway, Godfrey, 1865 or 6-1942
xCallaway, Godfrey.
Fellowship of the Veld: Sketches of Native Life
in South Africa. Negro U Pr.
Callaway, Joseph.
xCallaway, Joseph.
Energy Band Theory. Acad Pr.
ed. Quantum Theory of the Solid State. Acad
Pr.
Callaway, Morgan, 1862-1936
xCallaway, Morgan.
The Consecutive Subjunctive in Old English.
Kraus Repr.
Callcott, George H., 1929-
xCallcott, George H.

History in the United States, 1800-1860: Its
Practice & Purpose. Johns Hopkins.
Callcott, Margaret Law.
xCallcott, Margaret Law.
The Negro in Maryland Politics, 1870-1912.
Johns Hopkins.
Callcott, Wilfrid H. see Callcott, Wilfrid Hardy.
Callcott, Wilfrid Hardy, 1895-
xCallcott, Wilfrid H.
Caribbean Policy of the United States,
1890-1920. Octagon.
Church & State in Mexico, 1822-1857.
Octagon.
Callen, Anthea.
xCallen, Anthea.
Renoir. Two Continents.
Women Artists of the Arts & Crafts
Movement, 1870-1914. Pantheon.
Callen, Jeffrey P.
xCallen, Jeffrey P.
Manual of Dermatology: An Introduction to
Diagnosis & Treatment. Year Bk Med.
Callen, Larry.
xCallen, Larry.
The Deadly Mandrake. Little.
Sorrow's Song. Little.
Callender, Edward B. see Callender, Edward Belcher.
Callender, Edward Belcher, 1851-1917
xCallender, Edward B.
Thaddeus Stevens, Commoner. AMS Pr.
Calleo, David P., 1934-
xCalleo, David P.
Europe's Future: The Grand Alternatives.
Norton.
Callesen, Gerd.
xCallesen, Gerd.
Social-Demokraten & Internationalism: The
Copenhagen Social Democratic Newspaper's
Coverage of International Labor Affairs,
1871-1958. Kent Popular.
Callicott, Catherine D. see Callicott, Catherine Dorris.
Callicott, Catherine Dorris.
xCallicott, Catherine D.
In Praise of Dollhouses: The Story of a
Personal Collection. Morrow.
Callihan, E. L.
xCallihan, E. L.
Exercises & Tests for Journalists. Chilton.
Grammar for Journalists. Chilton.
Callis, Helmut G.
xCallis, Helmut G.
Foreign Capital in Southeast Asia. AMS Pr.
Foreign Capital in Southeast Asia. Arno.
Callis, Robert.
xCallis, Robert.
ed. Ethical Standards Casebook. Am Personnel.
Callison, Brian.
xCallison, Brian.
An Act of War. Dutton.
The Judas Ship. Dutton.
Trapp's Peace. Dutton.
Callison, C. H. see Callison, Charles.
Callison, Charles.
xCallison, C. H.
ed. America's Natural Resources. Wiley.
Callmann, Ellen.
xCallmann, Ellen.
Apollonio Di Giovanni. Oxford U Pr.
Callot, Jacques.
xCallot, Jacques.
Callot's Etchings. Dover.
Callow, Alexander B.
xCallow, Alexander B.
ed. The City Boss in America: An Interpretive
Reader. Oxford U Pr.
Tweed Ring. Oxford U Pr.
Callow, Clive.
xCallow, Clive.

Power from the Sea: The Search for North Sea
Oil & Gas. Verry.
Callow, James T.
xCallow, James T.
Guide to American Literature from Emily
Dickinson to the Present. B&N.
Guide to American Literature from Its
Beginnings Through Walt Whitman. B&N.
Callwood, June.
xCallwood, June.
Love, Hate, Fear, Anger, & the Other Lively
Emotions. Borgo Pr.
Love, Hate, Fear, Anger, & the Other Lively
Emotions. Newcastle Pub.
Calman, Kenneth C. *see* Calman, Kenneth Charles.
Calman, Kenneth Charles.
xCalman, Kenneth C.
Introduction to Cancer Medicine. Wiley.
Calmeil, Louis F. *see* Calmeil, Louis Florentin.
Calmeil, Louis Florentin, 1798-1895
xCalmeil, Louis F.
De la Paralysie Consideree Chez les Alienes.
Arno.
Calnan, T. D., 1914-
xCalnan, T. D.
Free As a Running Fox. Dial.
Calne, D. B. *see* Calne, Donald Brian.
Calne, Donald Brian.
xCalne, D. B.
ed. Dopaminergic Mechanisms. Raven.
ed. Progress in the Treatment of Parkinsonism.
Raven.
Calne, R. Y. *see* Calne, Roy Yorke.
Calne, Roy Yorke.
xCalne, R. Y.
Organ Grafts. Year Bk Med.
Calogero, F.
xCalogero, F.
Variable Phase Approach to Potential
Scattering. Acad Pr.
Calter, Paul.
xCalter, Paul.
Problem Solving with Computers. McGraw.
Calve, Emma, 1858-1942
xCalve, Emma.
My Life. Arno.
Calvert, Albert F. *see* Calvert, Albert Frederick.
Calvert, Albert Frederick, 1872-1946
xCalvert, Albert F.
German East Africa. Negro U Pr.
Nigeria & Its Tin Fields. Arno.
South-West Africa, During the German
Occupation, 1884-1914. Negro U Pr.
Calvert, George H. *see* Calvert, George Henry.
Calvert, George Henry, 1803-1889
xCalvert, George H.
Wordsworth: A Biographic Aesthetic Study.
Folcroft.
Calvert, J. M. *see* Calvert, Jack Maxwell.
Calvert, Jack Maxwell.
xCalvert, J. M.
Electronics. Wiley.
Calvert, Monte. *see* Calvert, Monte A.
Calvert, Monte A.
xCalvert, Monte.
The Mechanical Engineer in America,
1830-1910: Professional Cultures in Conflict.
Johns Hopkins.
Calvert, Peter.
xCalvert, Peter.
Study of Revolution. Oxford U Pr.
Calvert, Robert, 1922-
xCalvert, Robert.
Career Patterns of Liberal Arts Graduates.
Carroll Pr.
Calvert, Roger.
xCalvert, Roger.
Inland Waterways of Europe. Intl Pubns Serv.
Calverton, V. F. *see* Calverton, Victor Francis.
Calverton, Victor F. *see* Calverton, Victor Francis.

Calverton, Victor Francis, 1900-1940
xCalverton, V. F.
Bankruptcy of Marriage. Arno.
xCalverton, Victor F.
The Liberation of American Literature.
Octagon.
Calvez, Jean Yves, 1927-
xCalvez, Jean-Yves.
Politics & Society in the Third World. Orbis
Bks.
Calvez, Jean-Yves. *see* Calvez, Jean Yves.
Calvin College Faculty Committee. *see* Calvin College,
Grand Rapids. Curriculum Study Committee.
**Calvin College, Grand Rapids. Curriculum Study
Committee.**
xCalvin College Faculty Committee.
Christian Liberal Arts Education. Eerdmans.
Calvin, Jean, 1509-1564

xCalvin, John.

Concerning Scandals. Eerdmans.
On God & Political Duty. Bobbs.
On the Christian Faith: Selections from the
Institutes, Commentaries & Tracts. Bobbs.
Sermons from Job. Baker Bk.

Calvin, John. *see* Calvin, Jean.
Calvino, Italo.
xCalvino, Italo.
The Baron in the Trees. HarBraceJ.
The Castle of Crossed Destinies. HarBraceJ.
The Castle of Crossed Destinies. HarBraceJ.
Cosmicomics. HarBraceJ.
The Path to the Nest of Spiders. Ecco Pr.
T Zero. HarBraceJ.
Calvocoressi, M. D. *see* Calvocoressi, Michel D.
Calvocoressi, Michel D.
xCalvocoressi, M. D.
Mussorgsky. Biblio Dist.
Mussorgsky. Littlefield.
The Principles & Methods of Musical
Criticism. Da Capo.
A Survey of Russian Music. Greenwood.
xCalvocoressi, Michel D.
Masters of Russian Music. Johnson Repr.
The Principles & Methods of Musical
Criticism. Hyperion Conn.
Cam, Helen. *see* Cam, Helen Maud.
Cam, Helen Maud, 1885-
xCam, Helen.
Law-Finders & Law Makers in Medieval
England: Collected Studies in Legal &
Constitutional History. Kelley.
Camac, C. N. *see* Camac, Charles Nicoll Bancker.
Camac, Charles Nicoll Bancker, 1868-1940
xCamac, C. N.
Imhotep to Harvey: Backgrounds of Medical
History. Longwood Pr.
Camara, J. Mattoso. *see* Camara, Joaquim Mattoso.
Camara, Joaquim Mattoso.
xCamara, J. Mattoso.
The Portuguese Language. U of Chicago Pr.
Camarillo, Albert.
xCamarillo, Albert.
Chicanos in a Changing Society: From
Mexican Pueblos to American Barrios in
Santa Barbara & Southern California,
1848-1930. Harvard U Pr.
Cambon, Glauco.
xCambon, Glauco.
Dante's Craft: Studies in Language & Style. U
of Minn Pr.
Giuseppe Ungaretti. Columbia U Pr.
The Inclusive Flame: Studies in Modern
American Poetry. Peter Smith.
Cambridge Research Institute.
xCambridge Research Institute.

Omnibus Copyright Revision: Comparative
Analysis of the Issues. Am Soc Info Sci.
Trends Affecting the U. S. Banking System.
Ballinger Pub.
The Cambridge Songs.
xCambridge Songs.
The Cambridge Songs, a Goliard's Song Book
of the 11th Century. AMS Pr.
Cambridge Summer School in Mathematical Logic.
xCambridge Summer School in Mathematical
Logic, 1971.
Proceedings. Springer-Verlag.
Cambridge. University. Fitzwilliam Museum.
xFitzwilliam Museum.
All for Art: The Ricketts & Shannon
Collection. Cambridge U Pr.
Drawings & Watercolours by Peter De Wint.
Cambridge U Pr.
Cambridge. University. Institute of Criminology.
xInstitute of Criminology, University of Cambridge,
England.
The Library Catalogue of the Radzinowicz
Library. G K Hall.
Cambridge. University. Library.
xCambridge University Library.
Early English Printed Books in the University
Library. Johnson Repr.
Cambridge University Library. *see* Cambridge. University.
Library. Venn Collection.
Cambridge. University. Library. Venn Collection.
xCambridge University Library.
Catalog of a Collection of Books on Logic
Presented to the Library by John Venn. B
Franklin.
Cambridge. University. Trinity College Library.
xCambridge. University. Trinity College. Library.
Catalogue of the Books Presented by Edward
Capell to the Library of Trinity College in
Cambridge. Folcroft.
Camden, Carroll.
xCamden, Carroll.
ed. Restoration & Eighteenth-Century
Literature: Essays in Honor of Alan Dugald
McKillop. U of Chicago Pr.
Camden, William, 1551-1623
xCamden, William.
History of the Most Renowned & Victorious
Princess Elizabeth Late Queen of England:
Selected Chapters. U of Chicago Pr.
Camejo, Peter.
xCamejo, Peter.
Racism, Revolution, Reaction 1861-1877: The
Rise & Fall of Radical Reconstruction.
Monad Pr.
Camellion, Richard.
xCamellion, Richard.
Assassination: Theory & Practice. Paladin Ent.
Cameron, A. *see* Cameron, Alastair.
Cameron, A. V. *see* Cameron, Alice Virginia.
Cameron, Ad.
xCameron, Ad.
ed. Bird Families of the World. Abrams.
Cameron, Alan.
xCameron, Alan.
Circus Factions: Blues & Greens at Rome &
Byzantium. Oxford U Pr.
Porphyrius the Charioteer. Oxford U Pr.
Cameron, Alastair.
xCameron, A.
Principles of Lubrication. Longman.
Cameron, Alice Virginia, 1902-
xCameron, A. V.
Influence of Ariosto's Epic & Lyric Poetry on
Ronsard & His Group. Johnson Repr.
Cameron, Alison S. *see* Cameron, Alison Stilwell.
Cameron, Alison Stilwell.
xCameron, Alison S.
Chinese Painting Techniques. C E Tuttle.
Cameron, Angus.
xCameron, Angus.

Nightwatchers. Schol Bk Serv.
Cameron, Ann, 1943-
  xCameron, Ann.
    The Angel Book. Ballantine.
Cameron, David. *see* Cameron, David R.
Cameron, David R.
  xCameron, David.
    The Social Thought of Rousseau & Burke: A
      Comparative Study. U of Toronto Pr.
Cameron, E. *see* Cameron, Ewan.
Cameron, Eleanor.
  xCameron, Eleanor.
    The Court of the Stone Children. Avon.
    The Court of the Stone Children. Dutton.
    The Green & Burning Tree: On the Writing &
      Enjoyment of Children's Books. Little.
    Stowaway to the Mushroom Planet. Little.
    Stowaway to the Mushroom Planet. Schol Bk
      Serv.
    The Wonderful Flight to the Mushroom Planet.
      Little.
Cameron, Elisabeth.
  xCameron, Elisabeth.
    Potters on Pottery. St Martin.
Cameron, Ewan.
  xCameron, E.
    Hyaluronidase & Cancer. Pergamon.
Cameron, G. C. *see* Cameron, George Glenn.
Cameron, George G. *see* Cameron, George Glenn.
Cameron, George Glenn, 1905-
  xCameron, G. C.
    History of Early Iran. Gordon Pr.
  xCameron, George G.
    History of Early Iran. Greenwood.
    History of Early Iran. U of Chicago Pr.
Cameron, H. M. *see* Cameron, Hector MacDonald.
Cameron, Hector MacDonald.
  xCameron, H. M.
    ed. Liver Cell Cancer. Elsevier.
Cameron, Ivan L.
  xCameron, Ivan L.
    ed. Acidic Proteins of the Nucleus. Acad Pr.
    ed. Cellular & Molecular Renewal in the
      Mammalian Body. Acad Pr.
    ed. Developmental Aspects of the Cell Cycle.
      Acad Pr.
Cameron, J. M. *see* Cameron, James Malcolm.
Cameron, J. R. *see* Cameron, John R.
Cameron, James, 1914-
  xCameron, James.
    From the Inside Out: A Lynching in the
      North. That New Pub.
Cameron, James B.
  xCameron, James B.
    Advanced Accounting: Theory & Practice.
      HM.
Cameron, James M. *see* Cameron, James Munro.
Cameron, James Malcolm.
  xCameron, J. M.
    Forensic Dentistry. Churchill.
Cameron, James Munro, 1910-
  xCameron, J. M.
    On the Idea of a University. U of Toronto Pr.
  xCameron, James M.
    Images of Authority: A Consideration of the
      Concepts of "Regnum" & "Sacerdotium". Yale
      U Pr.
Cameron, James R. *see* Cameron, James Reese.
Cameron, James Reese, 1929-
  xCameron, James R.
    Frederick William Maitland & the History of
      English Law. Greenwood.
Cameron, Jenks, 1879-1957
  xCameron, Jenks.

The Bureau of Dairy Industry: Its History,
  Activities & Organization. AMS Pr.
The Development of Governmental Forest
  Control in the United States. Da Capo.
Development of Governmental Forest Control
  in the United States. Irvington.
The National Park Service: Its History,
  Activities & Organization. AMS Pr.
Cameron, John, 1914-
  xCameron, John.
    Development of Education in East Africa.
      Tchrs Coll.
    If Mice Could Fly. Atheneum.
Cameron, John R.
  xCameron, J. R.
    Thermoluminescent Dosimetry. U of Wis Pr.
  xCameron, John R.
    Medical Physics. Wiley.
Cameron, Kate.
  xCameron, Kate.
    Music from the Past. Nordon Pubns.
Cameron, Kenneth. *see* Cameron, Kenneth M.
Cameron, Kenneth M.
  xCameron, Kenneth.
    Power Play. Popular Lib.
  xCameron, Kenneth M.
    The Enjoyment of Theatre. Macmillan.
    Guide to Theatre Study. Macmillan.
    Our Jo: A Chronicle of a Coming Man.
      Macmillan.
Cameron, Kenneth N. *see* Cameron, Kenneth Neill.
Cameron, Kenneth Neill.
  xCameron, Kenneth N.
    Humanity & Society: A World History.
      Monthly Rev.
    Marx & Engels Today: A Modern Dialogue on
      Philosophy and History. Exposition.
Cameron, Lou.
  xCameron, Lou.
    The Cascade Ghost. Popular Lib.
    Code Seven. Berkley Pub.
    The Spirit Horses. Ballantine.
Cameron, Mary A. *see* Cameron, Mary Ann.
Cameron, Mary Ann.
  xCameron, Mary A.
    ed. Snow Tours in Washington. Signpost Bk
      Pub.
Cameron, Meribeth E. *see* Cameron, Meribeth Elliott.
Cameron, Meribeth Elliott, 1905-
  xCameron, Meribeth E.
    Reform Movement in China, 1898-1912. AMS
      Pr.
Cameron, Nigel.
  xCameron, Nigel.
    The Face of China As Seen by Photographers
      or Travelers: 1860-1930. Aperture.
    From Bondage to Liberation: East Asia
      1860-1952. Oxford U Pr.
Cameron, Norman. *see* Cameron, Norman Alexander.
Cameron, Norman Alexander, 1896-
  xCameron, Norman.
    Personality Development & Psychopathology:
      A Dynamic Approach. HM.
Cameron, Norman E. *see* Cameron, Norman Eustace.
Cameron, Norman Eustace.
  xCameron, Norman E.
    Evolution of the Negro. Negro U Pr.
Cameron, P. J.
  xCameron, P. J.
    Graph Theory, Coding Theory & Block
      Designs. Cambridge U Pr.
    Parallelisms of Complete Designs. Cambridge
      U Pr.
Cameron, Paul.
  xCameron, Paul.
    Sexual Gradualism: A Solution to the Sexual
      Dilemma of Teenagers & Young Adults.
      HumLife.
Cameron, Polly.
  xCameron, Polly.

Green Machine. Coward.
Cameron, Sharon.
  xCameron, Sharon.
    Lyricitme: Dickinson & the Limits of Genre.
      Johns Hopkins.
Cameron, Sheila M. *see* Cameron, Sheila MacNiven.
Cameron, Sheila MacNiven.
  xCameron, Sheila M.
    Homemade Ice Cream & Sherbet. C E Tuttle.
Cameron, Verney L. *see* Cameron, Verney Lovett.
Cameron, Verney Lovett, 1844-1894
  xCameron, Verney L.
    Across Africa. Johnson Repr.
    Across Africa. Negro U Pr.
Cameron, William B. *see* Cameron, William Bruce.
Cameron, William Bruce.
  xCameron, William B.
    Informal Sociology: A Casual Introduction to
      Sociological Thinking. Phila Bk Co.
Cameron, William W.
  xCameron, Wm.
    ed. Operation & Maintenance of Sewage
      Treatment Plants. Technomic.
Cameron, Wm. *see* Cameron, William W.
Cametti, Alberto, 1871-1935
  xCametti, Alberto.
    Palestrina. AMS Pr.
Camfield, William A.
  xCamfield, William A.
    Francis Picabia: His Art, Life & Times.
      Princeton U Pr.
Cammack, Floyd M.
  xCammack, Floyd M.
    Community College Library Instruction:
      Training for Self-Reliance in Basic Library
      Use. Shoe String.
Cammaert, Lorna P.
  xCammaert, Lorna P.
    A Woman's Choice: A Guide to Decision
      Making. Res Press.
Cammaerts, Emile.
  xCammaerts, Emile.
    The Laughing Prophet: The Seven Virtues & G.
      K. Chesterton. Folcroft.
Cammarata, Bernard, 1928-
  xCammarata, Bernard.
    Brother, Stranger. Paddington.
Cammell, C. R. *see* Cammell, Charles Richard.
Cammell, Charles Richard.
  xCammell, C. R.
    Aleister Crowley: The Man - the Mage - the
      Poet. Krishna Pr.
Cammett, John M. *see* Cammett, John McKay.
Cammett, John McKay, 1927-
  xCammett, John M.
    Antonio Gramsci & the Origins of Italian
      Communism. Stanford U Pr.
Camougis, George, 1930-
  xCamougis, George.
    Nerves, Muscles, & Electricity: An
      Introductory Manual of Electrophysiology.
      Plenum Pub.
Camp, Anthony J.
  xCamp, Anthony J.
    Everyone Has Roots: An Introduction to
      English Genealogy. Genealog Pub.
Camp, Catherine C. De. *see* De Camp, Catherine C.
Camp, Charles W. *see* Camp, Charles Wellner.
Camp, Charles Wellner, 1895-
  xCamp, Charles W.
    The Artisan in Elizabethan Literature.
      Octagon.
Camp, Helen. *see* Camp, Helen B.
Camp, Helen B., 1909-
  xCamp, Helen.
    Archaeological Excavations at Pemaquid,
      Maine. Maine St Mus.
Camp, L. S. De. *see* De Camp, L. S.
Camp, L. Sprague De. *see* De Camp, L. Sprague.
Camp, Maxime Du. *see* Du Camp, Maxime.

Campbell, James E. *see* Campbell, James Edward.
Campbell, James Edward.
  xCampbell, James E.
    ed. Pottery & Ceramics: A Guide to
      Information Sources. Gale.
Campbell, James Marshall, 1895-
  xCampbell, James.
    Greek Fathers. Cooper Sq.
Campbell, James W.
  xCampbell, James W.
    America in Her Centennial Year 1876. U Pr of
      Amer.
Campbell, Jeffrey.
  xCampbell, Jeffrey.
    The Homing. Putnam.
Campbell, Joan, 1929-
  xCampbell, Joan.
    The German Werkbund: The Politics of
      Reform in the Applied Arts. Princeton U Pr.
Campbell, John. *see* Campbell, John Franklin.
Campbell, John A.
  xCampbell, John A.
    Obstetrical Diagnosis by Radiographic,
      Ultrasonic & Nuclear Methods. Williams &
      Wilkins.
Campbell, John C. *see* Campbell, John Charles.
Campbell, John Campbell, Baron, 1779-1861
  xCampbell, John L.
    The Lives of the Chief Justices of England:
      From the Norman Conquest till the Death of
      Lord Tenterden. Arno.
Campbell, John Charles, 1867-1919
  xCampbell, John C.
    The Southern Highlander & His Homeland.
      Reprint.
    The Southern Highlander & His Homeland. U
      Pr of Ky.
Campbell, John Creighton.
  xCampbell, John C.
    Contemporary Japanese Budget Politics. U of
      Cal Pr.
Campbell, John F.
  xCampbell, John F.
    History & Bibliography of the New American
      Practical Navigator & the American Coast
      Pilot. Peabody Mus Salem.
Campbell, John Francis, 1822-1885
  xCampbell, J. F.
    The Celtic Dragon Myth. Newcastle Pub.
Campbell, John Franklin, 1940-
  xCampbell, John.
    Foreign Affairs Fudge Factory. Basic.
Campbell, John G. *see* Campbell, John Gregorson.
Campbell, John Gregorson.
  xCampbell, John G.
    Clan Traditions & Popular Tales of the
      Western Highlands & Islands. AMS Pr.
Campbell, John Kennedy.
  xCampbell, J. K.
    Honour, Family & Patronage: A Study of
      Institutions & Moral Values in a Greek
      Mountain Community. Oxford U Pr.
Campbell, John L. *see* Campbell, John Lorne.
Campbell, John Lorne, 1906-
  xCampbell, John L.
    Highland Songs of the Forty-Five. Arno.
Campbell, John S. *see* Campbell, John Scott.
Campbell, John Scott.
  xCampbell, John S.
    Improve Your Technical Communication. G S
      E Pubns.
Campbell, John W.
  xCampbell, John W.
    The Ultimate Weapon. Ace Bks.
Campbell, John W. *see* Campbell, John Wood.
Campbell, John Wood, 1910-1971
  xCampbell, John W.

    Cloak of Aesir. Hyperion-Conn.
Campbell, Joseph, 1904-
  xCampbell, Joseph.
    The Masks of God: Occidental Mythology.
      Penguin.
Campbell, Judith.
  xCampbell, Judith.
    The World of the Horse. A & W Pubs.
Campbell, June. *see* Campbell, June Blankenship.
Campbell, June Blankenship.

  xCampbell, June.
    Laboratory Mathematics: Medical & Biological
      Applications. Mosby.
Campbell, Karlyn K. *see* Campbell, Karlyn Kohrs.
Campbell, Karlyn Kohrs.
  xCampbell, Karlyn K.
    Critiques of Contemporary Rhetoric.
      Wadsworth Pub.
Campbell, Keith O.
  xCampbell, Keith O.
    Food for the Future: How Agriculture Can
      Meet the Challenge. U of Nebr Pr.
Campbell, Leslie. *see* Campbell, Leslie Caine.
Campbell, Leslie Caine, 1932-
  xCampbell, Leslie.
    Two Hundred Years of Pharmacy in
      Mississippi. U Pr of Miss.
Campbell, Lewis.
  xCampbell, Lewis.
    Life of James Clerk Maxwell. Johnson Repr.
    Religion in Greek Literature: A Sketch in
      Outline. Arno.
Campbell, Lily. *see* Campbell, Lily Bess.
Campbell, Lily B. *see* Campbell, Lily Bess.
Campbell, Lily Bess, 1883-1967
  xCampbell, Lily.
    The Grotesque in the Poetry of Robert
      Browning. Arden Lib.
  xCampbell, Lily B.
    Divine Poetry & Drama in Sixteenth-Century
      England. U of Cal Pr.
    Grotesque in the Poetry of Robert Browning.
      Folcroft.
Campbell, Lyle.
  xCampbell, Lyle.
    ed. The Languages of Native America:
      Historical & Comparative Assessment. U of
      Tex Pr.
    Quichean Linguistic Pre-History. U of Cal Pr.
Campbell, Margaret.
  xCampbell, Margaret.
    Dolmetsch: The Man & His Work. U of Wash
      Pr.
    The Spectral Bride. NAL.
Campbell, Margaret W.
  xCampbell, Margaret W.
    Paper Toy Making. Dover.
Campbell, Maria. *see* Campbell, Maria (Hull).
Campbell, Maria (Hull), 1788-1845
  xCampbell, Maria.
    ed. Revolutionary Services & Civil Life of
      General William Hull. Mss Info.
Campbell, Marie, 1907-
  xCampbell, Marie.
    Tales from the Cloud Walking Country.
      Greenwood.
Campbell, Mavis C. *see* Campbell, Mavis Christine.
Campbell, Mavis Christine.
  xCampbell, Mavis C.
    The Dynamics of Change in a Slave Society: A
      Sociopolitical History of the Free Colored's
      of Jamaica, 1800-1865. Fairleigh Dickinson.
Campbell, Mildred. *see* Campbell, Mildred Lucile.
Campbell, Mildred Lucile, 1897-
  xCampbell, Mildred.

    English Yeoman Under Elizabeth & the Early
      Stuarts. Kelley.
Campbell, Olwen (Ward).
  xCampbell, Olwen W.
    Thomas Love Peacock. Arno.
Campbell, Olwen W. *see* Campbell, Olwen (Ward).
Campbell, Oscar J. *see* Campbell, Oscar James.
Campbell, Oscar James, 1879-
  xCampbell, Oscar J.
    Comedies of Holberg. Arno.
    Comicall Satyre & Shakespeare's Troilus &
      Cressida. Huntington Lib.
    English Poetry of the Nineteenth Century.
      Greenwood.
    ed. Great English Poets. Arno.
Campbell, P. J. *see* Campbell, Patrick James.
Campbell, Patricia, 1901-
  xCampbell, Patricia.
    Cedarhaven. Popular Lib.
Campbell, Patrick James.
  xCampbell, P. J.
    The Ebb & Flow of Battle. St Martin.
Campbell, Persia C. *see* Campbell, Persia Crawford.
Campbell, Persia Crawford, 1898-
  xCampbell, Persia C.
    Chinese Coolie Emigration to Countries Within
      the British Empire. Biblio Dist.
    Chinese Coolie Emigration to Countries Within
      the British Empire. Chinese Materials.
    Chinese Coolie Emigration to Countries Within
      the British Empire. Negro U Pr.
Campbell, R.
  xCampbell, Robert.
    London Tradesman. Kelley.
Campbell, R. C. *see* Campbell, Richard Colin.
Campbell, R. H. *see* Campbell, Roy Hutcheson.
Campbell, R. Wright.
  xCampbell, R. Wright.
    Circus Couronne. G K Hall.
    The Spy Who Sat & Waited. PB.
    Where Pigeons Go to Die. Rawson Wade.
Campbell, Reginald J. *see* Campbell, Reginald John.
Campbell, Reginald John, 1867-1956
  xCampbell, Reginald J.
    Livingstone. Greenwood.
Campbell, Richard Colin.
  xCampbell, R. C.
    Statistics for Biologists. Cambridge U Pr.
Campbell, Richard L.
  xCampbell, Richard L.
    Historical Sketches of Colonial Florida. U
      Presses Fla.
Campbell, Rita R. *see* Campbell, Rita Ricardo.
Campbell, Rita Ricardo.
  xCampbell, Rita R.
    Drug Lag: Federal Government Decision
      Making. Hoover Inst Pr.
    Food Safety Regulation: A Study of the Use &
      Limitations of Cost-Benefit Analysis. Am
      Enterprise.
Campbell, Roald F. *see* Campbell, Roald Fay.
Campbell, Roald Fay.
  xCampbell, Roald F.
    Introduction to Educational Administration.
      Allyn.
    The Organization & Control of American
      Schools. Merrill.
    ed. Strengthening State Departments of
      Education. U Chicago Midwest Admin.
  xCampbell, Ronald F.
    The Organization & Control of American
      Schools. Merrill.
Campbell, Robert.
  xCampbell, Robert.
    The Enigma of the Mind. Time-Life.
    The Enigma of the Mind. Silver.
Campbell, Robert. *see* Campbell, R.
Campbell, Robert C.
  xCampbell, Robert C.

The Gospel of Paul. Judson.
Campbell, Robert Edward, 1931-
xCampbell, Robert.
Career Guidance: A Handbook of Methods.
Merrill.
Campbell, Robert W. *see* Campbell, Robert Wellington.
Campbell, Robert Wellington.
xCampbell, Robert W.
The Economics of Soviet Oil & Gas. Johns
Hopkins.
Soviet-Type Economies: Performance &
Evolution. HM.
Campbell, Rodney.
xCampbell, Rodney.
The Luciano Project: The Secret Wartime
Collaboration of the Mafia & the U.S. Navy.
McGraw.
Campbell, Ronald F. *see* Campbell, Roald Fay.
Campbell, Roy, 1901-1957
xCampbell, Roy.
Adamastor. Greenwood.
Flaming Terrapin. Scholarly.
Flowering Reeds: Poems. Scholarly.
Lorca: An Appreciation of His Poetry. Haskell.
Portugal. Arden Lib.
Campbell, Roy Hutcheson.
xCampbell, R. H.
Source Book of Scottish Economic & Social
History. Biblio Dist.
Campbell, Sheldon.
xCampbell, Sheldon.
Lifeboats to Ararat. McGraw.
Lifeboats to Ararat. Times Bks.
Campbell, Stephen K. *see* Campbell, Stephen Kent.
Campbell, Stephen Kent.
xCampbell, Stephen K.
Flaws & Fallacies in Statistical Thinking. P-H.
Campbell, Stu.
xCampbell, Stu.
Build Your Own Solar Water Heater. Garden
Way Pub.
The Mulch Book: A Guide for the Family
Food Gardener. Garden Way Pub.
Campbell, T. E. *see* Campbell, Thomas Elliott.
Campbell, Tessa.
xCampbell, Tessa.
Children's Picture Atlas. EMC.
Campbell, Thomas.
xCampbell, Thomas.
Complete Poetical Works of Thomas Campbell.
Haskell.
Campbell, Thomas Elliott.
xCampbell, T. E.
Colonial Caroline: A History of Caroline
County, Virginia. Dietz.
Campbell, Thomas F.
xCampbell, Thomas F.
Daniel E. Morgan, 1877-1949: The Good
Citizen in Politics. UPBS.
Campbell, Tim.
xCampbell, Tim.
The Do-It-Yourself Weather Book. Oxmoor
Hse.
Campbell, W. Reason.
xCampbell, W. Reason.
Dead Man Walking: Teaching in a Maximum
Security Prison. McGraw.
Campbell, Will D.
xCampbell, Will D.
Brother to a Dragonfly. Continuum.
Brother to a Dragonfly. Seabury.
Campbell, William A.
xCampbell, William A.
ed. North Carolina Guidebook for Registers of
Deeds. U of NC Inst Gov.
Campbell, William E. *see* Campbell, William Edward.
Campbell, William Edward, 1875-
xCampbell, William E.

More's Utopia & His Social Teaching. Russell.
Campbell-Johnson, Alan, 1913-
xCampbell-Johnson, Alan.
Eden: The Making of a Statesman. Greenwood.
Campbell-Jones, Suzanne, 1941-
xCampbell-Jones, Suzanne.
In Habit: A Study of Working Nuns. Pantheon.
Campion, Gilbert F. *see* Campion, Gilbert Francis
Montriou Campion.
Campion, Gilbert Francis Montriou Campion.
xCampion, Gilbert F.
European Parliamentary Procedure: A
Comparative Handbook. Hyperion Conn.
Campion, Thomas.
xCampion, Thomas.
Campion's Works. Oxford U Pr.
Songs & Masques: With Observations in the
Art of English Poesy. Folcroft.
Campione, Michael J.
xCampione, Michael J.
Anti-"Black" Magic. Campione.
Camplin, Jamie, 1947-
xCamplin, Jamie.
The Rise of the Rich. St Martin.
Campo, Michael R.
xCampo, Michael R.
ed. Pirandello, Moravia & Italian Poetry:
Intermediate Readings in Italian. Macmillan.
Campolo, Anthony.
xCampolo, Anthony.
A Denomination Looks at Itself. Judson.
Campos, Joachim J. *see* Campos, Joachim Joseph A.
Campos, Joachim Joseph A.
xCampos, Joachim J.
History of the Portuguese in Bengal. AMS Pr.
Campos Da Paz, Arthur.
xCampos Da Paz, Arthur.
Intro. by Human Reproduction. Igaku-Shoin.
Camrass, Zoe.
xCamrass, Zoe.
The Only Cookbook You'll Ever Need. Rand.
Camurati, Mireya.
xCamurati, Mireya.
Ideas y Motivos De Conversacion y
Composicion En Espanol. Heath.
Camus, Albert, 1913-1960
xCamus, Albert.
Exile & the Kingdom. Knopf.
Exile & the Kingdom. Random.
Fall. Knopf.
Fall. Random.
Notebooks: 1935-1942. Modern Lib.
Stranger. Knopf.
Stranger. Random.
Cana Conference of Chicago.
xCana Conference of Chicago.
Marriage: Discoveries and Encounters.
Delaney.
Perspectives on Money. Delaney.
Pre-Cana Packet. Delaney.
Cana, Frank R. *see* Cana, Frank Richardson.
Cana, Frank Richardson, 1865-1935
xCana, Frank R.
South Africa from the Great Trek to the
Union. Negro U Pr.
Canada. *see* Canada, Ralph.
Canada, John R.
xCanada, John R.
Capital Investment Decision Analysis for
Management & Engineering. P-H.
Canada, Lena.
xCanada, Lena.
To Elvis, with Love. Everest Hse.
To Elvis with Love. Schol Bk Serv.
Canada. Public Archives.
xCanada-Public Archives.
Documents Relating to Canadian Currency,
Exchange & Finance During the French
Period. B Franklin.
xPublic Archives of Canada.

Archives: Mirror of Canada Past - Miroir Du
Canada Passe. U of Toronto Pr.
Catalogue of the Public Archives of Canada:
Collection of Published Material with a
Chronological List of Pamphlets. G K Hall.
xPublic Archives of Canada (Ottawa).
Catalogue of the National Map Collection. G K
Hall.
Canada, Ralph.
xCanada.
Surviving the First Year of Law School. Lord
Pub.
Canada. Statistics Canada.
xStatistics Canada.
Canada Handbook: The 48th Annual
Handbook of Present Conditions & Recent
Progress. U of Wash Pr.
Canada-Public Archives. *see* Canada. Public Archives.
Canaday, Frank H., 1896-1976
xCanaday, Frank H.
Triumph in Color: The Life and Art of Molly
Morpeth Canaday. Phoenix Pub.
Canaday, John. *see* Canaday, John Edwin.
Canaday, John Edwin, 1907-
xCanaday, John.
The Artful Avocado. Cornerstone.
Lives of the Painters. Norton.
What Is Art?: An Introduction to Painting,
Sculpture, & Architecture. Knopf.
Canaday, Lee.
xCanaday, Lee.
Victim of Love. Dell.
Canaday, Nicholas.
xCanaday, Nicholas.
Melville & Authority. U Presses Fla.
**Canadian-American Conference on Parkinson'S Disease,
2d, Princeton, N.J., 1973.**
xCanadian-American Conference on Parkinson's
Disease, 2nd.
Parkinson's Disease: Advances in Neurology.
Raven.
Canadian Broadcasting Corporation.
xCanadian Broadcasting Corporation.
Thirty-Four Biographies of Canadian
Composers. Scholarly.
**Canadian Cancer Research Conference, 10th, Honey
Harbour, Ontario, 1973.**
xCanadian Cancer Research Conference, 10th,
1973.
Proceedings. U of Toronto Pr.
Canadian Mathematical Congress.
xBiennial Seminar of the Canadian Mathematical
Congress, 14th Univ. of Western Ontario, August
1973.
Optimal Control Theory & Its Applications:
Proceedings. Springer-Verlag.
Canadian Press Association.
xCanadian Press Association.
A History of Canadian Journalism in the
Several Portions of the Dominion. AMS Pr.
Canady, Robert L. *see* Canady, Robert Lynn.
Canady, Robert Lynn.
xCanady, Robert L.
How Parent-Teacher Conferences Build
Partnerships. Phi Delta Kappa.
Canal Zone Library-Museum. *see* Canal Zone,
Library-Museum, Balboa Heights.
Canal Zone, Library-Museum, Balboa Heights.
xCanal Zone Library-Museum.
Subject Catalog of the Special Panama
Collection of the Canal Zone Library
Museum. G K Hall.
Canart, Paul.
xCanart, Paul.
Studies in Comparative Semantics. St Martin.
Canary, Brenda. *see* Canary, Brenda Brown.
Canary, Brenda Brown.
xCanary, Brenda.
Home to the Mountain. Walker & Co.
Canary, Robert. *see* Canary, Robert H.

Canary, Robert H.
  xCanary, Robert.
    The Cabell Scene. Revisionist Pr.
  xCanary, Robert H.
    George Bancroft. Twayne.
    Robert Graves. Twayne.
Canavan, P. Joseph.
  xCanavan, P. Joseph.
    Paragraphs & Themes. Heath.
    Rhetoric & Literature. McGraw.
Canavor, Natalie, 1942-
  xCanavor, Natalie.
    Sell Your Photographs: The Complete
      Marketing Strategy for the Freelancer.
      Madrona Pubs.
Canaway, W. H.
  xCanaway, W. H.
    Crows in a Green Tree. State Mutual Bk.
Canby, Henry S. see Canby, Henry Seidel.
Canby, Henry Seidel, 1878-1961
  xCanby, Henry S.
    American Estimates. Kennikat.
    American Memoir. Greenwood.
    Classic Americans: A Study of Eminent
      American Writers from Irving to Whitman.
      Russell.
    College Sons & College Fathers. Arno.
    Thoreau. Peter Smith.
    Turn West, Turn East: Mark Twain & Henry
      James. Biblo.
Canby, Jeanny. see Canby, Jeanny Vorys.
Canby, Jeanny Vorys.
  xCanby, Jeanny.
    Ancient Near East in the Walters Art Gallery.
      Walters Art.
Canby, Vincent.
  xCanby, Vincent.
    Living Quarters. Ballantine.
    Living Quarters. Knopf.
Cancer Care, Inc.
  xCancer Care, Inc.
    Listen to the Children: A Study of the Impact
      on the Mental Health of Children of a
      Parent's Catastrophic Illness. Cancer Care.
Cancian, Frank.
  xCancian, Frank.
    Economics & Prestige in a Maya Community:
      The Religious Cargo System in Zinacantan.
      Stanford U Pr.
    The Innovator's Situation: Upper-Middle-Class
      Conservatism in Agricultural Communities.
      Stanford U Pr.
Cancro, R. see Cancro, Robert.
Cancro, Robert.
  xCancro, R.
    ed. Strategic Intervention in Schizophrenia:
      Current Developments in Treatment. Human
      Sci Pr.
  xCancro, Robert.
    ed. Progress in Functional Psychoses. Spectrum
      Pub.
Candelaria, Nash.
  xCandelaria, Nash.
    Memories of the Alhambra. Cibola.
Candland, Douglas. see Candland, Douglas K.
Candland, Douglas K.
  xCandland, Douglas.
    Psychology: The Experimental Approach.
      McGraw.
  xCandland, Douglas K.
    Psychology: The Experimental Approach.
      McGraw.
Candler, Allen D. see Candler, Allen Daniel.
Candler, Allen Daniel.
  xCandler, Allen D.
    ed. Georgia, Comprising Sketches of Counties,
      Towns, Events, Institutions, & Persons,
      Arranged in Cyclopedic Form. Reprint.
Candler, Teresa. see Candler, Teresa Gilardi.

Candler, Teresa Gilardi.
  xCandler, Teresa.
    The Northern Italian Cookbook. McGraw.
Candlin, Enid S. see Candlin, Enid Saunders.
Candlin, Enid Saunders.
  xCandlin, Enid S.
    The Breach in the Wall: A Memoir of the Old
      China. Macmillan.
Candlish, R. S. see Candlish, Robert Smith.
Candlish, Robert Smith, 1806-1873
  xCandlish, R. S.
    First Epistle of John. Kregel.
Candoli. see Candoli, I. Carl.
Candoli, I. Carl.
  xCandoli.
    School Business Administration: A Planning
      Approach. Allyn.
Cane, Melville, 1879-
  xCane, Melville.
    All & Sundry: An Oblique Autobiography.
      HarBraceJ.
Canetti, Elias, 1905-
  xCanetti, Elias.
    Auto-Da-Fe. Continuum.
    The Conscience of Words. Continuum.
    Crowds & Power. Continuum.
    Earwitness: Fifty Characters. Continuum.
    The Human Province. Continuum.
    The Tongue Set Free: Remembrance of a
      European Childhood. Continuum.
Caney, Steven.
  xCaney, Steven.
    Steven Caney's Playbook. Workman Pub.
Canfield, Cass, 1897-
  xCanfield, Cass.
    The Incredible Pierpont Morgan: Financier &
      Art Collector. Har-Row.
Canfield, D. Lincoln. see Canfield, Delos Lincoln.
Canfield, Delos Lincoln.
  xCanfield, D. Lincoln.
    An Introduction to Romance Linguistics. S Ill
      U Pr.
Canfield, Dorothy.
  xCanfield, Dorothy.
    Understood Betsy. Harmony & Co.
Canfield, J. Douglas. see Canfield, John Douglas.
Canfield, Jane W. see Canfield, Jane White.
Canfield, Jane White.
  xCanfield, Jane W.
    Frog Prince: A True Story. Har-Row.
    Swan Cove. Har-Row.
Canfield, John Douglas, 1941-
  xCanfield, J. Douglas.
    Nicholas Rowe & Christian Tragedy. U Presses
      Fla.
Canfield, Leon H. see Canfield, Leon Hardy.
Canfield, Leon Hardy, 1886-
  xCanfield, Leon H.
    The Early Persecutions of the Christians. AMS
      Pr.
Canfield, William W. see Canfield, William Walker.
Canfield, William Walker, 1855-1937
  xCanfield, William W.
    Legends of the Iroquois. Kennikat.
Cang, Joel.
  xCang, Joel.
    Silent Millions: A History of the Jews in the
      Soviet Union. Taplinger.
Cangelosi, Vincent E.
  xCangelosi, Vincent E.
    Basic Statistics: A Real World Approach. West
      Pub.
Cangemi, Joseph P.
  xCangemi, Joseph P.
    Higher Education & the Development of
      Self-Actualizing Personalities. Philos Lib.
Canham, Erwin D.
  xCanham, Erwin D.

    Ethics of United States Foreign Relations. U of
      Mo Pr.
Canjar, Lawrence. see Canjar, Lawrence Nicholas.
Canjar, Lawrence Nicholas.
  xCanjar, Lawrence.
    Thermodynamic Properties & Reduced
      Correlations for Gases. Gulf Pub.
Cannan, Edwin, 1861-1935
  xCannan, Edwin.
    History of the Theories of Production &
      Distribution in English Political Economy
      from 1776 to 1848. Kelley.
    Review of Economic Theory. Biblio Dist.
    Review of Economic Theory. Kelley.
Cannata, Sam.
  xCannata, Sam.
    Truth on Trial. Broadman.
Cannell, David.
  xCannell, David.
    Modern Development in Yacht Design. Dodd.
Cannell, J. see Cannell, John Clucas.
Cannell, J. C. see Cannell, John Clucas.
Cannell, John Clucas.
  xCannell, J.
    Secrets of Houdini. Wehman.
  xCannell, J. C.
    The Secrets of Houdini. Dover.
    Secrets of Houdini. Gale.
    The Secrets of Houdini. Peter Smith.
Cannie, Joan K. see Cannie, Joan Koob.
Cannie, Joan Koob.
  xCannie, Joan K.
    The Woman's Guide to Management Success:
      How to Win Power in the Real
      Organizational World. P-H.
Canning, Victor.
  xCanning, Victor.
    The Crimson Chalice. Acc Bks.
    The Crimson Chalice. Morrow.
    The Doomsday Carrier. Charter Bks.
    The Doomsday Carrier. Morrow.
    Flight of the Grey Goose. Morrow.
    The Satan Sampler. Morrow.
Cannom, Robert. see Cannom, Robert C.
Cannom, Robert C.
  xCannom, Robert.
    Van Dyke & the Mythical City Hollywood.
      Garland Pub.
Cannon, Bill. see Cannon, William.
Cannon, Bryan J. see Cannon, Bryan Jay.
Cannon, Bryan Jay.
  xCannon, Bryan J.
    Celebrate Yourself: The Secret to a Life of
      Hope & Joy. Word Bks.
Cannon, Carl L. see Cannon, Carl Leslie.
Cannon, Carl Leslie, 1888-
  xCannon, Carl L.
    American Book Collectors & Collecting from
      Colonial Times to the Present. Greenwood.
Cannon, Don L.
  xCannon, Don L.
    Understanding Microprocessors. Tex Instr Inc.
Cannon, Elaine.
  xCannon, Elaine.
    The Mighty Change. Deseret Bk.
    Putting Life in Your Life Story. Deseret Bk.
Cannon, Garland. see Cannon, Garland Hampton.
Cannon, Garland Hampton, 1924-
  xCannon, Garland.
    An Integrated Transformational Grammar of
      the English Language. Humanities.
Cannon, Grant G.
  xCannon, Grant G.
    Great Men of Modern Agriculture. Macmillan.
Cannon, J. see Cannon, John Ashton.
Cannon, James P. see Cannon, James Patrick.
Cannon, James Patrick.
  xCannon, James P.

Letters from Prison. Path Pr NY.
Notebook of an Agitator. Path Pr NY.
Speeches for Socialism. Path Pr NY.
The Struggle for a Proletarian Party. Path Pr
NY.

Cannon, Joe. see Cannon, Joseph Gurney.

Cannon, John Ashton.
xCannon, J.
Parliamentary Reform: 1640-1832. Cambridge
U Pr.

Cannon, Joseph Gurney.
xCannon, Joe.
Uncle Joe Cannon: The Story of a Pioneer
American. Scholarly.

Cannon, Joseph L, 1927-
xCannon, Joseph L.
For Missionaries Only. Baker Bk.

Cannon, Le Grand. see Cannon, le Grand Bouton.

Cannon, le Grand Bouton, 1815-1906
xCannon, Le Grand.
Personal Reminiscences of the Rebellion
1861-1866. Arno.

Cannon, Lee.
xCannon, Lee.
Quick & Easy Cookbook. Oxmoor Hse.

Cannon, Mary A. see Cannon, Mary Agnes.

Cannon, Mary Agnes, 1870-
xCannon, Mary A.
The Education of Women During the
Renaissance. Hyperion Conn.

Cannon, Minuha, 1912-
xCannon, Minuha.
The Fructose Cookbook. East Woods.

Cannon, Robert H.
xCannon, Robert H.
Dynamics of Physical Systems. McGraw.

Cannon, William, 1919-
xCannon, Bill.
How to Cast Small Metal & Rubber Parts.
TAB Bks.

Cannon, William R. see Cannon, William Ragsdale.

Cannon, William Ragsdale, 1916-
xCannon, William R.
Jesus the Servant: From the Gospel of Mark.
Upper Room.

Canon, Claudia Von. see Von Canon, Claudia.

Canon, M. see Canon, Michael D.

Canon, Michael D.
xCanon, M.
Theory of Optimal Control & Mathematical
Programming. McGraw.

Canovan, Margaret.
xCanovan, Margaret.
G. K. Chesterton: Radical Populist. HarBraceJ.

Cantarella, M. see Cantarella, Michele.

Cantarella, Michele, 1899-
xCantarella, M.
Prosatori Del Novecento. HR&W.

Cantarow, Ellen.
xCantarow, Ellen.
Moving the Mountain: Women Working for
Social Change. Feminist Pr.

Cantelon, Willard.
xCantelon, Willard.
Money Master of the World. Logos.
New Money or None. Logos.

Canter, David. see Canter, David V.

Canter, David V.
xCanter, David.
Psychology for Architects. Halsted Pr.
The Psychology of Place. Intl Pubns Serv.
The Psychology of Place. St Martin.

·, Larry W.
Canter, Larry W.
Handbook of Variables for Environmental
Impact Assessment. Ann Arbor Science.
Water Resources Assessment: Methodology &
Technology Sourcebook. Ann Arbor Science.

E. Ray.
·bery, E. Ray.

The Making of Economics. Wadsworth Pub.

Canterbury, Eng. (Province). Prerogative Court.
xCanterbury England Prerogative Court.
Wills from Doctors' Commons, 1495-1695.
Johnson Repr.

Canterbury England Prerogative Court. see Canterbury,
Eng. (Province). Prerogative Court.

Cantin, Donald. see Cantin, Donald W.

Cantin, Donald W.
xCantin, Donald.
Care & Maintenance of Small Boats. Manor
Bks.
xCantin, Donald W.
Turn Your Ideas into Money. Dutton.

Cantor, Edward B.
xCantor, Edward B.
Female Urinary Stress Incontinence. C C
Thomas.

Cantor, Leon.
xCantor, Lon.
How to Select & Install Antennas. Hayden.

Cantor, Leonard M. see Cantor, Leonard Martin.

Cantor, Leonard Martin.
xCantor, Leonard M.
Further Education in England & Wales.
Routledge & Kegan.

Cantor, Lon. see Cantor, Leon.

Cantor, Milton.
xCantor, Milton.
ed. American Workingclass Culture:
Explorations in American Labor & Social
History. Greenwood.
ed. Class, Sex, & the Woman Worker.
Greenwood.
The Divided Left: American Radicalism,
1900-1975. Hill & Wang.
Max Eastman. Irvington.

Cantor, Norman F.
xCantor, Norman F.
Church, Kingship & Lay Investiture in
England, 1089-1135. Octagon.
History of Popular Culture. Macmillan.
How to Study History. AHM Pub.
Medieval World: 300-1300. Macmillan.

Cantor, Robert C. see Cantor, Robert Chernin.

Cantor, Robert Chernin.
xCantor, Robert C.
And a Time to Live: Toward Emotional
Well-Being During the Crisis of Cancer.
Har-Row.
And a Time to Live: Toward Emotional
Well-Being During the Crisis of Cancer.
Har-Row.

Cantor, Robert D.
xCantor, Robert D.
American Government. Har-Row.
Introduction to International Politics. Peacock
Pubs.

Cantore, Enrico.
xCantore, Enrico.
Atomic Order: An Introduction to the
Philosophy of Microphysics. MIT Pr.

Cantow, M. J. see Cantow, Manfred J. R.

Cantow, Manfred J. R.
xCantow, M. J.
ed. Polymer Fractionation. Acad Pr.

Cantrell, Leon. see Cantrell, Leon Nicolas.

Cantrell, Leon Nicolas, 1943-
xCantrell, Leon.
Bards, Bohemians & Bookmen: Essays in
Australian Literature. U of Queensland Pr.

Cantril, Hadley.
xCantril, Hadley.

Gauging Public Opinion. Kennikat.
The Pattern of Human Concerns. Rutgers U Pr.
The Psychology of Social Movements. Core
Collection.
The Psychology of Social Movements. Krieger.
Reflections on the Human Venture. NYU Pr.

Cantu, Caesar C.
xCantu, Caesar C.
Cortes & the Fall of the Aztec Empire.
Modern World.

Cantu, Robert. see Cantu, Robert C.

Cantu, Robert C.
xCantu, Robert.
Toward Fitness: Guided Exercise for Those
with Health Problems. Human Sci Pr.

Cantwell, George. see Cantwell, George E.

Cantwell, George E.
xCantwell, George.
ed. Insect Diseases. Dekker.

Cantwell, J. D. see Cantwell, John D.

Cantwell, John D.
xCantwell, J. D.
Modern Cardiology. Butterworths.
xCantwell, John D.
Stay Young at Heart. Nelson Hall.

Cantwell, Zita M.
xCantwell, Zita M.
Instructional Technology: An Annotated
Bibliography. Scarecrow.

Canudo, Eugene R.
xCanudo, Eugene R.
Criminal Law of New York. Gould.

Capablanca, J. R. see Capablanca, Jose Raul.

Capablanca, Jose R. see Capablanca, Jose Raul.

Capablanca, Jose Raul, 1888-1942
xCapablanca, J. R.
A Primer of Chess. HarBraceJ.
xCapablanca, Jose R.
Chess Fundamentals. HarBraceJ.
Chess Fundamentals. McKay.
Primer of Chess. HarBraceJ.
World's Championship Matches: 1921 & 1927.
Dover.

Capachi, Nick, 1934-
xCapachi, Nick.
Excavation & Grading Handbook. Craftsman.

Capaldi. see Capaldi, Roderick A.

Capaldi, Frederick P. see Capaldi, Fredrick.

Capaldi, Fredrick.
xCapaldi, Frederick P.
Stepfamilies: A Cooperative Responsibility.
New Viewpoints.

Capaldi, Nicholas.
xCapaldi, Nicholas.
The Art of Deception. Prometheus Bks.
David Hume. Twayne.

Capaldi, Roderick A.
xCapaldi.
Membrane Proteins in Energy Transduction.
Dekker.

Caparosa, Ralph J.
xCaparosa, Ralph J.
An Atlas of Surgical Anatomy & Techniques of
the Temporal Bone. C C Thomas.

Capek, Karel, 1890-1938
xCapek, Karel.
The Absolute at Large. Garland Pub.
Absolute at Large. Hyperion Conn.
Money & Other Stories. Arno.

Capell, Edward, 1713-1781
xCapell, Edward.
Notes & Various Readings to Shakespeare.
AMS Pr.
ed. Notes & Various Readings to Shakespeare.
B Franklin.

Capell, Elizabeth A.
xCapell, Elizabeth A.

Constitutional Officers, Agencies, Boards &
Commissions in California State Government:
1849-1975. Inst Gov Stud Berk.
Capelle, Friedrich W.
xCapelle, Friedrich W.
Professional Perspective Drawing for Architects
& Engineers. McGraw.
Capen, Edward W. *see* Capen, Edward Warren.
Capen, Edward Warren, 1870-
xCapen, Edward W.
Historical Development of the Poor Law of
Connecticut. AMS Pr.
Capes, Bernard. *see* Capes, Bernard Edward Joseph.
Capes, Bernard Edward Joseph, d. 1918
xCapes, Bernard.
Historical Vignettes. Branden.
Historical Vignettes. Lib Serv Inc.
**Capital Conference on Graph Theory and Combination,
George Washington University, 1973.**
xCapital Conference on Graph Theory &
Conbinatorics, George Washington University,
June 18-22, 1973.
Graphs & Combinatorics: Proceedings.
Springer-Verlag.
Caplan. *see* Caplan, Ronald M.
Caplan, David.
xCaplan, David.
Biological Studies of Mental Processes. MIT
Pr.
Caplan, Frank.
xCaplan, Frank.
The Power of Play. Doubleday.
Caplan, Gerald, M.d.
xCaplan, Gerald.
An Approach to Community Mental Health.
Grune.
Arab & Jew in Jerusalem: Explorations in
Community Mental Health. Harvard U Pr.
Principles of Preventive Psychiatry. Basic.
Theory & Practice of Mental Health
Consultation. Basic.
Caplan, H. H.
xCaplan, H. H.
ed. The Classified Directory of Artists'
Signatures, Symbols, & Monograms. Gale.
Caplan, Neil.
xCaplan, Neil.
Palestine Jewry & the Arab Question,
1917-1925. Biblio Dist.
Caplan, Patricia.
xCaplan, Patricia.
ed. Women United, Women Divided:
Comparative Studies of Ten Contemporary
Cultures. Ind U Pr.
Caplan, Ronald.
xCaplan, Ronald.
Down North: The Book of Cape Breton's
Magazine. Doubleday.
Caplan, Ronald M.
xCaplan.
Advances in Obstetrics & Gynecology.
Williams & Wilkins.
Capley, M. J.
xCapley, M. J.
More Bible Puzzles & Games. Revell.
Caplovitz, David.
xCaplovitz, David.
Consumers in Trouble: Study of Debtors in
Default. Free Pr.
Making Ends Meet: How Families Cope with
Inflation & Recession. Sage.
Poor Pay More: Consumer Practices of Low
Income Families. Free Pr.
The Religious Drop-Outs: Apostasy Among
College Graduates. Sage.
Caplow, Theodore.
xCaplow, Theodore.

The Academic Marketplace. Arno.
Sociology. P-H.
The Sociology of Work. Greenwood.
Capon, Brian.
xCapon, Brian.
ed. Neighboring Group Participation. Plenum
Pub.
Capon, Robert F. *see* Capon, Robert Farrar.
Capon, Robert Farrar.
xCapon, Robert F.
Party Spirit: Some Entertaining Principles.
Morrow.
The Supper of the Lamb: A Culinary
Reflection. HarBracej.
Capon, Robin.
xCapon, Robin.
Paper Collage. Branford.
Caponi, Anthony.
xCaponi, Anthony.
Boulders & Pebbles of Poetry & Prose.
Independence Pr.
Caponigri, A. Robert. *see* Caponigri, Aloysius Robert.
Caponigri, Aloysius R. *see* Caponigri, Aloysius Robert.
Caponigri, Aloysius Robert, 1913-
xCaponigri, A. Robert.
tr. Contemporary Spanish Philosophy: An
Anthology. U of Notre Dame Pr.
xCaponigri, Aloysius R.
ed. Modern Catholic Thinkers. Arno.
Capote, Truman, 1924-
xCapote, Truman.
Christmas Memory. Random.
The Dogs Bark: Public People & Private
Places. NAL.
Other Voices Other Rooms. NAL.
Other Voices, Other Rooms. Random.
The Thanksgiving Visitor. Random.
Capotosto, John.
xCapotosto, John.
Basic Carpentry. Reston.
Capotosto, Rosario.
xCapotosto, Rosario.
The Complete Book of Woodworking.
Har-Row.
Cappelluzzo, Emma. *see* Cappelluzzo, Emma M.
Cappelluzzo, Emma M.
xCappelluzzo, Emma.
Guidance & the Migrant Child. HM.
Cappon, Daniel.
xCappon, Daniel.
Health & the Environment. Pergamon.
Cappon, Lester. *see* Cappon, Lester Jesse.
Cappon, Lester J. *see* Cappon, Lester Jesse.
Cappon, Lester Jesse, 1900-
xCappon, Lester.
ed. Atlas of Early American History: The
Revolutionary Era, 1769-1790. Newberry.
xCappon, Lester J.
American Genealogical Periodicals: A
Bibliography with a Chronological
Finding-List. NY Pub Lib.
Atlas of Early American History: The
Revolutionary Era, 1760-1790. Princeton U
Pr.
Capps, Benjamin, 1922-
xCapps, Benjamin.
The White Man's Road. Ace Bks.
White Man's Road. Har-Row.
Woman Chief. Doubleday.
Capps, Clifford S. *see* Capps, Clifford Sheats.
Capps, Clifford Sheats.
xCapps, Clifford S.
Colonial Georgia. Elsevier-Nelson.
Capps, Donald.
xCapps, Donald.
Pastoral Care: A Thematic Approach.
Westminster.
ed. Psychology of Religion: A Guide to
Information Sources. Gale.
xCapps, Donald E.

ed. Religious Personality. Wadsworth Pub.
Capps, Donald E. *see* Capps, Donald.
Capps, Jack L.
xCapps, Jack L.
ed. As I Lay Dying: A Concordance to the
Novel. Univ Microfilms.
Caprio, Betsy.
xCaprio, Betsy.
Star Trek: Good News in Modern Images.
Andrews & McMeel.
Caprio, Dennis.
xCaprio, Dennis.
Appliance Repair. Reston.
Caprio, Frank B. *see* Caprio, Frank Samuel.
Caprio, Frank S. *see* Caprio, Frank Samuel.
Caprio, Frank Samuel, 1906-
xCaprio, Frank B.
jt. auth. Parents & Teenagers. Citadel Pr.
xCaprio, Frank S.
Add Life to Your Years. Citadel Pr.
Female Homosexuality: A Psychodynamic
Study of Lesbianism. Citadel Pr.
How to Avoid a Nervous Breakdown. Dutton.
Parents & Teenagers. Citadel Pr.
Power of Sex. Citadel Pr.
Variations in Sexual Behavior. Citadel Pr.
Capron, J. Hugh.
xCapron, J. Hugh.
Wood Laminating. McKnight.
Capstick, Peter H. *see* Capstick, Peter Hathaway.
Capstick, Peter Hathaway.
xCapstick, Peter H.
Death in the Long Grass. St Martin.
Capt, E. Raymond.
xCapt, E. Raymond.
Stonehenge & Druidism. Artisan Sales.
Capua, A. G. De. *see* De Capua, A. G.
Capurro, L. R. *see* Capurro, Luis R. A.
Capurro, Luis R. *see* Capurro, Luis R. A.
Capurro, Luis R. A.
xCapurro, L. R.
ed. Contributions on the Physical
Oceanography of the Gulf of Mexico. Gulf
Pub.
xCapurro, Luis R.
Oceanography for Practicing Engineers. CBI
Pub.
Capute, Arnold J., 1923-
xCapute, Arnold J.
Primitive Reflex Profile. Univ Park.
Caputi, Anthony. *see* Caputi, Anthony Francis.
Caputi, Anthony Francis, 1924-
xCaputi, Anthony.
Buffo: The Genius of Vulgar Comedy. Wayne
St U Pr.
Caputo, David A., 1943-
xCaputo, David A.
ed. The Politics of Policy Making in America:
Five Case Studies. W H Freeman.
Revenue Sharing: Methodological Approaches
& Problems. Lexington Bks.
Caputo, Robert.
xCaputo, Robert.
Hyena Day. Coward.
Carafoli, E. *see* Carafoli, Ernesto.
Carafoli, Ernesto.
xCarafoli, E.
ed. Membrane Biochemistry: A Laboratory
Manual on Transport & Bioenergetics.
Springer-Verlag.
Caraley, Demetrios.
xCaraley, Demetrios.
City Governments & Urban Problems: A New
Introduction to Urban Politics. P-H.
Politics of Military Unification: A Study of
Conflict & the Policy Process. Columbia U
Pr.
Carano, Paul.
xCarano, Paul.

A Complete History of Guam. C E Tuttle.
Caras, Roger. *see* Caras, Roger A.
Caras, Roger A.
 xCaras, Roger.
  Dogs: Records, Stars, Feats, & Facts.
   HarBraceJ.
  The Forest. HM.
  The Forest. HR&W.
  Going to the Zoo with Roger Caras.
   HarBraceJ.
  Panther!. Penguin.
  The Roger Caras Dog Book. HR&W.
  Sockeye: The Life of a Pacific Salmon. Dial.
  Venomous Animals of the World. P-H.
  The Wonderful World of Mammals:
   Adventuring with Stamps. HarBraceJ.
 xCaras, Roger A.
  Yankee: The Inside Story of a Champion
   Bloodhound. Putnam.
Carasov, Victor, 1904-
 xCarasov, Victor.
  Two Gentlemen to See You, Sir: The
   Autobiography of a Villain. Taplinger.
Carbaugh, Robert J., 1946-
 xCarbaugh, Robert J.
  International Economics. Winthrop.
Carberry, M. *see* Carberry, M. S.
Carberry, M. S.
 xCarberry, M.
  Foundations of Computer Science. Computer
   Sci.
Carbo, Dorothy.
 xCarbo, Dorothy.
  Fix It Guide for Women. Arco.
Carby-Hall, Joseph R. *see* Carby-Hall, Joseph Roger.
Carby-Hall, Joseph Roger.
 xCarby-Hall, Joseph R.
  Worker Participation in Europe. Rowman.
Carchedi, Guglielmo.
 xCarchedi, Guglielmo.
  On the Economic Identification of Social
   Classes. Routledge & Kegan.
Carcione, Joe.
 xCarcione, Joe.
  The Greengrocer Cookbook. Celestial Arts.
Carcopino, Jerome, 1881-1970
 xCarcopino, Jerome.
  Cicero, the Secrets of His Correspondence.
   Greenwood.
Card, Leslie E. *see* Card, Leslie Ellsworth.
Card, Leslie Ellsworth.
 xCard, Leslie E.
  jt. auth. Poultry Production. Lea & Febiger.
Card, Orson S. *see* Card, Orson Scott.
Card, Orson Scott.
 xCard, Orson S.
  A Planet Called Treason. Dell.
  A Planet Called Treason. St Martin.
  Songmaster. Dial.
Cardamone, Tom.
 xCardamone, Tom.
  Advertising Agency & Studio Skills: A Guide
   to the Preparation of Art & Mechanicals for
   Reproduction. Watson-Guptill.
Carden, Karen W.
 xCarden, Karen W.
  The Persecuted Prophets. A S Barnes.
Carden, Patricia.
 xCarden, Patricia.
  The Art of Isaac Babel. Cornell U Pr.
Cardenal, Ernesto.
 xCardenal, Ernesto.
  Apocalypse, & Other Poems. New Directions.
  The Gospel in Solentiname. Orbis Bks.
  Homage to the American Indians. Johns
   Hopkins.
  In Cuba. New Directions.
Cardenas. *see* Cardenas, Alfonso F.
Cardenas, Alfonso F.
 xCardenas.

Data Base Management Systems. Allyn.
 xCardenas, Alfonso F.
  Computer Science. Wiley.
Cardiff, Gray E. *see* Cardiff, Gray Emerson.
Cardiff, Gray Emerson.
 xCardiff, Gray E.
  The Coming Real Estate Crash. Arlington Hse.
Cardiff, Sara.
 xCardiff, Sara.
  The Speaking Stones. Fawcett.
Cardinal, Roger.
 xCardinal, Roger.
  Primitive Painters 1835-1975. St Martin.
Cardinale, Hyginus E. *see* Cardinale, Igino.
Cardinale, Igino.
 xCardinale, Hyginus E.
  The Holy See & the International Order.
   Humanities.
Cardinall, Allan W. *see* Cardinall, Allan Wolsey.
Cardinall, Allan Wolsey, 1887-
 xCardinall, Allan W.
  In Ashanti & Beyond: The Record of a
   Resident Magistrate's Many Years in
   Tropical Africa. Johnson Repr.
  Tales Told in Togoland. Negro U Pr.
Carding, David K. *see* Carding, David Kellett.
Carding, David Kellett.
 xCarding, David K.
  The Home Medical Guide. Merrimack Bk Serv.
Cardiovascular Conference, 3rd, Aspen, Colo., 1972.
 xCardiovascular Conference, 3rd, Aspen, Colo.,
  Jan. 1972.
  Myocardial Infarction: A New Look at an Old
   Subject. S Karger.
Cardiovascular Conference, 4th, Aspen, Colo., Jan. 1973.
 see Conference on Cardiovascular Disease, 4th, Aspen,
 Colo., 1973.
Cardiovascular Conference, 5th, Snowmass-at-Aspen,
 Colorado, Jan. 1974. *see* Conference on
 Cardiovascular Disease, 5th, Aspen, Colo., 1974.
Cardiovascular Disease Conference, 1st,
 Snowmass-at-Aspen, Colorado, 1970. *see* Conference
 on Cardiovascular Disease, 1st, Aspen, Colo., 1970.
Cardiovascular Disease 6th Conference in Snowmass at
 Aspen, Colorado, January 1975. *see* Conference on
 Cardiovascular Disease, 6th, Aspen, Colo., 1975.
Cardona, George, 1926-
 xCardona, George.
  On Haplology in Indo-European. U of Pa Pr.
Cardona, Giorgio R. *see* Cardona, Giorgio Raimondo.
Cardona, Giorgio Raimondo.
 xCardona, Giorgio R.
  Standard Italian. Mouton.
Cardoso, Fernando E. *see* Cardoso, Fernando Henrique.
Cardoso, Fernando Henrique.
 xCardoso, Fernando E.
  Dependency & Development in Latin America.
   U of Cal Pr.
Cardozo, Benjamin N. *see* Cardozo, Benjamin Nathan.
Cardozo, Benjamin Nathan, 1870-1938
 xCardozo, Benjamin N.
  The Growth of the Law. Greenwood.
  Nature of the Judicial Process. Yale U Pr.
  Paradoxes of Legal Science. Greenwood.
Cardozo, Jacob L. *see* Cardozo, Jacob Lopes.
Cardozo, Jacob Lopes.
 xCardozo, Jacob L.
  The Contemporary Jew in the Elizabethan
   Drama. B Franklin.
Cardozo, Jacob N. *see* Cardozo, Jacob Newton.
Cardozo, Jacob Newton.
 xCardozo, Jacob N.
  Notes on Political Economy. Kelley.
  Notes on Political Economy. Scholarly.
Cardozo, Michael H., 1910-
 xCardozo, Michael H.

Diplomats in International Cooperation:
 Stepchildren of the Foreign Service. Cornell
 U Pr.
Cardus, Neville, Sir, 1889-1975
 xCardus, Neville.
  Autobiography. Greenwood.
  Talking of Music. Greenwood.
Cardwell, Charles E.
 xCardwell, Charles E.
  Argument & Inference: An Introduction to
   Symbolic Logic. Merrill.
Cardwell, D. S. *see* Cardwell, Donald Stephen Lowell.
Cardwell, Donald Stephen Lowell.
 xCardwell, D. S.
  From Watt to Clausius: The Rise of
   Thermodynamics in the Early Industrial Age.
   Cornell U Pr.
Cardwell, Jerry D. *see* Cardwell, Jerry Delmas.
Cardwell, Jerry Delmas.
 xCardwell, Jerry D.
  Readings in Social Psychology: A Symbolic
   Interaction Perspective. AHM Pub.
Careers Research & Advisory Centre. *see* Careers
 Research and Advisory Centre.
Careers Research and Advisory Centre.
 xCareers Research & Advisory Centre.
  Graduate Studies Nineteen Seventy-Nine to
   Nineteen Eighty. Intl Pubns Serv.
  Graduate Studies, 1978-79. Intl Pubns Serv.
Carefoot, Thomas, 1938-
 xCarefoot, Thomas.
  Pacific Seashores: A Guide to Intertidal
   Ecology. U of Wash Pr.
Carek, Donald J.
 xCarek, Donald J.
  Principles of Child Psychotherapy. C C
   Thomas.
Careless, Anthony. *see* Careless, Anthony G. S.
Careless, Anthony G. S.
 xCareless, Anthony.
  Initiative and Response: The Adaptation of
   Canadian Federalism to Regional Economic
   Development. McGill-Queens U Pr.
Careless, James M. *see* Careless, James Maurice
 Stockford.
Careless, James Maurice Stockford, 1919-
 xCareless, James M.
  Canada: A Story of Challenge. St Martin.
Carels, Edward. *see* Carels, Edward J.
Carels, Edward J.
 xCarels, Edward.
  The Physician & Cost Control. Oelgeschlager.
Carew, Anthony, 1943-
 xCarew, Anthony.
  Democracy & Government in European Trade
   Unions. Allen Unwin.
Carew, Dorothy.
 xCarew, Dorothy.
  Portugal. Macmillan.
Carew, Henry.
 xCarew, Henry.
  The Vampires of the Andes. Arno.
Carew, J. *see* Carew, Jean V.
Carew, Jan.
 xCarew, Jan.
  The Third Gift. Little.
Carew, Jean V.
 xCarew, J.
  Observing Intelligence in Young Children:
   Eight Case Studies. P-H.
 xCarew, Jean V.
  Beyond Bias: Perspectives on Classrooms.
   Harvard U Pr.
Carew, Jocelyn.
 xCarew, Jocelyn.
  Golden Sovereigns. Avon.
Carew, Richard.
 xCarew, Richard.

The Survey of Cornwall. Walter J Johnson.

Carew, Rod.
xCarew, Rod.
Carew. S&S.

Carey, Floyd D.
xCarey, Floyd D.
ed. Sunday School Basics. Pathway Pr.

Carey, Gary.
xCarey, Gary.
Grapes of Wrath Notes. Cliffs.
Lenny, Janis & Jimi. PB.
Of Mice & Men Notes. Cliffs.

Carey, George.
xCarey, George.
I Believe in Man. Eerdmans.

Carey, George. see Carey, George Gibson.

Carey, George G. see Carey, George Gibson.

Carey, George Gibson, 1934-
xCarey, George.
A Faraway Time & Place: Lore of the Eastern
Shore. Arno.
xCarey, George G.
Maryland Folklore & Folklife. Cornell
Maritime.

Carey, Henry C. see Carey, Henry Charles.

Carey, Henry Charles, 1793-1879
xCarey, Henry C.
Credit System in France, Great Britain & the
United States. Kelley.
Past, the Present, & the Future. Kelley.

Carey, Howard R. see Carey, Howard Ray.

Carey, Howard Ray.
xCarey, Howard R.
Journey into Light & Joy. De Vorss.

Carey, Iskandar, 1924-
xCarey, Iskandar.
Orang Asli: The Aboriginal Tribes of
Peninsular Malaysia. Oxford U Pr.

Carey, James T., 1925-
xCarey, James T.
Introduction to Criminology. P-H.
Sociology & Public Affairs: The Chicago
School. Sage.

Carey, John.
xCarey, John.
Thackeray: Prodigal Genius. Merrimack Bk
Serv.

Carey, John L., 1904-
xCarey, John L.
Getting Acquainted with Accounting. HM.

Carey, M. V.
xCarey, M. V.
Alfred Hitchcock & the Three Investigators in
the Mystery of the Flaming Footprints.
Random.

Carey, Mary.
xCarey, Mary.
Compiled by Grandmothers Are Very Special
People. Gibson.

Carey, Mathew.
xCarey, Mathew.
Autobiographical Sketches. Arno.

Carey, Nadine C.
xCarey, Nadine C.
On Wings of Song. Branden.

Carey, Neil G.
xCarey, Neil G.
A Guide to the Queen Charlotte Islands.
Alaska Northwest.

Carey, R. J. see Carey, R. J. P.

Carey, R. J. P.
xCarey, R. J.
Library Guiding: A Program for Exploiting
Library Resources. Shoe String.

Carey, Robert L. see Carey, Robert Lincoln.

Carey, Robert Lincoln, 1898-1962
xCarey, Robert L.
Daniel Webster As an Economist. AMS Pr.

Carey Jones, N S.
xCarey Jones, N S.

The Pattern of a Dependent Economy: The
National Income of British Honduras.
Greenwood.

Carey-Jones, N. S.
xCarey-Jones, N. S.
Politics, Public Enterprise & the Industrial
Development Agency: Industrialisation
Policies & Practices. Holmes & Meier.

Cargan, Leonard.
xCargan, Leonard.
Sociological Footprints: Introductory Readings
in Sociology. HM.

Cargas, Harry J.
xCargas, Harry J.
Daniel Berrigan & Contemporary Protest
Poetry. Coll & U Pr.
David's Decision: Betrayal or Trust?.
Concordia.
The Holocaust: An Annotated Bibliography.
Cath Lib Assn.
Religious Experience & Process Theology: The
Pastoral Implications of a Major Modern
Movement. Paulist Pr.

Cargill, Jennifer S.
xCargill, Jennifer S.
Practical Approval Plan Management. Oryx Pr.

Cargill, Morris.
xCargill, Morris.
A Gallery of Nazis. Lyle Stuart.

Cargill, Oscar, 1898-
xCargill, Oscar.
Drama & Liturgy. Octagon.
Intellectual America: Ideas on the March.
Cooper Sq.
Toward a Pluralistic Criticism. S Ill U Pr.

Cargill, Thomas F.
xCargill, Thomas F.
Money, the Financial System, & Monetary
Policy. P-H.

Cargo, Douglas B, 1943
xCargo, Douglas B.
Solid Wastes: Factors Influencing Generation
Rates. U Chicago Dept Geog.

Cargo, Robert T.
xCargo, Robert T.
A Concordance to Baudelaire's "les Fleurs Du
Mal". Greenwood.

Carhart, Alfreda. see Carhart, Alfreda (Post).

Carhart, Alfreda (Post).
xCarhart, Alfreda.
Masoud the Bedouin. Arno.

Carhart, Margaret S. see Carhart, Margaret Sprague.

Carhart, Margaret Sprague, 1877-
xCarhart, Margaret S.
The Life & Work of Joanna Baillie. R West.
Life & Work of Joanna Baillie. Shoe String.

Carico, Charles. see Carico, Charles C.

Carico, Charles C.
xCarico, Charles.
Systems of Linear Equations & Inequalities.
Wadsworth Pub.
xCarico, Charles C.
Algebraic Expressions. Wadsworth Pub.
Exponential & Logarithmic Functions.
Wadsworth Pub.
Functions & Relations. Wadsworth Pub.
The Real Number System. Wadsworth Pub.

Carigan, William.
xCarigan, William.
Flying Game. Juniper Pubs.

Carin, Arthur. see Carin, Arthur A.

Carin, Arthur A.
xCarin, Arthur.
Teaching Science Through Discovery. Merrill.
xCarin, Arthur A.
Teaching Science Through Discovery. Merrill.

Carington, Whately, 1892-1947
xCarington, Whately.
Matter, Mind & Meaning. Arno.

Carini, E. see Carini, Edward.

Carini, Edward.
xCarini, E.
Take Another Look. P-H.

Carini, Geraldine. see Carini, Geraldine K.

Carini, Geraldine K.
xCarini, Geraldine.
Traction Made Manageable: A Self Learning
Module. McGraw.

Carkhuff, Robert R.
xCarkhuff, Robert R.
GETAJOB. Human Res Dev Pr.
How to Help Yourself: The Art of Program
Development. Human Res Dev Pr.

Carlander, Kenneth D. see Carlander, Kenneth Dixon.

Carlander, Kenneth Dixon, 1915-
xCarlander, Kenneth D.
Handbook of Freshwater Fishery Biology. Iowa
St U Pr.

Carlberg, David M.
xCarlberg, David M.
Essentials of Bacterial & Viral Genetics. C C
Thomas.

Carle, Eric.
xCarle, Eric.
illus. Do You Want to Be My Friend?. T Y
Crowell.
illus. The Grouchy Ladybug. T Y Crowell.
illus. I See a Song. T Y Crowell.
illus. Very Hungry Caterpillar. Philomel.

Carleton, Frances B. see Carleton, Frances Bridges.

Carleton, Frances Bridges.
xCarleton, Frances B.
The Dramatic Monologue: Vox Humana.
Humanities.

Carleton, H. M. see Carleton, Harry Montgomerie.

Carleton, Harry Montgomerie.
xCarleton, H. M.
Carleton's Histological Technique. Oxford U
Pr

Carleton, Mark T.
xCarleton, Mark T.
Politics & Punishment: A History of the
Louisiana State Penal System. La State U Pr.

Carleton, Patrick.
xCarleton, Patrick.
Buried Empires: The Earliest Civilizations of
The Middle East. Hyperion Conn.

Carleton, R. Milton.
xCarleton, R. Milton.
Vegetables for Today's Gardens. Wilshire.

Carleton, William, 1794-1869
xCarleton, William.
Stories from Carleton. Humanities.
Traits & Stories of the Irish Peasantry. Garland
Pub.
Works of William Carleton. Arno.

Carley, Keith W.
xCarley, Keith W.
Ezekiel Among the Prophets: A Study of
Ezekiel's Place in Prophetic Tradition.
Allenson.

Carley, L.
xCarley, Lionel.
Delius: A Life in Pictures. Oxford U Pr.

Carley, Lionel. see Carley, L.

Carley, V. A. see Carley, Verna Adeline.

Carley, Verna Adeline, 1900-
xCarley, V. A.
Student Aid in the Secondary Schools of the
United States. AMS Pr.

Carley, Wayne.
xCarley, Wayne.
Charley the Mouse Finds Christmas. Garrard.
Color My World. Garrard.
Percy the Parrot Passes the Puck. Garrard.
Percy the Parrot Strikes Out. Garrard.
Percy the Parrot Yelled Quiet!. Garrard.
Puppy Love. Garrard.

Carlgren, M. W. see Carlgren, W. M.

Carlgren, W. M.
  xCarlgren, M. W.
    Swedish Foreign Policy During the Second
      World War. St Martin.
Carli, Franco De. see De Carli, Franco.
Carlier, Auguste, 1803-1890
  xCarlier, Auguste.
    Marriage in the United States. Arno.
Carlile, Clark S. see Carlile, Clark Stiles.
Carlile, Clark Stiles, 1912-
  xCarlile, Clark S.
    Project Text for Public Speaking. Har-Row.
Carlile, William. see Carlile, William Warrand.
Carlile, William W. see Carlile, William Warrand.
Carlile, William Warrand.
  xCarlile, William.
    Evolution of Modern Money. Kelley.
  xCarlile, William W.
    Evolution of Modern Money. B Franklin.
Carlin, Harriette L.
  xCarlin, Harriette L.
    Medical Secretary Medi-Speller: A
      Transcription Aid. C C Thomas.
Carlin, Jerome E. see Carlin, Jerome Edward.
Carlin, Jerome Edward, 1927-
  xCarlin, Jerome E.
    Lawyers on Their Own: A Study of Individual
      Practitioners in Chicago. Rutgers U Pr.
Carline, Richard.
  xCarline, Richard.
    Stanley Spencer at War. Merrimack Bk Serv.
Carlinsky, Dan.
  xCarlinsky, Dan.
    The Jewish Quiz Book. Doubleday.
Carlisle, Anthony, Sir, 1768-1840
  xCarlisle, Anthony.
    An Essay on the Disorders of Old Age, & on
      the Means for Prolonging Human Life. Arno.
Carlisle, Earl.
  xCarlisle, Earl C.
    Little Known Facts & Secrets About Real
      Estate. Carlisle Indus.
Carlisle, Earl C. see Carlisle, Earl.
Carlisle, Howard M.
  xCarlisle, Howard M.
    Management Essentials: Concepts &
      Applications. SRA.
Carlisle, Norman. see Carlisle, Norman V.
Carlisle, Norman V.
  xCarlisle, Norman.
    Where to Live for Your Health. HarBraceJ.
Carlisle, Olga. see Carlisle, Olga Andreyev.
Carlisle, Olga Andreyev.
  xCarlisle, Olga.
    Island in Time: A Memoir of Childhood.
      HR&W.
    Solzhenitsyn & the Secret Circle. HR&W.
Carlisle, Rodney P.
  xCarlisle, Rodney P.
    Hearst & the New Deal - The Progressive As
      Reactionary. Garland Pub.
Carll, Barbara.
  xCarll, Barbara.
    One Piece of the Puzzle: A School Readiness
      Manual. Athena Pubns.
Carlon, Patricia.
  xCarlon, Patricia.
    Illinois Supplement for Real Estate Principles
      and Practices. Merrill.
Carlsen. see Carlsen, Robert D.
Carlsen, Darvey. see Carlsen, Darvey E.
Carlsen, Darvey E.
  xCarlsen, Darvey.
    Graphic Arts. Bennett Co.
Carlsen, G. R. see Carlsen, G. Robert.
Carlsen, G. Robert.
  xCarlsen, G. R.
    British & Western Literature. McGraw.
    Focus: Themes in Literature. McGraw.
  xCarlsen, G. Robert.

    American Literature: Themes & Writers.
      McGraw.
    ed. American Literature: Themes & Writers.
      McGraw.
    Books & the Teenage Reader: A Guide for
      Teachers, Librarians & Parents. Har-Row.
    Focus: Themes in Literature. McGraw.
    Insights: Themes in Literature. McGraw.
    ed. Insights: Themes in Literature. McGraw.
Carlsen, James C.
  xCarlsen, James C.
    Melodic Perception: A Program for
      Self-Instruction. McGraw.
Carlsen, Robert D.
  xCarlsen.
    Encyclopedia of Business Charts. P-H.
Carlsen, Ruth C. see Carlsen, Ruth Christoffer.
Carlsen, Ruth Christoffer.
  xCarlsen, Ruth C.
    Half-Past Tomorrow. HM.
Carlson, Andrew R.
  xCarlson, Andrew R.
    German Foreign Policy, 1890-1914 & Colonial
      Policy to 1914: A Handbook & Annotated
      Bibliography. Scarecrow.
Carlson, B. C. see Carlson, Bille Chandler.
Carlson, Bernice W. see Carlson, Bernice Wells.
Carlson, Bernice Wells.
  xCarlson, Bernice W.
    Do It Yourself: Tricks, Stunts & Skits.
      Abingdon.
    Funny Bone Dramatics. Abingdon.
    Quick Wits & Nimble Fingers. Abingdon.
    Right Play for You. Abingdon.
Carlson, Betty.
  xCarlson, Betty.
    From the Mountains of L'Abri. Good News.
    No One's Perfect. Good News.
    Reflections from a Small Chalet. Good News.
Carlson, Bille Chandler, 1924-
  xCarlson, B. C.
    ed. Special Functions of Applied Mathematics.
      Acad Pr.
Carlson, Carole C.
  xCarlson, Carole C.
    Established in Eden. Revell.
Carlson, Chuck.
  xCarlson, Dale.
    The Plant People. Dell.
Carlson, Dale. see Carlson, Dale Bick.
Carlson, Dale Bick.
  xCarlson, Dale.
    Baby Needs Shoes. Atheneum.
    The Human Apes. Atheneum.
    The Shining Pool. Atheneum.
    Triple Boy. Atheneum.
Carlson, Edgar M. see Carlson, Edgar Magnus.
Carlson, Edgar Magnus, 1908-
  xCarlson, Edgar M.
    The Classic Christian Faith. Augsburg.
    The Future of Church-Related Higher
      Education. Augsburg.
Carlson, Frederic Paul, 1938-
  xCarlson, Paul F.
    ed. Introduction to Applied Optics for
      Engineers. Acad Pr.
Carlson, G. Raymond.
  xCarlson, G. Raymond.
    The Acts Story. Gospel Pub.
    The Life Worth Living. Gospel Pub.
    Preparing to Teach God's Word. Gospel Pub.
Carlson, George. see Carlson, George L.
Carlson, George L.
  xCarlson, George.
    illus. Oodles of Riddles. Platt.
Carlson, Jean, 1935-
  xCarlson, Jean.
    Enjoying Soccer. Madrona Pubs.
Carlson, Loraine.
  xCarlson, Loraine.

    TraveLeer Guide to Yucatan & Guatemala.
      Upland Pr.
Carlson, Lucile.
  xCarlson, Lucile.
    Africa's Lands & Nations. McGraw.
Carlson, Margaret B. see Carlson, Margaret Bresnahan.
Carlson, Margaret Bresnahan.
  xCarlson, Margaret B.
    How to Get Your Car Repaired Without
      Getting Gypped. Har-Row.
Carlson, Marvin. see Carlson, Marvin A.
Carlson, Marvin A., 1935-
  xCarlson, Marvin.
    The French Stage in the Nineteenth Century.
      Scarecrow.
  xCarlson, Marvin A.
    Goethe & the Weimar Theatre. Cornell U Pr.
Carlson, Mary C. see Carlson, Mary Callery.
Carlson, Mary Callery.
  xCarlson, Mary C.
    Some People. Tyndale.
Carlson, Natalie. see Carlson, Natalie (Savage).
Carlson, Natalie (Savage).
  xCarlson, Natalie.
    The Family Under the Bridge. Schol Bk Serv.
  xCarlson, Natalie S.
    Brother for the Orphelines. Har-Row.
    Carnival in Paris. Har-Row.
    Family Under the Bridge. Har-Row.
    The Half Sisters. Har-Row.
    King of the Cats & Other Tales. Doubleday.
    The Night the Scarecrow Walked. Scribner.
Carlson, Paul F. see Carlson, Frederic Paul.
Carlson, Peter S.
  xCarlson, Peter S.
    The Biology of Crop Productivity. Acad Pr.
Carlson, Raymond.
  xCarlson, Raymond.
    ed. National Directory of Free Vacation &
      Travel Information. Pilot Bks.
    ed. National Directory of Low-Cost Tourist
      Attractions. Pilot Bks.
    ed. National Directory of Theme Parks &
      Amusement Areas. Pilot Bks.
Carlson, Richard O.
  xCarlson, Richard O.
    Adoption of Educational Innovations. Ctr Educ
      Policy Mgmt.
Carlson, Rick J.
  xCarlson, Rick J.
    The End of Medicine. Wiley.
Carlson, Robert A.
  xCarlson, Robert A.
    Educational Television in Its Cultural & Public
      Affairs Dimension: A Selected Literature
      Review of Public Television As an Issue in
      Adult Education. Syracuse U Cont Ed.
Carlson, Robert E. see Carlson, Robert Eugene.
Carlson, Robert Eugene.
  xCarlson, Robert E.
    Liverpool & Manchester Railway Project,
      1821-1831. Kelley.
Carlson, Ronald L., 1934-
  xCarlson, Ronald L.
    Criminal Justice Procedure for Police.
      Anderson Pub Co.
Carlson, Roy, 1927-
  xCarlson, Roy.
    ed. Contemporary Northwest Writing: A
      Collection of Poetry & Fiction. Oreg St U Pr.
Carlson, Ruth K. see Carlson, Ruth Kearney.
Carlson, Ruth Kearney.
  xCarlson, Ruth K.
    Speaking Aids Through the Grades. Tchrs Coll.
Carlson, Sevinc.
  xCarlson, Sevinc.

Indonesia's Oil. Westview.

Carlson, Sune, 1909-
  xCarlson, Sune.
    Study on the Pure Theory of Production.
      Kelley.
Carlson, Theodore L. *see* Carlson, Theodore Leonard.
Carlson, Theodore Leonard, 1905-
  xCarlson, Theodore L.
    The Illinois Military Tract. Arno.
Carlson, Thorsten R. *see* Carlson, Thorsten Robert.
Carlson, Thorsten Robert.
  xCarlson, Thorsten R.
    Administrators & Reading. HarBraceJ.
Carlsson, A. *see* Carlsson, Arvid.
Carlsson, Arvid.
  xCarlsson, A.
    ed. Current Topics in Extrapyramidal
      Disorders. Springer-Verlag.
Carlston, Charles E.
  xCarlston, Charles E.
    The Parables of the Triple Tradition. Fortress.
Carlston, Kenneth S. *see* Carlston, Kenneth Smith.
Carlston, Kenneth Smith, 1904-
  xCarlston, Kenneth S.
    Law & Organization in World Society. U of Ill
      Pr.
    The Process of International Arbitration.
      Greenwood.
Carlton. *see* Carlton, Lessie.
Carlton, David.
  xCarlton, David.
    ed. The Dynamics of the Arms Race. Halsted
      Pr.
Carlton, Eric.
  xCarlton, Eric.
    Ideology & Social Order. Routledge & Kegan.
Carlton, Frank T. *see* Carlton, Frank Tracy.
Carlton, Frank Tracy, 1873-
  xCarlton, Frank T.
    Economic Influences Upon Educational
      Progress in the United States 1820-1850.
      Tchrs Coll.
Carlton, Lessie.
  xCarlton.
    Reading, Self-Directive Dramatization &
      Self-Concept. Merrill.
Carlut, C. *see* Carlut, Charles.
Carlut, Charles.
  xCarlut, C.
    France De Nos Jours. Macmillan.
  xCarlut, Charles.
    A Concordance to Flaubert's La Tentation de
      Saint Antoine. Garland Pub.
    French for Oral & Written Review. HR&W.
Carlyle, Alexander, 1722-1805
  xCarlyle, Alexander.
    Anecdotes & Characters of the Times. Oxford
      U Pr.
Carlyle, Alexander J. *see* Carlyle, Alexander James.
Carlyle, Alexander James, 1861-1943
  xCarlyle, Alexander J.
    Christian Church & Liberty. B Franklin.
Carlyle, Jane B. *see* Carlyle, Jane Baillie (Welsh).
Carlyle, Jane Baillie (Welsh).
  xCarlyle, Jane B.
    Letters & Memorials of Jane Welsh Carlyle.
      AMS Pr.
Carlyle, Thomas, 1795-1881
  xCarlyle, Thomas.

Critical & Miscellaneous Essays. Scholarly.
    ed. Latter- Day Pamphlets. Arno.
    Letters of Thomas Carlyle. R West.
    Letters of Thomas Carlyle. Scholarly.
    Letters of Thomas Carlyle to John Stuart Mill,
      John Sterling & Robert Browning. Haskell.
    Letters of Thomas Carlyle: 1826-1936. R West.
    The Love Letters of Thomas Carlyle & Jane
      Welsh. AMS Pr.
    Montaigne & Other Essays, Chiefly
      Biographical. Scholarly.
    Past & Present. Dutton.
    Past & Present. NYU Pr.
    Reminiscences. R West.
    Reminiscences. Scholarly.
    Works of Thomas Carlyle. AMS Pr.
    The Works of Thomas Carlyle. R West.
Carman, Bliss.
  xCarman, Bliss.
    Compiled by Canadian Poetry in English.
      Greenwood.
    Songs from Vagabondia. Gordon Pr.
    Songs from Vagabondia. Greenwood.
    Songs from Vagabondia. Johnson Repr.
Carman, Harry J. *see* Carman, Harry James.
Carman, Harry James, 1884-1964
  xCarman, Harry J.
    Street Surface Railway Franchises of New
      York City. AMS Pr.
Carman, J. Neale. *see* Carman, Justice Neale.
Carman, John S. *see* Carman, John Stanley.
Carman, John Stanley.
  xCarman, John S.
    Obstacles to Mineral Development: A
      Pragmatic View. Pergamon.
Carman, Justice Neale, 1897-
  xCarman, J. Neale.
    A Study of the Pseudo-Map Cycle of Arthurian
      Romance to Investigate Its
      Historico-Geographic Background & to
      Provide a Hypothesis As to Its Fabrication.
      Regents Pr KS.
Carman, Robert A.
  xCarman, Robert A.
    Quick Arithmetic. Wiley.
    Study Skills: A Student's Guide for Survival.
      Wiley.
Carmen, Ira H.
  xCarmen, Ira H.
    Power & Balance: An Introduction to
      American Constitutional Government.
      HarBraceJ.
Carmen, Richard.
  xCarmen, Richard.
    Our Endangered Hearing: Understanding &
      Coping with Hearing Loss. G K Hall.
Carmer, Carl. *see* Carmer, Carl Lamson.
Carmer, Carl Lamson.
  xCarmer, Carl.
    The Boy Drummer of Vincennes. Harvey.
Carmichael, A. C.
  xCarmichael, A. C.
    Domestic Manners & Social Condition of the
      White, Coloured, & Negro Population of the
      West Indies. Negro U Pr.
Carmichael, A. Douglas. *see* Carmichael, Alexander
  Douglas.
Carmichael, Alexander, 1832-1912
  xCarmichael, Alexander.
    Celtic Invocations: Selections from Volume I of
      Carmina Gadelica. Seabury.
Carmichael, Alexander Douglas, 1929-
  xCarmichael, A. Douglas.
    Ocean Engineering Power Systems. Cornell
      Maritime.
Carmichael, Ava.
  xCarmichael, Ava.
    From White Knuckles to Cockpit Cool. Aero.
Carmichael, Calum M.
  xCarmichael, Calum M.

The Laws of Deuteronomy. Cornell U Pr.
Carmichael, Carrie.
  xCarmichael, Carrie.
    Non-Sexist Childraising. Beacon Pr.
    Secrets of the Great Magicians. Raintree Pubs.
Carmichael, D. Erskine. *see* Carmichael, Daniel Erskine.
Carmichael, Daniel Erskine, 1932-
  xCarmichael, D. Erskine.
    The Pap Smear: Life of George N.
      Papanicolaou. C C Thomas.
Carmichael, H. T. *see* Carmichael, Hugh Thompson.
Carmichael, Hoagy, 1899-
  xCarmichael, Hoagy.
    Stardust Road. Greenwood.
Carmichael, Hugh Thompson.
  xCarmichael, H. T.
    Prospects & Proposals: Lifetime Learning for
      Psychiatrists, 1972. Am Psychiatric.
Carmichael, Ian S. *see* Carmichael, Ian S. E.
Carmichael, Ian S. E.
  xCarmichael, Ian S.
    Igneous Petrology. McGraw.
Carmichael, Joel.
  xCarmichael, Joel.
    Arabs Today. Doubleday.
    Open Letter to Moses & Mohammed.
      Heineman.
Carmichael, Leonard.
  xCarmichael, Leonard.
    Reading & Visual Fatigue. Greenwood.
Carmichael, Oliver C. *see* Carmichael, Oliver Cromwell.
Carmichael, Oliver Cromwell, 1891-1966
  xCarmichael, Oliver C.
    Graduate Education: A Critique & a Program.
      Greenwood.
Carmichael, Peter A. *see* Carmichael, Peter Archibald.
Carmichael, Peter Archibald.
  xCarmichael, Peter A.
    Reasoning: A Textbook of Elementary Logic.
      Philos Lib.
Carmichael, R. D. *see* Carmichael, Robert Daniel.
Carmichael, Robert D. *see* Carmichael, Robert Daniel.
Carmichael, Robert Daniel, 1879-1967
  xCarmichael, R. D.
    The Logic of Discovery. Arno.
  xCarmichael, Robert D.
    Mathematical Tables & Formulas. Dover.
Carmody, Denise L. *see* Carmody, Denise Lardner.
Carmody, Denise Lardner, 1935-
  xCarmody, Denise L.
    Women & World Religions. Abingdon.
Carmody, John, 1939-
  xCarmody, John.
    The Progressive Pilgrim: The Challenge of
      Living Religiously Today. Fides Claretian.
Carnac, Nicholas.
  xCarnac, Nicholas.
    Tournament of Shadows. Scribner.
Carnacina, Luigi, 1888-
  xCarnacina, Luigi.
    Great Italian Cooking: La Grande Cucina
      Internazionale. Abrams.
Carnahan, David H. *see* Carnahan, David Hobart.
Carnahan, David Hobart, 1874-
  xCarnahan, David H.
    Prologue in the Old French & Provencal
      Mystery. Haskell.
Carnap, Rudlof.
  xCarnap, Rudolf.
    Two Essays on Entropy. U of Cal Pr.
Carnap, Rudolf, 1891-1970
  xCarnap, Rudolf.
    Philosophy & Logical Syntax. AMS Pr.
    ed. Studies in Inductive Logic & Probability. U
      of Cal Pr.
Carnap, Rudolf. *see* Carnap, Rudlof.
Carnduff, John.
  xCarnduff, John.

An Introduction to Organic Chemistry. Wiley.

Carne, Barbara.
  xCarne, Barbara.
    A Basic Guide to Horse Care & Management.
    Arco.

Carne-Ross, D. S.
  xCarne-Ross, D. S.
    Instaurations: Essays in & Out of Literature,
    Pindar to Pound. U of Cal Pr.

Carnegie Commission on Higher Education.
  xCarnegie Commission on Higher Education.
    Academic Degree Structures: Innovative
    Approaches. McGraw.
    The Academic Melting Pot: Catholics & Jews
    in American Higher Education. McGraw.
    The Academic System in American Society.
    McGraw.
    Academic Transformation: Seventeen
    Institutions Under Pressure. McGraw.
    American College & American Culture.
    McGraw.
    American Learned Societies in Transition: The
    Impact of Dissent & Disruption. McGraw.
    Antibias Regulations of Universities: Faculty
    Problems & Their Solutions. McGraw.
    Any Person, Any Study: An Essay on Higher
    Education in the United States. McGraw.
    Beginning of the Future: A Historical
    Approach to Graduation in the Arts &
    Sciences. McGraw.
    Between Two Worlds: A Profile of Negro
    Higher Education. McGraw.
    Breaking the Access Barriers: A Profile of
    Two-Year Colleges. McGraw.
    Bridges to Understanding: International
    Programs of American Colleges &
    Universities. McGraw.
    Campus & the City: Maximizing Assets &
    Reducing Liabilities. McGraw.
    The Capitol & the Campus: State
    Responsibility for Postsecondary Education.
    McGraw.
    Centers of Learning: Britain, France, Germany,
    United States. McGraw.
    Change in University Organization: 1964-1971.
    McGraw.
    Colleges of the Forgotten Americans: A Profile
    of State Colleges & Regional Universities.
    McGraw.
    Computers & the Learning Process in Higher
    Education. McGraw.
    Content & Context: Essays on College
    Education. McGraw.
    Continuity & Discontinuity: Higher Education
    & the Schools. McGraw.
    Credit for College: Public Policy for Student
    Loans. McGraw.
    Degree & What Else? Correlates &
    Consequences of a College Education.
    McGraw.
    Demand & Supply in U. S. Higher Education.
    McGraw.
    A Digest of Reports of the Carnegie
    Commission on Higher Education. McGraw.
    Dissent & Disruption: Proposals for
    Consideration by the Campus. McGraw.
    The Divided Academy: Professors & Politics.
    McGraw.
    Education & Evangelism: A Profile of the
    Protestant Colleges. McGraw.
    Education & Politics at Harvard. McGraw.
    Education for the Professions of Medicine,
    Law, Theology, & Social Welfare. McGraw.
    Education, Income & Human Behavior.
    McGraw.
    Efficiency in Liberal Education. McGraw.
    The Emerging Technology: Instructional Uses
    of the Computer in Higher Education.
    McGraw.
    Faculty Bargaining: Change & Conflict.

    McGraw.
    The Fourth Revolution: Instructional
    Technology in Higher Education. McGraw.
    From Backwater to Mainstream: A Profile of
    Catholic Higher Education. McGraw.
    From Isolation to Mainstream: Problems of the
    Colleges Founded for Negroes. McGraw.
    Future of Higher Education: Some Speculation
    & Suggestions. McGraw.
    Governance of Higher Education: Six Priority
    Problems. McGraw.
    Higher Education & Earnings: College As an
    Investment & a Screening Device. McGraw.
    Higher Education & the Nation's Health:
    Policies for Medical & Dental Education.
    McGraw.
    Higher Education in Nine Countries. McGraw.
    Higher Education: Who Pays? Who Benefits?
    Who Should Pay?. McGraw.
    The Home of Science: The Role of the
    University. McGraw.
    Institutions in Transition: A Profile of Change
    in Higher Education. McGraw.
    Invisible Colleges: A Profile of Small, Private
    Colleges with Limited Resources. McGraw.
    Leadership & Ambiguity: The American
    College President. McGraw.
    Less Time, More Options: Education Beyond
    the High School. McGraw.
    Models & Mavericks: A Profile of Private
    Liberal Arts Colleges. McGraw.
    The More Effective Use of Resources: An
    Imperative for Higher Education. McGraw.
    Multicampus University: A Study of Academic
    Governance. McGraw.
    New Depression in Higher Education: A Study
    of the Financial Conditions at 41 Colleges &
    Universities. McGraw.
    New Directions in Legal Education. McGraw.
    New Students & New Places: Policies for the
    Future Growth & Development of America's
    Higher Education. McGraw.
    The Nonprofit Research Institute: Its Origin,
    Operation, Problems & Prospects. McGraw.
    Open Door Colleges: Policies for the
    Community Colleges. McGraw.
    Opportunities for Women in Higher Education:
    Their Current Participation, Prospects for the
    Future & Recommendations for Action.
    McGraw.
    Priorities for Action. McGraw.
    Professional Education: Some New Directions.
    McGraw.
    The Purposes & the Performance of Higher
    Education in the U. S.: Approaching the Year
    2000. McGraw.
    Quality & Equality: New Levels of Federal
    Responsibility for Higher Education.
    McGraw.
    Quality & Equality: Revised Recommendations:
    New Levels of Federal Responsibility for
    Higher Education. McGraw.
    Reform on Campus: Changing Students,
    Changing Academic Programs. McGraw.
    Reports. McGraw.
    The Rise of the Arts on the American Campus.
    McGraw.
    The Sponsored Research of the Carnegie
    Commission on Higher Education. McGraw.
    A Statistical Portrait of Higher Education.
    McGraw.
    Teachers & Students: Aspects of American
    Higher Education. McGraw.
    Toward a Learning Society: Alternative
    Channels to Life, Work & Service. McGraw.
    The University & the City: Eight Cases of
    Involvement. McGraw.
    The University As an Organization. McGraw.
    The Useful Arts & the Liberal Tradition.
    McGraw.

    Where Colleges Are & Who Attends: Effects of
    Accessability on College Attendance.
    McGraw.
    Women & the Power to Change. McGraw.

Carnegie Council on Policy Studies in Higher Education.
  xCarnegie Council on Policy Studies in Higher
  Education.
    Faculty Bargaining in Public Higher Education:
    A Report & Two Essays. Jossey-Bass.
    The Federal Role in Postsecondary Education:
    Unfinished Business, 1975-1980. Jossey-Bass.
    Giving Youth a Better Chance: Options for
    Education, Work, & Service. Jossey-Bass.
    Low or No Tuition: The Feasibility of a
    National Policy for the First Two Years of
    College. Jossey-Bass.
    Making Affirmative Action Work in Higher
    Education: An Analysis of Institutional &
    Federal Policies with Recommendations.
    Jossey-Bass.
    Next Steps for the Nineteen Eighties in
    Student Financial Aid: A Fourth Alternative.
    Jossey-Bass.
    Progress & Problems in Medical & Dental
    Education: Federal Support Versus Federal
    Control. Jossey-Bass.
    Selective Admissions in Higher Education:
    Comment & Recommendations & Two
    Reports. Jossey-Bass.
    The States & Private Higher Education:
    Problems & Policies in a New Era.
    Jossey-Bass.
    Three Thousand Futures: The Next Twenty
    Years for Higher Education. Jossey-Bass.

Carnegie, Dale, 1888-1955
  xCarnegie, Dale.
    How to Develop Self-Confidence & Influence
    People by Public Speaking. PB.
    How to Win Friends & Influence People. PB.
    How to Win Friends & Influence People. S&S.

Carnegie Endowment for Internatioal Peace. see Carnegie
  Endowment for International Peace.

Carnegie Endowment for International Peace.
  xCarnegie Endowment for Internatioal Peace.
    American Labor in a Changing World
    Economy. Praeger.
  xCarnegie Endowment for International Peace.
    A Repertoire of League of Nations Documents,
    1919-1947. Oceana.
    Treaties & Agreements with, & Concerning
    China, 1919-29. Hyperion Conn.
    United Nations Studies. Greenwood.

**Carnegie Endowment for International Peace. Division
of International Law.**
  xCarnegie Endowment for International Peace,
  Division of International Law.
    The Sino-Japanese Negotiations of 1915:
    Japanese & Chinese Documents & Chinese
    Official Statement. AMS Pr.

Carnegie Foundation for the Advancement of Teaching.
  xCarnegie Foundation for the Advancement of
  Teaching.
    The Financial Status of the Professor in
    America & in Germany. Arno.
    Missions of the College Curriculum: A
    Contemporary Review with Suggestions.
    Jossey-Bass.
    More Than Survival: Prospects for Higher
    Education in a Period of Uncertainty.
    Jossey-Bass.
  xTheCarnegie Foundation for the Advancement of
  Teaching.
    The States & Higher Education: A Proud Past
    & Vital Future. Jossey-Bass.

Carnegie Institute of Technology. see Carnegie Institute
  of Technology, Pittsburgh.

Carnegie Institute of Technology Department of English.
  see Carnegie Institute of Technology, Pittsburgh.
  Department of English.

Carnegie Institute of Technology, Pittsburgh.
  xCarnegie Institute of Technology.
    Studies in Faulkner. Arno.
Carnegie Institute of Technology, Pittsburgh.
  Department of English.
  xCarnegie Institute of Technology Department of
    English.
    ed. Lovers Meeting: Discussions of Five Plays
      by Shakespeare. Arno.
    ed. Six Novelists: Stendhal, Dostoevski,
      Tolstoy, Hardy, Dreiser & Proust. Arno.
    Six Satirists. Arno.
Carnegie Institution of Washington.
  xCarnegie Institution of Washington.
    Additions to the Palaeontology of the Pacific
      Coast & Great Basin Regions of North
      America. Johnson Repr.
    Ancient Maya Paintings of Bonampak Mexico.
      Carnegie Inst.
    Contributions to American Archaeology. AMS
      Pr.
    Contributions to Paleontology. Johnson Repr.
    Eocene Flora of Western America. Johnson
      Repr.
    Marine Mammals. Johnson Repr.
    Miocene & Pliocene Floras of Western North
      America. Johnson Repr.
    Papers Concerning the Palaeontology of
      California, Arizona & Idaho. Johnson Repr.
    Papers Concerning the Palaeontology of
      California, Nevada & Oregon. Johnson Repr.
    Papers Concerning the Palaeontology of
      California, Oregon & the Northern Great
      Basin Province. Johnson Repr.
    Papers Concerning the Palaeontology of the
      Cretaceous & Later Tertiary of Oregon, of
      the Pliocene of North-Western Nevada, & of
      the Late Miocene & Pleistocene of California.
      Johnson Repr.
    Papers Concerning the Palaeontology of the
      Pleistocene of California & the Tertiary of
      Oregon. Johnson Repr.
    Studies of Tertiary & Quaternary Mammals of
      North America. Johnson Repr.
    Studies of the Pleistocene Palaeobotany of
      California. Johnson Repr.
    Studies of the Pliocene Palaeobotany of
      California. Johnson Repr.
    Studies on Cenozoic Vertebrates of Western
      America. Johnson Repr.
    Studies on the Fossil Flora & Fauna of the
      Western United States. Johnson Repr.
**Carnegie Institution of Washington. Department of
  Meridian Astrometry.**
  xCarnegie Institution Of Washington - Dept. Of
    Meridian Astronomy.
    General Catalogue of Thirty Three Thousand
      Three Hundred Forty-Two Stars for the
      Epoch 1950. Johnson Repr.
Carnell, C. Mitchell.
  xCarnell, C. Mitchell.
    Development, Management, & Evaluation of
      Community Speech & Hearing Centers. C C
      Thomas.
Carner, Chas.
  xCarner, Chas.
    Tawny. Macmillan.
Carner, Mosco.
  xCarner, Mosco.
    Alban Berg: The Man & the Work. Holmes &
      Meier.
    Puccini: A Critical Biography. Holmes &
      Meier.
Carnevale, Thomas.
  xCarnevale, Thomas.
    Encounters with Arithmetic. HarBraceJ.
Carnevali, Doris L.
  xCarnevali, Doris L.

    ed. Nursing Management for the Elderly.
      Lippincott.
Carney, Edward M.
  xCarney, Edward M.
    The American Business Manual. Arno.
Carney, George O.
  xCarney, George O.
    The Sounds of People & Places: Readings in
      the Geography of Music. U Pr of Amer.
Carney, Gerard J.
  xCarney, Gerard J.
    The Complete Field Sales Program. Am Mgmt.
Carney, James.
  xCarney, James.
    Medieval Irish Lyrics. U of Cal Pr.
Carney, James D. *see* Carney, James Donald.
Carney, James Donald.
  xCarney, James D.
    Fundamentals of Logic. Macmillan.
Carney, John P.
  xCarney, John P.
    Nation of Change: The American Democratic
      System. Har-Row.
Carney, Louis P.
  xCarney, Louis P.
    Corrections & the Community. P-H.
    Introduction to Correctional Science. McGraw.
    Probation & Parole: Legal & Social
      Dimensions. McGraw.
Carney, Thomas.
  xCarney, Thomas.
    Daylight Moon. NAL.
Carney, Thomas P.
  xCarney, Thomas P.
    Instant Evolution: We'd Better Get Good at It.
      U of Notre Dame Pr.
Carnochan, W. B.
  xCarnochan, W. B.
    Confinement & Flight: An Essay on English
      Literature of the Eighteenth Century. U of
      Cal Pr.
Carnovale, Norbert, 1932-
  xCarnovale, Norbert.
    Twentieth-Century Music for Trumpet &
      Orchestra: An Annotated Bibliography. Brass
      Pr.
Carnoy, Martin.
  xCarnoy, Martin.
    Education & Employment: A Critical
      Appraisal. Unipub.
    Education As Cultural Imperialism. Longman.
    Industrialization in a Latin American Common
      Market. Brookings.
    ed. The Limits of Educational Reform.
      Longman.
Caro, C. G. *see* Caro, Colin Gerald.
Caro, Colin Gerald.
  xCaro, C. G.
    The Mechanics of the Circulation. Oxford U
      Pr.
Caro, Elme M. *see* Caro, Elme Marie.
Caro, Elme Marie, 1826-1887
  xCaro, Elme M.
    George Sand. Kennikat.
    George Sand. R West.
Caro, Francis G., 1936-
  xCaro, Francis G.
    ed. Readings in Evaluation Research. Russell
      Sage.
Caroe, Olaf K. *see* Caroe, Olaf Kirkpatrick.
Caroe, Olaf Kirkpatrick, Sir, 1892-
  xCaroe, Olaf K.
    Soviet Empire: The Turks of Central Asia &
      Stalinism. St Martin.
Caroline, Nancy. *see* Caroline, Nancy L.
Caroline, Nancy L.
  xCaroline, Nancy.
    Emergency Care in the Streets. Little.
Carone, Pasquale A.
  xCarone, Pasquale A.

    Drug Abuse in Industry. C C Thomas.
Caroselli, Remus F.
  xCaroselli, Remus F.
    The Mystery Cottage in Left Field. Putnam.
Carosso, Vincent P.
  xCarosso, Vincent P.
    ed. The Survival of Small Business. Arno.
Carothers, Gibson.
  xCarothers, Gibson.
    Slanguage: America's Second Language.
      Sterling.
Carothers, L. *see* Carothers, Leslie A.
Carothers, Leslie A.
  xCarothers, L.
    The Public Accommodations Law of 1964:
      Arguments, Issues, & Attitudes in a Legal
      Debate. Smith Coll.
Carothers, Merlin. *see* Carothers, Merlin R.
Carothers, Merlin R.
  xCarothers, Merlin.
    Praise Works!. Logos.
Carothers, Neil, 1884-
  xCarothers, Neil.
    Fractional Money: A History of the Small
      Coins & Fractional Paper Currency of the
      United States. Kelley.
Carp, Frances M. *see* Carp, Francis Merchant.
Carp, Francis Merchant.
  xCarp, Frances M.
    Retirement. Human Sci Pr.
Carpelan, Bo. *see* Carpelan, Bo Gustaf Bertelsson.
Carpelan, Bo Gustaf Bertelsson, 1926-
  xCarpelan, Bo.
    Bow Island. Delacorte.
Carpenter. *see* Carpenter, Philip Lee.
Carpenter, Allan. *see* Carpenter, John Allan.
Carpenter, Allen. *see* Carpenter, John Allan.
Carpenter, Andrew.
  xCarpenter, Andrew.
    ed. Place, Personality & the Irish Writer. B&N.
Carpenter, C. R. *see* Carpenter, Clarence Ray.
Carpenter, Cecelia S. *see* Carpenter, Cecelia Svinth.
Carpenter, Cecelia Svinth.
  xCarpenter, Cecelia S.
    They Walked Before: The Indians of
      Washington State. Wash St Hist Soc.
Carpenter, Charles A.
  xCarpenter, Charles A.
    Modern British Drama. AHM Pub.
Carpenter, Charles B.
  xCarpenter, Charles B.
    ed. Clinical Histocompatibility Testing. Grune.
Carpenter, Clarence Ray, 1905-
  xCarpenter, C. R.
    Naturalistic Behavior of Nonhuman Primates.
      Pa St U Pr.
Carpenter, Edmund. *see* Carpenter, Edmund Snow.
Carpenter, Edmund Snow.
  xCarpenter, Edmund.
    ed. Explorations in Communication: An
      Anthology. Beacon Pr.
Carpenter, Edward.
  xCarpenter, Edward.
    Psychology of the Poet Shelley. Folcroft.
    Psychology of the Poet Shelley. Haskell.
Carpenter, F. Lynn.
  xCarpenter, F. Lynn.
    Ecology & Evolution of an Andean
      Hummingbird (Oreotrochilus Estella). U of
      Cal Pr.
Carpenter, Frances.
  xCarpenter, Frances.
    Tales of a Chinese Grandmother. C E Tuttle.
    Tales of a Korean Grandmother. C E Tuttle.
  xCarpenter, Francis.
    Tales of a Chinese Grandmother. Am
      Repr-Rivercity Pr.
Carpenter, Francis. *see* Carpenter, Frances.
Carpenter, Frederic I. *see* Carpenter, Frederic Ives.

Carpenter, Frederic Ives, 1903-
xCarpenter, Frederic I.
Eugene O'Neill. Coll & U Pr.
Eugene O'Neill. G K Hall.
Eugene O'neill. Twayne.
Carpenter, Gene B.
xCarpenter, Gene B.
Principles of Crystal Structure Determination.
Benjamin-Cummings.
Carpenter, Humphrey.
xCarpenter, Humphrey.
Jesus. Hill & Wang.
Carpenter, J. Estlin. *see* Carpenter, Joseph Estlin.
Carpenter, Jesse T. *see* Carpenter, Jesse Thomas.
Carpenter, Jesse Thomas.
xCarpenter, Jesse T.
Competition & Collective Bargaining in the
Needle Trades, 1910-1967. NY Sch Indus
Rel.
Carpenter, John Allan, 1917-
xCarpenter, Allan.
Alaska. Childrens.
Arizona. Childrens.
Arkansas. Childrens.
Burundi. Childrens.
California. Childrens.
Connecticut. Childrens.
District of Columbia. Childrens.
Far-Flung America. Childrens.
Florida. Childrens.
Gabon. Childrens.
Georgia. Childrens.
Ghana. Childrens.
Guinea. Childrens.
Hawaii. Childrens.
Idaho. Childrens.
Illinois. Childrens.
Indiana. Childrens.
Kansas. Childrens.
Kentucky. Childrens.
Lesotho. Childrens.
Liberia. Childrens.
Louisiana. Childrens.
Maine. Childrens.
Maryland. Childrens.
Massachusetts. Childrens.
Mauritania. Childrens.
Montana. Childrens.
Nebraska. Childrens.
Nevada. Childrens.
New Hampshire. Childrens.
New Jersey. Childrens.
Niger. Childrens.
Nigeria. Childrens.
North Carolina. Childrens.
North Dakota. Childrens.
Oklahoma. Childrens.
Oregon. Childrens.
Pennsylvania. Childrens.
Rhode Island. Childrens.
Rhodesia. Childrens.
Sierra Leone. Childrens.
South Carolina. Childrens.
South Dakota. Childrens.
Sudan. Childrens.
Swaziland. Childrens.
Tanzania. Childrens.
Tennessee. Childrens.
Texas. Childrens.
Uganda. Childrens.
Utah. Childrens.
Vermont. Childrens.
Washington. Childrens.
West Virginia. Childrens.
Wyoming. Childrens.
xCarpenter, Allen.
Iowa. Childrens.
Carpenter, Joseph E. *see* Carpenter, Joseph Estlin.
Carpenter, Joseph Estlin, 1844-1927
xCarpenter, J. Estlin.

Theism in Medieval India. Intl Pubns Serv.
xCarpenter, Joseph E.
Theism in Medieval India. AMS Pr.
Carpenter, Malcolm B.
xCarpenter, Malcolm B.
Core Text of Neuroanatomy. Williams &
Wilkins.
Carpenter, Mary, 1807-1877
xCarpenter, Mary.
Our Convicts. Patterson Smith.
Carpenter, Nan Cooke.
xCarpenter, Nan Cooke.
Music in the Medieval & Renaissance
Universities. Da Capo.
Carpenter, Niles, 1891-
xCarpenter, Niles.
Immigrants & Their Children, 1920. Arno.
Nationality, Color, & Economic Opportunity in
the City of Buffalo. Negro U Pr.
Carpenter, Philip L. *see* Carpenter, Philip Lee.
Carpenter, Philip Lee.
xCarpenter.
Plants in the Landscape. Thomson Pub CA.
xCarpenter, Philip L.
Plants in the Landscape. W H Freeman.
Carpenter, R. E. *see* Carpenter, Roger Edwin.
Carpenter, Rhys, 1889-
xCarpenter, Rhys.
Esthetic Basis of Greek Art of the Fifth &
Fourth Centuries, B.C. Peter Smith.
Greek Sculpture: A Critical Review. U of
Chicago Pr.
Greeks in Spain. AMS Pr.
Humanistic Value of Archaeology. Greenwood.
Carpenter, Richard. *see* Carpenter, Richard C.
Carpenter, Richard C.
xCarpenter, Richard.
Thomas Hardy. St Martin.
xCarpenter, Richard C.
Thomas Hardy. Twayne.
Carpenter, Robert D., 1923-
xCarpenter, Robert D.
Thanks Doctor. RDC Pubs.
Carpenter, Roger Edwin.
xCarpenter, R. E.
A Comparison of Thermoregulation & Water
Metabolism in the Kangaroo Rats
Dypodomys agilis & Dipodomys merriami. U
of Cal Pr.
Carpenter, Samuel T.
xCarpenter, Samuel T.
Structural Mechanics. Krieger.
Carpenter, Walter H. *see* Carpenter, Walter Hull.
Carpenter, Walter Hull.
xCarpenter, Walter H.
Small Business & Pattern Bargaining. Arno.
Carpenter, William. *see* Carpenter, William Seal.
Carpenter, William S. *see* Carpenter, William Seal.
Carpenter, William Seal, 1890-1957
xCarpenter, William.
The Unfinished Business of Civil Service
Reform. Kennikat.
xCarpenter, William S.
The Development of American Political
Thought. Hyperion Conn.
The Unfinished Business of Civil Service
Reform. Greenwood.
Carpenter, William W. *see* Carpenter, William Weston.
Carpenter, William Weston, 1889-
xCarpenter, William W.
Certain Phases of the Administration of High
School Chemistry. AMS Pr.
Carpentier, Alejo, 1904-
xCarpentier, Alejo.
The Lost Steps. Avon.
Lost Steps. Knopf.
Carpentier, Michael H. *see* Carpentier, Michel H.
Carpentier, Michel H.
xCarpentier, Michael H.

Radars - New Concepts. Gordon.
Carper, Dean. *see* Carper, L. Dean.
Carper, Jean.
xCarper, Jean.
Brand Name Nutrition Counter. Bantam.
Carper, L. Dean.
xCarper, Dean.
Sound of Drums. Herald Hse.
Carpozi, George.
xCarpozi, George.
The John Wayne Story. Arlington Hse.
Ordeal by Trial: The Alice Crimmins Case.
Walker & Co.
Son of Sam: The .44 Caliber Killer. Manor Bks.
Carr, Albert H. Z.
xCarr, Albert Z.
Business As a Game. NAL.
xCarr, Walter H.
The World & William Walker. Greenwood.
Carr, Albert Z. *see* Carr, Albert H. Z.
Carr, Anna, 1955-
xCarr, Anna.
Rodale's Color Handbook of Garden Insects.
Rodale Pr Inc.
Carr, Anne.
xCarr, Anne.
The Theological Method of Karl Rahner.
Scholars Pr Ca.
Carr, Archie. *see* Carr, Archie Fairly.
Carr, Archie Fairly.
xCarr, Archie.
The Everglades. Silver.
The Everglades. Time-Life.
Carr, Cecil T. *see* Carr, Cecil Thomas.
Carr, Cecil Thomas, Sir, 1878-
xCarr, Cecil T.
Concerning English Administrative Law. AMS
Pr.
Carr, David.
xCarr, David.
The Beginners Guide to Good Gardening.
Sterling.
Carr, Donald E. *see* Carr, Donald Eaton.
Carr, Donald Eaton, 1903-
xCarr, Donald E.
Deadly Feast of Life. Doubleday.
Death of the Sweet Waters. Norton.
Energy & the Earth Machine. Norton.
The Forgotten Senses. Doubleday.
Carr, E. H. *see* Carr, Edward Hallett.
Carr, Edward H. *see* Carr, Edward Hallett.
Carr, Edward Hallett, 1892-
xCarr, E. H.
Dostoevsky. Allen Unwin.
Foundations of a Planned Economy.
Macmillan.
Foundations of a Planned Economy 1926-1929.
Macmillan.
The Soviet Impact on the Western World.
Fertig.
xCarr, Edward H.
Foundations of a Planned Economy.
Macmillan.
Twenty Years' Crisis, 1919-1939: An
Introduction to the Study of International
Relations. Har-Row.
Carr, Elizabeth B. *see* Carr, Elizabeth Ball.
Carr, Elizabeth Ball.
xCarr, Elizabeth B.
Da Kine Talk: From Pidgin to Standard
English in Hawaii. U Pr of Hawaii.
Carr, George S. *see* Carr, George Shoobridge.
Carr, George Shoobridge, 1837-
xCarr, George S.
Formulas & Theorems in Pure Mathematics.
Chelsea Pub.
Carr, Harvey, 1873-1954
xCarr, Harvey A.
Introduction to Space Perception. Hafner.
Carr, Harvey A. *see* Carr, Harvey.

Carr, Ian. see Carr, Ian Archibald.
Carr, Ian Archibald.
    xCarr, Ian.
        Lymphoreticular Disease: An Introduction for
            the Pathologist & Oncologist. Lippincott.
Carr, J. G.
    xCarr, J. G.
        Aroma & Flavour in Wine Making.
            Transatlantic.
Carr, Jack, 1921-
    xCarr, Jack.
        Advanced Table Tennis. A S Barnes.
        Advanced Table Tennis. Cornerstone.
Carr, Jacquelyn B., 1923-
    xCarr, Jacquelyn B.
        Communicating & Relating.
            Benjamin-Cummings.
        Communicating with Myself: A Journal.
            Benjamin-Cummings.
Carr, Jayge.
    xCarr, Jayge.
        Leviathan's Deep. Doubleday.
        Leviathan's Deep. Playboy Pbks.
Carr, Jess.
    xCarr, Jess.
        Millie & Cleve. Nordon Pubns.
        The Moonshiners. Sherbourne.
        Ship Ride Down the Spring Branch & Other
            Stories. Moore Pub Co.
Carr, Jo.
    xCarr, Jo.
        Trouble with Tikki. Lantern.
Carr, John C. see Carr, John Charles.
Carr, John Charles.
    xCarr, John C.
        Pygmalion or Frankenstein?: Alternative
            Schooling in American Education. A-W.
Carr, John D. see Carr, John Dickson.
Carr, John Dickson.
    xCarr, John D.
        Arabian Nights Murder. Macmillan.
        Case of the Constant Suicides. Macmillan.
        Corpse in the Waxworks. Macmillan.
        Crooked Hinge. Macmillan.
        The Crooked Hinge. Pubs Inc.
        Death Watch. Macmillan.
        The Murder of Sir Edmund Godfrey. Hyperion
            Conn.
Carr, Joseph. see Carr, Joseph J.
Carr, Joseph J.
    xCarr, Joseph.
        Elements of Electronic Instrumentation &
            Measurement. Reston.
        Op Amp Circuit Design & Applications. TAB
            Bks.
        Z-80 User's Manual. Reston.
    xCarr, Joseph J.
        Antenna Data Reference Manual-Including
            Dimension Tables. TAB Bks.
        How to Design & Build Electronic
            Instrumentation. TAB Bks.
        How to Troubleshoot & Repair Amateur Radio
            Equipment. TAB Bks.
Carr, Larry.
    xCarr, Larry.
        Four Fabulous Faces: Swanson, Garbo,
            Crawford, Dietrich. Penguin.
Carr, Lois G. see Carr, Lois Green.
Carr, Lois Green.
    xCarr, Lois G.
        Maryland's Revolution of Government,
            1689-1692. Cornell U Pr.
Carr, Patrick.
    xCarr, Patrick.
        ed. The Illustrated History of Country Music.
            Doubleday.
Carr, R. see Carr, Rachel E.
Carr, Rachel E.
    xCarr, R.

        See & Be: Yoga & Creative Movement for
            Children. P-H.
Carr, Raymond.
    xCarr, Raymond.
        Spain 1808-1939. Oxford U Pr.
Carr, Reg.
    xCarr, Reg.
        Anarchism in France: The Case of Octave
            Mirbeau. McGill-Queens U Pr.
Carr, Robert K. see Carr, Robert Kenneth.
Carr, Robert Kenneth, 1908-
    xCarr, Robert K.
        Supreme Court & Judicial Review. Greenwood.
Carr, Robyn.
    xCarr, Robyn.
        Chelynne. Little.
Carr, Roy.
    xCarr, Roy.
        Fleetwood Mac: Rumours N'Fax. Crown.
Carr, Samuel, 1913-
    xCarr, Samuel.
        The Batsford Book of Country Verse. David &
            Charles.
        Poetry of the Railways. David & Charles.
Carr, T. R.
    xCarr, T. R.
        Quantitative Research in Public Administration
            & Policy Analysis: A Methodologically
            Annotated Bibliography. Univ OK Gov Res.
Carr, Terry.
    xCarr, Terry.
        ed. Classic Science Fiction: The First Golden
            Age. Har-Row.
        ed. Creatures from Beyond: Nine Stories of
            Science Fiction & Fantasy. Elsevier-Nelson.
        ed. The Ides of Tomorrow: Original Science
            Fiction Tales of Horror. Little.
        ed. The Infinite Arena: Seven Science Fiction
            Stories About Sports. Elsevier-Nelson.
        ed. Worlds Near & Far: Nine Stories of
            Science Fiction & Fantasy. Elsevier-Nelson.
        ed. Year's Finest Fantasy. Berkley Pub.
        ed. Year's Finest Fantasy. Berkley Pub.
Carr, Virginia Spencer.
    xCarr, Virginia Spencer.
        The Lonely Hunter: A Biography of Carson
            McCullers. Doubleday.
Carr, Walter H. see Carr, Albert H. Z.
Carr, William, 1921-
    xCarr, William.
        Hitler: A Study in Personality & Politics. St
            Martin.
Carr, William H. see Carr, William H. A.
Carr, William H. A.
    xCarr, William H.
        Hollywood Tragedy. Fawcett.
Carr-Ruffino, N. see Carr-Ruffino, Norma.
Carr-Ruffino, Norma.
    xCarr-Ruffino, N.
        Writing Short Business Reports. McGraw.
Carra, Andrew J.
    xCarra, Andrew J.
        ed. The Complete Guide to Hiking &
            Backpacking. Winchester Pr.
Carranco, Lynwood.
    xCarranco, Lynwood.
        Logging the Redwoods. Caxton.
Carras, Mary C.
    xCarras, Mary C.
        Dynamics of Indian Political Factions: A Study
            of District Councils in the State of
            Maharashtra. Cambridge U Pr.
Carre, Antonio.
    xCarre, Antonio.
        Necker et la question des grains a la fin du
            XVIIIe siecle. B Franklin.
Carre, J. J. see Carre, Jean Jacques.
Carre, Jean Jacques.
    xCarre, J. J.

        French Economic Growth. Stanford U Pr.
Carre, Jean M. see Carre, Jean Marie.
Carre, Jean Marie, 1887-1958
    xCarre, Jean M.
        A Season in Hell: The Life of Arthur Rimbaud.
            AMS Pr.
Carre, John Le. see Le Carre, John.
Carrell, A. see Carrell, Al.
Carrell, Al.
    xCarrell, A.
        Super Handyman's Encyclopedia of Home
            Repair Hints: Better, Faster, Cheaper, &
            Easier Ideas for House & Workshop. P-H.
Carrell, Norman.
    xCarrell, Norman.
        Bach the Borrower. Greenwood.
Carreno, Josephine.
    xCarreno, Josephine.
        ed. Spanish for Hospital Personnel. Med Exam.
Carretto, Carlo.
    xCarretto, Carlo.
        The God Who Comes. Orbis Bks.
        God Who Comes. Pillar Bks.
        In Search of the Beyond. Doubleday.
        In Search of the Beyond. Orbis Bks.
        Letters from the Desert. Pillar Bks.
        Love Is for Living. Orbis Bks.
        Summoned by Love. Orbis Bks.
Carrey, Dixieann W.
    xCarrey, Dixieann W.
        First Impressions: A Guide to More Profitable
            Direct Mail Advertising. D W Carrey.
Carrick, Carol.
    xCarrick, Carol.
        The Accident. HM.
        Brook. Macmillan.
        Clearing in the Forest. Dial.
        The Crocodiles Still Wait. HM
        Dirt Road. Macmillan.
        The Foundling. HM.
        The Highest Balloon on the Common.
            Greenwillow.
        Lost in the Storm. HM.
        Octopus. HM.
        Paul's Christmas Birthday. Greenwillow.
        Pond. Macmillan.
        A Rabbit for Easter. Greenwillow.
        Some Friend!. HM.
        Swamp Spring. Macmillan.
Carrick, Donald.
    xCarrick, Donald.
        The Deer in the Pasture. Greenwillow.
        illus. Drip, Drop. Macmillan.
Carrick, Edward, 1905-
    xCarrick, Edward.
        ed. Art & Design in the British Film: A
            Pictorial Directory of British Art Directors &
            Their Work. Arno.
Carrick, Malcolm.
    xCarrick, Malcolm.
        I Can Squash Elephants!: A Masai Tale About
            Monsters. Viking Pr.
        illus. Mr. Tod's Trap. Har-Row.
Carrick, Peter.
    xCarrick, Peter.
        Story of Honda Motor Cycles. Aztex.
Carrick, R. J. see Carrick, Roger John.
Carrick, Roger John, 1937-
    xCarrick, R. J.
        East-West Technology Transfer in Perspective.
            U of Cal Intl St.
Carrier Air Conditioning Co. see Carrier Corporation.
Carrier Corporation.
    xCarrier Air Conditioning Co.
        Handbook of Air Conditioning System Design.
            McGraw.
Carrier, Fred. see Carrier, Fred J.
Carrier, Fred J., 1936-
    xCarrier, Fred.

Catholic History of Alabama & the Floridas. Arno.

Carroll, Peter. *see* Carroll, Peter N.

Carroll, Peter N.
xCarroll, Peter.
The Restless Centuries: A History of the American People. Burgess.
xCarroll, Peter N.
The Free & the Unfree: A New History of the United States. Penguin.
The Other Samuel Johnson: A Psychohistory of Early New England. Fairleigh Dickinson.
Puritanism & the Wilderness: The Intellectual Significance of the New England Frontier, 1629-1700. Columbia U Pr.

Carroll, Phil, 1895-
xCarroll, Phil.
Practical Production & Inventory Control. McGraw.

Carroll Press.
xThe Carroll Press Staff.
Career Guide to Professional Associations: A Directory of Organizations by Occupational Field. Carroll Pr.

The Carroll Press Staff. *see* Carroll Press.

Carroll, Robert. *see* Carroll, Robert Lynn.

Carroll, Robert Lynn.
xCarroll, Robert.
The Order Microsauria. Am Philos.

Carroll, Ruth. *see* Carroll, Ruth Robinson.

Carroll, Ruth Robinson, 1899-
xCarroll, Ruth.
illus. What Whiskers Did. Schol Bk Serv.

Carroll, Sidney W. *see* Carroll, Sydney Wentworth.

Carroll, Stephen J.
xCarroll, Stephen J.
Organizational Behavior. Wiley.

Carroll, Sydney W. *see* Carroll, Sydney Wentworth.

Carroll, Sydney Wentworth, 1877-1958
xCarroll, Sidney W.
Some Dramatic Opinions. Kennikat.
xCarroll, Sydney W.
Some Dramatic Opinions. R West.

Carroll, Theodus, 1928-
xCarroll, Theodus.
Firsts Under the Wire: The World's Fastest Horses (1900-1950). Silver.
xCarroll, Theodus C.
The Lost Christmas Star. Garrard.

Carroll, Theodus C. *see* Carroll, Theodus.

Carroll, Vern.
xCarroll, Vern.
ed. Adoption in Eastern Oceania. U Pr of Hawaii.
ed. Pacific Atoll Populations. U Pr of Hawaii.

Carroll, W. H. *see* Carroll, William H.

Carroll, William, 1915-
xCarroll, Bill.
ed. Mazda Rotary Engine Manual. Auto Bk.

Carroll, William H.
xCarroll, W. H.
How to Put Money in Your Pockets Every Day. Merritt Pubs.

Carrott, Richard G.
xCarrott, Richard G.
The Egyptian Revival: Its Sources, Monuments, & Meaning, 1808-1858. U of Cal Pr.

Carrouges, Michel, 1910-
xCarrouges, Michel.
Andre Breton & the Basic Concepts of Surrealism. U of Ala Pr.

Carrow, Milton M. *see* Carrow, Milton Michael.

Carrow, Milton Michael, 1913-
xCarrow, Milton M.
Licensing Power in New York City. Rothman.

Carrubba, Eugene R.
xCarrubba, Eugene R.
Assuring Product Integrity. Lexington Bks.

Carrubba, Joseph La. *see* La Carrubba, Joseph.

Carrubba, Robert W.
xCarrubba, Robert W.
ed. Directory of College & University Classicists in the United States & Canada. Pa St U Pr.

Carruth, Gorton.
xCarruth, Gorton.
ed. The Encyclopedia of American Facts & Dates. T Y Crowell.

Carruth, William H. *see* Carruth, William Herbert.

Carruth, William Herbert, 1859-1924
Verse Writing: A Practical Handbook for College Classes & Private Guidance. R West.
Verse Writing: A Practical Handbook for College Classes & Private Guidance. Folcroft.

Carruthers, Peter A., 1935-
xCarruthers, Peter A.
Spin & Isospin in Particle Physics. Gordon.

Carruthers, W.
xCarruthers, W.
Some Modern Methods of Organic Synthesis. Cambridge U Pr.

Carryl, Guy W. *see* Carryl, Guy Wetmore.

Carryl, Guy Wetmore.
xCarryl, Guy W.
Grimm Tales Made Gay. Irvington.

Carsberg, Bryan V.
xCarsberg, Bryan V.
Introduction to Mathematical Programming for Accountants. Kelley.

Carse, Adam. *see* Carse, Adam Von Ahn.

Carse, Adam V. *see* Carse, Adam Von Ahn.

Carse, Adam Von Ahn, 1878-1958
xCarse, Adam.
The History of Orchestration. Dover.
History of Orchestration. Peter Smith.
Musical Wind Instruments. A History of the Wind Instruments Used in European Orchestras & Wind Bands, from the Later Middle Ages up to the Present Time. Da Capo.
xCarse, Adam V.
The History of Orchestration. Gordon Pr.

Carse, James P.
xCarse, James P.
Death & Existence: A Conceptual History of Human Mortality. Wiley.

Carslaw, Horatio S. *see* Carslaw, Horatio Scott.

Carslaw, Horatio Scott.
xCarslaw, Horatio S.
Conduction of Heat in Solids. Oxford U Pr.

Carson. *see* Carson, Albert Ben.

Carson, Ada. *see* Carson, Ada Lou.

Carson, Ada Lou.
xCarson, Ada.
Royall Tyler. Twayne.

Carson, Albert Ben.
xCarson.
Accounting Essentials for Career Secretaries. SW Pub.

Carson, Arthur B. *see* Carson, Arthur Brinton.

Carson, Arthur Brinton.
xCarson, Arthur B.
Foundation Construction. McGraw.

Carson, C. Deane. *see* Carson, Deane.

Carson, Clarence B. *see* Carson, Clarence Buford.

Carson, Clarence Buford.
xCarson, Clarence B.
American Tradition. Foun Econ Ed.
Fateful Turn: From Individual Liberty to Collectivism, 1880-1960. Foun Econ Ed.
Flight from Reality. Foun Econ Ed.

Carson, Deane.
xCarson, C. Deane.
Money & Finance: Readings in Theory, Policy & Institutions. Wiley.

Carson, Edward.
xCarson, Edward.
The Ancient & Rightful Customs: A History of the English Customs Service. Shoe String.

Carson, Gerald.
xCarson, Gerald.
Cornflake Crusade. Arno.
The Golden Egg: The Personal Income Tax, Where It Came from, How It Grew. HM.
Men, Beasts & Gods: A History of Cruelty & Kindness to Animals. Scribner.
The Polite Americans: A Wide-Angle View of Our More or Less Good Manners Over 300 Years. Greenwood.

Carson, Gordon B.
xCarson, Gordon B.
ed. Production Handbook. Ronald Pr.

Carson, Herbert L.
xCarson, Herbert L.
Steps in Successful Speaking. Van Nos Reinhold.

Carson, Josephine, 1919-
xCarson, Josephine.
Where You Goin', Girlie?. Dial.

Carson, Linwood.
xCarson, Linwood.
The Avenging Angels. Nordon Pubns.

Carson, M. A. *see* Carson, Michael A.

Carson, Michael A.
xCarson, M. A.
Hillslope Form & Process. Cambridge U Pr.

Carson, Patricia.
xCarson, Patricia.
Materials for West African History in the Archives of Belgium & Holland. Humanities.

Carson, Rachael. *see* Carson, Rachel Louise.

Carson, Rachel. *see* Carson, Rachel Louise.

Carson, Rachel Louise.
xCarson, Rachael.
Silent Spring. Fawcett.
xCarson, Rachel.
Silent Spring. HM.
Under the Sea Wind: A Naturalist's Picture of Ocean Life. Oxford U Pr.

Carson, Ray F., 1939-
xCarson, Ray F.
Counter Control for Championship Wrestling. A S Barnes.
The Encyclopedia of Championship Wrestling Drills. A S Barnes.
Principles of Championship Wrestling. A S Barnes.
Principles of Championship Wrestling. Cornerstone.
Systematic Championship Wrestling. A S Barnes.

Carson, Richard B. *see* Carson, Richard Burns.

Carson, Richard Burns, 1944-
xCarson, Richard B.
The Olympian Cars. Knopf.

Carson, Robert B. *see* Carson, Robert Barry.

Carson, Robert Barry, 1934-
xCarson, Robert B.
American Economy in Conflict. Heath.

Carson, Robert C., 1930-
xCarson, Robert C.
Interaction Concepts of Personality. Beresford Bk Serv.

Carson, Russell M. L. *see* Carson, Russell Mack Little.

Carson, Russell Mack Little.
xCarson, Russell M. L.
Peaks & People of the Adirondacks. ADK Mtn Club.

Carstairs, G. M. *see* Carstairs, G. Morris.

Carstairs, G. Morris.
xCarstairs, G. M.

The Great Universe of Kota: Stress, Change & Mental Disorder in an Indian Village. U of Cal Pr.

Carsten, F. L. *see* Carsten, Francis Ludwig.

Carsten, Francis Ludwig.
 xCarsten, F. L.
  Revolution in Central Europe, 1918-1919. U of Cal Pr.
 xCarsten, Francis T.
  Fascist Movements in Austria: From Schonerer to Hitler. Sage.

Carsten, Francis T. *see* Carsten, Francis Ludwig.

Carstensen, Jens T. *see* Carstensen, Jens Thur.

Carstensen, Jens Thur, 1926-
 xCarstensen, Jens T.
  Theory of Pharmaceutical Systems. Acad Pr.

Carstensen, Vernon. *see* Carstensen, Vernon Rosco.

Carstensen, Vernon Rosco, 1907-
 xCarstensen, Vernon.
  Farms of Forests. Arno.
  ed. Public Lands: Studies in the History of the Public Domain. U of Wis Pr.

Carswell, C. *see* Carswell, Catherine Macfarlane.

Carswell, Catherine. *see* Carswell, Catherine Macfarlane.

Carswell, Catherine Macfarlane, 1879-1946
 xCarswell, C.
  The Life of Robert Burns. Gordon Pr.
 xCarswell, Catherine.
  Life of Robert Burns. Gale.
  The Life of Robert Burns. R West.

Carswell, John.
 xCarswell, John.
  Lives & Letters: A. R. Orage-Beatrice Hastings-Katherine Mansfield-John Middleton Murray-S. S. Koteiliansky. New Directions.

Cartellieri, Otto, 1872-1930
 xCartellieri, Otto.
  Court of Burgundy. Haskell.

Carter. *see* Carter, Donald.

Carter, A. E. *see* Carter, Alfred Edward.

Carter, Alberta S. *see* Carter, Alberta Simpson.

Carter, Alberta Simpson.
 xCarter, Alberta S.
  Fool's Proof. Popular Lib.

Carter, Alfred Edward.
 xCarter, A. E.
  Charles Baudelaire. Twayne.

Carter, Alice C. *see* Carter, Alice Clare.

Carter, Alice Clare.
 xCarter, Alice C.
  Dutch Republic in Europe in the Seven Years War. U of Miami Pr.
  Getting, Spending & Investing in Early Modern Times: Essays on Dutch, English & Huguenot Economic History. Humanities.

Carter, Angela, 1940-
 xCarter, Angela.
  The Bloody Chamber. Har-Row.
  The Sadeian Woman: And the Ideology of Pornography. Pantheon.

Carter, Anne.
 xCarter, Anne.
  God Loved the Muddle. Concordia.

Carter, Anne P., 1925-
 xCarter, Anne P.
  Structural Change in the American Economy. Harvard U Pr.

Carter, Annette.
 xCarter, Annette.
  Exploring from the Chesapeake Bay to the Poconos. Lippincott.

Carter, April.
 xCarter, April.

Authority & Democracy. Routledge & Kegan.
  Direct Action & Liberal Democracy. Har-Row.
  Direct Action & Liberal Democracy. Routledge & Kegan.

Carter, Arnold.
 xCarter, Arnold.
  Communicate Effectively!. Pelican.

Carter, Ashley.
 xCarter, Ashley.
  Master of Blackoaks. Fawcett.
  Panama. Fawcett.
  Sword of the Golden Stud. Fawcett.
  Taproots of Falconhurst. Fawcett.

Carter, Barbara.
 xCarter, Barbara.
  Organizing School Volunteer Programs. Schol Bk Serv.

Carter, C. E. *see* Carter, Charles Ernest Owen.

Carter, C. Eric.
 xCarter, C. E.
  Case Studies in East African Geography. Transatlantic.

Carter, C. M. *see* Carter, Gwendolen Margaret.

Carter, C. O. *see* Carter, Cedric O.

Carter, Carrol J. *see* Carter, Carrol Joe.

Carter, Carrol Joe.
 xCarter, Carrol J.
  Pike in Colorado. Old Army.

Carter, Cedric O.
 xCarter, C. O.
  The Genetics of Locomotor Disorders. Oxford U Pr.

Carter, Charles E. *see* Carter, Charles Ernest Owen.

Carter, Charles Ernest Owen, 1887-
 xCarter, C. E.
  Principles of Astrology. Theos Pub Hse.
 xCarter, Charles E.
  Principles of Astrology. Theos Pub Hse.

Carter, Charles F. *see* Carter, Charles Franklin.

Carter, Charles Franklin.
 xCarter, Charles F.
  Stories of the Old Missions of California. Arno.

Carter, Charles H.
 xCarter, Charles H.
  Medical Aspects of Mental Retardation. C C Thomas.

Carter, Clarence E. *see* Carter, Clarence Edwin.

Carter, Clarence Edwin, 1881-1961
 xCarter, Clarence E.
  Great Britain & the Illinois Country 1763-74. Arno.
  Great Britain & the Illinois Country, 1763-1774. Kennikat.

Carter, Codell K. *see* Carter, Kay Codell.

Carter, Conrad. *see* Carter, Conrad C.

Carter, Conrad C.
 xCarter, Conrad.
  The Production & Staging of Plays. Arco.

Carter, Dan T.
 xCarter, Dan T.
  Scottsboro: A Tragedy of the American South. La State U Pr.

Carter, David C.
 xCarter, David C.
  Action Techniques for the Take-Charge Sales Manager. P-H.
  Take Charge & Sell. P-H.

Carter, David E.
 xCarter, David E.
  ed. Corporate Identity Manuals. Art Dir.
  ed. Designing Corporate Symbols. Art Dir.

Carter, Del.
 xCarter, Del.
  Good News for Grimy Gulch. Judson.

Carter, Dilford C.
 xCarter, Dilford C.

Catalogue of Type Specimens of Neotropical Bats in Selected European Museums. Tex Tech Pr.

Carter, Donald.
 xCarter.
  Backgammon: How to Play & Win. Borden.
 xCarter, Donald.
  Backgammon: How to Play & Win. Holloway.

Carter, E. Dale.
 xCarter, E. Dale.
  ed. Antologia Del Realismo Magico: Ocho Cuentos Hispanoamericanos. Odyssey Pr.

Carter, E. F. *see* Carter, Ernest Frank.

Carter, Edward, 1929-
 xCarter, Edward.
  Response in Christ: A Study of the Christian Life. Alba Bks.

Carter, Edward C. *see* Carter, Edward Carlos.

Carter, Edward Carlos.
 xCarter, Edward C.
  ed. Enterprise & Entrepreneurs in Nineteenth & Twentieth Century France. Johns Hopkins.

Carter, Eleanor-Jean.
 xCarter, Eleanor-Jean.
  Doll Modes & Doll Fashions & Patterns. Carter Craft.

Carter, Elizabeth.
 xCarter, Elizabeth.
  Letters from Mrs. Elizabeth Carter to Mrs. Montagu Between the Years 1755-1800. AMS Pr.

Carter, Elizabeth E. *see* Carter, Elizabeth Eliot.

Carter, Elizabeth Eliot.
 xCarter, Elizabeth E.
  Valley of the Kings: A Novel of Tutankhamun. Dutton.

Carter, Ernest F. *see* Carter, Ernest Frank.

Carter, Ernest Frank, 1899-
 xCarter, E. F.
  Dictionary of Inventions and Discoveries. Crane-Russak Co.
 xCarter, Ernest F.
  Let's Look at Trains. A Whitman.

Carter, Ernestine R. *see* Carter, Ernestine Russell.

Carter, Ernestine Russell.
 xCarter, Ernestine R.
  Gymnastics for Girls & Women. P-H.

Carter, Evelyn.
 xCarter, Evelyn.
  No Ground. Logos.

Carter, Forrest.
 xCarter, Forrest.
  The Education of Little Tree. Delacorte.
  The Education of Little Tree. Dell.
  Gone to Texas. Delacorte.
  The Vengeance Trail of Josey Wales. Delacorte.
  The Vengeance Trail of Josey Wales. Dell.

Carter, Frances Monet.
 xCarter, Francis M.
  Psychosocial Nursing: Theory & Practice in Hospital & Community Mental Health. Macmillan.

Carter, Francis M. *see* Carter, Frances Monet.

Carter, Frederick.
 xCarter, Frederick.
  D. H. Lawrence & the Body Mystical. Arden Lib.
  D. H. Lawrence & the Body Mystical. Haskell.
 xCarter, Frederick D.
  D. H. Lawrence - the Body Mystical. Folcroft.

Carter, Frederick D. *see* Carter, Frederick.

Carter, G. R. *see* Carter, Gordon R.

Carter, G. S. *see* Carter, George Stuart.

Carter, George F. *see* Carter, George Francis.

Carter, George Francis, 1912-
 xCarter, George F.

Earlier Than You Think: A Personal View of
Man in America. Tex A&M Univ Pr.
Carter, George Stuart.
xCarter, G. S.
Structure & Habit in Vertebrate Evolution. U
of Wash Pr.
Carter, Giles F.
xCarter, Giles F.
Principles of Physical & Chemical Metallurgy.
ASM.
Carter, Gordon R.
xCarter, G. R.
Diagnostic Procedures in Veterinary
Bacteriology & Mycology. C C Thomas.
Carter, Gwendolen. *see* Carter, Gwendolen Margaret.
Carter, Gwendolen M. *see* Carter, Gwendolen Margaret.
Carter, Gwendolen Margaret.
xCarter, C. M.
ed. African One-Party States. Brown Bk.
xCarter, Gwendolen.
Five African States: Responses to Diversity -
the Congo, Dahomey, the Cameroun Federal
Republic, the Rhodesias & Nyasaland, South
Africa. Cornell U Pr.
xCarter, Gwendolen M.
ed. African One-Party States. Cornell U Pr.
Government of the Soviet Union. HarBraceJ.
Government of the United Kingdom.
HarBraceJ.
ed. Southern Africa in Crisis. Ind U Pr.
ed. Southern Africa: The Continuing Crisis. Ind
U Pr.
Which Way Is South Africa Going?. Ind U Pr.
xCarter, Gwendolyn.
The Politics of Inequality: South Africa Since
1948. Octagon.
Carter, Gwendolyn. *see* Carter, Gwendolen Margaret.
Carter, Harold.
xCarter, Harold.
The Study of Urban Geography. Halsted Pr.
Carter, Harold A.
xCarter, Harold A.
Myths That Mire the Ministry. Judson.
The Prayer Tradition of Black People. Judson.
Carter, Harvey L. *see* Carter, Harvey Lewis.
Carter, Harvey Lewis, 1904-
xCarter, Harvey L.
Far Western Frontiers. Am Hist Assn.
Carter, Hobart C. *see* Carter, Hobart Clinton.
Carter, Hobart Clinton, 1907-
xCarter, Hobart C.
Modern Basic Mathematics. Irvington.
Carter, Hodding, 1907-
xCarter, Hodding.
The Angry Scar: The Story of Reconstruction.
Greenwood.
Doomed Road of Empire: The Spanish Trail of
Conquest. McGraw.
First Person Rural. Greenwood.
South Strikes Back. Negro U Pr.
Southern Legacy. La State U Pr.
Their Words Were Bullets: The Southern Press
in War, Reconstruction & Peace. U of Ga Pr.
Carter, Howard.
xCarter, Howard.
The Discovery of the Tomb of Tutankhamen.
Dover.
The Discovery of the Tomb of Tutankhamen.
Peter Smith.
Carter, Hugh, 1895-
xCarter, Hugh.
Social Theories of L. T. Hobhouse. Kennikat.
Carter, Hugh. *see* Carter, Hugh Alton.
Carter, Hugh Alton.
xCarter, Hugh.
Cousin Beedie & Cousin Hot: My Life with the
Carter Family of Plains, Georgia. P-H.
Carter, J. Ted.
xCarter, J. Ted.

Patterned Fast-Break Basketball. P-H.
Carter, James E., 1935-
xCarter, James E.
Following Jesus: The Nature of Christian
Discipleship. Broadman.
Carter, Jimmy.
xCarter, Jimmy.
A Government As Good As Its People. PB.
A Government As Good As Its People. S&S.
Carter, Joan H. *see* Carter, Joan Haselman.
Carter, Joan Haselman.
xCarter, Joan H.
Standards of Nursing Care: A Guide for
Evaluation. Springer Pub.
Carter, John F. *see* Carter, John Franklin.
Carter, John Franklin, 1897-1967
xCarter, John F.
What We Are About to Receive. Arno.
Carter, John H. *see* Carter, John Henton.
Carter, John Henton.
xCarter, John H.
Log of Commodore Rollingpin: His Adventures
Afloat & Ashore. Scholarly.
Carter, John M. *see* Carter, John Mack.
Carter, John Mack.
xCarter, John M.
How to Be Outrageously Successful with
Women. Ballantine.
Carter, Kay Codell.
xCarter, Codell K.
A Contemporary Introduction to Logic with
Applications. Glencoe.
Carter, L. R.
xCarter, L. R.
A Practical Approach to Computer Simulation
in Business. Halsted Pr.
Carter, Lanie.
xCarter, Lanie.
Congratulations! You're Going to Be a
Grandmother. Oak Tree Pubns.
Carter, Lief H.
xCarter, Lief H.
The Limits of Order. Lexington Bks.
Reason in Law. Little.
Carter, Lillian.
xCarter, Lillian.
Away from Home: Letters to My Family. S&S.
Away from Home: Letters to My Family.
Warner Bks.
Carter, Lin.
xCarter, Lin.
As the Green Star Rises. DAW Bks.
The Barbarian of World's End. DAW Bks.
The City Outside the World. Berkley Pub.
Dreams from R'lyeh. Arkham.
The Immortal of World's End. DAW Bks.
The Pirate of World's End. DAW Bks.
Renegade of Callisto. Dell.
Thongor & the Wizard of Lemuria. Berkley
Pub.
The Valley Where Time Stood Still. Popular
Lib.
Carter, Linda B. *see* Carter, Linda Broadus.
Carter, Linda Broadus.
xCarter, Linda B.
Fundamentals of Nursing Review. Arco.
Carter, Lynne C.
xCarter, Lynne C.
Guide to Cellular Energetics. W H Freeman.
Carter, Mary E. *see* Carter, Mary Ellen.
Carter, Mary Ellen.
xCarter, Mary E.
Edgar Cayce on Prophecy. Warner Bks.
Carter, Melvin W.
xCarter, Melvin W.
ed. Management of Low-Level Radioactive
Waste. Pergamon.
Carter, Michael, 1946-
xCarter, Michael.

Crafts of China. Doubleday.
Carter, Nick.
xCarter, Nick.
The Pamplona Affair. Charter Bks.
Carter, Paul A. *see* Carter, Paul Allen.
Carter, Paul Allen, 1926-
xCarter, Paul A.
The Creation of Tomorrow: Fifty Years of
Magazine Science Fiction. Columbia U Pr.
Decline & Revival of the Social Gospel: Social
& Political Liberalism in American Protestant
Churches, 1920-1940. Shoe String.
Little America: Town at the End of the World.
Columbia U Pr.
Twenties in America. AHM Pub.
Carter, Peter.
xCarter, Peter.
Mao. Viking Pr.
Under Goliath. Oxford U Pr.
Carter, R. L.
xCarter, Robert L.
Reinsurance. Kluwer Boston.
Carter, R. W. *see* Carter, Roger William.
Carter, Randolph.
xCarter, Randolph.
The World of Flo Ziegfeld. Merrimack Bk
Serv.
Carter, Robert C.
xCarter, Robert C.
Introduction to Electrical Circuit Analysis.
Krieger.
Carter, Robert E. *see* Carter, Robert Edward.
Carter, Robert Edward, 1919-
xCarter, Robert E.
Arson Investigation. Glencoe.
Carter, Robert L. *see* Carter, R. L.
Carter, Robert M.
xCarter, Robert M.
Back on the Street: The Diversion of Juvenile
Offenders. P-H.
ed. Communication in Organizations: An
Annotated Bibliography & Sourcebook. Gale.
Carter, Robert M. *see* Carter, Robert Melvin.
Carter, Robert Melvin.
xCarter, Robert M.
ed. Correctional Institutions. Har-Row.
Corrections in America. Har-Row.
ed. Probation, Parole, & Community
Corrections. Wiley.
Carter, Roger William.
xCarter, R. W.
Simple Groups of Lie Type. Wiley.
Carter, Ronald L.
xCarter, Ronald L.
The Criminal's Image of the City. Pergamon.
Carter, Russell G. *see* Carter, Russell Gordon.
Carter, Russell Gordon.
xCarter, Russell G.
A Patriot Lad of Old Cape Cod. W S Sullwold.
Carter, S. E. *see* Carter, Stephan E.
Carter, Samuel, 1904-
xCarter, Samuel.
Incredible Great White Fleet. Macmillan.
The Siege of Atlanta, 1864. Ballantine.
Carter, Stephan E.
xCarter, S. E.
ed. Fundamental & Clinical Studies of
Bleomycin. Univ Park.
Carter, Stephen.
xCarter, Stephen.
The Politics of Solzhenitsyn. Holmes & Meier.
Carter, Stephen K.
xCarter, Stephen K.
Chemotherapy of Cancer. Wiley.
Carter, Thomas P.
xCarter, Thomas P.
Mexican Americans in School: A Decade of
Change. College Bd.
Carter, Vernon G. *see* Carter, Vernon Gill.

Carter, Vernon Gill.
  xCarter, Vernon G.
    Topsoil & Civilization. U of Okla Pr.
Carter, W. J.
  xCarter, W. J.
    Papermachine Clothing. Halsted Pr.
Carter, Walter, 1897-
  xCarter, Walter.
    Insects in Relation to Plant Disease. Wiley.
Carter, William E.
  xCarter, William E.
    The First Book of South America. Watts.
Carter-Ruck, Peter. *see* Carter-Ruck, Peter Frederick.
Carter-Ruck, Peter. *see* Carter-Ruck, Peter.
Carter-Ruck, Peter Frederick, 1914-
  xCarter-Ruck, Peter.
    Libel & Slander. Shoe String.
Cartier, John O.
  xCartier, John O.
    The Modern Deer Hunter. T Y Crowell.
Cartland, Barbara, 1902-
  xCartland, Barbara.
    Bride to the King. Bantam.
    Bride to the King. Dutton.
    Castle Made for Love. Brodart.
    Dawn of Love. Dutton.
    The Dragon & the Pearl. Brodart.
    The Drums of Love. Brodart.
    Duke & the Preacher's Daughter. Brodart.
    Journey to Paradise. Dutton.
    Judgement of Love. Brodart.
    The Light of Love: Lines to Live by, Day by
      Day. Dell.
    The Light of Love: Lines to Live by Day by
      Day. Elsevier-Nelson.
    Lights of Love. BJ Pub Group.
    Look, Listen & Love. Brodart.
    Lord Ravenscar's Revenge. Brodart.
    Love & the Loathsome Leopard. Brodart.
    Love in the Clouds. Dutton.
    Love Leaves at Midnight. Brodart.
    Love Pirate. Brodart.
    Lovers in Paradise. Brodart.
    Marquis Who Hated Women. Brodart.
    Outrageous Lady. Brodart.
    Prince & the Pekingese. Brodart.
    Princess in Distress. Brodart.
    Punishment of a Vixen. Brodart.
    Race for Love. Brodart.
    A Runaway Star. Brodart.
    The Sign of Love. Brodart.
    Touch of Love. Brodart.
Cartlidge, David R.
  xCartlidge, David R.
    Documents for the Study of the Gospels.
      Fortress.
Cartlidge, Michelle.
  xCartlidge, Michelle.
    Pippin & Pod. Pantheon.
Cartmell. *see* Cartmell, Edward.
Cartmell, Edward.
  xCartmell.
    Valency & Molecular Structure. Butterworths.
  xCartmell, Edward.
    Valency & Molecular Structure. Van Nos
      Reinhold.
Cartmell, Ronald.
  xCartmell, Ronald.
    Wood Sculpture. Taplinger.
Cartmill, Matt.
  xCartmill, Matt.
    Primate Origins. Burgess.
The Cartographic Department of Oxford University
  Press. *see* Oxford University Press.
Cartter, Allan M. *see* Cartter, Allan Murray.
Cartter, Allan Murray.
  xCartter, Allan M.
    Theory of Wages & Employment. Greenwood.
Cartwright, Ann.
  xCartwright, Ann.

    How Many Children?. Routledge & Kegan.
    Life Before Death. Routledge & Kegan.
    Parents & Family Planning Services. Beresford
      Bk Serv.
Cartwright, Carol. *see* Cartwright, Carol A.
Cartwright, Carol A.
  xCartwright, Carol.
    Exceptional Previews: A Self-Evaluation
      Handbook for Special Education Students.
      Wadsworth Pub.
  xCartwright, Carol A.
    Developing Observation Skills. McGraw.
Cartwright, Colbert S., 1924-
  xCartwright, Colbert S.
    The Lord's Prayer Comes Alive. Bethany Pr.
Cartwright, Desmond. *see* Cartwright, Desmond S.
Cartwright, Desmond S., 1924-
  xCartwright, Desmond.
    Introduction to Personality. Rand.
  xCartwright, Desmond S.
    Theories & Models of Personality. Wm C
      Brown.
Cartwright, Donald. *see* Cartwright, Donald I.
Cartwright, Donald I., 1949-
  xCartwright, Donald.
    Extensions of Positive Operators Between
      Banach Lattices. Am Math.
Cartwright, Dorwin.
  xCartwright, Dorwin.
    ed. Group Dynamics: Research & Theory.
      Har-Row.
Cartwright, John, 1740-1824
  xCartwright, John.
    Commonwealth in Danger. B Franklin.
    Life & Correspondence of Major Cartwright. B
      Franklin.
    Life & Correspondence of Major Cartwright.
      Kelley.
Cartwright, John M. *see* Cartwright, John Macdonald.
Cartwright, John Macdonald.
  xCartwright, John M.
    Farm & Ranch Real Estate Law. Lawyers
      Co-Op.
    Glossary of Real Estate Law. Lawyers Co-Op.
Cartwright, John R.
  xCartwright, John R.
    Political Leadership in Sierra Leone. U of
      Toronto Pr.
Cartwright, Joseph H., 1939-
  xCartwright, Joseph H.
    The Triumph of Jim Crow: Tennessee Race
      Relations in the 1880s. U of Tenn Pr.
Cartwright, Justin.
  xCartwright, Justin.
    The Horse of Darius. Macmillan.
Cartwright, Peter.
  xCartwright, Peter.
    Autobiography of Peter Cartwright: The
      Backwoods Preacher. Arno.
Cartwright, Rosalind D. *see* Cartwright, Rosalind
Dymond.
Cartwright, Rosalind Dymond.
  xCartwright, Rosalind D.
    Night Life: Explorations in Dreaming. P-H.
    Primer on Sleep & Dreaming. A-W.
Cartwright, Sally.
  xCartwright, Sally.
    Animal Homes. Coward.
    Sunlight. Coward.
    What's in a Map?. Coward.
Cartwright, William H. *see* Cartwright, William Holman.
Cartwright, William Holman.
  xCartwright, William H.
    ed. The Reinterpretation of American History
      & Culture. Coun Soc Studies.
Carty, Sally C. *see* Carty, Sally Clarke.
Carty, Sally Clarke.
  xCarty, Sally C.

    How to Make Braided Rugs. McGraw.
Carus, Paul.
  xCarus, Paul.
    Gospel of Buddha. Auromere.
    The Gospel of Buddha. Gordon Pr.
    The Gospel of Buddha. Omen Pr.
    Gospel of Buddha. Open Court.
Carus-Wilson, E. M. *see* Carus-Wilson, Eleanora Mary.
Carus-Wilson, Eleanora Mary.
  xCarus-Wilson, E. M.
    Pref. by & ed. The Overseas Trade of Bristol in
      the Later Middle Ages. Kelley.
Caruso, Domenick.
  xCaruso, Domenick.
    Creating Contexts: A Practical Approach to
      Writing. Norton.
Caruso, Peter, 1886-
  xCaruso, Peter.
    Destination. Philos Lib.
Caruth, Donald L.
  xCaruth, Donald L.
    Work Measurement for Commercial Banks.
      Bankers.
Caruthers, J. W. *see* Caruthers, Jerald W.
Caruthers, Jerald W.
  xCaruthers, J. W.
    Fundamentals of Marine Acoustics. Elsevier.
Carvajal, Manuel J.
  xCarvajal, Manuel J.
    ed. Population Growth & Human Productivity.
      U Presses Fla.
Carvell, Fred J.
  xCarvell, Fred J.
    Human Relations in Business. Macmillan.
Carver, D. K.
  xCarver, D. K.
    Introduction to Business Data Processing: With
      Basic, Fortran & Cobol Programming. Wiley.
  xCarver, D. Keith.
    Beginning Basic. Brooks-Cole.
Carver, D. Keith. *see* Carver, D. K.
Carver, George, 1888-1949
  xCarver, George.
    ed. Periodical Essays of the Eighteenth
      Century. Arno.
Carver, Humphrey.
  xCarver, Humphrey.
    Cities in the Suburbs. U of Toronto Pr.
    Compassionate Landscape. U of Toronto Pr.
Carver, John N.
  xCarver, John N.
    The Family of the Retarded Child. Syracuse U
      Pr.
Carver, Michael. *see* Carver, Richard Michael Power.
Carver, Raymond.
  xCarver, Raymond.
    Furious Seasons & Other Stories. Capra Pr.
    Put Yourself in My Shoes. Capra Pr.
Carver, Richard Michael Power, Baron Carver, 1915-
  xCarver, Michael.
    The Apostles of Mobility: The Theory &
      Practice of Armoured Warfare. Holmes &
      Meier.
Carver, Robert E., 1931-
  xCarver, Robert E.
    ed. Procedures in Sedimentary Petrology.
      Wiley.
Carver, Thomas N. *see* Carver, Thomas Nixon.
Carver, Thomas Nixon, 1865-1961
  xCarver, Thomas N.
    The Distribution of Wealth. Hyperion Conn.
Carver, Tina K. *see* Carver, Tina Kasloff.
Carver, Tina Kasloff.
  xCarver, Tina K.
    A Conversation Book: English in Everyday
      Life. P-H.
Carver, Vida.
  xCarver, Vida.

Disability & the Environment. Schocken.

Carvic, Heron.
xCarvic, Heron.
Odds on Miss Seeton. Har-Row.
Odds on Miss Seeton. Popular Lib.

Carwardine, William H. *see* Carwardine, William Horace.

Carwardine, William Horace, 1855-1929
xCarwardine, William H.
The Pullman Strike. C H Kerr.

Cary, Alice.
xCary, Alice.
Ballads for Little Folk. Arno.

Cary, Barbara.
xCary, Barbara.
Meet Abraham Lincoln. Random.

Cary, Bob.
xCary, Bob.
Winter Camping. Greene.

Cary, Diana S. *see* Cary, Diana Serra.

Cary, Diana Serra, 1918-
xCary, Diana S.
Hollywood's Children: An Inside Account of
the Child Star Era. HM.

Cary, Edward, 1840-1917
xCary, Edward.
George William Curtis. Folcroft.
George William Curtis. Greenwood.
George William Curtis. Scholarly.

Cary, Elisabeth Luther, 1867-1936
xCary, Elizabeth L.
Browning, Poet & Man: A Survey. R West.
Browning, Poet & Man: A Survey. Scholarly.

Cary, Elizabeth L. *see* Cary, Elisabeth Luther.

Cary, Emily.
xCary, Emily.
My High Love Calling. Bouregy.

Cary, Henry F. *see* Cary, Henry Francis.

Cary, Henry Francis, 1772-1844
xCary, Henry F.
The Early French Poets. Arden Lib.
The Early French Poets. Century Bookbindery.
The Early French Poets. Kennikat.

Cary, Howard B.
xCary, Howard B.
Modern Welding Technology. P-H.

Cary, Jane R. *see* Cary, Jane Randolph.

Cary, Jane Randolph.
xCary, Jane R.
How to Create Interiors for the Disabled: A
Guidebook for Family & Friends. Pantheon.
Storage: Cabinets, Closets & Wall Systems.
Har-Row.

Cary, Joyce, 1888-
xCary, Joyce.
Prisoner of Grace. Queens Hse.

Cary, Lee J.
xCary, Lee J.
ed. Community Development As a Process. U
of Mo Pr.

Cary, Mara.
xCary, Mara.
Useful Baskets. HM.

Cary, Max, 1881-1958
xCary, Max.
Documentary Sources of Greek History.
Greenwood.
A History of the Greek World: 323-146 B.C..
Methuen Inc.

Cary, Otis, 1851-1932
xCary, Otis.
A History of Christianity in Japan: Roman
Catholic & Greek Orthodox Missions. C E
Tuttle.

Cary, Richard, 1909-
xCary, Richard.
Early Reception of Edwin Arlington Robinson:
The First Twenty Years. Colby.
Mary N. Murfree. Coll & U Pr.
Mary N. Murfree. Irvington.

Cary, Willie M. *see* Cary, Willie Mae.

Cary, Willie Mae.
xCary, Willie M.
Worse Than Silence: The Black Child's
Dilemma. Vantage.

Casad, Robert C.
xCasad, Robert C.
Expropriation in Central America & Panama:
Processes & Procedures. W S Hein.

Casaldaliga, Pedro.
xCasaldaliga, Pedro.
I Believe in Justice & Hope. Fides Claretian.

Casale, Antonio.
xCasale, Antonio.
Polymer Stress Reactions. Acad Pr.

Casale, Joan T.
xCasale, Joan T.
The Diet Food Finder. Bowker.

Casanova, Richard L.
xCasanova, Richard L.
Illustrated Guide to Fossil Collecting.
Naturegraph.

Casarett, Alison P.
xCasarett, Alison P.
Radiation Biology. P-H.

Casaubon, Meric.
xCasaubon, Meric.
A Letter of Meric Casaubon to Peter du
Moulin Concerning Natural Experimental
Philosophie.. Schol Facsimiles.

Casavis, James N.
xCasavis, James N.
Christmas Morning. J N Casavis.
Principal's Guidelines for Action in Parent
Conferences. P-H.

Casazza, Giulio Gatti. *see* Gatti-Casazza, Giulio.

Casciano-Savignano, C. Jennie.
xCasciano-Savignano, C. Jennie.
Systems Approach to Curriculum &
Instructional Improvement. Merrill.

Cascio, Wayne F.
xCascio, Wayne F.
Applied Psychology in Personnel Management.
Reston.

Case, Arthur E. *see* Case, Arthur Ellicott.

Case, Arthur Ellicott, 1894-
xCase, Arthur E.
Four Essays on Gulliver's Travels. Peter Smith.

Case, Brian.
xCase, Brian.
The Illustrated Encyclopedia of Jazz. Crown.

Case, Clarence M. *see* Case, Clarence Marsh.

Case, Clarence Marsh, 1874-1946
xCase, Clarence M.
Non-Violent Coercion: A Study in Methods of
Social Pressure. Ozer.

Case, D. H. *see* Case, Denis Henry Vaughan.

Case, Denis Henry Vaughan.
xCase, D. H.
Modern Mathematical Topics. Philos Lib.

Case, Emsan.
xCase, Ensan.
Wingmen. Avon.

Case, Ensan. *see* Case, Emsan.

Case, Fred. *see* Case, Frederick E.

Case, Frederick E.
xCase, Fred.
Real Estate Brokerage. P-H.
xCase, Frederick E.
Real Estate Financing. Wiley.

Case, James H., 1940-
xCase, James H.
Economics & the Competitive Process. NYU
Pr.

Case, John.
xCase, John.
ed. Co-Ops, Communes, & Collectives:
Experiments in Social Change in the 1960s &
1970s. Pantheon.

Case, Karl E.
xCase, Karl E.

Property Taxation: The Need for Reform.
Ballinger Pub.

Case, Lynn M. *see* Case, Lynn Marshall.

Case, Lynn Marshall, 1903-
xCase, Lynn M.
French Opinion on War & Diplomacy During
the Second Empire. Octagon.

Case, Patricia A. *see* Case, Patricia Ann.

Case, Patricia Ann.
xCase, Patricia A.
How to Write Your Autobiography: Preserving
Your Family Heritage. Woodbridge Pr.

Case, Robert H. *see* Case, Robert Hope.

Case, Robert Hope, 1857-1944
xCase, Robert H.
English Epithalamies. Folcroft.

Case, Shirley J. *see* Case, Shirley Jackson.

Case, Shirley Jackson, 1872-1947
xCase, Shirley J.
The Social Triumph of the Ancient Church.
Arno.

Case, Walter H. *see* Case, Walter Hodgin.

Case, Walter Hodgin, 1882-
xCase, Walter H.
History of Long Beach & Vicinity. Arno.

Casebier, Allan.
xCasebier, Allan.
Film Appreciation. HarBraceJ.

Casebier, Dennis G.
xCasebier, Dennis G.
Camp Rock Spring California. Tales Mojave
Rd.
Fort Pah-Ute California. Tales Mojave Rd..

Casella, Dolores.
xCasella, Dolores.
World of Baking. D White.
World of Breads. D White.

Caserio, Robert L., 1944-
xCaserio, Robert L.
Plot, Story, & the Novel: From Dickens & Poe
to the Modern Period. Princeton U Pr.

Casewit, Curtis W.
xCasewit, Curtis W.
America's Tennis Book. Scribner.
Freelance Photography: Advice from the Pros.
Macmillan.
The Stop Smoking Book for Teens. Messner.

Casey, Betty.
xCasey, Betty.
The Complete Book of Square Dancing (&
Round Dancing). Doubleday.

Casey, Douglas R.
xCasey, Douglas R.
The Expatriate Investor. Everest Hse.
The International Man: The Complete
Guidebook to the World's Last Frontiers for
Freedom Seekers, Investors, Adventurers,
Speculators & Expatriates. Alexandria Hse.

Casey, Edward S., 1939-
xCasey, Edward S.
Imagining: A Phenomenological Study. Ind U
Pr.

Casey, J. *see* Casey, James.

Casey, James, 1944-
xCasey, J.
The Kingdom of Valencia in the Seventeenth
Century. Cambridge U Pr.

Casey, John.
xCasey, John.
Testimony & Demeanor. Knopf.

Casey, Juanita.
xCasey, Juanita.
The Circus. Longship Pr.

Casey, Lydian.
xCasey, Lydian.
Outdoor Gardening. Lerner Pubns.

Casey, Ralph D. *see* Casey, Ralph Droz.

Casey, Ralph Droz, 1890-
xCasey, Ralph D.

ed. Press in Perspective. La State U Pr.
Casey, Richard G. *see* Casey, Richard Gardiner.
Casey, Richard Gardiner, 1890-
    xCasey, Richard G.
        Friends & Neighbors. Mich St U Pr.
Casey, T. A. *see* Casey, Thomas Aquinas.
Casey, Thomas Aquinas.
    xCasey, T. A.
        ed. Corneal Grafting. Butterworths.
Cash, Anthony, 1933-
    xCash, Anthony.
        Lenin. Viking Pr.
Cash, Audrey.
    xCash, Audrey.
        The Southern Literary Cookbook. Hope Ent
        Fla.
Cash, Grace, 1915-
    xCash, Grace.
        Promise Unto Death. Herald Pr.
Cash, Joseph H.
    xCash, Joseph H.
        Working the Homestake. Iowa St U Pr.
Cash, June C. *see* Cash, June Carter.
Cash, June Carter, 1929-
    xCash, June C.
        Among My Klediments. Zondervan.
Cash, Kevin. *see* Cash, Kevin Richard.
Cash, Kevin Richard, 1926-
    xCash, Kevin.
        Who the Hell Is William Loeb?. Amoskeag Pr.
Cash, Philip.
    xCash, Philip.
        Medical Men at the Siege of Boston, April,
        1775 - April, 1776: Problems of the
        Massachusetts & Continental Armies. Am
        Philos.
Cashdan, Sheldon.
    xCashdan, Sheldon.
        Abnormal Psychology. P-H.
Cashin, Edward J.
    xCashin, Edward J.
        Augusta & the American Revolution: Events in
        the Georgia Back Country, 1773-1783.
        Richmond Cty Hist Soc.
Cashin, Herschel V.
    xCashin, Herschel V.
        Under Fire with the Tenth U. S. Cavalry.
        Arno.
Cashman, Thomas J.
    xCashman, Thomas J.
        Data Processing & Computer Programming: A
        Modular Approach. Har-Row.
Cashmore, Ernest.
    xCashmore, Ernest.
        Rastaman: The Rastafarian Movement in
        England. Allen Unwin.
Casida, L. E. *see* Casida, Lester Earl.
Casida, Lester Earl, 1904-
    xCasida, L. E.
        Industrial Microbiology. Wiley.
Caskey, John H. *see* Caskey, John Homer.
Caskey, John Homer, 1895-
    xCaskey, John H.
        The Life & Works of Edward Moore. Shoe
        String.
Caskey, Marie, 1945-
    xCaskey, Marie.
        Chariot of Fire: Religion & the Beecher
        Family. Yale U Pr.
Casler, Darwin J.
    xCasler, Darwin J.
        Evolution of CPA Ethics: A Profile of
        Professionalization. Mich St U Busn.
Casler, John O. *see* Casler, John Overton.
Casler, John Overton.
    xCasler, John O.
        Four Years in the Stonewall Brigade. Pr of
        Morningside.
Caso, Adolph.
    xCaso, Adolph.

America's Italian Founding Fathers. Branden.
America's Italian Founding Fathers:
    1770-1780. Dante Univ Bkshlf.
Caso, Alfonso, 1896-
    xCaso, Alfonso.
        Aztecs, People of the Sun. U of Okla Pr.
Cason, Eloise M. *see* Cason, Eloise May (Boeker).
Cason, Eloise May (Boeker), 1901-
    xCason, Eloise M.
        Mechanical Methods for Increasing the Speed
        of Reading: An Experimental Study at the
        Third Grade Level. AMS Pr.
Cason, Marjorie.
    xCason, Marjorie.
        The Art of Bolivian Highland Weaving.
        Watson-Guptill.
Caspari, Irene E.
    xCaspari, Irene E.
        Troublesome Children in Class. Routledge &
        Kegan.
Caspary, Gerard E.
    xCaspary, Gerard E.
        Politics & Exegesis: Origen & the Two Swords.
        U of Cal Pr.
Caspary, Vera.
    xCaspary, Vera.
        The Dreamers. PB.
        Laura. Queens Hse.
        The Secrets of Grownups. McGraw.
Casper, Barry M.
    xCasper, Barry M.
        Revolutions in Physics. Norton.
Casper, Jonathan D.
    xCasper, Jonathan D.
        Lawyers Before the Warren Court: Civil
        Liberties & Civil Rights, 1957-66. U of Ill Pr.
Casper, Leonard, 1923-
    xCasper, Leonard.
        A Lion Unannounced: Twelve Stories & a
        Fable. SMU Press.
Casper, M. E.
    xCasper, M. E.
        Energy-Saving Techniques for the Food
        Industry. Noyes.
Caspers, W. J.
    xCaspers, W. J.
        Theory of Spin Relaxation. Krieger.
Cass, David.
    xCass, David.
        ed. The Hamiltonian Approach to Dynamic
        Economics. Acad Pr.
Cass, James.
    xCass, James.
        Counselors' Comparative Guide to American
        Colleges, 1976. Har-Row.
Cass, Loretta K.
    xCass, Loretta K.
        Childhood Pathology & Later Adjustment: The
        Question of Prediction. Wiley.
Cass, M. T. *see* Cass, Marion T.
Cass, Marion T.
    xCass, M. T.
        Speech Habilitation in Cerebral Palsy. Hafner.
Cass, Zoe.
    xCass, Zoe.
        The Silver Leopard. Popular Lib.
Cassady, Carolyn.
    xCassady, Carolyn.
        Heart Beat: My Life with Jack & Neal.
        Creative Arts Bk.
Cassady, Ralph, 1900-
    xCassady, Ralph.
        Auctions & Auctioneering. U of Cal Pr.
Cassara, Ernest, 1925-
    xCassara, Ernest.
        The Enlightenment in America. Twayne.
        ed. History of the United States of America: A
        Guide to Information Sources. Gale.
Cassard, Daniel W.
    xCassard, Daniel W.

Approved Practices in Feeds & Feeding.
    Interstate.
Cassata, Mary B.
    xCassata, Mary B.
        ed. The Administrative Aspects of Education
        for Librarianship: A Symposium. Scarecrow.
        Mass Communication: Principles & Practices.
        Macmillan.
        ed. Reader in Library Communication.
        IHS-PDS.
Cassedy, Sylvia.
    xCassedy, Sylvia.
        In Your Own Words: A Beginner's Guide to
        Writing. Doubleday.
Cassel, Claes-Magnus.
    xCassel, Claes-Magnus.
        Foundations of Inference in Survey Sampling.
        Wiley.
Cassel, Gustav, 1866-1945
    xCassel, Gustav.
        Foreign Investments. Arno.
        Fundamental Thoughts in Economics.
        Kennikat.
        Money & Foreign Exchange After 1914. Arno.
        Nature & Necessity of Interest. Kelley.
        Theory of Social Economy. Kelley.
Cassel, Russell N. *see* Cassel, Russell Napoleon.
Cassel, Russell Napoleon, 1911-
    xCassel, Russell N.
        Drug Abuse Education. Chris Mass.
        ed. Leadership Development: Theory &
        Practice. Chris Mass.
        The Psychology of Decision Making. Chris
        Mass.
Cassell, Eric J., 1928-
    xCassell, Eric J.
        The Healer's Art: A New Approach to the
        Doctor-Patient Relationship. Lippincott.
Cassell, Joan.
    xCassell, Joan.
        A Group Called Women: Sisterhood &
        Symbolism in the Feminist Movement.
        Longman.
Cassell, Richard A., 1921-
    xCassell, Richard A.
        Ford Madox Ford: A Study of His Novels.
        Greenwood.
Cassell, Sylvia.
    xCassell, Sylvia.
        Nature Games & Activities. Har-Row.
Cassells. *see* Salus, Naomi Panush.
Casselman, Robert C.
    xCasselman, Robert C.
        Continuum: How Science, Psychology &
        Mysticism Point to a Life Beyond...& to an
        Extraordinary Kind of God. Marek.
Cassels, Alan, 1929-
    xCassels, Alan.
        Mussolini's Early Diplomacy. Princeton U Pr.
Cassels, Donald E.
    xCassels, Donald E.
        The Ductus Arteriosus. C C Thomas.
Cassels, J. W. *see* Cassels, John William Scott.
Cassels, John William Scott.
    xCassels, J. W.
        Introduction to Diophantine Approximation.
        Hafner.
Cassels, Louis.
    xCassels, Louis.
        Forbid Them Not. Independence Pr.
        The Reality of God. Herald Pr.
Cassen, R. *see* Cassen, Robert.
Cassen, Robert.
    xCassen, R.
        Planning for Growing Populations. OECD.
Casserley, H. C.
    xCasserley, H. C.

Outline of Irish Railway History. David & Charles.

Casserly, John J., 1927-
xCasserly, John J.
The Ford Whitehouse: The Diary of a Speechwriter. Colo Assoc.

Cassese, John-Marie Foreword by. *see* Bacigalupo, Leonard.

Cassiday, Bruce.
xCassiday, Bruce.
The Complete Solar House. Dodd.
The Complete Solar House. Warner Bks.
Dinah!: A Biography. Watts.
Home Guide to Lawns & Landscaping. Har-Row.
How to Choose Your Vacation House. Dodd.
xCassiday, Neil.
Betty Ford: Woman of Courage. Dale Books Inc.

Cassiday, Doris.
xCassiday, Doris.
Careers in the Beauty Industry. Watts.
Fashion Industry Careers. Watts.

Cassiday, Neil. *see* Cassiday, Bruce.

Cassidy, F. G. *see* Cassidy, Frederic Gomes.

Cassidy, Frederic Gomes.
xCassidy, F. G.
ed. Dictionary of Jamaican English. Cambridge U Pr.

Cassidy, John A.
xCassidy, John A.
Algernon C. Swinburne. Twayne.

Cassidy, Norma C. *see* Cassidy, Norma Cronin.

Cassidy, Norma Cronin.
xCassidy, Norma C.
Favorite Novenas & Prayers. Paulist Pr

Cassidy, Sheila, 1937-
xCassidy, Sheila.
Audacity to Believe. Collins Pubs.

Cassie, Dhyan.
xCassie, Dhyan.
Auditory Training Handbook for Good Listeners. Interstate.

Cassileth, Barrie R.
xCassileth, Barrie R.
ed. The Cancer Patient: Social & Medical Aspects of Care. Lea & Febiger.

Cassill, R. V. *see* Cassill, Ronald Verlin.

Cassill, Ronald V. *see* Cassill, Ronald Verlin.

Cassill, Ronald Verlin, 1919-
xCassill, R. V.
Hoyt's Child. PB.
xCassill, Ronald V.
In an Iron Time: Statements & Reiterations. Purdue.

Cassin, Maxine.
xCassin, Maxine.
A Touch of Recognition. AMS Pr.

Cassin-Scott, Jack.
xCassin-Scott, Jack.
Ceremonial Uniforms of the World. Arco.
Ceremonial Uniforms of the World. Hippocrene Bks.

Cassinari, Valentino.
xCassinari, Valentino.
Central Pain: A Neurosurgical Survey. Harvard U Pr.

Cassinelli, C. W.
xCassinelli, C. W.
Total Revolution: A Comparative Study of Germany Under Hitler, the Soviet Union Under Stalin, & China Under Mao. ABC-Clio.

Cassirer, Ernst, 1874-1945
xCassirer, Ernst.

Problem of Knowledge: Philosophy, Science, & History Since Hegel. Yale U Pr.
Symbol, Myth & Culture: Essays & Lectures of Ernst Cassirer 1935-45. Yale U Pr.

Cassity, Turner.
xCassity, Turner.
Steeplejacks in Babel. Godine.

Cassola, Carlo, 1917-
xCassola, Carlo.
Fausto & Anna. Greenwood.

Casson, H. *see* Casson, Herbert Newton.

Casson, Herbert N. *see* Casson, Herbert Newton.

Casson, Herbert Newton, 1869-
xCasson, H.
History of the Telephone. Gordon Pr.
xCasson, Herbert N.
The History of the Telephone. Arno.

Casson, Lionel, 1914
xCasson, Lionel.
Ancient Egypt. Time-Life.
Ancient Egypt. Silver.
tr. & ed. Masters of Ancient Comedy: Selections from Aristophanes, Menander, Plautus & Terence. T Y Crowell.

Casson, Mark.
xCasson, Mark.
Alternatives to the Multinational Enterprise. Holmes & Meier.

Casson, Michael.
xCasson, Michael.
The Craft of the Potter. Barron.

Casson, Stanley, 1889-1944
xCasson, Stanley.
Some Modern Sculptors. Arno.

Cassorla, Albert, 1949-
xCassorla, Albert.
The Suntan Book. Running Pr.

Castagno, Margaret, 1922-
xCastagno, Margaret F.
Historical Dictionary of Somalia. Scarecrow.

Castagno, Margaret F. *see* Castagno, Margaret.

Castagnoli, Ferdinando.
xCastagnoli, Ferdinando.
Orthogonal Town Planning in Antiquity. MIT Pr.

Castaing, C. *see* Castaing, Charles.

Castaing, Charles.
xCastaing, C.
Convex Analysis & Measurable Multifunctions. Springer-Verlag.

Castaneda, Alfredo.
xCastaneda, Alfredo.
The Educational Needs of Minority Groups. Prof Educ Pubn.

Castaneda, Carlos.
xCastaneda, Carlos.
The Second Ring of Power. S&S.
The Second Ring of Power. PB.

Castaneda, James A.
xCastaneda, James A.
Agustin Moreto. Twayne.

Castaneda, Jorge.
xCastaneda, Jorge.
Legal Effects of United Nations Resolutions. Columbia U Pr.

Castano, Francis A.
xCastano, Francis A.
ed. Handbook of Clinical Dental Auxiliary Practice. Lippincott.

Castano, J. B.
xCastano, John B.
Naval Officers Uniform Guide. Naval Inst Pr.

Castano, John B. *see* Castano, J. B.

Casteel, J. Doyle.
xCasteel, J. Doyle.
Value Clarification in the Classroom: A Primer. Goodyear.

Castel, Albert. *see* Castel, Albert E.

Castel, Albert E.
xCastel, Albert.

General Sterling Price & the Civil War in the West. La State U Pr.
The Presidency of Andrew Johnson. Regents Pr KS.

Castellucis, Richard L.
xCastellucis, Richard L.
Pulse & Logic Circuits. Delmar.
Pulse & Logic Circuits. Van Nos Reinhold.

Castetter, Edward F. *see* Castetter, Edward Franklin.

Castetter, Edward Franklin.
xCastetter, Edward F.
The Ethnobiology of the Papago Indians. AMS Pr.

Castetter, William B. *see* Castetter, William Benjamin.

Castetter, William Benjamin, 1914-
xCastetter, William B.
Personnel Function in Educational Administration. Macmillan.
Planning the Financial Compensation of School Administrative Personnel. Interstate.

Castex, Pierre. *see* Castex, Pierre Georges.

Castex, Pierre Georges, 1915-
xCastex, Pierre.
Nightmare Rally. Abelard.

Casti, J. L.
xCasti, John.
Imbedding Methods in Applied Mathematics. A-W.
xCasti, John L.
ed. Dynamical Systems & Their Applications: Linear Theory. Acad Pr.

Casti, John. *see* Casti, J. L.

Casti, John L. *see* Casti, J. L.

Castiglia, Julie.
xCastiglia, Julie.
Jill the Pill. Atheneum.

Castiglioni, Arturo, 1874-1953
xCastiglioni, Arturo
A History of Medicine. Aronson.

Castile, George. *see* Castile, George Pierre.

Castile, George Pierre.
xCastile, George.
North American Indians: An Introduction to the Chichimeca. McGraw.

Castille, Vernon De. *see* De Castille, Vernon.

Castillo, Michel Del. *see* Del Castillo, Michel.

Castino, Ruth. *see* Castino, Ruth A.

Castino, Ruth A.
xCastino, Ruth.
Spinning & Dyeing the Natural Way. Van Nos Reinhold.

Castle, Beatrice H. *see* Castle, Beatrice Hanscom.

Castle, Beatrice Hanscom, 1867-1950
xCastle, Beatrice H.
The Grand Island Story. Marquette Cnty Hist.

Castle, Coralie.
xCastle, Coralie.
Hors d'oeuvre, Etc.. One Hund One Prods.

Castle, David.
xCastle, David.
Toward Caring: People Building in the Family. Friends United.

Castle, Emery N.
xCastle, Emory N.
Farm Business Management: The Decision-Making Process Macmillan.

Castle, Emory N. *see* Castle, Emery N.

Castle, Frank.
xCastle, Frank.
Dakota Boomtown. Fawcett.

Castle, Irene. *see* Castle, Irene Foote.

Castle, Irene Foote, 1893-1963
xCastle, Irene.
My Husband. Da Capo.

Castle, Jeffery Lloyd.
xCastle, Jeffrey Lloyd.
How Not to Lose at Poker. Wilshire.

Castle, Jeffery Lloyd. *see* Castle, Jeffery Lloyd.

Castle, John, Pseud.
xCastle, John.

The Password Is Courage. Bantam.
Castle, Mary.
xCastle, Mary.
Hospital Infection Control. Wiley.
Castle, Sue.
xCastle, Sue.
The Complete Guide to Preparing Baby Foods
at Home. Doubleday.
Face Talk, Hand Talk, Body Talk. Doubleday.
Castle, Winifred M. see Castle, Winifred Mary.
Castle, Winifred Mary.
xCastle, Winifred M.
Statistics in Small Doses. Churchill.
Castleman, Harry.
xCastleman, Harry.
All Together Now: First Complete Beatles
Discography, 1961-75. Pierian.
All Together Now: The First Complete Beatles
Discography, 1961-1975. Ballantine.
Castleman, Kenneth R.
xCastleman, Kenneth R.
Digital Image Processing. P-H.
Castles, Alex C. see Castles, Alexander Cuthbert.
Castles, Alexander Cuthbert.
xCastles, Alex C.
Australia: A Chronology & Fact Book. Oceana.
Castles, Francis G. see Castles, Francis Geoffrey.
Castles, Francis Geoffrey.
xCastles, Francis G.
Politics & Social Insight. Sage.
Pressure Groups & Political Culture: A
Comparative Study. Humanities.
The Social Democratic Image of Society: A
Study of the Achievements & Origins of
Scandinavian Social Democracy in
Comparative Perspective. Routledge &
Kegan.
Castles, Mary R. see Castles, Mary Reardon.
Castles, Mary Reardon.
xCastles, Mary R.
Dying in an Institution: Nurse Patient
Perspectives. ACC.
Castles, Stephen.
xCastles, Stephen.
Immigrant Workers & Class Structure in
Western Europe. Oxford U Pr.
Castor, Henry.
xCastor, Henry.
America's First World War: General Pershing
& the Yanks. Random.
First Book of the War with Mexico. Watts.
Castore, George F.
xCastore, George F.
Action Language in Junior High School
Groups. Vantage.
Castro, Americo, 1885-1972
xCastro, Americo.
An Idea of History: Selected Essays of
Americo Castro. Ohio St U Pr.
The Spaniards: An Introduction to Their
History. U of Cal Pr.
Castro, Daniel.
xCastro, Daniel.
Looking at Life. Journey Pubns.
Castro, Fidel, 1927-defendant
xCastro, Fidel.
History Will Absolve Me. Lyle Stuart.
Castro, J. E. see Castro, John E.
Castro, John E.
xCastro, J. E.
Immunological Aspects of Cancer. Univ Park.
Castro y Rossi, Adolfo De, 1823-1898
xCastro Y Rossi, Aldolfo De.
The History of the Jews in Spain: From the
Time of Their Settlement in That Country till
the Commencement of the Present Century.
Greenwood.
Castro Y Rossi, Aldolfo De. see Castro y Rossi, Adolfo
De.
Casty, A. see Casty, Alan.

Casty, Alan.
xCasty, A.
Mass Media & Mass Man. HR&W.
xCasty, Alan.
Act of Writing & Reading: A Combined Text.
P-H.
Development of the Film: An Interpretive
History. HarBraceJ.
Dramatic Art of the Film. Har-Row.
The Films of Robert Rossen. Museum Mod
Art.
Let's Make It Clear!: A Workbook &
Anthology for Concrete & Accurate Writing.
HarBraceJ.
Caswall, Henry, 1810-1870
xCaswall, Henry.
America, & the American Church. Arno.
Caswell, Christopher.
xCaswell, Christopher.
Championship Dinghy Sailing. Norton.
Caswell, Hollis L. see Caswell, Hollis Leland.
Caswell, Hollis Leland, 1901-
xCaswell, Hollis L.
City School Surveys: An Interpretation &
Appraisal. AMS Pr.
Catalano, Joseph S.
xCatalano, Joseph S.
A Commentary of Jean-Paul Sartre's "Being &
Nothingness". U of Chicago Pr.
Catalano, Ralph, 1946-
xCatalano, Ralph.
Health, Behavior & the Community: An
Ecological Perspective. Pergamon.
Cataldo, Bernard F.
xCataldo, Bernard F.
Introduction to Law & the Legal Process.
Wiley.
Cataldo, John W.
xCataldo, John W.
Lettering: A Guide for Teachers. Davis Mass.
Catanese, Anthony J. see Catanese, Anthony James.
Catanese, Anthony James.
xCatanese, Anthony J.
Introduction to Urban Planning. McGraw.
Personality, Politics & Planning: How City
Planners Work. Sage.
Catania, A. Charles.
xCatania, A. Charles.
ed. Handbook of Applied Behavior Analysis:
Social & Instructional Processes. Halsted Pr.
Learning. P-H.
xCatania, Charles A.
Contemporary Research in Operant Behavior.
Scott F.
Catania, Charles A. see Catania, A. Charles.
Catcheside, D. G.
xCatcheside, D. G.
The Genetics of Recombination. Univ Park.
Catchpole, Brian.
xCatchpole, Brian.
A Map History of Modern China. Heinemann
Ed.
Catchpole, Clive.
xCatchpole, Clive.
Owls. McGraw.
Catchpole, W. L.
xCatchpole, W. L.
Business Guide to Insurance. Intl Pubns Serv.
Catchpool, Corder, 1883-1952
xCatchpool, Corder.
On Two Fronts: Letters of a Conscientious
Objector. Garland Pub.
Cate, Curtis, 1924-
xCate, Curtis.
George Sand: A Biography. Avon.
George Sand: A Biography. HM.
Ides of August: The Berlin Wall Crisis - 1961.
M Evans.
Cate, Dick.
xCate, Dick.

Flying Free. Elsevier-Nelson.
Cate, James L. see Cate, James Lea.
Cate, James Lea.
xCate, James L.
Medieval & Historiographical Essays in Honor
of James Westfall Thompson. Kennikat.
Cateora, Philip R.
xCateora, Philip R.
International Marketing. Irwin.
Cater, Douglas. see Cater, Douglass.
Cater, Douglass.
xCater, Douglas.
Politics of Health. Krieger.
xCater, Douglass.
ed. The Future of Public Broadcasting. Praeger.
Cater, Fred W. see Cater, Frederick William.
Cater, Frederick William, 1912-
xCater, Fred W.
Cloudy Pass Epizonal Batholith & Associated
Subvolcanic Rocks. Geol Soc.
Cates, Edwin H.
xCates, Edwin H.
English in America. Lerner Pubns.
Catford, J. C. see Catford, John Cunnison.
Catford, John Cunnison, 1917-
xCatford, J. C.
Fundamental Problems in Phonetics. Ind U Pr.
Cathcart, James.
xCathcart, James.
Multiple-Continuous Offense for High School
Basketball. P-H.
Cathcart, Robert S.
xCathcart, Robert S.
Small Group Communication: A Reader. Wm
C Brown.
Cather, Willa. see Cather, Willa Sibert.
Cather, Willa Sibert, 1873-1947
xCather, Willa.
A Lost Lady. Knopf.
A Lost Lady. Random.
Lucy Gayheart. Random.
Not Under Forty. Knopf.
Obscure Destinies. Random.
Old Beauty & Others. Knopf.
The Old Beauty & Others. Random.
One of Ours. Knopf.
One of Ours. Random.
The Professor's House. Random.
The Song of the Lark. U of Nebr Pr.
Uncle Valentine & Other Stories: Willa
Cather's Uncollected Short Fiction,
1915-1929. U of Nebr Pr.
Catherall, Arthur, 1906-
xCatherall, Arthur.
Camel Caravan. HM.
Death of an Oil Rig. S G Phillips.
Last Horse on the Sands. Lothrop.
Night of the Black Frost. Lothrop.
Strange Intruder. Lothrop.
Catherwood, Mary (Hartwell), 1847-1902
xCatherwood, Mary H.
The Queen of the Swamp & Other Plain
Americans. Mss Info.
Catherwood, Mary H. see Catherwood, Mary (Hartwell).
Catholic Church. Pope.
xMonks Of Solesmes.
ed. Liturgy: One Hundred & Sixty-Nine
Pronouncements from Benedict Fourteenth to
John Twenty-Third. Dghtrs St Paul.
ed. Our Lady: Eight Hundred & Sixty-Eight
Pronouncements from Benedict Fourteenth to
John Twenty-Third. Dghtrs St Paul.
ed. Woman in the Modern World: Six Hundred
& Thirty-Seven Pronouncements from Leo
Thirteenth to Pius Twelfth. Dghtrs St Paul.
Catholic Hospital Association.
xCatholic Hospital Association.

Guidebook. Cath Health.
Guidelines on Roles & Relationships of Board,
Chief Executive Officer, & Medical Staff of
Catholic Hospital & Long Term Care
Facilities. Cath Health.
xTheCatholic Hospital Association.
Math Primer for Students in Radiologic
Technology. Cath Health.
Catholic Library Association.
xCatholic Library Association.
C L A: Handbook & Membership Directory.
Cath Lib Assn.
Catholic Theological Society of America.
xTheCatholic Theological Society of America.
Human Sexuality: New Directions in American
Catholic Thought. Doubleday.
Catholic University of America.
xCatholic University Of America.
Catholic University Studies in German. AMS
Pr.
Catholic University Studies in Romance
Languages & Literatures. AMS Pr.
Catholic University Of America - School Of Law. see
Catholic University of America. Columbus School of
Law.
**Catholic University of America. Columbus School of
Law.**
xCatholic University Of America - School Of Law.
Jubilee Law Lectures. Arno.
Catlett, Robert H.
xCatlett, Robert H.
Readings in Animal Energetics. Mss Info.
Catlin, Alberta P.
xCatlin, Alberta P.
Practical Nursing: PreTest Self-Assessment &
Review. McGraw-Pretest.
Catlin, George, 1796-1872
xCatlin, George.
Letters & Notes on the Manners, Customs &
Conditions of the North American Indians.
Dover.
Letters & Notes on the Manners, Customs,&
Conditions of the North American Indians.
Scholarly.
Catlin, George. see Catlin, George Edward Gordon.
Catlin, George Edward Gordon, Sir, 1896-
xCatlin, George.
The Story of the Political Philosophers. Gordon
Pr.
Catlin, Warren B. see Catlin, Warren Benjamin.
Catlin, Warren Benjamin, 1881-
xCatlin, Warren B.
Progress of Economics: A History of Economic
Thought. Cyrco Pr.
The Progress of Economics: A History of
Economic Thought. Irvington.
Catling, Patrick S. see Catling, Patrick Skene.
Catling, Patrick Skene.
xCatling, Patrick S.
Exterminator. Trident.
Cato, Nancy.
xCato, Nancy.
All the Rivers Run. NAL.
All the Rivers Run. St Martin.
Cato, Nathaniel J. Le. see Le Cato, Nathaniel J.
Catoe, Lynn E.
xCatoe, Lynn E.
ed. UFOs & Related Subjects: An Annotated
Bibliography. Gale.
Catoir, John. see Catoir, John T.
Catoir, John T.
xCatoir, John.
Catholics & Broken Marriage. Ave Maria.
Catron, Donald G., 1938-
xCatron, Donald G.
The Anesthesiologists Handbook. Univ Park.
Catsimpoolas, Nicholas.
xCatsimpoolas, Nicholas.

Immunological Aspects of Food. AVI.
Cattell, Ann, 1893-
xCattell, Ann.
Dictionary of Esoteric Words. Citadel Pr.
Cattell, David T. see Cattell, David Tredwell.
Cattell, David Tredwell, 1923-
xCattell, David T.
Communism & the Spanish Civil War. Johnson
Repr.
Soviet Diplomacy & the Spanish Civil War.
Johnson Repr.
Cattell, Nancy G.
xCattell, Nancy G.
College & Career: Adjusting to College &
Selecting an Occupation. Irvington.
Cattell, Psyche.
xCattell, Psyche.
Raising Children with Love & Limits.
Nelson-Hall.
Cattell, Raymond B. see Cattell, Raymond Bernard.
Cattell, Raymond Bernard.
xCattell, Raymond B.
ed. Human Affairs. Arno.
Catterall, Calvin D.
xCatterall, Calvin D.
Strategies for Helping Students. C C Thomas.
Catton, Bruce, 1899-
xCatton, Bruce.
America Goes to War. Columbia U Pr.
ed. American Heritage Short History of the
Civil War. Dell.
Banners at Shenandoah. Queens Hse.
Grant Moves South. Little.
Grant Takes Command. Little.
Stillness at Appomattox. Doubleday.
Catton, Bruce. see Catton, Bruce Charles.
Catton, Bruce Charles, 1899-
xCatton, Bruce.
Coming Fury. Doubleday.
The Coming Fury. PB.
Catton, William. see Catton, William Bruce.
Catton, William Bruce.
xCatton, William.
Two Roads to Sumter. McGraw.
Catudal, Honore M. see Catudal, Honore Marc.
Catudal, Honore Marc, 1944-
xCatudal, Honore M.
The Exclave Problem of Western Europe. U of
Ala Pr.
Catullus. see Catullus, C. Valerius.
Catullus, C. Valerius.
xCatullus.
The Catullus of William Hull. InterCulture.
xCatullus, Gaius V.
Complete Poetry. U of Mich Pr.
Catullus, Gaius V. see Catullus, C. Valerius.
Cauchie, Maurice, 1882-
xCauchie, Maurice.
Thematic Index of the Works of Francois
Couperin. AMS Pr.
Caudill, Harry M., 1922-
xCaudill, Harry M.
A Darkness at Dawn: Appalachian Kentucky &
the Future. U Pr of Ky.
My Land Is Dying. Dutton.
Night Comes to the Cumberlands: Biography of
a Depressed Area. Little.
Caudill, R. Paul.
xCaudill, R. Paul.
Ephesians: A Translation with Notes.
Broadman.
Caudill, Rebecca.
xCaudill, Rebecca.
Certain Small Shepherd. HR&W.
Contrary Jenkins. HR&W.
Somebody Go & Bang a Drum. Dutton.
Caudill, William. see Caudill, William Wayne.
Caudill, William W. see Caudill, William Wayne.

Caudill, William Wayne.
xCaudill, William.
Memos from Egypt: Joint U.S. Egyptian Study
Group on Building Materials & Building
Technology. CBI Pub.
xCaudill, William W.
Architecture & You: How to Experience &
Enjoy Buildings. Watson-Guptill.
Caughey, John. see Caughey, John Walton.
Caughey, John W. see Caughey, John Walton.
Caughey, John Walton.
xCaughey, John.
The California Gold Rush. U of Cal Pr.
Los Angeles: Biography of a City. U of Cal Pr.
xCaughey, John W.
California: A Remarkable State's Life History.
P-H.
Hubert Howe Bancroft, Historian of the West.
Russell.
Caughill, Rita E.
xCaughill, Rita E.
The Dying Patient: A Supportive Approach.
Little.
Caughley, Graeme.
xCaughley, Graeme.
Analysis of Vertebrate Populations. Wiley.
Caulcott, Evelyn.
xCaulcott, Evelyn.
Significance Tests. Routledge & Kegan.
Cauldwell, Samuel M. see Cauldwell, Samuel Milbank.
Cauldwell, Samuel Milbank, 1862-1916
xCauldwell, Samuel M.
Chocolate Cake & Black Sand & Two Other
Plays. Core Collection.
Cauley, Lorinda B. see Cauley, Lorinda Bryan.
Cauley, Lorinda Bryan.
xCauley, Lorinda B.
illus. The Animal Kids. Putnam.
The Bake-Off. Putnam.
Pease Porridge Hot: A Mother Goose
Cookbook. Putnam.
illus. The Ugly Duckling. HarBraceJ.
The Ugly Duckling. HarBraceJ.
Caulfield, H. J. see Caulfield, Henry John.
Caulfield, Henry John.
xCaulfield, H. J.
The Applications of Holography. Krieger.
Caulfield, Sean.
xCaulfield, Sean.
The Experience of Praying. Paulist Pr.
Cauman, Samuel.
xCauman, Samuel.
The Living Museum: Experiences of an Art
Historian & Museum Director--Alexander
Dorner. NYU Pr.
Cauro, Roland.
xCauro, Roland.
Stringcraft. Sterling.
Causey, Denzil Y.
xCausey, Denzil Y.
Accounting for Decision Making. Grid Pub.
Causey, Don.
xCausey, Don.
Killer Insects. Watts.
Cautela, Joseph R.
xCautela, Joseph R.
Relaxation: A Comprehensive Manual for
Adults, Children, & Children with Special
Needs. Res Press.
Cauthen, John K, 1906-
xCauthen, John K.
Speaker Blatt: His Challenges Were Greater. U
of SC Pr.
Caux, Len De. see De Caux, Len.
Cava, Esther Laden.
xCava, Esther Laden.
Parents Guide to Successful Child Rearing:
How to Say No Without Guilt. Exposition.
Cava, Michael P. see Cava, Michael Patrick.

Cava, Michael Patrick.
  xCava, Michael P.
    Cyclobutadiene & Related Compounds. Acad
      Pr.
Cavaiani, Mabel.
  xCavaiani, Mabel.
    The Low Cholesterol Cookbook. Har-Row.
    Simplified Quantity Regional Recipes. Hayden.
Cavalier, Julian, 1931-
  xCavalier, Julien.
    Classic American Railroad Stations. A S
      Barnes.
Cavalier, Julien. see Cavalier, Julian.
Cavalier, Robert J.
  xCavalier, Robert J.
    Ludwig Wittgenstein's Tractatus
      Logico-Philosophicus: A Transcendental
      Critique of Ethics. U Pr of Amer.
Cavaliero, Glen, 1927-
  xCavaliero, Glen.
    Paradise Stairway. Persea Bks.
Cavalli-Sforza, L. L. see Cavalli-Sforza, Luigi Luca.
Cavalli-Sforza, Luigi Luca.
  xCavalli-Sforza, L. L.
    The Genetics of Human Populations. W H
      Freeman.
Cavallo, Diana, 1931-
  xCavallo, Diana.
    Lower East Side: A Portrait in Time.
      Macmillan.
Cavallo, Robert M.
  xCavallo, Robert M.
    Photography: What's the Law. Crown.
Cavan, R. S. see Cavan, Ruth Shonle.
Cavan, Ruth S. see Cavan, Ruth Shonle.
Cavan, Ruth Shonle, 1896-
  xCavan, R. S.
    Marriage & Family in the Modern World: A
      Book of Readings. Har-Row.
  xCavan, Ruth S.
    Family & the Depression: A Study of One
      Hundred Chicago Families. Arno.
    Personal Adjustment in Old Age. Arno.
    ed. Readings in Juvenile Delinquency.
      Har-Row.
Cavanagh, Denis.
  xCavanagh, Denis.
    Obstetric Emergencies. Har-Row.
Cavanagh, Helen M. see Cavanagh, Helen Marie.
Cavanagh, Helen Marie, 1904-
  xCavanagh, Helen M.
    Funk of Funk's Grove. Ill St Hist Soc.
Cavanah, Frances.
  xCavanah, Frances.
    Abe Lincoln Gets His Chance. Schol Bk Serv.
    Holiday Roundup. Macrae.
    The Truth About the Man Behind the Book
      That Sparked the War Between the States.
      Westminster.
Cavanaugh, Joan.
  xCavanaugh, Joan.
    More of Jesus, Less of Me. Logos.
Cavanaugh, Joseph H. see Cavanaugh, Joseph Hubert.
Cavanaugh, Joseph Hubert, 1917-
  xCavanaugh, Joseph H.
    Evidence for Our Faith. U. of Notre Dame Pr.
Cavanaugh, Tom R.
  xCavanaugh, Tom R.
    Bannerstone House: A Frank Lloyd Wright
      House, Springfield, Illinois. C C Thomas.
Cavanna, Betty, 1909-
  xCavanna, Betty.

    Almost Like Sisters. Morrow.
    Ballet Fever. Westminster.
    Boy Next Door. Berkley Pub.
    The Boy Next Door. Morrow.
    Catchpenny Street. Westminster.
    Country Cousin. Morrow.
    Love, Laurie. Westminster.
    Spice Island Mystery. Morrow.
    Touch of Magic. Westminster.
    Two's Company. Westminster.
Cave, Cyril.
  xCave, Cyril.
    A Survey of Recent Research in Special
      Education. Humanities.
Cave, Emma.
  xCave, Emma.
    Blood Bond. Har-Row.
Cave, Marion S. see Cave, Marion Stilwell.
Cave, Marion Stilwell, 1904-
  xCave, Marion S.
    Chromosomes of the California Liliaceae. U of
      Cal Pr.
Cave, Richard.
  xCave, Richard A.
    A Study of the Novels of George Moore.
      B&N.
Cave, Richard A. see Cave, Richard.
Cavell, Stanley, 1926-
  xCavell, Stanley.
    The World Viewed: Reflections on the
      Ontology of Film. Harvard U Pr.
Cavelti, Peter. see Cavelti, Peter C.
Cavelti, Peter C., 1947-
  xCavelti, Peter.
    How to Invest in Gold. Follett.
Caven, Brian, 1921-
  xCaven, Brian.
    The Punic Wars. St Martin.
Cavenagh, F. A. see Cavenagh, Francis Alexander.
Cavenagh, Francis Alexander, 1884-1946
  xCavenagh, F. A.
    James & John Stuart Mill on Education.
      Greenwood.
Cavendish, Richard.
  xCavendish, Richard.
    A History of Magic. Taplinger.
    King Arthur & the Grail: The Arthurian
      Legends & Their Meaning. Taplinger.
Caveney, Philip.
  xCaveney, Philip.
    The Sins of Rachel Ellis. Berkley Pub.
    The Sins of Rachel Ellis. St Martin.
Cavert, C. Edward.
  xCavert, C. Edward.
    An Approach to the Design of Mediated
      Instruction. Assn Ed Comm Tech.
Cavert, Samuel M. see Cavert, Samuel Mccrea.
Cavert, Samuel McCrea, 1888-
  xCavert, Samuel M.
    On the Road to Christian Unity: An Appraisal
      of the Ecumenical Movement. Greenwood.
Caves, Richard E.
  xCaves, Richard E.
    Air Transport & Its Regulators: An Industry
      Study. Harvard U Pr.
    American Industry-Structure, Conduct,
      Performance. P-H.
    Britain's Economic Prospects. Brookings.
    Industrial Organization in Japan. Brookings.
    World Trade & Payments: An Introduction.
      Little.
Cavin, Bram.
  xCavin, Bram.
    How to Run a Successful Florist & Plant Store.
      Wiley.
Cavin, Ruth.
  xCavin, Ruth.

    A Matter of Money: What Do You Do with a
      Dollar?. S G Phillips.
Cavitch, David.
  xCavitch, David.
    D. H. Lawrence & the New World. Oxford U
      Pr.
    D. H. Lawrence & the New World. Oxford U
      Pr.
Cawelti, John G.
  xCawelti, John G.
    Apostles of the Self-Made Man. U of Chicago
      Pr.
  xCawelti, John O.
    Apostles of the Self-Made Man. U of Chicago
      Pr.
Cawelti, John O. see Cawelti, John G.
Cawley, James. see Cawley, James S.
Cawley, James S.
  xCawley, James.
    Exploring the Housatonic River & Valley. A S
      Barnes.
    Tales of Old Grafton. A S Barnes.
Cawley, Leo P.
  xCawley, Leo P.
    Electrophoresis & Immunochemical Reactions
      in Gels: Techniques & Interpretation. Am
      Soc Clinical.
Caws, Mary A. see Caws, Mary Ann.
Caws, Mary Ann.
  xCaws, Mary A.
    ed. About French Poetry from Dada to "Tel
      Quel": Text & Theory. Wayne St U Pr.
  xCaws, Mary Ann.
    The Presence of Rene Char. Princeton U Pr.
    Rene Char. Twayne.
Caws, Peter.
  xCaws, Peter.
    Sartre. Routledge & Kegan.
Cawson, R. A.
  xCawson, R. A.
    Clinical Pharmacology in Dentistry. Churchill.
Cawston, Vee.
  xCawston, Vee.
    Matuk, the Eskimo Boy. Lantern.
Cawte, John.
  xCawte, John.
    Medicine Is the Law: Studies in Psychiatric
      Anthropology of Australian Tribal Societies.
      U Pr of Hawaii.
Caxton, William.
  xCaxton, William.
    Prologues & Epilogues of William Caxton. B
      Franklin.
Cay, Donald F.
  xCay, Donald F.
    Curriculum: Design for Learning. Bobbs.
Cayce, Edgar E. see Cayce, Edgar Evans.
Cayce, Edgar Evans.
  xCayce, Edgar E.
    Edgar Cayce on Atlantis. Warner Bks.
Cayer, N. Joseph.
  xCayer, N. Joseph.
    Public Personnel Administration in the United
      States. St Martin.
Cayeux, Lucien, 1864-1944
  xCayeux, Lucien.
    Past & Present Causes in Geology. Hafner.
Cayford, John E.
  xCayford, John E.
    Underwater Work: A Manual of Scuba
      Commercial Salvage & Construction
      Operations. Cornell Maritime.
Cayou, Dolores K. see Cayou, Dolores Kirton.
Cayou, Dolores Kirton.
  xCayou, Dolores K.
    Modern Jazz Dance. Mayfield Pub.
Cazalas, Mary W.
  xCazalas, Mary W.

Nursing & the Law. Aspen Systems.
Cazalet-Keir, Thelma.
　xCazalet-Keir, Thelma.
　　ed. Homage to P. G. Wodehouse. Humanities.
Cazamian, Louis F. *see* Cazamian, Louis Francois.
Cazamian, Louis Francois, 1877-1965
　xCazamian, Louis F.
　　Criticism in the Making. Folcroft.
Cazden, C. B. *see* Cazden, Courtney B.
Cazden, Courtney B.
　xCazden, C. B.
　　Child Language & Education. HR&W.
　xCazden, Courtney B.
　　ed. Functions of Language in the Classroom.
　　Tchrs Coll.
Cazemajou, Jean.
　xCazemajou, Jean.
　　Stephen Crane. U of Minn Pr.
Cazziol, R. J. *see* Cazziol, Roger J.
Cazziol, Roger J.
　xCazziol, R. J.
　　Paul et Remi. Cambridge U Pr.
　xCazziol, Roger J.
　　Vacances Au Senegal. Cambridge U Pr.
Cazzola, Gus, 1934-
　xCazzola, Gus.
　　A Chisel for Ezekiel. Concordia.
Cb Test Labs.
　xCB Test Labs Staff.
　　How to Select & Install CB Antennas. Hayden.
CB Test Labs Staff. *see* Cb Test Labs.
Ccm Information Corporation.
　xMacmillan Information Division.
　　Environmental Pollution: A Guide to Current
　　Research. Macmillan Info.
Ceaser, James W.
　xCeaser, James W.
　　Presidential Selection: Theory & Development.
　　Princeton U Pr.
Cebeci, Tuncer.
　xCebeci, Tuncer.
　　Analysis of Turbulent Boundary Layers. Acad
　　Pr.
Cebik, L. B.
　xCebik, L. B.
　　Seven Steps to Designing Your Own Ham
　　Equipment. Sams.
Cebula, Richard J.
　xCebula, Richard J.
　　The Determinants of Human Migration.
　　Lexington Bks.
Cebulash, Mel.
　xCebulash, Mel.
　　The Champion's Jacket. Creative Ed.
　　Football Players Do Amazing Things. Random.
Ceccato, Silvio.
　xCeccato, Silvio.
　　ed. Linguistic Analysis & Programming for
　　Mechanical Translation. Gordon.
Cecchetti, Giovanni, 1922-
　xCecchetti, Giovanni.
　　Giovanni Verga. Twayne.
Cecchettini, Philip A. *see* Cecchettini, Philip Alan.
Cecchettini, Philip Alan.
　xCecchettini, Philip A.
　　Art America: Resource Manual. McGraw.
Cecco, Marcello De. *see* De Cecco, Marcello.
Cecil, David, Lord, 1902-
　xCecil, David.
　　Melbourne. Bobbs.
　　Melbourne. Crown.
　　Melbourne. Greenwood.
　　A Portrait of Jane Austen. FS&G.
　　A Portrait of Jane Austen. Hill & Wang.
　　Reading As One of the Fine Arts. Arden Lib.
　　Reading As One of the Fine Arts. Folcroft.
Cecil, George.
　xCecil, George.

Digging. Watts.
Cecil, Lamar.
　xCecil, Lamar.
　　Albert Ballin: Business & Politics in Imperial
　　Germany, 1888-1918. Princeton U Pr.
　　The German Diplomatic Service 1871-1914.
　　Princeton U Pr.
Cecil, Mirabel.
　xCecil, Mirabel.
　　Zig Zag the Bee: A Summer Story. McGraw.
Cecil, P. B. *see* Cecil, Paula B.
Cecil, Paula B.
　xCecil, P. B.
　　Word Processing in the Modern Office. A-W.
　xCecil, Paula B.
　　Word Processing in the Modern Office.
　　Benjamin-Cummings.
Cedar. *see* Cedar, Paul.
Cedar, Paul.
　xCedar.
　　Becoming a Lover. Tyndale.
Ceder, Jack. *see* Ceder, Jack Gary.
Ceder, Jack G. *see* Ceder, Jack Gary.
Ceder, Jack Gary.
　xCeder, Jack.
　　Trigonometry: A Modern Approach. HR&W.
　xCeder, Jack G.
　　Calculus. Allyn.
Cedergren, Harry R.
　xCedergren, Harry R.
　　Drainage of Highway & Airfield Pavements.
　　Wiley.
Cehelsky, Marta.
　xCehelsky, Marta.
　　Land Reform in Brazil: The Management of
　　Social Change. Westview.
Ceitin, G. S.
　xCeitin, G. S.
　　Fourteen Papers on Logic, Geometry,
　　Topology, & Algebra. Am Math.
Celce-Murcia, Marianne.
　xCelce-Murcia, Marianne.
　　ed. Teaching English As a Second or Foreign
　　Language. Newbury Hse.
Celender, Donald. *see* Celender, Donald D.
Celender, Donald D.
　xCelender, Donald.
　　Musical Instruments in Art. Lerner Pubns.
Celieres, Andre.
　xCelieres, Andre.
　　Prose Style of Emerson. Folcroft.
　　The Prose Style of Emerson. Gordon Pr.
Celli, Angelo, 1857-1914
　xCelli, Angelo.
　　The History of Malaria in the Roman
　　Campagna from Ancient Times. AMS Pr.
Cellini. *see* Cellini, Benvenuto.
Cellini, Benvenuto, 1500-1571
　xCellini.
　　Autobiography. Penguin.
Cember, H. *see* Cember, Herman.
Cember, Herman.
　xCember, H.
　　Introduction to Health Physics. Pergamon.
Cement Admixtures Association.
　xCement Admixtures Association Ltd.
　　Concrete Admixtures: Use & Applications.
　　Longman.
Cement Admixtures Association Ltd. *see* Cement
　Admixtures Association.
Cendrars, Blaise, 1887-1961
　xCendrars, Blaise.
　　Complete Postcards from the Americas: Poems
　　of Road & Sea. U of Cal Pr.
　　Selected Writings of Blaise Cendrars.
　　Greenwood.
Censer, Jack Richard.
　xCenser, Jack Richard.

Prelude to Power: The Parisian Radical Press,
　1789-1791. Johns Hopkins.
Censoni, Robert.
　xCensoni, Robert.
　　Cowgirl Kate. Holiday.
Center, Allen H.
　xCenter, Allen H.
　　Public Relations Practices: Case Studies. P-H.
Center for Applied Linguistics.
　xCenter for Applied Linguistics, Washington D.C.
　　Dictionary Catalog of the Library of the Center
　　for Applied Linguistics, Washington, D. C..
　　G K Hall.
Center for Applied Linguistics, Washington D.C. *see*
　Center for Applied Linguistics.
Center for Arts Information.
　xCenter for Arts Information.
　　Directory for the Arts. Ctr for Arts Info.
Center for Attitudinal Healing. *see* Center for Attitudinal
　Healing, Tiburon, California.
Center for Attitudinal Healing, Tiburon, California.
　xCenter for Attitudinal Healing.
　　There Is a Rainbow Behind Every Dark Cloud.
　　Celestial Arts.
Center for Blood Research.
　xSponsored by the Center for Blood Research.
　　The Chemistry & Physiology of the Human
　　Plasma Proteins: Proceedings of a Conference
　　Held November 19-21 1978 in Boston,
　　Massachusetts, USA. Pergamon.
Center for Compliance Information. *see* Aspen Systems
　Corporation. Center for Compliance Information.
Center for Curriculum Design.
　xTheCenter for Curriculum Design.
　　ed. Somewhere Else: A Living-Learning
　　Catalog. Swallow.
Center for Environmental & Consumer Justice. *see*
　Center for Environmental and Consumer Justice.
Center for Environmental and Consumer Justice.
　xCenter for Environmental & Consumer Justice.
　　Discrimination in Private Employment in
　　Puerto Rico (Color, Sex & National Origin).
　　U of PR Pr.
Center For Programmed Learning For Business. *see*
　Michigan. University. Center for Programmed
　Learning of Business.
**Center for Science in the Public Interest. Simple
Lifestyle Team.**
　xCenter for Science in the Public Interest.
　　Household Pollutant Guide. Doubleday.
　　Ninety Nine Ways to a Simple Lifestyle.
　　Doubleday.
　　Ninety-Nine Ways to a Simple Lifestyle. Ind U
　　Pr.
Center for Southern Folklore.
　xCenter for Southern Folklore.
　　American Folklore Films & Videotapes: an
　　Index. Ctr South Folklore.
Center for Strategic & International Studies, Georgetown
　University. *see* Georgetown University, Washington,
　D.C. Center for Strategic and International Studies.
Center for the Study of Democratic Institutions.
　xCenter for the Study of Democratic Institutions.
　　Challenges to Democracy: The Next Ten
　　Years. Arno.
　　The Corporation & the Economy. Greenwood.
　　Natural Law & Modern Society. Arno.
Centers, Richard.
　xCenters, Richard.
　　Psychology of Social Classes: A Study of Class
　　Consciousness. Russell.
Centra, John A.
　xCentra, John A.
　　Determining Faculty Effectiveness: Assessing
　　Teaching, Research, & Service for Personnel
　　Decisions & Improvement. Jossey-Bass.
Central Conference of American Rabbis.
　xCentral Conference of American Rabbis.
　　A Passover Haggadah. Penguin.
　xTheCentral Conference of American Rabbis.

299

A Passover Haggadah. Viking Pr.
Central Electric Railfans' Association.
  xCentral Electric Railfans' Association.
    Chicago's Rapid Transit: Rolling Stock,
    1892-1947. Central Electric.
    Indiana Railroad System. Central Electric.
Central Electricity Generating Board.
  xCentral Electricity Generating Board.
    ed. Phraseology for Civil Engineering. Intl
    Ideas.
Central Intelligence Agency. *see* United States. Central
  Inteligence Agency.
Centre De Mathematique Sociale Ecole Des Hautes
  Etudes En Sciences Sociales. *see* Paris. Ecole Pratique
  Des Hautes Etudes.
**Centre for Information on Language Teaching and
Research.**
    xCentre for Information on Language Teaching &
    Research.
    ed. Language Teaching & Linguistics.
    Cambridge U Pr.
Centre for Middle Eastern & Islamic Studies, University
  of Durham, England. *see* Centre for Middle Eastern
  and Islamic Studies.
Centre for Middle Eastern and Islamic Studies.
  xCentre for Middle Eastern & Islamic Studies,
  University of Durham, England.
    The Middle East Yearbook 1978. Watts.
Centre National de la Recherche Scientifique. *see*
  Colloque International Sur les Methodes De
  Spectroscopie Instrumentale, Orsay, France, 1966.
Centuori, Walter J.
  xCentuori, Walter J.
    A Concordance to the Poets of the Dolce Stil
    Novo. U of Nebr Pr.
    A Concordance to the Poets of the Dolce Stil
    Novo. Univ Microfilms.
Century Association, New York.
  xCentury Association, New York.
    Robert Henri & Five of His Pupils: Loan
    Exhibition of Paintings, April 5, to June 1,
    1946. Arno.
CEP. *see* Council on Economic Priorities.
Ceperley, Gordon. *see* Ceperley, Gordon G.
Ceperley, Gordon G.
  xCeperley, Gordon.
    A Promised Land for a Chosen People. Friends
    Israel-Spearhead Pr.
Ceplair, Larry.
  xCeplair, Larry S.
    The Inquisition in Hollywood: Politics in the
    Film Community, 1930-1960. Doubleday.
Ceplair, Larry S. *see* Ceplair, Larry.
Ceramists' Conference, First, Oct. 1963. *see* British
  Ceramic Research Association.
Ceravolo, Joseph, 1934-
  xCeravolo, Joseph.
    Transmigration Solo. Toothpaste.
Cercignani, Carlo.
  xCercignani, Carlo.
    Mathematical Methods in Kinetic Theory.
    Plenum Pub.
Cerepak, John R.
  xCerepak, John R.
    Accounting for Business. Merrill.
Cerf, Bennett. *see* Cerf, Bennett Alfred.
Cerf, Bennett A. *see* Cerf, Bennett Alfred.
Cerf, Bennett Alfred, 1898-1971
  xCerf, Bennett.
    At Random: The Reminiscences of Bennett
    Cerf. Random.
    Stories to Make You Feel Better. G K Hall.
    Stories to Make You Feel Better. Random.
  xCerf, Bennett A.
    More Riddles. Beginner.
Cermak, Laird S.
  xCermak, Laird S.

Improving Your Memory. McGraw.
Improving Your Memory. Norton.
Levels of Processing in Human Memory.
  Halsted Pr.
Cermak, V. *see* Cermak, Vladimir.
Cermak, Vladimir.
  xCermak, V.
    ed. Terrestrial Heat Flow in Europe.
    Springer-Verlag.
Cerminara, Gina.
  xCerminara, Gina.
    Many Lives, Many Loves. NAL.
    Many Mansions. Morrow.
    Many Mansions. NAL.
    The Mark Twain Proposition. Donning Co.
    The World Within. Morrow.
Cerney, J. *see* Cerney, J. V.
Cerney, J. V.
  xCerney, J.
    Modern Magic of Natural Healing with Water
    Therapy. P-H.
  xCerney, J. V.
    Acupuncture Without Needles. Cornerstone.
    Acupuncture Without Needles. P-H.
    Dynamic Laws of Thinking Rich. P-H.
    Dynamic Laws of Thinking Rich. P-H.
    Talk Your Way to Success with People. P-H.
Cernica, J. N. *see* Cernica, John N.
Cernica, John N.
  xCernica, J. N.
    Strength of Materials. HR&W.
  xCernica, John N.
    Fundamentals of Reinforced Concrete. A-W.
Cernik, Sheridan L. *see* Cernik, Sheridan Lee.
Cernik, Sheridan Lee, 1942-
  xCernik, Sheridan L.
    Preventative Medicine & Management for the
    Horse. A S Barnes.
Cerny, Charlene.
  xCerny, Charlene.
    Navajo Pictorial Weaving. Museum NM Pr.
Cerny, Jaroslav, Paleographer.
  xCerny, Jaroslav.
    Ancient Egyptian Religion. Greenwood.
    Coptic Etymological Dictionary. Cambridge U
    Pr.
Cerreto, Frank.
  xCerreto, Frank.
    Power Skills in Mathematics II. McGraw.
Certo, Samuel C.
  xCerto, Samuel C.
    Principles of Modern Management: Functions
    & Systems. Wm C Brown.
Cerutti, Toni.
  xCerutti, Toni.
    Guide to Composition in Italian. Cambridge U
    Pr.
Cervantes Saavedra. *see* Cervantes Saavedra, Miguel De.
Cervantes Saavedra, Miguel De, 1547-1616
  xCervantes Saavedra.
    The Portable Cervantes. Penguin.
Cervenka, Jaroslav.
  xCervenka, Jaroslav.
    Chromosomes in Human Cancer. C C Thomas.
Cesaire, Aime.
  xCesaire, Aime.
    Discourse on Colonialism. Monthly Rev.
Cesari, L. *see* Cesari, Lamberto.
Cesari, Lamberto.
  xCesari, L.
    Asymptotic Behavior & Stability Problems in
    Ordinary Differential Equations.
    Springer-Verlag.
    Surface Area. Kraus Repr.
  xCesari, Lamberto.
    ed. Nonlinear Functional Analysis &
    Differential Equations: Proceedings of the
    Michigan State University Conference.
    Dekker.
Cescinsky, H. *see* Cescinsky, Herbert.

Cescinsky, Herbert, 1875-
  xCescinsky, H.
    Gentle Art of Faking Furniture. Peter Smith.
  xCescinsky, Herbert.
    Gentle Art of Faking Furniture. Dover.
Ceserani, Victor.
  xCeserani, Victor.
    Practical Cookery. Intl Ideas.
Cespedes, Alba De, 1911-
  xCespedes, Alba de.
    Remorse. Greenwood.
Cevasco, G. A. *see* Cevasco, George A.
Cevasco, George A.
  xCevasco, G. A.
    Oscar Wilde, British Author, Poet & Wit.
    SamHar Pr.
    The Population Problem. SamHar Pr.
Ch'En, Paul H. *see* Ch'En, Paul Heng-Chao.
Ch'En, Paul Heng-Chao, 1944-
  xCh'En, Paul H.
    Chinese Legal Tradition Under the Mongols:
    The Code of 1291 As Reconstructed.
    Princeton U Pr.
Ch'U, T'Ung-Tsu.
  xCh'u, T'ung-tsu.
    Local Government in China Under the Ch'ing.
    Stanford U Pr.
Chabbert, Rosy.
  xChabbert, Rosy.
    Leonella. Delacorte.
Chabod, Federico.
  xChabod, Federico.
    A History of Italian Fascism. Fertig.
Chabon, Irwin.
  xChabon, Irwin.
    Awake & Aware: Participating in Childbirth
    Through Psychoprophylaxis. Delacorte.
Chace, G. Earl.
  xChace, G. Earl.
    Wonders of Prairie Dogs. Dodd.
    Wonders of Rattlesnakes. Dodd.
    Wonders of the Pronghorn. Dodd.
Chachra, V. *see* Chachra, Vinod.
Chachra, Vinod.
  xChachra, V.
    Applications of Graph Theory Algorithms.
    Elsevier.
Chacko, David.
  xChacko, David.
    Price. St Martin.
Chacko, G. K. *see* Chacko, George Kuttickal.
Chacko, George K. *see* Chacko, George Kuttickal.
Chacko, George Kuttickal, 1930-
  xChacko, G. K.
    ed. Health Handbook: An International
    Reference on Care & Cure. Elsevier.
  xChacko, George K.
    Management Information Systems. Petrocelli.
Chaconas, D. J. *see* Chaconas, Doris J.
Chaconas, Doris J.
  xChaconas, D. J.
    Danger in the Swamp. Lantern.
Chaconas, Spiro J.
  xChaconas, Spiro J.
    ed. Orthodontics. PSG Pub.
Chaconas, Stephen G. *see* Chaconas, Stephen George.
Chaconas, Stephen George, 1913-
  xChaconas, Stephen G.
    Adamantios Korais: A Study in Greek
    Nationalism. AMS Pr.
Chadam, J. M.
  xChadam, J. M.
    ed. Nonlinear Partial Differential Equations &
    Applications: Proceedings of a Special
    Seminar Held at Indiana University,
    1976-1977. Springer-Verlag.
Chadbourne, Richard M. *see* Chadbourne, Richard
  Mcclain.
Chadbourne, Richard Mcclain.
  xChadbourne, Richard M.

Charles-Augustin Sainte Beuve. Twayne.
Chaddock, D. H.
xChaddock, D. H.
Introduction to Fastening Systems. Oxford U Pr.
Chadsey, Charles E. *see* Chadsey, Charles Ernest.
Chadsey, Charles Ernest, 1870-
xChadsey, Charles E.
Struggle Between President Johnson & Congress Over Reconstruction. AMS Pr.
Chadsey, Charles P.
xChadsey, Charles P.
ed. The Grosset Webster Large-Type Dictionary. G&D.
Chadwick, Bill.
xChadwick, Bill.
Illustrated Ice Hockey Rules. Doubleday.
Chadwick, Esther A. *see* Chadwick, Esther Alice.
Chadwick, Esther Alice.
xChadwick, Esther A.
In the Footsteps of the Brontes. Haskell.
In the Footsteps of the Brontes. R West.
Chadwick, French E. *see* Chadwick, French Ensor.
Chadwick, French Ensor.
xChadwick, French E.
ed. Graves Papers & Other Documents Relating to the Naval Operations of the Yorktown Campaign, July to October 1781. Arno.
ed. The Graves Papers & Other Documents Relating to the Naval Operations of the Yorktown Campaign, July to October 1781: New York Historical Society. U Pr of Va.
Chadwick, George. *see* Chadwick, George F.
Chadwick, George F.
xChadwick, George.
A Systems View of Planning: Towards a Theory of the Urban and Regional Planning Process. Pergamon.
Chadwick, H. M. *see* Chadwick, Hector Munro.
Chadwick, H. Munro. *see* Chadwick, Hector Munro.
Chadwick, Hector Munro.
xChadwick, H. M.
Early Scotland: The Picts, the Scots & the Welsh of Southern Scotland. Octagon.
Studies in Old English. Arden Lib.
Studies in Old English. Folcroft.
xChadwick, H. Munro.
The Nationalities of Europe & the Growth of National Ideologies. Cooper Sq.
Chadwick, Henry, 1920-
xChadwick, Henry.
Priscillian of Avila: The Occult & the Charismatic in the Early Church. Oxford U Pr.
Chadwick, John, 1920-
xChadwick, John.
Decipherment of Linear B. Cambridge U Pr.
Chadwick, John W. *see* Chadwick, John White.
Chadwick, John White.
xChadwick, John W.
ed. Lovers' Treasury of Verse. Arno.
Chadwick, Lee.
xChadwick, Lee.
Cuba Today. Lawrence Hill.
Chadwick, M. J. *see* Chadwick, Michael J.
Chadwick, Michael J.
xChadwick, M. J.
The Ecology of Resource Degradation & Renewal. Halsted Pr.
Chadwick, Nora. *see* Chadwick, Nora Kershaw.
Chadwick, Nora K. *see* Chadwick, Nora Kershaw.
Chadwick, Nora Kershaw, 1891-1972
xChadwick, Nora.
The British Heroic Age: The Welsh & the Men of the North. Verry.
xChadwick, Nora K.
Oral Epics of Central Asia. Cambridge U Pr.
Chadwick, Owen.
xChadwick, Owen.

Acton & Gladstone. Humanities.
Reformation. Penguin.
Chadwick, P. *see* Chadwick, Peter.
Chadwick, Peter, 1931-
xChadwick, P.
Continuum Mechanics: Concise Theory & Problems. Halsted Pr.
Chadwick, Roxane.
xChadwick, Roxane.
Don't Shoot. Lerner Pubns.
Chadwick, William J.
xChadwick, William J.
The Annotated Fiduciary: Materials on Fiduciary Responsibility and Prohibited Transactions Under ERISA. Intl Found Employ.
Regulation of Employee Benefits: Erisa & Other Federal Laws. Intl Found Employ.
Chaet, Bernard.
xChaet, Bernard.
The Art of Drawing. HR&W.
An Artist's Notebook: Techniques & Materials. HR&W.
Chafe, Wallace L.
xChafe, Wallace L.
The Caddoan, Iroquoian, & Siouan Languages. Mouton.
Meaning & Structure of Language. U of Chicago Pr.
Meaning & the Structure of Language. U of Chicago Pr.
Chafe, William H. *see* Chafe, William Henry.
Chafe, William Henry.
xChafe, William H.
American Woman: Her Changing Social, Economic & Political Roles, 1920-1970. Oxford U Pr.
Civilities & Civil Rights: Greensboro, North Carolina, & the Black Struggle for Freedom. Oxford U Pr.
Chafee, Zechariah.
xChafee, Zechariah.
Third Degree. Arno.
Chafer, Lewis S. *see* Chafer, Lewis Sperry.
Chafer, Lewis Sperry, 1871-1952
xChafer, Lewis S.
Systematic Theology. Zondervan.
Chafetz, Janet S. *see* Chafetz, Janet Saltzman.
Chafetz, Janet Saltzman.
xChafetz, Janet S.
A Primer on the Construction & Testing of Theories in Sociology. Peacock Pubs.
Chaffee, Ellen E.
xChaffee, Ellen E.
Basic Physiology & Anatomy. Lippincott.
Chaffee, S. *see* Chaffee, Steven H.
Chaffee, Steven H.
xChaffee, S.
Using the Mass Media: Communication Problems in American Society. McGraw.
Chaffee, Wilber A.
xChaffee, Wilber A.
Dissertations on Latin America by U. S. Historians, 1960-1970: A Bibliography. U of Tex Pr.
Chaffer, John.
xChaffer, John.
History & the History Teacher. Allen Unwin.
Chaffin, Lillie D.
xChaffin, Lillie D.
Freeman. Macmillan.
Chaffin, Verner F., 1918-
xChaffin, Verner F.
Studies in the Georgia Law of Decedents' Estates & Future Interests. Michie.
Chagall, David.
xChagall, David.
Diary of a Deaf Mute. Millenium Hse.
Chagnon, Napoleon A.
xChagnon, Napoleon A.

Evolutionary Biology & Human Social Behavior: An Anthropological Perspective. Duxbury Pr.
Chai, Ch'U. *see* Chai, Chu.
Chai, Chu.
xChai, Ch'U.
Changing Society of China. NAL.
xChai, Chu.
The Story of Chinese Philosophy. Greenwood.
Chai, Winberg.
xChai, Winberg.
Confucianism. Barron.
ed. Essential Works of Chinese Communism. Universe.
Chaij, Fernando.
xChaij, Fernando.
The Impending Drama. Southern Pub.
Chaiken, William E.
xChaiken, William E.
Mainstreaming the Learning Disabled Adolescent: A Staff Development Guide. C C Thomas.
Chaikin, Joseph, 1935-
xChaikin, Joseph.
The Presence of the Actor. Atheneum.
Chaikin, Miriam.
xChaikin, Miriam.
I Should Worry, I Should Care. Har-Row.
Chaillou, Jacques.
xChaillou, Jacques.
Hyperbolic Differential Polynomials & Their Singular Perturbations. Kluwer Boston.
Chair, Somerset De. *see* De Chair, Somerset.
Chaison, Gary N.
xChaison, Gary N.
ed. Readings in Canadian Industrial Relations. Mss Info.
Chaitow, Leon.
xChaitow, Leon.
The Acupuncture Treatment of Pain. Arco.
Chajes, Alexander, 1930-
xChajes, Alexander.
Principles of Structural Stability Theory. P-H.
Chakrabarti, Kisor K. *see* Chakrabarti, Kisor Kumar.
Chakrabarti, Kisor Kumar.
xChakrabarti, Kisor K.
The Logic of Gotama. U Pr of Hawaii.
Chakrabarty, A. M. *see* Chakrabarty, Ananda M.
Chakrabarty, Ananda M., 1938-
xChakrabarty, A. M.
Genetic Engineering. CRC Pr.
Chakrabarty, S. C.
xChakrabarty, S. C.
Imagery of Physical Beauty in Tennyson. Arden Lib.
Chakravarti, Anand.
xChakravarti, Anand.
Contradiction & Change: Emerging Patterns of Authority in a Rajasthan Village. Oxford U Pr.
Chakravarty, Suhash.
xChakravarty, Suhash.
From Khyber to Oxus: A Study in Imperial Expansion. South Asia Bks.
Chakravarty, Sukhamoy.
xChakravarty, Sukhamoy.
Capital & Development Planning. MIT Pr.
Chalazonitis, N. *see* Chalazonitis, Nicolas.
Chalazonitis, Nicolas.
xChalazonitis, N.
ed. Abnormal Neuronal Discharges. Raven.
Chalfant, H. Paul, 1979-
xChalfant, H. Paul.
Sociological Aspects of Poverty: A Bibliography. Vance Biblios.
Chalfant, Stuart A.
xChalfant, Stuart A.

Aboriginal Territory of the Nez Perce Indians. Clearwater Pub.

Chalfant, William B. see Chalfant, William Bergen.

Chalfant, William Bergen.
xChalfant, William B.
Primer of Free Government. Philos Lib.

Chaliand, Gerard, 1934-
xChaliand, Gerard.
Armed Struggle in Africa: With the Guerrillas in Portuguese Guinea. Monthly Rev.

Chalklin, C. W.
xChalklin, C. W.
The Provincial Towns of Georgian England: A Study of the Building Process, 1740-1820. McGill-Queens U Pr.

Challa, Krishna, 1947-
xChalla, Krishna.
Investment & Returns in Exploration & the Impact on the Supply of Oil & Natural Gas Reserves. Arno.

Challener, Richard D.
xChallener, Richard D.
French Theory of the Nation in Arms, 1866-1939. Russell.

Challice, C. E.
xChallice, C. E.
ed. Ultrastructure of the Mammalian Heart. Acad Pr.

Challifour, John L., 1939-
xChallifour, John L.
Generalized Functions & Fourier Analysis: An Introduction. Benjamin-Cummings.

Challinor, John.
xChallinor, John.
Geology Explained in North Wales. David & Charles.

Challinor, Raymond.
xChallinor, Raymond.
The Origins of British Bolshevism. Rowman.

Challis, A. J.
xChallis, Aidan J.
Motueka: An Archaeological Survey. Longman.

Challis, Aidan J. see Challis, A. J.

Chalmers, Alexander.
xChalmers, Alexander.
The Works of English Poets, from Chaucer to Cowper. Adler.
ed. Works of the English Poets from Chaucer to Cowper. Greenwood.

Chalmers, Bruce.
xChalmers, Bruce.
Principles of Solidification. Krieger.

Chalmers, David M. see Chalmers, David Mark.

Chalmers, David Mark.
xChalmers, David M.
The Muckrake Years. Krieger.

Chalmers, Edlen. see Chalmers, Elden M.

Chalmers, Elden M.
xChalmers, Edlen.
Making the Most of Family Living. Pacific Pr Pub Assn.

Chalmers, George, 1742-1825
xChalmers, George.
Another Account of the Incidents, from Which the Title, & a Part of the Story of Shakspeare's Tempest Were Derived. AMS Pr.
The Life of Daniel De Foe. Arden Lib.
Life of Daniel De Foe. Folcroft.

Chalmers, Harvey.
xChalmers, Harvey.
Tales of the Mohawk: Stories of Old New York State from Colonial Times to the Age of Homespun, 1st & 2nd Ser. Friedman.

Chalmers, Helena.
xChalmers, Helena.
Clothes, on & off the Stage: A History of Dress from the Earliest Times to the Present Day. Gale.

Chalmers, James A. see Chalmers, James Anderson.

Chalmers, James Anderson.
xChalmers, James A.
Economic Principles: Macroeconomic Theory & Policy. Macmillan.

Chalmers, Margaret T. see Chalmers, Margaret Taylor.

Chalmers, Margaret Taylor.
xChalmers, Margaret T.
Colonial Fireplace Cooking & Early American Recipes. Eberly Pr.

Chalmers, T. W. see Chalmers, Thomas Wightman.

Chalmers, Thomas Wightman.
xChalmers, T. W.
Historic Researches: Chapters in the History of Physical & Chemical Discovery. Dawson Pub.

Chalmers, W. E. see Chalmers, William Ellison.

Chalmers, William Ellison.
xChalmers, W. E.
ed. Racial Conflict & Negotiations: Perspectives & First Case Studies. U of Mich Inst Labor.

Chaloner, John. see Chaloner, John Seymour.

Chaloner, John Seymour.
xChaloner, John.
To the Manner Born. St Martin.

Chalpin, Lila. see Chalpin, Lila K.

Chalpin, Lila K.
xChalpin, Lila.
William Sansom. Twayne.

Chamber of Commerce of the United States of America.
xChamber of Commerce of the United States.
Analysis of Workers' Compensation Laws. Chamber Comm US.

Chamberlain, Barbara.
xChamberlain, Barbara.
The Prisoners' Sword. Cook.

Chamberlain, Betty.
xChamberlain, Betty.
The Artist's Guide to His Market. Watson-Guptill.

Chamberlain, Elwyn M.
xChamberlain, Elwyn M.
Gates of Fire. Grove.

Chamberlain, Houston S. see Chamberlain, Houston Stewart.

Chamberlain, Houston Stewart, 1855-1927
xChamberlain, Houston S.
Foundations of the Nineteenth Century. Fertig.

Chamberlain, John, 1903-
xChamberlain, John.
The Enterprising Americans: A Business History of the United States. Har-Row.
Farewell to Reform: The Rise, Life & Decay of the Progressive Mind in America. Times Bks.
The Letters of John Chamberlain. Greenwood.

Chamberlain, Lawrence, 1878-
xChamberlain, Lawrence.
The Work of the Bond House. Arno.

Chamberlain, Lawrence H. see Chamberlain, Lawrence Henry.

Chamberlain, Lawrence Henry, 1906-
xChamberlain, Lawrence H.
Loyalty & Legislative Action: A Survey of Activity by the New York State Legislature 1919-1949. Johnson Repr.
President, Congress & Legislation. AMS Pr.

Chamberlain, Narcissa. see Chamberlain, Narcissa G.

Chamberlain, Narcissa G.
xChamberlain, Narcissa.
French Menus for Parties. Hastings.
Omelette Book. Knopf.
The Omelette Book. McGraw.

Chamberlain, Neil. see Chamberlain, Neil W.

Chamberlain, Neil W.
xChamberlain, Neil.
The Labor Sector. McGraw.
xChamberlain, Neil W.
Collective Bargaining. McGraw.
ed. Contemporary Economic Issues. Irwin.
The Labor Sector. McGraw.
The Limits of Corporate Responsibility. Basic.

Chamberlain, Neville, 1869-1940
xChamberlain, Neville.
In Search of Peace. Arno.

Chamberlain, Nugent F., 1916-
xChamberlain, Nugent F.
The Practice of NMR Spectroscopy: With Spectra-Structure Correlations for Hydrogen-One. Plenum Pub.

Chamberlain, Peter.
xChamberlain, Peter.
Allied Combat Tanks. Arco.
Anti-Aircraft Guns. Arco.
Axis Combat Tanks. Arco.
Infantry, Mountain, & Airborne Guns. Arco.

Chamberlain, Robert S. see Chamberlain, Robert Stoner.

Chamberlain, Robert Stoner, 1903-
xChamberlain, Robert S.
Conquest & Colonization of Honduras, 1502-1550. Octagon.
Conquest & Colonization of Yucatan, 1517-1550. Octagon.

Chamberlain, Samuel.
xChamberlain, Samuel.
The Chamberlain Selection of New England Rooms, 1639-1863. Hastings.
Clementine in the Kitchen. Hastings.
Etched in Sunlight: Fifty Years in the Graphic Arts. Boston Public Lib.
ed. Fair Is Our Land. Hastings.
Soft Skies of France. Hastings.
Stroll Through Historic Salem. Hastings.
A Tour of Old Sturbridge Village. Hastings.

Chamberlain, Valerie. see Chamberlain, Valerie M.

Chamberlain, Valerie M.
xChamberlain, Valerie.
Creative Home Economics Instruction. McGraw.
xChamberlain, Valerie M.
Creative Home Economics Instruction. McGraw.

Chamberlain, W. H. see Chamberlain, William Henry Jason.

Chamberlain, Walter.
xChamberlain, Walter.
The Thames & Hudson Manual of Etching & Engraving. Thames Hudson.
The Thames & Hudson Manual of Wood Engraving. Thames Hudson.

Chamberlain, William Henry Jason.
xChamberlain, W. H.
Adams' Revolvers. Barrie & Jenkins.

Chamberlin, E. R. see Chamberlin, Eric Russell.

Chamberlin, Edward, 1899-
xChamberlin, Edward H.
Theory of Monopolistic Competition: A Re-Orientation of the Theory of Value. Harvard U Pr.

Chamberlin, Edward H. see Chamberlin, Edward.

Chamberlin, Edwin M. see Chamberlin, Edwin Martin.

Chamberlin, Edwin Martin, 1835-1892
xChamberlin, Edwin M.
The Sovereigns of Industry. Hyperion Conn.

Chamberlin, Eric Russell.
xChamberlin, E. R.

Librarian & His World. Philos Lib.
Marguerite of Navarre. Dial.
The Sack of Rome. David & Charles.

Chamberlin, Everett.
xChamberlin, Everett.
Chicago & Its Suburbs. Arno.

Chamberlin, Joseph E. *see* Chamberlin, Joseph Edgar.

Chamberlin, Joseph Edgar, 1851-1935
xChamberlin, Joseph E.
Boston Transcript: A History of Its First Hundred Years. Arno.

Chamberlin, Judi.
xChamberlin, Judi.
On Our Own: Patient-Controlled Alternatives to the Mental Health System. McGraw.

Chamberlin, L. J. *see* Chamberlin, Leslie J.

Chamberlin, Leslie J.
xChamberlin, L. J.
Improving School Discipline. C C Thomas.

Chamberlin, Waldo, 1905-
xChamberlin, Waldo.
The Chronology & Fact Book of the United Nations: 1941-1979. Oceana.

Chamberlin, Willard J. *see* Chamberlin, Willard Joseph.

Chamberlin, Willard Joseph, 1890-
xChamberlin, Willard J.
Entomological Nomenclature & Literature. Greenwood.

Chamberlin, William H. *see* Chamberlin, William Henry.

Chamberlin, William Henry, 1897-
xChamberlin, William H.
America's Second Crusade. R Myles.
Soviet Planned Economic Order. AMS Pr.
Soviet Planned Economic Order. Greenwood.

Chambers, Aidan.
xChambers, Aidan.
Breaktime. Har-Row.

Chambers, Bradford.
xChambers, Bradford.
ed. Right On: An Anthology of Black Literature. NAL.

Chambers, C.
xChambers, C.
Modern Inorganic Chemistry: An Intermediate Text. Butterworths.

Chambers, Clarke A.
xChambers, Clarke A.
Paul U. Kellogg & the Survey: Voices for Social Welfare & Social Justice. U of Minn Pr.

Chambers, D. S. *see* Chambers, David Sanderson.

Chambers, David L.
xChambers, David L.
Making Fathers Pay: The Enforcement of Child Support. U of Chicago Pr.

Chambers, David Sanderson.
xChambers, D. S.
The Imperial Age of Venice: 1380-1580. HarBraceJ.

Chambers, Donald L.
xChambers, Donald L.
How to Gold-Leaf Antiques & Other Art Objects. Crown.

Chambers, E. K. *see* Chambers, Edmund Kerchever.

Chambers, Edmund K. *see* Chambers, Edmund Kerchever.

Chambers, Edmund Kerchever.
xChambers, E. K.
English Pastorals. Arno.
xChambers, Edmund K.

Early English Lyrics, Amorous, Divine, Moral & Trivial. AMS Pr.
English Pastorals. Arden Lib.
English Pastorals. Folcroft.
Matthew Arnold: A Study. Russell.
Mediaeval Stage. Oxford U Pr.
Notes on the History of the Revels Office Under the Tudors. B Franklin.
ed. Oxford Book of Sixteenth Century Verse. Oxford U Pr.
Samuel Taylor Coleridge: A Biographical Study. Greenwood.

Chambers, Frank M.
xChambers, Frank M.
Proper Names in the Lyrics of the Troubadours. U of NC Pr.

Chambers, Frank P. *see* Chambers, Frank Pentland.

Chambers, Frank Pentland, 1900-
xChambers, Frank P.
History of Taste: An Account of the Revolutions of Art Criticism & Theory in Europe. Greenwood.

Chambers, H. *see* Chambers, Harold L.

Chambers, H. E. *see* Chambers, Henry Edward.

Chambers, Harold L.
xChambers, H.
Drafting & Manual Programming for Numerical Control. P-H.

Chambers, Henry E. *see* Chambers, Henry Edward.

Chambers, Henry Edward, 1860-1929
xChambers, H. E.
Constitutional History of Hawaii. Johnson Repr.
xChambers, Henry E.
Constitutional History of Hawaii. AMS Pr.

Chambers, James.
xChambers, James.
The Devil's Horsemen. Atheneum.

Chambers, Jane.
xChambers, Jane.
Burning. BJ Pub Group.

Chambers, John.
xChambers, John.
Fritzi's Winter. Atheneum.

Chambers, John C. *see* Chambers, John Carlton.

Chambers, John Carlton.
xChambers, John C.
An Executive's Guide to Forecasting. Wiley.

Chambers, John M.
xChambers, John M.
Computational Methods for Data Analysis. Wiley.

Chambers, Jonathan D. *see* Chambers, Jonathan David.

Chambers, Jonathan David.
xChambers, Jonathan D.
Population, Economy, & Society in Pre-Industrial England. Oxford U Pr.
The Workshop of the World: British Economic History from 1820 to 1880. Oxford U Pr.

Chambers, Kenneth. *see* Chambers, Kenneth A.

Chambers, Kenneth A.
xChambers, Kenneth.
The Country Lover's Guide to Wildlife: Mammals, Amphibians, & Reptiles of the Northeastern United States. Johns Hopkins.

Chambers, M. M. *see* Chambers, Merritt Madison.

Chambers, Marilyn.
xChambers, Marilyn.
Marilyn Chambers: My Story. Warner Bks.

Chambers, Merritt M. *see* Chambers, Merritt Madison.

Chambers, Merritt Madison, 1899-
xChambers, M. M.
Above High School. Interstate.
Colleges & the Courts: Faculty & Staff Before the Bench. Interstate.
Higher Education & State Governments, 1970-1975. Interstate.
Higher Education in the Fifty States. Interstate.
xChambers, Merritt M.

Chance & Choice in Higher Education. Interstate.

Chambers, Mortimer.
xChambers, Mortimer.
Ancient Greece. Am Hist Assn.
ed. Fall of Rome: Can It Be Explained?. HR&W.

Chambers, Oswald, 1874-1917
xChambers, Oswald.
Daily Thoughts for Disciples. Zondervan.

Chambers, R. *see* Chambers, Robert.

Chambers, R. W. *see* Chambers, Raymond Wilson.

Chambers, Raymond J.
xChambers, Raymond J.
Accounting, Evaluation & Economic Behavior. Scholars Bk.

Chambers, Raymond L.
xChambers, R.
Buyers Handbook: A Guide to Defensive Shopping. P-H.

Chambers, Raymond W. *see* Chambers, Raymond Wilson.

Chambers, Raymond Wilson, 1874-1942
xChambers, R. W.
The Text of Piers Plowman. Arden Lib.
Text of Piers Plowman. Folcroft.
xChambers, Raymond W.
England Before the Norman Conquest. Greenwood.
The Teaching of English in the Universities of England. Folcroft.
Thomas More. U of Mich Pr.

Chambers, Richard D.
xChambers, Richard D.
Fluorine in Organic Chemistry. Wiley.

Chambers, Richard L.
xChambers, Richard L.
ed. Contemporary Turkish Short Stories: An Intermediate Reader. Bibliotheca

Chambers, Robert, 1802-1871
xChambers, R.
Popular Rhymes of Scotland. Gordon Pr.
xChambers, Robert.
Popular Rhymes of Scotland. Gale.
Popular Rhymes of Scotland. Quaker City.

Chambers, Robert W. *see* Chambers, Robert William.

Chambers, Robert William, 1865-1933
xChambers, Robert W.
The Gay Rebellion. Arno.
In Search of the Unknown. Hyperion Conn.

Chambers, Roger R.
xChambers, Roger R.
Plain Truth About Armstrongism. Baker Bk.

Chambers, Ross.
xChambers, Ross.
Meaning & Meaningfulness: Studies in the Analysis & Interpretation of Texts. French Forum.

Chambers, Selma L. *see* Chambers, Selma Lola.

Chambers, Selma Lola.
xChambers, Selma L.
The Golden Book of Words. Western Pub.

Chambers, Theodore F. *see* Chambers, Theodore Frelinghuysen.

Chambers, Theodore Frelinghuysen, 1849-1916
xChambers, Theodore F.
Early Germans of New Jersey: Their History, Churches & Genealogies. Genealog Pub.

Chambers, Wicke.
xChambers, Wicke.
The Lip-Smackin', Joke-Crackin' Cookbook for Kids. Western Pub.

Chambers, William, 1800-1883
xChambers, William.
American Slavery & Colour. Metro Bks.
American Slavery & Colour. Negro U Pr.
Things As They Are in America. Negro U Pr.

Chambers, William N. *see* Chambers, William Nisbet.

Chambers, William Nisbet, 1916-
xChambers, William N.

Political Parties in a New Nation: The American Experience, 1776-1809. Oxford U Pr.
Chambliss, J. J. *see* Chambliss, Joseph James.
Chambliss, Joseph James, 1929-
xChambliss, J. J.
Boyd H. Bode's Philosophy of Education. Ohio St U Pr.
Chambliss, Rollin.
xChambliss, Rollin.
Social Thought: From Hammurabi to Comte. Irvington.
Chambliss, William J.
xChambliss, William J.
Crime & the Legal Process. McGraw.
Criminal Law in Action. Wiley.
Law, Order & Power. A-W.
On the Take: From Petty Crooks to Presidents. Ind U Pr.
ed. Problems of Industrial Society. A-W.
Chambliss, William J. *see* Chambliss, William Jones.
Chambliss, William Jones.
xChambliss, William J.
ed. Sociological Readings in the Conflict Perspective. A-W.
Chamelin, Neil C.
xChamelin, Neil C.
Criminal Law for Policemen. P-H.
Introduction to Criminal Justice. P-H.
Chametzky, Jules.
xChametzky, Jules.
From the Ghetto: The Fiction of Abraham Cahan. U of Mass Pr.
Champernowne, D. G. *see* Champernowne, David Gawen.
Champernowne, David Gawen.
xChampernowne, D. G.
The Distribution of Income Between Persons. Cambridge U Pr.
Champigny, Robert, 1922-
xChampigny, Robert.
What Will Have Happened: A Philosophical & Technical Essay on Mystery Stories. Ind U Pr.
Champion, Dean J.
xChampion, Dean J.
The Sociology of Organizations. McGraw.
Champion, Ivan F.
xChampion, Ivan F.
Across New Guinea from the Fly to the Sepik. AMS Pr.
Champion, J. M. *see* Champion, John M.
Champion, James J. *see* Champion, James Joseph.
Champion, James Joseph.
xChampion, James J.
The Periphrastic Futures Formed by the Romance Reflexes of Vado (ad) Plus Infinite. U of NC Pr.
Champion, John M.
xChampion, J. M.
General Hospital: A Model. Univ Park.
xChampion, John M.
Critical Incidents in Management. Irwin.
Predicting Academic Success of Business Administration Students. Ga St U Busn Pub.
Champion, Larry S.
xChampion, Larry S.
Evolution of Shakespeare's Comedy: A Study in Dramatic Perspective. Harvard U Pr.
Perspective in Shakespeare's English Histories. U of Ga Pr.
Champlin, John. *see* Champlin, John Denison.
Champlin, John Denison.
xChamplin, John.
Cyclopedia of Painters & Paintings. Gordon Pr.
Champlin, John R. *see* Champlin, John Rittenhouse.
Champlin, John Rittenhouse.
xChamplin, John R.

ed. Power. Lieber-Atherton.
Champlin, Joseph M.
xChamplin, Joseph M.
Alone No Longer. Ave Maria.
Chan, Esther.
xChan, Esther.
Authentic Chinese Cooking. Peter Smith.
Chan, Lois M. *see* Chan, Lois Mai.
Chan, Lois Mai.
xChan, Lois M.
ed. Marlowe Criticism: A Bibliography. G K Hall.
Chan, Shu-Park.
xChan, Shu-Park.
Analysis of Linear Networks & Systems: A Matrix-Oriented Approach with Computer Applications. A-W.
Chan, Wing-Tsit, 1901-
xChan, Wing-Tsit.
Historical Charts of Chinese Philosophy. Far Eastern Pubns.
An Outline & Annotated Bibliography of Chinese Philosophy. Far Eastern Pubns.
Religious Trends in Modern China. Octagon.
Chanan, Gabriel.
xChanan, Gabriel.
ed. Frontiers of Classroom Research. Humanities.
Chanan, Michael.
xChanan, Michael.
Chilean Cinema. NY Zoetrope.
The Dream That Kicks: The Prehistory & Early Years of Cinema in Britain. Routledge & Kegan.
Chanana, Charanjit.
xChanana, Charanjit.
Computers in Asia. Intl Pubns Serv.
Chance, Britton.
xChance, Britton.
ed. Control of Energy Metabolism. Acad Pr.
ed. Probes of Structure & Function of Macromolecules & Membranes. Acad Pr.
Chance, Burton, 1868-
xChance, Burton.
Ophthalmology. AMS Pr.
Ophthalmology. Hafner.
Chance, John K.
xChance, John K.
Race & Class in Colonial Oaxaca. Stanford U Pr.
Chance, Paul.
xChance, Paul.
Learning & Behavior. Wadsworth Pub.
Chance, Stephen.
xChance, Stephen.
The Stone of Offering: A Septimus Mystery. Elsevier-Nelson.
Chancellor, Betty.
xChancellor, Betty.
A Child's Christmas Cookbook. Evergreen.
A Child's Christmas Cookbook. Harvey.
Chancellor, E. Beresford. *see* Chancellor, Edwin Beresford.
Chancellor, Edwin B. *see* Chancellor, Edwin Beresford.
Chancellor, Edwin Beresford, 1868-1937
xChancellor, E. Beresford.
Literary Types, Being Essays in Criticism. Folcroft.
xChancellor, Edwin B.
Dickens & His Times. Folcroft.
Chand, B.
xChand, Bool.
Our Earth & the Universe. Asia.
Chand, Bool. *see* Chand, B.
Chandavarkar, Sumana.
xChandavarkar, Sumana.
Children of India. Lothrop.
Chander, Romesh.
xChander, Romesh.

Planning for Satellite Broadcasting: The Indian Instructional Television Experiment. Unipub.
Chandler, Alfred D. *see* Chandler, Alfred Dupont.
Chandler, Alfred Dupont.
xChandler, Alfred D.
ed. Managerial Hierarchies: Comparative Perspectives on the Rise of Modern Industrial Enterprise. Harvard U Pr.
Chandler, Alice.
xChandler, Alice.
Dream of Order: The Medieval Ideal in Nineteenth-Century English Literature. U of Nebr Pr.
Chandler, Allison.
xChandler, Allison.
When Oklahoma Took the Trolley. Interurban.
Chandler, Anna C. *see* Chandler, Anna Curtis.
Chandler, Anna Curtis.
xChandler, Anna C.
Story-Lives of Master Artists. Lippincott.
Chandler, Arthur.
xChandler, Arthur.
Stereo Views. Troubador Pr.
Chandler, Billy J. *see* Chandler, Billy Jaynes.
Chandler, Billy Jaynes.
xChandler, Billy J.
The Bandit King: Lampiao of Brazil. Tex A&M Univ Pr.
The Feitosas & the Sertao Dos Inhamuns: The History of a Family & a Community in Northeast Brazil, 1700-1930. U Presses Fla.
Chandler, Caroline A. *see* Chandler, Caroline Augusta.
Chandler, Caroline Augusta.
xChandler, Caroline A.
Early Child Care: The New Perspectives. Beresford Bk Serv.
Chandler, Charles D. *see* Chandler, Charles Deforest.
Chandler, Charles Deforest.
xChandler, Charles D.
How Our Army Grew Wings. Arno.
Chandler, Charlotte.
xChandler, Charlotte.
Hello, I Must Be Going: Groucho & His Friends. Penguin.
Chandler, D. L. *see* Chandler, David Leon.
Chandler, David.
xChandler, David.
The Aphrodite. Ballantine.
The Aphrodite. Morrow.
Chandler, David. *see* Chandler, David G.
Chandler, David G.
xChandler, David.
The Art of Warfare in the Age of Marlborough. Hippocrene Bks.
Dictionary of the Napoleonic Wars. Macmillan.
Marlborough As Military Commander. Hippocrene Bks.
Chandler, David L.
xChandler, David L.
Life on Mars. Dutton.
Chandler, David Leon.
xChandler, D. L.
One Hundred Tons of Gold. Dell.
Chandler, Edna W. *see* Chandler, Edna Walker.
Chandler, Edna Walker.
xChandler, Edna W.
Cowboy Andy. Beginner.
Indian Paintbrush. A Whitman.
Popcorn Patch. A Whitman.
Chandler, Elizabeth L. *see* Chandler, Elizabeth Lathrop.
Chandler, Elizabeth Lathrop.
xChandler, Elizabeth L.
A Study of the Sources of the Tales & Romances Written by Nathaniel Hawthorne Before 1853. Arden Lib.
Chandler, Evan.
xChandler, Evan.
Dying Light. NAL.
Chandler, Frank W. *see* Chandler, Frank Wadleigh.

Chandler, Frank Wadleigh, 1873-1947
 xChandler, Frank W.
  Aspects of Modern Drama. R West.
  Aspects of Modern Drama. Scholarly.
  The Literature of Roguery. Arden Lib.
  Literature of Roguery. B Franklin.
  Modern Continental Playwrights. R West.
Chandler, George, 1915-
 xChandler, George.
  Libraries in the East: An International &
   Comparative Study. Acad Pr.
Chandler, Joan M.
 xChandler, Joan M.
  America Since Independence. Oxford U Pr.
Chandler, Lester. see Chandler, Lester Vernon.
Chandler, Lester V. see Chandler, Lester Vernon.
Chandler, Lester Vernon, 1905-
 xChandler, Lester.
  Inflation in the United States 1940-1948. Da
   Capo.
 xChandler, Lester V.
  The Economics of Money & Banking.
   Har-Row.
  The Monetary-Financial System. Har-Row.
Chandler, Paul A.
 xChandler, Paul A.
  ed. Glaucoma. Lea & Febiger.
Chandler, Peleg W. see Chandler, Peleg Whitman.
Chandler, Peleg Whitman, 1816-1889
 xChandler, Peleg W.
  American Criminal Trials. AMS Pr.
  American Criminal Trials. Arno.
Chandler, Raymond, 1888-1959
 xChandler, Raymond.
  Chandler Before Marlowe: Raymond
   Chandler's Early Prose & Poetry 1908-1912.
   U of SC Pr.
  The Long Goodbye. Ballantine.
  Raymond Chandler Speaking. Arno.
  Simple Art of Murder. Ballantine.
Chandler, Robert.
 xChandler, Robert.
  The Magic Ring & Other Russian Folktales.
   Merrimack Bk Serv.
Chandler, Robert F. see Chandler, Robert Flint.
Chandler, Robert Flint, 1907-
 xChandler, Robert F.
  Rice in the Tropics: A Guide to Development
   of National Programs. Westview.
Chandler, Russell.
 xChandler, Russell.
  The Overcomers. Revell.
Chandler, T. J. see Chandler, Tony John.
Chandler, Tony John.
 xChandler, T. J.
  The Climate of the British Isles. Longman.
Chandler, Zelphs E. see Chandler, Zilpha Emma.
Chandler, Zilpha Emma, 1894-
 xChandler, Zelphs E.
  Analysis of the Stylistic Technique of Addison,
   Johnson, Hazlitt & Pater. Folcroft.
Chandoha, Walter.
 xChandoha, Walter.
  The Literary Cat. Lippincott.
Chandor, Anthony.
 xChandor, Anthony.
  ed. Dictionary of Computers. Penguin.
Chandra, Kananur V.
 xChandra, Kananur V.
  The Adjustment & Attitudes of East Indian
   Students in Canada. R & E Res Assoc.
Chandra, Moti.
 xChandra, Moti.
  ed. Studies in Early Indian Painting. Asia.
  Trade & Trade Routes in Ancient India. South
   Asia Bks.
Chandras, Kananur V., 1939-
 xChandras, Kananur V.

Arab, Armenian, Syrian, Lebanese, East Indian,
 Pakistani & Bangla Deshi Americans: A
 Study Guide & Source Book. R & E Res
 Assoc.
Four Thousand Years of Indian Education: A
 Short History of the Hindu, Buddhist &
 Moslem Periods. R & E Res Assoc.
ed. Racial Discrimination Against
 Neither-White-nor-Black American
 Minorities. R & E Res Assoc.
Chandrasekhar, S. see Chandrasekhar, Subrahmanyan.
Chandrasekhar, Sivaramakrishna, 1930-
 xChandrasekhar, S.
  Liquid Crystals. Cambridge U Pr.
Chandrasekhar, Sripati, 1917-
 xChandrasekhar, S.
  Infant Mortality, Population Growth & Family
   Planning in India. U of NC Pr.
 xChandrasekhar, Sripati.
  ed. Asia's Population Problems: With a
   Discussion of Population & Immigration in
   Australia. Greenwood.
Chandrasekhar, Subrahmanyan.
 xChandrasekhar, S.
  Illumination & Polarization of the Sunlit Sky
   on Rayleigh Scattering. Am Philos.
 xChandrasekhar, Subrahmanyan.
  Radiative Transfer. Dover.
Chandrasekharan, K. see Chandrasekharan, Komaravolu.
Chandrasekharan, Komaravolu, 1920-
 xChandrasekharan, K.
  Arithmetical Functions. Springer-Verlag.
Chaneles, Sol.
 xChaneles, Sol.
  Collecting Movie Memorabilia. Arco.
Chaney, Charles L.
 xChaney, Charles L.
  Design for Church Growth. Broadman.
Chaney, Margaret S. see Chaney, Margaret Stella.
Chaney, Margaret Stella.
 xChaney, Margaret S.
  Nutrition. HM.
Chaney, Robert. see Chaney, Robert Galen.
Chaney, Robert Galen, 1913-
 xChaney, Robert.
  Adventures in ESP. Astara.
  The Inner Way. Astara.
Chaney, William A., 1922-
 xChaney, William A.
  The Cult of Kingship in Anglo-Saxon England:
   The Transition from Paganism to
   Christianity. U of Cal Pr.
Chang, Arnold.
 xChang, Arnold.
  Painting in the People's Republic of China:
   The Politics of Style. Westview.
Chang, C. W.
 xChang, C. W.
  Increasing Food Production Through
   Education, Research & Extension. Unipub.
Chang, Chin-Liang.
 xChang, Chin-Liang.
  Symbolic Logic & Mechanical Theorem
   Proving. Acad Pr.
Chang, Constance D.
 xChang, Constance D.
  Chinese Menu Cookbook. Doubleday.
Chang, Dae H.
 xChang, Dae H.
  ed. Crime & Delinquency. Schenkman.
  Introduction to Criminal Justice: Theory &
   Application. Kendall-Hunt.
Chang, Hao.
 xChang, Hao.
  Liang Ch'i-Ch'ao & Intellectual Transition in
   China, 1890-1907. Harvard U Pr.
Chang, Herbert Y.
 xChang, Herbert Y.

Fault Diagnosis of Digital Systems. Krieger.
Chang, John K.
 xChang, John K.
  Industrial Development in Pre-Communist
   China: A Quantitative Analysis. Beresford Bk
   Ser.
Chang, Jolan.
 xChang, Jolan.
  The Tao of Love & Sex: The Ancient Chinese
   Way to Ecstasy. Dutton.
Chang, K. C. see Chang, Kwang-Chih.
Chang, Kwang-Chih.
 xChang, K. C.
  Early Chinese Civilization: Anthropological
   Perspectives. Harvard U Pr.
  ed. Food in Chinese Culture: Anthropological
   & Historical Perspectives. Yale U Pr.
 xChang, Kwang-Chih.
  The Archaeology of Ancient China. Yale U Pr.
  Fengpitou, Tapenkeng & the Prehistory of
   Taiwan. Yale U Anthro.
  Shang Civilization. Yale U Pr.
Chang, Louis W.
 xChang, Louis W.
  A Color Atlas & Manual for Applied
   Histochemistry. C C Thomas.
Chang, N. P. see Chang, Ngee-Pong.
Chang, Ngee-Pong.
 xChang, N. P.
  ed. Five Decades of Weak Interactions. NY
   Acad Sci.
Chang, P'Eng-Ch'Un. see Chang, Peng-Chun.
Chang, Parris H., 1936-
 xChang, Parris H.
  Power & Policy in China. Pa St U Pr.
Chang, Peng-Chun, 1892-1957
 xChang, P'Eng-Ch'Un.
  Education for Modernization in China: A
   Search for Criteria of Curriculum
   Construction in View of the Transition in
   National Life, with Special Reference to
   Secondary Education. AMS Pr.
Chang, Raymond.
 xChang, Raymond.
  Basic Principles of Spectroscopy. Krieger.
  Speaking of Chinese. Norton.
Chang, Richard T.
 xChang, Richard T.
  Historians & Meiji Statesmen. U Presses Fla.
Chang, S. T. see Chang, Shu-Ting.
Chang, Shu-Ting.
 xChang, S. T.
  ed. The Biology & Cultivation of Edible
   Mushrooms. Acad Pr.
Chang, Wonona W.
 xChang, Wonona W.
  Encyclopedia of Chinese Food & Cooking.
   Crown.
Change Institute, University of Maryland.
 xChange Institute. University of Maryland.
  Frontiers in Librarianship: Proceedings of
   Change Institute 1969. Greenwood.
Chanin, Abe.
 xChanin, Abe.
  This Land, These Voices: A Different View of
   Arizona History in Words of Those Who
   Lived It. Northland.
Chankin, Donald O., 1934-
 xChankin, Donald O.
  Anonymity & Death: The Fiction of B. Traven.
   Pa St U Pr.
Chanler, Julie. see Chanler, Julie (Olin).
Chanler, Julie (Olin), 1882-1961
 xChanler, Julie.
  His Messengers Went Forth. Arno.
Chanlett, Emil T.
 xChanlett, Emil T.
  Environmental Protection. McGraw.

Channels, Vera G.
  xChannels, Vera G.
    Career Education in Home Economics.
      Interstate.
    Experiences in Interpersonal Relationships.
      Interstate.
Channels, Vera G. *see* Channels, Vera.
Channing, Edward, 1856-1931
  xChanning, Edward.
    A History of the United States. Octagon.
Channing, Edward T. *see* Channing, Edward Tyrrel.
Channing, Edward Tyrrel.
  xChanning, Edward T.
    Lectures Read to the Seniors in Harvard
      College. S Ill U Pr.
Channing, Mark.
  xChanning, Mark.
    White Python: Adventure & Mystery in Tibet.
      Arno.
Channing, William. *see* Channing, William Ellery.
Channing, William E. *see* Channing, William Ellery.
Channing, William Ellery, 1780-1842
  xChanning, William.
    Character & Writings of John Milton. Folcroft.
  xChanning, William E.
    The Character & Writings of John Milton.
      Arden Lib.
    Discourses on War. Garland Pub.
    Discourses on War. Gordon Pr.
    Discourses on War. Ozer.
    Thoreau: The Poet-Naturalist, with Memorial
      Verses. Scholarly.
Channon, Derek F.
  xChannon, Derek F.
    The Strategy & Structure of British Enterprise.
      Harvard Busn.
Channon, Howard.
  xChannon, Howard.
    Portrait of Liverpool. Intl Pubns Serv.
Chansler, Walter S.
  xChansler, Walter S.
    Successful Trapping Methods: A Guide to
      Good Trapping. Van Nos Reinhold.
Chant, Joy.
  xChant, Joy.
    The Grey Mane of Morning. Allen Unwin.
Chantikian, Kosrof.
  xChantikian, Kosrof.
    Imaginations & Self-Discoveries: Poems
      1971-73. KOSMOS.
    Prophecies & Transformations. KOSMOS.
Chao, Kang, 1929-
  xChao, Kang.
    Capital Formation in Mainland China,
      1952-1965. U of Cal Pr.
    The Development of Cotton Textile Production
      in China. Harvard U Pr.
Chao, Kuo-Chun.
  xChao, Kuo-Chun.
    Agrarian Policies of Mainland China: A
      Documentary Study, 1949-56. Harvard U Pr.
    Economic Planning & Organization in
      Mainland China: A Documentary Study,
      1949-1957. Harvard U Pr.
Chao, Lincoln L.
  xChao, Lincoln L.
    Introduction to Statistics. Brooks-Cole.
    Statistics for Management. Brooks-Cole.
Chao Liu, Jung. *see* Liu, Jung Chao.
Chao, Shu-Li.
  xChao, Shu-Li.
    Tale of Li Youcai's Rhymes. Cambridge U Pr.
Chao, Yuen R. *see* Chao, Yuen Ren.
Chao, Yuen Ren.
  xChao, Yuen R.
    Concise Dictionary of Spoken Chinese.
      Harvard U Pr.
  xChao, Yuen Ren.

    A Grammar of Spoken Chinese. U of Cal Pr.
Chapian, Marie.
  xChapian, Marie.
    Holy Spirit & Me. Creation Hse.
    I Learn About the Gifts of the Holy Spirit.
      Creation Hse.
    Intro. by Of Whom the World Was Not
      Worthy. Bethany Fell.
Chapin, Bradley.
  xChapin, Bradley.
    Provincial America, 1600-1763. Free Pr.
Chapin, Chester F. *see* Chapin, Chester Fisher.
Chapin, Chester Fisher, 1922-
  xChapin, Chester F.
    Personification in Eighteenth-Century English
      Poetry. Octagon.
Chapin, Cynthia.
  xChapin, Cynthia.
    Clean Streets, Clean Water, Clean Air. A
      Whitman.
Chapin, Edwin H. *see* Chapin, Edwin Hubbell.
Chapin, Edwin Hubbell, 1814-1880
  xChapin, Edwin H.
    Humanity in the City. Arno.
Chapin, F. Stuart. *see* Chapin, Francis Stuart.
Chapin, Francis S. *see* Chapin, Francis Stuart.
Chapin, Francis Stuart, 1888-
  xChapin, F. Stuart.
    Field Work & Social Research. Arno.
    Human Activity Patterns in the City: Things
      People Do in Time & in Space. Wiley.
    Urban Land Use Planning. U of Ill Pr.
  xChapin, Francis S.
    Experimental Designs in Sociological Research.
      Greenwood.
Chapin, June R.
  xChapin, June R.
    Teaching Social Studies Skills. Little.
Chapin, Robert C. *see* Chapin, Robert Coit.
Chapin, Robert Coit, 1863-
  xChapin, Robert C.
    Standard of Living Among Workingmen's
      Families in New York City. Arno.
Chapin, Suzy.
  xChapin, Suzy.
    The Adjustable Diet Cookbook. T Y Crowell.
Chaplen, Frank.
  xChaplen, Frank.
    Paragraph Writing. Oxford U Pr.
Chaplin, Annabel.
  xChaplin, Annabel.
    The Bright Light of Death. De Vorss.
Chaplin, Charles, 1889-
  xChaplin, Charles.
    My Autobiography. S&S.
Chaplin, Charles C. *see* Chaplin, Charles C. G.
Chaplin, Charles C. G., 1906-
  xChaplin, Charles C.
    Fishwatcher's Guide to West Atlantic Coral
      Reefs. Harrowood Bks.
Chaplin, David.
  xChaplin, David.
    ed. Population Policies & Growth in Latin
      America. Irvington.
Chaplin, J. P. *see* Chaplin, James Patrick.
Chaplin, James P.
  xChaplin, J. P.
    The Dictionary of the Occult & Paranormal.
      Dell.
Chaplin, James P. *see* Chaplin, James Patrick.
Chaplin, James Patrick, 1919-
  xChaplin, J. P.
    Dictionary of Psychology. Dell.
    Systems & Theories of Psychology. HR&W.
  xChaplin, James P.
    Primer of Neurology & Neurophysiology.
      Wiley.
Chaplin, Jane (Dunbar), 1819-1884
  xChaplin, Jane D.

    Out of the Wilderness. Arno.
Chaplin, Jane D. *see* Chaplin, Jane (Dunbar).
Chaplin, Mary.
  xChaplin, Mary.
    Gardening for the Physically Handicapped &
      Elderly. David & Charles.
Chapman. *see* Chapman, George.
Chapman, Arthur G. *see* Chapman, Arthur Glenn.
Chapman, Arthur Glenn.
  xChapman, Arthur G.
    Christmas Trees for Pleasure & Profit. Rutgers
      U Pr.
Chapman, Berlin. *see* Chapman, Berlin Basil.
Chapman, Berlin B. *see* Chapman, Berlin Basil.
Chapman, Berlin Basil.
  xChapman, Berlin.
    Education in Central West Virginia, 1910-1975.
      McClain.
  xChapman, Berlin B.
    Federal Management & Disposition of the
      Lands of Oklahoma Territory, 1866-1907.
      Arno.
Chapman, Blanche A. *see* Chapman, Blanche Adams.
Chapman, Blanche Adams, 1895-
  xChapman, Blanche A.
    Marriages of Isle of Wight County, Virginia,
      1628-1800. Genealog Pub.
Chapman, Brian.
  xChapman, Brian.
    Introduction to French Local Government.
      Greenwood.
    Introduction to French Local Government.
      Hyperion Conn.
    The Profession of Government: The Public
      Service in Europe. Greenwood.
Chapman, Carleton A. *see* Chapman, Carleton Abramson.
Chapman, Carleton Abramson, 1911-
  xChapman, Carleton A.
    Geology of Acadia National Park. Chatham Pr.
Chapman, Carleton B.
  xChapman, Carleton B.
    Dartmouth Medical School: The First 175
      Years. U Pr of New Eng.
Chapman, Carol.
  xChapman, Carol.
    Ig Lives in a Cave. Dutton.
Chapman, Carol. *see* Chapman, Carol A.
Chapman, Carol A.
  xChapman, Carol.
    Barney Bipple's Magic Dandelions. Dutton.
Chapman, Charles E. *see* Chapman, Charles Edward.
Chapman, Charles Edward, 1880-1941
  xChapman, Charles E.
    The Founding of Spanish California: The
      Northwestward Expansion of New Spain,
      1687-1783. Octagon.
    A History of the Cuban Republic: A Study in
      Hispanic American Politics. Gordon Pr.
Chapman, Claire.
  xChapman, Claire.
    Teaching Squash. Soccer.
Chapman, Coolidge O. *see* Chapman, Coolidge Otis.
Chapman, Coolidge Otis.
  xChapman, Coolidge O.
    An Index of Names in Pearl, Purity, Patience
      & Gawain. Greenwood.
Chapman, Dennis.
  xChapman, Dennis.
    Introduction to Practical High Resolution
      Nuclear Magnetic Resonance Spectroscopy.
      Acad Pr.
Chapman, Dorothy H.
  xChapman, Dorothy H.
    Index to Black Poetry. G K Hall.
Chapman, E. N. *see* Chapman, Elwood N.
Chapman, Elizabeth. *see* Chapman, Elizabeth K.
Chapman, Elizabeth K.
  xChapman, Elizabeth.

Visually Handicapped Children & Young
People. Routledge & Kegan.
xChapman, Elizabeth K.
Visually Handicapped Children & Young
People. Routledge & Kegan.
Chapman, Elizabeth R. *see* Chapman, Elizabeth Rachel.
Chapman, Elizabeth Rachel.
xChapman, Elizabeth R.
A Companion to "in Memoriam". Arden Lib.
A Companion to "in Memoriam". Folcroft.
Chapman, Elwood N.
xChapman, E. N.
Getting into Business. Wiley.
xChapman, Elwood N.
College Survival: Find Yourself. Find a Career.
SRA.
From Campus to Career Success. SRA.
Supervisor's Survival Kit: A Mid-Management
Primer. SRA.
Chapman, F. B. *see* Chapman, Frederick Bennett.

Chapman, Frederick Bennett, 1887-
xChapman, F. B.
Flute Technique. Oxford U Pr.

Chapman, Gary. *see* Chapman, Gary D.

Chapman, Gary D., 1938-
xChapman, Gary.
Toward a Growing Marriage. Moody.

Chapman, George.
xChapman.
Bussy D'ambois. Norton.
xChapman, George.
All Fools. U of Nebr Pr.
Bussy D'ambois. Johns Hopkins.
Bussy D'ambois. U of Nebr Pr.
Gentleman Usher. U of Nebr Pr.

Chapman, Guy.
xChapman, Guy.
The Dreyfus Case: A Reassessment.
Greenwood.
Chapman, Helen E.
xChapman, Helen E.
Paul Brewster & Son. Arno.
Chapman, Hester. *see* Chapman, Hester W.
Chapman, Hester W., 1899-1976
xChapman, Hester.
Four Fine Gentlemen. U of Nebr Pr.
Chapman, Ian M.
xChapman, Ian M.
Do a Loving Thing. Judson.
Chapman, James C. *see* Chapman, James Crosby.
Chapman, James Crosby, 1889-1925
xChapman, James C.
Individual Differences in Ability &
Improvement & Their Correlations. AMS Pr.
Chapman, Jane R.
xChapman, Jane R.
ed. Economic Independence for Women: The
Foundation for Equal Rights. Sage.
Chapman, Jean.
xChapman, Jean.
Moon Eyes. McGraw.
Chapman, John, 1944-
xChapman, John.
Adult English One. P-H.
Adult English Three. P-H.
Adult English Two. P-H.
Chapman, John A. *see* Chapman, John Alexander.
Chapman, John Alexander, 1875-
xChapman, John A.
Wordsworth & Literary Criticism. Folcroft.
Chapman, John B. *see* Chapman, John Bisset.
Chapman, John Bisset.
xChapman, John B.
Horace & His Poetry. AMS Pr.
Chapman, John J. *see* Chapman, John Jay.

Chapman, John Jay, 1862-1933
xChapman, John J.
Causes & Consequences. Gordon Pr.
Learning, & Other Essays. Arno.
Memories & Milestones. Arno.
Practical Agitation. Johnson Repr.
xChapman, John Jay.
The Collected Works of John Jay Chapman.
M&S Pr.
Chapman, John M. *see* Chapman, John Martin.
Chapman, John Martin.
xChapman, John M.
Licensed Lending in New York. Columbia U
Pr.
Chapman, John S. *see* Chapman, John Stewart.
Chapman, John Stewart.
xChapman, John S.
The Atypical Mycobacteria & Human
Mycobacteriosis. Plenum Pub.
Byron & the Honourable Augusta Leigh. Yale
U Pr.
Chapman, Kenneth G. *see* Chapman, Kenneth Garnier.
Chapman, Kenneth Garnier, 1927-
xChapman, Kenneth G.
Graded Readings & Exercises in Old Icelandic.
U of Cal Pr.
Chapman, Kenneth M. *see* Chapman, Kenneth Milton.
Chapman, Kenneth Milton.
xChapman, Kenneth M.
The Pottery of San Ildefonso Pueblo. U of NM
Pr.
Chapman, L. R.
xChapman, L. R.
The Process of Learning Mathematics.
Pergamon.
Chapman, Laura H.
xChapman, Laura H.
Approaches to Art in Education. HarBraceJ.
Chapman, M. Winslow. *see* Chapman, Mary Winslow.
Chapman, Maria. *see* Chapman, Maria (Weston).
Chapman, Maria (Weston), 1806-1885
xChapman, Maria.
Right & Wrong in Massachusetts. Negro U Pr.
Chapman, Marie. *see* Chapman, Marie M.
Chapman, Marie M.
xChapman, Marie.
Successful Teaching Ideas. Standard Pub.
xChapman, Marie M.
Puppet Animals Tell Bible Stories. Accent Bks.
Chapman, Mary L. *see* Chapman, Mary Lewis.
Chapman, Mary Lewis.
xChapman, Mary L.
ed. Literary Landmarks: A Guide to Homes &
Memorials of American Writers Which Are
Open to the Public. Literary Sketches.
Chapman, Mary Winslow.
xChapman, M. Winslow.
Gelded Centaur. Golden Quill.
Chapman, N. B. *see* Chapman, Norman Bellamy.
Chapman, Norman Bellamy.
xChapman, N. B.
ed. Advances in Linear Free-Energy
Relationships. Plenum Pub.
Chapman, O. L. *see* Chapman, Orville L.
Chapman, Orville L.
xChapman, O. L.
ed. Organic Photochemistry. Dekker.
Chapman, R. F. *see* Chapman, Reginald Frederick.
Chapman, Raymond.
xChapman, Raymond.
Linguistics & Literature: An Introduction to
Literary Stylistics. Littlefield.
Chapman, Reginald Frederick.
xChapman, R. F.
The Insects: Structure & Function. Elsevier.
Chapman, Robert D. *see* Chapman, Robert Dewitt.
Chapman, Robert Dewitt, 1937-
xChapman, Robert D.
Discovering Astronomy. W H Freeman.
Chapman, Robert W. *see* Chapman, Robert William.

Chapman, Robert William, 1881-1960
xChapman, Robert W.
Johnsonian & Other Essays & Reviews.
Scholarly.
Chapman, Roger.
xChapman, Roger.
No Time on Our Side. Norton.
Chapman, S. *see* Chapman, Sydney.
Chapman, Samuel, 1859-1943
xChapman, Samuel.
The Postage Stamps of Mexico 1856-1868.
Quarterman.
Chapman, Samuel G.
xChapman, Samuel G.
A Descriptive Profile of the Assault Incident.
Univ OK Gov Res.
Chapman, Stanley D.
xChapman, Stanley D.
ed. History of Working-Class Housing: A
Symposium. Rowman.
Chapman, Stephen R.
xChapman, Stephen R.
Crop Production: Principles & Practices. W H
Freeman.
Chapman, Suzanne E.
xChapman, Suzanne E.
ed. Early American Design Motifs. Dover.
Historic Floral & Animal Designs for
Embroiderers & Craftsmen. Dover.
Historic Floral & Animal Designs for
Embroiderers & Craftsmen. Peter Smith.
Chapman, Sydney.
xChapman, S.
Atmospheric Tides: Thermal & Gravitational.
Kluwer Boston.
Chapman, V. J. *see* Chapman, Valentine Jackson.
Chapman, Valentine Jackson.
xChapman, V. J.
Coastal Vegetation. Pergamon.
Chapman, Vera.
xChapman, Vera.
The Green Knight. Avon.
Chappel, Bernice M.
xChappel, Bernice M.
Listening & Learning: Practical Activities for
Developing Listening Skills. Pitman Learning.
Chappell, A. F. *see* Chappell, Arthur Fred.
Chappell, Arthur Fred.
xChappell, A. F.
The Enigma of Rabelais: An Essay in
Interpretation. Folcroft.
Chappell, Clovis G.
xChappell, Clovis G.
Chappell's Special Day Sermons. Baker Bk.
Faces About the Cross. Baker Bk.
Feminine Faces. Baker Bk.
Chappell, J. B. *see* Chappell, John Brian.
Chappell, Jeannette.
xChappell, Jeannette.
Destination Uncharted. Golden Quill.
Chappell, John Brian.
xChappell, J. B.
ATP. Carolina Biological.
Chappell, Wallace D.
xChappell, Wallace D.
All for Jesus!. Broadman.
Clovis Chappell: Preacher of the Word.
Broadman.
Chappell, Warren, 1904-
xChappell, Warren.
The Living Alphabet. U Pr of Va.
Chapple, Eliot D. *see* Chapple, Eliot Dismore.
Chapple, Eliot Dismore.
xChapple, Eliot D.
Principles of Anthropology. Krieger.
Chapple, Steve.
xChapple, Steve.

Don't Mind Dying: A Novel of Country Lust
& Urban Decay. Doubleday.
Char, Devron H.
xChar, Devron H.
Immunology of Uveitis & Ocular Tumors.
Grune.
Char, Rene, 1907-
xChar, Rene.
Leaves of Hypnos. SBD.
Charalambous, George.
xCharalambous, George.
ed. Analysis of Foods & Beverages: Headspace
Techniques. Acad Pr.
ed. Flavor of Foods & Beverages: Chemistry &
Technology. Acad Pr.
Charalambous, J.
xCharalambous, J.
Mass Spectrometry of Metal Compounds.
Butterworths.
Charbeneau, Gerald T.
xCharbeneau, Gerald T.
ed. Principles & Practice of Operative
Dentistry. Lea & Febiger.
Charbonneau, Harvey C.
xCharbonneau, Harvey C.
Industrial Quality Control. P-H.
Charcot, Jean M. *see* Charcot, Jean Martin.
Charcot, Jean Martin, 1825-1893
xCharcot, Jean M.
Clinical Lectures on Senile & Chronic Diseases.
Arno.
Chard, Chester S.
xChard, Chester S.
Northeast Asia in Prehistory. U of Wis Pr.
Chard, T.
xChard, T.
An Introduction to Radioimmunoassay &
Related Techniques. Elsevier.
Charell, Ralph.
xCharell, Ralph.
How I Turn Ordinary Complaints into
Thousands of Dollars: The Diary of a Tough
Customer. Stein & Day.
How to Get the Upper Hand. Avon.
How to Make Things Go Your Way. Watts.
Chari, M. V. *see* Chari, M. V. K.
Chari, M. V. K.
xChari, M. V.
ed. Finite Elements in Electrical & Magnetic
Field Problems. Wiley.
Charig, Alan. *see* Charig, Alan Jack.
Charig, Alan Jack.
xCharig, Alan.
A New Look at Dinosaurs. Mayflower Bks.
Charland, William A., 1937-
xCharland, William A.
Decide to Live. Westminster.
Charles, Allegra.
xCharles, Allegra.
How to Win at Ladies Doubles. Arco.
Charles, C. M.
xCharles, C. M.
Individualizing Instruction. Mosby.
The Special Student: Practical Help for the
Classroom Teacher. Mosby.
Charles, Donald.
xCharles, Donald.
illus. Calico Cat Looks Around. Childrens.
Calico Cat Meets Bookworm. Childrens.
illus. Calico Cat's Rainbow. Childrens.
illus. Count on Calico Cat. Childrens.
Fat Fat Calico Cat. Childrens.
The Jolly Pancake. Childrens.
illus. Letters from Calico Cat. Childrens.
illus. Shaggy Dog's Animal Alphabet.
Childrens.
illus. Shaggy Dog's Tall Tale. Childrens.
Charles, Edgar D.
xCharles, Edgar D.

ed. Social & Economic Impacts of Coronary
Artery Disease. Lexington Bks.
Charles, Elizabeth.
xCharles, Elizabeth.
How to Keep Your Pet Healthy. Macmillan.
Charles, Iona.
xCharles, Iona.
Grenencourt. Popular Lib.
Charles River Assoc. *see* Charles River Associates.
Charles River Associates.
xCharles River Assoc.
International Cartels: Policy Implications for
the United States. Praeger.
Charles, Robert.
xCharles, Robert.
The Hour of the Wolf. Pinnacle Bks.
Charles, Robert H. *see* Charles, Robert Henry.
Charles, Robert Henry, 1855-1931
xCharles, Robert H.
Religious Development Between the Old &
New Testaments. Folcroft.
Charles, Vera K. *see* Charles, Vera Katherine.
Charles, Vera Katherine.
xCharles, Vera K.
Introduction to Mushroom Hunting. Dover.
Introduction to Mushroom Hunting. Peter
Smith.
Charleston Free Library. *see* Charleston, South Carolina.
Free Library.
Charleston, South Carolina. Free Library.
xCharleston Free Library.
Index to Wills of Charleston County, South
Carolina 1671-1868. Genealog Pub.
Charlesworth, Arthur R.
xCharlesworth, Arthur R.
Paradise Found. Philos Lib.
Charlesworth, James C. *see* Charlesworth, James Clyde.
Charlesworth, James Clyde, 1900-
xCharlesworth, James C.
ed. Contemporary Political Analysis. Free Pr.
Governmental Administration. Greenwood.
Charlesworth, James H.
xCharlesworth, James H.
The Odes of Solomon. Scholars Pr Ca.
Charlesworth, Max. *see* Charlesworth, Maxwell John.
Charlesworth, Maxwell John.
xCharlesworth, Max.
The Existentialists & Jean-Paul Sartre. St
Martin.
Charlier, Roger H. *see* Charlier, Roger Henri.
Charlier, Roger Henri.
xCharlier, Roger H.
Marine Science & Technology: An Introduction
to Oceanography. U Pr of Amer.
Charlip, Remy.
xCharlip, Remy.
illus. Fortunately. Schol Bk Serv.
illus. Fortunately. Schol Bk Serv.
Hooray for Me!. Schol Bk Serv.
Thirteen. Schol Bk Serv.
Where Is Everybody?. A-W.
Charlot, G. *see* Charlot, Gaston.
Charlot, Gaston.
xCharlot, G.
Chemical Reactions in Solvents & Melts.
Pergamon.
Charlot, Jean, 1898-
xCharlot, Jean.
Art from the Mayans to Disney. Arno.
An Artist on Art: Collected Essays of Jean
Charlot. U Pr of Hawaii.
Charlton, Elizabeth.
xCharlton, Elizabeth.
Jeremy & the Ghost. Dandelion Pr.
Things I See. Dandelion Pr.

Charlton, Michael.
xCharlton, Michael.
Many Reasons Why: The American
Involvement in Vietnam. Hill & Wang.
Charlton, Sue E. *see* Charlton, Sue Ellen M.
Charlton, Sue Ellen M.
xCharlton, Sue E.
The French Left & European Integration. U of
Denver Intl.
Charm, Stanley E.
xCharm, Stanley E.
Fundamentals of Food Engineering. AVI.
Charmatz, Bill.
xCharmatz, Bill.
illus. Cat's Whiskers. Macmillan.
illus. Little Duster. Macmillan.
illus. The Troy St. Bus. Macmillan.
Charmine, Susan E.
xCharmine, Susan E.
The Complete Raw Juice Therapy. Baronet.
Charnay, Desire, 1828-1915
xCharnay, Desire.
The Ancient Cities of the New World: Being
Voyages & Explorations in Mexico & Central
America from 1857 to 1882. AMS Pr.
Charnes, A. *see* Charnes, Abraham.
Charnes, Abraham.
xCharnes, A.
ed. Management Science Approaches to
Manpower Planning & Organizational
Design. Elsevier.
Charney, George.
xCharney, George.
A Long Journey. Times Bks.
Charney, Len.
xCharney, Len.
Build a Yurt: The Low-Cost Mongolian Round
House. Macmillan.
Build a Yurt: The Low Cost Mongolian Round
House. Macmillan.
Charney, Maurice.
xCharney, Maurice.
Comedy High & Low: An Introduction to the
Experience of Comedy. Oxford U Pr.
How to Read Shakespeare. McGraw.
Charney, Ted.
xCharney, Ted.
Student Chemist Explores Organic Compounds.
Rosen Pr.
Charniak, Eugene.
xCharniak, Eugene.
ed. Artificial Intelligence Programming. L
Erlbaum Assocs.
Charnley, J. *see* Charnley, John.
Charnley, John.
xCharnley, J.
Low Friction Arthroplasty of the Hip: Theory
& Practice. Springer-Verlag.
xCharnley, John.
Closed Treatment of Common Fractures.
Churchill.
Charnley, Mitchell V. *see* Charnley, Mitchell Vaughn.
Charnley, Mitchell Vaughn.
xCharnley, Mitchell V.
Reporting. HR&W.
Charnock, Richard S. *see* Charnock, Richard Stephen.
Charnock, Richard Stephen, 1820-1904 or 5
xCharnock, Richard S.
Ludus Patronymicus: Or, the Etymology of
Curious Surnames. Gale.
Charny, Israel W.
xCharny, Israel W.
Strategies Against Violence: Design for
Nonviolent Change. Westview.
Charon, J. *see* Charon, Joel M.
Charon, Joel M., 1939-
xCharon, J.

Symbolic Interactionism: An Introduction, an
Interpretation, an Integration. P-H.
xCharon, Joel M.
The Meaning of Sociology. Alfred Pub.
ed. The Meaning of Sociology: A Reader.
Alfred Pub.

Charosh, Mannis.
xCharosh, Mannis.
Mathematical Games for One or Two. T Y
Crowell.
Straight Lines, Parallel Lines, Perpendicular
Lines. T Y Crowell.

Charques, R. D. *see* Charques, Richard Denis.
Charques, Richard. *see* Charques, Richard Denis.
Charques, Richard Denis, 1899-
xCharques, R. D.
Contemporary Literature & Social Revolution.
Haskell.
xCharques, Richard.
The Twilight of Imperial Russia. Oxford U Pr.

Charriere, Henri, 1906-
xCharriere, Henri.
Papillon. Morrow.
Papillon. PB.

Charron, Jean D. *see* Charron, Jean Daniel.
Charron, Jean Daniel.
xCharron, Jean D.
The Wisdom of Pierre Charron: An Original &
Orthodox Code of Morality. Greenwood.

Charteris, Evan. *see* Charteris, Evan Edward.
Charteris, Evan Edward.
xCharteris, Evan.
The Life & Letters of Sir Edmund Gosse.
Haskell.
The Life & Letters of Sir Edmund Gosse. R
West.

Charteris, Leslie, 1907-
xCharteris, Leslie.
Follow the Saint. Am Repr Rivercity Pr.
Holy Terror. Arno.
The Saint & the Templar Treasure. Doubleday.

Charters, A. *see* Charters, Alexander N.
Charters, Alexander N.
xCharters, A.
Hill & the Valley: The Story of University
College at Syracuse University Through 1964.
Syracuse U Cont Ed.
xCharters, Alexander N.
Toward the Educative Society. Syracuse U
Cont Ed.

Charters, Ann.
xCharters, Ann.
I Love: The Story of Vladimir Mayakovsky &
Lili Brik. FS&G.

Charters, Margaret.
xCharters, Margaret.
Consumer Education Programming in
Continuing Education. Syracuse U Cont Ed.

Charters, Samuel.
xCharters, Samuel.
From a Swedish Notebook. SBD.

Charters, Samuel. *see* Charters, Samuel Barclay.
Charters, Samuel B. *see* Charters, Samuel Barclay.
Charters, Samuel Barclay.
xCharters, Samuel.
The Roots of the Blues: An African Search.
Merrimack Bk Serv.
Sweet As the Showers of Rain. Music Sales.
xCharters, Samuel B.
The Country Blues. Da Capo.

Charters, W. W. *see* Charters, Werrett Wallace.
Charters, Werrett Wallace, 1875-1952
xCharters, W. W.
Curriculum Construction. Arno.

Chartham, Robert.
xChartham, Robert.
Advice to Women. NAL.

Chartier, Armand B.
xChartier, Armand B.

Barbey D'Aurevilly. Twayne.
Chartrand, Gary.
xChartrand, Gary.
Graphs As Mathematical Models. Prindle.

Chartrand, Robert L. *see* Chartrand, Robert Lee.
Chartrand, Robert Lee.
xChartrand, Robert L.
Computers & Political Campaigning. Chartrand.
ed. Computers in the Service of Society.
Pergamon.
Information Technology Serving Society.
Pergamon.

Charvat, William, 1905-
xCharvat, William.
Literary Publishing in America, 1790-1850. U
of Pa Pr.
Origins of American Critical Thought,
1810-1835. A S Barnes.
Origins of American Critical Thought,
1810-1835. Russell.
Profession of Authorship in America,
1800-1870: The Papers of William Charvat.
Ohio St U Pr.

Charyn, Jerome.
xCharyn, Jerome.
The Catfish Man: A Conjured Life. Arbor Hse.
The Education of Patrick Silver. Arbor Hse.
The Education of Patrick Silver. Avon.
ed. Troubled Vision: An Anthology of
Contemporary Short Novels & Passages.
Macmillan.

Chase, Alice E. *see* Chase, Alice Elizabeth.
Chase, Alice Elizabeth.
xChase, Alice E.
Looking at Art. T Y Crowell.

Chase, Allan, 1913-
xChase, Allan.
The Legacy of Malthus: The Social Costs of
the New Scientific Racism. U of Ill Pr.
xChase, Allen.
The Legacy of Malthus: The Social Costs of
the New Scientific Racism. Knopf.

Chase, Allen. *see* Chase, Allan.
Chase, Catherine.
xChase, Catherine.
An Alphabet Book. Dandelion Pr.
Baby Mouse Learns His ABC's. Dandelion Pr.
Duncan McTavish in Switzerland. Dandelion
Pr.
Feet. Dandelion Pr.
Hot & Cold. Dandelion Pr.
The Miracles at Cana. Dandelion Pr.
The Mouse in My House. Dandelion Pr.
My Balloon. Dandelion Pr.
Noah's Ark. Dandelion Pr.
See the Fly Fly. Dandelion Pr.

Chase, Clinton I.
xChase, Clinton I.
Measurement for Educational Evaluation. A-W.

Chase, Cochrane.
xChase, Cochrane.
Marketing Problem Solver. Chilton.

Chase, Deborah.
xChase, Deborah.
The Medically-Based No-Nonsense Beauty
Book. Knopf.
The Medically Based No-Nonsense Beauty
Book. PB.

Chase, Donald.
xChase, Donald.
Filmmaking: The Collaborative Art. Little.

Chase, Edward T. *see* Chase, Edward Tinsley.
Chase, Edward Tinsley.
xChase, Edward T.
Covering the Court. Doubleday.

Chase, Francis S. *see* Chase, Francis Seabury.
Chase, Francis Seabury, 1890-
xChase, Francis S.

Education Faces New Demands. U of
Pittsburgh Pr.

Chase, George H. *see* Chase, George Henry.
Chase, George Henry.
xChase, George H.
A History of Sculpture. Greenwood.

Chase, Gilbert, 1906-
xChase, Gilbert.
ed. American Composer Speaks: A Historical
Anthology, 1770-1965. La State U Pr.

Chase, Glen.
xChase, Glen.
Greek Fire. Nordon Pubns.
In a Bind. Nordon Pubns.
Lights! Action! Murder!. Nordon Pubns.
Where the Action Is. Nordon Pubns.

Chase, Harold W. *see* Chase, Harold William.
Chase, Harold William.
xChase, Harold W.
American Government in Comparative
Perspective. New Viewpoints.

Chase, Heman.
xChase, Heman.
More Than Land: Stories of New England
Country Life & Surveying. Bauhan.

Chase, Ilka, 1905-
xChase, Ilka.
Dear Intruder. PB.

Chase, John, 1953-
xChase, John.
The Sidewalk Companion to Santa Cruz
Architecture. Western Tanager.

Chase, John. *see* Chase, John Churchill.
Chase, John Churchill.
xChase, John.
Frenchmen, Desire, Good Children & Other
Streets of New Orleans. Crager.

Chase, Larry.
xChase, Larry.
The Other Side of the Report Card: A
How-to-Do-It Program in Affective
Education. Goodyear.

Chase, Lewis.
xChase, Lewis.
A Sense of Values. Philos Lib.

Chase, Lewis N. *see* Chase, Lewis Nathaniel.
Chase, Lewis Nathaniel, 1873-1937
xChase, Lewis N.
English Heroic Play: A Critical Description of
the Rhymed Tragedy of the Restoration.
Russell.

Chase, Lucien B. *see* Chase, Lucien Bonaparte.
Chase, Lucien Bonaparte, 1817-1864
xChase, Lucien B.
English Serfdom & American Slavery: Or,
Ourselves As Others See Us. Arno.

Chase Manhattan Bank. *see* Chase Manhattan Bank,
New York.
Chase Manhattan Bank, New York.
xChase Manhattan Bank.
The Cashier. McGraw.

Chase, Mary E. *see* Chase, Mary Ellen.
Chase, Mary Ellen, 1887-
xChase, Mary E.
Journey to Boston. Norton.
Mary Peters. Macmillan.
Silas Crockett. Macmillan.

Chase, Mildred L.
xChase, Mildred L.
Housekeeping Management for Health Care
Facilities. Cath Health.

Chase, Naomi F. *see* Chase, Naomi Feigelson.
Chase, Naomi Feigelson.
xChase, Naomi F.
A Child Is Being Beaten: Violence Against
Children, an American Tragedy. McGraw.

Chase, Pattie.
xChase, Pattie.

The Contemporary Quilt: New American
Quilts & Fabric Art. Dutton.
Chase, Richard. see Chase, Richard Volney.
Chase, Richard B.
xChase, Richard B.
Production & Operations Management: A Life
Cycle Approach. Irwin.
Chase, Richard V. see Chase, Richard Volney.
Chase, Richard Volney, 1914-1962
xChase, Richard.
The American Novel & Its Tradition. Gordian.
The American Novel & Its Tradition. Johns
Hopkins.
ed. Melville: A Collection of Critical Essays.
P-H.
xChase, Richard V.
Quest for Myth. Greenwood.
Chase, Robert A. see Chase, Robert Arthur.
Chase, Robert Arthur, 1928-
xChase, Robert A.
Atlas of Hand Surgery. Saunders.
Chase, Salmon P. see Chase, Salmon Portland.
Chase, Salmon Portland.
xChase, Salmon P.
Diary & Correspondence of Salmon P. Chase.
Da Capo.
Chase, Samuel. see Chase, Samuel B.
Chase, Samuel B.
xChase, Samuel.
Asset Prices in Economic Analysis. U of Cal
Pr.
Chase, Stuart, 1888-
xChase, Stuart.
American Credos. Greenwood.
The Economy of Abundance. Arno.
Economy of Abundance. Kennikat.
For This We Fought: Guide Lines to America's
Future As Reported to the Twentieth
Century Fund. Greenwood.
Goals for America: A Budget of Our Needs &
Resources: Guide Lines to America's Future
As Reported to the Twentieth Century Fund.
Greenwood.
Government in Business. Greenwood.
Power of Words. HarBraceJ.
The Proper Study of Mankind. Greenwood.
Tyranny of Words. HarBraceJ.
Chase, Thomas N. see Chase, Thomas Newell.
Chase, Thomas Newell.
xChase, Thomas N.
ed. Huntington's Disease. Raven.
Chase, W. Linwood. see Chase, Willard Linwood.
Chase, Willard Linwood.
xChase, W. Linwood.
A Guide for the Elementary Social Studies
Teacher. Allyn.
Chase-Riboud, Barbara.
xChase-Riboud, Barbara.
Sally Hemings. Avon.
Sally Hemings. Viking Pr.
Chasen, Sylvan H., 1926-
xChasen, Sylvan H.
Geometric Principles & Procedures for
Computer Graphic Applications. P-H.
Chasin, Helen.
xChasin, Helen.
Casting Stones. Little.
Chasis, David A., 1938-
xChasis, David A.
Plastic Piping Systems. Indus Pr.
Chassan, J. B.
xChassan, J. B.
Research Design in Clinical Psychology &
Psychiatry. Halsted Pr.
Chasseguet-Smirgel, J. see Chasseguet-Smirgel, Janine.
Chasseguet-Smirgel, Janine, 1928-
xChasseguet-Smirgel, J.

Female Sexuality: New Psychoanalytic Views.
U of Mich Pr.
Chastain, Kenneth.
xChastain, Kenneth.
Spanish Grammar in Review: Patterns for
Communication. Rand.
Chastain, Madye L. see Chastain, Madye Lee.
Chastain, Madye Lee.
xChastain, Madye L.
illus. Bright Days. HarBraceJ.
Chastain, Thomas.
xChastain, Thomas.
High Voltage. Doubleday.
Chasteen, Joseph E., 1943-
xChasteen, Joseph E.
Four-Handed Dentistry in Clinical Practice.
Mosby.
Chasteen, Joseph E. see Chasteen, Joseph E.
Chasteen, Joseph E., 1943-
xChasteen, Joseph E.
Essentials of Clinical Dental Assisting. Mosby.
Chatagnier, Louis J.
xChatagnier, Louis J.
Images de la France contemporaine. Intl Film.
Chateaubriand, Francois Auguste Rene.
xChateaubriand, Francois R.
The Natchez: An Indian Tale. Fertig.
xChateaubriand, Francois-Rene de.
Atala & Rene. U of Cal Pr.
Chateaubriand, Francois R. see Chateaubriand, Francois
Auguste Rene.
Chateaubriand, Francois-Rene de. see Chateaubriand,
Francois Auguste Rene.
Chatelain, Emile L. see Chatelain, Emile Louis Marie.
Chatelain, Emile Louis Marie, 1851-1933
xChatelain, Emile L.
Introduction a la lecture des notes tironiennes.
B Franklin.
Chatelain, Maurice.
xChatelain, Maurice.
Our Ancestors Came from Outer Space. Dell.
Our Ancestors Came from Outer Space.
Doubleday.
Chatelet, Albert.
xChatelet, Albert.
Impressionist Painting. McGraw.
Chatfield, Charles, 1934-
xChatfield, Charles.
ed. Peace Movements in America. Schocken.
Chatfield, Christopher.
xChatfield, Christopher.
Statistics for Technology: A Course in Applied
Statistics. Methuen Inc.
Chatfield, Hale.
xChatfield, Hale.
At Home. Ashland Poetry.
Chatfield, Mark.
xChatfield, Mark.
Churches the Victorians Forgot. Eastview.
Chatfield, Michael.
xChatfield, Michael.
ed. The English View of Accountants Duties &
Responsibilities: 1881-1902. Arno.
A History of Accounting Thought. Krieger.
Chatham, Russell.
xChatham, Russell.
Striped Bass on the Fly: A Guide to California
Waters. Cal Living Bks.
Chatman, Seymour. see Chatman, Seymour Benjamin.
Chatman, Seymour B. see Chatman, Seymour Benjamin.
Chatman, Seymour Benjamin, 1928-
xChatman, Seymour.
Story & Discourse: Narrative Structure in
Fiction & Film. Cornell U Pr.
Theory of Meter. Mouton.
xChatman, Seymour B.
Story & Discourse: Narrative Structure in
Fiction & Film. Cornell U Pr.
Chatt, Orville K., 1924-
xChatt, Orville K.

Design Is Where You Find It. Iowa St U Pr.
Chatten, Elizabeth N.
xChatten, Elizabeth N.
Samuel Foote. Twayne.
Chattergy, R.
xChattergy, Rahul.
Top-Down Modular Programming in Fortran
with Watfiv. Winthrop.
Chattergy, Rahul. see Chattergy, R.
Chatterjee, Biswanath.
xChatterjee, Biswanath.
Propagation of Radio Waves. Asia.
Pulse Circuits. Asia.
Chatterjee, S. N. see Chatterjee, Satya N.
Chatterjee, Samprit.
xChatterjee, Samprit.
Regression Analysis by Example. Wiley.
Chatterjee, Satya N.
xChatterjee, S. N.
Manual of Renal Transplantation.
Springer-Verlag.
Chatterton, Betty.
xChatterton, Betty J.
Grandma's Down-Home Recipes. Chatterton
Pr.
Chatterton, Betty J. see Chatterton, Betty.
Chatterton, E. Keble. see Chatterton, Edward Keble.
Chatterton, Edward Keble, 1878-1944
xChatterton, E. Keble.
Q-Ships & Their Story. Arno.
Chatterton, Pauline.
xChatterton, Pauline.
Coordinated Crafts for the Home. Marek.
Gobelin Stitch Embroidery. Scribner.
Patchwork & Applique. Dial.
Chatterton, Thomas.
xChatterton, Thomas.
Works of Thomas Chatterton. AMS Pr.
Chatterton, Wayne.
xChatterton, Wayne.
Alexander Woollcott. Twayne.
Chattopadhyaya, D. P. see Chattopadhyaya, Debiprasad.
Chattopadhyaya, Debiprasad.
xChattopadhyaya, D. P.
Individuals & Worlds: Essays in
Anthropological Rationalism. Oxford U Pr.
Chattopadhyaya, H. see Chattopadhyaya, Harindranath.
Chattopadhyaya, Harindranath, 1898-
xChattopadhyaya, H.
Masks & Farewells. Asia.
Chaturvedi, M. S.
xChaturvedi, M. S.
History of the Indian Air Force. Advent Bk.
Chatwin, Bruce. see Chatwin, C. Bruce.
Chatwin, C. Bruce.
xChatwin, Bruce.
In Patagonia. Summit Bks.
Chaucer, Geoffrey.
xChaucer, Geoffrey.

The Canterbury Tales. Bobbs.
Canterbury Tales. Dutton.
Canterbury Tales. Johnson Repr.
Canterbury Tales. Oxford U Pr.
Canterbury Tales. Random.
Canterbury Tales. Doubleday.
Canterbury Tales. Penguin.
The Canterbury Tales: A Facsimile &
   Transcription of the Hengwrt Manuscript
   with Variants from the Ellesmere Manuscript.
   U of Okla Pr.
Canterbury Tales: A Selection. NAL.
Chanticleer & the Fox. T Y Crowell.
The Complete Poetry & Prose of Geoffrey
   Chaucer. HR&W.
General Prologue to the Canterbury Tales.
   Cambridge U Pr.
Troilus & Criseyde. Dutton.
Troilus & Criseyde. Penguin.
Works of Geoffrey Chaucer. Arno.
Works of Geoffrey Chaucer. HM.

Chauchard, Paul, 1912-
   xChauchard, Paul.
   Our Need of Love. Kenedy.

Chaudhry, M. Hanif.
   xChaudhry, M. Hanif.
   Applied Hydraulic Transients. Van Nos
      Reinhold.

Chaudhuri, Haridas.
   xChaudhuri, Haridas.
   Evolution of Integral Consciousness. Theos Pub
      Hse.
   Mastering the Problems of Living. Theos Pub
      Hse.

Chaudhuri, Joyotpaul.
   xChaudhuri, Joyotpaul.
   ed. The Non-Lockean Roots of American
      Democratic Thought. U of Ariz Pr.

Chaudhuri, K. N.
   xChaudhuri, K. N.
   ed. Economy & Society: Essays in Indian
      Economic & Social History. Oxford U Pr.
   English East India Company: Study of the
      Early Joint-Stock Company, 1600-1640.
      Biblio Dist.
   English East India Company: The Study of an
      Early Jointstock Company 1600-1640. Kelley.

Chaudhuri, Nirad C, 1897-
   xChaudhuri, Nirad C.
   The Autobiography of an Unknown Indian. U
      of Cal Pr.

Chaudhuri, Pramit.
   xChaudhuri, Pramit.
   The Indian Economy: Poverty & Development.
      St Martin.

Chauhan, Shivadan Singh.
   xChauhan, Shivdan Singh.
   Nationalities Question in USA & USSR: A
      Comparative Study. Verry.
Chauhan, Shivdan Singh. see Chauhan, Shivadan Singh.

Chauncey, George A., 1927-
   xChauncey, George A.
   Decisions! Decisions!. John Knox.
Chauncey, Marlin R. see Chauncey, Marlin Ray.

Chauncey, Marlin Ray, 1891-
   xChauncey, Marlin R.
   The Educational & Occupational Preferences of
      College Seniors: Their Significance for
      College Achievement. AMS Pr.
Chaunu, P. see Chaunu, Pierre.

Chaunu, Pierre.
   xChaunu, P.
   European Expansion in the Later Middle Ages.
      Elsevier.

Chavarria, Jesus, 1935-
   xChavarria, Jesus.
   Jose Carlos Mariategui & the Rise of Modern
      Peru, 1890-1930. U of NM Pr.
Chavel, I. see Chavel, Isaac.

Chavel, Isaac.
   xChavel, I.
   Riemannian Symmetric Spaces of Rank One.
      Dekker.

Chaves, Jonathan, 1943-
   xChaves, Jonathan.
   Mei Yao-Ch'en & the Development of Early
      Sung Poetry. Columbia U Pr.

Chavez, Angelico.
   xChavez, Fray A.
   Song of Francis. Northland.

Chavez, Carlos.
   xChavez, Carlos.
   Toward a New Music: Music & Electricity. Da
      Capo.
Chavez, Fray A. see Chavez, Angelico.

Chavin, Walter.
   xChavin, Walter.
   Responses of Fish to Environmental Changes.
      C C Thomas.

Chawla, Hector B.
   xChawla, Hector B.
   Simple Eye Diagnosis. Churchill.

Chawla, Sudershan.
   xChawla, Sudershan.
   ed. Changing Patterns of Security & Stability in
      Asia. Praeger.
   ed. Southeast Asia Under the New Balance of
      Power. Praeger.

Chayes, Abram, 1922-
   xChayes, Abram.
   The Cuban Missile Crisis. Oxford U Pr.

Chayes, Felix, 1916-
   xChayes, Felix.
   Ratio Correlation: A Manual for Students of
      Petrology & Geochemistry. U of Chicago Pr.
Chaytor, H. J. see Chaytor, Henry John.
Chaytor, Henry J. see Chaytor, Henry John.

Chaytor, Henry John, 1871-1954
   xChaytor, H. J.
   From Script to Print: An Introduction to
      Medieval Vernacular Literature. British Am
      Bks.
   The Troubadours. R West.
   xChaytor, Henry J.
   History of Aragon & Catalonia. AMS Pr.
   The Troubadours of Dante: Being Selections
      from the Works of the Provencal Poets
      Quoted by Dante, with Introduction, Notes,
      Concise Grammar & Glossary. AMS Pr.

Chazan, Barry I.
   xChazan, Barry I.
   ed. Moral Education. Tchrs Coll.

Chazan, Robert.
   xChazan, Robert.
   Church, State & Jew in the Middle Ages.
      Behrman.
   Medieval Jewry in Northern France: A
      Political & Social History. Johns Hopkins.
   ed. Modern Jewish History: A Source Reader.
      Schocken.
Chazarain, J. see Chazarain, Jacques.

Chazarain, Jacques, 1942-
   xChazarain, J.
   Fourier Integral Operators & Partial
      Differential Equations. Springer-Verlag.

Cheales, Alan B.
   xCheales, Alan B.
   Proverbial Folk-Lore. Arden Lib.
   Proverbial Folk-Lore. Folcroft.

Cheape, Charles W., 1945-
   xCheape, Charles W.
   Moving the Masses: Urban Public Transit in
      New York, Boston, & Philadelphia, 1880 to
      1912. Harvard U Pr.
Cheatham, K. Follis. see Cheatham, Karyn Follis.

Cheatham, Karyn Follis, 1943-
   xCheatham, K. Follis.

Life on a Cool Plastic Ice Floe. Westminster.

Cheatham, Lillian.
   xCheatham, Lillian.
   Portrait of Emma. Popular Lib.
Cheek. see Cheek, Carl.

Cheek, Carl.
   xCheek.
   Drawing Hands. G&D.
   Quick Sketching. G&D.

Cheek, David B.
   xCheek, David B.
   Clinical Hypnotherapy. Grune.

Cheek, Donald B.
   xCheek, Donald B.
   ed. Fetal & Postnatal Cellular Growth:
      Hormones & Nutrition. Wiley.
   ed. Human Growth: Body Composition, Cell
      Growth, Energy & Intelligence. Lea &
      Febiger.

Cheek, Donald K.
   xCheek, Donald K.
   Assertive Black-Puzzled White. Impact Pubs
      Cal.
Cheek, Martha C. see Cheek, Martha Collins.

Cheek, Martha Collins.
   xCheek, Martha C.
   Diagnostic & Prescriptive Reading Instruction:
      A Guide for Classroom Teachers. Wm C
      Brown.
Cheek, N. H. see Cheek, Neil H.

Cheek, Neil H.
   xCheek, N. H.
   Leisure & Recreation Places. Ann Arbor
      Science.

Cheeks, James.
   xCheeks, James E.
   How to Compensate Executives. Dow
      Jones-Irwin.
Cheeks, James E. see Cheeks, James.

Cheesman, Paul R.
   xCheesman, Paul R.
   Great Leaders of the Book of Mormon.
      Promised Land.
   The World of the Book of Mormon. Deseret
      Bk.

Cheetham, Juliet.
   xCheetham, Juliet.
   Social Work with Immigrants. Routledge &
      Kegan.
Cheever, George B. see Cheever, George Barrell.

Cheever, George Barrell, 1807-1890
   xCheever, George B.
   God Against Slavery. Arno.

Cheever, John.
   xCheever, John.
   Falconer. Ballantine.
   Falconer. G K Hall.
   Falconer. Knopf.
   Some People, Places, & Things That Will Not
      Appear in My Next Novel. Arno.
   The Stories of John Cheever. Ballantine.
   The Stories of John Cheever. Knopf.
   World of Apples. Knopf.
   World of Apples. Warner Bks.

Cheever, Susan.
   xCheever, Susan.
   Looking for Work. S&S.

Cheffers, John.
   xCheffers, John T.
   Introduction to Physical Education: Concepts
      of Human Movement. P-H.
Cheffers, John T. see Cheffers, John.

Chek-Chart.
   xChek-Chart.
   Tune-up Service. Bobbs.

Cheke, Marcus, Sir.
   xCheke, Marcus.

The Coed Killer. Walker & Co.
Meanwhile Farm. Les Femmes Pub.
Cheney, Mary A. *see* Cheney, Mary A. (Bushnell).
Cheney, Mary A. (Bushnell).
xCheney, Mary A.
Life & Letters of Horace Bushnell. Arno.
Cheney, Roberta. *see* Cheney, Roberta Carkeek.
Cheney, Roberta C. *see* Cheney, Roberta Carkeek.
Cheney, Roberta Carkeek.
xCheney, Roberta.
Music, Saddles & Flapjacks: Dudes at the Oto Ranch. Mountain Pr.
xCheney, Roberta C.
The Big Missouri Winter Count. Naturegraph.
Cheney, Sheldon, 1886-
xCheney, Sheldon.
Stage Decoration. Arno.
Cheney, Theodore. *see* Cheney, Theodore A.
Cheney, Theodore A.
xCheney, Theodore.
Camping by Backpack & Canoe. T Y Crowell.
Cheney, Thomas. *see* Cheney, Thomas E.
Cheney, Thomas E.
xCheney, Thomas.
ed. Lore of Faith & Folly. U of Utah Pr.
Cheney, Winifred G. *see* Cheney, Winifred Green.
Cheney, Winifred Green.
xCheney, Winifred G.
The Southern Hospitality Cookbook. Oxmoor Hse.
Chenfeld, Mimi B. *see* Chenfeld, Mimi Brodsky.
Chenfeld, Mimi Brodsky.
xChenfeld, Mimi B.
Teaching Language Arts Creatively. HarBraceJ.
Cheng, Bin, 1921-
xCheng, Bin.
The Law of International Air Transport. Oceana.
Cheng, Charles W.
xCheng, Charles W.
Altering Collective Bargaining: Citizen Participation in Educational Decision Making. Praeger.
Cheng, Chin-Chuan.
xCheng, Chin-Chuan.
A Synchronic Phonology of Mandarin Chinese. Mouton.
Cheng, Hou-Tien.
xCheng, Hou-Tien.
The Chinese New Year. HR&W.
Cheng, J. C. *see* Cheng, James Chester.
Cheng, James Chester, 1926-
xCheng, J. C.
Chinese Sources for the Taiping Rebellion, 1850-1864. Paragon.
Cheng, Julia C. *see* Cheng, Julia Chih.
Cheng, Julia Chih, 1931-
xCheng, Julia C.
Chinese Home Cooking. Kodansha.
xCheng, Julia Chih.
Chinese Home Cooking. Kodansha.
Cheng, P. C. *see* Cheng, Philip C.
Cheng, Peter, 1930-
xCheng, Peter P.
A Chronology of the People's Republic of China from October 1, 1949. Littlefield.
Cheng, Peter P. *see* Cheng, Peter.
Cheng, Philip C., 1925-
xCheng, P. C.
Steamship Accounting. Cornell Maritime.
xCheng, Phillip C.
Financial Management in the Shipping Industry. Cornell Maritime.
Cheng, Phillip C. *see* Cheng, Philip C.
Cheng, T. C. *see* Cheng, Thomas Clement.
Cheng, Thomas C. *see* Cheng, Thomas Clement.
Cheng, Thomas Clement.
xCheng, T. C.

ed. Aspects of the Biology of Symbiosis. Univ Park.
xCheng, Thomas C.
General Parasitology. Acad Pr.
Cheng, Ying-Wan.
xCheng, Ying-Wan.
Postal Communication in China & Its Modernization, 1860-1896. Harvard U Pr.
Chenier, Blanche.
xChenier, Blanche.
Regency Row. Fawcett.
Summer Masquerade. Fawcett.
Chennakesavan, Sarasvati, 1918-
xChennakesavan, Sarasvati.
Concepts of Indian Philosophy. South Asia Bks.
xChennakesavan, Saraswati.
A Critical Study of Hinduism. Asia.
Chennakesavan, Saraswati. *see* Chennakesavan, Sarasvati.
Chenoweth, Clyde G.
xChenoweth, Clyde Garfield.
Our Tragic Inflation Orgy & What to Do About It: An Introduction to the Fascinating Economics of Tomorrow. Exposition.
Chenoweth, Clyde Garfield. *see* Chenoweth, Clyde G.
Chenoweth, Don W.
xChenoweth, Don W.
Soviet Civil Procedure: History & Analysis. Am Philos.
Chenoweth, Patricia.
xChenoweth, Patricia.
How to Raise & Train a Lhasa Apso. TFH Pubns.
Chenu, M. D. *see* Chenu, Marie Dominique.
Chenu, Marie Dominique, 1895-
xChenu, M. D.
Nature, Man & Society in the Twelfth Century: Essays on New Theological Perspectives in the Latin West. U of Chicago Pr.
Cherel, Albert, 1880-
xCherel, Albert O.
Spanish Without Toil. French & Eur.
Cherel, Albert O. *see* Cherel, Albert.
Cheremisinoff, Nicholas P.
xCheremisinoff, Nicholas P.
ed. Fiberglass-Reinforced Plastics Deskbook. Ann Arbor Science.
Fundamentals of Wind Energy. Ann Arbor Science.
Gasohol for Energy Production. Ann Arbor Science.
Industrial & Hazardous Wastes Impoundment. Ann Arbor Science.
Wood for Energy Production. Ann Arbor Science.
Cheremisinoff, P. H. *see* Cheremisinoff, Paul N.
Cheremisinoff, Paul. *see* Cheremisinoff, Paul N.
Cheremisinoff, Paul N.
xCheremisinoff, P. H.
Woodwastes Utilization & Disposal. Technomic.
xCheremisinoff, Paul.
ed. Air Pollution Control & Design Handbook. Dekker.
xCheremisinoff, Paul N.

ed. Air Pollution Control & Design Handbook. Dekker.
ed. Carbon Adsorption Handbook. Ann Arbor Science.
Environmental Assessment & Impact Statement Handbook. Ann Arbor Science.
Geothermal Energy Technology Assessment. Technomic.
Industrial Noise Control Handbook. Ann Arbor Science.
Pollution Engineering Practice Handbook. Ann Arbor Science.
Principles & Applications of Solar Energy. Ann Arbor Science.
Cherepov, George, 1909-
xCherepov, George.
Discovering Oil Painting. Watson-Guptill.
Cherescavich, Gertrude D.
xCherescavich, Gertrude D.
A Textbook for Nursing Assistants. Mosby.
Cherington, Paul T. *see* Cherington, Paul Terry.
Cherington, Paul Terry, 1876-
xCherington, Paul T.
Advertising As a Business Force: A Compilation of Experience Records. Arno.
Cherkas, Selma.
xCherkas, Selma.
Dining with Celebrities. C E Tuttle.
Cherkin, Arthur.
xCherkin, Arthur.
ed. Physiology & Cell Biology of Aging. Raven.
Chermet, J.
xChermet, J.
Venography of the Inferior Vena Cava & Its Branches. Springer-Verlag.
Chern, S. S.
xChern, S. S.
ed. Studies in Global Geometry & Analysis. Math Assn.
Chern, S. S. *see* Chern, Shiing-Shen.
Chern, Shiing-Shen, 1911-
xChern, S. S.
Selected Papers. Springer-Verlag.
Chernaik, Judith.
xChernaik, Judith.
The Daughter: A Novel Based on the Life of Eleanor Marx. Har-Row.
Chernenko, Konstantin U. *see* Chernenko, Konstantin Ustinovich.
Chernenko, Konstantin Ustinovich.
xChernenko, Konstantin U.
Soviet Democracy: Principles & Practice. Vantage.
Chernetsov, V. N. *see* Chernetsov, Valerii Nikolaevich.
Chernetsov, Valerii Nikolaevich.
xChernetsov, V. N.
Prehistory of Western Siberia. McGill-Queens U Pr.
Chernev, Irving, 1900-
xChernev, Irving.
Chessboard Magic!: A Collection of 160 Brilliant Chess Endings. Dover.
Combinations: The Heart of Chess. Dover.
Logical Chess: Move by Move. S&S.
Wonders & Curiosities of Chess. Dover.
Cherniack, Reuben M.
xCherniack, Reuben M.
Pulmonary Function Testing. Saunders.
xCherniack, Rueben M.
Respiration in Health & Disease. Saunders.
Cherniack, Rueben M. *see* Cherniack, Reuben M.
Cherniak, Laurence.
xCherniak, Laurence.
The Great Books of Hashish. And-or Pr.
Cherniavsky, Michael.
xCherniavsky, Michael.

ed. Social Textures of Western Civilization:
  The Lower Depths. Wiley.
Chernik, Vladimir P., 1930-
  xChernik, Vladimir P.
    The Consumer's Guide to Insurance Buying.
      Sherbourne.
Cherniss, Harold. *see* Cherniss, Harold Fredrik.
Cherniss, Harold F. *see* Cherniss, Harold Fredrik.
Cherniss, Harold Fredrik, 1904-
  xCherniss, Harold.
    Aristotle's Criticism of Presocratic Philosophy.
      Octagon.
  xCherniss, Harold F.
    Aristotle's Criticism of Plato & the Academy.
      Russell.
    Platonism of Gregory of Nyssa. B Franklin.
Chernoff, Goldie T. *see* Chernoff, Goldie Taub.
Chernoff, Goldie Taub.
  xChernoff, Goldie T.
    Clay-Dough, Play-Dough. Walker & Co.
    Clay Dough, Play Dough. Schol Bk Serv.
    Easy Costumes You Don't Have to Sew. Schol
      Bk Serv.
    Easy Costumes You Don't Have to Sew. Schol
      Bk Serv.
Chernoff, P. R. *see* Chernoff, Paul R.
Chernoff, Paul R., 1942-
  xChernoff, P. R.
    Properties of Infinite Dimensional Hamiltonian
      Systems. Springer-Verlag.
  xChernoff, Paul R.
    Product Formulas, Nonlinear Semigroups &
      Addition of Unbounded Operators. Am
      Math.
Chernow, C. *see* Chernow, Fred B.
Chernow, F. *see* Chernow, Fred B.
Chernow, Fred B.
  xChernow, C.
    jt. auth. Teaching the Culturally Disadvantaged
      Child. P-H.
  xChernow, F.
    Teaching the Culturally Disadvantaged Child.
      P-H.
Cherns, Albert.
  xCherns, Albert.
    Using the Social Sciences. Routledge & Kegan.
Cherny, Robert W.
  xCherny, Robert W.
    Populism & the Election of 1896. Viking Pr.
Cheronis, Nicholas D. *see* Cheronis, Nicholas Dimitrius.
Cheronis, Nicholas Dimitrius.
  xCheronis, Nicholas D.
    Identification of Organic Compounds: A
      Students Text Using Semimicro Techniques.
      Wiley.
Cherrett, J. M.
  xCherrett, J. M.
    The Control of Injurious Animals. St Martin.
Cherrier, Francois.
  xCherrier, Francois.
    Fascinating Experiments in Chemistry. Sterling.
    Fascinating Experiments in Physics. Sterling.
Cherrington, B. E.
  xCherrington, B. E.
    Gaseous Electronics & Gas Lasers. Pergamon.
Cherrington, Ernest H. *see* Cherrington, Ernest Hurst.
Cherrington, Ernest Hurst, 1877-1950
  xCherrington, Ernest H.
    Evolution of Prohibition in the United States of
      America: A Chronological History of the
      Liquor Problem & the Temperance Reform in
      the United States from the Earliest
      Settlements to the Consumation of National
      Prohibition. Patterson Smith.
Cherry, C. *see* Cherry, C. Conrad.
Cherry, C. Conrad, 1937-
  xCherry, C.

God's New Israel: Religious Interpretations of
  American Destiny. P-H.
Theology of Jonathan Edwards: A Reappraisal.
  Peter Smith.
Cherry, Colin.
  xCherry, Colin.
    On Human Communication: A Review, a
      Survey & a Criticism. MIT Pr.
    ed. Pragmatic Aspects of Human
      Communication. Kluwer Boston.
Cherry, Elaine C.
  xCherry, Elaine C.
    Fluorescent Light Gardening. Van Nos
      Reinhold.
Cherry, George W. *see* Cherry, George William.
Cherry, George William, 1929-
  xCherry, George W.
    Pascal Programming Structures: An
      Introduction to Systematic Programming.
      Reston.
Cherry, Mike, 1934-
  xCherry, Mike.
    On High Steel: The Education of an
      Ironworker. Ballantine.
    On High Steel: The Education of an
      Ironworker. Times Bks.
Cherry, Raymond.
  xCherry, Raymond.
    Leathercrafting: Procedures & Projects.
      McKnight.
Cherry, Richard L.
  xCherry, Richard L.
    ed. A Return to Vision. HM.
Cherry, Rona B.
  xCherry, Rona B.
    The World of American Business: An
      Introduction. Har-Row.
Cherry, Sheldon. *see* Cherry, Sheldon H.
Cherry, Sheldon H.
  xCherry, Sheldon.
    For Women of All Ages: A Gynecologist's
      Guide to Modern Female Health Care. NAL.
    Understanding Pregnancy & Childbirth.
      Bantam.
  xCherry, Sheldon H.
    For Women of All Ages: A Gynecologist's
      Guide to Modern Female Health Care.
      Macmillan.
    Understanding Pregnancy & Childbirth.
      Bantam.
    Understanding Pregnancy & Childbirth. Bobbs.
Cherryh, C. J.
  xCherryh, C. J.
    Brothers of Earth. DAW Bks.
    Fires of Azeroth. DAW Bks.
    Gate of Ivrel. DAW Bks.
Cherryholmes, Lynn.
  xCherryholmes, Lynn.
    Learning About People. McGraw.
Chertkov, Vladimir G. *see* Chertkov, Vladimir
  Grigorevich.
Chertkov, Vladimir Grigorevich, 1854-1936
  xChertkov, Vladimir G.
    The Last Days of Tolstoy. Kraus Repr.
Chervin, Ronda.
  xChervin, Ronda.
    The Woman's Tale: A Journal of Inner
      Exploration. Seabury.
Chesapeake Research Consortium.
  xChesapeake Research Consortium.
    Effects of Tropical Storm Agnes on the
      Chesapeake Bay Estuarine System. Johns
      Hopkins.
Chesarek, Frank.
  xChesarek, Frank.
    jt. auth. Montana: Two Lane Highway in a
      Four Lane World. Mountain Pr.
Chesbro, George. *see* Chesbro, George C.
Chesbro, George C.
  xChesbro, George.

An Affair of Sorcerers. NAL.
An Affair of Sorcerers. S&S.
City of Whispering Stone. NAL.
  xChesbro, George C.
    City of Whispering Stone. S&S.
Chesebro. *see* Chesebro, James W.
Chesebro, James W.
  xChesebro.
    Orientations to Public Communication. SRA.
Chesen, Eli S.
  xChesen, Eli S.
    Religion May Be Hazardous to Your Health.
      Macmillan.
Chesher, Richard H.
  xChesher, Richard H.
    The Systematics of Sympatric Species in West
      Indian Spatangoids: A Revision of the
      Genera Brissopsis, Plethotaenia,
      Paleopneustes, & Saviniaster. U Miami
      Marine.
Cheshire, D. F.
  xCheshire, D. F.
    Music Hall in Britain. Fairleigh Dickinson.
Cheshire, David. *see* Cheshire, David F.
Cheshire, David F.
  xCheshire, David.
    The Book of Movie Photography. Knopf.
Cheshire, Maxine.
  xCheshire, Maxine.
    Maxine Cheshire, Reporter. HM.
Cheshire, N. M. *see* Cheshire, Neil M.
Cheshire, Neil M.
  xCheshire, N. M.
    The Nature of Psychodynamic Interpretation.
      Wiley.
Cheskin, Louis, 1907-
  xCheskin, Louis.
    Color for Profit. Liveright.
    Secrets of Marketing Success. Trident.
Chesler, Phyllis.
  xChesler, Phyllis.
    About Men. Bantam.
    About Men. S&S.
Chesneau, Roger.
  xChesneau, Roger.
    ed. Scale Models in Plastic. Scribner.
Chesneaux, Jean.
  xChesneaux, Jean.
    China: The People's Republic, 1949-1976.
      Pantheon.
    Pasts & Futures: Or What Is History for?.
      Thames Hudson.
    Peasant Revolts in China 1840-1949. Norton.
    ed. Popular Movements & Secret Societies in
      China, 1840-1950. Stanford U Pr.
Chesnut, D. B., 1932-
  xChesnut, D. B.
    Finite Groups & Quantum Theory. Wiley.
Chesnut, Mary B. *see* Chesnut, Mary Boykin (Miller).
Chesnut, Mary Boykin (Miller).
  xChesnut, Mary B.
    A Diary from Dixie. Harvard U Pr.
    Diary from Dixie. HM.
    A Diary from Dixie. Peter Smith.
Chesnutt, C. *see* Chesnutt, Charles Waddell.
Chesnutt, Charles W. *see* Chesnutt, Charles Waddell.
Chesnutt, Charles Waddell, 1858-1932
  xChesnutt, Charles.
    House Behind the Cedars. Macmillan.
  xChesnutt, Charles W.

Colonel's Dream. Arno.
The Colonel's Dream. Irvington.
Colonel's Dream. Mnemosyne.
Colonel's Dream. Negro U Pr.
The Conjure Woman. Scholarly.
Conjure Woman. U of Mich Pr.
Marrow of Tradition. AMS Pr.
Marrow of Tradition. Arno.
The Marrow of Tradition. Dynamic Learn
    Corp.
The Marrow of Tradition. Irvington.
The Marrow of Tradition. U of Mich Pr.
Marrow of Tradition. U of Mich Pr.

Chesnutt, Helen M.
    xChesnutt, Helen M.
        Charles Waddell Chesnutt: Pioneer of the
            Color Line. U of NC Pr.
Chesnutt, N. P.
    xChesnutt, N. P.
        Southern Union. Mangan Bks.
Chess, Stella.
    xChess, Stella.
        An Introduction to Child Psychiatry. Grune.
        ed. Psychiatric Disorders of Children with
            Congenital Rubella. Brunner-Mazel.
Chess, Victoria.
    xChess, Victoria.
        Alfred's Alphabet Walk. Greenwillow.
Chesser, Eustace, 1902-
    xChesser, Eustace.
        When & How to Quit Smoking. Emerson.
Chessex, Jacques.
    xChessex, Jacques.
        A Father's Love. Nordon Pubns.
Chessick, Richard. see Chessick, Richard D.
Chessick, Richard D., 1931-
    xChessick, Richard.
        Intensive Psychotherapy of the Borderline
            Patient. Aronson.
    xChessick, Richard D.
        Great Ideas in Psychotherapy. Aronson.
Chessman, G. Wallace.
    xChessman, G. Wallace.
        Theodore Roosevelt & the Politics of Power.
            Little.
Chessmore, Roy A.
    xChessmore, Roy A.
        Profitable Pasture Management. Interstate.
Chester, Carole.
    xChester, Carole.
        Germany. Rand.
        New York. David & Charles.
        New York. Hippocrene Bks.
Chester, Daniel N. see Chester, Daniel Norman.
Chester, Daniel Norman.
    xChester, Daniel N.
        ed. Lessons of the British War Economy.
            Greenwood.
Chester, Deborah.
    xChester, Deborah.
        A Love So Wild. Coward.
Chester, Edward M.
    xChester, Edward M.
        The Ocular Fundus in Systemic Disease: A
            Clinical Pathological Correlation. Year Bk
            Med.
Chester, Edward W.
    xChester, Edward W.
        Clash of Titans: Africa & U. S. Foreign Policy.
            Orbis Bks.
        A Guide to Political Platforms. Shoe String.
        Sectionalism, Politics & American Diplomacy.
            Scarecrow.
Chester, Eng. Diocese. see Chester, England. (Diocese).
Chester, England. (Diocese).
    xChester, Eng. Diocese.
        Child-Marriages, Divorces, & Ratifications Etc.
            1561-66. Kraus Repr.
Chester, Lewis.
    xChester, Lewis.

The Secret Life of Jeremy Thorpe: The Scandal
    of the Century. Times Bks.
Chester, Michael.
    xChester, Michael.
        Deeper Than Speech: Frontiers of Language &
            Communication. Macmillan.
        Particles: An Introduction to Particle Physics.
            NAL.
        Particles: An Introduction to Particle Physics.
            Macmillan.
Chester, R. see Chester, Robert.
Chester, Robert.
    xChester, R.
        ed. Divorce in Europe. Kluwer Boston.
Chester, W.
    xChester, W.
        Mechanics. Allen Unwin.
Chester, William L.
    xChester, William L.
        One Against a Wilderness. DAW Bks.
Chesterfield, Lord. see Chesterfield, Philip Dormer
    Stanhope.
Chesterfield, Philip Dormer Stanhope.
    xChesterfield, Lord.
        Some Unpublished Letters of Lord
            Chesterfield. R West.
Chesterman, Charles W. see Chesterman, Charles Wesley.
Chesterman, Charles Wesley.
    xChesterman, Charles W.
        The Audubon Society Field Guide to North
            American Rocks & Minerals. Knopf.
Chesterman, James.
    xChesterman, James.
        Classical Terracotta Figures. Overlook Pr.
Chesterton, G. K. see Chesterton, Gilbert Keith.
Chesterton, Gilbert K. see Chesterton, Gilbert Keith.
Chesterton, Gilbert Keith, 1874-1936
    xChesterton, G. K.
        All Is Grist: A Book of Essays. Scholarly.
        All Things Considered. Folcroft.
        Appreciations & Criticisms of the Works of
            Charles Dickens. Folcroft.
        Appreciations & Criticisms of the Works of
            Charles Dickens. R West.
        As I Was Saying. Folcroft.
        Charles Dickens. Folcroft.
        Chaucer. Folcroft.
        The Everlasting Man. Doubleday.
        The Everlasting Man. Greenwood.
        George Bernard Shaw. Folcroft.
        The Innocence of the Father Brown. Garland
            Pub.
        Napoleon of Notting Hill. Paulist Pr.
        Orthodoxy. Doubleday.
        Thackeray. Folcroft.
        Thomas Carlyle. Folcroft.
        Thomas Carlyle. Haskell.
        Twelve Modern Apostles & Their Creeds.
            Arno.
    xChesterton, Gilbert K.
        All Is Grist: A Book of Essays. Arno.
        All Things Considered. Arno.
        All Things Considered. Dufour.
        As I Was Saying. Arno.
        Chaucer. Greenwood.
        Come to Think of It. Arno.
        Defendant. Arno.
        George Bernard Shaw. Arden Lib.
        Leo Tolstoy. Folcroft.
        Lunacy & Letters. Arno.
        Orthodoxy. Darby Bks.
        Orthodoxy. Greenwood.
        Thomas Carlyle. Arden Lib.
        Twelve Types. AMS Pr.
        Utopia of Usurers, & Other Essays. Arno.
        Varied Types. Arno.
        Varied Types. Scholarly.
Chestnut, Harold.
    xChestnut, Harold.

Systems Engineering Methods. Wiley.
Systems Engineering Tools. Wiley.
Cheston, Stephen T. see Cheston, T. Stephen.
Cheston, T. Stephen.
    xCheston, Stephen T.
        ed. Aspects of Soviet Policy Toward Latin
            America. Mss Info.
Chethimattam, John B.
    xChethimattam, John B.
        Patterns of Indian Thought. Orbis Bks.
Chetwynd-Hayes, R.
    xChetwynd-Hayes, R.
        Dominique. Belmont-Tower.
Cheung, Dominic.
    xCheung, Dominic.
        Feng Chih. G K Hall.
Cheung, Y. K.
    xCheung, Y. K.
        Finite Strip Method in Structural Analysis.
            Pergamon.
Chevalier, Jack.
    xChevalier, Jack.
        The Broad Street Bullies: The Incredible Story
            of the Philadelphia Flyers. Macmillan.
Chevalier, Michael. see Chevalier, Michel.
Chevalier, Michel, 1806-1879
    xChevalier, Michael.
        Society, Manners & Politics in the United
            States: Letters on North America. Peter
            Smith.
Chevalier, Pierre, Explorer.
    xChevalier, Pierre.
        Subterranean Climbers: Twelve Years in the
            World's Deepest Chasm. Zephyrus Pr.
Chevalier-Skolnikoff, Suzanne.
    xChevalier-Skolnikoff, Suzanne.
        ed. Primate Bio-Social Development:
            Biological, Social & Ecological Determinants.
            Garland Pub.
Chevalley, Claude, 1909-
    xChevalley, Claude.
        Theory of Lie Groups. Princeton U Pr.
Cheville, N. F. see Cheville, Norman F.
Cheville, Norman F., 1934-
    xCheville, N. F.
        Cytopathology in Viral Diseases. S Karger.
    xCheville, Norman F.
        Cell Pathology. Iowa St U Pr.
Cheviot, A. see Cheviot, Andrew.
Cheviot, Andrew.
    xCheviot, A.
        Proverbs, Proverbial Expressions & Popular
            Rhymes of Scotland. Gordon Pr.
    xCheviot, Andrew.
        ed. Proverbs, Proverbial Expressions, & Popular
            Rhymes of Scotland. Gale.
Chevrot, Georges.
    xChevrot, Georges.
        Simon Peter. Scepter Pubs.
Chew. see Chew, Ruth.
Chew, Allen F.
    xChew, Allen F.
        An Atlas of Russian History: Eleven Centuries
            of Changing Borders. Yale U Pr.
Chew, Peter.
    xChew, Peter.
        The Inner World of the Middle-Aged Man.
            Macmillan.
Chew, Ruth.
    xChew.
        Trouble with Magic. Schol Bk Serv.
    xChew, Ruth.

Insights: A Selection of Creative Literature About Children. Aronson.

Child Study Association of America. Wel-Met.
xChildren's Book Committee of CSAA, Wel-Met Inc.
Children's Books of the Year 1976. Child Study.

Child Study Association Of America. *see* Chilton Book Company. Automotive Editorial Dept.

Child Welfare League of America.
xChild Welfare League of America Staff.
CWLA Standards for Child Protective Service. Child Welfare.

Child Welfare League of America Staff. *see* Child Welfare League of America.

Child, William H. *see* Child, William Henry.

Child, William Henry, 1832-
xChild, William H.
History of the Town of Cornish New Hampshire with Genealogical Record, 1763-1910. Reprint.

Childe, V. Gordon. *see* Childe, Vere Gordon.

Childe, Vera G. *see* Childe, Vere Gordon.

Childe, Vere G. *see* Childe, Vere Gordon.

Childe, Vere Gordon, 1892-1957
xChilde, V. Gordon.
Prehistoric Communities of the British Isles. Arno.
xChilde, Vera G.
Progress & Archaeology. Greenwood.
xChilde, Vere G.
Bronze Age. Biblo.
The Danube in Prehistory. AMS Pr.
Prehistoric Communities of the British Isles. Greenwood.
Society & Knowledge. Greenwood.

Childerhose, R. J.
xChilderhose, R. J.
Pacific Salmon & Steelhead Trout. U of Wash Pr.

Childers, Donald G.
xChilders, Donald G.
Digital Filtering & Signal Processing. West Pub.

Childers, James W. *see* Childers, James Wesley.

Childers, James Wesley, 1906-
xChilders, James W.
Tales from Spanish Picaresque Novels: A Motif-Index. State U NY Pr.

Children''S TV Workshop. *see* Children'S Television Workshop.

Children's Allowance Conference, 1967. *see* Children'S Allowances Conference, Warrenton, Va., 1967.

Children's Allowances Conference, Warrenton, Va., 1967.
xChildren's Allowance Conference, 1967.
Children's Allowance & the Economic Welfare of Children: The Report of a Conference. Arno.

Children's Book Committee of CSAA, Wel-Met Inc. *see* Child Study Association of America. Wel-Met.

Children's Books International, 1st, Boston Public Librayy.
xChildrens Book International Symposium, 1st, Boston Public Library, 1975.
Childrens Books International I: Proceedings. Boston Public Lib.

Children's Hospital Medical Center, the Health Education Department, Boston, Mass. *see* Boston. Children'S Hospital Medical Center.

Children's Television Workshop.
xChildren''S TV Workshop.
ed. Sesame Street Book of People & Things. NAL.
xChildren's Television Workshop.
The Best of the Electric Company. G&D.
The Electric Company Crazy Cut-Ups. G&D.
xChildren'S TV Workshop.

Sesame Street Begins at Home. S&S.
ed. Sesame Street Book of Letters. NAL.
ed. Sesame Street Book of Puzzlers. NAL.
ed. Sesame Street Book of Shapes. NAL.
xChildrens'S TV Workshop.
ed. Sesame Street Book of Numbers. NAL.

Children'S TV Workshop. *see* Children'S Television Workshop.

Childrens Book International Symposium, 1st, Boston Public Library, 1975. *see* Children'S Books International, 1st, Boston Public Librayy.

Childrens'S TV Workshop. *see* Children'S Television Workshop.

Childress, Alice.
xChildress, Alice.
Let's Hear It for the Queen. Coward.
A Short Walk. Coward.

Childress, James F.
xChildress, James F.
Civil Disobedience & Political Obligation: A Study in Christian Social Ethics. Yale U Pr.

Childress, R. L. *see* Childress, Robert L.

Childress, Robert L.
xChildress, R. L.
Fundamentals of Finite Mathematics. P-H.
xChildress, Robert L.
Calculus for Business & Economics. P-H.

Childress, William.
xChildress, William.
Lobo. Barlenmir.

Childs, Brevard S.
xChilds, Brevard S.
Introduction to the Old Testament As Scripture. Fortress.

Childs, David.
xChilds, David.
ed. The Changing Face of Western Communism. St Martin.

Childs, Edmund. *see* Childs, Edmund Lunness.

Childs, Edmund Lunness.
xChilds, Edmund.
William Caxton: A Portrait in a Background. St Martin.

Childs, Frances Sergeant, 1901-
xChilds, Frances
French Refugee Life in the United States, 1790-1800: An American Chapter of the French Revolution. Porcupine Pr.

Childs, Frances *see* Childs, Frances Sergeant.

Childs, Harwood L. *see* Childs, Harwood Lawrence.

Childs, Harwood Lawrence.
xChilds, Harwood L.
Reference Guide to the Study of Public Opinion. Gale.

Childs, J. *see* Childs, John Farnsworth.

Childs, James B. *see* Childs, James Bennett.

Childs, James Bennett.
xChilds, James B.
ed. Government Document Bibliography in the United States & Elsewhere. Johnson Repr.

Childs, James J.
xChilds, James J.
Principles of Numerical Control. Indus Pr.

Childs, James M., 1939-
xChilds, James M.
Christian Anthropology & Ethics. Fortress.

Childs, James R. *see* Childs, James Rives.

Childs, James Rives, 1893-
xChilds, James R.
American Foreign Service. Kennikat.

Childs, John Farnsworth.
xChilds, J.
Encyclopedia of Long Term Financing & Capital Management. P-H.

Childs, John L. *see* Childs, John Lawrence.

Childs, John Lawrence, 1889-
xChilds, John L.

Education & Morals: An Experimentalist Philosophy of Education. Arno.
Education & the Philosophy of Experimentalism. Arno.
Education & the Philosophy of Experimentalism. Telegraph Bks.

Childs, L. N. *see* Childs, Lindsay.

Childs, Lindsay.
xChilds, L. N.
A Concrete Introduction to Higher Algebra. Springer-Verlag.

Childs, Marquis. *see* Childs, Marquis William.

Childs, Marquis W. *see* Childs, Marquis William.

Childs, Marquis William.
xChilds, Marquis.
The Farmer Takes a Hand: The Electric Power Revolution in Rural America. Da Capo.
xChilds, Marquis W.
Ethics in a Business Society. Greenwood.

Childs, Timothy, 1941-
xChilds, Timothy.
Cold Turkey. Har-Row.

Chiles, Paul N. *see* Chiles, Paul Nelson.

Chiles, Paul Nelson, 1910-
xChiles, Paul N.
The Puerto Rican Press Reaction to the United States, 1888-1898. Arno.

Chiles, Webb.
xChiles, Webb.
Storm Passage: Alone Around Cape Horn. Times Bks.

Chilimidos, R. S. *see* Chilimidos, Robert S.

Chilimidos, Robert S.
xChilimidos, R. S.
Auto Theft Investigation. Legal Bk Corp.

Chill, Abraham.
xChill, Abraham.
The Minhagim: The Customs & Ceremonies of Judaism, Their Origins & Rationale. Hermon.

Chill, Dan S.
xChill, Dan S.
The Arab Boycott of Israel: Economic Aggression and World Reaction. Praeger.

Chillingworth, H. R.
xChillingworth, H. R.
Complex Variables. Pergamon.

Chillingworth, William, 1602-1644
xChillingworth, William.
Works of William Chillingworth. AMS Pr.

Chilton Book Company Auto. Ed. Dept. *see* Chilton Book Company. Automotive Editorial Dept.

Chilton Book Company. Automotive Editorial Dept.
xChild Study Association Of America.
Round About the City: Stories You Can Read to Yourself. T Y Crowell.
xChilton Book Company Auto. Ed. Dept.
Chilton's Motorcycle Troubleshooting Guide. Chilton.
xChilton Book Company. Automotive Editorial Dept.
Chilton's Repair & Tune-up Guide: For Blazer-Jimmy, 1969-1977. Chilton.
xChilton's Automotive Ed. Dept.

Chilton's Auto Repair Manual 1978. Chilton.

Chilton's Auto Repair Manual 1979. Chilton.

Chilton's Import Automotive Repair Manual. Chilton.

Chilton's Repair & Tune-up Guide for Aspen-Volare, 1976-1978. Chilton.

Chilton's Repair & Tune-up Guide for Chevelle, el Camino, Monte Carlo 1964-1977. Chilton.

Chilton's Repair & Tune-up Guide for Chevrolet-GMC Vans 1967-1978. Chilton.

Chilton's Repair & Tune-Up Guide for Camaro 1967-1979. Chilton.

Chilton's Repair & Tune-up Guide for Chevy 2 & Nova, 1962-1977. Chilton.

Chilton's Repair & Tune-up Guide for Cutlass-442, 1970-1977. Chilton.

Chilton's Repair & Tune-up Guide for Dodge-Plymouth Vans 1967-1977. Chilton.

Chilton's Repair & Tune-up Guide for Dodge 1968-1977. Chilton.

Chilton's Repair & Tune-up Guide for Datsun 240-260-280z, 1970-1977. Chilton.

Chilton's Repair & Tune-up Guide for Ford Courier 1972-78. Chilton.

Chilton's Repair & Tune-up Guide for Ford Vans 1966-1977. Chilton.

Chilton's Repair & Tune-up Guide for Fiat 1969-1978. Chilton.

Chilton's Repair & Tune-up Guide for Granada-Monarch, 1975-1977. Chilton.

Chilton's Repair & Tune-Up Guide for Honda 350-550, 1972-1977. Chilton.

Chilton's Repair & Tune-up Guide for Honda 750 1969-1977. Chilton.

Chilton's Repair & Tune-up Guide for Jeep Wagoneer, Commando & Cherokee 1966-79. Chilton.

Chilton's Repair & Tune-up Guide for Maverick & Comet 1970-1977. Chilton.

Chilton's Repair & Tune-up Guide for Mazda 1971-78. Chilton.

Chilton's Repair & Tune-up Guide for Pinto 1971-1977. Chilton

Chilton's Repair & Tune-up Guide for Rabbit-Scirocco 1975-1978. Chilton.

Chilton's Repair & Tune-up Guide for Toyota 1970-1977. Chilton.

Chilton's Repair & Tune-up Guide for Volkswagen 1970-1977. Chilton.

Chilton's Repair & Tune-up Guide for Yamaha 360-400 1976-78. Chilton.

xChilton's Automotive Editorial Department.

Chevy Two & Nova, Nineteen Sixty-Two to Nineteen Seventy-Nine. Chilton.

Chilton Automotive Multi-Guide, Spring Nineteen Thirty-One. Chilton.

Chilton's Auto Repair Manual Nineteen-Eighty. Chilton.

Chilton's Auto Repair Manual, 1940-1953 Ed.. Chilton.

Chilton's Auto Repair Manual, 1954-1963 Ed.. Chilton.

Chilton's Auto Repair Manual, 1964-1971. Chilton.

Chilton's Foreign Car Repair Manual: Vol. 1, German, Swedish & Italian Cars. Chilton.

Chilton's Foreign Car Repair Manual: Vol. 2, French, British & Japanese Cars. Chilton.

Chilton's Guide to Emission Controls & How They Work. Chilton.

Chilton's Motor Age Manual Profesional De Aire Acordicionado De 1973: Automoviles Americanos Desde 1966 Hasta 1973. Chilton.

Chilton's Motorcycle Repair Manual. Chilton.

Chilton's Repair & Tune-up Guide, Bronco 1966-1973. Chilton.

Chilton's Repair & Tune-up Guide for Amx & Javelin: 1968-1971. Chilton.

Chilton's Repair & Tune-up Guide for Audi, 1970-1973. Chilton.

Chilton's Repair & Tune-up Guide for Barracuda & Challenger: 1965-1972. Chilton.

Chilton's Repair & Tune-up Guide for Bultaco, Montesa, & Ossa 1963-1972. Chilton.

Chilton's Repair & Tune-up Guide for Bmw Motorcycle Through 1972. Chilton.

Chilton's Repair & Tune-up Guide for BSA Thru 1972. Chilton.

Chilton's Repair & Tune-Up Guide for BMW: 1959-1970. Chilton.

Chilton's Repair & Tune-up Guide for BMW 2, 1969-1974. Chilton.

Chilton's Repair & Tune-up Guide for Charger, Coronet 1971-1975. Chilton.

Chilton's Repair & Tune-up Guide for Chevrolet-GMC Vans, 1967-1974. Chilton.

Chilton's Repair & Tune-up Guide for Corvette Stingray, 1963-1976. Chilton.

ed. Chilton's Repair & Tune-up Guide for Corvair, 1960-1969. Chilton.

Chilton's Repair & Tune-up Guide for Camaro, 1967-69. Chilton.

Chilton's Repair & Tune-up Guide for Dodge Charger: 1967-1970. Chilton.

Chilton's Repair & Tune-up Guide for Dodge Dart & Demon: 1965-1972. Chilton.

Chilton's Repair & Tune-up Guide for Datsun: 1961-1972. Chilton.

Chilton's Repair & Tune-up Guide for Datsun 2, 1973-1975. Chilton.

Chilton's Repair & Tune-up Guide for Datsun, 240-260z, 1970-1974. Chilton.

Chilton's Repair & Tune-up Guide for Ford Courier, 1972-1975. Chilton.

Chilton's Repair & Tune-up Guide for Firebird, 1967-1974. Chilton.

Chilton's Repair & Tune-up Guide for Fiat, 1970-73. Chilton.

Chilton's Repair & Tune-up Guide for Gremlin & Hornet, 1970-1974. Chilton.

Chilton's Repair & Tune-up Guide for Harley-Davidson Singles, 1947-1972. Chilton.

Chilton's Repair & Tune-up Guide for Harley Davidson V Twins, 1965-1974. Chilton.

Chilton's Repair & Tune-up Guide for Honda Elsinores, 1973-1975. Chilton.

Chilton's Repair & Tune-up Guide for Honda Fours, 1969-1972. Chilton.

Chilton's Repair & Tune-up Guide for Honda Singles, 1963-1972. Chilton.

Chilton's Repair & Tune-up Guide for Honda Twins, 1966-1972. Chilton.

Chilton's Repair & Tune-up Guide for Honda XL Series, 1970-1975. Chilton.

Chilton's Repair & Tune-up Guide for Hodaka, 1964-1973. Chilton.

Chilton's Repair & Tune-up Guide for Honda 125-200 Twins, 1969-1976. Chilton.

Chilton's Repair & Tune-up Guide for Honda 350-360 Twins, 1968-1975. Chilton.

Chilton's Repair & Tune-up Guide for Honda 450-500, 1966-1976. Chilton.

Chilton's Repair & Tune-up Guide for Inboard-Outdrives: 1968-1972. Chilton.

Chilton's Repair & Tune-up Guide for International Scout, 1967-1973: International Scout. Chilton.

ed. Chilton's Repair & Tune-up Guide for Jeep Universal, 1953-1976. Chilton.

Chilton's Repair & Tune-up Guide for Jaguar, 1960-1969. Chilton.

Chilton's Repair & Tune-up Guide for Kawasaki Triples, 1969-1975. Chilton.

Chilton's Repair & Tune-up Guide for Kawasaki, 1966-1972. Chilton.

Chilton's Repair & Tune-up Guide for Kawasaki 900 Z1, 1973-1974. Chilton.

Chilton's Repair & Tune-up Guide for Mercedes-Benz: 1961-1970. Chilton.

Chilton's Repair & Tune-up Guide for Mercedes Benz 2, 1968-1973. Chilton.

Chilton's Repair & Tune-up Guide for Moto Guzzi, 1966-1972. Chilton.

Chilton's Repair & Tune-up Guide for Mazda Pick-up, 1972-1975. Chilton.

Chilton's Repair & Tune-up Guide for Mustang: 1965-1973. Chilton.

Chilton's Repair & Tune-up Guide for Norton 750 & 850, 1966-1973. Chilton.

Chilton's Repair & Tune-up Guide for Outboard Motors Under 30 Horsepower, 1966-1972. Chilton.

Chilton's Repair & Tune-up Guide for Outboard Motors 30 Horsepower & Over: 1966-1972. Chilton.

Chilton's Repair & Tune-up Guide for Opel: 1964-1970. Chilton.

Chilton's Repair & Tune-up Guide for Porsche: 1950-68. Chilton.

Chilton's Repair & Tune-up Guide for Porsche 2, 1969-1973. Chilton.

Chilton's Repair & Tune-up Guide for Ramcharger - Trailduster, 1974-1975. Chilton.

Chilton's Repair & Tune-up Guide for Rebel-Matador, 1967-1974. Chilton.

Chilton's Repair & Tune-up Guide for Road Runner, Satellite, Belvedere, GTX, 1968-1973. Chilton.

Chilton's Repair & Tune-up Guide for Renault: 1964-72. Chilton.

Chilton's Repair & Tune-up Guide for Suzuki Singles & Twins, 1970-1974. Chilton.

Chilton's Repair & Tune-up Guide for Suzuki Triples, 1972-1974. Chilton.

Chilton's Repair & Tune-up Guide for Suzuki, 1963-1972. Chilton.

Chilton's Repair & Tune-up Guide for Snowmobiles: 1965-72. Chilton.

Chilton's Repair & Tune-up Guide for Tempest, GTO & Le Mans, 1968-1973. Chilton.

Chilton's Repair & Tune-up Guide for Toyota Hi Lux, 1970-1974. Chilton.

Chilton's Repair & Tune-up Guide for Toyota Land Cruiser, 1966-1974. Chilton.

Chilton's Repair & Tune-up Guide for Triumph Motorcycle Through 1972. Chilton.

Chilton's Repair & Tune-up Guide for Triumph: 1963-1970. Chilton.

Chilton's Repair & Tune-up Guide for Triumph 2, 1969-1973. Chilton.

Chilton's Repair & Tune-up Guide for Valiant & Duster: 1963-1972. Chilton.

Chilton's Repair & Tune-up Guide for Volkswagen: 1949-1971. Chilton.

Chilton's Repair & Tune-up Guide for Winnebago Motor Homes, 1968-1974. Chilton.

Chilton's Repair & Tune-up Guide for Yamaha Enduros, 1968-1974. Chilton.

Chilton's Repair & Tune-up Guide for Yamaha Four-Strokes, 1970-1974. Chilton.

Chilton's Repair & Tune-up Guide for Yamaha Street 2-Stroke Bikes, 1967-1975. Chilton.

Guia Chilton Pare la Diagnosis De Averias En el Automovil. Chilton.

Guia Pare la Reparacion y Afinacion Del Volkswagen 1, 1949-1971. Chilton.

xChilton's Automotive Editorial Dept.

Chevette, Nineteen Seventy-Six to Nineteen Eighty. Chilton.

Chevrolet Mid-Size Nineteen Sixty-Four to Nineteen Seventy-Nine. Chilton.

Chevrolet, Nineteen Sixty-Eight to Nineteen Seventy-Nine. Chilton.

ed. Chilton's Auto Repair Manual, 1977. Chilton.

Chilton's Basic Auto Maintenance. Chilton.

Chilton's Chevrolet Luv: 1972-1979, Repair & Tune-up Guide. Chilton.

Chilton's Datsun Pick-Ups: 1970-1979 Repair & Tune-up Guide. Chilton.

Chilton's Jeep CJ: 1953-1979, Repair & Tune-up Guide. Chilton.

Chilton's Mercedes-Benz: 1974-1979, Repair & Tune-up Guide. Chilton.

Chilton's Motorcycle Owner's Handbook. Chilton.

ed. Chilton's Motorcycle Repair Manual. Chilton.

Chilton's Mustang II: 1974-1978, Repair & Tune-up Guide. Chilton.

Chilton's Pinto-Bobcat: 1971-1979, Repair & Tune-up Guide. Chilton.

Chilton's Repair & Tune-up Guide for Chevrolet Luv, 1972-1975. Chilton.

Chilton's Repair & Tune-up Guide for Dodge Dart & Demon, 1968-1976. Chilton.

Chilton's Repair & Tune-up Guide for Datson Pick-Ups, 1970-1975. Chilton.

Chilton's Repair & Tune-up Guide for Fairlane & Torino, 1962-1975. Chilton.

Chilton's Repair & Tune-up Guide for Honda Civic, 1973-1976. Chilton.

Chilton's Repair & Tune-up Guide for MG, 1961-1975. Chilton.

Chilton's Repair & Tune-up Guide for Valiant & Duster, 1968-1976. Chilton.

Chilton's Small Engines: Repair & Tune-up Guide. Chilton.

Ford Fiesta, 1978 to 1980. Chilton.

Ford, 1968 to 1979. Chilton.

Omni & Horizon, Nineteen Seventy-Eight to Nineteen Eighty. Chilton.

Toyota, 1970-1979. Chilton.

Volkswagen, Nineteen Seventy to Nineteeen Seventy-Nine. Chilton.

Yamaha Six Fifty, Nineteen Seventy to Seventy-Nine. Chilton.

Chilton, Carl S., 1923-
xChilton, Carl S.
Successful Small Client Accounting Practice. P-H.

Chilton's Automotive Ed. Dept. see Chilton Book Company. Automotive Editorial Dept.

Chilton's Automotive Editorial Department. see Chilton Book Company. Automotive Editorial Dept.

Chilton's Automotive Editorial Dept. see Chilton Book Company. Automotive Editorial Dept.

Chilver, G. E. see Chilver, Guy Edward Farquhar.

Chilver, Guy Edward Farquhar.
xChilver, G. E.
A Historical Commentary on Tacitus' Histories I & II. Oxford U Pr.

Chilver, J. W. see Chilver, Joseph.

Chilver, Joseph.
xChilver, J. W.
The Human Aspects of Management: A Case Study Approach. Pergamon.

Chilver, Peter.
xChilver, Peter.
Designing a School Play. Taplinger.

Chimbos, Peter D.
xChimbos, Peter D.
Marital Violence: A Study of Interspouse Homicide. R & E Res Assoc.

Chimenti, Frances. see Chimenti, Francesca.

Chimenti, Francesca.
xChimenti, Frances.
The Web of Deception. Dell.

Chin, Felix, 1937-
xChin, Felix.
Cable Television: A Selected Bibliography. Vance Biblios.

China Institute of International Affairs.
xChina Institute of International Affairs.
China & the United Nations. Greenwood.

Chinard, Gilbert, 1881-
xChinard, Gilbert.
Thomas Jefferson: The Apostle of Americanism. U of Mich Pr.

Chinchilla, Anastasio.
xChinchilla, Anastasio.
Anales Historicos De la Medicina En General y Biografico-Bibliograficos De la Espanola En Particular. Johnson Repr.

Chinery, Michael.
xChinery, Michael.
Animals in the Zoo. Taplinger.
Concise Color Encyclopedia of Nature. T Y Crowell.
Life in the Zoo. Taplinger.

Chinese Art Appraisers Association.
xChinese Art Appraisers Association.
Concepts in Dating Chinese Paintings. Chinese Art App.

Ching, Doris C., 1930-
xChing, Doris C.
Reading & the Bilingual Child. Intl Reading.

Ching, Frank, 1943-
xChing, Frank.
Architectural Graphics. Van Nos Reinhold.

Ching, Marvin K. see Ching, Marvin K. L.

Ching, Marvin K. L.
xChing, Marvin K.
ed. Linguistic Perspectives on Literature. Routledge & Kegan.

Chiggaltai.
xChinggaltai.
Grammar of the Mongol Language. Ungar.

Chinggaltai. see Chiggaltai.

Chinitz, Benjamin.
xChinitz, Benjamin.
ed. Central City Economic Development. Abt Assoc.
The Declining Northeast: Demographic & Economic Analyses. Praeger.

Chinn, L. J. see Chinn, Leland J.

Chinn, Leland J.
xChinn, L. J.
Chemistry & Biochemistry of Steroids. Geron-X.

Chinn, Peggy L.
xChinn, Peggy L.
Child Health Maintenance: A Guide to Clinical Assessment. Mosby.

Chinn, Philip C.
xChinn, Philip C.

Mental Retardation: A Life Cycle Approach. Mosby.

Chinn, William G.
xChinn, William G.
Arithmetic & Calculators: How to Deal with Arithmetic in the Calculator Age. W H Freeman.

Chinnici, Joseph P.
xChinnici, Joseph P.
The English Catholic Enlightenment: John Lingard & the Cisalpine Movement, 1780 to 1850. Patmos Pr.

Chinook, Nipi.
xChinook, Nipi.
The Ski Bum's Guide to Mountain Wildlife. Bowery Pub.

Chinoy, Ely.
xChinoy, Ely.
Sociological Perspective. Peter Smith.
xChinoy, Ely S.
Society: An Introduction to Sociology. Random.

Chinoy, Ely S. see Chinoy, Ely.

Chintamani, Chirravoori Yajneswara, Sir, 1880-1941
xChintamani, Shirroavoore Y.
Indian Politics Since the Mutiny: Being an Account of the Development of Public Life & Political Institutions of Prominent Local Political Personalities. Hyperion Conn.

Chintamani, Shirroavoore Y. see Chintamani, Chirravoori Yajneswara.

Chiogioji. see Chiogioji, Melvin H.

Chiogioji, Melvin H., 1939-
xChiogioji.
Industrial Energy Conservation. Dekker.

Chipman, John S. see Chipman, John Somerset.

Chipman, John Somerset, 1926-
xChipman, John S.
ed. Preferences, Utility, & Demand: A Minnesota Symposium. HarBraceJ.
The Theory of Inter-Sectoral Money Flows & Income Formation. AMS Pr.

Chipp, Herschel B. see Chipp, Herschel Browning.

Chipp, Herschel Browning.
xChipp, Herschel B.
Theories of Modern Art: A Source Book by Artists & Critics. U of Cal Pr.

Chipp, Sylvia A.
xChipp, Sylvia A.
ed. Asian Women in Transition. Pa St U Pr.

Chippendale, P. R. see Chippendale, Peter Richard.

Chippendale, Peter Richard.
xChippendale, P. R.
ed. Accountability in Education. U of Queensland Pr.

Chippendale, Thomas, 1718-1779
xChippendale, Thomas.
Gentleman & Cabinet-Maker's Director. Dover.
Gentleman & Cabinet-Makers Director. Peter Smith.

Chipperfield, Mary.
xChipperfield, Mary.
Lions. Raintree Pubs.

Chippindale, Warren.
xChippindale, Warren.
ed. Current Value Accounting: A Practical Guide for Business. Am Mgmt.

Chirgwin, F. J. see Chirgwin, F. John.

Chirgwin, F. John.
xChirgwin, F. J.
The Library Assistant's Manual. Shoe String.

Chirigos, Michael A.
xChirigos, Michael A.
ed. Control of Neoplasia by Modulation of the Immune System. Raven.
ed. Immune Modulation & Control of Neoplasia by Adjuvant Therapy. Raven.

Chirkov, Iurii Ivanovich.
xChirkov, Y. I.

Agrometeorology. Springer-Verlag.

Chirkov, Y. I. *see* Chirkov, Iurii Ivanovich.

Chiro, Giovoanni Di. *see* Di Chiro, Giovanni.

Chirol, Valentine, Sir, 1852-1929
xChirol, Valentine.
India. Arno.

Chironis, Nicholas P.
xChironis, Nicholas P.
Mechanisms, Linkages, & Mechanical Controls.
McGraw.

Chisholm, Alan R. *see* Chisholm, Alan Rowland.

Chisholm, Alan Rowland, 1888-
xChisholm, Alan R.
Towards Herodiade: A Literary Genealogy.
AMS Pr.

Chisholm, Derrick M.
xChisholm, Derrick M.
Introduction to Oral Medicine. Saunders.

Chisholm, E. *see* Chisholm, Erik.

Chisholm, Erik, 1904-1965
xChisholm, E.
Operas of Leos Janacek. Pergamon.

Chisholm, J. S. *see* Chisholm, John Stephen Roy.

Chisholm, John Stephen Roy.
xChisholm, J. S.
Vectors in Three-Dimensional Space.
Cambridge U Pr.

Chisholm, M. *see* Chisholm, Michael.

Chisholm, Margery M.
xChisholm, Margery M.
Psychiatric Community Mental Health Nursing
Case Studies. Med Exam.

Chisholm, Michael.
xChisholm, M.
Freight Flows & Spatial Aspects of the British
Economy. Cambridge U Pr.
ed. Spatial Policy Problems of the British
Economy. Cambridge U Pr.

Chisholm, Roderick. *see* Chisholm, Roderick M.

Chisholm, Roderick M.
xChisholm, Roderick.
Theory of Knowledge. P-H.
xChisholm, Roderick M.
Perceiving: A Philosophical Study. Cornell U
Pr.

Chisholm, Roger. *see* Chisholm, Roger K.

Chisholm, Roger K.
xChisholm, Roger.
Principles of Economics. Scott F.
Principles of Macroeconomics. Scott F.
Principles of Microeconomics. Scott F.

Chislett, William.
xChislett, William.
George Meredith: A Study & an Appraisal.
Haskell.

Chisman, Forrest P., 1944-
xChisman, Forrest P.
Attitude Psychology & the Study of Public
Opinion. Pa St U Pr.

Chisnall, Peter M.
xChisnall, Peter M.
Effective Industrial Marketing. Longman.

Chissell, Joan.
xChissell, Joan.
Brahms. Merrimack Bk Serv.

Chissom, Brad S.
xChissom, Brad S.
ed. Readings for Educational Research. Mss
Info.

Chiswick, Barry R.
xChiswick, Barry R.
Income Inequality: Regional Analyses Within a
Human Capital Framework. Natl Bur Econ
Res.

Chitayat, Gideon.
xChitayat, Gideon.
Trade Union Mergers & Labor Conglomerates.
Praeger.

Chiteji, Frank M.
xChiteji, Frank M.

The Development & Socio-Economic Impact of
Transportation in Tanzania Eighteen
Eighty-Four - Present. U Pr of Amer.

Chittenden, Margaret.
xChittenden, Margaret.
The Mystery of the Missing Pony. Garrard.

Chittick, William O.
xChittick, William O.
The Analysis of Foreign Policy Outputs.
Merrill.

Chittister, Joan.
xChittister, Joan.
Climb Along the Cutting Edge: An Analysis of
Change in Religious Life. Paulist Pr.

Chittock, Derek.
xChittock, Derek.
Portrait Painting Techniques. Larousse.

Chittum, Ida.
xChittum, Ida.
Farmer Hoo & the Baboons. Delacorte.
The Ghost Boy of el Toro. Independence Pr.
The Secrets of Madam Renee. Independence
Pr.

Chitwood, B. *see* Chitwood, Benjamin Goodwin.

Chitwood, B. J. *see* Chitwood, Billy J.

Chitwood, Benjamin Goodwin.
xChitwood, B.
Introduction to Nematology. Univ Park.

Chitwood, Billy J.
xChitwood, B. J.
Meet the Real Jesus. Broadman.

Chiu, Hungdah, 1936-
xChiu, Hungdah.
China & the Taiwan Issue. Praeger.
People's Republic of China & the Law of
Treaties. Harvard U Pr.

Chiu, Tony.
xChiu, Tony.
Port Arthur Chicken. Morrow.

Chivers, D. J. *see* Chivers, David John.

Chivers, David John.
xChivers, D. J.
The Siamang in Malaya: A Field Study of a
Primate in Tropical Rain Forest. S Karger.

Chloros, A. G.
xChloros, A. G.
Codification in a Mixed Jurisdiction: The Civil
Commercial Law of Seychelles. Elsevier.

Cho, Cheng. *see* Cho, Cheng T.

Cho, Cheng T.
xCho, Cheng.
Pediatric Infectious Diseases. Med Exam.

Cho, Emily.
xCho, Emily.
Looking Terrific: Express Yourself Through the
Language of Clothing. Putnam.

Cho, Lee-Jay.
xCho, Lee-Jay.
ed. Fertility Transition of East Asian
Populations. U Pr of Hawaii.

Cho, Y. H. *see* Cho, Yong Hyo.

Cho, Yong Hyo, 1934-
xCho, Y. H.
Public Policy & Urban Crime. Ballinger Pub.

Choate, Joseph H. *see* Choate, Joseph Hodges.

Choate, Joseph Hodges, 1832-1917
xChoate, Joseph H.
American Addresses. Arno.

Choate, Judith.
xChoate, Judith.
Awful Alexander. Doubleday.
Patchwork. Doubleday.

Choay, Francoise.
xChoay, Francoise.

Le Corbusier. Braziller.

Chochem, Corinne.
xChochem, Corinne.
Palestine Dances: Folk Dances of Palestine.
Greenwood.

Chodes, John. *see* Chodes, John J.

Chodes, John J.
xChodes, John.
Corbitt: The Story of Ted Corbitt, Long
Distance Runner. Tafnews.

Chodorow, Stanley.
xChodorow, Stanley.
Christian Political Theory & Church Politics in
the Mid-Twelfth Century: The Ecclesiology
of Gratian's Decretum. U of Cal Pr.

Chodzko, Aleksander Borejko, 1804-1891
xChodzko, Alexander B.
Compiled by Specimens of the Popular Poetry
of Persia: As Found in the Adventures and
Improvisations of Kurroglu, the
Bandit-Minstrel of Northern Persia. B
Franklin.

Chodzko, Alexander B. *see* Chodzko, Aleksander
Borejko.

Choi, Frederick D. *see* Choi, Frederick D. S.

Choi, Frederick D. S.
xChoi, Frederick D.
Introduction to Multinational Accounting. P-H.

Choi, Woonsang, 1925-
xChoi, Woonsang.
Fall of the Hermit Kingdom. Oceana.

Cholakian, Patricia F. *see* Cholakian, Patricia Francis.

Cholakian, Patricia Francis.
xCholakian, Patricia F.
ed. The Early French Novella: An Anthology
of Fifteenth & Sixteenth Century Tales. State
U NY Pr.

Cholawski, Shalom.
nCholawski, Shalom.
Soldiers from the Ghetto: Jewish Armed
Resistance in the East, 1941-1945. A S
Barnes.

Cholmeley, Katharine.
xCholmeley, Katharine.
Margery Kempe, Genius & Mystic. Folcroft.

Chomsky, Noam.
xChomsky, Noam.
American Power & the New Mandarins.
Pantheon.
American Power & the New Mandarins.
Random.
Aspects of the Theory of Syntax. MIT Pr.
Cartesian Linguistics: A Chapter in the History
of Rationalist Thought. Har-Row.
Current Issues in Linguistic Theory. Mouton.
The Logical Structure of Linguistic Theory.
Plenum Pub.
Morphophonemics of Modern Hebrew. Garland
Pub.
Peace in the Middle East?: Reflections on
Justice & Nationhood. Random.
Reflections on Language. Pantheon.
Rules & Representations. Columbia U Pr.
The Sound Pattern of English. Har-Row.

Chonko, Lawrence B.
xChonko, Lawrence B.
Selling & Sales Management: A Bibliography.
Am Mktg.

Chopin, Fryderyk. *see* Chopin, Fryderyk Franciszek.

Chopin, Fryderyk Franciszek.
xChopin, Fryderyk.
Selected Correspondence of Fryderyk Chopin.
Da Capo.

Chopin, K. *see* Chopin, Kate O'Flaherty.

Chopin, Kate. *see* Chopin, Kate O'Flaherty.

Chopin, Kate O'Flaherty.
xChopin, K.
Awakening & Other Stories. HR&W.
xChopin, Kate.

The Awakening. Avon.
The Awakening. Gordon Pr.
The Awakening. Norton.
Awakening & Other Stories. Peter Smith.
A Night in Acadie. Gordon Pr.
A Night in Acadie. Mss Info.
Choppin, Bruce.
xChoppin, Bruce.
ed. Admission to Higher Education: A Select
Annotated Bibliography. Humanities.
Aptitude Testing at Eighteen Plus. Humanities.
Choppin, G. *see* Choppin, Gregory R.
Choppin, Gregory R.
xChoppin, G.
ed. Nuclear Chemistry: Theory & Applications.
Pergamon.
Chopra, Kasturi L., 1933-
xChopra, Kasturi L.
Thin Film Phenomena. Krieger.
Chopra, P. N. *see* Chopra, Pran Nath.
Chopra, Pran, 1921-
xChopra, Pran.
India's Second Liberation. Advent Bk.
India's Second Liberation. Intl Bk Dist.
India's Second Liberation. MIT Pr.
On an Indian Border. Asia.
Uncertain India: A Political Profile of Two
Decades of Freedom. MIT Pr.
Chopra, Pran Nath.
xChopra, P. N.
Life & Letters Under the Mughals. South Asia
Bks.
Chopra, S. N. *see* Chopra, Surendranath.
Chopra, Surendranath, 1916-
xChopra, S. N.
India: An Area Study. Intl Pubns Serv.
xChopra, Surendranath.
India: An Area Study. Verry.
Choquet, Gustav. *see* Choquet, Gustave.
Choquet, Gustave.
xChoquet, Gustav.
Topology. Acad Pr.
Chorafas, Dimitris N.
xChorafas, Dimitrius N.
Control Systems Functions & Programming
Approaches. Acad Pr.
Chorafas, Dimitrius N. *see* Chorafas, Dimitris N.
Chorao, Kay.
xChorao, Kay.
The Baby's Lap Book. Dutton.
illus. Ida Makes a Movie. HM.
illus. Lester's Overnight. Dutton.
Molly's Lies. HM.
illus. The Repair of Uncle Toe. FS&G.
Chorin, A. J. *see* Chorin, Alexandre Joel.
Chorin, Alexandre J. *see* Chorin, Alexandre Joel.
Chorin, Alexandre Joel.
xChorin, A. J.
A Mathematical Introduction to Fluid
Mechanics. Springer-Verlag.
xChorin, Alexandre J.
Lectures on Turbulence Theory. Publish or
Perish.
Chorlton, F.
xChorlton, Frank.
ed. Textbook of Dynamics. Halsted Pr.
Chorlton, Frank. *see* Chorlton, F.
Choron, Jacques.
xChoron, Jacques.
Death & Western Thought. Macmillan.
Death & Western Thought. Macmillan.
Suicide. Scribner.
Chorover, Stephan. *see* Chorover, Stephan L.
Chorover, Stephan L.
xChorover, Stephan.
From Genesis to Genocide: The Meaning of
Human Nature & the Power of Behavior
Control. MIT Pr.
Chottiner, Sherman.
xChottiner, Sherman.

Mathematics for Modern Management.
Har-Row.
Chotzinoff, Samuel, 1889-1964
xChotzinoff, Samuel.
A Lost Paradise: Early Reminiscences. Arno.
Toscanini: An Intimate Portrait. Da Capo.
Chotzner, J. *see* Chotzner, Joseph.
Chotzner, Joseph, 1844-1914
xChotzner, J.
Hebrew Humour & Other Essays. Arden Lib.
Hebrew Humour & Other Essays. Folcroft.
Hebrew Humour & Other Essays. R West.
Chou, Calvin.
xChou, Calvin.
The Hollow Line in Dating Chinese Porcelains.
Chinese Art App.
Chou, Hung-Hsiang.
xChou, Hung-hsiang.
Oracle Bone Collections in the United States.
U of Cal Pr.
Chou, Shelley N.
xChou, Shelley N.
ed. Spinal Deformities & Neurological
Dysfunction. Raven.
Chou, Te-Chuan.
xChou, Techuan.
Clinical Vectorcardiography. Grune.
Chou, Techuan. *see* Chou, Te-Chuan.
Chou, Ya-Lun, 1922-
xChou, Ya-Lun.
Probability & Statistics for Decision-Making.
HR&W.
Choubey, B. N. *see* Choubey, Bishwa Nath.
Choubey, Bishwa Nath, 1930-
xChoubey, B. N.
Principles & Practice of Cooperative Banking
in India. Asia.
Choucri, Nazli.
xChoucri, Nazli.
ed. Forecasting in International Relations:
Theory, Methods, Problems, Prospects. W H
Freeman.
Nations in Conflict: National Growth &
International Violence. W H Freeman.
Population Dynamics & International Violence:
Propositions, Insights & Evidence. Lexington
Bks.
Choudhury, Bikram.
xChoudhury, Bikram.
Bikram's Beginning Yoga Class. J P Tarcher.
Choudhury, G. W. *see* Choudhury, Golam Wahed.
Choudhury, Golam Wahed.
xChoudhury, G. W.
The Last Days of United Pakistan. Ind U Pr.
Chouinard, Yvon, 1938-
xChouinard, Yvon.
Climbing Ice. Sierra.
Choukas, Michael, 1901-
xChoukas, Michael.
Propaganda Comes of Age. Pub Aff Pr.
Choukri, Mohamed, 1935-
xChoukri, Mohamed.
Tennessee Williams in Tangier. Cadmus Eds.
Chouraqui, Andre, 1917-
xChouraqui, Andre.
Letter to an Arab Friend. U of Mass Pr.
The People & the Faith of the Bible. U of Mass
Pr.
Chow, Brian G.
xChow, Brian G.
The Liquid Metal Fast Breeder Reactor: An
Economic Analysis. Am Enterprise.
Chow, Chuen-Yen, 1932-
xChow, Chuen-Yen.
An Introduction to Computational Fluid
Mechanics. Wiley.
Chow, Marilyn P.
xChow, Marilyn P.

Handbook of Pediatric Primary Care. Wiley.
Chow, Willard T.
xChow, Willard T.
The Reemergence of an Inner City: The Pivot
of Chinese Settlement in the East Bay Region
of the San Francisco Bay Area. R & E Res
Assoc.
Chow, Woo F. *see* Chow, Woo Foung.
Chow, Woo Foung, 1922-
xChow, Woo F.
Principles of Tunnel Diode Circuits. Krieger.
Chowla, S. *see* Chowla, Sarvadaman.
Chowla, Sarvadaman, 1907-
xChowla, S.
Riemann Hypothesis & Hilberts Tenth
Problem. Gordon.
Chown, John F., 1929-
xChown, John F.
Taxation & Multinational Enterprise. Longman.
Choy, Bong Youn, 1914-
xChoy, Bong-Yong.
Koreans in America. Nelson-Hall.
Choy, Bong-Yong. *see* Choy, Bong Youn.
Chreitzberg, Abel M. *see* Chreitzberg, Abel Mckee.
Chreitzberg, Abel Mckee, 1820-1908
xChreitzberg, Abel M.
Early Methodism in the Carolinas. Reprint.
Chrimes, Stanley B. *see* Chrimes, Stanley Bertram.
Chrimes, Stanley Bertram, 1907-
xChrimes, Stanley B.
English Constitutional History. Oxford U Pr.
English Constitutional Ideas in the Fifteenth
Century. AMS Pr.
Chrislock, Carl H. *see* Chrislock, Carl Henry.
Chrislock, Carl Henry.
xChrislock, Carl H.
The Progressive Era in Minnesota, 1899-1918.
Minn Hist.
Chrisman, Berna H. *see* Chrisman, Berna Hunter.
Chrisman, Berna Hunter, 1877-1963
xChrisman, Berna H.
When You & I Were Young, Nebraska.
Purcells.
Chrispeels, Maarten J.
xChrispeels, Maarten J.
Plants, Food, & People. W H Freeman.
Chrispin, A. R., 1930-
xChrispin, A. R.
Diagnostic Imaging of the Kidney & Urinary
Tract in Children. Springer-Verlag.
Christ, Carl F.
xChrist, Carl F.
Measurement in Economics: Studies in
Mathematical Economics & Econometrics in
Memory of Yehuda Grunfeld. Stanford U Pr.
Christ, Carol. *see* Christ, Carol P.
Christ, Carol P.
xChrist, Carol.
Diving Deep & Surfacing: Women Writers on
Spiritual Quest. Beacon Pr.
xChrist, Carol P.
Diving Deep & Surfacing: Women Writers on
Spiritual Quest. Beacon Pr.
Womanspirit Rising: A Feminist Reader in
Religion. Har-Row.
Christ, William.
xChrist, William.
Introduction to Materials & Structure of Music.
P-H.
Materials & Structure of Music. P-H.
xChrist, William B.
Materials & Structure of Music. P-H.
Christ, William B. *see* Christ, William.
Christ-Janer, Albert, 1910-
xChrist-Janer, Albert.
Eliel Saarinen: Finnish-American Architect &
Educator. U of Chicago Pr.
Christakes, George.
xChristakes, George.

Ethics in Counseling: Problem Situations. U of
Ariz Pr.
Study Power: Better Study Skills-Greater
Success in College. P Juul Pr.
Christiansen, Monty L., 1941-
xChristiansen, Monty L.
Park Planning Handbook: Fundamentals of
Physical Planning for Parks & Recreation
Areas. Wiley.
Christiansen, Nels W. see Christiansen, Nels Woodruff.
Christiansen, Nels Woodruff, 1893-
xChristiansen, Nels W.
The Relation of Supervision & Other Factors
to Certain Phases of Musical Achievement in
the Rural Schools of Utah. AMS Pr.
Christiansen, Pauline. see Christiansen, Pauline Grabill.
Christiansen, Pauline Grabill.
xChristiansen, Pauline.
From Inside Out: Writing from Subjective to
Objective. Winthrop.
Christiansen, Reidar T. see Christiansen, Reidar Thoralf.
Christiansen, Reidar Thoralf, 1886-
xChristiansen, Reidar T.
ed. Folktales of Norway. U of Chicago Pr.
Christiansen, Sigurd. see Christiansen, Sigurd Wesley.
Christiansen, Sigurd Wesley, 1891-1947
xChristiansen, Sigurd.
Two Living & One Dead. Greenwood.

Christie, Agatha. see Christie, Agatha (Miller) Agatha
Mary Clarissa (Miller) Christie Mallowan.

Christie, Agatha (Miller) Agatha Mary Clarissa (Miller)
Christie Mallowan, Dame, 1891-1976

xChristie, Agatha.
And Then There Were None. PB.
And Then There Were None. WSP.
Appointment with Death. Dell.
The Boomerang Clue. Dell.
Cards on the Table. Dell.
Cards on the Table. Dodd.
A Caribbean Mystery. PB.
Crooked House. Dodd.
Crooked House. PB.
Dead Man's Mirror. Dell.
Death Comes As the End. PB.
Evil Under the Sun. PB.
Funerals Are Fatal. PB.
Halloween Party. PB.
Mrs. McGinty's Dead. PB.
Murder at the Vicarage. Dodd.
Murder in Retrospect. Dell.
Murder in Three Acts. Popular Lib.
Murder Is Announced. Dodd.
Murder Is Announced. PB.
The Murder of Roger Ackroyd. Dodd.
The Murder of Roger Ackroyd. Garland Pub.
Murder of Roger Ackroyd. PB.
Murder on the Links. Dell.
Murder with Mirrors. PB.
The Mysterious Mr. Quinn. Dell.
Nemesis. Dodd.
Nemesis. PB.
The Pale Horse. PB.
Postern of Fate. Bantam.
The Postern of Fate. Dodd.
Postern of Fate. G K Hall.
The Regatta Mystery. Dell.
Surprise Surprise. Dell.
Surprise, Surprise: A Collection of Mystery
Stories with Unexpected Endings. Dodd.
Ten Little Indians. Dodd.
There Is a Tide. Dell.
They Came from Baghdad. Dodd.
They Came to Baghdad. Dell.
The Third Girl. PB.
Christie, Archibald H.
xChristie, Archibald H.

Pattern Design: An Introduction to the Study
of Formal Ornament. Dover.
Pattern Design: An Introduction to the Study
of Formal Ornament. Peter Smith.
Christie, John A. see Christie, John Aldrich.
Christie, John Aldrich.
xChristie, John A.
Thoreau As World Traveler. Columbia U Pr.
Christie, O. F. see Christie, Octavius Francis.
Christie, Octavius F. see Christie, Octavius Francis.
Christie, Octavius Francis, 1867-
xChristie, O. F.
Johnson, the Essayist: His Opinions of Men,
Morals & Manners. Haskell.
Johnson, the Essayist: His Opinions of Men,
Morals & Manners. R West.
xChristie, Octavius F.
Dickens & His Age. Phaeton.
Christie, Richard.
xChristie, Richard.
Studies in Machiavellianism. Acad Pr.
Christine, Charles T.
xChristine, Charles T.
Practical Guide to Curriculum & Instruction.
P-H.
Christman, Elizabeth.
xChristman, Elizabeth.
Flesh & Spirit. Morrow.
A Nice Italian Girl. Dodd.
Christman, Ernest H.
xChristman, Ernst H.
Primer on Refraction. C C Thomas.
Christman, Ernst H. see Christman, Ernest H.
Christman, Raymond J. see Christman, Raymond John.
Christman, Raymond John, 1919-
xChristman, Raymond J.
Sensory Experience. Har-Row.
Christofides, Nicos.
xChristofides, Nicos.
ed. Combinatorial Optimization. Wiley.
Christoph, James B. see Christoph, James Bernard.
Christoph, James Bernard.
xChristoph, James B.
ed. Cases in Comparative Politics. Little.
Christopher, 1950-
xChristopher.
Our New Age: Words for the People. World
Light.
Christopher, A. J.
xChristopher, A. J.
Southern Africa. Shoe String.
Christopher, James W. see Christopher, James William.
Christopher, James William.
xChristopher, James W.
Conflict in the Far East: American Diplomacy
in China from 1928-1933. Arno.
Christopher, John.
xChristopher, John.
City of Gold & Lead. Macmillan.
City of Gold & Lead. Macmillan.
Dom & Va. Macmillan.
Guardians. Macmillan.
Guardians. Macmillan.
Lotus Caves. Macmillan.
Lotus Caves. Macmillan.
Pool of Fire. Macmillan.
Pool of Fire. Macmillan.
Prince in Waiting. Macmillan.
Prince in Waiting. Macmillan.
The Sword of the Spirits. Macmillan.
The Sword of the Spirits. Macmillan.
White Mountains. Macmillan.
White Mountains. Macmillan.
Christopher, Martin.
xChristopher, Martin.
Customer Service & Distribution Strategy.
Halsted Pr.
Christopher, Matt. see Christopher, Matthew F.
Christopher, Matthew F.
xChristopher, Matt.

Catch That Pass!. Archway.
Catch That Pass. PB.
Catch That Pass!. Little.
Catcher with a Glass Arm. Little.
Dirt Bike Racer. Little.
The Dog That Stole Football Plays. Little.
Face-off. Little.
Football Fugitive. Little.
The Fox Steals Home. Little.
Front Court Hex. Little.
Glue Fingers. Little.
Ice Magic. Little.
Johnny Long Legs. Little.
Johnny No Hit. Little.
Look Who's Playing First Base. Little.
No Arm in Left Field. Little.
Power Play. Little.
Stranded. Little.
The Submarine Pitch. Little.
Touchdown for Tommy. Little.
Tough to Tackle. Little.
The Twenty-One Mile Swim. Little.
Christopher, Milbourne.
xChristopher, Milbourne.
Houdini: A Pictorial Life. T Y Crowell.
Houdini: the Untold Story. PB.
The Illustrated History of Magic. T Y Crowell.
Mediums, Mystics & the Occult. T Y Crowell.
Panorama of Magic. Dover.
Search for the Soul. T Y Crowell.
Christopher, Peter.
xChristopher, Peter.
Images of Spain. Norton.
Christy, Arthur, 1899-1946
xChristy, Arthur.
Orient in American Transcendentalism: A
Study of Emerson, Thoreau & Alcott.
Octagon.
Christy, Dennis T., 1947-
xChristy, Dennis T.
Essentials of Precalculus Mathematics.
Har-Row.
Christy, G. A. see Christy, George A.
Christy, George.
xChristy, George.
Los Angeles Underground Gourmet. S&S.
Christy, George A.
xChristy, G. A.
Introduction to Investments. McGraw.
Christy, Jim, 1945-
xChristy, Jim.
Rough Road to the North: Travels Along the
Alaska Highway. Doubleday.
Christy, Joe.
xChristy, Joe.
The Complete Guide to Single-Engine
Beechcrafts. TAB Bks.
The Complete Guide to Single-Engine Cessnas.
TAB Bks.
How to Buy a Used Airplane. TAB Bks.
How to Install & Finish Synthetic Aircraft
Fabrics. TAB Bks.
Lear Jet. TAB Bks.
Maintenance Overhaul Guide to Lycoming
Aircraft Engines. TAB Bks.
Christy, John.
xChristy, John.
The Complete MG Guide Model by Model.
TAB Bks.
Chroman, Eleanor.
xChroman, Eleanor.
The Potter's Primer. Dutton.
Chronicles of England.
xChronicles of England.
The Brut: Part II. Kraus Repr.
Chruden, Herbert J.
xChruden, Herbert J.

Personnel Management. SW Pub.
Readings in Personnel Management. SW Pub.

Chu, Arthur.
xChu, Arthur.
The Collectors Book of Jade. Crown.

Chu, Daniel.
xChu, Daniel.
The Glorious Age in Africa: The Story of
Three Great African Empires. Doubleday.
Passage to the Golden Gate: A History of the
Chinese in America to 1910. Doubleday.

Chu, Don-Chean, 1910-
xChu, Don-Chean.
Chairman Mao: Education of the Proletariat.
Philos Lib.

Chu, Godwin. see Chu, Godwin C.

Chu, Godwin C., 1927-
xChu, Godwin.
Radical Change Through Communication in
Mao's China. U Pr of Hawaii.

Chu, Louis, 1915-
xChu, Louis.
Eat a Bowl of Tea. U of Wash Pr.

Chu, Wesley W.
xChu, Wesley W.
ed. Advances in Computer Communications.
Artech Hse.

Chu, Yaohan, 1920-
xChu, Yaohan.
Digital Computer Design Fundamentals.
McGraw.
Digital Simulation of Continuous Systems.
McGraw.

Chua, Leon O., 1936-
xChua, Leon O.
Introduction to Nonlinear Network Theory.
Krieger.

Chuan, Helen.
xChuan, Helen.
ed. Medical-Surgical Nursing: Pretest
Self-Assessment & Review. McGraw-Pretest.

Chubb, Basil.
xChubb, Basil.
The Government & Politics of Ireland.
Stanford U Pr.

Chubb, Bruce A.
xChubb, Bruce A.
How to Operate Your Model Railroad.
Kalmbach.

Chubb, Edwin W. see Chubb, Edwin Watts.

Chubb, Edwin Watts, 1865-1959
xChubb, Edwin W.
Masters of English Literature. Arno.
Stories of Authors, British & American. Arno.

Chubb, Thomas C. see Chubb, Thomas Caldecot.

Chubb, Thomas Caldecot, 1899-
xChubb, Thomas C.
Life of Giovanni Boccaccio. Kennikat.
The Life of Giovanni Boccaccio. R West.
White God & Other Poems. AMS Pr.
The White God & Other Poems. Elliots Bks.

Chudacoff, Howard P.
xChudacoff, Howard P.
Evolution of American Urban Society. P-H.

Chudoba, Bohdan.
xChudoba, Bohdan.
Spain & the Empire: 1519-1643. Octagon.

Chue, S. H.
xChue, S. H.
Thermodynamics: A Rigorous Postulatory
Approach. Wiley.

Chui, Edward F.
xChui, Edward F.
Golf. Goodyear.

Chuinard, E. G.
xChuinard, Eldon G.
Only One Man Died: The Medical Aspects of
the Lewis & Clark Expedition. A H Clark.

Chuinard, Eldon G. see Chuinard, E. G.

Chun, Ki-Taek.
xChun, Ki-Taek.
Measures for Psychological Assessment: A
Guide to 3,000 Original Sources & Their
Applications. U of Mich Soc Res.

Chung. see Chung, An-Min.

Chung, An-Min, 1921-
xChung.
Linear Programming. Merrill.

Chung, E. K. see Chung, Edward K.

Chung, Edward K.
xChung.
Artificial Cardiac Pacing: Practical Approach.
Williams & Wilkins.
xChung, E. K.
Ambulatory Electrocardiography: Holter
Monitor Electrocardiography.
Springer-Verlag.
xChung, Edward K.
Cardiac Arrhythmias: Self-Assessment.
Williams & Wilkins.
ed. Cardiac Emergency Care. Lea & Febiger.
Exercise Electrocardiography: Practical
Approach. Williams & Wilkins.
ed. Non-Invasive Cardiac Diagnosis. Lea &
Febiger.
Quick Reference to Cardiovascular Diseases.
Lippincott.

Chung, Henry.
xChung, Henry.
Oriental Policy of the United States. Arno.
The Oriental Policy of the United States.
Chinese Materials.

Chung, Joseph S. see Chung, Joseph Sang-Hoon.

Chung, Joseph Sang-Hoon, 1929-
xChung, Joseph S.
The North Korean Economy: Structure &
Development. Hoover Inst Pr.

Chung, K. L. see Chung, Kai Lai.

Chung, Kai L. see Chung, Kai Lai.

Chung, Kai Lai, 1917-
xChung, K. L.
Elementary Probability Theory with Stochastic
Processes. Springer-Verlag.
Lectures on Boundary Theory for Markov
Chains. Princeton U Pr.
xChung, Kai L.
A Course in Probability Theory. Acad Pr.

Chung, Sandra.
xChung, Sandra.
Case Marking & Grammatical Relations in
Polynesian. U of Tex Pr.

Chung, T. J.
xChung, T. J.
Finite Element Analysis in Fluid Dynamics.
McGraw.

Churba, Joseph.
xChurba, Joseph.
Politics of Defeat: America's Decline in the
Middle-East. Cyrco Pr.
The Politics of Defeat: America's Decline in
the Middle East. Irvington.

Church, A. Hamilton. see Church, Alexander Hamilton.

Church, Albert M.
xChurch, Albert M.
Statistics & Computers in the Appraisal
Process. Intl Assess.

Church, Alexander H. see Church, Alexander Hamilton.

Church, Alexander Hamilton, 1866-
xChurch, A. Hamilton.
The Proper Distribution of Expense Burden.
Arno.
xChurch, Alexander H.
Production Factors in Cost Accounting &
Works Management. Arno.

Church, Alfred J. see Church, Alfred John.

Church, Alfred John, 1829-1912
xChurch, Alfred J.
Early Britain. Dynamic Learn Corp.
xChurch, Alfred S.

Early Britain. Folcroft.

Church, Alfred S. see Church, Alfred John.

Church, Alonzo, 1903-
xChurch, Alonzo.
Calculi of Lambda Conversion. Kraus Repr.
Introduction to Mathematical Logic. Kraus
Repr.
Introduction to Mathematical Logic. Princeton
U Pr.

Church, Archibald G. see Church, Archibald George.

Church, Archibald George, 1886-
xChurch, Archibald G.
East Africa, a New Dominion: A Crucial
Experiment in Tropical Development & Its
Significance to the British Empire. Negro U
Pr.

Church, Arthur H. see Church, Arthur Henry.

Church, Arthur Henry, 1865-1937
xChurch, Arthur H.
On the Interpretation of Phenomena of
Phyllotaxis. Hafner.
Thalassiophyta & the Subaerial Transmigration.
Hafner.

Church, Austin H. see Church, Austin Harris.

Church, Austin Harris, 1906-
xChurch, Austin H.
Mechanical Vibrations. Wiley.

Church, J. W.
xChurch, J. W.
Deep in Piney Woods. Arno.

Church, James C., 1911-
xChurch, James C.
Practical Plumbing Design Guide. McGraw.

Church, Joseph.
xChurch, Joseph.
Understanding Your Child from Birth to Three:
A Guide to Your Child's Psychological
Development. Random.

Church, Margaret.
xChurch, Margaret.
Don Quixote: The Knight of La Mancha. NYU
Pr.

Church of England.
xChurch of England.
Articles to Be Inquired of, in the First
Metropoliticall Visitation of the Most
Reverand Father, Richarde...Archbishop of
Canterbury. Walter J Johnson.

Church of Scotland.
xChurch of Scotland.
The First & Second Booke of Discipline:
Together with Some Acts of the Generall
Assemblies. Walter J Johnson.
Register of Ministers, Exhorters & Readers &
of Their Stipends. AMS Pr.

Church Of Scotland - General Assembly - Committee On
Public Worship And Aids To Devotion. see Church of
Scotland. General Assembly. Committee on Public
Worship and Aids to Devotion.

**Church of Scotland. General Assembly. Committee on
Public Worship and Aids to Devotion.**
xChurch Of Scotland - General Assembly -
Committee On Public Worship And Aids To
Devotion.
Prayers for the Christian Year. Oxford U Pr.

Church of South India.
xChurch Of South India.
Book of Common Worship. Oxford U Pr.
Order for the Lord's Supper or the Holy
Eucharist. Oxford U Pr.
Ordinal: Orders for the Ordination of Deacons,
the Ordination of Presbyters, the
Consecration of Bishops. Oxford U Pr.

Church, R. W. see Church, Richard William.

Church, Richard, 1893-
xChurch, Richard.

The Collected Poems of Richard Church. AMS
    Pr.
Eight for Immortality. Arno.
Eight for Immortality. Folcroft.
Five Boys in a Cave. John Day.
French Lieutenant: A Ghost Story. John Day.
Mary Shelley. Arden Lib.
Mary Shelley. Folcroft.
Church, Richard W. see Church, Richard William.
Church, Richard William, 1815-1890
    xChurch, R. W.
    The Oxford Movement: Twelve Years
        1833-1845. Norwood Edns.
    Oxford Movement: Twelve Years, 1833-1845.
        U of Chicago Pr.
    xChurch, Richard W.
    Bacon. AMS Pr.
    Bacon. Folcroft.
    Dante & Other Essays. Folcroft.
    Dante & Other Essays. Kennikat.
    Spenser. AMS Pr.
    Spenser. Folcroft.
    Spenser. Gale.
Church, Robert. see Church, Robert J.
Church, Robert J.
    xChurch, Robert.
    Turtles. TFH Pubns.
Church, Ronald J. see Church, Ronald James Harrison.
Church, Ronald James Harrison.
    xChurch, Ronald J.
    Modern Colonization. Hyperion Conn.
Church, Roy A.
    xChurch, Roy A.
    Economic & Social Change in a Midland
        Town: Victorian Nottingham, 1815-1900.
        Biblio Dist.
    Economic & Social Change in a Midland
        Town: Victorian Nottingham, 1815-1900.
        Kelley.
Church, Ruth E. see Church, Ruth Ellen.
Church, Ruth Ellen.
    xChurch, Ruth E.
    Entertaining with Wine. Rand.
Church, Vivian.
    xChurch, Vivian.
    Colors Around Me. Afro Am.
Church, William F. see Church, William Farr.
Church, William Farr, 1912-
    xChurch, William F.
    Richelieu & Reason of State. Princeton U Pr.
Churchill, David.
    xChurchill, David.
    It, Us & the Others. Har-Row.
Churchill, E. Richard. see Churchill, Elmer Richard.
Churchill, Elmer Richard.

    xChurchill, E. Richard.

    Holiday Hullabaloo!: Facts, Jokes, & Riddles.
        Watts.

Churchill, George B. see Churchill, George Bosworth.
Churchill, George Bosworth, 1866-1925
    xChurchill, George B.
    Richard the Third up to Shakespeare. Johnson
        Repr.
    Richard the Third up to Shakespeare. Rowman.
Churchill, Henry S. see Churchill, Henry Stern.
Churchill, Henry Stern.
    xChurchill, Henry S.
    City Is the People. Norton.
Churchill, James E., 1934-
    xChurchill, James E.
    The Backyard Building Book. Stackpole.
    The Backyard Building Book II. Stackpole.
    The Homesteader's Handbook. Random.

Churchill, Lindsey, 1935-
    xChurchill, Lindsey.

Questioning Strategies in Sociolinguistics.
    Newbury Hse.
Churchill, Rogers P. see Churchill, Rogers Platt.
Churchill, Rogers Platt, 1902-
    xChurchill, Rogers P.
    The Anglo-Russian Convention of 1907. Arno.
    The Anglo-Russian Convention of 1907. R S
        Barnes.
    xChurchill, Rogers Platt.
    The Anglo-Russian Convention of 1907.
        Octagon.
Churchill, Ruel V. see Churchill, Ruel Vance.
Churchill, Ruel Vance, 1899-
    xChurchill, Ruel V.
    Complex Variables & Applications. McGraw.
    Operational Mathematics. McGraw.
Churchill, Sallie R.
    xChurchill, Sallie R.
    ed. No Child Is Unadoptable: A Reader on
        Adoption of Children with Special Needs.
        Sage.
Churchill, Sam. see Churchill, Samuel.
Churchill, Samuel, 1911-
    xChurchill, Sam.
    Don't Call Me Ma. Doubleday.
Churchill, Stuart W. see Churchill, Stuart Winston.
Churchill, Stuart Winston, 1920-
    xChurchill, Stuart W.
    The Interpretation & Use of Rate Data: The
        Rate Concept. Hemisphere Pub.
Churchill, William, 1859-1920
    xChurchill, William.
    Beach-la-Mar, the Jargon or Trade Speech of
        the Western Pacific. AMS Pr.
Churchill, Winston, 1871-1947
    xChurchill, Winston.
    Coniston. Folcroft.
    Coniston. Irvington.
    The Crisis. Folcroft.
Churchill, Winston Leonard Spencer, Sir, 1874-1965
    xChurchill, Winston S.
    Great Contemporaries. Arno.
    Great Contemporaries. U of Chicago Pr.
    Liberalism & the Social Problem. Haskell.
    People's Rights. Taplinger.
    While England Slept: A Survey of World
        Affairs 1932-8. Arno.
Churchill, Winston S. see Churchill, Winston Leonard
    Spencer.
Churchland, P. M. see Churchland, Paul M.
Churchland, Paul M., 1942-
    xChurchland, P. M.
    Scientific Realism & the Plasticity of Mind.
        Cambridge U Pr.
Churchman, C. West. see Churchman, Charles West.
Churchman, Charles West, 1913-
    xChurchman, C. West.
    Systems Approach. Dell.
    The Systems Approach & Its Enemies. Basic.
    Thinking for Decisions: Deductive Quantitative
        Methods. SRA.
Churchman, P. H. see Churchman, Philip Hudson.
Churchman, Philip H. see Churchman, Philip Hudson.
Churchman, Philip Hudson.
    xChurchman, P. H.
    A Survey of the Influence of Sir Walter Scott
        in Spain. Folcroft.
    xChurchman, Philip H.
    A Survey of the Influence of Sir Walter Scott
        in Spain. Arden Lib.
Churchward, L. G.
    xChurchward, L. G.
    Contemporary Soviet Government. Elsevier.
Churg, Jacob.
    xChurg, Jacob.
    Kidney Disease: Present Status. Williams &
        Wilkins.
Churgin, Jonah R.
    xChurgin, Jonah R.

The New Woman & the Old Academe: Sexism
    & Higher Education. Libra.
Chused, Richard H., 1943-
    xChused, Richard H.
    A Modern Approach to Property: Cases,
        Notes, Materials. West Pub.
Chusid, Joseph G.
    xChusid, Joseph G.
    Correlative Neuroanatomy & Functional
        Neurology. Lange.
Chute, B. J. see Chute, Beatrice Joy.
Chute, Beatrice Joy.
    xChute, B. J.
    Greenwillow. Dutton.
    Story of a Small Life. Dutton.
Chute, G. M. see Chute, George M.
Chute, George M.
    xChute, G. M.
    Electronics in Industry. McGraw.
    xChute, George M.
    Electronics in Industry. McGraw.
Chute, Marchette. see Chute, Marchette Gaylord.
Chute, Marchette Gaylord, 1909-
    xChute, Marchette.
    Geoffrey Chaucer of England. Dutton.
    The Green Tree of Democracy. Dutton.
    Introduction to Shakespeare. Dutton.
    Stories from Shakespeare. NAL.
    Stories from Shakespeare. Philomel.
    Wonderful Winter. Dutton.
Chute, William J. see Chute, William Joseph.
Chute, William Joseph.
    xChute, William J.
    Damn Yankee: The First Career of Frederick
        A. P. Barnard. Kennikat.
Chyatte, Sam L. see Chyatte, Samuel B.
Chyatte, Samuel B.
    xChyatte, Sam L.
    ed. Rehabilitation in Chronic Renal Failure.
        Williams & Wilkins.
Chyet, Stanley F.
    xChyet, Stanley F.
    Lopez of Newport: Colonial American
        Merchant Prince. Wayne St U Pr.
Chyzowych, Walter.
    xChyzowych, Walter.
    The Official Soccer Book of the United States
        Soccer Federation. Rand.
Ciarcia, Steve.
    xCiarcia, Steve.
    Ciarcia's Circuit Cellar. McGraw.
Ciardi, John.
    xCiardi, John.
    For Instance. Norton.
    How Does a Poem Mean. HM.
    The Little That Is All. Rutgers U Pr.
    Lives of X. Rutgers U Pr.
    This Strangest Everything. Rutgers U Pr.
Ciarlet, P. G. see Ciarlet, Philippe G.
Ciarlet, Philippe G.
    xCiarlet, P. G.
    The Finite Element Method for Elliptic
        Problems. Elsevier.
Ciba Foundation.
    xCIBA Foundation.

ed. Acute Diarrhea. Elsevier.
Aromatic Amino Acids in the Brain:
  Proceedings. Elsevier.
Atherogenesis; Initiating Factors: Proceedings.
  Elsevier.
Biochemistry & Pharmacology of Platelets.
  Elsevier.
Carbon-Fluorine Compounds. Elsevier.
Cell Patterning. Elsevier.
Chlorophyll Organization & Energy Transfer in
  Photosynthesis. Elsevier.
ed. Ciba Foundation Symposium No. 48.
  Elsevier.
CIBA Foundation Symposium 49: Health &
  Disease in Tribal Societies. Elsevier.
CIBA Foundation Symposium 51: Iron
  Metabolism. Elsevier.
CIBA Foundation Symposium 52: The Freezing
  of Mammalian Embryos. Elsevier.
CIBA Foundation Symposium 54: Respiratory
  Tract Mucus. Elsevier.
CIBA Foundation Symposium 55:
  Hepatotrophic Factors & the Liver. Elsevier.
CIBA Foundation Symposium 56: Cerebral
  Vascular Smooth Muscle & Its Control.
  Elsevier.
Civilization & Science. Elsevier.
Congenital Disorders of Erythroposesis.
  Elsevier.
Corneal Graft Failure. Elsevier.
ed. Embryogenesis in Mammals. Elsevier.
Energy Transformation in Biological Systems.
  Elsevier.
Enzyme Defects & Immune Dysfunction.
  Elsevier.
Extrasensory Perception. Citadel Pr.
ed. The Future As an Academic Discipline.
  Elsevier.
Future 0f Philanthropic Organizations. Elsevier.
Haemopoietic Stem Cells. Elsevier.
Hard Tissue Growth, Repair &
  Remineralization. Elsevier.
Health Care in a Changing Setting: The U. K.
  Experience. Elsevier.
Human Genetics: Possibilities & Realities.
  Elsevier.
Immunopotentiation: Proceedings. Elsevier.
Intrauterine Infection. Elsevier.
Law & Ethics of A.I.D. & Embryo Transfer.
  Elsevier.
Lipids, Malnutrition, & the Developing Brain.
  Elsevier.
Locomotion of the Tissue Cells. Elsevier.
Lung Liquids. Elsevier.
Medical Care of Prisoners & Detainees.
  Elsevier.
Medical Research Systems in Europe:
  Proceedings. Elsevier.
ed. Monoamine Oxidase & Its Inhibition.
  Elsevier.
Ontogeny of Acquired Immunity. Elsevier.
ed. Outcome of Severe Damage to the Central
  Nervous System. Elsevier.
Pathogenic Mycoplasmas. Elsevier.
Peptide Transport in Bacteria & Mammalian
  Gut. Elsevier.
Physiology, Emotion & Psychosomatic Illness.
  Elsevier.
Polymerization in Biological Systems. Elsevier.
ed. Polypeptide Hormones: Molecular &
  Cellular Aspects. Elsevier.
Pregnancy Metabolism, Diabetes & the Fetus.
  Elsevier.
Protein Turnover. Elsevier.
ed. Research & Medical Practice: Their
  Interaction. Elsevier.
Sex, Hormones & Behaviour. Elsevier.
Size at Birth. Elsevier.
The Structure & Function of Chromatin.
  Elsevier.

Submolecular Biology & Cancer. Elsevier.
Trypanosomiasis & Leishmaniasis with Special
  Reference to Chigas' Disease: Proceedings.
  Elsevier.
xCiba Founndation.
  The Poisoned Patient: The Role of the
  Laboratory. Elsevier.
Ciba Founndation. *see* Ciba Foundation.
Cicchetti, Charles J.
  xCicchetti, Charles J.
    The Costs of Congestion: An Econometric
    Analysis of Wilderness Recreation. Ballinger
    Pub.
    The Marginal Cost & Pricing of Electricity: An
    Applied Approach. Ballinger Pub.
Ciccolella, Cathy.
  xCiccolella, Cathy.
    A Buyer's Guide to Videocassette Recorders.
    Sterling.
Ciccorella, Aubra Dair.
  xCiccorella, Patricia L.
    Crossing the Crest. Branden.
Ciccorella, Patricia L. *see* Ciccorella, Aubra Dair.
Cicero. *see* Cicero, Marcus Tullius.
Cicero, M. T. *see* Cicero, Marcus Tullius.
Cicero, Marcus T. *see* Cicero, Marcus Tullius.
Cicero, Marcus Tullius.
  xCicero.
    Cicero on Oratory & Orators. S Ill U Pr.
    Cicero's Letters to Atticus. Cambridge U Pr.
    Murder Trials. Penguin.
    Nature of the Gods. Penguin.
    Pro Milone. Cambridge U Pr.
    Thirty-Five Letters of Cicero. Oxford U Pr.
    Tusculan Disputations. Harvard U Pr.
  xCicero, M. T.
    On Old Age & on Friendship. U of Mich Pr.
  xCicero, Marcus T.
    Letters of Cicero: A Selection in Translation.
    Norton.
Cicourel, Aaron V. *see* Cicourel, Aaron Victor.
Cicourel, Aaron Victor, 1928-
  xCicourel, Aaron V.
    Theory & Method in a Study of Argentine
    Fertility. Krieger.
Ciferri, A.
  xCiferri, A.
    ed. Ultra-High Modulus Polymers. Burgess-Intl
    Ideas.
Cikovsky, Nicolai.
  xCikovsky, Nicolai.
    The Life & Work of George Inness. Garland
    Pub.
Cilingiroglu, Ayhan.
  xCilingiroglu, Ayhan.
    Manufacture of Heavy Electrical Equipment in
    Developing Countries. Johns Hopkins.
Cillie, Francois S. *see* Cillie, Francois Stephanus.
Cillie, Francois Stephanus, 1908-
  xCillie, Francois S.
    Centralization or Decentralization?: A Study in
    Educational Adaptation. AMS Pr.
Cimasoni, G.
  xCimasoni, Geneve.
    The Crevicular Fluid. S Karger.
Cimasoni, Geneve. *see* Cimasoni, G.
Cimerman, V. *see* Cimerman, Vjekoslav.
Cimerman, Vjekoslav.
  xCimerman, V.
    Atlas of Photogrammetric Instruments.
    Elsevier.
Ciminero, Anthony R.
  xCiminero, Anthony R.
    ed. Handbook of Behavioral Assessment.
    Wiley.
Cinader, Bernard. *see* Cinader, Bernhard.
Cinader, Bernhard.
  xCinader, Bernard.

ed. Immunology of Receptors. Dekker.
Cincinnati University.
  xUniversity of Cincinnati.
    Modern Greek Collection. G K Hall.
Cincura, Andrew, 1917-
  xCincura, Andrew.
    ed. An Anthology of Slovak Literature. Univ
    Hardcovers.
Cinlar, E. *see* Cinlar, Erhan.
Cinlar, Erhan, 1941-
  xCinlar, E.
    Introduction to Stochastic Processes. P-H.
Cinnamon, Kenneth. *see* Cinnamon, Kenneth M.
Cinnamon, Kenneth M.
  xCinnamon, Kenneth.
    Cults & Cons: The Exploitation of the
    Emotional Growth Consumer. Nelson-Hall.
Cioffari, Bernard.
  xCioffari, Bernard.
    Experiments in College Physics. Heath.
Cioffari, Vincenzo, 1905-
  xCioffari, Vincenzo.
    Beginning Italian. Heath.
Cioran, Samuel D. *see* Cioran, Samuel David.
Cioran, Samuel David, 1941-
  xCioran, Samuel D.
    The Apocalyptic Symbolism of Andrej Belyj.
    Mouton.
Cioranescu, Alexandre.
  xCioranescu, Alexandre.
    Vasile Alecsandri. Irvington.
Cipel, Louis.
  xCipel, Louis.
    Radiology of the Acute Abdomen in the
    Newborn: A Self-Teaching Manual. Grune.
Cipolla, Carlo. *see* Cipolla, Carlo M.
Cipolla, Carlo M.
  xCipolla, Carlo.
    Economic History of World Population.
    Penguin.
  xCipolla, Carlo M.
    Before the Industrial Revolution: European
    Society & Economy, 1000-1700. Norton.
    Clocks & Culture, 1300-1700. Norton.
    Cristofano & the Plague: A Study in the
    History of Public Health in the Age of
    Galileo. U of Cal Pr.
    The Economic History of World Population.
    B&N.
    Faith, Reason & the Plague in
    Seventeenth-Century Tuscany. Cornell U Pr.
    Guns, Sails & Empires: Technological
    Innovation & the Early Phases of European
    Expansion 1400-1700. T Y Crowell.
Cipriano, Anthony J.
  xCipriano, Anthony J.
    America's Journeys into Space: The Astronauts
    of the United States. Messner.
Cirese, Sarah.
  xCirese, Sarah.
    Quest: A Search for Self. HR&W.
Ciria, Alberto.
  xCiria, Alberto.
    Parties & Power in Modern Argentina,
    1930-1946. State U NY Pr.
Cirillo, R. *see* Cirillo, Renato.
Cirillo, Renato.
  xCirillo, R.
    The Economics of Vilfredo Pareto. Biblio Dist.
Cirker, Hayward.
  xCirker, Hayward.
    Monograms & Alphabetic Devices. Dover.
    Monograms & Alphabetic Devices. Peter
    Smith.
Cirlot, J. E. *see* Cirlot, Juan Eduardo.
Cirlot, Juan Eduardo.
  xCirlot, J. E.
    A Dictionary of Symbols. Philos Lib.
Cise, Jerrold G. Van. *see* Van Cise, Jerrold G.
Cise, Philip S. Van. *see* Van Cise, Philip S.

Ciske, Karen. see Ciske, Karen L.
Ciske, Karen L.
   xCiske, Karen.
     ed. Primary Nursing. Nursing Res.
Cismaru, Alfred, 1929-
   xCismaru, Alfred.
     Boris Vian. Twayne.
     Marguerite Duras. Twayne.
     Marivaux & Moliere: A Comparison. Tex Tech
       Pr.
Cissell, Robert.
   xCissell, Robert.
     Mathematics of Finance. HM.
Cissley, Charles H.
   xCissley, Charles H.
     Systems & Data Processing in Insurance
       Companies. LOMA.
Citati, Pietro.
   xCitati, Pietro.
     Goethe. Dial.
Citizens Board of Inquiry into Health Services for
   Americans. see Citizens' Board of Inquiry into Health
   Services for Americans.
Citizens' Association Of New York. see Citizens'
   Association of New York. Council of Hygiene and
   Public Health.
**Citizens' Association of New York. Council of Hygiene
   and Public Health.**
   xCitizens' Association Of New York.
     Report of the Council of Hygiene & Public
       Health of the Citizens' Association of New
       York Upon the Sanitary Condition of the
       City. Arno.
**Citizens' Board of Inquiry into Health Services for
   Americans.**
   xCitizens Board of Inquiry into Health Services for
     Americans.
     Heal Yourself. Am Pub Health.
Citizens' Research Foundation.
   xCitizens' Research Foundation.
     Model State Statute: Politics, Elections &
       Public Office. CRF.
     Money & Politics: A Report of the Citizens'
       Research Foundation Conference. CRF.
   xCitizens' Research Foundtion.
     Political Contributors & Lenders of 10.000
       Dollars or More in 1972. CRF.
   xCitizens's Research Foundation.
     Political Contributors of 500 Dollars or More
       in 1972 to Candidates & Committees in
       Twelve States. CRF.
Citizens' Research Foundtion. see Citizens' Research
   Foundation.
Citizens's Research Foundation. see Citizens' Research
   Foundation.
Citizenship Education Study. see Citizenship Education
   Study, Detroit.
Citizenship Education Study, Detroit.
   xCitizenship Education Study.
     Curriculum for Citzenship: A Total School
       Approach. Greenwood.
   xCitizenship Education Study Staff.
     Problem Solving. Wayne St U Pr.
Citizenship Education Study Staff. see Citizenship
   Education Study, Detroit.
Citrine, W. M. see Citrine, Walter Mclennan Citrine.
Citrine, Walter McLennan Citrine, Baron, 1887-
   xCitrine, W. M.
     Men & Work: An Autobiography. Greenwood.
City Literary Institute Of London. see London. City
   Literary Institute.
Ciupik, Larry A.
   xCiupik, Larry A.
     Space Machines. Raintree Pubs.
Civic Federation of Chicago, Chicago Conference on
   Trusts, Sept. 1899. see Chicago Conference on Trusts,
   1899.
Claerbaut, David.
   xClaerbaut, David P.

     Black Student Alienation: A Study. R & E Res
       Assoc.
Claerbaut, David P. see Claerbaut, David.
Claerbout, Jon F.
   xClaerbout, Jon F.
     Fundamentals of Geophysical Data Processing:
       With Applications to Petroleum Prospecting.
       McGraw.
Claessen, H. J. M.
   xClaessen, Henri J.
     ed. The Early State. Mouton.
Claessen, Henri J. see Claessen, H. J. M.
Clagett, Helen L. see Clagett, Helen Lord.
Clagett, Helen Lord.
   xClagett, Helen L.
     A Guide to the Law & Legal Literature of
       Argentina. Gordon Pr.
     A Guide to the Law & Legal Literature of the
       Mexican States. Gordon Pr.
Clagett, John.
   xClagett, John.
     Orange R. Popular Lib.
Clagett, Marshall, 1916-
   xClagett, Marshall.
     Greek Science in Antiquity. Arno.
Claghorn, Kate. see Claghorn, Kate Holladay.
Claghorn, Kate Holladay, 1863-1938
   xClaghorn, Kate.
     Immigrant's Day in Court. Arno.
Clague, Ewan.
   xClague, Ewan.
     Statistics & Economic Policy. U Cal LA Indus
       Rel.
Claiborne, Craig.
   xClaiborne, Craig.
     The Chinese Cookbook. Lippincott.
     Classic French Cooking. Silver.
     Cooking with Herbs & Spices. Bantam.
     Cooking with Herbs & Spices. Har-Row.
     Craig Claiborne's Favorites from the New
       York Times. Times Bks.
     Craig Claiborne's Favorites from The New
       York Times. Warner Bks.
     Craig Claiborne's Kitchen Primer. Knopf.
     Craig Claiborne's Kitchen Primer. Random.
     Craig Claiborne's New New York Times
       Cookbook. Times Bks.
     Veal Cookery. Har-Row.
Claiborne, Robert.
   xClaiborne, Robert.
     The First Americans. Time-Life.
     The First Americans. Silver.
     God or Beast: Evolution & Human Nature.
       Norton.
Clair, Leonard St. see St. Clair, Leonard.
Clair, Rene, 1898-
   xClair, Rene.
     Cinema Yesterday & Today. Peter Smith.
Claire, Keith.
   xClaire, Keith.
     The Otherwise Girl. HR&W.
Claire, Rosine, 1911-
   xClaire, Rosine.
     French Gourmet Vegetarian Cookbook.
       Celestial Arts.
     French Vegetarian Cosmetics. Strawberry Hill.
Claire, Vivian.
   xClaire, Vivian.
     Linda Ronstadt. Music Sales.
Clairmont, Claire. see Clairmont, Clara Mary Jane.
Clairmont, Clara Mary Jane.
   xClairmont, Claire.
     The Journals of Claire Clairmont. Harvard U
       Pr.
Clamp, Betty A. see Clamp, Betty Ann.
Clamp, Betty Ann.
   xClamp, Betty A.
     Cooking with Low Cost Proteins. Arco.
Clancey, K. see Clancey, Kevin.

Clancey, Kevin, 1944-
   xClancey, K.
     Seminormal Operators. Springer-Verlag.
Clanchy, M. T.
   xClanchy, M. T.
     From Memory to Written Record in England,
       1066-1307. Harvard U Pr.
Clancy, Ambrose, 1948-
   xClancy, Ambrose.
     Blind Pilot. Morrow.
Clancy, John.
   xClancy, John.
     Clancy's Oven Cookery. Delacorte.
     John Clancy's Fish Cookery. HR&W.
Clancy, Judith. see Clancy, Judith S.
Clancy, Judith S.
   xClancy, Judith.
     Last Look at the Old Met. Synergistic Pr.
Clancy, Laurie, 1942-
   xClancy, Laurie.
     A Collapsible Man. St Martin.
Clancy, Leo.
   xClancy, Leo.
     Fix. Knopf.
Clancy, Thomas H.
   xClancy, Thomas H.
     The Conversational Word of God: A
       Commentary on the Doctrine of St. Ignatius
       of Loyola Concerning Spiritual Conversation,
       with Four Early Jesuit Texts. Inst Jesuit.
     An Introduction to Jesuit Life: The
       Constitutions & History Through 435 Years.
       Inst Jesuit.
Claparede, Edouard, 1873-1940
   xClaparede, Edouard.
     Experimental Pedagogy & the Psychology of
       the Child. Arno.
Clapham, Arthur R. see Clapham, Arthur Roy.
Clapham, Arthur Roy.
   xClapham, Arthur R.
     Excursion Flora of the British Isles. Cambridge
       U Pr.
     Flora of the British Isles. Cambridge U Pr.
Clapham, C. R. see Clapham, C. R. J.
Clapham, C. R. J.
   xClapham, C. R.
     Introduction to Mathematical Analysis.
       Routledge & Kegan.
Clapham, J. H. see Clapham, John Harold.
Clapham, John.
   xClapham, John.
     Dvorak. Norton.
Clapham, John H. see Clapham, John Harold.
Clapham, John Harold, Sir, 1873-1946
   xClapham, J. H.
     Causes of the War of 1792. Octagon.
   xClapham, John H.
     Economic Development of France & Germany
       1815-1914. Cambridge U Pr.
Clapham, Sidney.
   xClapham, Sidney.
     Primulas. A S Barnes.
Clapham, W. B. see Clapham, Wentworth B.
Clapham, Wentworth B., 1942-
   xClapham, W. B.
     Natural Ecosystems. Macmillan.
Clapp, Charles L.
   xClapp, Charles L.
     The Congressman: His Work As He Sees It.
       Greenwood.
Clapp, Elsie R. see Clapp, Elsie Ripley.
Clapp, Elsie Ripley.
   xClapp, Elsie R.
     Community Schools in Action. Arno.
Clapp, Henry A. see Clapp, Henry Austin.
Clapp, Henry Austin, 1841-1904
   xClapp, Henry A.

Reminiscences of a Dramatic Critic: With an
Essay on the Art of Henry Irving. Arno.
Clapp, Jane.
xClapp, Jane.
Art Censorship: A Chronology of Proscribed &
Prescribed Art. Scarecrow.
Professional Ethics & Insignia. Scarecrow.
Clapp, Patricia.
xClapp, Patricia.
I'm Deborah Sampson: A Soldier in the War of
the Revolution. Lothrop.
Clar, C. Raymond.
xClar, C. Raymond.
Out of the River Mist. Forest Hist Soc.
Clar, Eric. see Clar, Erich Julius.
Clar, Erich Julius, 1902-
xClar, Eric.
The Aromatic Sextet. Wiley.
Clar, Lawrence. see Clar, Lawrence M.
Clar, Lawrence M.
xClar, Lawrence.
Calculus with Analytic Geometry for the
Technologies. P-H.
Mathematics for the Technologies with
Calculus. P-H.
xClar, Lawrence M.
Mathematics for Business & Consumers.
Macmillan.
Mathematics for the Technologies. P-H.
Clara, Louise P.
xClara, Louise P.
Solving Writing Problems: A Self-Paced
Workbook. HR&W.
Clardy, Jesse V.
xClardy, Jesse V.
The Superfluous Man in Russian Letters. U Pr
of Amer.
Clare, Anthony.
xClare, Anthony.
Psychiatry in Dissent: Controversial Issues in
Thought & Practice. Inst Study Human.
Clare, Christopher R.
xClare, Christopher R.
Designing Logic Systems Using State
Machines. McGraw.
Clare, Dollie.
xClare, Dollie.
The Tantalizing Disclosures of a Welsh Girl.
Philos Lib.
Clare, John.
xClare, John.
The Midsummer Cushion. Persea Bks.
Clare, Paul. see Clare, Paul K.
Clare, Paul K.
xClare, Paul.
Introduction to American Corrections.
Holbrook.
Clare, Wallace.
xClare, Wallace.
A Guide to Copies & Abstracts of Irish Wills.
Genealog Pub.
Claremon, Neil.
xClaremon, Neil.
Borderland. Knopf.
Easy Favors. McGraw.
Clareson, Thomas D.
xClareson, Thomas D.
Many Futures, Many Worlds: Theme and
Form in Science Fiction. Kent St U Pr.
Claretie, Jules, 1840-1913
xClaretie, Jules.
The Crime of the Boulevard. Arno.
Clarfield, Gerard H.
xClarfield, Gerard H.
Timothy Pickering & the American Republic.
U of Pittsburgh Pr.
Clarie, Thomas C., 1943-
xClarie, Thomas C.

Occult Bibliography: An Annotated List of
Books Published in English, 1971 Through
1975. Scarecrow.
Clarizio, Harvey F., 1934-
xClarizio, Harvey F.
Toward Positive Classroom Discipline. Wiley.
Clark. see Clark, A. F.
Clark, A. F.
xClark.
ed. Nonmetallic Materials & Composites at
Low Temperatures. Plenum Pub.
Clark, A. P.
xClark, A. P.
Advanced Data-Transmission Systems. Halsted
Pr.
Principles of Digital Data Transmission.
Halsted Pr.
Clark, Admont G. see Clark, Admont Gulick.
Clark, Admont Gulick.
xClark, Admont G.
The Real Imagination: An Introduction to
Poetry. SRA.
Clark, Albert C. see Clark, Albert Curtis.
Clark, Albert Curtis, 1859-1937
xClark, Albert C.
Descent of Manuscripts. Oxford U Pr.
Clark, Alfred, 1909-
xClark, Alfred.
Theory of Adsorption & Catalysis. Acad Pr.
Clark, Alice.
xClark, Alice.
Working Life of Women in the Seventeenth
Century. Biblio Dist.
Working Life of Women in the Seventeenth
Century. Kelley.
Clark, Ann L.
xClark, Ann L.
Childbearing: A Nursing Perspective. Davis Co.
A Short Course in Pediatric Care. West Pub.
Clark, Ann N. see Clark, Ann Nolan.
Clark, Ann Nolan, 1898-
xClark, Ann N.
All This Wild Land. Viking Pr.
Clark, Anne.
xClark, Anne.
Australian Adventure: Letters from an
Ambassador's Wife. U of Tex Pr.
Historic Homes of San Augustine. Encino Pr.
Homesteading in Urban U. S. A.. Praeger.
Clark, Annie M. see Clark, Annie Maria Lawrence.
Clark, Annie Maria Lawrence, 1835-1912
xClark, Annie M.
The Alcotts in Harvard. Folcroft.
Clark, Arthur M. see Clark, Arthur Melville.
Clark, Arthur Melville, 1895-
xClark, Arthur M.
The Realistic Revolt in Modern Poetry.
Folcroft.
Realistic Revolt in Modern Poetry. Haskell.
Studies in Literary Modes. Folcroft.
Thomas Heywood, Playwright & Miscellanist.
Russell.
Clark, Barrett H. see Clark, Barrett Harper.
Clark, Barrett Harper, 1890-1953
xClark, Barrett H.
Maxwell Anderson: The Man & His Plays.
Folcroft.
Paul Green. Haskell.
Clark, Bill.
xClark, Bill.
A Paper Ark. Everest Hse.
Clark, Brian.
xClark, Brian.
Whose Life Is It Anyway?. Avon.
Whose Life Is It Anyway?. Dodd.
Clark, Bruce B. see Clark, Bruce Budge.
Clark, Bruce Budge.
xClark, Bruce B.

Favorite Selections from Out of the Best
Books. Deseret Bk.
Clark, Burton R.
xClark, Burton R.
Academic Power in Italy: Bureaucracy &
Oligarchy in National University System. U
of Chicago Pr.
Clark, C. E. Frazer.
xClark, C. Frazer.
Nathaniel Hawthorne: A Descriptive
Bibliography. U of Pittsburgh Pr.
Clark, C. Frazer. see Clark, C. E. Frazer.
Clark, Cal.
xClark, Cal.
Comparative Patterns of Foreign Policy &
Trade: The Communist Balkans & Politics.
Intl Development.
Clark, Carolyn C. see Clark, Carolyn Chambers.
Clark, Carolyn Chambers.
xClark, Carolyn C.
Classroom Skills for Nurse Educators. Springer
Pub.
The Nurse As Continuing Educator. Springer
Pub.
Clark, Champ.
xClark, Champ.
The Badlands. Time-Life.
The Badlands. Silver.
Clark, Charles H. see Clark, Charles Heber.
Clark, Charles Heber, 1841-1915
xClark, Charles H.
Random Shots. Arno.
Clark, Charles M. see Clark, Charles Manning Hope.
Clark, Charles Manning Hope.
xClark, Charles M.
History of Australia. Intl Schol Bk Serv.
Clark, Charles T. see Clark, Charles Tallifero.
Clark, Charles Tallifero.
xClark, Charles T.
Statistical Analysis for Administrative
Decisions. SW Pub.
Clark, Chester W. see Clark, Chester Wells.
Clark, Chester Wells.
xClark, Chester W.
Franz Joseph & Bismarck: The Diplomacy of
Austria Before the War of 1866. Russell.
Clark, Colin, 1905-
xClark, Colin.
Population Growth & Land Use. St Martin.
Starvation or Plenty?. Taplinger.
Value of Agricultural Land. Pergamon.
Clark, Colin. see Clark, Colin Grant.
Clark, Colin Grant, 1905-
xClark, Colin.
National Income & Outlay. Biblio Dist.
National Income & Outlay. Kelley.
National Income, 1924-1931. Biblio Dist.
Clark, Colin W. see Clark, Colin Whitcomb.
Clark, Colin Whitcomb, 1931-
xClark, Colin.
The Theoretical Side of Calculus. Krieger.
xClark, Colin W.
Mathematical Bioeconomics: The Optimal
Management of Renewable Resources. Wiley.
Clark, Cumberland, 1862-
xClark, Cumberland.
Astronomy in the Poets. Folcroft.
Charles Dickens & the Begging-Letter Writer.
Haskell.
Charles Dickens & the Yorkshire Schools, with
His Letter to Mrs. Hall. Folcroft.
The Dogs in Dickens. Haskell.
Shakespeare & Costume. Folcroft.
A Study of Macbeth. Folcroft.
A Study of Shakespeare's Henry VIII. Folcroft.
Clark, D. Cecil.
xClark, D. Cecil.
Using Instructional Objectives in Teaching.
Scott F.
Clark, D. H. see Clark, David H.

Clark, D. T. *see* Clark, David Thomas.
Clark, David. *see* Clark, David Hazell.
Clark, David Allen.
  xClark, David Allen.
    Jokes, Puns, & Riddles. Doubleday.
Clark, David H.
  xClark, D. H.
    ed. Historical Supernovae. Pergamon.
Clark, David Hazell.
  xClark, David.
    Social Therapy in Psychiatry. Aronson.
Clark, David K.
  xClark, David K.
    The Pantheism of Alan Watts. Inter-Varsity.
Clark, David L. *see* Clark, David Leigh.
Clark, David Leigh.
  xClark, David L.
    Conodonts & Zonation of the Upper Devonian
      in the Great Basin. Geol Soc.
Clark, David Thomas.
  xClark, D. T.
    Polymer Surfaces. Wiley.
Clark, Don. *see* Clark, Donald Henry.
Clark, Donald B. *see* Clark, Donald Bettice.
Clark, Donald Bettice.
  xClark, Donald B.
    Alexander Pope. Twayne.
    English Literature: A College Anthology.
      Macmillan.
Clark, Donald Henry.
  xClark, Don.
    Humanistic Teaching. Merrill.
    Living Gay. Celestial Arts.
    Loving Someone Gay. Celestial Arts.
    Loving Someone Gay. NAL.
Clark, Donald L. *see* Clark, Donald Lemen.
Clark, Donald Lemen, 1888-
  xClark, Donald L.
    Rhetoric in Greco-Roman Education.
      Greenwood.
Clark, Duvie.
  xClark, Duvie.
    The Peculiar Truth. Atheneum.
Clark, Edna M. *see* Clark, Edna Maria.
Clark, Edna Maria.
  xClark, Edna M.
    Ohio Art & Artists. Gale.
Clark, Eleanor, 1913-
  xClark, Eleanor.
    The Bitter Box. AMS Pr.
    Dr. Heart: A Novella & Other Stories.
      Pantheon.
    Eyes, Etc.: A Memoir. Pantheon.
Clark, Electa.
  xClark, Electa.
    Leading Ladies: An Affectionate Look at
      American Women of the Twentieth Century.
      Stein & Day.
Clark, Ella E. *see* Clark, Ella Elizabeth.
Clark, Ella Elizabeth, 1896-
  xClark, Ella E.
    Indian Legends from the Northern Rockies. U
      of Okla Pr.
    Indian Legends of the Pacific Northwest. U of
      Cal Pr.
Clark, Ellery H. *see* Clark, Ellery Harding.
Clark, Ellery Harding, 1909-
  xClark, Ellery H.
    Boston Red Sox: 75th Anniversary History,
      1901-1975. Exposition.
    Red Sox Fever. Exposition.
Clark, Eric, fl. 1969-
  xClark, Eric.
    The Sleeper. Atheneum.
Clark, Evans, 1888-
  xClark, Evans.
    Financing the Consumer. Arno.
Clark, Felton G. *see* Clark, Felton Grandison.
Clark, Felton Grandison, 1903-
  xClark, Felton G.

    The Control of State-Supported
      Teacher-Training Programs for Negroes.
      AMS Pr.
Clark, Francis E. *see* Clark, Francis Edward.
Clark, Francis Edward, 1851-1927
  xClark, Francis E.
    Our Italian Fellow Citizens in Their Old
      Homes & Their New. Arno.
Clark, Frank.
  xClark, Frank.
    Contemporary Math. Watts.
Clark, Frank J. *see* Clark, Frank James.
Clark, Frank James, 1922-
  xClark, Frank J.
    Mathematics for Data Processing. Reston.
Clark, Fred E. *see* Clark, Fred Emerson.
Clark, Fred Emerson, 1890-
  xClark, Fred E.
    Principles of Marketing. Arno.
Clark, Fred M.
  xClark, Fred M.
    Objective Methods for Testing Authenticity &
      the Study of Ten Doubtful "Comedias"
      Attributed to Lope de Vega. U of NC Pr.
Clark, Freda, 1978-
  xClark, Freda.
    Secretary's Desk Book of Shortcuts &
      Timesavers. P-H.
Clark, G. *see* Clark, Garth.
Clark, Gail.
  xClark, Gail.
    The Baroness of Bow Street. PB.
    The Baroness of Bow Street. Putnam.
    Dulcie Bligh. PB.
Clark, Garth.
  xClark, G.
    Potters of Southern Africa. Verry.
Clark, George.
  xClark, George.
    Primer in Neurological Staining Procedures. C
      C Thomas.
Clark, George N. *see* Clark, George Norman.
Clark, George Norman, Sir, 1890-
  xClark, George N.
    Dutch Alliance & the War Against French
      Trade, 1688-1697. Russell.
    History of the Royal College of Physicians of
      London. Oxford U Pr.
    Later Stuarts, 1660-1714. Oxford U Pr.
Clark, Gilbert.
  xClark, Gilbert.
    Art-Design: Communicating Visually. Art
      Educ.
Clark, Gordon H. *see* Clark, Gordon Haddon.
Clark, Gordon Haddon.
  xClark, Gordon H.
    Dewey. Presby & Reformed.
    Religion, Reason & Revelation. Presby &
      Reformed.
Clark, Grahame. *see* Clark, John Grahame Douglas.
Clark, Grover.
  xClark, Grover.
    Balance Sheets of Imperialism: Facts & Figures
      on Colonies. Russell.
    The Great Wall Crumbles. Arno.
Clark, H. *see* Clark, Hylton.
Clark, Harold. *see* Clark, Harold Willard.
Clark, Harold F. *see* Clark, Harold Florian.
Clark, Harold Florian, 1899-
  xClark, Harold F.
    The Cost of Government & the Support of
      Education: An Intensive Study of New York
      State with Results Applicable Over the Entire
      Country. AMS Pr.
    Economic Theory & Correct Occupational
      Distribution. Arno.
Clark, Harold Willard, 1891-
  xClark, Harold.

    The New Creationism. Southern Pub.
Clark, Harry, 1917-
  xClark, Harry.
    A Venture in History: The Production,
      Publication, & Sale of the Works of Hubert
      Howe Bancroft. U of Cal Pr.
Clark, Henry W.
  xClark, Henry W.
    History of Alaska. Arno.
Clark, Herbert H.
  xClark, Herbert H.
    Psychology & Language: An Introduction to
      Psycholinguistics. HarBraceJ.
Clark, Hylton.
  xClark, H.
    First Course in Quantum Mechanics. Van Nos
      Reinhold.
Clark, J. H. *see* Clark, James H.
Clark, James A. *see* Clark, James Anthony.
Clark, James Anthony, 1907-
  xClark, James A.
    The Chronological History of the Petroleum &
      Natural Gas Industries. Gulf Pub.
Clark, James D'A., 1901-
  xClark, James d'A.
    Pulp Technology & Treatment for Paper. Miller
      Freeman.
Clark, James H.
  xClark, J. H.
    Female Sex Steroids: Receptors & Function.
      Springer-Verlag.
Clark, James I.
  xClark, James I.
    Shortcut to Peril. Raintree Pubs.
    Steel Coffin at Forty Fathoms. Raintree Pubs.
Clark, James L. *see* Clark, James Lippitt.
Clark, James Lippitt, 1883-
  xClark, James L.
    The Great Arc of the Wild Sheep. U of Okla
      Pr.
Clark, James M. *see* Clark, James Milford.
Clark, James Milford, 1930-
  xClark, James M.
    Teachers & Politics in France: A Pressure
      Group Study of the Federation de
      l'Education Nationale. Syracuse U Pr.
Clark, Joan.
  xClark, Joan.
    Thomasina & the Trout Tree. Tundra Bks.
Clark, John, 1935-
  xClark, John.
    Businesses Today: Successes & Failures.
      Random.
Clark, John G. *see* Clark, John Grahame Douglas.
Clark, John Grahame Douglas.
  xClark, Grahame.
    Aspects of Prehistory. U of Cal Pr.
    Stone Age Hunters. McGraw.
  xClark, John G.
    Prehistoric Societies. Phila Bk Co.
  xClark, John Grahame Douglas.
    World Prehistory in New Perspective.
      Cambridge U Pr.
Clark, John J.
  xClark, John J.
    Capital Budgeting: The Planning & Control of
      Capital Expenditures. P-H.
    Financial Management: A Capital Market
      Approach. Holbrook.
  xClark, Margaret T.
    jt. auth. Financial Management: A Capital
      Market Approach. Holbrook.
Clark, John M., Jr
  xClark, John M.
    Experimental Biochemistry. W H Freeman.
Clark, John M. *see* Clark, John Maurice.
Clark, John Maurice, 1884-
  xClark, John M.

Competition As a Dynamic Process.
Greenwood.
Costs of the World War to the American
People. Kelley.
Economics of Planning Public Works. Kelley.
Standards of Reasonableness in Local Freight
Discriminations. AMS Pr.
Clark, John P. see Clark, John Pepper.
Clark, John Pepper, 1935-
xClark, John P.
America, Their America. Holmes & Meier.
Clark, John R., 1927-
xClark, John R.
Coastal Ecosystem Management: A Technical
Manual for the Conservation of Coastal Zone
Resources. Wiley.
Form & Frenzy in Swift's Tale of a Tub.
Cornell U Pr.
Clark, John W. see Clark, John William.
Clark, John William, 1925-
xClark, John W.
Religion & the Moral Standards of American
Businessmen. SW Pub.
Clark, Jon.
xClark, Jon.
Physical Data Base Record Design. QED Info
Sci.
Clark, Kenneth.
xClark, Kenneth.
The Gothic Revival: An Essay in the History
of Taste. Har-Row.
Clark, Kenneth. see Clark, Kenneth Mckenzie.
Clark, Kenneth B. see Clark, Kenneth Bancroft.
Clark, Kenneth Bancroft, 1914-
xClark, Kenneth B.
The American Revolution: Democratic Politics
& Popular Education. Am Enterprise.
The Pathos of Power. Har-Row.
Pathos of Power. Har-Row.
Prejudice & Your Child. Beacon Pr.
Prejudice & Your Child. Peter Smith.
Relevant War Against Poverty: A Study of
Community Action Programs & Observable
Social Change. Har-Row.
Clark, Kenneth McKenzie, Baron Clark, 1903-
xClark, Kenneth.
Another Part of the Wood: A Self Portrait.
Ballantine.
Another Part of the Wood: A Self-Portrait.
Har-Row.
An Introduction to Rembrandt. Har-Row.
Leonardo Da Vinci: An Account of His
Development As an Artist. Gannon.
The Other Half: A Self-Portrait. Har-Row.
Rembrandt & the Italian Renaissance. Norton.
Rembrandt & the Italian Renaissance. NYU Pr.
Clark, L. R.
xClark, L. R.
The Ecology of Insect Populations in Theory &
Practice. Methuen Inc.
Clark, La Verne H. see Clark, Laverne Harrell.
Clark, Laura V. see Clark, Laura Veach.
Clark, Laura Veach, 1886-
xClark, Laura V.
A Study of the Relationship Between the
Vocational Home Economics Teacher
Training Curricula of a Group of Women's
Colleges & Expected Responsibilities of
Beginning Teachers. AMS Pr.
Clark, Laverne Harrell.
xClark, La Verne H.
They Sang for Horses: The Impact of the
Horse on Navajo & Apache Folklore. U of
Ariz Pr.
Clark, Le Mon, 1897-
xClark, LeMon.

Where Do Babies Come from? & How to Keep
Them There!: What a Teenager Should Know
About Sex, Love, Marriage & Birth Control.
Exposition.
Clark, LeMon. see Clark, le Mon.
Clark, Leonard. see Clark, Leonard Francis.
Clark, Leonard Francis.
xClark, Leonard.
The Marching Wind. Arden Lib.
Clark, Leonard H.
xClark, Leonard H.
The American Secondary School Curriculum.
Macmillan.
Strategies & Tactics in Secondary School
Teaching: A Book of Readings. Macmillan.
Clark, Leta. see Clark, Leta W.
Clark, Leta W.
xClark, Leta.
How to Open Your Own Shop or Gallery. St
Martin.
xClark, Leta W.
How to Open Your Own Shop or Gallery.
Penguin.
Clark, Linda. see Clark, Linda A.
Clark, Linda A.
xClark, Linda.
Face Improvement Through Exercise &
Nutrition. Keats.
The New Way to Eat. Celestial Arts.
Rejuvenation. Devin.
xClark, Linda A.
Secrets of Health & Beauty: How to Make
Yourself Over. Devin.
Clark, Lorenne. see Clark, Lorenne M. G.
Clark, Lorenne M. G.
xClark, Lorenne.
ed. The Sexism of Social & Political Theory:
Women & Reproduction from Plato to
Nietzsche. U of Toronto Pr.
Clark, M. Gardner. see Clark, Mills Gardner.
Clark, M. M. see Clark, Margaret Macdonald.
Clark, M. R. see Clark, Marjorie Ruth.
Clark, M. Ursula. see Clark, Mary Ursula.
Clark, Marden J., 1916-
xClark, Marden J.
Modern & Classic: The "Wooing Both Ways".
Brigham.
Clark, Margaret G. see Clark, Margaret Goff.
Clark, Margaret Goff.
xClark, Margaret G.
Barney & the UFO. Dodd.
Death at Their Heels. Dodd.
Clark, Margaret Macdonald.
xClark, M. M.
Teaching Left-Handed Children. Verry.
Clark, Margaret T. see Clark, John J.
Clark, Margery. see Clark, Margery Pseud.
Clark, Margery Pseud.
xClark, Margery.
Poppy Seed Cakes. Doubleday.
Clark, Marjorie A.
xClark, Marjorie A.
Captive on the Ho Chi Minh Trail. Moody.
Party Fun for Juniors. Moody.
Clark, Marjorie R. see Clark, Marjorie Ruth.
Clark, Marjorie Ruth, 1899-
xClark, M. R.
Organized Labor in Mexico. Gordon Pr.
xClark, Marjorie R.
A History of the French Labor Movement,
1910-1928. Johnson Repr.
Organized Labor in Mexico. Russell.
Clark, Mark W. see Clark, Mark Wayne.
Clark, Mark Wayne, 1896-
xClark, Mark W.
From the Danube to the Yalu. Greenwood.
Clark, Martin.
xClark, Martin.

Antonio Gramsci & the Revolution That
Failed. Yale U Pr.
Clark, Mary Ann.
xClark, Mary Ann.
Great American Catholics. Ave Maria.
Clark, Mary Cowles Illus. by. see Baum, L. Frank.
Clark, Mary E.
xClark, Mary E.
Contemporary Biology. Saunders.
Clark, Mary H. see Clark, Mary Higgins.
Clark, Mary Higgins.
xClark, Mary H.
The Cradle Will Fall. S&S.
A Stranger Is Watching. Dell.
A Stranger Is Watching. G K Hall.
A Stranger Is Watching. S&S.
Where Are the Children. Dell.
Where Are the Children?. S&S.
Clark, Mary Ursula, Sister, 1897-
xClark, M. Ursula.
Cult of Enthusiasm in French Romanticism.
AMS Pr.
Clark, Mavis T. see Clark, Mavis Thorpe.
Clark, Mavis Thorpe.
xClark, Mavis T.
The Hundred Islands. Macmillan.
If the Earth Falls In. HM.
Spark of Opal. Macmillan.
Clark, Miles. see Clark, Miles Morton.
Clark, Miles Morton.
xClark, Miles.
Glenn Clark: His Life & Writings. Abingdon.
Clark, Mills Gardner, 1917-
xClark, M. Gardner.
The Development of China's Steel Industry &
Soviet Technical Aid. NY Sch Indus Rel.
Clark, Nancy Fairchild.
xClark, Nancy Fairchild.
Normal Conduction System & the
Electrocardiogram: A Programmed
Instruction Unit. Davis Co.
Clark, Norma L. see Clark, Norma Lee.
Clark, Norma Lee.
xClark, Norma L.
Mallory. Fawcett.
Sophia & Augusta. Fawcett.
Clark, Paul O. see Clark, Paul Odell.
Clark, Paul Odell.
xClark, Paul O.
Gulliver Dictionary. Haskell.
Clark, Peter.
xClark, Peter.
English Provincial Society from the
Reformation to the Revolution: Religion,
Politics & Society in Kent, 1500-1640.
Fairleigh Dickinson.
Clark, Peter A.
xClark, Peter A.
Action Research & Organizational Change.
Har-Row.
Clark, R. E. see Clark, Robert Edward David.
Clark, R. L. see Clark, Robert Louis.
Clark, R. T. see Clark, Robert Thomas Rundle.
Clark, Ralph D.
xClark, Ralph D.
Case Studies in Echocardiography: A
Diagnostic Workbook. Saunders.
Clark, Rebecca.
xClark, Rebecca.
Breakthrough. Unity Bks.
Clark, Robert B. see Clark, Robert Bernard.
Clark, Robert Bernard.
xClark, Robert B.
Dynamics in Metazoan Evolution: The Origin
of the Coelom & Segments. Oxford U Pr.
Clark, Robert Edward David.
xClark, R. E.
God Beyond Nature. Pacific Pr Pub Assn.
Clark, Robert J. see Clark, Robert Judson.

Clark, Robert Judson.
  xClark, Robert J.
    ed. The Arts & Crafts Movement in America.
    Princeton U Pr.
Clark, Robert L.
  xClark, Robert L.
    ed. Archive-Library Relations. Bowker.
Clark, Robert Louis.
  xClark, R. L.
    The Economics of Individual & Population
    Aging. Cambridge U Pr.
Clark, Robert M. *see* Clark, Robert Maurice.
Clark, Robert Maurice.
  xClark, Robert M.
    Analysis of Urban Solid Waste Services: A
    Systems Approach. Ann Arbor Science.
Clark, Robert P.
  xClark, Robert P.
    Power & Policy in the Third World. Wiley.
Clark, Robert S., 1916-
  xClark, Robert S.
    Fundamentals of Criminal Justice Research.
    Lexington Bks.
Clark, Robert Thomas Rundle.
  xClark, R. T.
    Myth & Symbol in Ancient Egypt. Thames
    Hudson.
Clark, Rodney, 1945-
  xClark, Rodney.
    The Japanese Company. Yale U Pr.
Clark, Ronald W. *see* Clark, Ronald William.
Clark, Ronald William.
  xClark, Ronald W.
    The Life of Bertrand Russell. Knopf.
Clark, Roy P. *see* Clark, Roy Peter.
Clark, Roy Peter.
  xClark, Roy P.
    ed. Best Newspaper Writing. 1979: Winners of
    the American Society of Newspaper Editors
    Competition. Mod Media Inst.
    ed. Best Newspaper Writing: 1980 Winners of
    the American Society of Newspaper Editors
    Competition. Mod Media Inst.
Clark, Rufus W. *see* Clark, Rufus Wheelwright.
Clark, Rufus Wheelwright, 1813-1886
  xClark, Rufus W.
    African Slave Trade. Arno.
Clark, S. H. *see* Clark, Solomon Henry.
Clark, S. J.
  xClark, S. J.
    Structure Drill in Indonesian. C E Tuttle.
Clark, Sam.
  xClark, Sam.
    Designing & Building Your Own House Your
    Own Way. HM.
Clark, Samuel, 1945-
  xClark, Samuel.
    Social Origins of the Irish Land War. Princeton
    U Pr.
Clark, Samuel D. *see* Clark, Samuel Delbert.
Clark, Samuel Delbert, 1910-
  xClark, Samuel D.
    Church & Sect in Canada. U of Toronto Pr.
    Suburban Society. U of Toronto Pr.
Clark, Solomon Henry, 1861-1927
  xClark, S. H.
    ed. Handbook of Best Readings. Arno.
Clark, Stephen.
  xClark, Stephen.
    ed. The Incredible Illustrated Tool Book.
    Pathmark Bks.
Clark, Stephen B.
  xClark, Stephen B.
    Building Christian Communities: Strategy for
    Renewing the Church. Ave Maria.
Clark, Stephen R. *see* Clark, Stephen R. L.
Clark, Stephen R. L.
  xClark, Stephen R.

Aristotle's Man: Speculations Upon
  Aristotelian Anthropology. Oxford U Pr.
  The Moral Status of Animals. Oxford U Pr.
Clark, Steve, 1943-
  xClark, Steve.
    The Complete Book of Baseball Cards. G&D.
    Illustrated Basketball Dictionary for Young
    People. P-H.
    Illustrated Basketball Dictionary for Young
    People. Harvey.
Clark, Sydney P. *see* Clark, Sydney Procter.
Clark, Sydney Procter, 1929-
  xClark, Sydney P.
    Structure of the Earth. P-H.
Clark, T. *see* Clark, Tim.
Clark, T. J. *see* Clark, Timothy John Hayes.
Clark, Ted.
  xClark, Ted.
    The Oppression of Youth. Peter Smith.
Clark, Terry N.
  xClark, Terry N.
    ed. Citizen Preferences & Urban Public Policy:
    Models, Measures, Uses. Sage.
    Community Power & Policy Outputs: A
    Review of Urban Research. Sage.
    ed. Comparative Community Politics. Halsted
    Pr.
Clark, Thomas C. *see* Clark, Thomas Curtis.
Clark, Thomas Curtis.
  xClark, Thomas C.
    ed. One Hundred Poems of Peace: An
    Anthology. Arno.
Clark, Thomas D. *see* Clark, Thomas Dionysius.
Clark, Thomas Dionysius, 1903-
  xClark, Thomas D.
    Agrarian Kentucky. U Pr of Ky.
    Historic Maps of Kentucky. U Pr of Ky.
    The Southern Country Editor. Peter Smith.
Clark, Tim.
  xClark, T.
    Psychopath: The Case of Patrick Mackay.
    Routledge & Kegan.
Clark, Timothy.
  xClark, Timothy R.
    ed. The World Wars Remembered: Personal
    Recollections of Heroes, Hello Girls, Flying
    Aces, Prisoners, Survivors & Those on the
    Homefront...from the Pages of Yankee
    Magazine. Yankee Bks.
Clark, Timothy John Hayes.
  xClark, T. J.
    ed. Asthma. Saunders.
Clark, Timothy R. *see* Clark, Timothy.
Clark, Tom, 1941-
  xClark, Tom.
    At Malibu. Kulchur Foun.
    The Great Naropa Poetry Wars. Cadmus Eds.
    When Things Get Tough on Easy Street:
    Selected Poems 1963-1978. Black Sparrow.
Clark, Truman R., 1935-
  xClark, Truman R.
    Puerto Rico & the United States, 1917-1933. U
    of Pittsburgh Pr.
Clark, Victor S. *see* Clark, Victor Selden.
Clark, Victor Selden, 1868-1946
  xClark, Victor S.
    Porto Rico & Its Problems. Arno.
Clark, Vivian V. *see* Clark, Vivian Vreeland.
Clark, Vivian Vreeland.
  xClark, Vivian V.
    Outpatient Services Journal Articles. Med
    Exam.
Clark, W. E. *see* Clark, Wilfrid Edward le Gros.
Clark, W. Edmund, 1947-
  xClark, W. Edmund.
    Socialist Development & Public Investment in
    Tanzania, 1964-73. U of Toronto Pr.
Clark, W. Hartley. *see* Clark, William Hartley.
Clark, Wallace H.
  xClark, Wallace H.

    ed. Human Malignant Melanoma. Grune.
Clark, Walter E. *see* Clark, Walter Ernest.
Clark, Walter Ernest, 1873-1955
  xClark, Walter E.
    Josiah Tucker, Economist: A Study in the
    History of Economics. AMS Pr.
Clark, Walter V. *see* Clark, Walter Van Tilburg.
Clark, Walter Van Tilburg, 1909-
  xClark, Walter V.
    Ox-Bow Incident. Peter Smith.
    Ox Bow Incident. NAL.
Clark, Wesley C. *see* Clark, Wesley Clarke.
Clark, Wesley Clarke, 1907-
  xClark, Wesley C.
    ed. Journalism Tomorrow. Syracuse U Pr.
Clark, Wilfrid Edward le Gros, Sir.
  xClark, W. E.
    The Antecedents of Man: An Introduction to
    the Evolution of Primates. Times Bks.
    The Fossil Evidence for Human Evolution: An
    Introduction to the Study of
    Paleoanthropology. U of Chicago Pr.
Clark, William. *see* Clark, William D.
Clark, William D.
  xClark, William.
    Death Valley: The Story Behind the Scenery. K
    C Pubns.
Clark, William Hartley.
  xClark, W. Hartley.
    The Politics of the Common Market.
    Greenwood.
Clark, William J., 1840-1889
  xClark, William J.
    Great American Sculptures. Garland Pub.
Clark, Wilson.
  xClark, Wilson.
    Energy for Survival: The Alternative to
    Extinction. Doubleday.
    Energy for Survival: The Alternative to
    Extinction. Doubleday.
Clarke. *see* Clarke, Robert B.
Clarke, A. B. *see* Clarke, A. Bruce.

Clarke, A. Bruce.
  xClarke, A. B.
    Probability & Random Processes for Engineers
    & Scientists. Wiley.

Clarke, Ann M. *see* Clarke, Ann Margaret.

Clarke, Ann Margaret.

  xClarke, Ann M.
    ed. Early Experience: Myth & Evidence. Free
    Pr.
Clarke, Arthur C.
  xClarke, Arthur C.
    Dolphin Island. Berkley Pub.
    Earthlight. Ballantine.
Clarke, Arthur C. *see* Clarke, Arthur Charles.
Clarke, Arthur Charles, 1917-
  xClarke, Arthur C.

Against the Fall of Night. BJ Pub Group.
Boy Beneath the Sea. Har-Row.
Childhood's End. Ballantine.
Childhood's End. HarBraceJ.
Deep Range. HarBraceJ.
The Deep Range. NAL.
Expedition to Earth. Ballantine.
Expedition to Earth. HarBraceJ.
The Exploration of Space. PB.
Fall of Moondust. NAL.
The Fountains of Paradise. Ballantine.
The Fountains of Paradise. G K Hall.
The Fountains of Paradise. HarBraceJ.
Glidepath. NAL.
Imperial Earth. G K Hall.
Imperial Earth. HarBraceJ.
Prelude to Space. HarBraceJ.
Profiles of the Future: An Inquiry into the
	Limits of the Possible. Har-Row.
Promise of Space. Har-Row.
Reach for Tomorrow. Ballantine.
Reach for Tomorrow. HarBraceJ.
Rendezvous with Rama. Ballantine.
Rendezvous with Rama. G K Hall.
Rendezvous with Rama. HarBraceJ.
Tales from the White Hart. Ballantine.
Tales from the White Hart. HarBraceJ.
Tales of Ten Worlds. NAL.
Tales of Ten Worlds. HarBraceJ.
Voices from the Sky. PB.
Clarke, Arthur G., 1887-
	xClarke, Arthur G.
	Analytical Studies in the Psalms. Kregel.
Clarke, Austin, 1896-
	xClarke, Austin.
	Celtic Twilight & the Nineties. Dufour.
	The Collected Poems of Austin Clarke. AMS
		Pr.
	Echo at Coole & Other Poems. Dufour.
Clarke, Beverley.
	xClarke, Beverly.
	Graphic Design in Educational Television.
		Watson-Guptill.
Clarke, Beverly. *see* Clarke, Beverley.
Clarke, Brenda.
	xClarke, Brenda.
	The Lofty Banners. Popular Lib.
Clarke, Brian, 1953-
	xClarke, Brian.
	Architectural Stained Glass. McGraw.
Clarke, C. A. *see* Clarke, Cyril Astley.
Clarke, Charles F. *see* Clarke, Charles Frederick Orme.
Clarke, Charles Frederick Orme.
	xClarke, Charles F.
	Britain Today: A Review of Current Political &
		Social Trends. Greenwood.
Clarke, Charles G. *see* Clarke, Charles Galloway.
Clarke, Charles Galloway.
	xClarke, Charles G.
	ed. American Cinematographer Manual. Am
		Soc Cine.
Clarke, Colin C. *see* Clarke, Colin Campbell.
Clarke, Colin Campbell.
	xClarke, Colin C.
	Romantic Paradox: An Essay on the Poetry of
		Wordsworth. Greenwood.
Clarke, Cyril Astley.
	xClarke, C. A.
	Human Genetics & Medicine. St Martin.
Clarke, D. *see* Clarke, Dennis.
Clarke, David H.
	xClarke, David H.
	Exercise Physiology. P-H.
Clarke, David L.
	xClarke, David L.
	Analytical Archaeology. Columbia U Pr.
Clarke, Dennis.
	xClarke, D.

Computer Aided Structural Design. Wiley.
Clarke, Desmond.
	xClarke, Desmond.
	Dublin. David & Charles.
Clarke, Donald.
	xClarke, Donald.
	ed. Encyclopedia of How It's Built. A & W
		Pubs.
	The Encyclopedia of How It's Made. A & W
		Pubs.
Clarke, Duncan L.
	xClarke, Duncan L.
	Politics of Arms Control: The Role &
		Effectiveness of the U. S. Arms Control &
		Disarmament Agency. Free Pr.
Clarke, Edward H. *see* Clarke, Edward Hammond.
Clarke, Edward Hammond, 1820-1877
	xClarke, Edward H.
	Century of American Medicine, 1776-1876. B
		Franklin.
Clarke, Frank H.
	xClarke, Frank H.
	ed. How Modern Medicines Are Developed.
		Futura Pub.
Clarke, G. M. *see* Clarke, Geoffrey Mallin.
Clarke, Geoffrey Mallin.
	xClarke, G. M.
	Statistics & Experimental Design. Univ Park.
Clarke, H. *see* Clarke, Harold D.
Clarke, H. Edwards.
	xClarke, H. Edwards.
	The Greyhound. Soccer.
Clarke, H. Harrison. *see* Clarke, Henry Harrison.
Clarke, Harold. *see* Clarke, Joy Harold.
Clarke, Harold D.
	xClarke, H.
	Political Choice in Canada. McGraw.
Clarke, Helen.
	xClarke, Helen.
	Vikings. Watts.
Clarke, Helen A. *see* Clarke, Helen Archibald.
Clarke, Helen Archibald, d. 1926
	xClarke, Helen A.
	Browning & His Century. Haskell.
	xClarke, Hellen A.
	Browning & His Century. R West.
Clarke, Hellen A. *see* Clarke, Helen Archibald.
Clarke, Henry B. *see* Clarke, Henry Butler.
Clarke, Henry Butler, 1863-1904
	xClarke, Henry B.
	The Cid Campeador & the Waning of the
		Crescent in the West. AMS Pr.
Clarke, Henry Harrison, 1902-
	xClarke, H. Harrison.
	Application of Measurement to Health &
		Physical Education. P-H.
Clarke, I. F. *see* Clarke, Ignatius Frederick.
Clarke, Ignatius Frederick.
	xClarke, I. F.
	The Pattern of Expectation. Basic.
Clarke, Isabel C. *see* Clarke, Isabel Constance.
Clarke, Isabel Constance.
	xClarke, Isabel C.
	Maria Edgeworth: Her Family & Friends.
		Arden Lib.
	Maria Edgeworth: Her Family & Friends.
		Folcroft.
Clarke, J. F. *see* Clarke, John Frederick.
Clarke, J. Harold. *see* Clarke, Joy Harold.
Clarke, J. I. *see* Clarke, John Innes.
Clarke, James F. *see* Clarke, James Freeman.
Clarke, James Freeman, 1810-1888
	xClarke, James F.

Anti-Slavery Days: A Sketch of the Struggle
	Which Ended in the Abolition of Slavery in
	the United States. AMS Pr.
Anti Slavery Days: A Sketch of the Struggle
	Which Ended in the Abolition of Slavery in
	the United States. Negro U Pr.
Nineteenth Century Questions. Arno.
Clarke, James M. *see* Clarke, James Mitchell.
Clarke, James Mitchell.
	xClarke, James M.
	The Life & Adventures of John Muir. Sierra.
	The Life & Adventures of John Muir. Word
		Shop.
Clarke, John.
	xClarke, John.
	High School Drop Out. Doubleday.
Clarke, John Frederick.
	xClarke, J. F.
	Dynamics of Relaxing Gases. Butterworths.
Clarke, John H. *see* Clarke, John Henry.
Clarke, John Henrik, 1915-
	xClarke, John H.
	ed. American Negro Short Stories. Hill &
		Wang.
	ed. Marcus Garvey & the Vision of Africa.
		Random.
Clarke, John Henry, 1852-1931
	xClarke, John H.
	From Copernicus to William Blake. Folcroft.
	God of Shelley & Blake. Folcroft.
	God of Shelley & Blake. Haskell.
Clarke, John Innes.
	xClarke, J. I.
	Population Geography. Pergamon.
	Population Geography & Developing Countries.
		Pergamon.
	Populations of the Middle East & North
		Africa: A Geographical Approach. Holmes &
		Meier.
Clarke, John J. *see* Clarke, John Joseph.
Clarke, John Joseph, 1879-
	xClarke, John J.
	A History of Local Government of the United
		Kingdom. Greenwood.
Clarke, John R., 1913-
	xClarke, John.
	Executive Power: How to Use It Effectively.
		P-H.
	xClarke, John R.
	Roman Black & White Figural Mosaics. NYU
		Pr.
Clarke, Joseph F.
	xClarke, Joseph F.
	Pseudonyms: The Names Behind the Names.
		Elsevier-Nelson.
Clarke, Joy Harold, 1899-
	xClarke, Harold.
	Growing Berries & Grapes at Home. Dover.
	xClarke, J. Harold.
	Growing Berries & Grapes at Home. Peter
		Smith.
Clarke, M. L. *see* Clarke, Martin Lowther.
Clarke, M. P. *see* Clarke, Mary Patterson.
Clarke, Martin Lowther.
	xClarke, M. L.
	Richard Porson: A Biographical Essay. Arden
		Lib.
Clarke, Mary Patterson, 1879-1959
	xClarke, M. P.
	Parliamentary Privilege in the American
		Colonies. Da Capo.
Clarke, Mary S. *see* Clarke, Mary Stetson.
Clarke, Mary Stetson.
	xClarke, Mary S.
	The Limner's Daughter. Hilltop Pr.
	Women's Rights in the United States. Viking
		Pr.
Clarke, Mary W. *see* Clarke, Mary Whatley.
Clarke, Mary Whatley.
	xClarke, Mary W.

Swenson Saga, & the SMS Ranches. Jenkins.
Clarke, Maude V. see Clarke, Maude Violet.
Clarke, Maude Violet, 1892-1935
 xClarke, Maude V.
  Medieval Representation & Consent: A Study
  of Early Parliaments in England & Ireland,
  with Special Reference to the Modus Tenendi
  Parliamentum. Russell.
Clarke, Nina H.
 xClarke, Nina H.
  History of the Black Public Schools of
  Montgomery County, Maryland 1872-1961.
  Vantage.
Clarke, P. see Clarke, Peter.
Clarke, P. H. see Clarke, Patricia H.
Clarke, Patricia H.
 xClarke, P. H.
  ed. Genetics & Biochemistry of Pseudomonas.
  Wiley.
Clarke, Pauline, 1921-
 xClarke, Pauline.
  Torolv the Fatherless. Merrimack Bk Serv.
Clarke, Peter, 1942-
 xClarke, P.
  Liberals & Social Democrats. Cambridge U Pr.
Clarke, Philip S.
 xClarke, Philip S.
  Calculus & Analytic Geometry. Heath.
Clarke, R. F. see Clarke, Ronald F.
Clarke, Raymond, 1938-
 xClarke, Raymond.
  Innovative Faculty Team Programs: An
  Administrator's Handbook. P-H.
Clarke, Richard F. see Clarke, Richard Frederick.
Clarke, Richard Frederick, 1839-1900
 xClarke, Richard F.
  ed. Cardinal Lavigerie & the African Slave
  Trade. Negro U Pr.
Clarke, Robert B.
 xClarke.
  Statistical Reasoning & Procedures. Merrill.
Clarke, Ron.
 xClarke, Ron.
  Successful Track & Field. Sterling.
Clarke, Ronald F.
 xClarke, R. F.
  Growth & Nature of Drama. Cambridge U Pr.
Clarke, Terence.
 xClarke, Terence.
  The Englewood Readings. Dustbooks.
Clarke, Tom E.
 xClarke, Tom E.
  Alaska Challenge. Lothrop.
Clarke, W. E.
 xClarke, W. E.
  Reminiscences of Robert Louis Stevenson.
  Arden Lib.
  Reminiscences of Robert Louis Stevenson.
  Folcroft.
Clarke, William C.
 xClarke, William C.
  Place & People: An Ecology of a New Guinean
  Community. U of Cal Pr.
Clarke, William K. see Clarke, William Kendall.
Clarke, William Kendall.
 xClarke, William K.
  The Robber Baroness. St Martin.
Clarke, Winifred.
 xClarke, Winifred.
  George Bernard Shaw: An Appreciation &
  Interpretation. Arden Lib.
Clarkson, Bayard.
 xClarkson, Bayard.
  ed. Control of Proliferation in Animal Cells.
  Cold Spring Harbor.
Clarkson, E. N. see Clarkson, Euan Neilson Kerr.
Clarkson, Edith Margaret, 1915-
 xClarkson, Margaret.

Clarkson, Euan Neilson Kerr, 1937-
 xClarkson, E. N.
  Invertebrate Palaeontology & Evolution. Allen
  Unwin.
Clarkson, Ewan.
 xClarkson, Ewan.
  Wolves. Raintree Pubs.
Clarkson, Henry E.
 xClarkson, Henry E.
  Yachtsman's A-Z. Arco.
Clarkson, James D.
 xClarkson, James D.
  The Cultural Ecology of a Chinese Village:
  Cameron Highlands, Malaysia. U Chicago
  Dept Geog.
Clarkson, Jesse D. see Clarkson, Jesse Dunsmore.
Clarkson, Jesse Dunsmore, 1897-
 xClarkson, Jesse D.
  History of Russia. Random.
Clarkson, Kenneth W.
 xClarkson, Kenneth W.
  Food Stamps & Nutrition. Am Enterprise.
  Inflated Unemployment Statistics: The Effects
  of Welfare Work Registration Requirements.
  Law & Econ U Miami.
Clarkson, Leslie A.
 xClarkson, Leslie A.
  Death, Disease & Famine in Pre-Industrial
  England. St Martin.
Clarkson, Margaret. see Clarkson, Edith Margaret.
Clarkson, Paul S. see Clarkson, Paul Stephen.
Clarkson, Paul Stephen.
 xClarkson, Paul S.
  Law of Property in Shakespeare & the
  Elizabethan Drama. Gordian.
Clarkson, Rosetta E.
 xClarkson, Rosetta E.
  The Golden Age of Herbs & Herbalists. Dover.
  The Golden Age of Herbs & Herbalists. Peter
  Smith.
Clarkson, Stephen.
 xClarkson, Stephen.
  The Soviet Theory of Development: India &
  the Third World in Marxist-Leninist
  Scholarship. U of Toronto Pr.
Clarkson, Thomas, 1760-1846
 xClarkson, Thomas.
  History of the Rise, Progress &
  Accomplishment of the Abolition of the
  African Slave-Trade by the British
  Parliament. Biblio Dist.
  Strictures on a Life of William Wilberforce.
  Arno.
Clarneau, William.
 xClarneau, William.
  Do-It Yourselfer's Guide to Home Planning &
  Construction. TAB Bks.
Clary, Jack. see Clary, Jack T.
Clary, Jack T.
 xClary, Jack.
  The Captains. Atheneum.
Clason, George S. see Clason, George Samuel.
Clason, George Samuel, 1874-
 xClason, George S.
  Richest Man in Babylon. Dutton.
Class, Edward C. see Class, Edward Christian.
Class, Edward Christian, 1896-
 xClass, Edward C.
  Prescription & Election in Elementary-School
  Teacher-Training Curricula in State Teachers
  Colleges. AMS Pr.
Class, Robert A. see Class, Robert Allan.
Class, Robert Allan.
 xClass, Robert A.
  ed. Current Techniques in Architectural
  Practice. McGraw.
Classen, Ernest, 1881-
 xClassen, Ernest.

Outlines of the History of the English
  Language. Greenwood.
Clastres, Pierre, 1934-
 xClastres, Pierre.
  Society Against the State. Urizen Bks.
Claude, Inis L.
 xClaude, Inis L.
  National Minorities: An International Problem.
  Greenwood.
  Power & International Relations. Random.
  Swords into Plowshares: The Problems &
  Progress of International Organization.
  Random.
Claude, Richard, 1934-
 xClaude, Richard P.
  The Supreme Court & the Electoral Process.
  Johns Hopkins.
Claude, Richard P. see Claude, Richard.
Claudel, Paul, 1868-1955
 xClaudel, Paul.
  Claudel on the Theatre. U of Miami Pr.
  Eye Listens. Kennikat.
Claudia, Susan.
 xClaudia, Susan.
  A Silent Voice. NAL.
Claudin, Fernando.
 xClaudin, Fernando.
  The Communist Movement: From Comintern
  to Cominform. Monthly Rev.
Claus, Karen E.
 xClaus, Karen E.
  Power & Influence in Health Care:: A New
  Approach to Leadership. Mosby.
Claus, R. see Claus, Reinhart.
Claus, Reinhart.
 xClaus, R.
  Light Scattering by Phonon Polaritons.
  Springer-Verlag.
Claus, Tom.
 xClaus, Tom.
  ed. Christian Leadership in Indian America.
  Moody.
Claus, V. see Claus, Volker.
Claus, Volker, 1944-
 xClaus, V.
  ed. Graph-Grammars & Their Application to
  Computer Science & Biology: Proceedings,
  International Workshop, Bad Honnef,
  October 30-November 3, 1978.
  Springer-Verlag.
Clausen, Aage R.
 xClausen, Aage R.
  How Congressmen Decide: A Policy Focus. St
  Martin.
Clausen, Chris A.
 xClausen, Chris A.
  Principles of Industrial Chemistry. Wiley.
Clausen, Joy. see Clausen, Joy Princeton.
Clausen, Joy Princeton.
 xClausen, Joy.
  Maternity Nursing Today. McGraw.
Clausen, Lucy W. see Clausen, Lucy Wilhelmine.
Clausen, Lucy Wilhelmine, 1909-
 xClausen, Lucy W.
  Insect Fact & Folklore. Macmillan.
Clauser, Suzanne.
 xClauser, Suzanne.
  A Girl Named Sooner. Avon.
  A Girl Named Sooner. Doubleday.
Clauss, Francis J. see Clauss, Francis Jacob.

Clauss, Francis Jacob, 1926-
xClauss, Francis J.
Solid Lubricants & Self-Lubricating Solids.
Acad Pr.
Clauss, Roy H.
xClauss, Roy H.
Remediable Arterial Disease. Grune.
Clavelin, Maurice.
xClavelin, Maurice.
The Natural Philosophy of Galileo: Essay on
the Origins & Formation of Classical
Mechanics. MIT Pr.
Claveloux, Nicole.
xClaveloux, Nicole.
Private Eye Grabote. Quist.
Clawson, Marion, 1905-
xClawson, Marion.
Decision Making in Timber Production,
Harvest, & Marketing. Johns Hopkins.
The Economics of National Forest
Management. Johns Hopkins.
Economics of Outdoor Recreation. Johns
Hopkins.
The Economics of U. S. Nonindustrial Private
Forests. Resources Future.
ed. Natural Resources & International
Development. AMS Pr.
Planning & Urban Growth: An
Anglo-American Comparison. Johns Hopkins.
Suburban Land Conversion in the United
States: An Economic & Governmental
Process. Johns Hopkins.
Uncle Sam's Acres. Greenwood.
The Western Range Livestock Industry. Arno.
Claxton, Guy.
xClaxton, Guy.
The Little Ed Book. Routledge & Kegan.
Clay, C. J. see Clay, Charles John Jervis.
Clay, Charles John Jervis.
xClay, C. J.
ed. Modern Merchant Banking: A Guide to the
Workings of the Accepting Houses of the
City of London & Their Services to Industry
& Commerce. Herman Pub.
Clay, Christopher.
xClay, Christopher.
Public Finance & Private Wealth: The Career
of Sir Stephen Fox, 1627-1716. Oxford U Pr.
Clay, Clarence S. see Clay, Clarence Samuel.
Clay, Clarence Samuel.
xClay, Clarence S.
Acoustical Oceanography: Principles &
Applications. Wiley.
Clay, George. see Clay, George R.
Clay, George R.
xClay, George.
Family Occasions. G K Hall.
Family Occasions. Random.
Clay, Henry, Sir, 1883-1954
xClay, Henry.
Lord Norman. Arno.
Private Correspondence of Henry Clay. Arno.
Clay, Horace F. see Clay, Horace Freestone.
Clay, Horace Freestone.
xClay, Horace F.
Tropical Exotics. U Pr of Hawaii.
Tropical Shrubs. U Pr of Hawaii.
Clay, James H. see Clay, James Hubert.
Clay, James Hubert.
xClay, James H.
Theatrical Image. McGraw.
Clay, James W.
xClay, James W.
ed. North Carolina Atlas: Portrait of a
Changing Southern State. U of NC Pr.
Clay, Lucius D. see Clay, Lucius Dubignon.
Clay, Lucius Dubignon, 1897-
xClay, Lucius D.

Decision in Germany. Greenwood.
Clay, Patrick.
xClay, Patrick.
Sgt. Hawk. Nordon Pubns.
Clay, R. M. see Clay, Rotha Mary.
Clay, Reginald S. see Clay, Reginald Stanley.
Clay, Reginald Stanley.
xClay, Reginald S.
The History of the Microscope. Longwood Pr.
The History of the Microscope. Saifer.
Clay, Rotha Mary.
xClay, R. M.
Mediaeval Hospitals of England. Biblio Dist.
Clay, William C. see Clay, William Caldwell.
Clay, William Caldwell, 1915-
xClay, William C.
The Dow Jones-Irwin Guide to Estate
Planning. Dow Jones-Irwin.
Clayburn, Barbara B., 1930-
xClayburn, Barbara B.
Prairie Stationmaster: The Story of One Man's
Railroading Career in Nebraska 1917-1963.
Harlo Pr.
Claycombe, William W.
xClaycombe, William W.
Foundations of Mathematical Programming.
Reston.
Claydon, L. F. see Claydon, Leslie F.
Claydon, Leslie F.
xClaydon, L. F.
Renewing Urban Teaching. Cambridge U Pr.
Clayes, S. see Clayes, Stanley A.
Clayes, Stanley. see Clayes, Stanley A.
Clayes, Stanley A.
xClayes, S.
Contexts for Composition. P-H.
xClayes, Stanley.
Contexts for Composition. P-H
xClayes, Stanley A.
ed. Contemporary Drama: Thirteen Plays.
Scribner.
Drama & Discussion. P-H.
Claypool, John.
xClaypool, John.
Stages: The Art of Living the Expected. Word
Bks.
Clayton, Barbara.
xClayton, Barbara.
Guide to New Bedford. Globe Pequot.
Clayton, Bernard.
xClayton, Bernard.
The Complete Book of Breads. S&S.
Clayton, Donald D.
xClayton, Donald D.
The Dark Night Sky: A Personal Adventure in
Cosmology. Times Bks.
Principles of Stellar Evolution &
Nucleosynthesis. McGraw.
Clayton, Ellen C. see Clayton, Ellen Creathorne.
Clayton, Ellen Creathorne, 1834-1900
xClayton, Ellen C.
Queens of Song: Being Memoirs of Some of
the Most Celebrated Female Vocalists. Arno.
Clayton, G. see Clayton, George Burbridge.
Clayton, George Burbridge.
xClayton, G.
Operational Amplifiers. Butterworths.
Clayton, Jo.
xClayton, Jo.
Diadem from the Stars. DAW Bks.
Clayton, John, 1892-
xClayton, John.
ed. Illinois Fact Book & Historical Almanac,
1673-1968. S Ill U Pr.
Clayton, John J. see Clayton, John Jacob.
Clayton, John Jacob.
xClayton, John J.

Saul Bellow: In Defense of Man. Ind U Pr.
What Are Friends for?. Little.
Clayton, Kenneth C.
xClayton, Kenneth C.
Solid Wastes Management: The Regional
Approach. Ballinger Pub.
Clayton, Powell, 1833-1914
xClayton, Powell.
Aftermath of the Civil War, in Arkansas.
Negro U Pr.
Clayton, R. F.
xClayton, R. F.
Monitoring of Radioactive Contamination on
Surfaces. Unipub.
Clayton, Richard R.
xClayton, Richard R.
Family Marriage & Social Change. Heath.
Clayton, Robert.
xClayton, Robert.
Central & East Africa. John Day.
U.S.S.R. John Day.
Clayton, Robert D.
xClayton, Robert D.
Concepts & Careers in Physical Education.
Burgess.
Clayton, Roderick K.
xClayton, Roderick K.
Light & Living Matter: A Guide to the Study
of Photobiology. Krieger.
Clayton, Victoria V. see Clayton, Victoria Virginia
(Hunter).
Clayton, Victoria Virginia (Hunter).
xClayton, Victoria V.
White & Black Under the Old Regime. Arno.
Clear, Val.
xClear, Val.
ed. Marriage & the Family Through Science
Fiction. St Martin.
Cleare, John.
xCleare, John.
World Guide to Mountains & Mountaineering.
Mayflower Bks.
Cleary, A. see Cleary, Alan.
Cleary, Alan.
xCleary, A.
Educational Technology: Implications for Early
& Special Education. Wiley.
xCleary, Alan.
Instrumentation for Psychology. Wiley.
Cleary, Beverly.
xCleary, Beverly.

Beezus & Ramona. Morrow.
Beezus & Ramona. Dell.
Ellen Tebbits. Morrow.
Ellen Tebbits. Dell.
Fifteen. Morrow.
Fifteen. Dell.
Henry & Ribsy. Dell.
Henry & Ribsy. Morrow.
Henry & the Clubhouse. Morrow.
Henry Huggins. Morrow.
Henry Huggins. Dell.
The Luckiest Girl. Dell.
The Luckiest Girl. Morrow.
Otis Spofford. Dell.
Otis Spofford. Morrow.
Ramona & Her Father. Morrow.
Ramona & Her Mother. Dell.
Ramona & Her Mother. Morrow.
Ramona the Brave. Morrow.
Ramona the Brave. Schol Bk Serv.
Ramona the Pest. Morrow.
Ramona the Pest. Schol Bk Serv.
The Real Hole. Morrow.
Ribsy. Archway.
Ribsy. Morrow.
Socks. Dell.
Socks. Morrow.
Two Dog Biscuits. Morrow.

Cleary, Denis J.
xCleary, Denis J.
The Capricorn Run. Playboy Pbks.
Cleary, E. J. see Cleary, Esmond John.
Cleary, Edward J. see Cleary, Edward John.
Cleary, Edward John.
xCleary, Edward J.
The ORSANCO Story: Water Quality
Management in the Ohio Valley Under an
Interstate Compact. Johns Hopkins.
Cleary, Esmond John.
xCleary, E. J.
The Building Society Movement. Merrimack
Bk Serv.
Cleary, Jon, 1917-
xCleary, Jon.
The Beaufort Sisters. Fawcett.
The Beaufort Sisters. Morrow.
The Liberators. Morrow.
A Sound of Lightning. Morrow.
The Sundowners. Scribner.
A Very Private War. Morrow.
Cleaton, Irene.
xCleaton, Irene.
Books & Battles: American Literature,
1920-1930. Cooper Sq.
Cleaton-Jones, Peter.
xCleaton-Jones, Peter.
Essential Medicine for Dental Practice. C C
Thomas.
Cleaveland, Agnes M. see Cleaveland, Agnes Morley.
Cleaveland, Agnes Morley, 1874-
xCleaveland, Agnes M.
No Life for a Lady. Gannon.
No Life for a Lady. U of Nebr Pr.
Cleaveland, Frederic N.
xCleaveland, Frederic N.
Congress & Urban Problems: A Casebook on
the Legislative Process. Brookings.

Cleaver, Dale G.
xCleaver, Dale G.
Art: An Introduction. HarBraceJ.
Art & Music: An Introduction. HarBraceJ.
Cleaver, Eldridge, 1935-
xCleaver, Eldridge.
Soul on Fire. Word Bks.
Soul on Ice. Dell.
Soul on Ice. McGraw.
Cleaver, Elizabeth, 1939-
xCleaver, Elizabeth.

illus. & Retold by Petrouchka. Atheneum.
Cleaver, Harry, 1944-
xCleaver, Harry.
Reading CAPITAL Politically. U of Tex Pr.
Cleaver, James.
xCleaver, James.
A History of Graphic Art. Charles River Bks.
History of Graphic Art. Greenwood.
Cleaver, Vera.

xCleaver, Vera.

Delpha Green & Company. NAL.
Delpha Green & Company. Lippincott.
Dust of the Earth. NAL.
Dust of the Earth. Lippincott.
Grover. NAL.

jt. auth. Grover. Lippincott.
I Would Rather Be a Turnip. NAL.
I Would Rather Be a Turnip. Lippincott.
A Little Destiny. Lothrop.
Me Too. NAL.
Me Too. Lippincott.
Queen of Hearts. Bantam.
Where the Lilies Bloom. NAL.
Where the Lilies Bloom. Lippincott.
Cleaves, Cheryl S.
xCleaves, Cheryl S.
Mathematics of the Business World. A-W.
Cleaves, Peter S.
xCleaves, Peter S.
Bureaucratic Politics & Administration in
Chile. U of Cal Pr.
Clebsch, Alfred, 1833-1872
xClebsch, Alfred.
Theorie De L'elasticite Des Corps Solides.
Johnson Repr.
Clebsch, William. see Clebsch, William A.
Clebsch, William A.
xClebsch, William.
Christianity in European History. Oxford U Pr.
xClebsch, William A.
American Religious Thought: A History. U of
Chicago Pr.
Christian Interpretations of the Civil War.
Fortress.
Clecak, Peter.
xClecak, Peter.
Crooked Paths: Reflections on Socialism,
Conservatism, & the Welfare State. Har-Row.
Crooked Paths: Reflections on Socialism,
Conservatism & the Welfare State. Har-Row.
Cleckley, Franklin D.
xCleckley, Franklin D.
Handbook on Evidence for West Virginia
Lawyers. Michie.
Cleef, E. Van. see Van Cleef, E.
Cleeton, Claud E. see Cleeton, Claud Edwin.
Cleeton, Claud Edwin, 1907-
xCleeton, Claud E.
Strategies for the Options Trader. Wiley.
Cleeve, Brian. see Cleeve, Brian Talbot.
Cleeve, Brian Talbot, 1921-
xCleeve, Brian.
Hester. Coward.
Judith. Berkley Pub.
Judith. Coward.
Clegg, A. B. see Clegg, Alexander Bradshaw.
Clegg, Alexander Bradshaw, Sir, 1904-
xClegg, A. B.
The Changing Primary School: Teachers Speak
on Adapting to New Ways. Schocken.
The Excitement of Writing. Schocken.
Clegg, Edward. see Clegg, Edward Marshall.
Clegg, Edward Marshall.
xClegg, Edward.
Race & Politics: Partnership in the Federation
of Rhodesia & Nyasaland. Greenwood.
Clegg, Jerry S.
xClegg, Jerry S.

The Structure of Plato's Philosophy. Bucknell
U Pr.
Clegg, Reed K.
xClegg, Reed K.
Probation & Parole: Principles & Practices. C C
Thomas.
Clegg, Stewart.
xClegg, Stewart.
Organization, Class & Control. Routledge &
Kegan.
The Theory of Power & Organization.
Routledge & Kegan.
Cleland, Charles C. see Cleland, Charles Carr.
Cleland, Charles Carr.
xCleland, Charles C.
The Profoundly Mentally Retarded. P-H.
Cleland, Charles E. see Cleland, Charles Edward.
Cleland, Charles Edward.
xCleland, Charles E.
ed. For the Director: Research Essays in
Honor of James B. Griffin. U Mich Mus
Anthro.
Cleland, David I.
xCleland, David I.
The Origin & Development of a Philosophy of
Long-Range Planning in American Business.
Arno.
Systems Analysis & Project Management.
McGraw.
Cleland, John.
xCleland, John.
The Memoirs of a Coxcomb. Garland Pub.
Clem, Orlie M. see Clem, Orlie Martin.
Clem, Orlie Martin, 1891-
xClem, Orlie M.
Detailed Factors in Latin Prognosis. AMS Pr.
Clem, Ralph S.
xClem, Ralph S.
ed. No Room for Man: Population & the
Future Through Science-Fiction. Littlefield.
ed. No Room for Man: Population & the
Future Through Science Fiction. Rowman.
Clemen, Rudolf A. see Clemen, Rudolf Alexander.
Clemen, Rudolf Alexander.
xClemen, Rudolf A.
The American Livestock & Meat Industry.
Johnson Repr.
Clemen, Wolfgang.
xClemen, Wolfgang H.
The Development of Shakespeare's Imagery.
Methuen Inc.
Clemen, Wolfgang H. see Clemen, Wolfgang.
Clemenceau, Georges E. see Clemenceau, Georges
Eugene Benjamin.
Clemenceau, Georges Eugene Benjamin.
xClemenceau, Georges E.
Surprises of Life. Arno.
Clemens, Bryan T.
xClemens, Bryan T.
The Counselor & Religious Questioning &
Conflicts. HM.
Clemens, Clara.
xClemens, Clara.
My Father, Mark Twain. AMS Pr.
Clemens, Cyril.
xClemens, Cyril.
A Chat with Robert Frost. Folcroft.
Chesterton As Seen by His Contemporaries.
Gordon Pr.
Chesterton As Seen by His Contemporaries.
Haskell.
Mark Twain & Harry S. Truman. Arden Lib.
Mark Twain & Harry S. Truman. Folcroft.
Mark Twain Wit & Wisdom. Folcroft.
My Cousin Mark Twain. Arden Lib.
My Cousin Mark Twain. Folcroft.
My Cousin, Mark Twain. Haskell.
Clemens, Dale.
xClemens, Dale P.

Educational Psychology. Vantage.
Cleveland, Jess M. see Cleveland, Jesse M.
Cleveland, Jesse M.
xCleveland, Jess M.
The Chemistry of Plutonium. Am Nuclear Soc.
Cleveland Museum of Art.
xCleveland Museum of Art.
Japonisme: Japanese Influence on French Art
1854-1910. C E Tuttle.
xCleveland Museum of Art Staff.
Handbook of the Cleveland Museum of Art.
Ind U Pr.
Selected Works: The Cleveland Museum of
Art. Ind U Pr.
Cleveland Museum of Art Staff. see Cleveland Museum
of Art.
Cleveland Public Library - John G. White Department.
see Cleveland Public Library. John G. White
Department.
Cleveland Public Library. John G. White Department.
xCleveland Public Library - John G. White
Department.
Catalog of the Chess Collection, Including
Checkers. G K Hall.
xCleveland Public Library, John G. White
Department.
Catalog of Folklore & Folk Songs. G K Hall.
Clevenger, Theodore.
xClevenger, Theodore.
The Speech Communication Process. Scott F.
Cleverdon, Douglas.
xCleverdon, Douglas.
The Growth of Milk Wood. New Directions.
Cleverley, William O.
xCleverley, William O.
Essentials of Hospital Finance. Aspen Systems.
Financial Management of Health Care
Facilities. Aspen Systems.
Clewes, Howard, 1912-
xClewes, Howard.
I, the King. Morrow.
Clewlow, C. William.
xClewlow, C. William.
ed. Four Rock Art Studies. Ballena Pr.
Clews, Henry, 1836-1923
xClews, Henry.
Fifty Years in Wall Street. Arno.
Clews, Roy.
xClews, Roy.
The Drums of War. St Martin.
Cliburn, Alan.
xCliburn, Alan.
All This, & Mrs. Calucci Too!. Accent Bks.
Click, J. W.
xClick, J. W.
Magazine Editing & Production. Wm C Brown.
Click, Phyllis.
xClick, Phyllis.
Administration of Schools for Young Children.
Delmar.
Cliffe. see Cliffe, Lionel.
Cliffe, Lionel.
xCliffe.
Government & Rural Development in East
Africa: Essays on Political Penetration.
Kluwer Boston.
Clifford, A. Jerome. see Clifford, Albert Jerome.
Clifford, Albert Jerome, 1918-
xClifford, A. Jerome.
Independence of the Federal Reserve System.
U of Pa Pr.
Clifford, Brian. see Clifford, Brian R.
Clifford, Brian R.
xClifford, Brian.
The Psychology of Person Identification.
Routledge & Kegan.
Clifford, David. see Clifford, David Leonard.
Clifford, David Leonard.
xClifford, David.

The Two Jerusalems in Prophecy. Loizeaux.
Clifford, Deborah. see Clifford, Deborah Pickman.
Clifford, Deborah Pickman.
xClifford, Deborah.
Mine Eyes Have Seen the Glory: A Biography
of Julia Ward Howe. Little.
Clifford, Eth, 1915-
xClifford, Eth.
illus. The Curse of the Moonraker. HM.
Help! I'm a Prisoner in the Library. HM.
Clifford, Francis.
xClifford, Francis.
Drummer in the Dark. Ballantine.
Clifford, H. T. see Clifford, Harold Trevor.
Clifford, Harold Trevor.
xClifford, H. T.
Identifying Grasses: Data, Methods &
Illustrations. U of Queensland Pr.
Clifford, Hugh C. see Clifford, Hugh Charles.
Clifford, Hugh Charles, Sir, 1866-1941
xClifford, Hugh C.
In Days That Are Dead. Arno.
Clifford, James L. see Clifford, James Lowry.
Clifford, James Lowry, 1901-
xClifford, James L.
Dictionary Johnson: The Middle Years of
Samuel Johnson. McGraw.
ed. Eighteenth-Century English Literature:
Modern Essays in Criticism. Oxford U Pr.
From Puzzles to Portraits: Problems of a
Literary Biographer. U of NC Pr.

Clifford, Jerrold R.

xClifford, Jerrold R.
Basic Woodworking & Carpentry...with
Projects. Tab Bks.

Clifford, John G. see Clifford, John Garry.
Clifford, John Garry.
xClifford, John G.
The Citizen Soldiers: The Plattsburg Training
Camp Movement, 1913-1920. U Pr of Ky.
Clifford, Martin, 1910-
xClifford, Martin.
Basic Drafting. TAB Bks.

Clifford, Nicholas. see Clifford, Nicholas Rowland.
Clifford, Nicholas Rowland.
xClifford, Nicholas.
Retreat from China: British Policy in the Far
East, 1937-1941. Da Capo.
Clifford, Richard J.
xClifford, Richard J.
The Cosmic Mountain in Canaan & the Old
Testament. Harvard U Pr.
Clifford, Tom M. see Clifford, Tom N.
Clifford, Tom N.
xClifford, Tom M.
Review of African Granulites & Related Rocks.
Geol Soc.
Clifford, W., 1918-
xClifford, W.
Primer of Social Case Work in Africa. Oxford
U Pr.
Clifford, W. G.
xClifford, William G.
Books in Bottles: The Curious in Literature.
Gale.
Clifford, William, 1918-
xClifford, William.
Planning Crime Prevention. Lexington Bks.
Clifford, William G. see Clifford, W. G.
Clifford, William K. see Clifford, William Kingdon.
Clifford, William Kingdon, 1845-1879
xClifford, William K.
Lectures & Essays. Chelsea Pub.
Lectures & Essays. Scholarly.
Mathematical Papers. Chelsea Pub.
Clift, Jeannette.
xClift, Jeannette.

Some Run with Feet of Clay. Revell.
Clift, Roland.
xClift, Roland.
Bubbles, Drops & Particles. Acad Pr.
Clift, W. D. see Clift, W. Dale.
Clift, W. Dale.
xClift, W. D.
ARRL Technician-General Q & A Book. Am
Radio.
Clifton. see Clifton, Harold Dennis.
Clifton, D. see Clifton, Harold Dennis.
Clifton, David S.
xClifton, David S.
Project Feasibility Analysis: A Guide to
Profitable New Ventures. Wiley.
Clifton, H. D. see Clifton, Harold Dennis.
Clifton, Harold Dennis.
xClifton.
Accounting & Computer Systems. Beekman
Pubs.
xClifton, D.
Business Data Systems. P-H.
xClifton, H. D.
Accounting & Computer Systems. Van Nos
Reinhold.
Choosing & Using Computers: Assessing Data
Processing Requirements for Smaller
Companies. Beekman Pubs.
Systems Analysis for Business Data Processing.
Van Nos Reinhold.
Clifton, Lucille.
xClifton.
My Friend Jacob. Dutton.
xClifton, Lucille.
All Us Come Cross the Water. HR&W.
Amifika. Dutton.
The Boy Who Didn't Believe in Spring.
Dutton.
Don't You Remember?. Dutton.
The Lucky Stone. Delacorte.
Clifton, Robert. see Clifton, Robert L.
Clifton, Robert L.
xClifton, Robert.
Grassroots Administration: A Handbook for
Staff & Directors of Small Community Based
Social-Service Agencies. Brooks-Cole.
Clifton, Robert T.
xClifton, Robert T.
Barbs, Prongs, Points, Prickers, & Stickers:
Complete & Illustrated Catalogue of Antique
Barbed Wire. U of Okla Pr.
Clignet, Remi.
xClignet, Remi.
The Africanization of the Labor Market:
Educational & Occupational Segmentations in
the Camerouns. U of Cal Pr.
Clinard, Marshall B. see Clinard, Marshall Barron.
Clinard, Marshall Barron.
xClinard, Marshall B.
Anomie & Deviant Behavior: A Discussion &
Critique. Free Pr.
Crime in Developing Countries: A Comparative
Perspective. Wiley.
Sociology of Deviant Behavior. HR&W.
Clinard, Turner N. see Clinard, Turner Norman.
Clinard, Turner Norman.
xClinard, Turner N.
Responding to God: The Life of Stewardship.
Westminster.
Cline, C. see Cline, Clarence Lee.
Cline, C. L. see Cline, Clarence Lee.
Cline, C. Terry.
xCline, C. Terry.
Cross Current. Fawcett.
Damon. Fawcett.
Death Knell. Fawcett.
Cline, Clarence L. see Cline, Clarence Lee.
Cline, Clarence Lee.
xCline, C.

Byron, Shelley & Their Pisan Circle. R West.
xCline, C. L.
ed. The Owl & the Rossettis: Letters of Charles
A. Howell & Dante Gabriel, Christina, &
William Michael Rossetti. Pa St U Pr.
xCline, Clarence L.
Byron, Shelley & Their Pisan Circle. Russell.
Cline, Gloria G. see Cline, Gloria Griffen.
Cline, Gloria Griffen.
xCline, Gloria G.
Exploring the Great Basin. U of Okla Pr.
Cline, Gloria S. see Cline, Gloria Stark.
Cline, Gloria Stark.
xCline, Gloria S.
An Index to Criticisms of British & American
Poetry. Scarecrow.
Cline, Howard F. see Cline, Howard Francis.
Cline, Howard Francis.
xCline, Howard F.
ed. Latin American History: Essays on Its
Study & Teaching, 1898-1965. U of Tex Pr.
Provisional Historical Gazeteer with Locational
Notes on Florida Colonial Communities,
1700-1823. Clearwater Pub.
Cline, Martin J., 1934-
xCline, Martin J.
Cancer Chemotherapy. Saunders.
The White Cell. Harvard U Pr.
Cline, Ray S.
xCline, Ray S.
Secrets, Spies & Scholars: Blueprint of the
Essential CIA. Acropolis.
World Power Assessment: A Calculus of
Strategic Drift. CSI Studies.
Cline, Victor B.
xCline, Victor B.
ed. Where Do You Draw the Line?: An
Exploration into Media Violence,
Pornography, & Censorship. Brigham.
Cline, Walter B. see Cline, Walter Buchanan.
Cline, Walter Buchanan, 1904-
xCline, Walter B.
Notes on the People of Siwah & El Garah in
the Libyan Desert. AMS Pr.
Clinebell, Charlotte H.
xClinebell, Charlotte H.
Counseling for Liberation. Fortress.
Meet Me in the Middle: On Becoming Human
Together. Har-Row.
Clinebell, Howard. see Clinebell, Howard John.
Clinebell, Howard J. see Clinebell, Howard John.
Clinebell, Howard John, 1922-
xClinebell, Howard.
Growth Groups: Marriage & Family
Enrichment, Creative Singlehood, Human
Liberation, Youth Work, Social Change.
Abingdon.
xClinebell, Howard J.
Growth Counseling for Marriage Enrichment:
Pre-Marriage & the Early Years. Fortress.
Growth Counseling for Mid-Years Couples.
Fortress.
**Clinic on Library Applications of Data Processing, 12th,
Champaign, Illinois, 1975.**
xClinic on Library Applications of Data Processing
Proceedings, 1975.
The Use of Computers in Literature Searching
& Related Reference Activities in Libraries.
U of Ill Lib Sci.
**Clinic on Library Applications of Data Processing,
University of Illinois.**
xClinic on Library Applications of Data
Processing, 1964.

Applications of Minicomputers to Library &
Related Problems. U of Ill Lib Sci.
The Economics of Library Automation. U of Ill
Lib Sci.
MARC Uses & Users. U of Ill Lib Sci.
Networking & Other Forms of Cooperation. U
of Ill Lib Sci.
Proceedings. U of Ill Lib Sci.
Clinton, Alan.
xClinton, Alan.
The Trade Union Rank & File: Trades Councils
in Britain, 1900-1940. Rowman.
Clinton, Charles A. see Clinton, Charles Anthony.
Clinton, Charles Anthony, 1939-
xClinton, Charles A.
Local Success & Federal Failure: A Study of
Community Development & Educational
Change in the Rural South. Abt Assoc.
Clinton, Daniel J. see Clinton, Daniel Joseph.
Clinton, Daniel Joseph, 1900-
xClinton, Daniel J.
Gomez, Tyrant of the Andes. Greenwood.
Clinton, George.
xClinton, George.
Memoirs of the Life & Writings of Lord Byron.
Folcroft.
Clinton, Henry F. see Clinton, Henry Fynes.
Clinton, Henry Fynes, 1781-1852
xClinton, Henry F.
Fasti Romani: The Civil & Literary Chronology
of Rome & Constantinople from the Death of
Augustus to the Death of Justin the 2nd. B
Franklin.
Clipper, Lawrence J.
xClipper, Lawrence J.
G. K. Chesterton. Twayne.
Clippinger, John H. see Clippinger, John Henry.
Clippinger, John Henry.
xClippinger, John H.
Meaning & Discourse: A Computer Model of
Psychoanalytic Speech & Cognition. Johns
Hopkins.
Clipson, Colin W.
xClipson, Colin W.
Planning for Cardiac Care: A Guide to the
Planning & Design of Cardiac Care Facilities.
Health Admin Pr.
Clissold, Stephen.
xClissold, Stephen.
The Barbary Slaves. Rowman.
Spain. Walker & Co.
Clive, Alan, 1944-
xClive, Alan.
State of War: Michigan in World War II. U of
Mich Pr.
Clive, William, 1924-
xClive, William.
The Tune That They Play. PB.
Clizbe, John A.
xClizbe, John A.
A Chance for Change: Confronting Student
Under Achievement. Exposition.
Cloak, F. T. see Cloak, Frank Theodore.
Cloak, Frank Theodore.
xCloak, F. T.
A Natural Order of Cultural Adoption & Loss
in Trinidad. U NC Inst Res Soc Sci.
Cloar, Carroll.
xCloar, Carroll.
Hostile Butterflies & Other Paintings. Memphis
St Univ.
Clock, Herbert.
xClock, Herbert.
The Light in the Sky. Arno.
Clodd, Edward, 1840-1930
xClodd, Edward.

Story of the Alphabet. Gale.
The Story of the Alphabet. R West.
Thomas Henry Huxley. AMS Pr.
Thomas Henry Huxley. Folcroft.
Clodfelter, Michael.
xClodfelter, Michael D.
The Pawns of Dishonor. Branden.
Clodfelter, Michael D. see Clodfelter, Michael.
Clogg, Clifford C.
xClogg, Clifford C.
Measuring Underemployment: Demographic
Indicators for the United States. Acad Pr.
Clogg, R. see Clogg, Richard.
Clogg, Richard, 1939-
xClogg, R.
A Short History of Modern Greece. Cambridge
U Pr.
xClogg, Richard.
ed. The Struggle for Greek Independence:
Essays to Mark the 150th Anniversary of the
Greek War of Independence. Shoe String.
Cloke, Marjane.
xCloke, Marjane.
Modern Business Letter-Writer's Manual.
Doubleday.
The Modern Business Letter Writer's Manual.
Doubleday.
Cloke, Richard, 1916-
xCloke, Richard.
Jerry the Put. Kent Pubns.
Vector-Lee. Kent Pubns.
Clokey, Richard M., 1936-
xClokey, Richard M.
William H. Ashley: Enterprise & Politics in the
Trans-Mississippi West. U of Okla Pr.
Clontz, Ralph C.
xClontz, Ralph C.
Equal Credit Opportunity Manual. Warren
Cloonan, William J., 1942-
xCloonan, William J.
Racine's Theatre: The Politics of Love.
Romance.
Clopper, Edward N. see Clopper, Edward Nicholas.
Clopper, Edward Nicholas, 1879-1953
xClopper, Edward N.
Child Labor in City Streets. AMS Pr.
Child Labor in City Streets. Arno.
Clopper, Lawrence M., 1941-
xClopper, Lawrence M.
ed. Chester. U of Toronto Pr.
Clor, Harry M., 1929-
xClor, Harry M.
Obscenity & Public Morality: Censorship in a
Liberal Society. U of Chicago Pr.
Close, Charles M.
xClose, Charles M.
Analysis of Linear Circuits. HarBraceJ.
Close, Guy C.
xClose, Guy C.
Work Improvement. Wiley.
Close, J. Robert. see Close, John R.
Close, John R., 1912-
xClose, J. Robert.
Functional Anatomy of the Extremities: Some
Electronic & Kinematic Methods of Study. C
C Thomas.
Close, Paul D. see Close, Paul Dunham.
Close, Paul Dunham.
xClose, Paul D.
Sound Control & Thermal Insulation of
Buildings. Van Nos Reinhold.
Close, R. A.
xClose, Reg A.
A Reference Grammar for Students of English.
Longman.
Close, Reg A. see Close, R. A.
Close, Richard W.
xClose, Richard W.

Practical Swimming Officiating. Dolphin
Aquatics.
Closs, Hannah. *see* Closs, Hannah Priebsch.
Closs, Hannah Priebsch.
xCloss, Hannah.
The Silent Tarn. Popular Lib.
Silent Tarn. Vanguard.
Tristan. Popular Lib.
Closson, Ernest, 1870-1950
xClosson, Ernest.
History of the Piano. Scholarly.
Clotfelter, Beryl E., 1926-
xClotfelter, Beryl E.
Reference Systems & Inertia: The Nature of
Space. Iowa St U Pr.
Clotfelter, Cecil F.
xClotfelter, Cecil F.
ed. Camping & Backpacking: A Guide to
Information Sources. Gale.
Hunting & Fishing. Libs Unl.
Clothey, Fred W.
xClothey, Fred W.
The Many Faces of Murukan: The History &
Meaning of a South Indian God. Mouton.
Clothier, Peter, 1936-
xClothier, Peter.
Parapoems. Horizon.
Clouard, Henri.
xClouard, Henri.
ed. French Writers of Today. Oxford U Pr.
Cloud, Patricia.
xCloud, Patricia.
This Willing Passion. Berkley Pub.
Cloudsley-Thompson, J. L.
xCloudsley-Thompson, J. L.
Animal Twilight, Man & Game in Eastern
Africa. Dufour.
Spiders & Scorpions. McGraw.
xCloudsley-Thompson, John.
Animal Migration. Putnam.
Camels. Raintree Pubs.
Cloudsley-Thompson, John. *see* Cloudsley-Thompson, J.
L.

Clough, Dick B.

xClough, Dick B.
A Handbook of Effective Techniques for
Teacher Aides. C C Thomas.

Utilizing Teacher Aides in the Classroom. C C
Thomas.

Clough, Eric. *see* Clough, Eric A.
Clough, Eric A.
xClough, Eric.
ed. A Public Library Service for Ethnic
Minorities in Great Britain. Greenwood.
Clough, Jeffory.
xClough, Jeffory J.
Azoth. Windy Row.
Clough, Jeffory J. *see* Clough, Jeffory.
Clough, Ralph N., 1916-
xClough, Ralph N.
East Asia & U. S. Security. Brookings.
Clough, Richard H. *see* Clough, Richard Hudson.
Clough, Richard Hudson.
xClough, Richard H.
Construction Contracting. Wiley.
Construction Project Management. Wiley.
Clough, Shepard B. *see* Clough, Shepard Bancroft.
Clough, Shepard Bancroft, 1901-
xClough, Shepard B.
Century of American Life Insurance: A History
of the Mutual Life Insurance Company of
New York, 1843-1943. Greenwood.
Clouse, Robert G.
xClouse, Robert G.

ed. Protest & Politics: Christianity &
Contemporary Affairs. Attic Pr.
Clouston, A. E. *see* Clouston, Arthur E.
Clouston, Arthur E., 1908-
xClouston, A. E.
The Dangerous Skies. Arno.
Clouston, William A. *see* Clouston, William Alexander.
Clouston, William Alexander, 1843-1896
xClouston, William A.
Flowers from a Persian Garden & Other
Papers. Arno.
A Group of Eastern Romances & Stories, from
the Persian, Tamil & Urdu. Folcroft.
Clout, H. *see* Clout, Hugh D.
Clout, Hugh. *see* Clout, Hugh D.
Clout, Hugh D.
xClout, H.
The Regional Problem in Western Europe.
Cambridge U Pr.
xClout, Hugh.
Franco-Belgian Border Region. Oxford U Pr.
The Massif Central. Oxford U Pr.
xClout, Hugh D.
The Geography of Post-War France: A Social
& Economic Approach. Pergamon.
ed. Regional Development in Western Europe.
Wiley.
Clouzet, Maryse. *see* Clouzet, Maryse Choisy.
Clouzet, Maryse Choisy, 1903-
xClouzet, Maryse.
Sigmund Freud: A New Appraisal. Greenwood.
Clover, Vernon T.
xClover, Vernon T.
Business Research Methods. Grid Pub.
Clovis, Albert I. *see* Clovis, Albert L.
Clovis, Albert L.
xClovis, Albert I.
ed. Consumer Protection: A Symposium. Da
Capo.
Clow, Barbara.
xClow, Barbara.
Stained Glass: A Basic Manual. Little.
Cloward, Richard A.
xCloward, Richard A.
Delinquency & Opportunity: A Theory of
Delinquent Gangs. Free Pr.
Clower, Jerry.
xClower, Jerry.
Ain't God Good. Word Bks.
Let the Hammer Down. PB.
Let the Hammer Down. Word Bks.
Clowers, Myles L.
xClowers, Myles L.
Understanding American Politics Through
Fiction. McGraw.
Clowers, Norman L.
xClowers, Norman L.
Patrolman Patterns, Problems, & Procedures. C
C Thomas.
Clowney, Edmund P.
xClowney, Edmund P.
Preaching & Biblical Theology. Presby &
Reformed.
Club Managers Association. *see* Club Managers
Association of America.
Club Managers Association of America.
xClub Managers Association.
Club Management Operations. Kendall-Hunt.
Clubb, Louise G. *see* Clubb, Louise George.
Clubb, Louise George.
xClubb, Louise G.
Giambattista Della Porta: Dramatist. Princeton
U Pr.
Clubbe, John.
xClubbe, John B.
Two Reminiscences of Thomas Carlyle. Duke.
Clubbe, John B. *see* Clubbe, John.
Cluett, Robert.
xCluett, Robert.

Prose Style & Critical Reading. Tchrs Coll.
Cluff, Charles E.
xCluff, Charles E.
Parapsychology & the Christian Faith. Judson.
Cluff, Leighton E.
xCluff, Leighton E.
Clinical Problems with Drugs. Saunders.
Clugston, Richard.
xClugston, Richard.
Estimating Manufacturing Costs. CBI Pub.
Cluley, J. C. *see* Cluley, John Charles.
Cluley, John C. *see* Cluley, John Charles.
Cluley, John Charles.
xCluley, J. C.
Programming for Minicomputers. Crane-Russak
Co.
xCluley, John C.
Computer Interfacing & On-Line Operation.
Crane-Russak Co.
Clum, John M.
xClum, John M.
Paddy Chayefsky. Twayne.
Ridgely Torrence. Twayne.
Clum, W. *see* Clum, Woodworth.
Clum, Woodworth.
xClum, W.
Apache Agent: The Story of John P. Clum.
Gordon Pr.
xClum, Woodworth.
Apache Agent: The Story of John P. Clum. U
of Nebr Pr.
Clurman, David, 1927-
xClurman, David.
The Business Condominium: A New Form of
Business Property Ownership. Wiley.
Clurman, Harold, 1901-
xClurman, Harold.
The Divine Pastime: Theatre Essays.
Macmillan.
The Fervent Years: The Story of the Group
Theatre & the Thirties. HarBraceJ.
Ibsen. Macmillan.
Ibsen. Macmillan.
ed. Nine Plays of the Modern Theater. Grove.
Intro. by On Directing. Macmillan.
On Directing. Macmillan.
Cluster, Dick.
xCluster, Dick.
Shrinking Dollars, Vanishing Jobs: Why the
Economy Isn't Working for You. Beacon Pr.
Clutter, Mary E.
xClutter, Mary E.
ed. Dormancy & Developmental Arrest:
Experimental Analysis in Plants & Animals.
Acad Pr.
Clutterbuck, Richard. *see* Clutterbuck, Richard L.
Clutterbuck, Richard L.
xClutterbuck, Richard.
Kidnap & Ransom: The Response. Merrimack
Bk Serv.
Clutton-Brock, A. *see* Clutton-Brock, Arthur.
Clutton-Brock, Arthur, 1868-1924
xClutton-Brock, A.
More Essays on Books. R West.
Necessity of Art. Arno.
xClutton-Brock, Arthur.
More Essays on Books. Arno.
More Essays on Religion. Arno.
Clyde, James E., 1901-
xClyde, James E.
Construction Inspection: A Field Guide to
Practice. Wiley.
Clyde, Sheri.
xClyde, Sheri.
A Child's Library of Dreams. Celestial Arts.
Clyde, William M. *see* Clyde, William M'Callum.
Clyde, William M'Callum.
xClyde, William M.

Antonio Machado. Twayne.
Contemporary Spanish Poetry: 1898-1963. Twayne.
Federico Garcia Lorca. Twayne.

Cobb, Charlie, 1943-
xCobb, Charlie.
Everywhere Is Yours. Third World.

Cobb, Edith, 1895-
xCobb, Edith.
The Ecology of Imagination in Childhood. Columbia U Pr.

Cobb, Henry V. see Cobb, Henry Van Zandt.

Cobb, Henry Van Zandt.
xCobb, Henry V.
The Forecast of Fulfillment: A Review of Research on Predictive Assessment of the Adult Retarded for Social & Vocational Adjustment. Tchrs Coll.

Cobb, Hubbard H., 1917-
xCobb, Hubbard H.
Improvements That Increase the Value of Your House. McGraw.

Cobb, Irvin S. see Cobb, Irvin Shrewsbury.

Cobb, Irvin Shrewsbury, 1876-1944
xCobb, Irvin S.
Exit Laughing. Gale.
Those Times & These. Arno.

Cobb, J. E. see Cobb, Jesse E.

Cobb, J. Stanley.
xCobb.
Marine Ecology: Selected Readings. Univ Park.

Cobb, Jesse E., 1890-1971
xCobb, J. E.
Cobb's Baptist Church Manual. Baptist Pub Hse.

Cobb, John B.
xCobb, John B.
Christ in a Pluralistic Age. Westminster.
God & the World. Westminster.
Process Theology: An Introductory Exposition. Westminster.
Theology & Pastoral Care. Fortress.

Cobb, Louise S. see Cobb, Louise Staples.

Cobb, Louise Staples, 1897-
xCobb, Louise S.
A Study of the Functions of Physical Education in Higher Education. AMS Pr.

Cobb, Mary Ann.
xCobb, Mary Ann.
Lorie: A Story of Hope. Nelson.

Cobb, Richard. see Cobb, Richard Charles.

Cobb, Richard C. see Cobb, Richard Charles.

Cobb, Richard Charles, 1917-
xCobb, Richard.
Paris & Its Provinces 1792-1802. Oxford U Pr.
Streets of Paris. Pantheon.
Tour de France. Holmes & Meier.
xCobb, Richard C.
Reactions to the French Revolution. Oxford U Pr.

Cobb, Robert. see Cobb, Robert A.

Cobb, Robert A.
xCobb, Robert.
Contemporary Philosophies of Physical Education & Athletics. Merrill.

Cobb, Roger W.
xCobb, Roger W.
Participation in American Politics: The Dynamics of Agenda-Building. Johns Hopkins.

Cobb, Sidney.
xCobb, Sidney.
Frequency of the Rheumatic Diseases. Harvard U Pr.

Cobb, Thomas R. see Cobb, Thomas Read Rootes.

Cobb, Thomas Read Rootes, 1823-1862
xCobb, Thomas R.

Historical Sketch of Slavery, from the Earliest Periods. Arno.

Cobb, Vicki.
xCobb, Vicki.
Arts & Crafts You Can Eat. Lippincott.
Bet You Can't!: Science Impossibilities to Fool You. Lothrop.
How the Doctor Knows You're Fine. Lippincott.
The Long & Short of Measurement. Enslow Pubs.
More Science Experiments You Can Eat. Lippincott.
Truth on Trial: The Story of Galileo Galilei. Coward.

Cobb, Wilton P. see Cobb, Addie Davis.

Cobban, A. see Cobban, Alfred.

Cobban, Alfred.
xCobban, A.
The Nation State & National Self Determination. Watts.
xCobban, Alfred.
Ambassadors & Secret Agents: The Diplomacy of the First Earl of Malmesbury at the Hague. Hyperion Conn.
Aspects of the French Revolution. Braziller.
Dictatorship: Its History & Theory. Haskell.
Edmund Burke & the Revolt Against the Eighteenth Century: A Study of the Political & Social Thinking of Burke, Wordsworth, Coleridge, & Southey. Arden Lib.
Edmund Burke & the Revolt Against the Eighteenth Century: A Study of the Political & Social Thinking of Burke, Wordsworth, Coleridge, & Southey. Arden Lib.
A History of Modern France. Braziller.

Cobbe, James.
xCobbe, James.
Governments & Mining Companies in Developing Countries. Westview.

Cobbett, William, 1763-1835
xCobbett, William.
ed. Cobbett's Parliamentary History of England from the Norman Conquest in 1066 to the Year 1803. AMS Pr.

Cobden, Richard, 1804-1865
xCobden, Richard.
England, Ireland, & America. Inst Study Human.
The Political Writings of Richard Cobden. Gordon Pr.
Political Writings of Richard Cobden. Kraus Repr.

Coben, Stanley.
xCoben, Stanley.
ed. Reform, War, & Reaction: 1912-1932. U of SC Pr.

Cober, Alan E.
xCober, Alan E.
Cober's Choice. Dutton.

Coblans, H. see Coblans, Herbert.

Coblans, Herbert.
xCoblans, H.
ed. The Use of Physics Literature. Butterworths.

Coble, A. B. see Coble, Arthur Byron.

Coble, Arthur Byron, 1878-
xCoble, A. B.
Algebraic Geometry & Theta Functions. Am Math.

Cobleigh, Ira. see Cobleigh, Ira U.

Cobleigh, Ira U.
xCobleigh, Ira.
The Dowbeaters: How to Buy Stocks That Go up. Macmillan.

Coblentz, Stanton. see Coblentz, Stanton A.

Coblentz, Stanton A.
xCoblentz, Stanton.
Lord of Tranerica. Bouregy.

Coblentz, Stanton A. see Coblentz, Stanton Arthur.

Coblentz, Stanton Arthur, 1896-
xCoblentz, Stanton.
Avarice: A History. Pub Aff Pr.
xCoblentz, Stanton A.
In Caverns Below. Garland Pub.
Literary Revolution. AMS Pr.
The Literary Revolution. Johnson Repr.
Literary Revolution. Scholarly.
ed. Modern British Lyrics: An Anthology. Arno.
ed. The Music Makers: An Anthology of Recent American Poetry. Granger Bk.
When the Birds Fly South. Arno.
When the Birds Fly South. Borgo Pr.
When the Birds Fly South. Newcastle Pub.

Coburn, Alvin F. see Coburn, Alvin Frederick.

Coburn, Alvin Frederick, 1899-
xCoburn, Alvin F.
Commitment Total. Walker & Co.

Coburn, Andrew.
xCoburn, Andrew.
The Baby Sitter. PB.
The Babysitter. Norton.
The Babysitter. PB.
Off Duty. Norton.

Coburn, John. see Coburn, John B.

Coburn, John B.
xCoburn, John.
A Life to Live - a Way to Pray. Seabury.
xCoburn, John B.
Christ's Life, Our Life. Seabury.
Deliver Us from Evil: The Prayer of Our Lord. Seabury.
The Hope of Glory: Exploring the Mystery of Christ in You. Seabury.
Prayer & Personal Religion. Westminster.

Coburn, Kathleen.
xCoburn, Kathleen.
Experience into Thought: Perspectives in the Coleridge Notebooks. U of Toronto Pr.
In Pursuit of Coleridge. Rowman.

Coburn, Louis, 1915-
xCoburn, Louis.
Library Media Center Problems - Case Studies. Oceana.

Coburn, Walt.
xCoburn, Walt.
Drift Fence. Belmont-Tower.
The Night Branders. Belmont-Tower.

Coca, Arthur F. see Coca, Arthur Fernandez.

Coca, Arthur Fernandez, 1875-
xCoca, Arthur F.
Pulse Test. Arc Bks.
Pulse Test. Lyle Stuart.

Coceani, Flavio.
xCoceani, Flavio.
ed. Prostaglandins & Perinatal Medicine. Raven.

Cochin, Augustin, 1823-1872
xCochin, Augustin.
Results of Emancipation. Arno.
Results of Slavery. Arno.
Results of Slavery. Negro U Pr.

Cochin, Ira.
xCochin, Ira.
Analysis & Design of Dynamic Systems. Har-Row.

Cochran, J. A. see Cochran, James Alan.

Cochran, Jacqueline.
xCochran, Jacqueline.
The Stars at Noon. Arno.

Cochran, James Alan.
xCochran, J. A.
Analysis of Linear Integral Equations. McGraw.

Cochran, John A.
xCochran, John A.
Money, Banking & the Economy. Macmillan.

Cochran, Mickey.
xCochran, Mickey.

Introduction to Ordinary Differential
Equations. P-H.
Theory of Ordinary Differential Equations.
McGraw.
Code, Grant. *see* Code, Grant Hyde.
Code, Grant Hyde.
xCode, Grant.
This Undying Quest. Stanton & Lee.
Code, Joseph B. *see* Code, Joseph Bernard.
Code, Joseph Bernard, 1899-
xCode, Joseph B.
Great American Foundresses. Arno.
Codevilla, Angelo, 1943-
xCodevilla, Angelo.
Modern France. Open Court.
Codex Theodosianus.
xCodex Theodosianus.
Theodosian Code & Novels, & the Sirmondian
Constitutions. Greenwood.
Codner, Bernard.
xCodner, Bernard.
Income Producing Services. Natl Ret Merch.
Cody, Al.
xCody, Al.
Broken Wheels. Manor Bks.
Forbidden River. Bouregy.
Forbidden River. Manor Bks.
The Fort at the Dry. Bouregy.
Guns on the Bitterroot. Assoc Bk.
Gunsong at Twilight. Manor Bks.
Once a Sheriff. Manor Bks.
The Outcasts. Manor Bks.
Return to Fort Yavapa. Bouregy.
Cody, Martin L., 1941-
xCody, Martin L.
Competition & the Structure of Bird
Communities. Princeton U Pr.
ed. Ecology & Evolution of Communities.
Harvard U Pr.
Coe, Charles N. *see* Coe, Charles Norton.
Coe, Charles Norton.
xCoe, Charles N.
Wordsworth & the Literature of Travel.
Octagon.
Coe, Evan.
xCoe, Evan.
ed. Images of America: Selected Readings
Based on Alistair Cooke's America. Knopf.
Coe, George A. *see* Coe, George Albert.
Coe, George Albert, 1862-1951
xCoe, George A.
Am I Getting an Education?. AMS Pr.
Social Theory of Religious Education. Arno.
Coe, Joffre L. *see* Coe, Joffre Lanning.
Coe, Joffre Lanning.
xCoe, Joffre L.
The Formative Cultures of the Carolina
Piedmont. Univ Microfilms.
Coe, Mary Lee.
xCoe, Mary Lee.
Growing with Community Gardening.
Countryman.
Coe, Michael D.
xCoe, Michael D.
The Maya. Thames Hudson.
The Maya Scribe & His World. Grolier Club.
The Maya Scribe & His World. U Pr of Va.
Coe, Michele. *see* Coe, Michelle E.
Coe, Michelle E.
xCoe, Michele.
How to Write for Television. Crown.
xCoe, Michelle E.
How to Write for Television. Crown.
Coe, Ralph T.
xCoe, Ralph T.
Dale Eldred: Sculpture into Environment.
Regents Pr KS.
Coe, Richard N.
xCoe, Richard N.

Samuel Beckett. Grove.
Samuel Beckett. Univ Microfilms.
Coe, Rodney M.
xCoe, Rodney M.
Preventive Health Care for Adults: A Study of
Medical Practice. Coll & U Pr.
Sociology of Medicine. McGraw.
Coe, Samuel P.
xCoe, Samuel P.
Contemporary Psychology in Marx & Engels.
Am Inst Marxist.
Coe, W. E.
xCoe, W. E.
Engineering Industry of the North of Ireland.
Kelley.
Coe, Wesley R. *see* Coe, Wesley Roswell.
Coe, Wesley Roswell, 1869-1960
xCoe, Wesley R.
Starfishes, Serpent Stars, Sea Urchins & Sea
Cucumbers of the Northeast. Peter Smith.
Coen, Franklin.
xCoen, Franklin.
The Plunderers. Coward.
Coen, Luciano.
xCoen, Luciano.
The Oriental Rug. Har-Row.
Coen, Rena N. *see* Coen, Rena Neumann.
Coen, Rena Neumann.
xCoen, Rena N.
American History in Art. Lerner Pubns.
Medicine in Art. Lerner Pubns.
Painting & Sculpture in Minnesota, 1820-1914.
U of Minn Pr.
Coens, Mary X. *see* Coens, Mary Xavier.
Coens, Mary Xavier.
xCoens, Mary X.
G. I. Nun. Kenedy.
Coerne, Louis A. *see* Coerne, Louis Adolphe.
Coerne, Louis Adolphe, 1870-1922
xCoerne, Louis A.
The Evolution of Modern Orchestration. AMS
Pr.
Coes, Donald V., 1943-
xCoes, Donald V.
The Impact of Price Uncertainty: A Study of
Brazilian Exchange Rate Policy. Garland
Pub.
Coes, L. *see* Coes, Loring.
Coes, Loring, 1915-
xCoes, L.
Abrasives. Springer-Verlag.
Coester, Alfred. *see* Coester, Alfred Lester.
Coester, Alfred Lester, 1874-1958
xCoester, Alfred.
Literary History of Spanish America. Cooper
Sq.
Coetzee, J. F. *see* Coetzee, Johannes Francois.
Coetzee, Johannes. *see* Coetzee, Johannes Francois.
Coetzee, Johannes Francois.
xCoetzee, J. F.
ed. Solute-Solvent Interactions. Dekker.
xCoetzee, Johannes.
Solute-Solvent Interactions. Dekker.
Cofer, Charles N. *see* Cofer, Charles Norval.
Cofer, Charles Norval.
xCofer, Charles N.
ed. The Structure of Human Memory. W H
Freeman.
Coffeehouse Jones.
xCoffeehouse Jones.
Cook in Your Coffeepot. Survey Pub Co.
Coffer, William E.
xCoffer, William E.
Phoenix: The Decline & Rebirth of the Indian
People. Van Nos Reinhold.
Coffey. *see* Coffey, Wayne R.
Coffey, Alan.
xCoffey, Alan.

Human Relations: Law Enforcement in a
Changing Community. P-H.
xCoffey, Alan R.
The Prevention of Crime & Delinquency. P-H.
Process & Impact of Justice. Glencoe.
Coffey, Alan R. *see* Coffey, Alan.
Coffey, D. J.
xCoffey, David J.
Dolphins, Whales & Porpoises: The
Encyclopedia of Sea Mammals. Macmillan.
The Encyclopedia of Aquarium Fishes. Arco.
Coffey, David J. *see* Coffey, D. J.
Coffey, Frank.
xCoffey, Frank.
The Pride of Portland: The Story of the Trail
Blazers. Everest Hse.
The Shaman. St Martin.
Coffey, J. I. *see* Coffey, Joseph I.
Coffey, John W., 1943-
xCoffey, John W.
Political Realism in American Thought.
Bucknell U Pr.
Coffey, Joseph I.
xCoffey, J. I.
Strategic Power & National Security. U of
Pittsburgh Pr.
Coffey, Kenneth J.
xCoffey, Kenneth J.
Manpower for Military Mobilization. Am
Enterprise.
Coffey, Peter.
xCoffey, Peter.
ed. The Economic Policies of the Common
Market. St Martin.
World Monetary Crisis. St Martin.
Coffey, Thomas M.
xCoffey, Thomas M.
The Long Thirst: Prohibition in America
1920-1933. Norton.
Coffey, Wayne R.
xCoffey.
How We Choose a Congress. St Martin.
Coffin, Charles C. *see* Coffin, Charles Carleton.
Coffin, Charles Carleton, 1823-1896
xCoffin, Charles C.
Four Years of Fighting. Arno.
Coffin, George. *see* Coffin, George Sturgis.
Coffin, George S. *see* Coffin, George Sturgis.
Coffin, George Sturgis, 1903-
xCoffin, George.
Bridge Summary Complete. Branden.
xCoffin, George S.
Bridge Play from A to Z. Dover.
Coffin, Harold G.
xCoffin, Harold G.
Fossils in Focus. Zondervan.
Coffin, Henry S. *see* Coffin, Henry Sloane,
Coffin, Henry Sloane, 1877-1954
xCoffin, Henry S.
Religion Yesterday & Today. Arno.
Some Christian Convictions: A Practical
Restatement in Terms of Present-Day
Thinking. Arno.
Coffin, Joseph, 1899-
xCoffin, Joseph.
Complete Book of Coin Collecting. Coward.
Coffin, Levi, 1798-1877
xCoffin, Levi.
Reminiscences of Levi Coffin, the Reputed
President of the Underground Railroad.
Arno.
Coffin, Mark T. *see* Coffin, Mark Tristram.
Coffin, Mark Tristram.
xCoffin, Mark T.
American Narrative Obituary Verse & Native
American Balladry. Folcroft.
Coffin, Robert P. *see* Coffin, Robert Peter Tristram.
Coffin, Robert Peter Tristram, 1892-1955
xCoffin, Robert P.

Lost Paradise: A Boyhood on a Maine Coast Farm. Scholarly.
Maine Doings. Thorndike Pr.
Strange Holiness. Thorndike Pr.

Coffin, Royce A.
xCoffin, Royce A.
The Communicator. Am Mgmt.
The Communicator. B&N.
The Negotiator: A Manual for Winners. Am Mgmt.
The Negotiator: A Manual for Winners. B&N.
Coffin, Tristam P. *see* Coffin, Tristram Potter.
Coffin, Tristan P. *see* Coffin, Tristram Potter.
Coffin, Tristram P.
xCoffin, Tristram P.
The British Traditional Ballad in North America. U of Tex Pr.
Coffin, Tristram P. *see* Coffin, Tristram Potter.
Coffin, Tristram Potter, 1922-
xCoffin, Tristam P.
The Female Hero in Folklore & Legend. Continuum.
xCoffin, Tristan P.
Illustrated Book of Christmas Folklore. Continuum.
xCoffin, Tristram P.
The Female Hero in Folklore & Legend. PB.
The Illustrated Book of Baseball Folklore. Continuum.
ed. Indian Tales of North America: An Anthology for the Adult Reader. U of Tex Pr.
A Proper Book of Sexual Folklore. Continuum.
Uncertain Glory: Folklore & the American Revolution. Gale.
Coffman, Edward G. *see* Coffman, Edward Grady.
Coffman, Edward Grady.
xCoffman, Edward G.
ed. Computer & Job-Shop Scheduling Theory. Wiley.
Operating Systems Theory. P-H.
Coffman, Edward M.
xCoffman, Edward M.
Hilt of the Sword: The Career of Peyton C. March. U of Wis Pr.
Coffman, Ralph J.
xCoffman, Ralph J.
Solomon Stoddard. Twayne.
Coffman, Tom.
xCoffman, Tom.
Catch a Wave: A Case Study of Hawaii's New Politics. U Pr of Hawaii.
Coffman, Virginia.
xCoffman, Virginia.
The Cliffs of Dread. NAL.
The Dark Palazzo. Arbor Hse.
The Dark Palazzo. Fawcett.
High Terrace. NAL.
The House at Sandalwood. Fawcett.
The House on the Moat. NAL.
Hyde Place. Arbor Hse.
Hyde Place. Fawcett.
Night at Sea Abbey. NAL.
The Rest Is Silence. NAL.
Coffman, William E. *see* Coffman, William Eugene.
Coffman, William Eugene, 1913-
xCoffman, William E.
Frontiers of Educational Measurement & Information Systems. HM.
Coffron, James.
xCoffron, James W.
Getting Started in Digital Troubleshooting. Reston.
Coffron, James W. *see* Coffron, James.
Cogan, David G. *see* Cogan, David Glendenning.
Cogan, David Glendenning, 1908-
xCogan, David G.

Ophthalmic Manifestations of Systemic Vascular Disease. Saunders.
Cogan, Morris L.
xCogan, Morris L.
Clinical Supervision. HM.
Cogan, Morton.
xCogan, Morton.
Imperialism & Religion: Assyria, Judah and Israel in the Eighth and Seventh Centuries B.C.E.. Scholars Pr Ca.
Coger, Leslie I. *see* Coger, Leslie Irene.
Coger, Leslie Irene.
xCoger, Leslie I.
Readers Theatre Handbook: A Dramatic Approach to Literature. Scott F.
Coger, Rick.
xCoger, Rick.
Developing Effective Instructional Systems. Chris Mass.
Coggan, Donald. *see* Coggan, Frederick Donald.
Coggan, Frederick Donald, 1909-
xCoggan, Donald.
Great Words of the Christian Faith. Abingdon.
Cogger, H. G. *see* Cogger, Harold G.
Cogger, Harold G.
xCogger, H. G.
Australian Reptiles in Colour. U Pr of Hawaii.
Coggins, Gordon.
xCoggins, Gordon.
A Guide to Writing Essays & Research Papers. Van Nos Reinhold.
Coggins, Jack.
xCoggins, Jack.
Arms & Equipment of the Civil War. Doubleday.
Horseman's Bible. Doubleday.
illus. Prepare to Dive: The Story of Man Undersea. Dodd.
Coggins, Wade T.
xCoggins, Wade I.
ed. Evangelical Missions Tomorrow. William Carey Lib.
Coghill, George E. *see* Coghill, George Ellett.
Coghill, George Ellett, 1872-1941
xCoghill, George E.
Early Embryonic Somatic Movements in Birds & Mammals Other Than Man. Kraus Repr.
Coghill, Nevill.
xCoghill, Nevill.
The Pardon of Piers Plowman. Arden Lib.
Pardon of Piers Plowman. Folcroft.
Coghlan. *see* Coghlan, David A.
Coghlan, David A., 1929-
xCoghlan.
Vehicle Chassis Systems. Duxbury Pr.
Cogley, John.
xCogley, John.
A Canterbury Tale: Experiences & Reflections: 1916-1976. Seabury.
Catholic America. Doubleday.
Cogniat, Raymond, 1896-
xCogniat, Raymond.
Chagall. Crown.
Soutine. Crown.
Cohan, George M. *see* Cohan, George Michael.
Cohan, George Michael, 1878-1942
xCohan, George M.
Twenty Years on Broadway & the Years It Took to Get There: The True Story of a Trouper's Life from the Cradle to the Closed Shop. Greenwood.
Cohan, Tony.
xCohan, Tony.
ed. Outlaw Visions. Acrobat.
Cohen. *see* Cohen, Henry A.

Cohen, Aaron.
xCohen, Aaron.
Designing & Space Planning for Libraries: A Behavioral Guide. Bowker.

Cohen, Abner.
xCohen, Abner.
Custom & Politics in Urban Africa: A Study of Hausa Migrants in Yoruba Towns. U of Cal Pr.

Cohen, Abraham, 1887-
xCohen, Abraham.
Everyman's Talmud. Dutton.
Everyman's Talmud. Schocken.

Cohen, Alan S.
xCohen, Alan S.
ed. Medical Emergencies: Diagnostic & Management Procedures from Boston City Hospital. Little.
ed. Rheumatology & Immunology. Grune.
Cohen, Albert K. *see* Cohen, Albert Kircidel.
Cohen, Albert Kircidel.
xCohen, Albert K.
ed. Prison Violence. Lexington Bks.
Cohen, Allan R.
xCohen, Allan R.
Effective Behavior in Organizations: Learning from the Interplay of Cases, Concepts & Student Experiences. Irwin.
Cohen, Annabelle, 1920-
xCohen, Annabelle.
Handbook of Cellular Chemistry. Mosby.
Cohen, Arthur A. *see* Cohen, Arthur Allen.
Cohen, Arthur A.
xCohen, Arthur A.
Communism of Mao Tse-Tung. U of Chicago Pr.
Cohen, Arthur A. *see* Cohen, Arthur Allen.
Cohen, Arthur Allen, 1928-
xCohen, Arhtur A.
Acts of Theft. HarBraceJ.
xCohen, Arthur A.
The Natural & the Supernatural Jew: An Historical and Theological Introduction. Behrman.
Sonia Delaunay. Abrams.
Cohen, Arthur M.
xCohen, Arthur M.
The Critical Incident in Growth Groups: A Manual for Group Leaders. Univ Assocs.
The Two-Year College Instructor Today. Praeger.
Cohen, Arthur R. *see* Cohen, Arthur Robert.
Cohen, Arthur Robert, 1927-1963
xCohen, Arthur R.
Attitude Change & Social Influence. Basic.
Cohen, B. *see* Cohen, Bernard P.
Cohen, B. Bernard. *see* Cohen, Benjamin Bernard.
Cohen, Barbara.
xCohen.
R My Name Is Rosie. Schol Bk Serv.
xCohen, Barbara.
The Carp in the Bath Tub. Dell.
The Carp in the Bathtub. Lothrop.
I Am Joseph. Lothrop.
The Innkeeper's Daughter. Lothrop.
R My Name Is Rosie. Lothrop.
Thank You, Jackie Robinson. Lothrop.
Unicorns in the Rain. Atheneum.
Where's Florrie?. Lothrop.
Cohen, Benjamin Bernard, 1922-
xCohen, B. Bernard.
Literature for Understanding. Scott F.
Cohen, Benjamin I.
xCohen, Benjamin I.
Multinational Firms & Asian Exports. Yale U Pr.
Cohen, Benjamin J.
xCohen, Benjamin J.

The Question of Imperialism: The Political
Economy of Dominance & Dependence.
Basic.
Cohen, Bernard, 1906-
xCohen, Bernard.
Sociocultural Changes in American Jewish Life
As Reflected in Selected Jewish Literature.
Fairleigh Dickinson.
Cohen, Bernard C. *see* Cohen, Bernard Cecil.
Cohen, Bernard Cecil, 1926-
xCohen, Bernard C.
Press & Foreign Policy. Princeton U Pr.
The Public's Impact on Foreign Policy. Little.
Cohen, Bernard P.
xCohen, B.
Developing Sociological Knowledge: Theory &
Method. P-H.
xCohen, Bernard P.
Conflict, Conformity & Social Status. Elsevier.
Cohen, Bernice H.
xCohen, Bernice H.
Genetic Issues in Public Health & Medicine. C
C Thomas.
Cohen, Beth.
xCohen, Beth.
Attic Bilingual Vases & Their Painters. Garland
Pub.
Cohen, Boaz, 1899-1968
xCohen, Boaz.
Law & Tradition in Judaism. Ktav.
Cohen, Bruce J., 1938-
xCohen, Bruce J.
ed. Crime in America: Perspectives on Criminal
& Delinquent Behavior. Peacock Pubs.
Cohen, Burton.
xCohen, Burton.
Nelson Makes a Face. Lothrop.
Cohen, Carl, 1931-
xCohen, Carl.
Democracy. Free Pr.
Democracy. U of Ga Pr.
Cohen, Chapman, 1868-
xCohen, Chapman.
Primitive Survivals in Modern Thought. Arno.
Cohen, D. *see* Cohen, David.
Cohen, D. E. *see* Cohen, Daniel E.
Cohen, Dan.
xCohen, Dan.
The Case of the Battling Ball Clubs. Carolrhoda
Bks.
The Case of the Long Lost Twin. Carolrhoda
Bks.
The Case of the Runaway Rabbit. Carolrhoda
Bks.
The Mystery of the Hidden Camera.
Carolrhoda Bks.
The Mystery of the Locked Door. Carolrhoda
Bks.
The Mystery of the Marked Money.
Carolrhoda Bks.
Undefeated: The Life of Hubert H. Humphrey.
Lerner Pubns.
Cohen, Dan. *see* Cohen, Daniel.
Cohen, Daniel.
xCohen, Dan.
The Case of the Missing Poodle. Carolrhoda
Bks.
The Mystery of the Faded Footprint.
Carolrhoda Bks.
xCohen, Daniel.

The Ancient Visitors. Doubleday.
Animal Territories. Hastings.
illus. Ceremonial Magic. Schol Bk Serv.
Curses, Hexes, & Spells. Lippincott.
Dealing with the Devil. Dodd.
Dreams, Visions & Drugs: A Search for Other
Realities. Watts.
Famous Curses. Dodd.
Frauds & Hoaxes & Swindles. Dell.
Frauds, Hoaxes, & Swindles. Watts.
Ghostly Animals. Doubleday.
Great Mistakes. M Evans.
The Greatest Monsters in the World. Archway.
The Greatest Monsters in the World. Dodd.
Greatest Monsters in the World. PB.
The Human Side of Computers. McGraw.
In Search of Ghosts. Dodd.
Masters of the Occult. Dodd.
Meditation: What It Can Do for You. Dodd.
Missing: Stories of Strange Disappearances. PB.
Missing: Stories of Strange Disappearances.
Dodd.
Modern Look at Monsters. Dodd.
Monsters You Never Heard of. Dodd.
Real Ghosts. Archway.
Real Ghosts. Dodd.
Real Ghosts. PB.
Supermonsters. Archway.
Supermonsters. Dodd.
Supermonsters. PB.
Talking with the Animals. Dodd.
The Tomb Robbers. McGraw.
Vaccination & You. Messner.
What's Happening to Our Weather. M Evans.
The World's Most Famous Ghosts. Archway.
The World's Most Famous Ghosts. Dodd.
The World's Most Famous Ghosts. PB.
xCohen, Daniel E.
The Far Side of Consciousness. Dodd.
Cohen, Daniel E.
xCohen, D. E.
Groups of Cohomological Dimension One.
Springer-Verlag.
Cohen, Daniel E. *see* Cohen, Daniel.
Cohen, David, 1932-
xCohen, D.
How to Win Criminal Cases by Establishing a
Reasonable Doubt. P-H.
xCohen, David.
J. B. Watson-the Founder of Behaviourism: A
Biography. Routledge & Kegan.
ed. Multi-Ethnic Media: Selected
Bibliographies in Print. ALA.
Psychologists on Psychology. Taplinger.
Cohen, David. *see* Cohen, David Steven.
Cohen, David Steven, 1943-
xCohen, David.
The Ramapo Mountain People. Rutgers U Pr.
Cohen, David W. *see* Cohen, David William.
Cohen, David William.
xCohen, David W.
ed. Neither Slave nor Free: The Freedman of
African Descent in the Slave Societies of the
New World. Johns Hopkins.
Womunafu's Bunafu: A Study of Authority in a
Nineteenth-Century African Community.
Princeton U Pr.
Cohen, Dorothy. *see* Cohen, Dorothy H.
Cohen, Dorothy H.
xCohen, Dorothy.
The Learning Child. Pantheon.
xCohen, Dorothy H.
The Learning Child. Random.
Observing & Recording the Behavior of Young
Children. Tchrs Coll.
Cohen, Edmund D.
xCohen, Edmund D.

C. G. Jung & the Scientific Attitude.
Littlefield.
C. G. Jung & the Scientific Attitude. Philos
Lib.
Cohen, Edward E.
xCohen, Edward E.
Ancient Athenian Maritime Courts. Princeton
U Pr.
Cohen, Edward H.
xCohen, Edward H.
Ebenezer Cooke: The Sot-Weed Canon. U of
Ga Pr.
Cohen, Edward R., 1939-
xCohen, Edward R.
Materials for a Basic Course in Property. West
Pub.
Cohen, Edwin, 1931-
xCohen, Edwin.
Oral Interpretation: The Communication of
Literature. SRA.

Cohen, Elaine P. *see* Cohen, Elaine Pear.
Cohen, Elaine Pear.
xCohen, Elaine P.
Art, Another Language for Learning. Schol Bk
Serv.
Cohen, Eliot A.
xCohen, Eliot A.
Commandos & Politicians: Elite Military Units
in Modern Democracies. Harvard U Intl Aff.
Cohen, Ellis N.
xCohen, Ellis N.
Anesthetic Exposure in the Workplace. PSG
Pub.
Cohen, Emmeline. *see* Cohen, Emmeline W.
Cohen, Emmeline W.
xCohen, Emmeline.
Growth of the British Civil Service, 1780-1939.
Biblio Dist.
Cohen, F. R. *see* Cohen, Frederick Ronald.
Cohen, Florence C. *see* Cohen, Florence Chanock.
Cohen, Florence Chanock.
xCohen, Florence C.
The Monkey Puzzle Tree. Story Pr.
Cohen, Fred.
xCohen, Fred.
Standards Relating to Dispositional Procedures.
Ballinger Pub.
Cohen, Frederick Ronald.
xCohen, F. R.
The Homology of Iterated Loop Spaces.
Springer-Verlag.
Cohen, Gail A.
xCohen, Gail A.
ed. Teaching Abroad. Inst Intl Educ.
Cohen, Gary G.
xCohen, Gary G.
Weep Not for Me. Moody.
Cohen, H. Hirsch.
xCohen, H. Hirsch.
The Drunkenness of Noah. U of Ala Pr.
Cohen, Hennig.
xCohen, Hennig.
ed. A Concordance to Melville's Moby Dick.
Univ Microfilms.
Cohen, Henry A, 1895-
xCohen.
Public Construction Contracts & the Law.
McGraw.
Cohen, Herbert J. *see* Cohen, Herbert Jesse.
Cohen, Herbert Jesse.
xCohen, Herbert J.
Urban Community Care for the
Developmentally Disabled. C C Thomas.
Cohen, Howard, 1944-
xCohen, Howard.
Equal Rights for Children. Littlefield.
Equal Rights for Children. Rowman.
Cohen, Howard M. *see* Cohen, Howard Martin.

Cohen, Howard Martin.
xCohen, Howard M.
The Relationship of the Prison Program to
Changes in Attitudes & Self Concepts of
Inmates. R & E Res Assoc.
Cohen, I. Bernard, 1914-
xCohen, I. Bernard.
Birth of a New Physics. Doubleday.
Introduction to Newton's Principia. Harvard U
Pr.
Cohen, J. see Cohen, Jacob.
Cohen, J. M. see Cohen, John Michael.
Cohen, J. W. see Cohen, Jacob Willem.
Cohen, Jacob, 1918-
xCohen, J.
Special Bibliography in Monetary Economics &
Finance. Gordon.
Cohen, Jacob Willem.
xCohen, J. W.
On Regenerative Processes in Queueing
Theory. Springer-Verlag.
Cohen, Jamey.
xCohen, Jamey.
Dmitri. Seaview Bks.
Cohen, Jane R., 1938-
xCohen, Jane R.
Charles Dickens & His Original Illustrators.
Ohio St U Pr.
Cohen, Jay O.
xCohen, Jay O.
The Staphylococci. Krieger.
Cohen, Jerome A. see Cohen, Jerome Alan.
Cohen, Jerome Alan.
xCohen, Jerome A.
ed. Contemporary Chinese Law: Research
Problems & Perspectives. Harvard U Pr.
ed. Criminal Process in the People's Republic
of China, 1949-1963: An Introduction.
Harvard U Pr.
ed. The Dynamics of China's Foreign
Relations. Harvard U Pr.
ed. Essays on China's Legal Tradition.
Princeton U Pr.
Cohen, Jerome B. see Cohen, Jerome Bernard.
Cohen, Jerome Bernard.
xCohen, Jerome B.
Guide to Intelligent Investing. Dow
Jones-Irwin.
Personal Finance. Irwin.
Cohen, Joan L. see Cohen, Joan Lebold.
Cohen, Joan Lebold.
xCohen, Joan L.
China Today & Her Ancient Treasures.
Abrams.
Cohen, Joan Mandel.
xCohen, Joan Mandel.
Form & Realism in Six Novels of Anthony
Trollope. Mouton.
Cohen, Joel E.
xCohen, Joel E.
Casual Groups of Monkeys & Men: Stochastic
Models of Elemental Social Systems. Harvard
U Pr.
Food Webs & Niche Space. Princeton U Pr.
Cohen, Joel H.
xCohen, Joel H.
Steve Garvey: Storybook Star. Putnam.
Cohen, John.
xCohen, John.
Medicine, Mind, & Man: An Introduction to
Psychology for Students of Medicine &
Allied Professions. W H Freeman.
Cohen, John Michael.
xCohen, J. M.
Penguin Dictionary of Modern Quotations.
Penguin.
xCohen, M. J.

jt. auth. Penguin Dictionary of Modern
Quotations. Penguin.
Cohen, Jon S.
xCohen, Jon S.
Finance & Industrialization in Italy, 1894-1914.
Arno.
Cohen, Joseph, 1926-
xCohen, Joseph.
Journey to the Trenches: The Life of Isaac
Rosenberg, 1890-1918. Basic.
Cohen, Joseph J.
xCohen, Joseph J.
In Quest of Heaven: The Story of the Sunrise
Cooperative Farm Community. Porcupine Pr.
Cohen, Joseph W.
xCohen, Joseph W.
Superior Student in American Higher
Education. McGraw.
Cohen, Jules A.
xCohen, Jules A.
How to Computerize Your Small Business.
P-H.
Cohen, Julius H. see Cohen, Julius Henry.
Cohen, Julius Henry, 1873-
xCohen, Julius H.
They Builded Better Than They Knew. Arno.
Cohen, Kalman J.
xCohen.
Management Science in Banking. Warren.
xCohen, Kalman J.
Theory of the Firm: Resource Allocation in a
Market Economy. P-H.
Cohen, Lawrence.
xCohen, Lawrence.
ed. Oral Diagnosis & Treatment Planning. C C
Thomas.
A Synopsis of Medicine in Dentistry. Lea &
Febiger.
Cohen, Leo E.
xCohen, Leo E.
Cohen's Complete Book of Gin Rummy. Ace
Bks.
Cohen, Leon W. see Cohen, Leon Warren.
Cohen, Leon Warren.
xCohen, Leon W.
The Structure of the Real Number System.
Krieger.
Cohen, Leonard, 1934-
xCohen, Leonard.
Death of a Lady's Man. Penguin.
Death of a Lady's Man. Viking Pr.
Cohen, Lily Y. see Cohen, Lily Young.
Cohen, Lily Young.
xCohen, Lily Y.
Lost Spirituals. Arno.
Cohen, Louis.
xCohen, Louis.
Research Methods in Education. Biblio Dist.
Cohen, M. J. see Cohen, John Michael.
Cohen, M. M. see Cohen, Marshall M.
Cohen, M. R. see Cohen, Morris Raphael.
Cohen, Marilyn. see Cohen, Marilyn A.
Cohen, Marilyn A.
xCohen, Marilyn.
The Developmental Resource: Behavioral
Sequences for Assessment & Program
Planning. Grune.
Cohen, Mark N. see Cohen, Mark Nathan.
Cohen, Mark Nathan.
xCohen, Mark N.
ed. Biosocial Mechanisms of Population
Regulation. Yale U Pr.
The Food Crisis in Prehistory: Over Population
& Origins of Agriculture. Yale U Pr.
Cohen, Marshall M.
xCohen, M. M.
A Course in Simple Homotopy Theory.
Springer-Verlag.
Cohen, Martin A.
xCohen, Martin A.

The Martyr: The Story of a Secret Jew & the
Mexican Inquisition in the Sixteenth Century.
Jewish Pubn.
Cohen, Marvin.
xCohen, Marvin.
The Monday Rhetoric of the Love Club &
Other Parables. New Directions.
Cohen, Matt. see Cohen, Matthew.
Cohen, Matthew, 1942-
xCohen, Matt.
Colors of War. Methuen Inc.
Night Flights: Stories New & Selected.
Doubleday.
Cohen, Matthew M., 1949-
xCohen, Matthew M.
Instructions for Parents. ACC.
Cohen, Michael J. see Cohen, Michael Jay.
Cohen, Michael Jay.
xCohen, Michael J.
ed. Drugs & the Special Child. Halsted Pr.
Cohen, Michael Joseph, 1940-
xCohen, Michael J.
Palestine, Retreat from the Mandate: The
Making of British Policy, 1936-45. Holmes &
Meier.
Cohen, Miriam.
xCohen, Miriam.
Lost in the Museum. Greenwillow.
No Good in Art. Greenwillow.
Tough Jim. Macmillan.
When Will I Read?. Greenwillow.
Cohen, Morris R. see Cohen, Morris Raphael.
Cohen, Morris Raphael, 1880-1947
xCohen, M. R.
Preface to Logic. Peter Smith.
xCohen, Morris R.
A Dreamer's Journey: The Autobiography of
Morris Raphael Cohen. Arno.
Introduction to Logic. HarBraceJ.
Law & the Social Order: Essays in Legal
Philosophy. Shoe String.
A Preface to Logic. Dover.
Cohen, Myron L., 1937-
xCohen, Myron L.
House United, House Divided: The Chinese
Family in Taiwan. Columbia U Pr.
Cohen, Naomi W. see Cohen, Naomi Wiener.
Cohen, Naomi Wiener, 1927-
xCohen, Naomi W.
Not Free to Desist: The American Jewish
Committee, 1906-1966. Jewish Pubn.
Cohen, Nathan E. see Cohen, Nathan Edward.
Cohen, Nathan Edward.
xCohen, Nathan E.
ed. Social Work & Social Problems. Natl Assn
Soc Wkrs.
Cohen, Paul.
xCohen, Paul.
Realm of the Submarine. Macmillan.
Cohen, Paul A.
xCohen, Paul A.
China & Christianity: The Missionary
Movement & the Growth of Chinese
Antiforeignism, 1860-1870. Harvard U Pr.
ed. Reform in Nineteenth-Century China.
Harvard U Pr.
Cohen, Peter, 1939-
xCohen, Peter.
The Gospel According to the Harvard Business
School. Penguin.
Cohen, Peter. see Cohen, Peter Zachary.
Cohen, Peter Z. see Cohen, Peter Zachary.
Cohen, Peter Zachary.
xCohen, Peter.
Morena. Atheneum.
xCohen, Peter Z.

Foal Creek. Atheneum.
Morena. Atheneum.
Muskie Hook. Atheneum.
Cohen, Philip, 1945-
xCohen, Philip.
Control of Enzyme Activity. Halsted Pr.
Cohen, Philip K., 1943-
xCohen, Philip K.
The Moral Vision of Oscar Wilde. Fairleigh
Dickinson.
Cohen, R. J. *see* Cohen, Ronald Jay.
Cohen, Raymond, 1947-
xCohen, Raymond.
Threat Perception in International Crisis. U of
Wis Pr.
Cohen, Richard. *see* Cohen, Richard M.
Cohen, Richard M.
xCohen, Richard.
World Series. Dial.
xCohen, Richard M.
The World Series. Dial.
Cohen, Robert, 1938-
xCohen, Robert.
Acting Professionally: Raw Facts About
Careers in Acting. B&N.
Creative Play Direction. P-H.
Giraudoux: Three Faces of Destiny. U of
Chicago Pr.
Cohen, Robert D. *see* Cohen, Robert Douglas.
Cohen, Robert Douglas.
xCohen, Robert D.
Freshman Seminar: A New Orientation.
Westview.
Cohen, Roberta G.
xCohen, Roberta G.
Therapeutic Group Work for Health
Professionals. Springer Pub.
Cohen, Robin.
xCohen, Robin.
ed. Peasants & Proletarians: The Struggles of
Third World Workers. Monthly Rev.
Cohen, Ronald.
xCohen, Ronald.
ed. Comparative Political Systems: Studies in
the Politics of Pre-Industrial Societies. U of
Tex Pr.
ed. Origins of the State: The Anthropology of
Political Evolution. Inst Study Human.
Cohen, Ronald. *see* Cohen, Ronald D.
Cohen, Ronald D.
xCohen, Ronald.
The Paradox of Progressive Education: The
Gary Plan & Urban Schooling. Kennikat.
Cohen, Ronald Jay.
xCohen, R. J.
Binge!: It's Not a State of Hunger...It's a State
of Mind. Macmillan.
Cohen, Rose. *see* Cohen, Rose (Gallup).
Cohen, Rose (Gallup), 1880-
xCohen, Rose.
Out of the Shadow. Ozer.
Cohen, S. *see* Cohen, Stanley.
Cohen, Sara K. *see* Cohen, Sara Kay.
Cohen, Sara Kay.
xCohen, Sara K.
Whoever Said Life Is Fair?. Scribner.
Cohen, Sarah B. *see* Cohen, Sarah Blacher.
Cohen, Sarah Blacher.
xCohen, Sarah B.
ed. Comic Relief: Humor in Contemporary
American Literature. U of Ill Pr.
Cohen, Saul B. *see* Cohen, Saul Bernard.
Cohen, Saul Bernard.
xCohen, Saul B.
Geography & Politics in a World Divided.
Oxford U Pr.
Cohen, Selma J. *see* Cohen, Selma Jeanne.
Cohen, Selma Jeanne, 1920-
xCohen, Selma J.

ed. Dance As a Theatre Art: Source Readings
in Dance History from 1581 to the Present.
Har-Row.
ed. The Modern Dance: Seven Statements of
Belief. Columbia U Pr.
Cohen, Sherry S. *see* Cohen, Sherry Suib.
Cohen, Sherry Suib.
xCohen, Sherry S.
Tough Gazoobies on That. Ashley Bks.
Cohen, Shirley.
xCohen.
Special People: A Brighter Future for Everyone
with Physical, Mental & Emotional
Disabilities. P-H.
Cohen, Sidney, 1910-
xCohen, Sidney.
ed. Drug Abuse & Alcoholism: Current Critical
Issues. Haworth Pr.
The Drug Dilemma. McGraw.
Cohen, Sol.
xCohen, Sol.
Education in the United States: A
Documentary History. Random.
Cohen, Stanley.
xCohen, S.
Mechanisms of Immunopathology. Wiley.
xCohen, Stanley.
ed. Biology of the Lymphokines. Acad Pr.
Law Enforcement Guide to United States
Supreme Court Decisions. C C Thomas.
Psychological Survival: The Experience of
Long-Term Imprisonment. Irvington.
Cohen, Stephen.
xCohen, Stephen.
Pathways of the Pulp. Mosby.
Cohen, Stephen F.
xCohen, Stephen F.
Bukharin & the Bolshevik Revolution: A
Political Biography, 1888-1938. Oxford U Pr.
ed. The Soviet Union Since Stalin. Ind U Pr.
Cohen, Stephen P., 1936-
xCohen, Stephen P.
The Indian Army: Its Contribution to the
Development of a Nation. U of Cal Pr.
Cohen, Stephen S.
xCohen, Stephen S.
Modern Capitalist Planning: The French
Model. U of Cal Pr.
Cohen, Stephen Z.
xCohen, Stephen Z.
The Other Generation Gap: The Middle-Aged
& Their Aging Parents. Follett.
Cohen, Stewart.
xCohen, Stewart.
ed. Child Development: Contemporary
Perspectives. Peacock Pubs.
Cohen, Stuart J.
xCohen, Stuart J.
ed. New Directions in Patient Compliance.
Lexington Bks.
Cohen, Sydney.
xCohen, Sydney.
Immunology of Parasitic Infections. Mosby.
Cohen, William A., 1937-
xCohen, William A.
The Executive's Guide to Finding a Superior
Job. Am Mgmt.
Principles of Technical Management. Am
Mgmt.
Cohen, William B., 1941-
xCohen, William B.
The French Encounter with Africans: White
Response to Blacks, 1530 to 1880. Ind U Pr.
Cohen, William S.
xCohen, William S.
Of Sons & Seasons. S&S.
Cohen, Yehoshua S., 1937-
xCohen, Yehoshua S.

Diffusion of an Innovation in an Urban System:
The Spread of Planned Regional Shopping
Centers in the United States, 1949-1968. U
Chicago Dept Geog.
Spatial Components of Manufacturing Change,
1950-1960.. U Chicago Dept Geog.
Cohn, Alfred.
xCohn, Alfred.
Criminal Justice System & Its Psychology. Van
Nos Reinhold.
Cohn, Alvin W.
xCohn, Alvin W.
Criminal Justice Planning & Development.
Sage.
The Future of Policing. Sage.
Cohn, Angelo.
xCohn, Angelo.
First Book of the Netherlands. Watts.
Wonderful World of Paper. Abelard.
Cohn, Arthur, 1910-
xCohn, Arthur.
The Collector's Twentieth-Century Music in
the Western Hemisphere. Da Capo.
Twentieth-Century Music in Western Europe:
The Compositions & Recordings. Da Capo.
Cohn, David. *see* Cohn, David L.
Cohn, David L.
xCohn, David.
Step by Step Introduction to 8080
Microprocessor Systems. Intl Schol Bk Serv.
xCohn, David L.
A Step by Step Introduction to 8080
Microprocessor Systems. Dilithium Pr.
Cohn, David Lewis, 1896-1960
xCohn, David.
Where I Was Born & Raised. U of Notre
Dame Pr.
Cohn, Elchanan.
xCohn, Elchanan.
Economics of Education. Ballinger Pub.
Input-Output Analysis in Public Education.
Ballinger Pub.
Cohn, Frederick, 1932-
xCohn, Frederick.
Understanding Human Sexuality. P-H.
Cohn, H. *see* Cohn, Harvey.
Cohn, Harvey.
xCohn, H.
A Classical Invitation to Algebraic Numbers &
Class Fields. Springer-Verlag.
Cohn, Henry J.
xCohn, Henry J.
Government of the Rhine Palatinate in the
Fifteenth Century. Oxford U Pr.
Cohn, Jan, 1933-
xCohn, Jan.
Improbable Fiction: The Life of Mary Roberts
Rinehart. U of Pittsburgh Pr.
Cohn, Keith.
xCohn, Keith.
Coming Back: A Guide to Recovering from
Heart Attack & Living Confidently with
Coronary Disease. A-W.
Cohn, L. *see* Cohn, Leslie.
Cohn, Laurence S., 1939-
xCohn, Laurence S.
Effective Use of ANS COBOL Computer
Programming Language. Wiley.
Cohn, Lawrence H.
xCohn, Lawrence H.
The Treatment of Acute Myocardial Ischemia:
An Integrated Medical-Surgical Approach.
Futura Pub.
Cohn, Leslie, 1943-
xCohn, L.
Analytic Theory of the Harishchandra
C-Function. Springer-Verlag.
Cohn, Marvin.
xCohn, Marvin.

Helping Your Teen-Age Student: What Parents
Can Do to Improve Reading & Study Skills.
NAL.
Cohn, P. M. see Cohn, Paul Moritz.
Cohn, Paul Moritz.
xCohn, P. M.
Algebra. Wiley.
Linear Equations. Routledge & Kegan.
Solid Geometry. Routledge & Kegan.
Cohn, Peter. see Cohn, Peter F.
Cohn, Peter F.
xCohn, Peter.
Diagnosis & Therapy of Coronary Artery
Disease. Little.
Cohn, Richard M.
xCohn, Richard M.
Difference Algebra. Krieger.
Cohn, Robert G. see Cohn, Robert Greer.
Cohn, Robert Greer.
xCohn, Robert G.
Toward the Poems of Mallarme. U of Cal Pr.
Cohn, Ruby.
xCohn, Ruby.
Back to Beckett. Princeton U Pr.
ed. A Casebook on Waiting for Godot. Grove.
Currents in Contemporary Drama. Ind U Pr.
Cohn, Stanley H. see Cohn, Stanley Harold.
Cohn, Stanley Harold, 1922-
xCohn, Stanley H.
Economic Development in the Soviet Union.
Heath.
Economic Development in the Soviet Union.
Irvington.
Cohn, Theodore.
xCohn, Theodore.
Compensating Key Executives in the Smaller
Company. Am Mgmt.
Cohn, Theodore H., 1940-
xCohn, Theodore H.
Canadian Food Aid: Domestic & Foreign
Policy Implications. U of Denver Intl.
Cohn, W. see Cohn, Werner.
Cohn, Werner, 1926-
xCohn, W.
The Gypsies. A-W.
xCohn, Werner.
The Gypsies. Benjamin-Cummings.
Cohn, William, 1880-1961
xCohn, William.
Chinese Painting. Hacker.
Cohodas, Marvin.
xCohodas, Marvin.
The Great Ball Court of Chichen Itza, Yucatan,
Mexico. Garland Fub.
Cohon, Jared L.
xCohon, Jared L.
Multiobjective Programming & Planning. Acad
Pr.
Cohrssen, John J.
xCohrssen, John J.
The Organization of the United Nations to
Deal with Drug Abuse. Drug Abuse.
Coigney, Virginia.
xCoigney, Virginia.
Children Are People Too: How We Fail Our
Children & How We Can Love Them.
Morrow.
Coil, Henry W. see Coil, Henry Wilson.
Coil, Henry Wilson.
xCoil, Henry W.
A Comprehensive View of Freemasonry.
Macoy Pub.
Coit, Daniel W. see Coit, Daniel Wadsworth.
Coit, Daniel Wadsworth, 1787-1876
xCoit, Daniel W.
Digging for Gold Without a Shovel: Letters of
Daniel Wadsworth Coit from Mexico &
California. Old West.
Coit, Margaret L.
xCoit, Margaret L.

Andrew Jackson. HM.
Fight for Union. HM.
The Growing Years, 1789-1829. Silver.
The Sweep Westward, 1829-1849. Silver.
Coit, Stanton, 1857-1944
xCoit, Stanton.
Neighbourhood Guilds: An Instrument of
Social Reform. Arno.
Coke, Desmond, 1879-
xCoke, Desmond.
Art of Silhouette. Gale.
Coke, Roger, fl. 1696
xCoke, Roger.
Discourse of Trade. Arno.
A Discourse of Trade. Johnson Repr.
Coke, Van Deren, 1921-
xCoke, Van Deren.
The Painter & the Photograph: From Delacroix
to Warhol. U of NM Pr.
Cokelet, Giles R.
xCokelet, Giles R.
ed. Erythrocyte Mechanics & Blood Flow. A R
Liss.
Coker, Jerry.
xCoker, Jerry.
Improvising Jazz. P-H.
Listening to Jazz. P-H.
Coker, William C. see Coker, William Chambers.
Coker, William Chambers, 1872-1953
xCoker, William C.
The Club & Coral Mushrooms (Clavarias) of
the United States & Canada. Peter Smith.
The Gasteromycetes of the Eastern United
States & Canada. Dover.
Colahan, John.
xColahan, John.
Australian Opal Safari. Intl Pubns Serv.
Colander, David C.
xColander, David C.
ed. Solutions to Inflation. HarBraceJ.
Colangelo, Nicholas.
xColangelo, Nicholas.
Multicultural Nonsexist Education: A Human
Relations Approach. Kendall-Hunt.
New Voices in Counseling the Gifted.
Kendall-Hunt.
Colas, Alain, 1943-
xColas, Alain.
Around the World Alone. Barron.
Colavita, Francis B.
xColavita, Francis B.
Sensory Changes in the Elderly. C C Thomas.
Colberg, Marshall R. see Colberg, Marshall Rudolph.
Colberg, Marshall Rudolph.
xColberg, Marshall R.
Business Economics: Principles & Cases. Irwin.
The Consumer Impact of Repeal of 14(B).
Heritage Found.
Colbert, Douglas A.
xColbert, Douglas A.
Computers & Management for Business. Van
Nos Reinhold.
Colbert, Edwin H. see Colbert, Edwin Harris.
Colbert, Edwin Harris, 1905-
xColbert, Edwin H.
Age of Reptiles. Norton.
The Dinosaur World. Stravon.
Colbert, Evelyn. see Colbert, Evelyn Speyer.
Colbert, Evelyn S. see Colbert, Evelyn Speyer.
Colbert, Evelyn Speyer, 1918-
xColbert, Evelyn.
Southeast Asia in International Politics,
1941-1956. Cornell U Pr.
xColbert, Evelyn S.
The Left Wing in Japanese Politics.
Greenwood.
Colbert, J. C. see Colbert, James Canfield.
Colbert, James Canfield, 1899-
xColbert, J. C.

Sugar Esters: Preparation & Applications.
Noyes.
Colbert, Roman.
xColbert, Roman.
Brief French Reference Grammar. Van Nos
Reinhold.
Brief Spanish Reference Grammar. D Van
Nostrand.
Colborn, J. G., 1939-
xColborn, J. G.
The Thermal Structure of the Indian Ocean. U
Pr of Hawaii.
Colborne, C. L.
xColborne, C. L.
Practical Boat Handling on Rivers & Canals.
David & Charles.
Colburn. see Colburn, C. William.
Colburn, C. William.
xColburn.
An Orientation to Listening & Audience
Analysis. SRA.
Colburn, David R.
xColburn, David R.
ed. America & the New Ethnicity. Kennikat.
Colburn, Robert E.
xColburn, Robert E.
Fire Protection & Suppression. McGraw.
Colby, Anthony. see Colby, Anthony Owen.
Colby, Anthony O. see Colby, Anthony Owen.
Colby, Anthony Owen.
xColby, Anthony.
Healing Time. Seaview Bks.
xColby, Anthony O.
A Doctor's Book on Smoking & How to Quit.
Contemp Bks.
Healing Time. Playboy Pbks.
Colby, Averil.
xColby, Averil.
Patchwork Quilts. David & Charles.
Patchwork Quilts. Scribner.
Quilting. David & Charles.
Quilting. Scribner.
Colby, Benjamin N.
xColby, Benjamin N.
Ethnic Relations in the Chiapas Highlands of
Mexico. Museum NM Pr.
Colby, C. B. see Colby, Carroll B.
Colby, Carrol B.
xColby, C. B.
Atom at Work: How Nuclear Power Can
Benefit Man. Coward.
Colby, Carroll B.
xColby, C. B.

The Sikhs: Their Religious Beliefs & Practices.
Routledge & Kegan.
Cole-Whittaker, Terry, 1939-
xCole-Whittaker, Terry.
What You Think of Me Is None of My
Business. Oak Tree Pubns.
Colean, Miles L. *see* Colean, Miles Lanier.
Colean, Miles Lanier, 1898-
xColean, Miles L.
Renewing Our Cities. Kraus Repr.
Coleberd, Frances.
xColeberd, Frances.
Adventures in California: A Seasonal Guide to
the Golden State. Chronicle Bks.
Colebrook, Joan.
xColebrook, Joan.
Innocents of the West: Travels Through the
Sixties. Basic.
Colecchia, Francesca. *see* Colecchia, Francesca Maria.
Colecchia, Francesca Maria, 1927-
xColecchia, Francesca.
Paisajes Y Personajes Latinoamericanos. Van
Nos Reinhold.
Repaso Oral. Heath.
Coleman. *see* Coleman, Ronny J.
Coleman, A. D. *see* Coleman, Allan D.
Coleman, Alan D. *see* Coleman, Allan D.
Coleman, Alexander.
xColeman, Alexander.
Eca De Queiros & European Realism. NYU
Pr.
xColeman, John A.
Other Voices: A Study of the Late Poetry of
Luis Cernuda. U of NC Pr.
Coleman, Allan D.
xColeman, A. D.
Light Readings: A Photography Critic's
Writings 1968-1978. Oxford U Pr.
xColeman, Alan D.
The Grotesque in Photography. Summit Bks.
Coleman, Almand R.
xColeman, Almand R.
Financial Accounting: A General Management
Approach. Wiley.
Coleman, Arthur P. *see* Coleman, Arthur Prudden.
Coleman, Arthur Philemon, 1852-1939
xColeman, Arthur P.
Ice Ages Recent & Ancient. AMS Pr.
The Last Million Years: A History of the
Pleistocene in North America. AMS Pr.
Coleman, Arthur Prudden, 1897-
xColeman, Arthur P.
Humor in the Russian Comedy from Catherine
to Gogol. AMS Pr.
Coleman, B. I. *see* Coleman, Bruce Ivor.
Coleman, Bruce Ivor.
xColeman, B. I.
ed. The Idea of the City in Nineteenth-Century
Britain. Routledge & Kegan.
Coleman, D. C. *see* Coleman, Donald Cuthbert.
Coleman, D. G. *see* Coleman, Dorothy Gabe.
Coleman, David, 1937-
xColeman, David.
For the Long Term. Concept Pub.
Coleman, Donald C. *see* Coleman, Donald Cuthbert.
Coleman, Donald Cuthbert.
xColeman, D. C.
The Economy of England 1450-1750. Oxford
U Pr.
xColeman, Donald C.
The British Paper Industry, 1495-1860: A
Study in Industrial Growth. Greenwood.
Coleman, Donald G.
xColeman, Donald G.
Woodworking Factbook: Basic Information on
Wood for Wood Carvers, Home Woodshop
Craftsmen, Tradesmen & Instructors. Speller.
Coleman, Dorothy Gabe.
xColeman, D. G.

Rabelais: A Critical Study in Prose Fiction.
Cambridge U Pr.
Coleman, Dorothy S.
xColeman, Dorothy S.
The Collector's Book of Dolls' Clothes:
Costumes in Miniature, 1700-1929. Crown.
Collector's Encyclopedia of Dolls. Crown.
Coleman, Eleanor S.
xColeman, Eleanor S.
Cross & the Sword of Cortes. S&S.
Coleman, Emily.
xColeman, Emily.
Brief Encounters. Doubleday.
Brief Encounters. Doubleday.
Coleman, Eric.
xColeman, Eric.
Dinghies for All Waters: Safe Family Cruising
& Day Sailing. Transatlantic.
Coleman, F. *see* Coleman, Frances.
Coleman, Frances, 1913-
xColeman, F.
Guide to Surgical Terminology. Med
Economics.
xColeman, Francis.
Guide to Surgical Terminology. Van Nos
Reinhold.
Coleman, Francis. *see* Coleman, Frances.
Coleman, Frank M., 1937-
xColeman, Frank M.
Hobbes & America: Exploring the
Constitutional Foundations. U of Toronto Pr.
Coleman, Frederic. *see* Coleman, Frederic Abernethy.
Coleman, Frederic Abernethy, 1876-
xColeman, Frederic.
The Far East Unveiled: An Inner History of
Events in Japan & China in the Year 1916.
Scholarly Res Inc.
Coleman, Herbert T. *see* Coleman, Herbert Thomas John.
Coleman, Herbert Thomas John, 1872-
xColeman, Herbert T.
Public Education in Upper Canada. AMS Pr.
Coleman, Howard W.
xColeman, Howard W.
Case Studies in Broadcast Management.
Hastings.
ed. Color Television: The Business of
Colorcasting. Hastings.
Coleman, J. M. *see* Coleman, James M.
Coleman, J. Winston. *see* Coleman, John Winston.
Coleman, James C. *see* Coleman, James Covington.
Coleman, James Covington.
xColeman, James C.
Abnormal Psychology & Modern Life. Scott F.
Contemporary Psychology & Effective
Behavior. Scott F.
Coleman, James K. *see* Coleman, James Karl.
Coleman, James Karl, 1897-
xColeman, James K.
State Administration in South Carolina. AMS
Pr.
Coleman, James M.
xColeman, J. M.
Deltas: Processes of Deposition & Models for
Exploration. Burgess.
Coleman, James S.
xColeman, James S.
Nigeria: Background to Nationalism. U of Cal
Pr.
Power & the Structure of Society. Norton.
Coleman, James S. *see* Coleman, James Samuel.
Coleman, James Samuel.
xColeman, James S.

Equality of Educational Opportunity. Arno.
Information Systems & Performance Measures
in Schools. Educ Tech Pubns.
Introduction to Mathematical Sociology. Free
Pr.
Mathematics of Collective Action. Beresford
Bk Serv.
Coleman, James Smoot.
xColeman, James S.
ed. Education & Political Development.
Princeton U Pr.
ed. Political Parties & National Integration in
Tropical Africa. U of Cal Pr.
Coleman, James W. *see* Coleman, James William.
Coleman, James William.
xColeman, James W.
Social Problems. Har-Row.
Coleman, John A. *see* Coleman, John Aloysius.
Coleman, John Aloysius, 1937-
xColeman, John A.
The Evolution of Dutch Catholicism,
1958-1974. U of Cal Pr.
Coleman, John C.
xColeman, John C.
Relationships in Adolescence. Routledge &
Kegan.
Coleman, John Winston, 1898-
xColeman, J. Winston.
Famous Kentucky Duels. Henry Clay.
Historic Kentucky. Henry Clay.
Coleman, Joseph.
xColeman, Joseph.
Your Career in Law Enforcement. Arco.
Coleman, Kenneth.
xColeman, Kenneth.
Colonial Georgia: A History. Kraus Intl.
Georgia History in Outline. U of Ga Pr.
A History of Georgia. U of Ga Pr.
Coleman, Kenneth M.
xColeman, Kenneth M.
Public Opinion in Mexico City About the
Electoral System. U of NC Pr.
Coleman, Laurence V. *see* Coleman, Laurence Vail.
Coleman, Laurence Vail.
xColeman, Laurence V.
Historic House Museums. Gale.
Coleman, Lonnie.
xColeman, Lonnie.
Look Away Beulah Land. Dell.
Look Away, Beulah Land. Doubleday.
Orphan Jim. Doubleday.
Coleman, Lucien E.
xColeman, Lucien E.
How to Teach the Bible. Broadman.
Coleman, Mcalister, 1889-
xColeman, McAlister.
Men & Coal. Arno.
Coleman, Neville, 1938-
xColeman, Neville.
Australian Fisherman's Fish Guide: Angler's
Aid to Identification, Location, Habits &
Eating Qualities of Australian Sea Fishes. Intl
Pubns Serv.
Coleman, R. G. *see* Coleman, Robert Griffin.
Coleman, R. V. *see* Coleman, Robert Vincent.
Coleman, Robert, 1915-1941
xColeman, Robert.
The Development of Informal Geometry. AMS
Pr.
Coleman, Robert E. *see* Coleman, Robert Emerson.
Coleman, Robert Emerson, 1928-
xColeman, Robert E.
Evangelism in Perspective. Chr Pubns.
Coleman, Robert Griffin, 1923-
xColeman, R. G.
Ophiolites: Ancient Oceanic Lithosphere.
Springer-Verlag.
Coleman, Robert Vincent.
xColeman, R. V.

ed. Illustrations of Early English Popular
Literature. Arno.
ed. Illustrations of Old English Literature.
Arno.
Memoirs of the Principal Actors in the Plays of
Shakespeare. AMS Pr.
Collier, John William, 1906-
xCollier, J. W.
Wood Finishing. Pergamon.
Collier, Joseph. *see* Collier, Joseph M.
Collier, Joseph M.
xCollier, Joseph.
ed. Forces in the Shaping of American Culture.
Hwong Pub.
Collier, K. G. *see* Collier, Kenneth Gerald.
Collier, Keith, 1927-
xCollier, Keith.
Construction Contracts. Reston.
Fundamentals of Construction Estimating &
Cost Accounting. P-H.
Collier, Kenneth Gerald.
xCollier, K. G.
ed. Innovation in Higher Education.
Humanities.
Collier, Larry.
xCollier, Larry.
How to Fly Helicopters. TAB Bks.
Collier, Peter.
xCollier, Peter.
ed. Dilemmas of Democracy: Readings in
American Government. HarBraceJ.
When Shall They Rest?: The Cherokees' Long
Struggle with America. HR&W.
Collier, R. *see* Collier, Robert Jacob.
Collier, Raymond O. *see* Collier, Raymond Oliver.
Collier, Raymond Oliver.
xCollier, Raymond O.
ed. Experimental Design & Interpretation.
McCutchan.
Collier, Richard, 1924-
xCollier, Richard.
Bridge Across the Sky: The Berlin Blockade &
Airlift. McGraw.
Collier, Robert J. *see* Collier, Robert Jacob.
Collier, Robert Jacob.
xCollier, R.
ed. Optical Holography. Acad Pr.
xCollier, Robert J.
Optical Holography. Acad Pr.
Collier, Sophia, 1956-
xCollier, Sophia.
Soul Rush: The Odyssey of a Young Woman of
the '70s. Morrow.
Collieu, A. *see* Collieu, Anthony Mcbain.
Collieu, Anthony Mcbain.
xCollieu, A.
The Mechanical & Thermal Properties of
Materials. Crane-Russak Co.
Colligan, Douglas.
xColligan, Douglas.
Creative Insomnia. McGraw.
Creative Insomnia. Watts.
Colligan, Elsa.
xColligan, Elsa.
The Aerialist. Barlenmir.
Collin, Mary A.
xCollin, Mary A.
Medical Terminology & the Body Systems.
Har-Row.
Collin, Robert E.
xCollin, Robert E.
Antenna Theory. McGraw.
Field Theory of Guided Waves. McGraw.
Foundations for Microwave Engineering.
McGraw.
Collin, W. E. *see* Collin, William Edwin.
Collin, William Edwin.
xCollin, W. E.

White Savannahs. U of Toronto Pr.
Colling, Aubrey.
xColling, Aubrey.
ed. Coronary Care in the Community. Biblio
Dist.
Colling, Susan.
xColling, Susan.
Frogmorton. Knopf.
Collingwood, Edward. *see* Collingwood, Edward Foyle.
Collingwood, Edward Foyle.
xCollingwood, Edward.
Theory of Cluster Sets. Cambridge U Pr.
Collingwood, R. G. *see* Collingwood, Robin George.
Collingwood, Robin G. *see* Collingwood, Robin George.
Collingwood, Robin George, 1889-1943
xCollingwood, R. G.
tr. Autobiography. Arno.
xCollingwood, Robin G.
Autobiography. Oxford U Pr.
Idea of History. Oxford U Pr.
Idea of Nature. Oxford U Pr.
Collingwood, Thomas R.
xCollingwood, Tom.
Get Fit for Living. Human Res Dev Pr.
Collingwood, Tom. *see* Collingwood, Thomas R.
Collingwood, William G. *see* Collingwood, William
Gershom.
Collingwood, William Gershom, 1854-1932
xCollingwood, William G.
The Art Teaching of John Ruskin. Folcroft.
Collins. *see* Collins, A. G.
Collins, A. Frederick. *see* Collins, Archie Frederick.
Collins, A. G.
xCollins.
Geochemistry of Oilfield Waters. Elsevier.
Collins, A. S. *see* Collins, Arthur Simons.
Collins, Adela Y. *see* Collins, Adela Yarbro.
Collins, Adela Yarbro.
xCollins, Adela Y.
The Combat Myth in the Book of Revelation.
Scholars Pr Ca.
Collins, Adrian A. *see* Collins, Adrian Anthony.
Collins, Adrian Anthony.
xCollins, Adrian A.
Federal Income Taxation of Employee Benefits.
Boardman.
Collins, Alice. *see* Collins, Alice H.
Collins, Alice H.
xCollins, Alice.
The Human Services: An Introduction.
Odyssey Pr.
xCollins, Alice H.
Family Day Care: A Practical Guide for
Parents, Caregivers, & Professionals. Beacon
Pr.
The Lonely & Afraid: Counseling the Hard to
Reach. Odyssey Pr.
Natural Helping Networks: A Strategy for
Prevention. Natl Assn Soc Wkrs.
Collins, Archie Frederick, 1869-
xCollins, A. Frederick.
The Radio Amateur's Handbook. T Y Crowell.
Collins, Arthur, 1682?-1760
xCollins, Arthur.
Letters & Memorials of State, in the Reigns of
Queen Mary, Queen Elizabeth, King James,
King Charles the First, Part of the Reign of
King Charles the Second, & Oliver's
Usurpation. AMS Pr.
Collins, Arthur Simons, 1899-
xCollins, A. S.
Profession of Letters: A Study of the Relation
of Author to Patron Publisher, & Public
1780-1832. Kelley.
Collins, Camilla. *see* Collins, Camilla Holben.
Collins, Camilla Holben.
xCollins, Camilla.
In the Hollow of His Hand. Herald Hse.
Collins, Charles H. *see* Collins, Charles Henry.

Collins, Charles Henry, Sir, 1887-
xCollins, Charles H.
Public Administration in Hong Kong. AMS Pr.
Collins, Charles W.
xCollins, Charles W.
ed. Atlas of Wisconsin. Am Pub Co WI.
Collins, D. *see* Collins, Desmond.
Collins, D. Ray.
xCollins, D. Ray.
Comprehensive Guide to Sports Skills Tests &
Measurement. C C Thomas.
Collins, David, 1932-
xCollins, David.
Daydreams: Making Your Fantasies Work for
You. Watts.
Collins, David. *see* Collins, David R.
Collins, David R.
xCollins, David.
Joshua Poole Hated School. Broadman.
A Spirit of Giving. Broadman.
xCollins, David R.
Abraham Lincoln. Mott Media.
Football Running Backs: Three Ground
Gainers. Garrard.
If I Could, I Would. Garrard.
Collins, Desmond.
xCollins, D.
Background to Archaeology: Britain in Its
European Setting. Cambridge U Pr.
Collins, Donald R. *see* Collins, Donald Reiszner.
Collins, Donald Reiszner, 1933-
xCollins, Donald R.
The Collins Guide to Dog Nutrition. Howell
Bk.
Collins, Douglas, 1945-
xCollins, Douglas.
Sartre As Biographer. Harvard U Pr.
Collins, Edward A.
xCollins, Edward A.
Experiments in Polymer Science. Wiley.
Collins, Erlene L.
xCollins, Erlene L.
Evaluating the Effectiveness of Alternative
Treatment Strategies in a Comprehensive
Alcoholism Treatment Center. R & E Res
Assoc.
Collins, F. Thomas. *see* Collins, Frank Thomas.
Collins, Fletcher.
xCollins, Fletcher.
Production of Medieval Church Music-Drama.
U Pr of Va.
Collins, Floyd, 1951-
xCollins, Floyd.
Scarecrow. St Luke TN.
Collins, Frank Thomas, 1916-
xCollins, F. Thomas.
Building with Tilt Up. Know How.
Design of Tilt up Buildings. Know How.
Manual of Tilt up Construction. Know How.
Collins, Gary. *see* Collins, Gary R.
Collins, Gary R.
xCollins, Gary.
Family Talk. Vision Hse.
You Can Profit from Stress. Vision Hse.
xCollins, Gary R.
ed. Facing the Future: Church & Family
Together. Word Bks.
Collins, George R. *see* Collins, George Roseborough.
Collins, George Roseborough, 1917-
xCollins, George R.
Antonio Gaudi. Braziller.
Collins, George W. *see* Collins, George William.
Collins, George William, 1937-
xCollins, George W.
The Virial Theorem in Stellar Astrophysics.
Pachart Pub Hse.
Collins, Harold W.
xCollins, Harold W.

Educational Measurement & Evaluation: A
   Worktext. Scott F.
Collins, Henry H. *see* Collins, Henry Hill.
Collins, Henry Hill.
   xCollins, Henry H.
   Familiar Garden Birds of America. Har-Row.
Collins, J. C. *see* Collins, John Churton.
Collins, J. Churton. *see* Collins, John Churton.
Collins, J. Lawton. *see* Collins, Joseph Lawton.
Collins, Jackie.
   xCollins, Jackie.
   The Hollywood Zoo. Pinnacle Bks.
   Lovehead. Warner Bks.
   Lovers & Gamblers. G&D.
   Lovers & Gamblers. Warner Bks.
Collins, James C.
   xCollins, James C.
   Accident Reconstruction. C C Thomas.
Collins, James D. *see* Collins, James Daniel.
Collins, James Daniel.
   xCollins, James D.
   The Existentialists: A Critical Study.
      Greenwood.
   God in Modern Philosophy. Greenwood.
Collins, James P. *see* Collins, James Potter.
Collins, James Potter.
   xCollins, James P.
   Autobiography of a Revolutionary Soldier.
      Arno.
Collins, Jim.
   xCollins, Jim.
   The Strange Story of Uri Geller. Raintree Pubs.
Collins, John C. *see* Collins, John Churton.
Collins, John Churton, 1848-1908
   xCollins, J. C.
   Posthumous Essays of John Churton Collins.
      Folcroft.
   xCollins, J. Churton.
   Greek Influence on English Poetry. Haskell.
   xCollins, John C.
   Greek Influence on English Poetry. Folcroft.
   Illustrations of Tennyson. AMS Pr.
   Illustrations of Tennyson. Folcroft.
   Jonathan Swift: A Biographical & Critical
      Study. Folcroft.
   Jonathan Swift: A Biographical & Critical
      Study. Gordon Pr.
   Studies in Poetry & Criticism. Folcroft.
Collins, John J., 1938-
   xCollins, John J.
   Primitive Religion. Littlefield.
   Primitive Religion. Rowman.
Collins, John J. *see* Collins, John James.
Collins, John James, 1909-
   xCollins, John J.
   Bargaining at the Local Level. Fordham.
Collins, John Joseph.
   xCollins, John J.
   The Apocalyptic Vision of the Book of Daniel.
      Scholars Pr Ca.
   The Sibylline Oracles of Egyptian Judaism.
      Scholars Pr Ca.
Collins, John M.
   xCollins, John M.
   Imbalance of Power: Shifting U.S.-Soviet
      Military Strengths. Presidio Pr.
Collins, John W.
   xCollins, John W.
   Maxims of Chess. McKay.
Collins, Joseph Lawton, 1896-
   xCollins, J. Lawton.
   Lightning Joe: An Autobiography. La State U
      Pr.
Collins, Joseph T.
   xCollins, Joseph T.
   Amphibians & Reptiles in Kansas. U of KS
      Mus Nat Hist.
Collins, K. J. *see* Collins, Kenneth John.
Collins, Kenneth John.
   xCollins, K. J.

Human Adaptability: A History &
   Compendium of Research in the International
   Biological Program. St Martin.
Collins, Larry.
   xCollins, Larry.
   Freedom at Midnight. Avon.
   Freedom at Midnight. S&S.
   Or I'll Dress You in Mourning. NAL.
Collins, Leo C.
   xCollins, Leo C.
   Hercules Seghers. Hacker.
Collins, Lyndhurst.
   xCollins, Lyndhurst.
   ed. Locational Dynamics of Manufacturing
      Activity. Wiley.
   ed. The Use of Models in the Social Sciences.
      Westview.
Collins, Margaret.
   xCollins, Margaret.
   ed. Theater Wagon Plays of Place & Any
      Place. U Pr of Va.
Collins, Marjorie A.
   xCollins, Marjorie A.
   Manual for Accepted Missionary Candidates.
      William Carey Lib.
Collins, Maurice.
   xCollins, Maurice.
   Kith & Kids: Self-Help for Families of the
      Handicapped. Intl Schol Bk Serv.
Collins, Max.
   xCollins, Max.
   The Broker's Wife. Berkley Pub.
Collins, Meghan.
   xCollins, Meghan R.
   Maiden Crown. HM.
Collins, Meghan R. *see* Collins, Meghan.
Collins, Norman, 1907-
   xCollins, Norman.
   The Husband's Story. Atheneum.
Collins, Norman R.
   xCollins, Norman R.
   Concentration & Price-Cost Margins in
      Manufacturing Industries. U of Cal Pr.
Collins, Orvis. *see* Collins, Orvis F.
Collins, Orvis F.
   xCollins, Orvis.
   Interaction & Social Structure. Mouton.
Collins, P. D. *see* Collins, P. D. B.
Collins, P. D. B.
   xCollins, P. D.
   An Introduction to Regge Theory &
      High-Energy Physics. Cambridge U Pr.
   Regge Poles in Particle Physics.
      Springer-Verlag.
Collins, Patricia.
   xCollins, Patricia.
   My Friend Andrew. P-H.
   Your Daughter Is Brain Damaged: A Mother's
      Story. Dutton.
   Your Daughter Is Brain Damaged: A Mother's
      Story. Paddington.
Collins, R. Douglas.
   xCollins, R. Douglas.
   Illustrated Diagnosis of Localized Diseases.
      Lippincott.
   Illustrated Manual of Fluid & Electrolyte
      Disorders. Lippincott.
   Illustrated Manual of Neurologic Diagnosis.
      Lippincott.
Collins, Randall.
   xCollins, Randall.
   Conflict Sociology: Toward an Explanatory
      Science. Acad Pr.
   The Credential Society: A Historical Sociology
      of Education & Stratification. Acad Pr.
   The Discovery of Society. Random.
Collins, Richard. *see* Collins, Richard L.
Collins, Richard L., 1933-
   xCollins, Richard.

Flying the Weathermap. Delacorte.
   xCollins, Richard L.
   Flying IFR. Delacorte.
   Flying Safely. Delacorte.
Collins, Robert O.
   xCollins, Robert O.
   African History: Text & Readings. Phila Bk
      Co.
   Egypt & the Sudan. P-H.
Collins, Sheila D.
   xCollins, Sheila D.
   A Different Heaven & Earth. Judson.
Collins, T. *see* Collins, Thomas.
Collins, Thomas.
   xCollins, T.
   Complete Guide to Retirement. P-H.
Collins, Varnum L. *see* Collins, Varnum Lansing.
Collins, Varnum Lansing, 1870-1936
   xCollins, Varnum L.
   ed. Brief Narrative of the Ravages of the
      British & Hessians at Princeton in 1776-1777.
      Arno.
   President Witherspoon. Arno.
Collins, Vincent J., 1914-
   xCollins, Vincent J.
   Principles of Anesthesiology. Lea & Febiger.
Collins, Vincent P. *see* Collins, Vincent Paul.
Collins, Vincent Paul, 1915-
   xCollins, Vincent P.
   Me, Myself & You. Abbey.
Collins, Virgil D. *see* Collins, Virgil Dewey.
Collins, Virgil Dewey, 1898-
   xCollins, Virgil D.
   World Marketing. Arno.
Collins, Wilkie, 1824-1889
   xCollins, Wilkie.
   Armadale. Dover.
   Armadale. Merrimack Bk Serv.
   Armadale. Scholarly.
   The Dead Secret. Dover.
   Little Novels. Dover.
   Little Novels. Peter Smith.
   The Moonstone. Am Repr-Rivercity Pr.
   Moonstone. Dutton.
   Moonstone. Har-Row.
   Moonstone. Oxford U Pr.
   Moonstone. Penguin.
   Moonstone. Airmont.
   No Name. Dover.
   Poor Miss Finch: A Novel. Scholarly.
   The Queen of Hearts. Arno.
   Tales of Terror & the Supernatural. Dover.
   Tales of Terror & the Supernatural. Peter
      Smith.
   Works of Wilkie Collins. AMS Pr.
Collinson, Francis. *see* Collinson, Francis M.
Collinson, Francis M.
   xCollinson, Francis.
   The Bagpipe: The History of a Musical
      Instrument. Routledge & Kegan.
Collinson, Richard, Sir, 1811-1883
   xCollinson, Richard.
   Journal of H.M.S. Enterprise on the Expedition
      in Search of Sir John Franklin's Ships by
      Behring Strait: 1850-55. AMS Pr.
Collipp, P. J.
   xCollipp, Platon J.
   ed. Childhood Obesity. PSG Pub.
Collipp, Platon J. *see* Collipp, P. J.
Collis, John S. *see* Collis, John Stewart.
Collis, John Stewart, 1900-
   xCollis, John S.
   Christopher Columbus. Stein & Day.
   Living with a Stranger: A Discourse on the
      Human Body. Braziller.
   Worm Forgives the Plough. Braziller.
Collis, Maurice, 1889-
   xCollis, Maurice.

First Holy One. Greenwood.
Great Within. Arno.
Collison, David.
   xCollison, David.
     Stage Sound. Drama Bk.
Collison, Robert L. *see* Collison, Robert Lewis.
Collison, Robert Lewis.
   xCollison, Robert L.
     ed. Dictionary of Dates. Greenwood.
     Directory of Libraries & Special Collections on
      Asia & North Africa. Shoe String.
     ed. Progress in Library Science, 1966. Shoe
      String.
     ed. Progress in Library Science, 1967. Shoe
      String.
Collman, Charles A. *see* Collman, Charles Albert.
Collman, Charles Albert, 1868-
   xCollman, Charles A.
     Our Mysterious Panics, 1830-1930: A Story of
      Events & the Men Involved. Greenwood.
Collmann, Robin D. *see* Collmann, Robin Dickinson.
Collmann, Robin Dickinson, 1896-
   xCollmann, Robin D.
     The Psychogalvanic Reactions of Exceptional
      & Normal School Children. AMS Pr.
Colloms, Brenda.
   xColloms, Brenda.
     The Mayflower Pilgrims. St Martin.
Colloms, Martin.
   xColloms, Martin.
     High Performance Loudspeakers. Halsted Pr.
Collons, Rodger D.
   xCollons, Roger D.
     An Algorithm for the Coefficient of
      Concordance. Ga St U Busn Pub.
Collons, Roger D. *see* Collons, Rodger D.
Colloque De Topologie Differentielle, Dijon, 1974.
   xColloquium Held at Dijon, June 17-22, 1974.
     Differential Topology & Geometry!
     Proceedings. Springer-Verlag.
**Colloque International Sur les Methodes De
Spectroscopie Instrumentale, Orsay, France, 1966.**
   xCentre National de la Recherche Scientifique.
     New Methods of Instrumental Spectroscopy.
     Gordon.
Colloque Sur la Programmation, Paris, 9-11 April, 1974.
   see Programming Symposium, Paris, 1974.
Colloquium Held at Dijon, June 17-22, 1974. *see*
   Colloque De Topologie Differentielle, Dijon, 1974.
Colloquium of the Workshop for Biological Chemistry,
   April 29 - May 1, 1976, Mosbach-Baden. *see*
   Gesellschaft Fuer Biologische Chemie.
Colloquium on Automata, Languages & Programming,
   2nd, University of Saarbrucken, 1974. *see* Colloquium
   on Automata, Languages and Programming, 2d,
   University of Saarbrucken.
**Colloquium on Automata, Languages and Programming,
2d, University of Saarbrucken.**
   xColloquium on Automata, Languages &
     Programming, 2nd, University of Saarbrucken,
     1974.
     Proceedings. Springer-Verlag.
**Colloquium on Mathematical Analysis, Jyvaskyla,
Finland, 1970.**
   xColloquium on Mathematical Analysis, Jyvaskyla,
     1970.
     Topics in Analysis: Proceedings.
     Springer-Verlag.
**Colloquium on Methods of Optimization, Novosibirsk,
1968.**
   xColloquium on Methods of Optimization,
     Novosibirsk USSR, 1968.
     Proceedings. Springer-Verlag.
Colloquium on Myth in Literature, Bucknell &
   Susquehanna Universities, Mar. 21-2, 1974. *see*
   Bucknell-Susquehanna Colloquium on Myth in
   Literature, 1974.

**Colloquium on Numerical Analysis, Lausanne,
Switzerland, 1976.**
   xProceedings of the Colloquium on Numerical
     Analysis, Lausanne, Oct. 11-13, 1976.
     Numerical Analysis. Birkhauser.
Colloquy on Celtic Art, Oxford, England, 1972.
   xColloquy, Oxford Maison Francaise, 1972.
     Celtic Art in Ancient Europe - Five
      Protohistoric Centuries: Proceedings. Acad
      Pr.
Colloquy, Oxford Maison Francaise, 1972. *see* Colloquy
   on Celtic Art, Oxford, England, 1972.
Collyer, David J.
   xCollyer, David J.
     Fly-Dressing. David & Charles.
Colm, Hanna.
   xColm, Hanna.
     The Existentialist Approach to Psychotherapy
      with Adults & Children. Grune.
Colman. *see* Colman, Hila.
Colman, Arthur D.
   xColman, Arthur D.
     Love & Ecstasy. Continuum.
Colman, Hila.
   xColman.
     The Amazing Miss Laura. Schol Bk Serv.
   xColman, Hila.
     After the Wedding. Morrow.
     The Amazing Miss Laura. Morrow.
     Bride at Eighteen. Morrow.
     The Case of the Stolen Bagels. Crown.
     Chicano Girl. Morrow.
     Claudia, Where Are You?. Archway.
     Claudia, Where Are You?. Morrow.
     Claudia, Where Are You?. PB.
     Daughter of Discontent. Morrow.
     Diary of a Frantic Kid Sister. Crown.
     Diary of a Frantic Kid Sister. Archway.
     Diary of a Frantic Kid Sister. PB.
     Ellie's Inheritance. Morrow.
     The Family & the Fugitive. Morrow.
     Friends & Strangers on Location. Morrow.
     The Girl from Puerto Rico. Morrow.
     Nobody Has to Be a Kid Forever. Crown.
     Nobody Has to Be a Kid Forever. Archway.
     Rachel's Legacy. Morrow.
     Sometimes I Don't Love My Mother. Morrow.
     Sometimes I Don't Love My Mother. Schol Bk
      Serv.
     That's the Way It Is, Amigo. T Y Crowell.
     What's the Matter with Dobsons?. Crown.
Colman, Louis.
   xColman, Louis.
     Lumber. AMS Pr.
Colman, Raphael.
   xColman, Raphael.
     How to Develop the Learning Powers of the
      Child & of the Teenager. Am Classical Coll
      Pr.
Colman, Samuel.
   xColman, Samuel.
     Nature's Harmonic Unity: A Treatise on Its
      Relation to Proportional Form. Arno.
Colman, William G.
   xColman, William G.
     Cities, Suburbs & States: Governing &
      Financing Urban America. Free Pr.
Colmer, John.
   xColmer, John.
     Coleridge to Catch 22: Images of Society. St
      Martin.
Colodner, Solomon, 1908-
   xColodner, Solomon.
     Concepts & Values. Shengold.
Colodny, Robert G. *see* Colodny, Robert Garland.
Colodny, Robert Garland.
   xColodny, Robert G.
     ed. Logic, Laws, & Life: Some Philosophical
      Complications. U of Pittsburgh Pr.
Colojoara, I. *see* Colojoara, Ion.

Colojoara, Ion.
   xColojoara, I.
     Theory of Generalized Spectral Operators.
      Gordon.
Colomb, P. *see* Colomb, Philip Howard.
Colomb, Philip Howard, 1831-1899
   xColomb, P.
     The Great War of 189-: A Forecast. Arno.
Colombo, Attilio.
   xColombo, Attilio.
     Fantastic Photographs. Pantheon.
Colombo, John R. *see* Colombo, John Robert.
Colombo, John Robert, 1936-
   xColombo, John R.
     Colombo's Canadian References. Oxford U Pr.
     ed. Popcorn in Paradise: The Wit & Wisdom of
      Hollywood. HR&W.
Colonial Dames Of America - Chapter 1 Baltimore. *see*
   Colonial Dames of America. Chapter 1, Baltimore.
Colonial Dames of America. Chapter 1, Baltimore.
   xColonial Dames Of America - Chapter 1
     Baltimore.
     Ancestral Records & Portraits: A Compilation
      from the Archives. Genealog Pub.
Colonial Williamsburg. *see* Colonial Williamsburg
   Foundation.
Colonial Williamsburg Foundation.
   xColonial Williamsburg.
     Gardens of Williamsburg. HR&W.
     Legacy from the Past. HR&W.
     A Window on Williamsburg. HR&W.
   xColonial Williamsburg Foundation Staff.
     Colonial Williamsburg Official Guidebook &
      Map. Williamsburg.
     Gardens of Williamsburg. Williamsburg.
     Legacy from the Past. Williamsburg.
     The Williamsburg Collection of Antique
      Furnishings. Williamsburg.
Colonial Williamsburg Foundation Staff. *see* Colonial
   Williamsburg Foundation.
Colonias, John S.
   xColonias, John S.
     Particle Accelerator Design Computer
      Programs. Acad Pr.
Colonna, Francesco.
   xColonna, Francesco.
     Hypnerotomachia Poliphili. Garland Pub.
     Hypnerotomachia: The Strife of Love in a
      Dreame (1592).. Schol Facsimiles.
     Hypnerotomachia: The Strife of Love in a
      Dreame. Walter J Johnson.
Colony, Horatio, 1900-
   xColony, Horatio.
     The Antique Thorn. Branden.
     Demon in Love. Branden.
     Early Land. Branden.
     ed. Flower Myth. Branden.
     Some Phoenix Blood. Branden.
Colorado, Antonio J.
   xColorado, Antonio J.
     The First Book of Puerto Rico. Watts.
     The First Book of Puerto Rico. Watts.
Colorado School of Mines. *see* Colorado. School of
   Mines, Golden.
Colorado. School of Mines, Golden.
   xColorado School of Mines.
     ed. Subject Catalog of the Arthur Lakes
      Library, Colorado School of Mines. G K
      Hall.
Colquhoun, Archibald.
   xColquhoun, Archibald.
     Manzoni & His Times: A Biography of the
      Author of The Betrothed (I Promessi Sposi).
      Hyperion Conn.
Colson, Charles. *see* Colson, Charles W.
Colson, Charles W.
   xColson, Charles.

Born Again. Bantam.
Born Again. Chosen Bks Pub.
Born Again. G K Hall.
Born Again. Revell.
xColson, Charles W.
Life Sentence. Chosen Bks Pub.
Colson, Howard P., 1910-
xColson, Howard P.
I Recommend the Bible. Broadman.
Colson, Percy, 1873-1952
xColson, Percy.
Their Ruling Passions. Arno.
Colston, Lowell G.
xColston, Lowell G.
Pastoral Care with Handicapped Persons.
Fortress.
Colter, Cyrus.
xColter, Cyrus.
The Hippodrome. Popular Lib.
The Hippodrome: A Novel. Swallow.
Colter, Janet.
xColter, Rudyard.
Favorite Vermont Ski Inns & Lodging Guide.
McGraw.
Colter, Rudyard. *see* Colter, Janet.
Coltey, Roger W., 1931-
xColtey, Roger W.
Survey of Medical Technology. Mosby.
Coltharp, Bruce R.
xColtharp, Bruce R.
When They Crucified Our Lord. Broadman.
Coltman, Irene.
xColtman, Irene.
Private Men & Public Causes: Philosophy &
Politics in the English Civil War. Allenson.
Coltman, M. *see* Coltman, Michael M.
Coltman, Michael M., 1930-
xColtman, M.
Food & Beverage Cost Control. P-H.
xColtman, Michael M.
Financial Management for the Hospitality
Industry. CBI Pub.
Hospitality Management Accounting. CBI Pub.
Colton, Arthur W. *see* Colton, Arthur Willis.
Colton, Arthur Willis, 1868-1943
xColton, Arthur W.
Delectable Mountains. Arno.
Colton, C. C. *see* Colton, Charles Caleb.
Colton, Calvin.
xColton, Calvin.
Abolition a Sedition. AMS Pr.
History & Character of American Revivals of
Religion. AMS Pr.
Public Economy for the United States. Kelley.
Colton, Charles C. *see* Colton, Charles Caleb.
Colton, Charles Caleb.
xColton, C. C.
Remarks on Don Juan. Arden Lib.
xColton, Charles C.
Remarks on Don Juan. Folcroft.
Colton, Harold S. *see* Colton, Harold Sellers.
Colton, Harold Sellers.
xColton, Harold S.
Handbook of Northern Arizona Pottery Wares.
AMS Pr.
Colton, Helen.
xColton, Helen.
Our Sexual Evolution. Watts.
Colton, Joel. *see* Colton, Joel G.
Colton, Joel G.
xColton, Joel.
Twentieth Century. Silver.
Colton, Judith, 1943-
xColton, Judith.
The Parnasse Francois: Titon Du Tillet & the
Origins of the Monument to Genius. Yale U
Pr.
Colton, Theodore.
xColton, Theodore.

Statistics in Medicine. Little.
Colton, Timothy J., 1947-
xColton, Timothy J.
Commissars, Commanders, & Civilian
Authority: The Structure of Soviet Military
Politics. Harvard U Pr.
Coltrane, James.
xColtrane, James.
Talon: A Novel of Suspense. Bobbs.
Colum, Mary. *see* Colum, Mary Maguire.
Colum, Mary Maguire.
xColum, Mary.
From These Roots: The Ideas That Have Made
Modern Literature. Kennikat.
Our Friend James Joyce. Peter Smith.
Colum, Padraic, 1881-
xColum, Padraic.
Collected Poems. Devin.
Girl Who Sat by the Ashes. Macmillan.
Homage to James Joyce. Folcroft.
On James Stephens. Folcroft.
Columbia Law Review.
xColumbia Law Review.
Essays on International Law. Oceana.
Essays on Jurisprudence from the Columbia
Law Review. Greenwood.
Columbia University.
xColumbia University.
Avery Index to Architectural Periodicals. G K
Hall.
Avery Index to Architectural Periodicals: Third
Supplement. G K Hall.
Avery Obituary Index of Architects & Artists.
G K Hall.
Catalog of the Avery Memorial Architectural
Library. G K Hall.
Catalog of the Avery Memorial Architectural
Library, Columbia University, Suppl. 2. G K
Hall.
Catalog of the Avery Memorial Architectural
Library, First Supplement. G K Hall.
Catalog of the Avery Memorial Architectural
Library, Second Edition, Fourth Supplement.
G K Hall.
Columbia University Contributions to Oriental
History & Philology. AMS Pr.
Columbia University Germanic Studies, Old
Ser.. AMS Pr.
Columbia University Indo-Iranian Ser.. AMS
Pr.
Columbia University Oriental Studies. AMS Pr.
Columbia University Studies in Romance
Philology & Literature. AMS Pr.
Columbia University Studies in the Social
Sciences. AMS Pr.
Dictionary Catalog of the Library of the School
of Library Service. G K Hall.
Dictionary Catalog of the Teachers College
Library. G K Hall.
Dictionary Catalog of the Teachers College
Library, First Supplement. G K Hall.
Dictionary Catalog of the Teachers College
Library, Second Supplement. G K Hall.
Lectures on Literature. Arno.
Quarter Century of Learning, 1904-1929. Arno.
Spinoza Bibliography. G K Hall.
xColumbia University, New York.
Compiled by Cumulative Author Index to
Psychological Index, 1894 to 1935, &
Psychological Abstracts, 1927 to 1958. G K
Hall.
**Columbia University. Bureau of Applied Social
Research.**
xBureau of Applied Social Research, Columbia
University.
The People Look at Radio. Arno.
Columbia University: Center for Advanced Research in

Urban & Environmental Affairs. *see* Columbia
University. Center for Advanced Research in Urban
and Environmental Affairs.
**Columbia University. Center for Advanced Research in
Urban and Environmental Affairs.**
xColumbia University Center for Advanced
Research in Enviornmental Affairs.
Fifteen Families in Akcalan. Pr of Nova Scotia.
Working Paper 2.. Pr of Nova Scotia.
xColumbia University: Center for Advanced
Research in Urban & Environmental Affairs.
The New York Federal Archive Building: A
Proposal for Mixed Re-Use. Pr of Nova
Scotia.
Columbia University. Dept. of Philosophy.
xColumbia University, Dept. of Philosophy.
ed. Studies in the History of Ideas. AMS Pr.
Columbia University Law Library, New York. *see*
Columbia University. Library. Law Library.
Columbia University Legislative Drafting Research Fund.
see Columbia University. Library. Law Library.
Columbia University, New York. *see* Columbia
University.
Columbia University. Libraries. East Asiatic Library.
xColumbia University, East Asian Library, New
York. 1962.
Index to Learned Chinese Periodicals. G K
Hall.
Columbia University. Library. Law Library.
xColumbia University Law Library, New York.
Dictionary Catalog of the Columbia University
Law Library. G K Hall.
Dictionary Catalog of the Columbia University
Law Library, First Supplement. G K Hall.
xColumbia University Legislative Drafting
Research Fund.
Constitutions of the United States, 1974-76:
National & State. Oceana.
Columbia University Press.
xColumbia University Press.
The New Columbia Encyclopedia. Lippincott.
Columbia University. School of Social Work.
xColumbia University School of Social Work.
Counseling in Abortion Services: Physician -
Nurse - Social Worker. Univ Bk Serv.
Columbia University. Teachers College.
xColumbia University. Teachers College.
Contributions to Education: Numbers 1-974.
AMS Pr.
Columbia University. Teachers College. Library.
xColumbia University, Teachers College Library.
Dictionary Catalog of the Teachers College
Library, Columbia University, Third
Supplement. G K Hall.
Columbu, Anita.
xColumbu, Anita.
jt. auth. Weight Training for Young Athletes.
Contemp Bks.
Columbu, Franco.
xColumbu, Franco.
Coming on Strong. Contemp Bks.
Starbodies: The Women's Weight Training
Book. Dutton.
Weight Training & Body Building: A Complete
Guide for Young Athletes. Wanderer Bks.
Weight Training for Young Athletes. Contemp
Bks.
Winning Weight Lifting & Powerlifting.
Contemp Bks.
Colver, Anne, 1908-
xColver, Anne.
Borrowed Treasure. Knopf.
Colvin, Ian D. *see* Colvin, Ian Duncan.
Colvin, Ian Duncan, 1877-
xColvin, Ian D.
Germans in England, 1066-1598. Kennikat.
Colwell, A. R. *see* Colwell, Arthur R.
Colwell, Arthur R.
xColwell, A. R.

Understanding Your Diabetes. C C Thomas.
Colwell, Ernest C. *see* Colwell, Ernest Cadman.
Colwell, Ernest Cadman, 1901-
xColwell, Ernest C.
Study of the Bible. U of Chicago Pr.
Colwell, John A.
xColwell, John A.
Clinical Recognition & Treatment of Diabetic
Vascular Disease. C C Thomas.
Colwell, Peter.
xColwell, Peter.
Introduction to Complex Variables. Merrill.
Colwell, R. *see* Colwell, Rita R.
Colwell, Richard.
xColwell, Richard.
Concepts for a Musical Foundation. P-H.
xColwell, Richard J.
Teaching of Instrumental Music. P-H.
xColwell, Ruth.
jt. auth. Concepts for a Musical Foundation.
P-H.
Colwell, Richard J. *see* Colwell, Richard.
Colwell, Rita R., 1934-
xColwell, R.
Marine & Estuarine Microbiology Laboratory
Manual. Univ Park.
Colwell, Robert.
xColwell, Robert.
Guide to Bicycle Trails. Stackpole.
Introduction to Backpacking. Stackpole.
Introduction to Foot Trails in America. B&N.
Colwell, Ruth. *see* Colwell, Richard.
Colwin, Laurie.
xColwin, Laurie.
Happy All the Time. G K Hall.
Happy All the Time. Knopf.
Happy All the Time. PB.
Passion & Affect. Avon.
Colyer, Frank. *see* Colyer, James Frank.
Colyer, James Frank, Sir, 1866-1954
xColyer, Frank.
Old Instruments Used for Extracting Teeth.
Longwood Pr.
Coma, Anthony S.
xComa, Anthony S.
Preparing the Thoroughbred: A Trainer's
Guide. Arco.
Coman, Katharine, 1857-1915
xComan, Katharine.
The Industrial History of the United States.
Arno.
Coman, Peter.
xComan, Peter W.
Catholics & the Welfare State. Longman.
Coman, Peter W. *see* Coman, Peter.
Comanor, William S.
xComanor, William S.
Advertising & Market Power. Harvard U Pr.
Comaromi, John P. *see* Comaromi, John Phillip.
Comaromi, John Phillip, 1937-
xComaromi, John P.
The Eighteen Editions of the Dewey Decimal
Classification. Forest Pr.
Comas, Juan, 1900-
xComas, Juan.
Racial Myths. Greenwood.
Comay, Joan.
xComay, Joan.
The World's Greatest Story: The Epic of the
Jewish People in Biblical Times. HR&W.
Combe, E. C.
xCombe, Edward C.
Notes on Dental Materials. Churchill.
Combe, Edward C. *see* Combe, E. C.
Combe, George, 1788-1858
xCombe, George.

The Constitution of Man Considered in
Relation to External Objects. Schol
Facsimiles.
Notes on the United States of North America
During a Phrenological Visit in 1838-1940.
Arno.
Combe, Iris.
xCombe, Iris.
Border Collies. Merrimack Bk Serv.
Comblin, Jose. *see* Comblin, Joseph.
Comblin, Joseph, 1923-
xComblin, Jose.
The Church & the National Security State.
Orbis Bks.
Sent from the Father: Meditations on the
Fourth Gospel. Orbis Bks.
Combs. *see* Combs, F. Michael.
Combs, Ann, 1935-
xCombs, Ann.
Helter Shelter. Lippincott.
Combs, Arthur W. *see* Combs, Arthur Wright.
Combs, Arthur Wright.
xCombs, Arthur W.
Myths in Education: Beliefs That Hinder
Progress & Their Alternatives. Allyn.
Perceptual Psychology: A Humanistic
Approach to the Study of Persons. Har-Row.
Professional Education of Teachers: A
Humanistic Approach to Teacher
Preparation. Allyn.
Combs, B. *see* Combs, Barbara J.
Combs, Barbara. *see* Combs, Barbara J.
Combs, Barbara J.
xCombs, B.
An Invitation to Health: Your Personal
Responsibility. A-W.
xCombs, Barbara.
An Invitation to Health: Your Personal
Responsibility. Benjamin-Cummings.
Combs, F. Michael.
xCombs.
Percussion Manual. Wadsworth Pub.
Combs, H. C. *see* Combs, Homer Carroll.
Combs, Homer Carroll.
xCombs, H. C.
Concordance to the English Poems of John
Donne. Haskell.
Combs, James E.
xCombs, Jim.
Dimensions of Political Drama. Goodyear.
Combs, Jim.
xCombs, Jim.
Chevrolet Tune-up Maintenance: All Models,
1966-1977. Clymer Pubns.
Dodge Omni: 1978 Shop Manual. Clymer
Pubns.
Honda Service Repair Handbook: Accord,
1976-77. Clymer Pubns.
Mazda GLC Shop Manual: 1977-1978. Clymer
Pubns.
Combs, Jim. *see* Combs, James E.
Combs, Paul H.
xCombs, Paul H.
Handbook of International Purchasing. CBI
Pub.
Combs, Steve.
xCombs, Steve.
Winning Wrestling. Contemp Bks.
Combs, W. V.
xCombs, W. V.
First Federal Issue 1798-1801: U. S. Embossed
Revenue Stamped Paper. Am Philatelic.
Comenius, Johann Amos.
xComenius, John A.
The Great Didactic of John Amos Comenius.
Russell.
Orbis Pictus of John Amos Comenius. Gale.
Comenius, John A. *see* Comenius, Johann Amos.
Comer, Cornelia A. *see* Comer, Cornelia Atwood (Pratt).

Comer, Cornelia Atwood (Pratt).
xComer, Cornelia A.
Preliminaries, & Other Stories. Arno.
Comer, David J.
xComer, David J.
Modern Electronic Circuit Design. A-W.
Comer, John P. *see* Comer, John Preston.
Comer, John Preston, 1888-
xComer, John P.
Legislative Functions of National
Administrative Authorities. AMS Pr.
Comerchero, Victor.
xComerchero, Victor.
Nathanael West: The Ironic Prophet. U of
Wash Pr.
Comfort, A. *see* Comfort, Alexander.
Comfort, Alex. *see* Comfort, Alexander.
Comfort, Alexander, 1920-
xComfort, A.
The Biology of Senescence. Elsevier.
xComfort, Alex.
The Facts of Love. Crown.
A Good Age. Crown.
A Good Age. S&S.
I & That. Crown.
Poems for Jane. Crown.
Comfort, Richard A.
xComfort, Richard A.
Revolutionary Hamburg: Labor Politics in the
Early Weimar Republic. Stanford U Pr.
Comfort, W. W. *see* Comfort, William Wistar.
Comfort, William Wistar.
xComfort, W. W.
Continuous Pseudometrics. Dekker.
Comini, Alessandra.
xComini, Alessandra.
Egon Schiele's Portraits. Braziller.
Egon Schiele's Portraits. U of Cal Pr.
The Fantastic Art of Vienna. Knopf.
Comins, Ethel M.
xComins, Ethel M.
Under a Dancing Star. Bouregy.
Comins, Jeremy.
xComins, Jeremy.
Art from Found Objects. Lothrop.
Chinese & Japanese Crafts & Their Cultural
Backgrounds. Lothrop.
Totems, Decoys, & Covered Wagons:
Cardboard Constructions from Early
American Life. Lothrop.
Comish, Newel W.
xComish, Newel W.
Effective Leadership of Voluntary
Organizations. Anna Pub.
Comitas, Lambros.
xComitas, Lambros.
Caribbeana, 1900-1965: A Topical
Bibliography. U of Wash Pr.
The Complete Caribbeana 1900-1975: A
Bibliographic Guide to the Scholarly
Literature. Kraus Intl.
Comito, Terry, 1935-
xComito, Terry.
The Idea of the Garden in the Renaissance.
Rutgers U Pr.
Commager, Henry S. *see* Commager, Henry Steele.
Commager, Henry Steele, 1902-
xCommager, Henry S.

The American Mind: An Interpretation of
American Thought & Character Since the
1800's. Yale U Pr.
Empire of Reason: How Europe Imagined &
America Realized the Enlightenment.
Doubleday.
ed. Fifty Basic Civil War Documents. Van Nos
Reinhold.
First Book of American History. Watts.
Freedom & Order: A Commentary on the
American Political Scene. NAL.
Freedom, Loyalty, Dissent. Oxford U Pr.
The People & Their Schools. Phi Delta Kappa.
ed. Struggle for Racial Equality: A
Documentary Record. Peter Smith.
xCommager, Steele.
Odes of Horace: A Critical Study. Ind U Pr.
Commager, Steele. *see* Commager, Henry Steele.
Commander, Lydia K. *see* Commander, Lydia Kingsmill.
Commander, Lydia Kingsmill.
xCommander, Lydia K.
The American Idea. Arno.
Commerce Clearing House.
xCommerce Clearing House.
American Stock Exchange Directory, Revised
to July 1, 1979. Commerce.
Australian Master Tax Guide: 1979.
Commerce.
Canadian Income Tax Act with Regulations.
Commerce.
Canadian Master Tax Guide. Commerce.
Common Market Reporter: Court Decisions,
1961-1966. Commerce.
Federal Estate & Gift Taxes Code &
Regulations As of April 1980. Commerce.
Federal Estate & Gift Taxes Explained,
Including Estate Planning: 1979 Edition.
Commerce.
Federal Graduated Withholding Tax, Effective
January 1, 1980. Commerce.
Federal Tax Computation 1980. Commerce.
Federal Tax Return Manual, 1981. Commerce.
Guide to New Zealand Estate & Gift Duties.
Commerce.
Guidebook to Fair Employment Practices:
1979. Commerce.
Guidebook to Florida Taxes: 1980. Commerce.
Guidebook to Illinois Taxes: 1981. Commerce.
Guidebook to Labor Relations: 1980.
Commerce.
Guidebook to Massachusettes Taxes: 1981.
Commerce.
Guidebook to Michigan Taxes: 1981.
Commerce.
Guidebook to New Jersey Taxes: 1981.
Commerce.
Guidebook to New York Taxes: 1981.
Commerce.
Guidebook to Occupational Safety & Health:
1977. Commerce.
Income Tax Regulations, As of Febuary 1980.
Commerce.
Individual's Filled-in Tax Return Forms: 1981
Edition. Commerce.
Mexican Labor Law, As of January 1, 1978.
Commerce.
National Association of Securities Dealers, Inc.
Reprint of the Manual As of September,
1979. Commerce.
New York Stock Exchange Inc. Directory,
Revised to September 28, 1979. Commerce.
New Zealand Master Tax Guide: 1980.
Commerce.
Nineteen Eighty Pocket-Tax. Commerce.
Ontario Securities Legislation. Commerce.
Pacific Stock Exchange Constitution & Rules
As of October, 1979. Commerce.
Real Estate Settlement Costs. Commerce.
Real Estate Settlement Procedures. Commerce.
Sales Tax Guide, Canada: 1979-80. Commerce.

Singapore Master Tax Guide. Commerce.
State Tax Handbook, As of Oct. 1, 1979.
Commerce.
Stock Values & Dividends for Nineteen
Eighty-One Tax Purposes. Commerce.
Tax Law of the State of New York: 1979
Edition. Commerce.
Ten Forty Preparation: 1980. Commerce.
U. S. Master Tax Guide: 1981 Edition.
Commerce.
U.S. Excise Tax Guide, 1979: 1980.
Commerce.
xCommerce Clearing House Editorial Staff.
Common Market Reporter: Court Decisions
1967-1970. Commerce.
Commerce Clearing House Editorial Staff. *see* Commerce
Clearing House.
Commerce Clearing House, Inc. *see* Commerce Clearing
House, Inc. (New Jersey).
Commerce Clearing House, Inc. (New Jersey).
xCommerce Clearing House, Inc.
Small Business Investment Companies. Arno.
Commisiion on Critical Choices. *see* Commission on
Critical Choices for Americans.
**Commission of Inquiry into the Charges Made Against
Leon Trotsky in the Moscow Trials. Preliminary
Commission, Coyoacan, Mexico, 1937.**
xPreliminary Commission of Inquiry.
Case of Leon Trotsky: Report of Hearings on
the Charges Made Against Him in the
Moscow Trials. Path Pr NY.
Commission of the European Communities.
xCommission of the European Communities.
Conference on the Quality of the Environment
& the Iron & Steel Industry: 24-26 Sept.
1974. Pergamon.
Criteria (Dose-Effect Relationships) for
Radium. Pergamon.
Energy Research & Development Programme.
Kluwer Boston.
ed. Energy Research & Development
Programme, Status Report 1977. Kluwer
Boston.
Organophosphorus Pesticides Criteria
(Dose-Effect Relationships) for
Organophosphorus Compounds. Pergamon.
Plasma Wall Interaction: Proceedings of the
International Symposium EUR 5782e,
Kernsfoschungsanlage Julich, 1976.
Pergamon.
Public Health Risks of Exposure to Asbestos.
Pergamon.
Commission On Campus Unrest. *see* United States.
Commission on Campus Unrest.
Commission on Cancer Control, Cancer Detection
Committee. *see* International Union Against Cancer.
Commission on Cancer Control. Cancer Detection
Committee.
Commission on Country Life. *see* United States. Country
Life Commission.
Commission on Critical Choice. *see* Commission on
Critical Choices for Americans.
Commission on Critical Choices. *see* Commission on
Critical Choices for Americans.
Commission on Critical Choices for Americans.
xCommisiion on Critical Choices.
The Soviet Empire: Expansion & Detente.
Lexington Bks.
xCommission on Critical Choice.
How Others See Us. Lexington Bks.
xCommission on Critical Choices.
Southern Asia: The Politics of Poverty &
Peace. Lexington Bks.
Vital Resources. Lexington Bks.
xCommission on Education for Health
Administration.

Selected Papers of the Commission on
Education for Health Administration. Health
Admin Pr.
Commission on Education for Health Administration. *see*
Commission on Critical Choices for Americans.
Commission On Education In Agriculture And Natural
Resources. *see* Conference on Undergraduate
Education in the Biological Sciences for Students in
Agriculture and Natural Resources, Washington, D.C.,
1966.
Commission On English. *see* College Entrance
Examination Board. Commission on English.
Commission on Foundations & Private Philanthropy. *see*
Commission on Foundations and Private Philanthropy.
Commission on Foundations and Private Philanthropy.
xCommission on Foundations & Private
Philanthropy.
Foundations: Private Giving & Public Policy. U
of Chicago Pr.
Commission on Natural Resources, National Research
Council. *see* National Research Council. Commission
on Natural Resources.
Commission on Non-Traditional Study.
xCommission on Non-Traditional Study.
Diversity by Design. Jossey-Bass.
**Commission on the Government of the University of
Toronto.**
xCommission on the Organization of the Illinois
General Assembly.
Improving the State Legislature: Report. U of
Ill Pr.
Commission on the Organization of the Illinois General
Assembly. *see* Commission on the Government of the
University of Toronto.
Commission on the Teaching of Bioethics.
xCommission on the Teaching of Bioethics.
The Teaching of Bioethics: Report. Hastings
Ctr Inst Soc.
Commission on U. S.-Latin American Relations. *see*
Commission on United States-Latin American
Relations.
Commission on United States-Latin American Relations.
xCommission on U. S.-Latin American Relations.
The Americas in a Changing World. Times
Bks.
xCommission on U.S.-Latin American Relations.
The Americas in a Changing World. Arno.
Commission on U.S.-Latin American Relations. *see*
Commission on United States-Latin American
Relations.
Commission to Study the Organisation of the Peace.
xCommission to Study the Organization of Peace.
Building Peace: Reports of the Commission to
Study the Organization of Peace, 1939-1972.
Scarecrow.
New Dimensions for the United Nations.
Oceana.
Organizing Peace in the Nuclear Age.
Greenwood.
Strengthening the United Nations. Greenwood.
United Nations & Human Rights. Oceana.
The United Nations: The Next Twenty Five
Years. Oceana.
Commission to Study the Organization of Peace. *see*
Commission to Study the Organisation of the Peace.
Committee for a New England Bibliography.
xCommittee for a New England Bibliography Inc.
the Bibliographies of New England History.
ed. Massachusetts: A Bibliography of Its
History. G K Hall.
Committee for Economic Development.
xCommittee for Economic Development.

Achieving Energy Independence. Comm Econ Dev.

An Approach to Federal Urban Policy. Comm Econ Dev.

Assisting Development in Low Income Countries. Comm Econ Dev.

Broadcasting & Cable Television: Policies for Diversity & Change. Comm Econ Dev.

Budgeting for National Objectives. Comm Econ Dev.

Building a National Health-Care System. Comm Econ Dev.

Community Economic Development Efforts: Five Case Studies. Comm Econ Dev.

Congressional Decision Making for National Security. Comm Econ Dev.

Development Assistance to Southeast Asia. Comm Econ Dev.

Economic Development Issues: Latin America. Comm Econ Dev.

Economic Growth in the United States-Its Past & Future. Comm Econ Dev.

Educating Tomorrow's Managers. Comm Econ Dev.

Education for the Urban Disadvantaged from Preschool to Employment. Comm Econ Dev.

Fighting Inflation & Promoting Growth. Comm Econ Dev.

Financing a Better Election System. Comm Econ Dev.

Financing the Nation's Housing Needs. Comm Econ Dev.

Fiscal & Monetary Policies for Steady Economic Growth. Comm Econ Dev.

Fiscal Issues in the Future of Federalism. Comm Econ Dev.

Further Weapons Against Inflation. Comm Econ Dev.

Helping Insure Our Energy Future: A Program for Developing Synthetic Fuel Plants Now. Comm Econ Dev.

High Employment Without Inflation: A Positive Program for Economic Stabilization. Comm Econ Dev.

Improving Executive Management in the Federal Government. Comm Econ Dev.

Improving Federal Program Performance. Comm Econ Dev.

Improving Management of the Public Work Force: The Challenge to State & Local Government. Comm Econ Dev.

Improving Productivity in State & Local Government. Comm Econ Dev.

Improving the Public Welfare System. Comm Econ Dev.

Innovation in Education: New Directions for the American School. Comm Econ Dev.

International Economic Consequences of High-Priced Energy. Comm Econ Dev.

Jobs for the Hard-to-Employ: New Directions for a Public Private Partnership. Comm Econ Dev.

Making Congress More Effective. Comm Econ Dev.

The Management & Financing of Colleges. Comm Econ Dev.

Military Manpower & National Security. Comm Econ Dev.

Modernizing Local Government. Comm Econ Dev.

Modernizing State Government. Comm Econ Dev.

More Effective Programs for a Cleaner Environment. Comm Econ Dev.

A New Trade Policy Toward Communist Countries. Comm Econ Dev.

New U. S. Farm Policy for Changing World Food Needs. Comm Econ Dev.

Nontariff Distortions of Trade. Comm Econ Dev.

Nuclear Energy & National Security. Comm Econ Dev.

Redefining Government's Role in the Market System. Comm Econ Dev.

Reducing Crime & Assuring Justice. Comm Econ Dev.

Reshaping Government in Metropolitan Areas. Comm Econ Dev.

Social Responsibilities of Business Corporations. Comm Econ Dev.

Stimulating Technological Progress. Comm Econ Dev.

Strengthening the World Monetary System. Comm Econ Dev.

Toward a New International Economic System: A Joint Japanese-American View. Comm Econ Dev.

Training & Jobs for the Urban Poor. Comm Econ Dev.

Training & Jobs Programs in Action: Case Studies in Private-Sector Initiatives for the Hard-To-Employ. Comm Econ Dev.

Committee for International Environmental Programs. see Environmental Studies Board. Committee for International Environmental Programs.

Committee For The Survey Of Chemistry. see National Research Council. Panel on Basic Chemical Research in Government Laboratories.

Committee of Education & Total Employment. see Forum of Education. Committee on Education and Total Employment.

Committee of London Clearing Banks. see Committee on London Clearing Bankers.

Committee of RSD, ALA. see American Library Association. Ad Hoc Reference Books Review Committee.

Committee of the Children's Services Division. see American Library Association. Library Service to the Disadvantaged Child Committee.

Committee of the President's Conference on Unemployment. see Conference on Unemployment, Washington, D.C., 1921. Committee on Unemployment and Business Cycles.

Committee of the Young Adult Services Division, ALA. see American Library Association. Young Adult Services Division. Research Committee.

Committee On Agricultural Land Use And Wildlife Resources. see National Research Council. Committee on Agriculture Land Use and Wildlife Resources.

Committee On Animal Health. see National Research Council. Subcommittee on Prenatal and Postnatal Mortality in Bovines.

Committee on Animal Nutrition. see National Research Council. Committee on Animal Nutrition. Subcommittee on Fluorosis.

Committee on Animal Nutrition, Agricultural Board. see National Research Council. Committee on Animal Nutrition. Subcommittee on Feed Composition.

Committee on Animal Nutrition Board on Agriculture & Renewable Resources, Natl Research Council. see National Research Council. Subcommittee on Beef Cattle Nutrition.

Committee On Atmospheric Sciences. see National Research Council. Committee on Atmospheric Sciences.

Committee on Banking & Currency, U. S. Senate, 1934. see United States. Congress. House. Committee on Banking and Currency.

Committee On Banking And Currency - Staff Report. see United States. Congress. House. Committee on Banking and Currency.

Committee on Biologic Effects of Atmosphere Pollutants. see National Research Council. Committee on Biologic Effects of Atmospheric Pollutants.

Committee On Biological Effects Of Atmospheric Pollutants. see National Research Council. Committee on Biologic Effects of Atmospheric Pollutants.

Committee On Data For Science And Technology Of The International Council Of Scientific Unions. see

International Council of Scientific Unions. Committee on Data for Science and Technology.

Committee on Education & Labor, U.S. Senate, 76th Congress, 3rd Session. see United States. Congress. Senate. Committee on Education and Labor.

Committee on Federal Agency Evaluation Research, National Research Council. see National Research Council. Committee on Federal Agency Evaluation Research.

Committee On Food Protection. see National Research Council. Food Protection Committee.

Committee on Food Protection, NRC. see National Research Council. Food Protection Committee.

Committee On Foreign Relations. see National Research Council. Committee on Foreign Relations.

Committee on Hazardous Materials. see National Research Council. Committee on Hazardous Materials, Advisory to the United States Coast Guard.

Committee On Interplay Of Engineering With Biology And Medicine. see National Academy of Engineering. Task Group on Industrial Activity.

Committee on London Clearing Bankers.
　　xCommittee of London Clearing Banks.
　　　　London Clearing Banks' Evidence to the
　　　　　　Wilson Committee. Longman.

Committee on Medical and Biologic Effects of Environmental Pollutants, National Research Council. see National Research Council. Committee on Medical and Biologic Effects of Environmental Pollutants.

Committee on Mineral Resources & Environment, National Research Council. see National Research Council. Committee on Mineral Resources and the Environment.

Committee on Mineral Resources & the Environment, National Research Council. see National Research Council. Committee on Mineral Resources and the Environment.

Committee on Nuclear Science. see National Research Council. Committee on Nuclear Sciences.

Committee On Nuclear Sciences. see National Research Council. Committee on Nuclear Sciences.

Committee On Oceanography. see National Research Council. Committee on Oceanography.

Committee On Pollution. see National Research Council. Committee on Pollution.

Committee on Power Plant Siting. see National Academy of Engineering. Committee on Power Plant Siting.

Committee on Pre & Postoperative Care American College of Surgeons. see American College of Surgeons. Committee on Pre and Postoperative Care.

Committee on Prosthetics Research & Development. see Symposium on the Child with an Acquired Amputation, Toronto, 1970.

Committee On Research In The Life Sciences. see National Academy of Sciences. Washington, D.C., Committe on Research in the Life Sciences.

Committee On Salmonella - Division Of Biology And Agriculture. see National Research Council. Committee on Salmonella.

Committee on Salmonellosis & Arizonosis of the American Assn. of Vet. Lab Diagnosticians. see American Association of Veterinary Laboratory Diagnosticians. Committee on Salmonellosis and Arizonosis.

Committee on Scholarly Communication with the People's Republic of China (CSCPRC). see American Insect Control Delegation.

Committee on Seismology. see National Research Council. Panel on Seismograph Networks.

Committee On Social And Behavioral Urban Research - Division Of Behavioral Sciences. see National Research Council. Committee on Social and Behavioral Urban Research.

Committee on Space Research, Seattle, Wash. see International Council of Scientific Unions. Committee on Space Research.

Committee on Taxation, Resources, & Economic Development. see Committee on Taxation Resources and Economic Development.

Committee on Taxation Resources and Economic Development.
    xCommittee on Taxation, Resources, & Economic Development.
        Land Use & Public Policy. U of Wis Pr.
Committee on the Alaska Earthquake. *see* National Research Council. Committee on the Alaska Earthquake.
Committee on the Costs of Medical Care.
    xCommittee on the Costs of Medical Care, October 1932.
        Medical Care for the American People: The Final Report of the Committee on the Costs of Medical Care. Arno.
Committee on Transportation, Assembly of Engineering, Natl. Research Council. *see* National Research Council. Committee on Transportaion.
Committee On Underwater Telecommunications Division Of Physical Sciences. *see* National Research Council. Committee on Transportaion.
Committee On Urban Technology - Division Of Engineering. *see* National Fire Protection Association. Sectional Committee on Protective Equipment for Fire Fighters.
Committee on Vocational Education Research & Development, National Research Council. *see* National Research Council. Committee on Vocational Education Research and Development.
Common Council for American Unity.
    xCommon Council for American Unity.
        The Alien & the Immigration Law. Greenwood.
Commons, John R. *see* Commons, John Rogers.
Commons, John Rogers, 1862-1945
    xCommons, John R.
        Industrial Goodwill. Arno.
        Industrial Government. Arno.
        Legal Foundations of Capitalism. Kelley.
        Legal Foundations of Capitalism. U of Wis Pr.
        Principles of Labor Legislation. Folcroft.
        Principles of Labor Legislation. Kelley.
        Principles of Labor Legislation. Quest Edns.
        Races & Immigrants in America. Kelley.
Commonwealth Relations Office - London. *see* India Office Library.
Commonwealth Secretariat.
    xCommonwealth Secretariat.
        Meat. Intl Pubns Serv.
        Plantation Crops. Intl Pubns Serv.
Commonwealth Spaceflight Symposium, 1st, London, 1959.
    xCommonwealth Spaceflight Symposium Of The British Interplanetary Society - 1st - 1959.
        Spaceflight Technology: Proceedings. Acad Pr.
Commune de Paris, 1789-1794. *see* Paris. Commune, 1789-1794.
Communications Research Machines, Inc. *see* Communications-Research-Machines, Inc.
Communications-Research-Machines, Inc.
    xCommunications Research Machines, Inc.
        Abnormal Psychology: Current Perspectives. Random.
        Life & Health. Random.
Communist Party of America. *see* Communist Party of the United States of America.
Communist Party of the United States of America.
    xCommunist Party of America.
        Communist. Greenwood.
Community Management Corporation.
    xCommunity Management Corporation.
        Financial Management of Condominium & Homeowner's Associations. Urban Land.
Community Service Society of New York.
    xCommunity Service Society of New York.
        Family in a Democratic Society. Arno.
        Social Agency Research - What's Involved?. Family Serv.
Community Work Group.
    xCommunity Work Group.

Current Issues in Community Work. Routledge & Kegan.
Comoss, Patricia M. *see* Comoss, Patricia Mccall.
Comoss, Patricia Mccall.
    xComoss, Patricia M.
        Cardiac Rehabilitation: A Comprehensive Nursing Approach. Lippincott.
Compaine, Benjamin M.
    xCompaine, Benjamin M.
        ed. Who Owns the Media?: Concentration of Ownership in the Mass Communication Industry. Crown.
        ed. Who Owns the Media?: Concentration of Ownership in the Mass Communications Industry. Knowledge Indus.
Companion, Audrey. *see* Companion, Audrey L.
Companion, Audrey L.
    xCompanion, Audrey.
        Chemical Bonding. McGraw.
    xCompanion, Audrey L.
        Chemical Bonding. McGraw.
Company for Propagation of the Gospel in New England and the Parts Adjacent in America.
    xCompany for the Propagation of the Gospel in New England & the Parts Adjacent in America, London.
        Some Correspondence Between the Governors & Treasurers of the New England Company in London & the Commissioners of the United Colonies in America the Missionaries of the Company & Others Between the Years 1657 & 1712. B Franklin.
Company for the Propagation of the Gospel in New England & the Parts Adjacent in America, London. *see* Company for Propagation of the Gospel in New England and the Parts Adjacent in America.
Compayre, Gabriel, 1843-1913
    xCompayre, Gabriel.
        Abelard & the Origin & Early History of the Universities. AMS Pr.
        Abelard & the Origin & Early History of the Universities. Greenwood.
        Abelard & the Origin & Early History of the Universities. Scholarly.
        History of Pedagogy. AMS Pr.
        The History of Pedagogy. R West.
        History of Pedagogy. Scholarly.
        Montaigne & Education of the Judgment. R West.
Comper, Frances M. *see* Comper, Frances Margaret Mary.
Comper, Frances Margaret Mary.
    xComper, Frances M.
        The Life of Richard Rolle. Scholarly.
Compere, Edward L. *see* Compere, Edward Lyon.
Compere, Edward Lyon, 1901-
    xCompere, Edward L.
        Orthopaedic Surgery. Year Bk Med.
Compere, Newton L.
    xCompere, Newton L.
        How to Raise & Train a German Wirehaired Pointer. TFH Pubns.
Comprone, Joseph J.
    xComprone, Joseph J.
        Form & Substance: The Modern Essay. Wm C Brown.
Compton, Arthur H. *see* Compton, Arthur Holly.
Compton, Arthur Holly, 1892-1962
    xCompton, Arthur H.
        Freedom of Man. Greenwood.
Compton, Beulah. *see* Compton, Beulah Roberts.
Compton, Beulah Roberts.
    xCompton, Beulah.
        Social Work Processes. Dorsey.
Compton, Charles, 1917-
    xCompton, Charles.
        Inside Chemistry. McGraw.
Compton, D. G.
    xCompton, D. G.

Synthajoy. Berkley Pub.
        Synthajoy. Gregg.
Compton, D. G. *see* Compton, David Guy.
Compton, David Guy.
    xCompton, D. G.
        Farewell, Earth's Bliss. Borgo Pr.
        The Steel Crocodile. Gregg.
        The Steel Crocodile. PB.
        A Usual Lunacy. Borgo Pr.
        Windows. Berkley Pub.
Compton, Eric N., 1925-
    xCompton, Eric N.
        Inside Commercial Banking. Wiley.
Compton, Herbert. *see* Compton, Herbert Eastwick.
Compton, Herbert Eastwick, 1853-1906
    xCompton, Herbert.
        A Particular Account of the European Military Adventurers of Hindustan: From 1784 to 1803. Oxford U Pr.
Compton, Linda, 1940-
    xCompton, Linda F.
        Andalusian Lyrical Poetry & Old Spanish Love Songs: The "Muwashshah" & Its "Kharja". NYU Pr.
Compton, Linda F. *see* Compton, Linda.
Compton, Thelma J.
    xCompton, Thelma J.
        The Glass Tree. Commonwealth Pr.
Compton-Burnett, Ivy, 1892-
    xCompton-Burnett, Ivy.
        Present & the Past. Intl Pubns Serv.
Compton-Rickett, Arthur, 1869-1937
    xCompton-Rickett, Arthur.
        Personal Forces in Modern Literature. AMS Pr.
        Personal Forces in Modern Literature. Arno.
        Personal Forces in Modern Literature. Folcroft.
Computer Consultants Limited.
    xComputer Consultants Ltd.
        British Commercial Computer Digest. Pergamon.
        European Computer Survey Nineteen Sixty-Eight to Sixty-Nine. Pergamon.
        European Computer Survey Nineteen Sixty-Nine to Seventy. Pergamon.
        European Computer Users Handbook, 1969-70. Pergamon.
Computer Consultants Ltd. *see* Computer Consultants Limited.
Computer Usage Co., Inc. *see* Computer Usage Company, Inc., New York.
Computer Usage Company Inc. *see* Computer Usage Company, Inc., New York.
Computer Usage Company, Inc., New York.
    xComputer Usage Co., Inc.
        Computer Usage - Applications. McGraw.
        Computer Usage - Fundamentals. McGraw.
    xComputer Usage Company Inc.
        Computer Usage - Three Sixty Fortran Programming. McGraw.
Comroe, Julius H. *see* Comroe, Julius Hiram.
Comroe, Julius Hiram, 1911-
    xComroe, Julius H.
        Retrospectroscope: Insights into Medical Discovery. Von Gehr.
Comstock, John H. *see* Comstock, John Henry.
Comstock, John Henry, 1849-1931
    xComstock, John H.
        Introduction to Entomology. Comstock.
Comte, August. *see* Comte, Auguste.
Comte, Auguste.
    xComte, August.
        Introduction to Positive Philosophy. Bobbs.
    xComte, Auguste.

Auguste Comte & Positivism: The Essential
  Writings. Har-Row.
The Catechism of Positive Religion. Kelley.
General View of Positivism. Irvington.
General View of Positivism. Speller.
Positive Philosophy. AMS Pr.
Positivist Library of Auguste Comte,
  1798-1854. B Franklin.
Comtet, L. see Comtet, Louis.
Comtet, Louis.
  xComtet, L.
    Advanced Combinatorics: The Art of Finite &
      Infinite Expansions. Kluwer Boston.
Comtre Corp. see Comtre Corporation.
Comtre Corporation.
  xComtre Corp.
    Multiprocessors & Parallel Processing. Wiley.
Conacher, J. B.
  xConacher, J. B.
    Aberdeen Coalition, 1852-1855: A Study in
      Mid-Nineteenth-Century Party Politics.
      Cambridge U Pr.
Conan Doyle, Arthur. see Doyle, Arthur Conan.
Conant, Charles A. see Conant, Charles Arthur.
Conant, Charles Arthur.
  xConant, Charles A.
    A History of Modern Banks of Issue. Folcroft.
    History of Modern Banks of Issue. Kelley.
    A History of Modern Banks of Issue. Quest
      Edns.
Conant, James B. see Conant, James Bryant.
Conant, James Bryant, 1893-
  xConant, James B.
    The Citadel of Learning. Greenwood.
    Comprehensive High School: A Second Report
      to Interested Citizens. McGraw.
    Education in a Divided World: The Function
      of the Public Schools in Our Unique Society.
      Greenwood.
    ed. Overthrow of the Phlogiston Theory: The
      Chemical Revolution of 1775-1789. Harvard
      U Pr.
    ed. Pasteur's & Tyndall's Study of Spontaneous
      Generation. Harvard U Pr.
    Thomas Jefferson & the Development of
      American Public Education. U of Cal Pr.
Conant, Kenneth J. see Conant, Kenneth John.
Conant, Kenneth John, 1894-
  xConant, Kenneth J.
    Carolingian & Romanesque Architecture:
      800-1200. Penguin.
    Carolingian & Romanesque Architecture.
      Viking Pr.
Conant, Martha P. see Conant, Martha Pike.
Conant, Martha Pike.
  xConant, Martha P.
    Oriental Tale in England in the Eighteenth
      Century. Octagon.
Conant, Melvin.
  xConant, Melvin.
    The Long Polar Watch: Canada & the Defense
      of North America. Greenwood.
Conant, Ralph W. see Conant, Ralph Wendell.
Conant, Ralph Wendell, 1926-
  xConant, Ralph W.
    The Conant Report: A Study of the Education
      of Librarians. MIT Pr.
Conant, Roger, 1909-
  xConant, Roger.
    A Field Guide to Reptiles & Amphibians of
      Eastern & Central North America. HM.
Conant, T. J. see Conant, Thomas Jefferson.
Conant, Thomas Jefferson, 1802-1891
  xConant, T. J.
    Meaning & Use of Baptizein. Kregel.
Conard, Henry S. see Conard, Henry Shoemaker.
Conard, Henry Shoemaker.
  xConard, Henry S.

How to Know the Mosses & Liverworts. Wm
  C Brown.
Conaway, J. C.
  xConaway, J. C.
    Garden of Unicorns. Ballantine.
    The Magician's Sleeve. Fawcett.
Conaway, James.
  xConaway, James.
    World's End. Bantam.
    World's End. Morrow.
Conaway, Jim.
  xConaway, Jim.
    They Do It with Mirrors. Belmont-Tower.
Conaway, Judith, 1948-
  xConaway, Judith.
    City Crafts from Secret Cities. Follett.
    The Discovery Book of Inside & Outside.
      Raintree Pubs.
    The Discovery Book of Size. Raintree Pubs.
    The Discovery Book of Time. Raintree Pubs.
    The Discovery Book of Up & Down. Raintree
      Pubs.
    Great Outdoor Games from Trash & Other
      Things. Raintree Pubs.
    I Dare You!. Raintree Pubs.
    I'll Get Even. Raintree Pubs.
    Sometimes It Scares Me. Raintree Pubs.
Concetta, Sister, D.s.p, 1916-
  xConcetta.
    In the Light of the Bible. Dghtrs St Paul.
Conconi, Charles.
  xConconi, Charles.
    The Washington Sting. Coward.
Concord, Mass. Antiquarian Museum.
  xMuseum of Concord Antiquarian Society.
    An Olde Concorde Christmas. St Martin.
Condax, Kate D. see Condax, Kate Delano.
Condax, Kate Delano.
  xCondax, Kate D.
    Horse Sense: The Cause & Correction of
      Problems. Winchester Pr.
Conde, J. C.
  xConde, Jesse C.
    Sugar Trains Pictorial. Glenwood.
Conde, Jesse C. see Conde, J. C.
Conder, John. see Conder, John J.
Conder, John J.
  xConder, John.
    Formula of His Own: Henry Adam's Literary
      Experiment. U of Chicago Pr.
Conder, Susan.
  xConder, Susan.
    Growing Indoors. Viking Pr.
Condie, K. C. see Condie, Kent C.
Condie, Kent C.
  xCondie, K. C.
    Plate Tectonics & Crustal Evolution.
      Pergamon.
Condit, Carl W.
  xCondit, Carl W.
    The Railroad & the City: A Technological &
      Urbanistic History of Cincinnati. Ohio St U
      Pr.
Condon, E. U. see Condon, Edward Uhler.
Condon, Edward Uhler.
  xCondon, E. U.
    Atomic Structure. Cambridge U Pr.
Condon, Geneal.
  xCondon, Geneal.
    The Complete Book of Flower Preservation.
      P-H.
Condon, John C.
  xCondon, John C.
    An Introduction to Intercultural
      Communication. Bobbs.
Condon, Richard.
  xCondon, Richard.

Abandoned Woman. Dial.
Bandicoot. Dial.
Money Is Love. Ballantine.
Money Is Love. Dial.
Condon, Robert. see Condon, Robert J.
Condon, Robert E.
  xCondon, Robert E.
    ed. Surgical Care: A Physiologic Approach to
      Clinical Management. Lea & Febiger.
Condon, Robert J., 1934-
  xCondon, Robert.
    Data Processing with Applications. Reston.
  xCondon, Robert J.
    Data Processing Systems Analysis & Design.
      Reston.
    Data Processing with Applications. Reston.
Condorcet, Marie J. see Condorcet, Marie Jean Antoinne
  Nicolas Caritat.
**Condorcet, Marie Jean Antoinne Nicolas Caritat,
Marquis De, 1743-1794**
  xCondorcet, Marie J.
    Sketch for a Historical Picture of the Progress
      of the Human Mind. Hyperion Conn.
Condry, William M.
  xCondry, William M.
    Thoreau. Dufour.
Cone, Arthur L.
  xCone, Arthur L.
    The Complete Guide to Hunting. Follett.
    Complete Guide to Hunting. Macmillan.
    Fishing Made Easy. Macmillan.
    Fishing Made Easy. Macmillan.
Cone, Cynthia A.
  xCone, Cynthia A.
    Guide to Cultural Anthropology. Scott F.
Cone, Edward T.
  xCone, Edward T.
    The Composer's Voice. U of Cal Pr.
    Musical Form & Musical Performance. Norton.
Cone, James. see Cone, James H.
Cone, James H.
  xCone, James.
    God of the Oppressed. Seabury.
Cone, Molly.
  xCone, Molly.
    About Learning. UAHC.
    The Amazing Memory of Harvey Bean. HM.
    Annie Annie. HM.
    Call Me Moose. HM.
    Dance Around the Fire. HM.
    Leonard Bernstein. T Y Crowell.
    Mishmash & the Sauerkraut Mystery.
      Archway.
    Mishmash & the Sauerkraut Mystery. PB.
    Mishmash & the Sauerkraut Mystery. HM.
    Mishmash & the Venus Flytrap. HM.
    Mishmash & the Venus Flytrap. Archway.
    Mishmash & the Venus Flytrap. PB.
    Other Side of the Fence. HM.
    Promise Is a Promise. HM.
    Purim. T Y Crowell.
    Who Knows Ten: Children's Tales of the Ten
      Commandments. UAHC.
Cone, Richard A.
  xCone, Richard A.
    ed. Membrane Transduction Mechanisms.
      Raven.
Cone, William F.
  xCone, William F.
    Supervising Employees Effectively. A-W.
Conely, James.
  xConely, James.
    A Guide to Improvisation: An Introductory
      Handbook for Church Organists. Abingdon.
Coney, John C. see Coney, John Charles.
Coney, John Charles.
  xConey, John C.

Conference on Hokan Languages, 1st, San Diego, Calif., 1970.
 xConference on Hokan Languages, San Diego, California, April, 1970.
  Hokan Studies: Proceedings. Mouton.
Conference on Inflammation, Princeton University, 1972.
 xConference on Inflammation, Princeton, 1972.
  Conference on Inflammation, Princeton, 1972: Mechanisms & Control. Acad Pr.
Conference on Information Theory. Statistical Decision Functions. Random Processes.
 xConference on Information Theory, Statistical Decision Functions, Random Processes - 3rd, Liblice, 1962.
  Information Theory, Statistical Decision Functions, Random Processes. Acad Pr.
Conference on Intellectual Trends in Latin America, University of Texas, 1945.
 xConference on Intellectual Trends in Latin America, University of Texas, 1945.
  Papers. Greenwood.
Conference on Isobaric Spin in Nuclear Physics, Tallahassee, 1966.
 xConference On Isobaric Spin In Nuclear Physics - Tallahassee - 1966.
  Isobaric Spin in Nuclear Physics: Proceedings. Acad Pr.
Conference on Issues in Educational Measurement, 2nd, Carmel, Cal., 1974. see Ctb-Mcgraw-Hill Conference on Issues in Educational Measurement, 2d, Carmel, California, 1973.
Conference on K-Theory & Operator Algebras, University of Georgia, Athens, Ga., Apr. 21-25, 1975. see Conference on K-Theory and Operator Algebras, University of Georgia, 1975.
Conference on K-Theory and Operator Algebras, University of Georgia, 1975.
 xConference on K-Theory & Operator Algebras, University of Georgia, Athens, Ga., Apr. 21-25, 1975.
  K-Theory & Operator Algebras: Proceedings. Springer-Verlag.
Conference on Latin America, 4th, University of Houston, 1969.
 xFourth Annual Conference on Latin America, April 17-19, 1969.
  Intro. by Contemporary Latin America: Proceedings. Lat Am Stud.
Conference on Latin-American Fine Arts, Texas University, College of Fine Arts. see Texas. University. College of Fine Arts.
Conference on Local Fields - NUFFIC Summer School - Driebergen - 1966. see Conference on Local Fields, Driebergen, Netherlands, 1966.
Conference on Local Fields, Driebergen, Netherlands, 1966.
 xConference on Local Fields - NUFFIC Summer School - Driebergen - 1966.
  Proceedings. Springer-Verlag.
Conference on Magnetism & Magnetic Materials 20th, Dec 3-6, 1974 San Francisco. see Conference on Magnetism and Magnetic Materials.
Conference on Magnetism and Magnetic Materials.
 xConference on Magnetism & Magnetic Materials 20th, Dec 3-6, 1974 San Francisco.
  Magnetism & Magnetic Materials: Proceedings. Am Inst Physics.
Conference on Management Problems in Serials Work, Florida Atlantic University, 1973.
 xFlorida Atlantic University Conference.
  Management Problems in Serials Work: Proceedings. Greenwood.
Conference on Marmosets in Experimental Medicine, Oak Ridge, Tenn., 1977.
 xConference on Marmosets in Experimental Medicine, Oak Ridge Tenn., March 16-18, 1977.

 Marmosets in Experimental Medicine: Proceedings. S Karger.
Conference on Medical Education, Pietermaritzburg, 1964.
 xUniversity of Natal-Conference on Medical Education Durban - July 1964.
  Medical Education in South Africa: Proceedings. Verry.
Conference on Numerical Methods for Non-Linear Optimization, University of Dundee, 1971.
 xConference on Numerical Methods for Non-Linear Optimization, University of Dundee, Scotland, June-July, 1971.
  Numerical Methods in Non-Linear Optimization. Acad Pr.
Conference on Operator Theory, Dalhousie University, 1973.
 xConference on Operator Theory, Dalhousie Univ., Halifax, 1973.
  Proceedings. Springer-Verlag.
Conference on Optimization in Action, University of Bristol, 1975.
 xConference on Optimization in Action, Institute of Mathematics & Its Applications, University of Bristol, England, January 1975.
  Optimization in Action: Proceedings. Acad Pr.
Conference on Ordinary and Partial Differential Equations, 4th, Dundee, Scotland, 1976.
 xFourth Conference Held at Dundee, Scotland, Mar 30-Apr 2, 1976.
  Ordinary & Partial Differential Equations, Dundee 1976: Proceedings. Springer-Verlag.
Conference on Origins of Life, 3rd, California, 1970. see Conference on Origins of Life, 3rd, Pacific Palisades, Calif., 1970.
Conference on Origins of Life, 3rd, Pacific Palisades, Calif., 1970.
 xConference on Origins of Life, 3rd, California, 1970.
  Planetary Astronomy: Proceedings. Springer-Verlag.
Conference on Particle Physics, University of California, Irvine, 1971.
 xAIP Conference, Univ. of California at Irvine, Dec., 1971.
  Particle Physics 1971: Proceedings. Am Inst Physics.
Conference on Poverty in America. see Conference on Poverty in America, University of California, Berkeley, 1965.
Conference on Poverty in America, University of California, Berkeley, 1965.
 xConference on Poverty in America.
  Poverty in America. Arno.
Conference on Probabilistic Methods in Differential Equations, University of Victoria, 1974.
 xProbabilistic Conference, the University of Victoria, August 1974.
  Probabilistic Methods in Differential Equations: Proceedings. Springer-Verlag.
Conference on Psychiatry & Medical Education, Atlanta, 1967. see Conference on Psychiatry and Medical Education, Atlanta, 1967.
Conference on Psychiatry and Medical Education, Atlanta, 1967.
 xConference on Psychiatry & Medical Education, Atlanta, 1967.
  Psychiatry & Medical Education Two. Am Psychiatric.
  Teaching Psychiatry in Medical School: Proceedings. Am Psychiatric.
Conference on Qualitative Theory of Nonlinear Differential and Integral Equations, University of Wisconsin, 1968.
 xConference on Qualitative Theory of Nonlinear Differential & Integral Equations, Wisconsin.

 Studies in Applied Mathematics Five: Advances in Differential & Integral Equations. Proceedings. Soc Indus-Appl Math.
Conference on Quantitative Flourescence Techniques As Applied to Cell Biology, Seattle, Wash. see Conference on Quantitative Fluorescence Techniques As Applied to Cell Biology, Battelle Seattle Research Center, 1972.
Conference on Quantitative Fluorescence Techniques As Applied to Cell Biology, Battelle Seattle Research Center, 1972.
 xConference on Quantitative Flourescence Techniques As Applied to Cell Biology, Seattle, Wash.
  Fluorescence Techniques in Cell Biology: Proceedings. Springer-Verlag.
Conference On Radiation Effects In Semiconductors - Sante Fe. see Santa Fe Conference on Radiation Effects in Semiconductors.
Conference On Reading - University Of Chicago. see Conference on Reading, University of Chicago, 1965.
Conference on Reading, University of Chicago, 1965.
 xConference On Reading - University Of Chicago.
  Reading: Seventy-Five Years of Progress. U of Chicago Pr.
  Recent Developments in Reading. U of Chicago Pr.
Conference on Regional Economic Development, 1st, Bellagio, Italy, 1960.
 xBellagio Conference.
  Regional Economic Planning: Proceedings. OECD.
Conference on Research Designs in General Semantics, 1st, Pennsylvania State University, 1969.
 xConference on Research Designs in General Semantics, 1st, Pennsylvania State University. Proceedings. Gordon.
Conference on Research in Income & Wealth. see Conference on Research in Income and Wealth.
Conference on Research in Income and Wealth.
 xConference on Research in Income & Wealth.
  Input-Output Analysis: An Appraisal. Arno.
  Problems of Capital Formation: Concepts, Measurement, & Controlling Factors. Arno.
  Trends in the American Economy in the Nineteenth Century. Arno.
 xConference On Research In Income And Wealth.
  Long-Range Economic Projection. Natl Bur Econ Res.
  Output, Input & Productivity Measurement. Natl Bur Econ Res.
Conference On Science - Philosophy And Religion - 6th Symposium. see Conference on Science, Philosophy and Religion in Their Relation to the Democratic Way of Life.
Conference on Science and Agribusiness in the Seventies, London, 1974.
 xAgribusiness Council.
  Agriculture Initiative in the Third World. Lexington Bks.
Conference on Science, Philosophy & Religion in Their Relation to the Democratic Way of Life, 3rd. see Conference on Science, Philosophy and Religion in Their Relation to the Democratic Way of Life.
Conference on Science, Philosophy and Religion in Their Relation to the Democratic Way of Life.
 xConference On Science - Philosophy And Religion - 6th Symposium.
  Approaches to Group Understanding. Cooper Sq.
  Conflicts of Power in Modern Culture. Cooper Sq.
 xConference on Science, Philosophy & Religion in Their Relation to the Democratic Way of Life, 3rd.

Approaches to Group Understanding:
Proceedings. Kraus Repr.
Science, Philosophy, & Religion: Proceedings.
Kraus Repr.
xConference on Science-Philosphy & Religion in
Their Relation to the Democratic Way of Life -
4th.
Approaches to World Peace: Proceedings.
Kraus Repr.
Goals for American Education: Proceedings.
Kraus Repr.
xConference on Science-Philosphy & Religion in
Their Relation to the Democratic Way of Life -
5th.
Approaches to National Unity: Proceedings.
Kraus Repr.

**Conference on Science, Philosophy and Religion in Their
Relation to the Democratic Way of Life, 11th,
Columbia University, 1950.**
xConference on Science-Philosphy & Religion in
Their Relation to the Democratic Way of Life,
11th.
Foundations of World Organization: A Political
& Cultural Appraisal: Proceeding. Kraus
Repr.

**Conference on Science, Philosophy and Religion in Their
Relation to the Democratic Way of Life, 12th,
Columbia University, 1951.**
xConference on Science-Philosphy & Religion in
Their Relation to the Democratic Way of Live,
12th, New York.
Freedom & Authority in Our Time:
Proceeding. Kraus Repr.

**Conference on Science, Philosophy and Religion in Their
Relation to the Democratic Way of Life, 13th,
Columbia University, 1952.**
xConference On Science - Philosophy And
Religion - 13th Symposium.
Symbols & Values. Cooper Sq.

**Conference on Science, Philosophy and Religion in Their
Relation to the Democratic Way of Life, 14th,
Harvard University, 1954.**
xConference On Science - Philosophy And
Religion - 14th Symposium.
Symbols & Society. Cooper Sq.

**Conference on Science, Philosophy and Religion in Their
Relation to the Democratic Way of Life, 16th, Jewish
Theological Seminary of America, 1960.**
xConference on Science-Philosphy & Religion in
Their Religion to the Democratic Way of Life,
New York.
Ethics & Bigness: Proceedings. Kraus Repr.
Conference on Science-Philosphy & Religion in Their
Relation to the Democratic Way of Life - 4th. see
Conference on Science, Philosophy and Religion in
Their Relation to the Democratic Way of Life.
Conference on Science-Philosphy & Religion in Their
Relation to the Democratic Way of Life - 5th. see
Conference on Science, Philosophy and Religion in
Their Relation to the Democratic Way of Life.

**Conference on Semiconductor Nuclear-Particle
Detectors and Circuits, Gatlinburg, Tenn., 1967.**
xNational Academy Of Sciences Division Of
Physical Sciences.
Semiconductor Nuclear-Particle Detectors &
Circuits. Natl Acad Pr.
Conference on Silicon Carbide, 3rd, 1973. see
International Conference on Silicon Carbide, 3d,
Miami Beach, Fla. 1973.
Conference On Social Psychology - University Of
Oklahoma - 1950. see Conference on Social
Psychology at Crossroads, University of Oklahoma,
1950.

**Conference on Social Psychology at Crossroads,
University of Oklahoma, 1950.**
xConference On Social Psychology - University Of
Oklahoma - 1950.

Social Psychology at the Crossroads. Arno.
**Conference on Some Economic Aspects of Postwar
Inter-American Relations, University of Texas, 1946.**
xConference On Some Economic Aspects Of
Postwar Inter-American Relations - University
Of Texas - 1946.
Papers. Greenwood.

**Conference on Statistical Computation, University of
Wisconsin, 1969.**
xConference On Statistical Computation - Univ. Of
Wis. 1969.
Statistical Computation. Acad Pr.

**Conference on Tensions in Development, Oxford
University, 1961.**
xConference on Tensions in Development, Oxford
Univ.
Restless Nations: A Study of World Tensions
& Development. Greenwood.
Conference on the Aging, 4th, University of Michican,
1951. see Conference on Aging, 4th, University of
Michigan, 1951.

**Conference on the Biology of Normal and Atypical
Pigment Cell Growth, 3rd, New York, 1951.**
xConference On The Biology Of Normal And
A-Typical Pigment Cell Growth - 3rd - New
York - 1951.
Pigment Cell Growth: Proceedings. Acad Pr.
Conference On The Biology Of Normal And A-Typical
Pigment Cell Growth - 4th - Houston - Texas - 1957.
see International Pigment Cell Conference. 4th,
Houston, Tex., 1957.

**Conference on the Care of Dependent Children,
Washington, D.C., 1909.**
xConference On The Care Of Dependent Children.
Proceedings of the Conference of the Care of
Dependent Children. Arno.

**Conference on the Family in the Caribbean, 1st, St.
Thomas, V.I., 1968.**
xConference on the Family in the Caribbean, 2nd,
Aruba, Netherlands Antilles, Dec. 1-5, 1969.
The Family in the Caribbean: Proceedings. Intl
Pubns Serv.

**Conference on the Formal Aspects of Cognitive
Processes, Ann Arbor, Michigan, 1973.**
xInterdisciplinary Conference, Ann Arbor, March
1973.
Formal Aspects Cognitive Processes:
Proceedings. Springer-Verlag.

Conference on the Myocardium, Canberra, 1973.
xConference on Canberra, 1973.
The Myocardium: Proceedings. S Karger.

**Conference on the Numerical Solution of Differential
Equations, Dundee, Scot., 1973.**
xConference on the Numerical Solution of
Differential Equations.
Proceedings. Springer-Verlag.

**Conference on the Public Land Law Review Commission
Report, San Francisco, 1970.**
xConference on the Public Land Law Review
Commission Report, Dec. 1970.
America's Public Lands: Politics, Economics, &
Administration. Inst Gov Stud Berk.

**Conference on the Theory of Ordinary and Partial
Differential Equations, Dundee, Scot., 1972.**
xConference on the Theory of Ordinary & Partial
Differential Equations, Dundee, Scotland, 1972.
Proceedings. Springer-Verlag.

**Conference on the Undergraduate and Lifetime Reading
Interest, University of Michigan, 1958.**
xConference On The Undergraduate And Lifetime
Reading Interest.
Reading for Life: Developing the College
Student's Lifetime Reading Interest.
Greenwood.

Conference on the Universe of Vedanta, Delhi, 1975.
xConference on "the Universe of Vedanta," 6-7
May, 1975.

Marxism on Vedanta: Papers. South Asia Bks.
**Conference on the Use of Orbiting Spacecraft in
Geographic Research, Houston, Tex., 1965.**
xConference On The Use Of Orbiting Spacecraft
In Geographic Research - Houston - Tex 1965.
Spacecraft in Geographic Research. Natl Acad
Pr.

**Conference on Training in Child Psychiatry,
Washington, D.C., 1963.**
xConference on Training in Child Psychiatry,
1963.
Career Training in Child Psychiatry. Am
Psychiatric.

**Conference on Undergraduate Education in the
Biological Sciences for Students in Agriculture and
Natural Resources, Washington, D.C., 1966.**
xCommission On Education In Agriculture And
Natural Resources.
Undergraduate Education in the Biological
Sciences for Students in Agriculture &
Natural Resources. Natl Acad Pr.

**Conference on Undergraduate Teaching in the Animal
Sciences, Washington, D.C., 1966.**
xCommission On Education In Agriculture And
Natural Resources.
Undergraduate Teaching in the Animal
Sciences. Natl Acad Pr.

**Conference on Undergraduate Teaching in the Plant and
Soil Sciences, Washington, D.C., 1967.**
xCommission On Education In Agriculture And
Natural Resources.
Undergraduate Education in the Plant & Soil
Sciences. Natl Acad Pr.
Conference On Unemployment - Washington D. C. -
1921. see Conference on Unemployment, Washington,
D.C., 1921.

Conference on Unemployment, Washington, D.C., 1921.
xConference On Unemployment - Washington D.
C. - 1921.
Recent Economic Changes in the United
States. Johnson Repr.

**Conference on Unemployment, Washington, D.C., 1921.
Committee on Unemployment and Business Cycles.**
xCommittee of the President's Conference on
Unemployment.
Business Cycles & Unemployment:
Proceedings. Arno.
Conference On Value Inquiry - 3rd. see Conference on
Value Inquiry, 3rd, State University of New York,
College at Geneseo, 1969.

**Conference on Value Inquiry, 3rd, State University of
New York, College at Geneseo, 1969.**
xConference On Value Inquiry - 3rd.
Human Values & Natural Science: Proceedings.
Gordon.
Conference on Visual Prosthesis - 2nd. see Conference on
Visual Prosthesis, 2nd, University of Chicago, 1969.

**Conference on Visual Prosthesis, 2nd, University of
Chicago, 1969.**
xConference on Visual Prosthesis - 2nd.
Visual Prosthesis: The Interdisciplinary
Dialogue, Proceedings. Acad Pr.
Conference, Rosa Marni, Italy, June 1973. see
International Conference on the Biogenesis of
Mitochondria, Rosa Marina, Italy, 1973.
Conford, Ella. see Conford, Ellen.
Conford, Ellen.
xConford, Ella.
And This Is Laura. Archway.
xConford, Ellen.

The Alfred G. Graebner Memorial High School
    Handbook of Rules & Regulations. Archway.
The Alfred G. Graebner Memorial High School
    Handbook of Rules & Regulations. Little.
Alfred G. Graebner Memorial High School
    Handbook of Rules & Regulations: A Novel.
    PB.
And This Is Laura. Little.
And This Is Laura. PB.
Anything for a Friend. Little.
Dear Lovey Hart: I Am Desperate. Little.
Dreams of Victory. Dell.
Dreams of Victory. Little.
Eugene the Brave. Little.
Felicia, the Critic. Archway.
Felicia the Critic. Little.
Felicia the Critic. PB.
Hail, Hail Camp Timberwood. Little.
Hail, Hail, Camp Timberwood. Archway.
Hail, Hail Camp Timberwood. PB.
Impossible Possum. Little.
The Luck of Pokey Bloom. Archway.
The Luck of Pokey Bloom. Little.
Me & the Terrible Two. Archway.
Me & the Terrible Two. Little.
Me & the Terrible Two. PB.
The Revenge of the Incredible Dr. Rancid &
    His Youthful Assistant, Jeffrey. Little.
We Interrupt This Semester for an Important
    Bulletin. Little.

Confucius.
    xConfucius.
    Analects of Confucius. Paragon.
Congalton, A. A. see Congalton, Athol Alexander.
Congalton, Athol Alexander.
    xCongalton, A. A.
    Status & Prestige in Australia. Verry.
Congdon, Howard K., 1941-
    xCongdon, Howard K.
    The Pursuit of Death. Abingdon.
Congdon, Kirby.
    xCongdon, Kirby.
    Contemporary Poets in American Anthologies
        1960-1977. Scarecrow.
Congdon, S. Perry.
    xCongdon, S. Perry.
    Frwd. by The Drama Reader: Full-Length
        Plays for the Secondary School. Odyssey Pr.
Conger, Flora S. see Conger, Flora Stabler.
Conger, Flora Stabler.
    xConger, Flora S.
    Child Care Aide Skills. McGraw.
Conger, George P. see Conger, George Perrigo.
Conger, George Perrigo, 1884-
    xConger, George P.
    Ideologies of Religion. Arno.
    Theories of Macrocosms & Microcosms in the
        History of Philosophy. Russell.
Conger, John J. see Conger, John Janeway.
Conger, John Janeway.
    xConger, John J.
    Adolescence & Youth: Psychological
        Development in a Changing World. Har-Row.
    Contemporary Issues in Adolescent
        Development. Har-Row.
Congleton, Henry B. see Congleton, Henry Brooke
    Parnell.
Congleton, Henry Brooke Parnell, Baron, 1776-1842
    xCongleton, Henry B.
    On Financial Reform. Kelley.
Congleton, J. E. see Congleton, James Edmund.
Congleton, James Edmund.
    xCongleton, J. E.
    Theories of Pastoral Poetry in England,
        1684-1798. Haskell.
Congress For Cultural Freedom - Berlin - 1960. see
    Congress for Cultural Freedom, Berlin, 1960.
Congress for Cultural Freedom, Berlin, 1960.
    xCongress For Cultural Freedom - Berlin - 1960.

History & Hope. Arno.
**Congress of American-Soviet Friendship, 2d, New York,
1973.**
    xNational Council of American Soviet Friendship.
    Science in Soviet Russia. Arno.
Congress of EUCARPIA, 7th, Budapest, 1974. see
    European Association for Research on Plant Breeding.
Congress of International College of Psychosomatic
    Medicine, 2nd, Amsterdam, June 18-21, 1973. see
    International College of Psychosomatic Medicine.
Congress of Neurological Surgeons.
    xCongress of Neurological Surgeons.
    Clinical Neurosurgery. Williams & Wilkins.
Congress of Pediatric Dermatology, 2nd, Mexico City,
    October 20-23, 1976. see International Congress of
    Pediatric Dermatology.
Congress of Polish-American Scholars & Scientists, 1st.
    see Congress of Scholars and Scientists, 1st, Columbia
    University, 1966.
**Congress of Scholars and Scientists, 1st, Columbia
University, 1966.**
    xCongress of Polish-American Scholars &
        Scientists, 1st.
    Program & Abstracts of Papers. Polish Inst
        Arts.
**Congress of the European Society for Pediatric
Neurosurgery.**
    xCongress of the European Society for Pediatric
        Neurosurgery, 5th, Stresa, September, October
        1976.
    Pediatric Neurosurgery: Proceedings. S Karger.
Congress of the International Astronautical Federation,
    22nd, Brussels, Sept. 1971. see International
    Astronautical Federation.
Congress of the World Federation of Haemophilia, 7th,
    Teheran 1971. see World Federation of Hemophilia.
Congress On Africa. see Congress on Africa, Atlanta,
    1895.
Congress on Africa, Atlanta, 1895.
    xCongress On Africa.
    Africa & the American Negro. Arno.
Congress, 75th, 1st Session, House Document No. 360.
    see United States. National Resources Committee.
    Science Committee.
Congressional Information Service.
    xCongressional Information Service.
    CIS U.S. Congressional Committee Prints
        Index. Cong Info.
    xCongressional Information Service, Inc.
    American Statistics Index Fourth Annual
        Supplement. Cong Info.
Congressional Information Service, Inc. see Congressional
    Information Service.
Congressional Quarterley Staff. see Congressional
    Quarterly, Inc.
Congressional Quarterly. see Congressional Quarterly,
    Inc.
Congressional Quarterly, Inc.
    xCongressional Quarterley Staff.
    Congressional Ethics. Congr Quarterly.
    xCongressional Quarterly.
    ed. Defense Policy. Congr Quarterly.
    Elections '80. Congr Quarterly.
    ed. ERR: Foreign Policy. Congr Quarterly.
    Federal Regulatory Directory. Congr Quarterly.
    Guide to the Supreme Court. Congr Quarterly.
    Health Policy. Congr Quarterly.
    Historic Documents: Nineteen Seventy-Nine.
        Congr Quarterly.
    Inside Congress. Congr Quarterly.
    Middle East: U. S. Policy, Israel, Oil & the
        Arabs. Congr Quarterly.
    ed. National Party Conventions: Seventeen
        Thirty-One to Nineteen Seventy-Eight. Congr
        Quarterly.
    ed. Politics in America. Congr Quarterly.
    Spring Guide to Current American
        Government 1980. Congr Quarterly.
    Washington Lobby. Congr Quarterly.
    xCongressional Quarterly Inc.

Candidates Nineteen Eighty. Congr Quarterly.
    ed. China. Congr Quarterly.
    Congressional Quarterly Almanac, 1979. Congr
        Quarterly.
    Federal Regulatory Directory Nineteen Eighty
        to Eighty One. Congr Quarterly.
    Guide to Current American Government Fall
        Nineteen Eighty. Congr Quarterly.
    Nineteen Seventy Nine Guide to Current
        Amerian Government. Congr Quarterly.
    President Carter Nineteen Seventy Nine.
        Congr Quarterly.
    Roll Call 1979. Congr Quarterly.
    Washington Information Directory Nineteen
        Eighty to Eighty One. Congr Quarterly.
xCongressional Quarterly Staff.
    Complete Watergate: Chronology of a Crisis.
        Congr Quarterly.
    Congressional Quarterly Almanac, 1977. Congr
        Quarterly.
    Congressional Quarterly Almanac: 1978. Congr
        Quarterly.
    Congressional Quarterly's Guide to the
        Congress of the United States. Congr
        Quarterly.
    Congressional Roll Call, 1969. Congr
        Quarterly.
    Congressional Roll Call, 1970. Congr
        Quarterly.
    Congressional Roll Call 1971. Congr Quarterly.
    Congressional Roll Call 1973. Congr Quarterly.
    Congressional Roll Call 1974. Congr Quarterly.
    Congressional Roll Call, 1975. Congr
        Quarterly.
    Congressional Roll Call, 1976. Congr
        Quarterly.
    Congressional Roll Call, 1977. Congr
        Quarterly.
    Congressional Roll Call: 1978. Congr
        Quarterly.
    ed. Consumer Protection: Gains & Setbacks.
        Congr Quarterly.
    Continuing Energy Crisis in America. Congr
        Quarterly.
    Crime & Justice: Trends & Directions. Congr
        Quarterly.
    Editorial Research Reports on the Women's
        Movement. Congr Quarterly.
    Education for a Nation. Congr Quarterly.
    Energy Policy. Congr Quarterly.
    ERR: Advances in Science. Congr Quarterly.
    ERR: Rights Revolution. Congr Quarterly.
    Guide to Current American Government:
        Spring 1981 Edition. Congr Quarterly.
    Guide to U. S. Elections, 1789-1974. Congr
        Quarterly.
    Historic Documents. Congr Quarterly.
    ed. Historic Documents of 1977. Congr
        Quarterly.
    Historic Documents: 1978. Congr Quarterly.
    Members of Congress Since 1789. Congr
        Quarterly.
    The Middle East: U. S. Policy, Israel, Oil & the
        Arabs. Congr Quarterly.
    National Party Conventions from 1831-1972.
        Congr Quarterly.
    Nixon: The Fifth Year of His Presidency.
        Congr Quarterly.
    Nixon: The Fourth Year. Congr Quarterly.
    Origins & Development Congress. Congr
        Quarterly.
    Powers of Congress. Congr Quarterly.
    Presidency: Nineteen Seventy-Eight. Congr
        Quarterly.
    Presidency, Nineteen Seventy-Five. Congr
        Quarterly.
    Presidency, Nineteen Seventy-Four. Congr
        Quarterly.
    ed. Presidency, Nineteen Seventy-Seven. Congr
        Quarterly.

Presidency, Seventy-Six. Congr Quarterly.
Presidential Election Since Seventeen
    Eighty-Nine. Congr Quarterly.
Supreme Court & Individual Rights. Congr
    Quarterly.
The Supreme Court, Justice & the Law. Congr
    Quarterly.
Taxes, Jobs, & Inflation. Congr Quarterly.
Urban America: Policies & Problems. Congr
    Quarterly.
U.S. Defense Policy: Weapons, Strategy &
    Commitments. Congr Quarterly.
Washington Information Directory. Times Bks.
Congressional Quarterly Service. *see* Congressional
    Quarterly Service, Washington, D.C.
Congressional Quarterly Service, Washington, D.C.
    xCongressional Quarterly Service.
    Congressional Districts in the Nineteen
        Seventies. Congr Quarterly.
    Historic Documents, Volume Four. Congr
        Quarterly.
    Nixon: The First Year of His Presidency.
        Congr Quarterly.
    Nixon: The Third Year. Congr Quarterly.
Congressional Quarterly Staff. *see* Congressional
    Quarterly, Inc.
Congreve. *see* Congreve, William.
Congreve, William.
    xCongreve.
    Love for Love. Norton.
    xCongreve, William.
    Love for Love. Hill & Wang.
    Love for Love. U of Nebr Pr.
Coninx, Raymond G. *see* Coninx, Raymond G. F.
Coninx, Raymond G. F.
    xConinx, Raymond G.
    Foreign Exchange Today. Halsted Pr.
    Foreign Exchange Today. Wiley.
Conkin, Paul A. *see* Conkin, Paul Keith.
Conkin, Paul K. *see* Conkin, Paul Keith.
Conkin, Paul Keith.
    xConkin, Paul A.
    A History of Recent America. AHM Pub.
    xConkin, Paul K.
    Puritans & Pragmatists: Eight Eminent
        American Thinkers. Ind U Pr.
Conklin, Drue K.
    xConklin, Drue K.
    ed. The Official Scrabble Players Handbook.
        Crown.
Conklin, Gladys. *see* Conklin, Gladys (Plemon).
Conklin, Gladys (Plemon).
    xConklin, Gladys.
    Chimpanzee Roams the Forest. Holiday.
    Fairy Rings & Other Mushrooms. Holiday.
    Giraffe Lives in Africa. Holiday.
    How Insects Grow. Holiday.
    If I Were a Bird. Holiday.
    Lucky Ladybugs. Holiday.
    Tarantula, the Giant Spider. Holiday.
    When Insects Are Babies. Holiday.
Conklin, Gladys Plemon.
    xConklin, Gladys.
    Black Widow Spider -- Danger!. Holiday.
    The Bug Club Book: A Handbook for Young
        Bug Collectors. Holiday.
    I Caught a Lizard. Holiday.
    I Like Beetles. Holiday.
    I Watch Flies. Holiday.
    Journey of the Gray Whales. Holiday.
    The Llamas of South America. Holiday.
    The Octopus & Other Cephalopods. Holiday.
Conklin, Harold C.
    xConklin, Harold C.
    Folk Classification: A Topically Arranged
        Bibliography of Contemporary & Background
        References Through 1971. Yale U Anthro.
Conklin, John E.
    xConklin, John E.

The Impact of Crime. Macmillan.
Conklin, Marie E. *see* Conklin, Marie Eckhardt.
Conklin, Marie Eckhardt, 1908-
    xConklin, Marie E.
    Genetic & Biochemical Aspects of the
        Development of Datura. S Karger.
Conklin, Mike.
    xConklin, Mike.
    Inside Football. Contemp Bks.
Conklin, Paul S. *see* Conklin, Paul Salisbury.
Conklin, Paul Salisbury, 1895-
    xConklin, Paul S.
    History of Hamlet Criticism 1601-1821.
        Humanities.
Conklin, Robert.
    xConklin, Robert.
    How to Get People to Do Things. Contemp
        Bks.
Conkling, J. Christopher.
    xConkling, J. Christopher.
    Joseph Smith Chronology. Deseret Bk.
Conley, C. H. *see* Conley, Carey Herbert.
Conley, Carey Herbert, 1879-
    xConley, C. H.
    First English Translators of the Classics.
        Kennikat.
Conley, John, 1912 (june 1)-
    xConley, John.
    Face-Lift Operation. C C Thomas.
    Regional Flaps of the Head & Neck. Saunders.
Conley, John. *see* Conley, John J.
Conley, John J.
    xConley, John.
    Complications of Head & Neck Surgery.
        Saunders.
Conley, Patrick T.
    xConley, Patrick T.
    Catholicism in Rhode Island: The Formative
        Era. Ri Pubns Soc.
Conley, Thomas H.
    xConley, Tom.
    Pastoral Care for Personal Growth. Judson.
Conley, Tom. *see* Conley, Thomas H.
Conley, Virginia C.
    xConley, Virginia C.
    Curriculum & Instruction in Nursing. Little.
Conley, William, 1948-
    xConley, William.
    Computer Optimization Techniques. McGraw.
    Computer Optimization Techniques. Petrocelli.
Conlin, Joseph R. *see* Conlin, Joseph Robert.
Conlin, Joseph Robert.
    xConlin, Joseph R.
    American Anti-War Movements. Glencoe.
    The American Radical Press: 1880-1960.
        Greenwood.
Conlon, Frank F.
    xConlon, Frank F.
    A Caste in a Changing World: The Chitrapur
        Saraswat Brahmans, 1700-1935. U of Cal Pr.
Conlon, Kathleen, 1943-
    xConlon, Kathleen.
    A Move in the Game. Fawcett.
    A Move in the Game. Stein & Day.
Conlon, V. M. *see* Conlon, Vera M.
Conlon, Vera M.
    xConlon, V. M.
    Camera Techniques in Archaeology. St Martin.
Conn. *see* Conn, Harold O.
Conn, Bruce C.
    xConn, Bruce C.
    Horror of Cabrini-Green. Holloway.
Conn, Charles P. *see* Conn, Charles Paul.
Conn, Charles Paul.
    xConn, Charles P.
    A Faith to Keep. Pathway Pr.
    The Meaning of Marriage. Pathway Pr.
    The Relevant Record. Pathway Pr.
    The Winner's Circle. Berkley Pub.
    xConn, Charles W.

jt. auth. The Relevant Record. Pathway Pr.
    xConn, Paul.
    The Possible Dream. Berkley Pub.
    The Winner's Circle. Revell.
Conn, Charles W.
    xConn, Charles W.
    Highlights of Hebrew History. Pathway Pr.
Conn, Charles W. *see* Conn, Charles Paul.
Conn, Eric E.
    xConn, Eric E.
    Outlines of Biochemistry. Wiley.
Conn, George H. *see* Conn, George Harold.
Conn, George Harold, 1890-
    xConn, George H.
    The Arabian Horse in America. Arco.
    ed. The Arabian Horse in Fact, Fantasy &
        Fiction. Arco.
    How to Get a Horse & Live with It. Arco.
Conn, Hadley L.
    xConn, Hadley L.
    ed. Cardiac & Vascular Diseases. Lea &
        Febiger.
Conn, Harold O.
    xConn.
    The Hepatic Coma Syndromes & Lactulose.
        Williams & Wilkins.
Conn, Jack F., 1952-
    xConn, Jack F.
    Non-Abelian Minimal Closed Ideals of
        Transitive Lie Algebras. Princeton U Pr.
Conn, Martha O. *see* Conn, Martha Orr.
Conn, Martha Orr.
    xConn, Martha O.
    Crazy to Fly. Atheneum.
Conn, Paul. *see* Conn, Charles Paul.
Conn, Stewart.
    xConn, Stewart.
    Ambush & Other Poems. Macmillan.
Connah, Graham.
    xConnah, Graham.
    The Archaeology of Benin: Excavations &
        Other Researches in & Around Banin City,
        Nigeria. Oxford U Pr.
Connatser, Larry A. *see* Connatser, Larry Allen.
Connatser, Larry Allen, 1947-
    xConnatser, Larry A.
    The Effect of an Academic Program on the
        Moral Development of Incarcerated Young
        Adults. R & E Res Assoc.
Connaughton, Howard W.
    xConnaughton, Howard W.
    Craftsmen in Business: A Guide to Financial
        Management & Taxes. Am Craft.
Connecticut. General Assembly.
    xConnecticut General Assembly.
    Minutes of the Testimony Taken Before John
        Q. Wilson, Joseph Eaton, & Morris
        Woodruff, Committee from the General
        Assembly, to Inquire into the Condition of
        the Connecticut State Prison. Arno.
Connecticut Historical Society. *see* Connecticut
    Historical Society, Hartford.
Connecticut Historical Society, Hartford.
    xConnecticut Historical Society.
    Collections of the Connecticut Historical
        Society. AMS Pr.
Connell, Candace.
    xConnell, Candace.
    The Red Turrets of Orne. Doubleday.
Connell, Evan. *see* Connell, Evan S.
Connell, Evan S, 1924-
    xConnell, Evan.
    Double Honeymoon. Avon.
    xConnell, Evan S.
    Anatomy Lesson, & Other Stories. Arno.
    The Connoisseur. Knopf.
    A Long Desire. HR&W.
    The White Lantern. HR&W.
Connell, John.
    xConnell, John.

Assessing Village Labour Situations in
Developing Countries. Oxford U Pr.
The End of Tradition: Country Life in Central
Surrey. Routledge & Kegan.
Connell, Kenneth H. *see* Connell, Kenneth Hugh.
Connell, Kenneth Hugh.
xConnell, Kenneth H.
The Population of Ireland, 1750-1845.
Greenwood.
Connell, R. W. *see* Connell, Robert William.
Connell, Richard E. *see* Connell, Richard Edward.
Connell, Richard Edward, 1893-1949
xConnell, Richard E.
Apes & Angels. Arno.
Connell, Robert William.
xConnell, R. W.
The Childs Construction of Politics. Intl Schol
Bk Serv.
Connell, W. F. *see* Connell, William Fraser.
Connell, William F. *see* Connell, William Fraser.
Connell, William Fraser.
xConnell, W. F.
A History of Education in the Twentieth
Century World. Tchrs Coll.
Studying the Local Community: Education in
Action. Allen Unwin.
xConnell, William F.
Educational Thought & Influence of Matthew
Arnold. Greenwood.
Connellan, Leo.
xConnellan, Leo.
Another Poet in New York. Living Poets.
Crossing America. Penmaen Pr.
First Selected Poems. U of Pittsburgh Pr.
Connellan, Thomas K., 1942-
xConnellan, Thomas K.
The Brontosaurus Principle: A Manual for
Corporate Survival. P-H.
Connelly, J. A. *see* Connelly, Joseph Alvin.
Connelly, James F. *see* Connelly, James Francis.
Connelly, James Francis.
xConnelly, James F.
Precalculus Mathematics: A Functional
Approach. Macmillan.
Connelly, Joseph Alvin.
xConnelly, J. A.
Analog Integrated Circuits: Devices, Circuits,
Systems & Applications. Wiley.
Connelly, Thomas L. *see* Connelly, Thomas Lawrence.
Connelly, Thomas Lawrence.
xConnelly, Thomas L.
Army of the Heartland: The Army of
Tennessee, 1861-1862. La State U Pr.
Autumn of Glory: The Army of Tennessee,
1862-1865. La State U Pr.
Civil War Tennessee: Battles and Leaders. U of
Tenn Pr.
The Marble Man: Robert E Lee & His Image
in American Society. Knopf.
The Marble Man: Robert E. Lee & His Image
in American Society. La State U Pr.
The Politics of Command: Factions & Ideas in
Confederate Strategy. La State U Pr.
Connely, Willard, 1888-
xConnely, Willard.
Laurence Sterne As Yorick. Greenwood.
Conner, Berenice G. *see* Conner, Berenice Gillette.
Conner, Berenice Gillette.
xConner, Berenice G.
Dyes from Your Garden. E A Seemann.
Conner, Daniel E. *see* Conner, Daniel Ellis.
Conner, Daniel Ellis, 1837-1920
xConner, Daniel E.
Confederate in the Colorado Gold Fields. U of
Okla Pr.
Conner, Frederick W. *see* Conner, Frederick William.
Conner, Frederick William, 1909-
xConner, Frederick W.

Cosmic Optimism: A Study of the
Interpretation of Evolution by American
Poets from Emerson to Robinson. Octagon.
Conner, J. Richard. *see* Conner, James Richard.
Conner, James Richard.
xConner, J. Richard.
ed. Economics & Decision Making for
Environmental Quality. U Presses Fla.
Conner, Michael.
xConner, Michael.
I Am Not the Other Houdini. Har-Row.
I Am Not the Other Houdini. Har-Row.
Conner, P. E. *see* Conner, Pierre E.
Conner, Patrick, 1947-
xConner, Patrick.
Oriental Architecture in the West. Thames
Hudson.
Savage Ruskin. Wayne St U Pr.
Conner, Pierre E.
xConner, P. E.
Differentiable Periodic Maps. Springer-Verlag.
xConner, Pierre E.
Lectures on the Action of a Finite Group.
Springer-Verlag.
Conner, Ross F.
xConner, Ross F.
Attorneys As Activists: Evaluating the
American Bar Association's BASICS
Program. Sage.
Conners, Kenneth W. *see* Conners, Kenneth Wray.
Conners, Kenneth Wray.
xConners, Kenneth W.
Lord, Have You Got a Minute?. Judson.
Connery, R. H. *see* Connery, Robert Howe.
Connery, Robert H. *see* Connery, Robert Howe.
Connery, Robert Hough, 1907-
xConnery, Robert Howe.
The Navy & the Industrial Mobilization in
World War II. Da Capo.
Connery, Robert Howe.
xConnery, R. H.
The Federal Government & Metropolitan
Areas. Arno.
xConnery, Robert H.
Governmental Problems in Wild Life
Conservation. AMS Pr.
The National Energy Problem. Lexington Bks.
Politics of Mental Health: Organizing
Community Mental Health in Metropolitan
Areas. Columbia U Pr.
Rockefeller of New York: Executive Power in
the Statehouse. Cornell U Pr.
Connery, Robert Howe. *see* Connery, Robert Hough.
Connett, W. C.
xConnett, W. C.
The Theory of Ultraspherical Multipliers. Am
Math.
Conningham, Frederic A. *see* Conningham, Frederic
Arthur.
Conningham, Frederic Arthur.
xConningham, Frederic A.
Currier & Ives Prints: An Illustrated Check
List. Crown.
Connolly, Cyril, 1903-
xConnolly, Cyril.
The Evening Colonnade. HarBraceJ.
Connolly, Eileen.
xConnolly, Eileen.
Tarot: A New Handbook for the Apprentice.
Borgo Pr.
The Tarot: A New Handbook for the
Apprentice. Newcastle Pub.
Connolly, Harold X.
xConnolly, Harold X.
A Ghetto Grows in Brooklyn. NYU Pr.
Connolly, James B. *see* Connolly, James Brendan.
Connolly, James Brendan, 1868-1957
xConnolly, James B.

Out of Gloucester. Arno.
Connolly, James E.
xConnolly, James E.
Public Speaking As Communication. Burgess.
Connolly, Thomas E. *see* Connolly, Thomas Edmund.
Connolly, Thomas Edmund, 1918-
xConnolly, Thomas E.
Swinburne's Theory of Poetry. State U NY Pr.
Connolly, Walter B.
xConnolly, Walter B.
Work Stoppages & Union Responsibility. PLI.
Connor, Anna T. *see* Connor, Anna Thomas.
Connor, Anna Thomas.
xConnor, Anna T.
Corncraft. A S Barnes.
Connor, Frances P.
xConnor, Frances P.
Education of Homebound or Hospitalized
Children. Tchrs Coll.
Connor, James P.
xConnor, James P.
Classroom Activities for Helping Hyperactive
Children. Ctr Appl Res.
Connor, Jerome J.
xConnor, Jerome J.
Analysis of Structural Member Systems. Wiley.
Connor, John W.
xConnor, John W.
Acculturation & the Retention of an Ethnic
Identity in Three Generations of Japanese
Americans. R & E Res Assoc.
A Study of the Marital Stability of Japanese
War Brides. R & E Res Assoc.
Connor, Patrick E.
xConnor, Patrick E.
Dimensions in Modern Management. HM.
Connor, R. D. *see* Connor, Robert Diggs Wimberly.
Connor, Robert Diggs Wimberly, 1878-1950
xConnor, R. D.
Ante-Bellum Builders of North Carolina.
Reprint.
Race Elements in the White Population of
North Carolina. Reprint.
Revolutionary Leaders of North Carolina.
Reprint.
Connor, Seymour V.
xConnor, Seymour V.
Broadcloth & Britches: The Santa Fe Trade.
Tex A&M Univ Pr.
Connor, Tony.
xConnor, Tony.
In the Happy Valley: Poems. Oxford U Pr.
The Memoirs of Uncle Harry: Poems. Oxford
U Pr.
Connor, Walter D.
xConnor, Walter D.
Public Opinion in European Socialist Systems.
Praeger.
Socialism, Politics & Equality: Hierarchy &
Change in Eastern Europe & the USSR.
Columbia U Pr.
Connors, Andree.
xConnors, Andree.
Amateur People. Fiction Coll.
Connors, Eugene T.
xConnors, Eugene T.
Student Discipline & the Law. Phi Delta
Kappa.
Connors, Kenneth A. *see* Connors, Kenneth Antonio.
Connors, Kenneth Antonio, 1932-
xConnors, Kenneth A.
Reaction Mechanisms in Organic Analytical
Chemistry. Wiley.
A Textbook of Pharmaceutical Analysis. Wiley.
Connors, Richard J., 1927-
xConnors, Richard J.
A Cycle of Power: The Career of Jersey City
Mayor Frank Hague. Scarecrow.
Connors, Tracy D.
xConnors, Tracy D.

The Nonprofit Organization Handbook.
  McGraw.
Conolly, Brian.
  xConolly, Brian.
    Lecture Notes in Queueing Systems. Halsted
    Pr.
Conot, Robert. *see* Conot, Robert E.
Conot, Robert E.
  xConot, Robert.
    A Streak of Luck. Bantam.
Conover, Herbert S.
  xConover, Herbert S.
    Grounds Maintenance Handbook. McGraw.
Conover, Mary B. *see* Conover, Mary H.
Conover, Mary H.
  xConover, Mary B.
    Understanding Electrocardiography:
    Physiological & Interpretive Concepts.
    Mosby.
Conover, Milton, 1890-
  xConover, Milton.
    The General Land Office: Its History,
    Activities & Organization. AMS Pr.
    The Office of Experiment Stations: Its History,
    Activities & Organization. AMS Pr.
Conover, Paul H.
  xConover, Paul H.
    Asia & Africa: Introductory Studies of
    Non-Western Societies. Merrill.
Conover, W. J.
  xConover, W. J.
    Practical Nonparametric Statistics. Wiley.
  xConover, William J.
    Practical Nonparametric Statistics. Wiley.
Conover, William J. *see* Conover, W. J.
Conquest, Robert.
  xConquest, Robert.
    Arias from a Love Opera: Other Poems.
    Macmillan.
    The Politics of Ideas in the U.S.S.R..
    Greenwood.
Conrad, Barnaby.
  xConrad, Barnaby.
    Endangered. Berkley Pub.
    Endangered. Putnam.
Conrad, Clifford L.
  xConrad, Clifford L.
    Computer Mathematics. Hayden.
Conrad, Daniel L. *see* Conrad, Daniel Lynn.
Conrad, Daniel Lynn.
  xConrad, Daniel L.
    Successful Fund Raising Techniques. Public
    Management.
Conrad, David R., 1937-
  xConrad, David R.
    Education for Transformation: Implications in
    Lewis Mumford's Ecohumanism. ETC Pubns.
Conrad, Jessie. *see* Conrad, Jessie (George).
Conrad, Jessie (George).
  xConrad, Jessie.
    Joseph Conrad As I Knew Him. Arno.
    Joseph Conrad As I Knew Him. R West.
    Joseph Conrad As I Knew Him. Scholarly.
Conrad, John P.
  xConrad, John P.
    Future of Corrections. Am Acad Pol Soc Sci.
Conrad, John P. *see* Conrad, John Phillips.
Conrad, John Phillips.
  xConrad, John P.
    Crime & Its Correction: An International
    Survey of Attitudes & Practices. U of Cal Pr.
    ed. The Evolution of Criminal Justice: A Guide
    for Practical Criminologists. Sage.
    In Fear of Each Other: Studies of
    Dangerousness in America. Lexington Bks.
Conrad, John W.
  xConrad, John W.
    Contemporary Ceramic Techniques. P-H.
Conrad, Joseph, 1857-1924
  xConrad, Joseph.

Almayer's Folly. Bentley.
Almayer's Folly. Buccaneer Bks.
Almayer's Folly. Penguin.
Conrad's Prefaces to His Works. Arno.
Conrad's Prefaces to His Works. Haskell.
The Inheritors. Gregg.
Joseph Conrad on Fiction. U of Nebr Pr.
Last Essays. Arno.
Lord Jim. Bentley.
Lord Jim. Buccaneer Bks.
Lord Jim. Dutton.
Lord Jim. HM.
Lord Jim. NAL.
Lord Jim. Penguin.
Lord Jim. Pendulum Pr.
Lord Jim. AMSCO Sch.
Lord Jim. Doubleday.
Lord Jim. Norton.
Lord Jim. Airmont.
Nostromo. NAL.
Nostromo. Penguin.
Notes on Life & Letters. Arno.
Portable Conrad. Penguin.
Tales of Unrest. Gordon Pr.
Tales of Unrest. Penguin.
Typhoon & Youth. Heinemann Ed.
Conrad, Peter.
  xConrad, Peter.
    Imagining America. Oxford U Pr.
    Shandyism: The Character of Romantic Irony.
    B&N.
Conrad, Robert, 1928-
  xConrad, Robert.
    The Destruction of Brazilian Slavery,
    1850-1888. U of Cal Pr.
Conrad, Susan P. *see* Conrad, Susan Phinney.
Conrad, Susan Phinney.
  xConrad, Susan P.
    Perish the Thought: Intellectual Women in
    Romantic America 1830-1860. Citadel Pr.
    Perish the Thought: Intellectual Women in
    Romantic America, 1830-1860. Oxford U Pr.
Conrads, Ulrich.
  xConrads, Ulrich.
    ed. Programs & Manifestoes on 20th-Century
    Architecture. MIT Pr.
Conradt, David P.
  xConradt, David P.
    The German Polity. Longman.
Conran, Shirley.
  xConran, Shirley.
    Superwoman. Bantam.
Conrat, Maisie.
  xConrat, Maisie.
    The American Farm: A Photographic History.
    HM.
Conron, John.
  xConron, John.
    ed. The American Landscape: A Critical
    Anthology of Prose & Poetry. Oxford U Pr.
Conroy, Al.
  xConroy, Al.
    Last Train to Bannock. Dell.
Conroy, Barbara.
  xConroy, Barbara.
    Library Staff Development & Continuing
    Education: Principles & Practices. Libs Unl.
Conroy, Francis Hilary, 1919-
  xConroy, Hilary.
    The Japanese Frontier in Hawaii, 1868-1898.
    Arno.
Conroy, Frank, 1936-
  xConroy, Frank.
    Stop-Time. Penguin.
Conroy, G. C. *see* Conroy, Glenn C.
Conroy, Glenn C.
  xConroy, G. C.
    Primate Postcranial Remains from the
    Oligocene of Egypt. S Karger.
Conroy, Hilary. *see* Conroy, Francis Hilary.

Conroy, Jack, 1899-
  xConroy, Jack.
    The Disinherited. Bentley.
    The Disinherited. Hill & Wang.
Conroy, Mary.
  xConroy, Mary.
    Common Sense Self-Defense: A Practical
    Manual for Students & Teachers. Mosby.
    The Rational Woman's Guide to Self-Defense.
    G&D.
Conroy, Pat.
  xConroy, Pat.
    The Great Santini. Avon.
    The Great Santini. HM.
Conservation Education Assn. *see* Conservation
  Education Association.
Conservation Education Association.
  xConservation Education Assn.
    Environmental Conservation Education: A
    Selected Annotated Bibliography-1977
    Supplement. Interstate.
  xConservation Education Association.
    Critical Index of Films on Man & His
    Environment. Interstate.
    ed. Environmental Conservation Education: A
    Selected Annotated Bibliography-1976
    Supplement. Interstate.
    Environmental Conservation Education: 1975
    Supplement. Interstate.
Conservation Foundation.
  xConservation Foundation.
    Conservation & New Economic Realities.
    Conservation Foun.
    National Parks for the Future. Conservation
    Foun.
    ed. Paying for Pollution: Water Quality &
    Effluent Charges. Conservation Foun.
    Toward Clean Water: A Guide to Citizen
    Action. Conservation Foun.
Considine, Douglas M. *see* Considine, Douglas Maxwell.
Considine, Douglas Maxwell.
  xConsidine, Douglas M.
    ed. Van Nostrand's Scientific Encyclopedia.
    Van Nos Reinhold.
Considine, Tim.
  xConsidine, Tim.
    The Photographic Dictionary of Soccer.
    Warner Bks.
Constable, Betty.
  xConstable, Betty.
    Squash Basics for Men & Women. Dutton.
Constable, G. *see* Constable, Giles.
Constable, George.
  xConstable, George.
    The Neanderthals. Silver.
    The Neanderthals. Time-Life.
Constable, Giles.
  xConstable, G.
    ed. Libellus De Diversis Ordinibus et
    Professionibus Qui Sunt in Aecclesia: Orders
    & Callings of the Church. Oxford u Pr.
  xConstable, Giles.
    Medieval Monasticism: A Select Bibliography.
    U of Toronto Pr.
Constable, J. W. *see* Constable, John W.
Constable, John W., 1922-
  xConstable, J. W.
    Church Since Pentecost. Concordia.
Constable, W. G. *see* Constable, William George.
Constable, William George, 1887-
  xConstable, W. G.
    The Painter's Workshop. Dover.
Constance, John D. *see* Constance, John Dennis.
Constance, John Dennis, 1909-
  xConstance, John D.
    How to Become a Professional Engineer.
    McGraw.
    Mechanical Engineering for Professional
    Engineers' Examinations. McGraw.
Constans, H. Philip. *see* Constans, Henry Philip.

Constans, Henry Philip, 1928-
xConstans, H. Philip.
Fit for Freedom. U Pr of Amer.
Constans, Jacques.
xConstans, Jacques A.
Marine Sources of Energy. Pergamon.
Constans, Jacques A. *see* Constans, Jacques.
Constant, Constantine.
xConstant, Constantine.
The Student Earth Scientist Explores Weather.
Rosen Pr.
Constant, James.
xConstant, James N.
Gravitational Action. Pioneer Pub Co.
Introduction to Defense Radar Systems
Engineering. Hayden.
Constant, James N. *see* Constant, James.
Constant, Jules.
xConstant, Jules.
Learning Electrocardiography: A Complete
Course. Little.
Constantelos, Demetrios J.
xConstantelos, Demetrios J.
Greek Orthodox Church: Faith, History, &
Practice. Seabury.
Constantin, James A.
xConstantin, James A.
Marketing Strategy & Management. Business
Pubns.
Constantine, Eddie, 1917-
xConstantine, Eddie.
The God-Player. Ballantine.
Constantine, Larry L.
xConstantine, Larry L.
Group Marriage; A Study of Contemporary
Multilateral Marriage. Macmillan.
Constantine, Mildred.
xConstantine, Mildred.
Revolutionary Soviet Film Posters. Johns
Hopkins.
Constantinescu, C. *see* Constantinescu, Corneliu.
Constantinescu, Corneliu.
xConstantinescu, C.
Duality in Measure Theory. Springer-Verlag.
Potential Theory on Harmonic Spaces.
Springer-Verlag.
Constantinescu, F. *see* Constantinescu, Florin.
Constantinescu, Florin.
xConstantinescu, F.
Problems in Quantum Mechanics. Pergamon.
Constantino, Ernesto, 1930-
xConstantino, Ernesto.
Ilokano Dictionary. U Pr of Hawaii.
Constantino, Renato.
xConstantino, Renato.
Neocolonial Identity & Counter-Consciousness:
Essays on Cultural Decolonization. M E
Sharpe.
Constiner, Merle.
xConstiner, Merle.
Sumatra Alley. Elsevier-Nelson.
Constitutional Convention of the State of Nevada. *see*
Nevada. Constitutional Convention, 1864.
Construction Labor Reporter Editorial Staff. *see* Bureau
of National Affairs, Washington, D.C.
Consumer Credit Project.
xConsumer Credit Project.
New Credit Rights for Women. Consumer
Credit Proj.
Consumer Guide.
xConsumer Guide.

Add-a-Room. S&S.
The Complete Book of War Games. S&S.
ed. The Complete Consumer Guide for
Travelers. PB.
ed. Consumer Guide to a Flatter Stomach. PB.
The Fastest, Cheapest, Best Way to Clean
Everything. S&S.
The Food Processor Bread Cookbook. S&S.
ed. Safer More Successful Suntanning. PB.
ed. The Tool Catalog. Har-Row.
xConsumer Guide Editorial Staff.
ed. Consumer Guide Fix-It. S&S.
xConsumer Guide Editors.
The Basic Book of Ham Radio. S&S.
Blue Ribbon Canning & Preserving. S&S.
Bromeliads & Orchids. S&S.
Cacti & Other Succulents. S&S.
ed. Cars, Nineteen Swdenty Three: Best Buys,
Test Reports, & Dealer Prices. PB.
ed. CB Operator's Manual & Log. S&S.
Clay Cookery. S&S.
ed. Complete Book of CB Citizens Band Radio
& Equipment. PB.
The Complete Book of Citizen Band Radio. PB.
The Complete Book of Vans. PB.
Complete Book of Walking. S&S.
ed. Consumer Buying Guide, 1973: Best Buys
& Discount Prices. PB.
The Consumer Guide: Guns. PB.
ed. Consumer Guide: Photographic Equipment.
PB.
Consumer Guide the Food Preserver. S&S.
The Cook's Store. S&S.
Cut Flowers. S&S.
Decorating Your Office for Success. Har-Row.
Designing with Indoor Plants. S&S.
The Energy Savers Catalog. Putnam.
Food Preserver. S&S.
Food Processor Cookbook. S&S.
Gas Savers Guide. Fawcett.
ed. Getting Pests to Bug off. Crown.
Getting Your Share: Social Security, Medicare,
Government Benefits. S&S.
Hanging Plants. S&S.
The Home Energy Saver. Fawcett.
The Joy of Making Your Own. S&S.
The Pressure Cooker Cookbook. S&S.
ed. Smoke Cookery. Crown.
Special Report: How to Make Money During
Inflation-Recession. Har-Row.
Thrill Sports Catalog. Dutton.
ed. The Tool Catalog. Har-Row.
Van Ideas & Plans. S&S.
ed. Vans. S&S.
The Whole Bath Catalog. S&S.
Whole Boating Book. S&S.
Whole Car Catalog. S&S.
Whole Fishing Catalog. S&S.
Whole House Catalog. S&S.
Whole Kitchen Catalog. S&S.
Whole Kitchen Catalog. S&S.
Whole Stereo Catalog. S&S.
Your Home Is Money: Managing Your Home
for Profit. McGraw.
xConsumer Guide Magazine.
ed. Spectators Guide to Sports: Rules, Scoring,
Strategy & Competing. NAL.
xConsumer Guide Magazine Editors.

ed. Consumer Guide---Complete Guide to
Fishing Equipment. NAL.
ed. Consumer Guide---Complete Guide to
Golfing Equipment. NAL.
Consumer Guide-Complete Buying Guide to
Stereo & Tape Recorders. NAL.
Consumer Guide: Photographic Equipment
Test Reports. NAL.
Miniatures. Har-Row.
Model Airplanes. Har-Row.
Model Cars. Har-Row.
Model Military Toys. Har-Row.
Model Trains. Har-Row.
xConsumer's Guide Editors.
Caring for Your Child: A Complete Medical
Guide. Crown.
The Complete Book of Mopeds. Warner Bks.
xConsumers Guide.
ed. The Complete Book of Roller Skating. PB.
xConsumers Guide Editors.
Food Processor Cookbook. PB.
Consumer Guide Editorial Staff. *see* Consumer Guide.
Consumer Guide Editors. *see* Consumer Guide.
Consumer Guide Magazine. *see* Consumer Guide.
Consumer Guide Magazine Editors. *see* Consumer Guide.
Consumer Reports.
xConsumer Reports.
ed. Funerals: Consumers' Last Rights. Norton.
xConsumer Reports Editors.
Consumer Reports Guide to Used Cars: Model
Years 1974 Through 1977. Doubleday.
Consumer Reports Money Saving Guide to
Energy in the Home. Doubleday.
The Medicine Show. Pantheon.
Consumer Reports Editors. *see* Consumer Reports.
Consumer's Guide Editors. *see* Consumer Guide.
Consumers Guide. *see* Consumer Guide.
Consumers Guide Editors. *see* Consumer Guide.
Consumers Power Company.
xConsumers Power Company.
Fundamentals of Natural Gas. A-W.
Conta, Marcia M. *see* Conta, Marica Maher.
Conta, Marica Maher.
xConta, Marcia M.
Women for Human Rights. Raintree Pubs.
Conte, Joseph Le. *see* Le Conte, Joseph.
Conte, Sylvester B.
xConte, Sylvester B.
Positioning & Technique Handbook for
Radiologic Technologists. Mosby.
Contemporary China Institute. *see* London. University.
Contemporary China Institute.
Contemporary Programs, Inc.
xContemporary Programs Inc.
Woman's Contemporary Image: A Personal &
Professional Guide. P-H.
Contenau, G. *see* Contenau, Georges.
Contenau, Georges.
xContenau, G.
Everyday Life in Babylon & Assyria. St
Martin.
xContenau, Georges.
Everyday Life in Babylon & Assyria. Norton.
Conti, Philip M., 1916-
xConti, Philip M
The Pennsylvania State Police Force
1905-1977. Stackpole.
Contoski, Victor.
xContoski, Victor.
Broken Treaties. SBD.
Contreras, H. *see* Contreras, Heles.
Contreras, Heles.
xContreras, H.
A Theory of Word Order with Special
Reference to Spanish. Elsevier.
**Convention of Friends of Agricultural Education,
Chicago, 1871.**
xConvention of Friends of Agricultural Education,
Chicago.

Early View of the Land-Grant Colleges. U of
  Ill Pr.
Converse, A. O. see Converse, Alvin O.
Converse, Alvin O., 1932-
  xConverse, A. O.
    Optimization. Krieger.
Converse, Gordon. see Converse, Gordon N.
Converse, Gordon N.
  xConverse, Gordon.
    Come See the Place: The Holy Land Jesus
      Knew. P-H.
Converse, Philip E., 1928-
  xConverse, Philip E.
    American Social Attitudes Data Sourcebook:
      1947-1978. Harvard U Pr.
Conveyor Equipment Manufacturers Association.
  xConveyor Equipment Manufacturers Assoc.
    Belt Conveyors for Bulk Materials. CBI Pub.
Conway, Barbara L. see Conway, Barbara Lang.
Conway, Barbara Lang, 1945-
  xConway, Barbara L.
    Pediatric Neurologic Nursing. Mosby.
Conway, Darlyne.
  xConway, Darlyne.
    Depression Era Glass Handbook & Pricing
      Guide. Educator Bks.
Conway, David.
  xConway, David.
    Ritual Magic: An Occult Primer. Dutton.
Conway, Donald.
  xConway, Donald J.
    ed. Human Response to Tall Buildings. DH&R.
Conway, Donald J. see Conway, Donald.
Conway, H. McKinley. see Conway, Hobart Mckinley.
Conway, Hobart Mckinley, 1920-
  xConway, H. McKinley.
    Legislative Climates for Economic
      Development. Conway Pubns.
    New Industries of the Seventies. Conway
      Pubns.
    Pitfalls in Development. Conway Pubns.
Conway, J. B. see Conway, John B.
Conway, James A.
  xConway, James A.
    Understanding Communities. P-H.
Conway, Jim.
  xConway, Jim.
    Men in Mid-Life Crisis. Cook.
Conway, John B.
  xConway, J. B.
    A Functional Calculus for Subnormal
      Operators, II. Am Math.
    Functions of One Complex Variable.
      Springer-Verlag.
Conway, Joseph B.
  xConway, J. B.
    Creep-Rupture Data for the Refractory Metals
      to High Temperatures. Gordon.
Conway, M. D. see Conway, Moncure Daniel.
Conway, Michael.
  xConway, Michael.
    Films of Greta Garbo. Citadel Pr.
    Films of Jean Harlow. Citadel Pr.
    Films of Marilyn Monroe. Citadel Pr.
Conway, Mimi.
  xConway, Mimi.
    Rise Gonna Rise: A Portrait of Southern
      Textile Workers. Doubleday.
    Rise Gonna Rise: A Portrait of Southern
      Textile Workers. Doubleday.
Conway, Moncure D. see Conway, Moncure Daniel.
Conway, Moncure Daniel, 1832-1907
  xConway, M. D.
    Omitted Chapters of History Disclosed in the
      Life & Papers of Edmund Randolph. Da
      Capo.
  xConway, Moncure D.

Golden Hour. Negro U Pr.
Life of Nathaniel Hawthorne. Folcroft.
Life of Nathaniel Hawthorne. Haskell.
Solomon & Solomonic Literature. Haskell.
Solomon & Solomonic Literature. R West.
Thomas Carlyle. Folcroft.
Thomas Carlyle. Norwood Edns.
Conway, Richard. see Conway, Richard Walter.
Conway, Richard A.
  xConway, Richard A.
    Handbook of Industrial Waste Disposal. Van
      Nos Reinhold.
Conway, Richard Walter.
  xConway, Richard.
    Programming for Poets: A Gentle Introduction
      Using Pascal. Winthrop.
Conway, Steve.
  xConway, Steve.
    Logging Practices: Principles of Timber
      Harvesting Systems. Miller Freeman.
    Timber Cutting Practices. Miller Freeman.
Conway, Theresa.
  xConway, Theresa.
    Crimson Glory. Fawcett.
    Gabrielle. Fawcett.
Conway, William M. see Conway, William Martin
  Conway.
Conway, William Martin Conway, Baron, 1856-1937
  xConway, William M.
    The Van Eycks & Their Followers. AMS Pr.
Conwell. see Conwell, Russell Herman.
Conwell, Russell H. see Conwell, Russell Herman.
Conwell, Russell Herman, 1843-1925
  xConwell.
    Acres of Diamonds. Revell.
  xConwell, Russell H.
    Acres of Diamonds. BJ Pub Group.
    Acres of Diamonds. Har-Row.
Conybeare, C. E. see Conybeare, C. E. B.
Conybeare, C. E. B.
  xConybeare, C. E.
    Geomorphology of Oil & Gas Fields in
      Sandstone Bodies. Elsevier.
Conybeare, W. J. see Conybeare, William John.
Conybeare, William John.
  xConybeare, W. J.
    Life & Epistles of St. Paul. Eerdmans.
    The Life & Epistles of St. Paul. Gordon Pr.
Conyngham, William J.
  xConyngham, William J.
    Industrial Management in the Soviet Union:
      The Role of the CPSU in Industrial
      Decision-Making, 1917-1970. Hoover Inst Pr.
Conze, Edward, 1904-
  xConze, Edward.
    ed. Buddhist Texts Through the Ages.
      Har-Row.
Conze, Werner.
  xConze, Werner.
    The Shaping of the German Nation: A
      Historical Analysis. St Martin.
Conzelmann, Hans.
  xConzelmann, Hans.
    History of Primitive Christianity. Abingdon.
Coodley, Eugene L., 1920-
  xCoodley, Eugene L.
    ed. Diagnostic Enzymology. Lea & Febiger.
Coody, Betty.
  xCoody, Betty F.
    Using Literature with Young Children. Wm C
      Brown.
Coody, Betty F. see Coody, Betty.
Coogan, Michael D. see Coogan, Michael David.
Coogan, Michael David.
  xCoogan, Michael D.
    ed. Stories from Ancient Canaan. Westminster.
Coogler, J. Gordon.
  xCoogler, J. Gordon.
    Purely Original Verse. C H Neuffer.
Cook, A. H. see Cook, Alan H.

Cook, Adrian.
  xCook, Adrian.
    The Alabama Claims: American Politics &
      Anglo-American Relations, 1865-1872.
      Cornell U Pr.
    The Armies of the Streets: The New York City
      Draft Riots of 1863. U Pr of Ky.
Cook, Alan H.
  xCook, A. H.
    Celestial Masers. Cambridge U Pr.
Cook, Albert. see Cook, Albert Spaulding.
Cook, Albert S. see Cook, Albert Stanburrough.
Cook, Albert Spaulding.
  xCook, Albert.
    Meaning of Fiction. Wayne St U Pr.
Cook, Albert Stanburrough, 1853-1927
  xCook, Albert S.
    Chaucerian Papers. AMS Pr.
    Concordance to Beowulf. Folcroft.
    Concordance to Beowulf. Gale.
    Concordance to Beowulf. Haskell.
    A Concordance to English Poems of Thomas
      Gray. Folcroft.
    A Concordance to the English Poems of
      Thomas Gray. Peter Smith.
    Historical Background of Chaucer's Knight.
      Haskell.
    Last Months of Chaucer's Earliest Patron.
      AMS Pr.
    A Literary Middle English Reader. Folcroft.
Cook, Alice H. see Cook, Alice Hanson.
Cook, Alice Hanson.
  xCook, Alice H.
    Introduction to Japanese Trade Unionism. NY
      Sch Indus Rel.
    The Working Mother: A Survey of Problems &
      Programs in Nine Countries. NY Sch Indus
      Rel.
Cook, Ann.
  xCook, Ann.
    What Was It Like?: When Your Grandparents
      Were Your Age. Pantheon.
Cook, Anna M. see Cook, Anna Maria Green.
Cook, Anna Maria Green, 1844-1936
  xCook, Anna M.
    History of Baldwin County Georgia. Reprint.
Cook, Arthur N. see Cook, Arthur Norton.
Cook, Arthur Norton, 1896-
  xCook, Arthur N.
    British Enterprise in Nigeria. Biblio Dist.
Cook, B. F.
  xCook, B. F.
    ed. Greek & Roman Art in the British
      Museum. Barron.
Cook, Barbara, 1939-
  xCook, Barbara.
    How to Raise Good Kids. Bethany Fell.
Cook, Barbara I.
  xCook, Barbara I.
    Counseling Women. HM.
Cook, Bernadine.
  xCook, Bernadine.
    Looking for Susie. A-W.
Cook, Bruce, 1932-
  xCook, Bruce.
    Listen to the Blues. Scribner.
Cook, Charles E.
  xCook, Charles E.
    Radar Signals: An Introduction to Theory &
      Application. Acad Pr.
Cook, Chris.
  xCook, Chris.
    By-Elections in British Politics. St Martin.
    jt. auth. English Historical Facts, 1485-1603.
      Rowman.
  xCook, Christopher.

History of the Great Trains. HarBraceJ.
Longman Atlas of Modern British History: A
  Visual Guide to British Society & Politics,
  1700-1970. Longman.
Cook, Christopher. see Cook, Chris.
Cook, Clarence. see Cook, Clarence Chatham.
Cook, Clarence Chatham, 1828-1900
  xCook, Clarence.
    The House Beautiful: Essays on Beds & Tables,
      Stools & Candlesticks. Caroline Hse.
    The House Beautiful: Essays on Beds & Tables,
      Stools & Candlesticks. North River.
Cook, Constance E. see Cook, Constance Ewing.
Cook, Constance Ewing.
  xCook, Constance E.
    Nuclear Power & Legal Advocacy: The
      Environmentalists & the Courts. Lexington
      Bks.
Cook, D. B. see Cook, David B.
Cook, David, fl. 1965-
  xCook, David.
    African Literature: A Critical View. Longman.
Cook, David B.
  xCook, D. B.
    Ab Initio Valence Calculations in Chemistry.
      Halsted Pr.
    Structures & Approximations for Electrons in
      Molecules. Halsted Pr.
Cook, David M. see Cook, David Marsden.
Cook, David Marsden, 1938-
  xCook, David M.
    The Theory of the Electromagnetic Field. P-H.
Cook, David R.
  xCook, David R.
    Guide to Educational Research. Allyn.
Cook, E. T. see Cook, Edward Tyas.
Cook, Edward. see Cook, Edward Tyas.
Cook, Edward M., 1944-
  xCook, Edward M.
    The Fathers of the Towns: Leadership &
      Community Structure in Eighteenth Century
      New England. Johns Hopkins.
Cook, Edward T. see Cook, Edward Tyas.
Cook, Edward Tyas, Sir, 1857-1919
  xCook, E. T.
    The Life of John Ruskin. Arden Lib.
  xCook, Edward.
    More Literary Recreations. R West.
  xCook, Edward T.
    Life of John Ruskin. Haskell.
    Literary Recreations. Arno.
    More Literary Recreations. Arno.
Cook, Eleanor.
  xCook, Eleanor.
    Browning's Lyrics: An Exploration. U of
      Toronto Pr.
Cook, Fay L. see Cook, Fay Lomax.
Cook, Fay Lomax.
  xCook, Fay L.
    Who Should Be Helped?: Public Support for
      Social Services. Sage.
Cook, Francis H.
  xCook, Francis H.
    Hua-Yen Buddhism: The Jewel Net of Indra.
      Pa St U Pr.
Cook, Fred J.
  xCook, Fred J.

American Political Bosses & Machines. Watts.
    City Cop. Doubleday.
    The Cuban Missile Crisis, October 1962: The
      U. S. & Russia Face a Nuclear Showdown.
      Watts.
    Lobbying in American Politics. Watts.
    Privateers of Seventy Six. Bobbs.
    Storm Before Dawn. Condor Pub Co.
    A Two-Dollar Bet Means Murder. Greenwood.
    The U-2 Incident, May, 1960: An American
      Spy-Plane Downed Over Russia Intensifies
      the Cold War. Watts.
Cook (G. and D.) and Company, New Haven.
  xCook, G. D., & Co.
    Illustrated Catalogue of Carriages & Special
      Business Advertiser. Dover.
Cook, G. C. see Cook, Gordon Charles.
Cook, G. D., & Co. see Cook (G. and D.) and Company,
  New Haven.
Cook, Gail C. see Cook, Gail C. A.
Cook, Gail C. A.
  xCook, Gail C.
    ed. Opportunity for Choice: A Goal for
      Women in Canada. Unipub.
Cook, Gerhard A. see Cook, Gerhard Albert.
Cook, Gerhard Albert, 1907-
  xCook, Gerhard A.
    A Survey of Modern Industrial Chemistry. Ann
      Arbor Science.
Cook, Gillian. see Cook, Gillian P.
Cook, Gillian P.
  xCook, Gillian.
    Spatial Dynamics of Business Growth in the
      Witwatersrand. U Chicago Dept Geog.
Cook, Gladys F. see Cook, Gladys Emerson.
Cook, Gladys Emerson, 1899-
  xCook, Gladys E.
    Drawing Dogs. G&D.
Cook, Gordon Charles.
  xCook, G. C.
    Tropical Gastroenterology. Oxford U Pr.
Cook, Graeme.
  xCook, Graeme.
    Commandos in Action. Taplinger.
    None but the Valiant: Exciting True War
      Stories in the Air & at Sea. Taplinger.
Cook, Harold J. see Cook, Harold James.
Cook, Harold James, 1887-
  xCook, Harold J.
    Tales of the 04 Ranch: Recollections of Harold
      J. Cook, 1887-1909. U of Nebr Pr.
Cook, Harvey R.
  xCook, Harvey R.
    More Profits Through Advertising. Sterling.
Cook, J. see Cook, James Wilfred.
Cook, J. E. see Cook, Jimmie E.
Cook, J. M. see Cook, John M.
Cook, James. see Cook, James Graham.
Cook, James G. see Cook, James Gordon.
Cook, James Gordon.
  xCook, James G.
    Our Astonishing Atmosphere. Dial.
    Our Living Soil. Dial.
Cook, James Graham, 1925-
  xCook, James.
    Remedies & Rackets: The Truth About Patent
      Medicines Today. Arno.
Cook, James Wilfred, 1900-
  xCook, J.
    Progress in Organic Chemistry. Plenum Pub.
Cook, Jan. see Cook, Joseph J.
Cook, Jan L. see Cook, Jan Leslie.
Cook, Jan Leslie.
  xCook, Jan L.
    The Mysterious Undersea World. Natl Geog.
Cook, Jeffrey.
  xCook, Jeffrey.
    The Architecture of Bruce Goff. Har-Row.
Cook, Jerry.
  xCook, Jerry.

Love, Acceptance & Forgiveness. Regal.
Cook, Jimmie E.
  xCook, J. E.
    Remediating Reading Disabilities: Simple
      Things That Work. Aspen Systems.
Cook, Joan M. see Cook, Joan Marble.
Cook, Joan Marble.
  xCook, Joan M.
    In Defense of Homo Sapiens. Dell.
    In Defense of Homo Sapiens. FS&G.
Cook, John E.
  xCook, John E.
    What You Should Know About Data
      Processing. Oceana.
Cook, John H. see Cook, John Harrison.
Cook, John Harrison, 1881-
  xCook, John H.
    A Study of the Mill Schools of North Carolina.
      AMS Pr.
Cook, John M.
  xCook, J. M.
    The Troad: An Archaeological & Topographical
      Study. Oxford U Pr.
Cook, John P. see Cook, John Philip.
Cook, John Philip.
  xCook, John P.
    Composite Construction Methods. Wiley.
Cook, John W. see Cook, John William.
Cook, John William.
  xCook, John W.
    Auditing: Philosophy & Technique. HM.
Cook, Joseph. see Cook, Joseph J.
Cook, Joseph J.
  xCook, Jan.
    jt. auth. Coastal Fishing for Beginners. Dodd.
  xCook, Joseph.
    Nightmare World of the Shark. Dodd.
  xCook, Joseph J.
    Coastal Fishing for Beginners. Dodd.
    The Incredible Atlantic Herring. Dodd.
    Nocturnal World of the Lobster. Dodd.
    Wonders of the Pelican World. Dodd.
Cook, Kenneth.
  xCook, Kenneth.
    Play Little Victims. Pergamon.
Cook, L. M. see Cook, Laurence Martin.
Cook, Laurence Martin.
  xCook, L. M.
    Population Genetics. Methuen Inc.
Cook, Lloyd A. see Cook, Lloyd Allen.
Cook, Lloyd Allen.
  xCook, Lloyd A.
    ed. Toward Better Human Relations. Arno.
Cook, M. see Cook, Michael Garnet.
Cook, Michael Garnet.
  xCook, M.
    Archives Administration: A Manual for
      Intermediate & Smaller Organizations & for
      Local Government. Dawson Pub.
Cook, Myra B.
  xCook, Myra B.
    Dynamic Teaching in the Elementary School.
      P-H.
Cook, N. H. see Cook, Nathan H.
Cook, Nathan H.
  xCook, N. H.
    Manufacturing Analysis. A-W.
Cook, Peter.
  xCook, Peter.
    ed. The Complete Book of Sailing. Doubleday.
Cook, Ray L. see Cook, Ray Lewis.
Cook, Ray Lewis.
  xCook, Ray L.
    Soil Management for Conservation &
      Production. Wiley.
Cook, Raymond A. see Cook, Raymond Allen.
Cook, Raymond Allen.
  xCook, Raymond A.

Fire from the Flint: The Amazing Careers of
Thomas Dixon. Blair.
Cook, Reginald L. *see* Cook, Reginald Lansing.
Cook, Reginald Lansing, 1903-
xCook, Reginald L.
Passage to Walden. Russell.
Cook, Richard I.
xCook, Richard I.
Sir Samuel Garth. Twayne.
Cook, Richard J.
xCook, Richard J.
Rails Across the Midlands. Golden West.
Super Power Steam Locomotives. Golden
West.
Cook, Richard M.
xCook, Richard M.
Carson McCullers. Ungar.
Cook, Robert A., 1912-
xCook, Robert A.
Walk with the King Today. Christian Herald.
Cook, Robin, 1940-
xCook, Robin.
Sphinx. NAL.
Sphinx. Putnam.
Sphinx. G K Hall.
Cook, S. T. *see* Cook, Stephen T.
Cook, Samuel F. *see* Cook, Samuel Fletcher.
Cook, Samuel Fletcher, 1842-
xCook, Samuel F.
Drummond Island: The Story of the British
Occupation 1815-1828. Black Letter.
Cook, Scott.
xCook, Scott.
ed. Markets in Oaxaca. U of Tex Pr.
Cook, Sherburne F. *see* Cook, Sherburne Friend.
Cook, Sherburne Friend, 1896-1974
xCook, Sherburne F.
The Conflict Between the California Indian &
White Civilization. AMS Pr.
The Conflict Between the California Indian &
White Civilization. U of Cal Pr.
The Population of Central Mexico in the
Sixteenth Century. AMS Pr.
The Population of the California Indians
1769-1970. U of Cal Pr.
Cook, Shirley.
xCook, Shirley.
illus. Diary of a Fat Housewife. Accent Bks.
Diary of a Jogging Housewife. Accent Bks.
Cook, Stanley A. *see* Cook, Stanley Arthur.
Cook, Stanley Arthur, 1873-1949
xCook, Stanley A.
An Introduction to the Bible. Greenwood.
Cook, Stephen T.
xCook, S. T.
ed. Current Issues in Fiscal Policy. Biblio Dist.
Cook, Susan.
xCook, Susan.
The Alvin Ailey American Dance Theater.
Morrow.
Cook, Sylvia J. *see* Cook, Sylvia Jenkins.
Cook, Sylvia Jenkins, 1943-
xCook, Sylvia J.
From Tobacco Road to Route 66: The
Southern Poor White in Fiction. U of NC Pr.
Cook, T. M. *see* Cook, Trevor Morgan.
Cook, Terri.
xCook, Terri.
Family Guide to Honolulu & the Island of
Oahu. Hawaiian Serv.
Cook, Thomas D.
xCook, Thomas D.
ed. Qualitative & Quantitative Methods in
Evaluation Research. Sage.
Cook, Thomas M.
xCook, Thomas M.
Introduction to Management Science. P-H.
Cook, Tim. *see* Cook, Timothy.
Cook, Timothy.
xCook, Tim.

Vagrant Alcoholics. Routledge & Kegan.
Cook, Trevor Morgan.
xCook, T. M.
Chemical Plant & Its Operation. Pergamon.
Cook, W. Robert.
xCook, W. Robert.
The Theology of John. Moody.
Cook, Walter A. *see* Cook, Walter Anthony.
Cook, Walter Anthony, 1922-
xCook, Walter A.
Case Grammar: The Development of the
Matrix Model(1970-1976). Georgetown U Pr.
Introduction to Tagmemic Analysis.
Georgetown U Pr.
Introduction to Tagmemic Analysis. Irvington.
Cook, Walter L.
xCook, Walter L.
Table Prayers for Children. Bethany Pr.
Cook, Wanda D.
xCook, Wanda D.
Adult Literacy Education in the United States.
Intl Reading.
Cook, Warren L.
xCook, Warren L.
Flood Tide of Empire: Spain & the Pacific
Northwest, 1543-1819. Yale U Pr.
Cook, William H., 1931-
xCook, William H.
Success, Motivation, & the Scriptures.
Broadman.
Cook, William W. *see* Cook, William Wallace.
Cook, William Wallace, 1867-1933
xCook, William W.
Adrift in the Unknown: Queer Adventures in a
Queer Realm. Arno.
Cast Away at the Pole. Arno.
Cooke, Alistair, 1908-
xCooke, Alistair.
Alistair Cooke's America. Knopf.
The Americans. Berkley Pub.
The Americans. G K Hall.
Six Men. Berkley Pub.
Six Men. G K Hall.
Six Men. Knopf.
Talk About America. Knopf.
xCooke, Alistar.
Six Men. Berkley Pub.
Cooke, Alistar. *see* Cooke, Alistair.
Cooke, Ann.
xCooke, Ann.
Giraffes at Home. T Y Crowell.
Cooke, Barclay.
xCooke, Barclay.
Championship Backgammon: Learning Through
Master Play. P-H.
Cooke, Bernard. *see* Cooke, Bernard J.
Cooke, Bernard J.
xCooke, Bernard.
Formation of Faith. Loyola.
Cooke, Cynthia W.
xCooke, Cynthia W.
MS. Guide to a Woman's Health: The Most
up-to-Date Guide to Woman's Health & Well
Being. Doubleday.
Cooke, David C. *see* Cooke, David Coxe.
Cooke, David Coxe, 1917-
xCooke, David C.
How Money Is Made. Dodd.
Taiwan--Island China. Dodd.
Cooke, Deryck.
xCooke, Deryck.
I Saw the World End: A Study of Wagner's
Ring. Oxford U Pr.
Cooke, Donald E. *see* Cooke, Donald Ewin.
Cooke, Donald Ewin, 1916-
xCooke, Donald E.

America's Great Document - the Constitution.
Hammond Inc.
Atlas of the Presidents. Hammond Inc.
Presidents in Uniform. Hastings.
Cooke, Dwight.
xCooke, Dwight.
There Is No Asia. Kennikat.
Cooke, Edward F. *see* Cooke, Edward Francis.
Cooke, Edward Francis, 1923-
xCooke, Edward F.
Detailed Analysis of the Constitution.
Littlefield.
Guide to Pennsylvania Politics. Greenwood.
Cooke, Gerald, 1943-
xCooke, Gerald.
The Role of the Forensic Psychologist. C C
Thomas.
Cooke, Grace M. *see* Cooke, Grace Macgowan.
Cooke, Grace Macgowan, 1863-1944
xCooke, Grace M.
The Grapple. AMS Pr.
Cooke, Hereward Lester.
xCooke, Hereward Lester.
Painting Techniques of the Masters.
Watson-Guptill.
Cooke, John D. *see* Cooke, John Daniel.
Cooke, John Daniel.
xCooke, John D.
English Literature of the Victorian Period.
Russell.
Cooke, Marjorie B. *see* Cooke, Marjorie Benton.
Cooke, Marjorie Benton, 1876-1920
xCooke, Marjorie B.
Dramatic Episodes. Core Collection.
Cooke, Michael. *see* Cooke, Michael G.
Cooke, Michael G.
xCooke, Michael.
Acts of Inclusion: Studies Bearing on an
Elementary Theory of Romanticism. Yale U
Pr.
Cooke, Nelson M. *see* Cooke, Nelson Magor.
Cooke, Nelson Magor.
xCooke, Nelson M.
Arithmetic Review for Electronics. McGraw.
Cooke, P. St. George. *see* Cooke, Philip St. George.
Cooke, Philip P. *see* Cooke, Philip Pendleton.
Cooke, Philip Pendleton, 1816-1850
xCooke, Philip P.
Froissart Ballads, & Other Poems. Arno.
Cooke, Philip St. George, 1809-1895
xCooke, P. St. George.
Conquest of New Mexico & California.
Sullivan Bks Intl.
Cooke, Robert, 1935-
xCooke, Robert.
Improving on Nature: The Brave New World
of Genetic Engineering. Times Bks.
Cooke, Robert W.
xCooke, Robert W.
Designing with Light on Paper & Film. Davis
Mass.
Cooke, Roderic.
xCooke, Roderic C.
Fungi, Man & His Environment. Longman.
Cooke, Roderic C. *see* Cooke, Roderic.
Cooke, Ronald U.
xCooke, Ronald U.
Arroyos & Environmental Change in the
American South-West. Oxford U Pr.
Geomorphology in Deserts. U of Cal Pr.
Cooke, Rose. *see* Cooke, Rose (Terry).
Cooke, Rose (Terry), 1827-1892
xCooke, Rose.

Huckleberries Gathered from New England
Hills. Mss Info.
Huckleberries Gathered from New England
Hills. Somerset Pub.
Somebody's Neighbors. Mss Info.
The Sphinx's Children & Other People. Mss
Info.
Cooke, Thomas D. see Cooke, Thomas Darlington.
Cooke, Thomas Darlington.
xCooke, Thomas D.
ed. The Humor of the Fabliaux: A Collection
of Critical Essays. U of Mo Pr.
The Old French & Chaucerian Fabliaux: A
Study of Their Comic Climax. U of Mo Pr.
Cooke, W. Bridge. see Cooke, William Bridge.
Cooke, William Bridge.
xCooke, W. Bridge.
Ecology of Fungi. CRC Pr.
Cookenboo, Leslie. see Cookenboo, Leslie J.
Cookenboo, Leslie J.
xCookenboo, Leslie.
Crude Oil Pipe Lines & Competition in the Oil
Industry & Costs of Operating Crude Oil
Pipe Lines. Arno.
Cookey, S. J. see Cookey, Sylvanus John Sodienye.
Cookey, Sylvanus John Sodienye, 1934-
xCookey, S. J.
Britain & the Congo Question, 1885-1913.
Humanities.
Cookson, Catherine.
xCookson, Catherine.
Color Blind. NAL.
The Devil & Mary Ann. Morrow.
Dwelling Place. Bobbs.
The Garment. NAL.
Glass Virgin. Bobbs.
A Grand Man. Morrow.
The Husband. NAL.
Life & Mary Ann. Morrow.
The Long Corridor. NAL.
The Lord & Mary Ann. Morrow.
Love & Mary Ann. Morrow.
Marriage & Mary Ann. Morrow.
Mary Ann & Bill. Morrow.
Mary Ann's Angels. Morrow.
Matty Doolin. NAL.
Mrs. Flannagan's Trumpet. Lothrop.
Nipper. Bobbs.
Our John Willie. NAL.
The Unbaited Trap. NAL.
Cookson, J. E.
xCookson, J. E.
Lord Liverpool's Administration: The Crucial
Years, 1815-1822. Shoe String.
Cookson, John.
xCookson, John.
Survey of Chemical & Biological Warfare.
Monthly Rev.
Cool, J. see Cool, Steven J.
Cool, Steven J.
xCool, J.
ed. Frontiers in Visual Science: Proceedings of
the University of Houston College of
Optometry Dedication Symposium, Houston
Texas, March, 1977. Springer-Verlag.
Coole, Arthur B. see Coole, Arthur Braddan.
Coole, Arthur Braddan, 1900-
xCoole, Arthur B.
The Early Coins of the Chou Dynasty.
Quarterman.
Spade Coin Types of the Chou Dynasty.
Quarterman.
Cooley, Adelaide N.
xCooley, Adelaide N.
The Monument Maker: A Biography of
Frederick Ernst Triebel. Exposition.
Cooley, Henry S. see Cooley, Henry Scofield.
Cooley, Henry Scofield.
xCooley, Henry S.

A Study of Slavery in New Jersey. AMS Pr.
A Study of Slavery in New Jersey. Johnson
Repr.
Cooley, Leland F. see Cooley, Leland Frederick.
Cooley, Leland Frederick.
xCooley, Leland F.
The Richest Poor Folks. St Martin.
Cooley, Marilyn. see Cooley, Marilyn H.
Cooley, Marilyn H.
xCooley, Marilyn.
Checklist for a Working Wife. Doubleday.
Cooley, Peter, 1940-
xCooley, Peter.
The Room Where Summer Ends.
Carnegie-Mellon.
Cooley, R. H.
xCooley, R. H.
Complete Metalworking Manual. Arco.
Cooley, Robert N.
xCooley, Robert N.
Radiology of the Heart & Great Vessels.
Williams & Wilkins.
Cooley, Thomas, 1942-
xCooley, Thomas.
Educated Lives: The Rise of Modern
Autobiography in America. Ohio St U Pr.
ed. The Norton Sampler: Short Essays for
Composition. Norton.
Cooley, William W.
xCooley, William W.
Multivariate Data Analysis. Wiley.
Coolidge, Dane.
xCoolidge, Dane.
The Navajo Indians. AMS Pr.
Coolidge, Guy O. see Coolidge, Guy Omeron.
Coolidge, Guy Omeron.
xCoolidge, Guy O.
The French Occupation of the Champlain
Valley: From 1609-1759. Harbor Hill Bks.
Coolidge, Louis A. see Coolidge, Louis Arthur.
Coolidge, Louis Arthur, 1861-1925
xCoolidge, Louis A.
Ulysses S. Grant. AMS Pr.
Coolidge, Mary E. see Coolidge, Mary Elizabeth
Burroughs Roberts Smith.
**Coolidge, Mary Elizabeth Burroughs Roberts Smith,
1860-1945**
xCoolidge, Mary E.
The Rain-Makers: Indians of Arizona & New
Mexico. AMS Pr.
Coolidge, Olivia. see Coolidge, Olivia E.
Coolidge, Olivia E.
xCoolidge, Olivia.
The Apprenticeship of Abraham Lincoln.
Scribner.
Gandhi. HM.
Golden Days of Greece. T Y Crowell.
Legends of the North. HM.
Lives of Famous Romans. HM.
Trojan War. HM.
Cooling, B. Franklin.
xCooling, B. Franklin.
Symbol, Sword, & Shield: Defending
Washington During the Civil War. Shoe
String.
Cools, A. R. see Cools, Alexander Rudolf.
Cools, Alexander Rudolf.
xCools, A. R.
ed. Psychobiology of the Striatum. Elsevier.
Coomaraswamy, A. K. see Coomaraswamy, Ananda
Kentish.
Coomaraswamy, Ananda. see Coomaraswamy, Ananda
Kentish.
Coomaraswamy, Ananda K. see Coomaraswamy, Ananda
Kentish.
Coomaraswamy, Ananda Kentish, 1877-1947
xCoomaraswamy, A. K.

History of Indian & Indonesian Art. Peter
Smith.
History of Indian & Indonesian Art. Verry.
xCoomaraswamy, Ananda.
Buddha & the Gospel of Buddhism. Folcroft.
Buddha & the Gospel of Buddhism. Univ Bks.
xCoomaraswamy, Ananda K.
The Arts & Crafts of India & Ceylon. FS&G.
Buddha & the Gospel of Buddhism. South Asia
Bks.
Christian & Oriental Philosophy of Art. Dover.
Christian & Oriental Philosophy of Art. Peter
Smith.
Hinduism & Buddhism. Greenwood.
The History of Indian & Indonesian Art.
Dover.
History of Indian & Indonesian Art. Intl Pubns
Serv.
Origin of the Buddha Image. Intl Pubns Serv.
Coomber, D. I.
xCoomber, D. I.
ed. Radiochemical Methods in Analysis.
Plenum Pub.
Coombes, Archie J. see Coombes, Archie James.
Coombes, Archie James.
xCoombes, Archie J.
Some Australian Poets. Arno.
Coombes, David. see Coombes, David L.
Coombes, David L.
xCoombes, David.
ed. The Power of the Purse: A Symposium on
the Role of European Parliaments in
Budgetary Decisions. Praeger.
Coombs, Charles. see Coombs, Charles Ira.
Coombs, Charles Ira, 1914-
xCoombs, Charles.
Auto Racing. Morrow.
Mopeding. Morrow.
Passage to Space: The Shuttle Transportation
System. Morrow.
Project Apollo: Mission to the Moon. Morrow.
Spacetrack, Watchdog of the Skies. Morrow.
Tankers, Giants of the Sea. Morrow.
Coombs, Clyde. see Coombs, Clyde Hamilton.
Coombs, Clyde F.
xCoombs, Clyde F.
Printed Circuits Handbook. McGraw.
Coombs, Clyde H. see Coombs, Clyde Hamilton.
Coombs, Clyde Hamilton.
xCoombs, Clyde.
Mathematical Psychology: An Elementary
Introduction. P-H.
xCoombs, Clyde H.
A Theory of Psychological Scaling.
Greenwood.
Coombs, Orde.
xCoombs, Orde.
ed. Do You See My Love for You Growing?.
Dodd.
Coombs, Patricia.
xCoombs, Patricia.
illus. Dorrie & the Amazing Magic Elixir.
Lothrop.
Dorrie & the Birthday Eggs. Lothrop.
Dorrie & the Blue Witch. Dell.
Dorrie & the Blue Witch. Lothrop.
Dorrie & the Dreamyard Monsters. Lothrop.
Dorrie & the Fortune Teller. Lothrop.
illus. Dorrie & the Goblin. Lothrop.
Dorrie & the Halloween Plot. Lothrop.
illus. Dorrie & the Screebit Ghost. Lothrop.
illus. Dorrie & the Weather-Box. Lothrop.
illus. Dorrie & the Witch Doctor. Lothrop.
Dorrie & the Witch's Imp. Lothrop.
illus. Dorrie & the Wizard's Spell. Lothrop.
Coombs, Philip H. see Coombs, Philip Hall.
Coombs, Philip Hall.
xCoombs, Philip H.

Attacking Rural Poverty: How Non-Formal
  Education Can Help. Johns Hopkins.
Coombs, Robert. see Coombs, Robert H.
Coombs, Robert H.
  xCoombs, Robert.
    ed. Socialization in Drug Abuse. Schenkman.
  xCoombs, Robert H.
    Mastering Medicine: Professional Socialization
      in Medical School. Free Pr.
    ed. Psychosocial Aspects of Medical Training.
      C C Thomas.
Coombs, W. E. see Coombs, William E.
Coombs, William E.
  xCoombs, W. E.
    Construction Accounting & Financial
      Management. McGraw.
Coon, Betty, 1947-
  xCoon, Betty.
    Seaward. Berkeley Poets.
Coon, C. S. see Coon, Carleton Stevens.
Coon, Carleton S. see Coon, Carleton Stevens.
Coon, Carleton Stevens, 1904-
  xCoon, C. S.
    Caravan: The Story of the Middle East.
      Krieger.
    A Reader in Cultural Anthropology. Krieger.
  xCoon, Carleton S.
    The Hunting Peoples. Merrimack Bk Serv.
    A North Africa Story: An Anthropologist As
      OSS Agent, 1941-1943. Gambit.
    The Races of Europe. Greenwood.
Coon, Dennis.
  xCoon, Dennis L.
    Essentials of Psychology: Exploration &
      Application. West Pub.
Coon, Dennis L. see Coon, Dennis.
Coon, Glenn. see Coon, Glenn A.
Coon, Glenn A.
  xCoon, Glenn.
    Lovely Lord of the Lord's Day. Pacific Pr Pub
      Assn.
Coon, Nelson.
  xCoon, Nelson.
    The Complete Book of Violets. A S Barnes.
    Dictionary of Useful Plants. Rodale Pr Inc.
    Using Wayside Plants. Dover.
    Using Wayside Plants. Hearthside.
Coonen, L. P.
  xCoonen, Lester P.
    Genesis of Biology. Thomist.
Coonen, Lester P. see Coonen, L. P.
Cooney. see Cooney, David O.
Cooney, Barbara, 1917-
  xCooney, Barbara.
    illus. Christmas. T Y Crowell.
    illus. Little Prayer. Hastings.
Cooney, Caroline B.
  xCooney, Caroline B.
    Rear-View Mirror. Random.
    Safe As the Grave. Coward.
Cooney, Cyprian.
  xCooney, Cyprian.
    Understanding the New Theology. Macmillan.
Cooney, David O.
  xCooney.
    Activated Charcoal: Antidotal & Other
      Medical Uses. Dekker.
    Advances in Biomedical Engineering. Dekker.
  xCooney, David O.
    ed. Advances in Biomedical Engineering.
      Dekker.
Cooney, John D. see Cooney, John Ducey.
Cooney, John Ducey.
  xCooney, John D.
    Amarna Reliefs from Hermopolis in American
      Collections. Bklyn Mus.
Coonley, Douglas R.
  xCoonley, Douglas R.

Wind: Making It Work for You. Franklin Inst
  Pr.
Coons, John E.
  xCoons, John E.
    Education by Choice: The Case for Family
      Control. U of Cal Pr.
Coontz, Otto.
  xCoontz, Otto.
    The Quiet House. Little.
    illus. A Real Class Clown. Little.
Coontz, Sydney H.
  xCoontz, Sydney H.
    Productive Labour & Effective Demand,
      Including a Critique of Keynesian Economics.
      Kelley.
Coop, Richard H.
  xCoop, Richard H.
    Psychological Concepts in the Classroom.
      Har-Row.
Cooper. see Cooper, James Fenimore.
Cooper, A. M. see Cooper, Alfred M.
Cooper, Al.
  xCooper, Al.
    World of Logotypes. Art Dir.
Cooper, Alfred M.
  xCooper, A. M.
    How to Supervise People. McGraw.
Cooper, Alice P. see Cooper, Page.
Cooper, B. E. see Cooper, Brian Edward.
Cooper, Brian, 1919-
  xCooper, Brian.
    Murder of Mary Steers. Vanguard.
Cooper, Brian Edward.
  xCooper, B. E.
    Statistics for Experimentalists. Pergamon.
Cooper, C. see Cooper, Cary L.
Cooper, Cary L.
  xCooper, C.
    Behavioral Problems in Organizations. P-H.
  xCooper, Cary L.
    ed. Developing Social Skills in Managers:
      Advances in Group Training. Halsted Pr.
    ed. The Quality of Working Life in Western &
      Eastern Europe. Greenwood.
    Theories of Group Processes. Wiley.
    Understanding Executive Stress. Petrocelli.
Cooper, Cary L. see Cooper, Gary L.
Cooper, Chester L.
  xCooper, Chester L.
    ed. Growth in America. Greenwood.
Cooper, Clara. see Cooper, Clara (Chassell).
Cooper, Clara (Chassell), 1893-
  xCooper, Clara.
    The Relation Between Morality & Intellect: A
      Compendium of Evidence Contributed by
      Psychology, Criminology, & Sociology. AMS
      Pr.
Cooper, Clare C.
  xCooper, Clare C.
    Easter Hill Village: Some Social Implications of
      Design. Free Pr.
Cooper, Darien. see Cooper, Darien B.
Cooper, Darien B.
  xCooper, Darien.
    How to Be Happy Though Young. Revell.
Cooper, David D.
  xCooper, David D.
    The Lesson of the Scaffold: The Public
      Execution Controversy in Victorian England.
      Ohio U Pr.
Cooper, David E. see Cooper, David Edward.
Cooper, David Edward.
  xCooper, David E.
    Presupposition. Mouton.
Cooper, David G.
  xCooper, David G.
    Architectural & Engineering Salesmanship.
      Wiley.
Cooper, Derek.
  xCooper, Derek.

The Gullibility Gap. Routledge & Kegan.
    Road to the Isles: Travellers in the Hebrides,
      1770-1914. Routledge & Kegan.
Cooper, Dominic, 1944-
  xCooper, Dominic.
    The Dead of Winter. St Martin.
    Men at Axlir. St Martin.
Cooper, Douglas.
  xCooper, Douglas.
    Living God's Joy. Pacific Pr Pub Assn.
    Living God's Love. Pacific Pr Pub Assn.
Cooper, Duff, 1890-1954
  xCooper, Duff.
    Talleyrand. Stanford U Pr.
Cooper, Edmund, 1926-
  xCooper, Edmund.
    The Overman Culture. Berkley Pub.
Cooper, Elizabeth, 1877-1945
  xCooper, Elizabeth.
    The Women of Egypt. Hyperion Conn.
Cooper, Elizabeth K.
  xCooper, Elizabeth K.
    Discovering Chemistry. HarBraceJ.
    Fish from Japan. HarBraceJ.
Cooper, Emmanuel.
  xCooper, Emmanuel.
    Glazes for the Potter. Scribner.
Cooper, F. T. see Cooper, Frederic Taber.
Cooper, Frederic T. see Cooper, Frederic Taber.
Cooper, Frederic Taber, 1864-1937
  xCooper, F. T.
    Some American Story Tellers. Gordon Pr.
    Some English Story Tellers: A Book of the
      Younger Novelists. Gordon Pr.
  xCooper, Frederic T.
    Some American Story Tellers. Arno.
Cooper, Frederick, 1947-
  xCooper, Frederick.
    Plantation Slavery on the East Coast of Africa.
      Yale U Pr.
Cooper, G. Arthur. see Cooper, Gustav Arthur.
Cooper, Gale.
  xCooper, Gale.
    jt. auth. Anatomy of the Guinea Pig. Harvard
      U Pr.
    Inside Animals. Little.
Cooper, Gary L.
  xCooper, Cary L.
    Learning from Others in Groups: Experimental
      Learning Approaches. Greenwood.
Cooper, Gayle.
  xCooper, Gayle.
    Checklist of American Imprints. Scarecrow.
Cooper, George, 1937-
  xCooper, George.
    Voluntary Tax: New Perspectives on
      Sophisticated Estate Tax Avoidance.
      Brookings.
Cooper, George H. see Cooper, George Henderson.
Cooper, George Henderson, 1894-
  xCooper, George H.
    Building Construction Estimating. McGraw.
Cooper, George R.
  xCooper, George R.
    Probabilistic Methods of Signal & System
      Analysis. HR&W.
Cooper, Grace C.
  xCooper, Grace C.
    Guide to Teaching Early Child Development:
      A Comprehensive Curriculum. Child Welfare.
Cooper, Grosvenor.
  xCooper, Grosvenor.
    Learning to Listen: A Handbook for Music. U
      of Chicago Pr.
Cooper, Gustav Arthur, 1902-
  xCooper, G. Arthur.

Brachiopods from the Caribbean Sea & Adjacent Waters. U Miami Marine.

Cooper, H. B. *see* Cooper, Hal B. H.

Cooper, Hal B. H.
xCooper, H. B.
Source Testing for Air Pollution Control. McGraw.

Cooper, Helen.
xCooper, Helen.
Great Grandmother Goose. Greenwillow.
Pastoral: Mediaeval into Renaissance. Rowman.

Cooper, Henry S. *see* Cooper, Henry S. F.

Cooper, Henry S. F.
xCooper, Henry S.
A House in Space. HR&W.

Cooper, Herbert K.
xCooper, Herbert K.
ed. Cleft Palate & Cleft Lip: A Team Approach to Clinical Management & Rehabilitation of the Patient. Saunders.

Cooper, Herman. *see* Cooper, Hermann.

Cooper, Hermann, 1895-
xCooper, Herman.
An Accounting of Progress & Attendance of Rural School Children in Delaware. AMS Pr.

Cooper, I. S. *see* Cooper, Irving Spencer.

Cooper, Irving. *see* Cooper, Irving Spencer.

Cooper, Irving S. *see* Cooper, Irving Spencer.

Cooper, Irving Spencer, 1922-
xCooper, I. S.
ed. Cerebellar Stimulation in Man. Raven.
Living with Chronic Neurologic Disease: A Handbook for Patient & Family. Norton.
xCooper, Irving.
ed. The Cerebellum, Epilepsy & Behavior. Plenum Pub.
xCooper, Irving S.
The Pulvinar-LP Complex. C C Thomas.

Cooper, Irving Steiger, Bp, 1882-1935
xCooper, Irving S.
Theosophy Simplified. Gordon Pr.
Theosophy Simplified. Theos Pub Hse.

Cooper, J. C., fl. 1972-
xCooper, J. C.
An Illustrated Encyclopaedia of Traditional Symbols. Thames Hudson.

Cooper, J. David. *see* Cooper, James David.

Cooper, J. F. *see* Cooper, James Fenimore.

Cooper, J. T. *see* Cooper, James Thomas.

Cooper, James David, 1942-
xCooper, J. David.
The What & How of Reading Instruction. Merrill.

Cooper, James F. *see* Cooper, James Fenimore.

Cooper, James Fenimore, 1789-1851
xCooper.
The Pathfinder. McDougal-Littell.
xCooper, J. F.
Gleanings in Europe. Kraus Repr.
xCooper, James F.

Chain Bearer: Or, the Littlepage Manuscripts. AMS Pr.
Correspondence of James Fenimore Cooper. Arno.
Correspondence of James Fenimore Cooper. Haskell.
Last of the Mohicans. NAL.
The Last of the Mohicans. Pendulum Pr.
Last of the Mohicans. Airmont.
Last of the Mohicans. AMSCO Sch.
Last of the Mohicans. Dodd.
Pathfinder. Lighthouse Pr NY.
Pathfinder. NAL.
Pathfinder. Airmont.
The Pathfinder. Regents Pub.
The Pioneers. Lighthouse Pr NY.
The Pioneers. State U NY Pr.
Pioneers. NAL.
Pioneers. Airmont.

Cooper, James R.
xCooper, James R.
Real Estate & Urban Land Analysis. Lexington Bks.

Cooper, James Thomas.
xCooper, J. T.
Dr. Cooper's Fabulous Fructose Diet. Fawcett.
Dr. Cooper's Fabulous Fructose Diet. M Evans.
The Fabulous Fructose Recipe Book. M Evans.

Cooper, Jerry M.
xCooper, Jerry M.
The Army & Civil Disorder: Federal Military Intervention in Labor Disputes, 1877-1900. Greenwood.

Cooper, Jilly.
xCooper, Jilly.
How to Stay Married. Taplinger.

Cooper, John C. *see* Cooper, John Charles.

Cooper, John Charles.
xCooper, John C.
Living, Loving, & Letting Go: The Art of Being a Parent. Word Bks.

Cooper, John L., 1936-
xCooper, John L.
The Police & the Ghetto. Kennikat.
The Seventh Decade: A Study of the Women's Liberation Movement. Kendall-Hunt.

Cooper, John M. *see* Cooper, John Montgomery.

Cooper, John Madison, 1939-
xCooper, John M.
Reason & Human Good in Aristotle. Harvard U Pr.

Cooper, John Miller.
xCooper, John M.
The Theory & Science of Basketball. Lea & Febiger.

Cooper, John Montgomery, 1881-1949
xCooper, John M.
The Northern Algonquian Supreme Being. AMS Pr.

Cooper, John O.
xCooper, John O.
Measurement & Analysis of Behavioral Techniques. Merrill.
Parenting: Strategies & Educational Methods. Merrill.

Cooper, Joseph. *see* Cooper, Joseph David.

Cooper, Joseph David.
xCooper, Joseph.
Cameras & Operating Techniques. Amphoto.
Close-Up Photography & Copying. Amphoto.
Lenses & Lens Systems. Amphoto.
Special Effects, Shooting Situations, & Darkroom Techniques. Amphoto.

Cooper, Judith.
xCooper, Judith.
Ubu Roi: An Analytical Study. Tulane Romance Lang.

Cooper, Kay.
xCooper, Kay.

All About Goldfish As Pets. Messner.
All About Rabbits As Pets. Messner.
A Chipmunk's Inside-Outside World. Messner.

Cooper, Ken.
xCooper, Ken.
Nonverbal Communication for Business Success. Am Mgmt.

Cooper, Kenneth. *see* Cooper, Kenneth H.

Cooper, Kenneth H.
xCooper, Kenneth.
Aerobics. Bantam.
xCooper, Kenneth H.
Aerobics. M Evans.
The Aerobics Way: New Data on the Worlds Most Popular Exercise Program. M Evans.

Cooper, L. G. *see* Cooper, Lloyd G.

Cooper, Lane, 1875-1959
xCooper, Lane.
ed. Art of the Writer: Essays, Excerpts, & Translations. Arno.
Late Harvest: Sketches of Cook, Adams, & Kleist: the College President; with Philosophical Reviews, & Papers on Coleridge, Wordsworth, & Byron. Cornell U Pr.
Prose Poetry of Thomas De Quincey. Folcroft.

Cooper, Laura G.
xCooper, Laura G.
Standard Fortran: A Problem-Solving Approach. HM.

Cooper, Lee.
xCooper, Lee.
Chinese Language for Beginners. C E Tuttle.
Fun with French. Little.
Fun with German. Little.
Fun with Spanish. Little.
More Fun with Spanish. Little.

Cooper, Lloyd G., 1935-
xCooper, L. G.
Professional Library in Education Collection. Brodart.

Cooper, Louise F. *see* Cooper, Louise Field.

Cooper, Louise Field, 1905-
xCooper, Louise F.
Breakaway. Knopf.

Cooper, Lynna.
xCooper, Lynna.
Forgotten Love. NAL.
Offer of Marriage. NAL.
Substitute Bride. NAL.

Cooper, M. D. *see* Cooper, Max D.

Cooper, M. H. *see* Cooper, Michael H.

Cooper, M. K. *see* Cooper, Mae Klein.

Cooper, Mae Klein.
xCooper, M. K.
Private Lies. Fawcett.
Private Lies. S&S.

Cooper, Margaret. *see* Cooper, Margaret Rice.

Cooper, Margaret Rice.
xCooper, Margaret.
Great Bone Hunt. Macmillan.

Cooper, Martin, 1910-
xCooper, Martin.
French Music: From the Death of Berlioz to the Death of Faure. Oxford U Pr.
Georges Bizet. Greenwood.

Cooper, Matthew.
xCooper, Matthew.
The Nazi War Against Soviet Partisans. Stein & Day.

Cooper, Max D.
xCooper, M. D.
ed. Immune Deficiency. Springer-Verlag.
xCooper, Max D.
ed. Development of Host Defenses. Raven.

Cooper, Michael, 1943-
xCooper, Michael.
Things to Make & Do for George Washington's Birthday. Watts.

Cooper, Michael. *see* Cooper, Michael H.

Cooper, Michael D. *see* Cooper, Michael David.
Cooper, Michael David.
    xCooper, Michael D.
        California's Demand for Librarians: Projecting
            Future Requirements. Inst Gov Stud Berk.
Cooper, Michael H.
    xCooper, M. H.
        Prices & Profits in the Pharmaceutical
            Industry. Pergamon.
    xCooper, Michael.
        Rationing Health Care. Halsted Pr.
Cooper, Michele F.
    xCooper, Michele F.
        Freshman Writer. Har-Row.
Cooper, Morton.
    xCooper, Morton.
        Approaches to Vocal Rehabilitation. C C
            Thomas.
        Rich People. M Evans.
Cooper, Murray S. *see* Cooper, Murray Sam.
Cooper, Murray Sam.
    xCooper, Murray S.
        ed. Quality Control in the Pharmaceutical
            Industry. Acad Pr.
Cooper, Norman W. *see* Cooper, W. Norman.
Cooper, Page, 1891-1958
    xCooper, Alice P.
        Authors & Others. Arno.
Cooper, Parley J.
    xCooper, Parley J.
        Dark Desires. PB.
Cooper, Paul.
    xCooper, Paul.
        Perspectives in Music Theory: An
            Historical-Analytical Approach. Har-Row.
Cooper, Paulette.
    xCooper, Paulette.
        ed. Growing up Puerto Rican. Arbor Hse.
        ed. Growing up Puerto Rican. NAL.
        Let's Find Out About Halloween. Watts.
Cooper, Philip, 1908-
    xCooper, Philip.
        The Craft of Surgery. Little.
Cooper, Philip. *see* Cooper, Philip D.
Cooper, Philip D., 1942-
    xCooper, Philip.
        Health Care Marketing: Issues & Trends.
            Aspen Systems.
Cooper, Phyllis.
    xCooper, Phyllis.
        Feminine Gymnastics. Burgess.
Cooper, Robert D.
    xCooper, Robert D.
        A Study of Current Collection Practices,
            Procedures & Problems. Intl Found Employ.
Cooper, Samuel W. *see* Cooper, Samuel Williams.
Cooper, Samuel Williams, 1860-1939
    xCooper, Samuel W.
        Think & Thank: A Tale. Arno.
Cooper, Signe S. *see* Cooper, Signe Skott.
Cooper, Signe Skott.
    xCooper, Signe S.
        Contemporary Nursing Practice: A Guide for
            the Returning Nurse. McGraw.
        Continuing Nursing Education. McGraw.
Cooper, Simon.
    xCooper, Simon.
        The Dirt Sandwich. Dial.
Cooper, Susan.
    xCooper, Susan.

        The Dark Is Rising. Atheneum.
        The Dark Is Rising. Atheneum.
        Dawn of Fear. HarBraceJ.
        Greenwitch. Atheneum.
        Greenwitch. Atheneum.
        The Grey King. Atheneum.
        The Grey King. Atheneum.
        Jethro & the Jumbie. Atheneum.
        Over Sea, Under Stone. HarBraceJ.
        Over Sea, Under Stone. HarBraceJ.
        Preparing, Designing & Leading Workshops: A
            Humanistic Approach. CBI Pub.
        Silver on the Tree. Atheneum.
        Silver on the Tree. Atheneum.
Cooper, Terry T. *see* Cooper, Terry Touff.
Cooper, Terry Touff.
    xCooper, Terry T.
        Many Hands Cooking: An International
            Cookbook for Girls & Boys. T Y Crowell.
Cooper, Theodore W., 1923-
    xCooper, Theodore W.
        By Popular Choice: Why Not Vocalize the
            Silent Majority?. Technicon Pubs.
Cooper, Thomas, 1759-1839
    xCooper, Thomas.
        Lectures on the Elements of Political
            Economy. Kelley.
Cooper, Thomas M.
    xCooper, Thomas M.
        Applied Practice Management: A Strategy for
            Stress Control. Mosby.
Cooper, W. F. *see* Cooper, William Fordham.
Cooper, W. Norman.
    xCooper, Norman W.
        Finding Your Self. De Vorss.
        Love That Heals. De Vorss.
Cooper, Walter G. *see* Cooper, Walter Gerald.
Cooper, Walter Gerald, 1860-
    xCooper, Walter G.
        Official History of Fulton County. Reprint.
Cooper, Wendy.
    xCooper, Wendy.
        Don't Change: A Biological Revolution for
            Women. Stein & Day.
Cooper, William B., 1911-
    xCooper, William B.
        Licensed Operator's Key to Refrigeration. Busn
            News.
Cooper, William Fordham.
    xCooper, W. F.
        Electrical Safety Engineering. Butterworths.
Cooper, William J. *see* Cooper, William James.
Cooper, William James, 1940-
    xCooper, William J.
        South & the Politics of Slavery, 1828-1856. La
            State U Pr.
Cooper, William S. *see* Cooper, William Skinner.
Cooper, William Skinner, 1884-
    xCooper, William S.
        Coastal Dunes of California. Geol Soc.
        Coastal Sand Dunes of Oregon & Washington.
            Geol Soc.
Cooper, Wyatt.
    xCooper, Wyatt.
        Families: A Memoir & a Celebration. Har-Row.
Cooperation in Documentation & Communication. *see*
    Cooperation in Documentation and Communication
    (Organisation).
**Cooperation in Documentation and Communication
    (Organisation).**
    xCooperation in Documentation &
        Communication.
        Bibliographical Notes for Understanding the
            Transnational Corporations & the Third
            World. CoDoC.
Cooperman, Avram M.
    xCooperman, Avram M.

        Surgery of the Pancreas: A Text & Atlas.
            Mosby.
Cooperman, Hasye.
    xCooperman, Hasye.
        Aesthetics of Stephane Mallarme. Russell.
Coover, Robert.
    xCoover, Robert.
        The Origin of the Brunists. Viking Pr.
Coox, Alvin D.
    xCoox, Alvin D.
        The Anatomy of a Small War: The
            Soviet-Japanese Struggle for
            Changkufeng-Khasan, 1938. Greenwood.
        ed. China & Japan: Search for Balance Since
            World War I. ABC-Clio.
Cope, Dwight W.
    xCope, Dwight W.
        Plastics. Goodheart.
Cope, Edward D. *see* Cope, Edward Drinker.
Cope, Edward Drinker, 1840-1897
    xCope, Edward D.
        The Origin of the Fittest: Essays on Evolution
            & the Primary Factors of Organic Evolution.
            Arno.
Cope, Jackson. *see* Cope, Jackson I.
Cope, Jackson I.
    xCope, Jackson.
        The Metaphoric Structure of Paradise Lost.
            Octagon.
Cope, Jeff.
    xCope, Jeff.
        Weaponless Control: For Law Enforcement &
            Security Personnel. C C Thomas.
Cope, Oliver, 1902-
    xCope, Oliver.
        Breast: Its Problems - Benign & Malignant -
            How to Deal with Them. HM.
Cope, Thomas P. *see* Cope, Thomas Pym.
Cope, Thomas Pym.
    xCope, Thomas P.
        Philadelphia Merchant: The Diary of Thomas
            P. Cope, 1800-1851. Regnery-Gateway.
Cope, Zachary.
    xCope, Zachary.
        Cope's Early Diagnosis of the Acute Abdomen.
            Oxford U Pr.
        History of the Acute Abdomen. Oxford U Pr.
Copeland, Adrian D.
    xCopeland, Adrian D.
        Textbook of Adolescent Psychopathology &
            Treatment. C C Thomas.
Copeland, Bonnie.
    xCopeland, Bonnie C.
        Lady of Moray. Atheneum.
Copeland, Bonnie C. *see* Copeland, Bonnie.
Copeland, Hannah C. *see* Copeland, Hannah Case.
Copeland, Hannah Case.
    xCopeland, Hannah C.
        Art & the Artist in the Works of Samuel
            Beckett. Mouton.
Copeland, Herbert F. *see* Copeland, Herbert Faulkner.
Copeland, Herbert Faulkner.
    xCopeland, Herbert F.
        Classification of Lower Organisms. Pacific Bks.
Copeland, Irene.
    xCopeland, Irene.
        The Flea Market & Garage Sale Handbook.
            Popular Lib.
Copeland, J. C.
    xCopeland, James C.
        ed. Regulatory Biology. Ohio St U Pr.
Copeland, James.
    xCopeland, James.
        For the Love of Ann. Ballantine.
Copeland, James C. *see* Copeland, J. C.
Copeland, Lawrence O., 1936-
    xCopeland, Lawrence O.

Principles of Seed Science & Technology.
Burgess.
Copeland, Lewis.
xCopeland, Lewis.
ed. High School Subjects Self Taught.
Doubleday.
ed. World's Great Speeches. Dover.
Copeland, Marion W.
xCopeland, Marion W.
Charles Alexander Eastman (Ohiyesa). Boise St
Univ.
Copeland, Melvin T. *see* Copeland, Melvin Thomas.
Copeland, Melvin Thomas, 1884-
xCopeland, Melvin T.
Cotton Manufacturing Industry of the United
States. Kelley.
Principles of Merchandising. Arno.
Copeland, Mildred.
xCopeland, Mildred.
Occupational Therapy for Mentally Retarded
Children: Guidelines for Occupational
Therapy Aides & Certified Occupational
Therapy Assistants. Univ Park.
Copeland, Pamela C.
xCopeland, Pamela C.
The Five George Masons: Patriots & Planters
of Virginia & Maryland. U Pr of Va.
Copeland, Peter F.
xCopeland, Peter F.
Working Dress in Colonial & Revolutionary
America. Greenwood.
Copeland, Richard W.
xCopeland, Richard W.
Mathematics & the Elementary Teacher.
HR&W.
Copeland, Thomas E.
xCopeland, Thomas E.
Financial Theory & Corporate Policy. A-W.
Copeland, Wilfred, 1941-
xCopeland, Wilfred.
The World Monetary Chaos & the Cowardice
of the United States & of the World Bankers.
Inst Econ Pol.
Copeland, William C.
xCopeland, William C.
Obtaining Federal Money for Children's
Services. Child Welfare.
Copenhaver, Brian. *see* Copenhaver, Brian P.
Copenhaver, Brian P.
xCopenhaver, Brian.
Symphorien Champier & the Reception of the
Occultist Tradition in Renaissance France.
Mouton.
Copi, Irving M.
xCopi, Irving M.
Introduction to Logic. Macmillan.
Symbolic Logic. Macmillan.
Copland, Aaron, 1900-
xCopland, Aaron.
Copland on Music. Da Capo.
Copland on Music. Norton.
Music & Imagination. Harvard U Pr.
What to Listen for in Music. McGraw.
What to Listen for in Music. NAL.
Copland, Douglas B. *see* Copland, Douglas Berry.
Copland, Douglas Berry, Sir, 1894-
xCopland, Douglas B.
Australia in the World Crisis, 1929-1933. AMS
Pr.
Copleston, F. C. *see* Copleston, Frederick Charles.
Copleston, Frederick. *see* Copleston, Frederick Charles
John Paul.
Copleston, Frederick Charles.
xCopleston, F. C.
History of Medieval Philosophy. Har-Row.
Copleston, Frederick Charles John Paul.
xCopleston, Frederick.
On the History of Philosophy. B&N.
Copley, Esther. *see* Copley, Esther Hewlett.

Copley, Esther Hewlett.
xCopley, Esther.
History of Slavery & Its Abolition. Scholarly.
Copley, Frank B. *see* Copley, Frank Barkley.
Copley, Frank Barkley.
xCopley, Frank B.
Frederick W. Taylor, Father of Scientific
Management. Kelley.
Copley, John S. *see* Copley, John Singleton.
Copley, John Singleton.
xCopley, John S.
Letters & Papers of John Singleton Copley &
Henry Pelham, 1739-1776. Da Capo.
Coplin, William D.
xCoplin, William D.
Everyman's Prince: A Guide to Understanding
Your Political Problems. Duxbury Pr.
Introduction to International Politics. P-H.
Copman, Louis.
xCopman, Louis.
The Cuckold. Ashley Bks.
Copp, Dewitt S.
xCopp, Dewitt S.
A Different Kind of Rain. Norton.
Copp, Henry N. *see* Copp, Henry Norris.
Copp, Henry Norris, 1843-1912
xCopp, Henry N.
Public Land Laws. Arno.
United States Mineral Lands. Arno.
Coppa, Frank J.
xCoppa, Frank J.
The Immigrant Experience in America.
Twayne.
Planning, Protectionism & Politics in Liberal
Italy: Economics & Politics in the Giolittian
Age. Intl Schol Bk Serv.
ed. Screen & Society: The Impact of Television
Upon Aspects of Contemporary Civilization.
Nelson-Hall.
Coppard, Alfred E. *see* Coppard, Alfred Edgar.
Coppard, Alfred Edgar, 1878-1957
xCoppard, Alfred E.
Adam & Eve & Pinch Me: Tales. Arno.
The Collected Tales of A. E. Coppard. Arno.
Ninepenny Flute: Twenty-One Tales. Arno.
Coppel, Alfred.
xCoppel, Alfred.
The Dragon. HarBraceJ.
Thirty-Four East. Popular Lib.
Coppel, W. A.
xCoppel, W. A.
Dichotomies in Stability Theory.
Springer-Verlag.
Disconjugacy. Springer-Verlag.
Coppell, W. G.
xCoppell, William G.
World Catalogue of Theses & Dissertations
About the Australian Aborigines & Torres
Strait Islanders. Intl Schol Bk Serv.
Coppell, W. G. *see* Coppell, William George.
Coppell, William G. *see* Coppell, W. G.
Coppell, William George.
xCoppell, W. G.
Australia in Figures: A Handbook of
Economic, Political & Social Statistics. U of
Queensland Pr.
Coppen, H. E. *see* Coppen, Helen Elizabeth.
Coppen, Helen Elizabeth.
xCoppen, H. E.
Aids to Teaching & Learning. Pergamon.
Coppens, Peter R. De. *see* De Coppens, Peter R.
Coppens, Yves.
xCoppens, Yves.
ed. Earliest Man & Environments in the Lake
Rudolf Basin: Stratigraphy, Paleoecology, &
Evolution. U of Chicago Pr.
Copper, Basil.
xCopper, Basil.

Voices of Doom. St Martin.
Copper, Marcia S.
xCopper, Marcia S.
The Horseman's Etiquette Book. Scribner.
Copperman, Paul.
xCopperman, Paul.
The Literacy Hoax: The Decline of Reading,
Writing & Learning in the Public Schools &
What We Can Do About It. Morrow.
The Literacy Hoax: The Decline of Reading,
Writing, & Learning in the Public Schools &
What We Can Do About It. Morrow.
Copperud, Carol.
xCopperud, Carol.
The Test Design Handbook. Educ Tech Pubns.
Coppin, Ezra.
xCoppin, Ezra.
Guns, Guts, & God!. Prod Hse.
Guns, Guts & God. Reward Bks.
Coppleson, Malcolm.
xCoppleson, Malcolm.
Colposcopy: A Scientific & Practical Approach
to the Cervix in Health & Disease. C C
Thomas.
Coppock, J. O. *see* Coppock, John O.
Coppock, J. T. *see* Coppock, John Terence.
Coppock, John O.
xCoppock, J. O.
North Atlantic Policy: The Agricultural Gap.
Kraus Repr.
Coppock, John Terence.
xCoppock, J. T.
The Spatial Dimensions of Public Policy.
Pergamon.
Coppock, Joseph D. *see* Coppock, Joseph David.
Coppock, Joseph David, 1909-
xCoppock, Joseph D.
International Trade Instability. Lexington Bks.
Coppola, Andrew J. *see* Coppola, Andrew Joseph.
Coppola, Andrew Joseph.
xCoppola, Andrew J.
Law of Business Contracts. Littlefield.
The Law of Commercial Paper. Littlefield.
Materials in the Law of Agency. Littlefield.
Coppola, Eleanor.
xCoppola, Eleanor.
Notes. PB.
Notes. S&S.
Copson, E. T. *see* Copson, Edward Thomas.
Copson, Edward T. *see* Copson, Edward Thomas.
Copson, Edward Thomas, 1901-
xCopson, E. T.
Partial Differential Equations. Cambridge U Pr.
xCopson, Edward T.
Asymptotic Expansions. Cambridge U Pr.
Coptic Church.
xCoptic Church.
Coptic Morning Service for the Lord's Day.
AMS Pr.
xCopyright Society Of The United States.
Studies on Copyright. Rothman.
Copyright Society of the United States. *see* Coptic
Church.
Coral Gables Conference on Physical Principles of
Biological Membranes, University of Miami, 1968.
xCoral Gables Conference On Physical Principles
Of Biological Membranes - University Of Miami
- 1968.
Proceedings. Gordon.
Coran, Arnold G.
xCoran, Arnold G.
Surgery of the Neonate. Little.
Corbeiller, Philippe E. Le. *see* Le Corbeiller, Philippe E.
Corbet, H. *see* Corbet, Hugh.
Corbet, Hugh.
xCorbet, H.
ed. In Search of a New World Economic
Order. Halsted Pr.
Corbett, E. V. *see* Corbett, Edmund V.

Corbett, Edith.
  xCorbett, Edith O.
    The Playtime Shoebox. Messner.
Corbett, Edith O. *see* Corbett, Edith.
Corbett, Edmund V.
  xCorbett, E. V.
    Introduction to Librarianship. Philos Lib.
Corbett, Edward P. *see* Corbett, Edward P. J.
Corbett, Edward P. J.
  xCorbett, Edward P.
    The Little English Handbook: Choices &
      Conventions. Wiley.
    The Little Rhetoric. Wiley.
    The Little Rhetoric & Handbook. Wiley.
    Rhetorical Analyses of Literary Works. Oxford
      U Pr.
Corbett, J. A. *see* Corbett, James Arthur.
Corbett, J. Elliott. *see* Corbett, Jack Elliott.
Corbett, Jack Elliott, 1920-
  xCorbett, J. Elliott.
    Prophets on Main Street. John Knox.
Corbett, James Arthur.
  xCorbett, J. A.
    The Papacy: A Brief History. Peter Smith.
Corbett, James Edward, 1875-1955
  xCorbett, Jim.
    My India. Century Bookbindery.
Corbett, Jan.
  xCorbett, Jan.
    Creative Youth Leadership. Judson.
Corbett, Jim. *see* Corbett, James Edward.
Corbett, John P. *see* Corbett, John Patrick.
Corbett, John Patrick, 1916-
  xCorbett, John P.
    Europe & the Social Order. Hyperion Conn.
Corbett, Julian. *see* Corbett, Julian Stafford.
Corbett, Julian S. *see* Corbett, Julian Stafford.
Corbett, Julian Stafford, Sir, 1854-1922
  xCorbett, Julian.
    Monk. Arno.
  xCorbett, Julian S.
    The Campaign of Trafalgar. AMS Pr.
    ed. Fighting Instructions, 1530-1816. B
      Franklin.
    ed. Papers Relating to the Navy During the
      Spanish War 1585-1587. B Franklin.
    Some Principles of Maritime Strategy. AMS Pr.
    Successors of Drake. B Franklin.
Corbett, Margery.
  xCorbett, Margery.
    The Comely Frontispiece: The Emblematic
      Title-Page in England, 1550-1660. Routledge
      & Kegan.
Corbett, Nancy Ann.
  xCorbett, Nancy Ann.
    Clinical Simulations in Nursing Practice.
      Saunders.
Corbett, Pearson H. *see* Corbett, Pearson Harris.
Corbett, Pearson Harris, 1900-
  xCorbett, Pearson H.
    Hyrum Smith, Patriarch. Deseret Bk.
Corbett, Percy E. *see* Corbett, Percy Ellwood.
Corbett, Percy Ellwood, 1892-
  xCorbett, Percy E.
    Growth of World Law. Princeton U Pr.
Corbett, Scott.
  xCorbett, Scott.

    The Boy Who Walked on Air. Little.
    Bridges. Schol Bk Serv.
    Captain Butcher's Body. Little.
    The Case of the Burgled Blessing Box. Little.
    The Case of the Fugitive Firebug. Little.
    The Case of the Silver Skull. Little.
    The Case of the Ticklish Tooth. Little.
    Cop's Kid. Little.
    The Disappearing Dog Trick. Little.
    The Discontented Ghost. Dutton.
    Dr. Merlin's Magic Shop. Little.
    The Donkey Planet. Dutton.
    The Foolish Dinosaur Fiasco. Little.
    The Great Custard Pie Panic. Little.
    The Great Custard Pie Panic. Schol Bk Serv.
    The Great McGoniggle Rides Shotgun. Little.
    The Great McGoniggle's Gray Ghost. Little.
    Great McGoniggle's Gray Ghost. Dell.
    The Great McGoniggle's Key Play. Little.
    The Hairy Horror Trick. Little.
    Here Lies the Body. Dell.
    Here Lies the Body. Little.
    The Hockey Girls. Dutton.
    The Hockey Trick. Little.
    The Home Run Trick. Little.
    The Mysterious Zetabet. Little.
    Steady, Freddie. Dutton.
    Take a Number. Dutton.
    The Turnabout Trick. Little.
Corbett, Thomas H.
  xCorbett, Thomas H.
    Cancer & Chemicals. Nelson-Hall.
Corbin. *see* Corbin, Floyd.
Corbin, Charles B.
  xCorbin, Charles B.
    Concepts in Physical Education with
      Laboratories & Experiments. Wm C Brown.
    A Textbook of Motor Development. Wm C
      Brown.
Corbin, Cheryl.
  xCorbin, Cheryl.
    Nutrition. HR&W.
Corbin, David R., 1944-
  xCorbin, David R.
    Discover Swaging. Stackpole.
Corbin, Floyd.
  xCorbin.
    How to Relax in a Busy World. Borden.
Corbin, H. Dan.
  xCorbin, H. Dan.
    Education for Leisure. P-H.
Corbin, Henry.
  xCorbin, Henry.
    Creative Imagination in the Sufism of
      Ibn'Arabi. Princeton U Pr.
Corbin, Marie.
  xCorbin, Marie.
    ed. The Couple. Penguin.
Corbin, Patricia.
  xCorbin, Patricia.
    All About Wicker. Dutton.
Corbitt, Helen.
  xCorbitt, Helen.
    Helen Corbitt's Greenhouse Cookbook. HM.
Corbman, B. P. *see* Corbman, Bernard P.
Corbman, Bernard P.
  xCorbman, B. P.
    Textiles: Fiber to Fabric. McGraw.
  xCorbman, Bernard P.
    Mathematics of Retail Merchandising. Ronald
      Pr.
    Textiles: Fiber to Fabric. McGraw.
Corbridge, D. E. C.
  xCorbridge, S.
    The Structural Chemistry of Phosphorus.
      Elsevier.
Corbridge, S. *see* Corbridge, D. E. C.
Corcao, Gustavo.
  xCorcao, Gustavo.

    Who If I Cry Out. U of Tex Pr.
Corcoran, A. Wayne.
  xCorcoran, A. Wayne.
    Costs: Accounting, Analysis & Control. Wiley.
Corcoran, Barbara.
  xCorcoran, Barbara.
    All the Summer Voices. Atheneum.
    Cabin in the Sky. Atheneum.
    The Clown. Atheneum.
    A Dance to Still Music. Atheneum.
    A Dance to Still Music. Atheneum.
    Don't Slam the Door When You Go.
      Atheneum.
    The Faraway Island. Atheneum.
    Long Journey. Atheneum.
    Meet Me at Tamerlane's Tomb. Atheneum.
    Rising Damp. Atheneum.
    This Is a Recording. Atheneum.
Corcoran, J. W. *see* Corcoran, John W.
Corcoran, John W.
  xCorcoran, J. W.
    ed. Mechanism of Action of Antimicrobial &
      Antitumor Agents. Springer-Verlag.
Corcoran, Paul E., 1944-
  xCorcoran, Paul E.
    Political Language & Rhetoric. U of Tex Pr.
Corcoran, Thomas H.
  xCorcoran, Thomas H.
    Latin Prose & Poetry: Selections for the
      Classroom. Univ Microfilms.
Corcos, Lucille, 1908-
  xCorcos, Lucille.
    illus. The City Book. Western Pub.
Cord, Barry.
  xCord, Barry.
    Gun Junction. Nordon Pubns.
    The Gun Shy Kid. Belmont Tower.
    Last Chance at Devil's Canyon. Nordon Pubns.
    The Third Rider. Belmont-Tower.
Cord, R. *see* Cord, Robert L.
Cord, Robert L.
  xCord, R.
    Protest, Dissent & the Supreme Court.
      Winthrop.
  xCord, Robert L.
    Political Science: An Introduction. P-H.
Cordasco, Francesco.
  xCordasco, Francesco.
    ed. Bilingual Education in American Schools:
      A Guide to Information Sources. Gale.
    ed. History of American Education: A Guide
      to Information Sources. Gale.
    Immigrant Children in American Schools: A
      Classified & Annotated Bibliography with
      Selected Source Documents. Kelley.
    ed. Medical Education in the United States: A
      Guide to Information Sources. Gale.
    The Puerto Rican Experience: A Sociological
      Sourcebook. Littlefield.
    The Puerto Rican Experience: A Sociological
      Sourcebook. Rowman.
    Puerto Ricans on the United States Mainland:
      A Bibliography of Reports, Texts, Critical
      Studies & Related Materials. Rowman.
    The Puerto Ricans, 1493-1973: A Chronology
      & Fact Book. Oceana.
    ed. Sociology of Education: A Guide to
      Information Sources. Gale.
Corday, Eliot.
  xCorday, Eliot.
    ed. Controversies in Cardiology. Davis Co.
Cordell, A. Robert. *see* Cordell, Alfred Robert.
Cordell, Alexander.
  xCordell, Alexander.
    This Sweet & Bitter Earth. St Martin.
Cordell, Alfred Robert.
  xCordell, A. Robert.
    Complications of Intrathoracic Surgery. Little.
Corden, W. M. *see* Corden, Warner Max.

Corden, Warner Max.
  xCorden, W. M.
    ed. Public Assistance to Industry: Protection &
      Subsidies in Britain & Germany. Westview.
    Theory of Protection. Oxford U Pr.
Corder, Frederick, 1852-1932
  xCorder, Frederick.
    Ferencz (Francois) Liszt. AMS Pr.
Corder, Jim W. *see* Corder, Jimmie Wayne.
Corder, Jimmie Wayne.
  xCorder, Jim W.
    Contemporary Writing: Process & Practice.
      Scott F.
    Finding a Voice. Scott F.
Cordes, Alfred.
  xCordes, Alfred.
    The Descent of the Doves: Camus's Journey to
      the Spirit. U Pr of Amer.
Cordes, H. O. *see* Cordes, Heinz Otto.
Cordes, Heinz Otto, 1925-
  xCordes, H. O.
    Elliptic Pseudo-Differential Operators: An
      Abstract Theory. Springer-Verlag.
Cordier, Andrew W. *see* Cordier, Andrew Wellington.
Cordier, Andrew Wellington.
  xCordier, Andrew W.
    ed. Columbia Essays in International Affairs:
      The Dean's Papers. Columbia U Pr.
    ed. Paths to World Order. Columbia U Pr.
Cordier, Sherwood S.
  xCordier, Sherwood S.
    Calculus of Power: The Current
      Soviet-American Conventional Military
      Balance in Central Europe. U Pr of Amer.
Cordingly, David.
  xCordingly, David.
    Marine Painting in England, 1700-1900. Potter.
Cordle, Thomas, 1918-
  xCordle, Thomas.
    Andre Gide. St Martin.
    Andre Gide. Twayne.
Cordova-Ferrer, Jacqueline.
  xCordova-Ferrer, Jacqueline.
    Legal Documents on Bilingual Education. Polis
      Pr.
Cordry, Eugene A. *see* Cordry, Eugene Allen.
Cordry, Eugene Allen, 1926-
  xCordry, Eugene A.
    History of New Lebanon, Cooper County,
      Missouri. VKM.
Corduneanu, C.
  xCorduneanu, Constantin.
    Integral Equations & Stability of Feedback
      Systems. Acad Pr.
    Principles of Differential & Integral Equations.
      Chelsea Pub.
Corduneanu, Constantin. *see* Corduneanu, C.
Cordwell, Miriam.
  xCordwell, Miriam.
    Hair Design & Fashion: Principles &
      Relationships. Crown.
Cordy, Don.
  xCordy, Don.
    The Protein Book. Naturegraph.
Core, Earl L. *see* Core, Earl Lemley.
Core, Earl Lemley, 1902-
  xCore, Earl L.
    Chronicles of Core. McClain.
    Vegetation of West Virginia. McClain.
Core, H. A.
  xCore, Harold.
    Wood Structure & Identification. Syracuse U
      Pr.
Core, Harold. *see* Core, H. A.
Corelli, Marie, 1855-1924
  xCorelli, Marie.

    Cameos. Arno.
    Free Opinions Freely Expressed on Certain
      Phases of Modern Social Life & Conduct.
      AMS Pr.
    Song of Miriam: And Other Stories. Arno.
Coren, Alan.
  xCoren, Alan.
    Arthur & the Great Detective. Little.
    Arthur the Kid. Little.
    Arthur's Last Stand. Little.
    Buffalo Arthur. Little.
    Golfing for Cats. St Martin.
    Klondike Arthur. Little.
    Railroad Arthur. Little.
Coren, Stanley.
  xCoren, Stanley.
    Seeing Is Deceiving: The Psychology of Visual
      Illusions. Halsted Pr.
    Sensation & Perception. Acad Pr.
Cores, Lucy. *see* Cores, Lucy Michaella.
Cores, Lucy Michaella, 1914-
  xCores, Lucy.
    Katya. St Martin.
Corey, Dallas.
  xCorey, Dallas.
    The Christmas Legend of Monkey Joe.
      Monkey Joe Ent.
Corey, Dorothy.
  xCorey, Dorothy.
    Everybody Takes Turns. A Whitman.
Corey, E. Raymond.
  xCorey, E. Raymond.
    ed. Industrial Marketing: Cases & Concepts.
      P-H.
Corey, Gerald. *see* Corey, Gerald F.
Corey, Gerald F.
  xCorey, Gerald.
    Groups: Process & Practice. Brooks-Cole.
    I Never Knew I Had a Choice. Brooks-Cole.
    Professional & Ethical Issues in Counseling &
      Psychotherapy. Brooks-Cole.
  xCorey, Gerald F.
    Theory & Practice of Counseling &
      Psychotherapy. Brooks-Cole.
Corey, Irene.
  xCorey, Irene.
    The Mask of Reality: An Approach to Design
      for Theatre. Anchorage.
Corey, Lawrence.
  xCorey, Lawrence.
    Medicine in a Changing Society. Mosby.
Corey, Lewis.
  xCorey, Lewis.
    The Decline of American Capitalism. Arno.
Corey, Paul, 1903-
  xCorey, Paul.
    Are Cats People?: Notes of a Cat-Watcher.
      Contemp Bks.
    Do Cats Think?: Notes of a Cat-Watcher.
      Contemp Bks.
    How to Build Country Homes on a Budget. T
      Y Crowell.
Corfe, T. *see* Corfe, Thomas Howell.
Corfe, Thomas Howell.
  xCorfe, T.
    St. Patrick & Irish Christianity. Cambridge U
      Pr.
  xCorfe, Tom.
    The Murder of Archbishop Thomas. Lerner
      Pubns.
    St. Patrick & Irish Christianity. Lerner Pubns.
Corfe, Tom. *see* Corfe, Thomas Howell.
Coriell, Ron.
  xCoriell, Ron.
    Listen, Look & Live. Revell.
Corinth, K. *see* Corinth, Katherine (Clary).
Corinth, Katherine (Clary).
  xCorinth, K.

    Fashion Showmanship: Everything You Need
      to Know to Give a Fashion Show. Textile Bk.
  xCorinth, Kay.
    Fashion Showmanship: Everything You Need
      to Know to Give a Fashion Show. Wiley.
Corinth, Kay. *see* Corinth, Katherine (Clary).
Corkery, Daniel, 1878-1964
  xCorkery, Daniel.
    Hounds of Banba. Arno.
Corkhill, Thomas.
  xCorkhill, Thomas.
    The Complete Dictionary of Wood. Stein &
      Day.
Corkill, W. A.
  xCorkill, W. A.
    Railway Modelling: An Introduction. David &
      Charles.
Corkran, Herbert, 1924-
  xCorkran, Herbert.
    Patterns of International Cooperation in the
      Caribbean, 1942-1969. SMU Press.
Corle, Edwin, 1906-1956
  xCorle, Edwin.
    Billy the Kid. U of NM Pr.
    Fig Tree John. Liveright.
    Fig Tree John. PB.
    Igor Stravinsky. Arno.
Corlett, P. N. *see* Corlett, Peter Norman.
Corlett, Peter Norman.
  xCorlett, P. N.
    Practical Programming. Cambridge U Pr.
Corlett, William.
  xCorlett, William.
    Christ Story. Bradbury Pr.
    The Dark Side of the Moon. Bradbury Pr.
    The Gate of Eden. Bradbury Pr.
    The Islamic Space. Bradbury Pr.
    The Judaic Law. Bradbury Pr.
    Return to the Gate. Bradbury Pr.
Corlett, William T. *see* Corlett, William Thomas.
Corlett, William Thomas, 1854-1948
  xCorlett, William T.
    The Medicine-Man of the American Indian &
      His Cultural Background. AMS Pr.
Corley, Edwin.
  xCorley, Edwin.
    Air Force One. Dell.
    Air Force One. Doubleday.
Corley, R. H. *see* Corley, R. H. V.
Corley, R. H. V.
  xCorley, R. H.
    Oil Palm Research. Elsevier.
Corley, Robert N. *see* Corley, Robert Neil.
Corley, Robert Neil.
  xCorley, Robert N.
    Fundamentals of Business Law. P-H.
    The Legal Environment of Business. McGraw.
    Principles of Business Law. P-H.
Corliss, John O.
  xCorliss, John O.
    The Ciliated Protozoa: Characterization,
      Classification & Guide to the Literature.
      Pergamon.
Corliss, Richard.
  xCorliss, Richard.
    Talking Pictures: Screenwriters in the
      American Cinema. Overlook Pr.
Corliss, William R.
  xCorliss, William R.

Ancient Man: A Handbook of Puzzling
Artifacts. Sourcebook.
Mysterious Universe: A Handbook of
Astronomical Anomalies. Sourcebook.
Strange Artifacts: A Sourcebook on Ancient
Man. Sourcebook.
Strange Life: A Sourcebook on the Mysteries
of Organic Nature. Sourcebook.
Strange Minds: A Sourcebook of Unusual
Mental Phenomena. Sourcebook.
Strange Planet: A Sourcebook of Unusual
Geological Facts. Sourcebook.
Strange Universe: A Sourcebook of Curious
Astronomical Observations. Sourcebook.
Cormack, Margaret L. see Cormack, Margaret Lawson.
Cormack, Margaret Lawson, 1912-
xCormack, Margaret L.
The Hindu Woman. Greenwood.
Cormack, Maribelle, 1902-
xCormack, Maribelle B.
First Book of Stones. Watts.
Cormack, Maribelle B. see Cormack, Maribelle.
Cormack, R. M. see Cormack, Richard Melville.
Cormack, Richard Melville.
xCormack, R. M.
ed. Spatial & Temporal Analysis in Ecology.
Intl Co-Op.
Corman, Avery.
xCorman, Avery.
Oh, God!. Bantam.
Corman, Calvin W.
xCorman, Calvin W.
Commercial Law: Cases & Materials. Little.
Corman, Cid.
xCorman, Cid.
Sun Rock Man. New Directions.
Cormican, John.
xCormican, John.
A Guidebook for Teaching About the English
Language. Allyn.
Cormier, Frank.
xCormier, Frank.
Presidents Are People Too. Pub Aff Pr.
Cormier, Henri, 1909-
xCormier, Henri.
The Humor of Jesus. Alba.
Cormier, Robert.
xCormier, Robert.
After the First Death. Avon.
After the First Death. Pantheon.
The Chocolate War. Dell.
The Chocolate War. Pantheon.
Cormier, William H.
xCormier, William H.
Interviewing Strategies for Helpers: A Guide to
Assessment, Treatment & Evaluation.
Brooks-Cole.
Corn, Wanda. see Corn, Wanda M.
Corn, Wanda M.
xCorn, Wanda.
ed. Art of Andrew Wyeth. NYGS.
xCorn, Wanda M.
ed. The Art of Andrew Wyeth. NYGS.
Cornaby, W. Arthur. see Cornaby, William Arthur.
Cornaby, William Arthur, 1860-1921
xCornaby, W. Arthur.
A String of Chinese Peach-Stones. Gale.
Cornacchia, Harold J.
xCornacchia, Harold J.
Drugs in the Classroom: A Conceptual Model
for School Programs. Mosby.
Health in the Elementary Schools. Mosby.
Cornaro, Luigi, 1475-1566
xCornaro, Luigi.
The Art of Living Long. Arno.
Cornblath, Marvin.
xCornblath, Marvin.

Disorders of Carbohydrate Metabolism in
Infancy. Saunders.
Cornehls, James V.
xCornehls, James V.
ed. Economic Development & Economic
Growth. New Viewpoints.
Corneille, Pierre.
xCorneille, Pierre.
Le Cid. French & Eur.
Le Cid. La State U Pr.
Le Cid. Larousse.
Le Cid. AHM Pub.
Cid. Barron.
Pompee. Oxford U Pr.
Cornelia. see Cornelia, Nicholas J.
Cornelia, Nicholas J.
xCornelia.
Office Machines Course. SW Pub.
Cornelisen, Ann, 1926-
xCornelisen, Ann.
Strangers & Pilgrims: The Last Italian
Migration. HR&W.
Cornelius. see Cornelius, Ethelwyn G.
Cornelius, Carol.
xCornelius, Carol.
Polka Dots, Checks, & Stripes. Childs World.
Cornelius, Ethelwyn G.
xCornelius.
Food Service Careers. Bennett Co.
Cornelius, Janet.
xCornelius, Janet.
Constitution Making in Illinois, 1818 to 1970.
U of Ill Pr.
Cornelius, Wayne A., 1945-
xCornelius, Wayne A.
Politics & the Migrant Poor in Mexico City.
Stanford U Pr.
**Cornell Agricultural Waste Management Conference,
8th, 1976.**
xCornell Waste Management Conference, 8th.
Land As a Waste Management Alternative.
Ann Arbor Science.
Cornell, Alexander.
xCornell, Alexander H.
The Decision-Maker's Handbook. P-H.
Cornell, Alexander H. see Cornell, Alexander.
Cornell, Francis G. see Cornell, Francis Griffith.
Cornell, Francis Griffith, 1906-
xCornell, Francis G.
A Measure of Tax-Paying Ability of Local
School Administrative Units. AMS Pr.
Cornell, James.
xCornell, James.
The Great International Disaster Book. PB.
The Great International Disaster Book.
Scribner.
xCornell, James C.
Lost Lands & Forgotten People. Sterling.
Nature at Its Strangest: True Stories from the
Files of the Smithsonian Institution's Center
for Short-Lived Phenomena. Sterling.
Cornell, James C. see Cornell, James.
Cornell, Jane.
xCornell, Jane.
Successful Custom Interiors. Structures Pub.
Successful Family & Recreation Rooms.
Structures Pub.
Cornell, John B. see Cornell, John Bilheimer.
Cornell, John Bilheimer, 1921-
xCornell, John B.
Two Japanese Villages: Matsunagi, a Japanese
Mountain Community, Kurusu, a Japanese
Agricultural Community. Greenwood.
Cornell, Kenneth. see Cornell, William Kenneth.
Cornell, Robert J.
xCornell, Robert J.
Anthracite Coal Strike of 1902. Russell.
Cornell University.
xCornell University.

Cornell University Libraries: Southeast Asia
Catalog. G K Hall.
Third Supplement to the Cumulation of the
Library Catalogsupplements of the New York
State School of Industrial & Labor Relations.
G K Hall.
Cornell University. Libraries.
xCornell University Libraries.
Catalogue of the Witchcraft Collection in the
Cornell University Library. Kraus Intl.
Petrarch: Catalogue of the Petrarch Collection
in Cornell University Library. Kraus Intl.
**Cornell University. New York State School of Industrial
and Labor Relations.**
xCornell University, New York State School of
Industrial & Labor Ralations.
Cumulation of the Library Catalog Supplements
of Martin P. Catherwood Library of the New
York State School of Industrial & Labor
Relations. G K Hall.
Library Catalog of the Martin P. Catherwood
Library of the New York State School of
Industrial & Labor Relations. G K Hall.
Cornell Waste Management Conference, 8th. see Cornell
Agricultural Waste Management Conference, 8th,
1976.
Cornell, William A.
xCornell, William A.
Our Pennsylvania Heritage. Penns Valley.
Cornell, William K. see Cornell, William Kenneth.
Cornell, William Kenneth.
xCornell, Kenneth.
Post-Symbolist Period: French Poetic Currents,
1900-1920. Shoe String.
Symbolist Movement. Shoe String.
xCornell, William K.
Adolphe Rette, 1863-1930. AMS Pr.
Corner, E. J. see Corner, Edred John Henry.
Corner, Edred John Henry.
xCorner, E. J.
A Monograph of Clavaria & Allied Genera.
Dawson Pub.
Monograph of Clavaria & Allied Genera.
Lubrecht & Cramer.
Corner, George W. see Corner, George Washington.
Corner, George Washington, 1889-
xCorner, George W.
Anatomy. AMS Pr.
Anatomy. Hafner.
Ourselves Unborn: An Embryologist's Essay on
Man. R West.
Ourselves Unborn: An Embryologist's Essay on
Man. Shoe String.
Corney, Alan.
xCorney, Alan.
Atomic & Laser Spectroscopy. Oxford U Pr.
Cornfeld, Gaalyah. see Cornfeld, Gaalyahu.
Cornfeld, Gaalyahu, 1902-
xCornfeld, Gaalyah.
Archaeology of the Bible: Book by Book.
Har-Row.
Cornford, F. M. see Cornford, Francis MacDonald.
Cornford, Francis M. see Cornford, Francis MacDonald.
Cornford, Francis MacDonald, 1874-1943
xCornford, F. M.
Principium Sapientiae: The Origins of Greek
Philosophical Thought. Peter Smith.
xCornford, Francis M.
ed. Greek Religious Thought from Homer to
the Age of Alexander. AMS Pr.
Corning Museum of Glass. see Corning, N.Y. Museum of
Glass.
Corning, N.Y. Museum of Glass.
xCorning Museum of Glass.
A Survey of Glassmaking from Ancient Egypt
to the Present. U of Chicago Pr.
xTheCorning Museum of Glass.

Glass from the Corning Museum of Glass-a
Guide to the Collections. Corning.

Cornish, Sam.
xCornish, Sam.
Grandmother's Pictures. Avon.
Grandmother's Pictures. Bookstore Pr.
Grandmother's Pictures. Bradbury Pr.

Cornish-Bowden, Athel.
xCornish-Bowden, Athel.
Fundamentals of Enzyme Kinetics.
Butterworths.

Corns, Marshall C.
xCorns, Marshall C.
Practical Operations & Management of a Bank.
Bankers.

Cornuelle, Richard. see Cornuelle, Richard C.

Cornuelle, Richard C., 1927-
xCornuelle, Richard.
De-Managing America: The Final Revolution.
Random.

Cornwall, E. Judson.
xCornwall, Judson.
Let Us Abide. Revell.
Let Us Be Holy. Logos.
Let Us Draw Near. Logos.
Let Us Enjoy Forgiveness. Revell.

Cornwall, John.
xCornwall, John.
Growth & Stability in a Mature Economy.
Biblio Dist.
Modern Capitalism: Its Growth &
Transformation. St Martin.

Cornwall, Judson. see Cornwall, E. Judson.

Cornwall, Julian.
xCornwall, Julian C.
Revolt of the Peasantry, 1549. Routledge &
Kegan.

Cornwall, Julian C. see Cornwall, Julian

Cornwell, Elmer E.
xCornwell, Elmer E.
Presidential Leadership of Public Opinion.
Greenwood.

Cornwell, H. Campbell. see Cornwell, H. J. Campbell.

Cornwell, H. J. Campbell.
xCornwell, H. Campbell.
Forty Years of Caledonian Locomotives
1882-1922. David & Charles.

Cornwell, Keith.
xCornwell, Keith.
The Flow of Heat. Van Nos Reinhold.

Corpus Juris Civilis.
xCorpus Juris Civilis.
Institutes of Justinian. Greenwood.

Corpus, Severino F.
xCorpus, Severino F.
An Analysis of the Racial Adjustment
Activities & Problems of the
Filipino-American Christian Fellowship in
Los Angeles. R & E Res Assoc.

Corr, Edwin G.
xCorr, Edwin G.
The Political Process in Colombia. U of Denver
Intl.

Corr, Francis A.
xCorr, Francis A.
Government Services for Consumers.
Pendulum Pr.

Corradi, Lou.
xCorradi, Lou.
The Set-up. Fawcett.

Corradini, Enrico, 1868-1931
xCorradini, Enrico.
Discorsi Politici: 1902-1923. AMS Pr.

Corre, Alan D.
xCorre, Allan.
Understanding the Talmud. Ktav.

Corre, Allan. see Corre, Alan D.

Correa, Hector.
xCorrea, Hector.

Integrated Economic Accounting: Theory &
Applications to National, Real, & Financial
Economic Planning. Lexington Bks.

Correale, William H.
xCorreale, William H.
A Building Code Primer. McGraw.

Correll, Donovan S. see Correll, Donovan Stewart.

Correll, Donovan Stewart.
xCorrell, Donovan S.
Aquatic & Wetland Plants of Southwestern
United States. Stanford U Pr.
Native Orchids of North America North of
Mexico. Stanford U Pr.

Correll, Marsha M.
xCorrell, Marsha M.
Teaching the Gifted & Talented. Phi Delta
Kappa.

Corrie, Bruce. see Corrie, Bruce A.

Corrie, Bruce A.
xCorrie, Bruce.
The Atlantic Coast Conference: Silver
Anniversary, 1953-1978. Carolina Acad Pr.

Corriere, Richard.
xCorriere, Richard.
The Dream Makers: Discovering Your
Breakthrough Dreams. T Y Crowell.

Corrigan, Barbara, 1922-
xCorrigan, Barbara.
How to Make Pants & Jeans That Really Fit.
Doubleday.
How to Make Something Out of Practically
Nothing: New Fashions from Old Clothes.
Doubleday.
I Love to Sew. Doubleday.
Of Course You Can Sew: Basics of Sewing for
the Young Beginner. Doubleday.

Corrigan, Beatrice.
xCorrigan, Beatrice.
ed. Curious Annals: New Documents Relating
to Browning's Roman Murder Story. U of
Toronto Pr.

Corrigan, Eileen. see Corrigan, Eileen M.

Corrigan, Eileen M.
xCorrigan, Eileen.
Problem Drinkers Seeking Treatment. Rutgers
Ctr Alcohol.
xCorrigan, Eileen M.
Alcoholic Women in Treatment. Oxford U Pr.

Corrigan, John E.
xCorrigan, John E.
Growing up Christian: Penance & the Moral
Development of Children. Pflaum Pr.

Corrigan, John T.
xCorrigan, John T.
Guide for the Organization & Operation of a
Religious Resource Center. Cath Lib Assn.

Corrigan, Philip. see Corrigan, Philip Richard D.

Corrigan, Philip Richard D.
xCorrigan, Philip.
Socialist Construction & Marxist Theory:
Bolshevism & Its Critique. Monthly Rev.

Corrigan, Robert. see Corrigan, Robert Willoughby.
Corrigan, Robert W. see Corrigan, Robert Willoughby.

Corrigan, Robert Willoughby, 1927-
xCorrigan, Robert.
The Theatre in Search of a Fix. Delacorte.
xCorrigan, Robert W.
The World of the Theatre. Scott F.

Corris, Peter.
xCorris, Peter.
Passage, Port & Plantation: A History of
Solomon Islands Labour Migration
1870-1914. Intl Schol Bk Serv.

Corrothers, James D. see Corrothers, James David.

Corrothers, James David, 1869-1917
xCorrothers, James D.
In Spite of the Handicap: An Autobiography.
Negro U Pr.

Corruccini, Robert S.
xCorruccini, Robert S.

ed. Anthropological Studies Related to Health
Problems of North American Indians. Mss
Info.

Corry, John.
xCorry, John.
Golden Clan: The Murrays, the McDonnells, &
the Irish American Aristocracy. HM.

Corry, Joseph.
xCorry, Joseph.
Observations Upon the Windward Coast of
Africa: Religion, Character, Customs, Etc., of
the Natives. Biblio Dist.

Cors, Paul B., 1913-
xCors, Paul B.
Railroads. Libs Unl.

Corsa, Leslie.
xCorsa, Leslie.
Population Planning. U of Mich Pr.

Corse, Carl D.
xCorse, Carl D.
Introduction to Shipboard Weapons. Naval Inst
Pr.

Corsini, Raymond J.
xCorsini, Raymond J.
ed. Current Personality Theories. Peacock
Pubs.
Current Psychotherapies. Peacock Pubs.
The Practical Parent: The ABC's of Child
Discipline. Har-Row.
ed. Readings in Current Personality Theories.
Peacock Pubs.

Corson, James C. see Corson, James Clarkson.

Corson, James Clarkson.
xCorson, James C.
ed. Notes & Index to Sir Herbert Grierson's
Edition of the Letters of Sir Walter Scott.
Oxford U Pr.

Corson, John J. see Corson, John Jay.

Corson, John Jay.
xCorson, John J.
Economic Needs of Older People. Kraus Repr.
The Governance of Colleges & Universities:
Modernizing Structure & Processes. McGraw.

Corson, Richard, 1918-
xCorson, Richard.
Champions at Speed. Dodd.
Stage Makeup. P-H.

Corson, S. A. see Corson, Samuel Abraham.

Corson, Samuel Abraham.
xCorson, S. A.
Ethology & Nonverbal Communication in
Mental Health: An Interdisciplinary
Biopsychosocial Exploration. Pergamon.

Corson, William R.
xCorson, William R.
The Consequences of Failure. Norton.

Cort, David, 1904-
xCort, David.
The Sin of Henry R. Luce: An Anatomy of
Journalism. Lyle Stuart.

Cort, Louise A. see Cort, Louise Allison.

Cort, Louise Allison, 1944-
xCort, Louise A.
Shigaraki, Potters' Valley. Kodansha.

Cort, Margaret.
xCort, Margaret.
Little Oleg. Carolrhoda Bks.

Cortada, James W.
xCortada, James W.
ed. Spain in the Twentieth-Century World:
Essays on Spanish Diplomacy, 1898-1978.
Greenwood.
Two Nations Over Time: Spain & the United
States, 1776-1977. Greenwood.

Cortazar, Julio.
xCortazar, Julio.
Hopscotch. Avon.

Cortes, Carlos E.
xCortes, Carlos E.

Gaucho Politics in Brazil: The Politics of Rio
Grande do Sul 1930-1964. U of NM Pr.
Cortes, F. see Cortes, Fernando.
Cortes, Fernando.
xCortes, F.
Systems Analysis for Social Scientists. Wiley.
Cortes, Juan B.
xCortes, Juan B.
Delinquency & Crime, a Biopsychosocial
Approach: Empirical, Theoretical, & Practical
Aspects of Criminal Behavior. Acad Pr.
Cortes, Rosario M. see Cortes, Rosario Mendoza.
Cortes, Rosario Mendoza.
xCortes, Rosario M.
Pangasinan, 1572-1800. Cellar.
Corti, E. see Corti, Egon Caesar.
Corti, Egon C. see Corti, Egon Caesar.
Corti, Egon Caesar, Conte, 1886-1953
xCorti, E.
Reign of the House of Rothschild. Gordon Pr.
xCorti, Egon C.
Maximilian & Charlotte of Mexico. Gordon Pr.
Corti, Maria.
xCorti, Maria.
An Introduction to Literary Semiotics. Ind U
Pr.
Cortina, Frank M. see Cortina, Frank Michael.
Cortina, Frank Michael.
xCortina, Frank M.
Face to Face. Columbia U Pr.
Stroke a Slain Warrior. Columbia U Pr.
Cortissoz, Royal, 1869-1948
xCortissoz, Royal.
American Artists. AMS Pr.
American Artists. Arno.
Personalities in Art. Arno.
Cortland, Philip Van. see Van Cortlandt, Philip.
Cortner, Richard C.
xCortner, Richard C.
Constitutional Law & Politics: Three Arizona
Case-Studies. U of Ariz Pr.
Cortot, Alfred, 1877-1962
xCortot, Alfred.
French Piano Music. Da Capo.
In Search of Chopin. Greenwood.
Corum, J. M.
xCorum, J. M.
ed. Pressure Vessels & Piping: Verification &
Qualification of Inelastic Analysis Computer
Programs. ASME.
Corvin, R O.
xCorvin, R. O.
David & His Mighty Men. Arno.
Corwin. see Corwin, Lawrence J.
Corwin, Arthur F.
xCorwin, Arthur F.
ed. Immigrants--& Immigrants: Perspectives on
Mexican Labor Migration to the United
States. Greenwood.
Corwin, B. R.
xCorwin, B. R.
A Trip to the Rockies. Arno.
Corwin, E. S. see Corwin, Edward Samuel.
Corwin, Edward S. see Corwin, Edward Samuel.
Corwin, Edward Samuel, 1878-1963
xCorwin, E. S.
French Policy & the American Alliance of
1778. Peter Smith.
xCorwin, Edward S.

Constitution & World Organization. Arno.
Constitutional Revolution, Ltd.. Greenwood.
Edward S. Corwin's, the Constitution & What
It Means Today. Princeton U Pr.
French Policy & the American Alliance of
1778. B Franklin.
Higher Law Background of American
Constitutional Law. Cornell U Pr.
Liberty Against Government: The Rise,
Flowering, & Decline of a Famous Judicial
Concept. Greenwood.
National Supremacy: Treaty Power Vs. State
Power. Peter Smith.
The President: Office & Powers, 1787-1957:
History & Analysis of Practice & Opinion.
NYU Pr.
Presidential Power & the Constitution: Essays.
Cornell U Pr.
Twilight of the Supreme Court: A History of
Our Constitutional Theory. Shoe String.
Corwin, Lawrence J.
xCorwin.
Calculus in Vector Spaces. Dekker.
Corwin, Norman. see Corwin, Norman Lewis.
Corwin, Norman Lewis, 1910-
xCorwin, Norman.
Holes in a Stained Glass Window. Lyle Stuart.
Corwin, R. D. see Corwin, R. David.
Corwin, R. David.
xCorwin, R. D.
Racial Minorities in Banking: New Workers in
the Banking Industry. Coll & U Pr.
Corwin, Ronald G.
xCorwin, Ronald G.
Education in Crisis: A Sociological Analysis of
Schools & Universities in Transition. Wiley.
Corwin, Ruthann, 1945-
xCorwin, Ruthann.
Environmental Impact Assessment. Freeman C.
Cory, George.
xCory, George.
Head-on with Hurricane Camille. Raintree
Pubs.
Cory, Irene. see Cory, Irene E.
Cory, Irene E.
xCory, Irene.
Pawdie. Vanguard.
Cory, Lloyd.
xCory, Lloyd.
Quote Unquote. Victor Bks.
Coryell, Julie.
xCoryell, Julie.
Jazz Rock Fusion, the People, the Music. Dell.
Cosentino, Geraldine.
xCosentino, Geraldine.
Carnival Glass. Western Pub.
Coser, L. see Coser, Lewis A.
Coser, Lewis. see Coser, Lewis A.
Coser, Lewis A., 1913-
xCoser, L.
Georg Simmel. P-H.
xCoser, Lewis.
Masters of Sociological Thought: Ideas in
Historical & Social Context. HarBraceJ.
xCoser, Lewis A.
Continuities in the Study of Social Conflict.
Free Pr.
Functions of Social Conflict. Free Pr.
Masters of Sociological Thought: Ideas in
Historical & Social Context. HarBraceJ.
Coser, Rose L. see Coser, Rose Laub.
Coser, Rose Laub, 1916-
xCoser, Rose L.
The Family: Its Structure & Functions. St
Martin.
Life in the Ward. Mich St U Pr.
Cosgrave, Patrick.
xCosgrave, Patrick.

Public Poetry of Robert Lowell. Taplinger.
Cosgriff, James H.
xCosgriff, James H.
The Practice of Emergency Nursing.
Lippincott.
Cosgriff, John.
xCosgriff, John W.
Lower Triassic Temnospondyli of Tasmania.
Geol Soc.
Cosgriff, John W. see Cosgriff, John.
Cosgrove, Cornelius B. see Cosgrove, Cornelius Burton.
Cosgrove, Cornelius Burton.
xCosgrove, Cornelius B.
Caves of the Upper Gila & Hueco Areas in
New Mexico & Texas. Kraus Repr.
Cosgrove, Margaret.
xCosgrove, Margaret.
illus. Eggs & What Happens Inside Them.
Dodd.
illus. Wonders of the Tree World. Dodd.
illus. Wonders of Your Senses. Dodd.
illus. Your Muscles & Ways to Exercise Them.
Dodd.
Cosgrove, Richard A., 1941-
xCosgrove, Richard A.
The Rule of Law: Albert Venn Dicey, Victorian
Jurist. U of NC Pr.
Cosgrove, Stephen.
xCosgrove, Stephen.
Catundra. Creative Ed.
Catundra. Price Stern.
Catundra. Soc for Visual.
Creole. Creative Ed.
The Dream Tree. Price Stern.
Kartusch. Price Stern.
Kartusch. Creative Ed.
Little Mouse on the Prairie. Creative Ed.
Little Mouse on the Prairie. Price Stern.
Little Mouse on the Prairie. Soc for Visual.
Muffin Muncher. Price Stern.
xCosgrove, Steve.
Bangalee. Creative Ed.
Dream Tree. Creative Ed.
Gnome from Nome. Creative Ed.
Hucklebug. Creative Ed.
In Search of Saveopotamas. Creative Ed.
Leo the Lop. Creative Ed.
Muffin Muncher. Creative Ed.
Serendipity. Creative Ed.
Wheedle on the Needle. Creative Ed.
xCosgrove, Steven.
Gnome from Nome. Price Stern.
Cosgrove, Steve. see Cosgrove, Stephen.
Cosgrove, Steven. see Cosgrove, Stephen.
Cosi, Liliana.
xCosi, Liliana.
The Young Ballet Dancer. Stein & Day.
Cosic, Dobrica, 1921-
xCosic, Dobrica.
Reach to Eternity. HarBraceJ.
Coskey, Evelyn, 1932-
xCoskey, Evelyn.
Christmas Crafts for Everyone. Abingdon.
Easter Eggs for Everyone. Abingdon.
Cosman, Anna.
xCosman, Anna.
How to Read & Write Poetry. Watts.
Cosman, Carol.
xCosman, Carol.
ed. The Penguin Book of Women Poets.
Penguin.
ed. The Penguin Book of Women Poets. Viking
Pr.
Cosman, Madeleine P. see Cosman, Madeleine Pelner.
Cosman, Madeleine Pelner.
xCosman, Madeleine P.
Fabulous Feasts: Medieval Cookery &
Ceremony. Braziller.
Cosmas, Graham A.
xCosmas, Graham A.

An Army for Empire: The United States Army in the Spanish American War. U of Mo Pr.

Cosner, Ron, 1940-
xCosner, Ron.
Football's Multiple Pro-I Offense. P-H.

COSPAR-IAU-IUTAM Symposium, Sao Paulo, Brazil, June 19-21, 1974. *see* Symposium on Satellite Dynamics, 4th, Sao Paulo, Brazil, 1974.

Cossa, Luigi, 1831-1896
xCossa, Luigi.
Introduction to the Study of Political Economy. Hyperion Conn.

Cossi, Olga.
xCossi, Olga.
Fire Mate. Independence Pr.

Cossons, Neil.
xCossons, Neil.
The BP Book of Industrial Archaeology. David & Charles.

Costa, C. D. *see* Costa, Charles Desmond Nuttall.

Costa, Charles Desmond Nuttall.
xCosta, C. D.
ed. Horace. Routledge & Kegan.

Costa De Beauregard, Oliver. *see* Costa De Beauregard, Olivier.

Costa, E. *see* Costa, Erminio.

Costa, Erminio.
xCosta, E.
ed. The Endorphins. Raven.
ed. Mechanism of Action of Benzodiazepines. Raven.
ed. Nonstriatal Dopaminergic Neurons. Raven.

Costa, Richard H. *see* Costa, Richard Hauer.

Costa, Richard Hauer.
xCosta, Richard H.
H. G. Wells. Twayne.

Costa, Sylvia. *see* Costa, Sylvia Allen.

Costa, Sylvia Allen.
xCosta, Sylvia.
How to Prepare a Production Budget for Film & Video Tape. TAB Bks.

Costa De Beauregard, Olivier.
xCosta De Beauregard, Oliver.
Precis of Special Relativity. Acad Pr.

Costain, Thomas B.
xCostain, Thomas B.
High Towers. Doubleday.
Silver Chalice. PB.
Silver Chalice. Doubleday.
White & the Gold. Doubleday.

Costain, Thomas B. *see* Costain, Thomas Bertram.

Costain, Thomas Bertram, 1885-
xCostain, Thomas B.
The Conquering Family. Doubleday.
The Conquering Family. Popular Lib.
The Last Plantagenets. Doubleday.
Last Plantagenets. Popular Lib.

Costantini, Costanzo.
xCostantini, Costanzo.
Are All Italians Lousy Lovers. Lyle Stuart.

Costanza, Betty.
xCostanza, Betty.
Women's Track & Field. Dutton.

Costas, O. E. *see* Costas, Orlando E.

Costas, Orlando E.
xCostas, O. E.
Theology of the Crossroads in Contemporary Latin America: Missiology in Mainline Proestantism 1969-1974. Humanities.
xCostas, Orlando E.
The Church and Its Mission: A Shattering Critique from the Third World. Tyndale.
The Integrity of Mission: The Inner Life & Outreach of the Church. Har-Row.

Costello, Anita C. *see* Costello, Anita Coles.

Costello, Anita Coles.
xCostello, Anita C.
Picasso's "Vollard Suite". Garland Pub.

Costello, C. G. *see* Costello, Charles Gerard.

Costello, Charles G. *see* Costello, Charles Gerard.

Costello, Charles Gerard, 1929-
xCostello, C. G.
Symptoms of Psychopathology: A Handbook. Wiley.
xCostello, Charles G.
Anxiety & Depression: The Adaptive Emotions. McGill-Queens U Pr.

Costello, David F. *see* Costello, David Francis.

Costello, David Francis, 1904-
xCostello, David F.
The Desert World. T Y Crowell.
Prairie World. T Y Crowell.
The Prairie World. U of Minn Pr.
The Seashore World. Lippincott & Crowell.
World of the Gull. Lippincott.
World of the Porcupine. Lippincott.
World of the Prairie Dog. Lippincott.

Costello, Don.
xCostello, Don.
For Inner Peace & Strength. Dghtrs St Paul.

Costello, Gerald M.
xCostello, Gerald M.
Mission to Latin America: The Successes & Failures of a Twentieth-Century Crusade. Orbis Bks.

Costello, Mark.
xCostello, Mark.
The Murphy Stories. U of Ill Pr.

Costello, Maurice J.
xCostello, Maurice J.
Palms & Soles in Medicine. C C Thomas.

Costello, Patty.
xCostello, Patty.
Bowling. Van Nos Reinhold.

Costello, Peter.
xCostello, Peter.
In Search of Lake Monsters. Berkley Pub.
The Magic Zoo. St Martin.

Costello, Timothy. *see* Costello, Timothy W.

Costello, Timothy W.
xCostello, Timothy.
Psychology in Administration: Research Orientation Text with Integrated Readings. P-H.

Coster, Charles H. *see* Coster, Charles Henry.

Coster, Charles Henry.
xCoster, Charles H.
Late Roman Studies. Harvard U Pr.

Costich, Julia F.
xCostich, Julia F.
Antonin Artaud. Twayne.

Costigan, Daniel M.
xCostigan, Daniel M.
Electronic Delivery of Documents & Graphics. Van Nos Reinhold.

Costigan, Giovanni.
xCostigan, Giovanni.
A History of Modern Ireland: With a Sketch of Earlier Times. Pegasus.

Costin, Lela B.
xCostin, Lela B.
The Licensing of Family Homes in Child Welfare: A Guide for Instructors & Trainees. Wayne St U Pr.

Costin, Michael.
xCostin, Michael.
Racing & Sports Car Chassis Design. Bentley.

Costley, Dan L.
xCostley, Dan L.
Human Relations in Organizations. West Pub.

Costner, Herbert L., 1930-
xCostner, Herbert L.
ed. Sociological Methodology 1971. Jossey-Bass.
ed. Sociological Methodology 1972. Jossey-Bass.
ed. Sociological Methodology 1973-74. Jossey-Bass.

Coston, William H. *see* Coston, William Hilary.

Coston, William Hilary.
xCoston, William H.
The Spanish-American War Volunteer. Arno.

Costonis, John. *see* Costonis, John J.

Costonis, John J.
xCostonis, John.
The Puerto Rico Plan: Environmental Protection Through Development Rights Transfer. Urban Land.
xCostonis, John J.
Regulation V. Compensation in Land Use Control: A Recommended Accommodation, a Critique, & an Interpretation. Inst Gov Stud Berk.
Space Adrift: Landmark Preservation & the Marketplace. U of Ill Pr.

Costonis, Maureen.
xCostonis, Maureen.
ed. Therapy in Motion. U of Ill Pr.

Cotchett, Joseph W.
xCotchett, Joseph W.
Federal Courtroom Evidence. Parker & Son.

Cotes, Rosemary A.
xCotes, Rosemary A.
Dante's Garden, with Legends of the Flowers. Folcroft.

Cotgreave, Alfred, 1849-1911
xCotgreave, Alfred.
Contents-Subject Index to General & Periodical Literature. Gale.

Cotham, Perry C.
xCotham, Perry C.
Politics, Americanism & Christianity. Baker Bk.

Cothen, Grady C.
xCothen, Grady C.
Unto All the World: Bold Mission. Broadman.

Cothenet, Edouard.
xCothenet, Edouard.
Imitating Christ Abbey.

Cotler, Harold I., 1946-
xCotler, Harold J.
Encyclopedic Deskbook of Teaching Ideas & Classroom Activities. P-H.

Cotler, Harold J. *see* Cotler, Harold I.

Cotlow, Lewis. *see* Cotlow, Lewis N.

Cotlow, Lewis N.
xCotlow, Lewis.
The Twilight of the Primitive. Ballantine.

Cotner, Robert. *see* Cotner, Robert Crawford.

Cotner, Robert C. *see* Cotner, Robert Crawford.

Cotner, Robert Crawford.
xCotner, Robert.
tr. Theodore Foster's Minutes of the Convention Held at South Kingstown, R.I. in March, 1790. RI Hist Soc.
xCotner, Robert C.
Readings in American History. HM.

Cotran, E. *see* Cotran, Eugene.

Cotran, Eugene.
xCotran, E.
ed. Readings in African Law. Biblio Dist.

Cotroneo, Ross R. *see* Cotroneo, Ross Ralph.

Cotroneo, Ross Ralph.
xCotroneo, Ross R.
History of the Northern Pacific Land Grant, 1900-1952. Arno.

Cott, Allan, 1910-
xCott, Allan.
The Orthomolecular Approach to Learning Disabilities. Acad Therapy.

Cott, Jonathan.
xCott, Jonathan.
Forever Young. Random.

Cottam, Richard W.
xCottam, Richard W.
Nationalism in Iran. U of Pittsburgh Pr.

Cotte, Sabine.
xCotte, Sabine.
Claude Lorrain. Braziller.

Cotter, James F. *see* Cotter, James Finn.

Cotter, James Finn.
  xCotter, James F.
    Inscape: The Christology & Poetry of Gerard
     Manley Hopkins. U of Pittsburgh Pr.
Cotter, Joseph S. see Cotter, Joseph Seamon.
Cotter, Joseph Seamon, 1861-
  xCotter, Joseph S.
    Collected Poems of Joseph S. Cotter, Sr.. Arno.
    Negro Tales. Arno.
    A White Song & a Black One. AMS Pr.
Cotterell, Arthur.
  xCotterell, Arthur.
    A Dictionary of World Mythology. Putnam.
Cotterill, R. S. see Cotterill, Robert Spencer.
Cotterill, Robert Spencer, 1884-
  xCotterill, R. S.
    The Southern Indians: The Story of the
     Civilized Tribes Before Removal. U of Okla
     Pr.
Cottesloe, Gloria, Baroness.
  xCottesloe, Gloria.
    The Story of the Battersea Dogs' Home. David
     & Charles.
Cottin, Lou.
  xCottin, Lou.
    Elders in Rebellion: A Guide to Senior
     Activism. Doubleday.
Cottingham, Clive.
  xCottingham, Clive.
    Game of Billiards. Lippincott.
Cottle, Charles R.
  xCottle, Charles R.
    Sunrise. Visage Pr.
Cottle, Thomas. see Cottle, Thomas J.
Cottle, Thomas J.
  xCottle, Thomas.
    Readings in Personality & Adjustment.
     Har-Row.
  xCottle, Thomas J.
    Busing. Beacon Pr.
    College: Reward & Betrayal. U of Chicago Pr.
    Hidden Survivors: Portraits of Poor Jews in
     America. P-H.
    Private Lives & Public Accounts. New
     Viewpoints.
    Private Lives & Public Accounts. U of Mass
     Pr.
    Readings in Adolescent Psychology:
     Contemporary Perspectives. Har-Row.
Cottle, William C.
  xCottle, William C.
    Preparation for Counseling. P-H.
Cottler, Joseph, 1899-
  xCottler, Joseph.
    Champions of Democracy. Arno.
Cottom, Truman W.
  xCottom, Truman W.
    Building & Construction Desk Book, with
     Forms. P-H.
Cotton. see Cotton, Horace.
Cotton, Albert F. see Cotton, Frank Albert.
Cotton, F. A. see Cotton, Frank Albert.
Cotton, F. Albert. see Cotton, Frank Albert.
Cotton, Frank Albert.
  xCotton, Albert F.
    Progress in Inorganic Chemistry. Krieger.
  xCotton, F. A.
    Chemistry: An Investigative Approach. HM.
  xCotton, F. Albert.
    Advanced Inorganic Chemistry: A
     Comprehensive Text. Wiley.
    Chemical Applications of Group Theory.
     Wiley.
Cotton, H. see Cotton, Horace.
Cotton, Henry, 1789-1879
  xCotton, Henry.
    The Typographical Gazetteer. Gale.
Cotton, Horace, 1907-
  xCotton.

Medical Practice Management. Van Nos
  Reinhold.
  xCotton, H.
    Medical Practice Management. Med
     Economics.
Cotton, Norris.
  xCotton, Norris.
    In the Senate: Amidst Conflict & Turmoil.
     Dodd.
Cotton, Walter A. see Cotton, Walter Aidan.
Cotton, Walter Aidan.
  xCotton, Walter A.
    Race Problem in South Africa. Negro U Pr.
Cottrell, A. H. see Cottrell, Alan Howard.
Cottrell, Alan. see Cottrell, Alan Howard.
Cottrell, Alan Howard.
  xCottrell, A. H.
    The Mechanical Properties of Matter. Krieger.
  xCottrell, Alan.
    An Introduction to Metallurgy. Crane-Russak
     Co.
Cottrell, Alvin J.
  xCottrell, Alvin J.
    Military Forces in the Persian Gulf. Sage.
Cottrell, Donald P. see Cottrell, Donald Peery.
Cottrell, Donald Peery, 1902-
  xCottrell, Donald P.
    Instruction & Instructional Facilities in the
     Colleges of the United Lutheran Church in
     America. AMS Pr.
Cottrell, Edyth Y. see Cottrell, Edyth Young.
Cottrell, Edyth Young.
  xCottrell, Edyth Y.
    Stretching the Food Dollar Cookbook.
     Woodbridge Pr.
    Sugar-Coated Teddy. Woodbridge Pr.
Cottrell, Fred, 1903-
  xCottrell, Fred W.
    The Railroader. Irvington.
Cottrell, Fred W. see Cottrell, Fred.
Cottrell, James E.
  xCottrell, James E.
    Anesthesia & Neurosurgery. Mosby.
Cottrell, Jane E.
  xCottrell, Jane E.
    Alberto Moravia. Ungar.
Cottrell, Leonard.
  xCottrell, Leonard.
    Anvil of Civilization. NAL.
Cottrell, Leonard S. see Cottrell, Leonard Slater.
Cottrell, Leonard Slater.
  xCottrell, Leonard S.
    American Opinion on World Affairs in the
     Atomic Age. Greenwood.
Cottrell, Robert D.
  xCottrell, Robert D.
    Colette. Ungar.
    Simone De Beauvoir. Ungar.
Cottrell, Sue.
  xCottrell, Sue.
    Hoof Beats North & South: Horses &
     Horsemen of the Civil War. Exposition.
Cottrell, T. L. see Cottrell, Tom Leadbetter.
Cottrell, Tom Leadbetter.
  xCottrell, T. L.
    Chemistry. Oxford U Pr.
Cottrell, William F. see Cottrell, William Frederick.
Cottrell, William Frederick, 1903-
  xCottrell, William F.
    Energy & Society: The Relation Between
     Energy, Social Change & Economic
     Development. Greenwood.
Cotz, Victor. see Cotz, Victor J.
Cotz, Victor J., 1919-
  xCotz, Victor.
    Plant Engineers Manual & Guide. P-H.
Cotzias, G. see Cotzias, George C.
Cotzias, George C.
  xCotzias, G.

    ed. Developments in Treatment for Parkinson's
     Disease. Krieger.
Couasnon, Charles.
  xCouasnon, Charles.
    The Church of the Holy Sepulchre in
     Jerusalem. Oxford U Pr.
Couch, Houston B.
  xCouch, Houston B.
    Diseases of Turfgrasses. Krieger.
Couch, Jean. see Couch, Jean M.
Couch, Jean M.
  xCouch, Jean.
    Runner's World Yoga Book. Anderson World.
Couch, William T. see Couch, William Terry.
Couch, William Terry, 1901-
  xCouch, William T.
    ed. Culture in the South. Negro U Pr.
    The Human Potential: An Essay on Its
     Cultivation. Duke.
Coudenhove-Kalergi, Heinrich J. see
  Coudenhove-Kalergi, Heinrich Johann Maria.
Coudenhove-Kalergi, Heinrich Johann Maria.
  xCoudenhove-Kalergi, Heinrich J.
    Anti-Semitism Throughout the Ages.
     Greenwood.
Coudert, Jo.
  xCoudert, Jo.
    Advice from a Failure. Stein & Day.
    The Alcoholic in Your Life. Warner Bks.
    The I Never Cooked Before Cookbook. NAL.
Coues, Elliott, 1842-1899
  xCoues, Elliott.
    Fur-Bearing Animals of North America. Arno.
Couffer, Jack.
  xCouffer, Jack.
    Canyon Summer. Putnam.
Couffignal, Robert.
  xCouffignal, Robert.
    Apollinaire. U of Ala Pr.
Couger, J. D. see Couger, J. Daniel.
Couger, J. Daniel.
  xCouger, J. D.
    A First Course in Data Processing. Wiley.
  xCouger, J. Daniel.
    Fortran IV: A Programmed Instruction
     Approach. Irwin.
    Introduction to Computer-Based Information
     Systems. Wiley.
    ed. System Analysis Techniques. Wiley.
Coughlan, Michael P.
  xCoughlan, Michael P.
    Molybdenum & Molybdenum-Containing
     Enzymes. Pergamon.
Coughlan, Robert, 1914-
  xCoughlan, Robert.
    The Private World of William Faulkner.
     Cooper Sq.
    World of Michelangelo. Time-Life.
Coughlin. see Coughlin, Raymond F.
Coughlin, Caroline M.
  xCoughlin, Caroline M.
    ed. Recurring Library Issues: A Reader.
     Scarecrow.
Coughlin, Edward V.
  xCoughlin, Edward V.
    Adelardo Lopez De Ayala. Twayne.
Coughlin, George G. see Coughlin, George Gordon.
Coughlin, George Gordon.
  xCoughlin, George G.
    Your Introduction to Law. Har-Row.
Coughlin, R. see Coughlin, Robert F.
Coughlin, Raymond F.
  xCoughlin.
    Applied Calculus. Allyn.
Coughlin, Richard J.
  xCoughlin, Richard J.
    Double Identity: The Chinese in Modern
     Thailand. Greenwood.
Coughlin, Robert. see Coughlin, Robert F.

Coughlin, Robert F.
  xCoughlin, R.
    Operational Amplifiers & Linear Integrated
      Circuits. P-H.
  xCoughlin, Robert.
    Principles & Applications of Semiconductors &
      Circuits. P-H.
Couhig, Marcelle R. *see* Couhig, Marcelle Reese.
Couhig, Marcelle Reese.
  xCouhig, Marcelle R.
    Asphodel Plantation Cookbook. Pelican.
Couldrey, Vivienne.
  xCouldrey, Vivienne.
    Swans of Brhyadr. Coward.
    The Swans of Brhyadr. Fawcett.
Coull, Bruce C.
  xCoull, Bruce C.
    ed. Ecology of Marine Benthos. U of SC Pr.
Coulling, Sidney.
  xCoulling, Sidney.
    Matthew Arnold & His Critics: A Study of
      Arnold's Controversies. Ohio U Pr.
Couloumbis, T. A. *see* Couloumbis, Theodore A.
Couloumbis, Theodore A.
  xCouloumbis, T. A.
    Foreign Interference in Greek Politics: An
      Historical Perspective. Pella Pub.
  xCouloumbis, Theodore A.
    Greek Political Reaction to American &
      NATO Influences. Yale U Pr.
Coulson, Charles A. *see* Coulson, Charles Alfred.
Coulson, Charles Alfred.
  xCoulson, Charles A.
    Valence. Oxford U Pr.
Coulson, Juanita.
  xCoulson, Juanita.
    Dark Priestess. Ballantine.
Coulson, N. J. *see* Coulson, Noel James.
Coulson, Noel. *see* Coulson, Noel James.
Coulson, Noel James.
  xCoulson, N. J.
    Succession in the Muslim Family. Cambridge U
      Pr.
  xCoulson, Noel.
    A History of Islamic Law. Columbia U Pr.
Coulson, Walter F.
  xCoulson, Walter F.
    ed. Surgical Pathology. Lippincott.
Coulson, William D. *see* Coulson, William D. E.
Coulson, William D. E., 1942-
  xCoulson, William D.
    An Annotated Bibliography of Greek & Roman
      Art, Architecture, & Archaeology. Garland
      Pub.
Coulston, Frederick.
  xCoulston, Frederick.
    ed. Human Epidemiology & Animal Laboratory
      Correlations in Chemical Carcinogens. Ablex
      Pub.
    ed. The Potential Carcinogenicity of
      Nitrosatable Drugs. Ablex Pub.
Coulter, E. Merton. *see* Coulter, Ellis Merton.
Coulter, Ellis Merton, 1890-
  xCoulter, E. Merton.
    Confederate States of America. La State U Pr.
    Daniel Lee, Agriculturist: His Life North &
      South. U of Ga Pr.
    ed. A List of the Early Settlers of Georgia. U
      of Ga Pr.
Coulter, Harris L.
  xCoulter, Harris L.
    Homoeopathic Medicine. Formur Intl.
Coulter, James. *see* Coulter, James A.
Coulter, James A.
  xCoulter, James.
    The Literary Microcosm: Theories of
      Interpretation of the Later Neoplatonists.
      Humanities.
Coulter, Jeff.
  xCoulter, Jeff.

Approaches to Insanity: A Philosophical &
  Sociological Study. Biblio Dist.
The Social Construction of Mind: Studies in
  Ethnomethodology & Linguistic Philosophy.
  Rowman.
Coulter, John W. *see* Coulter, John Wesley.
Coulter, John Wesley, 1893-
  xCoulter, John W.
    Drama of Fiji: A Contemporary History. C E
      Tuttle.
Coulter, Merle C. *see* Coulter, Merle Crowe.
Coulter, Merle Crowe, 1894-1958
  xCoulter, Merle C.
    Story of the Plant Kingdom. U of Chicago Pr.
Coulter, W. Alan.
  xCoulter, W. Alan.
    ed. Adaptive Behavior: Concepts &
      Measurements. Grune.
Coulthard, A. R.
  xCoulthard, A. R.
    The Writer's Craft: A Concise Rhetoric &
      Handbook. Wadsworth Pub.
Coulthard, Malcolm. *see* Coulthard, Richard Malcolm.
Coulthard, Richard Malcolm.
  xCoulthard, Malcolm.
    Introduction to Discourse Analysis. Longman.
Coulton, Claudia J.
  xCoulton, Claudia J.
    Social Work Quality Assurance Programs: A
      Comparative Analysis. Natl Assn Soc Wkrs.
Coulton, G. G. *see* Coulton, George Gordon.
Coulton, George G. *see* Coulton, George Gordon.
Coulton, George Gordon, 1858-1947
  xCoulton, G. G.
    Five Centuries of Religion. Octagon.
    Inquisition & Liberty. Peter Smith.
    Inquisition & Liberty. R West.
    Medieval Panorama: The English Scene from
      Conquest to Reformation. Norton.
  xCoulton, George G.
    Art & the Reformation. Shoe String.
    The Chronicler of European Chivalry. R West.
    Inquisition. Folcroft.
    Life in the Middle Ages. Cambridge U Pr.
    Medieval Scene: An Informal Introduction to
      the Middle Ages. Peter Smith.
    Studies in Medieval Thought. Russell.
Coulton, J. J.
  xCoulton, J. J.
    Ancient Greek Architects at Work: Problems
      of Structure & Design. Cornell U Pr.
Coulton, J. J. *see* Coulton, John James.
Coulton, Jill.
  xCoulton, Jill.
    Women's Gymnastics. Charles River Bks.
    Women's Gymnastics. Sterling.
Coulton, John James.
  xCoulton, J. J.
    Architectural Development of the Greek Stoa.
      Oxford U Pr.
Council for Exceptional Children.
  xCouncil for Exceptional Children.
    Abilities of Young Children. Coun Exc Child.
    Brain Damage in School Age Children. Coun
      Exc Child.
    Exceptional Children Research Review. Coun
      Exc Child.
    Helping Young Children Develop Language
      Skills: A Book of Activities. Coun Exc Child.
Council for High Blood Pressure Research.
  xCouncil for High Blood Research, 1972.
    Blood Pressure - Regulation & Control:
      Proceedings. Am Heart.
Council for High Blood Research, 1972. *see* Council for
  High Blood Pressure Research.
Council for National Cooperation in Aquatics.
  xCouncil for National Cooperation in Aquatics.
    The New Science of Skin & Scuba Diving.
      Follett.
  xNational Council for Cooperation in Aquatics.

The New Science of Skin & Scuba Diving.
  Follett.
**Council of Biology Editors. Committee on Form and
Style.**
  xCouncil of Biology Editors Committee on Form &
    Style.
    CBE Style Manual. Coun Biology Eds.
Council of Europe.
  xCouncil of Europe.
    ed. Collected Edition of the "Travaux
      Preparatories" of the European Convention
      on Human Rights. Kluwer Boston.
    ed. Collected Edition of the "Travaux
      Preparatoires of the European Convention on
      Human Rights": Vol. V Legal Committee-Ad
      Hoc Joint Committee-Committee of
      Ministers-Consultative Assembly 23 June -
      28 August 1950. Kluwer Boston.
    ed. Monument Protection in Europe. Kluwer
      Boston.
    ed. Population Decline in Europe: Implications
      of a Declining or Stationary Population. St
      Martin.
    Yearbook of the European Convention on
      Human Rights. Kluwer Boston.
    Yearbook of the European Convention on
      Human Rights, 1978. Intl Pubns Serv.
Council of State Governments.
  xCouncil of State Governments.
    Federal Grants-in-Aid. Arno.
    Federal-State Relations. Arno.
    The Handbook of Interstate Crime Control.
      Greenwood.
    Reorganizing State Government. Greenwood.
  xExecutive Offices Of The National Academy Of
    Sciences - National Academy Of Engineering.
    Impact of Science & Technology on Regional
      Economic Development. Natl Acad Pr.
  xTheCouncil of State Governments.
    ed. Suggested State Legislation, 1941-1978. W
      W Gaunt.
Council on Economic Priorities.
  xCEP.
    Cleaning up: The Cost of Refinery Pollution
      Control. CEP.
    Cracking Down: Oil Refining & Pollution
      Control. CEP.
    Military Maneuvers. CEP.
    Minding the Corporate Conscience 1978:
      Public Interest Organizations & Corporate
      Social Accountability. CEP.
    Power Plant Performance: Nuclear & Coal
      Capacity Factors & Economics. CEP.
    The Price of Power Update: Electric Utilities &
      the Environment. CEP.
    Shortchanged Update: Minorities & Women in
      Banking. CEP.
  xCouncil on Economic Priorities.
    Cleaning Up: The Cost of Refinery Pollution
      Control. Praeger.
    Jobs & Energy: The Employment & Economic
      Impacts of Nuclear Power, Conservation, &
      Other Energy Options. CEP.
    Paper Profits: Pollution in the Pulp & Paper
      Industry. MIT Pr.
    The Price of Power: Electric Utilities & the
      Environment. MIT Pr.
    Women & Minorities in Banking:
      Shortchanged-Update. Praeger.
Council on Foreign Relations.
  xCouncil on Foreign Relations Inc., New York.
    Catalog of the Foreign Relations Library. G K
      Hall.
Council on Foreign Relations Inc., New York. *see*
  Council on Foreign Relations.
Council on International Educational Exchange.
  xCouncil on International Educational Exchange.

The Budget Traveler's Latin America: 1979-80. Dutton.
Where to Stay USA. Frommer-Pasmantier.
The Whole World Handbook, 1974-1975. Frommer-Pasmantier.
Counselman, Mary E. *see* Counselman, Mary Elizabeth.
Counselman, Mary Elizabeth, 1911-
xCounselman, Mary E.
Half in Shadow. Arkham.
Counsilman, James E.
xCounsilman, James E.
The Complete Book of Swimming. Atheneum.
Country Beautiful.
xCountry Beautiful.
ed. The Great American Circus. Country Beautiful.
xCountry Beautiful Editors.
ed. America in the Words of Her Great Poets. Country Beautiful.
America the Beautiful in the Words of Henry Wadsworth Longfellow. Country Beautiful.
America the Beautiful in the Words of John F. Kennedy. Country Beautiful.
America the Beautiful in the Words of Robert F. Kennedy. Country Beautiful.
America the Beautiful in the Words of Ralph Waldo Emerson. Country Beautiful.
ed. America's Great Adventure: The Spirit of Freedom. Country Beautiful.
ed. America's Great National Forests. Country Beautiful.
ed. America's Great Wilderness. Country Beautiful.
ed. Antique & Decorator Bottles: A Collector's Guide. Country Beautiful.
The Beauty of America in Great American Art. Country Beautiful.
ed. The Civil War Years: A House Divided Cannot Stand. Country Beautiful.
Famous Battlefields of North America. Country Beautiful.
ed. Four-Hundred Landmarks of America: Where to Go & What to See. Country Beautiful.
ed. The Four Seasons. Country Beautiful.
ed. The Great American West. Country Beautiful.
Great Art Treasures in America's Museums. Country Beautiful.
ed. Great Mountains of North America. Country Beautiful.
ed. Houses of Great Americans. Country Beautiful.
ed. Landmarks of the USA: Our 51 Capitols. Country Beautiful.
ed. Lincoln: His Words & His World. Country Beautiful.
Love. Country Beautiful.
Love in the Words & Life of Jesus. Country Beautiful.
ed. The Majestic Wonders of America. Country Beautiful.
A Man of Destiny: Winston S. Churchill. Country Beautiful.
ed. The Meaning & Mystery of Love. Country Beautiful.
ed. The Most Amazing American: Benjamin Franklin. Country Beautiful.
ed. National Parks of America. Country Beautiful.
ed. Nostalgic Treasures from America's Past. Country Beautiful.
One Hundred One Wonders of America. Country Beautiful.
The Spirit of Early America: The Life & Words of Benjamin Franklin. Country Beautiful.
The Story of America. Country Beautiful.
This Beautiful Land in the Words of Walt Whitman. Country Beautiful.
ed. Thoreau's Walden. Country Beautiful.

Country Beautiful Editors. *see* Country Beautiful.
Country Women's Council of the U.S.A.
xCountry Women's Council of the USA.
The USA, Our Way of Life. North Plains.
Countryman, Kathleen. *see* Countryman, Kathleen M.
Countryman, Kathleen M.
xCountryman, Kathleen.
Development & Implementation of a Patient's Bill of Rights in Hospitals. Am Hospital.
Countryman, Vern.
xCountryman, Vern.
Cases & Materials on Debtor & Creditor. Little.
Law in Contemporary Society: The Orgain Lectures. U of Tex Pr.
The Lawyer in Modern Society. Little.
Counts, Bill.
xCounts, Bill.
Called to Be Free. Revell.
Counts, George S. *see* Counts, George Sylvester.
Counts, George Sylvester, 1889-
xCounts, George S.
The Challenge of Soviet Education. Greenwood.
Country of the Blind: The Soviet System of Mind Control. Greenwood.
Dare the School Build a New Social Order?. S Ill U Pr.
Education & American Civilization. Greenwood.
Couper, A. D.
xCouper, A. D.
The Geography of Sea Transport. Humanities.
Couper, Heather.
xCouper, Heather.
Space Frontiers. Viking Pr.
Couper, J. M. *see* Couper, John Mill.
Couper, John Mill, 1914-
xCouper, J. M.
Looking for a Wave. Bradbury Pr.
Coupland, R. E. *see* Coupland, Rex E.
Coupland, Reginald, Sir, 1884-1952
xCoupland, Reginald.
Exploitation of East Africa, 1856-1890: The Slave Trade & the Scramble. Northwestern U Pr.
Coupland, Rex E.
xCoupland, R. E.
ed. Peripheral Neuroendocrine Interaction. Springer-Verlag.
Courant, R. *see* Courant, Richard.
Courant, Richard.
xCourant, R.
Supersonic Flow & Shock Waves. Springer-Verlag.
xCourant, Richard.
Introduction to Calculus & Analysis. Wiley.
Courlander, Harold, 1908-
xCourlander, Harold.
The Drum & the Hoe: Life & Lore of the Haitian People. U of Cal Pr.
Haiti Singing. Cooper Sq.
The Mesa of Flowers. Popular Lib.
Negro Folk Music, U.S.A. Columbia U Pr.
Olode the Hunter & Other Tales from Nigeria. HarBraceJ.
Tales of Yoruba Gods & Heroes. Crown.
Cournos, John, 1881-1966
xCournos, John.
The Mask. AMS Pr.
Cournot, Antoine Augustin, 1801-1877
xCournot, Augustin.
Revue Sommaire Des Doctrines Economiques. Kelley.
Cournot, Augustin. *see* Cournot, Antoine Augustin.
Cournoyer. *see* Cournoyer, Norman G.
Cournoyer, Norman G.
xCournoyer.

Hotel, Restaurant & Travel Law. Duxbury Pr.
Couro, Ted.
xCouro, Ted.
Let's Talk 'Iipay Aa: An Introduction to the Mesa Grande Diegueno Language. Ballena Pr.
Let's Talk 'Iipay Aa: An Introduction to the Mesa Grande Diegueno Language. Malki Mus Pr.
Coursault, Jesse H. *see* Coursault, Jesse Harliaman.
Coursault, Jesse Harliaman, 1871-
xCoursault, Jesse H.
The Learning Process: Educational Theory Implied in Theory of Knowledge. AMS Pr.
Course, Edwin.
xCourse, Edwin.
Railways Then & Now. David & Charles.
Coursen, Herbert R.
xCoursen, Herbert R.
Christian Ritual & the World of Shakespeare's Tragedies. Bucknell U Pr.
Coursey, Robert D.
xCoursey, Robert D.
ed. Program Evaluation for Mental Health: Methods, Strategies and Participants. Grune.
Courtenay, Thomas P. *see* Courtenay, Thomas Peregrine.
Courtenay, Thomas Peregrine, 1782-1841
xCourtenay, Thomas P.
Commentaries on the Historical Plays of Shakspeare. AMS Pr.
Courthion, Pierre.
xCourthion, Pierre.
Impressionism. Abrams.
Courthope, W. J. *see* Courthope, William John.
Courthope, William J. *see* Courthope, William John.
Courthope, William John, 1842-1917
xCourthope, W. J.
Liberal Movement in English Literature. Folcroft.
xCourthope, William J.
Addison. AMS Pr.
Addison. Folcroft.
History of English Poetry. Russell.
Liberal Movement in English Literature. AMS Pr.
Courtine, Robert. *see* Courtine, Robert J.
Courtine, Robert J.
xCourtine, Robert.
The Hundred Glories of French Cooking. FS&G.
Courtis, Stuart A. *see* Courtis, Stuart Appleton.
Courtis, Stuart Appleton, 1874-
xCourtis, Stuart A.
Courtis-Watters Illustrated Golden Dictionary for Young Readers. Western Pub.
Courtney, C. P. *see* Courtney, Cecil Patrick.
Courtney, Caroline.
xCourtney, Caroline.
Duchess in Disguise. Warner Bks.
Duchess in Disguise. G K Hall.
A Wager for Love. G K Hall.
A Wager for Love. Warner Bks.
A Wager for Love. G K Hall.
Courtney, Cecil Patrick.
xCourtney, C. P.
Montesquieu & Burke. Greenwood.
Courtney, Damien A.
xCourtney, Damien A.
Statistical Demography. St Martin.
Courtney, E. Wayne.
xCourtney, E. Wayne.
ed. Applied Research in Education. Littlefield.
Courtney, Gerald. *see* Courtney, Gerry.
Courtney, Gerry, 1951-
xCourtney, Gerald.
High Pressure Center. Ashley Bks.
Courtney, Leonard.
xCourtney, Leonard.

ed. Reading Interaction: The Teacher, the
Pupil, the Materials. Intl Reading.
Courtney, Margaret A. *see* Courtney, Margaret Ann.
Courtney, Margaret Ann, 1834-1920
xCourtney, Margaret A.
Cornish Feasts & Folk-Lore. Folcroft.
Cornish Feasts & Folklore. Rowman.
Courtney, W. L. *see* Courtney, William Leonard.
Courtney, William Leonard, 1850-1928
xCourtney, W. L.
The Feminine Note in Fiction. Folcroft.
Courtney, William P. *see* Courtney, William Prideaux.
Courtney, William Prideaux, 1845-1913
xCourtney, William P.
Eight Friends of the Great. Folcroft.
Secrets of Our National Literature: Chapters in
the History of the Anonymous &
Pseudonymous Writings of Our Countrymen.
Gale.
Courtright, Gordon.
xCourtright, Gordon.
Trees & Shrubs for Western Gardens. Intl
Schol Bk Serv.
Courville, Selme.
xCourville, Selme.
Master Chef Sam's Acadiana Country
Cookbook. Vantage.
Courvoisier, Karl, 1846-
xCourvoisier, Karl.
Technics of Violin Playing. Longwood Pr.
Technics of Violin Playing. Scholarly.
Coury, F. F. *see* Coury, Fred F.
Coury, Fred F., 1940-
xCoury, F. F.
A Practical Guide to Minicomputer
Applications. Wiley.
xCoury, Fred F.
ed. A Practical Guide to Minicomputer
Applications. Inst Electrical.
Couser, G. Thomas.
xCouser, G. Thomas.
American Autobiography: The Prophetic Mode.
U of Mass Pr.
Cousins, Albert N.
xCousins, Albert N.
Urban Life: The Sociology of Cities & Urban
Society. Wiley.
Cousins, Frank.
xCousins, Frank.
Wood Carver of Salem: Samuel McIntire, His
Life & Work. AMS Pr.
Cousins, Geoffrey, 1900-
xCousins, Geoffrey.
Lords of the Links: The Story of Professional
Golf. Merrimack Bk Serv.
Cousins, Norman.
xCousins, Norman.
Anatomy of an Illness As Perceived by the
Patient: Reflections on Healing &
Regeneration. Norton.
Dr. Schweitzer of Lambarene. Greenwood.
Cousteau, Jacques. *see* Cousteau, Jacques Yves.
Cousteau, Jacques Y. *see* Cousteau, Jacques-Yves.
Cousteau, Jacques Yves.
xCousteau, Jacques.
The Art of Motion. Abrams.
Attack & Defense. Abrams.
Instinct & Intelligence. Abrams.
Intro. by Outer & Inner Space. Abrams.
Provinces of the Sea. Abrams.
Quest for Food. Abrams.
Intro. by Riches of the Sea. Abrams.
xCousteau, Jacques Y.
The Act of Life. Abrams.
xCousteau, Jacques-Yves.
Diving for Sunken Treasure. A & W Pubs.
Diving for Sunken Treasure. Doubleday.
The Silent World. Har-Row.
Cousteau, Jacques-Yves.
xCousteau, Jacques Y.

Dolphins. A & W Pubs.
xCousteau, Jacques-Yves.
Dolphins. Doubleday.
Life & Death in a Coral Sea. A & W Pubs.
Life & Death in a Coral Sea. Doubleday.
Cousteau, Jacques-Yves. *see* Cousteau, Jacques Yves.
Coutant, Helen.
xCoutant, Helen.
First Snow. Knopf.
Coutarelli, Spiro A., 1943-
xCoutarelli, Spiro A.
Venture Capital in Europe. Praeger.
Coutinho, Afranio.
xCoutinho, Alfranio.
Introduction to Literature in Brazil. Columbia
U Pr.
Coutinho, Alfranio. *see* Coutinho, Afranio.
Coutinho, John De S.
xCoutinho, John De S.
Advanced Systems Development Management.
Wiley.
Coutsouradis, D.
xCoutsouradis, D.
ed. High Temperature Alloys for Gas Turbines.
Burgess-Intl Ideas.
Coutts, T. J. *see* Coutts, Timothy J.
Coutts, Timothy J.
xCoutts, T. J.
ed. Active & Passive Thin Film Devices. Acad
Pr.
Coutts-Smith, Kenneth, 1929-
xCoutts-Smith, Kenneth.
The Dream of Icarus. Braziller.
Couvaras, Costa G., 1911-
xCouvaras, Costa G.
Photo Album of the Greek Resistance. Wire
Pr.
Couzens, Gerald S. *see* Couzens, Gerald Secor.
Couzens, Gerald Secor.
xCouzens, Gerald S.
A Baseball Album. Lippincott & Crowell.
Couzens, Reginald C.
xCouzens, Reginald C.
Stories of the Months & Days. Gale.
Cove, D. J.
xCove, D. J.
Genetics. Cambridge U Pr.
Cove, Mary K.
xCove, Mary K.
Regarding Religious Education. Religious Educ.
Covell, Jon C. *see* Covell, Jon Etta Hastings Carter.
Covell, Jon Etta Hastings Carter, 1910-
xCovell, Jon C.
Under the Seal of Sesshu. Hacker.
Covelli, Pasquale. *see* Covelli, Pat.
Covelli, Pat.
xCovelli, Pasquale.
Borrowing Time: Growing up with Juvenile
Diabetes. T Y Crowell.
Coveney, P. J. *see* Coveney, Peter.
Coveney, Peter.
xCoveney, P. J.
ed. France in Crisis, 1620-1675. Rowman.
xCoveney, Peter.
Image of Childhood: The Individual & Society,
a Study of the Theme in English Literature.
Gannon.
Covensky, Milton, 1916-
xCovensky, Milton.
The Ancient Near Eastern Tradition. Har-Row.
Cover, John H. *see* Cover, John Higson.
Cover, John Higson, 1891-
xCover, John H.
Neighborhood Distribution & Consumption of
Meat in Pittsburgh: As Related to Other
Social & Economic Factors. Arno.
Coverdale, G. M.
xCoverdale, G. M.

Planning Education in Relation to Rural
Development. Unipub.
Coverdale, Joan.
xCoverdale, Joan.
I Share This Marsh. Whale & Eagle.
Coverdale, John F., 1940-
xCoverdale, John F.
The Political Transformation of Spain After
Franco. Praeger.
Covert, Alice L. *see* Covert, Alice Lent.
Covert, Alice Lent, 1913-
xCovert, Alice L.
The Distant Drum. Bouregy.
The Glass House. Bouregy.
Covert, Paul.
xCovert, Paul.
Cages. Liveright.
Covey, Stephen R.
xCovey, Stephen R.
How to Succeed with People. Deseret Bk.
Covici, Pascal, Jr, 1930-
xCovici, Pascal.
Mark Twain's Humor: The Image of a World.
SMU Press.
Covill, William E.
xCovill, William E.
Ink Bottles & Inkwells. W S Sullwold.
Coville, Alfred.
xCoville, Alfred.
ed. Studies in Anglo-French History During
the Eighteenth, Nineteenth & Twentieth
Centuries. Arno.
Coville, Bruce.
xCoville, Bruce.
The Foolish Giant. Lippincott.
Sarah's Unicorn. Lippincott
Coville, Walter J.
xCoville, Walter J.
Abnormal Psychology. Har-Row.
Covin, Theron M.
xCovin, Theron M.
ed. Readings in the Psychology of Early
Childhood. Mss Info.
Covina, Gina.
xCovina, Gina.
The Ouija Book. S&S.
Covington, A. K. *see* Covington, Arthur Kenneth.
Covington, Arthur Kenneth.
xCovington, A. K.
ed. Ion Selective Electrode Methodology. CRC
Pr.
Covington, W. A.
xCovington, W. A.
History of Colquitt County. Reprint.
Covino, Benjamin G.
xCovino, Benjamin G.
Local Anesthetics: Mechanisms of Action &
Clinical Use. Grune.
Covino, Frank.
xCovino, Frank.
Discover Acrylics with Frank Covino: An
Academic Approach. North Light Pub.
Covvey, H. Dominic.
xCovvey, H. Dominic.
Computer Consciousness: Surviving the
Automated Eighties. A-W.
Computers in the Practice of Medicine. A-W.
Cowan, David.
xCowan, David.
Introduction to Modern Literary Arabic.
Cambridge U Pr.
Cowan, Evelyn.
xCowan, Evelyn.
Spring Remembered: A Scottish Jewish
Childhood. Taplinger.
Cowan, Frank, 1844-1905
xCowan, Frank.

Revi-Lona: A Romance of Love in a Marvelous
Land. Arno.
Cowan, Geoffrey.
xCowan, Geoffrey.
Fun with Magic. G&D.
Cowan, Gregory.
xCowan, Gregory.
Plain English Please: A Rhetoric. Random.
Plain English Rhetoric & Reader. Random.
Cowan, H. J. see Cowan, Henry J.
Cowan, Henry J.
xCowan, H. J.
An Historical Outline of Architectural Science.
Elsevier.
xCowan, Henry J.
A Dictionary of Architectural Science. Halsted
Pr.
The Master Builders: A History of Structural &
Environmental Design from Ancient Egypt to
the Nineteenth Century. Wiley.
Cowan, James.
xCowan, James.
Daybreak: A Romance of an Old World. Arno.
Fairy Folk Tales of the Maori. AMS Pr.
Cowan, Laing G. see Cowan, Laing Gray.
Cowan, Laing Gray.
xCowan, Laing G.
France & the Saar, 1680-1948. AMS Pr.
Local Government in West Africa. AMS Pr.
Cowan, Marian M. see Cowan, Marion M.
Cowan, Marion M.
xCowan, Marian M.
Tzotzil Grammar. Summer Inst Ling.
Cowan, Paul.
xCowan, Paul.
The Tribes of America. Doubleday.
Cowan, Peter, 1929-
xCowan, Peter.
ed. The Future of Planning. Sage.
Cowan, Rachel.
xCowan, Rachel.
illus. Growing Up Yanqui. Viking Pr.
Cowan, Robert G. see Cowan, Robert Granniss.
Cowan, Robert Granniss.
xCowan, Robert G.
Backward Glance: Los Angeles 1901-1915.
Cowan.
Ranchos of California: A List of Spanish
Concessions & Mexican Grants. Cowan.
Cowan, S. T. see Cowan, Samuel Tertius.
Cowan, Sada.
xCowan, Sada.
Pomp & Other Plays. Core Collection.
Cowan, Samuel Tertius.
xCowan, S. T.
Cowan & Steel's Manual for the Identification
of Medical Bacteria. Cambridge U Pr.
A Dictionary of Microbial Taxonomy.
Cambridge U Pr.
Coward, E. Walter.
xCoward, E. Walter.
ed. Irrigation & Agricultural Development in
Asia: Perspectives from the Social Sciences.
Cornell U Pr.
Coward, Noel. see Coward, Noel Pierce.
Coward, Noel P. see Coward, Noel Pierce.
Coward, Noel Pierce, Sir, 1899-1973
xCoward, Noel.
Present Indicative: An Autobiography. Da
Capo.
xCoward, Noel P.
Star Quality: Six Stories. Greenwood.
Cowardin, David. see Cowardin, David H.
Cowardin, David H.
xCowardin, David.
Handling Elevator Emergencies. Natl Fire Prot.
Cowart, Andrew T.
xCowart, Andrew T.

Decisions, Politics & Change: A Study of
Norwegian Urban Budgeting. Universitet.
Cowd, M. A.
xCowd, M. A.
Revision Chemistry. Butterworths.
Cowden, Dudley J. see Cowden, Dudley Johnstone.
Cowden, Dudley Johnstone, 1899-
xCowden, Dudley J.
Measures of Exports of the United States.
AMS Pr.
Cowe, Eileen G. see Cowe, Eileen Grace.
Cowe, Eileen Grace.
xCowe, Eileen G.
A Study of Kindergarten Activities for
Language Development. R & E Res Assoc.
Cowell, F. A. see Cowell, Frank Alan.
Cowell, Frank Alan.
xCowell, F. A.
Measuring Inequality: Techniques for the Social
Sciences. Halsted Pr.
Cowell, Frank R. see Cowell, Frank Richard.
Cowell, Frank Richard, 1897-
xCowell, Frank R.
History, Civilization & Culture: An
Introduction to the Historical & Social
Philosophy of Pitirum A. Sorokin. Hyperion
Conn.
Cowell, Henry.
xCowell, Henry.
Charles Ives & His Music. Oxford U Pr.
Cowell, Henry J. see Cowell, Henry John.
Cowell, Henry John, 1871-
xCowell, Henry J.
Robert Louis Stevenson: An Englishman's
Restudy After Fifty Years, of R. L. S. the
Man. Folcroft.
Cowell, Joe. see Cowell, Joseph.
Cowell, Joseph, 1792-1863
xCowell, Joe.
Thirty Years Passed Among the Players in
England & America. Shoe String.
Cowell, Raymond.
xCowell, Raymond.
The Critical Enterprise: English Studies in
Higher Education. Rowman.
ed. Critics on Yeats. U of Miami Pr.
Cowen, Claudine L. see Cowen, Claudine La Haye.
Cowen, Claudine La Haye.
xCowen, Claudine L.
The Virginia Gardener's Calendar. U Pr of Va.
Cowen, Painton.
xCowen, Painton.
Rose Windows. Chronicle Bks.
Cowen, Philip, 1853-1943
xCowen, Philip.
Memories of an American Jew. Arno.
Cowen, R. see Cowen, Richard.
Cowen, Richard.
xCowen, R.
History of Life. McGraw.
xCowen, Richard.
Controversies in the Earth Sciences: A Reader.
West Pub.
Cowen, Roy C., 1930-
xCowen, Roy C.
Christian Dietrich Grabbe. Twayne.
Cowen, Zelman.
xCowen, Zelman.
American-Australian Private International Law.
Oceana.
British Commonwealth of Nations in a
Changing World: Law, Politics & Prospects.
Northwestern U Pr.
Cowie, A. T. see Cowie, Alfred T.
Cowie, Alfred T.
xCowie, A. T.
Hormonal Control of Lactation.
Springer-Verlag.
Cowie, Donald.
xCowie, Donald.

Antique Collector's Dictionary. Arc Bks.
Cowie, Ian.
xCowie, Ian.
Growing Knowing Jesus. John Knox.
Cowie, James B.
xCowie, James B.
An Ethnography of a Chiropractic Clinic:
Definitions of a Deviant Situation. Free Pr.
Cowie, Peter.
xCowie, Peter.
Eighty Years of Cinema. A S Barnes.
ed. Fifty Major Film-Makers. A S Barnes.
Finnish Cinema. A S Barnes.
ed. Hollywood, 1920-1970. A S Barnes.
Cowing, Thomas G.
xCowing, Thomas G.
The Economics of Local Public Service
Consolidation. Lexington Bks.
Cowle, Jerry.
xCowle, Jerry.
Discover the Trees. Sterling.
Cowles, Ginny.
xCowles, Ginny.
Nicholas. HM.
Cowles, Laurence G.
xCowles, Laurence G.
Analysis & Design of Transistor Circuits.
Krieger.
xCowles, Lawrence G.
A Sourcebook of Modern Transistor Circuits.
P-H.
Cowles, Lawrence G. see Cowles, Laurence G.
Cowles, Raymond B. see Cowles, Raymond Bridgman.
Cowles, Raymond Bridgman.
xCowles, Raymond B.
Desert Journal: A Naturalist Reflects on Arid
California. U of Cal Pr.
Cowles, Virginia. see Cowles, Virginia Spencer.
Cowles, Virginia Spencer.
xCowles, Virginia.
The Astors. Knopf.
Cowley, Au-Deane S.
xCowley, Au-Deane S.
Family Integration & Mental Health. R & E
Res Assoc.
Cowley, Charles R., 1934-
xCowley, Charles R.
Theory of Stellar Spectra. Gordon.
Cowley, F. G. see Cowley, Frederick George.
Cowley, Fraser.
xCowley, Fraser.
Critique of British Empiricism. St Martin.
Cowley, Frederick George.
xCowley, F. G.
The Monastic Order in South Wales,
1066-1349. Verry.
Cowley, Joy.
xCowley, Joy.
The Growing Season. Doubleday.
Cowley, Malcolm.
xCowley, Malcolm.
And I Worked at the Writer's Trade: Chapters
of Literary History, 1918-1978. Penguin.
ed. Books That Changed Our Minds. Arno.
The Faulkner-Cowley File: Letters &
Memories, 1944-1962. Penguin.
Many-Windowed House: Collected Essays on
American Writers & American Writing. S Ill
U Pr.
A Second Flowering: Works & Days of the
Lost Generation. Penguin.
A Second Flowering: Works & Days of the
Lost Generation. Viking Pr.
Cowley, W. H. see Cowley, William Harold.
Cowley, William Harold.
xCowley, W. H.

Presidents, Professors, & Trustees: The
   Evolution of American Academic
   Government. Jossey-Bass.
Cowling, Elizabeth.
   xCowling, Elizabeth.
     The Cello. Scribner.
Cowling, George H. see Cowling, George Herbert.
Cowling, George Herbert, 1881-1946
   xCowling, George H.
     Chaucer. Arno.
     Music on the Shakespearian Stage. AMS Pr.
Cowling, Keith.
   xCowling, Keith.
     Advertising & Economic Behaviour. Holmes &
      Meier.
Cowling, M. see Cowling, Maurice.
Cowling, Maurice.
   xCowling, M.
     The Impact of Hitler: British Politics & British
      Policy 1933-1940. Cambridge U Pr.
   xCowling, Maurice.
     The Impact of Hitler: British Politics & British
      Policy, 1933-1940. U of Chicago Pr.
Cowling, T. M.
   xCowling, T. M.
     Sub-Regional Planning Studies: An Evaluation.
      Pergamon.
Cowper, H. S. see Cowper, Henry Swainson.
Cowper, Henry Swainson, 1865-1941
   xCowper, H. S.
     The Art of Attack: Being a Study in the
      Development of Weapons & Appliances of
      Offence, from the Earliest Times to the Age
      of Gunpowder. Rowman.
Cowper, Richard.
   xCowper, Richard.
     Clone. PB.
Cowper, William.
   xCowper, William.
     The Poetical Works of William Cowper. AMS
      Pr.
Cowperthwait, John H. see Cowperthwait, John Howard.
Cowperthwait, John Howard.
   xCowperthwait, John H.
     Money, Silver & Finance. Greenwood.
Cox, Albert W.
   xCox, Albert W.
     Sonar & Underwater Sound. Lexington Bks.
Cox, Allan J.
   xCox, Allan J.
     Confessions of a Corporate Headhunter.
      Trident.
Cox, Archibald.
   xCox, Archibald.
     Civil Rights, the Constitution & the Courts.
      Harvard U Pr.
     Law & the National Labor Policy. U Cal LA
      Indus Rel.
Cox, Benjamin G. see Cox, Benjamin Gould.
Cox, Benjamin Gould.
   xCox, Benjamin G.
     Care & Rehabilitation of the Stroke Patient. C
      C Thomas.
Cox, Bernard, 1929-
   xCox, Bernard.
     Paddle Steamers. Sterling.
Cox, Beverly, 1945-
   xCox, Beverly.
     Minceur Italienne: Slimming Gourmet Menus
      & Recipes. Vanguard.
Cox, C. B.
   xCox, C. B.
     ed. The Twentieth-Century Mind: History,
      Ideas, & Literature in Britain, Vol. I:
      Nineteen Hundred to Nineteen Eighteen.
      Oxford U Pr.
   xCox, Charles B.

     ed. Dylan Thomas: A Collection of Critical
      Essays. P-H.
Cox, C. Robinson.
   xCox, C. Robinson.
     Criminal Justice: Improving Police Report
      Writing. Interstate.
Cox, Charles B. see Cox, C. B.
Cox, D. see Cox, R. David.
Cox, D. R. see Cox, David Roxbee.
Cox, David R. see Cox, David Roxbee.
Cox, David Roxbee.
   xCox, D. R.
     Problems & Solutions in Theoretical Statistics.
      Methuen Inc.
     Renewal Theory. Methuen Inc.
     Theoretical Statistics. Methuen Inc.
   xCox, David R.
     Planning of Experiments. Wiley.
Cox, E. Aubrey.
   xCox, E. Aubrey.
     Bottoms Up with a Rear Admiral. Moore Pub
      Co.
Cox, Edwin.
   xCox, Edwin.
     Changing Aims in Religious Education.
      Humanities.
Cox, Eli P.
   xCox, Eli P.
     Marketing Research: Information for Decision
      Making. Har-Row.
     Retail Decentralization. Mich St U Busn.
Cox, Erle.
   xCox, Erle.
     Out of the Silence. Hyperion Conn.
Cox, Frank D.
   xCox, Frank D.
     Human Intimacy: Marriage, the Family & Its
      Meaning. West Pub.
Cox, Fred M.
   xCox, Fred M.
     ed. Tactics & Techniques of Community
      Practice. Peacock Pubs.
Cox, George. see Cox, George Gurney.
Cox, George Gurney, 1901-
   xCox, George.
     Lindbergh: An American Epic. Golden Quill.
Cox, George W.
   xCox, George W.
     Agricultural Ecology: An Analysis of World
      Food Production Systems. W H Freeman.
     ed. Readings in Conservation Ecology.
      Goodyear.
Cox, Harold E.
   xCox, Harold E.
     Early Electric Cars of Philadelphia 1885-1911.
      Cox.
Cox, Harvey.
   xCox, Harvey.
     God's Revolution & Man's Responsibility.
      Judson.
Cox, Harvey. see Cox, Harvey Gallagher.
Cox, Harvey Gallagher.
   xCox, Harvey.
     Feast of Fools: A Theological Essay on
      Festivity & Fantasy. Harvard U Pr.
Cox, Helen.
   xCox, Helen.
     Cooking Under Pressure. Merrimack Bk Serv.
     The Floral Art Book of Reference. Pergamon.
Cox, J. P. see Cox, John P.
Cox, James A.
   xCox, James A.
     A Century of Light. Benjamin Co.
     A Century of Light. Larousse.
Cox, James M. see Cox, James Melville.
Cox, James Melville, 1925-
   xCox, James M.
     Mark Twain: The Fate of Humor. Princeton U
      Pr.
Cox, James W. see Cox, James William.

Cox, James William, 1923-
   xCox, James W.
     A Guide to Biblical Preaching. Abingdon.
     Learning to Speak Effectively. Baker Bk.
     Surprised by God. Broadman.
     ed. The Twentieth-Century Pulpit. Abingdon.
Cox, Joan.
   xCox, Joan.
     Mindsong. Avon.
Cox, John, 1935-
   xCox, John.
     Overkill: Weapons of the Nuclear Age. T Y
      Crowell.
Cox, John H. see Cox, la Wanda C. (Fenlason).
Cox, John P.
   xCox, J. P.
     Theory of Stellar Pulsation. Princeton U Pr.
Cox, Joseph W.
   xCox, Joseph W.
     Champion of Southern Federalism: Robert
      Goodloe Harper of South Carolina. Kennikat.
Cox, K. G. see Cox, Keith Gordon.
Cox, K. R. see Cox, Kevin R.
Cox, Keith Gordon.
   xCox, K. G.
     Interpretation of Igneous Rocks. Allen Unwin.
Cox, Keith K. see Cox, Keith Kohn.
Cox, Keith Kohn.
   xCox, Keith K.
     ed. Readings in Market Research. Irvington.
Cox, Kenyon, 1856-1919
   xCox, Kenyon.
     Classic Point of View: Six Lectures on
      Painting. Arno.
Cox, Kevin. see Cox, Kevin R.
Cox, Kevin R.
   xCox, K. R.
     ed. Locational Approaches to Power &
      Conflict. Halsted Pr.
   xCox, Kevin.
     ed. Locational Approaches to Power &
      Conflict. Krieger.
   xCox, Kevin R.
     Location & Public Problems: A Political
      Geography of the Contemporary World.
      Maaroufa Pr.
Cox, la Wanda C. (Fenlason).
   xCox, John H.
     Politics, Principle & Prejudice 1865-1866:
      Dilemma of Reconstruction in America.
      Atheneum.
   xCox, Lawanda.
     jt. auth. Politics, Principle & Prejudice
      1865-1866: Dilemma of Reconstruction in
      America. Atheneum.
Cox, Lawanda. see Cox, la Wanda C. (Fenlason).
Cox, Lee S. see Cox, Lee Sheridan.
Cox, Lee Sheridan.
   xCox, Lee S.
     Figurative Design in "Hamlet": The
      Significance of the Dumb Show. Ohio St U
      Pr.
Cox, Leonard.
   xCox, Leonard.
     Arte or Crafte of Rhethoryke. AMS Pr.
     Arte or Crafte of Rhethoryke. Folcroft.
Cox, Martha H. see Cox, Martha Heasley.
Cox, Martha Heasley.
   xCox, Martha H.
     Maxwell Anderson Bibliography. Arden Lib.
Cox, Oliver C. see Cox, Oliver Cromwell.
Cox, Oliver Cromwell, 1901-1974
   xCox, Oliver C.
     Race Relations: Elements & Social Dynamics.
      Wayne St U Pr.
Cox, Palmer, 1840-1924
   xCox, Palmer.

illus. Another Brownie Book. Dover.
illus. The Brownies at Home. Dover.
illus. The Brownies: Their Book. Dover.
Cox, R. David.
  xCox, D.
    Student Critic: Thinking & Writing About
      Literature. Winthrop.
Cox, R. Merritt. *see* Cox, Ralph Merritt.
Cox, Ralph Merritt, 1939-
  xCox, R. Merritt.
    Eighteenth Century Spanish Literature.
      Twayne.
Cox, Richard H.
  xCox, Richard H.
    ed. Religious Systems & Psychotherapy. C C
      Thomas.
Cox, Robert V., 1927-
  xCox, Robert V.
    Deadly Pursuit. Ballantine.
Cox, Robert W.
  xCox, Robert W.
    The Anatomy of Influence: Decision Making in
      International Organization. Yale U Pr.
Cox, Samuel S. *see* Cox, Samuel Sullivan.
Cox, Samuel Sullivan, 1824-1889
  xCox, Samuel S.
    Orient Sunbeams: From the Porte to the
      Pyramids, by Way of Palestine. Arno.
Cox, T. *see* Cox, Tom.
Cox, Thomas S., 1944-
  xCox, Thomas S.
    Civil-Military Relations in Sierra Leone: A
      Case Study of African Soldiers in Politics.
      Harvard U Pr.
Cox, Tom, 1906-
  xCox, T.
    Stress. Univ Park.
  xCox, Tom.
    Damned Englishman: A Study of Erskine
      Childers (1870-1922). Exposition.
Cox, Victoria.
  xCox, Victoria.
    Nature's Assistant. Western Pub.
  xCox, Virginia.
    Nature's Carpet Sweeper. Western Pub.
Cox, Virginia. *see* Cox, Victoria.
Cox, William E. *see* Cox, William Edwin.
Cox, William Edwin, 1930-1978
  xCox, William E.
    Industrial Marketing Research. Wiley.
Cox, William R. *see* Cox, William Robert.
Cox, William Robert, 1901-
  xCox, William R.
    The Backyard Five. Dodd.
    Game, Set, & Match. Dodd.
    Gunner on the Court. Dodd.
    Home Court Is Where You Find It. Dodd.
    Trouble at Second Base. Dodd.
    The Unbeatable Five. Dodd.
Cox-Gedmark, Jan, 1950-
  xCox-Gedmark, Jan.
    Coping with Physical Disability. Westminster.
Coxe, George H. *see* Coxe, George Harmon.
Coxe, George Harmon, 1901-
  xCoxe, George H.
    Double Identity. Manor Bks.
    No Place for Murder. G K Hall.
    The Silent Witness. Manor Bks.
Coxe, Louis. *see* Coxe, Louis Osborne.
Coxe, Louis O. *see* Coxe, Louis Osborne.
Coxe, Louis Osborne, 1918-
  xCoxe, Louis.
    Nikal Seyn & Decoration Day: A Poem & a
      Play. Vanderbilt U Pr.
    Passage: Selected Poems, 1943-1978. U of Mo
      Pr.
  xCoxe, Louis O.
    Edwin Arlington Robinson. U of Minn Pr.
Coxe, Weld.
  xCoxe, Weld.

Marketing Architectural & Engineering
    Services. Krieger.
Coxeter, H. S. *see* Coxeter, Harold Scott MacDonald.
Coxeter, Harold S. *see* Coxeter, Harold Scott MacDonald.
Coxeter, Harold Scott MacDonald.
  xCoxeter, H. S.
    Generators & Relations for Discrete Groups.
      Springer-Verlag.
    Introduction to Geometry. Wiley.
    Projective Geometry. U of Toronto Pr.
    Regular Complex Polytopes. Cambridge U Pr.
    Regular Polytopes. Dover.
    Regular Polytopes. Peter Smith.
  xCoxeter, Harold S.
    Real Projective Plane. Cambridge U Pr.
Coxhead, Nona.
  xCoxhead, Nona.
    Mindpower. Penguin.
    Mindpower. St Martin.
    The Richest Girl in the World: An American
      Odyssey. Doubleday.
Coxon, Anthony P. *see* Coxon, Anthony Peter
Macmillan.
Coxon, Anthony Peter Macmillan.
  xCoxon, Anthony P.
    Class & Hierarchy: The Social Meaning of
      Occupations. St Martin.
Coxon, J. M.
  xCoxon, J. M.
    Organic Photochemistry. Cambridge U Pr.
Coxon, Philip.
  xCoxon, Philip.
    The World of an Island. Merrimack Bk Serv.
Coxon, Roger.
  xCoxon, Roger.
    Chesterfield & His Critics. Folcroft.
Coy, Harold.
  xCoy, Harold.
    Chicano Roots Go Deep. Dodd.
    First Book of Hospitals. Watts.
    First Book of Presidents. Watts.
Coy, Kendrick.
  xCoy, Kendrick.
    Multi-Sensory Educational Aids from Scrap. C
      C Thomas.
Coyaud, Maurice.
  xCoyaud, Maurice.
    Introduction a l'Etude Des Langages
      Documentaires. U of Ala Pr.
Coyle, David C. *see* Coyle, David Cushman.
Coyle, David Cushman, 1887-
  xCoyle, David C.
    Breakthrough to the Great Society. Oceana.
    Ordeal of the Presidency. Greenwood.
    Ordeal of the Presidency. Pub Aff Pr.
Coyle, Jeanette.
  xCoyle, Jeanette.
    A Field Guide to the Common & Interesting
      Plants of Baja California. Nat Hist Pub Co.
Coyle, John J. *see* Coyle, John Joseph.
Coyle, John Joseph.
  xCoyle, John J.
    The Management of Business Logistics. West
      Pub.
Coyle, Lee.
  xCoyle, Lee.
    George Ade. Irvington.
  xCoyle, Lee P.
    George Ade. Coll & U Pr.
Coyle, Lee P. *see* Coyle, Lee.
Coyle, William.
  xCoyle, William.
    Research Papers. Bobbs.
    Research Papers. Odyssey Pr.
Coyne, John.
  xCoyne, John.

How to Make Upside-Down Dolls. Bobbs.
    ed. The Penland School of Crafts Book of
      Jewelry Making. Bobbs.
    The Piercing. Berkley Pub.
    The Piercing. Putnam.
Coyne, John R.
  xCoyne, John R.
    Fall in & Cheer. Doubleday.
Coyne, Thomas J. *see* Coyne, Thomas Joseph.
Coyne, Thomas Joseph.
  xCoyne, Thomas J.
    Readings in Managerial Economics. Business
      Pubns.
Coynik, David, 1946-
  xCoynik, David.
    Film: Real to Reel. Har-Row.
    Film: Real to Reel. McDougal-Littell.
Coysh, A. W. *see* Coysh, Arthur Wilfred.
Coysh, Arthur Wilfred.
  xCoysh, A. W.
    British Art Pottery, 1870-1940. C E Tuttle.
Coysh, Victor.
  xCoysh, Victor.
    Alderney. David & Charles.
    Channel Islands: A New Study. David &
      Charles.
Cozad, R. L. *see* Cozad, Robert L.
Cozad, Robert L.
  xCozad, R. L.
    ed. The Speech Clinician & the
      Hearing-Impaired Child. C C Thomas.
Cozen, L. *see* Cozen, Lewis Nathan.
Cozen, Lewis. *see* Cozen, Lewis Nathan.
Cozen, Lewis Nathan, M.d, 1910-
  xCozen, L.
    Office Orthopedics. C C Thomas.
  xCozen, Lewis.
    An Atlas of Orthopedic Surgery. Lea &
      Febiger.
Cozzens, Frederic S. *see* Cozzens, Frederick Swartwout.
Cozzens, Frederick Swartwout, 1818-1869
  xCozzens, Frederic S.
    Sparrowgrass Papers. Arno.
Cozzens, James G. *see* Cozzens, James Gould.
Cozzens, James Gould, 1903-
  xCozzens, James G.
    By Love Possessed. Fawcett.
    By Love Possessed. HarBraceJ.
    By Love Possessed. HarBraceJ.
    Castaway. HarBraceJ.
    Guard of Honor. HarBraceJ.
    Men & Brethren. HarBraceJ.
  xCozzens, James Gould.
    A Flower in Her Hair. Bruccoli.
Cozzi, Angelo, 1934-
  xCozzi, Angelo.
    photos by Innocence in the Mirror. Morrow.
Crabb, John H., 1922-
  xCrabb, John H.
    Legal System of Congo-Kinshasa. Michie.
Crabbe, Buster.
  xCrabbe, Buster.
    Buster Crabbe's Arthritis Exercise Book. S&S.
Crabbe, David.
  xCrabbe, David.
    ed. World Energy Book: A-Z Atlas &
      Statistical Source Book. Nichols Pub.
    ed. The World Energy Book: An A-Z, Atlas, &
      Statistical Sourcebook. MIT Pr.
Crabbe, George.
  xCrabbe, George.
    Poems. AMS Pr.
    Poems. Scholarly.
Crabbe, Pierre.
  xCrabbe, Pierre.
    ORD & CD in Chemistry & Biochemistry: An
      Introduction. Acad Pr.
    ed. Prostaglandin Research. Acad Pr.
Crabbs, Lelah M. *see* Crabbs, Lelah Mae.

Crabbs, Lelah Mae, 1885-
xCrabbs, Lelah M.
Measuring Efficiency in Supervision &
Teaching. AMS Pr.
Crabites, Pierre, 1877-1943
xCrabites, Pierre.
Gordon, the Sudan & Slavery. Negro U Pr.
Crable, Richard E.
xCrable, Richard E.
Argumentation As Communication: Reasoning
with Receivers. Merrill.
Crabtree, Koby T.
xCrabtree, Koby T.
Fundamental Experiments in Microbiology.
HR&W.
Crackanthorpe, David.
xCrackanthorpe, David.
Hubert Crackanthorpe & English Realism in
the 1890s. U of Mo Pr.

Crackanthorpe, Hubert. see Crackanthorpe, Hubert
Montague.

Crackanthorpe, Hubert Montague, 1870-1896
xCrackanthorpe, Hubert.
Collected Stories, 1893-1897.. Schol Facsimiles.

Cracknell, A. P. see Cracknell, Arthur P.

Cracknell, Arthur P.
xCracknell, A. P.
Applied Group Theory. Pergamon.
ed. Kronecker Product Tables. IFI Plenum.
Ultrasonics. Crane-Russak Co.

Craddock, Denis.
xCraddock, Denis.
Obesity & Its Management. Churchill.

Craddock, Fred B.
xCraddock, Fred B.
As One Without Authority. Abingdon.
Overhearing the Gospel. Abingdon.

Craddock, Jerry R. see Craddock, Jerry Russell.

Craddock, Jerry Russell.
xCraddock, Jerry R.
Latin Legacy Versus Substratum Residue: The
Unstressed Derivational Suffixes in the
Romance Vernaculars of the Western
Mediterranean. U of Cal Pr.

Craddock, Thomas.
xCraddock, Thomas.
Charles Lamb. Arden Lib.
Charles Lamb. Folcroft.
Charles Lamb. Norwood Edns.

Craft, Ann.
xCraft, Ann.
Handicapped Married Couples: A Welsh Study
of Couples Handicapped from Birth by
Mental, Physical of Personality Disorder.
Routledge & Kegan.

Craft, Berniece. see Craft, Berniece Robinette.

Craft, Berniece Robinette.
xCraft, Berniece.
An Introduction to Legal Typing. Bobbs.

Craft, Harvey M., 1925-
xCraft, Harvey M.
Logic, Style, & Arrangement: Literature for
Composition. Glencoe.

Craft, James E. see Craft, James Elliott.

Craft, James Elliott, 1902-
xCraft, James E.
Wheels on the Mountains. McClain.

Craft, M. see Craft, Michael John.

Craft, Michael John.
xCraft, M.
ed. Psychopathic Disorders. Pergamon.

Craft, Robert.
xCraft, Robert.

Current Convictions: Views & Reviews. Knopf.
Craft, Ruth.
xCraft, Ruth.
Carrie Hepple's Garden. Atheneum.
The King's Collection. Doubleday.
Crafts, Roger C. see Crafts, Roger Conant.
Crafts, Roger Conant, 1911-
xCrafts, Roger C.
A Textbook of Human Anatomy. Wiley.
Cragg. see Cragg, Kenneth.
Cragg, Ernest E.
xCragg, Ernest E.
The Cragg Commentaries. Farnswth Pub.
Cragg, Gerald R. see Cragg, Gerald Robertson.
Cragg, Gerald Robertson.
xCragg, Gerald R.
Church & the Age of Reason. Penguin.
The Church & the Age of Reason 1648-1789.
Eerdmans.
Cragg, Gordon. see Cragg, Gordon M. L.
Cragg, Gordon M. L.
xCragg, Gordon.
Organoboranes in Organic Synthesis. Dekker.
Cragg, Kenneth.
xCragg.
House of Islam. Duxbury Pr.
xCragg, Kenneth.
The House of Islam. Dickenson.
Islam from Within: Anthology of a Religion.
Duxbury Pr.
Cragg, Sheila, 1938-
xCragg, Sheila.
Tantrums, Toads, & Teddy Bears. Herald Pr.
Cragoe, Elizabeth.
xCragoe, Elizabeth.
Buttercups & Daisy. St Martin.
Craig, A. C. see Craig, Archibald C.
Craig, Alec.
xCraig, Alec.
Above All Liberties. Arno.
The Banned Books of England & Other
Countries: A Study of the Conception of
Literary Obscenity. Greenwood.
Craig, Alexander S.
xCraig, Alexander S.
Dictionary of Rubber Technology. Philos Lib.
Craig, Allan.
xCraig, Allan.
Counting Things & Magic Rings. Branden.
Craig, Archibald C.
xCraig, A. C.
Christian Faith & Practice. Outlook.
Craig, Charlotte.
xCraig, Charlotte.
Christoph Martin Wieland As the Originator of
the Modern Travesty in German Literature.
U of NC Pr.
Craig, Clarence T. see Craig, Clarence Tucker.
Craig, Clarence Tucker, 1895-1953
xCraig, Clarence T.
ed. Challenge of Our Culture. Arno.
Craig, Colette G. see Craig, Colette Grinevald.
Craig, Colette Grinevald.
xCraig, Colette G.
The Structure of Jacaltec. U of Tex Pr.
Craig, David.
xCraig, David.
Extreme Situations: Literature & Crisis from
the Great War to the Atom Bomb. B&N.
Craig, E. Quita. see Craig, Evelyn Quita.
Craig, Edward G. see Craig, Edward Gordon.
Craig, Edward Gordon, 1872-
xCraig, Edward G.
Books & Theatres. Arno.
Theatre Advancing. Arno.
The Theatre-Advancing. R West.
xCraig, Gordon.
On the Art of the Theatre. Theatre Arts.
Craig, Eleanor.
xCraig, Eleanor.

One, Two, Three: The Story of Matt, a Feral
Child. McGraw.
One, Two, Three: The Story of Matt a Feral
Child. NAL.
Craig, Evelyn Quita, 1917-
xCraig, E. Quita.
Black Drama of the Federal Theatre Era:
Beyond the Formal Horizons. U of Mass Pr.
Craig, G. see Craig, Grace J.
Craig, Gary.
xCraig, Gary.
ed. Jobs & Community Action. Routledge &
Kegan.
Craig, Gerald M.
xCraig, Gerald M.
ed. Early Travellers in the Canadas: 1791-1867.
Greenwood.
Craig, Gerald S. see Craig, Gerald Spellman.
Craig, Gerald Spellman, 1893-
xCraig, Gerald S.
Certain Techniques Used in Developing a
Course of Study in Science for the Horace
Mann Elementary School. AMS Pr.
Craig, Gordon. see Craig, Edward Gordon.
Craig, Grace J.
xCraig, G.
Child Development. P-H.
Human Development. P-H.
xCraig, Grace J.
Human Development. P-H.
Craig, Hardin, 1875-1968
xCraig, Hardin.
English Religious Drama of the Middle Ages.
Greenwood.
Freedom & Renaissance. Kennikat.
Literary Study & the Scholarly Profession.
Arno.
Craig, J. W. see Craig, John W.
Craig, James, 1930-
xCraig, James.
Production for the Graphic Designer.
Watson-Guptill.
Craig, James R. see Craig, James Richard.
Craig, James Richard.
xCraig, James R.
Methods of Psychological Research. HR&W.
Craig, Jean.
xCraig, Jean.
Story of Musical Notes. Lerner Pubns.
Craig, John, 1921-
xCraig, John.
All G.O.D.'s Children. Morrow.
Track & Field. Watts.
Craig, John W.
xCraig, J. W.
Design of Lossy Filters. MIT Pr.
Craig, M. Jean.
xCraig, M. Jean.
Dinosaurs & More Dinosaurs. Schol Bk Serv.
Dinosaurs & More Dinosaurs. Schol Bk Serv.
The Donkey Prince. Doubleday.
The Donkey Prince. Doubleday.
Little Monsters. Schol Bk Serv.
Little Monsters. Dial.
Questions & Answers About Weather. Schol
Bk Serv.
Craig, Margaret (Maze).
xCraig, Margaret M.
Marsha. Berkley Pub.
Trish. Berkley Pub.
Craig, Margaret M. see Craig, Margaret (Maze).
Craig, Richard B.
xCraig, Richard B.
Bracero Program: Interest Groups & Foreign
Policy. U of Tex Pr.
Craig, Robert. see Craig, Robert W.
Craig, Robert C.
xCraig, Robert C.

Psychology of Learning in the Classroom.
Macmillan.
Craig, Robert G. *see* Craig, Robert George.
Craig, Robert George.
xCraig, Robert G.
ed. Dental Materials: A Problem Oriented
Approach. Mosby.
Restorative Dental Materials. Mosby.
Craig, Robert W.
xCraig, Robert.
Storm & Sorrow in the High Pamirs. S&S.
Craig, Ruth H.
xCraig, Ruth H.
Learning the Nemeth Braille Code: A Manual
for Teachers. Brigham.
Craig, Sidney D., 1927-
xCraig, Sidney D.
Raising Your Child, Not by Force But by
Love. Westminster.
Craig, W. *see* Craig, William Henry.
Craig, Warren, 1924-
xCraig, Warren.
Sweet & Lowdown: America's Popular Song
Writers. Scarecrow.
Craig, William, 1929-
xCraig, William.
The Fall of Japan. Penguin.
The Strasbourg Legacy. Berkley Pub.
Craig, William D.
xCraig, William D.
Coins of the World, 1750-1850. Wehman.
Craig, William H. *see* Craig, William Henry.
Craig, William Henry, 1835-
xCraig, W.
Doctor Johnson & the Fair Sex: A Study of
Contrasts. Gordon Pr.
xCraig, William H.
Doctor Johnson & the Fair Sex: A Study of
Contrasts. Folcroft.
Craige, Betty Jean.
xCraige, Betty Jean.
Lorca's "Poet in New York": The Fall into
Consciousness. U Pr of Ky.
Craighead, Frank C. *see* Craighead, Frank Cooper.
Craighead, Frank Cooper, 1916-
xCraighead, Frank C.
Track of the Grizzly. Sierra.
Craigie, W. A. *see* Craigie, William Alexander.
Craigie, William A. *see* Craigie, William Alexander.
Craigie, William Alexander, Sir, 1867-1957
xCraigie, W. A.
The Religion of Ancient Scandinavia. Gordon
Pr.
xCraigie, William A.
The Growth of American English. Folcroft.
Growth of American English. Greenwood.
The Icelandic Sagas. Folcroft.
Icelandic Sagas. Kraus Repr.
The Northern Element in English Literature.
Folcroft.
Northern Words in Modern English. Norwood
Edns.
Religion of Ancient Scandinavia. Arno.
Some Anomalies of Spelling. Folcroft.
Craigin, Elisabeth.
xCraigin, Elisabeth.
Either Is Love. Arno.
Craik, Elizabeth M.
xCraik, Elizabeth M.
The Dorian Aegean. Routledge & Kegan.
Craik, George L. *see* Craik, George Lillie.
Craik, George Lillie, 1798-1866
xCraik, George L.
Spenser & His Poetry. AMS Pr.
Craik, Harry. *see* Craik, Henry.
Craik, Henry, Sir, 1846-1927
xCraik, Harry.
Life of Jonathan Swift. B Franklin.
Life of Jonathan Swift. R West.
Craik, Kenneth. *see* Craik, Kenneth H.

Craik, Kenneth H.
xCraik, Kenneth.
ed. Perceiving Environmental Quality:
Research & Applications. Plenum Pub.
Craik, Kenneth J. *see* Craik, Kenneth James Williams.
Craik, Kenneth James Williams.
xCraik, Kenneth J.
Nature of Explanation. Cambridge U Pr.
Crain, Darrell C.
xCrain, Darrell C.
The Arthritis Handbook. Arc Bks.
Crain, Ernest.
xCrain, Ernest.
The Challenge of Texas Politics: Text with
Readings. West Pub.
Crain, Jim.
xCrain, Jim.
Camping Around California. Random.
Camping Around New England. Random.
Camping Around Washington. Random.
Crain, Robert L.
xCrain, Robert L.
Discrimination, Personality & Achievement: A
Survey of Northern Negroes. Acad Pr.
The Politics of Community Conflict: The
Fluoridation Decision. Bobbs.
The Politics of Community Conflict: The
Fluoridation Decision. Irvington.
Politics of School Desegregation: Comparative
Case Studies of Community Structure &
Policy-Making. NORC.
Crain, W. Mark.
xCrain, W. Mark.
Vehicle Safety Inspection Systems: How
Effective?. Am Enterprise.
Crain, William W.
xCrain, William W.
The Psycho Squad. PB.
Craine, Eugene R.
xCraine, Eugene R.
ed. Chronicles of Michoacan. U of Okla Pr.
ed. The Codex Perez & The Book of Chilam
Balam of Mani. U of Okla Pr.
Cram, Donald J.
xCram, Donald J.
Fundamentals of Carbanion Chemistry. Acad
Pr.
Cram, Mildred, 1889-
xCram, Mildred.
Stranger Things. Arno.
Cram, R. A. *see* Cram, Ralph Adams.
Cram, Ralph A. *see* Cram, Ralph Adams.
Cram, Ralph Adams, 1863-1942
xCram, R. A.
Impressions of Japanese Architecture & the
Allied Arts. Peter Smith.
xCram, Ralph A.
Convictions & Controversies. Arno.
Cramblit, Joella.
xCramblit, Joella.
Flowers Are for Keeping: How to Dry Flowers
& Make Gifts & Decorations. Messner.
Cramer, Gail L.
xCramer, Gail L.
Agricultural Economics & Agribusiness: An
Introduction. Wiley.
Cramer, H. *see* Cramer, Heinrich.
Cramer, Harald, 1893-
xCramer, Harald.
Structural & Statistical Problems for a Class of
Stochastic Processes. Princeton U Pr.
Cramer, Heinrich.
xCramer, H.
ed. Cyclic Nucleotides: Mechanisms of Action.
Wiley.
Cramer, James A.
xCramer, James A.
tr. Preventing Crime. Sage.
Cramer, Phebe.
xCramer, Phebe.

Word Association. Acad Pr.
Cramer, Raymond L., 1908-
xCramer, Raymond L.
Psychology of Jesus & Mental Health.
Zondervan.
Cramlet, Ross C.
xCramlet, Ross C.
Woodturning Visualized. Glencoe.
Woodwork Visualized. Glencoe.
Crampton, Beecher.
xCrampton, Beecher.
Grasses in California. U of Cal Pr.
Crampton, E. W. *see* Crampton, Earle Wilcox.
Crampton, Earle Wilcox, 1895-
xCrampton, E. W.
Applied Animal Nutrition: The Use of
Feedstuffs in the Formulation of Livestock
Rations. W H Freeman.
Crampton, Georgia R. *see* Crampton, Georgia Ronan.
Crampton, Georgia Ronan.
xCrampton, Georgia R.
The Condition of Creatures: Suffering & Action
in Chaucer & Spenser. Yale U Pr.
Cranch, Christopher P. *see* Cranch, Christopher Pearse.
Cranch, Christopher Pearse.
xCranch, Christopher P.
The Life & Letters of Christopher Pearse
Cranch. AMS Pr.
Crandall, Andrew W. *see* Crandall, Andrew Wallace.
Crandall, Andrew Wallace.
xCrandall, Andrew W.
The Early History of the Republican Party.
Peter Smith.
Crandall, Hugh.
xCrandall, Hugh.
Grand Teton: The Story Behind the Scenery. K
C Pubns.
Crandall, Jo Ann.
xCrandall, Jo Ann.
Adult Vocational ESL. Ctr Appl Ling.
Crandall, Joy M.
xCrandall, Joy M.
Early to Learn. Dodd.
Crandall, Stephen H.
xCrandall, Stephen H.
Dynamics of Mechanical & Electromechanical
Systems. McGraw.
Engineering Analysis: A Survey of Numerical
Procedures. McGraw.
Crandall, Thomas D.
xCrandall, Thomas D.
ed. FTC Door-to-Door Sales Rule. Community
Law.
Crane. *see* Crane, Stephen.
Crane, Aimee.
xCrane, Aimee.
ed. Art in the Armed Forces. Garland Pub.
Crane, Burton.
xCrane, Burton.
Practical Economist. Macmillan.
Crane, Chilton.
xCrane, Chilton.
Procedures in Vascular Surgery. Little.
Crane, Edgar G., 1941-
xCrane, Edgar G.
Legislative Review of Government Programs:
Tools for Accountability. Praeger.
Crane, Florence.
xCrane, Florence.
Gypsy Secret. G&D.
Crane, George W. *see* Crane, George Washington.
Crane, George Washington, 1901-
xCrane, George W.
Psychology Applied. Hopkins.
Crane, Hewitt D.
xCrane, Hewitt D.

The New Social Marketplace: Notes on
  Effecting Social Change in America's Third
  Century. Ablex Pub.
Crane, John.
  xCrane, John.
    Laboratory Experiments for Microprocessor
      Systems. P-H.
Crane, John K.
  xCrane, John K.
    T. H. White. Twayne.
Crane, Jules M.
  xCrane, Jules M.
    Introduction to Marine Biology (a Laboratory
      Text). Merrill.
Crane, Julia G.
  xCrane, Julia G.
    Field Projects in Anthropology: A Student
      Handbook. Scott F.
Crane, Lucy, 1842-1882
  xCrane, Lucy.
    Art & the Formation of Taste. Garland Pub.
Crane, P. W.
  xCrane, P. W.
    Worked Examples in Basic Electronics.
      Pergamon.
Crane, Philip M., 1930-
  xCrane, Philip M.
    The Sum of Good Government. Green Hill.
    Surrender in Panama: The Case Against the
      Treaty. Dale Books Inc.
    Surrender in Panama: The Case Against the
      Treaty. Green Hill.
Crane, R. K. *see* Crane, Robert K.
Crane, R. S. *see* Crane, Ronald Salmon.
Crane, Rhonda J.
  xCrane, Rhonda J.
    The Politics of International Standards: France
      & the Color TV War. Ablex Pub.
Crane, Robert, 1938-
  xCrane, Robert.
    Understanding Today's Economics. Watts.
Crane, Robert D. *see* Crane, Robert Dickson.
Crane, Robert Dickson.
  xCrane, Robert D.
    Planning the Future of Saudi Arabia: A Model
      for Achieving National Priorities. Praeger.
Crane, Robert I.
  xCrane, Robert I.
    Aspects of Political Mobilization in South Asia.
      Maxwell Schl Citizen.
    A History of South Asia. Am Hist Assn.
Crane, Robert K.
  xCrane, R. K.
    ed. Gastrointestinal Physiology II. Univ Park.
Crane, Ronald S. *see* Crane, Ronald Salmon.
Crane, Ronald Salmon.
  xCrane, R. S.
    Census of British Newspapers & Periodicals,
      1620-1800. Saifer.
    Critical & Historical Principles of Literary
      History. U of Chicago Pr.
  xCrane, Ronald S.
    A Census of British Newspapers & Periodicals:
      1620-1800. Johnson Repr.
    ed. A Collection of English Poems, 1660-1800.
      Granger Bk.
Crane, Stephen.
  xCrane.
    The Red Badge of Courage. McDougal-Littell.
  xCrane, Stephen.

The Complete Poems of Stephen Crane.
  Cornell U Pr.
Maggie, a Girl of the Streets: A Story of New
  York. Schol Facsimiles.
Men, Women & Boats. Arno.
Notebook of Stephen Crane. U Pr of Va.
The Portable Stephen Crane. Penguin.
The Portable Stephen Crane. Viking Pr.
The Red Badge of Courage. Andor Pub.
The Red Badge of Courage. Biblio Dist.
The Red Badge of Courage. Brown Bk.
Red Badge of Courage. Fleet.
The Red Badge of Courage. G K Hall.
Red Badge of Courage. Modern Lib.
Red Badge of Courage. Modern Lib.
Red Badge of Courage. Peter Pauper.
Red Badge of Courage. Schol Facsimiles.
The Red Badge of Courage. Western Pub.
The Red Badge of Courage. Pendulum Pr.
Red Badge of Courage. Watts.
Red Badge of Courage. Airmont.
Red Badge of Courage. AMSCO Sch.
Red Badge of Courage. Schol Bk Serv.
The Red Badge of Courage. Bantam.
Red Badge of Courage. Dodd.
Red Badge of Courage. Macmillan.
The Red Badge of Courage. PB.
The Red Badge of Courage. Regents Pub.
The Third Violet. Scholarly.
Whilomville Stories. Mss Info.
Whilomville Stories. Scholarly.
Crane, Theodore R. *see* Crane, Theodore Rawson.
Crane, Theodore Rawson, 1929-
  xCrane, Theodore R.
    ed. Colleges & the Public 1787-1862. Tchrs
      Coll.
    The Dimensions of American Education. A-W
Crane, Verner. *see* Crane, Verner Winslow.
Crane, Verner W. *see* Crane, Verner Winslow.
Crane, Verner Winslow, 1889-
  xCrane, Verner.
    The Southern Frontier, 1670-1732. Greenwood.
  xCrane, Verner W.
    The Southern Frontier 1670-1732. Norton.
Crane, Walter, 1845-1915
  xCrane, Walter.
    Artist's Reminiscences. Gale.
    Ideals in Art. Garland Pub.
    Of the Decorative Illustration of Books Old &
      New. Gale.
Crane, Warren E. *see* Crane, Warren Eugene.
Crane, Warren Eugene.
  xCrane, Warren E.
    Delectable Desserts. Hayden.
Crane, William C. *see* Crane, William Carey.
Crane, William Carey, 1816-1885
  xCrane, William C.
    Life & Select Literary Remains of Sam
      Houston of Texas. Arno.
Cranfield, Geoffrey A. *see* Cranfield, Geoffrey Alan.
Cranfield, Geoffrey Alan.
  xCranfield, Geoffrey A.
    The Press & Society: From Caxton to
      Northcliffe. Longman.
Cranfill, Thomas M. *see* Cranfill, Thomas Mabry.
Cranfill, Thomas Mabry.
  xCranfill, Thomas M.
    Anatomy of the Turn of the Screw. Gordian.
Cranin, A. Norman, 1927-
  xCranin, A. Norman.
    Modern Family Guide to Dental Health. Stein
      & Day.
    Oral Implantology. C C Thomas.
Crank, J. *see* Crank, John.
Crank, John.
  xCrank, J.
    The Mathematics of Diffusion. Oxford U Pr.
  xCrank, John.

ed. Diffusion in Polymers. Acad Pr.
Crankshaw, Edward.
  xCrankshaw, Edward.
    The Forsaken Idea: A Study of Viscount
      Milner. Greenwood.
    Joseph Conrad: Some Aspects of the Art of the
      Novel. Russell.
Crano, William D.
  xCrano, William D.
    Principles of Research in Social Psychology.
      McGraw.
Cranor, Henry D. *see* Cranor, Henry Downes.
Cranor, Henry Downes.
  xCranor, Henry D.
    Marriage Licenses of Caroline County,
      Maryland, 1774-1815. Genealog Pub.
Cranor, Phoebe.
  xCranor, Phoebe.
    How Am I Supposed to Love Myself?. Bethany
      Fell.
Crapanzano, V. *see* Crapanzano, Vincent.
Crapanzano, Vincent.
  xCrapanzano, V.
    Case Studies in Spirit Possession. Wiley.
  xCrapanzano, Vincent.
    The Hamadsha: A Study in Moroccan
      Ethnopsychiatry. U of Cal Pr.
Crapol, Edward P.
  xCrapol, Edward P.
    America for Americans: Economic Nationalism
      & Anglophobia in the Late Nineteenth
      Century. Greenwood.
Crary, Catherine S.
  xCrary, Catherine S.
    Price of Loyalty: Tory Writings from the
      Revolutionary Era. McGraw.
Crashaw, Richard.
  xCrashaw, Richard.
    The Complete Works of Richard Crashaw
      AMS Pr.
Crasilneck, Harold B. *see* Crasilneck, Harold Bernard.
Crasilneck, Harold Bernard.
  xCrasilneck, Harold B.
    Clinical Hypnosis: Principles & Applications.
      Grune.
Craton, Michael.
  xCraton, Michael.
    Roots & Branches: Current Directions in Slave
      Studies. Pergamon.
Cratty, B. *see* Cratty, Bryant J.
Cratty, Bryant J.
  xCratty, B.
    Teaching Motor Skills. P-H.
  xCratty, Bryant J.
    Active Learning: Games to Enhance Academic
      Abilities. P-H.
    Career Potentials in Physical Activity. P-H.
    Psycho-Motor Behavior in Education & Sport:
      Selected Papers. C C Thomas.
    Remedial Motor Activity for Children. Lea &
      Febiger.
Craven, Avery. *see* Craven, Avery Odelle.
Craven, Avery O. *see* Craven, Avery Odelle.
Craven, Avery Odelle, 1886-
  xCraven, Avery.
    Historian & the Civil War. U of Chicago Pr.
  xCraven, Avery O.
    Civil War in the Making, 1815-1860. La State
      U Pr.
    Edmund Ruffin, Southerner: A Study in
      Secession. La State U Pr.
    Growth of Southern Nationalism, 1848-1861.
      La State U Pr.
    Rachel of Old Louisiana. La State U Pr.
    Soil Exhaustion As a Factor in the Agricultural
      History of Virginia and Maryland, 1606-1860.
      Peter Smith.
Craven, B. D. *see* Craven, Bruce Desmond.
Craven, Bruce Desmond.
  xCraven, B. D.

Mathematical Programming & Control Theory.
Methuen Inc.

Craven, George M., 1929-
xCraven, George M.
Object & Image: An Introduction to
Photography. P-H.

Craven, John. *see* Craven, John A.

Craven, John A.
xCraven, John.
Distribution of the Product. Allen Unwin.

Craven, John P.
xCraven, John.
Ocean Engineering Systems. MIT Pr.

Craven, Margaret.
xCraven, Margaret.
Again Calls the Owl. G K Hall.
Again Calls the Owl. Putnam.
I Heard the Owl Call My Name. Dell.
I Heard the Owl Call My Name. Doubleday.
I Heard the Owl Call My Name. G K Hall.
Walk Gently This Good Earth. Dell.
Walk Gently This Good Earth. G K Hall.
Walk Gently This Good Earth. Putnam.

Craven, Roy C.
xCraven, Roy C.
Ceremonial Centers of the Maya. U Presses
Fla.
A Concise History of Indian Art. Oxford U Pr.

Craven, Wesley F. *see* Craven, Wesley Frank.

Craven, Wesley Frank, 1905-
xCraven, Wesley F.
The Colonies in Transition, 1660-1713.
Har-Row.
Colonies in Transition, 1660-1713. Har-Row.
Dissolution of the Virginia Company: The
Failure of a Colonial Experiment. Peter
Smith.
Legend of the Founding Fathers. Cornell U Pr.
White, Red, & Black: The Seventeenth-Century
Virginian. Norton.
White, Red, & Black: The Seventeenth Century
Virginian. U Pr of Va.

Cravens, David W.
xCravens, David W.
Marketing Decision Making: Concepts &
Strategy. Irwin.

Cravens, Gwyneth.
xCravens, Gwyneth.
Speed of Light. S&S.

Cravens, Hamilton.
xCravens, Hamilton.
Triumph of Evolution: American Scientists &
the Heredity-Environment Controversy,
1900-1941. U of Pa Pr.

Cravens, Richard. *see* Cravens, Richard H.

Cravens, Richard H.
xCravens, Richard.
Vines. Silver.
xCravens, Richard H.
Vines. Time-Life.

Cravioto, Joaquin.
xCravioto, Joaquin.
ed. Early Malnutrition & Mental Development.
Humanities.

Crawford. *see* Crawford, Theodore.

Crawford, Annie L. *see* Crawford, Annie Laurie.

Crawford, Annie Laurie.
xCrawford, Annie L.
Psychiatric Nursing: A Basic Manual. Davis
Co.

Crawford, Charles. *see* Crawford, Charles P.

Crawford, Charles P.
xCrawford, Charles.
Bad Fall. Har-Row.
Letter Perfect. Archway.
xCrawford, Charles P.
Letter Perfect. Dutton.

Crawford, Clan, 1927-
xCrawford, Clan.

Strategy & Tactics in Municipal Zoning. P-H.

Crawford, David A. *see* Crawford, David Alexander
Edward Lindsay.

Crawford, David Alexander Edward Lindsay, 1871-1940
xCrawford, David A.
Evolution of Italian Sculpture. B Franklin.

Crawford, E. *see* Crawford, Elisabeth T.

Crawford, Elisabeth T.
xCrawford, E.
ed. Sociological Praxis: Current Roles &
Settings. Sage.

Crawford, Emmanuel J. *see* Crawford, Emmanuel James.

Crawford, Emmanuel James.
xCrawford, Emmanuel J.
Oil & the Changed Structure of the World at
the Beginning of the 21st Century. Inst Econ
Pol.

Crawford, Francis M. *see* Crawford, Francis Marion.

Crawford, Francis Marion, 1854-1909
xCrawford, Francis M.
Marzio's Crucifix. AMS Pr.
Marzio's Crucifix. Scholarly.

Crawford, Hubert H.
xCrawford, Hubert H.
Crawford's Encyclopedia of Comic Books. A &
W Pubs.
Crawford's Encyclopedia of Comic Books.
Jonathan David.

Crawford, J. Wickersham. *see* Crawford, James Pyle
Wickersham.

Crawford, James.
xCrawford, James.
The Creation of States in International Law.
Oxford U Pr.

Crawford, James F. *see* Crawford, James Franklin.

Crawford, James Franklin, 1920-
xCrawford, James F.
Readings in Modern Economics. HR&W.

Crawford, James P. *see* Crawford, James Pyle
Wickersham.

Crawford, James Pyle Wickersham.
xCrawford, J. Wickersham.
Spanish Pastoral Drama. Folcroft.
xCrawford, James P.
Spanish Drama Before Lope de Vega.
Greenwood.

Crawford, Jay B. *see* Crawford, Jay Boyd.

Crawford, Jay Boyd.
xCrawford, Jay B.
Credit Mobilier of America: Its Origin &
History, Its Work of Constructing the Union
Pacific Railroad & the Relation of Congress
Therewith. Greenwood.

Crawford, Joanna.
xCrawford, Joanna.
Primrose. HarBraceJ.

Crawford, John E. *see* Crawford, John Edmund.

Crawford, John Edmund.
xCrawford, John E.
Children with Subtle Perceptual-Motor
Difficulties. Stanwix.

Crawford, John R.
xCrawford, John R.
How to Be a Consistent Winner in the Most
Popular Card Games. Doubleday.

Crawford, John W.
xCrawford, John W.
Discourse: Essay on English & American
Literature. Humanities.

Crawford, Kenneth G. *see* Crawford, Kenneth Gale.

Crawford, Kenneth Gale, 1902-
xCrawford, Kenneth G.
The Pressure Boys: The Inside Story of
Lobbying in America. Arno.

Crawford, Kenneth Grant.
xCrawford, Kenneth G.
Canadian Municipal Government. U of
Toronto Pr.

Crawford, Linda.
xCrawford, Linda.

Something to Make Us Happy. Ballantine.
Something to Make Us Happy. G K Hall.
Something to Make Us Happy. S&S.

Crawford, Lucy C.
xCrawford, Lucy C.
Organization & Administration of Distributive
Education. Merrill.

Crawford, Martin.
xCrawford, Martin.
Air Pollution Control Theory. McGraw.

Crawford, Mary C. *see* Crawford, Mary Caroline.

Crawford, Mary Caroline, 1874-1932
xCrawford, Mary C.
Goethe & His Woman Friends. Haskell.
In the Days of the Pilgrim Fathers. Gale.

Crawford, Max, 1938-
xCrawford, Max.
The Backslider. Avon.
The Backslider. FS&G.
The Bad Communist. HarBraceJ.

Crawford, Mel.
xCrawford, Mel.
The Bambi Book. Western Pub.
illus. The Turtle Book. Western Pub.

Crawford, Michael. *see* Crawford, Michael H.

Crawford, Michael H., 1939-
xCrawford, Michael.
The Roman Republic. Humanities.

Crawford, Nelson A. *see* Crawford, Nelson Antrim.

Crawford, Nelson Antrim, 1888-
xCrawford, Nelson A.
Ethics of Journalism. Greenwood.
The Ethics of Journalism. Johnson Repr.
Ethics of Journalism. Scholarly.

Crawford, Osbert G. *see* Crawford, Osbert Guy
Stanhope.

Crawford, Osbert Guy Stanhope, 1886-1957
xCrawford, Osbert G.
The Fung Kingdom of Sennar: With a
Geographical Account of the Middle Nile
Region. AMS Pr.

Crawford, Patricia, 1933-
xCrawford, Patricia.
Homesteading. Macmillan.

Crawford, R. M. *see* Crawford, Raymond Maxwell.

Crawford, Raymond Maxwell, 1906-
xCrawford, R. M.
Australia. Humanities.

Crawford, Richard.
xCrawford, Richard.
American Studies & American Musicology: A
Point of View & a Case in Point. Inst Am
Music.
Men, Women & Bridge: Startling Tales of the
Bridge Table. Sterling.

Crawford, Richard P.
xCrawford, Richard P.
ed. Bovine Brucellosis: An International
Symposium. Tex A&M Univ Pr.

Crawford, Rudd.
xCrawford, Rudd.
Achievement in Mathematics. Allyn.

Crawford, Stanley. *see* Crawford, Stanley G.

Crawford, Stanley G., 1937-
xCrawford, Stanley.
Some Instructions. Knopf.

Crawford, T. S.
xCrawford, T. S.
History of the Umbrella. Taplinger.

Crawford, Tad, 1946-
xCrawford, Tad.
Legal Guide for the Visual Artist. Dutton.

Crawford, Teri.
xCrawford, Teri.
The First Wild West Rodeo. Silver.

Crawford, Theodore, Sir.
xCrawford.
Pathology of Ischaemic Heart Disease.
Butterworths.

Crawford, Vaughn E. *see* Crawford, Vaughn Emerson.

Crawford, Vaughn Emerson.
xCrawford, Vaughn E.
Sumerian Economic Texts from the First
Dynasty of Isin. AMS Pr.
Crawford, Virginia M. *see* Crawford, Virginia Mary
(Smith).
Crawford, Virginia Mary (Smith), 1862?-
xCrawford, Virginia M.
Studies in Foreign Literature. Kennikat.
Crawford, Walter B. *see* Crawford, Walter Byron.
Crawford, Walter Byron.
xCrawford, Walter B.
ed. Reading Coleridge: Approaches &
Applications. Cornell U Pr.
Crawford, William, 1948-
xCrawford, William.
The Keepers of Light: A History & Working
Guide to Early Photographic Processes.
Morgan.
Crawford, William P., 1922-
xCrawford, William P.
Mariner's Weather. Norton.
Crawhall, Joseph, 1821-1896
xCrawhall, Joseph.
Quaint Cuts in the Chap Book Style. Dover.
Quaint Cuts in the Chap Book Style. Peter
Smith.
Crawley, C. W. *see* Crawley, Charles William.
Crawley, Charles William.
xCrawley, C. W.
The Question of Greek Independence: A Study
of British Policy in the Near East,
1821-1833. Fertig.
Crawley, Gerald M. *see* Crawley, Gerard M.
Crawley, Gerard M.
xCrawley, Gerald M.
Energy. Macmillan.
Crawley, Stanley M. *see* Crawley, Stanley W.
Crawley, Stanley W.
xCrawley, Stanley M.
Steel Buildings: Analysis & Design. Wiley.
Cray, Ed.
xCray, Ed.
Levi's. HM.
Crayder, Dorothy.
xCrayder, Dorothy.
The Riddles of Mermaid House. Atheneum.
Craze, Michael.
xCraze, Michael.
The Life & Lyrics of Andrew Marvell. B&N.
Creagh-Osborne, Richard.
xCreagh-Osborne, Richard.
Dinghy Building. De Graff.
Creamer, Daniel. *see* Creamer, Daniel Barnett.
Creamer, Daniel Barnett.
xCreamer, Daniel.
Overseas Research & Development by United
States Multinationals, 1966-1975: Estimates
of Expenditures & a Statistical Profile.
Conference Bd.
Creasey, John.
xCreasey, John.
Danger for the Baron. Manor Bks.
Department of Death. Popular Lib.
The League of Dark Men. Popular Lib.
A Plague of Demons. HR&W
A Sharp Rise in Crime. Scribner.
Creasey, William A.
xCreasey, William A.
Drug Disposition in Humans: The Basis of
Clinical Pharmacology. Oxford U Pr.
Creasy, Donna N. *see* Creasy, Donna Newberry.
Creasy, Donna Newberry.
xCreasy, Donna N.
Food Careers. P-H.
Creative Editors. *see* Creative Educational Society,
Mankato, Minnesota.
Creative Education, Inc., Mankato, Minnesota.
xCreative Editors.

How to Have Fun Making Dinner. Creative
Ed.
How to Have Fun Making Lunch. Creative Ed.
How to Have Fun with a Flower Garden.
Creative Ed.
How to Have Fun with a Vegetable Garden.
Creative Ed.
Creative Educational Society Editors. *see* Creative
Educational Society, Mankato, Minnesota.
Creative Educational Society, Mankato, Minnesota.
xCreative Editors.
Our Natural Environment. Creative Ed.
xCreative Educational Society Editors.
How to Have Fun Baking Cookies & Cakes.
Creative Ed.
How to Have Fun Building a Sailboat. Creative
Ed.
How to Have Fun Knitting. Creative Ed.
How to Have Fun Making a Kite. Creative Ed.
How to Have Fun Making Bird Feeders & Bird
Houses. Creative Ed.
How to Have Fun Making Breakfast. Creative
Ed.
How to Have Fun Making Christmas
Decorations. Creative Ed.
How to Have Fun Making Mobiles. Creative
Ed.
How to Have Fun Making Puppets. Creative
Ed.
How to Have Fun Sewing. Creative Ed.
How to Have Fun Weaving. Creative Ed.
How to Have Fun with an Indoor Garden.
Creative Ed.
How to Have Fun with Macrame. Creative Ed.
How to Have Fun with Needlepoint. Creative
Ed.
Creaton, David.
xCreaton, David.
Beasts & Babies. St Martin.
Beasts Go West. St Martin.
Crebillon, Claude P. *see* Crebillon, Claude Prosper Jolyot
De.
Crebillon, Claude Prosper Jolyot De, 1707-1777
xCrebillon, Claude P.
Letters from the Marchioness De M to the
Count De R. Garland Pub.
Creed, Charles.
xCreed, Charles.
The Art of the Affair. Ellis Pr.
Creed, R. S. *see* Creed, Richard Stephen.
Creed, Richard Stephen, 1898-
xCreed, R. S.
Reflex Activity of the Spinal Cord. Oxford U
Pr.
Creed, Virginia.
xCreed, Virginia.
France. Fideler.
Creedman, Theodore S.
xCreedman, Theodore S.
Historical Dictionary of Costa Rica. Scarecrow.
Creegan, Charles C. *see* Creegan, Charles Cole.
Creegan, Charles Cole.
xCreegan, Charles C.
Great Missionaries of the Church. Arno.
Creel, George, 1876-1953
xCreel, George.
How We Advertised America. Arno.
Creel, Herrlee G. *see* Creel, Herrlee Glessner.
Creel, Herrlee Glessner.
xCreel, Herrlee G.
Chinese Thought from Confucius to Mao
Tse-Tung. U of Chicago Pr.
Confucius, the Man & the Myth. Greenwood.
Creel, J. Luke.
xCreel, Luke.
Folk Tales of Liberia. Denison.
Creel, Luke. *see* Creel, J. Luke.
Creel, Richard. *see* Creel, Richard E.
Creel, Richard E., 1940-
xCreel, Richard.

Religion & Doubt: Toward a Faith of Your
Own. P-H.
Creeley, Bobbie. *see* Creeley, Robert.
Creeley, Robert, 1926-
xCreeley, Bobbie.
illus. Thirty Things. Black Sparrow.
xCreeley, Robert.
Charm: Early & Uncollected Poems. Four
Seasons Foun.
Later. New Directions.
Thirty Things. Black Sparrow.
Creer, Thomas L.
xCreer, Thomas L.
Asthma Therapy: A Behavioral Health Care
System for Respiratory Disorders. Springer
Pub.
Creese, Thomas M.
xCreese, Thomas M.
Differential Equations for Engineers. McGraw.
Creeth, Edmund.
xCreeth, Edmund.
ed. Tudor Plays: An Anthology of Early
English Drama. Norton.
Cregier, Don M., 1930-
xCregier, Don M.
Bounder from Wales: Lloyd George's Career
Before the First World War. U of Mo Pr.
Creigh, Dorothy W. *see* Creigh, Dorothy Weyer.
Creigh, Dorothy Weyer.
xCreigh, Dorothy W.
Intro. by A Primer for Local Historical
Societies. AASLH.
Creighton, David.
xCreighton, David.
Deeds of Gods & Heroes. St Martin.
Creighton, Helen, 1914-
xCreighton, Helen.
Law Every Nurse Should Know. Saunders.
Songs & Ballads from Nova Scotia. Peter
Smith.
Creighton, Joanne V.
xCreighton, Joanne V.
Joyce Carol Oates. Twayne.
Creizenach, Wilhelm. *see* Creizenach, Wilhelm Michael
Anton.
Creizenach, Wilhelm Michael Anton.
xCreizenach, Wilhelm.
The English Drama in the Age of Shakespeare.
Dynamic Learn Corp.
English Drama in the Age of Shakespeare.
Folcroft.
English Drama in the Age of Shakespeare.
Haskell.
English Drama in the Age of Shakespeare.
Russell.
Crelin, Edmund S., 1923-
xCrelin, Edmund S.
Anatomy of the Newborn: An Atlas. Lea &
Febiger.
Functional Anatomy of the Newborn. Yale U
Pr.
Cremin, Lawrence A. *see* Cremin, Lawrence Arthur.
Cremin, Lawrence Arthur, 1925-
xCremin, Lawrence A.
The Genius of American Education. U of
Pittsburgh Pr.
Public Education. Basic.
Crena De Iongh, Daniel, 1888-
xCrena De Iongh, Daniel.
Byzantine Aspects of Italy. Norton.
Crenner, James.
xCrenner, James.
Aging Ghost. Golden Quill.
Crenshaw, James. *see* Crenshaw, James L.
Crenshaw, James L.
xCrenshaw, James.
Gerhard von Rad. Word Bks.
xCrenshaw, James L.

Prophetic Conflict: Its Effect Upon Israelite
Religion. De Gruyter.
Studies in Ancient Israelite Wisdom. Ktav.
Crenson, Matthew A., 1943-
xCrenson, Matthew A.
The Federal Machine: Beginnings of
Bureaucracy in Jacksonian America. Johns
Hopkins.
Cresci, M. see Cresci, Martha W.
Cresci, Martha W., 1907-
xCresci, M.
How to Put Yourself Across with Key Words
& Phrases. P-H.
xCresci, Martha W.
Complete Book of Model Business Letters.
P-H.
Crescimbeni, Joseph.
xCrescimbeni, Joseph.
Language Enrichment Activities for the
Elementary School. P-H.
Cresser, Malcolm S.
xCresser, Malcolm S.
Solvent Extraction in Flame Spectroscopic
Analysis. Butterworths.
Cressey, Donald R. see Cressey, Donald Ray.
Cressey, Donald Ray, 1919-
xCressey, Donald R.
Other People's Money: A Study in the Social
Psychology of Embezzlement. Patterson
Smith.
Theft of the Nation: The Structure &
Operations of Organized Crime in America.
Har-Row.
Cressey, George B. see Cressey, George Babcock.
Cressey, George Babcock, 1896-
xCressey, George B.
Soviet Potentials: A Geographic Appraisal.
Syracuse U Pr.
Cressey, James.
xCressey, James.
The Dragon & George. P-H.
Fourteen Rats & a Rat Catcher. P-H.
Max the Mouse. P-H.
Cressey, Paul G. see Cressey, Paul Goalby.
Cressey, Paul Goalby.
xCressey, Paul G.
Taxi-Dance Hall: A Sociological Study in
Commercialized Recreation & City Life.
Greenwood.
Taxi-Dance Hall: A Sociological Study in
Commercialized Recreation & City Life.
Patterson Smith.
Cressey, William W.
xCressey, William W.
Spanish Phonology & Morphology: A
Generative View. Georgetown U Pr.
Cressman, L. S. see Cressman, Luther Sheeleigh.
Cressman, Luther Sheeleigh, 1897-
xCressman, L. S.
Prehistory of the Far West: Homes of Vanished
Peoples. U of Utah Pr.
Cresswell, Helen.
xCresswell, Helen.
Absolute Zero. Avon.
A Game of Catch. Macmillan.
Night Watchmen. Macmillan.
Ordinary Jack. Avon.
Cresswell, Nicholas, 1750-1804
xCresswell, Nicholas.
Journal of Nicholas Cresswell, 1774-1777.
Kennikat.
Cressy, David.
xCressy, David.
Education in Tudor & Stuart England. St
Martin.
Cressy, Earl H. see Cressy, Earl Herbert.
Cressy, Earl Herbert.
xCressy, Earl H.

Daughters of Changing Japan. Greenwood.
Creston, Paul, 1906-
xCreston, Paul.
Rational Metric Notation: The Mathematical
Basis of Meters, Symbols, a Note-Values.
Exposition.
Creswell, Clifford J.
xCreswell, Clifford J.
Spectral Analysis of Organic Compounds: An
Introductory Programmed Text. Burgess.
Creswell, John.
xCreswell, John.
Generals & Admirals: The Story of Amphibious
Command. Greenwood.
Creswell, K. A. see Creswell, Keppel Archibald Cameron.
Creswell, Keppel Archibald Cameron, 1879-
xCreswell, K. A.
Muslim Architecture of Egypt. Hacker.
Cretan, Gladys Y. see Cretan, Gladys Yessayan.
Cretan, Gladys Yessayan.
xCretan, Gladys Y.
A Hole, a Box & a Stick. Lothrop.
Lobo. Lothrop.
Lobo & Brewster. Lothrop.
Creteau, Paul G., 1925-
xCreteau, Paul G.
Principles of Real Estate Law. Castle Pub Co.
Creutzfeldt, W. see Creutzfeldt, Werner.
Creutzfeldt, Werner.
xCreutzfeldt, W.
ed. The Genetics of Diabetes Mellitus.
Springer-Verlag.
Creux, Francois Du. see Du Creux, Francois.
Crevea, Rafael Altamira Y. see Altamira Y Crevea,
Rafael.
Creveld, Martin L. Van. see Van Creveld, Martin L.
Crew, Michael A.
xCrew, Michael A.
ed. Problems in Public-Utility Economics &
Regulation. Lexington Bks.
Public Utility Economics. St Martin.
Crew, P. Mack. see Crew, Phyllis Mack.
Crew, Phyllis Mack, 1939-
xCrew, P. Mack.
Calvinist Preaching & Iconoclasm in the
Netherlands, 1544-1569. Cambridge U Pr.
Crews, Cecil. see Crews, Cecil Robert.
Crews, Cecil Robert.
xCrews, Cecil.
History of the Michigan Credit Union League.
Wayne St U Pr.
Crews, Donald.
xCrews, Donald.
Freight Train. Greenwillow.
Truck. Greenwillow.
Crews, Frederick. see Crews, Frederick C.
Crews, Frederick C.
xCrews, Frederick.
Out of My System: Psychoanalysis, Ideology,
& Critical Method. Oxford U Pr.
The Random House Handbook. Random.
xCrews, Frederick C.
Pooh Perplex: A Freshman Casebook. Dutton.
Crews, Harry, 1935-
xCrews, Harry.
Blood & Grits. Har-Row.
Childhood, the Biography of a Place. G K Hall.
A Feast of Snakes. Ballantine.
The Gypsy's Curse. PB.
The Gypsy's Curse. Ultramarine Pub.
Crews, William.
xCrews, William.
Four Causes of Reality. Philos Lib.
Cribb, C. C.
xCribb, C. C.

The Coming Kingdom. Manhattan Ltd NC.
The Devil's Empire. Manhattan Ltd NC.
Getting Ready for Heaven. Manhattan Ltd
NC.
The Horrified & the Glorified. Manhattan Ltd
NC.
Spinning Straw into Gold. Manhattan Ltd NC.
Staking Your Claim on Healing. Manhattan
Ltd NC.
Cribbin, James J.
xCribbin, James J.
Effective Managerial Leadership. Am Mgmt.
Crichton, Ian.
xCrichton, Ian.
The Art of Dying. Humanities.
Crichton, Michael, 1942-
xCrichton, Michael.
The Andromeda Strain. Dell.
Andromeda Strain. Knopf.
Five Patients: The Hospital Explained. Knopf.
The Great Train Robbery. Bantam.
The Great Train Robbery. G K Hall.
The Great Train Robbery. Knopf.
Crichton, Robert.
xCrichton, Robert.
The Camerons. Warner Bks.
Crick, Bernard. see Crick, Bernard R.
Crick, Bernard R.
xCrick, Bernard.
In Defence of Politics. U of Chicago Pr.
Crickmay, Marie C.
xCrickmay, Marie C.
Speech Therapy & the Bobath Approach to
Cerebral Palsy. C C Thomas.
Criep, Leo H. see Criep, Leo Hermann.
Criep, Leo Hermann, 1896-
xCriep, Leo H.
Allergy & Clinical Immunology. Grune.
Clinical Immunology & Allergy. Grune.
Crihfield, Liza.
xCrihfield, Liza.
Ko-Uta: Little Songs of the Geisha World. C E
Tuttle.
Crile, George, 1907-
xCrile, George.
Surgery: Your Choices Your Alternatives.
Delacorte.
Surgery: Your Choices, Your Alternatives. G K
Hall.
What Women Should Know About the Breast
Cancer Controversy. Macmillan.
Crim, John W. see Crim, John Winthrop.
Crim, John Winthrop, 1924-
xCrim, John W.
Compensating Non-Supervisory Professional
Employees. Univ Microfilms.
Cripe, Helen.
xCripe, Helen.
American Manuscripts, 1763-1815: An Index
to Documents Described in Auction Records
& Dealers' Catalogs. Scholarly Res Inc.
Thomas Jefferson & Music. U Pr of Va.
Crippen, Raymond C.
xCrippen, Raymond C.
Identification of Organic Compounds with the
Aid of Gas Chromatography. McGraw.
Crippen, Thomas G. see Crippen, Thomas George.
Crippen, Thomas George.
xCrippen, Thomas G.
Christmas & Christmas Lore. Gale.
Christmas & Christmas Lore. Gordon Pr.
Cripps. see Cripps, Martin.
Cripps, Martin.
xCripps.
Introduction to Computer Hardware. Winthrop.
Crisafulli, Alessandro S.
xCrisafulli, Alessandro S.
ed. Linguistic & Literary Studies in Honor of
Helmut A. Hatzfeld. Intl Schol Bk Serv.
Crisafulli, Allesandro S. see Crisafulli, Alessandro S.

Criscuolo, Nicholas P.
    xCriscuolo, Nicholas P.
        Supervising the Reading Program. Pendell Pub.
Crisler, Lois.
    xCrisler, Lois.
        Arctic Wild. Har-Row.
        Arctic Wild. Har-Row.
        Captive Wild. Har-Row.
Crisp, N. J.
    xCrisp, N. J.
        The London Deal. St Martin.
        The Odd Job Man. St Martin.
Crispen, Margaret.
    xCrispen, Margaret.
        How Any Woman Can Get Rich Fast in Real
          Estate. Andrews & McMeel.
Crispin, John.
    xCrispin, John.
        Pedro Salinas. Twayne.
Criss, Lillian M.
    xCriss, Lillian M.
        That Tent by the Sawdust Pile. Pacific Pr Pub
          Assn.
Crist, Evamae B. see Crist, Evamae Barton.
Crist, Evamae Barton.
    xCrist, Evamae B.
        Take This House. Herald Pr.
Cristescu, Romulus.
    xCristescu, Romulus.
        Ordered Vector Spaces & Linear Operators.
          Intl Schol Bk Serv.
Cristiani, Leon, 1879-
    xCristiani, Leon.
        Evidence of Satan in the Modern World. TAN
          Bks Pubs.
Criswell, Cloyd. see Criswell, Cloyd Mann.
Criswell, Cloyd Mann.
    xCriswell, Cloyd.
        Arrow by Day. M Jones.
Criswell, W. A.
    xCriswell, W. A.
        Expository Sermons on Revelation. Zondervan.
Criswell, W. A. see Criswell, Wallie A.
Criswell, Wallie A.
    xCriswell, W. A.
        Did Man Just Happen?. Moody.
        Expository Sermons on the Book of Daniel.
          Zondervan.
        Expository Sermons on the Epistle of James.
          Zondervan.
        The Holy Spirit in Today's World. Zondervan.
        What to Do Until Jesus Comes Back.
          Broadman.
        With a Bible in My Hand. Broadman.
Critchfield, Howard J.
    xCritchfield, Howard J.
        General Climatology. P-H.
Critchfield, Richard.
    xCritchfield, Richard.
        The Golden Bowl Be Broken: Peasant Life in
          Four Cultures. Ind U Pr.
Critchley, J. S., 1942-
    xCritchley, John.
        Feudalism. Allen Unwin.
Critchley, John. see Critchley, J. S.
Critchley, Macdonald.
    xCritchley, Macdonald.
        Dyslexia Defined. C C Thomas.
        Music & the Brain: Studies in the Neurology of
          Music. C C Thomas.
        Silent Language. Butterworths.
    xCritchley, McDonald.
        Parietal Lobes. Hafner.
Critchley, McDonald. see Critchley, Macdonald.
Critchley, T. A. see Critchley, Thomas Alan.
Critchley, Thomas Alan, 1919-
    xCritchley, T. A.

        The Conquest of Violence: Order & Liberty in
          Britain. Schocken.
Critchlow, Keith.
    xCritchlow, Keith.
        Order in Space: A Design Source Book. Viking
          Pr.
Crites, Stephen.
    xCrites, Stephen.
        In the Twilight of Christendom: Hegel Vs.
          Kierkegaard on Faith & History. Scholars Pr
          Ca.
Crittenden, Mabel, 1917-
    xCrittenden, Mabel.
        The Fern Book. Celestial Arts.
Croall, Stephen.
    xCroall, Stephen.
        The Anti-Nuclear Handbook. Pantheon.
Croan, Melvin.
    xCroan, Melvin.
        East Germany: The Soviet Connection. Sage.
Croat, Thomas B.
    xCroat, Thomas B.
        Flora of Barro Colorado Island. Stanford U Pr.
Croce, Arlene.
    xCroce, Arlene.
        Afterimages. Knopf.
        Afterimages. Random.
Croce, Benedetto, 1866-1952
    xCroce, Benedetto.
        Autobiography. Arno.
        Goethe. Kennikat.
        The History of the Kingdom of Naples. U of
          Chicago Pr.
Crocetti, Guido M.
    xCrocetti, Guido M.
        Contemporary Attitudes Toward Mental
          Illness. U of Pittsburgh Pr..
Crocker, Helen B. see Crocker, Helen Bartter.
Crocker, Helen Bartter.
    xCrocker, Helen B.
        The Green River of Kentucky. U Pr of Ky.
Crocker, Lester G.
    xCrocker, Lester G.
        Diderot's Chaotic Order: Approach to
          Synthesis. Princeton U Pr.
Crocker, Malcolm J.
    xCrocker, Malcolm J.
        Noise & Noise Control. CRC Pr.
Crocker, Richard L.
    xCrocker, Richard L.
        The Early Medieval Sequence. U of Cal Pr.
        History of Musical Style. McGraw.
Crocker, Walter. see Crocker, Walter Russell.
Crocker, Walter R. see Crocker, Walter Russell.
Crocker, Walter Russell, 1902-
    xCrocker, Walter.
        Nigeria: A Critique of British Colonial
          Administration. Gordon Pr.
    xCrocker, Walter R.
        Nigeria: A Critique of British Colonial
          Administration. Arno.
Crockett, Candace, 1945-
    xCrockett, Candace.
        Card Weaving. Watson-Guptill.
        The Complete Spinning Book. Watson-Guptill.
Crockett, J. S.
    xCrockett, J. S.
        For Those Who Sell (and Who the Hell
          Doesn't?!). Farnswth Pub.
Crockett, J. S. Dave. see Crockett, J. S.
Crockett, James U. see Crockett, James Underwood.
Crockett, James Underwood.
    xCrockett, James U.

        Annuals. Time-Life.
        Annuals. Silver.
        Crockett's Indoor Garden. Little.
        Crockett's Tool Shed. Little.
        Evergreens. Time-Life.
        Evergreens. Silver.
        Flowering House Plants. Silver.
        Flowering House Plants. Time-Life.
        Flowering Shrubs. Time-Life.
        Flowering Shrubs. Silver.
        Foliage House Plants. Time-Life.
        Lawns & Ground Covers. Time-Life.
        Perennials. Time-Life.
        Perennials. Silver.
        Vegetables & Fruits. Silver.
        Vegetables & Fruits. Time-Life.
    xCrockett, James Underwood.
        Greenhouse Gardening As a Hobby.
          Doubleday.
    xCrockett, James V.
        Foliage House Plants. Silver.
        Lawns & Ground Covers. Silver.
Crockett, James V. see Crockett, James Underwood.
Crockett, Jim.
    xCrockett, Jim.
        ed. The Guitar Player Book. Grove.
Crockett, Joseph P.
    xCrockett, Joseph P.
        Federal Tax System of the United States: A
          Survey of Law & Administration.
          Greenwood.
Crockett, Norman L.
    xCrockett, Norman L.
        The Black Towns. Regents Pr KS.
Crockett, S. R. see Crockett, Samuel Rutherford.
Crockett, Samuel R. see Crockett, Samuel Rutherford.
Crockett, Samuel Rutherford, 1860-1914
    xCrockett, S. R.
        Tales of Our Coast. Arno.
    xCrockett, Samuel R.
        Adventurer in Spain. Arno.
        Love Idylls. Arno.
Crockett, W. David. see Crockett, William David.
Crockett, William David, 1919-
    xCrockett, W. David.
        Promotion & Publicity for Churches.
          Morehouse.
Crockett, William S. see Crockett, William Shillinglaw.
Crockett, William Shillinglaw, 1866-1945
    xCrockett, William S.
        Footsteps of Scott. Folcroft.
Croes, Martin.
    xCroes, Martin.
        Marijuana Reappraised: Two Personal
          Accounts. Myrin Institute.
Croft, A. J. see Croft, Antony Julian.
Croft, Antony Julian, 1925-
    xCroft, A. J.
        Cryogenic Laboratory Equipment. Plenum Pub.
Croft, Doreen. see Croft, Doreen J.
Croft, Doreen J.
    xCroft, Doreen.
        Activities Handbook for Teachers of Young
          Children. HM.
    xCroft, Doreen J.
        Parents & Teachers. A Resource Book for
          Home, School & Community Relations.
          Wadsworth Pub.
Croft, F. Max.
    xCroft, F. Max.
        Information Systems: A Management Science
          Approach. Van Nos Reinhold.
Croft, J. see Croft, Julian.
Croft, J. H.
    xCroft, J. H.
        Going Metric in Catering. Pergamon.
Croft, Julian, 1941-
    xCroft, J.
        T. H. Jones. Verry.
Croft, K. see Croft, Kenneth.

Diplomacy During the American Civil War.
Wiley.
xCrook, David P.
American Democracy in English Politics,
1815-1850. Oxford U Pr.
Crook, J. A. see Crook, John Anthony.
Crook, John Anthony.
xCrook, J. A.
Law & Life of Rome. Cornell U Pr.
Crook, Roger H.
xCrook, Roger H.
An Open Book to the Christian Divorcee.
Broadman.
Crookall, Robert, 1890-
xCrookall, Robert.
Out-of-the Body Experiences: A Fourth
Analysis. Citadel Pr.
Crookenden, Napier, Sir.
xCrookenden, Napier.
Airborne at War. Scribner.
Crookes, William, Sir, 1832-1919
xCrookes, William.
The Wheat Problem. Arno.
Crooks, James B.
xCrooks, James B.
Politics & Progress: The Rise of Urban
Progressivism in Baltimore, 1895-1911. La
State U Pr.
Crooks, Lois. see Crooks, Lois C.
Crooks, Lois C.
xCrooks, Lois.
Operating Room Techniques for the Surgical
Team. Little.
Crooks, R. see Crooks, Robert.
Crooks, Robert.
xCrooks, R.
Our Sexuality. A-W.
xCrooks, Robert.
Our Sexuality. Benjamin Cummings.
Crookston, Stephanie, 1947-
xCrookston, Stephanie.
Creative Cakes. Random.
Croome, Angela.
xCroome, Angela.
Hovercraft. Astor-Honor.
Croome, D. J. see Croome, Derek J.
Croome, Derek J.
xCroome, D. J.
Air Conditioning & Ventilation of Buildings.
Pergamon.
ed. Quality & Total Cost in Buildings &
Services Design. Longman.
Cropsey, Joseph.
xCropsey, Joseph.
Political Philosophy & the Issues of Politics. U
of Chicago Pr.
Polity & Economy: An Interpretation of the
Principles of Adam Smith. Greenwood.
Crosbie, John S., 1920-
xCrosbie, John S.
Crosbie's Book of Punned Haiku. Workman
Pub.
Crosbie's Dictionary of Riddles. Crown.
Crosbie, Paul V.
xCrosbie, Paul V.
Interaction in Small Groups. Macmillan.
Crosbie, Sylvia K., 1938-
xCrosbie, Sylvia K.
A Tacit Alliance: France & Israel from the
Suez to the Six Day War. Princeton U Pr.
Crosby, Alfred W.
xCrosby, Alfred W.
The Columbian Exchange: Biological and
Cultural Consequences of 1492. Greenwood.
Crosby, C. A.
xCrosby, Cynthia A.
Historical Dictionary of Malawi. Scarecrow.
Crosby, Caresse, 1892-
xCrosby, Caresse.

The Passionate Years. Ecco Pr.
Crosby, Cynthia A. see Crosby, C. A.
Crosby, Donald F., 1933-
xCrosby, Donald F.
God, Church, & Flag: Senator Joseph R.
McCarthy & the Catholic Church,
1950-1957. U of NC Pr.
Crosby, Ernest. see Crosby, Ernest Howard.
Crosby, Ernest H. see Crosby, Ernest Howard.
Crosby, Ernest Howard, 1856-1907
xCrosby, Ernest.
Garrison the Non-Resistant. Ozer.
xCrosby, Ernest H.
Captain Jinks, Hero. Irvington.
Crosby, Everett U. see Crosby, Everett Uberto.
Crosby, Everett Uberto.
xCrosby, Everett U.
ed. The Past as Prologue: Sources & Studies in
European Civilization. Irvington.
Crosby, Harry, 1926-
xCrosby, Harry.
The Cave Paintings of Baja California: The
Great Murals of an Unknown People. Copley
Bks.
Crosby, John.
xCrosby, John.
An Affair of Strangers. Stein & Day.
An Affair of Strangers. Warner Bks.
Dear Judgement. PB.
Dear Judgment. Stein & Day.
Crosby, Josiah, Sir, 1880-
xCrosby, Josiah.
Siam: The Crossroads. AMS Pr.
Crosby, Philip B.
xCrosby, Philip B.
The Art of Getting Your Own Sweet Way.
Dutton.
The Art of Getting Your Own Sweet Way.
McGraw.
Quality Is Free: The Art of Making Quality
Certain. NAL.
Crosby, Ruth.
xCrosby, Ruth.
From an Old Leather Trunk. Chris Mass.
I Was a Summer Boarder. Chris Mass.
Crosby, Sumner M. see Crosby, Sumner Mcknight.
Crosby, Sumner Mcknight, 1909-
xCrosby, Sumner M.
The Apostle Bas-Relief at Saint-Denis. Yale U
Pr.
Crosby, Sylvester S. see Crosby, Sylvester Sage.
Crosby, Sylvester Sage, d. 1914
xCrosby, Sylvester S.
The Early Coins of America. Quarterman.
Crosignani, P. G. see Crosignani, Piergiorgio.
Crosignani, Piergiorgio.
xCrosignani, P. G.
Prolactin & Human Reproduction. Acad Pr.
Crosland, Charles A. see Crosland, Charles Anthony
Raven.
Crosland, Charles Anthony Raven, 1918-
xCrosland, Charles A.
The Future of Socialism. Greenwood.
Crosland, Jessie (Raven).
xCrosland, Jessie.
tr. Medieval French Literature. Greenwood.
Old French Epic. Haskell.
Crosland, M. P. see Crosland, Maurice P.
Crosland, Maurice P.
xCrosland, M. P.
Historical Studies in the Language of
Chemistry. Dover.
Crosland, T. W. see Crosland, Thomas William Hodgson.
Crosland, Thomas William Hodgson, 1865-1924
xCrosland, T. W.

English Sonnet. Folcroft.
Cross, Aleene.
xCross, Aleene.
Home Economics Evaluation. Merrill.
xCross, Aleene A.
ed. Vocational Instruction. Am Voc Assn.
Cross, Aleene A. see Cross, Aleene.
Cross, Alfred Rupert Neale, Sir.
xCross, Rupert.
Precedent in English Law. Oxford U Pr.
Cross, Amanda.
xCross, Amanda.
The Question of Max. Avon.
The Question of Max. G K Hall.
The Question of Max. Knopf.
The Theban Mysteries. Avon.
Cross, Arthur L. see Cross, Arthur Lyon.
Cross, Arthur Lyon, 1873-1940
xCross, Arthur L.
Anglican Episcopate & the American Colonies.
Shoe String.
Cross, Colin.
xCross, Colin.
The Liberals in Power: 1905-1914. Greenwood.
Cross, Dolores E.
xCross, Dolores E.
ed. Teaching in a Multicultural Society:
Perspectives & Professional Strategies. Free
Pr.
Cross, Donna W. see Cross, Donna Woolfolk.
Cross, Donna Woolfolk.
xCross, Donna W.
Word Abuse: How the Words We Use, Use Us.
Coward.
Cross, F. L. see Cross, Frank Leslie.
Cross, Frank B. see Cross, Frank Bernard.
Cross, Frank Bernard.
xCross, Frank B.
Illustrated Guide to Fishes in Kansas. U of KS
Mus Nat Hist.
Cross, Frank L.
xCross, Frank L.
Corporate Communicators Guide for
Environmental Control. Technomic.
ed. Industrial Plant Siting. Technomic.
Cross, Frank Leslie, 1900-
xCross, F. L.
The Oxford Dictionary of the Christian
Church. Oxford U Pr.
Cross, Frank M. see Cross, Frank Moore.
Cross, Frank Moore.
xCross, Frank M.
The Ancient Library of Qumran & Modern
Biblical Studies. Baker Bk.
The Ancient Library of Qumran & Modern
Biblical Studies. Greenwood.
Canaanite Myth & Hebrew Epic: Essays in the
History of the Religion of Israel. Harvard U
Pr.
ed. Qumran & the History of the Biblical Text.
Harvard U Pr.
Cross, Gary P.
xCross, Gary P.
Conflict & Human Interaction. Kendall-Hunt.
Cross, Gilbert B.
xCross, Gilbert B.
Next Week East Lynne: Domestic Drama in
Performance, 1820-1874. Bucknell U Pr.
Cross, Gordon R.
xCross, Gordon R.
The Psychology of Learning: An Introduction
for Students of Education. Pergamon.
Cross, Hardy, 1885-1959
xCross, Hardy.
Arches, Continuous Frames, Columns, &
Conduits: Selected Papers. U of Ill Pr.
Cross, Helen R. see Cross, Helen Reeder.
Cross, Helen Reeder.
xCross, Helen R.

A Curiosity for the Curious. Coward.
The Real Tom Thumb. Schol Bk Serv.
Cross, Jack L. *see* Cross, Jack Lee.
Cross, Jack Lee, 1921-
xCross, Jack L.
London Mission: The First Critical Years.
Mich St U Pr.
Cross, Jean.
xCross, Jean.
In Grandmother's Day: A Legacy of Recipes,
Remedies & Country Wisdom from 100
Years Ago. P-H.
Cross, Jeanne.
xCross, Jeanne.
illus. Simple Printing Methods. S G Phillips.
Cross, Jennifer.
xCross, Jennifer.
The Supermarket Trap: The Consumer & the
Food Industry. Ind U Pr.
Cross, John. *see* Cross, John G.
Cross, John G.
xCross, John.
Social Traps. U of Mich Pr.
Cross, K. Patricia. *see* Cross, Kathryn Patricia.
Cross, Kathryn Patricia.
xCross, K. Patricia.
The Missing Link: Connecting Adult Learners
to Learning Resources. College Bd.
Cross, Luther S.
xCross, Luther S.
Story Sermons for Children. Baker Bk.
Cross, Martin.
xCross, Martin.
Local Government & Politics. Longman.
Cross, R. C. *see* Cross, Robert Craigie.
Cross, Ralph D.
xCross, Ralph D.
ed. Atlas of Mississippi. U Pr of Miss.
Cross, Richard K., 1940-
xCross, Richard K.
Flaubert & Joyce: The Rite of Fiction.
Princeton U Pr.
Cross, Robert Craigie.
xCross, R. C.
Plato's Republic: A Philosophical Commentary.
St Martin.
Cross, Robert D.
xCross, Robert D.
ed. The Church and the City: 1865-1910.
Irvington.
Cross, Rupert. *see* Cross, Alfred Rupert Neale.
Cross, Tom P. *see* Cross, Tom Peete.
Cross, Tom Peete.
xCross, Tom P.
ed. Ancient Irish Tales. B&N.
Cross, W. L. *see* Cross, Wilbur Lucius.
Cross, Wilbur.
xCross, Wilbur.
Kids & Booze: What You Must Know to Help
Them. Dutton.
Cross, Wilbur L. *see* Cross, Wilbur Lucius.
Cross, Wilbur Lucius, 1862-1948
xCross, W. L.
Four Contemporary Novelists. AMS Pr.
xCross, Wilbur L.
The Development of the English Novel. Arden
Lib.
Development of the English Novel.
Greenwood.
Four Contemporary Novelists. Arno.
Crossan, Greg.
xCrossan, Gregory D.
A Relish for Eternity: The Process of
Divinization in the Poetry of John Clare.
Humanities.
Crossan, Gregory D. *see* Crossan, Greg.
Crossan, John D. *see* Crossan, John Dominic.
Crossan, John Dominic.
xCrossan, John D.

Cliffs of Fall: Paradox & Polyvalence in the
Parables of Jesus. Seabury.
Finding Is the First Act: Trove Folktales &
Jesus' Treasure Parable. Fortress.
Crossan, R. M. *see* Crossan, Richard M.
Crossan, Richard M.
xCrossan, R. M.
Master Standard Data: The Economic
Approach to Work Measurement. McGraw.
Crosse, Howard. *see* Crosse, Howard D.
Crosse, Howard D.
xCrosse, Howard.
Management Policies for Commercial Banks.
P-H.
Crosser, P. K. *see* Crosser, Paul K.
Crosser, Paul K.
xCrosser, P. K.
East-West Dialogues: Foundations & Problems
of Revolutionary Praxis. Humanities.
xCrosser, Paul K.
Economic Fictions: A Critique of Subjectivistic
Economic Theory. Greenwood.
Prolegomena to All Future Metaeconomics:
Formation & Deformation of Economic
Thought. Green.
Crossfield, A. Scott. *see* Crossfield, Albert Scott.
Crossfield, Albert Scott.
xCrossfield, A. Scott.
Always Another Dawn: The Story of a Rocket
Test Pilot. Arno.
Crossick, Geoffrey.
xCrossick, Geoffrey.
ed. The Lower-Middle Class in Britain,
1870-1914. St Martin.
Crosskey, W. W. *see* Crosskey, William Winslow.
Crosskey, William W. *see* Crosskey, William Winslow.
Crosskey, William Winslow.
xCrosskey, W. W.
Politics & Constitution in the History of the
United States. U of Chicago Pr.
xCrosskey, William W.
Politics & the Constitution in the History of
the United States. U of Chicago Pr.
Crossland, John R. *see* Crossland, John Redgwick.
Crossland, John Redgwick, 1892-
xCrossland, John R.
ed. The Book of Ballads. Arno.
ed. The Book of Ballads. Granger Bk.
Crossley, Anthony.
xCrossley, Anthony.
Training the Young Horse: The First Two
Years. Arco.
Crossley, David J.
xCrossley, David J.
How to Argue: An Introduction to Logical
Thinking. Random.
Crossley, Patricia G.
xCrossley, Patricia G.
Let's Learn Astrology: The First Astrology
Workbook for Beginners. Exposition.
Crossley-Holland, Kevin.
xCrossley-Holland, Kevin.
Pedlar of Swaffham. HM.
xCrossley-Holland, Kevin C.
Green Blades Rising: The Anglo-Saxons. HM.
Crossley-Holland, Kevin C. *see* Crossley-Holland, Kevin.
Crossman, Richard. *see* Crossman, Richard Howard
Stafford.
Crossman, Richard H. *see* Crossman, Richard Howard
Stafford.
Crossman, Richard Howard Stafford, 1907-1974
xCrossman, Richard.
Palestine Mission: A Personal Record. Arno.
xCrossman, Richard H.

Government & the Governed: A History of
Political Ideas & Political Practice. Core
Collection.
Government & the Governed: A History of
Political Ideas & Political Practice.
Greenwood.
Crosson, Frederick J. *see* Crosson, Frederick James.
Crosson, Frederick James, 1926-
xCrosson, Frederick J.
ed. Human & Artificial Intelligence. Irvington.
Crosten, William L. *see* Crosten, William Loran.
Crosten, William Loran, 1909-
xCrosten, William L.
French Grand Opera: An Art & a Business. Da
Capo.
Croswell, Anne.
xCroswell, Anne.
Some of My Best Friends Are Runners. St
Martin.
Crotch, W. Walter. *see* Crotch, William Walter.
Crotch, Walter. *see* Crotch, William Walter.
Crotch, Walter W. *see* Crotch, William Walter.
Crotch, William Walter, 1874-1947
xCrotch, W. Walter.
The Pageant of Dickens. Haskell.
xCrotch, Walter.
The Soul of Dickens. Haskell.
xCrotch, Walter W.
The Soul of Dickens. R West.
Crothers, Edward J.
xCrothers, Edward J.
Paragraph Structure Inference. Ablex Pub.
Crothers, George D. *see* Crothers, George Dunlap.
Crothers, George Dunlap, 1909-
xCrothers, George D.
German Elections of 1907. AMS Pr.
Crothers, J. Frances. *see* Crothers, J. Francis.
Crothers, J. Francis.
xCrothers, J. Frances.
Puppeteer's Library Guide: A Bibliographic
Index to the Literature of the World Puppet
Theatre. Scarecrow.
Crothers, Samuel M. *see* Crothers, Samuel Mcchord.
Crothers, Samuel Mcchord, 1857-1927
xCrothers, Samuel M.
Cheerful Giver: Essays. Arno.
Pardoner's Wallet. Arno.
Crotty, William. *see* Crotty, William J.
Crotty, William J.
xCrotty, William.
ed. The Party Symbol: Readings on Political
Parties. W H Freeman.
xCrotty, William J.
American Parties in Decline. Little.
Crouch, Austin.
xCrouch, Austin.
Bright Side of Death. Broadman.
Crouch, Colin.
xCrouch, Colin.
ed. Resurgence of Class Conflict in Western
Europe Since 1968. Holmes & Meier.
ed. State & Economy in Contemporary
Capitalism. St Martin.
Crouch, Harold. *see* Crouch, Harold A.
Crouch, Harold A., 1940-
xCrouch, Harold.
The Army & Politics in Indonesia. Cornell U
Pr.
Crouch, James E. *see* Crouch, James Ensign.
Crouch, James Ensign, 1908-
xCrouch, James E.
Functional Human Anatomy. Lea & Febiger.
Human Anatomy & Physiology. Wiley.
Crouch, Milton.
xCrouch, Milton.
ed. Directory of State & Local History
Periodicals. ALA.
Crouch, Ralph. *see* Crouch, Ralph.
Crouch, Ralph.
xCrouch, R.

Preparatory Mathematics for Elementary
    Teachers. Krieger.
    xCrouch, Ralph B.
    Finite Mathematics with Statistics for Business.
      McGraw.
Crouch, Ralph B. *see* Crouch, Ralph.
Crouch, Robert L.
    xCrouch, Robert L.
    Human Behavior: An Economic Approach.
      Duxbury Pr.
Crouch, Steve.
    xCrouch, Steve.
    Steinbeck Country. Crown.
Crouch, W. W. *see* Crouch, Winston Winford.
Crouch, Winston W. *see* Crouch, Winston Winford.
Crouch, Winston Winford, 1907-
    xCrouch, W. W.
    California Government & Politics. P-H.
    Guide for Modern Personnel Commissions. Intl
      Personnel Mgmt.
    xCrouch, Winston W.
    California Government & Politics. P-H.
    Organized Civil Servants: Public
      Employer-Employee Relations in California.
      U of Cal Pr.
    Southern California Metropolis: A Study in
      Development of Government for a
      Metropolitan Area. U of Cal Pr.
Crouse, Nellis M. *see* Crouse, Nellis Maynard.
Crouse, Nellis Maynard, 1884-
    xCrouse, Nellis M.
    French Pioneers in the West Indies, 1624-1664.
      Octagon.
Crouse, Timothy.
    xCrouse, Timothy.
    The Boys on the Bus. Random.
Crouse, William H. *see* Crouse, William Harry.
Crouse, William Harry, 1907-
    xCrouse, William H.
    The Auto Book. McGraw.
    Automotive Body Repair & Refinishing.
      McGraw.
    Automotive Electronics & Electrical
      Equipment. McGraw.
    Automotive Emission Control. McGraw.
    Automotive Engine Design. McGraw.
    Automotive Engines. McGraw.
    Automotive Mechanics. McGraw.
    Automotive Mechanics. McGraw.
    Automotive Mechanics. McGraw.
    Automotive Technician's Handbook. McGraw.
    Automotive Tools, Fasteners, and
      Measurements: A Text-Workbook. McGraw.
    Small Engine Mechanics. McGraw.
Crouthers, David D.
    xCrouthers, David D.
    Flags of American History. Hammond Inc.
Crouzet, Maurice.
    xCrouzet, Maurice.
    The European Renaissance Since 1945.
      HarBraceJ.
Crovitz, Elaine.
    xCrovitz, Elaine.
    Courage Knows No Sex. Chris Mass.
Crow, Carl, 1883-1945
    xCrow, Carl.
    Great American Customer. Arno.
Crow, Charles S. *see* Crow, Charles Sumner.
Crow, Charles Sumner, 1880-
    xCrow, Charles S.
    Evaluation of English Literature in the High
      School. AMS Pr.
Crow, D. R. *see* Crow, David Richard.
Crow, David Richard.
    xCrow, D. R.
    Principles & Applications of Electrochemistry.
      Methuen Inc.
Crow, Duncan.
    xCrow, Duncan.

The Edwardian Woman. St Martin.
    ed. Modern Battle Tanks. Arco.
Crow, James F.
    xCrow, James F.
    Genetic Distance. Plenum Pub.
    An Introduction to Population Genetics
      Theory. Burgess.
Crow, Jeffrey J.
    xCrow, Jeffrey J.
    ed. The Southern Experience in the American
      Revolution. U of NC Pr.
    ed. Writing North Carolina History. U of NC
      Pr.
Crow, John A. *see* Crow, John Armstrong.
Crow, John Armstrong.
    xCrow, John A.
    Se Habla Espanol. Har-Row.
Crow, L. D. *see* Crow, Lester Donald.
Crow, Lester C. *see* Crow, Lester Donald.
Crow, Lester D. *see* Crow, Lester Donald.
Crow, Lester Donald.
    xCrow, L. D.
    Human Development & Learning. Krieger.
    xCrow, Lester C.
    Introduction to Guidance: Basic Principles &
      Practices. Krieger.
    xCrow, Lester D.
    Human Development & Adjustment. Littlefield.
    New Approaches to the Psychology of
      Childhood and Adolescence. Exposition.
Crow, Martha F. *see* Crow, Martha Foote.
Crow, Martha Foote, 1854-1924
    xCrow, Martha F.
    The American Country Girl. Arno.
Crowder, Michael, 1934-
    xCrowder, Michael.
    Colonial West Africa: Collected Essays. Biblio
      Dist.
    Revolt in Bussa: A Study of British Native
      Administration in Nigerian Dorgu,
      1902-1935. Northwestern U Pr.
    The Story of Nigeria. Merrimack Bk Serv.
Crowder, Richard.
    xCrowder, Richard.
    Carl Sandburg. Coll & U Pr.
    Carl Sandburg. Twayne.
    No Featherbed to Heaven: A Biography of
      Michael Wigglesworth 1631-1705. Mich St U
      Pr.
Crowdis, David G.
    xCrowdis, David G.
    Concepts of Calculus with Applications to
      Business & Economics. Glencoe.
    Introduction to Mathematical Ideas. McGraw.
Crowe. *see* Crowe, Percy Robert.
Crowe, Cecily.
    xCrowe, Cecily.
    Abbey Gate. PB.
    The Talisman. St Martin.
Crowe, Eyre, 1824-1910
    xCrowe, Eyre.
    Thackeray's Haunts & Homes. Folcroft.
Crowe, Frederick E.
    xCrowe, Frederick E.
    Theology of the Christian Word: A Study in
      History. Paulist Pr.
Crowe, John H.
    xCrowe, John H.
    ed. Anhydrobiosis. Acad Pr.
    ed. Dry Biological Systems. Acad Pr.
Crowe, Keith J.
    xCrowe, Keith J.
    A History of the Original Peoples of Northern
      Canada. McGill-Queens U Pr.
Crowe, Kenneth C.
    xCrowe, Kenneth C.
    America for Sale. Doubleday.
Crowe, P. R. *see* Crowe, Percy Robert.
Crowe, Patrick H.
    xCrowe, Patrick H.

How to Teach School & Make a Living at the
    Same Time. Andrews & McMeel.
Crowe, Percy Robert.
    xCrowe.
    Concepts in Climatology. Longman.
    xCrowe, P. R.
    Concepts in Climatology. St Martin.
Crowe, Robert L.
    xCrowe, Robert L.
    Clyde Monster. Dutton.
Crowe-Carraco, Carol, 1943-
    xCrowe-Carraco, Carol.
    Big Sandy. U Pr of Ky.
Crowell, Alfred A.
    xCrowell, Alfred A.
    Creative News Editing. Wm C Brown.
Crowell, Ivan H. *see* Crowell, Ivan Herrett.
Crowell, Ivan Herrett, 1904-
    xCrowell, Ivan H.
    Chip Carving Patterns & Designs. Dover.
    Chip Carving Patterns & Designs. Gannon.
Crowell, Marnie R. *see* Crowell, Marnie Reed.
Crowell, Marnie Reed.
    xCrowell, Marnie R.
    North to the St. Lawrence. Raquette Pr.
Crowell, Muriel B.
    xCrowell, Muriel B.
    The Fine Art of Needlepoint. T Y Crowell.
Crowell, Richard A.
    xCrowell, Richard A.
    Stock Market Strategy. McGraw.
Crowell, Thomas L. *see* Crowell, Thomas Lee.
Crowell, Thomas Lee, Jr.
    xCrowell, Thomas L.
    Index to Modern English. McGraw.
    Modern English Essays. McGraw.
Crowest, Frederick. *see* Crowest, Frederick James.
Crowest, Frederick J. *see* Crowest, Frederick James.
Crowest, Frederick James, 1850-1927
    xCrowest, Frederick.
    Great Tone-Poets: Being Short Memoirs of the
      Greater Musical Composers. Arno.
    xCrowest, Frederick J.
    Musicians' Wit, Humour, & Anecdote. Gale.
Crowhurst, Norman H.
    xCrowhurst, Norman H.
    How to Select & Install Your Own Speakers.
      TAB Bks.
Crowhurst, P. *see* Crowhurst, Patrick.
Crowhurst, Patrick.
    xCrowhurst, P.
    The Defence of British Trade, 1689-1815.
      Dawson Pub.
Crowle, Alfred J.
    xCrowle, Alfred J.
    Immunodiffusion. Acad Pr.
Crowley, Aleister, 1875-1947
    xCrowley, Aleister.
    The Argonauts. Krishna Pr.
    Clouds Without Water. Krishna Pr.
    Clouds Without Water. Yoga.
    Diary of a Drug Fiend. Krishna Pr.
    Diary of a Drug Fiend. Weiser.
    Songs of the Spirit. Krishna Pr.
    The Soul of the Desert. Thelema Pubns.
    The Star & the Garter. Krishna Pr.
    The Stratagem & Other Stories. Krishna Pr.
    Tannhauser: A Story of All Time. Krishna Pr.
Crowley, Arthur.
    xCrowley, Arthur.
    Bonzo Beaver. HM.
Crowley, Charles B.
    xCrowley, Charles B.
    Universal Mathematics in
      Aristotelian-Thomistic Philosophy: The
      Hermeneutics of Aristotelian Texts Relative
      to Universal Mathematics. U Pr of Amer.
Crowley, Dale.
    xCrowley, Dale.

Soon Coming of Our Lord. Loizeaux.

Crowley, Ellen T.
xCrowley, Ellen T.
ed. Trade Names Dictionary: Company Index. Gale.

Crowley, Frances G.
xCrowley, Frances G.
Domingo Faustino Sarmiento. Twayne.

Crowley, Francis Keble.
xCrowley, Frank.
ed. A New History of Australia. Holmes & Meier.

Crowley, Frank. *see* Crowley, Francis Keble.

Crowley, J. E., 1943-
xCrowley, J. E.
This Sheba, Self: The Conceptualization of Economic Life in Eighteenth-Century America. Johns Hopkins.

Crowley, John.
xCrowley, John.
Engine Summer. Doubleday.

Crowley, John W. *see* Crowley, John William.

Crowley, John William, 1945-
xCrowley, John W.
George Cabot Lodge. Twayne.

Crowley, Kitty A.
xCrowley, Kitty A.
First Women of the Skies. Silver.

Crowley, Mary C.
xCrowley, Mary C.
Think Mink!. Revell.
Women Who Win. Revell.
You Can Too. Revell.

Crowley, Maude.
xCrowley, Maude.
Azor & the Blue-Eyed Cow. Gregg.

Crowley, T. *see* Crowley, Terry.

Crowley, Terry.
xCrowley, T.
The Middle Clarence Dialects of Bandjalang. Humanities.

Crowley, Thomas H.
xCrowley, Thomas H.
Modern Communications. Columbia U Pr.

Crown, David A.
xCrown, David A.
Forensic Examination of Paints & Pigments. C C Thomas.

Crown, Fenya.
xCrown, Fenya.
How to Recycle Old Clothes into New Fashions. P-H.

Crown, S. *see* Crown, Sidney.

Crown, Sidney.
xCrown, S.
Essential Principles of Psychiatry. Raven.

Crowne, Douglas P.
xCrowne, Douglas P.
The Approval Motive: Studies in Evaluative Dependence. Greenwood.
The Experimental Study of Personality. Halsted Pr.

Crowne, John.
xCrowne, John.
City Politiques. U of Nebr Pr.

Crowningshield, Gerald. *see* Crowningshield, Gerald R.

Crowningshield, Gerald R.
xCrowningshield, Gerald.
Cost Accounting: Principles & Managerial Applications. HM.

Crowson, Lydia.
xCrowson, Lydia.
The Esthetic of Jean Cocteau. U Pr of New Eng.

Crowson, P. C. *see* Crowson, Philip C. F.

Crowson, P. S. *see* Crowson, Paul.

Crowson, Paul.
xCrowson, P. S.

Tudor Foreign Policy. St Martin.

Crowson, Philip C. F.
xCrowson, P. C.
Economics for Managers. Intl Ideas.

Crowther, Duane S.
xCrowther, Duane S.
Prophetic Warnings to Modern America. Horizon Utah.
Prophets & Prophecies of the Old Testament. Horizon Utah.

Crowther, J. G. *see* Crowther, James Gerald.

Crowther, James Gerald, 1899-
xCrowther, J. G.
The Cavendish Laboratory: 1874-1974. N Watson.

Crowther-Hunt, Norman. *see* Crowther-Hunt, Norman Crowther-Hunt.

Crowther-Hunt, Norman Crowther-Hunt, Baron, 1920-
xCrowther-Hunt, Norman.
Two Early Political Associations: The Quakers & the Dissenting Deputies in the Age of Sir Robert Walpole. Greenwood.

Croxton, C. *see* Croxton, C. A.

Croxton, C. A.
xCroxton, C.
Introduction to Liquid State Physics. Wiley.

Croxton, Clive A.
xCroxton, Clive A.
ed. Progress in Liquid Physics. Wiley.

Croy, Homer, 1883-1965
xCroy, Homer.
How Motion Pictures Are Made. Arno.
How Motion Pictures Are Made. Dynamic Learn Corp.

Croy, O. R. *see* Croy, Otto R.

Croy, Otto R, 1902-
xCroy, O. R.
Camera Copying & Reproduction. Focal Pr.
The Complete Art of Printing & Enlarging. Focal Pr.
Design by Photography. Focal Pr.
Design by Photography. Hastings.
Graphic Effects by Photography. Focal Pr.

Croy, Peter.
xCroy, Peter.
Graphic Design & Reproduction Techniques. Focal Pr.

Crozier, Brian.
xCrozier, Brian.
Strategy of Survival. Arlington Hse.
Struggle for the Third World. Dufour.

Crozier, Michel.
xCrozier, Michel.
Bureaucratic Phenomenon. U of Chicago Pr.
The Crisis of Democracy: Report on the Governability of Democracies to the Trilateral Commission. NYU Pr.
The World of the Office Worker. Schocken.
World of the Office Worker. U of Chicago Pr.

Crozier, William A. *see* Crozier, William Armstrong.

Crozier, William Armstrong, 1864-1913
xCrozier, William A.
Crozier's General Armory: A Registry of American Families Entitled to Coat Armor. Genealog Pub.

Cruden, Alexander.
xCruden, Alexander.
Cruden's Pocket Dictionary of Bible Terms. Baker Bk.

Cruden, Robert.
xCruden, Robert.
Many & One: A Social History of the United States. P-H.

Crue, Benjamin. *see* Crue, Benjamin L.

Crue, Benjamin L.
xCrue, Benjamin.

ed. Chronic Pain: Further Observations from City of Hope National Medical Center. Spectrum Pub.

Cruess, Richard L.
xCruess, Richard L.
ed. Surgical Management of Degenerative Arthritis of the Lower Limb. Lea & Febiger.

Cruickshank, J. G. *see* Cruickshank, James George.

Cruickshank, James George.
xCruickshank, J. G.
Soil Geography. Halsted Pr.

Cruickshank, John.
xCruickshank, John.
Albert Camus & the Literature of Revolt. Greenwood.

Cruickshank, William M.
xCruickshank, William M.
ed. Cerebral Palsy: A Developmental Disability. Syracuse U Pr.
Education of Exceptional Children & Youth. P-H.
ed. Learning Disabilities in Home, School, & Community. Syracuse U Pr.
Learning Disabilities: The Struggle from Adolescence Toward Adulthood. Syracuse U Pr.
Preparation of Teachers of Brain-Injured Children. Syracuse U Pr.
ed. Teacher of Brain Injured Children: A Discussion of the Bases for Competency. Syracuse U Pr.

Cruikshank, Douglas E.
xCruikshank, Douglas E.
Young Children Learning Mathematics. Allyn.

Cruikshank, George.
xCruikshank, George.
Graphic Works of George Cruikshank. Dover.

Cruikshank, Margaret.
xCruikshank, Margaret L.
Thomas Babington Macaulay. Twayne.

Cruikshank, Margaret L. *see* Cruikshank, Margaret.

Crum, Lawrence E., 1942-
xCrum, Lawrence E.
Classroom Activities & Experiments for Life Science. P-H.

Crum, Mason, 1887-
xCrum, Mason.
Gullah: Negro Life in the Carolina Sea Islands. Negro U Pr.

Crum, Milton.
xCrum, Milton.
Manual on Preaching. Judson.

Crum, Walter E. *see* Crum, Walter Ewing.

Crum, Walter Ewing, 1865-
xCrum, Walter E.
ed. Coptic Dictionary. Oxford U Pr.

Crumb, R.
xCrumb, R.
The Complete Fritz the Cat. Belier Pr.

Crumbley, D. Larry.
xCrumbley, D. Larry.
Organizing, Operating & Terminating Subchapter S Corporations, Law, Taxation & Accounting. Lawyers & Judges.
A Practical Guide to Preparing a Federal Gift Tax Return. Lawyers & Judges.
Readings in Oil Industry Accounting. Pennwell Pub.

Crummell, Alexander, 1819-1898
xCrummell, Alexander.
Africa & America: Addresses & Discourses. Negro U Pr.
Africa & America: Addresses & Discourses. Scholarly.

Crummey, Robert O.
xCrummey, Robert O.
Old Believers & the World of Antichrist: The Vyg Community & the Russian State, 1694-1855. U of Wis Pr.

Crump, Charles G. *see* Crump, Charles George.

Crump, Charles George, 1862-1935
  xCrump, Charles G.
    History & Historical Research. B Franklin.
Crump, Elaine C. see Crump, Elaine Carmichael.
Crump, Elaine Carmichael.
  xCrump, Elaine C.
    Chinaberry Beads. Pelican.
Crump, Geoffrey H. see Crump, Geoffrey Herbert.
Crump, Geoffrey Herbert, 1891-
  xCrump, Geoffrey H.
    A Guide to the Study of Shakespeare's Plays.
      Folcroft.
    Speaking Poetry. Folcroft.
Crump, Ian A. see Crump, Ian Alan.
Crump, Ian Alan.
  xCrump, Ian A.
    Australian Scientific Societies & Professional
      Associations. Intl Schol Bk Serv.
Crump, Irving, 1887-
  xCrump, Irving.
    Our Merchant Marine Academy, Kings Point.
      Greenwood.
    Our United States Coast Guard Academy.
      Greenwood.
Crump, J. I. see Crump, James Irving.
Crump, James Irving.
  xCrump, J. I.
    ed. Chinese & Japanese Music-Dramas. U of
      Mich Ctr Chinese.
    Chinese Theater in the Days of Kublai Khan.
      U of Ariz Pr.
Crump, Spencer.
  xCrump, Spencer.
    Fundamentals of Journalism. McGraw.
    Ride the Big Red Cars: How Trolleys Helped
      Build Southern California. Trans-Anglo.
Crunden, Robert M. see Crunden, Robert Morse.
Crunden, Robert Morse.
  xCrunden, Robert M.
    ed. Superfluous Men: Conservative Critics of
      American Culture, 1900-1945. U of Tex Pr.
Cruse, Amy, 1870-
  xCruse, Amy.
    After the Victorians. Scholarly.
Cruse, Harold.
  xCruse, Harold.
    The Crisis of the Negro Intellectual. Morrow.
Cruse, Julius M., 1937-
  xCruse, Julius M.
    Immunology Examination Review Book. Med
      Exam.
Crutchfield, James A. see Crutchfield, James Arthur.
Crutchfield, James Arthur.
  xCrutchfield, James A.
    The Pacific Salmon Fisheries: A Study of
      Irrational Conservation. Johns Hopkins.
Crutchley, Brooke.
  xCrutchley, Brooke.
    Preparation of Manuscripts & Correction of
      Proofs. Cambridge U Pr.
Crutsinger, George M. see Crutsinger, George Mahan.
Crutsinger, George Mahan, 1886-
  xCrutsinger, George M.
    Survey Study of Teacher Training in Texas, &
      a Suggested Program. AMS Pr.
Cruttenden, Alan, 1936-
  xCruttenden, Alan.
    Language in Infancy & Childhood: A Linguistic
      Introduction to Language Acquisition. St
      Martin.
Cruttwell, Charles R. see Cruttwell, Charles Robert
  Mowbray Fraser.
Cruttwell, Charles Robert Mowbray Fraser, 1887-
  xCruttwell, Charles R.
    History of the Great War, 1914-1918. Oxford
      U Pr.
Cruttwell, Maud.
  xCruttwell, Maud.

    Donatello. Arno.
    Luca Signorelli. Scholarly.
Cruz, Daniel Da. see Da Cruz, Daniel.
Cruz, J. B. see Cruz, Jose Bejar.
Cruz, Joan C. see Cruz, Joan Carroll.
Cruz, Joan Carroll, 1931-
  xCruz, Joan C.
    Desires of Thy Heart. NAL.
    Desires of Thy Heart. Tandem Pr.
Cruz, Jose B. see Cruz, Jose Bejar.
Cruz, Jose Bejar.
  xCruz, J. B.
    ed. System Sensitivity Analysis. Acad Pr.
  xCruz, Jose B.
    Signals in Linear Circuits. HM.
Cruz Costa, Joao.
  xCruz Costa, Joao.
    A History of Ideas in Brazil: The Development
      of Philosophy in Brazil & the Evolution of
      National History. U of Cal Pr.
Cruzic, Kay.
  xCruzic, Kay.
    Toward a Better Life: The Resource Guide for
      the Disabled. Sovereign Bks.
Cryan, John. see Cryan, John R.
Cryan, John R.
  xCryan, John.
    Early Childhood Education: Foundations for
      Lifelong Learning. Phi Delta Kappa.
Cryer, Philip E.
  xCryer, Philip E.
    Diagnostic Endocrinology. Oxford U Pr.
Crystal, D. see Crystal, David.
Crystal, David, 1941-
  xCrystal, D.
    Prosodic Systems & Intonation in English.
      Cambridge U Pr.
  xCrystal, David
    Child Language Learning & Linguistics: An
      Overview for the Teaching & Therapeutic
      Professions. Intl Ideas.
    Linguistics. Penguin.
    Systems of Prosodic & Paralinguistic Features
      in English. Mouton.
Crystal, Graef S.
  xCrystal, Graef S.
    Executive Compensation: Money, Motivation
      & Imagination. Am Mgmt.
    Financial Motivation for Executives. Am
      Mgmt.
Csaky, T. Z.
  xCsaky, T. Z.
    Introduction to General Pharmacology. ACC.
Csanady, G. T.
  xCsanady, G. T.
    Turbulent Diffusion in the Environment.
      Kluwer Boston.
Csath, Geza.
  xCsath, Geza.
    Intro. by The Magician's Garden & Other
      Stories. Columbia U Pr.
Csikos-Nagy, Bela.
  xCsikos-Nagy, Bela.
    Socialist Economic Policy. St Martin.
**Ctb-Mcgraw-Hill Conference on Issues in Educational
  Measurement, 2d, Carmel, California, 1973.**
  xConference on Issues in Educational
    Measurement, 2nd, Carmel, Cal., 1974.
    Aptitude - Achievement Distinction:
      Proceedings. CTB McGraw-Hill.
Cua, A. S. see Cua, Antonio S.
Cua, Antonio S.
  xCua, A. S.
    Dimensions of Moral Creativity: Paradigms,
      Principles, & Ideals. Pa St U Pr.
Cuatrecasas, J. see Cuatrecasas, Jose.
Cuatrecasas, Jose.
  xCuatrecasas, J.

    Brunelliaceae. Hafner.
Cuatrecasas, P.
  xCuatrecasas, P.
    ed. Receptors & Recognition, Ser. B, Vol. 1:
      The Specificity & Action of Animal Bacterial
      & Plant Toxins. Methuen Inc.
Cuban Economic Research Project, University of Miami.
  see Grupo Cubano De Investigaciones Economicas.
Cubberley, Ellwood P. see Cubberley, Ellwood Patterson.
Cubberley, Ellwood Patterson, 1868-1941
  xCubberley, Ellwood P.
    ed. Readings in Public Education in the United
      States: A Collection of Sources & Readings
      to Illustrate the History of Educational
      Practice & Progress in the United States.
      Greenwood.
Cubitt, G. S. see Cubitt, Gerald S.
Cubitt, Gerald S.
  xCubitt, G. S.
    South West. Verry.
Cudahy, Brian J.
  xCudahy, Brian J.
    Rails Under the Mighty Hudson. Greene.
    Under the Sidewalks of New York: The Story
      of the Greatest Subway System in the World.
      Greene.
Cudahy, Sheila.
  xCudahy, Sheila.
    The Bristle Cone Pine & Other Poems.
      HarBraceJ.
    The Trojan Gold. Har-Row.
Cudd, John M. see Cudd, John Michael.
Cudd, John Michael, 1942-
  xCudd, John M.
    The Chicopee Manufacturing Company.
      Scholarly Res Inc.
Cuddihy, John M. see Cuddihy, John Murray.
Cuddihy, John Murray.
  xCuddihy, John M.
    No Offense: Civil Religion & Protestant Taste.
      Seabury.
Cuddon, J. A. see Cuddon, John A.
Cuddon, John A.
  xCuddon, J. A.
    A Dictionary of Literary Terms. Doubleday.
    The International Dictionary of Sports &
      Games. Schocken.
Cudkowicz, Leon, 1923-
  xCudkowicz, Leon.
    The Human Bronchial Circulation in Health &
      Disease. Krieger.
Cudlipp, Edythe.
  xCudlipp, Edythe.
    Vitamins. G&D.
Cudworth, Ralph, 1617-1688
  xCudworth, Ralph.
    True Intellectual System of the Universe.
      Adler.
    The True Intellectual System of the Universe.
      Garland Pub.
Cuevas, Santos.
  xCuevas, Santos.
    The Greatest Help. Branden.
Cuff, E. C.
  xCuff, E. C.
    ed. Perspectives in Sociology. Allen Unwin.
Culbert, Samuel A.
  xCulbert, Samuel A.
    The Invisible War: Pursuing Self-Interests at
      Work. Wiley.
Culbert, T. Patrick.
  xCulbert, T. Patrick.
    ed. The Classic Maya Collapse. U of NM Pr.
    Lost Civilization: The Story of the Classic
      Maya. Har-Row.
Culbertson, John M. see Culbertson, John Mathew.
Culbertson, John Mathew, 1921-
  xCulbertson, John M.

Money & Banking. McGraw.

Culbertson, Judi.
    xCulbertson, Judi.
        Games Christians Play: An Irreverent Guide to
            Religion Without Tears. Har-Row.

Culbertson, Manie.
    xCulbertson, Manie.
        May I Speak?: The Diary of a Crossover
            Teacher. Pelican.

Culin, Charlotte.
    xCulin, Charlotte.
        Cages of Glass, Flowers of Time. Bradbury Pr.

Culin, Stewart, 1858-1929
    xCulin, Stewart.
        Chess & Playing-Cards. Arno.
        Games of the North American Indians. Dover.

Culinary Arts Institute.
    xCulinary Arts Institute.
        The Budget Cookbook. PB.
        ed. Nutrition Cookbook. Delair.
    xCulinary Arts Institute Arts Staff.
        ed. The Budget Cookbook. Delair.
    xCulinary Arts Institute Staff.
        ed. Bread & Soup Cookbook. Delair.
        ed. The Cookie Jar. Delair.
        ed. Crockery Cooking. Delair.
        ed. The Dessert Book. Delair.
        ed. Italian Cookbook. Delair.
        ed. Mexican Cookbook. Delair.
        ed. Microwave Cooking. Delair.
        ed. The New World Encyclopedia of Cooking.
            Delair.
        ed. Polish Cookbook. Delair.
        Wok, Fondue, & Chafing Dish. Delair.
    xTheCulinary Arts Institute.
        The Canning & Freezing Book. PB.
Culinary Arts Institute Arts Staff. see Culinary Arts
    Institute.
Culinary Arts Institute Staff. see Culinary Arts Institute.

Cull, John G.
    xCull, John G.
        ed. Administrative Techniques of Rehabilitation
            Facility Operations. C C Thomas.
        ed. Alcohol Abuse & Rehabilitation
            Approaches. C C Thomas.
        ed. Career Guidance for Black Adolescents: A
            Guide to Selected Professional Occupations.
            C C Thomas.
        ed. Counseling & Rehabilitating the Diabetic. C
            C Thomas.
        ed. Counseling High School Students: Special
            Problems & Approaches. C C Thomas.
        Counseling Strategies with Special Populations.
            C C Thomas.
        ed. Deciding on Divorce: Personal & Family
            Considerations. C C Thomas.
        ed. Fundamentals of Criminal Behavior &
            Correctional Systems. C C Thomas.
        ed. Law Enforcement & Correctional
            Rehabilitation. C C Thomas.
        ed. The Neglected Older American: Social &
            Rehabilitation Services. C C Thomas.
        ed. Organization & Administration of Drug
            Abuse Treatment Programs. C C Thomas.
        ed. Problems of Disadvantaged & Deprived
            Youth. C C Thomas.
        ed. Problems of Runaway Youth. C C Thomas.
        ed. Rehabilitation Facility Approaches in
            Severe Disabilities. C C Thomas.
        ed. Rehabilitation of the Urban Disadvantaged.
            C C Thomas.
        ed. Rehabilitation Techniques in Severe
            Disability: Case Studies. C C Thomas.
        ed. Types of Drug Abusers & Their Abuses. C
            C Thomas.
        ed. Understanding Disability for Social &
            Rehabilitation Services. C C Thomas.

Cullen, Charles G.
    xCullen, Charles G.

Matrices & Linear Transformations. A-W.

Cullen, Countee, 1903-1946
    xCullen, Countee.
        ed. Caroling Dusk: An Anthology of Verse by
            Negro Poets. Har-Row.
        ed. Caroling Dusk: An Anthology of Verse by
            Negro Poets. Irvington.
        Color. Arno.
        One Way to Heaven. AMS Pr.

Cullen, Donald E.
    xCullen, Donald E.
        National Emergency Strikes. NY Sch Indus
            Rel.

Cullen, Gordon, 1914-
    xCullen, Gordon.
        Concise Townscape. Van Nos Reinhold.
Cullen, I. G. see Cullen, Ian.

Cullen, Ian.
    xCullen, I. G.
        ed. Analysis & Decision in Regional Policy.
            Methuen Inc.
Cullen, Joseph. see Cullen, Joseph Warren.

Cullen, Joseph Warren.
    xCullen, Joseph.
        ed. Legacies in the Study of Behavior: The
            Wisdom & Experience of Many. C C
            Thomas.
Cullen, M. O. see Cullen, Max O'Rell.

Cullen, Max O'Rell, 1903-
    xCullen, M. O.
        How to Carve Meat, Game & Poultry. Dover.
        How to Carve Meat, Game & Poultry. Peter
            Smith.

Cullen, Patrick, 1940-
    xCullen, Patrick.
        The Infernal Triad: The Flesh, the World & the
            Devil in Spenser & Milton. Princeton U Pr.
        Spenser, Marvell, & Renaissance Pastoral.
            Harvard U Pr.

Cullen, Seamus.
    xCullen, Seamus.
        Astra & Flondrix. Pantheon.
        Astra & Flondrix. PB.
Cullen, Stuart C. see Cullen, Stuart Chester.

Cullen, Stuart Chester.
    xCullen, Stuart C.
        Essentials of Anesthetic Practice. Year Bk
            Med.

Cullen, T. R.
    xCullen, T. R.
        The Ego & the Machine. Gottlieb & Allen.
Culler, Arthur D. see Culler, Arthur Dwight.

Culler, Arthur Dwight.
    xCuller, Arthur D.
        Imaginative Reason: The Poetry of Matthew
            Arnold. Greenwood.

Culler, Jonathan.
    xCuller, Jonathan.
        Structuralist Poetics: Structuralism, Linguistics
            & the Study of Literature. Cornell U Pr.
Culler, Jonathan. see Culler, Jonathan D.

Culler, Jonathan D.
    xCuller, Jonathan.
        Ferdinand De Saussure. Penguin.
        Flaubert: The Uses of Uncertainty. Cornell U
            Pr.

Culler, R. D.
    xCuller, R. D.
        The Spray: Building & Sailing a Replica of
            Joshua Slocum's Famous Vessel. Intl Marine.
Culleton, R. Gerald. see Culleton, Richard Gerald.

Culleton, Richard Gerald, 1902-1950
    xCulleton, R. Gerald.
        The Reign of Anti-Christ. TAN Bks Pubs.

Culligan, Matthew J., 1918-
    xCulligan, Matthew J.
        How to Be a Billion Dollar Persuader. St
            Martin.

Cullinan, Bernice E.
    xCullinan, Bernice E.

ed. Literature & Young Children. NCTE.

Cullinan, Douglas.
    xCullinan, Douglas.
        Special Education for Adolescents: Issues &
            Perspectives. Merrill.

Culliney, John, 1942-
    xCulliney, John L.
        Forests of the Sea: Life & Death on the
            Continental Shelf. Doubleday.
        The Forests of the Sea: Life & Death on the
            Continental Shelf. Sierra.
Culliney, John L. see Culliney, John.
Culling, L. T. see Culling, Louis T.

Culling, Louis T.
    xCulling, L. T.
        Incredible I Ching. Weiser.

Cullingworth, J. B.
    xCullingworth, J. B.
        Essays on Housing Policy: The British Scene.
            Allen Unwin.
Cullison, Arthur E. see Cullison, Arthur Edison.

Cullison, Arthur Edison, 1914-
    xCullison, Arthur E.
        Feeds & Feeding. Reston.

Cullity, Bernard Dennis.
    xCullity, Berrard D.
        Introduction to Magnetic Materials. A-W.
Cullity, Berrard D. see Cullity, Bernard Dennis.

Cullmann, Oscar.
    xCullmann, Oscar.
        Christ & Time: The Primitive Christian
            Conception of Time & History. Westminster.
        Christology of the New Testament.
            Westminster.
        Early Christian Worship. Westminster.
Cullom, Shelby. see Cullom, Shelby Moore.

Cullom, Shelby Moore, 1829-1914
    xCullom, Shelby.
        Fifty Years of Public Service: Personal
            Recollections of Shelby M. Cullom. Da Capo.

Cullop, Charles P.
    xCullop, Charles P.
        Confederate Propaganda in Europe, 1861-1865.
            U of Miami Pr.

Cullum, Albert.
    xCullum, Albert.
        Murphy, Molly, Max & Me. Quist.

Cullum, Elizabeth.
    xCullum, Elizabeth.
        Cottage Herbal. David & Charles.

Cully, Iris V.
    xCully, Iris V.
        Christian Child Development. Har-Row.
        ed. Process & Relationship: Issues in Theology,
            Philosophy, & Religious Education. Religious
            Educ.

Culotta, Charles A.
    xCulotta, Charles A.
        Respiration & the Lavoisier Tradition: Theory
            & Modification, 1777-1850. Am Philos.

Culp, Archie W.
    xCulp, Archie W.
        Principles of Energy Conversion. McGraw.
Culp, D. W. see Culp, Daniel Wallace.
Culp, Daniel W. see Culp, Daniel Wallace.

Culp, Daniel Wallace.
    xCulp, D. W.
        ed. Twentieth Century Negro Literature. Arno.
    xCulp, Daniel W.
        ed. Twentieth Century Negro Literature. Arno.

Culp, G. Richard.
    xCulp, Richard G.
        Remember Thy Creator. Baker Bk.

Culp, John H.
    xCulp, John H.
        Oh, Valley Green!. Popular Lib.
Culp, Richard G. see Culp, G. Richard.

Culshaw, John.
    xCulshaw, John.

The Concerto. Greenwood.

Culver, Charles A. *see* Culver, Charles Aaron.

Culver, Charles Aaron, 1875-
xCulver, Charles A.
Musical Acoustics. McGraw.

Culver, John H.
xCulver, John H.
Power & Politics in California. Wiley.

Culver, Raymond B. *see* Culver, Raymond Benjamin.

Culver, Raymond Benjamin, 1887-1938
xCulver, Raymond B.
Horace Mann & Religion in the Massachusetts Public Schools. Arno.

Culver, Robert. *see* Culver, Robert Duncan.

Culver, Robert D.
xCulver, Robert D.
jt. auth. Daniel & the Latter Days. Moody.
Toward a Biblical View of Civil Government. Moody.

Culver, Robert D. *see* Culver, Robert Duncan.

Culver, Robert Duncan.
xCulver, Robert.
The Living God. Victor Bks.
xCulver, Robert D.
Life of Christ. Baker Bk.

Culver, Roger B.
xCulver, Roger B.
Astronomy. Har-Row.
The Gemini Syndrome: Star Wars of the Oldest Kind. Pachart Pub Hse.

Culver, Timothy. *see* Culver, Timothy J.

Culver, Timothy J.
xCulver, Timothy.
Ex Officio. M Evans.

Culver, Vivian M.
xCulver, Vivian M.
Modern Bedside Nursing. Saunders.

Culwick, Arthur T. *see* Culwick, Arthur Theodore.

Culwick, Arthur Theodore.
xCulwick, Arthur T.
Ubena of the Rivers. AMS Pr.

Culyer, A. J. *see* Culyer, Anthony J.

Culyer, Anthony J.
xCulyer, A. J.
ed. Economic Policies & Social Goals: Aspects of Public Choice. St Martin.
Measuring Health: Lessons for Ontario. U of Toronto Pr.
Need & the National Health Service: Economics & Social Choice. Rowman.

Cumberland, David.
xCumberland, David.
Death & Justice Frescoes. Bookstore Pr.

Cumbler, John T.
xCumbler, John T.
Working-Class Community in Industrial America: Work, Leisure, & Struggle in Two Industrial Cities, 1880-1930. Greenwood.

Cumerford, William R.
xCumerford, William R.
Fund Raising: A Professional Guide. F E Peters.

Cumes, J. W. *see* Cumes, J. W. C.

Cumes, J. W. C., 1922-
xCumes, J. W.
Inflation: A Study in Stability. Pergamon.

Cumming, Charles G. *see* Cumming, Charles Gordon.

Cumming, Charles Gordon, 1885-
xCumming, Charles G.
Assyrian & Hebrew Hymns of Praise. AMS Pr.

Cumming, John.
xCumming, John.
Ego & Milieu: Theory & Practice of Environmental Therapy. Aldine Pub.

Cumming, Patricia.
xCumming, Patricia.
Afterwards. Alicejamesbooks.

Cumming, Robert D. *see* Cumming, Robert Denoon.

Cumming, Robert Denoon, 1917-
xCumming, Robert D.

Human Nature & History: A Study of the Development of Liberal Political Thought. U of Chicago Pr.
Starting Point: An Introduction to the Dialectic of Existence. U of Chicago Pr.

Cumming, W. P. *see* Cumming, William Patterson.
Cumming, William P. *see* Cumming, William Patterson.

Cumming, William Patterson.
xCumming, W. P.
The Discovery of North America. Merrimack Bk Serv.
xCumming, William P.
British Maps of Colonial America. U of Chicago Pr.

Cummings, A. L. *see* Cummings, Abbott Lowell.
Cummings, Abbott L. *see* Cummings, Abbott Lowell.

Cummings, Abbott Lowell.
xCummings, A. L.
The Crowninshield-Bentley House. Essex Inst.
xCummings, Abbott L.
The Framed Houses of Massachusetts Bay, 1625-1725. Harvard U Pr.

Cummings, Bernice.
xCummings, Bernice.
Women Organizing: An Anthology. Scarecrow.

Cummings, Betty S. *see* Cummings, Betty Sue.

Cummings, Betty Sue.
xCummings, Betty S.
Let a River Be. Atheneum.
Now, Ameriky. Atheneum.

Cummings, E. E. *see* Cummings, Edward Estlin.

Cummings, Edward Estlin, 1894-1962
xCummings, E. E.
Complete Poems. Liveright.
Enormous Room. Liveright.
Him. Bantam.
Him. Liveright.
No Thanks. Liveright.

Cummings, Jack 1940-
xCummings, Jack.
Complete Guide to Real Estate Financing. P-H.

Cummings, L. L. *see* Cummings, Larry L.

Cummings, Larry L.
xCummings, L. L.
Performance in Organizations: Determinants & Appraisal. Scott F.
Readings in Organizational Behavior & Human Performance. Irwin.

Cummings, Mary L. *see* Cummings, Mary Lou.

Cummings, Mary Lou.
xCummings, Mary L.
ed. Full Circle: Stories of Mennonite Women. Faith & Life.

Cummings, Milton C.
xCummings, Milton C.
Democracy Under Pressure: An Introduction to the American Political System. HarBraceJ.

Cummings, Paul.
xCummings, Paul.
Artists in Their Own Words. St Martin.
ed. Dictionary of Contemporary American Artists. St Martin.
ed. Fine Arts Market Place. Bowker.

Cummings, Ray.
xCummings, Ray.
A Brand New World. Ace Bks.
Girl in the Golden Atom. Hyperion Conn.
Insect Invasion. Boureqy.
Tarrano the Conqueror. Garland Pub.
xCummings, Raymond.
Girl in the Golden Atom. Lighthouse Pr NY.

Cummings, Raymond. *see* Cummings, Ray.

Cummings, Richard.
xCummings, Richard.
Contemporary Selling. Rand.

Cummings, Richard L.
xCummings, Richard L.

Educational Innovations in Latin America. Scarecrow.

Cummings, Thomas G.
xCummings, Thomas G.
Improving Productivity & the Quality of Work Life. Praeger.

Cummings, Thomas S. *see* Cummings, Thomas Seir.

Cummings, Thomas Seir, 1804-1894
xCummings, Thomas S.
Historic Annals of the National Academy of Design. Da Capo.

Cummings, William K.
xCummings, William K.
Changes in the Japanese University: A Comparative Perspective. Praeger.
Education & Equality in Japan. Princeton U Pr.

Cummins, D. Duane.
xCummins, D. Duane.
The American Revolution. Glencoe.
xCummins, Duane D.
Origins of the Civil War. Glencoe.

Cummins, Duane D. *see* Cummins, D. Duane.

Cummins, J. David.
xCummins, J. David.
Development of Life Insurance Surrender Values in the United States. Huebner Foun Insur.

Cummins, J. G. *see* Cummins, John G.

Cummins, John G.
xCummins, J. G.
The Spanish Traditional Lyric. Pergamon.

Cummins, Marsha Hirsch.
xCummins, Marsha Z.
Writing the Research Paper: A Guide & Sourcebook. HM.

Cummins, Marsha Z. *see* Cummins, Marsha Hirsch.
Cummins, Robert A. *see* Cummins, Robert Alexander.

Cummins, Robert Alexander, 1874-
xCummins, Robert A.
Improvement & Distribution of Practice. AMS Pr.

Cummins, Roger W.
xCummins, Roger W.
Humorous but Wholesome: A History of Palmer Cox & the Brownies, 1974. Century Hse.

Cumont, Franz. *see* Cumont, Franz Valery Marie.

Cumont, Franz Valery Marie, 1868-1947
xCumont, Franz.
Astrology & Religion Among the Greeks & Romans. Dover.
Astrology & Religion Among the Greeks & Romans. Peter Smith.
Oriental Religions in Roman Paganism. Dover.
Oriental Religions in Roman Paganism. Peter Smith.

Cumper, G. E. *see* Cumper, George Edward.

Cumper, George Edward.
xCumper, G. E.
ed. The Economy of the West Indies. Greenwood.

Cumpston, I. M.
xCumpston, I. M.
ed. The Growth of the British Commonwealth: 1880-1932. St Martin.

Cumpston, I M.
xCumpston, I. M.
Indians Overseas in British Territories: 1839-1854. Beekman Pubs.
Indians Overseas in British Territories, 1834-54. Dawson Pub.

Cundiff, Edward. *see* Cundiff, Edward W.

Cundiff, Edward W.
xCundiff, Edward.
Fundamentals of Modern Marketing. P-H.
xCundiff, Edward W.

Fundamentals of Modern Marketing. P-H.
Marketing Doctoral Dissertation Abstracts,
1978. Am Mktg.
Cundy, Henry M. *see* Cundy, Henry Martyn.
Cundy, Henry Martyn.
xCundy, Henry M.
Mathematical Models. Oxford U Pr.
Cuneo, Mary L. *see* Cuneo, Mary Louise Hector.
Cuneo, Mary Louise Hector.
xCuneo, Mary L.
Inside a Sand Castle & Other Secrets. HM.
Cunha. *see* Cunha, Tony J.
Cunha, Tony J.
xCunha.
ed. Swine Feeding & Nutrition. Acad Pr.
Cuniberti, John M. *see* Cuniberti, John Michael.
Cuniberti, John Michael, 1931-
xCuniberti, John M.
The Birth of a Nation: A Formal Shot-by-Shot
Analysis Together with Microfiche. Res
Pubns Conn.
Cunitz, Jonathan A.
xCunitz, Jonathan A.
Computer Cases in Accounting. P-H.
Cunliffe, Barry. *see* Cunliffe, Barry W.
Cunliffe, Barry W.
xCunliffe, Barry.
Hengistbury Head. Merrimack Bk Serv.
Cunliffe, Frederick.
xCunliffe, Frederick.
Criminalistics & Scientific Investigation. P-H.
Cunliffe, John W. *see* Cunliffe, John William.
Cunliffe, John William, 1865-1946
xCunliffe, John W.
Leaders of the Victorian Revolution. Kennikat.
Leaders of the Victorian Revolution. Russell.
Cunliffe, Marcus.
xCunliffe, Marcus.
Chattel Slavery & Wage Slavery: The
Anglo-American Context, 1830-1860. U of
Ga Pr.
ed. Pastmasters: Some Essays on American
Historians. Greenwood.
ed. Pastmasters: Some Essays on American
Historians. Peter Smith.
Cunliffe, W. Gordon. *see* Cunliffe, William Gordon.
Cunliffe, W. J. *see* Cunliffe, William James.
Cunliffe, William Gordon.
xCunliffe, W. Gordon.
Gunter Grass. Twayne.
Cunliffe, William James.
xCunliffe, W. J.
The Acnes: Clinical Features, Pathogenesis &
Treatment. Saunders.
Cunniff, P. F.
xCunniff, Patrick F.
Environmental Noise Pollution. Wiley.
Cunniff, Patrick F. *see* Cunniff, P. F.
Cunningham, A. J.
xCunningham, A. J.
ed. The Generation of Antibody Diversity: A
New Look. Acad Pr.
Cunningham, Allan, 1784-1842
xCunningham, Allan.
Life & Land of Burns. AMS Pr.
Cunningham, Ben.
xCunningham, Ben.
Green Eyes. Ballantine.
Cunningham, Bess V. *see* Cunningham, Bess Virginia.
Cunningham, Bess Virginia, 1882-
xCunningham, Bess V.
The Prognostic Value of a Primary Group Test:
A Study of Intelligence & Relative
Achievement in the First Grade. AMS Pr.
Cunningham, Bill.
xCunningham, William.
Blacks in the Performing Arts. Shoe String.
Cunningham, Bronnie.
xCunningham, Bronnie.

Best Book of Riddles, Puns & Jokes.
Doubleday.
Compiled by Funny Business. Penguin.
Cunningham, Charles B.
xCunningham, Charles B.
Simple Studies in Romans. Baker Bk.
Cunningham, Chet.
xCunningham, Chet.
The Gold & the Glory. Nordon Pubns.
The Power & the Prize. Nordon Pubns.
Rainbow Saga. Nordon Pubns.
This Splendid Land. Nordon Pubns.
Cunningham, Cliff. *see* Cunningham, Clifford Charles.
Cunningham, Clifford Charles.
xCunningham, Cliff.
Helping Your Exceptional Baby: A Practical &
Honest Approach to Raising a Mentally
Handicapped Child. Pantheon.
Cunningham, Dixon C.
xCunningham, Dixon C.
Cases on Financial Institutions. Grid Pub.
Cunningham, Donald H.
xCunningham, Donald H.
ed. A Reading Approach to Professional Police
Writing. C C Thomas.
ed. The Teaching of Technical Writing. NCTE.
Cunningham, Donna, 1942-
xCunningham, Donna.
An Astrological Guide to Self-Awareness.
CRCS Pubns WA.
Cunningham, Frank.
xCunningham, Frank.
Objectivity in Social Science. U of Toronto Pr.
Cunningham, Gary M. *see* Cunningham, Gary Mac.
Cunningham, Gary Mac, 1941-
xCunningham, Gary M.
An Accounting Research Framework for
Multinational Enterprises. Univ Microfilms.
Cunningham, Gerry.
xCunningham, Gerry.
Light Weight Camping Equipment & How to
Make It. Scribner.
Cunningham, Gustavus W. *see* Cunningham, Gustavus
Watts.
Cunningham, Gustavus Watts, 1881-
xCunningham, Gustavus W.
Five Lectures on the Problem of the Mind.
AMS Pr.
Idealistic Argument in Recent British &
American Philosophy. Arno.
Idealistic Argument in Recent British &
American Philosophy. Greenwood.
Cunningham, H. H. *see* Cunningham, Horace Herndon.
Cunningham, Harry A. *see* Cunningham, Harry Allen.
Cunningham, Harry Allen, 1891-
xCunningham, Harry A.
Material Facilities Needed in the Training of
Intermediate Grade Teachers in Science.
AMS Pr.
Cunningham, Horace Herndon, 1913-
xCunningham, H. H.
Doctors in Gray: The Confederate Medical
Service. Peter Smith.
Cunningham, J. *see* Cunningham, James B.
Cunningham, J. V. *see* Cunningham, James Vincent.
Cunningham, James, 1938-
xCunningham, James.
Sources of Finance for Higher Education in
America. U Pr of Amer.
Cunningham, James. *see* Cunningham, James W.
Cunningham, James B., 1938-
xCunningham, J.
Teaching Metrics Simplified. P-H.
Cunningham, James F. *see* Cunningham, James
Frederick.
Cunningham, James Frederick.
xCunningham, James F.

Uganda & Its Peoples: Notes on the
Protectorate of Uganda, Especially the
Anthropology & Ethnology of Its Indigenous
Races. Metro Bks.
Cunningham, James Vincent.
xCunningham, J. V.
Collected Essays of J. V. Cunningham.
Swallow.
Exclusions of a Rhyme: Poems & Epigrams.
Swallow.
Cunningham, James W.
xCunningham, James.
Middle & Secondary School Reading.
Longman.
xCunningham, Patricia.
jt. auth. Middle & Secondary School Reading.
Longman.
Cunningham, Jere.
xCunningham, Jere.
Hunter's Blood. Fawcett.
The Legacy. Fawcett.
The Visitor. St Martin.
Cunningham, John, 1938-
xCunningham, J.
Complex Variable Methods in Science &
Technology. Van Nos Reinhold.
xCunningham, John.
Handbook of Remote Control & Automation
Techniques. TAB Bks.
Cunningham, John. *see* Cunningham, John Edward.
Cunningham, John E. *see* Cunningham, John Edward.
Cunningham, John Edward, 1923-
xCunningham, John.
Understanding & Using the VOM & EVM.
TAB Bks.
xCunningham, John E.
Building & Installing Electronic Intrusion
Alarms. Sams.
The Complete Broadcast Antenna Handbook:
Design, Installation, Operation &
Maintenance. TAB Bks.
Security Electronics. Sams.
Cunningham, John J. *see* Cunningham, John James.
Cunningham, John James.
xCunningham, John J.
Common Plants: Botanical & Colloquial
Nomenclature. Garland Pub.
Cunningham, John T.
xCunningham, John T.
This Is New Jersey. Rutgers U Pr.
Cunningham, Joyce I.
xCunningham, Joyce I.
A Concordance to Andre Gide's la Symphonie
Pastorale. Garland Pub.
Cunningham, Julia.
xCunningham, Julia.
Burnish Me Bright. Dell.
Burnish Me Bright. Pantheon.
Come to the Edge. Avon.
Come to the Edge. Pantheon.
Dorp Dead. Avon.
Dorp Dead. Pantheon.
Far in the Day. Dell.
Far in the Day. Pantheon.
Macaroon. Dell.
Macaroon. Pantheon.
Tuppenny. Dutton.
Cunningham, Kenneth S. *see* Cunningham, Kenneth
Stewart.
Cunningham, Kenneth Stewart, 1890-
xCunningham, Kenneth S.
The Measurement of Early Levels of
Intelligence. AMS Pr.
Cunningham, Laura.
xCunningham, Laura.
Sweet Nothings. Avon.
Cunningham, Louis. *see* Cunningham, Louis M.
Cunningham, Louis M.
xCunningham, Louis.

Counseling Theories: A Selective Examination for School Counselors. Merrill.

Cunningham, Luvern L.
xCunningham, Luvern L.
Governing Schools: New Approaches to Old Issues. Merrill.

Cunningham, Madelyn.
xCunningham, Madelyn.
Monique. BJ Pub Group.

Cunningham, Maggi, 1916-
xCunningham, Maggi.
Black Hawk. Dillon.

Cunningham, Maggi. *see* Cunningham, Margaret.

Cunningham, Margaret, 1916-
xCunningham, Maggi.
Little Turtle. Dillon.

Cunningham, Mary S. *see* Cunningham, Mary Smith.

Cunningham, Mary Smith.
xCunningham, Mary S.
The Woman's Club of EL Paso: Its First Thirty Years. Tex Western.

Cunningham, Noble E., 1926-
xCunningham, Noble E.
ed. Early Republic: 1789-1828. U of SC Pr.
The Process of Government Under Jefferson. Princeton U Pr.

Cunningham, Patricia. *see* Cunningham, James W.
Cunningham, Patricia M. *see* Cunningham, Patricia Marr.

Cunningham, Patricia Marr.
xCunningham, Patricia M.
Classroom Reading Instruction, K-5: Alternative Approaches. Heath.

Cunningham, Richard B.
xCunningham, Richard B.
Creative Stewardship. Abingdon.

Cunningham, Robert. *see* Cunningham, Robert Maris.

Cunningham, Robert L., 1926-
xCunningham, Robert L.
ed. Liberty & the Rule of Law. Tex A&M Univ Pr.

Cunningham, Robert M. *see* Cunningham, Robert Maris.

Cunningham, Robert Maris, 1909-
xCunningham, Robert.
Governing Hospitals: Trustees & the New Accountabilities. Am Hospital.
xCunningham, Robert M.
Asking & Giving: A Report on Hospital Philanthropy. Am Hospital.

Cunningham, Robert S. *see* Cunningham, Robert Stanley.

Cunningham, Robert Stanley.
xCunningham, Robert S.
Rationale. Mojave Bks.

Cunningham, W. J.
xCunningham, W. J.
Agony at Galloway: One Church's Struggle with Social Change. U Pr of Miss.

Cunningham, W. Patrick.
xCunningham, William P.
The Music Locator. Resource Pubns.

Cunningham, William, 1849-1919
xCunningham, William.
Alien Immigrants to England. Biblio Dist.
Alien Immigrants to England. Kelley.
Growth of the English Industry & Commerce. Biblio Dist.

Cunningham, William. *see* Cunningham, Bill.
Cunningham, William P. *see* Cunningham, W. Patrick.
Cunnington, C. W. *see* Cunnington, Cecil Willett.
Cunnington, C. Willett. *see* Cunnington, Cecil Willett.

Cunnington, Cecil Willett.
xCunnington, C. W.
The History of Underclothes. Gordon Pr.
Why Women Wear Clothes. Gordon Pr.
xCunnington, C. Willett.

Handbook of English Costume in the Eighteenth Century. Plays.
Handbook of English Costume in the Nineteenth Century. Plays.
Handbook of English Costume in the Sixteenth Century. Plays.

Cunnington, Phillis. *see* Cunnington, Phillis Emily.

Cunnington, Phillis Emily, 1887-
xCunnington, Phillis.
Medieval & Tudor Costume. Plays.

Curatorial Staff, Metropolitan Museum of Art. *see* New York (City). Metropolitan Museum of Art.

Curcic, Slobodan.
xCurcic, Slobodan.
Gracanica: King Milutin's Church & Its Place in Late Byzantine Architecture. Pa St U Pr.

Curfman, F. L. *see* Curfman, Frederick Lester.

Curfman, Frederick Lester.
xCurfman, F. L.
Automotive Radiator Construction & Restoration for Antique & Classic. Post-Era.

Curl, James C.
xCurl, James C.
Developmental Arithmetic: An Individualized Approach. McGraw.

Curl, Tom.
xCurl, Tom.
Beef Cattle Book: A Working Guide for Cattlemen. Oxmoor Hse.

Curl, Vega.
xCurl, Vega.
Pasteboard Masks: Fact As Spiritual Symbol in the Novels of Hawthorne & Melville. Folcroft.

Curle, Adam.
xCurle, Adam.
Planning for Education in Pakistan: A Personal Case Study. Harvard U Pr.

Curle, N.
xCurle, N.
Applied Differential Equations. Van Nos Reinhold.

Curle, Richard, 1883-
xCurle, Richard.
Aspects of George Meredith. R West.
Joseph Conrad & His Characters: A Study of Six Novels. Russell.
Joseph Conrad: The History of His Books. Folcroft.
Last Twelve Years of Joseph Conrad. R West.
Last Twelve Years of Joseph Conrad. Russell.
Life Is a Dream. Arno.
xCurle, Richard H.
Aspects of George Meredith. Haskell.
Aspects of George Meredith. Phaeton.

Curle, Richard H. *see* Curle, Richard.

Curlee-Salisbury, Joan.
xCurlee-Salisbury, Joan.
When the Woman You Love Is an Alcoholic. Abbey.

Curley, Anthony J.
xCurley, Anthony J.
Investment Analysis & Management. Har-Row.

Curley, Daniel.
xCurley, Daniel.
Ann's Spring. T Y Crowell.
Billy Beg & the Bull. T Y Crowell.
Hilarion. HM.
In the Hands of Our Enemies: Stories. U of Ill Pr.

Curley, Dorothy N. *see* Curley, Dorothy Nyren.

Curley, Dorothy Nyren.
xCurley, Dorothy N.
ed. Modern American Literature. Ungar.

Curley, E. M. *see* Curley, Edwin M.

Curley, Edwin M.
xCurley, E. M.

Descartes Against the Skeptics. Harvard U Pr.
Spinoza's Metaphysics: An Essay in Interpretation. Harvard U Pr.

Curley, James M. *see* Curley, James Michael.

Curley, James Michael, 1874-
xCurley, James M.
I'd Do It Again: A Record of All My Uproarious Years. Arno.

Curley, Michael J., 1942-
xCurley, Michael J.
tr. Physiologus. U of Tex Pr.

Curley, Michael J. *see* Curley, Michael Joseph.

Curley, Michael Joseph, 1900-1972
xCurley, Michael J.
Church & State in the Spanish Floridas (1783-1822). AMS Pr.

Curling, Audrey.
xCurling, Audrey.
Enthusiasts in Love. Popular Lib.

Curling, Bill.
xCurling, Bill.
All the Queen's Horses. Merrimack Bk Serv.

Curno, Paul.
xCurno, Paul.
ed. Political Issues & Community Work. Routledge & Kegan.

Curr, John, 1756-1823
xCurr, John.
Coal Viewer & Engine Builder's Practical Companion. Biblio Dist.
Coal Viewer & Engine Builder's Practical Companion. Kelley.

Curran. *see* Curran, Jan Goldberg.

Curran, Charles E.
xCurran, Charles E.
ed. Absolutes in Moral Theology?. Greenwood.
Catholic Moral Theology in Dialogue. U of Notre Dame Pr.
Themes in Fundamental Moral Theology. U of Notre Dame Pr.
Transition & Tradition in Moral Theology. U of Notre Dame Pr.

Curran, Desmond.
xCurran, Desmond.
Psychological Medicine: An Introduction to Psychiatry. Churchill.

Curran, Dolores.
xCurran, Dolores.
In the Beginning There Were the Parents. Winston Pr.
Who, Me Teach My Child Religion?. Winston Pr.

Curran, Francis X. *see* Curran, Francis Xavier.

Curran, Francis Xavier, 1914-
xCurran, Francis X.
Catholics in Colonial Law. Loyola.

Curran, Jan Goldberg.
xCurran.
The Statue of Liberty Is Cracking up: A Guide to Loving, Leaving, & Living Again. HarBraceJ.

Curran, Joseph M. *see* Curran, Joseph Maroney.

Curran, Joseph Maroney, 1932-
xCurran, Joseph M.
The Birth of the Irish Free State, 1921-1923. U of Ala Pr.

Curran, June, 1923-
xCurran, June.
Drawing Home Plans: A Simplified Drafting System for Planning & Design. Brooks Pub Co.

Curran, Patrick J. *see* Curran, Patrick J. T.

Curran, Patrick J. T., 1931-
xCurran, Patrick J.
Principles & Procedures of Tour Management. CBI Pub.

Curran, R. C. *see* Curran, Robert Crowe.

Curran, Robert Crowe.
xCurran, R. C.

Color Atlas of Histopathology. Oxford U Pr.
Curran, Samuel C. *see* Curran, Samuel Crowe.
Curran, Samuel Crowe.
xCurran, Samuel C.
Energy & Human Needs. Halsted Pr.
Curran, Ward S., 1935-
xCurran, Ward S.
Principles of Financial Management. McGraw.
Curran, William, 1921-
xCurran, William.
Beautiful Wisconsin. Beautiful Am.
Colorful Northern California. Beautiful Am.
xCurran, William C.
Beautiful Los Angeles. Beautiful Am.
Beautiful Washington D. C.. Beautiful Am.
Curran, William C. *see* Curran, William.
Curran, William J.
xCurran, William J.
Law, Medicine & Forensic Science. Little.
Currell, David.
xCurrell, David.
Puppetry for School Children. Branford.
Curren, Polly.
xCurren, Polly.
I Know an Electrician. Putnam.
Pea Patch Island. Western Pub.
Current, Richard N. *see* Current, Richard Nelson.
Current, Richard Nelson.
xCurrent, Richard N.
Daniel Webster & the Rise of National
Conservatism. Little.
Essentials of American History. Knopf.
Essentials of American History. Knopf.
A History of the United States. Knopf.
History of the United States. Knopf.
Lincoln & the First Shot. Har-Row.
The Lincoln Nobody Knows. Greenwood.
The Lincoln Nobody Knows. Hill & Wang.
Current, William.
xCurrent, William.
Greene & Greene: Architects in the Residential
Style. Morgan.
Pueblo Architecture of the Southwest: A
Photographic Essay. U of Tex Pr.
xCurrent, William R.
Greene & Greene: Architects in the Residential
Style. Amon Carter.
Current, William R. *see* Current, William.
Currey, Cecil B.
xCurrey, Cecil B.
Reason & Revelation: John Duns Scotus on
Natural Theology. Franciscan Herald.
Curriculum Adaption Network for Bilingual Bicultural
Education. *see* Curriculum Adaptation Network for
Bilingual Bicultural Education.
**Curriculum Adaptation Network for Bilingual Bicultural
Education.**
xCurriculium Adaption Network for Bilingual
Bicultural Education.
ESL Reader: Un Nino Llamado Manuel.
Barron.
xCurriculum Adaptation Network for Bilingual
Bicultural Education.
A Boy Named Manuel, ESL Reader. Barron.
Curriculum Dev. Unit. *see* Curriculum Development
Unit.
Curriculum Development Unit.
xCurriculum Dev. Unit.
ed. The World of Stone: Life, Folklore &
Legends of Aran - Island Life Ser.. Irish Bk
Ctr.
xCurriculum Development Unit.
The Celtic Way of Life. Humanities.
Dublin Divided City: Portrait of Dublin 1913.
Humanities.
A World of Stone: Life , Folklore & Legends
of the Aran Islands. Humanities.
Curriculum Theory Conference, University of Wisconsin,
Milwaukee, November 11-14, 1976. *see* Milwaukee

Curriculum Theory Conference, University of
Wisconsin-Milwaukee, 1976.
Currie, David M., 1918-
xCurrie, David M.
Come, Let Us Worship God: A Handbook of
Prayers for Leaders of Worship. Westminster.
Currie, David P.
xCurrie, David P.
ed. Federalism & the New Nations of Africa. U
of Chicago Pr.
Currie, Dorothy H.
xCurrie, Dorothy H.
How to Organize a Children's Library. Oceana.
Currie, Harold W.
xCurrie, Harold W.
Eugene V. Debs. Twayne.
Currie, I. G. *see* Currie, Iain G.
Currie, Iain G.
xCurrie, I. G.
ed. Fundamental Mechanics of Fluids.
McGraw.
Currie, Lauchlin. *see* Currie, Lauchlin Bernard.
Currie, Lauchlin Bernard.
xCurrie, Lauchlin.
Taming the Megalopolis: A Design for Urban
Growth. Pergamon.
Currie, Robert.
xCurrie, Robert.
Industrial Politics. Oxford U Pr.
Currie, Thomas W. *see* Currie, Thomas White.
Currie, Thomas White.
xCurrie, Thomas W.
Austin Presbyterian Theological Seminary: A
Seventy-Fifth Anniversary History. Trinity U
Pr.
Currier, Dean P.
xCurrier, Dean P.
Elements of Research in Physical Therapy.
Williams & Wilkins.
Currier, John J. *see* Currier, John James.
Currier, John James, 1834-1912
xCurrier, John J.
History of Newburyport, Massachusetts. NH
Pub Co..
Currier, Richard L.
xCurrier, Richard L.
Coins of the Ancient World. Lerner Pubns.
Retold by Pottery in Ancient Times. Lerner
Pubns.
Curry. *see* Curry, Hiram B.
Curry, Barbara. *see* Curry, Barbara A.
Curry, Barbara A.
xCurry, Barbara.
Model Aircraft. Watts.
Curry, E. R. *see* Curry, Earl R.
Curry, Earl R., 1933-
xCurry, E. R.
Hoover's Dominican Diplomacy & the Origins
of the Good Neighbor Policy. Garland Pub.
Curry, Gene.
xCurry, Gene.
A Dirty Way to Die. Belmont-Tower.
Wildcat Woman. Belmont Tower.
Curry, Haskell B. *see* Curry, Haskell Brooks.
Curry, Haskell Brooks, 1900-
xCurry, Haskell B.
Foundations of Mathematical Logic. Dover.
Foundations of Mathematical Logic. Peter
Smith.
Theory of Formal Deducibility. U of Notre
Dame Pr.
Curry, Hiram B.
xCurry.
Twenty Years of Community Medicine: A
Hunterdon Medical Center Symposium.
Columbia Pub.
Curry, Jane L. *see* Curry, Jane Louise.
Curry, Jane Louise.
xCurry, Jane L.

Daybreakers. HarBraceJ.
The Ice Ghosts Mystery. Atheneum.
The Ice Ghosts Mystery. Atheneum.
The Lost Farm. Atheneum.
Over the Sea's Edge. HarBraceJ.
Poor Tom's Ghost. Atheneum.
Curry, Kenneth.
xCurry, Kenneth.
Southey. Routledge & Kegan.
Curry, Peggy (Simson).
xCurry, Peggy S.
Creating Fiction from Experience. Writer.
Curry, Peggy S. *see* Curry, Peggy (Simson).
Curry, Richard A., 1939-
xCurry, Richard A.
Ramon De Mesonero Romanos. Twayne.
Curry, Richard O. *see* Curry, Richard Orr.
Curry, Richard Orr.
xCurry, Richard O.
ed. Radicalism, Racism, & Party Realignment:
The Border States during Reconstruction.
Johns Hopkins.
Curry, Robert. *see* Curry, Robert Arthur.
Curry, Robert Arthur.
xCurry, Robert.
Bahamian Lore. Gordon Pr.
Curry, Roy W. *see* Curry, Roy Watson.
Curry, Roy Watson.
xCurry, Roy W.
Woodrow Wilson & Far Eastern Policy,
1913-1921. Octagon.
Curry, S. S. *see* Curry, Samuel Silas.
Curry, Samuel Silas, 1847-1921
xCurry, S. S.
Vocal & Literary Interpretation of the Bible. R
West.
Curry, Walter C. *see* Curry, Walter Clyde.
Curry, Walter Clyde, 1887-
xCurry, Walter C.
Demonic Metaphysics of Macbeth. Haskell.
Curry-Lindahl, Kai.
xCurry-Lindahl, Kai.
Let Them Live: A Worldwide Survey of
Animals Threatened with Extinction.
Morrow.
Curson, Julie P.
xCurson, Julie P.
A Guide's Guide to Philadelphia. Curson Hse.
Curtain, R. F. *see* Curtain, Ruth F.
Curtain, Ruth F.
xCurtain, R. F.
Infinite Dimensional Linear Systems Theory.
Springer-Verlag.
Curti, Merle. *see* Curti, Merle Eugene.
Curti, Merle E. *see* Curti, Merle Eugene.
Curti, Merle Eugene, 1897-
xCurti, Merle.
Human Nature in American Thought: A
History. U of Wis Pr.
Probing Our Past. Peter Smith.
xCurti, Merle E.
Bryan & World Peace. Garland Pub.
Bryan & World Peace. Octagon.
History of American Civilization. Arno.
Peace or War: The American Struggle
1635-1936. Canner.
Peace or War: The American Struggle,
1636-1936. Ozer.
Prelude to Point Four: American Technical
Missions Overseas Eighteen Thirty-Eight to
Nineteen Thirty-Eight. Greenwood.
Curties, T. J. *see* Curties, T. J. Horsley.
Curties, T. J. Horsley.
xCurties, T. J.
The Monk of Udolpho: A Romance. Arno.
Curtin, Dennis.
xCurtin, Dennis.

The Darkroom Handbook: A Complete Guide
to the Best Design, Construction &
Equipment. Curtin & London.
Curtin, Jeremiah, 1835-1906
xCurtin, Jeremiah.
The Mongols: A History. Greenwood.
Curtin, Mary E. see Curtin, Mary Ellen.
Curtin, Mary Ellen.
xCurtin, Mary E.
ed. Symposium on Love. Human Sci Pr.
Curtin, Philip D.
xCurtin, Philip D.
ed. Africa Remembered: Narratives by West
Africans from the Era of the Slave Trade. U
of Wis Pr.
Atlantic Slave Trade: A Census. U of Wis Pr.
Economic Change in Pre-Colonial Africa:
Senegambia in the Era of the Slave Trade. U
of Wis Pr.
Image of Africa: British Ideas & Action,
1780-1850. U of Wis Pr.
ed. Imperialism. Walker & Co.
Precolonial African History. Am Hist Assn.
Two Jamaicas: The Role of Ideas in a Tropical
Colony, 1830-1865. Greenwood.
Curtin, Richard T.
xCurtin, Richard T.
Income Equity Among U. S. Workers: The
Bases & Consequences of Deprivation.
Praeger.
Curtin, Sharon R.
xCurtin, Sharon R.
Nobody Ever Died of Old Age. Little.
Curtis. see Curtis, Leonard F.
Curtis, A. see Curtis, Arthur B.
Curtis, Anthony.
xCurtis, Anthony.
The Pattern of Maugham: A Critical Portrait.
Taplinger.
Somerset Maugham. Macmillan.
Curtis, Arthur B.
xCurtis, A.
Mathematics of Accounting. P-H.
Curtis, Audrey.
xCurtis, Audrey.
My World. Humanities.
Curtis, Charles J.
xCurtis, Charles J.
Contemporary Protestant Thought. Glencoe.
Curtis, Charles W.
xCurtis, Charles W.
Linear Algebra: An Introductory Approach.
Allyn.
Curtis, Charlotte.
xCurtis, Charlotte.
The Rich & Other Atrocities. Har-Row.
Curtis, Chris. see Curtis, Christopher.
Curtis, Christopher.
xCurtis, Chris.
Be Your Own Chimney Sweep. Garden Way
Pub.
Curtis, D. B. see Curtis, Dan B.
Curtis, Dan B.
xCurtis, D. D.
Communication for Problem-Solving. Wiley.
Curtis, David, 1942-
xCurtis, David.
Experimental Cinema. Dell.
Curtis, Donald.
xCurtis, Donald.
The Christ-Based Teachings. Unity Bks.
Daily Power for Joyful Living. Wilshire.
How to Be Happy & Successful. CSA Pr.
Live It up. CSA Pr.
Master Meditations. CSA Pr.
Curtis, Edmund, 1881-1943
xCurtis, Edmund.

History of Ireland. Methuen Inc.
A History of Medieval Ireland from 1086 to
1513. Gordon Pr.
Curtis, Edward. see Curtis, Edward S.
Curtis, Edward E. see Curtis, Edward Ely.
Curtis, Edward Ely.
xCurtis, Edward E.
Organization of the British Army in the
American Revolution. AMS Pr.
The Organization of the British Army in the
American Revolution. Scholarly.
Curtis, Edward S.
xCurtis, Edward.
Edward Sheriff Curtis: Visions of a Vanishing
Race. T Y Crowell.
xCurtis, Edward S.
Portraits from North American Indian Life. A
& W Pubs.
Curtis, Foley.
xCurtis, Foley.
The Little Book of Big Tongue Twisters.
Harvey.
Curtis, Francis D. see Curtis, Francis Day.
Curtis, Francis Day, 1888-
xCurtis, Francis D.
Some Values Derived from Extensive Reading
of General Science. AMS Pr.
Curtis, George W. see Curtis, George William.
Curtis, George William, 1824-1892
xCurtis, George W.
From the Easy Chair. Greenwood.
From the Easy Chair. R West.
Literary & Social Essays. Kennikat.
Literary & Social Essays. R West.
Potiphar Papers. AMS Pr.
The Potiphar Papers. R West.
Potiphar Papers. Scholarly.
Curtis, Helena.
xCurtis, Helena.
Marvelous Animals: An Introduction to the
Protozoa. Natural Hist.
Curtis, Jack H.
xCurtis, Jack H.
Sociology: An Introduction. Glencoe.
Curtis, James C.
xCurtis, James C.
Andrew Jackson & the Search for Vindication.
Little.
The Fox at Bay: Martin Van Buren & the
Presidency, 1837-1841. U Pr of Ky.
Curtis, James F.
xCurtis, James F.
ed. Processes & Disorders of Human
Communication. Har-Row.
Curtis, James M., 1940-
xCurtis, James M.
Culture As Polyphony: An Essay on the
Nature of Paradigms. U of Mo Pr.
Curtis, Jane.
xCurtis, Jane.
Welcome the Birds to Your Home. Greene.
Curtis, Jean, 1939-
xCurtis, Jean.
Working Mothers. S&S.
Curtis, L. Perry. see Curtis, Lewis Perry.
Curtis, Leonard F.
xCurtis.
Soils in the British Isles. Longman.
Curtis, Lewis Perry, 1932-
xCurtis, L. Perry.
Apes & Angels: The Irishman in Victorian
Caricature. Smithsonian.
Curtis, Lindsay R.
xCurtis, Lindsay R.
Pregnant & Lovin' It. H P Bks.
Curtis, Lionel, 1872-1955
xCurtis, Lionel.
Capital Question of China. Kennikat.
Curtis, M. L. see Curtis, Morton Landers.

Curtis, Michael.
xCurtis, Michael.
ed. The Palestinians: People, History, Politics.
Transaction Bks.
Totalitarianism. Transaction Bks.
Curtis, Morton Landers, 1921-
xCurtis, M. L.
Matrix Groups. Springer-Verlag.
Curtis, P. C. see Curtis, Philip Chadsey.
Curtis, Philip C. see Curtis, Philip Chadsey.
Curtis, Philip Chadsey, 1928-
xCurtis, P. C.
Multivariate Calculus with Linear Algebra.
Krieger.
xCurtis, Philip C.
Calculus with an Introduction to Vectors.
Krieger.
Curtis, Richard.
xCurtis, Richard.
Genial Idiots: The American Saga As Seen by
Our Humorists. Macmillan.
Life of Malcolm X. Macrae.
Curtis, Robert. see Curtis, Robert H.
Curtis, Robert H.
xCurtis, Robert.
On ESP. P-H.
xCurtis, Robert H.
Medical Talk for Beginners. Messner.
Questions & Answers About Alcoholism. P H.
Curtis, Roger W. see Curtis, Roger William.
Curtis, Roger William, 1910-
xCurtis, Roger W.
Color in Outdoor Painting. Watson-Guptill.
Curtis, Stanley J. see Curtis, Stanley James.
Curtis, Stanley James.
xCurtis, Stanley J.
History of Education in Great Britain.
Greenwood.
Curtis, Thomas E.
xCurtis, Thomas E.
Curriculum & Instruction for Emerging
Adolescents. A-W.
Curtis, W. Robert, 1943-
xCurtis, W. Robert.
Area Based Human Services. Social Matrix.
The Integration of Health & Social Services.
Social Matrix.
Curtis, William E. see Curtis, William Eleroy.
Curtis, William Eleroy, 1850-1911
xCurtis, William E.
The Capitals of Spanish America. Gordon Pr.
Children of the Sun. AMS Pr.
Curtis-Prior, P. B.
xCurtis-Prior, P. B.
ed. Prostaglandins: An Introduction to Their
Biochemistry, Physiology and Pharmacology.
Elsevier.
Curtiss, David R. see Curtiss, David Raymond.
Curtiss, David Raymond, 1878-
xCurtiss, David R.
Analytic Functions of a Complex Variable.
Math Assn.
Curtiss, Ellen T.
xCurtiss, Ellen T.
Corporate Responsibilities & Opportunities to
1990. Lexington Bks.
Curtiss, John S. see Curtiss, John Shelton.
Curtiss, John Shelton, 1899-
xCurtiss, John S.
Russia's Crimean War. Duke.
Curtiss, Lora L. see Curtiss, Lora Lee.
Curtiss, Lora Lee.
xCurtiss, Lora L.
Who Wants to Wear Boots?. Denison.
Curtiss, Mina. see Curtiss, Mina Stein Kirstein.
Curtiss, Mina Stein Kirstein, 1896-
xCurtiss, Mina.
Other People's Letters: A Memoir. HM.
Curtiss, Richard D.
xCurtiss, Richard D.

Thomas E. Williams & the Fine Arts Press.
Dawsons.
Curtiss, Ursula.
xCurtiss, Ursula.
Letter of Intent. Dodd.
Curtius, E. R. *see* Curtius, Ernst Robert.
Curtius, Ernst Robert, 1886-
xCurtius, E. R.
European Literature & the Latin Middle Ages.
Princeton U Pr.
Curtius, H. C. *see* Curtius, Hans-Christoph.
Curtius, Hans-Christoph.
xCurtius, H. C.
ed. Clinical Biochemistry: Principles &
Methods. De Gruyter.
Curwen, Samuel.
xCurwen, Samuel.
The Journal of Samuel Curwen, Loyalist.
Harvard U Pr.
Curwin, Richard. *see* Curwin, Richard L.
Curwin, Richard L.
xCurwin, Richard.
The Discipline Book: A Complete Guide to
School & Classroom Management. Reston.
Curwood, James O. *see* Curwood, James Oliver.
Curwood, James Oliver, 1878-1927
xCurwood, James O.
Courage of Captain Plum. AMS Pr.
Nomads of the North: A Story of Romance &
Adventure Under the Open Stars. AMS Pr.
Curzon, Daniel.
xCurzon, Daniel.
Something You Do in the Dark. Ashley Bks.
Cusack, Isabel L. *see* Cusack, Isabel Langis.
Cusack, Isabel Langis.
xCusack, Isabel L.
Ivan the Great. T Y Crowell.
Cuschieri, A. *see* Cuschieri, Alfred.
Cuschieri, Alfred.
xCuschieri, A.
Introduction to Research in Medical Sciences.
Churchill.
Cusens, A. R. *see* Cusens, Anthony Ralph.
Cusens, Anthony Ralph.
xCusens, A. R.
Bridge Deck Analysis. Wiley.
Cushenbery, Donald C.
xCushenbery, Donald C.
Effective Reading Instruction for Slow
Learners. C C Thomas.
Reading & the Gifted Child: A Guide for
Teachers. C C Thomas.
Reading Improvement Through Diagnosis,
Remediation & Individualized Instruction.
P-H.
Cushing, Barry E.
xCushing, Barry E.
Accounting Information Systems & Business
Organizations. A-W.
ed. Frontiers of Auditing Research. U of Tex
Busn Res.
Cushing, D. H.
xCushing, D. H.
Detection of Fish. Pergamon.
Fisheries Biology: A Study in Population
Dynamics. U of Wis Pr.
Marine Ecology & Fisheries. Cambridge U Pr.
xCushing, David H.
Fisheries Resources of the Sea & Their
Management. Oxford U Pr.
Cushing, David H. *see* Cushing, D. H.
Cushing, Frank H. *see* Cushing, Frank Hamilton.
Cushing, Frank Hamilton, 1857-1900
xCushing, Frank H.
My Adventures in Zuni. Filter.
Outlines of Zuni Creation Myths. AMS Pr.
Zuni: Selected Writings of Frank Hamilton
Cushing. U of Nebr Pr.
Cushing, Harry A. *see* Cushing, Harry Alonzo.

Cushing, Harry Alonzo, 1870-1955
xCushing, Harry A.
History of the Transition from Provincial to
Commonwealth Government in
Massachusetts. AMS Pr.
Cushing, James T., 1937-
xCushing, James T.
Applied Analytical Mathematics for Physical
Scientists. Wiley.
Cushing, Mary Fitch Watkins.
xCushing, Mary W.
The Rainbow Bridge. Arno.
Cushing, Mary W. *see* Cushing, Mary Fitch Watkins.
Cushing, Richard J. *see* Cushing, Richard James.
Cushing, Richard James, Cardinal, 1895-
xCushing, Richard J.
Mary. Dghtrs St Paul.
Meditations for Religious. Dghtrs St Paul.
Cushing, Thomas, b. 1821
xCushing, Thomas.
ed. A Genealogical & Biographical History of
Allegheny County, Pennsylvania. Genealog
Pub.
Cushion, John P.
xCushion, John P.
Pottery & Porcelain Tablewares. Morrow.
Cushman, Dan.
xCushman, Dan.
Stay Away, Joe. Stay Away.
Cushman, Horatio B. *see* Cushman, Horatio Bardwell B.
Cushman, Horatio Bardwell B, b. 1882
xCushman, Horatio B.
History of the Choctaw, Chickasaw & Natchez
Indians. Russell.
Cushman, Joseph A. *see* Cushman, Joseph Augustine.
Cushman, Joseph Augustine, 1881-1949
xCushman, Joseph A.
Foraminifera: Their Classification & Economic
Use. Harvard U Pr.
Cushman, Keith.
xCushman, Keith.
D. H. Lawrence at Work: The Emergence of
the Prussian Officer Stories. U Pr of Va.
Cushman, M. L. *see* Cushman, Martelle L.
Cushman, Martelle L., 1908-
xCushman, M. L.
Governance of Teacher Education. McCutchan.
The Governance of Teacher Education. Phi
Delta Kappa.
Cushman, Robert E. *see* Cushman, Robert Earl.
Cushman, Robert Earl.
xCushman, Robert E.
Therapeia: Plato's Conception of Philosophy.
Greenwood.
Cushman, Robert Eugene.
xCushman, Robert E.
The Independent Regulatory Commissions.
Octagon.
xCushman, Robert F.
Cases in Civil Liberties. P-H.
Cases in Constitutional Law. P-H.
Leading Constitutional Decisions. P-H.
Cushman, Robert F. *see* Cushman, Robert Eugene.
Cusick, P. *see* Cusick, Philip A.
Cusick, Philip A.
xCusick, P.
Inside High School: The Students World.
HR&W.
Cussans, John E. *see* Cussans, John Edwin.
Cussans, John Edwin, 1837-1899
xCussans, John E.
The History of Hertfordshire. Rowman.
Cussianovich, Alejandro.
xCussianovich, Alejandro.
Religious Life & the Poor: Liberation Theology
Perspectives. Orbis Bks.
Cussler, Clive.
xCussler, Clive.

Iceberg. Bantam.
Iceberg. Dodd.
The Mediterranean Caper. Bantam.
Raise the Titanic. Bantam.
Cussler, E. L.
xCussler, E. L.
Multicomponent Diffusion. Elsevier.
Cust, Edward, Sir, Bart, 1794-1878
xCust, Edward.
Lives of the Warriors of the Civil Wars of
France & England: Warriors of the
Seventeenth Century. Arno.
Lives of the Warriors of the Thirty Years' War:
Warriors of the Seventeenth Century. Arno.
Custance, Arthur C.
xCustance, Arthur C.
The Doorway Papers. Zondervan.
The Flood: Local or Global?. Zondervan.
Noah's Three Sons: Human History in Three
Dimensions. Zondervan.
Science & Faith. Zondervan.
Custance, Reginald. *see* Custance, Reginald Neville.
Custance, Reginald Neville, Sir, 1847-1935
xCustance, Reginald.
Study of War. Kennikat.
Custer, R. Philip. *see* Custer, Richard Philip.
Custer, Richard Philip.
xCuster, R. Philip.
ed. Atlas of the Blood & Bone Marrow.
Saunders.
Custodio, Maurice.
xCustodio, Maurice.
ed. Peace & Pieces: An Anthology of
Contemporary American Poetry. SF Arts &
Letters.
Cutak, Ladislaus.
xCutak, Ladislaus.
Cactus Guide. Van Nos Reinhold.
Cuthbert, Arthur A.
xCuthbert, Arthur A.
The Life & World-Work of Thomas Lake
Harris, Written from Direct Personal
Knowledge. AMS Pr.
Cuthbert, Clifton, 1907-
xCuthbert, Clifton.
Another Such Victory. AMS Pr.
Cuthbertson, Gilbert M. *see* Cuthbertson, Gilbert Morris.
Cuthbertson, Gilbert Morris.
xCuthbertson, Gilbert M.
Political Power. Rice Univ.
Cuthbertson, Tom.
xCuthbertson, Tom.
Anybody's Bike Book: An Original Manual of
Bicycle Repairs. Ten Speed Pr.
Anybody's Roller-Skating Book. Bantam.
Cutino, Peter. *see* Cutino, Peter J.
Cutino, Peter J.
xCutino, Peter.
ed. Polo: The Manual for Coach & Player.
Swimming.
Cutler, Anne G.
xCutler, Anne G.
Indexing Methods & Theory. Williams &
Wilkins.
Cutler, Anthony.
xCutler, Antony.
Marx's Capital & Capitalism Today. Routledge
& Kegan.
Cutler, Antony. *see* Cutler, Anthony.
Cutler, B. D. *see* Cutler, Bradley Dwyane.
Cutler, Bradley D. *see* Cutler, Bradley Dwyane.
Cutler, Bradley Dwyane.
xCutler, B. D.
Modern British Authors: Their First Editions.
Arden Lib.
xCutler, Bradley D.
Modern British Authors: Their First Editions.
Folcroft.
Cutler, Carol.
xCutler, Carol.

The Woman's Day Low-Calorie Dessert
Cookbook. HM.
Cutler, D. F. see Cutler, David Frederick.
Cutler, David Frederick, 1939-
xCutler, D. F.
Applied Plant Anatomy. Longman.
Cutler, Ebbitt.
xCutler, Ebbitt.
I Once Knew an Indian Woman. HM.
Cutler, G. Ripley.
xCutler, G. Ripley.
Of Battles Long Ago: Memoirs of an American
Ambulance Driver in World War I.
Exposition.
Cutler, Hugh C. see Cutler, Hugh Carson.
Cutler, Hugh Carson.
xCutler, Hugh C.
Corn, Cucurbits & Cotton from Glen Canyon.
AMS Pr.
Cutler, Irving.
xCutler, Irving.
Chicago: Metropolis of the Mid-Continent.
Kendall-Hunt.
Cutler, Ivor.
xCutler, Ivor.
The Animal House. Morrow.
Cutler, Jervis.
xCutler, Jervis.
Topographical Description of the State of Ohio,
Indiana Territory, & Louisiana. Arno.
A Topographical Description of the State of
Ohio, Indiana Territory, & Louisiana.
Garland Pub.
Cutler, Katherine. see Cutler, Katherine N.
Cutler, Katherine N.
xCutler, Katherine.
Growing a Garden Indoors or Out. Lothrop.
xCutler, Katherine N.
Crafts for Christmas. Lothrop.
Creative Shellcraft. Lothrop.
From Petals to Pinecones: A Nature Art &
Craft Book. Lothrop.
Cutler, Laurence S.
xCutler, Lawrence.
Handbook of Housing Systems for Designers &
Developers. Van Nos Reinhold.
Cutler, Lawrence. see Cutler, Laurence S.
Cutler, Merritt D. see Cutler, Merritt Dana.
Cutler, Merritt Dana, 1898-
xCutler, Merritt D.
How to Cut Drawings on Scratchboard.
Watson-Guptill.
Cutler, Roland.
xCutler, Roland.
The Gates of Sagittarius. Dial.
Cutler, Wade E.
xCutler, Wade E.
Triple Your Reading Speed. Arco.
Cutler, William W.
xCutler, William W.
ed. The Divided Metropolis: Social & Spatial
Dimensions of Philadelphia, 1800-1975.
Greenwood.
Cutlip, Scott H. see Cutlip, Scott M.
Cutlip, Scott M.
xCutlip, Scott H.
Effective Public Relations. P-H.
Cutright, Paul R. see Cutright, Paul Russell.
Cutright, Paul Russell, 1897-
xCutright, Paul R.
Great Naturalists Explore South America.
Arno.
A History of the Lewis & Clark Journals. U of
Okla Pr.
Cutright, Phillips.
xCutright, Phillips.
Impact of Family Planning Programs on
Fertility: The U. S. Experience. Praeger.
Cutter, Robert A. see Cutter, Robert Arthur.

Cutter, Robert Arthur, 1930-
xCutter, Robert A.
The Model Car Handbook. TAB Bks.
Cutting, Mary S. see Cutting, Mary Stewart (Doubleday).
Cutting, Mary Stewart (Doubleday), 1851-1924
xCutting, Mary S.
Little Stories of Courtship. Arno.
Little Stories of Married Life. Arno.
More Stories of Married Life. Arno.
Refractory Husbands. Arno.
Cuttle, Constance.
xCuttle, Constance.
Completely Cheese. Jonathan David.
Cutts, David R.
xCutts, David R.
That's How It Works. Vantage.
Cutts, Edward L. see Cutts, Edward Lewes.
Cutts, Edward Lewes, 1824-1901
xCutts, Edward L.
Parish Priests & Their People in the Middle
Ages in England. Ams Pr.
Cutul, Ann-Marie.
xCutul, Ann-Marie.
ed. Twentieth-Century European Painting: A
Guide to Information Sources. Gale.
Cuvier, Georges, Baron, 1769-1832
xCuvier, Georges.
Memoirs on Fossil Elephants & on
Reconstruction of the Genera Palaeotherium
& Anoplotherium. Arno.
Cuyler, Lewis. see Cuyler, Lewis C.
Cuyler, Lewis C.
xCuyler, Lewis.
Short Bike Rides in the Berkshires. Globe
Pequot.
Cuyler, Louise. see Cuyler, Louise Elvira.
Cuyler, Louise Elvira, 1908-
xCuyler, Louise.
The Symphony. HarBraceJ.
Cwiklo, William E.
xCwiklo, William E.
Computers in Litigation Support. McGraw.
ed. Computers in Litigation Support. Petrocelli.
Cyca, Robert.
xCyca, Robert.
Exploring Manning Park. Mountaineers.
Cynewulf.
xCynewulf.
Christ of Cynewulf: A Poem in Three Parts,
the Advent, the Ascension, & the Last
Judgment. Arno.
Cyphers, Emma H. see Cyphers, Emma Hodkinson.
Cyphers, Emma Hodkinson.
xCyphers, Emma H.
Fruit & Vegetable Arrangements. Hearthside.
Cyr, Frank W. see Cyr, Frank William.
Cyr, Frank William, 1900-
xCyr, Frank W.
Responsibility for Rural-School Administration:
Allocation of Responsibilities in the
Administration of Schools in Rural Areas.
AMS Pr.
Cyr, Helen.
xCyr, Helen W.
A Filmography of the Third World: An
Annotated List of 16mm Films. Scarecrow.
Cyr, Helen W. see Cyr, Helen.
Czaczkes, J. W.
xCzaczkes, J. W.
Chronic Hemodialysis As a Way of Life.
Brunner-Mazel.
Czaja, Bruce.
xCzaja, Bruce.
How to Take Great Sports Action Photos. TAB
Bks.
Czajka, Peter A.
xCzajka, Peter A.
Poisoning Emergencies: A Guide for
Emergency Medical Personnel. Mosby.
Czamanski, Stan. see Czamanski, Stanislaw.

Czamanski, Stanislaw.
xCzamanski, Stan.
Regional & Interregional Social Accounting.
Lexington Bks.
Czarnecki, Jan.
xCzarnecki, Jan.
Compiled by Soviet Union, 1917-1967: An
Annotated Bibliography of Soviet
Semicentennial Publications in the Collection
of the University of Miami at Coral Gables,
Florida. U of Miami Pr.
Czarnowski, M. S.
xCzarnowski, M. S.
Productive Capacity of Locality As a Function
of Soil & Climate with Particular Reference
to Forest Land. La State U Pr.
Czech, Josef.
xCzech, Josef.
Oscilloscope Measuring Technique: Principles
& Applications of Modern Cathode Ray
Oscilloscopes. Springer-Verlag.
Czempiel, Ernst Otto.
xCzempiel, Ernst-Otto.
ed. The Euro-American System: Economic &
Political Relations Between North America &
Western Europe. Westview.
Czempiel, Ernst-Otto. see Czempiel, Ernst Otto.
Czompo, Ann I.
xCzompo, Ann I.
Recreational Jazz Dance. AC Pubns.
Czudnowski, Moshe M., 1924-
xCzudnowski, Moshe M.
Comparing Political Behavior. Sage.
D'Abernon, Edgar V. see D'Abernon, Edgar Vincent, 1st
Viscount.
D'Agapeyeff, Alexander.
xD'Agapeyeff, Alexander.
Codes & Ciphers. Gale
D'Agostino, Giovanna.
xD'Agostino, Giovanna.
Mama D's Pasta & Pizza. Western Pub.
D'Agostino, Guido, 1910-
xD'Agostino, Guido.
Olives on the Apple Tree. Arno.
D'Alessandro, Robert.
xD'Alessandro, Robert.
Glory. Morgan.
D'Alton, Martina.
xD'Alton, Martina.
The Runner's Guide to the U. S. A. Summit
Bks.
D'Amato, Jane. see D'Amato, Janet.
D'Amato, Janet.
xD'Amato, Jane.
Algonquian & Iroquois Crafts for You to Make.
Messner.
xD'Amato, Janet.
jt. auth. African Animals Through African
Eyes. Messner.
jt. auth. African Crafts for You to Make.
Messner.
Colonial Crafts for You to Make. Messner.
jt. auth. Indian Crafts. Lion.
jt. auth. More Colonial Crafts for You to
Make. Messner.
D'Amato, M. R., 1922-
xD'Amato, M. R.
Experimental Psychology: Methodology,
Psychophysics & Learning. McGraw.
D'Ambrosio, Charles. see D'Ambrosio, Charles A.
D'Ambrosio, Charles A.
xD'Ambrosio, Charles.
Guide to Successful Investing. P-H.
xD'Ambrosio, Charles A.
Principles of Modern Investments. SRA.
D'Ambrosio, Richard. see D'Ambrosio, Richard
Anthony.
D'Ambrosio, Richard Anthony.
xD'Ambrosio, Richard.

Leonora. McGraw.

D'Ambrosio, Vinnie-Marie.
xD'Ambrosio, Vinnie-Marie.
Life of Touching Mouths. NYU Pr.

D'Amelio, Joseph.
xD'Amelio, Joseph.
Perspective Drawing Handbook. L Amiel Pub.

D'Angelo, Edward, 1932-
xD'Angelo, Edward.
The Teaching of Critical Thinking. Humanities.

D'Angelo, F. *see* D'Angelo, Frank J.
D'Angelo, Frank H. *see* D'Angelo, Frank J.

D'Angelo, Frank J.
xD'Angelo, F.
Process & Thought in Composition. Winthrop.
xD'Angelo, Frank H.
Process & Thought in Composition. P-H.
xD'Angelo, Frank J.
Process & Thought in Composition. Winthrop.

D'Antonio, William V.
xD'Antonio, William V.
Influentials in Two Border Cities: A Study in Community Decision-Making. U of Notre Dame Pr.

D'Aprix, Roger M.
xD'Aprix, Roger M.
In Search of a Corporate Soul. Am Mgmt.

D'Arbeloff, Natalie.
xD'Arbeloff, Natalie.
Designing with Natural Forms. Watson-Guptill.

D'Arcangelo. *see* D'Arcangelo, Bartholomew.

D'Arcangelo, Bartholomew.
xD'Arcangelo.
Mathematics for Plumbers & Pipefitters. Delmar.

D'Arcy, Ella.
xD'Arcy, Ella.
Monochromes. Garland Pub.

D'Arcy, Martin C.
xD'Arcy, Martin C.
Revelation & Love's Architecture. Charles River Bks.

D'Arcy, Martin C. *see* D'Arcy, Martin Cyril.

D'Arcy, Martin Cyril.
xD'Arcy, Martin C.
The Meeting of Love & Knowledge: Perennial Wisdom. Greenwood.
The Nature of Belief. Arno.
xD'Arcy, Martin S.
The Nature of Belief. Greenwood.

D'Arcy, Martin Cyrill, 1888-
xD'Arcy, Martin C.
Communism & Christianity. Devin.

D'Arcy, Martin S. *see* D'Arcy, Martin Cyril.

D'Arcy, Paula, 1947-
xD'Arcy, Paula.
Song for Sarah: A Young Mother's Journey Through Grief, & Beyond. Shaw Pubs.

D'Atri, J. E.
xD'Atri, J. E.
Naturally Reductive Metrics & Einstein Metrics on Compact Lie Groups. Am Math.

D'Augustine, Charles H.
xD'Augustine, Charles H.
Multiple Methods of Teaching Mathematics in the Elementary School. Har-Row.

D'Aulaire, Emily.
xD'Aulaire, Emily.
Chimps & Baboons. Natl Wildlife.

D'Aulaire, Ingri.
xD'Aulaire, Ingri.
jt. auth. D'Aulaires' Trolls. Doubleday.

D'Azzo, John J. *see* D'Azzo, John Joachim.

D'Azzo, John Joachim.
xD'Azzo, John J.
Feedback Control System Analysis & Synthesis. McGraw.

D'Cruz, J. V.
xD'Cruz, J. V.

ed. The Renewal of Australian Schools: A Changing Perspective in Educational Planning. Verry.

D'Ermo, Dominique, 1927-
xD'Ermo, Dominique.
The Chef's Dessert Cookbook. Atheneum.

D'Estout, Henri G. *see* D'Estout, Henri Georges.

D'Estout, Henri Georges, 1907-
xD'Estout, Henri G.
Aircraft Weight & Balance Control. Aero.

D'Imperio, Dan.
xD'Imperio, Dan.
The Country Antiques Companion. Dodd.

D'Orsay, Laurence R.
xD'Orsay, Laurence R.
Stories You Can Sell. Arno.

D'Souza, Austin A. *see* D'Souza, Austin Anthony.

D'Souza, Austin Anthony.
xD'Souza, Austin A.
Anglo-Indian Education: A Study of Its Origins & Growth in Bengal up to 1960. Oxford U Pr.

D'Urso, S.
xD'Urso, S.
ed. Changes, Issues & Prospects in Australian Education. U of Queensland Pr.

Da Cruz, Daniel, 1921-
xDa Cruz, Daniel.
The Captive City. Ballantine.

Da Silva, Zenia S. *see* Da Silva, Zenia Sacks.

Da Silva, Zenia Sacks.
xDa Silva, Zenia S.
Spanish: A Short Course. Har-Row.

Daaku, K. Yeboa. *see* Daaku, Kwame Yeboa.

Daaku, Kwame Yeboa.
xDaaku, K. Yeboa.
Osei Tutu & the Asante. Heinemann Ed.

Daane, James.
xDaane, James.
Preaching with Confidence: A Theological Essay on the Power of the Pulpit. Eerdmans.

Dabbs, Jack A. *see* Dabbs, Jack Autrey.

Dabbs, Jack Autrey.
xDabbs, Jack A.
The French Army in Mexico, 1861-67: A Study in Military Government. Mouton.
Word Frequency in Newspaper Bengali. Tex A & M Lang.

Dabbs, James M. *see* Dabbs, James Mcbride.

Dabbs, James Mcbride, 1896-1970
xDabbs, James M.
The Southern Heritage. Greenwood.

D'Abernon, Edgar Vincent, 1st Viscount, 1857-1941
xD'Abernon, Edgar V.
The Eighteenth Decisive Battle of the World: Warsaw, 1920. Hyperion-Conn.

Dabney, Lancaster E. *see* Dabney, Lancaster Eugene.

Dabney, Lancaster Eugene, 1898-
xDabney, Lancaster E.
Claude Billard, Minor French Dramatist of the Early Seventeenth Century. Johnson Repr.

Dabney, Lewis M.
xDabney, Lewis M.
The Indians of Yoknapatawpha: A Study in Literature & History. La State U Pr.

Dabney, Robert L. *see* Dabney, Robert Lewis.

Dabney, Robert Lewis, 1820-1898
xDabney, Robert L.
Lectures in Systematic Theology. Zondervan.

Dabney, Virginius, 1901-
xDabney, Virginius.
Dry Messiah: The Life of Bishop Cannon. Greenwood.
Liberalism in the South. AMS Pr.
Richmond: The Story of a City. U Pr of Va.

Dabrowski, Roman, fl. 1948-
xDabrowski, Roman.
Mussolini, Twilight & Fall. Hyperion Conn.

Dace, Wallace, 1920-
xDace, Wallace.

A Proposal for a National Theater. Rosen Pr.

Dacey. *see* Dacey, Norman F.
Dacey, John. *see* Dacey, John S.

Dacey, John S.
xDacey, John.
Adolescents Today. Goodyear.

Dacey, Michael F., 1932-
xDacey, Michael F.
One-Dimensional Central Place Theory. Northwestern U Pr.

Dacey, Norman F.
xDacey.
What's Wrong with Your Life Insurance. Macmillan.
xDacey, Norman F.
How to Avoid Probate. Crown.
How to Avoid Probate Updated. Crown.
What's Wrong with Your Life Insurance. Macmillan.

Dacie, J. V. *see* Dacie, John Vivian.

Dacie, John Vivian.
xDacie, J. V.
Practical Haematology. Churchill.

DaCosta, Frank.
xDaCosta, Frank.
How to Build Your Own Working Robot Pet. TAB Bks.

Dacque, Edgar, 1878-1945
xDacque, Edgar.
Vergleichende Biologische Formenkunde der Fossilen Niederen Tiere: Biological Comparative Morphology of Lower Fossil Animals. Arno.

Dacre, Charlotte, b. 1782
xDacre, Charlotte.
The Libertine. Arno.
The Passions. Arno.

Dadant , C. P. *see* Dadant, Camille Pierre.
Dadant, C. P. *see* Dadant, Camille Pierre.

Dadant, Camille Pierre.
xDadant , C. P.
ed. First Lessons in Beekeeping. Dadant & Sons.
xDadant, C. P.
First Lessons in Beekeeping. Scribner.

Daddow, Viv. *see* Daddow, Vivian.

Daddow, Vivian.
xDaddow, Viv.
The Puffing Pioneers & Queensland's Railway Builders. U of Queensland Pr.

Dadi, M. M.
xDadi, M. M.
Income Share of Factory Labour in India. Intl Pubns Serv.

Daehlin, Reidar A.
xDaehlin, Reidar A.
The Family of the Forgiven. Concordia.

Daellenbach, Hans G.
xDaellenbach, Hans G.
Introduction to Operations Research Techniques. Allyn.

Daemmrich, Horst S.
xDaemmrich, Horst S.
ed. The Challenge of German Literature. Wayne St U Pr.

Daffner. *see* Daffner, Richard H.

Daffner, Richard H.
xDaffner.
Case Studies in Radiology. ACC.

Dafoe, John W. *see* Dafoe, John Wesley.

Dafoe, John Wesley, 1866-1944
xDafoe, John W.
Clifford Sifton in Relation to His Times. Arno.

Daganzo, Carlos. *see* Daganzo, Carlos F.

Daganzo, Carlos F.
xDaganzo, Carlos.
Multinomial Probit: The Theory & Its Application to Demand Forecasting. Acad Pr.

Daggett, Stuart, 1881-
xDaggett, Stuart.

Chapters on the History of the Southern
    Pacific. Kelley.
Principles of Inland Transportation.
    Greenwood.
Railroad Reorganization. Johnson Repr.
Railroad Reorganization. Kelley.
Daglish. see Daglish, Eric Fitch.
Daglish, E. Fitch. see Daglish, Eric Fitch.
Daglish, Eric Fitch.
    xDaglish.
        Dog Breeding. Arco.
    xDaglish, E. Fitch.
        Dog Breeding. Palmetto Pub.
Dagostino, Frank R.
    xDagostino, Frank R.
        Estimating in Building Construction. Reston.
Dahl, Borghild. see Dahl, Borghild Margarethe.
Dahl, Borghild Margarethe.
    xDahl, Borghild.
        Good News. Dutton.
        I Wanted to See. Macmillan.
        Under This Roof. Dutton.
Dahl, Dale C.
    xDahl, Dale C.
        Market & Price Analysis: The Agricultural
            Industries. McGraw.
Dahl, Georg, 1905-
    xDahl, George.
        Two Children's Stories for Physicians & Other
            Wise Men. U of Minn Bell.
Dahl, George. see Dahl, Georg.
Dahl, Gerald L.
    xDahl, Gerald L.
        Why Christian Marriages Are Breaking up.
            Nelson.
Dahl, Gordon.
    xDahl, Gordon.
        Work, Play, & Worship in a Leisure-Oriented
            Society. Augsburg.
Dahl, Mogen. see Dahl, Mogens H.
Dahl, Mogens H.
    xDahl, Mogen.
        Garden Pests & Diseases of Flowers & Shrubs.
            Macmillan.
Dahl, Norman.
    xDahl, Norman.
        Build & Sail Your Own Boat. Merrimack Bk
            Serv.
Dahl, Norman C.
    xDahl, Norman C.
        ed. World Change & World Security. MIT Pr.
Dahl, Paul. see Dahl, Poul.
Dahl, Poul.
    xDahl, Paul.
        Introduction to Electron & Ion Optics. Acad
            Pr.
Dahl, Richard C.
    xDahl, Richard C.
        Effective Speaking for Lawyers. W S Hein.
Dahl, Roald.
    xDahl, Roald.
        Charlie & the Chocolate Factory. Knopf.
        Charlie & the Chocolate Factory. Bantam.
        Charlie & the Chocolate Factory. Knopf.
        Charlie & the Great Glass Elevator: The
            Further Adventures of Charlie Bucket &
            Willie Wonka, the Chocolate-Maker
            Extraordinaire. Knopf.
        Danny the Champion of the World. Bantam.
        The Enormous Crocodile. Knopf.
        My Uncle Oswald. Knopf.
        Someone Like You. Knopf.
        Switch Bitch. Knopf.
        Switch Bitch. Warner Bks.
    xDahl, Ronald.
        Fantastic Mr. Fox. Bantam.
Dahl, Robert A. see Dahl, Robert Alan.
Dahl, Robert Alan, 1915-
    xDahl, Robert A.

After the Revolution: Authority in a Good
    Society. Yale U Pr.
Preface to Democratic Theory. U of Chicago
    Pr.
ed. Regimes & Oppositions. Yale U Pr.
Who Governs: Democracy & Power in an
    American City. Yale U Pr.
Dahl, Ronald. see Dahl, Roald.
Dahl, Svend, 1887-1963
    xDahl, Svend.
        History of the Book. Scarecrow.
Dahlberg, Charles C. see Dahlberg, Charles Clay.
Dahlberg, Charles Clay.
    xDahlberg, Charles C.
        Stroke: A Doctor's Personal Story of His
            Recovery. Norton.
Dahlberg, Edward, 1900-
    xDahlberg, Edward.
        Bottom Dogs. AMS Pr.
        Confessions of Edward Dahlberg. Braziller.
        Edward Dahlberg Reader. New Directions.
        The Flea of Sodom. Haskell.
        Leafless American. Beacham.
        Those Who Perish. AMS Pr.
Dahlberg, Edwin T. see Dahlberg, Edwin Theodore.
Dahlberg, Edwin Theodore, 1892-
    xDahlberg, Edwin T.
        I Pick up Hitchhikers. Judson.
Dahlberg, Kenneth A.
    xDahlberg, Kenneth A.
        ed. Beyond the Green Revolution: The Ecology
            & Politics of Global Agricultural
            Development. Plenum Pub.
Dahlberg, Michael. see Dahlberg, Michael D.
Dahlberg, Michael D., 1940-
    xDahlberg, Michael.
        Guide to Coastal Fishes of Georgia & Nearby
            States. U of Ga Pr.
Dahle, John.
    xDahle, John.
        ed. Library of Christian Hymns. AMS Pr.
Dahlem, Glenn G.
    xDahlem, Glenn G.
        Effective Pupil Personnel Services. Ctr Appl
            Res.
**Dahlem Workshop on Neoplastic Transformation
    Mechanisms and Consequences, Berlin, Germany,
    1977.**
    xDahlem Workshop on Neoplastic Transformation.
        Neoplastic Transformation: Mechanisms &
            Consequences, Report. Dahlem.
Dahlen, Beverly.
    xDahlen, Beverly.
        Out of the Third. Momos.
Dahlhaus, Carl, 1928-
    xDahlhaus, Carl.
        Richard Wagner's Music Dramas. Cambridge
            U Pr.
Dahlin, David C.
    xDahlin, David C.
        Bone Tumors: General Aspects & Data on
            6,221 Cases. C C Thomas.
Dahlke, Paul, 1865-1928
    xDahlke, Paul.
        Buddhist Stories. Arno.
Dahlman, O. see Dahlman, Ola.
Dahlman, Ola.
    xDahlman, O.
        Monitoring Underground Nuclear Explosions.
            Elsevier.
Dahlstedt, Marden.
    xDahlstedt, Marden.
        The Stopping Place. Schol Bk Serv.
Dahlstrom, Carl E. see Dahlstrom, Carl Enoch William
    Leonard.
Dahlstrom, Carl Enoch William Leonard.
    xDahlstrom, Carl E.
        Strindberg's Dramatic Expressionism. Arno.
Dahlstrom, J. see Dahlstrom, Jo Ann Wolf.

Dahlstrom, Jo Ann Wolf.
    xDahlstrom, J.
        Promises to Keep: Reading & Writing About
            Values. P-H.
Dahlstrom, W. Grant. see Dahlstrom, William Grant.
Dahlstrom, William Grant.
    xDahlstrom, W. Grant.
        ed. Basic Readings on the MMPI: A New
            Selection on Personality Measurement. U of
            Minn Pr.
Dahm, Bernhard.
    xDahm, Bernhard.
        Sukarno & the Struggle for Indonesian
            Independence. Cornell U Pr.
Dahm, Thomas E. Van. see Van Dahm, Thomas E.
Dahms, Alan M.
    xDahms, Alan M.
        Thriving: Beyond Adjustment. Brooks-Cole.
Dahmus, Joseph H. see Dahmus, Joseph Henry.
Dahmus, Joseph Henry, 1909-
    xDahmus, Joseph H.
        Prosecution of John Wyclyf. Shoe String.
Dahrendorf, Ralf.
    xDahrendorf, Ralf.
        Class & Class Conflict in Industrial Society.
            Stanford U Pr.
        Life Chances: Approaches to Social & Political
            Theory. U of Chicago Pr.
        Society & Democracy in Germany.
            Greenwood.
        Society & Democracy in Germany. Norton.
Dai, Bingham, 1899-
    xDai, Bingham.
        Opium Addiction in Chicago. Patterson Smith.
Daiches. see Daiches, David.
Daiches, D. see Daiches, David.
Daiches, David, 1912-
    xDaiches.
        Critical Approaches to Literature. Longman.
    xDaiches, D.
        A Critical History of English Literature. Wiley.
    xDaiches, David.
        D. H. Lawrence. Folcroft.
        D. H. Lawrence. R West.
        ed. Idea of a New University: An Experiment
            in Sussex. MIT Pr.
        Literary Essays. U of Chicago Pr.
        Literary Landscapes of the British Isles: A
            Narrative Atlas. Paddington.
        Literature & Society. Haskell.
        Literature & Society. Somerset Pub.
        More Literary Essays. U of Chicago Pr.
        The Place of Meaning in Poetry. Arden Lib.
        The Place of Meaning in Poetry. Folcroft.
        Stevenson & the Art of Fiction. Darby Bks.
        Stevenson & the Art of Fiction. Folcroft.
        Two Studies. Folcroft.
        Two Studies. R West.
        Virginia Woolf. Greenwood.
Daigh, Ralph.
    xDaigh, Ralph.
        Maybe You Should Write a Book. P-H.
Daigon, Arthur.
    xDaigon, Arthur.
        Put It in Writing. HarBraceJ.
Daiker, Donald A.
    xDaiker, Donald A.
        The Writer's Options: College Sentence
            Combining. Har-Row.
Dailey, Janet.
    xDailey, Janet.
        Touch the Wind. PB.
Daily, Benjamin W. see Daily, Benjamin William.
Daily, Benjamin William, 1883-
    xDaily, Benjamin W.
        Ability of High School Pupils to Select
            Essential Data in Solving Problems. AMS Pr.
Daily, Jay E. see Daily, Jay Elwood.
Daily, Jay Elwood.
    xDaily, Jay E.

The Anatomy of Censorship. Dekker.

Daim, Wilfried.
xDaim, Wilfried.
Christianity, Judaism, & Revolution. Ungar.
Vatican & Eastern Europe. Ungar.

Daines, David R. see Daines, David Rainey.

Daines, David Rainey.
xDaines, David R.
Legislacion de Aguas en los Paises del Grupo
Andino. Utah St U Pr.

Daintith, John.
xDaintith, John.
A Dictionary of Physical Sciences. Universe.

Dair, Carl.
xDair, Carl.
Design with Type. U of Toronto Pr.

Daitch, Paul B.
xDaitch, Paul B.
Introduction to College Engineering. A-W.

Daitzman, Reid J.
xDaitzman, Reid J.
Mental Jogging. Marek.

Dake, Charles R. see Dake, Charles Romyn.

Dake, Charles Romyn.
xDake, Charles R.
A Strange Discovery. Gregg.

Dake, L. P.
xDake, L. P.
Fundamentals of Reservoir Engineering.
Elsevier.

Dakin, Douglas.
xDakin, Douglas.
The Greek Struggle for Independence,
1821-1833. U of Cal Pr.
Turgot & the Ancien Regime in France.
Octagon.

Dakin, H. S.
xDakin, H. S.
High-Voltage Photography. H S Dakin.

Dal Fabbro, Mario, 1913-
xDal Fabbro, Mario.
How to Build Modern Furniture. McGraw.
How to Make Children's Furniture & Play
Equipment. McGraw.

Dalaba, Oliver V.
xDalaba, Oliver V.
That None Be Lost. Gospel Pub.

Dalal, Minakshi L., 1925-
xDalal, Minakshi L.
Conflict in Sanskrit Drama. Intl Pubns Serv.

Dalbiez, Roland.
xDalbiez, Roland.
Psychoanalytical Method & the Doctrine of
Freud. Arno.

Dalby, Michael T.
xDalby, Michael T.
Bureaucracy in Historical Perspective. Scott F.

Dalcho, Frederick, 1770?-1836
xDalcho, Frederick.
An Historical Account of the Protestant
Episcopal Church, in South Carolina, from
the First Settlement of the Province, to the
War of the Revolution. Arno.

Dale, Arbie.
xDale, Arbie M.
Change Your Job, Change Your Life. Playboy
Pbks.
Change Your Job, Change Your Life. Wideview
Bks.
Twenty Minutes a Day to a More Powerful
Intelligence. Playboy Pbks.

Dale, Arbie M. see Dale, Arbie.

Dale, Celia.
xDale, Celia.
Act of Love. Belmont-Tower.
The Deception. Har-Row.

Dale, D. C. see Dale, Dion Murray Crosbie.

Dale, Delbert A.
xDale, Delbert A.
Trumpet Technique. Oxford U Pr.

Dale, Dion Murray Crosbie.
xDale, D. C.
Applied Audiology for Children. C C Thomas.

Dale, Duane.
xDale, Duane.
Beyond Experts: A Guide for Citizen Group
Training. Citizen Involve.
Planning, for a Change: A Citizen's Guide to
Creative Planning & Program Development.
Citizen Involve.
xDale, Duane D.
How to Make Citizen Involvement Work:
Strategies for Developing Clout. Citizen
Involve.

Dale, Duane D. see Dale, Duane.

Dale, Edgar, 1900-
xDale, Edgar.
Building a Learning Environment. Phi Delta
Kappa.
Content of Motion Pictures. Arno.
The Good Mind. Phi Delta Kappa.
How to Appreciate Motion Pictures. Arno.
The Humane Leader. Phi Delta Kappa.
The Word Game: Improving Communications.
Phi Delta Kappa.

Dale, Edward E. see Dale, Edward Everett.

Dale, Edward Everett, 1879-
xDale, Edward E.
Cow Country. U of Okla Pr.
Cross Timbers: Memories of a North Texas
Boyhood. U of Tex Pr.

Dale, Ernest, 1917-
xDale, Ernest.
Readings in Management: Landmarks & New
Frontiers. McGraw.

Dale, Johannes, 1923-
xDale, Johannes.
Stereochemistry & Conformational Analysis.
Verlag Chemie.

Dale, Kathleen.
xDale, Kathleen.
Brahms: A Biography, with a Survey of Books,
Editions & Recordings. Shoe String.

Dale, Robert D.

xDale, Robert D.
Making Good Marriages Better. Broadman.

Dale Yarn Co. see Dale Yarn Company.

Dale Yarn Company.
xDale Yarn Co.
Knit Your Own Norwegian Sweaters. Dover.
Knit Your Own Norwegian Sweaters: Complete
Instructions for 50 Authentic Sweaters, Hats,
Mittens, Gloves, Caps, Etc.. Peter Smith.

Dalen, James E., 1932-
xDalen, James E.
Pulmonary Embolism. Krieger.

Dales, Richard C.
xDales, Richard C.
The Intellectual Life of Western Europe in the
Middle Ages. U Pr of Amer.

Daley, Brian.
xDaley, Brian.
The Doomfarers of Coramonde. Ballantine.
Han Solo's Revenge. Ballantine.

Daley, Eliot A.
xDaley, Eliot A.

Father Feelings. Morrow.
Father Feelings. PB.

Daley, Henry O.
xDaley, Henry O.
Problems in Chemistry. Dekker.

Daley, Maxime. see Daley, Maxine.

Daley, Maxine.
xDaley, Maxime.
How to Get a Man After You're Forty.
Har-Row.

Daley, Robert.
xDaley, Robert.
The Fast One. Ballantine.
Prince of the City: The True Story of the Cop
Who Knew Too Much. HM.

Dalgado, D. G. see Dalgado, Daniel Gelanio.

Dalgado, Daniel Gelanio.
xDalgado, D. G.
Lord Byron's Childe Harold's Pilgrimage to
Portugal. Folcroft.

Dalgliesh, Alice, 1893-
xDalgliesh, Alice.
Courage of Sarah Noble. Scribner.
The Fourth of July Story. Scribner.
Little Wooden Farmer. Macmillan.
Little Wooden Farmer. Macmillan.
Thanksgiving Story. Scribner.

Dalglish, Doris N.
xDalglish, Doris N.
People Called Quakers. Arno.

Dali, Salvador, 1904-
xDali, Salvador.
Open Letter to Salvador Dali. Heineman.

Dalinka, M. K. see Dalinka, Murray K.

Dalinka, Murray K.
xDalinka, M. K.
Arthrography. Springer-Verlag.

Dalis, G. see Dalis, Gus T.

Dalis, Gus T.
xDalis, G.
Teaching Strategies for Values Awareness &
Decision-Making in Health Education. C B
Slack.

Dallas, Richard J.
xDallas, Richard J.
Clerical & Secretarial Systems for the Office.
P-H.

Dallas, Sandra.
xDallas, Sandra.
Cherry Creek Gothic: Victorian Architecture in
Denver. U of Okla Pr.
No More Than Five in a Bed: Colorado Hotels
in the Old Days. U of Okla Pr.
Vail. Pruett.

Dallek, Robert.
xDallek, Robert.
Franklin D. Roosevelt & American Foreign
Policy: 1932-1945. Oxford U Pr.

Dallenbach-Hellweg, G. see Dallenbach-Hellweg, Gisela.

Dallenbach-Hellweg, Gisela.
xDallenbach-Hellweg, G.
ed. Functional Morphologic Changes in Female
Sex Organs Induced by Exogenous
Hormones. Springer-Verlag.
Histopathology of the Endometrium.
Springer-Verlag.

Dallin, Alexander.
xDallin, Alexander.
ed. Diversity in International Communism: A
Documentary Record. Columbia U Pr.
Political Terror in Communist Systems.
Stanford U Pr.
The Soviet Union at the United Nations: An
Inquiry into Soviet Motives & Objectives.
Greenwood.
ed. The Twenty-Fifth Congress of the CPSU:
Assessment & Context. Hoover Inst Pr.

Dallin, David J.
xDallin, David J.

Forced Labor in Soviet Russia. Octagon.
Soviet Foreign Policy After Stalin. Greenwood.
Soviet Russia & the Far East. Shoe String.

Dallin, Leon.
xDallin, Leon.
Foundations in Music Theory. Wadsworth Pub.
Listeners Guide to Musical Understanding.
Wm C Brown.

Dallman, John C.
xDallman, John C.
Investigation of Separated Flow Model in
Annular Gas-Liquid Two-Phase Flows.
Garland Pub.

Dallmayr, Fred R.
xDallmayr, Fred R.
ed. Understanding & Social Inquiry. U of
Notre Dame Pr.

Dallos, Peter.
xDallos, Peter.
The Auditory Periphery: Biophysics &
Physiology. Acad Pr.

Dally, James W.
xDally, James W.
Experimental Stress Analysis. McGraw.

Dalmais, Anne Marie.
xDalmais, Anne-Marie.
The Adventures of Little Rabbit. Western Pub.
Dalmais, Anne-Marie. see Dalmais, Anne Marie.
Dalrymple, Bryon. see Dalrymple, Byron W.
Dalrymple, Byron. see Dalrymple, Byron W.

Dalrymple, Byron W.
xDalrymple, Bryon.
How to Call Wildlife. T Y Crowell.
xDalrymple, Byron.
The Complete Book of Deer Hunting. Follett.
Fishing for Fun. G K Hall.
Fishing for Fun. Winchester Pr.
North American Game Animals. Crown.
Survival in the Outdoors. Dutton.
xDalrymple, Byron W.
Complete Book of Deer Hunting. Winchester
Pr.
How to Rig & Fish Natural Baits. T Y Crowell.

Dalrymple, Glenn V.
xDalrymple, Glenn V.
ed. Radiology in Primary Care. Mosby.

Dalsgaard, Per.
xDalsgaard, Per.
Bright Ideas for Your Home. Har-Row.
Dalton, A. J. see Dalton, Albert Joseph.
Dalton, Albert J. see Dalton, Albert Joseph.

Dalton, Albert Joseph.
xDalton, A. J.
Ultrastructure of the Kidney. Acad Pr.
xDalton, Albert J.
ed. Membranes. Acad Pr.
Ultrastructure of Animal Viruses &
Bacteriophages: An Atlas. Acad Pr.

Dalton, David.
xDalton, David.
ed. Rolling Stones. Music Sales.

Dalton, Gene W.
xDalton, Gene W.
The Distribution of Authority in Formal
Organizations. MIT Pr.
ed. Organizational Change & Development.
Irwin.
ed. Organizational Structure & Design. Irwin.

Dalton, Hugh, 1887-
xDalton, Hugh.
Principles of Public Finance. Kelley.
Dalton, John. see Dalton, John W.

Dalton, John W., 1942-
xDalton, John.
The Professional Cosmetologist. West Pub.
Dalton, K. C. see Dalton, Kenneth Godfrey.

Dalton, Katharina, 1916-
xDalton, Katharina.

Once a Month. Hunter Hse.

Dalton, Kenneth Godfrey.
xDalton, K. C.
Geography of Sierra Leone. Cambridge U Pr.
Dalton, R. see Dalton, Richard.

Dalton, Richard.
xDalton, R.
The Provincial Token-Coinage of the 18th
Century. Quarterman.

Dalven, Rae.
xDalven, Rae.
tr. & ed. Modern Greek Poetry. Russell.

Dalven, Richard.
xDalven, Richard.
Introduction to Applied Solid State Physics:
Topics on the Applications of
Semiconductors, Superconductors, & the
Nonlinear Optical Properties of Solids.
Plenum Pub.

Daly, Bruce.
xDaly, Bruce.
The Psychological Theory of the Voluptuous
Woman. Gloucester Art.
Daly, Carroll J. see Daly, Carroll John.

Daly, Carroll John, 1889-1958
xDaly, Carroll J.
Murder from the East: A Race Williams Story.
Intl Polygonics.
Daly, Charles P. see Daly, Charles Patrick.

Daly, Charles Patrick, 1816-1899
xDaly, Charles P.
First Theater in America: When Was the
Drama First Introduced in America?. B
Franklin.

Daly, D. J.
xDaly, D. J.
Tariff & Science Policies: Applications of a
Model of Nationalism. U of Toronto Pr

Daly, Donald F.
xDaly, Donald F.
Aim for a Job in Air Conditioning &
Refrigeration. Arco.
Aim for a Job in Air Conditioning &
Refrigeration. Rosen Pr.
Aim for a Job in the Building Trades. Rosen
Pr.

Daly, Dorothy.
xDaly, Dorothy.
Italy. Rand.

Daly, Herman E.
xDaly, Herman E.
Economics, Ecology, Ethics: Essays Toward a
Steady-State Economy. W H Freeman.
Steady-State Economics: The Economics of
Biophysical Equilibrium & Moral Growth. W
H Freeman.
Toward a Steady-State Economy. W H
Freeman.

Daly, Howell V.
xDaly, Howell V.
An Introduction to Insect Biology & Diversity.
McGraw.

Daly, James, 1932-
xDaly, James.
Cosmic Harmony & Political Thinking in Early
Stuart England. Am Philos.
Sir Robert Filmer & English Political Thought.
U of Toronto Pr.
Daly, James J. see Daly, James Jeremiah.

Daly, James Jeremiah, 1872-
xDaly, James J.
Cheerful Ascetic, & Other Essays. Arno.

Daly, Jay.
xDaly, Jay.
Walls. Har-Row.

Daly, Kathleen N.
xDaly, Kathleen N.

A Child's Book of Animals. Doubleday.
A Child's Book of Flowers. Doubleday.

Daly, Marsha.
xDaly, Marsha.
Peter Frampton. G&D.

Daly, Maurice.
xDaly, Maurice.
Daly's Billiard Book. Peter Smith.
Daly, Muriel D. see Daly, Muriel De B.

Daly, Muriel De B.
xDaly, Muriel D.
Ants' Nest. Arno.
Daly, Peter M. see Daly, Peter Maurice.

Daly, Peter Maurice.
xDaly, Peter M.
Literature in the Light of the Emblem:
Structural Parallels Between the Emblem &
Literature in the Sixteenth & Seventeenth
Centuries. U of Toronto Pr.
Daly, Reginald A. see Daly, Reginald Aldworth.

Daly, Reginald Aldworth, 1871-1957
xDaly, Reginald A.
Igneous Rocks & the Depths of the Earth.
Hafner.
Strength & Structure of the Earth. Hafner.
Daly, Richard T. see Daly, Richard Timon.

Daly, Richard Timon.
xDaly, Richard T.
Applications of the Mathematical Theory of
Linguistics. Mouton.

Daly, Robert.
xDaly, Robert.
God's Altar: The World & the Flesh in Puritan
Poetry. U of Cal Pr.

Daly, Robert J., 1933-
xDaly, Robert J.
Christian Sacrifice: The Judaeo-Christian
Background Before Origen. Intl Schol Bk
Serv.
The Origins of the Christian Doctrine of
Sacrifice. Fortress.
Daly, T. A. see Daly, Thomas Augustine.

Daly, Thomas Augustine, 1871-1948
xDaly, T. A.
ed. Little Book of American Humorous Verse.
Arno.
ed. A Little Book of American Humorous
Verse. Granger Bk.

Daly, Victor.
xDaly, Victor.
Not Only War: A Story of Two Great
Conflicts. AMS Pr.
Dalyell, John G. see Dalyell, John Graham.

Dalyell, John Graham, Sir, Bart, 1775-1851
xDalyell, John G.
The Darker Superstitions of Scotland. Folcroft.
The Darker Superstitions of Scotland. R West.
Musical Memoirs of Scotland, with Historical
Annotations. Folcroft.
Musical Memoirs of Scotland with Historical
Annotations. Norwood Edns.
Dalzell, J. Ralph. see Dalzell, James Ralph.

Dalzell, James Ralph, 1900-
xDalzell, J. Ralph.
Repairing & Remodeling Guide for Home
Interiors: Planning, Materials, Methods.
McGraw.

Dalzell, Robert F.
xDalzell, Robert F.
Daniel Webster & the Trial of American
Nationalism, 1843-1852. Norton.

Dam, Kenneth W.
xDam, Kenneth W.
Oil Resources: Who Gets What How?. U of
Chicago Pr.
Damachi, U. G. see Damachi, Ukandi Godwin.
Damachi, Ukandi G. see Damachi, Ukandi Godwin.

Damachi, Ukandi Godwin.
xDamachi, U. G.

ed. Industrial Relations in Africa. St Martin.
xDamachi, Ukandi G.
   Development Paths in Africa & China.
      Westview.
   Human Resources & African Development.
      Praeger.
   Leadership Ideology in Africa: Attitudes
      Toward Socioeconomic Development.
      Praeger.
Damane, M.
xDamane, M.
   jt. ed. & ed. Lithoko: Sotho Praise Poems.
      Oxford U Pr.
Damaskin, Boris B. *see* Damaskin, Boris Borisovich.
Damaskin, Boris Borisovich.
xDamaskin, Boris B.
   Adsorption of Organic Compounds on
      Electrodes. Plenum Pub.
Damer, Eyre, 1854-
xDamer, Eyre.
   When the Ku Klux Rode. Arno.
   When the Ku Klux Rode. Negro U Pr.
Damer, T. Edward.
xDamer, T. Edward.
   Attacking Faulty Reasoning. Wadsworth Pub.
Damerst, William A.
xDamerst, William A.
   Clear Technical Reports. HarBraceJ.
Dames, Michael.
xDames, Michael.
   The Avebury Cycle. Thames Hudson.
   The Silbury Treasure: The Great Goddess
      Rediscovered. Thames Hudson.
Damiani, Bruno M. *see* Damiani, Bruno Mario.
Damiani, Bruno Mario.
xDamiani, Bruno M.
   Francisco Lopez De Ubeda. Twayne.
Damico, Alfonso J., 1942-
xDamico, Alfonso J.
   Democracy & the Case for Amnesty. U Presses
      Fla.
Damjan, Mischa.
xDamjan, Mischa.
   The False Flamingoes. Scroll Pr.
   Little Green Man. Schol Bk Serv.
Damjanov, Ivan.
xDamjanov, Ivan.
   General Pathology. Med Exam.
Damm, Helene Van. *see* Von Damm, Helene.
Damm, Helene Von. *see* Von Damm, Helene.
Damon, Albert, 1918-1973
xDamon, Albert.
   Human Biology & Ecology. Norton.
Damon, S. Foster. *see* Damon, Samuel Foster.
Damon, Samuel Foster.
xDamon, S. Foster.
   A Note on the Discovery of a New Page of
      Poetry in William Blake's Milton. Folcroft.
Damon, William, 1944-
xDamon, William.
   The Social World of the Child. Jossey-Bass.
Damore, Leo.
xDamore, Leo.
   The Crime of Dorothy Sheridan. Arbor Hse.
Damrosch, Leopold.
xDamrosch, Leopold.
   The Uses of Johnson's Criticism. U Pr of Va.
Dan, Uri.
xDan, Urid.
   Carlos Must Die. Nordon Pubns.
Dan, Urid. *see* Dan, Uri.
Dana, Barbara.
xDana, Barbara.
   Crazy Eights. Har-Row.
Dana, Charles A. *see* Dana, Charles Anderson.
Dana, Charles Anderson, 1819-1897
xDana, Charles A.
   Art of Newspaper Making. Arno.
   ed. Household Book of Poetry. Arno.
Dana, H. W. *see* Dana, Henry Wadsworth Longfellow.

Dana, Henry Wadsworth Longfellow, 1881-1950
xDana, H. W.
   Intro. by Seven Soviet Plays. Greenwood.
Dana, Julian, 1907-
xDana, Julian.
   Sutter of California: A Biography. Greenwood.
Dana, Katharine (Floyd), 1835-1886
xDana, Katherine F.
   Our Phil, & Other Stories. Arno.
Dana, Katherine F. *see* Dana, Katharine (Floyd).
Dana, Richard. *see* Dana, Richard Henry.
Dana, Richard H. *see* Dana, Richard Henry.
Dana, Richard Henry, 1815-1882
xDana, Richard.
   The Seaman's Friend. Schol Facsimiles.
xDana, Richard H.
   Two Years Before the Mast. Dutton.
   Two Years Before the Mast. Pitman Learning.
   Two Years Before the Mast. Pendulum Pr.
   Two Years Before the Mast. Airmont.
Dana, Samuel T. *see* Dana, Samuel Trask.
Dana, Samuel Trask.
xDana, Samuel T.
   California Lands. Arno.
Dana, William F. *see* Dana, William Franklin.
Dana, William Franklin, 1863-
xDana, William F.
   The Optimism of Ralph Waldo Emerson.
      Folcroft.
   The Optimism of Ralph Waldo Emerson.
      Gordon Pr.
Danaceau, Paul.
xDanaceau, Paul.
   Pot Luck in Texas: Changing a Marijuana Law.
      Drug Abuse.
Danaher, Kevin.
xDanaher, Kevin.
   Folktales of the Irish Countryside. D White.
Danaher, Mary A., 1938-
xDanaher, Mary A.
   The Commemorative Coinage of Modern
      Sports. A S Barnes.
Danandjaja, James.
xDanandjaja, James.
   An Annotated Bibliography of Javanese
      Folklore. Cellar.
Dance, Daryl C. *see* Dance, Daryl Cumber.
Dance, Daryl Cumber.
xDance, Daryl C.
   Shuckin' & Jivin': Folklore from Contemporary
      Black Americans. Ind U Pr.
Dance, F. R.
xDance, F. R.
   Broadcast Training Techniques. Unipub.
Dance, S. Peter.
xDance, S. Peter.
   The Art of Natural History: Animal Illustrators
      & Their Work. Overlook Pr.
Dance, Stanley.
xDance, Stanley.
   The World of Earl Hines. Scribner.
Danckwerts, P. V., 1916-
xDanckwerts, P. V.
   Gas Liquid Reactions. McGraw.
Dando, William A.
xDando, William A.
   The Geography of Famine. Halsted Pr.
Dandre, Victor.
xDandre, Victor E.
   Anna Pavlova in Art & Life. Arno.
Dandre, Victor E. *see* Dandre, Victor.
Dandy, Walter E. *see* Dandy, Walter Edward.
Dandy, Walter Edward, 1886-1946
xDandy, Walter E.
   The Brain. Har-Row.
Dane, Les.
xDane, Les.
   Strike - It - Rich Sales Prospecting. P-H.
Daneke, Gregory A.
xDaneke, Gregory A.

   Energy Policy & Public Administration.
      Lexington Bks.
Danford, John W.
xDanford, John W.
   Wittgenstein & Political Philosophy: A
      Re-Examination of the Foundation of Social
      Science. U of Chicago Pr.
Danforth Foundation. *see* Danforth Foundation, St.
   Louis. Commission on Church Colleges and
   Universities.
**Danforth Foundation, St. Louis. Commission on Church
   Colleges and Universities.**
xDanforth Foundation.
   School & the Democratic Environment.
      Columbia U Pr.
Danforth, William H.
xDanforth, William H.
   I Dare You. I Dare You.
Danger, Eric P. *see* Danger, Eric Paxton.
Danger, Eric Paxton.
xDanger, Eric P.
   How to Use Color to Sell. CBI Pub.
Dangerfield, George, 1904-
xDangerfield, George.
   Awakening of American Nationalism,
      1815-1828. Har-Row.
   Awakening of American Nationalism,
      1815-1828. Har-Row.
   The Damnable Question: A Study in
      Anglo-Irish Relations. Little.
   The Damnable Question: A Study of
      Anglo-Irish Relations. Little.
   Strange Death of Liberal England. Peter Smith.
   Strange Death of Liberal England, 1910-1914.
      Putnam.
Dangott, Lilliam. *see* Dangott, Lillian R.
Dangott, Lillian R.
xDangott, Lilliam.
   A Time to Enjoy: The Pleasures of Aging. P-H.
Danhauer, Jeffrey L.
xDanhauer, Jeffrey L.
   Multidimensional Speech Perception by the
      Hearing Impaired: A Treatise on Distinctive
      Features. Univ Park.
Danhof, Clarence H., 1911-
xDanhof, Clarence H.
   Government Contracting & Technological
      Change. Greenwood.
Daniel, A. R. *see* Daniel, Albert R.
Daniel, Albert R.
xDaniel, A. R.
   Up-to-Date Confectionery. Burgess-Intl Ideas.
Daniel, Anita.
xDaniel, Anita.
   Story of Albert Schweitzer. Random.
Daniel, Charles S.
xDaniel, Charles S.
   Ai: A Social Vision. Arno.
Daniel, Cuthbert.
xDaniel, Cuthbert.
   Applications of Statistics to Industrial
      Experimentation. Wiley.
   Fitting Equations to Data: Computer Analysis
      of Multifactor Data. Wiley.
   Fitting Equations to Data: Computer Analysis
      of Multifactor Data for Scientists &
      Engineers. Wiley.
Daniel, G. *see* Daniel, Glyn.
Daniel, George B. *see* Daniel, George Bernard.
Daniel, George Bernard.
xDaniel, George B.
   ed. Renaissance & Other Studies in Honor of
      William Leon Wiley. U of NC Pr.
Daniel, Glenda.
xDaniel, Glenda.
   Dune Country: A Guide for Hikers &
      Naturalists. Swallow.
Daniel, Glyn.
xDaniel, G.

A Hundred & Fifty Years of Archaeology.
Harvard U Pr.
Daniel, Glyn. see Daniel, Glyn Edmund.
Daniel, Glyn Edmund.
xDaniel, Glyn.
First Civilizations: The Archaeology of Their
Origins. T Y Crowell.
Daniel, Iulii Markovich, 1925-
xDaniel, Yuli.
Prison Poems. O'Hara.
Daniel, James W.
xDaniel, James W.
Computation & Theory in Ordinary Differential
Equations. W H Freeman.
Daniel, Norman.
xDaniel, Norman.
The Arabs & Mediaeval Europe. Longman.
Daniel, Pete.
xDaniel, Pete.
Deep'n As It Come: The 1927 Mississippi
River Flood. Oxford U Pr.
Deep'n As It Come: The 1927 Mississippi
River Flood. Oxford U Pr.
Daniel, Peter A. see Daniel, Peter Augustin.
Daniel, Peter Augustin.
xDaniel, Peter A.
Notes & Conjectural Emendations of Certain
Doubtful Passages in Shakespeare's Plays.
AMS Pr.
Daniel, Robert P. see Daniel, Robert Prentiss.
Daniel, Robert Prentiss, 1902-1968
xDaniel, Robert P.
Psychological Study of Delinquent &
Non-Delinquent Negro Boys. AMS Pr.
Daniel, Theodore W.
xDaniel, Theodore W.
Principles of Silviculture. McGraw.
Daniel, Walter G. see Daniel, Walter Green.
Daniel, Walter Green, 1905-
xDaniel, Walter G.
Reading Interests & Needs of Negro College
Freshmen Regarding Social Science
Materials. AMS Pr.
Daniel, Wayne W., 1929-
xDaniel, Wayne W.
Applied Nonparametric Statistics. HM.
Business Statistics: Basic Concepts &
Methodology. HM.
ed. Collecting Sensitive Data by Randomized
Response: An Annotated Bibliography. Ga St
U Busn Pub.
Daniel, William A. see Daniel, William Andrew.
Daniel, William Andrew, 1914-
xDaniel, William A.
Adolescents in Health & Disease. Mosby.
Education of Negro Ministers. Negro U Pr.
Daniel Yankelovich, Inc.
xDaniel Yankelovich, Inc.
Changing Values on Campus: Political &
Personal Attitudes of Today's College
Students. WSP.
Daniel, Yuli. see Daniel, Iulii Markovich.
Daniele, Joseph. see Daniele, Joseph William.
Daniele, Joseph W. see Daniele, Joseph William.
Daniele, Joseph William.
xDaniele, Joseph.
Building Masterpiece Miniatures. Stackpole.
xDaniele, Joseph W.
Building Colonial Furnishings, Miniatures, &
Folk Art. Stackpole.
Building Early American Furniture. Stackpole.
Early American Metal Projects. McKnight.
Daniell, Jere R.
xDaniell, Jere R.
Experiment in Republicanism: New Hampshire
Politics & the American Revolution,
1741-1794. Harvard U Pr.
Daniell, Rosemary.
xDaniell, Rosemary.

Fatal Flowers: On Sin, Sex & Suicide in the
Deep South. HR&W.
Danielli, James F. see Danielli, James Frederic.
Danielli, James Frederic, 1911-
xDanielli, James F.
Cell Physiology & Pharmacology. Hafner.
Danielou, Alain.
xDanielou, Alain.
Hindu Polytheism. Princeton U Pr.
Danielou, Jean.
xDanielou, Jean.
The Dead Sea Scrolls & Primitive Christianity.
Greenwood.
Prayer As a Political Problem. Guild Bks.
Daniels, A. see Daniels, Arthur.
Daniels, A. R. see Daniels, A. Richard.
Daniels, A. Richard.
xDaniels, A. R.
Introduction to Electrical Machines. Intl Schol
Bk Serv.
Daniels, Alfred.
xDaniels, Alfred.
Drawing for Fun. Doubleday.
Daniels, Arthur.
xDaniels, A.
Music. HR&W.
Daniels, Arthur S. see Daniels, Arthur Simpson.
Daniels, Arthur Simpson.
xDaniels, Arthur S.
Adapted Physical Education. Har-Row.
Daniels, Aruna C.
xDaniels, Aruna C.
ed. Essentials of Surgical Pathology: A
Programmed Text. Little.
Daniels, David, 1942-
xDaniels, David.
The Golden Age of Contract Bridge. Stein &
Day.
Orchestral Music: A Source Book. Scarecrow.
Daniels, Dorothy.
xDaniels, Dorothy.
The Apollo Fountain. Warner Bks.
Darkhaven. Warner Bks.
Illusion at Haven's Edge. PB.
Perrine. Warner Bks.
Portrait of a Witch. PB.
The Two Worlds of Peggy Scott. PB.
Whistle in the Wind. PB.
Daniels, Douglas H. see Daniels, Douglas Henry.
Daniels, Douglas Henry.
xDaniels, Douglas H.
Pioneer Urbanites: A Social & Cultural History
of Black San Francisco. Temple U Pr.
Daniels, Draper.
xDaniels, Draper.
Giants, Pigmies & Other Advertising People.
Crain Bks.
Daniels, Else.
xDaniels, Else.
Vacation at Sea: A Travel Guide for Cruises.
Cornerstone.
Vacation at Sea: A Travel Guide for Cruises.
S&S.
Daniels, Elva S.
xDaniels, Elva S.
Performing for Others. Ctr Appl Res.
Daniels, Farrington, 1889-
xDaniels, Farrington.
Direct Use of the Sun's Energy. Ballantine.
Direct Use of the Sun's Energy. Yale U Pr.
Experimental Physical Chemistry. McGraw.
Daniels, George, 1926-
xDaniels, George.
The Art of Breguet. Biblio Dist.
Daniels, George. see Daniels, George Emery.
Daniels, George Emery, 1914-
xDaniels, George.

Home Guide to Plumbing, Heating, & Air
Conditioning. B&N.
Home Guide to Plumbing, Heating, & Air
Conditioning. Har-Row.
How to Be Your Own Home Electrician. B&N.
How to Be Your Own Home Electrician.
Har-Row.
How to Use Hand & Power Tools. Har-Row.
Daniels, George H.
xDaniels, George H.
American Science in the Age of Jackson.
Columbia U Pr.
ed. Nineteenth-Century American Science: A
Reappraisal. Northwestern U Pr.
Daniels, Harold M., 1927-
xDaniels, Harold M.
What to Do with Sunday Morning.
Westminster.
Daniels, Harold R.
xDaniels, Harold R.
ed. Mechanical Press Handbook. Herman Pub.
Daniels, Harvey, 1936-
xDaniels, Harvey.
Printmaking. Viking Pr.
Daniels, James M. see Daniels, James Maurice.
Daniels, James Maurice.
xDaniels, James M.
Oriented Nuclei: Polarized Targets & Beams.
Acad Pr.
Daniels, John, 1881-
xDaniels, John.
In Freedom's Birthplace: A Study of Boston
Negroes. Arno.
In Freedom's Birthplace: A Study of the
Boston Negroes. Johnson Repr.
In Freedom's Birthplace: A Study of the
Boston Negroes. Negro U Pr.
Daniels, John D.
xDaniels, John D.
International Business: Environments &
Operations. A-W.
Daniels, Jonathan, 1902-
xDaniels, Jonathan.
The End of Innocence. Da Capo.
Frontier on the Potomac. Da Capo.
The Gentlemanly Serpent & Other Columns
from a Newspaperman in Paradise. U of SC
Pr.
Prince of Carpetbaggers. Greenwood.
Intro. by A Southerner Discovers the South.
Da Capo.
Daniels, Josephus.
xDaniels, Josephus.
Editor in Politics. Greenwood.
Life of Woodrow Wilson, 1856-1924.
Greenwood.
Life of Woodrow Wilson, 1856-1924. Scholarly.
Tar Heel Editor. Greenwood.
Daniels, Les.
xDaniels, Les.
The Silver Skull: A Novel of Sorcery. Scribner.
ed. Thirteen Tales of Terror. Scribner.
Daniels, Les. see Daniels, Leslie R.
Daniels, Leslie R.
xDaniels, Leslie R.
Learning How to Paint in Oils: Illustrated Step
by Step on TV Storyboard. Doubleday.
Daniels, Mary, 1937-
xDaniels, Mary.
Cat Astrology. Avon.
Cat Astrology. Morrow.
Daniels, May.
xDaniels, May.
The French Drama of the Unspoken.
Greenwood.
Daniels, Norman, 1942-
xDaniels, Norman.

Thomas Reid's Inquiry: The Geometry of
Visibles & the Case for Realism. B Franklin.
Wyndward Fury. Warner Bks.

Daniels, Patricia.
xDaniels, Patricia.
Aladdin & the Magic Lamp. Raintree Child.
Ali Baba & the Forty Thieves. Raintree Child.
Beauty & the Beast. Raintree Child.
Cinderella. Raintree Child.
Rumpelstiltskin. Raintree Child.
Sinbad the Sailor. Raintree Child.
Sleeping Beauty. Raintree Child.

Daniels, Patrick.
xDaniels, Patrick.
Early Photography. St Martin.

Daniels, R. Balfour. *see* Daniels, Robertson Balfour.

Daniels, Richard W., 1942-
xDaniels, Richard W.
Approximation Methods for Electronic Filter
Design: With Applications to Passive, Active
& Digital Networks. McGraw.

Daniels, Robertson Balfour, 1900-
xDaniels, R. Balfour.
Some Seventeenth-Century Worthies in a
Twentieth-Century Mirror. Russell.

Daniels, Robin, 1941-
xDaniels, Robin.
Conversations with Menuhin. St Martin.

Daniels, Roger.
xDaniels, Roger.
The Decision to Relocate the Japanese
Americans. Har-Row.
Politics of Prejudice: The Anti-Japanese
Movement in California & the Struggle for
Japanese Exclusion. Atheneum.
The Politics of Prejudice: The Anti-Japanese
Movement in California & the Struggle for
Japanese Exclusion. Peter Smith.
The Politics of Prejudice: The Anti-Japanese
Movement in California & the Struggle for
Japanese Exclusion. U of Cal Pr.
Racism in California: A Reader in the History
of Oppression. Macmillan.
ed. Two Monographs on Japanese Canadians.
Arno.

Daniels, Stuart R.
xDaniels, Stuart R.
Inelastic Steel Structures. U of Tenn Pr.

Daniels, Velma. *see* Daniels, Velma Seawell.
Daniels, Velma S. *see* Daniels, Velma Seawell.

Daniels, Velma Seawell.
xDaniels, Velma.
Patches of Joy. Pelican.
xDaniels, Velma S.
Patches of Joy. Pelican.

Danielson, Dorothy.
xDanielson, Dorothy.
Reading in English: For Students of English As
a Second Language. P-H.

Danielson, Henry.
xDanielson, Henry.
Arthur Machen: A Bibliography. Folcroft.
Arthur Machen: A Bibliography. Gale.

Danielson, Michael N.
xDanielson, Michael N.
Politics of Exclusion. Columbia U Pr.

Danielson, Roswell S.
xDanielson, Roswell S.
Cuban Medicine. Transaction Bks.

Danielsson, Robert.
xDanielsson, Robert.
Chess for People Who Can't Even Play
Checkers. Van Nos Reinhold.

Danilov, A. D. *see* Danilov, Aleksei Dmitrievich.

Danilov, Aleksei Dmitrievich.
xDanilov, A. D.
Chemistry of the Ionosphere. Plenum Pub.

Dank, Milton, 1920-
xDank, Milton.

The Dangerous Game. Lippincott.
The Dangerous Game. Dell.
Game's End. Lippincott.

Dankenbring, William F.
xDankenbring, William F.
The First Genesis: A New Case for Creation.
Triumph Pub.

Danker, Frederick W.
xDanker, Frederick W.
Luke. Fortress.
Multipurpose Tools for Bible Study. Concordia.
No Room in the Brotherhood: The Preus-Otten
Purge of Missouri. Clayton Pub Hse.

Dankert, Clyde E. *see* Dankert, Clyde Edward.

Dankert, Clyde Edward, 1901-
xDankert, Clyde E.
Adam Smith: Man of Letters & Economist.
Exposition.
ed. Hours of Work. Greenwood.

Dankleff, Richard.
xDankleff, Richard.
Popcorn Girl. Oreg St U Pr.

Danks, Rabindra.
xDanks, Rabindra.
Night Fell: Poems & Drawings. Pygmalion Pr.

Dann, Colin.
xDann, Colin.
The Animals of Farthing Wood.
Elsevier-Nelson.

Dann, D. *see* Dann, David J.

Dann, David J.
xDann, D.
Forms in Your Life. Monarch Pr.

Dann, Jack.
xDann, Jack.
Timetipping. Doubleday.

Dann, John C.
xDann, John C.
The Revolution Remembered: Eyewitness
Accounts of the War for Independence. U of
Chicago Pr.

Dann, Sam.
xDann, Sam.
The Third Body. Popular Lib.

Dannen, Kent, 1946-
xDannen, Kent.
Listen to the Sparrow's Song. Bethany Pr.

Dannenberg, Linda.
xDannenberg, Linda.
The Paris Way of Beauty. S&S.

Dannenfeldt, Karl H.
xDannenfeldt, Karl H.
Leonhard Rauwolf: Sixteenth-Century
Physician, Botanist, & Traveler. Harvard U
Pr.

Danner, Douglas.
xDanner, Douglas.
Pattern Deposition Checklists. Lawyers Co-Op.
Pattern Interrogatories: 1970-73. Lawyers
Co-Op.

Dannett, Sylvia G. *see* Dannett, Sylvia G. L.

Dannett, Sylvia G. L.
xDannett, Sylvia G.
The Low Blood Sugar Gourmet Cookbook.
Har-Row.

Dannhauser, Werner J.
xDannhauser, Werner J.
Nietzsche's View of Socrates. Cornell U Pr.

Danoff, Judith.
xDanoff, Judith.
Open for Children: For Those Interested in
Early Childhood Education. McGraw.

Danon, J.
xDanon, J.
Lectures on the Mossbauer Effect. Gordon.

Danowski, T. S.
xDanowski, T. S.

Diabetes As a Way of Life. Coward.
Sustained Weight Control: The Individual
Approach. Davis Co.

Danowski, T S.
xDanowski, T. S.
Outline of Endocrine Gland Syndromes.
Williams & Wilkins.

Danskin, J. M. *see* Danskin, John Moffatt.

Danskin, John Moffatt, 1923-
xDanskin, J. M.
Theory of Max-Min, & Its Application to
Weapons Allocation Problems.
Springer-Verlag.

Dante Alighieri.
xDante Alighieri.
Dante's Inferno. Ind U Pr.
Dante's Inferno. Schocken.
Divine Comedy. Columbia U Pr.
The Divine Comedy. Norton.
The Divine Comedy. Rowman.
The Divine Comedy. AHM Pub.
Literary Criticism of Dante Alighieri. U of
Nebr Pr.
Portable Dante. Penguin.

Danto, Arthur. *see* Danto, Arthur Coleman.

Danto, Arthur Coleman, 1924-
xDanto, Arthur.
Nietzsche As Philosopher. Columbia U Pr.

Danton, G L.
xDanton, G. L.
The Theory & Practice of Seamanship.
Routledge & Kegan.
xDanton, Graham.
Theory & Practice of Seamanship. Routledge &
Kegan.

Danton, George H. *see* Danton, George Henry.

Danton, George Henry, 1880-
xDanton, George H.
Nature Sense in the Writings of Ludwig Tieck.
AMS Pr.

Danton, Graham. *see* Danton, G L.

Danton, J. Periam, 1908-
xDanton, J. Periam.
Dimensions of Comparative Librarianship.
ALA.
ed. Index to Festschriften in Librarianship.
Bowker.

Dantzic, C. *see* Dantzic, Cynthia Maris.
Dantzic, Cynthia M. *see* Dantzic, Cynthia Maris.

Dantzic, Cynthia Maris.
xDantzic, C.
Stop Dropping Breadcrumbs on My Yacht.
P-H.
xDantzic, Cynthia M.
Sounds of Silents. P-H.

Dantzig, G. B. *see* Dantzig, George Bernard.
Dantzig, George B. *see* Dantzig, George Bernard.

Dantzig, George Bernard, 1914-
xDantzig, G. B.
ed. Studies in Optimization. Math Assn.
xDantzig, George B.
Linear Programming & Extensions. Princeton
U Pr.

Danysh, Joseph.
xDanysh, Joseph.
Stop Without Quitting. Intl Gen Semantics.

Danzig, Alan. *see* Danzig, Allan.

Danzig, Allan.
xDanzig, Alan.
Thesis: Rhetoric of the Essay. Wadsworth Pub.

Danzig, Allison.
xDanzig, Allison.
ed. The Fireside Book of Tennis. S&S.

Danziger, Carl.
xDanziger, Carl.
Unmarried Heterosexual Cohabitation. R & E
Res Assoc.

Danziger, Edmund J. *see* Danziger, Edmund Jefferson.

Danziger, Edmund Jefferson, 1938-
xDanziger, Edmund J.

The Chippewas of Lake Superior. U of Okla Pr.
Indians & Bureaucrats: Administering the
Reservation Policy During the Civil War. U
of Ill Pr.

Danziger, Edward G, 1893-
xDanziger, Edward G.
Papa D: A Saga of Love & Cooking. Blair.

Danziger, Kurt.
xDanziger, Kurt.
Readings in Child Socialization. Pergamon.

Danziger, Marlies K.
xDanziger, Marlies K.
The Critical Reader: Analyzing & Judging
Literature. Ungar.
Oliver Goldsmith & Richard Brinsley Sheridan.
Ungar.

Danziger, Paula, 1944-
xDanziger, Paula.
The Cat Ate My Gymsuit. Dell.
The Cat Ate My Gymsuit. Dell.
The Cat Ate My Gymsuit. Delacorte.

Danziger, Raphael.
xDanziger, Raphael.
Abd al-Qadir & the Algerians: Resistance to
the French & Internal Consolidation. Holmes
& Meier.

Daoud, Hesham O.
xDaoud, Hesham O.
Daoud's Aviation Dictionary. Aviation.

Darack, Arthur.
xDarack, Arthur.
The Consumers Digest Automobile Repair
Book. McGraw.
The Guide to Home Appliance Repair.
McGraw.
Outdoor Power Equipment: How It Works,
How to Fix It. Stein & Day.

Darbee, Harry.
xDarbee, Harry.
Catskill Flytier: My Life, Times, & Techniques.
Lippincott.

Darbelnet, John, 1904-
xDarbelnet, John.
Pensee & Structure. Scribner.

Darbishire, Helen, 1881-1961
xDarbishire, Helen.
ed. Early Lives of Milton. Scholarly.
The Poet Wordsworth. Greenwood.

Darby, Catherine.
xDarby, Catherine.
A Dream of Fair Serpents. Popular Lib.
Falcon to the Lure. Popular Lib.

Darby, H. C. see Darby, Henry Clifford.

Darby, Henry Clifford, 1909-
xDarby, H. C.
ed. Domesday England. Cambridge U Pr.
Domesday Gazetteer. Cambridge U Pr.

Darby, Joseph J.
xDarby, Joseph J.
tr. Alternative Draft of a Penal Code for the
Federal Republic of Germany. Rothman.

Darby, McIhael. see Darby, Michael R.

Darby, Michael R.
xDarby, McIhael.
Intermediate Macroeconomics. McGraw.

Darby, Michele L. see Darby, Michele Leonardi.

Darby, Michele Leonardi.
xDarby, Michele L.
Research Methods for Oral Health
Professionals: An Introduction. Mosby.

Darcy, Claire.
xDarcy, Clare.
Cressida. G K Hall.
Cressida. NAL.
Cressida. Walker & Co.

Darcy, Clare.
xDarcy, Clare.

Allegra. NAL.
Allegra. Walker & Co.
Eugenia. G K Hall.
Eugenia. Walker & Co.
Eugenia. NAL.
Gwendolen. NAL.
Gwendolen. G K Hall.
Regina. G K Hall.
Regina. NAL.

Darcy, Clare. see Darcy, Claire.

Darden, Ellington, 1943-
xDarden, Ellington.
Conditioning for Football. Anna Pub.
The Nautilus Book: An Illustrated Guide to
Physical Fitness the Nautilus Way. Contemp
Bks.
Nutrition for Athletes. Anna Pub.
Olympic Athletes Ask Questions About
Exercise & Nutrition. Anna Pub.

Darden, Norma.
xDarden, Norma Jean.
Spoonbread & Strawberry Wine: Recipes &
Reminiscences of a Family. Doubleday.

Darden, Norma Jean. see Darden, Norma.

Dardig, Jill. see Dardig, Jill C.

Dardig, Jill C.
xDardig, Jill.
Sign Here: A Contracting Book for Children
and Their Parents. Behaviordelia.

Darell-Brown, Susan.
xDarell-Brown, Susan.
The Mississippi. Silver.

Dargan, E. Preston. see Dargan, Edwin Preston.

Dargan, Edwin C. see Dargan, Edwin Charles.

Dargan, Edwin Charles, 1852-1930
xDargan, Edwin C.
History of Preaching. B Franklin.

Dargan, Edwin P. see Dargan, Edwin Preston.

Dargan, Edwin Preston
xDargan, E. Preston.
ed. The Evolution of Balzac's Comedie
Humaine. Cooper Sq.
xDargan, Edwin P.
ed. Studies in Balzac's Realism. Russell.

Dargan, Marion.
xDargan, Marion.
Guide to American Biography. Greenwood.

Darian, Steven G.
xDarian, Steven G.
English As a Foreign Language: History,
Development, & Methods of Teaching. U of
Okla Pr.
The Ganges in Myth & History. U Pr of
Hawaii.

Darilek, Richard E.
xDarilek, Richard E.
A Loyal Opposition in Time of War: The
Republican Party & the Politics of Foreign
Policy from Pearl Harbor to Yalta.
Greenwood.

Daringer, Helen F. see Daringer, Helen Fern.

Daringer, Helen Fern, 1892-
xDaringer, Helen F.
Adopted Jane. HarBraceJ.

Dark, Harris E. see Dark, Harris Edward.

Dark, Harris Edward, 1922-
xDark, Harris E.
Auto Engines of Tomorrow: Power
Alternatives for Cars to Come. Ind U Pr.

Dark, Harry.
xDark, Harry.
The Greatest Ozarks Guidebook. Chicago
Review.
The Greatest Ozarks Guidebook. Greatest
Graphics.

Dark, Philip J. see Dark, Philip John Crosskey.

Dark, Philip John Crosskey.
xDark, Philip J.

An Introduction to Benin Art & Technology.
Oxford U Pr.

Dark, Sidney, 1874-1947
xDark, Sidney.
Charles Dickens. Arden Lib.
Charles Dickens. Folcroft.
Charles Dickens. Haskell.
Twelve Bad Men. Arno.
Twelve Bad Men. Folcroft.
Twelve Royal Ladies. Arno.

Darke, Majorie. see Darke, Marjorie.

Darke, Marjorie.
xDarke, Majorie.
A Question of Courage. T Y Crowell.

Darley, Frederic L.
xDarley, Frederic L.
Diagnosis & Appraisal of Communication
Disorders. P-H.
Evaluation of Appraisal Techniques in Speech
& Language Pathology. A-W.

Darling, Ada W., 1880-
xDarling, Ada W.
Antique Jewelry Identification with Price
Guide. Wallace-Homestead.

Darling, Donald B.
xDarling, Donald B.
Radiography of Infants & Children: A Problem
Oriented Manual of Radiographic &
Fluoroscopic Procedures. C C Thomas.

Darling, Erik.
xDarling, Erik.
Chords for Guitar. Schirmer Bks.

Darling, Frank C.
xDarling, Frank C.
Thailand & the United States. Pub Aff Pr.
The Westernization of Asia: A Comparative
Political Analysis. G K Hall.
The Westernization of Asia: A Comparative
Political Analysis. Schenkman

Darling, Kathy.
xDarling, Kathy.
Bug Circus. Garrard.
The Easter Bunny's Secret. Garrard.
Games Gorillas Play. Garrard.
Little Bat's Secret. Garrard.
Paul & His Little-Big Dog. Garrard.
Pecos Bill Finds a Horse. Garrard.

Darling, Lois.

xDarling, Lois.
illus. Worms. Morrow.

Darling, Rosalyn B. see Darling, Rosalyn Benjamin.

Darling, Rosalyn Benjamin.
xDarling, Rosalyn B.
Families Against Society: A Study of Reactions
to Children with Birth Defects. Sage.

Darlington, C. D. see Darlington, Cyril Dean.

Darlington, C. Leroy.
xDarlington, C. LeRoy.
The Chemical World: Activities &
Explorations. HM.

Darlington, Cyril Dean, 1903-
xDarlington, C. D.
Chromosome Botany & the Origins of
Cultivated Plants. Allen Unwin.
Chromosome Botany & the Origins of
Cultivated Plants. Hafner.
Evolution of Man & Society. S&S.
Evolution of Man & Society. S&S.
The Little Universe of Man. Allen Unwin.

Darlington, Joy, 1947-
xDarlington, Joy.
Fast Friends. Berkley Pub.
Fast Friends. Doubleday.

Darlington, Mary C. see Darlington, Mary Carson
(O'Hara).

Darlington, Mary Carson (O'Hara), 1824-1915
xDarlington, Mary C.

ed. Fort Pitt & Letters from the Frontier. Arno.

Darlington, William A. *see* Darlington, William Aubrey.

Darlington, William Aubrey, 1890-
xDarlington, William A.
Literature in the Theatre, & Other Essays. Arno.

Darmady, E. M. *see* Darmady, Edward Michael.

Darmady, Edward Michael.
xDarmady, E. M.
Renal Pathology. Butterworths.

Darnell, A. W. *see* Darnell, Anthony William.

Darnell, Anthony William, 1880-
xDarnell, A. W.
illus. Orchids for the Outdoor Garden: A Descriptive List of the World's Orchids for the Use of Amateur Gardeners. Dover.
Orchids for the Outdoor Garden: A Descriptive List of the World's Orchids for the Use of Amateur Gardeners. Peter Smith.
Unfamiliar Flowers for Your Garden. Dover.
Unfamiliar Flowers for Your Garden. Peter Smith.

Darnell, D. K. *see* Darnell, Donald K.

Darnell, Donald K.
xDarnell, D. K.
Persons Communicating. P-H.

Darnton, Robert.
xDarnton, Robert.
The Business of Enlightenment: A Publishing History of the Encyclopedie, 1775-1800. Harvard U Pr.

Darr, Jack.
xDarr, Jack.
Fix Your Small Appliances. Sams.
The Home Appliance Clinic: Controls, Cycle Timers, Wiring & Repair. TAB Bks.
How to Test Almost Everything Electronic. TAB Bks.

Darr, Richard K.
xDarr, Richard K.
A History of the Nashua & Lowell Railroad Corporation, 1835-1880. Arno.

Darrah, D. D. *see* Darrah, Delmar Duane.

Darrah, Delmar Duane.
xDarrah, D. D.
History & Evolution of Freemasonry. Wehman.
xDarrah, Delmore D.
History & Evolution of Freemasonry. Powner.

Darrah, Delmore D. *see* Darrah, Delmar Duane.

Darrah, William C. *see* Darrah, William Culp.

Darrah, William Culp, 1909-
xDarrah, William C.
The World of Stereographs. W C Darrah.

Darrell, Elizabeth.
xDarrell, Elizabeth.
The Jade Alliance. Putnam.

Darrell, Margery.
xDarrell, Margery.
Once Upon a Time: The Fairy-Tale World of Arthur Rackham. Viking Pr.

Darroch, Dorothy B. *see* Darroch, Dorothy Broom.

Darroch, Dorothy Broom.
xDarroch, Dorothy B.
Doing Sociology: Chapter Guides, Projects, Tool Kit. Har-Row.

Darroch, Nadina.
xDarroch, Nadina.
Cooking with Coffee. A & W Pubs.

Darrow, Clarence. *see* Darrow, Clarence Seward.

Darrow, Clarence S. *see* Darrow, Clarence Seward.

Darrow, Clarence Seward, 1857-1938
xDarrow, Clarence.
An Eye for an Eye. Moore Pub Co.
A Persian Pearl & Other Essays. Haskell.
xDarrow, Clarence S.
Marx Versus Tolstoy: A Debate. Ozer.

Darrow, Gerald F., 1931-
xDarrow, Gerald F.

Four Decades of Choral Training. Scarecrow.

Darrow, Ralph C.
xDarrow, Ralph C.
House Journal Editing. Interstate.

Darst, David M., 1947-
xDarst, David M.
The Complete Bond Book: A Guide to All Types of Fixed-Income Securities. McGraw.

Dart, Peter.
xDart, Peter.
Pudovkin's Films & Film Theory. Arno.

Dart, Thurston, 1921-
xDart, Thurston.
Editing Early Music: Notes on the Preparation of Printer's Copy. Oxford U Pr.

Dartmouth College. Library.
xDartmouth College Library-Hanover, N. H.
Dictionary Catalog of the Stefansson Collection on the Polar Regions. G K Hall.

Dartmouth College Library-Hanover, N. H. *see* Dartmouth College. Library.

Darton, F. Harvey. *see* Darton, Frederick Joseph Harvey.

Darton, F. J. *see* Darton, Frederick Joseph Harvey.

Darton, Frederick J. *see* Darton, Frederick Joseph Harvey.

Darton, Frederick Joseph Harvey.
xDarton, F. Harvey.
From Surtees to Sassoon: Some English Contrasts 1838-1928. Folcroft.
xDarton, F. J.
Arnold Bennett. Haskell.
xDarton, Frederick J.
Arnold Bennett. Scholarly.

Darton, Nelson H. *see* Darton, Nelson Horatio.

Darton, Nelson Horatio, 1865-1948
xDarton, Nelson H.
Catalogue & Index of Contributions to North American Geology: 1732-1891. Arno.

Darvill, Fred T., 1927-
xDarvill , Fred T.
North Cascades Highway Guide. Darvill Outdoor.

Darwin, Charles. *see* Darwin, Charles Robert.

Darwin, Charles R. *see* Darwin, Charles Robert.

Darwin, Charles Robert.
xDarwin, Charles.
Autobiographies. Oxford U Pr.
Autobiography & Selected Letters. Dover.
Autobiography & Selected Letters. Peter Smith.
The Descent of Man & Selection in Relation to Sex. Gale.
Expression of the Emotions in Man & Animals. U of Chicago Pr.
Fertilization of Orchids by Insects. E M Coleman Ent.
The Illustrated Origin of the Species. Hill & Wang.
Journal of Researches into the Natural History & Geology of the Countries Visited During the Voyage of H. M. S. "Beagle" Round the World, Under the Command of Capt. Fitz Roy, R. A.. Norwood Edns.
Origin of Species. Macmillan.
Origin of Species. NAL.
The Origin of Species. Norton.
The Origin of Species. Ungar.
The Origin of the Species. Rowman.
The Voyage of Charles Darwin. Mayflower Bks.
xDarwin, Charles R.

The Descent of Man & Selection in Relation to Sex. Intl Pubns Serv.
The Different Forms of Flowers on Plants of the Same Species. Intl Pubns Serv.
The Effects of Cross & Self Fertilisation in the Vegetable Kingdom. R West.
Evolution by Natural Selection. Johnson Repr.
The Expression of Emotions in Man & Animals. R West.
Expression of the Emotions in Man & Animals. AMS Pr.
Expression of the Emotions in Man & Animals. Greenwood.
Insectivorous Plants. AMS Pr.
Journal of Researches into the Geology & Natural History of the Various Countries Visited by H. M. S. Beagle Under the Command of Captain Fitzroy, R. N. from 1832 to 1836. Intl Pubns Serv.
The Origin of Species. R West.
Origin of Species. Penguin.
The Variation of Animals & Plants Under Domestication. Intl Pubns Serv.

Darwin, Francis D. *see* Darwin, Francis Darwin Swift.

Darwin, Francis Darwin Swift.
xDarwin, Francis D.
The English Mediaeval Recluse. Folcroft.

Dary, David.
xDary, David.
The Buffalo Book: The Full Saga of the American Animal. Swallow.
How to Write News for Broadcast & Print Media. TAB Bks.
True Tales of the Old-Time Plains. Crown.

Daryanani, Gobind.
xDaryanani, Gobind.
Principles of Active Network Synthesis & Design. Wiley.

Das, Bhagavan, 1869-1958
xDas, Bhagavan.
Essential Unity of All Religions. Theos Pub Hse.

Das, Binod S. *see* Das, Binod Sankar.

Das, Binod Sankar.
xDas, Binod S.
Studies in the Economic History of Orissa from Ancient Times to 1833. South Asia Bks.

Das, Braja. *see* Das, Braja M.

Das, Braja M., 1941-
xDas, Braja.
Introduction to Soil Mechanics. Iowa St U Pr.

Das, G. K.
xDas, G. K.
E. M. Forster's India. Rowman.

Das, J. P. *see* Das, Jagannath Prasad.

Das, Jagannath Prasad.
xDas, J. P.
Simultaneous & Successive Cognitive Processes. Acad Pr.

Das, M. N. *see* Das, Mihir Nath.

Das, Mihir Nath.
xDas, M. N.
Design & Analysis of Experiments. Halsted Pr.

Das, S. K. *see* Das, Satyendra Kumar.

Das, S. Sunder, 1924-
xDas, S. Sunder.
General Psychology. Asia.

Das, Satyendra Kumar.
xDas, S. K.
Cynewulf & the Cynewulf Canon. Gordon Pr.

Das, Veena.
xDas, Venna.
Structure & Cognition: Aspects of Hindu Caste & Ritual. Oxford U Pr.

Das, Venna. *see* Das, Veena.

Dasch. *see* Dasch, Clement E.

Dasch, Clement E.
xDasch.

Neotropic Mesochorinae - Hymenoptera,
Ichneumonidae. Am Entom Inst.
Dasent, G. W. *see* Dasent, George Webbe.
Dasent, George Webbe.
xDasent, G. W.
The Cat on the Dovrefell: A Christmas Tale.
Putnam.
Dasent, W. E.
xDasent, W. E.
Nonexistent Compounds: Compounds of Low
Stability. Dekker.
Dasgupta, A. K. *see* Dasgupta, Ajit Kumar.
Dasgupta, Ajit K. *see* Dasgupta, Ajit Kumar.
Dasgupta, Ajit Kumar.
xDasgupta, A. K.
Economic Theory & the Developing Countries.
St Martin.
xDasgupta, Ajit K.
Agriculture & Economic Development in India.
Intl Bk Dist.
Economic Freedom, Technology & Planning
for Growth. Intl Bk Dist.
Dasgupta, Biplab. *see* Dasgupta, Biplap.
Dasgupta, Biplap.
xDasgupta, Biplab.
The Naxalite Movement. Intl Pubns Serv.
Dasgupta, Somesh.
xDasgupta, Somesh.
Come, Solitude, Speak to Me. InterCulture.
Dasgupta, Subhayu.
xDasgupta, Subhayu.
Hindu Ethos & the Challenge of Change.
Humanities.
Hindu Ethos & the Challenge of Change.
Verry.
Dasgupta, Sugata, 1926-
xDasgupta, Sugata.
Social Work & Social Change: A Case Study of
Indian Village Development. Porter Sargent.
Dash, Joan.
xDash, Joan.
Summoned to Jerusalem: The Life of Henrietta
Szold. Har-Row.
Dash, Samuel.
xDash, Samuel.
Eavesdroppers. Da Capo.
Dashefsky, Arnold.
xDashefsky, Arnold.
ed. Ethnic Identity in Society. Rand.
Dasmann, R. F. *see* Dasmann, Raymond Frederick.
Dasmann, Raymond F. *see* Dasmann, Raymond
Frederick.
Dasmann, Raymond Frederick, 1919-
xDasmann, R. F.
Environmental Conservation. Wiley.
xDasmann, Raymond F.
Destruction of California. Macmillan.
Different Kind of Country. Macmillan.
Ecological Principles for Economic
Development. Wiley.
No Further Retreat: The Fight to Save Florida.
Macmillan.
Dasso, Jerome. *see* Dasso, Jerome J.
Dasso, Jerome J.
xDasso, Jerome.
Fundamentals of Real Estate. P-H.
Datar, Asha L. *see* Datar, Asha Laxman.
Datar, Asha Laxman.
xDatar, Asha L.
India's Economic Relations with the USSR &
Eastern Europe, 1953-54 to 1969-70.
Cambridge U Pr.
Date, C. J.
xDate, C. J.
Introduction to Database Systems. A-W.
Datesman, Susan K.
xDatesman, Susan K.
ed. Women, Crime & Justice. Oxford U Pr.
Dathorne, O. R.
xDathorne, O. R.

African Literature in the Twentieth Century. U
of Minn Pr.
Datig, Fred A., 1925-
xDatig, Fred A.
Cartridges for Collectors. Borden.
Datta, Lois-Ellin.
xDatta, Lois-Ellin.
ed. Improving Evaluations. Sage.
Datta, S. C. *see* Datta, Subhash Chandra.
Datta, Subhash Chandra, 1931-
xDatta, S. C.
Introduction to Gymnosperms. Asia.
Dattaray, Rajatbaran.
xDattaray, Rajatbaran.
A Critical Survey of the Life & Works of
Ksemendra. South Asia Bks.
Dau, Frederick W., 1880-
xDau, Frederick W.
Florida Old & New. Gale.
Daub, Edward E.
xDaub, Edward E.
Comprehending Technical Japanese. U of Wis
Pr.
Fire. Raintree Child.
Daube, David.
xDaube, David.
The Exodus Pattern in the Bible. Greenwood.
Forms of Roman Legislation. Greenwood.
Daube, Jasper R.
xDaube, Jasper R.
Medical Neurosciences: An Approach to
Anatomy, Pathology, & Physiology by
Systems & Levels. Little.
Dauben, Joseph W. *see* Dauben, Joseph Warren.
Dauben, Joseph Warren, 1944-
xDauben, Joseph W.
Georg Cantor: His Mathematics & Philosophy
of the Infinite. Harvard U Pr.
Daubenmire, Rexford. *see* Daubenmire, Rexford F.
Daubenmire, Rexford F., 1909-
xDaubenmire, Rexford.
Plant Geography: With Special Reference to
North America. Acad Pr.
Plants & Environment: A Textbook of Plant
Autecology. Wiley.
xDaubenmire, Rexford F.
Plant Communities: A Textbook of Plant
Synecology. Har-Row.
Daubier, Jean.
xDaubier, Jean.
History of the Chinese Cultural Revolution.
Random.
Daudel, R. *see* Daudel, Raymond.
Daudel, Raymond.
xDaudel, R.
Quantum Theory of Chemical Reactivity.
Kluwer Boston.
xDaudel, Raymond.
Quantum Theory of the Chemical Bond.
Kluwer Boston.
Daudet, Alphonse, 1840-1897
xDaudet, Alphonse.
Letters from My Windmill. Penguin.
Lettres De Mon Moulin. French & Eur.
Monday Tales. Arno.
Tartarin De Tarascon. French & Eur.
Daudistel, Howard. *see* Daudistel, Howard C.
Daudistel, Howard C.
xDaudistel, Howard.
Criminal Justice: Situations & Decisions.
HR&W.
Dauer, Carl C. *see* Dauer, Carl Calvin.
Dauer, Carl Calvin.
xDauer, Carl C.
Infectious Diseases. Harvard U Pr.
Dauer, Manning J. *see* Dauer, Manning Julian.
Dauer, Manning Julian, 1909-
xDauer, Manning J.

The Adams Federalists. Johns Hopkins.
Dauer, Rosamond.
xDauer, Rosamond.
Bullfrog & Gertrude Go Camping.
Greenwillow.
Bullfrog Builds a House. Greenwillow.
Bullfrog Grows up. Greenwillow.
Mrs. Piggery Snout. Har-Row.
My Friend, Jasper Jones. Schol Bk Serv.
Dauer, Victor. *see* Dauer, Victor Paul.
Dauer, Victor Paul.
xDauer, Victor.
Dynamic Physical Education for Elementary
School Children. Burgess.
Daugherty, Harry M. *see* Daugherty, Harry Micajah.
Daugherty, Harry Micajah.
xDaugherty, Harry M.
The Inside Story of the Harding Tragedy.
Arno.
Inside Story of the Harding Tragedy. Western
Islands.
Daugherty, James. *see* Daugherty, James Henry.
Daugherty, James Henry, 1889-
xDaugherty, James.
illus. Andy & the Lion. Viking Pr.
Daughters of St. Paul.
xDaughters Of St. Paul.
Alive in the Spirit. Dghtrs St Paul.
All or Nothing. Dghtrs St Paul.
Always with Jesus. Dghtrs St Paul.
Bible for Children. Dghtrs St Paul.
The Bible for Young People: New Testament.
Dghtrs St Paul.
ed. Bible for Young Readers. Dghtrs St Paul.
ed. Bible Stories for Everyone. Dghtrs St Paul.
A Brief Catholic Dictionary for Young People.
Dghtrs St Paul.
Brief Review for Confirmation. Dghtrs St Paul.
Brief Summary of the Ten Commandments.
Dghtrs St Paul.
ed. Catechism of Modern Man. Dghtrs St Paul.
Catherine of Siena. Dghtrs St Paul.
Choose Your Tomorrow. Dghtrs St Paul.
Christ Lives in Me. Dghtrs St Paul.
Christ of Vatican Two. Dghtrs St Paul.
Christ: Our Way to the Father. Dghtrs St Paul.
Christ's Law of Love. Dghtrs St Paul.
ed. Church's Amazing Story. Dghtrs St Paul.
Communicators for Christ. Dghtrs St Paul.
ed. Dimensions of the Priesthood. Dghtrs St
Paul.
Documents on Renewal for Religious. Dghtrs
St Paul.
Drawing Near Him with Confidence. Dghtrs St
Paul.
Eight Celebrations of the Word. Dghtrs St
Paul.
Everyman's Challenge. Dghtrs St Paul.
Faces of Courage. Dghtrs St Paul.
Faith We Live By. Dghtrs St Paul.
Fifty-Seven Saints for Boys & Girls. Dghtrs St
Paul.
Gentle Revolutionary. Dghtrs St Paul.
God the Father Sent His Son. Dghtrs St Paul.
God's People on the Move. Dghtrs St Paul.
Heaven. Dghtrs St Paul.
His Saving Love. Dghtrs St Paul.
Holy Bible Illustrated. Dghtrs St Paul.
I Learn About Jesus. Dghtrs St Paul.
I Learn About Jesus: Projects & Activities for
Pre-Schoolers. Dghtrs St Paul.
I Pray with Jesus. Dghtrs St Paul.
Into the Woods & Other Favorite Verses.
Dghtrs St Paul.
Introductions to the Books of the New
Testament. Dghtrs St Paul.
Live the Mass. Dghtrs St Paul.
Live the Truth-Give the Truth. Dghtrs St Paul.
Living & Growing Through the Eucharist.
Dghtrs St Paul.

Mary, Queen of Apostles. Dghtrs St Paul.
Mass Means of Communication. Dghtrs St
  Paul.
Master Plan Revealed. Dghtrs St Paul.
Moments for Prayer. Dghtrs St Paul.
Moments of Decision. Dghtrs St Paul.
Mother Cabrini. Dghtrs St Paul.
Mother Seton. Dghtrs St Paul.
My Favorite Prayers & Reflections. Dghtrs St
  Paul.
My Massbook. Dghtrs St Paul.
My Prayer Book. Dghtrs St Paul.
Obedience: The Greatest Freedom. Dghtrs St
  Paul.
ed. One Family Under God. Dghtrs St Paul.
Pinocchio. Dghtrs St Paul.
Really Living. Dghtrs St Paul.
Religion for the People of Today. Dghtrs St
  Paul.
Religious Life in the Light of Vatican 2. Dghtrs
  St Paul.
St. Bernadette. Dghtrs St Paul.
St. Paul Mass Book for Children. Dghtrs St
  Paul.
St. Rita of Cascia: Saint of the Impossible.
  Dghtrs St Paul.
Saints for Young People for Every Day. Dghtrs
  St Paul.
Sixteen Documents of Vatican Two. Dghtrs St
  Paul.
Sunday Liturgy Themes. Dghtrs St Paul.
Teachings & Miracles of Jesus. Dghtrs St Paul.
Thoughts of the Servant of God, Mother
  Thecla Merlo. Dghtrs St Paul.
We Make a Promise. Dghtrs St Paul.
When Jesus Was Born. Dghtrs St Paul.
Where the Gospel Meets the World. Dghtrs St
  Paul.
Wind & Shadows. Dghtrs St Paul.
Woman of Faith. Dghtrs St Paul.
Women of the Bible. Dghtrs St Paul.
Women of the Gospel. Dghtrs St Paul.
tr. Yes to Life. Dghtrs St Paul.
Your Right to Be Informed. Dghtrs St Paul.
xDaughters of St. Paul Editorial Staff.
  Looking Ahead to Marriage. Dghtrs St Paul.
xDaughters St. Paul.
  Preparing to Recieve Jesus Christ. Dghtrs St
    Paul.
Daughters of St. Paul Editorial Staff. see Daughters of St.
  Paul.
Daughters of the American Revolution. Alabama.
  xAlabama Society, DAR.
    Index to Alabama Wills, 1808-1870. Genealog
      Pub.
Daughters of the American Revolution. Georgia.
  xGeorgia Chapters, D. A. R.
    The Historical Collections Georgia Chapters,
      D. A. R.: Old Bible Records & Land
      Lotteries. Southern Hist Pr.
    Historical Collections of the Georgia Chapters,
      Daughters of the American Revolution.
      Southern Hist Pr.
**Daughters of the American Revolution. Georgia. Joeseph
Habersham Chapter, Atlanta.**
  xDaughters Of The American Revolution -
    Georgia.
    Historical Collections of the Joseph Habersham
      Chapter. Genealog Pub.
Daughters St. Paul. see Daughters of St. Paul.
Daumal, Rene, 1908-1944
  xDaumal, Rene.
    A Night of Serious Drinking. Shambhala
      Pubns.
Dauney, William.
  xDauney, William.
    Ancient Scotish Melodies. AMS Pr.
Dauten, Carl A. see Dauten, Carl Anton.
Dauten, Carl Anton.
  xDauten, Carl A.

Business Cycles & Forecasting. SW Pub.
Dauven, Jean.
  xDauven, Jean.
    The Powers of Hypnosis. Stein & Day.
Dauvillier, A. see Dauvillier, Alexandre.
Dauvillier, Alexandre.
  xDauvillier, A.
    Cosmic Dust. Philos Lib.
Dauw, Dean C.
  xDauw, Dean C.
    Stranger in Your Bed: A Guide to Emotional
      Intimacy. Nelson-Hall.
Dauwer, Leo P.
  xDauwer, Leo P.
    I Remember Southie: A Boston Bicentennial
      Celebration. Chris Mass.
Davar, R. S. see Davar, Rustom S.
Davar, Rustom S.
  xDavar, R. S.
    Personnel Management & Industrial Relations
      in India. Intl Bk Dist.
  xDavar, Rustom S.
    Personnel Management & Industrial Relations
      in India. Intl Pubns Serv.
Davaras, Costis.
  xDavaras, Costis.
    Guide to Cretan Antiquities. Noyes.
Davenport, Basil, 1905-1966
  xDavenport, Basil.
    ed. Portable Roman Reader. Penguin.
Davenport, Charles B. see Davenport, Charles Benedict.
Davenport, Charles Benedict.
  xDavenport, Charles B.
    Race Crossing in Jamaica. Negro U Pr.
Davenport, Diana.
  xDavenport, Diana.
    The Desperate Season. Fawcett.
Davenport, Donald H. see Davenport, Donald Hills.
Davenport, Donald Hills.
  xDavenport, Donald H.
    Index to Business Indices. Gale.
Davenport, E. H. see Davenport, Ernest Harold.
Davenport, Ernest Harold.
  xDavenport, E. H.
    The Oil Trusts & Anglo-American Relations.
      Hyperion Conn.
Davenport, F. M. see Davenport, Frederick Morgan.
Davenport, Frances G. see Davenport, Frances Gardiner.
Davenport, Frances Gardiner, 1870-1927
  xDavenport, Frances G.
    A Classified List of Printed Original Materials
      for English Manorial & Agrarian History
      During the Middle Ages. B Franklin.
    Economic Development of a Norfolk Manor,
      1086-1565. Biblio Dist.
    Economic Development of a Norfolk Manor,
      1085-1585. Kelley.
  xDavenport, Frances G.
    ed. European Treaties Bearing on the History
      of the United States & Its Dependencies to
      1815. Peter Smith.
Davenport, Francis G. see Davenport, Frances Gardiner.
Davenport, Frederick Morgan, 1866-1956
  xDavenport, F. M.
    Primitive Traits in Religious Revivals: A Study
      in Mental & Social Evolution. Gordon Pr.
Davenport, Herbert J. see Davenport, Herbert Joseph.
Davenport, Herbert Joseph, 1861-1931
  xDavenport, Herbert J.
    Economics of Alfred Marshall. Kelley.
    Economics of Enterprise. Kelley.
    Outlines of Economic Theory. Kelley.
Davenport, Horace W. see Davenport, Horace Willard.
Davenport, Horace Willard, 1912-
  xDavenport, Horace W.

ABC of Acid-Base Chemistry: The Elements of
  Physiological Blood-Gas Chemistry for
  Medical Students & Physicians. U of Chicago
  Pr.
A Digest of Digestion. Year Bk Med.
Davenport, John W. see Davenport, John Warner.
Davenport, John Warner, 1931-
  xDavenport, John W.
    Baseball Graphics. First Impressions.
Davenport, Richard, 1930-
  xDavenport, Richard.
    Outline of Animal Development. A-W.
Davenport, Robert, fl. 1623
  xDavenport, Robert.
    Works of Robert Davenport. Arno.
Davenport, Russell W. see Davenport, Russell Wheeler.
Davenport, Russell Wheeler, 1899-1954
  xDavenport, Russell W.
    The Dignity of Man. Greenwood.
Davenport, T. C.
  xDavenport, T. C.
    ed. The Rheology of Lubricants. Halsted Pr.
Davenport, T. R. see Davenport, T. R. H.
Davenport, T. R. H.
  xDavenport, T. R.
    South Africa: A Modern History. U of Toronto
      Pr.
Davenport, W. see Davenport, William P.
Davenport, W. A. see Davenport, William Anthony.
Davenport, W. H. see Davenport, William Henry.
Davenport, Walter.
  xDavenport, W.
    Frwd. by Power & Glory: The Life of Boies
      Penrose. Scholarly.
  xDavenport, Walter.
    Power & Glory: The Life of Boies Penrose.
      Scholarly.
Davenport, Wilbur B.
  xDavenport, W.
    Probability & Random Processes: An
      Introduction for Applied Scientists &
      Engineers. McGraw.
Davenport, William. see Davenport, William Wyatt.
Davenport, William Anthony, 1935-
  xDavenport, W. A.
    The Art of the Gawain-Poet. Humanities.
Davenport, William Henry, 1908-
  xDavenport, W. H.
    The One Culture. Pergamon.
Davenport, William P.
  xDavenport, W.
    Modern Data Communication: Concepts,
      Language & Media. Hayden.
Davenport, William W. see Davenport, William Wyatt.
Davenport, William Wyatt.
  xDavenport, W.
    Athens. Silver.
  xDavenport, William.
    Athens. Time-Life.
  xDavenport, William W.
    Gyro!: The Life & Times of Lawrence Sperry.
      Scribner.
Daves, Francis M.
  xDaves, Francis M.
    Cherokee Woman. Branden.
Davey, Cyril. see Davey, Cyril James.
Davey, Cyril James.
  xDavey, Cyril.
    Fifty Lives for God. Judson.
Davey, Harold W.
  xDavey, Harold W.
    Contemporary Collective Bargaining. P-H.
Davey, Henry, 1853-1929
  xDavey, Henry.
    History of English Music. Da Capo.
Davey, Homer C.
  xDavey, Homer C.
    Financing Real Estate in California. Har-Row.
Davey, Patrick J.
  xDavey, Patrick J.

Defenses Against Unnegotiated Cash Tender
Offers. Conference Bd.

Daviau, Donald G.
xDaviau, Donald G.
The Ariadne Auf Naxos of Hugo von
Hofmannsthal & Richard Strauss. U of NC
Pr.

David, Alfred, 1929-
xDavid, Alfred.
The Strumpet Muse: Art & Morals in
Chaucer's Poetry. Ind U Pr.
ed. Twelve Dancing Princesses & Other Fairy
Tales. Ind U Pr.

David, Arie E.
xDavid, Arie E.
The Strategy of Treaty Termination: Lawful
Breaches & Retaliations. Yale U Pr.

David, D. J. see David, Donald Joseph.

David, David S.
xDavid, David S.
Calcium Metabolism in Renal Failure &
Nephrolithiasis. Wiley.

David, Deborah S. see David, Deborah Sarah.

David, Deborah Sarah.
xDavid, Deborah S.
Forty-Nine Percent Majority: The Male Sex
Role. A-W.

David, Donald Joseph, 1930-
xDavid, D. J.
Gas Chromatographic Detectors. Wiley.

David, Edward E.
xDavid, Edward E.
Human Communication: A Unified View.
McGraw.

David, Elizabeth, 1913-
xDavid, Elizabeth.
English Bread & Yeast Cookery. Viking Pr.
French Country Cooking. Penguin.
French Provincial Cooking. Penguin.

David, Eugene.
xDavid, Eugene.
Crystal Magic. P-H.

David, F. N. see David, Florence Nightingale.
David, Florence N. see David, Florence Nightingale.

David, Florence Nightingale, 1909-
xDavid, F. N.
A First Course in Statistics. Hafner.
xDavid, Florence N.
Games, Gods & Gambling: The Origins &
History of Probability & Statistical Ideas from
the Earliest Times to the Newtonian Era.
Hafner.

David, H. see David, Heinz.
David, H. A. see David, Herbert Aron.

David, Heinz.
xDavid, H.
Submicroscopic Ortho- & Patho-Morphology of
the Liver. Pergamon.

David, Henry P. see David, Henry Philip.

David, Henry Philip, 1923-
xDavid, Henry P.
ed. Abortion in Psychosocial Perspective:
Trends in Transnational Research. Springer
Pub.

David, Herbert Aron.
xDavid, H. A.
ed. Order Statistics. Wiley.

David, Jay.
xDavid, Jay.
ed. Growing up Black. S&S.
Growing up Black. PB.

David, Kenneth. see David, Kenneth H.

David, Kenneth H.
xDavid, Kenneth.
ed. The New Wind: Changing Identities in
South Asia. Beresford Bk Serv.

David, Lester.
xDavid, Lester.

The Lonely Lady of San Clemente: The Story
of Pat Nixon. T Y Crowell.
Richard & Elizabeth. Ballantine.

David, M. see David, Michel.

David, Michel, 1945-
xDavid, M.
Geostatistical Ore Reserve Estimation.
Elsevier.

David, Myriam.
xDavid, M.
Early Child Care in France. Gordon.

David, P. see David, Pierre.
David, Paul T. see David, Paul Theodore.

David, Paul Theodore.
xDavid, Paul T.
Barriers to Youth Employment. Arno.
Executives for Government: Central Issues of
Federal Personnel Administration.
Greenwood.
Party Strength in the United States 1872-1970.
U Pr of Va..
ed. The Presidential Election & Transition of
1960-61: Brookings Lectures & Additional
Papers. Brookings.

David, Pedro R.
xDavid, Pedro R.
ed. The World of the Burglar: Five Criminal
Lives. U of NM Pr.

David, Pierre.
xDavid, P.
Propagation of Waves. Pergamon.

David, R. see David, Richard.

David, Richard.
xDavid, R.
Shakespeare in the Theatre. Cambridge U Pr.

David-Neel, Alexandra.
xDavid-Neel, Alexandra.
The Superhuman Life of Gesar of Ling. Arno.

Davidge, R. W., 1936
xDavidge, R. W.
Mechanical Behaviour of Ceramics. Cambridge
U Pr.

Davidman, Joy.
xDavidman, Joy.
Letter to a Comrade. AMS Pr.

Davidoff, L. see Davidoff, Linda L.

Davidoff, Leonore.
xDavidoff, Leonore.
A Day in the Life of a Victorian Domestic
Servant. Allen Unwin.

Davidoff, Linda L.
xDavidoff, L.
Introduction to Psychology. McGraw.
xDavidoff, Linda L.
Introduction to Psychology. McGraw.

Davidoff, Zino.
xDavidoff, Zino.
Connoisseur's Book of the Cigar. McGraw.

Davidovits, P. see Davidovits, Paul.

Davidovits, Paul.
xDavidovits, P.
ed. Alkali Halide Vapors: Structure, Spectra, &
Reaction Dynamics. Acad Pr.

Davidow, Mike.
xDavidow, Mike.
Cities Without Crisis. Intl Pub Co.

Davids, Anthony.
xDavids, Anthony.
ed. Child Personality & Psychopathology:
Current Topics. Krieger.
ed. Child Personality & Psychopathology:
Current Topics. Wiley.
Children in Conflict: A Casebook. Wiley.

Davids, L. E. see Davids, Lewis E.

Davids, Lewis E.
xDavids, L. E.
Instant Business Dictionary. Watts.
xDavids, Lewis E.

Dictionary of Banking & Finance. Littlefield.
Dictionary of Banking & Finance. Rowman.
Dictionary of Insurance. Littlefield.
Instant Business Dictionary. Career Inst.

Davids, T. Rhys. see Davids, T. W. Rhys.

Davids, T. W. Rhys.
xDavids, T. Rhys.
Lectures on the Origin & Growth of Religion
As Illustrated by Some Points in the History
of Indian Buddhism. Verry.

Davids, Thomas W. see Davids, Thomas William Rhys.

Davids, Thomas William Rhys, 1843-1922
xDavids, Thomas W.
Buddhist India. Arno.
Buddhist India. Intl Pubns Serv.

Davidsohn, A.
xDavidsohn, A.
Synthetic Detergents. Halsted Pr.

Davidson. see Davidson, R. Theodore.

Davidson, Abraham A.
xDavidson, Abraham A.
The Eccentrics & Other American Visionary
Painters. Dutton.
Story of American Painting. Abrams.

Davidson, Alan, 1924-
xDavidson, Alan.
Fish and Fish Dishes of Laos. C E Tuttle.
North Atlantic Seafood. Viking Pr.

Davidson, Alan J.
xDavidson, Alan J.
Radiologic Diagnosis of Renal Parenchymal
Disease. Saunders.

Davidson, Alastair, 1939-
xDavidson, Alastair.
Antonio Gramsci: Towards an Intellectual
Biography. Carrier Pigeon.

Davidson, Avram.
xDavidson, Avram.
Masters of the Maze. Manor Bks.

Davidson, Basil, 1914-
xDavidson, Basil.
Africa in History: Themes & Outlines.
Macmillan.
African Kingdoms. Time-Life.
African Kingdoms. Silver.
African Slave Trade: Pre-Colonial History,
1450-1850. Little.
History of East & Central Africa to the Late
Nineteenth Century. Peter Smith.
A History of West Africa 1000-1800.
Longman.
Let Freedom Come: Africa in Modern History.
Little.
The Lost Cities of Africa. Little.

Davidson, Bill. see Davidson, William.

Davidson, Bill R., 1928-
xDavidson, Bill R.
To Keep & Bear Arms. Sycamore Island.

Davidson, Carson.
xDavidson, Carson.
Fast-Talking Dolphin. Dodd.
Fast Talking Dolphin. Schol Bk Serv.

Davidson, Cathy N.
xDavidson, Cathy N.
ed. The Lost Tradition: Mothers & Daughters
in Literature. Ungar.

Davidson, Charles S. see Davidson, Charles Sprecher.

Davidson, Charles Sprecher, 1910-
xDavidson, Charles S.
Liver Pathophysiology: Its Relevance to
Human Disease. Little.
ed. Problems in Liver Diseases.
Thieme-Stratton.

Davidson, Clarissa S. see Davidson, Clarissa Start.

Davidson, Clarissa Start.
xDavidson, Clarissa S.
God's Man: The Story of Pastor Niemoeller.
Greenwood.

Davidson, Clifford.
xDavidson, Clifford.

Drama & Art: An Introduction to the Use of
Evidence from the Visual Arts for the Study
of Early Drama. Medieval Inst.
Davidson, Dan A.
xDavidson, Dana.
A Breakthrough to New Free Energy Sources.
R & E Res Assoc.
Davidson, Dana. *see* Davidson, Dan A.
Davidson, Donald, 1893-
xDavidson, Donald.
Southern Writers in the Modern World. U of
Ga Pr.
Tennessee: The Old River, Frontier to
Secession. HR&W.
Davidson, Elizabeth H. *see* Davidson, Elizabeth Huey.
Davidson, Elizabeth Huey, 1902-
xDavidson, Elizabeth H.
Establishment of the English Church in
Continental American Colonies. AMS Pr.
Davidson, Ellen P. *see* Davidson, Ellen Prescott.
Davidson, Ellen Prescott.
xDavidson, Ellen P.
For Always Only. Norton.
Davidson, Eric H., 1937-
xDavidson, Eric H.
Gene Activity in Early Development. Acad Pr.
Davidson, Georgie.
xDavidson, Georgie.
Origami. Larousse.
Davidson, Glen W.
xDavidson, Glen W.
ed. The Hospice: Development &
Administration. Hemisphere Pub.
Living with Dying. Augsburg.
Davidson, Gordon C. *see* Davidson, Gordon Charles.
Davidson, Gordon Charles, 1884-
xDavidson, Gordon C.
North West Company. Russell.
Davidson, Gustav, 1895-1971
xDavidson, Gustav.
All Things Are Holy. Dragons Teeth.
Davidson, H. Ellis. *see* Davidson, Hilda Roderick (Ellis).
Davidson, H. R. *see* Davidson, Hilda Roderick (Ellis).
Davidson, H. W. *see* Davidson, Hugh Wilson.
Davidson, Hilda E. *see* Davidson, Hilda Roderick Ellis.
Davidson, Hilda Roderick (Ellis).
xDavidson, H. Ellis.
Gods & Myths of Northern Europe. Penguin.
xDavidson, H. R.
Gods & Myths of Northern Europe. Gannon.
Davidson, Hilda Roderick Ellis.
xDavidson, H. R.
ed. The Journey to the Other World. Rowman.
xDavidson, Hilda E.
Patterns of Folklore. Rowman.
Davidson, Homer L.
xDavidson, Homer L.
Admiral Color TV Service Manual. TAB Bks.
Admiral Monochrome TV Service Manual.
TAB Bks.
Davidson, Hugh M. *see* Davidson, Hugh Mccullough.
Davidson, Hugh Mccullough, 1918-
xDavidson, Hugh M.
Audience, Words, & Art: Studies in
Seventeenth-Century French Rhetoric. Ohio
St U Pr.
A Concordance to Pascal's "Les Provinciales".
Garland Pub.
Davidson, Hugh Wilson.
xDavidson, H. W.
Manufactured Carbon. Pergamon.
Davidson, Ian.
xDavidson, Ian D.
Britain & the Making of Europe. St Martin.
Davidson, Ian D. *see* Davidson, Ian.
Davidson, Isobel, 1869-
xDavidson, Isobel.

Real Stories from Baltimore County History.
Gale.
Davidson, Israel, 1870-1939
xDavidson, Israel.
Parody in Jewish Literature. AMS Pr.
Davidson, J. A. *see* Davidson, James.
Davidson, J. F. *see* Davidson, John Frank.
Davidson, J. K. *see* Davidson, John Knight.
Davidson, J. W. *see* Davidson, James Wightman.
Davidson, James, 1922-
xDavidson, J. A.
Indo-China-Signposts in the Storm. Longman.
Davidson, James D. *see* Davidson, James Dale.
Davidson, James Dale.
xDavidson, James D.
The Squeeze. PB.
The Squeeze. S&S.
The Squeeze. Summit Bks.
Davidson, James R. *see* Davidson, James Robert.
Davidson, James Robert, 1942-
xDavidson, James R.
A Dictionary of Protestant Church Music.
Scarecrow.
Davidson, James W. *see* Davidson, James West.
Davidson, James West.
xDavidson, James W.
The Complete Wilderness Paddler. Knopf.
The Logic of Millennial Thought:
Eighteenth-Century New England. Yale U
Pr.
Davidson, James Wightman, 1915-
xDavidson, J. W.
Northern Rhodesian Legislative Council.
Greenwood.
Davidson, Jane P.
xDavidson, Jane P.
David Teniers the Younger. Westview.
Davidson, Jeffrey L.
xDavidson, Jeffrey L.
Political Partnerships: Neighborhood Residents
& Their Council Members. Sage.
Davidson, Jim.
xDavidson, Jim.
How to Plan Your Life. Pelican.
Davidson, Joan.
xDavidson, Joan.
Planning & the Rural Environment. Pergamon.
Davidson, John, 1947-
xDavidson, John.
The Long Road North. Doubleday.
Davidson, John Frank.
xDavidson, J. F.
ed. Fluidization. Acad Pr.
ed. Fluidization. Cambridge U Pr.
Davidson, John Knight.
xDavidson, J. K.
Aseptic Necrosis of Bone. Elsevier.
Davidson, John P. *see* Davidson, John Pirnie.
Davidson, John Pirnie, 1924-
xDavidson, John P.
Collective Models of the Nucleus. Acad Pr.
Davidson, Kerry.
xDavidson, Kerry.
Twentieth Century Civilization. Har-Row.
Davidson, L. *see* Davidson, Les.
Davidson, Laura. *see* Davidson, Laurie.
Davidson, Laurie.
xDavidson, Laura.
The Sociology of Gender. Rand.
Davidson, Leon, 1922-
xDavidson, Leon.
Flying Saucers: An Analysis of the Air Force
Project Blue Book Special Report No. 14
Including the C.I.A. & the Saucers. Blue
Book.
Davidson, Les.
xDavidson, L.
Using the Magic of Word Power to Multiply
Real Estate Sales. P-H.
Davidson, Levette J. *see* Davidson, Levette Jay.

Davidson, Levette Jay, 1894-1957
xDavidson, Levette J.
Guide to American Folklore. Greenwood.
Literature of the Rocky Mountain West
1803-1903. Kennikat.
Davidson, Leybourne Stanley Patrick.
xDavidson, Stanley.
Human Nutrition & Dietetics. Churchill.
Davidson, Lionel.
xDavidson, Lionel.
Murder Games. Coward.
The Night of Wenceslas. Penguin.
The Sun Chemist. Knopf.
The Sun Chemist. Penguin.
Davidson, Margaret.
xDavidson, Margaret.
Successful Studios & Work Centers. Structures
Pub.
Wild Animal Families. Hastings.
Davidson, Marion.
xDavidson, Marion.
Making It Legal: A Law Primer for the
Craftmaker, Visual Artist, & Writer.
McGraw.
Davidson, Marshall. *see* Davidson, Marshall B.
Davidson, Marshall B.
xDavidson, Marshall.
Life in America. HM.
Davidson, Michael, 1944-
xDavidson, Michael.
Mutabilities (& the Foul Papers). Sand Dollar.
Davidson, Mickie.
xDavidson, Mickie.
Adventures of George Washington. Schol Bk
Serv.
Pirate Book. Random.
Davidson, Muriel.
xDavidson, Muriel.
Hot Spot. Marek.
The Thursday Woman. Atheneum.
The Thursday Woman. Berkley Pub.
Davidson, Neil.
xDavidson, Neil A.
Abstract Algebra: An Active Learning
Approach. HM.
Davidson, Neil A. *see* Davidson, Neil.
Davidson, Park O. *see* Davidson, Park Olof.
Davidson, Park Olof.
xDavidson, Park O.
ed. Behavioral Medicine: Changing Health
Lifestyles. Brunner Mazel.
Davidson, Paul.
xDavidson, Paul.
Money & the Real World. Halsted Pr.
Davidson, Philip. *see* Davidson, Philip Grant.
Davidson, Philip G. *see* Davidson, Philip Grant.
Davidson, Philip Grant, 1902-
xDavidson, Philip.
Propaganda in the American Revolution.
Norton.
xDavidson, Philip G.
Propaganda & the American Revolution,
1763-1789. U of NC Pr.
Davidson, Phillip L.
xDavidson, Phillip L.
SWAT (Special Weapons & Tactics). C C
Thomas.
Davidson, R. Theodore.
xDavidson.
Chicano Prisoners: The Key to San Quentin.
HR&W.
Davidson, Ralph. *see* Davidson, Ralph Howard.
Davidson, Ralph Howard.
xDavidson, Ralph.
Insect Pests of Farm, Garden, & Orchard.
Wiley.
Davidson, Richard L.
xDavidson, Richard L.

Somatic Cell Hybridization. Raven.
Davidson, Robin.
  xDavidson, Robin.
    Cornwall. David & Charles.
Davidson, Roger H.
  xDavidson, Roger H.
    Congress Against Itself. Ind U Pr.
    The Politics of Comprehensive Manpower
      Legislation. Johns Hopkins.
Davidson, Ronald C.
  xDavidson, Ronald C.
    Theory of Nonneutral Plasmas.
      Benjamin-Cummings.
Davidson, Roslyn.
  xDavidson, Roslyn.
    Rehabilitation Administrative Procedures for
      Extended Care Facilities. C C Thomas.
Davidson, Sara.
  xDavidson, Sara.
    Loose Change: Three Women of the Sixties.
      Doubleday.
    Real Property. Doubleday.
Davidson, Sharon V. see Davidson, Sharon Van Sell.
Davidson, Sharon Van Sell, 1944-
  xDavidson, Sharon V.
    PSRO: Utilization & Audit in Patient Care.
      Mosby.
Davidson, Sidney.
  xDavidson, Sidney.
    Fundamentals of Accounting. Dryden Pr.
    Inflation Accounting: A Guide for the
      Accountant & the Financial Analyst.
      McGraw.
  xDavidson, Sydney.
    Accounting: The Language of Business. T
      Horton & Dghts.
Davidson, Stanley. see Davidson, Leybourne Stanley
  Patrick.
Davidson, Stephen M.
  xDavidson, Stephen M.
    The Cost of Living Longer National Health
      Insurance & the Elderly. Lexington Bks.
Davidson, Sydney. see Davidson, Sidney.
Davidson, Thomas, 1840-1900
  xDavidson, Thomas.
    Aristotle & Ancient Educational Ideals. B
      Franklin.
    Aristotle & Ancient Educational Ideals. R
      West.
    Aristotle & Ancient Educational Ideals.
      Scholarly.
    Education of the Greek People, & Its Influence
      on Civilization. AMS Pr.
    The Education of the Greek People & Its
      Influence on Civilization. Scholarly.
    Education of the Wage-Earners: Contribution
      Toward Solution of Educational Problems of
      Democracy. B Franklin.
    History of Education. AMS Pr.
    History of Education. B Franklin.
    A History of Education. R West.
Davidson, Victor, 1889-
  xDavidson, Victor.
    History of Wilkinson County. Reprint.
Davidson, W. F.
  xDavidson, W. F.
    The Country Life Picture Book of Scotland.
      Arco.
Davidson, W. R. see Davidson, William R.
Davidson, William, 1918-
  xDavidson, Bill.
    Collura: Actor with a Gun. PB.
Davidson, William L. see Davidson, William Leslie.
Davidson, William Leslie, 1848-1929
  xDavidson, William L.
    Political Thought in England: The Utilitarians,
      from Bentham to J. S. Mill. Hyperion Conn.
    The Stoic Creed. Arno.
Davidson, William R.
  xDavidson, W. R.

Retailing Management. Wiley.
Davidson, William V.
  xDavidson, William V.
    Historical Geography of the Bay Islands,
      Honduras: Anglo-Hispanic Conflict in the
      Western Caribbean. Southern U Pr.
Davie, Cedric T. see Davie, Cedric Thorpe.
Davie, Cedric Thorpe, 1913-
  xDavie, Cedric T.
    Musical Structure & Design. Dover.
Davie, Donald.
  xDavie, Donald.
    Articulate Energy: An Inquiry into the Syntax
      of English Poetry. Scholarly.
    ed. Augustan Lyric. Heinemann Ed.
    Ezra Pound. Viking Pr.
    A Gathered Church: The Literature of the
      English Dissenting Interest, 1700-1930.
      Oxford U Pr.
    Thomas Hardy & British Poetry. Oxford U Pr.
    Trying to Explain. U of Mich Pr.
Davie, Maurice R. see Davie, Maurice Rea.
Davie, Maurice Rea, 1893-
  xDavie, Maurice R.
    Evolution of War: A Study of Its Role in Early
      Societies. Elliots Bks.
Davies, A. see Davies, Arthur Powell.
Davies, A. Mervyn. see Davies, Alfred Mervyn.
Davies, Alan. see Davies, Alan T.
Davies, Alan T.
  xDavies, Alan.
    ed. Antisemitism & the Foundations of
      Christianity. Paulist Pr.
Davies, Alfred Mervyn.
  xDavies, A. Mervyn.
    Presbyterian Heritage. John Knox.
Davies, Alice I.
  xDavies, Alice I.
    Allart van Everdingen. Garland Pub.
Davies, Andrew.
  xDavies, Andrew.
    Fantastic Feats of Doctor Boox. Bradbury Pr.
    The Fantastic Feats of Doctor Boox. Schol Bk
      Serv.
Davies, Aneirin T. see Davies, Aneirin Talfan.
Davies, Aneirin Talfan.
  xDavies, Aneirin T.
    Dylan: Druid of the Broken Body. Humanities.
Davies, Arthur Powell.
  xDavies, A.
    Meaning of the Dead Sea Scrolls. NAL.
Davies, B. see Davies, Blodwen.
Davies, Benjamin.
  xDavies, Benjamin.
    ed. Baker's Pocket Harmony of the Gospels.
      Baker Bk.
Davies, Bernard. see Davies, Bernard David.
Davies, Bernard David.
  xDavies, Bernard.
    Use of Groups in Social Work Practice.
      Routledge & Kegan.
Davies, Bettilu D.
  xDavies, Bettilu D.
    The Secret of the Hidden Cave. Zondervan.
Davies, Blodwen.
  xDavies, B.
    String of Amber: The Heritage of the
      Mennonites. Heinman.
Davies, Brian, 1937-
  xDavies, B.
    Integral Transforms & Their Applications.
      Springer-Verlag.
  xDavies, Brian.
    An Introduction to Clinical Psychiatry. Intl
      Schol Bk Serv.
Davies, C. see Davies, Cyril.
Davies, C. N. see Davies, Charles Norman.
Davies, C. W. see Davies, Cecil Whitfield.
Davies, Cecil Whitfield.
  xDavies, C. W.

Dictionary of Electrochemistry. Halsted Pr.
Davies, Charles M. see Davies, Charles Maurice.
Davies, Charles Maurice, 1828-1910
  xDavies, Charles M.
    Broad Church. Garland Pub.
Davies, Charles Norman, 1910-
  xDavies, C. N.
    Air Filtration. Acad Pr.
Davies, Cyril.
  xDavies, C.
    Organization for Program Management. Wiley.
Davies, D. I. see Davies, David Ian.
Davies, D. M. see Davies, David Margerison.
Davies, D. R. see Davies, David Richard.
Davies, D. S. see Davies, Duncan.
Davies, D. W. see Davies, David William.
Davies, David. see Davies, David William.
Davies, David Ian.
  xDavies, D. I.
    Free Radicals in Organic Synthesis.
      Springer-Verlag.
Davies, David Margerison.
  xDavies, D. M.
    ed. Textbook of Adverse Drug Reactions.
      Oxford U Pr..
Davies, David Richard, 1889-1958
  xDavies, D. R.
    Reinhold Niebuhr: Prophet from America.
      Arno.
Davies, David Roy.
  xDavies, D. R.
    Human Vigilance Performance. Elsevier.
Davies, David W.
  xDavies, David W.
    World of the Elseviers. Greenwood.
Davies, David W. see Davies, David William.
Davies, David William.
  xDavies, D. W.
    Dutch Influences on English Culture,
      1558-1625. Folger Bks.
  xDavies, David.
    The Evergreen Tree. Grant Dahlstrom.
  xDavies, David W.
    ed. Concordance to the Essays of Francis
      Bacon. Gale.
    Public Libraries As Culture & Social Centers:
      The Origin of the Concept. Scarecrow.
Davies, Derek A. C., 1943-
  xDavies, Derek A. C.
    Greek Islands. Kodansha.
Davies, Donald Watts.
  xDavies, D. W.
    Communication Networks for Computers.
      Wiley.
    Computer Networks & Their Protocols. Wiley.
Davies, Duncan.
  xDavies, D. S.
    The Humane Technologist. Oxford U Pr.
Davies, E. B. see Davies, Edward Brian.
Davies, Edward Brian.
  xDavies, E. B.
    ed. Quantum Theory of Open Systems. Acad
      Pr.
Davies, Eirian.
  xDavies, Eirian.
    On the Semantics of Syntax: Mood &
      Condition in English. Humanities.
Davies, Emily, 1830-1921
  xDavies, Emily.
    Higher Education of Women. AMS Pr.
Davies, Eryl.
  xDavies, Eryl.
    Ocean Frontiers. Viking Pr.
Davies, Godfrey, 1892-1957
  xDavies, Godfrey.
    Early Stuarts, 1603-1660. Oxford U Pr.
Davies, Gordon L.
  xDavies, Gordon L.

The Earth in Decay: A History of British
    Geomorphology 1578-1878. N Watson.
Davies, Henry W. *see* Davies, Henry Walford.
Davies, Henry Walford.
    xDavies, Henry W.
    Music & Worship. AMS Pr.
Davies, Horton.
    xDavies, Horton.
    Great South African Christians. Greenwood.
    Compiled by Prayers & Other Resources for
    Public Worship. Abingdon.
Davies, Hugh S. *see* Davies, Hugh Sykes.
Davies, Hugh Sykes, 1909-
    xDavies, Hugh S.
    Browning & the Modern Novel. Folcroft.
Davies, I. K. *see* Davies, Ivor Kevin.
Davies, Ivor. *see* Davies, Ivor Kevin.
Davies, Ivor K. *see* Davies, Ivor Kevin.
Davies, Ivor Kevin.
    xDavies, I. K.
    Objectives in Curriculum Design. McGraw.
    xDavies, Ivor.
    ed. Contributions to an Educational
        Technology. Nichols Pub.
    xDavies, Ivor K.
    ed. Contributions to an Educational
        Technology. Crane-Russak Co.
Davies, J. A. *see* Davies, James Arthur.
Davies, J. Clarence.
    xDavies, J. Clarence.
    Neighborhood Groups & Urban Renewal.
        Columbia U Pr.
    The Politics of Pollution. Pegasus.
Davies, J. G. *see* Davies, John Gordon.
Davies, J. H.
    xDavies, J. H.
    Musicalia: Sources of Information in Music.
        Pergamon.
Davies, J. K. *see* Davies, John Kenyon.
Davies, J. Kenneth. *see* Davies, Joseph Kenneth.
Davies, J. T. *see* Davies, John Tasman.
Davies, James Arthur.
    xDavies, J. A.
    Education in a Welsh Rural County,
        1870-1973. Verry.
Davies, James C. *see* Davies, James Chowning.
Davies, James Chowning, 1918-
    xDavies, James C.
    Human Nature in Politics: The Dynamics of
        Political Behavior. Greenwood.
Davies, John, Sir, 1569-1626
    xDavies, John.
    Orchestra: Or a Poem of Dancing. Scholarly.
Davies, John B. *see* Davies, John Booth.
Davies, John Booth.
    xDavies, John B.
    The Psychology of Music. Stanford U Pr.
Davies, John G. *see* Davies, John Gordon.
Davies, John Gordon, 1919-
    xDavies, J. G.
    Christians, Politics & Violent Revolution. Orbis
        Bks.
    The Early Christian Church. Baker Bk.
    ed. The Westminster Dictionary of Worship.
        Westminster.
    xDavies, John G.
    Daily Life of Early Christians. Greenwood.
    The Early Christian Church. Greenwood.
Davies, John Kenyon.
    xDavies, J. K.
    Democracy & Classical Greece. Humanities.
Davies, John L. *see* Davies, John Lloyd.
Davies, John Lloyd.
    xDavies, John L.
    Geographical Variation in Coastal
        Development. Longman.
Davies, John Tasman, 1924-
    xDavies, J. T.

Turbulence Phenomena: An Introduction to the
    Eddy Transfer of Momentum, Mass & Heat,
    Particularly at Interfaces. Acad Pr.
Davies, Jonathan C. *see* Davies, Jonathan Ceredig.
Davies, Jonathan Ceredig, 1859-1932
    xDavies, Jonathan C.
    Folk-Lore of West & Mid-Wales. Norwood
        Edns.
    Folklore of West & Mid Wales. Folcroft.
Davies, Joseph E. *see* Davies, Joseph Earl.
Davies, Joseph Earl, 1901-1938
    xDavies, Joseph E.
    Fundamentals of Housing Study: A
        Determination of Factors Basic to an
        Understanding of American Housing
        Problems. AMS Pr.
Davies, Joseph Kenneth.
    xDavies, J. Kenneth.
    Economics & the American System. Lippincott.
Davies, Julian.
    xDavies, Julian.
    Elementary Biochemistry: An Introduction to
        the Chemistry of Living Cells. P-H.
Davies, K. G. *see* Davies, Kenneth Gordon.
Davies, Kenneth Gordon.
    xDavies, K. G.
    The North Atlantic World in the Seventeenth
        Century. U of Minn Pr.
Davies, Laurence.
    xDavies, Laurence.
    Cesar Franck & His Circle. Da Capo.
    Ravel Orchestral Music. U of Wash Pr.
Davies, Margaret (Gay).
    xDavies, Margaret G.
    Enforcement of English Apprenticeship: A
        Study in Applied Mercantilism, 1563-1642.
        Harvard U Pr.
Davies, Margaret G. *see* Davies, Margaret (Gay).
Davies, Margaret L. *see* Davies, Margaret Llewelyn.
Davies, Margaret Llewelyn, 1861-
    xDavies, Margaret L.
    ed. Life As We Have Known It. Norton.
Davies, Martin.
    xDavies, Martin.
    Prisoners of Society: Attitudes & After-Care.
        Routledge & Kegan.
    Support Systems in Social Work. Routledge &
        Kegan.
Davies, Nigel, 1920-
    xDavies, Nigel.
    The Toltec Heritage: From the Fall of Tula to
        the Rise of Tenochtitlan. U of Okla Pr.
Davies, Oliver.
    xDavies, Oliver.
    Roman Mines in Europe. Arno.
Davies, P. C. *see* Davies, P. C. W.
Davies, P. C. W.
    xDavies, P. C.
    The Forces of Nature. Cambridge U Pr.
    xDavies, P. W.
    Space & Time in the Modern Universe.
        Cambridge U Pr.
    xDavies, Paul.
    The Runaway Universe. Har-Row.
    The Runaway Universe. Penguin.
Davies, P. W. *see* Davies, P. C. W.
Davies, Paul. *see* Davies, P. C. W.
Davies, Penelope.
    xDavies, Penelope.
    Tutankhamun's Egypt. St Martin.
Davies, Peter.
    xDavies, Peter.
    Fly Away Paul. Crown.
Davies, R.
    xDavies, R.
    Forgotten Railways: Chilterns & Cotswolds.
        David & Charles.
Davies, R. G. *see* Davies, Richard Gareth.
Davies, R. R.
    xDavies, R. R.

Lordship & Society in the March of Wales
    1282-1400. Oxford U Pr.
Davies, R. W. *see* Davies, Robert William.
Davies, Reg. *see* Davies, Reginald Thorne.
Davies, Reginald Thorne.
    xDavies, Reg.
    ed. Literature of the Romantic Period,
        1750-1850. B&N.
Davies, Richard Gareth.
    xDavies, R. G.
    Computer Programming in Quantitative
        Biology. Acad Pr.
Davies, Richard O.
    xDavies, Richard O.
    Housing Reform During the Truman
        Administration. U of Mo Pr.
Davies, Robert W. *see* Davies, Robert William.
Davies, Robert William.
    xDavies, R. W.
    The Soviet Collective Farm: 1929-1930.
        Harvard U Pr.
    ed. The Soviet Union. Allen Unwin.
    xDavies, Robert W.
    The Development of the Soviet Budgetary
        System. Greenwood.
Davies, Robertson. *see* Davies, William Robertson.
Davies, Ross L. *see* Davies, Rosser Llewelyn.
Davies, Rosser Llewelyn.
    xDavies, Ross L.
    Marketing Geography with Special Reference
        to Retailing. Methuen Inc.
Davies, Rupert E. *see* Davies, Rupert Eric.
Davies, Rupert Eric, 1909-
    xDavies, Rupert E.
    ed. Approach to Christian Education. Philos
        Lib.
Davies, Ruth A. *see* Davies, Ruth Ann.
Davies, Ruth Ann.
    xDavies, Ruth A.
    The School Library Media Program:
        Instructional Force for Excellence. Bowker.
Davies, S. *see* Davies, Stephen.
Davies, Samuel, 1723-1761
    xDavies, Samuel.
    Collected Poems. Schol Facsimiles.
Davies, Stephen, 1948-
    xDavies, S.
    The Diffusion of Process Innovations.
        Cambridge U Pr.
Davies, Stevie.
    xDavies, Stevie.
    Renaissance Views of Man. B&N.
Davies, T. L. *see* Davies, Thomas Lewis Owen.
Davies, Thomas.
    xDavies, Thomas.
    Memoirs of the Life of David Garrick. Arno.
Davies, Thomas L. *see* Davies, Thomas Lewis Owen.
Davies, Thomas Lewis Owen.
    xDavies, T. L.
    A Supplementary English Glossary. R West.
    xDavies, Thomas L.
    Supplementary English Glossary. Gale.
Davies, Thomas M.
    xDavies, Thomas M.
    Indian Integration in Peru: A Half Century of
        Experience, 1900-1948. U of Nebr Pr.
Davies, Trevor H., 1871-
    xDavies, Trevor H.
    Spiritual Voices in Modern Literature. Folcroft.
Davies, W. D. *see* Davies, William David.
Davies, W. J. *see* Davies, W. J. K.
Davies, W. J. K.
    xDavies, W. J.
    Ravenglass & Eskdale Railway. Kelley.
Davies, William David, 1911-
    xDavies, W. D.

Christian Origins & Judaism. Arno.
The Gospel & the Land: Early Christianity &
Jewish Territorial Doctrine. U of Cal Pr.

Davies, William Robertson, 1913-
xDavies, Robertson.
Fifth Business. Penguin.
One Half of Robertson Davies. Penguin.
One Half of Robertson Davies. Viking Pr.
World of Wonders. Penguin.
World of Wonders. Viking Pr.

Davin, D. M. see Davin, Daniel Marcus.

Davin, Daniel Marcus, 1913-
xDavin, D. M.
Closing Times. Oxford U Pr.

Davinson, Donald.
xDavinson, Donald.
Academic & Legal Deposit Libraries. Shoe
String.

Davinson, Donald. see Davinson, Donald Edward.

Davinson, Donald Edward.
xDavinson, Donald.
The Periodicals Collection. Westview.
Theses & Dissertations As Information Sources.
Shoe String.

Davio, Marc.
xDavio, Marc.
Discrete & Switching Functions. McGraw.

Davis, A. L. see Davis, Alva Leroy.

Davis, Adelle.
xDavis, Adelle.
Let's Cook It Right. Formur Intl.
Let's Cook It Right. HarBraceJ.
Let's Cook It Right. NAL.
Let's Eat Right to Keep Fit. Formur Intl.
Let's Eat Right to Keep Fit. HarBraceJ.
Let's Eat Right to Keep Fit. NAL.
Let's Get Well. Formur Intl.
Let's Get Well. HarBraceJ.
Let's Get Well. NAL.

Davis, Alan. see Davis, Alan G.

Davis, Alan G.
xDavis, Alan.
ed. Medical Encounters: The Experience of
Illness & Treatment. St Martin.
Relationships Between Doctors & Patients.
Lexington Bks.

Davis, Albert Roy.
xDavis, Albert Roy.
The Magnetic Blueprint of Life. Exposition.

Davis, Alec.
xDavis, Alec.
Graphics: Design into Production. Merrimack
Bk Serv.

Davis, Allen F.
xDavis, Allen F.
The Peoples of Philadelphia: A History of
Ethnic Groups & Lower Class Life,
1790-1940. Temple U Pr.

Davis, Allen F. see Davis, Allen Freeman.

Davis, Allen Freeman.
xDavis, Allen F.
Conflict & Consensus in Early American
History. Heath.
Conflict & Consensus in Modern American
History. Heath.
Spearheads for Reform: The Social Settlements
& the Progressive Movement, 1890-1914.
Oxford U Pr.

Davis, Allison.
xDavis, Allison.
Deep South: A Social Anthropological Study of
Caste & Class. U of Chicago Pr.
Psychology of the Child in the Middle Class. U
of Pittsburgh Pr.

Davis, Alva Leroy.
xDavis, A. L.
ed. Culture, Class, & Language Variety: A
Resource Book for Teachers. NCTE.

Davis, Angela. see Davis, Angela Yvonne.

Davis, Angela Yvonne, 1944-
xDavis, Angela.
If They Come in the Morning: Voices of
Resistance. Okpaku Communications.

Davis, Anne M. see Davis, Anne Mallard.

Davis, Anne Mallard.
xDavis, Anne M.
None to Comfort Me. Blair.

Davis, Anthony.
xDavis, Anthony.
Tackle Motorcycle Sport This Way. Soccer.

Davis, Arthur P. see Davis, Arthur Paul.

Davis, Arthur Paul.
xDavis, Arthur P.
ed. Cavalcade: Negro American Writing from
1760 to the Present. HM.
From the Dark Tower: Afro-American Writers
from 1900 to 1960. Howard U Pr.

Davis, Audrey B.
xDavis, Audrey B.
Circulation Physiology & Medical Chemistry in
England, 1650-1680. Coronado Pr.

Davis, B. see Davis, Brian.

Davis, Barbara.
xDavis, Barbara.
Learning Science & Metric Through Cooking.
Sterling.

Davis, Barbara K. see Davis, Barbara Kerr.

Davis, Barbara Kerr.
xDavis, Barbara K.
Letters to My Husband's Analyst. Dutton.

Davis, Bertram H. see Davis, Bertram Hylton.

Davis, Bertram Hylton.
xDavis, Bertram H.
Proof of Eminence: The Life of Sir John
Hawkins. Ind U Pr.

Davis, Bob, 1944-
xDavis, Bob.
photos by Faces of Japan. Kodansha.

Davis, Bob J.
xDavis, Bob J.
ed. Information Sources in Transportation,
Material Management, & Physical
Distribution: An Annotated Bibliography &
Guide. Greenwood.

Davis, Brian, Miee.
xDavis, B.
The Selection of Database Software. Intl Pubns
Serv.
xDavis, Brian.
The Selection of Database Software. Hayden.

Davis, Brian L.
xDavis, Brian L.
German Army Uniforms & Insignia,
1933-1945. Arco.

Davis, Britton, 1860-
xDavis, Britton.
The Truth About Geronimo. U of Nebr Pr.

Davis, Bruce.
xDavis, Bruce.
Hugs & Kisses. Workman Pub.

Davis, Bruce L.
xDavis, Bruce L.
Compiled by Criminological Bibliographies:
Uniform Citations to Bibliographies, Indexes,
& Review Articles of the Literature of Crime
Study in the United States. Greenwood.

Davis, Burke.
xDavis, Burke.
George Washington & the American
Revolution. Random.
Old Hickory: A Life of Andrew Jackson. Dial.
The Summer Land. Mockingbird Bks.

Davis, Calvin V. see Davis, Calvin Victor.

Davis, Calvin Victor.
xDavis, Calvin V.
Handbook of Applied Hydraulics. McGraw.

Davis, Carl S.
xDavis, Carl S.

ed. Differential Treatment of Drug & Alcohol
Abusers. ETC Pubns.

Davis, Carol B. see Davis, Carol Beery.

Davis, Carol Beery.
xDavis, Carol B.
Home Is North. Golden Quill.

Davis, Charles B. see Davis, Charles Belmont.

Davis, Charles Belmont, 1866-1926
xDavis, Charles B.
Borderland of Society. Arno.
Stage Door. Arno.
Tales of the Town. Arno.

Davis, Charles H. see Davis, Charles Henry Stanley.

Davis, Charles Hargis.
xDavis, Charles H.
Guide to Information Science. Greenwood.
Illustrative Computer Programming for
Libraries: Selected Examples for Information
Specialists. Greenwood.
Information Retrieval & Documentation in
Chemistry. Greenwood.

Davis, Charles Henry Stanley, 1840-1917
xDavis, Charles H.
Early Families of Wallingford, Connecticut.
Genealog Pub.

Davis, Charles S. see Davis, Charles Shepard.

Davis, Charles Shepard, 1910-
xDavis, Charles S.
The Cotton Kingdom in Alabama. Porcupine
Pr.

Davis, Christopher.
xDavis, Christopher.
Plains Indians. Watts.

Davis, Chuck, 1935-
xDavis, Chuck.
ed. The Vancouver Book. Intl Schol Bk Serv.

Davis, Cos H.
xDavis, Cos H.
Children & the Christian Faith. Broadman.

Davis, Cullom.
xDavis, Cullom.
Oral History: From Tape to Type. ALA.
ed. The Public & the Private Lincoln:
Contemporary Perspectives. S Ill U Pr.

Davis, Curtis C. see Davis, Curtis Carroll.

Davis, Curtis Carroll, 1916-
xDavis, Curtis C.
Revolution's Godchild: The Birth, Death &
Regeneration of the Society of the Cincinnati
in North Carolina. U of NC Pr.

Davis, Cushman K. see Davis, Cushman Kellogg.

Davis, Cushman Kellogg, 1838-1900
xDavis, Cushman K.
Law in Shakespeare. AMS Pr.

Davis, D. Russell. see Davis, Derek Russell.

Davis, Daniel S.
xDavis, Daniel S.
Marcus Garvey. Watts.
Struggle for Freedom: The History of Black
Americans. HarBraceJ.

Davis, Daphne.
xDavis, Daphne.
The Baby Animal Book. Western Pub.

Davis, Dave.
xDavis, David.
Strike Power. Contemp Bks.

Davis, David. see Davis, Dave.

Davis, David B. see Davis, David Brion.

Davis, David Brion.
xDavis, David B.
ed. Ante-Bellum Reform. Har-Row.
Antebellum American Culture: An Interpretive
Anthology. Heath.
Homicide in American Fiction, 1798-1860: A
Study in Social Values. Cornell U Pr.
The Problem of Slavery in an Age of
Revolution, 1770-1823. Cornell U Pr.
The Problem of Slavery in the Age of
Revolution: 1770-1823. Cornell U Pr.

Davis, David H. see Davis, David Howard.

Davis, David Howard.
  xDavis, David H.
    Energy Politics. St Martin.
Davis, Derek Russell.
  xDavis, D. Russell.
    An Introduction to Psychopathology. Oxford U
    Pr.
Davis, Don. *see* Davis, Donald Bast.
Davis, Donald Bast.
  xDavis, Don.
    Sound System Engineering. Sams.
Davis, Donald G.
  xDavis, Donald G.
    The Association of American Library Schools,
    1915-1968: An Analytical History.
    Scarecrow.
Davis, Dorothy B. *see* Davis, Dorothy Brandt.
Davis, Dorothy Brandt.
  xDavis, Dorothy B.
    The Little Man. Brethren.
Davis, Douglas. *see* Davis, Douglas F.
Davis, Douglas F.
  xDavis, Douglas.
    There's an Elephant in the Garage. Dutton.
  xDavis, Douglas F.
    The Lion's Tail. Atheneum.
    The White Redwoods: Ghosts of the Forest.
    Naturegraph.
Davis, Douglas M.
  xDavis, Douglas.
    Artculture: Essays on the Post-Modern.
    Har-Row.
Davis, E. Dale. *see* Davis, Elwood Dale.
Davis, Edith. *see* Davis, Edith Atwood.
Davis, Edith (Smith), 1859-1917
  xDavis, Edith S.
    Whether White or Black, a Man. Arno.
Davis, Edith Atwood.
  xDavis, Edith.
    Parent Education: A Survey of the Minnesota
    Program. Greenwood.
Davis, Edith S. *see* Davis, Edith (Smith).
Davis, Edwin W. *see* Davis, Edwin Wallace.
Davis, Edwin Wallace, 1903-
  xDavis, Edwin W.
    Functional Pattern Technique for Classification
    of Jobs. AMS Pr.
Davis, Eleanor H.
  xDavis, Eleanor H.
    Abraham Fornander: A Biography. U Pr of
    Hawaii.
Davis, Eliza T. *see* Davis, Eliza Timberlake.
Davis, Eliza Timberlake.
  xDavis, Eliza T.
    Frederick County, Virginia, Marriages,
    1771-1825. Genealog Pub.
    Frederick County, Virginia Marriages,
    1771-1825. Va Bk.
Davis, Ellen N., 1937-
  xDavis, Ellen N.
    The Vapheio Cups & Aegean Gold & Silver
    Ware. Garland Pub.
Davis, Elmer. *see* Davis, Elmer Holmes.
Davis, Elmer H. *see* Davis, Elmer Holmes.
Davis, Elmer Holmes.

  xDavis, Elmer.
    History of the New York Times, 1851-1921.
    Scholarly.

  xDavis, Elmer H.
    But We Were Born Free. Greenwood.
    By Elmer Davis. Arno.
    History of the New York Times, 1851-1921.
    Greenwood.
    Not to Mention the War. Arno.

Davis, Elwood Dale.
  xDavis, E. Dale.

Teaching Reading in the Secondary School.
  Kendall-Hunt.
Davis, Esther G. *see* Davis, Esther Gonzales.
Davis, Esther Gonzales.
  xDavis, Esther G.
    A Taste of Mexico: A Primer of Mexican
    Cooking. Rand-Tofua.
Davis, Evangeline.
  xDavis, Evangeline.
    Rebel Raider: A Biography of Admiral
    Semmes. Lippincott.
Davis, F. James. *see* Davis, Floyd James.
Davis, F. T.
  xDavis, Frank T.
    Business Acquisitions Desk Book, with
    Checklists & Forms. Inst Busn Plan.
Davis, Fei-Ling.
  xDavis, Fei-Ling.
    Primitive Revolutionaries of China: A Study of
    Secret Societies in the Late Nineteenth
    Century. U Pr of Hawaii.
Davis, Ferdinand.
  xDavis, Ferdinand.
    Essentials of Counterpoint. U of Okla Pr.
Davis, Flora.
  xDavis, Flora.
    Inside Intuition: What We Know About
    Nonverbal Communication. NAL.
Davis, Floyd James, 1920-
  xDavis, F. James.
    Understanding Minority Dominant Relations:
    Sociological Contributions. AHM Pub.
Davis, Forest K., 1918-
  xDavis, Forest K.
    Journey Among Mountains. Adamant Pr.
    Return from Enlightenment. Adamant Pr.
Davis, Francis W.
  xDavis, Francis W.
    Horse Packing in Pictures. Scribner.
Davis, Francyne.
  xDavis, Francyne.
    The Low Blood Sugar Cookbook. Bantam.
Davis, Frank. *see* Davis, Frank Cecil.
Davis, Frank Cecil, 1892-
  xDavis, Frank.
    The Plain Man's Guide to Second Hand
    Furniture. Merrimack Bk Serv.
    The Plain Man's Guide to Second-Hand
    Furniture. Transatlantic.
Davis, Frank M. *see* Davis, Frank Marshall.
Davis, Frank Marshall, 1905-
  xDavis, Frank M.
    I Am the American Negro. Arno.
Davis, Frank T. *see* Davis, F. T.
Davis, Fred, 1948-
  xDavis, Fred.
    Country Tools: Essential Hardware & Livery.
    Oliver Pr.
    Yearning for Yesterday: A Sociology of
    Nostalgia. Free Pr.
Davis, Gary. *see* Davis, Gary A.
Davis, Gary A.
  xDavis, Gary.
    Training Creative Thinking. Krieger.
  xDavis, Gary A.
    Psychology of Education: New Looks. Heath.
Davis, Genevieve, 1923-
  xDavis, Genevieve.
    A Passion in the Blood. S&S.
Davis, Genny W. *see* Davis, Genny Wright.
Davis, Genny Wright.
  xDavis, Genny W.
    The Lovers Book: Your Secret Source of Love.
    Macmillan.
Davis, George E. *see* Davis, George Earl.
Davis, George Earl, 1889-
  xDavis, George E.
    Radiation & Life. Iowa St U Pr.
Davis, George T. *see* Davis, George Theron.

Davis, George Theron, 1899-1944
  xDavis, George T.
    A Navy Second to None: The Development of
    Modern American Naval Policy. Greenwood.
Davis, Gordon B.
  xDavis, Gordon B.
    Introduction to Electronic Computers.
    McGraw.
Davis, Gordon B. *see* Davis, Gordon Bitter.
Davis, Gordon Bitter.
  xDavis, Gordon B.
    Auditing & EDP. Am Inst CPA.
    Computer Data Processing. McGraw.
    Readings in Management Information Systems.
    McGraw.
Davis, Grania.
  xDavis, Grania.
    Dr. Grass. Avon.
Davis, Grant M. *see* Davis, Grant Miller.
Davis, Grant Miller.
  xDavis, Grant M.
    Increasing Motor Carrier Productivity: An
    Empirical Analysis. Praeger.
Davis, H. L. *see* Davis, Harold Lenoir.
Davis, H. S. *see* Davis, Herbert Spencer.
Davis, Hank.
  xDavis, Hank.
    ed. Operant-Pavlovian Interactions. Halsted Pr.
Davis, Harold E. *see* Davis, Harold Eugene.
Davis, Harold Eugene, 1902-
  xDavis, Harold E.
    Hinsdale of Hiram: The Life of Burke Aaron
    Hinsdale, Pioneer Educator 1837-1900. U Pr
    of Wash.
    Latin American Diplomatic History: An
    Introduction. La State U Pr.
    Latin American Leaders. Cooper Sq.
    Latin American Thought: A Historical
    Introduction. Free Pr.
    Latin American Thought: A Historical
    Introduction. La State U Pr.
    Revolutionaries, Traditionalists & Dictators in
    Latin America. Cooper Sq.
    Teaching of Philosophy in Universities of the
    United States. OAS.
  xDavis, Harold Eugene.
    Latin American Foreign Policies: An Analysis.
    Johns Hopkins.
Davis, Harold Lenoir, 1896-
  xDavis, H. L.
    Honey in the Horn. Avon.
    Honey in the Horn. Larlin Corp.
Davis, Harold T. *see* Davis, Harold Thayer.
Davis, Harold Thayer, 1892-
  xDavis, Harold T.
    Analysis of Economic Time Series. Trinity U
    Pr.
    Introduction to Nonlinear Differential &
    Integral Equations. Dover.
    Summation of Series. Trinity U Pr.
Davis, Harry F.
  xDavis, Harry F.
    Introduction to Vector Analysis. Allyn.
Davis, Harwell G. *see* Davis, Harwell Goodwin.
Davis, Harwell Goodwin, 1882-
  xDavis, Harwell G.
    The Legend of Landsee. Strode.
Davis, Hazel, 1900-
  xDavis, Hazel.
    Personnel Administration in Three
    Non-Teaching Services of the Public Schools.
    AMS Pr.
Davis, Henry M. *see* Davis, Henry McVey.
Davis, Henry McVey, 1896-
  xDavis, Henry M.
    Use of State High School Examinations As an
    Instrument for Judging the Work of Teachers.
    AMS Pr.
Davis, Henry W. *see* Davis, Henry William Carless.

Davis, Henry William Carless, 1874-1928
xDavis, Henry W.
The Political Thought of Heinrich Von Treitschke. Greenwood.
Davis, Herbert. *see* Davis, Herbert John.
Davis, Herbert J. *see* Davis, Herbert John.
Davis, Herbert John.
xDavis, Herbert.
Nineteenth-Century Studies. Folcroft.
xDavis, Herbert J.
ed. Nineteenth Century Studies. Greenwood.
The Satire of Jonathan Swift. Greenwood.
Davis, Herbert Spencer, 1875-
xDavis, H. S.
Culture & Diseases of Game Fishes. U of Cal Pr.
Davis, Hiram S. *see* Davis, Hiram Simmons.
Davis, Hiram Simmons, 1903-
xDavis, Hiram S.
Productivity Accounting. Indus Res Unit-Wharton.
Davis, Horace, 1831-1916
xDavis, Horace.
American Constitutions: The Relations of the Three Departments As Adjusted by a Century. AMS Pr.
American Constitutions: The Relations of the Three Departments As Adjusted by a Century. Johnson Repr.
Davis, Horace B. *see* Davis, Horace Bancroft.
Davis, Horace Bancroft, 1898-
xDavis, Horace B.
Toward a Marxist Theory of Nationalism. Monthly Rev.
Davis, Howard H.
xDavis, Howard H.
Beyond Class Images: Explorations in the Structure of Social Consciousness. Biblio Dist.
Davis, Hubert J.
xDavis, Hubert J.
Christmas in the Mountains: Southwest Virginia Christmas Customs & Their Origins. Johnson NC.
The Silver Bullet & Other American Witch Stories. Jonathan David.
Davis, J. Ronnie.
xDavis, J. Ronnie.
An Analysis of Market Failure: Externalities , Public Goods, & Mixed Goods. U Presses Fla.
Evaluating Educational Investment. Lexington Bks.
Davis, Jacquelyn K.
xDavis, Jacquelyn K.
Salt II & U. S.-Soviet Strategic Forces. Inst Foreign Policy Anal.
Davis, James C. *see* Davis, James Cushman.
Davis, James Cushman.
xDavis, James C.
The Decline of the Venetian Nobility As a Ruling Class. AMS Pr.
A Venetian Family & Its Fortune, 1500-1900: The Dona & the Conservation of Their Wealth. Am Philos.
Davis, James E.
xDavis, James E.
ed. Dealing with Censorship. NCTE.
Davis, James E. *see* Davis, James Edward.
Davis, James Edward, 1940-
xDavis, James E.
Frontier America, 1800-1840: A Comparative Demographic Analysis of the Settlement Process. A H Clark.
Davis, James H., 1932-
xDavis, James H.
Group Performance. A-W.
Davis, James H. *see* Davis, James Hill.
Davis, James Herbert.
xDavis, James H.

Fenelon. Twayne.
Davis, James Hill.
xDavis, James H.
Racial Transition in the Church. Abingdon.
Davis, James W., 1920-
xDavis, James W.
Presidential Primaries: Road to the White House. Greenwood.
Davis, Jeff C. *see* Davis, Jefferson C.
Davis, Jefferson.
xDavis, Jefferson.
Papers of Jefferson Davis. La State U Pr.
Davis, Jefferson C.
xDavis, Jeff C.
Advanced Physical Chemistry: Molecules, Structure, & Spectra. Wiley.
Davis, Jerome, 1891-
xDavis, Jerome.
Citizens of One World. Citadel Pr.
Disarmament: A World View. Citadel Pr.
Davis, Jerry S.
xDavis, Jerry S.
Guide to the Literature of Student Financial Aid. College Bd.
Davis, Jesse.
xDavis, Jesse.
Classics of the Royal Ballet. Coward.
Davis, Jessica M. *see* Davis, Jessica Milner.
Davis, Jessica Milner.
xDavis, Jessica M.
Farce. Methuen Inc.
Davis, Joan.
xDavis, Joan E.
Neurologic Critical Care. Van Nos Reinhold.
Davis, Joan E. *see* Davis, Joan.
Davis, Joe.
xDavis, Joe.
Complete Snooker. Transatlantic.
Davis, Joe L. *see* Davis, Joe Lee.
Davis, Joe Lee.
xDavis, Joe L.
Sons of Ben: Jonsonian Comedy in Caroline England. Wayne St U Pr.
Davis, John. *see* Davis, John Hagy.
Davis, John F. *see* Davis, John Francis.
Davis, John Francis, Sir, Bart, 1795-1890
xDavis, John F.
China, During the War & Since the Peace. Scholarly Res Inc.
Davis, John G. *see* Davis, John Gordon.
Davis, John Gordon.
xDavis, John G.
Leviathan. Fawcett.
Taller Than Trees. PB.
Davis, John H. *see* Davis, John Herbert.
Davis, John H. R.
xDavis, John.
People of the Mediterranean: An Essay in Comparative Social Anthropology. Routledge & Kegan.
Davis, John Hagy, 1929-
xDavis, John.
Venice. Newsweek.
xDavis, John H.
The Guggenheims: An American Epic. Morrow.
Guggenheims: An American Epic. Morrow.
Davis, John Herbert, 1904-
xDavis, John H.
Evasive Peace: A Study of the Zionist - Arab Problem. Intl Pubns Serv.
Davis, John J. *see* Davis, John James.
Davis, John James, 1936-
xDavis, John J.

Conquest & Crisis: Studies in Joshua, Judges & Ruth. BMH Bks.
Mummies, Men & Madness. Baker Bk.
Mummies, Men & Madness. BMH Bks.
Paradise to Prison: Studies in Genesis. Baker Bk.
Paradise to Prison: Studies in Genesis. BMH Bks.
Davis, John T., 1948-
xDavis, John T.
Walking!. Andrews & McMeel.
Walking!. Bantam.
Davis, John W. *see* Davis, John William.
Davis, John William, 1917-
xDavis, John W.
ed. Infectious & Parasitic Diseases of Wild Birds. Iowa St U Pr.
ed. Parasitic Diseases of Wild Mammals. Iowa St U Pr.
Davis, Joseph C.
xDavis, Joseph C.
Buying Your House: A Complete Guide to Inspection & Evaluation. Emerson.
Davis, Joseph S. *see* Davis, Joseph Stancliffe.
Davis, Joseph Stancliffe, 1885-
xDavis, Joseph S.
Wheat & the AAA. Da Capo.
The World between the Wars, 1919-39: An Economist's View. Johns Hopkins.
Davis, Judy.
xDavis, Judy.
Cardiac Rehabilitation for the Patient & Family. Reston.
Davis, Julie.
xDavis, Julie.
The Gathering Passion. Nordon Pubns.
Davis, Karen.
xDavis, Karen.
National Health Insurance: Benefits, Costs, & Consequences. Brookings.
Davis, Katharine B. *see* Davis, Katharine Bement.
Davis, Katharine Bement, 1860-1935
xDavis, Katharine B.
Factors in the Sex Life of Twenty-Two Hundred Women. Arno.
xDavis, Katherine B.
Factors in the Sex Life of Twenty-Two Hundred Women. R West.
Davis, Katherine B. *see* Davis, Katharine Bement.
Davis, Keith.
xDavis, Keith.
The Challenge of Business. McGraw.
Organizational Behavior: A Book of Readings. McGraw.
Davis, Ken.
xDavis, Ken.
Kids & Cash: Solving a Parent's Dilemma. Oak Tree Pubns.
Davis, Kenneth.
xDavis, Kenneth.
Restoring Furniture. Arco.
Davis, Kenneth C. *see* Davis, Kenneth Culp.
Davis, Kenneth Culp.
xDavis, Kenneth C.
Discretionary Justice: A Preliminary Inquiry. Greenwood.
Discretionary Justice: A Preliminary Inquiry. U of Ill Pr.
Discretionary Justice in Europe & America. U of Ill Pr.
Davis, Kenneth L.
xDavis, Kenneth L.
ed. Brain Acetylcholine & Neuropsychiatric Disease. Plenum Pub.
Davis, Kenneth R. *see* Davis, Kenneth Rexton.
Davis, Kenneth Rexton, 1921-
xDavis, Kenneth R.
Marketing Management. Wiley.
Davis, Kenneth S. *see* Davis, Kenneth Sydney.

Davis, Kenneth Sydney, 1912-
  xDavis, Kenneth S.
    ed. Paradox of Poverty in America. Wilson.
Davis, Kim. *see* Davis, Kimberly Scott.
Davis, Kimberly Scott.
  xDavis, Kim.
    Reading & Writing About Language.
    Wadsworth Pub.
Davis, King E.
  xDavis, King E.
    Fund Raising in the Black Community:
    History, Feasibility, & Conflict. Scarecrow.
Davis, L. Irby.
  xDavis, L. Irby.
    A Field Guide to the Birds of Mexico &
    Central America. U of Tex Pr.
Davis, Lance. *see* Davis, Lance Edwin.
Davis, Lance E. *see* Davis, Lance Edwin.
Davis, Lance Edwin.
  xDavis, Lance.
    Institutional Change & American Economic
    Growth. Cambridge U Pr.
  xDavis, Lance E.
    American Economic Growth: An Economist's
    History of the United States. Har-Row.
Davis, Lawrence. *see* Davis, Lawrence Howard.
Davis, Lawrence B.
  xDavis, Lawrence B.
    Immigrants, Baptists & the Protestant Mind in
    America. U of Ill Pr.
Davis, Lawrence Howard, 1943-
  xDavis, Lawrence.
    Theory of Action. P-H.
Davis, Lawrence M.
  xDavis, Lawrence M.
    Studies in Linguistics in Honor of Raven I.
    McDavid Jr. U of Ala Pr.
Davis Lecture Committee. *see* Illinois University. Davis
  Lecture Committee.
Davis, Lee N. *see* Davis, Lee Niedringhaus.
Davis, Lee Niedringhaus, 1947-
  xDavis, Lee N.
    Frozen Fire: Where Will It Happen Next?.
    Friends Earth.
Davis, Lenwood G.
  xDavis, Lenwood G.
    Black Artists in the United States: An
    Annotated Bibliography of Books, Articles, &
    Dissertations on Black Artists, Seventeen
    Seventy-Nine to Nineteen Seventy-Nine.
    Greenwood.
    I Have a Dream: The Life & Times of Martin
    Luther King, Jr.. Greenwood.
Davis, Louis E.
  xDavis, Louis E.
    ed. Design of Jobs. Goodyear.
Davis, Louise. *see* Davis, Louise Littleton.
Davis, Louise Littleton.
  xDavis, Louise.
    Frontier Tales of Tennessee. Pelican.
Davis, M. *see* Davis, Marian L.
Davis, M. H. *see* Davis, M. H. A.
Davis, M. H. A.
  xDavis, M. H.
    Linear Estimation & Stochastic Control.
    Methuen Inc.
Davis, Marcella Z. *see* Davis, Marcella Zaleski.
Davis, Marcella Zaleski.
  xDavis, Marcella Z.
    Living with Multiple Sclerosis: A Social
    Psychological Analysis. C C Thomas.
Davis, Marian L., 1934-
  xDavis, M.
    Visual Design in Dress. P-H.
Davis, Marilyn K. *see* Davis, Marilyn Kornreich.
Davis, Marilyn Kornreich.
  xDavis, Marilyn K.
    Music Dictionary. Doubleday.
Davis, Martha.
  xDavis, Martha.

    Understanding Body Movement: An Annotated
    Bibliography. Arno.
Davis, Martin, 1928-
  xDavis, M.
    ed. The Undecidable: Basic Papers on
    Undecidable Propositions, Unsolvable
    Problems & Computable Functions. Raven.
  xDavis, Martin.
    Applied Nonstandard Analysis. Wiley.
    A First Course in Functional Analysis. Gordon.
    Lectures on Modern Mathematics. Gordon.
Davis, Mary.
  xDavis, Mary.
    Careers with a Telephone Company. Lerner
    Pubns.
Davis, Mary. *see* Davis, Mary Lee.
Davis, Mary H. *see* Davis, Mary Hayes.
Davis, Mary Hayes.
  xDavis, Mary H.
    Chinese Fables & Folk Stories.. Folcroft.
Davis, Mary K. *see* Davis, Mary Kay.
Davis, Mary Kay.
  xDavis, Mary K.
    More Needlepoint from America's Great Quilt
    Designs. Workman Pub.
    Needlepoint from America's Great Quilt
    Designs. Workman Pub.
Davis, Mary L.
  xDavis, Mary L.
    Polly & the President. Lerner Pubns.
Davis, Mary Lee.
  xDavis, Mary.
    Careers in a Bank. Lerner Pubns.
    Careers in a Medical Center. Lerner Pubns.
    Careers in Baseball. Lerner Pubns.
    Careers in Printing. Lerner Pubns.
Davis, Melinda.
  xDavis, Melinda.
    Storage. Pantheon.
Davis, Melton S.
  xDavis, Milton S.
    Who Defends Rome: The Forty-Five Days,
    July 25 - September 8, 1943. Dial.
Davis, Merrell R.
  xDavis, Merrell R.
    Melville's Mardi: A Chartless Voyage. Shoe
    String.
Davis, Michael, 1940-
  xDavis, M.
    Multiaxial Actions on Manifolds.
    Springer-Verlag.
  xDavis, Michael.
    The Image of Lincoln in the South. U of Tenn
    Pr.
Davis, Michael M. *see* Davis, Michael Marks.
Davis, Michael Marks, 1879-1971
  xDavis, Michael M.
    Paying Your Sickness Bills. Arno.
    Psychological Interpretations of Society. AMS
    Pr.
Davis, Mildred.
  xDavis, Mildred.
    The Dark Place. PB.
    They Buried a Man. PB.
Davis, Mildred. *see* Davis, Mildred B.
Davis, Mildred B.
  xDavis, Mildred.
    Lucifer Land. Popular Lib.
    Lucifer Land. Random.
    Scorpion. PB.
    Scorpion. Random.
Davis, Milton S. *see* Davis, Melton S.
Davis, Myrna.
  xDavis, Myrna.
    The Potato Book. Morrow.
    The Potato Book. Morrow.
Davis, Nanette J.
  xDavis, Nanette J.

    Sociological Constructions of Deviance:
    Perspectives & Issues in the Field. Wm C
    Brown.
Davis, Norah D. *see* Davis, Norah Deakin.
Davis, Norah Deakin.
  xDavis, Norah D.
    At Home in the Sun: An Open-House Tour of
    Solar Homes in the United States. Garden
    Way Pub.
Davis, Norman, 1913-
  xDavis, Norman.
    A Chaucer Glossary. Oxford U Pr.
    ed. Non-Cycle Plays & Fragments. Oxford U
    Pr.
    ed. Paston Letters & Papers of the Fifteenth
    Century. Oxford U Pr.
Davis, Norman M., 1936-
  xDavis, Norman M.
    The Complete Book of United States Coin
    Collecting. Macmillan.
Davis, Nuel P. *see* Davis, Nuel Pharr.
Davis, Nuel Pharr, 1915-
  xDavis, Nuel P.
    Lawrence & Oppenheimer. S&S.
Davis, O. B.
  xDavis, O. B.
    Introduction to Biblical Literature. Hayden.
    Workouts in Reading & Writing. Hayden.
Davis, Oswald H. *see* Davis, Oswald Harcourt.
Davis, Oswald Harcourt, 1882-1962
  xDavis, Oswald H.
    The Master: A Study of Arnold Bennett.
    Folcroft.
Davis, P. H. *see* Davis, Peter Hadland.
Davis, P. J. *see* Davis, Philip J.
Davis, P. Michael.
  xDavis, P. Michael.
    A Practical Guide to Preparing a Fiduciary
    Income Tax Return. Lawyers & Judges.
Davis, Pat.
  xDavis, Pat.
    Badminton Complete. A S Barnes.
Davis, Patricia. *see* Davis, Patricia Talbot.
Davis, Patricia Talbot.
  xDavis, Patricia.
    End of the Line: Alexander J. Cassatt &
    Pennsylvania Railroad. N Watson.
Davis, Paxton.
  xDavis, Paxton.
    Ned. Atheneum.
    Three Days. Atheneum.
Davis, Pearce.
  xDavis, Pearce.
    Development of the American Glass Industry.
    Russell.
Davis, Peter Hadland.
  xDavis, P. H.
    Principles of Angiosperm Taxonomy. Krieger.
Davis, Phil.
  xDavis, Phil.
    Photography. Wm C Brown.
Davis, Philip.
  xDavis, Philip.
    The Field of Social Service. Milford Hse.
Davis, Philip. *see* Davis, Philip E.
Davis, Philip E.
  xDavis, Philip.
    Introduction to Moral Philosophy. Merrill.
  xDavis, Philip E.
    Dialogues of Modern Philosophy. Allyn.
    ed. Moral Duty & Legal Responsibility: A
    Philosophical-Legal Casebook. Irvington.
Davis, Philip J., 1923-
  xDavis, P. J.
    The Lore of Large Numbers. Math Assn.
    The Mathematics of Matrices: A First Book of
    Matrix Theory & Linear Algebra. Wiley.
  xDavis, Philip J.

Circulant Matrices. Wiley.

Davis, Polly.
 xDavis, Polly.
  English Structure in Focus. Newbury Hse.
Davis, R. H. *see* Davis, Ralph H.
Davis, R. Hunt.
 xDavis, R. Hunt.
  Bantu Education & the Education of Africans
  in South Africa. Ohio U Ctr Intl.
Davis, Ralph C. *see* Davis, Ralph Currier.
Davis, Ralph Currier.
 xDavis, Ralph C.
  Fundamentals of Top Management. Arno.
  Principles of Business Organization &
  Operation. Hive Pub.
Davis, Ralph H.
 xDavis, R. H.
  The Normans & Their Myth. Thames Hudson.
Davis, Rebecca (Harding), 1831-1910
 xDavis, Rebecca H.
  Silhouettes of American Life. Mss Info.
Davis, Rebecca H. *see* Davis, Rebecca (Harding).
Davis, Richard A. *see* Davis, Richard Albert.
Davis, Richard Albert, 1937-
 xDavis, Richard A.
  Principles of Oceanography. A-W.
Davis, Richard B. *see* Davis, Richard Beale.
Davis, Richard Beale.
 xDavis, Richard B.
  Compiled by American Literature Through
  Bryant. AHM Pub.
  A Colonial Southern Bookshelf: Reading in the
  Eighteenth Century. U of Ga Pr.
  Intellectual Life in the Colonial South,
  1585-1763. U of Tenn Pr.
  Literature & Society in Early Virginia,
  1608-1840. La State U Pr.
Davis, Richard C.
 xDavis, Richard C.
  Compiled by North American Forest History.
  A Guide to Archives & Manuscripts in the
  United States & Canada. ABC-Clio.
Davis, Richard F.
 xDavis, Richard F.
  Modern Dairy Cattle Management. P-H.
Davis, Richard H.
 xDavis, Richard H.
  ed. Aging: Prospects & Issues. USC Andrus
  Geron.
Davis, Richard H. *see* Davis, Richard Harding.
Davis, Richard Harding, 1864-1916
 xDavis, Richard H.
  About Paris. Irvington.
  Bar Sinister. AMS Pr.
  Bar Sinister. Greenwood.
  Bar Sinister. Scholarly.
  Gallegher & Other Stories. AMS Pr.
  Gallegher & Other Stories. Mss Info.
  Gallegher & Other Stories. Scholarly.
  Lion & the Unicorn. Arno.
  Ranson's Folly. Arno.
  Soldiers of Fortune. Irvington.
  Soldiers of Fortune. Scholarly.
  Stories for Boys. Arno.
  Van Bibber, & Others. Arno.
Davis, Richard W.
 xDavis, Richard W.
  ed. Disraeli. Little.
Davis, Robert. *see* Davis, Robert P.
Davis, Robert E. *see* Davis, Robert Edward.
Davis, Robert Edward.
 xDavis, Robert E.
  Response to Innovation: A Study of Popular
  Argument About New Mass Media. Arno.
Davis, Robert G., 1941-
 xDavis, Robert G.
  Elementary Physical Education: A Systematic
  Approach. Hunter NC.
Davis, Robert G. *see* Davis, Robert Gorham.

Davis, Robert Gorham.
 xDavis, Robert G.
  C. P. Snow. Columbia U Pr.
Davis, Robert H. *see* Davis, Robert Henry.
Davis, Robert Henry.
 xDavis, Robert H.
  ed. Historical Dictionary of Colombia.
  Scarecrow.

Davis, Robert M. *see* Davis, Robert Murray.
Davis, Robert Murray.
 xDavis, Robert M.
  Intro. by Evelyn Waugh: A Checklist of
  Primary & Secondary Material. Whitston
  Pub.
  Modern British Short Novels. Scott F.
  ed. Steinbeck: A Collection of Critical Essays.
  P-H.
Davis, Robert P.
 xDavis, Robert.
  Control Tower. Putnam.
 xDavis, Robert P.
  Cat Five. Morrow.
  Cat Five. PB.
Davis, Robert R. *see* Davis, Robert Ralph.
Davis, Robert Ralph.
 xDavis, Robert R.
  Lexicon of Historical & Political Terms.
  Monarch Pr.
Davis, Robert S. *see* Davis, Robert Scott.
Davis, Robert Scott, 1954-
 xDavis, Robert S.
  Georgia Citizens & Soldiers of the American
  Revolution. Southern Hist Pr.
Davis, Rodney. *see* Davis, Rodney E.
Davis, Rodney E.
 xDavis, Rodney.
  Real Estate. McGraw.
Davis, S. *see* Davis, S. G.
Davis, S. G., 1907-
 xDavis, S.
  Hong Kong in Its Geographical Setting. AMS
  Pr.
Davis, S. Rufus. *see* Davis, Solomon.
Davis, Sam.
 xDavis, Sam.
  The Form of Housing. Van Nos Reinhold.
Davis, Sandra T. *see* Davis, Sandra T. W.
Davis, Sandra T. W.
 xDavis, Sandra T.
  Intellectual Change & Political Development in
  Early Modern Japan: Ono Azusa, a Case
  Study. Fairleigh Dickinson.
Davis, Sharon.
 xDavis, Sharon.
  Vocational Education of Handicapped Students:
  A Guide for Policy Development. Coun Exc
  Child.
Davis, Solomon.
 xDavis, S. Rufus.
  The Federal Principle: A Journey Through
  Time in Quest of Meaning. U of Cal Pr.
Davis, Stanley. *see* Davis, Stanley Nelson.
Davis, Stanley M.
 xDavis, Stanley M.
  Matrix. A-W.
  ed. Workers & Managers in Latin America.
  Heath.
Davis, Stanley N. *see* Davis, Stanley Nelson.
Davis, Stanley Nelson.
 xDavis, Stanley.
  Geology: Our Physical Environment. McGraw.
 xDavis, Stanley N.
  Hydrogeology. Wiley.
Davis, Stephen C. *see* Davis, Stephen Chapin.
Davis, Stephen Chapin, 1833-1856
 xDavis, Stephen C.

  California Gold Rush Merchant: The Journal of
  Stephen Chapin Davis. Greenwood.
Davis, Stephen T., 1940-
 xDavis, Stephen T.
  The Debate About the Bible: Inerrancy Versus
  Infallibility. Westminster.
Davis, Steven I.
 xDavis, Steven I.
  The Management Function in International
  Banking. Halsted Pr.
Davis, Terence, 1924-
 xDavis, Terence.
  The Gothick Taste. Fairleigh Dickinson.
Davis, Thomas B. *see* Davis, Thomas Brabson.
Davis, Thomas Brabson.
 xDavis, Thomas B.
  Carlos de Alvear, Man of Revolution: The
  Diplomatic Career of Argentina's First
  Minister to the United States. Greenwood.
Davis, Vincent.
 xDavis, Vincent.
  ed. The Post-Imperial Presidency. Transaction
  Bks.
Davis, W. Jackson. *see* Davis, William Jackson.
Davis, W. M. *see* Davis, William Morris.
Davis, W. R. *see* Davis, William Robert.
Davis, Walter A. *see* Davis, Walter Albert.
Davis, Walter Albert, 1942-
 xDavis, Walter A.
  The Act of Interpretation: A Critique of
  Literary Reason. U of Chicago Pr.
Davis, William. *see* Davis, William Thomas.
Davis, William C., 1946-
 xDavis, William C.
  Breckinridge: Statesman, Soldier & Symbol. La
  State U Pr.
  The Orphan Brigade: The Kentucky
  Confederates Who Couldn't Go Home.
  Doubleday.
Davis, William Edmund, 1937-
 xDavis, William F.
  Educator's Resource Guide to Special
  Education: Terms-Laws-Tests-Organizations.
  Allyn.
Davis, William F. *see* Davis, William Edmund.
Davis, William Jackson, 1942-
 xDavis, W. Jackson.
  The Seventh Year: Industrial Civilization in
  Transition. Norton.
Davis, William M. *see* Davis, William Morris.
Davis, William Morris, 1850-1934
 xDavis, W. M.
  The Coral Reef Problem. Krieger.
 xDavis, William M.
  Coral Reef Problem. AMS Pr.
Davis, William R. *see* Davis, William Riley.
Davis, William Riley, 1886-
 xDavis, William R.
  Development & Present Status of Negro
  Education in East Texas. AMS Pr.
Davis, William Robert, 1929-
 xDavis, W. R.
  Classical Fields, Particles & the Theory of
  Relativity. Gordon.
Davis, William S., 1943-
 xDavis, William S.
  Business Data Processing. A-W.
  Information Age. A-W.
  Information Processing Systems: An
  Introduction to Modern Computer-Based
  Information Systems. A-W.
  Operating Systems: A Systematic View. A-W.
Davis, William Thomas, 1822-1907
 xDavis, William.
  History of the Judiciary of Massachusetts. Da
  Capo.
Davis, William V. *see* Davis, William Virgil.
Davis, William Virgil, 1940-
 xDavis, William V.

One Way to Reconstruct the Scene. Yale U Pr.
Davis, William W. see Davis, William Watts Hart.
Davis, William Watts Hart, 1820-1910
  xDavis, William W.
    Fries Rebellion, 1798-1799. Arno.
    A Genealogical & Personal History of Bucks
     County, Pennsylvania. Genealog Pub.
Davis-Goff, Annabel.
  xDavis-Goff, Annabel.
    Night Tennis. Coward.
Davison, A. see Davison, Alec.
Davison, Alec.
  xDavison, A.
    Games & Simulations in Action. Biblio Dist.
Davison, Charles, 1858-1940
  xDavison, Charles.
    The Founders of Seismology. Arno.
Davison, Gerald C.
  xDavison, Gerald C.
    Abnormal Psychology: An Experimental
     Clinical Approach. Wiley.
Davison, Graeme. see Davison, Graeme John.
Davison, Graeme John, 1940-
  xDavison, Graeme.
    The Rise & Fall of Marvellous Melbourne. Intl
     Schol Bk Serv.
Davison, Ian, 1939-
  xDavison, Ian.
    Values, Ends & Society. U of Queensland Pr.
Davison, Jean.
  xDavison, Jean.
    The Golden Torrent. Doubleday.
Davison, Kenneth E.
  xDavison, Kenneth E.
    The Presidency of Rutherford B. Hayes.
     Greenwood.
Davison, Peter.
  xDavison, Peter.
    The Breaking of the Day & Other Poems.
     AMS Pr.
Davison, Peter. see Davison, Peter Hobley.
Davison, Peter Hobley.
  xDavison, Peter.
    Intro. by & ed. Literature & Society. Somerset
     Hse.
    Intro. by & ed. Mass Media & Mass
     Communication. Somerset Hse.
Davison, Ronald C.
  xDavison, Ronald C.
    Astrology. Arc Bks.
Davison, Stanley Roland.
  xDavison, Stanley S.
    Leadership of the Reclamation Movement,
     1875-1902. Arno.
Davison, Stanley S. see Davison, Stanley Roland.
Davisson, Charles N. see Davisson, Charles Nelson.
Davisson, Charles Nelson.
  xDavisson, Charles N.
    Economic Effects of the Wage-Price
     Guideposts. U Mich Busn Div Res.
Davisson, William I.
  xDavisson, William I.
    Computer-Assisted Instruction in Economics. U
     of Notre Dame Pr.
Davitz, Joel. see Davitz, Joel Robert.
Davitz, Joel R. see Davitz, Joel Robert.
Davitz, Joel Robert.
  xDavitz, Joel.
    Love & Understanding. Paulist Pr.
    Psychology of the Educational Process.
     McGraw.
  xDavitz, Joel R.
    The Communication of Emotional Meaning.
     Greenwood.
Davitz, Lois J. see Davitz, Lois Jean.
Davitz, Lois Jean.
  xDavitz, Lois J.
    The Psychiatric Patient: Case Histories.
     Springer Pub.
Davson. see Davson, Hugh.

Davson, Hugh.
  xDavson.
    The Eye. Acad Pr.
  xDavson, Hugh.
    ed. Eye. Acad Pr.
Davy, Charles.
  xDavy, Charles.
    ed. Footnotes to the Film. Arno.
Davy, Don, 1927-
  xDavy, Don.
    Anatomy & Life Drawing. Taplinger.
    Drawing Animals & Birds. Taplinger.
Davy, Humphry.
  xDavy, Humphry B.
    The Collected Works of Sir Humphry Davy.
     Johnson Repr.
Davy, Humphry B. see Davy, Humphry.
Davydov, A. S. see Davydov, Aleksandr Sergeevich.
Davydov, Aleksandr Sergeevich.
  xDavydov, A. S.
    Quantum Mechanics. Pergamon.
    Theory of Molecular Excitons. Plenum Pub.
  xDavydov, Alexandre S.
    Quantum Mechanics. Neo Pr.
Davydov, Alexandre S. see Davydov, Aleksandr
  Sergeevich.
Davydov, Gavriil. see Davydov, Gavriil Ivanovich.
Davydov, Gavriil Ivanovich.
  xDavydov, Gavriil.
    Two Voyages to Russian America, 1802-1807.
     Limestone Pr.
Dawe, Donald G.
  xDawe, Donald G.
    ed. Christian Faith in a Religiously Plural
     World. Orbis Bks.
Dawe, Jessamon.
  xDawe, Jessamon.
    Functional Business Communication. P-H.
Dawe, R. D.
  xDawe, R. D.
    Collation & Investigation of Manuscripts of
     Aeschylus. Cambridge U Pr.
Dawes, Charles G. see Dawes, Charles Gates.
Dawes, Charles Gates, 1865-1951
  xDawes, Charles G.
    Journal As Ambassador to Great Britain.
     Greenwood.
Dawes, Clinton J.
  xDawes, Clinton J.
    Marine Algae of the West Coast of Florida. U
     of Miami Pr.
Dawes, Francis Edward, 1910-
  xDawes, Frank.
    Not in Front of the Servants: A True Portrait
     of English Upstairs-Downstairs Life.
     Taplinger.
Dawes, Frank. see Dawes, Francis Edward.
Dawes, J. N. see Dawes, John Nicholas Irwin.
Dawes, John Nicholas Irwin.
  xDawes, J. N.
    Citizen to Soldier: Australia Before the Great
     War: Recollections of Members of the First
     A.I.F.. Intl Schol Bk Serv.
Dawes, Nathaniel T.
  xDawes, Nathaniel T.
    The Packard: 1942-1962. A S Barnes.
Dawes, William M.
  xDawes, William M.
    The Circle & the Conic Curves. Branden.
    The Hyperbola & the Parabola. Branden.
Dawidoff, Robert.
  xDawidoff, Robert.
    The Education of John Randolph. Norton.
Dawidowicz, Lucy. see Dawidowicz, Lucy S.
Dawidowicz, Lucy S.
  xDawidowicz, Lucy.
    Holocaust Reader. Behrman.
Dawisha, Karen.
  xDawisha, Karen.

    Soviet Foreign Policy Towards Egypt. St
     Martin.
Dawkins, J. V.
  xDawkins, J. V.
    ed. Developments in Polymer Characterisation.
     Burgess-Intl Ideas.
Dawkins, John.
  xDawkins, John.
    Syntax & Readability. Intl Reading.
Dawkins, Richard M. see Dawkins, Richard Mcgillivray.
Dawkins, Richard Mcgillivray, 1871-1955
  xDawkins, Richard M.
    tr. & ed. Modern Greek Folktales. Greenwood.
    tr. & ed. More Greek Folktales. Greenwood.
Dawley, Alan, 1943-
  xDawley, Alan.
    Class & Community: The Industrial Revolution
     in Lynn. Harvard U Pr.
Dawn, C. Ernest.
  xDawn, C. Ernest.
    From Ottomanism to Arabism: Essays on the
     Origins of Arab Nationalism. U of Ill Pr.
Dawson, A. J. see Dawson, Alec John.
Dawson, Adele. see Dawson, Adele Godchaux.
Dawson, Adele Godchaux, 1905-
  xDawson, Adele.
    Health, Happiness & the Pursuit of Herbs.
     Greene.
Dawson, Alec John, 1872-1951
  xDawson, A. J.
    Finn the Wolfhound. HarBraceJ.
Dawson, Amy.
  xDawson, Amy.
    Bobbin Lacemaking for Beginners. Sterling.
Dawson, Anthony B.
  xDawson, Anthony B.
    Indirections: Shakespeare & the Art of Illusion.
     U of Toronto Pr.
Dawson, Carl.
  xDawson, Carl.
    His Fine Wit: A Study of Thomas Love
     Peacock. U of Cal Pr.
    Victorian Noon: English Literature in 1850.
     Johns Hopkins.
Dawson, Christopher. see Dawson, Christopher Biron
  Stewart.
Dawson, Christopher Biron Stewart.
  xDawson, Christopher.
    Tackle Sailing This Way. Soccer.
Dawson, Christopher H. see Dawson, Christopher Henry.
Dawson, Christopher Henry, 1889-
  xDawson, Christopher H.
    The Historic Reality of Christian Culture: A
     Way to the Renewal of Human Life.
     Greenwood.
    Medieval Essays. Arno.
    Religion & the Rise of Western Culture. AMS
     Pr.
Dawson, Christopher Mounsey.
  xDawson, M.
    ed. Studies in Latin Poetry. Cambridge U Pr.
Dawson, E. Yale. see Dawson, Elmer Yale.
Dawson, Elmer Y. see Dawson, Elmer Yale.
Dawson, Elmer Yale, 1918-
  xDawson, E. Yale.
    Cacti of California. U of Cal Pr.
  xDawson, Elmer Y.
    Marine Botany: An Introduction. HR&W.
Dawson, Fielding, 1930-
  xDawson, Fielding.
    Two Penny Lane. Black Sparrow.
Dawson, Henry B. see Dawson, Henry Barton.
Dawson, Henry Barton, 1821-1889
  xDawson, Henry B.
    Sons of Liberty in New York. Arno.
Dawson, J. William. see Dawson, John William.
Dawson, Jerry F.
  xDawson, Jerry F.

Friedrich Schleiermacher: The Evolution of a
   Nationalist. U of Tex Pr.
Dawson, John. *see* Dawson, John Philip.
Dawson, John A.
   xDawson, John A.
      Computing for Geographers. Crane-Russak Co.
      ed. The Marketing Environment. St Martin.
Dawson, John C. *see* Dawson, John Charles.
Dawson, John Charles, 1876-
   xDawson, John C.
      Toulouse in the Renaissance: The Floral
      Games, University & Student Life: Etienne
      Dolet. AMS Pr.
Dawson, John J.
   xDawson, John W.
      The Cancer Patient. Augsburg.
Dawson, John P. *see* Dawson, John Philip.
Dawson, John Philip.
   xDawson, John.
      Cases on Restitution. Michie.
   xDawson, John P.
      The Oracles of the Law. Greenwood.
Dawson, John W. *see* Dawson, John J.
Dawson, John William, Sir, 1820-1899
   xDawson, J. William.
      Modern Ideas of Evolution. N Watson.
Dawson, Joseph M. *see* Dawson, Joseph Martin.
Dawson, Joseph Martin, 1879-
   xDawson, Joseph M.
      America's Way in Church, State & Society.
      Greenwood.
      Baptists & the American Republic. Arno.
Dawson, M. *see* Dawson, Christopher Mounsey.
Dawson, Peter E., 1930-
   xDawson, Peter E.
      Evaluation, Diagnosis, & Treatment of Occlusal
      Problems. Mosby.
Dawson, Philip.
   xDawson, Philip.
      ed. French Revolution. P-H.
Dawson, Raymond. *see* Dawson, Raymond Stanley.
Dawson, Raymond Stanley.
   xDawson, Raymond.
      An Introduction to Classical Chinese. Oxford
      U Pr.
Dawson, Robert M. *see* Dawson, Robert Macgregor.
Dawson, Robert Macgregor, 1895-1958
   xDawson, Robert M.
      Democratic Government in Canada. U of
      Toronto Pr.
      ed. Development of Dominion Status,
      1900-1936. Biblio Dist.
      Government of Canada. U of Toronto Pr.
Dawson, Robert O.
   xDawson, Robert O.
      Standards Relating to Adjudication. Ballinger
      Pub.
Dawson, Thomas H.
   xDawson, Thomas H.
      Theory & Practice of Solid Mechanics. Plenum
      Pub.
Dawson, Townes L. *see* Dawson, Townes Loring.
Dawson, Townes Loring.
   xDawson, Townes L.
      Business Law: Text & Cases. Heath.
Dawson, William J. *see* Dawson, William James.
Dawson, William James, 1854-1928
   xDawson, William J.
      Literary Leaders of Modern England. Folcroft.
Day, A. C. *see* Day, A. Colin.
Day, A. Colin.
   xDay, A. C.
      Compatible Fortran. Cambridge U Pr.
Day, A. Grove. *see* Day, Arthur Grove.
Day, Alan. *see* Day, Alan Edwin.
Day, Alan E. *see* Day, Alan Edwin.
Day, Alan Edwin.
   xDay, Alan.
      History: A Reference Handbook. Shoe String.
   xDay, Alan E.

      ed. Archaeology: A Reference Handbook. Shoe
      String.
Day, Arthur Grove, 1904-
   xDay, A. Grove.
      Books About Hawaii: Fifty Basic Authors. U Pr
      of Hawaii.
      Pacific Islands Literature: One Hundred Basic
      Books. U Pr of Hawaii.
Day, Avanelle. *see* Day, Avanelle S.
Day, Avanelle S.
   xDay, Avanelle.
      Spice Cookbook. D White.
Day, Barbara, 1938-
   xDay, Barbara.
      Open Learning in Early Childhood. Macmillan.
Day, Bradford M.
   xDay, Bradford M.
      ed. The Checklist of Fantastic Literature in
      Paperbound Books. Arno.
      ed. The Supplemental Checklist of Fantastic
      Literature. Arno.
Day Care & Child Development Council of America. *see*
   Day Care and Child Development Council of
   America.
Day Care and Child Development Council of America.
   xDay Care & Child Development Council of
   America.
      Alternatives in Quality Child Care. Acropolis.
Day, Charles E.
   xDay, Charles E.
      ed. Low Density Lipoproteins. Plenum Pub.
Day, Clarence.
   xDay, Clarence.
      Life with Father. Knopf.
Day, Clarence A. *see* Day, Clarence Albert.
Day, Clarence Albert.
   xDay, Clarence A.
      Ezekiel Holmes, Father of Maine Agriculture.
      U Maine Orono.
Day, Clarence B. *see* Day, Clarence Burton.
Day, Clarence Burton.
   xDay, Clarence B.
      The Birth Pangs of Pakistan. Chinese Materials.
Day, Cyrus L. *see* Day, Cyrus Lawrence.
Day, Cyrus Lawrence, 1900-
   xDay, Cyrus L.
      Art of Knotting & Splicing. Naval Inst Pr.
Day, David, fl. 1973-
   xDay, David.
      Brass Rubbings. Persea Bks.
      ed. Many Voices: An Anthology of
      Contemporary Canadian Indian Poetry. Intl
      Schol Bk Serv.
Day, Douglas.
   xDay, Douglas.
      Journey of the Wolf. PB.
Day, Edmund E. *see* Day, Edmund Ezra.
Day, Edmund Ezra, 1883-1951
   xDay, Edmund E.
      Education for Freedom & Responsibility:
      Selected Essays. Arno.
Day, Eugene D.
   xDay, Eugene D.
      Advanced Immunochemistry. Krieger.
Day, Frank.
   xDay, Frank.
      If You Can Walk, You Can Ski. Macmillan.
Day, G. S. *see* Day, George S.
Day, George E. *see* Day, George Edward.
Day, George Edward, 1815-1872
   xDay, George E.
      A Practical Treatise on the Domestic
      Management & Most Important Diseases of
      Advanced Life. Arno.
Day, George F.
   xDay, George F.
      The Uses of History in the Novels of Vardis
      Fisher. Revisionist Pr.
Day, George S.
   xDay, G. S.

      Buyer Attitudes and Brand Choice Behavior.
      Free Pr.
Day, Harvey.
   xDay, Harvey.
      Encyclopaedia of Natural Health & Healing.
      Woodbridge Pr.
Day, Howard D.
   xDay, Howard D.
      A Guide for Adult School Crossing Guards. C
      C Thomas.
Day, J. S. *see* Day, John S.
Day, James, Writer on Music.
   xDay, James.
      Literary Background of Bach's Cantatas.
      Dufour.
      Vaughan Williams. Biblio Dist.
      Vaughan Williams. Littlefield.
Day, James W. *see* Day, James Wentworth.
Day, James Wentworth, 1899-
   xDay, James W.
      In Search of Ghosts. Taplinger.
Day, Janis K. *see* Day, Janis Kathleen.
Day, Janis Kathleen.
   xDay, Janis K.
      A Working Approach to Human Relations in
      Organizations. Brooks-Cole.
Day, Jo Anne C. *see* Day, Joanne C.
Day, Joanne C.
   xDay, Jo Anne C.
      ed. Decorative Silhouettes of the Twenties for
      Designers & Craftsmen. Dover.
   xDay, JoAnne C.
      Decorative Silhouettes of the Twenties for
      Designers & Craftsmen. Peter Smith.
Day, John, 1902-
   xDay, John.
      An Economic History of Athens Under Roman
      Domination. Arno.
Day, John S.
   xDay, J. S.
      Subcontracting Policy in the Airframe Industry.
      Pergamon.
Day, Leroy J.
   xDay, LeRoy J.
      Dynamic Christian Fellowship. Judson.
Day, Lewis F. *see* Day, Lewis Foreman.
Day, Lewis Foreman, 1845-1910
   xDay, Lewis F.
      Alphabets Old & New for the Use of
      Craftsmen. Gale.
      The Anatomy of Pattern. Garland Pub.
      The Application of Ornament. Garland Pub.
      Art in Needlework. Garland Pub.
      Instances of Accessory Art. Garland Pub.
      Nature & Ornament: Nature the Raw Material
      of Design. Gale.
      Nature in Ornament. Gale.
      Nature in Ornament. Garland Pub.
      The Planning of Ornament. Garland Pub.
Day, Marion C. *see* Day, Marion Clyde.
Day, Marion Clyde.
   xDay, Marion C.
      Theoretical Inorganic Chemistry. Van Nos
      Reinhold.
Day, Owen T.
   xDay, Owen T.
      The Hallelujah Hole: The Story of a Frontier
      Preacher. Judson.
Day, Peter R., 1928-
   xDay, Peter R.
      Genetics of Host-Parasite Interaction. W H
      Freeman.
Day, Peter R. *see* Day, Peter Russell.
Day, Peter Russell, 1933-
   xDay, Peter R.
      Communication in Social Work. Pergamon.
Day, R. A. *see* Day, Reuben Alexander.
Day, R. B. *see* Day, Richard B.
Day, R. H.
   xDay, Ross H.

Studies in Perception. Intl Schol Bk Serv.

Day, Reuben Alexander.
xDay, R. A.
General Chemistry. P-H.
Quantitative Analysis. P-H.

Day, Richard, 1928-
xDay, Richard.
Easy Things to Make with Concrete & Masonry. Arco.
The Home Owner Handbook of Plumbing & Heating. Crown.
How to Build Patios & Decks. Har-Row.
How to Remodel Your Attic or Basement. Arco.
How to Service & Repair Your Own Car. Har-Row.

Day, Richard B.
xDay, R. B.
Leon Trotsky & the Politics of Economic Isolation. Cambridge U Pr.

Day, Robert. *see* Day, Robert A.

Day, Robert A., 1924-
xDay, Robert.
How to Write & Publish a Scientific Paper. ISI Pr.

Day, Ross H. *see* Day, R. H.
Day, Satis B. *see* Day, Satis Biswas.

Day, Satis Biswas.
xDay, Satis B.
A Hindu Interpretation of the Hand & Its Portents As Practiced by the Palmists of India. U of Minn Bell.
xDay, Stacey B.
jt. auth. A Hindu Interpretation of the Hand & Its Portents As Practiced by the Palmists of India. U of Minn Bell.

Day, Stacey. *see* Day, Stacey B.

Day, Stacey B.
xDay, Stacey.
ed. A Companion to the Life Sciences. Van Nos Reinhold.
xDay, Stacey B.
ed. Cancer Invasion & Metastasis: Biologic Mechanisms & Therapy. Raven.
Health Communications. Intl Found Biosocial Dev.

Day, Stacey B. *see* Day, Satis Biswas.

Day, Thomas.
xDay, Thomas.
The History of Sandford & Merton. Garland Pub.

Day, W. A. *see* Day, William Alan.

Day, William, 1928-
xDay, William.
Genesis on Planet Earth: The Search for Life's Beginning. Hse of Talos.

Day, William Alan.
xDay, W. A.
The Thermodynamics of Simple Materials with Fading Memory. Springer-Verlag.

Day-Lewis, Cecil, 1904-1972
xDay-Lewis, Cecil.
Revolution in Writing. Folcroft.

Dayan, Moshe, 1915-
xDayan, Moshe.
Diary of the Sinai Campaign. Greenwood.
Diary of the Sinai Campaign. Schocken.
Living with the Bible. Morrow.

Dayan, Ruth.
xDayan, Ruth.
And Perhaps: The Story of Ruth Dayan. HarBraceJ.
Crafts of Israel. Macmillan.

Dayan, Yael, 1939-
xDayan, Yael.
Three Weeks in October. Delacorte.
Three Weeks in October. Dell.

Dayhoff, M. O. *see* Dayhoff, Margaret O.

Dayhoff, Margaret O.
xDayhoff, M. O.
ed. Atlas of Protein Sequence & Structure 1972. Natl Biomedical.

Daynes, Byron W.
xDaynes, Byron W.
Contemporary Readings in American Government. Heath.

Dayrell, Elphinstone, 1869-1917
xDayrell, Elphinstone.
Folk Stories from Southern Nigeria, West Africa. Negro U Pr.

Dayton. *see* Dayton, Howard Lape.
Dayton, C. M. *see* Dayton, Chauncey Mitchell.

Dayton, Chauncey Mitchell.
xDayton, C. M.
Design of Educational Experiments. McGraw.

Dayton, Donald W.
xDayton, Donald W.
Discovering an Evangelical Heritage. Har-Row.

Dayton, Edward R.
xDayton, Edward R.
Strategy for Leadership. Revell.

Dayton, Howard Lape, 1943-
xDayton.
Your Money: Frustration or Freedom?. Tyndale.

Dayton, Irene, 1922-
xDayton, Irene.
In Oxbow of Time's River. Windy Row.

Dayton, Mona.
xDayton, Mona.
Earth & Sky. Har-Row.

Dayton, O. W. *see* Dayton, O. William.

Dayton, O. William, 1914-
xDayton, O. W.
Athletic Training & Conditioning. Wiley.

Dayton, Seymour, 1923-
xDayton, Seymour.
Controlled Clinical Trial of a Diet High in Unsaturated Fat in Preventing Complications of Atherosclerosis. Am Heart.

Dazai, Osamu, Pseud.
xDazai, Osamu.
No Longer Human. New Directions.

DC Comics Editors. *see* DC Comics, Inc.

DC Comics, Inc.
xDC Comics Editors.
American at War: The Best of DC Wars Comics. S&S.

De , Beauregard, Oliver Costa. *see* Costa De Beauregard, Oliver.
De , Biran, Pierre Maine. *see* Maine De Biran, Pierre.
De , Camp, L. Sprague. *see* De Camp, L. Sprague.
De , Chardin, Pierre Teilhard. *see* Teilhard De Chardin, Pierre.
De , Figueroa, Martin Fernandez. *see* Fernandez De Figueroa, Martin.
De , Iongh, Daniel Crena. *see* Crena De Iongh, Daniel.
De , Lenval, Helena Lubienska. *see* Lubienska De Lenval, Helena.
De , Vate, Dwight Van. *see* Van De Vate, Dwight.
De , Vazquez, Margot Arce. *see* Arce de Vazquez, Margot.
De Alvarez, Russell R. *see* De Alvarez, Russell Ramon.
De Angeli, Marguerite. *see* De Angeli, Marguerite Lofft.
De, Anil K. *see* De, Anil Kumar.

De, Anil Kumar.
xDe, Anil K.
Solvent Extraction of Metals. Van Nos Reinhold.

De Alvarez, Russell Ramon.
xDe Alvarez, Russell R.
ed. Textbook of Gynecology. Lea & Febiger.

De Angeli, Marguerite Lofft, 1889-
xDe Angeli, Marguerite.

Fiddlestrings. Doubleday.
The Lion in the Box. Doubleday.
Whistle for the Crossing. Doubleday.

De Aragon, Ray J. *see* De Aragon, Ray John.

De Aragon, Ray John.
xDe Aragon, Ray J.
Padre Martinez & Bishop Lamy. Pan-Am Publishing Co.

De Armond, R. N.
xDe Armond, R. N.
ed. Early Visitors to Southeastern Alaska: Nine Accounts. Alaska Northwest.

De, Assis, Joaquim M. Machado. *see* Machado de Assis, Joaquim M.

De Avila, Fernando B. *see* Avila, Fernando B. de.

De, Ayala, Ramon Perez. *see* Perez de Ayala, Ramon.

De Azevedo, Fernando. *see* Azevedo, Fernando De.

De Balzac, Honore. *see* Balzac, Honore De.

De Barthe, Joe. *see* De Barthe, Joseph.

De Barthe, Joseph.
xDe Barthe, Joe.
Life & Adventures of Frank Grouard. U of Okla Pr.

De Bary, W. Theodore. *see* De Bary, William Theodore.

De Bary, William T. *see* De Bary, William Theodore.

De Bary, William Theodore.
xDe Bary, W. Theodore.
ed. Principle & Practicality: Essays in Neo-Confucianism & Practical Learning. Columbia U Pr.
xDe Bary, William T.
ed. Sources of Chinese Tradition. Columbia U Pr.

De Beaumont, Marguerite.
xDe Beaumont, Marguerite.
Horses & Ponies: Their Breeding, Feeding & Management. J A Allen.

De Berdt, Dennys.
xDe Berdt, Dennys.
Letters of Dennys De Berdt, 1757-70. Arno.

De Bilio, Beth.
xDe Bilio, Beth.
The Widow's Escort. Dell.

De Blasis, Celeste.
xDe Blasis, Celeste.
The Proud Breed. Fawcett.

De Blij, Harm J.
xDe Blij, Harm J.
Geography: Regions & Concepts. Wiley.
Human Geography: Culture, Society, & Space. Wiley.
Systematic Political Geography. Wiley.

De Boer, John J. *see* De Boer, John James.

De Boer, John James.
xDe Boer, John J.
Teaching Secondary English. Greenwood.

De Bono, Edward, 1933-
xDe Bono, Edward.
The Dog Exercising Machine. S&S.

De Boor, C. *see* De Boor, Carl.

De Boor, Carl.
xDe Boor, C.
A Practical Guide to Splines. Springer-Verlag.

De Bougainville, Louis A. *see* Bougainville, Louis A. De.

De Breffny, Brian.
xDe Breffny, Brian.
Castles of Ireland. Thames Hudson.
The Churches & Abbeys of Ireland. Norton.
Land of Ireland. Abrams.
The Synagogue. Macmillan.

De Camp, Catherine C. *see* De Camp, Catherine Crook.

De Camp, Catherine Crook.
xDe Camp, Catherine C.

ed. Creatures of the Cosmos. Westminster.
Teach Your Child to Manage Money: A Guide for Tots Through Teens. US News & World.
De Camp, L. S. *see* De Camp, Lyon Sprague.
De Camp, L. Sprague. *see* De Camp, Lyon Sprague.
De Camp, Lyon Sprague.
xDe Camp, L. S.
Darwin & His Great Discovery. Macmillan.
xDe Camp, L. Sprague.
Citadels of Mystery. Ballantine.
The Compleat Enchanter: The Magical Misadventures of Harold Shea. Ballantine.
The Great Fetish. Doubleday.
The Great Fetish. PB.
Lest Darkness Fall. Ballantine.
Literary Swordsmen & Sorcerers: The Makers of Heroic Fantasy. Arkham.
Lost Continents: The Atlantis Theme in History, Science & Literature. Dover.
Lost Continents: The Atlantis Theme in History, Science, & Literature. Peter Smith.
Lovecraft: A Biography. Ballantine.
De Capriles, Miguel A, 1906-
xDe Capriles, Miguel A.
Modern Financial Accounting. Rothman.
De Capua, A. G. *see* De Capua, Angelo George.
De Capua, Angelo George, 1924-
xDe Capua, A. G.
German Baroque Poetry: Interpretive Readings. State U NY Pr.
De Carli, Franco.
xDe Carli, Franco.
The World of Fish. Abbeville Pr.
De Castille, Vernon.
xDe Castille, Vernon.
How to Gain Tranquillity & the Pleasures of Internal Contentment & Emotional Balance Without the Taking of Pills. Am Classical Coll Pr.
De Castro Y Rossi, Adolfo. *see* Castro Y Rossi, Adolfo De.
De Caux, Len, 1899-
xDe Caux, Len.
The Living Spirit of the Wobblies. Intl Pub Co.
De Cecco, Marcello.
xDe Cecco, Marcello.
Money & Empire: The International Gold Standard 1890-1914. Rowman.
De Chair, Somerset Struben, 1911-
xDe Chair, Somerset.
Legend of the Yellow River. St Martin.
De Chair, Somerset. *see* De Chair, Somerest Struben.
De Chant, John A., 1917-
xDe Chant, John M.
Devilbirds: The Story of the United States Marine Corps Aviation in World War II. Zenger Pub.
De Chant, John M. *see* De Chant, John A.
De. Chardin, Pierre Teilhard. *see* Teilhard De Chardin, Pierre.
De Chateaubriand, Francois-Rene. *see* Chateaubriand, Francois-Rene de.
De Coppens, Peter R. *see* De Coppens, Peter Roche.
De Coppens, Peter Roche, 1938-
xDe Coppens, Peter R.
Ideal Man in Classical Sociology: The Views of Comte, Durkheim, Pareto, & Weber. Pa St U Pr.
De Dienes, Andre, 1913-
xDe Dienes, Andre.
Sun-Warmed Nudes. Elysium.
De Fer, Hugo.
xDe Fer, Hugo.
The Art & Science of Stimulating the Force & Daring of Your Inventiveness Faculties.. Am Classical Coll Pr.
De Fleur, Melvin L. *see* De Fleur, Melvin Lawrence.

De Fleur, Melvin Lawrence, 1923-
xDe Fleur, Melvin L.
Theories of Mass Communication. Longman.
De Forest, Ernest Grant.
xDe Forest, Grant E.
God in the American Schools: Religious Education in a Pluralistic Society. Am Classical Coll Pr.
De Forest, Grant E. *see* De Forest, Ernest Grant.
De France, Joseph J.
xDe France, Joseph J.
Communications Electronics Circuits. HR&W.
De Francis, John. *see* De Francis, John Francis.
De Francis, John Francis, 1911-
xDe Francis, John.
Nationalism & Language Reform in China. Octagon.
De, Gamboa, Pedro Sarmiento. *see* Sarmiento De Gamboa, Pedro.
De Garmo, Charles, 1849-1934
xDe Garmo, Charles.
Herbart & the Herbartians. Folcroft.
De Gast, Robert, 1936-
xDe Gast, Robert.
The Lighthouses of the Chesapeake. Johns Hopkins.
De Gasztold, Carmen B. *see* De Gasztold, Carmen Bernos.
De Gasztold, Carmen Bernos.
xDe Gasztold, Carmen B.
Prayers from the Ark & The Creatures' Choir. Penguin.
De Goncourt, Edmond L. *see* Goncourt, Edmond L. de.
De Gorog, Ralph. *see* De Gorog, Ralph Paul.
De Gorog, Ralph Paul, 1922-
xDe Gorog, Ralph.
Lexique Francais Moderne - Ancien Francais. U of Ga Pr.
De Gouy, Louis P. *see* De Gouy, Louis Pullig.
De Gouy, Louis Pullig, 1869-1947
xDe Gouy, Louis P.
The Bread Tray: Nearly 600 Recipes for Homemade Breads, Rolls, Muffins, & Biscuits. Dover.
The Soup Book: 770 Recipes. Peter Smith.
De Grange, McQuilkin, 1880-
xDe Grange, McQuilkin.
Nature & Elements of Sociology. Greenwood.
De Grazia, Alfred.
xDe Grazia, Alfred.
Eight Bads - Eight Goods: The American Contradictions. Peter Smith.
Politics for Better or Worse. Scott F.
De Grazia, Edward.
xDe Grazia, Edward.
Censorship Landmarks. Bowker.
De Grazia, Sebastian.
xDe Grazia, Sebastian.
Of Time, Work & Leisure. Kraus Repr.
De Graziani, Vincenzo G. *see* De Graziani, Vincenzo Gustavo.
De Graziani, Vincenzo Gustavo.
xDe Graziani, Vincenzo G.
The Franco-German Coalition & the Emergence of a New International Superpower: Its Effects Upon the Future Course of History. Inst Econ Pol.
De Groat, Diane.
xDe Groat, Diane.
illus. Alligator's Toothache. Crown.
De Groot, Roy A. *see* De Groot, Roy Andries.
De Groot, Roy Andries, 1912-
xDe Groot, Roy A.
Cooking with the Cuisinart Food Processor. McGraw.
Feasts for All Seasons. McGraw.
Pressure Cookery Perfected. Summit Bks.
Revolutionary French Cooking. McGraw.
De Haan, Martin. *see* De Haan, Martin Ralph.
De Haan, Martin R. *see* De Haan, Martin Ralph.

De Haan, Martin Ralph, 1891-
xDe Haan, Martin.
Genesis & Evolution. Zondervan.
xDe Haan, Martin R.
Law or Grace. Zondervan.
De Haas, Elsa, 1901-
xDe Haas, Elsa.
Antiquities of Bail: Origin & Historical Development in Criminal Cases to the Year 1275. AMS Pr.
De Harven, Emile, 1924-
xDe Harven, Emile.
Caminos Peligrosos. EMC.
Gefahrliche Wege. EMC.
De Haven, Tom.
xDe Haven, Tom.
Freaks' Amour. Morrow.
De Hollanda, Francisco. *see* Hollanda, Francisco De.
De Jaeger, Charles.
xDe Jaeger, Charles.
photos by Paul Is a Maltese Boy. Hastings.
De Jong, Dola, 1911-
xDe Jong, Dola.
By Marvelous Agreement. Knopf.
House on Charlton Street. Scribner.
De Jong, Gerald F. *see* De Jong, Gerald Francis.
De Jong, Gerald Francis, 1921-
xDe Jong, Gerald F.
The Dutch in America, 1609-1974. Twayne.
De Jong, Kees A.
xDe Jong, Kees A.
ed. Gravity & Tectonics. Wiley.
De Jong, Meindert.
xDe Jong, Meindert.
The Easter Cat. Macmillan.
Easter Cat. Macmillan.
De Jong, Ralph.
xDe Jong, Ralph.
The Life of Mary Magdalene in the Paintings of the Great Masters. Gloucester Art.
De Jong, Rudolph H., 1928-
xDe Jong, Rudolph H.
Local Anesthetics. C C Thomas.
De Jong, W.
xDe Jong, W.
ed. Hypertension & Brain Mechanisms. Elsevier.
De Jonge, Alex, 1938-
xDe Jonge, Alex.
Dostoevsky & the Age of Intensity. St Martin.
De Jonge, Alfred R. *see* De Jonge, Alfred Robert Willy.
De Jonge, Alfred Robert Willy.
xDe Jonge, Alfred R.
Gottfried Kinkel As Political & Social Thinker. AMS Pr.
De Kadt, Emanuel. *see* De Kadt, Emanuel Jehuda.
De Kadt, Emanuel Jehuda.
xDe Kadt, Emanuel.
Catholic Radicals in Brazil. Oxford U Pr.
ed. Sociology & Development. Methuen Inc.
De Kay, James T.
xDe Kay, James T.
Meet Christopher Columbus. Random.
Meet Martin Luther King Jr. Random.
De Kay, Ormonde.
xDe Kay, Ormonde.
Adventures of Lewis & Clark. Random.
Meet Andrew Jackson. Random.
Meet Theodore Roosevelt. Random.
De Kiewiet, Cornelis W. *see* De Kiewiet, Cornelius William.
De Kiewiet, Cornelius William, 1902-
xDe Kiewiet, Cornelis W.
Imperial Factor in South Africa: A Study in Politics & Economics. Russell.
De Kunffy, Charles, 1936-
xDe Kunffy, Charles.
Creative Horsemanship. A S Barnes.
De la Fontaine, Jean. *see* La Fontaine, Jean De.
De La Mare, Walter. *see* De la Mare, Walter John.

De la Mare, Walter John, 1873-1956
   xDe La Mare, Walter.
      Lewis Carroll. Folcroft.
      Lewis Carroll. Haskell.
      Lewis Carroll. Porter.
      The Return. Arno.
      Songs of Childhood. Garland Pub.
      Songs of Childhood. Peter Smith.
      Songs of Childhood. Dover.

De la Nuez, Manuel.
   xDe La Nuez, Manual.
      Eduardo Marquina. Twayne.

De la Roche, Mazo, 1885-
   xDe La Roche, Mazo.
      Mary Wakefield. Fawcett.
      Mary Wakefield. Little.
      Variable Winds at Jalna. Fawcett.
      Variable Winds at Jalna. Little.
      Whiteoak Heritage. Little.
      Whiteoaks of Jalna. Fawcett.

De la Torre, Jose R.
   xDe La Torre, Jose.
      Exports of Manufactured Goods from
         Developing Countries: Marketing Factors &
         the Role of Foreign Enterprise. Arno.

De la Vega, Garcilaso. *see* Garcilaso de la Vega.

De Laguna, Frederica, 1906-
   xDe Laguna, Frederica.
      The Archaeology of Cook Inlet, Alaska. AMS
         Pr.
      The Story of a Tlingit Community: Problem in
         the Relationship Between Archaeological,
         Ethnological & Historical Methods.
         Scholarly.

De Larrabeiti, Michael.
   xDe Larrabeiti, Michael.
      The Borribles. Macmillan.

De Laubenfels, David J., 1925-
   xDe Laubenfels, David J.
      Mapping the World's Vegetation:
         Regionalization of Formations & Flora.
         Syracuse U Pr.

De Leeuw, Adele. *see* De Leeuw, Adele Louise.

De Leeuw, Adele Louise, 1899-
   xDe Leeuw, Adele.
      Barred Road. Macmillan.
      The Boy with Wings. Galloway.
      Paul Bunyan & His Blue Ox. Garrard.

De Leeuw, Frank.
   xDe Leeuw, Frank.
      Operating Costs in Public Housing: A Financial
         Crisis. Urban Inst.

De Leiris, Alain.
   xDe Leiris, Alain.
      The Drawings of Edouard Manet. U of Cal Pr.

De Leon, Daniel.
   xDe Leon, Daniel.
      Industrial Unionism: Selected Editorials. NY
         Labor News.

De Leon, Thomas Cooper, 1839-1914
   xDe Leon, Thomas C.
      Four Years in Rebel Capitals. Reprint.
      ed. South Songs. Greenwood.

De Lima, Agnes.
   xDe Lima, Agnes.
      Our Enemy the Child. Arno.

De Longueville, Thomas. *see* Longueville, Thomas de.

De Luca, Anthony J.
   xDe Luca, Anthony.
      Freud & Future Religious Experience. Philos
         Lib.
   xDe Luca, Anthony J.
      Freud & Future Religious Experience.
         Littlefield.

De Luca, Louis J.
   xDe Luca, Louis J.

      Calculus: A First Course. P-H.

De Luna, Frederick A., 1928-
   xDe Luna, Frederick A.
      French Republic Under Cavaignac 1848.
         Princeton U Pr.

De Madariaga, Salvador. *see* Madariaga, Salvador De.
De Madariaga, Salvadore. *see* Madariaga, Salvadore De.
De Maistre, Joseph M. *see* Maistre, Joseph M. De.
De Mare, Eric. *see* De Mare, Eric Samuel.

De Mare, Eric Samuel.
   xDe Mare, Eric.
      London's River: The Story of a City.
         Merrimack Bk Serv.

De Mare, George.
   xDe Mare, George.
      Communicating at the Top: What You Need to
         Know About Communicating to Run an
         Organization. Wiley.

De Maria, Gary, 1954-
   xDe Maria, Gary.
      The Closet. Strawberry Hill.

De Menil, Alexander N. *see* De Menil, Alexander
   Nicolas.

De Menil, Alexander Nicolas, 1849-1928
   xDe Menil, Alexander N.
      Literature of the Louisiana Territory. B
         Franklin.

De Mente, Boye.
   xDe Mente, Boye.
      Eros' Revenge: The Brave New World of
         American Sex. Phoenix Bks.
      Tourist & the Real Japan: How to Avoid
         Pitfalls & Get the Most Out of Your Trip. C
         E Tuttle.

De Mille, A. B. *see* De Mille, Alban Bertram.

De Mille, Agnes.
   xDe Mille, Agnes.
      Speak to Me, Dance with Me. Popular Lib.
      Where the Wings Grow. Doubleday.

De Mille, Alban Bertram, 1873-
   xDe Mille, A. B.
      Literature in the Century. Folcroft.

De Mille, George E. *see* De Mille, George Edmed.

De Mille, George Edmed, 1898-
   xDe Mille, George E.
      Literary Criticism in America: A Preliminary
         Survey. Russell.

De Mille, James, 1837-1880
   xDe Mille, James.
      A Strange Manuscript Found in a Copper
         Cylinder. Arno.

De Mille, Richard, 1922-
   xDe Mille, Richard.
      Castaneda's Journey: The Power & the
         Allegory. Capra Pr.
      ed. The Don Juan Papers: Further Castaneda
         Controversies. Ross-Erikson.

De Moll, Lane.
   xDe Moll, Lane.
      ed. Stepping Stones: Appropriate Technology &
         Beyond. Schocken.

De Moncrif, Francois A. *see* Moncrif, Francois A. De.
De Montesquieu, C. *see* Montesquieu, C. de.

De Montreville, Doris.
   xDe Montreville, Doris.
      ed. Third Book of Junior Authors. Wilson.

De Morgan, Augustus.
   xDe Morgan, Augustus.
      Budget of Paradoxes. Arno.
      The Encyclopedia of Eccentrics. Open Court.

De Neufville, Richard, 1939-
   xDe Neufville, Richard.
      Airport Systems Planning: A Critical Look at
         the Methods & Experience. MIT Pr.

De Palma, A. F. *see* De Palma, Anthony F.

De Palma, Anthony F.
   xDe Palma, A. F.
      Surgery of the Shoulder. Lippincott.

De Paola. *see* De Paola, Thomas Anthony.

De Paola, Thomas Anthony.
   xDe Paola.
      Things to Make & Do for Valentine's Day.
         Schol Bk Serv.
   xDe Paola, Tomie.
      Flicks. HarBraceJ.
      The Kids' Cat Book. Holiday.
      The Knight & the Dragon. Putnam.
      illus. The Lady of Guadalupe. Holiday.
      illus. Oliver Button Is a Sissy. HarBraceJ.
      illus. Oliver Button Is a Sissy. HarBraceJ.
      illus. Pancakes for Breakfast. HarBraceJ.
      The Popcorn Book. Holiday.
      The Popcorn Book. Schol Bk Serv.
      The Quicksand Book. Holiday.
      Songs of the Fog Maiden. Holiday.
      illus. Things to Make & Do for Valentine's
         Day. Watts.
      When Everyone Was Fast Asleep. Holiday.
      illus. When Everyone Was Fast Asleep.
         Penguin.

De Paola, Tomie. *see* De Paola, Thomas Anthony.

De Paor, Maire.
   xDe Paor, Maire.
      Early Christian Ireland. Thames Hudson.

De Pauw, John W. *see* De Pauw, John Whylen.

De Pauw, John Whylen, 1937-
   xDe Pauw, John W.
      Soviet-American Trade Negotiations. Praeger.

De Pauw, Linda G. *see* De Pauw, Linda Grant.

De Pauw, Linda Grant.
   xDe Pauw, Linda G.
      Founding Mothers: Women of America in the
         Revolutionary Era. HM.

De Polnay, Peter, 1906-
   xDe Polnay, Peter.
      The Stuffed Dog. St Martin.

De Quincey, Thomas.
   xDe Quincey, Thomas.
      Confessions of an English Opium-Eater &
         Other Writings. NAL.

De Regniers, Beatrice S. *see* De Regniers, Beatrice
   Schenk.

De Regniers, Beatrice Schenk.
   xDe Regniers, Beatrice S.
      Abraham Lincoln Joke Book. Random.
      A Bunch of Poems & Verses. HM.
      Circus. Viking Pr.
      Laura's Story. Atheneum.
      Little House of Your Own. HarBraceJ.
      Little Sister & the Month Brothers. HM.
      May I Bring a Friend. Atheneum.
      May I Bring a Friend?. Atheneum.
      Who Likes the Sun. HarBraceJ.

De Renzo, D. *see* De Renzo, D. J.

De Renzo, D. J.
   xDe Renzo, D.
      Energy from Bioconversion of Waste Materials.
         Noyes.
   xDe Renzo, D. J.
      ed. European Technology for Obtaining Energy
         from Solid Waste. Noyes.
      ed. Nitrogen Control & Phosphorus Removal in
         Sewage Treatment. Noyes.
      Unit Operations for Treatment of Hazardous
         Industrial Wastes. Noyes.
      Wind Power: Recent Developments. Noyes.

De Reyna, Rudy, 1914-
   xDe Reyna, Rudy.
      How to Draw What You See. Watson-Guptill.
      Magic Realist Oil Painting. Watson-Guptill.
      Painting in Opaque Watercolor.
         Watson-Guptill.

De Rico, Ul, 1944-
   xDe Rico, Ul.
      The Rainbow Goblins. Thames Hudson.
      Rainbow Goblins. Warner Bks.

De River, J. Paul. *see* De River, Joseph Paul.

De River, Joseph Paul.
   xDe River, J. Paul.

Archaeology at the National Greek Orthodox
    Shrine, St. Augustine, Florida. U Presses Fla.
Deagon, Ann, 1930-
    xDeagon, Ann.
    There Is No Balm in Birmingham. Godine.
Deak, Etienne.
    xDeak, Etienne.
    Dictionary of Colorful French Slanguage &
        Colloquialisms. Dutton.
Deak, Francis.
    xDeak, Francis.
    ed. A Collection of Neutrality Laws,
        Regulations & Treaties of Various Countries.
        Greenwood.
    ed. A Collection of Neutrality Laws,
        Regulations & Treaties of Various Countries.
        Kraus Repr.
Deak, Gloria-Gilda, 1930-
    xDeak, Gloria-Gilda.
    American Views: Prospects & Vistas. NY Pub
        Lib.
Deakin, James, 1929-
    xDeakin, James.
    Lobbyists. Pub Aff Pr.
Deakin, Mary H. *see* Deakin, Mary Hannah.
Deakin, Mary Hannah.
    xDeakin, Mary H.
    The Early Life of George Eliot. R West.
Deal, Borden, 1922-
    xDeal, Borden.
    Adventure. Doubleday.
Deal, William S.
    xDeal, William S.
    Christian's Daily Manna. Deal Pubns.
    Counseling Christian Parents. Deal Pubns.
    Daily Christian Living. Deal Pubns.
    Problems of the Spirit-Filled Life. Deal Pubns.
Dealey, Ted, 1892-
    xDealey, Ted.
    Diaper Days of Dallas. SMU Press.
Dean, Anabel.
    xDean, Anabel.
    Animal Defenses. Messner.
    Animals That Fly. Messner.
    How Animals Communicate. Messner.
    Plants That Eat Insects: A Look at Carnivorous
        Plants. Lerner Pubns.
    Up, Up, & Away!: The Story of Ballooning.
        Westminster.
Dean, Audrey Vincente.
    xDean, Audrey Vincente.
    Wooden Spoon Puppets. Plays.
Dean, B. V. *see* Dean, Burton Victor.
Dean, Bessie.
    xDean, Bessie.
    Let's Love One Another. Horizon Utah.
Dean, Britten.
    xDean, Britten.
    China & Great Britain: The Diplomacy of
        Commercial Relations, 1860-1864. Harvard U
        Pr.
Dean, Burton Victor.
    xDean, B. V.
    Mathematics for Modern Management.
        Krieger.
Dean, D. L. *see* Dean, Donald Lee.
Dean, Donald Lee, 1926-
    xDean, D. L.
    Discrete Field Analysis of Structural Systems.
        Springer-Verlag.
Dean, Geoffrey.
    xDean, Geoffrey.
    The Porphyrias: A Story of Inheritance &
        Environment. State Mutual Bk.
Dean, H. *see* Dean, Harvey R.__.
Dean, H. B. *see* Dean, Herschel B.
Dean, Harvey R.__, 1943-
    xDean, H.

Manufacturing: Industry & Careers. P-H.
Dean, Herschel B.
    xDean, H. B.
    Gleanings from God's Word. Standard Pub.
Dean, J. Robert. *see* Dean, John Robert.
Dean, John A. *see* Dean, John Aurie.
Dean, John Aurie, 1921-
    xDean, John A.
    Chemical Separation Methods. Van Nos
        Reinhold.
Dean, John Robert.
    xDean, J. Robert.
    A Land Called California. Pacific Sun.
Dean, Leonard F. *see* Dean, Leonard Fellows.
Dean, Leonard Fellows.
    xDean, Leonard F.
    ed. Play of Language. Oxford U Pr.
Dean, Nancy.
    xDean, Nancy.
    ed. In the Looking Glass: Twenty-One Modern
        Short Stories by Women. Putnam.
Dean, Nell M. *see* Dean, Nell Marr.
Dean, Nell Marr.
    xDean, Nell M.
    Society Doctor. Assoc Bk.
Dean, R. D. *see* Dean, Robert D.
Dean, R. T.
    xDean, R. T.
    Cellular Degradative Processes. Methuen Inc.
Dean, Ralph.
    xDean, Ralph.
    The Real Estate Manual for Successful
        Investing. Dean & Assocs.
Dean, Robert. *see* Dean, Robert James.
Dean, Robert D.
    xDean, R. D.
    Spatial Economic Theory. Free Pr.
Dean, Robert J. *see* Dean, Robert James.
Dean, Robert James, 1932-
    xDean, Robert.
    How Can We Believe?. Broadman.
    xDean, Robert J.
    First Corinthians for Today. Broadman.
Dean, Robert W.
    xDean, Robert W.
    Nationalism & Political Change in Eastern
        Europe: The Slovak Question & the
        Czechoslovak Reform Movement. U of
        Denver Intl.
Dean, Stanley R.
    xDean, Stanley R.
    Psychiatry & Mysticism. Nelson-Hall.
Dean, Thomas, 1938-
    xDean, Thomas.
    Post-Theistic Thinking: The Marxist-Christian
        Dialogue in Radical Perspective. Temple U
        Pr.
Dean, Thomas S. *see* Dean, Thomas Scott.
Dean, Thomas Scott.
    xDean, Thomas S.
    Thermal Storage. Franklin Inst Pr.
Dean, Vera. *see* Dean, Vera Micheles.
Dean, Vera (Micheles), 1903-
    xDean, Vera M.
    Nature of the Non-Western World. NAL.
Dean, Vera M. *see* Dean, Vera (Micheles).
Dean, Vera Micheles, 1903-1972
    xDean, Vera.
    Europe & the United States. Greenwood.
Dean, Warren.
    xDean, Warren.
    Latin America: The Struggle Against Poverty.
        Macmillan.
Dean, William F. *see* Dean, William Frishe.
Dean, William Frishe.
    xDean, William F.
    General Dean's Story. Greenwood.
Dean, Winton.
    xDean, Winton.

Bizet. Biblio Dist.
    Bizet. Hyperion Conn.
    Bizet. Littlefield.
Deandrea, William L.
    xDeAndrea, William L.
    The Hog Murders. Avon.
    Killed in the Ratings. Avon.
Deane, Cecil V. *see* Deane, Cecil Victor.
Deane, Cecil Victor.
    xDeane, Cecil V.
    Dramatic Theory & the Rhymed Heroic Play.
        Arden Lib.
    Dramatic Theory & the Rhymed Heroic Play.
        Biblio Dist.
    Dramatic Theory & the Rhymed Heroic Play.
        Folcroft.
Deane, Dorothy N. *see* Deane, Dorothy Newell.
Deane, Dorothy Newell.
    xDeane, Dorothy N.
    Sierra Railway. Howell-North.
Deane, Phillis. *see* Deane, Phyllis.
Deane, Phyllis.
    xDeane, Phillis.
    The Evolution of Economic Ideas. Cambridge
        U Pr.
    xDeane, Phyllis.
    Colonial Social Accounting. Shoe String.
    The First Industrial Revolution. Cambridge U
        Pr.
Deane, Tony.
    xDeane, Tony.
    The Folklore of Cornwall. Rowman.
Deane, Wallace.
    xDeane, Wallace.
    Fijian Society: Or, The Sociology & Psychology
        of the Fijians. AMS Pr.
Deangelis, Anthony M.
    xDeAngelis, Anthony M.
    Surgical Anatomy of Peripheral Nerves. Futura
        Pub.
Deangelis, Catherine.
    xDeAngelis, Catherine.
    Pediatric Primary Care. Little.
Deanin, Rudolph D.
    xDeanin, Rudolph D.
    Polymer Structure, Properties & Applications.
        CBI Pub.
Dearborn, Ned H. *see* Dearborn, Ned Harland.
Dearborn, Ned Harland, 1893-
    xDearborn, Ned H.
    Oswego Movement in American Education.
        AMS Pr.
    Oswego Movement in American Education.
        Arno.
Dearden, C. W.
    xDearden, C. W.
    The Stage of Aristophanes. Humanities.
Dearden, Harold, 1882-
    xDearden, Harold.
    Devilish but True: The Doctor Looks at
        Spiritualism. Beekman Pubs.
    Devilish but True: The Doctor Looks at
        Spiritualism. Rowman.
Dearden, John.
    xDearden, John.
    Financial Accounting & Reporting: A
        Contemporary Emphasis. P-H.
Dearden, M. *see* Dearden, Michael.
Dearden, Michael.
    xDearden, M.
    A Modern Course in Biology. Pergamon.
Dearden, R. F.
    xDearden, R. F.

ed. Education & the Development of Reason. Routledge & Kegan.

Problems in Primary Education. Routledge & Kegan.

Dearing, Charles L. *see* Dearing, Charles Lee.

Dearing, Charles Lee.
  xDearing, Charles L.
    National Transportation Policy. Greenwood.

Dearing, Trevor, 1933-
  xDearing, Trevor.
    Supernatural Healing Today. Logos.
    Supernatural Superpowers. Logos.

Dearing, Vinton A. *see* Dearing, Vinton Adams.

Dearing, Vinton Adams, 1920-
  xDearing, Vinton A.
    Principles & Practice of Textual Analysis. U of Cal Pr.

Dearmond, Stephen J.
  xDeArmond, Stephen J.
    Structure of the Human Brain: A Photographic Atlas. Oxford U Pr.

Deason, Hilary J.
  xDeason, Hilary J.
    Compiled by AAAS Science Book List for Children. AAAS.

Deasy, C. M.
  xDeasy, C. M.
    Design for Human Affairs. Halsted Pr.

Deasy, Mary, 1914-
  xDeasy, Mary.
    The Hour of Spring. Arno.

Deatherage, F. E. *see* Deatherage, Fred E.

Deatherage, Fred E., 1913-
  xDeatherage, F. E.
    Food for Life. Plenum Pub.

Deathridge, John.
  xDeathridge, John.
    Wagner's Rienzi: A Reappraisal Based on a Study of Sketches & Drafts. Oxford U Pr.

Deaton, A. *see* Deaton, Angus.

Deaton, Angus.
  xDeaton, A.
    Economics & Consumer Behavior. Cambridge U Pr.

Deaton, John G.
  xDeaton, John G.
    Book of Family Medical Questions. Random.

Deats, Randy.
  xDeats, Randy.
    Dancing Disco. Morrow.

Debaigts, Jacques.
  xDebaigts, Jacques.
    The Modern Fireplace. Van Nos Reinhold.

DeBakey. *see* Debakey, Michael Ellis.

DeBakey, Michael. *see* Debakey, Michael Ellis.

Debakey, Michael Ellis.
  xDeBakey.
    Living Heart. G&D.
  xDeBakey, Michael.
    The Living Heart. Charter Bks.

DeBenedetti, Charles.
  xDeBenedetti, Charles.
    The Origins of the Modern American Peace Movement, 1915-1929. Kraus Intl.
    Peace Reform in American History. Ind U Pr.

DeBenedictis, Daniel J.
  xDeBenedictis, Daniel J.
    The Complete Real Estate Adviser. S&S.
    The Complete Real Estate Advisor. PB.

DeBlassie, Richard R.
  xDeBlassie, Richard R.
    ed. Measuring & Evaluating Pupil Progress. Mss Info.

Debo, Angie, 1890-
  xDebo, Angie.

And Still the Waters Run. Gordian.

Geronimo: The Man, His Time, His Place. U of Okla Pr.

History of the Indians of the United States. U of Okla Pr.

Prairie City: The Story of an American Community. Gordian.

Debo, Harvey V.
  xDebo, Harvey V.
    Construction Superintendent's Job Guide. Wiley.

Debo, Richard K., 1938-
  xDebo, Richard K.
    Revolution & Survival: The Foreign Policy of Soviet Russia, 1917-1918. U of Toronto Pr.

DeBoer, John C.
  xDeBoer, John C.
    Let's Plan: A Guide to the Planning Process for Voluntary Organizations. Pilgrim NY.

Deboo, Gordon J.
  xDeboo, Gordon J.
    Integrated Circuits & Semiconductor Devices: Theory & Application. McGraw.

Debray, Regis.
  xDebray, Regis.
    Revolution in the Revolution?: Armed Struggle and Political Struggle in Latin America. Greenwood.

Debre, Moses.
  xDebre, Moses.
    Image of the Jew in French Literature from 1800 to 1908. Ktav.

Debreczeny, Paul.
  xDebreczeny, Paul.
    tr. Literature & National Identity: Nineteenth-Century Russian Critical Essays. U of Nebr Pr.
    Nikolay Gogol & His Contemporary Critics. Am Philos.

Debreu, Gerard.
  xDebreu, Gerard.
    Theory of Value: An Axiomatic Analysis of Economic Equilibrium. Yale U Pr.

Debrum. *see* Debrum, Seraphim Joseph.

Debrum, Seraphim Joseph.
  xDebrum.
    General Business for Economic Understanding. SW Pub.

Debs, Eugene V. *see* Debs, Eugene Victor.

Debs, Eugene Victor, 1855-1926
  xDebs, Eugene V.
    Eugene V. Debs Speaks. Path Pr NY.

Debus, A. G. *see* Debus, Allen G.

Debus, Allen G.
  xDebus, A. G.
    Man & Nature in the Renaissance. Cambridge U Pr.

Decalo, Samuel.
  xDecalo, Samuel.
    Coups & Army Rule in Africa: Studies in Military Style. Yale U Pr.
    Historical Dictionary of Chad. Scarecrow.
    Historical Dictionary of Niger. Scarecrow.
    Historical Dictionary of Togo. Scarecrow.

Decaprio, Annie.
  xDeCaprio, Annie.
    A Modern Approach to Business Spelling. Bobbs.

Decaro, Matthew.
  xDeCaro, Matthew V.
    Gray's Anatomy Coloring Book. Running Pr.

DeCaro, Matthew V. *see* Decaro, Matthew.

Dechant, Emarld V. *see* Dechant, Emerald V.

Dechant, Emerald. *see* Dechant, Emerald V.

Dechant, Emerald V.
  xDechant, Emarld V.
    Psychology in Teaching Reading. P-H.
  xDechant, Emerald.

How to Be Happily Married. Alba.

Improving the Teaching of Reading. P-H.

Reading Improvement in the Secondary School. P-H.

Deci, Edward L.
  xDeci, Edward L.
    Readings in Industrial & Organizational Psychology. McGraw.

Decker, Beatrice.
  xDecker, Beatrice.
    After the Flowers Have Gone. Zondervan.

Decker, Benton W. *see* Decker, Benton Weaver.

Decker, Benton Weaver.
  xDecker, Benton W.
    Return of the Black Ships. Vantage.

Decker, Donald M.
  xDecker, Donald M.
    Luis Durand. Irvington.

Decker, Duane. *see* Decker, Duane Walter.

Decker, Duane Walter, 1910-
  xDecker, Duane.
    Fast Man on a Pivot. Morrow.
    Long Ball to Left Field. Morrow.
    Rebel in Right Field. Morrow.
    Third-Base Rookie. Morrow.

Decker, James A. *see* Decker, James Arthur.

Decker, James Arthur, 1917-
  xDecker, James A.
    What Will You Have?. Unity Bks.

Decker, John P. *see* Decker, John Peter.

Decker, John Peter, 1915-
  xDecker, John P.
    Solving Personality Clashes with Time-Zero Synecology.

Decker, Leslie E. *see* Decker, Leslie Edward.

Decker, Leslie Edward, 1930-
  xDecker, Leslie E.
    Railroads, Lands & Politics: The Taxation of the Railroad Land Grants, 1864-1897. Brown U Pr.

Decker, Malcolm.
  xDecker, Malcolm.
    Brink of Revolution: New York in Crisis, 1765-1776. Argosy.

Decker, Randall E.
  xDecker, Randall E.
    Patterns of Exposition. Little.

Decker, Robert.
  xDecker, Robert.
    The Proud Mexicans. Regents Pub.

Declue, Denise.
  xDeClue, Denise.
    Women Shaping History. Raintree Pubs.

Deconninck, G.
  xDeconninck, G.
    Introduction to Radioanalytical Physics. Elsevier.

DeCoster, Cyrus Cole, 1914-
  xDeCoster, Cyrus C.
    Pedro Antonio de Alarcon. Twayne.

Decoster, D. T. *see* Decoster, Don T.

Decoster, Don T.
  xDecoster, D. T.
    Accounting for Managerial Decision Making. Wiley.

DeCourcy, Peter.
  xDeCourcy, Peter.
    A Silent Tragedy: Child Abuse in the Community. Alfred Pub.

Decroly, J. C.
  xDecroly, J. C.
    Parametric Amplifiers. Halsted Pr.

Dedek, John F., 1929-
  xDedek, John F.
    Contemporary Medical Ethics. Andrews & McMeel.

Dedera, Don.
  xDedera, Don.

Goodbye, Garcia, Adios. Northland.
Navajo Rugs: How to Find, Evaluate, Buy &
     Care for Them. Northland.
Dedijer, V. see Dedijer, Vladimir.
Dedijer, Vladimir.
     xDedijer, V.
     History of Yugoslavia. McGraw.
Dee, John, 1527-1608
     xDee, John.
     Private Diary of Dr. John Dee & the Catalogue
          of His Library of Manuscripts. AMS Pr.
     Private Diary of Dr. John Dee & the Catalogue
          of His Library of Manuscripts. Johnson Repr.
     Stagger Lee. Manor Bks.
Deeb, Marius.
     xDeeb, Marius.
     The Lebanese Civil War. Praeger.
Deedy, John. see Deedy, John G.
Deedy, John G.
     xDeedy, John.
     Literary Places: A Guided Pilgrimage; New
          York & New England. Andrews & McMeel.
Deegan, Arthur X.
     xDeegan, Arthur X.
     Coaching: A Management Skill for Improving
          Individual Performance. A-W.
Deegan, James F.
     xDeegan, James F.
     An Econometric Model of the Gulf Coast Oil
          & Gas Exploration Industry. Arno.
Deegan, Paul. see Deegan, Paul J.
Deegan, Paul J.
     xDeegan, Paul.
     Hospital: Life in a Medical Center. Creative
          Ed.
     xDeegan, Paul J.
     Almost a Champion. Creative Ed.
     Bunting & Baserunning. Creative Ed.
     Close but Not Quite. Creative Ed.
     Dan Moves up. Creative Ed.
     Hitting the Baseball. Creative Ed.
     Important Decision. Creative Ed.
     Passing the Football. Creative Ed.
     Placekicking & Punting. Creative Ed.
     Stickhandling & Passing. Creative Ed.
     Tournaments. Creative Ed.
Deeken, Alfons.
     xDeeken, Alfons.
     Process & Permanence in Ethics: Max
          Scheler's Moral Philosophy. Paulist Pr.
Deeley, Lilla.
     xDeeley, Lilla.
     Favorite Hungarian Recipes. Dover.
     Favorite Hungarian Recipes. Peter Smith.
Deely, John N.
     xDeely, John N.
     The Problem of Evolution: A Study of the
          Philosophical Repercussions of Evolutionary
          Science. Hackett Pub.
Deem, Bill. see Deem, William.
Deem, Rosemary.
     xDeem, Rosemary.
     Women & Schooling. Routledge & Kegan.
Deem, William.
     xDeem, Bill.
     Digital Computer Circuits & Concepts. Reston.
Deeming, Sue.
     xDeeming, Sue.
     Bean Cookery. H P Bks.
Deems, Betty.
     xDeems, Betty.
     Easy-to-Make Felt Ornaments for Christmas
          and Other Occasions. Dover.
Deeney, Daniel.
     xDeeney, Daniel.

Peasant Lore from Gaelic Ireland. Folcroft.
Peasant Lore from Gaelic Ireland. Porter.
Deep, Samuel D.
     xDeep, Samuel D.
     Human Relations in Management. Glencoe.
     Introduction to Business: A Systems Approach.
          P-H.
Dees, Benjamin.
     xDees, Benjamin.
     E. A. Baratynsky. Twayne.
Deese, James. see Deese, James Earle.
Deese, James Earle, 1921-
     xDeese, James.
     Psychology As Science & Art. HarBraceJ.
Deeson, A. F. see Deeson, A. F. L.
Deeson, A. F. L.
     xDeeson, A. F.
     An Illustrated History of Steamships.
          Transatlantic.
Deetz, James. see Deetz, James J. F.
Deetz, James J. F.
     xDeetz, James.
     In Small Things Forgotten: The Archaeology of
          Early American Life. Doubleday.
Defant, Albert, 1884-
     xDefant, Albert.
     Ebb & Flow: The Tides of Earth, Air & Water.
          U of Mich Pr.
Defelice, James.
     xDeFelice, James.
     Filmguide to Odd Man Out. Ind U Pr.
Defelitta, Frank.
     xDeFelitta, Frank.
     Audrey Rose. Putnam.
Deferrari, Roy J. see Deferrari, Roy Joseph.
Deferrari, Roy Joseph, 1890-
     xDeferrari, Roy J.
     Memoirs of the Catholic University of America
          1918-1960. Dghtrs St Paul.
     Some Problems of Catholic Higher Education
          in the United States. Dghtrs St Paul.
DeFleur, Melvin L. see Defleur, Melvin Lawrence.
Defleur, Melvin Lawrence.
     xDeFleur, Melvin L.
     Sociology: Human Society. Scott F.
Defoe, Daniel, 1616?-1731
     xDefoe, Daniel.
     Account of the Conduct & Proceedings of the
          Pirate Gow: The Original of Sir Walter
          Scott's Captain Cleveland. B Franklin.
     Complete English Tradesman. B Franklin.
     Complete English Tradesman. Kelley.
     The Earlier Life & Chief Earlier Works of
          Daniel Defoe. B Franklin.
     The Farther Adventures of Robinson Crusoe,
          Being the Second & Last Part of His Life.
          AMS Pr.
     The Fortunes & Misfortunes of the Famous
          Moll Flanders. AMS Pr.
     The Four Years Voyages of Captain George
          Roberts. Garland Pub.
     A General History of the Pyrates. U of SC Pr.
     The History of the Life & Adventures of Mr.
          Duncan Campbell. AMS Pr.
     Life, Adventures & Pyracies of the Famous
          Captain Singleton. Oxford U Pr.
     Street-Robberies Consider'd: The Reason of
          Their Being So Frequent. Carolingian.
     A System of Magick. Rowman.
     Tour Through the Whole Island of Great
          Britain. Penguin.
Deforges, Regine.
     xDeforges, Regine.
     Confessions of O: Conversations with Pauline
          Reage. Viking Pr.
Defourneaux, Marcelin.
     xDefourneaux, Mercelin.
     Daily Life in Spain in the Golden Age.
          Stanford U Pr.
Defourneaux, Mercelin. see Defourneaux, Marcelin.

Defrancesco, Henry F.
     xDefrancesco, Henry F.
     Quantitative Analysis Methods for Substantive
          Analysts. Krieger.
DeFrancis, John. see Defrancis, John Francis.
DeFrancis, John Francis, 1911-
     xDeFrancis, John.
     Things Japanese in Hawaii. U Pr of Hawaii.
Defren, Burton J.
     xDefren, Burton J.
     Partnership Desk Book. Inst Busn Plan.
Defries, Esther P. see Defries, Esther Phoebe.
Defries, Esther Phoebe.
     xDefries, Esther P.
     Browning Primer. Kennikat.
     A Browning Primer. R West.
Degani, Meir H.
     xDegani, Meir H.
     Astronomy Made Simple. Doubleday.
Degas, Hilaire. see Degas, Hilaire Germain Edgar.
Degas, Hilaire Germain Edgar.
     xDegas, Hilaire.
     Degas. G&D.
Degelius, Gunnar. see Degelius, Gunnar Bror Fritiof.
Degelius, Gunnar Bror Fritiof, 1903-
     xDegelius, Gunnar.
     Further Studies on the Epiphytic Vegetation on
          Twigs. Humanities.
Degen, Bruce.
     xDegen, Bruce.
     Aunt Possum & the Pumpkin Man. Har-Row.
     illus. The Little Witch & the Riddle. Har-Row.
Degen, Marie L. see Degen, Marie Louise.
Degen, Marie Louise.
     xDegen, Marie L.
     The History of the Woman's Peace Party.
          AMS Pr.
     The History of the Woman's Peace Party. B
          Franklin.
Degenkolb, Oris H., 1918-
     xDegenkolb, Oris H.
     Concrete Box Girder Bridges. ACI.
     Concrete Box Girder Bridges. Iowa St U Pr.
Degens, T.
     xDegens, T.
     The Game on Thatcher Island. Viking Pr.
Degenshein, Joan.
     xDegenshein, Joan.
     Successful Cosmetic Selling. Lebhar Friedman.
Degh, Linda.
     xDegh, Linda.
     ed. Folktales of Hungary. U of Chicago Pr.
Degler, Carl N.
     xDegler, Carl N.
     The Age of the Economic Revolution:
          1876-1900. Scott F.
     At Odds: Women & the Family in America.
          from the Revolution to the Present. Oxford U
          Pr.
     The Democratic Experience: A Short American
          History. Scott F.
     Out of Our Past: The Forces That Shaped
          Modern America. Har-Row.
     Out of Our Past: The Forces That Shaped
          Modern America. Har-Row.
     Place Over Time: The Continuity of Southern
          Distinctiveness. La State U Pr.
DeGraaf, Richard M.
     xDeGraaf, Richard M.
     Trees, Shrubs, & Vines for Attracting Birds: A
          Manual for the Northeast. U of Mass Pr.
Degravelles, William D.
     xDegravelles, William D.
     Injuries Following Rear-End Automobile
          Collisions. C C Thomas.
Degrazia, Joseph, 1883-
     xDegrazia, Joseph.
     Math Is Fun. Emerson.
     More Math Teasers. B&N.
Degremont. see Degremont, S.A.

Degremont, S.A.
 xDegremont.
  Water Treatment Handbook. Halsted Pr.
DeGrood, David H.
 xDeGrood, David H.
  Consciousness & Social Life. Humanities.
  Radical Currents in Contemporary Philosophy.
   Fireside Bks.
  Radical Currents in Contemporary Philosophy.
   Green.
DeGroot, Leslie J.
 xDeGroot, Leslie J.
  ed. Endocrinology. Grune.
  Radiation Associated Thyroid Carcinoma.
   Grune.
Degroot, Morris. see Degroot, Morris H.
Degroot, Morris H., 1931-
 xDegroot, Morris.
  Probability & Statistics. A-W.
DeHaan, Martin R. see Dehaan, Martin Ralph.
DeHaan, Martin Ralph, 1891-
 xDeHaan, Martin R.
  Pentecost & After. Zondervan.
Dehart, Florence E.
 xDeHart, Florence E.
  The Librarian's Psychological Commitments:
   Human Relations in Librarianship.
   Greenwood.
DeHaven, Edna P.
 xDeHaven, Edna P.
  Teaching & Learning the Language Arts. Little.
Dehn, Adolf Arthur.
 xDehn, Virginia.
  ed. Adolf Dehn Drawings. U of Mo Pr.
Dehn, Virginia. see Dehn, Adolf Arthur.
Dehoney, Waane. see Dehoney, Wayne.
Dehoney, Wayne.
 xDehoney, Waane.
  Preaching to Change Lives. Broadman.
 xDehoney, Wayne.
  An Evangelical's Guidebook to the Holy Land.
   Broadman.
Deibel, Terry L.
 xDeibel, Terry L.
  Culture & Information: Two Foreign Policy
   Functions. Sage.
Deichmann, Paul, 1898-
 xDeichmann, Paul.
  German Air Force Operations in Support of
   the Army. Arno.
Deighton, Lee C.
 xDeighton, Lee C.
  Handbook of American English Spelling.
   HarBraceJ.
Deighton, Len.
 xDeighton, Len.
  Airshipwreck. HR&W.
  The Billion Dollar Brain. Berkley Pub.
  Blitzkrieg: From the Rise of Hitler to the Fall
   of Dunkirk. Knopf.
  Catch a Falling Spy. PB.
  An Expensive Place to Die. Berkley Pub.
  Fighter: The True Story of the Battle of
   Britain. Knopf.
Deimling, K. see Deimling, Klaus.
Deimling, Klaus, 1943-
 xDeimling, K.
  Ordinary Differential Equations in Banach
   Spaces. Springer-Verlag.
Deindorfer, Scott.
 xDeindorfer, Scott.
  Dear Scott. Workman Pub.
Deiss, Lucien.
 xDeiss, Lucien.

  Springtime of the Liturgy: Liturgical Texts of
   the First Four Centuries. Liturgical Pr.
Deitch, Lillian.
 xDeitch, Lillian.
  Prepaid Legal Services: Socio-Economic
   Impacts. Lexington Bks.
Deitchman, Seymour J.
 xDeitchman, Seymour J.
  New Technology & Military Power: General
   Purpose Military Forces for the 1980's &
   Beyond. Westview.
Deitel, Harvey M., 1945- `
 xDeitel, Harvey M.
  Introduction to Computer Programming with
   the Basic Language. P-H.
Deitz, Samuel M.
 xDeitz, Samuel M.
  Discipline in the Schools: A Guide to Reducing
   Misbehavior. Educ Tech Pubns.
Deitzer, Bernard. see Deitzer, Bernard A.
Deitzer, Bernard A.
 xDeitzer, Bernard.
  Incidents in Modern Business. Merrill.
 xDeitzer, Bernard A.
  Contemporary Management Concepts. Grid
   Pub.
  Contemporary Management Incidents. Grid
   Pub.
DeJ Ellis, Maria. see Ellis, Maria deJ.
Dejerine, Joseph J. see Dejerine, Joseph Jules.
Dejerine, Joseph Jules.
 xDejerine, Joseph J.
  Psychoneuroses & Their Treatment by
   Psychotherapy. Arno.
Dejon, William L.
 xDejon, William L.
  Policy Formulation. CBI Pub.
  Principles of Management. Tent & Case.
   Benjamin-Cummings.
DeJong, Peter.
 xDeJong, Peter.
  Husband & Wife: The Sexes in Scripture &
   Society. Zondervan.
  Patterns of Intergenerational Occupational
   Mobility of American Females. R & E Res
   Assoc.
Dejours, Pierre.
 xDejours, Pierre.
  Respiration. Oxford U Pr.
Deju, Raul. see Deju, Raul A.
Deju, Raul A.
 xDeju, Raul.
  The Environment & Its Resources. Gordon.
 xDeju, Raul A.
  Regional Hydrology Fundamentals. Gordon.
Dekker. see Dekker, Thomas.
Dekker, George.
 xDekker, George.
  Coleridge & the Literature of Sensibility. B&N.
Dekker, H. C.
 xDekker, H. C.
  Planning in a Dutch & a Yugoslav Steelworks:
   A Comparative Study. Humanities.
Dekker, Thomas.
 xDekker.
  The Shoemaker's Holiday. Norton.
 xDekker, Thomas.
  Gull's Hornbook. AMS Pr.
  The Gull's Hornbook. Folcroft.
  The Plague Pamphlets of Thomas Dekker. R
   West.
  The Plague Pamphlets of Thomas Dekker.
   Scholarly.
  Shoemaker's Holiday. Cambridge U Pr.
  The Shoemakers Holiday. Johns Hopkins.
  Shoemaker's Holiday. Barron.
Dekmejian, R. Hrair, 1933-
 xDekmejian, R. Hrair.

  Egypt Under Nasir: A Study in Political
   Dynamics. State U NY Pr.
  Patterns of Political Leadership: Egypt, Israel,
   Lebanon. State U NY Pr.
DeKock, R. L. see Dekock, Roger L.
Dekock, Roger L.
 xDeKock, R. L.
  Chemical Structure & Bonding. A-W.
 xDeKock, Roger L.
  Chemical Structure & Bonding.
   Benjamin-Cummings.
DeKornfeld, Thomas J.
 xDeKornfeld, Thomas J.
  Respiratory Care Case Studies. Med Exam.
DeKorte, Juliann.
 xDeKorte, Juliann.
  Finally Home. Revell.
DeKruyter, Arthur H.
 xDeKruyter, Arthur H.
  Complete Candlelight Services for Christmas.
   Zondervan.
Del , Castillo, Bernal Diaz. see Diaz Del Castillo, Bernal.
Del Bueno, Dorothy J.
 xDel Bueno, Dorothy J.
  Case Studies in Pharmacology. Little.
Del Castillo, Michel, 1933-
 xDel Castillo, Michel.
  Child of Our Time. Knopf.
Del Chiaro, Mario A. see Del Chiaro, Mario Aldo.
Del Chiaro, Mario Aldo, 1925-
 xDel Chiaro, Mario A.
  Etruscan Red-Figured Vase-Painting at Caere.
   U of Cal Pr.
Del Guercio, Louis R. see Del Guercio, Louis R. M.
Del Guercio, Louis R. M.
 xDel Guercio, Louis R.
  Multilingual Manual for Medical
   History-Taking. Little.
Del Mazza, Valentino.
 xDel Mazza, Valentino.
  Our Lady Among Us. Dghtrs St Paul.
Del Plaine, Frances K. see Del Plaine, Frances Kelley.
Del Plaine, Frances Kelley.
 xDel Plaine, Frances K.
  ed. College Readings in Poetry: English &
   American. Granger Bk.
Del Pulgar, Fernando. see Pulgar, Fernando Del.
Del Re, Gerard.
 xDel Re, Gerard.
  The Christmas Almanack. Doubleday.
Del Rey, Judy-Lynn.
 xDel Rey, Judy-Lynn.
  ed. Stellar Science Fiction Stories. Ballantine.
  ed. Stellar Short Novels. Ballantine.
Del Rey, Lester, 1915-
 xDel Rey, Lester.
  Attack from Atlantis. Ballantine.
  Early Del Rey. Ballantine.
  Moon of Mutiny. Ballantine.
  Moon of Mutiny. Gregg.
  Outpost of Jupiter. Ballantine.
  Tunnel Through Time. Schol Bk Serv.
Del Sesto, Steven L.
 xDel Sesto, Steven L.
  Science, Politics & Controversy: Civilian
   Nuclear Power in the United States,
   1946-1974. Westview.
Del Toro, Vincent.
 xDel Toro, Vincent.
  Principles of Electrical Engineering. P-H.
Del Vecchio, Alfred.
 xDel Vecchio, Alfred.
  ed. Concise Dictionary of Atomics. Philos Lib.
Delaat, Adrian N. see Delaat, Adrian N. C.
Delaat, Adrian N. C.
 xDelaat, Adrian N.
  A Primer of Serology. Har-Row.
 xDelaat, Adrian N. C.

Microbiology for the Allied Health Professions.
Lea & Febiger.
Delacato, Carl H.
xDelacato, Carl H.
Diagnosis & Treatment of Speech & Reading
Problems. C C Thomas.
Delacroix, Eugene.
xDelacroix, Eugene.
Delacroix. G&D.
The Journal of Eugene Delacroix. Cornell U
Pr.
DeLage, Ida.
xDeLage, Ida.
ABC Christmas. Garrard.
ABC Easter Bunny. Garrard.
ABC Fire Dogs. Garrard.
ABC Halloween Witch. Garrard.
ABC Pigs Go to Market. Garrard.
ABC Pirate Adventure. Garrard.
ABC Santa Claus. Garrard.
Am I a Bunny?. Garrard.
A Bunny Ride. Garrard.
Bunny School. Garrard.
Frannie's Flower. Garrard.
Good Morning, Lady. Garrard.
Old Witch & Her Magic Basket. Garrard.
The Old Witch & the Dragon. Garrard.
The Old Witch Finds a New House. Garrard.
The Pilgrim Children on the Mayflower.
Garrard.
The Squirrel's Tree Party. Garrard.
Delahay, Paul.
xDelahay, Paul.
Advances in Electrochemistry &
Electrochemical Engineering. Krieger.
DeLamater, John.
xDeLamater, John.
Premarital Sexuality: Attitudes, Relationships,
Behavior. U of Wis Pr.
Delamont, Vic.
xDelamont, Victor L.
The Ministry of Music in the Church. Moody.
Delamont, Victor L. see Delamont, Vic.
Delamotte, Philip H. see Delamotte, Philip Henry.
Delamotte, Philip Henry, 1821-1889
xDelamotte, Philip H.
The Practice of Photography. Arno.
Deland, Frank H., 1921-
xDeland, Frank H.
Cerebral Radionuclide Angiography. Saunders.
Deland, Margaret. see Deland, Margaret Wade
(Campbell).
Deland, Margaret W. see Deland, Margaret Wade
(Campbell).
Deland, Margaret Wade (Campbell), 1857-1945
xDeland, Margaret.
The Awakening of Helena Richie. Irvington.
xDeland, Margaret W.
Old Chester Days. Arno.
Delaney, A.
xDelaney, A.
illus. The Butterfly. Delacorte.
Delaney, C. F. see Delaney, Cyril.
Delaney, Cornelius F.
xDelaney, C. F.
ed. Rationality & Religious Belief. U of Notre
Dame Pr.
The Synoptic Vision: Essays on the Philosophy
of Wilfrid Sellars. U of Notre Dame Pr.
Delaney, Cyril, 1925-
xDelaney, C. F.
Electronics for the Physicist with Applications.
Halsted Pr.
Delaney, Edmund T.
xDelaney, Edmund T.
Greenwich Village: A Photographic Guide.
Dover.
Delaney, Gayle. see Delaney, Gayle M. V.
Delaney, Gayle M. V.
xDelaney, Gayle.

Living Your Dreams. Har-Row.
Delaney, Jack J.
xDelaney, Jack J.
The Media Program in the Elementary and
Middle School: Its Organization &
Administration. Shoe String.
Delaney, Janice.
xDelaney, Janice.
The Curse: A Cultural History of Menstruation.
NAL.
Delaney, John J.
xDelaney, John J.
ed. Why Catholic. Doubleday.
ed. Why Catholic. Doubleday.
Delaney, Laurence.
xDelaney, Laurence.
The Triton Ultimatum. Dell.
The Triton Ultimatum. T Y Crowell.
Delaney, Mary M. see Delaney, Mary Murray.
Delaney, Mary Murray, 1912-
xDelaney, Mary M.
Of Irish Ways. Dillon.
Of Irish Ways. Har-Row.
Delaney, Ned.
xDelaney, Ned.
Bert & Barney. HM.
illus. One Dragon to Another. HM.
illus. Two Strikes, Four Eyes. HM.
illus. A Worm for Dinner. HM.
Delaney, Patrick J. see Delaney, Patrick J. V.
Delaney, Patrick J. V.
xDelaney, Patrick J.
Geology & Geomorphology of the Coastal
Plain of Rio Grande Do Sul, Brazil &
Northern Uruguay. La State U Pr.
Quaternary Geologic History of the Coastal
Plain of Rio Grande Do Sul, Brazil. La State
U Pr.
Delange, F. see Delange, Francois.
Delange, Francois.
xDelange, F.
Endemic Goitre & Thyroid Function in Central
Africa. S Karger.
Delange, Jacqueline, 1923-
xDelange, Jacqueline.
The Art & Peoples of Black Africa. Dutton.
Delanglez, Jean, 1896-1949
xDelanglez, Jean.
The French Jesuits in Lower Louisiana
(1700-1763). AMS Pr.
Delano, Anne. see Delano, Anne Lee.
Delano, Anne Lee.
xDelano, Anne.
Field Hockey. Wm C Brown.
Delano, Hugh.
xDelano, Hugh.
Eddie. Atheneum.
Delano, Isaac O.
xDelano, Isaac O.
The Soul of Nigeria. AMS Pr.
Delany, Mary. see Delany, Mary Granville Pendarves.
Delany, Mary Granville Pendarves.
xDelany, Mary.
Autobiography & Correspondence of Mary
Granville, Mrs. Delany. AMS Pr.
Delany, Paul.
xDelany, Paul.
D. H. Lawrence's Nightmare: The Writer &
His Circle in the Years of the Great War.
Basic.
Delany, Samuel. see Delany, Samuel R.
Delany, Samuel R.
xDelany, Samuel.
Einstein Intersection. Ace Bks.
xDelany, Samuel R.

The Ballad of Beta-2. Gregg.
Dhalgren. Gregg.
Driftglass. Gregg.
The Fall of the Towers. Gregg.
The Jewel-Hinged Jaw: Notes on the Language
of Science Fiction. Dragon Pr.
Triton. Bantam.
Triton. Gregg.
Delany, Selden P. see Delany, Selden Peabody.
Delany, Selden Peabody, 1874-1935
xDelany, Selden P.
Married Saints. Arno.
Delany, Sheila.
xDelany, Sheila.
Chaucer's House of Fame: The Poetics of
Skeptical Fideism. U of Chicago Pr.
Delany, Vincent T. see Delany, Vincent Thomas
Hyginns.
Delany, Vincent Thomas Hyginns.
xDelany, Vincent T.
ed. Frederic William Maitland Reader. Oceana.
DeLapp, G. Leslie.
xDeLapp, G. Leslie.
In the World. Herald Hse.
Delattre, Pierre, 1930-
xDelattre, Pierre.
Tales of a Dalai Lama. Creative Arts Bk.
Walking on Air. HM.
Delauney, Rachel.
xDelauney, Rachel.
Fleur. Warner Bks.
Delaunois, A. L.
xDelaunois, A. L.
ed. Biostatistics in Pharmacology. Pergamon.
Delavenay, Emile.
xDelavenay, Emile.
D. H. Lawrence & Edward Carpenter: A Study
in Edwardian Transition. Taplinger.
Delbanco, Nicholas.
xDelbanco, Nicholas.
Possession. Morrow.
Delbecq, Andre. see Delbecq, Andre L.
Delderfield, Eric R.
xDelderfield, Eric R.
Inns and Their Signs: Fact and Fiction. David
& Charles.
Delderfield, R. F. see Delderfield, Ronald Frederick.
Delderfield, Ronald F. see Delderfield, Ronald Frederick.
Delderfield, Ronald Frederick, 1912-1972
xDelderfield, R. F.
All Over the Town. S&S.
Charlie, Come Home. S&S.
Diana. PB.
Farewell the Tranquil Mind. PB.
Long Summer Day. PB.
Napoleon in Love. S&S.
Post of Honor. PB.
Stop at a Winner. S&S.
Theirs Was the Kingdom. PB.
xDelderfield, Ronald F.
Charlie, Come Home. G K Hall.
Horseman Riding By. S&S.
Delear, Frank J.
xDelear, Frank J.
Famous First Flights Across the Atlantic.
Dodd.
Igor Sikorsky, His Three Careers in Aviation.
Dodd.
Delbecq, Andre L.
xDelbecq, Andre.
Group Techniques for Program Planning: A
Guide to Nominal Group & Delphi
Processes. Scott F.

Deleeuw, Diane.
  xDeleeuw, Dianne.
    Figure Skating. Atheneum.

Deleeuw, Dianne. *see* Deleeuw, Diane.

Deleon, David.
  xDeLeon, David.
    The American As Anarchist: Reflections on
    Indigenous Radicalism. Johns Hopkins.

DeLeon, Thomas C. *see* Deleon, Thomas Cooper.

Deleuze, Gilles.
  xDeleuze, Gilles.
    Proust & Signs. Braziller.

Delevoryas, Theodore, 1929-
  xDelevoryas, Theodore.
    Plant Diversification. HR&W.

Delevoy, Robert L.
  xDelevoy, Robert L.
    Early Flemish Painting. McGraw.
    Symbolists & Symbolism. Rizzoli Intl.

Deleyne, Jan.
  xDeleyne, Jan.
    The Chinese Economy. Har-Row.

Delf, George.
  xDelf, George.
    Jomo Kenyatta: Towards Truth About "the
    Light of Kenya". Greenwood.

Delfgaauw, Bernard. *see* Delfgaauw, Bernardus Marie
Ignatius.

Delfgaauw, Bernardus Marie Ignatius.
  xDelfgaauw, Bernard.
    Twentieth Century Philosophy. Magi Bks.

Delfinado, Mercedes D.
  xDelfinado, Mercedes D.
    A Catalog of the Diptera of the Oriental
    Region. U Pr of Hawaii.

Delhaye, J. M.
  xDelhaye, J. M.
    Thermohydraulics of Two-Phase Systems for
    Industrial Design & Nuclear Engineering.
    McGraw.

Delhom, L. A. *see* Delhom, Louis A.

Delhom, Louis A.
  xDelhom, L. A.
    Design & Application of Transistor Switching
    Circuits. McGraw.

Delille, Edward.
  xDelille, Edward.
    Some French Writers. Arno.

Delillo, Don.
  xDeLillo, Don.
    Ratner's Star. Knopf.
    Ratner's Star. Random.
    Running Dog. Knopf.
    Running Dog. Random.

Delisi, C. *see* Delisi, Charles.

Delisi, Charles, 1941-
  xDelisi, C.
    Antigen Antibody Interactions.
    Springer-Verlag.

Dell, Catherine.
  xDell, Catherine.
    The Magic of Ballet. Rand.

Dell, Christopher, 1927-
  xDell, Christopher.
    Lincoln & the War Democrats: The Grand
    Erosion of Conservative Tradition. Fairleigh
    Dickinson.

Dell, Ethel M. *see* Dell, Ethel May.

Dell, Ethel May, d. 1939
  xDell, Ethel M.

    Swindler & Other Stories. Arno.

Dell, Floyd, 1887-1969
  xDell, Floyd.
    Homecoming: An Autobiography. Kennikat.
    Love in the Machine Age: A Psychological
    Study of the Transition from Patriarchal
    Society. Octagon.

Dell, Sidney. *see* Dell, Sidney Samuel.

Dell, Sidney Samuel.
  xDell, Sidney.
    The Balance of Payments Adjustment Process
    in Developing Countries. Pergamon.
    The Inter-American Development Bank: A
    Study in Development Financing. Irvington.

Dell'Isola, Frank.
  xDell'Isola, Frank.
    Thomas Merton: A Bibliography. Kent St U Pr.

Della Femina, Jerry.
  xDella Femina, Jerry.
    An Italian Grows in Brooklyn. Little.

Della, Mirandola, Giovanni Pico. *see* Pico della
Mirandola, Giovanni.

Della-Piana, Gabriel M. *see* Della-Piana, Gabriel Mario.

Della-Piana, Gabriel Mario, 1926-
  xDella-Piana, Gabriel M.
    How to Talk with Children & Other People.
    Wiley.
    Reading Diagnosis & Prescription: An
    Introduction. HR&W.

Dellenbaugh, Frederick S. *see* Dellenbaugh, Frederick
Samuel.

Dellenbaugh, Frederick Samuel, 1853-1935
  xDellenbaugh, Frederick S.
    The North-Americans of Yesterday: A
    Comparative Study of North-American
    Indian Life, Customs, & Products, on the
    Theory of the Ethnic Unity of Race. AMS
    Pr.

Deller, Anthony W. *see* Deller, Anthony William.

Deller, Anthony William.
  xDeller, Anthony W.
    Deller's Walker on Patents: 1964-76. Lawyers
    Co-Op.
    Patent Claims. Lawyers Co-Op.

Dellmann, Horst-Dieter.
  xDellmann, Horst-Dieter.
    ed. Textbook of Veterinary Histology. Lea &
    Febiger.

Delman, David.
  xDelman, David.
    The Nice Murderers. Morrow.

Delmar, Vina.
  xDelmar, Vina.
    Freeways. HarBraceJ.
    Freeways. Manor Bks.

Delmonte, Diana.
  xDelmonte, Diana.
    Dynamics in the Arts. Speller.

Delone, Richard. *see* Delone, Richard Peter.

Delone, Richard Peter.
  xDelone, Richard.
    Aspects of Twentieth-Century Music. P-H.

Delong, Deanna.
  xDeLong, Deanna.
    How to Dry Foods. H P Bks.

Delong, Fred J.
  xDelong, Fred J.
    Aim for a Job in Drafting. Rosen Pr.

Delong, Howard, 1936-
  xDeLong, Howard.
    Profile of Mathematical Logic. A-W.

Delora, Joann S.
  xDeLora, Joann S.
    Understanding Human Sexuality. HM.
    Understanding Sexual Interaction. HM.

Deloria, Ella. *see* Deloria, Ella Cara.

Deloria, Ella C. *see* Deloria, Ella Cara.

Deloria, Ella Cara.
  xDeloria, Ella.

    Dakota Texts. AMS Pr.
  xDeloria, Ella C.
    Dakota Texts. Dakota Pr.
    Speaking of Indians. Dakota Pr.

Deloria, Vine.
  xDeloria, Vine.
    God Is Red. Dell.
    The Indian Affair. Friend Pr.
    Of Utmost Good Faith. S&S.

Delozier, M. Wayne.
  xDelozier, M. Wayne.
    Experiential Learning Exercises in Marketing.
    Goodyear.
    The Marketing Communications Process.
    McGraw.
    Marketing Management: Strategies & Cases.
    Merrill.

Delp, Paul S.
  xDelp, Paul S.
    The Gentle Way. Philos Lib.

Delpar, Helen.
  xDelpar, Helen.
    The Discoverers: An Encyclopedia of Explorers
    & Exploration. McGraw.
    Encyclopedia of Latin America. McGraw.

Delph, Edward W. *see* Delph, Edward William.

Delph, Edward William.
  xDelph, Edward W.
    The Silent Community: Public Homosexual
    Encounters. Sage.

Delphine, Freda.
  xDelphine, Freda.
    I Promise You Tomorrow. Pacesetter Pr.

Delsol, Paula.
  xDelsol, Paula.
    Chinese Astrology. Warner Bks.

Delson, Donn.
  xDelson, Donn.
    The Dictionary of Marketing & Related Terms
    in the Motion Picture Industry. Bradson.

Delson, Roberta M. *see* Delson, Roberta Marx.

Delson, Roberta Marx.
  xDelson, Roberta M.
    New Towns for Colonial Brazil: Spatial &
    Social Planning of the Eighteenth Century.
    Univ Microfilms.

Delton, Judy.
  xDelton, Judy.
    The Best Mom in the World. A Whitman.
    Brimhall Comes to Stay. Lothrop.
    Brimhall Turns to Magic. Lothrop.
    Kitty in the Middle. Dell.
    Kitty in the Middle. HM.
    Lee Henry's Best Friend. A Whitman.
    On a Picnic. Doubleday.
    Penny-Wise, Fun-Foolish. Crown.
    Rabbit Finds a Way. Crown.
    Rabbit's New Rug. Parents.
    Two Good Friends. Crown.
    Two Is Company. Crown.

Delu, Christian. *see* Delu, Christian Roland.

Delu, Christian Roland.
  xDelu, Christian.
    French Provincial Cuisine. Barron.

Deluca, Charles.
  xDeLuca, Charles J.
    Pacific Marine Life: A Survey of Pacific Ocean
    Invertebrates. C E Tuttle.

DeLuca, Charles J. *see* Deluca, Charles.

DeLuca, H. F. *see* Deluca, Hector F.

Deluca, Hector F., 1930-
  xDeLuca, H. F.
    Vitamin D: Metabolism & Function.
    Springer-Verlag.

Deluca, Sam.
  xDeLuca, Sam.
    The Football Handbook. Jonathan David.
    The Football Playbook. Jonathan David.

Delucchi, V. L. *see* Delucchi, Vittorio.

Delucchi, Vittorio.
 xDelucchi, V. L.
  ed. Studies in Biological Control. Cambridge U
  Pr.
Delumeau, Jean.
 xDelumeau, Jean.
  Catholicism Between Luther & Voltaire: A
  New View of the Counter-Reformation.
  Westminster.
Delzell, Charles F.
 xDelzell, Charles F.
  ed. Mediterranean Fascism, 1919-1949. Walker
  & Co.
DeMan, J. M., 1925-
 xDeMan, J. M.
  Principles of Food Chemistry. AVI.
  ed. Rheology & Texture in Food Quality. AVI.
Demaray, Donald E.
 xDemaray, Donald E.
  Introduction to Homiletics. Baker Bk.
DeMarco, Thomas J., 1942-
 xDeMarco, Thomas J.
  Clinical Dental Sciences Review. Arco.
DeMarco, Tom.
 xDeMarco, Tom.
  Concise Notes on Software Engineering.
  Yourdon.
  Structured Analysis & System Specification.
  Yourdon.
Demaree, Albert L. *see* Demaree, Albert Lowther.
Demaree, Albert Lowther, 1894-
 xDemaree, Albert L.
  The American Agricultural Press: 1819-1860.
  Porcupine Pr.
Demarest, David P.
 xDemarest, David P.
  ed. From These Hills, From These Valleys:
  Selected Fiction About Western
  Pennsylvania. U of Pittsburgh Pr.
Demarest, Gary. *see* Demarest, Gary W.
Demarest, Gary W.
 xDemarest, Gary.
  Colossians: The Mystery of Christ in Us. Word
  Bks.
Demarest, Robert J.
 xDemarest, Robert J.
  Conception, Birth & Contraception: A Visual
  Presentation. McGraw.
DeMarre. *see* Demarre, Dean A.
DeMarre, Dean A., 1936-
 xDeMarre.
  Applied Biomedical Electronics for
  Technicians. Dekker.
DeMause, Lloyd.
 xDeMause, Lloyd.
  ed. The History of Childhood. Har-Row.
  ed. The History of Childhood. Psychohistory
  Pr.
Demazure, M. *see* Demazure, Michel.
Demazure, Michel.
 xDemazure, M.
  Lectures on P-Divisible Groups.
  Springer-Verlag.
Dember, Sol.
 xDember, Sol.
  Complete Airbrush Techniques for Commercial,
  Technical, & Industrial Applications. Bobbs.
  Drawing & Painting the World of Animals.
  Sams.
Dember, William. *see* Dember, William Norton.
Dember, William Norton, 1928-
 xDember, William.
  Psychology of Perception. HR&W.
Dembner, S. Arthur.
 xDembner, S. Arthur.
  Modern Circulation Methods. Krieger.
Dembo, L. S.
 xDembo, L. S.

  ed. Criticism: Speculative & Analytical Essays.
  U of Wis Pr.
Dembo, Myron H.
 xDembo, Myron H.
  Teaching for Learning: Applying Educational
  Psychology in the Classroom. Goodyear.
Dembowski, P. *see* Dembowski, Peter.
Dembowski, Peter.
 xDembowski, P.
  Finite Geometries. Springer-Verlag.
Dembroski, T. M. *see* Dembroski, Theodore M.
Dembroski, Theodore M.
 xDembroski, T. M.
  ed. Coronary Prone Behavior. Springer-Verlag.
Demby, William.
 xDemby, William.
  Love Story Black. Reed & Cannon.
Demcy, Arthur I., 1904-
 xDemcy, Arthur I.
  How to Cope with United States Customs.
  Oceana.
Deme, Laszlo, 1933-
 xDeme, Laszlo.
  jt. auth. The Radical Left in the Hungarian
  Revolution of 1848. East Eur Quarterly.
 xDeme, Lazlo.
  The Radical Left in the Hungarian Revolution
  of 1848. East Eur Quarterly.
Deme, Lazlo. *see* Deme, Laszlo.
Dement, William C. *see* Dement, William Charles.
Dement, William Charles, 1928-
 xDement, William C.
  Some Must Watch While Some Must Sleep. SF
  Bk Co.
Demerath, N. J. *see* Demerath, Nicholas Jay.
Demerath, Nicholas Jay.
 xDemerath, N. J.
  Dynamics of Idealism: White Activists in a
  Black Movement. Jossey-Bass.
Demers, Laurence. *see* Demers, Laurence M.
Demers, Laurence M.
 xDemers, Laurence.
  ed. Evaluation of Liver Function: A
  Multifaceted Approach to Clinical Diagnosis.
  Urban & S.
Demers, Ralph M.
 xDemers, Ralph M.
  The Circuit. Ballantine.
Demeter, Richard L.
 xDemeter, Richard L.
  Primer, Presses, & Composing Sticks: Women
  Printers of the Colonial Period. Exposition.
Demetillo, Ricaredo.
 xDemetillo, Ricaredo.
  Lazarus, Troubadour. Cellar.
Demetrios, George, 1896-
 xDemetrios, George.
  When Greek Meets Greek. Arno.
Demetz, Peter, 1922-
 xDemetz, Peter.
  Postwar German Literature: A Critical
  Introduction. Irvington.
  Postwar German Literature: A Critical
  Introduction. Schocken.
Demidoff, Lorna B.
 xDemidoff, Lorna B.
  The Complete Siberian Husky. Howell Bk.
Demillo, Richard A.
 xDemillo, Richard A.
  ed. Foundations of Secure Computation. Acad
  Pr.
Deming, Philander, 1829-1915
 xDeming, Philander.
  Adirondack Stories. Mss Info.
  Story of a Pathfinder. Arno.
Deming, Richard.
 xDeming, Richard.

  The Paralegal: A New Career. Elsevier-Nelson.
  Women: The New Criminals. Elsevier-Nelson.
Deming, Robert H.
 xDeming, Robert H.
  Ceremony & Art: Robert Herrick's Poetry.
  Mouton.
Deming, Romine R.
 xDeming, Romine R.
  Divergent Corrections. R & E Res Assoc.
Demko, George J.
 xDemko, George J.
  jt. ed. & ed. Geographical Perspectives in the
  Soviet Union: A Selection of Readings. Ohio
  St U Pr.
Demmon, E. L. *see* Demmon, Elwood Leonard.
Demmon, Elwood Leonard, 1892-
 xDemmon, E. L.
  Opportunities in Forestry Careers. Natl Textbk.
Demolen, Richard L.
 xDemolen, Richard L.
  Meaning of the Renaissance & Reformation.
  HM.
DeMond, Robert O. *see* Demond, Robert Orley.
DeMond, Robert Orley, 1889-
 xDeMond, Robert O.
  The Loyalists in North Carolina During the
  Revolution. Genealog Pub.
Demone, Harold. *see* Demone, Harold W.
Demone, Harold W.
 xDemone, Harold.
  ed. A Handbook of Human Service
  Organizations. Human Sci Pr.
 xDemone, Harold W.
  The Planning & Administration of Human
  Services. Human Sci Pr.
DeMont, Bill.
 xDeMont, Billie C.
  Accountability: An Action Model for the
  Public Schools. ETC Pubns.
DeMont, Billie C. *see* Demont, Bill.
DeMont, Roger.
 xDeMont, Roger.
  Busing, Taxes & Desegregation. Interstate.
Demorest, Steve.
 xDemorest, Steve.
  Alice Cooper. Popular Lib.
Demoro, Harre W.
 xDemoro, Harre W.
  Southern Pacific Bay Area Steam. Chatham
  Pub CA.
Demos, George D.
 xDemos, George D.
  An Introduction to Counseling: A Handbook.
  Western Psych.
Demos, John.
 xDemos, John.
  Little Commonwealth: Family Life in Plymouth
  Colony. Oxford U Pr.
Demosthenes.
 xDemosthenes.
  Demosthenes Against Androtion & Against
  Timocrates. Arno.
  On the Peace: Second Philippic on Chersonesus
  & Third Philippic. Arno.
  Select Private Orations of Demosthenes. Arno.
  The Speech of Demosthenes Against the Law
  of Leptines. Arno.
Demott, Robert.
 xDemott, Robert J.
  ed. Artful Thunder - Versions of the Romantic
  Tradition in American Literature - in Honor
  of Howard P. Vincent. Kent St U Pr.
Demott, Robert J. *see* Demott, Robert.
Demouzon. *see* Demouzon, Alain.
Demouzon, Alain, 1945-
 xDemouzon.
  The First-Born of Egypt. Peebles Pr.
Dempsey, Al.
 xDempsey, Al.

Dog Kill. P-H.
Dempsey, David. *see* Dempsey, David K.
Dempsey, David K.
xDempsey, David.
Psychology & You. Scott F.
Dempsey, Hugh A. *see* Dempsey, Hugh Aylmer.
Dempsey, Hugh Aylmer, 1929-
xDempsey, Hugh A.
Charcoal's World. U of Nebr Pr.
Dempsey, Jack.
xDempsey, Jack.
Dempsey. Har-Row.
Dempsey, James M.
xDempsey, James M.
Fiber Crops. U Presses Fla.
Dempsey, John J., 1935-
xDempsey, John J.
Community Services for Retarded Children:
The Consumer-Provider Relationship. Univ
Park.
Dempsey, Paul.
xDempsey, Paul.
Complete Guide to Outboard Motor Service &
Repair. TAB Bks.
Complete Handbook of Lawnmower Repair.
TAB Bks.
The Complete Snowmobile Repair Handbook.
TAB Bks.
How to Repair Briggs & Stratton Engines. TAB
Bks.
How to Repair Diesel Engines. TAB Bks.
How to Repair Lift Trucks. TAB Bks.
How to Repair Small Gasoline Engines. TAB
Bks.
Moped Repair Handbook. TAB Bks.
Vega. TAB Bks.
xDempsey, Paul K.
Power Tuning Your Car, Truck, Van or RV.
TAB Bks.
Dempsey, Paul K. *see* Dempsey, Paul.
Dempsey, T.
xDempsey, T.
Delphic Oracle: Its Early History, Influence &
Fall. Arno.
Dempster, Lauramay T., 1905-
xDempster, Lauramay T.
The Genus Galium (Rubiaceae) in Mexico &
Central America. U of Cal Pr.
The Polygamous Species of the Genus Galium
(Rubiaceae), Section Lophogalium, of Mexico
& Southwestern United States. U of Cal Pr.
Dempster, Stuart.
xDempster, Stuart.
The Modern Trombone: A Definition of Its
Idioms. U of Cal Pr.
Demske, Dick. *see* Demske, Richard.
Demske, Richard.
xDemske, Dick.
Exterior Home Repairs. Delair.
Home Comfort. Delair.
Home Repairs Made Easy. Delair.
Interior Home Repairs. Delair.
Demski, Joel S.
xDemski, Joel S.
Information Analysis. A-W.
Demura, Fumio.
xDemura, Fumio.
Advanced Nunchaku. Ohara Pubns.
Advanced Nunchaku. Wehman.
Demus, Otto.
xDemus, Otto.
Byzantine Art & the West. NYU Pr.
Byzantine Mosaic Decoration: Aspects of
Monumental Art in Byzantium. Caratzas
Bros.
Demuth, Norman, 1898-1968
xDemuth, Norman.

Albert Roussel: A Study. Hyperion Conn.
An Anthology of Musical Criticism.
Greenwood.
Ravel. Hyperion Conn.
DeMyer, Marian K.
xDeMyer, Marian K.
Parents & Children in Autism. Halsted Pr.
Den Hartog, Jacob P. *see* Den Hartog, Jacob Pieter.
Den Hartog, Jacob Pieter, 1901-
xDen Hartog, Jacob P.
Mechanics. Dover.
Strength of Materials. Dover.
Den Ouden, Bernard. *see* Ouden, Bernard D.
Denan, Jay.
xDenan, Jay.
Burnout: Funny Car Races. Troll Assocs.
Hot on Wheels: The Rally Scene. Troll Assocs.
Denbeaux, Fred J.
xDenbeaux, Fred J.
Understanding the Bible. Westminster.
Denber, Herman C. *see* Denber, Herman C. B.
Denber, Herman C. B.
xDenber, Herman C.
Textbook of Clinical Psychopharmacology.
Thieme-Stratton.
Denbow, William.
xDenbow, William.
Chandler. Belmont-Tower.
Denburg, Joseph K. Van. *see* Van Denburg, Joseph K.
Denby, David.
xDenby, David.
ed. Awake in the Dark: An Anthology of
American Film Criticism, 1915 to the
Present. Random.
Denby, Edwin, 1903-
xDenby, Edwin.
Collected Poems. Full Court NY.
Looking at the Dance. Popular Lib.
Dence, Joseph B.
xDence, Joseph B.
Mathematical Techniques in Chemistry. Wiley.
Dendel, Esther W. *see* Dendel, Esther Warner.
Dendel, Esther Warner, 1910-
xDendel, Esther W.
African Fabric Crafts: Sources of African
Design & Technique. Taplinger.
Designing from Nature: A Source Book for
Artists & Craftsmen. Taplinger.
Dendy, Arthur, 1865-1925
xDendy, Arthur.
ed. Problems of Modern Science: A Series of
Lectures Delivered at King's College
(University of London). Arno.
Dendy, William, 1942-
xDendy, William.
Lost Toronto. Oxford U Pr.
Denenberg, Herbert S.
xDenenberg, Herbert S.
A Consumer's Guide to Bankruptcy. Pilot Bks.
Denenberg, Victor H.
xDenenberg, Victor H.
ed. Education of the Infant & Young Child.
Acad Pr.
Denes, Magda, 1934-
xDenes, Magda.
In Necessity & Sorrow: Life & Death in an
Abortion Hospital. Basic.
In Necessity & Sorrow: Life & Death in an
Abortion Hospital. Penguin.
Denes, Peter B.
xDenes, Peter B.
The Speech Chain: The Physics & Biology of
Spoken Language. Doubleday.
Denevan, William M.
xDenevan, William
ed. The Native Population of the Americas in
1492. U of Wis Pr.
Denevan, William *see* Denevan, William M.
Denevi, Marco.
xDenevi, Marco.

Ceremonia Secreta y Otros Cuentos.
Macmillan.
Deng, F. M. *see* Deng, Francis Mading.
Deng, Francis M. *see* Deng, Francis Mading.
Deng, Francis Mading, 1938-
xDeng, F. M.
Dinka of the Sudan. HR&W.
xDeng, Francis M.
The Dinka & Their Songs. Oxford U Pr.
Dengler, Mariana. *see* Dengler, Marianna.
Dengler, Marianna.
xDengler, Mariana.
A Pebble in Newcomb's Pond. G&D.
xDengler, Marianna.
Catch the Passing Breeze. HR&W.
A Pebble in Newcomb's Pond. HR&W.
Dengler, Sandy.
xDengler, Sandy.
Getting into the Bible. Moody.
The Horse Who Loved Picnics. Moody.
The Melon Hound. Moody.
Dengrove, Edward.
xDengrove, Edward.
Hypnosis & Behavior Therapy. C C Thomas.
Denham, Bertie, Baron, 1927-
xDenham, Bertie.
The Man Who Lost His Shadow. Scribner.
Denham, H. M.
xDenham, H. M.
The Aegean: A Sea-Guide to Its Coasts &
Islands. Norton.
Southern Turkey, the Levant & Cyprus: A
Sea-Guide to the Coasts & Islands. Norton.
Denham, Hardy R.
xDenham, Hardy R.
Living Toward a Vision. Broadman.
Denham, Ken.
xDenham, Ken.
My Learn to Fish Book. Western Pub.
Denham, Robert D.
xDenham, Robert D.
Northrop Frye: An Enumerative Bibliography.
Scarecrow.
Northrop Frye & Critical Method. Pa St U Pr.
Denhardt, D. T.
xDenhardt, D. T.
ed. The Single-Stranded DNA Phages. Cold
Spring Harbor.
Denhardt, J. *see* Denhardt, J. G.
Denhardt, J. G.
xDenhardt, J.
Complete Guide to Estate Accounting &
Taxes. P-H.
xDenhardt, J. G.
Complete Guide to Estate Accounting &
Taxes. P-H.
Complete Guide to Trust Accounting & Trust
Income Taxation. P-H.
Everyone's Guide to Estate Planning. Contemp
Bks.
Denhardt, Robert M. *see* Denhardt, Robert Moorman.
Denhardt, Robert Moorman, 1912-
xDenhardt, Robert M.
Foundation Sires of the American Quarter
Horse. U of Okla Pr.
The Horse of the Americas. U of Okla Pr.
Denholtz, Melvin.
xDenholtz, Melvin.
How to Save Your Teeth & Your Money: A
Consumer's Guide to Better, Less Costly
Dental Care. Van Nos Reinhold.
Deniker, Joseph, 1852-1918
xDeniker, Joseph.
The Races of Man: Outline of Anthropology &
Ethnography. Arno.
Denikin, Anton. *see* Denikin, Anton Ivanovich.

Denikin, Anton I. *see* Denikin, Anton Ivanovich.
Denikin, Anton Ivanovich, 1872-1947
  xDenikin, Anton.
    The White Army. Gordon Pr.
  xDenikin, Anton I.
    The Career of a Tsarist Officer: Memoirs,
      1872-1916. U of Minn Pr.
    The White Army. Academic Intl.
    The White Army. Hyperion Conn.
Dening, Walter, 1846-1913
  xDening, Walter.
    Japan in Days of Yore. Great Eastern.
Denis, Christopher.
  xDenis, Christopher.
    The Films of Shirley Maclaine. Citadel Pr.
Denis, Pierre, 1883-1951
  xDenis, Pierre.
    The Argentine Republic, Its Development &
      the Progress. AMS Pr.
Denisen, Ervin L.
  xDenisen, Ervin L.
    Principles of Horticulture. Macmillan.
Denisoff, R. Serge.
  xDenisoff, R. Serge.
    An Introduction to Sociology. Macmillan.
    Theories & Paradigms in Contemporary
      Sociology. Peacock Pubs.
  xDenisoff, Serge R.
    The Sociology of Dissent. HarBraceJ.
Denisoff, Serge R. *see* Denisoff, R. Serge.
Denison, Edward F. *see* Denison, Edward Fulton.
Denison, Edward Fulton.
  xDenison, Edward F.
    Accounting for United States Economic
      Growth: 1929-1969. Brookings.
    How Japan's Economy Grew So Fast: The
      Sources of Postwar Expansion. Brookings.
Denison, Mary A. *see* Denison, Mary Andrews.
Denison, Mary Andrews, 1826-1911
  xDenison, Mary A.
    Out of Prison. Arno.
Denisov, E. T. *see* Denisov, Evgenii Timofeevich.
Denisov, Evgenii Timofeevich.
  xDenisov, E. T.
    Liquid-Phase Oxidation of Oxygen -
      Containing Compounds. Plenum Pub.
    Liquid-Phase Reaction Rate Constants. IFI
      Plenum.
Denisov, P. N. *see* Denisov, Petr Nikitich.
Denisov, Petr Nikitich.
  xDenisov, P. N.
    Principles of Constructing Linguistic Models.
      Mouton.
Denitch, Bogdan D. *see* Denitch, Bogdan Denis.
Denitch, Bogdan Denis.
  xDenitch, Bogdan D.
    The Legitimation of a Revolution: The
      Yugoslav Case. Yale U Pr.
Denitto, Dennis.
  xDeNitto, Dennis.
    Film & the Critical Eye. Macmillan.
Denker, Ellen.
  xDenker, Ellen.
    jt. auth. The Rocking Chair Book. Mayflower
      Bks.
Denker, H. W. *see* Denker, Hans-Werner.
Denker, Hans-Werner, 1941-
  xDenker, H. W.
    Implantation: The Role of Proteinases, &
      Blockage of Implantation Through Proteinase
      Inhibitors. Springer-Verlag.
Denker, Henry.
  xDenker, Henry.

    The Actress. PB.
    The Actress. S&S.
    The Director. PB.
    The Experiment. PB.
    The Experiment. S&S.
    Horowitz & Mrs. Washington. Berkley Pub.
    Horowitz & Mrs. Washington. Putnam.
    The Scofield Diagnosis. PB.
    The Scofield Diagnosis. S&S.
    The Starmaker. PB.
    The Starmaker. S&S.
Denker, M. *see* Denker, Manfred.
Denker, Manfred.
  xDenker, M.
    ed. Ergodic Theory: Proceedings, Oberwolfach,
      Germany, 11-17 June 1978. Springer-Verlag.
Denlinger, Milo G. *see* Denlinger, Milo Grange.
Denlinger, Milo Grange, 1890-
  xDenlinger, Milo G.
    Complete Boxer. Howell Bk.
    The Complete Siamese Cat. Howell Bk.
Denmark, Florence.
  xDenmark, Florence.
    Who Discriminates Against Women. Sage.
Denn, M. *see* Denn, Morton M.
Denn, Morton M., 1939-
  xDenn, M.
    Process Fluid Mechanics. P-H.
  xDenn, Morton M.
    Optimization by Variational Methods. Krieger.
Dennemeyer, Rene.
  xDennemeyer, Rene.
    Introduction to Partial Differential Equations &
      Boundary Value Problems. McGraw.
Dennes, William R. *see* Dennes, William Ray.
Dennes, William Ray.
  xDennes, William R.
    Some Dilemmas of Naturalism. Arno.
Dennett, D. C. *see* Dennett, Daniel Clement.
Dennett, Daniel Clement.
  xDennett, D. C.
    Content & Consciousness. Humanities.
Denney, Martyn.
  xDenney, Martyn.
    London's Waterways. David & Charles.
    London's Waterways. Hippocrene Bks.
Denney, Myron K.
  xDenney, Myron K.
    Second Opinion. G&D.
Denney, Reuel, 1913-
  xDenney, Reuel.
    The Astonished Muse. U of Chicago Pr.
    Connecticut River & Other Poems. AMS Pr.
    Conrad Aiken. U of Minn Pr.
Denning. *see* Denning, Melita.
Denning, Melita.
  xDenning.
    Apparel of High Magick. Llewellyn Pubns.
    Triumph of Light. Llewellyn Pubns.
Dennis, Brian.
  xDennis, Brian.
    Experimental Music in Schools: Towards a
      New World of Sound. Oxford U Pr.
Dennis, Charles, 1946-
  xDennis, Charles.
    Somebody Just Grabbed Annie. St Martin.
Dennis, Charles H. *see* Dennis, Charles Henry.
Dennis, Charles Henry, 1860-1943
  xDennis, Charles H.
    Eugene Field's Creative Years. R West.
    Eugene Field's Creative Years. Scholarly.
Dennis, Earle S.
  xDennis, Earle S.
    Marriage Bonds of Bedford County, Virginia,
      1755-1800. Genealog Pub.
Dennis, Ervin A.
  xDennis, Erwin A.
    Comprehensive Graphic Arts. Bobbs.
Dennis, Erwin A. *see* Dennis, Ervin A.
Dennis, Everette. *see* Dennis, Everette E.

Dennis, Everette E.
  xDennis, Everette.
    Enduring Issues in Mass Communication. West
      Pub.
  xDennis, Everette E.
    The Media Society: Evidence About Mass
      Communication in America. Wm C Brown.
Dennis, J. Richard.
  xDennis, J. Richard.
    Fractions Are Parts of Things. T Y Crowell.
Dennis, Jan P.
  xDennis, Jan P.
    ed. The How-to Book: Loving God, Loving
      Others. Good News.
Dennis, John.
  xDennis, John.
    The Age of Pope. Arno.
    The Age of Pope. Folcroft.
    Dr. Johnson. Folcroft.
Dennis, John G. *see* Dennis, John Gordon.
Dennis, John Gordon, 1920-
  xDennis, John G.
    Structural Geology. Wiley.
Dennis, John V.
  xDennis, John V.
    A Complete Guide to Bird Feeding. Knopf.
Dennis, Landt.
  xDennis, Landt.
    Catch the Wind: A Book of Windmills &
      Windpower. Schol Bk Serv.
    Collecting Photographs: A Guide to the New
      Art Boom. Dutton.
Dennis, Lane T.
  xDennis, Lane T.
    A Reason for Hope. Revell.
Dennis, Lawrence, 1893-
  xDennis, Lawrence.
    Coming American Fascism. AMS Pr.
    Operational Thinking for Survival. R Myles.
Dennis, Lisl.
  xDennis, Lisl.
    photos by Catch the Wind: A Book of
      Windmills & Windpower. Schol Bk Serv.
    jt. auth. Collecting Photographs: A Guide to
      the New Art Boom. Dutton.

    How to Take Better Travel Photos. H P Bks.

Dennis, Lorraine B. *see* Dennis, Lorraine Bradt.
Dennis, Lorraine Bradt.
  xDennis, Lorraine B.
    Psychology of Human Behavior for Nurses.
      Saunders.
Dennis, Marshall W.
  xDennis, Marshall W.
    Fundamentals of Mortgage Lending. Reston.
Dennis, Nigel.
  xDennis, Nigel.
    Cards of Identity. Vanguard.
Dennis, Nigel F. *see* Dennis, Nigel Forbes.
Dennis, Nigel Forbes, 1912-
  xDennis, Nigel F.
    Dramatic Essays. Greenwood.
Dennis, Patrick.
  xDennis, Patrick.
    Auntie Mame. Popular Lib.
    Auntie Mame. Vanguard.
Dennis, Paul.
  xDennis, Paul.
    The Marijuana Catalogue. Playboy Pbks.
Dennis, Peter.
  xDennis, Peter.
    Decision by Default: Peacetime Conscription &
      British Defence, 1919 - 1939. Duke.
Dennis, Ralph.
  xDennis, Ralph.

Down Among the Jocks. Popular Lib.
MacTaggart's War. Popular Lib.
Murder's Not an Odd Job. Popular Lib.
Working for the Man. Popular Lib.
Dennis, Robert. *see* Dennis, Robert C.
Dennis, Robert C.
xDennis, Robert.
Conversations with a Corpse. Ballantine.
Dennis, Robert L. *see* Dennis, Robert Lee.

Dennis, Robert Lee.
xDennis, Robert L.
jt. auth. The Complete Handbook for Medical
Secretaries & Assistants. Little.
Dennis, Wayne, 1905-

xDennis, Wayne.
The Hopi Child. Arno.
The Intellectually Gifted: An Overview. Grune.
ed. Readings in General Psychology. Arno.
Dennis, Wesley.
xDennis, Wesley.
illus. Tumble: The Story of a Mustang.
Hastings.

Dennis, William J. *see* Dennis, William Jefferson.
Dennis, William Jefferson, 1886-
xDennis, William J.
Tacna & Arica: An Account of the Chile-Peru
Boundary Dispute & of the Arbitrations by
the United States. Shoe String.
Dennison, A. Dudley. *see* Dennison, Alfred Dudley.
Dennison, Alfred Dudley, 1914-
xDennison, A. Dudley.
Contemporary Illustrations for Speakers &
Teachers. Zondervan.
Dennison, Darwin.
xDennison, Darwin.
Alcohol & Behavior: An Activated Education
Approach. Mosby.
Dennison, George, 1925-
xDennison, George.
Oilers & Sweepers & Other Stories. Random.
Dennison, Henry S. *see* Dennison, Henry Sturgis.
Dennison, Henry Sturgis, 1877-1952
xDennison, Henry S.
Organization Engineering. Hive Pub.
Dennison, John *see* Dennison, John M.
Dennison, John M.
xDennison, John
Analysis of Geologic Structures. Norton.
Denniston, John D. *see* Denniston, John Dewar.
Denniston, John Dewar.
xDenniston, John D.
Greek Literary Criticism. AMS Pr.
Greek Literary Criticism. Kennikat.
Greek Prose Style. Greenwood.
Denniston, Lyle W.
xDenniston, Lyle W.
The Reporter & the Law: Techniques of
Covering the Courts. Hastings.
Denny, Don.
xDenny, Don.
The Annunciation from the Right: From Early
Christian Times to the Sixteenth Century.
Garland Pub.
Denny, Harold N. *see* Denny, Harold Norman.
Denny, Harold Norman, 1889-
xDenny, Harold N.
Dollars for Bullets: The Story of American
Rule in Nicaragua. Greenwood.
Denny, M. Ray. *see* Denny, Maurice Ray.
Denny, Maurice Ray, 1918-
xDenny, M. Ray.
Comparative Psychology: An Evolutionary
Analysis of Animal Behavior. Wiley.
Denny, Walter B.
xDenny, Walter B.

The Ceramics of the Mosque of Rustem Pasha
& the Environment of Change. Garland Pub.
Denomme, Robert T. *see* Denomme, Robert Thomas.
Denomme, Robert Thomas.
xDenomme, Robert T.
The French Parnassian Poets. S Ill U Pr.
Leconte de Lisle. Twayne.
Nineteenth-Century French Romantic Poets. S
Ill U Pr.
Denonn, Lester E. *see* Denonn, Lester Eugene.
Denonn, Lester Eugene, 1901-
xDenonn, Lester E.
Secured Transactions Under the Original & the
Revised UCC. PLI.
Denoon, David.
xDenoon, David B.
ed. The New International Economic Order: A
U. S. Response. NYU Pr.
Denoon, David B. *see* Denoon, David.
Denoon, Donald.
xDenoon, Donald.
A Grand Illusion: The Failure of Imperial
Policy in the Transvaal Colony During the
Period of Reconstruction, 1900-1905.
Longman.
Southern Africa Since 1800. Longman.
Denore, Rochel.
xDeNore, Rochel.
An Innocent Heart. Ace Bks.
A Love So Proud. Ace Bks.
Denova, Charles C., 1928-
xDenova, Charles C.
Establishing a Training Function: A Guide for
Management. Educ Tech Pubns.
Test Construction for Training Evaluation. Van
Nos Reinhold.
Densley, Barbara.
xDensley, Barbara.
The ABC's of Home Food Dehydration.
Horizon Utah.
Denslow, Van Buren.
xDenslow, Van Buren.
Principles of the Economic Philosophy of
Society, Government & Industry. Garland
Pub.
Densmore, Frances, 1867-1957
xDensmore, Frances.
American Indians & Their Music. Johnson
Repr.
Chippewa Customs. Johnson Repr.
Chippewa Customs. Minn Hist.
Chippewa Customs. Scholarly.
Chippewa Music. Da Capo.
Chippewa Music. Ross.
Choctaw Music. Da Capo.
How Indians Use Wild Plants for Food,
Medicine & Crafts. Dover.
How Indians Use Wild Plants for Food,
Medicine & Crafts. Peter Smith.
Menominee Music. Da Capo.
Menominee Music. Scholarly.
Music of Acoma, Isleta, Cochiti, & Zuni
Pueblos. Da Capo.
Music of the Indians of British Columbia. Da
Capo.
Nootka & Quileute Music. Da Capo.
Northern Ute Music. Da Capo.
Papago Music. Da Capo.
Pawnee Music. Da Capo.
Pawnee Music. Scholarly.
xDensmore, Francis.
Chippewa Music. Scholarly.
Densmore, Francis. *see* Densmore, Frances.
Dent, Alan.
xDent, Alan.
Mrs. Patrick Campbell. Greenwood.
Preludes & Studies. Kennikat.
The World of Shakespeare. Taplinger.
Dent, E. J. *see* Dent, Edward Joseph.
Dent, Edward J. *see* Dent, Edward Joseph.

Dent, Edward Joseph.
xDent, E. J.
The Rise of Romantic Opera. Cambridge U Pr.
xDent, Edward J.
The Rise of Romantic Opera. Cambridge U Pr.
A Theatre for Everybody: The Story of the Old
Vic & Sadler's Wells. Hyperion Conn.
Dent, H. C. *see* Dent, Harold Collett.
Dent, Harold Collett, 1894-
xDent, H. C.
Education in England & Wales. Shoe String.
Dent, Joseph B.
xDent, Joseph B.
Fundamentals of Engineering Graphics.
Macmillan.
Dent, W. *see* Dent, William.
Dent, William.
xDent, W.
Practical Cataloguing. Philos Lib.
Dentan, Robert K. *see* Dentan, Robert Knox.
Dentan, Robert Knox, 1936-
xDentan, Robert K.
The Semai: A Nonviolent People of Malaya.
HR&W.
Dente, Leonard A.
xDente, Leonard A.
Veblen's Theory of Social Change. Arno.
Dentler, Robert A.
xDentler, Robert A.
ed. Readings in Educational Psychology:
Contemporary Perspectives. Har-Row.
Denton, John A.
xDenton, John A.
Medical Sociology. HM.
Denton, T. E. *see* Denton, Thomas E.
Denton, Thomas E.
xDenton, T. E.
Fish Chromosome Methodology. C C Thomas.
Denton, Wallace.
xDenton, Wallace.
Family Problems & What to Do About Them.
Westminster.
Denver. Art Museum.
xDenver Art Museum.
Colorado Collects: A Panorama of World Art
from Private Collections. Denver Art Mus.
Guide to the Denver Art Museum. Denver Art
Mus.
xDenver Art Museum Staff.
Twenty Colorado Artists. Denver Art Mus.
Denver Art Museum Staff. *see* Denver. Art Museum.
Denver. Public Library.
xDenver Public Library.
Catalog of the Conservation Library. G K Hall.
Catalog of the Western History Department,
Denver Public Library. G K Hall.
Catalog of the Western History Department,
Denver Public Library, 1st Suppl. G K Hall.
Denvir, John, 1843-1916
xDenvir, John.
The Life Story of an Old Rebel. Biblio Dist.
Denza, Eileen, 1937-
xDenza, Eileen.
Diplomatic Law: Commentary on the Vienna
Convention on Diplomatic Relations. Oceana.
Denzel, Justin F.
xDenzel, Justin F.
Sampson, Yankee Stallion. Garrard.
Denzin, Norman K.
xDenzin, Norman K.
ed. Children & Their Caretakers. Transaction
Bks.
Sociological Methods: A Sourcebook. McGraw.
ed. The Values of Social Science. Transaction
Bks.

Deo, Narsingh, 1936-
xDeo, Narsingh.
Graph Theory with Applications to
Engineering & Computer Science. P-H.

Castlereagh. St Martin.
Derry, T. K. *see* Derry, Thomas Kingston.
Derry, Thomas K. *see* Derry, Thomas Kingston.
Derry, Thomas Kingston, 1905-
xDerry, T. K.
A History of Modern Norway, 1814-1972.
Oxford U Pr.
xDerry, Thomas K.
A Short History of Norway. Greenwood.
Dershimer, Richard A.
xDershimer, Richard A.
The Federal Government & Educational R&D.
Lexington Bks.
Derthick, Martha.
xDerthick, Martha.
Influence of Federal Grants: Public Assistance
in Massachusetts. Harvard U Pr.
Policymaking for Social Security. Brookings.
Uncontrollable Spending for Social Services
Grants. Brookings.
xDerthick, Martha A.
National Guard in Politics. Harvard U Pr.
Derthick, Martha A. *see* Derthick, Martha.
Dertouzos, Michael L.
xDertouzos, Michael L.
ed. The Computer Age: A Twenty-Year View.
MIT Pr.
Derven, Ronald.
xDerven, Ronald.
How to Cut Your Energy Bills. Structures Pub.
Successful Vacation Homes. Structures Pub.
Des Jarlait, Patrick.
xDes Jarlait, Patrick.
Patrick Des Jarlait: The Story of an American
Indian Artist. Lerner Pubns.
Des Lauriers, Austin M.
xDes Lauriers, Austin M.
The Experience of Reality in Childhood
Schizophrenia. Intl Univs Pr.
Des Pres, Terrence.
xDes Pres, Terrence.
The Survivor: An Anatomy of Life in the
Death Camps. Oxford U Pr.
The Survivor: An Anatomy of Life in the
Death Camps. Oxford U Pr.
Desai, A. R. *see* Desai, Akshayakumar Ramanlal.
Desai, Akshayakumar Ramanlal.
xDesai, A. R.
ed. Peasant Struggles in India. Oxford U Pr.
Desai, Anita, 1937-
xDesai, Anita.
Fire on the Mountain. Har-Row.
Desai, Ashok V.
xDesai, Ashok V.
Real Wages in Germany, 1871-1913. Oxford U
Pr.
Desai, C. S. *see* Desai, Chandrakant S.
Desai, Chandrakant S.
xDesai, C. S.
Elementary Finite Element Method. P-H.
Desai, Meghnad.
xDesai, Meghnad.
Marxian Economic Theory. Biblio Dist.
Marxian Economics. Littlefield.
Marxian Economics. Rowman.
xDesai, Megnad.
Applied Econometrics. McGraw.
Desai, Megnad. *see* Desai, Meghnad.
Desai, Morarji *see* Desai, Morarji Ranchodji.
Desai, Morarji Ranchodji, 1896-
xDesai, Morarji.
The Story of My Life. Pergamon.
The Story of My Life. South Asia Bks.
Desan, W. *see* Desan, Wilfrid.
Desan, Wilfrid.
xDesan, W.
The Marxism of Jean-Paul Sartre. Peter Smith.
Desatnick, R. L. *see* Desatnick, Robert L.
Desatnick, Robert L.
xDesatnick, R. L.

Innovative Human Resource Management. Am
Mgmt.
xDesatnick, Robert L.
The Expanding Role of the Human Resources
Manager. Am Mgmt.
Human Resource Management in the
Multinational Company. Nichols Pub.
Desautels, Paul. *see* Desautels, Paul E.
Desautels, Paul E.
xDesautels, Paul.
The Gem Kingdom. Random.
xDesautels, Paul E.
The Gem Kingdom. Random.
Desbarats, Peter.
xDesbarats, Peter.
Gabrielle & Selena. HarBraceJ.
Gabrielle & Selena. HarBraceJ.
Desberg, Dan.
xDesberg, Dan.
Modern French. HarBraceJ.
Desborough, Vincent R. *see* Desborough, Vincent Robin
d'Arba.
Desborough, Vincent Robin d'Arba.
xDesborough, Vincent R.
The Greek Dark Ages. St Martin.
Descargues, Pierre.
xDescargues, Pierre.
Perspective. Abrams.
Descartes, Rene, 1596-1650
xDescartes, Rene.
Discourse on Method. Bobbs.
Discourse on Method. Hackett Pub.
Meditations on First Philosophy. Bobbs.
Meditations on First Philosophy. Hackett Pub.
Rene Descartes: Essential Writings. Har-Row.
Deschler, Lewis.
xDeschler, Lewis.
Deschler's Rules of Order. P-H.
Deschner, Donald.
xDeschner, Donald.
The Films of Cary Grant. Citadel Pr.
The Films of Spencer Tracy. Citadel Pr.
Films of W. C. Fields. Citadel Pr.
Descola, Jean.
xDescola, Jean.
Conquistadors. Kelley.
Desfosses, Helen.
xDesfosses, Helen.
ed. Socialism in the Third World. Praeger.
Deshen, Shlomo. *see* Deshen, Shlomo A.
Deshen, Shlomo A.
xDeshen, Shlomo.
The Predicament of Homecoming: Cultural &
Social Life of North African Immigrants in
Israel. Cornell U Pr.
Deshimaru, Roshi T. *see* Deshimaru, Taisen.
Deshimaru, Taisen.
xDeshimaru, Roshi T.
The Voice of the Valley: Zen Teachings. Bobbs.
Deshmukh, C. D. *see* Deshmukh, Chintaman
Dwarkanath.
Deshmukh, Chintaman Dwarkanath, 1896-
xDeshmukh, C. D.
Reflections on Finance, Education & Society.
Orient Bk Dist.
Desikachar, T. K. *see* Desikachar, T. K. V.
Desikachar, T. K. V.
xDesikachar, T. K.
Religiousness in Yoga: Lectures on Theory &
Practice. U Pr of Amer.
Deskins, Barbara B.
xDeskins, Barbara B.
Everyone's Guide to Better Food & Nutrition.
Jonathan David.
Desmarest, Marie A. *see* Desmarest, Marie-Anne.
Desmarest, Marie-Anne.
xDesmarest, Marie A.
Torrents. NAL.
Desmedt, J. E. *see* Desmedt, John E.

Desmedt, John E.
xDesmedt, J. E.
ed. Attention, Voluntary Contraction &
Event-Related Cerebral Potentials. S Karger.
ed. Language & Hemispheric Specialization in
Man: Cerebral Event-Related Potentials. S
Karger.
Desmond, Adrian J., 1947-
xDesmond, Adrian J.
The Ape's Reflexion. Dial.
Desmond, Alice (Curtis), 1897-
xDesmond, Alice C.
Marie Antoinette's Daughter. Dodd.
Desmond, Alice C. *see* Desmond, Alice (Curtis).
Desmond, Glenn M.
xDesmond, Glenn M.
Business Valuation Handbook. Valuation.
Desmond, John F.
xDesmond, John F.
ed. A Still Moment: Essays on the Art of
Eudora Welty. Scarecrow.
Desmond, Robert W. *see* Desmond, Robert William.
Desmond, Robert William, 1900-
xDesmond, Robert W.
The Information Process: World News
Reporting to the Twentieth Century. U of
Iowa Pr.
The Press & World Affairs. Arno.
Desnick, Shirley G.
xDesnick, Shirley G.
Geriatric Contentment: A Guide to Its
Achievement in Your Home. C C Thomas.
Desnuelle, P. *see* Desnuelle, Pierre.
Desnuelle, Pierre.
xDesnuelle, P.
ed. Structure-Function Relationships of
Proteolytic Enzymes: Proceedings. Acad Pr.
DeSouza, Glenn R.
xDeSouza, Glenn R.
System Methods for Socio-Economic &
Environmental Impact Analysis. Lexington
Bks.
Despert, J. Louis. *see* Despert, Juliette Louise.
Despert, J. Louise. *see* Despert, Juliette Louise.
Despert, Juliette Louise, 1892-
xDespert, J. Louis.
Children of Divorce. Doubleday.
xDespert, J. Louise.
The Inner Voices of Children. S&S.
Desroche, Henri.
xDesroche, Henri.
The Sociology of Hope. Routledge & Kegan.
Desrosier, Norman W.
xDesrosier, Norman W.
Economics of New Food Product
Development. AVI.
Fundamentals of Food Freezing. AVI.
Dessau, Hermann, 1856-1931
xDessau, Hermann.
Geschichte der Romischen Kaiserzeit. Arno.
Dessau, Joanna.
xDessau, Joanna.
Absolute Elizabeth. St Martin.
The Red-Haired Brat. St Martin.
Dessert, Nan.
xDessert, Nan.
Seconds, Please. Strode.
Dessi, Giuseppe, 1909-
xDessi, Giuseppe.
The Forests of Norbio. HarBraceJ.
Dessi, Guiseppe. *see* Dessi, Giuseppe.
Dessler, G. *see* Dessler, Gary.
Dessler, Gary, 1942-
xDessler, G.
Organization Theory: Integrating Structure &
Behavior. P-H.
xDessler, Gary.

The Development of Children's Concepts of
Causal Relations. Greenwood.

Deutscher, Isaac, 1907-1967
xDeutscher, Isaac.
Lenin's Childhood. Oxford U Pr.
Marxism in Our Time. Ramparts.
On Socialist Man. Path Pr NY.
Prophet Unarmed: Trotsky, 1921-1929. Oxford
U Pr.
The Prophet Unarmed: Trotsky, 1921-1929.
Oxford U Pr.
Soviet Trade Unions: Their Place in Soviet
Labour Policy. Hyperion Conn.
Stalin: A Political Biography. Oxford U Pr.

Deutscher, Tamara.
xDeutscher, Tamara.
ed. Not by Politics Alone: The Other Lenin.
Lawrence Hill.

Deutschman, Deborah.
xDeutschman, Deborah.
Signals. Playboy Pbks.
Signals. Seaview Bks.

Devall, William S. see Devall, William Sigure.

Devall, William Sigure.
xDevall, William S.
Junior High School Art Curriculum. U Pr of
Amer.

Devane, Richard S.
xDevane, Richard S.
The Failure of Individualism: A Documented
Essay. Greenwood.

DeVane, William C. see DeVane, William Clyde.

Devane, William Clyde, 1898-
xDeVane, William C.
American University in the Twentieth Century.
La State U Pr.

Devaney, John.
xDevaney, John.
Great Upsets of Stanley Cup Hockey. Garrard.
Star Pass Receivers of the NFL. Random.
The Story of Basketball. Random.

Devaraja, N. K. see Devaraja, Nand Kishore.

Devaraja, Nand Kishore, 1917-
xDevaraja, N. K.
Hinduism & Christianity. Asia.
ed. Indian Philosophy Today. South Asia Bks.

Dever, Alan. see Dever, G. E. Alan.

Dever, G. E. Alan.
xDever, Alan.
Community Health Analysis: A Holistic
Approach. Aspen Systems.

Dever, Joseph, 1919-
xDever, Joseph.
Cushing of Boston: A Candid Portrait.
Branden.

Dever, Richard B. see Dever, Richard Bernard.

Dever, Richard Bernard, 1934-
xDever, Richard B.
Talk: Teaching the American Language to
Kids. Merrill.

Dever, William G.
xDever, William G.
A Manual of Field Excavation: A Handbook
for Field Archaeologists. Ktav.

Deveraux, Jude.
xDeveraux, Jude.
The Enchanted Land. Avon.

Deverell, William.
xDeverell, William.
Needles. Bantam.
xDeverell, William H.
Needles. Little.

Deverell, William H. see Deverell, William.

Devereux, Frederick L.
xDevereux, Frederick L.

Backyard Pony: Selecting & Owning a Horse.
Watts.
Horseback Riding. Watts.
Horses. Watts.
Practical Navigation for the Yachtsman.
Norton.
Ride Your Pony Right. Dodd.

Devereux, George, 1908-
xDevereux, George.
Ethnopsychoanalysis: Psychoanalysis &
Anthropology As Complementary Frames of
Reference. U of Cal Pr.

Devereux, Hugo B. see Devereux, Hugo Bernard.

Devereux, Hugo Bernard.
xDevereux, Hugo B.
The Small State As the Major Troublemaker in
History & the Need to Eliminate Its
Existence for the Peace of the World. Inst
Econ Pol.

Devereux, James P. see Devereux, James Patrick Sinnott.

Devereux, James Patrick Sinnott, 1903-
xDevereux, James P.
Wake Island. Major Bks.

Devignes, Antoine.
xDevignes, Antoine.
How to Recognize 30 Edible Mushrooms.
Barron.

Deville, Lawrence.
xDeville, Lawrence.
American Foreign Policy & American Business:
The Two Worlds in Conflict. Am Classical
Coll Pr.

DeVille, Roberta.
xDeVille, Roberta.
Lovers for Life: The Key to a Loving &
Lasting Marriage. Morrow.

Devine, Bob.
xDevine, Bob.
Born a Snake Fighter. Moody.
The Feathered Trip Hammer. Moody.
The Oyster Thief. Moody.
The Soil Factory. Moody.
The Trap Door Spider. Moody.

Devine, Charles J. see Devine, Charles Joseph.

Devine, Charles Joseph.
xDevine, Charles J.
Urology in Practice. Little.

Devine, Dominic, 1920-
xDevine, Dominic.
Sunk Without a Trace. St Martin.

Devine, Donald F.
xDevine, Donald F.
Mathematics for Elementary Education. Wiley.

Devine, Donald J. see Devine, Donald John.

Devine, Donald John, 1937-
xDevine, Donald J.
Does Freedom Work: Liberty & Justice in
America. Green Hill.

Devine, Edward T. see Devine, Edward Thomas.

Devine, Edward Thomas, 1867-1948
xDevine, Edward T.
Principles of Relief. Arno.

Devine, George.
xDevine, George.
ed. A World More Human - a Church More
Christian. Alba.

Devine, Marjorie M.
xDevine, Marjorie M.
Dimensions of Food: An Introductory
Laboratory Manual. Har-Row.

Devine, P. J.
xDevine, P. J.
An Introduction to Industrial Economics. Allen
Unwin.

Devine, Philip E., 1944-
xDevine, Philip E.
The Ethics of Homicide. Cornell U Pr.

Devinney, Edward J.
xDevinney, Edward J.

Contemporary Astronomy. Merrill.

Devino, W. Stanley. see Devino, William Stanley.

Devino, William Stanley.
xDevino, W. Stanley.
A Study of Textile Mill Closings in Selected
New England Communities. U Maine Orono.

DeVito, Alfred.
xDeVito, Alfred.
Creative Sciencing: A Practical Approach.
Little.

DeVito, Joseph. see Devito, Joseph A.

DeVito, Joseph A., 1938-
xDeVito, Joseph.
Psychology of Speech & Language: An
Introduction to Psycholinguistics. Random.
xDeVito, Joseph A.
Communicology: An Introduction to the Study
of Communication. Har-Row.
The Interpersonal Communication Book.
Har-Row.
Psycholinguistics. Bobbs.

Devlin, C. B.
xDevlin, C. B. Duke.
The Horseman's Dictionary: Medical &
General. A S Barnes.

Devlin, C. B. Duke. see Devlin, C. B.

Devlin, Christopher.
xDevlin, Christopher.
Life of Robert Southwell, Poet & Martyr.
Greenwood.

Devlin, John C.
xDevlin, John C.
The World of Roger Tory Peterson: An
Authorized Biography. Times Bks.

Devlin, K. see Devlin, Keith J.

Devlin, K. J. see Devlin, Keith J.

Devlin, Keith J.
xDevlin, K.
Fundamentals of Contemporary Set Theory.
Springer-Verlag.
xDevlin, K. J.
Aspects of Constructibility. Springer-Verlag.
The Axiom of Constructibility: A Guide for the
Mathematician. Springer-Verlag.
The Souslin Problem. Springer-Verlag.

Devlin, Patrick, Baron, 1905-
xDevlin, Patrick.
Enforcement of Morals. Oxford U Pr.
The Judge. Oxford U Pr.

Devlin, Polly.
xDevlin, Polly.
The Vogue Book of Fashion Photography. S&S.

Devlin, Robert M.
xDevlin, Robert M.
Plant Physiology. D Van Nostrand.

Devlin, Wende.
xDevlin, Wende.
Cranberry Mystery. Schol Bk Serv.
Cranberry Thanksgiving. Schol Bk Serv.
Hang on Hester!. Lothrop.
How Fletcher Was Hatched. Schol Bk Serv.
Old Black Witch!. Schol Bk Serv.

Devol, Jerry B.
xDevol, Terry B.
Establishment of the First U. S. Government
Post Offices in the Northwest Territory. Am
Philatelic.

Devol, Terry B. see Devol, Jerry B.

Devons, Ely.
xDevons, Ely.
Essays in Economics. Greenwood.

DeVos, Ton, 1926-
xDeVos, Ton.
Introduction to Politics. Winthrop.

Devreese, J. T. see Devreese, Jozef T.

Devreese, Jozef T.
xDevreese, J. T.

ed. Highly Conducting One Dimensional
   Solids. Plenum Pub.
Devries, David L.
   xDevries, David L.
      Teams-Games-Tournament: The Team
      Learning Approach. Educ Tech Pubns.
Dew, Edward.
   xDew, Edward.
      Politics in the Altiplano: The Dynamics of
      Change in Rural Peru. U of Tex Pr.
Dewan, S. B.
   xDewan, Shashi.
      Power Semiconductor Circuits. Wiley.
Dewan, Shashi. *see* Dewan, S. B.
Dewar, Margaret.
   xDewar, Margaret.
      Labour Policy in U. S. S. R. 1917-1928.
      Octagon.
      Soviet Trade with Eastern Europe. Greenwood.
Dewar, Michael.
   xDewar, Michael.
      Internal Security Weapons & Equipment of the
      World. Scribner.
Dewar, Michael J. *see* Dewar, Michael James Steuart.
Dewar, Michael James Steuart.
   xDewar, Michael J.
      Introduction to Modern Chemistry. Oxford U
      Pr.
Dewdney, John C.
   xDewdney, John C.
      Geography of the Soviet Union. Pergamon.
Dewees, Donald N.
   xDewees, Donald N.
      Economics & Public Policy: The Automobile
      Pollution Case. MIT Pr.
Dewees, Jacob.
   xDewees, Jacob.
      Great Future of America & Africa. Arno.
      Great Future of America & Africa. Scholarly.
Deweese, Charles W.
   xDeweese, Charles W.
      A Community of Believers. Judson.
      The Emerging Role of Deacons. Broadman.
Deweese, David D. *see* Deweese, David Downs.
Deweese, David Downs.
   xDeweese, David D.
      Textbook of Otolaryngology. Mosby.
DeWeese, Paul N. *see* DeWeese, Paul Nathan.
DeWeese, Paul Nathan, 1955-
   xDeWeese, Paul N.
      Hope in an Age of Nihilism. Greeno Hadden.
Dewey, Ariane.
   xDewey, Ariane.
      The Fish Peri. Macmillan.
Dewey, Clive.
   xDewey, Clive.
      The Imperial Impact: Studies in the Economic
      History of Africa & India. Humanities.
Dewey, Davis R. *see* Dewey, Davis Rich.
Dewey, Davis Rich, 1858-1942
   xDewey, Davis R.
      Financial History of the United States. Kelley.
Dewey, Donald.
   xDewey, Donald.
      Modern Capital Theory. Columbia U Pr.
      Monopoly in Economics & Law. Greenwood.
      Theory of Imperfect Competition: A Radical
      Reconstruction. Columbia U Pr.
Dewey, Edward R.
   xDewey, Edward R.
      Cycles: The Mysterious Forces That Trigger
      Events. Dutton.
Dewey, George, 1837-1917
   xDewey, George.

Autobiography of George Dewey: Admiral of
   the Navy. Scholarly.
Dewey, Godfrey, 1887-
   xDewey, Godfrey.
      English Spelling: Roadblock to Reading. Tchrs
      Coll.
      Relative Frequency of English Spellings. Tchrs
      Coll.
Dewey, Jackie, 1923-
   xDewey, Jackie.
      Of Life & Breath: A Holistic Approach. Beta
      Bk.
Dewey, John, 1859-1952
   xDewey, John.
      Creative Intelligence: Essays in the Pragmatic
      Attitude. Octagon.
      Dictionary of Education. Greenwood.
      Education Today. Greenwood.
      Experience & Nature. Dover.
      Experience & Nature. Open Court.
      Experience & Nature. Peter Smith.
      How We Think: A Restatement of the Relation
      of Reflective Thinking to the Educative
      Process. Heath.
      Lectures in China, 1919-1920. U Pr of Hawaii.
      Moral Principles in Education. S Ill U Pr.
      Outlines of a Critical Theory of Ethics.
      Greenwood.
      Problems of Men. Greenwood.
      Public & Its Problems. Swallow.
      The School & Society. S Ill U Pr.
      Theory of the Moral Life. Irvington.
Dewey, Melvil.
   xDewey, Melvil.
      A Classification & Subject Index for
      Cataloguing & Arranging the Books &
      Pamphlets of a Library. Gordon Pr.
Dewey, Robert E.
   xDewey, Robert E.
      Introduction to Ethics. Macmillan.
Dewhirst, Martin.
   xDewhirst, Martin.
      ed. The Soviet Censorship. Scarecrow.
Dewhurst, C. Kurt.
   xDewhurst, C. Kurt.
      Artists in Aprons: Folk Art by American
      Women. Dutton.
Dewhurst, D. J.
   xDewhurst, D. J.
      An Introduction to Biomedical
      Instrumentation. Pergamon.
Dewhurst, Kenneth.
   xDewhurst, Kenneth.
      Friedrich Schiller--Medicine, Psychology, &
      Literature: With the First English Edition of
      His Complete Medical & Psychological
      Writings. U of Cal Pr.
Dewhurst, R. *see* Dewhurst, Robin.
Dewhurst, Robin.
   xDewhurst, R.
      Approaching Retirement. State Mutual Bk.
DeWitt, Bryce S. *see* Dewitt, Bryce Seligman.
DeWitt, Bryce Seligman, 1923-
   xDeWitt, Bryce S.
      Dynamical Theory of Groups & Fields.
      Gordon.
Dewitt, David M. *see* Dewitt, David Miller.
Dewitt, David Miller, 1837-1912
   xDewitt, David M.
      Assassination of Abraham Lincoln & Its
      Expiation. Arno.
      The Impeachment & Trial of Andrew Johnson,
      Seventeenth President of the U.S.. Scholarly.
DeWitt, Frances B. *see* Dewitt, Frances Borum.
DeWitt, Frances Borum.
   xDeWitt, Frances B.
      Our Educational Challenge: Specific Learning
      Disabled Adolescents. Acad Therapy.
Dewitt, Howard A.
   xDeWitt, Howard A.

California Civilization: An Interpretation.
   Kendall-Hunt.
DeWolfe. R. H. *see* Dewolfe, Robert H.
DeWolfe, Robert H.
   xDeWolfe, R. H.
      Carboxylic Ortho Acid Derivatives: Preparation
      & Synthetic Applications. Acad Pr.
Dewsbury, Donald A., 1939-
   xDewsbury, Donald A.
      Comparative Animal Behavior. McGraw.
Dexler, Paul R.
   xDexler, Paul R.
      Yesterday's Cars. Lerner Pubns.
Dexter, Beverly L. *see* Dexter, Beverly Liebherr.
Dexter, Beverly Liebherr.
   xDexter, Beverly L.
      Special Education & the Classroom Teacher:
      Concepts, Perspectives & Strategies. C C
      Thomas.
Dexter, Colin.
   xDexter, Colin.
      The Silent World of Nicholas Quinn. St
      Martin.
Dexter, Elisabeth Williams (Anthony), 1887-
   xDexter, Elizabeth W.
      Career Women of America. Kelley.
Dexter, Elizabeth W. *see* Dexter, Elisabeth Williams
   (Anthony).
Dexter, Henry M. *see* Dexter, Henry Martyn.
Dexter, Henry Martyn.
   xDexter, Henry M.
      The England & Holland of the Pilgrims.
      Genealog Pub.
Dexter, Lewis A. *see* Dexter, Lewis Anthony.
Dexter, Lewis Anthony.
   xDexter, Lewis A.
      ed. People, Society & Mass Communications.
      Free Pr.
   xDexter, Lewis Anthony.
      How Organizations Are Represented in
      Washington. Bobbs.
Dexter, N C.
   xDexter, N. C.
      Liberal Studies: An Outline Course. Pergamon.
Dexter, Pat E. *see* Dexter, Pat Egan.
Dexter, Pat Egan.
   xDexter, Pat E.
      Arrow in the Wind. Elsevier-Nelson.
      The Boy Who Snuck in. Concordia.
Dexter, Stephen C.
   xDexter, Stephen C.
      Handbook of Oceanographic Engineering
      Materials. Wiley.
Dexter, Walter, 1877-1944
   xDexter, Walter.
      Days in Dickensland. Haskell.
      Dickens: The Story of the Life of the World's
      Favourite Author. Folcroft.
Dextreit. *see* Dextreit, Raymond.
Dextreit, Raymond.
   xDextreit.
      ed. Our Earth Our Cure. Bolder Bks.
Deyl, Z. *see* Deyl, Zdenek.
Deyl, Zdenek.
   xDeyl, Z.
      ed. Liquid Column Chromatography: A Survey
      of Modern Techniques & Applications.
      Elsevier.
Deyneka, Anita.
   xDeyneka, Anita.
      Alexi & the Mountain Treasure. Cook.
      Christians in the Shadow of the Kremlin. Cook.
      Tanya & the Border Guard. Cook.
Deyoe, George P. *see* Deyoe, George Percy.
Deyoe, George Percy, 1901-
   xDeyoe, George P.

Certain Trends in Curriculum Practices &
Policies in State Normal Schools & Teachers
Colleges. AMS Pr.

Dezettel, Louis M.
xDezettel, Louis M.
Masons & Builders Library. Audel.

Dhalla, Maneckji N. *see* Dhalla, Maneckji Nusservanji.

Dhalla, Maneckji Nusservanji, 1875-1956
xDhalla, Maneckji N.
History of Zoroastrianism. AMS Pr.
Our Perfecting World: Zarathushtra's Way of
Life. AMS Pr.

Dhamija, Jasleen, 1933-
xDhamija, Jasleen.
Living Tradition of Iran's Crafts. Advent Bk.
Living Tradition of Iran's Crafts. Biblio Dist.

Dhar, Prithvi N. *see* Dhar, Prithvi Nath.

Dhar, Prithvi Nath.
xDhar, Prithvi N.
Demand for Energy in North-West India. Asia.

Dhar, Sudhir K. *see* Dhar, Sudhir Kumar.

Dhar, Sudhir Kumar, 1920-
xDhar, Sudhir K.
Astrophysical Enigmas. Asia.

Dhar, T. N. *see* Dhar, Trilok N.

Dhar, Trilok N.
xDhar, T. N.
Education & Employment in India: The Policy
Nexus. South Asia Bks.

Dharan, Murali.
xDharan, Murali.
Total Quality Control in the Clinical
Laboratory. Mosby.

Dhavamony, Mariasusai.
xDhavamony, Mariasusai.
Love of God According to Saiva Siddhanta: A
Study in the Mysticism & Theology of
Saivism. Oxford U Pr.

Dhrymes, P. J. *see* Dhrymes, Phoebus J.

Dhrymes, Phoebus J., 1932-
xDhrymes, P. J.
Mathematics for Econometrics.
Springer-Verlag.

Di Cesare, Mario A.
xDi Cesare, Mario A.
ed. A Concordance to the Complete Writings
of George Herbert. Cornell U Pr.

Di Chiro, Giovanni, 1926-
xDi Chiro, Giovanni.
Atlas of Detailed Normal
Pneumoencephalographic Anatomy. C C
Thomas.

Di Donato, Georgia, 1932-
xDi Donato, Georgia.
Woman of Justice. Doubleday.

Di Giacomo, Melchior.
xDi Giacomo, Melchior.
The Tennis Experience. Larousse.

Di Napoli, Peter J. *see* Di Napoli, Peter John.

Di Napoli, Peter John, 1905-
xDi Napoli, Peter J.
Homework in New York City Elementary
Schools. AMS Pr.

Di Noto, Andrea.
xDi Noto, Andrea.
Anytime, Anywhere, Anybody Games.
Western Pub.

Di Palma, Giuseppe.
xDi Palma, Giuseppe.
Political Syncretism in Italy: Historical
Coalition Strategies & the Present Crisis. U
of Cal Intl St.

Di Prima, Diane.
xDi Prima, Diane.
Loba. Wingbow Pr.
Revolutionary Letters Etc. City Lights.

Di Tommaso, Andrea.
xDi Tommaso, Andrea.
Structure & Ideology in Boiardo's "Orlando
Innamorato". U of NC Pr.

Di Tullo, Frank.
xDi Tullo, Frank.
Hypno Weight Control: How to Lose Weight &
Discover Yourself Through Self-Hypnosis.
Exposition.

Diack, Hunter.
xDiack, Hunter.
Reading & the Psychology of Perception.
Greenwood.

Diagram Group.
xDiagram Group.
Child's Body. Bantam.
Child's Body: A Parent's Manual. Paddington.
Comparisons. St Martin.
Enjoying Combat Sports. Paddington.
Enjoying Gymnastics. Paddington.
Enjoying Racquet Sports. Paddington.
Enjoying Skating. Paddington.
Enjoying Soccer. Paddington.
Enjoying Swimming & Diving. Paddington.
Man's Body. Bantam.
Man's Body: An Owner's Manual. Paddington.
Mothers. Paddington.
Pets: Every Owner's Encyclopedia.
Paddington.
Rules of the Game. Bantam.
The Way to Play. Bantam.
Woman's Body: An Owner's Manual. Bantam.
xTheDiagram Group.
The Body Manual: A Complete Family Guide.
Paddington.
The Complete Encyclopedia of Exercises.
Paddington.
Enjoying Track & Field Sports. Paddington.
Musical Instruments of the World. Bantam.
Musical Instruments of the World: An
Illustrated Encyclopedia. Paddington.
The Official World Encyclopedia of Sports &
Games: The Rules, Techniques of Play &
Equipment for Over 400 Sports & 1000
Games. Paddington.
Woman's Body: An Owner's Manual.
Paddington.

Dial, Hertha.
xDial, Hertha.
Little Blue Heaven. De Vorss.

Dial, Joan.
xDial, Joan.
Lovers & Warriors. Fawcett.
Susanna. Fawcett.

Dial, O. E. *see* Dial, O. Eugene.

Dial, O. Eugene.
xDial, O. E.
Privacy, Security, & Computers: Guidelines for
Municipal & Other Public Information
Systems. Praeger.

Diaman, N. A.
xDiaman, N. A.
The Fourth Wall. Persona Pr.

Diamant, Lincoln.
xDiamant, Lincoln.
ed. The Broadcast Communications Dictionary.
Hastings.

Diamant, R. M. *see* Diamant, Rudolph Maximilian
Eugen.

Diamant, Rudolph Maximilian Eugen, 1925-
xDiamant, R. M.
Total Energy. Pergamon.

Diamond. *see* Diamond, Seymour.

Diamond, Ann C. *see* Diamond, Ann Cynthia.

Diamond, Ann Cynthia.
xDiamond, Ann C.
Bride's Magazine Guide to Today's Marriage.
S&S.

Diamond, Arlyn.
xDiamond, Arlyn.
ed. The Authority of Experience: Essays in
Feminist Criticism. U of Mass Pr.

Diamond, Arthur S. *see* Diamond, Arthur Sigismund.

Diamond, Arthur Sigismund.
xDiamond, Arthur S.
The Evolution of Law & Order. Greenwood.

Diamond, Charles.
xDiamond, Charles.
The Facial Nerve. Oxford U Pr.

Diamond, Donna.
xDiamond, Donna.
Adapted by & illus. Swan Lake. Holiday.

Diamond, Dorothy. *see* Diamond, Dorothy M.

Diamond, Dorothy M.
xDiamond, Dorothy.
Musical Instruments. Raintree Child.

Diamond, Frank B.
xDiamond, Frank B.
Increase Your Profits in the Stock Market.
Cornerstone.

Diamond, Harold J., 1934-
xDiamond, Harold J.
Music Criticism: An Annotated Guide to the
Literature. Scarecrow.

Diamond, J. *see* Diamond, Jay.

Diamond, Jay.
xDiamond, J.
Introduction to Contemporary Business. P-H.
xDiamond, Jay.
Mathematics of Business. P-H.
Principles of Marketing. P-H.
Retail Buying. P-H.

Diamond, Malcolm L. *see* Diamond, Malcolm Luria.

Diamond, Malcolm Luria.
xDiamond, Malcolm L.
Contemporary Philosophy & Religious
Thought: An Introduction to the Philosophy
of Religion. McGraw.
Martin Buber: Jewish Existentialist. Oamon.

Diamond, Marian C. *see* Diamond, Marian Cleeves.

Diamond, Marian Cleeves.
xDiamond, Marian C.
ed. Hormonal Contraceptives, Estrogens &
Human Welfare. Acad Pr.

Diamond, Peter. *see* Diamond, Peter A.

Diamond, Peter A.
xDiamond, Peter.
ed. Uncertainty in Economics: Readings &
Exercises. Acad Pr.

Diamond, Robert M.
xDiamond, Robert M.
Amateur Psychologist's Dictionary. Arc Bks.
The Amateur Psychologist's Dictionary. Arco.
Instructional Development for Individualized
Learning in Higher Education. Educ Tech
Pubns.

Diamond, Seymour.
xDiamond.
The Practicing Physicians Approach to
Headache. Williams & Wilkins.
xDiamond, Seymour.
More Than Two Aspirin: Hope for Your
Headache Problem. Avon.
ed. Vasoactive Substances Relevant to
Migraine. C C Thomas.

Diamond, Stanley, 1922-
xDiamond, Stanley.
Culture in History: Essays in Honor of Paul
Radin. Octagon.
ed. Primitive Views of the World. Columbia U
Pr.
ed. Toward a Marxist Anthropology: Problems
& Perspectives. Mouton.

Diamond, Walter H.
xDiamond, Walter H.
Comparative State Income Tax Guide with
Forms. Oceana.

Diamonstein, Barbaralee.
xDiamonstein, Barbaralee.

Inside New York's Art World. Rizzoli Intl.
Dias, Robert Vas. *see* Vas Dias, Robert.
Diat, Louis, 1885-1957
xDiat, Louis.
French Country Cooking for Americans.
Dover.
French Country Cooking for Americans. Peter
Smith.
Diaz, Janet. *see* Diaz, Janet Winecoff.
Diaz, Janet Winecoff, 1934-
xDiaz, Janet.
Ana Maria Matute. Irvington.
Diaz Del Castillo, Bernal.
xDiaz Del Castillo, Bernal.
Conquest of New Spain. Penguin.
Dib, Albert.
xDib, Albert.
Forms & Agreements for Architects, Engineers
& Contractors. Boardman.
Dibacco, Thomas V.
xDibacco, Thomas V.
ed. Presidential Power in Latin American
Politics. Praeger.
DiBattista, Maria, 1947-
xDiBattista, Maria.
Virginia Woolf's Major Novels: The Fables of
Anon. Yale U Pr.
Dibble, Vernon K.
xDibble, Vernon K.
The Legacy of Albion Small. U of Chicago Pr.
Dibden, Arthur J. *see* Dibden, Arthur James.
Dibden, Arthur James, 1919-
xDibden, Arthur J.
ed. Academic Deanship in American Colleges
& Universities. S Ill U Pr.
Dibdin, Michael.
xDibdin, Michael.
The Last Sherlock Holmes Story. Ballantine.
The Last Sherlock Holmes Story. Pantheon.
Dibdin, Thomas J. *see* Dibdin, Thomas John.
Dibdin, Thomas John, 1771-1841
xDibdin, Thomas J.
Reminiscences of Thomas Dibdin. AMS Pr.
Dibelius, Martin, 1883-1947
xDibelius, Martin.
Fresh Approach to the New Testament &
Early Christian Literature. Greenwood.
Dibell, Ansen.
xDibell, Anson.
Pursuit of the Screamer. DAW Bks.
Dibell, Anson. *see* Dibell, Ansen.
Dibernard, Barbara, 1948-
xDibernard, Barbara.
Alchemy & Finnegans Wake. State U NY Pr.
Dible, Don M. *see* Dible, Donald M.
Dible, Donald M.
xDible, Don M.
ed. How to Plan & Finance a Growing
Business. Entrepreneur Pr.
Dibner, Martin.
xDibner, Martin.
The Deep Six. Pinnacle Bks.
Ransom Run. Ballantine.
The Trouble with Heroes. Pinnacle Bks.
Dibner, S. S. *see* Dibner, Susan Schmidt.
Dibner, Susan Schmidt.
xDibner, S. S.
Integration or Segregation for the Physically
Handicapped Child?. C C Thomas.
DiCara, Leo V., 1937-
xDiCara, Leo V.
ed. Limbic & Autonomic Nervous Systems
Research. Plenum Pub.
Dicey, Albert V. *see* Dicey, Albert Venn.
Dicey, Albert Venn, 1835-1922
xDicey, Albert V.

Lectures on the Relation Between Law &
Public Opinion in England, During the
Nineteenth Century. AMS Pr.
The Privy Council. Hyperion Conn.
Dichter, Ernest, 1907-
xDichter, Ernest.
Handbook of Consumer Motivations: The
Psychology of the World of Objects.
McGraw.
Total Self-Knowledge. Stein & Day.
Dichter, Harry.
xDichter, Harry.
Handbook of Early American Sheet Music:
1768-1889. Peter Smith.
Dick, Bernard F.
xDick, Bernard F.
The Anatomy of Film. St Martin.
Billy Wilder. Twayne.
Dick, David.
xDick, David.
All Modern Slavery Indefensible: Intended for
All Places Where Slavery Does Exist. Arno.
Dick, Everett.
xDick, Everett.
Vanguards of the Frontier: A Social History of
the Northern Plains & Rocky Mountains
from the Fur Traders to the Sod Busters. U
of Nebr Pr.
Dick, Everett. *see* Dick, Everett Newfon.
Dick, Everett Newfon, 1898-
xDick, Everett.
The Sod-House Frontier: A Social History of
the Northern Plains from the Creation of
Kansas & Nebraska to the Admission of the
Dakotas. U of Nebr Pr.
Dick, George.
xDick, George.
Immunisation. Update Pub Intl.
Dick, H. Lenox H.
xDick, Lenox.
The Art & Science of Fly Fishing. Citadel Pr.
Art & Science of Fly Fishing. Winchester Pr.
Dick, H. M. *see* Dick, Heather M.
Dick, Heather M.
xDick, H. M.
ed. Histocompatibility Techniques. Elsevier.
Dick, James C.
xDick, James C.
Violence & Oppression. U of Ga Pr.
Dick, James G. *see* Dick, James Gardiner.
Dick, James Gardiner.
xDick, James G.
Analytical Chemistry. Krieger.
Dick, Jane.
xDick, Jane.
Volunteers & the Making of Presidents. Dodd.
Dick, John H. *see* Dick, John Henry.
Dick, John Henry, 1919-
xDick, John H.
Other Edens: The Sketchbook of an
Artist-Naturalist. Devin.
Dick, Lenox. *see* Dick, H. Lenox H.
Dick, Philip. *see* Dick, Philip K.
Dick, Philip K.
xDick, Philip.
Clans of the Alphane Moon. Dell.
xDick, Philip K.
Clans of the Alphane Moon. Gregg.
Counter-Clock World. Gregg.
Eye in the Sky. Ace Bks.
Eye in the Sky. Gregg.
The Ganymede Takeover. Ace Bks.
The Solar Lottery. Gregg.
The Three Stigmata of Palmer Eldritch. Gregg.
Ubik. Gregg.
Vulcan's Hammer. Gregg.
The World Jones Made. Gregg.
Dick, Robert C.
xDick, Robert C.

Argumentation & Rational Debating. Wm C
Brown.
Dick, W. Carson. *see* Dick, William Carson.
Dick, Walter.
xDick, Walter.
The Systematic Design of Instruction. Scott F.
Dick, William.
xDick, William.
Byron & His Poetry. AMS Pr.
Byron & His Poetry. Folcroft.
Byron & His Poetry. Haskell.
Dick, William B. *see* Dick, William Brisbane.
Dick, William Brisbane, 1827-1901
xDick, William B.
Compiled by Dick's Festival Reciter:
Containing Appropriate Pieces & Programs,
Original & Selected for Washington's
Birthday, Memorial Day.... Arno.
Dick, William Carson.
xDick, W. Carson.
An Introduction to Clinical Rheumatology.
Churchill.
Dick-Read, Grantly, 1890-1959
xDick-Read, Grantly.
Childbirth Without Fear: The Original
Approach to Natural Childbirth. Har-Row.
Dickason, David H. *see* Dickason, David Howard.
Dickason, David Howard.
xDickason, David H.
Daring Young Men: The Story of the
American Pre-Raphaelites. Arno.
Dickason, Elizabeth J.
xDickason, Jean.
Maternal & Infant Care. McGraw.
Maternal & Infant Drugs & Nursing
Intervention. McGraw.
Dickason, Jean. *see* Dickason, Elizabeth J.
Dicke, Robert H. *see* Dicke, Robert Henry.
Dicke, Robert Henry.
xDicke, Robert H.
Gravitation & the Universe. Am Philos.
Theoretical Significance of Experimental
Relativity. Gordon.
Dickens, A. G. *see* Dickens, Arthur Geoffrey.
Dickens, Arthur Geoffrey.
xDickens, A. G.
Reformation & Society in Sixteenth Century
Europe. HarBraceJ.
Dickens, Charles, 1812-1870
xDickens, Charles.

Adventures of Oliver Twist. Beekman Pubs.
Adventures of Oliver Twist. Oxford U Pr.
Barnaby Rudge. Dutton.
Barnaby Rudge. Penguin.
Character Portraits from Dickens. Haskell.
The Christmas Books. Penguin.
A Christmas Carol. Doubleday.
A Christmas Carol. Harmony & Co.
A Christmas Carol. St Martin.
Christmas Carol. Macmillan.
A Christmas Carol. Pendulum Pr.
A Christmas Carol. Peter Pauper.
Christmas Carol. Airmont.
Christmas Carol. Lippincott.
A Christmas Carol. PB.
Christmas Stories. Dutton.
Classic Ghost Stories. Dover.
David Copperfield. Dell.
David Copperfield. Dodd.
David Copperfield. Dutton.
David Copperfield. NAL.
David Copperfield. HM.
David Copperfield. Macmillan.
David Copperfield. Airmont.
David Copperfield. PB.
David Copperfield. Penguin.
Dombey & Son. NAL.
Dombey & Son. Oxford U Pr.
Dombey & Son. Penguin.
Great Expectations. Bobbs.
Great Expectations. Dutton.
Great Expectations. Heinemann Ed.
Great Expectations. HR&W.
Great Expectations. Macmillan.
Great Expectations. Odyssey Pr.
Great Expectations. Oxford U Pr.
Great Expectations. PB.
Great Expectations. St Martin.
Great Expectations. NAL.
Great Expectations. Pendulum Pr.
Great Expectations. Watts.
Great Expectations. Airmont.
Great Expectations. AMSCO Sch.
Great Expectations. Penguin.
Letters of Charles Dickens to Wilkie Collins
    1851-1870. R West.
Little Dorrit. NAL.
Little Dorrit. Oxford U Pr.
Little Dorrit. Penguin.
Martin Chuzzlewit. Dutton.
Martin Chuzzlewit. NAL.
Old Curiosity Shop. Dutton.
The Old Curiosity Shop. Penguin.
Personal History, Adventures, Experience, &
    Observation of David Copperfield, the
    Younger, of Blunderstone Rookery. AMS Pr.
The Public Readings. Oxford U Pr.
Reminiscences of My Father. Haskell.
Tale of Two Cities. Dell.
Tale of Two Cities. Dutton.
A Tale of Two Cities. G K Hall.
Tale of Two Cities. Macmillan.
Tale of Two Cities. Oxford U Pr.
Tale of Two Cities. Penguin.
Tale of Two Cities. Pitman Learning.
Tale of Two Cities. WSP.
Tale of Two Cities. NAL.
Tale of Two Cities. G&D.
A Tale of Two Cities. Raintree Pubs.
A Tale of Two Cities. Pendulum Pr.
Tale of Two Cities. Watts.
Tale of Two Cities. AMSCO Sch.
Tale of Two Cities. Airmont.
Two Tale of Two Cities. Macmillan.
Dickens, E. Larry. *see* Dickens, Edwin Larry.
Dickens, Edwin Larry.
    xDickens, E. Larry.

Fundamentals of Texas Government. Sterling
    Swift.
Dickens, Frank.
    xDickens, Frank.
    Albert Herbert Hawkins, the Naughtiest Boy in
        the World, & the Space Rocket. Doubleday.
    ed. Carbohydrate Metabolism & Its Disorders.
        Acad Pr.
    Fly Away Peter. Scroll Pr.
Dickens, Henry F. *see* Dickens, Henry Fielding.
Dickens, Henry Fielding, Sir, 1849-1933
    xDickens, Henry F.
    Memories of My Father. Haskell.
Dickens, Homer.
    xDickens, Homer.
    Films of Gary Cooper. Citadel Pr.
    The Films of Ginger Rogers. Citadel Pr.
    The Films of Katharine Hepburn. Citadel Pr.
    Films of Marlene Dietrich. Citadel Pr.
    xDickens, Homer C.
    The Films of Ginger Rogers. Citadel Pr.
Dickens, Homer C. *see* Dickens, Homer.
Dickens, Mamie. *see* Dickens, Mary.
Dickens, Mary, 1838-1896
    xDickens, Mamie.
    My Father As I Recall Him. Haskell.
Dickens, Michael.
    xDickens, Michael.
    The World of Butterflies. Macmillan.
Dickens, Milton.
    xDickens, Milton.
    Guidebook for Speech Communication.
        HarBraceJ.
    Speech: Dynamic Communication. HarBraceJ.
Dickens, Roy S., 1938-
    xDickens, Roy S.
    Cherokee Prehistory: The Pisgah Phase in the
        Appalachian Summit Region. U of Tenn Pr.
Dickenson, John P.
    xDickenson, John P.
    Brazil. Westview.
Dickenson, Luella.
    xDickenson, Luella.
    Reminiscences of a Trip Across the Plains in
        1846 & Early Days in California. Ye Galleon.
Dickerman, Pat.
    xDickerman, Pat.
    Adventure Travel. Adventure Guides.
Dickerson, F. Reed. *see* Dickerson, Frederick Reed.
Dickerson, Frederick Reed, 1909-
    xDickerson, F. Reed.
    Legislative Drafting. Greenwood.
    xDickerson, Reed.
    Products Liability & the Food Consumer.
        Greenwood.
Dickerson, John.
    xDickerson, John.
    Raku Handbook: A Practical Approach to
        Ceramic Art. Van Nos Reinhold.
Dickerson, O. M. *see* Dickerson, Oliver Morton.
Dickerson, Oliver M. *see* Dickerson, Oliver Morton.
Dickerson, Oliver Morton, 1875-1966
    xDickerson, O. M.
    The Navigation Acts & the American
        Revolution. Octagon.
    xDickerson, Oliver M.
    The Navigation Acts & the American
        Revolution. U of Pa Pr.
Dickerson, Reed. *see* Dickerson, Frederick Reed.
Dickerson, Richard E. *see* Dickerson, Richard Earl.
Dickerson, Richard Earl.
    xDickerson, Richard E.
    Chemical Principles. Benjamin-Cummings.
    The Structure & Action of Proteins.
        Benjamin-Cummings.
Dickey, Charley.
    xDickey, Charley.

Charley Dickey's Bobwhite Quail Hunting.
    Oxmoor Hse.
Charley Dickey's Deer Hunting. Oxmoor Hse.
Dickey, George E. *see* Dickey, George Edward.
Dickey, George Edward.
    xDickey, George E.
    Money, Prices & Growth: The American
        Experience, 1869-1896. Arno.
Dickey, Glenn.
    xDickey, Glenn.
    The History of American League Baseball.
        Stein & Day.
    History of National League Baseball. Stein &
        Day.
Dickey, James.
    xDickey, James.
    Babel to Byzantium: Poets & Poetry Now.
        Octagon.
    Buckdancer's Choice. Columbia U Pr.
    Deliverance. Dell.
    God's Images: The Bible: a New Vision.
        Oxmoor Hse.
    illus. In Pursuit of the Grey Soul. Bruccoli.
    The Strength of Fields. Doubleday.
Dickey, John Sloan.
    xDickey, John Sloan.
    Canada & the American Presence: The United
        States Interest in an Independent Canada.
        NYU Pr.
Dickey, John W.
    xDickey, John W.
    Analytic Techniques in Urban & Regional
        Planning: With Applications in Public
        Administration & Affairs. McGraw.
Dickey, Lawrence D.
    xDickey, Lawrence D.
    Clinical Ecology. C C Thomas.
Dickey, R. I. *see* Dickey, Robert Irvine.
Dickey, R. P., 1936-
    xDickey, R. P.
    Acting Immortal: Poems. U of Mo Pr.
Dickey, Robert Irvine, 1909-
    xDickey, R. I.
    Accountants Cost Handbook. Wiley.
Dickey, William.
    xDickey, William.
    More Under Saturn. Columbia U Pr.
    Of the Festivity. AMS Pr.
    The Rainbow Grocery. U of Mass Pr.
Dickie, George.
    xDickie, George.
    Aesthetics: A Critical Anthology. St Martin.
    Art & the Aesthetic: An Institutional Analysis.
        Cornell U Pr.
Dickie, James.
    xDickie, James.
    ed. The Undead. PB.
Dickins, Anthony. *see* Dickins, Anthony Stewart
    Mackay.
Dickins, Anthony Stewart Mackay, 1914-
    xDickins, Anthony.
    Guide to Fairy Chess. Dover.
Dickins, Bruce.
    xDickins, Bruce.
    ed. The Dream of the Rood. Irvington.
Dickinson. *see* Dickinson, Emily.
Dickinson, A. K. *see* Dickinson, Alaric Keith.
Dickinson, Alan E. *see* Dickinson, Alan Edgar Frederic.
Dickinson, Alan Edgar Frederic.
    xDickinson, Alan E.
    A Study of Mozart's Last Three Symphonies.
        Scholarly.
Dickinson, Alaric Keith.
    xDickinson, A. K.
    ed. History Teaching & Historical
        Understanding. Heinemann Ed.
Dickinson, Alice.
    xDickinson, Alice.

Charles Darwin & Natural Selection. Watts.
The Colony of Massachusetts. Watts.
First Book of Prehistoric Animals. Watts.
Taken by the Indians: True Tales of Captivity.
   Watts.
Dickinson, Arthur L. *see* Dickinson, Arthur Lowes.
Dickinson, Arthur Lowes, Sir, 1859-1935
   xDickinson, Arthur L.
   Accounting Practice & Procedure. Scholars Bk.
Dickinson, C. H.
   xDickinson, C. H.
   Plant Pathology & Plant Pathogens. Halsted Pr.
   xDickinson, Colin.
   The Encyclopedia of Mushrooms. Putnam.
Dickinson, Colin. *see* Dickinson, C. H.
Dickinson, Edward, 1853-1946
   xDickinson, Edward.
   Music in the History of the Western Church.
      AMS Pr.
   Music in the History of the Western Church.
      Haskell.
Dickinson, Emily, 1830-1886
   xDickinson.
   Love Poems. Peter Pauper.
   xDickinson, Emily.
   Final Harvest: Emily Dickinson's Poems.
      Little.
   Letters. Harvard U Pr.
   Two Poems. Walker & Co.
Dickinson, G. C. *see* Dickinson, Gordon Cawood.
Dickinson, G. Lowes. *see* Dickinson, Goldsworthy
   Lowes.
Dickinson, Goldsworthy L. *see* Dickinson, Goldsworthy
   Lowes.
Dickinson, Goldsworthy Lowes, 1862-1936
   xDickinson, G. Lowes.
   The Greek View of Life. Quality Lib.
   Greek View of Life. U of Mich Pr.
   Letters from a Chinese Official: Being an
      Eastern View of Western Civilization. R
      West.
   xDickinson, Goldsworthy L.
   Causes of International War. Garland Pub.
Dickinson, Gordon Cawood.
   xDickinson, G. C.
   Maps & Air Photographs: Images of Earth.
      Halsted Pr.
Dickinson, H. T.
   xDickinson, H. T.
   Liberty & Property: Political Ideology in
      Eighteenth-Century Britain. Holmes & Meier.
   ed. Politics & Literature in the Eighteenth
      Century. Rowman.
Dickinson, Henry D. *see* Dickinson, Henry Douglas.
Dickinson, Henry Douglas.
   xDickinson, Henry D.
   Economics of Socialism. Arno.
Dickinson, J. C. *see* Dickinson, John Compton.
Dickinson, John.
   xDickinson, John.
   Political Writings of John Dickinson,
      1764-1774. Da Capo.
Dickinson, John C. *see* Dickinson, John Compton.
Dickinson, John Compton.
   xDickinson, J. C.
   The Later Middle Ages: From the Norman
      Conquest to the Eve of the Reformation.
      B&N.
   xDickinson, John C.
   Monastic Life in Medieval England.
      Greenwood.
Dickinson, L. T. *see* Dickinson, Leon Townsend.
Dickinson, Leon Townsend, 1912-
   xDickinson, L. T.
   A Guide to Literary Study. HR&W.
Dickinson, Peter, 1927-
   xDickinson, Peter.

Annerton Pit. Little.
Chance, Luck & Destiny. Little.
The Dancing Bear. Little.
The Gift. Little.
One Foot in the Grave. Pantheon.
Tulku. Dutton.
Dickinson, Peter A.
   xDickinson, Peter A.
   The Complete Retirement Planning Book: Your
      Guide to Happiness, Health & Financial
      Security. Dutton.
Dickinson, Robert E. *see* Dickinson, Robert Eric.
Dickinson, Robert Eric, 1905-
   xDickinson, Robert E.
   The Population Problem of Southern Italy: An
      Essay in Social Geography. Greenwood.
   Regional Concept: The Anglo-American
      Leaders. Routledge & Kegan.
Dickinson, Thomas H. *see* Dickinson, Thomas Herbert.
Dickinson, Thomas Herbert, 1877-
   xDickinson, Thomas H.
   The Insurgent Theatre. Arno.
   Outline of Contemporary Drama. Biblo.
Dickinson, Thorold.
   xDickinson, Thorold.
   A Discovery of Cinema. Oxford U Pr.
   Soviet Cinema. Arno.
Dickinson, W. Croft. *see* Dickinson, William Croft.
Dickinson, W. J. *see* Dickinson, William J.
Dickinson, William Croft.
   xDickinson, W. Croft.
   Scotland from the Earliest Times to 1603.
      Oxford U Pr.
Dickinson, William J.
   xDickinson, W. J.
   Gene-Enzyme Systems in Drosophila.
      Springer-Verlag.
Dickman, Byron A.
   xDickman, Byron A.
   You're Fired. Gracelaine.
Dickman, R. Thomas.
   xDickman, R. Thomas.
   In God We Should Trust. Libra.
Dickmeyer, Lowell A.
   xDickmeyer, Lowell A.
   Basketball Is for Me. Lerner Pubns.
   Football Is for Me. Lerner Pubns.
   Ice Skating Is for Me. Lerner Pubns.
   Swimming Is for Me. Lerner Pubns.
   Track Is for Me. Lerner Pubns.
Dicks, Brian.
   xDicks, Brian.
   Corfu. David & Charles.
Dicks, Brian. *see* Dicks, Thomas Richard Brian.
Dicks, D. R.
   xDicks, D. R.
   Early Greek Astronomy to Aristotle. Cornell U
      Pr.
Dicks, Thomas Richard Brian.
   xDicks, Brian.
   The Ancient Persians: How They Lived &
      Worked. David & Charles.
   The Isle of Wight. David & Charles.
Dicksee, Lawrence R. *see* Dicksee, Lawrence Robert.
Dicksee, Lawrence Robert.
   xDicksee, Lawrence R.
   Goodwill & Its Treatment in Accounts. Arno.
Dickson, Carter.
   xDickson, Carter.
   Death in Five Boxes. Belmont-Tower.
Dickson, David R. *see* Dickson, David Ross.
Dickson, David Ross.
   xDickson, David R.
   Human Vocal Anatomy. C C Thomas.
Dickson, David T.
   xDickson, David T.
   Tax Shelters for the Not-So-Rich. Contemp
      Bks.
Dickson, Edward M.
   xDickson, Edward M.

The Hydrogen Energy Economy: A Realistic
   Appraisal of Prospects & Impacts. Praeger.
Dickson, Felice, 1943-
   xDickson, Felice.
   Growing Food in South Florida. Banyan Bks.
Dickson, Gordon R.
   xDickson, Gordon R.
   The Far Call. Dell.
   The Far Call. Dial.
   Hour of the Horde. DAW Bks.
   The Lifeship. Har-Row.
   Masters of Everon. Ace Bks.
   Necromancer. DAW Bks.
   None but Man. DAW Bks.
   The R-Master. Lippincott.
   Soldier, Ask Not. Ace Bks.
   Soldier, Ask Not. DAW Bks.
   Tactics of Mistake. DAW Bks.
Dickson, Harris, 1868-1946
   xDickson, Harris.
   Story of King Cotton. Negro U Pr.
Dickson, J. H. *see* Dickson, James Holms.
Dickson, James G., 1938-
   xDickson, James G.
   Law & Politics: The Office of Attorney
      General in Texas. Sterling Swift.
Dickson, James Holms, 1937-
   xDickson, J. H.
   Bryophytes of the Pleistocene: The British
      Record & Its Chorological & Ecological
      Implications. Cambridge U Pr.
Dickson, Keith A.
   xDickson, Keith A.
   Towards Utopia: A Study of Brecht. Oxford U
      Pr.
Dickson, L. E. *see* Dickson, Leonard Eugene.
Dickson, Leonard E. *see* Dickson, Leonard Eugene.
Dickson, Leonard Eugene.
   xDickson, L. E.
   Linear Algebras. Hafner.
   xDickson, Leonard E.
   Collected Mathematical Papers. Chelsea Pub.
   History of the Theory of Numbers. Chelsea
      Pub.
   Plane Trigonometry with Practical
      Applications. Chelsea Pub.
Dickson, Mimi.
   xDickson, Mimi.
   Learning Joy: A Book for Parents & Teachers
      Who Want to Help Children Find
      Themselves--& Joy. Whitmore.
Dickson, Naida.
   xDickson, Naida.
   illus. I'd Like . . .. Denison.
   illus. In the Meadow. Denison.
   illus. The Littlest Helper. Denison.
Dickson, P. *see* Dickson, Peter W.
Dickson, Paul.
   xDickson, Paul.
   Chow: A Cook's Tour of Military Food. NAL.
   The Future File. Avon.
   The Great American Ice Cream Book.
      Atheneum.
   Mature Person's Guide to Kites, Yoyos,
      Frisbees & Other Childlike Diversions. NAL.
   The Official Rules. Delacorte.
   Out of This World. Dell.
Dickson, Peter W.
   xDickson, P.
   Kissinger & the Meaning of History.
      Cambridge U Pr.
Dickson, Roy W. *see* Dickson, Roy Ward.
Dickson, Roy Ward.
   xDickson, Roy W.
   The Greatest Quiz Book Ever. Har-Row.
   The Greatest Quiz Book Ever. Bantam.
Dickson, Stanley, 1927-
   xDickson, Stanley.

Communication Disorders: Remedial Principles & Practices. Scott F.

Dickson, T. R. see Dickson, Thomas R.

Dickson, Thomas R.
xDickson, T. R.
The Computer & Chemistry: An Introduction to Programming & Numerical Methods. W H Freeman.
Introduction to Chemistry. Wiley.

Dickson, W. K. see Dickson, William Kennedy Laurie.

Dickson, William J.
xDickson, William J.
No One Was Looking. Concordia.

Dickson, William Kennedy Laurie.
xDickson, W. K.
History of the Kinetograph, Kinetoscope & Kinetophonograph. Arno.

Dickstein, Morris.
xDickstein, Morris.
Gates of Eden: American Culture in the Sixties. Basic.

DiClerico, Robert. see DiClerico, Robert E.

DiClerico, Robert E.
xDiClerico, Robert.
The American President. P-H.

Dictionary of Early Modern English Pronunciation Symposium, Edinburgh, October 23-26, 1974. see Symposium on the Proposed Dictionary of Early Modern English Pronunciation, Edinburgh, 1974.

Didactic Systems Staff. see International Symposium on Long Range Planning for Management, Paris, 1965.

Didday, Rich. see Didday, Richard L.

Didday, Rich L. see Didday, Richard L.

Didday, Richard L.
xDidday, Rich.
Fortran for Humans. West Pub.
xDidday, Rich L.
Fortran for Business People. West Pub.

Didear, Hedwig K. see Didear, Hedwig Krell.

Didear, Hedwig Krell.
xDidear, Hedwig K.
Compiled by History of Karnes County & Old Helena. Jenkins.

Diderot, Denis, 1713-1784
xDiderot, Denis.
Dialogues. Kennikat.
Dialogues. R West.
Diderot, Interpreter of Nature: Selected Writings. Hyperion Conn.
Diderot's Early Philosophical Works. AMS Pr.
Diderot's Early Philosophical Works. B Franklin.
Diderot's Thoughts on Art & Style. B Franklin.
Rameau's Nephew & D'Alembert's Dream. Penguin.

Didion, Joan.
xDidion, Joan.
Slouching Towards Bethlehem. FS&G.
The White Album. PB.
The White Album. S&S.

DiDonno, Lupe.
xDiDonno, Lupe.
How to Design & Build Your Own House. Knopf.

Diebold Group. see Diebold Group, Inc. New York.

Diebold Group, Inc. New York.
xDiebold Group.
Automatic Data Processing Handbook. McGraw.

Diebold, William.
xDiebold, William.
Industrial Policy As an International Issue. McGraw.

Diederich, Bernard.
xDiederich, Bernard.
Trujillo: The Death of the Goat. Little.

Diederich, Paul B. see Diederich, Paul Bernard.

Diederich, Paul Bernard.
xDiederich, Paul B.

Measuring Growth in English. NCTE.

Diedrich, Richard C.
xDiedrich, Richard C.
Guidance Personnel & Other Professionals. HM.

Diefendorf, Jeffry M., 1945-
xDiefendorf, Jeffry M.
Businessmen & Politics in the Rhineland, 1789-1834. Princeton U Pr.

Diehl, Carl, 1947-
xDiehl, Carl.
Americans & German Scholarship, 1770-1870. Yale U Pr.

Diehl, Charles, 1859-1944
xDiehl, Charles.
History of the Byzantine Empire. AMS Pr.

Diehl, Gaston.
xDiehl, Gaston.
Derain. Crown.
The Fauves. Abrams.
Pascin. Crown.
Van Dongen. Crown.
Vasarely. Crown.

Diehl, James M.
xDiehl, James M.
Paramilitary Politics in Weimar Germany. Ind U Pr.

Diehl, Marcy O. see Diehl, Marcy Otis.

Diehl, Marcy Otis.
xDiehl, Marcy O.
Medical Transcribing: Techniques & Procedures. Saunders.

Diehl, William.
xDiehl, William.
Sharky's Machine. Delacorte.
Sharky's Machine. Dell.

Diehl, William E.
xDiehl, William E.
Christianity & Real Life. Fortress.

Diehr, George.
xDiehr, George.
Business Programming with BASIC. Wiley.

Diemer, Hugo.
xDiemer, Hugo.
Factory Organization & Administration. Arno.
Industrial Organization & Management. Hive Pub.

Diener, Edward.
xDiener, Edward.
Ethics in Social & Behavioral Research. U of Chicago Pr.

Diener, Royce.
xDiener, Royce.
How to Finance a Growing Business. Fell.

Diener, Theodor O. see Diener, Theodore Otto.

Diener, Theodore Otto, 1921-
xDiener, Theodor O.
Viroids & Viroid Diseases. Wiley.

Dienes, Andre De. see De Dienes, Andre.

Dienes, C. Thomas.
xDienes, C. Thomas.
Law, Politics, & Birth Control. U of Ill Pr.

Dienes, Leslie.
xDienes, Leslie.
Locational Factors & Locational Developments in the Soviet Chemical Industry. U Chicago Dept Geog.
The Soviet Energy System: Resource Use & Policies. Halsted Pr.

Dienhart, Charlotte M.
xDienhart, Charlotte M.
Basic Human Anatomy & Physiology. Saunders.

Dienstein, William, 1909-
xDienstein, William.
How to Write a Narrative Investigation Report. C C Thomas

Dienstfrey, Patricia.
xDienstfrey, Patricia.

Newspaper Stories & Other Poems. Berkeley Poets.

Diep, Bridgette. see Diep, Brigitte.

Diep, Brigitte.
xDiep, Bridgette.
Trip Through Cambodia. Scroll Pr.

Dierauf, E. see Dierauf, Edward J.

Dierauf, Edward J.
xDierauf, E.
Unified Concepts in Applied Physics. P-H.

Dieringer, Beverly.
xDieringer, Beverly.
The Paper Bead Book. McKay.

Dierker, E. see Dierker, Egbert.

Dierker, Egbert.
xDierker, E.
Topological Methods in Walrasian Economics. Springer-Verlag.

Dierks, Jack C. see Dierks, Jack Cameron.

Dierks, Jack Cameron.
xDierks, Jack C.
Leap to Arms: The Cuban Campaign of 1898. Lippincott.

Diers, Donna.
xDiers, Donna.
Research in Nursing Practice. Lippincott.

Dies, Auguste, 1875-1958
xDies, Auguste.
Autour de Platon: Essais de Critique et d'Histoire. Arno.

Dies, Martin, 1901-1972
xDies, Martin.
The Trojan Horse in America. Arno.

Diesing, Paul.
xDiesing, Paul.
Reason in Society: Five Types of Decisions & Their Social Conditions. Greenwood.
xDiesing, Paul R.
Patterns of Discovery in the Social Sciences. Aldine Pub.

Diesing, Paul R. see Diesing, Paul.

Diestel. see Diestel, Joseph.

Diestel, Joseph.
xDiestel.
Vector Measures. Am Math.

Dietary Allowances Committee. see National Academy of Sciences, Washington, D.C.

Dietary Consultants of the Iowa State Department of Health. see Iowa. State Department of Health.

Dieter, George. see Dieter, George Ellwood.

Dieter, George Ellwood.
xDieter, George.
Mechanical Metallurgy. McGraw.

Dieterich, Daniel, 1945-
xDieterich, Daniel.
ed. Teaching About Doublespeak. NCTE.

Dietiker, Simone R. see Dietiker, Simone Renaud.

Dietiker, Simone Renaud.
xDietiker, Simone R.
Franc-Parler. Heath.

Dietmeyer. see Dietmeyer, Donald Leo.

Dietmeyer, Donald Leo, 1932-
xDietmeyer.
Logic Design of Digital Systems. Allyn.

Dietrich, B. C.
xDietrich, B. C.
Death, Fate & the Gods: The Development of a Religious Idea in Greek Popular Belief & in Homer. Humanities.
The Origins of Greek Religion. De Gruyter.

Dietrich, C. F. see Dietrich, Cornelius Frank.

Dietrich, Cornelius Frank.
xDietrich, C. F.
Uncertainty, Calibration & Probability: The Statistics of Scientific & Industrial Measurement. Krieger.

Dietrich, Dorothy. see Dietrich, Dorothy M.

Dietrich, Dorothy M.
xDietrich, Dorothy.

ed. Reading & Revolution: Role of Reading in
    Today's Society. Intl Reading.
Dietrich, R. F.
    xDietrich, R. F.
        Portrait of the Artist As a Young Superman: A
            Study of Shaw's Novels. Brown Bk.
        Portrait of the Artist As a Young Superman: A
            Study of Shaw's Novels. U Presses Fla.
Dietrich, R. F. see Dietrich, Richard.
Dietrich, Richard.
    xDietrich, R. F.
        The Art of Fiction. HR&W.
Dietrich, Richard. see Dietrich, Richard F.
Dietrich, Richard F., 1936-
    xDietrich, Richard.
        ed. Realities of Literature. Wiley.
Dietrich, Richard V. see Dietrich, Richard Vincent.
Dietrich, Richard Vincent, 1924-
    xDietrich, Richard V.
        Geology & Virginia. U Pr of Va.
        Rocks & Rock Minerals. Wiley.
Dietz, Albert G. see Dietz, Albert George Henry.
Dietz, Albert George Henry.
    xDietz, Albert G.
        ed. Industrialized Building Systems for
            Housing. MIT Pr.
Dietz, Betty W. see Dietz, Elisabeth Hoffmann (Warner).
Dietz, David.
    xDietz, David.
        Stars & the Universe. Random.
Dietz, Elisabeth Hoffmann (Warner).
    xDietz, Betty W.
        Musical Instruments of Africa: Their Nature,
            Use & Place in the Life of a Deeply Musical
            People. John Day.
Dietz, Frederick C. see Dietz, Frederick Charles.
Dietz, Frederick Charles, 1888-
    xDietz, Frederick C.
        The Industrial Revolution. Greenwood.
Dietz, Henry A.
    xDietz, Henry A.
        Political Participation in a Non-Electoral
            Setting: The Urban Poor in Lima, Peru. Ohio
            U Ctr Intl.
Dietz, Lew, 1906-
    xDietz, Lew.
        The Allagash. Thorndike Pr.
        Jeff White: Young Trapper. Thorndike Pr.
Dietz, Peter. see Dietz, Peter O.
Dietz, Peter O.
    xDietz, Peter.
        Pension Funds: Measuring Investment
            Performance. Free Pr.
Dietze, Gottfried.
    xDietze, Gottfried.
        America's Political Dilemma: From Limited to
            Unlimited Democracy. Johns Hopkins.
        In Defense of Property. Inst Humane.
        Two Concepts of the Rule of Law. Liberty
            Fund.
Diffie, Bailey W. see Diffie, Bailey Wallys.
Diffie, Bailey Wallys.
    xDiffie, Bailey W.
        Foundations of the Portuguese Empire,
            1415-1850. U of Minn Pr.
        Prelude to Empire: Portugal Overseas Before
            Henry the Navigator. U of Nebr Pr.
Difloe, D. see Difloe, Donna.
Difloe, Donna.
    xDifloe, D.
        How to Buy Furniture. Macmillan.
DiGaetani, John L. see DiGaetani, John Louis.
DiGaetani, John Louis, 1943-
    xDiGaetani, John L.
        ed. Penetrating Wagner's Ring: An Anthology.
            Fairleigh Dickinson.
Digby, Anne.
    xDigby, Anne.
        Pauper Palaces. Routledge & Kegan.
Digges, Thomas A. see Digges, Thomas Atwood.

Digges, Thomas Atwood, 1741-1821
    xDigges, Thomas A.
        Adventures of Alonso. Irvington.
Diggins, Dean.
    xDiggins, Dean.
        The Human Personality. Little.
Diggins, John P.
    xDiggins, John P.
        The Bard of Savagery: Thorstein Veblen &
            Modern Social Theory. Continuum.
        Mussolini & Fascism: The View from America.
            Princeton U Pr.
Diggle, John. see Diggle, John W.
Diggle, John W.
    xDiggle, John.
        ed. Oxides & Oxide Films. Dekker.
    xDiggle, John W.
        ed. Oxides & Oxide Films. Dekker.
Diggory, Peter.
    xDiggory, Peter.
        Planning or Prevention: The New Face of
            Family Planning. Merrimack Bk Serv.
Diggs, Dorothy C.
    xDiggs, Dorothy C.
        Working Manual for Altar Guilds. Morehouse.
DiGiacomo, James.
    xDiGiacomo, James.
        Meet the Lord: Encounters with Jesus.
            Winston Pr.
DiGiulio, Robert C., 1949-
    xDiGiulio, Robert C.
        Effective Parenting: What's Your Style. Follett.
        When You Are a Single Parent. Abbey.
Dignan, Patrick J. see Dignan, Patrick Joseph.
Dignan, Patrick Joseph, 1905-
    xDignan, Patrick J.
        A History of the Legal Incorporation of
            Catholic Church Property in the United
            States (1784-1932). AMS Pr.
DiIorio, Gino J. see DiIorio, Gino Joseph.
DiIorio, Gino Joseph.
    xDiIorio, Gino J.
        Direct Physical Measurement of Mass Yields in
            Thermal Fission of Uranium. Garland Pub.
Dijkstra, Edsger Wybe.
    xDijkstra, Edward W.
        A Discipline of Programming. P-H.
Dijkstra, Edward W. see Dijkstra, Edsger Wybe.
Dik, S. C. see Dik, Simon C.
Dik, Simon C.
    xDik, S. C.
        Functional Grammar. Elsevier.
Diket, A. L.
    xDiket, A. L.
        Wha' Hae Wi' (Pender) Bled. Vantage.
Dikstein, S.
    xDikstein, S.
        ed. Fundamentals of Cell Pharmacology. C C
            Thomas.
Diles, David L.
    xDiles, David L.
        Twelfth Man in the Huddle. Word Bks.
Dilke, O. A. W. see Dilke, Oswald Ashton Wentworth.
Dilke, Oswald Ashton Wentworth.
    xDilke, O. A. W.
        The Ancient Romans: How They Lived &
            Worked. Dufour.
Dilker, Barbara, 1947-
    xDilker, Barbara.
        Stage Management Forms & Formats. Drama
            Bk.
Dill, John R.
    xDill, John R.
        Child Psychology in Contemporary Society.
            Allyn.
Dill, Marshall.
    xDill, Marshall.
        Germany: A Modern History. U of Mich Pr.
Dill, William R.
    xDill, William R.

Organization for Forecasting & Planning:
    Experience in the Soviet Union & the United
    States. Wiley.
Running the American Corporation. P-H.
Dilla, Harriette M. see Dilla, Harriette May.
Dilla, Harriette May, 1886-
    xDilla, Harriette M.
        Politics of Michigan 1865-1878. AMS Pr.
Dillard, Annie.
    xDillard, Annie.
        Holy the Firm. G K Hall.
        Holy the Firm. Har-Row.
Dillard, J. L. see Dillard, Joey Lee.
Dillard, Joey Lee, 1924-
    xDillard, J. L.
        All American English. Random.
        All-American English. Random.
        American Talk: Where Our Words Came from.
            Random.
Dillaway, Newton, 1904-
    xDillaway, Newton.
        Consent. Unity Bks.
Dille, Robert C.
    xDille, Robert C.
        ed. The Collected Works of Buck Rogers in the
            25th Century. A & W Pubs.
Dillenberger, John.
    xDillenberger, John.
        Protestant Thought & Natural Science: A
            Historical Interpretation. Greenwood.
Diller. see Diller, Mary Black.
Diller, Aubrey, 1903-
    xDiller, Aubrey.
        Race Mixture Among the Greeks Before
            Alexander. Greenwood.
Diller, Mary Black, 1899-
    xDiller.
        Drawing for Young Artists. G&D.
Diller, Robert.
    xDiller, Robert.
        Farm Ownership, Tenancy, & Land Use in the
            Nebraska Community. Arno.
Dilley, Frank B. see Dilley, Frank Brown.
Dilley, Frank Brown, 1886-
    xDilley, Frank B.
        Teacher Certification in Ohio & a Proposed
            Plan of Reconstruction. AMS Pr.
Dilley, Marjorie R. see Dilley, Marjorie Ruth.
Dilley, Marjorie Ruth, 1903-
    xDilley, Marjorie R.
        British Policy in Kenya Colony. Biblio Dist.
Dilligan, Robert J.
    xDilligan, Robert J.
        ed. Concordance to the English Poetry of
            Gerard Manley Hopkins. U of Wis Pr.
Dillingham, Pegge.
    xDillingham, Pegge.
        Sound Comics. P-H.
Dillingham, William B.
    xDillingham, William B.
        An Artist in the Rigging: The Early Work of
            Herman Melville. U of Ga Pr.
        Melville's Short Fiction, 1853-1856. U of Ga
            Pr.
Dillistone, Frederick W. see Dillistone, Frederick
    William.
Dillistone, Frederick William, 1903-
    xDillistone, Frederick W.
        The Christian Understanding of Atonement.
            Westminster.
Dillner, Martha H.
    xDillner, Martha H.
        Personalizing Reading Instruction in Middle,
            Junior & Senior High Schools. Macmillan.
Dillon, Bert.
    xDillon, Bert.
        A Chaucer Dictionary: Proper Names &
            Allusions Excluding Place Names. G K Hall.
Dillon, Catherine.
    xDillon, Catherine.

Beloved Captive. NAL.
Constantine Cay. NAL.
White Fires Burning. NAL.
The White Khan. NAL.

Dillon, George L., 1944-
xDillon, George L.
Introduction to Contemporary Linguistic
Semantics. P-H.

Dillon, J. B. see Dillon, Joseph B.

Dillon, Jacquelyn. see Dillon, Jacquelyn A.

Dillon, Jacquelyn A.
xDillon, Jacquelyn.
How to Design & Teach a Successful School
String & Orchestra Program. Kjos.

Dillon, John B. see Dillon, John Brown.

Dillon, John Brown, 1808?-1879
xDillon, John B.
History of Indiana from Its Earliest Exploration
by Europeans to the Close of Territorial
Government in 1816. Arno.

Dillon, John L.
xDillon, John L.
The Analysis of Response in Crop & Livestock
Production. Pergamon.

Dillon, Joseph B.
xDillon, J. B.
Thermal Insulation: Recent Developments.
Noyes.

Dillon, L. S. see Dillon, Lawrence S.

Dillon, Lawrence S.
xDillon, L. S.
The Genetic Mechanism & the Origin of Life.
Plenum Pub.
xDillon, Lawrence S.
Animal Variety: An Evolutionary Account.
Wm C Brown.

Dillon, Mark.
xDillon, Mark.
American Race Car Drivers. Lerner Pubns.

Dillon, Merton L. see Dillon, Merton Lynn.

Dillon, Merton Lynn, 1924-
xDillon, Merton L.
The Abolitionists: The Growth of a Dissenting
Minority. Norton.
The Abolitionists: The Growth of a Dissenting
Minority. N Ill U Pr.

Dillon, Michael, Dr.
xDillon, Michael.
A Dictionary of Chinese History. Biblio Dist.

Dillon, Myles, 1900-1972
xDillon, Myles.
The Cycles of the Kings. Folcroft.
Early Irish Literature. U of Chicago Pr.
tr. & Compiled by There Was a King in
Ireland: Five Tales from Oral Tradition. U of
Tex Pr.

Dillon, Ray. see Dillon, Ray D.

Dillon, Ray D.
xDillon, Ray.
Zero Base Budgeting for Health Care
Institutions. Aspen Systems.

Dillon, Richard. see Dillon, Richard H.

Dillon, Richard H.
xDillon, Richard.
High Steel. Celestial Arts.

Dillon, Richard S.
xDillon, Richard S.
Handbook of Endocrinology: Diagnosis &
Management of Endocrine & Metabolic
Disorders. Lea & Febiger.

Dillon, Roy. see Dillon, Roy D.

Dillon, Roy D.
xDillon, Roy.
Working with Animal Supplies & Services.
McGraw.

Dillow, Jody. see Dillow, Joseph.

Dillow, Joseph.
xDillow, Jody.

Speaking in Tongues. Zondervan.

Dillow, Joseph C.
xDillow, Joseph C.
Solomon on Sex. Nelson.

Dillow, Linda.
xDillow, Linda.
Creative Counterpart. Nelson.

Dilly, Martin.
xDilly, Martin.
This Is Model Flying. Transatlantic.

Dilman, Ilham.
xDilman, Ilham.
Morality & Inner Life: A Study in Plato's
"Gorgias". B&N.

Dilman, Vladimir M. see Dilman, Vladimir Mikhailovich.

Dilman, Vladimir Mikhailovich.
xDilman, Vladimir M.
Law of Deviation of Homeostasis & Diseases
of Aging. PSG Pub.

Dilts, Preston V.
xDilts, Preston V.
Core Studies in Obstetrics & Gynecology.
Williams & Wilkins.

Dilworth, James. see Dilworth, James B.

Dilworth, James B., 1939-
xDilworth, James.
Production & Operations Management:
Manufacturing & Nonmanufacturing.
Random.

Dimaras, C. T. see Dimaras, C. Th.

Dimaras, C. Th, 1904-
xDimaras, C. T.
History of Modern Greek Literature. State U
NY Pr.

DiMascio, Alberto.
xDiMascio, Alberto.
ed. Clinical Handbook of Psychopharmacology.
Aronson.

Dimbleby, Richard.
xDimbleby, Richard.
Elizabeth Our Queen. Greenwood.

DiMento, Joseph F.
xDiMento, Joseph F.
The Consistency Doctrine & the Limits of
Planning. Oelgeschlager.

Dimick, Kenneth M.
xDimick, Kenneth M.
Ladies in Waiting: Behind Prison Walls. Accel
Devel.

Dimier, Louis, 1865-1943
xDimier, Louis.
French Painting in the Sixteenth Century.
Arno.

Dimitrijevic, Dimitrije.
xDimitrijevic, Dimitrije.
Money & Finance in Contemporary
Yugoslavia. Irvington.

Dimitrovsky, H. Z. see Dimitrovsky, Hayim Zalman.

Dimitrovsky, Hayim Zalman.
xDimitrovsky, H. Z.
Exploring the Talmud. Ktav.

Dimmack, Max.
xDimmack, Max.
Noel Counihan. Intl Schol Bk Serv.

Dimmick, Robert L.
xDimmick, Robert L.
An Introduction to Experimental Aerobiology.
Krieger.

Dimmitt, Richard B. see Dimmitt, Richard Bertrand.

Dimmitt, Richard Bertrand.
xDimmitt, Richard B.
Actor Guide to the Talkies, 1949-1964.
Scarecrow.

Dimnet, Ernest, 1866-1954
xDimnet, Ernest.
The Art of Thinking. Fawcett.
The Art of Thinking. Folcroft.

Dimock, Edward C.
xDimock, Edward C.

The Literatures of India: An Introduction. U of
Chicago Pr.
Place of the Hidden Moon: Erotic Mysticism
in the Vaisnava-Sahajiya Cult of Bengal. U of
Chicago Pr.
tr. & ed. Thief of Love: Bengali Tales from
Court & Village. U of Chicago Pr.

Dimock, Marshall. see Dimock, Marshall E.

Dimock, Marshall E., 1907-
xDimock, Marshall.
Games Cats Play & Other Scrivelsby Tales.
Countryman.

Dimock, Marshall E. see Dimock, Marshall Edward.

Dimock, Marshall Edward, 1903-
xDimock, Marshall E.
Congressional Investigating Committees. AMS
Pr.
Free Enterprise & the Administrative State.
Greenwood.

DiMona, Joe. see Dimona, Joseph.

DiMona, Joseph.
xDiMona, Joe.
To the Eagle's Nest. Morrow.

Dimond, Paul R.
xDimond, Paul R.
Dilemma of Local Government: Discrimination
in the Provision of Public Services. Lexington
Bks.

Dimond, S. J. see Dimond, Stuart J.

Dimond, Stanley E. see Dimond, Stanley Ellwood.

Dimond, Stanley Ellwood.
xDimond, Stanley E.
Civics for Citizens. Lippincott.
Our American Government. Lippincott.

Dimond, Stuart J.
xDimond, S. J.
Neuropsychology: A Textbook of Systems &
Psychological Functions of the Human Brain.
Butterworths
xDimond, Stuart J.
ed. Evolution & Lateralization of the Brain.
NY Acad Sci.

Dimondstein, Geraldine.
xDimondstein, Geraldine.
Children Dance in the Classroom. Macmillan.
Exploring the Arts with Children. Macmillan.

Dimsdale, Marcus S. see Dimsdale, Marcus Southwell.

Dimsdale, Marcus Southwell.
xDimsdale, Marcus S.
A History of Latin Literature. Arno.

Dincauze, Dena F. see Dincauze, Dena Ferran.

Dincauze, Dena Ferran.
xDincauze, Dena F.
Cremation Cemeteries in Eastern
Massachusetts. Peabody Harvard.

Dinculeanu, N. see Dinculeanu, Nicolae.

Dinculeanu, Nicolae.
xDinculeanu, N.
Vector Measures. Pergamon.

Diner, Hasia R.
xDiner, Hasia R.
In the Almost Promised Land: American Jews
& Blacks, 1915-1935. Greenwood.

Diner, Steven J., 1944-
xDiner, Steven J.
A City & Its Universities: Public Policy in
Chicago, 1892-1919. U of NC Pr.

Dingerson, A. Gary.
xDingerson, Arthur G.
Practice Management in Preventive Dentistry.
Lippincott.

Dingerson, Arthur G. see Dingerson, A. Gary.

Dingle, H. see Dingle, Hugh.

Dingle, Hugh.
xDingle, H.
ed. Evolution of Insect Migration & Diapause.
Springer-Verlag.

Dingman, Roger.
xDingman, Roger.

Power in the Pacific: The Origins of Naval
Arms Limitation, 1914-1922. U of Chicago
Pr.
Dingwall, Eric J. *see* Dingwall, Eric John.
Dingwall, Eric John.
xDingwall, Eric J.
The American Woman: A Historical Study.
Octagon.
Frwd. by Racial Pride & Prejudice.
Greenwood.
Racial Pride & Prejudice. Negro U Pr.
Dingwall, John.
xDingwall, John.
Sunday Too Far Away!. Heinemann Ed.
Dingwall, Robert.
xDingwall, Robert.
Aspects of Illness. St Martin.
Readings in the Sociology of Nursing.
Churchill.
Dingwall, Robert J.
xDingwall, Robert J.
The Garden Answers. Cadillac.
Dingwall, William O. *see* Dingwall, William Orr.
Dingwall, William Orr.
xDingwall, William O.
A Survey of Linguistic Science. Greylock Pubs.
Dinham, Sarah M.
xDinham, Sarah M.
Exploring Statistics: An Introduction for
Psychology & Education. Brooks-Cole.
Dinitz, Simon.
xDinitz, Simon.
ed. Deviance: Studies in Definition,
Management, & Treatment. Oxford U Pr.
Dinkel, John J.
xDinkel, John J.
Management Science: Text & Applications.
Irwin.
Dinkin, Eleanor.
xDinkin, Eleanor.
Parallel Play for Parents: A Guide to
Playground Exercise. Nelson-Hall.
Dinkmeyer, Don. *see* Dinkmeyer, Don C.
Dinkmeyer, Don C.
xDinkmeyer, Don.
jt. auth. Adlerian Counseling & Psychotherapy.
Brooks-Cole.
The Encouragement Book: Becoming a Positive
Person. P-H.
xDinkmeyer, Don C.
Group Counseling: Theory & Practice. Peacock
Pubs.
Dinneen, Francis P.
xDinneen, Francis P.
An Introduction to General Linguistics.
Georgetown U Pr.
An Introduction to General Linguistics.
Irvington.
Dinnerstein, L. *see* Dinnerstein, Leonard.
Dinnerstein, Leonard.
xDinnerstein, L.
Leo Frank Case. Columbia U Pr.
xDinnerstein, Leonard.
ed. American Vistas. Oxford U Pr.
Natives & Strangers: Ethnic Groups & the
Building of America. Oxford U Pr.
ed. Uncertain Americans: Readings in Ethnic
History. Oxford U Pr.
Dinnsen, Daniel A.
xDinnsen, Daniel A.
ed. Current Approaches to Phonological
Theory. Ind U Pr.
Dinsdale, Tim.
xDinsdale, Tim.
Loch Ness Monster. Routledge & Kegan.
Dinsmoor, William B. *see* Dinsmoor, William Bell.
Dinsmoor, William Bell, 1886-
xDinsmoor, William B.

Athenian Archon List in the Light of Recent
Discoveries. Greenwood.
Dinsmore, Charles A. *see* Dinsmore, Charles Allen.
Dinsmore, Charles Allen, 1860-1941
xDinsmore, Charles A.
Great Poets & the Meaning of Life. Arno.
The Great Poets & the Meaning of Life. R
West.
Dinsmore, Francis W.
xDinsmore, Francis W.
Developing Tomorrow's Managers Today. Am
Mgmt.
Dinsmore, M. H. *see* Dinsmore, Maret H.
Dinsmore, Maret H.
xDinsmore, M. H.
What Really Happened When Christ Died.
Accent Bks.
Dintiman, George B.
xDintiman, George B.
Comprehensive Manual of Physical Education
Activities for Men. P-H.
Dinwiddy, Bruce.
xDinwiddy, Bruce.
Promoting African Enterprise. Verry.
Diomedi, Alexander.
xDiomedi, Alexander.
Sketches of Indian Life in the Pacific
Northwest. Ye Galleon.
Dion, Leon, 1923-
xDion, Leon.
Quebec: The Unfinished Revolution.
McGill-Queens U Pr.
Dion, Paula, 1939-
xDion, Paula.
Wings of Desire. Ballantine.
Dionetti, Michelle.
xDionetti, Michelle.
The Day Eli Went Looking for Bear. A-W.
Thalia Brown & the Blue Bug. A-W.
DiOrio, Al, 1950-
xDiOrio, Al.
Little Girl Lost: The Life & Hard Times of
Judy Garland. Manor Bks.
DiOrio, Dorothy M.
xDiOrio, Dorothy M.
Leconte De Lisle: A Hundred & Twenty Years
of Criticism, 1850-1970. Romance.
DiPalma, Raymond.
xDiPalma, Raymond.
Gallery Goers. SBD.
DiPerna, Antoinette R.
xDiPerna, Antoinette R.
Creativity for Your Child. Branden.
DiPerna, Paula.
xDiPerna, Paula.
The Complete Travel Guide to Cuba. St
Martin.
DiPorta, Leo.
xDiPorta, Leo.
Zen Running. Everest Hse.
Dippie, Brian. *see* Dippie, Brian W.
Dippie, Brian W.
xDippie, Brian.
Custer's Last Stand. Viking Pr.
Dirac, P. A. *see* Dirac, Paul Adrien Maurice.
Dirac, Paul A. *see* Dirac, Paul Adrien Maurice.
Dirac, Paul Adrien Maurice, 1902-
xDirac, P. A.
Spinors in Hilbert Space. Plenum Pub.
xDirac, Paul A.
General Theory of Relativity. Wiley.
Dircks, Richard.
xDircks, Richard.
Richard Cumberland. Twayne.
Dirheimer, Y. *see* Dirheimer, Yves.
Dirheimer, Yves, 1934-
xDirheimer, Y.

The Craniovertebral Region in Chronic
Inflammatory Rheumatic Diseases.
Springer-Verlag.
Dirks, Gerald E.
xDirks, Gerald E.
Canada's Refugee Policy: Indifference or
Opportunism?. McGill-Queens U Pr.
Dirks, John E. *see* Dirks, John Edward.
Dirks, John Edward, 1919-
xDirks, John E.
Critical Theology of Theodore Parker.
Greenwood.
Dirksen, Charles J.
xDirksen, Charles J.
Advertising Principles & Problems. Irwin.
Dirlam, Joel B.
xDirlam, Joel B.
Fair Competition: The Law & Economics of
Antitrust Policy. Greenwood.
Dirlik, Arif.
xDirlik, Arif.
Revolution & History: Origins of Marxist
Historiography in China, 1919-1937. U of Cal
Pr.
Dirsztay, Patricia.
xDirsztay, Patricia.
Church Furnishings: The Nadfas Guide.
Routledge & Kegan.
DiSaia, Philip J.
xDiSaia, Philip J.
Synopsis of Gynecologic Oncology. Wiley.
Disch, Thomas.
xDisch, Thomas.
Getting into Death. PB.
Disch, Thomas M.
xDisch, Thomas M.
ed. Bad Moon Rising. Ultramarine Pub.
The Early Science Fiction Stories of Thomas
M. Disch (1963-1966). Gregg.
The Genocides. Gregg.
The Genocides. PB.
On Wings of Song. Bantam.
On Wings of Song. St Martin.
ed. Strangeness. Avon.
Disend, Michael, 1945-
xDisend, Michael.
Stomping the Goyim. SBD.
Disher, Maurice W. *see* Disher, Maurice Willson.
Disher, Maurice Willson, 1893-
xDisher, Maurice W.
Clowns & Pantomimes. Arno.
Disick, Renee S.
xDisick, Renee S.
Individualizing Language Instruction: Strategies
& Methods. HarBraceJ.
Diska, Pat.
xDiska, Pat.
Andy Says Bonjour. Vanguard.
Disley, John.
xDisley, John.
Orienteering. Stackpole.
Disney, A. R. *see* Disney, Anthony R.
Disney, Anthony R., 1938-
xDisney, A. R.
Twilight of the Pepper Empire: Portuguese
Trade in Southwest India in the Early
Seventeenth Century. Harvard U Pr.
Disney, Doris D. *see* Disney, Doris Miles.
Disney, Doris M. *see* Disney, Doris Miles.
Disney, Doris Miles.
xDisney, Doris D.
At Some Forgotten Door. Manor Bks.
xDisney, Doris M.
Look Back on Murder. Ace Bks.
Only Couples Need Apply. NAL.
Disney (Walt) Productions.
xWalt Disley Studio.
illus. Walt Disney's Nursery Tales. Western
Pub.
xWalt Disney.

Donald Duck: Instant Millionaire. Western
Pub.
Mickey Mouse & Goofy: The Big Bear Scare.
Western Pub.
xWalt Disney Productions.
ABC. Western Pub.
The Aristocats. Random.
Black Hole. Western Pub.
The Black Hole. Western Pub.
Black Hole. Western Pub.
Black Hole. Western Pub.
The Black Hole Storybook. Random.
The Book of Tall Tales: Featuring "The Shaggy
Dog". Random.
Brer Rabbit & His Friends. Random.
Cars! Cars! Cars!: Featuring "The Love Bug" &
Other Fun on Wheels. Random.
The Circus Book Featuring "Toby Tyler".
Random.
Counting. Western Pub.
The Detective Book Featuring "Emil & the
Detectives". Random.
Donald Duck & the Super-Sticky Situation.
Western Pub.
Donald Duck Goes Camping. Western Pub.
Friends to Find. Western Pub.
Goofy Keeps Fit. Western Pub.
Goofy Presents the Olympics: A Fun &
Exciting History of the Olympics from the
Ancient Games to Today. Random.
Hidden Pictures. Western Pub.
How It Happens. Western Pub.
If I Met Winnie the Pooh. G&D.
The Love Bug. Random.
Magic Tricks. Western Pub.
Mickey & the Beanstalk. Random.
The Mickey Mouse Birthday Book. Random.
The Mickey Mouse Magic Book. Random.
The Mickey Mouse Make-It Book. Random.
Nursery Rhymes. Western Pub.
The Outdoor Adventure Book. Random.
People You See. Western Pub.
Puzzles. Western Pub.
The Rescuers. Western Pub.
Robin Hood & the Great Coach Robbery.
Random.
The Sorcerer's Apprentice. Random.
The Underwater Adventure Book Featuring
"20,000 Leagues Under the Sea". Random.
Walt Disney Characters Needlepoint
Workbook. Random.
Walt Disney Productions Presents Goofy's
Gags. Random.
Walt Disney Productions Presents "The Black
Hole". Random.
Walt Disney Productions Presents "the
Rescuers". Random.
Walt Disney Productions Presents "The Small
One". Random.
Walt Disney's Cinderella. Random.
Walt Disney's Mickey Mouse & Donald Duck
at the Circus. Random.
Walt Disney's Peter & the Wolf. Random.
Walt Disney's the Brave Little Tailor. Random.
Walt Disney's the Haunted House. Random.
Walt Disney's Winnie the Pooh & Tigger Too.
Random.
Walt Disney's 101 Dalmations. Random.
xWalt Disney Studio.

Bambi, Friends of the Forest. Western Pub.
Bambi's Fragrant Forest. Western Pub.
Brer Rabbit & the Tar Baby. Western Pub.
Donald Duck & the Witch Next Door.
Western Pub.
The Haunted Mansion. Western Pub.
Heidi. Western Pub.
Mickey Mouse & the Marvelous Smell
Machine. Western Pub.
Pooh & Piglet's Book of Big & Little. Western
Pub.
Pooh Sleepytime Stories. Western Pub.
Tigger & Winnie-the-Pooh. Western Pub.
The Walt Disney Song Book. Western Pub.
Walt Disney's Alice in Wonderland. Western
Pub.
Walt Disney's Bambi. Western Pub.
Walt Disney's Cinderella. Western Pub.
Walt Disney's Mickey Mouse: The Kitten
Sitters. Western Pub.
illus. Walt Disney's Mother Goose. Western
Pub.
Walt Disney's Peter & the Wolf. Western Pub.
Walt Disney's Pinocchio. Western Pub.
Walt Disney's Snow White & the Seven
Dwarfs. Western Pub.
Walt Disney's Story Land. Western Pub.
xWalt Disney Studios.
Bambi Saves the Day. Dutton.
Bambi's Big Day. Dutton.
Donald Duck & the Magic Mailbox. Western
Pub.
Donald Duck, It's Play Time!. Western Pub.
Donald Duck: The Play Along Book. Western
Pub.
Donald's Camping Adventure. Dutton.
Dumbo. Western Pub.
Giant Walt Disney Word Book. Western Pub.
Gingerbread Man. Western Pub.
Hello, Winnie-the-Pooh!. Western Pub.
If I Met Mickey Mouse. G&D.
The Jungle Book. Western Pub.
Mickey Mouse & the Great Lot Plot. Western
Pub.
Mickey Mouse & the Sunken Treasure. Dutton.
Mickey Mouse, Hideaway Island. Western Pub.
Mickey Mouse Takes a Vacation. Dutton.
Mickey's Circus Adventure. Dutton.
Old MacDonald Duck Had a Farm. Dutton.
Pinocchio & the Puppet Theater. Dutton.
Scrooge McDuck & the Vacant Lot. Dutton.
Snow White & the Seven Dwarfs. Western Pub.
Snow White's Party. Dutton.
illus. Uncle Remus Brer Rabbit Stories.
Western Pub.
Walt Disney's Christmas Parade. Western Pub.
Walt Disney's Li'l Bad Wolf Stories. Western
Pub.
illus. Walt Disney's Mickey & His Friends.
Western Pub.
Walt Disney's Pooh's Schoolhouse. Western
Pub.
Walt Disney's Winnie-the-Pooh Meets Tigger.
Western Pub.
Winnie the Pooh: Hungry for Money. Western
Pub.
Dison, Norma. see Dison, Norma Greenler.
Dison, Norma Greenler.
xDison, Norma.
Clinical Nursing Techniques. Mosby.
Simplified Drugs & Solutions for Nurses,
Including Arithmetic. Mosby.
Dispenza, Joseph.
xDispenza, Joseph.
The House of Alarcon. Coward.
Disque, Jerry.
xDisque, Jerry.

In Between: The Adolescents' Struggle for
Independence. Phi Delta Kappa.
Disque, Robert O.
xDisque, Robert O.
Applied Plastic Design in Steel. Krieger.
Dissemination Center-Bilingual-Bicultural Education. see
Dissemination Center for Bilingual Bicultural
Education.
Dissemination Center for Bilingual Bicultural Education.
xDissemination Center for Bilingual-Bicultural
Education.
Guide to Title Vii Esea Bilingual Bicultural
Projects: 1973-1974. Arno.
xDissemination Center-Bilingual-Bicultural
Education.
Mundo Fisico: Physical Science Worktext.
Barron.
Dissemination Center for Bilingual-Bicultural Education.
see Dissemination Center for Bilingual Bicultural
Education.
Dissent.
xDissent (Periodical).
Voices of Dissent. Arno.
Dissent (Periodical). see Dissent.
Disston, Harry, 1899-
xDisston, Harry.
Beginning the Rest of Your Life: A Guide to
an Active Retirement. A S Barnes.
Distad, Audree.
xDistad, Audree.
Come to the Fair. Har-Row.
Dakota Sons. Har-Row.
The Dream Runner. Har-Row.
The Dream Runner. Har-Row.
Distad, N. Merrill.
xDistad, N. Merrill.
Guessing at Truth: The Life of Julius Charles
Hare 1795-1855. Patmos Pr
DiStasio, J. I.
xDiStasio, J. I.
ed. Ultrasonics As a Medical Diagnostic Tool.
Noyes.
Distefano, Nestor.
xDistefano, Nestor.
Nonlinear Processes in Engineering: Dynamic
Programming, Invariant Imbedding,
Quasilinearization, Finite Element, System
Identification & Optimization. Acad Pr.
District of Columbia. Juvenile Court.
xU.S. Senate, Juvenile Court of the District of
Columbia.
Message from the President of the United
States Transmitting a Letter from the Judge
of the Juvenile Court of the District of
Columbia: A Report Covering the Work of
the Juvenile Court During the Period from
July 1, 1906 to June 30, 1926. Arno.
Ditchfield, P. H. see Ditchfield, Peter Hampson.
Ditchfield, Peter H. see Ditchfield, Peter Hampson.
Ditchfield, Peter Hampson, 1854-1930
xDitchfield, P. H.
Books Fatal to their Authors. Folcroft.
Books Fatal to Their Authors. Gordon Pr.
xDitchfield, Peter H.
Books Fatal to Their Authors. B Franklin.
Ditlea, Steve.
xDitlea, Steve.
A Simple Guide to Home Computers. A & W
Pubs.
Ditmanson, Harold H.
xDitmanson, Harold H.
Grace in Experience & Theology. Augsburg.
Ditmars, Raymond. see Ditmars, Raymond Lee.
Ditmars, Raymond L. see Ditmars, Raymond Lee.
Ditmars, Raymond Lee, 1876-1942
xDitmars, Raymond.
Strange Animals I Have Known. HarBraceJ.
xDitmars, Raymond L.

Confessions of a Scientist. Arno.
Strange Animals I Have Known. HarBraceJ.

Dittberner, Job L., 1939-
xDittberner, Job L.
End of Ideology & American Social Thought:
1930 to 1960. Univ Microfilms.

Dittman, Richard.
xDittman, Richard.
Physics in Everyday Life. McGraw.

Dittmar, Heinrich, 1870-
xDittmar, Heinrich.
Aischines von Sphettos: Studien zur
Literaturgeschichte der Sokratiker. Arno.

Dittmar, Norbert.
xDittmar, Norbert.
A Critical Survey of Sociolinguistics: Theory &
Application. St Martin.

Dittmer, Lowell.
xDittmer, Lowell.
Liu Shao-Ch'i & the Chinese Cultural
Revolution: The Politics of Mass Criticism. U
of Cal Pr.

Dittrick, Mark.
xDittrick, Mark.
The Bedbook. HarBraceJ.

Ditzel, Paul. see Ditzel, Paul C.

Ditzel, Paul C.
xDitzel, Paul.
Railroad Yard. Messner.

Diubaldo, Richard J.
xDiubaldo, Richard J.
Stefansson & the Canadian Arctic.
McGill-Queens U Pr.

Div. of Earth Sciences. see National Academy of
Sciences, Washington, D.C.

Divac, Ivan.
xDivac, Ivan.
ed. The Neostriatum: Proceedings of a
Workshop Sponsored by the European Brain
& Behaviour Society, Denmark, 17-19 April
1978. Pergamon.

Divari, Nikolai B. see Divari, Nikolai Borisovich.

Divari, Nikolai Borisovich.
xDivari, Nikolai B.
ed. Atmospheric Optics. Plenum Pub.

Dively, George S., 1902-
xDively, George S.
Power of Professional Management. Am Mgmt.

DiVincenti, Marie.
xDiVincenti, Marie.
Administering Nursing Service. Little.

Divine, James. see Divine, James H.

Divine, James H.
xDivine, James.
How to Beat Test Anxiety & Score Higher on
Your Exams. Barron.

Divine, Robert A.
xDivine, Robert A.
ed. American Foreign Policy. NAL.
ed. Cuban Missile Crisis. New Viewpoints.
Illusion of Neutrality. U of Chicago Pr.
The Reluctant Belligerent: American Entry into
World War II. Krieger.
The Reluctant Belligerent: American Entry into
World War II. Wiley.

Division Of Behavioral Sciences. see National Academy
of Sciences, Washington, D.C.

Division of Biology & Agriculture. see National Academy
of Sciences, Washington, D.C.

Division Of Biology And Agriculture. see National
Academy of Sciences, Washington, D.C.

Division of Chemistry & Chemical Technology. see
National Academy of Sciences, Washington, D.C.

Division of Chemistry and Chemical Technology. see
National Academy of Sciences, Washington, D.C.

Division Of Earth Sciences. see National Academy of
Sciences, Washington, D.C.

Division Of Engineering. see National Academy of
Sciences, Washington, D.C.

Division of Mathematics - Committee on Support of

Research in Mathematical Sciences. see National
Academy of Sciences, Washington, D.C.

Division of Medical Sciences. see National Academy of
Sciences, Washington, D.C.

Division of Medical Sciences, Assembly of Life Sciences,
National Research Council. see National Academy of
Sciences, Washington, D.C.

Division of Medical Sciences, National Research Council.
see National Academy of Sciences, Washington, D.C.

Division of Medical Sciences, NRC. see National
Academy of Sciences, Washington, D.C.

Division of Physical Sciences. see National Academy of
Sciences, Washington, D.C.

DIVO Institut fuer Wirtschaftsforschung, Sozialforschung
und angewandte Mathematik. see DIVO-Institut,
Frankfurt-Am-Main.

DIVO-Institut, Frankfurt-Am-Main.
xDIVO Institut fuer Wirtschaftsforschung,
Sozialforschung und angewandte Mathematik.
German Election Study, October 1965. ICPSR.

Divry, George C. see Divry, George Constantopoulos.

Divry, George Constantopoulos, 1890-
xDivry, George C.
Divry's English-To-Greek Phrase &
Conversation Pronouncing Manual. Divry.

Diwan, Romesh.
xDiwan, Romesh K.
Alternative Development Strategies &
Appropriate Technology: Science Policy for
an Equitable World Order. Pergamon.

Diwan, Romesh K. see Diwan, Romesh.

Dix, Carol.
xDix, Carol.
The Camargue. Verry.

Dix, Carol. see Dix, Carol M.

Dix, Carol M.
xDix, Carol.
D. H. Lawrence & Women. Rowman.

Dix, Dorothea L. see Dix, Dorothea Lynde.

Dix, Dorothea Lynde, 1802-1887
xDix, Dorothea L.
On Behalf of the Insane Poor: Selected Reports
1843-1852. Arno.

Dix, Ernest R. see Dix, Ernest Reginald McClintock.

Dix, Ernest Reginald McClintock, 1857-1936
xDix, Ernest R.
Catalogue of Early Dublin Printed Books,
1601-1700. B Franklin.
Printing in Dublin Prior to 1601. B Franklin.

Dix, Samuel M.
xDix, Samuel M.
Energy: A Critical Decision for the United
States Economy. Energy Educ.

Dixit, A. K. see Dixit, Avinash K.

Dixit, Avinash. see Dixit, Avinash K.

Dixit, Avinash K.
xDixit, A. K.
Optimization in Economic Theory. Oxford U
Pr.
xDixit, Avinash.
The Theory of Equilibrium Growth. Oxford U
Pr.

Dixon. see Dixon, Franklin W.

Dixon, C. Willis. see Dixon, Cyril Willis.

Dixon, Conrad.
xDixon, Conrad.
Navigation by Pocket Calculator. Scribner.

Dixon, Cyril Willis.
xDixon, C. Willis.
Colonial Administrations of Sir Thomas
Maitland. Kelley.

Dixon, Franklin W.
xDixon.
The Pentagon Spy. Wanderer Bks.
xDixon, Franklin W.

The Apeman's Secret. Wanderer Bks.
Arctic Patrol Mystery. G&D.
The Clue in the Embers. G&D.
Clue of the Broken Blade. G&D.
The Clue of the Hissing Serpent. G&D.
Clue of the Screeching Owl. G&D.
Crisscross Shadow. G&D.
Danger on Vampire Trail. G&D.
Disappearing Floor. G&D.
Flickering Torch Mystery. G&D.
Footprints Under the Window. G&D.
Great Airport Mystery. G&D.
Hardy Boys Handbook: Seven Stories of
Survival. Wanderer Bks.
Hooded Hawk Mystery. G&D.
House on the Cliff. G&D.
Hunting for Hidden Gold. G&D.
Mark on the Door. G&D.
The Masked Monkey. G&D.
Melted Coins. G&D.
The Mystery of the Samurai Sword. S&S.
Night of the Werewolf. S&S.
Sign of the Crooked Arrow. G&D.
The Sting of the Scorpion. G&D.
Twisted Claw. G&D.
While the Clock Ticked. G&D.

Dixon, J C.
xDixon, J. C.
ed. Continuing Education in the Later Years. U
Presses Fla.

Dixon, James M. see Dixon, James Main.

Dixon, James Main, 1856-1933
xDixon, James M.
Matthew Arnold. Folcroft.

Dixon, Janice T.
xDixon, Janice T.
Preserving Your Past: A Painless Guide to
Writing Your Autobiography & Family
History. Doubleday.

Dixon, Jeane.
xDixon, Jeane.
The Call to Glory: Jeane Dixon Speaks of
Jesus. Morrow.
Horoscopes for Dogs. HM.

Dixon, John D.
xDixon, John D.
Problems in Group Theory. Dover.

Dixon, John R.
xDixon, John R.
Design Engineering: Inventiveness, Analysis &
Decision Making. McGraw.
A Programmed Introduction to Probability.
Krieger.

Dixon, John W.
xDixon, John W.
Art & Theological Imagination. Seabury.
The Physiology of Faith: A Theory of
Theological Relativity. Har-Row.

Dixon, Keith.
xDixon, Keith.
Sociological Theory: Pretence & Possibility.
Routledge & Kegan.

Dixon, Lyle J.
xDixon, Lyle J.
Mathematics for Elementary Teachers. Merrill.

Dixon, M. see Dixon, Maynard.

Dixon, Marlene.
xDixon, Marlene.
Health Care in Crisis: Essays on Health
Services Under Capitalism. Synthesis Pubns.
Women in Class Struggle. Synthesis Pubns.

Dixon, Maynard.
xDixon, M.
Maynard Dixon Sketch Book. Northland.

Dixon, Norman.
xDixon, Norman.
Georgian Pistols: The Art & Craft of the
Flintlock Pistol, 1715-1840. Shumway.
xDixon, Norman F.

On the Psychology of Military Incompetence.
Basic.
Dixon, Norman F. *see* Dixon, Norman.
Dixon, Pahl.
xDixon, Pahl.
Hot Skateboarding. Warner Bks.
Dixon, Paige.
xDixon, Paige.
Lion on the Mountain. Atheneum.
May I Cross Your Golden River. Atheneum.
Silver Wolf. Atheneum.
Silver Wolf. Atheneum.
Summer of the White Goat. Atheneum.
Dixon, R. *see* Dixon, Robert T.
Dixon, R. A. *see* Dixon, R. A. N.
Dixon, R. A. N.
xDixon, R. A.
Spain. Rand.
Dixon, R. J.
xDixon, R. J.
Regional Growth & Unemployment in the
United Kingdom. Holmes & Meier.
Dixon, R. L. *see* Dixon, Robert L.
Dixon, R. M. *see* Dixon, Robert M. W.
Dixon, Robert. *see* Dixon, Robert L.
Dixon, Robert G. *see* Dixon, Robert Galloway.
Dixon, Robert Galloway.
xDixon, Robert G.
Standards Development in the Private Sector:
Thoughts on Interest Representation &
Procedural Fairness. Natl Fire Prot.
Dixon, Robert L.
xDixon, R. L.
Executive's Accounting Primer. McGraw.
xDixon, Robert.
Essentials of Accounting. Macmillan.
Dixon, Robert M. W.
xDixon, R. M.
A Grammar of Yidin. Cambridge U Pr.
ed. Grammatical Categories in Australian
Languages. Humanities.
Handbook of Australian Languages.
Humanities.
Dixon, Robert S.
xDixon, Robert S.
A Master List of Nonstellar Optical
Astronomical Objects. Ohio St U Pr.
Dixon, Robert T.
xDixon, R.
Dynamic Astronomy. P-H.
xDixon, Robert.
Dynamic Astronomy. P-H.
Physical Science: A Dynamic Approach. P-H.
Dixon, Roland B. *see* Dixon, Roland Burrage.
Dixon, Roland Burrage, 1875-1934
xDixon, Roland B.
Oceanic Mythology. Cooper Sq.
Dixon, Samuel L., 1934-
xDixon, Samuel L.
Working with People in Crisis: Theory &
Practice. Mosby.
Dixon, Stephen, 1936-
xDixon, Stephen.
No Relief. Street Fiction.
Work. Street Fiction.
Dixon, Thomas, 1864-1946
xDixon, Thomas.
The Clansman: An Historical Romance of the
Ku Klux Klan. U Pr of Ky.
The Fall of a Nation: Sequel to the Birth of a
Nation. Arno.
Dixon, W. J. *see* Dixon, Wilfrid Joseph.
Dixon, W. Macneile. *see* Dixon, William Macneile.
Dixon, W. T.
xDixon, W. T.
Theory & Interpretation of Magnetic
Resonance Spectra. Plenum Pub.
Dixon, Wilfrid J. *see* Dixon, Wilfrid Joseph.
Dixon, Wilfrid Joseph.
xDixon, W. J.

Exploring Data Analysis: The Computer
Revolution in Statistics. U of Cal Pr.
xDixon, Wilfrid J.
Introduction to Statistical Analysis. McGraw.
Dixon, William H. *see* Dixon, William Hepworth.
Dixon, William Hepworth, 1821-1879
xDixon, William H.
White Conquest. Arno.
Dixon, William M. *see* Dixon, William Macneile.
Dixon, William Macneile, 1866-1945
xDixon, W. Macneile.
The Edinburgh Book of Scottish Verse.
Folcroft.
ed. Edinburgh Book of Scottish Verse,
1300-1900. AMS Pr.
English Epic & Heroic Poetry. Haskell.
The Human Situation. Folcroft.
The Human Situation. Gordon Pr.
xDixon, William M.
An Apology for the Arts. Arden Lib.
Edinburgh Book of Scottish Verse, 1300-1900.
AMS Pr.
English Epic & Heroic Poetry. AMS Pr.
Dixson, Robert J. *see* Dixson, Robert James.
Dixson, Robert James.
xDixson, Robert J.
Practical Guide to the Teaching of English As
a Foreign Language. Regents Pub.
Dixson, Zella. *see* Dixson, Zella (Allen).
Dixson, Zella (Allen), Mrs, 1858-1924
xDixson, Zella.
Comprehensive Subject Index to Universal
Prose Fiction. Folcroft.
A Comprehensive Subject Index to Universal
Prose Fiction. Gordon Pr.
Dizenzo, Patricia.
xDizenzo, Patricia.
An American Girl. Avon.
Dizikes, John, 1932-
xDizikes, John.
Britain, Roosevelt & the New Deal: British
Opinion, 1932-1938. Garland Pub.
Djamour, Judith.
xDjamour, Judith.
Muslim Matrimonial Court in Singapore.
Humanities.
Djerassi, Carl.
xDjerassi, Carl.
The Politics of Contraception. Norton.
Djindjian, R. *see* Djindjian, Rene.
Djindjian, Rene.
xDjindjian, R.
Super-Selective Arteriography of the External
Carotid Artery. Springer-Verlag.
Dlab, Vlastimil.
xDlab, Vlastimil.
Indecomposable Representations of Graphs &
Algebras. Am Math.
Dlugatch, Irving, 1910-
xDlugatch, Irving.
Dynamic Cost Reduction. Wiley.
Dlugosch, Sharon.
xDlugosch, Sharon.
Folding Table Napkins: A New Look at a
Traditional Craft. Brighton Pubns.
Dmytryshyn, Basil, 1925-
xDmytryshyn, Basil.
A History of Russia. P-H.
Imperial Russia: A Source Book 1700-1917.
HR&W.
ed. Medieval Russia: A Source Book,
900-1700. HR&W.
U.S.S.R.: A Concise History. Scribner.
Doak, G. O. *see* Doak, George Osmore.
Doak, George Osmore.
xDoak, G. O.
Organometallic Compounds of Arsenic,
Antimony, & Bismuth. Krieger.
Doan, Daniel, 1914-
xDoan, Daniel.

Dan Doan's Fitness Program for Hikers &
Cross-Country Skiers. NH Pub Co.
Doan, Robert L.
xDoan, Robert L.
Arts & Crafts Achievement Activities. Ctr
Appl Res.
Number Readiness Achievement Activities. Ctr
Appl Res.
Science Discovery Achievement Activities. Ctr
Appl Res.
Social Living Achievement Activities. Ctr Appl
Res.
Doane Agricultural Service. *see* Doane Agricultural
Service, St. Louis.
Doane Agricultural Service, St. Louis.
xDoane Agricultural Service.
Potawatomie Reserve Lands in Kansas, Sold by
the Prairie Band, Potawatomie Indians to the
Santa Fe Railroad, 1868: Appraisal.
Clearwater Pub.
Doane, Donald C. *see* Doane, Donald Calvin.
Doane, Donald Calvin, 1906-
xDoane, Donald C.
Needs of Youth: An Evaluation for Curriculum
Purposes. AMS Pr.
Doane, Doris C. *see* Doane, Doris Chase.
Doane, Doris Chase.
xDoane, Doris C.
How to Read Tarot Cards. T Y Crowell.
xDoane, Doris Chase.
How to Read Tarot Cards. B&N.
Dobb, Maurice. *see* Dobb, Maurice Herbert.
Dobb, Maurice H. *see* Dobb, Maurice Herbert.
Dobb, Maurice Herbert, 1900-
xDobb, Maurice.
Capitalism, Yesterday & Today. Beekman Pubs.
On Economic Theory & Socialism. Collected
Papers. Routledge & Kegan.
Soviet Economic Development Since 1917.
Routledge & Kegan.
xDobb, Maurice H.
Capitalist Enterprise & Social Progress.
Hyperion Conn.

Dobbert, John.

xDobbert, John.

Dear Dawn, Dear Dad. Revell.
Give Yourself a Chance. Revell.
If Being a Christian Is So Great, Why Do I
Have the Blahs?. Regal.

Dobbins, Bill.
xDobbins, Bill.
The Gold's Gym Weight-Training Book:
Building a Beautiful, Strong, & Healthy Body.
J P Tarcher.
Dobbins, Gaines S. *see* Dobbins, Gaines Stanley.
Dobbins, Gaines Stanley, 1886-
xDobbins, Gaines S.
Learning to Lead. Broadman.
Dobbins, Richard A.
xDobbins, Richard A.
Atmospheric Motion & Air Pollution: An
Introduction for Students of Engineering &
Science. Wiley.
Dobbs, Archibald E. *see* Dobbs, Archibald Edward.
Dobbs, Archibald Edward, 1882-
xDobbs, Archibald E.
Education & Social Movements 1700-1850.
Kelley.
Dobbs, D. E. *see* Dobbs, David E.
Dobbs, David E.
xDobbs, D. E.
Cech Cohomological Dimensions for
Commutative Rings. Springer-Verlag.
Dobbs, Frank W.
xDobbs, Frank W.

Age of the Molecule: Chemistry in the World
& Society. Har-Row.
Dobby, E. H. see Dobby, Ernest Henry George.
Dobby, Ernest Henry George.
xDobby, E. H.
Southeast Asia. Verry.
Dobell, Bertram, 1842-1914
xDobell, Bertram.
Catalogue of Books Printed for Private
Circulation. Gale.
Sidelights on Charles Lamb. Folcroft.

Dobelstein, A. see Dobelstein, Andrew W.

Dobelstein, Andrew W.
xDobelstein, A.
Politics, Economics, & the Public Welfare. P-H.

Dober, Richard P.
xDober, Richard P.
Environmental Design. Krieger.

Dobereiner, Peter.
xDobereiner, Peter.
Golf Explained: How to Take Advantage of the
Rules. Sterling.

Dobie, Ann B.
xDobie, Ann B.
Comprehension & Composition: An
Introduction to the Essay. Macmillan.

Dobie, G. Vera.
xDobie, G. Vera.
Alphonse Daudet. Folcroft.

Dobie, J. Frank. see Dobie, James Frank.

Dobie, James Frank, 1888-1964
xDobie, J. Frank.
Apache Gold & Yaqui Silver. Little.
Apache Gold & Yaqui Silver. U of NM Pr.
ed. Coffee in the Gourd. SMU Press.
Coronado's Children: Tales of Lost Mines &
Buried Treasures of the Southwest. U of Tex
Pr.
Cow People. Little.
ed. Follow De Drinkin' Gou'd. SMU Press.
I'll Tell You a Tale. Little.
ed. Legends of Texas. SMU Press.
The Mustangs. Little.
Prefaces. Little.
ed. Rainbow in the Morning. SMU Press.
Rattlesnakes. Little.
Some Part of Myself. Little.
Some Part of Myself. U of Tex Pr.
ed. Southwestern Lore. SMU Press.
ed. Straight Texas. SMU Press.
Tales of Old-Time Texas. Little.

Dobin, Abraham, 1907-
xDobin, Abraham.
Fertile Fields: Recollections & Reflections of a
Busy Life. A S Barnes.

Dobkin, Alexander, 1908-
xDobkin, Alexander.
Principles of Figure Drawing. T Y Crowell.

Dobkowski, Michael N.
xDobkowski, Michael N.
The Tarnished Dream: The Basis of American
Anti-Semitism. Greenwood.

Dobler, Lavinia. see Dobler, Lavinia G.

Dobler, Lavinia G.
xDobler, Lavinia.
Arrow Book of the United Nations. Schol Bk
Serv.

Doblin, Alfred, 1878-1957
xDoblin, Alfred.
Men Without Mercy. Fertig.

Doblin, Jay, 1920-
xDoblin, Jay.
Perspective: A New System for Designers.
Watson-Guptill.

Dobree, Bonamy, 1891-
xDobree, Bonamy.

Alexander Pope. Greenwood.
Amateur & the Theatre. Folcroft.
The Broken Cistern. Haskell.
English Essayists. Folcroft.
English Literature in the Early Eighteenth
Century, 1700-1740. Oxford U Pr.
ed. Five Heroic Plays. Greenwood.
Histriophone: A Dialogue on Dramatic Diction.
Folcroft.

Dobrian, Walter A.
xDobrian, Walter A.
Conversational Spanish. Har-Row.

Dobrin, Arnold.
xDobrin, Arnold.
A Life for Israel: The Story of Golda Meir.
Dial.

Dobroszycki, Lucjan.
xDobroszycki, Lucjan.
Image Before My Eyes: A Photographic
History of Jewish Life in Poland, 1864-1939.
Schocken.

Dobson, Austin, 1840-1921
xDobson, Austin.
Eighteenth Century Vignettes. Folcroft.
Eighteenth Century Vignettes. Scholarly.
Fielding. AMS Pr.
Fielding. Darby Bks.
Fielding. Norwood Edns.
Life of Oliver Goldsmith. Arno.
Life of Oliver Goldsmith. R West.
Richard Steele. R West.
Richard Steele. Scholarly.
Thomas Bewick & His Pupils. Gale.

Dobson, Christopher.
xDobson, Christopher.
The Carlos Complex: A Study in Terror.
Putnam.
The Cruelest Night. Little.
The Terrorists: Their Weapons, Leaders &
Tactics. Facts on File.

Dobson, E. J. see Dobson, Eric John.

Dobson, Eric John.
xDobson, E. J.
Moralities on the Gospels: A New Source of
Ancrene Wisse. Oxford U Pr.
The Origins of Ancrene Wisse. Oxford U Pr.

Dobson, J. F. see Dobson, John Frederic.

Dobson, James, 1936-
xDobson, James.
Dare to Discipline. Bantam.
Dare to Discipline. Tyndale.

Dobson, James. see Dobson, James C.

Dobson, James C., 1936-
xDobson, James.
Hide or Seek. Revell.
Preparing for Adolescence. Bantam.
Preparing for Adolescence. Vision Hse.
What Wives Wish Their Husbands Knew
About Women. Tyndale.

Dobson, John F. see Dobson, John Frederic.

Dobson, John Frederic, 1875-1947
xDobson, J. F.
The Greek Orators. Ares.
The Greek Orators. R West.
xDobson, John F.
Ancient Education & Its Meaning for Us.
Cooper Sq.
Greek Orators. Arno.

Dobson, John H.
xDobson, John H.
A Guide to the Book of Exodus. Judson.

Dobson, John M.
xDobson, John M.
America's Ascent: The United States Becomes
a Great Power, 1880-1914. N Ill U Pr.

Dobson, Margaret J.
xDobson, Margaret J.
Softball for Girls. Krieger.

Dobson, Narda.
xDobson, Narda.

History of Belize. Longman.
Dobson, Rosemary.
xDobson, Rosemary.
tr. Seven Russian Poets: Imitations. U of
Queensland Pr.
Dobson, Theodore. see Dobson, Theodore Elliott.
Dobson, Theodore Elliott.
xDobson, Theodore.
Inner Healing: God's Great Assurance. Paulist
Pr.
Dobson, W. A. see Dobson, W. A. C. H.
Dobson, W. A. C. H.
xDobson, W. A.
Late Han Chinese: A Study of the Archaic-Han
Shift. U of Toronto Pr.
Doby, John T. see Doby, John Thomas.
Doby, John Thomas, 1920-
xDoby, John T.
Introduction to Social Psychology. Irvington.
Introduction to Social Research. Irvington.
Doby, T. see Doby, Tibor.
Doby, Tibor.
xDoby, T.
Development of Angiography & Cardiovascular
Catheterization. Psg Pub.
Dobyns, Henry F.
xDobyns, Henry F.
Peasants, Power, & Applied Social Change:
Vicos As a Model. Sage.
Spanish Colonial Tucson: A Demographic
History. U of Ariz Pr.
Dobzhansky, Theodosius. see Dobzhansky, Theodosius
Grigorievich.
Dobzhansky, Theodosius Grigorievich, 1900-1975
xDobzhansky, Theodosius.
Evolution. W H Freeman.
Genetic Diversity & Human Equality. Basic.
Genetics & the Origin of Species. Columbia U
Pr.
Genetics of the Evolutionary Process.
Columbia U Pr.
Doche, Viviane.
xDoche, Viviane.
Cedars by the Mississippi: The
Lebanese-Americans in the Twin-Cities. R &
E Res Assoc.
Docherty, Thomas Henderson.
xDocherty, Tommy.
ABC of Soccer Sense: Strategy & Tactics in
Modern Soccer. Arco.
Docherty, Tommy. see Docherty, Thomas Henderson.
Dock, V. Thomas.
xDock, V. Thomas.
Principles of Business Data Processing. SRA.
Dockery, Wallene T.
xDockery, Wallene T.
Gabby's Christmas Wish. Shoal Creek Pub.
Dockstader, Frederick J.
xDockstader, Frederick J.
Great North American Indians: Profiles in Life
& Leadership. Van Nos Reinhold.
Weaving Arts of the North American Indian. T
Y Crowell.
Doctoroff, Michael.
xDoctoroff, Michael.
Synergistic Management: Creating the Climate
for Superior Performance. Am Mgmt.
Doctorow, E. L., 1931-
xDoctorow, E. L.
Ragtime. Bantam.
Ragtime. G K Hall.
Ragtime. Random.
Dodd. see Dodd, Lawrence C.
Dodd, C. H. see Dodd, Charles Harold.
Dodd, Charles H. see Dodd, Charles Harold.
Dodd, Charles Harold, 1884-
xDodd, C. H.
The Meaning of Paul for Today. Collins Pubs.
Parables of the Kingdom. Scribner.
xDodd, Charles H.

Founder of Christianity. Macmillan.
Historical Tradition in the Fourth Gospel.
Cambridge U Pr.
Meaning of Paul for Today. NAL.
Dodd, Clement Henry.
xDodd, C. H.
Politics & Government in Turkey. U of Cal Pr.
Dodd, Donald B.
xDodd, Donald B.
Historical Atlas of Alabama. U of Ala Pr.
Dodd, Edward. *see* Dodd, Edward Howard.
Dodd, Edward Howard, 1905-
xDodd, Edward.
Polynesia's Sacred Isle. Dodd.
Dodd, George, 1808-1881
xDodd, George.
Days at the Factories. Kelley.
The Food of London. Arno.
Dodd, George G.
xDodd.
ed. Computer Vision & Sensor-Based Robots.
Plenum Pub.
Dodd, Gerald D.
xDodd, Gerald D.
Radiology of the Nose, Paranasal Sinuses &
Nasopharynx. Williams & Wilkins.
Dodd, Harold.
xDodd, Harold.
The Pathology and Surgery of the Veins of the
Lower Limb. Churchill.
Dodd, John D. *see* Dodd, John Durrance.
Dodd, John Durrance.
xDodd, John D.
Course Book in General Botany. Iowa St U Pr.
Dodd, Lawrence C., 1946-
xDodd.
Congress Reconsidered. Congr Quarterly.
xDodd, Lawrence C.
Coalitions in Parliamentary Government.
Princeton U Pr.
Congress & the Administrative State. Wiley.
Congress Reconsidered. HR&W.
Dodd, Lynley.
xDodd, Lynley.
The Nickle Nackle Tree. Macmillan.
Dodd, Marguerite.
xDodd, Marguerite.
America's Cook Book. Scribner.
Dodd, Marylin J.
xDodd, Marylin J.
Oncology Nursing Case Studies. Med Exam.
Dodd Mead & Co. *see* Dodd, Mead and Company,
Publishers, New York.
Dodd, Mead and Company, Publishers, New York.
xDodd Mead & Co.
One Hundred Twenty Fifth Anniversary
Anthology. Dodd.
Dodd, William E. *see* Dodd, William Edward.
Dodd, William Edward, 1869-1940
xDodd, William E.
The Life of Nathaniel Macon. Scholarly.
Life of Nathaniel Macon 1757-1837. B
Franklin.
Doddridge, Joseph, 1769-1826
xDoddridge, Joseph.
Notes, on the Settlement & Indian Wars, of the
Western Parts of Virginia & Pennsylvania,
from the Year 1763 Until the Year 1783
Inclusive. Garland Pub.
Dodds, Annie E. *see* Dodds, Annie Edwards Powell.
Dodds, Annie Edwards Powell.
xDodds, Annie E.
The Romantic Theory of Poetry: An
Examination in the Light of Croce's
Aesthetic. AMS Pr.
Dodds, E. D. *see* Dodds, Elisabeth D.
Dodds, E. R. *see* Dodds, Eric Robertson.
Dodds, Elisabeth D.
xDodds, E. D.

illus. Marriage to a Difficult Man: The
Uncommon Union of Jonathan & Sarah
Edwards. Westminster.
xDodds, Elizabeth D.
Marriage to a Difficult Man: The Uncommon
Union of Jonathan & Sarah Edwards.
Westminster.
Dodds, Elizabeth D. *see* Dodds, Elisabeth D.
Dodds, Eric R. *see* Dodds, Eric Robertson.
Dodds, Eric Robertson, 1893-
xDodds, E. R.
Missing Persons: An Autobiography. Oxford U
Pr.
Pagan & Christian in an Age of Anxiety: Some
Aspects of Religious Experience from Marcus
Aurelius to Constantine. Norton.
xDodds, Eric R.
The Greeks & the Irrational. U of Cal Pr.
Dodds, Harold W. *see* Dodds, Harold Willis.
Dodds, Harold Willis, 1889-
xDodds, Harold W.
The Academic President: Educator or
Caretaker?. Greenwood.
Dodds, J. C.
xDodds, J. C.
The Investment Behaviour of British Life
Insurance Companies. Biblio Dist.
Dodds, J. W. *see* Dodds, John Wendell.
Dodds, John W. *see* Dodds, John Wendell.
Dodds, John Wendell, 1902-
xDodds, J. W.
Thomas Southerne Dramatist. Century
Bookbindery.
xDodds, John W.
Age of Paradox: A Biography of England,
1841-1851. Greenwood.
Doder, Dusko.
xDoder, Dusko.
The Yugoslavs. Random.
The Yugoslavs. Random.
Dodes, Irving A. *see* Dodes, Irving Allen.
Dodes, Irving Allen.
xDodes, Irving A.
Introduction to Statistical Analysis: A Modern
Computational Approach. Hayden.
Dodge, Arthur F. *see* Dodge, Arthur Farwell.
Dodge, Arthur Farwell, 1882-
xDodge, Arthur F.
Occupational Ability Patterns. AMS Pr.
Dodge, Bayard.
xDodge, Bayard.
Muslim Education in Medieval Times. Mid
East Inst.
Dodge, Bertha S. *see* Dodge, Bertha Sanford.
Dodge, Bertha Sanford, 1902-
xDodge, Bertha S.
The Story of Nursing. Little.
Dodge Building Cost Services. *see* McGraw-Hill
Publishing Company, Inc.
Dodge, Carroll W. *see* Dodge, Carroll William.
Dodge, Carroll William, 1895-
xDodge, Carroll W.
Lichen Flora of the Antarctic Continent &
Adjacent Islands. Phoenix Pub.
Dodge, Doris J. *see* Dodge, Doris Jansen.
Dodge, Doris Jansen.
xDodge, Doris J.
Agricultural Policy & Performance in Zambia:
History, Prospects, & Proposals for Change.
U of Cal Intl St.
Dodge, H. Robert, 1929-
xDodge, Robert H.
Field Sales Management: Text & Cases.
Business Pubns.
Dodge, Mary A. *see* Dodge, Mary Abigail.
Dodge, Mary Abigail, 1833-1896
xDodge, Mary A.
Twelve Miles from a Lemon. Arno.
Dodge, Natt N. *see* Dodge, Natt Noyes.

Dodge, Natt Noyes, 1900-
xDodge, Natt N.
Flowers of the Southwest Deserts. SW Pks
Mnmts.
Dodge, Nicholas A.
xDodge, Nicholas A.
A Climbing Guide to Oregon. Touchstone Pr
Ore.
Dodge, Richard H.
xDodge, Richard H.
How to Read & Write in College: A Complete
Course. Har-Row.
Dodge, Richard I. *see* Dodge, Richard Irving.
Dodge, Richard Irving, 1827-1895
xDodge, Richard I.
Our Wild Indians: Thirty Three Years'
Personal Experience Among the Red Men of
the Great West. Arno.
Dodge, Robert H. *see* Dodge, H. Robert.
Dodgson, Charles L. *see* Dodgson, Charles Lutwidge.
Dodgson, Charles Lutwidge, 1832-1898
xDodgson, Charles L.
The Diaries of Lewis Carroll. Greenwood.
Lewis Carroll Picture Book: A Selection from
the Unpublished Writings & Drawings of
Lewis Carroll, Together with Reprints from
Scare & Unacknowledged Work. Gale.
Dodman, Frank E. *see* Dodman, Frank Ellerton.
Dodman, Frank Ellerton, 1908-
xDodman, Frank E.
The Observer's Book of Ships. Scribner.
Dodsley, Robert, 1703-1764
xDodsley, Robert.
A Collection of Poems. Scholarly.
Dodson, Edward O. *see* Dodson, Edward Ottway.
Dodson, Edward Ottway.
xDodson, Edward O.
Evolution: Process & Product. D Van
Nostrand.
Dodson, Fitzhugh.
xDodson, Fitzhugh.
The Carnival Kidnap Caper. Oak Tree Pubns.
How to Father. NAL.
I Wish I Had a Computer That Makes Waffles:
Teaching Your Child with Modern Nursery
Rhymes. Oak Tree Pubns.
Dodson, Laura S. *see* Dodson, Laura Sue.
Dodson, Laura Sue.
xDodson, Laura S.
Family Counseling: A Systems Approach.
Accel Devel.
Dodson, Owen.
xDodson, Owen.
Come Home Early, Child. Popular Lib.
Dodson, Susan.
xDodson, Susan.
The Creep. Archway.
The Creep. Schol Bk Serv.
Dodwell, Charles Reginald.
xDodwell, P. C.
Painting in Europe 800-1200. Viking Pr.
Dodwell, P. C. *see* Dodwell, Charles Reginald.
Doe, Bruce R.
xDoe, Bruce R.
Lead Isotopes. Springer-Verlag.
Doe, Paul.
xDoe, Paul.
Tallis. Oxford U Pr.
Doebelin, Ernest O.
xDoebelin, Ernest O.
Measurement Systems: Application & Design.
McGraw.
Doeker, Gunther.
xDoeker, Gunther.

Federal Republic of Germany & German
Democratic Republic in International
Relations. Oceana.
Doell, Charles E. *see* Doell, Charles Edward.
Doell, Charles Edward.
xDoell, Charles E.
Elements of Park & Recreation Administration.
Burgess.
Doelle, H. W.
xDoelle, H. W.
Bacterial Metabolism. Acad Pr.
Doenecke, Justus D.
xDoenecke, Justus D.
Not to the Swift: The "Old" Isolationists in the
Cold War Era. Bucknell U Pr.
Not to the Swift: The Old Isolationists in the
Cold War Era. Inst Humane.
Doenicke, A. *see* Doenicke, Alfred.
Doenicke, Alfred.
xDoenicke, A.
ed. Etomidate: An Intravenous Hypnotic
Agent. First Report on Clinical &
Experimental Experience. Springer-Verlag.
Doerffler, Alfred, 1884-
xDoerffler, Alfred.
The Burden Made Light. Concordia.
Open the Meeting with Prayer. Concordia.
Doering, George G.
xDoering, George G.
Clinical Dermatology of Small Animals: A
Stereoscopic Presentation. Mosby.
Doermann, Humphrey.
xDoermann, Humphrey.
Toward Equal Access. College Bd.
Doerner, Cynthia.
xDoerner, Cynthia.
Winning Tennis Doubles. Contemp Bks.
Doerr, Arthur H.
xDoerr, Arthur H.
Principles of Physical Geography. Barron.
Doetsch, R. *see* Doetsch, Raymond Nicholas.
Doetsch, Raymond N. *see* Doetsch, Raymond Nicholas.
Doetsch, Raymond Nicholas.
xDoetsch, R.
Introduction to Bacteria & Their Ecobiology.
Univ Park.
xDoetsch, Raymond N.
Journey to the Green & Golden Lands: The
Epic of Survival on the Wagon Trail.
Kennikat.
Doezema, Linda P. *see* Doezema, Linda Pegman.
Doezema, Linda Pegman.
xDoezema, Linda P.
ed. Dutch Americans: A Guide to Information
Sources. Gale.
Doggett, Frank. *see* Doggett, Frank A.
Doggett, Frank A.
xDoggett, Frank.
ed. Wallace Stevens: A Celebration. Princeton
U Pr.
Doggett, R. G.
xDoggett, R. G.
ed. Pseudomonas Aeruginosa: Clinical
Manifestations of Infection & Current
Therapy. Acad Pr.
Doherty, Catherine D. *see* Doherty, Catherine de
Hueck.
Doherty, Catherine de Hueck, 1900-
xDoherty, Catherine D.
Dear Father: A Message of Love to Priests.
Alba.
The Gospel Without Compromise. Ave Maria.
I Live on an Island. Ave Maria.
Strannik: The Call to Pilgrimage for Western
Man. Ave Maria.
xDoherty, Catherine de Hueck.
Fragments of My Life. Ave Maria.
Doherty, Dennis.
xDoherty, Dennis.

Dimensions of Human Sexuality. Doubleday.
Doherty, Michael E.
xDoherty, Michael E.
Asking Questions About Behavior: An
Introduction to What Psychologists Do. Scott
F.
Doherty, Robert E. *see* Doherty, Robert Emmett.
Doherty, Robert Emmett, 1923-
xDoherty, Robert E.
Industrial & Labor Relations Terms: A
Glossary. NY Sch Indus Rel.
Doherty, William T.
xDoherty, William T.
Louis Houck: Missouri Historian &
Entrepreneur. U of Mo Pr.
Dohm, Hedwig, 1833-1919
xDohm, Hedwig.
Women's Nature & Privilege. Hyperion Conn.
Dohrman, H. T.
xDohrman, H. T.
California Cult: The Story of Mankind United.
AMS Pr.
Doi, Takeo, 1920-
xDoi, Takeo.
The Anatomy of Dependence. Kodansha.
Doi, Teruo.
xDoi, Teruo.
ed. Patent & Know-How Licensing in Japan &
the United States. U of Wash Pr.
Doig, Ivan.
xDoig, Ivan.
The Streets We Have Come Down: Literature
of the City. Hayden.
This House of Sky: Landscapes of a Western
Mind. HarBraceJ.
This House of Sky: Landscapes of a Western
Mind. HarBraceJ.
Utopian America: Dreams & Realities. Hayden.
Dolaghan, Thomas.
xDolaghan, Thomas.
The Navajos Are Coming to Jesus. William
Carey Lib.
Dolan. *see* Dolan, Edward F.
Dolan, Edward. *see* Dolan, Edward F.
Dolan, Edward F.
xDolan.
The Bermuda Triangle & Other Mysteries of
Nature. Watts.
Child Abuse. Watts.
xDolan, Edward.
Engines Work Like This. McGraw.
xDolan, Edward F.
Archie Griffin. Archway.
Archie Griffin. Doubleday.
The Complete Beginner's Guide to Bowling.
Doubleday.
The Complete Beginner's Guide to
Gymnastics. Doubleday.
The Complete Beginners Guide to Ice Skating.
Doubleday.
Fred Lynn: The Hero from Boston. Doubleday.
Gun Control: A Decision for Americans.
Watts.
Martina Navratilova. Doubleday.
Matthew Henson, Black Explorer. Dodd.
Starting Soccer: A Handbook for Boys & Girls.
Har-Row.
Dolan, Edwin G.
xDolan, Edwin G.
Basic Economics. Dryden Pr.
Dolan, Jack, 1933-
xDolan, Jack.
I Wonder Who's in Charge. Theos Pub Hse.
Dolan, Jay P., 1936-
xDolan, Jay P.
The Immigrant Church: New York's Irish &
German Catholics, 1815-1865. Johns
Hopkins.
Dolan, Joseph M.
xDolan, Joseph M.

Give Comfort to My People. Paulist Pr.
Dolan, Josephine A.
xDolan, Josephine A.
Nursing in Society: A Historical Perspective.
Saunders.
Dolan, Paul J.
xDolan, Paul J.
ed. Introduction to Drama. Wiley.
ed. Introduction to Fiction. Wiley.
Of War & War's Alarms: Fiction & Politics in
the Modern World. Free Pr.
Dolan, Sheila.
xDolan, Sheila.
The Wishing Bottle. HM.
Dolan, Winthrop W., 1909-
xDolan, Winthrop W.
A Choice of Sundials. Greene.
Dolbeare, Kenneth. *see* Dolbeare, Kenneth M.
Dolbeare, Kenneth M.
xDolbeare, Kenneth.
Institutions, Policies, & Goals: A Reader in
American Politics. Heath.
ed. Public Policy Evaluation. Sage.
xDolbeare, Kenneth M.
American Ideologies: The Competing Political
Beliefs of the 1970's. Rand.
American Politics: Policies, Power, & Change.
Heath.
Dolby. *see* Dolby, J. L.
Dolby, J. L.
xDolby.
The Statistics CumIndex. R & D Pr.
xDolby, J. L.
Compiled by The Statistics CumIndex. R & D
Pr.
Dolce, Philip C.
xDolce, Phillip C.
ed. Suburbia: The American Dream &
Dilemma. Doubleday.
Dolce, Phillip C. *see* Dolce, Philip C.
Dolch, Edward W. *see* Dolch, Edward William.
Dolch, Edward William.
xDolch, Edward W.
Dog Pals. Garrard.
Friendly Birds. Garrard.
I Like Cats. Garrard.
In the Woods. Garrard.
Monkey Friends. Garrard.
On the Farm. Garrard.
Once There Was a Bear. Garrard.
Once There Was a Cat. Garrard.
Once There Was a Dog. Garrard.
Once There Was a Monkey. Garrard.
Once There Was a Rabbit. Garrard.
Once There Was an Elephant. Garrard.
Psychology & Teaching of Reading.
Greenwood.
Some Are Small. Garrard.
Stories from Alaska. Garrard.
Stories from Hawaii. Garrard.
Stories from Italy. Garrard.
Stories from Mexico. Garrard.
Dolch, Marguerite P. *see* Dolch, Marguerite Pierce.
Dolch, Marguerite Pierce.
xDolch, Marguerite P.
Animal Stories from Africa. Garrard.
Once There Was a Coyote. Garrard.
Stories from Africa. Garrard.
Dolciani, Mary P.
xDolciani, Mary P.
Modern Introductory Analysis. HM.
Dold, A. *see* Dold, Albrecht.
Dold, Albrecht.
xDold, A.

Lectures on Algebraic Topology.
Springer-Verlag.
Dole, Malcolm, 1903-
xDole, Malcolm.
ed. The Radiation Chemistry of
Macromolecules. Acad Pr.
Dolensek, Nancy.
xDolensek, Nancy.
Mutt. Potter.
Dolezal, V. *see* Dolezal, Vaclav.
Dolezal, V. J. *see* Dolezal, Vaclav.
Dolezal, Vaclav.
xDolezal, V.
Nonlinear Networks. Elsevier.
xDolezal, V. J.
Monotone Operators & Applications in Control
& Network Theory. Elsevier.
Dolge, Alfred, 1848-
xDolge, Alfred.
Men Who Have Made Piano History. Vestal.
Dolgoff, Ralph.
xDolgoff, Ralph.
Understanding Social Welfare. Har-Row.
Dolgoff, Sam, 1902-
xDolgoff, Sam.
ed. The Anarchist Collectives: Workers'
Self-Management in the Spanish Revolution
(1936 to 1939). Free Life.
Dolgun, Alexander.
xDolgun, Alexander.
Alexander Dolgun's Story: An American in the
Gulag. Knopf.
Dolhinow, P. J. *see* Dolhinow, Phyllis.
Dolhinow, Phyllis.
xDolhinow, P. J.
Primate Patterns. HR&W.
Dolit, Alan, 1934-
xDolit, Alan.
You Can Lose Weight. Caroline Hse.
You Can Lose Weight. Nellen Pub.
Doll, John P.
xDoll, John P.
Production Economics: Theory with
Applications. Grid Pub.
Doll, Ronald C.
xDoll, Ronald C.
Curriculum Improvement: Decision Making &
Process. Allyn.
Dollaghan, Helen.
xDollaghan, Helen.
Helen Dollaghan's Best Main Dishes. McGraw.
Dollar, Charles M.
xDollar, Charles M.
Historian's Guide to Statistics: Quantitative
Analysis & Historical Research. Krieger.
Dollar, Truman.
xDollar, Truman.
How to Carry Out God's Stewardship Plan.
Nelson.
xDollar, Truman S.
Teenage Rebellion. Revell.
Dollar, Truman S. *see* Dollar, Truman.
Dollard, John.
xDollard, John.
Fear in Battle. AMS Pr.
Fear in Battle. Greenwood.
Frustration & Aggression. Greenwood.
Dollen, Charles.
xDollen, Charles J.
Abortion in Context: A Select Bibliography.
Scarecrow.
Dollen, Charles J. *see* Dollen, Charles.
Dollfus, A. *see* Dollfus, Audouin.
Dollfus, Audouin.
xDollfus, A.
Surfaces & Interiors of Planets & Satellites.
Acad Pr.
Dollinger, Johann J. von. *see* Dollinger, Johann Joseph
Ignaz von.

Dollinger, Johann Joseph Ignaz von, 1799-1890
xDollinger, Johann J. von.
Lectures on the Reunion of the Churches.
Allenson.
Dollinger, Philippe.
xDollinger, Philippe.
The German Hansa. Stanford U Pr.
Dolloff, Francis W.
xDolloff, Francis W.
How to Care for Works of Art on Paper. Mus
Fine Arts Boston.
Dolman, John.
xDolman, John.
The Art of Play Production. Har-Row.
Dolmetsch, Mabel.
xDolmetsch, Mabel.
Dances of England & France from 1450-1600:
With Their Music & Authentic Manner of
Performance. Da Capo.
Personal Recollections of Arnold Dolmetsch.
Da Capo.
Dolphin, David.
xDolphin, David.
Tabulation of Infrared Spectral Data. Wiley.
Dolphin, Robert.
xDolphin, Robert.
Analysis of Economic & Personal Factors
Leading to Consumer Bankruptcy. Mich St U
Busn.
Dolto, Francoise. *see* Dolto, Francoise Marette.
Dolto, Francoise Marette.
xDolto, Francoise.
The Jesus of Psychoanalysis: A Freudian
Interpretation of the Gospel. Doubleday.
Dolukhanov, Paul M. *see* Dolukhanov, Pavel Markovich.
Dolukhanov, Pavel Markovich.
xDolukhanov, Paul M.
Ecology & Economy in Neolithic Eastern
Europe. St Martin.
Doman, Glenn. *see* Doman, Glenn J.
Doman, Glenn J.
xDoman, Glenn.
Teach Your Baby Math. S&S.
Domandi, Agnes K. *see* Domandi, Agnes Korner.
Domandi, Agnes Korner.
xDomandi, Agnes K.
ed. Modern German Literature. Ungar.
Domanska, Janina.
xDomanska, Janina.
Din Dan Don It's Christmas. Greenwillow.
I Saw a Ship A-Sailing. Macmillan.
illus. If All the Seas Were One Sea. Macmillan.
King Krakus & the Dragon. Greenwillow.
illus. Marilka. Macmillan.
The Tortoise & the Tree. Greenwillow.
illus. Turnip. Macmillan.
Dombroski, Robert S.
xDombroski, Robert S.
ed. Critical Perspectives on the "Decameron".
B&N.
Dombrow, Bernard A. *see* Dombrow, Bernard Albert.
Dombrow, Bernard Albert, 1908-
xDombrow, Bernard A.
Polyurethanes. Krieger.
Dombrowski, James, 1897-
xDombrowski, James.
Early Days of Christian Socialism in America.
Octagon.
Domesday Commemoration, 1866.
xDomesday Commemoration, 1886.
Domesday Studies. B Franklin.
Domesday Commemoration, 1886. *see* Domesday
Commemoration, 1866.
Domett, Henry W. *see* Domett, Henry Williams.
Domett, Henry Williams.
xDomett, Henry W.
History of the Bank of New York, 1784-1884.
Greenwood.
Domhoff, G. William.
xDomhoff, G. William.

ed. C. Wright Mills & "The Power Elite".
Beacon Pr.
Higher Circles: The Governing Class in
America. Random.
ed. Power Structure Research. Sage.
The Powers That Be: Processes of Ruling Class
Domination in America. Random.
Who Rules America?. P-H.
Dominguez, George S.
xDominguez, George S.
The Business Guide to Tosca: Effects &
Actions. Wiley.
Dominguez, John R., 1937-
xDominguez, John R.
Capital Flows in Minority Areas. Lexington
Bks.
Venture Capital. Lexington Bks.
Dominguez, Jorge I., 1945-
xDominguez, Jorge L.
Cuba: Order & Revolution. Harvard U Pr.
Dominguez, Jorge L. *see* Dominguez, Jorge I.
Dominian, J. *see* Dominian, Jacob.
Dominian, Jacob.
xDominian, J.
Marital Breakdown. Franciscan Herald.
Dominic, R. B.
xDominic, R. B.
The Attending Physician. Har-Row.
Dominowski, R. *see* Dominowski, Roger L.
Dominowski, Roger L., 1939-
xDominowski, R.
Research Methods. P-H.
Dominy, Eric.
xDominy, Eric.
Teach Yourself Judo. Emerson.
Teach Yourself Karate. Emerson.
Teach Yourself Self-Defense. Emerson.
Dommel, Paul R., 1933-
xDommel, Paul R.
The Politics of Revenue Sharing. Ind U Pr.
Dommermuth, William P.
xDommermuth, William P.
Pref. by The Use of Sampling in Marketing
Research. Am Mktg.
Dommisse, G. F.
xDommisse, G. F.
Arteries & Veins of the Human Spinal Cord
from Birth. Churchill.
Domville, Eric, 1929-
xDomville, Eric.
ed. A Concordance to the Plays of W. B.
Yeats. Cornell U Pr.
Don Nanjira, Daniel D. *see* Don Nanjira, Daniel D. C.
Don Nanjira, Daniel D. C.
xDon Nanjira, Daniel D.
The Status of Aliens in East Africa: Asians &
Europeans in Tanzania, Uganda, & Kenya.
Praeger.
Donagan, Alan.
xDonagan, Alan.
Theory of Morality. U of Chicago Pr.
Donaghy, Peter.
xDonaghy, Peter.
In Search of Life. Franciscan Herald.
Donaho, M. *see* Donaho, Melvin W.
Donaho, Melvin W.
xDonaho, M.
How to Get the Job You Want: A Guide to
Resumes, Interviews & Job Hunting Strategy.
P-H.
Donahoe, Bernard. *see* Donahoe, Bernard F.
Donahoe, Bernard F.
xDonahoe, Bernard.
Private Plans & Public Dangers: The Story of
FDR's Third Nomination. U of Notre Dame
Pr.
Donahoe, James J.
xDonahoe, James J.

Dream Reality: The Conscious Creation of
Dream & Paranormal Experience. Bench Pr.
Enigma: Psychology, the Paranormal &
Self-Transformation. Bench Pr.

Donahoe, John W.
xDonahoe, John W.
Learning, Language, & Memory. Har-Row.

Donahoo, Clara A.
xDonahoo, Clare A.
Orthopedic Nursing. Little.

Donahoo, Clare A. *see* Donahoo, Clara A.

Donahue, J. E. *see* Donahue, James Edward.

Donahue, James Edward, 1947-
xDonahue, J. E.
Complementary Definitions of Programming
Language Semantics. Springer-Verlag.

Donahue, John.
xDonahue, John C.
ed. Five Plays from the Children's Theatre
Company of Minneapolis. U of Minn Pr.

Donahue, John C. *see* Donahue, John.

Donahue, Parnell.
xDonahue, Parnell.
Germs Make Me Sick: A Health Handbook for
Kids. Knopf.
Sports Doc: Medical Advice, Diet, Fitness
Tips, & Other Essential Hints for Young
Athletes. Knopf.

Donahue, Roy L. *see* Donahue, Roy Luther.

Donahue, Roy Luther.
xDonahue, Roy L.
Soils: An Introduction to Soils & Plant
Growth. P-H.

Donahue, Thomas J. *see* Donahue, Thomas John.

Donahue, Thomas John, 1943-
xDonahue, Thomas J.
The Theater of Fernando Arrabal: A Garden of
Earthly Delights. NYU Pr.

Donajgrodzki, A. P.
xDonajgrodzki, A. P.
ed. Social Control in Nineteenth Century
Britain. Rowman.

Donakowski, Conrad L., 1936-
xDonakowski, Conrad L.
A Muse for the Masses: Ritual & Music in an
Age of Democratic Revolution, 1770-1870. U
of Chicago Pr.

Donald, A. G. *see* Donald, Archibald Gordon.

Donald, Archibald Gordon.
xDonald, A. G.
Management, Information & Systems.
Pergamon.

Donald, David. *see* Donald, David Herbert.

Donald, David H. *see* Donald, David Herbert.

Donald, David Herbert, 1920-
xDonald, David.
Compiled by The Nation in Crisis, 1861-1877.
AHM Pub.
Politics of Reconstruction, 1863-1867. La State
U Pr.
xDonald, David H.
Liberty & Union. Heath.
Liberty & Union. Little.

Donald, Elsie B. *see* Donald, Elsie Burch.

Donald, Elsie Burch.
xDonald, Elsie B.
London Shopping Guide. Penguin.

Donald, Henderson H. *see* Donald, Henderson Hamilton.

Donald, Henderson Hamilton.
xDonald, Henderson H.
Negro Freedman: Life Conditions of the
American Negro in the Early Years After
Emancipation. Cooper Sq.

Donald, Vivian.
xDonald, Vivian.
Cathy's Choice. NAL.

Donaldson, Alfred G. *see* Donaldson, Alfred Gaston.

Donaldson, Alfred Gaston.
xDonaldson, Alfred G.

Some Comparative Aspects of Irish Law. Duke.

Donaldson, E. F. *see* Donaldson, Elvin Frank.

Donaldson, Elvin F. *see* Donaldson, Elvin Frank.

Donaldson, Elvin Frank, 1903-
xDonaldson, E. F.
Personal Finance. Wiley.
xDonaldson, Elvin F.
Corporate Finance. Wiley.
Personal Finance. Wiley.

Donaldson, Frances. *see* Donaldson, Frances Lonsdale.

Donaldson, Frances Lonsdale, Lady.
xDonaldson, Frances.
Edward VIII: The Road to Abdication.
Lippincott.

Donaldson, Gerald.
xDonaldson, Gerald.
The Walking Book. HR&W.

Donaldson, Gordon, 1926-
xDonaldson, Gordon.
Niagara: The Eternal Circus. Doubleday.
Northwards by Sea. Beekman Pubs.
Strategy for Financial Mobility. Harvard Busn.

Donaldson, Hamish.
xDonaldson, Hamish.
A Guide to the Successful Management of
Computer Projects. Halsted Pr.
A Guide to the Successful Management of
Computer Projects. Wiley.

Donaldson, Ian.
xDonaldson, Ian.
World Upside-Down: Comedy from Jonson to
Fielding. Oxford U Pr.

Donaldson, James H.
xDonaldson, James H.
Casualty Claim Practice. Irwin.

Donaldson, Les, 1928-
xDonaldson, Les.
Behavioral Supervision: Practical Ways to
Change Unsatisfactory Behavior & Increase
Productivity. A-W.
How to Use Psychological Leverage to Double
the Power of What You Say. P-H.

Donaldson, Margaret. *see* Donaldson, Margaret C.

Donaldson, Margaret C.
xDonaldson, Margaret.
Children's Minds. Norton.
Journey into War. Andre Deutsch.

Donaldson, Norman.
xDonaldson, Norman.
How Did They Die?. St Martin.

Donaldson, Peter, 1934-
xDonaldson, Peter.
Guide to the British Economy. Gannon.

Donaldson, Robert H.
xDonaldson, Robert H.
Soviet Policy Toward India: Ideology &
Strategy. Harvard U Pr.

Donaldson, Scott.
xDonaldson, Scott.
By Force of Will: The Life & Art of Ernest
Hemingway. Penguin.
Suburban Myth. Columbia U Pr.

Donaldson, Stephen R.
xDonaldson, Stephen R.
The Power That Preserves. Ballantine.

Donaldson, T. *see* Donaldson, Thomas.

Donaldson, Thomas.
xDonaldson, T.
Ethical Issues in Business: A Philosophical
Approach. P-H.

Donaldson, Thomas C. *see* Donaldson, Thomas Corwin.

Donaldson, Thomas Corwin, 1843-1898
xDonaldson, Thomas C.
Idaho of Yesterday. Greenwood.

Donat, Alexander.
xDonat, Alexander.

ed. The Death Camp Treblinka: A
Documentary. Schocken.
The Holocaust Kingdom: A Memoir. Schocken.

Donato, Anthony.
xDonato, Anthony.
Preparing Music Manuscript. Greenwood.

Donatus, Cornelius.
xDonatus, Cornelius.
How to Anticipate the Business Future
Without the Use of Computers. Am Classical
Coll Pr.

Donceel, Joseph F., 1906-
xDonceel, Joseph F.
The Searching Mind: An Introduction to a
Philosophy of God. U of Notre Dame Pr.

Donchess, Barbara.
xDonchess, Barbara.
How to Cope with His Horoscope. Vulcan Bks.

Donders, Joseph G.
xDonders, Joseph G.
Jesus, the Way: Reflections on the Gospel of
Luke. Orbis Bks.

Dondis, Donis A.
xDondis, Donis A.
A Primer of Visual Literacy. MIT Pr.

Dondo, Mathurin Marius.
xDondo, Muthurin.
Modern French Course. Heath.

Dondo, Muthurin. *see* Dondo, Mathurin Marius.

Done, J. N. *see* Done, John N.

Done, John N.
xDone, J. N.
Applications of High-Speed Liquid
Chromatography. Wiley.

Donegan, William L.
xDonegan, William L.
Cancer of the Breast. Saunders.

Donelan, Michael. *see* Donelan, Michael D.

Donelan, Michael D.
xDonelan, Michael.
ed. The Reason of States: A Study in
International Political Theory. Allen Unwin.

Donelson, Kenneth. *see* Donelson, Kenneth L.

Donelson, Kenneth L.
xDonelson, Kenneth.
ed. Students' Right to Read. NCTE.
xDonelson, Kenneth L.
Literature for Today's Young Adults. Scott F.

Doney, Willis.
xDoney, Willis.
ed. Descartes: A Collection of Critical Essays.
U of Notre Dame Pr.

Dong, Collin. *see* Dong, Collin H.

Dong, Collin H.
xDong, Collin.
The Arthritic's Cookbook. Bantam.

Donham, Wallace B. *see* Donham, Wallace Brett.

Donham, Wallace Brett, 1877-1954
xDonham, Wallace B.
Education for Responsible Living: The
Opportunity for Liberal Arts Colleges.
Greenwood.

Donhauser, Paul S.
xDonhauser, Paul S.
History of American Ceramics: The Studio
Potter. Kendall-Hunt.

Doniach, N. S. *see* Doniach, Nakdimon Shabbethay.

Doniach, Nakdimon Shabbethay.
xDoniach, N. S.
ed. Oxford English-Arabic Dictionary of
Current Usage. Oxford U Pr.

Doniach, S.
xDoniach, S.
Green's Functions for Solid State Physicists.
Benjamin-Cummings.

Donigan, Robert L.
xDonigan, Robert L.

Chemical Tests & the Law. Traffic Inst.
Evidence Handbook. Traffic Inst.
Doniger, Simon, ed.
xDoniger, Simon.
ed. The Nature of Man in Theological &
Psychological Perspective. Arno.
Donington, Robert.
xDonington, Robert.
The Opera. HarBraceJ.
A Performer's Guide to Baroque Music.
Scribner.
String Playing in Baroque Music. Scribner.
Donkin, R. A.
xDonkin, R. A.
Spanish Red: An Ethnogeographical Study of
Cochineal & the Opuntia Cactus. Am Philos.
Donlan, Walter.
xDonlan, Walter.
Intro. by The Classical World Bibliography of
Greek Drama & Poetry. Garland Pub.
Donleavy, J. P. *see* Donleavy, James Patrick.
Donleavy, James P. *see* Donleavy, James Patrick.
Donleavy, James Patrick.
xDonleavy, J. P.
A Fairy Tale of New York. Delacorte.
A Fairy Tale of New York. Dell.
The Ginger Man. Dell.
Meet My Maker, the Mad Molecule. Dell.
Schultz. Delacorte.
illus. The Unexpurgated Code: A Complete
Manual of Survival & Manners. Delacorte.
xDonleavy, James P.
Ginger Man. Astor-Honor.
The Ginger Man. Delacorte.
Donley, Marshall O., 1932-
xDonley, Marshall O.
The Future of Teacher Power in America. Phi
Delta Kappa.
Power to the Teacher. How America's
Educators Became Militant. Ind U Pr.
Donley, Michael B.
xDonley, Michael B.
The SALT Handbook. Heritage Found.
Donlon, T. A. *see* Donlon, Thomas F.
Donlon, Thomas F.
xDonlon, T. A.
A Feasibility Study of the SAT Performance of
High-Ability Students from 1960 to
1974(Valedictorian Study). College Bd.
Donna, Natalie.
xDonna, Natalie.
The Peanut Cookbook. Lothrop.
Donnachie, Ian. *see* Donnachie, Ian L.
Donnachie, Ian L.
xDonnachie, Ian.
Victorian & Edwardian Scottish Lowlands from
Historic Photographs. David & Charles.
xDonnachie, Ian L.
Old Galloway. David & Charles.
Donnan, Christopher B.
xDonnan, Christopher B.
Ancient Burial Patterns of the Moche Valley,
Peru. U of Tex Pr.
Donne, John.
xDonne, John.
Devotions Upon Emergent Occasions. Folcroft.
The Divine Poems. Oxford U Pr.
Donne's Prebend Sermons. Harvard U Pr.
Pseudo-Martyr. Schol Facsimiles.
Some Poems & a Devotion of John Donne.
Folcroft.
Donnell, Annie (Hamilton), 1862-
xDonnell, Annie H.
Rebecca Mary. Arno.
Donnell, Annie H. *see* Donnell, Annie (Hamilton).
Donnell, Marianne.
xDonnell, Marianne.

ed. Toponyms of Florida: An Alphabetical
Listing of Names Approved by the United
States Board on Geographic Names Through
1976, with 1977 Addendum. U Presses Fla.
Donnellan, T. *see* Donnellan, Thomas.
Donnellan, Thomas.
xDonnellan, T.
Lattice Theory. Pergamon.
Donnelly, Doris.
xDonnelly, Doris.
Learning to Forgive. Macmillan.
Donnelly, Francis P. *see* Donnelly, Francis Patrick.
Donnelly, Francis Patrick, 1869-1959
xDonnelly, Francis P.
Literature the Leading Educator. Arno.
Donnelly, I. *see* Donnelly, Ignatius.
Donnelly, Ignatius, 1831-1901
xDonnelly, I.
Ragnarok - the Age of Fire & Gravel. Univ
Bks.
xDonnelly, Ignatius.
The American People's Money. Hyperion
Conn.
Doctor Huguet. Arno.
The Golden Bottle. Irvington.
The Golden Bottle. Johnson Repr.
Donnelly, James. *see* Donnelly, James H.
Donnelly, James H.
xDonnelly, James.
Fundamentals of Management: Functions,
Behavior, Models. Business Pubns.
xDonnelly, James H.
Analysis for Marketing Decisions. Irwin.
Donnelly, John.
xDonnelly, John.
ed. Conscience. Alba.
ed. Language, Metaphysics, & Death. Fordham.
Donnelly, John P. *see* Donnelly, John Patrick.
Donnelly, John Patrick, 1934-
xDonnelly, John P.
Reform & Renewal. McGrath.
Donnelly, M. S. *see* Donnelly, Murray S.
Donnelly, Mabel C. *see* Donnelly, Mabel Collins.
Donnelly, Mabel Collins.
xDonnelly, Mabel C.
George Gissing, Grave Comedian. Kraus Repr.
Donnelly, Murray S.
xDonnelly, M. S.
The Government of Manitoba. U of Toronto
Pr.
Donnelly, Paul R.
xDonnelly, Paul R.
Guide for Developing a Hospital
Administrative Policy Manual. Cath Health.
Donnelly, R. J. *see* Donnelly, Richard Joseph.
Donnelly, Richard Joseph, 1919-
xDonnelly, R. J.
Active Games & Contests. Ronald Pr.
Donnelly, Russell J.
xDonnelly, Russell J.
Experimental Superfluidity. U of Chicago Pr.
Donner, Frederick W.
xDonner, Frederick W.
Compiled by A Preliminary Glossary of
Chinese Linguistic Terminology. Chinese
Materials.
Donner, Jorn.
xDonner, Jorn.
Personal Vision of Ingmar Bergman. Arno.
Donner, Wolf.
xDonner, Wolf.
The Five Faces of Thailand: An Economic
Geography. St Martin.
The Five Faces of Thailand: An Economic
Geography. Westview.
Donoghue, Charles.
xDonoghue, Charles.

Light Your Own Fire to Bigger Sales. Natl
Underwriter.
Donoghue, Denis.
xDonoghue, Denis.
Integrity of Yeats. Folcroft.
Donoghue, John D.
xDonoghue, John D.
Pariah Persistence in Changing Japan: A Case
Study. U Pr of Amer.
Donoghue, Mary A. *see* Donoghue, Mary Agnes.
Donoghue, Mary Agnes.
xDonoghue, Mary A.
Assassination: Murder in Politics. Major Bks.
Donoghue, Mildred R.
xDonoghue, Mildred R.
The Child & the English Language Arts. Wm
C Brown.
Second Languages in Primary Education.
Newbury Hse.
Donoghue, W. F. *see* Donoghue, William F.
Donoghue, William F., 1921-
xDonoghue, W. F.
Monotone Matrix Functions & Analytic
Continuation. Springer-Verlag.
xDonoghue, William F.
Distributions & Fourier Transforms. Acad Pr.
Donohue, J. W. *see* Donohue, Joseph W.
Donohue, Joseph. *see* Donohue, Joseph W.
Donohue, Joseph W., 1935-
xDonohue, J. W.
Dramatic Character in the English Romantic
Age. Princeton U Pr.
xDonohue, Joseph.
Theatre in the Age of Kean. Rowman.
Donohue, Mark.
xDonohue, Mark.
The Unfair Advantage. Dodd.
Donoso Cortes, Juan. *see* Donoso Cortes, Juan.
Donoso, E. *see* Donoso, Ephraim.
Donoso, Ephraim.
xDonoso, E.
ed. Acute Myocardial Infarction.
Thieme-Stratton.
ed. Angina Pectoris. Thieme-Stratton.
ed. Critical Cardiac Care. Thieme-Stratton.
Donoso, Jose, 1924-
xDonoso, Jose.
Charleston & Other Stories. Godine.
**Donoso Cortes, Juan, Marques de Valdegamas,
1809-1853**
xDonoso Cortes, Juan.
An Essay on Catholicism, Authority & Order
Considered in Their Fundamental Principles.
Hyperion Conn.
Donovan. *see* Donovan, Marilee Irvers.
Donovan, Bonnie.
xDonovan, Bonnie.
The Cesarean Birth Experience: A Practical,
Comprehensive, & Reassuring Guide for
Parents & Professionals. Beacon Pr.
Donovan, Frank. *see* Donovan, Frank Robert.
Donovan, Frank R. *see* Donovan, Frank Robert.
Donovan, Frank Robert.
xDonovan, Frank.
Let's Go Metric. McKay.
Prepare Now for a Metric Future. Popular Lib.
xDonovan, Frank R.
The Medal: The Story of the Medal of Honor.
Dodd.
Donovan, John.
xDonovan, John.
Good Old James. Har-Row.
Remove Protective Coating a Little at a Time.
Har-Row.
Donovan, John. *see* Donovan, John J.
Donovan, John C.
xDonovan, John C.

The Cold Warriors: A Policy-Making Elite. Heath.
The Politics of Poverty. Pegasus.
The Politics of Poverty. U Pr of Amer.

Donovan, John J.
xDonovan, John.
Systems Programming. McGraw.

Donovan, Joseph P. see Donovan, Joseph Patrick.

Donovan, Joseph Patrick, 1911-
xDonovan, Joseph P.
Pelagius & the Fifth Crusade. AMS Pr.

Donovan, Josephine, 1941-
xDonovan, Josephine.
ed. Feminist Literary Criticism: Explorations in Theory. U Pr of Ky.

Donovan, M. Denise. see Donovan, Mary Denise.

Donovan, Marilee Ivers.
xDonovan.
Cancer Care Nursing. ACC.

Donovan, Mary Denise.
xDonovan, M. Denise.
Parents & the First Grade. Dillon-Liederbach.

Donovan, Michael. see Donovan, R. Michael.

Donovan, Peter.
xDonovan, Peter.
Basic English for Science. Oxford U Pr.
Chinese Communist Materials at the Bureau of Investigation Archives, Taiwan. U of Mich Ctr Chinese.
Interpreting Religious Experience. Seabury.

Donovan, R. Michael.
xDonovan, Michael.
Planning & Controlling Manufacturing Resources. Am Mgmt.

Donovan, Robert E.
xDonovan, Robert E.
Hunting Whitetail Deer. Winchester Pr.
Hunting Wild Bees. Winchester Pr.

Donovan, Robert J.
xDonovan, Robert J.
Conflict & Crisis: The Presidency of Harry S. Truman, 1945-1948. Norton.

Donzelot, Jacques.
xDonzelot, Jacques.
The Policing of Families. Pantheon.

Doob, Joseph L.
xDoob, Joseph L.
Stochastic Processes. Wiley.

Doob, Leonard W. see Doob, Leonard William.

Doob, Leonard William, 1909-
xDoob, Leonard W.
Communication in Africa: A Search for Boundaries. Greenwood.
Panorama of Evil: Insights from the Behavioral Sciences. Greenwood.
Pathways to People. Yale U Pr.
Patriotism & Nationalism: Their Psychological Foundations. Greenwood.
Plans of Men. Shoe String.

Doob, Penelope B. see Doob, Penelope B. R.

Doob, Penelope B. R.
xDoob, Penelope B.
Nebuchadnezzar's Children: Conventions of Madness in Middle English Literature. Yale U Pr.

Doody, Margaret. see Doody, Margaret Anne.
Doody, Margaret A. see Doody, Margaret Anne.

Doody, Margaret Anne.
xDoody, Margaret.
Aristotle Detective. Har-Row.
xDoody, Margaret A.
A Natural Passion: A Study of the Novels of Samuel Richardson. Oxford U Pr.

Dooley, D. J. see Dooley, David Joseph.

Dooley, Daniel J., 1940-
xDooley, Daniel J.
Data-Conversion Integrated Circuits: IEEE Selected Reprints. Wiley.

Dooley, David Joseph, 1921-
xDooley, D. J.

Art of Sinclair Lewis. U of Nebr Pr.
Compton Mackenzie. Twayne.

Dooley, Dennis A.
xDooley, Dennis A.
ed. Index to State Bar Association Reports & Proceedings. W S Hein.

Dooley, Patrick K. see Dooley, Patrick Kiaran.

Dooley, Patrick Kiaran.
xDooley, Patrick K.
Pragmatism As Humanism: The Philosophy of William James. Nelson-Hall.

Dooley, Thomas A. see Dooley, Thomas Anthony.

Dooley, Thomas Anthony, 1927-1961
xDooley, Thomas A.
Night They Burned the Mountain. NAL.

Doolin, Dennis. see Doolin, Dennis J.

Doolin, Dennis J.
xDoolin, Dennis.
A Chinese-English Dictionary of Communist Chinese Terminology. Hoover Inst Pr.
xDoolin, Dennis J.
tr. Communist China: The Politics of Student Opposition. Hoover Inst Pr.

Dooling, D. M.
xDooling, D. M.
ed. A Way of Working. Doubleday.

Doolittle, Jerome.
xDoolittle, Jerome.
Canyons & Mesas. Silver.
The Southern Appalachians. Silver.
xDoolittle, Jerry.
Canyons & Mesas. Time-Life.

Doolittle, Jerry. see Doolittle, Jerome.

Dooner, Pierton W., 1844-1907?
xDooner, W. Pierton.
Last Days of the Republic. Arno.

Dooner, W. Pierton. see Dooner, Pierton W.

Doorn, Robert J., 1946-
xDoorn, Robert J.
A Blueprint for a New Nation: The Structure of the Na-Griamel Federation. Exposition.

Dopfer, Kurt.
xDopfer, Kurt.
The New Political Economy of Development: Integrated Theory & Asian Experience. St Martin.

Dopp, Peggy H. see Dopp, Peggy Hanson.

Dopp, Peggy Hanson.
xDopp, Peggy H.
Tomorrow Is a River. J Phunn.

Dopsch, Alfons, 1896-1953
xDopsch, Alfons.
The Economic & Social Foundations of European Civilization. Fertig.
Economic & Social Foundations of European Civilization. Gordon Pr.

Dor-El, David.
xDor-El, David.
The Clermont Book of Backgammon. Winchester Pr.

Doran, Charles F.
xDoran, Charles F.
The Politics of Assimilation: Hegemony & Its Aftermath. Johns Hopkins.

Doran, John, 1807-1878
xDoran, John.
History of Court Fools. Haskell.

Doran, Madeleine, 1905-
xDoran, Madeleine.
Text of King Lear. AMS Pr.
Text of King Lear. Folcroft.

Dore, Gustave, 1832-1883
xDore, Gustave.
Dore Bible Illustrations. Dover.
The Dore Bible Illustrations. Peter Smith.
Dore Gallery. Arco.
Dore's Illustrations for Rabelais: A Selection of 252 Illustrations. Dover.

Dore, R. P. see Dore, Ronald Philip.
Dore, Ronald P. see Dore, Ronald Philip.

Dore, Ronald Philip.
xDore, R. P.
Aspects of Social Change in Modern Japan. Princeton U Pr.
xDore, Ronald P.
The Diploma Disease: Education, Qualification, & Development. U of Cal Pr.

Doreian, Patrick.
xDoreian, Patrick-.
Mathematics & the Study of Social Relations. Schocken.

Doreian, Patrick-. see Doreian, Patrick.

Doremus, R. H.
xDoremus, Robert H.
Glass Science. Wiley.

Doremus, Robert H. see Doremus, R. H.
Doren, Carl C. Van. see Van Doren, Carl C.
Doren, Carl Van. see Van Doren, Carl C.
Doren, Carlton Van. see Van Doren, Carlton.
Doren, Mark Van. see Van Doren, Mark.

Dorey, T A.
xDorey, T. A.
ed. Latin Historians. Routledge & Kegan.

Dorey, T. A. see Dorey, Thomas Alan.

Dorey, Thomas Alan.
xDorey, T. A.
ed. Tacitus. Routledge & Kegan.

Dorf, Richard. see Dorf, Richard C.

Dorf, Richard C.
xDorf, Richard.
Introduction to Computers & Computer Science. Boyd & Fraser.
xDorf, Richard C.
Computers & Man. Boyd & Fraser.
Energy, Resources & Policy. A-W.
Modern Control Systems. A-W.

Dorfman, Eugene, 1917-
xDorfman, Eugene.
Narreme in the Medieval Romance Epic: An Introduction to Narrative Structures. U of Toronto Pr.

Dorfman, Gerald A. see Dorfman, Gerald Allen.

Dorfman, Gerald Allen, 1939-
xDorfman, Gerald A.
Government Versus Trade Unionism in British Politics Since 1968. Hoover Inst Pr.

Dorfman, John.
xDorfman, John.
Well-Being: An Introduction to Health. Scott F.

Dorfman, Leon.
xDorfman, Leon.
Student Biologist Explores Ecology. Rosen Pr.

Dorfman, Mark S., 1945-
xDorfman, Mark S.
Introduction to Insurance. P-H.

Dorfman, R. see Dorfman, Robert.

Dorfman, Robert.
xDorfman, R.
Linear Programming & Economic Analysis. McGraw.
xDorfman, Robert.
Economics of the Environment: Selected Readings. Norton.
Prices & Markets. P-H.

Dorian, Dith M.
xDorian, Edith M.
High-Water Cargo. Rutgers U Pr.

Dorian, Donald C. see Dorian, Donald Clayton.

Dorian, Donald Clayton, 1900-
xDorian, Donald C.
English Diodatis. AMS Pr.

Dorian, Edith M. see Dorian, Dith M.

Dorian, Frederick, 1902-
xDorian, Frederick.
Musical Workshop. Greenwood.

Dorian, Marguerite.
xDorian, Marguerite.

illus. When the Snow Is Blue. Lothrop.
Dorin, Patrick C.
xDorin, Patrick C.
Amtrak Trains & Travel. Superior Pub.
The Soo Line. Superior Pub.
Doring, P. F.
xDoring, P. F.
Colloquial German. Routledge & Kegan.
Dorio. *see* Dorio, Martin M.
Dorio, Martin M.
xDorio.
ed. Multiple Electron Resonance Spectroscopy.
Plenum Pub.
Doris, Lillian.
xDoris, Lillian.
Complete Secretary's Handbook. P-H.
Dorken, Hildegard.
xDorken, Hildegard.
Lord Byron's Subjektivismus in Seinem
Verhalten Zur Geschichte. Johnson Repr.
Dorland, Michael.
xDorland, Michael.
Double-Cross Circuit. G&D.
The Double-Cross Circuit. NAL.
Dorling. *see* Dorling, Alison Rosemary.
Dorling, Alison Rosemary.
xDorling.
Use of Mathematical Literature. Butterworths.
Dorman, C. C.
xDorman, C. C.
North Western Album. Soccer.
Dorman, Harry G. *see* Dorman, Harry Gaylord.
Dorman, Harry Gaylord, 1906-
xDorman, Harry G.
Toward Understanding Islam: Contemporary
Apologetic of Islam & Missionary Policy.
AMS Pr.
Dorman, Lynn.
xDorman, Lynn.
Growing Children. Brooks Cole.
Dorman, Marcus R. *see* Dorman, Marcus Roberts
Phipps.
Dorman, Marcus Roberts Phipps.
xDorman, Marcus R.
Journal of a Tour in the Congo Free State.
Negro U Pr.
Dorman, Michael.
xDorman, Michael.
Detectives of the Sky: Investigating Aviation
Tragedies. Watts.
Dorman, R. G. *see* Dorman, Richard George.
Dorman, Richard George.
xDorman, R. G.
Dust Control & Air Cleaning. Pergamon.
Dorman, Sonya.
xDorman, Sonya.
Planet Patrol. Coward.
Stretching Fence. Ohio U Pr.
Dormant, Diane.
xDormant, Diane.
Rolemaps. Educ Tech Pubns.
Dorn. *see* Dorn, Edwin.
Dorn, Edward.
xDorn, Edward.
The Cycle. Frontier Press Calif.
Gunslinger. Wingbow Pr.
Interviews. Four Seasons Foun.
Some Business Recently Transacted in the
White World. Frontier Press Calif.
Dorn, Edwin.
xDorn.
Rules & Racial Equality. Yale U Pr.
Dorn, Robert D.
xDorn, Robert D.
A Manual of the Vascular Plants of Wyoming.
Garland Pub.
Dorn, Sylvia O. *see* Dorn, Sylvia O'Neill.
Dorn, Sylvia O'Neill.
xDorn, Sylvia O.

Insider's Guide to Antiques, Art &
Collectibles. Cornerstone.
Dornan, James E.
xDornan, James E.
ed. United States National Security Policy in
the Decade Ahead. Crane-Russak Co.
Dornberg, John.
xDornberg, John.
Eastern Europe: A Communist Kaleidoscope.
Dial.
The Soviet Union Today. Dial.
The Two Germanys. Dial.
Dornburgh, Henry.
xDornburgh, Henry.
Why the Wilderness Is Called Adirondack: The
Earliest Account of Founding of the
MacIntyre Mine. Harbor Hill Bks.
Dorne, David.
xDorne, David.
Easy-to-Do Leathercraft Projects with Full Size
Templates. Dover.
Dorner, G. *see* Dorner, Gunter.
Dorner, Gunter.
xDorner, G.
Hormones & Brain Differentiation. Elsevier.
Dornette, William H. *see* Dornette, William H. L.
Dornette, William H. L.
xDornette, William H.
Legal Aspects of Anesthesia. Davis Co.
ed. Monitoring in Anesthesia. Davis Co.
Dornfeld, Ernst. *see* Dornfeld, Ernst John.
Dornfeld, Ernst John, 1911-
xDornfeld, Ernst.
Butterflies of Oregon. Intl Schol Bk Serv.
Dorny, C. Nelson, 1937-
xDorny, C. Nelson.
A Vector Space Approach to Models &
Optimization. Krieger.
Doroghi, Edwin. *see* Doroghi, Ervin.
Doroghi, Ervin, 1881-
xDoroghi, Edwin.
Grounds for Divorce in European Countries.
Kraus Repr.
Doron, Gideon.
xDoron, Gideon.
The Smoking Paradox: Public Regulation in the
Cigarette Industry. Abt Assoc.
Dorr, Donal.
xDorr, Donal.
Remove the Heart of Stone: Charismatic
Renewal & the Experience of Grace. Paulist
Pr.
Dorr, Eugene. *see* Dorr, Eugene L.
Dorr, Eugene L.
xDorr, Eugene.
Merchandising. McGraw.
Dorr, John A. *see* Dorr, John Adam.
Dorr, John Adam.
xDorr, John A.
Geology of Michigan. U of Mich Pr.
Dorr, Nell.
xDorr, Nell.
Of Night & Day. Scrimshaw Calif.
Dorr, Rheta C. *see* Dorr, Rheta Louise (Childe).
Dorr, Rheta Louise (Childe), 1872-1948
xDorr, Rheta C.
Inside the Russian Revolution. Arno.
Susan B. Anthony, the Woman Who Changed
the Mind of a Nation. AMS Pr.
Dorrance, G. S. *see* Dorrance, Graeme S.
Dorrance, Graeme S.
xDorrance, G. S.
National Monetary & Financial Analysis. St
Martin.
Dorset, Gerald.
xDorset, Gerald.
Adventure in Rich Port. New Earth.
Aristocrat of Intellect. Haskell.
Dorsett, Loyd G.
xDorsett, Loyd G.

Audio-Visual Teaching Machines. Educ Tech
Pubns.
Dorsett, Lyle. *see* Dorsett, Lyle W.
Dorsett, Lyle W.
xDorsett, Lyle.
The Queen City: A History of Denver. Pruett.
xDorsett, Lyle W.
Franklin D. Roosevelt & the City Bosses.
Kennikat.
The Queen City: A History of Denver. Pruett.
Dorsey, G. A. *see* Dorsey, George Amos.
Dorsey, George A. *see* Dorsey, George Amos.
Dorsey, George Amos, 1868-1931
xDorsey, G. A.
Cheyenne. Kraus Repr.
xDorsey, George A.
The Cheyenne. Ye Galleon.
Indians of the Southwest. AMS Pr.
Dorsey, James O. *see* Dorsey, James Owen.
Dorsey, James Owen, 1848-1895
xDorsey, James O.
Omaha Sociology. Johnson Repr.
Dorsey, Joan.
xDorsey, Joan.
Introducing Your Kids to the Outdoors. Stone
Wall Pr.
Dorsey, John M. *see* Dorsey, John Morris.
Dorsey, John Morris, 1900-
xDorsey, John M.
ed. The Growth of Self-Insight. Wayne St U
Pr.
Illness or Allness: Conversations of a
Psychiatrist. Wayne St U Pr.
University Professor John M. Dorsey. Wayne
St U Pr.
Dorso, Richard.
xDorso, Richard.
Thicker Than Water. HarBraceJ.
Dorson, Richard. *see* Dorson, Richard Mercer.
Dorson, Richard M. *see* Dorson, Richard Mercer.
Dorson, Richard Mercer, 1916-
xDorson, Richard.
ed. Folklore in the Modern World. Beresford
Bk Serv.
xDorson, Richard M.
ed. African Folklore. Ind U Pr.
American Folklore. U of Chicago Pr.
American Folklore & the Historian. U of
Chicago Pr.
ed. American Negro Folktales. Fawcett.
British Folklorists: A History. U of Chicago Pr.
Buying the Wind: Regional Folklore in the
United States. U of Chicago Pr.
ed. Davy Crockett American Comic Legend.
Greenwood.
Folklore & Fakelore: Essays Toward a
Discipline of Folk Studies. Harvard U Pr.
ed. Folklore & Folklife: An Introduction. U of
Chicago Pr.
Folktales Told Around the World. U of
Chicago Pr.
Negro Folktales in Michigan. Greenwood.
Negro Tales from Pine Bluff, Arkansas &
Calvin, Michigan. Kraus Repr.
Dorst, Jean.
xDorst, Jean.
Field Guide to the Larger Mammals of Africa.
HM.
The Life of Birds. Columbia U Pr.
Dorwart, Reinhold A. *see* Dorwart, Reinhold August.
Dorwart, Reinhold August, 1911-
xDorwart, Reinhold A.
Prussian Welfare State Before 1740. Harvard U
Pr.
Dorweiler, Paul.
xDorweiler, Paul.
Auto Stereo Service & Installation. TAB Bks.
Dory, John P. *see* Dory, John Paul.
Dory, John Paul, 1943-
xDory, John P.

The Domestic Diversifying Acquisition
  Decision. Univ Microfilms.
Dos Passos, John.
  xDos Passos, John.
    Adventures of a Young Man. Queens Hse.
    Brazil on the Move. Greenwood.
    Facing the Chair: Story of the Americanization
      of Two Foreign-Born Workmen. Da Capo.
    The Grand Design. Queens Hse.
    Manhattan Transfer. Bentley.
    Manhattan Transfer. HM.
    The Prospect Before Us. Greenwood.
    Theme Is Freedom. Arno.
    Tour of Duty. Greenwood.
Dos Santos, Joyce A. *see* Dos Santos, Joyce Audy.
Dos Santos, Joyce Audy.
  xDos Santos, Joyce A.
    Sand Dollar, Sand Dollar. Lippincott.
Doshay, Lewis J. *see* Doshay, Lewis Jacob.
Doshay, Lewis Jacob, 1896-
  xDoshay, Lewis J.
    Boy Sex Offender & His Later Career.
      Patterson Smith.
Doss, Helen. *see* Doss, Helen Grigsby.
Doss, Helen Grigsby.
  xDoss, Helen.
    The Family Nobody Wanted. Little.
    The Family Nobody Wanted. Schol Bk Serv.
Doss, M. *see* Doss, Manfred.
Doss, Manfred.
  xDoss, M.
    ed. Diagnosis & Therapy of Porphyrias & Lead
      Toxication. Springer-Verlag.
Doss, Margot P. *see* Doss, Margot Patterson.
Doss, Margot Patterson.
  xDoss, Margot P.
    Golden Gate Park at Your Feet. Presidio Pr.
Dossat, Roy J.
  xDossat, Roy J.
    Principles of Refrigeration. Wiley.
Dossick, Jesse J. *see* Dossick, Jesse John.
Dossick, Jesse John, 1911-
  xDossick, Jesse J.
    Doctoral Research at the School of Education,
      New York University, 1890-1970: A
      Classified List of 4,336 Dissertations with
      Some Critical & Statistical Analysis. NYU Pr.
    Doctoral Research on Russia & the Soviet
      Union. NYU Pr.
    Doctoral Research on Russia & the Soviet
      Union: 1960-1975. Garland Pub.
Dostal, Rudolf.
  xDostal, Rudolf.
    On Integration in Plants. Harvard U Pr.
Doster, William C.
  xDoster, William C.
    Differing Eye: An Introduction to Literature.
      Glencoe.
Dosumu-Johnson, T. O.
  xDosumu-Johnson, T. O.
    Reflections of an African Nationalist. Vantage.
Dott, Robert. *see* Dott, Robert H.
Dott, Robert H.
  xDott, Robert.
    Evolution of the Earth. McGraw.
Dottin, Paul, 1895-1965
  xDottin, Paul.
    Life & Strange & Surprising Adventures of
      Daniel DeFoe. Octagon.
Dotto, Lydia.
  xDotto, Lydia.
    The Ozone War. Doubleday.
Dotts, Maryann J.
  xDotts, Maryann J.
    The Church Resource Library: How to Start It
      & Make It Grow. Abingdon.
    When Jesus Was Born. Abingdon.
Doty, C. Stewart. *see* Doty, Charles Stewart.
Doty, Charles Stewart.
  xDoty, C. Stewart.

From Cultural Rebellion to Counterrevolution:
  The Politics of Maurice Barres. Ohio U Pr.
  ed. The Industrial Revolution. Krieger.
Doty, Harry L., 1911-
  xDoty, Harry L.
    Letters to Ron. Herald Hse.
Doty, Jean S. *see* Doty, Jean Slaughter.
Doty, Jean Slaughter.
  xDoty, Jean S.
    Can I Get There by Candlelight?. Macmillan.
    The Crumb. Greenwillow.
    The Crumb. Schol Bk Serv.
    Gabriel. Macmillan.
    Monday Horses. Archway.
    The Monday Horses. Greenwillow.
    The Monday Horses. PB.
    Summer Pony. Macmillan.
    Summer Pony. Macmillan.
Doty, Pamela.
  xDoty, Pamela.
    Guided Change of the American Health
      System: Where the Levers Are. Human Sci
      Pr.
Doty, Roy, 1922-
  xDoty, Roy.
    Gunga, Your Din-Din Is Ready: Son of Puns,
      Gags, Quips & Riddles. Doubleday.
    How Much Does America Cost?. Doubleday.
    Puns, Gags, Quips & Riddles: A Collection of
      Dreadful Jokes. Doubleday.
    Q's Are Weird O's: More Puns, Gags, Quips &
      Riddles. Doubleday.
    Where Are You Going with That Coal?.
      Doubleday.
    Where Are You Going with That Energy?.
      Doubleday.
    Where Are You Going with That Oil.
      Doubleday.
    ed. Wordless Workshop. Taplinger.
Doty, William F. *see* Doty, William Lodewick.
Doty, William G., 1939-
  xDoty, William G.
    Letters in Primitive Christianity. Fortress.
Doty, William L. *see* Doty, William Lodewick.
Doty, William Lodewick, 1919-
  xDoty, William F.
    Meet Your Pastor. Alba Bks.
  xDoty, William L.
    One Season Following Another: A Cycle of
      Faith. Franciscan Herald.
Dou, Alberto.
  xDou, Alberto.
    Lectures on Partial Differential Equations of
      First Order. U of Notre Dame Pr.
Doubleday, Abner, 1819-1893
  xDoubleday, Abner.
    Reminiscences of Forts Sumter & Moultrie in
      1860-61. Reprint.
Doubleday, Ellen.
  xDoubleday, Ellen.
    Two-Part Writing. Branden.
Doubleday, Neal F. *see* Doubleday, Neal Frank.
Doubleday, Neal Frank.
  xDoubleday, Neal F.
    Variety of Attempt: British & American Fiction
      in the Early Nineteenth Century. U of Nebr
      Pr.
Doubleday, Nelson.
  xDoubleday, Nelson.
    Encyclopedia of World Travel. Doubleday.
Doubleday, Thomas, 1790-1870
  xDoubleday, Thomas.
    Financial, Monetary & Statistical History of
      England, from the Revolution of 1688 to the
      Present Time. Greenwood.
Doucet, Lorraine D.
  xDoucet, Lorraine D.

Medical Technology Examination Review.
  Lippincott.
Doucette, John.
  xDoucette, John.
    Progress Tests for the Developmentally
      Disabled: An Evaluation. Abt Assoc.
Doudna, Martin K.
  xDoudna, Martin K.
    Concerned About the Planet: The Reporter
      Magazine & American Liberalism,
      1949-1968. Greenwood.
Dougall, Charles S. *see* Dougall, Charles Shirra.
Dougall, Charles Shirra.
  xDougall, Charles S.
    The Burns Country. Folcroft.
    The Burns Country. R West.
Dougall, Herbert E. *see* Dougall, Herbert Edward.
Dougall, Herbert Edward.
  xDougall, Herbert E.
    Capital Markets & Institutions. P-H.
Dougan, Michael B., 1944-
  xDougan, Michael B.
    Confederate Arkansas: The People & Policies
      of a Frontier State in Wartime. U of Ala Pr.
Dougherty, Adelyn.
  xDougherty, Adelyn.
    A Study of Rhythmic Structure in the Verse of
      William Butler Yeats. Mouton.
Dougherty, Betty. *see* Dougherty, Betty J.
Dougherty, Betty J.
  xDougherty, Betty.
    Green Gardener: How an Amateur Created a
      Wild Garden. David & Charles.
Dougherty, James E.
  xDougherty, James E.
    Contending Theories of International Relations.
      Har-Row.
Dougherty, James J., 1939-
  xDougherty, James J.
    The Politics of Wartime Aid: American
      Economic Assistance to France & French
      Northwest Africa, 1940-1946. Greenwood.
Dougherty, James L.
  xDougherty, James L.
    Union-Free Labor Relations: A Step-by-Step
      Guide to Staying Union Free. Gulf Pub.
Dougherty, Neil J.
  xDougherty, Neil J.
    Contemporary Approaches to the Teaching of
      Physical Education. Burgess.
Dougherty, William M.
  xDougherty, William M.
    Introduction to Hematology. Mosby.
Doughton, Morgan J.
  xDoughton, Morgan J.
    Peoplepower: An Alternative to 1984. Media
      America.
Doughty, Charles M. *see* Doughty, Charles Montagu.
Doughty, Charles Montagu, 1843-1926
  xDoughty, Charles M.
    Adam Cast Forth. AMS Pr.
    Travels in Arabia Deserta. Dover.
    Travels in Arabia Deserta. Peter Smith.
Doughty, Howard, 1904-
  xDoughty, Howard.
    Francis Parkman. Greenwood.
Doughty, Oswald.
  xDoughty, Oswald.
    English Lyric in the Age of Reason. Folcroft.
    English Lyric in the Age of Reason. Russell.
    Forgotten Lyrics of the Eighteenth Century.
      Folcroft.
    Forgotten Lyrics of the Eighteenth Century.
      Russell.
Doughty, Paul L.
  xDoughty, Paul L.
    Huaylas: An Andean District in Search of
      Progress. Cornell U Pr.
Douglas. *see* Douglas, Jack D.
Douglas, A. H. *see* Douglas, Arthur Henry.

Douglas, Alan. *see* Douglas, Alan Lockhart Monteith.
Douglas, Alan Lockhart Monteith.
  xDouglas, Alan.
    Sourcebook of Electronic Organ Circuits. TAB
    Bks.
Douglas, Alfred, 1942-
  xDouglas, Alfred.
    The Tarot: The Origins, Meaning & Uses of
    the Cards. Penguin.
Douglas, Alfred. *see* Douglas, Alfred Bruce.
Douglas, Alfred B. *see* Douglas, Alfred Bruce.
Douglas, Alfred Bruce, Lord, 1870-1945
  xDouglas, Alfred.
    Autobiography of Lord Alfred Douglas. Arno.
    Autobiography of Lord Alfred Douglas. R
    West.
    The Autobiography of Lord Alfred Douglas.
    Scholarly.
    True History of Shakespeare's Sonnets.
    Kennikat.
  xDouglas, Alfred B.
    Oscar Wilde: A Summing-up. Folcroft.
    Oscar Wilde & Myself. AMS Pr.
Douglas, Ann.
  xDouglas, Ann.
    Industrial Peacemaking. Columbia U Pr.
Douglas, Arthur Henry.
  xDouglas, A. H.
    An Approach to Engineering Mathematics.
    Pergamon.
Douglas, Colin, 1945-
  xDouglas, Colin.
    Bleeders Come First. Taplinger.
    The Greatest Breakthrough Since Lunchtime.
    Taplinger.
    The Houseman's Tale. Taplinger.
Douglas, David, 1799-1834
  xDouglas, David.
    Journal Kept by David Douglas During His
    Travels in North America, 1823 27. Lubrecht
    & Cramer.
Douglas, David C. *see* Douglas, David Charles.
Douglas, David Charles, 1898-
  xDouglas, David C.
    The Norman Achievement: 1050-1100. U of
    Cal Pr.
    The Norman Fate, 1100-1154. U of Cal Pr.
Douglas, Ellen, Pseud.
  xDouglas, Ellen.
    The Rock Cried Out. HarBraceJ.
    Where the Dreams Cross. Ultramarine Pub.
Douglas, Evan J., 1946-
  xDouglas, Evan J.
    Managerial Economics: Theory, Practice &
    Problems. P-H.
Douglas, Frederic H. *see* Douglas, Frederic Huntington.
Douglas, Frederic Huntington.
  xDouglas, Frederic H.
    Indian Art of the United States. Arno.
Douglas, Gawin, Bp. of Dunkeld, 1474?-1522
  xDouglas, Gawyn.
    Palice of Honour. AMS Pr.
    The Palice of Honour. Johnson Repr.
Douglas, Gawyn. *see* Douglas, Gawin.
Douglas, George B. *see* Douglas, George Brisbane.
Douglas, George Brisbane, Sir, Bart, 1856-1935
  xDouglas, George B.
    Contemporary Scottish Verse. AMS Pr.
Douglas, Gertrude, Lady.
  xDouglas, Gertrude.
    Linked Lives. Garland Pub.
Douglas, Gina.
  xDouglas, Gina.
    The Ganges. Silver.
Douglas, Ian.
  xDouglas, Ian.
    Humid Landforms. Mit Pr.
Douglas, J. *see* Douglas, Jim.
Douglas, J. D. *see* Douglas, Jack D.
Douglas, J. H. *see* Douglas, John Henry.

Douglas, Jack, 1908-
  xDouglas, Jack.
    Rubber Duck. Putnam.
Douglas, Jack D.
  xDouglas.
    Introduction to the Sociologies of Everyday
    Life. Allyn.
  xDouglas, J. D.
    ed. Existential Sociology. Cambridge U Pr.
  xDouglas, Jack D.
    ed. Crime & Justice in American Society.
    Irvington.
    ed. Deviance & Respectability: The Social
    Construction of Moral Meanings. Basic.
    ed. Impact of Sociology: Readings in the Social
    Sciences. Irvington.
    ed. Introduction to Sociology: Situations &
    Structures. Free Pr.
    ed. Official Deviance: Readings in Malfeasance,
    Misfeasance, & Other Forms of Corruption.
    Har-Row.
    ed. Relevance of Sociology. P-H.
Douglas, Jim.
  xDouglas, J.
    Collocation Methods for Parabolic Equations in
    a Single Space Variable: Based on C to the
    First Power-Piecewise-Polynomial Spaces.
    Springer-Verlag.
Douglas, John Henry.
  xDouglas, J. H.
    ed. Cassell's Concise French-English,
    English-French Dictionary. Macmillan.
Douglas, John S. *see* Douglas, John Scott.
Douglas, John Scott.
  xDouglas, John S.
    Story of the Oceans. Greenwood
Douglas, Johnson E.
  xDouglas, Johnson E.
    Successful Seed Programs: A Planning &
    Management Guide. Westview.
Douglas, Keith. *see* Douglas, Keith Castellain.
Douglas, Keith Castellain.
  xDouglas, Keith.
    Alamein to Zem Zem. Oxford U Pr.
Douglas, Lloyd C. *see* Douglas, Lloyd Cassel.
Douglas, Lloyd Cassel, 1877-1951
  xDouglas, Lloyd C.
    White Banners. PB.
Douglas, Lloyd V. *see* Douglas, Lloyd Virgil.
Douglas, Lloyd Virgil.
  xDouglas, Lloyd V.
    jt. auth. Teaching Business Subjects. P-H.
Douglas, Marjory S. *see* Douglas, Marjory Stoneman.
Douglas, Marjory Stoneman.
  xDouglas, Marjory S.
    Hurricane. Mockingbird Bks.
Douglas, Martha C.
  xDouglas, Martha C.
    Go for It: How to Get Your First Good Job.
    Chronicle Bks.
Douglas, Mary. *see* Douglas, Mary Tew.
Douglas, Mary P. *see* Douglas, Mary Teresa (Peacock).
Douglas, Mary Teresa (Peacock), 1903-
  xDouglas, Mary P.
    Pupil Assistant in the School Library. ALA.
Douglas, Mary Tew.
  xDouglas, Mary.
    Implicit Meanings: Essays in Anthropology.
    Routledge & Kegan.
Douglas, Neil H.
  xDouglas, Neil H.
    Freshwater Fishes of Louisiana. Claitors.
Douglas, Norman, 1868-1952
  xDouglas, Norman.

    In the Beginning. Scholarly.
    Late Harvest. AMS Pr.
    London Street Games. Gale.
    London Street Games. Johnson Repr.
    Old Calabria. Hyperion Conn.
Douglas, Norman. *see* Douglas, Norman George Norman
  Douglas.
Douglas, Norman George Norman Douglas.
  xDouglas, Norman.
    South Wind. Intl Pubns Serv.
    South Wind. Scholarly.
Douglas, Paul H. *see* Douglas, Paul Howard.
Douglas, Paul Howard, 1892-
  xDouglas, Paul H.
    American Apprenticeship & Industrial
    Education. AMS Pr.
    Ethics in Government. Greenwood.
    The Problem of Unemployment. Arno.
    Theory of Wages. Kelley.
    The Worker in Modern Economic Society.
    Arno.
Douglas, R. Gordon. *see* Douglas, Robert Gordon.
Douglas, Robert Gordon.
  xDouglas, R. Gordon.
    Operative Obstetrics. ACC.
Douglas, Roy, 1924-
  xDouglas, Roy.
    In the Year of Munich. St Martin.
Douglas, Roy. *see* Douglas, Roy Ian.
Douglas, Roy Ian.
  xDouglas, Roy.
    The History of the Liberal Party: 1895-1970.
    Fairleigh Dickinson.
Douglas, S. W.
  xDouglas, S. W.
    Principles of Veterinary Radiography. Lea &
    Febiger.
Douglas, Stephen A., 1938-
  xDouglas, Stephen A.
    Political Socialization & Student Activism in
    Indonesia. U of Ill Pr.
Douglas, Thorne.
  xDouglas, Thorne.
    Mustang Men. Fawcett.
Douglas, Tom.
  xDouglas, Tom.
    Group Processes in Social Work: A Theoretical
    Synthesis. Wiley.
    Groupwork Practice. Intl Univs Pr.
Douglas, W. A. *see* Douglas, William A. B.
Douglas, Walter B. *see* Douglas, Walter Bond.
Douglas, Walter Bond.
  xDouglas, Walter B.
    Manuel Lisa. Argosy.
Douglas, William A. B.
  xDouglas, W. A.
    Out of the Shadows: Canada in the Second
    World War. Oxford U Pr.
Douglas, William O. *see* Douglas, William Orville.
Douglas, William Orville.
  xDouglas, William O.
    America Challenged. Princeton U Pr.
    Douglas of the Supreme Court: A Selection of
    His Opinions. Greenwood.
    Of Men & Mountains. Seattle Bk.
    The Right of the People. Greenwood.
    Towards a Global Federalism. NYU Pr.

Douglas-Hamilton, Iain.
  xDouglas-Hamilton, Iain.
    Among the Elephants. Penguin.

Douglas-Young, John.
  xDouglas-Young, John.
    Complete Guide to Reading Schematic
    Diagrams. P-H.
    Practical Oscilloscope Handbook. P-H.

Douglass, Amanda H. *see* Douglass, Amanda Hart.

Douglass, Amanda Hart.
  xDouglass, Amanda H.
    Charlotte. Belmont-Tower.
Douglass, Barbara.
  xDouglass, Barbara.
    Skateboard Scramble. Westminster.
Douglass, D. H. *see* Douglass, David H.
Douglass, David H., 1932-
  xDouglass, D. H.
    ed. Superconductivity in d- & f- Band Metals.
    Plenum Pub.
Douglass, Earl L. *see* Douglass, Earl Leroy.
Douglass, Earl Leroy, 1888-
  xDouglass, Earl L.
    The Douglass Devotional. M Evans.
Douglass, Frederick, 1817?-1895
  xDouglass, Frederick.
    The Frederick Douglass Papers: Series One:
    Speeches, Debates, & Interviews Volume I:
    Eighteen Forty-One to Eighteen Forty-Six.
    Yale U Pr.
    My Bondage & My Freedom. Dover.
    My Bondage & My Freedom. Johnson Chi.
Douglass, Gordon K.
  xDouglass, Gordon K.
    The New Interdependence: The European
    Community & the United States. Lexington
    Bks.
Douglass, Harlan P. *see* Douglass, Harlan Paul.
Douglass, Harlan Paul, 1871-1953
  xDouglass, Harlan P.
    The Little Town; Especially in Its Rural
    Relationships. Arno.
    The Protestant Church As a Social Institution.
    Russell.
    Suburban Trend. Arno.
    The Suburban Trend. Johnson Repr.
Douglass, J. Harvey. *see* Douglass, James Harvey.
Douglass, James Harvey.
  xDouglass, J. Harvey.
    Projects in Wood Furniture. McKnight.
Douglass, Joseph D.
  xDouglass, Joseph D.
    Soviet Military Strategy in Europe. Pergamon.
    Soviet Strategy for Nuclear War. Hoover Inst
    Pr.
Douglass, Laura M. *see* Douglass, Laura Mae.
Douglass, Laura Mae.
  xDouglass, Laura M.
    The Effective Nurse: Leader & Manager.
    Mosby.
    Review of Leadership in Nursing. Mosby.
Douglass, Robert W.
  xDouglass, Robert W.
    Forest Recreation. Pergamon.
Douglass, William, 1691?-1752
  xDouglass, William.
    Summary, Historical & Political, of the First
    Planting, Progressive Improvements, &
    Present State of the British Settlements in
    North-America. Arno.
Douglass, William A.
  xDouglass, William A.
    Amerikanuak: Basques in the New World. U of
    Nev Pr.
  xDouglass, William S.
    Echalar & Murelaga: Opportunity & Rural
    Exodus in Two Spanish Basque Villages. St
    Martin.
Douglass, William S. *see* Douglass, William A.
Douhet, Giulio, 1869-1930
  xDouhet, Giulio.
    The Command of the Air. Arno.
Doukas, K. A. *see* Doukas, Kimon Apostolus.
Doukas, Kimon Apostolus, 1903-
  xDoukas, K. A.
    The French Railroads & the State. Octagon.
Doukhobor Research Committee.
  xDoukhobor Research Committee.

    The Doukhobors of British Columbia.
    Greenwood.
Doulis, Thomas.
  xDoulis, Thomas.
    George Theotokas. Twayne.
Doumato, Lamia.
  xDoumato, Lamia.
    ed. American Drawing: A Guide to
    Information Sources. Gale.
Doust, W. A.
  xDoust, W. A.
    The Ocean on a Plank. Vantage.
Douthwaite, Graham.
  xDouthwaite, Graham.
    Attorney's Guide to Restitution. A Smith Co.
Douty, Christopher M. *see* Douty, Christopher Morris.
Douty, Christopher Morris.
  xDouty, Christopher M.
    The Economics of Localized Disasters: The
    1906 San Francisco Catastrophe. Arno.
Douville, Leone.
  xDouville, Leone.
    Patient Care Services Policy Manual for the
    Nursing Department. Cath Health.
Douzou, P. *see* Douzou, Pierre.
Douzou, Pierre.
  xDouzou, P.
    Cryobiochemistry: An Introduction. Acad Pr.
Dove, W. F. *see* Dove, William F.
Dove, William F.
  xDove, W. F.
    ed. Growth & Differentiation in Physarum
    Polycephalum. Princeton U Pr.
Dover, K. J. *see* Dover, Kenneth James.
Dover, Kenneth James.
  xDover, K. J.
    Aristophanic Comedy. U of Cal Pr.
    Greek Homosexuality. Harvard U Pr.
    Greek Homosexuality. Random.
    Greek Popular Morality in the Time of Plato &
    Aristotle. U of Cal Pr.
Doveton, Dorothy M.
  xDoveton, Dorothy M.
    The Human Geography of Swaziland. AMS Pr.
Dovring, Karin.
  xDovring, Karin.
    Frontiers of Communication: The Americas in
    Search of Political Culture. Chris Mass.
Dow, A. B. *see* Dow, Alden B.
Dow, Alden B., 1904-
  xDow, A. B.
    Reflections. Northwood Inst.
Dow, George F. *see* Dow, George Francis.
Dow, George Francis, 1868-1936
  xDow, George F.
    Arts & Crafts in New England. 1704-1775. Da
    Capo.
    Pirates of the New England Coast 1630-1730.
    Argosy.
Dow, J. Kamal.
  xDow, J. Kamal.
    Colombia's Foreign Trade & Economic
    Integration in Latin America. U Presses Fla.
Dow, Jones & Co., New York. *see* Dow Jones and Co.,
  New York.
Dow Jones and Co., New York.
  xDow, Jones & Co., New York.
    Nineteen Seventy-Seven, the Dow Jones
    Securities Valuation Handbook. Dow Jones.
Dow, Paul E.
  xDow, Paul E.
    ed. Criminology in Literature. Longman.
Dow, R. *see* Dow, Ronald.
Dow, Robert A. *see* Dow, Robert Arthur.
Dow, Robert Arthur.
  xDow, Robert A.
    Learning Through Encounter. Judson.
Dow, Roger W.
  xDow, Roger W.

    Business English. Wiley.
Dow, Ronald.
  xDow, R.
    Marketing & Work Study. Pergamon.
Dow, Sterling, 1903-
  xDow, Sterling.
    Fifty Years of Sathers: The Sather
    Professorship of Classical Literature in the
    University of California, Berkeley,
    1913-14-1963-64. U of Cal Pr.
Dow, Steven.
  xDow, Steven.
    Breeding Angelfish for the Hobbyist &
    Professional. Palmetto Pub.
    Success with Corydoras Catfish. Arco.
    Success with Corydoras Catfish. Palmetto Pub.
Dowall, David E.
  xDowall, David E.
    Effects of Environmental Regulations on
    Housing Costs. CPL Biblios.
Dowbenko, George.
  xDowbenko, George.
    Homegrown Holography. Amphoto.
Dowd, Douglas F. *see* Dowd, Douglas Fitzgerald.
Dowd, Douglas Fitzgerald, 1919-
  xDowd, Douglas F.
    Modern Economic Problems in Historical
    Perspective. Heath.
Dowd, James J.
  xDowd, James J.
    Stratification Among the Aged. Brooks-Cole.
Dowd, Jerome, 1864-
  xDowd, Jerome.
    Negro in American Life. Negro U Pr.
    Negro Races: A Sociological Study. Metro Bks.
Dowd, Merle E.
  xDowd, Merle E.
    How to Earn a Fortune & Become Independent
    in Your Own Business. P-H.
Dowdell, Dorothy.
  xDowdell, Dorothy.
    Careers in Horticultural Sciences. Messner.
    Tahoe. Playboy Pbks.
Dowden, Ann O. *see* Dowden, Anne Ophelia Todd.
Dowden, Anne O. *see* Dowden, Anne Ophelia Todd.
Dowden, Anne Ophelia Todd, 1907-
  xDowden, Ann O.
    Look at a Flower. T Y Crowell.
  xDowden, Anne O.
    illus. Look at a Flower. T Y Crowell.
    illus. State Flowers. T Y Crowell.
Dowden, Edward, 1843-1913
  xDowden, Edward.
    The French Revolution & English Literature.
    Folcroft.
    French Revolution & English Literature.
    Kennikat.
    A History of French Literature. Arno.
    A History of French Literature. Folcroft.
    Introduction to Shakespeare. AMS Pr.
    Introduction to Shakespeare. Arno.
    Introduction to Shakespeare. Folcroft.
    Southey. AMS Pr.
    Southey. Folcroft.
Dowdey, Clifford, 1904-
  xDowdey, Clifford.
    Bugles Blow No More. Larlin Corp.
Dowdey, Landon G. *see* Dowdey, Landon Gerald.
Dowdey, Landon Gerald.
  xDowdey, Landon G.
    ed. Journey to Freedom: A Casebook with
    Music. Swallow.
Dowell, Arlene Taylor, 1941-
  xDowell, Arlene Taylor.
    Cataloging with Copy: A Decision-Makers
    Handbook. Libs Unl.
Dowell, Coleman.
  xDowell, Coleman.
    Mrs. October Was Here. New Directions.
Dowell, Eldridge F. *see* Dowell, Eldridge Foster.

Dowell, Eldridge Foster, 1905-
   xDowell, Eldridge F.
     A History of Criminal Syndicalism Legislation
       in the United States. AMS Pr.
     History of Criminal Syndicalism Legislation in
       the United States. Da Capo.
Dowell, L. see Dowell, Linus J.
Dowell, Linus J., 1930-
   xDowell, L.
     Strategies for Teaching Physical Education.
       P-H.
Dower, J. W. see Dower, John W.
Dower, John W.
   xDower, J. W.
     Empire & Aftermath: Yoshida Shigeru & the
       Japanese Experience, 1878-1954. Harvard U
       Pr.
Dowis, Edward. see Dowis, Edward Franklin.
Dowis, Edward Franklin, 1901-
   xDowis, Edward.
     How to Install Your Own Home or Mobile
       Electric Power Plant. TAB Bks.
Dowley, Jennifer.
   xDowley, Jennifer.
     ed. Money Business: Grants & Awards for
       Creative Artists. Artists Found.
Dowling, Harry F. see Dowling, Harry Filmore.
Dowling, Harry Filmore, 1904-
   xDowling, Harry F.
     Fighting Infection: Conquests of the Twentieth
       Century. Harvard U Pr.
Dowling, Jerry L.
   xDowling, Jerry L.
     Criminal Investigation. HarBraceJ.
Dowling, John. see Dowling, John Clarkson.
Dowling, John Clarkson, 1920-
   xDowling, John.
     Leandro Fernandez de Moratin. Twayne.
Dowling, John Malcolm.
   xDowling, M.
     ed. Readings in Econometric Theory. Colo
       Assoc.
Dowling, John R.
   xDowling, John R.
     Developing & Administering an Industrial
       Training Program. CBI Pub.
Dowling, M. see Dowling, John Malcolm.
Dowling, Marion.
   xDowling, Marion.
     The Modern Nursery. Longman.
Dowling, Theodore E. see Dowling, Theodore Edward.
Dowling, Theodore Edward, 1837-1921
   xDowling, Theodore E.
     Armenian Church. AMS Pr.
Dowling, Tom.
   xDowling, Tom.
     Coach: A Season with Lombardi. Norton.
     Coach: A Season with Lombardi. Popular Lib.
Dowling, William C.
   xDowling, William C.
     The Boswellian Hero. U of Ga Pr.
     The Critic's Hornbook: Reading for
       Interpretation. Har-Row.
Dowling, William L.
   xDowling, William L.
     Prospective Rate Setting. Aspen Systems.
Down, Goldie. see Down, Goldie M.
Down, Goldie M.
   xDown, Goldie.
     More Lives Than a Cat. Southern Pub.
   xDown, Goldie M.
     No Forty-Hour Week. Southern Pub.
Downer, Alan S.
   xDowner, Alan S.
     British Drama: A Handbook & Brief Chronicle.
       Irvington.
Downer, Alan S. see Downer, Alan Seymour.
Downer, Alan Seymour, 1912-
   xDowner, Alan S.

     ed. American Drama & Its Critics: A
       Collection of Critical Essays. U of Chicago
       Pr.
Downer, Ann H.
   xDowner, Ann H.
     Physical Therapy Procedures: Selected
       Techniques. C C Thomas.
Downer, Marion.
   xDowner, Marion.
     Long Ago in Florence: The Story of Della
       Robbia Sculpture. Lothrop.
Downes, D. M. see Downes, David M.
Downes, David. see Downes, David M.
Downes, David A. see Downes, David Anthony.
Downes, David Anthony, 1927-
   xDownes, David A.
     Ruskin's Landscape of Beatitude. Univ
       Microfilms.
Downes, David M.
   xDownes, D. M.
     Gambling, Work & Leisure: A Study Across
       Three Areas. Routledge & Kegan.
   xDownes, David.
     ed. Deviant Interpretations. B&N.
Downes, Edward.
   xDownes, Edward.
     Adventures in Symphonic Music. Kennikat.
Downes, Olin, 1886-1955
   xDownes, Olin.
     Symphonic Masterpieces. Arno.
     Symphonic Masterpieces. Scholarly.
Downes, William H. see Downes, William Howe.
Downes, William Howe, 1854-1941
   xDownes, William H.
     The Life & Works of Winslow Homer. B
       Franklin.
Downey, Fairfax D. see Downey, Fairfax Davis.
Downey, Fairfax Davis, 1893-
   xDowney, Fairfax D.
     Our Lusty Forefathers: Being Diverse
       Chronicles of the Fervors, Frolics, Fights,
       Festivities, & Failings of Our American
       Ancestors. Arno.

Downey, Glanville. see Downey, Glanville Robert Emory
  Glanville Downey.

**Downey, Glanville Robert Emory Glanville Downey,
  1908-**
   xDowney, Glanville.
     Gaza in the Early Sixth Century. U of Okla Pr.
     History of Antioch in Syria: From Seleucus to
       the Arab Conquest. Princeton U Pr.
     The Late Roman Empire. Krieger.
     Late Roman Empire. Peter Smith.
Downey, Jake.
   xDowney, Jake.
     Teach Your Child Badminton. Transatlantic.
Downey, James.
   xDowney, James.
     Eighteenth Century Pulpit: A Study of the
       Sermons of Butler, Berkeley, Secker, Sterne,
       Whitefield & Wesley. Oxford U Pr.
Downey, Meriel. see Downey, Meriel Elaine.
Downey, Meriel Elaine.
   xDowney, Meriel.
     Moral Education: Theory & Practice. Har-Row.
Downey, Murray W.
   xDowney, Murray W.
     Art of Soul Winning. Baker Bk.
Downey, W. K. see Downey, William Kevin.
Downey, William Kevin.
   xDowney, W. K.
     ed. Food Quality & Nutrition: Research
       Priorities for Thermal Processing. Burgess-Intl
       Ideas.
Downie, Don.
   xDownie, Don.
     Cockpit Navigation Guide. TAB Bks.
Downie, N. M. see Downie, Norville Morgan.

Downie, Norville M. see Downie, Norville Morgan.
Downie, Norville Morgan.
   xDownie, N. M.
     Descriptive & Inferential Statistics. Har-Row.
   xDownie, Norville M.
     Types of Test Scores. HM.
Downing, A. B.
   xDowning, A. B.
     ed. Euthanasia & the Right to Death: The Case
       for Voluntary Euthanasia. Humanities.
Downing, A. F. see Downing, Antoinette Forrester.
Downing, Antoinette Forrester.
   xDowning, A. F.
     Architectural Heritage of Newport, Rhode
       Island: 1640-1915. Potter.
Downing, David.
   xDowning, David.
     The Devil's Virtuosos: German Generals at
       War, 1940-1945. St Martin.
Downing, Elisabeth, 1933-
   xDowning, Elizabeth.
     Keeping Rabbits. Merrimack Bk Serv.
Downing, Elizabeth. see Downing, Elisabeth.
Downing, George.
   xDowning, George.
     Massage & Meditation. Random.
     Massage Book. Bookworks.
Downing, Henry F. see Downing, Henry Francis.
Downing, Henry Francis, 1851-
   xDowning, Henry F.
     The American Cavalryman: A Liberian
       Romance. AMS Pr.
Downing, Paul B.
   xDowning, Paul B.
     ed. Air Pollution & the Social Sciences:
       Formulating & Implementing Control
       Programs. Irvington.
Downing, Richard I. see Downing, Richard Ivan.
Downing, Richard Ivan.
   xDowning, Richard I.
     National Income & Social Accounts: An
       Australian Study. Intl Schol Bk Serv.
Downs, Anthony.
   xDowns, Anthony.
     Economic Theory of Democracy. Har-Row.
     Inside Bureaucracy. Little.
     Opening up the Suburbs: An Urban Strategy
       for America. Yale U Pr.
     Who Are the Urban Poor?. Comm Econ Dev.
Downs, Brian W. see Downs, Brian Westerdale.
Downs, Brian Westerdale, 1893-
   xDowns, Brian W.
     A Study of Six Plays by Ibsen. Octagon.
Downs, Cal W.
   xDowns, Cal W.
     The Organizational Communicator. Har-Row.
     Professional Interviewing. Har-Row.
Downs, Florence S.
   xDowns, Florence S.
     ed. Issues in Nursing Research. ACC.
     A Source Book of Nursing Research. Davis Co.
Downs, George W.
   xDowns, George W.
     Bureaucracy, Innovation & Public Policy.
       Lexington Bks.
Downs, Hugh.
   xDowns, Hugh.
     Thirty Dirty Lies About Old. Argus Comm.
     Thirty Dirty Lies About Old. G K Hall.
Downs, Hugh R.
   xDowns, Hugh R.
     Rhythms of a Himalayan Village. Har-Row.
Downs, James. see Downs, James Chesterfield.
Downs, James Chesterfield, 1905-
   xDowns, James.
     Principles of Real Estate Management. Inst
       Real Estate.
Downs, James F.
   xDowns, James F.

Cultures in Crisis. Glencoe.
Human Nature: An Introduction to Cultural
    Anthropology. Glencoe.
Human Variation: An Introduction to Physical
    Anthropology. Glencoe.
The Navajo. HR&W.
Two Worlds of the Washo: An Indian Tribe of
    California & Nevada. HR&W.

Downs, Robert B. *see* Downs, Robert Bingham.

Downs, Robert Bingham, 1903-
    xDowns, Robert B.
    Books & History. U of Ill Lib Sci.
    Books That Changed America. Macmillan.
    Books That Changed the South. Littlefield.
    Books That Changed the South. U of NC Pr.
    Books That Changed the World. ALA.
    Books That Changed the World. NAL.
    Famous Books: Great Writings in the History
        of Civilization. Littlefield.
    ed. First Freedom: Liberty & Justice in the
        World of Books & Reading. ALA.
    Friedrich Froebel. Twayne.
    How to Do Library Research. U of Ill Pr.

Downs, Robert C. *see* Downs, Robert C. S.

Downs, Robert C. S.
    xDowns, Robert C.
    Peoples. Bobbs.

Downs, Roger M.
    xDowns, Roger M.
    Maps in Minds: Reflections on Cognitive
        Mapping. Har-Row.

Downs, Rose G. *see* Downs, Rose Genevieve.

Downs, Rose Genevieve.
    xDowns, Rose G.
    Dietary Policy & Procedure Manual. Cath
        Health.

Downs, Theodore, 1919-
    xDowns, Theodore.
    Fossil Vertebrates of Southern California. U of
        Cal Pr.

Dowse, R. E. *see* Dowse, Robert Edward.

Dowse, Robert Edward.
    xDowse, R. E.
    Political Sociology. Wiley.

Dowsey-Magog, Paul.
    xDowsey-Magog, Paul.
    Overland Through Asia: An Underground
        Guide. New Glide.

Dowson, D.
    xDowson, Duncan.
    A History of Tribology. Longman.
Dowson, Duncan. *see* Dowson, D.
Dowson, Ernest. *see* Dowson, Ernest Christopher.
Dowson, Ernest Christopher.
    xDowson, Ernest.
    The Letters of Ernest Dowson. Fairleigh
        Dickinson.
    The Stories of Ernest Dowson. Gordon Pr.
Dowson, H. R. *see* Dowson, Henry R.
Dowson, Henry R.
    xDowson, H. R.
    Spectral Theory of Linear Operators. Acad Pr.
Dowson, John, 1820-1881
    xDowson, John.
    Classical Dictionary of Hindu Mythology,
        Religion, Geography, History & Literature.
        Verry.
Dowst, Somerby R.
    xDowst, Somerby R.
    More Basics for Buyers. CBI Pub.
Dox, Ida.
    xDox, Ida.
    Melloni's Illustrated Medical Dictionary.
        Williams & Wilkins.
Doxat, John, 1914-
    xDoxat, John.

Stirred, Not Shaken: The Dry Martini.
    Merrimack Bk Serv.
Doxey, G. V.
    xDoxey, G. V.
    The Industrial Colour Bar in South Africa.
        Greenwood.
Doxey, Roy W. *see* Doxey, Roy Watkins.
Doxey, Roy Watkins.
    xDoxey, Roy W.
    Latter-Day Prophets & the Doctrine &
        Covenants. Deseret Bk.
Doxey, William S.
    xDoxey, William S.
    Espionage. Belmont-Tower.
Doyal, Robert N.
    xDoyal, Robert N.
    Counseling Approaches with Elementary
        School Children. HM.
Doyen, John T.
    xDoyen, John T.
    Systematics of the Genus Coelocnemis
        (Coleoptera: Tenebrionidae: A Quatitative
        Study of Variation. U of Cal Pr.
Doyle, A. Conan. *see* Doyle, Arthur Conan.
Doyle, Adrian C. *see* Doyle, Adrian Conan.
Doyle, Adrian Conan.
    xDoyle, Adrian C.
    Exploits of Sherlock Holmes. Random.
Doyle, Arthur C. *see* Doyle, Arthur Conan.

Doyle, Arthur Conan Doyle, Sir, 1859-1930
    xDoyle, A. Conan.
    The Sign of the Four. Ballantine.
    xDoyle, Arthur C.
    Adventures of Sherlock Holmes. Har-Row.
    Best Supernatural Tales of Arthur Conan
        Doyle. Dover.
    The History of Spiritualism. Arno.
    Hound of the Baskervilles. Buccaneer Bks.
    The Hound of the Baskervilles. Oxford U Pr.
    The Lost World. Buccaneer Bks.
    The Memoirs of Sherlock Holmes. Ballantine.
    Memoirs of Sherlock Holmes. Penguin.
    Sign of the Four. Buccaneer Bks.
    Tales of Terror & Mystery. Penguin.
    Valley of Fear. Buccaneer Bks.
    xDoyle, Arthur Conan.
    Adventures of Sherlock Holmes. Macmillan.
    The Hound of the Baskervilles. Garland Pub.
    The Valley of Fear. Berkley Pub.
Doyle, Arthur Conan. *see* Doyle, Arthur Conan Doyle.

Doyle, Bertram W. *see* Doyle, Bertram Wilbur.

Doyle, Bertram Wilbur, 1897-
    xDoyle, Bertram W.
    The Etiquette of Race Relations in the South:
        A Study in Social Control. Schocken.
    Etiquette of Race Relations in the South.
        Kennikat.

Doyle, Dennis M.
    xDoyle, Dennis M.
    Efficient Accounting & Record Keeping. Wiley.

Doyle, J. *see* Doyle, John M.

Doyle, Jack, 1928-
    xDoyle, Jack.
    The American Indian from Beginning to End.
        Vantage.
Doyle, James, 1937-
    xDoyle, James.
    Annie Howells & Achille Frechette. U of
        Toronto Pr.
    Not Above the Law: The Battles of Watergate
        Prosecutors Cox & Jaworski. Morrow.
Doyle, James M.
    xDoyle, James M.
    Reference Resources: A Systematic Approach.
        Scarecrow.
Doyle, Jean M. *see* Doyle, Jean Monty.

Doyle, Jean Monty.
    xDoyle, Jean M.
    The Complete Handbook for Medical
        Secretaries & Assistants. Little.
Doyle, John.
    xDoyle, John.
    The Auto Repair Book. Doubleday.
Doyle, John M.
    xDoyle, J.
    Introduction to Electrical Wiring. Reston.
    Spelling Reference for Business & School.
        Reston.
    xDoyle, John M.
    Digital Switching & Timing Circuits. Duxbury
        Pr.
Doyle, John R. *see* Doyle, John Robert.

Doyle, John Robert.
    xDoyle, John R.
    Arthur Shearly Cripps. Twayne.
    Thomas Pringle. Twayne.

Doyle, Kenneth O.
    xDoyle, Kenneth O.
    Student Evaluation of Instruction. Lexington
        Bks.

Doyle, L. B. *see* Doyle, Lauren B.

Doyle, L. E. *see* Doyle, Lawrence E.

Doyle, Lauren B.
    xDoyle, L. B.
    Information Retrieval & Processing. Wiley.

Doyle, Lawrence E.
    xDoyle, L. E.
    Manufacturing Processes & Materials for
        Engineers. P-H.

Doyle, Mary P. *see* Doyle, Mary Peter.
Doyle, Mary Peter, Sister, 1898-
    xDoyle, Mary P.
    Study of Play Selection in Women's Colleges.
        AMS Pr.
Doyle, Michael P.
    xDoyle, Michael P.
    Experimental Organic Chemistry. Wiley.
Doyle, P. A. *see* Doyle, Paul A.
Doyle, Paul A.
    xDoyle, P. A.
    Guide to Basic Information Sources in English
        Literature. J Norton Pubs.
    xDoyle, Paul A.
    Liam O'Flaherty. Twayne.
    Paul Vincent Carroll. Bucknell U Pr.
    Pearl S. Buck. Coll & U Pr.
    Pearl S. Buck. Twayne.
Doyle, Peter.
    xDoyle, Peter.
    Analytical Marketing Management. Har-Row.
Doyle, Phyllis B.
    xDoyle, Phyllis B.
    Helping the Severely Handicapped Child: A
        Guide for Parents & Teachers. T Y Crowell.
Doyle, Rodger P.
    xDoyle, Rodger P.
    The Complete Food Handbook. Grove.
Doyle, Rosa, Sister.
    xDoyle, Rosa.
    Catholic Atmosphere in Marie Von Ebner
        Eschenbach: Its Use As a Literary Device.
        AMS Pr.
Doyle, Ruth M. *see* Doyle, Ruth Moses.
Doyle, Ruth Moses.
    xDoyle, Ruth M.
    Soft Toys Made with Love....and the Help of
        30 Full Size Patterns. Howard Doyle.
Doyle, Stephen C.
    xDoyle, Stephen C.

Covenant Renewal in Religious Life: Biblical
Reflections. Franciscan Herald.

Doz, Yves L.
xDoz, Yves L.
Government Control & Multinational Strategic
Management: Power Systems &
Telecommunication Equipment. Praeger.

Dozier, Edward P.
xDozier, Edward P.
Pueblo Indians of North America. HR&W.

Dozois, Gardner.
xDozois, Gardner.
Strangers. Berkley Pub.

Drabble, Margaret, 1939-
xDrabble, Margaret.
For Queen & Country: Victorian England. HM.
The Garrick Year. Popular Lib.
The Genius of Thomas Hardy. Knopf.
The Ice Age. Knopf.
The Ice Age. Popular Lib.
The Realms of Gold. Knopf.
The Realms of Gold. Popular Lib.
A Writer's Britain: Landscape in Literature.
Knopf.

Drabble, Phil.
xDrabble, Phil.
Badgers at My Window. Merrimack Bk Serv.
Badgers at My Window. Taplinger.

Drabeck, Bernard A.
xDrabeck, Bernard A.
Structures for Composition. HM.

Drabek, Ann Gordon.
xDrabek, Anne G.
The Politics of African & Middle Eastern
States: An Annotated Bibliography.
Pergamon.
Drabek, Anne G. see Drabek, Ann Gordon.
Drabkin, David L. see Drabkin, David Lion.

Drabkin, David Lion, 1899-
xDrabkin, David L.
Fundamental Structure: Nature's Architecture.
U of Pa Pr.

Drabkin, Marjorie.
xDrabkin, Marjorie.
Word Mastery: A Guide to the Understanding
of Words. Barron.

Drachkovitch, Mildred M.
xDrachkovitch, Milorad M.
ed. Fifty Years of Communism in Russia. Pa St
U Pr.
Drachkovitch, Milorad M. see Drachkovitch, Mildred M.

Drachsler, Julius, 1889-1927
xDrachsler, Julius.
Democracy & Assimilation: The Blending of
Immigrant Heritages in America. Negro U
Pr.

Drackett, Phil.
xDrackett, Phil.
ed. Encyclopedia of the Motor Car. Crown.

Draeger, Alain.
xDraeger, Alain.
Brazil. Overlook Pr.

Draeger, Donn F.
xDraeger, Donn F.
Asian Fighting Arts. Berkley Pub.
Asian Fighting Arts. Kodansha.
Asian Fighting Arts. Wehman.

Classical Budo. Weatherhill.

Classical Bujutsu. Weatherhill.

Modern Bujutsu & Budo. Weatherhill.

Draganic, Ivan G.
xDraganic, Ivan G.
The Radiation Chemistry of Water. Acad Pr.

Dragnich, Alex N.
xDragnich, Alex N.

The Development of Parliamentary
Government in Serbia. East Eur Quarterly.
Drago, Harry S. see Drago, Harry Sinclair.

Drago, Harry Sinclair, 1888-
xDrago, Harry S.
Great Range Wars: Violence on the Grasslands.
Dodd.

Drago, Russell S.
xDrago, Russell S.
Experiments in General Chemistry. Allyn.
Principles of Chemistry with Practical
Perspectives. Allyn.

Dragonwagon, Crescent.
xDragonwagon, Crescent.
Stevie Wonder. Music Sales.
When Light Turns into Night. Har-Row.

Dragoumis, Julia D., 1858-
xDragoumis, Julia D.
Tales of a Greek Island. Arno.

Dragsted, Ove.
xDragsted, Ove.
Gems & Jewelry in Color. Macmillan.

Drahms, August, 1849-1927
xDrahms, August.
Criminal, His Personnel & Environment: A
Scientific Study. Patterson Smith.

Drake, Albert.
xDrake, Albert.
In the Time of Surveys & Other Stories of
Americans Abroad. White Ewe.
One Summer. White Ewe.

Drake, Alvin W.
xDrake, Alvin W.
ed. Analysis of Public Systems. MIT Pr.
Fundamentals of Applied Probability Theory.
McGraw.
Drake, Charles. see Drake, Charles L.

Drake, Charles L.
xDrake, Charles.
Oceanography. HR&W.

Drake, David.
xDrake, David.
The Dragon Lord. Berkley Pub.
The Dragon Lord. Putnam.

Drake, Debbie.
xDrake, Debbie.
Debbie Drake's Secrets of Perfect Figure
Development. P-H.

Drake, Durant, 1878-1933
xDrake, Durant.
Problems of Religion: An Introductory Survey.
Greenwood.
Drake, Francis S. see Drake, Francis Samuel.

Drake, Francis Samuel, 1828-1885
xDrake, Francis S.
Tea Leaves: Being a Collection of Letters &
Documents Relating to the Shipment of Tea
to the American Colonies in the Year 1773,
by the East India Tea Company. Gale.

Drake, Fred W., 1939-
xDrake, Fred W.
China Charts the World: Hsu Chi-Yu & His
Geography of 1848. Harvard U Pr.
Drake, George. see Drake, George R.

Drake, George R., 1938-
xDrake, George.
Everyone's Book of Hand & Small Power
Tools. Reston.
Repair & Maintenance of Small Gasoline
Engines. Reston.
xDrake, George R.
The Repair & Servicing of Small Appliances.
Reston.

Drake, James, 1667-1707
xDrake, James.
The Antient & Modern Stages Survey'd.
Garland Pub.

Drake, John W.
xDrake, John W.

The Administration of Transportation Modeling
Projects. Lexington Bks.

Drake, Michael.
xDrake, Michael.
Population & Society in Norway, 1735-1865.
Cambridge U Pr.

Drake, Milton.
xDrake, Milton.
Almanacs of the United States. Scarecrow.

Drake, Paul W., 1944-
xDrake, Paul W.
Socialism & Populism in Chile, 1932-52. U of
Ill Pr.

Drake Publishers.
xDrake Publishers Editors.
The Complete Carpenter's Handbook. Sterling.
Drake Publishers Editors. see Drake Publishers.
Drake, Raleigh M. see Drake, Raleigh Moseley.

Drake, Raleigh Moseley.
xDrake, Raleigh M.
Abnormal Psychology. Littlefield.

Drake, Robert, 1930-
xDrake, Robert.
The Burning Bush & Other Stories. Aurora
Pubs.

Drake, Rollen H.
xDrake, Rollen H.
A Comparative Study of the Mentality &
Achievement of Mexican & White Children.
R & E Res Assoc.

Drake, Russell.
xDrake, Russell.
How to Make Electronic Music. Crown.
Drake, Samuel A. see Drake, Samuel Adams.

Drake, Samuel Adams, 1833-1905
xDrake, Samuel A.
Historic Mansions & Highways Around Boston.
C E Tuttle.
Nooks & Corners of the New England Coast.
Gale.
Old Boston Taverns & Tavern Clubs. Gale.
Drake, Samuel G. see Drake, Samuel Gardner.

Drake, Samuel Gardner, 1798-1875
xDrake, Samuel G.
Particular History of the Five Years French &
Indian War in New England & Parts
Adjacent. Arno.
Result of Some Researches Among the British
Archives for Information Relative to the
Founders of New England. Genealog Pub.

Drake, Stillman.
xDrake, Stillman.
Galileo at Work: His Scientific Biography. U of
Chicago Pr.
tr. Mechanics in Sixteenth-Century Italy:
Selections from Tartaglia, Benedetti, Guido
Ubaldo, & Galileo. U of Wis Pr.
Drake, Thomas E. see Drake, Thomas Edward.

Drake, Thomas Edward, 1907-
xDrake, Thomas E.
Quakers & Slavery in America. Peter Smith.

Drake, W. Raymond.
xDrake, W. Raymond.
Gods & Spacemen of the Ancient Past. NAL.

Drake, William A, 1899-
xDrake, William A.
Contemporary European Writers. Gordon Pr.
Drake, William D. see Drake, William Daniel.

Drake, William Daniel, 1941-
xDrake, William D.
The Connoisseur's Handbook of Marijuana.
S&S.

Drakeford, John W.
xDrakeford, John W.

A Christian View of Homosexuality. Broadman.
Counseling for Church Leaders. Broadman.
Experiential Bible Study. Broadman.
Games Husbands & Wives Play. Broadman.
How to Manipulate Your Mate. Nelson.

jt. auth. In Praise of Women: A Christian
Approach to Love, Marriage, & Equality.
Har-Row.

Mothers Are Special. Broadman.
People to People Therapy. Har-Row.

A Proverb a Day Keeps the Troubles Away.
Broadman.
Psychology in Search of a Soul. Broadman.

Drakeford, Robina.
xDrakeford, Robina.
In Praise of Women: A Christian Approach to
Love, Marriage, & Equality. Har-Row.

Dramesi, John A.
xDramesi, John A.
Code of Honor. Norton.
Drane, James. *see* Drane, James F.
Drane, James F.
xDrane, James.
Authority & Institution: A Study in Church
Crisis. Glencoe.
xDrane, James F.
The Possibility of God. Littlefield.
Religion & Ethics. Paulist Pr.
Dranov, Paula.
xDranov, Paula.
Inside the Music Publishing Industry.
Knowledge Indus.
Dransfield, John E. *see* Dransfield, John Edgar.
Dransfield, John Edgar, 1887-
xDransfield, John E.
Administration of Enrichment to Superior
Children in a Typical Classroom. AMS Pr.
Draper. *see* Draper, Mary Wanda.
Draper, Cena C. *see* Draper, Cena Christopher.
Draper, Cena Christopher.
xDraper, Cena C.
Dandy & the Mystery of the Locked Room.
Independence Pr.
The Worst Hound Around. Westminster.
Draper, James T.
xDraper, James T.
The Church Christ Approves. Broadman.
Foundations of Biblical Faith. Broadman.
Titus, Patterns for Church Living. Tyndale.
Draper, John W. *see* Draper, John William.
Draper, John William, 1893-
xDraper, John W.
Eighteenth Century English Aesthetics: A
Bibliography. Intl Pubns Serv.
Eighteenth Century English Aesthetics: A
Bibliography. Octagon.
Funeral Elegy & the Rise of English
Romanticism. Octagon.
Funeral Elegy & the Rise of English
Romanticism. Phaeton.
Hamlet of Shakespeare's Audience. Octagon.
Orientalia & Shakespeareana. Vantage.
Othello of Shakespeare's Audience. Octagon.
Stratford to Dogberry: Studies in Shakespeare's
Earlier Plays. Arno.
The Twelfth Night of Shakespeare's Audience.
Octagon.
Draper, Mary Wanda.
xDraper.
Caring for Children. Bennett Co.
Steps in Clothing Skills. Bennett Co.
Draper, N. R. *see* Draper, Norman Richard.
Draper, Norman. *see* Draper, Norman Richard.
Draper, Norman Richard.
xDraper, N. R.

Applied Regression Analysis. Wiley.
xDraper, Norman.
Applied Regression Analysis. Wiley.
Draper, Ronald P., 1928-
xDraper, Ronald P.
D. H. Lawrence. St Martin.
D. H. Lawrence. Twayne.

Drath, V. H. *see* Drath, Viola Herms.

Drath, Viola Herms.

xDrath, V. H.
Typisch Deutsch. HR&W.

Dravid, P. S. *see* Dravid, Purushottam Shrikrishna.

Dravid, Purushottam Shrikrishna, 1933-
xDravid, P. S.
Analysis of Continuous Beams & Rigid Frames.
Asia.
Dray, William H.
xDray, William H.
Laws & Explanation in History. Greenwood.
Draycott, A. P.
xDraycott, A. P.
Sugar-Beet Nutrition. Halsted Pr.
Drayer, Adam M.
xDrayer, Adam M.
Problems in Middle & High School Teaching:
A Handbook for Student Teachers &
Beginning Teachers. Allyn.
Drayton, Michael, 1563-1631
xDrayton, Michael.
Muses Elizium. B Franklin.
Drazan, Joseph G. *see* Drazan, Joseph Gerald.
Drazan, Joseph Gerald, 1943-
xDrazan, Joseph G.
The Nightmare: A Checklist of the World
Literature to 1976. R & E Res Assoc.
The Pacific Northwest: An Index to People &
Places in Books. Scarecrow.
Dreben, Burton.
xDreben, Burton.
Decision Problem: Solvable Classes of
Quantificational Formulas. A-W.
Dreeben, Robert.
xDreeben, Robert.
ed. Issues in Microanalysis. Ballinger Pub.
On What Is Learned in School. A-W.
Drees, Jack.
xDrees, Jack.
Where Is He Now?: Sports Heroes of
Yesterday Revisited. Jonathan David.
Dregne, H. E. *see* Dregne, Harold E.
Dregne, Harold E.
xDregne, H. E.
Soils of Arid Regions. Elsevier.
Dreier, John C.
xDreier, John C.
ed. The Alliance for Progress: Problems and
Perspectives. Johns Hopkins.
Dreikurs, Rudolf.
xDreikurs, Rudolf.
Parent's Guide to Child Discipline. Dutton.
Psychodynamics, Psychotherapy & Counseling:
Collected Papers. A Adler Inst.
Psychology in the Classroom: A Manual for
Teachers. Har-Row.
Dreisbach. *see* Dreisbach, John Franklin.
Dreisbach, John Franklin, 1915-
xDreisbach.
Balsa Wood & Its Properties. Columbia
Graphs.
Dreisbach, Robert H. *see* Dreisbach, Robert Hastings.
Dreisbach, Robert Hastings, 1916-
xDreisbach, Robert H.
Handbook of Poisoning: Prevention, Diagnosis,
& Treatment. Lange.
Dreiser, Theodore, 1871-1945
xDreiser, Theodore.

An American Tragedy. Bentley.
An American Tragedy. NAL.
Financier. NAL.
Fine Furniture. Folcroft.
Fine Furniture. Haskell.
Free & Other Stories. Scholarly.
A Hoosier Holiday. Greenwood.
Notes on Life. U of Ala Pr.
Theodore Dreiser: A Selection of Uncollected
Prose. Wayne St U Pr.
Twelve Men. Scholarly.
Drendel, Lou, 1937-
xDrendel, Lou.
Air War in Viet Nam. Arco.
Drennan, Robert D.
xDrennan, Robert D.
ed. Prehistoric Social, Political, & Economic
Development in the Area of the Tehuacan
Valley: Some Results of the Palo Blanco
Project. U Mich Mus Anthro.
Drenth, Wiendelt.
xDrenth, Wiendelt.
Kinetics Applied to Organic Reactions. Dekker.
Dresch, Stephen P.
xDresch, Stephen P.
An Economic Perspective on the Evolution of
Graduate Education: A Technical Report
Presented to the National Board on Graduate
Education. Natl Acad Pr.
Drescher, Joan. *see* Drescher, Joan E.
Drescher, Joan E.
xDrescher, Joan.
illus. Your Family, My Family. Walker & Co.
Drescher, John M.
xDrescher, John M.
If I Were Starting My Family Again.
Abingdon.
Meditations for the Newly Married. Herald Pr.
Spirit Fruit. Herald Pr.
What Should Parents Expect?. Abingdon.
When Opposites Attract. Abbey.
Drescher, Seymour.
xDrescher, Seymour.
Dilemmas of Democracy: Tocqueville &
Modernization. U of Pittsburgh Pr.
Econocide: British Slavery in the Era of
Abolition. U of Pittsburgh Pr.
Dresher, Melvin.
xDresher, Melvin.
ed. Advances in Game Theory. Princeton U Pr.
Dresner. *see* Dresner, Samuel H.
Dresner, Samuel. *see* Dresner, Samuel H.
Dresner, Samuel H.
xDresner.
Levi Yitzhak of Berditchev: Portrait of a
Hasidic Master. Hartmore.
xDresner, Samuel.
Judaism: The Way of Sanctification. United
Syn Bk.
Dressel, Paul L. *see* Dressel, Paul Leroy.
Dressel, Paul Leroy.
xDressel, Paul L.
Higher Education as a Field of Study: The
Emergence of a Profession. Jossey-Bass.
Institutional Research in the University: A
Handbook. Jossey-Bass.
Dresselhaus, Richard L.
xDresselhaus, Richard L.
The Deacon & His Ministry. Gospel Pub.
Teaching for Decision. Gospel Pub.
Dresser, Christopher.
xDresser, Christopher.
Art of Decorative Design. Am Life Foun.
The Art of Decorative Design. Garland Pub.
Dresser, Peter Van. *see* Van Dresser, Peter.
Dressler, David.
xDressler, David.

Practice & Theory of Probation & Parole.
Columbia U Pr.
Readings in Criminology & Penology.
Columbia U Pr.

Dressler, William, 1890-
xDressler, William.
Clinical Aids in Cardiac Diagnosis. Grune.

Dretke, James P., 1931-
xDretke, James P.
A Christian Approach to Muslims: Reflections
from West Africa. William Carey Lib.

Drevdahl, Elmer R.
xDrevdahl, Elmer R.
Fundamentals of Excavation Equipment for
Engineering & Technology. Roadrunner
Tech.

Drever, James, 1873-1950
xDrever, James.
A Dictionary of Psychology. Gannon.
Dictionary of Psychology. Penguin.

Drever, James I.
xDrever, James I.
ed. Sea Water: Cycles of the Major Elements.
Acad Pr.

Drew, Clifford J., 1943-
xDrew, Clifford J.
Introduction to Designing & Conducting
Research. Mosby.
Drew, Donald. *see* Drew, Donald J.

Drew, Donald B.
xDrew, Donald B.
Uncle Don's Down East Cookbook. Stein &
Day.

Drew, Donald J.
xDrew, Donald.
Images of Man: A Critique of the
Contemporary Cinema. Inter-Varsity.

Drew, E. A.
xDrew, E. A.
ed. Underwater Research. Acad Pr.

Drew, Edwin P.
xDrew, Edwin P.
The Complete Light-Pack Camping &
Trail-Food Cookbook. McGraw.

Drew, Elizabeth.
xDrew, Elizabeth.
American Journal: The Events of 1976.
Random.
Senator. S&S.

Drew, Elizabeth A.
xDrew, Elizabeth A.
Directions in Modern Poetry. Gordian.
Discovering Drama. Kennikat.
Discovering Poetry. Norton.

Drew, John.
xDrew, Jon S.
Doing Business in the European Community.
Butterworths.
Drew, Jon S. *see* Drew, John.
Drew, Katherine F. *see* Drew, Katherine Fischer.

Drew, Katherine Fischer.
xDrew, Katherine F.
ed. The Barbarian Invasions: Catalyst of a New
Order. Krieger.
Studies in History. Rice Univ.

Drew, Philip, 1943-
xDrew, Philip.
Frei Otto: Form & Structure. Westview.

Drew, Ralph.
xDrew, Ralph.
Professional Ophthalmic Dispensing. Prof
Press.
Drew, Thomas B. *see* Drew, Thomas Bradford.

Drew, Thomas Bradford, 1902-
xDrew, Thomas B.
ed. Advances in Chemical Engineering. Acad
Pr.

Drewes, Marilyn.
xDrewes, Marilyn.

Your Bull Terrier. Denlingers.
Drewry, William S. *see* Drewry, William Sidney.
Drewry, William Sidney, 1870-
xDrewry, William S.
Southampton Insurrection. Johnson NC.
Drews, Elizabeth M. *see* Drews, Elizabeth Monroe.
Drews, Elizabeth Monroe, 1915-
xDrews, Elizabeth M.
The Higher Levels of Human Growth. Philos
Lib.
Drews, J. *see* Drews, Jurgen.
Drews, Jurgen.
xDrews, J.
ed. R-Factors: Their Properties & Possible
Control: Symposium, Baden Near Vienna,
April 27-29, 1977. Springer-Verlag.
Drexler, Arthur.
xDrexler, Arthur.
ed. The Architecture of the Ecole des
Beaux-Arts. MIT Pr.
Ludwig Mies Van Der Rohe. Braziller.
Drexler, Rosalyn.
xDrexler, Rosalyn.
Alex: Portrait of a Teenage Prostitute.
Ballantine.
The Cosmopolitan Girl. M Evans.
The Cosmopolitan Girl. Warner Bks.
Drey, Rudolf E. *see* Drey, Rudolf E. A.
Drey, Rudolf E. A.
xDrey, Rudolf E.
Apothecary Jars: Pharmaceutical Pottery &
Porcelain in Europe & the East 1150-1850.
Merrimack Bk Serv.
Dreyer, Jacob S.
xDreyer, Jacob S.
Composite Reserve Assets in the International
Monetary System. Jai Pr.
Dreyer, Sharon. *see* Dreyer, Sharon O.
Dreyer, Sharon O.
xDreyer, Sharon.
A Guide to Nursing Management of
Psychiatric Patients. Mosby.
Dreyfus, Alfred.
xDreyfus, Alfred.
The Dreyfus Case. Fertig.
Dreyfus, Edward A.
xDreyfus, Edward A.
Adolescence: Theory & Experience. Merrill.
Dreyfus, Stuart E.
xDreyfus, Stuart E.
Dynamic Programming & the Calculus of
Variations. Acad Pr.
Dreyfuss, Henry, 1904-
xDreyfuss, Henry.
ed. Symbol Sourcebook: An Authoritative
Guide to International Graphic Symbols.
McGraw.
Dreyfuss, J. *see* Dreyfuss, Jack R.
Dreyfuss, Jack R.
xDreyfuss, J.
Radiologic Examination of the Colon. Krieger.
xDreyfuss, Jack R.
Radiology of the Colon. Williams & Wilkins.
Dreyfuss, Joel.
xDreyfuss, Joel.
The Bakke Case: The Politics of Inequality.
HarBraceJ.
The Bakke Case: The Politics of Inequality.
HarBraceJ.
Drezner, Stephen M.
xDrezner, Stephen M.
A Planning Guide for Voluntary Human
Service Delivery Agencies. Family Serv.
Driberg, Jack H. *see* Driberg, Jack Herbert.
Driberg, Jack Herbert.
xDriberg, Jack H.
People of the Small Arrow. Arno.
Dridzo, Solomon A. *see* Dridzo, Solomon Abramovich.
Dridzo, Solomon Abramovich, 1878-
xDridzo, Solomon A.

Marx & the Trade Unions. Greenwood.
Driesch, Hans. *see* Driesch, Hans Adolf Eduard.
Driesch, Hans Adolf Eduard, 1867-1941
xDriesch, Hans.
Psychical Research: The Science of the
Super-Normal. Arno.
Driggers, B. Carlisle.
xDriggers, Carlisle.
Compiled by Models of Metropolitan Ministry.
Broadman.
Driggers, Carlisle. *see* Driggers, B. Carlisle.
Driggs, Louise.
xDriggs, Louise.
Soups & Stews the World Over. Hastings.
Drimmer, Frederick.
xDrimmer, Frederick.
Compiled by A Friend Is Someone Special.
Gibson.
Drinan, Robert F.
xDrinan, Robert F.
Honor the Promise: America's Commitment to
Israel. Doubleday.
Religion, the Courts, & Public Policy.
Greenwood.
Drinker, Henry S. *see* Drinker, Henry Sandwith.
Drinker, Henry Sandwith, 1880-1965
xDrinker, Henry S.
The Chamber Music of Johannes Brahms.
Greenwood.
Drinker, Sophie L. *see* Drinker, Sophie Lewis
Hutchinson.
Drinker, Sophie Lewis Hutchinson.
xDrinker, Sophie L.
Music & Women: The Story of Women in
Their Relation to Music. Zenger Pub.
Drinkwater, John, 1882-1937
xDrinkwater, John.
The Life & Adventures of Carl Laemmle.
Arno.
Patriotism in Literature. Norwood Edns.
Dripps, Robert D. *see* Dripps, Robert Dunning.
Dripps, Robert Dunning.
xDripps, Robert D.
Introduction to Anesthesia: The Principles of
Safe Practice. Saunders.
Driscoll, Charles B. *see* Driscoll, Charles Benedict.
Driscoll, Charles Benedict, 1885-1951
xDriscoll, Charles B.
The Life of O. O. McIntyre. Beekman Pubs.
Driscoll, Edward F.
xDriscoll, Edward F.
Industrial Electronics: Devices, Circuits &
Applications. Am Technical.
Driscoll, Edward J.
xDriscoll, Edward J.
Minnesota Supplement for Modern Real Estate
Practice. Real Estate Ed Co.
Driscoll, Fred. *see* Driscoll, Frederick F.
Driscoll, Frederick. *see* Driscoll, Frederick F.
Driscoll, Frederick F., 1943-
xDriscoll, Fred.
Solid State Devices & Applications. P-H.
xDriscoll, Frederick.
Analysis of Electric Circuits. P-H.
Driscoll, Lucy.
xDriscoll, Lucy.
Chinese Calligraphy. Paragon.
Driscoll, Peter, 1942-
xDriscoll, Peter.
In Connection with Kilshaw. Lippincott.
In Connection with Kilshaw. Popular Lib.
Pangolin. Lippincott.
Pangolin. Popular Lib.
The White Lie Assignment. Lippincott.
The White Lie Assignment. Popular Lib.
Driskell, Jeanette.
xDriskell, Jeanette.
A Guide to Tutoring. U Pr of Idaho.
Driskill, Linda.
xDriskill, Linda.

Decisive Writing: An Improvement Program.
  Oxford U Pr.
Driver, Edwin D.
  xDriver, Edwin D.
    Differential Fertility in Central India. Princeton
      U Pr.
    The Sociology & Anthropology of Mental
      Illness: A Reference Guide. U of Mass Pr.
Driver, Harold E. *see* Driver, Harold Edson.
Driver, Harold Edson, 1907-
  xDriver, Harold E.
    ed. Americas on the Eve of Discovery.
      Greenwood.
    Classification & Development of North
      American Indian Cultures: A Statistical
      Analysis of the Driver-Massey Sample. Am
      Philos.
    Indians of North America. U of Chicago Pr.
Driver, Helen I. *see* Driver, Helen Irene.
Driver, Helen Irene, 1904-
  xDriver, Helen I.
    Counseling & Learning Through Small-Group
      Discussion. Monona.
Driver, John, 1924-
  xDriver, John.
    Community & Commitment. Herald Pr.
Driver, Leota S. *see* Driver, Leota Stultz.
Driver, Leota Stultz.
  xDriver, Leota S.
    Fanny Kemble. Negro U Pr.
Driver, R. *see* Driver, Rodney David.
Driver, Robienetta.
  xDriver, Robienetta.
    The Revolution in Medical Technology
      Education. C C Thomas.
Driver, Rodney D. *see* Driver, Rodney David.
Driver, Rodney David, 1932-
  xDriver, R.
    Ordinary & Delay Differential Equations.
      Springer-Verlag.
  xDriver, Rodney D.
    Introduction to Ordinary Differential
      Equations. Har-Row.
Driver, Tom F. *see* Driver, Tom Faw.
Driver, Tom Faw, 1925-
  xDriver, Tom F.
    Patterns of Grace: Human Experience As
      Word of God. Har-Row.
Driver, Walter E.
  xDriver, Walter E.
    Plastics Chemistry & Technology. Van Nos
      Reinhold.
Driz, Ovsei. *see* Driz, Ovsei Ovseevich.
Driz, Ovsei Ovseevich.
  xDriz, Ovsei.
    The Boy & the Tree. P-H.
Drohan, N. T. *see* Drohan, Neville Thomas.
Drohan, Neville Thomas.
  xDrohan, N. T.
    Australian Economic Framework. Intl Pubns
      Serv.
Drollinger, William C.
  xDrollinger, William C.
    Tax Shelters & Tax-Free Income for Everyone.
      Epic Pubns.
Droms, William G., 1944-
  xDroms, William G.
    Finance & Accounting for Non-Financial
      Managers. A-W.
Dronberger, Ilse.
  xDronberger, Ilse.
    Political Thought of Max Weber: In Quest of
      Statesmanship. Irvington.
Drone, Jeanette M. *see* Drone, Jeanette Marie.
Drone, Jeanette Marie, 1940-
  xDrone, Jeanette M.
    Index to Opera, Operetta & Musical Comedy
      Synopses in Collections & Periodicals.
      Scarecrow.
Dronke, P. *see* Dronke, Peter.

Dronke, Peter.
  xDronke, P.
    The Medieval Lyric. Cambridge U Pr.
  xDronke, Peter.
    Medieval Latin & the Rise of the European
      Love Lyric. Oxford U Pr.
Drooker, Penelope B.
  xDrooker, Penelope B.
    Embroidering with the Loom: Creative
      Combinations of Weaving & Stitchery. Van
      Nos Reinhold.
Droop, M. *see* Droop, M. R.
Droop, M. R.
  xDroop, M.
    ed. Advances in Microbiology of the Sea. Acad
      Pr.
Drooyan, Irving.
  xDrooyan, Irving.
    Elementary Algebra for College Students.
      Wiley.
    Essentials of Trigonometry. Macmillan.
    Trigonometry: An Analytic Approach.
      Macmillan.
Dror, Y. *see* Dror, Yehezkel.
Dror, Yehezkel, 1928-
  xDror, Y.
    Design for Policy Sciences. Elsevier.
Drost, Walter H.
  xDrost, Walter H.
    David Snedden & Education for Social
      Efficiency. U of Wis Pr.
Drost-Hansen, W.
  xDrost-Hansen, W.
    ed. Cell-Associated Water. Acad Pr.
Drotning, Jayne.
  xDrotning, Jayne.
    Creative Woodworking. Contemp Bks.
Droz, R. *see* Droz, Remy.
Droz, Remy.
  xDroz, R.
    Understanding Piaget. Intl Univs Pr.
Dru, Ricki.
  xDru, Ricki.
    The First Blue Jeans. Silver.
Drubert, John.
  xDrubert, John.
    Nifty Number Nine. P-H.
Drucker, H. M. *see* Drucker, Henry Matthew.
Drucker, Henry Matthew.
  xDrucker, H. M.
    Doctrine & Ethos in the Labour Party. Allen
      Unwin.
Drucker, Malka.
  xDrucker, Malka.
    The George Foster Story. Holiday.
Drucker, Peter. *see* Drucker, Peter Ferdinand.
Drucker, Peter F. *see* Drucker, Peter Ferdinand.
Drucker, Peter Ferdinand, 1909-
  xDrucker, Peter.
    People & Performance: The Best of Peter
      Drucker on Management. Har-Row.
  xDrucker, Peter F.
    Adventures of a Bystander. Har-Row.
    Adventures of a Bystander. Har-Row.
    Age of Discontinuity: Guidelines to Our
      Changing Society. Har-Row.
    America's Next Twenty Years. Arno.
    Effective Executive. Har-Row.
    The Future of Industrial Man: A Conservative
      Approach. Greenwood.
    Managing in Turbulent Times. Har-Row.
    Practice of Management. Har-Row.
Drucker, Philip, 1911-
  xDrucker, Philip.
    Cultures of the North Pacific Coast. Har-Row.
Drucker, Saul.
  xDrucker, Saul.
    Children Astray. Arno.
Drucker-Colin, Rene. *see* Drucker-Colin, Rene Raul.

Drucker-Colin, Rene Raul.
  xDrucker-Colin, Rene.
    ed. The Functions of Sleep. Acad Pr.
Drug Abuse Council. *see* Drug Abuse Council,
  Washington, D.C.
Drug Abuse Council, Washington, D.C.
  xDrug Abuse Council.
    Altered States of Consciousness. Drug Abuse.
  xTheDrug Abuse Council.
    The Facts About "Drug Abuse". Free Pr.
Druks, Herbert.
  xDruks, Herbert.
    The U. S. & Israel. Speller.
Drum, David J.
  xDrum, David J.
    Outreach in Counseling: Applying the Growth
      & Prevention Model in Schools & Colleges.
      Carroll Pr.
    Structured Groups for Facilitating
      Development: Acquiring Life Skills,
      Resolving Life Themes, & Making Life
      Transitions. Human Sci Pr.
Drum, Karl, 1893-
  xDrum, Karl.
    Airpower & Russian Partisan Warfare. Arno.
Drumheller, Sidney J.
  xDrumheller, Sidney J.
    Handbook of Curriculum Design for
      Individualized Instruction: A Systems
      Approach (How to Develop Curriculum
      Materials from Rigorously Defined
      Behavioral Objectives).. Educ Tech Pubns.
    Teacher's Handbook for a Functional
      Behavior-Based Curriculum: Models &
      Guides for Classroom Use. Educ Tech Pubns.
Drummond. *see* Drummond, Harold D.
Drummond, A. H.
  xDrummond, A. H.
    Complete Beginner's Guide to Sailing.
      Doubleday.
Drummond, Andrew H.
  xDrummond, Andrew H.
    American Opera Librettos. Scarecrow.
Drummond, Don.
  xDrummond, Don.
    Reading: A Source Book. Heinemann Ed.
Drummond, Harold D.
  xDrummond.
    The Western Hemisphere. Allyn.
  xDrummond, Harold D.
    The Eastern Hemisphere. Allyn.
Drummond, Henry.
  xDrummond, Henry.
    Greatest Thing in the World. Collins Pubs.
    Greatest Thing in the World. G&D.
    Greatest Thing in the World. Revell.
    Tropical Africa. Negro U Pr.
Drummond, Ivor.
  xDrummond, Ivor.
    The Diamonds of Loreta. St Martin.
    The Necklace of Skulls. Dell.
    The Necklace of Skulls. St Martin.
    Stench of Poppies. Dell.
    A Stench of Poppies. St Martin.
    Tank of Sacred Eels. Dell.
    A Tank of Sacred Eels. St Martin.
Drummond, Lewis. *see* Drummond, Lewis A.
Drummond, Lewis A.
  xDrummond, Lewis.
    Leading Your Church in Evangelism.
      Broadman.
Drummond, Mansford E., 1930-
  xDrummond, Mansford E.
    Evaluation & Measurement Techniques for
      Digital Computer Systems. P-H.
Drummond, Michael.
  xDrummond, Michael.

photos by Montreal & Its Countryside. Oxford
    U Pr.
Drummond, Robert R. *see* Drummond, Robert
    Rutherford.
Drummond, Robert Rutherford.
    xDrummond, Robert R.
        Early German Music in Philadelphia. AMS Pr.
        Early German Music in Philadelphia. Da Capo.
Drumwright, Huber L.
    xDrumwright, Huber L.
        An Introduction to New Testament Greek.
          Broadman.
        Prayer Rediscovered. Broadman.
Druon, Maurice.
    xDruon, Maurice.
        The Ardent Infidels. Ace Bks.
Drury, Allen.
    xDrury, Allen.
        Advise & Consent. Avon.
        Advise & Consent. Doubleday.
        Come Nineveh, Come Tyre. Avon.
        Come Nineveh, Come Tyre. Doubleday.
        A God Against the Gods. Doubleday.
        Mark Coffin, U. S. S.: A Novel of Capitol Hill.
          Doubleday.
        Preserve & Protect. Doubleday.
        Preserve & Protect. Popular Lib.
        The Promise of Joy. Avon.
        The Promise of Joy. Doubleday.
        Return to Thebes. Dell.
        Return to Thebes. Doubleday.
Drury, Blanche J. *see* Drury, Blanche Jessen.
Drury, Blanche Jessen.
    xDrury, Blanche J.
        Posture & Figure Control Through Physical
          Education. Mayfield Pub.
Drury, Clifford. *see* Drury, Clifford M.
Drury, Clifford M.
    xDrury, Clifford.
        Nine Years with Spokane Indians: Diary of
          Elkanah Walker. A H Clark.
Drury, James W. *see* Drury, James Westbrook.
Drury, James Westbrook, 1919-
    xDrury, James W.
        The Government of Kansas. Regents Pr KS.
Drury, John, 1898-
    xDrury, John.
        Historic Midwest Houses. U of Chicago Pr.
        Old Illinois Houses. U of Chicago Pr.
Drury, Nevill, 1947-
    xDrury, Nevill.
        Don Juan, Mescalito & Modern Magic: The
          Mythology of Inner Space. Routledge &
          Kegan.
        Inner Visions: Explorations in Magical
          Consciousness. Routledge & Kegan.
        The Occult Sourcebook. Routledge & Kegan.
Drury, Richard S.
    xDrury, Richard S.
        My Secret War. Aero.
Drury, Roger. *see* Drury, Roger Wolcott.
Drury, Roger Wolcott.
    xDrury, Roger.
        The Champion of Merrimack County. Dell.
        The Champion of Merrimack County. Little.
Druten, John Van. *see* Van Druten, John.
Druxman, Michael B., 1941-
    xDruxman, Michael B.
        The Musical: From Broadway to Hollywood. A
          S Barnes.
Drvota, Mojmir.
    xDrvota, Mojmir.
        Triptych. SBD.
Dry, Florence. *see* Dry, Florence Swinton.
Dry, Florence S. *see* Dry, Florence Swinton.
Dry, Florence Swinton.
    xDry, Florence.
        Sources of Wuthering Heights. Folcroft.
    xDry, Florence S.

        The Sources of "Jane Eyre". Folcroft.
Dryburgh, Bob.
    xDryburgh, Robert.
        How You Can Be Sure You Are a Christian.
          Keats.
Dryburgh, Robert. *see* Dryburgh, Bob.
Dryden, Edgar A.
    xDryden, Edgar A.
        Nathaniel Hawthorne: The Poetics of
          Enchantment. Cornell U Pr.
Dryden, John, 1631-1700
    xDryden, John.
        Aureng-Zebe. U of Nebr Pr.
        Literary Criticism of John Dryden. U of Nebr
          Pr.
        Songs of John Dryden. Russell.
Drygas, H. *see* Drygas, Hilmar.
Drygas, Hilmar.
    xDrygas, H.
        Coordinate-Free Approach to Gauss-Markov
          Estimation. Springer-Verlag.
Drysdale, Rosemary.
    xDrysdale, Rosemary.
        The Art of Blackwork Embroidery. Scribner.
        Pulled Work on Canvas & Linen. Scribner.
Du Bartas, Guillaume de Salluste.
    xDu Bartas, Sieur.
        The Divine Weeks & Works of Guillaume de
          Saluste, Sieur du Bartas. Oxford U Pr.
Du Bartas, Sieur. *see* Du Bartas, Guillaume de Salluste.
Du Bois, W. E. *see* Du Bois, William Edward Burghardt.
Du Bois, W. E. B. *see* Du Bois, William Edward
    Burghardt.
Du Bois, William E. *see* Du Bois, William Edward
    Burghardt.
Du Bois, William Edward Burghardt, 1868-1963
    xDu Bois, W. E.
        The Negro. Kraus Repr.
        The Negro American Family. Kraus Repr.
        ed. Negro American Family. Negro U Pr.
        Suppression of the African Slave Trade to the
          United States of America, 1638-1870.
          Russell.
        The World & Africa: An Inquiry into the Part
          Which Africa Has Played in World History.
          Kraus Repr.
    xDu Bois, W. E. B.
        In Battle for Peace: The Story of My 83rd
          Birthday. Kraus Repr.
    xDu Bois, William E.
        The Suppression of the African Slave Trade to
          the United States of America, 1638-1870.
          Kraus Repr.
        The Suppression of the African Slave Trade to
          the United States of America 1638-1870.
          Schocken.
        World & Africa: Inquiry into the Part Which
          Africa Has Played in World History. Intl Pub
          Co.
Du Bos, Charles, 1882-1939
    xDu Bos, Charles.
        Byron & the Need of Fatality. Haskell.
Du Camp, Maxime, 1822-1894
    xDu Camp, Maxime.
        Theophile Gautier. Arden Lib.
        Theophile Gautier. Arno.
        Theophile Gautier. Kennikat.
        Theophile Gautier. R West.
Du Cann, Charles G. *see* Du Cann, Charles Garfield
    Lott.
Du Cann, Charles Garfield Lott, 1889-
    xDu Cann, Charles G.
        The Love-Lives of Charles Dickens.
          Greenwood.
Du Creux, Francois, 1596?-1666
    xDu Creux, Francois.
        History of Canada, or New France.
          Greenwood.
Du Jardin, Rosamond. *see* Du Jardin, Rosamond (Neal).

Du Jardin, Rosamond (Neal), 1902-
    xDu Jardin, Rosamond.
        Boy Trouble. Lippincott.
        Class Ring. Lippincott.
        Double Date. Lippincott.
        Double Feature. Lippincott.
        Double Feature. Berkley Pub.
        Double Wedding. Lippincott.
        One of the Crowd. Lippincott.
        Real Thing. Lippincott.
        Someone to Count On. Lippincott.
Du Jonchay, Ivan.
    xDu Jonchay, Yvan.
        Handbook of World Transport. Facts on File.
Du Jonchay, Yvan. *see* Du Jonchay, Ivan.
Du Mas, Frank. *see* Du Mas, Frank M.
Du Mas, Frank M.
    xDu Mas, Frank.
        Gay Is Not Good. Nelson.
Du Maurier, Daphne, Dame, 1907-
    xDu Maurier, Daphne.
        Frenchman's Creek. Bentley.
        Hungry Hill. Bentley.
        The Loving Spirit. Bentley.
        My Cousin Rachel. Bentley.
        The Parasites. Bentley.
        Rebecca. Avon.
        Rebecca. Doubleday.
Du Maurier, George. *see* Du Maurier, George Louis
    Palmella Busson.
Du Maurier, George Louis Palmella Busson, 1834-1896
    xDu Maurier, George.
        The Martian: A Novel. Century Bookbindery.
Du Plessis, N. *see* Du Plessis, Nicolaas.
Du Plessis, Nicolaas.
    xDu Plessis, N.
        Introduction to Potential Theory. Hafner.
Du Plessix Gray, Francine. *see* Gray, Francine Du
    Plessix.
Du Pont, Diane.
    xDu Pont, Diane.
        The French Passion. Fawcett.
Du Toit, Brian M., 1935-
    xDu Toit, Brian M.
        Drug Use & South African Students. Ohio U
          Ctr Intl.
        ed. Ethnicity in Modern Africa. Westview.
Du Val, Miles P. *see* Du Val, Miles Percy.
Du Val, Miles Percy, 1896-
    xDu Val, Miles P.
        And the Mountains Will Move: The Story of
          the Building of the Panama Canal.
          Greenwood.
Du Vall, Dean. *see* Du Vall, Dean F. V.
Du Vall, Dean F.
    xDu Vall, Dean F.
        How I'm Creating a Fortune in Real Estate
          Using Other People's Money, Time & Talent.
          Du Vall Financial.
Du Vall, Dean F. V.
    xDu Vall, Dean.
        The Big Dream. Lyle Stuart.
Duane, Allan.
    xDuane, Allan.
        The Hadrian Ransom. Popular Lib.
        The Hadrian Ransom. Putnam.
Duane, William.
    xDuane, William.
        ed. Letters to Benjamin Franklin, from His
          Family & Friends, 1751-1790. Arno.
Dubard, Etoile.
    xDubard, Etoile.
        Teaching Aphasics & Other Language
          Deficient Children: Theory & Application of
          the Association Method. U Pr of Miss.
Dubay, Thomas.
    xDubay, Thomas.
        A Call to Virginity?. Our Sunday Visitor.
Dubbel, S. Earl.
    xDubbel, S. Earl.

Daughter of the Plain Folk. Moody.
Dubbert, Joe L.
xDubbert, Joe L.
A Man's Place: Masculinity in Transition. P-H.
Dubbey, J. M. *see* Dubbey, John Michael.
Dubbey, John Michael, 1934-
xDubbey, J. M.
Development of Modern Mathematics.
Crane-Russak Co.
The Mathematical Work of Charles Babbage.
Cambridge U Pr.
Dubbs. *see* Dubbs, Patrick J.
Dubbs, Chris.
xDubbs, Chris.
The Easy Art of Smoking Food. Winchester Pr.
Dubbs, Patrick J.
xDubbs.
Cultural Contexts: An Introduction to the
Anthropological Perspective. Allyn.
Dube, Anthony.
xDube, Anthony.
Structure & Meaning: An Introduction to
Literature. HM.
Dube, Shiv K.
xDube, Shiv K.
ed. Immediate Care of the Sick & Injured
Child. Mosby.
Dubelman, Richard. *see* Dubelman, Richard S.
Dubelman, Richard S.
xDubelman, Richard.
The Adventures of Holly Hobbie. Delacorte.
Duberman, Lucile, 1926-
xDuberman, Lucile.
Gender & Sex in Society. HR&W.
Sociology: Focus on Society. Scott F.
Duberman, Martin. *see* Duberman, Martin B.
Duberman, Martin B.
xDuberman, Martin.
ed. Antislavery Vanguard: New Essays on the
Abolitionists. Princeton U Pr.
Dubie, Norman, 1945-
xDubie, Norman.
The City of the Olesha Fruit. Doubleday.
The Everlastings. Doubleday.
The Illustrations. Braziller.
In the Dead of the Night. U of Pittsburgh Pr.
Dubillard, Roland.
xDubillard, Roland.
Naives Hirondelles. Grove.
Dubin, Arthur D. *see* Dubin, Arthur Detmers.
Dubin, Arthur Detmers.
xDubin, Arthur D.
More Classic Trains. Kalmbach.
Some Classic Trains. Kalmbach.
Dubin, D. A.
xDubin, D. A.
Solvable Models in Algebraic Statistical
Mechanics. Oxford U Pr.
Dubin, F. S. *see* Dubin, Fred S.
Dubin, Fred S.
xDubin, F. S.
How to Save Energy & Cut Costs in Existing
Industrial & Commercial Buildings-an Energy
Conservation Manual. Noyes.
Dubin, N. *see* Dubin, Neil.
Dubin, Neil, 1949-
xDubin, N.
A Stochastic Model for Immunological
Feedback in Carcinogenesis: Analysis &
Approximations. Springer-Verlag.
Dubin, Robert.
xDubin, Robert.
Theory Building. Free Pr.
Dubinsky, David.
xDubinsky, David.
David Dubinsky: A Life with Labor. S&S.
Dubinsky, E. *see* Dubinsky, Ed.
Dubinsky, Ed.
xDubinsky, E.

The Structure of Nuclear Frechet Spaces.
Springer-Verlag.
Dubinsky, Irwin.
xDubinsky, Irwin.
Reform in Trade Union Discrimination in the
Construction Industry: Operation Dig & Its
Legacy. Irvington.
Dubisch, Roy, 1917-
xDubisch, Roy.
Introduction to Abstract Algebra. Krieger.
Dubitsky, Cora M. *see* Dubitsky, Cora Marie.
Dubitsky, Cora Marie.
xDubitsky, Cora M.
Building the Faith Community. Paulist Pr.
Duble, Richard.
xDuble, Richard.
Southern Lawns & Groundcovers. Pacesetter
Pr.
Dublin, Jack.
xDublin, Jack.
Credit Unions: Theory & Practice. Wayne St U
Pr.
Dublin, Louis I. *see* Dublin, Louis Israel.
Dublin, Louis Israel.
xDublin, Louis I.
The Money Value of a Man. Arno.
Dublin. University.
xDublin University.
Catalogue of Fifteenth Century Books in the
Library of Trinity College, Dublin, & in
Marsh's Library, Dublin, with a Few from
Other Collections. B Franklin.
Dubner, Barry H. *see* Dubner, Barry Hart.
Dubner, Barry Hart, 1940-
xDubner, Barry H.
The Law of International Sea Piracy. Kluwer
Boston.
DuBoff, Leonard D.
xDuBoff, Leonard D.
ed. Art Law, Domestic & International.
Rothman.
Dubofsky, Melvyn, 1934-
xDubofsky, Melvyn.
When Workers Organize: New York City in
the Progressive Era. U of Mass Pr.
DuBois, Armand B. *see* DuBois, Armand Budington.
DuBois, Armand Budington.
xDuBois, Armand B.
English Business Company After the Bubble
Act, 1720-1800. Octagon.
Dubois, Edward N.
xDubois, Edward N.
Essential Methods in Business Statistics.
McGraw.
DuBois, Ellen C. *see* DuBois, Ellen Carol..
DuBois, Ellen Carol, 1947-
xDuBois, Ellen C.
Feminism & Suffrage: The Emergence of an
Independent Women's Movement in America
Eighteen Forty-Eight to Eighteen Sixty-Nine.
Cornell U Pr.
DuBois, J. Harry. *see* DuBois, John Harry.
DuBois, John Harry, 1903-
xDuBois, J. Harry.
Plastics History, U. S. A. CBI Pub.
DuBois, Nelson. *see* DuBois, Nelson F.
DuBois, Nelson F.
xDuBois, Nelson.
Educational Psychology & Instructional
Decisions. Dorsey.
Dubois, P. *see* Dubois, Pierre.
Dubois, Paul. *see* Dubois, Paul M.
Dubois, Paul M.
xDubois, Paul.
The Hospice Way of Death. Human Sci Pr.
Dubois, Pierre.
xDubois, P.
Plastics in Agriculture. Intl Ideas.
Dubos, Rene. *see* Dubos, Rene Jules.
Dubos, Rene J. *see* Dubos, Rene Jules.

Dubos, Rene Jules, 1901-
xDubos, Rene.
A God Within. Irvington.
A God Within. Scribner.
Mirage of Health: Utopias, Progress, &
Biological Change. Har-Row.
The Professor, the Institute, & DNA.
Rockefeller.
xDubos, Rene J.
Dreams of Reason: Science & Utopias.
Columbia U Pr.
DuBose, Francias M. *see* DuBose, Francis M.
DuBose, Francis M.
xDuBose, Francias M.
How Churches Grow in an Urban World.
Broadman.
xDuBose, Francis M.
ed. Classics of Christian Missions. Broadman.
Dubose, Joel C. *see* Dubose, Joel Campbell.
Dubose, Joel Campbell, 1855-
xDubose, Joel C.
ed. Notable Men of Alabama: Personal &
Genealogical with Portraits. Reprint.
Dubovsky, Steven L.
xDubovsky, Steven L.
Clinical Psychiatry in Primary Care. Williams
& Wilkins.
DuBovy, Joseph.
xDuBovy, Joseph L.
Introduction to Biomedical Electronics.
McGraw.
DuBovy, Joseph L. *see* DuBovy, Joseph.
Dubowitz, Lilly M. *see* Dubowitz, Lilly M. S.
Dubowitz, Lilly M. S.
xDubowitz, Lilly M.
Gestational Age of the Newborn: A Clinical
Manual. A-W.
Dubowitz, Victor.
xDubowitz, Victor.
jt. auth. Gestational Age of the Newborn: A
Clinical Manual. A-W.
Muscle Biopsy: A Modern Approach. Saunders.
Muscle Disorders in Childhood. Saunders.
DuBreuil, Linda.
xDuBreuil, Linda.
Poppy. Nordon Pubns.
The Sunday Seducer. Nordon Pubns.
DuBrin, Andrew J.
xDuBrin, Andrew J.
Effective Business Psychology. Reston.
Human Relations: A Job Oriented Approach.
Reston.
The Practice of Supervision: Achieving Results
Through People. Business Pubns.
Survival in the Office: How to Move Ahead or
Hang On. Van Nos Reinhold.
Winning at Office Politics. Ballantine.
Winning at Office Politics. Van Nos Reinhold.
Dubrov. *see* Dubrov, Aleksandr Petrovich.
Dubrov, Aleksandr Petrovich.
xDubrov.
The Geomagnetic Field & Life:
Geomagnetobiology. Plenum Pub.
Dubrovin, Vivian.
xDubrovin, Vivian.
A Chance to Win. EMC.
Dubus, Andre, 1936-
xDubus, Andre.
Adultery & Other Choices. Godine.
Duby, Georges.
xDuby, Georges.

The Chivalrous Society. U of Cal Pr.
The Early Growth of the European Economy:
Warriors & Peasants from the Seventh to the
Twelfth Centuries. Cornell U Pr.
Medieval Marriage: Two Models from
Twelfth-Century France. Johns Hopkins.
Duc, Robert.
xDuc, Robert.
Renald, the Adventurer. Ashley Bks.
Ducasse, C. J. see Ducasse, Curt John.
Ducasse, Curt John, 1881-
xDucasse, C. J.
Critical Examination of the Belief in a Life
After Death. C C Thomas.
Nature, Mind & Death. Open Court.
Duce, Ivy O. see Duce, Ivy Oneita.
Duce, Ivy Oneita.
xDuce, Ivy O.
How a Master Works. Dodd.
How a Master Works. Sufism Reoriented.
Ducey, Michael H.
xDucey, Michael H.
Sunday Morning: Aspects of Urban Ritual.
Free Pr.
Duchac, Joseph.
xDuchac, Joseph.
The Poems of Emily Dickinson: An Annotated
Guide to Commentary Published in English,
1890-1977. G K Hall.
Duchacek, Ivo D., 1913-
xDuchacek, Ivo D.
Nations & Men: An Introduction to
International Politics. HR&W.
Duchaufour, Philippe, 1912-
xDuchaufour, Philippe.
Ecological Atlas of Soils of the World. Masson
Pub.
Duchein, Michel.
xDuchein, Michel.
Compiled by Basic International Bibliography
of Archive Administration. K G Saur.
Duck, Stephen W. see Duck, Steven W.
Duck, Steve. see Duck, Steven W.
Duck, Steven. see Duck, Steven W.
Duck, Steven W.
xDuck, Stephen W.
Personal Relationships & Personal Constructs:
A Study of Friendship Formation. Wiley.
xDuck, Steve.
ed. Theory & Practice in Interpersonal
Attraction. Acad Pr.
xDuck, Steven.
The Study of Acquaintance. Lexington Bks.
Duckett, Eleanor S. see Duckett, Eleanor Shipley.
Duckett, Eleanor Shipley.
xDuckett, Eleanor S.
Anglo-Saxon Saints & Scholars. Shoe String.
Catullus in English Poetry. Arden Lib.
Catullus in English Poetry. R West.
ed. Catullus in English Poetry. Russell.
Death & Life in the Tenth Century. U of Mich
Pr.
Latin Writers of the Fifth Century. Shoe String.
Duckett, Kenneth W.
xDuckett, Kenneth W.
Modern Manuscripts: A Practical Manual for
Their Management, Care & Use. AASLH.
Duckett, Margaret.
xDuckett, Margaret.
Mark Twain & Bret Harte. U of Okla Pr.
Duckles, Vincent. see Duckles, Vincent Harris.
Duckles, Vincent Harris, 1913-
xDuckles, Vincent.
Music Reference & Research Materials: An
Annotated Bibliography. Free Pr.
Duckworth, Alistair M., 1936-
xDuckworth, Alistair M.

The Improvement of the Estate: A Study of
Jane Austen's Novels. Johns Hopkins.
Duckworth, Derek.
xDuckworth, Derek.
The Continuing Swing?: Pupils' Reluctance to
Study Science. Humanities.
Duckworth, Henry T. see Duckworth, Henry Thomas
Forbes.
Duckworth, Henry Thomas Forbes, 1868-
xDuckworth, Henry T.
The Church of the Holy Sepulchre. AMS Pr.
Duckworth, Jane. see Duckworth, Jane C.
Duckworth, Jane C.
xDuckworth, Jane.
MMPI Interpretation Manual for Counselors &
Clinicians. Accel Devel.
Duckworth, Paul.
xDuckworth, Paul.
Creative Photographic Effects Simplified.
Amphoto.
Duckworth, R. A. see Duckworth, Roger Alan.
Duckworth, Roger Alan.
xDuckworth, R. A.
Mechanics of Fluids. Longman.
Duckworth, Walter E. see Duckworth, Walter Eric.
Duckworth, Walter Eric.
xDuckworth, Walter E.
A Guide to Operational Research. Methuen
Inc.
Duckworth, William.
xDuckworth, William.
Theoretical Foundations of Music. Wadsworth
Pub.
Duclaud-Williams, Roger H.
xDuclaud-Williams, Roger H.
The Politics of Housing in Britain & France.
Heinemann Ed.
Duclaux, Agnes Mary Frances (Robinson), 1857-1944
xDuclaux, Mary.
Life of Racine. Kennikat.
Life of Racine. R West.
Duclaux, Mary. see Duclaux, Agnes Mary Frances
(Robinson).
Ducros, Louis, 1846-
xDucros, Louis.
French Society in the Eighteenth Century. B
Franklin.
Ducrot, Oswald.
xDucrot, Oswald.
Encyclopedic Dictionary of the Sciences of
Language. Johns Hopkins.
Duczynska, Ilona.
xDuczynska, Ilona.
Workers in Arms: The Austrian Schutzbund &
the Civil War of 1934. Monthly Rev.
Dudden, Arthur P. see Dudden, Arthur Power.
Dudden, Arthur Power, 1921-
xDudden, Arthur P.
Joseph Fels & the Single - Tax Movement.
Temple U Pr.
Pardon Us, Mr. President!: American Humor
on Politics. A S Barnes.
Duddington, C. L.
xDuddington, C. L.
Instructions in Biology. Soccer.
Dudeney, Henry E. see Dudeney, Henry Ernest.
Dudeney, Henry Ernest, 1857-1930
xDudeney, Henry E.
Amusements in Mathematics. Dover.
Duderstadt, James. see Duderstadt, James J.
Duderstadt, James J.
xDuderstadt, James.
Nuclear Power: Technology on Trial. U of
Mich Pr.
Dudick, Thomas S.
xDudick, Thomas S.

Cost Controls for Industry. P-H.
How to Improve Profitability Through More
Effective Planning. Wiley.
Inventory Control for the Financial Executive.
Ronald Pr.
Dudko, Dmitrii.
xDudko, Dmitrii.
Our Hope. St Vladimirs.
Dudley, Barbara.
xDudley, Barbara H.
Where Is God?: Three Church Dramas.
Augsburg.
Dudley, Barbara H. see Dudley, Barbara.
Dudley, Brian A. see Dudley, Brian A. C.
Dudley, Brian A. C.
xDudley, Brian A.
Mathematical & Biological Interrelations.
Wiley.
Dudley, Carl S., 1932-
xDudley, Carl S.
Where Have All Our People Gone?: New
Choices for Old Churches. Pilgrim NY.
Dudley, Darle W.
xDudley, Darle W.
ed. Gear Handbook: The Design, Manufacture
& Application of Gears. McGraw.
Dudley, Donald L.
xDudley, Donald L.
How to Survive Being Alive. Doubleday.
xDudley, Donald M.
How to Survive Being Alive. NAL.
Dudley, Donald M. see Dudley, Donald L.
Dudley, Donald R. see Dudley, Donald Reynolds.
Dudley, Donald Reynolds.
xDudley, Donald R.
Civilization of Rome. NAL.
Dudley, Ernest.
xDudley, Ernest.
For Love of a Wild Thing. Eriksson.
Dudley, Guilford, 1932-
xDudley, Guilford.
Religion on Trial: Mircea Eliade & His Critics.
Temple U Pr.
Dudley, Guilford A., 1921-
xDudley, Guilford A.
A History of Eastern Civilizations. Wiley.
Dudley, H. C. see Dudley, Horace Chester.
Dudley, Horace Chester, 1909-
xDudley, H. C.
The Morality of Nuclear Planning??. Kronos
Pr.
Dudley, Hugh. see Dudley, Hugh Arnold Freeman.
Dudley, Hugh Arnold Freeman.
xDudley, Hugh.
The Presentation of Original Work in Medicine
& Biology. Churchill.
Dudley, Louise.
xDudley, Louise.
The Humanities. McGraw.
The Humanities. McGraw.
Dudley, Owen Francis, 1882-1952
xDudley, Owen Francis.
Will Men Be Like Gods?: Humanitarianism of
Human Happiness. Franciscan Herald.
Dudley, Patricia L. see Dudley, Patricia Louise.
Dudley, Patricia Louise, 1929-
xDudley, Patricia L.
Development & Systematics of Some Pacific
Marine Symbiotic Copepods: A Study of the
Biology of the Notodelphyidae, Associates of
Ascidians. U of Wash Pr.
Dudley, Ruth H. see Dudley, Ruth Hubbell.
Dudley, Ruth Hubbell.
xDudley, Ruth H.
Our American Trees. T Y Crowell.
Dudley, Stuart.
xDudley, Stuart.
Taking the Ache Out of Gardening. Soccer.
Dudman, Richard.
xDudman, Richard.

Forty Days with the Enemy. Liveright.

Dudycha, George J. *see* Dudycha, George John.

Dudycha, George John, 1903-
  xDudycha, George J.
    Psychology for Law Enforcement Officers. C C
    Thomas.

Due, John F. *see* Due, John Fitzgerald.

Due, John Fitzgerald.
  xDue, John F.
    Indirect Taxation in Developing Economies:
    The Role & Structure of Customs Duties,
    Excises, & Sales Taxes. Johns Hopkins.
    Theory of Incidence of Sales Taxation. Russell.

Due, Linnea A.
  xDue, Linnea A.
    High & Outside. Har-Row.

Dueker, Christopher W. *see* Dueker, Christopher Wayne.

Dueker, Christopher Wayne, 1929-
  xDueker, Christopher W.
    Medical Aspects of Sport Diving. A S Barnes.

Dueker, Joyce. *see* Dueker, Joyce S.

Dueker, Joyce S.
  xDueker, Joyce.
    The Old Fashioned Homemade Ice Cream
    Cookbook. B&N.
    jt. auth. The Old Fashioned Homemade
    Ice-Cream Cookbook. Bobbs.

Duell, Marie.
  xDuell, Marie.
    Countess of Sedgwick. McGraw.

Duenk, Lester G.
  xDuenk, Lester G.
    Auto Body Repair. Scribner.
    Autobody Repair. Bennett Co.

Duerr, Edwin, 1906-
  xDuerr, Edwin.
    Radio & Television Acting: Criticism, Theory
    & Practice. Greenwood.

Duerr, Michael. *see* Duerr, Michael G.

Duerr, Michael G.
  xDuerr, Michael.
    Organization & Control of International
    Operations. Conference Bd.
  xDuerr, Michael G.
    Are Today's Schools Preparing Tomorrow's
    Business Leaders?: A Worldwide Survey of
    Chief Executives. Conference Bd.
    The Expanded E E C & U.S. Business.
    Conference Bd.
    Impact of Commodity Shortages: A World
    Survey. Conference Bd.
    Problems Facing International Management.
    Conference Bd.
    What Troubles the World's Business Leaders.
    Conference Bd.

Duerr, William A. *see* Duerr, William Allen.

Duerr, William Allen.
  xDuerr, William A.
    Fundamentals of Forestry Economics.
    McGraw.

Duesenberry, J. S. *see* Duesenberry, James Stemble.

Duesenberry, James. *see* Duesenberry, James Stemble.

Duesenberry, James S. *see* Duesenberry, James Stemble.

Duesenberry, James Stemble, 1918-
  xDuesenberry, J. S.
    ed. The Brookings Model: Some Further
    Results. Elsevier.
  xDuesenberry, James.
    Money & Credit: Impact & Control. P-H.
  xDuesenberry, James S.

Business Cycles & Economic Growth.
    Greenwood.
Income, Saving & the Theory of Consumer
    Behavior. Harvard U Pr.

Dufau, Maria. *see* Dufau, Maria L.

Dufau, Maria L.
  xDufau, Maria.
    ed. Hormone Binding & Target Cell Activation
    in the Testis. Plenum Pub.

Duff, A. M. *see* Duff, John Wight.

Duff, Charles. *see* Duff, Charles St. Lawrence.

Duff, Charles St. Lawrence.
  xDuff, Charles.
    German for Beginners. Har-Row.

Duff, David, 1912-
  xDuff, David.
    Eugenie & Napoleon III. Morrow.
    Hessian Tapestry: The Hesse Family & British
    Royalty. David & Charles.

Duff, E. Gordon. *see* Duff, Edward Gordon.

Duff, Edward Gordon, 1863-1924
  xDuff, E. Gordon.
    Early Printed Books. Haskell.
    The Printers, Stationers, & Book-Binders of
    Westminster & London from 1476 to 1535.
    Arno.

Duff, John R.
  xDuff, John R.
    Alternating Current Fundamentals. Van Nos
    Reinhold.
    Alternating Current Fundamentals. Delmar.

Duff, John W. *see* Duff, John Wight.

Duff, John Wight.
  xDuff, John W.
    A Literary History of Rome in the Silver Age:
    From Tiberius to Hadrian. Greenwood.

Duff, P. W. *see* Duff, Patrick William.

Duff, Patrick W. *see* Duff, Patrick William.

Duff, Patrick William, 1901-
  xDuff, P. W.
    Personality in Roman Private Law. Rothman.
  xDuff, Patrick W.
    Personality in Roman Private Law. Kelley.

Duff, Robert A. *see* Duff, Robert Alexander.

Duff, Robert Alexander.
  xDuff, Robert A.
    Spinoza's Political & Ethical Philosophy.
    Kelley.
    Spinoza's Political & Ethical Philosophy. R
    West.

Duff, William, 1732-1815
  xDuff, William.
    Letters on the Intellectual & Moral Character
    of Women. Garland Pub.

Duff-Gordon, Lucie. *see* Duff-Gordon, Lucie (Austin).

Duff-Gordon, Lucie (Austin), Lady, 1821-1869
  xDuff-Gordon, Lucie.
    Letters from Egypt, 1863-65. AMS Pr.

Duffee, David.
  xDuffee, David.
    An Introduction to Corrections: A Policy &
    Systems Approach. Goodyear.
  xDuffee, David E.
    Correctional Management: Change & Control
    in Correctional Organizations. P-H.

Duffee, David E. *see* Duffee, David.

Duffett-Smith, Peter.
  xDuffett-Smith, Peter.
    Practical Astronomy with Your Calculator.
    Cambridge U Pr.

Duffey, Bernard I., 1917-
  xDuffey, Bernard I.
    The Chicago Renaissance in American Letters:
    A Critical History. Greenwood.

Duffey, Dave. *see* Duffey, David Michael.

Duffey, David M. *see* Duffey, David Michael.

Duffey, David Michael.
  xDuffey, Dave.
    Hunting Dog Know-How. Winchester Pr.
  xDuffey, David M.
    Expert Advice on Gun Dog Training.
    Winchester Pr.

Duffey, Eric.
  xDuffey, Eric.
    Grassland Ecology & Wildlife Management.
    Methuen Inc.

Duffie, J. A. *see* Duffie, John A.

Duffie, John A.
  xDuffie, J. A.
    Solar Energy Thermal Processes. Wiley.

Duffield, Anne, 1895-
  xDuffield, Anne.
    Dusty Dawn. Berkley Pub.
    Forever Tomorrow. Berkley Pub.
    The Grand Duchess. Berkley Pub.

Duffield, Guy P., 1909-
  xDuffield, Guy P.
    Handbook of Bible Lands. Regal.

Duffin, Henry C. *see* Duffin, Henry Charles.

Duffin, Henry Charles, 1884-
  xDuffin, Henry C.
    The Quintessence of Bernard Shaw. Folcroft.

Duffus, Robert L. *see* Duffus, Robert Luther.

Duffus, Robert Luther, 1888-
  xDuffus, Robert L.
    The Innocents at Cedro: A Memoir Thorstein
    Veblen and Some Others. Kelley.

Duffy, Charles G. *see* Duffy, Charles Gavan.

Duffy, Charles Gavan, Sir, 1816-1903
  xDuffy, Charles G.
    ed. The Ballad Poetry of Ireland. Schol
    Facsimiles.

Duffy, Christopher, 1936-
  xDuffy, Christopher.
    Austerlitz 1805. Shoe String.
    Fire & Stone: The Science of Fortress Warfare
    1660-1860. Hippocrene Bks.
    Siege Warfare: The Fortress in the Early
    Modern World, 1494-1660. Routledge &
    Kegan.

Duffy, Clinton T.
  xDuffy, Clinton T.
    From Heroin to San Quentin. Java Bks.

Duffy, Edward.
  xDuffy, Edward.
    Rousseau in England: The Context for
    Shelley's Critique of the Enlightenment. U of
    Cal Pr.

Duffy, Gerald G.
  xDuffy, Gerald G.
    How to Teach Reading Systematically.
    Har-Row.
    ed. Reading in the Middle School. Intl
    Reading.
    Systematic Reading Instruction. Har-Row.

Duffy, J. J.
  xDuffy, John J.
    Peaceman. Branden.

Duffy, John, 1915-
  xDuffy, John.
    The Healers: A History of American Medicine.
    U of Ill Pr.
    History of Public Health in New York City,
    1625-1866. Russell Sage.
    Sword of Pestilence: The New Orleans Yellow
    Fever Epidemic of 1853. La State U Pr.

Duffy, John C.
  xDuffy, John C.
    ed. Child Psychiatry. Med Exam.

Duffy, John J. *see* Duffy, J. J.

Duffy, Pat.
  xDuffy, Pat.
    All American Chinese Cookbook. Harbor Hse
    Pub.

Duffy, Robert E.
  xDuffy, Robert E.

Art Law: Representing Artists, Dealers &
Collectors. PLI.
Duffy, Thomas J. *see* Duffy, Thomas Joseph.
Duffy, Thomas Joseph.
xDuffy, Thomas J.
California Toxic Fungi. Mycological.
Duffy, William.
xDuffy, William.
Sugar Blues. Warner Bks.
Dufrechou, Carole.
xDufrechou, Carole.
Neil Young. Music Sales.
Dufrenne, Mikel.
xDufrenne, Mikel.
ed. Main Trends in Aesthetics & the Sciences
of Art. Holmes & Meier.
Dufresne, Edward R.
xDufresne, Edward R.
Partnership: Marriage & the Committed Life.
Paulist Pr.
Duft, Ken. *see* Duft, Kenneth D.
Duft, Kenneth D.
xDuft, Ken.
Principles of Management in Agribusiness.
Reston.
Dugan, Alan.
xDugan, Alan.
Collected Poems. Yale U Pr.
Dugan, Daniel O.
xDugan, Daniel O.
Faith for Tomorrow. Pflaum Pr.
Dugan, James, 1912-
xDugan, James.
Undersea Explorer: Story of Captain Cousteau.
Har-Row.
Dugan, John R. *see* Dugan, John Raymond.
Dugan, John Raymond.
xDugan, John R.
Illusion & Reality. A Study of Descriptive
Techniques in the Works of Guy de
Maupassant. Mouton.
Dugan, Thomas, 1938-
xDugan, Tom.
Photography Between Covers: Interviews with
Photo Book Makers. Light Impressions.
Dugan, Tom. *see* Dugan, Thomas.
Dugan, William.
xDugan, William.
illus. The Bug Book. Western Pub.
Dugard, C. J. R.
xDugard, John.
Human Rights & the South African Legal
Order. Princeton U Pr.
Dugard, John. *see* Dugard, C. J. R.
Dugdale, J. S. *see* Dugdale, Jack Stuart.
Dugdale, Jack Stuart.
xDugdale, J. S.
Teach Yourself Economic & Social History.
Dover.
Dugdale, Kathleen.
xDugdale, Kathleen.
Manual on Writing Research. Dugdale.
Duggan, Anne S. *see* Duggan, Anne Schley.
Duggan, Anne Schley, 1905-
xDuggan, Anne S.
Comparative Study of Undergraduate Women
Majors & Non-Majors in Physical Education
with Respect to Certain Personal Traits.
AMS Pr.
The Complete Tap Dance Book. U Pr of Amer.
Duggan, Ervin S.
xDuggan, Ervin S.
Against All Enemies. Avon.
Duggan, Francis X.
xDuggan, Francis X.
Paul Elmer More. Coll & U Pr.
Duggan, Joseph J.
xDuggan, Joseph J.

ed. Oral Literature: Seven Essays. B&N.
Duggan, Moira.
xDuggan, Moira.
Horses. Western Pub.
Duggan, Stephen P. *see* Duggan, Stephen Pierce Hayden.
Duggan, Stephen Pierce Hayden, 1870-1950
xDuggan, Stephen P.
A Professor at Large. Arno.
Duggan, William R. *see* Duggan, William Redman.
Duggan, William Redman.
xDuggan, William R.
A Socioeconomic Profile of South Africa.
Irvington.
Tanzania & Nyerere: A Study of Ujamaa &
Nationhood. Orbis Bks.
Duggins, James.
xDuggins, James.
Teaching Reading for Human Values in High
School. Merrill.
Duguit, Leon, 1859-1928
xDuguit, Leon.
Law in the Modern State. Fertig.
Dugundji, James.
xDugundji, James.
Topology. Allyn.
Duhamel, Jean.
xDuhamel, Jean.
Fifty Days: Napoleon in England. U of Miami
Pr.
Duignan, Peter.
xDuignan, Peter.
Guide to Research & Reference Works on
Sub-Saharan Africa. Hoover Inst Pr.
Handbook of American Resources for African
Studies. Hoover Inst Pr.
Duiker, William J., 1932-
xDuiker, William J.
The Comintern & Vietnamese Communism.
Ohio U Ctr Intl.
Duing, Walter.
xDuing, Walter.
Monsoon Regime of the Currents in the Indian
Ocean. U Pr of Hawaii.
Duis, Perry.
xDuis, Perry.
Chicago: Creating New Traditions. U of
Chicago Pr.
Dukas, Peter.
xDukas, Peter.
Hotel Front Office Management & Operation.
Wm C Brown.
How to Plan & Operate a Restaurant. Hayden.
Planning Profits in the Food and Lodging
Industry. CBI Pub.
Dukas, Vytas, 1923-
xDukas, Vytas.
tr. & ed. Twelve Contemporary Russian
Stories. Fairleigh Dickinson.
Duke, Basil W. *see* Duke, Basil Wilson.
Duke, Basil Wilson, 1838-1916
xDuke, Basil W.
History of Morgan's Cavalry. Kraus Repr.
Duke, C. B., 1938-
xDuke, C. B.
Tunneling in Solids. Acad Pr.
Duke, Charles R.
xDuke, Charles R.
Creative Dramatics & English Teaching.
NCTE.
Duke, Daniel. *see* Duke, Daniel Linden.
Duke, Daniel Linden.
xDuke, Daniel.
Managing Student Behavior Problems. Tchrs
Coll.
Duke, Judith S.
xDuke, Judith S.
Children's Books & Magazines: A Market
Study. Knowledge Indus.
Duke, Maurice.
xDuke, Maurice.

James Branch Cabell: A Reference Guide. G K
Hall.
Duke University. *see* Duke University, Durham, N. C.
Duke University - Durham - North Carolina - Americana
Club. *see* Duke University, Durham, North Carolina.
Americana Club.
Duke University, Durham, N. C.
xDuke University.
In Memoriam, William Kenneth Boyd. AMS
Pr.
Trinity College Historical Society Historical
Papers, Ser. 1-32. AMS Pr.
Trinity College Historical Society Papers, Ser.
1: Reconstruction & State Biography. AMS
Pr.
Trinity College Historical Society Papers, Ser.
11: 1915. AMS Pr.
Trinity College Historical Society Papers, Ser.
2: Legal & Biographical Studies. AMS Pr.
Trinity College Historical Society Papers, Ser.
3: Gov. W. W. Holden & Revolutionary
Documents. AMS Pr.
Trinity College Historical Society Papers, Ser.
4: 1900. AMS Pr.
Trinity College Historical Society Papers, Ser.
5: 1905. AMS Pr.
Trinity College Historical Society Papers, Ser.
6: 1906. AMS Pr.
Trinity College Historical Society Papers, Ser.
7: 1907. AMS Pr.
Trinity College Historical Society Papers, Ser.
8: 1908-1909. AMS Pr.
Trinity College Historical Society Papers, Ser.
9: 1912. AMS Pr.
Utopia Collection of the Duke University
Library. Folcroft.
**Duke University, Durham, North Carolina. Americana
Club.**
xDuke University - Durham - North Carolina -
Americana Club.
American Studies in Honor of William
Kenneth Boyd. Arno.
Duke University, Durham, North Carolina. Library.
xDuke University Library.
Dante Gabriel Rossetti. AMS Pr.
Duke University Library. *see* Duke University, Durham,
North Carolina. Library.
Duker, Sam, 1905-
xDuker, Sam.
Individualized Instruction in Mathematics.
Scarecrow.
Dukes, Ashley, 1885-1959
xDukes, Ashley.
Modern Dramatists. Arno.
Modern Dramatists. Folcroft.
Dukes, Ona B. *see* Dukes, Ona Brigham.
Dukes, Ona Brigham.
xDukes, Ona B.
Lord, What Are You Doing Next Tuesday?.
Bethany Pr.
Dukes, Paul, 1934-
xDukes, Paul.
October & the World: Perspectives on the
Russian Revolution. St Martin.
Dukhin, S. S. *see* Dukhin, Stanislav Samuilovich.
Dukhin, Stanislav Samuilovich.
xDukhin, S. S.
Dielectric Phenomena & the Double Layer in
Disperse Systems & Polyelectrolytes. Halsted
Pr.
Dukore, Bernard F. *see* Dukore, Bernard Frank.
Dukore, Bernard Frank.
xDukore, Bernard F.

ed. Documents for Drama & Revolution.
Irvington.
Money & Politics in Ibsen, Shaw, & Brecht. U
of Mo Pr.
Where Laughter Stops: Pinter's Tragicomedy.
U of Mo Pr.

Dulaney, Paul S.
xDulaney, Paul S.
The Architecture of Historic Richmond. U Pr
of Va.

Dulany, Don E. *see* Dulany, Don Edwin.

Dulany, Don Edwin, 1928-
xDulany, Don E.
Contributions to Modern Psychology: Selected
Readings in General Psychology. Oxford U
Pr.

Dulieu, Jean.
xDulieu, Jean.
Paulus & the Dragon. Crossing Pr.

Dulin, John J., 1921-
xDulin, John J.
Modern Electronic Calculations. G S E Pubns.

Duling, Dennis C.
xDuling, Dennis C.
Jesus Christ Through History. HarBraceJ.

Duling, Gretchen A.
xDuling, Gretchen A.
Adopting Joe: A Black Vietnamese Child. C E
Tuttle.

Dull, Jonathan R., 1942-
xDull, Jonathan R.
The French Navy & American Independence:
A Study of Arms & Diplomacy, 1774-1787.
Princeton U Pr.

Dulles, Allen.
xDulles, Allen.
The Craft of Intelligence. Greenwood.

Dulles, Allen. *see* Dulles, Allen Welsh.

Dulles, Allen W. *see* Dulles, Allen Welsh.

Dulles, Allen Welsh.
xDulles, Allen.
ed. Great Spy Stories from Fiction. Har-Row.
xDulles, Allen W.
Can We Be Neutral?. Arno.
Germany's Underground. Greenwood.

Dulles, Avery, 1918-
xDulles, Avery.
Church Membership As a Catholic &
Ecumenical Problem. Marquette.
Models of the Church. Doubleday.

Dulles, Eleanor L. *see* Dulles, Eleanor Lansing.

Dulles, Eleanor Lansing, 1895-
xDulles, Eleanor L.
Eleanor Lansing Dulles: Chances of a Lifetime:
A Memoir. P-H.
The French Franc: 1914-1928. Arno.
One Germany or Two: The Struggle at the
Heart of Europe. Hoover Inst Pr.

Dulles, Foster R. *see* Dulles, Foster Rhea.

Dulles, Foster Rhea, 1900-
xDulles, Foster R.
America's Rise to World Power, 1898-1954.
Har-Row.
America's Rise to World Power: 1898-1954.
Har-Row.
Civil Rights Commission 1957-1965. Mich St
U Pr.
A History of Recreation: America Learns to
Play. Irvington.
History of Recreation: America Learns to Play.
P-H.
Old China Trade. AMS Pr.
Prelude to World Power: American Diplomatic
History, 1860-1900. Macmillan.

Dulles, John W. *see* Dulles, John W. F.

Dulles, John W. F.
xDulles, John W.

Anarchists & Communists in Brazil, 1900-1935.
U of Tex Pr.
Castello Branco: The Making of a Brazilian
President. Tex A&M Univ Pr.
Vargas of Brazil: A Political Biography. U of
Tex Pr.

Duly, Colin.
xDuly, Colin.
The Houses of Mankind. Thames Hudson.

Dumas, Alexander, 1802-1870
xDumas, Alexandre.
Count of Monte Cristo. Lighthouse Pr NY.
The Count of Monte Cristo. Bantam.
Count of Monte Cristo. Dodd.

Dumas, Alexandre, 1824-1895
xDumas, Alexandre.
Camille. Arno.
The Great Lover & Other Plays. Ungar.

Dumas, Alexandre. *see* Dumas, Alexander.

Dumas, Andre.
xDumas, Andre.
Political Theology & the Life of the Church.
Westminster.

Dumas, Claire.
xDumas, Claire.
The Stranger. Ballantine.

Dumas, Enoch.
xDumas, Enoch.
Arithmetic Games. Pitman Learning.
Math Activities for Child Involvement. Allyn.

Dumas, F. M.
xDumas, F. M.
Gunfighter's Choice. Bouregy.

Dumas, Henry, 1934-1968
xDumas, Henry.
Jonoah & the Green Stone. Random.
Play Ebony Play Ivory. Random.

Dumas, Philippe.
xDumas, Philippe.
illus. The Story of Edward. Schol Bk Serv.

Dumazedier, Joffre.
xDumazedier, Joffre.
Sociology of Leisure. Elsevier.

Dumbarton Oaks.
xDumbarton Oaks Collections.
Byzantine Art. U of Chicago Pr.
Pre-Columbian Art. U of Chicago Pr.

Dumbarton Oaks Collections. *see* Dumbarton Oaks.

Dumbauld, Edward, 1905-
xDumbauld, Edward.
The Bill of Rights & What It Means Today.
Greenwood.
Constitution of the United States. U of Okla
Pr.
Life & Legal Writings of Hugo Grotius. U of
Okla Pr.
Thomas Jefferson & the Law. U of Okla Pr.

Dumbleton, John H.
xDumbleton, John H.
An Introduction to Orthopaedic Materials. C C
Thomas.

Dumezil, Georges, 1898-
xDumezil, Georges.
Destiny of a King. U of Chicago Pr.
Destiny of the Warrior. U of Chicago Pr.
Gods of the Ancient Northmen. U of Cal Pr.

Dumitriu, Anton.
xDumitriu, Anton.
History of Logic. Intl Schol Bk Serv.

Dummer, G. W. *see* Dummer, Geoffrey William Arnold.

Dummer, Geoffrey William Arnold.
xDummer, G. W.
Materials for Conductive & Resistive
Functions. Hayden.

Dummer, Jeremiah, 1681-1739
xDummer, Jeremiah.
Defence of the New-England Charters. Arno.

Dummett, Michael. *see* Dummett, Michael A. E.

Dummett, Michael A. E.
xDummett, Michael.

Truth & Other Enigmas. Harvard U Pr.

Dummett, Nanci L. *see* Dummett, Nanci Lee.

Dummett, Nanci Lee.
xDummett, Nanci L.
Self-Paced Business Mathematics. Wadsworth
Pub.

Dumoga, John, 1924-
xDumoga, John.
Africa Between East & West. Dufour.

Dumond, Dwight L. *see* Dumond, Dwight Lowell.

Dumond, Dwight Lowell, 1895-
xDumond, Dwight L.
Antislavery Origins of the Civil War in the
United States. Greenwood.
Antislavery Origins of the Civil War in the
United States. U of Mich Pr.
Antislavery: The Crusade for Freedom in
America. Norton.
Antislavery: The Crusade for Freedom in
America. U of Mich Pr.
ed. Southern Editorials on Secession. Peter
Smith.

Dumont, Jean Louis.
xDumont, Jean-Louis.
Paroles Du Terroir. Van Nos Reinhold.

Dumont, Jean-Louis. *see* Dumont, Jean Louis.

Dumont, Jean-Paul, 1940-
xDumont, Jean-Paul.
Under the Rainbow: Nature & Supernature
Among the Panare Indians. U of Tex Pr.

Dumont, Louis, 1911-
xDumont, Louis.
From Mandeville to Marx: Genesis & Triumph
of Economic Ideology. U of Chicago Pr.
From Mandeville to Marx: The Genesis &
Triumph of Economic Ideology. U of
Chicago Pr.
Homo Hierarchicus: The Caste System & Its
Implications. U of Chicago Pr.

Dumont, Rene, 1904-
xDumont, Rene.
Utopia or Else.... Universe.

Dumoulin, Heinrich.
xDumoulin, Heinrich.
Intro. by & ed. Buddhism in the Modern
World. Macmillan.
Intro. by Buddhism in the Modern World.
Macmillan.
Christianity Meets Buddhism. Open Court.
xDumoulin, Henrich.
ed. Buddhism in the Modern World.
Macmillan.

Dumoulin, Henrich. *see* Dumoulin, Heinrich.

Dunavent, James. *see* Dunavent, Jim.

Dunavent, Jim.
xDunavent, James.
How to Draw Airplanes. TAB Bks.

Dunaway, John M., 1945-
xDunaway, John M.
The Metamorphoses of the Self: The Mystic,
the Sensualist, & the Artist in the Works of
Julien Green. U Pr of Ky.

Dunaway, Wayland F. *see* Dunaway, Wayland Fuller.

Dunaway, Wayland Fuller, 1875-
xDunaway, Wayland F.
History of the James River & Kanawha
Company. AMS Pr.
The Scotch-Irish of Colonial Pennsylvania.
Genealog Pub.

Dunbabin, Katherine M. *see* Dunbabin, Katherine M. D.

Dunbabin, Katherine M. D.
xDunbabin, Katherine M.
The Mosaics of Roman North Africa: Studies
in Iconography & Patronage. Oxford U Pr.

Dunbabin, Thomas J. *see* Dunbabin, Thomas James.

Dunbabin, Thomas James.
xDunbabin, Thomas J.

The Greeks & Their Eastern Neighbours:
   Studies in the Relations Between Greece &
   the Countries of the Near East in the Eighth
   & Seventh Centuries B. C.. Greenwood.

Dunbar, Anthony.
   xDunbar, Tony.
   Our Land Too. Pantheon.

Dunbar, Carl O. *see* Dunbar, Carl Owen.

Dunbar, Carl Owen.
   xDunbar, Carl O.
   Historical Geology. Wiley.
   Principles of Stratigraphy. Wiley.

Dunbar, Charles F. *see* Dunbar, Charles Franklin.

Dunbar, Charles Franklin.
   xDunbar, Charles F.
   ed. Laws of the United States Relating to
   Currency, Finance & Banking from 1789 to
   1891. Greenwood.
   Compiled by Laws of the United States
   Relating to Currency Finance & Banking
   1789-1896. Kelley.

Dunbar, Ernest.
   xDunbar, Ernest.
   Nigeria. Watts.

Dunbar, Janet.
   xDunbar, Janet.
   The Early Victorian Woman: Some Aspects of
   Her Life, 1837-1857. Hyperion Conn.

Dunbar, Louise B. *see* Dunbar, Louise Burnham.

Dunbar, Louise Burnham, 1894-
   xDunbar, Louise B.
   A Study of "Monarchical" Tendencies in the
   United States from 1776 to 1801. Johnson
   Repr.
   Study of Monarchical Tendencies in the United
   States from 1776 to 1801. Scholarly.

Dunbar, M. J. *see* Dunbar, Maxwell John.

Dunbar, Maurice, 1928-
   xDunbar, Maurice.
   Fundamentals of Book Collecting. Hermes.
   xDunbar, Maury.
   Books & Collectors. Book Nest.

Dunbar, Maury. *see* Dunbar, Maurice.

Dunbar, Maxwell John.
   xDunbar, M. J.
   ed. Marine Production Mechanisms. Cambridge
   U Pr.

Dunbar, Nancy J.
   xDunbar, Nancy J.
   Compiled by Images of Sport in Early Canada:
   Les images du sport dans le Canada
   d'autrefois. McGill-Queens U Pr.

Dunbar, Paul L. *see* Dunbar, Paul Laurence.

Dunbar, Paul Laurence, 1872-1906
   xDunbar, Paul L.

Candle-Lightin' Time. AMS Pr.
The Complete Poems of Paul Laurence
   Dunbar. Dodd.
Fanatics. Arno.
Fanatics. Mnemosyne.
Fanatics. Negro U Pr.
Folks from Dixie. Arno.
Folks from Dixie. Irvington.
Folks from Dixie. Negro U Pr.
Howdy, Honey, Howdy. AMS Pr.
Howdy Honey Howdy. Arno.
In Old Plantation Days. Negro U Pr.
Li'l Gal. AMS Pr.
Li'l Gal. Scholarly.
Li'l'gal. Arno.
Love of Landry. Arno.
The Love of Landry. Irvington.
Love of Landry. Mnemosyne.
Love of Landry. Negro U Pr.
Speakin' O' Christmas & Other Christmas &
   Special Poems. AMS Pr.
Uncalled. AMS Pr.
Uncalled. Arno.
The Uncalled. Irvington.
Uncalled. Mnemosyne.
Uncalled: A Novel. Negro U Pr.
When Malindy Sings. AMS Pr.
When Malindy Sings. Arno.

Dunbar, Tony. *see* Dunbar, Anthony.
Dunbar, Willis F. *see* Dunbar, Willis Frederick.

Dunbar, Willis Frederick.
   xDunbar, Willis F.
   Michigan: A History of the Wolverine State.
   Eerdmans.

Duncan, A. S. *see* Duncan, Archibald Sutherland.
Duncan, Acheson J. *see* Duncan, Acheson Johnston.

Duncan, Acheson Johnston, 1904-
   xDuncan, Acheson J.
   Quality Control & Industrial Statistics. Irwin.

Duncan, Andrew, 1940-
   xDuncan, Andrew.
   Money Rush. Doubleday.

Duncan, Archibald Sutherland.
   xDuncan, A. S.
   ed. Dictionary of Medical Ethics. Humanities.
   Dictionary of Medical Ethics. State Mutual Bk.

Duncan, Beverly.
   xDuncan, Beverly.
   Sex Typing & Social Roles: A Research Report.
   Acad Pr.

Duncan, Bingham.
   xDuncan, Bingham.
   Whitelaw Reid: Journalist, Politician, Diplomat.
   U of Ga Pr.

Duncan, C. J. *see* Duncan, Christopher John.

Duncan, Charles.
   xDuncan, Charles.
   The Art of Classical Guitar Playing. Summy.

Duncan, Christopher John.
   xDuncan, C. J.
   ed. Calcium in Biological Systems. Cambridge
   U Pr.

Duncan, D. *see* Duncan, Douglas J. M.

Duncan, David D. *see* Duncan, David Douglas.

Duncan, David Douglas.
   xDuncan, David D.
   The Silent Studio. Norton.

Duncan, Douglas J. M.
   xDuncan, D.
   Ben Jonson & the Lucianic Tradition.
   Cambridge U Pr.

Duncan, E. H.
   xDuncan, E. H.
   Night Duty Social Worker. Elsevier-Nelson.

Duncan, E. R.
   xDuncan, Elwin R.

   ed. Dimensions of World Food Problems. Iowa
   St U Pr.

Duncan, Edmondstoune, 1866-1920
   xDuncan, Edmondstoune.
   Story of Minstrelsy. Gale.
   Story of the Carol. Gale.

Duncan, Elmer H.
   xDuncan, Elmer H.
   Soren Kierkegaard. Word Bks.

Duncan, Elwin R. *see* Duncan, E. R.

Duncan, F. *see* Duncan, Fraser G.

Duncan, Fraser G., 1932-
   xDuncan, F.
   Microprocessor Programming & Software
   Development. P-H.

Duncan, George B.
   xDuncan, George B.
   The Person & Work of the Holy Spirit in the
   Life of the Believer. John Knox.

Duncan, Hannibal G. *see* Duncan, Hannibal Gerald.

Duncan, Hannibal Gerald, 1885-
   xDuncan, Hannibal G.
   Race & Population Problems. Negro U Pr.

Duncan, Helen A.
   xDuncan, Helen A.
   Duncan's Dictionary for Nurses. Springer Pub.

Duncan, Hugh D. *see* Duncan, Hugh Dalziel.

Duncan, Hugh Dalziel.
   xDuncan, Hugh D.
   Symbols & Social Theory. Oxford U Pr.

Duncan, Ida R. *see* Duncan, Ida Riley.

Duncan, Ida Riley.
   xDuncan, Ida R.
   Complete Book of Progressive Knitting.
   Liveright.

Duncan, Isadora.
   xDuncan, Isadora.
   Art of the Dance. Theatre Arts.
   My Life. Liveright.

Duncan, James E.
   xDuncan, James E.
   The Reason for Joy. Broadman.
   Relax & Let God . . .. Broadman.

Duncan, James P.
   xDuncan, James P.
   Your Future in Foreign Service Careers. Rosen
   Pr.

Duncan, Jane.
   xDuncan, Jane.
   Brave Janet Reachfar. HM.
   Letter from Reachfar. St Martin.
   My Friends George & Tom. G K Hall.
   My Friends the Misses Kindness. St Martin.

Duncan, Jeffrey L.
   xDuncan, Jeffrey L.
   The Power & Form of Emerson's Thought. U
   Pr of Va.

Duncan, Julia C. *see* Duncan, Julia Coley.

Duncan, Julia Coley.
   xDuncan, Julia C.
   Halfway Home. Popular Lib.
   xDuncan, Julia Coley.
   Halfway Home. St Martin.

Duncan, Julian S. *see* Duncan, Julian Smith.

Duncan, Julian Smith, 1896-
   xDuncan, Julian S.
   Public & Private Operation of Railways in
   Brazil. AMS Pr.

Duncan, Kathleen M.
   xDuncan, Kathleen M.
   Crispin's Castle. Zondervan.
   Sally & the Shepherdess. Zondervan.

Duncan, Lois, 1934-
   xDuncan, Lois.

Daughters of Eve. Dell.
Daughters of Eve. Little.
Down a Dark Hall. NAL.
Down a Dark Hall. Little.
A Gift of Magic. Little.
A Gift of Magic. Archway.
Gift of Magic. PB.
Hotel for Dogs. Avon.
How to Write & Sell Your Personal
    Experiences. Writers Digest.
I Know What You Did Last Summer.
    Archway.
I Know What You Did Last Summer. Little.
I Know What You Did Last Summer. PB.
Peggy. Little.
Summer of Fear. Dell.
Summer of Fear. Little.

Duncan, Louis C. see Duncan, Louis Caspar.

Duncan, Louis Caspar, 1869-
    xDuncan, Louis C.
    Medical Men in the American Revolution
        1775-1783. Kelley.

Duncan, Robert.
    xDuncan, Robert.
    The Story of the Edinburgh Burns Relics with
        Fresh Facts About Burns & His Family.
        Folcroft.

Duncan, Robert. see Duncan, Robert Edward.

Duncan, Robert Edward, 1919-
    xDuncan, Robert.
    Opening of the Field. New Directions.
Duncan, Robert I.
    xDuncan, Robert I.
    Architectural Graphics & Communication.
        Kendall-Hunt.
Duncan, Robert L. see Duncan, Robert Lipscomb.
Duncan, Robert Lipscomb, 1927-
    xDuncan, Robert L.
    Brimstone. Morrow.
    The Day the Sun Fell. Ballantine.
    Fire Storm. Morrow.
Duncan, S. Blackwell.
    xDuncan, S. Blackwell.
    The Build-It Book of Cabinets & Built-Ins.
        TAB Bks.
    The Complete Handbook of Electrical & House
        Wiring. TAB Bks.
    The Dream House Think Book. TAB Bks.
    How to Build Your Own Log Home & Cabin
        from Scratch. TAB Bks.
    How to Make Your Own Camping & Hiking
        Gear. TAB Bks.
    xDuncan, Stuart B.
    The Complete Book of Outdoor Masonry. TAB
        Bks.

Duncan, Stuart B. see Duncan, S. Blackwell.
Duncan, T. Roger.
    xDuncan, T. Roger.
    You're Divorced, but Your Children Aren't.
        P-H.
Duncan, W. Jack. see Duncan, Walter Jack.
Duncan, W. R. see Duncan, W. Raymond.
Duncan, W. Raymond, 1936-
    xDuncan, W. R.
    ed. Soviet Policy in Developing Countries.
        Krieger.
    xDuncan, W. Raymond.
    ed. Soviet Policy in Developing Countries.
        Krieger.
Duncan, W. Raymond. see Duncan, Walter Raymond.
Duncan, Walter Jack.
    xDuncan, W. Jack.

Essentials of Management. Dryden Pr.
    Organizational Behavior. HM.
Duncan, Walter Raymond.
    xDuncan, W. Raymond.
    ed. The Quest for Change in Latin America:
        Sources for a Twentieth Century Analysis.
        Oxford U Pr.
Duncan, Wilbur H. see Duncan, Wilbur Howard.
Duncan, Wilbur Howard, 1910-
    xDuncan, Wilbur H.
    Woody Vines of the Southeastern United
        States. U of Ga Pr.
Duncan, William J. see Duncan, William James.
Duncan, William James, 1811-1885
    xDuncan, William J.
    ed. Notices & Documents Illustrative of the
        Literary History of Glasgow During the
        Greater Part of Last Century. AMS Pr.
Duncan, William R.
    xDuncan, William R.
    Thailand: A Complete Guide. C E Tuttle.
Duncan-Clark, S. J. see Duncan-Clark, Samuel John.
Duncan-Clark, Samuel John, 1875-1938
    xDuncan-Clark, S. J.
    Progressive Movement, Its Principles & Its
        Programme. AMS Pr.
Dunckel, E. B. see Dunckel, Earl B.
Dunckel, Earl B.
    xDunckel, E. B.
    Business Environment of the Seventies: A
        Trend Analysis for Business Planning.
        McGraw.
Duncker, Karl, 1903-
    xDuncker, Karl.
    On Problem-Solving. Greenwood.
Duncombe, Herbert S. see Duncombe, Herbert Sydney.
Duncombe, Herbert Sydney.
    xDuncombe, Herbert S.
    Modern County Government. Natl Assn
        Counties.
Duncombe, Sydney.
    xDuncombe, Sydney.
    Idaho State & Local Government. Caxton.
Dundas, James L.
    xDundas, James L.
    Heating Service. Kendall-Hunt.
Dundee Biennial Conference on Numerical Analysis.
    xBiennial Conference, Dundee, Great Britain, June
        28-July 1, 1977.
    Numerical Analysis: Proceedings.
        Springer-Verlag.
Dundes, Alan.
    xDundes, Alan.
    Analytic Essays in Folklore. Mouton.
    Interpreting Folklore. Ind U Pr.
    Work Hard & You Shall Be Rewarded: Urban
        Folklore from the Paperwork Empire. Ind U
        Pr.
    xDundes, Alen.
    ed. Varia Folklorica. Beresford Bk Serv.
Dundes, Alen. see Dundes, Alan.
Dundy, Elaine.
    xDundy, Elaine.
    Finch, Bloody Finch: The Life of Peter Finch.
        HR&W.
Dunes of Dare Garden Club.
    xDunes of Dare Garden Club.
    Wildflowers of the Outer Banks: Kitty Hawk to
        Hatteras. U of NC Pr.
Dunetz, Martin. see Dunetz, Martin R.
Dunetz, Martin R.
    xDunetz, Martin.
    How to Finance Your Retirement. Reston.
Dunfee, Maxine.
    xDunfee, Maxine.
    Teaching for Social Values in Social Studies.
        ACEI.
Dunfee, Thomas W.
    xDunfee, Thomas W.

Business Law: Key Issues & Concepts. Grid
    Pub.
Modern Business Law. Grid Pub.
Modern Business Law: An Introduction to
    Government & Business. Grid Pub.
Modern Business Law: An Introduction to the
    Legal Environment of Business. Grid Pub.
Modern Business Law: Contracts. Grid Pub.
Dunglison, Robley, 1798-1869
    xDunglison, Robley.
    Human Health. Arno.
Dunham, Aileen.
    xDunham, Aileen.
    Political Unrest in Upper Canada, 1815-1836.
        Greenwood.
Dunham, Arthur L. see Dunham, Arthur Louis.
Dunham, Arthur Louis.
    xDunham, Arthur L.
    Anglo-French Treaty of Commerce of 1860 &
        the Progress of the Industrial Revolution in
        France. Russell.
    xDunham, Arthur Louis.
    The Industrial Revolution in France,
        1815-1848. Exposition.
Dunham, Chester F. see Dunham, Chester Forrester.
Dunham, Chester Forrester, 1891-1959
    xDunham, Chester F.
    The Attitude of the Northern Clergy Toward
        the South 1860-1865. Porcupine Pr.
Dunham, Clarence. see Dunham, Clarence Whiting.
Dunham, Clarence W. see Dunham, Clarence Whiting.
Dunham, Clarence Whiting.
    xDunham, Clarence.
    Contracts, Specifications & Law for Engineers.
        McGraw.
    xDunham, Clarence W.
    Theory & Practice of Reinforced Concrete.
        McGraw.
Dunham, Dows.
    xDunham, Dows.
    The Barkal Temples. Mus Fine Arts Boston.
Dunham, H. Warren. see Dunham, Henry Warren.
Dunham, Harold H. see Dunham, Harold Hathaway.
Dunham, Harold Hathaway, 1903-
    xDunham, Harold H.
    Government Handout: A Study in the
        Administration of the Public Lands
        1875-1891. Da Capo.
Dunham, Henry Warren, 1906-
    xDunham, H. Warren.
    ed. City in Mid-Century: Prospects for Human
        Relations in the Urban Environment. Russell.
Dunham, James H. see Dunham, James Henry.
Dunham, James Henry, 1870-1953
    xDunham, James H.
    Religion of Philosophers. Arno.
Dunham, Montrew.
    xDunham, Montrew.
    Anne Bradstreet: Young Puritan Poet. Bobbs.
Dunham, Philip J.
    xDunham, Philip J.
    Experimental Psychology: Theory & Practice.
        Har-Row.
Dunham, William H. see Dunham, William Huse.
Dunham, William Huse, 1901-
    xDunham, William H.
    Lord Hastings' Indentured Retainers,
        1461-1483: The Lawfulness of Livery &
        Retaining Under the Yorkists & Tudors. Shoe
        String.
Duniway, Abigail (Scott), 1834-1915
    xDuniway, Abigail S.
    Path Breaking: An Autobiographical History of
        the Equal Suffrage Movement in the Pacific
        Coast States. Schocken.
Duniway, Abigail S. see Duniway, Abigail (Scott).
Duniway, Clyde A. see Duniway, Clyde Augustus.
Duniway, Clyde Augustus, 1866-1944
    xDuniway, Clyde A.

The Development of Freedom of the Press in
Massachusetts. B Franklin.
Dunkel, Wilbur D. see Dunkel, Wilbur Dwight.
Dunkel, Wilbur Dwight.
xDunkel, Wilbur D.
Dramatic Technique of Thomas Middleton in
His Comedies of London Life. Russell.
Dunkell, Samuel.
xDunkell, Samuel.
Lovelives: How We Make Love. Morrow.
Lovelives: How We Make Love. NAL.
Dunkels, Marjorie.
xDunkels, Marjorie.
Donkey Wrinkles & Tales. J A Allen.
Dunkerley, David.
xDunkerley, David.
Foreman: Aspects of Task & Structure.
Routledge & Kegan.
Occupations & Society. Routledge & Kegan.
The Study of Organizations. Routledge &
Kegan.
Dunkin, M. see Dunkin, M. J.
Dunkin, M. J.
xDunkin, M.
The Study of Teaching. HR&W.
Dunkin, Paul S. see Dunkin, Paul Shaner.
Dunkin, Paul Shaner, 1905-
xDunkin, Paul S.
How to Catalog a Rare Book. ALA.
Dunkle, William F. see Dunkle, William Frederick.
Dunkle, William Frederick.
xDunkle, William F.
Companion to the Book of Worship. Abingdon.
Dunklin, Howard T. see Dunklin, Howard Thomas.
Dunklin, Howard Thomas, 1899-
xDunklin, Howard T.
Prevention of Failure in First Grade Reading
by Means of Adjusted Instruction. AMS Pr.
Dunkling, Leslie.
xDunkling, Leslie.
The Nightmare. Newbury Hse.
xDunkling, Leslie A.
First Names First. Universe.
Dunkling, Leslie A. see Dunkling, Leslie.
Dunkman, William E. see Dunkman, William Edward.
Dunkman, William Edward, 1903-
xDunkman, William E.
Qualitative Credit Control. AMS Pr.
Dunlap, A. R. see Dunlap, Arthur Ray.
Dunlap, Arthur Ray.
xDunlap, A. R.
Dutch & Swedish Place-Names in Delaware. U
Delaware Pr.
Dunlap, G. D., 1923-
xDunlap, G. Dale.
Successful Celestial Navigation with H.O. 229.
Intl Marine.
Dunlap, G. Dale. see Dunlap, G. D.
Dunlap, George A. see Dunlap, George Arthur.
Dunlap, George Arthur, 1893-
xDunlap, George A.
Black, White & Red: The Problem of Shawnee
College. Dorrance.
Dunlap, Jan.
xDunlap, Jan.
Personal & Professional Success for Women
P-H.
Dunlap, Leslie W. see Dunlap, Leslie Whittaker.
Dunlap, Leslie Whittaker, 1911-
xDunlap, Leslie W.
American Historical Societies: 1790-1860.
Porcupine Pr.
Dunlap Society.
xDunlap Society.
Biennial Reports of the Treasurer & Secretary
of the Dunlap Society. B Franklin.
Dunlap, William, 1766-1839
xDunlap, William.

Andre: A Tragedy in Five Acts. B Franklin.
Four Plays, 1789-1812. Schol Facsimiles.
History of the Rise & Progress of the Arts of
Design in the United States. Arno.
Dunleavy, Gareth W.
xDunleavy, Gareth W.
The O'Conor Papers: A Descriptive Catalog &
Surname Register of the Materials at Clonalis
House. Univ Microfilms.
Dunlop, Burton D. see Dunlop, Burton David.
Dunlop, Burton David.
xDunlop, Burton D.
The Growth of Nursing Home Care. Lexington
Bks.
Dunlop, D. M.
xDunlop, Douglas.
Arab Civilization to A.D. 1500. Intl Bk Ctr.
Dunlop, Douglas. see Dunlop, D. M.
Dunlop, Eileen.
xDunlop, Eileen.
Fox Farm. HR&W.
The House on Mayferry Street. HR&W.
Dunlop, Ian, 1925-
xDunlop, Ian.
Chateaux of the Loire. Taplinger.
Dunlop, John. see Dunlop, John Thomas.
Dunlop, John B.
xDunlop, John B.
ed. Aleksandr Solzhenitsyn: Critical Essays &
Documentary Materials. Macmillan.
ed. Aleksandr Solzhenitsyn: Critical Essays &
Documentary Materials. Nordland Pub.
Dunlop, John C. see Dunlop, John Colin.
Dunlop, John Colin.
xDunlop, John C.
History of Prose Fiction. AMS Pr.
ed. History of Prose Fiction. B Franklin.
Dunlop, John T. see Dunlop, John Thomas.
Dunlop, John Thomas, 1914-
xDunlop, John.
ed. Labor in the Twentieth Century. Acad Pr.
xDunlop, John T.
Industrial Relations Systems. S Ill U Pr.
Dunlop, Richard.
xDunlop, Richard.
Backpacking & Outdoor Guide. Rand.
Wheels West. Rand.
Dunlop, Stewart.
xDunlop, Stewart.
Farming & the Countryside. Heinemann Ed.
Dunmore, Spencer, 1928-
xDunmore, Spencer.
Ashley Landing. Morrow.
The Last Hill. Morrow.
Means of Escape. Coward.
Dunn, Alan, 1900-
xDunn, Alan.
Architecture Observed. McGraw.
Dunn, Allan J. see Dunn, Joseph Allan Elphinstone.
Dunn, Arthur W. see Dunn, Arthur Wallace.
Dunn, Arthur Wallace, 1859-1926
xDunn, Arthur W.
Gridiron Nights: Humorous & Satirical Views
of Politics & Statesmen, Presented by the
Dining Club.. Arno.
Dunn, Branson E.
xDunn, Branson E.
Prayers for Country Living. Judson.
Dunn, Delmer D.
xDunn, Delmer D.
Financing Presidential Campaigns. Brookings.
Public Officials & the Press. A-W.
Dunn, Dennis J.
xDunn, Dennis J.

The Catholic Church & the Soviet
Government. East Eur Quarterly.
Detente & Papal-Communist Relations,
1962-1978. Westview.
Religion & Modernization in the Soviet Union.
Westview.
Dunn, Douglas.
xDunn, Douglas.
Barbarians. Merrimack Bk Serv.
ed. The Poetry of Scotland. David & Charles.
Two Decades of Irish Writing: A Critical
Survey. Dufour.
ed. Two Decades of Irish Writing: A Critical
Survey. Persea Bks.
Dunn, Edgar S. see Dunn, Edgar Streeter.
Dunn, Edgar Streeter.
xDunn, Edgar S.
Economic & Social Development: A Process of
Social Learning. Johns Hopkins.
Dunn, Esther C. see Dunn, Esther Cloudman.
Dunn, Esther Cloudman, 1891-
xDunn, Esther C.
Literature of Shakespeare's England. Cooper
Sq.
Dunn, Frederick S. see Dunn, Frederick Sherwood.
Dunn, Frederick Sherwood, 1893-1962
xDunn, Frederick S.
Practice & Procedure of International
Conferences. AMS Pr.
Dunn, George E.
xDunn, George E.
ed. Gilbert & Sullivan Dictionary. Da Capo.
A Gilbert & Sullivan Dictionary. Folcroft.
Dunn, Hampton.
xDunn, Hampton.
Re-Discover Florida. Trend House.
Dunn, Harold.
xDunn, Harold.
Our Hysterical Heritage: The American
Presidential Election Process, Out of the
Mouths of Babes. Stemmer Hse.
Dunn, I. S. see Dunn, Irving S.
Dunn, Irving S.
xDunn, I. S.
Fundamentals of Geotechnical Analysis. Wiley.
Dunn, J. see Dunn, John.
Dunn, Jacob P. see Dunn, Jacob Piatt.
Dunn, Jacob Piatt, 1855-1924
xDunn, Jacob P.
Indiana: A Redemption from Slavery. AMS Pr.
Dunn, James T. see Dunn, James Taylor.
Dunn, James Taylor.
xDunn, James T.
The St. Croix: Midwest Border River. Minn
Hist.
Dunn, Jane.
xDunn, Jane.
Moon in Eclipse: A Life of Mary Shelley. St
Martin.
Dunn, Jerry G.
xDunn, Jerry G
God Is for the Alcoholic. Moody.
Dunn, Joan.
xDunn, Joan.
Retreat from Learning: Why Teachers Can't
Teach, a Case History. Greenwood.
Dunn, John, 1940-
xDunn, J.
Western Political Theory in the Face of the
Future. Cambridge U Pr.
Dunn, John. see Dunn, John Petrie.
Dunn, John Petrie, 1878-1931
xDunn, John.

Ornamentation in the Works of Frederick
Chopin. Da Capo.
Dunn, Joseph Allan Elphinstone, 1872-1941
xDunn, Allan J.
The Flower of Fate. Arno.
Dunn, Judy.
xDunn, Judy.
Distress & Comfort. Harvard U Pr.

Dunn, Lynn P.

xDunn, Lynn P.
American Indians: A Study Guide & Source
Book. R & E Res Assoc.
Asian Americans: A Study Guide & Source
Book. R & E Res Assoc.
Chicanos: A Study Guide & Source Book. R &
E Res Assoc.

Dunn, Nell, 1936-

xDunn, Nell.
Talking to Women. Intl Pubns Serv.

Dunn, P. see Dunn, Phoebe.
Dunn, P. D. see Dunn, Peter.

Dunn, Paul H.

xDunn, Paul H.
Discovering the Quality of Success. Deseret
Bk.
The Osmonds: The Official Story of the
Osmond Family. Avon.

Dunn, Peter, 1927-
xDunn, P. D.
Appropriate Technology: Technology with a
Human Face. Schocken.
Dunn, Peter N.
xDunn, Peter N.
Spanish Picaresque Novel. Twayne.
Dunn, Phoebe.
xDunn, P.
Animal Friends. Creative Ed.
jt. photog. Friends. Creative Ed.
Dunn, R. see Dunn, Rita Stafford.
Dunn, Richard S.
xDunn, Richard S.
Puritans & Yankees: The Winthrop Dynasty of
New England, 1630-1717. Norton.
Sugar & Slaves: The Rise of the Planter Class
in the English West Indies, 1624-1713.
Norton.
Sugar & Slaves: The Rise of the Planter Class
in the English West Indies, 1624-1713. U of
NC Pr.
Dunn, Rita. see Dunn, Rita Stafford.

Dunn, Rita Stafford.

xDunn, R.
jt. auth. Practical Approaches to Individualizing
Instruction: Contracts & Other Effective
Teaching Strategies. P-H.
xDunn, Rita.
Administrator's Guide to New Programs for
Faculty Management & Evaluation. P-H.
Teaching Students Through Their Individual
Learning Styles: A Practical Approach.
Reston.
Dunn, S. Watson. see Dunn, Samuel Watson.
Dunn, Samuel Watson.
xDunn, S. Watson.
How Fifteen Transnational Corporations
Manage Public Affairs. Crain Bks.
International Advertising & Marketing. Grid
Pub.

Dunn, Waldo H. see Dunn, Waldo Hilary.

Dunn, Waldo Hilary, 1882-1969
xDunn, Waldo H.
English Biography. AMS Pr.
Froude & Carlyle: A Study of the Froude -
Carlyle Controversy. Kennikat.
R. D. Blackmore: The Author of "Lorna
Doone"; a Biography. Greenwood.
Dunn, William. see Dunn, William J.
Dunn, William J.
xDunn, William.
Enjoy Europe by Car. Scribner.
xDunn, William J.
Enjoy Europe by Train. Scribner.
Dunnahoo, Terry.
xDunnahoo, Terry.
This Is Espie Sanchez. Dutton.
Who Cares About Espie Sanchez?. Dutton.
Who Needs Espie Sanchez?. Dutton.
Dunnam, Maxie. see Dunnam, Maxie D.
Dunnam, Maxie D.
xDunnam, Maxie.
Barefoot Days of the Soul. Upper Room.
xDunnam, Maxie D.
Barefoot Days of the Soul. Word Bks.
Workbook of Intercessory Prayer. Upper
Room.
Dunne, Charles.
xDunne, Charles.
Outboard Boat & Motor Maintenance &
Repair. Oxmoor Hse.
Dunne, Finley P. see Dunne, Finley Peter.
Dunne, Finley Peter, 1867-1936
xDunne, Finley P.
Dissertations by Mr. Dooley. Irvington.
Dissertations by Mr. Dooley. Scholarly.
Observations by Mr. Dooley. Folcroft.
Observations by Mr. Dooley. Gordon Pr.
Observations by Mr. Dooley. Greenwood.
Observations by Mr. Dooley. Scholarly.
Dunne, George. see Dunne, George Harold.
Dunne, George Harold, 1905-
xDunne, George.
The Right to Development. Paulist Pr.
Dunne, Gerald T.
xDunne, Gerald T.
Hugo Black & the Judicial Revolution.
Irvington.
Hugo Black & the Judicial Revolution. S&S.
Hugo Black & the Judicial Revolution. S&S.
Dunne, Howard W.
xDunne, Howard W.
ed. Diseases of Swine. Iowa St U Pr.
Dunne, John G. see Dunne, John Gregory.
Dunne, John Gregory, 1932-
xDunne, John G.
Quintana & Friends. Dutton.
The Studio. FS&G.
Vegas: A Memoir of a Dark Season. Warner
Bks.
Dunne, John S., 1929-
xDunne, John S.
The Reasons of the Heart: A Journey into
Solitude & Back Again into the Human
Circle. U of Notre Dame Pr.
Dunne, Lee, 1934-
xDunne, Lee.
The Ringleader. S&S.
Dunne, P. M.
xDunne, P. M.
Engineering Drawing for Advanced Students.
Pergamon.
Dunne, Philip, 1908-
xDunne, Philip.
Take Two: A Life in Movies & Politics.
McGraw.
Dunnell, R. C. see Dunnell, Robert C.
Dunnell, Robert C., 1942-
xDunnell, R. C.

The Prehistory of Fishtrap, Kentucky. Yale U
Anthro.
Dunnett, Dorothy.
xDunnett, Dorothy.
Checkmate. Popular Lib.
Disorderly Knights. Popular Lib.
Game of Kings. Popular Lib.
Pawn in Frankincense. Popular Lib.
Dunnett, Rosalind.
xDunnett, Rosalind.
The Trinovantes. Humanities.
Dunnette, Marvin D.
xDunnette, Marvin D.
Handbook of Industrial & Organizational
Psychology. Rand.
Personnel Selection & Placement. Brooks-Cole.
Psychology Applied to Industry. P-H.
Work & Non-Work in the Year 2001.
Brooks-Cole.
Dunnigan, James F.
xDunnigan, James F.
The Complete Wargames Handbook: How to
Play, Design, & Find Them. Morrow.
Dunnill, M. S.
xDunnill, Michael.
Pathological Basis of Renal Disease. Saunders.
Dunnill, Michael. see Dunnill, M. S.
Dunning, Eric.
xDunning, Eric.
Barbarians, Gentlemen & Players: A
Sociological Study of the Development of
Rugby Football. NYU Pr.
Dunning, H. R. see Dunning, Henry R.
Dunning, Henry R.
xDunning, H. R.
Pressure Sensitive Adhesives: Formulations &
Technology. Noyes.
Dunning, James M. see Dunning, James Morse.
Dunning, James Morse.
xDunning, James M.
Dental Care for Everyone: Problems &
Proposals. Harvard U Pr.
Principles of Dental Public Health. Harvard U
Pr.
Dunning, John, 1942-
xDunning, John.
Denver. Times Bks.
Looking for Ginger North. Fawcett.
Tune in Yesterday: The Ultimate Encyclopedia
of Old-Time Radio, 1925-1976. P-H.
Dunning, N. A. see Dunning, Nelson A.
Dunning, Nelson A.
xDunning, N. A.
ed. The Farmers' Alliance History &
Agricultural Digest. Arno.
Dunning, Stephen.
xDunning, Stephen.
Literature for Adolescents: Teaching Poems,
Stories, Novels, & Plays. Scott F.
ed. Some Haystacks Don't Even Have Any
Needle: And Other Complete Modern
Poems. Lothrop.
Teaching Literature to Adolescents: Poetry.
Scott F.
Dunninger, Joseph, 1896-
xDunninger, Joseph.
Dunninger's Complete Encyclopedia of Magic.
Lyle Stuart.
Dunninger's Monument to Magic. Lyle Stuart.
Dunphy, J. Englebert. see Dunphy, John Englebert.
Dunphy, Jack.
xDunphy, Jack.
Nightmovers. Yankee Peddler.
Dunphy, John Englebert.
xDunphy, J. Englebert.
ed. Current Surgical Diagnosis & Treatment.
Lange.
Dunphy, Philip W.
xDunphy, Philip W.

ed. Career Development for the College
  Student. Carroll Pr.
ed. Career Development for the College
  Student. Carroll Pr.
Dunsany, Edward J. *see* Dunsany, Edward John Moreton
  Drax Plunkett.
**Dunsany, Edward John Moreton Drax Plunkett, Baron,
  1878-1957**
  xDunsany, Edward J.
    Book of Wonder. Arno.
    Dreamer's Tales. Arno.
    Last Book of Wonder. Arno.
  xDunsany, Lord.
    The Charwoman's Shadow. Ballantine.
    A Dreamer's Tales. Owlswick Pr.
    Gods, Men & Ghosts: The Best Supernatural
      Fiction of Lord Dunsany. Dover.
    Tales of Three Hemispheres. Owlswick Pr.
Dunsany, Lord. *see* Dunsany, Edward John Moreton
  Drax Plunkett.
Dunscomb, S. Whitney. *see* Dunscomb, Samuel Whitney.
Dunscomb, Samuel Whitney, 1868-1936
  xDunscomb, S. Whitney.
    Bankruptcy: A Study in Comparative
      Legislation. AMS Pr.
Dunseath, T. K.
  xDunseath, T. K.
    Spenser's Allegory of Justice in Book Five of
      "The Faerie Queene". Greenwood.
Dunsire, A.
  xDunsire, A.
    Administration: The Word & the Science.
      Halsted Pr.
Dunson, Josh, 1941-
  xDunson, Josh.
    Freedom in the Air: Song Movements of the
      Sixties. Greenwood.
Dunstan, Bernard, 1920-
  xDunstan, Bernard.
    Learning to Paint. Watson-Guptill.
    Painting Methods of the Impressionists.
      Watson-Guptill.
Dunstan, Elizabeth.
  xDunstan, Elizabeth.
    Twelve Nigerian Languages. Holmes & Meier.
Dunstan, J. Leslie. *see* Dunstan, John Leslie.
Dunstan, John.
  xDunstan, John.
    Paths to Excellence & the Soviet School.
      Humanities.
Dunstan, John Leslie, 1901-
  xDunstan, J. Leslie.
    ed. Protestantism. Braziller.
Dunstan, Mary J. *see* Dunstan, Maryjane.
Dunstan, Maryjane.
  xDunstan, Mary J.
    Worlds in the Making: Probes for Students of
      the Future. P-H.
Dunstan, Ralph, 1857-1933
  xDunstan, Ralph.
    A Cyclopaedic Dictionary of Music. Da Capo.
    A Cyclopaedic Dictionary of Music. Scholarly.
Dunton, Darlene.
  xDunton, Darlene.
    Complete Bonsai Handbook. Stein & Day.
Duplaix, Nicole.
  xDuplaix, Nicole.
    World Guide to Mammals. Crown.
Duplessis, Yves, 1912-
  xDuplessis, Yves.
    Surrealism. Greenwood.
Dupont, Henry, 1921-
  xDupont, Henry.
    ed. Educating Emotionally Disturbed Children:
      Readings. HR&W.
DuPre, Flint O.
  xDuPre, Flint O.
    Your Career in Federal Civil Service. Har-Row.
Dupre, Henri, d. 1929
  xDupre, Henri.

Purcell. AMS Pr.
Dupre, J. Stefan. *see* Dupre, Joseph Stefan.
Dupre, Joseph Stefan.
  xDupre, J. Stefan.
    Federalism & Policy Development: The Case of
      Adult Occupational Training in Ontario. U of
      Toronto Pr.
Dupree. *see* Dupree, Garland Crowe.
Dupree, A. Hunter.
  xDupree, A. Hunter.
    Science in the Federal Government: A History
      of Policies & Activities to 1940. Arno.
Dupree, Garland Crowe.
  xDupree.
    Legal Office Typing. SW Pub.
Dupree, Louis, 1925-
  xDupree, Louis.
    Prehistoric Research in Afghanistan. Am
      Philos.
Duprey, Kenneth.
  xDuprey, Kenneth.
    Old Houses on Nantucket. Architectural.
    Old Houses on Nantucket. Hastings.
Dupuis, Adrian M. *see* Dupuis, Adrian Maurice.
Dupuis, Adrian Maurice.
  xDupuis, Adrian M.
    ed. Nature, Aims & Policy. U of Ill Pr.
Dupuy, Eliza A. *see* Dupuy, Eliza Ann.
Dupuy, Eliza Ann, 1814?-1881
  xDupuy, Eliza A.
    The Cancelled Will. Arno.
    Dethroned Heiress. Arno.
Dupuy, Ernest R. *see* Dupuy, Richard Ernest.
Dupuy, Richard Ernest.
  xDupuy, Ernest R.
    An Outline History of the American
      Revolution. Har-Row.

Dupuy, Trevor N. *see* Dupuy, Trevor Nevitt
Dupuy, Trevor Nevitt.
  xDupuy, Trevor N.
    ed. Almanac of World Military Power. Presidio
      Pr.
    ed. Holidays: Days of Significance for All
      Americans. Watts.
    jt. auth. An Outline History of the American
      Revolution. Har-Row.
    Compiled by People & Events of the American
      Revolution. Bowker.
Duquoc, Christian.
  xDuquoc, Christian.
    ed. Dimensions of Spirituality. Seabury.
    Gift of Joy. Paulist Pr.
    Opportunities for Belief & Behavior. Paulist Pr.
    ed. The Prayer Life. Seabury.
    Secularization & Spirituality. Paulist Pr.
Duram, James C., 1939-
  xDuram, James C.
    Norman Thomas. Twayne.
Duran, Cheli.
  xDuran, Cheli.
    Kindling. Greenwillow.
Duran, Daniel F. *see* Duran, Daniel Flores.
Duran, Daniel Flores, 1946-
  xDuran, Daniel F.
    Latino Materials: A Multimedia Guide for
      Children & Young Adults. ABC-Clio.
Duran, Leo, 1883-
  xDuran, Leo.
    ed. Plays of Old Japan. Core Collection.
    Plays of Old Japan. Folcroft.
Duran, Livie I. *see* Duran, Livie Isauro.
Duran, Livie Isauro.
  xDuran, Livie I.
    Introduction to Chicano Studies: A Reader.
      Macmillan.
Duran, Manuel, 1925-
  xDuran, Manuel.

Cervantes. Twayne.
Luis de Leon. Irvington.
Durand, Robert.
  xDurand, Robert.
    The Ages of J. Christopher's Bks.
Durang, Christopher, 1950-
  xDurang, Christopher.
    A History of the American Film. Avon.
Durant, Jack D. *see* Durant, Jack Davis.
Durant, Jack Davis, 1930-
  xDurant, Jack D.
    Richard Brinsley Sheridan. Twayne.
Durant, John.
  xDurant, John.
    Highlights of College Football. Hastings.
    Highlights of the World Series. Hastings.
Durant, John R.
  xDurant, John R.
    The Chronic Leukemias: Chemistry,
      Pathophysiology & Treatment. C C Thomas.
Durant, Mary. *see* Durant, Mary B.
Durant, Mary B.
  xDurant, Mary.
    On the Road with John James Audubon.
      Dodd.
Durant, Will. *see* Durant, William James.
Durant, William James.
  xDurant, Will.
    Lessons of History. S&S.
Durante, Francesco.
  xDurante, Francesco.
    Western Europe & the Development of the
      Law of the Sea. Oceana.
Durantis, Gulielmus, Bp. of Mende, ca. 1237-1296
  xDurantis, Gulielmus.
    Symbolism of Churches & Church Ornaments:
      A Translation of the First Book of the
      Rationale Divinorum Officiorum. AMS Pr.
Duras, Marguerite.
  xDuras, Marguerite.
    Amante Anglaise. French & Eur.
    Destroy, She Said. Grove.
    India Song. French & Eur.
    India Song. Grove.
Durasoff, Steve.
  xDurasoff, Steve.
    Pentecost Behind the Iron Curtain. Logos.
Durbin, John R.
  xDurbin, John R.
    Modern Algebra: An Introduction. Wiley.
Durbin, Richard L.
  xDurbin, Richard L.
    Organization & Administration of Health Care:
      Theory, Practice, Environment. Mosby.
Durdag, M. *see* Durdag, Mete.
Durdag, Mete.
  xDurdag, M.
    Some Problems of Development Financing: A
      Case Study of the Turkish First Five-Year
      Plan 1963-1967. Kluwer Boston.
Durant, Robert F. *see* Durden, Robert Franklin.
Durden, Robert Franklin.
  xDurden, Robert F.
    The Gray & the Black: The Confederate
      Debate on Emancipation. La State U Pr.
Durdin, Tillman.
  xDurdin, Tillman.
    Southeast Asia. Atheneum.
Durel, Marie.
  xDurel, Marie.
    Speak English: A Practical Course for Foreign
      Students. Har-Row.
Duren, Lista.
  xDuren, Lista.
    Frame It: A Complete Do-It-Yourself Guide to
      Picture Framing. HM.
Duren, Ryne.
  xDuren, Ryne.

The Comeback. Lorenz Pr.

Durer, Albrecht.
  xDurer, Albrecht.
    The Complete Engravings, Etchings &
      Drypoints of Albrecht Durer. Peter Smith.
    Complete Engravings, Etchings, & Dry Points
      of Albrecht Durer. Dover.
    The Human Figure: The Complete 'Dresden
      Sketchbook'. Peter Smith.
    Maximilian's Triumphal Arch. Dover.
Durfee. *see* Durfee, Harold Allen.
Durfee, David A.
  xDurfee, David A.
    Power in American Society: Burden or
      Blessing. Allyn.
Durfee, Harold Allen, 1920-
  xDurfee.
    Analytic Philosophy & Phenomenology. Kluwer
      Boston.
Durfee, W. H. *see* Durfee, William H.
Durfee, William H.
  xDurfee, W. H.
    Calculus & Analytic Geometry. McGraw.
Durgnat, Raymond.
  xDurgnat, Raymond.
    Films & Feelings. MIT Pr.
    Franju. U of Cal Pr.
    Luis Bunuel. U of Cal Pr.
Durham, Bill.
  xDurham, Bill.
    Canoes & Kayaks of Western America. Shorey.
Durham, Mary E. *see* Durham, Mary Edith.
Durham, Mary Edith, 1863-1944
  xDurham, Mary E.
    Some Tribal Origins, Laws & Customs of the
      Balkans. AMS Pr.
Durham, Philip.
  xDurham, Philip.
    ed. Frontier in American Literature. Odyssey
      Pr.
Durham, Willard H. *see* Durham, Willard Higley.
Durham, Willard Higley, 1883-
  xDurham, Willard H.
    ed. Critical Essays of the Eighteenth Century,
      1700-1725. Russell.
Durka, Gloria.
  xDurka, Gloria.
    Aesthetic Dimensions of Religious Education.
      Paulist Pr.
Durken, Daniel.
  xDurken, Daniel.
    ed. Blow the Trumpet at the New Moon: A
      Sisters Today Jubilee. Liturgical Pr.
Durkheim, Emile, 1858-1917
  xDurkheim, Emile.
    Evolution of Educational Thought: Lectures on
      the Formation & Development of Secondary
      Education in France. Routledge & Kegan.
    Primitive Classification. U of Chicago Pr.
    Sociology & Philosophy. Free Pr.
Durkin, Catherine A.
  xDurkin, Catherine A.
    So You Want to Plan a Birthday Party.
      Atheneum.
Durkin, Dolores.
  xDurkin, Dolores.
    Strategies for Identifying Words: A Workbook
      for Teachers & Those Preparing to Teach.
      Allyn.
Durkin, Helen. *see* Durkin, Helen Elise.
Durkin, Helen Elise, 1901-
  xDurkin, Helen.
    The Group in Depth. Intl Univs Pr.
Durkin, Mary. *see* Durkin, Mary Sutro.
Durkin, Mary Brian.
  xDurkin, Mary Brian.
    Dorothy L. Sayers. Twayne.
Durkin, Mary G., 1934-
  xDurkin, Mary G.

The Suburban Woman: Her Changing Role in
  the Church. Seabury.
Durkin, Mary Sutro.
  xDurkin, Mary.
    The Natural Foods Diet Book. G&D.
Durkin, Ned.
  xDurkin, Ned.
    An Introduction to Medical Science: A
      Comprehensive Guide to Anatomy,
      Biochemistry & Physiology. Lippincott.
Durlach, Theresa M. *see* Durlach, Theresa Mayer.
Durlach, Theresa Mayer, 1891-
  xDurlach, Theresa M.
    The Relationship Systems of the Tlingit, Haida,
      & Tsimshian. AMS Pr.
Durney, C. H. *see* Durney, Carl H.
Durney, Carl H.
  xDurney, C. H.
    Introduction to Modern Electromagnetics.
      McGraw.
Durocher, Leo. *see* Durocher, Leo Ernest.
Durocher, Leo Ernest.
  xDurocher, Leo.
    Nice Guys Finish Last. PB.
    Nice Guys Finish Last. S&S.
Durost, Walter N. *see* Durost, Walter Nelson.
Durost, Walter Nelson, 1906-
  xDurost, Walter N.
    Children's Collecting Activity Related to Social
      Factors. AMS Pr.
Durr, Eleanor.
  xDurr, Eleanor.
    Lakeside Lore: Ohio's Chautauqua
      Vacationland. Exposition.
Durran, J. H.
  xDurran, J. H.
    Statistics & Probability. Cambridge U Pr.
Durrant, A. E.
  xDurrant, A. E.
    Australian Steam. David & Charles.
    Steam Locomotives of Eastern Europe. Kelley.
Durrell, Gerald. *see* Durrell, Gerald Malcolm.
Durrell, Gerald Malcolm, 1925-
  xDurrell, Gerald.
    Fauna & Family. S&S.
    Fillets of Plaice. Penguin.
    Golden Bats & Pink Pigeons. S&S.
    Menagerie Manor. Penguin.
    The Talking Parcel. Lippincott.
    Two in the Bush. Penguin.
    The Whispering Land. Penguin.
Durrell, Lawrence.
  xDurrell, Lawrence.
    Balthazar. Dutton.
    Balthazar. PB.
    Clea. Dutton.
    Clea. PB.
    The Dark Labyrinth. Penguin.
    Monsieur. Viking Pr.
    Nunquam: A Novel. Penguin.
    The Plant-Magic Man. Capra Pr.
    Sicilian Carousel. Penguin.
    Sicilian Carousel. Viking Pr.
    Tunc: A Novel. Penguin.
    Vega & Other Poems. Overlook Pr.
    White Eagles Over Serbia. S G Phillips.
Durrenmatt, Friedrich.
  xDurrenmatt, Friedrich.
    An Angel Comes to Babylon & Romulus the
      Great. Grove.
Durst, F.
  xDurst, Franz.
    jt. ed. & ed. Two-Phase Momentum, Heat &
      Mass Transfer in Chemical, Process, &
      Energy Engineering Systems. Hemisphere
      Pub.
Durst, Franz. *see* Durst, F.
Durst, H. Dupont.
  xDurst, H. Dupont.

Experimental Organic Chemistry. McGraw.
Dury, G. H.
  xDury, G. H.
    ed. Studies in Australian Geography.
      Humanities.
Dusen, Willian D. Van. *see* Van Dusen, William D.
Dusky, Lorraine.
  xDusky, Lorraine.
    Birthmark. M Evans.
Dussault, Gilles.
  xDussault, Gilles.
    Theory of Supervision in Teacher Education.
      Tchrs Coll.
Dussourd, J. L.
  xDussourd, J. L.
    ed. Fluid Mechanics of Combustion. ASME.
Dustoor, P. E. *see* Dustoor, Phiroze Edulji.
Dustoor, Phiroze Edulji, 1898-
  xDustoor, P. E.
    World of Words. Asia.
Duthie, Alexander.
  xDuthie, Alexander.
    The Greek Mythology: A Reader's Handbook.
      Greenwood.
Dutourd, Jean, 1920-
  xDutourd, Jean.
    The Horrors of Love. Greenwood.
Dutt, Ashok K.
  xDutt, Ashok K.
    India in Maps. Kendall-Hunt.
Dutt, Gargi.
  xDutt, Gargi.
    China's Cultural Revolution. Asia.
Dutt, Romesh C. *see* Dutt, Romesh Chunder.
Dutt, Romesh Chunder, 1848-1909
  xDutt, Romesh C.
    Economic History of India. Intl Pubns Serv.
    Economic History of India. Kelley.
Dutt, Shoshee C. *see* Dutt, Shoshee Chunder.
Dutt, Shoshee Chunder, 1824-1885
  xDutt, Shoshee C.
    Historical Studies & Recreations. Arno.
Dutt, Sukumar, 1891-
  xDutt, Sukumar.
    Supernatural in English Romantic Poetry.
      Folcroft.
Dutta, S. *see* Dutta, Satrajit.
Dutta, Satrajit.
  xDutta, S.
    Affect & Memory: A Reformulation.
      Pergamon.
Dutton, Bertha P. *see* Dutton, Bertha Pauline.
Dutton, Bertha Pauline, 1903-
  xDutton, Bertha P.
    The Pueblos. P-H.
Dutton, Geoffrey.
  xDutton, Geoffrey.
    Patrick White. Folcroft.
    Queen Emma of the South Seas. St Martin.
Dutton, Joan P. *see* Dutton, Joan Parry.
Dutton, Joan Parry.
  xDutton, Joan P.
    The Flower World of Williamsburg.
      Williamsburg.
Dutton, John A.
  xDutton, John A.
    The Ceaseless Wind: An Introduction to the
      Theory of Atmospheric Motion. McGraw.
Dutton, Margit S. *see* Dutton, Margit Stoll.
Dutton, Margit Stoll.
  xDutton, Margit S.
    The German Pastry Bakebook. Chilton.
Duty, Guy, 1907-
  xDuty, Guy.
    Divorce & Remarriage. Bethany Fell.
    God's Covenants & Our Time. Bethany Fell.
    If Ye Continue. Bethany Fell.
Duus, Peter, 1933-
  xDuus, Peter.

Feudalism in Japan. Knopf.

Duval, Elizabeth W.
  xDuval, Elizabeth W.
    T. E. Lawrence: A Bibliography. Haskell.

DuVal, F. Alan. *see* Duval, Francis Alan.

DuVal, Francis Alan, 1916-
  xDuVal, F. Alan.
    Moderne Deutsche Sprachlehre. Random.

Duval, Hanson R. *see* Duval, Hanson Rawlings.

Duval, Hanson Rawlings.
  xDuval, Hanson R.
    Aldous Huxley: A Bibliography. Folcroft.

Duval, Jean Jacques, 1930-
  xDuval, Jean-Jacques.
    Working with Stained Glass: Fundamental
    Techniques & Applications. T Y Crowell.

Duval, Jean-Jacques. *see* Duval, Jean Jacques.

Duval, Shelley.
  xDuval, Shelley.
    A Theory of Objective Self Awareness. Acad
    Pr.

Duvall, Evelyn. *see* Duvall, Evelyn Ruth Millis.

Duvall, Evelyn Ruth Millis, 1906-
  xDuvall, Evelyn.
    Evelyn Duvall's Handbook for Parents.
    Broadman.

Duvall, Sylvanus M. *see* Duvall, Sylvanus Milne.

Duvall, Sylvanus Milne, 1900-
  xDuvall, Sylvanus M.
    Men, Women, & Morals. Greenwood.

Duveneck, Josephine W. *see* Duveneck, Josephine
  Whitney.

Duveneck, Josephine Whitney, 1891-
  xDuveneck, Josephine W.
    Life on Two Levels: An Autobiography. W
    Kaufmann.

Duvignaud, Jean.
  xDuvignaud, Jean.
    Change at Shebika: Report from a North
    African Village. U of Tex Pr.

Duvoisin, Roger. *see* Duvoisin, Roger Antoine.

Duvoisin, Roger Antoine, 1904-
  xDuvoisin, Roger.
    illus. House of Four Seasons. Lothrop.
    illus. Our Veronica Goes to Petunia's Farm.
    Knopf.
    illus. Periwinkle. Knopf.
    illus. Snowy & Woody. Knopf.
    illus. Two Lonely Ducks: A Counting Book.
    Knopf.

Duvoisin, Roger C.
  xDuvoisin, Roger C.
    Parkinson's Disease: A Guide for Patient &
    Family. Raven.

Duyn, J. Van. *see* Van Duyn, J.

Duzee, Mabel Van. *see* Van Duzee, Mabel.

Duzer, Henry S. Van. *see* Van Duzer, Henry S.

Dvorak, M. *see* Dvorak, Milan.

Dvorak, Milan.
  xDvorak, M.
    Differentiation of Rat Ova During Cleavage.
    Springer-Verlag.

Dvorin, Eugene P.
  xDvorin, Eugene P.
    Government in American Society. A-W.
    Governments Within the States. A-W.

Dvorkin, David.
  xDvorkin, David.
    At Home with Solar Energy: A Consumer's
    Guide. Nelson.

Dvornik, Francis, 1893-
  xDvornik, Francis.
    Byzantium & the Roman Primacy. Fordham.

Dwan, Lois.
  xDwan, Lois.
    Los Angeles Restaurant Guide. J P Tarcher.

Dwarakanath, T. *see* Dwarakanath, Tandur.

Dwarakanath, Tandur.
  xDwarakanath, T.

Guide to Practicals in Electronics. Asia.

Dwek, Joe, 1938-
  xDwek, Joe.
    Backgammon for Profit. Stein & Day.

Dwiggins, B. *see* Dwiggins, Boyce H.

Dwiggins, Boyce. *see* Dwiggins, Boyce H.

Dwiggins, Boyce H.
  xDwiggins, B.
    Automotive Air Conditioning. Delmar.
  xDwiggins, Boyce.
    Automobile Repair Guide. Audel.
  xDwiggins, Boyce H.
    Automotive Air Conditioning. Van Nos
    Reinhold.

Dwiggins, Don.
  xDwiggins, Don.
    The Asteroid War. Childrens.
    Jimmy Fox & the Mountain Rescue. Childrens.
    Low-Horsepower Fun Aircraft You Can Build.
    TAB Bks.
    Man-Powered Aircraft. TAB Bks.
    Restoration of Antique & Classic Planes. TAB
    Bks.

Dwight, John A.
  xDwight, John A.
    How to Write a Research Paper. Learn
    Concepts OH.

Dwight, Timothy, 1752-1817
  xDwight, Timothy.
    Conquest of Canaan: A Poem in Eleven Books.
    Greenwood.
    Greenfield Hill. AMS Pr.
    Remarks on the Review of Inchiquin's Letters.
    Mss Info.

Dwivedi, Basant K.
  xDwivedi, Basant K.
    ed. Low Calorie & Special Dietary Foods. CRC
    Pr.

Dworkin, Andrea.
  xDworkin, Andrea.
    The New Womans Broken Heart: Short Stories.
    Frog in Well.
    Our Blood: Prophecies & Discourses on Sexual
    Politics. Har-Row.

Dworkin, Floss.
  xDworkin, Floss.
    Floss & Stan's "Why Are My Leaves Turning
    Yellow & Falling Off" Answer Book. Dutton.

Dworkin, Ronald.
  xDworkin, Ronald.
    Taking Rights Seriously. Harvard U Pr.

Dworsky, Lawrence N., 1943-
  xDworsky, Lawrence N.
    Modern Transmission Line Theory &
    Applications. Wiley.

Dwoskin, Robert P.
  xDwoskin, Robert P.
    The Rights of the Public Employee. ALA.

Dwoskin, Stephen.
  xDwoskin, Stephen.
    Film Is: The International Free Cinema.
    Overlook Pr.

Dwyer, Francis.
  xDwyer, Francis.
    On Seats & Saddles, Bits & Bitting, and the
    Prevention & Cure of Restiveness in Horses.
    North River.

Dwyer, James.
  xDwyer, James.
    Private Pilot's Blue Book. Macmillan.
    The Private Pilot's Blue Book. Stein & Day.

Dwyer, James L.
  xDwyer, James L.
    Contamination Analysis & Control. Van Nos
    Reinhold.

Dwyer, John. *see* Dwyer, John M.

Dwyer, John M.
  xDwyer, John.

ed. Medicine: PreTest Self-Assessment &
  Review. McGraw-Pretest.

Dwyer, Robert C.
  xDwyer, Robert C.
    Teaching Children Through Natural
    Mathematics. P-H.

Dwyer, Terence.
  xDwyer, Terence.
    Composing with Tape Recorders: Musique
    Concrete for Beginners. Oxford U Pr.
    Teaching Musical Appreciation. Oxford U Pr.

Dwyer-Joyce, Alice.
  xDwyer-Joyce, Alice.
    The Glitter-Dust. St Martin.
    The House of Jackdaws. St Martin.
    Lachlan's Woman. St Martin.
    The Master of Jethart. G K Hall.
    The Master of Jethart. St Martin.
    The Storm of Wrath. St Martin.
    The Swiftest Eagle. St Martin.

Dyak, Miriam, 1946-
  xDyak, Miriam.
    Dying. New Victoria Pubs.

Dyal, James. *see* Dyal, James Albert.

Dyal, James Albert.
  xDyal, James.
    Readings in Psychology: The Search for
    Alternatives. McGraw.

Dybek, Stuart, 1942-
  xDybek, Stuart.
    Brass Knuckles. U of Pittsburgh Pr.

Dybwad, Gunnar.
  xDybwad, Gunnar.
    Challenges in Mental Retardation. Columbia U
    Pr.

Dyce, Alexander.
  xDyce, Alexander.
    Reminiscences of Alexander Dyce. Ohio St U
    Pr
    Strictures on Mr. Colliers New Edition of
    Shakespeare, 1858. AMS Pr.

Dyck, Arthur J., 1932-
  xDyck, Arthur J.
    On Human Care: An Introduction to Ethics.
    Abingdon.

Dyck, Cornelius J.
  xDyck, Cornelius J.
    Twelve Becoming, Biographies of Mennonite
    Disciples from the Sixteenth to the Twentieth
    Century. Faith & Life.

Dydak, J. *see* Dydak, Jerzy.

Dydak, Jerzy.
  xDydak, J.
    Shape Theory: An Introduction.
    Springer-Verlag.

Dyde, Walter F. *see* Dyde, Walters Farrell.

Dyde, Walters Farrell, 1890-
  xDyde, Walter F.
    Public Secondary Education in Canada. AMS
    Pr.

Dye, Allan.
  xDye, H. Allan.
    Gestalt Approaches to Counseling. HM.

Dye, Daniel S. *see* Dye, Daniel Sheets.

Dye, Daniel Sheets.
  xDye, Daniel S.
    Chinese Lattice Designs. Dover.
    Chinese Lattice Designs. Peter Smith.

Dye, Gilian.
  xDye, Gillian.
    Bobbin Lace Braid. Branford.

Dye, Gillian. *see* Dye, Gilian.

Dye, H. Allan. *see* Dye, Hershel Allan.

Dye, Harold. *see* Dye, Harold Eldon.

Dye, Harold E. *see* Dye, Harold Eldon.

Dye, Harold Eldon, 1907-
  xDye, Harold.
    The Touch of Friendship. Broadman.
  xDye, Harold E.

No Rocking Chair for Me!. Broadman.
Dye, Hershel Allan.
　xDye, H. Allan.
　　Fundamental Group Procedures for School
　　　Counselors. HM.
Dye, John S. see Dye, John Smith.
Dye, John Smith.
　xDye, John S.
　　History of the Plots & Crimes of the Great
　　　Conspiracy to Overthrow Liberty in America.
　　　Arno.
Dye, T. see Dye, Thomas R.
Dye, Thomas. see Dye, Thomas R.
Dye, Thomas R.
　xDye, T.
　　Who's Running America: The Carter Years.
　　　P-H.
　xDye, Thomas.
　　ed. The Determinants of Public Policy.
　　　Lexington Bks.
　xDye, Thomas R.
　　Politics in States & Communities. P-H.
　　Understanding Public Policy. P-H.
Dyer, Adrian F.
　xDyer, Andrian F.
　　Investigating Chromosomes. Halsted Pr.
Dyer, Albion M. see Dyer, Albion Morris.
Dyer, Albion Morris.
　xDyer, Albion M.
　　First Ownership of Ohio Lands. Genealog Pub.
Dyer, Alvin R.
　xDyer, Alvin R.
　　Challenge. Deseret Bk.
Dyer, Andrian F. see Dyer, Adrian F.
Dyer, Anne.
　xDyer, Anne.
　　Design Your Own Stuffed Toys. Branford.
　　Dyes from Natural Sources. Branford.
Dyer, Brainard. see Dyer, Brainerd.
Dyer, Brainerd, 1901-
　xDyer, Brainard.
　　The Public Career of William M. Evarts. R S
　　　Barnes.
Dyer, Ceil.
　xDyer, Ceil.
　　Best Recipes from the Backs of Boxes, Bottles,
　　　Cans & Jars. McGraw.
　　The Carter Family Favorites Cookbook.
　　　Delacorte.
　　The Chopped, Minced & Ground Meat
　　　Cookbook. Arbor Hse.
　　Coffee Cookery. H P Bks.
　　The Eat to Lose Cookbook. G K Hall.
　　Freezer to Oven to Table. Arbor Hse.
Dyer, Charles A.
　xDyer, Charles A.
　　Preparing for Computer Assisted Instruction.
　　　Educ Tech Pubns.
Dyer, Colin. see Dyer, Colin L.
Dyer, Colin L.
　xDyer, Colin.
　　Population & Society in Twentieth Century
　　　France. Holmes & Meier.
Dyer, E. see Dyer, Eldon.
Dyer, Eldon, 1929-
　xDyer, E.
　　Cohomology Theories. Benjamin-Cummings.
Dyer, Esther R., 1950-
　xDyer, Esther R.
　　Cooperation in Library Service to Children.
　　　Scarecrow.
　　Cultural Pluralism & Children's Media. ALA.
Dyer, Everett D. see Dyer, Everett Dixon.
Dyer, Everett Dixon, 1918-
　xDyer, Everett D.
　　The American Family: Variety & Change.
　　　McGraw.
Dyer, G. W.
　xDyer, G. W.

Democracy in the South Before the Civil War.
　　Arno.
Dyer, George, 1755-1841
　xDyer, George.
　　Poems. Garland Pub.
Dyer, Henry, 1848-1918
　xDyer, Henry.
　　The Evolution of Industry. Arno.
Dyer, Henry. see Dyer, Henry S.
Dyer, Henry S.
　xDyer, Henry.
　　How to Achieve Accountability in the Public
　　　Schools. Phi Delta Kappa.
Dyer, Irwin A. see Dyer, Irwin Allen.
Dyer, Irwin Allen.
　xDyer, Irwin A.
　　ed. The Feedlot. Lea & Febiger.
Dyer, Jean R. see Dyer, Jean Royer.
Dyer, Jean Royer, 1941-
　xDyer, Jean R.
　　Understanding & Evaluating Educational
　　　Research. A-W.
Dyer, Keith R.
　xDyer, Keith R.
　　Estuaries: A Physical Introduction. Wiley.
Dyer, Lee.
　xDyer, Lee.
　　Project Management: An Annotated
　　　Bibliography. NY Sch Indus Rel.
Dyer, Mary L. see Dyer, Mary Lee.
Dyer, Mary Lee.
　xDyer, Mary L.
　　Practical Bookkeeping for the Small Business.
　　　Contemp Bks.
Dyer, Mike.
　xDyer, Mike.
　　Getting into Pro Baseball. Watts.
Dyer, Pete.
　xDyer, Pete.
　　Flip Flop Offense in High School Football.
　　　P-H.
Dyer, Ruth C. see Dyer, Ruth Caroline.
Dyer, Ruth Caroline.
　xDyer, Ruth C.
　　The Indians' Land Title in California: A Case
　　　in Federal Equity, 1851-1942. R & E Res
　　　Assoc.
Dyer, T. A. see Dyer, Thomas A.
Dyer, Thomas A.
　xDyer, T. A.
　　The Whipman Is Watching. HM.
Dyer, Walter A. see Dyer, Walter Alden.
Dyer, Walter Alden, 1878-1943
　xDyer, Walter A.
　　Early American Craftsmen. B Franklin.
　　Many Dogs There Be. Arno.
Dyer, Wayne. see Dyer, Wayne W.
Dyer, Wayne W.
　xDyer, Wayne.
　　Pulling Your Own Strings. G K Hall.
　xDyer, Wayne W.
　　Pulling Your Own Strings. Avon.
　　Pulling Your Own Strings. T Y Crowell.
Dyer, William G.
　xDyer, William G.
　　Insight to Impact: Strategies for Interpersonal
　　　& Organizational Change. Brigham.
Dyer, William P. see Dyer, William Penn.
Dyer, William Penn, 1874-
　xDyer, William P.
　　Activities of the Elementary School Principal
　　　for the Improvement of Instruction: The Kind
　　　of Supervisory Program Which a City
　　　Superintendent of Schools Should Set up for
　　　His Elementary School Principals. AMS Pr.
Dyet, James T.
　xDyet, James T.
　　Getting Through to Adults. Accent Bks.
Dygard, Thomas J.
　xDygard, Thomas J.

Point Spread. Morrow.
　　Winning Kicker. Morrow.
Dyk, Fay B. Van. see Van Dyk, Fay B.
Dyke, Dick Van. see Van Dyke, Dick.
Dyke, Henry Van. see Van Dyke, Henry.
Dyke, John, 1935-
　xDyke, John.
　　Pigwig. Methuen Inc.
　illus. Pigwig & the Pirates. Methuen Inc.
Dyke, John C. Van. see Van Dyke, John C.
Dyke, Paul Van. see Van Dyke, Paul.
Dyke, Vernon Van. see Van Dyke, Vernon.
Dykeman, Wilma.
　xDykeman, Wilma.
　　Prophet of Plenty: The First Ninety Years of
　　　W. D. Weatherford. U of Tenn Pr.
　　Tall Woman. HR&W.
Dyken, Paul.
　xDyken, Paul D.
　　Facial Features in Neurologic Syndromes.
　　　Mosby.
Dyken, Paul D. see Dyken, Paul.
Dyker, David A.
　xDyker, David A.
　　The Soviet Economy. St Martin.
Dykes, William R. see Dykes, William Rickatson.
Dykes, William Rickatson, 1877-1925
　xDykes, William R.
　　The Genus Iris. Dover.
　　A Handbook of Garden Irises. Theophrastus.
Dykhuizen, George, 1899-
　xDykhuizen, George.
　　Life & Mind of John Dewey. S Ill U Pr.
Dykstra, Robert R., 1930-
　xDykstra, Robert R.
　　Cattle Towns. Atheneum.
Dylan, Bob, 1941-
　xDylan, Bob.
　　Tarantula. Penguin.
Dym, H.
　xDym, H.
　　Fourier Series & Integrals. Acad Pr.
Dyment, Alan R.
　xDyment, Alan R.
　　ed. The Literature of the Film: A
　　　Bibliographical Guide to the Film As Art &
　　　Entertainment 1936-1970. Gale.
Dymov, A. M. see Dymov, Aleksandr Maksimovich.
Dymov, Aleksandr Maksimovich.
　xDymov, A. M.
　　Analytical Chemistry of Gallium. Halsted Pr.
Dymsza, W. see Dymsza, William A.
Dymsza, William A.
　xDymsza, W.
　　Multinational Business Strategy. McGraw.
Dynamic Aspects of Cerebral Edema International
　　Workshop, 3rd, Montreal June 25-9, 1976. see
　　International Workshop on Dynamic Aspects of
　　Cerebral Edema, 3rd, Montreal, Quebec, 1976.
Dynes, Wayne.
　xDynes, Wayne.
　　The Illuminations of the Stavelot Bible.
　　　Garland Pub.
Dyos, H. J. see Dyos, Harold James.
Dyos, Harold James.
　xDyos, H. J.
　　Study of Urban History. St Martin.
Dyson, A. E.
　xDyson, A. E.
　　ed. Education & Democracy. Routledge &
　　　Kegan.
　　Masterful Images: English Poetry from
　　　Metaphysicals to Romantics. B&N.
　xDyson, Anthony E.
　　The Crazy Fabric: Essays in Irony. Arno.
Dyson, Anthony E. see Dyson, A. E.
Dyson, Freeman J.
　xDyson, Freeman J.

ed. Symmetry Groups in Nuclear & Particle
    Physics: A Lecture Note & Reprint Volume.
    Benjamin-Cummings.
Dyson, Geoffrey H. *see* Dyson, Geoffrey H. G.
Dyson, Geoffrey H. G.
    xDyson, Geoffrey H.
        The Mechanics of Athletics. Holmes & Meier.
Dyson, George, Sir, 1883-1964
    xDyson, George.
        Progress of Music. Arno.
Dyson, John, 1943-
    xDyson, John.
        The Hot Arctic. Little.
Dyson, Ketaki K. *see* Dyson, Ketaki Kushari.
Dyson, Ketaki Kushari, 1940-
    xDyson, Ketaki K.
        A Various Universe: A Study of the Journals &
        Memoirs of British Men & Women in the
        Indian Subcontinent Seventeen Sixty Five to
        Eighteen Fifty Six. Oxford U Pr.
Dyson, Robert D.
    xDyson, Robert D.
        Cell Biology: A Molecular Approach. Allyn.
        Essentials of Cell Biology. Allyn.
Dyson, S. L., Mrs
    xDyson, S. L.
        The Stories of the Trees. Gale.
Dyson, Verne, 1879-
    xDyson, Verne.
        Anecdotes & Events in Long Island History.
        Friedman.
Dziewanowski, M. K.
    xDziewanowski, M. K.
        A History of Soviet Russia. P-H.
    xDziewanowski, Marian K.
        Communist Party of Poland: An Outline of
        History. Harvard U Pr.
Dziewanowski, Marian K. *see* Dziewanowski, M. K.
Dzik, Stanley J.
    xDzik, Stanley J.
        Aircraft Hardware Standards Manual &
        Engineering Reference. Aviation.
Dzulynski, Stanislaw, 1926-
    xDzulynski, Stanislaw.
        Current Marks on Firm Mud Bottoms. Shoe
        String.
E. E. E. Editors. *see* Eee.
E R C Editorial Staff. *see* Executive Reports
    Corporation, Englewood Cliffs, New Jersey.
Eade, Alfred T. *see* Eade, Alfred Thompson.
Eade, Alfred Thompson.
    xEade, Alfred T.
        Expanded Panorama Bible Study Course.
        Revell.
Eades, J. S. *see* Eades, Jeremy Seymour.
Eades, Jeremy Seymour, 1945-
    xEades, J. S.
        The Yoruba Today. Cambridge U Pr.
Eadie. *see* Eadie, William F.
Eadie, John W. *see* Eadie, John William.
Eadie, John William.
    xEadie, John W.
        ed. The Conversion of Constantine. Krieger.
Eadie, William F.
    xEadie.
        Orientations to Interpersonal Communication.
        SRA.
Eads, George C., 1942-
    xEads, George C.
        The Local Service Airline Experiment.
        Brookings.
Eager, Alan R.
    xEager, Alan R.
        A Guide to Irish Bibliographical Material: A
        Bibliography of Irish Bibliographies and
        Sources of Information. Greenwood.
Eager, Edward. *see* Eager, Edward McMaken.
Eager, Edward McMaken.
    xEager, Edward.

Half Magic. HarBraceJ.
        Half Magic. HarBraceJ.
        Magic or Not?. HarBraceJ.
Eager, Fred.
    xEager, Fred.
        Italic Handwriting for Young People.
        Macmillan.
Eagle, Chester.
    xEagle, Chester.
        Who Could Love the Nightingale?. David &
        Charles.
Eagle, Dorothy.
    xEagle, Dorothy.
        The Oxford Literary Guide to the British Isles.
        Oxford U Pr.
Eagle, M. R.
    xEagle, M. R.
        Introduction to Basic. Transatlantic.
Eagles, Juanita. *see* Eagles, Juanita Archibald.
Eagles, Juanita Archibald.
    xEagles, Juanita.
        Handbook of Normal & Therapeutic Nutrition.
        Raven.
Eagleson, John.
    xEagleson, John.
        The Radical Bible. Orbis Bks.
Eaglestone, Arthur A. *see* Eaglestone, Arthur Archibald.
Eaglestone, Arthur Archibald, 1892-
    xEaglestone, Arthur A.
        Plain Man & the Novel. Kennikat.
Eagleton, Clyde, 1891-1958
    xEagleton, Clyde.
        Analysis of the Problem of War. Arno.
        Analysis of the Problem of War. Garland Pub.
Eagleton, Terence, 1943-
    xEagleton, Terry.
        Criticism & Ideology: A Study in Marxist
        Literary Theory. Schocken.
        Marxism & Literary Criticism. U of Cal Pr.
Eagleton, Terry. *see* Eagleton, Terence.
Eagly, Robert V.
    xEagly, Robert V.
        Structure of Classical Economic Theory.
        Oxford U Pr.
Eagon, Angelo.
    xEagon, Angelo.
        Catalog of Published Concert Music by
        American Composers. Scarecrow.
Eakin, Richard M. *see* Eakin, Richard Marshall.
Eakin, Richard Marshall, 1910-
    xEakin, Richard M.
        Great Scientists Speak Again. U of Cal Pr.
Eames, A. J. *see* Eames, Arthur Johnson.
Eames, Arthur Johnson.
    xEames, A. J.
        Introduction to Plant Anatomy. Krieger.
Eames, Charles.
    xEames, Charles.
        A Computer Perspective. Harvard U Pr.
Eames, Edwin.
    xEames, Edwin.
        Anthropology of the City: An Introduction to
        Urban Anthropology. P-H.
Eames, Emma, 1865-1952
    xEames, Emma.
        Some Memories & Reflections. Arno.
Eames, James P.
    xEames, James P.
        Turbine & Jet-Propelled Aircraft Powerplants.
        Chartwell.
Eames, S. Morris. *see* Eames, Samuel Morris.
Eames, Samuel Morris, 1916-
    xEames, S. Morris.
        Pragmatic Naturalism: An Introduction. S Ill U
        Pr.
Eardley-Wilmot, John, 1750-1815
    xEardley-Wilmot, John.

Historical View of the Commission for
        Enquiring into the Losses, Services, & Claims
        of American Loyalists at the Close of the
        War Between England & Her Colonies in
        1783, with an Account of the Compensation
        Granted to Them by Parliament in 1785 &
        1788. Irvington.
Eareckson, Joni.
    xEareckson, Joni.
        Joni. Bantam.
        Joni. World Wide Pubs.
        Joni. Zondervan.
        A Step Further. Zondervan.
Eargle, John.
    xEargle, John.
        Sound Recording. Van Nos Reinhold.
Earhart, Amelia, 1898-1937
    xEarhart, Amelia.
        The Fun of It: Random Records of My Own
        Flying & of Women in Aviation. Gale.
Earhart, Lida B. *see* Earhart, Lida Belle.
Earhart, Lida Belle, 1864-
    xEarhart, Lida B.
        Systematic Study in the Elementary Schools.
        AMS Pr.
Earickson, Robert.
    xEarickson, Robert.
        Spatial Behavior of Hospital Patients: A
        Behavioral Approach to Spatial Interaction in
        Metropolitan Chicago. U Chicago Dept
        Geog.
Earl, Boyd.
    xEarl, Boyd.
        Introduction to Probability: A Programmed
        Unit in Modern Mathematics. McGraw.
Earl, Donald A. *see* Earl, Donald C.
Earl, Donald C.
    xEarl, Donald A.
        Moral & Political Tradition of Rome. Cornell
        U Pr.
Earl, George W. *see* Earl, George Windsor.
Earl, George Windsor.
    xEarl, George W.
        The Native Races of the Indian Archipelago:
        Papuans. AMS Pr.
Earl, John, fl. 1977-
    xEarl, John.
        Understanding Hi-Fi- Specifications. Intl Pubns
        Serv.
Earl, Paul H.
    xEarl, Paul H.
        ed. Analysis of Inflation. Lexington Bks.
        Inflation & the Structure of Industrial Prices.
        Lexington Bks.
Earlam, Richard.
    xEarlam, Richard.
        Clinical Tests of Oesophageal Function. Grune.
Earle, Alice M. *see* Earle, Alice Morse.
Earle, Alice Morse, 1851-1911
    xEarle, Alice M.

Child-Life in Colonial Days. Arden Lib.
Child Life in Colonial Days. Darby Bks.
Child Life in Colonial Days. Folcroft.
China Collecting in America. C E Tuttle.
China Collecting in America. Gale.
Colonial Days in Old New York. Gale.
Curious Punishments of Bygone Days. Gale.
Curious Punishments of Bygone Days.
    Patterson Smith.
Curious Punishments of Bygone Days. C E
    Tuttle.
Customs & Fashions in Old New England.
    Arden Lib.
Customs & Fashions in Old New England. C E
    Tuttle.
Customs & Fashions in Old New England.
    Corner Hse.
Customs & Fashions in Old New England.
    Gale.
Home & Child Life in Colonial Days.
    Macmillan.
Home Life in Colonial Days. Berkshire
    Traveller.
Home Life in Colonial Days. Jonathan David.
Margaret Winthrop. Reprint.
Two Centuries of Costume in America. Arno.
Two Centuries of Costume in America,
    1620-1820. Peter Smith.

Earle, Carville.
    xEarle, Carville V.
        The Evolution of a Tidewater Settlement
        System: All Hallow's Parish, Maryland,
        1650-1783. U Chicago Dept Geog.
Earle, Carville V. see Earle, Carville.
Earle, Edward M. see Earle, Edward Mead.
Earle, Edward Mead, 1894-
    xEarle, Edward M.
        ed. Modern France: Problems of the Third &
        Fourth Republics. Russell.
        ed. Nationalism & Internationalism: Essays
        Inscribed to Carlton J. H. Hayes. Octagon.
Earle, J. H. see Earle, James H.
Earle, James H.
    xEarle, J. H.
        Design Drafting. A-W.
    xEarle, James H.
        Descriptive Geometry. A-W.
        Engineering Design Graphics. A-W.
Earle, John, 1824-1903
    xEarle, John.
        Anglo-Saxon Literature. AMS Pr.
        Anglo-Saxon Literature. R West.
        Anglo-Saxon Literature. Scholarly.
        Microcosmography: Or, a Piece of the World
        Discovered in Essays & Characters.
        Scholarly.
Earle, Olive L. see Earle, Olive Lydia.
Earle, Olive Lydia.
    xEarle, Olive L.
        jt. auth. Animals & Their Ears. Morrow.
        illus. Camels & Llamas. Morrow.
        illus. Peas, Beans, & Licorice. Morrow.
        illus. Strange Companions in Nature. Morrow.
Earle, Peter, 1937-
    xEarle, Peter.
        Treasure of the Concepcion: The Wreck of the
        Almiranta. Viking Pr.
        The World of Defoe. Atheneum.
Earle, Peter G.
    xEarle, Peter G.
        Prophet in the Wilderness: The Works of
        Ezequiel Martinez Estrada. U of Tex Pr.
Earle, Ralph.
    xEarle, Ralph.
        How We Got Our Bible. Nazarene.
        What the Bible Says About the Second
        Coming. Baker Bk.
Earle, Ralph B.
    xEarle, Ralph B.

        ed. PSI & Political Science: Using the
        Personalized System of Instruction to Teach
        American Politics. Am Political.
Earle, Richard A.
    xEarle, Richard A.
        ed. Classroom Practice in Reading. Intl
        Reading.
        Teaching Reading & Mathematics. Intl
        Reading.
Earle, William, 1919-
    xEarle, William.
        Public Sorrows & Private Pleasures. Ind U Pr.
Earley, Stephen C. see Earley, Steven C.
Earley, Steven C.
    xEarley, Stephen C.
        An Introduction to American Movies. NAL.
Earls, Michael, 1873-1937
    xEarls, Michael.
        Manuscripts & Memories: Chapters in Our
        Literary Tradition. Arno.
Early, Margaret. see Early, Margaret Abigail Holt.
Early, Margaret Abigail Holt, 1896-
    xEarly, Margaret.
        Holt-Bennett Family History. McClain.
Early, Paul J.
    xEarly, Paul J.
        Textbook of Nuclear Medicine Technology.
        Mosby.
Earn, Josephine.
    xEarn, Josephine.
        Looking at Canada. Lippincott.
Earnshaw, A. see Earnshaw, Alan.
Earnshaw, Alan.
    xEarnshaw, A.
        The Chemistry of the Transition Elements.
        Oxford U Pr.
Earnshaw, Brian.
    xEarnshaw, Brian.
        Dragonfall 5 & the Royal Beast. Lothrop.
Earp, Frank R. see Earp, Frank Russell.
Earp, Frank Russell, 1871-
    xEarp, Frank R.
        Style of Aeschylus. Russell.
        Style of Sophocles. Russell.
Earp, Josephine. see Earp, Josephine Sarah Marcus.
Earp, Josephine Sarah Marcus.
    xEarp, Josephine.
        I Married Wyatt Earp: The Recollections of
        Josephine Sarah Marcus Earp. U of Ariz Pr.
Earthy, E. Dora. see Earthy, Emily Dora.
Earthy, Emily Dora, 1874-
    xEarthy, E. Dora.
        Valenge Women: The Social & Economic Life
        of the Valenge Women of Portuguese East
        Africa. Biblio Dist.
Easey, Ben.
    xEasey, Ben.
        Practical Organic Gardening. Merrimack Bk
        Serv.

Easley, G. M. see Easley, Grady M.
Easley, Grady M.
    xEasley, G. M.
        Primer for Small Systems Management.
        Winthrop.
Easlick, Kenneth A. see Easlick, Kenneth Alexander.
Easlick, Kenneth Alexander, 1893-
    xEaslick, Kenneth A.
        ed. Communicating in Dentistry: Sources &
        Evaluation of Information & Preparation of
        Manuscripts, Oral Reports, & Proposals for
        Research. C C Thomas.
Easson, Angus.
    xEasson, Angus.
        Elizabeth Gaskell. Routledge & Kegan.
Easson, Eric C. see Easson, Eric Craig.
Easson, Eric Craig.
    xEasson, Eric C.

        Cancer of the Uterine Cervix. Saunders.
Easson, William M., 1931-
    xEasson, William M.
        Dying Child: The Management of the Child or
        Adolescent Who Is Dying. C C Thomas.
        Psychiatry Examination Review. Arco.
        Psychiatry: Patient Management Review. Arco.
East, Dennis.
    xEast, Dennis.
        CIO & the Labor Movement. Viking Pr.
East, Frank Reynolds.
    xEast, Frank Reynolds.
        The Entity Process: The Accumulation of a
        Physical Property As a Function of Mortality
        & Magnitude of Rank.. Exposition.
East India Company. see East India Company (English).
East India Company (English).
    xEast India Company.
        The Petition & Remonstrance of the Governor
        & Company, Etc.. Walter J Johnson.
    xEast India Company & English.
        Dawn of British Trade to the East Indies. B
        Franklin.
    xEast India Company Library.
        Catalogue of the Library of the Honorable East
        India Company. B Franklin.
East India Company & English. see East India Company
    (English).
East India Company Library. see East India Company
    (English).
East, N. B.
    xEast, N. B.
        ed. African Theatre: A Checklist of Critical
        Materials. Holmes & Meier.
East, Robert. see East, Robert Abraham.
East, Robert A. see East, Robert Abraham.
East, Robert Abraham, 1909-
    xEast, Robert.
        John Adams. Twayne.
    xEast, Robert A.
        Business Enterprise in the American
        Revolutionary Era. AMS Pr.
        Business Enterprise in the American
        Revolutionary Era. Peter Smith.
        ed. The Loyalist Americans: A Focus on
        Greater New York. Sleepy Hollow.
East, W. G. see East, William Gordon.
East, William Gordon.
    xEast, W. G.
        The Soviet Union. Van Nos Reinhold.
Eastaugh, Kenneth.
    xEastaugh, Kenneth.
        The Carry-on Book. David & Charles.
Easterbrook, Don J., 1935-
    xEasterbrook, Don J.
        Principles of Geomorphology. McGraw.
Easterling, Jack.
    xEasterling, Jack.
        Confront, Construct, Complete: A
        Comprehensive Approach to Writing.
        Hayden.
Eastern Analytical Symposium, New York, 1966.
    xEastman Kodak Company.
        Adventures in Color - Slide Photography.
        Eastman Kodak.
        Kodak Professional Photoguide. Eastman
        Kodak.
        Photocomposition with Kodak Phototypesetting
        Products. Eastman Kodak.
        Photolab Design. Eastman Kodak.
Eastham, Barry C. see Eastham, Barry Caulfield.
Eastham, Barry Caulfield.
    xEastham, Barry C.
        Chinese Art Ivory. Ars Ceramica.
Eastham, R. D. see Eastham, Robert Duncan.
Eastham, Robert Duncan.
    xEastham, R. D.
        Clinical Hematology. Year Bk Med.
Eastlake, Charles. see Eastlake, Charles Locke.
Eastlake, Charles L. see Eastlake, Charles Locke.

Eastlake, Charles Locke, 1833-1906
xEastlake, Charles.
History of the Gothic Revival. Am Life Foun.
History of the Gothic Revival. Humanities.
xEastlake, Charles L.
Hints on Household Taste in Furniture,
Upholstery & Other Details. Arno.
Hints on Household Taste in Furniture,
Upholstery & Other Details. Peter Smith.
Eastlake, Elizabeth R. see Eastlake, Elizabeth Rigby.
Eastlake, Elizabeth Rigby, Lady, 1809-1893
xEastlake, Elizabeth R.
Journals & Correspondence of Lady Eastlake.
AMS Pr.
Eastlake, William.
xEastlake, William.
The Bronc People. U of NM Pr.
Go in Beauty. U of NM Pr.
Eastland, Terry.
xEastland, Terry.
Counting by Race: Equality from the Founding
Fathers to Bakke. Basic.
Eastman, Carol H. see Eastman, Carol M.
Eastman, Carol M., 1941-
xEastman, Carol H.
Aspects of Language & Culture. Chandler &
Sharp.
xEastman, Carol M.
Linguistic Theory & Language Description.
Har-Row.
Eastman, Charles. see Eastman, Charles Alexander.
Eastman, Charles A. see Eastman, Charles Alexander.
Eastman, Charles Alexander, 1858-1939
xEastman, Charles.
Indian Boyhood. Rio Grande.
xEastman, Charles A.
From the Deep Woods to Civilization:
Chapters in the Autobiography of an Indian.
U of Nebr Pr.
Indian Boyhood. Peter Smith.
Indian Boyhood. Dover.
Indian Scout Craft & Lore. Dover.
The Soul of the Indian: An Interpretation. U of
Nebr Pr.
Eastman, Charles M.
xEastman, Charles M.
ed. Spatial Synthesis in Computer-Aided
Building Design. Halsted Pr.
Eastman, Crystal, 1881-
xEastman, Crystal.
Work Accidents & the Law. Arno.
Eastman, Dick.
xEastman, Dick.
No Easy Road: Inspirational Thoughts on
Prayer. Baker Bk.
Eastman, Fred, 1886-
xEastman, Fred.
Christ in the Drama: A Study of the Influence
of Christ on the Drama of England &
America. Arno.
Eastman, Hope.
xEastman, Hope.
Lobbying: A Constitutionally Protected Right.
Am Enterprise.
Eastman, Jerry R. see Eastman, Terry R.
Eastman Kodak Company.
xKodak.
Printing Color Slides & Larger Transparencies.
Eastman Kodak.
xStaff of Eastman Kodak Co.,.
ed. Close-up Photography &
Photomacrography. Eastman Kodak.
Eastman Kodak Company. see Eastern Analytical
Symposium, New York, 1966.
Eastman, Lloyd E.
xEastman, Lloyd E.
The Abortive Revolution: China Under
Nationalist Rule, 1927-1937. Harvard U Pr.
Eastman, Margaret.
xEastman, Margaret.

Planning & Building Your Fireplace. Garden
Way Pub.
Eastman, Mary. see Eastman, Mary (Henderson).
Eastman, Mary (Henderson), 1818-1890
xEastman, Mary.
Aunt Phillis's Cabin: Or, Southern Life As It
Is. Irvington.
xEastman, Mary H.
Aunt Phillis's Cabin: Or, Southern Life As It
Is. Negro U Pr.
Eastman, Mary H. see Eastman, Mary (Henderson).
Eastman, Max, 1883-1969
xEastman, Max.
Literary Mind: Its Place in an Age of Science.
Octagon.
xEastman, Max. F.
Marx, Lenin & the Science of Revolution.
Hyperion Conn.
Since Lenin Died. Hyperion Conn.
Eastman, Max. F. see Eastman, Max.
Eastman, Nicholas J. see Eastman, Nicholson Joseph.
Eastman, Nicholson Joseph.
xEastman, Nicholas J.
Expectant Motherhood. Little.
Eastman, P. F. see Eastman, Peter F.
Eastman, Peter F.
xEastman, P. F.
Advanced First Aid Afloat. Cornell Maritime.
Advanced First Aid for All Outdoors. Cornell
Maritime.
Eastman, Philip D.
xEastman, Philip D.
Are You My Mother?. Beginner.
illus. Flap Your Wings. Random.
Go, Dog, Go. Beginner.
Eastman, Richard M.
xEastman, Richard M.
Style: Writing & Reading As the Discovery of
Outlook. Oxford U Pr.
Eastman, Robert.
xEastman, Robert.
The Pendulum. HarBraceJ.
Eastman, Roger.
xEastman, Roger.
ed. Coming of Age in Philosophy. Har-Row.
Eastman School of Music. see Eastman School of Music,
Rochester, New York.
Eastman School of Music, Rochester, New York.
xEastman School of Music.
Sibley Music Library Catalog of Sound
Recordings. G K Hall.
Eastman, Terry R.
xEastman, Jerry R.
Radiographic Fundamentals & Technique
Guide. Mosby.
Easton, Allan, 1916-
xEaston, Allan.
Complex Managerial Decisions Involving
Multiple Objectives. Krieger.
Decision Making: A Short Course in Problem
Solving for Professionals. Wiley.
Easton, David, 1917-
xEaston, David.
A Framework for Political Analysis. U of
Chicago Pr.
A Systems Analysis of Political Life. U of
Chicago Pr.
Easton, Robert. see Easton, Robert Olney.
Easton, Robert Olney.
xEaston, Robert.
Lord of Beasts: The Saga of Buffalo Jones. U of
Nebr Pr.
Easton, Stewart C. see Easton, Stewart Copinger.
Easton, Stewart Copinger.
xEaston, Stewart C.
The Era of Charlemagne: Frankish State &
Society. Krieger.
Easton, Thomas A.
xEaston, Thomas A.

Bioscope. Mayfield Pub.
Eastwick, Ivy O.
xEastwick, Ivy O.
In & Out the Windows: Happy Poems for
Children. Plough.
Eastwood, Bruce. see Eastwood, Bruce S.
Eastwood, Bruce S.
xEastwood, Bruce.
Directory of Audio-Visual Sources: History of
Science, Medicine & Technology. N Watson.
Eastwood, Dorothea, 1912-
xEastwood, Dorothea.
Story of Our Gardens. Dufour.
The Story of Our Gardens. Intl Schol Bk Serv.
Eastwood, F. W. see Eastwood, Frank Warburton.
Eastwood, Frank Warburton.
xEastwood, F. W.
Organic Chemistry: A First University Course
in Twelve Programs. Cambridge U Pr.
Eastwood, Mary, 1930-
xEastwood, Mary.
Fighting Job Discrimination: Three Federal
Approaches. Today News.
Easum, Chester V. see Easum, Chester Verne.
Easum, Chester Verne.
xEasum, Chester V.
Prince Henry of Prussia, Brother of Frederick
the Great. Greenwood.
Easwaran, Eknath.
xEaswaran, Eknath.
Gandhi the Man. Nilgiri Pr.
Meditation: Commonsense Directions for an
Uncommon Life. Nilgiri Pr.
Eaton, Anne T. see Eaton, Annie Thaxter.
Eaton, Annie Thaxter.
xEaton, Anne T.
ed. The Animals' Christmas. Viking Pr.
Eaton, Arthur W. see Eaton, Arthur Wentworth
Hamilton.
Eaton, Arthur Wentworth Hamilton, 1849-1937
xEaton, Arthur W.
The Famous Mather Byles: Noted Boston Tory
Preacher, Poet, & Wit 1707-1788. Arno.
Eaton, Charlotte.
xEaton, Charlotte.
A Last Memory of Robert Louis Stevenson.
Arden Lib.
A Last Memory of Robert Louis Stevenson.
Folcroft.
Stevenson at Manasquan. Folcroft.
Eaton, Clement, 1898-
xEaton, Clement.
A History of the Old South. Macmillan.
History of the Southern Confederacy. Free Pr.
A History of the Southern Confederacy.
Macmillan.
ed. Leaven of Democracy: The Growth of the
Democratic Spirit in the Time of Jackson.
Braziller.
Eaton, Clement. see Eaton, Clement William Clement
Eaton.
Eaton, Clement William Clement Eaton, 1898-
xEaton, Clement.
The Growth of Southern Civilization,
1790-1860. Har-Row.
Growth of Southern Civilization, 1790-1860.
Har-Row.
Eaton, Evelyn. see Eaton, Evelyn Sybil Mary.
Eaton, Evelyn Sybil Mary, 1902-
xEaton, Evelyn.
I Send a Voice. Theos Pub Hse.
Eaton, Faith.
xEaton, Faith.
Dolls in Color. Macmillan.
Eaton, Frank.
xEaton, Frank.
Pistol Pete - Veteran of the Old West. Evans
Pubns.
Eaton, Gareth R.
xEaton, Gareth R.

NMR Studies of Boron Hydrides & Related
Compounds. Benjamin-Cummings.
Eaton, Harriette G. *see* Eaton, Harriette Grace.
Eaton, Harriette Grace.
xEaton, Harriette G.
Bunya-Bunya Magic. Creative Pr.
Eaton, Jonathan, 1950-
xEaton, Jonathan.
Four Essays in the Theory of Uncertainty &
Portfolio Choice. Garland Pub.
Eaton, Marge.
xEaton, Marge.
Flower Pressing. Lerner Pubns.
Eaton, Quaintance.
xEaton, Quaintance.
The Boston Opera Company. Da Capo.
Eaton, Randall L., 1943-
xEaton, Randall L.
The Cheetah: The Biology, Ecology, &
Behavior of an Endangered Species. Krieger.
Eaton, S. Boyd. *see* Eaton, Stanley Boyd.
Eaton, Seymour.
xEaton, Seymour.
The Roosevelt Bears: Their Travels &
Adventures. Dover.
Eaton, Stanley Boyd.
xEaton, S. Boyd.
Radiology of the Pancreas & Duodenum.
Saunders.
Eaton, Theodore H. *see* Eaton, Theodore Hildreth.
Eaton, Theodore Hildreth, 1907-
xEaton, Theodore H.
Evolution. Norton.
Study of Organization & Method of the Course
of Study in Agriculture in Secondary Schools.
AMS Pr.
Eaton, Trevor.
xEaton, Trevor.
Theoretical Semics. Mouton.
Eaton, Walter P. *see* Eaton, Walter Prichard.
Eaton, Walter Prichard, 1878-1957
xEaton, Walter P.
Penguin Persons & Peppermints. Arno.
Eaton, William. *see* Eaton, William W.
Eaton, William E. *see* Eaton, William Edward.
Eaton, William Edward, 1943-
xEaton, William E.
The American Federation of Teachers,
1916-1961: A History of the Movement. S Ill
U Pr.
Eaton, William W.
xEaton, William.
The Sociology of Mental Disorders. Praeger.
Eaves, Edgar D.
xEaves, Edgar D.
Introductory Mathematical Analysis. Allyn.
Eavey, Charles B. *see* Eavey, Charles Benton.
Eavey, Charles Benton, 1889-
xEavey, Charles B.
History of Christian Education. Moody.
Eban, Abba. *see* Eban, Abba Solomon.
Eban, Abba Solomon, 1915-
xEban, Abba.
Abba Eban: An Autobiography. Random.
Promised Land. Nelson.
Ebaugh, Helen R. *see* Ebaugh, Helen Rose Fuchs.
Ebaugh, Helen Rose Fuchs, 1942-
xEbaugh, Helen R.
Out of the Cloister: A Study of Organizational
Dilemmas. U of Tex Pr.
Ebbeck, F. N.
xEbbeck, F. N.
ed. Education & the Child. Bks Australia.
Ebbesson, Sven. *see* Ebbesson, Sven O. E.
Ebbesson, Sven O. E.
xEbbesson, Sven.
ed. Comparative Neurology of the
Telencephalon. Plenum Pub.
Ebbighausen, E. G. *see* Ebbighausen, Edwin George
Garlef.

Ebbighausen, Edward G. *see* Ebbighausen, Edwin George
Garlef.
Ebbighausen, Edwin George Garlef, 1911-
xEbbighausen, E. G.
Astronomy. Merrill.
xEbbighausen, Edward G.
Astronomy. Merrill.
Ebbinghaus, Hermann, 1850-1909
xEbbinghaus, Hermann.
Psychology: An Elementary Text-Book. Arno.
Ebdon, David.
xEbdon, David.
Statistics in Geography: A Practical Approach.
Biblio Dist.
Ebel, Robert. *see* Ebel, Robert L.
Ebel, Robert L.
xEbel, Robert.
The Uses of Standardized Testing. Phi Delta
Kappa.
xEbel, Robert L.
Essentials of Educational Measurement. P-H.
Practical Problems in Educational
Measurement. Heath.
Ebeling, Gerhard, 1912-
xEbeling, Gerhard.
On Prayer: The Lord's Prayer in Today's
World. Fortress.
The Study of Theology. Fortress.
Ebenstein, William, 1910-
xEbenstein, William.
American Democracy in World Perspective.
Har-Row.
Fascism at Work. AMS Pr.
Fascist Italy. Russell.
The Nazi State. Octagon.
Pure Theory of Law. Kelley.
Pure Theory of Law. Rothman.
Eberhard, Wolfram, 1909-
xEberhard, Wolfram.
Chinese Fairy Tales & Folk Tales. Folcroft.
Chinese Festivals. E Langstaff.
tr. Folktales of China. U of Chicago Pr.
ed. Folktales of China. PB.
A History of China. U of Cal Pr.
Studies in Chinese Folklore & Related Essays.
Res Ctr Lang Semiotic.
Eberhart, Dikkon.
xEberhart, Dikkon.
On the Verge. Stemmer Hse.
Eberhart, George M.
xEberhart, George M.
Compiled By A Geo-Bibliography of
Anomalies: Primary Access to Observations
of UFOs, Ghosts, & Other Mysterious
Phenomena. Greenwood.
Eberhart, Mignon E. *see* Eberhart, Mignon Good.
Eberhart, Mignon Good, 1899-
xEberhart, Mignon E.
Five Passengers from Lisbon. Popular Lib.
xEberhart, Mignon G.
Another Woman's House. Popular Lib.
The Bayou Road. Popular Lib.
The Bayou Road. Random.

Call After Midnight. Popular Lib.
Casa Madrone. Random.

The Chiffon Scarf. Amereon Ltd.
The Chiffon Scarf. Popular Lib.

Danger in the Dark. Amereon Ltd.
Danger Money. Popular Lib.

The Dark Garden. Amereon Ltd.
Family Fortune. Popular Lib.
Family Fortune. Random.
The House on the Roof. Amereon Ltd.
Hunt with the Hounds. Popular Lib.
While the Patient Slept. Amereon Ltd.
The White Dress. Popular Lib.
Eberhart, Richard, 1904-
xEberhart, Richard.
Fields of Grace. Oxford U Pr.
Of Poetry & Poets. U of Ill Pr.
Quarry: New Poems. Oxford U Pr.
Eberle, Irmengarde, 1898-
xEberle, Irmengarde.
Modern Medical Discoveries. T Y Crowell.
Prairie Dogs in Prairie Dog Town. T Y
Crowell.
Eberlein, Patrick, 1944-
xEberlein, Patrick.
Geodesics & Ends in Certain Surfaces Without
Conjugate Points. Am Math.
Eberling, Ernest J. *see* Eberling, Ernest Jacob.
Eberling, Ernest Jacob, 1894-
xEberling, Ernest J.
Congressional Investigations: A Study of the
Origin & Development of the Power of
Congress to Investigate & Punish for
Contempt. Octagon.
Eberly, Carole.
xEberly, Carole.
Our Michigan: Ethnic Tales & Recipes. Eberly
Pr.
Eberly, Ralph D. *see* Eberly, Ralph Dunbar.
Eberly, Ralph Dunbar, 1917-
xEberly, Ralph D.
Moonfire. Libra.
Ebersohn, Wessel.
xEbersohn, Wessel.
A Lonely Place to Die. Pantheon.
A Lonely Place to Die. Random.
Ebersole, Dennis.
xEbersole, Dennis C.
Shop Mathematics. P-H.
Ebersole, Dennis C. *see* Ebersole, Dennis.
Ebersole, Frank B.
xEbersole, Frank B.
Things We Know: Fourteen Essays on
Problems of Knowledge. U of Oreg Bks.
Eberson, L. *see* Eberson, Lennart.
Eberson, Lennart.
xEberson, L.
Organic Electrochemistry. Springer-Verlag.
Ebert, Alan.
xEbert, Alan.
The Homosexuals. Macmillan.
Ebert, Friedrich A. *see* Ebert, Friedrich Adolf.
Ebert, Friedrich Adolf, 1791-1834
xEbert, Friedrich A.
General Bibliographical Dictionary. Gale.
Ebert, J. D. *see* Ebert, James David.
Ebert, James D. *see* Ebert, James David.
Ebert, James David.
xEbert, J. D.
Mechanisms of Cell Change. Wiley.
xEbert, James D.
Interacting Systems in Development. HR&W.
Ebert, M. *see* Ebert, Michael.
Ebert, Michael.
xEbert, M.
ed. Current Topics in Radiation Research.
Elsevier.
xEbert, Michael.

ed. Current Topics in Radiation Research.
Elsevier.
Ebert, Richard.
xEbert, Richard.
Lawrence of Arabia. Raintree Child.
Ebertin, Elsbeth. *see* Ebertin, Elsbeth Paula (Schmidt).
Ebertin, Elsbeth Paula (Schmidt), 1880-1944
xEbertin, Elsbeth.
Astrology & Romance. ASI Pubs Inc.
Eberwein, Robert T., 1940-
xEberwein, Robert T.
A Viewer's Guide to Film Theory & Criticism.
Scarecrow.
Ebey, George W. *see* Ebey, George William.
Ebey, George William, 1907-
xEbey, George W.
Adaptability Among the Elementary Schools of
an American City. AMS Pr.
Ebihara, May.
xEbihara, May.
ed. Papers in Anthropology & Linguistics. NY
Acad Sci.
Ebin, Victoria.
xEbin, Victoria.
The Body Decorated. Thames Hudson.
Ebinger, Charles K.
xEbinger, Charles K.
International Politics of Nuclear Energy. Sage.
Eble, Kenneth. *see* Eble, Kenneth Eugene.
Eble, Kenneth E. *see* Eble, Kenneth Eugene.
Eble, Kenneth Eugene.
xEble, Kenneth.
F. Scott Fitzgerald. Twayne.
xEble, Kenneth E.
The Craft of Teaching: A Guide to Mastering
the Professor's Art. Jossey-Bass.
F. Scott Fitzgerald. Coll & U Pr.
ed. F. Scott Fitzgerald. McGraw.
ed. Howells: A Century of Criticism. SMU
Press
Professors as Teachers. Jossey-Bass.
Ebner, James H.
xEbner, James H.
God Present As Mystery: A Search for
Personal Meaning in Contemporary
Theology. St Marys.
Ebner, Maria.
xEbner, Maria.
Connective Tissue Massage: Theory &
Therapeutic Application. Krieger.
Ebner, Michael H.
xEbner, Michael H.
ed. The Age of Urban Reform: New
Perspectives on the Progressive Era.
Kennikat.
Eboch, Sidney C.
xEboch, Sidney C.
Operating Audio-Visual Equipment. Har-Row.
Ebon, Martin.
xEbon, Martin.
ed. The Amazing Uri Geller. NAL.
Cloning of Man: A Brave New Hope---or
Horror?. NAL.
Prophecy in Our Time. Wilshire.
ed. The Riddle of the Bermuda Triangle. NAL.
Ebony.
xEbony Editors.
Black Revolution: An Ebony Special Issue.
Johnson Chi.
Martin Luther King, Jr.. Johnson Chi.
White Problem in America. Johnson Chi.
Ebony Editors. *see* Ebony.
Ebrahim, G. J.
xEbrahim, G. J.
Breast Feeding: The Biological Option.
Schocken.
Eby, Louise S. *see* Eby, Louise Saxe.
Eby, Louise Saxe.
xEby, Louise S.

Quest for Moral Law. Arno.
Eca de Queiroz. *see* Eca De Queiroz, Jose Maria De.
Eca De Queiroz, Jose Maria De, 1845-1900
xEca de Queiroz.
The Illustrious House of Ramires. Ohio U Pr.
Eccles, F. Y. *see* Eccles, Francis Yvon.
Eccles, Francis Yvon, 1871-
xEccles, F. Y.
Racine in England. Folcroft.
Eccles, John. *see* Eccles, John Carew.
Eccles, John C. *see* Eccles, John Carew.
Eccles, John Carew.
xEccles, John.
The Human Mystery. Springer-Verlag.
xEccles, John C.
Cerebellum As a Neuronal Machine.
Springer-Verlag.
Facing Reality: Philosophical Adventures by a
Brain Scientist. Springer-Verlag.
The Understanding of the Brain. McGraw.
Eccles, Mark.
xEccles, Mark.
Christopher Marlowe in London. Octagon.
Eccles, W. J. *see* Eccles, William John.
Eccles, William John.
xEccles, W. J.
Canadian Frontier, 1534-1760. U of NM Pr.
France in America. Har-Row.
Eccli, Eugene.
xEccli, Eugene.
ed. Low-Cost, Energy-Efficient Shelter for the
Owner & Builder. Rodale Pr Inc.
Echanis, Michael D.
xEchanis, Michael D.
Basic Stick Fighting for Combat. Ohara Pubns.
Knife Fighting, Knife Throwing for Combat.
Ohara Pubns.
Echeruo, Michael J. C.
xEcheruo, Michael J. C.
Joyce Cary & the Dimensions of Order. B&N.
Echols, Allan K.
xEchols, Allan K.
Dead Man's Range. Nordon Pubns.
Echols, John M.
xEchols, John M.
An English-Indonesian Dictionary. Cornell U
Pr.
Preliminary Checklist of Indonesian Imprints
During the Japanese Period: March 1962 -
August 1945. Cornell Mod Indo.
Eck, Marcel.
xEck, Marcel.
Lies & Truth. Macmillan.
Eck, Roger D.
xEck, Roger D.
Operations Research for Business. Wadsworth
Pub.
Eckard, Joseph D., 1942-
xEckard, Joseph D.
Professional Engineer's License Guide: What
You Need to Know & Do to Obtain PE
(&EIT) Registration. Herman Pub.
Eckardt, Wolf Von. *see* Von Eckardt, Wolf.
Eckberg, Douglas L. *see* Eckberg, Douglas Lee.
Eckberg, Douglas Lee.
xEckberg, Douglas L.
Intelligence & Race: The Origins & Dimensions
of the IQ Controversy. Praeger.
Eckbo, Garrett.
xEckbo, Garrett.
Art of Home Landscaping. McGraw.
Home Landscape: The Art of Home
Landscaping. McGraw.
Pref. by Public Landscape: Six Essays on
Government & Environmental Design in the
San Francisco Bay Area. Inst Gov Stud Berk.
Eckbo, Paul L. *see* Eckbo, Paul Leo.
Eckbo, Paul Leo.
xEckbo, Paul L.

The Future of World Oil. Ballinger Pub.
Ecke, Gustav.
xEcke, Gustav.
Chinese Domestic Furniture. C E Tuttle.
Ecke, Wolfgang, 1927-
xEcke, Wolfgang.
Flight Toward Home. Macmillan.
Eckener, Hugo, 1868-1954
xEckener, Hugo.
My Zeppelins. Arno.
Eckenrode, Hamilton J. *see* Eckenrode, Hamilton James.
Eckenrode, Hamilton James, 1881-
xEckenrode, Hamilton J.
Revolution in Virginia. Shoe String.
Eckenstein, Lina, d. 1931
xEckenstein, Lina.
Comparative Studies in Nursery Rhymes. Gale.
Comparative Studies in Nursery Rhymes.
Gordon Pr.
Spell of Words: Studies in Language Bearing on
Custom. Gale.
Spell of Words: Studies in Language Bearing on
Custom. R West.
Ecker, Gunter, 1924-
xEcker, Gunter.
Theory of Fully Ionized Plasmas. Acad Pr.
Ecker-Racz, L. L. *see* Ecker-Racz, L. Laszlo.
Ecker-Racz, L. Laszlo.
xEcker-Racz, L. L.
Politics & Economics of State & Local Finance.
P-H.
Eckert, Allan W.
xEckert, Allan W.
The Court-Martial of Daniel Boone. Little.
Incident at Hawk's Hill. Little.
xEckert, Allen.
Incident at Hawk's Hill. Dell.
Eckert, Allen. *see* Eckert, Allan W.
Eckert, Edward K., 1943-
xEckert, Edward K.
The Navy Department in the War of 1812. U
Presses Fla.
Eckert, Ernest R. *see* Eckert, Ernst R. G.
Eckert, Ernst R. G.
xEckert, Ernest R.
Analysis of Heat & Mass Transfer. McGraw.
Eckert, Helen M.
xEckert, Helen M.
Intro. by Practical Measurement of Physical
Performance. Lea & Febiger.
Eckert, John A. *see* Eckert, John Alfred.
Eckert, John Alfred, 1919-
xEckert, John A.
Cry, Try Again. Wisdom.
Eckert, Robert P. *see* Eckert, Robert Paul.
Eckert, Robert Paul, 1903-
xEckert, Robert P.
Edward Thomas: A Biography & a
Bibliography. Folcroft.
Edward Thomas: A Biography & a
Bibliography. Norwood Edns.
Eckert, Roger.
xEckert, Roger.
Animal Physiology. W H Freeman.
Eckert, Ross D.
xEckert, Ross D.
Airports & Congestion: A Problem of
Misplaced Subsidies. Am Enterprise.
Eckert, William G., 1926-
xEckert, William G.
Introduction to Forensic Sciences. Mosby.
Eckes, Alfred E., 1942-
xEckes, Alfred E.
The United States & the Global Struggle for
Minerals. U of Tex Pr.
Eckhardt, Caroline D., 1942-
xEckhardt, Caroline D.

ed. Essays in the Numerical Criticism of
Medieval Literature. Bucknell U Pr.
The Wiley Reader: Designs for Writing. Wiley.

Eckhardt, Robert B.
xEckhardt, Robert B.
The Study of Human Evolution. McGraw.

Eckhardt, William.
xEckhardt, William.
Governments Under Fire: Civil Conflict &
Imperialism. HRAFP.

Eckhart, Ludwig, 1890-
xEckhart, Ludwig.
Four-Dimensional Space. Ind U Pr.

Eckhaus, Viktor. *see* Eckhaus, Wiktor.

Eckhaus, W. *see* Eckhaus, Wiktor.

Eckhaus, Wiktor.
xEckhaus, Viktor.
Studies in Non-Linear Stability Theory.
Springer-Verlag.
xEckhaus, W.
Asymptotic Analysis of Singular Perturbations.
Elsevier.

Eckhouse, Richard H.
xEckhouse, Richard H.
Minicomputer Systems: Organization,
Programming & Applications (PDP-11). P-H.

Eckler, A. Ross. *see* Eckler, Albert Ross.

Eckler, Albert Ross, 1927-
xEckler, A. Ross.
Word Recreations: Games & Diversions from
Word Ways. Dover.

Eckles, Robert B.
xEckles, Robert B.
Purdue Pharmacy: The First Century. Purdue
Res Foun.
Purdue Pharmacy: The First Century. Purdue
Univ Bks.

Eckles, Robert W.
xEckles, Robert W.
Supervisory Management: A Short Course in
Supervision. Wiley.

Eckley, Grace.
xEckley, Grace.
Edna O'Brien. Bucknell U Pr.

Eckley, Wilton.
xEckley, Wilton.
T. S. Stribling. Twayne.

Eckman, Fred R.
xEckman, Fred R.
ed. Current Themes in Linguistics:
Bilingualism, Experimental Linguistics, &
Language Typologies. Halsted Pr.

Eckman, Lester. *see* Eckman, Lester Samuel.

Eckman, Lester Samuel.
xEckman, Lester.
The History of the Musar Movement
1840-1945. Shengold.
Soviet Policy Towards Jews & Israel. Shengold.

Eckschlager, Karel.
xEckschlager, Karel.
Information Theory As Applied to Chemical
Analysis. Wiley.

Eckstein, A. *see* Eckstein, Alexander.

Eckstein, Alexander, 1915-
xEckstein, A.
China's Economic Revolution. Cambridge U
Pr.
xEckstein, Alexander.
China's Economic Development: The Interplay
of Scarcity & Ideology. U of Mich Pr.
ed. Comparison of Economic Systems:
Theoretical & Methodological Approaches. U
of Cal Pr.
ed. Economic Trends in Communist China.
Beresford Bk Serv.
Quantitative Measures of China's Economic
Output. U of Mich Pr.

Eckstein, Artis A. *see* Eckstein, Artis Aleene.

Eckstein, Artis Aleene.
xEckstein, Artis A.

How to Make Treasures from Trash.
Hearthside.

Eckstein, Harry.
xEckstein, Harry.
Division & Cohesion in Democracy: A Study
of Norway. Princeton U Pr.
Patterns of Authority: A Structural Basis for
Political Inquiry. Wiley.

Eckstein, Jerome.
xEckstein, Jerome.
Platonic Method: An Interpretation of the
Dramatic-Philosophic Aspects of the Meno.
Greenwood.

Eckstein, Otto.
xEckstein, Otto.
Public Finance. P-H.

Eckstein, S. *see* Eckstein, Susan.

Eckstein, Stephen D. *see* Eckstein, Stephen Daniel.

Eckstein, Stephen Daniel.
xEckstein, Stephen D.
History of the Churches of Christ in Texas
1824-1950. Firm Foun Pub.

Eckstein, Susan, 1942-
xEckstein, S.
The Poverty of Revolution: The State & the
Urban Poor in Mexico. Princeton U Pr.

Eckstorm, Fannie. *see* Eckstorm, Fannie (Hardy).

Eckstorm, Fannie (Hardy), 1865-1946
xEckstorm, Fannie.
Penobscot Man. Arno.
xEckstorm, Fannie H.
The Penobscot Man. Juniper Maine.

Eckstorm, Fannie H. *see* Eckstorm, Fannie (Hardy).

Eckstrom, Lawrence J.
xEckstrom, Lawrence J.
Licensing in Foreign & Domestic Operations.
Boardman.

Eco, Umberto.
xEco, Umberto.
A Theory of Semiotics. Ind U Pr.

Economic Commission for Latin America. *see* United
Nations. Economic Commission for Latin America.

Economics Division FAO. *see* Food and Agriculture
Organization of the United Nations.

Economist (London).
xEconomist Editors.
Economist, 1843-1943: A Centenary Volume.
Arno.

Economist Editors. *see* Economist (London).

Economou, E. N., 1940-
xEconomou, E. N.
Green's Functions in Quantum Physics.
Springer-Verlag.

Economou, George.
xEconomou, George.
ed. Geoffrey Chaucer: A Collection of
Criticism. McGraw.
xEconomou, George D.
The Goddess Natura in Medieval Literature.
Harvard U Pr.

Economou, George D. *see* Economou, George.

Ecroyd, Donald. *see* Ecroyd, Donald H.

Ecroyd, Donald H.
xEcroyd, Donald.
Communicate Through Oral Reading. McGraw.

Edberg, Rolf, 1912-
xEdberg, Rolf.
At the Foot of the Tree: A Wanderer's
Musings Before the Fall. U of Ala Pr.
The Dream of Kilimanjaro. Pantheon.
On the Shred of a Cloud: Notes in a Travel
Book. U of Ala Pr.

Eddings, Claire N. *see* Eddings, Claire Neff.

Eddings, Claire Neff.
xEddings, Claire N.
Secretary's Complete Model Letter Handbook.
P-H.

Eddington, Arthur. *see* Eddington, Arthur Stanley.

Eddington, Arthur S. *see* Eddington, Arthur Stanley.

Eddington, Arthur Stanley, Sir, 1882-1944
xEddington, Arthur.
Science & the Unseen World. Folcroft.
xEddington, Arthur S.
The Mathematical Theory of Relativity.
Chelsea Pub.
Science & the Unseen World. Arden Lib.
Science & the Unseen World. Folcroft.

Eddington, Thomas.
xEddington, Thomas.
Contemporary Art & the Metaphysics of the
Art Expression. Gloucester Art.

Eddison, Eric R. *see* Eddison, Eric Rucker.

Eddison, Eric Rucker, 1882-1945
xEddison, Eric R.
Styrbiorn the Strong. Arno.

Eddleman, Floyd E. *see* Eddleman, Floyd Eugene.

Eddleman, Floyd Eugene.
xEddleman, Floyd E.
ed. American Drama Criticism: Interpretations,
1890-1977. Shoe String.

Eddowes, Maurice.
xEddowes, Maurice.
Crop Production in Europe. Oxford U Pr.

Eddowes, Michael.
xEddowes, Michael.
The Oswald File. Crown.

Eddy, George S. *see* Eddy, George Sherwood.

Eddy, George Sherwood, 1871-
xEddy, George S.
Pathfinders of the World Missionary Crusade.
Arno.

Eddy, John, 1932-
xEddy, John.
The Teacher & the Drug Scene. Phi Delta
Kappa.

Eddy, Paul.
xEddy, Paul.
Destination Disaster. Ballantine.
Destination Disaster. Times Bks.

Eddy, R. Lee. *see* Eddy, Robert Lee.

Eddy, Robert Lee, 1945-
xEddy, R. Lee.
What You Should Know About Marriage,
Divorce, Annulment, Separation &
Community Property in La.. Exposition.

Eddy, S. *see* Eddy, Samuel.

Eddy, Samuel.
xEddy, S.
Atlas of Drawings for Vertebrate Anatomy.
Wiley.

Eddy, William A. *see* Eddy, William Alfred.

Eddy, William Alfred, 1896-
xEddy, William A.
Gulliver's Travels: A Critical Study. Russell.

Ede, D. A.
xEde, Donald A.
An Introduction to Developmental Biology.
Halsted Pr.

Ede, Donald A. *see* Ede, D. A.

Edel, Abraham. *see* Edel, May (Mandelbaum).

Edel, Leon, 1907-
xEdel, Leon.
Bloomsbury: A House of Lions. Avon.
Bloomsbury: A House of Lions. Lippincott.
Prefaces of Henry James. Folcroft.

Edel, M. M. *see* Edel, May (Mandelbaum).

Edel, Matthew.
xEdel, Matthew.
Economies & the Environment. P-H.
Readings in Urban Economics. Macmillan.

Edel, May. *see* Edel, May (Mandelbaum).

Edel, May (Mandelbaum).
xEdel, Abraham.
Anthropology & Ethics: The Quest for Moral
Understanding. Transaction Bks.
xEdel, M. M.
The Chiga of Western Uganda. Dawson Pub.
xEdel, May.

jt. auth. Anthropology & Ethics: The Quest for
 Moral Understanding. Transaction Bks.
Edel, Wilbur.
 xEdel, Wilbur.
  The State Department, the Public & the United
   Nations. Vantage.
Edelberg, Guillermo S.
 xEdelberg, Guillermo S.
  The Procurement of Practices of the Mexican
   Affiliates of Selected United States
   Automobile Firms.. Arno.
Edelby, Neophytos.
 xEdelby, Neophytos.
  Future of Canon Law. Paulist Pr.
Edelen, D. G. *see* Edelen, Dominic G. B.
Edelen, Dominic G. B.
 xEdelen, D. G.
  An Introduction to Linear Algebra for Science
   & Engineering. Elsevier.
  Relativity & the Question of Discretization in
   Astronomy. Springer-Verlag.
Edelhart, Michael.
 xEdelhart, Michael.
  College Knowledge. Doubleday.
Edelhertz, Herbert.
 xEdelhertz, Herbert.
  The White-Collar Challenge to Nuclear
   Safeguards. Lexington Bks.
Edelman, Elaine.
 xEdelman, Elaine.
  Noeva: Three Women Poets. Dakota Pr.
Edelman, Gerald M.
 xEdelman, Gerald M.
  ed. Cellular Selection & Regulation in the
   Immune Response. Raven.
Edelman, J. *see* Edelman, Jack.
Edelman, Jack.
 xEdelman, J.
  Basic Biochemistry: A Visual Approach for
   College & University Students. Heinemann
   Ed.
Edelman, Jacob Murray, 1919-
 xEdelman, Murray.
  The Symbolic Uses of Politics. U of Ill Pr.
Edelman, Maurice, 1911-
 xEdelman, Maurice.
  Disraeli Rising. Stein & Day.
Edelman, Murray. *see* Edelman, Jacob Murray.
Edelman, Robert, 1945-
 xEdelman, Robert.
  Gentry Politics on the Eve of the Russian
   Revolution: The Nationalist Party,
   1907-1917. Rutgers U Pr.
Edelmann, Chester . *see* Edelmann, Chester M.
Edelmann, Chester M.
 xEdelmann, Chester .
  Pediatric Kidney Disease. Little.
Edelson, Edward, 1932-
 xEdelson, Edward.
  The Funny Men of the Movies. Doubleday.
  Funny Men of the Movies. Archway.
  Great Animals of the Movies. Doubleday.
  Great Kids of the Movies. Doubleday.
  Great Monsters of the Movies. Archway.
  Great Monsters of the Movies. PB.
  Great Monsters of the Movies. Doubleday.
  Great Movie Spectaculars. Doubleday.
  Great Movie Spectaculars. Archway.
  Tough Guys & Gals of the Movies. Doubleday.
  Who Goes There?: The Search for Intelligent
   Life in the Universe. Doubleday.
  Who Goes There: The Search for Intelligent
   Life in the Universe. McGraw.
Edelson, Marshall, 1928-
 xEdelson, Marshall.
  Idea of a Mental Illness. Yale U Pr.
  Sociotherapy & Psychotherapy. U of Chicago
   Pr.
Edelstein, Alex S.
 xEdelstein, Alex S.

ed. Information Societies: Comparing the
 Japanese & American Experiences. Intl
 Comm Ctr.
Information Societies: Comparing the Japanese
 & American Experiences. U of Wash Pr.
Edelstein, Arthur.
 xEdelstein, Arthur.
  ed. Images & Ideas in American Culture: The
   Functions of Criticism - Essays in Memory of
   Philip Rahv. U Pr of New Eng.
Edelstein, Barbara, 1931-
 xEdelstein, Barbara.
  The Woman Doctor's Diet for Teen-Age Girls.
   P-H.
Edelstein, Emma J. *see* Edelstein, Emma Jeannette Levy.
Edelstein, Emma Jeannette Levy.
 xEdelstein, Emma J.
  Asclepius: A Collection & Interpretation of the
   Testimonies. Arno.
Edelstein, J. D. *see* Edelstein, J. David.
Edelstein, J. David.
 xEdelstein, J. D.
  A Comparative Union Democracy:
   Organization & Opposition in British &
   American Unions. Halsted Pr.
 xEdelstein, J. David.
  Comparative Union Democracy: Organization
   & Opposition in British & American Union.
   Transaction Bks.
Edelstein, Ludwig, 1902-1965
 xEdelstein, Ludwig.
  Meaning of Stoicism. Harvard U Pr.
Edelstein, Stefan.
 xEdelstein, Stefan.
  Creating Curriculum in Music. A-W.
Edelstein, Tilden G., 1931-
 xEdelstein, Tilden G.
  Strange Enthusiasm: A Life of Thomas
   Wentworth Higginson. Yale U Pr.
  Strange Enthusiasm: A Life of Thomas
   Wentworth Higginson, 1823-1911. Atheneum.
Edelwich, Jerry.
 xEdelwich, Jerry.
  Burnout: Stages of Disillusionment in the
   Helping Professions. Human Sci Pr.
Eden, Alvin N.
 xEden, Alvin N.
  Growing up Thin. Berkley Pub.
Eden, Anthony, 1897-
 xEden, Anthony.
  Days for Decision. Kraus Repr.
Eden, Dorothy, 1912-
 xEden, Dorothy.
  An Afternoon Walk. Coward.
  An Afternoon Walk. Fawcett.
  Bridge of Fear. Ace Bks.
  Darkwater. Fawcett.
  The Deadly Travellers. Ace Bks.
  The House on Hay Hill. Fawcett.
  Listen to Danger. Ace Bks.
  The Marriage Chest. Fawcett.
  Melbury Square. Fawcett.
  The Salamanca Drum. Coward.
  The Salamanca Drum. Fawcett.
  The Salamanca Drum. G K Hall.
  Speak to Me of Love. Coward.
  Speak to Me of Love. Fawcett.
  The Storrington Papers. Coward.
  The Storrington Papers. Fawcett.
  The Storrington Papers. G K Hall.
  Whistle for the Crows. Ace Bks.
Eden, Helen. *see* Eden, Helen (Parry).
Eden, Helen (Parry), 1885-
 xEden, Helen (Parry).
  Whistles of Silver, & Other Stories. Arno.
Eden, Jerome.
 xEden, Jerome.

Animal Magnetism & the Life Energy.
 Exposition.
Eden, John.
 xEden, John.
  The Eye Book. Penguin.
  The Eye Book. Viking Pr.
Eden, Lynn.
 xEden, Lynn.
  Crisis in Watertown: The Polarization of an
   American Community. U of Mich Pr.
Eden, Richard J. *see* Eden, Richard John.
Eden, Richard John.
 xEden, Richard J.
  Analytic S-Matrix. Cambridge U Pr.
Eden, T. *see* Eden, Thomas.
Eden, Thomas, 1897-
 xEden, T.
  Tea. Longman.
Edens, David G.
 xEdens, David G.
  Oil & Development in the Middle East.
   Praeger.
Edens, W. *see* Edens, Walter.
Edens, Walter.
 xEdens, W.
  Teaching Shakespeare. Princeton U Pr.
Eder, G. *see* Eder, George Jackson.
Eder, George Jackson, 1900-
 xEder, G.
  What's Behind Inflation & How to Beat It.
   P-H.
Eder, Josef M. *see* Eder, Josef Maria.
Eder, Josef Maria, 1855-1944
 xEder, Josef M.
  History of Photography. Dover.
  History of Photography. Peter Smith.
Eder, Phanor J. *see* Eder, Phanor James.
Eder, Phanor James, 1880-
 xEder, Phanor J.
  American-Colombian Private International
   Law. Oceana.
Edera, Bruno.
 xEdera, Bruno.
  Full Length Animated Feature Films. Focal Pr.
  ed. Full Length Animated Feature Films.
   Hastings.
Edey, Maitland. *see* Edey, Maitland Armstrong.
Edey, Maitland A. *see* Edey, Maitland Armstrong.
Edey, Maitland Armstrong.
 xEdey, Maitland.
  Lost World of the Aegean. Silver.
  The Northeast Coast. Silver.
 xEdey, Maitland A.
  The Northeast Coast. Time-Life.
Edgar, Frank.
 xEdgar, Frank.
  ed. & Compiled by Hausa Tales & Traditions:
   An English Translation of Tatsuniyoyi Na
   Hausa. Univ Microfilms.
Edgar, Irving I. *see* Edgar, Irving Iskowitz.
Edgar, Irving Iskowitz, 1902-
 xEdgar, Irving I.
  Meditations in an Anatomy Laboratory &
   Other Poems. Philos Lib.
Edgar, Neal L., 1927-
 xEdgar, Neal L.
  A History & Bibliography of American
   Magazines: 1810-1820. Scarecrow.
Edgar, Patricia.
 xEdgar, Patricia.
  Children & Screen Violence. U of Queensland
   Pr.
Edgar, Pelham, 1871-1948
 xEdgar, Pelham.
  Art of the Novel from 1700 to the Present
   Time. Russell.
Edgar Stern Family Fund.
 xStern Family Fund.
  Recognition of Excellence. Free Pr.
Edgar, William C. *see* Edgar, William Crowell.

Edgar, William Crowell, 1865-1932
xEdgar, William C.
The Story of a Grain of Wheat. Arden Lib.
Story of a Grain of Wheat. Arno.
Edgcumbe, Richard, 1843-1937
xEdgcumbe, Richard.
Byron, the Last Phase. Haskell.
Edge, David.
xEdge, David.
ed. The Formative Years: How Children
Become Members of Their Society.
Schocken.
Edge, David. see Edge, David O.
Edge, David O.
xEdge, David.
Astronomy Transformed: The Emergence of
Radio Astronomy in Britain. Wiley.
Edge, Findley B, 1916-
xEdge, Findley B.
Teaching for Results. Broadman.
Edge, Frederick M. see Edge, Frederick Milnes.
Edge, Frederick Milnes.
xEdge, Frederick M.
The Exploits & Triumphs in Europe of Paul
Morphy, the Chess Champion. Dover.
Edgell, Stephen.
xEdgell, Stephen.
Middle Class Couples: A Study of Segregation,
Domination & Inequality in Marriage. Allen
Unwin.
Edgerton, Franklin, 1885-
xEdgerton, Franklin.
Buddhist Hybrid Sanskrit Grammar &
Dictionary. Verry.
Edgerton, Harold E. see Edgerton, Harold Eugene.
Edgerton, Harold Eugene, 1903-
xEdgerton, Harold E.
Electronic Flash-Strobe. MIT Pr.
ed. Moments of Vision: The Stroboscopic
Revolution on Photography. MIT Pr.
Edgerton, Henry. see Edgerton, Henry White.
Edgerton, Henry White.
xEdgerton, Henry.
Freedom in the Balance: Opinions of Judge
Henry W. Edgerton Relating to Civil
Liberties. Greenwood.
Edgerton, Robert B.
xEdgerton, Robert B.
The Cloak of Competence: Stigma in the Lives
of the Mentally Retarded. U of Cal Pr.
The Individual in Cultural Adaptation: A Study
of Four East African Peoples. U of Cal Pr.
Mental Retardation. Harvard U Pr.
Edgerton, Samuel Y., 1926-
xEdgerton, Samuel Y.
Renaissance Rediscovery of Linear Perspective.
Har-Row.
A Renaissance Rediscovery of Linear
Perspective: 1300-1450. Basic.
Edgett, James D., 1903-
xEdgett, James D.
How to Manage Your Way to the Top. P-H.
Edgeworth, Francis Y. see Edgeworth, Francis Ysidro.
Edgeworth, Francis Ysidro, 1845-1926
xEdgeworth, Francis Y.
Papers Relating to Political Economy. B
Franklin.
Edgeworth, Maria, 1767-1849
xEdgeworth, Maria.
The Absentee. Garland Pub.
Castle Rackrent. Garland Pub.
Castle Rackrent. Norton.
An Essay on Irish Bulls. Garland Pub.
Letters for Literary Ladies. Garland Pub.
The Life & Letters of Maria Edgeworth. Arno.
Moral Tales for Young People. Garland Pub.
The Parent's Assistant. Garland Pub.
Tales & Novels. Adler.
Tales & Novels. AMS Pr.

Edgmand, M. see Edgmand, Michael R.
Edgmand, Michael R.
xEdgmand, M.
Macroeconomics: Theory & Policy. P-H.

Edie, James M.
xEdie, James M.
Speaking & Meaning: The Phenomenology of
Language. Ind U Pr.

Ediger, Max, 1946-
xEdiger, Max.
A Vietnamese Pilgrimage. Faith & Life.
Ediger, Peter J.
xEdiger, Peter J.
The Prophets' Report on Religion in North
America. Faith & Life.
Edinborough, Arnold.
xEdinborough, Arnold.
Canada. French & Eur.
The Enduring Word: A Centennial History of
Wycliffe College. U of Toronto Pr.
Edinburg. see Edinburg, Golda M.
Edinburg, Golda M.
xEdinburg.
Clinical Interviewing & Counseling: Principles
& Techniques. ACC.
Edinburgh.
xEdinburgh Festival.
Douglas Sirk. NY Zoetrope.
Edinburgh Festival. see Edinburgh.
Edinburgh. University.
xEdinburgh University.
Catalogue of the Graduates. AMS Pr.
Pharmacological Experiments on Intact
Preparations. Churchill.
Pharmacological Experiments on Isolated
Preparations. Churchill.
Edinburgh. University. Library.
xEdinburgh University Library.
Index to Manuscripts. G K Hall.
Edinger, Lewis J. see Edinger, Lewis Joachim.
Edinger, Lewis Joachim, 1922-
xEdinger, Lewis J.
Politics in West Germany. Little.
Edington, G. M. see Edington, George Miller.
Edington, George Miller.
xEdington, G. M.
Pathology in the Tropics. Year Bk Med.
Edington, J. M. see Edington, John M.
Edington, John M.
xEdington, J. M.
Ecology & Environmental Planning. Methuen
Inc.
Edison Electric Institute.
xThe Edison Electric Institute.
ed. The Transitional Storm. Edison Elec.
xTheEdison Electric Institute.
Economic Growth in the Future: 1976-2000.
McGraw.
Edison, Michael.
xEdison, Michael.
Public Opinion Polls. Watts.
Edison, Thomas A. see Edison, Thomas Alva.
Edison, Thomas Alva, 1847-1931
xEdison, Thomas A.
Diary of Thomas A. Edison. Chatham Pr.
Editorial Research Report Staff. see Editorial Research
Reports.
Editorial Research Reports.
xEditorial Research Report Staff.
Editorial Research Reports on America's
Changing World Role. Congr Quarterly.
Editorial Research Reports on Political
Instability Abroad. Congr Quarterly.
Editorial Research Reports on the U. S.
Economy Under Stress. Congr Quarterly.
xEditorial Research Reports.

America in the 1980's. Congr Quarterly.
xEditorial Research Reports Staff.
Editorial Research Reports on Earth, Energy &
Environment. Congr Quarterly.
Editorial Research Reports Staff. see Editorial Research
Reports.
Editorial Staff. see Christian Service Society.
Editors of Advertising Age. see Advertising Age.
Editors of Farm Journal. see Farm Journal (Philadelphia,
1956-).
Editors of The National Notary Magazine of the
National Notary Assn. see National Notary
Association.
Editors of the Overseas Assignment Directory. see
Overseas Assignment Directory Service.
Editors of Time-Life Books. see Time-Life Books.
Edkins, J. see Edkins, Joseph.
Edkins, Joseph, 1823-1905
xEdkins, J.
Chinese Buddhism: A Volume of Sketches,
Historical, Descriptive & Critical. Paragon.
xEdkins, Joseph.
Chinese Buddhism: A Volume of Sketches,
Historical, Descriptive, & Critical. Chinese
Materials.
The Revenue & Taxation of the Chinese
Empire. Garland Pub.
Edler, Friedrich.
xEdler, Friedrich.
Dutch Republic & the American Revolution.
AMS Pr.
Edlin, Herbert L. see Edlin, Herbert Leeson.
Edlin, Herbert Leeson.
xEdlin, Herbert L.
Atlas of Plant Life. T Y Crowell.
What Wood Is That?: A Manual of Wood
Identification. Viking Pr.
Woodland Crafts in Britain: An Account of the
Traditional Uses of Trees & Timbers in the
British Countryside. David & Charles.
Edman, Irwin, 1896-1954
xEdman, Irwin.
Adam, the Baby, & the Man from Mars. Arno.
Contemporary & His Soul. Kennikat.
Edman, Marion. see Edman, Marion L.
Edman, Marion L.
xEdman, Marion.
ed. The Horizons of Man. Wayne St U Pr.
Edman, V. Raymond.
xEdman, V. Raymond.
But God!. Zondervan.
Edmands, Allen. see Edmands, Dodie.
Edmands, Dodie.
xEdmands, Allen.
jt. auth. The Children's Astrologer. Dutton.
xEdmands, Dodie.
The Children's Astrologer. Dutton.
Edmister, Wayne C.
xEdmister, Wayne C.
Applied Hydrocarbon Thermodynamics. Gulf
Pub.
Edmond, J. B. see Edmond, Joseph Bailey.
Edmond, Joseph Bailey, 1896-
xEdmond, J. B.
Fundamentals of Horticulture. McGraw.
The Magnificent Charter: The Origin & Role of
the Morrill Land-Grant Colleges &
Universities. Exposition.
Edmonds, Helen G.
xEdmonds, Helen G.
The Negro & Fusion Politics in North
Carolina, 1894-1901. Russell.
Edmonds, I. G.
xEdmonds, I. G.

Automotive Tune-Ups for Beginners. Macrae.
BMX! Bicycle Motocross for Beginners.
  HR&W.
Buddhism. Watts.
China's Red Rebel: The Story of Mao
  Tse-Tung. Macrae.
Drag Racing for Beginners. Bobbs.
Hinduism. Watts.
Hot Rodding for Beginners. Macrae.
Edmonds, Robin.
  xEdmonds, Robin.
    Soviet Foreign Policy 1962-1973: The Paradox
      of Super Power. Oxford U Pr.
    Soviet Foreign Policy 1962-1973: The Paradox
      of Super Power. Oxford U Pr.
Edmonds, Walter D. see Edmonds, Walter Dumaux.
Edmonds, Walter Dumaux.
  xEdmonds, Walter D.
    The Story of Richard Storm. Little.
Edmonds, C. Earl. see Edmondson, Clifton Earl.
Edmondson, Clifton Earl, 1937-
  xEdmondson, C. Earl.
    The Heimwehr & Austrian Politics. U of Ga
      Pr.
Edmondson, Jolee.
  xEdmondson, Jolee.
    The Woman Golfer's Catalogue. Stein & Day.
Edmondson, Kitty.
  xEdmondson, Kitty.
    The Pointer. Merrimack Bk Serv.
Edmonson, Harold. see Edmonson, Harold A.
Edmonson, Harold A.
  xEdmonson, Harold.
    Famous Spaceships of Fact & Fantasy.
      Kalmbach.
  xEdmonson, Harold A.
    ed. The Railroad Station Planbook. Kalmbach.
Edmonston, Barry.
  xEdmonston, Barry.
    Population Distribution in American Cities.
      Lexington Bks.
Edmonston, Louis Philippe.
  xEdmonston, Phil.
    Lemon-Aid. McKay.
Edmonston, Phil. see Edmonston, Louis Philippe.
Edmonston, William E.
  xEdmonston, William E.
    ed. Conceptual & Investigative Approaches to
      Hypnosis & Hypnotic Phenomena. NY Acad
      Sci.
Edmunds, Arthur.
  xEdmunds, Arthur.
    Fiberglass Boat Survey Manual. De Graff.
Edmunds, E. W. see Edmunds, Edward William.
Edmunds, Edward W. see Edmunds, Edward William.
Edmunds, Edward William.
  xEdmunds, E. W.
    Chaucer & His Poetry. Folcroft.
    A Historical Summary of English Literature.
      Folcroft.
    Pope & His Poetry. Folcroft.
    Pope & His Poetry. Haskell.
  xEdmunds, Edward W.
    Chaucer & His Poetry. AMS Pr.
    An Historical Summary of English Literature.
      Norwood Edns.
    Pope & His Poetry. AMS Pr.
Edmunds, G. see Edmunds, George.
Edmunds, George.
  xEdmunds, G.
    The Measurement of Human Aggressiveness.
      Halsted Pr.
Edmunds, George F.
  xEdmunds, George F.
    The Mayflies of North & Central America. U
      of Minn Pr.
Edmunds, H. Tudor. see Edmunds, Henry Tudor.
Edmunds, Henry Tudor.
  xEdmunds, H. Tudor.

Intro. by Some Unrecognized Factors in
  Medicine. Theos Pub Hse.
Edmunds, Lowell.
  xEdmunds, Lowell.
    Chance & Intelligence in Thucydides. Harvard
      U Pr.
Edmunds, Murrell, 1898-
  xEdmunds, Murrell.
    Dim Footprints along a Hazardous Trail. A S
      Barnes.
Edmunds, Stahrl.
  xEdmunds, Stahrl W.
    ed. Geothermal Energy & Regional
      Development: The Case of Imperial County,
      California. Praeger.
Edmunds, Stahrl W. see Edmunds, Stahrl.
Edmundson, Joseph.
  xEdmundson, Joseph.
    New Art of Keeping Fit: Modern Methods for
      Men. Emerson.
Edom, Clifton C. see Edom, Clifton Cedric.
Edom, Clifton Cedric.
  xEdom, Clifton C.
    Photojournalism: Principles & Practices. Wm C
      Brown.
Edsall, Marian S.
  xEdsall, Marian S.
    Library Promotion Handbook. Oryx Pr.
Edson, Charles L.
  xEdson, Charles L.
    Practical Guide to Low & Moderate-Income
      Housing. BNA.
Edson, Gary, 1937-
  xEdson, Gary.
    Mexican Market Pottery. Watson-Guptill.
Edson, Lee.
  xEdson, Lee.
    How We Learn. Silver.
    How We Learn. Time-Life.
Edson, Russell.
  xEdson, Russell.
    The Clam Theater. Columbia U Pr.
    The Reason Why the Closet-Man Is Never
      Sad. Columbia U Pr.
Edstrom, Lars-Olof.
  xEdstrom, Lars-Olof.
    Mass Education: Studies in Adult Education &
      Teaching by Correspondence in Some
      Developing Countries. Holmes & Meier.
Education & Training Systems Division of the Robert J.
  Brady Co. see Robert J. Brady Company.
Education Development Center Introductory Physical
  Science Group. see Education Development Center.
  I.P.S Group.
Education Development Center. I.P.S Group.
  xEducation Development Center Introductory
    Physical Science Group.
    College Introductory Physical Science. P-H.
Education Policies Commission. see Educational Policies
  Commission.
Education Resources Information Center. see Educational
  Resources Information Center.
Educational Broadcasting Corp. see The Educational
  Broadcasting Corporation.
The Educational Broadcasting Corporation.
  xEducational Broadcasting Corp.
    VD Blues. Avon.
Educational Challenges, Inc.
  xEducational Challenges, Inc.
    Carwash Corner. McCormick-Mathers.
    Caves of No Return. McCormick Mathers.
    The CB Mystery. McCormick-Mathers.
    The Chimp Who Makes Good...Pictures.
      McCormick-Mathers.
    Christie Caper. McCormick-Mathers.
    The Magic Arm. McCormick-Mathers.
    Magic Does the Trick. McCormick-Mathers.
    Strange Vibrations. McCormick-Mathers.
Educational Development Corporation.
  xEducational Development Corporation.

Spell-Write. Bowmar-Noble.
Educational Policies Commission. see Educational
  Policies Commission.
Educational Policies Commission.
  xEducation Policies Commission.
    School Athletics: Problems & Policies.
      Greenwood.
  xEducational Policies Commission.
    Research Memorandum on Education in the
      Depression. Arno.
Educational Research Council. see Educational Research
  Council of America.
Educational Research Council of America.
  xEducational Research Council.
    The Age of Western Expansion. Allyn.
    Agriculture: People & the Land. Allyn.
    Ancient Civilization. Allyn.
    The Challenge of Change. Allyn.
    Concepts & Inquiry: The Educational Research
      Council Social Science Program. Allyn.
    Four World Views. Allyn.
    Greek & Roman Civilization. Allyn.
    Industry: People & the Machine. Allyn.
    The Interaction of Cultures. Allyn.
  xEducational Research Council of America.
    Accountant. Changing Times.
    Actress. Changing Times.
    Advertising Copy Writer. Changing Times.
    Airplane Machinist. Changing Times.
    Analytical Testing Manager. Changing Times.
    Architect. Changing Times.
    Assistant Bank Manager. Changing Times.
    Astrophysicist. Changing Times.
    Auto Body Repairman. Changing Times.
    Baker. Changing Times.
    Beautician. Changing Times.
    Blacksmith. Changing Times.
    Boat Builders. Changing Times.
    Boot Maker. Changing Times.
    Building Maintenance Worker. Changing
      Times.
    Cabinetmaker. Changing Times.
    Camera Technician. Changing Times.
    Carpenter. Changing Times.
    Carpet Maker. Changing Times.
    Cellist. Changing Times.
    Ceramic Worker. Changing Times.
    Chef. Changing Times.
    Chemical Technicians. Changing Times.
    Child-Care Attendants. Changing Times.
    Children's Librarian. Changing Times.
    Choices & Decisions: Economics & Society.
      Allyn.
    Citrus Grower. Changing Times.
    Civil Engineers. Changing Times.
    Coal Miner. Changing Times.
    Coast Guard Petty Officer. Changing Times.
    Commercial Airline Pilot. Changing Times.
    Computer Operator. Changing Times.
    Congresswoman. Changing Times.
    Contract Cleaner. Changing Times.
    Corporate Lawyer. Changing Times.
    Corrugated Box Worker. Changing Times.
    Costume Maker. Changing Times.
    Dentist. Changing Times.
    Dredge Operator. Changing Times.
    Dressmaker. Changing Times.
    Dry Cleaners. Changing Times.
    Ecologist. Changing Times.
    Economist. Changing Times.
    Electrician. Changing Times.
    Electronic Repairer. Changing Times.
    Employee Counselor. Changing Times.
    Estimator. Changing Times.
    Executive Housekeeper. Changing Times.
    Fashion Designer. Changing Times.
    FDA Investigator. Changing Times.
    Firearms Examiner. Changing Times.
    Firefighters. Changing Times.
    Fish Biologist. Changing Times.

Edwards, Allen.
xEdwards, Allen.
Flawed Words & Stubborn Sounds: A Conversation with Elliott Carter. Norton.
Edwards, Allen D. *see* Edwards, Allen David.
Edwards, Allen David.
xEdwards, Allen D.
ed. Community & Community Development. Mouton.
Edwards, Allen L. *see* Edwards, Allen Louis.
Edwards, Allen Louis.
xEdwards, Allen L.
Experimental Design in Psychological Research. HR&W.
An Introduction to Linear Regression & Correlation. W H Freeman.
Multiple Regression & the Analysis of Variance & Covariance. W H Freeman.
Edwards, Anne, 1927-
xEdwards, Anne.
Child of Night. Popular Lib.
Exploring the Purcell Wilderness. Mountaineers.
The Great Houdini. Putnam.
The Inn & Us. Random.
Survivors. Dell.
Edwards, Anthony William Fairbank, 1935-
xEdwards, A. W.
Foundations of Mathematical Genetics. Cambridge U Pr.
Likelihood: An Account of the Statistical Concept of Likelihood & Its Application to Scientific Inference. Cambridge U Pr.
Edwards, Arthur C.
xEdwards, Arthur C.
String Ensemble Method: Beginning Class Instruction in Violin, Viola, Cello & Bass. Wm C Brown.
Edwards, Audrey.
xEdwards, Audrey.
Muhammad Ali: The Peoples Champ. Little.
Edwards, Bateman, 1898-
xEdwards, Bateman.
Classification of the Manuscripts of Gui De Cambrai's Vengement Alixandre. Kraus Repr.
Edwards, Bernard.
xEdwards, Bernard.
Sources of Social Statistics. Intl Pubns Serv.
Edwards, Bill.
xEdwards, Bill.
Northwood, King of Carnival Glass. Collector Bks.
Rarities in Carnival Glass. Collector Bks.
Edwards, Brian.
xEdwards, Brian.
Si Vis Pacem...Preparations for Change in the National Health Service. Oxford U Pr.
Edwards, C. A. *see* Edwards, Clive Arthur.
Edwards, C. H. *see* Edwards, Charles Henry.
Edwards, Charles E. *see* Edwards, Charles Edward.
Edwards, Charles Edward.
xEdwards, Charles E.
Dynamics of the United States Automobile Industry. U of Sc Pr.
Edwards, Charles Henry, 1937-
xEdwards, C. H.
Advanced Calculus of Several Variables. Acad Pr.
Edwards, Charlotte W. *see* Edwards, Charlotte Walrath.
Edwards, Charlotte Walrath.
xEdwards, Charlotte W.
Let Yourself Go: Try Creative Sunday School. Morehouse.
Edwards, Christine.
xEdwards, Christine.
The Stanislavsky Heritage: Its Contribution to the Russian & American Theatre. NYU Pr.
Edwards, Christopher, 1954-
xEdwards, Christopher.

Crazy for God. P-H.
Edwards, Clifford H.
xEdwards, Clifford H.
Planning, Teaching & Evaluating: A Competency Approach. Nelson-Hall.
Edwards, Clifford Q.
xEdwards, Clifford Q.
Summer at Sea. Word Bks.
Edwards, Clive Arthur, 1925-
xEdwards, C. A.
ed. Environmental Pollution by Pesticides. Plenum Pub.
xEdwards, Clive E.
Persistent Pesticides in the Environment. CRC Pr.
Edwards, Clive E. *see* Edwards, Clive Arthur.
Edwards, Corwin D., 1901-
xEdwards, Corwin D.
Big Business & the Policy of Competition. Greenwood.
Edwards, D. K. *see* Edwards, Donald Kenneth.
Edwards, David C.
xEdwards, David C.
General Psychology. Macmillan.
Edwards, David L. *see* Edwards, David Lawrence.
Edwards, David Lawrence.
xEdwards, David L.
The Last Things Now. Judson.
A Reason to Hope. Collins Pubs.
Edwards, David V.
xEdwards, David V.
The American Political Experience: An Introduction to Government. P-H.
Edwards, Don.
xEdwards, Don.
End - A New Beginning. Excelsior.
Edwards, Don A.
xEdwards, Don A.
Paths to Writing: Developing Prose Power Exposition.
Edwards, Donald Kenneth.
xEdwards, D. K.
Solar Collector Design. Franklin Inst Pr.
Edwards, E. B. *see* Edwards, Edward Bartholomew.
Edwards, E. D. *see* Edwards, Evangeline Dora.
Edwards, E. H.
xEdwards, E. H.
Fire & Sword in Shansi: The Story of the Martyrdom of Foreigners & Chinese Christians. Arno.
Edwards, E. W. *see* Edwards, Ernest Wood.
Edwards, Edgar O.
xEdwards, Edgar O.
Accounting for Economic Events. Scholars Bk.
Edwards, Edward, 1812-1886
xEdwards, Edward.
Libraries & Founders of Libraries. B Franklin.
Edwards, Edward A. *see* Edwards, Edward Allen.
Edwards, Edward Allen.
xEdwards, Edward A.
Operative Anatomy of Abdomen & Pelvis. Lea & Febiger.
Operative Anatomy of the Thorax. Lea & Febiger.
Edwards, Edward B. *see* Edwards, Edward Bartholomew.
Edwards, Edward Bartholomew, 1873-1948
xEdwards, E. B.
Pattern & Design with Dynamic Symmetry. Peter Smith.
xEdwards, Edward B.
Pattern & Design with Dynamic Symmetry. Dover.
Edwards, Eliezer, 1815-1891
xEdwards, Eliezer E.
Words, Facts & Phrases: A Dictionary of Curious, Quaint, & Out-of-the-Way Matters. Gale.
Edwards, Eliezer E. *see* Edwards, Eliezer.
Edwards, Elwyn H. *see* Edwards, Elwyn Hartley.

Edwards, Elwyn Hartley.
xEdwards, Elwyn H.
The Essentials of Horsemanship. Arco.
The Larousse Guide to Horses & Ponies of the World. Larousse.
Edwards, Ernest W. *see* Edwards, Ernest Wood.
Edwards, Ernest Wood.
xEdwards, E. W.
The Orlando Furioso & Its Predecessor. R West.
xEdwards, Ernest W.
The Orlando Furioso & Its Predecessor. Folcroft.
Edwards, Evangeline D. *see* Edwards, Evangeline Dora.
Edwards, Evangeline Dora, 1888-
xEdwards, E. D.
The Dragon Book. Folcroft.
xEdwards, Evangeline D.
The Dragon Book. Norwood Edns.
Edwards, Frank.
xEdwards, Frank.
Strange People. NAL.
Strange World. Lyle Stuart.
Strange World of Frank Edwards. Lyle Stuart.
Stranger Than Science. Lyle Stuart.
Strangest of All. NAL.
Edwards, Frederick G. *see* Edwards, Frederick George.
Edwards, Frederick George, 1853-1909
xEdwards, Frederick G.
The History of Mendelssohn's Oratorio Elijah. AMS Pr.
Edwards, Frederick H.
xEdwards.
Principles of Switching Circuits. Gordon.
xEdwards, Frederick H.
The Principles of Switching Circuits. MIT Pr.
Edwards, Gabrielle. *see* Edwards, Gabrielle I.
Edwards, Gabrielle I.
xEdwards, Gabrielle.
Man & Woman: Inside Homo Sapiens. Rosen Pr.
The Student Biologist Explores Drug Abuse. Rosen Pr.
Edwards, Gene.
xEdwards.
How to Have a Soul Winning Church. Rusthoi.
xEdwards, Gene.
How to Have a Soul Winning Church. Gospel Pub.
Edwards, George C.
xEdwards, George C.
Presidential Influence in Congress. W H Freeman.
Edwards, George J. *see* Edwards, George John.
Edwards, George John, 1875-
xEdwards, George J.
Grand Jury. AMS Pr.
Edwards, George W. *see* Edwards, George William.
Edwards, George William, 1891-
xEdwards, George W.
Evolution of Finance Capitalism. Kelley.
Edwards, Gladys B. *see* Edwards, Gladys Brown.
Edwards, Gladys Brown.
xEdwards, Gladys B.
Anatomy & Conformation of the Horse. Dreenan Pr.
Edwards, Goronwy. *see* Edwards, John Goronwy.
Edwards, Gus.
xEdwards, Gus.
The Offering: A Play in Two Acts. Dramatists Play.
Edwards, Harold M.
xEdwards, Harold M.
Riemann's Zeta Function. Acad Pr.
Edwards, Harry, 1942-
xEdwards, Harry.
Revolt of the Black Athlete. Free Pr.
Edwards, Harry S. *see* Edwards, Harry Stillwell.
Edwards, Harry Stillwell, 1855-1938
xEdwards, Harry S.

His Defense & Other Stories. Mss Info.
Two Runaways & Other Stories. Mss Info.

Edwards, Henry Sutherland, 1828-1906
xEdwards, Sutherland.
History of the Opera: From Monteverdi to
Donizetti. Da Capo.

Edwards, I. E. *see* Edwards, Iorwerth Eiddon Stephen.

Edwards, Iorwerth Eiddon Stephen.
xEdwards, I. E.
Tutankhamun's Jewelry. Metro Mus Art.

Edwards, J. H. *see* Edwards, John Hilton.

Edwards, James. *see* Edwards, James C.

Edwards, James C.
xEdwards, James.
Occasions for Philosophy. P-H.

Edwards, James D. *see* Edwards, James Don.

Edwards, James Don.
xEdwards, James D.
College Accounting: Principles & Procedures.
Irwin.
Contributions of Four Accounting Pioneers:
Kohler, Littleton, May, Paton. Mich St U
Busn.
Financial Accounting: A Programmed Text.
Irwin.
History of Public Accounting in the United
States. U of Ala Pr.

Edwards, Jane. *see* Edwards, June.

Edwards, Jesse E.
xEdwards, Jesse E.
Illustrated Coronary Fact Book. Arc Bks.

Edwards, John.
xEdwards, John.
Guide to Non-Ferrous Metals & Their
Markets. Nichols Pub.

Edwards, John Goronwy, Sir, 1891-1976
xEdwards, Goronwy.
The Second Century of the English Parliament.
Oxford U Pr.

Edwards, John H.
xEdwards, John H.
A Preliminary Checklist of the Writings of
Ezra Pound, Especially His Contributions to
Periodicals. Folcroft.

Edwards, John Hilton.
xEdwards, J. H.
Human Genetics. Methuen Inc.

Edwards, Jonathan, 1703-1758
xEdwards, Jonathan.
Freedom of the Will. Irvington.
Freedom of the Will. Yale U Pr.
Images or Shadows of Divine Things.
Greenwood.
Nature of True Virtue. U of Mich Pr.
Original Sin. Yale U Pr.
Works of President Edwards. B Franklin.

Edwards, Josephine C. *see* Edwards, Josephine
Cunnington.

Edwards, Josephine Cunnington.
xEdwards, Josephine C.
Malinki of Malawi. Pacific Pr Pub Assn.
Swift Arrow. Pacific Pr Pub Assn.
With an Holy Calling. Pacific Pr Pub Assn.

Edwards, June.
xEdwards, Jane.
Adapted by Treasure Island. Raintree Pubs.
xEdwards, June.
Adapted by Huckleberry Finn. Raintree Pubs.

Edwards, Lauton.
xEdwards, Lauton.
Industrial Arts Plastics. Scribner.
Industrial Arts Plastics. Bennett Co.

Edwards, Lawrence. *see* Edwards, Lawrence E.

Edwards, Lawrence E.
xEdwards, Lawrence.
Lover: The Confessions of a One-Night Stand.
FS&G.

Edwards, Linden F. *see* Edwards, Linden Forest.

Edwards, Linden Forest, 1899-
xEdwards, Linden F.

Concise Anatomy. McGraw.

Edwards, Lyford P. *see* Edwards, Lyford Paterson.

Edwards, Lyford Paterson, 1882-
xEdwards, Lyford P.
Natural History of Revolution. U of Chicago
Pr.

Edwards, Lynne.
xEdwards, Lynne.
Dead As the Dodo. Schol Bk Serv.

Edwards, Malcolm.
xEdwards, Malcolm.
Alien Landscapes. Mayflower Bks.

Edwards, Marie.
xEdwards, Marie.
The Challenge of Being Single. NAL.

Edwards, Michael M.
xEdwards, Michael M.
Growth of the British Cotton Trade,
1780-1815. Kelley.

Edwards, N. A. *see* Edwards, Norman A.

Edwards, Ninian W. *see* Edwards, Ninian Wirt.

Edwards, Ninian Wirt.
xEdwards, Ninian W.
History of Illinois, from 1778 to 1833: And
Life & Times of Ninian Edwards. Arno.

Edwards, Norman A.
xEdwards, N. A.
Cellular Biochemistry & Physiology. McGraw.

Edwards, Page.
xEdwards, Page.
The Mules That Angels Ride. Merrimack Bk
Serv.
Touring. Merrimack Bk Serv.

Edwards, Paul K. *see* Edwards, Paul Kenneth.

Edwards, Paul Kenneth, 1898-1959
xEdwards, Paul K.
The Southern Urban Negro As a Consumer.
Johnson Repr.
Southern Urban Negro As a Consumer. Negro
U Pr.

Edwards, Perry.
xEdwards, Perry.
Data Processing: Computers in Action.
Wadsworth Pub.
Data Processing: Computers in Action with
Fortran. Wadsworth Pub.
Flowcharting & BASIC. HarBraceJ.
Flowcharting & Fortran IV. McGraw.

Edwards, Peter, 1943-
xEdwards, Peter.
Illustrated Guide to the Seaweeds & Sea
Grasses in the Vicinity of Port Aransas,
Texas. U of Tex Pr.

Edwards, Philip R.
xEdwards, Philip R.
Identification of Enterobacteriaceae. Burgess.

Edwards, Phoebe.
xEdwards, Phoebe.
Anyone Can Quilt. Benjamin Co.

Edwards, R. Dudley. *see* Edwards, Robert Dudley.

Edwards, R. E. *see* Edwards, Robert E.

Edwards, R. G.
xEdwards, R. G.
ed. Immunobiology of Trophoblast. Cambridge
U Pr.

Edwards, Rachelle.
xEdwards, Rachelle.
Miranda's Folly. Fawcett.
The Silken Net. Fawcett.

Edwards, Raymond.
xEdwards, Raymond.
Chess Tactics & Attacking Techniques.
Routledge & Kegan.

Edwards, Reginald.
xEdwards, Reginald.
ed. Relevant Methods in Comparative
Education. Unipub.

Edwards, Rem B. *see* Edwards, Rem Blanchard.

Edwards, Rem Blanchard.
xEdwards, Rem B.

Pleasures & Pains: A Theory of Qualitative
Hedonism. Cornell U Pr.

Edwards, Rhoda.
xEdwards, Rhoda.
Fortune's Wheel. Doubleday.

Edwards, Richard, 1523?-1566
xEdwards, Richard.
Damon & Pithias. AMS Pr.

Edwards, Richard A. *see* Edwards, Richard Alan.

Edwards, Richard Alan.
xEdwards, Richard A.
A Concordance to Q. Scholars Pr Ca.
Sign of Jonah in the Theology of the
Evangelists & Q. Allenson.
A Theology of Q, a: Eschatology, Prophecy,
Wisdom. Fortress.

Edwards, Richard C.
xEdwards, Richard C.
The Capitalist System: A Radical Analysis of
American Society. P-H.

Edwards, Richard H. *see* Edwards, Richard Henry.

Edwards, Richard Henry, 1877-1954
xEdwards, Richard H.
Popular Amusements. Arno.

Edwards, Robert Dudley.
xEdwards, R. Dudley.
Church & State in Tudor Ireland: A History of
Penal Laws Against Irish Catholics
1534-1603. Russell.
ed. The Great Famine: Studies in Irish History,
1845-1852. Russell.

Edwards, Robert E.
xEdwards, R. E.
ed. Integration & Harmonic Analysis on
Compact Groups. Cambridge U Pr.
Littlewood-Paley & Multiplier Theory.
Springer-Verlag.

Edwards, Ron. *see* Edwards, Ronald George.

Edwards, Ronald George.
xEdwards, Ron.
Australian Traditional Bush Crafts. Schocken.

Edwards, Ronald J.
xEdwards, Ronald J.
In-Service Training in British Libraries: Its
Development & Present Practice. Gaylord
Prof Pubns.

Edwards, Ruth D. *see* Edwards, Ruth Dudley.

Edwards, Ruth Dudley.
xEdwards, Ruth D.
An Atlas of Irish History. Methuen Inc.
Patrick Pearse: The Triumph of Failure.
Taplinger.

Edwards, Stewart, 1937-
xEdwards, Stewart.
ed. The Communards of Paris, 1871. Cornell U
Pr.

Edwards, Sutherland. *see* Edwards, Henry Sutherland.

Edwards, Tilden.
xEdwards, Tilden.
Living Simply Through the Day: Spiritual
Survival in a Complex Age. Paulist Pr.

Edwards, Viv.
xEdwards, Viv.
The West Indian Language Issue in British
Schools: Challenges & Responses. Routledge
& Kegan.

Edwards, William H.
xEdwards, William H.
ed. Vascular Surgery. Univ Park.

Edwards, William J. *see* Edwards, William James.

Edwards, William James, 1869-
xEdwards, William J.
Twenty-Five Years in the Black Belt. Negro U
Pr.

Edwin, B., Dr
xEdwin, B.

Psycho-Yoga: The Practice of Mind Control.
Citadel Pr.
Psycho-Yoga: The Practice of Mind Control.
Newcastle Pub.

Eee.
xE. E. E. Editors.
Electronic Circuit Design Handbook. TAB Bks.

Eells, Hastings, 1895-
xEells, Hastings.
Martin Bucer. Russell.

Eells, John S. *see* Eells, John Shepard.

Eells, John Shepard.
xEells, John S.
Touchstones of Matthew Arnold. AMS Pr.
The Touchstones of Matthew Arnold. Coll & U
Pr.

Eells, Richard. *see* Eells, Richard Sedric Fox.

Eells, Richard Sedric Fox.
xEells, Richard.
Conceptual Foundations of Business. Irwin.
Global Corporations: The Emerging System of
World Economic Power. Free Pr.
Government of Corporations. Free Pr.

Eells, Robert.
xEells, Robert.
Lonely Walk: The Life of Senator Mark
Hatfield. Christian Herald.

Eells, Walter C. *see* Eells, Walter Crosby.

Eells, Walter Crosby, 1886-1962
xEells, Walter C.
Communism in Education in Asia, Africa, &
the Far Pacific. Greenwood.

Effinger, George A. *see* Effinger, George Alec.

Effinger, George Alec.
xEffinger, George A.
Felicia. Berkley Pub.
Heroics. Doubleday.
xEffinger, George Alec.
Death in Florence. Doubleday.
Fifty Fifty. Doubleday.

Effross, Harris I. *see* Effross, Harris Ira.

Effross, Harris Ira.
xEffross, Harris I.
County Governing Bodies in New Jersey:
Reorganization & Reform on Boards of
Chosen Freeholders, 1798-1974. Rutgers U
Pr.

Efird, James M.
xEfird, James M.
Jeremiah--Prophet Under Siege. Judson.
The New Testament Writings: History,
Literature, Interpretation. John Knox.
These Things Are Written: An Introduction to
the Religious Ideas of the Bible. John Knox.

Efron, Alexander, 1897-
xEfron, Alexander.
Exploring Heat. Hayden.
Exploring Matter & Nuclear Energy. Hayden.
Teaching of Physical Sciences in the Secondary
Schools of the United States, France & Soviet
Russia. AMS Pr.

Efron, Benjamin.
xEfron, Benjamin.
Currents & Trends in Contemporary Jewish
Thought. Ktav.

Efron, Edith, 1922-
xEfron, Edith.
How CBS Tried to Kill a Book. Manor Bks.

Efros, Israel I. *see* Efros, Israel Isaac.

Efros, Israel Isaac, 1890-
xEfros, Israel I.
Studies in Medieval Jewish Philosophy.
Columbia U Pr.

Eftekhar, Nas S. *see* Eftekhar, Nas Ser.

Eftekhar, Nas Ser, 1935-
xEftekhar, Nas S.
Principles of Total Hip Arthroplasty. Mosby.

Egami, Tomi, 1899-
xEgami, Tomi.

Rice Recipes from Around the World.
Kodansha.

Egan, Donald F., 1916-
xEgan, Donald F.
Fundamentals of Respiratory Therapy. Mosby.

Egan, F. *see* Egan, Ferol.

Egan, Ferol.
xEgan, F.
El Dorado Trail: The Story of the Gold Rush
Routes Across Mexico. McGraw.
xEgan, Ferol.
The Taste of Time. McGraw.

Egan, Gerard.
xEgan, Gerard.
Face to Face: The Small Group Experience &
Interpersonal Growth. Brooks-Cole.

Egan, Joseph J.
xEgan, Joseph J.
History of Clan Egan: The Birds of the Forest
of Wisdom. Univ Microfilms.

Egan, Kieran.
xEgan, Kieran.
Educational Development. Oxford U Pr.

Egan, M. David.
xEgan, M. David.
Concepts in Architectural Acoustics. McGraw.
Concepts in Thermal Comfort. P-H.

Egan, Walter G.
xEgan, Walter G.
Optical Properties of Inhomogeneous Materials:
Applications to Geology, Astronomy,
Chemistry & Engineering. Acad Pr.

Egbert, Alvin C. *see* Egbert, Alvin Charles.

Egbert, Alvin Charles.
xEgbert, Alvin C.
A Development Model for the Agricultural
Sector of Portugal. Johns Hopkins.

Egbert, Donald D. *see* Egbert, Donald Drew.

Egbert, Donald Drew.
xEgbert, Donald D.
The Beaux-Arts Tradition in French
Architecture. Princeton U Pr.

Egdahl, Richard H. *see* Egdahl, Richard Harrison.

Egdahl, Richard Harrison.
xEgdahl, Richard H.
ed. A Core Textbook of Surgery. Grune.
ed. Quality Assurance in Health Care. Aspen
Systems.
ed. Quality Health Care: The Role of
Continuing Medical Education. Aspen
Systems.
ed. Readings in Modern Surgery. Grune.

Ege, Lennart.
xEge, Lennart.
Balloons & Airships. Macmillan.

Egede, H. P. *see* Egede, Hans Poulsen.

Egede, Hans Poulsen, 1686-1758
xEgede, H. P.
A Description of Greenland. Kraus Repr.

Egelstaff, P. A. *see* Egelstaff, Peter A.

Egelstaff, Peter A.
xEgelstaff, P. A.
ed. Thermal Neutron Scattering. Acad Pr.

Egenter, Richard, 1902-
xEgenter, Richard.
Desecration of Christ. Franciscan Herald.
Moral Problems & Mental Health. Alba.

Eger, Edmond I.
xEger, Edmond I.
Anesthetic Uptake & Action. Williams &
Wilkins.

Egermeier, Elsie E. *see* Egermeier, Elsie Emilie.

Egermeier, Elsie Emilie.
xEgermeier, Elsie E.

Egermeier's Bible Story Book. Warner Pr.

Egerton, George W.
xEgerton, George W.
Great Britain & the Creation of the League of
Nations: Strategy, Politics, & International
Organization, 1914-1919. U of NC Pr.

Eggan, Lawrence C.
xEggan, Lawrence C.
Mathematics: Models & Applications. Heath.

Egge, Mandus A.
xEgge, Mandus A.
ed. Hymns, How to Sing Them. Augsburg.

Egge, Ruth S. *see* Egge, Ruth Stearns.

Egge, Ruth Stearns.
xEgge, Ruth S.
Recycled with Flair: How to Remodel Old
Furniture & Flea Market Finds. Coward.

Eggeling, H. F. *see* Eggeling, Hans F.

Eggeling, Hans F.
xEggeling, H. F.
Dictionary of Modern German Prose Usage.
Oxford U Pr.

Eggen, Paul. *see* Eggen, Paul D.

Eggen, Paul D.
xEggen, Paul.
Strategies for Teachers: Information Processing
Models in the Classroom. P-H.

Eggenberger, David.
xEggenberger, David.
Dictionary of Battles. T Y Crowell.
Flags of the U.S.A.. T Y Crowell.

Eggenschwiler, David, 1936-
xEggenschwiler, David.
The Christian Humanism of Flannery
O'Connor. Wayne St U Pr.

Egger, Rowland. *see* Egger, Rowland Andrews.

Egger, Rowland Andrews, 1908
xEgger, Rowland.
The President of the United States. McGraw.

Eggerichs, Fred. *see* Eggerichs, Fred W.

Eggerichs, Fred W., 1912-
xEggerichs, Fred.
A Bag Without Holes: How to Prepare for
Your Family, Your Finances, Your Future.
Bethany Fell.

Eggers, Philip.
xEggers, Philip.
Writing Skillful Sentences. Random.

Eggert, Jim, 1943-
xEggert, Jim.
Investigating Microeconomics. W Kaufmann.

Eggert, Richard.
xEggert, Richard.
Backpack Hiking: The First Steps. Stackpole.
Fish & Hunt the Backcountry. Stackpole.

Egginton, Joyce.
xEgginton, Joyce.
The Poisoning of Michigan. Norton.

Eggleston. *see* Eggleston, Edward.

Eggleston, Edward, 1837-1902
xEggleston.
The Hoosier Schoolmaster. McDougal-Littell.
xEggleston, Edward.
End of the World: A Love Story. AMS Pr.
Graysons: A Story of Illinois. AMS Pr.
The Hoosier School-Master. Hill & Wang.
The Hoosier Schoolmaster. Folcroft.
Hoosier Schoolmaster. Peter Smith.
The Hoosier Schoolmaster. Regents Pub.
Queer Stories for Boys & Girls. Core
Collection.
Ultimate Solution of the American Negro
Problem. AMS Pr.

Eggleston, John.
xEggleston, John.

ed. Contemporary Research in the Sociology of
Education. Methuen Inc.
Developments in Design Education.
Humanities.
The Sociology of the School Curriculum.
Routledge & Kegan.

Eggum, Tom.
xEggum, Tom.
Feeling Good. Nelson.
Eglar, Zekiye S. *see* Eglar, Zekiye Suleyman.
Eglar, Zekiye Suleyman, 1910-
xEglar, Zekiye S.
Punjabi Village in Pakistan. Columbia U Pr.
Egle, William H. *see* Egle, William Henry.
Egle, William Henry, 1830-1901
xEgle, William H.
Pennsylvania Women in the American
Revolution. Polyanthos.
Egleton, Clive.
xEgleton, Clive.
Backfire. Atheneum.
Eglinton, Guy, 1896-1928
xEglinton, Guy.
Reaching for Art. Arno.
Egoff, Sheila. *see* Egoff, Sheila A.
Egoff, Sheila A.
xEgoff, Sheila.
ed. Only Connect: Readings on Children's
Literature. Oxford U Pr.
Egret, Jean.
xEgret, Jean.
The French Pre-Revolution, 1787-1788. U of
Chicago Pr.
Egri, Lajos.
xEgri, Lajos.
Art of Creative Writing. Citadel Pr.
Egstrom, Glen H.
xEgstrom, Glen H.
Volleyball. Wm C Brown.
Ehlers, Henry J.
xEhlers, Henry J.
Crucial Issues in Education. HR&W.
Logic: Modern & Traditional. Merrill.
Ehlers, Walter H.
xEhlers, Walter H.
Administration for the Human Services: An
Introductory Programmed Text. Har-Row.
Ehman, Lee.
xEhman, Lee.
ed. Toward Effective Instruction in Secondary
Social Studies. HM.
Ehmann, Wilhelm.
xEhmann, Wilhelm.
Choral Directing. Augsburg.
Ehninger, Douglas.
xEhninger, Douglas.
Decision by Debate. Har-Row.
Influence, Belief, & Argument: An Introduction
to Responsible Persuasion. Scott F.
Principles & Types of Speech Communication.
Scott F.
Principles of Speech Communication. Scott F.
Ehre, Milton, 1933-
xEhre, Milton.
Oblomov & His Creator: The Life & Art of
Ivan Goncharov. Princeton U Pr.
Ehrenberg, Victor, 1891-
xEhrenberg, Victor.
Alexander & the Greeks. Hyperion Conn.
Aspects of the Ancient World: Essays &
Reviews. Arno.
The Greek State. Methuen Inc.
Greek State. Norton.
xEhrenberg, Victor L.
Society & Civilization in Greece & Rome.
Harvard U Pr.
Ehrenberg, Victor L. *see* Ehrenberg, Victor.
Ehrenburg, Ilia Grigorevich, 1891-1967
xEhrenburg, Ilya.

The Life of the Automobile. Urizen Bks.
Ninth Wave. Greenwood.
xEhrenburg, Ilya G.
Love of Jeanne Ney. Greenwood.
Ehrenburg, Ilya. *see* Ehrenburg, Ilia Grigorevich.
Ehrenburg, Ilya G. *see* Ehrenburg, Ilia Grigorevich.
Ehrenfeld, David W.
xEhrenfeld, David W.
The Arrogance of Humanism. Oxford U Pr.
Ehrenpreis, Andreas.
xEhrenpreis, Andreas.
Brotherly Community, the Highest Command
of Love: Two Anabaptist Documents of 1650
& 1560. Plough.
Ehrenpreis, Anne H. *see* Ehrenpreis, Anne Henry.
Ehrenpreis, Anne Henry.
xEhrenpreis, Anne H.
ed. Literary Ballad. U of SC Pr.
Ehrenpreis, Irvin, 1920-
xEhrenpreis, Irvin.
Literary Meaning & Augustan Values. U Pr of
Va.
The "Types Approach" to Literature. Folcroft.
Ehrenpreis, Leon.
xEhrenpreis, Leon.
Fourier Analysis in Several Complex Variables.
Wiley.
Ehrenreich, Barbara.
xEhrenreich, Barbara.
Complaints & Disorders: The Sexual Politics of
Sickness. Feminist Pr.
For Her Own Good: 150 Years of Expert's
Advice to Women. Doubleday.
Long March, Short Spring: The Student
Uprising at Home & Abroad. Monthly Rev.
Ehrenreich, John, 1943-
xEhrenreich, John.
ed. The Cultural Crisis of Modern Medicine.
Monthly Rev.
Ehrensaft, Philip.
xEhrensaft, W. Phillip.
Anatomies of America: Sociological
Perspectives. Macmillan.
Ehrensaft, W. Phillip. *see* Ehrensaft, Philip.
Ehrensperger, Harold A. *see* Ehrensperger, Harold
Adam.
Ehrensperger, Harold Adam, 1897-1973
xEhrensperger, Harold A.
Religious Drama: Ends & Means. Greenwood.
Ehrenwald, Jan, 1900-
xEhrenwald, Jan.
The ESP Experience: A Psychiatric Validation.
Basic.
ed. The History of Psychotherapy: From
Healing Magic to Encounter. Aronson.
Ehrenzweig, Albert A. *see* Ehrenzweig, Albert Armin.
Ehrenzweig, Albert Armin.
xEhrenzweig, Albert A.
Jurisdiction in a Nutshell, State & Federal.
West Pub.
Ehresmann, Donald L., 1937-
xEhresmann, Donald L.
Applied & Decorative Arts: A Bibliographic
Guide to Basic Reference Works, Histories, &
Handbooks. Libs Unl.
Fine Arts: A Bibliographic Guide to Basic
Reference Works, Histories & Handbooks.
Libs Unl.
Ehret, Christopher.
xEhret, Christopher.
Southern Nilotic History: Linguistic
Approaches to the Study of the Past.
Northwestern U Pr.
Ehrhardt, Arnold.
xEhrhardt, Arnold A.
Framework of the New Testament Stories.
Harvard U Pr.
Ehrhardt, Arnold A. *see* Ehrhardt, Arnold.
Ehrhardt, Roy.
xEhrhardt, Roy.

Clock Identification & Price Guide. Heart Am
Pr.
Ehrich, Robert W.
xEhrich, Robert W.
ed. Chronologies in Old World Archaeology. U
of Chicago Pr.
Ehrlich, Amy.
xEhrlich, Amy.
The Everyday Train. Dial.
Retold by Thumbelina. Dial.
Ehrlich, Ann. *see* Ehrlich, Ann Beard.
Ehrlich, Ann Beard.
xEhrlich, Ann.
Business Administration for the Dental
Assistant. Colwell Co.
Ehrlich, Eugen, 1862-1922
xEhrlich, Eugen.
Fundamental Principles of the Sociology of
Law. Arno.
Ehrlich, Eugene. *see* Ehrlich, Eugene H.
Ehrlich, Eugene H.
xEhrlich, Eugene.
How to Study Better & Get Higher Marks. T
Y Crowell.
xEhrlich, Eugene H.
Art of Technical Writing: A Manual for
Scientists, Engineers, & Students. T Y
Crowell.
How to Study Better & Get Higher Marks. T
Y Crowell.
Ehrlich, George E.
xEhrlich, George E.
Rehabilitation Management of Rheumatic
Conditions. Williams & Wilkins.
Total Management of the Arthritic Patient.
Lippincott.
Ehrlich, Howard J.
xEhrlich, Howard J.
Reinventing Anarchy: What Are Anarchists
Thinking These Days?. Routledge & Kegan.
Ehrlich, Jack.
xEhrlich, Jack.
Rebellion at Cripple Creek. PB.
Ehrlich, Jeffrey.
xEhrlich, Jeffrey.
The Carpenter's Manifesto. HR&W.
Ehrlich, Max. *see* Ehrlich, Max Simon.
Ehrlich, Max Simon, 1909-
xEhrlich, Max.
Reincarnation in Venice. Ace Bks.
Reincarnation in Venice. S&S.
The Reincarnation of Peter Proud. Bantam.
Ehrlich, Paul. *see* Ehrlich, Paul R.
Ehrlich, Paul R.
xEhrlich, Paul.
How to Be a Survivor. Am Repr-Rivercity Pr.
xEhrlich, Paul R.
Ecoscience: Population, Resources,
Environment. W H Freeman.
The End of Affluence: A Blueprint for Your
Future. Ballantine.
Evolution. McGraw.
The Population Bomb. Am Repr-Rivercity Pr.
The Process of Evolution. McGraw.
The Race Bomb: Skin Color, Prejudice, &
Intelligence. Times Bks.
Ehrlich, Thomas.
xEhrlich, Thomas.
Going to Law School?: Readings on a Legal
Career. Little.
Ehrlich, Walter, 1921-
xEhrlich, Walter.
They Have No Rights: Dred Scott's Struggle
for Freedom. Greenwood.
Ehrlichman, John.
xEhrlichman, John.
The Whole Truth. Popular Lib.
Whole Truth. S&S.
Ehrman, Edith.
xEhrman, Edith.

Students, Teachers & the Third World in the American College Curriculum. Learn Res Intl Stud.

Ehrman, Kenneth. see Ehrman, Kenneth A.

Ehrman, Kenneth A.
xEhrman, Kenneth.
Taxing California Property. Bull Pub.

Ehrmann, Henry W. see Ehrmann, Henry Walter.

Ehrmann, Henry Walter, 1908-
xEhrmann, Henry W.
Comparative Legal Cultures. P-H.
French Labor from Popular Front to Liberation. Russell.

Ehrmann, Herbert B. see Ehrmann, Herbert Brutus.

Ehrmann, Herbert Brutus, 1891-
xEhrmann, Herbert B.
The Case That Will Not Die: Commonwealth Vs. Sacco & Vanzetti. Little.

Eibl-Eibesfeldt, Irenaus.
xEibl-Eibesfeldt, Irenaus.
Love & Hate: The Natural History of Behavior Patterns. Schocken.

Eichelberger, Clark M. see Eichelberger, Clark Mell.

Eichelberger, Clark Mell, 1896-
xEichelberger, Clark M.
Organizing for Peace: A Personal History of the Founding of the United Nations. Har-Row.

Eichelberger, Clayton L., 1925-
xEichelberger, Clayton L.
Guide to Critical Reviews of United States Fiction, 1870-1910. Scarecrow.
Published Comment on William Dean Howells Through 1920: A Research Bibliography. G K Hall.

Eichelberger, Rosa K. see Eichelberger, Rosa Kohler.

Eichelberger, Rosa Kohler.
xEichelberger, Rosa K.
Big Fire in Baltimore. Stemmer Hse.

Eichenberg, Fritz, 1901-
xEichenberg, Fritz.
illus. Ape in a Cape: An Alphabet of Odd Animals. HarBraceJ.
illus. Ape in a Cape: An Alphabet of Odd Animals. HarBraceJ.
illus. Dancing in the Moon: Counting Rhymes. HarBraceJ.
illus. Dancing in the Moon: Counting Rhymes. HarBraceJ.
Endangered Species, & Other Fables with a Twist. Stemmer Hse.
Lithography & Silkscreen: Art & Technique. Abrams.

Eichenlaub, John E., M.d
xEichenlaub, John E.
The Marriage Art. Dell.

Eicher, Carl K.
xEicher, Carl K.
ed. Growth & Development of the Nigerian Economy. Mich St U Pr.

Eicher, Don. see Eicher, Don L.

Eicher, Don L.
xEicher, Don.
History of the Earth. P-H.
xEicher, Don L.
Geologic Time. P-H.

Eicher, T. see Eicher, Theophil.

Eicher, Theophil, 1932-
xEicher, T.
Cyclic Compounds. Springer-Verlag.

Eichholz, G. G.
xEichholz, Geoffrey G.
Environmental Aspects of Nuclear Power. Ann Arbor Science.

Eichholz, Geoffrey G. see Eichholz, G. G.

Eichhorn. see Eichhorn, David Max.

Eichhorn, David Max.
xEichhorn.

Evangelizing the American Jew. Jonathan David.

Eichhorn, Gunther. see Eichhorn, Gunther Louis.

Eichhorn, Gunther Louis, 1927-
xEichhorn, Gunther.
ed. Inorganic Biochemistry. Elsevier.

Eichhorn, Heinrich.
xEichhorn, Heinrich.
Astronomy of Star Positions: A Critical Investigation of Star Catalogues, the Methods of Their Construction, & Their Purpose. Ungar.

Eichhorn, W. see Eichhorn, Wolfgang.

Eichhorn, Wolfgang.
xEichhorn, W.
Theory of the Price Index: Fisher's Test Approach & Generalizations. Springer-Verlag.

Eichler, Edward P.
xEichler, Edward P.
The Community Builders. U of Cal Pr.

Eichler, Margrit.
xEichler, Margrit.
Martin's Father. Lollipop Power.

Eichler, Martin.
xEichler, Martin.
Projective Varieties & Modular Forms. Springer-Verlag.

Eichler, Victor B.
xEichler, Victor B.
Atlas of Comparative Embryology: A Laboratory Guide to Invertebrate & Vertebrate Embryos. Mosby.

Eichner, Alfred S.
xEichner, Alfred S.
Controlling Social Expenditures: The Search for Output Measures. Allanheld.
ed. A Guide to Post-Keynesian Economics. M E Sharpe.
A Guide to Post-Keynesian Economics. Pantheon.

Eichner, Donald O. see Eichner, Donald Oscar.

Eichner, Donald Oscar.
xEichner, Donald O.
The Inter-American Nuclear Energy Commission: Its Goals & Achievements. Arno.

Eichner, James. see Eichner, James A.

Eichner, James A.
xEichner, James.
Thomas Jefferson: The Complete Man. Watts.
xEichner, James A.
The First Book of Local Government. Watts.

Eichrodt, Walther, 1890-
xEichrodt, Walther.
Ezekiel: A Commentary. Westminster.

Eickemeyer, Carl.
xEickemeyer, Carl.
Over the Great Navajo Trail. AMS Pr.

Eickmann, Paul E.
xEickmann, Paul E.
Wonderful Works of God. Northwest Pub.

Eide, Arvid R.
xEide, Arvid R.
Engineering Fundamentals & Problem Solving. McGraw.

Eide, Asbjorn. see Eide, Asbjrn.

Eide, Asbjrn.
xEide, Asbjorn.
ed. Problems of Contemporary Militarism. St Martin.

Eide, Harald, 1896-
xEide, Harald.
Alaska Adventures of a Norwegian Cheechako: Greenhorn with a Gold Pan. Alaska Northwest.

Eidelberg, Ludwig, 1898-
xEidelberg, Ludwig.
ed. Encyclopedia of Psychoanalysis. Free Pr.

Eidelberg, Paul.
xEidelberg, Paul.

A Discourse on Statesmanship: The Design & Transformation of the American Polity. U of Ill Pr.
On the Silence of the Declaration of Independence. U of Mass Pr.

Eidenier, Elon G.
xEidenier, Elon G.
Sonnets to Eurydice. Windy Row.

Eidlitz, Leopold, 1823-1908
xEidlitz, Leopold.
The Nature & Function of Art, More Especially as Architecture. Da Capo.

Eidsvik, Charles, 1943-
xEidsvik, Charles.
Cineliteracy: Film Among the Arts. Random.
xEidsvik, Charles V.
Cineliteracy: Film Among the Arts. Horizon.

Eidsvik, Charles V. see Eidsvik, Charles.

Eighme, Lloyd. see Eighme, Lloyd E.

Eighme, Lloyd E.
xEighme, Lloyd.
Insects You Have Seen. Southern Pub.

Eighmy, John L. see Eighmy, John Lee.

Eighmy, John Lee.
xEighmy, John L.
Churches in Cultural Captivity: A History of the Social Attitudes of Southern Baptists. U of Tenn Pr.

Eighty-Fifth Symposium of the International Astronomical Union, Victoria, B. C., Canada, August 27-30, 1979. see International Astronomical Union.

Eigner, Larry, 1927-
xEigner, Larry.
Anything on Its Side. SBD.
Things Stirring Together or Far Away. Black Sparrow.
The World & Its Streets, Places. Black Sparrow.

Eik-Nes, K. B. see Eik-Nes, Kristen B.

Eik-Nes, Kristen B.
xEik-Nes, K. B.
Gas Phase Chromatography of Steroids. Springer-Verlag.

Eikeland, Peter J., 1852-1927
xEikeland, Peter J.
Ibsen Studies. Haskell.

Eiland, Murray L.
xEiland, Murray L.
Chinese & Exotic Rugs. NYGS.
ed. Oriental Rugs: A Comprehensive Guide. NYGS.

Eilenberg, Howard.
xEilenberg, Howard.
What You Should Know About Research Techniques for Retailers. Oceana.

Eilenberg, Samuel.
xEilenberg, Samuel.
Automata, Languages, & Machines. Acad Pr.

Eilers, Robert D.
xEilers, Robert D.
The Attitudes & Anticipated Behavior of Dentists Under Various Reimbursement Arrangements. Irwin.
Regulation of Blue Cross & Blue Shield Plans Irwin.

Eilon, Samuel.
xEilon, Samuel.
Applied Productivity Analysis for Industry. Pergamon.
Aspects of Management. Pergamon.
Management Control. Pergamon.

Eimerl, Sarel.
xEimerl, Sarel.
Gulls. S&S.
The Primates. Silver.
Primates. Silver.

Ein, Claudia, 1943-
xEin, Claudia.

How to Design Your Own Clothes & Make Your Own Patterns. Doubleday.
How to Make Your Own Wedding Gown. Doubleday.

Einarsson, Stafan, 1897-
xEinarsson, Stefan.
History of Icelandic Prose Writers. Kraus Repr.
Einarsson, Stefan. *see* Einarsson, Stafan.

Einaudi, Mario, 1904-
xEinaudi, Mario.
Communism in Western Europe. Shoe String.
Early Rousseau. Cornell U Pr.
Einaudi, Paula F. *see* Einaudi, Paula Ferris.

Einaudi, Paula Ferris.
xEinaudi, Paula F.
A Grammar of Biloxi. Garland Pub.
Einbond, Bernard L. *see* Einbond, Bernard Lionel.

Einbond, Bernard Lionel, 1937-
xEinbond, Bernard L.
The Coming Indoors & Other Poems. C E Tuttle.

Einhorn, E.
xEinhorn, E. C.
Old French: A Concise Handbook. Cambridge U Pr.
Einhorn, E. C. *see* Einhorn, E.
Einhorn, Jessica P. *see* Einhorn, Jessica Pernitz.

Einhorn, Jessica Pernitz.
xEinhorn, Jessica P.
Expropriation Politics. Lexington Bks.

Einsel, Walter.
xEinsel, Walter.
Did You Ever See?. Schol Bk Serv.
Einstein. *see* Einstein, Charles.

Einstein, Albert.
xEinstein, Albert.
Einstein on Peace. Schocken.
Living Philosophies. AMS Pr.

Einstein, Alfred, 1880-1952
xEinstein, Alfred.
Greatness in Music. Da Capo.
Greatness in Music. Scholarly.

Einstein, Charles.
xEinstein.
Willie's Time: A Memoir. Berkley Pub.
xEinstein, Charles.
ed. The Baseball Reader: Favorites from the Fireside Books of Baseball. Lippincott.

Einstein, Lewis, 1877-1967
xEinstein, Lewis.
Diplomat Looks Back. Yale U Pr.
Divided Loyalties: Americans in England During the War of Independence. Russell.
Tudor Ideals. Russell.

Einstein, Stanley.
xEinstein, Stanley.
ed. The Community's Response to Drug Use. Pergamon.

Einzig, Paul, 1897-
xEinzig, Paul.
Bankers, Statesmen & Economists. Arno.
Behind the Scenes of International Finance. Arno.
Dynamic Theory of Forward Exchange. St Martin.
Exchange Control. AMS Pr.
History of Foreign Exchange. St Martin.
Textbook of Foreign Exchange. St Martin.
Eisberg, Robert. *see* Eisberg, Robert Martin.
Eisberg, Robert M. *see* Eisberg, Robert Martin.

Eisberg, Robert Martin.
xEisberg, Robert.
Countdown: Skydiver, Rocket & Satellite Motion on Programmable Calculators. Dilithium Pr.
Quantum Physics of Atoms, Molecules, Solids, Nuclei, & Particles. Wiley.
xEisberg, Robert M.

Applied Mathematical Physics with Programmable Pocket Calculators. McGraw.
Fundamentals of Modern Physics. Wiley.
Eisele, J. A. *see* Eisele, John A.

Eisele, James E.
xEisele, James E.
Computer Assisted Planning of Curriculum & Instruction: How to Use Computer Based Resource Units to Individualize Instruction. Educ Tech Pubns.

Eisele, John A.
xEisele, J. A.
Applied Matrix & Tensor Analysis. Wiley.

Eiselt, Horst A.
xEiselt, Horst A.
Operations Research Handbook: Standard Algorithms & Methods with Examples. De Gruyter.

Eiseman, Alberta.
xEiseman, Alberta.
From Many Lands. Atheneum.

Eiseman, Ben.
xEiseman, Ben.
Prognosis of Surgical Disease. Saunders.
Surgical Decision Making. Saunders.

Eisen, Jeffrey.
xEisen, Jeffrey.
Get the Right Job Now!. Lippincott.
Eisen, M. *see* Eisen, Martin M.

Eisen, Martin M.
xEisen, M.
Mathematical Models in Cell Biology & Cancer Chemotherapy. Springer Verlag.
xEisen, Martin M.
Probability & Its Applications. Quantum Pubs.

Eisenberg, Abne M.
xEisenberg, Abne M.
Argument: A Guide to Formal & Informal Debate. P-H.
Living Communication. P-H.
Nonverbal Communication. Bobbs.
Nonverbal Communication. Irvington.
Understanding Communication in Business & the Professions. Macmillan.

Eisenberg, Arlene.
xEisenberg, Arlene.
Alive & Well: Decisions in Health. McGraw.
Eisenberg, Azriel. *see* Eisenberg, Azriel Louis.

Eisenberg, Azriel Louis, 1903-
xEisenberg, Azriel.
Fill a Blank Page: A Biography of Solomon Schechter. United Syn Bk.
ed. Home at Last. Bloch.
Modern Jewish Life in Literature. United Syn Bk.
Eisenberg, David. *see* Eisenberg, David S.

Eisenberg, David S.
xEisenberg, David.
Structure & Properties of Water. Oxford U Pr.

Eisenberg, Dennis.
xEisenberg, Dennis.
Meyer Lansky: Mogul of the Mob. Paddington.
Eisenberg, E. Michael. *see* Eisenberg, M. Michael.

Eisenberg, Gerson G.
xEisenberg, Gerson G.
Learning Vacations: A Guide to College Seminars, Conference Centers, Festivals, Art Museums, & Educational Tours in the U.S. & Abroad. Acropolis.

Eisenberg, Helen.
xEisenberg, Helen.
Fun with Skits, Stunts, & Stories. Baker Bk.
How to Lead Group Singing. Greenwood.
jt. auth. Public Speaker's Handbook of Humor. Baker Bk.
xEisenberg, Larry.
Public Speaker's Handbook of Humor. Baker Bk.
Eisenberg, Larry. *see* Eisenberg, Helen.

Eisenberg, M. G.
xEisenberg, M. G.
Treatment of the Spinal Cord Injured: An Interdisciplinary Perspective. C C Thomas.

Eisenberg, M. Michael, 1931-
xEisenberg, E. Michael.
Ulcers. G K Hall.
Eisenberg, Melvin A. *see* Eisenberg, Melvin Aron.

Eisenberg, Melvin Aron.
xEisenberg, Melvin A.
The Structure of the Corporation: A Legal Analysis. Little.

Eisenberg, Mickey S.
xEisenberg, Mickey S.
Manual of Antimicrobial Therapy & Infectious Diseases. Saunders.

Eisenberg, Myron G.
xEisenberg, Myron G.
Communications in a Health Care Setting. C C Thomas.

Eisenberg, Peter L.
xEisenberg, Peter L.
The Sugar Industry in Pernambuco, 1840-1910: Modernization Without Change. U of Cal Pr.
Eisenberg, R. B. *see* Eisenberg, Rita B.

Eisenberg, Rita B.
xEisenberg, R. B.
Auditory Competence in Early Life: The Roots of Communicative Behavior. Univ Park.
Eisenberg, Ronald L. *see* Eisenberg, Ronald Lee.

Eisenberg, Ronald Lee.
xEisenberg, Ronald L.
The Iguana Corps of the Haganah. Bloch.

Eisenberg, Sheldon.
xEisenberg, Sheldon.
Helping Clients with Special Concerns. Rand.
Eisenberger, K. *see* Eisenberger, Kenneth.

Eisenberger, Kenneth.
xEisenberger, K.
The Expert Consumer: A Complete Handbook. P-H.

Eisenbud, Merril.
xEisenbud, Merril.
Environment, Technology & Health: Human Ecology in Historical Perspective. NYU Pr.

Eisendrath, Craig R.
xEisendrath, Craig R.
Out of Discontent: Visions of the Contemporary University. Schenkman.

Eisenhardt, Catheryn.
xEisenhardt, Catheryn T.
Applying Linguistics in the Teaching of Reading & the Language Arts. Merrill.
Eisenhardt, Catheryn T. *see* Eisenhardt, Catheryn.
Eisenhower, Dwight D. *see* Eisenhower, Dwight David.

Eisenhower, Dwight David.
xEisenhower, Dwight D.
Crusade in Europe. Da Capo.
Letters to Mamie. Doubleday.
Eisenhower, Julie N. *see* Eisenhower, Julie Nixon.

Eisenhower, Julie Nixon.
xEisenhower, Julie N.
Special People. Ballantine.
Special People. S&S.

Eisenkramer, Henry E.
xEisenkramer, Henry E.
Classroom Music. Mark Foster Mus.
Eisenman, G. *see* Eisenman, George.

Eisenman, George.
xEisenman, G.
ed. Glass Electrodes for Hydrogen & Other Cations: Principles & Practice. Dekker.

Eisenmenger, Robert W.
xEisenmenger, Robert W.
The Dynamics of Growth in New England's Economy, 1870-1964. Columbia U Pr.

Eisenson, Jon, 1907-
xEisenson, Jon.

Aphasia in Children. Har-Row.
   ed. Stuttering: A Second Symposium. Har-Row.
   Voice & Diction: A Program for Improvement.
     Macmillan.
Eisenstadt, Abraham S. *see* Eisenstadt, Abraham Seldin.
Eisenstadt, Abraham Seldin, 1920-
   xEisenstadt, Abraham S.
   Charles McLean Andrews: A Study in
     American Historical Writing. AMS Pr.
Eisenstadt, S. N., 1923-
   xEisenstadt, S. N.
   Revolution & the Transformation of Societies:
     A Comparative Study of Civilizations. Free
     Pr.
Eisenstadt, S. N. *see* Eisenstadt, Shmuel Noah.
Eisenstadt, Samuel N. *see* Eisenstadt, Shmuel Noah.
Eisenstadt, Shmuel Noah.
   xEisenstadt, S. N.
   The Form of Sociology: Paradigms & Crises.
     Wiley.
   ed. Intellectuals & Tradition. Humanities.
   ed. Readings in Social Evolution &
     Development. Pergamon.
   ed. Socialism & Tradition. Humanities.
   xEisenstadt, Samuel N.
   From Generation to Generation: Age Groups
     & Social Structure. Free Pr.
   Integration & Development in Israel.
     Transaction Bks.
Eisenstaedt, Alfred.
   xEisenstaedt, Alfred.
   Eisenstaedt's Guide to Photography. Viking Pr.
   Martha's Vineyard. Penguin.
   People. Penguin.
Eisenstein, Ferdinand Gotthold Max, 1823-1852
   xEisenstein, Gotthold F.
   Mathematische Werke. Chelsea Pub.
Eisenstein, Gotthold F. *see* Eisenstein, Ferdinand
   Gotthold Max.
Eisenstein, James.
   xEisenstein, James.
   Counsel for the United States: U.S. Attorneys
     in the Political & Legal Systems. Johns
     Hopkins.
   Felony Justice: An Organizational Analysis of
     Criminal Courts. Little.
   Politics & the Legal Process. Har-Row.
Eisenstein, Phyllis.
   xEisenstein, Phyllis.
   Born to Exile. Arkham.
   Born to Exile. Dell.
Eisenstein, S. M. *see* Eisenstein, Sergei Mikhailovich.
Eisenstein, Sergei. *see* Eisenstein, Sergei Mikhailovich.
Eisenstein, Sergei Mikhailovich, 1898-1948
   xEisenstein, S. M.
   Que Viva Mexico!. Arno.
   xEisenstein, Sergei.
   Notes of a Film Director. Dover.
   Notes of a Film Director. Peter Smith.
Eisenstein, Zillah R.
   xEisenstein, Zillah R.
   ed. Capitalist Patriarchy & the Case for
     Socialist Feminism. Monthly Rev.
Eisinger, Chester E.
   xEisinger, Chester E.
   Fiction of the Forties. U of Chicago Pr.
Eisler, Benita.
   xEisler, Benita.
   ed. The Lowell Offering: Writings by New
     England Mill Women, 1840-1845. Har-Row.
   ed. The Lowell Offering: Writings by New
     England Mill Women 1840-1845. Lippincott.
Eisler, Colin. *see* Eisler, Colin T.
Eisler, Colin T.
   xEisler, Colin.
   Master of the Unicorn: The Life & Work of
     Jean Duvet. Abaris Bks.
Eisler, Paul E., 1919-
   xEisler, Paul E.

Compiled by World Chronology of Music
   History. Oceana.
Eisler, Riane.
   xEisler, Riane T.
   The Equal Rights Handbook. Avon.
Eisler, Riane T. *see* Eisler, Riane.
Eisner, Elliot W.
   xEisner, Elliot W.
   Conflicting Conceptions of Curriculum.
     McCutchan.
   Educating Artistic Vision. Macmillan.
   English Primary Schools: Some Observations &
     Assessments. Natl Assn Child Ed.
Eisner, Harry, 1893-
   xEisner, Harry.
   Classroom Teachers' Estimation of Intelligence
     & Industry of High School Students. AMS
     Pr.
Eisner, Lotte. *see* Eisner, Lotte H.
Eisner, Lotte H.
   xEisner, Lotte.
   Murnau. U of Cal Pr.
Eisner, Robert.
   xEisner, Robert.
   Factors in Business Investment. Ballinger Pub.
Eisner, Sigmund, 1920-
   xEisner, Sigmund.
   Tale of Wonder: A Source Study for the Wife
     of Bath's Tale. B Franklin.
   Tristan Legend: A Study in Sources.
     Northwestern U Pr.
Eisner, Victor.
   xEisner, Victor.
   Dimensions of School Health. C C Thomas.
Eisner, Vivien. *see* Eisner, Vivienne.
Eisner, Vivienne.
   xEisner, Vivien.
   Crafting with Newspapers. Sterling.
   xEisner, Vivienne.
   Quick & Easy Holiday Costumes. Lothrop.
Eissler, K. R. *see* Eissler, Kurt Robert.
Eissler, Kurt R. *see* Eissler, Kurt Robert.
Eissler, Kurt Robert, 1908-
   xEissler, K. R.
   Talent & Genius: The Fictitious Case of Tausk
     Contra Freud. Times Bks.
   xEissler, Kurt R.
   Medical Orthodoxy & the Future of
     Psychoanalysis. Intl Univs Pr.
   The Psychiatrist & the Dying Patient. Intl
     Univs Pr.
Eister, Allan W.
   xEister, Allan W.
   ed. Changing Perspectives in the Scientific
     Study of Religion. Krieger.
Eitan, Israel, 1885-
   xEitan, Israel.
   Contribution to Biblical Lexicography. AMS
     Pr.
Eiteman, David K.
   xEiteman, David K.
   Multinational Business Finance. A-W.
Eiteman, Wilford J. *see* Eiteman, Wilford John.
Eiteman, Wilford John, 1902
   xEiteman, Wilford J.
   Essentials of Accounting Theory. Masterco Pr.
   Leading World Stock Exchanges: Trading
     Practices & Organization. U Mich Busn Div
     Res.
   Personal Finance & Investment. Masterco Pr.
Eitz, Maria.
   xEitz, Maria.
   Dark Rice. Country Beautiful.
Eitzen. *see* Eitzen, D. Stanley.
Eitzen, D. Stanley.
   xEitzen.
   Social Problems. Allyn.
   xEitzen, D. Stanley.

In Conflict & Order: Understanding Society.
   Allyn.
   The Sociology of American Sport. Wm C
     Brown.
   ed. Sport in Contemporary Society: An
     Anthology. St Martin.
Ekberg, Carl J.
   xEkberg, Carl J.
   The Failure of Louis XIV's Dutch War. U of
     NC Pr.
Ekelund, R. B.
   xEkelund, R. B.
   A History of Economic Theory & Method.
     McGraw.
Ekirch, Arthur A. *see* Ekirch, Arthur Alphonse.
Ekirch, Arthur Alphonse, 1915-
   xEkirch, Arthur A.
   Idea of Progress in America, 1815-1860. AMS
     Pr.
   Idea of Progress in America, 1815-1860. Peter
     Smith.
   Progressivism in America: A Study of the Era
     from Theodore Roosevelt to Woodrow
     Wilson. New Viewpoints.
Eklund, Gordon.
   xEklund, Gordon.
   The Grayspace Beast. PB.
   Inheritors of Earth. BJ Pub Group.
Ekman, Paul.
   xEkman, Paul.
   Darwin & Facial Expression: A Century of
     Research in Review. Acad Pr.
Ekstein, Rudolf.
   xEkstein, Rudolf.
   The Teaching & Learning of Psychotherapy.
     Intl Univs Pr.
Eksteins, Modris.
   xEksteins, Modris.
   The Limits of Reason: The German
     Democratic Press & the Collapse of Weimar
     Democracy. Oxford U Pr.
Ekundare, R. O. *see* Ekundare, R. Olufemi.
Ekundare, R. Olufemi.
   xEkundare, R. O.
   Economic History of Nigeria 1860-1960.
     Holmes & Meier.
Ekvall, R. B. *see* Ekvall, Robert Brainerd.
Ekvall, Robert B. *see* Ekvall, Robert Brainerd.
Ekvall, Robert Brainerd, 1898-
   xEkvall, R. B.
   Fields on the Hoof: Nexus of Tibetan Nomadic
     Pastoralism. HR&W.
   xEkvall, Robert B.
   Faithful Echo. Coll & U Pr.
   Tents Against the Sky. Good News.
Ekwall. *see* Ekwall, Eldon E.
Ekwall, Eilert, 1877-1964
   xEkwall, Eilert.
   American & British Pronunciation. Folcroft.
   A History of Modern English Sounds &
     Morphology. Rowman.
Ekwall, Eldon. *see* Ekwall, Eldon E.
Ekwall, Eldon E.
   xEkwall.
   Ekwall Reading Inventory. Allyn.
   xEkwall, Eldon.
   Locating & Correcting Reading Difficulties.
     Merrill.
   xEkwall, Eldon E.
   Diagnosis & Remediation of the Disabled
     Reader. Allyn.
Ekwensi, Cyprian.
   xEkwensi, Cyprian O.
   Trouble in Form Six. Cambridge U Pr.
Ekwensi, Cyprian O. *see* Ekwensi, Cyprian.
El Azhary, M. S.
   xEl Azhary, M. S.

Political Cohesion of American Jews in
American Politics: A Reappraisal of Their
Role in Presidential Elections. U Pr of Amer.

El Gammal, Taher.
xEl Gammal, Taher.
An Atlas of Polytome Pneumography: With
Particular Reference to the Midline
Ventricles of the Brain. C C Thomas.

El Guindi, Fadwa.
xEl Guindi, Fadwa.
Religion in Culture. Wm C Brown.

El-Ashry, Mohamed T.
xEl-Ashry, Mohamed T.
ed. Air Photography & Coastal Problems. Acad
Pr.

El-Hawary, M. E.
xEl-Hawary, M. E.
Optimal Economic Operation of Electric Power
Systems. Acad Pr.

El-Hinnawi, Essam E.
xEl-Hinnawi, Essam E.
ed. Nuclear Energy & the Environment.
Pergamon.

El-Hodiri, M. A. see El-Hodiri, Mohamed A.
El-Hodiri, Mohamed A.
xEl-Hodiri, M. A.
Constrained Extrema: Introduction to the
Differentiable Case with Economic
Applications. Springer-Verlag.

El-Khawas, Mohamed A.
xEl-Khawas, Mohamed A.
Compiled by American-Southern African
Relations: Bibliographic Essays. Greenwood.

El-Messidi, Kathy. see El-Messidi, Kathy Groehn.
El-Messidi, Kathy Groehn, 1946-
xEl-Messidi, Kathy.
The Bargain. Caroline Hse.

El-Najjar, Mahmond Y.
xEl-Najjar, Mahmoud Y.
Forensic Anthropology: The Structure,
Morphology, & Variation of Human Bone &
Dentition. C C Thomas.

El-Najjar, Mahmoud Y. see El-Najjar, Mahmond Y.
El-Namaki, M. S. see El-Namaki, M. S. S.
El-Namaki, M. S. S., 1941-
xEl-Namaki, M. S.
Problems of Management in a Developing
Environment: The Case of Tanzania (State
Enterprises Between 1967 & 1975). Elsevier.

El-Rashidi, Galal, 1930-
xEl-Rashidi, Galal.
Arabs & the World of the Seventies. Verry.

Elam, Houston G.
xElam, Houston G.
Marketing for the Non-Marketing Executive.
Am Mgmt.

Elam, Stanley. see Elam, Stanley Munson.
Elam, Stanley Munson.
xElam, Stanley.
ed. A Decade of Gallup Polls of Attitudes
Toward Education: 1969-1978. Phi Delta
Kappa.

Elandt-Johnson, Regina C., 1918-
xElandt-Johnson, Regina C.
Probability Models & Statistical Methods in
Genetics. Wiley.
Survival Models & Data Analysis. Wiley.

Elazar, Daniel J. see Elazar, Daniel Judah.
Elazar, Daniel Judah.
xElazar, Daniel J.
American Federalism: A View from the States.
Har-Row.
American Partnership: Intergovernmental
Cooperation in Nineteenth Century United
States. U of Chicago Pr.
Community & Polity: The Organizational
Dynamics of American Jewry. Jewish Pubn.
Politics of Belleville: A Profile of the Civil
Community. Temple U Pr.

Elbaz, Jean S. see Elbaz, Jean Sauveur.

Elbaz, Jean Sauveur.
xElbaz, Jean S.
Plastic Surgery of the Abdomen. Masson Pub.

Elbert, George, 1911-
xElbert, George.
Plants That Really Bloom Indoors. S&S.
Plants That Really Bloom Indoors. S&S.
xElbert, George A.
Indoor Light Gardening Book. Crown.

Elbert, George A. see Elbert, George.

Elbert, Joyce.
xElbert, Joyce.
Crazy Ladies. NAL.
Crazy Lovers. NAL.
Drunk in Madrid. Arbor Hse.

Elbert, Samuel H.
xElbert, Samuel H.
ed. Hawaiian Grammar. U Pr of Hawaii.

Elbert, Virginie.
xElbert, Virginie Fowler.
Grow a Plant Pet. Doubleday.

Elbert, Virginie Fowler. see Elbert, Virginie.

Elbin, Paul N. see Elbin, Paul Nowell.
Elbin, Paul Nowell, 1905-
xElbin, Paul N.
Improvement of College Worship. AMS Pr.

Elbogen, Ismar, 1874-1943
xElbogen, Ismar.
A Century of Jewish Life. Jewish Pubn.

Elbourne, Edward T. see Elbourne, Edward Tregaskiss.
Elbourne, Edward Tregaskiss.
xElbourne, Edward T.
Factory Administration & Accounts. Arno.

Elbow, Peter.
xElbow, Peter.
Oppositions in Chaucer. Columbia U Pr.

Elbualy, Musallam S.
xElbualy, Musallam S.
Handbook of Clinical Dermatoglyphs. U of
Miami Pr.

Elcock, H. J.
xElcock, Howard.
Political Behaviour. Methuen Inc.

Elcock, Howard. see Elcock, H. J.
Eldefonso, E. see Eldefonso, Edward.
Eldefonso, Edward.
xEldefonso, E.
Control Treatment & Rehabilitation of Juvenile
Offenders. Glencoe.
xEldefonso, Edward.
Principles of Law Enforcement. Wiley.
Process & Impact of the Juvenile Justice
System. Glencoe.
Readings in Criminal Justice. Glencoe.

Elder, Arlene A.
xElder, Arlene A.
The Hindered Hand: Cultural Implications of
Early African-American Fiction. Greenwood.

Elder, Carl A.
xElder, Carl A.
Values & Moral Development in Children.
Broadman.

Elder, Fred S. see Elder, Frederick Stanton.
Elder, Frederick Stanton, 1868-
xElder, Fred S.
Morals & Religion. Philos Lib.

Elder, Glen H. see Elder, Glen H. Jr.
Elder, Glen H. Jr.
xElder, Glen H.
Children of the Great Depression: Social
Change in Life Experience. U of Chicago Pr.

Elder, John, 1933-
xElder, John.
The Bowels of the Earth. Oxford U Pr.

Elder, Joseph.
xElder, Joseph.
Farthest Reaches. Trident.

Elder, Leon.
xElder, Leon.

Hot Tubs: How to Build, Maintain & Enjoy
Your Own. Random.

Elder, N. C. see Elder, Neil C. M.
Elder, Neil C. M.
xElder, N. C.
Government in Sweden: The Executive at
Work. Pergamon.

Elder, William, 1806-1885
xElder, William.
Conversations on the Principal Subjects of
Political Economy. Garland Pub.

Eldersveld, Samuel. see Eldersveld, Samuel James.
Eldersveld, Samuel James.
xEldersveld, Samuel.
Citizens & Politics: Mass Political Behavior in
India. U of Chicago Pr.

Elderton, W. P. see Elderton, William Palin.
Elderton, William Palin.
xElderton, W. P.
Systems of Frequency Curves. Cambridge U Pr.

Eldred, Gary W.
xEldred, Gary W.
House for Sale. Harbour Hse.

Eldred, Pat. see Eldred, Patricia Mulrooney.
Eldred, Patricia M. see Eldred, Patricia Mulrooney.
Eldred, Patricia Mulrooney.
xEldred, Pat.
Easy Money Making Projects. Creative Ed.
xEldred, Patricia M.
Diana Ross. Creative Ed.

Eldredge, W. Jay. see Eldredge, Walter Jay.
Eldredge, Walter Jay.
xEldredge, W. Jay.
ed. Current Problems in Congenital Heart
Disease. Spectrum Pub.

Eldridge, Albert F.
xEldridge, Albert F.
ed. Legislatures in Plural Societies: The Search
for Cohesion in National Development.
Duke.

Eldridge, Evelyn.
xEldridge, Evelyn.
Environmental Issues: Family Impact. Burgess.

Eldridge, F. P. see Eldridge, Frank R.
Eldridge, Frank R.
xEldridge, F. P.
Wind Machines. Solar Energy Info.
xEldridge, Frank R.
Wind Machines. Van Nos Reinhold.

Eldridge, Hope T. see Eldridge, Hope Tisdale.
Eldridge, Hope Tisdale.
xEldridge, Hope T.
The Materials of Demography: A Selected &
Annotated Bibliography. Greenwood.

Eldridge, J. E. see Eldridge, John E.
Eldridge, John E.
xEldridge, J. E.
A Sociology of Organisations. Allen Unwin.

Eldridge, P. J. see Eldridge, Philip John.
Eldridge, Philip John.
xEldridge, P. J.
The Politics of Foreign Aid in India. Schocken.

Eldridge, Roswell.
xEldridge, Roswell.
ed. Dystonia. Raven.

Electric Power Research Institute.
xElectric Power Research Institute.
Electric Utility Solar Energy Activities. Solar
Energy Info.

**Electron Beam Processing Seminar, 3rd,
Stratford-Upon-Avon, 1974.**
xElectron Beam Processing Seminar 3rd.
Proceedings. Univ Tech.

Electron Microscopy Society. see Electron Microscopy
Society of America.
Electron Microscopy Society of America.
xElectron Microscopy Society.
Proceedings. Claitors.

Electronic Design.
xElectronic Design.

Elbaz, Jean S. see Elbaz, Jean Sauveur.

Four Hundred Ideas for Design. Hayden.
Microprocessor Basics. Hayden.
Electronic Technician-Dealer.
  xET D Staff.
    Color TV Trouble Factbook: Problems &
    Solutions. Tab Bks.
  xETD Magazine Editors.
    Color TV Trouble Factbook. TAB Bks.
Electronics.
  xElectronics Magazine.
    Active Filters. McGraw.
    Applying Microprocessors. McGraw.
    Applying Microprocessors. McGraw.
    Basics of Data Communications. McGraw.
    Circuits for Electronics Engineers. McGraw.
    Design Techniques for Electronics Engineers.
    McGraw.
    Design Techniques for Electronics Engineers.
    McGraw.
    Large Scale Integration. McGraw.
    McGraw-Hill's Leader in Electronics.
    McGraw.
    Memory Design: Microcomputers to
    Mainframes. McGraw.
    Microelectronics Interconnection & Packaging.
    McGraw.
    Microprocessors. McGraw.
    Microprocessors. McGraw.
    New Product Trends in Electronics Number
    One. McGraw.
    Practical Applications of Data
    Communications: A User's Guide. McGraw.
Electronics Illustrated.
  xElectronics Illustrated Editors.
    Best Electronics Projects. Arco.
Electronics Illustrated Editors. see Electronics Illustrated.
Electronics Magazine. see Electronics.
Elegant, Robert. see Elegant, Robert S.
Elegant, Robert S.
  xElegant, Robert.
    Hong Kong. Silver.
    Hong Kong. Time-Life.
  xElegant, Robert S.
    China's Red Masters: Political Biographies of
    the Chinese Communist Leaders. Greenwood.
Elert, W. see Elert, Werner.
Elert, Werner, 1885-1954
  xElert, W.
    The Lord's Supper Today. Concordia.
Eleventh European Peptide Symposium, Vienna, April
  1971. see European Peptide Symposium, 11th, Vienna,
  1971.
Elevitch, Franklin R.
  xElevitch, Franklin R.
    Fluorometric Techniques in Clinical Chemistry.
    Little.
Eley, Geoffrey.
  xEley, Geoffrey.
    Home Poultry Keeping. Charles River Bks.
Elfenbein, Julien, 1897-
  xElfenbein, Julien.
    Business Journalism. Greenwood.
    ed. Businesspaper Publishing Practice.
    Greenwood.
Elfers, Robert A.
  xElfers, Robert A
    A Sojourn in Mosaic. Friend Pr.
Elfman, Blossom.
  xElfman, Blossom.
    Butterfly Girl. HM.
    The Girls of Huntington House. HM.
    The Girls of Huntington House. Bantam.
    A House for Jonnie O. HM.
    A House for Jonnie O.. Bantam.
Elford, Homer J. see Elford, Homer J. R.
Elford, Homer J. R.
  xElford, Homer J.
    Guide to Church Ushering. Abingdon.
Elgerd, Olle I. see Elgerd, Olle Ingemar.

Elgerd, Olle Ingemar, 1925-
  xElgerd, Olle I.
    Control Systems Theory. Krieger.
    Control Systems Theory. McGraw.
Elgin, Kathleen, 1923-
  xElgin, Kathleen.
    The Fall Down, Break a Bone, Skin Your Knee
    Book. Walker & Co.
    Twenty-Eight Days. McKay.
Elgin, Robert, 1921-
  xElgin, Robert.
    The Tiger Is My Brother. Morrow.
Elgin, S. see Elgin, Suzette Haden.
Elgin, Suzette H. see Elgin, Suzette Haden.
Elgin, Suzette Haden.
  xElgin, S.
    What Is Linguistics?. P-H.
  xElgin, Suzette H.
    Pouring Down Words. P-H.
    A Primer of Transformational Grammar for
    Rank Beginners. NCTE.
  xElgin, Suzette Haden.
    Star-Anchored, Star-Angered. Doubleday.
Elgood, Cyril, 1892-
  xElgood, Cyril.
    Medicine in Persia. AMS Pr.
Elgood, Robert.
  xElgood, Robert.
    ed. Islamic Arms & Armour. Biblio Dist.
Eliade, Mircea, 1907-
  xEliade, Mircea.
    Australian Religions: An Introduction. Cornell
    U Pr.
    The Forge & the Crucible: The Origins &
    Structures of Alchemy. U of Chicago Pr.
    From Primitives to Zen: A Thematic
    Sourcebook in the History of Religions.
    Har-Row.
    ed. History of Religions. Essays in
    Methodology. U of Chicago Pr.
    The Old Man & the Bureaucrats. U of Notre
    Dame Pr.
    Patanjali & Yoga. Schocken.
    The Two & the One. U of Chicago Pr.
Elias, Albert J.
  xElias, Albert J.
    The Sonora Mutation. Avon.
Elias, Hans. see Elias, Hans Michael.
Elias, Hans Michael.
  xElias, Hans.
    Histology & Human Microanatomy. Wiley.
Elias, John L., 1933-
  xElias, John L.
    Conscientization & Deschooling: Freire's &
    Illich's Proposals for Reshaping Society.
    Westminster.
Elias, Norbert.
  xElias, Norbert.
    The Civilizing Process. Urizen Bks.
Elias, T. O. see Elias, Taslim Olawale.
Elias, Taslim Olawale.
  xElias, T. O.
    The Modern Law of Treaties. Oceana.
Eliason, Alan. see Eliason, Alan L.
Eliason, Alan L.
  xEliason, Alan.
    Business Computer Systems & Applications.
    SRA.
Eliason, Claudia. see Eliason, Claudia Fuhriman.
Eliason, Claudia F. see Eliason, Claudia Fuhriman.
Eliason, Claudia Fuhriman.
  xEliason, Claudia.
    A Practical Guide to Early Childhood
    Curriculum. Mosby.
  xEliason, Claudia F.
    A Practical Guide to Early Childhood
    Curriculum. Mosby.
Eliason, Robert E.
  xEliason, Robert E.

Early American Brass Makers. Brass Pr.
Eliassen, Arnt.
  xEliassen, Arnt.
    Meteorology: An Introductory Course.
    Universitet.
Eliel, E. L. see Eliel, Ernest Ludwig.
Eliel, Ernest L. see Eliel, Ernest Ludwig.
Eliel, Ernest Ludwig, 1921-
  xEliel, E. L.
    Stereochemistry of Carbon Compounds.
    McGraw.
  xEliel, Ernest L.
    ed. Conformational Analysis. Wiley.
Elimelech, Baruch.
  xElimelech, Baruch.
    A Tonal Grammar of Etsako. U of Cal Pr.
Elinson. see Elinson, Samuil Vladimirovich.
Elinson, Samuil Vladimirovich.
  xElinson.
    Analytical Chemistry of Zirconium & Hafnium.
    Halsted Pr.
Elion. see Elion, Glenn R.
Elion, G. see Elion, Glenn R.
Elion, Glenn R.
  xElion.
    jt. auth. Electro-Optics Handbook. Dekker.
  xElion, G.
    Fiber Optics in Communications Systems.
    Dekker.
Eliopoulos, Charlotte.
  xEliopoulos, Charlotte K.
    Gerontological Nursing. Lippincott.
Eliopoulos, Charlotte K. see Eliopoulos, Charlotte.
Eliot, Alexander.
  xEliot, Alexander.
    Zen Edge. Continuum.
Eliot, Charles. see Eliot, Charles Norton Edgecumbe.
Eliot, Charles Norton Edgecumbe, Sir, 1862-1931
  xEliot, Charles.
    Hinduism & Buddhism: An Historical Sketch.
    Routledge & Kegan.
Eliot, Charles W. see Eliot, Charles William.
Eliot, Charles William, 1834-1926
  xEliot, Charles W.
    Four American Leaders. Arden Lib.
    Four American Leaders. Folcroft.
    Late Harvest: Miscellaneous Papers Written
    Between Eighty & Ninety. Arno.
Eliot, George, 1819-1880
  xEliot, George.
    Adam Bede. Buccaneer Bks.
    Adam Bede. Dutton.
    Adam Bede. Merrimack Bk Serv.
    Adam Bede. NAL.
    Adam Bede. Penguin.
    Adam Bede. HM.
    Adam Bede. Airmont.
    Daniel Deronda. Merrimack Bk Serv.
    Daniel Deronda. NAL.
    Daniel Deronda. Penguin.
    Daniel Deronda. Peter Smith.
    Early Essays. Folcroft.
    Early Essays. R West.
    Felix Holt, the Radical. Dutton.
    Felix Holt, the Radical. Penguin.
    George Eliot's Life As Related in Her Letters
    & Journals. Scholarly.
    Silas Marner. Heinemann Ed.
    Silas Marner. Merrimack Bk Serv.
    Silas Marner. Penguin.
    Silas Marner. NAL.
    Silas Marner. PB.
    Silas Marner. Airmont.
    Silas Marner. AMSCO Sch.
    Silas Marner: The Weaver of Raveloe. Dutton.
Eliot Hurst, Michael. see Eliot Hurst, Michael E.
Eliot, R. C. see Eliot, Robert C.
Eliot, Robert C.
  xEliot, R. C.

ed. Boiler Fuel Additives for Pollution
Reduction & Energy Saving. Noyes.
ed. Coal Desulfurization Prior to Combustion.
Noyes.
Eliot, Robert S.
xEliot, Robert S.
ed. Cardiac Emergencies. Futura Pub.
Stress & the Major Cardiovascular Disorders.
Futura Pub.
Eliot, T. S. *see* Eliot, Thomas Stearns.
Eliot, Thomas S. *see* Eliot, Thomas Stearns.
Eliot, Thomas Stearns, 1888-
xEliot, T. S.
Cocktail Party. HarBraceJ.
Collected Poems, 1909-1962. HarBraceJ.
Complete Poems & Plays, 1909-1950.
HarBraceJ.
Four Quartets. Aurora Pubs.
Four Quartets. HarBraceJ.
Murder in the Cathedral. HarBraceJ.
Notes Towards the Definition of Culture.
HarBraceJ.
On Poetry & Poets. FS&G.
On Poetry & Poets. Octagon.
xEliot, Thomas S.
Points of View. Hyperion Conn.
Eliot Hurst, Michael E.
xEliot Hurst, Michael.
I Came to the City: Essays & Comments on
the Urban Scene. HM.
Elisofon, Eliot.
xElisofon, Eliot.
The Sculpture of Africa. Hacker.
Elison, George.
xElison, George.
Deus Destroyed: The Image of Christianity in
Early Modern Japan. Harvard U Pr.
Elkana, Yehuda, 1934-
xElkana, Yehuda.
Discovery of the Conservation of Energy.
Harvard U Pr.
ed. Toward a Metric of Science: The Advent of
Science Indicators. Wiley.
Elkin, A. P. *see* Elkin, Adolphus Peter.
Elkin, Adolphus P. *see* Elkin, Adolphus Peter.
Elkin, Adolphus Peter, 1891-
xElkin, A. P.
Aboriginal Men of High Degree. St Martin.
xElkin, Adolphus P.
Studies in Australian Totemism. AMS Pr.
Elkin, Benjamin.
xElkin, Benjamin.
How the Tsar Drinks Tea. Schol Bk Serv.
Such Is the Way of the World. Schol Bk Serv.
Elkin, Judith L. *see* Elkin, Judith Laikin.
Elkin, Judith Laikin, 1928-
xElkin, Judith L.
Jews of the Latin American Republics. U of
NC Pr.
Elkin, P. K. *see* Elkin, Peter Kingsley.
Elkin, Peter Kingsley.
xElkin, P. K.
The Augustan Defence of Satire. Oxford U Pr.
ed. Australian Poems in Perspective: A
Collection of Poems & Critical
Commentaries. U of Queensland Pr.
Elkin, Stanley, 1930-
xElkin, Stanley.
Criers & Kibitzers, Kibitzers & Criers. NAL.
Criers & Kibitzers, Kibitzers & Criers. Warner
Bks.
Elkind, David, 1931-
xElkind, David.

Child Development & Education: A Piagetian
Perspective. Oxford U Pr.
The Child's Reality: Three Developmental
Themes. Halsted Pr.
Development of the Child. Wiley.
ed. Readings in Human Development:
Contemporary Perspectives. Har-Row.
Elkins, A. *see* Elkins, Arthur.
Elkins, Arthur.
xElkins, A.
Management: Structures, Functions, &
Practices. A-W.
Elkins, Deborah.
xElkins, Deborah.
Teaching Literature: Designs for Cognitive
Development. Merrill.
Elkins, Dov P. *see* Elkins, Dov Peretz.
Elkins, Dov Peretz.
xElkins, Dov P.
ed. Glad to Be Me: Building Self-Esteem in
Yourself & Others. P-H.
Humanizing Jewish Life. A S Barnes.
Jewish Consciousness Raising: A Handbook of
50 Experiential Exercises for Jewish Groups.
Growth Assoc.
ed. Self Concept Sourcebook: Ideas &
Activities for Building Self Esteem. Growth
Assoc.
xElkins, Dov Peretz.
Teaching People to Love Themselves: A
Leader's Handbook of Theory & Technique
for Self-Esteem & Affirmation Training.
Growth Assoc.
Elkins, Hervey.
xElkins, Hervey.
Fifteen Years in the Senior Order of Shakers:
A Narration of Facts, Concerning That
Singular People. AMS Pr.
Elkins, Pete.
xElkins, Pete.
Catching Freshwater Striped Bass: Fish of the
Future. EPM Pubns.
Elkins, W. F.
xElkins, W. F.
Street Preachers, Faith Healers & Herb
Doctors in Jamaica, 1890-1925. Revisionist
Pr.
Elkins, William R.
xElkins, William R.
Literary Reflections. McGraw.
Ellacombe, Henry N. *see* Ellacombe, Henry Nicholson.
Ellacombe, Henry Nicholson, 1821-1916
xEllacombe, Henry N.
Plant-Lore & Garden-Craft of Shakespeare.
AMS Pr.
Ellacott, S. E.
xEllacott, S. E.
illus. Spearman to Minuteman: The Story of
the Soldier: 2000 B.C. - 1783 A.D. Abelard.
Ellacuria, Ignacio.
xEllacuria, Ignacio.
Freedom Made Flesh: The Mission of Christ &
His Church. Orbis Bks.
Ellard, John.
xEllard, John.
Normal & Pathological Responses to
Bereavement. Mss Info.
Ellberg, John.
xEllberg, John.
Tales of a Rambler. Arno.
Elledge, Scott.
xElledge, Scott.
ed. Continental Model: Selected French
Critical Essays of the Seventeenth Century,
in English Translation. Cornell U Pr.
Elledge, W. Paul, 1938-
xElledge, W. Paul.
Byron & the Dynamics of Metaphor.
Vanderbilt U Pr.
Ellefson, Ashley C. *see* Ellefson, C. Ashley.

Ellefson, C. Ashley.
xEllefson, Ashley C.
The Higher Schooling in the United States.
Two Continents.
xEllefson, C. Ashley.
The Higher Schooling in the United States.
Schenkman.
Ellegard, Alvar.
xEllegard, Alvar.
Who Was Junius?. Greenwood.
Elleinstein, Jean.
xElleinstein, Jean.
The Stalin Phenomenon. Humanities.
Ellenberger, D. Fred.
xEllenberger, D. Fred.
History of the Basuto, Ancient & Modern.
Negro U Pr.
Ellenberger, Henri F., 1905-
xEllenberger, Henri F.
Discovery of the Unconscious: The History &
Evolution of Dynamic Psychiatry. Basic.
Ellenberger, W. *see* Ellenberger, Wilhelm.
Ellenberger, Wilhelm, 1848-1929
xEllenberger, W.
An Atlas of Animal Anatomy for Artists. Peter
Smith.
Atlas of Animal Anatomy for Artists. Dover.
Ellenbogen, Abraham.
xEllenbogen, Abraham.
Letter Perfect: A Business Person's Guide to
More Effective Correspondence. Macmillan.
Ellenburg, M. Kelly.
xEllenburg, M. Kelly.
Effanbee, the Dolls with the Golden Hearts.
Trojan Pr.
Ellenson, Ann, 1936-
xEllenson, Ann.
Human Relations. P-H.
Ellentuck, Albert B.
xEllentuck, Albert B.
Practical Merger Techniques for Buying &
Selling a Business: Successful Tax & Financial
Strategies. Commerce.
Eller, Ernest M. *see* Eller, Ernest McNeill.
Eller, Ernest McNeill, 1903-
xEller, Ernest M.
Soviet Sea Challenge. Contemp Bks.
Eller, Vernard.
xEller, Vernard.
Cleaning up the Christian Vocabulary.
Brethren.
The Outward Bound: Caravaning As the Style
of the Church. Eerdmans.
The Simple Life: The Christian Stance Toward
Possessions. Eerdmans.
Ellery, Eloise, 1874-
xEllery, Eloise.
Brissot De Warville: A Study in the History of
the French Revolution. AMS Pr.
Brissot De Warville: A Study in the History of
the French Revolution. B Franklin.
Ellet, Elizabeth F. *see* Ellet, Elizabeth Fries Lummis.
Ellet, Elizabeth Fries Lummis, 1818-1877
xEllet, Elizabeth F.
The Pioneer Women of the West. Arno.
The Pioneer Women of the West. Longwood
Pr.
Ellett, Marcella H. *see* Ellett, Marcella Howard.
Ellett, Marcella Howard.
xEllett, Marcella H.
Textiles for Teens. Burgess.
The World of Children. Burgess.
Ellfeldt, Lois.
xEllfeldt, Lois.
Exercises for the Mature Adult. C C Thomas.
Primer for Choreographers. Mayfield Pub.
This Is Ballroom Dance. Mayfield Pub.
xEllfeldt, Lois E.
Folk Dance. Wm C Brown.
Ellfeldt, Lois E. *see* Ellfeldt, Lois.

Elliff, Mary, 1897-
xElliff, Mary.
Some Relationships Between Supply &
Demand for Newly Trained Teachers: A
Survey of the Situation in a Selected
Representative State, Missouri. AMS Pr.
Elliff, Thomas D.
xElliff, Thomas D.
Praying for Others. Broadman.
Ellin, Stanley.
xEllin, Stanley.
The Eighth Circle. Gregg.
Star Light, Star Bright. Random.
Elling, Ray H., 1929-
xElling, Ray H.
ed. Cross National Study of Health Systems:
Concepts, Methods, & Data Sources: a Guide
to Information Sources. Gale.
ed. Medical Sociologists at Work. Transaction
Bks.
ed. National Health Care: Issues & Problems in
Socialized Medicine. Lieber-Atherton.
Ellinger, Charles W.
xEllinger, Charles W.
ed. Synopsis of Complete Dentures. Lea &
Febiger.
Ellinger, Esther P. *see* Ellinger, Esther Parker.
Ellinger, Esther Parker.
xEllinger, Esther P.
Southern War Poetry of the Civil War. B
Franklin.
Ellinger, Herbert E.
xEllinger, Herbert E.
Automotive Electrical Systems. P-H.
Automotive Engines. P-H.
Automotive Suspension, Steering & Brakes.
P-H.
Ellington, Duke, 1899-1974
xEllington, Duke.
Music Is My Mistress. Da Capo.
Ellington, Mercer.
xEllington, Mercer.
Duke Ellington in Person: An Intimate
Memoir. HM.
Ellington, R. T.
xEllington, R. T.
ed. Liquid Fuels from Coal. Acad Pr.
Ellinwood, Leonard. *see* Ellinwood, Leonard Webster.
Ellinwood, Leonard Webster, 1905-
xEllinwood, Leonard.
History of American Church Music. Da Capo.
Elliot, Bob. *see* Elliot, Robert O. E.
Elliot, Elisabeth.
xElliot, Elisabeth.
Love Has a Price Tag. Christian Herald.
These Strange Ashes. Har-Row.
These Strange Ashes. Har-Row.
Twelve Baskets of Crumbs. Abingdon.
Twelve Baskets of Crumbs. Christian Herald.
Elliot, Geraldine.
xElliot, Geraldine.
Where the Leopard Passes: A Book of African
Folk Tales. Schocken.
Elliot, Jeffrey M.
xElliot, Jeffrey M.
Literary Voices. Borgo Pr.
Elliot, Jonathan.
xElliot, Jonathan.
ed. Debates in the Several State Conventions
on the Adoption of the Federal Constitution.
B Franklin.
The Funding System of the United States &
Great Britain. B Franklin.
Funding System of the United States & Great
Britain. Kelley.
Elliot, Margaret E.
xElliot, Margaret E.
Play with a Purpose: A Movement Program for
Children. Har-Row.
Elliot, Robert H. *see* Elliot, Robert Henry.

Elliot, Robert Henry, 1864-
xElliot, Robert H.
A Treatise on Glaucoma. Krieger.
Elliot, Robert O. E., 1902-
xElliot, Bob.
Northeastern Bass Fishing. Stone Wall Pr.
Elliot, Samuel H. *see* Elliot, Samuel Hayes.
Elliot, Samuel Hayes, 1809-1869
xElliot, Samuel H.
Parish-Side. Arno.
Elliot, Sharon.
xElliot, Sharon A.
The Busy People's Naturally Nutritious,
Decidedly Delicious, Fast Foodbook. Fresh
Pr.
Elliot, Sharon A. *see* Elliot, Sharon.
Elliot, Sumner L. *see* Elliot, Sumner Locke.
Elliot, Sumner Locke.
xElliot, Sumner L.
Going, PB.
Elliot, Zena. *see* Elliot, Zena Marjorie.
Elliot, Zena Marjorie.
xElliot, Zena.
Working with Copper. Sterling.
Elliott. *see* Elliott, Rachel Page.
Elliott, Alan C.
xElliott, Alan C.
On Sunday the Wind Came. Morrow.
Elliott, Albert P. *see* Elliott, Albert Pettigrew.
Elliott, Albert Pettigrew, 1893-
xElliott, Albert P.
Fatalism in the Works of Thomas Hardy.
Folcroft.
Fatalism in the Works of Thomas Hardy.
Russell.
Elliott, C. K. *see* Elliott, Charles Kenneth.
Elliott, Charles. *see* Elliott, Charles Newton.
Elliott, Charles Kenneth.
xElliott, C. K.
Guide to the Documentation of Psychology.
Shoe String.
Elliott, Charles Newton, 1906-
xElliott, Charles.
Care of Game Meat & Trophies. T Y Crowell.
Elliott, Clark A.
xElliott, Clark A.
Biographical Dictionary of American Science:
The Seventeenth Through the Nineteenth
Centuries. Greenwood.
Elliott, David, 1949-
xElliott, David.
Rodchenko & the Arts of Revolutionary
Russia. Pantheon.
Elliott, David M.
xElliott, David M.
Education & Research in the Nuclear Fuel
Cycle. U of Okla Pr.
Elliott, David S. *see* Elliott, David Stewart.
Elliott, David Stewart.
xElliott, David S.
Last Raid of the Daltons: Reliable Recital of
the Battle with the Bandits at Coffeyville,
Kansas. Arno.
Elliott, David W., 1939-
xElliott, David W.
Listen to the Silence. NAL.

Elliott, Donald.
xElliott, Donald.
Frogs & Ballet. Gambit.
Elliott, Douglas. *see* Elliott, Douglas A.
Elliott, Douglas A.
xElliott, Douglas.
Any Christian Can: A Personal Guide to
Individual Ministry. Word Bks.
Elliott, Edward C. *see* Elliott, Edward Charles.
Elliott, Edward Charles.
xElliott, Edward C.

ed. Charters & Basic Laws of Selected
American Universities & Colleges. AMS Pr.
Charters & Basic Laws of Selected American
Universities & Colleges. Greenwood.
Some Fiscal Aspects of Public Education in
American Cities. AMS Pr.
Elliott, Emory, 1942-
xElliott, Emory.
Power & the Pulpit in Puritan New England.
Princeton U Pr.
Elliott, George R. *see* Elliott, George Roy.
Elliott, George Roy, 1883-1963
xElliott, George R.
Flaming Minister: A Study of Othello As
Tragedy of Love & Hate. AMS Pr.
Elliott, Graeme Maurice.
xElliott, Maurice.
The Psychic Life of Jesus. Gordon Pr.
Elliott, Harley, 1940-
xElliott, Harley.
All Beautyfull & Foolish Souls. Crossing Pr.
Elliott, J. F. *see* Elliott, James Franklin.
Elliott, J. H. *see* Elliott, John Huxtable.
Elliott, James, Sir, 1880-1959
xElliott, James S.
Outlines of Greek & Roman Medicine.
Longwood Pr.
Elliott, James Franklin, 1924-
xElliott, J. F.
Interception Patrol: An Examination of the
Theory of Random Patrol As a Municipal
Police Tactic. C C Thomas.
Elliott, James S. *see* Elliott, James.
Elliott, John E.
xElliott, John E.
Competing Philosophies in American Political
Economics: Selected Readings with Essays &
Editorial Commentaries. Goodyear.
Elliott, John G., 1908-
xElliott, John G.
Matter, Life & Evolution. Gibson Hiller.
Elliott, John Huxtable.
xElliott, J. H.
Imperial Spain 1469-1716. NAL.
Elliott, John R.
xElliott, John R.
ed. The Prince of Poets: Essays on Edmund
Spenser. NYU Pr.
Elliott, Larry P.
xElliott, Larry P.
The X-Ray Diagnosis of Congenital Heart
Disease in Infants, Children & Adults:
Pathologic, Hemodynamic, & Clinical
Correlations As Related to Chest Film. C C
Thomas.
Elliott, Martin A. *see* Elliott, Martin Anderson.
Elliott, Martin Anderson.
xElliott, Martin A.
ed. Chemistry of Coal Utilization: Second
Supplementary Volume 2. Wiley.
Elliott, Maud H. *see* Elliott, Maud Howe.
Elliott, Maud Howe, 1854-1948
xElliott, Maud H.
This Was My Newport. Arno.
Uncle Sam Ward & His Circle. Arno.
Elliott, Maurice. *see* Elliott, Graeme Maurice.

Elliott, Neil.
xElliott, Neil.
The Gods of Life. Macmillan.
Elliott, Norman. *see* Elliott, Norman K.
Elliott, Norman K.
xElliott, Norman.
How to Be the Lord's Prayer. Macalester.
How to Be the Lord's Prayer. Word Bks.
Elliott, Orrin Leslie, 1860-1940
xElliott, Orrin Leslie.

Stanford University: The First Twenty-Five
Years. Arno.

Elliott, Rachel Page.
xElliott.
Dogsteps: Illustrated Gait at a Glance. Howell
Bk.

Elliott, Raymond.
xElliott, Raymond.
Fundamentals of Music. P-H.

Elliott, Richard V.
xElliott, Richard V.
Last of the Steamboats: The Saga of the Wilson
Line. Cornell Maritime.

Elliott, Robert C., 1914-
xElliott, Robert C.
Power of Satire: Magic, Ritual, Art. Princeton
U Pr.

Elliott, Robert J. *see* Elliott, Robert James.

Elliott, Robert James.
xElliott, Robert J.
The Existence of Value in Differential Games.
Am Math.

Elliott, Robert K.
xElliott, Robert K.
Management Fraud: Detection & Deterrence.
McGraw.

Elliott, Ruth, 1888-
xElliott, Ruth.
Organization of Professional Training in
Physical Education in State Universities.
AMS Pr.

Elliott, Sarah M.
xElliott, Sarah M.
Our Dirty Land. Messner.
Our Dirty Water. Messner.

Elliott, Shelden D. *see* Elliott, Shelden Douglas.

Elliott, Shelden Douglas, 1906-
xElliott, Shelden D.
Opportunities in a Law Career. Natl Textbk.

Elliott, Stewart.
xElliott, Stewart.
Timber Frame Planning Book. Contemp Bks.

Elliott, Sydney R. *see* Elliott, Sydney Robert.

Elliott, Sydney Robert, 1902-
xElliott, Sydney R.
English Cooperatives. Greenwood.

Elliott, Walter, 1842-1928
xElliott, Walter.
The Life of Father Hecker. Arno.

Elliott, William M. *see* Elliott, William Marion.

Elliott, William Marion, Jr, 1903-
xElliott, William M.
Cure for Anxiety. John Knox.

Elliott-Binns, Leonard E. *see* Elliott-Binns, Leonard
Elliott.

Elliott-Binns, Leonard Elliott, 1885-
xElliott-Binns, Leonard E.
From Moses to Elisha: Israel to the End of the
Ninth Century B. C.. Greenwood.

Ellis, A. E.
xEllis, A. E.
The Rack. Penguin.

Ellis, A. J. *see* Ellis, Albert James.

Ellis, Albert, 1913
xEllis, Albert.

Art & Science of Love. Lyle Stuart.
Brief Psychotherapy in Medical & Health
Practice. Springer Pub.
Creative Marriage. Lyle Stuart.
Executive Leadership: A Rational Approach.
Citadel Pr.
Executive Leadership: A Rational Approach.
Rational Living.
ed. Growth Through Reason: Verbatim Cases
in Rational-Emotive Therapy. Sci &
Behavior.
Humanistic Psychotherapy: The
Rational-Emotive Approach. Crown.
Humanistic Psychotherapy: The
Rational-Emotive Approach. McGraw.
If This Be Sexual Heresy. Lyle Stuart.
Reason & Emotion in Psychotherapy. Citadel
Pr.
Reason & Emotion in Psychotherapy. Lyle
Stuart.
Theoretical & Empirical Foundations of
Rational-Emotive Therapy. Brooks-Cole.

Ellis, Albert James.
xEllis, A. J.
ed. Chemistry & Geothermal Systems. Acad
Pr.

Ellis, Alec.
xEllis, Alec.
A History of Children's Reading & Literature.
Pergamon.
How to Find Out About Children's Literature.
Pergamon.
Library Services for Young People in England
& Wales, 1830-1970. Pergamon.

Ellis, Alexander J. *see* Ellis, Alexander John.

Ellis, Alexander John, 1814-1890
xEllis, Alexander J.
The History of Musical Pitch. Longwood Pr.

Ellis, Alfred B. *see* Ellis, Alfred Burdon.

Ellis, Alfred Burdon, 1852-1894
xEllis, Alfred B.
History of the Gold Coast of West Africa.
Negro U Pr.

Ellis, Anne, 1875-1938
xEllis, Anne.
The Life of an Ordinary Woman. Arno.
The Life of an Ordinary Woman. U of Nebr
Pr.

Ellis, Arthur K.
xEllis, Arthur K.
Teaching & Learning Elementary Social
Studies. Allyn.

Ellis, Arthur L.
xEllis, Arthur L.
A Mind on Harlem. R & E Res Assoc.

Ellis, Audrey.
xEllis, Audrey.
Complete Book of Home Freezing.
Transatlantic.
Cooking for Your Freezer. Transatlantic.
Meals to Enjoy from Your Freezer.
Transatlantic.

Ellis, Brian. *see* Ellis, Brian David.

Ellis, Brian David, 1929-
xEllis, Brian.
Rational Belief Systems. Rowman.

Ellis, C. H. *see* Ellis, Charles Howard.

Ellis, Charles Howard, 1895-
xEllis, C. H.
The British "Intervention" in Transcaspia,
1918-1919. U of Cal Pr.

Ellis, Chris.
xEllis, Chris.
How to Make Model Aircraft. Arco.

Ellis, D. *see* Ellis, David Maldwyn.

Ellis, David. *see* Ellis, David J.

Ellis, David J.
xEllis, David.

ed. In God's Community: Essays on the
Church & Its Ministry. Shaw Pubs.

Ellis, David M. *see* Ellis, David Maldwyn.

Ellis, David Maldwyn.
xEllis, D.
New York: the Empire State. P-H.
xEllis, David M.
History of New York State. Cornell U Pr.

Ellis, E. Earle. *see* Ellis, Edward Earle.

Ellis, Edward Earle.
xEllis, E. Earle.
Paul & His Recent Interpreters. Eerdmans.

Ellis, Ella T. *see* Ellis, Ella Thorp.

Ellis, Ella Thorp.
xEllis, Ella T.
Sleepwalker's Moon. Atheneum.
xEllis, Ella Thorp.
Hallelujah. Atheneum.

Ellis, F. S. *see* Ellis, Frederick Startridge.

Ellis, Frederick S. *see* Ellis, Frederick Stephen.

Ellis, Frederick Startridge, 1830-1901
xEllis, F. S.
An Alphabetical Table of Contents to Shelley's
Poetical Works. AMS Pr.

Ellis, Frederick Stephen.
xEllis, Frederick S.
History of St. Tammany Parish. Pelican.

Ellis, Geoffrey U. *see* Ellis, Geoffrey Uther.

Ellis, Geoffrey Uther, 1891-
xEllis, Geoffrey U.
Thackeray. Haskell.

Ellis, George A., 1947-
xEllis, George A.
Inside Folsom Prison: Transcendental
Meditation & the TM-Sidhi Program.
Chicago Review.

Ellis, George E. *see* Ellis, George Edward.

Ellis, George Edward, 1814-1894
xEllis, George E.
Puritan Age & Rule in the Colony of the
Massachusetts Bay, 1629-1685. B Franklin.

Ellis, George W. *see* Ellis, George Washington.

Ellis, George Washington, 1875-1919
xEllis, George W.
Negro Culture in West Africa: A Social Study
of the Negro Group of Vai-Speaking People,
with Its Own Invented Alphabet & Written
Language. Johnson Repr.

Ellis, Gwyn P. *see* Ellis, Gwynn Pennant.

Ellis, Gwynn Pennant.
xEllis, Gwyn P.
Medicinal Chemistry Reviews: A Select
Bibliography. Shoe String.

Ellis, Harold M. *see* Ellis, Harold Milton.

Ellis, Harold Milton, 1885-1947
xEllis, Harold M.
Joseph Dennie & His Circle: A Study in
American Literature from 1792-1812.
Johnson Repr.

Ellis, Harry B.
xEllis, Harry B.
The Dilemma of Israel. Am Enterprise.
Ideals & Ideologies: Communism, Socialism &
Capitalism. NAL.

Ellis, Havelock, 1859-1939
xEllis, Havelock.
Affirmations. Longwood Pr.
Chapman. Arden Lib.
Chapman. Folcroft.
Chapman. R West.
Criminal. AMS Pr.
The Criminal. Longwood Pr.
Criminal. Patterson Smith.
The Dance of Life. Greenwood.
The Dance of Life. R West.
My Confessional. Arno.
The Soul of Spain. Greenwood.
The Task of Social Hygiene. Arden Lib.
The World of Dreams. Gale.

Ellis, Howard S. *see* Ellis, Howard Sylvester.

Ellis, Howard Sylvester, 1898-
　xEllis, Howard S.
　　ed. The Economy of Brazil. U of Cal Pr.
　　Exchange Control in Central Europe.
　　　Greenwood.
　　Private Enterprise & Socialism in the Middle
　　　East. Am Enterprise.
Ellis, Jack. *see* Ellis, John T.
Ellis, Jack C.
　xEllis, Jack.
　　The Film Book Bibliography: 1940-1975.
　　　Scarecrow.
　xEllis, Jack C.
　　A History of Film. P-H.
Ellis, James E., 1945-
　xEllis, James E.
　　Buying & Owning Your Own Airplane. Iowa St
　　　U Pr.
Ellis, Jane, 1951-
　xEllis, Jane.
　　tr. An Early Soviet Saint: The Life of Father
　　　Zachariah. Templegate.
Ellis, Janice R. *see* Ellis, Janice Rider.
Ellis, Janice Rider.
　xEllis, Janice R.
　　Modules for Basic Nursing Skills. HM.
Ellis, Jeffrey.
　xEllis, Jeffrey.
　　Towards a General Comparative Linguistics.
　　　Mouton.
Ellis, Jessie (Croft).
　xEllis, Jessie C.
　　Index to Illustrations. Faxon.
Ellis, Jessie C. *see* Ellis, Jessie (Croft).
Ellis, John, 1945-
　xEllis, John.
　　The Cavalry: The History of Mounted Warfare.
　　　Putnam.
Ellis, John H. *see* Ellis, John Hubert.
Ellis, John Hubert, 1931-
　xEllis, John H.
　　Medicine in Kentucky. U Pr of Ky.
Ellis, John M. *see* Ellis, John Martin.
Ellis, John Martin.
　xEllis, John M.
　　The Theory of Literary Criticism: A Logical
　　　Analysis. U of Cal Pr.
Ellis, John T., 1922-
　xEllis, Jack.
　　Guide to Real Estate License Examinations.
　　　P-H.
　xEllis, John T.
　　Guide to Real Estate License Examinations.
　　　P-H.
Ellis, Joseph J.
　xEllis, Joseph J.
　　After the Revolution: Profiles of Early
　　　American Culture. Norton.
Ellis, Joyce. *see* Ellis, Joyce K.
Ellis, Joyce K.
　xEllis, Joyce.
　　The Big Split. Nelson.
Ellis, Julie.
　xEllis, Julie.
　　Eden. Fawcett.
　　The Girl in White. PB.
　　The Hampton Heritage. Fawcett.
　　The Hampton Heritage. S&S.
Ellis, June.
　xEllis, June.
　　ed. West African Families in Britain: A
　　　Meeting of Two Cultures. Routledge &
　　　Kegan.
Ellis, Keith, 1935-
　xEllis, Keith.
　　Critical Approaches to Ruben Dario. U of
　　　Toronto Pr.
　　Number Power: In Nature, Art, & Everyday
　　　Life. St Martin.
Ellis, Lewis E. *see* Ellis, Lewis Ethan.

Ellis, Lewis Ethan, 1898-
　xEllis, Lewis E.
　　Frank B. Kellogg & American Foreign
　　　Relations, 1925-1929. Greenwood.
Ellis, Loudell O.
　xEllis, Loudell O.
　　Church Treasurer's Handbook. Judson.
　　Intermediate Accounting. McGraw.
Ellis, M. J. *see* Ellis, Michael J.
Ellis, M. Leroy. *see* Ellis, Marion Leroy.
Ellis, Marc. *see* Ellis, Marc H.
Ellis, Marc H.
　xEllis, Marc.
　　A Year at the Catholic Worker. Paulist Pr.
Ellis, Maria Dej.
　xEllis, Maria deJ.
　　Agriculture & the State in Ancient
　　　Mesopotamia: An Introduction to Problems
　　　of Land Tenure. Univ Mus of U PA.
Ellis, Marion Leroy, 1928-
　xEllis, M. Leroy.
　　ed. Prose Classique. Wiley.
Ellis, Merle, 1934-
　xEllis, Merle.
　　Cutting up the Kitchen: The Butcher's Guide
　　　to Saving Money on Meat & Poultry.
　　　Chronicle Bks.
Ellis, Michael J.
　xEllis, M. J.
　　Activity & Play of Children. P-H.
Ellis, P. B. *see* Ellis, Peter Berresford.
Ellis, P. Beresford. *see* Ellis, Peter Berresford.
Ellis, Peter B. *see* Ellis, Peter Berresford.
Ellis, Peter Berresford.
　xEllis, P. B.
　　The Cornish Language & Its Literature.
　　　Routledge & Kegan.
　xEllis, P. Beresford.
　　The History of the Irish Working Class.
　　　Braziller.
　xEllis, Peter B.
　　The Boyne Water: The Battle of the Boyne,
　　　1690. St Martin.
　　Caesar's Invasion of Britain. NYU Pr.
　　H. Rider Haggard: A Voice from the Infinite.
　　　Routledge & Kegan.
Ellis, Philip P.
　xEllis, Phillip P.
　　Ocular Therapeutics & Pharmacology. Mosby.
Ellis, Phillip P. *see* Ellis, Philip P.
Ellis, Richard N., 1939-
　xEllis, Richard N.
　　General Pope & U. S. Indian Policy. U of NM
　　　Pr.
Ellis, Robert.
　xEllis, Robert.
　　Calculus with Analytic Geometry. HarBraceJ.
　　Lectures on Topological Dynamics.
　　　Benjamin-Cummings.
Ellis, Robert L.
　xEllis, Robert L.
　　Essential Sociology. Scott F.
Ellis, Theodore J. *see* Ellis, Theodore John.
Ellis, Theodore John.
　xEllis, Theodore J.
　　The Potential Role of Oil Shale in the U. S.
　　　Energy Mix: Questions of Development &
　　　Policy Formulation in an Environment Age.
　　　Arno.
Ellis, William D. *see* Ellis, William Donohue.
Ellis, William Donohue.
　xEllis, William D.
　　Clarke of St. Vith: The Sergeants' General.
　　　Dillon-Liederbach.
　　The Cuyahoga. Landfall Pr.
Ellis, Willis D. *see* Ellis, Willis Davis.
Ellis, Willis Davis.
　xEllis, Willis D.

　　ed. Source Book of Gestalt Psychology.
　　　Humanities.
Ellis-Fermor, Una. *see* Ellis-Fermor, Una Mary.
Ellis-Fermor, Una M. *see* Ellis-Fermor, Una Mary.
Ellis-Fermor, Una Mary.
　xEllis-Fermor, Una.
　　Some Recent Research in Shakespeare's
　　　Imagery. Folcroft.
　xEllis-Fermor, Una M.
　　Some Recent Research in Shakespeare's
　　　Imagery. Haskell.
Ellisen, Stanley A.
　xEllisen, Stanley A.
　　Divorce & Remarriage in the Church.
　　　Zondervan.
Ellison, Constance.
　xEllison, Constance M.
　　Gropings & Hopings. Windy Row.
Ellison, Constance M. *see* Ellison, Constance.
Ellison, Curtis W.
　xEllison, Curtis W.
　　Charles W. Chesnutt: A Reference Guide. G K
　　　Hall.
Ellison, Earl Jerome, 1907-
　xEllison, Jerome.
　　The Last Third of Life Club. Pilgrim NY.
　　Life's Second Half: The Pleasures of Aging.
　　　Devin.
　　Life's Second Half: The Pleasures of Aging. G
　　　K Hall.
Ellison, Elsie. *see* Ellison, Elsie C.
Ellison, Elsie C.
　xEllison, Elsie.
　　Fun with Lines & Curves. Lothrop.
Ellison, Fred P.
　xEllison, Fred P.
　　Brazil's New Novel: Four Northeastern
　　　Masters: Jose Lins do Rego, Jorge Amado,
　　　Graciliano, Rachel de Queiroz. Greenwood.
Ellison, Harlan.
　xEllison, Harlan.
　　ed. Again, Dangerous Visions. NAL.
　　Approaching Oblivion: Road Signs on the
　　　Treadmill Toward Tomorrow. Walker & Co.
　　ed. Dangerous Visions. NAL.
　　Deathbird Stories. Dell.
　　Deathbird Stories. Har-Row.
　　Strange Wine: Fifteen New Stories from the
　　　Nightside of the World. Har-Row.
Ellison, James W. *see* Ellison, James Whitfield.
Ellison, James Whitfield.
　xEllison, James W.
　　Proud Rachel. Stein & Day.
Ellison, Jerome. *see* Ellison, Earl Jerome.
Ellison, Lee M. *see* Ellison, Lee Monroe.
Ellison, Lee Monroe.
　xEllison, Lee M.
　　The Early Romantic Drama at the English
　　　Court. Folcroft.
Ellison, Lucile W. *see* Ellison, Lucile Watkins.
Ellison, Lucile Watkins.
　xEllison, Lucile W.
　　Butter on Both Sides. Scribner.
Ellison, T. *see* Ellison, Thomas.
Ellison, Thomas, 1833-1904
　xEllison, T.
　　Cotton Trade of Great Britain, 1886. Biblio
　　　Dist.
　xEllison, Thomas.
　　Cotton Trade of Great Britain. Kelley.
Ellison, Virginia H.
　xEllison, Virginia H.
　　The Pooh Cook Book. Dell.
　　Pooh Cookbook. Dutton.
　　The Pooh Get-Well Book. Dell.
　　The Pooh Party Book. Dell.
Ellison, William H. *see* Ellison, William Henry.
Ellison, William Henry.
　xEllison, William H.

The Federal Indian Policy in California,
1846-1860. R & E Res Assoc.
Elliston, Frederick.
xElliston, Frederick.
ed. Heidegger's Existential Analytic. Mouton.
Ellithorpe, Paul.
xEllithorpe, Paul.
Five Notes on the Stranger. Sunburst Pr.
Ellman, M. *see* Ellman, Michael.
Ellman, Michael.
xEllman, M.
Planning Problems in the USSR: The
Contribution of Mathematical Economics to
Their Solution, 1960-1971. Cambridge U Pr.
Ellmann, Richard, 1918-
xEllmann, Richard.
The Consciousness of Joyce. Oxford U Pr.
Identity of Yeats. Oxford U Pr.
Identity of Yeats. Oxford U Pr.
ed. Norton Anthology of Modern Poetry.
Norton.
Ulysses on the Liffey. Oxford U Pr.
Ellmore, R. Terry.
xEllmore, R. Terry.
The Illustrated Dictionary of
Broadcast-CATV-Telecommunications. TAB
Bks.
Ellner, Paul D. *see* Ellner, Paul Daniel.
Ellner, Paul Daniel, 1925-
xEllner, Paul D.
Current Procedures in Clinical Bacteriology. C
C Thomas.
Ellory, J. C. *see* Ellory, J. Clive.
Ellory, J. Clive.
xEllory, J. C.
ed. Membrane Transport in Red Cells. Acad
Pr.
Ellrodt, Robert.
xEllrodt, Robert.
Neoplatonism in the Poetry of Spenser. Arden
Lib.
Neoplatonism in the Poetry of Spenser.
Folcroft.
Ellsberg, Commander Edward, 1891-
xEllsberg, Edward.
Under the Red Sea Sun. Greenwood.
Ellsberg, Daniel.
xEllsberg, Daniel.
Papers on the War. PB.
Ellsberg, Edward. *see* Ellsberg, Commander Edward.
Ellsworth, Adelaide F. *see* Ellsworth, Adelaide Heidi
Frost.
Ellsworth, Adelaide Heidi Frost.
xEllsworth, Adelaide F.
The North American Opossum: An Anatomical
Atlas. Krieger.
Ellsworth, Donald P. *see* Ellsworth, Donald Paul.
Ellsworth, Donald Paul.
xEllsworth, Donald P.
Christian Music in Contemporary Witness:
Historical Antecedents & Contemporary
Practices. Baker Bk.
Ellsworth, Edward W.
xEllsworth, Edward W.
Liberators of the Female Mind: The Shirreff
Sisters, Educational Reform, & the Women's
Movement. Greenwood.
Ellsworth, Frank L.
xEllsworth, Frank L.
Law on the Midway: The Founding of the
University of Chicago Law School. U of
Chicago Pr.
Ellsworth, Henry W. *see* Ellsworth, Henry William.
Ellsworth, Henry William, 1814-1864
xEllsworth, Henry W.
Valley of the Upper Wabash, Indiana. Arno.
Ellsworth, Lucius F.
xEllsworth, Lucius F.

Craft to National Industry in the Nineteenth
Century: A Case Study of the Transformation
of the New York State Tanning Industry.
Arno.
Ellsworth, Ralph E. *see* Ellsworth, Ralph Eugene.
Ellsworth, Ralph Eugene, 1907-
xEllsworth, Ralph E.
Planning Manual for Academic Library
Buildings. Scarecrow.
Ellsworth, S. George. *see* Ellsworth, Samuel George.
Ellsworth, Samuel George, 1916-
xEllsworth, S. George.
Utah's Heritage. Peregrine Smith.
Ellul, Jacques.
xEllul, Jacques.
Apocalypse: The Book of Revelation. Seabury.
The Ethics of Freedom. Eerdmans.
Hope in Time of Abandonment. Seabury.
Meaning of the City. Eerdmans.
The Politics of God & the Politics of Man.
Eerdmans.
Prayer & Modern Man. Seabury.
Presence of the Kingdom. Seabury.
Propaganda: The Formation of Men's
Attitudes. Knopf.
Propaganda: The Formation of Men's
Attitudes. Random.
Ellwanger, H. B. *see* Ellwanger, Henry B.
Ellwanger, Henry B.
xEllwanger, H. B.
The Rose. E M Coleman Ent.
Ellwood, Charles A. *see* Ellwood, Charles Abram.
Ellwood, Charles Abram, 1873-1946
xEllwood, Charles A.
History of Social Philosophy. AMS Pr.
Story of Social Philosophy. Arno.
Ellwood, Robert S., 1933-
xEllwood, Robert S.
Alternative Altars: Unconventional & Eastern
Spirituality in America. U of Chicago Pr.
The Eagle & the Rising Sun: Americans & the
New Religions of Japan. Westminster.
An Invitation to Japanese Civilization.
Duxbury Pr.
Mysticism & Religion. P-H.
ed. Readings on Religion: From Inside &
Outside. P-H.
Ellyson, Mary H. *see* Ellyson, Mary Holbert.
Ellyson, Mary Holbert.
xEllyson, Mary H.
Mud & Money. Vantage.
Elmaghraby, F. E. *see* Elmaghraby, Salah Eldin.
Elmaghraby, S. E. *see* Elmaghraby, Salah Eldin.
Elmaghraby, Salah Eldin, 1927-
xElmaghraby, F. E.
Activity Networks: Project Planning & Control
by Network Models. Wiley.
xElmaghraby, S. E.
Some Network Models in Management
Science. Springer-Verlag.
Elman, Richard M.
xElman, Richard M.
Ill-at-Ease in Compton. Ultramarine Pub.
Elman, Robert.
xElman, Robert.
ed. All About Deer Hunting in America.
Winchester Pr.
Discover the Outdoors. Lion.
First in the Field: America's Pioneering
Naturalists. Van Nos Reinhold.
The Fisherman's Field Guide to the
Freshwater & Saltwater Gamefish of North
America. Knopf.
The Hiker's Bible. Doubleday.
Elmen, Paul.
xElmen, Paul.
Wheat Flour Messiah: Eric Jansson of Bishop
Hill. S Ill U Pr.
Elmendorf, Mary. *see* Elmendorf, Mary Lindsay.

Elmendorf, Mary Lindsay.
xElmendorf, Mary.
Nine Mayan Women: A Village Faces Change.
Schenkman.
Elmer, Carlos. *see* Elmer, Carlos H.
Elmer, Carlos H.
xElmer, Carlos.
Arizona in Color. Hastings.
Elmer, Elizabeth.
xElmer, Elizabeth.
Children in Jeopardy: A Study of Abused
Minors & Their Families. U of Pittsburgh Pr.
Fragile Families, Troubled Children: The
Aftermath of Infant Trauma. U of Pittsburgh
Pr.
Elmer, Herbert C. *see* Elmer, Herbert Charles.
Elmer, Herbert Charles, 1860-
xElmer, Herbert C.
Studies in Latin Moods & Tenses. Johnson
Repr.
Elmer, William B.
xElmer, William B.
The Optical Design of Reflectors. Wiley.
Elmes, James, 1782-1862
xElmes, James.
Thomas Clarkson: A Monograph: Being a
Contribution Towards the History of the
Abolition of the Slave Trade & Slavery.
Arno.
Elmore, D. T. *see* Elmore, Donald Trevor.
Elmore, Donald Trevor.
xElmore, D. T.
Peptides & Proteins. Cambridge U Pr.
Elmore, Francis H. *see* Elmore, Francis Hapgood.
Elmore, Francis Hapgood.
xElmore, Francis H.
Ethnobotany of the Navajo. AMS Pr.
Shrubs & Trees of the Southwest Uplands. SW
Pks Mnmts.
Elmore, Vernon. *see* Elmore, Vernon O.
Elmore, Vernon O.
xElmore, Vernon.
Exploring the Christian Way. Broadman.
Elms, Alan C., 1938-
xElms, Allan C.
Personality in Politics. HarBraceJ.
Elms, Allan C. *see* Elms, Alan C.
Elms, D. *see* Elms, David George.
Elms, David George.
xElms, D.
An Introduction to Modern Structural
Analysis. Gordon.
Elmslie, Kenward.
xElmslie, Kenward.
Moving Right Along. Z Pr.
Tropicalism. Z Pr.
Elmstrom, George. *see* Elmstrom, George P.
Elmstrom, George P.
xElmstrom, George.
Advanced Management for Optometrists. Prof
Press.
Elnett, Elaine. *see* Elnett, Elaine Pasvolsky.
Elnett, Elaine Pasvolsky, 1886-
xElnett, Elaine.
Historic Origin & Social Development of
Family Life in Russia. AMS Pr.
Elo, Arpad E., 1903-
xElo, Arpad E.
The Rating of Chess Players Past & Present.
Arco.
Elonka, Stephen M. *see* Elonka, Stephen Michael.
Elonka, Stephen Michael.
xElonka, Stephen M.

Standard Boiler Operators' Questions & Answers. McGraw.
Standard Industrial Hydraulics Questions & Answers. McGraw.
Standard Plant Operators Manual. McGraw.
Standard Plant Operators' Manual. McGraw.

Elovitz, Mark H.
xElovitz, Mark H.
A Century of Jewish Life in Dixie: The Birmingham Experience. U of Ala Pr.

Elrick, Harold.
xElrick, Harold.
Living Longer & Better: Guide to Optimal Health. Anderson World.

Elsasser, Walter M., 1904-
xElsasser, Walter M.
Atom & Organism: A New Approach to Theoretical Biology. Princeton U Pr.

Elsberg, John.
xElsberg, John.
The Price of Reindeer. White Ewe.

Elsberg, Ted.
xElsberg, Ted.
Career Exploration: You & Your Future. Fairchild.

Elsbree, Willard S. see Elsbree, Willard Slingerland.

Elsbree, Willard Slingerland, 1897-
xElsbree, Willard S.
American Teacher: Evolution of a Profession in a Democracy. Greenwood.
Teacher Turnover in the Cities & Villages of New York State. AMS Pr.

Elsby, F. H. see Elsby, Frank H.

Elsby, Frank H.
xElsby, F. H.
Marketing Cases. Pergamon.

Else, Gerald F. see Else, Gerald Frank.

Else, Gerald Frank, 1908-
xElse, Gerald F.
Aristotle's Poetics: The Argument. Univ Microfilms.
The Origin & Early Form of Greek Tragedy. Norton.

Elser, Smoke.
xElser, Smoke.
Packin' in on Mules & Horses. Mountain Pr.

Elsom, John.
xElsom, John.
Post-War British Theatre. Routledge & Kegan.

Elson, Arthur, 1873-1940
xElson, Arthur.
Modern Composers of Europe. Longwood Pr.

Elson, Benjamin. see Elson, Benjamin Franklin.

Elson, Benjamin Franklin.
xElson, Benjamin.
An Introduction to Morphology & Syntax. Summer Inst Ling.

Elson, Louis. see Elson, Louis Charles.
Elson, Louis C. see Elson, Louis Charles.

Elson, Louis Charles, 1848-1920
xElson, Louis.
History of American Music. Gordon Pr.
xElson, Louis C.
Great Composers & Their Work. Arno.
Great Composers & Their Work. Longwood Pr.
History of American Music. B Franklin.
The National Music of America & Its Sources. Gale.

Elson, Mark.
xElson, Mark.
Concepts of Programming Languages. SRA.
Data Structures. SRA.

Elson, Robert. see Elson, Robert T.

Elson, Robert T.
xElson, Robert.
Prelude to War. Time-Life.
Prelude to War. Silver.

Elster, Jon, 1940-
xElster, Jon.

Logic & Society: Contradictions & Possible Worlds. Wiley.

Elting, Irving.
xElting, Irving.
Dutch Village Communities on the Hudson River. AMS Pr.
Dutch Village Communities on the Hudson River. Johnson Repr.

Elting, Mary.
xElting, Mary.
The Hopi Way. M Evans.
A Mongo Homecoming. M Evans.
Still More Answers. G&D.

Elton, C. S. see Elton, Charles Sutherland.
Elton, Charles. see Elton, Charles Isaac.
Elton, Charles I. see Elton, Charles Isaac.

Elton, Charles Isaac.
xElton, Charles.
The Great Book Collectors. Gordon Pr.
xElton, Charles I.
Great Book-Collectors. R West.

Elton, Charles Sutherland, 1900-
xElton, C. S.
Animal Ecology. Methuen Inc.
The Ecology of Invasions by Animals & Plants. Methuen Inc.

Elton, Edwain J. see Elton, Edwin J.

Elton, Edwin J.
xElton, Edwain J.
Finance As a Dynamic Process. P-H.

Elton, G. see Elton, G. R.

Elton, G. R.
xElton, G.
ed. Annual Bibliography of British & Irish History: Publications of 1979. Humanities.

Elton, G. R. see Elton, Geoffrey Rudolph.
Elton, Geoffrey R. see Elton, Geoffrey Rudolph.

Elton, Geoffrey Rudolph.
xElton, G. R.
England Under the Tudors. Methuen Inc.
Modern Historians on British History, 1485-1945: A Critical Bibliography, 1945-1969. Cornell U Pr.
xElton, Geoffrey R.
Tudor Constitution: Documents & Commentary. Cambridge U Pr.

Elton, Godfrey. see Elton, Godfrey Elton.
Elton, Godfrey E. see Elton, Godfrey Elton.

Elton, Godfrey Elton, Baron, 1892-
xElton, Godfrey.
The Revolutionary Idea in France, 1789-1871. Fertig.
xElton, Godfrey E.
Revolutionary Idea in France, 1789-1871. AMS Pr.

Elton, O. see Elton, Oliver.

Elton, Oliver, 1861-1945
xElton, O.
Dickens & Thackeray. Haskell.
xElton, Oliver.
The Augustan Ages. Arden Lib.
The Augustan Ages. Folcroft.
The Brownings. Haskell.
The Brownings. R West.
Dickens & Thackeray. Folcroft.
Dickens & Thackeray. Porter.
Introduction to Michael Drayton. B Franklin.
Introduction to Michael Drayton. Folcroft.
Wordsworth. Folcroft.

Eltzbacher, Paul, 1868-1928
xEltzbacher, Paul.
Anarchism: Exponents of the Anarchist Philosophy. Arno.

Eluard, Paul.
xEluard, Paul.
Last Love Poems of Paul Eluard. La State U Pr.

Elvin, Charles N. see Elvin, Charles Norton.

Elvin, Charles Norton.
xElvin, Charles N.

Hand-Book of Mottoes: Borne by the Nobility, Gentry, Cities, Public Companies. Gale.

Elvin, Herbert Lionel, 1905-
xElvin, Lionel.
The Place of Commonsense in Educational Thought. Allen Unwin.

Elvin, Lionel. see Elvin, Herbert Lionel.

Elvin, Mark.
xElvin, Mark.
Pattern of the Chinese Past: A Social & Economic Interpretation. Stanford U Pr.

Elving, Bruce F.
xElving, Bruce F.
FM Atlas & Station Directory. F M Atlas.

Elwang, William W. see Elwang, William Wilson.

Elwang, William Wilson.
xElwang, William W.
The Negroes of Columbia, Missouri: A Concrete Study of the Race Problem. Metro Bks.

Elwell, Clarence E. see Elwell, Clarence Edward.

Elwell, Clarence Edward, 1904-
xElwell, Clarence E.
Influence of the Enlightenment on the Catholic Theory of Religious Education in France, 1750-1850. Russell.

Elwell, D. see Elwell, Dennis.

Elwell, Dennis.
xElwell, D.
Man-Made Gemstones. Halsted Pr.

Elwell, W. T. see Elwell, William Thomas.

Elwell, William Thomas.
xElwell, W. T.
Atomic Absorption Spectrophotometry. Pergamon.

Elwell-Sutton, Laurence. see Elwell-Sutton, Laurence Paul.

Elwell-Sutton, Laurence P. see Elwell-Sutton, Laurence Paul.

Elwell-Sutton, Laurence Paul.
xElwell-Sutton, Laurence.
Persian Oil: A Study in Power Politics. Greenwood.
xElwell-Sutton, Laurence P.
Persian Oil: A Study in Power Politics. Hyperion Conn.

Elwin, Malcolm, 1902-
xElwin, Malcolm.
Charles Reade. Russell.
De Quincey. Kennikat.
De Quincey. R West.
Lord Byron's Wife. Humanities.
Old Gods Falling. Arno.
Old Gods Falling. R West.
Old Gods Falling. Russell.
Strange Case of Robert Louis Stevenson. Russell.
Victorian Wallflowers. Core Collection.

Elwin, Verrier, 1902-1964
xElwin, Verrier.
The Baiga. AMS Pr.

Elwood, J. Mark.
xElwood, J. Mark.
Epidemiology of Anencephalus & Spina Bifida. Oxford U Pr.

Elwood, J. Murray.
xElwood, J. Murray.
Growing Together in Marriage. Ave Maria.
Kindly Light: The Spiritual Vision of John Henry Newman. Ave Maria.
A Month with Christ. Ave Maria.

Elwood, Roger.
xElwood, Roger.

Future City. PB.
ed. Future City. Trident.
ed. The Gifts of Asti & Other Stories of Science Fiction. Follett.
ed. More Science Fiction Tales: Crystal Creatures, Bird-Things, & Other Wierdies. Rand.
The Other Side of Tomorrow: Original Science Fiction Stories About Young People of the Future. Random.
ed. Survival from Infinity: Original Science Fiction Stories for Young Readers. Watts.

Ely, James W., 1938-
xEly, James W.
The Crisis of Conservative Virginia: The Byrd Organization & the Politics of Massive Resistance. U of Tenn Pr.

Ely, John H. *see* Ely, John Hart.
Ely, John Hart, 1938-
xEly, John H.
Democracy & Distrust: A Theory of Judicial Review. Harvard U Pr.

Ely, Richard T. *see* Ely, Richard Theodore.
Ely, Richard Theodore, 1854-1943
xEly, Richard T.
ed. Foundations of National Prosperity: Studies in the Conservation of Permanent National Resources. Johnson Repr.
Ground Under Our Feet: An Autobiography. Arno.
The Past & Present of Political Economy. Johnson Repr.
The Past & the Present of Political Economy. AMS Pr.

Ely, Vivian. *see* Ely, Vivien King.
Ely, Vivien King.
xEly, Vivian.
Starting Your Own Marketing Business. McGraw.

Elyot, Thomas, Sir, 1490?-1546
xElyot, Thomas.
Four Political Treatises, 1533-1541. Schol Facsimiles.

Elze, Karl, 1821-1889
xElze, Karl.
Notes on Elizabethan Dramatists with Conjectural Emendations of the Text. AMS Pr.

Elzey, Freeman F.
xElzey, Freeman F.
A First Reader in Statistics. Brooks-Cole.
An Introduction to Statistical Methods in the Behavioral Sciences. Brooks-Cole.

Elzinga, Richard J., 1931-
xElzinga, Richard J.
Fundamentals of Entomology. P-H.

Emans, S. J. *see* Emans, S. Jean Herriot.
Emans, S. Jean Herriot.
xEmans, S. J.
Pediatric & Adolescent Gynecology. Little.

Emants, Marcellus, 1848-1923
xEmants, Marcellus.
A Posthumous Confession. Twayne.

Emanuel, James A.
xEmanuel, James A.
A Chisel in the Dark: Poems: Selected & New. Lotus.

Emanuel, Lynn, 1949-
xEmanuel, Lynn.
Oblique Light. Slow Loris.

Emanuel, N. M. *see* Emanuel, Nikolai Markovich.
Emanuel, Nikolai Markovich.
xEmanuel, N. M.
Clinical Oncology: A Quantitative Approach. Halsted Pr.

Emanuel, Pericles.
xEmanuel, Pericles.

Introduction to Feedback Control Systems. McGraw.

Emberley, Barbara.
xEmberley, Barbara.
Drummer Hoff. P-H.
Story of Paul Bunyan. P-H.

Emberley, Ed.
xEmberley, Ed.
Ed Emberley's Amazing Look Through Book. Little.
illus. Ed Emberley's Big Green Drawing Book. Little.
illus. Ed Emberley's Drawing Book of Faces. Little.
illus. Ed Emberley's Great Thumbprint Drawing Book. Little.
Green Says Go. Little.

Emberley, Michael.
xEmberley, Michael.
illus. Dinosaurs!: A Drawing Book. Little.

Embertson, Jane.
xEmbertson, Jane.
Pods: Wildflowers & Weeds in Their Final Beauty. Scribner.

Embleton, Clifford.
xEmbleton, Clifford.
ed. Geomorphology: Present Problems & Future Prospects. Oxford U Pr.
ed. Process in Geomorphology. Halsted Pr.

Embling, Jack. *see* Embling, John Francis.
Embling, John Francis.
xEmbling, Jack.
A Fresh Look at Higher Education: European Implications of the Carnegie Commission Reports. Elsevier.

Emboden, William. *see* Emboden, William A.
Emboden, William A.
xEmboden, William.
Narcotic Plants. Macmillan.
Narcotic Plants. Macmillan.

Embree, Ainslie. *see* Embree, Ainslie Thomas.
Embree, Ainslie T. *see* Embree, Ainslie Thomas.
Embree, Ainslie Thomas.
xEmbree, Ainslie.
ed. Pakistan's Western Borderlands: The Transformation of a Political Order. Carolina Acad Pr.
xEmbree, Ainslie T.
Charles Grant & British Rule in India. AMS Pr.
ed. The Hindu Tradition. Random.

Embree, John F. *see* Embree, John Fee.
Embree, John Fee, 1908-1950
xEmbree, John F.
Suye Mura: A Japanese Village. U of Chicago Pr.

Embury, David A. *see* Embury, David Augustus.
Embury, David Augustus, 1886-
xEmbury, David A.
Fine Art of Mixing Drinks. Doubleday.

Emeleus, H. J. *see* Emeleus, Harry Julius.
Emeleus, Harry Julius.
xEmeleus, H. J.
Chemistry of Fluorine & Its Compounds. Acad Pr.
Modern Aspects of Inorganic Chemistry. Halsted Pr.

Emenegger, Robert.
xEmenegger, Robert.
UFO's Past, Present & Future. Ballantine.

Emerick, Lon. *see* Emerick, Lon L.
Emerick, Lon L.
xEmerick, Lon.
Parent Interview: Guidelines for Student & Practicing Speech Clinicians. Interstate.
xEmerick, Lon L.

ed. The Client-Clinician Relationship: Essays on Interpersonal Sensitivity in the Therapeutic Transaction. C C Thomas.
Diagnosis & Evaluation in Speech Pathology. P-H.
Therapy for Young Stutterers. Interstate.

Emerick, Robert H. *see* Emerick, Robert Henderson.
Emerick, Robert Henderson.
xEmerick, Robert H.
Troubleshooters Handbook for Mechanical Systems. McGraw.

Emerson, Barbara.
xEmerson, Barbara.
Leopold II of the Belgians: King of Colonialism. St Martin.

Emerson, David, 1900-
xEmerson, David.
The Fate of Esther Fox. Merrimack Bk Serv.

Emerson, Edward W. *see* Emerson, Edward Waldo.
Emerson, Edward Waldo, 1844-1930
xEmerson, Edward W.
Early Years of the Saturday Club, 1855-1870. Arno.

Emerson, Everett. *see* Emerson, Everett H.
Emerson, Everett H., 1925-
xEmerson, Everett.
ed. Letters from New England: The Massachusetts Bay Colony, 1629-1638. U of Mass Pr.
Puritanism in America. Twayne.
xEmerson, Everett H.
Captain John Smith. Twayne.
English Puritanism from John Hooper to John Milton. Duke.

Emerson, Geraldine M.
xEmerson, Geraldine M.
ed. Aging. Acad Pr.

Emerson, Harrington, 1853-1931
xEmerson, Harrington.
Efficiency As a Basis for Operation & Wages. Arno.
Efficiency As a Basis for Operation & Wages. Hive Pub.
Twelve Principles of Efficiency. Hive Pub.

Emerson, James C. *see* Emerson, James Christopher.
Emerson, James Christopher, 1913-
xEmerson, James C.
ed. The Life of Christ in the Conception & Expression of Chinese & Oriental Artists. Gloucester Art.

Emerson, Lloyd. *see* Emerson, Lloyd S.
Emerson, Lloyd S.
xEmerson, Lloyd.
Fundamental Mathematics for the Management & Social Sciences. Allyn.

Emerson, Lucy.
xEmerson, Lucy.
Gold Record. Fountain Pub Co NY.

Emerson, Nathaniel B. *see* Emerson, Nathaniel Bright.
Emerson, Nathaniel Bright, 1839-1915
xEmerson, Nathaniel B.
Pele & Hiiaka: A Myth from Hawaii. AMS Pr.
Pele & Hiiaka: A Myth from Hawaii. C E Tuttle.

Emerson, O. B.
xEmerson, O. B.
ed. Southern Literary Culture: A Bibliography of Masters' & Doctors' Theses. U of Ala Pr.

Emerson, O. F. *see* Emerson, Oliver Farrar.
Emerson, Oliver F. *see* Emerson, Oliver Farrar.
Emerson, Oliver Farrar, 1860-1927
xEmerson, O. F.
The History of the English Language. R West.
xEmerson, Oliver F.

Chaucer - Essays & Studies: A Selection from
the Writings of Oliver Farrar Emerson,
1860-1927. R West.
History of the English Language. Gale.
An Outline History of the English Language.
Folcroft.
Emerson, Ralph W. see Emerson, Ralph Waldo.
Emerson, Ralph Waldo.
xEmerson, Ralph W.
Correspondence Between Ralph Waldo
Emerson & Herman Grimm. Kennikat.
Emerson's Literary Criticism. U of Nebr Pr.
Letters from Ralph Waldo Emerson to a
Friend, 1838-1853. Kennikat.
On Man & God. Peter Pauper.
ed. Parnassus. Arno.
Parnassus. R West.
Parnassus. Somerset Pub.
xEmerson, Ralph Waldo.
The Works of Ralph Waldo Emerson. R West.
Emerson, Robert.
xEmerson, Robert.
Actors Guide to Monologues. Drama Bk.
Emerson, Rupert.
xEmerson, Rupert.
Government & Nationalism in Southeast Asia.
AMS Pr.
State & Sovereignty in Modern Germany.
Hyperion Conn.
Emerson, Thomas I. see Emerson, Thomas Irwin.
Emerson, Thomas Irwin, 1907-
xEmerson, Thomas I.
System of Freedom of Expression. Random.
Emerton, Ephraim, 1851-1935
xEmerton, Ephraim.
Learning & Living: Academic Essays. Arno.
Mediaeval Europe (814-1300). Norwood Edns.
Emerton, James H. see Emerton, James Henry.
Emerton, James Henry, 1847-1930
xEmerton, James H.
Common Spiders of the United States. Dover.
Common Spiders of the United States. Peter
Smith.
Emery, Alan E. see Emery, Alan E. H.
Emery, Alan E. H.
xEmery, Alan E.
Antenatal Diagnosis of Genetic Disease.
Churchill.
Elements of Medical Genetics. Churchill.
Elements of Medical Genetics. U of Cal Pr.
Emery, Anne, 1907-
xEmery, Anne.
Carey's Fortune. Westminster.
Dinny Gordon, Freshman. Macrae.
Dinny Gordon, Senior. Macrae.
Dinny Gordon, Sophomore. Macrae.
First Love, True Love. Westminster.
Free Not to Love. Westminster.
Going Steady. Westminster.
Stepfamily. Westminster.
Sweet Sixteen. Macrae.
Emery, Carla.
xEmery, Carla.
The Old Fashioned Recipe Book: The
Encyclopedia of Country Living. Bantam.
Emery, Clark. see Emery, Clark Mixon
Emery, Clark Mixon, 1909-
xEmery, Clark.
Ideas into Action: A Study of Pound's Cantos.
U of Miami Pr.
World of Dylan Thomas. U of Miami Pr.
Emery, D. A. see Emery, David A.
Emery, David A.
xEmery, D. A.
The Compleat Manager: Combining the
Humanistic & Scientific Approaches to the
Management Job. McGraw.
Emery, Donald W. see Emery, Donald William.
Emery, Donald William.
xEmery, Donald W.

Handbook of English Fundamentals.
Macmillan.
Variant Spellings in Modern American
Dictionaries. NCTE.
Emery, E. R. see Emery, Eric Roy John.
Emery, Edwin.
xEmery, Edwin.
History of the American Newspaper Publishers
Association. Greenwood.
Emery, Emma Wilson.
xEmery, Emma Wilson.
Aunt Puss & Others: Old Days in the Piney
Woods. Encino Pr.
Emery, Eric Roy John.
xEmery, E. R.
Principles of Intensive Care. Arco.
Emery, Henry C. see Emery, Henry Crosby.
Emery, Henry Crosby, 1872-1924
xEmery, Henry C.
Speculation on the Stock & Produce Exchanges
of the United States. AMS Pr.
Speculation on the Stock & Produce Exchanges
of the United States. Greenwood.
Emery, Jared M.
xEmery, Jared M.
Phacoemulsification & Aspiration of Cataracts:
Surgical Techniques, Complications &
Results. Mosby.
Emery, Laura. see Emery, Laura Comer.
Emery, Laura Comer.
xEmery, Laura.
George Eliot's Creative Conflict: The Other
Side of Silence. U of Cal Pr.
Emery, Leslie.
xEmery, Leslie.
Horseshoeing Theory & Hoof Care. Lea &
Febiger.
Emery, Pierre Yves.
xEmery, Pierre-Yves.
Prayer at the Heart of Life. Orbis Bks.
Emery, Pierre-Yves. see Emery, Pierre Yves.
Emery, Sarah A. see Emery, Sarah Smith.
Emery, Sarah Smith.
xEmery, Sarah A.
Reminiscences of a Newburyport
Nonagenarian. Heritage Bk.
Emery, Stewart.
xEmery, Stewart.
Actualizations: You Don't Have to Rehearse to
Be Yourself. Doubleday.
Actualizations: You Don't Have to Rehearse to
Be Yourself. Irvington.
Emery, Walter Byron, 1907-
xEmery, Walter Byron.
Broadcasting & Government: Responsibilities &
Regulations. Mich St U Pr.
National & International Systems of
Broadcasting: Their History, Operation &
Control. Mich St U Pr.
Emhardt, William C. see Emhardt, William Chauncey.
Emhardt, William Chauncey.
xEmhardt, William C.
Eastern Church in the Western World. AMS
Pr.
Emile-Male, Gilberte.
xEmile-Male, Gilberte.
The Restorer's Handbook of Easel Painting.
Van Nos Reinhold.
Emley, E. F. see Emley, Edward F.
Emley, Edward F.
xEmley, E. F.
Principles of Magnesium Technology.
Pergamon.
Emmanuel, Arghiri.
xEmmanuel, Arghiri.
Unequal Exchange: A Study of the Imperialism
of Trade. Monthly Rev.
Emmel, Thomas C.
xEmmel, Thomas C.

Butterflies: Their World, Their Life Cycle,
Their Behavior. Knopf.
An Introduction to Ecology & Population
Biology. Norton.
Population Biology. Har-Row.
Worlds Within Worlds: An Introduction to
Biology. HarBraceJ.
Emmens, see Emmens, Carol A.
Emmens, Carol A.
xEmmens.
Album of Television. Watts.
xEmmens, Carol A.
ed. An Audio-Visual Guide to American
Holidays. Scarecrow.
Famous People on Film. Scarecrow.
Emmerich, Andre.
xEmmerich, Andre.
Sweat of the Sun & Tears of the Moon: Gold
& Silver in Pre-Columbian Art. Hacker.
Emmerich, Herbert.
xEmmerich, Herbert.
Federal Organization & Administrative
Management. U of Ala Pr.
Emmerich, J. Oliver.
xEmmerich, Oliver.
Two Faces of Janus: The Saga of Deep South
Change. U Pr of Miss.
Emmerich, Oliver. see Emmerich, J. Oliver.
Emmerich, Werner.
xEmmerich, Werner.
Energy Does Matter. Walker & Co.
Emmerichs, Jack.
xEmmerichs, Jack.
Superwumpus. McGraw.
Emmerson, Donald K.
xEmmerson, Donald K.
Indonesia's Elite: Political Culture & Cultural
Politics. Cornell U Pr.
Emmerton, Bill
xEmmerton, Bill.
Running for Your Life. Nordon Pubns.
Emmet, Dorothy. see Emmet, Dorothy Mary.
Emmet, Dorothy Mary, 1904-
xEmmet, Dorothy.
Function, Purpose & Powers: Some Concepts
in the Study of Individuals & Societies.
Temple U Pr.
The Moral Prism. St Martin.
Sociological Theory & Philosophical Analysis.
Macmillan.
Emmet, Eric E. see Emmet, Eric Revell.
Emmet, Eric R. see Emmet, Eric Revell.
Emmet, Eric Revell.
xEmmet, Eric E.
Puzzles for Pleasure. Emerson.
xEmmet, Eric R.
Brain Puzzler's Delight. Emerson.
Handbook of Logic. Littlefield.
Emminger, Otmar, 1911-
xEmminger, Otmar.
On the Way to a New International Monetary
Order. Am Enterprise.
Emmitt, Robert.
xEmmitt, Robert.
Actaeon Homeward: A Novel. Swallow.
Emmons, Chester W. see Emmons, Chester Wilson.
Emmons, Chester Wilson, 1900-
xEmmons, Chester W.
Medical Mycology. Lea & Febiger.
Emmons, David M.
xEmmons, David M.
Garden in the Grasslands: Boomer Literature
of the Central Great Plains. U of Nebr Pr.
Emmons, Frederick E. see Emmons, Frederick Earle.
Emmons, Frederick Earle, 1880-
xEmmons, Frederick E.
City School Attendance Service. AMS Pr.
Emmons, Helen B. see Emmons, Helen Keith Boulware.
Emmons, Helen Keith Boulware.
xEmmons, Helen B.

The Mature Heart. Abingdon.

Emmons, Michael L.
xEmmons, Michael L.
The Inner Source: A Guide to Meditative
Therapy. Impact Pubs Cal.

Emmons, Shirlee.
xEmmons, Shirlee.
The Art of the Song Recital. Schirmer Bks.

Emmons, William H. see Emmons, William Harvey.

Emmons, William Harvey, 1876-
xEmmons, William H.
Gold Deposits of the World: With a Section on
Prospecting. Arno.

Emory, C. William. see Emory, William.

Emory, Eric S.
xEmory, Eric S.
When to Sell Stocks Portfolio Liquidation: The
Key to Superior Performance Without Stock
Selection. Exposition.

Emory, William.
xEmory, C. William.
Business Research Methods. Irwin.

Empedocles.
xEmpedocles.
The Fragments of Empedocles. Open Court.

Emperor, J. B. see Emperor, John Bernard.

Emperor, John Bernard.
xEmperor, J. B.
The Catullian Influence in English Lyric
Poetry, Circa 1600-1650. Octagon.

Empey, Arthur G. see Empey, Arthur Guy.

Empey, Arthur Guy, 1883-1963
xEmpey, Arthur G.
Tales from a Dugout. Arno.

Empey, LaMar T. see Empey, Lamar Taylor.

Empey, Lamar Taylor.
xEmpey, LaMar T.
The Future of Childhood & Juvenile Justice. U
Pr of Va.
ed. Juvenile Justice: The Progressive Legacy &
Current Reforms. U Pr of Va.

Empie, Paul C.
xEmpie, Paul C.
ed. Papal Primacy & the Universal Church.
Augsburg.
ed. Teaching Authority & Infallibility in the
Church. Augsburg.

Empleton, Bernard E.
xEmpleton, Bernard E.
First Aid for Skin & Scuba Divers. Follett.

Empson, William, 1906-
xEmpson, William.
Structure of Complex Words. Rowman.

Emrich, Duncan, 1908-
xEmrich, Duncan.
American Folk Poetry: An Anthology. Little.
Folklore of the American Land. Little.
Folklore on the American Land. Little.
The Whim-Wham Book. Schol Bk Serv.

Emrich, Wilhelm.
xEmrich, Wilhelm.
Literary Revolution & Modern Society &
Other Essays. Ungar.

Emshoff, James R.
xEmshoff, James R.
Analysis of Behavioral Systems. Macmillan.

Emsley, Clive.
xEmsley, Clive.
ed. Conflict & Stability in Europe. Biblio Dist.

Emsley, J. W. see Emsley, James William.

Emsley, James William.
xEmsley, J. W.
High Resolution Nuclear Magnetic Resonance
Spectroscopy. Pergamon.
NMR Spectroscopy Using Liquid Crystal
Solvents. Pergamon.

Emtsev, Mikhail. see Emtsev, Mikhail Tikhonovich.

Emtsev, Mikhail Tikhonovich.
xEmtsev, Mikhail.

World Soul. Macmillan.

Emurian, Ernest K.
xEmurian, Ernest K.
Famous Stories of Inspiring Hymns. Baker Bk.
Living Stories of Famous Hymns. Baker Bk.

Emy, H. V.
xEmy, H. V.
Liberals, Radicals & Social Politics, 1892-1914.
Cambridge U Pr.

Enby, Gunnel, 1941-
xEnby, Gunnel.
Let There Be Love: Sex & the Handicapped.
Taplinger.

Encel, S.
xEncel, S.
Cabinet Government in Australia. Intl Schol
Bk Serv.

Encel, Solomon.
xEncel, Solomon.
ed. The Art of Anticipation: Values & Methods
in Forecasting. Universe.

Encinas, Lydia. see Encinas, Lydia Proenza.

Encinas, Lydia Proenza.
xEncinas, Lydia.
Raggedy Ann & Andy's Sewing Book. Bobbs.

Enciso, Jorge, 1879-1969
xEnciso, Jorge.
Design Motifs of Ancient Mexico. Dover.
Designs from Pre-Columbian Mexico. Dover.

Encyclopaedia Britannica.
xEncyclopedia Britannica.
The Britannica Book of Music. Doubleday.
xEncyclopedia Britannica Editors.
Catastrophe: When Man Loses Control.
Bantam.
Energy: The Fuel of Life. Bantam.
How Things Work: Aerosols to Zippers.
Bantam.
Law in America: How & Why It Works.
Bantam.

Encyclopedia Britannica. see Encyclopaedia Britannica.
Encyclopedia Britannica Editors. see Encyclopaedia
Britannica.

Encyclopedie Mensuelle D'Outre-Mer.
xEncyclopedie Mensuelle d'Outre-mer.
Tunisia Fifty-Four: Seventy-Two Years of
Franco-Tunisian Collaboration. Negro U Pr.

Endacott, G. B.
xEndacott, G. B.
Fragrant Harbour: A Short History of Hong
Kong. Greenwood.
A History of Hong Kong. Oxford U Pr.

Ende, Richard C. von. see Von Ende, Richard C.

Endelman, Todd M.
xEndelman, Todd M.
The Jews of Georgian England, 1714-1830:
Tradition & Change in a Liberal Society.
Jewish Pubn.

Enderton, Herbert B.
xEnderton, Herbert B.
A Mathematical Introduction to Logic. Acad
Pr.

Endicott, John E.
xEndicott, John E.
The Politics of East Asia: China, Japan, Korea.
Westview.

Endicott, Kirk. see Endicott, Kirk Michael.

Endicott, Kirk Michael.
xEndicott, Kirk.
Batek Negrito Religion: The World-View &
Rituals of a Hunting & Gathering People of
Peninsular Malaysia. Oxford U Pr.

Endler, John A., 1947-
xEndler, John A.
Geographic Variation, Speciation, & Clines.
Princeton U Pr.

Endler, O. see Endler, Otto.

Endler, Otto.
xEndler, O.

Valuation Theory. Springer-Verlag.

Endo, H. see Endo, Hideya.

Endo, Hideya.
xEndo, H.
ed. Chemistry & Biological Actions of
4-Nitroquinoline 1-Oxide. Springer-Verlag.

Endres, Jeannette. see Endres, Jeannette Brakhane.

Endres, Jeannette Brakhane.
xEndres, Jeannette.
Food, Nutrition, & the Young Child. Mosby.

Endress, Charles A.
xEndress, Charles A.
History of Europe, 1500-1848. B&N.

Enelow, Allen J.
xEnelow, Allen J.
Interviewing & Patient Care. Oxford U Pr.

Enemark, Donald C.
xEnemark, Donald C.
Feasibility Study & Design of an Antenna
Pointing System with an in-Loop, Time
Shared Digital Computer. Mgmt Info Serv.

Energy Information Administration. see United States.
Federal Energy Administration.

Energy Policy Project Staff. see Ford Foundation. Energy
Policy Project.

Enerson, Laura.
xEnerson, Laura.
Our Library Lives in a Bus. Cove Pub Co.

Engdahl, Sylvia L. see Engdahl, Sylvia Louise.

Engdahl, Sylvia Louise.
xEngdahl, Sylvia L.
The Far Side of Evil. Atheneum.
Far Side of Evil. Atheneum.
Our World Is Earth. Atheneum.
This Star Shall Abide. Atheneum.
This Star Shall Abide. Atheneum.
Tool for Tomorrow: New Knowledge About
Genes. Atheneum.

Enge, Harald A.
xEnge, Harald A.
Introduction to Atomic Physics. A-W.
Introduction to Nuclear Physics. A-W.

Engel, Barbara A. see Engel, Barbara Alpern.

Engel, Barbara Alpern.
xEngel, Barbara A.
ed. Five Sisters: Women Against the Tsar.
Knopf.

Engel, Bernard F.
xEngel, Bernard F.
Marianne Moore. Coll & U Pr.

Engel, Beth B. see Engel, Beth Bland.

Engel, Beth Bland, 1921-
xEngel, Beth B.
Ride the Pine Sapling. Har-Row.

Engel, Carl, 1883-1944
xEngel, Carl.
Discords Mingled: Essays on Music. Arno.
The Literature of National Music. AMS Pr.
The Literature of National Music. Longwood
Pr.
Music of the Most Ancient Nations,
Particularly of the Assyrians, Egyptians, &
Hebrews, with Special Reference to Recent
Discoveries in Western Asia & in Egypt.
Arno.
Musical Instruments. Longwood Pr.
Musical Myths & Facts. Longwood Pr.

Engel, Claire E. see Engel, Claire Eliane.

Engel, Claire Eliane.
xEngel, Claire E.
The History of Mountaineering in the Alps.
Greenwood.

Engel, David M.
xEngel, David M.
Code & Custom in a Thai Provincial Court:
The Interaction of Formal & Informal
Systems of Justice. U of Ariz Pr.

Engel, Dolores.
xEngel, Dolores.

Voyage of the Kon-Tiki. Raintree Child.

Engel, Eva J.
xEngel, Eva L.
ed. German Narrative Prose. Dufour.

Engel, Eva L. *see* Engel, Eva J.

Engel, George L. *see* Engel, George Libman.

Engel, George Libman, 1913-
xEngel, George L.
Psychological Development in Health &
Disease. Saunders.

Engel, Gertrude.
xEngel, Gertrude.
How to Make Ceramics. Arco.

Engel, Herbert.
xEngel, Herbert.
Handbook of Creative Learning Exercises. Gulf
Pub.

Engel, James F.
xEngel, James F.
Cases in Promotional Strategy. Irwin.
How Can I Get Them to Listen?. Zondervan.
Promotional Strategy. Irwin.

Engel, Lehman, 1910-
xEngel, Lehman.
The Critics. Macmillan.
Getting Started in the Theater. Macmillan.
Getting Started in the Theater. Macmillan.
This Bright Day. Macmillan.

Engel, Lorenz.
xEngel, Lorenz.
Among the Plains Indians. Lerner Pubns.

Engel, Lyle K. *see* Engel, Lyle Kenyon.

Engel, Lyle Kenyon.
xEngel, Lyle K.
The Complete Book of Flying. Schol Bk Serv.
Complete Book of Minibikes & Minicycles.
Arco.
The Complete Book of Mobile Home Living.
Arco.
The Complete Book of Motor Camping. Arco.
The Complete Book of Trailering. Arco.
xEngel, Lyle Kenyon.
The Incredible A. J. Foyt. Arco.

Engel, Madeline H.
xEngel, Madeline H.
The Drug Scene: A Sociological Perspective.
Hayden.

Engel, Marian.
xEngel, Marian.
The Glassy Sea. St Martin.

Engel, Mary.
xEngel, Mary.
Psychopathology in Childhood: Social,
Diagnostic, & Therapeutic Aspects.
HarBraceJ.

Engel, Monroe.
xEngel, Monroe.
ed. Uses of Literature. Harvard U Pr.

Engel, Peter. *see* Engel, Peter H.

Engel, Peter A.
xEngel, Peter A.
Impact Wear of Materials. Elsevier.

Engel, Peter H.
xEngel, Peter.
High Gloss. Berkley Pub.
High Gloss. St Martin.
xEngel, Peter H.
Over-Achievers. Popular Lib.
The Overachievers. Crain Bks.

Engel, Rudolf C. *see* Engel, Rudolf C. H.

Engel, Rudolf C. H.
xEngel, Rudolf C.
Abnormal Electroencephalograms in the
Neonatal Period. C C Thomas.

Engel, Salo.
xEngel, Salo.

ed. Law, State & International Legal Order:
Essays in Honor of Hans Kelsen. U of Tenn
Pr.

Engelbarts, Rudolf.
xEngelbarts, Rudolf.
Books in Stir: A Bibliographic Essay About
Prison Libraries & About Books Written by
Prisoners & Prison Employees. Scarecrow.

Engelbourg, Saul, 1927-
xEngelbourg, Saul.
Power & Morality: American Business Ethics,
1840-1914. Greenwood.

Engelbrektson, Sune.
xEngelbrektson, Sune.
Gravity at Work & Play. HR&W.

Engelfriet, J. *see* Engelfriet, Joost.

Engelfriet, Joost.
xEngelfriet, J.
Simple Program Schemes & Formal Languages.
Springer-Verlag.

Engelhardt, H. *see* Engelhardt, Heinz.

Engelhardt, Heinz.
xEngelhardt, H.
High Performance Liquid Chromatography.
Springer-Verlag.

Engelking, R. *see* Engelking, Ryszard.

Engelking, Ryszard.
xEngelking, R.
Dimension Theory. Elsevier.

Engelmann, Arthur, 1853-1912
xEngelmann, Arthur.
History of Continental Civil Procedure. Kelley.
History of Continental Civil Procedure.
Rothman.

Engelmann, Siegfried.
xEngelmann, Siegfried.
Direct Instruction. Educ Tech Pubns.
Preventing Failure in the Primary Grades.
SRA.

Engels, Donald W.
xEngels, Donald W.
Alexander the Great & the Logistics of the
Macedonian Army. U of Cal Pr.

Engels, Frederick, 1820-1895
xEngels, Frederick.
Socialism: Utopian & Scientific. China Bks.
Socialism: Utopian & Scientific. Intl Pub Co.
Socialism: Utopian & Scientific. Path Pr NY.

Engels, Frederick. *see* Engels, Friedrich.

Engels, Friedrich, 1820-1895
xEngels, Frederick.
The Condition of the Working Class in
England. Academy Chi Ltd.
On Historical Materialism. Beekman Pubs.
On Historical Materialism. Intl Pub Co.
Origin of the Family, Private Property, & the
State. Intl Pub Co.
xEngels, Friedrich.
The Condition of the Working Class in
England. Stanford U Pr.
On Historical Materialism. AMS Pr.

Engels, John.
xEngels, John.
Signals from the Safety Coffin. U of Pittsburgh
Pr.

Engelsma, David.
xEngelsma, David.
Marriage: The Mystery of Christ & the Church.
Kregel.

Engelsman, Coert, 1930-
xEngelsman, Coert.
Engelsman's General Construction Cost Guide
1977. Van Nos Reinhold.

Engelsman, Joan C. *see* Engelsman, Joan Chamberlain.

Engelsman, Joan Chamberlain, 1932-
xEngelsman, Joan C.
The Feminine Dimension of the Divine.
Westminster.

Engelsohn, Harold S.
xEngelsohn, Harold S.

Basic Mathematics: Algebra with Arithmetic.
Wiley.
Programming Programmable Calculators.
Hayden.

Engelson, Morris.
xEngelson, Morris.
Spectrum Analyzer Theory & Applications.
Artech Hse.

Enger, Eldon D.
xEnger, Eldon D.
Concepts in Biology. Wm C Brown.
Essentials of Allied Health Science. Wm C
Brown.

Enger, Norman L.
xEnger, Norman L.
Documentation Standards for Computer
Systems. Tech Pr Inc.

Enggass, Robert, 1921-
xEnggass, Robert.
Early Eighteenth-Century Sculpture in Rome:
An Illustrated Catalogue Raisonne. Pa St U
Pr.

Engineering Concepts Curriculum Project.
xEngineering Concepts Curriculum Project - State
University of New York.
Man & His Technology. McGraw.
Man-Made World. McGraw.

Engineering Employer's Federation. *see* Engineering
Employers' Federation.

Engineering Employers' Federation.
xEngineering Employer's Federation.
Business Performance & Industrial Relations.
Intl Pubns Serv.

Engineering Index, Inc.
xEngineering Index, Inc.
Engineering Index Thesaurus. Macmillan Info.

Engineering Industry Training Board.
xEngineering Industry Training Board.
ed. First Year Training for Craftsmen &
Technicians: An Introduction to General &
Special Skills. Intl Ideas.
ed. Model Schemes for the Training of Adult
Operators in Technical Trades. Intl Ideas.
ed. Static Electrical Equipment Winding &
Building. Intl Ideas.
ed. Training for Capstan, Turret, & Sequence
Controlled Lathe Setters & Operators. Intl
Ideas.
ed. Training for Drilling Machine Operators.
Intl Ideas.
ed. Training for Milling Machine Operators &
Setters. Intl Ideas.
ed. Training for Riggers-Erectors. Intl Ideas.

Engineering Societies Library, New York.
xEngineering Societies Library, New York.
Classed Subject Catalog of the Engineering
Societies Library, New York City, 6th
Supplement. G K Hall.

Engineering Staff of Texas Instruments. *see* Texas
Instruments Incorporated.

Engineers Joint Council.
xEngineers Joint Council Editors.
Directory of Engineering Societies & Related
Organizations. AAES.
Theasurus of Engineering & Scientific Terms.
AAES.
Who's Who in Engineering. AAES.

Engineers Joint Council Editors. *see* Engineers Joint
Council.

England, A. B., 1939-
xEngland, A. B.
Byron's "Don Juan" & Eighteenth-Century
Literature: A Study of Some Rhetorical
Continuities & Discontinuities. Bucknell U
Pr.
Energy & Order in the Poetry of Swift.
Bucknell U Pr.

England, Barbara R.
xEngland, Barbara R.

Agriculture. Macmillan.
Audio-Lingual English Series, 6 Workbks.
  Macmillan.
Aviation. Macmillan.
Aviation Mechanics. Macmillan.
Banking. Macmillan.
Black Tulip. Macmillan.
Buffalo Bill. Macmillan.
Cowboys in Alaska, & Other Stories.
  Macmillan.
Engineering. Macmillan.
English Grammar Exercises. Macmillan.
English Nine Hundred Series. Macmillan.
English Pronunciation: A Manual for Teachers.
  Macmillan.
English This Way. Macmillan.
Four Short Mysteries. Macmillan.
International Trade. Macmillan.
Island of Truth, & Other Stories. Macmillan.
Journalism. Macmillan.
Key to English Adjectives. Macmillan.
Key to English Figurative Expressions.
  Macmillan.
Key to English Nouns. Macmillan.
Key to English Prepositions. Macmillan.
Key to English Two-Word Verbs. Macmillan.
Key to English Verbs. Macmillan.
Key to English Vocabulary. Macmillan.
Love Letter. Macmillan.
Magazine Reader. Macmillan.
Medicine. Macmillan.
Mitchell Family. Macmillan.
Murder Now & Then. Macmillan.
People Speak, & Other Stories. Macmillan.
Practical English Grammar. Macmillan.
Presidency in Conflict. Macmillan.
Readings & Conversations: About the United
  States, Its People, Its History & Its Customs.
  Eng Language.
Russells of Hollytree Circle. Macmillan.
Scenes of America. Macmillan.
Silver Elephant, & Other Stories. Macmillan.
Stories to Surprise You. Macmillan.
Three Detective Stories. Macmillan.
Twelve Famous Americans. Macmillan.
Vanishing Lady, & Other Stories. Macmillan.
Virginian. Macmillan.
English, Oliver S. see English, Oliver Spurgeon.
English, Oliver Spurgeon.
  xEnglish, Oliver S.
  Introduction to Psychiatry. Norton.
English, Paul W. see English, Paul Ward.
English, Paul Ward.
  xEnglish, Paul W.
  World Regional Geography: A Question of
    Place. Har-Row.
English, Suzanne.
  xEnglish, Suzanne.
  Goodbye Mr. Valentine. Libra.
English, T. Saunders. see English, Thomas Saunders.
English, Thomas Saunders, 1928-
  xEnglish, T. Saunders.
  ed. Ocean Resources & Public Policy. U of
    Wash Pr.
English, Urma.
  xEnglish, Urma.
  Organizing a Middle School or Junior High
    School Student Council. Natl Assn Principals.
Englund, Vi.
  xEnglund, Violet V.
  The Strand. Golden Owl Pub.
Englund, Violet V. see Englund, Vi.
Engren, Edith.
  xEngren, Edith.
  Marcy Tarrant. Fawcett.
Engs, Ruth. see Engs, Ruth C.
Engs, Ruth C.
  xEngs, Ruth.

Teaching Health Education in the Elementary
    School. HM.
Engstrom, Robert E.
  xEngstrom, Robert E.
  Planning & Design of Townhouses &
    Condominiums. Urban Land.
Engstrom, Ted W. see Engstrom, Theodore Wilhelm.
Engstrom, Theodore Wilhelm.
  xEngstrom, Ted W.
  The Art of Management for Christian Leaders.
    Word Bks.
  What in the World Is God Doing?: The New
    Face of Missions. Word Bks.
  The Work Trap. Revell.
Engstrom, W. A., 1925-
  xEngstrom, W. A.
  Multi-Media in the Church: A Beginner's
    Guide for Putting It All Together. John
    Knox.
Enis, Ben. see Enis, Ben M.
Enis, Ben M.
  xEnis, Ben.
  Marketing Principles. Goodyear.
  Personal Selling: Foundations, Process, &
    Management. Goodyear.
Enkvist, Nils E. see Enkvist, Nils Erik.
Enkvist, Nils Erik.
  xEnkvist, Nils E.
  Caricatures of Americans on the English Stage
    Prior to 1870. Kennikat.
Enlander, Derek.
  xEnlander, Derek.
  ed. Computers in Laboratory Medicine. Acad
    Pr.
Enlow, Donald H.
  xEnlow, Donald H.
  A Handbook of Facial Growth. Saunders.
Enlow, Harold L.
  xEnlow, Harold L.
  How to Carve Folk Figures & a Cigar-Store
    Indian. Dover.
Ennen, E. see Ennen, Edith.
Ennen, Edith.
  xEnnen, E.
  The Medieval Town. Elsevier.
Ennes, Harold. see Ennes, Harold E.
Ennes, Harold E., 1911-
  xEnnes, Harold.
  Television Broadcasting: Systems Maintenance.
    Sams.
  xEnnes, Harold E.
  Boolean Algebra for Computer Logic. Sams.
  Television Broadcasting: Equipment, Systems,
    & Operating Fundamentals. Sams.
Ennew, Judith, 1944-
  xEnnew, Judith.
  The Western Isles Today. Cambridge U Pr.
Ennis, Bernice, 1911-
  xEnnis, Bernice.
  Guide to the Literature in Psychiatry.
    Partridge.
Ennis, Bruce. see Ennis, Bruce J.
Ennis, Bruce J., 1941-
  xEnnis, Bruce.
  Prisoners of Psychiatry. HarBraceJ.
Ennis, Thomas E. see Ennis, Thomas Edson.
Ennis, Thomas Edson.
  xEnnis, Thomas E.
  French Policy & Developments in Indochina.
    Russell.
Eno, Susan.
  xEno, Susan.
  The Truth About What Women Want in Men.
    Morrow.
Enoch, Yvonne.
  xEnoch, Yvonne.
  Creative Piano Teaching. Stipes.
  Group Piano-Teaching. Oxford U Pr.
Enos, Darryl. see Enos, Darryl D.

Enos, Darryl D.
  xEnos, Darryl.
  The Sociology of Health Care: Social,
    Economic & Political Perspectives. Praeger.
Enos, Paul.
  xEnos, Paul.
  Quaternary Sedimentation in South Florida.
    Geol Soc.
Enquist, per Olov.
  xEnquist, Per Olov.
  The Night of the Tribades: A Play from 1889.
    Hill & Wang.
Enrick, Norbert L. see Enrick, Norbert Lloyd.
Enrick, Norbert Lloyd, 1920-
  xEnrick, Norbert L.
  Management Handbook of Decision-Oriented
    Statistics. Krieger.
Enright, D. J. see Enright, Dennis Joseph.
Enright, Dennis Joseph.
  xEnright, D. J.
  Beyond Land's End. Merrimack Bk Serv.
  A Faust Book. Oxford U Pr.
  The Typewriter Revolution & Other Poems.
    Open Court.
Enright, Elizabeth, 1909-
  xEnright, Elizabeth.
  Gone-Away Lake. HarBraceJ.
  Return to Gone-Away. HarBraceJ.
  Thimble Summer. Dell.
  illus. Thimble Summer. HR&W.
Enriques, Federigo, 1871-1946
  xEnriques, Federigo.
  Historic Development of Logic: The Principles
    & Structure of Science in the Conception of
    Mathematical Thinkers. Russell.
Enriquez, Pablo.
  xEnriquez, Pablo.
  The Pathology of the Spleen: A Functional
    Approach. Am Soc Clinical.
Enroth, Ronald M.
  xEnroth, Ronald M.
  The Lure of the Cults. Christian Herald.
Ensanian, Minas.
  xEnsanian, Minas.
  Cosmic Biology. Philos Lib.
Enser, A. G. S.
  xEnser, A. G. S.
  Compiled by A Subject Bibliography of the
    Second World War: Books in English
    1929-1974. Westview.
Ensign, Forest C. see Ensign, Forest Chester.
Ensign, Forest Chester, 1867-
  xEnsign, Forest C.
  Compulsory School Attendance & Child Labor.
    Arno.
Ensign, Georgianne.
  xEnsign, Georgianne.
  Hunt for the Mastodon. Watts.
Ensinger, Earl W.
  xEnsinger, Earl W.
  Problems in Artistic Woodturning. Woodcraft
    Supply.
Enslin, Morton S. see Enslin, Morton Scott.
Enslin, Morton Scott, 1897-
  xEnslin, Morton S.
  Christian Beginnings. Har-Row.
  The Prophet from Nazareth. Schocken.
Enslin, Theodore.
  xEnslin, Theodore.
  Ranger. North Atlantic.
Ensminger, Douglas.
  xEnsminger, Douglas.
  Conquest of World Hunger & Poverty. Iowa St
    U Pr.
Ensminger, M. E. see Ensminger, M. Eugene.
Ensminger, M. Eugene.
  xEnsminger, M. E.

The Complete Book of Dogs. A S Barnes.
The Complete Encyclopedia of Horses. A S
    Barnes.
Dairy Cattle Science. Interstate.
Horses & Tack. HM.
Poultry Science. Interstate.
xEnsminger, M. Eugene.
    Animal Science. Interstate.
    Swine Science. Interstate.

Ensor, Allison.
xEnsor, Allison.
    Mark Twain & the Bible. U Pr of Ky.

Ensor, D. M.
xEnsor, D. M.
    The Comparative Endocrinology of Prolactin.
    Methuen Inc.

Ensor, James.
xEnsor, James.
    The Prints of James Ensor. Da Capo.

Ensor, Phyllis.
xEnsor, Phyllis G.
    Personal Health: Confronting Your Health
    Behavior. Allyn.
Ensor, Phyllis G. see Ensor, Phyllis.

Enteen, George M.
xEnteen, George M.
    Soviet Historians & the Study of Russian
    Imperialism. Pa St U Pr.
    The Soviet Scholar-Bureaucrat: M. N.
    Pokrovskii & the Society of Marxist
    Historians. Pa St U Pr.

Entelek, Inc.
xEntelek Inc.
    Theory of Income Determination. Macmillan.
Entelis, John P. see Entelis, John Pierre.

Entelis, John Pierre, 1941-
xEntelis, John P.
    Comparative Politics of North Africa: Algeria,
    Morocco, & Tunisia. Syracuse U Pr.
Entelis, S. G. see Entelis, Sergei Genrikhovich.

Entelis, Sergei Genrikhovich.
xEntelis, S. G.
    Reaction Kinetics in the Liquid Phase. Halsted
    Pr.
Enters, Agna. see Enters, Angna.

Enters, Angna, 1907-
xEnters, Agna.
    First Person Plural. Da Capo.

Enthoven, Alain C., 1930-
xEnthoven, Alain C.
    Health Plan: The Only Practical Solution to the
    Soaring Cost of Medical Care. A-W.
    ed. Pollution, Resources & the Environment.
    Norton.

Enthoven, Jacqueline.
xEnthoven, Jacqueline.
    Stitchery for Children: A Manual for Teachers,
    Parents, & Children. Van Nos Reinhold.
    Stitches of Creative Embroidery. Van Nos
    Reinhold.

Entomological Society of America.
xEntomological Society of America.
    Annual Meating Programs. Entomol Soc.

Entwisle, Doris R.
xEntwisle, Doris R.
    Word Associations of Young Children. Johns
    Hopkins.

Entwistle, Harold.
xEntwistle, Harold.
    Antonio Gramsci: Conservative Schooling for
    Radical Politics. Routledge & Kegan.
    Class, Culture & Education. Methuen Inc.
Entwistle, William J. see Entwistle, William James.

Entwistle, William James, 1895-1952
xEntwistle, William J.
    The Arthurian Legend in the Literatures of the
    Spanish Peninsula. Kraus Repr.
xEntwistle, William S.

The Arthurian Legend in the Literatures of the
    Spanish Peninsula. Phaeton.
Entwistle, William S. see Entwistle, William James.

Environmental Action Coalition.
xEnvironmental Action Coalition.
    It's Your Environment: Things to Think
    About, Things to Do. Scribner.

Environmental Communication.
xEnvironmental Communications.
    Big Art: Megamurals & Supergraphics. Running
    Pr.
Environmental Communications. see Environmental
Communication.

Environmental Science Services Corporation.
xEnvironmental Science Services Scientific Staff.
    Air Pollution Control Primer. Environ Sci Serv.
Environmental Science Services Scientific Staff. see
Environmental Science Services Corporation.

Environmental Studies Board.
xEnvironmental Studies Board.
    An Assessment of Mercury in the
    Environment. Natl Acad Pr.
    Chloroform, Carbon Tetrachloride & Other
    Halomethanes. Natl Acad Pr.
    Kepone, Mirex, Hexachlorocyclopentadiene.
    Natl Acad Pr.
    Polychlorinated Biphenyls. Natl Acad Pr.
    Underground Disposal of Coal Mine Wastes.
    Natl Acad Pr.
xEnvironmental Studies Board, National Research
Council.
    Contemporary Pest Control Practices &
    Prospects: Report of the Executive
    Committee. Natl Acad Pr.
xEnvironmental Studies Board, Natl Research
Council.
    Cotton Pest Control. Natl Acad Pr.
    Pest Control: An Assesssment of Present &
    Alternative Technologies. Natl Acad Pr.
    Pest Control & Public Health. Natl Acad Pr.
Environmental Studies Board Commission on Natural
Resources, National Research Council. see National
Research Council. Commission on Natural Resources.

**Environmental Studies Board. Committee for
International Environmental Programs.**
xCommittee for International Environmental
Programs.
    Institutional Arrangements for International
    Environmental Cooperation. Natl Acad Pr.
Environmental Studies Board, National Research
Council. see Environmental Studies Board.
Environmental Studies Board, Natl Research Council. see
Environmental Studies Board.

Enyedi, Gyorgy.
xEnyedi, Gyorgy.
    Hungary: An Economic Geography. Westview.
Enzensberger, Hans M. see Enzensberger, Hans Magnus.

Enzensberger, Hans Magnus.
xEnzensberger, Hans M.
    Mausoleum. Urizen Bks.
    Politics & Crime. Continuum.

Eoff, Sherman Hinkle, 1900-
xEoff, Sherman J.
    Review of Spanish. Macmillan.
Eoff, Sherman J. see Eoff, Sherman Hinkle.

Ephron, Nora.
xEphron, Nora.
    Crazy Salad: Some Things About Women.
    Bantam.
    Crazy Salad: Some Things About Women.
    Knopf.
    Scribble, Scribble: Notes on the Media.
    Bantam.

Ephrussi, Boris, 1901-
xEphrussi, Boris.
    Hybridization of Somatic Cells. Princeton U Pr.
Epinal. see Imagerie Pellerin, Epinal, France.

Epiotis, N. D., 1944-
xEpiotis, N. D.

Structural Theory of Organic Chemistry.
    Springer-Verlag.
    Theory of Organic Reactions. Springer-Verlag.

Epker, Bruce N.
xEpker, Bruce N.
    Dentofacial Deformities: Surgical-Orthodontic
    Correction. Mosby.
Eppel, Emanuel M. see Eppel, Emanuel Montague.

Eppel, Emanuel Montague.
xEppel, Emanuel M.
    Adolescents & Morality: A Study of Some
    Moral Values & Dilemmas of Working
    Adolescents in the Context of a Changing
    Climate of Opinion. Humanities.

Eppen, Gary.
xEppen, Gary D.
    ed. Energy: The Policy Issues. U of Chicago
    Pr.
Eppen, Gary D. see Eppen, Gary.

Epperson, Arlin.
xEpperson, Arlin.
    Leisure Counseling: An Aspect of Leisure
    Education. C C Thomas.

Epps, Charles H.
xEpps, Charles H.
    ed. Complications in Orthopaedic Surgery.
    Lippincott.

Epps, Edgar G., 1929-
xEpps, Edgar G.
    Cultural Pluralism. McCutchan.
Epstein. see Epstein, Elliott M.
Epstein, A. L. see Epstein, Arnold Leonard.

Epstein, Abraham, 1892-1942
xEpstein, Abraham.
    The Challenge of the Aged. Arno.
    Facing Old Age: A Study of Old Age
    Dependency in the United States & Old Age
    Pensions. Arno.
Epstein, Anne M. see Epstein, Anne Merrick.

Epstein, Anne Merrick.
xEpstein, Anne M.
    Good Stones. HM.

Epstein, Arnold Leonard.
xEpstein, A. L.
    ed. The Craft of Social Anthropology.
    Pergamon.
    ed. The Craft of Social Anthropology.
    Transaction Bks.
    Matupit: Land, Politics & Change Among the
    Tolai of New Britain. U of Cal Pr.

Epstein, Arthur W.
xEpstein, Arthur W.
    Anatomist's Dream of Love. Libra.

Epstein, Bertram, 1910-
xEpstein, Bertram.
    Immediate & Retention Effects of Interpolated
    Rest Periods on Learning Performance. AMS
    Pr.

Epstein, Charlotte.
xEpstein.
    Learning to Care for the Aged. Reston.
xEpstein, Charlotte.
    Classroom Management & Teaching: Persistent
    Problems & Rational Solutions. Reston.

Epstein, Cy, 1936 or 7-
xEpstein, Cy.
    How to Kill a College. Sherbourne.

Epstein, David G., 1943-
xEpstein, David G.
    Debtor-Creditor Law in a Nutshell. West Pub.
    Teaching Materials on Business Reorganization
    Under the Bankruptcy Code. West Pub.

Epstein, Dena J.
xEpstein, Dena J.
    Music Publishing in Chicago Before 1871: The
    Firm of Root & Cady, 1858-1871. Info
    Coord.
    Sinful Tunes & Spirituals: Black Folk Music to
    the Civil War. U of Ill Pr.
Epstein, Earl B. see Epstein, Earl Bruce.

Epstein, Earl Bruce.
xEpstein, Earl B.
No More Mr. Nice Guy: Business Karate for
Getting to the Top & Staying There.
Farnswth Pub.

Epstein, Edmund L.
xEpstein, Edmund L.
Language & Style. Methuen Inc.
The Ordeal of Stephen Dedalus: The Conflict
of the Generations in James Joyce's "A
Portrait of the Artist As a Young Man". S Ill
U Pr.

Epstein, Edward. see Epstein, Edwin M.

Epstein, Edward J. see Epstein, Edward Jay.

Epstein, Edward Jay, 1935-
xEpstein, Edward J.
Cartel. Putnam.

Epstein, Edwin M.
xEpstein, Edward.
Rationality, Legitimacy, Responsibility: Search
for New Directions in Business & Society.
Goodyear.

Epstein, Elliot. see Epstein, Elliott M.

Epstein, Elliott M.
xEpstein.
Barron's Guide to Law Schools. Barron.
xEpstein, Elliot.
Barron's Guide to Law Schools. Barron.

Epstein, H. see Epstein, Hellmut.

Epstein, Helen, 1947-
xEpstein, Helen.
Children of the Holocaust: Conversations with
Sons & Daughters of Survivors. Putnam.

Epstein, Hellmut, 1903-
xEpstein, H.
Domestic Animals of China. Holmes & Meier.
Domestic Animals of Nepal. Holmes & Meier.
Origin of the Domestic Animals of Africa.
Holmes & Meier.

Epstein, Herman T. see Epstein, Herman Theodore.

Epstein, Herman Theodore, 1920-
xEpstein, Herman T.
Strategy for Education. Oxford U Pr.

Epstein, Jacob.
xEpstein, Jacob.
Wild Oats. Little.
Wild Oats. PB.

Epstein, Joel J.
xEpstein, Joel J.
Francis Bacon: A Political Biography. Ohio U
Pr.

Epstein, Joseph, 1937-
xEpstein, Joseph.
Familiar Territory: Observations on American
Life. Oxford U Pr.

Epstein, Kathie.
xEpstein, Kathie.
The Quiet Riot. Revell.

Epstein, Klaus.
xEpstein, Klaus.
The Genesis of German Conservatism.
Princeton U Pr.
Matthias Erzberger & the Dilemma of German
Democracy. Fertig.

Epstein, Laura.
xEpstein, Laura.
Helping People: The Task-Centered Approach.
Mosby.

Epstein, Leon D.
xEpstein, Leon D.
Governing the University: The Campus & the
Public Interest. Jossey-Bass.
Political Parties in Western Democracies.
Transaction Bks.

Epstein, Leslie.
xEpstein, Leslie.
King of the Jews. Avon.
King of the Jews. Coward.
The Steinway Quintet: Plus Four. Little.

Epstein, M. A. see Epstein, Michael Anthony.

Epstein, Marc J.
xEpstein, Marc J.
The Effect of Scientific Management on the
Development of the Standard Cost System.
Arno.

Epstein, Michael Anthony.
xEpstein, M. A.
ed. The Epstein-Barr Virus. Springer-Verlag.

Epstein, Morris, 1922-
xEpstein, Morris.
All About Jewish Holidays & Customs. Ktav.

Epstein, Mortimer, 1880-1946
xEpstein, Mortimer.
Early History of the Levant Company. Kelley.

Epstein, Perle. see Epstein, Perle S.

Epstein, Perle S.
xEpstein, Perle.
Individuals All. Macmillan.
Pilgrimage: Adventures of a Wandering Jew.
HM.

Epstein, R. L. see Epstein, Richard L.

Epstein, Richard L., 1947-
xEpstein, R. L.
Degrees of Unsolvability: Structure & Theory.
Springer-Verlag.

Epstein, Roslyn.
xEpstein, Roslyn.
American Indian Needlepoint Designs for
Pillows, Belts, Handbags & Other Projects.
Dover.

Epstein, Sandra, 1931-
xEpstein, Sandra.
A Place Like Dairy-Anne. Avon.
A Place Like Dairy-Anne. Dial.

Epstein, Scarlett. see Epstein, Trude Scarlett.

Epstein, Seymour, 1917-
xEpstein, Seymour.
The Dream Museum. Avon.
Looking for Fred Schmidt. Popular Lib.
Love Affair. Doubleday.
Love Affair. Popular Lib.

Epstein, Sherrie S.
xEpstein, Sherrie S.
Penny the Medicine Maker: The Story of
Penicillin. Lerner Pubns.

Epstein, Trude Scarlett.
xEpstein, Scarlett.
Capitalism, Primitive & Modern: Some Aspects
of Tolai Economic Growth. Mich St U Pr.

Epstein, William, 1912-
xEpstein, William.
The Last Chance: Nuclear Proliferation &
Arms Control. Free Pr.

Epton, Nina. see Epton, Nina Consuelo.

Epton, Nina Consuelo.
xEpton, Nina.
Josephine: The Empress & Her Children.
Norton.

Equal Rights Amendment Project.
xEqual Rights Amendment Project.
Compiled by The Equal Rights Amendment: A
Bibliographic Study. Greenwood.

Equiano, Olaudah, b. 1745
xEquiano, Olaudah.
Life of Olaudah Equiano, Or, Gustavus Vassa,
the African. Negro U Pr.

Eranko, E. O. see Eranko, Olavi.

Eranko, Olavi.
xEranko, E. O.
ed. Histochemistry of Nervous Transmission.
Elsevier.

Erasmus. see Erasmus, Desiderius.

Erasmus, Charles J.
xErasmus, Charles J.
Contemporary Change in Traditional
Communities of Mexico & Peru. U of Ill Pr.
In Search of the Common Good: Utopian
Experiments Past and Future. Free Pr.

Erasmus, D. A. see Erasmus, David A.

Erasmus, David A.
xErasmus, D. A.
Electron Probe Microanalysis in Biology.
Methuen Inc.

Erasmus, Desiderius.
xErasmus.
The Praise of Folly. Hendricks House.
Praise of Folly. Penguin.
xErasmus, Desiderius.
Comparation of a Vyrgin & a Martyr, 1537.
Schol Facsimiles.
The Complaint of Peace. Open Court.
The Complaint of Peace. Schol Facsimiles.
The Complaint of Peace. Walter J Johnson.
De Contemptu Mundi. Schol Facsimiles.
Discourse on Free Will. Ungar.
Education of a Christian Prince. Norton.
tr. Education of a Christian Prince. Octagon.
The Praise of Folly. J Simon.
Praise of Folly. Princeton U Pr.
Praise of Folly. U of Mich Pr.
The Praise of Folly. Yale U Pr.

Erb, Alta M. see Erb, Alta Mae.

Erb, Alta Mae, 1891-
xErb, Alta M.
Christian Education in the Home. Herald Pr.

Erb, Paul, 1894-
xErb, Paul.
Orie O. Miller: The Story of a Man & an Era.
Herald Pr.

Erb, Richard D.
xErb, Richard D.
ed. Federal Reserve Policies & Public
Disclosure. Am Enterprise.

Erbstosser, Martin.
xErbstosser, Martin.
The Crusades. Universe.

Ercklentz, Enno W., 1931-
xErcklentz, Enno W.
Modern German Corporation Law. Oceana.

Erdahl, Lowell O.
xErdahl, Lowell O.
Authentic Living. Abingdon.
Preaching for the People. Abingdon.

Erdlen, John. see Erdlen, John D.

Erdlen, John D.
xErdlen, John.
Job Hunting for the College Graduate. Heath.

Erdman, J. see Erdman, Joseph.

Erdman, Joseph.
xErdman, J.
Complete Guide to the Marital Deduction in
Estate Planning. Inst Busn Plan.

Erdman, Loula G. see Erdman, Loula Grace.

Erdman, Loula Grace.
xErdman, Loula G.
Life Was Simpler Then. Dodd.
The Years of the Locust. Gregg.

Erdman, Paul. see Erdman, Paul Emil.

Erdman, Paul Emil, 1932-
xErdman, Paul.
The Silver Bears. PB.

Erdmann, Carl, 1898-1945
xErdmann, Carl.
The Origin of the Idea of Crusade. Princeton U
Pr.

Erdoes, Richard.
xErdoes, Richard.
illus. The Rain Dance People: The Pueblo
Indians, Their Past & Present. Knopf.
Saloons of the Old West. Knopf.
The Sun Dance People: The Plains Indians,
Their Past & Present. Knopf.

Erdos, P.
xErdos, Paul.
Probabilistic Methods in Combinatorics. Acad
Pr.

Erdos, P. L. see Erdos, Paul L.

Erdos, Paul. see Erdos, P.

Erdos, Paul L.
  xErdos, P. L.
    Professional Mail Surveys. McGraw.
Erdtmann, Gerhard.
  xErdtmann, Gerhard.
    The Gamma Rays of the Radionuclides: Tables
      for Applied Gamma Ray Spectrometry.
      Verlag Chemie.
Erdy, Miklos.
  xErdy, Miklos.
    The Sumerian, Ural-Altaic, Magyar
      Relationship: A History of Research, Pt. 1,
      the 19th Century. Gilgamesh Pub.
Eremenko, Valentin A. see Eremenko, Valentin
  Nikiforovich.
Eremenko, Valentin Nikiforovich.
  xEremenko, Valentin A.
    Liquid-Phase Sintering. Plenum Pub.
Erens, Patricia, 1938-
  xErens, Patricia.
    The Films of Shirley MacLaine. A S Barnes.
    Masterpieces: Famous Chicagoans & Their
      Paintings. P Erens.
    ed. Sexual Stratagems: The World of Women in
      Film. Horizon.
Erf, Robert K.
  xErf, Robert K.
    ed. Holographic Nondestructive Testing. Acad
      Pr.
    Speckle Metrology. Acad Pr.
Ergang, Robert. see Ergang, Robert Reinhold.
Ergang, Robert Reinhold, 1898-
  xErgang, Robert.
    Europe Since Waterloo. Heath.
Ergood, Bruce.
  xErgood, Bruce.
    ed. Appalachia: Social Context, Past & Present.
      Kendall-Hunt.
Erhard, Ludwig.
  xErhard, Ludwig.
    Prosperity Through Competition. Greenwood.
Erhart, Katherine P. see Erhart, Katherine Patricia.
Erhart, Katherine Patricia, 1950-
  xErhart, Katherine P.
    The Development of the Facing Head Motif on
      Greek Coins & Its Relation to Classical Art.
      Garland Pub.
ERIC. see Educational Resources Information Center.
ERIC (Educational Information Center). see Educational
  Resources Information Center.
ERIC (Educational Resources Information Center). see
  Educational Resources Information Center.
Ericksen, Ephraim E. see Ericksen, Ephraim Edward.
Ericksen, Ephraim Edward.
  xEricksen, Ephraim E.
    The Psychological & Ethical Aspects of
      Mormon Group Life. U of Utah Pr.
Erickson, Arvel B.
  xErickson, Arvel B.
    The Public Career of Sir James Graham.
      Greenwood.
Erickson, B. H. see Erickson, Bonnie H.
Erickson, Bonnie H.
  xErickson, B. H.
    Understanding Data. McGraw.
Erickson, Carlton W. see Erickson, Carlton W. H.
Erickson, Carlton W. H.
  xErickson, Carlton W.
    Administering Instructional Media Programs.
      Macmillan.
    Fundamentals of Teaching with Audiovisual
      Technology. Macmillan.
Erickson, Carolly, 1943-
  xErickson, Carolly.
    Civilization & Society in the West. Scott F.
    Great Harry. Summit Bks.
    The Medieval Vision: Essays in History &
      Perception. Oxford U Pr.
Erickson, Charlotte. see Erickson, Charlotte Helen
  Zimmer.

Erickson, Charlotte Helen Zimmer.
  xErickson, Charlotte.
    The Freezer Cookbook. Chilton.
    The Working Person's Cookbook. Chilton.
Erickson, Donald A.
  xErickson, Donald A.
    ed. The Principal in Metropolitan Schools.
      McCutchan.
    ed. Public Controls for Nonpublic Schools. U
      of Chicago Pr.
Erickson, Erling A., 1934-
  xErickson, Erling A.
    Banking in Frontier Iowa, 1836-1865. Iowa St
      U Pr.
Erickson, Gerald D.
  xErickson, Gerald D.
    Family Therapy: An Introduction to Theory &
      Technique. Brooks-Cole.
Erickson, Gustav.
  xErickson, Gustav.
    Balanced Distribution. Philos Lib.
Erickson, John.
  xErickson, John.
    Soviet Military Power & Performance. Shoe
      String.
Erickson, John R.
  xErickson, John R.
    Panhandle Cowboy. U of Nebr Pr.
Erickson, Keith.
  xErickson, Keith V.
    Intro. by & Compiled by Aristotle's Rhetoric:
      Five Centuries of Philological Research.
      Scarecrow.
Erickson, Keith V. see Erickson, Keith.
Erickson, Kenneth P. see Erickson, Kenneth Paul.
Erickson, Kenneth Paul.
  xErickson, Kenneth P.
    The Brazilian Corporative State &
      Working-Class Politics. U of Cal Pr.
Erickson, Lois J. see Erickson, Lois Johnson.
Erickson, Lois Johnson.
  xErickson, Lois J.
    tr. Songs from the Land of Dawn. Arno.
Erickson, Marcene L.
  xErickson, Marcene L.
    Assessment & Management of Developmental
      Changes in Children. Mosby.
Erickson, Marilyn T.
  xErickson, Marilyn T.
    Child Psychopathology: Assessment, Etiology
      & Treatment. P-H.
    ed. Readings in Behavior Modification. Mss
      Info.
    ed. Readings in Behavior Modification
      Research with Children. Mss Info.
Erickson, Millard.
  xErickson, Millard J.
    ed. Relativism in Contemporary Christian
      Ethics. Baker Bk.
Erickson, Millard J.
  xErickson, Millard J.
    Contemporary Options in Eschatology: A
      Study of the Millennium. Baker Bk.
    ed. Living God: Readings in Christian
      Theology. Baker Bk.
    ed. New Life: Readings in Christian Theology.
      Baker Bk.
    Salvation: God's Amazing Plan. Victor Bks.
Erickson, Millard J. see Erickson, Millard.
Erickson, Milton H.
  xErickson, Milton H.

    ed. Hypnotic Alteration of Sensory, Perceptual
      & Psychophysical Processes. Halsted Pr.
    ed. Hypnotic Investigation of Psychodynamic
      Processes. Halsted Pr.
    Hypnotic Realities: The Induction of Clinical
      Hypnosis & Forms of Indirect Suggestion.
      Irvington.
    ed. Innovative Hypnotherapy. Halsted Pr.
    ed. The Nature of Hypnosis & Suggestion.
      Halsted Pr.
Erickson, Paul A.
  xErickson, Paul A.
    Ecological Impact Assessment: Principles &
      Applications. Acad Pr.
Erickson, Rica.
  xErickson, Rica.
    The Dempsters. Intl Schol Bk Serv.
Erickson, Robert, 1917-
  xErickson, Robert.
    Sound Structure in Music. U of Cal Pr.
Erickson, Rosemary. see Erickson, Rosemary J.
Erickson, Rosemary J.
  xErickson, Rosemary.
    Paroled but Not Free. Human Sci Pr.
Erickson, Russell E.
  xErickson, Russell E.
    Warton & the Traders. Lothrop.
Ericson, Edward E.
  xEricson, Edward E.
    Radicals in the University. Hoover Inst Pr.
Ericson, Eric, 1925-
  xEricson, Eric.
    The Sorcerer. St Martin.
Ericson, Lois.
  xEricson, Lois.
    The Bag Book. Van Nos Reinhold.
Ericson, Richard V. see Ericson, Richard Victor.
Ericson, Richard Victor.
  xEricson, Richard V.
    Criminal Reactions: The Labelling Perspective.
      Lexington Bks.
Ericson, Stig, 1929-
  xEricson, Stig.
    Dan Henry in the Wild West. Delacorte.
Ericsson, Dag.
  xEricsson, Dag.
    Materials Administration. McGraw.
Eriksen. see Eriksen, Karin.
Eriksen, Karin, 1944-
  xEriksen.
    Human Services Today. Reston.
Erikson, Erik H. see Erikson, Erik Homburger.
Erikson, Erik Homburger, 1902-
  xErikson, Erik H.
    Childhood & Society. Norton.
    Dimensions of a New Identity. Norton.
    Identity & the Life Cycle. Norton.
    Identity & the Life Cycle: Selected Papers. Intl
      Univs Pr.
    Life History & the Historical Moment. Norton.
Erikson, Joan M. see Erikson, Joan Mowat.
Erikson, Joan Mowat.
  xErikson, Joan M.
    Activity, Recovery, Growth: The Communal
      Role of Planned Activities. Norton.
Erikson, Kai T.
  xErikson, Kai T.
    Everything in Its Path: Destruction of
      Community in the Buffalo Creek Flood. S&S.
Erikson, Paul.
  xErikson, Paul.
    The Money Wolves. Berkley Pub.
    The Money Wolves. Morrow.
Erikson, Robert S.
  xErikson, Robert S.
    American Public Opinion: Its Origins, Content,
      & Impact. Wiley.
Eriksson. see Eriksson, Torsten.
Eriksson, Torsten.
  xEriksson.

The Reformers: An Historical Survey of
Pioneer Experiments in the Treatment of
Criminals. Elsevier.

Eringen, A. Cemal.
xEringen, A. Cemal.
ed. Continuum Physics. Acad Pr.

Erlandson, Keith.
xErlandson, Keith.
Gundog Training. Barrie & Jenkins.
Home Smoking & Curing: How You Can
Smoke-Cure, Salt, & Preserve Fish, Meat,
Poultry & Game. Barrie & Jenkins.

Erlanger, Ellen.
xErlanger, Ellen.
Hubert H. Humphrey: The Happy Warrior.
Lerner Pubns.

Erlanger, Rachel.
xErlanger, Rachel.
Lucrezia Borgia: A Biography. Dutton.

Erler, Fritz.
xErler, Fritz.
Democracy in Germany. Harvard U Pr.

Erlewein, David L.
xErlewein, David L.
Instructions for Veterinary Clients. Saunders.

Erlich, Avi.
xErlich, Avi.
Hamlet's Absent Father. Princeton U Pr.

Erlich, Lillian.
xErlich, Lillian.
Money Isn't Important: The Life of Maurice
Gusman. E A Seemann.

Erlich, Victor, 1914-
xErlich, Victor.
ed. Pasternak: A Collection of Critical Essays.
P-H.
ed. Twentieth-Century Russian Literary
Criticism. Yale U Pr.

Erman, Adolf, 1854-1937
xErman, Adolf.
ed. Ancient Egyptians. A Source Book of Their
Writings. Peter Smith.
Life in Ancient Egypt. Dover.
xErman, Adolph.
Life in Ancient Egypt. Arno.
Life in Ancient Egypt. Peter Smith.
Erman, Adolph. *see* Erman, Adolf.

Ermann, M. David.
xErmann, M. David.
ed. Corporate & Governmental Deviance:
Problems of Organizational Behavior in
Contemporary Society. Oxford U Pr.
Ermeling, William. *see* Ermeling, William K.

Ermeling, William K.
xErmeling, William.
Home Owner's Workshop. S&S.

Ermolaev, Herman.
xErmolaev, Herman.
Soviet Literary Theories 1917-1934: The
Genesis of Socialist Realism. Octagon.

Ernenwein, Leslie.
xErnenwein, Leslie.
Bullet Barricade. Nordon Pubns.
Renegade Ramrod. Nordon Pubns.

Ernest, John, 1935-
xErnest, John.
Charting the Operator Terrain. Am Math.
Ernest, John. *see* Ernest, John W.

Ernest, John W., 1914-
xErnest, John.
Introduction to Business Mathematics.
Glencoe.
xErnest, John W.
Creative Selling. McGraw.

Ernest, P. Edward.
xErnest, P. Edward.
ed. Family Album of Favorite Poems. G&D.

Ernst, Bernard.
xErnst, Bernard.

The Body Buddies. Macmillan.
Ernst, Bernard M. *see* Ernst, Bernard Morris Lee.

Ernst, Bernard Morris Lee.
xErnst, Bernard M.
Houdini & Conan Doyle: The Story of a
Strange Friendship. Arno.
Ernst, Carl W. *see* Ernst, Carl Wilhelm.

Ernst, Carl Wilhelm, 1845-1919
xErnst, Carl W.
Postal Service in Boston 1639-1893. Boston
Public Lib.

Ernst, David.
xErnst, David.
The Evolution of Electronic Music. Schirmer
Bks.
Musique Concrete. Taplinger.
Ernst, Joseph A. *see* Ernst, Joseph Albert.

Ernst, Joseph Albert.
xErnst, Joseph A.
Money & Politics in America, 1755-1775: A
Study in the Currency Act of 1764 & the
Political Economy of Revolution. U of NC
Pr.
Ernst, Kathryn. *see* Ernst, Kathryn F.

Ernst, Kathryn F.
xErnst, Kathryn.
Owl's New Cards. Crown.
xErnst, Kathryn F.
Danny & His Thumb. P-H.
Indians: The First Americans. Watts.

Ernst, Ken.
xErnst, Ken.
TA Stories for Kids. Celestial Arts.
Ernst, M. L. *see* Ernst, Morris Leopold.

Ernst, Max.
xErnst, Max.
Max Ernst. Hippocrene Bks.

Ernst, Morris Leopold, 1888-
xErnst, M. L.
The First Freedom. Da Capo.
Intro. by First Freedom. S Ill U Pr.

Ernst, Rick C.
xErnst, Rick C.
Proven Listing Techniques: The Answer to
Real Estate Success. Ernst.
Ernst, W. *see* Ernst, Werner.
Ernst, W. G. *see* Ernst, Wallace Gary.

Ernst, Wallace Gary, 1931-
xErnst, W. G.
Comparative Study of Low-Grade
Metamorphism in the California Coast
Ranges & the Outer Metamorphic Belt of
Japan. Geol Soc.
Earth Materials. P-H.

Ernst, Werner, 1927-
xErnst, W.
Geochemical Facies Analysis. Elsevier.

Erny, Pierre.
xErny, Pierre.
Childhood & Cosmos: The Social Psychology
of the Black African Child. Inscape Corp.

Erofeev, Venedikt, 1933-
xErofeev, Venedikt.
Moscow to the End of the Line. Taplinger.

Eron, Judy.
xEron, Judy.
Charlie Rich. Creative Ed.

Eron, Leonard D.
xEron, Leonard D.
ed. Relation of Theory to Practice in
Psychotherapy. Irvington.
Errington, Paul L. *see* Errington, Paul Lester.

Errington, Paul Lester.
xErrington, Paul L.
Muskrats & Marsh Management. U of Nebr Pr.
Of Men & Marshes. Iowa St U Pr.
Of Predation & Life. Iowa St U Pr.

Erskine, Addine G.
xErskine, Addine G.

The Principles & Practice of Blood Grouping.
Mosby.

Erskine, Beatrice.
xErskine, Beatrice S.
Palestine of the Arabs. Hyperion Conn.
Erskine, Beatrice S. *see* Erskine, Beatrice.
Erskine, J. *see* Erskine, John.

Erskine, Jim.
xErskine, Jim.
illus. Bert & Susie's Messy Tale. Crown.
Fold a Banana: & 146 Other Things to Do
When You're Bored. Potter.
The Snowman. Crown.

Erskine, John, 1879-1951
xErskine, J.
Pref. by Literary Discipline. Scholarly.
xErskine, John.
Complete Life. Arno.
The Delight of Great Books. R West.
The Delight of Great Books. Somerset Pub.
Leading American Novelists. Arno.
The Literary Discipline. Arden Lib.
Literary Discipline. Arno.
The Literary Discipline. Dynamic Learn Corp.
Literary Discipline. Folcroft.
The Literary Discipline. Johnson Repr.
Literary Discipline. Scholarly.
Moral Obligation to Be Intelligent & Other
Essays. Arno.

Erskine-Hill, Howard.
xErskine-Hill, Howard.
The Art of Alexander Pope. B&N.

Erte.
xErte.
Erte's Theatrical Costumes in Full-Color.
Dover.

Ertel, Paul P.
xErtel, Paul Y.
Medical Peer Review: Theory & Practice.
Mosby.
Ertel, Paul Y. *see* Ertel, Paul P.
Erven, Lawrence. *see* Erven, Lawrence W.

Erven, Lawrence W.
xErven, Lawrence.
First Aid & Emergency Rescue. Glencoe.
xErven, Lawrence W.
Handbook of Emergency Care & Rescue.
Glencoe.

Ervin, Jean.
xErvin, Jean.
ed. The Minnesota Experience: An Anthology.
Adams Minn.
The Twin Cities Perceived: A Study in Words
& Drawings. U of Minn Pr.
Ervine, St. John G. *see* Ervine, St. John Greer.

Ervine, St. John Greer, 1883-
xErvine, St. John G.
Some Impressions of My Elders. Folcroft.
Erwe, F. *see* Erwe, Friedhelm.

Erwe, Friedhelm.
xErwe, F.
Differential & Integral Calculus. Hafner.

Erwin, Annabel.
xErwin, Annabel.
Aurielle. Warner Bks.
Liliane. Warner Bks.

Erwin, Betty K.
xErwin, Betty K.
Who Is Victoria?. Archway.
Who Is Victoria. Little.
Who Is Victoria?. PB.
Erwin, E. *see* Erwin, Edward.

Erwin, Edward, 1937-
xErwin, E.
Behavior Therapy: Scientific, Philosophical &
Moral Foundations. Cambridge U Pr.
xErwin, Edward.

The Concept of Meaninglessness. Johns
	Hopkins.
Erwin, Jean.
	xErwin, Jean.
		How to Choose & Use the Right Therapist for
		You. Andrews & McMeel.
Erwin, Joseph.
	xErwin, Joseph.
		Captivity & Behavior: Primates in Breeding
		Colonies, Laboratories, & Zoos. Van Nos
		Reinhold.
Erwin, Joseph A.
	xErwin, Joseph A.
		ed. Lipids & Biomembranes of Eukaryotic
		Microorganisms. Acad Pr.
Erwin, Mabel D. see Erwin, Mabel Deane.
Erwin, Mabel Deane.
	xErwin, Mabel D.
		Clothing for Moderns. Macmillan.
Esau, Katherine.
	xEsau, Katherine.
		Anatomy of Seed Plants. Wiley.
Esbensen, Thorwald.
	xEsbensen, Thorwald.
		Student Contracts. Educ Tech Pubns.
Escalona, Sibylle K. see Escalona, Sibylle Korsch.
Escalona, Sibylle Korsch, 1915-
	xEscalona, Sibylle K.
		Application of the Level of Aspiration
		Experiment to the Study of Personality. AMS
		Pr.
Escarpit, Robert, 1918-
	xEscarpit, Robert.
		Book Revolution. Unipub.
		Open Letter to God. Heineman.
		tr. Sociology of Literature. Biblio Dist.
Escarraz, Donald R. see Escarraz, Donald Ray.
Escarraz, Donald Ray.
	xEscarraz, Donald R.
		Price Theory of Value in Public Finance. U
		Presses Fla.
Esch, Dortha.
	xEsch, Dortha.
		Musculoskeletal Function: An Anatomy &
		Kinesiology Laboratory Manual. U of Minn
		Pr.
Esch, Gerald W.
	xEsch, Gerald W.
		ed. Regulation of Parasite Populations. Acad
		Pr.
Escher, M. C. see Escher, Maurits Cornelis.
Escher, Maurits Cornelis.
	xEscher, M. C.
		The World of M. C. Escher. Abrams.
		World of M. C. Escher. NAL.
Eschholz, Paul A.
	xEschholz, Paul A.
		ed. Subject & Strategy: A Rhetoric Reader. St
		Martin.
Eschner, Arthur R.
	xEschner, Arthur R.
		ed. Readings in Forest Hydrology. Mss Info.
Escott, Paul D., 1947-
	xEscott, Paul D.
		After Secession: Jefferson Davis & the Failure
		of Confederate Nationalism. La State U Pr.
		Slavery Remembered: A Record of Twentieth
		Century Slave Narratives. U of NC Pr.
Escott, T. H. see Escott, Thomas Hay Sweet.
Escott, Thomas H. see Escott, Thomas Hay Sweet.
Escott, Thomas Hay Sweet, 1844-1924
	xEscott, T. H.
		Anthony Trollope, His Public Services, Private
		Friends & Literary Originals. Kennikat.
	xEscott, Thomas H.

Great Victorians: Memories & Personalities.
	Folcroft.
Masters of English Journalism: A Study of
	Personal Forces. Greenwood.
Esdaile, Arundell. see Esdaile, Arundell James Kennedy.
Esdaile, Arundell J. see Esdaile, Arundell James
	Kennedy.
Esdaile, Arundell James Kennedy, 1880-1956
	xEsdaile, Arundell.
		List of English Tales & Prose Romances
		Printed Before 1740. Folcroft.
	xEsdaile, Arundell J.
		List of English Tales & Prose Romances
		Printed Before 1740. B Franklin.
Esdaile, Katharine Ada Mcdowall.
	xEsdaile, Katherine A.
		English Monumental Sculpture Since the
		Renaissance. Hyperion Conn.
Esdaile, Katherine A. see Esdaile, Katharine Ada
	Mcdowall.
Eshbach, Charles E., 1914-
	xEshbach, Charles E.
		Food Service Management. CBI Pub.
Eshbach, Ovid W. see Eshbach, Ovid Wallace.
Eshbach, Ovid Wallace, 1893-
	xEshbach, Ovid W.
		Handbook of Engineering Fundamentals.
		Wiley.
Eshbach, Warren M.
	xEshbach, Warren M.
		A Future with Hope. Brethren.
Esherick, Joseph.
	xEsherick, Joseph W.
		Reform & Revolution in China: The 1911
		Revolution in Hunan & Hubei. U of Cal Pr.
Esherick, Joseph W. see Esherick, Joseph.
Eshleman, Clayton.
	xEshleman, Clayton.
		Coils. Black Sparrow.
		The Gull Wall. Black Sparrow.
		What She Means. Black Sparrow.
Eshleman, H. Frank. see Eshleman, Henry Frank.
Eshleman, Henry Frank, 1869-
	xEshleman, H. Frank.
		Historic Background & Annals of the Swiss &
		German Pioneer Settlers of Southeastern
		Pennsylvania & of Their Remote Ancestors.
		Genealog Pub.
Eshleman, J. Ross.
	xEshleman, J. Ross.
		The Family: An Introduction. Allyn.
Eshleman, Ruthe.
	xEshleman, Ruthe.
		ed. American Heart Association Cookbook.
		McKay.
Eshmeyer, R. E. see Eshmeyer, Reinhart Ernest.
Eshmeyer, Reinhart Ernest.
	xEshmeyer, R. E.
		Ask Any Vegetable. P-H.
Eshom. see Eshom, Myreta.
Eshom, Myreta.
	xEshom.
		Medical Secretary's Manual. ACC.
Eskelin, N. see Eskelin, Neil.
Eskelin, Neil.
	xEskelin, N.
		How to Make Money Speaking in Public. P-H.
Eskenazi, Gerald.
	xEskenazi, Gerald.
		Thinking Man's Guide to Pro Soccer. Dutton.
Eskinazi, S. see Eskinazi, Salamon.
Eskinazi, Salamon.
	xEskinazi, S.
		Fluid Mechanics & Thermodynamics of Our
		Environment. Acad Pr.
	xEskinazi, Salamon.
		ed. Vector Mechanics of Fluids &
		Magneto-Fluids. Acad Pr.
Eskrigge, Anne P. see Eskrigge, Anne Paramoure.

Eskrigge, Anne Paramoure, 1902-
	xEskrigge, Anne P.
		Complete Miniature Schnauzer. Howell Bk.
ESLAB Symposium, 6th, Noordwijk, Netherlands, 1972.
	xESLAB Symposium, 6th, Noordwijk, the
		Netherlands, Sept. 1972.
		Photon & Particle Interactions with Surfaces in
		Space: Proceedings. Kluwer Boston.
ESLAB Symposium, 6th, Noordwijk, the Netherlands,
	Sept. 1972. see ESLAB Symposium, 6th, Noordwijk,
	Netherlands, 1972.
Esler, Anthony.
	xEsler, Anthony.
		Aspiring Mind of the Elizabethan Younger
		Generation. Duke.
		Babylon. Morrow.
		For Love of a Pirate. Fawcett.
		For Love of a Pirate. Morrow.
		Forbidden City. Fawcett.
		Forbidden City. Morrow.
Esler, William K.
	xEsler, William K.
		Teaching Elementary Science. Wadsworth Pub.
Esman, Milton J. see Esman, Milton Jacob.
Esman, Milton Jacob.
	xEsman, Milton J.
		Common Aid Effort: The Development
		Assistance Activities of the Organization for
		Economic Cooperation & Development. Ohio
		St U Pr.
Esmay, Merle L., 1920-
	xEsmay, Merle L.
		Principles of Animal Environment. AVI.
Esmond, Harriet.
	xEsmond, Harriet.
		Eye Stones. Delacorte.
Esomar.
	xEuropean Society for Opinion & Marketing
		Research, 25th Congress.
		Fieldwork, Sampling & Questionnaire Design,
		Parts 1 & 2. Intl Pubns Serv.
		Forecasting in Marketing. Intl Pubns Serv.
		From Market Research to Advertising Strategy
		& Vice Versa. Intl Pubns Serv.
		Glossary of Technical Terms for Market
		Researchers:
		English-German-Spanish-French-
		lian-Dutch. Intl Pubns Serv.
		Managing Market Research As a Business. Intl
		Pubns Serv.
		ed. Marketing in a Changing World - the Role
		of Market Research: Proceedings. Intl Pubns
		Serv.
		ed. Papers on Analysis of Data. Intl Pubns
		Serv.
		Proceedings. Intl Pubns Serv.
		ed. Proceedings: From Experience to
		Innovation. Intl Pubns Serv.
Eson, Morris E.
	xEson, Morris E.
		Psychological Foundations of Education.
		HR&W.
Espenshade, A. Howry. see Espenshade, Abraham
	Howry.
Espenshade, Abraham H. see Espenshade, Abraham
	Howry.
Espenshade, Abraham Howry, 1869-1948
	xEspenshade, A. Howry.
		Pennsylvania Place Names. Genealog Pub.
	xEspenshade, Abraham H.
		Pennsylvania Place Names. Gale.
Espenshade, Jean E.
	xEspenshade, Jean E.
		Staff Manual for Teaching Patients About
		Diabetes Mellitus. Am Hospital.
Espenshade, Thomas J.
	xEspenshade, Thomas J.

The Cost of Children in Urban United States. Greenwood.

   ed. The Economic Consequences of Slowing Population Growth. Acad Pr.

Esper, Erwin A. *see* Esper, Erwin Allen.

Esper, Erwin Allen, 1895-1972

   xEsper, Erwin A.

   Analogy & Association in Linguistics & Psychology. U of Ga Pr.

Espey, John J. *see* Espey, John Jenkins.

Espey, John Jenkins, 1913-

   xEspey, John J.

   Ezra Pound's Mauberley: A Study in Composition. U of Cal Pr.

Espina, Noni.

   xEspina, Noni.

   Repertoire for the Solo Voice: A Fully Annotated Guide to Works for the Solo Voice Published in Modern Editions and Covering Material from the 13th Century to the Present. Scarecrow.

Espiritu, Socorro C.

   xEspiritu, Socorro C.

   A Study of the Treatment of the Philippines in Selected Social Studies Textbooks Published in the U. S. for Use in Elementary & Secondary Schools. R & E Res Assoc.

Esposito, Anthony.

   xEsposito, Anthony.

   Fluid Power with Applications. P-H.

Esposito, Phil.

   xEsposito, Phil.

   Hockey Is My Life. Dodd.

Espy, Hilda C. *see* Espy, Hilda Cole.

Espy, Hilda Cole.

   xEspy, Hilda C.

   Another World: Central America. Viking Pr.

Espy, Richard.

   xEspy, Richard.

   The Politics of the Olympic Games. U of Cal Pr.

Espy, Willard R.

   xEspy, Willard R.

   An Almanac of Words at Play. Potter.

   The Life & Works of Mr. Anonymous. Avon.

   Say It My Way: How to Avoid Certain Pitfalls of Spoken English, Together with a Decidedly Informal History of How Language Rose (or Fell). Doubleday.

Esquenazi-Mayo, Roberto.

   xEsquenazi-Mayo, Roberto.

   ed. Latin American Scholarship Since World War II: Trends in History, Political Science, Literature, Geography, & Economics. U of Nebr Pr.

Esquerre, Paul Joseph, 1872-1934

   xEsquerre, Paul-Joseph.

   The Applied Theory of Accounts. Arno.

Esquerre, Paul-Joseph. *see* Esquerre, Paul Joseph.

Esquire

   xEsquire Drink Bk.

   Art of Mixing Drinks. Bantam.

   xEsquire Editors.

   Esquire World of Golf. Trident.

   xEsquire Magazine.

   First Sports Reader. Arno.

   xEsquire Magazine Editors.

   ed. What Every Young Man Should Know: An Unconventional Guide for the Perceptive Young Man. Geis.

Esquire Drink Bk. *see* Esquire.

Esquire Editors. *see* Esquire.

Esquire Magazine. *see* Esquire.

Esquire Magazine Editors. *see* Esquire.

Esro Summer School in Space Physics, 3rd, Alpach, Austria, 1965.

   xESRO Summer School in Space Physics, 3rd, Albach, Austria, July 19-August 13, 1965.

Electromagnetic Radiation in Space: Proceedings. Kluwer Boston.

Essame, H. *see* Essame, Hubert.

Essame, Hubert, 1896-

   xEssame, H.

   Patton: A Study in Command. Scribner.

Essary, Don, 1939-

   xEssary, Don.

   Training Quarter Horses. A S Barnes.

Esser, Cajetan. *see* Esser, Kajetan.

Esser, Kajetan.

   xEsser, Cajetan.

   Love's Reply. Franciscan Herald.

Esser, Karl.

   xEsser, Karl.

   Genetics of Fungi. Springer-Verlag.

Essex Institute. *see* Essex Institute, Salem, Mass.

Essex Institute Fair, Salem, September 4-8, 1860. *see* Essex Institute, Salem, Mass.

Essex Institute, Salem, Mass.

   xEssex Institute.

   Essex Institute Historical Collections. Johnson Repr.

   xEssex Institute Fair, Salem, September 4-8, 1860.

   The Weal-Reaf: Proceedings. Essex Inst.

Essick, Robert N.

   xEssick, Robert N.

   William Blake, Printmaker. Princeton U Pr.

Essig, Edward O. *see* Essig, Edward Oliver.

Essig, Edward Oliver, 1884-

   xEssig, Edward O.

   History of Entomology. Hafner.

Esslemont, J. E. *see* Esslemont, John Ebenezer.

Esslemont, John Ebenezer, 1874-1925

   xEsslemont, J. E.

   Baha'u'llah & the New Era: An Introduction to the Baha'i Faith. Baha'i.

Esslen, Rainer.

   xEsslen, Rainer.

   The Complete Book of International Investing: How to Buy Foreign Securities & Who's on the International investment Scene. McGraw.

Esslin, Martin.

   xEsslin, Martin.

   An Anatomy of Drama. Hill & Wang.

   Antonin Artaud. Penguin.

   Brecht: The Man & His Work. Norton.

   Theatre of the Absurd. Doubleday.

   The Theatre of the Absurd. Overlook Pr.

   Theatre of the Absurd. Viking Pr.

Essman, Walter B.

   xEssman, Walter B.

   ed. Neurotransmitters, Receptors, & Drug Action. Spectrum Pub.

Essoe, Gabe.

   xEssoe, Gabe.

   Films of Clark Gable. Citadel Pr.

Estabrook, Leigh.

   xEstabrook, Leigh.

   ed. Libraries in Post-Industrial Society. Oryx Pr.

Estabrooks, George H. *see* Estabrooks, George Hoben.

Estabrooks, George Hoben, 1895-

   xEstabrooks, George H.

   Hypnotism. Dutton.

Estafen, Bernard D.

   xEstafen, Bernard D.

   The Comparative Management of Firms in Chile. Ind U Busn Res.

   The Systems Transfer Characteristics of Firms in Spain: A Comparative Management Study of American & Spanish Business Organizations. Ind U Busn Res.

Estaver, Marguerite.

   xEstaver, Marguerite.

   A Symphony of Leaves. Golden Quill.

Estep, William R. *see* Estep, William Roscoe.

Estep, William Roscoe, 1920-

   xEstep, William R.

The Anabaptist Story. Eerdmans.

Esterer, Arnulf. *see* Esterer, Arnulf K.

Esterer, Arnulf K.

   xEsterer, Arnulf.

   The Occult World. Messner.

   xEsterer, Arnulf K.

   Saying It Without Words: Signs & Symbols. Messner.

Esterline, John H.

   xEsterline, John H.

   Inside Foreign Policy: The Department of State Political System & Its Subsystems. Mayfield Pub.

Esterly, Diana. *see* Esterly, Diana Eames.

Esterly, Diana Eames.

   xEsterly, Diana.

   Early One-Design Sailboats. Scribner.

Esterman, Ben.

   xEsterman, Ben.

   The Eye Book: A Specialist's Guide to Your Eyes & Their Care. Great Ocean.

Estes, Eleanor.

   xEstes, Eleanor.

   The Coat-Hanger Christmas Tree. Atheneum.

   The Coat Hanger Christmas Tree. Atheneum.

   illus. Ginger Pye. HarBraceJ.

   Ginger Pye. HarBraceJ.

   Hundred Dresses. HarBraceJ.

   The Hundred Dresses. HarBraceJ.

   The Lost Umbrella of Kim Chu. Atheneum.

   Middle Moffat. HarBraceJ.

   The Middle Moffat. HarBraceJ.

   The Middle Moffat. HarBraceJ.

   Tunnel of Hugsy Goode. HarBraceJ.

Estes, Hiawatha T. *see* Estes, Hiawatha Thompson.

Estes, Hiawatha Thompson.

   xEstes, Hiawatha T.

   Ranch & Modern Homes. H Estes.

Estes, J. Worth, 1934-

   xEstes, J. Worth.

   Hall Jackson & the Purple Foxglove: Medical Practice & Research in Revolutionary America, 1760-1820. U Pr of New Eng.

Estes, Jack C., 1922-1975

   xEstes, Jack C.

   Compound Interest & Annuity Tables. McGraw.

   Handbook of Interest & Annuity Tables. McGraw.

   Handbook of Loan Payment Tables. McGraw.

   Real Estate License Preparation Course for the Uniform Examinations: For Salesmen & Brokers. McGraw.

Estes, Nada J.

   xEstes, Nada J.

   Nursing Diagnosis of the Alcoholic Person. Mosby.

Estes, Nolan.

   xEstes, Nolan.

   Marshalling Community Leadership to Support the Public Schools. Phi Delta Kappa.

Estes, Ralph W.

   xEstes, Ralph W.

   Corporate Social Accounting. Ronald Pr.

Estes, Thomas H.

   xEstes, Thomas H.

   Reading & Learning in the Content Classroom: Diagnostic & Instructional Strategies. Allyn.

Estes, William K. *see* Estes, William Kaye.

Estes, William Kaye.

   xEstes, William K.

Learning Theory & Mental Development. Acad
Pr.

Estes, Winston M., 1917-
xEstes, Winston M.
A Streetful of People. Avon.

Estey, Dale.
xEstey, Dale.
A Lost Tale. St Martin.

Esthus, Raymond A.
xEsthus, Raymond A.
From Enmity to Alliance: U. S.-Australian
Relations, 1931-41. U of Wash Pr.
Theodore Roosevelt & Japan. U of Wash Pr.

Estill, A. D. see Estill, Adelaide Duncan.
Estill, Adelaide. see Estill, Adelaide Duncan.
Estill, Adelaide Duncan, 1911-
xEstill, A. D.
The Sources of Synge. Porter.
xEstill, Adelaide.
Sources of Synge. Folcroft.

Estlake, Allan.
xEstlake, Allan.
The Oneida Community: A Record of an
Attempt to Carry Out the Principles of
Christian Unselfishnes & Scientific
Race-Improvement. AMS Pr.

Estleman, Loren D.
xEstleman, Loren D.
Dr. Jekyll & Mr. Holmes. Doubleday.
Dr. Jekyll & Mr. Holmes. Penguin.
The Hider. Doubleday.
The Hider. PB.
The High Rocks. Doubleday.
The High Rocks. PB.
Motor City Blue. HM.
Stamping Ground. Doubleday.

Estoril, Jean.
xEstoril, Jean.
Drina Dances in Italy. Vanguard.

Estrin, Jack C.
xEstrin, Jack C.
American History Made Simple. Doubleday.
World History Made Simple. Doubleday.

Estrin, Mary L. see Estrin, Mary Lloyd.
Estrin, Mary Lloyd.
xEstrin, Mary L.
To the Manor Born. NYGS.

Esty, John. see Esty, John C.
Esty, John C.
xEsty, John.
Choosing a Private School. Dodd.

Eszterhas, Joe.
xEszterhas, Joe.
Thirteen Seconds: Confrontation at Kent State.
Dodd.

ET D Staff. see Electronic Technician-Dealer.
ETD Magazine Editors. see Electronic
Technician-Dealer.

Eterovich, Adam S.
xEterovich, Adam S.
A Guide & Bibliography to Research on
Yugoslavs in the United States & Canada. R
& E Res Assoc.
A Guide & Bibliography to Research on
Yugoslavs in the United States & Canada.
Ragusan Pr.

Eterovich, Francis H.
xEterovich, Francis H.
Aristotle's Nicomachean Ethics: Commentary
& Analysis. U Pr of Amer.

Etgen, Garret J.
xEtgen, Garret J.
An Introduction to Ordinary Differential
Equations: With Difference Equations,
Numerical Methods, & Applications.
Har-Row.

Etgen, William M.
xEtgen, William M.

Dairy Cattle Feeding & Management. Wiley.

Ethe, Jane.
xEthe, Jane.
Easy & Attractive Gifts You Can Sew:
Step-by-Step Instructions for 20 Presents.
Dover.

Ethell, Jeff.
xEthell, Jeffrey L.
Moving Up to Twin-Engine Airplanes. TAB
Bks.

Ethell, Jeffrey. see Ethell, Jeffrey L.
Ethell, Jeffrey L.
xEthell, Jeffrey.
Used Aircraft Guide. Scribner.

Ethell, Jeffrey L. see Ethell, Jeff.
Etheredge, Lloyd.
xEtheredge, Lloyd S.
A World of Men: The Private Sources of
American Foreign Policy. MIT Pr.

Etheredge, Lloyd S. see Etheredge, Lloyd.
Etherege, George.
xEtherege, George.
Dramatic Works of Sir George Etherege.
Scholarly.
Letters of Sir George Etherege. U of Cal Pr.

Etherington, J. R. see Etherington, John R.
Etherington, John R.
xEtherington, J. R.
Environment & Plant Ecology. Wiley.

Etherton, Percy T. see Etherton, Percy Thomas.
Etherton, Percy Thomas, 1879-
xEtherton, Percy T.
Crisis in China. Arno.
Pacific: A Forecast. Arno.

Ethridge, Willie (Snow).
xEthridge, Willie S.
Side by Each. Vanguard.
Strange Fires: The True Story of John Wesley's
Love Affair in Georgia. Vanguard.
There's Yeast in the Middle East. Vanguard.

Ethridge, Willie S. see Ethridge, Willie (Snow).
Ethyl Corporation.
xEthyl Corporation.
Food for America's Future. Arno.

Etienne, Gilbert.
xEtienne, Gilbert.
Studies in Indian Agriculture: The Art of the
Possible. U of Cal Pr.

Etkin, Bernard.
xEtkin, Bernard.
Dynamics of Atmospheric Flight. Wiley.

Etkin, Ruth.
xEtkin, Ruth.
The Rhythm Band Book. Sterling.

Etkind, Efim. see Etkind, Efim Grigorevich.
Etkind, Efim Grigorevich.
xEtkind, Efim.
Notes of a Non-Conspirator. Oxford U Pr.

Etmekjian, James.
xEtmekjian, James.
Pattern Drills in Language Teaching. NYU Pr.

Eton, William.
xEton, William.
A Survey of the Turkish Empire. Arno.

Etons, Ursula.
xEtons, Ursula.
Angel Dusted: A Family's Nightmare.
Macmillan.

Ets, M. H. see Ets, Marie Hall.
Ets, Marie H. see Ets, Marie Hall.
Ets, Marie Hall, 1895-
xEts, M. H.
jt. auth. Nine Days to Christmas. Viking Pr.
xEts, Marie H.

illus. Gilberto & the Wind. Viking Pr.
illus. Gilberto & the Wind. Penguin.
illus. Just Me. Viking Pr.
Just Me. Penguin.
Nine Days to Christmas. Viking Pr.
Play with Me. Penguin.
illus. Play with Me. Viking Pr.

Etter, Les.
xEtter, Les.
Cool Man on the Court. Hastings.
Fast Break Forward. Hastings.
The Game of Hockey. Garrard.
Get Those Rebounds!. Hastings.
Hockey's Masked Men: Three Great Goalies.
Garrard.

Etter, Mildred F. see Etter, Mildred Field.
Etter, Mildred Field.
xEtter, Mildred F.
Exercise for the Prone Patient. Wayne St U Pr.

Ettinger, Pete.
xEttinger, Pete.
Precision Aerobatics. TAB Bks.

Ettinger, Richard P. see Ettinger, Richard Prentice.
Ettinger, Richard Prentice.
xEttinger, Richard P.
Credits & Collections. P-H.

Ettinger, Stephen J.
xEttinger, Stephen J.
Canine Cardiology. Saunders.

Ettinghausen, Henry.
xEttinghausen, Henry.
Francisco de Quevedo & the Neostoic
Movement. Oxford U Pr.

Ettinghausen, Richard.
xEttinghausen, Richard.
ed. Highlights of Persian Art. Westview.

Ettorre, E. M.
xEttorre, E. M.
Lesbians, Women & Society. Routledge &
Kegan.

Ettre, Leslie. see Ettre, Leslie S.
Ettre, Leslie S.
xEttre, Leslie.
ed. Ancillary Techniques of Gas
Chromatography. Krieger.

Etzioni, Amitai.
xEtzioni, Amitai.
Demonstration Democracy. Gordon.
Genetic Fix: The Next Technological
Revolution. Har-Row.
Readings on Modern Organizations. P-H.
A Sociological Reader in Complex
Organizations. HR&W.
Sociological Reader on Complex Organizations.
HR&W.

Etzkowitz, Henry, 1940-
xEtzkowitz, Henry.
Is America Possible?: Social Problems from
Conservative, Liberal, & Socialist
Perspectives. West Pub.

Etzold, Thomas. see Etzold, Thomas H.
Etzold, Thomas H.
xEtzold, Thomas.
Containment: Documents on American Policy
& Strategy 1945-1950. Columbia U Pr.
xEtzold, Thomas H.
ed. Aspects of Sino-American Relations Since
1784. New Viewpoints.

Eubank, Keith.
xEubank, Keith.
Summit Conferences, 1919-1960. U of Okla Pr.

Eubank, Nancy.
xEubank, Nancy.
The Lindberghs: Three Generations. Minn Hist.

Eubanks, I. D. see Eubanks, I. Dwaine.
Eubanks, I. Dwaine.
xEubanks, I. D.
Chemistry in Civilization. Wiley.

Euler, Harrison L. see Euler, Harrison Leslie.

Euler, Harrison Leslie, 1891-
　xEuler, Harrison L.
　　County Unification in Kansas. AMS Pr.
Euler, Leonhard, 1707-1783
　xEuler, Leonhard.
　　Letters of Euler on Different Subjects in
　　Natural Philosophy. Arno.
Eunson, Dale.
　xEunson, Dale.
　　Day They Gave Babies Away. FS&G.
Eunson, Roby.
　xEunson, Roby.
　　The Soong Sisters. Watts.
　　When France Was De Gaulle. Watts.
Euripides.
　xEuripides.
　　Alcestis. Allen Unwin.
　　Alcestis. Oxford U Pr.
　　Andromache. Oxford U Pr.
　　The Bacchae. Allen Unwin.
　　Bacchae. Oxford U Pr.
　　Hippolytos. Oxford U Pr.
　　Hippolytus. Allen Unwin.
　　Hippolytus. Oxford U Pr.
　　The Iphigeneia at Aulis of Euripides. Arno.
　　The Medea. Allen Unwin.
　　Medea. Oxford U Pr.
　　The Phoenissae of Euripides. Arno.
　　Rhesos. Oxford U Pr.
**Euromech Colloquium on Gyrodynamics, University of
　Louvain, 1973.**
　xEuromech 38 Colloquium, Louvain-la-Neuve,
　　Belgium, 3-5 September, 1973.
　　Gyrodynamics: Proceedings. Springer-Verlag.
Euromech 38 Colloquium, Louvain-la-Neuve, Belgium,
　3-5 September, 1973. see Euromech Colloquium on
　Gyrodynamics, University of Louvain, 1973.
European Anatomical Congress.
　xEuropean Anatomical Congress, 4th.
　　Abstracts. S Karger.
European Anatomical Congress, 4th. see European
　Anatomical Congress.
European Association for Research on Plant Breeding.
　xCongress of EUCARPIA, 7th, Budapest, 1974.
　　Heterosis in Plant Breeding: Proceedings.
　　Elsevier.
European Association of Radiology.
　xTheEuropean Association of Radiology
　　Symposium, Mainz, 1970.
　　Angiography-Scintigraphy: Proceedings.
　　Springer-Verlag.
European Astronomical Meeting, 1st, Athens, 1972.
　xEuropean Astronomical Meeting, 1st, Athens,
　　1972.
　　Galaxies & Relativistic Astrophysics:
　　Proceedings, Vol. 3. Springer-Verlag.
　　Solar Activity & Related Interplanetary &
　　Terrestrial Phenomenon: Proceedings.
　　Springer-Verlag.
　　Stars & the Milky Way System: Proceedings.
　　Springer-Verlag.
European Commission for Control of Foot & Mouth
　Disease. see European Commission for the Control of
　Foot and Mouth Disease.
**European Commission for the Control of Foot and
　Mouth Disease.**
　xEuropean Commission for Control of Foot &
　　Mouth Disease.
　　Report: Twenty-First Session, Rome, April
　　8-11, 1975. Unipub.
　xEuropean Commission for the Control of Foot &
　　Mouth Disease, Twenty First Session, Rome,
　　Italy, April 8-11, 1975.
　　Report. Unipub.
**European Conference on Computational Physics, 2d,
　Max-Planck-Institut Fuer Plasmaphysik, 1976.**
　xEuropean Conference on Computational Physics,
　　2nd, Garching, Apr. 1976.

Computing in Plasma Physics: Proceedings.
　Elsevier.
**European Conference on Microcirculation, 7th,
　Aberdeen, Scot., 1972.**
　xEuropean Conference on Microcirculation, 7th,
　　Aberdeen, Aug.-Sept. 1972, Part I.
　　Clinical Aspects of Microcirculation:
　　Proceedings. S Karger.
　　Methodology in Microcirculation: Proceedings.
　　S Karger.
**European Conference on Microcirculation, 8th, le
　Touquet-Paris-Plage, 1974.**
　xEuropean Conference on Microcirculation, 8th, le
　　Touquet 1974.
　　Recent Advances in Critical Microcirculatory
　　Research. S Karger.
European Conference on Mixing.
　xEuropean Conference on Mixing, 3rd.
　　Proceedings. BHRA Fluid.
European Conference on Mixing, 3rd. see European
　Conference on Mixing.
**European Conference on Psychosomatic Research, 9th,
　Vienna, 1972.**
　xEuropean Conference on Psychosomatic
　　Research, 9th, Vienna, April 1972.
　　Topics of Psychosomatic Research:
　　Proceedings. S Karger.
**European Conference on the Management of Large
　Space Programs, Paris, 1970.**
　xCNES.
　　Large Space Programs Management. Gordon.
European Congress of Allergology & Clinical
　Immunology, 9th. see European Congress of
　Allergology and Clinical Immunology, 9th, London,
　1974.
**European Congress of Allergology and Clinical
　Immunology, 9th, London, 1974.**
　xEuropean Congress of Allergology & Clinical
　　Immunology, 9th.
　　Allergy. Beekman Pubs.
**European Congress of Allergology and Clinical
　Immunology, 9th, London, 1974.**
　xEuropean Congress, 9th.
　　Allergy Seventy-Four: Proceedings. Grune.
**European Congress of Anaesthesiology, 1st, Vienna,
　1962.**
　xEuropean Congress of Anaesthesiology of the
　　World Federation of Societies of
　　Anaesthesiologists, 1st, Vienna, 1962.
　　Hypnosis in Anaesthesiology: Proceedings.
　　Springer-Verlag.
　　Resuscitation Controversial Aspects:
　　Proceedings. Springer-Verlag.
European Congress of Neurosurgery.
　xEuropean Congress Of Neurosurgery - Rome -
　　1963.
　　Hypothermia in Neurosurgery: Proceedings.
　　Springer-Verlag.
European Congress Of Neurosurgery - Rome - 1963. see
　European Congress of Neurosurgery.
European Congress of Sleep Research, 1st Basel, Oct.
　1972. see European Congress on Sleep Research, 1st,
　Basel, 1972.
**European Congress on Molecular Spectroscopy, 12th,
　Strasbourg, 1975.**
　xEuropean Congress on Molecular Spectroscopy,
　　12th, Strasbourg, 1975.
　　Molecular Spectroscopy of Dense Phases:
　　Proceedings. Elsevier.
European Congress on Sleep Research, 1st, Basel, 1972.
　xEuropean Congress of Sleep Research, 1st Basel,
　　Oct. 1972.
　　Sleep: Physiology, Biochemistry, Psychology,
　　Pharmacology, Clinical Implications. S
　　Karger.
**European Congress on Thermography, 1st, Amsterdam,
　1974.**
　xEuropean Congress on Thermography, 1st,
　　Amsterdam, Jun 1974.

Thermography. S Karger.
European Congress, 9th. see European Congress of
　Allergology and Clinical Immunology, 9th, London,
　1974.
European Dialysis & Transplant Assoc., 1974, Tel Aviv.
　see European Dialysis and Transplant Association.
European Dialysis and Transplant Association.
　xEuropean Dialysis & Transplant Assoc., 1974, Tel
　　Aviv.
　　Dialysis, Transplantation & Nephrology:
　　Proceedings. Beekman Pubs.
European Meeting of Statisticians, Grenoble, 1976.
　xEuropean Meeting of Statisticians, Sept. 6-11
　　1976, Grenoble, France.
　　Recent Developments in Statistics:
　　Proceedings. Elsevier.
European Meeting of Statisticians, Sept. 6-11 1976,
　Grenoble, France. see European Meeting of
　Statisticians, Grenoble, 1976.
European Meeting, Vienna, 1972. see International
　Congress of Cybernetics and Systems, University of
　Oxford, 1972.
**European Molecular Biology International Workshop,
　5th, University of Malta, 1976.**
　xEuropean Molecular Biology International
　　Workshop, Fifth, Marine Biological Laboratory
　　of the University of Malta, Malta, August 2-4,
　　1976.
　　Structure & Function of Haemocyanin:
　　Proceedings in Life Sciences. Springer-Verlag.
European Nutrition Conference, 2nd, Munich, 1976. see
　European Nutritional Conference.
European Nutritional Conference.
　xEuropean Nutrition Conference, 2nd, Munich,
　　1976.
　　Abstracts. S Karger.
European Organization for Caries Research, Board. see
　European Organization for Research on Flourine and
　Dental Caries Prevention.
**European Organization for Research on Flourine and
　Dental Caries Prevention.**
　xEuropean Organization for Caries Research,
　　Board.
　　ed. Reports of ORCA on Water Fluoridation. S
　　Karger.
**European Organization for Research on Treatment of
　Cancer.**
　xEuropean Organization for Research on
　　Treatment of Cancer, Plenary Session, Paris,
　　1969.
　　Advances in the Treatment of Acute (Blastic)
　　Leukemias: Proceedings. Springer-Verlag.
　　Aseptic Environments & Cancer Treatment:
　　Proceedings. Springer-Verlag.
European Pacemaker Colloquium.
　xEuropean Pacemaker Colloquium, Brussels, 2nd,
　　April, 1977.
　　To Pace or Not to Pace, Controversial Subjects
　　on Cardiac Pacing: Proceedings. Kluwer
　　Boston.
European Pacemaker Colloquium, Brussels, 2nd, April,
　1977. see European Pacemaker Colloquium.
European Parliament.
　xEuropean Parliament - Translation Division.
　　Terminology of Environmental Hygiene:
　　English-French-Italian-German-Dutch. Intl
　　Pubns Serv.
European Parliament - Translation Division. see
　European Parliament.
European Peptide Symposium, 11th, Vienna, 1971.
　xEleventh European Peptide Symposium, Vienna,
　　April 1971.
　　Peptides: Proceedings. Elsevier.
European Regional Conference of the International
　Geographical Union, Budapest. see International
　Geographical Union, Urbanization in Europe.
**European Seminar on Computerised Axial Tomography
　in Clinical Practice, 1st, London, 1976.**
　xEuropean Seminar on Computerized Axial
　　Tomography in Clinical Practice, 1st.

Proceedings. Springer-Verlag.
European Seminar on Computerized Axial Tomography
in Clinical Practice, 1st. *see* European Seminar on
Computerised Axial Tomography in Clinical Practice,
1st, London, 1976.
European Society for Opinion & Marketing Research,
25th Congress. *see* Esomar.
European Symposium on Calcified Tissues.
xEuropean Symposium on Calcified Tissues - 8th,
Jerusalem, 1971.
Calcified Tissue. Acad Pr.
Calcium Metabolism, Bone & Metabolic Bone
Diseases: Proceedings. Springer-Verlag.
European Symposium on Medical Enzymology, 1960.
xEuropean Symposium On Medical Enzymology -
1st - Milan - 1960.
Proceedings. Acad Pr.
**European Symposium on Modern Anesthetic Agents,
1st, Hamburg, 1973.**
xSymposium on Modern Anesthetic Agents, 1st,
Hamburg, Nov. 9-10, 1973.
Ethrane: Proceedings. Springer-Verlag.
Eusden, John D. *see* Eusden, John Dykstra.
Eusden, John Dykstra.
xEusden, John D.
Puritans, Lawyers & Politics in Early
Seventeenth Century England. Shoe String.
Eustis, Helen.
xEustis, Helen.
The Horizontal Man. Garland Pub.
Euwe, M. *see* Euwe, Machgielis.
Euwe, Machgielis, 1901-
xEuwe, M.
Strategy & Tactics in Chess. McKay.
xEuwe, Max.
Bobby Fischer - the Greatest?. Sterling.
A Guide to Chess Endings. Dover.
Euwe, Max. *see* Euwe, Machgielis.
Evan, Paul.
xEvan, Paul.
Gunsmoke Over Sabado. Bouregy.
Evan, W. M. *see* Evan, William M.
Evan, William M.
xEvan, W. M.
Organization Theory: Structures, Systems, &
Environments. Wiley.
xEvan, William M.
Frontiers in Organization & Management.
Praeger.
ed. Law & Sociology: Exploratory Essays.
Greenwood.
Evanoff, Vlad.
xEvanoff, Vlad.
illus. Fishing Rigs for Fresh & Salt Water.
Har-Row.
Fresh-Water Fisherman's Bible. Doubleday.
How to Fish in Salt Water. A S Barnes.
Modern Fishing Tackle. A S Barnes.
Spin Fishing. A S Barnes.
Surf Fishing. Har-Row.
Evans, Alan, 1930-
xEvans, Alan.
Thunder at Dawn. Doubleday.
Evans, Alan W.
xEvans, Alan W.
The Economics of Residential Location. St
Martin.
Evans, Anthony.
xEvans, Anthony.
Aquariums. Palmetto Pub.
Care & Breeding of Goldfish. Dover.
Evans, Archibald A.
xEvans, Archibald A.
Hours of Work in Industrialised Countries. Intl
Labour Office.
Evans, Arthur R.
xEvans, Arthur R.
The Literary Art of Eugene Fromentin: A
Study in Style and Motif. Johns Hopkins.
Evans, B. Ifor. *see* Evans, Benjamin Ifor.

Evans, Barry. *see* Evans, Hayden Barry.
Evans, Benjamin I. *see* Evans, Benjamin Ifor.
Evans, Benjamin Ifor, Sir, 1899-
xEvans, B. Ifor.
Literature & Science. Folcroft.
xEvans, Benjamin I.
English Literature Between the Wars. Folcroft.
Evans, Bergen, 1904-
xEvans, Bergen.
The Psychiatry of Robert Burton. Octagon.
Evans, Bertrand, 1912-
xEvans, Bertrand.
Shakespeare's Tragic Practice. Oxford U Pr.
Evans, Bruce, 1944-
xEvans, Bruce.
The Swingback-Motion Offense for Winning
Football. P-H.
Evans, C. Stephen.
xEvans, C. Stephen.
Preserving the Person: A Look at the Human
Sciences. Inter-Varsity.
Evans, C. W. *see* Evans, Colin W.
Evans, Cerinda W.
xEvans, Cerinda W.
Collis Potter Huntington. U Pr of Va.
Evans, Charles H., 1831-1910
xEvans, Charles H.
ed. Exports, Domestic & Foreign from the
American Colonies to Great Britain, from
1697 to 1789. Arno.
Evans, Christopher. *see* Evans, Christopher Richie.
Evans, Christopher Richie.
xEvans, Christopher.
The Micro Millennium. Viking Pr.
Evans, Colin W.
xEvans, C. W.
Powdered & Particulate Rubber Technology.
Intl Ideas.
xEvans, Colin W.
Hose Technology. Burgess-Intl Ideas.
Evans, Colleen T. *see* Evans, Colleen Townsend.
Evans, Colleen Townsend.
xEvans, Colleen T.
Love Is an Everyday Thing. Revell.
xEvans, Colleen Townsend.
Start Loving: The Miracle of Forgiving.
Doubleday.
Evans, D. M. *see* Evans, David Maclean Demetrius.
Evans, D. MacLean. *see* Evans, David Maclean
Demetrius.
Evans, D. Morier. *see* Evans, David Morier.
Evans, D. R. *see* Evans, David Russell.
Evans, D. S. *see* Evans, David Stanley.
Evans, D. Wainwright. *see* Evans, David Wainwright.
Evans, David.
xEvans, David.
The Good Book. Price Stern.
Evans, David B. *see* Evans, David Beecher.
Evans, David Beecher, 1928-
xEvans, David B.
Leontius of Byzantium: An Origenist
Christology. Dumbarton Oaks.
Evans, David Maclean Demetrius.
xEvans, D. M.
Special Tests & Their Meanings. Merrimack Bk
Serv.
xEvans, D. MacLean.
Introduction to Medical Chemistry. Har-Row.
Evans, David Morier, 1819-1874
xEvans, D. Morier.
Speculative Notes & Notes on Speculation,
Ideal & Real. B Franklin.
Evans, David Russell, 1937-
xEvans, D. R.
Essential Interviewing: A Programmed
Approach to Effective Communication.
Brooks-Cole.
Evans, David Stanley.
xEvans, D. S.

Observation in Modern Astronomy. Elsevier.
Evans, David Wainwright.
xEvans, D. Wainwright.
Compiled by Cooking for Your Heart's
Content: 250 Gourmet Recipes to Keep Your
Heart Healthy. Paddington.
Evans, Donald. *see* Evans, Donald D.
Evans, Donald D.
xEvans, Donald.
Faith, Authenticity, & Morality. U of Toronto
Pr.
Struggle & Fulfillment: The Inner Dynamics of
Religion & Morality. Collins Pubs.
Evans, Donald P.
xEvans, Donald P.
Still Hooked on Harness Racing. A S Barnes.
Super Bird: The Story of Albatross. A S
Barnes.
Evans, Douglas B.
xEvans, Douglas B.
Auto Tour Guide to the Lake Mead National
Recreation Area. SW Pks Mnmts.
Evans, E. A. *see* Evans, Eustace Anthony.
Evans, E. Belle.
xEvans, E. Belle.
Day Care for Infants: The Case for Infant Day
Care & a Practical Guide. Beacon Pr.
Day Care: How to Plan, Develop & Operate a
Day Care Center. Beacon Pr.
Evans, E. P. *see* Evans, Edward Payson.
Evans, E. W. *see* Evans, Eric Wyn.
Evans, Edward Payson, 1831-1917
xEvans, E. P.
Animal Symbolism in Ecclesiastical
Architecture. Gordon Pr.
Evans, Elizabeth, 1935-
xEvans, Elizabeth.
Ring Lardner. Ungar.
Evans, Elizabeth E. *see* Evans, Elizabeth Edson Gibson.
Evans, Elizabeth Edson Gibson, 1832-1911
xEvans, Elizabeth E.
The Abuse of Maternity. Arno.
Evans, Ellis D.
xEvans, Ellis D.
Contemporary Influences in Early Childhood
Education. HR&W.
Evans, Eric J.
xEvans, Eric J.
The Contentious Tithe: The Tithe Problem &
English Agriculture, 1750-1850. Routledge &
Kegan.
ed. Social Policy 1830-1914: Individualism,
Collectivism & the Origins of the Welfare
State. Routledge & Kegan.
Evans, Eric Wyn.
xEvans, E. W.
ed. Industrial Conflict in Britain. Biblio Dist.
Evans, Ernest, 1950-
xEvans, Ernest.
Calling a Truce to Terror: The American
Response to International Terrorism.
Greenwood.
Evans, Eustace Anthony.
xEvans, E. A.
Tritium & Its Compounds. Krieger.
Evans, Evelyn.
xEvans, Evelyn.
House by an African Path. Broadman.
Evans, F. C.
xEvans, F. C.
The Bahamas. Cambridge U Pr.
Evans, F. Gaynor. *see* Evans, Francis Gaynor.
Evans, Francis Gaynor, 1907-
xEvans, F. Gaynor.
Mechanical Properties of Bone. C C Thomas.
Evans, Francis L.
xEvans, Francis L.
Ozone in Water & Wastewater Treatment. Ann
Arbor Science.
Evans, Frank B. *see* Evans, Frank Bernard.

Evans, Frank Bernard, 1927-
    xEvans, Frank B.
        Modern Archives & Manuscripts: A Select
            Bibliography. Soc Am Archivists.
Evans, Frederick W. see Evans, Frederick William.
Evans, Frederick William, 1808-1893
    xEvans, Frederick W.
        Autobiography of a Shaker, & Revelation of
            the Apocalypse. AMS Pr.
        Autobiography of a Shaker & Revelation of the
            Apocalypse. Porcupine Pr.
Evans, G. see Evans, Grose.
Evans, G. Clifford. see Evans, George Clifford.
Evans, G. Edward, 1937-
    xEvans, G. Edward.
        Developing Library Collections. Libs Unl.
Evans, G. Heberton. see Evans, George Heberton.
Evans, G. R. see Evans, Gillian.
Evans, Gareth.
    xEvans, Garth.
        ed. Truth & Meaning: Essays in Semantics.
            Oxford U Pr.
Evans, Garth. see Evans, Gareth.
Evans, George Bird.
    xEvans, George Bird.
        Troubles with Bird Dogs & What to Do About
            Them: Training Experiences with Actual
            Dogs Under the Gun. Winchester Pr.
Evans, George Clifford.
    xEvans, G. Clifford.
        The Quantitative Analysis of Plant Growth. U
            of Cal Pr.
Evans, George E. see Evans, George Ewart.
Evans, George Ewart.
    xEvans, George E.
        Horse Power & Magic. Merrimack Bk Serv.
Evans, George Heberton, 1927-
    xEvans, G. Heberton.
        Canoeing Wilderness Waters. A S Barnes
Evans, George W. see Evans, George William.
Evans, George William.
    xEvans, George W.
        Programming & Coding for Automatic Digital
            Computers. McGraw.
Evans, Geraint N. see Evans, Geraint Nantglyn Davies.
Evans, Geraint Nantglyn Davies.
    xEvans, Geraint N.
        Uncommon Obdurate: The Several Public
            Careers of J. F. W. Des Barres. Peabody Mus
            Salem.
Evans, Gillian.
    xEvans, G. R.
        Anselm & Talking About God. Oxford U Pr.
Evans, Glen.
    xEvans, Glen.
        The Family Circle Guide to Self-Help.
            Ballantine.
Evans, Grose.
    xEvans, G.
        Van Gogh. McGraw.
Evans, H. J. see Evans, Henry John.
Evans, Harold.
    xEvans, Harold.
        Pictures on a Page: Photojournalism & Picture
            Editing. Wadsworth Pub.
Evans, Hayden Barry, 1936-
    xEvans, Barry.
        ed. Prayer Book Renewal: Worship & the New
            Book of Common Prayer. Seabury.
Evans, Henry C. see Evans, Henry Clay.
Evans, Henry Clay, Jr.
    xEvans, Henry C.
        Chile & Its Relations with the United States.
            Johnson Repr.
Evans, Henry John.
    xEvans, H. J.
        Mutagen-Induced Chromosome Damage in
            Man. Yale U Pr.
Evans, Herbert A. see Evans, Herbert Arthur.

Evans, Herbert Arthur, 1846-
    xEvans, Herbert A.
        ed. English Masques. Arno.
        English Masques. Folcroft.
Evans, Hilary, 1929-
    xEvans, Hilary.
        The Art of Picture Research: A Guide to
            Current Practice, Procedure, Techniques &
            Resources. David & Charles.
        Harlots, Whores & Hookers: A History of
            Prostitution. Taplinger.
        Ribbonwork. Bobbs.
        Sources of Illustration, 1500-1900. Hastings.
Evans, Howard E. see Evans, Howard Ensign.
Evans, Howard Ensign.
    xEvans, Howard E.
        Life on a Little-Known Planet. Dutton.
Evans, Hugh E.
    xEvans, Hugh E.
        Perinatal Medicine. Har-Row.
Evans, Humphrey Ap. see Ap Evans, Humphrey.
Evans, Hywell.
    xEvans, Hywell.
        Governmental Regulation of Industrial
            Relations: A Comparative Study of United
            States & British Experience. NY Sch Indus
            Rel.
Evans, Idella M.
    xEvans, Idella M.
        Psychology for a Changing World. Wiley.
Evans, Ivor H. see Evans, Ivor Hugh Norman.
Evans, Ivor Hugh Norman.
    xEvans, Ivor H.
        Papers on the Ethnology & Archaeology of the
            Malay Peninsula. AMS Pr.
Evans, J. A. see Evans, James Allan Stewart.
Evans, J. D. see Evans, John David Gemmill.
Evans, J. Harvey.
    xEvans, J. Harvey.
        Ocean Engineering Structures. MIT Pr.
Evans, J. L.
    xEvans, J. L.
        Knowledge & Infallibility. St Martin.
Evans, J. M. see Evans, John Martin.
Evans, J. Martin. see Evans, John Martin.
Evans, J. Warren. see Evans, James Warren.
Evans, James Allan Stewart, 1931-
    xEvans, J. A.
        Procopius. Twayne.
Evans, James E.
    xEvans, James E.
        A Guide to Prose Fiction in the Tatler & the
            Spectator. Garland Pub.
Evans, James F.
    xEvans, James F.
        Communications in Agriculture: The American
            Farm Press. Iowa St U Pr.
Evans, James Warren, 1938-
    xEvans, J. Warren.
        The Horse. W H Freeman.
Evans, Joan, 1893-
    xEvans, Joan.
        Monastic Iconography in France from the
            Renaissance to the Revolution. Cambridge U
            Pr.
        Monastic Life at Cluny, 910-1157. Shoe String.
        Pattern: A Study of Ornament in Western
            Europe from 1180 to 1900. Hacker.
        Taste & Temperament: A Brief Study of
            Psychological Types in Their Relation to the
            Visual Arts. Hyperion Conn.
Evans, John C. see Evans, John Comstock.
Evans, John Comstock.
    xEvans, John C.
        Touch Typewriting. Har-Row.
Evans, John David Gemmill, 1942-
    xEvans, J. D.

Aristotle's Concept of Dialectic. Cambridge U
            Pr.
Evans, John G.
    xEvans, John G.
        An Introduction to Environmental
            Archaeology. Cornell U Pr.
Evans, John Martin.
    xEvans, J. M.
        Paradise Lost & the Genesis Tradition. Oxford
            U Pr.
    xEvans, J. Martin.
        America: The View from Europe. Norton.
        America: The View from Europe. SF Bk Co.
Evans, Judith L.
    xEvans, Judith L.
        Children in Africa: A Review of Psychological
            Research. Tchrs Coll.
Evans, K. M. see Evans, Kathleen Marianne.
Evans, Katherine, 1901-
    xEvans, Katherine.
        Boy Who Cried Wolf. A Whitman.
Evans, Kathleen Marianne.
    xEvans, K. M.
        Sociometry & Education. Humanities.
Evans, Kenneth. see Evans, Kenneth L.
Evans, Kenneth L.
    xEvans, Kenneth.
        A Feast for Spiders. NAL.
    xEvans, Kenneth L.
        A Feast for Spiders. T Y Crowell.
Evans, L. T.
    xEvans, L. T.
        ed. Induction of Flowering: Some Case
            Histories. Cornell U Pr.
Evans, Larry.
    xEvans, Larry.
        Chess in Ten Lessons. A S Barnes.
        How to Draw Monsters. Troubador Pr.
        How to Draw Prehistoric Monsters. Troubador
            Pr.
Evans, Laura.
    xEvans, Laura.
        Desolation River Guide: Green River
            Wilderness. Westwater.
Evans, Lawton B. see Evans, Lawton Bryan.
Evans, Lawton Bryan, 1862-1934
    xEvans, Lawton B.
        A History of Georgia for Use in Schools.
            Reprint.
Evans, Les.
    xEvans, Les.
        China After Mao. Path Pr NY.
    xEvans, Leslie.
        ed. China After Mao. Monad Pr.
Evans, Leslie. see Evans, Les.
Evans, Louis H. see Evans, Louis Hadley.
Evans, Louis Hadley, 1926-
    xEvans, Louis H.
        Creative Love. Fawcett.
Evans, M. E. see Evans, Michael Edwin Glyn.
Evans, Mari, 1923-
    xEvans, Mari.
        I Am a Black Woman. Morrow.
        I Look at Me. Third World.
        Jim Flying High. Doubleday.
Evans, Mark.
    xEvans, Mark.
        The Morality Gap. Alba Bks.
        Soundtrack: The Music of the Movies. Da
            Capo.
Evans, Mary, 1890-
    xEvans, Mary.
        How to Make Historic American Costumes.
            Gale.
Evans, Maurice.
    xEvans, Maurice.
        G. K. Chesterton. Haskell.
Evans, Max.
    xEvans, Max.

The White Shadow. Joyce Pr.

Evans, Medford.
xEvans, Medford.
Assassination of Joe McCarthy. Western Islands.

Evans, Medford S. *see* Evans, Medford Stanton.

Evans, Medford Stanton, 1934-
xEvans, Medford S.
Revolt on the Campus. Greenwood.

Evans, Michael Edwin Glyn.
xEvans, M. E.
The Life of Beetles. Allen Unwin.
The Life of Beetles. Hafner.

Evans, Michele.
xEvans, Michele.
American Cuisine Minceur Cookbook. Warner Bks.

Evans, Norma P. *see* Evans, Norma Pontiff.

Evans, Norma Pontiff, 1937-
xEvans, Norma P.
The Ancestry & Descendants of William Riley Shumate (1777-1979). N P Evans.

Evans, Paul D. *see* Evans, Paul Demund.

Evans, Paul Demund.
xEvans, Paul D.
Holland Land Company. Kelley.

Evans, Peter, 1944-
xEvans, Peter.
Dependent Development: The Alliance of Multinational, State, & Local Capital in Brazil. Princeton U Pr.
Mastering Your Migraine. Dutton.

Evans, Peter. *see* Evans, Peter Angus.

Evans, Peter Angus, 1929-
xEvans, Peter.
The Music of Benjamin Britten. U of Minn Pr.

Evans, R. E.
xEvans, R. E.
The American War of Independence. Lerner Pubns.

Evans, R. G. *see* Evans, Robert G.

Evans, Ralph M. *see* Evans, Ralph Merrill.

Evans, Ralph Merrill.
xEvans, Ralph M.
Eye, Film & Camera in Color Photography. Krieger.
The Perception of Color. Wiley.

Evans, Richard I. *see* Evans, Richard Isadore.

Evans, Richard Isadore, 1922-
xEvans, Richard I.
Carl Rogers: The Man & His Ideas. Dutton.
Dialogue with Erik Erikson. Dutton.

Evans, Richard J., 1935-
xEvans, Richard J.
Collecting & Restoring Old Steam Engines. TAB Bks.

Evans, Robert.
xEvans, Robert.
Revision Notes on Building Law. Butterworths.

Evans, Robert A.
xEvans, Robert A.
ed. Christian Theology: A Case Method Approach. Har-Row.
Introduction to Christianity: A Case Method Approach. John Knox.

Evans, Robert F.
xEvans, Robert F.
Pelagius: Inquiries & Reappraisals. Allenson.

Evans, Robert G.
xEvans, R. G.
Extending Canadian Health Insurance: Options for Pharmacare & Denticare. U of Toronto Pr.

Evans, Robert R., 1932-
xEvans, Robert R.
ed. Readings in Collective Behavior. Rand.

Evans, Robley D. *see* Evans, Robley Dunglison.

Evans, Robley Dunglison, 1907-
xEvans, Robley D.

Atomic Nucleus. McGraw.

Evans, Roger.
xEvans, Roger.
How to Play Guitar. St Martin.

Evans, Rupert. *see* Evans, Rupert Nelson.

Evans, Rupert Nelson.
xEvans, Rupert.
Foundations of Vocational Education. Merrill.

Evans, Sara.
xEvans, Sara.
Personal Politics: The Roots of Women's Liberation in the Civil Rights Movement & the New Left. Random.

Evans, Sharon.
xEvans, Sharon.
Reading Achievement Program for the Moderately & Severely Retarded. Interstate.

Evans, Stanley J.
xEvans, Stanley J.
Microprogramming Techniques with Sample Programs. Reston.

Evans, Tabor.
xEvans, Tabor.
Longarm. BJ Pub Group.
Longarm & the Molly Maguires. BJ Pub Group.

Evans, Tom.
xEvans, Tom.
Shunga: The Art of Love in Japan. Paddington.

Evans, Virginia M. *see* Evans, Virginia Moran.

Evans, Virginia Moran, 1909-
xEvans, Virginia M.
Eyes of the Tiger. Golden Quill.

Evans, W. Glyn. *see* Evans, William Glyn.

Evans, W. H. *see* Evans, W. Howard.

Evans, W. Howard.
xEvans, W. H.
Preparation & Characterisation of Mammalian Plasma Membranes. Elsevier.

Evans, W. McKee. *see* Evans, William Mckee.

Evans, Wilbur.
xEvans, Wilbur.
The Twelfth Man: A Story of Texas A & M Football. Strode.

Evans, William.
xEvans, William.
The Great Doctrines of the Bible. Moody.
How to Prepare Sermons. Moody.
Law for Gardens & Small Estates. David & Charles.

Evans, William Glyn.
xEvans, W. Glyn.
Daily with the King. Moody.
Profiles of Revival Leaders. Broadman.

Evans, William M. *see* Evans, William Mckee.

Evans, William Mckee.
xEvans, W. McKee.
Ballots & Fence Rails: Reconstruction on the Lower Cape Fear. Norton.
xEvans, William M.
Ballots & Fence Rails: Reconstruction on the Lower Cape Fear. U of NC Pr.

Evans-Pritchard, Edward E. *see* Evans-Pritchard, Edward Eban.

Evans-Pritchard, Edward Eban, 1902-
xEvans-Pritchard, Edward E.
Theories of Primitive Religion. Oxford U Pr.

Evansen, Virginia. *see* Evansen, Virginia Besaw.

Evansen, Virginia Besaw.
xEvansen, Virginia.
The Flea Market Mystery. Dodd.

Evarts, Hal G. *see* Evarts, Hal George.

Evarts, Hal George, 1915-
xEvarts, Hal G.
Highgrader. PB.
The Purple Eagle Mystery. Scribner.
Renegade of Rainbow Basin. PB.

Evatt, Herbert V. *see* Evatt, Herbert Vere.

Evatt, Herbert Vere, 1894-1965
xEvatt, Herbert V.

The Task of Nations. Greenwood.

Eve, Paul.
xEve, Paul.
Cooking with Rice. FS&G.

Eveleigh, Virgil. *see* Eveleigh, Virgil W.

Eveleigh, Virgil W.
xEveleigh, Virgil.
Introduction to Control Systems Design. McGraw.

Evely, Louis, 1910-
xEvely, Louis.
In the Christian Spirit. Doubleday.
Love Your Neighbor. Doubleday.
Suffering. Doubleday.
Teach Us How to Pray. Paulist Pr.
That Man Is You. Paulist Pr.

Evelyn, John.
xEvelyn, John.
Diary of John Evelyn. Dutton.
The Diary of John Evelyn. R West.

Even, Shimon.
xEven, Shimon.
Graph Algorithms. Computer Sci.

Evenson, Norma.
xEvenson, Norma.
Le Corbusier: The Machine & the Grand Design. Braziller.
Two Brazilian Capitals: Architecture & Urbanism in Rio de Janeiro & Brasilia. Yale U Pr.

Evenson, Robert E. *see* Evenson, Robert Edward.

Evenson, Robert Edward.
xEvenson, Robert E.
Agricultural Research & Productivity. Yale U Pr.

Evera, Maxine Van. *see* Van Evera, Maxine.

Everard. *see* Everard, Kenneth E.

Everard, Kenneth E.
xEverard.
jt. auth. Business Principles & Management. SW Pub.

Everding, H. Edward.
xEverding, H. Edward.
Decision Making & the Bible. Judson.

Everest, F. Alton. *see* Everest, Frederick Alton.

Everest, Frank K. *see* Everest, Frank Kendall.

Everest, Frank Kendall.
xEverest, Frank K.
The Fastest Man Alive. Arno.

Everest, Frederick Alton, 1909-
xEverest, F. Alton.
Acoustic Techniques for Home & Studio. TAB Bks.

Everest, Kelvin.
xEverest, Kelvin.
Coleridge's Secret Ministry: The Context of the Conversation Poems 1795-1798. B&N.

Everett, Alan.
xEverett, Alan.
Materials. Halsted Pr.

Everett, Alexander H. *see* Everett, Alexander Hill.

Everett, Alexander Hill, 1790-1847
xEverett, Alexander H.
America: Or a General Survey of the Political Situation of the Several Powers of the Western Continent. Kelley.
Europe: Or a General Survey of the Present Situation of the Principal Powers. Kelley.

Everett, Donald E.
xEverett, Donald E.
Trinity University: A Record of One Hundred Years. Trinity U Pr.

Everett, Edward, 1794-1865
xEverett, Edward.
Orations & Speeches, on Various Occasions. Arno.

Everett, Edwin M. *see* Everett, Edwin Mallard.

Everett, Edwin Mallard, 1902-
xEverett, Edwin M.

Party of Humanity: The Fortnightly Review &
Its Contributors, 1865-1874. Russell.

Everett, Jana M. see Everett, Jana Matson.

Everett, Jana Matson.
xEverett, Jana M.
Women & Social Change in India. St Martin.

Everett, John P. see Everett, John Phelps.

Everett, John Phelps, 1875-
xEverett, John P.
Fundamental Skills of Algebra. AMS Pr.

Everett, N. B. see Everett, Newton Bennie.

Everett, Newton Bennie.
xEverett, N. B.
Functional Neuroanatomy. Lea & Febiger.

Everett, Robinson O.
xEverett, Robinson O.
ed. Anti-Poverty Programs. Oceana.
ed. Housing. Oceana.

Everett, T. H. see Everett, Thomas H.

Everett, Thomas G.
xEverett, Thomas G.
Annotated Guide to Bass Trombone Literature.
Brass Pr.

Everett, Thomas H.
xEverett, T. H.
How to Grow Beautiful House Plants. Fawcett.
xEverett, Thomas H.
How to Grow Beautiful Houseplants. Arco.

Everett, Walter K.
xEverett, Walter K.
Faulkner's Art & Characters. Barron.

Evergates, Theodore.
xEvergates, Theodore.
Feudal Society in the Bailliage of Troyes under
the Counts of Champagne, 1152-1284. Johns
Hopkins.

Everhart, Jim.
xEverhart, Jim.
CB Slanguage Illustrated. Centennial
Illustrated Texas Dictionary of the English
Language. Cliffs.

Everhart, W. Harry. see Everhart, Watson Harry.

Everhart, Watson Harry.
xEverhart, W. Harry.
Principles of Fishery Science. Cornell U Pr.

Everitt, Arthur V.
xEveritt, Arthur V.
Hypothalamus, Pituitary & Aging. C C
Thomas.

Everitt, B. S.
xEveritt, B. S.
The Analysis of Contingency Tables. Methuen
Inc.

Everitt, Brian.
xEveritt, Brian.
Cluster Analysis. Halsted Pr.

Everling, W. see Everling, Wolfgang.

Everling, Wolfgang.
xEverling, W.
Exercises in Computer Systems Analysis.
Springer-Verlag.

Everly, George. see Everly, George Stotelmyer.

Everly, George Stotelmyer.
xEverly, George.
The Stress Mess Solution. R J Brady.

Evers, Alf.
xEvers, Alf.
The Catskills: From Wilderness to Woodstock.
Doubleday.

Evers, Dora. see Evers, Dora R.

Evers, Dora R.
xEvers, Dora.
Your Future in Exotic Occupations. Rosen Pr.

Eversley, David. see Eversley, David Edward Charles.

Eversley, David Edward Charles.
xEversley, David.
Social Theories of Fertility & the Malthusian
Debate. Greenwood.

Eversley, George J. see Eversley, George John
Shaw-Lefevre.

Eversley, George John Shaw-Lefevre, Baron, 1832-1928
xEversley, George J.
Gladstone & Ireland: The Irish Policy of
Parliament from 1850-1894. Greenwood.
The Turkish Empire. Fertig.

Eversole, Lewis R.
xEversole, Lewis R.
Clinical Outline of Oral Pathology: Diagnosis
& Treatment. Lea & Febiger.

Everson, Bill. see Everson, William K.

Everson, George, 1885-
xEverson, George.
The Story of Television: The Life of Philo T.
Farnsworth. Arno.

Everson, William K.
xEverson, Bill.
Films of Laurel & Hardy. Citadel Pr.
xEverson, William K.
American Silent Film. Oxford U Pr.
Bad Guys: A Pictorial History of the Movie
Villain. Citadel Pr.
Classics of the Horror Film. Citadel Pr.

Evert, Walter H.
xEvert, Walter H.
Aesthetic & Myth in the Poetry of Keats.
Princeton U Pr.

Evertts, Eldonna L.
xEvertts, Eldonna L.
ed. Aspects of Reading. NCTE.

Everwine, Peter.
xEverwine, Peter.
Collecting the Animals. Atheneum.

Every, Dale Van. see Van Every, Dale.

Eves, Howard. see Eves, Howard Whitley.

Eves, Howard Whitley, 1911-
xEves, Howard.
Survey of Geometry. Allyn.

Evetts, Echo.
xEvetts, Echo.
China Mending: A Guide to Repairing &
Restoration. Merrimack Bk Serv.

Evetts, Julia.
xEvetts, Julia.
The Sociology of Educational Ideas. Routledge
& Kegan.

Evgrafov, M. A. see Evgrafov, Marat Andreevich.

Evgrafov, Marat Andreevich.
xEvgrafov, M. A.
Analytic Functions. Dover.

Evola, Niccolo D. see Evola, Niccolo Domenico.

Evola, Niccolo Domenico.
xEvola, Niccolo D.
Origini e dottrina del fascismo. AMS Pr.

Evrard, Franklin H.
xEvrard, Franklin H.
Successful Parole. C C Thomas.

Evrie, John H. Van. see Van Evrie, John H.

Evslin, Bernard.
xEvslin, Bernard.
The Greek Gods. Schol Bk Serv.
Greeks Bearing Gifts: The Epics of Achilles &
Ulysses. Schol Bk Serv.

E.W. Beth Memorial Colloquium, Paris, 1964. see
Edward Wood and Company Limited.

Ewald, William B. see Ewald, William Bragg.

Ewald, William Bragg, 1925-
xEwald, William B.
Masks of Jonathan Swift. Russell.

Ewald, William R.
xEwald, William R.
ed. Environment & Policy: The Next Fifty
Years. Ind U Pr.
ed. Environment for Man: The Next Fifty
Years. Ind U Pr.

Ewart, Gavin.
xEwart, Gavin.
ed. The Batsford Book of Light Verse for
Children. David & Charles.

Ewart, Park J.
xEwart, Park J.

Probability for Statistical Decision Making.
P-H.

Ewart, W. D. see Ewart, William Dunlop.

Ewart, William Dunlop.
xEwart, W. D.
Building a Ship. Dufour.

Ewbank, Weeb.
xEwbank, Weeb.
Football Greats. Bethany Pr.

Ewen, Cecil. see Ewen, Cecil Henry L'Estrange.

Ewen, Cecil H. see Ewen, Cecil Henry L'Estrange.

Ewen, Cecil Henry L'Estrange, 1877-
xEwen, Cecil.
A Guide to the Origin of British Surnames.
Gordon Pr.
xEwen, Cecil H.
Guide to the Origin of British Surnames. Gale.
History of Surnames of the British Isles: A
Concise Account of Their Origin, Evolution,
Etymology & Legal Status. Gale.

Ewen, Dale.
xEwen, Dale.
Mathematics for Technical Education. P-H.

Ewen, David, 1907-
xEwen, David.
All the Years of American Popular Music. P-H.
Complete Book of Classical Music. P-H.
Composers of Tomorrow's Music: A
Non-Technical Introduction to the Musical
Avant-Garde Movement. Greenwood.
Dictators of the Baton. Core Collection.
ed. From Bach to Stravinsky: The History of
Music by Its Foremost Critics. AMS Pr.
ed. From Bach to Stravinsky: The History of
Music by Its Foremost Critics. Greenwood.
George Gershwin: His Journey to Greatness.
Greenwood
Men of Popular Music. Arno.
World of Twentieth Century Music. P-H.

Ewen, Frederic, 1899-
xEwen, Frederic.
Prestige of Schiller in England, 1788-1859.
AMS Pr.

Ewen, Lynda Ann, 1943-
xEwen, Lynda Ann.
Corporate Power & Urban Crisis in Detroit.
Princeton U Pr.

Ewen, R. see Ewen, Robert B.

Ewen, Robert B.
xEwen, R.
Opening Leads. P-H.
xEwen, Robert B.
Choosing the College for You. Watts.

Ewens, W. J. see Ewens, Warren John.

Ewens, Warren John.
xEwens, W. J.
Mathematical Population Genetics.
Springer-Verlag.

Ewer, R. F.
xEwer, R. F.
The Carnivores. Cornell U Pr.

Ewers, Hanns H. see Ewers, Hanns Heinz.

Ewers, Hanns Heinz, 1871-1943
xEwers, Hanns H.
Edgar Allan Poe. Folcroft.

Ewers, John C. see Ewers, John Canfield.

Ewers, John Canfield.
xEwers, John C.
Artists of the Old West. Doubleday.
Indian Life on the Upper Missouri. U of Okla
Pr.
Plains Indian Painting: A Description of
Aboriginal American Art. AMS Pr.

Ewers, William.
xEwers, William L.
Solar Energy: A Biased Guide. Quality Bks IL.

Ewers, William L. see Ewers, William.

Ewert, David, 1922-
xEwert, David.

And Then Comes the End. Herald Pr.
Ewing, A. C. see Ewing, Alfred Cyril.
Ewing, Alexander W. see Ewing, Alexander William
    Gordon.
Ewing, Alexander William Gordon, Sir.
    xEwing, Alexander W.
        Aphasia in Children. Hafner.
Ewing, Alfred C. see Ewing, Alfred Cyril.
Ewing, Alfred Cyril, 1899-
    xEwing, A. C.
        Ethics. McKay.
    xEwing, Alfred C.
        The Definition of Good. Hyperion Conn.
        Ethics. Free Pr.
        Fundamental Questions of Philosophy.
        Macmillan.
Ewing, Barbara.
    xEwing, Barbara.
        Strangers. Atheneum.
Ewing, C. E. see Ewing, Clair E.
Ewing, Charles P. see Ewing, Charles Patrick.
Ewing, Charles Patrick, 1949-
    xEwing, Charles P.
        Crisis Intervention As Psychotherapy. Oxford
        U Pr.
Ewing, Clair E.
    xEwing, C. E.
        Introduction to Geodesy. Elsevier.
Ewing, Cortez A. see Ewing, Cortez Arthur Milton.
Ewing, Cortez Arthur Milton, 1896-1962
    xEwing, Cortez A.
        Presidential Elections from Abraham Lincoln
        to Franklin D. Roosevelt. Greenwood.
        Primary Elections in the South: A Study in
        Uniparty Politics. Greenwood.
Ewing, David W.
    xEwing, David W.
        Freedom Inside the Organization: Bringing
        Civil Liberties to the Workplace. McGraw.
        ed. Long-Range Planning for Management.
        Har-Row.
        Writing for Results in Business, Government,
        the Sciences & the Professions. Wiley.
Ewing, Elizabeth.
    xEwing, Elizabeth.
        Dress & Undress: A History of Women's
        Underwear. Drama Bk.
        History of Children's Costume. Scribner.
        History of Twentieth-Century Fashion.
        Scribner.
Ewing, Fayette C. see Ewing, Fayette Clay.
Ewing, Fayette Clay, 1862-1956
    xEwing, Fayette C.
        Hamlet: An Analytic & Psychologic Study.
        Arden Lib.
        Hamlet: An Analytic & Psychologic Study.
        Folcroft.
Ewing, Galen W. see Ewing, Galen Wood.
Ewing, Galen Wood, 1914-
    xEwing, Galen W.
        Instrumental Methods of Chemical Analysis.
        McGraw.
Ewing, John A.
    xEwing, John A.
        ed. Drinking. Nelson-Hall.
Ewing, John M.
    xEwing, John M.
        Word Analysis for Teachers. Interstate.
Ewing, Juliana H. see Ewing, Juliana Horatia Gatty.
Ewing, Juliana Horatia Gatty, 1841-1885
    xEwing, Juliana H.
        Mrs. Overtheway's Remembrances. Garland
        Pub.
Ewing, Kathryn.
    xEwing, Kathryn.
        A Private Matter. HarBraceJ.
Ewing, Kristine L.
    xEwing, Kristine L.

Care & Maintenance of Paper Machine
    Clothing. Inst Paper Chem.
Ewing, Lucie L. see Ewing, Lucy Elizabeth Lee.
Ewing, Lucy Elizabeth Lee.
    xEwing, Lucie L.
        George Frederick Watts, Sandro Botticelli,
        Matthew Arnold. Folcroft.
Ewing, S. B. see Ewing, S. Blaine.
Ewing, S. Blaine, 1905-
    xEwing, S. B.
        Burtonian Melancholy in the Plays of John
        Ford. Octagon.
Ewing, Upton C. see Ewing, Upton Clary.
Ewing, Upton Clary.
    xEwing, Upton C.
        The Prophet of the Dead Sea Scrolls. Philos
        Lib.
Ewton, Ralph W., 1938-
    xEwton, Ralph W.
        The Literary Theories of August Wilhelm
        Schlegel. Mouton.
Ewusi, Kodwo.
    xEwusi, Kodwo.
        Economic Development Planning in Ghana.
        Exposition.
Ewy, Donna.
    xEwy, Donna.
        Preparation for Breastfeeding. Doubleday.
        Preparation for Childbirth: A Lamaze Guide.
        Formur Intl.
        Preparation for Childbirth: A Lamaze Guide.
        Pruett.
Executive Offices Of The National Academy Of Sciences
    - National Academy Of Engineering. see Council of
    State Governments.
**Executive Reports Corporation, Englewood Cliffs, New
    Jersey.**
        xE R C Editorial Staff.
            E R C's President's Guide. P-H.
            Executive's Credit & Collection Guide. P-H.
            Executive's Desk Manual for Profitable
            Employee Handling. P-H.
            Executive's Tax Desk Manual. P-H.
            Treasurer's Guide. P-H.
            Treasurer's Tax Desk Manual. P-H.
Exel, G. W. see Exel, Godfrey W.
Exel, Godfrey W.
    xExel, G. W.
        Live Happily with the Woman You Love.
        Moody.
Exiner, Johanna.
    xExiner, Johanna.
        Teaching Creative Movement. Plays.
Exley, Richard.
    xExley, Richard D.
        The Other God: Seeing God As He Really Is.
        Logos.
Exley, Richard D. see Exley, Richard.
Exline, Joseph D., 1935-
    xExline, Joseph D.
        Individualized Techniques for Teaching Earth
        Science. P-H.
Experimental Designs Committee of the Association for
    Counselor Education and Supervision. see Association
    for Counselor Education and Supervision.
    Experimental Design Committee.
Expert Consultation on Fishing for Squid & Other
    Cephalopods. see Food and Agriculture Organization
    of the United Nations.
**Exploratory Conference on the History of Nuclear
    Physics, 1st, 2nd, Brookline, Mass., 1967, 1969.**
        xAIP & American Academy of Arts & Sciences
        Joint Conference, Brookline, Mass., 1967 &
        1969.
            Exploring the History of Nuclear Physics:
            Proceedings. Am Inst Physics.
Exton, Harold.
    xExton, Harold.

Handbook of Hypergeometric Integrals: Theory
    Applications, Tables, Computer Programs.
    Halsted Pr.
Exum, Jack.
    xExum, Jack.
        How to Win Souls Today. Lambert Bk.
Eyck, Erich, 1878-1964
    xEyck, Erich.
        tr. Gladstone. Biblio Dist.
        Gladstone. Kelley.
Eyerly, Jeanette. see Eyerly, Jeannette.
Eyerly, Jeannette.
    xEyerly, Jeanette.
        Goodbye to Budapest. Lippincott.
    xEyerly, Jeannette.
        Drop-Out. Berkley Pub.
        Drop-Out. Lippincott.
        Girl Like Me. Berkley Pub.
        Girl Like Me. Lippincott.
        Good-Bye to Budapest. Berkley Pub.
        More Than a Summer Love. Lippincott.
        Phaedra Complex. PB.
        The Phaedra Complex. Archway.
        Radigan Cares. PB.
        Radigan Cares. Archway.
        Radigan Cares. Lippincott.
        World of Ellen March. Lippincott.
Eyers, A. S.
    xEyers, A. S.
        Practical Woodwork for Laboratory
        Technicians. Pergamon.
Eyestone, Robert, 1942-
    xEyestone, Robert.
        From Social Issues to Public Policy. Wiley.
Eyken, W. Van Der. see Van Der Eyken, W.
Eyler, Ellen C.
    xEyler, Ellen C.
        Early English Gardens & Garden Books.
        Folger Bks.
Eyler, John M.
    xEyler, John M.
        Victorian Social Medicine: The Ideas &
        Methods of William Farr. Johns Hopkins.
Eyles, Allen.
    xEyles, Allen.
        John Wayne. A S Barnes.
Eyman, Joy S.
    xEyman, Joy S.
        How to Convict a Rapist. Stein & Day.
        Prisons for Women: A Practical Guide to
        Administration Problems. C C Thomas.
Eyongetah, Tambi.
    xEyongetah, Tambi.
        A History of the Cameroon. Longman.
Eyre, John.
    xEyre, John.
        Computers & Systems: An Introduction for
        Librarians. Shoe String.
Eyre, S. R.
    xEyre, S. R.
        Vegetation & Soils: A World Picture. Beresford
        Bk Serv.
        ed. World Vegetation Types. Columbia U Pr.
Eyre, V. see Eyre, Vincent.
Eyre, Vincent, Sir, 1811-1881
    xEyre, V.
        Journal of an Afghanistan Prisoner. Routledge
        & Kegan.
Eyre-Todd, George, 1862-1937
    xEyre-Todd, George.
        ed. Mediaeval Scottish Poetry: King James the
        First, Robert Henryson, William Dunbar,
        Gavin Douglas. Greenwood.
Eyring, H.
    xEyring, Henry.
        ed. Annual Review of Physical Chemistry.
        Annual Reviews.
Eyring, Henry.
    xEyring, Henry.

Significant Liquid Structures. Krieger.
   ed. Theoretical Chemistry: Advances &
     Perspectives. Acad Pr.
   ed. Theoretical Chemistry: Advances in
     Perspectives. Acad Pr.
Eyring, Henry. *see* Eyring, H.
Eyring, Leroy.
   xEyring, LeRoy.
   ed. Advances in High Temperature Chemistry.
     Acad Pr.
Eysenck, H. J. *see* Eysenck, Hans Jurgen.
Eysenck, Hans. *see* Eysenck, Hans Jurgen.
Eysenck, Hans J. *see* Eysenck, Hans Jurgen.
Eysenck, Hans Jurgen, 1916-
   xEysenck, H. J.
   ed. Case Studies in Behaviour Therapy.
     Routledge & Kegan.
   Check Your Own I. Q.. Gannon.
   Check Your Own IQ. Penguin.
   ed. Encyclopedia of Psychology. Continuum.
   ed. Handbook of Abnormal Psychology. EDITS
     Pubs.
   The Measurement of Intelligence. Krieger.
   Personality Structure & Measurement. EDITS
     Pubs.
   ed. The Psychological Basis of Ideology. Univ
     Park.
   Psychology Is About People. Open Court.
   Reminiscence, Motivation, & Personality: A
     Case Study in Experimental Psychology.
     Plenum Pub.
   Sex, Violence & the Media. Har-Row.
   Sex, Violence & the Media. St Martin.
   The Structure & Measurement of Intelligence.
     Springer-Verlag.
   xEysenck, Hans.
   Psychoticism As a Dimension of Personality.
     Crane-Russak Co.
   xEysenck, Hans J.
   ed. Textbook of Human Psychology. Univ
     Park.

Eysenck, Michael W.
   xEysenck, Michael W.
   Human Memory: Theory, Research &
     Individual Differences. Pergamon.

Eyton, John S. *see* Eyton, John Seymour.

Eyton, John Seymour, 1890-
   xEyton, John S.
   Dancing Fakir & Other Stories. Arno.

Ezell, Douglas.
   xEzell, Douglas.
   Revelations on Revelation: New Sounds from
     Old Symbols. Word Bks.

Ezell, Macel D.
   xEzell, Macel D.
   Unequivocal Americanism: Right-Wing Novels
     in the Cold War Era. Scarecrow.
Ezrahi, Sidra D. *see* Ezrahi, Sidra Dekoven.
Ezrahi, Sidra Dekoven.
   xEzrahi, Sidra D.
   By Words Alone: The Holocaust in Literature.
     U of Chicago Pr.
Ezrin. *see* Ezrin, Calvin.
Ezrin, Calvin.
   xEzrin.
   Clinical Endocrinology: A Survey of Current
     Practice. ACC.
   xEzrin, Calvin.
   Systematic Endocrinology. Har-Row.
Ezzati, Ali.
   xEzzati, Ali.
   World Energy Markets & OPEC Stability.
     Lexington Bks.
F. W. Faxon Co. *see* Faxon (F.W.) Co. Inc., Boston.
F.A.A. *see* United States. Federal Aviation
   Administration.

Faaland, Just.
   xFaaland, Just.
   Bangladesh: The Test Case for Development.
     Westview.
Faas, Larry A.
   xFaas, Larry A.
   Children with Learning Problems: A Handbook
     for Teachers. HM.
Fabe, Marilyn.
   xFabe, Marilyn.
   Up Against the Clock: Career Women Speak
     on the Choice to Have Children. Warner Bks.
Fabe, Maxene.
   xFabe, Maxene.
   T V Game Shows. Doubleday.
Faber, Doris.
   xFaber, Doris.
   The Assassination of Martin Luther King, Jr..
     Watts.
   Dwight Eisenhower. Abelard.
   Enough: The Revolt of the American
     Consumer. FS&G.
   The Perfect Life: The Shakers in America.
     FS&G.
   The Presidents' Mothers. St Martin.
   Wall Street: A Story of Fortune & Finance.
     Har-Row.
Faber, Frederick W. *see* Faber, Frederick William.
Faber, Frederick William, 1814-1863
   xFaber, Frederick W.
   Spiritual Conferences. TAN Bks Pubs.
Faber, Geoffrey. *see* Faber, Geoffrey Cust.
Faber, Geoffrey C. *see* Faber, Geoffrey Cust.
Faber, Geoffrey Cust, Sir, 1889-1961
   xFaber, Geoffrey.
   Oxford Apostles: A Character Study of the
     Oxford Movement. Norwood Edns.
   xFaber, Geoffrey C.
   Oxford Apostles: A Character Study of the
     Oxford Movement. AMS Pr.
Faber, Harold.
   xFaber, Harold.
   American Heroes of the 20th Century.
     Random.
   The Book of Laws. Times Bks.
   From Sea to Sea: The Growth of the United
     States. FS&G.
   ed. Luftwaffe: A History. Times Bks.
Faber, Heije, 1907-
   xFaber, Heije.
   Pastoral Care in the Modern Hospital.
     Westminster.
   Psychology of Religion. Westminster.
Faber, John.
   xFaber, John.
   Great News Photos & the Stories Behind
     Them. Dover.
Faber, M. *see* Faber, Malte Michael.
Faber, Malte Michael.
   xFaber, M.
   Introduction to Modern Austrian Capital
     Theory. Springer-Verlag.
Faber, Melvin D.
   xFaber, Melvin D.
   ed. Design Within: Psychoanalytic Approaches
     to Shakespeare. Aronson.
Faber, Rodney B.
   xFaber, Rodney B.
   Applied Electricity & Electronics for
     Technology. Wiley.
   Introduction to Electronic Amplifiers. Merrill.
Faber, Stuart J.
   xFaber, Stuart J.
   California Sentencing Handbook. Lega Bks.
Fabes, Gilbert H. *see* Fabes, Gilbert Henry.
Fabes, Gilbert Henry, 1894-
   xFabes, Gilbert H.

D. H. Lawrence-His First Editions: Points &
     Values. Folcroft.
   Modern First Editions: Points & Values,
     Second Series. Folcroft.
Fabian, D. J. *see* Fabian, Derek J.
Fabian, Derek J.
   xFabian, D. J.
   ed. Band Structure Spectroscopy of Metals &
     Alloys. Acad Pr.
Fabian, Larry L.
   xFabian, Larry L.
   Soldiers Without Enemies: Preparing the
     United Nations for Peacekeeping. Brookings.
Fabian, Monroe. *see* Fabian, Monroe H.
Fabian, Monroe H.
   xFabian, Monroe.
   The Pennsylvania-German Decorated Chest.
     Universe.
Fabian Society - London. *see* Fabian Society, London.
Fabian Society - London - International Research
   Section. *see* Fabian Society, London. International
   Research Section.
Fabian Society, London.
   xFabian Society - London.
   Where Stands Democracy?. Arno.
Fabian Society, London. International Research Section.
   xFabian Society - London - International Research
     Section.
   Hitler's Route to Bagdad. Arno.
Fabilli, Mary.
   xFabilli, Mary.
   Aurora Bligh & Early Poems. SBD.
Fabisch, Judith.
   xFabisch, Judith.
   Not Ready to Walk Alone. Zondervan.
Fabos, Julius G. *see* Fabos, Julius Gy.
Fabos, Julius Gy.
   xFabos, Julius G
   Planning the Total Landscape: A Guide to
     Intelligent Land Use. Westview.
Fabre, J. Henri. *see* Fabre, Jean Henri Casimir.
Fabre, Jean H. *see* Fabre, Jean Henri Casimir.
Fabre, Jean Henri Casimir, 1823-1915
   xFabre, J. Henri.
   The Life of the Spider. Norwood Edns.
   xFabre, Jean H.
   Jean Henri Fabre's Insects. Scribner.
Fabre, Michel.
   xFabre, Michel.
   The Unfinished Quest of Richard Wright.
     Morrow.
Fabrega, Horacio.
   xFabrega, Horacio.
   Illness & Shamanistic Curing in Zinacantan: An
     Ethnomedical Analysis. Stanford U Pr.
Fabri, Charles L. *see* Fabri, Charles Louis.
Fabri, Charles Louis, 1899-1968
   xFabri, Charles L.
   History of the Art of Orissa. South Asia Bks.
Fabri, Ralph, 1894-
   xFabri, Ralph.
   Color: A Complete Guide for Artists.
     Watson-Guptill.
Fabricand, Burton. *see* Fabricand, Burton P.
Fabricand, Burton P.
   xFabricand, Burton.
   The Science of Winning: A Random Walk on
     the Road to Riches. Van Nos Reinhold.
Fabricant, Solomon, 1906-
   xFabricant, Solomon.
   The Output of Manufacturing Industries,
     1899-1937. Arno.
   A Primer on Productivity. Peter Smith.
Fabris, Alfred C.
   xFabris, Alfred C.
   A Prosecutor's Guide for California Peace
     Officers. Benjamin-Cummings.
Fabrizio, R. *see* Fabrizio, Raymond.
Fabrizio, Raymond.
   xFabrizio, R.

The Rhetoric of No. HR&W.
The Rhetoric of YES. HR&W.
Fabry, Joseph B.
xFabry, Joseph B.
The Pursuit of Meaning: Viktor Frankl,
Logotherapy, & Life. Har-Row.
Fabun, Don.
xFabun, Don.
Children of Change. Glencoe.
Fackenheim, Emil L.
xFackenheim, Emil L.
God's Presence in History: Jewish Affirmations
& Philosophical Reflections. NYU Pr.
Fackenthal, Frank D. see Fackenthal, Frank Diehl.
Fackenthal, Frank Diehl, 1883-1968
xFackenthal, Frank D.
Greater Power, & Other Addresses. Arno.
Facklam, Margery.
xFacklam, Margery.
From Cell to Clone: The Story of Genetic
Engineering. HarBraceJ.
Frozen Snakes & Dinosaur Bones: Exploring a
Natural History Museum. HarBraceJ.
Fackler, John P.
xFackler, John P.
ed. Symmetry in Chemical Theory: The
Application of Group Theoretical Techniques
to the Solution of Chemical Problems. Acad
Pr.
Symmetry in Coordination Chemistry. Acad Pr.
Fackre, Gabriel. see Fackre, Gabriel J.
Fackre, Gabriel J.
xFackre, Gabriel.
Youth Ministry: The Gospel & the People.
Judson.
Facter, Dolly.
xFacter, Dolly.
Doctrine of the Buddha. Philos Lib.
Factory Mutual Engineering Corporation.
xFactory Mutual System.
Handbook of Industrial Loss Prevention.
McGraw.
Factory Mutual System. see Factory Mutual Engineering
Corporation.
Facts on File Digest Staff. see Facts on File, Inc., New
York.
Facts on File, Inc., New York.
xFacts on File Digest Staff.
Yearbook, 1979. Facts on File.
Faculty of Comparative Literature, Livingston College.
see Livingston College.
Faculty of Law, University of Khartoum. see Sudan Law
Reports: Civil Cases.
Fadala, Sam.
xFadala, Sam.
The Complete Black Powder Handbook.
Follett.
Fadeev, Aleksandr A. see Fadeev, Aleksandr
Aleksandrovich.
Fadeev, Aleksandr Aleksandrovich, 1901-1956
xFadeev, Aleksandr A.
Leningrad in the Days of the Blockade.
Greenwood.
Fadely, Jack L.
xFadely, Jack L.
Confrontation in Adolescence. Mosby.
Understanding the Alpha Child at Home &
School: Left & Right Hemispheric Function
in Relation to Personality & Learning. C C
Thomas.
Faden, Arnold M., 1934-
xFaden, Arnold M.
Economics of Space & Time: The Measure
Theoretic Foundations of Social Science.
Iowa St U Pr.
Fader, Daniel N.
xFader, Daniel N.

Hooked on Books: Program & Proof. Berkley
Pub.
Fadiman, Clifton, 1904-
xFadiman, Clifton.
The Lifetime Reading Plan. T Y Crowell.
Fadiman, James.
xFadiman, James.
Personality & Personal Growth. Har-Row.
Fadiman, Jeffrey.
xFadiman, Jeffrey A.
The Moment of Conquest: Meru, Kenya, 1907.
Ohio U Ctr Intl.
Fadiman, Jeffrey A. see Fadiman, Jeffrey.
Fadiman, William.
xFadiman, William.
Hollywood Now. Liveright.
Fadner, Donald E. see Fadner, Donald Edward.
Fadner, Donald Edward.
xFadner, Donald E.
The Responsible God: A Study of the Christian
Philosophy of H. Richard Niebuhr. Scholars
Pr Ca.
Faegre, Torvald.
xFaegre, Torvald.
Tents: Architecture of the Nomads. Doubleday.
Faegri, K. see Faegri, Knut.
Faegri, Knut.
xFaegri, K.
The Principles of Pollination Ecology.
Pergamon.
xFaegri, Knut.
Textbook of Pollen Analysis. Hafner.
Fafunwa, A. Babs, 1923-
xFafunwa, A. Babs.
History of Education in Nigeria. Allen Unwin.
Fagan, Brian. see Fagan, Brian M.
Fagan, Brian M.
xFagan, Brian.
The Rape of the Nile: Tomb Robbers, Tourists,
and Archaeologists in Egypt. Scribner.
xFagan, Brian M.
Archaeology: A Brief Introduction. Little.
Intro. by Civilization: Readings from Scientific
American. W H Freeman.
Corridors in Time: A Reader in Introductory
Archaeology. Little.
Cruising Guide to the Channel Islands. Capra
Pr.
Cruising Guide to the Channel Islands.
Western Marine Ent.
In the Beginning: An Introduction to
Archaeology. Little.
People of the Earth: An Introduction to World
Prehistory. Little.
The Rape of the Nile: Tomb Robbers, Tourists,
& Archaeologists in Egypt. Scribner.
Return to Babylon: Travelers, Archaeologists &
Monuments in Mesopotamia. Little.
World Prehistory: A Brief Introduction. Little.
Fagan, Cyril, 1895-
xFagan, Cyril.
Astrological Origins. Llewellyn Pubns.
Fagan, Harry.
xFagan, Harry.
Empowerment: Skills for Parish Social Action.
Paulist Pr.
Fagan, Joen.
xFagan, Joen.
ed. Life Techniques in Gestalt Therapy.
Har-Row.
Fagan, John J.
xFagan, John J.
Earth Environment. P-H.
Fagan, John M. see Fagan, John Michael.
Fagan, John Michael, 1953-
xFagan, John M.
Beautiful North Carolina. Beautiful Am.
Fagan, Sean.
xFagan, Sean.

Has Sin Changed. Doubleday.
Has Sin Changed?. M Glazier.
Fagan, William T.
xFagan, William T.
Measures for Research & Evaluation in the
English Language Arts. NCTE.
Fage, J. D.
xFage, J. D.
Ghana: A Historical Interpretation. U of Wis
Pr.
A History of Africa. Knopf.
Papers in African Prehistory. Cambridge U Pr.
Fagen, Richard R.
xFagen, Richard R.
ed. Capitalism & the State in U. S. Latin
American Relations. Stanford U Pr.
Cubans in Exile: Disaffection & the Revolution.
Stanford U Pr.
Politics & Privilege in a Mexican City. Stanford
U Pr.
Fagen, Stanley J.
xFagen, Stanly.
Teaching Children Self-Control: Preventing
Emotional & Learning Problems in the
Elementary School. Merrill.
Fagen, Stanly. see Fagen, Stanley A.
Fagence, Michael.
xFagence, Michael.
Citizen Participation in Planning. Pergamon.
Fagerhaugh, Shizuko. see Fagerhaugh, Shizuko Y.
Fagerhaugh, Shizuko Y.
xFagerhaugh, Shizuko.
Politics of Pain Management: Staff-Patient
Interaction. A-W.
Fagerlie, Joan M.
xFagerlie, Joan M.
Late Roman & Byzantine Solidi Found in
Sweden & Denmark. Am Numismatic.
Fagerstrom, William H. see Fagerstrom, William Henry.
Fagerstrom, William Henry, 1893-
xFagerstrom, William H.
Mathematical Facts & Processes Prerequisite to
the Study of Calculus. AMS Pr.
Fagg, Christopher.
xFagg, Christopher.
Ancient Greece. Watts.
Ancient Rome. Watts.
Fagg, John E. see Fagg, John Edwin.
Fagg, John Edwin, 1916-
xFagg, John E.
Latin America: A General History. Macmillan.
Fagin, Claire M.
xFagin, Claire M.
ed. Readings in Child & Adolescent Psychiatric
Nursing. Mosby.
Fagin, Larry.
xFagin, Larry.
Rhymes of a Jerk. Kulchur Foun.
Fagles, Robert.
xFagles, Robert.
I, Vincent: Poems from the Pictures of Van
Gogh. Princeton U Pr.
Fagothey, Austin, 1901-
xFagothey, Austin.
Right & Reason: Ethics in Theory & Practice.
Mosby.
Faguet, E. see Faguet, Emile.
Faguet, Emile, 1847-1916
xFaguet, E.
On Reading Nietzsche. Gordon Pr.
xFaguet, Emile.
Balzac. Haskell.
Balzac. R West.
Politicians & Moralists of the Nineteenth
Century. Arno.
Fagyas, M.
xFagyas, Maria.
Court of Honor. Popular Lib.
Court of Honor. S&S.
Fagyas, Maria. see Fagyas, M.

Fahey, James J.
xFahey, James J.
Pacific War Diary, 1942-1945. Greenwood.

Fahey, John.
xFahey, John.
Ballyhoo Bonanza: Charles Sweeny & the Idaho Mines. U of Wash Pr.
The Days of the Hercules. U Pr of Idaho.
The Flathead Indians. U of Okla Pr.
Inland Empire: D. C. Corbin & Spokane. U of Wash Pr.

Fahey, Thomas D.
xFahey, Thomas D.
Getting Into Olympic Form. Butterick Pub.
Good-Time Fitness for Kids. Butterick Pub.
What to Do About Athletic Injuries. Butterick Pub.

Fahey, William A.
xFahey, William A.
F. Scott Fitzgerald & the American Dream. T Y Crowell.

Fahl, Ronald J.
xFahl, Ronald J.
North American Forest & Conservation History: A Bibliography. ABC-Clio.

Fahn, Abraham.
xFahn, Abraham.
Plant Anatomy. Pergamon.

Fahn, Stanley.
xFahn, Stanley.
ed. Cerebral Hypoxia & Its Consequences. Raven.

Fahnestock, Murray, 1885-1969
xFahnestock, Murray.
ed. Those Wonderful Unauthorized Accessories for Model A Ford. Post-Era.

Fahrney, Ralph R. see Fahrney, Ralph Ray.

Fahrney, Ralph Ray.
xFahrney, Ralph R.
Horace Greeley & the Tribune in the Civil War. Da Capo.

Fahs, Charles B. see Fahs, Charles Burton.

Fahs, Charles Burton.
xFahs, Charles B.
Government in Japan: Recent Trends in Its Scope & Operation. AMS Pr.

Fahy, Carole.
xFahy, Carole.
Cooking with Beer. Dover.
Cooking with Beer. Peter Smith.

Fahy, Christopher.
xFahy, Christopher.
Home Remedies: Fixing up Houses and Apartments, Mostly Old but Also Otherwise. Scribner.

Fahy, Everett.
xFahy, Everett.
Some Followers of Domenico Ghirlandajo. Garland Pub.

Fain, Stephen M.
xFain, Stephen M.
Teaching in America. Scott F.

Fain, Tyrus G.
xFain, Tyrus G.
ed. Federal Reorganization: The Executive Branch. Bowker.
ed. The Intelligence Community:: History, Organization, & Issues. Bowker.

Fainlight, Ruth.
xFainlight, Ruth.
Cages. Dufour.

Fainsod, Merle, 1907-
xFainsod, Merle.
How Russia Is Ruled. Harvard U Pr.

Fair, Charles M.
xFair, Charles M.
The Dying Self. Columbia U Pr.

Fair, John D.
xFair, John D.

British Interparty Conferences: A Study of the Procedure of Conciliation in British Politics, Eighteen Sixty-Seven to Nineteen Twenty-One. Oxford U Pr.

Fair, Marvin. see Fair, Marvin Luke.

Fair, Marvin L. see Fair, Marvin Luke.

Fair, Marvin Luke.
xFair, Marvin.
Transportation Regulation. Wm C Brown.
xFair, Marvin L.
Economics of Transportation & Logistics. Business Pubns.

Fair, Ronald L.
xFair, Ronald L.
Hog Butcher. HarBraceJ.
Many Thousand Gone: An American Fable. Chatham Bkseller.
World of Nothing: Two Novellas. Chatham Bkseller.

Fairbank, Harold Arthur Thomas.
xFairbank, T. J.
Fairbank's Atlas of General Affections of the Skeleton. Churchill.

Fairbank, John K. see Fairbank, John King.

Fairbank, John King, 1907-
xFairbank, John K.
Cambridge History of China. Cambridge U Pr.
China: The People's Middle Kingdom & the U. S. A. Harvard U Pr.
China: Tradition & Transformation. HM.
Chinese-American Interactions: A Historical Summary. Rutgers U Pr.
ed. Chinese Thought & Institutions. U of Chicago Pr.
ed. Chinese World Order: Traditional China's Foreign Relations. Harvard U Pr.
The United States & China. Harvard U Pr.

Fairbank, T. J. see Fairbank, Harold Arthur Thomas.

Fairbank, Wilma.
xFairbank, Wilma.
Adventures in Retrieval: Han Murals & Shang Bronze Molds. Harvard U Pr.

Fairbanks, Carol, 1935-
xFairbanks, Carol.
More Women in Literature: Criticism of the Seventies. Scarecrow.

Fairbanks, David R.
xFairbanks, David R.
A Statistical Study of Residential & Agricultural Land Assessed Valuations & Market Price Trends for the Towns of Holliston & Hopkinton, Massachusetts. Quarterman.

Fairbanks, Henry G. see Fairbanks, Henry George.

Fairbanks, Henry George, 1914-
xFairbanks, Henry G.
Louise Imogen Guiney: Laureate of the Lost. Magi Bks.

Fairbanks, Virgil F.
xFairbanks, Virgil F.
Clinical Disorders of Iron Metabolism. Grune.

Fairchild, Betty.
xFairchild, Betty.
Now That You Know: What Every Parent Should Know About Homosexuality. HarBraceJ.

Fairchild Camera & Instrument Co. see Fairchild Camera and Instrument Corporation.

Fairchild Camera and Instrument Corporation.
xFairchild Camera & Instrument Co.
Semiconductor & Integrated Circuit Fabrication Techniques. Reston.

Fairchild, Henry P. see Fairchild, Henry Pratt.

Fairchild, Henry Pratt, 1880-
xFairchild, Henry P.

Dictionary of Sociology & Related Sciences. Greenwood.
Dictionary of Sociology & Related Sciences. Littlefield.
The Melting-Pot Mistake. Arno.

Fairchild, Hoxie N. see Fairchild, Hoxie Neale.

Fairchild, Hoxie Neale, 1894-
xFairchild, Hoxie N.
Noble Savage: A Study in Romantic Naturalism. Russell.

Fairchild, Johnson E.
xFairchild, Johnson E.
ed. America Faces the Nuclear Age. Sheridan.

Fairchild Market Research Division. see Anderson, Daniel R.

Fairchild, Roy W.
xFairchild, Roy W.
Finding Hope Again: A Pastor's Guide to Counseling Depressed Persons. Har-Row.

Fairchilds, Cissie C.
xFairchilds, Cissie C.
Poverty & Charity in Aix-en-Provence, 1640-1789. Johns Hopkins.

Fairclough, Henry R. see Fairclough, Henry Rushton.

Fairclough, Henry Rushton, 1862-1938
xFairclough, Henry R.
Love of Nature Among the Greeks & Romans. Cooper Sq.

Faires, Virgil M. see Faires, Virgil Moring.

Faires, Virgil Moring, 1897-
xFaires, Virgil M.
Design of Machine Elements. Macmillan.
Problems on Thermodynamics. Macmillan.
Thermodynamics. Macmillan.

Fairfield, James G. T., 1926-
xFairfield, James G. T.
When You Don't Agree. Herald Pr.

Fairfield, Roy P.
xFairfield, Roy P.
ed. Humanistic Frontiers in American Education. Prometheus Bks.
Person-Centered Graduate Education. Prometheus Bks.

Fairhaven College.
xWilliam O. Douglas Symposium, Fairhaven College, 1977.
In Honor of Justice Douglas: A Symposium on Individual Freedom & the Government. Greenwood.

Fairholt, F. W. see Fairholt, Frederick William.

Fairholt, Frederick W. see Fairholt, Frederick William.

Fairholt, Frederick William, 1814-1866
xFairholt, F. W.
A Dictionary of Terms in Art. Gordon Pr.
xFairholt, Frederick W.
ed. Dictionary of Terms in Art. Gale.

Fairhurst, Janet P. see Fairhurst, Janet Perry.

Fairhurst, Janet Perry.
xFairhurst, Janet P.
Homes of the Signers of the Declaration. Hartt Pubns.

Fairley, Barker, 1887-
xFairley, Barker.
Goethe As Revealed in His Poetry. Folcroft.
Goethe As Revealed in His Poetry. Ungar.

Fairley, Lincoln.
xFairley, Lincoln.
Facing Mechanization: The West Coast Longshore Plan. U Cal LA Indus Rel.

Fairley, Peter, 1930-
xFairley, Peter.
The Conquest of Pain. Scribner.

Fairley, William.
xFairley, William B.
Statistics & Public Policy. A-W.

Fairley, William B. see Fairley, William.

Fairlie, Henry, 1924-
xFairlie, Henry.

The Parties: Republicans & Democrats in This
    Century. St Martin.
The Seven Deadly Sins Today. New Republic.
The Seven Deadly Sins Today. U of Notre
    Dame Pr.
Fairlie, John A. *see* Fairlie, John Archibald.
Fairlie, John Archibald, 1872-1947
    xFairlie, John A.
    Centralization of Administration in New York
        State. AMS Pr.
Fairman, Charles.
    xFairman, Charles.
    Fourteenth Amendment & the Bill of Rights:
        The Incorporation Theory. Da Capo.
Fairman, H. W. *see* Fairman, Herbert Walter.
Fairman, Herbert Walter, 1907-
    xFairman, H. W.
    tr. & ed. The Triumph of Horus: An Ancient
        Egyptian Sacred Drama. U of Cal Pr.
Fairman, Joan. *see* Fairman, Joan A.
Fairman, Joan A.
    xFairman, Joan.
    A Penny Saved. Lantern.
Fairman, Paula.
    xFairman, Paula.
    Forbidden Destiny. Pinnacle Bks.
Fairservis, Walter A. *see* Fairservis, Walter Ashlin.
Fairservis, Walter Ashlin, 1921-
    xFairservis, Walter A.
    Costumes of the East. Am Mus Natl Hist.
    Egypt, Gift of the Nile. Macmillan.
Fairweather, Alan M.
    xFairweather, Alan M.
    The Word As Truth: A Critical Examination of
        the Christian Doctrine of Revelation in the
        Writings of Thomas Aquinas & Karl Barth.
        Greenwood.
Fairweather, Graeme.
    xFairweather, Graeme.
    Finite Element Galerkin Methods for
        Differential Equations. Dekker.
Fairweather, Owen.
    xFairweather, Owen.
    Practice & Procedure in Labor Arbitration.
        BNA.
Fairweather, William.
    xFairweather, William.
    Among the Mystics. Arno.
Faison, Edmund W. *see* Faison, Edmund W. J.
Faison, Edmund W. J., 1926-
    xFaison, Edmund W.
    Advertising: A Behavioral Approach for
        Managers. Wiley.
Fait, Hollis F.
    xFait, Hollis F.
    Task & Resource Book: Physical Education for
        the Handicapped. HR&W.
Faith, William L. *see* Faith, William Lawrence.
Faith, William Lawrence.
    xFaith, William L.
    Air Pollution. Wiley.
Faithorne, W. *see* Faithorne, William.
Faithorne, William, 1616-1691
    xFaithorne, W.
    Art of Graveing & Etching. Da Capo.
Faivre, Milton I.
    xFaivre, Milton I.
    How to Raise Rabbits for Fun & Profit.
        Nelson-Hall.
Fakhry, Ahmed.
    xFakhry, Ahmed.
    Pyramids. U of Chicago Pr.
Fakinos, Aris, 1935-
    xFakinos, Aris.
    The Marked Men. Liveright.
Falb, P. L. *see* Falb, Peter L.
Falb, Peter L.
    xFalb, P. L.

Some Successive Approximation Methods in
    Control & Oscillation Theory. Acad Pr.
Falbe, J. *see* Falbe, Jurgen.
Falbe, Jurgen.
    xFalbe, J.
    Carbon Monoxide in Organic Synthesis.
        Springer-Verlag.
    ed. New Syntheses with Carbon Monoxide.
        Springer-Verlag.
Falberg, Howard.
    xFalberg, Howard.
    What You Should Know About Personnel
        Management. Oceana.
Falbo. *see* Falbo, Clement E.
Falbo, Clement E.
    xFalbo.
    Finite Mathematics Applied. Wadsworth Pub.
Falcaro, Joe.
    xFalcaro, Joe.
    Bowling for All. Wiley.
Falck, Frank J. *see* Falck, Frank James.
Falck, Frank James, 1925-
    xFalck, Frank J.
    Stuttering: Learned & Unlearned. C C Thomas.
Falco, Maria J.
    xFalco, Maria J.
    Truth & Meaning in Political Science: An
        Introduction to Political Inquiry. Merrill.
Falcoff, Mark.
    xFalcoff, Mark.
    ed. Prologue to Peron: Argentina in Depression
        & War, 1930-1943. U of Cal Pr.
Falconbridge, Alexander, d. 1792
    xFalconbridge, Alexander.
    Account of the Slave Trade on the Coast of
        Africa. AMS Pr.
Falconer, Douglas S. *see* Falconer, Douglas Scott.
Falconer, Douglas Scott.
    xFalconer, Douglas S.
    Introduction to Quantitative Genetics. Wiley.
Falconer, Mary W.
    xFalconer, Mary W.
    Aging Patients: A Guide for Their Care.
        Springer Pub.
    The Drug, the Nurse, the Patient. Saunders.
Fales, E. D. *see* Fales, Edward D.
Fales, Edward D.
    xFales, E. D.
    The Book of Expert Driving. Dutton.
Falk, Doris V.
    xFalk, Doris V.
    Eugene O'Neill & the Tragic Tension: An
        Interpretive Study of the Plays. Rutgers U Pr.
    Lillian Hellman. Ungar.
Falk, Edwin A. *see* Falk, Edwin Albert.
Falk, Edwin Albert, 1894-
    xFalk, Edwin A.
    From Perry to Pearl Harbor: The Struggle for
        Supremacy in the Pacific. Greenwood.
Falk, I. S. *see* Falk, Isidore Sydney.
Falk, Isidore S. *see* Falk, Isidore Sydney.
Falk, Isidore Sydney.
    xFalk, I. S.
    The Costs of Medical Care: A Summary of
        Investigations on the Economic Aspects of
        the Prevention & Care of Illness. Arno.
    xFalk, Isidore S.
    The Incidence of Illness & the Receipt & Costs
        of Medical Care Among Representative
        Families: Experiences in Twelve Consecutive
        Months During 1928-1931. Arno.
Falk, John R.
    xFalk, John R.
    The Complete Guide to Bird Dog Training.
        Winchester Pr.
Falk, Julia A. *see* Falk, Julia S.
Falk, Julia S.
    xFalk, Julia A.

Language & Linguistics: Bases for a
    Curriculum. Ctr Appl Ling.
Falk, Mervyn L.
    xFalk, Mervyn L.
    ed. Cleft Palate Team Addresses the Speech
        Clinician. C C Thomas.
Falk, Nicholas.
    xFalk, Nicholas.
    Planning the Social Services. Lexington Bks.
Falk, Peter, 1921-
    xFalk, Peter.
    The Growth of the Church in Africa.
        Zondervan.
Falk, Richard A.
    xFalk, Richard A.
    A Global Approach to National Policy.
        Harvard U Pr.
    ed. Regional Politics & World Order. W H
        Freeman.
    Status of Law in International Society.
        Princeton U Pr.
    This Endangered Planet: Prospects & Proposals
        for Human Survival. Random.
    ed. The War System: An Interdisciplinary
        Approach. Westview.
Falk, S. Uno.
    xFalk, S. Uno.
    Alkaline Storage Batteries. Wiley.
Falk, Signi L. *see* Falk, Signi Lenea.
Falk, Signi Lenea.
    xFalk, Signi L.
    Archibald MacLeish. Coll & U Pr.
Falkberget, Johan, 1879-1967
    xFalkberget, Johan.
    Fourth Night Watch. U of Wis Pr.
Falkmer, S.
    xFalkmer, S.
    Structure & Metabolism of the Pancreatic Islets
        - a Centennial of Paul Langerhan's
        Discovery. Pergamon.
Falkner, F. *see* Falkner, Frank Tardrew.
Falkner, Frank Tardrew, 1918-
    xFalkner, F.
    ed. Fundamentals of Mortality Risks During
        the Perinatal Period & Infancy. S Karger.
Falkner, Murry C., 1899-
    xFalkner, Murry C.
    Falkners of Mississippi: A Memoir. La State U
        Pr.
Falkner, Thomas, 1707-1784
    xFalkner, Thomas.
    A Description of Patagonia & the Adjoining
        Parts of South America. AMS Pr.
Falkowski, Lawrence S.
    xFalkowski, Lawrence S.
    ed. Psychological Models in International
        Politics. Westview.
Falkson, Joseph L.
    xFalkson, Joseph L.
    HMOs & the Politics of Health System
        Reform. Am Hospital.
Fall, Bernard B., 1926-1967
    xFall, Bernard B.
    Last Reflections on a War. Schocken.
Fall, Frieda K. *see* Fall, Frieda Kay.
Fall, Frieda Kay, 1913-
    xFall, Frieda K.
    Art Objects, Their Care & Preservation: A
        Handbook for Museums & Collectors.
        McGilvery.
Fallaci, Oriana.
    xFallaci, Oriana.
    Letter to a Child Never Born. S&S.
Fallding, H. *see* Fallding, Harold.
Fallding, Harold.
    xFallding, H.

Drinking, Community & Civilization: The Account of a New Jersey Interview Study. Rutgers Ctr Alcohol.

The Sociology of Religion: An Explanation of the Unity & Diversity in Religion. McGraw.

xFallding, Harold.
The Sociological Task. Irvington.

Fallers, Lloyd A.
xFallers, Lloyd A.
Bantu Bureaucracy: A Century of Political Evolution Among the Basoga of Uganda. U of Chicago Pr.
Law Without Precedent: Legal Ideas in Action in the Courts of Colonial Busoga. U of Chicago Pr.

Fallig, Ralph L.
xFallig, Ralph L.
Practical Guide to Bookkeeping & Accounting. G&D.

Fallon, Ann C. see Fallon, Ann Connerton.

Fallon, Ann Connerton.
xFallon, Ann C.
Katharine Tynan. Twayne.

Fallon, Dennis J.
xFallon, Dennis J.
The Art of Ballroom Dance. Burgess.

Fallon, E. B.
xFallon, E. B.
The Appraiser's Handbook: A Unique Guide to Appraising Land, Buildings & Machinery with Specialized Information for Industrial Engineers. Exposition.

Fallon, Peter.
xFallon, Peter.
ed. Soft Day: A Miscellany of Contemporary Irish Writing. U of Notre Dame Pr.

Fallowell, Duncan.
xFallowell, Duncan.
Drug Tales. St Martin.

Fallows, Marjorie R., 1926-
xFallows, Marjorie R.
Irish Americans: Identity & Assimilation. P-H.

Falls, Harold B.
xFalls, Harold B.
ed. Exercise Physiology. Acad Pr.
ed. Foundations of Conditioning. Acad Pr.

Falls, Joe.
xFalls, Joe.
The Boston Marathon. Macmillan.
The Boston Marathon. Macmillan.
Detroit Tigers. Macmillan.

Falls, Leota K. see Falls, Leota Kate.

Falls, Leota Kate.
xFalls, Leota K.
The Birthright with Love. Moore Pub Co.

Falnes, Oscar J. see Falnes, Oscar Julius.

Falnes, Oscar Julius, 1898-
xFalnes, Oscar J.
National Romanticism in Norway. AMS Pr.

Fals-Borda, Orlando.
xFals-Borda, Orlando.
Peasant Society in the Colombian Andes: A Sociological Study of Saucio. Greenwood.
Subversion & Social Change in Colombia. Columbia U Pr.

Faludi, Andreas.
xFaludi, Andreas.
ed. Essays on Planning Theory & Education. Pergamon.
Planning Theory. Pergamon.
ed. A Reader in Planning Theory. Pergamon.

Fama, E. see Fama, Eugene F.

Fama, Eugene F., 1939-
xFama, E.
Theory of Finance. HR&W.
xFama, Eugene F.
Foundations of Finance: Portfolio Decisions & Securities Prices. Basic.

Family Circle.
xFamily Circle.

ed. Family Circle Creative Needlecrafts. P-H.
xFamily Circle Editors.
ed. Family Circle Favorite Recipes Cookbook. Paramount.

Family Circle Editors. see Family Circle.

The Family Handyman.
xFamily Handyman Editors.
ed. The Family Handyman Handbook of Carpentry Plans Projects. TAB Bks.
Outdoor Projects for Home & Garden. TAB Bks.
xFamily Handyman Magazine.
Heating with Wood. Butterick Pub.
Total Home Security. Butterick Pub.
xFamily Handyman Magazine Editors.
The Family Handyman Encyclopedia of Do-It-Yourself Projects. TAB Bks.
The Family Handyman Handbook of Home Improvement & Remodeling. TAB Bks.
The Family Handyman Practical Book of Saving Home Energy. TAB Bks.
xFamily Handyman Magazine Staff.
The Furniture Maker's Handbook. Scribner.
xFamily Handyman Staff.
America's Handyman Book. Scribner.
The Early American Furniture-Making Handbook. Scribner.
Family Handyman Home Improvement Book. Scribner.

Family Handyman Editors. see The Family Handyman.

Family Handyman Magazine. see The Family Handyman.

Family Handyman Magazine Editors. see The Family Handyman.

Family Handyman Magazine Staff. see The Family Handyman.

Family Handyman Staff. see The Family Handyman.

Family Service Association of America.
xFamily Service Association Of America.
Detailed Instruction for a Time Analysis Family Serv.
A New Perspective on Social Work. Family Serv.
Past & Present Motifs in Social Casework. Family Serv.
Preparing for Time Analysis. Family Serv.
Salary Planning in Family Service Agencies with Salary Ranges. Family Serv.
Selecting Services, Service Elements & Activities. Family Serv.
Social Work Assistants in Family Service Agencies. Family Serv.
Trends in Field Work Instruction. Family Serv.
Using Results of a Time Analysis. Family Serv.
Who Spoke for the Poor?: 1880-1914. Family Serv.

Family Weekly. see Family Weekly Magazine.

Family Weekly Magazine.
xFamily Weekly.
Cooking by the Calendar: A Family Weekly Cookbook. Times Bks.

Family Welfare Assn. see Family Welfare Association, London.

Family Welfare Association, London.
xFamily Welfare Assn.
Guide to the Social Services 1978. Intl Pubns Serv.

Famine Inquiry Commission of India. see India. Famine Inquiry Commission.

Famularo, Joseph J.
xFamularo, Joseph J.
Organization Planning Manual. Am Mgmt.

Fan, Tin-Chiu.
xFan, Ting C.
Chinese Residents in Chicago. R & E Res Assoc.

Fan, Ting C. see Fan, Tin-Chiu.

Fan, Tsen-Chung. see Fan, Tsun-Chung.

Fan, Tsun-Chung.
xFan, Tsen-Chung.

Dr. Johnson & Chinese Culture. Folcroft.

Fancher, Betsy.
xFancher, Betsy.
Lost Legacy of Georgia's Golden Isles. Larlin Corp.

Fancher, Raymond E.
xFancher, Raymond E.
Pioneers in Psychology. Norton.
Pioneers of Psychology. Norton.
Psychoanalytic Psychology: The Development of Freud's Thought. Norton.

Fancher, Wilda.
xFancher, Wilda.
I Have Heard the Rainbow. Broadman.

Fane, Xenia F.
xFane, Xenia F.
Child Care Careers. P-H.

Fanelli, Maresa.
xFanelli, Maresa.
Aujourd'hui. Heath.

Fanfani, Amintore.
xFanfani, Amintore.
Catholicism, Protestantism & Capitalism. Arno.
Catholicism, Protestantism & Capitalism. Folcroft.

Fang, Hsien-T'Ing. see Fang, Hsien-Ting.

Fang, Hsien-Ting, 1902-
xFang, Hsien-T'Ing.
The Triumph of the Factory System in England. Porcupine Pr.

Fang, Irving. see Fang, Irving E.

Fang, Irving E.
xFang, Irving.
Those Radio Commentators. Iowa St U Pr.

Fang-Kuei, Li. see Li, Fang-Kuei.

Fanger, Donald.
xFanger, Donald.
The Creation of Nikolai Gogol. Harvard U Pr.
Dostoevsky & Romantic Realism: A Study of Dostoevsky in Relation to Balzac, Dickens, Gogol. U of Chicago Pr.

Fann, K T, 1937-
xFann, K. T.
ed. Ludwig Wittgenstein: The Man & His Philosophy. Humanities.

Fann, William E.
xFann, William E.
ed. Phenomenology & Treatment of Alcoholism. Spectrum Pub.
ed. Phenomenology & Treatment of Anxiety. Spectrum Pub.

Fannin, Alice.
xFannin, Alice.
Woman: An Affirmation. Heath.

Fannin, Allen.
xFannin, Allen.
Handloom Weaving Technology. Van Nos Reinhold.

Fanning, Anthony E. see Fanning, Antony Edward.

Fanning, Antony Edward.
xFanning, Anthony E.
Planets, Stars & Galaxies: Descriptive Astronomy for Beginners. Peter Smith.

Fanning, Buckner.
xFanning, Buckner.
Christ in Your Shoes. Broadman.

Fanning, Charles.
xFanning, Charles.
Finley Peter Dunne & Mr. Dooley: The Chicago Years. U Pr of Ky.

Fanning, John W.
xFanning, John W.
A Common Sense Approach to Community Living Arrangements for the Mentally Retarded. C C Thomas.

Fanning, Odom.
xFanning, Odom.

Opportunities in Environmental Careers. Natl
Textbk.

Fannon, Patrick, 1929-
xFannon, Patrick.
Changing Face of Theology. Macmillan.

Fanon, Frantz, 1925-1961
xFanon, Frantz.
Toward the African Revolution. Grove.

Fanshawe, David, 1942-
xFanshawe, David.
African Sanctus: A Story of Travel & Music.
Times Bks.

Fanshawe, Elizabeth.
xFanshawe, Elizabeth.
Rachel. Bradbury Pr.

Fanshel, David.
xFanshel, David.
Far from the Reservation: The Transracial
Adoption of American Indian Children.
Scarecrow.
Toward More Understanding of Foster Parents.
R & E Res Assoc.

Fansler, Dean S. see Fansler, Dean Spruill.

Fansler, Dean Spruill, 1885-
xFansler, Dean S.
Chaucer & the Roman De la Rose. Peter
Smith.
Chaucer & the Roman de la Rose. Somerset
Pub.

Fansler, Harriott (Ely).
xFansler, Harriott E.
Evolution of Technic in Elizabethan Tragedy.
Phaeton.

Fansler, Harriott E. see Fansler, Harriott (Ely).

Fant, Clyde E.
xFant, Clyde E.
Preaching for Today. Har-Row.

Fante, John, 1909-
xFante, John.
Ask the Dust. Black Sparrow.

Fantham, Elaine.
xFantham, Elaine.
Comparative Studies in Republican Latin
Imagery. U of Toronto Pr.

Fantini, Mario. see Fantini, Mario D.

Fantini, Mario D.
xFantini, Mario.
The People & Their Schools: Community
Participation. Phi Delta Kappa.
xFantini, Mario D.
ed. Alternative Education: A Sourcebook for
Parents, Teachers, Students &
Administrators. Doubleday.

Fantino, Edmund. see Fantino, Edmund J.

Fantino, Edmund J.
xFantino, Edmund.
The Experimental Analysis of Behavior: A
Biological Perspective. W H Freeman.
xFantino, Edmund J.
Introduction to Contemporary Psychology. W
H Freeman.

Fanu, J. S. Le. see Le Fanu, J. S.

FAO. see Food and Agriculture Organization of the
United Nations.

FAO - WHO Joint Expert Committee on Food
Additives. see Joint Fao-Who Expert Committee on
Food Additives.

FAO Conference, 10th Session, Rome, 1959. see Joint
Fao-Who Expert Committee on Food Additives.

FAO Conference, 11th Session, Rome, 1961. see Joint
Fao-Who Expert Committee on Food Additives.

FAO Conference, 12th Session, Rome, 1963. see Joint
Fao-Who Expert Committee on Food Additives.

FAO Conference, 13th Session, Rome, 1965. see Joint
Fao-Who Expert Committee on Food Additives.

FAO Conference, 14th Session, Rome, 1967. see Joint
Fao-Who Expert Committee on Food Additives.

FAO Conference, 15th Session, Rome, 1969. see Food
and Agriculture Organization of the United Nations.
Conference.

FAO Conference, 16th Session, Rome, 1971. see Food
and Agriculture Organization of the United Nations.
Conference.

FAO Conference, 17th Session, Rome, 1973. see Food
and Agriculture Organization of the United Nations.
Conference.

FAO Conference, 18th Session, Rome, Nov. 8-27,1975.
see Food and Agriculture Organization of the United
Nations. Conference.

FAO Executive Director. see World Food Programme.

FAO-WHO Expert Committee on Food Additives.
Rome, 1974, 18th. see Joint Fao-Who Expert
Committee on Food Additives.

FAO-WHO Expert Committee on Nutrition, Rome,
1974, 9th. see Joint Fao-Who Expert Committee on
Nutrition.

FAO-WHO Joint Committee Expert Committee on
Nutrition, 8th. see Joint Fao-Who Expert Committee
on Nutrition.

Fapso, Richard J.
xFapso, Richard J.
Norwegians in Wisconsin. State Hist Soc Wis.

**Far West Laboratory for Educational Research and
Development.**
xFar West Laboratory for Educational Research &
Development.
Minicourse: A Microteaching Approach to
Teacher Education. Macmillan.
Minicourse Eight: Organizing Indepedent
Learning Primary Level. Macmillan.
Minicourse Fifteen: Organizing Independent
Learning-Intermediate Level. Macmillan.
Minicourse Five: Individualizing Instruction in
Mathematics. Macmillan.
Minicourse in Your School. Macmillan.
Minicourse Nine: Higher Cognitive
Questioning. Macmillan.
Minicourse One: Effective Questioning, -
Elementary Level. Macmillan.
Minicourse Two: Developing Children's Oral
Language. Macmillan.
xFar Western Laboratory for Educational Research
& Development.
Minicourse Eighteen: Teaching Reading As
Decoding. Macmillan.

Far Western Laboratory for Educational Research &
Development. see Far West Laboratory for
Educational Research and Development.

Faraday, Ann.
xFaraday, Ann.
The Dream Game. Har-Row.
The Dream Game. Har-Row.
Dream Power. Berkley Pub.

Faraday, Michael, 1791-1867
xFaraday, Michael.
The Chemical History of a Candle. Larlin
Corp.

Faragher, John M. see Faragher, John Mack.

Faragher, John Mack, 1945-
xFaragher, John M.
Women & Men on the Overland Trail. Yale U
Pr.

Farago, Francis T.
xFarago, Francis T.
Abrasive Methods Engineering. Indus Pr.
Handbook of Dimensional Measurement. Indus
Pr.

Farago, John.
xFarago, John.
ed. The Family: Vital Force or Outworn
Institution?. PB.

Farago, Ladislas.
xFarago, Ladislas.
Aftermath. Avon.
Aftermath: Martin Bormann & the Fourth
Reich. S&S.
ed. German Psychological Warfare. Arno.
Patton: Ordeal & Triumph. Astor-Honor.

Farago, Peter. see Farago, Peter Joseph.

Farago, Peter Joseph.
xFarago, Peter.
Life in Action: Biochemistry Explained. Knopf.

Farah, Caesar E.
xFarah, Caesar E.
The Dhayl in Medieval Arabic Historiography.
Am Orient Soc.

Farallones Institute.
xFarallones Institute.
The Integral Urban House: Self-Reliant Living
in the City. Sierra.

Faraone, Joseph J.
xFaraone, Joseph J.
Paraclete Power: A Study Guide for the Acts
of the Apostles. Alba.

Fararo, T. J.
xFararo, Thomas J.
Mathematical Sociology: An Introduction to
Fundamentals. Krieger.

Fararo, Thomas J. see Fararo, T. J.

Farb, Nathan, 1941-
xFarb, Nathan.
The Russians. Barron.

Farb, Peter.
xFarb, Peter.
Ecology. Silver.
Face of North America: The Natural History
of a Continent. Har-Row.
Face of North America: The Natural History
of a Continent. Har-Row.
ed. Forest. Silver.
Humankind. Bantam.
Humankind. HM.
Insects. Silver.

Farb, Stanley N., 1935-
xFarb, Stanley N.
Otolaryngology. Med Exam.

Farber. see Farber, Emmanuel.

Farber, Bernard.
xFarber, Bernard.
Comparative Kinship Systems: A Method of
Analysis. Krieger.
Family & Kinship in Modern Society. Scott F.

Farber, Donald C.
xFarber, Donald C.
From Option to Opening. Drama Bk.

Farber, E. see Farber, Emmanuel.

Farber, Emmanuel.
xFarber
Toxic Injury of the Liver. Dekker.
xFarber, E.
ed. The Pathology of Transcription &
Translation. Dekker.

Farber, Evan I. see Farber, Evan Ira.

Farber, Evan Ira.
xFarber, Evan I.
Classified List of Periodicals for the College
Library. Faxon.

Farber, Joseph. see Farber, Joseph C.

Farber, Joseph C.
xFarber, Joseph.
photos by Portrait of Essex. Globe Pequot.

Farber, Leslie. see Farber, Leslie H.

Farber, Leslie H.
xFarber, Leslie.
Lying, Despair, Jealousy, Envy, Sex, Suicide,
Drugs, & the Good Life. Har-Row.

Farber, Marvin, 1901-
xFarber, Marvin.
Foundation of Phenomenology: Edmund
Husserl & the Quest for a Rigorous Science
of Philosophy. State U NY Pr.
Naturalism & Subjectivism. State U NY Pr.

Farber, Maurice L., 1912-
xFarber, Maurice L.
Theory of Suicide. Arno.

Farber, Norma.
xFarber, Norma.

How Does It Feel to Be Old?. Dutton.
How the Hibernators Came to Bethlehem.
Walker & Co.
How the Left-Behind Beasts Built Ararat.
Walker & Co.
Never Say Ugh! to a Bug. Greenwillow.
There Goes Feathertop!. Dutton.
There Once Was a Woman Who Married a
Man. A-W.
This Is the Ambulance Leaving the Zoo.
Dutton.
Where's Gomer. Dutton.
xFarber, Norman.
Up the Down Elevator. A-W.
Farber, Norman. see Farber, Norma.
Farber, Robert.
xFarber, Robert.
Images of Woman. Amphoto.
Professional Fashion Photography. Amphoto.
Farber, Samuel, 1939-
xFarber, Samuel.
Revolution & Reaction in Cuba, 1933-1960: A
Political Sociology from Machado to Castro.
Columbia U Pr.
Farber, Thomas, 1944-
xFarber, Thomas.
The Material Plane. Dutton.
Who Wrote the Book of Love?. Avon.
Who Wrote the Book of Love?. Norton.
Farberow, N. see Farberow, Norman L.
Farberow, Norman L.
xFarberow, N.
Suicide in Different Cultures. Univ Park.
xFarberow, Norman L.
ed. The Many Faces of Suicide: Indirect
Self-Destructive Behavior. McGraw.
Fardo, Stephen W.
xFardo, Stephen W.
Electrical Power Systems Technology. Sams.
Farer, Tom J.
xFarer, Tom J.
ed. Financing African Development. MIT Pr.
The Future of the Inter-American System.
Praeger.
War Clouds on the Horn of Africa: The
Widening Storm. Carnegie Endow.
Farfan, H. F.
xFarfan, H. F.
Mechanical Disorders of the Low Back. Lea &
Febiger.
Farge, John La. see La Farge, John.
Farge, Oliver La. see La Farge, Oliver.
Farge, Phyllis La. see La Farge, Phyllis.
Farge, W. E. La. see La Farge, W. E.
Farges, Albert M.
xFarges, Albert M.
By the End of the Century, Who Will Be
Number One?. Inst Econ Pol.
Faria, A. J.
xFaria, Anthony J.
Compete: A Dynamic Marketing Simulation.
Business Pubns.
Faria, Anthony J. see Faria, A. J.
Faria, L. E. see Faria, Lawrence E.
Faria, Lawrence E.
xFaria, L. E.
Protective Breathing Apparatus. R J Brady.
Faricy, Robert. see Faricy, Robert L.
Faricy, Robert L., 1926-
xFaricy, Robert.
Praying for Inner Healing. Paulist Pr.
Farina, A. see Farina, Amerigo.
Farina, Amerigo.
xFarina, A.
Abnormal Psychology. P-H.
Farina, John E. see Farina, John Edward George.
Farina, John Edward George, 1933-
xFarina, John E.

Quantum Theory of Scattering Processes.
Pergamon.
Farina, Mario V.
xFarina, Mario V.
Programming in BASIC: The Time-Sharing
Language. P-H.
Fariq, Khurshid A. see Fariq, Khurshid Ahmad.
Fariq, Khurshid Ahmad.
xFariq, Khurshid A.
History of Arabic Literature. Intl Pubns Serv.
Faris, E. see Faris, Esron Mcgruder.
Faris, Ellsworth.
xFaris, Ellsworth.
ed. Intelligent Philanthropy. Patterson Smith.
Nature of Human Nature & Other Essays in
Social Psychology. Arno.
Faris, Esron Mcgruder.
xFaris, E.
Accounting for Lawyers. Michie.
Faris, J. A. see Faris, John Acheson.
Faris, John Acheson.
xFaris, J. A.
Quantification Theory. Routledge & Kegan.
Faris, John T. see Faris, John Thomson.
Faris, John Thomson, 1871-1949
xFaris, John T.
Men Who Conquered. Arno.
Faris, Ralph. see Faris, Ralph M.
Faris, Ralph M.
xFaris, Ralph.
ed. Crisis & Consciousness. Humanities.
Farish, Margaret K.
xFarish, Margaret K.
ed. Orchestral Music in Print. Musicdata.
ed. Orchestral Music in Print: Educational
Section. Musicdata.
Farjeon, Annabel.
xFarjeon, Annabel.
Siege of Trapp's Mill. Atheneum.
Farjeon, Benjamin L. see Farjeon, Benjamin Leopold.
Farjeon, Benjamin Leopold, 1833-1903
xFarjeon, Benjamin L.
Devlin the Barber. Arno.
Farkas, M. see Farkas, Miklos.
Farkas, Miklos.
xFarkas, M.
ed. Differential Equations. Elsevier.
Farkas, Sandor.
xFarkas, Sandor B.
Journey in North America, 1831. ABC-Clio.
Farkas, Sandor B. see Farkas, Sandor.
Farley, Belmont M. see Farley, Belmont Mercer.
Farley, Belmont Mercer, 1891-
xFarley, Belmont M.
What to Tell the People About the Public
Schools: A Study of the Content of the
Public School Publicity Program. AMS Pr.
Farley, Carol. see Farley, Carol J.
Farley, Carol J.
xFarley, Carol.
Bunch on McKellahan Street. Watts.
The Garden Is Doing Fine. Atheneum.
Loosen Your Ears. Atheneum.
Farley, Edward, 1929-
xFarley, Edward.
Ecclesial Man: A Social Phenomenology of
Faith & Reality. Fortress.
Farley, Eugene J.
xFarley, Eugene J.
Barron's Getting Ready for the High School
Equivalency Examination: Beginning
Preparation in Reading & English. Barron.
Farley, Gordon K.
xFarley, Gordon K.

Handbook of Child & Adolescent Psychiatric
Emergencies. Med Exam.
Farley, Jennie.
xFarley, Jennie.
Affirmative Action & the Woman Worker:
Guidelines for Personnel Management. Am
Mgmt.
Farley, John U.
xFarley, John U.
ed. Control of "Error" in Market Research
Data. Lexington Bks.
Farley, Karin. see Farley, Karin Clafford.
Farley, Karin Clafford.
xFarley, Karin.
Canal Boy. Cook.
Farley, Lin.
xFarley, Lin.
Sexual Shakedown: The Sexual Harassment of
Women on the Job. McGraw.
Farley, Philip.
xFarley, Philip J.
Arms Across the Sea. Brookings.
Farley, Philip J. see Farley, Philip.
Farley, Walter, 1915-
xFarley, Walter.
The Black Stallion Picture Book. Random.
Great Dane Thor. Random.
The Great Dane Thor. Dell.
The Horse-Tamer. Random.
Horse Tamer. Random.
Little Black Goes to the Circus. Beginner.
Farley, William E.
xFarley, William E.
Practical Public Relations for the Businessman.
Fell.
Farley-Hills, David.
xFarley-Hills, David.
Rochester's Poetry. Rowman.
Farlie, Barbara. see Farlie, Barbara L.
Farlie, Barbara L.
xFarlie, Barbara.
Flower Craft. Bobbs.
Farlow, Helen.
xFarlow, Helen.
Publicizing & Promoting Programs. McGraw.
Farlow, W. G. see Farlow, William Gibson.
Farlow, William Gibson, 1814-1919
xFarlow, W. G.
Some Edible & Poisonous Fungi. Shorey.
Farm Foundation. see Farm Foundation, Chicago.
Farm Foundation, Chicago.
xFarm Foundation.
Land Economics Research: Papers Presented at
a Symposium Held at Lincoln, Nebraska,
June 16-23, 1961. AMS Pr.
Farm Journal (Philadelphia, 1956-).
xEditors of Farm Journal.
Listen to the Land. P-H.
xFarm Journal Editions.
Great Home Cooking in America. PB.
xFarm Journal Editors.
ed. Ada the Ayrshire. Farm Journal.
America's Best Vegetable Recipes. Doubleday.
Farm Journal's Complete Home Baking Book.
Doubleday.
A Homespun Christmas. Doubleday.
ed. Listen to the Land: A Farm Journal
Treasury. G K Hall.
Farm Journal Editions. see Farm Journal (Philadelphia,
1956-).
Farm Journal Editors. see Farm Journal (Philadelphia,
1956-).
Farma, William J. see Farma, William Joseph.
Farma, William Joseph.
xFarma, William J.
Prose, Poetry & Drama for Oral Interpretation.
R West.
Farmer, B. H. see Farmer, Bertram Hughes.
Farmer, Bertram Hughes.
xFarmer, B. H.

Agricultural Colonization in India Since
  Independence. Oxford U Pr.
Farmer, Charles. *see* Farmer, Charles J.
Farmer, Charles J.
  xFarmer, Charles.
    The Digest Book of Canoeing. Follett.
    The Digest Book of Outdoor Cooking. Follett.
  xFarmer, Charles J.
    Backpack Fishing. Jolex.
    The Digest Book of Canoes, Kayaks, & Rafts.
      Follett.
Farmer, D. H. *see* Farmer, David Hugh.
Farmer, David Hugh.
  xFarmer, D. H.
    ed. The Oxford Dictionary of Saints. Oxford U
      Pr.
Farmer, David L. *see* Farmer, David Leighton.
Farmer, David Leighton.
  xFarmer, David L.
    Britain & the Stuarts 1603-1714. Humanities.
Farmer, Edward L.
  xFarmer, Edward L.
    Early Ming Government: The Evolution of
      Dual Capitals. Harvard U Pr.
Farmer, F. M. *see* Farmer, Fannie Merritt.
Farmer, Fannie. *see* Farmer, Fannie Merritt.
Farmer, Fannie Merritt, 1857-1915
  xFarmer, F. M.
    Original Boston Cooking School Cookbook.
      NAL.
  xFarmer, Fannie.
    The Boston Cooking School Cook Book.
      Gordon Pr.
Farmer, H. G. *see* Farmer, Henry George.
Farmer, Henry G. *see* Farmer, Henry George.
Farmer, Henry George, 1882-
  xFarmer, H. G.
    Historical Facts for the Arabian Musical
      Influence. Scholarly.
  xFarmer, Henry G.
    Historical Facts for the Arabian Musical
      Influence. Arno.
    History of Music in Scotland. Da Capo.
Farmer, Herbert H. *see* Farmer, Herbert Henry.
Farmer, Herbert Henry, 1892-
  xFarmer, Herbert H.
    Revelation & Religion: Studies in the
      Theological Interpretation of Religious Types.
      AMS Pr.
Farmer, Joan.
  xFarmer, Joan.
    Sedona. St Martin.
Farmer, John S. *see* Farmer, John Stephen.
Farmer, John Stephen, 1845?-1915?
  xFarmer, John S.
    Musa Pedestris: Three Centuries of Canting
      Songs & Slang Rhymes, 1536-1896. Cooper
      Sq.
Farmer, Penelope.
  xFarmer, Penelope.
    Beginnings: Creation Myths of the World.
      Atheneum.
    A Castle of Bone. Atheneum.
    The Story of Persephone. Morrow.
Farmer, Philip J. *see* Farmer, Philip Jose.
Farmer, Philip Jose.
  xFarmer, Philip J.
    Dare. Berkley Pub.
    The Dark Design. Berkley Pub.
    Dark Is the Sun. Ballantine.
    The Gates of Creation. Ace Bks.
    The Green Odyssey. Gregg.
    Lord Tyger. NAL.
    The Lovers. Ballantine.
    Night of Light. Berkley Pub.
    Night of Light. Garland Pub.
    The Stone God Awakens. Ace Bks.
    Strange Relations. Avon.
  xFarmer, Phillip Jose.

The Dark Design. Berkley Pub.
Farmer, Phillip Jose. *see* Farmer, Philip Jose.
Farmer, R. D. *see* Farmer, Richard Donald Trafford.
Farmer, Richard. *see* Farmer, Richard E.
Farmer, Richard Donald Trafford.
  xFarmer, R. D.
    Lecture Notes on Community Medicine.
      Mosby.
Farmer, Richard E.
  xFarmer, Richard.
    Law Enforcement & Community Relations..
      Reston.
Farmer, Richard N.
  xFarmer, Richard N.
    Corporate Social Responsibility. SRA.
Farmer, Silas, 1839-1902
  xFarmer, Silas.
    History of Detroit & Wayne County & Early
      Michigan: A Chronological Cyclopedia of the
      Past & Present. Gale.
Farmer, W. D. *see* Farmer, William Davis.
Farmer, W. R. *see* Farmer, William Reuben.
Farmer, William Davis.
  xFarmer, W. D.
    Homes for Pleasant Living. W D Farmer.
Farmer, William Reuben.
  xFarmer, W. R.
    The Last Twelve Verses of Mark. Cambridge U
      Pr.
Farmilant, Eunice.
  xFarmilant, Eunice.
    The Natural Foods Sweet Tooth Cookbook. BJ
      Pub Group.
Farnam, Henry W. *see* Farnam, Henry Walcott.
Farnam, Henry Walcott.
  xFarnam, Henry W.
    Chapters in the History of Social Legislation in
      the United States to 1860. AMS Pr.
Farnell, Ida.
  xFarnell, Ida.
    Spanish Prose - Poetry, Old - New. Arno.
Farnell, L. R. *see* Farnell, Lewis Richard.
Farnell, Lewis Richard, 1856-1934
  xFarnell, L. R.
    Outline History of Greek Religion. Ares.
Farner, Donald S. *see* Farner, Donald Stanley.
Farner, Donald Stanley.
  xFarner, Donald S.
    Avian Biology. Acad Pr.
Farnham, Charles H. *see* Farnham, Charles Haight.
Farnham, Charles Haight, 1841-1929
  xFarnham, Charles H.
    Life of Francis Parkman. Greenwood.
    Life of Francis Parkman. Haskell.
    Life of Francis Parkman. Scholarly.
  xFarnham, Charles Haight.
    A Life of Francis Parkman. Folcroft.
Farnham, Eliza. *see* Farnham, Eliza Woodson (Burhans).
Farnham, Eliza W. *see* Farnham, Eliza Woodson
  (Burhans).
Farnham, Eliza Woodson (Burhans), 1815-1864
  xFarnham, Eliza.
    Life in Prairie Land. Humanities.
  xFarnham, Eliza W.
    Life in Prairie Land. Arno.
Farnham, Emily, 1912-
  xFarnham, Emily.
    Charles Demuth: Behind a Laughing Mask. U
      of Okla Pr.
Farnham, Marynia F. *see* Farnham, Marynia L. Foot.
Farnham, Marynia L. Foot, 1899-
  xFarnham, Marynia F.
    Adolescent. Macmillan.
Farnham-Diggory, Sylvia.
  xFarnham-Diggory, Sylvia.

ed. Information Processing in Children. Acad
  Pr.
Learning Disabilities: A Psychological
  Perspective. Harvard U Pr.
Farnie, D. A.
  xFarnie, D. A.
    The English Cotton Industry & the World
      Market 1815-1896. Oxford U Pr.
Farnsworth, M. W. *see* Farnsworth, Marjorie Whyte.
Farnsworth, Marjorie Whyte, 1921-
  xFarnsworth, M. W.
    Genetics. Har-Row.
Farnsworth, Mona.
  xFarnsworth, Mona.
    The Menace of Marble Hill. Manor Bks.
Farnsworth, Richard A. *see* Farnsworth, Richard Ashley.
Farnsworth, Richard Ashley.
  xFarnsworth, Richard A.
    Productivity & the Law. Lexington Bks.
Farnsworth, T. *see* Farnsworth, Terry.
Farnsworth, Terry.
  xFarnsworth, T.
    Developing Executive Talent: A Practical
      Guide. McGraw.
Farnworth, Warren.
  xFarnworth, Warren.
    Approaches to Collage. Taplinger.
Farquhar, Francis P. *see* Farquhar, Francis Peloubet.
Farquhar, Francis Peloubet, 1887-
  xFarquhar, Francis P.
    History of the Sierra Nevada. U of Cal Pr.
Farquhar, George.
  xFarquhar, George.
    Complete Works. Gordian.
Farquharson, Robin, 1930-
  xFarquharson, Robin.
    Theory of Voting. Yale U Pr.
Farr, A. D. *see* Farr, Alfred Derek.
Farr, Alfred Derek.
  xFarr, A. D.
    Let Not the Deep: Story of the Royal National
      Lifeboat Institution. Intl Pubns Serv.
Farr, Caroline.
  xFarr, Caroline.
    Island of Evil. NAL.
Farr, Finis.
  xFarr, Finis.
    Fair Enough: The Life of Westbrook Pegler.
      Arlington Hse.
Farr, James F.
  xFarr, James F.
    An Estate Planner's Handbook. Little.
Farr, Kenneth H. *see* Farr, Kenneth R.
Farr, Kenneth R.
  xFarr, Kenneth H.
    Personalism & Party Politics:
      Institutionalization of the Popular Democratic
      Party of Puerto Rico. Inter Am U Pr.
  xFarr, Kenneth R.
    Historical Dictionary of Puerto Rico & the U.S.
      Virgin Islands. Scarecrow.
Farr, Roger. *see* Farr, Roger C.
Farr, Roger C.
  xFarr, Roger.
    Measurement & Evaluation of Reading.
      HarBraceJ.
    Teaching a Child to Read. HarBraceJ.
Farraday, Chelsea.
  xFarraday, Chelsea.
    Disco. Nordon Pubns.
    Intimate Strangers. Nordon Pubns.
Farrall, Arthur W. *see* Farrall, Arthur William.
Farrall, Arthur William.
  xFarrall, Arthur W.
    Dictionary of Agricultural & Food Engineering.
      Interstate.
    Engineering for Dairy & Food Products.
      Krieger.
Farrand, Max.
  xFarrand, Max.

Pathology of Rheumatic Diseases.
Springer-Verlag.
Fassbender, William. *see* Fassbender, William V.
Fassbender, William V.
xFassbender, William.
You & Your Health. Wiley.
Fassler, D. *see* Fassler, Doris.
Fassler, Doris.
xFassler, D.
Encounter with a New World: A
Reading-Writing Text for Speakers of English
As a Second Language. P-H.
Fassler, Joan.
xFassler, Joan.
All Alone with Daddy. Human Sci Pr.
The Boy with a Problem. Human Sci Pr.
Don't Worry Dear. Human Sci Pr.
Howie Helps Himself. A Whitman.
My Grandpa Died Today. Human Sci Pr.
One Little Girl. Human Sci Pr.
Fast, Howard.
xFast, Howard.
April Morning. Crown.
April Morning. Bantam.
Last Frontier. NAL.
Fast, Howard. *see* Fast, Howard Melvin.
Fast, Howard Melvin, 1914-
xFast, Howard.
The Art of Zen Meditation. Peace Pr.
The Establishment. Dell.
Establishment. HM.
The Establishment. G K Hall.
Freedom Road. Crown.
Freedom Road. Bantam.
Freedom Road. AMSCO Sch.
The Immigrants. Dell.
The Immigrants. G K Hall.
The Immigrants. HM.
The Magic Door. Peace Pr.
The Magic Door. Avon.
My Glorious Brothers. Hebrew Pub.
Second Generation. Dell.
The Second Generation. HM.
Second Generation. G K Hall.
Time & the Riddle: Thirty-One Zen Stories.
HM.

Fast, Jonathan.
xFast, Jonathan.
The Inner Circle. Delacorte.
The Inner Circle. Dell.

Fast, Julius.
xFast, Julius.
Talking Between the Lines: How We Mean
More Than We Say. Viking Pr.

Fast, Norman, 1948-
xFast, Norman D.
The Rise & Fall of Corporate New Venture
Divisions. Univ Microfilms.

Fast, Norman D. *see* Fast, Norman.

Fasuyi, T. A.
xFasuyi, T. A.
Cultural Policy in Nigeria. Unipub.

Fateley, W. G. *see* Fateley, William G.

Fateley, William G.
xFateley, W. G.
Infrared & Raman Selection Rules for
Molecular & Lattice Vibrations. Krieger.

Fatemi, Nasrollah S. *see* Fatemi, Nasrollah Saifpour.

Fatemi, Nasrollah Saifpour, 1911-
xFatemi, Nasrollah S.

The Dollar Crisis: The United States Balance of
Payments & Dollar Stability. NYU Pr.
Love, Beauty, & Harmony in Sufism. A S
Barnes.
Multinational Corporations. A S Barnes.
Sufism: Message of Brotherhood, Harmony, &
Hope. A S Barnes.
Father of Candor.
xFather of Candor.
An Enquiry into the Doctrine, Lately
Propagated, Concerning Libels, Warrants, &
the Seizure of Papers. Da Capo.
Fatigati, Evelyn.
xFatigati, Evelyn.
BZZZ: A Beekeeper's Primer. Rodale Pr Inc.
Garden on Greenway Street. Rodale Pr Inc.
Fatout, Paul.
xFatout, Paul.
Mark Twain in Virginia City. Kennikat.
Fatteh, Abdullah.
xFatteh, Abdullah.
Handbook of Forensic Pathology. Lippincott.
xFatteh, Abdullah.
Medicolegal Investigation of Gunshot Wounds.
Lippincott.
Fatteh, Adbullah. *see* Fatteh, Abdullah.
Faubion, Nina L. *see* Faubion, Nina Lane.
Faubion, Nina Lane.
xFaubion, Nina L.
Some Edible Mushrooms & How to Cook
Them. Binford.
Fauci, Anthony S.
xFauci, Anthony S.
ed. Antibody Production in Man: In Vitro
Synthesis & Clinical Implications. Acad Pr.
Fauconnier, Gilles.
xFauconnier, Gilles.
Theoretical Implications of Some Global
Phenomena in Syntax. Garland Pub.
Faugsted, George E. *see* Faugsted, George Edward.
Faugsted, George Edward.
xFaugsted, George E.
The Chilenos in the California Gold Rush. R &
E Res Assoc.
Faul, Henry.
xFaul, Henry.
Ages of Rocks, Planets & Stars. McGraw.
Faules, Don F.
xFaules, Don F.
Communication & Social Behavior: A Symbolic
Interaction Perspective. A-W.
Directing Forensics. Morton Pub.
Faulhaber, Charles.
xFaulhaber, Charles.
Latin Rhetorical Theory in Thirteenth &
Fourteenth Century Castile. U of Cal Pr.
Faulk, Henry.
xFaulk, Henry.
Group Captives: The Re-Education of German
Prisoners of War in Britain, 1945-1948.
Humanities.
Faulk, Laura E.
xFaulk, Laura E.
The Australian Alternative. Arlington Hse.
Faulk, Odie B.
xFaulk, Odie B.
Arizona: A Short History. U of Okla Pr.
Destiny Road: The Gila Trail & the Opening of
the Southwest. Oxford U Pr.
Geronimo Campaign. Oxford U Pr.
Faulk, Terry R.
xFaulk, Terry R.
Simple Methods of Mining Gold. Filter.
Faulkenberry, Luces M.
xFaulkenberry, Luces M.
An Introduction to Operational Amplifiers.
Wiley.
Faulkner, B. *see* Faulkner, Blanche.
Faulkner, Blanche.
xFaulkner, B.

The Lively House. Crescent Pubns.
Faulkner, Bob.
xFaulkner, Robert.
Learn to Cross-Country Ski in One Day. Rand.
Faulkner, Claude W. *see* Faulkner, Claude Winston.
Faulkner, Claude Winston, 1916-
xFaulkner, Claude W.
Byron's Political Verse Satire. Folcroft.
Faulkner, Florence.
xFaulkner, Florence.
Clue to Romance. Bouregy
Faulkner, Georgene.
xFaulkner, Georgene.
Melindy's Medal. Messner.
Faulkner, Harold U. *see* Faulkner, Harold Underwood.
Faulkner, Harold Underwood, 1890-1968
xFaulkner, Harold U.
Chartism & the Churches: A Study in
Democracy. Biblio Dist.
The Decline of Laissez Faire 1897-1917. M E
Sharpe.
Politics, Reform & Expansion: 1890-1900.
Har-Row.
Faulkner, John, 1901-1963
xFaulkner, John.
Cabin Road. La State U Pr.
Faulkner, Joseph. *see* Faulkner, Joseph E.
Faulkner, Joseph E.
xFaulkner, Joseph.
Religion's Influence in Contemporary Society:
Readings in the Sociology of Religion.
Merrill.
xFaulkner, Joseph E.
Exercises in Sociology. Merrill.
Faulkner, Lynn L., 1941-
xFaulkner, Lynn L.
ed. Handbook of Industrial Noise Control.
Indus Pr.
Faulkner, Margaret.
xFaulkner, Margaret.
I Skate!. Little.
Faulkner, Max.
xFaulkner, Max.
Play Championship Golf All Your Life.
Transatlantic.
Faulkner, Peter.
xFaulkner, Peter.
Robert Bage. G K Hall.
Robert Bage. Twayne.
Faulkner, Peter T., 1933-
xFaulkner, Peter T.
ed. Silent Bomb: A Guide to the Nuclear
Energy Controversy. Random.
ed. The Silent Bomb: A Guide to the Nuclear
Energy Controversy. Random.
Faulkner, Ray. *see* Faulkner, Ray Nelson.
Faulkner, Ray Nelson.
xFaulkner, Ray.
Art Today: An Introduction to the Visual Arts.
HR&W.
Inside Today's Home. HR&W.
Faulkner, Robert. *see* Faulkner, Bob.
Faulkner, Sarah.
xFaulkner, Sarah.
Planning a Home: A Practical Guide to Interior
Design. HR&W.
Planning a Home: A Practical Guide to Interior
Design. HR&W.
Faulkner, William, 1897-1962
xFaulkner, William.

Absalom, Absalom. Modern Lib.
Absalom, Absalom. Modern Lib.
Absalom, Absalom. Random.
Absalom, Absalom!. Random.
As I Lay Dying. Modern Lib.
As I Lay Dying. Random.
As I Lay Dying. Random.
Collected Stories. Random.
Collected Stories of William Faulkner.
  Random.
Fable. Random.
Flags in the Dust. Random.
Flags in the Dust. Random.
Go Down, Moses. Modern Lib.
Go Down, Moses. Random.
Go Down, Moses. Random.
Hamlet. Random.
Hamlet. Random.
Light in August. Modern Lib.
Light in August. Modern Lib.
Light in August. Random.
Light in August. Random.
The Marionettes. U Pr of Va.
The Portable Faulkner. Viking Pr.
Portable Faulkner. Penguin.
Pylon. Random.
Sound & the Fury. Modern Lib.
Sound & the Fury. Modern Lib.
Sound & the Fury. Random.
Sound & the Fury. Random.

Faunce, William A.
xFaunce, William A.
  Problems of an Industrial Society. McGraw.
Faure, G. see Faure, Gunter.
Faure, Gunter.
xFaure, G.
  Strontium Isotope Geology. Springer-Verlag.
xFaure, Gunter.
  Principles of Isotope Geology. Wiley.
Fauriel, C. C. see Fauriel, Claude Charles.
Fauriel, Claude Charles.
xFauriel, C. C.
  History of Provencal Poetry. Haskell.
Faurot, Albert.
xFaurot, Albert.
  Concert Piano Repertoire: A Manual of Solo
    Literature for Artists & Performers.
    Scarecrow.
Fauset, Jessie R. see Fauset, Jessie Redmon.
Fauset, Jessie Redmon.
xFauset, Jessie R.
  Chinaberry Tree: A Novel of American Life.
    Negro U Pr.
  Comedy, American Style. AMS Pr.
  Comedy, American Style. Negro U Pr.
  There Is Confusion. AMS Pr.
Fausold, Martin L.
xFausold, Martin L.
  Gifford Pinchot, Bull Moose Progressive.
    Greenwood.
  ed. The Hoover Presidency: A Reappraisal.
    State U NY Pr.
Fausset, Hugh A. see Fausset, Hugh I'Anson.
Fausset, Hugh I'Anson, 1895-
xFausset, Hugh A.
  Flame & the Light: Meanings in Vedanta &
    Buddhism. Greenwood.
xFausset, Hugh L.
  Studies in Idealism. Kennikat.
Fausset, Hugh L. see Fausset, Hugh I'Anson.
Faust, A. B. see Faust, Albert Bernhardt.
Faust, Albert B. see Faust, Albert Bernhardt.
Faust, Albert Bernhardt, 1870-1951
xFaust, A. B.
  Guide to the Materials for American History in
    Swiss & Austrian Archives. Kraus Repr.
xFaust, Albert B.

German Element in the United States. Arno.
  Lists of Swiss Emigrants in the Eighteenth
    Century to the American Colonies. Genealog
    Pub.
Faust, Augustus F.
xFaust, Augustus F.
  Brazil: Education in an Expanding Economy.
    Greenwood.
Faust, David.
xFaust, David.
  Puppet Plays with a Point. Standard Pub.
Faust, Frederic L.
xFaust, Frederic L.
  Juvenile Justice Philosophy: Readings, Cases &
    Comments. West Pub.
Faust, Henri.
xFaust, Henri.
  Half-Light & Overtones. AMS Pr.
Faust, Irvin.
xFaust, Irvin.
  Newsreel. HarBraceJ.
Faust, Joan L. see Faust, Joan Lee.
Faust, Joan Lee.
xFaust, Joan L.
  The New York Times Book of Annuals &
    Perennials. Times Bks.
Faust, Karl I. see Faust, Karl Irving.
Faust, Karl Irving.
xFaust, Karl I.
  Campaigning in the Philippines. Arno.
Faust, Ron.
xFaust, Ron.
  The Long Count. Fawcett.
Faust, Verne.
xFaust, Verne.
  Establishing Guidance Programs in Elementary
    Schools. HM.
  I Know More About You Than You Ever
    Dreamed Possible. Thomas Paine Pr
Faux, I. D.
xFaux, I. D.
  Computational Geometry for Design &
    Manufacture. Halsted Pr.
Faux, Ian.
xFaux, Ian.
  Modern Lithography. Transatlantic.
Faux, Marian.
xFaux, Marian.
  The Complete Resume Guide. Monarch Pr.
Favaloro, Rene G., 1923-
xFavaloro, Rene G.
  Surgical Treatment of Coronary
    Arteriosclerosis. Krieger.
Favat, F. Andre.
xFavat, F. Andre.
  Child & Tale: The Origins of Interest. NCTE.
Favazza, Armando R.
xFavazza, Armando R.
  Anthropological & Cross-Cultural Themes in
    Mental Health: An Annotated Bibliography,
    1925-1974. U of Mo Pr.
Favell, Judith E.
xFavell, Judith E.
  The Power of Positive Reinforcement: A
    Handbook of Behavior Modification. C C
    Thomas.
Faverty, Frederic E. see Faverty, Frederic Everett.
Faverty, Frederic Everett, 1902-
xFaverty, Frederic E.
  Matthew Arnold the Ethnologist. AMS Pr.
Favreau, Donald F., 1919-
xFavreau, Donald F.
  Guidelines for Fire Service Education Programs
    in Community & Junior Colleges. Am Assn
    Comm Jr Coll.
Favretti, Rudy. see Favretti, Rudy J.
Favretti, Rudy J.
xFavretti, Rudy.

For Every House a Garden: A Guide for
    Reproducing Period Gardens. Globe Pequot.
xFavretti, Rudy J.
  Landscapes & Gardens for Historic Buildings:
    A Handbook for Reproducing & Creating
    Authentic Landscape Settings. AASLH.
Fawcett, Edgar, 1847-1904
xFawcett, Edgar.
  Hopeless Case. Arno.
Fawcett, James T., 1935-
xFawcett, James T.
  ed. Psychological Perspectives on Population.
    Basic.
  Psychology & Population: Behavioral Research
    Issues in Fertility & Family Planning.
    Population Coun.
Fawcett Publications Editors. see Fawcett Publications,
  Inc.
Fawcett Publications, Inc.
xFawcett Publications Editors.
  Manual of Home Repairs, Remodeling and
    Maintainance. G&D.
Fawdry, Marguerite.
xFawdry, Marguerite.
  Chinese Childhood. Barron.
Faxon (F.W.) Co. Inc., Boston.
xF. W. Faxon Co.
  Cumulated Dramatic Index, 1909-1949. G K
    Hall.
  Cumulated Magazine Subject Index,
    1907-1949. G K Hall.
Faxon, Nathaniel W. see Faxon, Nathaniel Wales.
Faxon, Nathaniel Wales.
xFaxon, Nathaniel W.
  Massachusetts General Hospital, 1935-1955.
    Harvard U Pr.
Fay, Bernard, 1893-
xFay, Bernard.
  Two Franklins, Fathers of American
    Democracy. Scholarly.
Fay, Bertrand.
xFay, Bertrand.
  Church at Eucharist. Glencoe.
Fay, Brian.
xFay, Brian.
  Social Theory & Political Practice. Allen
    Unwin.
Fay, Charles R. see Fay, Charles Ryle.
Fay, Charles Ryle, 1884-
xFay, Charles R.
  Imperial Economy & Its Place in the
    Formation of Economic Doctrine.
    Greenwood.
  World of Adam Smith. Kelley.
Fay, Don.
xFay, Don.
  Teaching the Bible with Games. Standard Pub.
Fay, Edward A. see Fay, Edward Allen.
Fay, Edward Allen, 1843-1923
xFay, Edward A.
  Concordance of the Divina Commedia. Haskell.
Fay, Eliot G. see Fay, Eliot Gilbert.
Fay, Eliot Gilbert, 1902-
xFay, Eliot G.
  Lorenzo in Search of the Sun: D. H. Lawrence
    in Italy, Mexico & the American Southwest.
    AMS Pr.
Fay, J. D. see Fay, John David.
Fay, Jay W. see Fay, Jay Wharton.
Fay, Jay Wharton.
xFay, Jay W.
  American Psychology Before William James.
    Octagon.
Fay, John David.
xFay, J. D.
  Theta Functions of Riemann Surfaces.
    Springer-Verlag.
Fay, Rimmon C.
xFay, Rimmon C.

Southern California's Deteriorating Marine Environment: An Evaluation of the Health of the Benthic Marine Biota of Ventura,Los Angeles & Orange Counties. Cal Inst Public.

Fay, Theodore S. see Fay, Theodore Sedgwick.

Fay, Theodore Sedgwick, 1807-1898
xFay, Theodore S.
Norman Leslie: A Tale of Present Times. AMS Pr.
Norman Leslie: A Tale of Present Times. Mss Info.

Faye, Eleanor E., 1923-
xFaye, Eleanor E.
Clinical Low Vision. Little.

Fayerweather, John.
xFayerweather, John.
Strategy & Negotiation for the International Corporation: Guidelines & Cases. Ballinger Pub.

Fazey, C.
xFazey, C.
The Aetiology of Psychoactive Substance Use: A Report & Critically Annotated Bibliography on Research into the Aetiology of Alcohol, Nicotine, Opiate & Other Psychoactive Substance Use. Unipub.

Feagin, Crawford.
xFeagin, Crawford.
Variation & Change in Alabama English: A Sociolinguistic Study of the White Community. Georgetown U Pr.

Feagin, Joe R.
xFeagin, Joe R.
Ghetto Social Structure: A Survey of Black Bostonians. R & E Res Assoc.
Racial & Ethnic Relations. P-H.
Subordinating the Poor: Welfare & American Beliefs. P-H.
ed. The Urban Scene: Myths & Realities. Random.

Feagles, Anita M. see Feagles, Anita Macrae.

Feagles, Anita Macrae.
xFeagles, Anita M.
Sophia Scarlotti & Ceecee. Atheneum.

Fear, David E.
xFear, David E.
Short English Handbook. Scott F.

Fear, Richard. see Fear, Richard A.

Fear, Richard A.
xFear, Richard.
The Evaluation Interview. McGraw.

Fearing, Jerome W.
xFearing, Jerry.
The Story of Minnesota. Minn Hist.

Fearing, Jerry. see Fearing, Jerome W.

Fearing, Kenneth, 1902-1961
xFearing, Kenneth.
Collected Poems of Kenneth Fearing. AMS Pr.

Fearnley. see Fearnley, Bernard.

Fearnley, Bernard.
xFearnley.
Child Photography. Focal Pr.

Fearnley, Charles, 1915-
xFearnley, Charles.
Where Have All the Textures Gone?. Intl Pubns Serv.

Fearnside, W. Ward.
xFearnside, W. Ward.
About Thinking. P-H.
Fallacy: The Counterfeit of Argument. P-H.

Fearon, P. see Fearon, Peter.

Fearon, Peter.
xFearon, P.
The Origins & Nature of the Great Slump, 1929-1932. Humanities.

Fears, J. Wayne, 1938-
xFears, J. Wayne.

Backcountry Cooking. East Woods.
Trout Fishing the Southern Appalachians. East Woods.

Fears, Jerry.
xFears, Jerry.
Boom, Cash, & Balderdash: A Different Look at Fairbanks During Pipeline Construction. That New Pub.

Feather, L. see Feather, Leonard G.
Feather, Leonard. see Feather, Leonard G.

Feather, Leonard G.
xFeather, L.
Inside Jazz. Da Capo.
xFeather, Leonard.
The Encyclopedia of Jazz in the Seventies. Horizon.
Encyclopedia of Jazz in the Sixties. Horizon.
From Satchmo to Miles. Stein & Day.

Feather, Norman T.
xFeather, Norman T.
Values in Education & Society. Free Pr.

Featherly, Henry I. see Featherly, Henry Ira.

Featherly, Henry Ira, 1893-
xFeatherly, Henry I.
Taxonomic Terminology of the Higher Plants. Hafner.

Featherstone, Donald. see Featherstone, Donald F.

Featherstone, Donald F.
xFeatherstone, Donald.
Wargaming Airborne Operations. Intl Pubns Serv.
Weapons & Equipment of the Victorian Soldier. Sterling.
xFeatherstone, Donald F.
Advanced War Games. Soccer.
Dancing Without Danger: The Prevention & Treatment of Ballet Dancing Injuries. A S Barnes.
Naval War Games: Fighting Sea Battles with Model Ships. Soccer.
Wargaming Airborne Operations. A S Barnes.

Featherstone, R. M. see Featherstone, Robert M.

Featherstone, Robert M.
xFeatherstone, R. M.
ed. A Guide to Molecular Pharmacology-Toxicology. Dekker.

Featherstonhaugh, George W. see Featherstonhaugh, George William.

Featherstonhaugh, George William, 1780-1866
xFeatherstonhaugh, George W.
Excursion Through the Slave States from Washington on the Potomac, to the Frontier of Mexico. Negro U Pr.

Feaver, William.
xFeaver, William.
The Art of John Martin. Oxford U Pr.

Febvre, Lucien. see Febvre, Lucien Paul Victor.

Febvre, Lucien Paul Victor.
xFebvre, Lucien.
The Coming of the Book: The Impact of Printing 1450-1800. Schocken.
Geographical Introduction to History. Greenwood.
Life in Renaissance France. Harvard U Pr.

Fecher, Charles A.
xFecher, Charles A.
Mencken: A Study of His Thought. Knopf.

Fecher, Constance, 1911-
xFecher, Constance.
The Leopard Dagger. FS&G.

Fechner, Gustav T. see Fechner, Gustav Theodor.

Fechner, Gustav Theodor, 1801-1887
xFechner, Gustav T.
The Little Book of Life After Death. Arno.

Fecht, Gerald. see Fecht, Gerald R.

Fecht, Gerald R.
xFecht, Gerald.

The Complete Parent's Guide to Soccer. Goodyear.

Fechter, Alan.
xFechter, Alan.
Forecasting the Impact of Technological Change on Manpower Utilization & Displacement: An Analytic Summary. Urban Inst.
Public Employment Programs. Am Enterprise.

Fechtner, Leopold, 1911-
xFechtner, Leopold.
Encyclopedia of Ad-Libs, Crazy Jokes, Insults & Wisecracks. P-H.

Fedder, Ruth, 1907-
xFedder, Ruth.
Girl Grows Up. McGraw.
Guidance in the Homeroom. Tchrs Coll.

Feddes, R. A.
xFeddes, R. A.
Simulation of Field Water Use & Crop Yield. Halsted Pr.

Feder, Bernard.
xFeder, Bernard.
The Complete Guide to Taking Tests. P-H.

Feder, J. see Feder, Jose.

Feder, Jane.
xFeder, Jane.
Beany. Pantheon.
The Night Light. Dial.

Feder, Jose.
xFeder, J.
Prayer for Each Day. Paulist Pr.

Feder, Judith. see Feder, Judith Morris.

Feder, Judith Morris.
xFeder, Judith.
Medicare: The Politics of Federal Hospital Insurance. Lexington Bks.

Feder, Lillian.
xFeder, Lillian.
Ancient Myth in Modern Poetry. Princeton U Pr.
Crowell's Handbook of Classical Literature. T Y Crowell.
Madness in Literature. Princeton U Pr.

Feder, Norman.
xFeder, Norman.
American Indian Art. Abrams.

Feder, Paula K. see Feder, Paula Kurzband.

Feder, Paula Kurzband.
xFeder, Paula K.
Where Does the Teacher Live?. Dutton.

Federal Architecture Project.
xStaff of the Federal Architecture Project.
The Federal Presence: Architecture, Politics, & Symbols in U. S. Government Building. MIT Pr.

Federal Aviation Administration. see United States. Federal Aviation Administration.

Federal Aviation Administration Staff. see United States. Federal Aviation Administration.

Federal Communications Commission. see United States. Federal Communications Commission.

Federal Council of the Churches of Christ in America.
xFederal Council of the Churches of Christ in America.
The Public Relations of the Motion Picture Industry: A Report by the Department of Research & Education. Ozer.

Federal Electric Corporation.
xFederal Electric Corporation.
How to Write Effective Reports. A-W.
Logarithms. Wiley.
A Programmed Introduction to PERT: Program Evaluation & Review Technique. Wiley.
Special Purpose Transistors: A Self-Instructional Programed Manual. P-H.

Federal Energy Administration. see United States. Federal Energy Administration.

Federal Judicial Center - Board Of Editors. see Federal Judicial Center. Board of Editors.

Federal Judicial Center. Board of Editors.
  xFederal Judicial Center - Board Of Editors.
    Manual of Complex Litigation. Boardman.
Federal Parliamentary Labor Party. *see* Federal
  Parliamentary Labour Party (Australia).
Federal Parliamentary Labour Party (Australia).
  xFederal Parliamentary Labor Party.
    Caucus Minutes Nineteen One to Nineteen
      Forty-Nine, Vol. 2: 1917-1931. Intl Schol Bk
      Serv.
    Caucus Minutes Nineteen One to Nineteen
      Forty-Nine, Vol. 3: 1932-1949. Intl Schol Bk
      Serv.
Federal Theatre. (New York).
  xUnited States Works Progress Administration.
    Federal Theatre Plays. Da Capo.
Federal Trade Commission. *see* United States. Federal
  Trade Commission.
Federal Trade Commission, United States. *see* United
  States. Federal Trade Commission.
Federal Writer's Project. *see* Federal Writers' Project.
Federal Writer's Project, Delaware. *see* Federal Writers'
  Project. Delaware.
Federal Writer's Project, Florida. *see* Federal Writers'
  Project. Florida.
Federal Writer's Project, Georgia. *see* Federal Writers'
  Project. Georgia.
Federal Writer's Project, Illinois. *see* Federal Writers'
  Project. Illinois.
Federal Writer's Project of the Works Project
  Administration. *see* Federal Writers' Project.
  Nebraska.
Federal Writers Project. *see* Federal Writers' Project.
Federal Writers Project, California. *see* Federal Writers'
  Project. California.
Federal Writers Project, Georgia. *see* Federal Writers'
  Project. Georgia.
Federal Writers Project, Illinois. *see* Federal Writers'
  Project. Illinois.
Federal Writers Project, Massachusetts. *see* Federal
  Writers' Project. Massachusetts.
Federal Writers Project, Mississippi. *see* Federal Writers'
  Project. Mississippi.
Federal Writers Project, New Jersey. *see* Federal Writers'
  Project. New Jersey.
Federal Writers Project, New York. *see* Federal Writers'
  Project. New York (State).
Federal Writers Project, Pennsylvania. *see* Federal
  Writers' Project. Pennsylvania.
Federal Writers' Project.
  xFederal Writer's Project.
    American Stuff. Da Capo.
  xFederal Writers Project.
    Idaho: A Guide in Word & Picture. Oxford U
      Pr.
    Illinois: A Descriptive & Historical Guide.
      Somerset Pub.
    New York: Guide to the Empire State. Oxford
      U Pr.
    North Dakota: Guide to the Northern Prairie
      State. Oxford U Pr.
    Oregon Trail: The Missouri River to the Pacific
      Ocean. Somerset Pub.
    Slave Narratives: A Folk History of Slavery in
      the U.S. from Interviews with Former Slaves.
      Somerset Pub.
    South Carolina: A Guide to the Palmetto State.
      Somerset Pub.
    These Are Our Lives. Norton.
  xFederal Writers' Project.

    Alabama: A Guide to the Deep South.
      Somerset Pub.
    Arizona: The Grand Canyon State. Somerset
      Pub.
    Delaware: A Guide to the First State. Somerset
      Pub.
    Hands That Built New Hampshire. AMS Pr.
    Here's New England: A Guide to
      Vacationland. Somerset Pub.
    Idaho: A Guide in Word & Picture. Somerset
      Pub.
    Indiana: A Guide to the Hoosier State.
      Somerset Pub.
    Iowa: A Guide to the Hawkeye State. Somerset
      Pub.
    Kansas: A Guide to the Sunflower State.
      Somerset Pub.
    Kentucky: A Guide to the Bluegrass State.
      Somerset Pub.
    Lay My Burden Down: A Folk History of
      Slavery. Somerset Pub.
    Los Angeles: A Guide to the City & Its
      Environs. Somerset Pub.
    Louisiana: A Guide to the State. Somerset Pub.
    Maine: A Guide Down East. Somerset Pub.
    Maryland: A Guide to the Old Line State.
      Somerset Pub.
    Massachusetts: A Guide to Its Places & People.
      Somerset Pub.
    Minnesota: A State Guide. Somerset Pub.
    Mississippi: A Guide to the Magnolia State.
      Somerset Pub.
    Montana: A State Guide Book. Somerset Pub.
    Nebraska: A Guide to the Cornhusker State.
      Somerset Pub.
    Nevada: A Guide to the Silver State. Somerset
      Pub.
    New Hampshire: A Guide to the Granite State.
      Somerset Pub.
    New Jersey: A Guide to Its Present & Past.
      Somerset Pub.
    New Mexico: A Guide to the Colorful State.
      Somerset Pub.
    New Orleans: A City Guide. Somerset Pub.
    New York: A City Guide. Somerset Pub.
    New York City Guide. Octagon.
    New York State: A Guide to the Empire State.
      Somerset Pub.
    North Carolina: A Guide to the Old North
      State. Somerset Pub.
    The Ohio Guide. Somerset Pub.
    Oklahoma: A Guide to the Sooner State.
      Somerset Pub.
    Oregon: End of the Trail. Somerset Pub.
    Rhode Island: A Guide to the Smallest State.
      Somerset Pub.
    San Francisco. Somerset Pub.
    San Francisco: A Guide to the Bay & Its
      Cities. Hastings.
    South Dakota: A Guide to the State. Somerset
      Pub.
    Tennessee: A Guide to the State. Somerset
      Pub.
    Texas: A Guide to the Lone Star State.
      Somerset Pub.
    Utah: A State Guide. Somerset Pub.
    Vermont: A Guide to the Green Mountain
      State. Somerset Pub.
    Washington: A Guide to the Evergreen State.
      Somerset Pub.
    Washington: City & Capital. Somerset Pub.
    Wisconsin: A State Guide. Somerset Pub.
    Wyoming: A Guide to Its History, Highways &
      People. Somerset Pub.
  xFederal Writers' Projects.
    U.S. One: Maine to Florida. Somerset Pub.
  xWPA Writers' Project Editors.
    These Are Our Lives. Arno.
Federal Writers' Project. California.
  xFederal Writers Project, California.

    San Diego: A California City. AMS Pr.
  xFederal Writers' Project, California.
    Berkeley, the First Seventy-Five Years. AMS
      Pr.
    Death Valley: A Guide. AMS Pr.
Federal Writers' Project. Delaware.
  xFederal Writer's Project, Delaware.
    New Castle on the Delaware. AMS Pr.
Federal Writers' Project. Dutchess Co., N.Y.
  xFederal Writers' Project, Dutchess Co., N. Y.
    Dutchess County. AMS Pr.
Federal Writers' Project. Florida.
  xFederal Writer's Project, Florida.
    Seeing St. Augustine. AMS Pr.
Federal Writers' Project. Georgia.
  xFederal Writer's Project, Georgia.
    Savannah. AMS Pr.
  xFederal Writers Project, Georgia.
    Augusta. AMS Pr.
Federal Writers' Project. Idaho.
  xFederal Writers' Project, Idaho.
    Idaho Lore. AMS Pr.
Federal Writers' Project. Illinois.
  xFederal Writer's Project, Illinois.
    Princeton Guide. AMS Pr.
  xFederal Writers Project, Illinois.
    Nauvoo Guide. AMS Pr.
  xFederal Writers' Project. Illinois.
    Cairo Guide. AMS Pr.
    Galena Guide. AMS Pr.
Federal Writers' Project, Indiana. *see* Writers' Program.
  Indiana.
Federal Writers' Project. Massachusetts.
  xFederal Writers Project, Massachusetts.
    The Berkshire Hills. AMS Pr.
  xFederal Writers' Project, Massachusetts.
    The Albanian Struggle in the Old World &
      New. AMS Pr.
    The Armenians in Massachusetts. AMS Pr.
    Boston Looks Seaward. AMS Pr.
Federal Writers' Project. Minnesota.
  xFederal Writers' Project, Minnesota.
    The Bohemian Flats. AMS Pr.
Federal Writers' Project. Mississippi.
  xFederal Writers Project, Mississippi.
    Mississippi Gulf Coast, Yesterday & Today,
      1699-1939. AMS Pr.
Federal Writers' Project. Montana.
  xFederal Writers' Project, Montana.
    Land of Nakoda. AMS Pr.
Federal Writers' Project. Nebraska.
  xFederal Writer's Project of the Works Project
    Administration.
    Nebraska: A Guide to the Cornhusker State. U
      of Nebr Pr.
Federal Writers' Project. New Jersey.
  xFederal Writers Project, New Jersey.
    Stories of New Jersey, Its Significant Places,
      People & Activities. AMS Pr.
  xFederal Writers' Project, New Jersey.
    The Swedes & Finns in New Jersey. AMS Pr.
Federal Writers' Project. New York (City).
  xW.P.A. Federal Writers Project.
    Italians of New York: A Survey. Arno.
Federal Writers' Project. New York (State).
  xFederal Writers Project, New York.
    Rochester & Monroe County. AMS Pr.
Federal Writers' Project. Pennsylvania.
  xFederal Writers Project, Pennsylvania.
    Erie: A Guide to the City & County. AMS Pr.
    Northhampton County Guide. AMS Pr.
Federal Writers' Project. South Carolina.
  xFederal Writers' Project, South Carolina.
    South Carolina Folktales. AMS Pr.
  xFederal Writers' Project, W. P. A.
    Palmetto Pioneers, Six Stories of Early South
      Carolinians. Reprint.
Federal Writers' Project. South Dakota.
  xFederal Writers' Project, South Dakota.

Legends of the Mighty Sioux. AMS Pr.
Federal Writers' Project, W. P. A. *see* Federal Writers'
    Project. South Carolina.
Federal Writers' Projects. *see* Federal Writers' Project.
Federated American Engineering Societies. *see* American
    Engineering Council.
Federer, H. *see* Federer, Herbert.
Federer, Herbert.
    xFederer, H.
    Geometric Measure Theory. Springer-Verlag.
Federer, Walter T. *see* Federer, Walter Theodore.
Federer, Walter Theodore, 1915-
    xFederer, Walter T.
    Statistics & Society: Data Collection &
        Interpretation. Dekker.
Federico, Ronald C.
    xFederico, Ronald C.
    The Social Welfare Institution: An
        Introduction. Heath.
    Sociology. A-W.
Federlin, K. *see* Federlin, Konrad.
Federlin, Konrad.
    xFederlin, K.
    Immunopathology of Insulin: Clinical &
        Experimental Studies. Springer-Verlag.
Federlin, Tom.
    xFederlin, Tom.
    A Comprehensive Bibliography on American
        Sign Language: A Resource Manual.
        Federlin.
Federman, Raymond.
    xFederman, Raymond.
    Journey to Chaos: Samuel Beckett's Early
        Fiction. U of Cal Pr.
    ed. Surfiction: Fiction Now & Tomorrow.
        Swallow.
Federn, Karl, 1868-1942
    xFedern, Karl.
    Dante & His Time. Haskell.
    Dante & His Time. Kennikat.
    Dante & His Time. R West.
    Materialist Conception of History: A Critical
        Analysis. Greenwood.
    Richelieu. Haskell.
Federoff, Alexander.
    xFederoff, Alexander.
    Side of the Angels. Astor-Honor.
Federspiel, Howard. *see* Federspiel, Howard M.
Federspiel, Howard M.
    xFederspiel, Howard.
    Persatuan Islam: Islamic Reform in Twentieth
        Century Indonesia. Cornell Mod Indo.
Fedida, Sam.
    xFedida, Sam.
    The Viewdata Revolution. Halsted Pr.
    The Viewdata Revolution. Wiley.
Fedigan, L. M. *see* Fedigan, Linda Maria.
Fedigan, Linda Maria.
    xFedigan, L. M.
    A Study of Roles in the Arashiyama West
        Troop of Japanese Monkeys (Macaca
        Fuscata). S Karger.
Fedler, Fred.
    xFedler, Fred.
    Reporting for the Print Media. HarBraceJ.
Fedor, Thomas S. *see* Fedor, Thomas Stanley.
Fedor, Thomas Stanley, 1943-
    xFedor, Thomas S.
    Patterns of Urban Growth in the Russian
        Empire During the Nineteenth Century. U
        Chicago Dept Geog.
Fedoroff, S.
    xFedoroff, S.
    ed. Cell, Tissue and Organ Cultures in
        Neurobiology. Acad Pr.
Fedorov, Fedor I. *see* Fedorov, Fedor Ivanovich.
Fedorov, Fedor Ivanovich.
    xFedorov, Fedor I.

Theory of Elastic Waves in Crystals. Plenum
    Pub.
Feduccia, Alan. *see* Feduccia, J. Alan.
Feduccia, J. Alan.
    xFeduccia, Alan.
    Structure & Evolution of Vertebrates: A
        Laboratory Text for Comparative Vertebrate
        Anatomy. Norton.
Feegel, John R.
    xFeegel, John R.
    Death Sails the Bay. Avon.
Feehan, John M., 1916-
    xFeehan, John M.
    The Wind That Round the Fastnet Sweeps.
        Irish Bk Ctr.
Feeley, Malcolm M.
    xFeeley, Malcolm M.
    The Process Is the Punishment: Handling Cases
        in a Lower Criminal Court. Russell Sage.
Feelings, Tom.
    xFeelings, Tom.
    Something on My Mind. Dial.
Feenberg, E. *see* Feenberg, Eugene.
Feenberg, Eugene.
    xFeenberg, E.
    Theory of Quantum Fluids. Acad Pr.
Feeney, Leonard, 1897-
    xFeeney, Leonard.
    London Is a Place. Ravengate Pr.
Feeney, Robert E. *see* Feeney, Robert Earl.
Feeney, Robert Earl.
    xFeeney, Robert E.
    ed. Food Proteins: Improvement Through
        Chemical & Enzymatic Modification. Am
        Chemical.
Feerick, John D.
    xFeerick, John D.
    From Failing Hands: The Story of Presidential
        Succession. Fordham.
Fegely, Thomas D.
    xFegely, Thomas D.
    Wonders of Geese & Swans. Dodd.
    Wonders of Wild Ducks. Dodd.
    The World of Freshwater Fish. Dodd.
    The World of the Woodlot. Dodd.
Fehl, Fred.
    xFehl, Fred.
    On Broadway. Da Capo.
Fehr, Lucy M.
    xFehr, Lucy M.
    Cross-Country Skiing: A Guide to America's
        Best Trails. Morrow.
Fehrenbach, C. G. *see* Fehrenbach, Charles Gervase.
Fehrenbach, Charles Gervase, 1909-
    xFehrenbach, C. G.
    Marriage in Wittenwiler's Ring. AMS Pr.
Fehrenbach, T. R.
    xFehrenbach, T. R.
    Lone Star: A History of Texas & the Texans.
        Macmillan.
    Lone Star: A History of Texas & the Texans.
        MacMillan.
Fehrenbacher, Don E. *see* Fehrenbacher, Don Edward.
Fehrenbacher, Don Edward, 1920-
    xFehrenbacher, Don E.
    Chicago Giant: A Biography of Long John
        Wentworth. Brown U Pr.
    The Leadership of Abraham Lincoln. Wiley.
    Prelude to Greatness: Lincoln in the 1850's.
        Stanford U Pr.
Fehrman, Carl. *see* Fehrman, Carl Abraham Daniel.
Fehrman, Carl Abraham Daniel, 1915-
    xFehrman, Carl.
    Poetic Creation: Inspiration or Craft. U of
        Minn Pr.
Fei, Hsiao-T'Ung.
    xFei, Hsiao-Tung.

Peasant Life in China: A Field Study of
    Country Life in the Yangtze Valley.
    Routledge & Kegan.
Fei, Hsiao-Tung. *see* Fei, Hsiao-T'Ung.
Fei, John. *see* Fei, John C. H.
Fei, John C. *see* Fei, John C. H.
Fei, John C. H.
    xFei, John.
    Growth with Equity: The Taiwan Case. Oxford
        U Pr.
    xFei, John C.
    jt. auth. Growth with Equity: The Taiwan Case.
        Oxford U Pr.
Feibleman, James K. *see* Feibleman, James Kern.
Feibleman, James Kern, 1904-
    xFeibleman, James K.
    Christianity, Communism & the Ideal Society:
        A Philosophical Approach to Modern
        Politics. AMS Pr.
    Great April. Horizon.
    In Praise of Comedy: A Study in Its Theory &
        Practice. Russell.
    Ontology. Greenwood.
    Reach of Politics: A New Look at
        Government. Horizon.
    Understanding Civilizations: The Shape of
        History. Horizon.
Feibleman, Peter S., 1930-
    xFeibleman, Peter S.
    Charlie Boy. Little.
    Cooking of Spain & Portugal. Time-Life.
    Cooking of Spain & Portugal. Silver.
Feidelson, Charles.
    xFeidelson, Charles N.
    Symbolism in American Literature. U of
        Chicago Pr.
Feidelson, Charles N. *see* Feidelson, Charles.
Feiden, Karen L.
    xFeiden, Karen L.
    Basket Weaving. Emerson.
Feider, Paul A., 1951-
    xFeider, Paul A.
    Arise & Walk: The Christian Search for
        Meaning in Suffering. Fides Claretian.
Feied, Frederick.
    xFeied, Frederick.
    No Pie in the Sky: The Hobo As American
        Cultural Hero in the Works of Jack London,
        John Dos Passos, & Jack Kerouac. Citadel
        Pr.
Feifel, Herman.
    xFeifel, Herman.
    ed. Meaning of Death. McGraw.
Feiffer, Jules.
    xFeiffer, Jules.
    Ackroyd. Avon.
    Ackroyd. S&S.
    The Great Comic Book Heroes. Dial.
    Tantrum. Knopf.
Feigenbaum, Harvey.
    xFeigenbaum, Harvey.
    Echocardiography. Lea & Febiger.
Feigl, Herbert.
    xFeigl, Herbert.
    ed. Concepts, Theories & the Mind-Body
        Problem. U of Minn Pr.
    ed. Foundations of Science & the Concepts of
        Psychology & Psychoanalysis. U of Minn Pr.
Feil, Hila.
    xFeil, Hila.
    The Ghost Garden. Atheneum.
Feild, Lance, 1927-
    xFeild, Lance.
    Exploring Nova Scotia. East Woods.
Feild, Reshad.
    xFeild, Reshad.
    The Invisible Way. Har-Row.
    The Last Barrier. Har-Row.
Feilen, John.
    xFeilen, John.

Dirt Track Speedsters. Crestwood Hse.
Motocross. Crestwood Hse..
Racing on the Water. Crestwood Hse.
Feiling, Keith G. see Feiling, Keith Grahame.
Feiling, Keith Grahame, Sir, 1884-
xFeiling, Keith G.
Life of Neville Chamberlain. Shoe String.
Fein, Albert.
xFein, Albert.
Frederick Law Olmsted & the American
Environmental Tradition. Braziller.
Fein, Bruce E.
xFein, Bruce E.
Significant Decisions of the Supreme Court,
1972-1973 Term. Am Enterprise.
Significant Decisions of the Supreme Court,
1971-72 Term. Am Enterprise.
Fein, Helen, 1934-
xFein, Helen.
Imperial Crime & Punishment: The Massacre
at Jallianwala Bagh & British Judgment,
1919-1920. U Pr of Hawaii.
Fein, Jay S., 1937-
xFein, Jay S.
Boundary Layers in Homogeneous &
Stratified-Rotating Fluids: Notes on Lectures
by Allan R. Robinson & Victor Barcilon.
Univ Microfilms.
Fein, Richard J., 1929-
xFein, Richard J.
Robert Lowell. Twayne.
Feinberg, Charles L. see Feinberg, Charles Lee.
Feinberg, Charles Lee.
xFeinberg, Charles L.
God Remembers: A Study of Zechariah.
Multnomah.
Feinberg, Gerald, 1933-
xFeinberg, Gerald.
Consequences of Growth: The Prospects for a
Limitless Future. Continuum.
Feinberg, H. see Feinberg, Hilda.
Feinberg, Hilda.
xFeinberg, H.
Cosmetics-Perfumery Thesaurus. Macmillan
Info.
Feinberg, Joel.
xFeinberg, Joel.
Liberty: Selected Readings. Dickenson.
Moral Philosophy: Classic Texts &
Contemporary Problems. Dickenson.
Feinberg, Leonard, 1914-
xFeinberg, Leonard.
Introduction to Satire. Iowa St U Pr.
The Secret of Humor. Humanities.
Feinberg, Mortimer. see Feinberg, Mortimer R.
Feinberg, Mortimer R.
xFeinberg, Mortimer.
Leavetaking: When & How to Say Goodbye.
S&S.
xFeinberg, Mortimer R.
Effective Psychology for Managers. P-H.
Feinberg, R.
xFeinberg, R.
ed. Modern Power Transformer Practice.
Halsted Pr.
Feinberg, Walter.
xFeinberg, Walter.
ed. Work, Technology & Education: Dissenting
Essays in the Intellectual Foundations of
American Education. U of Ill Pr.
Feineman, N. see Feineman, Neil.
Feineman, Neil.
xFeineman, N.
Persistence of Vision: The Films of Robert
Altman. Arno.
Feinendegen, L. E. see Feinendegen, Ludwig E.
Feinendegen, Ludwig E.
xFeinendegen, L. E.

Tritium Labeled Molecules in Biology &
Medicine. Acad Pr.
Feiner, Johannes.
xFeiner, Johannes.
ed. The Common Catechism: A Book of
Christian Faith. Seabury.
Feinerman, R. P. see Feinerman, Robert P.
Feinerman, Robert P.
xFeinerman, R. P.
Polynomial Approximation. Krieger.
Feingold, Barbara A.
xFeingold, Barbara A.
Developmental Disabilities of Early Childhood.
C C Thomas.
Feingold, Ben. see Feingold, Ben F.
Feingold, Ben F.
xFeingold, Ben.
The Feingold Cookbook for Hyperactive
Children & Others with Problems Associated
with Food Additives & Salicylates. Random.
xFeingold, Ben F.
Introduction to Clinical Allergy. C C Thomas.
Feingold, Carl.
xFeingold, Carl.
Fundamentals of Structured COBOL
Programming. Wm C Brown.
Introduction to Assembler Language
Programming. Wm C Brown.
Introduction to Data Processing. Wm C Brown.
Feingold, Henry L., 1931-
xFeingold, Henry L.
The Politics of Rescue: The Roosevelt
Administration & the Holocaust, 1938-1945.
Rutgers U Pr.
Feingold, S. Norman, 1914-
xFeingold, S. Norman.
A Counselor's Handbook: Readings in
Counseling, Student Aid & Rehabilitation.
Carroll Pr.
Feininger, Andreas, 1906-
xFeininger, Andreas.
The Anatomy of Nature. Dover.
Andreas Feininger: Experimental Work.
Amphoto.
Color Photo Book. P-H.
Complete Photographer. P-H.
The Creative Photographer. P-H.
Darkroom Techniques. P-H.
Perfect Photograph. Amphoto.
Principles of Composition in Photography.
Amphoto.
Successful Photography. P-H.
Feinman, Clarice.
xFeinman, Clarice.
Women in the Criminal Justice System.
Praeger.
Feinman, Jeffrey.
xFeinman, Jeffrey.
Collecting Tomorrow's Collectibles. Macmillan.
Freebies for Kids. Wanderer Bks.
How to Make Money in Your Kitchen.
Morrow.
How You Can Profit from Today's Gold Rush.
Doubleday.
The Purple Pages. Dutton.
Feinschreiber, Robert.
xFeinschreiber, Robert.
Domestic International Sales Corporations.
PLI.
Tax Incentives for U. S. Exports. Oceana.
Feinsilver, A. see Feinsilver, Alexander.
Feinsilver, Alexander, 1910-
xFeinsilver, A.
Aspects of Jewish Belief. Ktav.
Feinsilver, P. J. see Feinsilver, Philip J.
Feinsilver, Philip J., 1948-
xFeinsilver, P. J.
Special Functions, Probability Semigroups, &
Hamiltonian Flows. Springer-Verlag.
Feinstein, Alan R. see Feinstein, Alvan R.

Feinstein, Alan S.
xFeinstein, Alan S.
Folk Tales from Siam. A S Barnes.
Feinstein, Alvan R.
xFeinstein, Alan R.
Clinical Judgment. Krieger.
xFeinstein, Alvan R.
Clinical Biostatistics. Mosby.
Feinstein, C. H.
xFeinstein, C. H.
Domestic Capital Formation in the United
Kingdom. Cambridge U Pr.
National Income, Expenditure & Output of the
United Kingdom, 1855-1965. Cambridge U
Pr.
Statistical Tables of National Income
Expenditure & Output of the UK 1855-1965.
Cambridge U Pr.
Feinstein, Elaine.
xFeinstein, Elaine.
The Shadow Master. S&S.
Feinstein, George W., 1913-
xFeinstein, George W.
Programed Spelling Demons. P-H.
Feinstein, Karen W. see Feinstein, Karen Wolk.
Feinstein, Karen Wolk.
xFeinstein, Karen W.
ed. Working Women & Families. Sage.
Feirer. see Feirer, John Louis.
Feirer, John. see Feirer, John Louis.
Feirer, John L. see Feirer, John Louis.
Feirer, John Louis.
xFeirer.
Advanced Woodwork & Furniture Making.
Bennett Co.
Basic Drafting. Bennett Co.
Basic Metalwork. Bennett Co.
Basic Woodworking. Bennett Co.
SI Metric Handbook. Bennett Co.
xFeirer, John.
Advanced Woodwork & Furniture-Making.
Scribner.
Carpentry Building & Construction. Bennett
Co.
SI Metric Handbook. Scribner.
xFeirer, John L.
Drawing & Planning for the Industrial Arts.
Bennett Co.
General Metals. McGraw.
Industrial Arts Woodworking. Bennett Co.
Wood: Materials & Processes. Bennett Co.
Woodworking for Industry: Technology &
Practice. Scribner.
Feis, Herbert, 1893-
xFeis, Herbert.
Changing Pattern of International Economic
Affairs. Kennikat.
The China Tangle: The American Effort in
China from Pearl Harbor to the Marshall
Mission. Princeton U Pr.
Feiss, George J., 1950-
xFeiss, George J.
Mind Therapies, Body Therapies. Celestial
Arts.
Feist, Uwe.
xFeist, Uwe.
The Fighting One O Nine: A Pictorial History
of the Messerschmitt BF 109 in Action.
Doubleday.
Feit, Edward.
xFeit, Edward.

African Opposition in South Africa: The
Failure of Passive Resistance. Hoover Inst Pr.
Governments & Leaders: An Approach to
Comparative Politics. HM.
Workers Without Weapons: The South African
Congress of Trade Unions & the
Organization of the African Workers. Shoe
String.

Feit, Marvin D.
xFeit, Marvin D.
Management & Administration of Drug &
Alcohol Programs. C C Thomas.

Feit, Walter, 1930-
xFeit, Walter.
Characters of Finite Groups.
Benjamin-Cummings.

Feith, Herbert.
xFeith, Herbert.
ed. Indonesian Political Thinking, 1945-1965.
Cornell U Pr.

Feiveson, Harold A.
xFeiveson, Harold A.
Boundaries of Analysis: An Inquiry into the
Tocks Island Dam Controversy. Ballinger
Pub.

Feiwel, George R.
xFeiwel, George R.
The Soviet Quest for Economic Efficiency:
Issues, Controversies, & Reforms. Irvington.

Fejes, Claire, 1920-
xFejes, Claire.
People of the Noatak. Knopf.

Fejto, Francois, 1909-
xFejto, Francois.
French Communist Party & the Crisis of
International Communism. MIT Pr.

Felber, John E. *see* Felber, John Edward.

Felber, John Edward.
xFelber, John E.
American's Tourist Manual for the U.S.S.R.
Intl Intertrade.

Feld, Barry.
xFeld, Barry.
Standards Relating to Rights of Minors.
Ballinger Pub.

Feld, Maury D.
xFeld, Maury D.
The Structure of Violence: Armed Forces As
Social Systems. Sage.

Feld, Raoul.
xFeld, Raoul.
Organic Chemistry of Titanium. Plenum Pub.

Feld, Werner. *see* Feld, Werner J.

Feld, Werner J.
xFeld, Werner.
ed. Comparative Regional Systems: West &
East Europe, North America, the Middle
East & Developing Countries. Pergamon.
xFeld, Werner J.
Domestic Political Realities of European
Unification: A Study of Mass Public & Elites
in the European Community Countries.
Westview.
ed. The Foreign Policies of West European
Socialist Parties. Praeger.

Feldacker, Bruce S.
xFeldacker, Bruce S.
Labor Guide to Labor Law. Reston.

Feldbausch, Friedrich K.
xFeldbausch, Friedrich K.
Finance Dictionary, German-English,
English-German. Leviathan Hse.

Feldblum, E. Y. *see* Feldblum, Esther Yolles.

Feldblum, Esther Yolles, 1933-1974
xFeldblum, E. Y.
The American Catholic Press & the Jewish
State: 1917-1959. Ktav.

Feldbrugge, F. J. *see* Feldbrugge, Ferdinand Joseph
Maria.

Feldbrugge, Ferdinand Joseph Maria.
xFeldbrugge, F. J.
Encyclopedia of Soviet Law. Oceana.

Feldenkrais, Moshe, 1904-
xFeldenkrais, Moshe.
Awareness Through Movement: Health
Exercises for Personal Growth. Har-Row.
The Case of Nora: Body Awareness As Healing
Therapy. Har-Row.

Felder, Dell.
xFelder, Dell.
The Challenge of American Democracy 1974.
Allyn.

Felderman, Eric.
xFelderman, Eric.
Animal Book. Holmgangers.

Feldhusen, John. *see* Feldhusen, John Frederick.
Feldhusen, John F. *see* Feldhusen, John Frederick.

Feldhusen, John Frederick.
xFeldhusen, John.
Creative Thinking & Problem Solving in Gifted
Education. Kendall-Hunt.
xFeldhusen, John F.
The Three-Stage Model of Course Design.
Educ Tech Pubns.

Feldman, Abraham J. *see* Feldman, Abraham Jehiel.

Feldman, Abraham Jehiel, 1893-
xFeldman, Abraham J.
The American Jew: A Study of Backgrounds.
Greenwood.
A Companion to the Bible. Bloch.

Feldman, Alan, 1945-
xFeldman, Alan.
Frank O'Hara. Twayne.

Feldman, Allan, 1943-
xFeldman, Allan M.
Welfare Economics & Social Choice Theory.
Kluwer Boston.

Feldman, Allan M. *see* Feldman, Allan.

Feldman, Annette.
xFeldman, Annette.
Annette Feldman's Needlework for the Home.
P-H.
The Hat Book. Van Nos Reinhold.

Feldman, Anthony.
xFeldman, Anthony.
Scientists & Inventors. Facts on File.
Space. Facts on File.
Technology at Work. Facts on File.

Feldman, Asher, 1873-1950
xFeldman, Asher.
The Parables & Similes of the Rabbis,
Agricultural & Pastoral. Folcroft.

Feldman, Bernard.
xFeldman, Bernard.
Analytic Properties of Trigonometric
Functions. Wadsworth Pub.

Feldman, Carol F. *see* Feldman, Carol Fleisher.

Feldman, Carol Fleisher.
xFeldman, Carol F.
The Development of Adaptive Intelligence: A
Cross-Cultural Study. Jossey-Bass.

Feldman, David H. *see* Feldman, David Henry.

Feldman, David Henry.
xFeldman, David H.
Beyond Universals in Cognitive Development.
Ablex Pub.

Feldman, David M. *see* Feldman, David Michael.

Feldman, David Michael, 1929-
xFeldman, David M.
Birth Control in Jewish Law: Marital Relations,
Contraception, & Abortion As Set Forth in
the Classic Texts of Jewish Law. Greenwood.
Marital Relations, Birth Control, & Abortion in
Jewish Law. Schocken.

Feldman, Edmund B. *see* Feldman, Edmund Burke.

Feldman, Edmund Burke.
xFeldman, Edmund B.

Varieties of Visual Experience. Abrams.
Varieties of Visual Experience: Art As Image &
Idea. P-H.

Feldman, Edwin B.
xFeldman, Edwin B.
Building Design for Maintainability. McGraw.
Housekeeping Handbook for Institutions,
Business & Industry. Fell.
How to Use Your Time to Get Things Done.
Fell.

Feldman, Elane.
xFeldman, Elane.
Going Bananas: The Complete Banana
Cookbook. Hippocrene Bks.

Feldman, Ethel K.
xFeldman, Ethel K.
Cook Your Way Thin. Arco.

Feldman, Frances L. *see* Feldman, Frances Lomas.

Feldman, Frances Lomas.
xFeldman, Frances L.
The Family in Today's Money World. Family
Serv.

Feldman, Franklin.
xFeldman, Franklin.
Art Works: Law, Policy, Practice. PLI.

Feldman, Harold.
xFeldman, Harold.
Mathematics of Business Affairs. PAR Inc.

Feldman, Herbert.
xFeldman, Herbert.
The End & the Beginning: Pakistan 1969-197.
Oxford U Pr.

Feldman, Irving, 1928-
xFeldman, Irving.
New & Selected Poems. Penguin.
New & Selected Poems. Viking Pr.

Feldman, Jacob J.
xFeldman, Jacob J.
Dissemination of Health Information: A Case
Study in Adult Learning. NORC.

Feldman, Joseph.
xFeldman, Joseph.
Dynamics of the Film. Arno.

Feldman, Kenneth A., 1937-
xFeldman, Kenneth A.
ed. College & Student: Selected Readings in
the Social Psychology of Higher Education.
Pergamon.
The Impact of College on Students.
Jossey-Bass.

Feldman, Laurence P., 1932-
xFeldman, Laurence P.
Consumer Protection: Problems & Prospects.
West Pub.

Feldman, M. Philip. *see* Feldman, Maurice Philip.

Feldman, Marvin J.
xFeldman, Marvin J.
Fears Related to Death & Suicide. Mss Info.

Feldman, Maurice Philip.
xFeldman, M. Philip.
Criminal Behaviour: A Psychological Analysis.
Wiley.

Feldman, Ronald A.
xFeldman, Ronald A.
Contemporary Approaches to Group
Treatment: Traditional,
Behavior-Modification, & Group-Centered.
Jossey-Bass.

Feldman, Saul.
xFeldman, Saul.
The Administration of Mental Health Services.
C C Thomas.

Feldman, Seth. *see* Feldman, Seth R.

Feldman, Seth R.
xFeldman, Seth.
ed. The Canadian Film Reader. NY Zoetrope.

Feldman, Silvia.
xFeldman, Silvia.

Choices in Childbirth. Bantam.
Choices in Childbirth. G&D.
Feldman, Stanley. *see* Feldman, Stanley A.
Feldman, Stanley A.
xFeldman, Stanley.
Tracheostomy & Artificial Ventilation in
Treatment of Respiratory Failure. Williams &
Wilkins.
xFeldman, Stanley A.
Muscle Relaxants. Saunders.
Feldman, W. M. *see* Feldman, William Moses.
Feldman, William Moses, 1879-1939
xFeldman, W. M.
Rabbinical Mathematics & Astronomy.
Hermon.
Feldstein, Paul J.
xFeldstein, Paul J.
Health Care Economics. Wiley.
Feldstein, Stanley, 1937-
xFeldstein, Stanley.
Land That I Show You: Three Centuries of
Jewish Life in America. Doubleday.
Once a Slave: The Slaves' View of Slavery.
Morrow.
Feldt, Robert H.
xFeldt, Robert H.
ed. Atrioventricular Canal Defects. Saunders.
Felice, Cynthia.
xFelice, Cynthia.
Godsfire. PB.
Felice, Raymond.
xFelice, Raymond.
Successful Landscaping. Structures Pub.
Felix, H. *see* Felix, Heidi.
Felix, Heidi.
xFelix, H.
Dynamic Morphology of Leukemia Cells: A
Comparative Study by Scanning Electron
Microscopy & Microcinematography.
Springer-Verlag
Felix, J. L. *see* Felix, Joseph L.
Felix, Joseph L., 1931-
xFelix, J. L.
Parenting with Style. Our Sunday Visitor.
xFelix, Joseph L.
Lord Have Murphy!. Nelson.
Proud Parenthood. Abingdon.
Felix, Lucienne.
xFelix, Lucienne.
Modern Mathematics & the Teacher.
Cambridge U Pr.
Felix, Morton.
xFelix, Morton.
Octave Higher Than Grief. Libra.
Felkenes, George T.
xFelkenes, George T.
ed. Effective Police Supervision: A Behavioral
Approach. Justice Sys.
Law Enforcement: A Selected Bibliography.
Scarecrow.
Felker, Donald W.
xFelker, Donald W.
Building Positive Self-Concepts. Burgess.
Felker, Evelyn H.
xFelker, Evelyn H.
Foster Parenting Young Children: Guidelines
from a Foster Parent. Child Welfare.
Felkin, William.
xFelkin, William.
History of the Machine-Wrought Hosiery &
Lace Manufactures. B Franklin.
History of the Machine-Wrought Hosiery &
Lace Manufactures. Kelley.
Felknor, Bruce L.
xFelknor, Bruce L.
Dirty Politics. Greenwood.
Fell, Barry.
xFell, Barry.

Introduction to Marine Biology. Har-Row.
Saga America. Times Bks.
Fell, Derek.
xFell, Derek.
How I Planned to Plant the White House
Vegetable Garden. Exposition.
Fell, Doris E. *see* Fell, Doris Elaine.
Fell, Doris Elaine.
xFell, Doris E.
Lady of the Tboli. Christian Herald.
Fell, James E., 1944-
xFell, James E.
Ores to Metals: The Rocky Mountain Smelting
Industry. U of Nebr Pr.
Fell, John, 1721-1798
xFell, John.
Delegate from New Jersey: The Journal of
John Fell. Kennikat.
Fell, John L., 1927-
xFell, John L.
Film: An Introduction. Praeger.
Film & the Narrative Tradition. U of Okla Pr.
A History of Films. HR&W.
Fell, Marie L. *see* Fell, Marie Leonore.
Fell, Marie Leonore, Sister, 1907-
xFell, Marie L.
The Foundations of Nativism in American
Textbooks, 1783-1860. Ozer.
Feller, William, 1906-1970
xFeller, William.
An Introduction to Probability Theory & Its
Applications. Wiley.
Fellini, Federico.
xFellini, Frederico.
Fellini on Fellini. Delacorte.
Fellini on Fellini. Dell.
Fellini, Frederico. *see* Fellini, Federico.
Fellman, David, 1908-
xFellman, David.
Constitutional Right of Association. U of
Chicago Pr.
The Defendant's Rights Today. U of Wis Pr.
Defendant's Rights Under English Law. U of
Wis Pr.
The Limits of Freedom. Greenwood.
Religion in American Public Law. Holmes &
Meier.
Fellman, Michael.
xFellman, Michael.
The Unbounded Frame: Freedom &
Community in Nineteenth Century American
Utopianism. Greenwood.
Fellner, Rudolph.
xFellner, Rudolph.
Opera Themes & Plots. S&S.
Fellner, William. *see* Fellner, William John.
Fellner, William J. *see* Fellner, William John.
Fellner, William John, 1905-
xFellner, William.
ed. Contemporary Economic Problems: 1976.
Am Enterprise.
Problems to Keep in Mind When It Comes to
Tax Reform. Am Enterprise.
xFellner, William J.
ed. Contemporary Economic Problems: 1978.
Am Enterprise.
Fellowes, Edmund H. *see* Fellowes, Edmund Horace.
Fellowes, Edmund Horace, 1870-1951
xFellowes, Edmund H.
English Madrigal Composers. Oxford U Pr.
Orlando Gibbons & His Family: The Last of
the Tudor School of Musicians. Shoe String.
Fellows, B. J. *see* Fellows, Brian J.
Fellows, Brian J.
xFellows, B. J.
The Discrimination Process & Development.
Pergamon.
Fellows, Catherine.
xFellows, Catherine.

Leonora. Fawcett.
Fellows, Huge Price.
xFellows, Hugh P.
Art & Skill of Talking with People: A New
Guide to Personal & Business Success. P-H.
Fellows, Hugh P. *see* Fellows, Huge Price.
Fellows, Jay, 1940-
xFellows, Jay.
The Failing Distance: The Autobiographical
Impulse in John Ruskin. Johns Hopkins.
Fellows, Lawrence.
xFellows, Lawrence.
East Africa. Macmillan.
A Gentle War: The Story of the Salvation
Army. Macmillan.
Fellows of the Royal Society of Literature of the U.K.
see Royal Society of Literature of the United
Kingdom, London.
Fellows, Otis E. *see* Fellows, Otis Edward.
Fellows, Otis Edward.
xFellows, Otis E.
Buffon. Twayne.
Fellows, Reginald B. *see* Fellows, Reginald Bruce.
Fellows, Reginald Bruce, 1871-
xFellows, Reginald B.
London to Cambridge by Train, 1845-1938.
Oleander Pr.
Fellows, Ward J.
xFellows, Ward J.
Religions East & West. HR&W.
Felner, Joel M.
xFelner, Joel M.
Echocardiography: A Teaching Atlas. Grune.
Fels, George.
xFels, George.
Mastering Pool. Contemp Bks.
Pool Simplified--Somewhat. Contemp Bks.
Fels, Rendigs, 1917-
xFels, Rendigs.
American Business Cycles, 1865-1897.
Greenwood.
Felsen, Henry G. *see* Felsen, Henry Gregor.
Felsen, Henry Gregor, 1916-
xFelsen, Henry G.
Boy Gets Car. Random.
Hot Rod. Dutton.
Hot Rod. AMSCO Sch.
Living with Your First Motorcycle. Berkley
Pub.
Street Rod. Random.
Felsen, Jerry.
xFelsen, Jerry.
Decision Making Under Uncertainty: An
Artificial Intelligence Approach. CDS Pub.
How to Double Your Money in Less Than One
Year by Trading in Listed Options. CDS Pub.
Low-Cost, Personal-Computer-Based
Investment Decision Systems. CDS Pub.
Felsen, L. B. *see* Felsen, Leopold B.
Felsen, Leopold B.
xFelsen, L. B.
Radiation & Scattering of Waves. P-H.
Felsenfeld, Carl.
xFelsenfeld, Carl.
Simplified Consumer Credit Forms. Warren.
Felsenfeld, Oscar.
xFelsenfeld, Oscar.
The Cholera Problem. Green.
Felsenthal, Norman.
xFelsenthal, Norman.
Orientations to Mass Communication. SRA.
Felshin, Jan. *see* Felshin, Janet.
Felshin, Janet.
xFelshin, Jan.
More Than Movement: An Introduction to
Physical Education. Lea & Febiger.
Felson, Benjamin.
xFelson, Benjamin.

Chest Roentgenology. Saunders.
Felt, Jeremy P.
  xFelt, Jeremy P.
    Hostages of Fortune: Child Labor Reform in
    New York State. Syracuse U Pr.
Felt, Joseph B. see Felt, Joseph Barlow.
Felt, Joseph Barlow, 1789-1869
  xFelt, Joseph B.
    Customs of New England. B Franklin.
Feltham, Ralph. see Feltham, Ralph George.
Feltham, Ralph George.
  xFeltham, Ralph.
    Diplomatic Handbook. Longman.
Felton, Bruce.
  xFelton, Bruce.
    Felton & Fowler's Best, Worst & Most
    Unusual. Fawcett.
    Felton & Fowler's Best, Worst & Most
    Unusual. T Y Crowell.
    ed. Felton & Fowler's Famous Americans You
    Never Knew Existed. Stein & Day.
Felton, Ernest L.
  xFelton, Ernest L.
    California's Many Climates. Pacific Bks.
Felton, Harold W.
  xFelton, Harold W.
    Deborah Sampson, Soldier of the Revolution.
    Dodd.
    Edward Rose, Negro Trail Blazer. Dodd.
    Gib Morgan, Oil Driller. Dodd.
    Mumbet: The Story of Elizabeth Freeman.
    Dodd.
Felton, John R. see Felton, John Richard.
Felton, John Richard, 1917-
  xFelton, John R.
    The Economics of Freight Car Supply. U of
    Nebr Pr.
Feman, Stephen S.
  xFeman, Stephen S.
    Handbook of Pediatric Ophthalmology. Grune.
Femina, Jerry Della. see Della Femina, Jerry.
Fenbury, D. M.
  xFenbury, D. M.
    Practice Without Policy: Genesis of Local
    Government in Papua New Guinea. Bks
    Australia.
Fenby, Eric, 1906-
  xFenby, Eric.
    Delius As I Knew Him. Greenwood.
Fencl, Shirley. see Fencl, Shirley Crum.
Fencl, Shirley Crum.
  xFencl, Shirley.
    The Two R's: Paragraph to Essay. Wiley.
Fender, Kay.
  xFender, Kay.
    Odette: A Bird in Paris. P-H.
Fendler, Janos H.
  xFendler, Janos H.
    Catalysis in Micellar & Macromolecular
    Systems. Acad Pr.
Fenelon. see Fenelon, Francois De Salignac De la
Mothe-.
Fenelon, Fania.
  xFenelon, Fania.
    Playing for Time. Atheneum.
    Playing for Time. Berkley Pub.
**Fenelon, Francois De Salignac De la Mothe-, Abp,
1651-1715**
  xFenelon.
    The Adventures of Telemachus. Garland Pub.
Fenger, Diane.
  xFenger, Diane.
    The Standard Book of Dog Grooming.
    Denlingers.
Fenger, Frederic A. see Fenger, Frederic Abildgaard.
Fenger, Frederic Abildgaard, 1882-
  xFenger, Frederic A.
    Cruise of Diablesse. Wellington.
Fenhagen, James. see Fenhagen, James C.

Fenhagen, James C.
  xFenhagen, James.
    Mutual Ministry: New Vitality for the Local
    Church. Seabury.
  xFenhagen, James C.
    More Than Wanderers: Spiritual Disciplines for
    Christian Ministry. Seabury.
Fenichel, Allen H., 1936-
  xFenichel, Allen H.
    Quantitative Analysis of the Growth &
    Diffusion of Steam Power in Manufacturing
    in the U. S., 1919-1938. Arno.
Fenichel, Gerald M.
  xFenichel, Gerald M.
    Neonatal Neurology. Churchill.
Fenlon, Arlene.
  xFenlon, Arlene.
    Getting Ready for Childbirth: A Guide for
    Expectant Parents. P-H.
Fenn, Eleanor (Frere), Lady, 1743-1813
  xFenn, Ellenor F.
    Fables in Monosyllables. Johnson Repr.
Fenn, Ellenor F. see Fenn, Eleanor (Frere).
Fenn, Richard K.
  xFenn, Richard K.
    Toward a Theory of Secularization. Soc Sci
    Stud Rel.
Fenn, William W. see Fenn, William Wallace.
Fenn, William Wallace, 1862-1932
  xFenn, William W.
    Theism: The Implication of Experience.
    Bauhan.
Fenna, D. see Fenna, Donald.
Fenna, Donald.
  xFenna, D.
    The Stockholm County Medical Information
    System. Springer-Verlag.
Fennell, F. A. see Fennell, Tom A.
Fennell, James, 1766-1816
  xFennell, James.
    Apology for the Life of James Fennell. Arno.
Fennell, John. see Fennell, John Lister Illingworth.
Fennell, John Lister Illingworth.
  xFennell, John.
    ed. Historical Russian Reader: A Selection of
    Texts from the Eleventh to the Sixteenth
    Centuries. Oxford U Pr.
    ed. Nineteenth-Century Russian Literature:
    Studies of Ten Russian Writers. U of Cal Pr.
Fennell, Rosemary.
  xFennell, Rosemary.
    The Common Agricultural Policy of the
    European Community. Allanheld.
Fennell, Tom A.
  xFennell, F. A.
    Orchids for Home & Garden. HR&W.
Fennema, O. see Fennema, Owen R.
Fennema, Owen R.
  xFennema, O.
    ed. Low Temperature Preservation of Foods &
    Living Matter. Dekker.
Fenner, Carol.
  xFenner, Carol.
    Gorilla Gorilla. Random.
Fenner, Frank J. see Fenner, Frank John.
Fenner, Frank John.
  xFenner, Frank J.
    Medical Virology. Acad Pr.
Fenner, Phyllis. see Fenner, Phyllis Reid.
Fenner, Phyllis R. see Fenner, Phyllis Reid.
Fenner, Phyllis Reid, 1899-
  xFenner, Phyllis.
    Strange but True: Stories of Many Things. John
    Day.
    Compiled by Where Speed Is King: Stories of
    Racing Adventure. Morrow.
  xFenner, Phyllis R.

    ed. Crack of the Bat: Stories of Baseball.
    Knopf.
    Compiled by A Dog's Life: Stories of
    Champions, Hunters, & Faithful Friends.
    Morrow.
    Compiled by The Endless Dark: Stories of
    Underground Adventure. Morrow.
    ed. Feasts & Frolics: Special Stories for Special
    Days. Knopf.
    Compiled by Gentle Like a Cyclone: Stories of
    Horses & Their Riders. Morrow.
    ed. Keeping Christmas: Stories of the Joyous
    Season. Morrow.
Fenner, Sal.
  xFenner, Sal.
    Sea Machines. Raintree Child.
Fennimore, Keith J.
  xFennimore, Keith J.
    Booth Tarkington. Twayne.
Fenno, Richard F.
  xFenno, Richard F.
    Congressmen in Committees. Little.
    Home Style: House Members in Their
    Districts. Little.
Fenollosa, Ernest. see Fenollosa, Ernest Francisco.
Fenollosa, Ernest F. see Fenollosa, Ernest Francisco.
Fenollosa, Ernest Francisco.
  xFenollosa, Ernest.
    Notes by Classic Noh Theatre of Japan. New
    Directions.
  xFenollosa, Ernest F.
    The Classic Noh Theatre of Japan. Greenwood.
    East & West. Irvington.
Fenstad, J. E. see Fenstad, Jens Erik.
Fenstad, Jens Erik.
  xFenstad, J. E.
    General Recursion Theory: An Axiomatic
    Approach. Springer-Verlag.
Fenten, Barbara.
  xFenten, Barbara.
    Careers in the Sports Industry. Watts.
    Natural Foods. Watts.
Fenten, D. X.
  xFenten, D. X.
    Indoor Gardening. Watts.
    Ms. - Attorney. Westminster.
    Ms.-M. D.. Westminster.
    TV & Radio Careers. Watts.
Fenton, Carroll L. see Fenton, Carroll Lane.
Fenton, Carroll Lane.
  xFenton, Carroll L.
    Plants We Live On: The Story of Grains &
    Vegetables. John Day.
    Story of the Great Geologists. Arno.
Fenton, Charles A.
  xFenton, Charles A.
    Stephen Vincent Benet: The Life & Times of
    an American Man of Letters, 1898-1943.
    Greenwood.
Fenton, Judith A. see Fenton, Judith Alsofrom.
Fenton, Judith Alsofrom.
  xFenton, Judith A.
    The Fertility Handbook. Potter.
Fenton, Norman, 1895-
  xFenton, Norman.
    Human Relations in Adult Corrections. C C
    Thomas.
Fenton, Robert S.
  xFenton, Robert S.
    Chess for You: The Easy Book for Beginners.
    G&D.
Fenwick, C. see Fenwick, Charles Ghequiere.
Fenwick, Charles G. see Fenwick, Charles Ghequiere.
Fenwick, Charles Ghequiere, 1880-1973
  xFenwick, C.
    Foreign Policy & International Law. Oceana.
  xFenwick, Charles G.

American Neutrality, Trial & Failure.
Greenwood.

Fenwick, Daman C.
xFenwick, Deman C.
The Master Handbook of Boat & Marine
Repair. TAB Bks.
Fenwick, Deman C. *see* Fenwick, Daman C.

Fenwick, R. D.
xFenwick, R. D.
The Advocate Guide to Gay Health. Dutton.

Fenwick, Sheridan, 1942-
xFenwick, Sheridan.
Getting It: The Psychology of EST. Lippincott.

Fenyvesi, Charles, 1937-
xFenyvesi, Charles.
Splendor in Exile: The Ex-Majesties of Europe.
New Republic.

Feo, Francesco.
xFeo, Francesco.
Andromaca. Garland Pub.
Fer, Hugo De. *see* De Fer, Hugo.

Feravolo, Rocco V.
xFeravolo, Rocco V.
Wonders Beyond the Solar System. Dodd.

Ferber, Edna.
xFerber, Edna.
American Beauty. Doubleday.
American Beauty. Fawcett.
Cheerful, by Request. Arno.
Cimarron. Doubleday.
Cimarron. Fawcett.
Fanny Herself. Arno.
Giant. Doubleday.
Giant. Fawcett.
Great Son. Fawcett.
Half Portions. Arno.
Ice Palace. Doubleday.
Ice Palace. Fawcett.
One Basket. Doubleday.
Personality Plus: Some Experiences of Emma
McChesney & Her Son, Jock. Arno.

Ferber, Robert, 1922-
xFerber, Robert.
Handbook of Marketing Research. McGraw.
ed. Readings in Survey Research. Am Mktg.

Ferber, Steve.
xFerber, Steve.
ed. All About Rifle Hunting & Shooting in
America. Winchester Pr.
Ferdico, John M. *see* Ferdico, John N.

Ferdico, John N.
xFerdico, John M.
Criminal Procedure for the Law Enforcement
Officer. West Pub.

Ferejohn, John A.
xFerejohn, John A.
Pork Barrel Politics: Rivers & Harbors
Legislation, 1947-1968. Stanford U Pr.

Ferencz, Benjamin B., 1920-
xFerencz, Benjamin B.
Defining International Aggression-the Search
for World Peace: A Documentary History &
Analysis. Oceana.
Less Than Slaves: Jewish Forced Labor & the
Quest for Compensation. Harvard U Pr.

Feret, Barbara L., 1940-
xFeret, Barbara L.
Gastronomical & Culinary Literature: A Survey
& Analysis of Historically-Oriented
Collections in the U. S. A.. Scarecrow.

Fergus, Patricia M.
xFergus, Patricia M.
Spelling Improvement: A Program for
Self-Instruction. McGraw.
Ferguson, A. *see* Ferguson, Anne.
Ferguson, A. B. *see* Ferguson, Albert Barnett.

Ferguson, Adam, 1723-1816
xFerguson, Adam.

An Essay on the History of Civil Society.
Transaction Bks.
Principles of Moral & Political Science. AMS
Pr.
Principles of Moral & Political Science.
Garland Pub.

Ferguson, Albert Barnett.
xFerguson, A. B.
ABC's of Athletic Injuries & Conditioning.
Krieger.

Ferguson, Anne.
xFerguson, A.
ed. Immunological Aspects of the Liver &
Gastrointestinal Tract. Univ Park.

Ferguson, Arthur B.
xFerguson, Arthur B.
CLIO Unbound: Perception of the Social &
Cultural Past in Renaissance England. Duke.

Ferguson, Ben.
xFerguson, Ben E.
The Shaping of a Man of Faith. Victor Bks.
Ferguson, Ben E. *see* Ferguson, Ben.
Ferguson, C. E. *see* Ferguson, Charles E.

Ferguson, Charles D.
xFerguson, Charles D.
The Experiences of a Forty-Niner in California.
Arno.

Ferguson, Charles E.
xFerguson, C. E.
Neoclassical Theory of Production &
Distribution. Cambridge U Pr.
Ferguson, Charles W. *see* Ferguson, Charles Wright.

Ferguson, Charles Wright, 1901-
xFerguson, Charles W.
Fifty Million Brothers: A Panorama of
American Lodges & Clubs. Greenwood.

Ferguson, Clyde L.
xFerguson, Clyde L.
The Stars & the Bible. Exposition.
Ferguson, Donald N. *see* Ferguson, Donald Nivison.

Ferguson, Donald Nivison, 1882-
xFerguson, Donald N.
A History of Musical Thought. Greenwood.
Image & Structure in Chamber Music. Da
Capo.
Masterworks of the Orchestral Repertoire: A
Guide for Listeners. U of Minn Pr.
Music As Metaphor: The Elements of
Expression. Greenwood.
Ferguson, E. James. *see* Ferguson, Elmer James.
Ferguson, Elizabeth. *see* Ferguson, Elizabeth A.

Ferguson, Elizabeth A.
xFerguson, Elizabeth.
Social Work: An Introduction. Har-Row.

Ferguson, Elmer James.
xFerguson, E. James.
The American Revolution: A General History,
1763-1790. Dorsey.
Compiled by Confederation, Constitution, &
Early National Period, 1781-1815. AHM
Pub.
Power of the Purse: A History of American
Public Finance 1776-1790. U of NC Pr.

Ferguson, Estelle.
xFerguson, Estelle.
How to Raise & Train a Chihuahua. TFH
Pubns.

Ferguson, Everett, 1933-
xFerguson, Everett.
Early Christians Speak. Sweet.

Ferguson, Frances.
xFerguson, Frances.
Wordsworth: Language As Counter-Spirit. Yale
U Pr.

Ferguson, Francis.
xFerguson, Francis.
Architecture, Cities, & the Systems Approach.
Braziller.

Ferguson, Frank L.
xFerguson, Frank L.

Efficient Drug Store Management. Fairchild.
Ferguson, Franklin. *see* Ferguson, Franklin Fields.

Ferguson, Franklin Fields.
xFerguson, Franklin.
Intro. by Negro American: A History. Ann
Arbor Pubs.

Ferguson, George, 1910-
xFerguson, George.
Some Early Australian Bookmen. Bks
Australia.
Ferguson, George. *see* Ferguson, George Wells.
Ferguson, George O. *see* Ferguson, George Oscar.

Ferguson, George Oscar, 1885-1960
xFerguson, George O.
Psychology of the Negro: An Experimental
Study. Negro U Pr.
Ferguson, George W. *see* Ferguson, George Wright.

Ferguson, George Wells, 1899-
xFerguson, George.
Signs & Symbols in Christian Art. Oxford U
Pr.
Signs & Symbols in Christian Art. Oxford U
Pr.

Ferguson, George Wright.
xFerguson, George W.
Europe by Eurail: 1979-80. G W Ferguson.

Ferguson, Helen.
xFerguson, Helen S.
Bring on the Puppets. Morehouse.
Ferguson, Helen S. *see* Ferguson, Helen.
Ferguson, Henry L. *see* Ferguson, Henry Lee.

Ferguson, Henry Lee.
xFerguson, Henry L.
Fishers Island' N. Y., 1614-1925. Harbor Hill
Bks.
Ferguson, J. D. *see* Ferguson, John De Lancey.
Ferguson, James. *see* Ferguson, James Mecham.
Ferguson, James M. *see* Ferguson, James Mecham.

Ferguson, James Mecham.
xFerguson, James.
ed. Comprehensive Handbook of Behavioral
Medicine. Spectrum Pub.
xFerguson, James M.
A Change for Heart: Your Family & the Food
You Eat. Bull Pub.
Habits, Not Diets: The Real Way to Weight
Control. Bull Pub.

Ferguson, Jeanne.
xFerguson, Jeanne.
You're Speaking-Who's Listening?. SRA.

Ferguson, John, 1921-
xFerguson, John.
Aristotle. Twayne.
Clement of Alexandria. Twayne.
Greek & Roman Religion: A Source Book.
Noyes.
Libraries in France. Shoe String.
The Open University from Within. NYU Pr.
Pelagius: A Historical & Theological Study.
AMS Pr.
The Place of Suffering. Attic Pr.
Religions of the Roman Empire. Cornell U Pr.
Ferguson, John C. *see* Ferguson, John Calvin.

Ferguson, John Calvin, 1866-1945
xFerguson, John C.
Outlines of Chinese Art. Arno.
Ferguson, John D. *see* Ferguson, John De Lancey.

Ferguson, John De Lancey, 1888-
xFerguson, J. D.
American Literature in Spain. Gordon Pr.
xFerguson, John D.
American Literature in Spain. AMS Pr.
Ferguson, John H. *see* Ferguson, John Henry.

Ferguson, John Henry.
xFerguson, John H.
The American Federal Government. McGraw.
The American System of Government.
McGraw.
Ferguson, L. Kraeer. *see* Ferguson, Lewis Kraeer.

Ferguson, le Baron O., 1939-
  xFerguson, LeBaren O.
    Approximation by Polynomials with Integral
      Coefficients. Am Math.
Ferguson, LeBaren O. see Ferguson, le Baron O.
Ferguson, Lewis Kraeer.
  xFerguson, L. Kraeer.
    Explain It to Me, Doctor. Lippincott.
Ferguson, Linda.
  xFerguson, Linda.
    Canada. Scribner.
Ferguson, Lloyd N.
  xFerguson, Lloyd N.
    Textbook of Organic Chemistry. Van Nos
      Reinhold.
Ferguson, Lucy R. see Ferguson, Lucy Rau.
Ferguson, Lucy Rau, 1930-
  xFerguson, Lucy R.
    Personality Development. Brooks-Cole.
Ferguson, M. Carr.
  xFerguson, M. Carr.
    Federal Income Taxation of Estates &
      Beneficiaries. Little.
Ferguson, Marilyn.
  xFerguson, Marilyn.
    The Aquarian Conspiracy: Personal & Social
      Transformation in the 1980s. J P Tarcher.
    The Brain Revolution: The Frontiers of Mind
      Research. Taplinger.
Ferguson, Mary Ann. see Ferguson, Mary Anne.
Ferguson, Mary Anne.
  xFerguson, Mary Ann.
    Images of Women in Literature. HM.
Ferguson, Pamela.
  xFerguson, Pamela.
    Dominion. Atheneum.
Ferguson, Phil M. see Ferguson, Phil Moss.
Ferguson, Phil Moss, 1899-
  xFerguson, Phil M.
    Reinforced Concrete Fundamentals. Wiley.
Ferguson, Robert.
  xFerguson, Robert.
    Arctic Harpooner: A Voyage on the Schooner
      Abbie Bradford 1878-1879. E M Coleman
      Ent.
Ferguson, Robert A., 1932-
  xFerguson, Robert A.
    The Universal Law of Cosmic Cycles. P-H.
Ferguson, Robert J.
  xFerguson, Robert J.
    Polygraph for the Defense. C C Thomas.
  xFerguson, Robert T.
    The Polygraph in Court. C C Thomas.
Ferguson, Robert T. see Ferguson, Robert J.
Ferguson, Ronald D.
  xFerguson, Ronald D.
    An Algebra Primer: Abecedarian Mathematics
      for College Students. Macmillan.
Ferguson, Rowena.
  xFerguson, Rowena.
    Church's Ministry with Senior Highs.
      Abingdon.
    Editing the Small Magazine. Columbia U Pr.
Ferguson, Samuel, Sir, 1810-1886
  xFerguson, Samuel.
    Congal: A Poem in Five Books. AMS Pr.
    Lays of the Western Gael, & Other Poems.
      AMS Pr.
Ferguson, Thaddeus.
  xFerguson, Thaddeus.
    A History of the Romance Vowel Systems
      Through Paradigmatic Reconstruction.
      Mouton.
Ferguson, Thomas S. see Ferguson, Thomas Shelburne.
Ferguson, Thomas Shelburne, 1929-
  xFerguson, Thomas S.
    Mathematical Statistics: A Decision Theoretic
      Approach. Acad Pr.
Ferguson, Valerie.
  xFerguson, Valerie.

  ed. Sayings of the Week. David & Charles.
Ferguson, W. J. see Ferguson, William J.
Ferguson, William J.
  xFerguson, W. J.
    I Saw Booth Shoot Lincoln. Jenkins.
Ferguson, William S. see Ferguson, William Scott.
Ferguson, William Scott, 1875-1954
  xFerguson, William S.
    Athenian Archons of the Third & Second
      Centuries Before Christ. Johnson Repr.
    The Athenian Secretaries. Johnson Repr.
    Greek Imperialism. Biblo.
Fergusson, Francis.
  xFergusson, Francis.
    Idea of a Theater: A Study of Ten Plays, the
      Art of Drama in Changing Perspective.
      Princeton U Pr.
    Literary Landmarks: Essays on the Theory &
      Practice of Literature. Rutgers U Pr.
Fergusson, Harvey, 1890-
  xFergusson, Harvey.
    The Conquest of Don Pedro. U of NM Pr.
    Grant of Kingdom. U of NM Pr.
Fergusson, James, Sir, Bart, 1904-
  xFergusson, James.
    Balloon Tytler. Transatlantic.
Fergusson, Robert.
  xFergusson, Robert.
    Works of Robert Fergusson. AMS Pr.
Ferholt, J. Deborah. see Ferholt, J. Deborah Lott.
Ferholt, J. Deborah Lott.
  xFerholt, J. Deborah.
    Clinical Assessment of Children: A
      Comprehensive Approach to Primary
      Pediatric Care. Lippincott.
Fericano, Paul F.
  xFericano, Paul F.
    ed. Stoogism Anthology. Poor Souls Pr.
Ferkauf, Eugene, 1920-
  xFerkauf, Eugene.
    Going into Business: How to Do It, by the
      Man Who Did It. Chelsea Hse.
Ferkiss, Victor. see Ferkiss, Victor C.
Ferkiss, Victor C.
  xFerkiss, Victor.
    Foreign Aid: Moral & Political Aspects. Coun
      Rel & Intl.
    Future of Technological Civilization. Braziller.
  xFerkiss, Victor C.
    Africa's Search for Identity. Braziller.
Ferleger, Herbert R. see Ferleger, Herbert Ronald.
Ferleger, Herbert Ronald, 1914-
  xFerleger, Herbert R.
    David A. Wells & the American Revenue
      System 1865-1870. Porcupine Pr.
Ferling, John E.
  xFerling, John E.
    The Loyalist Mind: Joseph Galloway & the
      American Revolution. Pa St U Pr.
Ferlinghetti, Lawrence.
  xFerlinghetti, Lawrence.
    Back Roads to Far Places. New Directions.
    Landscapes of Living & Dying. New
      Directions.
    Northwest Ecolog. City Lights.
    Open Eye, Open Heart. New Directions.
    Tyrannus Nix?. New Directions.
    Who Are We Now?. New Directions.
Ferlita, Ernest.
  xFerlita, Ernest.
    The Parables of Lina Wertmuller. Paulist Pr.
Ferm, Vergilius. see Ferm, Vergilius Ture Anselm.
Ferm, Vergilius T. see Ferm, Vergilius Ture Anselm.
Ferm, Vergilius Ture Anselm, 1896-1974
  xFerm, Vergilius.

    An Encyclopedia of Religion. Greenwood.
    ed. History of Philosophical Systems.
      Littlefield.
    Toward an Expansive Christian Theology.
      Philos Lib.
  xFerm, Vergilius T.
    ed. History of Philosophical Systems. Arno.
    ed. Religion in the Twentieth Century.
      Greenwood.
    ed. Religion in Transition. Arno.
  xFerm, Virgiulius.
    Protestant Credo. Philos Lib.
Ferm, Virgiulius. see Ferm, Vergilius Ture Anselm.
Ferman, Ed. see Ferman, Edward L.
Ferman, Edward L.
  xFerman, Ed.
    Graven Images: Three Original Novellas of
      Science Fiction. Elsevier-Nelson.
Ferman, Louis A.
  xFerman, Louis A.
    Evaluating the War on Poverty. Am Acad Pol
      Soc Sci.
Fermi, Enrico, 1901-1954
  xFermi, Enrico.
    Notes on Thermodynamics & Statistics. U of
      Chicago Pr.
Fermi, Laura.
  xFermi, Laura.
    Illustrious Immigrants: The Intellectual
      Migration from Europe, 1930-41. U of
      Chicago Pr.
    Mussolini. U of Chicago Pr.
Fernald, L. Dodge. see Fernald, Lloyd Dodge.
Fernald, Lloyd Dodge.
  xFernald, L. Dodge.
    Basic Psychology. HM.
    Introduction to Psychology. HM.
Fernandes, Florestan.
  xFernandes, Florestan.
    Negro in Brazilian Society. Atheneum.
    Negro in Brazilian Society. Columbia U Pr.
Fernandez, J. W. see Fernandez, James W.
Fernandez, Jack E.
  xFernandez, Jack E.
    An Introduction to Chemical Principles.
      Macmillan.
    Modern Chemical Science. Macmillan.
Fernandez, James W.
  xFernandez, J. W.
    Fang Architectonics. Inst Study Human.
Fernandez, Jose A. see Fernandez, Jose Antonio.
Fernandez, Jose Antonio, 1898-
  xFernandez, Jose A.
    Architecture in Puerto Rico. Architectural.
    Architecture in Puerto Rico. Hastings.
Fernandez, Juan A. see Fernandez, Juan Antonio.
Fernandez, Juan Antonio.
  xFernandez, Juan A.
    Donana: Spain's Wildlife Wilderness.
      Taplinger.
Fernandez, Justino, 1904-
  xFernandez, Justino.
    Guide to Mexican Art: From Its Beginnings to
      the Present. U of Chicago Pr.
Fernandez, Ramon, 1894-1944
  xFernandez, Ramon.
    Moliere: The Man Seen Through the Plays.
      Octagon.
Fernandez, Ronald.
  xFernandez, Ronald.
    The I, Me, & You: An Introduction to Social
      Psychology. HR&W.
    The Promise of Sociology. HR&W.
Fernandez De Figueroa, Martin.
  xFernandez De Figueroa, Martin.
    Spaniard in the Portuguese Indies: The
      Narrative of Martin Fernandez De Figueroa.
      Harvard U Pr.
Fernandez Mendez, Eugenio.
  xFernandez Mendez, Eugenio.

Historia Cultural De Puerto Rico 1493-1968. U
of PR Pr.

Fernandez-Armesto, Felipe.
xFernandez-Armesto, Felipe.
Ferdinand & Isabella. Taplinger.

Fernbach, S. *see* Fernbach, Sidney.

Fernbach, Sidney.
xFernbach, S.
ed. Computers & Their Role in the Physical
Sciences. Gordon.

Ferner, Jack D., 1930-
xFerner, Jack D.
Successful Time Management. Wiley.

Fernow, Bernhard E. *see* Fernow, Bernhard Eduard.

Fernow, Bernhard Eduard, 1851-1923
xFernow, Bernhard E.
Economics of Forestry: A Reference Book for
Students of Political Economy & Professional
& Lay Students of Forestry. Arno.

Fernow, Berthold, 1837-1908
xFernow, Berthold.
Ohio Valley in Colonial Days. B Franklin.

Ferns, H. S. *see* Ferns, Henry Stanley.

Ferns, Henry Stanley, 1913-
xFerns, H. S.
The Disease of Government. St Martin.

Ferns, John, 1940-
xFerns, John.
A. J. M. Smith. Twayne.

Feroe, Paul.
xFeroe, Paul.
ed. Silent Voices: Recent American Poems on
Nature. Ally Pr.

Ferra, B. *see* Ferra, Bartolome.

Ferra, Bartolome, 1893-1946
xFerra, B.
Chopin & George Sand in Majorca. Haskell

Ferracuti, Franco.
xFerracuti, Franco.
Delinquents & Nondelinquents in the Puerto
Rican Slum Culture. Ohio St U Pr.

Ferrand, Georgina.
xFerrand, Georgina.
Dangerous Inheritance. Ballantine.

Ferrante, J. *see* Ferrante, Jeanne.

Ferrante, Jeanne.
xFerrante, J.
The Computational Complexity of Logical
Theories. Springer-Verlag.

Ferrante, Joan M.
xFerrante, Joan M.
ed. In Pursuit of Perfection: Courtly Love in
Medieval Literature. Kennikat.

Ferrar, Terry A.
xFerrar, Terry A.
Electric Energy Policy Issues. Ann Arbor
Science.

Ferrar, William L. *see* Ferrar, William Leonard.

Ferrar, William Leonard, 1893-
xFerrar, William L.
Advanced Mathematics for Science: A Sequel
to Mathematics for Science. Oxford U Pr.

Ferrara, Angelo.
xFerrara, Angelo.
Emergency Transfer of the High Risk Neonate:
A Working Manual for Medical, Nursing &
Administrative Personnel. Mosby.

Ferrari, Domenico, 1940-
xFerrari, Domenico.
Computer Systems Performance Evaluation.
P-H.

Ferrari, Michael R.
xFerrari, Michael R.
Profiles of American College Presidents. Mich
St U Busn.

Ferrarius Montanus, Joannes.
xFerrarius Montanus, Joannes.

A Work Touching the Good Ordering of a
Common Weal. Johnson Repr.

Ferraro, Armando, 1894-
xFerraro, Armando.
A Trilogy of Freud's Major Fallacies. Vantage.

Ferraro, John R., 1918-
xFerraro, John R.
Low-Frequency Vibrations in Inorganic &
Coordination Compounds. Plenum Pub.

Ferraro, Pat.
xFerraro, Pat.
Bottle Collector's Book. Past in Glass.

Ferrars, E. X.
xFerrars, E. X.
In at the Kill. Doubleday.
In at the Kill. Penguin.
Last Will & Testament. Doubleday.
Murders Anonymous. Doubleday.
The Pretty Pink Shroud. Doubleday.
The Pretty Pink Shroud. Penguin.

Ferre, Nels. *see* Ferre, Nels Frederick Solomon.

Ferre, Nels F. *see* Ferre, Nels Frederick Solomon.

Ferre, Nels Frederick Solomon, 1908-
xFerre, Nels.
The Christian Understanding of God.
Greenwood.
xFerre, Nels F.
The Finality of Faith, & Christianity Among
the World Religions. Greenwood.

Ferreira, Linda A.
xFerreira, Linda A.
Read on, Speak Out. Newbury Hse.

Ferrell, Mallory H. *see* Ferrell, Mallory Hope.

Ferrell, Mallory Hope.
xFerrell, Mallory H.
Tweetsie Country: The East Tennessee &
Western North Carolina Railroad. Pruett.

Ferrell, O. C.
xFerrell, O. C.
Public Policy Issues in Marketing. Lexington
Bks.

Ferrell, Oliver P.
xFerrell, Oliver P.
Confidential Frequency List. Gilfer.

Ferrell, Robert H.
xFerrell, Robert H.
ed. America As a World Power, 1872-1945. U
of SC Pr.
ed. America in a Divided World: 1945-1972. U
of SC Pr.
American Diplomacy in the Great Depression:
Hoover-Stimson Foreign Policy, 1929-1933.
Shoe String.
Peace in Their Time: The Origins of the
Kellogg-Briand Pact. Norton.
Peace in Their Time: The Origins of the
Kellogg-Briand Pact. Shoe String.

Ferrell, Wilfred A.
xFerrell, Wilfred A.
Strategies in Prose. HR&W.

Ferrer, Aldo.
xFerrer, Aldo.
The Argentine Economy. U of Cal Pr.

Ferrero, G. *see* Ferrero, Guglielmo.

Ferrero, Guglielmo, 1871-1942
xFerrero, G.
Four Years of Fascism. AMS Pr.
xFerrero, Guglielmo.
The Greatness & Decline of Rome. Arno.
The Life of Caesar. Greenwood.
Peace & War. Arno.
The Principles of Power: The Great Political
Crises of History. Arno.

Ferres, Antonio.
xFerres, Antonio.
Literatura Espanola Del Ultimo Exilio.
Gordian.

Ferres, John H.
xFerres, John H.

ed. Modern Commonwealth Literature. Ungar.

Ferretti, Fred.
xFerretti, Fred.
The Great American Book of Sidewalk, Stoop,
Dirt, Curb & Alley Games. Workman Pub.
The Great American Marble Book. Workman
Pub.

Ferretti, Paolo A. *see* Ferretti, Paolo Maria.

Ferretti, Paolo Maria, 1866-1938
xFerretti, Paolo A.
Estetica Gregoriana. Da Capo.

Ferretti, Val S.
xFerretti, Val S.
Death in Literature. McGraw.

Ferri, Elsa.
xFerri, Elsa.
Disadvantaged Families & Playgroups.
Humanities.

Ferri, Robert.
xFerri, Robert.
The Tax Organizer. McGraw.
The Tax Organizer. McGraw.

Ferri-Pisani, Camille.
xFerri-Pisani, Camille F.
Prince Napoleon in America, 1861: Letters
from His Aide-De-Camp. Kennikat.

Ferri-Pisani, Camille F. *see* Ferri-Pisani, Camille.

Ferrier, Lucy.
xFerrier, Lucy.
Diving the Great Barrier Reef. Troll Assocs.

Ferrier, Susan. *see* Ferrier, Susan Edmonstone.

Ferrier, Susan Edmonstone, 1782-1854
xFerrier, Susan.
Works of Susan Ferrier. AMS Pr.

Ferriman, David. *see* Ferriman, David George.

Ferriman, David George.
xFerriman, David.
Human Hair Growth in Health & Disease. C C
Thomas.

Ferrini, Vincent, 1913-
xFerrini, Vincent.
Know Fish. Univ Conn Lib.

Ferris, Clifford D.
xFerris, Clifford D.
Introduction to Bioelectrodes. Plenum Pub.

Ferris, Elvira B. *see* Ferris, Elvira Binello.

Ferris, Elvira Binello.
xFerris, Elvira B.
Body Structures & Functions. Van Nos
Reinhold.

Ferris, George.
xFerris, George.
ed. Readings in Australian Marketing. Univ
Microfilms.

Ferris, George T. *see* Ferris, George Titus.

Ferris, George Titus, b. 1840
xFerris, George T.
Great Italian & French Composers. Gordon Pr.
Great Violinists & Pianists. Arno.

Ferris, Louanne.
xFerris, Louanne.
I'm Done Crying. M Evans.

Ferris, Norman B., 1931-
xFerris, Norman B.
Desperate Diplomacy: William H. Seward's
Foreign Policy, 1861. U of Tenn Pr.

Ferris, Paul.
xFerris, Paul.
The City. Viking Pr.
Dylan Thomas. Penguin.
Talk to Me About England. Coward.
Talk to Me About England. Popular Lib.

Ferris, Robert W.
xFerris, Robert W.
Pupil Personnel Strategies & Systems. C C
Thomas.

Ferris, Roxana Judkins (Stinchfield), 1895-
xFerris, Roxana S.

Native Shrubs of the San Francisco Bay
Region. U of Cal Pr.
Ferris, Roxana S. see Ferris, Roxana Judkins
(Stinchfield).
Ferris, Seymour W. see Ferris, Seymour Washington.
Ferris, Seymour Washington, 1900-
xFerris, Seymour W.
Handbook of Hydrocarbons. Acad Pr.
Ferris, Timothy.
xFerris, Timothy.
The Red Limit: The Search for the Edge of the
Universe. Bantam.
The Red Limit: The Search for the Edge of the
Universe. Morrow.
Ferriss, Abbott L. see Ferriss, Abbott Lamoyne.
Ferriss, Abbott Lamoyne, 1915-
xFerriss, Abbott L.
Indicators of Change in the American Family.
Russell Sage.
Indicators of Trends in American Education.
Russell Sage.
Indicators of Trends in the Status of American
Women. Russell Sage.
Ferriss, G. see Ferriss, Gregory S.
Ferriss, Gregory S.
xFerriss, G.
ed. Treatment of Epilepsy Today. Med
Economics.
Ferro, Robert.
xFerro, Robert.
The Others. Scribner.
Ferrucci, Piero.
xFerrucci, Piero.
Psychosynthesis. Crown.
Ferry, David.
xFerry, David.
The Limits of Mortality: An Essay on
Wordsworth's Major Poems. Greenwood.
On the Way to the Island. Columbia U Pr.
Ferry, W. Hawkins.
xFerry, W. Hawkins.
The Buildings of Detroit: A History. Wayne St
U Pr.
Fersch, Ellsworth A.
xFersch, Ellsworth A.
Law, Psychology, & the Courts: Rethinking
Treatment of the Young & the Disturbed. C
C Thomas.
Ferstle, Jim.
xFerstle, Jim.
Contemporary Jogging. Contemp Bks.
Ferziger, Joel H.
xFerziger, Joel H.
Theory of Neutron Slowing Down in Nuclear
Reactors. MIT Pr.
Fesharaki, Fereidun.
xFesharaki, Fereidun.
Development of the Iranian Oil Industry:
International & Domestic Aspects. Praeger.
Feshbach, Seymour.
xFeshbach, Seymour.
ed. Aggression & Behavior Change: Biological
& Social Processes. Praeger.
Fesperman, John. see Fesperman, John T.
Fesperman, John T.
xFesperman, John.
Two Essays on Organ Design. Sunbury Pr.
Fessel, W. J.
xFessel, W. J.
Rheumatology for Clinicians. Thieme-Stratton.
Fessenden, Francis.
xFessenden, Francis.
Life & Public Services of William Pitt
Fessenden. Da Capo.
Fessenden, Ralph J.
xFessenden, Ralph J.

Chemical Principles for the Life Sciences.
Allyn.
Organic Chemistry. Prindle.
Fessler, Donald R., 1907-
xFessler, Donald R.
Facilitating Community Change: A Basic
Guide. Univ Assocs.
Fessler, Edward A. see Fessler, Edward Anthony.
Fessler, Edward Anthony.
xFessler, Edward A.
Directed-Energy Weapons: A Juridical
Analysis. Praeger.
Fessler, Stella L. see Fessler, Stella Lau.
Fessler, Stella Lau.
xFessler, Stella L.
Chinese Meatless Cooking. NAL.
Fest, C. see Fest, Christa.
Fest, Christa.
xFest, C.
The Chemistry of Organophosphorus
Pesticides: Reactivity-Synthesis-Mcde of
Action-Toxicology. Springer-Verlag.
Fest, Joachim C., 1926-
xFest, Joachim C.
The Face of the Third Reich: Portraits of the
Nazi Leadership. Pantheon.
Hitler. Random.
Fest, Wilfried, 1943-
xFest, Wilfried.
Dictionary of German History 1806-1945. St
Martin.
Peace or Partition: The Habsburg Monarchy &
British Policy, 1914-1918. St Martin.
Festa-McCormick, Diana.
xFesta-McCormick, Diane.
Honore De Balzac. Twayne.
Festa-McCormick, Diane. see Festa-McCormick, Diana.
Festing, Michael F. see Festing, Michael Francis Wogan.
Festing, Michael Francis Wogan.
xFesting, Michael F.
ed. Animal Models of Obesity. Oxford U Pr.
Inbred Strains in Biomedical Research. Oxford
U Pr.
Festing, Sally.
xFesting, Sally.
Fishermen. David & Charles.
Festinger, Leon, 1919-
xFestinger, Leon.
Conflict, Decision & Dissonance. Stanford U
Pr.
A Theory of Cognitive Dissonance. Stanford U
Pr.
Fetherling, Dale, 1941-
xFetherling, Dale.
Mother Jones, the Miners' Angel: A Portrait. S
Ill U Pr.
Fetridge, William H. see Fetridge, William Harrison.
Fetridge, William Harrison, 1906-
xFetridge, William H.
ed. Navy Reader. Arno.
Fetros, John G.
xFetros, John G.
Dictionary of Factual & Fictional Riders &
Their Horses. Exposition.
Fetscher, Iring.
xFetscher, Iring.
Marx & Marxism. Continuum.
Fetter, Bruce.
xFetter, Bruce.
ed. Colonial Rule in Africa: Readings from
Primary Sources. U of Wis Pr.
Fetter, Frank A. see Fetter, Frank Albert.
Fetter, Frank Albert, 1863-1949
xFetter, Frank A.
Capital, Interest & Rent: Essays in the Theory
of Distribution. Inst Humane.
Masquerade of Monopoly. Kelley.
Fetter, Frank W. see Fetter, Frank Whitson.
Fetter, Frank Whitson, 1899-
xFetter, Frank W.

Development of British Monetary Orthodoxy
1797-1875. Kelley.
Fetter, Richard L.
xFetter, Richard L.
Telluride: From Pick to Powder. Caxton.
Fetterley, Judith, 1938-
xFetterley, Judith.
The Resisting Reader: A Feminist Approach to
American Fiction. Ind U Pr.
Fetterman, Elsie.
xFetterman, Elsie.
Consumer Education in Practice. Wiley.
Money Management: Choices & Decisions.
HM.
Feucht, Oscar E.
xFeucht, Oscar E.
Learning to Use Your Bible. Concordia.
Feuchtwanger, E. J.
xFeuchtwanger, E. J.
Gladstone. St Martin.
Feuer, H. see Feuer, Henry.
Feuer, Henry, 1912-
xFeuer, H.
ed. Chemistry of the Nitro & Nitroso Groups.
Wiley.
Feuer, Lewis S. see Feuer, Lewis Samuel.
Feuer, Lewis Samuel, 1912-
xFeuer, Lewis S.
Psychoanalysis & Ethics. Greenwood.
Feuer, Mortimer.
xFeuer, Morton.
Personal Liabilities of Corporate Officers &
Directors. P-H.
Feuer, Morton. see Feuer, Mortimer.
Feuerlicht, Ignace.
xFeuerlicht, Ignace.
Alienation: From the Past to the Future.
Greenwood.
Thomas Mann. Twayne.
Feuerstein, Re'Uven.
xFeuerstein, Reuven.
The Dynamic Assessment of Retarded
Performers: The Learning Potential,
Assessment Device, Theory, Instruments &
Techniques. Univ Park.
Feuerstein, Reuven. see Feuerstein, Re'Uven.
Feuerwerger, Marvin C.
xFeuerwerger, Marvin C.
Congress & Israel: Foreign Aid
Decision-Making in the House of
Representatives, Nineteen Sixty-Nine to
Ninety Seventy-Six. Greenwood.
Feuerwerker, Albert.
xFeuerwerker, Albert.
Chinese Communist Studies of Modern
Chinese History. Harvard U Pr.
Economic Trends in the Republic of China,
1912-1949. U of Mich Ctr Chinese.
ed. Modern China. P-H.
Feuillerat, Albert, 1874-1953
xFeuillerat, Albert.
Comment Marcel Proust a Compose Son
Roman. AMS Pr.
Feuillet, Andre.
xFeuillet, Andre.
The Priesthood of Christ & His Ministers.
Doubleday.
Few, William P. see Few, William Preston.
Few, William Preston.
xFew, William P.
Papers & Addresses. Arno.
Fewer, Derek.
xFewer, Derek.
Brain Tumor Chemotherapy. C C Thomas.
Fewings, David R.
xFewings, David R.
Corporate Growth & Common Stock Risk. Jai
Pr.
Fewkes, Jesse W. see Fewkes, Jesse Walter.

Fewkes, Jesse Walter, 1850-1930
xFewkes, Jesse W.
Designs on Prehistoric Hopi Pottery. Dover.
Designs on Prehistoric Hopi Pottery. Peter
Smith.
Fey, Harold E., 1898-
xFey, Harold E.
ed. How My Mind Has Changed. Peter Smith.
Fey, James T. *see* Fey, James Taylor.
Fey, James Taylor.
xFey, James T.
Patterns of Verbal Communication in
Mathematics Classes. Tchrs Coll.
Fey, William R., 1942-
xFey, William R.
Faith & Doubt: The Unfolding of Newman's
Thought on Certainty. Patmos Pr.
Feydeau, Georges. *see* Feydeau, Georges Leon Jules
Marie.
Feydeau, Georges Leon Jules Marie, 1862-1921
xFeydeau, Georges.
Four Farces. U of Chicago Pr.
Feydy, Ann L. *see* Feydy, Anne Lindbergh.
Feydy, Anne Lindbergh.
xFeydy, Ann L.
Osprey Island. HM.
Feys, J. *see* Feys, Jan.
Feys, Jan, 1933-
xFeys, J.
The Life of a Yogi. South Asia Bks.
Ffrench, Florence.
xFfrench, Florence.
Compiled by Music & Musicians in Chicago.
AMS Pr.
xFfrench, Florence F.
Music & Musicians in Chicago. Da Capo.
Ffrench, Florence F. *see* Ffrench, Florence.
Ffrench, G. *see* Ffrench, Geoffrey E.
Ffrench, Geoffrey E.
xFfrench, G.
Occupational Health. Herman Pub.
Ffrench, Richard.
xFfrench, Richard.
A Guide to the Birds of Trinidad & Tobago.
Harrowood Bks.
Fibush, Esther.
xFibush, Esther.
Forgive Me No Longer: The Liberation of
Martha. Family Serv.
Fic, Victor M., 1922-
xFic, Victor M.
The Bolsheviks & the Czechoslovak Legion:
Origin of Their Armed Conflict. South Asia
Bks.
Ficat, Paul.
xFicat, R. Paul.
Disorders of the Patello-Femoral Joint.
Williams & Wilkins.
Ficat, R. Paul. *see* Ficat, Paul.
Ficchi, Rocco. *see* Ficchi, Rocco F.
Ficchi, Rocco F.
xFicchi, Rocco.
ed. Practical Design for Electromagnetic
Compatibility. Hayden.
Ficek. *see* Ficek, Edmund F.
Ficek, Edmund F.
xFicek.
Real Estate Principles & Practices. Merrill.
Fichtenau, Heinrich.
xFichtenau, Heinrich.
The Carolingian Empire. U of Toronto Pr.
Fichter, George S.
xFichter, George S.

Cats. Western Pub.
A Changing World for Wildlife. Western Pub.
The Florida Cookbook. E A Seemann.
Florida-in Pictures. Sterling.
The Future Sea. Sterling.
Insect Pests. Western Pub.
Insects. Western Pub.
Keeping Amphibians & Reptiles As Pets.
Watts.
Racquetball. Watts.
Snakes Around the World. Watts.
Working Dogs. Watts.
Fichter, Harold. *see* Fichter, Harold O.
Fichter, Harold O.
xFichter, Harold.
The Master Lawnmower Repair Book. TAB
Bks.
Fichter, Joseph H. *see* Fichter, Joseph Henry.
Fichter, Joseph Henry, 1908-
xFichter, Joseph H.
Sociology. U of Chicago Pr.
Fick, Leonard J.
xFick, Leonard J.
Light Beyond: A Study of Hawthorne's
Theology. Folcroft.
Ficker, Victor. *see* Ficker, Victor B.
Ficker, Victor B.
xFicker, Victor.
Deprivation in America. Glencoe.
xFicker, Victor B.
Values in Conflict: A Text Reader in Social
Problems. Heath.
Fickett, Harold L.
xFickett, Harold L.
Hope for Your Church: Ten Principles of
Church Growth. Regal.
Layman's Guide to Baptist Beliefs. Zondervan.
Fickett, Wildon.
xFickett, Wildon.
Detonation. U of Cal Pr.
Ficklen, John R. *see* Ficklen, John Rose.
Ficklen, John Rose, 1858-1907
xFicklen, John R.
History of Reconstruction in Louisiana:
Through 1868. Peter Smith.
Fiddian, Robin.
xFiddian, Robin.
Ignacio Aldecoa. G K Hall.
Fideler, Raymond. *see* Fideler, Raymond Edwin.
Fideler, Raymond Edwin.
xFideler, Raymond.
South America. Fideler.
Fidell, Oscar. *see* Fidell, Oscar H.
Fidell, Oscar H.
xFidell, Oscar.
Ideas in Poetry. P-H.
Fidfaddy, Frederick A. *see* Fidfaddy, Frederick Augustus.
Fidfaddy, Frederick Augustus, Pseud.
xFidfaddy, Frederick A.
The Adventures of Uncle Sam. Irvington.
Fiedler, F. *see* Fiedler, Fred Edward.
Fiedler, Fred E. *see* Fiedler, Fred Edward.
Fiedler, Fred Edward.
xFiedler, F.
Theory of Leadership Effectiveness. McGraw.
xFiedler, Fred E.
Leadership & Effective Management. Scott F.
Fiedler, Jean.
xFiedler, Jean.
Great American Heroes. Lion.
Fiedler, Judith.
xFiedler, Judith.
Field Research: A Manual for Logistics &
Management of Scientific Studies in Natural
Settings. Jossey-Bass.
Fiedler, Leslie. *see* Fiedler, Leslie A.
Fiedler, Leslie A.
xFiedler, Leslie.

Love & Death in the American Novel. Stein &
Day.
Return of the Vanishing American. Stein &
Day.
The Stranger in Shakespeare. Stein & Day.
xFiedler, Leslie A.
A Fiedler Reader. Stein & Day.
Fiedorowicz, Z. *see* Fiedorowicz, Zbigniew.
Fiedorowicz, Zbigniew.
xFiedorowicz, Z.
Homology of Classical Groups Over Finite
Fields & Their Associated Infinite Loop
Spaces. Springer-Verlag.
Fiegehen, Guy.
xFiegehen, Guy.
Poverty & Progress in Britain, 1953-1973: A
Statistical Study of Low Income Households.
Cambridge U Pr.
Field & Stream. *see* Field and Stream.
Field and Stream.
xField & Stream.
Field & Stream Reader. Arno.
Field, Anne E.
xField, Anne E.
On the Trail of Stoddard Glass. Bauhan.
Field, Barry C.
xField, Barry C.
ed. Environmental Economics: A Guide to
Information Sources. Gale.
Field, Charles K. *see* Field, Charles Kellogg.
Field, Charles Kellogg.
xField, Charles K.
Stanford Stories: Tales of a Young University.
Arno.
Field, Daniel, 1938-
xField, Daniel.
The End of Serfdom: Nobility & Bureaucracy
in Russia, 1855-1861. Harvard U Pr.
Field, David, 1936-
xField, David.
Free to Do Right. Inter-Varsity.
Field, E. J. *see* Field, Ephraim Joshua.
Field, Edwin. *see* Field, Edwin M.
Field, Edwin M.
xField, Edwin.
How to Get Rich Through OPN. P-H.
Field, Ephraim Joshua.
xField, E. J.
Multiple Sclerosis: A Critical Conspectus. Univ
Park.
Field, Ernest R.
xField, Ernest R.
Rich Man's Tax Guide. Hearthside.
Field, Eugene, 1850-1895
xField, Eugene.
Little Book of Profitable Tales. Arno.
A Little Book of Profitable Tales. Folcroft.
A Little Book of Western Verse. Folcroft.
A Little Book of Western Verse. Core
Collection.
Love Songs of Childhood. Arno.
Field, Frances. *see* Field, Michael.
Field, Frank, 1942-
xField, Frank.
ed. The Conscript Army: A Study of Britain's
Unemployed. Routledge & Kegan.
ed. The Wealth Report. Routledge & Kegan.
Field, Frank. *see* Field, Franks.
Field, Frank M. *see* Field, Frank McCoy.
Field, Frank McCoy.
xField, Frank M.
Where Jesus Walked: Through the Holy Land
with the Master. Arno.
Field, Franks.
xField, Frank.
ed. Education & the Urban Crisis. Routledge &
Kegan.
Field, Frederick V. *see* Field, Frederick Vanderbilt.
Field, Frederick Vanderbilt, 1905-
xField, Frederick V.

Pre-Hispanic Mexican Stamp Designs. Dover.
Pre-Hispanic Mexican Stamp Designs. Peter
Smith.
Field, G. see Field, George.
Field, G. Lowell. see Field, George Lowell.
Field, George, 1809 or 10-1883
xField, G.
Memoirs, Incidents, Reminiscences of the
Early History of the New Church in
Michigan, Indiana, Illinois, & Adjacent
States, & Canada. AMS Pr.
Field, George L. see Field, George Lowell.
Field, George Lowell, 1911-
xField, G. Lowell.
Syndical & Corporative Institutions of Italian
Fascism. AMS Pr.
xField, George L.
Comparative Political Development: The
Precedent of the West. Cornell U Pr.
Field, Hazel E. see Field, Hazel Elizabeth.
Field, Hazel Elizabeth.
xField, Hazel E.
Atlas of Cat Anatomy. U of Chicago Pr.
Field, Helen A. see Field, Helen Atwater.
Field, Helen Atwater, 1883-
xField, Helen A.
Extensive Individual Reading Versus Class
Reading: A Study of the Development of
Reading Ability in the Transition Grades.
AMS Pr.
Field, Henry, 1902-
xField, Henry.
Contributions to the Anthropology of Iran.
Kraus Repr.
Field, Henry M. see Field, Henry Martyn.
Field, Henry Martyn, 1822-1907
xField, Henry M.
Bright Skies & Dark Shadows. Arno.
History of the Atlantic Telegraph. Arno.
The Story of the Atlantic Telegraph. Arno.
Field, John P.
xField, John P.
Cases for Composition. Little.
Field, John W.
xField, John W.
Group Practice Development: A Practical
Handbook. Aspen Systems.
Field, Joseph M., 1810-1856
xField, Joseph M.
The Drama in Pokerville. Irvington.
Field, Kate, 1838-1896
xField, Kate.
Charles Albert Fechter. Arno.
Field, Margaret J. see Field, Margaret Joyce.
Field, Margaret Joyce.
xField, Margaret J.
Akim-Kotoku: An Oman of the Gold Coast.
Negro U Pr.
Field, Matthew C.
xField, Matthew C.
Matt Field on the Santa Fe Trail. U of Okla
Pr.
Field, Michael.
xField, Frances.
jt. auth. Quintet of Cuisines. Time-Life.
jt. auth. Quintet of Cuisines. Silver.
xField, Michael.
Cooking with Michael Field. HR&W.
Quintet of Cuisines. Time-Life.
Quintet of Cuisines. Silver.
Field, Michael J.
xField, Michael J.
Differential Calculus & Its Applications. Van
Nos Reinhold.
Field, Minna.
xField, Minna.
The Aged, the Family, & the Community.
Columbia U Pr.
Field, Peter.
xField, Peter.

Powder Valley Getaway. PB.
Powder Valley Ransom. PB.
Rattlesnake Range. PB.
Field, Rachel.
xField, Rachel.
All This, & Heaven Too. Macmillan.
Prayer for a Child. Macmillan.
xField, Rachel L.
Prayer for a Child. Macmillan.
Field, Rachel. see Field, Rachel Lyman.
Field, Rachel L. see Field, Rachel.
Field, Rachel Lyman, 1894-1942
xField, Rachel.
And Now Tomorrow. Ace Bks.
And Now Tomorrow. Macmillan.
Calico Bush. Macmillan.
Field Research Corporation.
xField Research Corporation.
Public Opinion of Criminal Justice in
California: A Survey Conducted by Field
Research Corporation. Inst Gov Stud Berk.
Field, Richard S.
xField, Richard S.
Jasper Johns: Prints 1970-1977. Columbia U
Pr.
Paul Gauguin: The Paintings of the First
Voyage to Tahiti. Garland Pub.
Field, Stanley.
xField, Stanley.
Professional Broadcast Writers Handbook. TAB
Bks.
Field, Stephen J. see Field, Stephen Johnson.
Field, Stephen Johnson, 1816-1899
xField, Stephen J.
Personal Reminiscences of Early Days in
California. Da Capo.
Field, X. see Field, Xenia.
Field, Xenia.
xField, X.
Growing Bulbs in the House. St Martin.
Fielden, Joan.
xFielden, Joan.
From Garden to Table: A Complete Guide to
Vegetable Growing & Cooking. McClelland.
Fielden, John, 1784-1849
xFielden, John.
Curse of the Factory System. Biblio Dist.
Curse of the Factory System. Kelley.
Fielder, Mildred.
xFielder, Mildred.
A Guide to Black Hills Ghost Mines. North
Plains.
Hiking Trails in the Black Hills. North Plains.
Plant Medicine & Folklore. Winchester Pr.
Fieldhouse, David K. see Fieldhouse, David Kenneth.
Fieldhouse, David Kenneth, 1925-
xFieldhouse, David K.
Unilever Overseas: The Anatomy of a
Multinational. Hoover Inst Pr.
Fieldhouse, Roger.
xFieldhouse, Roger.
Workers' Educational Association: Aims &
Achievements 1903-1977. Syracuse U Cont
Ed.
Fielding, Gordon J.
xFielding, Gordon J.
Geography As Social Science. Har-Row.
Fielding, Henry, 1707-1754
xFielding, Henry.
Adventures of Joseph Andrews. Oxford U Pr.
The Adventures of Joseph Andrews. R West.
Amelia. Dutton.
An Enquiry into the Causes of the Late
Increase of Robbers. Patterson Smith.
A Journey from This World to the Next. Arno.
Journey from This World to the Next. Dutton.
The Life of Mr. Jonathan Wild. Garland Pub.
Fielding, Mantle.
xFielding, Mantle.

Dictionary of American Painters, Sculptors &
Engravers. Modern Bks.
Dictionary of American Painters, Sculptors &
Engravers. Wallace-Homestead.
Fielding, Nancy.
xFielding, Nancy.
Fielding's Selective Shopping Guide to Europe
1980. Fielding.
jt. auth. Fielding's Selective Shopping Guide to
Europe, 1981. Morrow.
xFielding, Temple.
Fielding's Selective Shopping Guide to Europe,
1981. Morrow.
Fielding, P. M.
xFielding, P. M.
ed. A National Directory of Four Year
Colleges, Two Year Colleges & Post High
School Training Programs for Young People
with Learning Disabilities. PIP.
Fielding, Raymond.
xFielding, Raymond.
The March of Time: 1935-1951. Oxford U Pr.
Fielding, Sarah, 1710-1768
xFielding, Sarah.
The History of Ophelia. Garland Pub.
The History of the Countess of Dellwyn, 1759.
Garland Pub.
The Lives of Cleopatra & Octavia, 1757.
Garland Pub.
Fielding, Stuart.
xFielding, Stuart.
ed. Antidepressants. Futura Pub.
ed. Anxiolytics. Futura Pub.
ed. New Frontiers in Psychotropic Drug
Research. Futura Pub.
Fielding, Temple. see Fielding, Nancy.
Fields, A. A. see Fields, Annie Adams.
Fields, Anne. see Fields, Annie Adams.
Fields, Annie. see Fields, Annie Adams.
Fields, Annie Adams, 1834-1915
xFields, A. A.
Charles Dudley Warner. Arno.
xFields, Anne.
Authors & Friends. Scholarly.
xFields, Annie.
Authors & Friends. AMS Pr.
Authors & Friends. Folcroft.
Life & Letters of Harriet Beecher Stowe.
Arden Lib.
Life & Letters of Harriet Beecher Stowe. Gale.
Nathaniel Hawthorne. Folcroft.
Nathaniel Hawthorne. Haskell.
Fields, Craig, 1946-
xFields, Craig.
About Computers. Winthrop.
Fields, J. T. see Fields, James Thomas.
Fields, James T. see Fields, James Thomas.
Fields, James Thomas, 1816-1881
xFields, J. T.
Underbrush. R West.
xFields, James T.
In & Out of Doors with Charles Dickens. AMS
Pr.
Old Acquaintance: Barry Cornwall & Some of
His Friends. Folcroft.
Old Acquaintance: Barry Cornwall & Some of
His Friends. R West.
Fields, Jeff.
xFields, Jeff.
Cry of Angels. Atheneum.
A Cry of Angels. Ballantine.
Fields, Kenneth, 1939-
xFields, Kenneth.
Other Walker: A Book of Poems. Talisman
Research.
Fields, Louis.
xFields, Louis W.
Bookkeeping Made Simple. Doubleday.
Fields, Louis W. see Fields, Louis.
Fields, Marion. see Fields, Marion L.

Fields, Marion L.
xFields, Marion.
Fundamentals of Food Microbiology. AVI.
Fields, Rona M.
xFields, Rona M.
Society Under Siege: A Psychology of Northern Ireland. Temple U Pr.
Fields, Susan.
xFields, Susan H.
Getting Married Again. Dodd.
Fields, Susan H. *see* Fields, Susan.
Fields, Victor A. *see* Fields, Victor Alexander.
Fields, Victor Alexander, 1901-
xFields, Victor A.
Foundations of the Singer's Art. Vantage.
Training the Singing Voice: An Analysis of the Working Concepts Contained Contained in Recent Contributions to Vocal Pedagogy. Da Capo.
Fieler, Frank B.
xFieler, Frank B.
Compiled by The David McCandless McKell Collection: A Descriptive Catalog of Manuscripts, Early Printed Books & Children's Books. G K Hall.
Fielo, S. B. *see* Fielo, Sandra B.
Fielo, Sandra B.
xFielo, S. B.
A Summary of Integrated Nursing Theory. McGraw.
Fienberg, Stephen. *see* Fienberg, Stephen E.
Fienberg, Stephen E.
xFienberg, Stephen.
The Analysis of Cross-Classified Categorical Data. MIT Pr.
xFienberg, Stephen E.
The Analysis of Cross-Classified Categorical Data. MIT Pr.
Fiennes, R. N. *see* Fiennes, Richard.
Fiennes, Richard.
xFiennes, R. N.
The Environment of Man. St Martin.
Fiering, Myron B.
xFiering, Myron B.
ed. Synthetic Streamflows. Am Geophysical.
Fieser, Louis F. *see* Fieser, Louis Frederick.
Fieser, Louis Frederick, 1899-
xFieser, Louis F.
Organic Experiments. Heath.
Reagents for Organic Synthesis. Wiley.
Style Guide for Chemists. Krieger.
xFieser, Mary.
jt. auth. Reagents for Organic Synthesis. Wiley.
Fieser, Mary. *see* Fieser, Louis Frederick.
Fife, Austin. *see* Fife, Austin E.
Fife, Austin E.
xFife, Austin.
ed. Forms Upon the Frontier: Folklife & Folk Arts in the United States. Utah St U Pr.
Fife, Dale.
xFife, Dale.
Follow That Ghost!. Dutton.
The Little Park. A Whitman.
North of Danger. Schol Bk Serv.
North of Danger. Dutton.
What's the Prize, Lincoln?. Coward.
Who Goes There Lincoln?. Coward.
Fife, P. C. *see* Fife, Paul C.
Fife, Paul C.
xFife, P. C.
Mathematical Aspects of Reacting & Diffusing Systems. Springer-Verlag.
Fifield, Russell H. *see* Fifield, Russell Hunt.
Fifield, Russell Hunt, 1914-
xFifield, Russell H.
Woodrow Wilson & the Far East: The Diplomacy of the Shantung Question. Shoe String.
Fifoot, C. H. *see* Fifoot, Cecil Herbert Stuart.

Fifoot, Cecil Herbert Stuart, 1899-
xFifoot, C. H.
Frederic William Maitland: A Life. Harvard U Pr.
Fifth Intl. Conference on Numerical Methods in Fluid Dynamics. *see* International Conference on Numerical Methods in Fluid Dynamics,5th, Twente University of Technology, 1976.
Figgis, John N. *see* Figgis, John Neville.
Figgis, John Neville, 1866-1919
xFiggis, John N.
Churches in the Modern State. Russell.
The Divine Right of Kings. Peter Smith.
Figler, Homer R., 1923-
xFigler, Homer R.
Overcoming Executive Midlife Crisis. Wiley.
Figley, Charles R., 1944-
xFigley, Charles R.
ed. Stress Disorders Among Vietnam Veterans: Theory, Research, & Treatment Implications. Brunner-Mazel.
Figner, Vera N. *see* Figner, Vera Nikolaevna.
Figner, Vera Nikolaevna, 1852-1942
xFigner, Vera N.
Memoirs of a Revolutionist. Greenwood.
Filby, P. William, 1911-
xFilby, P. William.
American & British Genealogy & Heraldry: A Selected List of Books. ALA.
File, Norman.
xFile, Norman.
How to Beat the Establishment & Get That Job. Apple-One.
How to Beat the Establishment & Get That Job. Laurida.
Filene, Catherine.
xFilene, Catherine.
Careers for Women. Arno.
Careers for Women. Norwood Edns.
Filene, Edward A. *see* Filene, Edward Albert.
Filene, Edward Albert, 1860-1937
xFilene, Edward A.
Speaking of Change: A Selection of Speeches & Articles. Arno.
Filene, Peter G.
xFilene, Peter G.
Americans & the Soviet Experiment, 1917-1933. Harvard U Pr.
Filer, L. J.
xFiler, L. J.
ed. Glutamic Acid: Advances in Biochemistry & Physiology. Raven.
Filey, Michael.
xFiley, Michael.
Toronto Album: Glimpses of the City That Was. U of Toronto Pr.
Filho, Fernando Venancio. *see* Venancio Filho, Fernando.
Filipiniana Book Guild.
xFilipiniana Book Guild.
ed. German Travelers on the Cordillera (1860-1890). Cellar.
Filkins, James H.
xFilkins, James H.
Lexicon of American Business Terms. Monarch Pr.
Fillastre, Jean Paul.
xFillastre, Jean-Paul.
ed. Nephrotoxicity: Interaction of Drugs with Membranes Systems Mitochondria-Lyososomes. Masson Pub.
Fillastre, Jean-Paul. *see* Fillastre, Jean Paul.
Filler, Louis, 1911-
xFiller, Louis.

ed. Abolition & Social Justice in the Era of Reform. Har-Row.
Appointment at Armageddon: Muckraking & Progressivism in American Life. Greenwood.
The Crusade Against Slavery, 1830-1860. Har-Row.
Dictionary of American Social Reform. Greenwood.
ed. From Populism to Progressivism: Representative Selections. Krieger.
Progressivism & Muckraking. Bowker.
ed. The Removal of the Cherokee Nation: Manifest Destiny or National Dishonor?. Krieger.
Vanguards & Followers: Youth in the American Tradition. Nelson-Hall.
Filley, Alan C.
xFilley, Alan C.
The Compleat Manager: What Works When. Res Press.
Fillian, Barbie.
xFillian, Barbie.
Eat Yourself Thin: Secrets of the Harbor Island Spas. Fell.
Fillingham, Paul.
xFillingham, Paul.
The Complete Book of Canoeing & Kayaking. Sterling.
Pilot's Guide to the Lesser Antilles. McGraw.
Filliou, Robert.
xFilliou, Robert.
Ample Food for Stupid Thought. Ultramarine Pub.
Fillmore, Charles, 1854-1948
xFillmore, Charles.
Prosperity. Unity Bks.
Revealing Word. Unity Bks.
Teach Us to Pray. Unity Bks.
Fillmore, Charles F. *see* Fillmore, Charles J.
Fillmore, Charles J.
xFillmore, Charles F.
ed. Individual Differences in Language Ability & Language Behavior. Acad Pr.
xFillmore, Charles J.
ed. Studies in Linguistic Semantics. Irvington.
Filon, Augustin. *see* Filon, Pierre Marie Augustin.
Filon, Pierre Marie Augustin, 1841-1916
xFilon, Augustin.
English Stage: Being an Account of the Victorian Drama. Arno.
Filson, Brent.
xFilson, Brent.
The Puma. Doubleday.
Filson, Sidney.
xFilson, Sidney.
How to Protect Yourself & Survive: From One Woman to Another. Watts.
Filstead, William. *see* Filstead, William J.
Filstead, William J.
xFilstead, William.
ed. Adolescence & Alcohol. Ballinger Pub.
xFilstead, William J.
ed. Alcohol & Alcohol Problems: New Thinking & New Directions. Ballinger Pub.
Filter, Maynard D.
xFilter, Maynard D.
Communication Disorders: A Handbook for Educators. C C Thomas.
Speech-Language Clinician's Handbook. C C Thomas.
Financial Analysis Group Ltd.
xFinancial Analysis Group Ltd.
ed. Britain's Top One Thousand Private Companies, 1974-5. British Bk Ctr.
Cash & Carry Retailing in the United Kingdom. Intl Pubns Serv.
Major Food Manufacturing Companies of Europe. Intl Pubns Serv.
Financial Pub Editors. *see* Financial Publishing Company.

Financial Publications. see Financial Publishing
  Company.
Financial Publishing Co. see Financial Publishing
  Company.
Financial Publishing Company.
  xFinancial Pub Editors.
    ed. Financial Pass-Through Yield & Value
      Tables for GNMA Mortgage-Backed
      Securities No. 715. Finan Pub.
  xFinancial Publications.
    Financial Capitalization Rate Tables No. 73.
      Finan Pub.
    Financial Monthly Mortgage Handbook: 6 per
      Cent to 15 per Cent No. 158. Finan Pub.
  xFinancial Publishing Co.
    Advance Payments Table No. 12. Finan Pub.
    Balloons, Residuals, & Renewals Tables No. 14.
      Finan Pub.
    Bond Yield Tables, Four Percent to Fourteen
      Percent Nos. 154, 254. Finan Pub.
    Continuous Compounding Growth Tables No.
      733. Finan Pub.
    Coupon Interest Calendar - 360-Day Basis No.
      360. Finan Pub.
    Coupon Interest Calendar - 365-Day Basis No.
      365. Finan Pub.
    Discount & Equivalent Interest Tables No.
      948. Finan Pub.
    Eight Rate & Prepayment Mortgage Yield
      Table No. 56. Finan Pub.
    Expanded Bond Values Tables. Finan Pub.
    Financial Compound Interest & Annuity Tables
      No. 376. Finan Pub.
    Financial Constant Percent Amortization Table
      No. 287. Finan Pub.
    Financial Monthly Refun Table, 78's Method
      No. 227. Finan Pub.
    Financial Mortgage Guide No. 149. Finan Pub.
    Financial Simple Interest Table, 360 Day Basis,
      No. 243: 4 Percent to 10 Percent by
      One-Fourth Percent. Finan Pub.
    High Coupon Callable Bond Values Tables No.
      74. Finan Pub.
    Holdback Tables No. 13. Finan Pub.
    Monthly Payment Direct Reduction Loan
      Amortization Schedules No.185. Finan Pub.
    Mortgage Payment Table No. 291. Finan Pub.
    Mortgage Payment Tables Nos. 67, 77, 153,
      193, 581, 392. Finan Pub.
    Mortgage Values Tables No. 207. Finan Pub.
    Net Yield After Capital Gains Tax 25 Percent
      No. 344, 30 Percent No. 444, 48 Percent No.
      544. Finan Pub.
    Net Yield Table for Gnma Mortgage Backed
      Securities No. 710. Finan Pub.
    Prepayment Mortgage Yield Table No. 435.
      Finan Pub.
    Savings Growth & Withdrawal Table:
      Individual Rates. Finan Pub.
    Truth-In-Lending Tables. Finan Pub.
    U. S. Treasury Bills Table No. 66. Finan Pub.
    Yields If Prepaid, Seventy-Eight's Method No.
      841. Finan Pub.
  xFinancial Publishing Company Staff.
    The Cost of Personal Borrowing in the United
      States. Finan Pub.
Financial Publishing Company Staff. see Financial
  Publishing Company.
Finar, I. L. see Finar, Ivor Lionel.
Finar, Ivor Lionel.
  xFinar, I. L.
    Stereochemistry & the Chemistry of Natural
      Products. Halsted Pr.
Finch, A. see Finch, Arthur.
Finch, Arthur.
  xFinch, A.
    Chemical Applications of Far Infrared
      Spectroscopy. Acad Pr.
Finch, Christofer. see Finch, Christopher.

Finch, Christopher.
  xFinch, Christofer.
    Rainbow: The Stormy Life of Judy Garland.
      Ballantine.
  xFinch, Christopher.
    Gone Hollywood. Doubleday.
    Norman Rockwell's America. Abrams.
    Rainbow: The Stormy Life of Judy Garland.
      G&D.
Finch, Curtis R.
  xFinch, Curtis R.
    Curriculum Development in Vocational &
      Technical Education: Planning Content &
      Implementation. Allyn.
Finch, Frank, 1911-
  xFinch, Frank.
    The Los Angeles Dodgers: The First Twenty
      Years. Jordan & Co.
Finch, George A. see Finch, George Augustus.
Finch, George Augustus, 1884-1957
  xFinch, George A.
    The Sources of Modern International Law.
      Johnson Repr.
Finch, I. J. see Finch, Ian J.
Finch, Ian J.
  xFinch, I. J.
    General Studies: First Handbook for Technical
      Students. Pergamon.
Finch, Karen.
  xFinch, Karen.
    Caring for Textiles. Watson-Guptill.
Finch, Marianne.
  xFinch, Marianne.
    Englishwoman's Experience in America. Negro
      U Pr.
Finch, Peter, 1947-
  xFinch, Peter.
    Typewriter Poems. Ultramarine Pub.
Finch, Phillip.
  xFinch, Phillip.
    Birthright. Seaview Bks.
Finch, Stuart M.
  xFinch, Stuart M.
    Fundamentals of Child Psychiatry. Norton.
Finch, Vernor C. see Finch, Vernor Clifford.
Finch, Vernor Clifford.
  xFinch, Vernor C.
    Geography of the World's Agriculture.
      Kennikat.
Fincham, J. R. S.
  xFincham, J. R. S.
    Genetic Complementation.
      Benjamin-Cummings.
Fincher. see Fincher, Ernest Barksdale.
Fincher, E. B. see Fincher, Ernest Barksdale.
Fincher, Ernest B. see Fincher, Ernest Barksdale.
Fincher, Ernest Barksdale, 1910-
  xFincher.
    The Vietnam War. Watts.
  xFincher, E. B.
    Spanish-Americans As a Political Factor in
      New Mexico, 1912-1950. Arno.
  xFincher, Ernest B.
    Government of the United States. P-H.
Fincher, Terry.
  xFincher, Terry.
    Creative Techniques in Photo Journalism.
      Lippincott & Crowell.
Finck, Furman J., 1900-
  xFinck, Furman J.
    Complete Guide to Portrait Painting.
      Watson-Guptill.
Finck, H. T. see Finck, Henry Theophilus.
Finck, Henry T. see Finck, Henry Theophilus.
Finck, Henry Theophilus, 1854-1926
  xFinck, H. T.
    My Adventures in the Golden Age of Music.
      Da Capo.
  xFinck, Henry T.

Chopin, & Other Musical Essays. Arno.
Massenet & His Operas. AMS Pr.
Primitive Love & Love-Stories. Gordon Pr.
Songs & Song Writers. Gordon Pr.
Songs & Song Writers. Longwood Pr.
Finder, Morris, 1917-
  xFinder, Morris.
    Reason & Art in Teaching Secondary-School
      English. Temple U Pr.
Findlay, Alexander.
  xFindlay, Alexander.
    Hundred Years of Chemistry. Humanities.
Findlay, James F., 1930-
  xFindlay, James F.
    Dwight L. Moody, American Evangelist:
      1837-1899. U of Chicago Pr.
Findlay, Jessie P. see Findlay, Jessie Patrick.
Findlay, Jessie Patrick.
  xFindlay, Jessie P.
    Footprints of Robert Burns. Folcroft.
Findlay, John R. see Findlay, John Ritchie.
Findlay, John Ritchie, 1824-1898
  xFindlay, John R.
    Personal Recollections of Thomas De Quincey.
      Folcroft.
Findler, N. V.
  xFindler, Nicholas V.
    ed. Associative Networks: The Representation
      & Use of Knowledge by Computers. Acad Pr.
Findler, Nicholas V. see Findler, N. V.
Findley, Carter V., 1941-
  xFindley, Carter V.
    Bureaucratic Reform in the Ottoman Empire:
      The Sublime Porte, 1789-1922. Princeton U
      Pr.
Findley, Rowe.
  xFindley, Rowe.
    Great American Deserts. Natl Geog.
Findley, Warren. see Findley, Warren George.
Findley, Warren George.
  xFindley, Warren.
    The Pros & Cons of Ability Grouping. Phi
      Delta Kappa.
Findling, John E.
  xFindling, John E.
    Dictionary of American Diplomatic History.
      Greenwood.
Findlow, Virginia H. see Findlow, Virginia Hallam.
Findlow, Virginia Hallam.
  xFindlow, Virginia H.
    Hysterical Histories. Windy Row.
Fine, Anne.
  xFine, Anne.
    The Summer-House Loon. T Y Crowell.
Fine, Ben.
  xFine, Ben.
    Rereading Capital. Columbia U Pr.
Fine, Carla.
  xFine, Carla.
    The Complete Guide to Foreign Medical
      Schools. Barron.
Fine, David M., 1934-
  xFine, David M.
    The City, the Immigrant, & American Fiction,
      1880-1920. Scarecrow.
Fine, Jo Renee.
  xFine, Jo Renee.
    The Synagogues of New York's Lower East
      Side. NYU Pr.
Fine, Joan.
  xFine, Joan.
    I Carve Stone. T Y Crowell.
Fine, Leonard W.
  xFine, Leonard W.
    Chemistry. Williams & Wilkins.
    Chemistry Decoded. Oxford U Pr.
Fine, Linda.
  xFine, Linda S.

The Complete Book of Hair Care, Hairstyling, & Hairstylists. Arco.
Fine, Linda S. see Fine, Linda.
Fine, Louis L., 1940-
xFine, Louis L.
After All We've Done for Them: Understanding Adolescent Behavior. P-H.
Fine, M. J. see Fine, Marvin J.
Fine, Marvin J.
xFine, M. J.
Intervention with Hyperactive Children: A Case Study Approach. Spectrum Pub.
xFine, Marvin J.
Principles & Techniques of Intervention with Hyperactive Children. C C Thomas.
Fine, Peter H. see Fine, Peter Heath.
Fine, Peter Heath.
xFine, Peter H.
Night Trains. Charter Bks.
Night Trains. Lippincott.
Fine, Peter J.
xFine, Peter J.
ed. Deafness in Infancy & Early Childhood. Williams & Wilkins.
Fine, Reuben, 1914-
xFine, Reuben.
Development of Freud's Thought: From the Beginnings (1886-1899) Through Id Psychology (1900-1914) to Ego Psychology (1914-1939). Aronson.
Fifty Chess Masterpieces: 1941-1944. Dover.
Great Moments in Modern Chess. Peter Smith.
A History of Psychoanalysis. Columbia U Pr.
Ideas Behind Chess Openings. McKay.
The Intimate Hour. Avery Pub.
Practical Chess Openings. McKay.
The Psychology of the Chess Player. Dover.
The World's Great Chess Games. McKay.
Fine, Sidney.
xFine, Sidney.
The American Past: Conflicting Interpretations of Great Issues. Macmillan.
Fine, Sidney. see Fine, Sidney A.
Fine, Sidney A, 1920-
xFine, Sidney.
Automobile Under the Blue Eagle: Labor, Management, & the Automobile Manufacturing Code. U of Mich Pr.
Fine, Terrence L.
xFine, Terrence L.
Theories of Probability: An Examination of Foundations. Acad Pr.
Fine, William F., 1943-
xFine, William F.
Progressive Evolutionism & American Sociology, 1890-1920. Univ Microfilms.
Finean, J. B.
xFinean, J. B.
Membranes & Their Cellular Functions. Halsted Pr.
Finegan, Jack, 1908-
xFinegan, Jack.
Archaeological History of the Ancient Middle East. Westview.
Archeology of the New Testament: The Life of Jesus & the Beginning of the Early Church. Princeton U Pr.
Finegold, Wilfred J.
xFinegold, Wilfred J.
Artificial Insemination. C C Thomas.
Fineman, Mark. see Fineman, Mark B.
Fineman, Mark B.
xFineman, Mark.
The Home Darkroom. Amphoto.
Finer, Herman, 1898-1969
xFiner, Herman.
Theory & Practice of Modern Government. Greenwood.
Finer, S. E. see Finer, Samuel Edward.
Finer, Samuel E. see Finer, Samuel Edward.

Finer, Samuel Edward.
xFiner, S. E.
ed. Five Constitutions. Humanities.
xFiner, Samuel E.
A Primer of Public Administration. Greenwood.
Fines, John.
xFines, John.
The Drama of History: An Experiment in Cooperative Teaching. Shoe String.
Fineshriber, William H.
xFineshriber, William H.
Stendhal the Romantic Rationalist. Folcroft.
Fingerman, M. see Fingerman, Milton.
Fingerman, Milton, 1928-
xFingerman, M.
Animal Diversity. HR&W.
Fingesten, Peter.
xFingesten, Peter.
Eclipse of Symbolism. U of SC Pr.
Finholt, Richard.
xFinholt, Richard.
American Visionary Fiction: Mad Metaphysics As Salvation Psychology. Kennikat.
Finifter, Ada W., 1938-
xFinifter, Ada W.
ed. Alienation & the Social System. Wiley.
Finizio, N.
xFinizio, Norman.
Ordinary Differential Equations with Modern Applications. Wadsworth Pub.
Finizio, Norman. see Finizio, N.
Fink, A. see Fink, Arthur Emil.
Fink, A. M. see Fink, Arlington M.
Fink, Arlene.
xFink, Arlene.
An Evaluation Primer. Capitol Pubns.
An Evaluation Primer. Sage.
Fink, Arlington M., 1922
xFink, A. M.
Almost Periodic Differential Equations. Springer-Verlag.
Fink, Arthur Emil, 1903-
xFink, A.
The Field of Social Work. HR&W.
Fink, B. Raymond. see Fink, Bernard Raymond.
Fink, Bernard Raymond.
xFink, B. Raymond.
The Human Larynx: A Functional Study. Raven.
Fink, Burton W.
xFink, Burton W.
Congenital Heart Disease: A Deductive Approach to Its Diagnosis. Year Bk Med.
Fink, Gary M.
xFink, Gary M.
Prelude to the Presidency: The Political Character & Legislative Leadership Style of Governor Jimmy Carter. Greenwood.
Fink, Karl J.
xFink, Karl J.
ed. The Quest for the New Science: Language & Thought in Eighteenth-Century Science. S Ill U Pr.
Fink, L. Dee, 1940-
xFink, L. Dee.
Listening to the Learner: An Exploratory Study of Personal Meaning in College Geography Courses. U Chicago Dept Geog.
Fink, Lawrence A.
xFink, Lawrence A.
Honors Teaching in American History. Tchrs Coll.
Fink, Max.
xFink, Max.
Convulsive Therapy: Theory & Practice. Raven.
ed. Psychobiology of Convulsive Therapy. Halsted Pr.
Fink, Paul. see Fink, Paul F.

Fink, Paul F.
xFink, Paul.
Moral Philosophy: An Introduction. Dickenson.
Fink, Paul J. see Fink, Paul Jay.
Fink, Paul Jay.
xFink, Paul J.
ed. Psychiatry & the Internist. Grune.
Fink, S. see Fink, Stuart S.
Fink, Stuart S.
xFink, S.
Business Data Processing. P-H.
Finkbeiner, Daniel T. see Finkbeiner, Daniel Talbot.
Finkbeiner, Daniel Talbot, 1919-
xFinkbeiner, Daniel T.
Introduction to Matrices & Linear Transformations. W H Freeman.
Finke, Blythe F. see Finke, Blythe Foote.
Finke, Blythe Foote.
xFinke, Blythe F.
Our Besieged Environment: The Pollution Problem. SamHar Pr.
Finkel, Coleman.
xFinkel, Coleman.
Professional Guide to Successful Meetings. Herman Pub.
Finkel, Donald.
xFinkel, Donald.
Answer Back. Atheneum.
Finkel, Jules, 1932-
xFinkel, Jules.
Computer-Aided Experimentation: Interfacing to Minicomputers. Wiley.
Finkel, Marion J.
xFinkel, Marion J.
Factors Influencing Clinical Research Success. Futura Pub.
Finkel, Norman J.
xFinkel, Norman J.
Therapy & Ethics: The Courtship of Law & Psychology. Grune.
Finkel, Saul.
xFinkel, Saul.
The Circular Seesaw. Pulse-Finger.
Finkelhor, David.
xFinkelhor, David.
Sexually Victimized Children. Free Pr.
Finkelhor, Dorothy C., 1902-
xFinkelhor, Dorothy C.
The Triumph of Age: How to Feel Young & Happy in Retirement. Follett.
Finkelstein, Barbara, 1937-
xFinkelstein, Barbara.
ed. Regulated Children - Liberated Children: Education in Psychohistorical Perspective. Psychohistory Pr.
Finkelstein, Haim, 1940-
xFinkelstein, Haim N.
Surrealism & the Crisis of the Object. Univ Microfilms.
Finkelstein, Haim N. see Finkelstein, Haim.
Finkelstein, Louis, 1895-
xFinkelstein, Louis.
Akiba: Scholar, Saint & Martyr. Atheneum.
Finkelstein, Michael O.
xFinkelstein, Michael O.
Quantitative Methods in Law: Studies in the Application of Mathematical Probability & Statistics to Legal Problems. Free Pr.
Finkelstein, Robert J., 1916-
xFinkelstein, Robert J.
Nonrelativistic Mechanics. Benjamin-Cummings.
Finkelstein, Sidney. see Finkelstein, Sidney Walter.
Finkelstein, Sidney Walter, 1909-
xFinkelstein, Sidney.
How Music Expresses Ideas. Intl Pub Co.
Finkenaur, Robert G., 1936-
xFinkenaur, Robert G.

COBOL for Students: A Programming Primer.
    Winthrop.
Finkle, Robert B.
    xFinkle, Robert B.
        Assessing Corporate Talent: A Key to
            Managerial Manpower Planning. Wiley.
Finkle-Strauss, Linda.
    xFinkle-Strauss, Linda.
        House Plants: How to Keep 'em Fat & Happy.
            McGraw.
Finlay, Ian H. *see* Finlay, Ian Hamilton.
Finlay, Ian Hamilton.
    xFinlay, Ian H.
        Honey by the Water. Black Sparrow.
Finlay, John L.
    xFinlay, John L.
        Canada in the North Atlantic Triangle: Two
            Centuries of Social Change. Oxford U Pr.
Finlay, Robert, 1940-
    xFinlay, Robert.
        Politics in Renaissance Venice. Rutgers U Pr.
Finlay, Winifred.
    xFinlay, Winifred.
        illus. Danger at Black Dyke. S G Phillips.
Finlayson, Ann.
    xFinlayson, Ann.
        Champions at Bat: Three Power Hitters.
            Garrard.
        Colonial Maryland. Elsevier-Nelson.
        Decathlon Men: Greatest Athletes in the
            World. Garrard.
        Greenhorn on the Frontier. Warne.
        House Cat. Warne.
        Rebecca's War. Warne.
        The Silver Bullet. Elsevier-Nelson.
Finlayson, Roderick.
    xFinlayson, Roderick.
        D'Arcy Cresswell. Twayne.
Finler, Joel. *see* Finler, Joel Waldo.
Finler, Joel Waldo.
    xFinler, Joel.
        Stroheim. U of Cal Pr.
Finley, Glenna.
    xFinley, Glenna.
        Dare to Love. NAL.
        Holiday for Love. NAL.
        Love's Magic Spell. NAL.
        Master of Love. NAL.
        Storm of Desire. NAL.
        Surrender My Love. NAL.
        When Love Speaks. NAL.
        Wildfire of Love. NAL.
    xFinley, Glenne.
        Reluctant Maiden. NAL.
Finley, Glenne. *see* Finley, Glenna.
Finley, James B. *see* Finley, James Bradley.
Finley, James Bradley, 1781-1856
    xFinley, James B.
        Life Among the Indians: Or, Personal
            Reminiscences & Historical Incidents
            Illustrative of Indian Life & Character. Arno.
        Memorials of Prison Life. Arno.
Finley, John H. *see* Finley, John Huston.
Finley, John Huston, 1904-
    xFinley, John H.
        Homer's Odyssey. Harvard U Pr.
Finley, Joseph E.
    xFinley, Joseph E.
        White Collar Union: The Story of the OPEIU
            and Its People. Octagon.
Finley, Lewis M.
    xFinley, Lewis M.
        The Complete Guide to Getting Yourself Out
            of Debt. Fell.
Finley, Lorraine N. *see* Finley, Lorraine Noel.
Finley, Lorraine Noel.
    xFinley, Lorraine N.
        Forever in Eden. Golden Quill.
Finley, M. I. *see* Finley, Moses I.

Finley, Mike, 1950-
    xFinley, Mike.
        Lucky You. Litmus.
        The Movie Under the Blindfold. Vanilla.
Finley, Moses I.
    xFinley, M. I.
        Ancient Greeks. Penguin.
        Ancient Sicily. Rowman.
        Atlas of Classical Archaeology. McGraw.
        Early Greece: The Bronze & Archaic Ages.
            Norton.
        The Olympic Games: The First Thousand
            Years. Viking Pr.
    xFinley, Moses I.
        Studies in Land & Credit in Ancient Athens,
            500-200 B. C.: The Horos-Inscriptions. Arno.
Finn, Edward E.
    xFinn, Edward E.
        These Are My Rites: A Brief History of the
            Eastern Rites of Christianity. Liturgical Pr.
Finn, J. *see* Finn, Jeremy D.
Finn, James.
    xFinn, James.
        ed. Peace, the Churches & the Bomb. Coun Rel
            & Intl.
Finn, Jeremy D.
    xFinn, J.
        General Model for Multivariate Analysis.
            HR&W.
Finn, Molly.
    xFinn, Molly.
        Summer Feasts. S&S.
Finn, Richard. *see* Finn, Richard P.
Finn, Richard P.
    xFinn, Richard.
        Your Fortune in Franchises. Contemp Bks.
    xFinn, Richard P.
        Your Fortune in Franchises. Contemp Bks.
Finn, Sidney B. *see* Finn, Sidney Bernard.
Finn, Sidney Bernard, 1908-
    xFinn, Sidney B.
        Clinical Pedodontics. Saunders.
Finnegan, John P. *see* Finnegan, John Patrick.
Finnegan, John Patrick.
    xFinnegan, John P.
        Against the Specter of a Dragon: The
            Campaign for American Military
            Preparedness, 1914-1917. Greenwood.
Finnegan, Marcus B.
    xFinnegan, Marcus B.
        The Law & Business of Licensing. Boardman.
Finnegan, Patrick. *see* Finnegan, Patrick S.
Finnegan, Patrick S.
    xFinnegan, Patrick.
        Broadcast Engineering & Maintenance
            Handbook. TAB Bks.
Finnegan, Ruth. *see* Finnegan, Ruth H.
Finnegan, Ruth H.
    xFinnegan, Ruth.
        Oral Poetry: Its Nature, Significance Social
            Context. Cambridge U Pr.
        ed. A World Treasury of Oral Poetry. Ind U
            Pr.
Finneran, Richard J.
    xFinneran, Richard J.
        ed. Anglo-Irish Literature: A Review of
            Research. Modern Lang.
Finnerty, Adam, 1944-
    xFinnerty, Adam.
        No More Plastic Jesus: Global Justice &
            Christian Lifestyle. Orbis Bks.
Finney, Ben, 1900-
    xFinney, Ben.
        Once a Marine, Always a Marine. Crown.
Finney, Brian.
    xFinney, Brian.
        Christopher Isherwood: A Critical Biography.
            Oxford U Pr.
Finney, Claude L. *see* Finney, Claude Lee.

Finney, Claude Lee.
    xFinney, Claude L.
        Evolution of Keats's Poetry. Russell.
Finney, D. J. *see* Finney, David John.
Finney, David J. *see* Finney, David John.
Finney, David John.
    xFinney, D. J.
        An Introduction to Statistical Science in
            Agriculture. Halsted Pr.
        Probit Analysis. Cambridge U Pr.
    xFinney, David J.
        Experimental Design & Its Statistical Basis. U
            of Chicago Pr.
Finney, Gretchen L. *see* Finney, Gretchen Ludke.
Finney, Gretchen Ludke.
    xFinney, Gretchen L.
        Musical Backgrounds for English Literature
            1580-1650. Greenwood.
Finney, Jack.
    xFinney, Jack.
        The Night People. PB.
Finney, Patricia, 1958-
    xFinney, Patricia.
        The Crow Goddess. Putnam.
Finney, Theodore M. *see* Finney, Theodore Mitchell.
Finney, Theodore Mitchell, 1902-
    xFinney, Theodore M.
        A History of Music. Greenwood.
Finnie, W. Bruce, 1934-
    xFinnie, W. Bruce.
        Topographic Terms in the Ohio Valley
            1748-1800. U of Ala Pr.
Finnigan, J.
    xFinnigan, John.
        Right People in the Right Jobs. Beekman Pubs.
Finnigan, John. *see* Finnigan, J.
Finnin, William M.
    xFinnin, William M.
        ed. The Morality of Scarcity: Limited
            Resources & Social Policy. La State U Pr.
Finniston, H. M.
    xFinniston, H. M.
        ed. Structural Characteristics of Materials.
            Burgess-Intl Ideas.
Finocchiaro, Mary. *see* Finocchiaro, Mary Bonomo.
Finocchiaro, Mary Bonomo, 1913-
    xFinocchiaro, Mary.
        Teaching Children Foreign Languages.
            McGraw.
        Teaching English As a Second Language.
            Har-Row.
Finocchiaro, Maurice A., 1942-
    xFinocchiaro, Maurice A.
        History of Science As Explanation. Wayne St
            U Pr.
Finot, Jean, 1858-1922
    xFinot, Jean.
        Race Prejudice. Arno.
        Race Prejudice. Negro U Pr.
Finston, Irving L.
    xFinston, Irving L.
        Inside Badminton. Contemp Bks.
Fintel, Mark.
    xFintel, Mark.
        ed. Handbook of Concrete Engineering. Van
            Nos Reinhold.
Fioravanzo, Giuseppe, 1891-
    xFioravanzo, Giuseppe.
        A History of Naval Tactical Thought. Naval
            Inst Pr.
Fioravanzo, Guiseppe. *see* Fioravanzo, Giuseppe.
Fiore, Robert L.
    xFiore, Robert L.
        Drama & Ethos: Natural-Law Ethics in Spanish
            Golden Age Theater. U Pr of Ky.
Fiorentino, Mary R.
    xFiorentino, Mary R.

Normal & Abnormal Development: The
Influence of Primitive Reflexes on Motor
Development. C C Thomas.
Reflex Testing Methods for Evaluating C. N. S.
Development. C C Thomas.
Fiorenza, Elisabeth S. see Fiorenza, Elisabeth Schussler.
Fiorenza, Elisabeth Schussler, 1938-
xFiorenza, Elisabeth S.
ed. Aspects of Religious Propaganda in Judaism
& Early Christianity. U of Notre Dame Pr.
xFiorenza, Elizabeth S.
The Apocalypse. Franciscan Herald.
Fiorenza, Elizabeth S. see Fiorenza, Elisabeth Schussler.
Firchow, Evelyn S. see Firchow, Evelyn Scherabon.
Firchow, Evelyn Scherabon.
xFirchow, Evelyn S.
tr. & ed. Icelandic Short Stories. Am
Scandinavian.
Fireman, Janet R.
xFireman, Janet R.
The Spanish Royal Corps of Engineers in the
Western Borderlands: Instrument of Bourbon
Reform, 1764-1815. A H Clark.
Fireman, Judy.
xFireman, Judy.
ed. The Cat Catalog. Workman Pub.
Firenze, Robert J.
xFirenze, Robert J.
The Process of Hazard Control. Kendall-Hunt.
Fireside, Harvey, 1929-
xFireside, Harvey.
Icon & Swastika: The Russian Orthodox
Church Under Nazi & Soviet Control.
Harvard U Pr.
Soviet Psychoprisons. Norton.
Firestone, J. M. see Firestone, John Mitchell.
Firestone, John Mitchell.
xFirestone, J. M.
Federal Receipts & Expenditures During
Business Cycles, 1879-1958. Natl Bur Econ
Res.
Federal Receipts & Expenditures During
Business Cycles: 1879-1958. Princeton U Pr.
Firey, Walter. see Firey, Walter Irving.
Firey, Walter Irving, 1916-
xFirey, Walter.
The Study of Possible Societies. Firey.
Firkins, Oscar. see Firkins, Oscar W.
Firkins, Oscar W., 1864-1932
xFirkins, Oscar.
Power & Elusiveness in Shelley. Octagon.
xFirkins, Oscar W.
Two Passengers for Chelsea & Other Plays.
Core Collection.
Firmage, D. Allan. see Firmage, David Allan.
Firmage, David Allan.
xFirmage, D. Allan.
Fundamental Theory of Structures. Krieger.
Firmage, Edwin B. see Firmage, Edwin Brown.
Firmage, Edwin Brown.
xFirmage, Edwin B.
Paul & the Expansion of the Church Today.
Deseret Bk.
Firmin, Peter.
xFirmin, Peter.
Basil Brush Finds Treasure. P-H.
Basil Brush in the Jungle. Schol Bk Serv.
illus. Basil Brush in the Jungle. P-H.
Firor, Ruth A. see Firor, Ruth Anita.
Firor, Ruth Anita.
xFiror, Ruth A.
Folkways in Thomas Hardy. A S Barnes.
Folkways in Thomas Hardy. Russell.
First Advanced Seminar in Economic Development. see
Advanced Seminar in Economic Development, 1st,
University at Austin, 1971.
First Edition Club, London.
xFirst Edition Club, London.

Bibliographical Catalogue of Lord Byron.
Folcroft.
First Illinois Conference on Medical Information
Systems, October 1974, Urbana, IL. see Illinois
Conference on Medical Information Systems, 1st,
University of Illinois, 1974.
First International Conference on Drag Reduction. see
International Conference on Drag Reduction,
Cambridge, Eng. 1974.
First International Congress of Quantum Chemistry,
Menton, France, July 4-10, 1973. see International
Congress on Quantum Chemistry, 1st, Menton, 1973.
First International Symposium on Wave & Tidal Energy.
see International Symposium on Wave and Tidal
Energy, Canterbury, England, 1978.
First, J. see First, Julia.
First, Julia.
xFirst, J.
Getting Smarter. P-H.
xFirst, Julia.
Amy. P-H.
Flat on My Face. Avon.
First, Ruth.
xFirst, Ruth.
Libya: The Elusive Revolution. Holmes &
Meier.
South West Africa. Peter Smith.
First Stanford Symposium. see Standard Symposium on
Mathematical Methods in the Social Sciences,
Stanford University, 1959.
First World Filtration Congress, May 14-17, 1974. see
World Filtration Congress, 1st, Paris, 1974.
Firth, C. H. see Firth, Sir Charles Harding.
Firth, Charles H. see Firth, Charles Harding.
Firth, Charles Harding, Sir, 1857-1936
xFirth, Charles H.
Oliver Cromwell & the Rule of the Puritans in
England. Oxford U Pr.
Political Significance of Gulliver's Travels.
Folcroft.
The Political Significance of Gulliver's Travels.
Peter Smith.
Firth, Frank E.
xFirth, Frank E.
Encyclopedia of Marine Resources. Van Nos
Reinhold.
Firth, Grace.
xFirth, Grace.
A Natural Year. S&S.
Stillroom Cookery: The Art of Preserving
Foods Naturally, with Recipes, Menus &
Metric Measures. EPM Pubns.
Firth, Peter. see Firth, Peter J.
Firth, Peter J.
xFirth, Peter.
Lord of the Seasons. John Knox.
Firth, Raymond. see Firth, Raymond William.
Firth, Raymond W. see Firth, Raymond William.
Firth, Raymond William, 1901-
xFirth, Raymond.
Families & Their Relatives, Kinship in a
Middle-Class Sector of London: An
Anthropological Study. Humanities.
Primitive Polynesian Economy. Norton.
xFirth, Raymond W.
Art & Life in New Guinea. AMS Pr.
Firth, Sir Charles Harding, 1857-1936
xFirth, C. H.
Stuart Tracts. Cooper Sq.
Fisch, Charles.
xFisch, Charles.
Digitalis. Grune.
Fisch, Edith L.
xFisch, Edith L.
Fisch on New York Evidence. Lond Pubns.
Fisch, Harold.
xFisch, Harold.

Hamlet & the Word: Covenant Pattern in
Shakespeare. Ungar.
Fischbacher, Theodore, 1909-
xFischbacher, Theodore.
A Study of the Role of the Federal
Government in the Education of the
American Indian. R & E Res Assoc.
Fischer, Al.
xFischer, Al.
Chili-Lovers' Cook Book. Golden West Pub.
Fischer, Ann M. see Fischer, John L.
Fischer, Bela.
xFischer, Bela.
The Human Exile. Philos Lib.
Fischer, Christiane, 1947-
xFischer, Christiane.
ed. Let Them Speak for Themselves: Women in
the American West 1849-1900. Dutton.
Let Them Speak for Themselves: Women in
the American West,1849-1900. Shoe String.
Fischer, Constance T.
xFischer, Constance T.
ed. Client Participation in Human Services:
The Prometheus Principle. Transaction Bks.
Fischer, David H. see Fischer, David Hackett.
Fischer, David Hackett, 1935-
xFischer, David H.
Historians' Fallacies: Toward a Logic of
Historical Thought. Har-Row.
Fischer, Donald E.
xFischer, Donald E.
Security Analysis & Portfolio Management.
P-H.
Fischer, Edward.
xFischer, Edward.
Light in the Far East: Archbishop Harold
Henry's Forty-Two Years in Korea. Seabury.
Mindanao Mission: Archbishop Patrick
Cronin's Forty Years in the Phillipines.
Seabury.
Fischer, Eleanor.
xFischer, Eleanor.
Unfinished Things. Morrow.
Fischer, Eric.
xFischer, Eric.
A German & English Glossary of Geographical
Terms. Greenwood.
Fischer, Ernst, 1899-
xFischer, Ernst.
Art Against Ideology. Braziller.
Fischer, Fritz, 1908-
xFischer, Fritz.
Germany's Aims in the First World War.
Norton.
World Power or Decline: The Controversy
Over Germany's Aims in the First World
War. Norton.
Fischer, G. see Fischer, Gerd.
Fischer, George.
xFischer, George.
ed. Revival of American Socialism: Selected
Papers of the Socialist Scholars Conference.
Oxford U Pr.
ed. Revival of American Socialism: Selected
Papers of the Socialist Scholars Conference.
Oxford U Pr.
Fischer, Georges.
xFischer, Georges.
The Non-Proliferation of Nuclear Weapons.
Cyrco Pr.
The Non-Proliferation of Nuclear Weapons.
Irvington.
The Non-Proliferation of Nuclear Weapons.
State Mutual Bk.
Fischer, Gerd, 1939-
xFischer, G.
Complex Analytic Geometry. Springer-Verlag.
Fischer, Gretl. see Fischer, Gretl K.
Fischer, Gretl K.
xFischer, Gretl.

In Search of Jerusalem: Religion & Ethics in
the Writings of A. M. Klein. McGill-Queens
U Pr.

Fischer, Harry C.
xFischer, Harry C.
The Uses of Accounting in Collective
Bargaining. U Cal LA Indus Rel.

Fischer, Helmut A.
xFischer, Helmut A.
Autoradiography. De Gruyter.

Fischer, James A.
xFischer, James A.
God Said: Let There Be Woman: A Study of
Biblical Women. Alba.

Fischer, Joel.
xFischer, Joel.
Effective Casework Practice: An Eclectic
Approach. McGraw.
The Effectiveness of Social Casework. C C
Thomas.

Fischer, John I. see Fischer, John Irwin.

Fischer, John Irwin, 1940-
xFischer, John I.
On Swift's Poetry. U Presses Fla.

Fischer, John L.
xFischer, Ann M.
jt. auth. Eastern Carolines. HRAFP.
xFischer, John L.
Eastern Carolines. HRAFP.

Fischer, Josef E.
xFischer, Josef E.
Total Parenteral Nutrition. Little.

Fischer, Kathleen B.
xFischer, Kathleen B.
Political Ideology & Educational Reform in
Chile, 1964-1976. UCLA Lat Am Ctr.

Fischer, Louis, 1896-1970
xFischer, Louis.
Great Challenge. Kennikat.
Life of Mahatma Gandhi. Macmillan.
Men & Politics: An Autobiography.
Greenwood.
Soviet Journey. Greenwood.
The Story of Indonesia. Greenwood.
This Is Our World. Greenwood.

Fischer, Norman, 1943-
xFischer, Norman.
Economy & Self: Philosophy & Economics
from the Mercantilists to Marx. Greenwood.

Fischer, Pauline.
xFischer, Pauline.
Egyptian Designs in Modern Stitchery. Dutton.

Fischer, Peter, 1939-
xFischer, Peter.
A Collection of International Concessions &
Related Instruments. Oceana.

Fischer, Raymond L.
xFischer, Raymond L.
Speaking to Communicate: An Introduction to
Speech. Dickenson.

Fischer, Robert. see Fischer, Robert James.

Fischer, Robert James.
xFischer, Robert.
Hot Dog!. Messner.

Fischer, Stanley.
xFischer, Stanley.
ed. Rational Expectations & Economic Policy.
U of Chicago Pr.

Fischer-Galati, Stephen. see Fischer-Galati, Stephen A.

Fischer-Galati, Stephen A.
xFischer-Galati, Stephen.
Ottoman Imperialism & German Protestantism,
1521-1555. Octagon.
The Socialist Republic of Rumania. Johns
Hopkins.
Twentieth Century Rumania. Columbia U Pr.

Fischler, Stan.
xFischler, Stan.

Garry Unger & the Battling Blues. Dodd.
Getting into Pro Soccer. Watts.
Hockey's Great Rivalries. Random.

Fischman, Burton L.
xFischman, Burton L.
Business Report Writing. Par Inc.

Fischman, Walter. see Fischman, Walter Ian.

Fischman, Walter Ian.
xFischman, Walter.
Furniture Finishing. Bobbs.

Fish, C. R. see Fish, Carl Russell.
Fish, Carl R. see Fish, Carl Russell.

Fish, Carl Russell, 1876-1932
xFish, C. R.
Guide to the Materials for American History in
Roman & Other Italian Archives. Kraus
Repr.
xFish, Carl R.
Civil Service & the Patronage. Russell.

Fish, Enrica.
xFish, Enrica.
Cat in Art. Lerner Pubns.

Fish, Gertrude S. see Fish, Gertrude Sipperly.

Fish, Gertrude Sipperly.
xFish, Gertrude S.
ed. The Story of Housing. Macmillan.

Fish, Hamilton, 1888-
xFish, Hamilton.
An American Manifesto of Freedom in Answer
to the Manifesto on Communism (1848).
Vantage.
The American People Are Living on Top of a
Nuclear Volcano. Vantage.

Fish, Helen D. see Fish, Helen Dean.

Fish, Helen Dean.
xFish, Helen D.
Boy's Book of Verse: An Anthology.
Lippincott.

Fish, Lydia M.
xFish, Lydia M.
The Folklore of the Coal Miners of the
Northeast of England. Folcroft.

Fish, Marie Poland.
xFish, Marie Poland.
Sounds of Western North Atlantic Fishes: A
Reference File of Biological Underwater
Sounds. Johns Hopkins.

Fish, Peter G. see Fish, Peter Graham.

Fish, Peter Graham.
xFish, Peter G.
The Politics of Federal Judicial Administration.
Princeton U Pr.

Fish, Robert L.
xFish, Robert L.
Gold of Troy. Doubleday.
A Gross Carriage of Justice. Doubleday.
Pursuit: A Novel. Doubleday.

Fish, Roy J.
xFish, Roy J.
Giving a Good Invitation. Broadman.

Fish, Stanley E. see Fish, Stanley Eugene.

Fish, Stanley Eugene.
xFish, Stanley E.
The Living Temple: George Herbert &
Catechizing. U of Cal Pr.

Fishback, W. T. see Fishback, William Thompson.

Fishback, William Thompson.
xFishback, W. T.
Projective & Euclidean Geometry. Wiley.

Fishbane, Joyce D.
xFishbane, Joyce O.
Politics of the Purse: Revenue & Finance in the
Sixth Illinois Constitutional Convention. U of
Ill Pr.

Fishbane, Joyce O. see Fishbane, Joyce D.
Fishbein, Harold. see Fishbein, Harold D.

Fishbein, Harold D.
xFishbein, Harold.

Evolution, Development & Children's
Learning. Goodyear.

Fishbein, Justin.
xFishbein, Justin.
Intro. by A Question of Competence:
Language, Intelligence, & Learning to Read.
SRA.

Fishbein, L. see Fishbein, Lawrence.

Fishbein, Lawrence.
xFishbein, L.
Potential Industrial Carcinogens & Mutagens.
Elsevier.
xFishbein, Lawrence.
Chemical Mutagens: Environmental Effects on
Biological Systems. Acad Pr.

Fishbein, Martin.
xFishbein, Martin.
Readings in Attitude Theory & Measurement.
Wiley.

Fishbein, Morris, 1889-
xFishbein, Morris.
Dr. Fishbein's Popular Illustrated Medical
Encyclopedia. Doubleday.
ed. Doctors at War. Arno.

Fishbein, William.
xFishbein, William.
ed. Sleep, Dreams & Memory: Advances in
Sleep Research. Spectrum Pub.

Fishburn, Angela.
xFishburn, Angela.
The Complete Home Guide to Making Pillows,
Draperies, Lampshades, Quilts & Slipcovers.
Larousse.

Fishburn, Katherine, 1944-
xFishburn, Katherine.
Richard Wright's Hero: The Faces of a
Rebel-Victim. Scarecrow.

Fishburn, Peter C.
xFishburn, Peter C.
Mathematics of Decision Theory. Mouton.
The Theory of Social Choice. Princeton U Pr.
Utility Theory for Decision Making. Krieger.

Fishel, Andrew.
xFishel, Andrew.
National Politics & Sex Discrimination in
Education. Lexington Bks.

Fishel, Jeff.
xFishel, Jeff.
Intro. by Parties & Elections in an Anti-Party
Age: American Politics & the Crisis of
Confidence. Ind U Pr.

Fishel, Wesley R.
xFishel, Wesley R.
The End of Extraterritoriality in China.
Octagon.

Fisher. see Fisher, Frank David.
Fisher, A. see Fisher, A. James.

Fisher, A. Garth.
xFisher, A. Garth.
The Complete Book of Physical Fitness.
Brigham.
Jogging. Wm C Brown.

Fisher, A. James, 1939-
xFisher, A.
Security for Business & Industry. P-H.

Fisher, Aileen. see Fisher, Aileen Lucia.

Fisher, Aileen Lucia.
xFisher, Aileen.

ed. The Science of Life: Contributions of
    Biology to Human Welfare. Plenum Pub.

Fisher, Kenneth P.
  xFisher, Kenneth P.
    Franchising Justice: The Office of Economic
      Opportunity Legal Services Program &
      Traditional Legal Aid. Am Bar Foun.

Fisher, L. E. *see* Fisher, Lillian Estelle.

Fisher, Leonard E. *see* Fisher, Leonard Everett.

Fisher, Leonard Everett.
  xFisher, Leonard E.
    illus. Across the Sea from Galway. Schol Bk
      Serv.
    Alphabet Art: Thirteen Abcs from Around the
      World. Schol Bk Serv.
    illus. Doctors. Watts.
    The Factories. Holiday.
    The Homemakers. Watts.
    illus. The Hospitals. Holiday.
    illus. Papermakers. Watts.
    illus. Peddlers. Watts.
    illus. Potters. Watts.
    Printers. Watts.
    The Railroads. Holiday.
    illus. A Russian Farewell. Schol Bk Serv.
    illus. Silversmiths. Watts.
    illus. Tanners. Watts.
  xFisher, Leonard Everett.
    The Death of Evening Star: The Diary of a
      Young New England Whaler. Doubleday.
    Leonard Everett Fisher's Liberty Book.
      Doubleday.
    Noonan: A Novel About Baseball, ESP & Time
      Warps. Doubleday.
    Sweeney's Ghost. Doubleday.

Fisher, Lillian E. *see* Fisher, Lillian Estelle.

Fisher, Lillian Estelle, 1891-
  xFisher, L. E.
    The Background of the Revolution for Mexican
      Independence. Gordon Pr.
  xFisher, Lillian E.
    Background of the Revolution for Mexican
      Independence. Russell.
    Intendant System in Spanish America.
      Gordian.

Fisher, Lloyd.
  xFisher, Lloyd.
    Fixed Effects Analysis of Variance. Acad Pr.

Fisher, Lois. *see* Fisher, Lois H.

Fisher, Lois H., 1936-
  xFisher, Lois.
    A Literary Gazetteer of England. McGraw.

Fisher, Louis.
  xFisher, Louis.
    The Constitution Between Friends: Congress,
      the President, & the Law. St Martin.

Fisher, M. F. *see* Fisher, Mary Frances Kennedy.

Fisher, Mae. *see* Fisher, Mae Therese.

Fisher, Mae Therese, 1913-
  xFisher, Mae.
    Lipreading for a More Active Life. Alexander
      Graham.

Fisher, Margaret.
  xFisher, Margaret.
    Colonial America. Fideler.

Fisher, Margery M.
  xFisher, Margery M.
    One & One. Dial.

Fisher, Marvin. *see* Fisher, Marvin Junior.

Fisher, Marvin Junior, 1927-
  xFisher, Marvin.
    Going Under: Melville's Short Fiction & the
      American 1850's. La State U Pr.

Fisher, Mary, 1858-
  xFisher, Mary.
    A Group of French Critics. Arno.

Fisher, Mary Frances Kennedy, 1908-
  xFisher, M. F.

The Art of Eating. Random.
With Bold Knife & Fork. Putnam.

Fisher, Mildred L.
  xFisher, Mildred L.
    Albatross of Midway Island: A Natural History
      of the Laysan Albatross. S Ill U Pr.
    jt. auth. Wonders of the World of the
      Albatross. Dodd.

Fisher, Miles Mark, 1899-
  xFisher, Miles M.
    Negro Slave Songs in the United States.
      Citadel Pr.
    Negro Slave Songs in the United States.
      Russell.

Fisher, Morris.
  xFisher, Morris.
    Provinces & Provincial Capitals of the World.
      Scarecrow.

Fisher, Patty.
  xFisher, Patty.
    The Value of Food. Oxford U Pr.

Fisher, Peter.
  xFisher, Peter.
    Special Teachers-Special Boys. St Martin.

Fisher, R. V. *see* Fisher, Richard Virgil.

Fisher, Ralph E., 1920-
  xFisher, Ralph E.
    Vanishing Markers: Memories of Boston &
      Maine Railroading 1946-1952. Greene.

Fisher, Richard. *see* Fisher, Richard B.

Fisher, Richard B.
  xFisher, Richard.
    Joseph Lister. Stein & Day.
  xFisher, Richard B.
    A Dictionary of Drugs: The Medicines You
      Use. Schocken.
    Syrie Maugham. Biblio Dist.

Fisher, Richard Virgil, 1928-
  xFisher, R. V.
    Pyrogenic Mineral Stability, Lower Member of
      the John Day Formation, Eastern Oregon. U
      of Cal Pr.

Fisher, Robert.
  xFisher, Robert.
    Intensive Clerical & Civil Service Training. SW
      Pub.

Fisher, Robert C. *see* Fisher, Robert Charles.

Fisher, Robert Charles.
  xFisher, Robert C.
    Calculus & Analytic Geometry. P-H.

Fisher, Robert J.
  xFisher, Robert J.
    Learning How to Learn: The English Primary
      School & American Education. HarBraceJ.

Fisher, Robert T. *see* Fisher, Robert Thaddeus.

Fisher, Robert Thaddeus.
  xFisher, Robert T.
    Classical Utopian Theories of Education. Coll
      & U Pr.

Fisher, Roger. *see* Fisher, Roger Drummer.

Fisher, Roger Drummer, 1922-
  xFisher, Roger.
    Points of Choice. Oxford U Pr.

Fisher, Ronald. *see* Fisher, Ronald Aylmer.

Fisher, Ronald A. *see* Fisher, Sir Ronald Aylmer.

Fisher, Ronald Aylmer, Sir, 1890-1962
  xFisher, Ronald.
    The Genetical Theory of Natural Selection.
      Dover.

Fisher, Ronald M.
  xFisher, Ronald M.
    The Appalachian Trail. Natl Geog.

Fisher, S. G. *see* Fisher, Sydney George.

Fisher, Sethard.
  xFisher, Sethard.
    Black Elected Officials in California. R & E
      Res Assoc.

Fisher, Seymour.
  xFisher, Seymour.

What We Really Know About Childrearing:
    Science in Support of Effective Parenting.
    Basic.

Fisher, Sidney G. *see* Fisher, Sydney George.

Fisher, Sir Ronald Aylmer, 1890-
  xFisher, Ronald A.
    Theory of Inbreeding. Acad Pr.

Fisher, Sydney G. *see* Fisher, Sydney George.

Fisher, Sydney George, 1856-1927
  xFisher, S. G.
    Men, Women & Manners in Colonial Times.
      Gordon Pr.
  xFisher, Sidney G.
    The True History of the American Revolution.
      Irvington.
  xFisher, Sydney G.
    Men, Women & Manners in Colonial Times.
      Gale.
    The Struggle for American Independence.
      Arno.

Fisher, Sydney N. *see* Fisher, Sydney Nettleton.

Fisher, Sydney Nettleton.
  xFisher, Sydney N.
    ed. France & the European Community. Ohio
      St U Pr.
    The Middle East: A History. Knopf.
    Middle East: A History. Knopf.

Fisher, T. M.
  xFisher, T. M.
    Images. Ghost Dance.

Fisher, Terry.
  xFisher, Terry.
    A Class Act. Warner Bks.

Fisher, Timothy.
  xFisher, Timothy.
    Hammocks, Hassocks & Hideaways. A-W.

Fisher, Vardis.
  xFisher, Vardis.
    Gold Rushes & Mining Camps of the Early
      American West. Caxton.

Fisher, Wallace E.
  xFisher, Wallace E.
    Stand Fast in Faith: Finding Freedom Through
      Discipline in the Ten Commandments.
      Abingdon.
    Who Dares to Preach?: The Challenge of
      Biblical Preaching. Augsburg.

Fisher, Walter.
  xFisher, Walter.
    Human Services: The Third Revolution in
      Mental Health. Alfred Pub.

Fisher, Walter D. *see* Fisher, Walter Dummer.

Fisher, Walter Dummer, 1916-
  xFisher, Walter D.
    Clustering & Aggregation in Economics. Johns
      Hopkins.

Fisher, William A. *see* Fisher, William Arms.

Fisher, William Arms, 1861-1948
  xFisher, William A.
    Notes on Music in Old Boston. AMS Pr.

Fisher, William H. *see* Fisher, William Harvey.

Fisher, William Harvey, 1950-
  xFisher, William H.
    Free at Last: A Bibliography of Martin Luther
      King, Jr.. Scarecrow.
    The Invisible Empire: A Bibliography of the Ku
      Klux Klan. Scarecrow.

Fishlow, Albert.
  xFishlow, Albert.
    American Railroads & the Transformation of
      the Ante-Bellum Economy. Harvard U Pr.
    The Mature Neighbor Policy: A New United
      States Economic Policy for Latin America. U
      of Cal Intl St.

Fishman, Alfred P.
  xFishman, Alfred P.

ed. Heart Failure. McGraw.
ed. Pulmonary Circulation & Interstitial Space. U of Chicago Pr.

Fishman, George S.
xFishman, George S.
Principles of Discrete Event Simulation. Wiley.
Spectral Methods in Econometrics. Harvard U Pr.
Fishman, J. *see* Fishman, Joshua A.
Fishman, J. A. *see* Fishman, Joshua A.
Fishman, Joseph F. *see* Fishman, Joseph Fulling.

Fishman, Joseph Fulling.
xFishman, Joseph F.
Crucibles of Crime: The Shocking Story of the American Jail. Patterson Smith.

Fishman, Joshua A.
xFishman, J.
Advances in the Creation & Revision of Writing Systems. Mouton.
xFishman, J. A.
ed. Advances in the Study of Societal Multilingualism. Mouton.
xFishman, Joshua A.
Hungarian Language Maintenance in the United States. Res Ctr Lang Semiotic.
Language Loyalty in the United States. Arno.

Fishman, Ken.
xFishman, Ken.
Paradise. Dell.
Paradise. T Y Crowell.

Fishman, Lew.
xFishman, Lew.
ed. Golf Magazine's Shortcuts to Better Golf. Har-Row.

Fishman, Mark, 1947-
xFishman, Mark.
Manufacturing the News. U of Tex Pr.

Fishman, Morris.
xFishman, Morris.
The Actor in Training. Greenwood.

Fishman, Robert
xFishman, Robert.
Criminal Recidivism in New York City: An Evaluation of the Impact of Rehabilitation & Diversion Services. Praeger.

Fishman, Robert A.
xFishman, Robert A.
Cerebrospinal Fluid in Diseases of the Nervous System. Saunders.

Fishman, Sterling.
xFishman, Sterling.
ed. Teacher, Student, & Society: Perspectives on Education. Little.

Fishtein, Ruth.
xFishtein, Ruth.
Classroom Psychology. Book-Lab.

Fishwick, J. H., 1932-
xFishwick, J. H.
Applications of Lithium in Ceramics. CBI Pub.

Fishwick, Marshal William.
xFishwick, Marshall W.
Great Silver Crowns. Golden Quill.
Fishwick, Marshall W. *see* Fishwick, Marshal William.

Fishwick, Marshall William.
xFishwick, Marshall W.
ed. American Studies in Transition. U of Pa Pr.
Lee After the War. Greenwood.
Fisk, George M. *see* Fisk, George Mygatt.

Fisk, George Mygatt, 1864-1910
xFisk, George M.
Continental Opinion Regarding a Proposed Middle European Tariff-Union. AMS Pr.
Fisk, James W. *see* Fisk, James Waddingham.

Fisk, James Waddingham, 1926-
xFisk, James W.
A Practical Guide to Management of the Painful Neck & Back: Diagnosis, Manipulation, Exercises, Prevention. C C Thomas.
Fisk, Loretta Z. *see* Fisk, Lori.

Fisk, Lori.
xFisk, Loretta Z.
A Survival Guide for Teachers. Wiley.

Fisk, Milton.
xFisk, Milton.
Ethics & Society: A Marxist Interpretation of Value. NYU Pr.

Fisk, Nicholas.
xFisk, Nicholas.
Escape from Splatterbang. Macmillan.
Grinny: A Novel of Science Fiction. Elsevier-Nelson.
Monster Maker. Macmillan.
Space Hostages. Macmillan.

Fisk, Samuel.
xFisk, Samuel.
Divine Healing Under the Searchlight. Reg Baptist.
Divine Sovereignty & Human Freedom. Loizeaux.
Fisk University Library (Nashville). *see* Fisk University, Nashville. Library.

Fisk University, Nashville. Library.
xFisk University Library (Nashville).
Dictionary Catalog of the Negro Collection of the Fisk University Library. G K Hall.

Fisk University, Nashville. Social Science Institute.
xSocial Science Institute Fisk Univ.
Unwritten History of Slavery. IHS-PDS.

Fiske, Charles, Bp, 1868-1942
xFiske, Charles.
Confessions of a Puzzled Parson, & Other Pleas for Reality. Arno.
Fiske, Horace S. *see* Fiske, Horace Spencer.

Fiske, Horace Spencer, 1859-1940
xFiske, Horace S.
Provincial Types in American Fiction. Kennikat.

Fiske, John.
xFiske, John.
Reading Television. Methuen Inc.

Fiske, Loring.
xFiske, Loring.
How to Beat Better Tennis Players. Doubleday.
How to Beat Better Tennis Players. Wilshire.

Fiske, Roger.
xFiske, Roger.
English Theatre Music in the Eighteenth Century. Oxford U Pr.

Fiske, Stephen, 1840-1916
xFiske, Stephen.
Off-Hand Portraits of Prominent New Yorkers. Arno.

Fison, J. E.
xFison, J. E.
Understanding the Old Testament: The Way of Holiness. Greenwood.

Fisz, Marek.
xFisz, Marek.
Probability Theory & Mathematical Statistics. Krieger.

Fitch, A. A.
xFitch, A. A.
ed. Developments in Geophysical Exploration Methods. Burgess-Intl Ideas.
Fitch, Bob. *see* Fitch, Robert Beck.
Fitch, Charles M. *see* Fitch, Charles Marden.

Fitch, Charles Marden.
xFitch, Charles M.
The Complete Book of Houseplants. Dutton.
Complete Book of Houseplants. Dutton.
The Complete Book of Miniature Roses. Dutton.
The Complete Book of Miniature Roses. Dutton.
Fitch, E. C. *see* Fitch, Ernest C.

Fitch, Ernest C.
xFitch, E. C.
Introduction to Fluid Logic. McGraw.
Fitch, Florence M. *see* Fitch, Florence Mary.

Fitch, Florence Mary, 1875-
xFitch, Florence M.
Their Search for God: Ways of Worship in the Orient. Lothrop.
Fitch, George H. *see* Fitch, George Hamlin.

Fitch, George Hamlin, 1852-1925
xFitch, George H.
Comfort Found in Good Old Books. Arno.
Comfort Found in Good Old Books. Gordon Pr.
Great Spiritual Writers of America. Arno.
Great Spiritual Writers of America. Folcroft.
Great Spiritual Writers of America. Gordon Pr.
Fitch, Harry N. *see* Fitch, Harry Norton.

Fitch, Harry Norton, 1887-
xFitch, Harry N.
Analysis of the Supervisory Activities & Techniques of the Elementary School Training Supervisor in State Normal Schools & Teachers Colleges. AMS Pr.
Fitch, James M. *see* Fitch, James Marston.

Fitch, James Marston.
xFitch, James M.
American Building: The Environmental Forces That Shape It. Schocken.

Fitch, John, 1743-1798
xFitch, John.
The Original Steam-Boat Supported: Or, Reply to Mr. James Rumsey's Pamphlet. Arno.

Fitch, John E.
xFitch, John E.
Marine Food & Game Fishes of California. U of Cal Pr.
Fitch, Kenneth. *see* Fitch, Kenneth Leonard.

Fitch, Kenneth Leonard.
xFitch, Kenneth.
Human Life Science. HR&W.
Fitch, Lyle C. *see* Fitch, Lyle Craig.

Fitch, Lyle Craig.
xFitch, Lyle C.
ed. Agenda for a City: Issues Confronting New York. Sage.

Fitch, Richard D.
xFitch, Richard D.
Accidental or Incendiary. C C Thomas.

Fitch, Robert Beck, 1938-
xFitch, Bob.
My Eyes Have Seen. New Glide.
Fitch, Robert E. *see* Fitch, Robert Elliot.

Fitch, Robert Elliot, 1902-
xFitch, Robert E.
Certain Blind Man: And Other Essays on the American Mood. Arno.
Fitter, Richard. *see* Fitter, Richard Sidney Richmond.

Fitter, Richard Sidney Richmond.
xFitter, Richard.
Vanishing Wild Animals of the World. Watts.

Fitti, Charles J.
xFitti, Charles J.
Between God & Man. Philos Lib.
Fitting, James E. *see* Fitting, James Edward.

Fitting, James Edward.
xFitting, James E.
The Archaeology of Michigan: A Guide to the Prehistory of the Great Lakes Region. Cranbrook.

Fittipaldi, Silvio.
xFittipaldi, Silvio.
How to Pray Always Without Always Praying. Fides Claretian.
Fitton, A. O. *see* Fitton, Alan Ogden.

Fitton, Alan Ogden.
xFitton, A. O.
Practical Heterocyclic Chemistry. Acad Pr.

Fitts, Donald D.
xFitts, Donald D.
Vector Analysis in Chemistry. McGraw.

Fitts, Dudley.
xFitts, Dudley.

ed. Anthology of Contemporary Latin
American Poetry. Greenwood.
ed. Greek Plays in Modern Translation. Dial.
Fitts, Leroy.
xFitts, Leroy.
Lott Carey: First Black Missionary to Africa.
Judson.
Fitts, Paul M. *see* Fitts, Paul Morris.
Fitts, Paul Morris.
xFitts, Paul M.
Human Performance. Greenwood.
Fitz, Jean D. *see* Fitz, Jean Dewitt.
Fitz, Jean Dewitt.
xFitz, Jean D.
Devon Maze. Geron-X.
Fitz-Gibbon, Carol. *see* Fitz-Gibbon, Carol Taylor.
Fitz-Gibbon, Carol Taylor.
xFitz-Gibbon, Carol.
How to Calculate Statistics. Sage.
How to Design a Program Evaluation. Sage.
Fitz-Simons, Marian J. *see* Fitz-Simons, Marian
Josephine.
Fitz-Simons, Marian Josephine, 1895-
xFitz-Simons, Marian J.
Some Parent-Child Relationships As Shown in
Clinical Case Studies. AMS Pr.
Fitzgerald, Adolf A. *see* Fitzgerald, Adolf Alexander.
Fitzgerald, Adolf Alexander, Sir, 1890-
xFitzgerald, Adolf A.
Current Accounting Trends. Arno.
Fitzgerald, Adolphus L. *see* Fitzgerald, Adolphus Leigh.
Fitzgerald, Adolphus Leigh, 1840-
xFitzgerald, Adolphus L.
Thirty Years' War on Silver. Greenwood.
Fitzgerald, Arda F. *see* Fitzgerald, John M.
Fitzgerald, Brian.
xFitzgerald, Brian.
The Anglo-Irish: Three Representative Types,
Cork, Ormonde, Swift, 1602-1745. Folcroft.
Daniel Defoe: A Study in Conflict. Arden Lib.
Daniel Defoe: A Study in Conflict. Folcroft.
Daniel Defoe: A Study in Conflict. Somerset
Pub.
Fitzgerald, C. P. *see* Fitzgerald, Charles Patrick.
Fitzgerald, Cathleen.
xFitzGerald, Cathleen.
Let's Find Out About Bees. Watts.
Let's Find Out About Words. Watts.
Fitzgerald, Charles P. *see* Fitzgerald, Charles Patrick.
Fitzgerald, Charles Patrick, 1902-
xFitzgerald, C. P.
China: A Short Cultural History. Barrie &
Jenkins.
China: A Short Cultural History. Quaker City.
Son of Heaven: A Biography of Li Shih-Min,
Founder of the T'ang Dynasty. Chinese
Materials.
xFitzgerald, Charles P.
Mao Tse-Tung & China. Holmes & Meier.
Son of Heaven: A Biography of Li Shih-Min,
Founder of the T'ang Dynasty. AMS Pr.
Fitzgerald, David.
xFitzgerald, David.
photos by Oklahoma. Graphic Arts Ctr.
Fitzgerald, Donalie.
xFitzgerald, Donalie.
Edith L. Randall's Your Place in the Cards.
Bobbs.
Fitzgerald, Edmond J. *see* Fitzgerald, Edmond James.
Fitzgerald, Edmond James, 1912-
xFitzgerald, Edmond J.
Marine Painting in Watercolor. Watson-Guptill.
Fitzgerald, Edward.
xFitzgerald, Edward.

Dictionary of Madame De Sevigne. B Franklin.
Letters & Literary Remains of Edward
Fitzgerald. AMS Pr.
Letters & Literary Remains of Edward
Fitzgerald. Folcroft.
Letters of Edward Fitzgerald. Folcroft.
Letters of Edward Fitzgerald. S Ill U Pr.
Some New Letters of Edward Fitzgerald.
Folcroft.
Fitzgerald, Ernest A.
xFitzgerald, Ernest A.
How to Be a Successful Failure. Atheneum.
Fitzgerald, F. Scott.
xFitzgerald, F. Scott.
This Side of Paradise. Scribner.
Fitzgerald, F. Scott. *see* Fitzgerald, Francis Scott Key.
Fitzgerald, Frances, 1940-
xFitzGerald, Frances.
Fire in the Lake: The Vietnamese & the
Americans in Vietnam. Little.
Fire in the Lake: The Vietnamese & the
Americans in Vietnam. Random.
Fitzgerald, Francis Scott Key, 1896-1940
xFitzgerald, F. Scott.
Flappers & Philosophers. Scribner.
The Great Gatsby. Scribner.
Great Gatsby. Scribner.
Last Tycoon. Scribner.
The Notebooks of F. Scott Fitzgerald.
HarBraceJ.
The Notebooks of F. Scott Fitzgerald.
HarBraceJ.
The Price Was High: The Last Uncollected
Stories by F. Scott Fitzgerald. HarBraceJ.
Taps at Reveille. Scribner.
Tender Is the Night. Scribner.
Fitzgerald, Hiram E.
xFitzgerald, Hiram E.
ed. Developmental Psychology: Studies in
Human Development. Dorsey.
Fitzgerald, James A. *see* Fitzgerald, James Augustine.
Fitzgerald, James Augustine.
xFitzgerald, James A.
Teaching Reading & the Language Arts.
Glencoe.
Fitzgerald, Jerry.
xFitzGerald, Jerry.
Internal Controls for Computerized Systems.
FitzGerald & Assocs.
Fitzgerald, Jerry. *see* Fitzgerald, John M.
Fitzgerald, John D. *see* Fitzgerald, John Dennis.
Fitzgerald, John Dennis.
xFitzgerald, John D.
Great Brain. Dial.
Great Brain. Dell.
Great Brain at the Academy. Dell.
The Great Brain at the Academy. Dial.
The Great Brain Does It Again. Dial.
Great Brain Reforms. Dell.
The Great Brain Reforms. Dial.
Me & My Little Brain. Dell.
Me & My Little Brain. Dial.
More Adventures of the Great Brain. Dell.
More Adventures of the Great Brain. Dial.
Papa Married a Mormon. Western Epics.
The Return of the Great Brain. Dell.
The Return of the Great Brain. Dial.
Fitzgerald, John M.
xFitzgerald, Arda F.
jt. auth. Fundamentals of Systems Analysis.
Wiley.
xFitzgerald, Jerry.
Fundamentals of Data Communications. Wiley.
Fundamentals of Systems Analysis. Wiley.
xFitzgerald, John M.
The Fundamentals of Systems Analysis. Wiley.
FitzGerald, M. J. *see* Fitzgerald, M. J. T.
Fitzgerald, M. J. T.
xFitzGerald, M. J.

Human Embryology: A Regional Approach.
Har-Row.
Fitzgerald, Maragret M. *see* Fitzgerald, Margaret Mary.
Fitzgerald, Margaret Mary, 1916-
xFitzgerald, Maragret M.
First Follow Nature: Primitivism in English
Poetry, 1725-1750. Octagon.
Fitzgerald, Maurice J. *see* Fitzgerald, Maurice John.
Fitzgerald, Maurice John, 1901-
xFitzgerald, Maurice J.
Handbook of Criminal Investigation. Arco.
Fitzgerald, Mike.
xFitzgerald, Mike.
British Prisons. Biblio Dist.
Fitzgerald, Nancy.
xFitzgerald, Nancy.
Chelsea. Doubleday.
Chelsea. G K Hall.
Mayfair. Doubleday.
Mayfair. Popular Lib.
Fitzgerald, Patrick.
xFitzgerald, Patrick.
Industrial Combination in England. Arno.
Fitzgerald, Penelope.
xFitzgerald, Penelope.
The Golden Child. Scribner.
Fitzgerald, Percy. *see* Fitzgerald, Percy Hetherington.
Fitzgerald, Percy H. *see* Fitzgerald, Percy Hetherington.
Fitzgerald, Percy Hetherington, 1834-1925
xFitzgerald, Percy.
Charles Lamb: His Friends, His Haunts & His
Books. Folcroft.
Principles of Comedy & Dramatic Effect.
Folcroft.
xFitzgerald, Percy H.
Charles Lamb: His Friends, His Haunts & His
Books. Norwood Edns.
Charles Lamb: His Friends, His Haunts & His
Books. R West.
Fitzgerald, R. V., 1922-
xFitzgerald, R. V.
Conjoint Marital Therapy. Aronson.
Fitzgerald, R. W. *see* Fitzgerald, Robert W.
Fitzgerald, Randall.
xFitzgerald, Randall.
Complete Book of Extraterrestrial Encounters.
Macmillan.
Fitzgerald, Robert, 1910-
xFitzgerald, Robert.
In the Rose of Time: Poems, 1939-1956. New
Directions.
FitzGerald, Robert D. *see* Fitzgerald, Robert David.
Fitzgerald, Robert David, 1902-
xFitzGerald, Robert D.
Of Places & Poetry. U of Queensland Pr.
Fitzgerald, Robert W.
xFitzgerald, R. W.
Strength of Materials. A-W.
Fitzgerald, Ross, 1944-
xFitzgerald, Ross.
ed. Human Needs & Politics. Pergamon.
Fitzgerald, S. *see* Fitzgerald, Stephen.
Fitzgerald, Stephen.
xFitzgerald, S.
China & the Overseas Chinese: A Study of
Peking's Changing Policy, 1949-1970.
Cambridge U Pr.
Fitzgerald, Tamsin, 1950-
xFitzgerald, Tamsin.
Tamsin. Dial.
Tamsin. Popular Lib.
Fitzgerald, Theodore C., 1903-1967
xFitzgerald, Theodore C.
The Coturnix Quail: Anatomy & Histology.
Iowa St U Pr.
Fitzgibbon, Constantine.
xFitzgibbon, Constantine.
The Life of Dylan Thomas. Little.
Fitzgibbon, Louis, 1925-
xFitzgibbon, Louis.

Katyn. Noontide.

Fitzgibbon, Russell H. see Fitzgibbon, Russell Humke.

Fitzgibbon, Russell Humke, 1902-
xFitzgibbon, Russell H.
Cuba & the United States, 1900-1935. Russell.

Fitzhardinge, L. F.
xFitzhardinge, L. F.
The Spartans. Thames Hudson.

Fitzharris, Timothy L.
xFitzharris, Timothy L.
The Desirability of a Correctional Ombudsman.
Inst Gov Stud Berk.

Fitzhugh, Louise.
xFitzhugh, Louise.
The Long Secret. Dell.
The Long Secret. Dell.
Long Secret. Har-Row.
Nobodys Family Is Going to Change. Dell.
Nobody's Family Is Going to Change. FS&G.
Sport. Delacorte.
Sport. Dell.

Fitzley, George, 1938-
xFitzley, George.
ed. Growing & Preserving Your Own Fruits &
Vegetables. Jonathan David.

Fitzmaurice-Kelly, James.
xFitzmaurice-Kelly, James.
Lope De Vega & Spanish Drama. Haskell.
Some Masters of Spanish Verse. Arno.

Fitzmyer, Joseph A.
xFitzmyer, Joseph A.
The Dead Sea Scrolls: Major Publications &
Tools for Study. Scholars Pr Ca.
xFitzmyer, Joseph F.
Pauline Theology: A Brief Sketch. P-H.

Fitzmyer, Joseph F. see Fitzmyer, Joseph A.

Fitzpatrick, Daniel J.
xFitzpatrick, Daniel J.
Confusion, Call, Commitment: The Spiritual
Exercises & Religious Education. Alba.

FitzPatrick, E. A. see Fitzpatrick, Ewart Adsil.

Fitzpatrick, Edward A. see Fitzpatrick, Edward Augustus.

Fitzpatrick, Edward Augustus, 1884-1960
xFitzpatrick, Edward A.
Educational Views & Influence of DeWitt
Clinton. AMS Pr.
Educational Views & Influence of De Witt
Clinton. Arno.

Fitzpatrick, Ewart Adsil.
xFitzPatrick, E. A.
An Introduction to Soil Science. Longman.
xFitzpatrick, Ewart Adsil.
Pedology: A Systematic Approach to Soil
Science. Hafner.

Fitzpatrick, F. L. see Fitzpatrick, Frederick Linder.

Fitzpatrick, Frederick Linder.
xFitzpatrick, F. L.
Living Things. HR&W.
Modern Life Science. HR&W.
Modern Life Science. HR&W.

Fitzpatrick, H. M. see Fitzpatrick, Harry Morton.

Fitzpatrick, Harry Morton, 1886-
xFitzpatrick, H. M.
The Lower Fungi, Phycomycetes. Johnson
Repr.

Fitzpatrick, J. see Fitzpatrick, Joseph P.

Fitzpatrick, James F.
xFitzpatrick, James F.
The Law & Roadside Hazards. Michie.

Fitzpatrick, James K.
xFitzpatrick, James K.
Builders of the American Dream. Arlington
Hse.
How to Survive in Your Liberal School.
Arlington Hse.

Fitzpatrick, Janine.
xFitzpatrick, Janine.
The Dreamwalker. PB.

Fitzpatrick, Joseph P.
xFitzpatrick, J.

Puerto Rican Americans: The Meaning of
Migration to the Mainland. P-H.

Fitzpatrick, Malcolm S.
xFitzpatrick, Malcolm S.
Environmental Health Planning: Community
Development Based on Environmental &
Health Precepts. Ballinger Pub.

Fitzpatrick, Philip M. see Fitzpatrick, Philip Matthew.

Fitzpatrick, Philip Matthew.
xFitzpatrick, Philip M.
Principles of Celestial Mechanics. Acad Pr.

Fitzpatrick, Sheila.
xFitzpatrick, Sheila.
ed. Cultural Revolution in Russia, 1928-1931.
Ind U Pr.
Education & Social Mobility in the Soviet
Union: 1921-1934. Cambridge U Pr.

Fitzroy, Peter T.
xFitzroy, Peter T.
Analytical Methods for Marketing
Management. McGraw.

Fitzsimmons, S. J. see Fitzsimmons, Stephen J.

Fitzsimmons, Stephen J.
xFitzsimmons, S. J.
Guidance Manual to Providing Neighborhood
Services. Westview.

Fitzsimons, Christopher.
xFitzsimons, Christopher.
Early Warning. Viking Pr.

Fitzsimons, Raymond. see Fitzsimons, Raymund.

Fitzsimons, Raymund.
xFitzsimons, Raymond.
Edmund Kean: Fire from Heaven. Dial.

Fitzsimons, Ruth M.
xFitzsimons, Ruth M.
Let's Play Hide & Seek. Expression.

Fitzwater, Eva.
xFitzwater, Eva.
Pearl Notes. Cliffs.

Fitzwilliam Museum. see Cambridge University.
Fitzwilliam Museum.

Fivaz, Derek.
xFivaz, Derek.
ed. African Languages: A Genetic &
Decimalised Classification for Bibliographic &
General Reference. G K Hall.

Fix, Janet.
xFix, Janet.
For Singles Only. Revell.

Fix, William R., 1941-
xFix, William R.
Pyramid Odyssey. Mayflower Bks.

Fixel, Rowland W. see Fixel, Rowland Wells.

Fixel, Rowland Wells, 1887-
xFixel, Rowland W.
Law of Aviation. Michie.

Fixx, James. see Fixx, James F.

Fixx, James F.
xFixx, James.
More Games for the Super-Intelligent. Popular
Lib.
xFixx, James F.
The Complete Book of Running. Random.
Games for the Super-Intelligent. Popular Lib.
Games for the Superintelligent. Doubleday.
More Games for the Superintelligent.
Doubleday.

Fjelde, Rolf.
xFjelde, Rolf.
ed. Ibsen: A Collection of Critical Essays. P-H.

Flaccus, Louis W. see Flaccus, Louis William.

Flaccus, Louis William.
xFlaccus, Louis W.
Artists & Thinkers. Arno.

Flach, Frederic F.
xFlach, Frederic F.
The Nature & Treatment of Depression. Wiley.

Flack, Horace E. see Flack, Horace Edgar.

Flack, Horace Edgar, 1879-
xFlack, Horace E.

The Adoption of the Fourteenth Amendment.
AMS Pr.
Adoption of the Fourteenth Amendment. Peter
Smith.
Spanish-American Diplomatic Relations
Preceding the War of 1898. AMS Pr.

Flack, Marjorie.
xFlack, Marjorie.
Angus Lost. Doubleday.
Story About Ping. Viking Pr.
Story About Ping. Penguin.

Flad, H. D. see Flad, Hans-Dieter.

Flad, Hans-Dieter.
xFlad, H. D.
ed. Immunodiagnosis & Immunotherapy of
Malignant Tumors: Relevance to Surgery.
Proceedings of a Workshop Held at
Reisenburg, Nov. 2-4, 1977. Springer-Verlag.

Fladeland, Betty. see Fladeland, Betty Lorraine.

Fladeland, Betty Lorraine, 1919-
xFladeland, Betty.
Men & Brothers: Anglo-American Antislavery
Cooperation. U of Ill Pr.

Flader, Susan.
xFlader, Susan L.
Thinking Like a Mountain: Aldo Leopold &
the Evolution of an Ecological Attitude
Toward Deer, Wolves, & Forests. U of Mo
Pr.
Thinking Like a Mountain: Aldo Leopold &
the Evolution of an Ecological Attitude
Toward Deer, Wolves & Forests. U of Nebr
Pr.

Flader, Susan L. see Flader, Susan.

Flagg, Andrew S.
xFlagg, Andrew S.
The Story of Cape Cod Cooking. W S
Sullwold.

Flagg, Charles A. see Flagg, Charles Allcott.

Flagg, Charles Allcott, 1870-1920
xFlagg, Charles A.
Alphabetical Index of Revolutionary Pensioners
Living in Maine. Genealog Pub.
An Index of Pioneers from Massachusetts to
the West, Especially the State of Michigan.
Genealog Pub.

Flagg, Jared B. see Flagg, Jared Bradley.

Flagg, Jared Bradley, 1820-1899
xFlagg, Jared B.
Life & Letters of Washington Allston. Arno.
Life & Letters of Washington Allston. Da
Capo.

Flagg, John F. see Flagg, John Ferard.

Flagg, John Ferard, 1914-
xFlagg, John F.
ed. Chemical Processing of Reactor Fuels.
Acad Pr.

Flagg, William. see Flagg, William G.

Flagg, William G., 1934-
xFlagg, William.
The Clam Lover's Cookbook. Caroline Hse.
xFlagg, William G.
Clam Lover's Cookbook. Cookbooks Inc.
The Clam Lover's Cookbook. North River.

Flaherty, David H.
xFlaherty, David H.
Privacy in Colonial New England, 1630-1776.
U Pr of Va.

Flaherty, Frances H. see Flaherty, Frances Hubbard.

Flaherty, Frances Hubbard.
xFlaherty, Frances H.
Odyssey of a Film-Maker: Robert Flaherty's
Story. Arno.

Flaherty, Maureen O. see Flaherty, Maureen O'Brien.

Flaherty, Maureen O'Brien, 1933-
xFlaherty, Maureen O.
The Care of the Elderly Person: A Guide for
the Licensed Practical Nurse. Mosby.

Flake, Chad J.
xFlake, Chad J.

ed. A Mormon Bibliography, 1830-1930:
Books, Pamphlets, Periodicals, & Broadsides
Relating to the First Century of Mormonism.
U of Utah Pr.

Flakser, David.
xFlakser, David.
Marxism Ideology & Myths. Philos Lib.

Flam, Jack. *see* Flam, Jack D.

Flam, Jack D.
xFlam, Jack.
Bread & Butter. Viking Pr.

Flamholtz. *see* Flamholtz, Eric.

Flamholtz, Eric.
xFlamholtz.
Human Resource Accounting. Dickenson.
xFlamholtz, Eric.
Human Resource Accounting. CBI Pub.

Flammang, James M.
xFlammang, James M.
How to Make Your Old Car Run Like New.
TAB Bks.

Flammonde, Paris.
xFlammonde, Paris.
UFO Exist. Ballantine.

Flanagan, Cathleen C.
xFlanagan, Cathleen C.
American Folklore: A Bibliography, 1950-1974.
Scarecrow.

Flanagan, Geraldine. *see* Flanagan, Geraldine Lux.

Flanagan, Geraldine L. *see* Flanagan, Geraldine Lux.

Flanagan, Geraldine Lux.
xFlanagan, Geraldine.
First Nine Months of Life. S&S.
xFlanagan, Geraldine L.
The First Nine Months of Life. Intl Ideas.

Flanagan, Hallie. *see* Flanagan, Hallie (Ferguson).

Flanagan, Hallie (Ferguson), 1890-
xFlanagan, Hallie.
Arena: The History of the Federal Theatre.
Arno.

Flanagan, Henry E.
xFlanagan, Henry E.
Basic Lacrosse Strategy: An Introduction for
Young Players. Doubleday.

Flanagan, J. L. *see* Flanagan, James Loton.

Flanagan, James Loton, 1925
xFlanagan, J. L.
Speech Analysis, Synthesis & Perception.
Springer-Verlag.
ed. Speech Synthesis. Acad Pr.

Flanagan, John T. *see* Flanagan, John Theodore.

Flanagan, John Theodore, 1906-
xFlanagan, John T.
Edgar Lee Masters: The Spoon River Poet &
His Critics. Scarecrow.
ed. Folklore in American Literature.
Greenwood.
Profile of Vachel Lindsay. Merrill.

Flanagan, Richard.
xFlanagan, Richard.
The Hunting Variety. Popular Lib.

Flanagan, Thomas.
xFlanagan, Thomas.
Louis "David" Riel: "Prophet of the New
World". U of Toronto Pr.

Flandermeyer, Kenneth L.
xFlandermeyer, Kenneth L.
Clear Skin: A Step by Step Program to Stop
Pimples, Blackheads, Acne. Little.

Flanders, H. *see* Flanders, Harley.

Flanders, Harley.
xFlanders, H.
Calculus. Acad Pr.
xFlanders, Harley.
Algebra. Acad Pr.
Algebra & Trigonometry. Acad Pr.
A First Course in Calculus with Analytic
Geometry. Acad Pr.

Flanders, James P.
xFlanders, James P.

Practical Psychology. Har-Row.

Flanders, Jesse K. *see* Flanders, Jesse Knowlton.

Flanders, Jesse Knowlton, 1878-
xFlanders, Jesse K.
Legislative Control of the Elementary
Curriculum. AMS Pr.

Flanders, Ned A.
xFlanders, Ned A.
Analyzing Teaching Behavior. A-W.

Flanders, Robert B. *see* Flanders, Robert Bruce.

Flanders, Robert Bruce.
xFlanders, Robert B.
Nauvoo: Kingdom on the Mississippi. U of Ill
Pr.

Flandrau, Charles M. *see* Flandrau, Charles Macomb.

Flandrau, Charles Macomb, 1871-1938
xFlandrau, Charles M.
Loquacities. Arno.

Flanery, E. B.
xFlanery, E. B.
The Crack in the Bible. Ashley Bks.

Flanner, Janet, 1892-
xFlanner, Janet.
Cubical City. Popular Lib.
The Cubical City. S Ill U Pr.
Janet Flanner's World: Uncollected Writing's
1932-1975. HarBraceJ.
Men & Monuments. Arno.
Paris Was Yesterday. Popular Lib.

Flapan, Dorothy.
xFlapan, Dorothy.
Assessment of Early Child Development.
Aronson.
Children's Understanding of Social Interaction.
Tchrs Coll.

Flapan, Simha.
xFlapan, Simha.
Zionism & the Palestinians. B&N.

Flapan, Simha. *see* Flapan, Simpha.

Flapan, Simpha.
xFlapan, Simha.
ed. When Enemies Dare to Talk: An
Israeli-Palestinian Debate (5-6 September
1978) Organised by "New Outlook". Biblio
Dist.

Flatt, Adrian E.
xFlatt, Adrian E.
The Care of Minor Hand Injuries. Mosby.
The Care of the Rheumatoid Hand. Mosby.

Flatte, S. M. *see* Flatte, Stanley M.

Flatte, Stanley M.
xFlatte, S. M.
ed. Sound Transmission Through a Fluctuating
Ocean. Cambridge U Pr.

Flatter, Richard, 1891-1960
xFlatter, Richard.
Moor of Venice. Folcroft.

Flatto, Leopold.
xFlatto, Leopold.
Advanced Calculus. Krieger.

Flaubert, Gustave, 1821-1880
xFlaubert, Gustave.
Bouvard & Pecuchet. Greenwood.
Bouvard & Pecuchet. Penguin.
Bouvard et Pecuchet. French & Eur.
The First Sentimental Education. U of Cal Pr.

Flavell, John H.
xFlavell, John H.
Cognitive Development. P-H.
The Development of Role-Taking &
Communication Skills in Children. Krieger.

Flavier, Juan M.
xFlavier, Juan M.
My Friends in the Barrios. Cellar.

Flavin, Martin, 1883-1967
xFlavin, Martin.
Journey in the Dark. Greenwood.

Flaxman, John.
xFlaxman, John.

Flaxman's Illustrations to Homer. Dover.

Fleay, David. *see* Fleay, David Howells.

Fleay, David Howells, 1907-
xFleay, David.
Nightwatchmen of Bush & Plain: Australian
Owls & Owl-Like Birds. Taplinger.

Fleay, Frederick G. *see* Fleay, Frederick Gard.

Fleay, Frederick Gard, 1831-1909
xFleay, Frederick G.
Chronicle History of London Stage, 1559-1642.
B Franklin.
Guide to Chaucer & Spenser. AMS Pr.
Introduction to Shakespearian Study. AMS Pr.

Fleck, Henrietta. *see* Fleck, Henrietta Christina.

Fleck, Henrietta Christina, 1903-
xFleck, Henrietta.
Introduction to Nutrition. Macmillan.
Toward Better Teaching of Home Economics.
Macmillan.

Fleck, Ludwik.
xFleck, Ludwik.
Genesis & Development of a Scientific Fact. U
of Chicago Pr.

Fleck, Richard.
xFleck, Richard F.
Palms, Peaks & Prairies. Golden Quill.

Fleck, Richard F. *see* Fleck, Richard.

Fleckenstein, J. *see* Fleckenstein, Josef.

Fleckenstein, Josef.
xFleckenstein, J.
Early Medieval Germany. Elsevier.

Flecker, James E. *see* Flecker, James Elroy.

Flecker, James Elroy, 1884-1915
xFlecker, James E.
Collected Prose. AMS Pr.

Fleckner, John A., 1941-
xFleckner, John A.
Archives & Manuscripts: Surveys. Soc Am
Archivists.

Fleder. *see* Fleder, Laura W.

Fleder, Laura W.
xFleder.
How to Use French Verbs. Barron.

Fleege, Francis. *see* Fleege, Francis J.

Fleege, Francis J.
xFleege, Francis.
How to Eat: Chewing, Tooth Care & Diet.
Elsevier-Nelson.

Fleer, Gedaliah.
xFleer, Gedaliah.
Rabbi Nachman's Fire: An Introduction to
Breslover Chassidus. Hermon.

Fleet, F. R.
xFleet, F. R.
Theory of Wit & Humour. Kennikat.

Fleet, James Van. *see* Van Fleet, James.

Fleetwood, Hugh.
xFleetwood, Hugh.
The Beast. Atheneum.
A Conditional Sentence. PB.
Foreign Affairs. PB.
Foreign Affairs. Stein & Day.
The Girl Who Passed for Normal. PB.
The Girl Who Passed for Normal. Stein &
Day.
The Order of Death. S&S.
A Picture of Innocence. PB.

Flegg, H. Graham.
xFlegg, H. Graham.
From Geometry to Topology. Crane-Russak
Co.

Flegmann, A. W.
xFlegmann, G. W.
Soils & Other Growth Media. AVI.

Flegmann, G. W. *see* Flegmann, A. W.

Fleischer, Arthur C.
xFleischer, Arthur C.
Introduction to Diagnostic Sonography. Wiley.

Fleischer, Eugene B., 1931-
xFleischer, Eugene B.

A Style Manual for Citing Microform &
    Nonprint Media. ALA.
Fleischer, G. see Fleischer, Gerald.
Fleischer, Gerald, 1943-
    xFleischer, G.
    Evolutionary Principles of the Mammalian
        Middle Ear. Springer-Verlag.
Fleischer, Jane.
    xFleischer, Jane.
    Sitting Bull, Warrior of the Sioux. Troll Assocs.
Fleischer, Leonore.
    xFleischer, Leonore.
    The Chicken Soup Book. Taplinger.
    Joni Mitchell. Music Sales.
Fleischer, M. P. see Fleischer, Manfred P.
Fleischer, Manfred P., 1928-
    xFleischer, M. P.
    ed. The Decline of the West?. Krieger.
    xFleischer, Manfred P.
    Decline of the West. Peter Smith.
Fleischman, Albert Sidney.
    xFleischman, Sid.
    By the Great Horn Spoon. Little.
    Chancy & the Grand Rascal. Little.
    The Ghost in the Noonday Sun. Little.
    The Ghost on Saturday Night. Little.
    Humbug Mountain. Little.
    Me & the Man on the Moon Eyed Horse.
        Little.
    The Wooden Cat Man. Little.
Fleischman, H. Samuel.
    xFleischman, H. Samuel.
    Gang Girl. Doubleday.
Fleischman, Paul.
    xFleischman, Paul.
    The Birthday Tree. Har-Row.
    The Half-a-Moon Inn. Har-Row.
Fleischman, Sid. see Fleischman, Albert Sidney.
Fleischmann, Christa.
    xFleischmann, Christa.
    ed. Mark in Time: Portraits & Poetry-San
        Francisco. New Glide.
Fleisher, Belton M.
    xFleisher, Belton M.
    Labor Economics: Theory, Evidence & Policy.
        P-H.
    A Primer in Economics. Glencoe.
Fleisher, Michael. see Fleisher, Michael L.
Fleisher, Michael L.
    xFleisher, Michael.
    The Great Superman Book. Warner Bks.
    xFleisher, Michael L.
    Chasing Hairy. St Martin.
    The Great Superman Book. Crown.
Fleisher, Robbin.
    xFleisher, Robbin.
    Quilts in the Attic. Macmillan.
Fleishman, Avrom.
    xFleishman, Avrom.
    The English Historical Novel: Walter Scott to
        Virginia Woolf. Johns Hopkins.
    Fiction & the Ways of Knowing: Essays on
        British Novels. U of Tex Pr.
    A Reading of Mansfield Park. An Essay in
        Critical Synthesis. Johns Hopkins.
Fleisig, Heywood. see Fleisig, Heywood W.
Fleisig, Heywood W.
    xFleisig, Heywood.
    Long Term Capital Flows & the Great
        Depression: The Role of the United States,
        1927-1933. Arno.
Fleissner, Robert F.
    xFleissner, Robert F.
    Dickens & Shakespeare: A Study in Histrionic
        Contrasts. Haskell.
Fleming, Alice. see Fleming, Alice Mulcahey.
Fleming, Alice Mulcahey, 1928-
    xFleming, Alice.

Hosannah the Home Run: Poems About
    Sports. Little.
Psychiatry: What's It All About. Contemp Bks.
Something for Nothing: A History of
    Gambling. Delacorte.
Fleming, Berry, 1899-
    xFleming, Berry.
    Compiled by Autobiography of a City in Arms:
        Augusta, Georgia, 1861-1865. Richmond Cty
        Hist Soc.
    Two Tales for Autumn. Cotton Lane.
Fleming, Daniel J.
    xFleming, Daniel J.
    Calculus with Analytic Geometry. Har-Row.
Fleming, David A.
    xFleming, David A.
    ed. The Fire & the Cloud: An Anthology of
        Catholic Spirituality. Paulist Pr.
Fleming, Dick.
    xFleming, Dick.
    The Winning of Opie. Doubleday.
Fleming, George.
    xFleming, George.
    Computer Simulation Techniques in Hydrology.
        Elsevier.
Fleming, Gladys A. see Fleming, Gladys Andrews.
Fleming, Gladys Andrews.
    xFleming, Gladys A.
    Creative Rhythmic Movement: Boys & Girls
        Dancing. P-H.
Fleming, H. K. see Fleming, Horace Kingston.
Fleming, Horace Kingston.
    xFleming, H. K.
    The Day They Kidnapped Queen Victoria. St
        Martin.
Fleming, I. see Fleming, Ian.
Fleming, Ian.
    xFleming, I.
    Frontier Orbitals & Organic Chemical
        Reactions. Wiley.
    Spectroscopic Methods in Organic Chemistry.
        McGraw.
    Spectroscopic Methods of Organic Chemistry.
        McGraw.
    xFleming, Ian.
    Casino Royale. French & Eur.
    Diamonds Are Forever. BJ Pub Group.
    Diamonds Are Forever. French & Eur.
    Doctor No. BJ Pub Group.
    Doctor No. French & Eur.
    Doctor No. NAL.
    Octopussy. French & Eur.
    On Her Majesty's Secret Service. French &
        Eur.
    On Her Majesty's Secret Service. NAL.
Fleming, Jennifer B. see Fleming, Jennifer Baker.
Fleming, Jennifer Baker.
    xFleming, Jennifer B.
    For Better, for Worse: A Feminist Handbook
        on Marriage & Other Options. Scribner.
    Stopping Wife Abuse: A Guide to the
        Emotional, Psychological & Legal
        Implications for the Abused Woman & Those
        Helping Her. Doubleday.
Fleming, Jo.
    xFleming, Jo.
    His Affair. M Evans.
    His Affair. PB.
Fleming, John.
    xFleming, John E.
    The Case for Affirmative Action for Blacks in
        Higher Education. Howard U Pr.
Fleming, John A. see Fleming, John Arnold.
Fleming, John Arnold, 1871-
    xFleming, John A.
    The Troubadours of Provence.. Folcroft.
Fleming, John E. see Fleming, John.
Fleming, John G.
    xFleming, John G.

An Introduction to the Law of Torts. Oxford U
    Pr.
Fleming, June.
    xFleming, June.
    Games (& More!) for Backpackers. Victoria
        Hse.
    ed. The Outdoor Idea Book. Victoria Hse.
    The Well-Fed Backpacker. Victoria Hse.
Fleming, Karl.
    xFleming, Karl.
    The First Time. Berkley Pub.
    The First Time. S&S.
Fleming, Malcolm. see Fleming, Malcolm L.
Fleming, Malcolm L.
    xFleming, Malcolm.
    Instructional Message Design: Principles from
        the Behavioral Sciences. Educ Tech Pubns.
Fleming, Peter.
    xFleming, Peter.
    Brazilian Adventure. Norwood Edns.
    Brazilian Adventure. Scholars Ref Lib.
Fleming, Rita A., 1952-
    xFleming, Rita A.
    ed. Primary Care Techniques: Laboratory Tests
        in Ambulatory Facilities. Mosby.
Fleming, Robert L.
    xFleming, Robert L.
    Kathmandu Valley. Kodansha.
Fleming, S. J. see Fleming, Stuart James.
Fleming, Stuart James.
    xFleming, S. J.
    Authenticity in Art: The Scientific Detection of
        Forgery. Crane-Russak Co.
Fleming, Thomas J.
    xFleming, Thomas J.
    All Good Men. Arno.
Fleming, W. H. see Fleming, Wendell Helms.
Fleming, Wallace B. see Fleming, Wallace Bruce.
Fleming, Wallace Bruce, 1872-
    xFleming, Wallace B.
    History of Tyre. AMS Pr.
Fleming, Walter.
    xFleming, Walter.
    Algebra & Trigonometry. P-H.
    College Algebra. P-H.
    Plane Trigonometry. P-H.
Fleming, Walter L. see Fleming, Walter Lynwood.
Fleming, Walter Lynwood, 1874-1932
    xFleming, Walter L.
    Civil War & Reconstruction in Alabama. Peter
        Smith.
    Civil War & Reconstruction in Alabama.
        Reprint.
    Documentary History of Reconstruction:
        Political, Military, Social, Religious,
        Educational & Industrial. Peter Smith.
Fleming, Wendell Helms.
    xFleming, W. H.
    Deterministic & Stochastic Optimal Control.
        Springer-Verlag.
    Functions of Several Variables. Springer-Verlag.
Fleming, William, 1909-
    xFleming, William.
    Arts & Ideas. HR&W.
Fleming, William H. see Fleming, William Hansell.
Fleming, William Hansell, 1844-1915
    xFleming, William H.
    How to Study Shakespeare. AMS Pr.
    How to Study Shakespeare. Arden Lib.
Flemings, Merton. see Flemings, Merton C.
Flemings, Merton C., 1929-
    xFlemings, Merton.
    Solidification Processing. McGraw.
Flemion, Philip F.
    xFlemion, Philip F.
    Historical Dictionary of El Salvador.
        Scarecrow.
Flemming, J. S.
    xFlemming, John.

Inflation. Oxford U Pr.

Flemming, John. *see* Flemming, J. S.

Flemming, N. C. *see* Flemming, Nicholas Coit.

Flemming, Nicholas Coit.
  xFlemming, N. C.
    ed. The Undersea. Macmillan.

Flemyng, Francis P. *see* Flemyng, Francis Patrick.

Flemyng, Francis Patrick.
  xFlemyng, Francis P.
    Southern Africa: A Geography & Natural
      History of the Country, Colonies &
      Inhabitants from the Cape of Good Hope to
      Angola. Negro U Pr.

Flenley, J. R. *see* Flenley, John Roger.

Flenley, John Roger.
  xFlenley, J. R.
    The Equatorial Rain Forest: A Geological
      History. Butterworths.

Fles, Barthold, 1902-
  xFles, Barthold.
    East Germany. Watts.

Flesch, Carl. *see* Flesch, Karl.

Flesch, Karl, 1873-1944
  xFlesch, Carl.
    The Memoirs of Carl Flesch. Da Capo.

Flesch, Rudolf.
  xFlesch, Rudolf.
    The Art of Clear Thinking. Har-Row.
    The Art of Clear Thinking. Har-Row.

Flesch, Rudolf. *see* Flesch, Rudolf Franz.

Flesch, Rudolf F. *see* Flesch, Rudolf Franz.

Flesch, Rudolf Franz, 1911-
  xFlesch, Rudolf.
    Art of Readable Writing. Macmillan.
    How to Write, Speak & Think More
      Effectively. NAL.
    Look It up: A Deskbook of American Spelling
      & Style. Har-Row.
  xFlesch, Rudolf F.
    Marks of Readable Style: A Study in Adult
      Education. AMS Pr.

Flesher, Dale L.
  xFlesher, Dale L.
    Accounting for the Middle Manager. Van Nos
      Reinhold.
    Operations Auditing in Hospitals. Lexington
      Bks.

Fletcher, Aaron.
  xFletcher, Aaron.
    Bounty Hunter. Nordon Pubns.
    Love's Gentle Agony. Dell.
    Outback. Nordon Pubns.

Fletcher, Adele W. *see* Fletcher, Adele Whitely.

Fletcher, Adele Whitely.
  xFletcher, Adele W.
    How to Stretch Your Dollar. Benjamin Co.

Fletcher, Alan D.
  xFletcher, Alan D.
    Fundamentals of Advertising Research. Grid
      Pub.

Fletcher, Alan M. *see* Fletcher, Alan Mark.

Fletcher, Alan Mark.
  xFletcher, Alan M.
    Fishes & Their Young. A-W.
    Fishes That Hide. A-W.

Fletcher, Alice C. *see* Fletcher, Alice Cunningham.

Fletcher, Alice Cunningham, 1845-1923
  xFletcher, Alice C.
    Indian Story & Song from North America.
      AMS Pr.
    Indian Story & Song from North America.
      Johnson Repr.

Fletcher, Angus. *see* Fletcher, Angus John Stewart.

Fletcher, Angus John Stewart, 1930-
  xFletcher, Angus.
    The Prophetic Moment: An Essay on Spenser.
      U of Chicago Pr.

Fletcher, Anthony.
  xFletcher, Anthony.

A County Community in Peace & War: Sussex
  1600-1660. Longman.

Fletcher, C. Brunsdon. *see* Fletcher, Charles Brunsdon.

Fletcher, Charles Brunsdon, 1859-1946
  xFletcher, C. Brunsdon.
    Stevenson's Germany: The Case Against
      Germany in the Pacific. Arno.
    Stevenson's Germany: The Case Against
      Germany in the Pacific. R West.

Fletcher, Colin, Ph.d.
  xFletcher, Colin.
    Person in the Sight of Sociology. Routledge &
      Kegan.

Fletcher, David, 1940-
  xFletcher, David.
    Raffles. Popular Lib.
    A Respectable Woman. PB.

Fletcher, Frank T. *see* Fletcher, Frank Thomas Herbert.

Fletcher, Frank Thomas Herbert.
  xFletcher, Frank T.
    Montesquieu & English Politics (1750-1800).
      Porcupine Pr.

Fletcher, George P.
  xFletcher, George P.
    Rethinking Criminal Law. Little.

Fletcher, Gerald F.
  xFletcher, Gerald F.
    Exercise & Coronary Heart Disease: Role in
      Prevention, Diagnosis, Treatment. C C
      Thomas.
    Exercise in the Management of Coronary Heart
      Disease: A Guide for the Practicing
      Physician. C C Thomas.

Fletcher, Gilbert H. *see* Fletcher, Gilbert Hungerford.

Fletcher, Gilbert Hungerford, 1911-
  xFletcher, Gilbert H.
    ed. Textbook of Radiotherapy. Lea & Febiger.

Fletcher, Giles.
  xFletcher, Giles.
    Of the Russe Commonwealth 1591. Harvard U
      Pr.

Fletcher, H. *see* Fletcher, Harold.

Fletcher, Harold.
  xFletcher, H.
    Mathematics with Understanding. Pergamon.

Fletcher, Helen J. *see* Fletcher, Helen Jill.

Fletcher, Helen Jill.
  xFletcher, Helen J.
    Puzzles & Quizzles. Abelard.

Fletcher, Inglis.
  xFletcher, Inglis.
    Cormorant's Brood. Queens Hse.

Fletcher, Inglis. *see* Fletcher, Inglis Clark.

Fletcher, Inglis Clark, 1888-1969
  xFletcher, Inglis.
    Men of Albemarle. Bantam.
    Men of Albemarle. Queens Hse.
    Queen's Gift. Queens Hse.

Fletcher, J. *see* Fletcher, John.

Fletcher, J. S. *see* Fletcher, Joseph Smith.

Fletcher, Jefferson B. *see* Fletcher, Jefferson Butler.

Fletcher, Jefferson Butler, 1865-1946
  xFletcher, Jefferson B.
    Symbolism of the Divine Comedy. AMS Pr.

Fletcher, Jesse C.
  xFletcher, Jesse C.
    Living Sacrifices: A Missionary Odyssey.
      Broadman.
    Practical Discipleship. Broadman.

Fletcher, John, 1937-
  xFletcher, J.
    Use of Economics Literature. Butterworths.
  xFletcher, John.
    Claude Simon & Fiction Now. Humanities.
    ed. Forces in Modern French Drama: Studies
      in Variations on the Permitted Lie. Ungar.
    Two Noble Kinsmen. AMS Pr.
    The Two Noble Kinsmen. U of Nebr Pr.

Fletcher, John G. *see* Fletcher, John Gould.

Fletcher, John Gould, 1886-1950
  xFletcher, John G.
    Some Contemporary American Poets. Folcroft.

Fletcher, Joseph. *see* Fletcher, Joseph Francis.

Fletcher, Joseph Francis, 1905-
  xFletcher, Joseph.
    Humanhood: Essays in Biomedical Ethics.
      Prometheus Bks.

Fletcher, Joseph S. *see* Fletcher, Joseph Smith.

Fletcher, Joseph Smith, 1863-1935
  xFletcher, J. S.
    The Middle Temple Murder. Dover.
  xFletcher, Joseph S.
    At the Blue Bell Inn. Arno.
    Massingham Butterfly, & Other Stories. Arno.

Fletcher, Kenneth. *see* Fletcher, Kenneth R.

Fletcher, Kenneth R.
  xFletcher, Kenneth.
    Extend: Youth Reaching Youth. Augsburg.

Fletcher, Leon. *see* Fletcher, Leon C.

Fletcher, Leon C.
  xFletcher, Leon.
    How to Design & Deliver a Speech. Har-Row.

Fletcher, Leslie.
  xFletcher, Leslie.
    Florida's Fantastic Fauna & Flora. Beau Lac.

Fletcher, Lucille.
  xFletcher, Lucille.
    Eighty Dollars to Stamford. Penguin.

Fletcher, Margaret I. *see* Fletcher, Margaret Isabel.

Fletcher, Margaret Isabel, 1897-
  xFletcher, Margaret I.
    Adult & the Nursery School Child. U of
      Toronto Pr.

Fletcher, Max E. *see* Fletcher, Max Ellis.

Fletcher, Max Ellis, 1921-
  xFletcher, Max E.
    Economics & Social Problems. HM.

Fletcher, Mike.
  xFletcher, Mike.
    Tuning a Racing Yacht. Norton.

Fletcher, Neville H. *see* Fletcher, Neville Horner.

Fletcher, Neville Horner.
  xFletcher, Neville H.
    Chemical Physics of Ice. Cambridge U Pr.

Fletcher, Omar.
  xFletcher, Omar.
    Escape from Death Row. Holloway.

Fletcher, R. A., fl. 1978-
  xFletcher, R. A.
    The Episcopate in the Kingdom of Leon in the
      Twelfth Century. Oxford U Pr.

Fletcher, Robert H. *see* Fletcher, Robert Huntington.

Fletcher, Robert Huntington.
  xFletcher, Robert H.
    Arthurian Material in the Chronicles,
      Especially Those of Great Britain & France
      ... Expanded by a Bibliography & Critical
      Essay for the Period 1905-1965 by Roger
      Sherman Loomis. B Franklin.

Fletcher, Robert S. *see* Fletcher, Robert Samuel.

Fletcher, Robert Samuel, 1900-1959
  xFletcher, Robert S.
    History of Oberlin College: From Its
      Foundation Through the Civil War. Arno.

Fletcher, Ron. *see* Fletcher, Ron A.

Fletcher, Ron A.
  xFletcher, Ron.
    Every Body Is Beautiful. Lippincott.

Fletcher, Samuel G. *see* Fletcher, Samuel Glen.

Fletcher, Samuel Glen.
  xFletcher, Samuel G.
    Diagnosing Speech Disorders from Cleft Palate.
      Grune.

Fletcher, William C.
  xFletcher, William C.
    Religion & Soviet Foreign Policy, 1945-1970.
      Oxford U Pr.

Fletcher, William I., 1938-
  xFletcher, William I.

An Engineering Approach to Digital Design. P-H.

Fletcher, William Y. *see* Fletcher, William Younger.

Fletcher, William Younger.
xFletcher, William Y.
English Book Collectors. B Franklin.

Fleure, Herbert J. *see* Fleure, Herbert John.

Fleure, Herbert John, 1877-1969
xFleure, Herbert J.
The Peoples of Europe. AMS Pr.

Fleuter, D. L. *see* Fleuter, Douglas L.

Fleuter, Douglas L., 1921-
xFleuter, D. L.
The Workweek Revolution: A Guide to the Changing Workweek. A-W.

Flew, A. G. *see* Flew, Antony Garrard Newton.

Flew, Antony.
xFlew, Antony.
A Dictionary of Philosophy. St Martin.

Flew, Antony. *see* Flew, Antony Garrard Newton.

Flew, Antony Garrard Newton, 1923
xFlew, A. G.
ed. Logic & Language. Biblio Dist.
xFlew, Antony.
Thinking Straight. Prometheus Bks.

Flew, Josiah.
xFlew, Josiah.
Studies in Browning. Haskell.
Studies in Browning. R West.

Flew, R. Newton. *see* Flew, Robert Newton.

Flew, Robert Newton, 1886-
xFlew, R. Newton.
Idea of Perfection in Christian Theology: An Historical Study of the Christian Ideal for the Present Life. Humanities.

Flexner, Abraham, 1866-1959
xFlexner, Abraham.
Prostitution in Europe. Patterson Smith.

Flexner, Eleanor, 1908-
xFlexner, Eleanor.
Century of Struggle: The Woman's Rights Movement in the United States. Harvard U Pr.

Flexner, James. *see* Flexner, James Thomas.

Flexner, James Carey Thomas, 1908-
xFlexner, James T.
That Wilder Image: The Painting of America's Native School from Thomas Cole to Winslow Homer. Dover.

Flexner, James T. *see* Flexner, James Carey Thomas.

Flexner, James Thomas, 1908-
xFlexner, James.
World of Winslow Homer. Time-Life.
World of Winslow Homer. Silver.
xFlexner, James T.
Doctors on Horseback: Pioneers of American Medicine. Peter Smith.
The Light of Distant Skies: 1760-1835. Dover.
Lord of the Mohawks: A Biography of Sir William Johnson. Little.

Flexner, Stuart B. *see* Flexner, Stuart Berg.

Flexner, Stuart Berg.
xFlexner, Stuart B.
I Hear America Talking: An Illustrated Treasury of American Words & Phrases. Van Nos Reinhold.

Flick, Alexander C. *see* Flick, Alexander Clarence.

Flick, Alexander Clarence, 1869-1942
xFlick, Alexander C.
Decline of the Medieval Church. B Franklin.
Loyalism in New York During the American Revolution. AMS Pr.
Loyalism in New York During the American Revolution. Arno.

Flick, Art. *see* Flick, Arthur B.

Flick, Arthur B.
xFlick, Art.

ed. Art Flick's Master Fly-Tying Guide. Crown.
Art Flicks New Streamside Guide to Naturals & Their Imitations. Crown.

Flick, Carlos, 1927-
xFlick, Carlos T.
The Birmingham Political Union & the Movements for Reform in Britain, 1830-1839. Shoe String.

Flick, Carlos T. *see* Flick, Carlos.

Flick, E. W. *see* Flick, Ernest W.

Flick, Ernest W.
xFlick, E. W.
Adhesive & Sealant Compounds & Their Formulations. Noyes.
Solvent-Based Paint Formulations. Noyes.

Flicker, Barbara.
xFlicker, Barbara.
Standards for Juvenile Justice: A Summary & Analysis. Ballinger Pub.

Fliegel, Carl J. *see* Fliegel, Carl John.

Fliegel, Carl John.
xFliegel, Carl J.
Compiled by Index to the Records of the Moravian Mission Among the Indians of North America. Res Pubns Conn.

Fliegel, Dorian.
xFliegel, Dorian.
The Fix. HM.

Fliess, Peter J.
xFliess, Peter J.
Freedom of the Press in the German Republic, 1918-1933. Greenwood.

Fliess, Robert, 1895-1970
xFliess, Robert.
Symbol, Dream & Psychosis. Intl Univs Pr.

Flink, James J.
xFlink, James J.
The Car Culture. MIT Pr.

Flink, Salomon J.
xFlink, Salomon J.
Equity Financing of Small Manufacturing Companies in New Jersey. Arno.

Flinn, Avril.
xFlinn, Avril.
Come into My Parlor. Logos.

Flinn, Richard. *see* Flinn, Richard Aloysius.

Flinn, Richard A. *see* Flinn, Richard Aloysius.

Flinn, Richard Aloysius.
xFlinn, Richard.
Engineering Materials & Their Applications. HM.
xFlinn, Richard A.
Fundamentals of Metal Casting. A-W.

Flinn, Thomas A., 1925-
xFlinn, Thomas A.
Local Government & Politics: Analyzing Decision-Making Systems. Scott F.

Flint, Betty M. *see* Flint, Betty Margaret.

Flint, Betty Margaret.
xFlint, Betty M.
Child & the Institution: A Study of Deprivation & Recovery. U of Toronto Pr.

Flint, James.
xFlint, James.
Letters from America: Containing Observations on the Climate & Agriculture of the Western States, the Manners of the People & the Prospects of Emigrants. Johnson Repr.

Flint, Jerry, 1931-
xFlint, Jerry.
The Dream Machine: The Golden Age of American Automobiles 1945-1965. Times Bks.

Flint, Rachael H. *see* Flint, Rachael Heyhoe.

Flint, Rachael Heyhoe.
xFlint, Rachael H.
Field Hockey. Barron.

Flint, Richard F. *see* Flint, Richard Foster.

Flint, Richard Foster, 1902-
xFlint, Richard F.
Earth & Its History. Norton.
Glacial & Quaternary Geology. Wiley.

Flint, Robert, 1838-1910
xFlint, Robert.
Vico. Arno.

Flint, Timothy, 1780-1840
xFlint, Timothy.
Little Henry: the Stolen Child. Irvington.

Flipper, Henry O. *see* Flipper, Henry Ossian.

Flipper, Henry Ossian, 1856-1940
xFlipper, Henry O.
Colored Cadet at West Point. Arno.

Flippo, Edwin B.
xFlippo, Edwin B.
Principles of Personnel Management. McGraw.
Principles of Personnel Management. McGraw.

Flitter, Hessel H. *see* Flitter, Hessel Howard.

Flitter, Hessel Howard.
xFlitter, Hessel H.
An Introduction to Physics in Nursing. Mosby.

Floan, Howard R. *see* Floan, Howard Russell.

Floan, Howard Russell, 1918-
xFloan, Howard R.
The South in Northern Eyes. Haskell.

Floberg, Marilyn, 1932-
xFloberg, Marilyn.
Practice in Real Estate Mathematics. Har-Row.

Floethe, Louise L. *see* Floethe, Louise Lee.

Floethe, Louise Lee.
xFloethe, Louise L.
Fishing Around the World. Scribner.

Flohn, Hermann.
xFlohn, N.
Climate & Weather. McGraw.
Flohn, N. *see* Flohn, Hermann.

Flood, E. A. *see* Flood, Edward Alison.

Flood, Edward Alison, 1904-
xFlood, E. A.
ed. The Solid-Gas Interface. Dekker.

Flood, James E. *see* Flood, James Edward.

Flood, James Edward.
xFlood, James E.
Language-Reading Instruction for the Young Child. Macmillan.

Flood, Jeanne.
xFlood, Jeanne.
Brian Moore. Bucknell U Pr.

Flood, R. B. *see* Flood, Riefford B.

Flood, Riefford B., 1920-
xFlood, R. B.
Home Fruit & Vegetable Production. Scarecrow.

Flood, Robert.
xFlood, Robert.
Men Who Shaped America. Moody.

Flood, Robert J.
xFlood, Robert J.
Clay Tobacco Pipes in Cambridgeshire. Oleander Pr.

Flood, William Grattan. *see* Flood, William Henry Grattan.

Flood, William Henry Grattan, 1859-1928
xFlood, William Grattan.
The Story of the Bagpipe. Longwood Pr.
The Story of the Harp. Longwood Pr.

Flora, Cornelia B. *see* Flora, Cornelia Butler.

Flora, Cornelia Butler, 1943-
xFlora, Cornelia B.
Pentecostalism in Colombia: Baptism by Fire & Spirit. Fairleigh Dickinson.

Flora, James.
xFlora, James.

illus. The Day the Cow Sneezed. HarBraceJ.
illus. Fishing with Dad. HarBraceJ.
illus. The Great Green Turkey Creek Monster.
 Atheneum.
The Great Green Turkey Creek Monster.
 Atheneum.
illus. Little Hatchy Hen. HarBraceJ.
illus. Pishtosh, Bullwash & Wimple. Atheneum.
illus. Stewed Goose. Atheneum.

Flora, Joseph M.
 xFlora, Joseph M.
 Vardis Fisher. Coll & U Pr.
 Vardis Fisher. Twayne.

Flora, Paul.
 xFlora, Paul.
 Penthouse. Abrams.

Flora, Peter.
 xFlora, Peter.
 ed. Development of Welfare States in Europe
  & America. Transaction Bks.

Flora, Snowden D. *see* Flora, Snowden Dwight.

Flora, Snowden Dwight, 1879-
 xFlora, Snowden D.
 Tornadoes of the United States. U of Okla Pr.

Florance, Chris, 1910-
 xFlorance, Chris.
 Carolina Home Gardener. U of NC Pr.

Florea, J. H.
 xFlorea, J. H.
 The ABC of Poultry Raising: A Complete
  Guide for the Beginner or Expert. Dover.
 ABC of Poultry Raising: A Complete Guide for
  the Beginner or Expert. Peter Smith.

Floren, Lee.
 xFloren, Lee.
 Fighting Ramrod. Nordon Pubns.
 Night Riders. Nordon Pubns.
 Renegade Gambler. G K Hall.
 Rifles on the Range. Nordon Pubns.

Florence, Gene, 1944-
 xFlorence, Gene.
 Collector's Encyclopedia of Depression Glass.
  Collector Bks.

Florence, P. S. *see* Florence, Philip Sargant.
Florence, P. Sargant. *see* Florence, Philip Sargant.
Florence, Philip S. *see* Florence, Philip Sargant.

Florence, Philip Sargant, 1890-
 xFlorence, P. S.
 Atlas of Economic Structure & Policies.
  Pergamon.
 xFlorence, P. Sargant.
 The Logic of British & American Industry: A
  Realistic Analysis of Economic Structure &
  Government. Routledge & Kegan.
 xFlorence, Philip S.
 Economics of Fatigue & Unrest & the
  Efficiency of Labour in English & American
  Industry. Greenwood.
 Use of Factory Statistics in the Investigation of
  Industrial Fatigue. AMS Pr.

Florence, Ronald.
 xFlorence, Ronald.
 Marx's Daughters: Eleanor Marx, Rosa
  Luxemburg, Angelica Balabanoff. Dial.

Flores, Angel.
 xFlores, Angel.
 ed. Franz Kafka Today. Gordian.
 Lope De Vega: Monster of Nature. Kennikat.
 ed. Nineteenth Century French Tales. Ungar.
 ed. Spanish Writers in Exile. Porter.

Flores, Ivan.
 xFlores, Ivan.
 Data Structure & Management. P-H.

Flores, Janis.
 xFlores, Janis.
 Peregrine House. Dell.
 Peregrine House. Doubleday.

Flores, Solomon H. *see* Flores, Solomon Hernandez.

Flores, Solomon Hernandez.
 xFlores, Solomon H.

The Nature & Effectiveness of Bilingual
 Education Programs for the Spanish-Speaking
 Child in the United States. Arno.

Florey, Kitty B. *see* Florey, Kitty Burns.

Florey, Kitty Burns.
 xFlorey, Kitty B.
 Family Matters. Seaview Bks.

Florida Atlantic University Conference. *see* Conference
 on Management Problems in Serials Work, Florida
 Atlantic University, 1973.

**Florida Colloquium on Molecular Biology, University of
Florida, Gainesville, 1975.**
 xSymposium, University of Florida, Gainsville,
  March, 1975.
 Chromosomal Proteins & Their Role in the
  Regulation of Gene Expression: Proceedings.
  Acad Pr.

Florida. University, Gainesville.
 xUniversity of Florida.
 Catalog of the Latin American Collection,
  University of Florida Libraries, First
  Supplement. G K Hall.
 Libraries Catalog of the Latin American
  Library. G K Hall.

Floridi, Alexis U. *see* Floridi, Ulisse Alessio.

Floridi, Ulisse Alessio.
 xFloridi, Alexis U.
 The Uncertain Alliance: The Catholic Church
  & Labor in Latin America. AISI.

Florin, Lambert.
 xFlorin, Lambert F.
 California Ghost Towns. Superior Pub.

Florin, Lambert F. *see* Florin, Lambert.

Florinsky, Michael T., 1894-
 xFlorinsky, Michael T.
 End of the Russian Empire. Macmillan.
 Integrated Europe?. Greenwood.

Florio, A. E.
 xFlorio, A. E.
 Safety Education. McGraw.

Florio, Anthony.
 xFlorio, Anthony.
 Two to Get Ready. Victor Bks.

Florman, Samuel. *see* Florman, Samuel C.

Florman, Samuel C.
 xFlorman, Samuel.
 The Existential Pleasures of Engineering. St
  Martin.
 xFlorman, Samuel C.
 Engineering & the Liberal Arts: A
  Technologist's Guide to History, Literature,
  Philosophy, Art & Music. McGraw.
 The Existential Pleasures of Engineering. St
  Martin.

Flory, Jane.
 xFlory, Jane.
 The Bear on the Doorstep. HM.
 illus. The Golden Venture. HM.
 illus. The Liberation of Clementine Tipton.
  HM.
 The Lost & Found Princess. HM.
 The Unexpected Grandchildren. HM.

Flory, Paul J.
 xFlory, Paul J.
 Principles of Polymer Chemistry. Cornell U Pr.

Flory, Wendy S. *see* Flory, Wendy Stallard.

Flory, Wendy Stallard.
 xFlory, Wendy S.
 Ezra Pound & the Cantos: A Record of
  Struggle. Yale U Pr.

Floud, Roderick.
 xFloud, Roderick.
 Introduction to Quantitative Methods for
  Historians. Methuen Inc.

Flournoy, Francis R. *see* Flournoy, Francis Rosebro.

Flournoy, Francis Rosebro, 1884-
 xFlournoy, Francis R.

British Policy Towards Morocco in the Age of
 Palmerston, 1830-1865. Negro U Pr.

Flournoy, Valerie.
 xFlournoy, Valerie.
 The Best Time of Day. Random.

Flower, Benjamin O. *see* Flower, Benjamin Orange.

Flower, Benjamin Orange, 1858-1918
 xFlower, Benjamin O.
 Progressive Men, Women & Movements of the
  Past Twenty-Five Years. Hyperion Conn.

Flower, Elizabeth.
 xFlower, Elizabeth.
 A History of Philosophy in America. Hackett
  Pub.

Flower, Enola.
 xFlower, Enola.
 Child's History of California. Caxton.

Flower, Pat.
 xFlower, Pat.
 Odd Job. Stein & Day.

Flower, Phyllis.
 xFlower, Phyllis.
 The Barn Owl. Har-Row.

Flower, Raymond, 1921-
 xFlower, Raymond.
 Chianti: The Land, the People & the Wine.
  Universe.
 Lloyd's of London: An Illustrated History.
  Hastings.

Flowers, B. H. *see* Flowers, Brian Hilton.

Flowers, Brian Hilton.
 xFlowers, B. H.
 Properties of Matter. Wiley.

Flowers, John G. *see* Flowers, John Garland.

Flowers, John Garland, 1895-
 xFlowers, John G.
 Content of Student-Teaching Courses Designed
  for the Training of Secondary Teachers in
  State Teachers Colleges. AMS Pr.

Flowers, Montaville, 1868-1934
 xFlowers, Montaville.
 The Japanese Conquest of American Opinion.
  Arno.

Flowers, T. H. *see* Flowers, Thomas Harold.

Flowers, Thomas Harold.
 xFlowers, T. H.
 Introduction to Exchange Systems. Wiley.

Floyd, Ann.
 xFloyd, Ann.
 Cognitive Development in the School Years.
  Halsted Pr.

Floyd, Barry.
 xFloyd, Barry.
 Jamaica: An Island Microcosm. St Martin.

Floyd, Don E. *see* Floyd, Don Edgar.

Floyd, Don Edgar, 1918-
 xFloyd, Don E.
 Polyamide Resins. Van Nos Reinhold.

Floyd, Mary K.
 xFloyd, Mary K.
 Abortion Bibliography for 1970. Whitston Pub.
 Abortion Bibliography for 1971. Whitston Pub.
 Abortion Bibliography for 1972. Whitston Pub.
 Abortion Bibliography for 1973. Whitston Pub.
 Abortion Bibliography for 1974. Whitston Pub.
 Abortion Bibliography for 1976. Whitston Pub.
 Abortion Bibliography for 1977. Whitston Pub.

Floyd, Thomas L.
 xFloyd, Thomas L.
 Digital Logic Fundamentals. Merrill.

Floyd, Troy S.
 xFloyd, Troy S.
 The Columbus Dynasty in the Caribbean,
  1492-1526. U of NM Pr.

Floyd, Virginia.
 xFloyd, Virginia.
 ed. Eugene O'Neill: A World View. Ungar.

Floyd, W. F.
 xFloyd, W. F.

ed. Symposium on Fatigue & Symposium on
Human Factors in Equipment Design. Arno.

Fluck, Sandra.
xFluck, Sandra.
Experiential English. Glencoe.

Flugel, John C. *see* Flugel, John Carl.

Flugel, John Carl, 1884-1955
xFlugel, John C.
The Psychology of Clothes. AMS Pr.

Flugge, Wilhelm. *see* Flugge, Wilhelm Gottfried Wilhelm
Flugge.

Flugge, Wilhelm Gottfried Wilhelm Flugge, 1904-
xFlugge, Wilhelm.
ed. Handbook of Engineering Mechanics.
McGraw.

Fluharty, George. *see* Fluharty, George W.

Fluharty, George W.
xFluharty, George.
Public Speaking. Har-Row.

Fluharty, Vernon L. *see* Fluharty, Vernon Lee.

Fluharty, Vernon Lee.
xFluharty, Vernon L.
Dance of the Millions: Military Rule & the
Social Revolution in Colombia. Greenwood.

Flukinger, Roy.
xFlukinger, Roy.
Paul Martin: Victorian Photographer. U of Tex
Pr.

Flumiani, C. M. *see* Flumiani, Carlo Maria.

Flumiani, Carlo M. *see* Flumiani, Carlo Maria.

Flumiani, Carlo Maria.
xFlumiani, C. M.
The Gyrations of the Dollar & the Deceit of
Gold. Am Classical Coll Pr.
How to Make a Fortune in a Bear Market. Am
Classical Coll Pr.
How to Protect Your Money from the
Destructive Powers of Inflation, Business
Depressions, Political Turmoil, Wars,
Revolutions & How to Double Your
Patrimony Safely Every Five Years.. Am
Classical Coll Pr.
The Laws of History & the Caprice of Men.
Am Classical Coll Pr.
The Physiology & Pathology of Stock Market
Action. Inst Econ Finan.
The Power Anatomy of the Economic Forces
Dominating the Business & Political World.
Am Classical Coll Pr.
Power Anatomy of the Economic Forces
Dominating the Business & the Political
World. Inst Econ Finan.
Stock Market Mastery Through the
Application of the First Elliott Wave. Am
Classical Coll Pr.
xFlumiani, Carlo M.
illus. The Laws of History & the Caprice of
Men. Am Classical Coll Pr.
xFlumiani, Carlo Maria.
The Cylinder Theory & the Metaphysics of
Catastrophe. Inst Econ Finan.

Flury, Patricia A.
xFlury, Patricia A.
Environmental Health & Safety in the Hospital
Laboratory. C C Thomas.

Flygare, Thomas. *see* Flygare, Thomas J.

Flygare, Thomas J.
xFlygare, Thomas.
The Legal Rights of Students. Phi Delta Kappa.
xFlygare, Thomas J.
The Legal Rights of Teachers. Phi Delta
Kappa.

Flygt, Sten G. *see* Flygt, Sten Gunnar.

Flygt, Sten Gunnar, 1911-
xFlygt, Sten G.
Friedrich Hebbel's Conception of Movement in
the Absolute & in History. AMS Pr.

Flynn, Cleta, 1940-
xFlynn, Cleta.

The Parable: A Story of Jesus, Son of Joseph.
Donning Co.

Flynn, Dianne.
xFlynn, Dianne.
Portrait Drawing Techniques. Larousse.

Flynn, Elizabeth G. *see* Flynn, Elizabeth Gurley.

Flynn, Elizabeth Gurley.
xFlynn, Elizabeth G.
Alderson Story: My Life As a Political
Prisoner. Intl Pub Co.

Flynn, Elizabeth W.
xFlynn, Elizabeth W.
Designs in Affective Education: A Teacher
Resource Program for Junior & Senior High.
Paulist Pr.

Flynn, George, 1921-
xFlynn, George.
Transistor - Transistor Logic. Sams.
Transistor-Transistor Logic. Sams.

Flynn, Gerard. *see* Flynn, Gerard C.

Flynn, Gerard C.
xFlynn, Gerard.
Manuel Breton De los Herreros. Twayne.
Manuel Tamayo y Baus. Twayne.
Sor Juana Ines de la Cruz. Irvington.

Flynn, James R. *see* Flynn, James Robert.

Flynn, James Robert, 1934-
xFlynn, James R.
Humanism & Ideology: An Aristotelian View.
Routledge & Kegan.

Flynn, Jay.
xFlynn, Jay.
Trouble Is My Business. Nordon Pubns.

Flynn, Joe B.
xFlynn, Joe B.
The Design of Executive Protection Systems. C
C Thomas.

Flynn, John E. *see* Flynn, John Edward.

Flynn, John Edward.
xFlynn, John E.
Architectural Interior Systems: Lighting, Air
Conditioning, Acoustics. Van Nos Reinhold.

Flynn, John T. *see* Flynn, John Thomas.

Flynn, John Thomas, 1883-1964
xFlynn, John T.
As We Go Marching. Arno.
As We Go Marching. Free Life.
God's Gold: The Story of Rockefeller & His
Times. Greenwood.
xFlynn, John Thomas.
Country Squire in the White House. Da Capo.

Flynn, Leslie. *see* Flynn, Leslie B.

Flynn, Leslie B.
xFlynn, Leslie.
God's Will: You Can Know It. Victor Bks.
xFlynn, Leslie B.
Day of Resurrection. Baker Bk.
Great Church Fights. Victor Bks.

Flynn, Patricia A. *see* Flynn, Patricia Anne Randolph.

Flynn, Patricia Anne Randolph.
xFlynn, Patricia A.
Holistic Health: The Art & Science of Care. R
J Brady.

Flynn, Philip.
xFlynn, Philip.
Francis Jeffrey. U Delaware Pr.

Flynn, Robert J., 1923-
xFlynn, Robert J.
Parasites of Laboratory Animals. Iowa St U Pr.

Flynn, Thomas, 1944-
xFlynn, Thomas.
Tales for My Brothers' Keepers. Norton.

Flynt, Wayne, 1940-
xFlynt, Wayne.
Duncan Upshaw Fletcher: Dixie's Reluctant
Progressive. U Presses Fla.

Foa, Edna B.
xFoa, Edna B.

Handbook of Behavioral Interventions. Wiley.

Foa, Uriel G.
xFoa, Uriel G.
Societal Structures of the Mind. C C Thomas.

Fobel, Jim.
xFobel, Jim.
The Big Book of Fabulous, Fun'filled
Celebrations & Holiday Crafts. HR&W.

Foch, Ferdinand, 1851-1929
xFoch, Ferdinand.
Principles of War. AMS Pr.

Fochs, Arnold.
xFochs, Arnold.
Advertising That Won Elections. A J Pub.

Fochtman, Dianne.
xFochtman, Dianne.
Principles of Nursing Care for the Pediatric
Surgery Patient. Little.

Fodell, Beverly, 1930-
xFodell, Beverly.
Cesar Chavez & the United Farm Workers: A
Selective Bibliography. Wayne St U Pr.

Fodor, Janet D. *see* Fodor, Janet Dean.

Fodor, Janet Dean.
xFodor, Janet D.
The Linguistic Description of Opaque
Contexts. Garland Pub.

Fodor, Jerry A.
xFodor, Jerry A.
Psychological Explanation: An Introduction to
the Philosophy of Psychology. Random.

Fodor, Nandor.
xFodor, Nandor.
Encyclopaedia of Psychic Science. Citadel Pr.
Encyclopaedia of Psychic Science. Univ Bks.

Fodor, R. V.
xFodor, R. V,
Angry Waters: Floods & Their Control. Dodd.
Earth in Motion: The Concept of Plate
Tectonics. Morrow.
Growing Strong. Sterling.
Impact!. Nordon Pubns.
xFodor, Ronald V.
What to Eat & Why: The Science of Nutrition.
Morrow.

Fodor, Ronald V. *see* Fodor, R. V.

Foell, Wesley K.
xFoell, Wesley K.
Management of Energy-Environment Systems:
Methods & Case Studies. Wiley.

Foerster, Donald M. *see* Foerster, Donald Madison.

Foerster, Donald Madison, 1914-1961
xFoerster, Donald M.
Homer in English Criticism: The Historical
Approach in the Eighteenth Century. Shoe
String.

Foerster, Friedrich W. *see* Foerster, Friedrich Wilhelm.

Foerster, Friedrich Wilhelm, 1869-1966
xFoerster, Friedrich W.
Europe & the German Question. AMS Pr.

Foerster, H. Von. *see* Von Foerster, H.

Foerster, Norman, 1887-
xFoerster, Norman.
American Criticism: A Study in Literary
Theory from Poe to the Present. Russell.
ed. American Ideals. Arno.
ed. American Poetry & Prose. HM.
Future of the Liberal College. Arno.
Image of America: Our Literature from
Puritanism to the Space Age. U of Notre
Dame Pr.
The Intellectual Heritage of Thoreau. Folcroft.
ed. Introduction to American Poetry & Prose.
HM.

Foerster, Paul A.
xFoerster, Paul A.
Algebra & Trigonometry: Functions &
Applications. A-W.

Fogarty, Michael P. *see* Fogarty, Michael Patrick.

Fogarty, Michael Patrick.
   xFogarty, Michael P.
      Christian Democracy in Western Europe,
      1820-1953. Greenwood.
Fogarty, Robert S.
   xFogarty, Robert S.
      Dictionary of American Communal & Utopian
      History. Greenwood.
Fogel, Julianna A.
   xFogel, Julianna A.
      Wesley Paul, Marathon Runner. Lippincott.
Fogel, Marvin.
   xFogel, Marvin.
      The Medical School Admission Adviser.
      Dutton.
Fogel, Robert W. *see* Fogel, Robert William.
Fogel, Robert William.
   xFogel, Robert W.
      Railroads & American Economic Growth:
      Essays in Econometric History. Johns
      Hopkins.
Fogelin, Robert J.
   xFogelin, Robert J.
      Evidence & Meaning: Studies in Analytic
      Philosophy. Humanities.
      Understanding Arguments: An Introduction to
      Informal Logic. HarBraceJ.
Fogelman, K. R.
   xFogelman, K. R.
      Leaving the Sixth Form: A Selection of
      Opinions. Humanities.
Fogelson, Raymond D.
   xFogelson, Raymond D.
      ed. The Anthropology of Power: Ethnographic
      Studies from Asia, Oceania & New World.
      Acad Pr.
Fogelson, Robert. *see* Fogelson, Robert M.
Fogelson, Robert M.
   xFogelson, Robert.
      ed. Los Angeles Riots. Arno.
Fogerty, James E., 1945-
   xFogerty, James E.
      Compiled by Preliminary Guide to the
      Holdings of the Minnesota Regional Research
      Centers. Minn Hist.
Fogg, G. E. *see* Fogg, Gordon Elliott.
Fogg, Gordon Elliott.
   xFogg, G. E.
      Algal Cultures & Phytoplankton Ecology. U of
      Wis Pr.
Fogg, H. G. *see* Fogg, Harry George Witham.
Fogg, Harry George Witham.
   xFogg, H. G.
      History of Popular Garden Plants from A to Z.
      A S Barnes.
Fogg, Walter.
   xFogg, Walter.
      One Thousand Sayings of History, Presented
      As Pictures in Prose. Gale.
Fogh, Jorgen. *see* Fogh, Jorgen.
Fogh, Jorgen.
   xFogh, Jorgen.
      ed. Contamination in Tissue Culture. Acad Pr.
      ed. Human Tumor Cells in Vitro. Plenum Pub.
Fogle, Richard H. *see* Fogle, Richard Harter.
Fogle, Richard Harter.
   xFogle, Richard H.
      Idea of Coleridge's Criticism. Greenwood.
      Imagery of Keats & Shelley: A Comparative
      Study. U of NC Pr.
Fohl, Mark E.
   xFohl, Mark E.
      A Microprocessor Course. Petrocelli.
Fohrer, Georg.
   xFohrer, Georg.
      History of Israelite Religion. Abingdon.
Foin, Theodore C.
   xFoin, Theodore C.

      Ecological Systems & the Environment. HM.
Fokker, Anthony H. *see* Fokker, Anthony Herman
Gerard.
Fokker, Anthony Herman Gerard.
   xFokker, Anthony H.
      Flying Dutchman: The Life of Anthony
      Fokker. Arno.
Fokker, Nicolas, 1908-
   xFokker, Nicolas.
      The Tamer. Har-Row.
Folan, Lilias. *see* Folan, Lilias M.
Folan, Lilias M.
   xFolan, Lilias.
      Lilias, Yoga & You. Bantam.
Folb, Edith A.
   xFolb, Edith A.
      Runnin' Down Some Lines: The Language &
      Culture of Black Teenagers. Harvard U Pr.
Folda, Jaroslav.
   xFolda, Jaroslav.
      Crusader Manuscript Illumination at Saint-Jean
      D'acre, 1275-1291. Princeton U Pr.
Foldeak, Arpad. *see* Foldeak, Walter Arpad.
Foldeak, Walter Arpad.
   xFoldeak, Arpad.
      Chess Olympiads. Branden.
      Chess Olympiads: 1927-1968. Dover.
Foldvari, Maria V. *see* Foldvari, Maria Vogl.
Foldvari, Maria Vogl.
   xFoldvari, Maria V.
      Theory & Practice of Regional Geochemical
      Exploration. Heyden.
Foldvary, Fred E., 1946-
   xFoldvary, Fred E.
      The Soul of Liberty: The Universal Ethic of
      Freedom & Human Rights. Gutenberg.
Folejewski, Zbigniew, 1910-
   xFolejewski, Zbigniew.
      Maria Dabrowska. Irvington.
Foley, Bernard. *see* Foley, Bernard J.
Foley, Bernard J.
   xFoley, Bernard.
      Accounting Information Disclosure &
      Collective Bargaining. Holmes & Meier.
Foley, Bernice W. *see* Foley, Bernice Williams.
Foley, Bernice Williams.
   xFoley, Bernice W.
      Spaceships of the Ancients. Veritie Pr.
      Why the Cock Crows Three Times. Childrens.
      Why the Cock Crows Three Times. Childs
      World.
Foley, Charles, 1908-
   xFoley, Charles.
      The Struggle for Cyprus. Hoover Inst Pr.
Foley, Daniel J.
   xFoley, Daniel J.
      Ground Covers for Easier Gardening. Dover.
Foley, Donald L.
   xFoley, Donald L.
      Controlling London's Growth: Planning the
      Great Wen, 1940-1960. U of Cal Pr.
Foley, Henry A.
   xFoley, Henry A.
      Community Mental Health Legislation: The
      Formative Process. Lexington Bks.
Foley, James.
   xFoley, James.
      Foundations of Theoretical Phonology.
      Cambridge U Pr.
Foley, Lou. *see* Foley, Louise Munro.
Foley, Louise Munro.
   xFoley, Lou.
      Somebody Stole Second. Dell.
Foley, Vincent D.
   xFoley, Vincent D.
      An Introduction to Family Therapy. Grune.
Folger, John K.
   xFolger, John K.

      Education of the American Population. Arno.
      Human Resources & Higher Education: Staff
      Report of the Commission on Human
      Resources & Advanced Education. Russell
      Sage.
Folger Shakespeare Library, Washington, D.C.
   xFolger Shakespeare Library, Washington, D. C.
      Catalog of Manuscripts of the Folger
      Shakespeare Library. G K Hall.
      Catalog of Printed Books of the Folger
      Shakespeare Library. G K Hall.
      Catalog of Printed Books of the Folger
      Shakespeare Library, First Supplement. G K
      Hall.
      Folger Shakespeare Library: Catalog of the
      Shakespeare Collection. G K Hall.
Folinsbee, Lawrence J.
   xFolinsbee, Lawrence J.
      ed. Environmental Stress: Individual Human
      Adaptations. Acad Pr.
Folk, Ernest L.
   xFolk, Ernest L.
      The Delaware General Corporation Law: A
      Commentary & Analysis. Little.
Folk, G. Edgar. *see* Folk, George Edgar.
Folk, George Edgar, 1914-
   xFolk, G. Edgar.
      Hamster Guide. TFH Pubns.
Folkenflik, Robert, 1939-
   xFolkenflik, Robert.
      Samuel Johnson, Biographer. Cornell U Pr.
Folkman, David I.
   xFolkman, David I.
      The Nicaragua Route. U of Utah Pr.
Folkow, Bjoern. *see* Folkow, Bjorn.
Folkow, Bjorn.
   xFolkow, Bjoern.
      Circulation. Oxford U Pr.
Folks, Homer, 1867-1963
   xFolks, Homer.
      Care of Destitute, Neglected, & Delinquent
      Children. Arno.
      The Care of Destitute, Neglected & Delinquent
      Children. Natl Assn Soc Wkrs.
      The Care of the Destitute, Neglected &
      Delinquent Children. Johnson Repr.
Follendore, Joan S.
   xFollendore, Joan S.
      Compiled by From Our Immigrants with Love.
      Racz Pub.
Follett, Helen (Thomas).
   xFollett, Helen T.
      Arnold Bennett. Folcroft.
      Some Modern Novelists: Appreciations &
      Estimates. Arno.
      Some Modern Novelists: Appreciations &
      Estimates. R West.
   xFollett, Wilson.
      jt. auth. Some Modern Novelists: Appreciations
      & Estimates. Arno.
      jt. auth. Some Modern Novelists: Appreciations
      & Estimates. R West.
Follett, Helen T. *see* Follett, Helen (Thomas).
Follett, James, 1939-
   xFollett, James.
      The Wotan Warhead. Stein & Day.
Follett, Ken.
   xFollett, Ken.
      Eye of the Needle. Arbor Hse.
      Eye of the Needle. NAL.
Follett, Mary P. *see* Follett, Mary Parker.
Follett, Mary Parker, 1868-1933
   xFollett, Mary P.
      The Speaker of the House of Representatives.
      B Franklin.
Follett, Robert. *see* Follett, Robert J. R.
Follett, Robert J. R.
   xFollett, Robert.

How to Keep Score in Business. Follett.
What to Take Backpacking--& Why. Alpine
   Guild.
Follett, Wilson.
   xFollett, Wilson.
      Modern American Usage. Warner Bks.
Follett, Wilson. *see* Follett, Helen (Thomas).
Follette, Suzanne La. *see* La Follette, Suzanne.
Follis, John.
   xFollis, John.
      Architectural Signing & Graphics.
         Watson-Guptill.
Follmann, Joseph F. *see* Follmann, Joseph Francis.
Follmann, Joseph Francis, 1908-
   xFollmann, Joseph F.
      The Economics of Industrial Health: History,
         Theory, & Practice. Am Mgmt.
      Helping the Troubled Employee. Am Mgmt.
Folmsbee, Beulah.
   xFolmsbee, Beulah.
      Little History of the Horn-Book. Horn Bk.
Folprecht, William.
   xFolprecht, William.
      Superstars of Sports. Newbury Hse.
Folsom, Franklin, 1907-
   xFolsom, Franklin.
      The Life & Legend of George McJunkin: Black
         Cowboy. Elsevier-Nelson.
Folsom, James K.
   xFolsom, James K.
      ed. The Western: A Collection of Critical
         Essays. P-H.
Folsom, Kenneth E.
   xFolsom, Kenneth E.
      Friends, Guests & Colleagues: The Mufu
         System of the Late Ch'ing Period. U of Cal
         Pr.
Folsom, Merrill.
   xFolsom, Merrill.
      Great American Mansions & Their Stories.
         Hastings.
      More Great American Mansions & Their
         Stories. Hastings.
Folsom, Ralph H. *see* Folsom, Ralph Haughwout.
Folsom, Ralph Haughwout.
   xFolsom, Ralph H.
      Corporate Competition Law in the European
         Communities. Lexington Bks.
Folsom, Robert S. *see* Folsom, Robert Slade.
Folsom, Robert Slade.
   xFolsom, Robert S.
      Attic Black-Figured Pottery. Noyes.
      Attic Red-Figured Pottery. Noyes.
Folsome, Clair E. *see* Folsome, Clair Edwin.
Folsome, Clair Edwin, 1935-
   xFolsome, Clair E.
      The Origin of Life: A Warm Little Pond. W H
         Freeman.
Folta, J. *see* Folta, Jeannette R.
Folta, Jeannette R.
   xFolta, J.
      Sociological Framework for Patient Care.
         Wiley.
Foltin, Lore B. *see* Foltin, Lore Barbara.
Foltin, Lore Barbara.
   xFoltin, Lore B.
      ed. Paths to German Poetry: An Introductory
         Anthology. Har-Row.
Folts, Harold C.
   xFolts, Harold C.
      McGraw-Hill's Compilation of Data
         Communications Standards. McGraw.
Foltz, Mary J. *see* Foltz, Mary Jane.
Foltz, Mary Jane.
   xFoltz, Mary J.
      Awani. Morrow.
Fomon, Samuel J. *see* Fomon, Samuel Joseph.
Fomon, Samuel Joseph.
   xFomon, Samuel J.

      Infant Nutrition. Saunders.
Fondation des Sciences Politiques, Paris, France. *see*
   Fondation Nationale Des Sciences Politiques.
Fondation Nationale Des Sciences Politiques.
   xFondation des Sciences Politiques, Paris, France.
      Bibliographie Courante D'Articles de
         Periodiques Posterieurs a 1944 Sur les
         Problems Politiques, Economiques et Sociaux:
         Dixieme Supplement. G K Hall.
   xFondation Nationale des Sciences Politiques.
      Bibliographie Courante D' Articles De
         Periodiques Posterieurs a 1944 Sur les
         Problems Poliiques, Economiques, et Sociaux,
         Suppl 6. G K Hall.
      Bibliographie Courante d'Articles de
         Periodiques Posterieurs a 1944 sur les
         Problemes Politiques. Economiques et
         Sociaux. G K Hall.
Fondiller, Harvey V.
   xFondiller, Harvey V.
      ed. The Best of Popular Photography.
         Ziff-Davis Pub.
      ed. The Popular Photography Answer Book.
         Ziff-Davis Pub.
Foner, Ann. *see* Foner, Anne.
Foner, Anne.
   xFoner, Ann.
      Age in Society. Sage.
Foner, Eric.
   xFoner, Eric.
      ed. America's Black Past: A Reader in
         Afro-American History. Har-Row.
      Free Soil, Free Labor, Free Men: The Ideology
         of the Republican Party Before the Civil War.
         Oxford U Pr.
      ed. Nat Turner. P-H.
Foner, Nancy, 1945-
   xFoner, Nancy.
      Jamaica Farewell: Jamaican Migrants in
         London. U of Cal Pr.
      Status & Power in Rural Jamaica: A Study of
         Educational & Political Change. Tchrs Coll.
Foner, P. S. *see* Foner, Philip Sheldon.
Foner, Philip S. *see* Foner, Philip Sheldon.
Foner, Philip Sheldon, 1910-
   xFoner, P. S.
      The Autobiographies of the Haymarket
         Martyrs. Am Inst Marxist.
   xFoner, Philip S.
      ed. American Labor Songs of the Nineteenth
         Century. U of Ill Pr.
      American Socialism & Black Americans: From
         the Age of Jackson to World War II.
         Greenwood.
      Antonio Maceo: The "Bronze Titan" of Cuba's
         Struggle for Independence. Monthly Rev.
      ed. Autobiographies of the Hay Market
         Martyrs. Humanities.
      The Autobiographies of the Haymarket
         Martyrs. Monad Pr.
      Business & Slavery: The New York Merchants
         & the Irrepressible Conflict. Russell.
      Case of Joe Hill. Intl Pub Co.
      Great Labor Uprising of 1877. Monad Pr.
      Mark Twain: Social Critic. Intl Pub Co.
      Organized Labor & the Black Worker. Intl Pub
         Co.
      Women & the American Labor Movement:
         From Colonial Times to the Eve of World
         War I. Free Pr.
Fong, B. *see* Fong, Bernadine Chuck.
Fong, Bernadine. *see* Fong, Bernadine Chuck.
Fong, Bernadine Chuck.
   xFong, B.
      The Child: Development Through Adolescence.
         A-W.
   xFong, Bernadine.
      The Child: Development Through Adolescence.
         Benjamin-Cummings.
Fong, Peter. *see* Fong, Peter P.

Fong, Peter P.
   xFong, Peter.
      Statistical Theory of Nuclear Fission. Gordon.
Fonseca, John R.
   xFonseca, John R.
      Handling Consumer Credit Cases. Lawyers
         Co-Op.
Fontaine, A. *see* Fontaine, Andre.
Fontaine, Andre, 1910-
   xFontaine, A.
      The Art of Writing Nonfiction. Har-Row.
Fontaine, J. S. La. *see* La Fontaine, J. S.
Fontaine, Joan, 1917-
   xFontaine, Joan.
      No Bed of Roses. Berkley Pub.
      No Bed of Roses. Morrow.
Fontaine, John.
   xFontaine, John.
      Journal of John Fontaine: An Irish Huguenot
         Son in Spain & Virginia, 1710-1719. U Pr of
         Va.
Fontaine, Roger W.
   xFontaine, Roger W.
      The Andean Pact: A Political Analysis. Sage.
      On Negotiating with Cuba. Am Enterprise.
Fontana, Andrea.
   xFontana, Andrea.
      The Last Frontier: The Social Meaning of
         Growing Old. Sage.
Fontana, Bernard L.
   xFontana, Bernard L.
      Tarahumara: Where Night Is the Day of the
         Moon. Northland.
Fontana, D. C.
   xFontana, D. C.
      The Questor Tapes. Amereon Ltd.
      The Questor Tapes. Ballantine.
Fontana, Mars G. *see* Fontana, Mars Guy.
Fontana, Mars Guy.
   xFontana, Mars G.
      Corrosion Engineering. McGraw.
Fontana, Vincent J.
   xFontana, Vincent J.
      Maltreated Child: The Maltreatment Syndrome
         in Children - A Medical, Legal & Social
         Guide. C C Thomas.
      Somewhere a Child Is Crying:
         Maltreatment-Causes & Prevention. NAL.
Fontane, Theodor, 1819-1898
   xFontane, Theodor.
      Effi Briest. Penguin.
      Effi Briest. Suhrkamp.
      Effi Briest. Ungar.
Fontanetta, John.
   xFontanetta, John.
      Building & Using a Solar-Heated Geodesic
         Greenhouse. Garden Way Pub.
Fonteyn, Margot, Dame, 1919-
   xFonteyn, Margot.
      A Dancer's World: An Introduction for
         Parents & Students. Knopf.
      The Magic of Dance. Knopf.
      Margot Fonteyn: Autobiography. Knopf.
      Margot Fonteyn: Autobiography. Warner Bks.
Food & Agriculture Organization. *see* Food and
   Agriculture Organization of the United Nations.
Food & Agriculture Organization of the U.N. *see* Food
   and Agriculture Organization of the United Nations.
Food & Nutrition Board. *see* National Research Council.
   Food and Nutrition Board.
**Food and Agriculture Organization of the United
   Nations.**
   xEconomics Division FAO.
      Fishing Ports & Markets. State Mutual Bk.
   xExpert Consultation on Fishing for Squid & Other
      Cephalopods.
      Report: Supplement One. Unipub.
   xFAO.

Advances in Aquaculture. State Mutual Bk.
European Inland Water Fish. State Mutual Bk.
The Fish Resources of the Ocean. State Mutual
Bk.
xFood & Agriculture Organization.
Desert Locust Project: Final Report. Unipub.
Drought in the Sahel: International Relief
Operations, 1973-1975. Unipub.
FAO-UNDP Land & Water Resources Survey
in the Jebel Marra Area-the Sudan. Unipub.
Joint FAO-WHO Expert Committee on
Brucellosis: Fifth Report. Unipub.
Pesticide Residues in Food: Report of the Joint
FAO-Who Meeting, Rome, 1970. Unipub.
Pesticide Residues in Food: Report of the 1972
Joint FAO-WHO Meeting, Rome. Unipub.
A Review of Cheese Production, Consumption
& Trade in Some Developed Countries.
Unipub.
xFood & Agriculture Organization of the U.N.
Protection of the Public in the Event of
Radiation Accidents: Proceedings. World
Health.

**Food and Agriculture Organization of the United
Nations. Conference.**
xFAO Conference, 15th Session, Rome, 1969.
Report. Unipub.
xFAO Conference, 16th Session, Rome, 1971.
Report. Unipub.
xFAO Conference, 17th Session, Rome, 1973.
Report. Unipub.
xFAO Conference, 18th Session, Rome, Nov.
8-27,1975.
Report. Unipub.

Food and Nutrition Board - Division of Biology and
Agriculture. see National Research Council.
Committee on Maternal Nutrition.

Food Protection Committee. see National Research
Council. Food Protection Committee.

Fooshee, George.
xFooshee, George.
You Can Beat the Money Squeeze. Revell.

Foot, Philippa.
xFoot, Philippa R.
Virtues & Vices & Other Essays in Moral
Philosophy. U of Cal Pr.

Foot, Philippa R. see Foot, Philippa.

Foote, Andrew H. see Foote, Andrew Hull.

Foote, Andrew Hull, 1806-1863
xFoote, Andrew H.
Africa & the American Flag. Beekman Pubs.
Africa & the American Flag. Negro U Pr.
xFoote, H.
Africa & the American Flag. Dawson Pub.

Foote, Caleb.
xFoote, Caleb.
Cases & Materials on Family Law. Little.

Foote, Evelyn C. see Foote, Evelyn Carter.

Foote, Evelyn Carter.
xFoote, Evelyn C.
Time with God: Devotional Readings for
Youth. Broadman.

Foote, Gary L.
xFoote, Gary L.
Hydrologic Inventory of the Great Salt Lake
Desert Area. Utah St U Pr.

Foote, H. see Foote, Andrew Hull.

Foote, Mary H. see Foote, Mary Hallock.

Foote, Mary Hallock, 1847-1938
xFoote, Mary H.
Coeur D'Alene. AMS Pr.

Foote, Patricia.
xFoote, Patricia.
Girls Can Be Anything They Want. Messner.

Foote, Shelby.
xFoote, Shelby.
Follow Me Down. Random.

Foote, Timothy.
xFoote, Timothy.

The Great Ringtail Garbage Caper. HM.

Footman, David, 1895-
xFootman, David.
Civil War in Russia. Greenwood.
Ferdinand Lassalle, Romantic Revolutionary.
Greenwood.
Red Prelude: The Life of the Russian Terrorist
Zhelyabov. Hyperion Conn.

Footner, Hulbert, 1879-1944
xFootner, Hulbert.
Maryland Main & the Eastern Shore. Gale.

Foray, Cyril P., 1934-
xForay, Cyril P.
Historical Dictionary of Sierra Leone.
Scarecrow.

Forbes, Archibald, 1838-1900
xForbes, Archibald.
Life of Napoleon the Third. Kennikat.

Forbes, Bertie C. see Forbes, Bertie Charles.

Forbes, Bertie Charles.
xForbes, Bertie C.
Automotive Giants of America: Men Who Are
Making Our Motor Industry. Arno.
Men Who Are Making the West. Arno.

Forbes, Bryan, 1926-
xForbes, Bryan.
Stranger. Doubleday.

Forbes, Clarence A. see Forbes, Clarence Allen.

Forbes, Clarence Allen.
xForbes, Clarence A.
Greek Physical Education. AMS Pr.

Forbes, D. see Forbes, Duncan.

Forbes, David C. see Forbes, David Carl.

Forbes, David Carl.
xForbes, David C.
Successful Roach Fishing. David & Charles.

Forbes, Duncan, 1922-
xForbes, D.
Hume's Philosophical Politics. Cambridge U
Pr.
xForbes, Duncan.
Life Before Man: The Story of Fossils. Dufour.
Life Before Man: The Story of Fossils.
Transatlantic.

Forbes, Edward.
xForbes, Edward.
The Natural History of the European Seas.
Arno.

Forbes, Elizabeth.
xForbes, Elizabeth.
Opera from A to Z. A S Barnes.

Forbes, Eric G. see Forbes, Eric Gregory.

Forbes, Eric Gregory.
xForbes, Eric G.
A Source Book of Government-Owned
Biomedical Inventions. Quest Pub.

Forbes, Ernest R.
xForbes, Ernest R.
The Maritime Rights Movement, 1919-1927: A
Study in Canadian Regionalism.
McGill-Queens U Pr.

Forbes, Esther.
xForbes, Esther.
Paul Revere & the World He Lived In. HM.

Forbes, Gordon, 1934-
xForbes, Gordon.
A Handful of Summers. Mayflower Bks.

Forbes, J. T. see Forbes, John Thomas.

Forbes, Jack D.
xForbes, Jack D.
Apache, Navaho, & Spaniard. Greenwood.
Apache, Navaho, & Spaniard. U of Okla Pr.

Forbes, Jack E. see Forbes, Jack Edwin.

Forbes, Jack Edwin.
xForbes, Jack E.
Mathematics for Elementary Teachers. A-W.

Forbes, Jean.
xForbes, Jean.
Communications & Networks. Heinemann Ed.

Forbes, John R. see Forbes, John Ripley.

Forbes, John Ripley.
xForbes, John R.
In the Steps of the Great American Zoologist,
William Temple Hornaday. Natural Sci
Youth.

Forbes, John T. see Forbes, John Thomas.

Forbes, John Thomas.
xForbes, J. T.
Socrates. R West.
xForbes, John T.
Socrates. Norwood Edns.

Forbes, Malcolm S.
xForbes, Malcolm S.
Fact & Comment. Knopf.

Forbes, R. B. see Forbes, Robert B.

Forbes, R. J. see Forbes, Robert James.

Forbes, Robert B.
xForbes, R. B.
ed. Contributions to the Geology of the Bering
Sea Basin & Adjacent Regions. Geol Soc.

Forbes, Robert James.
xForbes, R. J.
More Studies in Early Petroleum History.
Hyperion Conn.
Studies in Early Petroleum History. Hyperion
Conn.

Forbes, Rosalind.
xForbes, Rosalind.
Life Stress. Doubleday.

Forbes, Stanton, 1923-
xForbes, Stanton.
Buried in So Sweet a Place. G K Hall.
The Will & Last Testament of Constance
Cobble. Doubleday.

Forbes, T. W. see Forbes, Theodore Watson.

Forbes, Theodore Watson, 1902-
xForbes, T. W.
ed. Human Factors in Highway Traffic Safety
Research. Krieger.

Forbes, Tom. see Forbes, Tom H.

Forbes, Tom H.
xForbes, Tom.
Quincy's Harvest. Lippincott.

Forbis, Judith.
xForbis, Judith.
The Classic Arabian Horse. Liveright.

Forcese, Dennis P.
xForcese, Dennis P.
Stages of Social Research: Contemporary
Perspectives. P-H.

Forche, Carolyn.
xForche, Carolyn.
Gathering the Tribes. Yale U Pr.

Forcione, Alban K., 1938-
xForcione, Alban K.
Cervantes, Aristotle, & the Persiles. Princeton
U Pr.

Ford. see Ford, John.

Ford, Amelia C. see Ford, Amelia Clewley.

Ford, Amelia Clewley.
xFord, Amelia C.
Colonial Precedents of Our National Land
System As It Existed in 1800. Porcupine Pr.

Ford, Anne.
xFord, Anne.
Davy Crockett. Putnam.

Ford, Barbara.
xFord, Barbara.
Animals That Use Tools. Messner.
Future Food: Alternate Protein for the Year
2000. Morrow.
The Island Ponies: An Environmental Study of
Their Life on Assateague. Morrow.
Why Does a Turtle Live Longer Than a Dog?:
A Report on Animal Longevity. Morrow.

Ford, Betty.
xFord, Betty.
The Times of My Life. Ballantine.
The Times of My Life. Har-Row.

Ford, C. Quentin. see Ford, Clarence Quentin.

Ford, Charles.
 xFord, Charles.
  ed. Making Musical Instruments: Strings &
   Keyboard. Pantheon.
Ford, Charles W.
 xFord, Charles W.
  Clinical Education for the Allied Health
   Professions. Mosby.
Ford, Clarence Quentin.
 xFord, C. Quentin.
  ed. Space Technology & Earth Problems. Am
   Astronaut.
Ford, Clebert.
 xFord, Clebert.
  A Guide to the Black Apple. L J Martin.
Ford, Clellan S. *see* Ford, Clellan Stearns.
Ford, Clellan Stearns.
 xFord, Clellan S.
  Patterns of Sexual Behavior. Greenwood.
  Patterns of Sexual Behavior. Har-Row.
Ford, D. W. *see* Ford, Douglas William Cleverley.
Ford, Dan, 1945-
 xFord, Dan.
  Pappy: The Life of John Ford. P-H.
Ford, David L.
 xFord, David L.
  ed. Readings in Minority-Group Relations.
   Univ Assocs.
Ford, Desmond.
 xFord, Desmond.
  Daniel. Southern Pub.
  Physicians of the Soul. Southern Pub.
Ford, Donald H.
 xFord, Donald H.
  Standard Fortran Programming. Irwin.
Ford, Donald H. *see* Ford, Donald Herbert.
Ford, Donald Herbert, 1921-
 xFord, Donald H.
  ed. Anatomy of the Central Nervous System in
   Review. Elsevier.
Ford, Doug.
 xFord, Doug.
  Start Golf Young. Sterling.
Ford, Douglas William Cleverley.
 xFord, D. W.
  The Ministry of the Word. Eerdmans.
Ford, Duane, 1945-
 xFord, Duane.
  Area Key Offense: A New Multiple Attack for
   Basketball. P-H.
Ford, E. B. *see* Ford, Edmund Briscoe.
Ford, E. H. *see* Ford, Edward Hugh Rawlinson.
Ford, Edmund Briscoe, 1901-
 xFord, E. B.
  Ecological Genetics. Methuen Inc.
Ford, Edsel.
 xFord, Edsel.
  Looking for Shiloh: Poems. U of Mo Pr.
Ford, Edward E.
 xFord, Edward E.
  Permanent Love: Practical Steps to a Lasting
   Relationship. Winston Pr.
Ford, Edward Hugh Rawlinson.
 xFord, E. H.
  Human Chromosomes. Acad Pr.
Ford, Emily E. *see* Ford, Emily Ellsworth (Fowler).
Ford, Emily Ellsworth (Fowler), 1826-1893
 xFord, Emily E.
  Notes on the Life of Noah Webster. B
   Franklin.
Ford, F. Madox. *see* Ford, Ford Madox.
Ford, Ford M. *see* Ford, Ford Madox.
Ford, Ford Madox, 1873-1939
 xFord, F. Madox.
  Parade's End. Knopf.
 xFord, Ford M.

Critical Attitude. Arno.
  Ford Madox Brown: A Record of His Life &
   Work. AMS Pr.
Ford Foundation. Energy Policy Project.
 xEnergy Policy Project Staff.
  A Time to Choose: America's Energy Future.
   Ballinger Pub.
Ford, Francis X. *see* Ford, Francis Xavier.
Ford, Francis Xavier, Bp, 1892-1952
 xFord, Francis X.
  Come Holy Spirit. Orbis Bks.
Ford, Franklin L. *see* Ford, Franklin Lewis.
Ford, Franklin Lewis, 1920-
 xFord, Franklin L.
  Strasbourg in Transition, 1648-1789. Norton.
Ford, George B. *see* Ford, George Barry.
Ford, George Barry.
 xFord, George B.
  A Degree of Difference. FS&G.
Ford, George H. *see* Ford, George Harry.
Ford, George Harry.
 xFord, George H.
  ed. The Dickens Critics. Greenwood.
  ed. Dickens Critics. Cornell U Pr.
Ford, Gerald R., 1913-
 xFord, Gerald R.
  A Time to Heal: The Autobiography of Gerald
   R. Ford. Har-Row.
Ford, H. L. *see* Ford, Herbert L.
Ford, Harold P.
 xFord, Harold P.
  ed. Ethics & Nuclear Strategy?. Orbis Bks.
Ford, Henry.
 xFord, Henry.
  My Life & Work. Arno.
Ford, Henry J. *see* Ford, Henry Jones.
Ford, Henry Jones, 1851-1925
 xFord, Henry J.
  The Natural History of the State: An
   Introduction to Political Science. Hyperion
   Conn.
Ford, Herbert.
 xFord, Herbert.
  Flee the Captor. Southern Pub.
Ford, Herbert L.
 xFord, H. L.
  Collation of the Ben Jonson Folios. Folcroft.
  Collation of the Ben Jonson Folios,
   1616-31-1640. Haskell.
Ford, Hilary.
 xFord, Hilary.
  Castle Malindine. Ballantine.
Ford, Horace A.
 xFord, Horace A.
  Archery, Its Theory & Practice. Shumway.
Ford, Isaac N. *see* Ford, Isaac Nelson.
Ford, Isaac Nelson, 1848-1912
 xFord, Isaac N.
  Tropical America. AMS Pr.
Ford, J. D. *see* Ford, Jeremiah Denis Matthias.
Ford, J. Massyngberd. *see* Ford, Josephine
 Massyngberde.
Ford, J. Massyngberde. *see* Ford, Josephine
 Massyngberde.
Ford, James A. *see* Ford, James Alfred.
Ford, James Alfred.
 xFord, James A.
  Analysis of Indian Village Site Collections from
   Louisiana & Mississippi. Kraus Repr.
  Ceramic Decoration Sequence at an Old Indian
   Village Site Near Sicily Island, Louisiana.
   Kraus Repr.
Ford, James L. *see* Ford, James Lorne.
Ford, James Lorne, 1939-
 xFord, James L.
  Ohlin-Heckscher Theory of the Basis & Effects
   of Commodity Trade. Asia.
Ford, Jeremiah Denis Matthias, 1873-
 xFord, J. D.

 ed. A Spanish Anthology: A Collection of
   Lyrics from the Thirteenth Century to the
   Present Time. Gordon Pr.
Ford, Jesse H. *see* Ford, Jesse Hill.
Ford, Jesse Hill.
 xFord, Jesse H.
  Conversion of Buster Drumwright: The
   Television & Stage Scripts. Vanderbilt U Pr.
  The Raider. Ballantine.
Ford, Jo Ann G. *see* Ford, Jo Ann Garofalo.
Ford, Jo Ann Garofalo.
 xFord, Jo Ann G.
  Applied Decision Making for Nurses. Mosby.
Ford, John.
 xFord.
  The Broken Heart. Norton.
 xFord, John.
  Broken Heart. U of Nebr Pr.
Ford, Josephine Massyngberde.
 xFord, J. Massyngberd.
  Pentecostal Experience. Paulist Pr.
 xFord, J. Massyngberde.
  The Hospital Prayer Book. Paulist Pr.
Ford, Julienne.
 xFord, Julienne.
  Paradigms & Fairy Tales: An Introduction to
   the Science of Meanings. Routledge & Kegan.
Ford, Kristina, 1946-
 xFord, Kristina.
  ed. Remote Sensing for Planners Ctr Urban
   Pol Res
Ford, Leroy.
 xFord, LeRoy.
  Primer for Teachers & Leaders. Broadman.
  Using the Lecture in Teaching & Training.
   Broadman.
Ford, Lewis S.
 xFord, Lewis S.
  ed. Two Process Philosophers: Hartshorne's
   Encounter with Whitehead. Scholars Pr Ca.
Ford, Marcia.
 xFord, Marcia.
  Linda's Champion Cocker. Assoc Bk.
Ford, Mary. *see* Ford, Mary Elizabeth Nestlerode.
Ford, Mary Elizabeth Nestlerode, 1907-
 xFord, Mary.
  The Application of the Rorschach Test to
   Young Children. Greenwood.
Ford, Murray J. *see* Ford, Murray J. S.
Ford, Murray J. S.
 xFord, Murray J.
  Planning, Preparing, Praising. Judson.
Ford, Newell F., 1912-
 xFord, Newell F.
  The Prefigurative Imagination of John Keats: A
   Study of the Beauty-Truth Identification &
   Its Implications. AMS Pr.
Ford, Norman D., 1921-
 xFord, Norman D.
  All of Mexico at Low Cost. Harian.
  Investing to Beat Inflation. Harian.
Ford, Paul L. *see* Ford, Paul Leicester.
Ford, Paul Leicester, 1865-1902
 xFord, Paul L.

Franklin Bibliography: A List of Books Written
by, or Relating to Benjamin Franklin.
Longwood Pr.

George Washington. Kennikat.

List of Some Briefs in Appeal Causes Which
Relate to America Tried Before the Lord
Commissioners of Appeals of Prize Causes of
His Majesty's Privy Council, 1736-58. B
Franklin.

The Many-Sided Franklin. Arno.

The Many Sided Franklin. R West.

Some Notes Towards an Essay on the
Beginnings of American Dramatic Literature,
1606-1789. B Franklin.

Tattletales of Cupid. Arno.

The True George Washington. Arden Lib.

The True George Washington. Arno.

Who Was the Mother of Franklin's Son?: An
Historical Conundrum, Hitherto Given
up-Now Partly Answered. B Franklin.

Ford, R. D.
xFord, R. D.
Introduction to Acoustics. Intl Ideas.

Ford, Richard.
xFord, Richard.
Children in the Cinema. Ozer.

Ford, Richard I.
xFord, Richard I.
ed. The Nature & Status of Ethnobotany. U
Mich Mus Anthro.

Ford, Robert, 1846-1905
xFord, Robert.
Children's Rhymes, Children's Games,
Children's Songs, Children's Stories. Gale.

Ford, Robert C. see Ford, Robert Clayton.

Ford, Robert Clayton.
xFord, Robert C.
Principles of Management: A Decision-Making
Approach. Reston.

Ford, Robert N.
xFord, Robert N.
Why Jobs Die & What to Do About It: Job
Redesign & Future Productivity. Am Mgmt.

Ford, S. F. see Ford, Susan F.

Ford, Sewell, 1868-1946
xFord, Sewell.
Horses Nine: Stories of Harness & Saddle.
Arno.
On with Torchy. Arno.

Ford, Stephen.
xFord, Stephen.
Acquisition of Library Materials. ALA.

Ford, Susan F.
xFord, S. F.
Summary of Validity Data from the
Admissions Testing Program Validity Study
Service. College Bd.

Ford, W. C. see Ford, Worthington Chauncey.

Ford, W. Herschel, D. D.
xFord, W. Herschel.
Simple Sermons for Funeral Services.
Zondervan.

Ford, W. Herschel. see Ford, William Herschel.

Ford, Willard S. see Ford, Willard Stanley.

Ford, Willard Stanley, 1890-
xFord, Willard S.
Some Administrative Problems of the High
School Cafeteria. AMS Pr.

Ford, William Herschel, 1900-
xFord, W. Herschel.

Simple Sermons for a Sinful Age. Zondervan.

Simple Sermons for a World in Crisis.
Zondervan.

Simple Sermons for Saints & Sinners.
Zondervan.

Simple Sermons for Sunday Evening.
Zondervan.

Simple Sermons for Time & Eternity.
Zondervan.

Simple Sermons for Times Like These.
Zondervan.

Simple Sermons for Twentieth Century
Christians. Zondervan.

Simple Sermons From the Gospel of Matthew.
Zondervan.

Simple Sermons on Conversion &
Commitment. Zondervan.

Simple Sermons on Evangelistic Themes.
Zondervan.

Simple Sermons on Grace & Glory. Zondervan.

Simple Sermons on Great Christian Doctrines.
Zondervan.

Simple Sermons on Heaven, Hell, & Judgment.
Zondervan.

Simple Sermons on New Testament Texts.
Zondervan.

Simple Sermons on Old Testament Texts.
Zondervan.

Simple Sermons on Prayer. Zondervan.

Simple Sermons on Prophetic Themes.
Zondervan.

Simple Sermons on the Christian Life.
Zondervan.

Simple Sermons on the Old Time Religion.
Zondervan.

Simple Talks for Christian Workers.
Zondervan.

Ford, William W. see Ford, William Webber.

Ford, William Webber, M.d., 1871-1941.
xFord, William W.
Bacteriology. AMS Pr.
Bacteriology. Hafner.

Ford, Worthington Chauncey, 1858-1941
xFord, W. C.
ed. Defences of Philadelphia in 1777. Da Capo.

Forde, Gerhard O.
xForde, Gerhard O.
Where God Meets Man: Luther's
Down-to-Earth Approach to the Gospel.
Augsburg.

Forde, Nels W.
xForde, Nels W.
Cato the Censor. Twayne.

Forde-Johnston, J. see Forde-Johnston, James L.

Forde-Johnston, James. see Forde-Johnston, James L.

Forde-Johnston, James L.
xForde-Johnston, J.
Hillforts of the Iron Age in England & Wales:
A Survey of the Surface Evidence. Rowman.
xForde-Johnston, James.
Great Medieval Castles of Britain. Merrimack
Bk Serv.

Forder, Anthony.
xForder, Anthony.
Concepts in Social Administration: A
Framework for Analysis. Routledge & Kegan.

Forder, Henry G. see Forder, Henry George.

Forder, Henry George, 1889-
xForder, Henry G.
Calculus of Extension. Chelsea Pub.

Fordham, Edward W. see Fordham, Edward Wilfrid.

Fordham, Edward Wilfrid.
xFordham, Edward W.
ed. Notable Cross-Examinations. Greenwood.

Fordham, Frieda.
xFordham, Frieda.

An Introduction to Jung's Psychology.
Gannon.
Introduction to Jung's Psychology. Penguin.

Fordham, Jim.
xFordham, Jim.
The Assault on the Sexes. Arlington Hse.

Fordham, Paul.
xFordham, Paul.
Learning Networks in Adult Education:
Non-Formal Education on a Housing Estate.
Routledge & Kegan.

Fordin, Hugh, 1935-
xFordin, Hugh.
Getting to Know Him: A Biography of Oscar
Hammerstein II. Random.

Fordney, Marilyn T. see Fordney, Marilyn Takahashi.

Fordney, Marilyn Takahashi.
xFordney, Marilyn T.
Insurance Handbook for the Medical Office.
Saunders.

Fordyce, Jack K.
xFordyce, Jack K.
Managing with People: A Manager's Handbook
of Organization Development. A-W.

Fordyce, Rachel.
xFordyce, Rachel.
ed. Caroline Drama: A Bibliographic History of
Criticism. G K Hall.
Children's Theatre & Creative Dramatics: An
Annotated Bibliography. G K Hall.

Forehand, G. A. see Forehand, Garlie Albert.

Forehand, Garlie Albert.
xForehand, G. A.
Psychology for Living. McGraw.

Foreign & Commonwealth Office, London. see Great
Britain. Colonial Office. Library.

Forell, George W. see Forell, George Wolfgang.

Forell, George Wolfgang.
xForell, George W.
Christian Lifestyle: Reflections on Romans 12
to 15. Fortress.
ed. Corporation Ethics: The Quest for Moral
Authority. Fortress.
ed. Crisis in Marriage. Fortress.
ed. God's Call to Public Responsibility.
Fortress.
The Protestant Faith. Fortress.
ed. Work As Praise. Fortress.

Foreman, Carolyn T. see Foreman, Carolyn Thomas.

Foreman, Carolyn Thomas, 1875-
xForeman, Carolyn T.
Indian Women Chiefs. Zenger Pub.

Foreman, Grant, 1869-1953
xForeman, Grant.
Five Civilized Tribes. U of Okla Pr.
Indian Removal: The Emigration of the Five
Civilized Tribes of Indians. U of Okla Pr.
Indians & Pioneers: The Story of the American
Southwest Before 1830. U of Okla Pr.
Last Trek of the Indians. Russell.

Foreman, J. K. see Foreman, James K.

Foreman, James K.
xForeman, J. K.
ed. Topics in Automatic Chemical Analysis.
Halsted Pr.

Foreman, John, 1945-
xForeman, John.
Prime of Life Beauty Book. Stein & Day.

Foreman, Kenneth J.
xForeman, Kenneth J.
From This Day Forward: Thoughts About a
Christian Marriage. Outlook.

Foreman, L. L.
xForeman, L. L.
Rawhiders of the Brasada. Ace Bks.

Foreman, Lewis.
xForeman, Lewis.
Systematic Discography. Shoe String.

Foreman, Michael, 1938-
xForeman, Michael.

All the King's Horses. Bradbury Pr.
Dinosaurs & All That Rubbish. T Y Crowell.
Moose. Pantheon.
illus. Two Giants. Pantheon.
Winter's Tales. Doubleday.
Foreman, Thomas E. *see* Foreman, Thomas Elton.
Foreman, Thomas Elton.
xForeman, Thomas E.
Discrimination Against the Negro in American
Athletics. R & E Res Assoc.
Foreman, Walter C., 1943-
xForeman, Walter C.
The Music of the Close: The Final Scenes of
Shakespeare's Tragedies. U Pr of Ky.
Foren, R. *see* Foren, Robert.
Foren, Robert.
xForen, R.
Authority in Social Casework. Pergamon.
Forest, Eva.
xForest, Eva.
From a Spanish Prison. Random.
Forest, Grant E. De. *see* De Forest, Grant E.
Forester, C. S. *see* Forester, Cecil Scott.
Forester, Cecil S. *see* Forester, Cecil Scott.
Forester, Cecil Scott.
xForester, C. S.
Admiral Hornblower in the West Indies. Little.
Admiral Hornblower in the West Indies.
Pinnacle Bks.
The African Queen. Queens Hse.
Brown on Resolution. Merrimack Bk Serv.
The Captain from Connecticut. Little.
Commodore Hornblower. Pinnacle Bks.
Commodore Hornblower. Little.
The Gun. Merrimack Bk Serv.
Hornblower & the Atropos. Little.
Hornblower & the Atropos. Pinnacle Bks.
Hornblower During the Crisis. Little.
Hornblower During the Crisis. Pinnacle Bks.
The Last Nine Days of the Bismarck. Little.
Lord Hornblower. Pinnacle Bks.
Lord Hornblower. Little.
Plain Murder. Merrimack Bk Serv.
xForester, Cecil S.
African Queen. Modern Lib.
Forester, Tom.
xForester, Tom.
The British Labour Party & the Working Class.
Holmes & Meier.
Forfar, John O.
xForfar, John O.
Textbook of Paediatrics. Churchill.
Forgan, Harry W.
xForgan, Harry W.
Read All About It!: Using Interests & Hobbies
to Motivate Young Readers. Goodyear.
Teaching Content Area Reading Skills: A
Modular Preservice & Inservice Program.
Merrill.
Forge, Andrew.
xForge, Andrew.
Rauschenberg. NAL.
Forge, Anthony.
xForge, Anthony.
ed. Primitive Art & Society. Oxford U Pr.
Forgie, George B.
xForgie, George B.
Patricide in the House Divided: A
Psychological Interpretation of Lincoln & His
Age. Norton.
Forgione, Albert G.
xForgione, Albert G.
Fear: Learning to Cope. Van Nos Reinhold.
Forgus, Ronald. *see* Forgus, Ronald H.
Forgus, Ronald H.
xForgus, Ronald.
Personality: A Cognitive View. P-H.
xForgus, Ronald H.

Perception: A Cognitive-Stage Approach.
McGraw.
Forisha, Bill E.
xForisha, Bill E.
Moral Development & Education. Prof Educ
Pubns.
Forkner, C. E. *see* Forkner, Claude Ellis.
Forkner, Claude Ellis, Jr., M.d, 1900-
xForkner, C. E.
Pseudomonas Aeruginosa Infections. Grune.
Forliti, John E.
xForliti, John E.
Program Planning for Youth Ministry. St
Marys.
Forman, Charles W.
xForman, Charles W.
ed. Christianity in the Non-Western World.
Arno.
ed. Christianity in the Non-Western World.
Gannon.
A Faith for the Nations. Westminster.
Forman, George E.
xForman, George E.
Cognitive Development: A Life-Span View.
Brooks Cole.
Forman, H. C. *see* Forman, Henry Chandlee.
Forman, Henry C. *see* Forman, Henry Chandlee.
Forman, Henry Chandlee, 1904-
xForman, H. C.
Maryland Architecture: A Short History from
1634 Through the Civil War. Cornell
Maritime.
xForman, Henry C.
The Architecture of the Old South: The
Medieval Style, 1585-1850. Russell.
Forman, Henry J. *see* Forman, Henry James.
Forman, Henry James, 1879-
xForman, Henry J.
In the Footprints of Heine. R West.
Our Movie Made Children. Arno.
Forman, James, 1928-
xForman, James.
The White Crow. FS&G.
xForman, James D.
Freedom's Blood. Watts.
Forman, James. *see* Forman, James D.
Forman, James D.
xForman, James.
A Ballad for Hogskin Hill. FS&G.
A Fine, Soft Day. FS&G.
Horses of Anger. FS&G.
Inflation. Watts.
The Life & Death of Yellow Bird. FS&G.
My Enemy, My Brother. Schol Bk Serv.
Nazism. Dell.
People of the Dream. FS&G.
Song of Jubilee. FS&G.
The Survivor. FS&G.
xForman, James D.
Communism: From Marx's Manifesto to 20th
Century Reality. Watts.
Nazism. Watts.
Forman, James D. *see* Forman, James.
Forman, Max L. *see* Forman, Max Leon.
Forman, Max Leon, 1909-
xForman, Max L.
ed. World's Greatest Quotations. Exposition.
Forman, R. C.
xForman, R. C.
Public Speaking Made Easy. Baker Bk.
Forman, Shepard, 1938-
xForman, Shepard.
The Brazilian Peasantry. Columbia U Pr.
Formanek, Ruth.
xFormanek, Ruth.
Charting Intellectual Development: A Practical
Guide to Piagetian Tasks. C C Thomas.
Fornari, Franco.
xFornari, Franco.

The Psychoanalysis of War. Lib Soc Sci.
Fornari, Harry, 1919-
xFornari, Harry.
Mussolini's Gadfly, Roberto Farinacci.
Vanderbilt U Pr.
Fornell, Claes.
xFornell, Claes.
Consumer Input for Marketing Decisions: A
Study of Corporate Departments for
Consumer Affairs. Praeger.
Forney, G. David.
xForney, G. David.
Concatenated Codes. MIT Pr.
Forney, J. W. *see* Forney, John Wien.
Forney, John Wien, 1817-1881
xForney, J. W.
Anecdotes of Public Men. Da Capo.
Forrai, Maria. *see* Forrai, Maria S.
Forrai, Maria S.
xForrai, Maria.
A Look at Divorce. Lerner Pubns.
A Look at Mental Retardation. Lerner Pubns.
A Look at Physical Handicaps. Lerner Pubns.
A Look at Prejudice & Understanding. Lerner
Pubns.
A Look at the Environment. Lerner Pubns.
Forrer, Gordon R., 1922-
xForrer, Gordon R.
Psychiatric Self-Help. Libra.
Forrest, A. C. *see* Forrest, Alfred Clinton.
Forrest, Alan. *see* Forrest, Alan I.
Forrest, Alan I.
xForrest, Alan.
Society & Politics in Revolutionary Bordeaux.
Oxford U Pr.
Forrest, Alfred Clinton, 1916-
xForrest, A. C.
The Unholy Land. Devin.
Forrest, D. W. *see* Forrest, Derek William.
Forrest, Derek William.
xForrest, D. W.
Francis Galton: The Life & Work of a
Victorian Genius. Taplinger.
Forrest, G. Topham. *see* Forrest, George Topham.
Forrest, Gary G.
xForrest, Gary G.
The Diagnosis & Treatment of Alcoholism. C
C Thomas.
Forrest, George Topham, 1872-1945
xForrest, G. Topham.
ed. The Parish of St. Margaret, Westminster.
AMS Pr.
Forrest, John C.
xForrest, John C.
Principles of Meat Science. W H Freeman.
Forrest, Richard, 1932-
xForrest, Richard.
The Death in the Willows. HR&W.
Death Through the Looking Glass. Bobbs.
Death Through the Looking Glass. PB.
Forrester, A. R.
xForrester, A. R.
Organic Chemistry of Stable Free Radicals.
Acad Pr.
Forrester, D. M. *see* Forrester, Deborah Macadam.
Forrester, David.
xForrester, David.
Listening with the Heart. Paulist Pr.
Forrester, David A. *see* Forrester, David A. R.
Forrester, David A. R.
xForrester, David A.
Schmalenbach & After: A Study of the
Evolution of German Business Economics.
Intl Schol Bk Serv.
Forrester, Deborah Macadam.
xForrester, D. M.
The Radiology of Joint Disease. Saunders.
Forrester, Donald J.
xForrester, Donald J.

ed. Pediatric Dental Medicine. Lea & Febiger.

Forrester, Gertrude, 1895-
  xForrester, Gertrude.
    Occupational Literature: An Annotated
     Bibliography. Wilson.

Forrester, Ian S.
  xForrester, Ian S.
    The German Legal System. Rothman.

Forrester, Jay. *see* Forrester, Jay Wright.

Forrester, Jay W. *see* Forrester, Jay Wright.

Forrester, Jay Wright.
  xForrester, Jay.
    World Dynamics. MIT Pr.
  xForrester, Jay W.
    Collected Papers of Jay W. Forrester. MIT Pr.
    Industrial Dynamics. MIT Pr.
    World Dynamics. MIT Pr.

Forrester, Rex, 1928-
  xForrester, Rex.
    Trout Fishing in New Zealand. Madrona Pubs.

Forsberg, Junius L. *see* Forsberg, Junius Leonard.

Forsberg, Junius Leonard, 1907-
  xForsberg, Junius L.
    Diseases of Ornamental Plants. U of Ill Pr.

Forsberg, Roberta J.
  xForsberg, Roberta J.
    Antoine De Saint-Exupery & David Beaty:
     Poets of a New Dimension. Twayne.
    The World of David Beaty: The Place of
     Images. Twayne.

Forseth, Kevin.
  xForseth, Kevin.
    Graphics for Architecture. Van Nos Reinhold.

Forsh, Ol'Ga Dmitrievna, 1873-1961
  xForsh, Olga D.
    Palace & Prison. Hyperion Conn.

Forsh, Olga D. *see* Forsh, Ol'Ga Dmitrievna.

Forshaw, Joseph M. *see* Forshaw, Joseph Michael.

Forshaw, Joseph Michael.
  xForshaw, Joseph M.
    Parrots of the World. TFH Pubns.

Forsling, Mary. *see* Forsling, Mary L.

Forsling, Mary L.
  xForsling, Mary.
    Anti-Diuretic Hormone. Eden Med Res.
  xForsling, Mary L.
    Anti-Diuretic Hormone. Eden Med Res.
    Antidiuretic Hormone. Eden Med Res.

Forsman, Bettie.
  xForsman, Bettie.
    From Lupita's Hill. Atheneum.

Forssell, Nils.
  xForssell, Nils.
    Fouche, the Man Napoleon Feared. AMS Pr.

Forst, Martin L. *see* Forst, Martin Lyle.

Forst, Martin Lyle.
  xForst, Martin L.
    Civil Commitment & Social Control. Lexington
     Bks.

Forst, Wendell.
  xForst, Wendell.
    Theory of Unimolecular Reactions. Acad Pr.

Forster, Arnold.
  xForster, Arnold.
    Cross-Currents. Greenwood.
    Danger on the Right. Greenwood.

Forster, Denis.
  xForster, Denis.
    ed. Homogeneous Catalysis-II. Am Chemical.

Forster, E. M. *see* Forster, Edward Morgan.

Forster, Edward M. *see* Forster, Edward Morgan.

Forster, Edward Morgan, 1879-1970
  xForster, E. M.

Abinger Harvest. HarBraceJ.
Aspects of the Novel. HarBraceJ.
Aspects of the Novel. Holmes & Meier.
Collected Tales of E. M. Forster. Knopf.
Goldsworthy Lowes Dickinson. HarBraceJ.
Goldsworthy Lowes Dickinson. Holmes &
  Meier.
Howards End. Holmes & Meier.
Longest Journey. Knopf.
Passage to India. HarBraceJ.
A Passage to India. Holmes & Meier.
A Room with a View. Holmes & Meier.
Room with a View. Knopf.
Two Cheers for Democracy. HarBraceJ.
Two Cheers for Democracy. Holmes & Meier.
  xForster, Edward M.
    Anonymity: An Enquiry. Folcroft.
    Howards End. Random.
    Longest Journey. Random.
    Room with a View. Random.

Forster, Francis M.
  xForster, Francis M.
    Clinical Neurology. Mosby.
    Reflex Epilepsy, Behavioral Therapy &
     Conditional Reflexes. C C Thomas.

Forster, John, 1812-1876
  xForster, John.
    Charles Dickens. Folcroft.
    The Life & Times of Oliver Goldsmith. Arden
     Lib.
    The Life & Times of Oliver Goldsmith.
     Scholarly.
    Life of Oliver Goldsmith. Greenwood.

Forster, Joseph.
  xForster, Joseph.
    Great Teachers: Burns, Shelley, Coleridge,
     Tennyson, Ruskin, Carlyle, Emerson,
     Browning. Folcroft.

Forster, Robert, 1926-
  xForster, Robert.
    The House of Saulx-Tavanes: Versailles &
     Burgundy, 1700-1830. Johns Hopkins.

Forster, Roger T.
  xForster, Roger T.
    God's Strategy in Human History. Tyndale.

Forstman, H. Jackson.
  xForstman, H. Jackson.
    Word & Spirit: Calvin's Doctrine of Biblical
     Authority. Stanford U Pr.

Forstner, Lorne J.
  xForstner, Lorne J.
    ed. Everlasting Universe: Readings on the
     Ecological Revolution. Heath.

Forsyth, Ella M. *see* Forsyth, Ella Marie.

Forsyth, Ella Marie.
  xForsyth, Ella M.
    Building a Chamber Music Collection: A
     Descriptive Guide to Published Scores.
     Scarecrow.

Forsyth, Frederick, 1938-
  xForsyth, Frederick.
    The Day of the Jackal. Bantam.
    The Devil's Alternative. Bantam.
    The Devil's Alternative. Viking Pr.
    The Dogs of War. Bantam.
    Dogs of War. G K Hall.
    The Dogs of War. Viking Pr.
    The Odessa File. Bantam.

Forsyth, George H.
  xForsyth, George H.
    The Monastery of Saint Catherine at Mount
     Sinai: The Church & Fortress of Justinian:
     Plates. U of Mich Pr.

Forsyth, James.
  xForsyth, James.
    Other Heart. Theatre Arts.

Forsyth, R. A. *see* Forsyth, Raymond Aubrey.

Forsyth, Raymond Aubrey, 1926-
  xForsyth, R. A.

The Lost Pattern: Essays on the Emergent City
  Sensibility in Victorian England. Intl Schol
  Bk Serv.

Forsyth, William.
  xForsyth, William.
    History of Trial by Jury. B Franklin.

Forsythe, Alexandra I.
  xForsythe, Alexandra I.
    Computer Science: A Primer. Wiley.

Forsythe, Charles E. *see* Forsythe, Charles Edward.

Forsythe, Charles Edward.
  xForsythe, Charles E.
    Administration of High School Athletics. P-H.

Forsythe, David P., 1941-
  xForsythe, David P.
    Humanitarian Politics: The International
     Committee of the Red Cross. Johns Hopkins.

Forsythe, George E. *see* Forsythe, George Elmer.

Forsythe, George Elmer.
  xForsythe, George E.
    Computer Methods for Mathematical
     Computations. P-H.
    Computer Solution of Linear Algebraic
     Systems. P-H.

Forsythe, Robert S. *see* Forsythe, Robert Stanley.

Forsythe, Robert Stanley, 1886-1941
  xForsythe, Robert S.
    Relations of Shirley's Plays to the Elizabethan
     Drama. Arno.

Forsythe, Sidney A., 1920-
  xForsythe, Sidney A.
    An American Missionary Community in China,
     1895-1905. Harvard U Pr.

Fort, Charles, 1874-1932
  xFort, Charles.
    LO!. Garland Pub.

Fort, Raymond C., 1929-
  xFort, Raymond C.
    ed. Adamantane: The Chemistry of Diamond
     Molecules. Dekker.

Forte, Allen.
  xForte, Allen.
    The Compositional Matrix. Da Capo.
    The Structure of Atonal Music. Yale U Pr.
    Tonal Harmony in Concept & Practice.
     HR&W.

Forte, David F.
  xForte, David F.
    The Supreme Court. Watts.

Forte, Imogene.
  xForte, Imogene.
    Comprehension Magic. Incentive Pubns.

Fortenbaugh, Samuel B., 1902-
  xFortenbaugh, Samuel B.
    In Order to Form a More Perfect Union: An
     Inquiry into the Origins of a College. Union
     Coll.

Fortes, Meyer.
  xFortes, Meyer.
    ed. Studies in African Social Anthropology.
     Acad Pr.

Fortescue, Adrian, 1874-1923
  xFortescue, Adrian.
    Lesser Eastern Churches. AMS Pr.
    The Orthodox Eastern Church. Arno.
    Orthodox Eastern Church. B Franklin.

Fortescue, J. A. *see* Fortescue, John A. C.

Fortescue, John.
  xFortescue, John.
    The Governance of England: Otherwise Called
     the Difference Between an Absolute & a
     Limited Monarchy. Hyperion Conn.
    De Laudibus Legum Anglie. Hyperion Conn.

Fortescue, John A. C.
  xFortescue, J. A.
    Environmental Geochemistry: A Holistic
     Approach. Springer-Verlag.

Fortescue, John W. *see* Fortescue, John William.

Fortescue, John William, Sir, 1859-1933
  xFortescue, John W.

History of British Army 1809-1810. AMS Pr.
History of British Army 1811-1812. AMS Pr.
History of British Army 1813-1815. AMS Pr.
History of British Army 1815-1838. AMS Pr.
History of British Army 1839-1852. AMS Pr.
History of British Army 1852-1870. AMS Pr.
A History of the British Army. AMS Pr.
Forthal, Sonya.
xForthal, Sonya.
Cogwheels of Democracy: A Study of the
Precinct Captain. Greenwood.
Fortier, Alcee.
xFortier, Alcee.
History of Louisiana. Claitors.
Fortier, Ed.
xFortier, Ed.
One Survived. Alaska Northwest.
Fortman, Edmund J., 1901-
xFortman, Edmund J.
Everlasting Life After Death. Alba.
Fortman, Jan. *see* Fortman, Janis L.
Fortman, Janis L., 1949-
xFortman, Jan.
Houdini & Other Masters of Magic. Raintree
Pubs.
Fortman, Marvin.
xFortman, Marvin.
The Legal Aspects of Doing Business in
Arizona. U of Ariz Pr.
Fortmann, Thomas E.
xFortmann, Thomas E.
Introduction to Linear Control Systems.
Dekker.
Fortnum, Charles D. *see* Fortnum, Charles Drury
Edward.
Fortnum, Charles Drury Edward, 1820-1899
xFortnum, Charles D.
Maiolica: A Historical Treatise on the Glazed
& Enamelled Earthenwares of Italy. Garland
Pub.
Fortunato, Connie.
xFortunato, Connie.
Music Is for Children. Cook.
Fortune.
xFortune Editorial Staff.
The Exploding Metropolis. Greenwood.
xFortune Editors.
ed. Fabulous Future: America in Nineteen
Eighty. Arno.
xFortune Magazine.
Fortune's Favorites: Portraits of Some
American Corporations, an Anthology. Arno.
U. S. A., the Permanent Revolution.
Greenwood.
xFortune Magazine Editors.
Markets of the Sixties. Arno.
Fortune Editorial Staff. *see* Fortune.
Fortune Editors. *see* Fortune.
Fortune Magazine. *see* Fortune.
Fortune Magazine Editors. *see* Fortune.
Fortune, Reo F. *see* Fortune, Reo Franklin.
Fortune, Reo Franklin, 1903-
xFortune, Reo F.
Arapesh. AMS Pr.
Omaha Secret Societies. AMS Pr.
Fortune, Robert, 1813-1880
xFortune, Robert.
Three Years' Wanderings in the Northern
Provinces of China. Garland Pub.
Fortune, Timothy T. *see* Fortune, Timothy Thomas.
Fortune, Timothy Thomas, 1856-1928
xFortune, Timothy T.
Dreams of Life: Miscellaneous Poems. Arno.
Fortune, William L.
xFortune, William L.
The Moment. Progeny Pr.
Forty, Ralph.
xForty, Ralph.

Sayonara Streetcar. Interurban.
The Forum.
xTheForum.
Forum Papers, Second Series. Arno.
**Forum of Education. Committee on Education and Total
Employment.**
xCommittee of Education & Total Employment.
ed. Educated Unemployment in India:
Challenge & Response. College Mktg Grp.
Forward, Robert L.
xForward, Robert L.
Dragon's Egg. Ballantine.
Forward, Susan.
xForward, Susan.
Betrayal of Innocence: Incest & Its
Devastation. J P Tarcher.
Betrayal of Innocence: Incest & Its
Devastation. Penguin.
Fosback, Norman G.
xFosback, Norman G.
Stock Market Logic: A Sophisticated Approach
to Profits on Wall Street. Inst Econmetric.
Fosburgh, Hugh, 1916-
xFosburgh, Hugh.
The Hunter. Belmont-Tower.
Fosdick, Harry E. *see* Fosdick, Harry Emerson.
Fosdick, Harry Emerson, 1878-1969
xFosdick, Harry E.
As I See Religion. Greenwood.
Great Time to Be Alive: Sermons on
Christianity in Wartime. Arno.
The Meaning of Prayer. Abingdon.
The Meaning of Prayer. Folcroft.
On Being a Real Person. Har-Row.
Fosdick, Lucian J. *see* Fosdick, Lucian John.
Fosdick, Lucian John, 1849-
xFosdick, Lucian J.
The French Blood in America. Genealog Pub.
Fosdick, Raymond B. *see* Fosdick, Raymond Blaine.
Fosdick, Raymond Blaine, 1883-
xFosdick, Raymond B.
American Police Systems. Patterson Smith.
European Police Systems. Patterson Smith.
Foshay, Arthur W. *see* Foshay, Arthur Wellesley.
Foshay, Arthur Wellesley.
xFoshay, Arthur W.
ed. Professional As Educator. Tchrs Coll.
Foshee, Howard. *see* Foshee, Howard B.
Foshee, Howard B., 1925-
xFoshee, Howard.
Broadman Church Manual. Broadman.
Foskett, A. C. *see* Foskett, Antony Charles.
Foskett, Antony Charles.
xFoskett, A. C.
The Subject Approach to Information. Shoe
String.
Foskett, D. J.
xFoskett, D. J.
Classification & Indexing in the Social
Sciences. Butterworths.
Foskett, Daphne.
xFoskett, Daphne.
A Dictionary of British Miniature Painters.
Merrimack Bk Serv.
Foss. *see* Foss, Christopher F.
Foss, Christopher. *see* Foss, Christopher F.
Foss, Christopher F.
xFoss.
Artillery of the World. Scribner.
xFoss, Christopher.
Artillery of the World. Scribner.
Infantry Weapons of the World. Scribner.
Jane's Pocket Book of Towed Artillery.
Macmillan.
Military Vehicles of the World. Scribner.
xFoss, Christopher F.
Armoured Fighting Vehicles of the World.
Scribner.
Foss, Clive.
xFoss, Clive.

Byzantine & Turkish Sardis. Harvard U Pr.
Foss, Dennis C.
xFoss, Dennis C.
The Value Controversy in Sociology: A New
Orientation for the Profession. Jossey-Bass.
Foss, Donald J.
xFoss, Donald J.
Psycholinguistics: An Introduction to the
Psychology of Language. P-H.
Foss, E. W. *see* Foss, Edward W.
Foss, Edward W.
xFoss, E. W.
Construction & Maintenance for Farm &
Home. Wiley.
Foss, Hubert. *see* Foss, Hubert James.
Foss, Hubert James, 1899-1953
xFoss, Hubert.
Ralph Vaughan Williams: A Study. Greenwood.
Foss, Martin, 1889-
xFoss, Martin.
Logic & Existence. Philos Lib.
Foss, Michael.
xFoss, Michael.
Age of Patronage: The Arts in England,
1660-1750. Cornell U Pr.
Foss, Mildred B.
xFoss, Mildred B.
Creative Embroidery with Your Sewing
Machine. P-H.
Foss, Phillip O.
xFoss, Phillip O.
Politics & Grass: The Administration of
Grazing on the Public Domain. Greenwood.
Foss, William O.
xFoss, William O.
The Norwegian Lady & the Wreck of the
Dictator. Donning Co.
Fossard, A. *see* Fossard, Andre.
Fossard, Andre.
xFossard, A.
Multivariable System Control. Elsevier.
Fossum, John A.
xFossum, John A.
Labor Relations: Development Structure
Process. Business Pubns.
Fossum, R. M. *see* Fossum, Robert M.
Fossum, Robert M.
xFossum, R. M.
The Divisor Class Group of a Krull Domain.
Springer-Verlag.
Trivial Extensions of Abelian Categories:
Homological Algebra of Trivial Extensions of
Abelian Categories with Applications to Ring
Theory. Springer-Verlag.
Fossum, Timothy V.
xFossum, Timothy V.
Calculus & the Computer: An Approach to
Problem Solving. Scott F.
Foster, Ahram J. *see* Foster, Abram John.
Foster, Abram John.
xFoster, Abram J.
The Coming of the Electrical Age to the
United States. Arno.
Foster, Adriance S. *see* Foster, Adriance Sherwood.
Foster, Adriance Sherwood.
xFoster, Adriance S.
Comparative Morphology of Vascular Plants.
W H Freeman.
Foster, Alan D. *see* Foster, Alan Dean.
Foster, Alan Dean.
xFoster, Alan D.

Alien. Warner Bks.

Dark Star. Ballantine.

The End of the Matter. Ballantine.

Icerigger. Ballantine.

Star Trek Log Nine. Amereon Ltd.

Star Trek Log Nine. Ballantine.

Star Trek Log One. Amereon Ltd.

Star Trek Log Seven. Ballantine.

Star Trek Log Six. Amereon Ltd.

Star Trek Log Six. Ballantine.

Foster, Albert B. *see* Foster, Albert Beryl.

Foster, Albert Beryl, 1906-

xFoster, Albert B.

Approved Practices in Soil Conservation. Interstate.

Foster, Arthur L. *see* Foster, Arthur Lorne.

Foster, Arthur Lorne, 1922-

xFoster, Arthur L.

ed. The House Church Evolving. Exploration Pr.

Foster Associates.

xFoster Associates.

Energy Prices, 1960-73. Ballinger Pub.

Foster, Augustus J. *see* Foster, Augustus John.

Foster, Augustus John.

xFoster, Augustus J.

Jeffersonian America: Notes on the United States of America Collected in the Years 1805-1807 & 1811-1812. Greenwood.

Foster, C. E.

xFoster, C. E.

How to Prepare Stamp Exhibits. Hobby Pub Serv.

Foster, Carol.

xFoster, Carol.

Developing Self-Control. F Fournies.

Foster, Catharine O. *see* Foster, Catharine Osgood.

Foster, Catharine Osgood, 1907-

xFoster, Catharine O.

Organic Flower Gardening. Rodale Pr Inc.

The Organic Gardener. Knopf.

xFoster, Catherine O.

Organic Flower Gardening. Rodale Pr Inc.

Foster, Catherine O. *see* Foster, Catharine Osgood.

Foster, Caxton C., 1929-

xFoster, Caxton C.

Computer Architecture. Van Nos Reinhold.

Content Addressable Parallel Processors. Van Nos Reinhold.

Programming a Microcomputer: 6502. A-W.

Foster, Charles.

xFoster, Charles.

Home Winemaking. Beekman Pubs.

Foster, Charles R. *see* Foster, Charles Richard.

Foster, Charles Richard, 1901-

xFoster, Charles R.

Editorial Treatment of Education in the American Press. AMS Pr.

Foster, Daniel. *see* Foster, Daniel W.

Foster, Daniel W.

xFoster, Daniel.

A Layman's Guide to Modern Medicine. S&S.

Foster, David. *see* Foster, David William.

Foster, David W. *see* Foster, David William.

Foster, David William.

xFoster, David.

ed. Latin American Government Leaders. ASU Lat Am St.

xFoster, David W.

Augusto Roa Bastos. Twayne.

ed. Chilean Literature: A Working Bibliography of Secondary Sources. G K Hall.

Christian Allegory in Early Hispanic Poetry. U Pr of Ky.

Currents in the Contemporary Argentine Novel: Arlt, Mallea, Sabato, & Cortazar. U of Mo Pr.

ed. Dictionary of Contemporary Latin American Authors. ASU Lat Am St.

Luis de Gongora. Twayne.

The Marques de Santillana. Irvington.

ed. Modern Latin American Literature. Ungar.

Studies in the Contemporary Spanish-American Short Story. U of Mo Pr.

Foster, Donald L. *see* Foster, Donald Leroy.

Foster, Donald Leroy, 1928-

xFoster, Donald L.

Prints in the Public Library. Scarecrow.

Foster, Douglas. *see* Foster, Douglas W.

Foster, Douglas W.

xFoster, Douglas.

Marketing Imperative. Beekman Pubs.

Foster, Edward.

xFoster, Edward.

Mary E. Wilkins Freeman. Hendricks House.

Foster, Edward H. *see* Foster, Edward Halsey.

Foster, Edward Halsey.

xFoster, Edward H.

Catharine Maria Sedgwick. Twayne.

Josiah Gregg & Lewis H. Garrard. Boise St Univ.

Susan & Anna Warner. Twayne.

Foster, Elizabeth R. *see* Foster, Elizabeth Read.

Foster, Elizabeth Read.

xFoster, Elizabeth R.

The Painful Labour of Mr. Elsyng. Am Philos.

Foster, Eugene S.

xFoster, Eugene S.

Understanding Broadcasting. A-W.

Foster, Frances S. *see* Foster, Frances Smith.

Foster, Frances Smith.

xFoster, Frances S.

ed. Witnessing Slavery: The Development of the Ante-Bellum Slave Narratives. Greenwood.

Foster, G. Allen.

xFoster, G. Allen.

Sunday in Centreville: The Battle of Bull Run, 1861. D White.

Foster, Genevieve. *see* Foster, Genevieve (Stump).

Foster, Genevieve (Stump), 1893-

xFoster, Genevieve.

illus. World of Captain John Smith. Scribner.

illus. World of William Penn. Scribner.

Foster, George. *see* Foster, George McClelland.

Foster, George E. *see* Foster, George Everett.

Foster, George Everett, 1849-

xFoster, George E.

Se-Quo-Yah, the American Cadmus & Modern Moses. AMS Pr.

Foster, George M. *see* Foster, George McClelland.

Foster, George McClelland, 1913-

xFoster, George.

ed. Long-Term Field Research in Social Anthropology. Acad Pr.

xFoster, George M.

Medical Anthropology. Wiley.

Foster, Harold M.

xFoster, Harold M.

The New Literacy: The Language of Film & Television. NCTE.

Foster, Herbert L.

xFoster, Herbert L.

Ribbin', Jivin', & Playin' the Dozens: The Unrecognized Dilemma of Inner-City Schools. Ballinger Pub.

Foster, J.

xFoster, J.

A Short Course in General Relativity. Longman.

Foster, J. R. *see* Foster, James Ralph.

Foster, J. W. *see* Foster, John Watson.

Foster, James H. *see* Foster, James Henry.

Foster, James Henry.

xFoster, James H.

Solid Liver Tumors. Saunders.

Foster, James Ralph, 1890-

xFoster, J. R.

History of the Pre-Romantic Novel in England. Kraus Repr.

Foster, Janet.

xFoster, Janet.

Working for Wildlife: The Beginning of Preservation in Canada. U of Toronto Pr.

Foster, John, 1929-

xFoster, John.

Discovery Learning in the Primary School. Routledge & Kegan.

xFoster, John L.

ed. A First Poetry Book. Oxford U Pr.

Foster, John L.

xFoster, John L.

National Policy Game: A Simulation of the American Political Process. Wiley.

Foster, John L. *see* Foster, John.

Foster, John T.

xFoster, John T.

The Flight of the Lone Eagle: Charles Lindbergh Flies Nonstop from New York to Paris. Watts.

The Gallant Gray Trotter. Dodd.

Foster, John W. *see* Foster, John Watson.

Foster, John Watson, 1836-1917

xFoster, J. W.

American Diplomacy in the Orient. Chinese Materials.

xFoster, John W.

American Diplomacy in the Orient. Da Capo.

Foster, K. Neil.

xFoster, K. Neill.

Revolution of Love. Bethany Fell.

Foster, K. Neill. *see* Foster, K. Neil.

Foster, Kenelm.

xFoster, Kenelm.

The Two Dantes & Other Studies. U of Cal Pr.

Foster, Laurence, 1903-1969

xFoster, Laurence.

Negro-Indian Relationships in the Southeast. AMS Pr.

Foster, Lawrence.

xFoster, Lawrence.

ed. Experience & Theory. U of Mass Pr.

Foster, Lee, 1943-

xFoster, Lee.

Adventures in California Country. Beautiful Am.

Foster, Lowell W.

xFoster, Lowell W.

Geo-Metrics: The Metric Application of Geometric Tolerancing. A-W.

Foster, M. A.

xFoster, M. A.

The Gameplayers of Zan. DAW Bks.

Foster, Martha. *see* Foster, Martha M.

Foster, Martha M.

xFoster, Martha.

Medical Office Practice. Bobbs.

Foster, Muriel, 1884-1963

xFoster, Muriel.

Muriel Foster's Fishing Diary. Viking Pr.

Foster, Norman, 1916-

xFoster, Norman.

Practical Tables for Building Construction. McGraw.

Foster, Orline (Dorman).

xFoster, Orline D.

Stimulating the Organization. Hive Pub.

Foster, Orline D. *see* Foster, Orline (Dorman).

Foster, Paul L.
xFoster, Paul L.
Bank Expansion in Virginia, 1962-1966: The Holding Company & the Direct Merger. U Pr of Va.

Foster, R. *see* Foster, Roy.

Foster, R. L.
xFoster, R. L.
The Nature of Enzymology. Halsted Pr.

Foster, Reginald F. *see* Foster, Reginald Francis.

Foster, Reginald Francis, 1896-
xFoster, Reginald F.
Famous Short Stories Analysed. Folcroft.

Foster, Richard B.
xFoster, Richard B.
ed. Strategy & Security in Northeast Asia. Crane-Russak Co.

Foster, Richard J.
xFoster, Richard J.
The Celebration of Discipline: Paths to Spiritual Growth. Har-Row.

Foster, Robert, 1949-
xFoster, Robert.
The Complete Guide to Middle Earth: From "the Hobbit" to "the Silmarillion". Ballantine.
A Guide to Middle Earth. Ballantine.

Foster, Robert J. *see* Foster, Robert John.

Foster, Robert John, 1929 (apr. 19)-
xFoster, Robert J.
General Geology. Merrill.
Geology. Merrill.
Physical Geology. Merrill.

Foster, Roy, 1928-
xFoster, R.
Organic Charge-Transfer Complexes. Acad Pr.

Foster, Ruth S
xFoster, Ruth S.
Homeowner's Guide to Landscaping That Saves Energy Dollars. McKay.

Foster, Stephen, 1942-
xFoster, Stephen.
Notes from the Caroline Underground: Alexander Leighton, the Puritan Triumvirate, & the Laudian Reaction to Nonconformity. Shoe String.
Their Solitary Way: The Puritan Social Ethic in the First Century of Settlement in New England. Yale U Pr.

Foster, Stephen C.
xFoster, Stephen C.
ed. Dada Spectrum: The Dialectics of Revolt. Coda Pr.

Foster, W. *see* Foster, William.

Foster, William, Sir, 1863-1951
xFoster, W.
ed. Early Travels in India, 1583-1619. Verry.

Foster, William. *see* Foster, William Murchison.

Foster, William Murchison, 1931-
xFoster, William.
Build-It Book of Solar Heating Projects. TAB Bks.
Homeowner's Guide to Solar Heating & Cooling. TAB Bks.

Foster, William T.
xFoster, William T.
Principles of Acute Coronary Care. ACC.

Foster, William Z. *see* Foster, William Zebulon.

Foster, William Zebulon, 1881-1961
xFoster, William Z.

Great Steel Strike & Its Lessons. Arno.
Great Steel Strike & Its Lessons. Da Capo.
History of the Communist Party of the United States. Greenwood.
History of the Three Internationals: The World Socialist & Communist Movements from 1848 to the Present. Greenwood.
Negro People in American History. Intl Pub Co.
Toward Soviet America. Educator Pubns.
Toward Soviet America. Hyperion Conn.

Foth, H. D.
xFoth, Henry D.
Fundamentals of Soil Science. Wiley.

Foth, Henry D. *see* Foth, H. D.

Fothergill, Augusta B. *see* Fothergill, Augusta Bridgland Middleton.

Fothergill, Augusta Bridgland Middleton.
xFothergill, Augusta B.
Marriage Records of Brunswick County, Virginia, 1730-1852. Genealog Pub.

Fothergill, Brian.
xFothergill, Brian.
Beckford of Fonthill. Merrimack Bk Serv.

Fothergill, Gerald.
xFothergill, Gerald.
List of Emigrant Ministers to America, 1690-1811. Genealog Pub.

Fothergill, John, 1712-1780
xFothergill, John.
Chain of Friendship: Selected Letters of Dr. John Fothergill of London, 1735-1780. Harvard U Pr.

Fotheringham, James.
xFotheringham, James.
Wordsworth's Prelude As a Study of Education. Folcroft.

Fotine, Larry.
xFotine, Larry.
Musicians & Other Noisemakers. Poly Tone.

Fotion, N.
xFotion, N.
Moral Situations. Kent St U Pr.

Fotitch, Tatiana. *see* Fotitch, Tatiana Zurunitch.

Fotitch, Tatiana Zurunitch, 1900-
xFotitch, Tatiana.
Anthology of Old Spanish. Intl Schol Bk Serv.

Fototeca Unione.
xUnione, Fototeca.
Ancient Roman Architecture. K G Saur.

Foucar, Emile C. *see* Foucar, Emile Charles Victor.

Foucar, Emile Charles Victor, 1894-
xFoucar, Emile C.
I Lived in Burma. Dufour.

Fouillee, A. *see* Fouillee, Alfred Jules Emile.

Fouillee, Alfred Jules Emile, 1838-1912
xFouillee, A.
Modern French Legal Philosophy. Kelley.
Modern French Legal Philosophy. Rothman.

Foulds, L. *see* Foulds, Leslie.

Foulds, Leslie.
xFoulds, L.
Neoplastic Development. Acad Pr.

Foulds, Sam.
xFoulds, Sam.
America's Soccer Heritage: A History of the Game. Soccer for Am.

Foulet, Alfred. *see* Foulet, Alfred Lucien.

Foulet, Alfred Lucien.
xFoulet, Alfred.
On Editing Old French Texts. Regents Pr KS.

Foulke, Patricia.
xFoulke, Patricia N.
Europe Under Canvas: A Guide to Camping for Singles, Couples & Families. P-H.

Foulke, Patricia N. *see* Foulke, Patricia.

Foulke, R. A. *see* Foulke, Roy Anderson.

Foulke, Robert.
xFoulke, Robert.

An Anatomy of Literature. HarBraceJ.

Foulke, Roy Anderson, 1896-
xFoulke, R. A.
Practical Financial Statement Analysis. McGraw.

Foulkes, David. *see* Foulkes, William David.

Foulkes, William David, 1935-
xFoulkes, David.
A Grammar of Dreams. Basic.
Psychology of Sleep. Scribner.

Foulks, Edward F.
xFoulks, Edward F.
ed. Current Perspectives in Cultural Psychiatry. Halsted Pr.

Fountain, Helen.
xFountain, Helen.
A Cage of Birds. Golden Quill.

Fountain, John C.
xFountain, John C.
Dictionary of Soda & Mineral Water Bottles. Old Time.

Fountaine, George La. *see* La Fountaine, George.

Fouque, Victor, b. 1802
xFouque, Victor.
The Truth Concerning the Invention of Photography: Nicephore Niepce-His Life, Letters, & Works (1867). Arno.

Fouraker, Lawrence E.
xFouraker, Lawrence E.
Bargaining Behavior. Greenwood.

Fourier, Francois M. *see* Fourier, Francois Marie Charles.

Fourier, Francois Marie Charles.
xFourier, Francois M.
Passions of the Human Soul, & Their Influence on Society & Civilization. Kelley.

Fourman, M. *see* Fourman, Maximilian.

Fourman, Maximilian.
xFourman, M.
Teach Yourself Russian. McKay.

Fournel, Paul, 1947-
xFournel, Paul.
Little Girls Breathe the Same Air As We Do. Braziller.

Fournier, Robert. *see* Fournier, Robert L.

Fournier, Robert L., 1915-
xFournier, Robert.
Illustrated Dictionary of Practical Pottery. Van Nos Reinhold.

Fournies, Ferdinand F.
xFournies, Ferdinand F.
Coaching for Improved Work Performance. Van Nos Reinhold.

Fourquin, G. *see* Fourquin, Guy.

Fourquin, Guy.
xFourquin, G.
The Anatomy of Popular Rebellion in the Middle Ages. Elsevier.
xFourquin, Guy.
Lordship & Feudalism in the Middle Ages. Universe.

Fourteen International Universitaetswochen Fuer Kernphysik 1975 der Karlfranzens-Universitaet at Schladming. *see* Internationale Universitatswochen Fuer Kernphysik der Karl-Franzens-Universitat Graz, 14th, Schladming, Austria, 1975.

Fourth Annual Conference on Latin America, April 17-19, 1969. *see* Conference on Latin America, 4th, University of Houston, 1969.

Fourth Conference Held at Dundee, Scotland, Mar 30-Apr 2, 1976. *see* Conference on Ordinary and Partial Differential Equations, 4th, Dundee, Scotland, 1976.

Fourth International Working-Meeting on Soil Micromorphology, 1973. *see* International Working-Meeting on Soil Micromorphology, 4th, Department of Geography, Queen'S University, 1973.

Fourth Lepetit Colloquium Held in Cocoyoc, Mex., Nov., 1972. *see* Lepetit Colloquium, 4th, Cocoyoc, Mexico, 1972.

Fourth Symposium, Oct. 22-25, 1975. *see* Nasw Professional Symposium on Social Work, 4th, Hollywood, Florida, 1975.

Fourth Symposium of the International Research Society for Children's Literature, Held at the University of Exeter, September 9-12, 1978. *see* International Research Society for Children's Literature.

Fourth Winter School on Probability, Karpacz, Poland, Jan. 1975. *see* Winter School on Probability, 4th, Karpacz, Poland, 1975.

Fousek, Peter G.
  xFousek, Peter G.
    Foreign Central Banking: The Instruments of Monetary Policy. Kennikat.

Fout, John C., 1937-
  xFout, John C.
    German History & Civilization - 1806-1914: A Bibliography of Scholarly Periodical Literature. Scarecrow.

Fowell, Frank.
  xFowell, Frank.
    Censorship in England. Arno.
    Censorship in England. B Franklin.

Fowkes, William C.
  xFowkes, William C.
    Clinical Assessment for the Nurse Practitioner. Mosby.

Fowler, Albert. *see* Fowler, Albert Vann.

Fowler, Albert Vann.
  xFowler, Albert.
    ed. Cranberry Lake from Wilderness to Adirondack Park. Syracuse U Pr.

Fowler, Carol.
  xFowler, Carol.
    Daisy Hooee Nampeyo. Dillon.

Fowler, Charles H., M.d
  xFowler, Charles H.
    Historical Romance of the American Negro. Johnson Repr.

Fowler, David C., 1921-
  xFowler, David C.
    Literary History of the Popular Ballad. Duke.

Fowler, Dorothy (Canfield), 1902-
  xFowler, Dorothy G.
    Cabinet Politician: The Postmasters General, 1829-1909. AMS Pr.

Fowler, Dorothy G. *see* Fowler, Dorothy (Canfield).

Fowler, Douglas.
  xFowler, Douglas.
    Reading Nabokov. Cornell U Pr.

Fowler, Earl. *see* Fowler, Earl P.

Fowler, Earl P.
  xFowler, Earl.
    Can Crafts. Chilton.

Fowler, Earle B. *see* Fowler, Earle Broadus.

Fowler, Earle Broadus.
  xFowler, Earle B.
    Spenser & the System of Courtly Love. Folcroft.
    Spenser & the System of Courtly Love. Phaeton.

Fowler, Elaine W.
  xFowler, Elaine W.
    English Sea Power in the Early Tudor Period, 1485-1558. Folger Bks.

Fowler, Ethel L.
  xFowler, Ethel L.
    ed. Daffodil Poetry Book. Arno.

Fowler, Flora C.
  xFowler, Flora C.
    ed. Reading Games for Middle & Upper Grades. Mss Info.

Fowler, Gene, 1931-
  xFowler, Gene.
    Fires. Thorp Springs.
    The Mighty Barnum. Garland Pub.

Fowler, George B. *see* Fowler, George Bingham.

Fowler, George Bingham, 1903-
  xFowler, George B.

Intellectual Interests of Engelbert of Admont. AMS Pr.

Fowler, H. W. *see* Fowler, Henry Weed.

Fowler, Harold N. *see* Fowler, Harold North.

Fowler, Harold North.
  xFowler, Harold N.
    Handbook of Greek Archaeology. AMS Pr.
    A Handbook of Greek Archaeology. R West.

Fowler, Henry T. *see* Fowler, Henry Thatcher.

Fowler, Henry Thatcher, 1867-1948
  xFowler, Henry T.
    The History & Literature of the New Testament. Greenwood.

Fowler, Henry W. *see* Fowler, Henry Weed.

Fowler, Henry Watson.
  xFowler, Henry W.
    Dictionary of Modern English Usage. Oxford U Pr.

Fowler, Henry Weed, 1878-1965
  xFowler, H. W.
    The Fishes of Oceania, 1927. Kraus Repr.
  xFowler, Henry W.
    The Fishes of Oceania. Johnson Repr.

Fowler, J. *see* Fowler, Jack.

Fowler, J. H. *see* Fowler, John Henry.

Fowler, Jack.
  xFowler, J.
    Patterns of Success: How to Discover & Follow Them. P-H.

Fowler, James W.
  xFowler, James W.
    Trajectories in Faith: Five Life Stories. Abingdon.
  xFowler, Jim.
    Life Maps: Conversations on the Journey to Faith. Winston Pr.

Fowler, Jim. *see* Fowler, James W.

Fowler, John Henry, 1861-1932
  xFowler, J. H.
    De Quincey As Literary Critic. Folcroft.

Fowler, John M.
  xFowler, John M.
    Energy & the Environment. McGraw.

Fowler, Kenneth, 1900-
  xFowler, Kenneth.
    Jackal's Gold. Doubleday.

Fowler, Murray E.
  xFowler, Murray E.
    Restraint & Handling of Wild & Domestic Animals. Iowa St U Pr.

Fowler, Noble O.
  xFowler, Noble O.
    Cardiac Diagnosis & Treatment. Har-Row.
    ed. Diagnostic Methods in Cardiology. Davis Co.

Fowler, Orson S. *see* Fowler, Orson Squire.

Fowler, Orson Squire, 1809-1887
  xFowler, Orson S.
    The Octagon House: A Home for All. Dover.

Fowler, P. J.
  xFowler, Peter J.
    Approaches to Archaeology. St Martin.

Fowler, Peter J. *see* Fowler, P. J.

Fowler, Raymond E., 1933-
  xFowler, Raymond E.
    The Andreasson Affair. Bantam.
    The Andreasson Affair. P-H.
    UFOs-Interplanetary Visitors: A UFO Investigator Reports on the Facts, Fables & Fantasies of the Flying Saucer Conspiracy. Exposition.

Fowler, Robert B. *see* Fowler, Robert Booth.

Fowler, Robert Booth.
  xFowler, Robert B.
    Contemporary Issues in Political Theory. Wiley.

Fowler, Robert H.
  xFowler, Robert H.

Jason McGee. Har-Row.

Fowler, Roger.
  xFowler, Roger.
    ed. A Dictionary of Modern Critical Terms. Routledge & Kegan.
    Language & Control. Routledge & Kegan.
    ed. Style & Structure in Literature: Essays in the New Stylistics. Cornell U Pr.
    Understanding Language: An Introduction to Linguistics. Routledge & Kegan.

Fowler, Stewart H. *see* Fowler, Stewart Hampton.

Fowler, Stewart Hampton, 1922-
  xFowler, Stewart H.
    Beef Production in the South. Interstate.

Fowler, Thomas, 1832-1904
  xFowler, Thomas.
    Locke. AMS Pr.
    Locke. R West.

Fowler, Truth M. *see* Fowler, Truth Mary.

Fowler, Truth Mary.
  xFowler, Truth M.
    Haiku for All Day. Golden Quill.

Fowler, W. B.
  xFowler, Wilton B.
    British-American Relations, 1917-1918: The Role of Sir William Wiseman. Princeton U Pr.

Fowler, William C. *see* Fowler, William Chauncey.

Fowler, William Chauncey, 1793-1881
  xFowler, William C.
    Local Law in Massachusetts & Connecticut. Arno.

Fowler, William M.
  xFowler, William M.
    The Baron of Beacon Hill: A Biography of John Hancock. HM.

Fowler, Wilton B.
  xFowler, Wilton B.
    American Diplomatic History Since 1890. AHM Pub.

Fowler, Wilton B. *see* Fowler, W. B.

Fowles, Grant. *see* Fowles, Grant R.

Fowles, Grant R.
  xFowles, Grant.
    Analytical Mechanics. HR&W.
  xFowles, Grant R.
    Introduction to Modern Optics. HR&W.

Fowles, Jib.
  xFowles, Jib.
    ed. Handbook of Futures Research. Greenwood.

Fowles, John, 1926-
  xFowles, John.
    The Aristos. Little.
    The Aristos. NAL.
    The Collector. Dell.
    The Collector. Little.
    Daniel Martin. Little.
    Daniel Martin. NAL.
    The Ebony Tower. Little.
    The Ebony Tower. NAL.
    The French Lieutenant's Woman. Little.
    French Lieutenant's Woman. NAL.
    Islands. Little.
    The Tree. Little.

Fowlie, Wallace, 1908-
  xFowlie, Wallace.
    Clowns & Angels: Studies in Modern French Literature. Cooper Sq.
    Journal of Rehearsals: A Memoir. Duke.
    Lautreamont. Twayne.
    Love in Literature: Studies in Symbolic Expression. Arno.
    A Reading of Proust. Peter Smith.
    A Reading of Proust. U of Chicago Pr.
    Stendhal. Macmillan.

Fowlkes, Martha R., 1940-
  xFowlkes, Martha R.

Behind Every Successful Man: Wives of
    Medicine & Academe. Columbia U Pr.
Fox. *see* Fox, David J.
Fox, A. F. *see* Fox, Anthony Francis.
Fox, Adam, 1883-
    xFox, Adam.
    Plato for Pleasure. Folcroft.
Fox, Aileen Mary (Henderson), Lady, 1907-
    xFox, Aileen.
    Prehistoric Maori Fortifications in the North
        Island of New Zealand. Longman.
Fox, Allen.
    xFox, Allen.
    If I'm the Better Player, Why Can't I Win?.
        Tennis Mag.
Fox, Annette Baker.
    xFox, Annette B.
    Canada & the United States: Transnational &
        Transgovernmental Relations. Columbia U Pr.
    xFox, Annette B.
        jt. auth. NATO & the Range of American
        Choice. Columbia U Pr.
    The Politics of Attraction: Four Middle Powers
        & the United States. Columbia U Pr.
Fox, Anthony Francis.
    xFox, A. F.
    World of Oil. Pergamon.
Fox, C. A. O.
    xFox, C. A.
    Notes on William Shakespeare & Robert Tofte.
        Folcroft.
Fox, Charles.
    xFox, Charles.
    Jazz on Record: A Critical Guide. Greenwood.
Fox, Charles J. *see* Fox, Charles James.
Fox, Charles James.
    xFox, Charles J.
    Memorials & Correspondence of Charles James
        Fox. AMS Pr.
Fox, Charles K. *see* Fox, Charles Kunkel.
Fox, Charles Kunkel, 1908-
    xFox, Charles K.
    Gettysburg. A S Barnes.
    This Wonderful World of Trout. Freshet Pr.
Fox, Charles P. *see* Fox, Charles Philip.
Fox, Charles Philip, 1904-
    xFox, Charles P.
    American Circus Posters in Full Color. Dover.
    Circus in America. Country Beautiful.
    The Great Circus Street Parade in Pictures.
        Dover.
    When Summer Comes. Contemp Bks.
Fox, Charlotte M. *see* Fox, Charlotte Milligan.
Fox, Charlotte Milligan, 1864-1916
    xFox, Charlotte M.
    Annals of the Irish Harpers. Lemma.
Fox, Cyril F. *see* Fox, Cyril Fred.
Fox, Cyril Fred.
    xFox, Cyril F.
    The Personality of Britain, Its Influence on
        Inhabitant & Invader in Prehistoric & Early
        Historic Times. AMS Pr.
Fox, Daniel M.
    xFox, Daniel M.
    Discovery of Abundance: Simon N. Patten &
        the Transformation of Social Theory. Cornell
        U Pr.
Fox, David J.
    xFox.
    Fundamentals of Research in Nursing. ACC.
Fox, Debbie Diane.
    xFox, Deborah D.
    A Face for Me. Wyden.
Fox, Deborah D. *see* Fox, Debbie Diane.
Fox, Dixon R. *see* Fox, Dixon Ryan.
Fox, Dixon Ryan, 1887-1945
    xFox, Dixon R.

The Decline of Aristocracy in the Politics of
    New York. AMS Pr.
    Yankees & Yorkers. Greenwood.
Fox, Donna R. *see* Fox, Donna Russell.
Fox, Donna Russell.
    xFox, Donna R.
    Clinical Management of Voice Disorders.
        Cliffs.
Fox, Douglas. *see* Fox, Douglas M.
Fox, Douglas A., 1927-
    xFox, Douglas A.
    The Vagrant Lotus: An Introduction to
        Buddhist Philosophy. Westminster.
Fox, Douglas M.
    xFox, Douglas.
    Managing the Public's Interest: A
        Results-Oriented Approach. HR&W.
Fox, Early L. *see* Fox, Early Lee.
Fox, Early Lee, 1890-1946
    xFox, Early L.
    American Colonization Society, 1817-1840.
        AMS Pr.
    xFox, Early Lee.
    American Colonization Society 1817-40.
        Scholarly.
Fox, Edward J.
    xFox, Edward J.
    Modern Marketing: Principles & Practice. Scott
        F.
Fox, Edward W. *see* Fox, Edward Whiting.
Fox, Edward Whiting.
    xFox, Edward W.
    Atlas of American History. Oxford U Pr.
Fox, Emmet.
    xFox, Emmet.
    Alter Your Life. Har-Row.
    Diagrams for Living: The Bible Unveiled.
        Har-Row.
Fox, Gardner. *see* Fox, Gardner F.
Fox, Gardner F.
    xFox, Gardner.
    Hurricane. Nordon Pubns.
    xFox, Gardner F.
    The Liberty Sword. Nordon Pubns.
Fox, Geoffrey E.
    xFox, Geoffrey E.
    Working-Class Emigres from Cuba. R & E Res
        Assoc.
Fox, George.
    xFox, George.
    The Journal of George Fox. Octagon.
Fox, Grace.
    xFox, Grace.
    ed. The Hairy Brown Angel & Other Animal
        Tails. Victor Bks.
Fox, Grace E. *see* Fox, Grace Estelle.
Fox, Grace Estelle, 1899-
    xFox, Grace E.
    British Admirals & Chinese Pirates, 1832-1869.
        Hyperion Conn.
Fox, H. *see* Fox, Harold.
Fox, Harold.
    xFox, H.
    Postgraduate Obstetrical & Gynaecological
        Pathology. Pergamon.
Fox, Harrison W.
    xFox, Harrison W.
    Congressional Staffs: The Invisible Force in
        American Lawmaking. Free Pr.
Fox, Harry W.
    xFox, Harry W.
    Master OP Amp Applications Handbook. TAB
        Bks.
Fox, Helen M. *see* Fox, Helen Morgenthau.
Fox, Helen Morgenthau.
    xFox, Helen M.
    Gardening with Herbs for Flavor & Fragrance.
        Dover.
Fox, Hugh, 1932-
    xFox, Hugh.

First Fire: Central & South American Indian
    Poetry. Doubleday.
    Honeymoon-Mom. December Pr.
    The Living Underground: A Critical Overview.
        Whitston Pub.
    ed. The Living Underground: An Anthology of
        Contemporary American Poetry. Whitston
        Pub.
Fox, I. *see* Fox, Irving.
Fox, Irving, 1912-
    xFox, I.
    Fleas of Eastern United States. Hafner.
Fox, John C. *see* Fox, John Charles.
Fox, John Charles, Sir, 1855-1943
    xFox, John C.
    The Byron Mystery. R West.
    The Byron Mystery. Scholarly.
Fox, Karl A. *see* Fox, Karl August.
Fox, Karl August, 1917-
    xFox, Karl A.
    ed. Economic Analysis for Educational
        Planning: Resource Allocation in Non
        Market Systems. Johns Hopkins.
Fox, Leslie.
    xFox, Leslie.
    Computing Methods for Scientists & Engineers.
        Oxford U Pr.
    Introduction to Numerical Linear Algebra.
        Oxford U Pr.
Fox, Lilla M. *see* Fox, Lilla Margaret.
Fox, Lilla Margaret.
    xFox, Lilla M.
    Folk Costume of Eastern Europe. Plays.
    Folk Costume of Southern Europe. Plays.
    Folk Costume of Western Europe. Plays.
Fox, M. *see* Fox, Marion Laffey.
Fox, M. W.
    xFox, M. W.
    Concepts in Ethology: Animal & Human
        Behavior. U of Minn Pr.
Fox, Marion. *see* Fox, Marion Laffey.
Fox, Marion Laffey.
    xFox, M.
    It's Your Body - Know What the Doctor
        Ordered: Your Complete Guide to Medical
        Testing. P-H.
    xFox, Marion.
    A Patient's Guide to Medical Testing. Charles.
Fox, Mary V. *see* Fox, Mary Virginia.
Fox, Mary Virginia.
    xFox, Mary V.
    Jane Fonda: Something to Fight for. Dillon.
Fox, Matthew, 1940-
    xFox, Matthew.
    On Becoming a Musical Mystical Bear:
        Spirituality American Style. Paulist Pr.
    A Spirituality Named Compassion, & the
        Healing of the Global Village, Humpty
        Dumpty, & Us. Winston Pr.
    ed. Western Spirituality: Historical Roots &
        Ecumenical Routes. Fides Claretian.
    Whee! We, Wee All the Way Home: A Guide
        to the New Sensual Spirituality. McGrath.
Fox, Michael W., 1937-
    xFox, Michael W.
    Integrative Development of Brain & Behavior
        in the Dog. U of Chicago Pr.
    Understanding Your Cat. Coward.
    Understanding Your Cat. Bantam.
Fox, Nell (Nathan), 1906-
    xFox, Nell N.
    How to Raise & Train an Australian Terrier.
        TFH Pubns.
Fox, Nell N. *see* Fox, Nell (Nathan).
Fox, Norman A.
    xFox, Norman A.
    Roughshod. Dell.
Fox, Paula.
    xFox, Paula.

Dear Prosper. D White.
The Little Swineherd & Other Tales. Dutton.
Maurice's Room. Macmillan.
Maurice's Room. Macmillan.
Stone-Faced Boy. Bradbury Pr.
Fox, Peter. *see* Fox, Peter F.
Fox, Peter F.
xFox, Peter.
Mantis. St Martin.
Fox, Ray E. *see* Fox, Ray Errol.
Fox, Ray Errol.
xFox, Ray E.
Angela Ambrosia. Knopf.
Angela Ambrosia. PB.
Fox, Renee C.
xFox, Renee C.
The Courage to Fail: A Social View of Organ
Transplants & Dialysis. U of Chicago Pr.
Essays in Medical Sociology: Journeys into the
Field. Wiley.
Fox, Richard L.
xFox, Richard L.
Optimization Methods for Engineering Design.
A-W.
Fox, Richard W. *see* Fox, Richard Wightman.
Fox, Richard Wightman, 1945-
xFox, Richard W.
So Far Disordered in Mind: Insanity in
California, 1870-1930. U of Cal Pr.
Fox, Robert.
xFox, Robert.
Caloric Theory of Gases from Lavoisier to
Regnault. Oxford U Pr.
Destiny News. December Pr.
Fox, Robert B. *see* Fox, Robert Barlow.
Fox, Robert Barlow, 1930-
xFox, Robert B.
Little Injun, Big Injun, Mormon Injun. Horizon
Utah.
Fox, Robert J. *see* Fox, Robert Joseph.
Fox, Robert Joseph, 1927-
xFox, Robert J.
The Marian Catechism. Our Sunday Visitor.
A Prayer Book for Young Catholics. Our
Sunday Visitor.
A World at Prayer. Our Sunday Visitor.
Fox, Robert W.
xFox, Robert W.
Introduction to Fluid Mechanics. Wiley.
Fox, Rodney.
xFox, Rodney.
Agricultural & Technical Journalism.
Greenwood.
Creative News Photography. Univ Microfilms.
Fox, Ruth. *see* Fox, Ruth A.
Fox, Ruth A.
xFox, Ruth.
The Tangled Chain: The Structure of Disorder
in the Anatomy of Melancholy. U of Cal Pr.
Fox, S. L. *see* Fox, Samuel.
Fox, Samuel, 1914-
xFox, S. L.
Industrial & Occupational Ophthalmology. C C
Thomas.
xFox, Samuel.
Management & the Law. Irvington.
Fox, Sanford.
xFox, Sanford.
Economic Control & Free Enterprise. Philos
Lib.
Fox, Seymour.
xFox, Seymour.
Freud & Education. C C Thomas.
Fox, Sidney A. *see* Fox, Sidney Albert.
Fox, Sidney Albert, 1898-
xFox, Sidney A.
Ophthalmic Plastic Surgery. Grune.
Surgery of Ptosis. Grune.
Surgery of Ptosis. Williams & Wilkins.
Fox, Siv C. *see* Fox, Siv Cedering.

Fox, Siv Cedering.
xFox, Siv C.
The Blue Horse & Other Night Poems. HM.
How to Eat a Fortune Cookie. SBD.
Fox, Sonny.
xFox, Sonny.
Jokes & Tips for the Joke Teller. Putnam.
Fox, Theodore, Sir, 1889-
xFox, Theodore.
Crisis in Communication: The Functions &
Future of Medical Journals. Humanities.
Fox, Vernon. *see* Fox, Vernon Brittain.
Fox, Vernon B. *see* Fox, Vernon Brittain.
Fox, Vernon Brittain, 1916-
xFox, Vernon.
Introduction to Criminology. P-H.
xFox, Vernon B.
Introduction to Corrections. P-H.
Fox, William S. *see* Fox, William Sherwood.
Fox, William Sherwood, 1878-
xFox, William S.
Greek & Roman Mythology. Cooper Sq.
Fox, William T. *see* Fox, William Thornton Rickert.
Fox, William Thornton Rickert.

xFox, William T.
ed. European Security & the Atlantic System.
Columbia U Pr.
ed. How Wars End. Am Acad Pol Soc Sci.
NATO & the Range of American Choice.
Columbia U Pr.
ed. Theoretical Aspects of International
Relations. U of Notre Dame Pr.
Fox-Davies, Arthur C. *see* Fox-Davies, Arthur Charles.
Fox-Davies, Arthur Charles, 1871-1928
xFox-Davies, Arthur C.
ed. Armorial Families: A Directory of
Gentlemen of Coat-Armour. C E Tuttle.
Fox-Genovese, Elizabeth, 1941-
xFox-Genovese, Elizabeth.
The Origins of Physiocracy: Economic
Revolution & Social Order in
Eighteenth-Century France. Cornell U Pr.
Fox-Lockert, Lucia, 1928-
xFox-Lockert, Lucia.
Women Novelists in Spain & Spanish America.
Scarecrow.
Foxall, Raymond.
xFoxall, Raymond.
The Dark Forest. PB.
The Silver Goblet. PB.
Foxe, John, 1516-1587
xFoxe, John.
The English Sermons of John Foxe. Schol
Facsimiles.
Foxhall, William B.
xFoxhall, William B.
Professional Construction Management &
Project Administration. McGraw.
Foxley, A. *see* Foxley, Alejandro.
Foxley, Alejandro.
xFoxley, A.
ed. Income Distribution in Latin America.
Cambridge U Pr.
Foxley, Cecilia H.
xFoxley, Cecilia H.
Locating, Recruiting, & Employing Women: An
Equal Opportunity Approach. Garrett Pk.
Foxley, Cecilia H. *see* Foxley, Cecilia H.
Foxley, Eric.
xFoxley, Eric.
First Course in ALGOL 60. A-W.
Foxon, David. *see* Foxon, David Fairwenther.
Foxon, David Fairwenther.
xFoxon, David.

Libertine Literature in England 1660-1745.
Univ Bks.
Foxworth, Jo.
xFoxworth, Jo.
Boss Lady: An Executive Woman Talks About
Making It. T Y Crowell.
Foy, Nancy.
xFoy, Nancy.
Computer Management: A Common Sense
Approach. Van Nos Reinhold.
Foy, Thomas.
xFoy, Thomas.
Richard Crashaw Poet & Saint. Folcroft.
Fozdar, Jamshed.
xFozdar, Jamshed.
The God of Buddha. Asia.
Fraassen, B. C. Van. *see* Van Fraassen, B. C.
Fracchia, Charles A.
xFracchia, Charles A.
Converted into Houses. Penguin.
Living Together Alone: The New American
Monasticism. Har-Row.
Fradin, Dennis.
xFradin, Dennis.
Alaska in Words & Pictures. Childrens.
California in Words & Pictures. Childrens.
Cara. Childrens.
Ohio in Words & Pictures. Childrens.
xFradin, Dennis B.
Bad Luck Tony. P-H.
Fradin, Dennis B.
xFradin, Dennis B.
Beyond the Mountain, Beyond the Forest.
Childrens.
The New Spear. Childrens.
Fradin, Dennis B. *see* Fradin, Dennis.
Fraenkel, A. A. *see* Fraenkel, Abraham Adolf.
Fraenkel, Abraham Adolf.
xFraenkel, A. A.
Abstract Set Theory. Elsevier.
Fraenkel, Eduard, 1888-
xFraenkel, Eduard.
Horace. Oxford U Pr.
Fraenkel, Jack R., 1932-
xFraenkel, Jack R.
Decision-Making in American Government.
Allyn.
How to Teach About Values: An Analytic
Approach. P-H.
Fraenkel, Peter.
xFraenkel, Peter.
Overland. David & Charles.
Frager, Dorothy.
xFrager, Dorothy.
Cloth Hats, Bags 'n Baggage. Chilton.
The Quilting Primer. Chilton.
Frahm, Robert.
xFrahm, Robert.
What's Happening in Minimum Competency
Testing. Phi Delta Kappa.
Fraiberg, Louis. *see* Fraiberg, Selma H.
Fraiberg, Louis Benjamin, 1913-
xFraiberg, Louis.
Psychoanalysis & American Literary Criticism.
Octagon.
Fraiberg, Selma H.
xFraiberg, Selma.
Every Child's Birthright: In Defense of
Mothering. Bantam.
Insights from the Blind: Comparative Studies of
Blind & Sighted Infants. NAL.
Frailey, Lester E. *see* Frailey, Lester Eugene.
Frailey, Lester Eugene, 1890-
xFrailey, Lester E.

Handbook of Business Letters. P-H.
Fraisse, Paul.
xFraisse, Paul.
The Psychology of Time. Greenwood.
Fraizer, Dale W. see Fraizer, Dale Watson.
Fraizer, Dale Watson, 1946-
xFraizer, Dale W.
Alain Robbe-Grillet: An Annotated
Bibliography of Critical Studies, 1953-1972.
Scarecrow.
Frakes, George E. see Frakes, George Edward.
Frakes, George Edward.
xFrakes, George E.
ed. Pollution Papers. Irvington.
Frakes, L. A. see Frakes, Lawrence A.
Frakes, Lawrence A.
xFrakes, L. A.
Climates Throughout Geologic Time. Elsevier.
Fraleigh, John B.
xFraleigh, John B.
A First Course in Abstract Algebra. A-W.
Fraley, E. S., 1889-
xFraley, Edgar.
Fragments & Splinters. Commonwealth Pr.
Fraley, Edgar. see Fraley, E. S.
Fram, E. H. see Fram, Eugene H.
Fram, Eugene H.
xFram, E. H.
What You Should Know About Small Business
Credit & Finance. Oceana.
Frame, Donald M. see Frame, Donald Murdoch.
Frame, Donald Murdoch, 1911-
xFrame, Donald M.
Montaigne in France, 1812-1852. Octagon.
Frame, Janet.
xFrame, Janet.
Living in the Maniototo. Braziller.
Frame, Jean.
xFrame, Jean.
How to Give a Party. Watts.
Frame, Paul, 1913-
xFrame, Paul.
Drawing Cats & Kittens. Watts.
Drawing Dogs & Puppies. Watts.
Frampton, Mary.
xFrampton, Mary.
Mary Frampton & Friends Rock & Roll
Recipes. Doubleday.
Franc, Miriam A. see Franc, Miriam Alice.
Franc, Miriam Alice.
xFranc, Miriam A.
Ibsen in England. Folcroft.
Franca, Oswaldo, 1936-
xFranca, Oswaldo.
The Long Haul. Dutton.
France, Anatole, 1844-1924
xFrance, Anatole.
Latin Genius. Arno.
Prefaces, Introductions & Other Uncollected
Papers. Kennikat.
Tales from a Mother-of-Pearl Casket. Arno.
France, Anna K. see France, Anna Kay.
France, Anna Kay.
xFrance, Anna K.
Boris Pasternak's Translations of Shakespeare.
U of Cal Pr.
France Armee Etat Major. see France. Armee.
Etat-Major. Service Historique.
France. Armee. Etat-Major. Service Historique.
xFrance Armee Etat Major.
Afrique Francaise du Nord: Bibliographie
Militaire des Ouvrages Francaise ou Traduits
en Francais et des Articles des Principales
Revues Francaises Relatifs a l'Algerie, a la
Tunisie et au Maroc de 1830-1926. AMS Pr.
France. Chambre Des Deputes, 1814-1848. see France.
Chambre Des Deputes, 1814-1848. Commission
Chargee D'Examiner la Proposition De M. De Tracy,
Relative Aux Esclaves De Colonies.

France. Chambre Des Desputes, 1814-1848. Commission Chargee D'Examiner la Proposition De M. De Tracy, Relative Aux Esclaves De Colonies.
xFrance. Chambre Des Deputes, 1814-1848.
Report Made to the Chamber of Deputies on
the Abolition of Slavery in the French
Colonies, July 23, 1839. Negro U Pr.
France, Dorothy. see France, Dorothy D.
France, Dorothy D.
xFrance, Dorothy.
Special Days of the Church Year. Bethany Pr.
France, Edward E.
xFrance, Edward E.
Some Aspects of the Migration of the Negro to
the San Francisco Bay Area Since 1940. R &
E Res Assoc.
France. Institut National De la Statistique et Des Etudes Economiques.
xInstitut National De la Statistique et Des Etudes
Economiques.
Annuaire Statistique De la France 1979. Intl
Pubns Serv.
France, Joseph J. De. see De France, Joseph J.
France. Ministere De la Guerre.
xFrance, Ministere de la Guerre.
Rules & Regulations for the Field Exercise &
Manoeuvres of the French Infantry: Issued
August 1, 1791. Greenwood.
France. Ministere De L'Interieur.
xFrance. Ministere de l'interieur.
Correspondance du ministre de l'interieur
relative au commerce, aux subsistances et a
l'administration generale. AMS Pr.
France. Ministere Des Affaires Etrangeres.
xFrance, Ministere Des Affaires Etrangeres.
Les Combattants Francais De la Guerre
Americaine, 1778-1783. Genealog Pub.
France, Rachel, 1936-
xFrance, Rachel.
ed. A Century of Plays by American Women.
Rosen Pr.
France, Richard, 1938-
xFrance, Richard.
The Theatre of Orson Welles. Bucknell U Pr.
Francesca, Rosina.
xFrancesca, Rosina.
How to Marry Somebody Else's Housebroken
Husband. Ashley Bks.
Franchere, Hoyt C.
xFranchere, Hoyt C.
Edwin Arlington Robinson. Twayne.
Franchere, Ruth.
xFranchere, Ruth.
Cesar Chavez. T Y Crowell.
Franchi, Eda.
xFranchi, Eda.
The Long Road Back. NAL.
Franchimont, Paul.
xFranchimont, Paul.
ed. Cancer Related Antigens: Proceedings of
the European Economic Communities
Symposium on Cancer Related Antigens,
Liege, May 3-4, 1976. Elsevier.
Francis, Alfred W. see Francis, Alfred West.
Francis, Alfred West.
xFrancis, Alfred W.
Critical Solution Temperatures. Am Chemical.
Francis, Arlene.
xFrancis, Arlene.
Arlene Francis: A Memoir. S&S.
Francis, Carl C., 1901-
xFrancis, Carl C.
Introduction to Human Anatomy. Mosby.
Francis, Charles E.
xFrancis, Charles E.
Tuskegee Airmen: The Story of the Negro in
the U. S. Air Force. Branden.
Francis, Clark. see Francis, Jack Clark.
Francis, Claude.
xFrancis, Claude.

The Book of Honey. Autumn Pr.
Francis, Convers, 1795-1863
xFrancis, Convers.
Life of John Eliot: The Apostle to the Indians.
Mss Info.
Life of John Eliot: The Apostle to the Indians.
Somerset Pub.
Francis, Dave.
xFrancis, Dave.
Improving Work Groups: A Practical Manual
for Team Building. Univ Assocs.
Francis, Dick.
xFrancis, Dick.
Bonecrack. Har-Row.
Bonecrack. PB.
Dead Cert. PB.
Flying Finish. PB.
For Kicks. PB.
Forfeit. PB.
High Stakes. Har-Row.
High Stakes. PB.
In the Frame. Har-Row.
In the Frame. PB.
Nerve. PB.
Odds Against. PB.
Rat Race. PB.
Trial Run. Har-Row.
Risk. Har-Row.
Risk. PB.
Trial Run. PB.
Whip Hand. Har-Row.
Francis, Dorothy Brenner.
xFrancis, Dorothy B.
The Flint Hills Foal. Abingdon.
The Legacy of Merton Manor. Bouregy.
xFrancis, Dorthy B.
The Flint Hills Foal. Schol Bk Serv.
Francis, Dorthy B. see Francis, Dorothy Brenner.
Francis, F. G. see Francis, F. J.
Francis, F. J.
xFrancis, F. G.
Food Colorimetry: Theory & Applications.
AVI.
Francis, Frank.
xFrancis, Frank.
Natasha's New Doll. O'Hara.
Francis, Fred O.
xFrancis, Fred O.
Conflict at Colossae: A Problem in the
Interpretation of Early Christianity,
Illustrated by Selected Modern Studies.
Scholars Pr Ca.
Francis, Gloria A.
xFrancis, Gloria A.
Compiled by Whitman at Auction. Bruccoli.
ed. Whitman at Auction: 1899-1972. Gale.
Francis, Gloria M.
xFrancis, Gloria M.
Promoting Psychological Comfort. Wm C
Brown.
Francis, Hazel.
xFrancis, Hazel.
Language in Teaching & Learning. Allen
Unwin.
Francis, J. A. see Francis, John.
Francis, Jack Clark.
xFrancis, Clark.
Portfolio Analysis. P-H.
Francis, John.
xFrancis, J. A.
History of the English Railway: Its Social
Relations & Revelations 1820-1845. David &
Charles.
Francis, John De. see De Francis, John.
Francis, Mabel.
xFrancis, Mable.
One Shall Chase a Thousand. Chr Pubns.
Francis, Mable. see Francis, Mabel.
Francis, Nelle.
xFrancis, Nelle.

Dostoevsky: The Seeds of Revolt, 1821-1849.
Princeton U Pr.

Frank, Kenneth A.
xFrank, Kenneth A.
ed. The Human Dimension in Psychoanalytic
Practice. Grune.

Frank, Larry. *see* Frank, Lawrence Phillip.

Frank, Lawrence K. *see* Frank, Lawrence Kelso.

Frank, Lawrence Kelso, 1890-1968
xFrank, Lawrence K.
Nature & Human Nature: Man's New Image
of Himself. Greenwood.

Frank, Lawrence Phillip.
xFrank, Larry.
Historic Pottery of the Pueblo Indians,
1660-1880. NYGS.
Indian Silver Jewelry of the Southwest
1868-1930. NYGS.

Frank, Marcella.
xFrank, Marcella.
Modern English: A Practical Reference Guide.
P-H.

Frank, Martin J.
xFrank, Martin J.
Cardiovascular Physical Diagnosis. Year Bk
Med.

Frank, Mel.
xFrank, Mel.
Marijuana Grower's Guide. And-or Pr.

Frank, P. M. *see* Frank, Paul M.

Frank, Pat.
xFrank, Pat.
Alas, Babylon. Bantam.
Alas, Babylon. Lippincott.

Frank, Paul M.
xFrank, P. M.
Introduction to System Sensitivity Theory.
Acad Pr.

Frank, Peter.
xFrank, Peter.
Brief Course in Calculus with Applications.
Har-Row.

Frank, Phil.
xFrank, Phil.
Subee Lives on a Houseboat. Messner.

Frank, Robert.
xFrank, Robert.
The Americans. Aperture.

Frank, Robert G. *see* Frank, Robert Gregg.

Frank, Robert Gregg, 1943-
xFrank, Robert G.
Harvey & the Oxford Physiologists: A Study of
Scientific Ideas & Social Interaction. U of Cal
Pr.

Frank, Robert W. *see* Frank, Robert Worth.

Frank, Robert Worth, 1914-
xFrank, Robert W.
Chaucer & the Legend of Good Women.
Harvard U Pr.

Frank, Roberta.
xFrank, Roberta.
ed. A Plan for the Dictionary of Old English.
U of Toronto Pr.

Frank, Ronald E. *see* Frank, Ronald Edward.

Frank, Ronald Edward.
xFrank, Ronald E.
The Public's Use of Television. Sage.

Frank, Samuel B.
xFrank, Samuel B.
Acne: Update for the Practitioner. Yorke Med.

Frank, Sid. *see* Frank, Sidney.

Frank, Sidney.
xFrank, Sid.
Presidents: Tidbits & Trivia. Hammond Inc.
xFrank, Sidney.
Presidents: Tidbits & Trivia. Hammond Inc.

Frank, Stuart. *see* Frank, Arthur.

Frank, Ted.
xFrank, Ted.
Basic Business & Professional Speech
Communication. P-H.

Frank, Tenney, 1876-1939
xFrank, Tenney.
Aspects of Social Behavior in Ancient Rome.
Cooper Sq.
Economic History of Rome. Gordon Pr.
An Economic Survey of Ancient Rome.
Octagon.

Frank, Waldo. *see* Frank, Waldo David.

Frank, Waldo D. *see* Frank, Waldo David.

Frank, Waldo David, 1889-1967
xFrank, Waldo.
ed. Tales from the Argentine. Gordon Pr.
Tales from the Argentine. R West.
xFrank, Waldo D.
City Block. AMS Pr.
The Death & Birth of David Markand: An
American Story. Johnson Repr.
In the American Jungle. Arno.
Our America. AMS Pr.
ed. Tales from the Argentine. Arno.

Frank-Stromborg, Marilyn.
xFrank-Stromborg, Marilyn.
Primary Care Assessment & Management Skills
for Nurses: A Self-Assessment Manual.
Lippincott.

Frankau, Gilbert, 1884-
xFrankau, Gilbert.
Men, Maids & Mustard-Pot: A Collection of
Tales. Arno.

Franke, Richard. *see* Franke, Richard W.

Franke, Richard W.
xFranke, Richard.
The Seeds of Famine: Ecological Destruction &
the Development Dilemma in the West
African Sahel. Allanheld.

Franke, Wolfgang, 1912-
xFranke, Wolfgang.
A Century of Chinese Revolution, 1851-1949.
U of SC Pr.
China & the West. U of SC Pr.
Reform & Abolition of the Traditional Chinese
Examination System. Harvard U Pr.

Frankel, Barbara.
xFrankel, Barbara.
Childbirth in the Ghetto: Folk Beliefs of Negro
Women in a North Philadelphia Hospital
Ward. R & E Res Assoc.

Frankel, Charles, 1917-
xFrankel, Charles.
Case for Modern Man. Arno.
Case for Modern Man. Beacon Pr.
ed. Controversies & Decisions: The Social
Sciences & Public Policy. Russell Sage.
Education & the Barricades. Norton.
Human Rights & Foreign Policy. Foreign
Policy.
The Neglected Aspect of Foreign Affairs:
American Educational & Cultural Policy
Abroad. Brookings.

Frankel, Fred H.
xFrankel, Fred H.
ed. Hypnosis: Trance As a Coping Mechanism.
Plenum Pub.

Frankel, Hans H. *see* Frankel, Hans Hermann.

Frankel, Hans Hermann, 1916-
xFrankel, Hans H.
Compiled by Catalogue of Translations from
the Chinese Dynastic Histories for the Period
220-960. Greenwood.
The Flowering Plum & the Palace Lady:
Interpretations of Chinese Poetry. Yale U Pr.

Frankel, Joseph.
xFrankel, Joseph.

International Relations in a Changing World.
Oxford U Pr.

Frankel, Leon A.
xFrankel, Leon A.
Gastric Surgery & the Dumping Syndrome:
The "Mirror-Image" Concept. C C Thomas.

Frankel, Martin R.
xFrankel, Martin R.
Inference from Survey Samples: An Empirical
Investigation. U of Mich Soc Res.

Frankel, Marvin. *see* Frankel, Marvin E.

Frankel, Marvin E.
xFrankel, Marvin.
The Grand Jury: An Institution on Trial. Hill
& Wang.
Partisan Justice. Hill & Wang.

Frankel, Max G.
xFrankel, Max G.
Functional Teaching of the Mentally Retarded.
C C Thomas.

Frankel, O. H. *see* Frankel, Otto Herzberg.

Frankel, Otto Herzberg.
xFrankel, O. H.
ed. Crop Genetic Resources for Today &
Tomorrow. Cambridge U Pr.

Frankel, Paul H.
xFrankel, Paul H.
Essentials of Petroleum: A Key to Oil
Economics. Biblio Dist.

Frankel, R. *see* Frankel, Rafael.

Frankel, Rafael.
xFrankel, R.
Pollination Mechanisms, Reproduction & Plant
Breeding. Springer-Verlag.

Frankel, Robert.
xFrankel, Robert.
Radiation Protection for Radiologic
Technologists. McGraw,

Frankel, S. Herbert. *see* Frankel, Sally Herbert.

Frankel, Sally Herbert.
xFrankel, S. Herbert.
Capital Investment in Africa: Its Course &
Effects. Fertig.
Two Philosophies of Money: The Conflict of
Trust & Authority. St Martin.

Frankel, Sidney, 1910-
xFrankel, Sidney.
Multiconductor Transmission Line Analysis.
Artech Hse.

Frankel, Theodore, 1929-
xFrankel, Theodore T.
Gravitational Curvature: An Introduction to
Einstein's Theory. W H Freeman.

Frankel, Theodore T. *see* Frankel, Theodore.

Frankel, Victor H.
xFrankel, Victor H.
ed. Basic Biomechanics of the Skeletal System.
Lea & Febiger.

Frankel, Virginia.
xFrankel, Virginia.
The Incredible, Wonderful, Flexible World of
Built-Ins. Scribner.
What Your House Tells About You. Trident.

Frankena, William K.
xFrankena, William K.
Ethics. P-H.

Frankenhoff, Charles A.
xFrankenhoff, Charles A.
Environmental Planning & Development in the
Caribbean. U of PR Pr.

Frankenstein, C. *see* Frankenstein, Carl.

Frankenstein, Carl.
xFrankenstein, C.
Impaired Intelligence: Pathology &
Rehabilitation. Gordon.
Varieties of Juvenile Delinquency. Gordon.
xFrankenstein, Carl.

They Think Again: Restoring Cognitive
Abilities Through Teaching. Van Nos
Reinhold.
Frankenstein, Marilyn.
xFrankenstein, Marilyn.
Basic Algebra. P-H.
Frankfather, Dwight, 1946-
xFrankfather, Dwight.
The Aged in the Community: Managing
Senility & Deviance. Praeger.
Frankfort, Ellen.
xFrankfort, Ellen.
Rosie: The Investigation of a Wrongful Death.
Dial.
Vaginal Politics. Times Bks.
Frankfort, Henri, 1897-1954
xFrankfort, Henri.
Ancient Egyptian Religion: An Interpretation.
Har-Row.
Ancient Egyptian Religion: An Interpretation.
Peter Smith.
Art & Architecture of the Ancient Orient.
Penguin.
Art & Architecture of the Ancient Orient.
Viking Pr.
Frankfort, Roberta, 1945-
xFrankfort, Roberta.
Collegiate Women: Domesticity & Career in
Turn of the Century America. NYU Pr.
Frankfurt, Harry G., 1929-
xFrankfurt, Harry G.
ed. Leibniz: A Collection of Critical Essays. U
of Notre Dame Pr.
Frankfurter, Felix.
xFrankfurter, Felix.
Business of the Supreme Court:: A Study in the
Federal Judicial System. Johnson Repr.
Felix Frankfurter Reminisces. Greenwood.
Of Law & Life & Other Things That Matter:
Papers & Addresses of Felix Frankfurter,
1956-1963. Atheneum.
Of Law & Life & Other Things That Matter:
Papers & Addresses of Felix Frankfurter,
1956-1963. Harvard U Pr.
Frankl, Victor. see Frankl, Viktor Emil.
Frankl, Viktor Emil.
xFrankl, Victor.
The Unconscious God. S&S.
Frankland, Phillip.
xFrankland, Phillip.
Atlas of Selected Iowa Services. U of Iowa Pr.
Franklin, A. J. see Franklin, Arnold J.
Franklin, Allan, 1938-
xFranklin, Allan.
The Principle of Inertia in the Middle Ages.
Colo Assoc.
Franklin, Arnold J.
xFranklin, A. J.
Cement and Mortar Additives. Noyes.
Franklin, B. A. see Franklin, Benjamin Alvey.
Franklin, Benjamin.
xFranklin, Benjamin.
Anais Nin: An Introduction. Ohio U Pr.
An Apology for Printers. Acropolis.
Autobiography of Benjamin Franklin.
Macmillan.
Autobiography of Benjamin Franklin. Yale U
Pr.
Autobiography of Benjamin Franklin. Watts.
Autobiography of Benjamin Franklin. Airmont.
ed. The Prose of the Minor Connecticut Wits.
Schol Facsimiles.
The Whistle. Lerner Pubns.
Franklin, Benjamin Alvey, 1869-
xFranklin, B. A.
The Industrial Executive. Hive Pub.
Franklin, Clay.
xFranklin, Clay.

Ten Plays of Terror: Dramatic Adaptations for
Amateur Players. A S Barnes.
Franklin, Colin.
xFranklin, Colin.
Private Presses. Dufour.
Franklin, D. A.
xFranklin, D. A.
A Guide to Medical Mathematics. Halsted Pr.
Franklin, Eric, 1929-
xFranklin, Eric.
Christ the Lord: A Study in the Purpose &
Theology of Luke-Acts. Westminster.
Franklin, Frank G. see Franklin, Frank George.
Franklin, Frank George.
xFranklin, Frank G.
Legislative History of Naturalization in the
United States: From the Revolutionary War
to 1861. Arno.
Franklin, Gene F.
xFranklin, Gene F.
Digital Control of Dynamic Systems. A-W.
Franklin, H. Bruce. see Franklin, Howard Bruce.
Franklin, Howard Bruce.
xFranklin, H. Bruce.
ed. Future Perfect: American Science Fiction
of the Nineteenth Century. Oxford U Pr.
Future Perfect: American Science Fiction of
the Nineteenth Century. Oxford U Pr.
Franklin, Jack L.
xFranklin, Jack L.
An Introduction to Program Evaluation. Wiley.
Franklin, Jerome L.
xFranklin, Jerome L.
Survey-Guided Development III: A Manual for
Concepts Training. Univ Assocs.
Franklin, Jessie M. see Franklin, Jessie Merle.
Franklin, Jessie Merle.
xFranklin, Jessie M.
Grandparents Are Special. Broadman.
Franklin, Jimmie L. see Franklin, Jimmie Lewis.
Franklin, Jimmie Lewis.
xFranklin, Jimmie L.
The Blacks in Oklahoma. U of Okla Pr.
Born Sober: Prohibition in Oklahoma,
1907-1959. U of Okla Pr.
Franklin, Joe.
xFranklin, Joe.
A Gift for People. M Evans.
Franklin, Joel N.
xFranklin, Joel N.
Matrix Theory. P-H.
Franklin, John H. see Franklin, John Hope.
Franklin, John Hope, 1915-
xFranklin, John H.
From Slavery to Freedom: A History of Negro
Americans. Knopf.
Racial Equality in America. U of Chicago Pr.
Franklin, Jon.
xFranklin, Jon.
Shocktrauma. St Martin.
Franklin, Julian H., comp
xFranklin, Julian H.
ed. Constitutionalism & Resistance in the
Sixteenth Century: Three Treatises by
Holtman, Beza & Mornay. Irvington.
tr. & ed. Constitutionalism & Resistance in the
Sixteenth Century: Three Treatises by
Heltman, Beza & Mornay. Pegasus.
Franklin, Linda. see Franklin, Linda Campbell.
Franklin, Linda Campbell.
xFranklin, Linda.
Antiques & Collectibles: A Bibliography of
Works in English, 16th Century to 1976.
Scarecrow.
Franklin, Marian P. see Franklin, Marian Pope.
Franklin, Marian Pope.
xFranklin, Marian P.

ed. Classroom Centers & Stations in America
& Britain. Mss Info.
Franklin, Max.
xFranklin, Max.
Baby Blue Marine. NAL.
The Dark. NAL.
Franklin, Miriam A. see Franklin, Miriam Anna.
Franklin, Miriam Anna.
xFranklin, Miriam A.
Rehearsal: The Principles & Practice of Acting
for the Stage. P-H.
Franklin, Raoul N.
xFranklin, Raoul N.
Plasma Phenomena in Gas Discharges. Oxford
U Pr.
Franklin, Shirley A.
xFranklin, Shirley A.
Perilous Homecoming. Bouregy.
Franklin, Thomas B. see Franklin, Thomas Bedford.
Franklin, Thomas Bedford.
xFranklin, Thomas B.
Climates in Miniature: A Study in
Micro-Climate & Environment. Greenwood.
Franklin, Ursula.
xFranklin, Ursula.
Anatomy of Poesis: The Prose Poems of
Stephane Mallarme. U of NC Pr.
The Rhetoric of Valery's Prose "Aubades". U
of Toronto Pr.
Franklin, Vincent P.
xFranklin, Vincent P.
The Education of Black Philadelphia: The
Social & Educational History of a Minority
Community, Nineteen Hundred to Nineteen
Fifty. U of Pa Pr.
Franklin, Wayne.
xFranklin, Wayne.
Discoverers, Explorers, Settlers: The Diligent
Writers of Early America. U of Chicago Pr.
Frankling, Eleanor.
xFrankling, Eleanor.
Practical Dog Breeding & Genetics. Arco.
Franklyn, Robert A. see Franklyn, Robert Alan.
Franklyn, Robert Alan.
xFranklyn, Robert A.
The Art of Staying Young. S&S.
Instant Beauty. Arc Bks.
Franko, Lawrence G.
xFranko, Lawrence G.
Developing Country Debt. Pergamon.
Franks. see Franks, Richard.
Franks, Arthur H. see Franks, Arthur Henry.
Franks, Arthur Henry, 1907-
xFranks, Arthur H.
Twentieth Century Ballet. Greenwood.
Franks, B. Don.
xFranks, B. Don.
Evaluating Performance in Physical Education.
Acad Pr.
Franks, C. E. see Franks, Charles Edward Selwyn.
Franks, Charles Edward Selwyn, 1936-
xFranks, C. E.
The Canoe & White Water: From Essential to
Sport. U of Toronto Pr.
Franks, Hugh.
xFranks, Hugh.
Will to Live. Routledge & Kegan.
Franks, J. R. see Franks, Julian R.
Franks, Julian R.
xFranks, J. R.
Modern Managerial Finance. Wiley.
Franks, Kenny A. see Franks, Kenny Arthur.
Franks, Kenny Arthur, 1945-
xFranks, Kenny A.
Stand Watie & the Agony of the Cherokee
Nation. Memphis St Univ.
Franks, Maurice R.
xFranks, Maurice R.
How to Avoid Alimony. NAL.
Franks, R. see Franks, Richard.

Franks, Richard.
xFranks.
Simplified Medical Dictionary. Van Nos Reinhold.
xFranks, R.
Simplified Medical Dictionary. Med Economics.
xFranks, Richard.
Simplified Medical Dictionary. Delmar.
Frankston, Jay.
xFrankston, Jay.
A Christmas Story. Summit Bks.
Franqui, Carlos, 1921-
xFranqui, Carlos.
Diary of the Cuban Revolution. Viking Pr. Twelve. Lyle Stuart.
Fransella, F. see Fransella, Fay.
Fransella, Fay.
xFransella, F.
Personal Change & Reconstruction: Research on a Treatment of Stuttering. Acad Pr.
Frantz, F. see Frantz, Forrest H.
Frantz, Forrest H.
xFrantz, F.
Successful Moonlighting Techniques That Can Make You Rich. P-H.
Frantz, Joe B. see Frantz, Joe Bertram.
Frantz, Joe Bertram.
xFrantz, Joe B.
Aspects of the American West: Three Essays. Tex A&M Univ Pr.
Frantz, Ray W. see Frantz, Ray William.
Frantz, Ray William.
xFrantz, Ray W.
English Traveller & the Movement of Ideas, 1660-1732. Octagon.
Frantzis, Nicholas, 1934-
xFrantzis, Nicholas.
The Seven Popular Games of Backgammon. Exposition.
Franz, Carl.
xFranz, Carl.
The People's Guide to Mexico. John Muir.
Franz, Maurice.
xFranz, Maurice.
ed. The Calendar of Organic Gardening: A Guidebook to Successful Gardening Through the Year. McGraw.
Franzen, Carl G. see Franzen, Carl Gustave Frederick.
Franzen, Carl Gustave Frederick, 1886-
xFranzen, Carl G.
Foundations of Secondary Education. Greenwood.
Franzen, Gosta, 1906-
xFranzen, Gosta.
Prose & Poetry of Modern Sweden: An Intermediate Swedish Reader. U of Nebr Pr.
Franzen, Greta.
xFranzen, Greta.
Great Ship Vasa. Hastings.
Franzen, Lavern G.
xFranzen, Lavern G.
Good News from Luke: Visual Messages for Children. Augsburg.
Franzen, Nils Olof.
xFranzen, Nils-Clof.
Agaton Sax & the Diamond Thieves. Andre Deutsch.
Franzen, Nils-Clof. see Franzen, Nils Olof.
Franzen, Raymond H. see Franzen, Raymond Hugh.
Franzen, Raymond Hugh, 1895-
xFranzen, Raymond H.
Accomplishment Ratio: A Treatment of the Inherited Determinants of Disparity in School Product. AMS Pr.
Franzwa, Gregory M.
xFranzwa, Gregory M.
The Oregon Trail Revisited. Patrice Pr.
Frary, Ihna T. see Frary, Ihna Thayer.

Frary, Ihna Thayer, 1873-
xFrary, Ihna T.
They Built the Capitol. Arno.
xFrary, L. T.
Early Homes of Ohio. Peter Smith.
Frary, L. T. see Frary, Ihna Thayer.
Frary, Michael.
xFrary, Michael.
Impressions of the Big Thicket. U of Tex Pr.
Impressions of the Texas Panhandle. Tex A&M Univ Pr.
Frasche, Dean F.
xFrasche, Dean F.
Southeast Asian Ceramics: Ninth Through Seventeenth Centuries. Weatherhill.
Frascino, Edward.
xFrascino, Edward.
Eddie Spaghetti. Har-Row.
Frascogna, X. M. see Frascogna, Xavier M.
Frascogna, Xavier M.
xFrascogna, X. M.
Successful Artist Management. Watson-Guptill.
Fraser, Alexander C. see Fraser, Alexander Campbell.
Fraser, Alexander Campbell, 1819-1914
xFraser, Alexander C.
Locke. Kennikat.
Philosophy of Theism. AMS Pr.
Rational Philosophy in History & in System: An Introduction to a Logical & Metaphysical Course. B Franklin.
Fraser, Allan.
xFraser, Allan.
The Bull. Scribner.
Fraser, Amy S. see Fraser, Amy Stewart.
Fraser, Amy Stewart.
xFraser, Amy S.
The Hills of Home. Routledge & Kegan.
In Memory Long. Routledge & Kegan.
Fraser, Anthea.
xFraser, Anthea.
Breath of Brimstone. Dodd.
Home Through the Dark. Dodd.
Home Through the Dark. G K Hall.
Island in Waiting. St Martin.
The Stone. St Martin.
Fraser, Antonia. see Fraser, Antonia Pakenham.
Fraser, Antonia Pakenham, Lady, 1932-
xFraser, Antonia.
ed. Love Letters: An Anthology. Knopf.
Mary Queen of Scots. Delacorte.
Quiet As a Nun. Ace Bks.
Royal Charles: Charles II & the Restoration. Knopf.
Fraser, C. M. see Fraser, Constance Mary.
Fraser, Chelsea. see Fraser, Chelsea Curtis.
Fraser, Chelsea Curtis, 1876-
xFraser, Chelsea.
Famous American Flyers. Arno.
Fraser, Colin, 1935-
xFraser, Colin.
Avalanches & Snow Safety. Scribner.
Fraser, Constance Mary.
xFraser, C. M.
Tyneside. David & Charles.
Fraser, D. see Fraser, Donald Alexander Stuart.
Fraser, David.
xFraser, David.
Blitz. Doubleday.
Fraser, Dean.
xFraser, Dean.
People Problem: What You Should Know About Growing Population & Vanishing Resources. Ind U Pr.
Fraser, Derek.
xFraser, Derek.
Power & Authority in the Victorian City. St Martin.
Fraser, Donald, 1870-1933
xFraser, Donald.

African Idylls: Portraits & Impressions of Life on a Central African Mission Station. Negro U Pr.
Future of Africa. Negro U Pr.
Fraser, Donald Alexander Stuart, 1925-
xFraser, D.
Structure of Inference. Krieger.
Fraser, Douglas.
xFraser, Douglas F.
Torres Straits Sculpture: A Study in Oceanic Primitive Art. Garland Pub.
Fraser, Douglas F. see Fraser, Douglas.
Fraser, F. Clarke.
xFraser, F. Clarke.
Genetics of Man. Lea & Febiger.
Fraser, G. S. see Fraser, George Sutherland.
Fraser, George. see Fraser, George MacDonald.
Fraser, George M. see Fraser, George MacDonald.
Fraser, George MacDonald, 1925-
xFraser, George.
Intro. by The World of the Public School. St Martin.
xFraser, George M.
Flashman in the Great Game. Knopf.
Flashman in the Great Game. NAL.
Flashman's Lady. Knopf.
Flashman's Lady. NAL.
Fraser, George R. see Fraser, George Robert.
Fraser, George Robert.
xFraser, George R.
The Causes of Blindness in Childhood: A Study of 776 Children with Severe Visual Handicaps. Johns Hopkins.
Fraser, George Sutherland, 1915-
xFraser, G. S.
Alexander Pope. Routledge & Kegan.
Lawrence Durrell: A Critical Study. Dutton.
Fraser, Gordon. see Fraser, Gordon Holmes.
Fraser, Gordon Holmes.
xFraser, Gordon.
Rain on the Desert. Moody.
Fraser, Ian F. see Fraser, Ian Forbes.
Fraser, Ian Forbes, 1907-1969
xFraser, Ian F.
Spirit of French Canada: A Study of the Literature. AMS Pr.
Fraser, J. M. see Fraser, John Munro.
Fraser, J. T.
xFraser, J. T.
Of Time, Passion & Knowledge: Reflections on the Strategy of Existence. Braziller.
Fraser, James. see Fraser, James Howard.
Fraser, James Howard.
xFraser, James.
ed. Childrens Authors & Illustrators: A Guide to Manuscript Collections in U. S. Libraries. K G Saur.
Fraser, John Munro.
xFraser, J. M.
Industrial Psychology. Pergamon.
Fraser, Marshall.
xFraser, Marshall.
College Algebra & Trigonometry: A Functions Approach. Benjamin-Cummings.
Intermediate Algebra. Burgess.
Intermediate Algebra. Page-Ficklin.
Fraser, Mowat G. see Fraser, Mowat Gjems.
Fraser, Mowat Gjems, 1898-
xFraser, Mowat G.
Education & Western Civilization-the Long View: An Attempt to Gain Perspective. Exposition.
Fraser, N. see Fraser, Nicholas.
Fraser, Nicholas, 1948-
xFraser, N.
Aristotle Onassis. Ballantine.
xFraser, Nicholas.
Aristotle Onassis. Lippincott.
Fraser, P. M. see Fraser, Peter Marshall.

Fraser, Peter, 1932-
xFraser, Peter.
Puppet Circus. Plays.
Fraser, Peter Marshall.
xFraser, P. M.
Rhodian Funerary Monuments. Oxford U Pr.
Fraser, Robert G.
xFraser, Robert G.
Diagnosis of Diseases of the Chest. Saunders.
Organ Physiology: Structure & Function of the
Lung with Emphasis on Roentgenology.
Saunders.
Fraser, Ronald, 1930-
xFraser, Ronald.
Blood of Spain: An Oral History of the Spanish
Civil War. Pantheon.
ed. Tajos: The Story of a Village on the Costa
Del Sol. Pantheon.
Fraser, Sylvia.
xFraser, Sylvia.
The Candy Factory. Little.
Fraser, Thomas M.
xFraser, Thomas M.
Culture & Change in India: The Barpali
Experiment. U of Mass Pr.
Fraser, William A. *see* Fraser, William Alexander.
Fraser, William Alexander, 1859-1933
xFraser, William A.
Brave Hearts. Arno.
Thirteen Men. Arno.
Frassanito, William A.
xFrassanito, William A.
Antietam: The Photographic Legacy of
America's Bloodiest Day. Scribner.
Frater, Charles.
xFrater, Charles.
Sound Recording for Motion Pictures. A S
Barnes.
Frates, Jeffrey.
xFrates, Jeffrey.
Introduction to the Computer: An Integrative
Approach. P-H.
Frattolillo, Rinaldo.
xFrattolillo, Salmieri.
American Grilles. HarBraceJ.
Frattolillo, Salmieri. *see* Frattolillo, Rinaldo.
Frauenfelder, Hans.
xFrauenfelder, Hans.
Subatomic Physics. P-H.
Fraunce, Abraham.
xFraunce, Abraham.
The Arcadian Rhetorike. Hyperion Conn.
Fraunfelder, F. T.
xFraunfelder, F. T.
Drug-Induced Ocular Side Effects & Drug
Interactions. Lea & Febiger.
Frautschi, R. L.
xFrautschi, Richard L.
Pour et Contre: Manuel De Conversations
Graduees. Har-Row.
Frautschi, Richard L. *see* Frautschi, R. L.
Frauwallner, Erich.
xFrauwallner, Erich.
History of Indian Philosophy. Humanities.
History of Indian Philosophy. Orient Bk Dist.
Frawley, Honora M. *see* Frawley, Honora Margaret.
Frawley, Honora Margaret, 1892-
xFrawley, Honora M.
Certain Procedures of Studying Poetry in the
Fifth Grade. AMS Pr.
Fray, G. I., 1928-
xFray, G. I.
The Chemistry of Cyclo-Octatetraene & Its
Derivatives. Cambridge U Pr.
Fraydas, Stan.
xFraydas, Stan.
Professional Cartooning: A Complete Course in
Graphic Humor. Krieger.
Frayne, Trent.
xFrayne, Trent.

Famous Hockey Players. Dodd.
Famous Women Tennis Players. Dodd.
Frazee, Charles A.
xFrazee, Charles A.
Orthodox Church in Independent Greece
1821-52. Cambridge U Pr.
Frazee, Steve.
xFrazee, Steve.
Many Rivers to Cross. Fawcett.
Frazer, J. Ronald.
xFrazer, J. Ronald.
Business Decision Simulation: A Time Sharing
Approach. Reston.
Introduction to Business Simulation. Reston.
Frazer, James E.
xFrazer, James E.
Tales of Pudding Hill: True Animal Stories
from New Hampshire. Exposition.
Frazer, James G. *see* Frazer, James George.
Frazer, James George.
xFrazer, James G.
Aftermath: A Supplement to The Golden
Bough. AMS Pr.
The Fear of the Dead in Primitive Religion.
Arno.
Growth of Plato's Ideal Theory: An Essay.
Russell.
Frazer, R. W. *see* Frazer, Robert Watson.
Frazer, Robert W. *see* Frazer, Robert Watson.
Frazer, Robert Walter, 1911-
xFrazer, Robert W.
Forts of the West: Military Forts & Presidios &
Posts Commonly Called Forts West of the
Mississippi to 1898. U of Okla Pr.
Frazer, Robert Watson, 1854-1921
xFrazer, R. W.
Literary History of India. Haskell.
xFrazer, Robert W.
British India. Arno.
Frazer, William J. *see* Frazer, William Johnson.
Frazer, William Johnson, 1924-
xFrazer, William J.
Crisis in Economic Theory: A Study of
Monetary Policy, Analysis, & Economic
Goals. U Presses Fla.
Liquidity Structure of Firms & Monetary
Economics. U Presses Fla.
Frazer, Winifred D. *see* Frazer, Winifred Dusenbury.
Frazer, Winifred Dusenbury.
xFrazer, Winifred D.
Love As Death in "The Iceman Cometh: A
Modern Treatment of an Ancient Theme. U
Presses Fla.
Frazer, Winifred L., 1916-
xFrazer, Winifred L.
E.G. & E.G.O. Emma Goldman & "The
Iceman Cometh". U Presses Fla.
Frazier, Alexander.
xFrazier, Alexander.
Open Schools for Children. Assn Supervision.
Teaching Children Today: An Informal
Approach. Har-Row.
Frazier, Claude. *see* Frazier, Claude Albee.
Frazier, Claude A. *see* Frazier, Claude Albee.
Frazier, Claude Albee, 1920-
xFrazier, Claude.
Mastering the Art of Winning Tennis: The
Psychology Behind Successful Strategy.
Pagurian.
xFrazier, Claude A.
ed. Games Doctors Play. C C Thomas.
Insect Allergy: Allergic & Toxic Reactions to
Insects & Other Arthropods. Green.
Occupational Asthma. Van Nos Reinhold.
Parents' Guide to Allergy in Children. G&D.
Sniff, Sniff Al-er-gee. Johnny Reads.
Frazier, E. Franklin. *see* Frazier, Edward Franklin.
Frazier, Edward F. *see* Frazier, Edward Franklin.
Frazier, Edward Franklin, 1894-1962
xFrazier, E. Franklin.

Negro Family in the United States. U of
Chicago Pr.
Race & Culture Contacts in the Modern
World. Beacon Pr.
xFrazier, Edward F.
Race & Culture Contacts in the Modern
World. Greenwood.
Frazier, James R.
xFrazier, James R.
ed. Readings on the Behavior Disorders of
Childhood. Mss Info.
Frazier, Neta (Lohnes), 1890-
xFrazier, Neta L.
Stout-Hearted Seven. HarBraceJ.
Frazier, Neta L. *see* Frazier, Neta (Lohnes).
Frazier, Robert C.
xFrazier, Robert C.
The Humanities: An American Experience.
Kendall-Hunt.
Frazier, Shervert. *see* Frazier, Shervert H.
Frazier, Shervert H.
xFrazier, Shervert.
An Introduction to Psychopathology. Aronson.
Frazier, William C. *see* Frazier, William Carroll.
Frazier, William Carroll.
xFrazier, William C.
Food Microbiology. McGraw.
Frcolumbia University, East Asian Library, New York.
1962. *see* Columbia University. Libraries. East Asiatic
Library.
Fream, W. C. *see* Fream, William C.
Fream, William C.
xFream, W. C.
Notes on Gynaecological Nursing. Churchill.
xFream, William C.
Notes on Medical Nursing. Churchill.
Notes on Obstetrics. Churchill.
Notes on Surgical Nursing. Churchill.
Freas, Frank K. *see* Freas, Frank Kelly.
Freas, Frank Kelly, 1922-
xFreas, Frank K.
Intro. by Frank Kelly Freas: The Art of
Science Fiction. Donning Co.
Frech, H. E.
xFrech, H. E.
Public Insurance in Private Medical Markets:
Some Problems of National Health Insurance.
Am Enterprise.
Frech, Mary. *see* Frech, Mary L.
Frech, Mary L.
xFrech, Mary.
ed. Chronology & Documentary Handbook of
the State of Colorado. Oceana.
Fredenslund. *see* Fredenslund, Aage.
Fredenslund, Aage.
xFredenslund.
Vapor-Liquid Equilibria Using UNIFAC: A
Group Contribution Method. Elsevier.
Frederic, Harold, 1856-1898
xFrederic, Harold.
The Copperhead. Mss Info.
Copperhead & Other Stories of the North
During the American War. AMS Pr.
The Damnation of Theron Ware. Harvard U
Pr.
Damnation of Theron Ware. HR&W.
Deserter & Other Stories: A Book of Two
Wars. Arno.
In the Sixties. AMS Pr.
In the Valley. Folcroft.
March Hares. Folcroft.
The Market Place. Folcroft.
Marsena & Other Stories of the Wartime.
Arno.
Frederick, A. Bruce.
xFrederick, A. Bruce.
Gymnastics for Men. Wm C Brown.
Frederick, Dean K.
xFrederick, Dean K.

Linear Systems in Communication & Control. Wiley.

Frederick E. Jones Memorial Symposium in Thoracic Surgery, Columbus, Ohio, 1976.
 xFrederick E. Jones Memorial Symposium in Thoracic Surgery, Columbus, Ohio, October 1976.
  Perspectives in Lung Cancer: Proceedings. S Karger.

Frederick, Faustulus. *see* Frederick, Faustulus Joseph.

Frederick, Faustulus Joseph.
 xFrederick, Faustulus.
  jt. auth. In Our Carib Indian Village. Lothrop.

Frederick, Filis.
 xFrederick, Filis.
  Design & Sell Toys, Games & Crafts. Chilton.

Frederick, J. George. *see* Frederick, Justus George.
Frederick, John H. *see* Frederick, John Hutchinson.

Frederick, John Hutchinson, 1896-
 xFrederick, John H.
  Industrial Marketing. Arno.

Frederick, Justus George.
 xFrederick, J. George.
  Long Island Seafood Cook Book. Peter Smith.
  The Long Island Seafood Cookbook. Dover.
  Pennsylvania Dutch Cook Book. Peter Smith.
  The Pennsylvania Dutch Cookbook. Dover.

Frederick, Portia M.
 xFrederick, Portia M.
  Medical Office Assistant: Administrative & Clinical. Saunders.

Frederick, Stella.
 xFrederick, Stella.
  I Can Be a Marine Biologist. Career Pub.

Fredericks, Carlton.
 xFredericks, Carlton.
  Breast Cancer: A Nutritional Approach. G&D.
  Carlton Frederick's High-Fiber Way to Total Health. PB.
  Look Younger, Feel Healthier. G&D.
  Low Blood Sugar & You. Charter Bks.
  Low Blood Sugar & You. G&D.
  Psycho-Nutrition. G&D.

Fredericks, H. D. *see* Fredericks, H. D. Bud.

Fredericks, H. D. Bud.
 xFredericks, H. D.
  The Teaching Research Curriculum for Moderately & Severely Handicapped. C C Thomas.
  The Teaching Research Curriculum for Moderately & Severely Handicapped: Gross & Fine Motor. C C Thomas.
  The Teaching Research Curriculum for Moderately & Severely Handicapped: Self-Help & Cognitive. C C Thomas.

Fredericks, Laura.
 xFredericks, Laura.
  Chastity Belt. Speller.

Fredericksen, Burton B.
 xFredericksen, Burton B.
  Census of Pre-Nineteenth-Century Italian Paintings in North American Public Collections. Harvard U Pr.

Fredericksen, Hazel.
 xFredericksen, Hazel.
  The Child & His Welfare. W H Freeman.

Frederickson, H. George.
 xFrederickson, H. George.
  ed. Public Administration & Public Policy. Lexington Bks.

Frederickson, Keville.
 xFrederickson, Keville.
  Opportunities in Nursing. Natl Textbk.

Fredman, Alice. *see* Fredman, Alice Green.
Fredman, Alice G. *see* Fredman, Alice Green.

Fredman, Alice Green, 1924-
 xFredman, Alice.
  Anthony Trollope. Columbia U Pr.
 xFredman, Alice G.

Diderot & Sterne. Octagon.

Fredman, John.
 xFredman, John.
  The Wolf of Masada. Avon.
  The Wolf of Masada. Morrow.

Fredman, L. E. *see* Fredman, Lionel E.

Fredman, Lionel E.
 xFredman, L. E.
  Australian Ballot: The Story of an American Reform. Mich St U Pr.

Fredman, Mike.
 xFredman, Mike.
  Kisses Leave No Fingerprints. St Martin.

Fredrich, Carl. *see* Fredrich, Carl Johann.

Fredrich, Carl Johann, 1871-1930
 xFredrich, Carl.
  Hippokratische Untersuchungen. Arno.

Fredrick, Laurence. *see* Fredrick, Laurence W.

Fredrick, Laurence W.
 xFredrick, Laurence.
  An Introduction to Astronomy. D Van Nostrand.
 xFredrick, Laurence W.
  Astronomy. Van Nos Reinhold.
  Introduction to Astronomy. D Van Nostrand.

Free, Anne R.
 xFree, Anne R.
  Social Usage. P-H.

Free, John B. *see* Free, John Brand.

Free, John Brand.
 xFree, John B.
  Insect Pollination of Crops. Acad Pr.

Freeborn, Brian.
 xFreeborn, Brian.
  Good Luck Mister Cain. St Martin.

Freeborn, Richard.
 xFreeborn, Richard.
  Turgenev: The Novelist's Novelist, a Study. Greenwood

Freeburg, Victor O. *see* Freeburg, Victor Oscar.

Freeburg, Victor Oscar, 1882-
 xFreeburg, Victor O.
  Art of Photoplay Making. Arno.

Freed, Earl X.
 xFreed, Earl X.
  An Alcoholic Personality?. C B Slack.

Freed, John B.
 xFreed, John B.
  The Friars & German Society in the Thirteenth Century. Medieval Acad.

Freed, Lewis.
 xFreed, Lewis.
  T. S. Eliot: Aesthetics & History. Open Court.

Freedberg, S. J. *see* Freedberg, Sydney Joseph.
Freedberg, Sydney J. *see* Freedberg, Sydney Joseph.

Freedberg, Sydney Joseph.
 xFreedberg, S. J.
  Painting in Italy: 1500 to 1600. Viking Pr.
  Painting in Italy: 1500-1600. Penguin.
 xFreedberg, Sydney J.
  Parmigianino: His Works in Painting. Greenwood.

Freedeman, Charles E. *see* Freedeman, Charles Eldon.

Freedeman, Charles Eldon, 1926-
 xFreedeman, Charles E.
  Conseil d'Etat in Modern France. AMS Pr.

Freeden, Michael.
 xFreeden, Michael.
  The New Liberalism: An Ideology of Social Reform. Oxford U Pr.

Freedgood, Lillian.
 xFreedgood, Lillian.
  An Enduring Image: American Painting from 1665. T Y Crowell.

Freedland, Mark R. *see* Freedland, Mark Robert.

Freedland, Mark Robert.
 xFreedland, Mark R.
  The Contract of Employment. Oxford U Pr.

Freedland, Michael, 1934-
 xFreedland, Michael.

The Two Lives of Errol Flynn. Bantam.
The Two Lives of Errol Flynn. Morrow.

Freedle, Roy O.
 xFreedle, Roy O.
  ed. Discourse Production & Comprehension. Ablex Pub.

Freedley, Edwin T. *see* Freedley, Edwin Troxell.

Freedley, Edwin Troxell, 1827-1904
 xFreedley, Edwin T.
  A Practical Treatise on Business. Arno.

Freedley, George.
 xFreedley, George.
  History of the Theatre. Crown.

Freedman, A. L.
 xFreedman, A. L.
  Real-Time Computer Systems. Crane-Russak Co.

Freedman, Alfred M.
 xFreedman, Alfred M.
  Comprehensive Textbook of Psychiatry. Williams & Wilkins.

Freedman, Audrey.
 xFreedman, Audrey.
  Managing Labor Relations. Conference Bd.
  Security Bargains Reconsidered: SUB
  Severance Pay Guaranteed Work. Conference Bd.

Freedman, Carol R.
 xFreedman, Carol R.
  Teaching Patients: A Practical Handbook for the Health Care Professional. Courseware.
  Teaching Patients: A Practical Handbook for the Health Care Professional. Irvington.

Freedman, Daniel G.
 xFreedman, Daniel G.
  Human Infancy: An Evolutionary Perspective. Halsted Pr.
  Human Sociobiology: A Holistic Approach. Free Pr.

Freedman, David, 1938-
 xFreedman, David.
  Statistics. Norton.
 xFreedman, David A.
  Approximating Countable Markov Chains. Holden-Day.

Freedman, David A. *see* Freedman, David.

Freedman, Florence B.
 xFreedman, Florence B.
  Two Tickets to Freedom: The True Story of Ellen & William Craft, Fugitive Slaves. S&S.

Freedman, H.
 xFreedman, H. F.
  Super Marriage, Super Sex. Ballantine.

Freedman, H. F. *see* Freedman, H.

Freedman, Jill.
 xFreedman, Jill.
  Circus Days. Crown.

Freedman, Leonard.
 xFreedman, Leonard.
  Power & Politics in America. Duxbury Pr.

Freedman, M. *see* Freedman, Maurice.
Freedman, M. H. *see* Freedman, Michael H.
Freedman, Marcia. *see* Freedman, Marcia K.

Freedman, Marcia K.
 xFreedman, Marcia.
  Process of Work Establishment. Columbia U Pr.

Freedman, Mark, 1943-
 xFreedman, Mark.
  Homosexuality & Psychological Functioning. Brooks-Cole.

Freedman, Maurice.
 xFreedman, M.
  Pref. by Chinese Lineage & Society: Fukien & Kwangtung. Humanities.
 xFreedman, Maurice.

Diary of a Nazi Lady. Ace Bks.

Freeman, H. MacKenzie. *see* Freeman, Hal Mackenzie.

Freeman, Hal Mackenzie.
xFreeman, H. MacKenzie.
Ocular Trauma. ACC.

Freeman, Harrop A. *see* Freeman, Harrop Arthur.

Freeman, Harrop Arthur, 1907-
xFreeman, Harrop A.
Counseling in the United States. Oceana.

Freeman, Howard E.
xFreeman, Howard E.
Handbook of Medical Sociology. P-H.
Social Problems: A Policy Perspective. Rand.

Freeman, J. B.
xFreeman, J. B.
Assignments in Mathematics. Asia.

Freeman, J. D.
xFreeman, J. D.
Iban Agriculture: A Report on the Shifting
Cultivation of Hill Rice by the Iban of
Sarawak. AMS Pr.

Freeman, J. Leiper. *see* Freeman, John Leiper.

Freeman, James M.
xFreeman, James M.
Untouchable: An Indian Life History. Stanford
U Pr.

Freeman, Jean T. *see* Freeman, Jean Todd.

Freeman, Jean Todd.
xFreeman, Jean T.
Diagnosis Positive. PB.

Freeman, Jo.
xFreeman, Jo.
The Politics of Women's Liberation: A Case
Study of an Emerging Social Movement & Its
Relation to the Policy Process. Longman.

Freeman, Joanna M., 1929-
xFreeman, Joanna M
Pref. by Basic Technical & Business Writing.
Iowa St U Pr.

Freeman, John, 1880-1929
xFreeman, John.
English Portraits & Essays. Folcroft.
English Portraits & Essays. Scholarly.
Portrait of George Moore in a Study of His
Work. Folcroft.
Portrait of George Moore in a Study of His
Work. Scholarly.

Freeman, John. *see* Freeman, John Charles.

Freeman, John Charles.
xFreeman, John.
ed. Prisons Past & Future. Heinemann Ed.

Freeman, John Leiper.
xFreeman, J. Leiper.
Political Process: Executive Bureau -
Legislative Committee Relations. Random.

Freeman, Joseph, 1897-1965
xFreeman, Joseph.
An American Testament: A Narrative of
Rebels & Romantics. R West.

Freeman, Kathleen.
xFreeman, Kathleen.
Ancilla to the Pre-Socratic Philosophers: A
Complete Translation of the Fragments in
Diels, Fragmente Der Vorsokratiker. Harvard
U Pr.
Greek City-States. Norton.
The Work & Life of Solon, with a Translation
of His Poems. Arno.

Freeman, Leonard M.
xFreeman, Leonard M.
ed. Clinical Scintillation Imaging. Grune.
Radioimmunoassay. Grune.
Radionuclide Studies of the Genitourinary
System. Grune.

Freeman, Linton C.
xFreeman, Linton C.

Patterns of Local Community Leadership.
Irvington.

Freeman, Lucy.
xFreeman, Lucy.
The Case on Cloud Nine. Arbor Hse.
The Psychiatrist Says Murder. Arbor Hse.
The Sorrow & the Fury: Overcoming Hurt &
Loss from Childhood to Old Age. P-H.
Too Deep for Tears. Dutton.
Who Is Sylvia?. Arbor Hse.

Freeman, M. A. *see* Freeman, Michael Alexander
Reykers.

Freeman, Mae. *see* Freeman, Mae (Blacker).

Freeman, Mae (Blacker), 1907-
xFreeman, Mae.
The Sun, the Moon, & the Stars. Random.
Undersea Base. Watts.
xFreeman, Mae B.
Finding Out About the Past. Random.
Fun with Ballet. Random.
Fun with Chemistry. Random.

Freeman, Mae B. *see* Freeman, Mae (Blacker).

Freeman, Mary E. *see* Freeman, Mary Eleanor (Wilkins).

Freeman, Mary Eleanor (Wilkins), 1852-1930
xFreeman, Mary E.
The Givers. Mss Info.
The Portion of Labor. Irvington.
Pot of Gold & Other Stories. Arno.

Freeman, Michael Alexander Reykers.
xFreeman, M. A.
Adult Articular Cartilage. Grune.
ed. Adult Articular Cartilage. Lippincott.

Freeman, Michelle A.
xFreeman, Michelle A.
The Poetics of Translatio Studii & Conjointure:
Chretien de Troyes's Cliges. French Forum.

Freeman, Milton M. *see* Freeman, Milton M. R.

Freeman, Milton M. R.
xFreeman, Milton M.
People Pollution: Sociologic & Ecologic
Viewpoints on the Prevalence of People.
McGill-Queens U Pr.

Freeman, Patricia, 1924-
xFreeman, Patricia.
Pathfinder: An Operational Guide for the
School Librarian. Har-Row.

Freeman, Peter.
xFreeman, Peter.
Software Systems Principles: A Survey. SRA.

Freeman, Ralph E. *see* Freeman, Ralph Evans.

Freeman, Ralph Evans.
xFreeman, Ralph E.
ed. Postwar Economic Trends in the United
States. Arno.

Freeman, Richard B. *see* Freeman, Richard Barry.

Freeman, Richard Barry, 1943-
xFreeman, Richard B.
Labor Economics. P-H.
Market for College-Trained Manpower: A
Study in the Economics of Career Choice.
Harvard U Pr.
ed. The Overeducated American. Acad Pr.

Freeman, Robert R.
xFreeman, Robert R.
ed. Information in the Language Sciences.
Elsevier.

Freeman, Roger. *see* Freeman, Roger Anthony.

Freeman, Roger A., 1904-
xFreeman, Roger A.
The Growth of American Government: A
Morphology of the Welfare State. Hoover
Inst Pr.

Freeman, Roger Anthony.
xFreeman, Roger.

Thunderbolt: A Documentary History of the
Republic P-47. Scribner.

Freeman, Roger L.
xFreeman, Roger L.
English-Spanish, Spanish-English Dictionary of
Communications & Electronic Terms.
Cambridge U Pr.

Freeman, Rosemary.
xFreeman, Rosemary.
English Emblem Books. Octagon.

Freeman, Ruth. *see* Freeman, Ruth Sunderlin.

Freeman, Ruth B.
xFreeman, Ruth B.
Community Health Nursing Practice. Saunders.

Freeman, Ruth Sunderlin.
xFreeman, Ruth.
Cavalcade of Dolls: A Basic Sourcebook for
Collectors. Century Hse.

Freeman, S. David.
xFreeman, S. David.
Energy: The New Era. Random.
Energy: The New Era. Walker & Co.

Freeman, Susan T. *see* Freeman, Susan Tax.

Freeman, Susan Tax.
xFreeman, Susan T.
Neighbors: The Social Contract in a Castilian
Hamlet. U of Chicago Pr.
The Pasiegos: Spaniards in No Man's Land. U
of Chicago Pr.

Freeman, Thomas, 1919-
xFreeman, Thomas.
Childhood Psychopathology & Adult
Psychoses. Intl Univs Pr.
Chronic Schizophrenia. Intl Univs Pr.
A Psychoanalytic Study of the Psychoses. Intl
Univs Pr.

Freeman, Tony.
xFreeman, Tony.
illus Beginning Surfing. Childrens.
Blimps. Childrens.
An Introduction to Radio-Controlled
Sailplanes. Childrens.

Freeman, Walter J.
xFreeman, Walter J.
Mass Action in the Nervous System:
Examination of the Neurophysiological Basis
of Adaptive Behavior Through the EEG.
Acad Pr.

Freeman, William, 1880-
xFreeman, William.
Concise Dictionary of English Idioms. Writer.
Compiled by Dictionary of Fictional
Characters. Writer.
The Human Approach to Literature. Folcroft.
Human Approach to Literature. Kennikat.
Human Approach to Literature. R West.
Incredible Defoe. Kennikat.
The Incredible Defoe. R West.

Freeman-Grenville, G. S. *see* Freeman-Grenville, Greville
Stewart Parker.

Freeman-Grenville, Greville Stewart Parker.
xFreeman-Grenville, G. S.
Chronology of World History: A Calendar of
Principal Events from 3000 BC to AD 1976.
Rowman.
A Modern Atlas of African History. Rowman.
The Muslim & Christian Calendars: Being
Tables for the Conversion of Muslim &
Christian Dates from the Hijra to the Year
A. D. 2000. Rowman.

Freemantle, Brian.
xFreemantle, Brian.
Charlie M. Ballantine.
Charlie M.. Doubleday.
The Inscrutable Charlie Muffin. Doubleday.

Freemon, Frank R.
xFreemon, Frank R.
Organic Mental Disease. Spectrum Pub.

Freer, Coburn.
xFreer, Coburn.

Music for a King: George Herbert's Style &
the Metrical Psalms. Johns Hopkins.

Freese, Arthur S.
xFreese, Arthur S.
The End of Senility. Arbor Hse.

Freese, Lee, 1942-
xFreese, Lee.
ed. Theoretical Methods in Sociology: Seven
Essays. U of Pittsburgh Pr.

Freese, R. S. *see* Freese, Ralph S.

Freese, Ralph S., 1946-
xFreese, R. S.
The Structure of Modular Lattices of Width
Four with Applications to Varieties of
Lattices. Am Math.

Freeze, R. Allan.
xFreeze, R. Allan.
Groundwater. P-H.

Frege, Gottlob.
xFrege, Gottlob.
Conceptual Notation & Related Articles.
Oxford U Pr.
Foundations of Arithmetic: A
Logico-Mathematical Enquiry into the
Concept of Numbers. Northwestern U Pr.
Logical Investigations. Yale U Pr.
Translations from the Philosophical Writings of
Gottlob Frege. Rowman.

Freggiaro, Naomi, 1944-
xFreggiaro, Naomi.
A Gathering of Thoughts. Beta Bk.

Fregly, Bert, 1922-
xFregly, Bert.
How to Cast Your Own Horoscope. Ashley
Bks.

Fregnac, Claude.
xFregnac, Claude.
The Great Houses of Paris. Viking Pr.

Fregosi, Claudia.
xFregosi, Claudia.
Are There Spooks in the Dark?. Schol Bk Serv.
A Gift. P-H.
Snow Maiden. P-H.
Sun Grumble. Macmillan.

Frei, Ernest J.
xFrei, Ernest J.
The Historical Development of the Philippine
National Language. AMS Pr.

Frei, Hans W.
xFrei, Hans W.
The Eclipse of Biblical Narrative: A Study in
Eighteenth & Nineteenth Century
Hermeneutics. Yale U Pr.
The Identity of Jesus Christ: The
Hermeneutical Bases of Dogmatic Theology.
Fortress.

Frei, R. W. *see* Frei, Roland W.

Frei, Roland W.
xFrei, R. W.
Diffuse Reflectance Spectroscopy in
Environmental Problem-Solving. CRC Pr.
xFrei, Roland W.
ed. Recent Advances in Environmental
Analysis. Gordon.

Freiberger. *see* Freiberger, Robert H.

Freiberger, Robert H.
xFreiberger.
Arthrography. ACC.

Freiberger, Stephen. *see* Freiberger, Stephen J.

Freiberger, Stephen J.
xFreiberger, Stephen.
Consumer's Guide to Personal Computing &
Microcomputers. Hayden.

Freidel, Frank. *see* Freidel, Frank Burt.

Freidel, Frank Burt.
xFreidel, Frank.
ed. The Golden Age of American History.
Braziller.
Our Country's Presidents. Natl Geog.

Freidenreich, Harriet P. *see* Freidenreich, Harriet Pass.

Freidenreich, Harriet Pass, 1947-
xFreidenreich, Harriet P.
The Jews of Yugoslavia: A Quest for
Community. Jewish Pubn.

Freides, Thelma.
xFreides, Thelma K.
Literature & Bibliography of the Social
Sciences. Wiley.

Freides, Thelma K. *see* Freides, Thelma.

Freidheim, Elizabeth A.
xFreidheim, Elizabeth A.
Sociological Theory in Research Practice.
Schenkman.

Freidson, E. *see* Freidson, Eliot.

Freidson, Eliot.
xFreidson, E.
Doctoring Together: A Study of Professional
Social Control. Elsevier.
xFreidson, Eliot.
Doctoring Together: A Study of Professional
Social Control. U of Chicago Pr.
ed. Hospital in Modern Society. Free Pr.
Profession of Medicine: A Study of the
Sociology of Applied Knowledge. Har-Row.
Professional Dominance: The Social Structure
of Medical Care. Aldine Pub.

Freidus, Alberta J. *see* Freidus, Alberta Joy.

Freidus, Alberta Joy, 1939-
xFreidus, Alberta J.
Sumatran Contributions to the Development of
Indonesian Literature, 1920-1942. U Pr of
Hawaii.

Freienmuth Von Helms, E. *see* Freienmuth Von Helms,
Ernst Eduard Paul.

Freienmuth Von Helms, Ernst Eduard Paul, 1901-
xFreienmuth Von Helms, E.
German Criticism of Gustave Flaubert. AMS
Pr.

Freifelder, Morris, 1907-
xFreifelder, Morris.
Catalytic Hydrogenation in Organic Synthesis:
Procedures & Commentary. Wiley.

Freilich, Gerald.
xFreilich, Gerald.
Calculus: A Short Course with Applications to
Business, Economics, & the Social Sciences.
W H Freeman.

Freilich, Joan. *see* Freilich, Joan S.

Freilich, Joan S.
xFreilich, Joan.
Paul Claudel's le Soulier De Satin: A Stylistic,
Structuralist, & Psychoanalytic Interpretation.
U of Toronto Pr.

Freilich, Morris.
xFreilich, Morris.
ed. Marginal Natives at Work: Anthropologists
in the Field. Halsted Pr.

Freilicher, Morton.
xFreilicher, Morton.
Estate Planning Handbook with Forms. P-H.

Freiman, G. A.
xFreiman, G. A.
Foundations of a Structural Theory of Set
Addition. Am Math.

Frein, Joseph P.
xFrein, Joseph P.
Handbook of Construction Management &
Organization. Van Nos Reinhold.

Freire, Paulo, 1921-
xFreire, Paulo.
Pedagogy in Process: The Letters to Guinea
Bissau. Continuum.
Pedagogy of the Oppressed. Continuum.

Freireich, Emil G. *see* Freireich, Emil J.

Freireich, Emil J.
xFreireich, Emil G.
ed. Leukemia & Lymphoma. Grune.

Freis. *see* Freis, Edward D.

Freis, Edward D.
xFreis.

Treatment of Hypertension. Univ Park.

Freivalds, John.
xFreivalds, John.
The Famine Plot. Stein & Day.

Fremantle, Alan F. *see* Fremantle, Alan Frederick.

Fremantle, Alan Frederick, 1877-
xFremantle, Alan F.
England in the Nineteenth Century. Kraus
Repr.

Fremantle, Anne. *see* Fremantle, Anne Jackson.

Fremantle, Anne Jackson, 1909-
xFremantle, Anne.
George Eliot. Haskell.
ed. Latin American Literature Today. NAL.

Fremgen, James M.
xFremgen, James M.
Accounting for Managerial Analysis. Irwin.

Fremlin, D. H.
xFremlin, D. H.
Topological Riesz Spaces & Measure Theory.
Cambridge U Pr.

Fremon, George.
xFremon, George.
Why Trade It In?: Your Mechanic Can Save
You Money. Liberty Pub.

Fremont, Herbert, 1924-
xFremont, Herbert.
Teaching Secondary Mathematics Through
Applications. Prindle.

Fremont, Theodore S.
xFremont, Theodore S.
Informal Diagnostic Assessment of Children. C
C Thomas.

Frenay, Agnes C. *see* Frenay, Agnes Clare.

Frenay, Agnes Clare.
xFrenay, Agnes C.
Understanding Medical Terminology. Cath
Health.

French, Alfred.
xFrench, Alfred.
The Growth of the Athenian Economy.
Greenwood.

French, Alfred. *see* French, Alfred P.

French, Alfred P.
xFrench, Alfred.
Depression in Children & Adolescents. Human
Sci Pr.
Disturbed Children & Their Families:
Innovations in Evaluation & Treatment.
Human Sci Pr.

French, Alice, 1850-1934
xFrench, Alice.
Book of True Lovers. Arno.
Stories of a Western Town. Mss Info.
Stories of a Western Town. Somerset Pub.

French, Allen, 1870-1946
xFrench, Allen.
The First Year of the American Revolution.
Octagon.
General Gage's Informers: New Material Upon
Lexington & Concord , Benjamin Thompson
As Loyalist & the Treachery of Benjamin
Church, Jr. Greenwood.
Siege of Boston. Reprint.

French, Anne. *see* French, Anne (Warner).

French, Anne (Warner), 1869-1913
xFrench, Anne.
Susan Clegg & Her Friend Mrs. Lathrop. Arno.
Susan Clegg & Her Neighbors' Affairs. Arno.

French, Anthony P. *see* French, Anthony Philip.

French, Anthony Philip.
xFrench, Anthony P.
Newtonian Mechanics. Norton.
Special Relativity. Norton.

French, Benjamin F. *see* French, Benjamin Franklin.

French, Benjamin Franklin, 1799-1877
xFrench, Benjamin F.

History of the Rise & Progress of the Iron
  Trade of the United States, 1621-1857.
  Kelley.
French, Bevan M.
  xFrench, Bevan M.
    The Moon Book. Penguin.
    Progressive Contact Metamorphism of the
      Biwabik Iron-Formation, Mesabi Range,
      Minnesota. Minn Geol Survey.
French, Brandon, 1944-
  xFrench, Brandon.
    On the Verge of Revolt: Women in American
      Films of the Fifties. Ungar.
French, Brian.
  xFrench, Brian.
    Practice of Collage. Transatlantic.
    Principles of Collage. Emerson.
French, Bryant M. see French, Bryant Morey.
French, Bryant Morey.
  xFrench, Bryant M.
    Mark Twain & the Gilded Age: The Book That
      Named an Era. SMU Press.
French, C. E. see French, Charles Ezra.
French, Charles Ezra, 1923-
  xFrench, C. E.
    Survival Strategies for Agricultural
      Cooperatives. Iowa St U Pr.
French, Charles F.
  xFrench, Charles F.
    American Guide to U.S. Coins. Trident.
French, David. see French, David G.
French, David G.
  xFrench, David.
    Working Communally: Patterns & Possibilities.
      Russell Sage.
French, Dorothy K. see French, Dorothy Kayser.
French, Dorothy Kayser.
  xFrench, Dorothy K.
    I Don't Belong Here. Westminster.
French, Dwight K.
  xFrench, Dwight K.
    National Survey of Family Growth, Cycle I:
      Sample Design, Estimation Procedures &
      Variance Estimation. Natl Ctr Health Stats.
French, E. L. see French, Edgar Lionel.
French, Edgar Lionel.
  xFrench, E. L.
    ed. Melbourne Studies in Education, 1961-62.
      Intl Schol Bk Serv.
    ed. Melbourne Studies in Education, 1963. Intl
      Schol Bk Serv.
    ed. Melbourne Studies in Education, 1964. Intl
      Schol Bk Serv.
    ed. Melbourne Studies in Education, 1965. Intl
      Schol Bk Serv.
    ed. Melbourne Studies in Education, 1966. Intl
      Schol Bk Serv.
    ed. Melbourne Studies in Education, 1967. Intl
      Schol Bk Serv.
    ed. Melbourne Studies in Education,
      1968-1969. Intl Schol Bk Serv.
    ed. Melbourne Studies in Education, 1970. Intl
      Schol Bk Serv.
    ed. Melbourne Studies in Education, 1971. Intl
      Schol Bk Serv.
French, Gilbert J. see French, Gilbert James.
French, Gilbert James, 1804-1866
  xFrench, Gilbert J.
    Life & Times of Samuel Crompton. Kelley.
French, Gilbert M. see French, Gilbert Morse.
French, Gilbert Morse, 1928-
  xFrench, Gilbert M.
    Cortical Functioning in Behavior: Research &
      Commentary. Scott F.
French, Giles.
  xFrench, Giles.

Cattle Country of Peter French. Binford.
French, Gordon.
  xFrench, Gordon.
    The Battered Bastards. Nordon Pubns.
French, H. W. see French, Henry Willard.
French, Harold W.
  xFrench, Harold W.
    The Swan's Wide Waters: Ramakrishna &
      Western Culture. Kennikat.
French, Harvey M.
  xFrench, Harvey M.
    The Anatomy of Arson. Arco.
French, Henry Willard, 1854-
  xFrench, H. W.
    Art & Artists in Connecticut. Da Capo.
French, Hollis.
  xFrench, Hollis.
    Silver Collector's Glossary & a List of Early
      American Silversmiths & Their Marks. Da
      Capo.
French, J. Milton. see French, Joseph Milton.
French, Jennie, 1947-
  xFrench, Jennie.
    Design for Stained Glass. Van Nos Reinhold.
French, Jennnie. see French, Jennie.
French, Jere S. see French, Jere Stuart.
French, Jere Stuart.
  xFrench, Jere S.
    Urban Space: A Brief History of the City
      Square. Kendall Hunt.
French, Joel.
  xFrench, Joel.
    War Beyond the Stars. New Leaf.
French, John C. see French, John Calvin.
French, John Calvin, 1875-
  xFrench, John C.
    Problem of the Two Prologues to Chaucer's
      Legend of Good Women. AMS Pr.
    Problem of the Two Prologues to Chaucer's
      Legend of Good Women. Folcroft.
    The Problem of the Two Prologues to
      Chaucer's Legend of Good Women. Gordon
      Pr.
French, John D.
  xFrench, John D.
    ed. Frontiers in Brain Research. Columbia U
      Pr.
French, Joseph L. see French, Joseph Lewis.
French, Joseph Lewis, 1858-1936
  xFrench, Joseph L.
    ed. Great Sea Stories: Second Series. Arno.
French, Joseph Milton, 1895-
  xFrench, J. Milton.
    ed. Life Records of John Milton 1608-1674.
      Gordian.
French, Laura.
  xFrench, Laura.
    Women in Business. Raintree Pubs.
French, Marilyn, 1929-
  xFrench, Marilyn.
    The Women's Room. BJ Pub Group.
    The Women's Room. Summit Bks.
French, Michael.
  xFrench, Michael.
    Abingdon's. Berkley Pub.
    Abingdon's. Doubleday.
    Rhythms. Doubleday.
    The Throwing Season. Delacorte.
French, N. R. see French, Norman R.
French, Norman R.
  xFrench, N. R.
    ed. Perspectives in Grassland Ecology: Results
      & Applications of the US-IBP Grassland
      Biome Study. Springer-Verlag.
French, Peter. see French, Peter A.
French, Peter A.
  xFrench, Peter.
    The Scope of Morality. U of Minn Pr.
    ed. Studies in Metaphysics. U of Minn Pr.
  xFrench, Peter A.

    ed. Contemporary Perspectives in the
      Philosophy of Language. U of Minn Pr.
    ed. Studies in Epistemology. U of Minn Pr.
    ed. Studies in Ethical Theory. U of Minn Pr.
French, R. A. see French, Richard Anthony.
French, Richard Anthony.
  xFrench, R. A.
    The Socialist City: Spatial Structure & Urban
      Policy. Wiley.
French, Ruth. see French, Ruth M.
French, Ruth M.
  xFrench, Ruth.
    Dynamics of Health Care. McGraw.
    Guide to Diagnostic Procedures. McGraw.
  xFrench, Ruth M.
    Dynamics of Health Care. McGraw.
French, Thomas E. see French, Thomas Ewing.
French, Thomas Ewing.
  xFrench, Thomas E.
    Engineering Drawing & Graphic Technology.
      McGraw.
    Engineering Drawing & Graphic Technology.
      McGraw.
    Graphic Science & Design. McGraw.
French, Warren.
  xFrench, Warren.
    Frank Norris. Coll & U Pr.
French, Warren. see French, Warren G.
French, Warren A.
  xFrench, Warren A.
    Views of Marketing: A Reader. Har-Row.
French, Warren G.
  xFrench, Warren.
    Filmguide to The Grapes of Wrath. Ind U Pr.
    ed. The Thirties: Fiction, Poetry, Drama.
      Everett-Edwards.
    ed. The Twenties: Fiction, Poetry, Drama.
      Everett-Edwards.
  xFrench, Warren G.
    ed. American Winners of the Nobel Literary
      Prize. U of Okla Pr.
    ed. Companion to the Grapes of Wrath. Kelley.
French, Wendell L.
  xFrench, Wendell L.
    Organization Development: Behavioral Science
      Interventions for Organization Improvement.
      P-H.
    The Personnel Management Process: Cases on
      Human Resources Administration. HM.
French, William B.
  xFrench, William B.
    Law of the Real Estate Business. Irwin.
    Real Estate Review's Guide to Real Estate
      Licensing Examinations for Salespersons &
      Brokers. Warren.
French, William M. see French, William Marshall.
French, William Marshall, 1907-
  xFrench, William M.
    America's Educational Tradition: An
      Interpretive History. Heath.
Freneau, Philip. see Freneau, Philip Morin.
Freneau, Philip M. see Freneau, Philip Morin.
Freneau, Philip Morin, 1752-1832
  xFreneau, Philip.
    Some Account of the Capture of the Ship
      Aurora. Arno.
  xFreneau, Philip M.
    A Collection of Poems on American Affairs &
      Variety of Other Subjects. Schol Facsimiles.
    The Last Poems of Philip Freneau. Greenwood.
Frenkel, Jacob A.
  xFrenkel, Jacob A.
    ed. International Economic Policy: Theory &
      Evidence. Johns Hopkins.
    ed. The Monetary Approach to the Balance of
      Payments. U of Toronto Pr.
Frenz, Horst, 1912-
  xFrenz, Horst.

Eugene O'Neill. Ungar.

Frenzel, Burkhard.
xFrenzel, Burkhard.
Climatic Fluctuations of the Ice Age. UPBS.

Frenzel, Louis E.
xFrenzel, Louis E.
Getting Acquainted with Microcomputers.
Sams.
Howard W. Sams Crash Course in
Microcomputers. Bobbs.
The Howard W. Sams Crash Course in
Microcomputers. Sams.

Frere, Richard, 1922-
xFrere, Richard.
Maxwell's Ghost: An Epilogue to Gavin
Maxwell's Camusfearna. Verry.

Frere, Sheppard. *see* Frere, Sheppard Sunderland.

Frere, Sheppard Sunderland.
xFrere, Sheppard.
Britannia: A History of Roman Britain.
Routledge & Kegan.

Frerking, Marvin E.
xFrerking, Marvin E.
Crystal Oscillator Design & Temperature
Compensation. Van Nos Reinhold.

Freschet, Berniece.
xFreschet, Berniece.
Five Fat Raccoons. Scribner.
Lizard Lying in the Sun. Scribner.
Moose Baby. Putnam.
Owl & the Prairie Dog. Scribner.
Porcupine Baby. Putnam.
Possum Baby. Putnam.
Pronghorn on the Powder River. T Y Crowell.
Turtle Pond. Scribner.
The Watersnake. Scribner.
Where's Henrietta's Hen?. Putnam.

Frese, Joseph R.
xFrese, Joseph R.
ed. Business Enterprise in Early New York.
Sleepy Hollow.

Fresener, Scott.
xFresener, Scott O.
ed. How to Print T-Shirts for Fun & Profit.
Southwest Screen Print.

Fresener, Scott O. *see* Fresener, Scott.

Fretter, William B.
xFretter, William B.
Introduction to Experimental Physics. Peter
Smith.

Fretwell, Stephen D.
xFretwell, Stephen D.
Populations in a Seasonal Environment.
Princeton U Pr.

Freuchen, Dagmar.
xFreuchen, Dagmar.
jt. auth. Dagmar Freuchen's Cookbook of the
Seven Seas. M Evans.

Freud, Anna, 1895-
xFreud, Anna.
Difficulties in the Path of Psychoanalysis: A
Confrontation of Past with Present
Viewpoints. Intl Univs Pr.
Ego & the Mechanisms of Defense. Intl Univs
Pr.
Infants Without Families: Reports on the
Hampstead Nurseries. Intl Univs Pr.
Introduction to Psychoanalysis: Lectures for
Child Analysts & Teachers. Intl Univs Pr.
Normality & Pathology in Childhood:
Assessments of Development. Intl Univs Pr.
Problems of Psychoanalytic Training,
Diagnosis, & the Technique of Therapy. Intl
Univs Pr.

Freud, Arthur.
xFreud, Arthur.
Of Human Sovereignty. Philos Lib.

Freud, Geza, 1922-
xFreud, Geza.

Orthogonal Polynomials. Pergamon.

Freud, Sigmund, 1856-1939
xFreud, Sigmund.
Autobiographical Study. Norton.
Civilization & Its Discontents. Norton.
Cocaine Papers. NAL.
Complete Introductory Lectures on
Psychoanalysis. Norton.
Dora: An Analysis of a Case of Hysteria.
Macmillan.
Ego & the Id. Norton.
Five Lectures on Psycho-Analysis. Norton.
The Future of an Illusion. Norton.
General Selection from the Works of Sigmund
Freud. Doubleday.
The History of the Psychoanalytic Movement.
Johnson Repr.
History of the Psychoanalytic Movement.
Macmillan.
Infantile Cerebral Paralysis. U of Miami Pr.
Inhibitions, Symptoms & Anxiety. Norton.
Letters of Sigmund Freud. Basic.
On the History of the Psychoanalytic
Movement. Norton.
Origins of Psycho-Analysis: Letters to Wilhelm
Fliess, Drafts & Notes, 1887-1902. Basic.
Psychoanalysis & Faith: The Letters of
Sigmund Freud & Oskar Pfister. Basic.
Psychopathology of Everyday Life. NAL.
Psychopathology of Everyday Life. Norton.
Studies in Parapsychology. Macmillan.

Freudenberger, C. Dean.
xFreudenberger, C. Dean.
A Christian Responsibility in a Hungry World.
Abingdon.

Freudenheim, Y. *see* Freudenheim, Yehoshu'A.

Freudenheim, Yehoshu'A.
xFreudenheim, Y.
Government in Israel. Oceana.

Freudenthal, H. *see* Freudenthal, Hans.

Freudenthal, Hans, 1905-
xFreudenthal, H.
Mathematics As an Educational Task. Kluwer
Boston.

Freudenthal, Ralph.
xFreudenthal, Ralph I.
ed. Polynuclear Aromatic Hydrocarbons:
Chemistry, Metabolism, & Carcinogenesis.
Raven.

Freudenthal, Ralph I. *see* Freudenthal, Ralph.

Freuler, F. *see* Freuler, Franz.

Freuler, Franz.
xFreuler, F.
Cast Manual for Adults & Children.
Springer-Verlag.

Freund, Ernst, 1864-1932
xFreund, Ernst.
Administrative Powers Over Persons &
Property: A Comparative Survey. B Franklin.
Legal Nature of Corporations. B Franklin.
The Legal Nature of Corporations. Gordon Pr.

Freund, Gisele.
xFreund, Gisele.
The World in My Camera. Dial.

Freund, H. R. *see* Freund, Herman Robert.

Freund, Herman Robert.
xFreund, H. R.
Principles of Head & Neck Surgery. ACC.

Freund, John E.
xFreund, John E.
College Mathematics with Business
Applications. P-H.
Mathematical Statistics. P-H.
Modern Elementary Statistics. P-H.

Freund, Paul A. *see* Freund, Paul Abraham.

Freund, Paul Abraham, 1908-
xFreund, Paul A.

On Law & Justice. Harvard U Pr.
On Understanding the Supreme Court: A
Series of Lectures Delivered Under the
Auspices of the Julius Rosenthal Foundation
at Northwestern University, School of Law.
Greenwood.

Freund, Philip, 1909-
xFreund, Philip.
Art of Reading the Novel. Macmillan.

Freundlich, August L.
xFreundlich, August L.
Richard Florsheim. A S Barnes.

Freundlich, Charles I.
xFreundlich, Charles I.
Workbook in Latin First Year. AMSCO Sch.

Freundlich, Irwin M.
xFreundlich, Irwin M.
Diffuse Pulmonary Disease: A Radiologic
Approach. Saunders.

Frey, Alexander H. *see* Frey, Alexander Hamilton.

Frey, Alexander Hamilton.
xFrey, Alexander H.
Cases & Materials on Corporations. Little.

Frey, Charles, 1935-
xFrey, Charles.
Shakespeare's Vast Romance: A Study of the
Winter's Tale. U of Mo Pr.

Frey, Charles F., 1929-
xFrey, Charles F.
ed. Initial Management of the Trauma Patient.
Lea & Febiger.

Frey, David G. *see* Frey, David Grove.

Frey, David Grove, 1915-
xFrey, David G.
ed. Limnology in North America. U of Wis Pr.

Frey, David H.
xFrey, David H.
Existential Theory for Counselors. HM.

Frey, David L.
xFrey, David L.
The First Tetralogy Shakespeare's Scrutiny of
the Tudor Myth: A Dramatic Exploration of
Devine Providence. Mouton.

Frey, Hank.
xFrey, Hank.
Diver Below: The Complete Guide to Skin &
Scuba Diving. Macmillan.

Frey, James H.
xFrey, James H.
ed. Contemporary Issues in Sport. Am Acad
Pol Soc.

Frey, Leonard H. *see* Frey, Leonard Hamilton.

Frey, Leonard Hamilton.
xFrey, Leonard H.
ed. Readings in Early English Language
History. Odyssey Pr.

Frey, Marguerite K. *see* Frey, Marguerite Kurth.

Frey, Marguerite Kurth.
xFrey, Marguerite K.
I Wonder, I Wonder. Concordia.

Frey, Paul R. *see* Frey, Paul Reheard.

Frey, Paul Reheard.
xFrey, Paul R.
Chemistry Problems & How to Solve Them.
Har-Row.

Frey, R. W. *see* Frey, Robert W.

Frey, Robert W.
xFrey, R. W.
ed. The Study of Trace Fossils: A Synthesis of
Principles, Problems, & Procedures in
Ichnology. Springer-Verlag.

Frey, Shaney.
xFrey, Shaney.
Complete Beginner's Guide to Skin Diving.
Doubleday.
The Complete Beginners Guide to Swimming.
Doubleday.

Frey-Wyssling, A. *see* Frey-Wyssling, Albert.

Frey-Wyssling, Albert, 1900-
xFrey-Wyssling, A.

Comparative Organellography of the Cytoplasm. Springer-Verlag.

Freyer, Grattan.
xFreyer, Grattan.
Peadar O'Donnell. Bucknell U Pr.

Freyhardt, H. C. see Freyhardt, Herbert C.

Freyhardt, Herbert C.
xFreyhardt, H. C.
ed. Growth & Properties. Springer-Verlag.

Freyn, Hubert, 1897-
xFreyn, Hubert.
Prelude to War: The Chinese Student Rebellion of 1935-1936. Hyperion Conn.

Freyre, Gilberto.
xFreyre, Gilberto.
The Mansions & the Shanties(Sobrados E Mucambos): The Making of Modern Brazil. Greenwood.
New World in the Tropics: The Culture of Modern Brazil. Greenwood.
Order & Progress: Brazil from Monarchy to Republic. Greenwood.

Freyre, Jorge F.
xFreyre, Jorge F.
External & Domestic Financing in the Economic Development of Puerto Rico. U of PR Pr.

Freytag, Gustav, 1816-1895
xFreytag, Gustav.
Martin Luther. AMS Pr.

Fribance, Austin E.
xFribance, Austin E.
Industrial Instrumentation Fundamentals. McGraw.

Friberg, L. see Friberg, Lars.

Friberg, Lars.
xFriberg, L.
ed. Handbook of the Toxicology of Metals. Elsevier.

Friberg, Stig, 1930-
xFriberg, Stig.
ed. Food Emulsions. Dekker.

Frick, C. H.
xFrick, C. H.
Comeback Guy. HarBraceJ.
Comeback Guy. HarBraceJ.
Five Against the Odds. HarBraceJ.
Patch. HarBraceJ.

Fricke, Charles W. see Fricke, Charles Williams.

Fricke, Charles Williams.
xFricke, Charles W.
California Criminal Evidence. Legal Bk Corp.
California Criminal Law. Legal Bk Corp.
California Criminal Procedure. Legal Bk Corp.

Frickey, Edwin, 1893-
xFrickey, Edwin.
Economic Fluctuations in the United States: A Systematic Analysis of Long-Run Trends & Business Cycles, 1866-1914. Russell.

Friday, Nancy.
xFriday, Nancy.
Men in Love: Men's Sexual Fantasies: The Triumph of Love Over Rage. Delacorte.

Friday, William.
xFriday, William.
How to Sell Your Product Through (Not to) Wholesalers. Prudent Pub Co.

Friddell, Guy.
xFriddell, Guy.
Colgate Darden: Conversations with Guy Friddell. U Pr of Va.

Fridkin, V. M. see Fridkin, Vladimir Mikhailovich.

Fridkin, Vladimir Mikhailovich.
xFridkin, V. M.
Photoferroelectrics. Springer-Verlag.

Fridrichsen, Anton. see Fridrichsen, Anton Johnson.

Fridrichsen, Anton Johnson, 1888-1953
xFridrichsen, Anton.

Problem of Miracle in Primitive Christianity. Augsburg.

Friebert, Stuart, 1931-
xFriebert, Stuart.
Dreaming of Floods: Poems. Vanderbilt U Pr.
A Field Guide to Contemporary Poetry & Poetics. Longman.

Fried, Alfred H. see Fried, Alfred Hermann.

Fried, Alfred Hermann, 1864-1921
xFried, Alfred H.
Restoration of Europe. Garland Pub.

Fried, Charles, 1935-
xFried, Charles.
Anatomy of Values: Problems of Personal & Social Choice. Harvard U Pr.
Right & Wrong. Harvard U Pr.

Fried, Edrita.
xFried, Edrita.
The Courage to Change: From Insight to Self-Innovation. Brunner-Mazel.

Fried, Edward R.
xFried, Edward R.
ed. Higher Oil Prices & the World Economy: The Adjustment Problem. Brookings.

Fried, Frederick.
xFried, Frederick.
America's Forgotten Folk Arts. Pantheon.

Fried, Ilana.
xFried, Ilana.
The Chemistry of Electrode Processes. Acad Pr.

Fried, Isaac.
xFried, Isaac.
Numerical Solution of Differential Equations. Acad Pr.

Fried, Jacob.
xFried, Jacob.
Technological & Social Change: A Transdisciplinary Model. Petrocelli.

Fried, John.
xFried, John H.
ed. Organic Reactions in Steroid Chemistry. Van Nos Reinhold.

Fried, John H. see Fried, John.

Fried, John J.
xFried, John J.
Life Along the San Andreas Fault. Dutton.

Fried, Lawrence A. see Fried, Lawrence A.

Fried, Lawrence A.
xFried, Lawrence A.
Anatomy of the Head, Neck, Face, & Jaws. Lea & Febiger.

Fried, Louis.
xFried, Louis.
Practical Data Processing Management. Reston.

Fried, Marc.
xFried, Marc.
The World of the Urban Working Class. Harvard U Pr.

Fried, Martha N. see Fried, Martha Nemes.

Fried, Martha Nemes.
xFried, Martha N.
Transitions: Four Rituals in Eight Cultures. Norton.

Fried, Maurice.
xFried, Maurice.
Soil-Plant System in Relation to Inorganic Nutrition. Acad Pr.

Fried, Robert, 1904-
xFried, Robert.
Introduction to Statistics. Halsted Pr.

Fried, Robert C.
xFried, Robert C.
Performance in American Bureaucracy. Little.

Friedan, Betty.
xFriedan, Betty.
The Feminine Mystique. Dell.
Feminine Mystique. Norton.

Friedberg, Charles K. see Friedberg, Charles Kaye.

Friedberg, Charles Kaye.
xFriedberg, Charles K.
ed. Angina Pectoris. Am Heart.
ed. Congestive Heart Failure. Grune.

Friedberg, Maruice. see Friedberg, Maurice.

Friedberg, Maurice, 1929-
xFriedberg, Maruice.
A Decade of Euphoria: Western Literature in Post-Stalin Russia, 1954-1964. Ind U Pr.

Friedberg, Stephen. see Friedberg, Stephen H.

Friedberg, Stephen H.
xFriedberg, Stephen.
Linear Algebra. P-H.

Friede, R. L. see Friede, Reinhard L.

Friede, Reinhard L.
xFriede, R. L.
Developmental Neuropathology. Springer-Verlag.
xFriede, Reinhard L.
Topographic Brain Chemistry. Acad Pr.

Friedel, R. A. see Friedel, Robert A.

Friedel, Robert A.
xFriedel, R. A.
Spectrometry of Fuels. Plenum Pub.

Frieden, Bernard J.
xFrieden, Bernard J.
The Environmental Protection Hustle. MIT Pr.
The Politics of Neglect: Urban Aid from Model Cities to Revenue Sharing. MIT Pr.

Frieden, Edward H.
xFrieden, Edward H.
Chemical Endocrinology. Acad Pr.

Friedenberg, Edgar Z. see Friedenberg, Edgar Zodiag.

Friedenberg, Edgar Zodiag.
xFriedenberg, Edgar Z.
Coming of Age in America: Growth & Acquiescence. Irvington.
R. D. Laing. Viking Pr.
Vanishing Adolescent. Beacon Pr.
The Vanishing Adolescent. Dell.

Friedenberg, Robert M.
xFriedenberg, Robert M.
Unexplored Model Systems in Modern Biology. Hafner.

Friedgut, Theodore H.
xFriedgut, Theodore H.
Political Participation in the USSR. Princeton U Pr.

Friedheim, Robert L.
xFriedheim, Robert L.
Understanding the Debate on Ocean Resources. U of Denver Intl.

Friedl, Ernestine, 1920-
xFriedl, Ernestine.
Vasilika: A Village in Modern Greece. HR&W.

Friedl, John.
xFriedl, John.
Anthropology: The Study of People. Har-Row.
Cultural Anthropology. Har-Row.

Friedl, Joseph, 1910-
xFriedl, Joseph.
A History of Education in McDowell County, West Virginia, 1858-1976. McClain.

Friedlaender, Ann F. see Friedlaender, Ann Fetter.

Friedlaender, Ann Fetter.
xFriedlaender, Ann F.
The Dilemma of Freight Transport Regulation. Brookings.

Friedlaender, Jonathan S. see Friedlaender, Jonathan Scott.

Friedlaender, Jonathan Scott.
xFriedlaender, Jonathan S.
Patterns of Human Variation: The Demography, Genetics, & Phenetics of the Bougainville Islanders. Harvard U Pr.

Friedlaender, Mitchell H.
xFriedlaender, Mitchell H.
Allergy & Immunology of the Eye. Har-Row.

Friedlaender, R. see Friedlaender, Walter F.

Friedlaender, Walter. see Friedlaender, Walter F.

Chemistry & Biochemistry of the Sulfhydryl
Group in Amino Acids, Peptides & Proteins.
Pergamon.
Friedman, Meyer.
xFriedman, Meyer.
Type A Behavior & Your Heart. Fawcett.
Type A Behavior & Your Heart. Knopf.
Friedman, Murray.
xFriedman, Murray.
ed. New Perspectives on School Integration.
Fortress.
Friedman, Myles. *see* Friedman, Myles I.
Friedman, Myles I., 1924-
xFriedman, Myles.
Rational Behavior: An Explanation of Behavior
That Is Especially Human. U of SC Pr.
xFriedman, Myles I.
Teaching Reading & Thinking Skills. Longman.
Friedman, Myra.
xFriedman, Myra.
Buried Alive: The Biography of Janis Joplin.
Morrow.
Friedman, Nathaniel A.
xFriedman, Nathaniel A.
Calculus & Mathematical Models. Prindle.
Friedman, Norman, 1946-
xFriedman, Norman.
Battleship Design & Development, 1905-1945.
Mayflower Bks.
ed. E. E. Cummings: A Collection of Critical
Essays. P-H.
Form & Meaning in Fiction. U of Ga Pr.
Friedman, Otto, 1905-
xFriedman, Otto.
Break-up of Czech Democracy. Greenwood.
Friedman, Philip, 1945-
xFriedman, Philip.
The Impact of Trade Destruction on National
Incomes: A Study of Europe 1924-1938. U
Presses Fla.
The Pilates Method of Physical & Mental
Conditioning. Doubleday.
Friedman, R. J. *see* Friedman, Raymond J.
Friedman, Ralph.
xFriedman, Ralph.
Oregon for the Curious. Caxton.
A Touch of Oregon. Comstock Edns.
Friedman, Raymond J.
xFriedman, R. J.
ed. The Psychology of Depression:
Contemporary Theory & Research. Halsted
Pr.
Friedman, Robert, 1925-
xFriedman, Robert.
ed. Family Roots of School Learning &
Behavior Disorders. C C Thomas.
Friedman, S. Marvin. *see* Friedman, Selwyn Marvin.
Friedman, Saul S., 1937-
xFriedman, Saul S.
Amcha: An Oral Testament of the Holocaust.
U Pr of Amer.
Incident at Massena: The Blood Libel in
America. Stein & Day.
Friedman, Selwyn Marvin.
xFriedman, S. Marvin.
ed. Biochemistry of Thermophily. Acad Pr.
Friedman, Sherwood.
xFriedman, Sherwood.
Modern Clerical Practice. Pitman Learning.
Friedman, W. F. *see* Friedman, Walter F.
Friedman, Walter F.
xFriedman, W. F.
Distribution Packaging. Krieger.
Friedman, Winifred H.
xFriedman, Winnifred H.
Boydell's Shakespeare Gallery. Garland Pub.
Friedman, Winnifred H. *see* Friedman, Winifred H.
Friedman, Yona, 1923-
xFriedman, Yona.

Toward a Scientific Architecture. MIT Pr.
Friedmann, Arnold.
xFriedmann, Arnold.
ed. Environmental Design Evaluation. Plenum
Pub.
Friedmann, Eugene A.
xFriedmann, Eugene A.
The Meaning of Work & Retirement. Arno.
Friedmann, Georges, 1902-
xFriedmann, Georges.
The Anatomy of Work: Labor, Leisure & the
Implications of Automation. Greenwood.
Friedmann, Lawrence W.
xFriedmann, Lawrence W.
The Psychological Rehabilitation of the
Amputee. C C Thomas.
The Surgical Rehabilitation of the Amputee. C
C Thomas.
Friedmann, Paul.
xFriedmann, Paul.
Anne Boleyn: A Chapter of English History,
1527-1536. AMS Pr.
Friedmann, Thomas.
xFriedmann, Thomas.
Hero - Azriel. Micah Pubns.
Friedmann, Wolfgang. *see* Friedmann, Wolfgang Gaston.
Friedmann, Wolfgang G. *see* Friedmann, Wolfgang
Gaston.
Friedmann, Wolfgang Gaston, 1907-
xFriedmann, Wolfgang.
The Future of the Oceans. Braziller.
ed. Public & Private Enterprise in Mixed
Economies. Columbia U Pr.
xFriedmann, Wolfgang G.
Law in a Changing Society. Columbia U Pr.
Friedrich, Barbara.
xFriedrich, Barbara.
Did Somebody Pack the Baby?: The Family
Moving Book. P-H.
Friedrich, Carl J. *see* Friedrich, Carl Joachim.
Friedrich, Carl Joachim.
xFriedrich, Carl J.
Age of Power. Cornell U Pr.
ed. Authority. Lieber-Atherton.
Constitutional Reason of State: The Survival of
the Constitutional Order. Brown U Pr.
The Impact of American Constitutionalism
Abroad. Holmes & Meier.
Inevitable Peace. Greenwood.
Pathology of Politics: Violence, Betrayal,
Corruption, Secrecy & Propaganda. Irvington.
Responsible Bureaucracy: A Study of the Swiss
Civil Service. Russell.
Friedrich, Johannes, 1893-
xFriedrich, Johannes.
Extinct Languages. Greenwood.
Extinct Languages. Philos Lib.
Friedrich, Lawrence W. *see* Friedrich, Lawrence William.
Friedrich, Lawrence William.
xFriedrich, Lawrence W.
ed. Nature of Physical Knowledge. Marquette.
Friedrich, Paul, 1927-
xFriedrich, Paul.
The Meaning of Aphrodite. U of Chicago Pr.
Friedrich, Priscilla.
xFriedrich, Priscilla.
Easter Bunny That Overslept. Lothrop.
Friedrich, Robert A.
xFriedrich, Robert A.
Energy Conservation for American Agriculture.
Ballinger Pub.
Friedrichs, Christopher R., 1947-
xFriedrichs, Christopher R.
Urban Society in an Age of War: Nordlingen,
1580-1720. Princeton U Pr.
Friedrichs, K. O. *see* Friedrichs, Kurt Otto.
Friedrichs, Kurt Otto.
xFriedrichs, K. O.

Special Topics in Fluid Dynamics. Gordon.
Spectral Theory of Operators in Hilbert Space.
Springer-Verlag.
Friedrichs, Robert W. *see* Friedrichs, Robert Winslow.
Friedrichs, Robert Winslow, 1923-
xFriedrichs, Robert W.
A Sociology of Sociology. Free Pr.
Friedson, Anthony M.
xFriedson, Anthony M.
Literature Through the Ages. Norwood Edns.
Friel, Brian.
xFriel, Brian.
Living Quarters. Merrimack Bk Serv.
Friend, Charles E.
xFriend, Charles E.
The Law of Evidence in Virginia. Michie.
Friend, David, 1899-
xFriend, David.
Creative Way to Paint. Watson-Guptill.
Friend, I. *see* Friend, Irwin.
Friend, Irwin.
xFriend, I.
Mutual Funds & Other Institutional Investors:
A New Perspective. McGraw.
Friend, John.
xFriend, John.
Coaching Youth League Football. Athletic Inst.
Friend, John. *see* Friend, John Kimball.
Friend, John K. *see* Friend, John Kimball.
Friend, John Kimball.
xFriend, John.
Public Planning: The Inter-Corporate
Dimension. Methuen Inc.
xFriend, John K.
Local Government & Strategic Choice: An
Operational Research Approach to the
Processes of Public Planning. Pergamon.
Friend, Morton.
xFriend, Morton.
The Vanishing Tungus: The Story of a
Remarkable Reindeer People. Dial.
Friend, Oscar. *see* Friend, Oscar Jerome.
Friend, Oscar Jerome, 1897-
xFriend, Oscar.
Lobo Brand. Bouregy.
Friend, Wayne Z.
xFriend, Wayne Z.
Corrosion of Nickel & Nickel-Base Alloys.
Wiley.
Friendly, Fred. *see* Friendly, Fred W.
Friendly, Fred W.
xFriendly, Fred.
The Good Guys, the Bad Guys & the First
Amendment: Free Speech Vs. Fairness in
Broadcasting. Random.
xFriendly, Fred W.
The Good Guys, the Bad Guys & the First
Amendment: Free Speech Vs. Fairness in
Broadcasting. Random.
Friendly, Henry J.
xFriendly, Henry J.
Federal Jurisdiction: A General View.
Columbia U Pr.
Friends Soc. Of Philadelphia. *see* Friends, Society Of.
Philadelphia Yearly Meeting.
Friends, Society Of.
xSociety Of Friends.
Exposition of the African Slave Trade from the
Year 1840 to 1850. AMS Pr.
**Friends, Society Of. American Friends Service
Committee.**
xAmerican Friends Service Committee.

Anatomy of Anti-Communism: A Report
   Prepared for the Peace Education Division of
   the American Friends Service Committee.
   Hill & Wang.
   Struggle for Justice: A Report on Crime &
   Punishment in America. Hill & Wang.
   Uncommon Controversy: Fishing Rights of the
   Muckleshoot, Puyallup, & Nisqually Indians.
   U of Wash Pr.
Friends, Society of. Philadelphia Yearly Meeting.
   xFriends Soc. Of Philadelphia.
   Exposition of the African Slave Trade.
   Scholarly.
Frier, Bruce W., 1943-
   xFrier, Bruce W.
   Landlords & Tenants in Imperial Rome.
   Princeton U Pr.
Frier, David A.
   xFrier, David A.
   Conflict of Interest in the Eisenhower
   Administration. Iowa St U Pr.
Frier, John P.
   xFrier, John P.
   Industrial Lighting Systems. McGraw.
Friermood, Elisabeth H. see Friermood, Elisabeth
Hamilton.
Friermood, Elisabeth Hamilton.
   xFriermood, Elisabeth H.
   Promises in the Attic. Landfall Pr.
Fries, Albert C.
   xFries, Albert C.
   Applied Secretarial Procedures. McGraw.
Fries, Charles C. see Fries, Charles Carpenter.
Fries, Charles Carpenter, 1887-
   xFries, Charles C.
   Linguistics & Reading. Irvington.
   Teaching & Learning English As a Foreign
   Language. U of Mich Pr.
Fries, Chloe.
   xFries, Chloe.
   The Full of the Moon. Creative Ed.
   No Place to Hide. Creative Ed.
Fries, James F.
   xFries, James F.
   Arthritis: A Comprehensive Guide. A-W.
   Systematic Lupus Erythematosus: A Clinical
   Analysis. Saunders.
Friesen, Duane. see Friesen, Duane K.
Friesen, Duane K.
   xFriesen, Duane.
   Moral Issues in the Control of Birth. Faith &
   Life.
Friesen, Stanley R. see Friesen, Stanley Richard.
Friesen, Stanley Richard, 1918-
   xFriesen, Stanley R.
   ed. Surgical Endocrinology: Clinical
   Syndromes. Lippincott.
Friesner, Arlyne.
   xFriesner, Arlyne.
   ed. Maternity Nursing. Med Exam.
Frigerio, A. see Frigerio, Alberto.
Frigerio, Alberto.
   xFrigerio, A.
   ed. Mass Spectrometry in Biochemistry &
   Medicine. Raven.
Friggens, Myriam.
   xFriggens, Myriam.
   Tales, Trails & Tommyknockers: Stories from
   Colorado's Past. Johnson Colo.
Frigidaire. see General Motors Corporation. Frigidaire
Division, Dayton, Ohio. Home Economics Dept.
Frings, Hubert.
   xFrings, Hubert.
   Animal Communication. U of Okla Pr.
Frink, Maurice, 1895-
   xFrink, Maurice.
   Cow Country Cavalcade: Eighty Years of the
   Wyoming Stock Growers Association. Old
   West.
Frinternational Symposium on X-Ray Optics & X-Ray

Microanalysis - 3rd - Stanford - California - 1962. see
International Symposium on X-Ray Optics and X-Ray
Microanalysis, 3d, Stanford, California, 1962.
Fripiat, J. J.
   xFripiat, J. J.
   ed. Data Handbook for Clay Materials & Other
   Non-Metallic Minerals. Pergamon.
Frisancho, A. Roberto, 1939-
   xFrisancho, A. Roberto.
   Human Adaptation: A Functional
   Interpretation. Mosby.
Frisbie, Charlotte J. see Frisbie, Charlotte Johnson.
Frisbie, Charlotte Johnson.
   xFrisbie, Charlotte J.
   ed. Southwestern Indian Ritual Drama. U of
   NM Pr.
Frisbie, Louise.
   xFrisbie, Louise K.
   Florida's Fabled Inns. Imperial Pub Co.
   Peace River Pioneers. Imperial Pub Co.
Frisbie, Louise K. see Frisbie, Louise.
Frisbie, W. Parker. see Frisbie, William Parker.
Frisbie, William Parker.
   xFrisbie, W. Parker.
   Sustenance Organization & Migration in
   Nonmetropolitan America. U of Iowa Pr.
Frisch, Joseph C.
   xFrisch, Joseph C.
   Extension & Comprehension in Logic. Philos
   Lib.
Frisch, K. C. see Frisch, Kurt Charles.
Frisch, Karl. see Frisch, Karl von.
Frisch, Karl von.
   xFrisch, Karl.
   Twelve Little Housemates. Pergamon.
Frisch, Kurt C. see Frisch, Kurt Charles.
Frisch, Kurt Charles.
   xFrisch, K. C.
   ed. Plastic Foams. Dekker.
   xFrisch, Kurt C.
   ed. Advances in Urethane Science &
   Technology. Technomic.
   Cyclic Monomers. Krieger.
   ed. Plastic Foams. Dekker.
   Polyelectrolytes. Technomic.
Frisch, Max, 1911-
   xFrisch, Max.
   Man in the Holocene. HarBraceJ.
   Montauk. HarBraceJ.
Frisch, Morton J.
   xFrisch, Morton J.
   ed. The Political Thought of American
   Statesmen: Selected Writings & Speeches.
   Peacock Pubs.
Frisch, O. R. see Frisch, Otto Robert.
Frisch, Otto R. see Frisch, Otto Robert.
Frisch, Otto Robert, 1904-
   xFrisch, O. R.
   What Little I Remember. Cambridge U Pr.
   xFrisch, Otto R.
   What Little I Remember. Cambridge U Pr.
Frisch, Ragnar. see Frisch, Ragnar Anton Kittil.
Frisch, Ragnar Anton Kittil, 1895-1973
   xFrisch, Ragnar.
   New Methods of Measuring Marginal Utility.
   Porcupine Pr.
Frisell, Anthony.
   xFrisell, Anthony.
   Baritone Voice. Taplinger.
Frishman, Austin M.
   xFrishman, Austin M.
   The Cockroach Combat Manual. Morrow.
   Preparation for Pesticide Certification
   Examinations: Questions & Answers for
   Commercial Pesticide Applicators. Arco.
Frisinger, Nellie.
   xFrisinger, Nellie.
   Jeff & Jenny & the Kidnapping. Accent Bks.
Frisken, William R.
   xFrisken, William R.

The Atmospheric Environment. Johns Hopkins.
Friskey, Margaret.
   xFriskey, Margaret.
   Chicken Little, Count-To-Ten. Childrens.
   Indian Two Feet & His Eagle Feather.
   Childrens.
   True Book of the Moon Ride Rock Hunt.
   Childrens.
   True Book of the Moonwalk Adventure.
   Childrens.
Friskin, James.
   xFriskin, James.
   Music for the Piano: A Handbook of Concert
   & Teaching Material from 1580 to 1952.
   Dover.
   Music for the Piano: A Handbook of Concert
   & Teaching Material from 1580 to 1952.
   Peter Smith.
Frison, George. see Frison, George C.
Frison, George C.
   xFrison, George.
   ed. The Casper Site: A Hell Gap Bison Kill on
   the High Plains. Acad Pr.
   xFrison, George C.
   Folsom Tools & Technology at the Hanson
   Site, Wyoming. U of NM Pr.
   Prehistoric Hunters of the High Plains. Acad
   Pr.
Friss, Istvan.
   xFriss, Istvan.
   ed. Essays on Economic Policy & Planning in
   Hungary. Intl Pubns Serv.
Frissel, M. J.
   xFrissel, M. J.
   Simulation of Accumulation and Leaching in
   Soils. Unipub.
Fristrup, Borge.
   xFristrup, Borge.
   The Greenland Ice Cap. U of Wash Pr.
Friters, Gerard M. see Friters, Gerard Martin.
Friters, Gerard Martin, 1911-
   xFriters, Gerard M.
   Outer Mongolia & Its International Position.
   Octagon.
Frith, Michael. see Frith, Michael K.
Frith, Michael K.
   xFrith, Michael.
   Some of Us Walk, Some Fly, Some Swim.
   Beginner.
Frith, Nigel.
   xFrith, Nigel.
   The Legend of Krishna. Schocken.
Fritsch, Bruno.
   xFritsch, Bruno.
   Growth Limitation and Political Power.
   Ballinger Pub.
Fritsch, Charles T. see Fritsch, Charles Theodore.
Fritsch, Charles Theodore, 1912-
   xFritsch, Charles T.
   Qumran Community: Its History & Scrolls.
   Biblo.
Fritschen, L. J. see Fritschen, Leo.
Fritschen, Leo.
   xFritschen, L. J.
   Environmental Instrumentation.
   Springer-Verlag.
Fritscher, John.
   xFritscher, John.
   Popular Witchcraft. Citadel Pr.
   xFritscher, John J.
   Popular Witchcraft. Bowling Green Univ.
Fritscher, John J. see Fritscher, John.
Fritschler, A. Lee.
   xFritschler, A. Lee.
   Executive's Guide to Government: How
   Washington Works. Winthrop.
Fritz, Dorothy B. see Fritz, Dorothy Bertolet.
Fritz, Dorothy Bertolet.
   xFritz, Dorothy B.

Indian Signs & Signals. Sterling.

Fror, Hans.
xFror, Hans.
I Will Tell You About God. Fortress.

Frosch, Thomas R.
xFrosch, Thomas R.
The Awakening of Albion: The Renovation of the Body in the Poetry of William Blake. Cornell U Pr.

Frost. *see* Frost, Peter J.

Frost, A. John. *see* Frost, Alfred John.

Frost, Alfred John.
xFrost, A. John.
Elliott Wave Principle: Key to Stock Market Profits. New Classics Lib.

Frost, Anne.
xFrost, Anne.
Representation & Administrative Tribunals. Routledge & Kegan.

Frost, Carol, 1948-
xFrost, Carol.
Liar's Dice. SBD.

Frost, Erica.
xFrost, Erica.
Harold & the Dinosaur Mystery. Troll Assocs.
Mystery of the Midnight Visitors. Troll Assocs.

Frost, Everett L. *see* Frost, Everett Lloyd.

Frost, Everett Lloyd.
xFrost, Everett L.
Archaeological Excavations of Fortified Sites on Taveuni, Fiji. U Pr of Hawaii.

Frost, F. J. *see* Frost, Frank J.

Frost, Frank J., 1929-
xFrost, F. J.
Democracy & the Athenians: Aspects of Ancient Politics. Wiley.
xFrost, Frank J.
Greek Society. Heath.

Frost, G. *see* Frost, Gavin.

Frost, Gavin.
xFrost, G.
Witch's Grimoire of Ancient Omens, Portents, Talismans, Amulets & Charms. P-H.
xFrost, Gavin.
Power Secrets from a Sorcerer's Private Magnum Arcanum. P-H.

Frost, Gerhard. *see* Frost, Gerhard E.

Frost, Gerhard E.
xFrost, Gerhard.
Homing in the Presence: Meditations for Daily Living. Winston Pr.
xFrost, Gerhard E.
Color of the Night: Reflections on the Book of Job. Augsburg.

Frost, H. Gordon.
xFrost, H. Gordon.
I'm Frank Hamer: The Life of a Texas Peace Officer. Jenkins.

Frost, J. L. *see* Frost, Joe L.

Frost, Jerry W. *see* Frost, Jerry William.

Frost, Jerry William.
xFrost, Jerry W.
The Keithian Controversy in Early Pennsylvania. Norwood Edns.

Frost, Joan Van Every.
xFrost, Joan Van Every.
Lisa. Nordon Pubns.

Frost, Joe L.
xFrost, J. L.
Early Childhood Education Rediscovered: Readings. HR&W.
xFrost, Joe L.
Children's Play & Playgrounds. Allyn.

Frost, John, 1800-1859
xFrost, John.
The American Speaker. Arno.

Frost, Kelman.
xFrost, Kelman.

Men of the Mirage. Lothrop.

Frost, Lawrence A.
xFrost, Lawrence A.
The Court Martial of General George Armstrong Custer. U of Okla Pr.
General Custer's Libbie. Superior Pub.

Frost, Marie.
xFrost, Marie.
Things Happen When Women Care. Standard Pub.

Frost, Norman, 1887-
xFrost, Norman.
Comparative Study of Achievement in Country & Town Schools. AMS Pr.

Frost, Peter.
xFrost, Peter.
Bakumatsu Currency Crisis. Harvard U Pr.

Frost, Peter J.
xFrost.
Organizational Reality: Reports from the Firing Line. Goodyear.

Frost, Raymond.
xFrost, Raymond.
The Backward Society. Greenwood.

Frost, Reuben B.
xFrost, Reuben B.
Administration of Physical Education & Athletics: Concepts & Practices. Wm C Brown.

Frost, Richard, 1929-
xFrost, Richard.
Getting Drunk with the Birds. Ohio U Pr.

Frost, Richard. *see* Frost, Richard Aylmer.

Frost, Richard Aylmer, 1905-
xFrost, Richard.
Race Against Time: Human Relations & Politics in Kenya Before Independence. Rowman.

Frost, Richard H.
xFrost, Richard H.
The Mooney Case. Stanford U Pr.

Frost, Robert, 1874-1963
xFrost, Robert.
In the Clearing. HR&W.
Stopping by Woods on a Snowy Evening. Dutton.

Frost, Robert. *see* Frost, Robert C.

Frost, Robert C., 1926-
xFrost, Robert.
Our Heavenly Father. Logos.

Frost, S. E.
xFrost, S. E.
Historical & Philosophical Foundations of Western Education. Merrill.

Frost, S. W. *see* Frost, Stuart Ward.

Frost, Stanley, 1881-1942
xFrost, Stanley.
Challenge of the Klan. AMS Pr.
Challenge of the Klan. Negro U Pr.

Frost, Stanley H.
xFrost, Stanley H.
Cenozoic Reef Biofacies: Tertiary Larger Foraminifera & Scleractinian Corals from Chiapas, Mexico. N Ill U Pr.

Frost, Stuart Ward, 1891-
xFrost, S. W.
Insect Life & Insect Natural History. Dover.

Frost, William, 1917-
xFrost, William.
Dryden & the Art of Translation. Shoe String.

Frostig, Marianne.
xFrostig, Marianne.
Education for Dignity. Grune.

Frothingham, Alice W. *see* Frothingham, Alice Wilson.

Frothingham, Alice Wilson.
xFrothingham, Alice W.

Spanish Glass. Hispanic Soc.

Frothingham, Octavius B. *see* Frothingham, Octavius Brooks.

Frothingham, Octavius Brooks, 1822-1895
xFrothingham, Octavius B.
George Ripley. AMS Pr.
Gerrit Smith: A Biography. Negro U Pr.

Frothingham, Paul R. *see* Frothingham, Paul Revere.

Frothingham, Paul Revere, 1864-1926
xFrothingham, Paul R.
All These. Arno.
All These. R West.
Confusion of Tongues. Arno.

Frothingham, Richard, 1812-1880
xFrothingham, Richard.
History of the Siege of Boston & of the Battles of Lexington, Concord & Bunker Hill. Da Capo.

Froud, Brian.
xFroud, Brian.
ed. Faeries. Abrams.
ed. Faeries. Bantam.

Froud, Nina.
xFroud, Nina.
The World Book of Soups. Ballantine.

Froude, James A. *see* Froude, James Anthony.

Froude, James Anthony, 1818-1894
xFroude, James A.
Bunyan. AMS Pr.
Bunyan. Folcroft.
English in Ireland in the Eighteenth Century. AMS Pr.
Froude's Life of Carlyle. Ohio St U Pr.
Lectures on the Council of Trent, Delivered at Oxford 1892-3. Kennikat.
Life & Letters of Erasmus. AMS Pr.
Life & Letters of Erasmus. R West.
Lord Beaconsfield. Arno.
Lord Beaconsfield. R West.
Spanish Story of the Armada & Other Essays. AMS Pr.

Frowen, S. F. *see* Frowen, Stephen.

Frowen, Stephen.
xFrowen, S. F.
ed. Monetary Policy & Economic Activity in West Germany. Halsted Pr.

Fruchtman, C. S. *see* Fruchtman, Caroline S.

Fruchtman, Caroline S.
xFruchtman, C. S.
Checklist of Vocal Chamber Works by Benedetto Marcello. Info Coord.

Frueh, Alfred J. *see* Frueh, Alfred Joseph.

Frueh, Alfred Joseph.
xFrueh, Alfred J.
Frueh on the Theatre: Theatrical Caricatures, 1906-1962. NY Pub Lib.

Fruehling, Rosemary T.
xFruehling, Rosemary T.
Working at Human Relations. McGraw.

Frum, Barbara.
xFrum, Barbara.
As It Happened. McClelland.

Fruman, Norman.
xFruman, Norman.
Coleridge, the Damaged Archangel. Braziller.

Frumkin, A. N. *see* Frumkin, Aleksandr Naumovich.

Frumkin, Aleksandr Naumovich.
xFrumkin, A. N.
ed. Progress in Electrochemistry of Organic Compounds. Plenum Pub.

Fruth, Florence K. *see* Fruth, Florence Knight.

Fruth, Florence Knight.
xFruth, Florence K.
Some Descendants of Richard Few of Chester County, Pennsylvania & Allied Lines 1682 -1976. F K Fruth.

Fruttero, Carl. *see* Fruttero, Carlo.

Fruttero, Carlo.
xFruttero, Carl.

The Sunday Woman. Avon.
xFruttero, Carlo.
The Sunday Woman. HarBraceJ.
Fry. *see* Fry, T. F.
Fry, Bernard M. *see* Fry, Bernard Mitchell.
Fry, Bernard Mitchell.
xFry, Bernard M.
Publishers & Libraries: The Study of Scholarly
& Research Journals. Lexington Bks.
Fry, Charles R. *see* Fry, Charles Rahn.
Fry, Charles Rahn.
xFry, Charles R.
Art Deco Interiors in Color. Dover.
Fry, D. B. *see* Fry, Dennis Butler.
Fry, Daniel W., 1908-
xFry, Daniel W.
The White Sands Incident. Best Bks.
Fry, Dennis Butler.
xFry, D. B.
The Physics of Speech. Cambridge U Pr.
Fry, Earl H.
xFry, Earl H.
Financial Invasion of the U. S. A.: A Threat to
American Society?. McGraw.
Fry, Edward. *see* Fry, Edward B.
Fry, Edward B.
xFry, Edward.
Reading Faster: Drillbook. Cambridge U Pr.
Teaching Faster Reading: A Manual.
Cambridge U Pr.
Fry, Edward Bernard, 1925-
xFry, Edward.
Reading Instruction for Classroom & Clinic.
McGraw.
Fry, Edward F.
xFry, Edward F.
Cubism. Oxford U Pr.
Fry, Edwin Maxwell.
xFry, Maxwell.
Architecture & the Environment. Allen Unwin.
Autobiographical Sketches. Merrimack Bk
Serv.
Fry, Eric C.
xFry, Eric C.
Shell Book of Practical & Decorative
Ropework. David & Charles.
Fry, Geoffrey K. *see* Fry, Geoffrey Kingdom.
Fry, Geoffrey Kingdom.
xFry, Geoffrey K.
The Growth of Government: The Development
of Ideas About the Role of the State & the
Machinery & Functions of Government in
Britain Since 1780. Biblio Dist.
Fry, Gladys-Marie, 1931-
xFry, Gladys-Marie.
Night Riders in Black Folk History. U of Tenn
Pr.
Fry, Henry P. *see* Fry, Henry Peck.
Fry, Henry Peck, 1881-
xFry, Henry P.
Modern Ku Klux Klan. Negro U Pr.
Fry, James.
xFry, James.
Employment & Income Distribution in the
African Economy. Biblio Dist.
Fry, John, 1930-
xFry, John.
Winners on the Ski Slopes. Watts.
Fry, Maxwell. *see* Fry, Edwin Maxwell.
Fry, P. S. *see* Fry, Peter George Robin Somerset.
Fry, Patricia L., 1940-
xFry, Patricia L.
Hints for the Backyard Rider. A S Barnes.
Fry, Paul H.
xFry, Paul H.
The Poet's Calling in the English Ode. Yale U
Pr.
Fry, Peter George Robin Somerset, 1931-
xFry, P. S.

World of Antiques. Intl Pubns Serv.
Fry, Richard, 1900-
xFry, Richard.
Bankers in West Africa: The Story of the Bank
of British West Africa Limited. Humanities.
Fry, Roger. *see* Fry, Roger Eliot.
Fry, Roger E. *see* Fry, Roger Eliot.
Fry, Roger Eliot, 1866-1934
xFry, Roger.
Art History As an Academic Study. Folcroft.
xFry, Roger E.
Georgian Art, 1760-1820: An Introductory
Review of English Painting, Architecture,
Sculpture During the Reign of George III.
AMS Pr.
Reflections on British Painting. Arno.
Fry, Rosalie K.
xFry, Rosalie K.
Mungo. FS&G.
Whistler in the Mist. FS&G.
Fry, Ruth T. *see* Fry, Ruth Thacker.
Fry, Ruth Thacker.
xFry, Ruth T.
Symbolic Profile. Gulf Pub.
Fry, Sam. *see* Fry, Samuel.
Fry, Samuel, 1909-
xFry, Sam.
Gin Rummy: How to Play & Win. Dover.
Fry, T. F.
xFry.
Further Computer Appreciation. Butterworths.
Fry, William F.
xFry, William F.
Sweet Madness: A Study of Humor. Pacific
Bks.
Fryckstedt, Olov W., 1920-
xFryckstedt, Olov W.
In Quest of America: A Study of Howells'
Early Development As a Novelist. Russell.
Frydland, Rachmiel.
xFrydland, Rachmiel.
When Being Jewish Was a Crime. Nelson.
Frye, Albert M. *see* Frye, Albert Myrton.
Frye, Albert Myrton.
xFrye, Albert M.
Rational Belief: An Introduction to Logic.
Greenwood.
Frye, Alton.
xFrye, Alton.
A Responsible Congress: The Politics of
National Security. McGraw.
Frye, Charles A.
xFrye, Charles A.
Towards a Philosophy of Black Studies. R & E
Res Assoc.
Values in Conflict: Blacks & the American
Ambivalence Toward Violence. U Pr of
Amer.
Frye, Fredric. *see* Frye, Fredric L.
Frye, Fredric L.
xFrye, Fredric.
Husbandry, Medicine & Surgery in Captive
Reptiles. Veterinary Med.
Frye, John, 1910-
xFrye, John.
The Men All Singing: The Story of Menhaden
Fishing. Donning Co.
Frye, Northrop.
xFrye, Northrop.

The Critical Path: An Essay on the Social
Context of Literary Criticism. Ind U Pr.
Educated Imagination. Ind U Pr.
Fables of Identity: Studies in Poetic
Mythology. HarBraceJ.
Fearful Symmetry: A Study of William Blake.
Princeton U Pr.
Fools of Time: Studies in Shakespearean
Tragedy. U of Toronto Pr.
Morality of Scholarship. Cornell U Pr.
Northrop Frye on Culture & Literature: A
Collection of Review Essays. U of Chicago
Pr.
The Practical Imagination: Stories, Poems,
Plays. Har-Row.
The Return of Eden: Five Essays on Milton's
Epics. U of Toronto Pr.
The Secular Scripture: A Study of the Structure
of Romance. Harvard U Pr.
ed. Sound & Poetry. Columbia U Pr.
Frye, Prosser H. *see* Frye, Prosser Hall.
Frye, Prosser Hall, 1866-1934
xFrye, Prosser H.
Literary Reviews & Criticisms. Arno.
Literary Reviews & Criticisms. Gordian.
Frye, William E. *see* Frye, William Emerson.
Frye, William Emerson.
xFrye, William E.
ed. Impact of Space Exploration on Society.
Am Astronaut.
Fryer, D. W. *see* Fryer, Donald W.
Fryer, Donald W.
xFryer, D. W.
Indonesia. Westview.
Fryer, Douglas. *see* Fryer, Douglas Henry.
Fryer, Douglas Henry.
xFryer, Douglas.
General Psychology. Har-Row.
Fryer, J. D.
xFryer, J. D.
Integrated Control of Weeds. Intl Schol Bk
Serv.
Fryer, Jonathan.
xFryer, Jonathan.
The Great Wall of China. A S Barnes.
Fryer, Judith.
xFryer, Judith.
The Faces of Eve: Women in the Nineteenth
Century American Novel. Oxford U Pr.
The Faces of Eve: Women in the Nineteenth
Century American Novel. Oxford U Pr.
How We Hear: The Story of Hearing. Lerner
Pubns.
Fryer, M. J. *see* Fryer, Michael John.
Fryer, Michael John.
xFryer, M. J.
An Introduction to Linear Programming &
Matrix Game Theory. Halsted Pr.
Fryman, Elizabeth D.
xFryman, Elizabeth D.
How to Raise & Train a Welsh Terrier. TFH
Pubns.
Fu, K. S. *see* Fu, King Sun.
Fu, King Sun, 1930-
xFu, K. S.
Syntactic Methods in Pattern Recognition.
Acad Pr.
Fu, Lo-Shu, 1920-
xFu, Lo-shu.
A Documentary Chronicle of Sino-Western
Relations, 1644-1820. U of Ariz Pr.
Fu, Shen.
xFu, Shen C. Y.
Traces of the Brush: Studies in Chinese
Calligraphy. Yale U Pr.
Fu, Shen C. Y. *see* Fu, Shen.
Fuchs, Arthur W. *see* Fuchs, Arthur Wolfram.
Fuchs, Arthur Wolfram, 1895-
xFuchs, Arthur W.

Principles of Radiographic Exposure &
Processing. C C Thomas.
Fuchs, Daniel, 1909-
xFuchs, Daniel.
The Apathetic Bookie Joint. Methuen Inc.
Comic Spirit of Wallace Stevens. Duke.
Fuchs, Erich, 1916-
xFuchs, Erich.
illus. Journey to the Moon. Delacorte.
Fuchs, J. W. *see* Fuchs, Johan Wilhelmus.
Fuchs, Jerome H.
xFuchs, Jerome H.
Computerized Cost Control Systems. P-H.
Computerized Inventory Control Systems. P-H.
Fuchs, Johan Wilhelmus.
xFuchs, J. W.
Classics Illustrated Dictionary. Oxford U Pr.
Fuchs, L. *see* Fuchs, Laszlo.
Fuchs, Laszlo.
xFuchs, L.
Infinite Abelian Groups. Acad Pr.
Fuchs, Peter C.
xFuchs, Peter C.
Epidemiology of Hospital Associated
Infections. Am Soc Clinical.
Fuchs, R. H. *see* Fuchs, Rudolf Herman.
Fuchs, Rudolf Herman, 1942-
xFuchs, R. H.
Dutch Painting. Oxford U Pr.
Fuchs, Stephen.
xFuchs, Stephen.
The Aboriginal Tribes of India. St Martin.
Fuchs, Victor R. *see* Fuchs, Victor Robert.
Fuchs, Victor Robert.
xFuchs, Victor R.
Determinants of Expenditures for Physicians'
Services in the United States. Natl Bur Econ
Res.
Economics of the Fur Industry. AMS Pr.
Fucik, S. *see* Fucik, Svatopluk.
Fucik, Svatopluk.
xFucik, S.
Spectral Analysis of Nonlinear Operators.
Springer-Verlag.
Fucilla, Joseph G. *see* Fucilla, Joseph Guerin.
Fucilla, Joseph Guerin.
xFucilla, Joseph G.
The Teaching of the Italian in the United States: A
Documentary History. Arno.
Fudge, Samuel R.
xFudge, Samuel R.
Living with Today's Teenagers. Moore Pub Co.
Fuehrer, Mary R. *see* Fuehrer, Mary Rosina.
Fuehrer, Mary Rosina, Sister, 1906-
xFuehrer, Mary R.
Study of the Relation of the Dutch Lancelot &
the Flemish Perchevael Fragments to the
Manuscripts of Chretien's Conte del Graal.
AMS Pr.
Fuellenbach, John.
xFuellenbach, John.
Ecclesiastical Office & the Primacy of Rome::
An Evaluation of Recent Theological
Discussion of First Clement. Intl Schol Bk
Serv.
Fuentes, Carlos.
xFuentes, Carlos.
Aura. FS&G.
A Change of Skin. FS&G.
The Death of Artemio Cruz. FS&G.
The Hydra Head. FS&G.
Fuerst, J. S.
xFuerst, J. S.
ed. Public Housing in Europe & America.
Halsted Pr.
Fuerst, Rene. *see* Fuerst, Walter Rene.
Fuerst, Walter Rene.
xFuerst, Rene.
ed. Twentieth Century Stage Decoration. Arno.
Fuess, Claude M. *see* Fuess, Claude Moore.

Fuess, Claude Moore, 1885-1963
xFuess, Claude M.
Calvin Coolidge: The Man from Vermont.
Greenwood.
Creed of a Schoolmaster. Arno.
Joseph B. Eastman, Servant of the People.
Greenwood.
Lord Byron As a Satirist in Verse. Haskell.
Fugard, Athol.
xFugard, Athol.
Dimetos & Two Early Plays. Oxford U Pr.
Fugate, Wilbur L. *see* Fugate, Wilbur Lindsay.
Fugate, Wilbur Lindsay.
xFugate, Wilbur L.
Foreign Commerce & the Antitrust Laws.
Little.
Fuglede, B. *see* Fuglede, Bent.
Fuglede, Bent.
xFuglede, B.
Finely Harmonic Functions. Springer-Verlag.
Fuguitt, Glenn V. *see* Fuguitt, Glenn Victor.
Fuguitt, Glenn Victor.
xFuguitt, Glenn V.
Growth & Change in Rural America. Urban
Land.
Fuhr, Mary T. *see* Fuhr, Mary Thomasina.
Fuhr, Mary Thomasina.
xFuhr, Mary T.
Clinical Experience Record & Nursing Care
Planning: A Guide for Student Nurses.
Mosby.
Fuhrmann, Joseph T., 1940-
xFuhrmann, Joseph T.
Origins of Capitalism in Russia: Industry &
Progress in the Sixteenth & Seventeenth
Centuries. Times Bks.
Fujii, John N.
xFujii, John N.
Puzzles & Graphs. NCTM.
Fujikawa, Gyo.
xFujikawa, Gyo.
illus. Babies. G&D.
illus. Baby Animals. G&D.
illus. Child's Book of Poems. G&D.
illus. Let's Grow a Garden. G&D.
illus. Surprise! Surprise!. G&D.
Fujioka, Michio.
xFujioka, Michio.
Angkor Wat. Kodansha.
Fujioka, Ryoichi, 1909-
xFujioka, Ryoichi.
Tea Ceremony Utensils. Weatherhill.
Fujita, H. *see* Fujita, Hiroshi.
Fujita, Hiroshi, 1922-
xFujita, H.
Mathematical Theory of Sedimentation
Analysis. Acad Pr.
Fujita, S. Neil.
xFujita, S. Neil.
illus. Aim for a Job in Graphic Design & Art.
Rosen Pr.
Fujiwara, Shizuo.
xFujiwara, Shizuo.
ed. Information Chemistry: Computer Assisted
Chemical Research Design. Intl Schol Bk
Serv.
Fukai, Shinji.
xFukai, Shinji.
Persian Glass. Weatherhill.
Fuks, Alexander, 1917-
xFuks, Alexander.
Ancestral Constitution: Four Studies in
Athenian Party Politics at the End of the
Fifth Century B. C.. Greenwood.
Fuks, B. A. *see* Fuks, Boris Abramovich.
Fuks, Boris A. *see* Fuks, Boris Abramovich.
Fuks, Boris Abramovich.
xFuks, B. A.

Theory of Analytic Functions of Several
Complex Variables. Am Math.
xFuks, Boris A.
Special Chapters in the Theory of Analytic
Functions of Several Complex Variables. Am
Math.
Fukuda, T. *see* Fukuda, Tetsuo.
Fukuda, Tetsuo.
xFukuda, T.
ed. World Issues in the Problems of
Schizophrenic Psychoses. Igaku-Shoin.
Fukuda, Tsuneari, 1912-
xFukuda, Tsuneari.
ed. Future of Japan & the Korean Peninsula.
Hollym Intl.
Fukui, Eiichir O, 1905-
xFukui, Eiichir O.
The Climate of Japan. Elsevier.
Fukui, K. *see* Fukui, Ken'Ichi.
Fukui, Ken'Ichi, 1918-
xFukui, K.
Theory of Orientation & Stereoselection.
Springer-Verlag.
Fukunaga, Keinosuke.
xFukunaga, Keinosuke.
Introduction to Statistical Pattern Recognition.
Acad Pr.
Fukurai, Shir O, 1920-
xFukurai, Shiro.
How Can I Make What I Cannot See?. Van
Nos Reinhold.
Fukurai, Shiro. *see* Fukurai, Shir O.
Fukurai, T. *see* Fukurai, Tomokichi.
Fukurai, Tomokichi.
xFukurai, T.
Clairvoyance & Thoughtography. Arno.
Fukushima, H. *see* Fukushima, Hiroyuki.
Fukushima, Hiroyuki.
xFukushima, H.
Index Guide to Drug Information Retrieval.
Elsevier.
Fukuzawa, Yukichi.
xFukuzawa, Yukichi.
Autobiography. Columbia U Pr.
Fulbright, Robert G.
xFulbright, Robert G.
Old Testament Friends: Men of Courage.
Broadman.
Fulcher, Jane M.
xFulcher, Jane M.
ed. Medical Librarian Examination Review
Book. Med Exam.
Fulda, Michael.
xFulda, Michael.
Oil & International Relations: Energy, Trade,
Technology & Politics. Arno.
Fulenwider, Claire K. *see* Fulenwider, Claire Knoche.
Fulenwider, Claire Knoche.
xFulenwider, Claire K.
Feminism in American Politics: A Study of
Ideological Influence. Praeger.
Fulghum, W. B. *see* Fulghum, Walter B.
Fulghum, Walter B.
xFulghum, W. B.
Dictionary of Biblical Allusions in English
Literature. Irvington.
Fulks, Watson.
xFulks, Watson.
Advanced Calculus: An Introduction to
Analysis. Wiley.
Full, Harold.
xFull, Harold.
Controversy in American Education: An
Anthology of Crucial Issues. Macmillan.
Fullard, Harold.
xFullard, Harold M.
ed. The Atlas of Canada & the World. Purnell
Ref Bks.
Fullard, Harold M. *see* Fullard, Harold.

Fuller, Anna, 1853-1916
   xFuller, Anna.
      Later Pratt Portraits: Sketched in a New
         England Suburb. Arno.
Fuller, Benjamin A. *see* Fuller, Benjamin Apthorp Gould.
Fuller, Benjamin Apthorp Gould, 1879-1956
   xFuller, Benjamin A.
      History of Greek Philosophy. Greenwood.
Fuller, C. J. *see* Fuller, Christopher J.
Fuller, Christopher J., 1949-
   xFuller, C. J.
      The Nayars Today. Cambridge U Pr.
Fuller, Claud E.
   xFuller, Claude E.
      Firearms of the Confederacy. Quarterman.
Fuller, Claude E. *see* Fuller, Claud E.
Fuller, David O. *see* Fuller, David Otis.
Fuller, David Otis, 1903-
   xFuller, David O.
      ed. Which Bible?. Kregel.
Fuller, Dudley D.
   xFuller, Dudley D.
      Theory & Practice of Lubrication for
         Engineers. Wiley.
Fuller, Edmund.
   xFuller, Edmund.
      ed. The Christian Idea of Education. Shoe
         String.
Fuller, Edward C., 1907-
   xFuller, Edward C.
      Chemistry & Man's Environment. HM.
Fuller, George W. *see* Fuller, George Washington.
Fuller, George Washington, 1876-1940
   xFuller, George W.
      A History of the Pacific Northwest. AMS Pr.
Fuller, Gordon, 1894-
   xFuller, Gordon.
      Algebra & Trigonometry. McGraw,
      Analytic Geometry. A-W
      Plane Trigonometry with Tables. McGraw.
Fuller, Harry J. *see* Fuller, Harry James.
Fuller, Harry James.
   xFuller, Harry J.
      General Botany. Har-Row.
Fuller, Henry B. *see* Fuller, Henry Blake.
Fuller, Henry Blake, 1857-1929
   xFuller, Henry B.
      The Chevalier of Pensieri Vani. Irvington.
      The Cliff-Dwellers. Irvington.
      Under the Skylights. Mss Info.
Fuller, Hoyt W.
   xFuller, Hoyt W.
      Journey to Africa. Third World.
Fuller, Hubert B. *see* Fuller, Hubert Bruce.
Fuller, Hubert Bruce, 1880-1957
   xFuller, Hubert B.
      The Speakers of the House. Arno.
Fuller, Iola.
   xFuller, Iola.
      Loon Feather. HarBraceJ.
      Loon Feather. HarBraceJ.
Fuller, Jack W.
   xFuller, Jack W.
      ed. Career Education: A Lifelong Process.
         Nelson-Hall.
      Continuing Education & the Community
         College. Nelson-Hall.
Fuller, James L.
   xFuller, James L.
      Concise Dental Anatomy & Morphology. Year
         Bk Med.
Fuller, Jan.
   xFuller, Jan.
      Space: The Scrapbook of My Divorce. Fawcett.
Fuller, Jean O. *see* Fuller, Jean Overton.
Fuller, Jean Overton.
   xFuller, Jean O.
      Swinburne: A Biography. Schocken.
Fuller, John. *see* Fuller, John Grant.
Fuller, John G. *see* Fuller, John Grant.

Fuller, John Grant, 1913-
   xFuller, John.
      The Ghost of Flight 401. Berkley Pub.
   xFuller, John G.
      The Airmen Who Would Not Die. Berkley
         Pub.
      The Airmen Who Would Not Die. Putnam.
      The Ghost of Flight 401. Berkley Pub.
      The Poison That Fell from the Sky. Berkley
         Pub.
Fuller, Kenneth G. *see* Fuller, Kenneth Gary.
Fuller, Kenneth Gary, 1904-
   xFuller, Kenneth G.
      An Experimental Study of Two Methods of
         Long Division. AMS Pr.
Fuller, Lon L.
   xFuller, Lon L.
      Anatomy of the Law. Greenwood.
      The Law in Quest of Itself. AMS Pr.
      Legal Fictions. Stanford U Pr.
      Morality of Law. Yale U Pr.
Fuller, Margaret.
   xFuller, Margaret.
      Trails of the Sawtooth & White Cloud
         Mountains. Signpost Bk Pub.
Fuller, Muriel, 1901-
   xFuller, Muriel.
      ed. More Junior Authors. Wilson.
Fuller, Nancy L. *see* Fuller, Nancy Lee.
Fuller, Nancy Lee.
   xFuller, Nancy L.
      illus. Fuffie's Problem. Denison.
Fuller, Nelson. *see* Fuller, Nelson W.
Fuller, Nelson W.
   xFuller, Nelson.
      Experiments for Electricity & Electronics.
         Bobbs.
Fuller, R. Buckminster. *see* Fuller, Richard Buckminster.
Fuller, Raymond G. *see* Fuller, Raymond Garfield.
Fuller, Raymond Garfield, 1886-
   xFuller, Raymond G.
      Child Labor & the Constitution. Arno.
Fuller, Reginald H. *see* Fuller, Reginald Horace.
Fuller, Reginald Horace.
   xFuller, Reginald H.
      The Formation of the Resurrection Narratives.
         Fortress.
      Foundations of New Testament Christology.
         Scribner.
Fuller, Richard Buckminster, 1895-
   xFuller, R. Buckminster.
      Earth, Inc.. Doubleday.
      Earth, Inc. Peter Smith.
      Operating Manual for Spaceship Earth. Dutton.
      Operating Manual for Spaceship Earth. S&S.
Fuller, Roy. *see* Fuller, Roy Broadbent.
Fuller, Roy Broadbent, 1912-
   xFuller, Roy.
      Owls & Artificers: Oxford Lectures on Poetry.
         Open Court.
Fuller, S. H. *see* Fuller, Samuel.
Fuller, Samuel, 1946-
   xFuller, S. H.
      Analysis of Drum & Disk Storage Units.
         Springer-Verlag.
Fuller, Thomas, 1608-1661
   xFuller, Thomas.
      History of the Worthies of England. AMS Pr.
      History of the Worthies of England. Church
         History.
Fuller, Wallace H. *see* Fuller, Wallace Hamilton.
Fuller, Wallace Hamilton.
   xFuller, Wallace H.
      Soils of the Desert Southwest. U of Ariz Pr.
Fuller, Wayne A.
   xFuller, Wayne A.
      Introduction to Statistical Time Series. Wiley.
Fuller, Wayne E. *see* Fuller, Wayne Edison.
Fuller, Wayne Edison, 1919-
   xFuller, Wayne E.

The American Mail: Enlarger of the Common
   Life. U of Chicago Pr.
   xFuller, Wayne F.
      The American Mail: Enlarger of the Common
         Life. U of Chicago Pr.
Fuller, Wayne F. *see* Fuller, Wayne Edison.
Fuller-Maitland, J. A. *see* Fuller-Maitland, John
   Alexander.
Fuller-Maitland, John A. *see* Fuller-Maitland, John
   Alexander.
Fuller-Maitland, John Alexander, 1856-1936
   xFuller-Maitland, J. A.
      Masters of German Music. Longwood Pr.
   xFuller-Maitland, John A.
      Spell of Music: An Attempt to Analyse the
         Enjoyment of Music. Arno.
Fullerton, George S. *see* Fullerton, George Stuart.
Fullerton, George Stuart, 1859-1925
   xFullerton, George S.
      System of Metaphysics. Greenwood.
      System of Metaphysics. Scholarly.
Fullerton, Gerald Lee, 1941-
   xFullerton, Lee.
      Historical Germanic Verb Morphology. De
         Gruyter.
Fullerton, Herbert H.
   xFullerton, Herbert H.
      Economic Simulation Model for Regional
         Development Planning. Ann Arbor Science.
Fullerton, James H.
   xFullerton, James H.
      Ice Hockey!: Playing & Coaching. Hastings.
Fullerton, Lee. *see* Fullerton, Gerald Lee.
Fullinwider, Robert K., 1942-
   xFullinwider, Robert K.
      The Reverse Discrimination Controversy: A
         Moral & Legal Analysis. Rowman.
Fullmer, Daniel W.
   xFullmer, Daniel W.
      Counseling: Group Theory & System. Carroll
         Pr.
      Family Consultation. HM.
Fulmer, Constance M. *see* Fulmer, Constance Marie.
Fulmer, Constance Marie.
   xFulmer, Constance M.
      George Eliot: A Reference Guide. G K Hall.
Fulmer, Robert M.
   xFulmer, Robert M.
      Practical Human Relations. Irwin.
Fulop-Miller, Rene, 1891-1963
   xFulop-Miller, Rene.
      Lenin & Gandhi. Arno.
      Rasputin the Holy Devil. Folcroft.
Fulton. *see* Fulton, Robert T.
Fulton, A. R. *see* Fulton, Albert Rondthaler.
Fulton, Albert Rondthaler, 1902-
   xFulton, A. R.
      Motion Pictures: The Development of an Art.
         U of Okla Pr.
Fulton, Chandler.
   xFulton, Chandler.
      Explorations in Developmental Biology.
         Harvard U Pr.
Fulton, Charles C. *see* Fulton, Charles Clarke.
Fulton, Charles Clarke, 1900
   xFulton, Charles C.
      Modern Microcrystal Tests for Drugs: The
         Identification of Organic Compounds by
         Microcrystalloscopic Chemistry. Wiley.
Fulton, Eileen.
   xFulton, Eileen.
      How My World Turns. Taplinger.
Fulton, Eleanore J. *see* Fulton, Eleanore Jane.
Fulton, Eleanore Jane.
   xFulton, Eleanore J.
      An Index to the Will Books & Intestate
         Records of Lancaster County, Pennsylvania,
         1729-1850. Genealog Pub.
Fulton, John F. *see* Fulton, John Farquhar.

Fulton, John Farquhar, 1899-1960
    xFulton, John F.
        The Great Medical Bibliographers: A Study in
        Humanism. Greenwood.
Fulton, Justin D. *see* Fulton, Justin Dewey.
Fulton, Justin Dewey, 1828-1901
    xFulton, Justin D.
        The Fight with Rome. Arno.
Fulton, Len.
    xFulton, Len.
        Dark Other Adam Dreaming. Dustbooks.
        ed. Directory of Small Magazine - Press
        Editors & Publishers. Dustbooks.
        ed. Directory of Small Magazine Press Editors
        & Publishers. Dustbooks.
        ed. Directory of Small Magazine Press Editors
        & Publishers: 1978-79. Dustbooks.
Fulton, Mary J.
    xFulton, Mary J.
        Detective Arthur, Master Sleuth. Western Pub.
        Detective Arthur on the Scent. Western Pub.
Fulton, Maurice G. *see* Fulton, Maurice Garland.
Fulton, Maurice Garland, 1877-1955
    xFulton, Maurice G.
        History of the Lincoln County War. U of Ariz
        Pr.
Fulton, R. *see* Fulton, Robert T.
Fulton, Richard M., 1940-
    xFulton, Richard M.
        ed. The Revolution That Wasn't: A
        Contemporary Assessment of 1776. Kennikat.
Fulton, Robert T.
    xFulton.
        Audiometry for the Retarded with Implications
        for the Difficult to Test. Krieger.
    xFulton, R.
        Auditory Stimulus-Response Control. Univ
        Park.
Fulweiler, Howard W.
    xFulweiler, Howard W.
        Letters from the Darkling Plain: Language &
        the Grounds of Knowledge in the Poetry of
        Arnold & Hopkins. U of Mo Pr.
Fulweiler, John H.
    xFulweiler, John H.
        How to Promote Your Shopping Center.
        Lebhar Friedman.
        Profitable Energy Management for Retailers &
        Shopping Centers. Lebhar Friedman.
Fulwell, Ulpian, fl. 1586
    xFulwell, Ulpian.
        Like Will to Like. AMS Pr.
Fulwiler, Kyle. *see* Fulwiler, Kyle D.
Fulwiler, Kyle D.
    xFulwiler, Kyle.
        The Apple Cookbook. Pacific Search.
Funai, Mamoru.
    xFunai, Mamoru.
        Cartoons for Kids. P-H.
Funchion, Michael F.
    xFunchion, Michael F.
        Chicago's Irish Nationalists, 1881-1890. Arno.
Fund for the Republic.
    xFund for the Republic, Inc.
        Digest of the Public Record of Communism in
        the United States.. Arno.
Fund for the Republic, Inc. *see* Fund for the Republic.
Fundaburk, Emma L. *see* Fundaburk, Emma Lila.
Fundaburk, Emma Lila.
    xFundaburk, Emma L.
        Art at Educational Institutions in the United
        States: A Handbook of Permanent,
        Semi-Permanent & Temporary Works of Art
        at Elementary & Secondary Schools, Colleges
        & Universities. Scarecrow.
        Reference Materials & Periodicals in
        Economics: An International List. Scarecrow.
Funes, Donald J.
    xFunes, Donald J.

        Musical Involvement: A Guide to Perceptive
        Listening. HarBraceJ.
Fung, Y. C. *see* Fung, Yuan-Cheng.
Fung, Yuan-Cheng, 1919-
    xFung, Y. C.
        Foundations of Solid Mechanics. P-H.
    xFung, Yuan-Cheng.
        A First Course in Continuum Mechanics. P-H.
Funigiello, Philip J.
    xFunigiello, Philip J.
        The Challenge to Urban Liberalism:
        Federal-City Relations During World War II.
        U of Tenn Pr.
        Toward a National Power Policy: The New
        Deal & the Electric Utility Industry,
        1933-1941. U of Pittsburgh Pr.
Funk, Arthur L. *see* Funk, Arthur Layton.
Funk, Arthur Layton, 1914-
    xFunk, Arthur L.
        The Politics of Torch: The Allied Landings &
        the Algiers Putsch, 1942. Regents Pr KS.
Funk, Charles E. *see* Funk, Charles Earle.
Funk, Charles Earle.
    xFunk, Charles E.
        jt. auth. Horsefeathers & Other Curious Words.
        Har-Row.
        Thereby Hangs a Tale: Stories of Curious Word
        Origins. Har-Row.
Funk, Hal D.
    xFunk, Hal D.
        ed. Learning to Teach in the Elementary
        School: Introductory Readings. Har-Row.
Funk, Robert W., 1937-
    xFunk, Robert W.
        Christopher Isherwood: A Reference Guide. G
        K Hall.
Funk, Tom.
    xFunk, Tom.
        illus. Horsefeathers & Other Curious Words.
        Har-Row.
        illus. I Read Signs. Holiday.
Funk, Wilfred. *see* Funk, Wilfred John.
Funk, Wilfred John, 1883-1965
    xFunk, Wilfred.
        Word Origins & Their Romantic Stories. T Y
        Crowell.
Funke, Mimi.
    xFunke, Mimi.
        Word Games. Doubleday.
Funke, U. H. *see* Funke, Ursula.
Funke, Ursula, 1939-
    xFunke, U. H.
        ed. Mathematical Models in Marketing: A
        Collection of Abstracts. Springer-Verlag.
Funkenstein, Daniel H.
    xFunkenstein, Daniel H.
        Medical Students, Medical Schools & Society
        During Five Eras: Factors Affecting the
        Career Choices of Physicians, 1958-1976.
        Ballinger Pub.
Funnell, Charles E.
    xFunnell, Charles E.
        By the Beautiful Sea: The Rise & High Times
        of That Great American Resort, Atlantic
        City. Knopf.
Funt, Marilyn, 1937-
    xFunt, Marilyn.
        Are You Anybody?: Conversations with Wives
        of Celebrities. Dial.
Fuori, W. *see* Fuori, William M.
Fuori, W. M. *see* Fuori, William M.
Fuori, William. *see* Fuori, William M.
Fuori, William M.
    xFuori, W.
        Introduction to Computer Operations. P-H.
    xFuori, W. M.

        Introduction to American National Standard
        Cobol. McGraw.
    xFuori, William.
        Introduction to Computer Operations.
        McGraw.
Fuoss, D. E. *see* Fuoss, Donald E.
Fuoss, Donald E.
    xFuoss, D. E.
        Creative Management Techniques in
        Interscholastic Athletics. Wiley.
Fuqua, Paul. *see* Fuqua, Paul Q.
Fuqua, Paul Q.
    xFuqua, Paul.
        Security Investigators Handbook. Gulf Pub.
Furbank, P. N. *see* Furbank, Philip Nicholas.
Furbank, Philip Nicholas.
    xFurbank, P. N.
        E. M. Forster: A Life. HarBraceJ.
Furchgott, Terry.
    xFurchgott, Terry.
        Phoebe & the Hot Water Bottles. Andre
        Deutsch.
Furer, Howard B., 1934-
    xFurer, Howard B.
        The Germans in America, 1607-1970: A
        Chronology & Factbook. Oceana.
Furfey, Paul H. *see* Furfey, Paul Hanly.
Furfey, Paul Hanly, 1896-
    xFurfey, Paul H.
        Love & the Urban Ghetto. Orbis Bks.
        Morality Gap. Macmillan.
Furlong, Marjorie.
    xFurlong, Marjorie.
        Edible? Incredible! Pondlife. Naturegraph.
Furlow, Elaine. *see* Furlow, Elaine Selcraig.
Furlow, Elaine Selcraig.
    xFurlow, Elaine.
        Love with No Strings: The Human Touch in
        Christian Social Ministries. Home Mission.
Furman, A. L. *see* Furman, Abraham Loew.
Furman, Abraham L. *see* Furman, Abraham Loew.
Furman, Abraham Loew, 1902-
    xFurman, A. L.
        ed. More Horse Stories. Archway.
        ed. More Horse Stories. PB.
    xFurman, Abraham L.
        ed. Everygirls Companion. Lantern.
        ed. More Teen-Age Ghost Stories. Lantern.
        ed. More Teen-Age Haunted Stories. Lantern.
Furman, Josh.
    xFurman, Josh.
        ed. Football Stories. PB.
Furman, S. *see* Furman, Seymour.
Furman, Seymour.
    xFurman, S.
        ed. Modern Cardiac Pacing: A Clinical
        Overview. Charles.
Furman, Victoria.
    xFurman, Victoria.
        Five in a Tent. Schol Bk Serv.
Furman, William B.
    xFurman, William B.
        Continuous Flow Analysis: Theory & Practice.
        Dekker.
Furmanov, Dmitrii Andreevich, 1891-1926
    xFurmanov, Dmitry A.
        Chapayev. Hyperion Conn.
Furmanov, Dmitry A. *see* Furmanov, Dmitrii
  Andreevich.
Furneaux, Barbara.
    xFurneaux, Barbara.
        ed. Autistic Children: Teaching, Community &
        Research Approaches. Routledge & Kegan.
Furneaux, Rupert.
    xFurneaux, Rupert.

Ancient Mysteries. Ballantine.
Great Treasure Hunts. Taplinger.
The Money Pit Mystery: The Costliest
Treasure Hunt Ever. Dodd.

Furner, Mary O.
xFurner, Mary O.
Advocacy & Objectivity: A Crisis in the
Professionalization of American Social
Science, 1865-1905. U Pr of Ky.

Furness, Edna L.
xFurness, Edna L.
Spelling for the Millions. Elsevier-Nelson.

Furness, Eric L., 1913-
xFurness, Eric L.
Money & Credit in Developing Africa. St
Martin.

Furnish, Dorothy J. see Furnish, Dorothy Jean.

Furnish, Dorothy Jean, 1921-
xFurnish, Dorothy J.
Exploring the Bible with Children. Abingdon.
Living the Bible with Children. Abingdon.

Furnish, Victor P. see Furnish, Victor Paul.

Furnish, Victor Paul.
xFurnish, Victor P.
The Moral Teaching of Paul. Abingdon.
Theology & Ethics in Paul. Abingdon.

Furniss, E. S. see Furniss, Edgar Stephenson.

Furniss, Edgar Stephenson, 1918-
xFurniss, E. S.
De Gaulle & the French Army: A Crisis in
Civil Military Relations. Kraus Repr.

Furniss, Norman.
xFurniss, Norman.
The Case for the Welfare State: From Social
Security to Social Equality. Ind U Pr.

Furnivall, Frederick James.
xFurnivall, J. F.
The Troublesome Reign of King John: Being
the Original of Shakespeare's "Life & Death
of King John". Folcroft.

Furnivall, J. F. see Furnivall, Frederick James.
Furnivall, J. S. see Furnivall, John Sydenham.
Furnivall, John S. see Furnivall, John Sydenham.

Furnivall, John Sydenham.
xFurnivall, J. S.
Colonial Policy & Practice: A Comparative
Study of Burma & Netherlands India. NYU
Pr.
xFurnivall, John S.
Progress & Welfare in Southeast Asia: A
Comparison of Colonial Policy & Practice.
AMS Pr.

Furrer, Jurg.
xFurrer, Jurg.
illus. Tortoise Island. A-W.

Furry, Margaret S. see Furry, Margaret Smith.

Furry, Margaret Smith.
xFurry, Margaret S.
Home Dyeing with Natural Dyes. Thresh
Pubns.

Furst, Alan.
xFurst, Alan.
The Paris Drop. Doubleday.

Furst, Arnold, 1918-
xFurst, Arnold.
How to Prepare & Administer Hypnotic
Prescriptions. Borden.
How to Prepare & Administer Hypnotic
Prescriptions. Magic Ltd.

Furst, Bruno.
xFurst, Bruno.
Stop Forgetting. Doubleday.

Furst, Charles.
xFurst, Charles.
Origins of the Mind: Mind-Brain Connections.
P-H.

Furst, Clyde. see Furst, Clyde Bowman.

Furst, Clyde Bowman, 1873-1931
xFurst, Clyde.

Observations of Professor Maturin. AMS Pr.

Furst, Lilian R.
xFurst, Lilian R.
The Contours of European Romanticism. U of
Nebr Pr.

Furst, Peter T.
xFurst, Peter T.
Hallucinogens & Culture. Chandler & Sharp.

Furstenberg, Egon von. see Von Furstenberg, Egon.

Furstenberg, George M. von. see Von Furstenberg,
George M.

Furtado, Celso.
xFurtado, Celso.
Diagnosis of the Brazilian Crisis. U of Cal Pr.

Furter, Pierre, 1931-
xFurter, Pierre.
Possibilities & Limitations of Functional
Literacy: The Iranian Experiment. Unipub.

Furth, Charlotte.
xFurth, Charlotte.
_ed._ The Limits of Change: Essays on
Conservative Alternatives in Republican
China. Harvard U Pr.

Furth, Hans G.
xFurth, Hans G.
Deafness & Learning: A Psycho-Social
Approach. Wadsworth Pub.
Thinking Goes to School: Piaget's Theory in
Practice. Oxford U Pr.

Furtwangler, A. see Furtwangler, Adolf.

Furtwangler, Adolf.
xFurtwangler, A.
Greek & Roman Sculpture. Longwood Pr.

Furtwangler, Wilhelm, 1886-1954
xFurtwangler, Wilhelm.
Concerning Music. Greenwood.

Fusco, Patricia S. see Fusco, Patricia Sayer.

Fusco, Patricia Sayer.
xFusco, Patricia S.
Marino & Ruby. Morrow.

Fusco, Peter.
xFusco, Peter.
The Romantics to Rodin: French
Nineteenth-Century Sculpture from North
American Collections. LA Co Art Mus.

Fuse, Katsuji.
xFuse, Katsuji.
Soviet Policy in the Orient. Hyperion Conn.

Fusfeld, Daniel R. see Fusfeld, Daniel Roland.

Fusfeld, Daniel Roland, 1922-
xFusfeld, Daniel R.
The Age of the Economist. Scott F.
Economics. Heath.

Fusi, Rolando.
xFusi, Rolando.
Looking at Florence. Intl Pubns Serv.

Fuson, Benjamin. see Fuson, Benjamin Willis.

Fuson, Benjamin Willis.
xFuson, Benjamin.
Browning & His English Predecessors in the
Dramatic Monolog. Folcroft.

Fuson, Henry H. see Fuson, Henry Harvey.

Fuson, Henry Harvey, 1876-
xFuson, Henry H.
Ballads of the Kentucky Highlands. Folcroft.

Fuson, Robert.
xFuson, Robert H.
Fundamental Place-Name Geography. Wm C
Brown.

Fuson, Robert H. see Fuson, Robert.

Fusonie, Alan.
xFusonie, Alan.
_ed._ International Agricultural Librarianship:
Continuity & Change. Greenwood.

Fussell, Edwin. see Fussell, Edwin S.

Fussell, Edwin S.
xFussell, Edwin.
Lucifer in Harness: American Meter, Metaphor
& Diction. Princeton U Pr.
xFussell, Edwin S.

Edwin Arlington Robinson: The Literary
Background of a Traditional Poet. Russell.

Fussell, G. E. see Fussell, George Edwin.

Fussell, George Edwin, 1889-
xFussell, G. E.
The Classical Tradition in West European
Farming. Fairleigh Dickinson.

Fussell, Paul, 1924-
xFussell, Paul.
The Great War & Modern Memory. Oxford U
Pr.
The Great War and Modern Memory. Oxford
U Pr.
Poetic Meter & Poetic Form. Random.
Poetic Meter & Poetic Form. Random.
Theory of Prosody in Eighteenth Century
England. Shoe String.

Fussell, Richard.
xFussell, Richard.
A Demographic Atlas of Birmingham. U of Ala
Pr.

Fussey, Joyce.
xFussey, Joyce.
Cows in the Corn. Merrimack Bk Serv.

Fussler, Herman H. see Fussler, Herman Howe.

Fussler, Herman Howe.
xFussler, Herman H.
Patterns in the Use of Books in Large Research
Libraries. U of Chicago Pr.

Fussner, F. Smith.
xFussner, F. Smith.
The Historical Revolution: English Historical
Writing & Thought 1580-1640. Greenwood.

Fusting, Eugene M.
xFusting, Eugene M.
Star-Sticks. Summer House.

Futas, Elizabeth
xFutas, Elizabeth.
_ed._ Library Acquisition Policies & Procedures.
Oryx Pr.

Futch, Ladell J.
xFutch, Ladell J.
Learning the New Testament. Judson.

Futrell. see Futrell, May Dipietro.

Futrell, May Dipietro.
xFutrell.
Primary Health Care of the Older Adult.
Duxbury Pr.

Futrelle, Jacques, 1875-1912
xFutrelle, Jacques.
Great Cases of the Thinking Machine. Dover.

Futuyma, Douglas J., 1942-
xFutuyma, Douglas J.
Evolutionary Biology. Sinauer Assoc.

Fux, Johann J. see Fux, Johann Joseph.

Fux, Johann Joseph.
xFux, Johann J.
Orfeo ed Euridice. Garland Pub.

Fuxe, K. see Fuxe, Kjell.

Fuxe, Kjell.
xFuxe, K.
_ed._ Dopaminergic Ergot Derivatives & Motor
Function: Proceedings of an International
Symposium, Stockholm, 1978. Pergamon.

Fuys, David J.
xFuys, David J.
Teaching Mathematics in the Elementary
School. Little.

Fyfe, Henry H. see Fyfe, Henry Hamilton.

Fyfe, Henry Hamilton, 1869-1951
xFyfe, Henry H.
Sir Arthur Pinero's Plays & Players.
Greenwood.

Fyfe, W. S.
xFyfe, W. S.

Fluids in the Earth's Crust: Their Significance
in Metamorphic, Tectonic, & Chemical
Transport Process. Elsevier.
Geochemistry of Solids: An Introduction.
McGraw.

Fyleman, Rose, 1877-1957
xFyleman, Rose.
Fairies & Chimneys. Core Collection.
ed. Here We Come A'piping. Granger Bk.
ed. Pipe & Drum. Core Collection.

Fyler, John M.
xFyler, John M.
Chaucer & Ovid. Yale U Pr.

Fymat, A. L. *see* Fymat, Alain L.

Fymat, Alain L.
xFymat, A. L.
Remote Sensing of the Atmosphere: Inversion
Methods & Applications. Elsevier.

Fynn, G. W.
xFynn, G. W.
The Cutting & Polishing of Electro-Optic
Materials. Halsted Pr.

Fyodorova, Victoria.
xFyodorova, Victoria.
Admiral's Daughter. Delacorte.
The Admiral's Daughter. Dell.

G. K. Hall & Co. *see* Hall, (G. K.) and Company.

Gaal, O.
xGaal, O.
Electrophoresis in the Separation of Biological
Macromolecules. Wiley.

Gaal, S. A. *see* Gaal, Steven A.

Gaal, Steven A.
xGaal, S. A.
Linear Analysis & Representation Theory.
Springer-Verlag.

Gaan, Margaret.
xGaan, Margaret.
Last Moments of a World. Norton.

Gaballa, G. A.
xGaballa, G. A.
The Memphite Tomb-Chapel of Mose. Intl
Schol Bk Serv.

Gabasov, R. *see* Gabasov, Rafail.

Gabasov, Rafail.
xGabasov, R.
The Qualitative Theory of Optimal Processes.
Dekker.

Gabb, M. H. *see* Gabb, Michael H.

Gabb, Michael. *see* Gabb, Michael H.

Gabb, Michael H.
xGabb, M. H.
Handbook of Laboratory Solutions. Chem Pub.
xGabb, Michael.
Creatures Great & Small. Lerner Pubns.
Everyday Science. Lerner Pubns.

Gabbard, Lucina Paquet.
xGabbard, Lucinda P.
The Dream Structure of Pinter's Plays: A
Psychoanalytic Approach. Fairleigh
Dickinson.

Gabbard, Lucinda P. *see* Gabbard, Lucina Paquet.

Gabbiani, Giulio.
xGabbiani, Giulio.
ed. The Cytoskeleton in Normal & Pathologic
Processes: Cell Biology. S Karger.
ed. The Cytoskeleton in Normal & Pathologic
Processes: Cell Physiopathology. S Karger.

Gabe, D. R. *see* Gabe, Dina Rufinovna.

Gabe, Dina Rufinovna.
xGabe, D. R.
Principles of Metal Surface Treatment &
Protection. Pergamon.

Gabel, Creighton.
xGabel, Creighton.
Analysis of Prehistoric Economic Patterns.
Irvington.

Gabel, Medard.
xGabel, Medard.

Ho-Ping Food for Everyone. Doubleday.

Gabel, Richard.
xGabel, Richard.
Development of Separations Principles in the
Telephone Industry. Mich St U Busn.

Gabel, Robert A.
xGabel, Robert A.
Signals & Linear Systems. Wiley.

Gabelnick, Henry L.
xGabelnick, Henry L.
Rheology of Biological Systems. C C Thomas.

Gabert, Glen.
xGabert, Glen.
In Hoc Signo?: A Brief History of Catholic
Parochial Education in America. Kennikat.

Gabin, Sanford B. *see* Gabin, Sanford Byron.

Gabin, Sanford Byron, 1936-
xGabin, Sanford B.
Judicial Review & the Reasonable Doubt Test.
Kennikat.

Gabiou, Alfrieda.
xGabiou, Alfrieda.
Gordon Lightfoot. Music Sales.

Gable, Fred B.
xGable, Fred B.
Opportunities in Pharmacy Careers. Natl
Textbk.
Psychosocial Pharmacy: The Synthetic Society.
Lea & Febiger.

Gable, John A.
xGable, John A.
The Bull Moose Years: Theodore Roosevelt &
the Progressive Party. Kennikat.

Gable, Richard W.
xGable, Richard W.
Administering Agricultural Development in
Asia: A Comparative Analysis of Four
National Programs. Westview.

Gabler, R. *see* Gabler, Robert E.

Gabler, Robert E.
xGabler, R.
Essentials of Physical Geography. HR&W.

Gablik, Suzi.
xGablik, Suzi.
Progress in Art. Rizzoli Intl.

Gabo, Naum, 1890-
xGabo, Naum.
Of Divers Arts. Princeton U Pr.

Gaboriau, Emile, 1835-1873
xGaboriau, Emile.
File No. 113. Arno.
Monsieur LeCoq. Dover.
Monsieur Lecoq. Peter Smith.

Gabriel, Joyce.
xGabriel, Joyce.
Having It All: A Practical Guide to
Overcoming the Career Woman's Blues. M
Evans.

Gabriel, Michael. *see* Gabriel, Michael R.

Gabriel, Michael R.
xGabriel, Michael.
Micrographics 1900-1977: A Bibliography.
Minn Scholarly.
xGabriel, Michael R.
The Microform Revolution in Libraries. Jai Pr.

Gabriel, Mordecai L. *see* Gabriel, Mordecai Lionel.

Gabriel, Mordecai Lionel.
xGabriel, Mordecai L.
ed. Great Experiments in Biology. P-H.

Gabriel, Philip L. *see* Gabriel, Philip Louis.

Gabriel, Philip Louis, 1908-
xGabriel, Philip L.
In the Ashes: The Story of Lebanon.
Whitmore.

Gabriel, Pierre.
xGabriel, Pierre.
Calculus of Fractions & Homotopy Theory.
Springer-Verlag.

Gabriel, Ralph H. *see* Gabriel, Ralph Henry.

Gabriel, Ralph Henry.
xGabriel, Ralph H.
ed. Christianity & Modern Thought. Elliots
Bks.
The Course of American Democratic Thought.
Wiley.

Gabriel, Richard A.
xGabriel, Richard A.
Crisis in Command: Mismanagement in the
Army. Hill & Wang.
xGabriel, Rochard A.
Program Evaluation: A Social Science
Approach. Mss Info.

Gabriel, Rochard A. *see* Gabriel, Richard A.

Gabriel, Roger.
xGabriel, Roger.
Medical Data Interpretation for MRCP.
Butterworths.
Postgraduate Nephrology. Butterworths.

Gabrieli, Francesco, 1904-
xGabrieli, Francesco.
ed. Arab Historians of the Crusades. U of Cal
Pr.

Gabrielsen, M. Alexander.
xGabrielsen, Milton A.
Aquatics Handbook. P-H.

Gabrielsen, Milton A. *see* Gabrielsen, M. Alexander.

Gackenbach, Dick.
xGackenbach, Dick.
Crackle Gluck & the Sleeping Toad. HM.
Do You Love Me?. Dell.
illus. Do You Love Me?. HM.
illus. Ida Fanfanny. Har-Row.
The Leatherman. HM.
More from Hound & Bear. HM.

Gadamer, Hans Georg, 1900-
xGadamer, Hans-Georg.
Dialogue & Dialectic: Eight Hermeneutical
Studies on Plato. Yale U Pr.

Gadamer, Hans-Georg. *see* Gadamer, Hans Georg.

Gadd, C. J. *see* Gadd, Cyril John.

Gadd, Cyril John, 1893-
xGadd, C. J.
History & Monuments of UR. Arno.

Gadd, Laurence.
xGadd, Laurence.
Deadly Beautiful: The World's Most Poisonous
Animals & Plants. Macmillan.

Gaddis, Ben. *see* Gaddis, Ben W.

Gaddis, Ben W.
xGaddis, Ben.
How to Repair Home Kitchen Appliances.
TAB Bks.
How to Repair Home Laundry Appliances.
TAB Bks.
xGaddis, Ben W.
Effective Troubleshooting with EVM & Scope.
TAB Bks.
Troubleshooting Solid-State Electronic Power
Supplies. TAB Bks.
Troubleshooting Solid State Wave-Generating
& Shaping Circuits. TAB Bks.

Gaddis, Vincent H.
xGaddis, Vincent H.
American Indian Myths & Mysteries. Chilton.
American Indian Myths & Mysteries. NAL.

Gaddy, C. Welton.
xGaddy, C. Welton.
In Awe of the Ordinary. Broadman.
Proclaim Liberty. Broadman.

Gaddy, Jerry J.
xGaddy, Jerry J.
Dust to Dust: Obituaries of the Gunfighters.
Presidio Pr.

Gaden, Eileen.
xGaden, Eileen.
Breads: Manna from Heaven. Christian Herald.

Gadler, Steve. *see* Gadler, Steve J.

Gadler, Steve J.
xGadler, Steve.

Sun Power: Facts About Solar Energy. Lerner
Pubns.
Gadney, Reg, 1941-
xGadney, Reg.
The Cage. Coward.
Gado, Otto.
xGado, Otto.
Reform of the Economic Mechanism in
Hungary: Development 1968-71. Intl Pubns
Serv.
Gadpaille, Warren J.
xGadpaille, Warren J.
Cycles of Sex. Scribner.
Gaeddert, Lou A. *see* Gaeddert, Louann Bigge.
Gaeddert, Lou Ann. *see* Gaeddert, Louann Bigge.
Gaeddert, LouAnn. *see* Gaeddert, Louann Bigge.
Gaeddert, Louann Bigge.
xGaeddert, Lou A.
Gustav the Gourmet Giant. Dial.
xGaeddert, Lou Ann.
Noisy Nancy & Nick. Doubleday.
Noisy Nancy Norris. Doubleday.
xGaeddert, LouAnn.
Gustav the Gourmet Giant. Dial.
Gaedeke, Ralph M.
xGaedeke, Ralph M.
ed. Marketing in Private & Public Nonprofit
Organizations: Perspectives & Illustrations.
Goodyear.
Gaer, J. *see* Gaer, Joseph.
Gaer, Joseph, 1897-
xGaer, J.
What the Great Religions Believe. Kazi Pubns.
xGaer, Joseph.
Ambrose Gwinett Bierce Bibliography &
Biographical Data. Darby Bks.
Bret Harte: Bibliography & Biographical Data.
B Franklin.
Holidays Around the World. Little.
Theatre of the Gold Rush Deende in San
Francisco. B Franklin.
What the Great Religions Believe. NAL.
Gafencu, Grigore, 1892-
xGafencu, Grigore.
Last Days of Europe: A Diplomatic Journey in
1939. Shoe String.
Gaff, Jerry G.
xGaff, Jerry G.
Toward Faculty Renewal: Advances in Faculty,
Instructional, & Organizational Development.
Jossey-Bass.
Gaff, Sally S. *see* Gaff, Sally Shake.
Gaff, Sally Shake.
xGaff, Sally S.
Professional Development: A Guide to
Resources. Change Mag.
Gaffey, John D. *see* Gaffey, John Dean.
Gaffey, John Dean, 1913-
xGaffey, John D.
Productivity of Labor in the Rubber Tire
Manufacturing Industry. AMS Pr.
Gaffney, James.
xGaffney, James.
Focus on Doctrine. Paulist Pr.
Moral Questions. Paulist Pr.
Newness of Life: A Modern Introduction to
Catholic Ethics. Paulist Pr.
Gaffney, M. P. *see* Gaffney, Matthew P.
Gaffney, Matthew P.
xGaffney, M. P.
Compiled by Annotated Bibliography of
Expository Writing in the Mathematical
Sciences. Math Assn.
Gafford, Phil E. *see* Gafford, Phil Ewing.
Gafford, Phil Ewing.
xGafford, Phil E.
Quo Vadis, America?. Huntleigh.
Gag, Wanda.
xGag, Wanda.

illus. ABC Bunny. Coward.
Jorinda & Joringel. Coward.
Gagan, David P. *see* Gagan, David Paul.
Gagan, David Paul, 1940-
xGagan, David P.
The Denison Family of Toronto. U of Toronto
Pr.
Gagarine, Marie.
xGagarine, Marie.
From Stolnoy to Spartanburg: The Two Worlds
of a Former Russian Princess. Sandlapper
Store.
Gage, Joy P.
xGage, Joy P.
When Parents Cry. Accent Bks.
Gage, Michael. *see* Gage, Michael Terence.
Gage, Michael Terence.
xGage, Michael.
ed. Design in Blockwork. Nichols Pub.
Gage, N. L. *see* Gage, Nathaniel Lees.
Gage, Nathaniel Lees.
xGage, N. L.
Educational Psychology. Rand.
Gager, Delaye, 1895-
xGager, Delaye.
French Comment on American Education.
AMS Pr.
Gagey, Edmond M. *see* Gagey, Edmond Mcadoo.
Gagey, Edmond Mcadoo, 1901-
xGagey, Edmond M.
Ballad Opera. Arno.
Gagliardi, Robert. *see* Gagliardi, Robert M.
Gagliardi, Robert M., 1934-
xGagliardi, Robert.
Introduction to Communications Engineering.
Wiley.
xGagliardi, Robert M.
Optical Communications. Wiley.
Gagliardo, John G.
xGagliardo, John G.
From Pariah to Patriot: The Changing Image of
the German Peasant, 1770-1840. U Pr of Ky.
Reich & Nation: The Holy Roman Empire As
Idea & Reality, 1763-1806. Ind U Pr.
Gagne, Robert M. *see* Gagne, Robert Mills.
Gagne, Robert Mills, 1916-
xGagne, Robert M.
The Conditions of Learning. HR&W.
Principles of Instructional Design. HR&W.
Gagnier, Ed.
xGagnier, Ed.
Inside Gymnastics. Contemp Bks.
Gagnon, John. *see* Gagnon, John H.
Gagnon, John H.
xGagnon, John.
Human Sexuality in Today's World. Little.
xGagnon, John H.
Human Sexualities. Scott F.
Life Designs: Individuals, Marriages, &
Families. Scott F.
Gahan, P. B.
xGahan, P. B.
ed. Autoradiography for Biologists. Acad Pr.
Gahn, Bessie W. *see* Gahn, Bessie Wilmarth (Brown).
Gahn, Bessie Wilmarth (Brown), 1885-
xGahn, Bessie W.
Original Patentees of Land at Washington Prior
to 1700. Genealog Pub.
Gaige, Frederick H.
xGaige, Frederick H.
Regionalism & National Unity in Nepal. U of
Cal Pr.
Gail, Marzieh.
xGail, Marzieh.
Dawn Over Mount Hira & Other Essays.
Baha'i.
Gailey, Harry A.
xGailey, Harry A.

Historical Dictionary of the Gambia.
Scarecrow.
Gaillard, Pieter J. *see* Gaillard, Pieter Johannes.
Gaillard, Pieter Johannes.
xGaillard, Pieter J.
ed. Parathyroid Glands: Ultrastructure,
Secretion & Function. U of Chicago Pr.
Gaimar, Geoffrey. *see* Gaimar, Geoffroy.
Gaimar, Geoffroy.
xGaimar, Geoffrey.
Anglo-Norman Metrical Chronicle of Geoffrey
Gaimar. B Franklin.
Gaine, Hugh, 1726 or 7-1807
xGaine, Hugh.
Journals of Hugh Gaine, Printer. Arno.
Gainer, Harold.
xGainer, Harold.
ed. Peptides in Neurobiology. Plenum Pub.
Gaines, Charles.
xGaines, Charles.
Dangler. S&S.
Gaines, Charles K. *see* Gaines, Charles Kelsey.
Gaines, Charles Kelsey, 1854-1943
xGaines, Charles K.
Gorgo: A Romance of Old Athens. Vanderbilt
U Pr.
Gaines, Ernest J., 1933-
xGaines, Ernest J.
Autobiography of Miss Jane Pittman. Dial.
The Autobiography of Miss Jane Pittman. G K
Hall.
The Autobiography of Miss Jane Pittman.
Bantam.
Catherine Carmier. Chatham Bkseller.
In My Father's House. Knopf.
Long Day in November. Dial.
Of Love & Dust. Norton.
Gaines, Glen A. *see* Gaines, Glenn A.
Gaines, Glenn A.
xGaines, Glen A.
Fire Fighting Operations in Garden
Apartments & Townhouses. R J Brady.
Gaines, James R.
xGaines, James R.
Wit's End: Days & Nights of the Algonquin
Round Table. HarBraceJ.
Wit's End: Days & Nights of the Algonquin
Round Table. HarBraceJ.
Gaines, M. C.
xGaines, M. C.
ed. Picture Stories from the Bible: The Old
Testament in Full-Color Comic-Strip Form.
Scarf Pr.
Gaines, Patricia E. *see* Gaines, Patricia Ellisor.
Gaines, Patricia Ellisor.
xGaines, Patricia E.
The Fabric Decoration Book. Morrow.
Soft: An Irresistible Collection of Pillows, Toys,
Bags, Objects to Sit on, Ornaments for the
Body, & Various Malleable Oddities... & How
to Make Them. Morrow.
Gaines, Stephen. *see* Gaines, Steven.
Gaines, Steven.
xGaines, Stephen.
The Club. Bantam.
xGaines, Steven.
The Club. Morrow.
Gaines, Wesley J. *see* Gaines, Wesley John.
Gaines, Wesley John, Bp, 1840-1912
xGaines, Wesley J.
African Methodism in the South: Or
Twenty-Five Years of Freedom. Metro Bks.
Negro & the White Man. Negro U Pr.
Gainham, Sarah.
xGainham, Sarah.
Night Falls on the City. Avon.
Gairdner, James.
xGairdner, James.

ed. Historical Collections of a Citizen of
London in the Fifteenth Century. Johnson
Repr.
Lollardy & the Reformation in England: An
Historical Survey. B Franklin.
Gaisberg, Frederick W. *see* Gaisberg, Frederick William.
Gaisberg, Frederick William.
xGaisberg, Frederick W.
The Music Goes Round. Arno.
Gaito, John.
xGaito, John.
ed. Introduction to Analysis of Variance
Procedures. Mss Info.
Gal, Allon.
xGal, Allon.
Brandeis of Boston. Harvard U Pr.
Gal, E.
xGal, E.
Human Congenital Malformations: The Design
of a Computer-Aided Study. Butterworths.
Gal, Hans, 1890-
xGal, Hans.
ed. The Musician's World: Letters of the Great
Composers. Thames Hudson.
Richard Wagner. Stein & Day.
Schumann Orchestral Music. U of Wash Pr.
Gal, Susan.
xGal, Susan.
Language Shift: Social Determinants of
Linguistic Change in Bilingual Austria. Acad
Pr.
Galambos, J. *see* Galambos, Janos.
Galambos, Janos.
xGalambos, J.
Characterizations of Probability Distributions:
A Unified Approach with an Emphasis on
Exponential & Related Models.
Springer-Verlag.
Galambos, John T.
xGalambos, John T.
Cirrhosis. Saunders.
Galambos, Louis.
xGalambos, Louis P.
The Public Image of Big Business in America,
1880-1940: A Quantitative Study in Social
Change. Johns Hopkins.
Galambos, Louis P. *see* Galambos, Louis.
Galanti, Anthony V.
xGalanti, Anthony V.
Polypropylene Fibers & Films. Plenum Pub.
Galarza, Ernesto, 1905-
xGalarza, Ernesto.
Barrio Boy. U of Notre Dame Pr.
Farm Workers & Agri-Business in California,
1947-1960. U of Notre Dame Pr.
Spiders in the House & Workers in the Field.
U of Notre Dame Pr.
Galasiewicz, Z. M. *see* Galasiewicz, Zygmunt M.
Galasiewicz, Zygmunt M.
xGalasiewicz, Z. M.
Superconductivity & Quantum Fluids.
Pergamon.
Galaskiewicz, Joseph.
xGalaskiewicz, Joseph.
Exchange Networks & Community Politics.
Sage.
Galassi, Merna D. *see* Galassi, Merna Dee.
Galassi, Merna Dee.
xGalassi, Merna D.
Assert Yourself: How to Be Your Own Person.
Human Sci Pr.
Galasso, F. S. *see* Galasso, Francis S.
Galasso, Francis S.
xGalasso, F. S.

Structure & Properties of Inorganic Solids.
Pergamon.
Galaty. *see* Galaty, Fillmore W.
Galaty, Fillmore W.
xGalaty.
Modern Real Estate Practice. Real Estate Ed
Co.
xGalaty, Fillmore W.
Modern Real Estate Practice. Follett.
Galavaris, George.
xGalavaris, George.
Bread & the Liturgy: The Symbolism of Early
Christian & Byzantine Bread Stamps. U of
Wis Pr.
Illustrations of the Liturgical Homilies of
Gregory Nazianzenus. Princeton U Pr.
Galaway, Burt.
xGalaway, Burt.
ed. Community Corrections: A Reader. C C
Thomas.
Galbraith. *see* Galbraith, James Ewen Kirkwood.
Galbraith, Catherine A. *see* Galbraith, Catherine Atwater.
Galbraith, Catherine Atwater.
xGalbraith, Catherine A.
India Now & Through Time. HM.
Galbraith, J. K. *see* Galbraith, John Kenneth.
Galbraith, James Ewen Kirkwood.
xGalbraith.
Basic Eye Surgery: A Manual for Surgeons in
Developing Countries. Churchill.
Galbraith, Jay.
xGalbraith, Jay.
Designing Complex Organizations. A-W.
Organization Design. A-W.
xGalbraith, Jay R.
Strategy Implementation: The Role of Structure
& Process. West Pub.
Galbraith, Jay R. *see* Galbraith, Jay.
Galbraith, John K. *see* Galbraith, John Kenneth.
Galbraith, John Kenneth, 1908-
xGalbraith, J. K.
China Passage. NAL.
xGalbraith, John K.
Affluent Society. NAL.
The Age of Uncertainty. G K Hall.
Age of Uncertainty. HM.
Almost Everyone's Guide to Economics.
Bantam.
Almost Everyone's Guide to Economics. HM.
Ambassador's Journal: A Personal Account of
the Kennedy Years. HM.
American Capitalism: The Concept of
Countervailing Power. M E Sharpe.
Annals of an Abiding Liberal. HM.
Economic Development. Harvard U Pr.
Liberal Hour. NAL.
The Nature of Mass Poverty. Harvard U Pr.
The New Industrial State. HM.
New Industrial State. HM.
The New Industrial State. NAL.
xGalbraith, John Kenneth.
Annals of an Abiding Liberal. NAL.
Galbraith, John S.
xGalbraith, John S.
Crown & Charter: The Early Years of the
British South Africa Company. U of Cal Pr.
Reluctant Empire: British Policy on the South
African Frontier, 1834-1854. Greenwood.
Galbraith, Kathryn O. *see* Galbraith, Kathryn Osebold.
Galbraith, Kathryn Osebold.
xGalbraith, Kathryn O.
Come Spring. Atheneum.
Galbraith, Madelyn, 1897-
xGalbraith, Madelyn.
There Is a Book. Herald Hse.
Galbraith, Vivian H. *see* Galbraith, Vivian Hunter.
Galbraith, Vivian Hunter, 1889-
xGalbraith, Vivian H.

Domesday Book: Its Place in Administrative
History. Oxford U Pr.
Galbraith, W O.
xGalbraith, W. O.
Colombia: A General Survey. Gordon Pr.
Galdames, Luis, 1881-
xGaldames, Luis.
History of Chile. Russell.
Galde, Dorothy. *see* Galde, Dorothy A.
Galde, Dorothy A.
xGalde, Dorothy.
Danger Comes to Squirrel Valley. Moody.
Galdone, Joanna.
xGaldone, Joanna.
Gertrude, the Goose Who Forgot. Watts.
Galdone, Paul.
xGaldone, Paul.
illus. & Retold by The Gingerbread Boy. HM.
illus. & ed. Hans in Luck. Parents.
illus. History of Mother Twaddle & the
Marvelous Achievements of Her Son Jack.
HM.
illus. Puss in Boots. HM.
Galdos, Benito Perez. *see* Perez Galdos, Benito.
Galdston, Iago, M.d, 1895-
xGaldston, Iago.
Medicine in Transition. U of Chicago Pr.
Psychoanalysis in Present-Day Psychiatry.
Brunner-Mazel.
Galdston, Olive.
xGaldston, Olive.
illus. Play with Puppets. Play Schs.
Gale, Bill.
xGale, Bill.
The Wonderful World of Walking. Morrow.
Gale, Cedric, 1905-
xGale, Cedric.
Building an Effective Vocabulary. Barron.
Gale, David.
xGale, David.
Theory of Linear Economic Models. McGraw.
Gale, Elizabeth W. *see* Gale, Elizabeth Wright.
Gale, Elizabeth Wright.
xGale, Elizabeth W.
I'm Glad. Judson.
Gale, Frank C.
xGale, Frank C.
Experiences with Plants for Young Children.
Pacific Bks.
Gale, Fred L.
xGale, Fred L.
Determining the Requirements for the Design
of Learner-Based Instruction. Merrill.
Gale, J. *see* Gale, Jack L.
Gale, Jack L.
xGale, J.
Listing Real Estate Successfully. P-H.
Gale, Raymond. *see* Gale, Raymond F.
Gale, Raymond F., 1918-
xGale, Raymond.
Who Are You??: The Psychology of Being
Yourself. P-H.
Gale Research Co. *see* Gale Research Company.
Gale Research Company.
xGale Research Co.
Library of Congress & National Union
Catalogue Author Lists, 1942-1962: A Master
Cummulation. Gale.
Gale, Robert L.
xGale, Robert L.
Charles Warren Stoddard. Boise St Univ.
Gale, Stephen.
xGale, Stephen.
ed. Philosophy in Geography. Kluwer Boston.
Gale, Steven H.
xGale, Steven H.
Butter's Going up: A Critical Analysis of
Harold Pinter's Work. Duke.
Gale, William.
xGale, William.

The Compound. Ballantine.
Galeano, Eduardo. *see* Galeano; Eduardo H.
Galeano, Eduardo H., 1940-
　xGaleano, Eduardo.
　　Open Veins of Latin America: Five Centuries
　　of the Pillage of a Continent. Monthly Rev.
Galenson, Walter, 1914-
　xGalenson, Walter.
　　ed. Comparative Labor Movements. Russell.
　　Danish System of Labor Relations: A Study in
　　Industrial Peace. Russell.
　　ed. Economic Growth & Structural Change in
　　Taiwan: The Postwar Experience of the
　　Republic of China. Cornell U Pr.
　　Primer on Employment & Wages. Phila Bk Co.
Galerie St. Etienne.
　xGalerie St. Etienne.
　　Egon Schiele: Watercolors & Drawings.
　　Johannes.
Galilei, Galileo.
　xGalilei, Galileo.
　　Dialogue Concerning the Two Chief World
　　Systems- Ptolemaic & Copernican. U of Cal
　　Pr.
　　Dialogue Concerning the Two Chief World
　　Systems-Ptolemaic & Copernican. U of Cal
　　Pr.
Galin, Saul.
　xGalin, Saul.
　　ed. Reference Books: How to Select & Use
　　Them. Random.
Galinsky, Ellen.
　xGalinsky, Ellen.
　　The Baby Cardinal. Putnam.
Galjart, B. F. *see* Galjart, Benno Franciscus.
Galjart, Benno Franciscus.
　xGaljart, B. F.
　　Peasant Mobilization & Solidarity. Humanities.
Gall, A. Le. *see* Le Gall, A.
Gall, Gretchen.
　xGall, Gretchen.
　　Touch Earth. Dakota Pr.
Gall, John, 1925-
　xGall, John.
　　Systemantics: How Systems Work and
　　Especially How They Fail. Times Bks.
Gall, Lorraine S.
　xGall, Lorraine S.
　　Instrumented Systems for Microbiological
　　Analysis of Body Fluids. CRC Pr.
Gall, Pirie M.
　xGall, Pirie M.
　　Municipal Development Programs in Latin
　　America: An Intercountry Evaluation.
　　Praeger.
Gallacher, Patrick J.
　xGallacher, Patrick J.
　　Love, the Word, & Mercury: A Reading of
　　John Gower's "Confessio Amantis". U of NM
　　Pr.
Gallager, H. Stephen, 1922-
　xGallager, H. Stephen.
　　ed. The Breast. Mosby.
Gallager, R. G. *see* Gallager, Robert G.
Gallager, Robert G.
　xGallager, R. G.
　　Information Theory & Reliable
　　Communication. Wiley.
Gallagher, Bernard J.
　xGallagher, Bernard J.
　　The Social World of Occupations.
　　Kendall-Hunt.
　　Sociology of Mental Illness. P-H.
Gallagher, Buell G. *see* Gallagher, Buell Gordon.
Gallagher, Buell Gordon, 1904-
　xGallagher, Buell G.
　　American Caste & the Negro College. Gordian.
Gallagher, Chuck.
　xGallagher, Chuck.

Hurrah for Parents. Liguori Pubns.
Gallagher, D. P. *see* Gallagher, David Patrick.
Gallagher, David Patrick.
　xGallagher, D. P.
　　Modern Latin American Literature. Oxford U
　　Pr.
Gallagher, Donald A.
　xGallagher, Donald A.
　　ed. Some Philosophers on Education: Papers
　　Concerning the Doctrines of Augustine,
　　Aristole, Aquinas & Dewey. Marquette.
Gallagher, Frank.
　xGallagher, Frank.
　　The Four Glorious Years. Johnson Repr.
Gallagher, I. J., 1930-
　xGallagher, I. J.
　　The Case of the Ancient Astronauts. Raintree
　　Pubs.
Gallagher, Joseph, 1929-
　xGallagher, Joseph.
　　Painting on Silence: An Orchestra of Poems.
　　Exposition.
Gallagher, Mary.
　xGallagher, Mary.
　　Spend It Foolishly. Atheneum.
Gallagher, Matthew P.
　xGallagher, Matthew P.
　　The Soviet History of World War II: Myths,
　　Memories & Realities. Greenwood.
Gallagher, Miriam.
　xGallagher, Miriam.
　　Let's Help Our Children Talk. Transatlantic.
Gallagher, Neil, 1941-
　xGallagher, Neil.
　　Don't Go Overseas Until You've Read This
　　Book. Bethany Fell.
　　How to Save Money on Almost Everything.
　　Bethany Fell.
Gallagher, Nora, 1949-
　xGallagher, Nora.
　　Parlor Games. A-W.
Gallagher, Patricia.
　xGallagher, Patricia.
　　Answer to Heaven. Avon.
　　Castles in the Air. Avon.
　　The Fires of Brimstone. Avon.
　　The Sons & the Daughters. PB.
Gallagher, R. H. *see* Gallagher, Richard M.
Gallagher, Rachel.
　xGallagher, Rachel.
　　Games in the Street. Schol Bk Serv.
Gallagher, Richard M.
　xGallagher, R. H.
　　Optimum Structural Design: Theory &
　　Applications. Wiley.
Gallagher, T. J.
　xGallagher, T. J.
　　Simple Dielectric Liquids: Mobility,
　　Conduction, & Breakdown. Oxford U Pr.
Gallagher, Thomas. *see* Gallagher, Thomas Michael.
Gallagher, Thomas Michael, 1918-
　xGallagher, Thomas.
　　Oona O'. HarBraceJ.
Gallaher, Art.
　xGallaher, Art.
　　ed. The Dying Community. U of NM Pr.
　　Plainville Fifteen Years Later. Columbia U Pr.
Gallaher, Grace M. *see* Gallaher, Grace Margaret.
Gallaher, Grace Margaret.
　xGallaher, Grace M.
　　Vassar Stories. Arno.
Gallahue, David L.
　xGallahue, David L.
　　A Conceptual Approach to Moving &
　　Learning. Wiley.
Galland, Joseph S. *see* Galland, Joseph Stanislaus.
Galland, Joseph Stanislaus.
　xGalland, Joseph S.

Historical & Analytical Bibliography of the
　Literature of Cryptology. AMS Pr.
Galland, Rene.
　xGalland, Rene.
　　George Meredith & British Criticism. Darby
　　Bks.
　　George Meredith & British Criticism. Folcroft.
Gallant, Donald M.
　xGallant, Donald M.
　　ed. Legal & Ethical Issues in Human Research
　　& Treatment-Psychopharmacologic
　　Consideraions. Halsted Pr.
Gallant, Gladys S.
　xGallant, Gladys S.
　　Living Image. Doubleday.
Gallant, Mavis.
　xGallant, Mavis.
　　From the Fifteenth District: A Novella & Eight
　　Short Stories. Random.
　　Other Paris: Stories. Arno.
Gallant, Roy A.
　xGallant, Roy A.
　　illus. Earth's Changing Climate. Schol Bk Serv.
　　Exploring the Universe. Doubleday.
　　Fires in the Sky: The Birth & Death of Stars.
　　Schol Bk Serv.
　　Memory: How It Works & How to Improve It.
　　Schol Bk Serv.
Gallarati-Scotti, Tommaso, Conte, 1878-1966
　xGallarati-Scotti, Tommaso.
　　Life of Antonio Fogazzaro. Kennikat.
Gallatin, Albert, 1761-1849
　xGallatin, Albert.
　　ed. Right of the United States of America to
　　the Northeastern Boundary Claimed by
　　Them. Arno.
Gallatin, Judith E., 1942-
　xGallatin, Judith E.
　　Adolescence & Individuality: A Conceptual
　　Approach to Adolescent Psychology.
　　Har-Row.
Gallaudet College Library, Washington, D. C. *see*
　Gallaudet College, Washington, D.C. Edward Miner
　Gallaudet Memorial Library.
Gallaudet College, Washington, D.C. Edward Miner
Gallaudet Memorial Library.
　xGallaudet College Library, Washington, D. C.
　　Dictionary Catalog on Deafness & the Deaf. G
　　K Hall.
Gallaway, Francis, 1903-
　xGallaway, Francis.
　　Reason, Rule & Revolt in English Classicism.
　　Octagon.
　　Reason, Rule & Revolt in English Classicism.
　　U Pr of Ky.
Gallen, John.
　xGallen, John.
　　ed. Christians at Prayer. U of Notre Dame Pr.
Gallender, Carolyn N. *see* Gallender, Carolyn Newton.
Gallender, Carolyn Newton.
　xGallender, Carolyn N.
　　Dietary Problems & Diets for the Handicapped.
　　C C Thomas.
Gallender, Demos.
　xGallender, Demos.
　　Eating Handicaps: Illustrated Techniques for
　　Feeding Disorders. C C Thomas.
　　Teaching Eating & Toileting Skills to the
　　Multi-Handicapped in the School Setting. C
　　C Thomas.
Galler, Meyer.
　xGaller, Meyer.
　　ed. Soviet Prison Camp Speech: A Survivor's
　　Glossary. U of Wis Pr.
Gallery, Daniel V.
　xGallery, Daniel V.

Brink. Warner Bks.
Cap'n Fatso. Warner Bks.
Clear the Decks. Warner Bks.
Stand By-y-y Start Engines. Warner Bks.

Galli, C.
xGalli, C.
ed. Dietary Lipids & Postnatal Development.
Raven.

Galli, Nicholas, 1945-
xGalli, Nicholas.
Foundations & Principles of Health Education.
Wiley.

Gallichan, Walter M. *see* Gallichan, Walter Matthew.

Gallichan, Walter Matthew, 1861-1946
xGallichan, Walter M.
Women Under Polygamy. AMS Pr.

Gallico, Paul, 1897-
xGallico, Paul.
The Boy Who Invented the Bubble Gun.
Delacorte.
Honorable Cat. Crown.
The House That Wouldn't Go Away.
Delacorte.
Matilda. Berkley Pub.
The Poseidon Adventure. Dell.

Gallie, W. B., 1912-
xGallie, W. B.
Peirce & Pragmatism. Greenwood.

Gallienne, Richard Le. *see* Le Gallienne, Richard.

Gallier, James.
xGallier, James.
Autobiography of James Gallier, Architect. Da
Capo.

Galligan, Michael.
xGalligan, Michael.
God & Evil. Paulist Pr.

Galliher, John F.
xGalliher, John F.
Criminology: Power, Crime & Criminal Law.
Dorsey.

Gallimore. *see* Gallimore, Ronald.

Gallimore, Ronald.
xGallimore.
Culture, Behavior & Education: A Study of
Hawaiian-Americans. Sage.

Gallin, Bernard.
xGallin, Bernard.
Hsin Hsing, Taiwan: A Chinese Village in
Change. U of Cal Pr.

Gallin, John I.
xGallin, John I.
ed. Leukocyte Chemotaxis: Methods,
Physiology, & Clinical Implications. Raven.

Gallistel, C. R., 1941-
xGallistel, C. R.
The Organization of Action: A New Synthesis.
Halsted Pr.

Gallivan, C. E.
xGallivan, C. E.
A Nation Under God?. Word Bks.

Gallo, Joseph D.
xGallo, Joseph D.
Shaping College Writing: Paragraph & Essay.
HarBraceJ.

Gallo, Rose A. *see* Gallo, Rose Adrienne.

Gallo, Rose Adrienne.
xGallo, Rose A.
F. Scott Fitzgerald. Ungar.

Gallob, Edward.
xGallob, Edward.
illus. City Rocks, City Blocks & the Moon.
Scribner.

Galloway, Charles.
xGalloway, Charles G.
Psychology for Learning & Teaching. McGraw.

Galloway, Charles G. *see* Galloway, Charles.

Galloway, Charles M.
xGalloway, Charles M.

Silent Language in the Classroom. Phi Delta
Kappa.

Galloway, Dale. *see* Galloway, Dale E.

Galloway, Dale E.
xGalloway, Dale.
How to Feel Like a Somebody Again. Harvest
Hse.

Galloway, David. *see* Galloway, David D.

Galloway, David D.
xGalloway, David.
Edward Lewis Wallant. Twayne.
A Family Album: A Novel. HarBraceJ.
xGalloway, David D.
Absurd Hero in American Fiction: Updike,
Styron, Bellow, Salinger. U of Tex Pr.

Galloway, David M.
xGalloway, David M.
Case Studies in Classroom Management.
Longman.
Educating Slow-Learning & Maladjusted
Children: Integration or Segregation?.
Longman.

Galloway, George B. *see* Galloway, George Barnes.

Galloway, George Barnes.
xGalloway, George B.
History of the House of Representatives. T Y
Crowell.

Galloway, J. *see* Galloway, John Crozier.

Galloway, John.
xGalloway, John.
ed. Criminal Justice & the Burger Court. Facts
on File.
The Gulf of Tonkin Resolution. Fairleigh
Dickinson.

Galloway, John Crozier.
xGalloway, J.
Origins of Modern Art, 1905-1914. McGraw.

Galloway, Joseph, 1731-1803
xGalloway, Joseph.
The Claim of the American Loyalists Reviewed
& Maintained Upon Incontrovertible
Principles of Law & Justice. Irvington.
Letters to a Nobleman, on the Conduct of the
War in the Middle Colonies. Irvington.
A Reply to the Observations of Lieut. Gen. Sir
William Howe, on a Pamphlet, Entitled
"Letters to a Nobleman": In Which His
Misrepresentations Are Detected. Irvington.

Galloway, Joseph H.
xGalloway, Joseph H.
Farm Animal Health & Disease Control. Lea &
Febiger.

Galloway, L. Thomas.
xGalloway, L. Thomas.
Recognizing Foreign Governments: The
Practice of the United States. Am Enterprise.

Galloway, Robert L. *see* Galloway, Robert Lindsay.

Galloway, Robert Lindsay, 1842-1908
xGalloway, Robert L.
History of Coal Mining in Great Britain.
Kelley.

Gallup, Dick, 1939-
xGallup, Dick.
Where I Hang My Hat. Full Court NY.
Where I Hang My Hat. Ultramarine Pub.

Gallup, George. *see* Gallup, George Horace.

Gallup, George H. *see* Gallup, George Horace.

Gallup, George Horace.
xGallup, George.
Sophisticated Poll Watcher's Guide. Princeton
Opinion.
xGallup, George H.
ed. The Gallup Poll: Public Opinion, 1978.
Scholarly Res Inc.
Pulse of Democracy: The Public-Opinion Poll
& How It Works. Greenwood.

Gallwey, W. Timothy.
xGallwey, W. Timothy.

The Inner Game of Tennis. Bantam.
The Inner Game of Tennis. Random.
Inner Skiing. Bantam.
Inner Skiing. Random.
Inner Tennis: Playing the Game. Random.

Galper, Jeffrey. *see* Galper, Jeffry H.

Galper, Jeffry H., 1942-
xGalper, Jeffrey.
The Politics of Social Services. P-H.
Social Work Practice: A Radical Perspective.
P-H.

Galpern, A. N., 1939-
xGalpern, A. N.
The Religions of the People in
Sixteenth-Century Champagne. Harvard U
Pr.

Galpin, A. M. *see* Galpin, Alfred Maurice.

Galpin, Alfred Maurice.
xGalpin, A. M.
French Prose: An Intermediate Reader.
Macmillan.

Galpin, Francis W. *see* Galpin, Francis Williams.

Galpin, Francis Williams, 1858-1945
xGalpin, Francis W.
Music of the Sumerians & Their Immediate
Successors, the Babylonians and Assyrians.
Arno.
Music of the Sumerians & Their Immediate
Successors, the Babylonians & Assyrians.
Greenwood.
The Music of the Sumerians & Their
Immediate Successors, the Babylonians &
Assyrians. Intl Pubns Serv.

Galpin, John.
xGalpin, John.
A Handbook of Goss China. State Mutual Bk.

Galston, A. *see* Galston, Arthur William.

Galston, Arthur W. *see* Galston, Arthur William.

Galston, Arthur William.
xGalston, A.
Life of the Green Plant. P-H.
xGalston, Arthur W.
Control Mechanisms in Plant Development.
P-H.

Galsworthy, John, 1867-1933
xGalsworthy, John.
Author & Critic. Folcroft.
Captures. Kelley.
Captures. Scholarly.
Dark Flower. Scholarly.
End of the Chapter. Scribner.
Five Tales. Scholarly.
Fraternity. Scholarly.
Letters from John Galsworthy 1900-1932.
Scholarly.
Modern Comedy. Scribner.

Galt, John, 1779-1839
xGalt, John.
The Life of Lord Byron. Folcroft.
The Life of Lord Byron. R West.

Galton, Arthur H. *see* Galton, Arthur Howard.

Galton, Arthur Howard, 1852-1921
xGalton, Arthur H.
Church & State in France, 1300-1907. B
Franklin.

Galton, Francis, Sir, 1822-1911
xGalton, Francis.
Finger Prints. Da Capo.
Hereditary Genius: An Inquiry into Its Laws &
Consequences. Peter Smith.
Inquiries into Human Faculty & Its
Development. AMS Pr.
Memories of My Life. AMS Pr.
Natural Inheritance. AMS Pr.

Galton, Lawrence.
xGalton, Lawrence.

The Complete Book of Symptoms & What
They Can Mean. S&S.
Complete Medical, Fitness & Health Guide for
Men. S&S.
Don't Give up on an Aging Parent. Crown.
How Long Will I Live?: And 434 Other
Questions Your Doctor Doesn't Have Time
to Answer & You Can't Afford to Ask.
Macmillan.
Medical Advances. Penguin.
The Silent Disease: Hypertension. NAL.
Galton, Ray. see Galton, Raymond Percy.
Galton, Raymond Percy.
xGalton, Ray.
Hancock's Half Hour. Biblio Dist.

Galtung, Johan.
xGaltung, Johan.
Members of Two Worlds: A Development
Study of Three Villages in Western Sicily.
Columbia U Pr.
Theory & Methods of Social Research.
Columbia U Pr.
The True Worlds: A Transnational Perspective.
Free Pr.

Galub, Jack.
xGalub, Jack.
The U. S. Air Force Academy Fitness Program
for Women. P-H.

Galus, Z. see Galus, Zbigniew.

Galus, Zbigniew.
xGalus, Z.
Fundamentals of Electrochemical Analysis.
Halsted Pr.

Galvin, Brendan.
xGalvin, Brendan.
No Time for Good Reasons. U of Pittsburgh
Pr.

Galvin, Patrick J.
xGalvin, Patrick J.
Finishing off. Structures Pub.

Galvin, Thomas J.
xGalvin, Thomas J.
Current Problems in Reference Service.
Bowker.

Gamage, J. R. see Gamage, James R.

Gamage, James R.
xGamage, J. R.
A Comprehensive Guide to the
English-Language Literature on Cannabis
(Marihuana). Stash.

Gamarnikow, Michael.
xGamarnikow, Michael.
Economic Reforms in Eastern Europe. Wayne
St U Pr.

Gambaccini, Paul.
xGambaccini, Paul.
The Rock Critic's Choice: The Top 200
Albums. Music Sales.

Gambaccini, Peter.
xGambaccini, Peter.
Bruce Springsteen. Music Sales.

Gamble, Andrew.
xGamble, Andrew.
Capitalism in Crisis: Inflation & the State.
Humanities.

Gamble, David P.
xGamble, David P.
A General Bibliography of the Gambia, up to
31 December 1977. G K Hall.

Gamble, Felton O.
xGamble, Felton O.
Clinical Foot Roentgenology. Krieger.

Gamble, Geoffrey.
xGamble, Geoffrey.
Wikchamni Grammar. U of Cal Pr.

Gamble, James L. see Gamble, James Lawder.

Gamble, James Lawder, 1883-
xGamble, James L.
Chemical Anatomy, Physiology & Pathology of
Extracellular Fluid: A Lecture Syllabus.
Harvard U Pr.

Gamble, John K. see Gamble, John King.

Gamble, John King.
xGamble, John K.
Global Marine Attributes. Ballinger Pub.
Marine Policy: A Comparative Approach.
Lexington Bks.

Gamble, Sidney D. see Gamble, Sidney David.

Gamble, Sidney David, 1890-
xGamble, Sidney D.
North China Villages: Social, Political &
Economic Activities Before 1933. U of Cal
Pr.

Gamble, Teri K. see Gamble, Teri Kwai.

Gamble, Teri Kwai.
xGamble, Teri K.
ed. Intermedia: Communication & Society.
Moore Pub Co.

Gamble, W. see Gamble, William.

Gamble, William, 1864-1933
xGamble, W.
Music Engraving & Printing: Historical &
Technical Treatise. Da Capo.
xGamble, William.
Music Engraving & Printing: Historical &
Technical Treatise. Arno.

Gambling, Trevor.
xGambling, Trevor.
A One Year Accounting Course. Pergamon.
Societal Accounting. Allen Unwin.

Gambordella, Theodore L.
xGambordella, Theodore L.
Seven Days to Self-Defense. Contemp Bks.

Gambrell, Herbert. see Gambrell, Herbert Pickens.

Gambrell, Herbert Pickens, 1898-
xGambrell, Herbert.
Anson Jones: The Last President of Texas. U
of Tex Pr.

Gambril, Donald L.
xGambril, Donald L.
Swimming. Goodyear.

Gambrill, Bessie L. see Gambrill, Bessie Lee.

Gambrill, Bessie Lee, 1883-
xGambrill, Bessie L.
College Achievement & Vocational Efficiency.
AMS Pr.

Gambs, John S. see Gambs, John Sake.

Gambs, John Sake, 1899-
xGambs, John S.
Decline of the I. W. W. Russell.

Gamer, Robert E., 1938-
xGamer, Robert E.
The Politics of Urban Development in
Singapore. Cornell U Pr.

Gamkrelidze, R. V.
xGamkrelidze, R. V.
Principles of Optimal Control Theory. Plenum
Pub.

Gammage, Allen Z.
xGammage, Allen Z.
Basic Criminal Law. McGraw.

Gammage, B. see Gammage, Bill.

Gammage, Bill.
xGammage, B.
An Australian in the First World War.
Cambridge U Pr.

Gammage, R. C. see Gammage, Robert George.

Gammage, Robert George, 1815-1888
xGammage, R. C.
History of the Chartist Movement. Carrier
Pigeon.

Gammans, Harold. see Gammans, Harold Winsor.

Gammans, Harold Winsor, 1885-
xGammans, Harold.
Lincoln Names & Epithets. Branden.

Gammill, Stephen L. see Gammill, Stephen Lane.

Gammill, Stephen Lane.
xGammill, Stephen L.
A Programmed Introduction to Upper
Gastrointestinal Radiology. Little.

Gammond, Peter.
xGammond, Peter.
ed. Duke Ellington: His Life & Music. Da
Capo.
The Illustrated Encyclopedia of Recorded
Opera. Crown.
Musical Instruments in Color. Macmillan.

Gammons, Homer P.
xGammons, Homer P.
Common Sense in Guidance. P-H.

Gamow, George.
xGamow, George.
Moon. Abelard.

Gamson, William A.
xGamson, William A.
Power & Discontent. Dorsey.
The Strategy of Social Protest. Dorsey.

Gamst, F. C. see Gamst, Frederick C.

Gamst, Frederick C.
xGamst, F. C.
Peasants in a Complex Society. HR&W.
xGamst, Frederick C.
Ideas of Culture: Sources & Uses. HR&W.

Gandhi, Mohandas K. see Gandhi, Mohandas
Karamchand.

Gandhi, Mohandas Karamchand, 1869-1948
xGandhi, Mohandas K.
Autobiography: The Story of My Experiments
with Truth. Beacon Pr.
Gandhi Reader: A Source Book of His Life &
Writings. AMS Pr.
Swaraj in One Year. AMS Pr.

Gandy, D. Ross. see Gandy, Daniel Ross.

Gandy, Daniel Ross, 1935-
xGandy, D. Ross.
Marx & History: From Primitive Society to the
Communist Future. U of Tex Pr.

Gandz, Solomon, 1887-1954
xGandz, Solomon.
Studies in Hebrew Astronomy & Mathematics.
Ktav.

Gane, C. see Gane, Christopher P.

Gane, Christopher P.
xGane, C.
Structured Systems Analysis: Tools &
Techniques. P-H.

Gane, Margaret D. see Gane, Margaret Drury.

Gane, Margaret Drury.
xGane, Margaret D.
Parade on an Empty Street. St Martin.
Parade on an Empty Street. G K Hall.

Gangel, Kenneth O.
xGangel, Kenneth O.
The Gospel & the Gay. Nelson.
Leadership for Church Education. Moody.
Understanding Teaching. Evang Tchr.

Gangemi, Kenneth, 1937-
xGangemi, Kenneth.
The Volcanoes from Puebla. Merrimack Bk
Serv.

Ganguli, B. N. see Ganguli, Birendranath.

Ganguli, Birendranath.
xGanguli, B. N.
Levels of Living in India: An Inter-State
Profile. Verry.

Ganguli, H. C. see Ganguli, Harish Chandra.

Ganguli, Harish Chandra, 1924-
xGanguli, H. C.
Some Thoughts on Planning in India. Asia.
Structure & Processes of Organization. Asia.

Ganguly, D. K. see Ganguly, Dilip Kumar.

Ganguly, Dilip Kumar, 1939-
xGanguly, D. K.

Aspects of Ancient Indian Administration.
South Asia Bks.
Ganin, Zvi.
xGanin, Zvi.
Truman, American Jewry, & Israel, 1945-1948.
Holmes & Meier.
Ganivet, Angel, 1865-1898
xGanivet, Angel.
Spain: An Interpretation. AMS Pr.
Gann, Ernest K. see Gann, Ernest Kellogg.
Gann, Ernest Kellog, 1910-
xGann, Ernest K.
Band of Brothers. S&S.
Gann, Ernest Kellogg, 1910-
xGann, Ernest K.
Fate Is the Hunter. S&S.
A Hostage to Fortune. Knopf.
Twilight for the Gods. PB.
Gann, L. H. see Gann, Lewis H.
Gann, Lewis. see Gann, Lewis H.
Gann, Lewis H.
xGann, L. H.
ed. African Proconsuls: European Governors in
Africa. Free Pr.
Burden of Empire: An Appraisal of Western
Colonialism in Africa South of the Sahara.
Hoover Inst Pr.
History of Northern Rhodesia: Early Days to
1953. Humanities.
History of Southern Rhodesia: Early Days to
1934. Humanities.
The Rulers of British Africa, 1870-1914.
Stanford U Pr.
South Africa: War, Revolution, or Peace?.
Hoover Inst Pr.
xGann, Lewis.
Guerrillas in History. Hoover Inst Pr.
xGann, Lewis H.
White Settlers in Tropical Africa. Greenwood.
Gann, Thomas. see Gann, Thomas William Francis.
Gann, Thomas William Francis, 1867-1938
xGann, Thomas.
In an Unknown Land. Arno.
Gannett, Ernest.
xGannett, Ernest.
Tanker Performance & Cost: Measurement,
Analysis & Management. Cornell Maritime.
Gannett, Henry, 1846-1914
xGannett, Henry.
A Gazetteer of Virginia & West Virginia.
Genealog Pub.
A Geographic Dictionary of Connecticut &
Rhode Island. Genealog Pub.
A Geographic Dictionary of New Jersey.
Genealog Pub.
Origin of Certain Place Names in the United
States. Gale.
The Origin of Certain Place Names in the
United States. Genealog Pub.
Gannon, Franklin R. see Gannon, Franklin Reid.
Gannon, Franklin Reid.
xGannon, Franklin R.
British Press & Germany, 1936-1939. Oxford U
Pr.
Gannon, Martin J.
xGannon, Martin J.
Organizational Behavior: A Managerial &
Organizational Perspective. Little.
Gannon, Robert.
xGannon, Robert.
Great Survival Adventures. Random.
How to Raise & Train an Irish Setter. TFH
Pubns.
Gannon, Robert I. see Gannon, Robert Ignatius.
Gannon, Robert Ignatius, 1893-
xGannon, Robert I.
After More Black Coffee. FS&G.
Gannon, Tom, 1944-
xGannon, Tom.

A Guide to Newport Rhode Island. Globe
Pequot.
Ganong, Joan. see Ganong, Joan M.
Ganong, Joan M.
xGanong, Joan.
jt. auth. Cases in Nursing Management. Aspen
Systems.
jt. auth. Nursing Management. Aspen Systems.
Ganong, Warren. see Ganong, Joan M.
Ganong, William F.
xGanong, William F.
The Nervous System. Lange.
Review of Medical Physiology. Lange.
Gans, Benjamin J.
xGans, Benjamin J.
Atlas of Oral Surgery. Mosby.
Gans, Eric L. see Gans, Eric Lawrence.
Gans, Eric Lawrence, 1941-
xGans, Eric L.
The Discovery of Illusion: Flaubert's Early
Works, 1835-1837. U of Cal Pr.
Gans, Herbert J.
xGans, Herbert J.
Deciding What's News: A Study of CBS
Evening News, NBC Nightly News,
Newsweek & Time. Pantheon.
Deciding What's News: A Study of CBS
Evening News, NBC Nightly News,
Newsweek & Time. Random.
More Equality. Pantheon.
More Equality. Random.
People & Plans: Essays on Urban Problems &
Solutions. Basic.
Gans, Roma.
xGans, Roma.
Caves. T Y Crowell.
Hummingbirds in the Garden. T Y Crowell.
Icebergs. T Y Crowell.
Gans, Stephen L.
xGans, Stephen L.
Surgical Pediatrics. Grune.
Gansberg, Judith M.
xGansberg, Judith M.
Stalag: U.S.A.: The Remarkable Story of
German POWs in America. T Y Crowell.
Ganshof, F. L. see Ganshof, Francois Louis.
Ganshof, Francois Louis, 1895-
xGanshof, F. L.
Carolingians & the Frankish Monarchy: Studies
in Carolingian History. Cornell U Pr.
Gant, Jonathan.
xGant, Jonathan.
Long Vendetta. Bouregy.
Gantenbein, James W. see Gantenbein, James Watson.
Gantenbein, James Watson, 1900-
xGantenbein, James W.
ed. The Evolution of Our Latin-American
Policy: A Documentary Record. Octagon.
Ganter. see Ganter, Grace.
Ganter, Grace.
xGanter.
Retrieval from Limbo: The Intermediary Group
Treatment of Inaccessible Children. Child
Welfare.
xGanter, Grace.
Human Behavior & the Social Environment: A
Perspective for Social Work Practice.
Columbia U Pr.
Ganton, Doris L., 1931-
xGanton, Doris L.
Breaking & Training the Driving Horse.
Wilshire.

Drive on: Training & Showing the Advanced
Driving Horse. A S Barnes.
Gantos, Jack.
xGantos, Jack.
Aunt Bernice. HM.
Fair-Weather Friends. HM.
Greedy Greeny. Doubleday.
The Perfect Pal. HM.
Willy's Raiders. Parents.
Worse Than Rotten, Ralph. HM.
Gantt, H. L. see Gantt, Henry Laurence.
Gantt, Henry Laurence, 1861-1919
xGantt, H. L.
Industrial Leadership. Hive Pub.
Organizing for Work. Hive Pub.
Work, Wages & Profits. Hive Pub.
Gantz, Charlotte O. see Gantz, Charlotte Orr.
Gantz, Charlotte Orr.
xGantz, Charlotte O.
A Naturalist in Southern Florida. U of Miami
Pr.
Ganz, A. W.
xGanz, A. W.
Berlioz in London. Hyperion Conn.
Ganz, Margaret.
xGanz, Margaret.
The Enduring Voice: Concerns in Literature
Present & Past. Macmillan.
Ganz, Raffael, 1923-
xGanz, Raffael.
ed. George Mikes Introduces Switzerland.
Transatlantic.
Ganzel, Dewey, 1927-
xGanzel, Dewey.
Mark Twain Abroad: The Cruise of the Quaker
City. U of Chicago Pr.
Ganzer, Nick.
xGanzer, Nick.
How to Prepare Rig & Fish Natural Baits for
Great Lakes Salmon & Trout. Merganzer Pr.
GAP Ad Hoc Committee. see Ad Hoc Committee on the
Report of the Joint Commission on the Mental Health
of Children.
GAP Committee on Adolescence. see Group for the
Advancement of Psychiatry. Committee on
Adolescence.
GAP Committee on Aging. see Group for the
Advancement of Psychiatry. Committee on Aging.
GAP Committee on Child Psychiatry. see Group for the
Advancement of Psychiatry. Committee on Child
Psychiatry.
GAP Committee on Family. see Group for the
Advancement of Psychiatry. Committee on the
Family.
GAP Committee on Governmental Agencies. see Group
for the Advancement of Psychiatry. Committee of
Governmental Agencies.
GAP Committee on International Relations. see Group
for the Advancement of Psychiatry. Committee on
International Relations.
GAP Committee on Med. Education. see Group for the
Advancement of Psychiatry. Committee on Medical
Education.
GAP Committee on Medical Education. see Group for
the Advancement of Psychiatry. Committee on
Medical Education.
GAP Committee on Mental Health Services. see Group
for the Advancement of Psychiatry. Committee on
Mental Health Services.
GAP Committee on Mental Retardation. see Group for
the Advancement of Psychiatry. Committee on Mental
Retardation.
GAP Committee on Preventive Psychiatry. see Group for
the Advancement of Psychiatry. Committee on
Preventive Psychiatry.
GAP Committee on Psychiatry & Religion. see Group
for the Advancement of Psychiatry. Committee on
Psychiatry and Religion.
GAP Committee on Psychiatry & Social Work. see

The Theory of Speech & Language.
Greenwood.
Gardiner, Alfred G. *see* Gardiner, Alfred George.
Gardiner, Alfred George, 1865-1946
xGardiner, Alfred G.
Many Furrows. Arno.
Many Furrows. Kennikat.
Portraits & Portents. Arno.
Portraits & Portents. R West.
Gardiner, C. Harvey. *see* Gardiner, Clinton Harvey.
Gardiner, Clinton H. *see* Gardiner, Clinton Harvey.
Gardiner, Clinton Harvey.
xGardiner, C. Harvey.
Naval Power in the Conquest of Mexico.
Greenwood.
xGardiner, Clinton H.
Martin Lopez. Conquistador Citizen of Mexico.
Greenwood.
Gardiner, G. F. *see* Gardiner, George Frederick.
Gardiner, George E.
xGardiner, George E.
Corinthian Catastrophe. Kregel.
Gardiner, George Frederick.
xGardiner, G. F.
Greenhouse Gardening. Chem Pub.
Gardiner, George H.
xGardiner, George H.
How I Sold a Million Dollars of Real Estate in
One Year. P-H.
Gardiner, Harold C. *see* Gardiner, Harold Charles.
Gardiner, Harold Charles, 1904-
xGardiner, Harold C.
ed. Fifty Years of the American Novel,
1900-1950: A Christian Appraisal. Gordian.
Gardiner, Harry N. *see* Gardiner, Harry Norman.
Gardiner, Harry Norman, 1855-1927
xGardiner, Harry N.
ed. Jonathan Edwards, a Retrospect. AMS Pr.
Gardiner, James J.
xGardiner, James J.
ed. Quest for a Black Theology. Pilgrim NY.
Gardiner, John A.
xGardiner, John A.
ed. Crime & Criminal Justice: Issues in Public
Policy Analysis. Heath.
Politics of Corruption: Organized Crime in an
American City. Russell Sage.
ed. Public Law & Public Policy. Praeger.
ed. Theft of the City: Readings on Corruption
in Urban America. Ind U Pr.
Gardiner, Leslie, 1921-
xGardiner, Leslie.
Curtain Calls: Travels in Albania, Romania &
Bulgaria. Biblio Dist.
Gardiner, M. James.
xGardiner, M. James.
Program Evaluation in Church Organization.
Anna Pub.
Gardiner, Mary S. *see* Gardiner, Mary Summerfield.
Gardiner, Mary Summerfield.
xGardiner, Mary S.
Principles of General Biology. Macmillan.
Gardiner, Muriel, 1901-
xGardiner, Muriel.
The Deadly Innocents: Portraits of Children
Who Kill. Basic.
Gardiner, Patrick.
xGardiner, Patrick.
Nature of Historical Explanation. Oxford U Pr.
Gardiner, Patrick. *see* Gardiner, Patrick L.
Gardiner, Patrick L., 1922-
xGardiner, Patrick.
ed. Nineteenth-Century Philosophy. Free Pr.
Gardiner, Samuel R. *see* Gardiner, Samuel Rawson.
Gardiner, Samuel Rawson, 1829-1902
xGardiner, Samuel R.

The Thirty Years' War: 1618-1648. Arden Lib.
The Thirty Years' War, 1618-1648. Haskell.
The Thirty Years' War: 1618-1648. Norwood
Edns.
Gardiner, Stephen.
xGardiner, Stephen.
Letters of Stephen Gardiner. Greenwood.
Obedience in Church & State: Three Political
Tracts. Greenwood.
Gardiner, W. C. *see* Gardiner, William Cecil.
Gardiner, W. Lambert.
xGardiner, W. Lambert.
Psychology: A Story of a Search. Brooks-Cole.
The Psychology of Teaching. Brooks-Cole.
Gardiner, William Cecil, 1933-
xGardiner, W. C.
Rates & Mechanisms of Chemical Reactions.
Benjamin-Cummings.
Gardiol, Rita M. *see* Gardiol, Rita Mazzetti.
Gardiol, Rita Mazzetti.
xGardiol, Rita M.
Ramon Gomez De la Serna. Twayne.
Gardner. *see* Gardner, Henry Alfred.
Gardner, Alfred L.
xGardner, Alfred L.
The Systematics of the Genus Didelphis
(Marsupialia : Didelphidae) in North &
Middle America. Tex Tech Pr.
Gardner, Allen H.
xGardner, Allen H.
A Primer on Planning an Estate. Lerner Law.
Gardner, Alvin F.
xGardner, Alvin F.
ed. Dental Examination Review Book. Med
Exam.
Pathology of Oral Manifestations of Systematic
Diseases. Hafner.
Synopsis of Pathology for the Allied Health
Professions. C C Thomas.
Gardner, Bernard.
xGardner, Bernard.
ed. Basic Surgery: A Symptom Oriented
Approach. ACC.
Gardner, Bruce. *see* Gardner, Bruce L.
Gardner, Bruce L.
xGardner, Bruce.
Optimal Stockpiling of Grain. Lexington Bks.
Gardner, Carl, 1931-
xGardner, Carl.
Andrew Young: A Biography. Sterling.
Gardner, Charles S. *see* Gardner, Charles Sidney.
Gardner, Charles Sidney, 1900-
xGardner, Charles S.
Chinese Traditional Historiography. Harvard U
Pr.
Gardner, Christina.
xGardner, Christina.
Effective Typesetting with IBM Tape
Composer. North Am Pub Co.
Gardner, David C.
xGardner, David C.
Careers & Disabilities: A Career Education
Approach. Greylock Pubs.
Gardner, David P.
xGardner, David P.
The California Oath Controversy. U of Cal Pr.
Gardner, E. A. *see* Gardner, Ernest Arthur.
Gardner, E. E. *see* Gardner, Emelyn Elizabeth.
Gardner, E. Stanley. *see* Gardner, Erle Stanley.
Gardner, Earl S. *see* Gardner, Erle Stanley.
Gardner, Edmund G. *see* Gardner, Edmund Garratt.
Gardner, Edmund Garratt, 1869-1935
xGardner, Edmund G.

Arthurian Legend in Italian Literature.
Octagon.
The Arthurian Legend in Italian Literature. R
West.
Dante's Ten Heavens: A Study of the Paradiso.
Arno.
Italian Literature. Folcroft.
Italian Literature. Norwood Edns.
Italian Literature. R West.
Gardner, Eldon J. *see* Gardner, Eldon John.
Gardner, Eldon John, 1909-
xGardner, Eldon J.
History of Biology. Burgess.
Principles of Genetics. Wiley.
Gardner, Elizabeth F. *see* Gardner, Elizabeth Frances.
Gardner, Elizabeth Frances.
xGardner, Elizabeth F.
Introduction to Literary Japanese. Far Eastern
Pubns.
Gardner, Emelyn Elizabeth.
xGardner, E. E.
Folklore from the Schoharie Hills, New York.
Arno.
Gardner, Erle S. *see* Gardner, Erle Stanley.
Gardner, Erle Stanley.
xGardner, E. Stanley.
The Case of the Careless Cupid. G K Hall.
xGardner, Earl S.
The Case of the Sulky Girl. Amereon Ltd.
The Case of the Velvet Claws. Amereon Ltd.
xGardner, Erle S.
The Case of the Bigamous Spouse. PB.
The Case of the Counterfeit Eye. Amereon
Ltd.
Case of the Counterfeit Eye. PB.
The Case of the Crooked Candle. Garland Pub.
The Case of the Curious Bride. Amereon Ltd.
Case of the Curious Bride. PB.
The Case of the Dangerous Dowager. Amereon
Ltd.
The Case of the Drowning Duck. Amereon
Ltd.
The Case of the Fabulous Fake. Morrow.
The Case of the Fenced-in Woman. Morrow.
Case of the Grinning Gorilla. PB.
The Case of the Haunted Husband. Amereon
Ltd.
The Case of the Horrified Heirs. Morrow.
The Case of the Lonely Heiress. PB.
Case of the Long Legged Models. PB.
The Case of the Lucky Legs. Amereon Ltd.
The Case of the Lucky Legs. PB.
Case of the Moth-Eaten Mink. PB.
The Case of the Negligent Nymph. PB.
The Case of the Nervous Accomplice. PB.
Case of the One-Eyed Witness. PB.
The Case of the Perjured Parrot. Amereon Ltd.
The Case of the Phantom Fortune. PB.
The Case of the Postponed Murder. G K Hall.
The Case of the Postponed Murder. Morrow.
The Case of the Postponed Murder. PB.
The. Case of the Queenly Contestant. Morrow.
The Case of the Shoplifter's Shoe. Amereon
Ltd.
The Case of the Shoplifter's Shoe. PB.
The Case of the Sleepwalker's Niece. Amereon
Ltd.
The Case of the Sleepwalker's Niece. PB.
The Case of the Stuttering Bishop. Amereon
Ltd.
The Case of the Substitute Face. Amereon Ltd.
Case of the Sun Bather's Diary. PB.
The Case of the Vagabond Virgin. PB.
Hovering Over Baja. Morrow.
Gardner, Ernest A. *see* Gardner, Ernest Arthur.
Gardner, Ernest Arthur, 1862-1939
xGardner, E. A.

Art of Greece. Cooper Sq.
xGardner, Ernest A.
Ancient Athens. Haskell.
Gardner, Floyd M. see Gardner, Floyd Martin.
Gardner, Floyd Martin, 1929-
xGardner, Floyd M.
Phaselock Techniques. Wiley.
Gardner, G. Peabody. see Gardner, George Peabody.
Gardner, George Peabody.
xGardner, G. Peabody.
Turkish Delight: A Cruise Along the Southern
Coast of Turkey. Peabody Mus Salem.
Gardner, Gerald. see Gardner, Gerald C.
Gardner, Gerald C.
xGardner, Gerald.
Who's in Charge Here?: 1980. Bantam.
Gardner, Helen. see Gardner, Helen Louise.
Gardner, Helen Louise, Dame.
xGardner, Helen.
The Composition of Four Quartets. Oxford U
Pr.
Noble Moor. Folcroft.
Reading of Paradise Lost. Oxford U Pr.
Religion & Literature. Oxford U Pr.
Gardner, Henry Alfred.
xGardner.
Paint Testing Manual: Physical & Chemical
Examination of Paints, Varnishes, Lacquers,
& Colors. ASTM.
Gardner, Horace J. see Gardner, Horace John.
Gardner, Horace John, 1895-
xGardner, Horace J.
Let's Celebrate Christmas: Parties, Plays,
Legends, Carols, Poetry, Stories. Ronald Pr.
Gardner, Howard.
xGardner, Howard.
Artful Scribbles: The Significance of Children's
Drawings. Basic.
The Arts & Human Development: A
Psychological Study of the Artistic Process.
Wiley.
Developmental Psychology: An Introduction.
Little.
The Quest for Mind: Piaget, Levi-Strauss, &
the Structuralist Movement. Knopf.
Gardner, Hugh.
xGardner, Hugh.
Children of Prosperity: Thirteen Modern
American Communes. St Martin.
Gardner, Isabella.
xGardner, Isabella.
Looking Glass: New Poems. U of Chicago Pr.
Gardner, James. see Gardner, James B.
Gardner, James B.
xGardner, James.
Illustrated Soccer Dictionary for Young People.
Harvey.
xGardner, James B.
Computerized Running Training Programs.
Tafnews.
Gardner, James E.
xGardner, James E.
Paraprofessional Work with Troubled Children.
Halsted Pr.
Safety Training for the Supervisor. A-W.
Training the New Supervisor. Am Mgmt.
Gardner, Jeanne.
xGardner, Jeanne.
A Grain of Mustard. Trident.
Gardner, John, 1905-
xGardner, John.
Building Classic Small Craft. Intl Marine.
Dory Book. Intl Marine.
The Werewolf Trace. G K Hall.
xGardner, John C.
The Resurrection. Ballantine.
Gardner, John. see Gardner, John Champlin.
Gardner, John C. see Gardner, John Champlin.
Gardner, John Champlin, 1933-
xGardner, John.

Freddy's Book. Knopf.
Gudgekin the Thistle Girl & Other Tales.
Bantam.
In the Suicide Mountains. HM.
Vlemk the Box-Painter. Lord John.
xGardner, John C.
The Complete Works of the Gawain Poet: In a
Modern English Version with a Critical
Introduction. U of Chicago Pr.
Grendel. Ballantine.
Grendel. Knopf.
Gudgekin the Thistle Girl & Other Tales.
Knopf.
In the Suicide Mountains. Knopf.
October Light. Ballantine.
October Light. Knopf.
On Moral Fiction. Basic.
The Sunlight Dialogues. Ballantine.
The Sunlight Dialogues. Knopf.
Gardner, John E.
xGardner, John.
The Nostradamus Traitor. Doubleday.
The Revenge of Moriarty. Berkley Pub.
Gardner, John F. see Gardner, John Fentress.
Gardner, John Fentress.
xGardner, John F.
The Experience of Knowledge: Essays on
American Education. Waldorf Pr.
Melville's Vision of America: A New
Interpretation of Moby Dick. Myrin Institute.
Gardner, John W. see Gardner, John William.
Gardner, John William, 1912-
xGardner, John.
Morale. Norton.
xGardner, John W.
Excellence: Can We Be Equal & Excellent Too.
Har-Row
In Common Cause. Norton.
Morale. Norton.
Gardner, Joseph M.
xGardner, Joseph M.
How to Sell Your Own Home Without a Real
Estate Agent & Save Thousands of Dollars.
Exposition.
Gardner, Judith K. see Gardner, Judith Krieger.
Gardner, Judith Krieger.
xGardner, Judith K.
ed. Readings in Developmental Psychology.
Little.
Gardner, K. L.
xGardner, K. L.
Programmed Vector Algebra. Oxford U Pr.
Gardner, Kenneth D.
xGardner, Kenneth D.
ed. Cystic Diseases of the Kidney. Wiley.
Gardner, Lloyd C., 1934-
xGardner, Lloyd C.
Architects of Illusion: Men & Ideas in
American Foreign Policy, 1941-1949. New
Viewpoints.
ed. The Great Nixon Turnaround: Americas
New Foreign Policy in the Post-Liberal Era.
New Viewpoints.
Imperial America: American Foreign Policy
Since 1898. HarBraceJ.
Looking Backward: A Reintroduction to
American History. McGraw.
ed. Origins of the Cold War. Wiley.
Gardner, Lucille.
xGardner, Lucille.
There Is Hope. Cook.
Gardner, Lytt I.
xGardner, Lytt I.
ed. Endocrine & Genetic Diseases of
Childhood & Adolescence. Saunders.
Gardner, Martin, 1914-
xGardner, Martin.

Codes, Ciphers, & Secret Writing. Archway.
Codes, Ciphers & Secret Writing. PB.
Codes, Ciphers & Secret Writing. S&S.
Fads & Fallacies in the Name of Science.
Dover.
The Flight of Peter Fromm. W Kaufmann.
The Incredible Dr. Matrix. Scribner.
Mathematics, Magic, & Mystery. Dover.
Mathematics, Magic & Mystery. Gannon.
Mathematics, Magic & Mystery. Peter Smith.
Perplexing Puzzles & Tantalizing Teasers.
Archway.
Perplexing Puzzles & Tantalizing Teasers. PB.
Space Puzzles: Curious Questions & Answers
About the Solar System. Archway.
Space Puzzles: Curious Questions & Answers
About the Solar System. PB.
Gardner, Mary A.
xGardner, Mary A.
The Press of Latin America: A Tentative &
Selected Bibliography in Spanish &
Portuguese. U of Tex Pr.
Gardner, Mary S. see Gardner, Mary Sewall.
Gardner, Mary Sewall.
xGardner, Mary S.
Public Health Nursing. Arno.
Gardner, Mercedes.
xGardner, Mercedes.
Scooter & the Magic Star. Dawne-Leigh.
Gardner, Paul, 1930-
xGardner, Paul.
The Simplest Game: The Intelligent
American's Guide to the World of Soccer.
Little.
Gardner, Paul F. see Gardner, Paul Vickers.
Gardner, Paul Vickers, 1908-
xGardner, Paul F.
Glass of Frederick Carder. Crown.
Gardner, Philip.
xGardner, Philip.
ed. E. M. Forster: The Critical Heritage.
Routledge & Kegan.
Gardner, R. P. see Gardner, Robin P.
Gardner, Richard. see Gardner, Richard A.
Gardner, Richard A.
xGardner, Richard.
The Parents Book About Divorce. Bantam.
xGardner, Richard A.
Dr. Gardner's Stories About the Real World.
Creative Therapeutics.
MBD: The Family Book About Minimal Brain
Dysfunction. Aronson.
The Objective Diagnosis of Minimal Brain
Dysfunction. Creative Therapeutics.
Psychotherapeutic Approaches to the Resistant
Child. Aronson.
Therapeutic Communication with Children:
The Mutual Storytelling Technique in Child
Psychotherapy. Aronson.
Gardner, Riley W.
xGardner, Riley W.
Cognitive Control: A Study of Individual
Consistencies in Cognitive Behavior. Intl
Univs Pr.
Personality Development at Preadolescence:
Explorations of Structure Formation. U of
Wash Pr.
Gardner, Robert.
xGardner, Robert.
This Is the Way It Works: A Collection of
Machines. Doubleday.
Gardner, Robin P.
xGardner, R. P.
Radioisotope Measurement Applications in
Engineering. Krieger.
Gardner, Sarah M. see Gardner, Sarah M. H.
Gardner, Sarah M. H.
xGardner, Sarah M.

Quaker Idyls. Arno.

Gardner, Sheldon.
xGardner, Sheldon.
The Care & Cultivation of Parents. Messner.

Gardner, Thomas J.
xGardner, Thomas J.
Criminal Law. West Pub.
Principles & Cases of the Law of Arrest,
Search, & Seizure. McGraw.

Gardner, W. H.
xGardner, W. H.
Some Thoughts on the Mayor of Casterbridge.
Folcroft.

Gardner, Wayland Downing, 1928-
xGardner, Wyland.
Government Finance: National, State & Local.
P-H.

Gardner, William.
xGardner, William.
Chemical Synonyms & Trade Names: A
Dictionary & Commercial Handbook. Intl
Pubns Serv.

Gardner, William I.
xGardner, William I.
Children with Learning & Behavior Problems:
A Behavior Management Approach. Allyn.
Learning & Behavior Characteristics of
Exceptional Children & Youth: A Humanistic
Behavioral Approach. Allyn.

Gardner, Wyland. see Gardner, Wayland Downing.

Gardner-Loulan, JoAnn.
xGardner-Loulan, JoAnn.
Period. New Glide.

Garduk, Edith L. see Garduk, Edith Levitov.

Garduk, Edith Levitov.
xGarduk, Edith L.
Immediate Effects on Patients of
Psychoanalytic Interpretations. Intl Univs Pr.

Gardyne, Alexander.
xGardyne, Alexander.
A Theatre of Scottish Worthies, & the Lyf,
Doings & Deathe of William Elphinston,
Bishop of Aberdee. Johnson Repr.

Gare, Fran.
xGare, Fran.
Dr. Atkins' Diet Cook Book. Bantam.

Gareau, Frederick H. see Gareau, Frederick Henry.

Gareau, Frederick Henry.
xGareau, Frederick H.
The Cold War, 1947-67: A Quantitative Study.
U of Denver Intl.

Garelick, May.
xGarelick, May.
About Owls. Schol Bk Serv.
Down to the Beach. Schol Bk Serv.
The Tremendous Tree Book. Schol Bk Serv.

Garfield, Brian. see Garfield, Brian Wynne.

Garfield, Brian Wynne, 1939-
xGarfield, Brian.
Hit. Macmillan.
Hopscotch. Fawcett.
Hopscotch. M Evans.
Line of Succession. Delacorte.
Line of Succession. Fawcett.
Valley of the Shadow. Belmont-Tower.
Wild Times. Dell.
Wild Times. S&S.

Garfield, Charles A.
xGarfield, Charles A.
Psychosocial Care of the Dying Patient.
McGraw.
ed. Stress & Survival: The Emotional Realities
of Life Threatening Illness. Mosby.

Garfield, David.
xGarfield, David.
A Player's Place: The Story of the Actors
Studio. Macmillan.

Garfield, Eugene.
xGarfield, Eugene.

Citation Indexing: Its Theory & Application in
Science, Technology & Humanities. Wiley.

Garfield, James A. see Garfield, James Abram.

Garfield, James Abram.
xGarfield, James A.
Works of James Abram Garfield. Arno.

Garfield, Leon.
xGarfield, Leon.
The Apprentices. Viking Pr.
The Confidence Man. Viking Pr.
The Ghost Downstairs. Pantheon.
The Golden Shadow. Pantheon.
Restless Ghost: Three Stories. Pantheon.
The Sound of Coaches. Popular Lib.
Strange Affair of Adelaide Harris. Pantheon.
ed. Strange Fish & Other Stories. Lothrop.

Garfield, Patricia. see Garfield, Patricia L.

Garfield, Patricia L.
xGarfield, Patricia.
Pathway to Ecstasy: The Way of the Dream
Mandala. HR&W.

Garfield, Paul. see Garfield, Paul J.

Garfield, Paul J.
xGarfield, Paul.
Public Utility Economics. P-H.

Garfinkel, Alan.
xGarfinkel, Alan.
Designs for Foreign Language Teacher
Education. Newbury Hse.

Garfinkel, Harold.
xGarfinkel, Harold.
Studies in Ethnomethodology. P-H.

Garfinkel, Irwin.
xGarfinkel, Irwin.
Earnings Capacity, Poverty & Inequality. Acad
Pr.

Garfinkel, Robert.
xGarfinkel, Robert.
Integer Programming. Wiley.

Garforth, Francis William.
xGarforth, Frank W.
John Stuart Mill's Theory of Education. B&N.

Garforth, Frank W. see Garforth, Francis William.

Garg, Jaynti P. see Garg, Jaynti Prasad.

Garg, Jaynti Prasad.
xGarg, Jaynti P.
Regionalism in International Politics. Intl
Pubns Serv.

Garg, Prem C., 1946-
xGarg, Prem C.
Optimal Economic Growth with Exhaustible
Resources. Garland Pub.

Garg, S. see Garg, Sabodh K.

Garg, Sabodh K.
xGarg, S.
Analysis of Structural Composite Materials.
Dekker.

Gargan, John J., 1934-
xGargan, John J.
The Complete Guide to Estate Planning. P-H.

Gargaz, Pierre Andre.
xGargaz, Pierre-Andre.
Project of Universal & Perpetual Peace.
Garland Pub.

Gargaz, Pierre-Andre. see Gargaz, Pierre Andre.

Gargi, Balwant, 1916-
xGargi, Balwant.
Nirankari Baba. Intl Pubns Serv.

Garibaldi, Gerald.
xGaribaldi, Gerald.
He Gave Himself to the Sea. Raintree Pubs.

Garinger, Elmer H. see Garinger, Elmer Henry.

Garinger, Elmer Henry, 1891-
xGaringer, Elmer H.
The Administration of Discipline in the High
School. AMS Pr.

Garis, Howard. see Garis, Howard Roger.

Garis, Howard R. see Garis, Howard Roger.

Garis, Howard Roger, 1873-
xGaris, Howard.

Uncle Wiggily's Happy Days. Platt.
xGaris, Howard R.
Uncle Wiggily & His Friends. Platt.

Garis, Roy L. see Garis, Roy Lawrence.

Garis, Roy Lawrence, 1897-
xGaris, Roy L.
Immigration Restriction: A Study of the
Opposition to & Regulation of Immigration
into the United States. Ozer.

Garlan, P. W. see Garlan, Patricia Wallace.

Garlan, Patricia Wallace.
xGarlan, P. W.
Star Sight: Visions of the Future. P-H.

Garland, Colden.
xGarland, Colden.
Developing Competence in Teaching Reading:
Instructional Modules in Reading Education.
Wm C Brown.

Garland, G. D. see Garland, George David.

Garland, George D. see Garland, George David.

Garland, George David, 1926-
xGarland, G. D.
Earth's Shape & Gravity. Pergamon.
xGarland, George D.
Introduction to Geophysics: Mantle, Core &
Crust. HR&W.

Garland, H. B. see Garland, Henry Burnand.

Garland, Hamlin, 1860-1940
xGarland, Hamlin.
The Captain of the Gray-Horse Troop.
Irvington.
Daughter of the Middle Border. Peter Smith.
Prairie Song & Western Story. Arno.
A Son of the Middle Border. U of Nebr Pr.

Garland, Harry.
xGarland, Harry.
Introduction to Microprocessor System Design.
McGraw.

Garland, Henry. see Garland, Henry Burnand.

Garland, Henry Burnand.
xGarland, H. B.
Concise Survey of German Literature. U of
Miami Pr.
xGarland, Henry.
ed. The Oxford Companion to German
Literature. Oxford U Pr.

Garland, Hugh A., 1805-1854
xGarland, Hugh A.
Life of John Randolph of Roanoke.
Greenwood.
Life of John Randolph of Roanoke. Haskell.
The Life of John Randolph of Roanoke.
Johnson Repr.

Garland, J. see Garland, J. D.

Garland, J. D., 1912-
xGarland, J.
National Electrical Code Reference Book. P-H.

Garland, James A. see Garland, James Albert.

Garland, James Albert, 1870-1906
xGarland, James A.
The Private Stable. North River.

Garland, John K.
xGarland, John K.
Chemistry of Our World. Macmillan.

Garland, John S.
xGarland, John S.
Financing Foreign Trade in Eastern Europe:
Problems of Bilateralism & Currency
Inconvertibility. Praeger.

Garland, Joseph E.
xGarland, Joseph E.
Boston's North Shore: Being an Account of
Life Among the Noteworthy, Fashionable,
Wealthy, Eccentric & Ordinary 1823-1890.
Little.
Centennial History of the Boston Medical
Library. F A Countway.
Lone Voyager. Nelson B Robinson.

Garland, Rosemary.
xGarland, Rosemary.

ed. My Bedtime Book of Two-Minute Stories.
   G&D.
Garland, Sarah.
   xGarland, Sarah.
   Potter Brownware. Scribner.
Garlick, Raymond.
   xGarlick, Raymond.
   Introduction to Anglo-Welsh Literature. Verry.
Garlin, Sender.
   xGarlin, Sender.
   William Dean Howells & the Haymarket Era.
      Am Inst Marxist.
Garliner, Daniel.
   xGarliner, Daniel.
   Swallow Right-or Else!. Green.
Garlington, Philip, 1943-
   xGarlington, Philip.
   Aces & Eights. M Evans.
Garlinski, Josef. *see* Garlinski, Jozef.
Garlinski, Jozef.
   xGarlinski, Josef.
   Hitler's Last Weapons: The Underground War
      Against the V1 & V2. Times Bks.
   xGarlinski, Jozef.
   Enigma War. Scribner.
Garma, Angel.
   xGarma, Angel.
   The Psychoanalysis of Dreams. Aronson.
Garman, E. Thomas.
   xGarman, E. Thomas.
   The Consumer's World, Buying, Money
      Management, & Issues: Resource. McGraw.
   The Consumer's World: Economic Issues &
      Money Management. McGraw.
Garmire, Bernard L.
   xGarmire, Bernard L.
   ed. Local Government Police Management. Intl
      City Mgt.
Garmo, Charles De. *see* De Garmo, Charles.
Garms, Walter I.
   xGarms, Walter I.
   Financing Community Colleges. Tchrs Coll.
Garn, Stanley M.
   xGarn, Stanley M.
   ed. Readings on Race. C C Thomas.
Garnand, Harry J. *see* Garnand, Harry Jennings.
Garnand, Harry Jennings, 1889-
   xGarnand, Harry J.
   Influence of Walter Scott on Works of Balzac.
      Octagon.
Garnell, P.
   xGarnell, P.
   Guided Weapon Control Systems. Pergamon.
Garner, Alan.
   xGarner, Alan.
   illus. The Aimer Gate. Philomel.
   Elidor. Philomel.
   Granny Reardun. Philomel.
   The Moon of Gomrath. Philomel.
   The Owl Service. Philomel.
   The Stone Book. Philomel.
   Tom Fobble's Day. Philomel.
Garner, Gerald W.
   xGarner, Gerald W.
   The Police Role in Alcohol-Related Crises. C C
      Thomas.
Garner, H. F.
   xGarner, H. F.
   Origin of Landscapes: A Synthesis of
      Geomorphology. Oxford U Pr.
Garner, Harry. *see* Garner, Harry Mason.
Garner, Harry Mason, Sir, 1891-
   xGarner, Harry.
   Chinese Lacquer. Merrimack Bk Serv.
   Oriental Blue & White. Merrimack Bk Serv.
Garner, Herschel W. *see* Garner, Herschel Whitaker.
Garner, Herschel Whitaker.
   xGarner, Herschel W.

Population Dynamics, Reproduction, &
   Activities of the Kangaroo Rat, Dipodomys
   Ordii, in Western Texas. Tex Tech Pr.
Garner, James W. *see* Garner, James Wilford.
Garner, James Wilford, 1871-1938
   xGarner, James W.
   Studies in Government & International Law.
      Greenwood.
Garner, John, 1920-
   xGarner, John.
   Franchise & Politics in British North America,
      1755-1867. U of Toronto Pr.
Garner, Philippe.
   xGarner, Philippe.
   ed. The Encyclopedia of Decorative Arts,
      1890-1940. Van Nos Reinhold.
   The Encyclopedia or Decorative Arts
      1890-1940. Litton Educ Pub.
Garner, Richard L.
   xGarner, Richard L.
   Columbus & Related Family Papers,
      1451-1902: An Inventory of the Boal
      Collection. Pa St U Pr.
Garner, Robert J. *see* Garner, Robert John.
Garner, Robert John, 1907-
   xGarner, Robert J.
   The Grafter's Handbook. Oxford U Pr.
Garner, S. Paul. *see* Garner, Samuel Paul.
Garner, Samuel Paul, 1910-
   xGarner, S. Paul.
   Evolution of Cost Accounting. U of Ala Pr.
Garner, W. R. *see* Garner, Wendell R.
Garner, Wendell R.
   xGarner, W. R.
   Uncertainty & Structure As Psychological
      Concepts. Krieger.
Garner, William R. *see* Garner, William Robert.
Garner, William Robert.
   xGarner, William R.
   Letters from California, 1846-1847. U of Cal
      Pr.
Garnes, Jane E.
   xGarnes, Jane E.
   The Complete Handbook of Leathercrafting.
      TAB Bks.
Garnett, Eve.
   xGarnett, Eve.
   illus. Further Adventures of the Family from
      One End Street. Vanguard.
Garnett, J. *see* Garnett, John.
Garnett, John, Ph.D.
   xGarnett, J.
   Analytic Capacity & Measure. Springer-Verlag.
Garnett, Lucy M. *see* Garnett, Lucy Mary Jane.
Garnett, Lucy Mary Jane, d. 1934
   xGarnett, Lucy M.
   Mysticism & Magic in Turkey: An Account of
      the Religious Doctrines, Monastic
      Organisation & Ecstatic Powers of the
      Dervish Orders. AMS Pr.
Garnett, R. *see* Garnett, Richard.
Garnett, R. C. *see* Garnett, Ronald George.
Garnett, Richard, 1835-1906
   xGarnett, R.
   The Age of Dryden. Arden Lib.
   xGarnett, Richard.
   The Age of Dryden. Arno.
   The Age of Dryden. R West.
   History of Italian Literature. R West.
   Life of John Milton. AMS Pr.
   Life of John Milton. Folcroft.
   Life of Ralph Waldo Emerson. Folcroft.
   Life of Thomas Carlyle. AMS Pr.
   Life of Thomas Carlyle. Arden Lib.
Garnett, Ronald George.
   xGarnett, R. C.
   Co-Operation & the Owenite Socialist
      Communities in Britain 1825-45. Humanities.
Garnett, Theodosia V.
   xGarnett, Theodosia V.

A Collection of Laboratory Specimens &
   Diagnostic Procedures. Littlefield.
Garoche, Pierre.
   xGaroche, Pierre.
   Dictionary of Commodities Carried by Ship.
      Cornell Maritime.
Garofalo, Raffaele.
   xGarofalo, Raffaele.
   Criminology. Patterson Smith.
Garoogian, Andrew.
   xGaroogian, Andrew.
   ed. Child Care Issues for Parents & Society: A
      Guide to Information Sources. Gale.
Garrad, Larch S. *see* Garrad, Larch Sylvia.
Garrad, Larch Sylvia.
   xGarrad, Larch S.
   The Naturalist in the Isle of Man. David &
      Charles.
Garraghan, Gilbert J. *see* Garraghan, Gilbert Joseph.
Garraghan, Gilbert Joseph, 1871-1942
   xGarraghan, Gilbert J.
   A Guide to Historical Method. Greenwood.
Garrand, Victor.
   xGarrand, Victor.
   Augustine Laure, S.J., Missionary to the
      Yakimas. Ye Galleon.
Garrard, J. G. *see* Garrard, John Gordon.
Garrard, John Gordon.
   xGarrard, J. G.
   ed. The Eighteenth Century in Russia. Oxford
      U Pr.
Garrard, Timothy F.
   xGarrard, Timothy H.
   Akan Weights & the Gold Trade. Longman.
Garrard, Timothy H. *see* Garrard, Timothy F.
Garratt, Colin. *see* Garratt, Colin Dennis.
Garratt, Colin Dennis.
   xGarratt, Colin.
   The Last of Steam. Swallow.
   A Popular Guide to the Preserved Steam
      Railways of Britain. Sterling.
   Veterans in Steam. Sterling.
Garraty, John A.
   xGarraty, John A.
   Unemployment in History: Economic Thought
      & Public Policy. Har-Row.
   Unemployment in History: Economic Thought
      & Public Policy. Har-Row.
Garraty, John A. *see* Garraty, John Arthur.
Garraty, John Arthur, 1920-
   xGarraty, John A.
   The American Nation: A History of the United
      States. Har-Row.
   From Main Street to the Left Bank: Students &
      Scholars Abroad. Mich St U Pr.
   Historical Viewpoints: Notable Articles from
      American Heritage. Har-Row.
   ed. Quarrels That Have Shaped the
      Constitution. Har-Row.
   Right-Hand Man: The Life of George W.
      Perkins. Greenwood.
   Silas Wright. AMS Pr.
   Woodrow Wilson: A Great Life in Brief.
      Greenwood.
Garrels, Robert M. *see* Garrels, Robert Minard.
Garrels, Robert Minard.
   xGarrels, Robert M.
   Chemical Cycles & the Global Environment:
      Assessing Human Influences. W Kaufmann.
   Evolution of Sedimentary Rocks. Norton.
Garren, John.
   xGarren, John.
   Oregon River Tours. Touchstone Pr Ore.
Garretson. *see* Garretson, Robert L.
Garretson, Oliver K. *see* Garretson, Oliver Kelleam.
Garretson, Oliver Kelleam, 1896-
   xGarretson, Oliver K.

Relationships Between Expressed Preferences
& Curricular Abilities of Ninth Grade Boys.
AMS Pr.

Garretson, R. L. *see* Garretson, Robert L.

Garretson, Robert L.
xGarretson.
Conducting Choral Music. Allyn.
xGarretson, R. L.
Music in Childhood Education. P-H.

Garrett, Albert.
xGarrett, Albert.
The History of British Wood Engraving.
Humanities.

Garrett, Charles. *see* Garrett, Charles L.

Garrett, Charles L.
xGarrett, Charles.
Electronic Prospecting. Ram Pub.
xGarrett, Charles L.
Successful Coin Hunting. Ram Pub.

Garrett, Clarke, 1935-
xGarrett, Clarke.
Respectable Folly: Millenarians and the French
Revolution in France and England. Johns
Hopkins.

Garrett, Eileen J. *see* Garrett, Eileen Jeanette Lyttle.

Garrett, Eileen Jeanette Lyttle, 1893-
xGarrett, Eileen J.
Awareness. Garrett-Helix.

Garrett, Florence. *see* Garrett, Florence Rome.

Garrett, Florence Rome.
xGarrett, Florence.
More Than the Quiet Pond. Golden Quill.

Garrett, Garet, 1878-
xGarrett, Garet.
The People's Pottage. Caxton.

Garrett, George, 1929-
xGarrett, George.
Cold Ground Was My Bed Last Night. U of
Mo Pr.

Garrett, H. E. *see* Garrett, Horace Edward.

Garrett, Henry E. *see* Garrett, Henry Edward.

Garrett, Henry Edward, 1894-
xGarrett, Henry E.
Great Experiments in Psychology. Irvington.

Garrett, Horace Edward.
xGarrett, H. E.
Surface Active Chemicals. Pergamon.

Garrett, Howard.
xGarrett, Howard.
ed. The Poster Book of Antique Auto Ads.
Citadel Pr.

Garrett, James. *see* Garrett, James F.

Garrett, James F.
xGarrett, James.
Rehabilitation Practices with the Physically
Disabled. Columbia U Pr.

Garrett, James J.
xGarrett, James J.
Antitrust Compliance: A Legal & Business
Guide. PLI.

Garrett, James L. *see* Garrett, James Leo.

Garrett, James Leo.
xGarrett, James L.
ed. Baptist Relations with Other Christians.
Judson.

Garrett, John, 1902-
xGarrett, John.
ed. More Talking of Shakespeare. Arno.
ed. Talking of Shakespeare. Arno.

Garrett, Leonard J.
xGarrett, Leonard J.
Production Management Analysis. HarBraceJ.

Garrett, Pat F. *see* Garrett, Patrick Floyd.

Garrett, Patrick Floyd.
xGarrett, Pat F.
Authentic Life of Billy, the Kid. U of Okla Pr.

Garrett, Patrick H.
xGarrett, Patrick H.

Analog Systems for Microprocessors &
Minicomputers. Reston.

Garrett, Peter K.
xGarrett, Peter K.
The Victorian Multiplot Novel: Studies in
Dialogical Form. Yale U Pr.

Garrett, Randall.
xGarrett, Randall.
Takeoff. Donning Co.

Garrett, Richard.
xGarrett, Richard.
Famous Characters of the Wild West. St
Martin.
Mrs. Simpson. St Martin.

Garrett, Romeo B.
xGarrett, Romeo B.
Famous First Facts About Negroes. Arno.

Garrett, S. D. *see* Garrett, Stephen Denis.

Garrett, Stephen Denis.
xGarrett, S. D.
Pathogenic Root-Infecting Fungi. Cambridge U
Pr.
Soil Fungi & Soil Fertility. Pergamon.

Garrett, Thomas M.
xGarrett, Thomas M.
Cases in Business Ethics. P-H.

Garrett, Thomas S. *see* Garrett, Thomas Samuel.

Garrett, Thomas Samuel.
xGarrett, Thomas S.
Christian Worship: An Introductory Outline.
Oxford U Pr.

Garrett, William J.
xGarrett, William J.
Ultrasound in Clinical Obstetrics. C C Thomas.

Garrey, M. M.
xGarrey, Matthew M.
Gynaecology Illustrated. Churchill.

Garrey, Matthew M. *see* Garrey, M. M.

Garrigue, Jean, 1912-
xGarrigue, Jean.
Animal Hotel. Eakins.
Chartres & Prose Poems. Eakins.
Studies for an Actress & Other Poems.
Macmillan.
Studies for an Actress & Other Poems.
Macmillan.

Garrison, Christian.
xGarrison, Christian.
The Dream Eater. Bradbury Pr.
Little Pieces of the West Wind. Bradbury Pr.

Garrison, Chuck.
xGarrison, Chuck.
Offshore Fishing in Southern California.
Chronicle Bks.

Garrison, Dee.
xGarrison, Dee.
Apostles of Culture: The Public Librarian &
American Society 1876-1920. Macmillan.

Garrison, James D.
xGarrison, James D.
Dryden & the Tradition of Panegyric. U of Cal
Pr.

Garrison, Jim, 1921-
xGarrison, Jim.
The Star-Spangled Contract. Warner Bks.

Garrison, Karl C. *see* Garrison, Karl Claudius.

Garrison, Karl Claudius, 1900-
xGarrison, Karl C.
Psychology of Adolescence. P-H.
The Psychology of Exceptional Children.
Wiley.

Garrison, Linda.
xGarrison, Linda.
Fitness & Figure Control: The Creation of You.
Mayfield Pub.

Garrison, Omar. *see* Garrison, Omar V.

Garrison, Omar V.
xGarrison, Omar.
Encyclopedia of Prophecy. Citadel Pr.
xGarrison, Omar V.

Encyclopedia of Prophecy. Citadel Pr.
Howard Hughes in Las Vegas. Lyle Stuart.

Garrison, Paul.
xGarrison, Paul.
Cross-Country Flying. TAB Bks.
How the Air Traffic Control System Works.
TAB Bks.
The Illustrated Encyclopedia of General
Aviation. TAB Bks.
Night-Flying in Single-Engine Airplanes. TAB
Bks.

Garrison, Peter.
xGarrison, Peter.
CV: Carrier Aviation. Presidio Pr.

Garrison, Ray H.
xGarrison, Ray H.
Managerial Accounting: Concepts for Planning,
Control, Decision Making. Business Pubns.

Garrison, W. L. *see* Garrison, William Lloyd.

Garrison, Webb. *see* Garrison, Webb B.

Garrison, Webb B.
xGarrison, Webb.
Lost Pages from American History. Stackpole.
Strange Facts About Death. Abingdon.
Strange Facts About the Bible. Abingdon.
Strange Facts About the Bible. Pillar Bks.
xGarrison, Webb B.
Codfish, Cats & Civilization. Kennikat.

Garrison, William L. *see* Garrison, William Lloyd.

Garrison, William Lloyd.
xGarrison, W. L.
The Letters of William Lloyd Garrison.
Harvard U Pr.
xGarrison, William L.
Sonnets. Irvington.
Thoughts on African Colonization. Arno.

Garrison, Winfred E. *see* Garrison, Winfred Ernest.

Garrison, Winfred Ernest, 1874-1969
xGarrison, Winfred E.
March of Faith: The Story of Religion in
America Since 1865. Greenwood.

Garrity, Richard. *see* Garrity, Richard G.

Garrity, Richard G.
xGarrity, Richard.
Canal Boatman: My Life on Upstate
Waterways. Syracuse U Pr.

Garrod, H. W. *see* Garrod, Heathcote William.

Garrod, Heathcote W. *see* Garrod, Heathcote William.

Garrod, Heathcote William, 1878-1960
xGarrod, H. W.
Collins. Octagon.
xGarrod, Heathcote W.
Collins. Folcroft.
Collins. Somerset Pub.
Profession of Poetry, & Other Lectures. Arno.
The Study of Poetry. Arden Lib.
The Study of Poetry. Folcroft.
Wordsworth: Lectures & Essays. Arden Lib.

Garrow, David J., 1953-
xGarrow, David J.
Protest at Selma: Martin Luther King, Jr., &
the Voting Rights Act of 1965. Yale U Pr.

Garry. *see* Garry, Ralph.

Garry, Ralph.
xGarry.
Guidance Techniques for Elementary Teachers.
Merrill.

Garsoian, N. G. *see* Garsoian, Nina G.

Garsoian, Nina G., 1923-
xGarsoian, N. G.
Paulician Heresy: A Study of the Origin &
Development of Paulicianism in Armenia &
the Eastern Provinces of the Byzantine
Empire. Mouton.

Garson, Arthur.
xGarson, Arthur.
A Guide to Cardiac Dysrhythmias in Children.
Grune.

Garson, Barbara.
xGarson, Barbara.

All the Livelong Day: The Meaning &
Demeaning of Routine Work. Penguin.
Garson, David. see Garson, G. David.
Garson, G. David.
xGarson, David.
Power & Politics in the United States: A
Political Economy Approach. Heath.
xGarson, G. David.
Group Theories of Politics. Sage.
ed. Worker Self-Management in Industry: The
West European Experience. Praeger.
Garson, Robert A.
xGarson, Robert A.
The Democratic Party & the Politics of
Sectionalism, 1941-1948. La State U Pr.
Garstka, W. U.
xGarstka, Walter U.
Water Resources & the National Welfare.
WRP.
Garstka, Walter U. see Garstka, W. U.
Garten, M. O. see Garten, Max Otto.
Garten, Max Otto.
xGarten, M. O.
Natural & Drugless Way for Better Health. Arc
Bks.
Natural & Drugless Way for Better Health.
P-H.
Gartenberg, Egon.
xGartenberg, Egon.
Johann Strauss: The End of an Era. Pa St U
Pr.
Gartenberg, Leo.
xGartenberg, Leo.
Torah Thoughts. Jonathan David.
Gartenberg, Michael.
xGartenberg, Michael.
Mathematics for Financial Analysis. Pergamon.
Gartenhaus, Jacob, 1896-
xGartenhaus, Jacob.
Famous Hebrew Christians. Baker Bk.
Garth, Samuel, Sir, 1661-1719
xGarth, Samuel.
The Dispensary: With a Short Account of the
Proceedings of the College of Physicians,
London, in Relation to the Sick Poor (1697)
& Claremont (1715). Schol Facsimiles.
Gartner. see Gartner, Alan.
Gartner, Alan.
xGartner.
Consumer Education in the Human Services.
Pergamon.
xGartner, Alan.
After Deschooling, What?. Har-Row.
ed. A Full Employment Program for the
1970's. Praeger.
How to Individualize Learning. Phi Delta
Kappa.
The Preparation of Human Service
Professionals. Human Sci Pr.
Gartner, Chloe.
xGartner, Chloe.
Anne Bonny. Zebra.
Garton, Jean S. see Garton, Jean Staker.
Garton, Jean Staker.
xGarton, Jean S.
Who Broke the Baby?. Bethany Fell.
Garve, Andrew.
xGarve, Andrew.
The Ashes of Loda. Har-Row.
The Cuckoo Line Affair. Har-Row.
No Tears for Hilda. Garland Pub.
No Tears for Hilda. Har-Row.
The Riddle of Samson. Har-Row.
Garven, Charles. see Garven, Charles M.
Garven, Charles M.
xGarven, Charles.
Student Journalist & Editing. Rosen Pr.
Garver. see Garver, Isobel M.
Garver, Isobel M.
xGarver.

Our Christian Heritage. Christs Mission.
Garver, Thomas H.
xGarver, Thomas H.
ed. Twelve Photographers of the American
Social Landscape. October.
Garvey, A. J. see Garvey, Amy Jacques.
Garvey, Amy J. see Garvey, Amy Jacques.
Garvey, Amy Jacques.
xGarvey, A. J.
Garvey & Garveyism. Macmillan.
xGarvey, Amy J.
Garvey & Garveyism. Octagon.
Garvey, Calixta, Sister.
xGarvey, M. Calixta.
Syntax of the Declinable Words in the Roman
De la Rose. AMS Pr.
Garvey, Catherine, 1930-
xGarvey, Catherine.
Play. Harvard U Pr.
Garvey, Chester R. see Garvey, Chester Roy.
Garvey, Chester Roy.
xGarvey, Chester R.
The Activity of Young Children During Sleep:
An Objective Study. Greenwood.
Garvey, Edward B.
xGarvey, Edward B.
Hiking Trails in the Mid-Atlantic States.
Contemp Bks.
Garvey, Gerald, 1935-
xGarvey, Gerald.
Constitutional Bricolage. Princeton U Pr.
Garvey, M. Calixta. see Garvey, Calixta.
Garvey, Michael.
xGarvey, Michael.
Confessions of a Catholic Worker. Thomas
More.
Garvey, Mona.
xGarvey, Mona.
Library Displays: Their Purpose, Construction
& Use. Wilson.
Garvie, A. F.
xGarvie, A. F.
Aeschylus' Supplices: Play & Trilogy.
Cambridge U Pr.
Garvin, Charles.
xGarvin, Charles.
The Work Incentive Experience. Allanheld.
Garvin, Harry. see Garvin, Harry Raphael.
Garvin, Harry Raphael, 1916-
xGarvin, Harry.
ed. Literature & History. Bucknell U Pr.
Garvin, Katherine, 1904-
xGarvin, Katherine.
The Great Tudors. Arden Lib.
The Great Tudors. Folcroft.
Garvin, Paul L.
xGarvin, Paul L.
A Prague School Reader on Esthetics, Literary
Structure & Style. Georgetown U Pr.
Garvy, George.
xGarvy, George.
Deposit Velocity & Its Significance.
Greenwood.
Money, Financial Flows & Credit in the Soviet
Union. Ballinger Pub.
Garvy, Helen.
xGarvy, Helen.
illus. How to Fix Your Bicycle. Shire Pr.
Garwood, Helen, 1876-
xGarwood, Helen.
Thomas Hardy: An Illustration of the
Philosophy of Schopenhauer. Folcroft.
Garwood, S. Gray.
xGarwood, S. Gray.
Educating Young Handicapped Children: A
Developmental Approach. Aspen Systems.
Gary, A. L.
xGary, A. L.

Eye Color, Sex, & Children's Behavior.
Nelson-Hall.
Gary, Charles L.
xGary, Charles L.
Flower Fables. EPM Pubns.
Garza, Eugenio D.
xGarza, Eugenio D.
Adolescent Mexican American Student
Attitudes of Self-Concept, Locus of Control
& Family Ideology in the Lower Rio Grande
Valley of Texas. R & E Res Assoc.
Garzilli, Enrico.
xGarzilli, Enrico.
Circles Without Center: Paths to the Discovery
& Creation of Self in Modern Literature.
Harvard U Pr.
Gas Dynamics Symposium.
xGas Dynamics Symposium - 2nd Biennial - 1958.
Transportation Properties in Gases:
Proceedings. Northwestern U Pr.
xGas Dynamics Symposium - 5th Biennial - 1964.
Physico-Chemical Diagnostics of Plasma:
Proceedings. Northwestern U Pr.
xGas Dynamics Symposium - 6th Biennial - 1967.
Advances in Plasma Dynamics: Proceedings.
Northwestern U Pr.
xGas Dynamics Symposium - 7th Biennial - 1968.
Energy: Proceedings. Northwestern U Pr.
Gas Dynamics Symposium - 2nd Biennial - 1958. see
Gas Dynamics Symposium.
Gas Dynamics Symposium - 5th Biennial - 1964. see Gas
Dynamics Symposium.
Gas Dynamics Symposium - 6th Biennial - 1967. see Gas
Dynamics Symposium.
Gas Dynamics Symposium - 7th Biennial - 1968. see Gas
Dynamics Symposium.
Gascoigne, Bamber.
xGascoigne, Bamber.
The Christians. Morrow.
Gascoigne, George.
xGascoigne, George.
Complete Works. Greenwood.
Complete Works. Scholarly.
Glass of Government. AMS Pr.
Gash, Jonathan.
xGash, Jonathan.
Gold by Gemini. Har-Row.
The Grail Tree. Har-Row.
Gash, Norman.
xGash, Norman.
Peel. Longman.
Politics in the Age of Peel: A Study in the
Technique of Parliamentary Representation,
1830-1850. Humanities.
Gasiorowicz, Stephen.
xGasiorowicz, Stephen.
Structure of Matter: A Survey of Modern
Physics. A-W.
xGasiorowicz, Stephen G.
Quantum Physics. Wiley.
Gasiorowicz, Stephen G. see Gasiorowicz, Stephen.
Gasiorowska, Xenia.
xGasiorowska, Xenia.
The Image of Peter the Great in Russian
Fiction. U of Wis Pr.
Gaskell, E. see Gaskell, Elizabeth Cleghorn (Stevenson).
Gaskell, Elizabeth. see Gaskell, Elizabeth Cleghorn
(Stevenson).
Gaskell, Elizabeth C. see Gaskell, Elizabeth Cleghorn
(Stevenson).
Gaskell, Elizabeth Cleghorn (Stevenson), 1810-1865
xGaskell, E.
The Letters of Mrs. Gaskell. State Mutual Bk.
xGaskell, Elizabeth.
Life of Charlotte Bronte. Dutton.
Life of Charlotte Bronte. Penguin.
North & South. Penguin.
North & South. Dutton.
xGaskell, Elizabeth C.

Grey Woman, & Other Tales. Arno.
Letters of Mrs. Gaskell. Harvard U Pr.
The Life of Charlotte Bronte. Oxford U Pr.
Lizzie Leigh, & Other Tales. Arno.
ed. North & South. Oxford U Pr.
North & South. Scholarly.
xGaskell, Mrs.
The Life of Charlotte Bronte. R West.
Gaskell, G. A. *see* Gaskell, George Arthur.
Gaskell, George Arthur.
xGaskell, G. A.
Dictionary of All Scriptures & Myths. Crown.
Gaskell, Jane, 1941-
xGaskell, Jane.
Atlan. PB.
Atlan. St Martin.
The City. PB.
The City. St Martin.
The Dragon. St Martin.
Some Summer Lands. PB.
Some Summer Lands. St Martin.
Gaskell, Mrs. *see* Gaskell, Elizabeth Cleghorn
(Stevenson).
Gaskell, Philip.
xGaskell, Philip.
From Writer to Reader: Studies in Editorial
Method. Oxford U Pr.
Gaskell, Ronald.
xGaskell, Ronald.
Drama & Reality: The European Theatre Since
Ibsen. Routledge & Kegan.
Gaskell, T. F. *see* Gaskell, Thomas Frohock.
Gaskell, Thomas Frohock.
xGaskell, T. F.
World Climate: The Weather, the Environment
& the Man. Thames Hudson.
Gaskill, Jack D.
xGaskill, Jack D.
Linear Systems, Fourier Transforms & Optics.
Wiley.
Gaskin, Catherine.
xGaskin, Catherine.
Property of a Gentleman. Fawcett.
The Summer of the Spanish Woman.
Doubleday.
The Summer of the Spanish Woman. Fawcett.
Gaskin, Ina May.
xGaskin, Ina May.
Spiritual Midwifery. Book Pub Co.
Gaskin, J. C. A. *see* Gaskin, John Charles Addison.
Gaskin, John Charles Addison.
xGaskin, J. C. A.
Hume's Philosophy of Religion. B&N.
Gaskin, Stephen.
xGaskin, Stephen.
Mind at Play. Book Pub Co.
Gasparini, Francesco.
xGasparini, Francesco.
The Practical Harmonist at the Harpsichord.
Da Capo.
Gasparini, Graziano.
xGasparini, Graziano.
Inca Architecture. Ind U Pr.
Gasque, W. Ward.
xGasque, W. Ward.
A History of the Criticism of the Acts of the
Apostles. Eerdmans.
Gasquet, Francis A. *see* Gasquet, Francis Aidan.
Gasquet, Francis Aidan, Cardinal, 1846-1929
xGasquet, Francis A.
English Monastic Life. Arno.
English Monastic Life. Kennikat.
xGasquet, Francis C.
Old English Bible & Other Essays. Kennikat.
Gasquet, Francis C. *see* Gasquet, Francis Aidan.
Gass, G. *see* Gass, Ian Graham.
Gass, Ian Graham.
xGass, G.

ed. Understanding the Earth: A Reader in the
Earth Sciences. MIT Pr.
Gass, Saul I.
xGass, Saul I.
Illustrated Guide to Linear Programming.
McGraw.
Gass, Sherlock B. *see* Gass, Sherlock Bronson.
Gass, Sherlock Bronson, 1878-1945
xGass, Sherlock B.
Criers of the Shops. Arno.
Gass, William H. *see* Gass, William H.
Gass, William H., 1924-
xGass, William.
On Being Blue: A Philosophical Inquiry.
Godine.
Gasser, Raymond. *see* Gasser, Raymond F.
Gasser, Raymond F.
xGasser, Raymond.
Atlas of Human Embryos. Har-Row.
Gasset, Jose Ortega y. *see* Ortega y Gasset, Jose.
Gassner, John.
xGassner, John.
ed. Reader's Encyclopedia of World Drama. T
Y Crowell.
ed. Twenty Best European Plays on the
American Stage. Crown.
Twenty Best Film Plays. Garland Pub.
Gasson, Raphael.
xGasson, Raphael.
Food for God's Children. Logos.
Gasster, Michael, 1930-
xGasster, Michael.
China's Struggle to Modernize. Knopf.
Gast, Kelly P.
xGast, Kelly P.
Paddy. Doubleday.
Gast, Robert de. *see* De Gast, Robert.
Gast, Ross H.
xGast, Ross H.
Contentious Consul: A Biography of John
Coffin Jones First United States Counselor
Agent at Hawai. Dawsons.
Gaster, Theodor H. *see* Gaster, Theodor Herzl.
Gaster, Theodor Herzl, 1906-
xGaster, Theodor H.
Festivals of the Jewish Year: A Modern
Interpretation & Guide. Morrow.
Thespis: Ritual, Myth, & Drama in the Ancient
Near East. Gordian.
Thespis: Ritual, Myth, & Drama in the Ancient
Near East. Norton.
Gastil, Raymond. *see* Gastil, Raymond D.
Gastil, Raymond D.
xGastil, Raymond.
Cultural Regions of the United States. U of
Wash Pr.
xGastil, Raymond D.
ed. Freedom in the World: Political Rights &
Civil Liberties. Transaction Bks.
Freedom in the World: Political Rights & Civil
Liberties, 1979. Freedom Hse.
ed. Freedom in the World: Political Rights &
Civil Liberties, 1978. G K Hall.
Gastineau, Clifford F. *see* Gastineau, Clifford Felix.
Gastineau, Clifford Felix.
xGastineau, Clifford F.
ed. Fermented Food Beverages in Nutrition.
Acad Pr.
Gastineau, Gary L.
xGastineau, Gary L.
The Stock Options Manual. McGraw.
Gastmann, Albert. *see* Gastmann, Albert L.
Gastmann, Albert L.
xGastmann, Albert.
Historical Dictionary of the French &
Netherlands Antilles. Scarecrow.
Gaston, E. Thayer.
xGaston, E. Thayer.

Music in Therapy. Macmillan.
Gaston, Edwin W.
xGaston, Edwin W.
Conrad Richter. Coll & U Pr.
Gaston, Herbert E. *see* Gaston, Herbert Earle.
Gaston, Herbert Earle, 1881-1956
xGaston, Herbert E.
The Nonpartisan League. Hyperion Conn.
Gaston, James C.
xGaston, James C.
London Poets & the American Revolution.
Whitston Pub.
Gaston, Jerry.
xGaston, Jerry.
Originality & Competition in Science: A Study
of the British High Energy Physics
Community. U of Chicago Pr.
The Reward System in British & American
Science. Wiley.
Gastonguay, Paul R., 1936-
xGastonguay, Paul R.
Evolution for Everyone. Pegasus.
Gastoue, Amedee, 1873-1943
xGastoue, Amedee.
Musique et Liturgie: Le Graduel et
l'Antiphonaire Romains; Histoire et
Description. AMS Pr.
Gastroenterological Symposium.
xGastroenterological Symposium, 3rd.
The Sphincter of Oddi: Proceedings. S Karger.
Gastroenterological Symposium, 3rd. *see*
Gastroenterological Symposium.
Gastwirt, Harold P.
xGastwirt, Harold P.
Fraud Corruption & Holiness: The Controversy
Over the Supervision of Jewish Dietary
Practice in New York City. Kennikat.
Gasztold, Carmen B. De. *see* De Gasztold, Carmen B.
Gatch, Jean.
xGatch, Jean.
School Makes Sense....Sometimes!. Human Sci
Pr.
Gatch, Milton McC.
xGatch, Milton McC.
Preaching & Theology in Anglo-Saxon
England: Aelfric & Wulfstan. U of Toronto
Pr.
Gatchel, Robert J.
xGatchel, Robert J.
ed. Clinical Applications of Biofeedback:
Appraisal & Status. Pergamon.
Gates, Bruce C.
xGates, Bruce C.
Chemistry of Catalytic Processes. McGraw.
Gates, Bruce L.
xGates, Bruce L.
Social Program Administration: The
Implementation of Social Policy. P-H.
Gates, D. M. *see* Gates, David Murray.
Gates, David.
xGates, David.
Type. Watson-Guptill.
Gates, David Murray.
xGates, D. M.
Atlas of Energy Budgets of Plant Leaves. Acad
Pr.
Gates, Doris.
xGates, Doris.
A Fair Wind for Troy. Viking Pr.
Little Vic. Viking Pr.
A Morgan for Melinda. Viking Pr.
Gates, Eleanor.
xGates, Eleanor.
The Poor Little Rich Girl. Garland Pub.
Gates, Frederick T. *see* Gates, Frederick Taylor.
Gates, Frederick Taylor, 1853-1929
xGates, Frederick T.
Chapters in My Life. Free Pr.
Gates, Frieda.
xGates, Frieda.

Easy to Make Costumes. Harvey.
Easy to Make Monster Masks & Disguises. Harvey.
Easy to Make Puppets. Harvey.
Glove, Mitten & Sock Puppets. Schol Bk Serv.
illus. Glove, Mitten & Sock Puppets. Walker & Co.
Gates, G. E. *see* Gates, Gordon Enoch.
Gates, Gary F.
xGates, Gary F.
Atlas of Abdominal Ultrasonography in Children. Churchill.
Gates, Gary P. *see* Gates, Gary Paul.
Gates, Gary Paul.
xGates, Gary P.
Air Time: The Inside Story of CBS News. Berkley Pub.
Air Time: The Inside Story of CBS News. Har-Row.
Gates, Gordon Enoch, 1897-
xGates, G. E.
Burmese Earthworms: An Introduction to the Systematics & Biology of Megadrile Oligochaetes with Special Reference to Southeast Asia. Am Philos.
Gates, Jean K. *see* Gates, Jean Key.
Gates, Jean Key.
xGates, Jean K.
Guide to the Use of Books & Libraries. McGraw.
Introduction to Librarianship. McGraw.
Gates, John D.
xGates, John D.
The Du Pont Family. Doubleday.
Gates, John E. *see* Gates, John Edward.
Gates, John Edward.
xGates, John E.
An Analysis of the Lexicographic Resources Used by American Biblical Scholars Today. Scholars Pr Ca.
Gates, Lewis E. *see* Gates, Lewis Edwards.
Gates, Lewis Edwards, 1860-1924
xGates, Lewis E.
Studies & Appreciations. Arno.
Gates, Paul W. *see* Gates, Paul Wallace.
Gates, Paul Wallace, 1901-
xGates, Paul W.
Fifty Million Acres. Arno.
Four Persistent Issues: Essays on California's Land Ownership Concentration, Water Deficits, Sub-State Regionalism, & Congressional Leadership. Inst Gov Stud Berk.
History of Public Land Law Development. Arno.
History of Public Land Law Development. Zenger Pub.
The Illinois Central Railroad & Its Colonization Work. Johnson Repr.
Gatewood, Willard B.
xGatewood, Willard B.
Eugene Clyde Brooks: Educator & Public Servant. Duke.
Gatewood, Worth.
xGatewood, Worth.
ed. Fifty Years-The New York Daily News in Pictures. Doubleday.
Gath, Dennis.
xGath, Dennis.
Child Guidance & Delinquency in a London Borough. Oxford U Pr.
Gathercole, P. W.
xGathercole, Peter.
Art of the Pacific Islands. Ind U Pr.
Gathercole, Peter. *see* Gathercole, P. W.
Gatheru, R. Mugo, 1925-
xGatheru, R. Mugo.
Child of Two Worlds: A Kikuyu's Story. NAL.
Gathje, Curtis.
xGathje, Curtis.

The Disco Kid. Watts.
Gathorne-Hardy, John. *see* Gathorne-Hardy, Jonathan.
Gathorne-Hardy, Jonathan.
xGathorne-Hardy, John.
Operation Peeg. Lippincott.
Gati, Charles.
xGati, Charles.
Caging the Bear: Containment & the Cold War. Bobbs.
ed. The Politics of Modernization in Eastern Europe: Testing the Soviet Model. Praeger.
Gatje, Helmut, 1927-
xGatje, Helmut.
The Qur'an & Its Exegesis: Selected Texts with Classical & Modern Muslim Interpretations. U of Cal Pr.
Gatlin, Lila L., 1928-
xGatlin, Lila L.
Information Theory & the Living System. Columbia U Pr.
Gattegno, Caleb.
xGattegno, Caleb.
The Common Sense of Teaching Mathematics. Ed Solutions.
Gatti, D. *see* Gatti, Daniel Jon.
Gatti, Daniel Jon.
xGatti, D.
Teacher & the Law. P-H.
xGatti, R.
jt. auth. Teacher & the Law. P-H.
Gatti, Guido M. *see* Gatti, Guido Maria.
Gatti, Guido Maria, 1892-
xGatti, Guido M.
Ildebrando Pizzetti. Hyperion Conn.
Gatti, R. *see* Gatti, Daniel Jon.
Gatti-Casazza, Giulio, 1869-1940
xGatti-Casazza, Giulio.
Memories of the Opera. Vienna Hse.
Gattiker, Irvin, 1916-
xGattiker, Irvin.
Complete Book of Rehearsal Techniques for the High School Orchestra. P-H.
Gatto, Joseph. *see* Gatto, Joseph A.
Gatto, Joseph A.
xGatto, Joseph.
Exploring Visual Design. Davis Mass.
xGatto, Joseph A.
Cities. Davis Mass.
Gatty, Harold, 1903-1957
xGatty, Harold.
Nature Is Your Guide: How to Find Your Way on Land & Sea. Penguin.
Gatty, Margaret. *see* Gatty, Margaret Scott.
Gatty, Margaret Scott.
xGatty, Margaret.
Parables from Nature. Garland Pub.
Gatzke, Hans W. *see* Gatzke, Hans Wilhelm.
Gatzke, Hans Wilhelm, 1915-
xGatzke, Hans W.
Stresemann & the Rearmament of Germany. Norton.
Gauch, Hugh. *see* Gauch, Hugh Gilbert.
Gauch, Hugh Gilbert, 1913-
xGauch, Hugh.
Inorganic Plant Nutrition. Acad Pr.
Gauch, Patricia L. *see* Gauch, Patricia Lee.
Gauch, Patricia Lee.
xGauch, Patricia L.
Aaron & the Green Mountain Boys. Coward.
Christina Katerina & the First Annual Grand Ballet. Coward.
Fridays. Putnam.
The Green of Me. Putnam.
The Impossible Major Rogers. Putnam.
On to Widecombe Fair. Putnam.
Once Upon a Dinkelsbuhl. Putnam.
Gaudiose, Dorothy. *see* Gaudiose, Dorothy M.
Gaudiose, Dorothy M., 1920-
xGaudiose, Dorothy.

Prophet of the People: A Biography of Padre Pio. Alba.
Gaudry, Eric.
xGaudry, Eric.
Anxiety & Educational Achievement. Wiley.
Gaughan, Edward.
xGaughan, Edward D.
College Algebra. Brooks-Cole.
Introduction to Analysis. Brooks-Cole.
Gaughan, Edward D. *see* Gaughan, Edward.
Gauguin, Paul.
xGauguin, Paul.
Drawings of Gauguin. Borden.
NOA-NOA. Archer Edns.
Noa Noa. FS&G.
Noa Noa. R West.
Gauld. *see* Gauld, Alan.
Gauld, Alan.
xGauld.
Human Action & Its Psychological Investigation. Routledge & Kegan.
xGauld, Alan.
The Founders of Psychical Research. Schocken.
Human Action & Its Psychological Investigation. Routledge & Kegan.
Poltergeists. Routledge & Kegan.
Gauldie, Sinclair.
xGauldie, Sinclair.
Architecture. Oxford U Pr.
Gault, Frank.
xGault, Frank.
Pele, the King of Soccer. Dell.
Gault, John C., 1945-
xGault, John C.
Public Utility Regulation of an Exhaustible Resource: The Case of Natural Gas. Garland Pub.
Gault, William C. *see* Gault, William Campbell.
Gault, William Campbell.
xGault, William C.
Cut-Rate Quarterback. Dutton.
Dirt Track Summer. Dutton.
Drag Strip. Berkley Pub.
Gasoline Cowboy. Dutton.
The Last Lap. Dutton.
Quarterback Gamble. Dutton.
Speedway Challenge. Berkley Pub.
Stubborn Sam. Dutton.
The Sunday Cycles. Dodd.
Thin Ice. Dutton.
Trouble at Second. Dutton.
Two-Wheeled Thunder. Schol Bk Serv.
Gaultier, Aloisius E. *see* Gaultier, Aloisius Edouard Camille.
Gaultier, Aloisius Edouard Camille, 1746?-1818
xGaultier, Aloisius E.
Amusing & Instructive Conversations for Children of Five Years. Johnson Repr.
Gaumann, T.
xGaumann, T.
ed. Aspects of Hydrocarbon Radiolysis. Acad Pr.
Gaunt, Larry D.
xGaunt, Larry D.
Examining Employers' Financial Capacity to Self-Insure Under Workmen's Compensation. Ga St U Busn Pub.
Gaunt, Leonard.
xGaunt, Leonard.
Commonsense Photography. Focal Pr.
The Focalguide to Darkroom. Focal Pr.
Lens Guide. Focal Pr.
ed. Pictorial Cyclopedia of Photography. Focal Pr.
Take Color. Focal Pr.
Gaunt, William, 1900
xGaunt, William.

Abortion Is a Blessing. Psych Dimensions.
Gaynes, Norman I.
    xGaynes, Norman I.
        Formulation of Organic Coatings. Van Nos
        Reinhold.
Gaynor, Frank, 1911-
    xGaynor, Frank.
        Dictionary of Mysticism. Citadel Pr.
Gaynor, James K.
    xGaynor, James K.
        Profile of the Law. BNA.
Gayton, Daniel F.
    xGayton, Daniel F.
        Butterball. Denison.
Gazda , George M. *see* Gazda, George Michael.
Gazda, George M. *see* Gazda, George Michael.
Gazda, George Michael, 1931-
    xGazda , George M.
        Theories & Methods of Group Counseling in
        the Schools. C C Thomas.
    xGazda, George M.
        Group Counseling: A Developmental
        Approach. Allyn.
        Innovations to Group Psychotherapy. C C
        Thomas.
Gazdar, Gerald.
    xGazdar, Gerald.
        Pragmatics: Implicature, Presupposition &
        Logical Form. Acad Pr.
Gazella, Jacqueline G. *see* Gazella, Jacqueline Gibson.
Gazella, Jacqueline Gibson.
    xGazella, Jacqueline G.
        Nutrition for the Childbearing Year. Woodland.
Gazes, Peter C.
    xGazes, Peter C.
        Clinical Cardiology: A Bedside Approach. Year
        Bk Med.
Gazley, John G. *see* Gazley, John Gerow.
Gazley, John Gerow, 1895-
    xGazley, John G.
        American Opinion of German Unification,
        1848-1871. AMS Pr.
        The Life of Arthur Young, 1741-1820. Am
        Philos.
Gazzaniga, Michael. *see* Gazzaniga, Michael S.
Gazzaniga, Michael S.
    xGazzaniga, Michael.
        Fundamentals of Psychology: An Introduction.
        Acad Pr.
    xGazzaniga, Michael S.
        Functional Neuroscience. Har-Row.
        The Integrated Mind. Plenum Pub.
Gbadamosi, T. G. *see* Gbadamosi, T. G. O.
Gbadamosi, T. G. O.
    xGbadamosi, T. G.
        The Growth of Islam Among the Yoruba:
        1841-1908. Humanities.
Geach, P. T. *see* Geach, Peter Thomas.
Geach, Peter T. *see* Geach, Peter Thomas.
Geach, Peter Thomas.
    xGeach, P. T.
        Logic Matters. U of Cal Pr.
        Reason & Argument. U of Cal Pr.
        Truth, Love, & Immortality: An Introduction
        to McTaggart's Philosophy. U of Cal Pr.
    xGeach, Peter T.
        Reference & Generality: An Examination of
        Some Medieval & Modern Theories. Cornell
        U Pr.
Geagan, Daniel J.
    xGeagan, Daniel J.
        The Athenian Constitution After Sulla. Am Sch
        Athens.
Geanakoplos, Deno J. *see* Geanakoplos, Deno John.
Geanakoplos, Deno John.
    xGeanakoplos, Deno J.

Byzantium & the Renaissance: Greek Scholars
        in Venice: Studies in the Dissemination of
        Greek Learning from Byzantium to Western
        Europe. Shoe String.
        Interaction of the "Sibling" Byzantine &
        Western Cultures in the Middle Ages &
        Italian Renaissance (330-1600). Yale U Pr.
Geaney, Dennis. *see* Geaney, Dennis J.
Geaney, Dennis J.
    xGeaney, Dennis.
        Full Church, Empty Rectory: Training Lay
        Ministers for Parishes Without Priests. Fides
        Claretian.
Geankoplis, Christie J.
    xGeankoplis, Christie J.
        Mass Transport Phenomena. Geankoplis.
Gear, C. William. *see* Gear, Charles William.
Gear, Charles William.
    xGear, C. William.
        Computer Organization & Programming.
        McGraw.
        Computer Organization & Programming.
        McGraw.
    xGear, G. W.
        Introduction to Computer Science. SRA.
Gear, Felix B.
    xGear, Felix B.
        Our Presbyterian Belief. John Knox.
Gear, G. W. *see* Gear, Charles William.
Gear, Josephine.
    xGear, Josephine.
        Masters or Servants?: A Study of Selected
        English Painters & Their Patrons of the Late
        18th & Early 19th Centuries. Garland Pub.
Gearhart, Elizabeth A.
    xGearhart, Elizabeth A.
        John Updike: A Comprehensive Bibliography
        with Selected Annotations. Folcroft.
        John Updike: A Comprehensive Bibliography
        with Selected Annotations. Norwood Edns.
Gearhart, Sally M. *see* Gearhart, Sally Miller.
Gearhart, Sally Miller, 1931-
    xGearhart, Sally M.
        The Wanderground: Stories of the Hill Women.
        Persephone.
Gearheart, B. R.
    xGearheart, B. R.
        Organization & Administration of Educational
        Programs for Exceptional Children. C C
        Thomas.
    xGearheart, Bill R.
        The Handicapped Student in the Regular
        Classroom. Mosby.
        Learning Disabilities: Educational Strategies.
        Mosby.
        The Trainable Retarded: A Foundations
        Approach. Mosby.
Gearheart, Bill R. *see* Gearheart, B. R.
Gearing, Catherine.
    xGearing, Catherine.
        Field Guide to Wilderness Living. Southern
        Pub.
Gearing, P. *see* Gearing, Philip J.
Gearing, Philip J.
    xGearing, P.
        Breaking into Print: How to Get Your Work
        Published. P-H.
Geary, D. P. *see* Geary, David Patrick.
Geary, David Patrick, 1928-
    xGeary, D. P.
        jt. auth. Community Relations & the
        Administration of Justice. Wiley.
Geary, Don.
    xGeary, Don.
        The How-to Book of Floors & Ceilings. TAB
        Bks.
        Step in the Right Direction: A Basic Map &
        Compass Book. Stackpole.
    xGeary, Donald.

How to Build Kitchen Cabinets, Counters, &
        Vanities. Reston.
        Interior & Exterior Painting. Reston.
Geary, Donald. *see* Geary, Don.
Geary, Gerald J. *see* Geary, Gerald Joseph.
Geary, Gerald Joseph, 1905-
    xGeary, Gerald J.
        The Secularization of the California Missions
        (1810-1846). AMS Pr.
Geary, Ida.
    xGeary, Ida.
        The Leaf Book: A Field Guide to Plants of
        Northern California. Tamal Land.
Geary, Michael.
    xGeary, Michael.
        Rand McNally Pictorial Encyclopedia of Dogs.
        Rand.
Geary, Patrick J., 1948-
    xGeary, Patrick J.
        Furta Sacra: Thefts of Relics in the Central
        Middle Ages. Princeton U Pr.
Geary, William M. *see* Geary, William Nevill
    Montgomerie.
**Geary, William Nevill Montgomerie, Sir, Bart,
    1859-1944**
    xGeary, William M.
        Nigeria Under British Rule. Biblio Dist.
Geba, Bruno A. *see* Geba, Bruno Hans.
Geba, Bruno Hans, 1927-
    xGeba, Bruno A.
        Breathe Away Your Tension. Bookworks.
Gebauer, Phyllis.
    xGebauer, Phyllis.
        The Pagan Blessing. Viking Pr.
Gebert, Kenneth. *see* Gebert, Kenneth L.
Gebert, Kenneth L.
    xGebert, Kenneth.
        National Electrical Code Blueprint Reading.
        Am Technical.
Gebhard, David.
    xGebhard, David.
        Charles F. A. Voysey, Architect. Hennessey.
        A Guide to Architecture in Los Angeles &
        Southern California. Peregrine Smith.
        Guide to Architecture in San Francisco &
        Northern California. Peregrine Smith.
Gebhard, Elizabeth R.
    xGebhard, Elizabeth R.
        The Theater at Isthmia. U of Chicago Pr.
Gebhardt, Chuck.
    xGebhardt, Chuck.
        Inside Death Valley. C Gebhardt.
Gebhardt, Richard H.
    xGebhardt, Richard H.
        ed. A Standard Guide to Cat Breeds. McGraw.
Gedat, Gustav Adolf.
    xGedat, Gustav-Adolf.
        They Built for Eternity. Arno.
Gedat, Gustav-Adolf. *see* Gedat, Gustav Adolf.
Geddes, Candida.
    xGeddes, Candida.
        ed. The Concise Book of the Horse. Arco.
Geddes, L. A. *see* Geddes, Leslie Alexander.
Geddes, Leslie Alexander.
    xGeddes, L. A.
        Principles of Applied Biomedical
        Instrumentation. Wiley.
Geddes, Paul.
    xGeddes, Paul.
        Code Name Hangman. Penguin.
Geddes, Robert N.
    xGeddes, Robert N.
        Owners Pictorial Guide for the Care &
        Understanding of the Mills Bell Slot
        Machine. Mead Co.
Geddes, Virgil, 1897-
    xGeddes, Virgil.
        Melodramadness of Eugene O'Neill. Folcroft.
Geddes, W. R. *see* Geddes, William Robert.

Geddes, William Robert.
  xGeddes, W. R.
    Nine Dayak Nights. Oxford U Pr.
Geddie, John, 1848-1937
  xGeddie, John.
    The Balladists. Folcroft.
Gedge, Pauline, 1945-
  xGedge, Pauline.
    Child of the Morning. Dial.
    Child of the Morning. Popular Lib.
Gedo, John E.
  xGedo, John E.
    ed. Freud: The Fusion of Science & Humanism:
      The Intellectual History of Psychoanalysis.
      Intl Univs Pr.
Gedzelman, Stanley D. see Gedzelman, Stanley David.
Gedzelman, Stanley David, 1944-
  xGedzelman, Stanley D.
    The Science & Wonders of the Atmosphere.
      Wiley.
Gee, Donald.
  xGee, Donald.
    The Fruit of the Spirit. Gospel Pub.
    This Is the Way. Gospel Pub.
    A Word to the Wise. Gospel Pub.
Gee, E. Gordon. see Gee, Elwood Gordon.
Gee, Elwood Gordon.
  xGee, E. Gordon.
    Education Law & the Public Schools: A
      Compendium. Allyn.
Gee, H. see Gee, Henry.
Gee, Henry.
  xGee, H.
    Documents Illustrative of English Church
      History. Kraus Repr.
Gee, Maurine H.
  xGee, Maurine H.
    Firestorm. Morrow.
Geel, Tyll Van. see Van Geel, Tyll.
Geen, Russell G., 1932-
  xGeen, Russell G.
    Personality: The Skein of Behavior. Mosby.
Geer, Dan, 1919-
  xGeer, Dan.
    Pro Rated Longshots: A Proven Method for
      Selecting Longshot Winners. P-H.
Geeraets, Walter J.
  xGeeraets, Walter J.
    Ocular Syndromes. Lea & Febiger.
Geerdes, Harold P.
  xGeerdes, Harold P.
    Planning & Equipping Educational Music
      Facilities. Music Ed.
Geering, R. G.
  xGeering, R. G.
    Christina Stead. Twayne.
Geertz, Clifford.
  xGeertz, Clifford.
    The Religion of Java. U of Chicago Pr.
Geffcken, J. see Geffcken, Johannes.
Geffcken, Johannes, 1861-1935
  xGeffcken, J.
    The Last Days of Greco-Roman Paganism.
      Elsevier.
Geffre, Claude.
  xGeffre, Claude.
    Humanism & Christianity. Seabury.
Gehlen, Arnold, 1904-
  xGehlen, Arnold.
    Man in the Age of Technology. Columbia U
      Pr.
Gehlen, Michael P.
  xGehlen, Michael P.
    The Politics of Coexistence: Soviet Methods &
      Motives. Greenwood.
Gehman, Clayton H., 1909-
  xGehman, Clayton H.
    Children of the Conestoga. Brethren.
Gehman, Richard.
  xGehman, Richard.

    Signet Book of Sausage. NAL.
Gehrels, T. see Gehrels, Thomas.
Gehrels, Thomas.
  xGehrels, T.
    ed. Asteroids. U of Ariz Pr.
Geibel, James.
  xGeibel, James.
    The Blond Brother. Putnam.
Geiger, Don, 1923-
  xGeiger, Don.
    Dramatic Impulse in Modern Poetics. La State
      U Pr.
Geiger, H. Kent.
  xGeiger, H. Kent.
    Family in Soviet Russia. Harvard U Pr.
    National Development 1776-1966: A Selective
      & Annotated Guide to the Most Important
      Articles in English. Scarecrow.
Geiger, Lura Jane.
  xGeiger, Lura Jane.
    Finding Hidden Treasure: TA Groups in the
      Church. Jalmar Pr.
Geiger, Maggy.
  xGeiger, Maggy.
    A Window Box Primer. Popular Lib.
Geiger, Maynard. see Geiger, Maynard J.
Geiger, Maynard J., 1901-
  xGeiger, Maynard.
    Franciscan Missionaries in Hispanic California
      1769-1848: A Biographical Dictionary.
      Huntington Lib.
Geiger, Rudolf, 1894-
  xGeiger, Rudolf.
    Climate Near the Ground. Harvard U Pr.
Geijer, Agnes.
  xGeijer, Agnes.
    A History of Textile Art. Biblio Dist.
Geikie, Roderick.
  xGeikie, Roderick.
    Dutch Barrier, 1705-1719. Greenwood.
Geil, Philip H. see Geil, Phillip Herbert.
Geil, Phillip Herbert, 1930-
  xGeil, Philip H.
    Polymer Single Crystals. Krieger.
Geiogamah, Hanay, 1945-
  xGeiogamah, Hanay.
    New Native American Drama: Three Plays. U
      of Okla Pr.
Geipel, John.
  xGeipel, John.
    Great Adventures of the Vikings. Rand.
Geiringer, Karl, 1899-
  xGeiringer, Karl.
    The Bach Family: Seven Generations of
      Creative Genius. Da Capo.
    Instruments in the History of Western Music.
      Oxford U Pr.
Geiringer, Paul L.
  xGeiringer, Paul L.
    Handbook of Heat Transfer Media. Krieger.
Geis, Darlene.
  xGeis, Darlene.
    Dinosaurs & Other Prehistoric Animals. G&D.
Geis, Gilbert.
  xGeis, Gilbert.
    Not the Law's Business: An Examination of
      Homosexuality, Abortion, Prostitution,
      Narcotics, & Gambling in the United States.
      Schocken.
    White-Collar Crime: Offenses in Business,
      Politics, & Professions. Free Pr.
    ed. White-Collar Crime: Theory & Research.
      Sage.
Geisberg, Max.
  xGeisberg, Max.
    The German Single-Leaf Woodcut: 1500-1550.
      Hacker.
Geiser, Robert L.
  xGeiser, Robert L.

    Hidden Victims: The Sexual Abuse of Children.
      Beacon Pr.
    The Illusion of Caring: Children in Foster Care.
      Beacon Pr.
Geisert, Paul.
  xGeisert, Paul.
    Genes & Populations. Ed Methods.
Geisinger, David L.
  xGeisinger, David L.
    Kicking It: The New Way to Stop Smoking
      Permanently. Grove.
    Kicking It: The New Way to Stop Smoking
      Permanently. NAL.
Geisler, Norman L.
  xGeisler, Norman L.
    General Introduction to the Bible. Moody.
    A Popular Survey of the Old Testament. Baker
      Bk.
Geismar, Ludwig L.
  xGeismar, Ludwig L.
    Families in an Urban Mold: Policy Implications
      of an Australian-U.S. Comparison. Pergamon.
    Family & Community Functioning: A Manual
      of Measurement for Social Work Practice &
      Policy. Scarecrow.
    Preventive Intervention in Social Work.
      Scarecrow.
Geiss, Imanuel.
  xGeiss, Imanuel.
    German Foreign Policy, 1871-1914. Routledge
      & Kegan.
    The Pan-African Movement: A History of
      Pan-Africanism in America, Europe & Africa.
      Holmes & Meier.
Geissler, Ludwig A.
  xGeissler, Ludwig A.
    Looking Beyond. Arno.
Geissman, T. A. see Geissman, Theodore Albert.
Geissman, Theodore A. see Geissman, Theodore Albert.
Geissman, Theodore Albert, 1908-
  xGeissman, T. A.
    Organic Chemistry of Secondary Plant
      Metabolism. Freeman C.
    Principles of Organic Chemistry. W H
      Freeman.
  xGeissman, Theodore A.
    Chemistry of Flavonoid Compounds.
      Macmillan.
Geist, Harold.
  xGeist, Harold.
    From Eminently Disadvantaged to Eminence.
      Green.
Geist, Otto W. see Geist, Otto William.
Geist, Otto William.
  xGeist, Otto W.
    Archaeological Excavations at Kukulik, St.
      Lawrence Island, Alaska. AMS Pr.
Geist, V. see Geist, Valerius.
Geist, Valerius.
  xGeist, V.
    Life Strategies, Human Evolution,
      Environmental Design: Toward a Biological
      Theory of Health. Springer-Verlag.
Geiwitz, P. James.
  xGeiwitz, P. James.
    Approaches to Personality: An Introduction to
      People. Brooks-Cole.
    Non-Freudian Personality Theories.
      Brooks-Cole.
Gekoski, R. A.
  xGekoski, R. A.
    Conrad: The Moral World of the Novelist.
      B&N.
Gelatt, H. B.
  xGelatt, H. B.
    Deciding. College Bd.
Gelatt, Roland, 1920-
  xGelatt, Roland.

Music Makers: Some Outstanding Musical
Performers of Our Day. Da Capo.
Gelb, Barbara L. *see* Gelb, Barbara Levine.
Gelb, Barbara Levine, 1931-
xGelb, Barbara L.
The Dictionary of Food & What's in It for
You. Ballantine.
A Dictionary of Food & What's in It for
You. Paddington.
Gelb, Bernard. *see* Gelb, Bernard A.
Gelb, Bernard A.
xGelb, Bernard.
Energy Use in Mining: Patterns & Prospects.
Ballinger Pub.
Gelb, Betsy D.
xGelb, Betsy D.
ed. Insights for Marketing Management.
Goodyear.
Marketing Is Everybody's Business. Goodyear.
Gelb, Gabriel. *see* Gelb, Gabriel M.
Gelb, Gabriel M.
xGelb, Gabriel.
Marketing Is Everybody's Business. Goodyear.
Gelb, Harold.
xGelb, Harold.
Clinical Management of Head, Neck & TMJ
Pain & Dysfunction: A Multi-Disciplinary
Approach to Diagnosis & Treatment.
Saunders.
Killing Pain Without Prescription. Har-Row.
Gelb, Ignace J, 1907-
xGelb, Ignace J.
Glossary of Old Akkadian. U of Chicago Pr.
Study of Writing. U of Chicago Pr.
Gelb, Leslie H.
xGelb, Leslie H.
The Irony of Vietnam: The System Worked.
Brookings.
Gelbart, S.
xGelbart, Stephen S.
Automorphic Forms & Adele Groups.
Princeton U Pr.
Gelbart, Stephen S. *see* Gelbart, S.
Gelbaum, Bernard R.
xGelbaum, Bernard R.
Counterexamples in Analysis. Holden-Day.
Geldard, Frank A. *see* Geldard, Frank Arthur.
Geldard, Frank Arthur.
xGeldard, Frank A.
Human Senses. Wiley.
Gelder, Lydia Van. *see* Van Gelder, Lydia.
Gelder, Patricia Van. *see* Van Gelder, Patricia.
Gelderman, Carol W.
xGelderman, Carol W.
George Fitzmaurice. G K Hall.
George Fitzmaurice. Twayne.
Geleerd, Elisabeth R.
xGeleerd, Elisabeth R.
ed. The Child Analyst at Work. Intl Univs Pr.
Gelender, Maxwell.
xGelender, Maxwell.
Review Text in Chemistry. AMSCO Sch.
Gelernt, Jules.
xGelernt, Jules.
World of Many Loves: The "Heptameron" of
Marguerite De Navarre. U of NC Pr.
Gelfand, Erwin W.
xGelfand, Erwin W.
ed. Biological Basis of Immunodeficiency.
Raven.
Gelfand, Izrail M. *see* Gelfand, Izrail Moiseevich.
Gelfand, Izrail Moiseevich.
xGelfand, Izrail M.
Calculus of Variations. P-H.
Gelfand, Mark I.
xGelfand, Mark I.
A Nation of Cities: The Federal Government &
Urban America 1933-1965. Oxford U Pr.
Gelinas, Paul. *see* Gelinas, Paul J.

Gelinas, Paul J.
xGelinas, Paul.
Coping with Anger. Rosen Pr.
Coping with Your Emotions. Rosen Pr.
Gelinas, Robert P.
xGelinas, Robert P.
How Teenagers Can Get Good Jobs. Rosen Pr.
Geline, Robert.
xGeline, Robert J.
The Practical Runner. Macmillan.
Geline, Robert J. *see* Geline, Robert.
Gelineau, Joseph.
xGelineau, Joseph.
The Liturgy Today & Tomorrow. Paulist Pr.
Gelineau, P. *see* Gelineau, R. Phyllis.
Gelineau, R. Phyllis.
xGelineau, P.
Experiences in Music. McGraw.
Songs in Action. McGraw.
Gella, Aleksander.
xGella, Aleksander.
ed. The Intelligentsia & the Intellectuals:
Theory, Method & Case Study. Sage.
Gellately, Robert, 1943-
xGellately, Robert.
The Politics of Economic Despair: Shopkeepers
& German Politics 1890-1914. Sage.
Geller, Arthur.
xGeller, Arthur.
Living Longer & Loving It. Hammond Inc.
Geller, D. *see* Geller, Dennis P.
Geller, Dennis P.
xGeller, D.
Structured Programming in APL. Winthrop.
Geller, Evelyn.
xGeller, Evelyn.
ed. Communism: End of the Monolith?
Wilson.
ed. Saving America's Cities. Wilson.
Geller, Lawrence D.
xGeller, Lawrence D.
The Books of the Pilgrims. Garland Pub.
Geller, Michael.
xGeller, Michael.
Mayhem on the Coney Beat. Belmont-Tower.
Geller, Ruth.
xGeller, Ruth.
Seed of a Woman. Imp Pr.
Geller, S. *see* Geller, Seymour.
Geller, Seymour, 1921-
xGeller, S.
ed. Solid Electrolytes. Springer-Verlag.
Gellermann, William, 1897-
xGellermann, William.
Martin Dies. Da Capo.
Gellert, Elizabeth.
xGellert, Elizabeth.
ed. Psychosocial Aspects of Pediatric Care.
Grune.
Gelles, Richard J.
xGelles, Richard J.
Family Violence. Sage.
Gellhorn, Ernst, 1893-
xGellhorn, Ernst.
Principles of Autonomic-Somatic Integrations:
Physiological Basis & Psychological &
Clinical Implications. U of Minn Pr.
Gellhorn, Martha, 1908-
xGellhorn, Martha.
Travels with Myself & Another. Dodd.
Weather in Africa. Dodd.
xGellhorn, Martha E.
Honeyed Peace: Stories. Arno.
Gellhorn, Martha E. *see* Gellhorn, Martha.
Gellhorn, Walter, 1906-
xGellhorn, Walter.

Federal Administrative Proceedings.
Greenwood.
Individual Freedom & Governmental
Restraints. Greenwood.
Sectarian College & the Public Purse: Fordham:
a Case Study. Oceana.
Security, Loyalty & Science. Johnson Repr.
When Americans Complain: Governmental
Grievance Procedures. Harvard U Pr.
Gelling, Margaret.
xGelling, Margaret.
Signposts to the Past: Place-Names & the
History of England. Biblio Dist.
Gellis, Roberta.
xGellis, Roberta.
The Dragon & the Rose. Playboy Pbks.
The Sword & the Swan. Playboy Pbks.
Gellner, E. *see* Gellner, Ernest.
Gellner, Ernest.
xGellner, E.
Legitimation of Belief. Cambridge U Pr.
xGellner, Ernest.
Cause & Meaning in the Social Sciences.
Routledge & Kegan.
Contemporary Thought & Politics. Routledge &
Kegan.
The Devil in Modern Philosophy. Routledge &
Kegan.
Spectacles & Predicaments: Essays in Social
Theory. Cambridge U Pr.
Thought & Change. U of Chicago Pr.
Words & Things: An Examination of, & an
Attack on, Linguistic Philosophy. Routledge
& Kegan.
Gelly, David.
xGelly, David.
The Facts About a Rock Group: Featuring
Whigs. Crown.
Gelman, Howard.
xGelman, Howard.
The Films of John Garfield. Citadel Pr.
Gelman, Rita. *see* Gelman, Rita Golden.
Gelman, Rita G. *see* Gelman, Rita Golden.
Gelman, Rita Golden.
xGelman, Rita.
Professor Coconut & the Thief. HR&W.
xGelman, Rita G.
Uncle Hugh: A Fishing Story. HarBraceJ.
Gelman, Rochel.
xGelman, Rochel.
The Child's Understanding of Number.
Harvard U Pr.
Gelman, Steve.
xGelman, Steve.
Evans of the Army. Doubleday.
Football Fury. Doubleday.
Gelpi, Donald L., 1934-
xGelpi, Donald L.
Charism & Sacrament: A Theology of Christian
Conversion. Paulist Pr.
Gelson, M. Aline. *see* Gelson, Mary Aline.
Gelson, Mary Aline, Sister, 1909-
xGelson, M. Aline.
Analysis of the Realistic Elements in the
Novels of Rene Bazin. AMS Pr.
Gelzer, Jay, Mrs, 1889-
xGelzer, Jay.
Street of a Thousand Delights. Arno.
Gemery, H. A.
xGemery, H. A.
ed. The Uncommon Market: Essays in the
Economic History of the Atlantic Slave
Trade. Acad Pr.
Gemignani, Michael C.
xGemignani, Michael C.
Axiomatic Geometry. A-W.
Gemme, Leila B.
xGemme, Leila B.

Hockey Is Our Game. Childrens.
Soccer Is Our Game. Childrens.
True Book of Spinoffs from Space. Childrens.
xGemme, Leila Boyle.
True Book of the Mars Landing. Childrens.
Gemme, Leila Boyle. *see* Gemme, Leila B.
Gemmill, Anna M. *see* Gemmill, Anna Murphy.
Gemmill, Anna Murphy, 1878-
xGemmill, Anna M.
Experimental Study at New York State
Teachers College at Buffalo to Determine a
Science Program for the Education of
Elementary Classroom Teachers. AMS Pr.
Gemming, Elizabeth.
xGemming, Elizabeth.
Lost City in the Clouds: The Discovery of
Machu Picchu. Coward.
Maple Harvest: The Story of Maple Sugaring.
Coward.
Wool Gathering: Sheep Raising in Old New
England. Coward.
Genazzani, E.
xGenazzani, E.
ed. Pharmacological Modulation of Steroid
Action. Raven.
Genders, Roy.
xGenders, Roy.
Greyhounds. Arco.
Greyhounds. Palmetto Pub.
Growing Old-Fashioned Flowers. A S Barnes.
Growing Soft Fruit. Merrimack Bk Serv.
Home-Grown Food: A Guide for Town
Gardeners. Transatlantic.
Simple Fruit Growing. Barron.
Gendlin, Eugene T., 1926-
xGendlin, Eugene T.
Focusing. Everest Hse.
Gendusa, Sam, 1939-
xGendusa, Sam.
Building Playground Sculpture & Homes.
Master Pr.
Gendzier, Irene L.
xGendzier, Irene L.
Practical Visions of Ya'qub Sanu'. Harvard U
Pr.
**Genealogical Society of the Church of Jesus Christ of
Latter-Day Saints.**
xGenealogical Society of the Church of Jesus
Christ of Latter-Day Saints.
jt. auth. A General Index to a Census of
Pensioners for Revolutionary or Military
Service, 1840. Genealog Pub.
General Agreement on Tariffs & Trade. *see* General
Agreement on Tariffs and Trade.
General Agreement on Tariffs and Trade.
xGeneral Agreement on Tariffs & Trade.
The Activities of GATT. Unipub.
General Anti-Slavery Convention, London, 1843. *see*
General Anti-Slavery Convention, 2d, London, 1843.
General Anti-Slavery Convention, 2d, London, 1843.
xGeneral Anti-Slavery Convention, London, 1843.
Proceedings. Arno.
General Assembly of the I.A.U., 16th, Grenoble, 1976.
see International Astronomical Union.
General Assembly 14th, Brighton, 1970. *see* International
Astronomical Union.
General Assembly 15th, Sydney, 1973. *see* International
Astronomical Union.
General Assembly, 13th, Prague, 1967. *see* International
Astronomical Union.
General Drafting Co. *see* General Drafting Company,
Inc.
General Drafting Company, Inc.
xGeneral Drafting Co.
Man's Domain: A Thematic Atlas of the
World. McGraw.
General Electric. *see* General Electric Company.
General Electric Company.
xGeneral Electric.

Solar Heating & Cooling of Buildings (Phase
O): Executive Summaries. Solar Energy Info.
xGeneral Electric Company.
G-MAP Training Manual. GE Train & Ed.
Responsibilities of Business Leadership: Talks
Presented at the Leadership Conference. Hive
Pub.
Solid Waste Management: Technology
Assessment. Van Nos Reinhold.
Work Effectiveness. GE Train & Ed.
xGeneral Electric Marketing Consulting Services.
Sales Situation Elements. GE Train & Ed.
General Electric Marketing Consulting Services. *see*
General Electric Company.
General Federation of Jewish Labour in Israel.
xGeneral Federation of Jewish Labour in Israel
Executive Committee.
Documents & Essays on Jewish Labour Policy
in Palestine. Greenwood.
General Fisheries Council for the Mediterranean.
xGeneral Fisheries Council for the Mediterranean.
Proceedings & Technical Papers. Unipub.
Report of the General Fisheries Council for the
Mediterranean: Report. Unipub.
General Foods. *see* General Foods Corporation.
General Foods Corporation.
xGeneral Foods.
Cora's Country Cookbook. Benjamin Co.
General Mills. *see* General Mills, Inc.
General Mills, Inc.
xGeneral Mills.
Betty Crocker's International Cookbook.
Random.
General Motors Corporation.
xGeneral Motors Corporation Research
Laboratories Symposium On Approximation Of
Functions - Warren Michigan - 1964.
Approximation of Functions, Proceedings.
Elsevier.
**General Motors Corporation. Frigidaire Division,
Dayton, Ohio. Home Economics Dept.**
xFrigidaire.
Microwave Cooking in Multiple Speeds.
Doubleday.
General Motors Corporation Research Laboratories
Symposium On Approximation Of Functions - Warren
Michigan - 1964. *see* General Motors Corporation.
Generous, William T.
xGenerous, William T.
Swords & Scales: The Development of the
Uniform Code of Military Justice. Kennikat.
Genesis Project.
xGenesis Project.
Jesus, His Life & Times. Morrow.
Genest. *see* Genest, Jacques.
Genest, Jacques.
xGenest.
Hypertension: Physiopathology & Treatment.
McGraw.
Genest, John, 1764-1839
xGenest, John.
Some Account of the English Stage from the
Restoration in 1660 to 1830. B Franklin.
Genet, Jean, 1910-
xGenet, Jean.
Funeral Rites. Grove.
Querelle. Grove.
Genette, Gerard, 1930-
xGenette, Gerard.
Narrative Discourse: An Essay in Method.
Cornell U Pr.
Geneva. Graduate Institute of International Studies.
xGraduate Institute Of International Studies -
Geneva.
World Crisis by the Professors of the Institute.
Arno.
Geneva Institute of International Relations.
xGeneva Institute Of International Relations.

Problems of Peace, Fifth Series. Arno.
Problems of Peace, First Ser. Arno.
Problems of Peace: Lectures. Eighth Series.
Arno.
Problems of Peace: Lectures. Second Series.
Arno.
Problems of Peace: Lectures. Third Series.
Arno.
Problems of Peace, Ninth Ser. Arno.
Problems of Peace, Thirteenth Ser. Arno.
Problems of Peace, Twelfth Ser. Arno.
Genevie, Louis. *see* Genevie, Louis E.
Genevie, Louis E.
xGenevie, Louis.
ed. Collective Behavior & Social Movements.
Peacock Pubs.
Genfan, Herb.
xGenfan, Herb.
How to Start Your Own Craft Business.
Watson-Guptill.
Gennard, John.
xGennard, John.
Job Security & Industrial Relations. OECD.
Genne, Elizabeth.
xGenne, Elizabeth S.
First of All Persons: A New Look at
Men-Women Relationships. Friend Pr.
Genne, William H. *see* Genne, Elizabeth.
Genne, Elizabeth S. *see* Genne, Elizabeth.
Genovese, Eugene D., 1930-
xGenovese, Eugene D.
From Rebellion to Revolution: Afro-American
Slave Revolts in the Making of the Modern
World. Random.
World the Slaveholders Made: Two Essays in
Interpretation. Random.
Genoways, Hugh H.
xGenoways, Hugh H.
Systematics & Evolutionary Relationships of
Spiny Pocket Mice, Genus Liomys. Tex Tech
Pr.
Genser, Cynthia, 1950-
xGenser, Cynthia.
Taking on the Local Color. Columbia U Pr.
Gensler, Kinereth. *see* Gensler, Kinereth D.
Gensler, Kinereth D.
xGensler, Kinereth.
The Poetry Connection: An Anthology of
Contemporary Poems with Ideas to Stimulate
Children's Writing. Tchrs & Writers Coll.
Gensler, M. Arthur.
xGensler, M. Arthur.
A Rational Approach to Office Planning. Am
Mgmt.
Gent, Peter.
xGent, Peter.
North Dallas Forty. Morrow.
North Dallas Forty. NAL.
Texas Celebrity Turkey Trot. Berkley Pub.
Texas Celebrity Turkey Trot. Morrow.
Genthe, Charles. *see* Genthe, Charles V.
Genthe, Charles V.
xGenthe, Charles.
Themes in American Literature. Heath.
Genthner, Henry. *see* Genthner, Henry J.
Genthner, Henry J.
xGenthner, Henry.
Automating Zero Base Budgeting. Petrocelli.
Gentil, Pierre Le. *see* Le Gentil, Pierre.
Gentilcore, R. Louis. *see* Gentilcore, Rocco Louis.
Gentilcore, Rocco Louis.
xGentilcore, R. Louis.
ed. Ontario. U of Toronto Pr.
Gentile, A. G. *see* Gentile, Adrian G.
Gentile, Adrian G.
xGentile, A. G.

In the Deserts of This Earth. HarBraceJ.
In the Deserts of This Earth. HarBraceJ.
George, Vic. *see* George, Victor.
George, Victor.
  xGeorge, Vic.
    Ideology & Social Welfare. Routledge & Kegan.
George Washington University, Biological Sciences
  Communication Project. *see* George Washington
  University, Washington, D.C. Biological Sciences
  Communication Project.
George Washington University, Washington, D.C.
  Biological Sciences Communication Project.
  xGeorge Washington University, Biological
    Sciences Communication Project.
    The Millets: A Bibliography of the World
      Literature Covering the Years 1930-1963.
      Scarecrow.
    Sorghum: A Bibliography of the World
      Literature Covering the Years 1930-1963.
      Scarecrow.
George, Wilfred R.
  xGeorge, Wilfred R.
    The Profit Box System of Forecasting Stock
      Prices. Dow Jones-Irwin.
George, Wilma. *see* George, Wilma B.
George, Wilma B.
  xGeorge, Wilma.
    Animals & Maps. U of Cal Pr.
Georges, Daniel E.
  xGeorges, Daniel E.
    The Geography of Crime & Violence: A Spatial
      & Ecological Perspective. Assn Am
      Geographers.
Georgescu-Roegen, Nicholas.
  xGeorgescu-Roegen, Nicholas.
    Entropy Law & the Economic Process.
      Harvard U Pr.
Georget, Etienne Jean, 1795-1828
  xGeorget, Etienne-Jean.
    De la Folie: Considerations Sur Cette Maladie.
      Arno.
Georget, Etienne-Jean. *see* Georget, Etienne Jean.
The Georgetown Law Journal.
  xGeorgetown Law Journal Editors.
    Frwd. by Georgetown Law Journal: Media &
      the First Amendment in a Free Society. U of
      Mass Pr.
Georgetown Law Journal Editors. *see* The Georgetown
  Law Journal.
Georgetown University, Washington, D.C. Center for
  Strategic and International Studies.
  xCenter for Strategic & International Studies,
    Georgetown University.
    Future of Business - Annual Review 1980-81:
      Practical Issues. Pergamon.
Georgi, Charlotte.
  xGeorgi, Charlotte.
    The Arts & the World of Business. Scarecrow.
Georgi, Jay R., 1928-
  xGeorgi, Jay R.
    Parasitology for Veterinarians. Saunders.
Georgia Chapters, D. A. R. *see* Daughters of the
  American Revolution. Georgia.
Georgia. General Assembly.
  xGeorgia General Assembly.
    Confederate Records of the State of Georgia,
      1860-1868. AMS Pr.
    Revolutionary Records of the State of Georgia,
      1769-1784. AMS Pr.
Georgia. General Assembly. Joint Committee to
  Investigate the Condition of the Georgia Penitentiary.
  xGeorgia General Assembly Joint Committee to
    Investigate the Condition of the Georgia
    Penitentiary.
    Proceedings. Arno.
Georgia Historical Society.
  xGeorgia Historical Society.

Index to United States Census of Georgia for
  1820. Genealog Pub.
Georgia. University. Department of Landscape
  Architecture.
  xLandscape Architecture Dept. of The Univ. of
    Georgia.
    Madison: A Visual Survey & Civic Design
      Study. U of Ga Pr.
Georgiade, Nicholas G., 1918-
  xGeorgiade, Nicholas G.
    Breast Reconstruction Following Mastectomy.
      Mosby.
Georgiades, Thrasybulos. *see* Georgiades, Thrasybulos
  Georgos.
Georgiades, Thrasybulos Georgos, 1907-
  xGeorgiades, Thrasybulos.
    Greek Music, Verse & Dance. Da Capo.
Georgiady, Nicholas P. *see* Georgiady, Nicholas Peter.
Georgiady, Nicholas Peter.
  xGeorgiady, Nicholas P.
    Gertie the Duck. Follett.
Georgiou, Constantine.
  xGeorgiou, Constantine.
    Children & Their Literature. P-H.
    The Clock. Harvey.
    Rani, Queen of the Jungle. P-H.
Georgopoulos, Basil S. *see* Georgopoulos, Basil Spyros.
Georgopoulos, Basil Spyros.
  xGeorgopoulos, Basil S.
    ed. Organization Research on Health
      Institutions. U of Mich Soc Res.
Gerald, Curtis F., 1915-
  xGerald, Curtis F.
    Applied Numerical Analysis. A-W.
  xGerald, Curtis G.
    Computers & the Art of Computation. A-W.
Gerald, Curtis G. *see* Gerald, Curtis F.
Gerald, J. Edward. *see* Gerald, James Edward.
Gerald, James Edward.
  xGerald, J. Edward.
    The British Press Under Government
      Economic Controls. Greenwood.
    The Press & the Constitution, 1931-1947. Peter
      Smith.
Gerald, John B. *see* Gerald, John Bart.
Gerald, John Bart, 1940-
  xGerald, John B.
    Conventional Wisdom. FS&G.
Gerani, Gary.
  xGerani, Gary.
    Fantastic Television. Crown.
Gerard, David E.
  xGerard, David E.
    ed. Libraries in Society: A Reader. K G Saur.
Gerard, Francois C., 1924-
  xGerard, Francois C.
    The Future of the Church: The Theology of
      Renewal of Willem Adolf Visser't Hooft.
      Pickwick.
Gerard, Ralph W. *see* Gerard, Ralph Waldo.
Gerard, Ralph Waldo, 1900-
  xGerard, Ralph W.
    ed. Food for Life. U of Chicago Pr.
Gerard, Yves.
  xGerard, Yves.
    ed. Thematic, Bibliographical & Critical
      Catalogue of the Works of Luigi Boccherini.
      Oxford U Pr.
Geras, Adele.
  xGeras, Adele.
    The Girls in the Velvet Frame. Atheneum.
Geraty, Lawrence. *see* Geraty, Lawrence T.
Geraty, Lawrence T.
  xGeraty, Lawrence.
    ed. God's Hand in My Life. Southern Pub.
Gerber, Dan. *see* Gerber, Daniel F.
Gerber, Daniel F.
  xGerber, Dan.

Revenant. Sumac Mich.
Gerber, Ellen W.
  xGerber, Ellen W.
    ed. Sport & the Body: A Philosophical
      Symposium. Lea & Febiger.
Gerber, Frederick H.
  xGerber, Frederick H.
    Indigo & the Antiquity of Dyeing. Arum Pr.
    Indigo & the Antiquity of Dyeing. Gerber
      Pubns.
Gerber, Israel J. *see* Gerber, Israel Joshua.
Gerber, Israel Joshua, 1918-
  xGerber, Israel J.
    Immortal Rebels: Freedom for the Individual in
      the Bible. Inst Jewish Stud.
Gerber, John A.
  xGerber, John A.
    Psychoneurosis Called Christianity. Libra.
Gerber, Philip L.
  xGerber, Philip L.
    Theodore Dreiser. Coll & U Pr.
    Theodore Dreiser. Twayne.
Gerber, Richard.
  xGerber, Richard.
    Utopian Fantasy: A Study of English Utopian
      Fiction Since the End of the Nineteenth
      Century. Folcroft.
    Utopian Fantasy: A Study of English Utopian
      Fiction Since the End of the Nineteenth
      Century. R West.
Gerber, Sanford E.
  xGerber, Sanford E.
    Audiometry in Infancy. Grune.
Gerber, Vicki.
  xGerber, Vicky.
    Find It, Sew It, Wear It!. Trident.
Gerber, Vicky. *see* Gerber, Vicki.
Gerberding, Keith A.
  xGerberding, Kieth A.
    How to Respond to Transcendental Meditation.
      Concordia.
Gerberding, Kieth A. *see* Gerberding, Keith A.
Gerbers, Teresa.
  xGerbers, Teresa.
    The Laughing Willows. Bouregy.
Gerbi, Antonello, 1904-
  xGerbi, Antonello.
    The Dispute of the New World: The History of
      a Polemic, 1750-1900. U of Pittsburgh Pr.
Gerbner. *see* Gerbner, George.
Gerbner, G. *see* Gerbner, George.
Gerbner, George.
  xGerbner.
    The Analysis of Communication Content:
      Developments in Scientific Theories &
      Computer Techniques. Krieger.
  xGerbner, G.
    Communications Technology & Social Policy:
      Understanding the New Cultural Revolution.
      Wiley.
  xGerbner, George.
    ed. Mass Media Policies in Changing Cultures.
      Wiley.
Gerbracht, Carl.
  xGerbracht, Carl.
    Understanding America's Industries.
      McKnight.
Gerbrandt, Gary L.
  xGerbrandt, Gary L.
    An Idea Book for Acting Out & Writing
      Language, K-8. NCTE.
Gerbrandy, Pieter S. *see* Gerbrandy, Pieter Sjoerds.
Gerbrandy, Pieter Sjoerds, 1885-
  xGerbrandy, Pieter S.
    Indonesia. AMS Pr.
Gerdeman, D. A.
  xGerdeman, D. A.

Arc Plasma Technology in Materials Science. Springer-Verlag.

Gerdts, William H.
  xGerdts, William H.
    American Impressionism. Henry Art.

Gere, Anne R. *see* Gere, Anne Ruggles.

Gere, Anne Ruggles.
  xGere, Anne R.
    Attitudes, Language, & Change. NCTE.

Gere, James M.
  xGere, James M.
    Analysis of Framed Structures. Van Nos Reinhold.

Gergely, Tibor, 1900-
  xGergely, Tibor.
    Busy Day, Busy People. Random.
    illus. Great Big Book of Bedtime Stories. Western Pub.

Gergen, K. J. *see* Gergen, Kenneth J.

Gergen, Kenneth J.
  xGergen, K. J.
    Concept of Self. HR&W.
  xGergen, Kenneth J.
    Psychology of Behavior Exchange. A-W.

Gerhard, Muriel.
  xGerhard, Muriel.
    Effective Teaching Strategies with the Behavioral Outcomes Approach. P-H.

Gerhard, Peter, 1920-
  xGerhard, Peter.
    The Southeast Frontier of New Spain. Princeton U Pr.

Gerhardsson, Birger.
  xGerhardsson, Birger.
    The Origins of the Gospel Traditions. Fortress.

Gerhardt, James M., 1930-
  xGerhardt, James M.
    Draft & Public Policy: Issues in Military Manpower Procurement, 1945-1970. Ohio St U Pr.

Gerhardt, Sidney.
  xGerhardt, Sidney.
    There Is a Better Way of Living!: A Sensible Approach to Personal & Family Growth. Continuum.

Gericke, Helmuth.
  xGericke, Helmuth.
    Lattice Theory. Ungar.

Gericke, Paul.
  xGericke, Paul.
    Crucial Experiences in the Life D. L. Moody. Insight Pr.

Gerin, Winifred.
  xGerin, Winifred.
    Charlotte Bronte: The Evolution of Genius. Oxford U Pr.
    Elizabeth Gaskell: A Biography. Oxford U Pr.
    Horatia Nelson. Oxford U Pr.

Gerkin, Charles V., 1922-
  xGerkin, Charles V.
    Crisis Experience in Modern Life: Theory & Theology for Pastoral Care. Abingdon.

Gerking, Shelby D. *see* Gerking, Shelby Delos.

Gerking, Shelby Delos, 1918-
  xGerking, Shelby D.
    ed. Ecology of Freshwater Fish Production. Halsted Pr.

Gerlach, Albert A., 1920-
  xGerlach, Albert A.
    Theory & Applications of Statistical Wave-Period Processing. Gordon.

Gerlach, Larry R.
  xGerlach, Larry R.
    Prologue to Independence: New Jersey in the Coming of the American Revolution. Rutgers U Pr.

Gerlach, Luther P.
  xGerlach, Luther P.

People, Power, Change: Movements of Social Transformation. Bobbs.

Gerlach, Rex.
  xGerlach, Rex.
    The Complete Book of Casting. Follett.
    The Complete Book of Casting. Winchester Pr.
    Creative Fly Tying & Fly Fishing. Follett.

Gerlach, Ronald. *see* Gerlach, Ronald A.

Gerlach, Ronald A.
  xGerlach, Ronald.
    Teaching About the Law. Anderson Pub Co.

Gerlach, Russel L., 1939-
  xGerlach, Russel L.
    Immigrants in the Ozarks: A Study in Ethnic Geography. U of Mo Pr.

Gerlach, Vernon S.
  xGerlach, Vernon S.
    Teaching & Media: A Systematic Approach. P-H.

Gerler, William R.
  xGerler, William R.
    Educator's Treasury of Humor for All Occasions. P-H.
    Compiled by A Pack of Riddles. Dutton.

Gerli, E. Michael.
  xGerli, E. Michael.
    Alfonso Martinez De Toledo. Twayne.

Gerlinger, Lorena.
  xGerlinger, Lorena.
    Baby Jesus. L Gerlinger.

Gerlings, Charlotte.
  xGerlings, Charlotte.
    Noah's Ark in Paper & Card. Taplinger.

Gerloch, M.
  xGerloch, M.
    Ligand-Field Parameters. Cambridge U Pr.

Germain, Carol P. *see* Germain, Carol P. Hanley.

Germain, Carol P. Hanley.
  xGermain, Carol P.
    A Cancer Unit: An Ethnography. Nursing Res.

Germain, Edward B.
  xGermain, Edward B.
    ed. English & American Surrealist Poetry. Penguin.

Germain, J. E. *see* Germain, Jean Eugene.

Germain, Jean Eugene.
  xGermain, J. E.
    Catalytic Conversion of Hydrocarbons. Acad Pr.

German, Don. *see* German, Donald R.

German, Donald R.
  xGerman, Don.
    Make Your Own Convenience Foods: How to Make Chemical Free Foods That Are Fast, Simple & Economical. Macmillan.
  xGerman, Donald R.
    Money & Banks. Dandelion Pr.

German Society for Documentation. *see* Deutsche Gesellschaft Fuer Dokumentation.

German Society for Neurosurgery, Dusseldorf, Nov 1971. *see* Deutsche Gesellschaft Fuer Neurochirurgie.

German War Office. *see* Great Britain. War Office. General Staff.

Germann, A. C.
  xGermann, A. C.
    Introduction to Law Enforcement & Criminal Justice. C C Thomas.

Germann, Donald R.
  xGermann, Donald R.
    The Anti-Cancer Diet. Wideview Bks.

Germany, Jo.
  xGermany, Jo.

City of Golden Cages. St Martin.
Devil Child. St Martin.

Germar, Herb.
  xGermar, Herb.
    Student Journalist & Photojournalism. Rosen Pr.

Germuth, Frederick G.
  xGermuth, Frederick G.
    Immunopathology of the Renal Glomerulus: Immune Complex Deposit & Antibasement Membrane Disease. Little.

Gernet, Louis, 1882-
  xGernet, Louis.
    L' Approvisionnement D'Athenes en ble au ve et au Ive Siecle. Arno.

Gernsback Library Staff. *see* Transistor Applications, Inc.

Gero, John S.
  xGero, John S.
    Design of Building Frames. Halsted Pr.

Geroch, Robert.
  xGeroch, Robert.
    General Relativity from A to B. U of Chicago Pr.

Gerold, William.
  xGerold, William.
    College Hill: A Photographic Study of Brown University in Its Two Hundredth Year. Brown U Pr.

Gerou, Nancy E., 1946-
  xGerou, Nancy E.
    Complete Guide to Administering the Intramural Program. P-H.

Gerould, Gordon H. *see* Gerould, Gordon Hall.

Gerould, Gordon Hall, 1877-
  xGerould, Gordon H.
    The Ballad of Tradition. Gordian.
    Chaucerian Essays. Russell.
    How to Read Fiction. Russell.
    ed. Old English & Medieval Literature. Arno.
    ed. Old English & Medieval Literature. Greenwood.
    ed. Old English & Medieval Literature. Scholarly.
    Patterns of English & American Fiction: A History. Russell.

Gerpen, Maurice Van. *see* Van Gerpen, Maurice.

Gerrard, A. *see* Gerrard, Anthony.

Gerrard, Anthony.
  xGerrard, A.
    Introduction to Matrix Methods in Optics. Wiley.

Gerrard, Brian.
  xGerrard, Brian.
    Interpersonal Skills for Health Professionals. Reston.

Gerrard, Don.
  xGerrard, Don.
    One Bowl: A Simple Concept for Controlling Body Weight. Random.

Gerrard, W. *see* Gerrard, William.

Gerrard, William.
  xGerrard, W.
    Organic Chemistry of Boron. Acad Pr.

Gerrish, Brian A. *see* Gerrish, Brian Albert.

Gerrish, Brian Albert, 1931-
  xGerrish, Brian A.
    Grace & Reason: A Study in the Theology of Luther. U of Chicago Pr.

Gerrish, Howard H.
  xGerrish, Howard H.
    Electricity & Electronics. Goodheart.

Gerrold, David.
  xGerrold, David.
    Deathbeast. Popular Lib.
    The Flying Sorcerers. Amereon Ltd.
    The Flying Sorcerers. Ballantine.
  xGerrold, M. David.
    Moonstar Odyssey. NAL.

Gerrold, M. David. *see* Gerrold, David.

Gerschenkron, Alexander.
 xGerschenkron, Alexander.
  Continuity in History & Other Essays. Harvard
   U Pr.
Gersh, Harry.
 xGersh, Harry.
  Animals Next Door: A Guide to Zoos &
   Aquariums of the Americas. Fleet.
  When a Jew Celebrates. Behrman.
Gersh, Marvin J.
 xGersh, Marvin J.
  How to Raise Children at Home in Your Spare
   Time. Fawcett.
  How to Raise Children at Home in Your Spare
   Time. Stein & Day.
Gershman, Herbert S.
 xGershman, Herbert S.
  The Surrealist Revolution in France. U of Mich
   Pr.
Gershon, Elliot S.
 xGershon, Elliot S.
  ed. The Impact of Biology on Modern
   Psychiatry. Plenum Pub.
Gershuny, J. see Gershuny, Jonathan.
Gershuny, Jonathan.
 xGershuny, J.
  After Industrial Society?: The Emerging
   Self-Service Economy. Humanities.
Gershuny, Theodore.
 xGershuny, Theodore.
  Soon to Be a Major Motion Picture: The
   Anatomy of an All-Star, Big-Budget,
   Multimillion-Dollar Disaster. HR&W.
Gersmehl, Philip.
 xGersmehl, Phillip.
  Physical Geography. HR&W.
Gersmehl, Phillip. see Gersmehl, Philip.
Gerson, Allan.
 xGerson, Allan.
  Israel, the West Bank & International Law.
   Biblio Dist.
Gerson, Corinne.
 xGerson, Corinne.
  Son for a Day. Atheneum.
  Tread Softly. Dial.
Gerson, Jack J.
 xGerson, Jacob J.
  Horatio Nelson Lay & Sino-British Relations,
   1854-1864. Harvard U Pr.
Gerson, Jacob J. see Gerson, Jack J.
Gerson, Joel.
 xGerson, Joel.
  Standard Textbook for Professional
   Estheticians. Milady.
Gerson, Louis L.
 xGerson, Louis L.
  Woodrow Wilson & the Rebirth of Poland,
   1914-1920: A Study in the Influence on
   American Policy of Minority Groups of
   Foreign Origin. Shoe String.
Gerson, Noel. see Gerson, Noel Bertram.
Gerson, Noel B.
 xGerson, Noel B.
  Daughter of Eve. Ace Bks.
Gerson, Noel B. see Gerson, Noel Bertram.
Gerson, Noel Bertram, 1914-
 xGerson, Noel.
  The Swamp Fox, Francis Marion. Mockingbird
   Bks.
 xGerson, Noel B.
  The Glorious Scoundrel: A Biography of
   Captain John Smith. Dodd.
  The Highwayman. Ace Bks.
  Neptune. Avon.
  Neptune. Dodd.
Gerson, Robert A., 1904-
 xGerson, Robert A.
  Music in Philadelphia. Greenwood.
Gerstein, Linda, 1938-
 xGerstein, Linda.

  Nikolai Strakhov. Harvard U Pr.
Gerstell, Vivian S.
 xGerstell, Vivian S.
  Silversmiths of Lancaster, Pennsylvania
   1730-1850. Sutter House.
Gersten, Leon.
 xGersten, Leon.
  Solutions to Your Writing Problems. Barron.
Gerstenberger, Erhard.
 xGerstenberger, Erhard S.
  Suffering. Abingdon.
Gerstenberger, Erhard S. see Gerstenberger, Erhard.
Gerstenfeld, Arthur, 1927-
 xGerstenfeld, Arthur.
  Innovation: A Study of Technological Policy. U
   Pr of Amer.
Gerster, Georg, 1928-
 xGerster, Georg.
  Flights of Discovery: The Earth from Above.
   Paddington.
Gerstinger, Heinz, 1919-
 xGerstinger, Heinz.
  Pedro Calderon De la Barca. Ungar.
Gerstl, Joel. see Gerstl, Joel Emery.
Gerstl, Joel Emery.
 xGerstl, Joel.
  ed. Professions for the People: The Politics of
   Skill. Halsted Pr.
  ed. Professions for the People: The Politics of
   Skill. Schenkman.
Gerstner, John H.
 xGerstner, John H.
  Reasons for Faith. Baker Bk.
Gerstner-Hirzel, Arthur.
 xGerstner-Hirzel, Arthur.
  Economy of Action & the Word in
   Shakespeare's Plays. AMS Pr.
  Economy of Action & the Word in
   Shakespeare's Plays. R West.
Gertsch, Willis J. see Gertsch, Willis John.
Gertsch, Willis John, 1906-
 xGertsch, Willis J.
  American Spiders. Van Nos Reinhold.
Gertzel, Cherry. see Gertzel, Cherry J.
Gertzel, Cherry J.
 xGertzel, Cherry.
  Politics of Independent Kenya. Northwestern U
   Pr.
Geruson, Richard T.
 xGeruson, Richard T.
  Cities & Urbanization. HR&W.
Gervais, David, 1943-
 xGervais, David.
  Flaubert & Henry James: A Study in Contrasts.
   B&N.
Gervasi, Tom.
 xGervasi, Tom.
  Arsenal of Democracy: American Weapons
   Available for Export. Grove.
Gervasutti, Giusto, 1909-1946
 xGervasutti, Giusto.
  Gervasutti's Climbs. Mountaineers.
Gerwin, Donald.
 xGerwin, Donald.
  Budgeting Public Funds: The Decision Process
   in the Urban School District. U of Wis Pr.
Gerwin, K. S. see Gerwin, Kenneth S.
Gerwin, Kenneth S.
 xGerwin, K. S.
  Detection of Hearing Loss & Ear Disease in
   Children. C C Thomas.
Gesch, Roy. see Gesch, Roy G.
Gesch, Roy G.
 xGesch, Roy.
  Lord of the Young Crowd. Concordia.
 xGesch, Roy G.
  God's World Through Young Eyes. Concordia.
  Help, I'm in College. Concordia.
Geschwender, James A., 1933-
 xGeschwender, James A.

  Racial Stratification in America. Wm C Brown.
Gesell, Arnold. see Gesell, Arnold Lucius.
Gesell, Arnold L. see Gesell, Arnold Lucius.
Gesell, Arnold Lucius.
 xGesell, Arnold.
  Infant & Child in the Culture of Today: The
   Guidance of Development in Home &
   Nursery School. Har-Row.
 xGesell, Arnold L.
  Infant Development: The Embryology of Early
   Human Behavior. Greenwood.
  Studies in Child Development. Greenwood.
Gesellschaft Deutscher Naturforscher und Arzte.
 xWissenschaftliche Konferenz der Gesellschaft
   Deutscher Naturforscher und Aerzte, 4th, Berlin,
   1967.
  Molecular Genetics: Proceedings.
   Springer-Verlag.
Gesellschaft Fuer Biologische Chemie.
 xColloquium of the Workshop for Biological
   Chemistry, April 29 - May 1, 1976,
   Mosbach-Baden.
  The Immune System: Proceedings.
   Springer-Verlag.
 xGesellschaft Fuer Biologische Chemie, 21st
   Colloquium, Mossbach-Baden, 1970.
  Biochemistry of Oxygen: Proceedings.
   Springer-Verlag.
  The Dynamic Structure of Cell Membranes:
   Proceedings. Springer-Verlag.
  Inhibitors: Tools in Cell Research Proceedings.
   Springer-Verlag.
  Mammalian Reproduction: Proceedings.
   Springer-Verlag.
  Regulation of Transcription & Translation in
   Eukaryotes: Proceedings. Springer-Verlag.
 xSymposium on the Biochemistry of Sensory
   Functions, Colloquium Mosbach, Apr. 1974.
   Proceedings. Springer-Verlag.
Gesellschaft Fuer Informatik.
 xGesellschaft fuer Informatik: 3 Jahrestagung,
   Hamburg 1973.
  Lecture Notes in Computer Science, Vol. 1.
   Springer Verlag.
Gesellschaft fuer Informatik: 3 Jahrestagung, Hamburg
 1973. see Gesellschaft Fuer Informatik.
Gesellschaft Fuer Nephrologie.
 xGesellschaft Fuer Nephrologie, 5th Symposium,
   Switzerland, 1967.
  Progress in Nephrology: Proceedings.
   Springer-Verlag.
Gesellschaft Fuer Nephrologie, 5th Symposium,
 Switzerland, 1967. see Gesellschaft Fuer Nephrologie.
**Gesellschaft Zur Bekampfung der Krebskrankheiten
Nordrhein-Westfalen.**
 xInternational Symposium of the "Gesellschaft Zur
   Bekampfung De Krebskran Kheiten
   Nordhrein-West-Falen E. V.", 7th, Dusseldorf,
   Oct. 1975.
  Tumors of the Male Genital System.
   Springer-Verlag.
 xInternational Symposium of the Gesellschraft Zur
   Bekaempfung der Krebskrankheiten
   Nordrhein-Westfalen E. V., Duesselford,
   Germany, October 17-18, 1974.
  Malignant Bone Tumors. Springer-Verlag.
Gess, Diane.
 xGess, Diane.
  Sunshine Porcupine. Oak Tree Pubns.
Gessford, John E. see Gessford, John Evans.
Gessford, John Evans.
 xGessford, John E.
  The Use of Reservoir Water for Hydroelectric
   Power Generation. Arno.
Gessner, Lynne.
 xGessner, Lynne.

Brother to the Navajo. Elsevier-Nelson.
Edge of Darkness. Walker & Co.
Navajo Slave. NAL.
Navajo Slave. Harvey.
Gessner, Robert, 1907-1968
xGessner, Robert.
Massacre: A Survey of Today's American
Indian. Da Capo.
Gest, Alexander P. *see* Gest, Alexander Purves.
Gest, Alexander Purves, 1853-
xGest, Alexander P.
Engineering. Cooper Sq.
Geston, Mark S.
xGeston, Mark S.
The Siege of Wonder. Ultramarine Pub.
Getchell, Bud, 1934-
xGetchell, Bud.
Physical Fitness: A Way of Life. Wiley.
Getchell, Robert.
xGetchell, Robert.
Alice Doesn't Live Here Anymore. Warner
Bks.
Getches, David H.
xGetches, David H.
Cases & Materials on Federal Indian Law.
West Pub.
Gethers, Peter.
xGethers, Peter.
The Dandy. Bantam.
xGethers, Peter S.
The Dandy. Dutton.
Gethers, Peter S. *see* Gethers, Peter.
Gething, Judith. *see* Gething, Judith R.
Gething, Judith R., 1940-
xGething, Judith.
Sex Discrimination & the Law in Hawaii: A
Guide to Your Legal Rights. U Pr of Hawaii.
Getman, Frederick H. *see* Getman, Frederick Hutton.
Getman, Frederick Hutton, 1877-1941
xGetman, Frederick H.
The Life of Ira Remsen. Arno.
Getoor, R. K. *see* Getoor, Ronald Kay.
Getoor, Ronald Kay, 1929-
xGetoor, R. K.
Markov Processes: Ray Processes & Right
Processes. Springer-Verlag.
Gettel, Ronald E., 1931-
xGettel, Ronald E.
Real Estate Guidelines & Rules of Thumb.
McGraw.
Gettens, Rutherford J. *see* Gettens, Rutherford John.
Gettens, Rutherford John.
xGettens, Rutherford J.
Two Early Chinese Bronze Weapons with
Meteoritic Iron Blades. Freer.
Gettinger, Stephen H.
xGettinger, Stephen H.
Sentenced to Die: The People, the Crimes &
the Controversy. Macmillan.
Gettings, Fred.
xGettings, Fred.
Arthur Rackham. Macmillan.
Palmistry Made Easy. Wilshire.
Gettleman, Marvin E.
xGettleman, Marvin E.
The Dorr Rebellion: A Study in American
Radicalism: 1833-1849. Krieger.
An Elusive Presence: The Discovery of John
H. Finley & His America. Nelson-Hall.
Gettleman, Susan.
xGettleman, Susan.
The Courage to Divorce. Ballantine.
The Courage to Divorce. S&S.
Gettmann, Royal A. *see* Gettmann, Royal Alfred.
Gettmann, Royal Alfred, 1904-
xGettmann, Royal A.
Turgenev in England & America. Greenwood.
Getty, Alice.
xGetty, Alice.

The Gods of Northern Buddhism. C E Tuttle.
Getty, J. Paul. *see* Getty, Jean Paul.
Getty, Jean Paul, 1892-
xGetty, J. Paul.
How to Be a Successful Executive. Playboy
Pbks.
Gettys, Joseph M. *see* Gettys, Joseph Miller.
Gettys, Joseph Miller.
xGettys, Joseph M.
How to Study I Corinthians. Attic Pr.
How to Study John. Attic Pr.
How to Study Luke. Attic Pr.
How to Study Philippians, Colossians, &
Philemon. Attic Pr.
Surveying the Historical Books. Attic Pr.
Surveying the Pentateuch. Attic Pr.
Getz, Arthur.
xGetz, Arthur.
illus. Hamilton Duck. Western Pub.
illus. Hamilton Duck's Springtime Story.
Western Pub.
Getz, Gene A.
xGetz, Gene A.
Audiovisual Media in Christian Education.
Moody.
Building up One Another. Victor Bks.
Measure of a Church. Regal.
Getz, George, 1906-
xGetz, George.
Business Law. Pitman Learning.
Getz, Malcolm.
xGetz, Malcolm.
Economics of the Urban Fire Department.
Johns Hopkins.
Getz, W. M. *see* Getz, Wayne Marcus.
Getz, Wayne Marcus.
xGetz, W. M.
ed. Mathematical Modelling in Biology &
Ecology: Proceedings of a Symposium Held
at the CSIR, Pretoria, July 1979.
Springer-Verlag.
Getzels, Jacob W.
xGetzels, Jacob W.
Educational Administration As a Social
Process: Theory, Research, Practice.
Har-Row.
Geuder, Patricia. *see* Geuder, Patricia A.
Geuder, Patricia A.
xGeuder, Patricia.
ed. They Really Taught Us How to Write.
NCTE.
Geumlek, Lois.
xGeumlek, Lois.
Stranger in Town. Bouregy.
Gewanter, Vera.
xGewanter, Vera.
A Passion for Vegetables: Recipes from
European Kitchens. Viking Pr.
Gewehr. *see* Gewehr, Wesley Marsh.
Gewehr, Wesley M. *see* Gewehr, Wesley Marsh.
Gewehr, Wesley Marsh, 1888-
xGewehr.
The Great Awakening in Virginia. Church
History.
xGewehr, Wesley M.
The Great Awakening in Virginia 1740-1790.
Peter Smith.
Gewehr, Wolf.
xGewehr, Wolf.
Reading German in the Humanities. Van Nos
Reinhold.
Reading German in the Natural Sciences. Van
Nos Reinhold.
Reading German in the Social Sciences. Van
Nos Reinhold.
Gewirth, Alan.
xGewirth, Alan.

Political Philosophy. Macmillan.
Reason & Morality. U of Chicago Pr.
Gewirtz, Herman.
xGewirtz, Herman.
Essentials of Physics. Barron.
How to Prepare for College Board
Achievement Tests -- Physics. Barron.
Gewirtz, J. L. *see* Gewirtz, Jacob L.
Gewirtz, Jacob L., 1924-
xGewirtz, J. L.
ed. Attachment & Dependency. Halsted Pr.
Geyer, R. A. *see* Geyer, Richard A.
Geyer, Richard A.
xGeyer, R. A.
Submersibles & Their Use in Oceanography &
Ocean Engineering. Elsevier.
Geyl, P. *see* Geyl, Pieter.
Geyl, Pieter, 1887-
xGeyl, P.
The Pattern of the Past: Can We Determine It.
Greenwood.
xGeyl, Pieter.
Debates with Historians. NAL.
Ghadar, Fariborz.
xGhadar, Fariborz.
The Evolution of OPEC Strategy. Lexington
Bks.
Ghali, A. *see* Ghali, Amin.
Ghali, Amin.
xGhali, A.
Structural Analysis: A Unified Classical &
Matrix Approach. Halsted Pr.
Ghandhi, Sorab K. *see* Ghandhi, Sorab Khushro.
Ghandhi, Sorab Khushro, 1928-
xGhandhi, Sorab K.
Theory & Practice of Microelectronics. Wiley.
Ghatak, A. K. *see* Ghatak, Ajoy K.
Ghatak, Ajoy K.
xGhatak, A. K.
ed. Contemporary Optics. Plenum Pub.
Introduction to Lattice Dynamics. A-W.
Ghatak, Subrata, 1939-
xGhatak, Subrata.
Development Economics. Longman.
Ghausi, M. S. *see* Ghausi, Mohammed Shuaib.
Ghausi, Mohammed Shuaib.
xGhausi, M. S.
Introduction to Distributed - Parameter
Networks: With Applications to Integrated
Circuits. Krieger.
Gheorghe, Alexandru.
xGheorghe, Alexandru.
Processing & Synthesis of Hydrogeological
Data. Intl Schol Bk Serv.
Gheorghiu, C. Virgil. *see* Gheorghiu, Constantin Virgil.
Gheorghiu, Constantin Virgil, 1916-
xGheorghiu, C. Virgil.
The Death of Kyralessa. Greenwood.
Ghering, W. L.
xGhering, W. L.
ed. Reference Data for Acoustic Noise Control.
Ann Arbor Science.
Ghertman, M. *see* Ghertman, Michel.
Ghertman, Michel.
xGhertman, M.
European Research in International Business.
Elsevier.
Ghez, Gilbert R.
xGhez, Gilbert R.
The Allocation of Time & Goods Over the Life
Cycle. Natl Bur Econ Res.
Ghezzi, Bert.
xGhezzi, Bert.
ed. Prayer Group Workshop. Servant.
Ghirelli, Michael.
xGhirelli, Michael.
ed. List of Emigrants from England to America
1682-1692. C E Tuttle.
Ghiselin, Brewster, 1903-
xGhiselin, Brewster.

Country of the Minotaur. U of Utah Pr.

Ghiselin, Micahel T., 1939-
xGhiselin, Michael T.
The Triumph of the Darwinian Method. U of
Cal Pr.

Ghiselin, Michael T., 1939-
xGhiselin, Michael T.
The Economy of Nature & the Evolution of
Sex. U of Cal Pr.

Ghiselin, Michael T. see Ghiselin, Micahel T.

Ghiselli, Edwin E. see Ghiselli, Edwin Ernest.

Ghiselli, Edwin Ernest, 1907-
xGhiselli, Edwin E.
Explorations in Managerial Talent. Goodyear.
Validity of Occupational Aptitude Tests.
Krieger.

Ghista, D. N. see Ghista, Dhanjoo N.

Ghista, Dhanjoo N.
xGhista, D. N.
ed. Theoretical Foundations of Cardiovascular
Processes. S Karger.

Ghizzetti, A. see Ghizzetti, Aldo.

Ghizzetti, Aldo.
xGhizzetti, A.
Quadrature Formulae. Acad Pr.
Quadrature Formulae. Birkhauser.

Ghosal. see Ghosal, A.

Ghosal, A.
xGhosal.
Applied Cybernetics: It's Relevance to
Operations Research. Gordon.
xGhosal, A.
jt. auth. Applied Cybernetics: It's Relevance to
Operations Research. Gordon.
Examples & Exercises in Operations Research.
Gordon.
xGhosal, Amitaval.
Some Aspects of Queueing & Storage Systems.
Springer-Verlag.

Ghosal, Amitaval. see Ghosal, A.

Ghose, Sankar, 1925-
xGhose, Sankar.
Socialism, Democracy & Nationalism in India.
Intl Pubns Serv.
Socialism, Democracy & Nationalism in India.
Paragon.

Ghose, Sisirkumar.
xGhose, Sisirkumar.
The Later Poems of Tagore. Greenwood.

Ghose, Zulfikar, 1935-
xGhose, Zulfikar.
Hamlet, Prufrock & Language. St Martin.

Ghosh, A. B. see Ghosh, Amiya Bhushan.

Ghosh, Amiya Bhushan.
xGhosh, A. B.
Price Trends & Policies in India. Intl Bk Dist.

Ghosh, Asok K.
xGhosh, Asok K.
Paleolithic Cultures of Singhbhum. Am Philos.

Ghosh, B. N.
xGhosh, B. N.
Disguised Unemployment in Underdeveloped
Countries, with Special Reference to India.
South Asia Bks.

Ghosh, Moni, 1892-
xGhosh, Moni.
Our Struggle: A Short History of Trade Union
Movement in Tisco Industry at Jamshedpur.
South Asia Bks.

Ghosh, Sanjib K. see Ghosh, Sanjib Kumar.

Ghosh, Sanjib Kumar, 1925-
xGhosh, Sanjib K.
Analytical Photogrammetry. Pergamon.

Ghosh, Sunanda.
xGhosh, Sunanda.
Legislative Committees in West Bengal. South
Asia Bks.

Ghosh, Tapan, 1928-
xGhosh, Tapan.

Gandhi Murder Trial. Asia.

Ghougassian, Joseph P.
xGhougassian, Joseph P.
Gordon W. Allport's Ontopsychology of the
Person. Philos Lib.

Ghurye, G. S. see Ghurye, Govind Sadashiv.

Ghurye, Govind Sadashiv, 1893-
xGhurye, G. S.
The Scheduled Tribes of India. Transaction
Bks.

Ghyka, Matila. see Ghyka, Matila Costiescu.

Ghyka, Matila Costiescu, 1881-1965
xGhyka, Matila.
The Geometry of Art & Life. Dover.

Giachino, J. W. see Giachino, Joseph William.

Giachino, Joseph W. see Giachino, Joseph William.

Giachino, Joseph William, 1906-
xGiachino, J. W.
Engineering - Technical Drafting. Am
Technical.
Everyday Sketching & Drafting. Am Technical.
Print Reading for Welders. Am Technical.
xGiachino, Joseph W.
Arc Welding. Am Technical.

Giacomo, Melchior Di. see Di Giacomo, Melchior.

Giallombardo, Rose.
xGiallombardo, Rose.
The Social World of Imprisoned Girls: A
Comparative Study of Institutions for
Juvenile Delinquents. Wiley.
Society of Women: A Study of a Women's
Prison. Wiley.

Giam, C. S.
xGiam, C. S.
Pollutant Effects on Marine Organisms.
Lexington Bks.

Giamatti, A. Barlett.
xGiamatti, A. Bartlett.
Earthly Paradise & the Renaissance Epic.
Princeton U Pr.

Giamatti, A. Bartlett. see Giamatti, A. Barlett.

Giambarba, Paul.
xGiambarba, Paul.
Surfmen & Lifesavers. Scrimshaw.

Giammattei, Victor M. see Giammattei, Victor Michael.

Giammattei, Victor Michael.
xGiammattei, Victor M.
Art of a Vanished Race: The Mimbres Classic
Black-on-White. Dillon-Tyler Pubs.

Gianakaris, C. J., 1934-
xGianakaris, C. J.
Foundations of Drama. HM.

Gianaris, Nicholas V.
xGianaris, Nicholas V.
Economic Development: Thought & Problems.
Chris Mass.

Giancoli, Douglas. see Giancoli, Douglas C.

Giancoli, Douglas C.
xGiancoli, Douglas.
Ideas of Physics. HarBraceJ.

Giangrande, Lawrence.
xGiangrande, Lawrence.
The Use of "Spoudaiogeloion" in Greek &
Roman Literature. Mouton.

Giangreco, C. Joseph.
xGiangreco, C. Joseph.
Education of the Hearing Impaired. C C
Thomas.

Giannelli, F.
xGiannelli, F.
Human Chromosomes DNA Synthesis. S
Karger.

Giannestras, Nicholas J.
xGiannestras, Nicholas J.
ed. Foot Disorders: Medical & Surgical
Management. Lea & Febiger.

Giannetti, Louis D.
xGiannetti, Louis D.

Understanding Movies. P-H.

Gianpietri, Peter.
xGianpietri, Peter.
The Successful Rules of Artistic Composition.
Gloucester Art.

Gianturco, Daniel T.
xGianturco, Daniel T.
The Promiscuous Teenager. C C Thomas.

Giarda, Christophoro. see Giarda, Cristoforo.

Giarda, Cristoforo, 1595-1649
xGiarda, Christophoro.
Bibliothecae Alexandrinae Icones Symbolicae.
Garland Pub.

Giardini, Fabio.
xGiardini, Fabio.
Loving Awareness of God's Presence in
Prayer. Alba.

Gibb, Carson, 1926-
xGibb, Carson.
Exposition & Literature. Macmillan.

Gibb, George S. see Gibb, George Sweet.

Gibb, George Sweet, 1916-
xGibb, George S.
The Whitesmiths of Taunton: A History of
Reed & Barton, 1824-1943. Arno.

Gibb, Hamilton A. see Gibb, Hamilton Alexander
Rosskeen.

Gibb, Hamilton Alexander Rosskeen, Sir, 1895-
xGibb, Hamilton A.
Arab Conquests in Central Asia. AMS Pr.
ed. Whither Islam?: A Survey of Modern
Movements in the Moslem World. AMS Pr.

Gibb, Jack R.
xGibb, Jack R.
Trust: A New View of Personal &
Organizational Development. Guild of
Tutors.

Gibb, Terence C. see Gibb, Terence Charles.

Gibb, Terence Charles.
xGibb, Terence C.
Principles of Mossbauer Spectroscopy. Halsted
Pr.
Principles of Mossbauer Spectroscopy.
Methuen Inc.

Gibbard, Graham S.
xGibbard, Graham S.
ed. Analysis of Groups: Contributions to
Theory, Research & Practice. Jossey-Bass.

Gibbard, Mark.
xGibbard, Mark.
Apprentices in Love. Morehouse.

Gibbens, T. C. see Gibbens, T. C. N.

Gibbens, T. C. N.
xGibbens, T. C.
Medical Remands in the Criminal Court.
Oxford U Pr.

Gibbes, Phoebe.
xGibbes, Phoebe.
The Life & Adventures of Mr. Francis Clive,
1764. Garland Pub.

Gibbes, Robert W. see Gibbes, Robert Wilson.

Gibbes, Robert Wilson, 1809-1866
xGibbes, Robert W.
Documentary History of the American
Revolution. Reprint.

Gibbia, S. W.
xGibbia, Salvatore W.
Wood Finishing & Refinishing. Van Nos
Reinhold.

Gibbia, Salvatore W. see Gibbia, S. W.

Gibbins, Neil L. see Gibbins, Neil Louis.

Gibbins, Neil Louis.
xGibbins, Neil L.
Law of Free Public Education in West Virginia:
A Handbook for School Personnel, Board
Members & Students. Interstate.

Gibbon, D. L. see Gibbon, Donald L.

Gibbon, Donald L.
xGibbon, D. L.

Aeration of Activated Sludge in Sewage
Treatment. Pergamon.
Gibbon, Edward, 1737-1794
xGibbon, Edward.
Autobiography. Oxford U Pr.
Decline & Fall of the Roman Empire. Dutton.
The Decline & Fall of the Roman Empire.
Modern Lib.
Gibbon's Decline & Fall of the Roman Empire.
Rand.
The History of the Decline & Fall of the
Roman Empire. AMS Pr.
Gibbon, John M. *see* Gibbon, John Murray.
Gibbon, John Murray.
xGibbon, John M.
Canadian Folk Songs (Old & New). Folcroft.
Gibbon, Peter.
xGibbon, Peter.
The Origins of Ulster Unionism: The
Formation of Popular Protestant Politics &
Ideology in Nineteenth-Century Ireland.
Rowman.
Gibbons, Barbara.
xGibbons, Barbara.
Diet Watchers Cookbook. Har-Row.
The Year-Round Turkey Cookbook: A Guide
to Delicious, Nutritious Dining with Today's
Versatile Turkey. McGraw.
Gibbons, Boyd.
xGibbons, Boyd.
Wye Island. Penguin.
Gibbons, D. E. *see* Gibbons, Don E.
Gibbons, Don.
xGibbons, Don.
The Clout. Avon.
Gibbons, Don. *see* Gibbons, Don C.
Gibbons, Don C.
xGibbons, Don.
The Criminological Enterprise: Theories &
Perspectives. P H.
xGibbons, Don C.
Criminal Justice Planning: An Introduction.
P-H.
Delinquent Behavior. P-H.
Gibbons, Don E.
xGibbons, D. E.
Applied Hypnosis & Hyperempiria. Plenum
Pub.
Gibbons, Euell.
xGibbons, Euell.
Euell Gibbons' Handbook of Edible Wild
Plants. Donning Co.
Feast on a Diabetic Diet. Fawcett.
jt. auth. Feast on a Diabetic Diet. McKay.
Stalking the Healthful Herbs. McKay.
Stalking the Wild Asparagus. McKay.
Gibbons, G. *see* Gibbons, Gerard.
Gibbons, Gail.
xGibbons, Gail.
illus. Clocks & How They Go. T Y Crowell.
illus. The Missing Maple Syrup Sap Mystery:
Or How Maple Syrup Is Made. Warne.
illus. Things to Make & Do for Columbus Day.
Watts.
illus. Things to Make & Do for Halloween.
Watts.
illus. Things to Make & Do for Your Birthday.
Watts.
Gibbons, Gerard.
xGibbons, G.
Avalanche - Diode Microwave Oscillators.
Oxford U Pr.
Gibbons, James, Cardinal, 1834-1921
xGibbons, James C.
A Retrospect of Fifty Years. Arno.
Gibbons, James C. *see* Gibbons, James.
Gibbons, Jean D. *see* Gibbons, Jean Dickinson.

Gibbons, Jean Dickinson, 1938-
xGibbons, Jean D.
Nonparametric Methods for Quantitative
Analysis. Am Sciences Pr.
Nonparametric Statistical Inference. McGraw.
Gibbons (Stanley) Ltd., London.
xStanley Gibbons Ltd.
ed. Stamps of the World. StanGib Ltd.
ed. Stanley Gibbons British Commonwealth.
StanGib Ltd.
Gibbs, A. J.
xGibbs, A. J.
Plant Virology: The Principles. Halsted Pr.
Gibbs and Cox Inc. *see* Gibbs and Cox, Inc., New York.
Gibbs and Cox, Inc., New York.
xGibbs and Cox Inc.
Marine Design Manual for Fiberglass
Reinforced Plastics. McGraw.
Gibbs, Benjamin.
xGibbs, Benjamin.
Freedom & Liberation. Humanities.
Freedom & Liberation. St Martin.
Gibbs, Frederic A. *see* Gibbs, Frederic Andrews.
Gibbs, Frederic Andrews.
xGibbs, Frederic A.
Medical Electroencephalography. A-W.
Gibbs, G. I.
xGibbs, G. I.
Handbook of Games & Simulation Exercises.
Sage.
Gibbs, George, 1815-1873
xGibbs, George.
Alphabetical Vocabulary of the Chinook
Language. AMS Pr.
Gibbs, Jack P.
xGibbs, Jack P.
Crime, Punishment, & Deterrence. Elsevier.
Gibbs, James A. *see* Gibbs, James Atwood.
Gibbs, James Atwood, 1922-
xGibbs, James A.
Oregon's Salty Coast. Superior Pub.
Gibbs, James L.
xGibbs, James L.
ed. Peoples of Africa. HR&W.
Gibbs, James W.
xGibbs, James W.
Dixie Clockmakers. Pelican.
Gibbs, John W. *see* Gibbs, John W. B.
Gibbs, John W. B.
xGibbs, John W.
Financial Decision-Making in Business:
Planning & Control Techniques to Increase
Your Profits. P-H.
Gibbs, M. *see* Gibbs, Martin.
Gibbs, M. E.
xGibbs, M. E.
Inhibition of Memory Formation. Plenum Pub.
Gibbs, Margaret S.
xGibbs, Margaret S.
Community Psychology: Theoretical &
Empirical Approaches. Halsted Pr.
Gibbs, Martin, 1922-
xGibbs, M.
ed. Structure & Function of Chloroplasts.
Springer-Verlag.
Gibbs, Mary A. *see* Gibbs, Mary Ann.
Gibbs, Mary Ann.
xGibbs, Mary A.
The Admiral's Lady. Fawcett.
Glass Palace. Fawcett.
Gibbs, R. Darnley. *see* Gibbs, Ronald Darnley.
Gibbs, R. S. *see* Gibbs, Ronald S.
Gibbs, Ronald Darnley, 1904-
xGibbs, R. Darnley.
Chemotaxonomy of Flowering Plants.
McGill-Queens U Pr.
Gibbs, Ronald J.
xGibbs, Ronald J.

Suspended Solids in Water. Plenum Pub.
Gibbs, Ronald S.
xGibbs, R. S.
Ambulatory Obstetrics: A Clinical Guide.
Wiley.
Gibbs, Sharon L.
xGibbs, Sharon L.
Greek & Roman Sundials. Yale U Pr.
Gibbs, Tony.
xGibbs, Tony.
Backpacking. Watts.
Navigation: Finding Your Way on Sea & Land.
Watts.
Practical Sailing. Hearst Bks.
Gibellini, Rosino.
xGibellini, Rosino.
ed. Frontiers of Theology in Latin America.
Orbis Bks.
Gibert, Stephen P.
xGibert, Stephen P.
Soviet Images of America. Crane-Russak Co.
Giblin, P. J.
xGiblin, P. J.
Graphs, Surfaces & Homology: An
Introduction to Algebraic Topology. Methuen
Inc.
Gibney, Frank.
xGibney, Frank.
Five Gentlemen of Japan: The Portrait of a
Nation's Character. C E Tuttle.
The Operators. Greenwood.
Gibor, Aharon.
xGibor, Aharon.
Intro. by Conditions for Life: Readings from
Scientific American. W H Freeman.
Gibra, Isaac. *see* Gibra, Isaac N.
Gibra, Isaac N.
xGibra, Isaac.
Probability & Statistical Inference for Scientists
& Engineers. P-H.
Gibran, Kahlil, 1883-1931
xGibran, Kahlil.
Broken Wings. Citadel Pr.
The Procession. Citadel Pr.
Prophet. Knopf.
Prose Poems. Knopf.
Thoughts & Meditations. Citadel Pr.
Gibson, Alexander D. *see* Gibson, Alexander Dunnett.
Gibson, Alexander Dunnett.
xGibson, Alexander D.
ed. Anthologie. Odyssey Pr.
Gibson, Althea, 1927-
xGibson, Althea.
I Always Wanted to Be Somebody. Har-Row.
Gibson, Arrell. *see* Gibson, Arrell Morgan.
Gibson, Arrell M. *see* Gibson, Arrell Morgan.
Gibson, Arrell Morgan.
xGibson, Arrell.
The American Indian: Prehistory to the
Present. Heath.
The Oklahoma Story. U of Okla Pr.
xGibson, Arrell M.
Life & Death of Colonel Albert Jennings
Fountain. U of Okla Pr.
Gibson, Arthur, 1922-
xGibson, Arthur.
The Silence of God: Creative Response to the
Films of Ingmar Bergman. E Mellen.
Gibson, Arthur H. *see* Gibson, Arthur Hopkin.
Gibson, Arthur Hopkin.
xGibson, Arthur H.
Artists of Early Michigan: A Biographical
Dictionary of Artists Native to or Active in
Michigan 1701-1900. Wayne St U Pr.
Gibson, C. G. *see* Gibson, Christopher G.
Gibson, Charles, 1920-
xGibson, Charles.

Monetary Economics: Readings on Current
Issues. McGraw.
Gibson, William M. *see* Gibson, William Merriam.
Gibson, William Merriam.
xGibson, William M.
A Bibliography of William Dean Howells.
Arden Lib.
ed. Bibliography of William Dean Howells.
Arno.
Bibliography of William Dean Howells.
Folcroft.
Gibson, William Peter Rea.
xGibson, W. P. R.
Essentials of Clinical Electric Response
Audiometry. Churchill.
Gibson-Jarvie, Clodagh.
xGibson-Jarvie, Clodagh.
The Loom & the Web. St Martin.
Giddens, Anthony.
xGiddens, Anthony.
Capitalism & Modern Social Theory: An
Analysis of the Writings of Marx, Durkheim
& Max Weber. Cambridge U Pr.
Central Problems in Social Theory: Action,
Structure & Contradiction in Social Analysis.
U of Cal Pr.
The Class Structure of the Advanced Societies.
Har-Row.
Emile Durkheim. Penguin.
Politics & Sociology in the Thought of Max
Weber. Humanities.
Giddens, Paul H. *see* Giddens, Paul Henry.
Giddens, Paul Henry, 1903-
xGiddens, Paul H.
Standard Oil Company (Indiana): Oil Pioneer
of the Middle West. Arno.
Giddings, Franklin H. *see* Giddings, Franklin Henry.
Giddings, Franklin Henry, 1855-1931
xGiddings, Franklin H.
Democracy & Empire: With Studies of Their
Psychological, Economic & Moral
Foundations. Arno.
Giddings, J. Calvin. *see* Giddings, John Calvin.
Giddings, James L. *see* Giddings, James Louis.
Giddings, James Louis, 1909-1964
xGiddings, James L.
Ancient Men of the Arctic. Knopf.
Archeology of Cape Denbigh. Brown U Pr.
Giddings, John Calvin, 1930-
xGiddings, J. Calvin.
Chemistry, Man, & Environmental Change: An
Integrated Approach. Har-Row.
Giddings, Joshua R. *see* Giddings, Joshua Reed.
Giddings, Joshua Reed, 1795-1864
xGiddings, Joshua R.
Speeches in Congress. Negro U Pr.
Gide, Andre. *see* Gide, Andre Paul Guillaume.
Gide, Andre P. *see* Gide, Andre Paul Guillaume.
Gide, Andre Paul Guillaume, 1896-1951
xGide, Andre.
Corydon. Octagon.
Immoralist. Knopf.
Immoralist. Random.
Notes on Chopin. Greenwood.
Oscar Wilde: A Study. Gordon Pr.
xGide, Andre P.
Dostoevsky. Greenwood.
Gide, Charles, 1847-1932
xGide, Charles.
Consumer's Cooperative Societies. Haskell.
Principles of Political Economy. AMS Pr.
Principles of Political Economy. Greenwood.
Gideonse, Harry D.
xGideonse, Harry D.
Against the Running Tide: Selected Essays on
Education & the Free Society. Cyrco Pr.
Gidley, M. *see* Gidley, Mick.
Gidley, Mick.
xGidley, M.

With One Sky Above Us: Life on an Indian
Reservation at the Turn of the Century.
Putnam.
Gie, Daphne.
xGie, Daphne.
Afghan Hounds: A Complete Guide. David &
Charles.
Giebink, Gerald A.
xGiebink, Gerald A.
Computer Projects in Health Care. Health
Admin Pr.
Giedion, Sigfried, 1888-1968
xGiedion, Sigfried.
Architecture & the Phenomena of Transition:
The Three Space Conceptions in
Architecture. Harvard U Pr.
Giedion-Welcker, Carola.
xGiedion-Welcker, Carola.
Compiled by In Memoriam James Joyce.
Folcroft.
xGiedion-Welcker, Carols.
Compiled By In Memoriam James Joyce.
Arden Lib.
Giedion-Welcker, Carols. *see* Giedion-Welcker, Carola.
Giegerich, W. *see* Giegerich, Wilhelm.
Giegerich, Wilhelm.
xGiegerich, W.
ed. Glass Machines: Construction & Operation
of Machines for the Forming of Hot Glass.
Springer-Verlag.
Gielgud, John, Sir, 1904-
xGielgud, John.
Stage Directions. Greenwood.
Stage Directions. Theatre Arts.
Gierach, John, 1946-
xGierach, John.
Signs of Life. Cherry Valley.
Gierc, Ronald N.
xGierc, Ronald N.
Understanding Scientific Reasoning. HR&W.
Giergielewicz, Mieczysaw.
xGiergielewicz, Mieczyslaw.
ed. Polish Civilization: Essays & Studies. NYU
Pr.
Giergielewicz, Mieczyslaw. *see* Giergielewicz,
Mieczysaw.
Gierl, Irmgard.
xGierl, Irmgard.
Cross Stitch Patterns. Scribner.
Gies, Joseph.
xGies, Joseph.
The Colonel of Chicago. Dutton.
The Ingenious Yankees. T Y Crowell.
Leonard of Pisa & the New Mathematics of the
Middle Ages. T Y Crowell.
Life in a Medieval Castle. Har-Row.
Life in a Medieval Castle. T Y Crowell.
Life in a Medieval City. T Y Crowell.
Giesbrecht, Johnny.
xGiesbrecht, Johnny.
The Angry Atheist. Moody.
Giesbrecht, Martin G. *see* Giesbrecht, Martin Gerhard.
Giesbrecht, Martin Gerhard, 1933-
xGiesbrecht, Martin G.
Using Economics. W Kaufmann.
Giese, Arthur C. *see* Giese, Arthur Charles.
Giese, Arthur Charles, 1904-
xGiese, Arthur C.
Cell Physiology. HR&W.
Living with Our Sun's Ultraviolet Rays.
Plenum Pub.
Giese, Frank S.
xGiese, Frank S.
French Lyric Poetry: An Anthology. Odyssey
Pr.
Giese, Roger W.
xGiese, Roger W.
Stereochemistry: An Introductory Programmed
Text. Burgess.
Giesecke, A. H. *see* Giesecke, Adolph Hartung.

Giesecke, Adolph Hartung, 1932-
xGiesecke, A. H.
ed. Anesthesia for the Surgery of Trauma.
Davis Co.
Giesecke, Frederick E. *see* Giesecke, Frederick Ernest.
Giesecke, Frederick Ernest.
xGiesecke, Frederick E.
Engineering Graphics. Macmillan.
Technical Drawing. Macmillan.
Giesecke, Minnie.
xGiesecke, Minnie.
The Genesis of Hand Preference. AMS Pr.
Genesis of Hand Preference. Kraus Repr.
Gieske, Millard. *see* Gieske, Millard L.
Gieske, Millard L.
xGieske, Millard.
Minnesota Farmer-Laborism: The Third Party
Alternative. U of Minn Pr.
Giessen, B. C.
xGiessen, B. C.
ed. Developments in the Structural Chemistry
of Alloy Phases. Plenum Pub.
Giff, Patricia. *see* Giff, Patricia Reilly.
Giff, Patricia G. *see* Giff, Patricia Reilly.
Giff, Patricia R. *see* Giff, Patricia Reilly.
Giff, Patricia Reilly.
xGiff, Patricia.
Today Was a Terrible Day. Viking Pr.
xGiff, Patricia G.
Next Year I'll Be Special. Dutton.
xGiff, Patricia R.
The Fourth Grade Celebrity. Dell.
Fourth Grade Celebrity. Delacorte.
The Girl Who Knew It All. Dell.
The Girl Who Knew It All. Delacorte.
Giffen, Lois Anita.
xGiffen, Lois Anita.
Theory of Profane Love Among the Arabs. The
Development of the Genre. NYU Pr.
Giffen, Robert, Sir, 1837-1910
xGiffen, Robert.
Growth of Capital. Kelley.
Giffin, Kim.
xGiffin, Kim.
Fundamentals of Interpersonal Communication.
Har-Row.
Gifford, Barry.
xGifford, Barry.
Jack's Book: An Oral Biography of Jack
Kerouac. Penguin.
Jack's Book: An Oral Biography of Jack
Kerouac. St Martin.
Landscape with Traveler: The Pillow Book of
Francis Reeves. Dutton.
Gifford, Denis.
xGifford, Denis.
The British Comic Catalogue, 1874-1974.
Greenwood.
The Illustrated Who's Who in British Films.
David & Charles.
Gifford, Henry.
xGifford, Henry.
ed. Leo Tolstoy: A Critical Anthology. Peter
Smith.
Gifford, James F.
xGifford, James F.
The Evolution of a Medical Center: A History
of Medicine at Duke University to 1941.
Duke.
ed. Undergraduate Medical Education & the
Elective System: Experience with the Duke
Curriculum, 1966-1975. Duke.
Gifford, John C. *see* Gifford, John Clayton.
Gifford, John Clayton.
xGifford, John C.
On Preserving Tropical Florida. Banyan Bks.
Gifford, Thomas.
xGifford, Thomas.

Hollywood Gothic. Ballantine.
Hollywood Gothic. Putnam.

Gifis, Steven H.
xGifis, Steven H.
Law Dictionary. Barron.

Gifkins, R. C., 1918-
xGifkins, R. C.
Optical Microscopy of Metals. Elsevier.

Gigch, John P. Van. *see* Van Gigch, John P.

Gigli, Beniamino, 1890-1957
xGigli, Beniamino.
The Memoirs of Beniamino Gigli. Arno.

Giglio, Giovanni.
xGiglio, Giovanni.
Triumph of Barabbas. AMS Pr.

Giglio, James M. *see* Giglio, James N.

Giglio, James N., 1939-
xGiglio, James M.
H. M. Daugherty & the Politics of Expediency.
Kent St U Pr.

Gijlstra, D. J.
xGijlstra, D. J.
ed. Leading Cases & Materials on the Law of
the European Communities. Kluwer Boston.

Gil, David. *see* Gil, David G.

Gil, David G.
xGil, David.
Beyond the Jungle: Essays on Human
Possibilities, Social Alternatives, & Radical
Practice. Schenkman.
xGil, David G.
Beyond the Jungle: Essays on Human
Possibilities, Social Alternatives, & Radical
Practice. G K Hall.
ed. Child Abuse & Violence. AMS Pr.

Gil, Federico. *see* Gil, Federico Guillermo.

Gil, Federico G. *see* Gil, Federico Guillermo.

Gil, Federico Guillermo.
xGil, Federico.
ed. Chile at the Turning Point: Lessons of the
Socialist Years, 1970-1973. Inst Study
Human.
xGil, Federico G.
Latin American-United States Relations.
HarBraceJ.

Gilb, Tom.
xGilb, Tom.
Humanized Input: Techniques for Reliable
Keyed Input. Winthrop.
Software Metrics. Winthrop.

Gilbart, James W. *see* Gilbart, James William.

Gilbart, James William, 1794-1863
xGilbart, James W.
History of Banking in America. Kelley.
History, Principles, & Practice of Banking.
Greenwood.

Gilbaugh, John W. *see* Gilbaugh, John Wesley.

Gilbaugh, John Wesley.
xGilbaugh, John W.
Teacher's Guide for Test Construction with
Percentage Tables for Computing Test Scores.
Modern Ed.

Gilbert, A. H. *see* Gilbert, Allan H.

Gilbert, Alan, 1944-
xGilbert, Alan.
ed. Development Planning & Spatial Structure.
Wiley.

Gilbert, Allan H., 1888-
xGilbert, A. H.
Dante's Conception of Justice. Gordon Pr.
A Geographical Dictionary of Milton. Gordon
Pr.
xGilbert, Allan H.

Dante & His Comedy. NYU Pr.
Dante's Conception of Justice. AMS Pr.
A Geographical Dictionary of Milton. Arden
Lib.
Geographical Dictionary of Milton. Folcroft.
Geographical Dictionary of Milton. Russell.
Symbolic Persons in the Masques of Ben
Jonson. AMS Pr.

Gilbert, Anna.
xGilbert, Anna.
A Family Likeness. St Martin.
Images of Rose. Delacorte.
The Leavetaking. St Martin.
The Look of Innocence. St Martin.
Remembering Louise. St Martin.

Gilbert, Anne, 1927-
xGilbert, Anne.
How to Be an Antiques Detective. G&D.

Gilbert, Annie.
xGilbert, Annie.
All My Afternoons: The Heart & Soul of the
TV Soap Opera. A & W Pubs.

Gilbert, Ariadne.
xGilbert, Ariadne.
More Than Conquerors. Arno.

Gilbert, Bentley B., 1924-
xGilbert, Bentley B.
British Social Policy, 1914-1939. Cornell U Pr.

Gilbert, Bil.
xGilbert, Bil.
How Animals Communicate. Pantheon.

Gilbert, Celia, 1932-
xGilbert, Celia.
Queen of Darkness. Viking Pr.

Gilbert, Christopher.
xGilbert, Christopher.
Late Georgian & Regency Furniture.
Transatlantic.

Gilbert, Colleen B., 1949-
xGilbert, Colleen B.
A Bibliography of the Works of Dorothy L.
Sayers. Shoe String.

Gilbert, Creighton.
xGilbert, Creighton.
Change in Piero Della Francesca. J J Augustin.
ed. Renaissance Art. Har-Row.

Gilbert, Doris (Wilcox).
xGilbert, Doris W.
Power & Speed in Reading. P-H.

Gilbert, Doris W. *see* Gilbert, Doris (Wilcox).

Gilbert, Doug, 1938-
xGilbert, Doug.
The Miracle Machine. Coward.

Gilbert, Douglas, 1889-
xGilbert, Douglas.
American Vaudeville: Its Life & Times. Peter
Smith.
Lost Chords: The Diverting Story of American
Popular Songs. Cooper Sq.

Gilbert, Edith.
xGilbert, Edith.
All About Parties. Jet'iquette.
Let's Set the Table with Edith Gilbert.
Jet'Iquette.
xGilbert, Edith W.
All About Parties. Hearthside.

Gilbert, Edith W. *see* Gilbert, Edith.

Gilbert, Edmund W. *see* Gilbert, Edmund William.

Gilbert, Edmund William, 1900-
xGilbert, Edmund W.
Brighton Old Ocean's Bauble. Intl Pubns Serv.

Gilbert, Enid F.
xGilbert, Enid F.
An Introduction to Pathology. Oxford U Pr.

Gilbert, Eugene.
xGilbert, Eugene.
The California to Remember. Copley Bks.

Gilbert, Everett E. *see* Gilbert, Everett Eddy.

Gilbert, Everett Eddy.
xGilbert, Everett E.

Sulfonation & Related Reactions. Krieger.

Gilbert, Felix, 1905-
xGilbert, Felix.
History: Choice & Commitment. Harvard U Pr.
ed. Norton History of Modern Europe. Norton.

Gilbert, G. M., 1911-
xGilbert, G. M.
The Psychology of Dictatorship: Based on an
Examination of the Leaders of Nazi
Germany. Greenwood.

Gilbert, George, 1922-
xGilbert, George.
Collecting Photographica: The Images &
Equipment of the First Hundred Years of
Photography. Dutton.
Collecting Photographica: The Images &
Equipment of the First Hundred Years of
Photography. Dutton.

Gilbert, Glenn G.
xGilbert, Glenn G.
ed. German Language in America: A
Symposium. U of Tex Pr.
Linguistic Atlas of Texas German. U of Tex Pr.
ed. Problems in Applied Educational
Sociolinguistics: Readings on Language &
Culture Problems of United States Ethnic
Groups. Mouton.

Gilbert, Gustav, 1843-1899
xGilbert, Gustav.
The Constitutional Antiquities of Sparta &
Athens. Humanities.

Gilbert, Isabel, 1917-
xGilbert, Isabel.
The No Smoking Book: How to Quit
Permanently. Presidio Pr.

Gilbert, Jack, 1915-
xGilbert, Jack.
Advanced Applications for Pocket Calculators.
TAB Bks.

Gilbert, James, 1935-
xGilbert, James.
The Flier's World. Random.
The World's Worst Aircraft. St Martin.

Gilbert, John T. *see* Gilbert, John Thomas.

Gilbert, John Thomas.
xGilbert, John T.
ed. History of the Irish Confederation & the
War in Ireland, 1641-1649, Containing a
Narrative of Affairs of Ireland. AMS Pr.

Gilbert, Lela.
xGilbert, Lela.
Just Five Days till Friday. Accent Bks.

Gilbert, M. *see* Gilbert, Martin.

Gilbert, Marilyn B.
xGilbert, Marilyn B.
Clear Writing. Wiley.

Gilbert, Martin.
xGilbert, M.
Lloyd George. P-H.
xGilbert, Martin.
British History Atlas. Macmillan.
Churchill. Doubleday.

Gilbert, Mercedes.
xGilbert, Mercedes.
Aunt Sara's Wooden God. AMS Pr.

Gilbert, Michael.
xGilbert, Michael.
Death Has Deep Roots. Har-Row.
The Night of the Twelfth. Penguin.

Gilbert, Michael. *see* Gilbert, Michael Francis.

Gilbert, Michael A.
xGilbert, Michael A.
How to Win an Argument. McGraw.

Gilbert, Michael Francis.
xGilbert, Michael.

Blood & Judgment. Har-Row.
The Danger Within. Har-Row.
The Empty House. Har-Row.
The Empty House. Penguin.
Fear to Tread. Har-Row.
The Killing of Katie Steelstock. Har-Row.

Gilbert, Milton, 1909-
xGilbert, Milton.
Currency Depreciation & Monetary Policy.
Arno.

Gilbert, Miriam.
xGilbert, Miriam.
Glory Be: The Career of a Young Hair Stylist.
Hastings.

Gilbert, N. see Gilbert, Neil.

Gilbert, Nan.
xGilbert, Nan.
Unchosen. Har-Row.
The Unchosen. Har-Row.

Gilbert, Neil.
xGilbert, N.
Planning for Social Welfare: Issues, Models &
Tasks. P-H.
xGilbert, Neil.
Coordinating Social Services: An Analysis of
Community, Organizational, & Staff
Characteristics. Praeger.
Dimensions of Social Welfare Policy. P-H.
Dynamics of Community Planning. Ballinger
Pub.
An Introduction to Social Work Practice. P-H.

Gilbert, Norma.
xGilbert, Norma.
Statistics. HR&W.

Gilbert, R. P. see Gilbert, Robert P.

Gilbert, Robert P., 1932-
xGilbert, R. P.
Function Theoretic Methods in Partial
Differential Equations. Acad Pr.

Gilbert, Sandra. see Gilbert, Sandra M.

Gilbert, Sandra M.
xGilbert, Sandra.
In the Fourth World: Poems. U of Ala Pr.
xGilbert, Sandra M.
Acts of Attention: The Poems of D. H.
Lawrence. Cornell U Pr.
ed. Shakespeare's Sisters: Feminist Essays on
Women Poets. Ind U Pr.

Gilbert, Sara. see Gilbert, Sara D.

Gilbert, Sara D.
xGilbert, Sara.
Feeling Good: A Book About You & Your
Body. Schol Bk Serv.
Ready, Set, Go: How to Find a Career That's
Right for You. Schol Bk Serv.

Gilbert, Stephen G.
xGilbert, Stephen G.
Atlas of General Zoology. Burgess.

Gilbert, Thomas F.
xGilbert, Thomas F.
Human Competence: Engineering Worthy
Performance. McGraw.
Thinking Metric. Wiley.

Gilbert, W. Kent.
xGilbert, W. Kent.
ed. Confirmation & Education. Fortress.

Gilbert, W. S. see Gilbert, William Schwenck.

Gilbert, William H.
xGilbert, William H.
ed. Public Relations in Local Government. Intl
City Mgt.

Gilbert, William J., 1941-
xGilbert, William J.
Modern Algebra with Applications. Wiley.

Gilbert, William Schwenck.
xGilbert, W. S.

Gilbert Before Sullivan: Six Comic Plays. U of
Chicago Pr.

Gilbertie, Sal.
xGilbertie, Sal.
Home Gardening at Its Best: Productive Ways
to Grow Your Own Fresh Vegetables.
Atheneum.

Gilbertson, Irvy.
xGilbertson, Irvy.
Practical Puppet Plays. Gospel Pub.

Gilbertson, Robert L.
xGilbertson, Robert L.
Fungi That Decay Ponderosa Pine. U of Ariz
Pr.

Gilbreath, Alice. see Gilbreath, Alice Thompson.

Gilbreath, Alice Thompson.
xGilbreath, Alice.
Fun with Weaving. Morrow.
Simple Decoupage: Having Fun with Cutouts.
Morrow.

Gilbreth, Frank B. see Gilbreth, Frank Bunker.

Gilbreth, Frank Bunker, 1868-1924
xGilbreth, Frank B.
Bricklaying System. Hive Pub.
Cheaper by the Dozen. T Y Crowell.
Cheaper by the Dozen. Bantam.
Field System. Hive Pub.
Primer of Scientific Management. Hive Pub.

Gilbreth, Terry J. see Gilbreth, Terry John.

Gilbreth, Terry John.
xGilbreth, Terry J.
Governing Geothermal Steam:
Intergovernmental Relations & Energy
Policy. Arno.

Gilby, Myriam.
xGilby, Myriam.
Free Weaving. Scribner.

Gilchrist. see Gilchrist, Anne (Burrows).

Gilchrist, Anne. see Gilchrist, Anne (Burrows).

Gilchrist, Anne (Burrows).
xGilchrist.
Mary Lamb. Sharon Hill.
xGilchrist, Anne.
The Letters of Anne Gilchrist & Walt
Whitman. Haskell.
Mary Lamb. AMS Pr.

Gilchrist, Elizabeth.
xGilchrist, Elizabeth.
Your Cheatin' Heart. Macmillan.
Your Cheatin' Heart. NAL.

Gilchrist, Francis G., 1895-
xGilchrist, Francis G.
Survey of Embryology. McGraw.

Gilchrist, J. D. see Gilchrist, James Duncan.

Gilchrist, James Duncan.
xGilchrist, J. D.
Extraction Metallurgy. Pergamon.
Fuels & Refractories. Pergamon.
Furnaces. Pergamon.

Gilchrist, Margaret.
xGilchrist, Margaret.
The Psychology of Creativity. Intl Schol Bk
Serv.

Gilchrist, Octavius. see Gilchrist, Octavius Graham.

Gilchrist, Octavius Graham, 1779-1823
xGilchrist, Octavius.
Examination of the Charges Maintained by
Messrs. Malone, Chalmers & Others, of Ben
Jonson's Enmity - Towards Shakespeare.
AMS Pr.

Gilchrist, Robert S.
xGilchrist, Robert S.
Curriculum Development: A Humanized
Systems Approach. Pitman Learning.

Gilchrist, Rupert.
xGilchrist, Rupert.
Dragonard Blood. Intl Schol Bk Serv.

Gilchrist, T. L. see Gilchrist, Thomas Lonsdale.

Gilchrist, Theo E.
xGilchrist, Theo E.

Halfway up the Mountain. Lippincott.

Gilchrist, Thomas Lonsdale.
xGilchrist, T. L.
Organic Reactions & Orbital Symmetry.
Cambridge U Pr.

Gildea, Marianna, Sister, 1907-
xGildea, Marianna.
Expressions of Religious Thought & Feeling in
the Chansons De Geste. AMS Pr.

Gildea, Ray. see Gildea, Ray Y.

Gildea, Ray Y.
xGildea, Ray.
Arsenic & Old Lead: A Layman's Guide to
Pollution & Conservation. U Pr of Miss.

Gilder, Eric.
xGilder, Eric.
The Dictionary of Composers & Their Music:
Every Listener's Companion. Facts on File.
A Dictionary of Composers & Their Music:
Every Listener's Companion Arranged
Chronologically & Alphabetically.
Paddington.

Gildersleeve, B. L. see Gildersleeve, Basil Lanneau.

Gildersleeve, Basil Lanneau, 1831-1924
xGildersleeve, B. L.
The Creed of the Old South. Gordon Pr.

Gildersleeve, Thomas. see Gildersleeve, Thomas Robert.

Gildersleeve, Thomas R. see Gildersleeve, Thomas
Robert.

Gildersleeve, Thomas Robert.
xGildersleeve, Thomas.
Successful Data Processing System Analysis.
P-H.
xGildersleeve, Thomas R.
Data Processing Project Management. Van Nos
Reinhold.
Decision Tables & Their Practical Application
in Data Processing. P-H.
Organizing & Documenting Data Processing
Information. Hayden.

Gildersleeve, Virginia C. see Gildersleeve, Virginia
Crocheron.

Gildersleeve, Virginia Crocheron, 1877-
xGildersleeve, Virginia C.
Government Regulation of the Elizabethan
Drama. Greenwood.

Gildner, Gary.
xGildner, Gary.
First Practice. U of Pittsburgh Pr.
ed. Out of This World: Poems from the
Hawkeye State. Iowa St U Pr.

Gildon, Charles, 1665-1724
xGildon, Charles.
The Post-Man Robb'd of His Mail: Or, the
Packet Broke Open. Garland Pub.

Giles, Carl H.
xGiles, Carl H.
Student Journalist & Feature Writing. Rosen
Pr.

Giles, Edward.
xGiles, Edward.
ed. Documents Illustrating Papal Authority,
A.D. 96-454. Hyperion Conn.

Giles, Eugene.
xGiles, Eugene.
ed. The Measures of Man: Methodologies in
Biological Anthropology. Peabody Harvard.

Giles, F. A. see Giles, Floyd.

Giles, Floyd.
xGiles, F. A.
Herbaceous Perennials. Reston.

Giles, H. A. see Giles, Herbert Allen.

Giles, Henry, 1809-1882
xGiles, Henry.
Illustrations of Genius, in Some of Its Relations
to Culture & Society. Folcroft.

Giles, Herbert. see Giles, Herbert Allen.

Giles, Herbert A.
xGiles, Herbert A.

A Glossary of Reference on Subjects
  Connected with Far East. Orient Bk Dist.
A Glossary of Reference on Subjects
  Connected with the Far East. Rowman.
Giles, Herbert A. *see* Giles, Herbert Allen.
Giles, Herbert Allen, 1845-1935
  xGiles, H. A.
    Confucianism & Its Rivals. Krishna Pr.
    The Religions of Ancient China. Gordon Pr.
  xGiles, Herbert.
    A History of Chinese Literature. R West.
  xGiles, Herbert A.
    Confucianism & Its Rivals. AMS Pr.
    History of Chinese Literature. Ungar.
    Religions of Ancient China. Arno.
    Religions of Ancient China. Folcroft.
  xGiles, Herbert G.
    A History of Chinese Literature. C E Tuttle.
Giles, Herbert G. *see* Giles, Herbert Allen.
Giles, James R. *see* Giles, James Richard.
Giles, James Richard, 1937-
  xGiles, James R.
    Claude McKay. Twayne.
Giles, Janice H. *see* Giles, Janice Holt.
Giles, Janice Holt.
  xGiles, Janice H.
    Hannah Fowler. Avon.
    Hannah Fowler. G K Hall.
    Hannah Fowler. G K Hall.
    Johnny Osage. Avon.
    Johnny Osage. G K Hall.
    The Kentuckians. Avon.
    The Kentuckians. G K Hall.
    Kentuckians. HM.
Giles, Raymond.
  xGiles, Raymond.
    Storm Over Sabrehill. Fawcett.
Giles, Tony.
  xGiles, Tony.
    The Farmer As Manager. Allen Unwin.
Gilfillan, Harriet W. *see* Gilfillan, Harriet Woodbridge.
Gilfillan, Harriet Woodbridge, 1909-
  xGilfillan, Harriet W.
    I Went to Pit College. AMS Pr.
Gilfillan, Merrill, 1945-
  xGilfillan, Merrill.
    Light Years: Selected Early Poems, 1969-1972.
      Blue Wind.
Gilfond, Henry.
  xGilfond, Henry.
    Favorite Short Stories. Walker & Co.
    Genealogy: How to Find Your Roots. Watts.
    Syria. Watts.
Gilge, Jeanette.
  xGilge, Jeanette.
    City-Kid Farmer. Cook.
    Growing-up Summer. Cook.
Gilgen, Albert R.
  xGilgen, Albert R.
    ed. Contemporary Scientific Psychology. Acad
      Pr.
Gilgoff, Alice.
  xGilgoff, Alice.
    Home Birth. Coward.
Gilhooley, Leonard.
  xGilhooley, Leonard.
    Contradiction & Dilemma: Orestes Brownson
      & the American Idea. Fordham.
Gilhuis, C.
  xGilhuis, C.
    Conversations on Growing Older. Eerdmans.
Gili, Elizabeth.
  xGili, Elizabeth.
    Apple Recipes from A to Z. Intl Pubns Serv.
Gilison, Jerome M., 1935-
  xGilison, Jerome M.
    The Soviet Image of Utopia. Johns Hopkins.
Gilkerson, William.
  xGilkerson, William.

The Scrimshander. Troubador Pr.
Gilkes, Martin.
  xGilkes, Martin.
    Introduction to Modern Poetry. Arden Lib.
    Introduction to Modern Poetry. Folcroft.
Gilkes, Patrick.
  xGilkes, Patrick.
    The Dying Lion: Feudalism & Modernization
      in Ethiopia. St Martin.
Gilkey, Langdon. *see* Gilkey, Langdon Brown.
Gilkey, Langdon Brown, 1919-
  xGilkey, Langdon.
    Message & Existence: An Introduction to
      Christian Theology. Seabury.
    Reaping the Whirlwind: A Christian
      Interpretation of History. Seabury.
Gilkey, Peter B.
  xGilkey, Peter B.
    The Index Theorem & the Heat Equation.
      Publish or Perish.
Gilkyson, Thomas W. *see* Gilkyson, Thomas Walter.
Gilkyson, Thomas Walter, 1880-
  xGilkyson, Thomas W.
    Oil. AMS Pr.
Gill, Arthur, 1930-
  xGill, Arthur.
    Applied Algebra for the Computer Sciences.
      P-H.
Gill, Bob, 1931-
  xGill, Bob.
    illus. I Keep Changing. Scroll Pr.
Gill, Brendan.
  xGill, Brendan.
    Summer Places. Methuen Inc.
Gill, Colin.
  xGill, Colin.
    Industrial Relations in the Chemical Industry.
      Renouf.
Gill, Crispin.
  xGill, Crispin.
    ed. Countryman's Britain. David & Charles.
    Countryman's Britain in Pictures. David &
      Charles.
    Mayflower Remembered: A History of the
      Plymouth Pilgrims. Taplinger.
  xGill, Grispin.
    Dartmoor. David & Charles.
Gill, Derek.
  xGill, Derek.
    Illegitimacy, Sexuality & the Status of Women.
      Biblio Dist.
Gill, Don.
  xGill, Don.
    Nature in the Urban Landscape: A Study of
      City Ecosystems. York Pr.
Gill, Eric, 1882-1940
  xGill, Eric.
    Autobiography. R West.
Gill, F. W. *see* Gill, Frederick W.
Gill, Flora, 1936-
  xGill, Flora.
    Economics & the Black Exodus: An Analysis
      of Negro Emigration from the Southern
      United States; 1910-70. Garland Pub.
Gill, Frederick W.
  xGill, F. W.
    Airline Competition: A Study of the Effects of
      Competition on the Quality & Price of
      Airline Service & the Self-Sufficiency of the
      United States Domestic Airlines. Pergamon.
Gill, G. B. *see* Gill, Gerald Byron.
Gill, Gerald Byron.
  xGill, G. B.
    Pericyclic Reactions. Methuen Inc.
Gill, Graeme J.
  xGill, Graeme J.
    Peasants & Government in the Russian
      Revolution. B&N.
Gill, Grispin. *see* Gill, Crispin.
Gill, Harold. *see* Gill, Harold B.

Gill, Harold B.
  xGill, Harold.
    The Apothecary in Colonial Virginia.
      Williamsburg.
  xGill, Harold B.
    Colonial Virginia. Elsevier-Nelson.
Gill, Jack C.
  xGill, Jack C.
    Mathematics & the Liberal Arts. Merrill.
Gill, Jerry H.
  xGill, Jerry H.
    Ian Ramsey: To Speak Responsibly of God.
      Allen Unwin.
Gill, Joan.
  xGill, Joan.
    Golden Retrievers. Arco.
    Golden Retrievers. Palmetto Pub.
Gill, John, 1924-
  xGill, John.
    Country Pleasures. Crossing Pr.
    Kiki. Little.
Gill, Joseph, 1901-
  xGill, Joseph.
    The Council of Florence. AMS Pr.
Gill, Merton M. *see* Gill, Merton Max.
Gill, Merton Max, 1914-
  xGill, Merton M.
    Topography & Systems in Psychoanalytic
      Theory. Intl Univs Pr.
Gill, Peter E. *see* Gill, Peter Edward.
Gill, Peter Edward, 1949-
  xGill, Peter E.
    Moral Judgments of Violence Among Irish &
      Swedish Adolescents. Humanities.
Gill, Richard. *see* Gill, Richard T.
Gill, Richard T.
  xGill, Richard.
    Economics & the Public Interest. Goodyear.
  xGill, Richard T.
    Economic Development: Past & Present. P-H.
    Economics & the Private Interest: An
      Introduction to Microeconomics. Goodyear.
    Economics & the Public Interest. Goodyear.
    ed. Great Debates in Economics. Goodyear.
Gill, Robert W.
  xGill, Robert W.
    Creative Perspective. Thames Hudson.
Gill, S. S. *see* Gill, Samuel Sidney.
Gill, Samuel Sidney, 1920-
  xGill, S. S.
    The Stress Analysis of Pressure Vessels &
      Pressure Vessel Components. Pergamon.
Gill, T. P. *see* Gill, Thomas Perrott.
Gill, Thomas Perrott.
  xGill, T. P.
    The Doppler Effect: An Introduction to the
      Theory of the Effect. Acad Pr.
Gilland, B. *see* Gilland, Bernard.
Gilland, Bernard.
  xGilland, B.
    The Next Seventy Years: Population, Food &
      Resources. Intl Schol Bk Serv.
Gillard, Quentin, 1947-
  xGillard, Quentin.
    Incomes & Accessibility: Metropolitan Labor
      Force Participation, Commuting, Income
      Differentials in the United States, 1960-1970.
      U Chicago Dept Geog.
Gillaspie, Beulah V. *see* Gillaspie, Beulah Vesta.
Gillaspie, Beulah Vesta, 1896-
  xGillaspie, Beulah V.
    Consumer Questions & Their Significance.
      AMS Pr.
Gillelan, G. Howard.
  xGillelan, G. Howard.

Archery at Home: How to Practice Daily &
Stay Sharp for Target Shooting, Field
Archery, & Bowhunting. McKay.
Complete Book of the Bow & Arrow.
Stackpole.

Gilleo, Alma.
xGilleo, Alma.
About Grams. Childs World.
About Liters. Childs World.
About Meters. Childs World.
About the Metric System. Childs World.
About the Thermometer. Childs World.
Air Travel from the Beginning. Childs World.
Communications from the Beginning. Childs
World.
Dinosaurs & Other Reptiles from the
Beginning. Childs World.

Giller, Norman M.
xGiller, Norman M.
An Adventure in Architecture. Virgo Pr.

Gillers, Stephen.
xGillers, Stephen.
Looking at Law School: A Student Guide from
the Society of American Law Teachers.
NAL.
ed. Looking at Law School: A Student Guide
from the Society of American Law Teachers.
Taplinger.
The Rights of Lawyers & Clients. Avon.

Gilles, Albert S.
xGilles, Albert S.
Comanche Days. SMU Press.

Gilles, Daniel.
xGilles, Daniel.
Alone. Sail Bks.

Gilles, R.
xGilles, R.
Mechanisms of Osmoregulation in Animals:
Maintenance of Cell Volume. Wiley.

Gillespie. see Gillespie, Sheena.

Gillespie, Alfred.
xGillespie, Alfred.
Gilliam Unbuttoned. Little.

Gillespie, Cecil. see Gillespie, Cecil Merie.

Gillespie, Cecil Merie.
xGillespie, Cecil.
Accounting Systems: Procedures & Methods.
P-H.

Gillespie, David. see Gillespie, David F.

Gillespie, David F.
xGillespie, David.
Organizational Response to Changing
Community Systems. Kent St U Pr.

Gillespie, Dizzy, 1917-
xGillespie, Dizzy.
To Be or Not to Bop: Memoirs. Doubleday.

Gillespie, Duncan.
xGillespie, Duncan.
Lighthearted Brewing. British Bk Ctr.

Gillespie, Gilbert.
xGillespie, Gilbert.
Public Access Cable Television in the United
States & Canada: With an Annotated
Bibliography. Praeger.

Gillespie, James E. see Gillespie, James Edward.

Gillespie, James Edward, 1887-
xGillespie, James E.
The Influence of Oversea Expansion on
England to 1700. Octagon.

Gillespie, John, 1921-
xGillespie, John.
The Musical Experience. Wadsworth Pub.

Gillespie, John T. see Gillespie, John Thomas.

Gillespie, John Thomas.
xGillespie, John T.

Creating a School Media Program. Bowker.
Paperback Books for Young People: An
Annotated Guide to Publishers &
Distributors. ALA.

Gillespie, Judith A.
xGillespie, Judith A.
Comparing Political Experiences. Am Political.

Gillespie, K. B. see Gillespie, Karen R.
Gillespie, Karen. see Gillespie, Karen R.

Gillespie, Karen R.
xGillespie, K. B.
Retail Business Management. McGraw.
xGillespie, Karen.
Retail Business Management. McGraw.

Gillespie, Neal C., 1933-
xGillespie, Neal C.
Collapse of Orthodoxy: The Intellectual Ordeal
of George Frederick Holmes. U Pr of Va.

Gillespie, Patricia H.
xGillespie, Patricia H.
Teaching Reading to the Mildly Retarded
Child. Merrill.

Gillespie, Robert.
xGillespie, Robert.
The Man Chain. SBD.

Gillespie, Sheena.
xGillespie.
Someone Like Me: Images for Writing.
Winthrop.
xGillespie, Sheena.
ed. Someone Like Me: Images for Writing.
Winthrop.

Gillet, Lev.
xGillet, Lev.
In Thy Presence. St Vladimirs.

Gillett, George W. see Gillett, George Willson.

Gillett, George Willson.
xGillett, George W.
An Experimental Study of the Genus Bidens
(Asteraceae) in the Hawaiian Islands. U of
Cal Pr.

Gillett, K. see Gillett, Keith.

Gillett, Keith.
xGillett, K.
Australian Seashores in Colour. C E Tuttle.

Gillett, Margaret.
xGillett, Margaret.
Foundation Studies in Education: Justifications
& New Directions: A Source Book.
Scarecrow.

Gillett, Mary.
xGillett, Mary.
Bugles at the Border. Blair.

Gillett, Philip.
xGillett, Philip W.
Introduction to Linear Algebra. HM.

Gillett, Philip W. see Gillett, Philip.

Gillette, Arnold S.
xGillette, Arnold S.
ed. Stage Scenery: Its Construction & Rigging.
Har-Row.

Gillette, Harriet E., 1914-
xGillette, Harriet E.
Systems of Therapy in Cerebral Palsy. C C
Thomas.

Gillette, J. Michael.
xGillette, J. Michael.
Designing with Light: An Introduction to Stage
Lighting. Mayfield Pub.

Gillette, King C. see Gillette, King Camp.

Gillette, King Camp, 1855-1932
xGillette, King C.
The Human Drift. Schol Facsimiles.

Gillette, Ned.
xGillette, Ned.
Cross-Country Skiing. Mountaineers.

Gillette, Paul.
xGillette, Paul.

Carmela. Arbor Hse.
Enjoying Wine. NAL.

Gillham, Nicholas W.
xGillham, Nicholas W.
Organelle Heredity. Raven.

Gilliam, Ann.
xGilliam, Ann.
ed. Voices for the Earth: A Treasury of the
Sierra Club Bulletin. Sierra.

Gilliard, Charles, 1879-
xGilliard, Charles.
A History of Switzerland. Greenwood.

Gilliard, E. Thomas. see Gilliard, Ernest Thomas.

Gilliard, Ernest Thomas, 1912-1965
xGilliard, E. Thomas.
Living Birds of the World. Doubleday.

Gilliatt, Penelope.
xGilliatt, Penelope.
The Cutting Edge. Coward.

Gillie, Christopher.
xGillie, Christopher.
Character in English Literature. Humanities.
A Preface to Jane Austen. Longman.

Gillies, Dee A. see Gillies, Dee Ann.

Gillies, Dee Ann.
xGillies, Dee A.
Patient Assessment & Management by the
Nurse Practitioner. Saunders.

Gillies, Emily.
xGillies, Emily.
Creative Dramatics for All Children. ACEI.

Gillies, Harold. see Gillies, Harold Delf.

Gillies, Harold Delf, Sir, 1919-
xGillies, Harold.
Principles & Art of Plastic Surgery. Little.

Gillies, Jerry, 1940-
xGillies, Jerry.
Friends: The Power & Potential of the
Company You Keep. Har-Row.

Gillies, John, 1925-
xGillies, John.
The Martyrs of Guanabara. Moody.

Gillies, John W. see Gillies, John Wallace.

Gillies, John Wallace.
xGillies, John W.
Principles of Pictorial Photography. Arno.

Gillies, M. T.
xGillies, M. T.
Animal Feeds from Waste Materials. Noyes.
Compressed Food Bars. Noyes.
ed. Drinking Water Detoxification. Noyes.
Fish & Shellfish Processing. Noyes.

Gillies, R. F. see Gillies, Robert Reid.
Gillies, R. R. see Gillies, Robert Reid.
Gillies, Robert P. see Gillies, Robert Pearse.

Gillies, Robert Pearse, 1788-1858
xGillies, Robert P.
Memoirs of a Literary Veteran: Including
Sketches & Anecdotes of the Most
Distinguished Literary Characters from
1794-1849. AMS Pr.

Gillies, Robert Reid.
xGillies, R. F.
Lecture Notes on Medical Microbiology.
Mosby.
xGillies, R. R.
Bacteriology Illustrated. Churchill.

Gillig, Harry.
xGillig, Harry.
Gillig's Guide to Turning Unprofitable Real
Estate into Moneymakers. Inst Busn Plan.
xGillig, Harry S.
Real Estate Investment for High Yield &
Profit. Inst Busn Plan.

Gillig, Harry S. see Gillig, Harry.

Gilligan, Gerald S.
xGilligan, Gerald S.
A Price Guide for Buying & Selling Rural
Acreage. McGraw.

Gilligan, Lawrence. see Gilligan, Lawrence G.

Gilligan, Lawrence G.
  xGilligan, Lawrence.
    Finite Mathematics: An Elementary Approach.
      Goodyear.
  xGilligan, Lawrence G.
    Finite Mathematics: An Elementary Approach.
      Goodyear.
Gilliland, Cleburne Hap.
  xGilliland, Hap.
    Practical Guide to Remedial Reading. Merrill.
Gilliland, Dolores S. *see* Gilliland, Dolores Scott.
Gilliland, Dolores Scott.
  xGilliland, Dolores S.
    Selected Women of the Scriptures of Stamina
      & Courage. Honor Bks.
Gilliland, Hap. *see* Gilliland, Cleburne Hap.
Gilliland, Marion S. *see* Gilliland, Marion Spjut.
Gilliland, Marion Spjut, 1918-
  xGilliland, Marion S.
    The Material Culture of Key Marco, Florida. U
      Presses Fla.
Gilliland, Martha W.
  xGilliland, Martha W.
    ed. Energy Analysis: A New Public Policy
      Tool. Westview.
Gillim, Marion H. *see* Gillim, Marion Hamilton.
Gillim, Marion Hamilton, 1909-
  xGillim, Marion H.
    Incidence of Excess Profits Taxation. AMS Pr.
Gillin, John L. *see* Gillin, John Lewis.
Gillin, John Lewis, 1871-1958
  xGillin, John L.
    Criminology & Penology. Greenwood.
    Criminology & Penology. Norwood Edns.
    The Dunkers: A Sociological Interpretation.
      AMS Pr.
    Taming the Criminal: Adventures in Penology.
      Patterson Smith.
Gillingham, John. *see* Gillingham, John Bennett.
Gillingham, John Bennett.
  xGillingham, John.
    Richard the Lionheart. Times Bks.
Gillingwater, David.
  xGillingwater, David.
    ed. The Regional Planning Process. Lexington
      Bks.
Gilliom, Richard D., 1934-
  xGilliom, Richard D.
    Introduction to Physical Organic Chemistry.
      A-W.
Gillis, Don, 1912-
  xGillis, Don.
    Unfinished Symphony Conductor. Jenkins.
Gillis, John R.
  xGillis, John R.
    The Development of European Society:
      1770-1870. HM.
    Prussian Bureaucracy in Crisis, 1840-1860:
      Origins of an Administrative Ethos. Stanford
      U Pr.
Gillis, Malcolm.
  xGillis, Malcolm.
    Taxation & Mining: Nonfuel Minerals in
      Bolivia & Other Countries. Ballinger Pub.
Gillis, William R. *see* Gillis, William Robert.
Gillis, William Robert, 1840-1929
  xGillis, William R.
    Gold Rush Days with Mark Twain. AMS Pr.
    Gold Rush Days with Mark Twain. Scholarly.
Gillispie, Charles C. *see* Gillispie, Charles Coulston.
Gillispie, Charles Coulston.
  xGillispie, Charles C.

    Edge of Objectivity: An Essay in the History
      of Scientific Ideas. Princeton U Pr.
    Genesis & Geology: A Study in the Relations
      of Scientific Thought, Natural Theology, &
      Social Opinion in Great Britain, 1790-1850.
      Gannon.
    Genesis & Geology: A Study in the Relations
      of Scientific Thought, Natural Theology &
      Social Opinion in Great Britain, 1790-1850.
      Harvard U Pr.
Gillman, Leonard.
  xGillman, Leonard.
    Calculus. Norton.
Gillman, Neil.
  xGillman, Neil.
    Gabriel Marcel on Religious Knowledge. U Pr
      of Amer.
Gillmor, C. Stewart, 1938-
  xGillmor, C. Stewart.
    Coulomb & the Evolution of Physics &
      Engineering in Eighteenth-Century France.
      Princeton U Pr.
Gillmor, Donald M.
  xGillmor, Donald M.
    Free Press & Fair Trial. Pub Aff Pr.
Gillon, Adam, 1921-
  xGillon, Adam.
    Conrad & Shakespeare & Other Essays. G K
      Hall.
    Conrad & Shakespeare & Other Essays.
      Hippocrene Bks.
Gillon, Edmund V. *see* Gillon, Edmund Vincent.
Gillon, Edmund Vincent.
  xGillon, Edmund V.
    Early Illustrations & Views of American
      Architecture. Dover.
    Early Illustrations & Views of American
      Architecture. Peter Smith.
    Early New England Gravestone Rubbings.
      Dover.
    Early New England Gravestone Rubbings.
      Peter Smith.
Gillquist, Peter E.
  xGillquist, Peter E.
    Let's Quit Fighting About the Holy Spirit.
      Zondervan.
    Love Is Now. Zondervan.
    The Physical Side of Being Spiritual.
      Zondervan.
Gillson, Margery. *see* Gillson, Margery (Stewart).
Gillson, Margery (Stewart), Mrs, 1892-
  xGillson, Margery.
    Developing a High School Chemistry Course
      Adapted to the Differentiated Needs of Boys
      & Girls. AMS Pr.
Gilluly, James, 1896-
  xGilluly, James.
    Principles of Geology. W H Freeman.
Gillum, P. E. *see* Gillum, Perry.
Gillum, Perry.
  xGillum, P. E.
    These Stones Speak. White Wing Pub.
Gilman, Benjamin I. *see* Gilman, Benjamin Ives.
Gilman, Benjamin Ives.
  xGilman, Benjamin I.
    Hopi Songs. AMS Pr.
Gilman, Chandler. *see* Gilman, Chandler Robbins.
Gilman, Chandler Robbins, 1802-1865
  xGilman, Chandler.
    Legends of a Log Cabin. Irvington.
Gilman, Charlotte P. *see* Gilman, Charlotte Perkins
  Stetson.
Gilman, Charlotte Perkins Stetson, 1860-1935
  xGilman, Charlotte P.

    His Religion & Hers: A Study of the Faith of
      Our Fathers & the Work of Our Mothers.
      Hyperion-Conn.
    The Living of Charlotte Perkins Gilman: An
      Autobiography. Arno.
Gilman, Daniel C. *see* Gilman, Daniel Coit.
Gilman, Daniel Coit, 1831-1908
  xGilman, Daniel C.
    The Launching of a University. Mss Info.
Gilman, Dorothy, 1923-
  xGilman, Dorothy.
    A New Kind of Country. Doubleday.
    A New Kind of Country. G K Hall.
    A Palm for Mrs. Pollifax. Doubleday.
    A Palm for Mrs. Pollifax. Fawcett.
    The Tightrope Walker. Doubleday.
    The Tightrope Walker. Fawcett.
    The Tightrope Walker. G K Hall.
    The Unexpected Mrs. Pollifax. Doubleday.
    Unexpected Mrs Pollifax. Fawcett.
Gilman, Ernest B. *see* Gilman, Ernest Bo.
Gilman, Ernest Bo., 1946-
  xGilman, Ernest B.
    The Curious Perspective: Literary & Pictorial
      Wit in the Seventeenth Century. Yale U Pr.
Gilman, George G.
  xGilman, George G.
    Gun Run. Pinnacle Bks.
    Paradise Loses. Pinnacle Bks.
Gilman, John J. *see* Gilman, John Joseph.
Gilman, John Joseph.
  xGilman, John J.
    Art & Science of Growing Crystals. Wiley.
Gilman, Lawrence, 1878-1939
  xGilman, Lawrence.
    Aspects of Modern Opera: Estimates &
      Inquiries. Haskell.
    Edward MacDowell: A Study. Da Capo.
    Nature in Music, & Other Studies in the Tone
      Poetry of Today. Arno.
Gilman, Nicholas P. *see* Gilman, Nicholas Paine.
Gilman, Nicholas Paine, 1849-1912
  xGilman, Nicholas P.
    Socialism & the American Spirit. Arno.
Gilman, Rhoda R.
  xGilman, Rhoda R.
    Red River Trails: Oxcart Routes between St.
      Paul & the Selkirk Settlement, 1820-1870.
      Minn Hist.
Gilman, Richard, 1925-
  xGilman, Richard.
    Decadence: The Strange Life of an Epithet.
      FS&G.
Gilman, Sander L.
  xGilman, Sander L.
    The Face of Madness: Hugh W. Diamond &
      the Origin of Psychiatric Photography.
      Brunner-Mazel.
Gilman, Stephen.
  xGilman, Stephen.
    The Art of la Celestina. Greenwood.
Gilman, William H. *see* Gilman, William Henry.
Gilman, William Henry, 1911-
  xGilman, William H.
    Melville's Early Life & Redburn. Russell.
Gilmartin, Brian G.
  xGilmartin, Brian G.
    The Gilmartin Report. Citadel Pr.
Gilmer, B. V. *see* Gilmer, Beverly Von Haller.
Gilmer, Beverly Von Haller.
  xGilmer, B. V.
    Industrial & Organizational Psychology.
      McGraw.
    Psychology. Har-Row.
Gilmer, Harry. *see* Gilmer, Harry Wesley.

Gilmer, Harry Wesley.
  xGilmer, Harry.
      The If-You Form an Israelite Law. Scholars Pr
      Ca.
Gilmer, R. W. *see* Gilmer, Robert W.
Gilmer, Robert W.
  xGilmer, R. W.
      Multiplicative Ideal Theory. Dekker.
Gilmore, Al-Tony.
  xGilmore, Al-Tony.
      Bad Nigger!: The National Impact of Jack
      Johnson. Kennikat.
      ed. Revisiting Blassingame's "The Slave
      Community": The Scholar's Respond.
      Greenwood.
Gilmore, Betty.
  xGilmore, Betty.
      The Needlepoint Primer. Chilton.
Gilmore, Cecile.
  xGilmore, Cecile.
      Hold Me Fast. Bouregy.
Gilmore, Charles. *see* Gilmore, Charles Minot.
Gilmore, Charles M. *see* Gilmore, Charles Minot.
Gilmore, Charles Minot, 1942-
  xGilmore, Charles.
      Understanding & Using Modern Signal
      Generators. TAB Bks.
  xGilmore, Charles M.
      Understanding & Using Modern Electronic
      Servicing Test Equipment. TAB Bks.
Gilmore, Christopher C. *see* Gilmore, Christopher Cook.
Gilmore, Christopher Cook.
  xGilmore, Christopher C.
      Atlantic City Proof. S&S.
Gilmore, Gene.
  xGilmore, Gene.
      ed. High School Journalism Today. Interstate.
      Modern Newspaper Editing. Boyd & Fraser.
Gilmore, Grant.
  xGilmore, Grant.
      The Ages of American Law. Yale U Pr.
      The Death of Contract. Ohio St U Pr.
Gilmore, H. William. *see* Gilmore, Homer William.
Gilmore, Homer William.
  xGilmore, H. William.
      Operative Dentistry. Mosby.
Gilmore, James R. *see* Gilmore, James Roberts.
Gilmore, James Roberts, 1822-1903
  xGilmore, James R.
      The Advance-Guard of Western Civilization.
      Reprint.
      Down in Tennessee & Back by Way of
      Richmond. Arno.
      Down in Tennessee, Back by Way of
      Richmond. Negro U Pr.
      The Rear-Guard of the Revolution. Reprint.
Gilmore, John V.
  xGilmore, John V.
      Productive Personality. Albion.
Gilmore, Joseph. *see* Gilmore, Joseph L.
Gilmore, Joseph L.
  xGilmore, Joseph.
      Rattlers. NAL.
Gilmore, Joseph P.
  xGilmore, Joseph P.
      Renal Physiology. Krieger.
Gilmore, Lee.
  xGilmore, Lee.
      Folk Instruments. Lerner Pubns.
Gilmore, Louis.
  xGilmore, Louis.
      For Sale by Owner. S&S.
Gilmore, Melvin R. *see* Gilmore, Melvin Randolph.
Gilmore, Melvin Randolph, 1868-1940
  xGilmore, Melvin R.
      Prairie Smoke. AMS Pr.
      Uses of Plants by the Indians of the Missouri
      River Region. U of Nebr Pr.
Gilmore, Myron P. *see* Gilmore, Myron Piper.

Gilmore, Myron Piper, 1910-
  xGilmore, Myron P.
      Argument from Roman Law in Political
      Thought, 1200-1600. Russell.
      World of Humanism, 1453-1517. Har-Row.
Gilmore, Robert, 1941-
  xGilmore, Robert.
      Lie Groups, Lie Algebras & Some of Their
      Applications. Wiley.
Gilmore, Robert L.
  xGilmore, Robert L.
      Caudillism & Militarism in Venezuela,
      1810-1910. Ohio U Pr.
Gilmore, Thomas B.
  xGilmore, Thomas B.
      ed. Early Eighteenth-Century Essays on Taste.
      Schol Facsimiles.
Gilmore, W. R. *see* Gilmore, William R.
Gilmore, William R.
  xGilmore, W. R.
      ed. Radioactive Waste Disposal: Low & High
      Level. Noyes.
Gilmour, Ian. *see* Gilmour, Ian Hedworth John Little.
Gilmour, Ian Hedworth John Little, 1926-
  xGilmour, Ian.
      Inside Right: A Study of Conservatism.
      Merrimack Bk Serv.
Gilmour, Peter.
  xGilmour, Peter.
      Praying Together. St Mary's.
Giloi, Wolfgang.
  xGiloi, Wolfgang K.
      Interactive Computer Graphics: Data
      Structures, Algorithms, Languages. P-H.
Giloi, Wolfgang K. *see* Giloi, Wolfgang.
Gilpatric, Guy, 1896-1950
  xGilpatric, Guy.
      Brownstone Front. Arno.
Gilpatrick, Eleanor G.
  xGilpatrick, Eleanor G.
      Structural Unemployment & Aggregate
      Demand: A Study of Employment &
      Unemployment in the United States
      1948-1964. Johns Hopkins.
Gilpin, Alan.
  xGilpin, Alan.
      Air Pollution. U of Queensland Pr.
      Dictionary of Economic Terms. Philos Lib.
      Dictionary of Environmental Terms. U of
      Queensland Pr.
Gilpin, Laura.
  xGilpin, Laura.
      Enduring Navaho. U of Tex Pr.
      The Hocus-Pocus of the Universe. Doubleday.
Gilpin, Michael. *see* Gilpin, Michael E.
Gilpin, Michael E., 1943-
  xGilpin, Michael.
      Group Selection in Predator-Prey
      Communities. Princeton U Pr.
Gilpin, Robert.
  xGilpin, Robert G.
      France in the Age of the Scientific State.
      Princeton U Pr.
Gilpin, Robert G. *see* Gilpin, Robert.
Gilpin, V. *see* Gilpin, Vincent.
Gilpin, Vincent.
  xGilpin, V.
      Pref. by The Good Little Ship. Sutter House.
  xGilpin, Vincent.
      Good Little Ship. Harrowood Bks.
      The Good Little Ship. Sutter House.
Gilpin, W. Clark.
  xGilpin, W. Clark.
      The Millenarian Piety of Roger Williams. U of
      Chicago Pr.
Gilreath, Esmarch S., 1904-
  xGilreath, Esmarch S.

      Experimental Procedures in Elementary
      Qualitative Analysis. McGraw.
Gilroy, John.
  xGilroy, John.
      Medical Neurology. Macmillan.
Gilson, Etienne H. *see* Gilson, Etienne Henry.
Gilson, Etienne Henry, 1884-
  xGilson, Etienne H.
      The Arts of the Beautiful. Greenwood.
      Elements of Christian Philosophy. Greenwood.
Gilson, Jamie.
  xGilson, Jamie.
      Dial Leroi Rupert, DJ. Lothrop.
Gilsvik, Bob.
  xGilsvik, Bob.
      The Complete Book of Trapping. Chilton.
      The Guide to Good Cheap Hunting. Stein &
      Day.
      The Modern Trapline: Methods & Materials.
      Chilton.
Gilula, N. B.
  xGilula, Norton B.
      ed. Membrane-Membrane Interactions. Raven.
Gilula, Norton B. *see* Gilula, N. B.
Gimbel, John.
  xGimbel, John.
      The American Occupation of Germany: Politics
      & the Military, 1945-1949. Stanford U Pr.
      The Origins of the Marshall Plan. Stanford U
      Pr.
Gimpel, James F.
  xGimpel, James F.
      Algorithms in SNOBOL 4. Wiley.
Gimpel, Jean.
  xGimpel, Jean.
      The Medieval Machine: The Industrial
      Revolution of the Middle Ages. Penguin.
Gimpl, Caroline Ann.
  xGimpl, Caroline Ann.
      The Correspondant & the Founding of the
      French Third Republic. Greenwood.
Ginat, J.
  xGinat, Joseph.
      Women in Muslim Rural Society. Transaction
      Bks.
Ginat, Joseph. *see* Ginat, J.
Gindely, Anton, 1829-1892
  xGindely, Anton.
      History of the Thirty Years War. Arno.
Gindick, Jon.
  xGindick, Jon.
      The Natural Blues & Country Western
      Harmonica. J Gindick.
Gindin, James. *see* Gindin, James Jack.
Gindin, James Jack, 1926-
  xGindin, James.
      The English Climate: An Excursion into a
      Biography of John Galsworthy. U of Mich
      Pr.
Ginell, R. *see* Ginell, Robert.
Ginell, Robert, 1912-
  xGinell, R.
      Association Theory: The Phases of Matter &
      Their Transformations. Elsevier.
Giner, Salvador.
  xGiner, Salvador.
      Sociology. Biblio Dist.
Gingell, Lesley. *see* Gingell, Lesley P.
Gingell, Lesley P., 1941-
  xGingell, Lesley.
      The ABCs of the Open Classroom. ETC Pubns.
Ginger, Ann F. *see* Ginger, Ann Fagan.
Ginger, Ann Fagan.
  xGinger, Ann F.
      ed. Human Rights Docket U.S. 1979.
      Meiklejohn Civ Lib.
Ginger, Ray.
  xGinger, Ray.

Ray Ginger's Jokebook About American
History. New Viewpoints.
Gingerich, Melvin, 1902-
xGingerich, Melvin.
The Christian & Revolution. Herald Pr.
Gingerich, Solomon F. *see* Gingerich, Solomon Francis.
Gingerich, Solomon Francis, 1875-
xGingerich, Solomon F.
Wordsworth. Folcroft.
Ginglend, David R.
xGinglend, David R.
Ready to Work?: Development of Occupational
Skills, Attitudes, & Behaviors with Mentally
Retarded Persons. Abingdon.
Gingras, Gustave, 1918-
xGingras, Gustave.
Feet Was I to the Lame. Intl Schol Bk Serv.
Gingras, Rosario C.
xGingras, Rosario C.
ed. Second-Language Acquisition & Foreign
Language Teaching. Ctr Appl Ling.
Gingrich, Donald.
xGingrich, Donald.
Relating the Arts. Ctr Appl Res.
Gingrich, Harold W.
xGingrich, Harold W.
Electrical Machinery, Transformers, & Control.
P-H.
Giniger, Kenneth S. *see* Giniger, Kenneth Seeman.
Giniger, Kenneth Seeman, 1919-
xGiniger, Kenneth S.
ed. The Compact Treasury of Inspiration.
Abingdon.
Ginott, Haim G.
xGinott, Haim G.
Group Psychotherapy with Children: The
Theory & Practice of Play-Therapy. McGraw.
Ginoux, Jean J.
xGinoux, Jean J.
Two Phase Flows & Heat Transfer with
Application to Nuclear Reactor Design
Problems. McGraw.
Ginsberg, Allen, 1926-
xGinsberg, Allen.
Howl & Other Poems. City Lights.
Journals: Early Fifties Early Sixties. Grove.
Planet News. City Lights.
Reality Sandwiches: 1953-1960. City Lights.
Ginsberg, Michael.
xGinsberg, Michael B.
Practical Guide to Antimicrobial Agents.
Williams & Wilkins.
Ginsberg, Michael B. *see* Ginsberg, Michael.
Ginsberg, Morris, 1889-
xGinsberg, Morris.
The Idea of Progress: A Reevaluation.
Greenwood.
Ginsborg, Paul.
xGinsborg, Paul.
Daniele Manin & the Venetian Revolution of
1848-49. Cambridge U Pr.
Ginsburg, Christian D. *see* Ginsburg, Christian David.
Ginsburg, Christian David, 1831-1914
xGinsburg, Christian D.
Massorah. Ktav.
Ginsburg, Douglas H., 1946-
xGinsburg, Douglas H.
Regulation of Broadcasting: Law & Policy
Towards Radio, Television & Cable
Communications. West Pub.
Ginsburg, G. P. *see* Ginsburg, Gerald Phillip.
Ginsburg, Gerald Phillip, 1932-
xGinsburg, G. P.
Emerging Strategies in Social Psychological
Research. Wiley.
Ginsburg, Herbert.
xGinsburg, Herbert.

Piaget's Theory of Intellectual Development.
P-H.
Ginsburg, Mirra.
xGinsburg, Mirra.
tr. Last Door to Aiya: A Selection of the Best
New Science Fiction from the Soviet Union.
S G Phillips.
tr. & ed. The Lazies: Tales of the Peoples of
Russia. Macmillan.
Little Rystu. Greenwillow.
Adapted by Mushroom in the Rain. Macmillan.
The Night It Rained Pancakes. Greenwillow.
Ookie-Spooky. Crown.
Where Does the Sun Go at Night?.
Greenwillow.
Ginsburg, Robert. *see* Ginsburg, Robert N.
Ginsburg, Robert N.
xGinsburg, Robert.
ed. Evolving Concepts in Sedimentology. Johns
Hopkins.
Ginsburg, Ruth R.
xGinsburg, Ruth R.
Nueva vista. Allyn.
Ginsburg, Seymour, 1927-
xGinsburg, Seymour.
An Introduction to Mathematical Machine
Theory. A-W.
Ginsburgs, George.
xGinsburgs, George.
Calendar of Diplomatic Affairs, Democratic
People's Republic of Korea. Oceana.
Soviet Foreign Policy Toward Western Europe.
Praeger.
xGinsburgs, George K.
Calendar of Diplomatic Affairs Democratic
People's Republic of Korea 1945-1975.
Symposia Pr.
Ginsburgs, George K. *see* Ginsburgs, George.
Ginter, Donald E.
xGinter, Donald E.
ed. Whig Organization in the General Election
of 1790: Selections from the Blair Adam
Papers. U of Cal Pr.
Ginther, John R. *see* Ginther, John Robert.
Ginther, John Robert, 1922-
xGinther, John R.
But You Look So Well!. Nelson-Hall.
Ginzberg, Eli, 1911-
xGinzberg, Eli.
ed. The Future of the Metropolis: People, Jobs,
Income. Olympus Pub Co.
Good Jobs, Bad Jobs, No Jobs. Harvard U Pr.
House of Adam Smith. Octagon.
Human Resources: The Wealth of a Nation.
Greenwood.
The Ineffective Soldier: Lessons for
Management & the Nation. Greenwood.
Men, Money & Medicine. Columbia U Pr.
ed. Values & Ideals of American Youth. Arno.
Ginzberg, Louis, 1873-1953
xGinzberg, Louis.
Legends of the Bible. Jewish Pubn.
Legends of the Jews. Jewish Pubn.
Ginzburg, Abraham.
xGinzburg, Abraham.
Algebraic Theory of Automata. Acad Pr.
Ginzburg, Carlo.
xGinzburg, Carlo.
The Cheese & the Worms: The Cosmos of a
Sixteenth Century Miller. Johns Hopkins.
Ginzburg, Eugenia S. *see* Ginzburg, Evgeniia Semenovna.
Ginzburg, Evgeniia Semenovna.
xGinzburg, Eugenia S.
Journey into the Whirlwind. HarBraceJ.
Ginzburg, V. L. *see* Ginzburg, Vitalii Lazarevich.
Ginzburg, Vitalii Lazarevich, 1916-
xGinzburg, V. L.
Propagation of Electromagnetic Waves in
Plasmas. Pergamon.
Gioello. *see* Gioello, Debbie Ann.

Gioello, Debbie A. *see* Gioello, Debbie Ann.
Gioello, Debbie Ann.
xGioello.
Fashion Production Terms. Fairchild.
xGioello, Debbie A.
Figure Types & Size Ranges. Fairchild.
Giono, Jean, 1895-1970
xGiono, Jean.
The Song of the World. Fertig.
Giora, Zvi.
xGiora, Zvi.
Psychopathology: A Cognitive View. Halsted
Pr.
Giordani, Igino, 1894-
xGiordani, Igino.
Christ, Hope of the World. Dghtrs St Paul.
Mary of Nazareth. Dghtrs St Paul.
Giorgi, A. *see* Giorgi, Amedeo.
Giorgi, Amedeo.
xGiorgi, A.
ed. Duquesne Studies in Phenomenological
Psychology. Duquesne.
xGiorgi, Amedeo.
Duquesne Studies in Phenomenological
Psychology. Humanities.
Psychology As a Human Science: A
Phenomenologically Based Approach.
Har-Row.
Giovacchini, Peter L.
xGiovacchini, Peter L.
Psychoanalysis of Character Disorders.
Aronson.
Giovannetti. *see* Giovannetti, Pericle.
Giovannetti, Pericle.
xGiovannetti.
Max. Atheneum.
Giovanni, Nikki.
xGiovanni, Nikki.
Gemini: An Extended Autobiographical
Statement on My First Twenty-Five Years of
Being a Black Poet. Penguin.
Vacation Time: Poems for Children. Morrow.
Giovannini, G. *see* Giovannini, Giovanni.
Giovannini, Giovanni, 1906-
xGiovannini, G.
Ezra Pound & Dante. Haskell.
Giovannitti, Len, 1920-
xGiovannitti, Len.
The Nature of the Beast. Random.
Giovannoni, Jeanne M.
xGiovannoni, Jeanne M.
Child Abuse & Neglect: An Examination from
the Perspective of Child Development
Knowledge. R & E Res Assoc.
Defining Child Abuse. Free Pr.
Gipson, Fred. *see* Gipson, Frederick Benjamin.
Gipson, Frederick Benjamin.
xGipson, Fred.
Curly & the Wild Boar. Har-Row.
Curly & the Wild Boar. Har-Row.
Gipson, Lawrence H. *see* Gipson, Lawrence Henry.
Gipson, Lawrence Henry, 1880-
xGipson, Lawrence H.
The Coming of the Revolution: 1763-1775.
Har-Row.
Coming of the Revolution: 1763-1775.
Har-Row.
Gipson, R. McCandless. *see* Gipson, Richard
Mccandless.
Gipson, Richard M. *see* Gipson, Richard Mccandless.
Gipson, Richard Mccandless.
xGipson, R. McCandless.
The Life of Emma Thursby. Da Capo.
xGipson, Richard M.
The Life of Emma Thursby, 1845-1931. U Pr
of Va.
Giragosian, N. *see* Giragosian, Newman H.
Giragosian, Newman H.
xGiragosian, N.

Successful Product & Business Development.
Dekker.
Girard, Joe.
xGirard, Joe.
How to Sell Anything to Anybody. S&S.
How to Sell Anything to Anybody. Warner
Bks.
How to Sell Yourself. S&S.
Girard, Louis J. *see* Girard, Louis Joseph.
Girard, Louis Joseph, 1919-
xGirard, Louis J.
Ultrasonic Fragmentation for Intraocular
Surgery. Mosby.
Girard, Pat.
xGirard, Pat.
Flying Machines. Raintree Child.
Girard, Rafael.
xGirard, Raphael.
Esotericism of the Popol Vuh. Theos U Pr.
Girard, Raphael. *see* Girard, Rafael.
Girard, Rene, 1923-
xGirard, Rene.
ed. Proust: A Collection of Critical Essays.
Greenwood.
Girard, Weldon, 1915-
xGirard, Weldon.
How to Make Big Money Selling Commercial
& Industrial Property. P-H.
Profit Opportunities in Commercial &
Industrial Real Estate. P-H.
Girardi, Giulio, 1926-
xGirardi, Guilio.
Marxism & Christianity. Macmillan.
Girardi, Guilio. *see* Girardi, Giulio.
Giraudoux, Jean, 1882-1944
xGiraudoux, Jean.
Ondine. French & Eur.
Provinciales. French & Eur.
Suzanne & the Pacific. Fortig.
Girault, Maurice.
xGirault, Maurice.
Stochastic Processes. Springer-Verlag.
Girault, V. *see* Girault, Vivette.
Girault, Vivette.
xGirault, V.
Finite Element Approximation of the
Navier-Stokes Equations. Springer-Verlag.
Girdano, Daniel A.
xGirdano, Daniel A.
Controlling Stress & Tension: A Holistic
Approach. P-H.
Girdano, Daniel A. *see* Girdano, Dorothy Dusek.
Girdano, Dorothy D. *see* Girdano, Dorothy Dusek.
Girdano, Dorothy Dusek.
xGirdano, Daniel A.
jt. auth. Drugs - A Factual Account. A-W.
xGirdano, Dorothy D.
Drugs - A Factual Account. A-W.
Girdler, Allan.
xGirdler, Allan.
Customizing Your Van. TAB Bks.
Girgus, Sam B., 1941-
xGirgus, Sam B.
Law of the Heart: Individualism & the Modern
Self in American Literature. U of Tex Pr.
Giri, V. V. *see* Giri, Varahagiri Venkata.
Giri, Varahagiri Venkata, 1894-
xGiri, V. V.
My Life & Times. Intl Pubns Serv.
My Life & Times. South Asia Bks.
Girion, Barbara.
xGirion, Barbara.
The Boy with the Special Face. Abingdon.
Joshua, the Czar, & the Chicken Bone Wish.
Scribner.
Misty & Me. Scribner.
Girl Scouts of the U. S. A. *see* Girl Scouts of the United
States of America.
Girl Scouts of the United States of America.
xGirl Scouts of the U. S. A.

Adventures in Careers. GS.
Every Girl Scout Camp an EQ Camp. GS.
Girl Scout Cookbook. Contemp Bks.
Guide to Helping Leaders - Design for
Learning. GS.
Hello Welcome to Girl Scouting. GS.
Leader's Workbook: Design for Learning. GS.
To Guide a Girl Scout Troop. GS.
What Is It Like to Be a Leader?. GS.
Worlds to Explore Handbook for Brownie &
Junior Girl Scouts. GS.
xGirl Scouts of the U.S.
Daisy Low of the Girl Scouts: The Story of
Juliette Gordon Low, Founder of the Girl
Scouts of United States of America. GS.
xGirl Scouts of the USA.
The Beginner's Cookbook. GS.
Being Aware. GS.
Brownies' Own Songbook. GS.
Cadette Girl Scout Handbook: For Cadettes.
GS.
Compass & Maps. GS.
Cooking Out-of-Doors: For Juniors, Brownies
Cadettes, Seniors & Leaders. GS.
A Council Guide to Eco-Action. GS.
Exploring the Hand Arts: For Juniors,
Cadettes, Seniors, & Leaders. GS.
Feeding a Crowd. GS.
Fun with Fundamentals. GS.
Games for Girl Scouts. GS.
Girl Scout Pocket Songbook: For Juniors,
Cadettes, Seniors, & Leaders. GS.
The Great Cookie Caper or, How to Discover
the World, Starting with a Cookie or
Anything Else. GS.
Handicapped Girls & Girl Scouting. GS.
Helping Leaders Help Girls Grow. GS.
Hiking-in Town or Country: For Juniors,
Cadettes, Seniors & Leaders. GS.
Hola!: Bienvenida a las Girl Scouts. GS.
How Girls Can Help Their Country. GS.
Moreabouts for Brownie Girl Scout Leaders.
GS.
Partnership in Planning. GS.
Planning Trips with Girl Scouts. GS.
Program Update. GS.
Safety-Wise: For Girls (Grade 7-12) & Adults
Who Work Directly with Girls. GS.
Sing Together: A Girl Scout Songbook. GS.
Skip to My Lou: For Brownies, Juniors,
Cadettes, Seniors & Leaders. GS.
The Story of the Four World Centres: For
Girls & Leaders. GS.
Training About Girl Scouting. GS.
Troop Financing in Dollars & Sense. GS.
Worlds to Explore Brownie & Junior Leaders
Guide. GS.
Worlds to Explore Junior Badges & Signs. GS.
xGirl Scouts of the U.S.A., Our Chalet Committee
of Wagggs.
Our Chalet Songbook. GS.
xGirl Scouts of the U.S.A. Program Dept.
Careers to Explore for Brownie & Junior Girl
Scouts. GS.
Let's Make It Happen. GS.
xGirl Scouts of U.S.
Let's Take a Walk: An Activity Picture Book
with Group Leader's Guide. GS.
Girl Scouts of the U.S. *see* Girl Scouts of the United
States of America.
Girl Scouts of the USA. *see* Girl Scouts of the United
States of America.
Girl Scouts of the U.S.A., Our Chalet Committee of
Wagggs. *see* Girl Scouts of the United States of
America.
Girl Scouts of the U.S.A. Program Dept. *see* Girl Scouts
of the United States of America.
Girl Scouts of U.S. *see* Girl Scouts of the United States
of America.

Girouard, Blanche, Lady.
xGirouard, Blanche M.
World Is for the Young: & Other Stories. Arno.
Girouard, Blanche M. *see* Girouard, Blanche.
Girouard, Mark, 1931-
xGirouard, Mark.
Sweetness & Light: The 'Queen Anne'
Movement, 1860-1900. Oxford U Pr.
Victorian Country House. Yale U Pr.
Giroux, Joan.
xGiroux, Joan.
The Haiku Form. C E Tuttle.
Girsanov, I. V. *see* Girsanov, Igor Vladimirovich.
Girsanov, Igor Vladimirovich.
xGirsanov, I. V.
Lectures on Mathematical Theory of
Extremum Problems. Springer-Verlag.
Girvan, Norman, 1941-
xGirvan, Norman.
Corporate Imperialism: Conflict &
Expropriation Transnational Corporations &
Economic Nationalism in the Third World.
M E Sharpe.
Corporate Imperialism: Conflict &
Expropriation. Transnational Corporations &
Economic Nationalism in the Third World.
Monthly Rev.
Gisborne, Thomas, 1758-1846
xGisborne, Thomas.
An Enquiry into the Duties of the Female Sex.
Garland Pub.
Gish, Arthur G.
xGish, Arthur G.
Living in Christian Community. Herald Pr.
Gish, Robert.
xGish, Robert.
Hamlin Garland. The Far West. Boise St Univ.
Gisselquist, David.
xGisselquist, David.
Oil Prices & Trade Deficits: U. S. Conflicts
with Japan & West Germany. Praeger.
Gissing, George. *see* Gissing, George Robert.
Gissing, George R. *see* Gissing, George Robert.
Gissing, George Robert, 1857-1903
xGissing, George.
Born in Exile: A Novel. AMS Pr.
In the Year of Jubilee. AMS Pr.
Letters of George Gissing to Gabrielle Fleury.
NY Pub Lib.
Letters of George Gissing to Members of His
Family. Haskell.
Life's Morning. AMS Pr.
A Life's Morning. R West.
Odd Women. AMS Pr.
Odd Women. Norton.
The Odd Women. R West.
Paying Guest. AMS Pr.
The Private Papers of Henry Ryecroft. Arden
Lib.
The Private Papers of Henry Ryecroft. R West.
Unclassed. AMS Pr.
Whirlpool. AMS Pr.
The Whirlpool. Fairleigh Dickinson.
xGissing, George R.
Letters of George Gissing to Members of His
Family. Scholarly.
Githens, Marianne.
xGithens, Marianne.
ed. A Portrait of Marginality: The Political
Behavior of the American Woman. Longman.
Gitin, David.
xGitin, David.
City Air. SBD.
Guitar Against the Wall. Panjandrum.
This Once: New & Selected Poems, 1965-1978.
Blue Wind.
Gitin, Maria.
xGitin, Maria.

Night Shift. Blue Wind.

Gitler, Ira.
xGitler, Ira.
Ice Hockey A to Z. Lothrop.

Gitlin, Todd.
xGitlin, Todd.
Campfires of the Resistance: Poetry from the
Movement. Bobbs.
The Whole World Is Watching: Mass Media in
the Making & Unmaking of the New Left. U
of Cal Pr.

Gitlow, Benjamin, 1891-
xGitlow, Benjamin.
Whole of Their Lives: Communism in America
- a Personal History & Intimate Portrayal of
Its Leaders. Arno.

Gitman, Larry. *see* Gitman, Lawrence J.

Gitman, Lawrence J.
xGitman, Larry.
Financial Management: Cases. West Pub.
xGitman, Lawrence J.
Principles of Managerial Finance. Har-Row.

Gitnick, Gary L.
xGitnick, Gary L.
ed. Current Gastroenterology & Hepatology.
HM Prof Med Div.

Gitsch, Eduard.
xGitsch, Eduard.
Gynecological Operative Anatomy: The Simple
& Radical Hysterectomy Atlas. De Gruyter.

Gittell, Marilyn.
xGittell, Marilyn.
ed. Educating an Urban Population. Sage.

Gittelsohn, Roland B. *see* Gittelsohn, Roland Bertram.

Gittelsohn, Roland Bertram, 1910-
xGittelsohn, Roland B.
Fire in My Bones: Essays on Judaism in a
Time of Crisis. Bloch.
Love, Sex & Marriage: A Jewish View. UAHC.
Love, Sex & Marriage: A Jewish View. UAHC.
The Modern Meaning of Judaism. Collins Pubs.

Gittelson, Bernard.
xGittelson, Bernard.
The Gittelson Biorhythm Code Book: Charts &
Compatibility Guides for 1978-1982. Arco.

Gittelson, Natalie.
xGittelson, Natalie.
Dominus: A Woman Looks at Men's Lives.
FS&G.
Dominus: A Woman Looks at Men's Lives.
HarBraceJ.

Gitter, Lena L.
xGitter, Lena L.
Montessori Approach to Art Education. Spec
Child.
Montessori Way. Spec Child.

Gittinger, J. Price. *see* Gittinger, James Price.

Gittinger, James Price.
xGittinger, J. Price.
Economic Analysis of Agricultural Projects.
Johns Hopkins.

Gittinger, Mattiebelle.
xGittinger, Mattiebelle.
Splendid Symbols: Textiles & Tradition in
Indonesia. Textile Mus.

Gittings, John.
xGittings, John.
A Chinese View of China. Pantheon.
Survey of the Sino-Soviet Dispute: A
Commentary & Extracts from the Recent
Polemics, 1963-1967. Oxford U Pr.

Gittings, Robert.
xGittings, Robert.
The Nature of Biography. U of Wash Pr.
Thomas Hardy's Later Years. Little.

Gittins, Anne.
xGittins, Anne.

Tales from the South Pacific Islands. Stemmer
Hse.

Gittins, H. Leigh, 1907-
xGittins, H. Leigh.
Idaho's Gold Road. U Pr of Idaho.

Gittleman, Arthur.
xGittleman, Arthur.
History of Mathematics. Merrill.

Gittleman, Edwin.
xGittleman, Edwin.
Jones Very: The Effective Years, 1833-1840.
Columbia U Pr.

Gittleman, Sol, 1934-
xGittleman, Sol.
From Shtetl to Suburbia: The Family in Jewish
Literary Imagination. Beacon Pr.

Gittus, Elizabeth.
xGittus, Elizabeth.
Flats, Families & the Under-Fives. Routledge &
Kegan.

Gittus, J. *see* Gittus, J. H.

Gittus, J. H.
xGittus, J.
Irradiation Effects in Crystalline Solids. Intl
Ideas.

Giudice, Giovanni.
xGiudice, Giovanni.
Developmental Biology of the Sea Urchin
Embryo. Acad Pr.

Giulio, Robert C. Di. *see* DiGiulio, Robert C.

Giuseppi, Montague S. *see* Giuseppi, Montague Spencer.

Giuseppi, Montague Spencer, 1869-
xGiuseppi, Montague S.
Naturalizations of Foreign Protestants in the
American & West Indian Colonies, Etc..
Genealog Pub.

Given, Barbara A.
xGiven, Barbara A.
Gastroenterology in Clinical Nursing. Mosby.

Given, James Buchanan.
xGiven, James Buchanan.
Society & Homicide in Thirteenth-Century
England. Stanford U Pr.

Givens, John.
xGivens, John.
A Friend in the Police. HarBraceJ.
Sons of the Pioneers. HarBraceJ.

Givner, A. *see* Givner, Abraham.

Givner, Abraham.
xGivner, A.
A Handbook of Behavior Modification for the
Classroom. HR&W.

Givone, D. D. *see* Givone, Donald D.

Givone, Donald D.
xGivone, D. D.
Introduction to Switching Circuit Theory.
McGraw.
xGivone, Donald D.
Microprocessors - Microcomputers: An
Introduction. McGraw.

Gjerset, Knut, 1865-1936
xGjerset, Knut.
History of the Norwegian People. AMS Pr.
Norwegian Sailors on the Great Lakes. Arno.

Gjessing, Dag T.
xGjessing, Dag T.
Remote Surveillance by Electromagnetic Waves
for Air-Water-Land. Ann Arbor Science.

Glaab, Charles N. *see* Glaab, Charles Nelson.

Glaab, Charles Nelson.
xGlaab, Charles N.
Factories in the Valley: Neenah-Menasha
1870-1915. State Hist Soc Wis.
A History of Urban America. Macmillan.

Glacken, Clarence J.
xGlacken, Clarence J.
The Great Loochoo: A Study of Okinawan
Village Life. Greenwood.

Glackens, Ira, 1907-
xGlackens, Ira.

A Measure of Sliding Sand. Eriksson.

Glackin, James J.
xGlackin, James J.
Improvised Munitions Systems. Paladin Ent.

Glad, Paul W.
xGlad, Paul W.
Trumpet Soundeth: William Jennings Bryan &
His Democracy, 1896-1912. U of Nebr Pr.

Gladden, E. N.
xGladden, E. N.
History of Public Administration. Biblio Dist.

Gladden, E. N. *see* Gladden, Edgar Norman.

Gladden, Edgar N. *see* Gladden, Edgar Norman.

Gladden, Edgar Norman.
xGladden, E. N.
Civil Services of the United Kingdom:
1885-1970. Biblio Dist.
xGladden, Edgar N.
Civil Services of the United Kingdom,
1855-1970. Kelley.

Gladden, Washington, 1836-1918
xGladden, Washington.
Applied Christianity: Moral Aspects of Social
Questions. Arno.
Who Wrote the Bible?: A Book for the People.
Arno.
xGladden, Washington T.
Working People & Their Employers. Arno.

Gladden, Washington T. *see* Gladden, Washington.

Gladfelter, Irl A.
xGladfelter, Irl A.
Dental Evidence: A Handbook for Police. C C
Thomas.

Gladstone, Bernard.
xGladstone, Bernard.
Complete Book of Garden & Outdoor Lighting.
Hearthside.
Hints & Tips for the Handyperson.
Cornerstone.

Gladstone, Francis.
xGladstone, Francis.
The Politics of Planning. Transatlantic.

Gladstone, Gary.
xGladstone, Gary.
Dune Buggies. Lippincott.

Gladstone, J. *see* Gladstone, John.

Gladstone, John.
xGladstone, J.
Mechanical Estimating Guidebook. McGraw.
xGladstone, John.
Air Conditioning Testing & Balancing: A Field
Practice Manual. Engineers Pr.
Correspondence on the Present State of Slavery
in the British West Indies and in the United
States of America. Humanities.
Florida Air Conditioning Contractor's
Handbook. Engineers Pr.
Journeyman General Mechanical Examination:
An Illustrated Review with Questions &
Answers. Engineers Pr.

Gladstone, M. J.
xGladstone, M. J.
A Carrot for a Nose: The Form of Folk
Sculpture on America's City Streets &
Country Roads. Scribner.

Gladstone, Meredith.
xGladstone, Meredith.
The Needlepoint Alphabet Book. Morrow.
Small Needlepoint Treasures: A Complete
How-to Workbook for Making Quick
Needlepoint Gifts. Morrow.

Gladstone, William E. *see* Gladstone, William Ewart.

Gladstone, William Ewart, 1809-1898
xGladstone, William E.
Arthur Henry Hallam. Folcroft.
Gleanings of Past Years, 1843-1878. AMS Pr.

Gladstone, William J.
xGladstone, William J.

Test Your Own Mental Health: A
Self-Evaluation Workbook. Arco.

Gladwell, I.
xGladwell, I.
ed. A Survey of Numerical Methods for Partial
Differential Equations. Oxford U Pr.

Gladwin, Ellis.
xGladwin, Ellis.
Living in the Changing Caribbean. Macmillan.

Gladwin, Thomas N.
xGladwin, Thomas N.
Environment, Planning & the Multinational
Corporation. Jai Pr.

Gladwyn, Hubert M. see Gladwyn, Hubert Miles
Gladwyn Jebb.

Gladwyn, Hubert Miles Gladwyn Jebb, Baron, 1900-
xGladwyn, Hubert M.
Europe After De Gaulle. Taplinger.

Glahe, F. see Glahe, Fred R.

Glahe, Fred R.
xGlahe, F.
ed. Adam Smith & the Wealth of Nations,
1776-1976: Bicentennial Essays. Colo Assoc.

Glaister, Stephen.
xGlaister, Stephen.
Mathematical Methods for Economists. Biblio
Dist.

Glamour.
xGlamour Magazine.
Glamour's "How to Do Anything Better" Book.
Rutledge Bks.
xGlamour Magazine Editors.
Glamour Beauty Book. S&S.
Glamour's Health & Beauty Book. S&S.

Glamour Magazine. see Glamour.

Glamour Magazine Editors. see Glamour.

Glansdorff, P.
xGlansdorff, P.
Thermodynamic Theory of Structure, Stability
& Fluctuations. Wiley.

Glantz, Stanton A.
xGlantz, Stanton A.
Mathematics for Biomedical Applications. U of
Cal Pr.

Glanville, Brian.
xGlanville, Brian.
A Book of Soccer. Oxford U Pr.
The Comic. Stein & Day.
History of the Soccer World Cup. Macmillan.
The Olympian. HM.

Glanville, Stephen R. see Glanville, Stephen Ranulph
Kingdom.

Glanville, Stephen Ranulph Kingdom, 1900-1956
xGlanville, Stephen R.
The Legacy of Egypt. Greenwood.

Glasby, G. P.
xGlasby, G. P.
ed. Marine Manganese Deposits. Elsevier.

Glasby, J. S. see Glasby, John Stephen.

Glasby, John S. see Glasby, John Stephen.

Glasby, John Stephen.
xGlasby, J. S.
Encyclopedia of the Alkaloids. Plenum Pub.
xGlasby, John S.
Boundaries of the Universe. Harvard U Pr.
The Nebular Variables. Pergamon.
xGlasby, S.
ed. Encyclopedia of the Alkaloids. Plenum Pub.

Glasby, S. see Glasby, John Stephen.

Glaser, Anton, 1924-
xGlaser, Anton.
History of Binary & Other Nondecimal
Numeration. A Glaser.
Neater by the Meter: An American Guide to
the Metric System. A Glaser.

Glaser, Barney G.
xGlaser, Barney G.

Awareness of Dying. Aldine Pub.
Discovery of Grounded Theory: Strategies for
Qualitative Research. Aldine Pub.
Organizational Scientists: Their Professional
Careers. Irvington.

Glaser, Daniel.
xGlaser, Daniel.
Effectiveness of a Prison & Parole System.
Bobbs.
ed. Handbook of Criminology. Rand.

Glaser, Diane. see Glaser, Dianne.

Glaser, Dianne.
xGlaser, Diane.
Diary of Trilby Frost. Dell.
xGlaser, Dianne.
Amber Wellington Daredevil. Dell.
Amber Wellington, Daredevil. Walker & Co.
The Case of the Missing Six. Holiday.
The Diary of Trilby Frost. Holiday.
Summer Secrets. Holiday.

Glaser, G. H. see Glaser, Gilbert H.

Glaser, Gilbert H.
xGlaser, G. H.
ed. Antiepileptic Drugs: Mechanisms of Action.
Raven.

Glaser, Herman. see Glaser, Hermann.

Glaser, Hermann.
xGlaser, Herman.
The Cultural Roots of National Socialism. U of
Tex Pr.

Glaser, Hy.
xGlaser, Hy.
How to Write Lyrics That Make Sense &
Dollars. Exposition.

Glaser, Lynn.
xGlaser, Lynn.
ed. Indians or Jews?: An Introduction...to a
Reprint of Manasseh Ben Israel's "the Hope
of Israel". D Franklin.

Glaser, Milton.
xGlaser, Milton.
The Underground Gourmet Cookbook. S&S.

Glaser, Robert, 1921-
xGlaser, Robert.
Adaptive Education: Individual Diversity &
Learning. HR&W.
Advances in Instructional Psychology. Halsted
Pr.

Glaser, Rollin. see Glaser, Rollin O.

Glaser, Rollin O.
xGlaser, Rollin.
Retail Personnel Management. Lebhar
Friedman.

Glaser, William A.
xGlaser, William A.
Pretrial Discovery & the Adversary System.
Russell Sage.

Glasgow, Aline.
xGlasgow, Aline.
Pair of Shoes. Dial.

Glasgow, Ellen. see Glasgow, Ellen Anderson Gholson.

Glasgow, Ellen Anderson Gholson, 1874-1945
xGlasgow, Ellen.
Barren Ground. Hill & Wang.
Barren Ground. Peter Smith.
The Freeman & Other Poems. Americanist.
The Freeman & Other Poems. AMS Pr.
Vein of Iron. HarBraceJ.

Glasgow, George, 1891-
xGlasgow, George.
Continental Statesmen. Kennikat.

Glasgow University Media Group.
xGlasgow University Media Group.
Bad News. Routledge & Kegan.
More Bad News. Routledge & Kegan.

Glashan, Roy. see Glashan, Roy R.

Glashan, Roy R., 1928-
xGlashan, Roy.

Compiled by American Governors &
Gubernatorial Elections, 1775-1978: A
Statistical Compilation. Meckler Bks.

Glashausser, Suellen.
xGlashausser, Suellen.
Plaiting Step-by-Step. Watson-Guptill.

Glasner, M. S. see Glasner, Shmuel.

Glasner, Peter. see Glasner, Peter E.

Glasner, Peter E.
xGlasner, Peter.
The Sociology of Secularisation: A Critique of
a Concept. Routledge & Kegan.

Glasner, Shmuel, 1945-
xGlasner, M. S.
Proximal Flows. Springer-Verlag.

Glass, Arnold L. see Glass, Arnold Lewis.

Glass, Arnold Lewis.
xGlass, Arnold L.
Cognition. A-W.

Glass, Bentley. see Glass, Hiram Bentley.

Glass, Bill. see Glass, William.

Glass, Carter, 1858-1946
xGlass, Carter.
An Adventure in Constructive Finance. Arno.

Glass, Charles.
xGlass, Charles.
Cacti & Succulents for the Amateur. Sterling.
Cacti & Succulents for the Amateur. Van Nos
Reinhold.

Glass, D. V. see Glass, David Victor.

Glass, David V. see Glass, David Victor.

Glass, David Victor.
xGlass, D. V.
ed. Introduction to Malthus. Biblio Dist.
xGlass, David V.
Population Policies & Movements in Europe.
Kelley.
xGlass, P. V.
Population Policies & Movements in Europe.
Biblio Dist.

Glass, Dick.
xGlass, Dick.
Service Shop Management Handbook. Sams.

Glass, Frankcina.
xGlass, Frankcina.
Marvin & Tige. Fawcett.
Marvin & Tige. St Martin.

Glass, Fred J. see Glass, Frederick James.

Glass, Frederick James, 1881-1930
xGlass, Fred J.
Paper Craft. Paragraph Pr.
Stencil Craft. Paragraph Pr.

Glass, Gene V.
xGlass, Gene V.
Design & Analysis of Time-Series Experiments.
Colo Assoc.
Statistical Methods in Education & Psychology.
P-H.

Glass, George B. see Glass, George B. Jerzy.

Glass, George B. Jerzy.
xGlass, George B.
ed. Gastrointestinal Hormones. Raven.
ed. Progress in Gastroenterology. Grune.

Glass, Hiram Bentley.
xGlass, Bentley.
ed. Forerunners of Darwin, 1745-1859. Johns
Hopkins.

Glass, Leslie.
xGlass, Leslie.
Getting Away with It. Avon.

Glass, Malcolm.
xGlass, Malcolm.
Bone Love. U Presses Fla.

Glass, Marion.
xGlass, Marion.
Integrated Studies in Patient Care. Delmar.
Integrated Studies in Patient Care. Van Nos
Reinhold.

Glass, Mary E. see Glass, Mary Ellen.

Glass, Mary Ellen.
 xGlass, Mary E.
  Silver & Politics in Nevada: 1892-1902. U of
   Nev Pr.
Glass, Montagu. *see* Glass, Montague Marsden.
Glass, Montague Marsden, 1877-1934
 xGlass, Montagu.
  Potash & Perlmutter: Their Co-Partnership
   Ventures & Adventures. Arno.
Glass, P. V. *see* Glass, David Victor.
Glass, Robert H.
 xGlass, Robert H.
  Office Gynecology. Williams & Wilkins.
Glass, Robert L., 1932-
 xGlass, Robert L.
  Software Reliability Guidebook. P-H.
Glass, Stuart. *see* Glass, Stuart M.
Glass, Stuart M.
 xGlass, Stuart.
  A Divorce Dictionary: A Book for You & Your
   Children. Little.
Glass, Thomas E.
 xGlass, Thomas E.
  Community Control in Education: A Study in
   Power Transition. Pendell Pub.
Glass, William.
 xGlass, Bill.
  Free at Last. Word Bks.
Glassburner, Bruce.
 xGlassburner, Bruce.
  ed. Economy of Indonesia: Selected Readings.
   Cornell U Pr.
Glassco, John.
 xGlassco, John.
  Memoirs of Montparnasse. Oxford U Pr.
Glasscock, Robin E. *see* Glasscock, Robin Edgar.
Glasscock, Robin Edgar.
 xGlasscock, Robin E.
  ed. The Lay Subsidy of 1334. Oxford U Pr.
Glasscote, R. M. *see* Glasscote, Raymond M.
Glasscote, Raymond M.
 xGlasscote, R. M.
  Halfway Houses for the Mentally Ill: A Study
   of Programs & Problems. Am Psychiatric.
Glasse, Hannah, fl. 1747
 xGlasse, Hannah.
  Art of Cookery Made Plain & Easy. Shoe
   String.
Glasse, James D.
 xGlasse, James D.
  The Art of Spiritual Snakehandling & Other
   Sermons. Abingdon.
  Putting It Together in the Parish. Abingdon.
Glasser, Alan J.
 xGlasser, Allen.
  Synthetic Feelings & Popular Culture. Ashley
   Bks.
Glasser, Allen. *see* Glasser, Alan J.
Glasser, Arthur F. *see* Glasser, Arthur Frederick.
Glasser, Arthur Frederick, 1914-
 xGlasser, Arthur F.
  ed. Crucial Dimensions in World
   Evangelization. William Carey Lib.
Glasser, Barbara.
 xGlasser, Barbara.
  Leroy, Oops. Contemp Bks.
Glasser, Hannelore.
 xGlasser, Hannelore.
  Artist's Contracts of the Early Renaissance.
   Garland Pub.
Glasser, Paul H.
 xGlasser, Paul H.
  Families in Crisis. Har-Row.
  ed. Individual Change Through Small Groups.
   Free Pr.
Glasser, William, 1925-
 xGlasser, William.

Identity Society. Har-Row.
Identity Society. Har-Row.
Positive Addiction. Har-Row.
Reality Therapy: A New Approach to
 Psychiatry. Har-Row.
Reality Therapy: A New Approach to
 Psychiatry. Har-Row.
Glassey, Lionel K. *see* Glassey, Lionel K. J.
Glassey, Lionel K. J.
 xGlassey, Lionel K.
  Politics & the Appointment of Justices of the
   Peace: 1675-1720. Oxford U Pr.
Glassey, Stanley C. *see* Glassey, Stanley Churchill.
Glassey, Stanley Churchill.
 xGlassey, Stanley C.
  Groundwork of Criticism: Judging Poetry.
   Greenwood.
Glassford, Robert G. *see* Glassford, Robert Gerald.
Glassford, Robert Gerald.
 xGlassford, Robert G.
  Application of a Theory of Games to the
   Transitional Eskimo Culture. Arno.
Glassgold, Peter, 1939-
 xGlassgold, Peter.
  ed. Living Space: Poems of the Dutch
   "Fifties". New Directions.
Glassie, Henry. *see* Glassie, Henry H.
Glassie, Henry H.
 xGlassie, Henry.
  Folk Housing in Middle Virginia: A Structural
   Analysis of Historic Artifacts. U of Tenn Pr.
  Pattern in the Material Folk Culture of the
   Eastern United States. U of Pa Pr.
Glassley, Ray. *see* Glassley, Ray Hoard.
Glassley, Ray Hoard, 1887-
 xGlassley, Ray.
  Indian Wars of the Pacific Northwest. Binford.
Glassman, Bernard, 1937-
 xGlassman, Bernard.
  Anti-Semitic Stereotypes Without Jews: Images
   of the Jews in England, 1290-1700. Wayne St
   U Pr.
Glassman, Carl.
 xGlassman, Carl.
  Hocus Focus: The World's Weirdest Cameras.
   Watts.
Glassman, Jon D.
 xGlassman, Jon D.
  Arms for the Arabs: The Soviet Union & War
   in the Middle East. Johns Hopkins.
Glassman, Judith.
 xGlassman, Judith.
  National Guide to Craft Supplies. Van Nos
   Reinhold.
Glassner, Barry.
 xGlassner, Barry.
  Clinical Sociology. Longman.
Glasson, William H. *see* Glasson, William Henry.
Glasson, William Henry, 1874-1946
 xGlasson, William H.
  History of Military Pension Legislation in the
   United States. AMS Pr.
Glassow, Michael A.
 xGlassow, Michael A.
  Prehistoric Agricultural Development in the
   Northern Southwest. Ballena Pr.
Glasstone, Richard.
 xGlasstone, Richard.
  Better Ballet. A S Barnes.
  Better Ballet. Soccer.
Glasstone, S. *see* Glasstone, Samuel.
Glasstone, Samuel.
 xGlasstone, S.
  Controlled Thermonuclear Reactions: An
   Introduction to Theory & Experiment.
   Krieger.
 xGlasstone, Samuel.

Sourcebook on Atomic Energy. Krieger.
Thermodynamics for Chemists. Krieger.
Glatstein, Jacob.
 xGlatstein, Jacob.
  Anthology of Holocaust Literature. Atheneum.
Glatt, M. M. *see* Glatt, Max Meier.
Glatt, Max Meier.
 xGlatt, M. M.
  A Guide to Addiction & Its Treatment.
   Halsted Pr.
Glatzer, Nahum N. *see* Glatzer, Nahum Norbert.
Glatzer, Nahum Norbert, 1903-
 xGlatzer, Nahum N.
  The Dimensions of Job: A Study & Selected
   Readings. Schocken.
  ed. Modern Jewish Thought: A Source Reader.
   Schocken.
Glatzer, Richard.
 xGlatzer, Richard.
  ed. Frank Capra: The Man & His Films. U of
   Mich Pr.
Glatzle, M. *see* Glatzle, Mary.
Glatzle, Mary.
 xGlatzle, M.
  Muggable Mary. P-H.
Glauber, Uta.
 xGlauber, Uta.
  illus. How the Willow Wren Became King.
   Abelard.
Glauert, M. B.
 xGlauert, M. B.
  Principles of Dynamics. Routledge & Kegan.
Glavin, John P.
 xGlavin, John P.
  Ferment in Special Education. Mss Info.
Glaz, Edit.
 xGlaz, Edith.
  Aldosterone. Pergamon.
Glaz, Edith. *see* Glaz, Edit.
Glazebrook, G. P. *see* Glazebrook, George Parkin De
 Twenebroker.
Glazebrook, George P. *see* Glazebrook, George Parkin
 Twenebroker.
Glazebrook, George Parkin De Twenebroker.
 xGlazebrook, G. P.
  Life in Ontario: A Social History. U of Toronto
   Pr.
  Story of Toronto. U of Toronto Pr.
Glazebrook, George Parkin Twenebroker.
 xGlazebrook, George P.
  History of Transportation in Canada.
   Greenwood.
Glazer, Lee.
 xGlazer, Lee.
  Cookie Becker Casts a Spell. Little.
Glazer, Nathan.
 xGlazer, Nathan.
  Affirmative Discrimination: Ethnic Inequality
   & Public Policy. Basic.
  American Judaism. U of Chicago Pr.
Glazer, Susan M.
 xGlazer, Susan M.
  Getting Ready to Read: Creating Readers from
   Birth Through Six. P-H.
Glazer, Tom.
 xGlazer, Tom.
  All About Your Name James, Jim, Jamie,
   Jimmy. Doubleday.
Glazier, Kenneth M.
 xGlazier, Kenneth M.
  Africa South of the Sahara: A Select &
   Annotated Bibliography, 1964-1968. Hoover
   Inst Pr.
Glazov, V. M. *see* Glazov, Vasilii Mikhailovich.
Glazov, Vasilii Mikhailovich.
 xGlazov, V. M.
  Liquid Semiconductors. Plenum Pub.
Gleason, Abbott.
 xGleason, Abbott.

European & Muscovite: Ivan Kireevsky & the
Origins of Slavophilism. Harvard U Pr.
Gleason, Gary M.
xGleason, Gary N.
Structured COBOL. Boyd & Fraser.
Gleason, Gary N. see Gleason, Gary M.
Gleason, H. A. see Gleason, Henry Allan.
Gleason, Henry A. see Gleason, Henry Allan.
Gleason, Henry Allan, 1917-
xGleason, H. A.
Plants of the Vicinity of New York. Hafner.
xGleason, Henry A.
Introduction to Descriptive Linguistics.
HR&W.
Manual of Vascular Plants of Northeastern
United States & Adjacent Canada. Van Nos
Reinhold.
Natural Geography of Plants. Columbia U Pr.
Gleason, Herbert W. see Gleason, Herbert Wendell.
Gleason, Herbert Wendell, 1855-1937
xGleason, Herbert W.
Thoreau Country. Sierra.
Gleason, James H. see Gleason, James Henry.
Gleason, James Henry.
xGleason, James H.
Beloved Sister: The Letters of James Henry
Gleason from Alta California & Hawaii,
1841-59. A H Clark.
Gleason, John J., 1934-
xGleason, John J.
Growing up to God: Eight Steps in Religious
Development. Abingdon.
Gleason, Judith I. see Gleason, Judith Illsley.
Gleason, Judith Illsley.
xGleason, Judith I.
This Africa: Novels by West Africans in
English & French. Northwestern U Pr.
Gleason, Philip.
xGleason, Philip.
ed. Contemporary Catholicism in the United
States. U of Notre Dame Pr.
Gleckner, Robert F.
xGleckner, Robert F.
Byron & the Ruins of Paradise. Greenwood.
Glegg, Gordon L. see Glegg, Gordon Lindsay.
Glegg, Gordon Lindsay.
xGlegg, Gordon L.
Design of Design. Cambridge U Pr.
Gleig, G. R. see Gleig, George Robert.
Gleig, George R. see Gleig, George Robert.
Gleig, George Robert, 1796-1888
xGleig, G. R.
The Life of Sir Walter Scott. Folcroft.
xGleig, George R.
The Campaigns of the British Army at
Washington & New Orleans. Rowman.
Gleim, William S.
xGleim, William S.
Meaning of Moby Dick. Russell.
Glemser, Bernard, 1908-
xGlemser, Bernard.
Departing Friends. Doubleday.
Glen, William.
xGlen, William.
Continental Drift & Plate Tectonics. Merrill.
Glenbow Historical Library, Glenbow-Alberta Institute.
see Glenbow-Alberta Institute. Library.
Glenbow-Alberta Institute. Library.
xGlenbow Historical Library, Glenbow-Alberta
Institute.
Catalogue of the Glenbow Historical Library.
G K Hall.
Glendening, P. J. see Glendening, P. J. T.
Glendening, P. J. T.
xGlendening, P. J.
Teach Yourself Icelandic. McKay.
Glendening, Parris N.
xGlendening, Parris N.

Pragmatic Federalism: An Intergovernmental
View of American Government. Palisades
Pub.
Glendinning, Nigel. see Glendinning, Oliver Nigel
Valentine.
Glendinning, Oliver Nigel Valentine.
xGlendinning, Nigel.
Goya & His Critics. Yale U Pr.
Glendinning, Richard.
xGlendinning, Richard.
Circus Days Under the Big Top. Garrard.
Glendinning, Victoria.
xGlendinning, Victoria.
Elizabeth Bowen. Avon.
Elizabeth Bowen. Knopf.
Glenister, S. H.
xGlenister, S. H.
Stories of Great Craftsmen. Arno.
Glenn. see Glenn, William W. L.
Glenn, Frank, 1901-
xGlenn, Frank.
Common Duct Stones. C C Thomas.
Glenn, Garrard.
xGlenn, Garrard.
Army & the Law. AMS Pr.
Glenn, Harold. see Glenn, Harold T.
Glenn, Harold T.
xGlenn, Harold.
Automechanics. Bennett Co.
xGlenn, Harold T.
Automobile Engine Rebuilding & Maintenance.
Chilton.
Exploring Power Mechanics. Bennett Co.
Glenn's Foreign Car Repair Manual. Chilton.
Glenn's Jaguar Repair & Tune-up Guide.
Chilton.
Glenn's Triumph Repair & Tune-up Guide.
Chilton.
Glenn's Volvo Repair & Tune-up Guide.
Chilton.
Glenn, Jerome. see Glenn, Jerome Clayton.
Glenn, Jerome Clayton.
xGlenn, Jerome.
Space Trek: The Endless Migration. Warner
Bks.
Glenn, Jerry.
xGlenn, Jerry.
Paul Celan. Twayne.
Glenn, Max E.
xGlenn, Max E.
ed. Appalachia in Transition. Bethany Pr.
Glenn, T. see Glenn, Thomas M.
Glenn, Thomas M.
xGlenn, T.
Steroids & Shock. Univ Park.
Glenn, William W. L.
xGlenn.
Thoracic & Cardiovascular Surgery with
Related Pathology. ACC.
Glennie, K. W.
xGlennie, K. W.
Desert Sedimentary Environments. Elsevier.
Glennon, James.
xGlennon, James.
Understanding Music. St Martin.
Glenny, Lyman A.
xGlenny, Lyman A.
ed. Funding Higher Education: A Six Nation
Analysis. Praeger.
Presidents Confront Reality: From Edifice
Complex to University Without Walls.
Jossey-Bass.
Gles, Margaret.
xGles, Margaret.
Come Play Hide & Seek. Garrard.
Gless, Darryl J., 1945-
xGless, Darryl J.

Measure for Measure, the Law & the Convent.
Princeton U Pr.
Glessing, Robert J.
xGlessing, Robert J.
Underground Press in America. Ind U Pr.
Glew, G. see Glew, George.
Glew, Geoffrey.
xGlew, Geoffrey.
Multiple Choice Questions in Psychiatry.
Butterworths.
Glew, George.
xGlew, G.
Catering Equipment & Systems Design.
Burgess-Intl Ideas.
Glew, Robert H.
xGlew, Robert H.
ed. Practical Enzymology of the
Sphingolipidoses. A R Liss.
Glick. see Glick, Robert A.
Glick, Ira D.
xGlick, Ira D.
Family Therapy & Research: An Annotated
Bibliography of Articles & Books, 1950-1970.
Grune.
Glick, Ira O. see Glick, Ira Oscar.
Glick, Ira Oscar.
xGlick, Ira O.
The First Year of Bereavement. Wiley.
Glick, Leonard.
xGlick, Leonard.
Introduction to Social Problems. A-W.
Glick, Leslie A. see Glick, Leslie Alan.
Glick, Leslie Alan.
xGlick, Leslie A.
Trading with Saudi Arabia: A Guide to the
Shipping, Trade, Investment & Tax Laws of
Saudi Arabia. Allanheld.
Glick, Paul C.
xGlick, Paul C.
American Families. Russell.
Glick, Phyllis. see Glick, Phyllis G.
Glick, Phyllis G., 1924-
xGlick, Phyllis.
The Mushroom Trail Guide. HR&W.
Glick, Robert A.
xGlick.
ed. Psychiatric Emergencies. Grune.
Glick, Ruth.
xGlick, Ruth.
Dollhouse Furniture You Can Make. A S
Barnes.
Glicken, Morley D.
xGlicken, Morley D.
ed. Toward Effective Social Work Practice.
Mss Info.
Glickman, Beatrice M. see Glickman, Beatrice Marden.
Glickman, Beatrice Marden.
xGlickman, Beatrice M.
Who Cares for the Baby?: Choices in Child
Care. Schocken.
Glickman, Carl D.
xGlickman, Carl D.
Leadership Guide for Elementary School
Improvement: Procedures for Assessment &
Change. Allyn.
Glickman, Esther.
xGlickman, Esther.
Child Placement Through Clinically Oriented
Casework. Columbia U Pr.
Glickman, Gladys, 1920-
xGlickman, Gladys.
Franchising. Bender.
Glickman, Harry.
xGlickman, Harry.
Promoter Ain't a Dirty Word. Intl Schol Bk
Serv.
Glickman, Jack.
xGlickman, Jack.

ed. Moral Philosophy: An Introduction. St
Martin.
Glickman, Norman J.
xGlickman, Norman J.
ed. Econometric Analysis of Regional Systems:
Explorations in Model Building & Policy
Analysis. Acad Pr.
The Growth & Management of the Japanese
Urban System. Acad Pr.
ed. Urban Impacts of Federal Policies. Johns
Hopkins.
Glickman, Richard, 1927-
xGlickman, Richard.
Complete Guide to Accounting & Financial
Methods & Controls for Service Businesses.
P-H.
Glickman, S. Craig.
xGlickman, S. Craig.
Knowing Christ. Moody.
Glicksberg, Charles. *see* Glicksberg, Charles Irving.
Glicksberg, Charles I. *see* Glicksberg, Charles Irving.
Glicksberg, Charles Irving, 1901-
xGlicksberg, Charles.
The Literature of Nihilism. Bucknell U Pr.
xGlicksberg, Charles I.
Literature & Religion: A Study in Conflict.
Greenwood.
The Literature of Commitment. Bucknell U Pr.
Modern Literary Perspectivism. SMU Press.
Glicksman, M. *see* Glicksman, Martin.
Glicksman, Martin.
xGlicksman, M.
Gum Technology in the Food Industry. Acad
Pr.
Glidewell, John C.
xGlidewell, John C.
Choice Points: Essays on the Emotional
Problems of Living with People. MIT Pr.
Glie, Rowen.
xGlie, Rowen.
ed. Speaking of Standards. CBI Pub.
Glieberman, Herbert A.
xGlieberman, Herbert A.
Confessions of a Divorce Lawyer. Ballantine.
Gliedman, John.
xGliedman, John.
The Unexpected Minority: Handicapped
Children in America. HarBraceJ.
Gligoric, S. *see* Gligoric, Svetozar.
Gligoric, Svetozar.
xGligoric, S.
The Sicilian Defence. Pergamon.
Glimcher, Arnold. *see* Glimcher, Arnold B.
Glimcher, Arnold B.
xGlimcher, Arnold.
Louise Nevelson. Dutton.
Gliner, Robert.
xGliner, Robert.
American Society As a Social Problem. Free
Pr.
Glines, Carroll V., 1920-
xGlines, Carroll V.
The Compact History of the United States Air
Force. Arno.
The Saga of the Air Mail. Arno.
Glinka, Mikhail I. *see* Glinka, Mikhail Ivanovich.
Glinka, Mikhail Ivanovich, 1804-1857
xGlinka, Mikhail I.
Memoirs. Greenwood.
Gloag, John, 1896-
xGloag, John.
The Architectural Interpretation of History. St
Martin.
Artorius Rex. St Martin.
Enjoying Architecture. Routledge & Kegan.
Gloag, Julian.
xGloag, Julian.
Our Mother's House. PB.
Glob, P. V. *see* Glob, Peter Vilhelm.

Glob, Peter Vilhelm, 1911-
xGlob, P. V.
Denmark: An Archaeological History from the
Stone Age to the Vikings. Cornell U Pr.
**Global Atmospheric Research Programme Joint
Organizing Committee.**
xJoint Organizing Committe,Eleventh Session.
GARP Report. Unipub.
Glock, Charles Y.
xGlock, Charles Y.
Adolescent Prejudice. Har-Row.
Adolescent Prejudice. Irvington.
Christian Beliefs & Anti-Semitism. Greenwood.
ed. Survey Research in the Social Sciences.
Russell Sage.
Glocker, Theodore W. *see* Glocker, Theodore Wesley.
Glocker, Theodore Wesley, 1881-
xGlocker, Theodore W.
The Government of American Trade Unions.
AMS Pr.
Government of American Trade Unions. Arno.
Glockling, Frank.
xGlockling, Frank.
Chemistry of Germanium. Acad Pr.
Glogau, Lillian.
xGlogau, Lillian.
Developing a Successful Elementary School
Media Center. P-H.
Gloge, Detlef.
xGloge, Detlef.
Optical Fiber Technology. Inst Electrical.
Optical Fiber Technology. Wiley.
Glorfeld, Louis E.
xGlorfeld, Louis E.
A Concise Guide for Writers. HR&W.
Glorig, Aram.
xGlorig, Aram.
ed. Audiometry: Principles & Practices.
Krieger.
Glorioso, Robert M.
xGlorioso, Robert M.
CMOS Designers' Primer & Handbook. E & L
Instru.
Engineering Cybernetics. Digital Pr.
Glos, George E. *see* Glos, George Ernest.
Glos, George Ernest.
xGlos, George E.
Comparative Law. Rothman.
Gloster, Hugh M. *see* Gloster, Hugh Morris.
Gloster, Hugh Morris, 1911-
xGloster, Hugh M.
Negro Voices in American Fiction. Russell.
Gloudemans, Robert J.
xGloudemans, Robert J.
Use-Value Farmland Assessments: Theory,
Practice & Impact. Intl Assess.
Glovach, Linda.
xGlovach, Linda.
illus. Let's Make a Deal. P-H.
Little Witch's Black Magic Book of Disguises.
P-H.
Little Witch's Black Magic Book of Games.
P-H.
illus. Little Witch's Black Magic Cookbook.
P-H.
illus. The Little Witch's Book of Yoga. P-H.
Little Witch's Christmas Book. P-H.
illus. Little Witch's Halloween Book. P-H.
The Little Witch's Thanksgiving Book. P-H.
Glover, Dennis W.
xGlover, Dennis W.
Respiratory Therapy: Basics for Nursing &
Allied Health Professions. Mosby.
Glover, Harry.
xGlover, Harry.
A Standard Guide to Pure Bred Dogs.
McGraw.
Glover, Jane.
xGlover, Jane.

Cavalli. St Martin.
Glover, Janet R. *see* Glover, Janet Reaveley.
Glover, Janet Reaveley.
xGlover, Janet R.
The Story of Scotland. Merrimack Bk Serv.
Glover, Janice.
xGlover, Janice.
Lighter Side of the Library. W S Sullwold.
Glover, John A.
xGlover, John A.
Behavior Modification: An Empirical Approach
to Self-Control. Nelson-Hall.
Glover, John D. *see* Glover, John Desmond.
Glover, John Desmond.
xGlover, John D.
ed. The Chief Executives Handbook. Dow
Jones-Irwin.
Public Loans to Private Business. Arno.
Glover, Jonathan.
xGlover, Jonathan.
Causing Death & Saving Lives. Penguin.
Responsibility. Humanities.
Glover, Michael, 1922-
xGlover, Michael.
The Napoleonic Wars: An Illustrated History.
David & Charles.
The Napoleonic Wars: An Illustrated History
1792-1815. Hippocrene Bks.
Glover, T. R. *see* Glover, Terrot Reaveley.
Glover, Terrot R. *see* Glover, Terrot Reaveley.
Glover, Terrot Reaveley, 1869-1943
xGlover, T. R.
Democracy in the Ancient World. Cooper Sq.
Jesus in the Experience of Men. Folcroft.
The Jesus of History. Folcroft.
Poets & Puritans. Folcroft.
Poets & Puritans. R West.
xGlover, Terrot R.
The Ancient World: A Beginning. Greenwood.
Challenge of the Greek: And Other Essays.
Arno.
Life & Letters in the Fourth Century. Russell.
Glowinski, R.
xGlowinski, R.
Energy Methods in Finite Element Analysis.
Wiley.
Gloyna, E. F. *see* Gloyna, Earnest F.
Gloyna, Earnest F.
xGloyna, E. F.
Principles of Radiological Health. Dekker.
xGloyna, Earnest F.
ed. Advances in Water Quality Improvement.
U of Tex Pr.
Glubb, John B. *see* Glubb, John Bagot.
Glubb, John Bagot, Sir, 1897-
xGlubb, John B.
The Story of the Arab Legion. Da Capo.
Glubok, Shirley.
xGlubok, Shirley.

Art of Africa. Har-Row.

The Art of America from Jackson to Lincoln. Macmillan.

The Art of America in the Early Twentieth Century. Macmillan.

The Art of America in the Gilded Age. Macmillan.

The Art of America Since World War II. Macmillan.

Art of Ancient Mexico. Har-Row.

Art of Ancient Rome. Har-Row.

Art of Colonial America. Macmillan.

The Art of Egypt Under the Pharaohs. Macmillan.

The Art of India. Macmillan.

The Art of Japan. Macmillan.

The Art of Photography. Macmillan.

The Art of the Comic Strip. Macmillan.

Art of the Etruscans. Har-Row.

The Art of the New American Nation. Macmillan.

Art of the North American Indian. Har-Row.

The Art of the Northwest Coast Indians. Macmillan.

Art of the Old West. Macmillan.

The Art of the Plains Indians. Macmillan.

The Art of the Southwest Indians. Macmillan.

The Art of the Spanish in the United States & Puerto Rico. Macmillan.

The Art of the Vikings. Macmillan.

ed. Digging in Assyria. Macmillan.

Dolls, Dolls, Dolls. Follett.

Fall of the Incas. Macmillan.

Olympic Games in Ancient Greece. Har-Row.

Gluck, Jay.

xGluck, Jay.

ed. Ukiyo: Stories of "The Floating World" of Postwar Japan. Vanguard.

Gluck, Louise, 1943-

xGluck, Louise.

The House on Marshland. Ecco Pr.

Gluck, Peter R.

xGluck, Peter R.

Cities in Transition: Social Changes & Institutional Responses in Urban Development. New Viewpoints.

Gluck, Sherna.

xGluck, Sherna.

ed. From Parlor to Prison: Five American Suffragists Talk About Their Lives. Octagon.

ed. From Parlor to Prison: Five American Suffragists Talk About Their Lives. Random.

Gluckman, Max, 1911-

xGluckman, Max.

Custom & Conflict in Africa. B&N.

The Ideas in Barotse Jurisprudence. Humanities.

Politics, Law & Ritual in Tribal Society. Biblio Dist.

Glucksmann, Alfred.

xGlucksmann, Alfred.

Sex Determination & Sexual Dimorphism in Mammals. Crane-Russak Co.

Glueck, Nelson, 1900-

xGlueck, Nelson.

Deities & Dolphins: The Story of the Nabataeans. FS&G.

Glueck, S. *see* Glueck, Sheldon.

Glueck, Sheldon.

xGlueck, S.

Of Delinquency & Crime: A Panorama of Years of Search & Research. C C Thomas.

xGlueck, Sheldon.

Delinquents & Nondelinquents in Perspective. Harvard U Pr.

Law & Psychiatry: Cold War or Entente Cordiale. Johns Hopkins.

Lives of Labor-Lives of Love: Fragments of Friendly Autobiographies. Exposition.

Toward a Typology of Juvenile Offenders: Implications for Therapy & Prevention. Grune.

xGlueck, Sheldon S.

Criminal Careers in Retrospect. Kraus Repr.

Five Hundred Criminal Careers. Kraus Repr.

Later Criminal Careers. Kraus Repr.

Glueck, Sheldon S. *see* Glueck, Sheldon.

Glueck, William F.

xGlueck, William F.

Foundations of Personnel. Business Pubns.

ed. Personnel: A Book of Readings. Business Pubns.

Personnel: A Diagnostic Approach. Business Pubns.

Readings in Business Policy from Business Week. McGraw.

xGlueck, William G.

Management. Dryden Pr.

Glueck, William G. *see* Glueck, William F.

Glusker, Irwin.

xGlusker, Irwin.

ed. A Southern Album: Recollections of Some People & Places & Times Gone By. Oxmoor Hse.

Glusker, Jenny P. *see* Glusker, Jenny Pickworth.

Glusker, Jenny Pickworth.

xGlusker, Jenny P.

Crystal Structure Analysis: A Primer. Oxford U Pr.

Glut, Donald F.

xGlut, Donald F.

Classic Movie Monsters. Scarecrow.

The Dinosaur Dictionary. Citadel Pr.

The Dracula Book. Scarecrow.

Gluyas, Constance, 1920-

xGluyas, Constance.

Born to Be King. BJ Pub Group.

The House on Twyford Street. NAL.

The King's Brat. Warner Bks.

My Lady Benbrook. Warner Bks.

Glymour, Clark. *see* Glymour, Clark N.

Glymour, Clark N.

xGlymour, Clark.

Theory & Evidence. Princeton U Pr.

Glynn, Jeanne D. *see* Glynn, Jeanne Davis.

Glynn, Jeanne Davis, 1932-

xGlynn, Jeanne D.

Answer Me, Answer Me. Glencoe.

Gnedenko, B. V. *see* Gnedenko, Boris Vladimirovich.

Gnedenko, Boris V. *see* Gnedenko, Boris Vladimirovich.

Gnedenko, Boris Vladimirovich, 1912-

xGnedenko, B. V.

Theory of Probability. Beekman Pubs.

xGnedenko, Boris V.

Theory of Probability. Chelsea Pub.

Gnedenko, Boris Vladimirovich.

xGnedenko, B. V.

Limit Distributions for Sums of Independent Random Variables. A-W.

Gnielinski, Stefan Von. *see* Von Gnielinski, Stefan.

Goadby, Edwin.

xGoadby, Edwin.

The England of Shakespeare. AMS Pr.

The England of Shakespeare. R West.

Gobel, Heinrich, 1879-

xGobel, Heinrich.

Tapestries of the Lowlands. Hacker.

Gober, Dom.

xGober, Dom.

Doomsday Squad. Holloway.

Goble, Danney, 1946-

xGoble, Danney.

Progressive Oklahoma: The Making of a New Kind of State. U of Okla Pr.

Goble, Frank G.

xGoble, Frank G.

A Third Force: The Psychology of Abraham Maslow. PB.

Goble, Neil.

xGoble, Neil.

Asimov Analyzed. Mirage Pr.

Goble, Paul.

xGoble, Paul.

jt. auth. Friendly Wolf. Bradbury Pr.

The Girl Who Loved Wild Horses. Bradbury Pr.

Lone Bull's Horse Raid. Bradbury Pr.

Goble, Phillip E., 1943-

xGoble, Phillip E.

Everything You Need to Grow a Messianic Synagogue. William Carey Lib.

Goblen, Peter.

xGoblen, Peter.

Journey Through the Light. Koheleth Pub.

Goblet D'Alviella, Eugene F. *see* Goblet D'Alviella, Eugene Felicien Albert.

Goblet, Y. M. *see* Goblet, Yann Morvran.

Goblet, Yann Morvran, 1881-1955

xGoblet, Y. M.

Twilight of Treaties. Kennikat.

Goblet D'Alviella, Eugene Felicien Albert, Comte, 1846-1925

xGoblet D'Alviella, Eugene F.

Lectures on the Origin & Growth of the Conception of God As Illustrated by Anthropology & History. AMS Pr.

Gocek, Matilda A.

xGocek, Matilda A.

Love Is a Challenge. Lib Res.

Orange County, New York: A Reader's Guide & Bibliography. Lib Res.

Gochros, Harvey L.

xGochros, Harvey L.

Treat Yourself to a Better Sex Life. P-H.

Gochros, Jean S.

xGochros, Jean S.

What to Say After You Clear Your Throat. Pr Pacifica.

Gockel, Herman W. *see* Gockel, Herman William.

Gockel, Herman William, 1906-

xGockel, Herman W.

Answer to Anxiety. Concordia.

Goda, Sidney, 1925-

xGoda, Sidney.

Articulation Therapy & Consonant Drill Book. Grune.

Godbey, Geoffrey.

xGodbey, Geoffrey.

Leisure Studies & Services: An Overview. HR&W.

Goddard, Alice L.

xGoddard, Alice L.

David, My Jewish Friend. Friend Pr.

Goddard, Anthea.

xGoddard, Anthea.

The Aztec Skull. Walker & Co.

Goddard, Carrie L. *see* Goddard, Carrie Lou.

Goddard, Carrie Lou.

xGoddard, Carrie L.

Jesus. Abingdon.

Goddard, Chris.

xGoddard, Chris.

Jazz Away from Home. Paddington.

Goddard, Donald.

xGoddard, Donald.

Easy Money. FS&G.

Easy Money. Popular Lib.

Goddard, Dwight, 1861-1939

xGoddard, Dwight.

ed. Buddhist Bible. Beacon Pr.

Goddard, Frederick O. *see* Goddard, Frederick Owen.

Goddard, Frederick Owen.
xGoddard, Frederick O.
Two-Sector Model of Economic Growth with
Technological Progress. U Presses Fla.
Goddard, H. C. see Goddard, Harold Clarke.
Goddard, Harold C. see Goddard, Harold Clarke.
Goddard, Harold Clarke, 1878-1950
xGoddard, H. C.
Studies in New England Transcendentalism. R
West.
xGoddard, Harold C.
Studies in New England Transcendentalism.
Humanities.
Goddard, Ives, 1941-
xGoddard, Ives.
Delaware Verbal Morphology: A Descriptive &
Comparative Study. Garland Pub.
Goddard, J. B.
xGoddard, John B.
Office Location in Urban & Regional
Development. Oxford U Pr.
Goddard, John, 1926-
xGoddard, John.
Kayaks Down the Nile. Brigham.
Goddard, John B. see Goddard, J. B.
Goddard, L. see Goddard, Leonard.
Goddard, Leonard.
xGoddard, L.
The Logic of Significance & Context. Halsted
Pr.
Goddard, Murray.
xGoddard, Murray.
How to Be Your Own Architect. TAB Bks.
Goddard, Pliny E. see Goddard, Pliny Earle.
Goddard, Pliny Earle, 1869-1928
xGoddard, Pliny E.
Indians of the Northwest Coast. Cooper Sq.
Indians of the Southwest. Cooper Sq.
Indians of the Southwest. Rio Grande.
Myths & Tales from the San Carlos Apache.
AMS Pr.
Goddard, Ruth, 1912-
xGoddard, Ruth.
Porfirio Salinas. Austin Pr.
Godden, Geoffrey. see Godden, Geoffrey A.
Godden, Geoffrey A.
xGodden, Geoffrey.
British Pottery: An Illustrated Guide. Potter.
Oriental Export Market Porcelain & Its
Influence on European Wares. Humanities.
xGodden, Geoffrey A.
British Porcelain: An Illustrated Guide.
Methuen Inc.
British Porcelain: An Illustrated Guide. Potter.
Oriental Export Market Porcelain & Its
Influence on European Wares. State Mutual
Bk.
Stevengraphs & Other Victorian Silk Pictures.
Fairleigh Dickinson.
Godden, Jon, 1906-
xGodden, Jon.
Ahmed & the Old Lady. G K Hall.
Ahmed & the Old Lady. Knopf.
Godden, Rumer, 1907-
xGodden, Rumer.
The Butterfly Lions: The Story of the
Pekingese in History, Legend & Art. Viking
Pr.
China Court. Avon.
The Diddakoi. Viking Pr.
Five for Sorrow, Ten for Joy. Viking Pr.
A Kindle of Kittens. Viking Pr.
Goddijn, Walter, 1921-
xGoddijn, Walter.
The Deferred Revolution: A Social Experiment
in Church Innovation in Holland, 1960-1970.
Elsevier.
Gode, Alexander, 1906-
xGode, Alexander.

French at Sight. Ungar.
Godefroy, Vincent.
xGodefroy, Vincent.
The Dramatic Genius of Verdi: Studies of
Selected Operas. St Martin.
Godel, Jules B., 1925-
xGodel, Jules B.
Sources of Construction Information: An
Annotated Guide to Reports, Books,
Periodicals, Standards, and Codes. Scarecrow.
Godelier, Maurice.
xGodelier, Maurice.
Rationality & Irrationality in Economics.
Monthly Rev.
Godet, Michel, 1948-
xGodet, Michel.
The Crisis in Forecasting & the Emergence of
the "Prospective" Approach: With Case
Studies in Energy & Air Transport.
Pergamon.
Godey, John, 1912-
xGodey, John.
The Talisman. Berkley Pub.
The Talisman. Putnam.
Godfrey, A. I. see Godfrey, Arthur I.
Godfrey, Arthur I.
xGodfrey, A. I.
Quantitative Methods for Managers. Intl Ideas.
Godfrey, Eleanor S. see Godfrey, Eleanor Smith.
Godfrey, Eleanor Smith.
xGodfrey, Eleanor S.
The Development of English Glassmaking,
1560-1640. U of NC Pr.
Godfrey, Lionel.
xGodfrey, Lionel.
The Life & Crimes of Errol Flynn. St Martin.
Godfrey, Richard T.
xGodfrey, Richard T.
Printmaking in Britain: A General History from
Its Beginnings to the Present Day. NYU Pr.
Godfrey, Robert K.
xGodfrey, Robert K.
Aquatic & Wetland Plants of Southeastern
States: Monocotyledons. U of Ga Pr.
Godfrey, Walter H. see Godfrey, Walter Hindes.
Godfrey, Walter Hindes, 1881-
xGodfrey, Walter H.
ed. Parish of Chelsea. AMS Pr.
Godin, Gabriel.
xGodin, Gabriel.
Analysis of Tides. U of Toronto Pr.
Godiwalla, Yezdi M. see Godiwalla, Yezdi Minoo.
Godiwalla, Yezdi Minoo.
xGodiwalla, Yezdi M.
Corporate Strategy & Functional Management.
Praeger.
Godkin, E. L. see Godkin, Edwin Lawrence.
Godkin, Edwin L. see Godkin, Edwin Lawrence.
Godkin, Edwin Lawrence, 1831-1902
xGodkin, E. L.
Unforeseen Tendencies of Democracy. Gordon
Pr.
xGodkin, Edwin L.
Life & Letters of Edwin Lawrence Godkin.
Greenwood.
Unforeseen Tendencies of Democracy. Arno.
Godlovitch, Stanley.
xGodlovitch, Stanley.
ed. Animals, Men & Morals: An Enquiry into
the Mal-Treatment of Non-Humans.
Taplinger.
Godsey, John D.
xGodsey, John D.
Preface to Bonhoeffer: The Man & Two of His
Shorter Writings. Fortress.
Godshalk, Fred I.
xGodshalk, Fred I.
Measurement of Writing Ability. College Bd.
Godshalk, William L. see Godshalk, William Leigh.

Godshalk, William Leigh.
xGodshalk, William L.
Patterning in Shakespearean Drama: Essays in
Criticism. Mouton.
Godson, Roy, 1942-
xGodson, Roy.
American Labor and European Politics: The
AFL As a Transnational Force. Crane-Russak
Co.
Godwin, Benjamin.
xGodwin, Benjamin.
Lectures on Slavery. Negro U Pr.
Godwin, Gail.
xGodwin, Gail.
The Odd Woman. Berkley Pub.
The Odd Woman. Warner Bks.
Godwin, George. see Godwin, George Stanley.
Godwin, George Stanley, 1889-
xGodwin, George.
The Great Mystics. Folcroft.
Godwin, John, 1928-
xGodwin, John.
Occult America. Doubleday.
Godwin, Joscelyn.
xGodwin, Joscelyn.
Athanasius Kircher: A Renaissance Man & the
Quest for Lost Knowledge. Thames Hudson.
Godwin, R. Kenneth.
xGodwin, R. Kenneth.
Comparative Policy Analysis: The Study of
Population Policy Determinants in
Developing Countries. Lexington Bks.
Godwin, William.
xGodwin, William.
Caleb Williams. Norton.
Caleb Williams. Oxford U Pr.
Memoirs of Mary Wollstonecraft. Gordon Pr.
Memoirs of Mary Wollstonecraft. Haskell.
Memoirs of the Author of a Vindication of the
Rights of Woman. Garland Pub.
Goebel, Julius, 1892-1973
xGoebel, Julius.
Felony & Misdemeanor: A Study in the
History of Criminal Law. U of Pa Pr.
Goedicke, Hans.
xGoedicke, Hans.
Re-used Blocks from the Pyramid of
Amenemhet I at Lisht. Metro Mus Art.
Goedicke, Patricia.
xGoedicke, Patricia.
Crossing the Same River. U of Mass Pr.
Goedsche, C. R. see Goedsche, Curt Rudolf.
Goedsche, Curt Rudolf, 1904-
xGoedsche, C. R.
Sag's Auf Deutsch: A First Book for German
Conversation. Irvington.
Goehlert, Robert. see Goehlert, Robert U.
Goehlert, Robert U.
xGoehlert, Robert.
City & Regional Planning: A Bibliography of
Journal Literature 1945-1975. Vance Biblios.
Congress & Law-Making: Researching the
Legislative Process. ABC-Clio.
Local Government: A Selected Bibliography of
Journal Literature. Vance Biblios.
Municipal Government: A Selected
Bibliography of Journal Literature. Vance
Biblios.
Reference Tools in Political Science. Vance
Biblios.
Goel, N. S.
xGoel, N. S.
On the Volterra & Other Nonlinear Models of
Interacting Populations. Acad Pr.
xGoel, Narendra.
Stochastic Models in Biology. Acad Pr.
Goel, Narendra. see Goel, N. S.
Goeldner, Christian T., 1933-
xGoeldner, Christian T.

The Thoroughbred Field Hunter. A S Barnes.
Goenner, M. E. *see* Goenner, Mary Ellen.
Goenner, Mary Ellen, Sister, 1905-
 xGoenner, M. E.
  Mary Verse of the Teutonic Knights. AMS Pr.
Goepfert, Paul, 1945-
 xGoepfert, Paul.
  Chiasma. Panjandrum.
Goerner, E. A. *see* Goerner, Edward Alfred.
Goerner, Edward Alfred.
 xGoerner, E. A.
  ed. Democracy in Crisis: New Challenges to
   Constitutional Democracy in the Atlantic
   Area. U of Notre Dame Pr.
Goertzel, Ted G. *see* Goertzel, Ted George.
Goertzel, Ted George.
 xGoertzel, Ted G.
  Political Society. Rand.
Goerzen, Janice L.
 xGoerzen, Janice L.
  Review of Maternal & Child Nursing. Mosby.
Goethals, George W.
 xGoethals, George W.
  ed. Experiencing Youth: First-Person Accounts.
   Little.
Goethe, Johann V. *see* Goethe, Johann Wolfgang Von.
Goethe, Johann von. *see* Goethe, Johann Wolfgang Von.
Goethe, Johann W. *see* Goethe, Johann Wolfgang Von.
Goethe, Johann W. Von. *see* Goethe, Johann Wolfgang
 Von.
Goethe, Johann Wolfgang Von.
 xGoethe, Johann V.
  Theory of Colours. Biblio Dist.
 xGoethe, Johann von.
  Goethe on Art. U of Cal Pr.
 xGoethe, Johann W.
  The Eternal Feminine: Selected Poems of
   Goethe. Ungar.
  Faust. French & Eur.
  Faust. Macmillan.
  Goethe's Plays. Ungar.
  Sufferings of Young Werther. Ungar.
  Theory of Colours. MIT Pr.
 xGoethe, Johann W. Von.
  Faust. Norton.
  Faust. Oxford U Pr.
Goetsch, H. B. *see* Goetsch, Helen Bertha.
Goetsch, Helen Bertha, 1902-
 xGoetsch, H. B.
  Parental Income & College Opportunities.
   AMS Pr.
Goetsch, Wilhelm, 1887-
 xGoetsch, Wilhelm.
  Ants. U of Mich Pr.
Goetz, Abraham.
 xGoetz, Abraham.
  Introduction to Differential Geometry. A-W.
Goetz, Delia.
 xGoetz, Delia.
  Deserts. Morrow.
  Neighbors to the South. HarBraceJ.
  Valleys. Morrow.
Goetz, Mary P. *see* Goetz, Mary Paul.
Goetz, Mary Paul.
 xGoetz, Mary P.
  Concept of Nobility in German Didactic
   Literature of the Thirteenth Century. AMS
   Pr.
Goetz, Raymond, 1922-
 xGoetz, Raymond.
  Tax Treatment of Pension Plans: Preferential or
   Normal?. Am Enterprise.
Goetz-Stankiewicz, Marketa.
 xGoetz-Stankiewicz, Marketa.
  The Silenced Theatre: Czech Playwrights
   Without a Stage. U of Toronto Pr.
Goetze, Rolf.
 xGoetze, Rolf.

Building Neighborhood Confidence: A
 Humanistic Strategy for Urban Housing.
 Ballinger Pub.
Goetzmann, William H.
 xGoetzmann, William H.
  Army Exploration in the American West,
   1803-1863. U of Nebr Pr.
  Exploration & Empire: The Explorer & the
   Scientist in the Winning of the American
   West. Norton.
  When the Eagle Screamed: The Romantic
   Horizon in American Diplomacy, 1800-1860.
   Wiley.
Goff, Beth.
 xGoff, Beth.
  Where Is Daddy: The Story of a Divorce.
   Beacon Pr.
Goff, Frederick R. *see* Goff, Frederick Richmond.
Goff, Frederick Richmond, 1916-
 xGoff, Frederick R.
  The Permanence of Johann Gutenberg. U of
   Tex Hum Res.
Goff, John H. *see* Goff, John Hedges.
Goff, John Hedges, 1899-1967
 xGoff, John H.
  Placenames of Georgia: Essays of John H.
   Goff. U of Ga Pr.
Goff, Paul E.
 xGoff, Paul E.
  Nature, Children & You. Exposition.
Goff, Richard D.
 xGoff, Richard D.
  Confederate Supply. Duke.
Goffart, Walter. *see* Goffart, Walter A.
Goffart, Walter A.
 xGoffart, Walter.
  Caput & Colonate: Towards a History of Late
   Roman Taxation. U of Toronto Pr.
 xGoffart, Walter A.
  Le Mans Forgeries: A Chapter from the
   History of Church Property in the Ninth
   Century. Harvard U Pr.
Goffer, Zvi.
 xGoffer, Zvi.
  Archaeological Chemistry: A Sourcebook on
   the Applications of Chemistry to
   Archaeology. Wiley.
Goffin, Robert, 1898-
 xGoffin, Robert.
  Horn of Plenty: The Story of Louis Armstrong.
   Da Capo.
Goffman, Erving.
 xGoffman, Erving.
  Asylums: Essays on the Social Situation of
   Mental Patients & Other Inmates. Aldine
   Pub.
  Asylums: Essays on the Social Situation of
   Mental Patients & Other Inmates.
   Doubleday.
  Frame Analysis: An Essay on the Organization
   of Experience. Har-Row.
  Frame Analysis: An Essay on the Organization
   of Experience. Harvard U Pr.
  Gender Advertisements. Har-Row.
  Gender Advertisements. Harvard U Pr.
  Interaction Ritual: Essays on Face-To-Face
   Behavior. Doubleday.
  Presentation of Self in Everyday Life.
   Doubleday.
  The Presentation of Self in Everyday Life.
   Overlook Pr.
Goffman, William.
 xGoffman, William.
  Scientific Information Systems & the Principle
   of Selectivity. Praeger.
Goffstein, M. B.
 xGoffstein, M. B.

Daisy Summerfields Style. Dell.
Daisy Summerfield's Style. Delacorte.
illus. Family Scrapbook. FS&G.
Fish for Supper. Dial.
illus. Goldie the Dollmaker. FS&G.
illus. A Little Schubert. Har-Row.
illus. Natural History. FS&G.
Neighbors. Har-Row.
Two Piano Tuners. FS&G.
The Underside of the Leaf. FS&G.
Gogarty, Oliver S. *see* Gogarty, Oliver St. John.
Gogarty, Oliver St. John.
 xGogarty, Oliver S.
  Many Lines to Thee: Letters to G. K. A. Bell
   from the Martello Tower at Sandycove,
   Rutland Square & Trinity College, Dublin,
   1904-7. Humanities.
Goggin, John M. *see* Goggin, John Mann.
Goggin, John Mann.
 xGoggin, John M.
  Spanish Majolica in the New World: Types of
   the Sixteenth to Eighteenth Centuries. Yale
   U Anthro.
Gogol, Nicolai V. *see* Gogol, Nikolai Vasilevich.
Gogol, Nikolai. *see* Gogol, Nikolai Vasilevich.
Gogol, Nikolai V. *see* Gogol, Nikolai Vasilevich.
Gogol, Nikolai Vasilevich, 1809-1852
 xGogol, Nicolai V.
  Dead Souls. Norton.
  The Overcoat, & Other Tales of Good & Evil.
   Bentley.
  Overcoat & Other Tales of Good & Evil.
   Norton.
 xGogol, Nikolai.
  Dead Souls. NAL.
  Dead Souls. Penguin.
  Dead Souls. Airmont.
 xGogol, Nikolai V.
  Dead Souls. Dutton.
Gogolak, Pete.
 xGogolak, Peter.
  Nothing to Kick About: The Autobiography of
   a Modern Immigrant. Dodd.
Gogolak, Peter. *see* Gogolak, Pete.
Goguel, Jean.
 xGoguel, Jean.
  Geothermics. McGraw.
Goguel, Maurice, 1880-1955
 xGoguel, Maurice.
  The Life of Jesus. AMS Pr.
Goguet, Antoine Y. *see* Goguet, Antoine Yves.
Goguet, Antoine Yves.
 xGoguet, Antoine Y.
  The Origin of Laws, Arts, & Sciences & Their
   Progress Among the Most Ancient Nations.
   AMS Pr.
Gohagan, John K. *see* Gohagan, John Kenneth.
Gohagan, John Kenneth.
 xGohagan, John K.
  Quantitative Analysis for Public Policy.
   McGraw.
Gohdes, Clarence.
 xGohdes, Clarence.
  American Literature in Nineteenth-Century
   England. S Ill U Pr.
Gohdes, Clarence. *see* Gohdes, Clarence Louis Frank.
Gohdes, Clarence L. *see* Gohdes, Clarence Louis Frank.
Gohdes, Clarence Louis Frank, 1901-
 xGohdes, Clarence.
  Literature & Theater of the States & Regions
   of the U. S. A: An Historical Bibliography.
   Duke.
  Periodicals of American Transcendentalism.
   AMS Pr.
 xGohdes, Clarence L.
  Periodicals of American Transcendentalism.
   Arno.
Goheen, Robert F.
 xGoheen, Robert F.

Human Nature of a University. Princeton U Pr.

Gohman, Fred.
xGohman, Fred.
illus. Spider Webb Mysteries. Lantern.

Gohmann, John W.
xGohmann, John W.
Air & Rail Labor Relations: A Judicial History of the Railway Labor Act. Kendall-Hunt.

Goilo, E. R.
xGoilo, E. R.
Papiamentu Textbook. Heinman.
Papiamentu Textbook. Intl Learn Syst.

Goin, Coleman J. *see* Goin, Coleman Jett.

Goin, Coleman Jett.
xGoin, Coleman J.
Introduction to Herpetology. W H Freeman.
Journey onto Land. Macmillan.

Goines, Donald.
xGoines, Donald.
Inner City Hoodlum. Holloway.
Street Players. Holloway.
Swamp Man. Holloway.
White Man's Justice: Black Man's Grief. Holloway.

Going, Allen J. *see* Going, Allen Johnston.

Going, Allen Johnston.
xGoing, Allen J.
Bourbon Democracy in Alabama, 1874-1890. Greenwood.

Going, Charles B. *see* Going, Charles Buxton.

Going, Charles Buxton, 1863-
xGoing, Charles B.
David Wilmot, Free Soiler: A Biography of the Great Advocate of the Wilmot Proviso. Peter Smith.
Principles of Industrial Engineering. Hive Pub.

Goings, Leslie F.
xGoings, Leslie F.
Automotive Air Conditioning. Am Technical.

Goist, Park D. *see* Goist, Park Dixon.

Goist, Park Dixon.
xGoist, Park D.
From Main Street to State Street: Town, City, & Community in America. Kennikat.

Goitein, S. D. *see* Goitein, Solomon Dob Fritz.

Goitein, Solomon Dob Fritz, 1900-
xGoitein, S. D.
ed. From the Land of Sheba: Tales of the Jews of Yemen. Schocken.
Letters of Medieval Jewish Traders. Princeton U Pr.
ed. Religion in a Religious Age. Ktav.

Gojmerac, Walter L.
xGojmerac, Walter L.
Bees, Bee Keeping, Honey & Pollination. AVI.

Gokak, V. K. *see* Gokak, Vinayak Krishna.

Gokak, Vinayak Krishna, 1909-
xGokak, V. K.
An Integral View of Poetry: An Indian Perspective. South Asia Bks.

Gokcen, N. A.
xGokcen, N. A.
Thermodynamics. Techscience Inc.

Gokhale, D. V. *see* Gokhale, Dattaprabhaker V.

Gokhale, Dattaprabhaker V.
xGokhale, D. V.
The Information in Contingency Tables. Dekker.

Gokhale, Narayan R., 1924-
xGokhale, Narayan R.
Hailstorms & Hailstone Growth. State U NY Pr.

Golab, Caroline.
xGolab, Caroline.
Immigrant Destinations. Temple U Pr.

Golan, Jonathan S.
xGolan, Jonathan S.
Localization of Noncommutative Rings. Dekker.

Golann, Stuart. *see* Golann, Stuart E.

Golann, Stuart E.
xGolann, Stuart.
ed. Handbook of Community Mental Health. Irvington.

Golant, Stephen M.
xGolant, Stephen M.
Location & Environment of Elderly Population. Halsted Pr.

Golant, William, 1937-
xGolant, William.
The Long Afternoon: British India 1601-1947. St Martin.

Golany, G. *see* Golany, Gideon.

Golany, Gideon.
xGolany, G.
ed. Strategy for New Community Development in the United States. DH&R.
xGolany, Gideon.
ed. Arid Zone Settlement Planning: The Israeli Experience. Pergamon.
ed. The Contemporary New Communities Movement in the United States. U of Ill Pr.
Innovations for Future Cities. Praeger.

Golay, Frank H.
xGolay, Frank H.
An Annotated Guide to Philippine Serials. Cornell SE Asia.
Underdevelopment and Economic Nationalism in Southeast Asia. Cornell U Pr.

Golay, M.
xGolay, M.
Introduction to Astronomical Photometry. Kluwer Boston.

Gold, Ann.
xGold, Anne.
Diet Watchers Gourmet Cookbook. G&D.
Diet Watcher's Guide. G&D.

Gold, Annalee.
xGold, Annalee.
How to Sell Fashion. Fairchild.

Gold, Anne. *see* Gold, Ann.

Gold, Arthur.
xGold, Arthur.
Misia. Knopf.

Gold, Artie.
xGold, Artie.
Some of the Cat Poems. Cross Country.

Gold, B. *see* Gold, Bernard.

Gold, Bela.
xGold, Bela.
Evaluating Technological Innovations: Methods, Expectattions, & Findings. Lexington Bks.

Gold, Bernard.
xGold, B.
Digital Processing of Signals. McGraw.

Gold, Diane E.
xGold, Diane E.
Housing Market Discrimination: Causes & Effects of Slum Formation. Praeger.

Gold, Don.
xGold, Don.
The Park: A Novel. Har-Row.

Gold, Doris B.
xGold, Doris B.
Honey in the Lion: Collected Poems. Biblio Pr.

Gold, Harvey J., 1932-
xGold, Harvey J.
Mathematical Modeling of Biological Systems: An Introductory Guidebook. Wiley.

Gold, John R. *see* Gold, John Robert.

Gold, John Robert.
xGold, John R.
An Introduction to Behavioural Geography. Oxford U Pr.

Gold, Joseph, 1912-
xGold, Joseph.
Fund Agreement in the Courts. Intl Monetary.
The Stand-By Arrangements of the International Monetary Fund: A Commentary on Their Formal, Legal & Financial Aspects. Intl Monetary.
Stature of Dickens: A Centenary Bibliography. U of Toronto Pr.

Gold, Ned.
xGold, Ned.
Eight Who Wrestled Death. Raintree Pubs.

Gold, Sharlya.
xGold, Sharlya.
Amelia Quackenbush. HM.

Gold, Sharon.
xGold, Sharon.
The Woman's Day Book of Beauty, Health & Fitness Hints. Morrow.

Gold, Steven D. *see* Gold, Steven David.

Gold, Steven David.
xGold, Steven D.
Property Tax Relief. Lexington Bks.

Gold, Thomas.
xGold, Thomas.
ed. Nature of Time. Cornell U Pr.

Goldbarth, Albert.
xGoldbarth, Albert.
Coprolites. SBD.

Goldbeck, Nikki.
xGoldbeck, Nikki.
The Dieter's Companion: A Guide to Nutritional Self-Sufficiency. McGraw.
The Dieter's Companion: A Guide to Nutritional Self-Sufficiency. NAL.

Goldbeck, W. B. *see* Goldbeck, Willis.

Goldbeck, Willis.
xGoldbeck, W. B.
A Business Perspective on Industry & Health Care. Springer-Verlag.

Goldbecker, William.
xGoldbecker, William.
This Is the German Shepherd. TFH Pubns.

Goldberg, Albert L. *see* Goldberg, Albert Leonard.

Goldberg, Albert Leonard.
xGoldberg, Albert L.
The Effects of Two Types of Sound Motion Pictures on Attitudes of Adults Toward Minority Groups. R & E Res Assoc.

Goldberg, Alfred, 1918-
xGoldberg, Alfred.
ed. History of the United States Air Force 1907-1957. Arno.

Goldberg, Barry B.
xGoldberg, Barry B.
Abdominal Gray Scale Ultrasonography. Wiley.
Diagnostic Uses of Ultrasound. Grune.

Goldberg, Bernard.
xGoldberg, Bernard.
ed. Communications Channels: Characterization & Behavior. Wiley.

Goldberg, Carl.
xGoldberg, Carl.
The Human Circle: An Existential Approach to the New Group Therapies. Nelson-Hall.
Therapeutic Partnership: Ethical Concerns in Psychotherapy. Springer Pub.

Goldberg, David E. *see* Goldberg, David Elliott.

Goldberg, David Elliott.
xGoldberg, David E.
College Chemistry. Macmillan.

Goldberg, Edward D.
xGoldberg, Edward D.
ed. Strategies for Marine Pollution Monitoring. Wiley.

Goldberg, Enid A.
xGoldberg, Enid A.
How to Run a School Newspaper. Lippincott.

Goldberg, Gerald J. *see* Goldberg, Gerald Jay.

Goldberg, Gerald Jay.
xGoldberg, Gerald J.

Fate of Innocence. P-H.
Goldberg, Gerry.
  xGoldberg, Gerry.
    A Strange Glory. St Martin.
Goldberg, Harriet L. *see* Goldberg, Harriet Labe.
Goldberg, Harriet Labe, 1906-
  xGoldberg, Harriet L.
    Child Offenders: A Study in Diagnosis &
     Treatment. Patterson Smith.
Goldberg, Homer.
  xGoldberg, Homer.
    Art of Joseph Andrews. U of Chicago Pr.
Goldberg, Isaac, 1887-1938
  xGoldberg, Isaac.
    Brazilian Literature. Core Collection.
    Brazilian Literature. Gordon Pr.
    Wonder of Words: An Introduction to
     Language for Every Man. Gale.
Goldberg, Jack L. *see* Goldberg, Jack Leonard.
Goldberg, Jack Leonard.
  xGoldberg, Jack L.
    Systems of Ordinary Differential Equations: An
     Introduction. Har-Row.
Goldberg, Joel, 1931-
  xGoldberg, Joel.
    Radio, Television & Sound System Repair: An
     Introduction. P-H.
Goldberg, Kalman, 1924-
  xGoldberg, Kalman.
    Our Changing Economy: An Introduction to
     Economics. Little.
Goldberg, Larry.
  xGoldberg, Larry.
    Goldberg's Diet Catalog. Macmillan.
    Goldberg's Diet Catalog. Macmillan.
Goldberg, Lawrence G.
  xGoldberg, Lawrence G.
    The Deregulation of the Banking & Securities
     Industries. Lexington Bks.
Goldberg, Lazer.
  xGoldberg, Lazer.
    Children & Science. Scribner.
    Learning to Choose: Stories & Essays About
     Science, Technology, & Human Values.
     Scribner.
Goldberg, Lester, 1924-
  xGoldberg, Lester.
    One More River: Stories. U of Ill Pr.
Goldberg, Louis, 1923-
  xGoldberg, Louis.
    Our Jewish Friends. Moody.
Goldberg, Marshall.
  xGoldberg, Marshall.
    The Anatomy Lesson. Berkley Pub.
Goldberg, Martin.
  xGoldberg, Martin.
    A Guide to Psychiatric Diagnosis &
     Understanding for the Helping Professions.
     Littlefield.
    A Guide to Psychiatric Diagnosis &
     Understanding for the Helping Professions.
     Nelson-Hall.
Goldberg, Maxwell H. *see* Goldberg, Maxwell Henry.
Goldberg, Maxwell Henry, 1907-
  xGoldberg, Maxwell H.
    Design in Liberal Learning. Jossey-Bass.
Goldberg, Milton S.
  xGoldberg, Milton S.
    Consent Decree: Its Formulation & Use. Mich
     St U Busn.
Goldberg, Morton F.
  xGoldberg, Morton F.
    ed. Genetic & Metabolic Eye Disease. Little.
Goldberg, Moses, 1940-
  xGoldberg, Moses.
    Children's Theatre: A Philosophy & a Method.
     P-H.
Goldberg, Philip.
  xGoldberg, Phillip.

Natural Sleep: How to Get Your Share. Rodale
  Pr Inc.
Goldberg, Phillip. *see* Goldberg, Philip.
Goldberg, Ray A. *see* Goldberg, Ray Allan.
Goldberg, Ray Allan, 1926-
  xGoldberg, Ray A.
    Agribusiness Coordination: A Systems
     Approach to the Wheat, Soybean & Florida
     Orange Economies. Ballinger Pub.
    Agribusiness Management for Developing
     Countries - Latin America. Ballinger Pub.
Goldberg, Richard H., 1943-
  xGoldberg, Richard H.
    Planting Your Money Tree: A Guide for the
     Small Investor. Chatham Sq.
Goldberg, Richard R.
  xGoldberg, Richard R.
    Fourier Transforms. Cambridge U Pr.
Goldberg, Robert L.
  xGoldberg, Robert L.
    A Systems Approach to Library Program
     Development. Scarecrow.
Goldberg, Rosamond (Webster), 1900-
  xGoldberg, Rosamond W.
    Occupational Diseases in Relation to
     Compensation & Health Insurance. AMS Pr.
Goldberg, Rosamond W. *see* Goldberg, Rosamond
  (Webster).
Goldberg, S. J. *see* Goldberg, Stan J.
Goldberg, Samuel.
  xGoldberg, Samuel.
    Introduction to Difference Equations: With
     Illustrative Examples from Economics,
     Psychology & Sociology. Wiley.
    Probability: An Introduction. P H.
Goldberg, Stan J.
  xGoldberg, S. J.
    Adventures of Stanley Kane. HarBraceJ.
Goldberg, Stanley J.
  xGoldberg, Stanley J.
    Pediatric & Adolescent Echocardiography: A
     Handbook. Year Bk Med.
Goldberg, Stella. *see* Goldberg, Stella R.
Goldberg, Stella R.
  xGoldberg, Stella.
    Life-Span Individual & Family Development.
     Brooks-Cole.
Goldberg, Steven.
  xGoldberg, Steven.
    The Inevitability of Patriarchy. Morrow.
Goldberg, Stuart C. *see* Goldberg, Stuart Charles.
Goldberg, Stuart Charles.
  xGoldberg, Stuart C.
    Private Placements & Restricted Securities.
     Boardman.
Goldberger, Anthony M. *see* Goldberger, Anthony Mark.
Goldberger, Anthony Mark, 1887-
  xGoldberger, Anthony M.
    Variability in Continuation School Populations:
     A Study of the Significance of Differences in
     the Proportions of Child Workers. AMS Pr.
Goldberger, Arthur S. *see* Goldberger, Arthur Stanley.
Goldberger, Arthur Stanley, 1930-
  xGoldberger, Arthur S.
    Econometric Theory. Wiley.
Goldberger, Emanuel, 1913-
  xGoldberger, Emanuel.
    A Primer of Water, Electrolyte & Acid-Base
     Syndromes. Lea & Febiger.
Goldberger, Judith M.
  xGoldberger, Judith M.
    The Looking Glass Factor. Dutton.
Goldberger, M. L. *see* Goldberger, Marvin L.
Goldberger, Marvin L.
  xGoldberger, M. L.
    Collision Theory. Krieger.
Goldberger, Paul.
  xGoldberger, Paul.

The City Observed - New York: A Guide to
  the Architecture of Manhattan. Random.
The City Observed-New York: A Guide to the
  Architecture of Manhattan. Random.
Goldblatt, Howard, 1939-
  xGoldblatt, Howard.
    Hsiao Hung. Twayne.
Goldblith, S. A. *see* Goldblith, Samuel A.
Goldblith, Samuel A.
  xGoldblith, S. A.
    ed. Freeze Drying & Advanced Food
     Technology. Acad Pr.
Golde, R. H. *see* Golde, Rudolf Heinrich.
Golde, Roger A.
  xGolde, Roger A.
    Muddling Through: The Art of Properly
     Unbusinesslike Management. Am Mgmt.
    What You Say Is What You Get. Dutton.
Golde, Rudolf Heinrich.
  xGolde, R. H.
    Lightning Protection. Chem Pub.
Goldemberg, Isaac, 1945-
  xGoldemberg, Isaac.
    The Fragmented Life of Don Jacobo Lerner.
     Persea Bks.
Golden, Charles J., 1949-
  xGolden, Charles J.
    Clinical Interpretation of Objective
     Psychological Tests. Grune.
    Diagnosis & Rehabilitation in Clinical
     Neuropsychology. C C Thomas.
    Learning Disabilities & Brain Dysfunction: An
     Introduction for Educators & Parents. C C
     Thomas.
Golden, Clinton S. *see* Golden, Clinton Strong.
Golden, Clinton Strong.
  xGolden, Clinton S.
    The Dynamics of Industrial Democracy. Da
     Capo.
Golden, Frederic.
  xGolden, Frederic.
    Colonies in Space: The Next Giant Step.
     HarBraceJ.
    Quasars, Pulsars, & Black Holes. PB.
Golden, Hal.
  xGolden, Hal.
    The Grant Seekers: The Foundation Fund
     Raising Manual. Oceana.
Golden, Harry. *see* Golden, Harry Lewis.
Golden, Harry Lewis, 1902-
  xGolden, Harry.
    Only in America. Greenwood.
Golden, Jack.
  xGolden, Jack.
    Environmental Impact Data Book. Ann Arbor
     Science.
Golden, James L.
  xGolden, James L.
    The Rhetoric of Western Thought. Kendall
     Hunt.
Golden, James Reed.
  xGolden, Jim.
    Economics & Public Policy: Principles,
     Problems & Applications. Avery Pub.
Golden, Jim. *see* Golden, James Reed.
Golden, Lawrence G.
  xGolden, Lawrence G.
    Effective Retailing. Rand.
Golden, Morris.
  xGolden, Morris.
    Fielding's Moral Psychology. U of Mass Pr.
Golden, Robert. *see* Golden, Robert E.
Golden, Robert E.
  xGolden, Robert.
    Flannery O'Connor & Caroline Gordon: A
     Reference Guide. G K Hall.
Golden, S. *see* Golden, Samuel A.
Golden, Samuel A.
  xGolden, S.

Frederick Goddard Tuckerman. Coll & U Pr.
xGolden, Samuel A.
Frederick Goddard Tuckerman. Irvington.
Frederick Goddard Tuckerman. Twayne.

Golden, Sidney.
xGolden, Sidney.
General University Chemistry: A
Developmental Approach. Oxford U Pr.

Goldenberg, Herbert.
xGoldenberg, Herbert.
Contemporary Clinical Psychology.
Brooks-Cole.

Goldenberg, I. Ira, 1936-
xGoldenberg, I. Ira.
Build Me a Mountain: Youth, Poverty, & the
Creation of New Settings. MIT Pr.

Goldensohn, Barry.
xGoldensohn, Barry.
Uncarving the Block. Vermont Crossroads.

Goldensohn, Eli S.
xGoldensohn, Eli S.
EEG Interpretation: Problems of Over-Reading
& Under-Reading. Futura Pub.

Goldenthal, Allan B.
xGoldenthal, Allan B.
Think Chinese, Speak Chinese. Regents Pub.

Goldenweiser, Alexander. *see* Goldenweiser, Alexander
A.

Goldenweiser, Alexander A., 1880-1940
xGoldenweiser, Alexander.
History, Psychology & Culture. Peter Smith.

Goldfarb, Jeffrey C.
xGoldfarb, Jeffrey C.
The Persistence of Freedom: The Sociological
Implications of Polish Student Theater.
Westview.

Goldfarb, Ronald L.
xGoldfarb, Ronald L.
After Conviction. S&S.
Contempt Power. Columbia U Pr.

Goldfeder, Cheryl. *see* Goldfeder, Cheryl Ann.

Goldfeder, Cheryl Ann.
xGoldfeder, Cheryl.
The Girl Who Wouldn't Talk. Natl Assn Deaf.

Goldfein, Donna, 1933-
xGoldfein, Donna.
Everywoman's Guide to Travel. Les Femmes
Pub.

Goldfeld, Stephen M.
xGoldfeld, Stephen M.
ed. Studies in Nonlinear Estimation. Ballinger
Pub.

Goldfield, David R.
xGoldfield, David R.
ed. The Enduring Ghetto: Sources & Readings.
Lippincott.
Urban America: From Downtown to No Town.
HM.

Goldfrank, Walter L.
xGoldfrank, Walter L.
The World-System of Capitalism: Past &
Present. Sage.

Goldfried, M. R. *see* Goldfried, Marvin R.

Goldfried, Marvin R.
xGoldfried, M. R.
Clinical Behavior Therapy. HR&W.

Goldgar, Bertrand A., 1927-
xGoldgar, Bertrand A.
The Curse of Party: Swift's Relations with
Addison & Steele. Folcroft.
The Curse of the Party: Swift's Relations with
Addison and Steele. Arden Lib.

Goldhaber, Gerald M.
xGoldhaber, Gerald M.
Organizational Communication. Wm C Brown.

Goldhaber, Jacob K.
xGoldhaber, Jacob K.
Algebra. Krieger.

Goldhamer, H. *see* Goldhamer, Herbert.

Goldhamer, Herbert, 1907-
xGoldhamer, H.
The Adviser. Elsevier.
xGoldhamer, Herbert.
The Foreign Powers in Latin America.
Princeton U Pr.
Psychosis & Civilization. Arno.
The Soviet Soldier: Soviet Military
Management at the Troop Level.
Crane-Russak Co.

Goldhor, Herbert.
xGoldhor, Herbert.
An Introduction to Scientific Research in
Librarianship. U of Ill Lib Sci.

Goldin, Augusta. *see* Goldin, Augusta R.

Goldin, Augusta R.
xGoldin, Augusta.
Bottom of the Sea. T Y Crowell.
Grass: The Everything, Everywhere Plant.
Elsevier-Nelson.
How to Release the Learning Power in
Children. P-H.
Let's Go to Build a Skyscraper. Putnam.
Spider Silk. T Y Crowell.
Spider Silk. T Y Crowell.
Sunlit Sea. T Y Crowell.
Where Does Your Garden Grow?. T Y
Crowell.

Goldin, Diana.
xGoldin, Diana.
A Tale of Two Williams. Metro Mus Art.

Goldin, Judah, 1914-
xGoldin, Judah.
Song at the Sea: Being a Commentary on a
Commentary in Two Parts. Yale U Pr.

Goldin, Marshall D., 1939-
xGoldin, Marshall D.
Intensive Care of the Surgical Patient. Year Bk
Med.

Golding, Claud.
xGolding, Claud.
Great Names in History, 356 B. C. to A. D.
1910. Arno.

Golding, William.
xGolding, William G.
Spire. HarBraceJ.

Golding, William. *see* Golding, William Gerald.

Golding, William G. *see* Golding, William Gerald.

Golding, William Gerald.
xGolding, William.
Free Fall. HarBraceJ.
Inheritors. PB.
xGolding, William G.
Inheritors. HarBraceJ.

Goldish, Dorothy M.
xGoldish, Dorothy M.
Basic Mathematics for Beginning Chemistry.
Macmillan.

Goldknopf, David, 1918-
xGoldknopf, David.
The Life of the Novel. U of Chicago Pr.

Goldman, Alan H., 1945-
xGoldman, Alan H.
Justice & Reverse Discrimination. Princeton U
Pr.

Goldman, Albert. *see* Goldman, Albert Harry.

Goldman, Albert Harry.
xGoldman, Albert.
Carnival in Rio. Dutton.
Disco. Dutton.
Grass Roots: Marijuana in America Today.
Har-Row.

Goldman, Alex J.
xGoldman, Alex J.
Judaism Confronts Contemporary Issues.
Shengold.

Goldman, Alvin I., 1938-
xGoldman, Alvin I.

Theory of Human Action. Princeton U Pr.

Goldman, Alvin L.
xGoldman, Alvin L.
The Supreme Court & Labor-Management
Relations Law. Lexington Bks.

Goldman, Bernard, 1922-
xGoldman, Bernard.
Reading & Writing in the Arts: A Handbook.
Wayne St U Pr.

Goldman, Bert A.
xGoldman, Bert A.
The Directory of Unpublished Experimental
Mental Measures,. Human Sci Pr.

Goldman, Dave.
xGoldman, Dave.
Full-Time Restless. Marek.

Goldman, David. *see* Goldman, David J.

Goldman, David J.
xGoldman, David.
Presidential Losers. Lerner Pubns.

Goldman, E. *see* Goldman, Earl.

Goldman, Earl.
xGoldman, E.
Intro. by Ice Cream Cookbook. Nitty Gritty.
xGoldman, Earl.
Ice Cream Cookbook. Nitty Gritty.

Goldman, Edward A., 1941-
xGoldman, Edward A.
ed. Jews in a Free Society: Challenges &
Opportunities. Ktav.

Goldman, Emma, 1869-1940
xGoldman, Emma.
Living My Life. AMS Pr.
Living My Life. Da Capo.
Living My Life. Dover.
Living My Life. NAL.
Living My Life. Peter Smith.
My Disillusionment in Russia. Gordon Pr.
My Disillusionment in Russia. Peter Smith.
The Psychology of Political Violence. Gordon
Pr.

Goldman, Eric. *see* Goldman, Eric Frederick.

Goldman, Eric Frederick, 1915-
xGoldman, Eric.
Rendezvous with Destiny: A History of
Modern American Reform. Random.

Goldman, Ethel.
xGoldman, Ethel.
I Like Fruit. Lerner Pubns.

Goldman, George D. *see* Goldman, George David.

Goldman, George David.
xGoldman, George D.
Innovations in Psychotherapy. C C Thomas.
Psychoanalytic Perspectives on Aggression.
Kendall-Hunt.
ed. Psychoanalytic Psychotherapy. A-W.

Goldman, Guido. *see* Goldman, Guido G.

Goldman, Guido G.
xGoldman, Guido.
German Political System. Random.

Goldman, Henry M. *see* Goldman, Henry Maurice.

Goldman, Henry Maurice, 1911-
xGoldman, Henry M.
ed. Current Therapy in Dentistry. Mosby.
Introduction to Periodontics. Mosby.
Periodontal Therapy. Mosby.

Goldman, Irving, 1911-
xGoldman, Irving.
Ancient Polynesian Society. U of Chicago Pr.

Goldman, James.
xGoldman, James.
Myself As Witness. Random.

Goldman, Jerry.
xGoldman, Jerry.
Ineffective Justice: Evaluating the Preappeal
Conference. Sage.

Goldman, Leo, 1920-
xGoldman, Leo.

Using Tests in Counseling. Goodyear.
Goldman, Leon, 1905-
   xGoldman, Leon M.
      Introduction to Modern Phototherapy. C C
      Thomas.
Goldman, Leon M. *see* Goldman, Leon.
Goldman, Mark.
   xGoldman, Mark.
      The Reader's Art: Virginia Woolf As Literary
      Critic. Mouton.
Goldman, Merle.
   xGoldman, Merle.
      Literary Dissent in Communist China.
      Atheneum.
      ed. Modern Chinese Literature in the May
      Fourth Era. Harvard U Pr.
   xGoldman, Merle R.
      Literary Dissent in Communist China. Harvard
      U Pr.
Goldman, Merle R. *see* Goldman, Merle.
Goldman, Mervin J.
   xGoldman, Mervin J.
      Principles of Clinical Electrocardiography.
      Lange.
Goldman, Michael.
   xGoldman, Michael.
      At the Edge: Poems. Macmillan.
Goldman, Morris, 1919-
   xGoldman, Morris.
      Fluorescent Antibody Methods. Acad Pr.
Goldman, Myer.
   xGoldman, Myer.
      A Radiographic Index. Year Bk Med.
Goldman, Norma.
   xGoldman, Norma.
      Latin Via Ovid: A First Course. Wayne St U
      Pr.
Goldman, Peter.
   xGoldman, Peter L.
      The Death & Life of Malcolm X. U of Ill Pr.
Goldman, Peter L. *see* Goldman, Peter.
Goldman, Ralph.
   xGoldman, Ralph.
      Principles of Medical Science. McGraw.
Goldman, Ralph M.
   xGoldman, Ralph M.
      Contemporary Perspectives on Politics.
      Transaction Bks.
Goldman, Ralph M. *see* Goldman, Ralph Morris.
Goldman, Ralph Morris.
   xGoldman, Ralph M.
      The Political Science Concept Inventory.
      ABC-Clio.
      Search for Consensus: The Story of the
      Democratic Party. Temple U Pr.
Goldman, Richard. *see* Goldman, Richard M.
Goldman, Richard M.
   xGoldman, Richard.
      ed. Looking at Children: Field Experiences in
      Child Study. Humanics Ltd.
Goldman, Ronald.
   xGoldman, Ronald.
      Angry Adolescents. Sage.
      Religious Thinking from Childhood to
      Adolescence. Humanities.
      Religious Thinking from Childhood to
      Adolescence. Seabury.
Goldman, Sheldon.
   xGoldman, Sheldon.
      ed. American Court Systems: Readings in
      Judicial Process & Behavior. W H Freeman.
      The Federal Courts As a Political System.
      Har-Row.
Goldman, Sherli E. *see* Goldman, Sherli Evens.
Goldman, Sherli Evens.
   xGoldman, Sherli E.
      Mary McCarthy: A Bibliography. HarBraceJ.
Goldman, Susan.
   xGoldman, Susan.

      ed. Cousins Are Special. A Whitman.
      Grandma Is Somebody Special. A Whitman.
      Grandpa & Me Together. A Whitman.
Goldman, William, 1931-
   xGoldman, William.
      Marathon Man. Delacorte.
      Marathon Man. Dell.
Goldman, Kjell.
   xGoldmann, Kjell.
      ed. Power, Capabilities, Interdependence:
      Problems in the Study of International
      Influence. Sage.
Goldmann, Lucien.
   xGoldmann, Lucien.
      Lukacs & Heidegger: Towards a New
      Philosophy. Routledge & Kegan.
Goldmann, Robert.
   xGoldmann, Robert B.
      A Work Experiment: Six Americans in a
      Swedish Plant. Ford Found.
Goldmann, Robert B. *see* Goldmann, Robert.
Goldmark, Josephine C. *see* Goldmark, Josephine Clara.
Goldmark, Josephine Clara, 1877-1950
   xGoldmark, Josephine C.
      Impatient Crusader: Florence Kelley's Life
      Story. Greenwood.
Goldmeier, Erich.
   xGoldmeier, Erich.
      Similarity in Visually Perceived Forms. Intl
      Univs Pr.
Goldner, Franz, 1903-
   xGoldner, Franz.
      Austrian Emigration: 1938-1945. Ungar.
Goldner, George R., 1943-
   xGoldner, George R.
      Niccolo & Piero Lamberti. Garland Pub.
Goldoni, Carlo, 1707-1793
   xGoldoni, Carlo.
      Comic Theatre: A Comedy in Three Acts. U of
      Nebr Pr.
      Liar. Theatre Arts.
      Memoirs of Carlo Goldoni. Greenwood.
      Memoirs of Carlo Goldoni. Sharon Hill.
Goldovsky, B. *see* Goldovsky, Boris.
Goldovsky, Boris.
   xGoldovsky, B.
      Bringing Opera to Life: Operatic Acting &
      Stage Direction. P-H.
   xGoldovsky, Boris.
      Accents on Opera: A Series of Brief Essays
      Stressing Known & Little Known Facts &
      Facets of a Familiar Art. Arno.
Goldreich, Gloria.
   xGoldreich, Gloria.
      Four Days. HarBraceJ.
      Lori. HR&W.
      Lori. Dell.
      What Can She Be?: A Computer Scientist.
      Lothrop.
Goldsborough, June.
   xGoldsborough, June.
      What's in the Woods?. P H.
Goldsbrough, Paul F.
   xGoldsbrough, Paul F.
      Microcomputer Interfacing with the 8255 PPI
      Chip. Sams.
Goldsby, Richard A.
   xGoldsby, Richard A.
      Biology. Har-Row.
      Cells & Energy. Macmillan.
      Race & Races. Macmillan.
Goldschmidt, Arthur, 1938-
   xGoldschmidt, Arthur.
      A Concise History of the Middle East.
      Westview.
Goldschmidt, E. P. *see* Goldschmidt, Ernst Philip.
Goldschmidt, Ernst Philip.
   xGoldschmidt, E. P.

      Medieval Texts & Their First Appearance in
      Print. Biblo.
Goldschmidt, Walter. *see* Goldschmidt, Walter Rochs.
Goldschmidt, Walter Rochs, 1913-
   xGoldschmidt, Walter.
      As You Sow: Three Studies in the Social
      Consequences of Agribusiness. Allanheld.
      Culture & Behavior of the Sebei: A Study in
      Continuity & Adaptation. U of Cal Pr.
      Exploring the Ways of Mankind. HR&W.
Goldschmidt, Y. *see* Goldschmidt, Yaaqov.
Goldschmidt, Yaaqov.
   xGoldschmidt, Y.
      Profit Measurement During Inflation:
      Accounting, Economic & Financial Aspects.
      Wiley.
Goldschmiedt, Henry.
   xGoldschmiedt, Henry.
      Practical Formulas for Hobby & Profit. Arco.
      Practical Formulas for Hobby or Profit. Chem
      Pub.
Goldsmith, Barbara.
   xGoldsmith, Barbara.
      Little Gloria...Happy at Last. Knopf.
      The Straw Man. FS&G.
Goldsmith, D. *see* Goldsmith, Donald.
Goldsmith, Donald.
   xGoldsmith, D.
      The Search for Life in the Universe. A-W.
   xGoldsmith, Donald.
      From the Black Hole to the Infinite Universe.
      Holden-Day.
      ed. Scientists Confront Velikovsky. Cornell U
      Pr.
      ed. Scientists Confront Velikovsky. Norton.
      The Search for Life in the Universe.
      Benjamin-Cummings.
Goldsmith, Elisabeth E. *see* Goldsmith, Elizabeth
   Edwards.
Goldsmith, Elizabeth E. *see* Goldsmith, Elizabeth
   Edwards.
Goldsmith, Elizabeth Edwards, 1860-
   xGoldsmith, Elisabeth E.
      Ancient Pagan Symbols. Gale.
   xGoldsmith, Elizabeth E.
      Ancient Pagan Symbols. AMS Pr.
Goldsmith, Gail.
   xGoldsmith, Gail.
      Ballad of Patty Hearst. Forsyth Gall.
Goldsmith, Joel. *see* Goldsmith, Joel S.
Goldsmith, Joel S., 1892-1964
   xGoldsmith, Joel.
      Conscious Union with God. Univ Bks.
      The Master Speaks. Citadel Pr.
      Master Speaks. Univ Bks.
   xGoldsmith, Joel S.
      Art of Meditation. Har-Row.
      Art of Spiritual Healing. Har-Row.
      Awakening Mystical Consciousness. Har-Row.
      Conscious Union with God. Citadel Pr.
      Consciousness Is What I Am. Har-Row.
      The Contemplative Life. Citadel Pr.
      Living Between Two Worlds. G K Hall.
      Living Between Two Worlds. Har-Row.
      Our Spiritual Resources. Har-Row.
      Parenthesis in Eternity. Har-Row.
      The World Is New. Har-Row.
Goldsmith, John, 1947-
   xGoldsmith, John.
      Voyage in the Beagle. Merrimack Bk Serv.
Goldsmith, John A., 1951-
   xGoldsmith, John A.
      Autosegmental Phonology. Garland Pub.
Goldsmith, Lawrence C., 1916-
   xGoldsmith, Lawrence C.
      Watercolor Bold & Free. Watson-Guptill.
Goldsmith, M. M.
   xGoldsmith, M. M.

Hobbes's Science of Politics. Columbia U Pr.

Goldsmith, Oliver, 1728-1774
xGoldsmith, Oliver.
Vicar of Wakefield. Dutton.
The Vicar of Wakefield. G K Hall.
Vicar of Wakefield. NAL.
Vicar of Wakefield. Oxford U Pr.
The Vicar of Wakefield. R West.
Vicar of Wakefield. Airmont.
Vicar of Wakefield. PB.

Goldsmith, Raymond W. see Goldsmith, Raymond William.

Goldsmith, Raymond William, 1904-
xGoldsmith, Raymond W.
Financial Intermediaries in the American Economy Since 1900. Arno.
The National Wealth of the United States in the Postwar Period. Arno.
Study of Saving in the United States. Greenwood.

Goldsmith, Seth B.
xGoldsmith, Seth B.
Prison Health: Travesty of Justice. N Watson.

Goldsmith, Ulrich K.
xGoldsmith, Ulrich K.
Stefan George. Columbia U Pr.

Goldsmith, William, 1938-
xGoldsmith, William.
Psychiatric Drugs for the Non - Medical Mental Health Worker. C C Thomas.

Goldsmith, William M.
xGoldsmith, William M.
ed. The Growth of Presidential Power: A Documented History. Chelsea Hse.

Goldstein, A. P. see Goldstein, Arnold P.

Goldstein, Abraham S.
xGoldstein, Abraham S.
The Insanity Defense. Greenwood.

Goldstein, Arnold P.
xGoldstein, A. P.
ed. Maximizing Treatment Gains: Transfer Enhancement in Psychotherapy. Acad Pr.
xGoldstein, Arnold P.
Changing Supervisor Behavior. Pergamon.
I Know What's Wrong, but I Don't Know What to Do About It. P-H.
Prescriptive Psychotherapies. Pergamon.
Psychotherapeutic Attraction. Pergamon.
Skillstreaming the Adolescent: A Structured Learning Approach to Teaching Prosocial Skills. Res Press.

Goldstein, Arnold S.
xGoldstein, Arnold S.
Case Problems in Community Pharmacy Management. Lea & Febiger.
Commercial Transactions Desk Book. Inst Busn Plan.
Strategies & Techniques for Saving the Financially-Distressed Small Business. Pilot Bks.

Goldstein, Avram.
xGoldstein, Avram.
Principles of Drug Action: The Basis of Pharmacology. Wiley.

Goldstein, Bernard.
xGoldstein, Bernard.
Children & Work: A Study of Socialization. Transaction Bks.

Goldstein, E. Bruce, 1941-
xGoldstein, E. Bruce.
Sensation & Perception. Wadsworth Pub.

Goldstein, Frances, 1940-
xGoldstein, Frances.
illus. Children's Treasure Hunt Travel Guide to Italy. Paper Tiger Pap.

Goldstein, Gersham.
xGoldstein, Gersham.
Index to Federal Tax Articles. Warren.

Goldstein, H. see Goldstein, Harry.

Goldstein, Harold.
xGoldstein, Harold.
ed. The Changing Environment for Library Services in the Metropolitan Area. U of Ill Lib Sci.

Goldstein, Harold M.
xGoldstein, Harold M.
Entry-Level Health Occupations: Development & Future. Johns Hopkins.
Utilization of Health Personnel: A Five Hospital Study. Aspen Systems.

Goldstein, Harriet I. see Goldstein, Harriet Irene.

Goldstein, Harriet Irene.
xGoldstein, Harriet I.
Art in Everyday Life. Macmillan.

Goldstein, Harry, 1911-
xGoldstein, H.
Reading & Listening Comprehension at Various Controlled Rates. AMS Pr.

Goldstein, Herbert, 1922-
xGoldstein, Herbert.
Classical Mechanics. A-W.
Fundamental Aspects of Reactor Shielding. Johnson Repr.

Goldstein, Israel, 1896-
xGoldstein, Israel.
Toward a Solution. Arno.

Goldstein, Jack.
xGoldstein, Jack.
Triumph Over Disease - by Fasting & Natural Diet. Arco.

Goldstein, Jeffrey H.
xGoldstein, Jeffrey H.
ed. The Psychology of Humor: Theoretical Perspectives & Empirical Issues. Acad Pr.
ed. Sports, Games & Play: Social & Psychological Viewpoints. Halsted Pr.

Goldstein, Jerome, 1931-
xGoldstein, Jerome.
Recycling: How to Re-Use Wastes in Home, Industry & Society. Schocken.

Goldstein, Jon H.
xGoldstein, Jon H.
Competition for Wetlands in the Midwest: An Economic Analysis. Johns Hopkins.

Goldstein, Jonathan A.
xGoldstein, Jonathan A.
Letters of Demosthenes. Columbia U Pr.

Goldstein, Joseph.
xGoldstein, Joseph.
Before the Best Interests of the Child. Free Pr.
Beyond the Best Interests of the Child. Free Pr.

Goldstein, Kenneth M.
xGoldstein, Kenneth M.
Cognitive Style: Five Approaches & Relevant Research. Wiley.

Goldstein, Kurt, 1878-
xGoldstein, Kurt.
Human Nature in the Light of Psychopathology. Schocken.

Goldstein, Larry. see Goldstein, Larry Joel.

Goldstein, Larry J. see Goldstein, Larry Joel.

Goldstein, Larry Joel.
xGoldstein, Larry.
Finite Mathematics & Its Applications. P-H.
Modern Mathematics & Its Applications. P-H.
xGoldstein, Larry J.
Abstract Algebra: A First Course. P-H.
Calculus & Its Applications. P-H.

Goldstein, Lee.
xGoldstein, Lee.
Communes, Law & Commonsense: A Legal Manual for Communities. New Community.

Goldstein, Leon.
xGoldstein, Leon.
Introduction to Comparative Physiology. HR&W.

Goldstein, Leon J.
xGoldstein, Leon J.

Historical Knowing. U of Tex Pr.

Goldstein, Loius A. see Goldstein, Louis A.

Goldstein, Louis A.
xGoldstein, Loius A.
Atlas of Orthopaedic Surgery. Mosby.
xGoldstein, Louis A.
Atlas of Orthopaedic Surgery. Mosby.

Goldstein, Malcolm.
xGoldstein, Malcolm.
George S. Kaufman: His Life, His Theater. Oxford U Pr.
Pope & the Augustan Stage. AMS Pr.

Goldstein, Menek.
xGoldstein, Menek.
Ergot Compounds & Brain Function: Neuroendocrine & Neuropsychiatric Aspects. Raven.

Goldstein, Michael J. see Goldstein, Michael Joseph.

Goldstein, Michael Joseph.
xGoldstein, Michael J.
ed. The Experience of Anxiety: A Casebook. Oxford U Pr.

Goldstein, Murray.
xGoldstein, Murray.
ed. Cerebrovascular Disorders & Stroke. Raven.

Goldstein, N. see Goldstein, Nathan.

Goldstein, Nathan.
xGoldstein, N.
Figure Drawing: Structure, Anatomy & Expressive Design of Human Form. P-H.
xGoldstein, Nathan.
The Art of Responsive Drawing. P-H.

Goldstein, Norman N.
xGoldstein, Norman N.
Foundations of Physiological Instrumentation: A Source Book with Experiments. C C Thomas.

Goldstein, Paul J.
xGoldstein, Paul J.
Prostitution & Drugs. Lexington Bks.

Goldstein, Philip, 1910-
xGoldstein, Philip.
Genetics Is Easy. Lantern.
Wonders of Parasites. Lantern.

Goldstein, Richard, 1942-
xGoldstein, Richard.
Spartan Seasons: How Baseball Survived the Second World War. Macmillan.

Goldstein, Robert J.
xGoldstein, Robert J.
Political Repression in Modern America. G K Hall.
Political Repression in Modern America. Two Continents.

Goldstein, Roberta B. see Goldstein, Roberta Butterfield.

Goldstein, Roberta Butterfield.
xGoldstein, Roberta B.
Cry Before Dawn. Golden Quill.
Fling Jeweled Pebbles. Golden Quill.
Wood Burns Red. Golden Quill.

Goldstein, Ronald E.
xGoldstein, Ronald E.
Esthetics in Dentistry. Lippincott.

Goldstein, Sidney, 1930-
xGoldstein, Sidney.
Sudden Death & Coronary Heart Disease. Futura Pub.

Goldstein, Stephen R., 1938-
xGoldstein, Stephen R.
Law & Public Education: Cases & Materials. Bobbs.

Goldstein, Susan B.
xGoldstein, Susan B.
The Communication Contract. C C Thomas.

Goldstein, Wallace L.
xGoldstein, Wallace L.
Teaching English As a Second Language: An Annotated Bibliography. Garland Pub.

Goldstein, Walter, 1930-
xGoldstein, Walter.

Dilemma of British Defense: The Imbalance Between Commitments & Resources. Ohio St U Pr.

Goldstein-Jackson, Kevin.
xGoldstein-Jackson, Kevin.
Things to Make with Everyday Objects. Atheneum.

Goldstene, Paul N., 1930-
xGoldstene, Paul N.
The Collapse of Liberal Empire: Science & Revolution in the Twentieth Century. Yale U Pr.
The Collapse of Liberal Empire: Science & the Revolution in the Twentieth Century. Chandler & Sharp.

Goldstine, Dora.
xGoldstine, Dora.
ed. Expanding Horizons in Medical Social Work. U of Chicago Pr.
ed. Readings in the Theory & Practice of Medical Social Work. U of Chicago Pr.

Goldstine, Herman H. *see* Goldstine, Herman Heine.

Goldstine, Herman Heine, 1913-
xGoldstine, Herman H.
The Computer from Pascal to Von Neumann. Princeton U Pr.

Goldston, Eli, 1920-
xGoldston, Eli.
The Quantification of Concern: Some Aspects of Social Accounting. Columbia U Pr.

Goldston, Robert. *see* Goldston, Robert C.

Goldston, Robert C.
xGoldston, Robert.
The Life & Death of Nazi Germany. Fawcett.
Life & Death of Nazi Germany. Bobbs.
Spain. Macmillan.
xGoldston, Robert C.
Spain. Watts.

Goldston, Will, 1877-1948
xGoldston, Will.
Exclusive Magical Secrets. Dover.

Goldstone, Richard A. *see* Goldstone, Richard Henry.

Goldstone, Richard Henry.
xGoldstone, Richard A.
Contexts of the Drama. McGraw.

Goldstucker, Jac L.
xGoldstucker, Jac L.
New Developments in Retail Trading Area Analysis & Site Selection. Ga St U Busn Pub.

Goldthorpe, J. E.
xGoldthorpe, J. E.
An Introduction to Sociology. Cambridge U Pr.

Goldwasser, Dan L.
xGoldwasser, Dan L.
A Guide to Rule 144. PLI.

Goldwasser, Janet.
xGoldwasser, Janet.
Huan-Ying: Workers' China. Monthly Rev.

Goldwater, Barry M. *see* Goldwater, Barry Morris.

Goldwater, Barry Morris, 1909-
xGoldwater, Barry M.
Why Not Victory?: A Fresh Look at American Foreign Policy. Greenwood.
With No Apologies: The Personal & Political Memoirs of United States Senator Barry M. Goldwater. Morrow.

Goldwin, Robert A.
xGoldwin, Robert A.
Left, Right & Center: Essays on Liberalism & Conservatism in the United States. Arno.
ed. Readings in American Foreign Policy. Oxford U Pr.

Goldwyn, Martin M.
xGoldwyn, Martin M.
You'd Better Believe It. Citadel Pr.

Goldwyn, Robert M.
xGoldwyn, Robert M.

Plastic & Reconstructive Surgery of the Breast. Little.
The Unfavorable Result in Plastic Surgery: Avoidance & Treatment. Little.

Gole, Susan, 1935-
xGole, Susan.
Early Maps of India. Humanities.

Goleman, Daniel.
xGoleman, Daniel.
The Varieties of the Meditative Experience. Dutton.
Varieties of the Meditative Experience. Halsted Pr.

Golemba, Henry L.
xGolemba, Henry L.
George Ripley. Twayne.

Golembiewski. *see* Golembiewski, Robert T.

Golembiewski, Robert. *see* Golembiewski, Robert T.

Golembiewski, Robert T.
xGolembiewski.
Approaches to Planned Change. Dekker.
xGolembiewski, Robert.
ed. Managerial Behavior & Organization Demands: Management As a Linking of Levels of Interaction. Peacock Pubs.
xGolembiewski, Robert T.
ed. Cases in Public Management. Rand.
ed. Public Administration: Readings in Institutions, Processes, Behavior, Policy. Rand.

Golenbock, Peter, 1946-
xGolenbock, Peter.
Dynasty: The New York Yankees 1949-1964. P-H.

Golf Digest.
xGolf Digest Editors.
ed. The Best of Golf Digest. S&S.
Better Golf. Intl Pubns Serv.
Better Golf. Soccer.
Better Golf for Boys. Dodd.
Touch System for Better Golf. S&S.
xGolf Digest Magazine Editors.
Instant Golf Lessons. Golf Digest Bks.

Golf Digest Editors. *see* Golf Digest.

Golf Digest Magazine Editors. *see* Golf Digest.

Golf Magazine.
xGolf Magazine Editors.
ed. Golf Magazine's Encyclopedia of Golf. Har-Row.
Golf Magazine's Tips from the Teaching Pros. Har-Row.

Golf Magazine Editors. *see* Golf Magazine.

Golffing, Francis.
xGolffing, Francis.
Likenesses. Typographeum.

Goliber, Paul F.
xGoliber, Paul F.
Refrigeration Servicing. Delmar.

Goligher, J. C.
xGoligher, J. C.
Surgery of the Anus, Rectum & Colon. Macmillan.

Golightly, Jean.
xGolightly, Jean.
Circuit Hikes in Virginia, West Virginia, Maryland & Pennsylvania. Potomac Appalach.

Golino, Carlo L. *see* Golino, Carlo Luigi.

Golino, Carlo Luigi, 1913-
xGolino, Carlo L.
ed. Contemporary Italian Poetry: An Anthology. Greenwood.

Goll, August, 1866-1936
xGoll, August.
Criminal Types in Shakespeare. Haskell.

Goll, Reinhold W. *see* Goll, Reinhold Weimar.

Goll, Reinhold Weimar.
xGoll, Reinhold W.

The Moon Twins & the Treasure. R W Goll.

Gollan, Anne.
xGollan, Anne.
The Tradition of Australian Cooking. Bks Australia.

Gollay, Elinor.
xGollay, Elinor.
Coming Back: The Community Experiences of Deinstitutionalized Mentally Retarded People. Abt Assoc.

Golledge, Reginald G.
xGolledge, Reginald G.
ed. Spatial Choice & Spatial Behavior: Geographic Essays on the Analysis of Preferences & Perceptions. Ohio St U Pr.

Goller, Nicholas.
xGoller, Nicholas.
Tomorrow's Silence. St Martin.

Golley, F. B. *see* Golley, Frank B.

Golley, Frank B.
xGolley, F. B.
ed. Tropical Ecological Systems: Trends in Terrestrial & Aquatic Research. Springer-Verlag.
xGolley, Frank B.
ed. Ecological Succession. Acad Pr.

Gollin, Gillian L. *see* Gollin, Gillian Lindt.

Gollin, Gillian Lindt.
xGollin, Gillian L.
Moravians in Two Worlds: A Study of Changing Communities. Columbia U Pr.

Gollin, James.
xGollin, James.
The Philomel Foundation. St Martin.

Gollin, Rita K., 1928-
xGollin, Rita K.
Nathaniel Hawthorne & the Truth of Dreams. La State U Pr.

Gollnick, Daniel A., 1940-
xGollnick, Daniel A.
Experimental Radiological Health Physics. Pergamon.

Gollock, Georgina A. *see* Gollock, Georgina Anne.

Gollock, Georgina Anne, 1861-1940
xGollock, Georgina A.
Daughters of Africa. Negro U Pr.
Lives of Eminent Africans. Negro U Pr.
Sons of Africa. Negro U Pr.

Gollwitzer, Helmut.
xGollwitzer, Helmut.
Song of Love: A Biblical Understanding of Sex. Fortress.

Golob, Eugene O. *see* Golob, Eugene Owen.

Golob, Eugene Owen, 1915-
xGolob, Eugene O.
Meline Tariff: French Agriculture & Nationalist Economic Policy. AMS Pr.

Gologor, Ethan.
xGologor, Ethan.
Psychodynamic Tennis: You, Your Opponent, & Other Obstacles to Perfection. Morrow.

Golomb, Louis, 1943-
xGolomb, Louis.
Brokers of Morality: Thai Ethnic Adaptation in a Rural Malaysian Setting. U Pr of Hawaii.

Golomshtok, I. N.
xGolomshtok, Igor.
Soviet Art in Exile. Random.

Golomshtok, Igor. *see* Golomshtok, I. N.

Golos, Natalie.
xGolos, Natalie.
Coping with Your Allergies. S&S.

Golovin, Nikolai N. *see* Golovin, Nikolai Nikolaevich.

Golovin, Nikolai Nikolaevich, 1875-1944
xGolovin, Nikolai N.
Problem of the Pacific in the Twentieth Century. Arno.

Golovkin, K. K. *see* Golovkin, Kirill Kapitonovich.

Golovkin, Kirill Kapitonovich.
xGolovkin, K. K.

Four Papers on Functions of Real Variables. Am Math.

Golub, Edward S., 1934-
xGolub, Edward S.
The Cellular Basis of the Immune Response: An Approach to Immunobiology. Sinauer Assoc.

Goluzin, G. M. *see* Goluzin, Gennadii Mikhailovich.

Goluzin, Gennadii Mikhailovich, 1906-1952
xGoluzin, G. M.
Geometric Theory of Functions of a Complex Variable. Am Math.

Golz, Lud.
xGolz, Lud.
A Daily Guide to Knowing God. Tyndale.

Golze, Alfred R., 1905-
xGolze, Alfred R.
ed. Handbook of Dam Engineering. Van Nos Reinhold.

Golzen, Godfrey.
xGolzen, Godfrey.
Changing Your Job. Intl Pubns Serv.

Gomaa, Ahamad M. *see* Gomaa, Ahmad M.

Gomaa, Ahmad M.
xGomaa, Ahamad M.
The Foundation of the League of Arab States: Wartime Diplomacy & Inter-Arab Politics 1941-1945. Longman.

Gomberg, Edith S.
xGomberg, Edith S.
ed. Gender & Disordered Behavior: Sex Differences in Psychopathology. Brunner Mazel.

Gombin, Richard, 1939-
xGombin, Richard.
The Radical Tradition: A Study in Modern Revolutionary Thought. St Martin.

Gombosi, Marilyn.
xGombosi, Marilyn.
A Day of Solemn Thanksgiving: Moravian Music for the Fourth of July, 1783, in Salem, North Carolina. U of NC Pr.

Gombrich, E. H. *see* Gombrich, Ernst Hans Josef.
Gombrich, Ernst H. *see* Gombrich, Ernst Hans Josef.

Gombrich, Ernst Hans Josef.
xGombrich, E. H.
Art, Perception & Reality. Johns Hopkins.
xGombrich, Ernst H.
The Sense of Order: A Study in the Psychology of Decorative Art. Cornell U Pr.

Gomer, R. *see* Gomer, Robert.

Gomer, Robert.
xGomer, R.
ed. Interactions on Metal Surfaces. Springer-Verlag.

Gomes, Leonard.
xGomes, Leonard.
International Economic Problems. St Martin.

Gomez, A. V. *see* Gomez, Al V.

Gomez, Al V., 1905-
xGomez, A. V.
The Foundation Stock. Vantage.

Gomez, Joan.
xGomez, Joan.
How Not to Die Young. Stein & Day.

Gomez, Joseph A.
xGomez, Joseph A.
Peter Watkins. Twayne.

Gomez, Manuel.
xGomez, Manuel.
At Work in Copper: Occupational Health & Safety in Copper Smelting. Inform.

Gomez, Manuel R.
xGomez, Manuel R.
ed. Tuberous Sclerosis. Raven.

Gomez, Thelma J.
xGomez, Thelma J.

ed. Independent Activities for Learning Centers. Mss Info.

Gomez, Victoria.
xGomez, Victoria.
Scream Cheese & Jelly!: Jokes, Riddles, & Puns. Lothrop.

Gomez-Moreno, Manuel, 1870-
xGomez-Moreno, Manuel.
Renaissance Sculpture in Spain. Hacker.

Gomme, A. W. *see* Gomme, Arnold Wycombe.

Gomme, Andor.
xGomme, Andor H.
Attitudes to Criticism. S Ill U Pr.

Gomme, Andor H. *see* Gomme, Andor.

Gomme, Arnold Wycombe.
xGomme, A. W.
Menander: A Commentary. Oxford U Pr.

Gomme, George L. *see* Gomme, George Laurence.

Gomme, George Laurence, Sir, 1853-1916
xGomme, George L.
Primitive Folk-Moots: Or, Open-Air Assemblies in Britain. Gale.

Gomori, George, 1934-
xGomori, George.
Cyprian Norwid. Twayne.

Gompel, C.
xGompel, C.
Pathology in Gynecology & Obstetrics. Lippincott.
xGompel, Claude.
Atlas of Diagnostic Cytology. Wiley.

Gompel, Claude. *see* Gompel, C.

Gompertz, Rolf.
xGompertz, Rolf.
Promotion & Publicity Handbook for Broadcasters. TAB Bks.

Goncharov, Ivan. *see* Goncharov, Ivan Aleksandrovich.
Goncharov, Ivan A. *see* Goncharov, Ivan Aleksandrovich.

Goncharov, Ivan Aleksandrovich.
xGoncharov, Ivan.
Oblomov. Bentley.
Oblomov. Penguin.
The Precipice. Fertig.
xGoncharov, Ivan A.
The Precipice. Hyperion Conn.

Goncourt, Edmond L. *see* Goncourt, Edmond Louis Antoine Huot De.
Goncourt, Edmond L. de. *see* Goncourt, Edmond Louis Antoins Huot De.

Goncourt, Edmond Louis Antoine Huot De.
xGoncourt, Edmond L.
Goncourt Journals, 1851-1870. Greenwood.

Goncourt, Edmond Louis Antoins Huot De.
xGoncourt, Edmond L. de.
Germinie. Greenwood.

Gondin, William R. *see* Gondin, William Richard.

Gondin, William Richard.
xGondin, William R.
Advanced Algebra & Calculus Made Simple. Doubleday.

Gonedes, Nicholas J.
xGonedes, Nicholas J.
Accounting for Common Stockholders: An Eclectic Decision-Making & Motivational Foundation. U of Tex Busn Res.

Gonen, Jay Y., 1934-
xGonen, Jay Y.
A Psychohistory of Zionism. NAL.

Gonzales, Laurence, 1947-
xGonzales, Laurence.
Jambeaux. HarBraceJ.

Gonzales, Ronald.
xGonzales, Ronald.
Understanding Your Car. Har-Row.

Gonzalez, Calos. *see* Gonzalez, Carlos.

Gonzalez, Carlos, 1936-
xGonzalez, Calos.

An Overview of the Mestizo Heritage: Implications for Teachers of Mexican-American Children. R & E Res Assoc.

Gonzalez, Carlos F.
xGonzalez, Carlos F.
Computed Brain & Orbital Tomography: Technique & Interpretation. Wiley.

Gonzalez, David J.
xGonzalez, David J.
Journey to the Third World. Indigena.

Gonzalez, Edward.
xGonzalez, Edward.
Cuba Under Castro: The Limits of Charisma. HM.

Gonzalez, Fernando L.
xGonzalez, Fernando L.
Disco-File: The Discographical Catalog of American Rock & Roll & Rhythm & Blues. F L Gonzalez.

Gonzalez, Gloria.
xGonzalez, Gloria.
Curtains. Dramatists Play.
Gaucho. Knopf.
The Glad Man. Dell.
The Glad Man. Knopf.

Gonzalez, Gustavo.
xGonzalez, Gustavo.
The Acquisition of Spanish Grammar by Native Spanish Speaking Children. Natl Clearinghse Bilingual Ed.

Gonzalez De Mendoza, Juan.
xGonzalez De Mendoza, Juan.
History of the Great & Mighty Kingdom of China & the Situation Thereof. B Franklin.

Gooch, Bob, 1919-
xGooch, Bob.
Land You Can Hunt. A S Barnes.

Gooch, Brad, 1952-
xGooch, Brad.
Daily News. Z Pr.

Gooch, Brison D. Foreword by. *see* Singh, R. John.
Gooch, Bryan N. *see* Gooch, Bryan N. S.

Gooch, Bryan N. S.
xGooch, Bryan N.
Musical Settings of Early & Mid-Victorian Literature: A Catalogue. Garland Pub.
Musical Settings of Late Victorian & Modern British Literature. Garland Pub.

Gooch, G. P. *see* Gooch, George Peabody.
Gooch, George P. *see* Gooch, George Peabody.

Gooch, George Peabody.
xGooch, G. P.
Century of British Foreign Policy. Kennikat.
Hobbes. Folcroft.
Under Six Reigns. Shoe String.
xGooch, George P.
Courts & Cabinets. Arno.
Franco-German Relations, 1871-1914. Russell.
ed. In Pursuit of Peace. Arno.
Studies in Diplomacy & Statecraft. Russell.
Studies in German History. Russell.
Studies in Modern History. Arno.

Gooch, John.
xGooch, John.
The Plans of War: The General Staff & British Military Strategy c. 1900-1916. Halsted Pr.

Gooch, Robert K. *see* Gooch, Robert Kent.

Gooch, Robert Kent, 1893-
xGooch, Robert K.
Parliamentary Government in France: Revolutionary Origins, 1789-1791. Russell.

Gooch, S. *see* Gooch, Stan.

Gooch, Stan.
xGooch, S.
Neanderthal Question. State Mutual Bk.
xGooch, Stan.

The Paranormal. Har-Row.
The Paranormal. Har-Row.
Good, Charles M.
xGood, Charles M.
Market Development in Traditionally
Marketless Societies. Ohio U Ctr Intl.
Good, Donald W.
xGood, Donald W.
Handbook. Macmillan.
Good, Harry G. *see* Good, Harry Gehman.
Good, Harry Gehman.
xGood, Harry G.
History of American Education. Macmillan.
History of Western Education. Macmillan.
Good Housekeeping.
xGood Housekeeping Editors.
Family Health & Medical Guide. Hearst Bks.
Good Housekeeping Editors. *see* Good Housekeeping.
Good Housekeeping Institute. *see* Good Housekeeping
Institute, London.
Good Housekeeping Institute, London.
xGood Housekeeping Institute.
Good Housekeeping's Children's Cook Book.
Intl Pubns Serv.
Good Housekeeping's Colour Cookery. Intl
Pubns Serv.
Good Housekeeping's Cookery Book. Intl
Pubns Serv.
Good Housekeeping's New Basic Cookery. Intl
Pubns Serv.
Good Housekeeping's New Picture Cookery.
Intl Pubns Serv.
Good, Merle.
xGood, Merle.
These People Mine. Herald Pr.
Good, Patricia Eileen King-Ellison.
xGood, Patricia K.
A Practical Guide to the MMPI: An
Introduction for Psychologists, Physicians,
Social Workers, & Other Professionals. U of
Minn Pr.
Good, Patricia K. *see* Good, Patricia Eileen King-Ellison.
Good, Paul.
xGood, Paul.
The Individual. Silver.
The Individual. Time-Life.
Good, R. A. *see* Good, Richard A.
Good, Ralph E.
xGood, Ralph E.
ed. Freshwater Wetlands: Ecological Processes
& Management Potential. Acad Pr.
Good, Richard A.
xGood, R. A.
Introduction to Mathematics. HarBraceJ.
Good, Ronald. *see* Good, Ronald D'Oyley.
Good, Ronald D'Oyley, 1896-
xGood, Ronald.
Features of Evolution in the Flowering Plants.
Dover.
Features of Evolution in the Flowering Plants.
Peter Smith.
Good, Shirley R. *see* Good, Shirley Ruth.
Good, Shirley Ruth.
xGood, Shirley R.
Analysis for Action: Nursing Care of the
Elderly. P-H.
Good, Susanna.
xGood, Susanna.
Burning Secrets. PB.
Good, Thomas L.
xGood, Thomas L.
Looking in Classrooms. Har-Row.
Teachers Make a Difference. HR&W.
Goodall, B. *see* Goodall, Brian.
Goodall, Blake.
xGoodall, Blake.

The Homilies of St. John Chrysostom on the
Letters of St. Paul to Titus & Philemon. U of
Cal Pr.
Goodall, Brian.
xGoodall, B.
The Economics of Urban Areas. Pergamon.
Goodall, Charles. *see* Goodall, Charles S.
Goodall, Charles S.
xGoodall, Charles.
Intro. by How to Train Your Own Gun Dog.
Howell Bk.
Goodall, Daphne M. *see* Goodall, Daphne Machin.
Goodall, Daphne Machin.
xGoodall, Daphne M.
Horses of the World. Macmillan.
Goodall, David. *see* Goodall, David W.
Goodall, David W.
xGoodall, David.
ed. Evolution of Desert Biota. U of Tex Pr.
Goodall, John. *see* Goodall, John A.
Goodall, John A.
xGoodall, John.
Heaven & Earth: Album Leaves from a Ming
Encyclopedia. Shambhala Pubns.
Goodall, John S.
xGoodall, John S.
illus. Ballooning Adventures of Paddy Pork.
HarBraceJ.
Creepy Castle. Atheneum.
An Edwardian Christmas. Atheneum.
An Edwardian Holiday. Atheneum.
illus. An Edwardian Summer. Atheneum.
Naughty Nancy. Atheneum.
Paddy Pork's Holiday. Atheneum.
illus. Paddy's Evening Out. Atheneum.
illus. The Story of an English Village.
Atheneum.
illus. The Surprise Picnic. Atheneum.
Goodall, Merrill. *see* Goodall, Merrill R.
Goodall, Merrill R.
xGoodall, Merrill.
California Water: A New Political Economy.
Allanheld.
Goodavage, Joseph. *see* Goodavage, Joseph F.
Goodavage, Joseph F.
xGoodavage, Joseph.
Storm on the Sun. NAL.
Goodban, W. T. *see* Goodban, William T.
Goodban, William T.
xGoodban, W. T.
Architectural Drawing & Planning. McGraw.
xGoodban, William T.
Architectural Drawing & Planning. McGraw.
Goodden, Robert.
xGoodden, Robert.
British Butterflies: A Field Guide. David &
Charles.
Silversmithing. Oxford U Pr.
Goode. *see* Goode, Stephen.
Goode, Clement G. *see* Goode, Clement Tyson.
Goode, Clement T. *see* Goode, Clement Tyson.
Goode, Clement Tyson.
xGoode, Clement G.
An Atlas of English Literature. Gordon Pr.
xGoode, Clement T.
An Atlas of English Literature. Arden Lib.
An Atlas of English Literature. Folcroft.
Byron As Critic. B Franklin.
Byron As Critic. Haskell.
Goode, Erich.
xGoode, Erich.
Deviant Behavior: An Interactionist Approach.
P-H.
Drugs in American Society. Knopf.
Goode, James M.
xGoode, James M.

Capital Losses: A Cultural History of
Washington's Destroyed Buildings.
Smithsonian.
Goode, John.
xGoode, John.
Turtles, Tortoises, Terrapins. Scribner.
Goode, Kenneth C. *see* Goode, Kenneth G.
Goode, Kenneth G.
xGoode, Kenneth C.
From Africa to the United States & Then: A
Concise Afro-American History. Scott F.
xGoode, Kenneth G.
California's Black Pioneers: A Brief Historical
Survey. McNally.
Goode, Richard. *see* Goode, Richard B.
Goode, Richard B.
xGoode, Richard.
The Individual Income Tax. Brookings.
Goode, Ruth.
xGoode, Ruth.
People of the First Cities. Macmillan.
People of the Ice Age. Macmillan.
Goode, Stephen.
xGoode.
Eurocommunism. Watts.
xGoode, Stephen.
Affluent Revolutionaries: A Portrait of the
New Left. New Viewpoints.
Assassination!: Kennedy, King, Kennedy.
Watts.
Guerrilla Warfare & Terrorism. Watts.
The National Defense System. Watts.
Goode, Stephen H., 1925- comp
xGoode, Stephen H.
ed. Index to Commonwealth Little Magazines
1964-65. Johnson Repr.
Index to Commonwealth Little Magazines,
1968-69. Whitston Pub.
Population & the Population Explosion: A
Bibliography for 1971. Whitston Pub.
Goode, W. *see* Goode, William Josiah.
Goode, William J. *see* Goode, William Josiah.
Goode, William Josiah.
xGoode, W.
The Family. P-H.
xGoode, William J.
The Celebration of Heroes: Prestige As a Social
Control System. U of Cal Pr.
Explorations in Social Theory. Oxford U Pr.
Principles of Sociology. McGraw.
Frwd. by Social Systems & Family Patterns: A
Propositional Inventory. Irvington.
World Revolution & Family Patterns. Free Pr.
Goodearl, K. R.
xGoodearl, K. R.
Dimension Theory for Nonsingular Injective
Modules. Am Math.
Goodell, Carol.
xGoodell, Carol.
ed. Changing Classroom. Ballantine.
Goodell, John S.
xGoodell, John S.
Libraries & Work Sampling. Libs Unl.
Goodell, William, 1792-1878
xGoodell, William.
American Slave Code in Theory & Practice: Its
Distinctive Features As Shown by Its
Statutes, Judicial Decisions, & Illustrative
Facts. Arno.
Goodenough, Erwin R. *see* Goodenough, Erwin
Ramsdell.
Goodenough, Erwin Ramsdell, 1893-1965
xGoodenough, Erwin R.
Church in the Roman Empire. Cooper Sq.
Goodenough, Florence. *see* Goodenough, Florence Laura.
Goodenough, Florence L. *see* Goodenough, Florence
Laura.
Goodenough, Florence Laura, 1886-
xGoodenough, Florence.

Anger in Young Children. Greenwood.
xGoodenough, Florence L.
    Measurement of Intelligence by Drawings.
    Arno.
Goodenough, George A. see Goodenough, George
    Alfred.
Goodenough, George Alfred, 1868-1929
xGoodenough, George A.
    Principles of Thermodynamics. Johnson Repr.
Goodenough, Ursula.
xGoodenough, Ursula.
    Genetics. HR&W.
Goodenough, Ward H.
xGoodenough, Ward H.
    Property, Kin & Community on Truk. Shoe
    String.
Goodenow, John M. see Goodenow, John Milton.
Goodenow, John Milton, 1782-1838
xGoodenow, John M.
    Historical Sketches of the Principles & Maxims
    of American Jurisprudence, in Contrast with
    the Doctrines of the English Common Law
    on the Subject of Crimes & Punishments.
    Arno.
Gooder, Eileen A.
xGooder, Eileen A.
    Latin for Local History: An Introduction.
    Longman.
Gooders, John.
xGooders, John.
    The Great Book of Birds. Dial.
Goodfellow, David M. see Goodfellow, David Martin.
Goodfellow, David Martin.
xGoodfellow, David M.
    Principles of Economic Sociology: The
    Economics of Primitive Life As Illustrated
    from the Bantu Peoples of South & East
    Africa. Negro U Pr.
Goodfellow, Ron.
xGoodfellow, Ron.
    Underwater Engineering. Pennwell Pub.
Goodfield, G. June.
xGoodfield, June.
    Playing God: Genetic Engineering & the
    Manipulation of Life. Random.
    The Siege of Cancer. Dell.
Goodfield, June. see Goodfield, G. June.
Goodfriend, Ronnie S. see Goodfriend, Ronnie
    Stephanie.
Goodfriend, Ronnie Stephanie.
xGoodfriend, Ronnie S.
    Power in Perception for the Young Child: A
    Comprehensive Program for the Development
    of Pre-Reading Visual Perceptual Skills. Tchrs
    Coll.
Goodgame, Louis R., 1927-
xGoodgame, Louis R.
    Delightful Discipline: Humorous Stories of
    Woodshed Wisdom & Biblical Principles.
    Mott Media.
Goodger, E. M.
xGoodger, E. M.
    Hydrocarbon Fuels: Production Properties &
    Performance of Liquids & Gases. Halsted Pr.
    Principles of Spaceflight Propulsion. Pergamon.
Goodglass, Harold.
xGoodglass, Harold.
    The Assessment of Aphasia & Related
    Disorders. Lea & Febiger.
    ed. Psycholinguistics & Aphasia. Johns
    Hopkins.
Goodgold, Edwin.
xGoodgold, Edwin.
    The Compleat Beatles Quiz Book. Warner Bks.
Goodhart, Arthur L. see Goodhart, Arthur Lehman.
Goodhart, Arthur Lehman, Sir, 1891-
xGoodhart, Arthur L.
    Law of the Land. U Pr of Va.
Goodheart, Eugene.
xGoodheart, Eugene.

Cult of the Ego: The Self in Modern Literature.
    U of Chicago Pr.
Culture & the Radical Conscience. Harvard U
    Pr.
The Failure of Criticism. Harvard U Pr.
Utopian Vision of D. H. Lawrence. U of
    Chicago Pr.
Goodheart, Pat.
xGoodheart, Pat.
    The Translator. HR&W.
Goodin, Robert E.
xGoodin, Robert E.
    The Politics of Rational Man. Wiley.
Goodlad. see Goodlad, John I.
Goodlad, John I.
xGoodlad.
    The Conventional & the Alternative in
    Education. McCutchan.
xGoodlad, John I.
    Early Schooling in the United States. McGraw.
    Facing the Future: Issues in Education &
    Schooling. McGraw.
    Nongraded Elementary School. HarBraceJ.
    What Schools Are For. Phi Delta Kappa.
Goodland, Norman L.
xGoodland, Norman L.
    Coronary Care. Year Bk Med.
Goodlin, Robert C.
xGoodlin, Robert C.
    Care of the Fetus. Masson Pub.
Goodloe, Abbie C. see Goodloe, Abbie Carter.
Goodloe, Abbie Carter, 1867-
xGoodloe, Abbie C.
    At the Foot of the Rockies. Arno.
Goodloe, William H.
xGoodloe, William H.
    Coconut Palm Frond Weaving. C E Tuttle.
Goodman, A. Harold, 1924-
xGoodman, A. Harold.
    Instrumental Music Guide. Brigham.
Goodman, A. W. see Goodman, Adolph Winkler.
Goodman, Adolph W. see Goodman, Adolph Winkler.
Goodman, Adolph Winkler, 1915-
xGoodman, A. W.
    Analytic Geometry & the Calculus. Macmillan.
    Concise Review of Algebra and Trigonometry.
    HR&W.
    Finite Mathematics with Applications.
    Macmillan.
    Mainstream of Algebra & Trigonometry. HM.
    Mathematics for Management & Social
    Sciences. HR&W.
xGoodman, Adolph W.
    Modern Calculus with Analytic Geometry.
    Macmillan.
Goodman, Allan E., 1944-
xGoodman, Allan E.
    The Lost Peace: America's Search for a
    Negotiated Settlement of the Vietnam War.
    Hoover Inst Pr.
    Politics in War: The Bases of Political
    Community in South Vietnam. Harvard U Pr.
Goodman, Anthony, 1936-
xGoodman, Anthony.
    A History of England from Edward II to James
    I. Longman.
Goodman, Bernice, 1927-
xGoodman, Bernice.
    The Lesbian: A Celebration of Difference. Out
    & Out.
Goodman, Cary.
xGoodman, Cary.
    Choosing Sides: Playground & Street Life on
    the Lower East Side. Schocken.
Goodman, David M. see Goodman, David Michael.
Goodman, David Michael.
xGoodman, David M.

Arizona Odyssey: Bibliographic Adventures in
    Nineteenth Century Magazines. AZ Hist
    Foun.
Goodman, David S.
xGoodman, David S.
    Emotional Well-Being Through Rational
    Behavior Training. C C Thomas.
Goodman, Elaine.
xGoodman, Elaine.
    jt. auth. The Family: Yesterday, Today,
    Tomorrow. FS&G.
xGoodman, Walter.
    The Family: Yesterday, Today, Tomorrow.
    FS&G.
Goodman, Ellen.
xGoodman, Ellen.
    Close to Home. S&S.
    Turning Points. Doubleday.
Goodman, Frank O.
xGoodman, Frank O.
    Dynamics of Gas-Surface Scattering. Acad Pr.
Goodman, Grant K. see Goodman, Grant Kohn.
Goodman, Grant Kohn, 1924-
xGoodman, Grant K.
    American Occupation of Japan: A
    Retrospective View. Paragon.
Goodman, Isidore.
xGoodman, Isidore.
    Funding Under ERISA. Commerce.
    Vesting Under ERISA. Commerce.
Goodman, Jack.
xGoodman, Jack.
    ed. While You Were Gone: A Report on
    Wartime Life in the United States. Da Capo.
Goodman, James A.
xGoodman, James A.
    ed. Dynamics of Racism in Social Work
    Practice. Natl Assn Soc Wkrs.
Goodman, Jay S.
xGoodman, Jay S.
    Democrats & Labor in Rhode Island,
    1952-1962: Changes in the Old Alliance.
    Brown U Pr.
    The Dynamics of Urban Government &
    Politics. Macmillan.
Goodman, Jeffrey.
xGoodman, Jeffrey.
    Psychic Archeology: Time Machine to the
    Past. Berkley Pub.
Goodman, John C.
xGoodman, John C.
    Economics of Public Policy: The Micro View.
    West Pub.
Goodman, Jonathan.
xGoodman, Jonathan.
    The Last Sentence. St Martin.
Goodman, Joseph I.
xGoodman, Joseph I.
    Diabetes Without Fear. Arbor Hse.
    Diabetes Without Fear. Avon.
Goodman, Joseph W.
xGoodman, Joseph W.
    Introduction to Fourier Optics. McGraw.
Goodman, Kenneth S.
xGoodman, Kenneth S.
    Choosing Materials to Teach Reading. Wayne
    St U Pr.
    Frwd. by & ed. The Psycholinguistic Nature of
    the Reading Process. Wayne St U Pr.
Goodman, L. A. see Goodman, Leo A.
Goodman, L. J. see Goodman, Louis J.
Goodman, Lawrence R.
xGoodman, Lawrence R.
    Intensive Care Radiology: Imaging of the
    Critically Ill. Mosby.
Goodman, Leo A.
xGoodman, L. A.
    Measures of Association for Cross
    Classifications. Springer-Verlag.
xGoodman, Leo A.

Analyzing Qualitative-Categorical Data:
Log-Linear Models & Latent-Structure
Analysis. Abt Assoc.

Goodman, Leonard H.
xGoodman, Leonard H.
ed. Current Career & Occupational Literature.
Wilson.
ed. Current Career & Occupational Literature,
1977-1979. Wilson.

Goodman, Libby.
xGoodman, Libby.
Learning Disabilities in the Secondary School:
Issues & Practices. Grune.

Goodman, Linda.
xGoodman, Linda.
Linda Goodman's Love Signs: A New
Approach to the Human Heart. Har-Row.

Goodman, Louis J.
xGoodman, L. J.
ed. Low-Cost Housing Technology: An
East-West Perspective. Pergamon.
xGoodman, Louis J.
ed. Geothermal Energy Projects: Planning &
Management. Pergamon.
ed. Management of Development Projects: An
International Case Study Approach.
Pergamon.

Goodman, Marguerite.
xGoodman, Marguerite.
Christmas Comes in Assorted Sizes. Ashley
Bks.

Goodman, Marjorie S. *see* Goodman, Marjorie Smith.

Goodman, Marjorie Smith.
xGoodman, Marjorie S.
Exercises in Physical Geography. Wayne St U
Pr.

Goodman, Mary E. *see* Goodman, Mary Ellen.

Goodman, Mary Ellen, 1911-1969
xGoodman, Mary E.
Culture of Childhood: Child's-Eye Views of
Society & Culture. Tchrs Coll.
Race Awareness in Young Children.
Macmillan.

Goodman, Michael J. *see* Goodman, Michael Jeffrey.

Goodman, Michael Jeffrey.
xGoodman, Michael J.
Ulcerative Colitis. Wiley.

Goodman, Morris C.
xGoodman, Morris C.
Modern Numerology. Wilshire.

Goodman, Murray.
xGoodman, Murray.
Organic Molecules in Action. Gordon.

Goodman, Nelson.
xGoodman, Nelson.
Problems & Projects. Hackett Pub.

Goodman, Norman.
xGoodman, Norman.
Society Today. Random.

Goodman, Paul, 1911-1972
xGoodman, Paul.
Collected Poems. Random.
Collected Poems. Random.
Creator Spirit Come!: The Literary Essays of
Paul Goodman. Dutton.
Creator Spirit Come: The Literary Essays of
Paul Goodman. Free Life.
Don Juan: Or, the Continuum of the Libido.
Black Sparrow.
Drawing the Line: The Political Essays of Paul
Goodman. Dutton.
Drawing the Line: The Political Essays of Paul
Goodman. Free Life.
ed. The Federalists Vs. the Jeffersonian
Republicans. Krieger.
Structure of Literature. U of Chicago Pr.

Goodman, Paul S.
xGoodman, Paul S.

Assessing Organizational Change: Rushton
Quality of Work Experiment. Wiley.

Goodman, Percival.
xGoodman, Percival.
The Double E. Doubleday.

Goodman, Philip, 1911-
xGoodman, Philip.
ed. Passover Anthology. Jewish Pubn.
ed. Purim Anthology. Jewish Pubn.
ed. The Sukkot & Simhat Torah Anthology.
Jewish Pubn.

Goodman, Raymond J.
xGoodman, Raymond J.
Management of Service for the Restaurant
Manager. Wm C Brown.

Goodman, Richard M. *see* Goodman, Richard Merle.

Goodman, Richard Merle.
xGoodman, Richard M.
Atlas of the Face in Genetic Disorders. Mosby.
ed. Genetic Diseases Among Ashkenazi Jews.
Raven.
Genetic Disorders Among the Jewish People.
Johns Hopkins.

Goodman, Robert, 1936-
xGoodman, Robert.
After the Planners. S&S.
After the Planners. S&S.

Goodman, Robert. *see* Goodman, Robert L.

Goodman, Robert L.
xGoodman, Robert.
General Electric Color TV Service Manual.
TAB Bks.
Troubleshooting with the Dual-Trace Scope.
TAB Bks.
xGoodman, Robert L.
General Electric Color TV Service Manual.
TAB Bks.
How to Repair Video Games. TAB Bks.
How to Use Color TV Test Instruments. TAB
Bks.
Indexed Guide to Modern Electronic Circuits.
TAB Bks.
Practical Troubleshooting with Modern
Electronic Test Instruments. TAB Bks.
Practical Troubleshooting with the Modern
Oscilloscope. TAB Bks.
Simplified TV Trouble Diagnosis. TAB Bks.
Troubleshooting Microprocessors & Digital
Logic. TAB Bks.

Goodman, Ryah T. *see* Goodman, Ryah Tumarkin.

Goodman, Ryah Tumarkin.
xGoodman, Ryah T.
Suddenly It's Evening. Bauhan.

Goodman, S. L. *see* Goodman, Saul Lederman.

Goodman, Sam R.
xGoodman, Sam R.
Controller's Handbook. Dow Jones-Irwin.
Financial Manager's Manual & Guide. P-H.

Goodman, Saul Lederman, 1901-
xGoodman, S. L.
The Faith of Secular Jews. Ktav.

Goodman, W. *see* Goodman, William.

Goodman, Walter.
xGoodman, Walter.
Committee: The Extraordinary Career of the
House Committee on un-American Activities.
FS&G.

Goodman, Walter. *see* Goodman, Elaine.

Goodman, William, 1915-
xGoodman, W.
Party System in America. P-H.

Goodman, Yetta M.
xGoodman, Yetta M.
Reading Strategies: Focus on Comprehension.
HR&W.

Goodnough, David.
xGoodnough, David.

Cherry Valley Massacre, November 11, 1778:
The Frontier Atrocity That Shocked a Young
Nation. Watts.
The Colony of New York. Watts.

Goodnow, Frank J. *see* Goodnow, Frank Johnson.

Goodnow, Frank Johnson, 1859-1939
xGoodnow, Frank J.
City Government in the United States. Arno.
Politics & Administration: A Study in
Government. Russell.

Goodnow, Jacqueline, 1924-
xGoodnow, Jacqueline.
Children Drawing. Harvard U Pr.

Goodpaster, Andrew J. *see* Goodpaster, Andrew Jackson.

Goodpaster, Andrew Jackson, 1915-
xGoodpaster, Andrew J.
For the Common Defense. Lexington Bks.

Goodpaster, Kenneth E.
xGoodpaster, Kenneth E.
ed. Ethics & Problems of the 21st Century. U
of Notre Dame Pr.

Goodrich, Carter, 1897-
xGoodrich, Carter.
Government Promotion of American Canals &
Railroads, 1800-1890. Greenwood.

Goodrich, Carter. *see* Goodrich, Carter Lyman.

Goodrich, Carter Lyman, 1897-
xGoodrich, Carter.
Canals & American Economic Development.
Kennikat.

Goodrich, Frances C.
xGoodrich, Frances C.
Third Adam. Philos Lib.

Goodrich, Frank C. *see* Goodrich, Frank Chauncey.

Goodrich, Frank Chauncey.
xGoodrich, Frank C.
A Primer of Quantum Chemistry. Krieger.

Goodrich, Frederick W. *see* Goodrich, Frederick Warren.

Goodrich, Frederick Warren, 1915-
xGoodrich, Frederick W.
Preparing for Childbirth: A Manual for
Expectant Parents. P-H.

Goodrich, Leland M. *see* Goodrich, Leland Matthew.

Goodrich, Leland Matthew.
xGoodrich, Leland M.
Charter of the United Nations: Commentary &
Documents. Columbia U Pr.
Korea: A Study of U. S. Policy in the United
Nations. Greenwood.
Korea: A Study of U. S. Policy in the United
Nations. Kraus Repr.

Goodrich, Marcus.
xGoodrich, Marcus.
Delilah. Popular Lib.

Goodrich, Norma L. *see* Goodrich, Norma Lorre.

Goodrich, Norma Lorre.
xGoodrich, Norma L.
Ancient Myths. NAL.
Medieval Myths. NAL.

Goodrich, Wallace, 1871-1952
xGoodrich, Wallace.
The Organ in France. Dunn & Webster.
The Organ in France. Longwood Pr.

Goodridge, Janet.
xGoodridge, Janet.
Creative Drama & Improvised Movement for
Children. Plays.

Goodsell, Jane.
xGoodsell, Jane.
Daniel Inouye. T Y Crowell.
Mayo Brothers. T Y Crowell.

Goodsell, Willystine, 1870-1962
xGoodsell, Willystine.
Conflict of Naturalism & Humanism. AMS Pr.
A History of Marriage & the Family. AMS Pr.

Goodson, Felix. *see* Goodson, Felix E.

Goodson, Felix E., 1922-
xGoodson, Felix.
Sweet Salt. C E Tuttle.

Goodson, J. M. *see* Goodson, Jo Max.

Goodson, Jo Max.
 xGoodson, J. M.
  Analysis of Human Mandibular Movement. S
  Karger.
Goodspeed, Donald J. *see* Goodspeed, Donald James.
Goodspeed, Donald James, 1919-
 xGoodspeed, Donald J.
  The German Wars 1914-1945. HM.
Goodspeed, Edgar J. *see* Goodspeed, Edgar Johnson.
Goodspeed, Edgar Johnson, 1871-1962
 xGoodspeed, Edgar J.
  Buying Happiness. Arno.
  Full History of the Wonderful Career of
   Moody & Sankey, in Great Britain &
   America. AMS Pr.
  History of Early Christian Literature. U of
   Chicago Pr.
  A Life of Jesus. Greenwood.
  Strange New Gospels. Arden Lib.
  Strange New Gospels. Arno.
  Things Seen & Heard. Arno.
Goodspeed, George S. *see* Goodspeed, George Stephen.
Goodspeed, George Stephen, 1860-1905
 xGoodspeed, George S.
  A History of the Babylonians & the Assyrians.
   Folcroft.
Goodstein, Leonard D. *see* Goodstein, Leonard David.
Goodstein, Leonard David.
 xGoodstein, Leonard D.
  Adjustment, Behavior, & Personality. A-W.
  Consulting with Human Service Systems. A-W.
Goodstein, R. L. *see* Goodstein, Reuben Louis.
Goodstein, Reuben Louis.
 xGoodstein, R. L.
  Fundamental Concepts of Mathematics.
   Pergamon.
Goodstone, Tony.
 xGoodstone, Tony.
  ed. The Pulps: Fifty Years of American Pop
   Culture. Chelsea Hse.
Goodwin, Albert.
 xGoodwin, Albert.
  The Friends of Liberty: The English
   Democratic Movement in the Age of the
   French Revolution. Harvard U Pr.
Goodwin, B. *see* Goodwin, Brian C.
Goodwin, B. L. *see* Goodwin, Brian L.
Goodwin, Brian C.
 xGoodwin, B.
  ed. Analytical Physiology of Cells &
   Developing Organisms. Acad Pr.
Goodwin, Brian L.
 xGoodwin, B. L.
  Handbook of Intermediate Metabolism of
   Aromatic Compounds. Methuen Inc.
Goodwin, Carole.
 xGoodwin, Carole.
  The Oak Park Strategy: Community Control of
   Racial Change. U of Chicago Pr.
Goodwin, Craufurd D. *see* Goodwin, Craufurd D. W.
Goodwin, Craufurd D. W.
 xGoodwin, Craufurd D.
  Canadian Economic Thought: The Political
   Economy of a Developing Nation,
   1814-1914. Duke.
  Exhortation & Controls: The Search for a
   Wage - Price Policy, 1945-1971. Brookings.
Goodwin, Derek.
 xGoodwin, Derek.
  Birds of Man's World. Cornell U Pr.
  Crows of the World. Cornell U Pr.
Goodwin, Donald W.
 xGoodwin, Donald W.
  ed. Alcoholism & Affective Disorders: Clinical,
   Genetic, & Biochemical Studies with
   Emphasis on Alcohol-Lithium Interaction.
   Spectrum Pub.
  Psychiatric Diagnosis. Oxford U Pr.
Goodwin, Gary C., 1940-
 xGoodwin, Gary C.

Cherokees in Transition: A Study of Changing
 Culture & Environment Prior to 1775. U
 Chicago Dept Geog.
Goodwin, George.
 xGoodwin, George.
  The Little Legislatures: Committees of
   Congress. U of Mass Pr.
Goodwin, John R., 1929-
 xGoodwin, John R.
  Business Law: Principles, Documents & Cases.
   Irwin.
  Travel & Lodging Law. Grid Pub.
Goodwin, John W.
 xGoodwin, John W.
  Agricultural Economics. Reston.
Goodwin, Leonard, 1929-
 xGoodwin, Leonard.
  Can Social Science Help Resolve National
   Problems?: Welfare, a Case in Point. Free Pr.
  Do the Poor Want to Work?: A
   Social-Psychological Study of Work
   Orientations. Brookings.
Goodwin, Maud (Wilder), 1856-1935
 xGoodwin, Maud W.
  ed. Historic New York. Friedman.
Goodwin, Maud W. *see* Goodwin, Maud (Wilder).
Goodwin, Stephen.
 xGoodwin, Stephen.
  The Blood of Paradise. Dutton.
Goodwin, T. W. *see* Goodwin, Trevor Walworth.
Goodwin, Trevor Walworth.
 xGoodwin, T. W.
  Introduction to Plant Biochemistry. Pergamon.
Goodwin, William L. *see* Goodwin, William Lawrence.
Goodwin, William Lawrence.
 xGoodwin, William L.
  Facilitating Student Learning: An Introduction
   to Educational Psychology. Har-Row.
  Handbook for Measurement & Evaluation in
   Early Childhood Education: Issues, Measures,
   & Methods. Jossey-Bass.
Goodwin, William W. *see* Goodwin, William Watson.
Goodwin, William Watson.
 xGoodwin, William W.
  Greek Grammar. St Martin.
Goodwin-Gill, Guy.
 xGoodwin-Gill, Guy S.
  International Law & the Movement of Persons
   Between States. Oxford U Pr.
Goodwin-Gill, Guy S. *see* Goodwin-Gill, Guy.
Goodwyn, Floyd L. *see* Goodwyn, Floyd Lowell.
Goodwyn, Floyd Lowell.
 xGoodwyn, Floyd L.
  Image Pattern & Moral Vision in John
   Webster. Humanities.
Goodwyn, Lawrence.
 xGoodwyn, Lawrence.
  Democratic Promise: The Populist Moment in
   America. Oxford U Pr.
  The Populist Moment: A Short History of the
   Agrarian Revolt in America. Oxford U Pr.
  The Populist Moment: A Short History of the
   Agrarian Revolt in America. Oxford U Pr.
Goody, J. R. *see* Goody, John Rankine.
Goody, Jack R. *see* Goody, John Rankine.
Goody, John Rankine.
 xGoody, J. R.
  Bridewealth & Dowry. Cambridge U Pr.
 xGoody, Jack R.
  ed. Literacy in Traditional Societies. Cambridge
   U Pr.
Goody, R. M.
 xGoody, Richard.
  Atmospheres. P-H.
Goody, Richard. *see* Goody, R. M.
Goodyear, F. H. *see* Goodyear, Frank Haigh.
Goodyear, Frank Haigh.
 xGoodyear, F. H.

 Archaeological Site Science. Elsevier.
Googe, Barnabe, 1540-1594
 xGooge, Barnabe.
  Eglogs, Epytaphes, & Sonettes, (1563). Schol
   Facsimiles.
Gooijer, C.
 xGooijer, C.
  The Interaction Between Alkali Cations &
   Azaaromatic Radical Anions: An ESR Study.
   Humanities.
Gookin, Daniel, 1612-1687
 xGookin, Daniel.
  Historical Account of the Doings & Sufferings
   of the Christian Indians in New England in
   the Years 1675, 1676, 1677. Arno.
Goolrick, Robert M.
 xGoolrick, Robert M.
  Public Policy Toward Corporate Growth: The
   ITT Merger Cases. Kennikat.
Goolrick, William. *see* Goolrick, William K.
Goolrick, William K.
 xGoolrick, William.
  The Battle of the Bulge. Time-Life.
Goolsby, Sam.
 xGoolsby, Sam.
  Great Southern Wild Game Cookbook. Pelican.
Gooneratne, Y. *see* Gooneratne, Yasmine.
Gooneratne, Yasmine, 1935-
 xGooneratne, Y.
  Alexander Pope. Cambridge U Pr.
Goossens, Eugene, Sir, 1893-1962
 xGoossens, Eugene.
  Overture & Beginners: A Musical
   Autobiography. Greenwood.
Gootnick, David.
 xGootnick, David.
  Getting a Better Job. McGraw.
Gootzeit, Michael J., 1939-
 xGootzeit, Michael J.
  David Ricardo. Columbia U Pr.
Gopal, Brij.
 xGopal, Brij.
  Elements of Ecology. Advent Bk.
Gopal, M. H. *see* Gopal, Mysore Hatti.
Gopal, Madan.
 xGopal, Madan.
  Munshi Premchand: A Literary Biography.
   Asia.
Gopal, Mysore Hatti, 1904-
 xGopal, M. H.
  Introduction to Research Procedure in Social
   Sciences. Asia.
Gopal, R.
 xGopal, R.
  ed. Energy Conservation in Building Heating &
   Air Conditioning Systems. ASME.
Gopalakrishnan, P.
 xGopalakrishnan, P.
  Computers in India: An Overview.
   InterCulture.
Gopalan, S. *see* Gopalan, Subramania.
Gopalan, Subramania, 1935-
 xGopalan, S.
  Outlines of Jainism. Halsted Pr.
Gopnik, Myrna.
 xGopnik, Myrna.
  Linguistic Structures in Scientific Texts.
   Mouton.
Goran, Horris. *see* Goran, Morris Herbert.
Goran, Morris. *see* Goran, Morris Herbert.
Goran, Morris H. *see* Goran, Morris Herbert.
Goran, Morris Herbert, 1916-
 xGoran, Horris.
  A Preface to Astronomy. Technomic.
 xGoran, Morris.

Fact, Fraud, & Fantasy: The Occult &
Pseudosciences. A S Barnes.
Fact, Fraud, & Fantasy: The Occult &
Pseudosciences. Littlefield.
Story of Fritz Haber. U of Okla Pr.
xGoran, Morris H.
Experimental Astronautics. Sams.
Gorbachev, V. M. see Gorbachev, Valentin Matveevich.
Gorbachev, Valentin Matveevich.
xGorbachev, V. M.
Nuclear Reactions in Heavy Elements: A Data
Handbook. Pergamon.
Gorbet, Larry.
xGorbet, Larry P.
A Grammar of Diegueno Nominals. Garland
Pub.
Gorbet, Larry P. see Gorbet, Larry.
Gorchakov, Nikolai A. see Gorchakov, Nikolai
Aleksandrovich.
Gorchakov, Nikolai Aleksandrovich, 1901-
xGorchakov, Nikolai A.
Theater in Soviet Russia. Arno.
Gordimer, Nadine.
xGordimer, Nadine.
Burger's Daughter. Penguin.
Burger's Daughter. Viking Pr.
Gordis, R. see Gordis, Robert.
Gordis, Robert, 1908-
xGordis, R.
The Book of Job: Commentary, New
Translation & Special Studies. Ktav.
xGordis, Robert.
Faith for Moderns. Bloch.
Understanding Conservative Judaism. Ktav.
The Word & the Book: Studies in Biblical
Language & Literature. Ktav.
Gordon. see Gordon, Gordon.
Gordon, Alvin. see Gordon, Alvin J.
Gordon, Alvin J.
xGordon, Alvin.
Inherit the Earth: Stories from Mexican Ranch
Life. U of Ariz Pr.
Of Vines & Missions. Northland.
Gordon, Andrew.
xGordon, Andrew M.
An American Dreamer: A Psychoanalytic
Study of the Fiction of Norman Mailer.
Fairleigh Dickinson.
Gordon, Andrew M. see Gordon, Andrew.
Gordon, Arnold J.
xGordon, Arnold J.
Chemist's Companion: A Handbook of
Practical Data, Techniques, & References.
Wiley.
Gordon, Arthur E.
xGordon, Arthur E.
The Inscribed Fibula Praenestina: Problems of
Authenticity. U of Cal Pr.
Gordon, Arthur E. see Gordon, Arthur Ernest.
Gordon, Arthur Ernest, 1902-
xGordon, Arthur E.
The Letter Names of the Latin Alphabet. U of
Cal Pr.
Gordon, Audrey. see Gordon, Audrey K.
Gordon, Audrey K.
xGordon, Audrey.
They Need to Know: How to Teach Children
About Death. P-H.
Gordon, Barbara, 1935-
xGordon, Barbara.
I'm Dancing As Fast As I Can. Bantam.
I'm Dancing As Fast As I Can. Har-Row.
Gordon, Bernard. see Gordon, Bernard L.
Gordon, Bernard L.
xGordon, Bernard.
Once There Was a Giant Sea Cow. McKay.
xGordon, Bernard L.

ed. Energy from the Sea: Marine Resource
Readings. U Pr of Amer.
ed. Hurricane in Southern New England: An
Analysis of the Great Storm of 1938. Book &
Tackle.
If an Auk Could Talk. Walck.
ed. Marine Careers: Selected Papers. Book &
Tackle.
Once There Was a Giant Sea Cow. McKay.
Gordon, Bertram. see Gordon, Bertram M.
Gordon, Bertram M., 1945-
xGordon, Bertram.
Collaborationism in France During the Second
World War. Cornell U Pr.
Gordon, Beverly.
xGordon, Beverly.
Feltmaking: Traditions, Techniques &
Contemporary Explorations. Watson-Guptill.
Shaker Textile Arts. U Pr of New Eng.
Gordon, C. G. see Gordon, Charles George.
Gordon, C. W. see Gordon, Charlotte W.
Gordon, Caroline, 1895-
xGordon, Caroline.
Aleck Maury, Sportsman. Cooper Sq.
Aleck Maury, Sportsman: A Novel. S Ill U Pr.
Garden of Adonis. Cooper Sq.
Green Centuries. Cooper Sq.
None Shall Look Back. Cooper Sq.
Penhally. Cooper Sq.
Strange Children. Cooper Sq.
Gordon, Charles George.
xGordon, C. G.
Colonel Gordon in Central Africa, 1874-1879.
Kraus Repr.
Gordon, Charlotte W.
xGordon, C. W.
Handbook of Astronomy, Astrophysics, &
Geophysics. Gordon
Gordon, Colin.
xGordon, Colin.
A Richer Dust: Echoes from an Edwardian
Album. Lippincott.
Gordon, Cosmo, Sir, 1777-1867
xGordon, Cosmo.
Life & Genius of Lord Byron. Folcroft.
Gordon, Cyrus.
xGordon, Cyrus H.
Common Background of Greek & Hebrew
Civilizations. Norton.
Gordon, Cyrus H. see Gordon, Cyrus.
Gordon, Cyrus Herzl, 1908-
xGordon, Cyrus H.
Homer & Bible: The Origin & Character of
East Mediterranean Literature. Ventnor.
Gordon, David C. see Gordon, David Cole.
Gordon, David Cole.
xGordon, David C.
Overcoming the Fear of Death. Macmillan.
Gordon, David J.
xGordon, David J.
Literary Art & the Unconscious. La State U Pr.
Gordon, David M.
xGordon, David M.
Problems in Political Economy: An Urban
Perspective. Heath.
Gordon, Donald C. see Gordon, Donald Craigie.
Gordon, Donald Craigie, 1911-
xGordon, Donald C.
Australian Frontier in New Guinea, 1870-1885.
AMS Pr.
Gordon, Douglas H. see Gordon, Douglas Hamilton.
Gordon, Douglas Hamilton.
xGordon, Douglas H.
The Pre-Historic Background of Indian Culture.
Greenwood.
Gordon, Edmund I.
xGordon, Edmund I.

Sumerian Proverbs: Glimpses of Everyday Life
in Ancient Mesopotamia. Greenwood.
Gordon, Edwin.
xGordon, Edwin.
Intro. by & ed. Experimental Research in the
Psychology of Music. U of Iowa Pr.
Psychology of Music Teaching. P-H.
Gordon, Elinor.
xGordon, Elinor.
Collecting Chinese Export Porcelain. Universe.
Gordon, Ethel E. see Gordon, Ethel Edison.
Gordon, Ethel Edison.
xGordon, Ethel E.
The French Husband. T Y Crowell.
Gordon, Everett J.
xGordon, Everett J.
Practical Medico-Legal Guide for the
Physician. C C Thomas.
Gordon, F. see Gordon, Francine E.
Gordon, Francine E.
xGordon, F.
Bringing Women into Management. McGraw.
Gordon, Frank S.
xGordon, Frank S.
The Legal Word Book. HM.
Gordon, Geoffrey.
xGordon, Geoffrey.
System Simulation. P-H.
Gordon, George. see Gordon, George J.
Gordon, George B. see Gordon, George Byron.
Gordon, George Byron, 1870-1927
xGordon, George B.
In the Alaskan Wilderness. AMS Pr.
Gordon, George G.
xGordon, George G.
Managing Management Climate. Lexington
Bks.
Gordon, George J.
xGordon, George.
Public Administration in America. St Martin.
Gordon, George N.
xGordon, George N.
Classroom Television: New Frontiers in ITV.
Hastings.
ed. Communications & Media: Constructing a
Cross-Discipline. Hastings.
The Communications Revolution: A History of
Mass Media in the United States. Hastings.
Erotic Communications: Studies in Sex, Sin &
Censorship. Hastings.
Idea Invaders. Hastings.
Gordon, George S. see Gordon, George Stuart.
Gordon, George Stuart, 1881-1942
xGordon, George S.
English Literature & the Classics. Folcroft.
ed. English Literature & the Classics. Russell.
Lives of Authors. Arno.
Lives of the Authors. R West.
Gordon, Gilbert.
xGordon, Gilbert.
Quantitative Decision-Making for Business.
P-H.
Gordon, Gordon.
xGordon.
Ordeal. Berkley Pub.
Gordon, Harold J.
xGordon, Harold J.
Hitler & the Beer Hall Putsch. Princeton U Pr.
Gordon, Herbert. see Gordon, I. Herbert.
Gordon, I. Herbert.
xGordon, Herbert.
The Canoe Book. McGraw.
Gordon, I. R. see Gordon, I. R. F.
Gordon, I. R. F.
xGordon, I. R.
A Preface to Pope. Longman.
Gordon, Ira J.
xGordon, Ira J.

Baby Learning Through Baby Play: A Parent's
Guide for the First Two Years. St Martin.
Child Learning Through Child Play: Learning
Activities for Two & Three-Year-Olds. St
Martin.
Human Development: A Transactional
Perspective. Har-Row.
Gordon, Irving L., 1915-
xGordon, Irving L.
American Studies: A Conceptual Approach.
AMSCO Sch.
Review Text in American History. AMSCO
Sch.
Review Text in World History. AMSCO Sch.
Gordon, Jan, 1882-1944
xGordon, Jan.
Modern French Painters. Arno.
Gordon, John, 1925-
xGordon, John.
The Ghost on the Hill. Viking Pr.
Gordon, John. see Gordon, John Frazer.
Gordon, John E., 1931-
xGordon, John E.
How to Succeed in Organic Chemistry. Wiley.
The Organic Chemistry of Electrolyte
Solutions. Wiley.
Gordon, John F. see Gordon, John Frazer.
Gordon, John Frazer.
xGordon, John.
The Alaskan Malamute. Arco.
Borzoi. Arco.
xGordon, John F.
The German Shepherd. Arco.
Gordon, John M.
xGordon, John M.
Resurrection Messages. Baker Bk.
Gordon, Katharine.
xGordon, Katharine.
The Emerald Peacock. Morrow.
Gordon, Larry.
xGordon, Larry.
Barely Audible: A History of the Denver
Broncos. Graphic Impress.
Gordon, Leonard.
xGordon, Leonard.
Sociology & American Social Issues. HM.
Gordon, Leonard A.
xGordon, Leonard A.
Syllabus of Indian Civilization. Columbia U Pr.
Gordon, Leonard H. see Gordon, Leonard H. D.
Gordon, Leonard H. D., 1928-
xGordon, Leonard H.
ed. Taiwan: Studies in Chinese Local History.
Columbia U Pr.
Gordon, Lincoln.
xGordon, Lincoln.
Growth Policies & the International Order.
McGraw.
Gordon, Louise.
xGordon, Louise.
How to Draw the Human Figure: An
Anatomical Approach. Penguin.
Gordon, M. see Gordon, Mitchell.
Gordon, M. J. see Gordon, Michael J. C.
Gordon, Malcolm S.
xGordon, Malcolm S.
Animal Physiology: Principles & Adaptations.
Macmillan.
Gordon, Margaret, 1939-
xGordon, Margaret.
illus. A Paper of Pins. HM.
Gordon, Margaret S.
xGordon, Margaret S.
Economics of Welfare Policies. Columbia U Pr.
Gordon, Marshall.
xGordon, Marshall.
A First Course in Statistics. Macmillan.
Gordon, Mary.
xGordon, Mary.

Final Payments. Ballantine.
Final Payments. Random.
Gordon, Maurice B. see Gordon, Maurice Bear.
Gordon, Maurice Bear, 1916-
xGordon, Maurice B.
Naval & Maritime Medicine During the
American Revolution. Ventnor.
Gordon, Michael.
xGordon, Michael.
The American Family in Social-Historical
Perspective. St Martin.
Gordon, Michael J. C., 1948-
xGordon, M.
Edinburgh LCF: A Mechanised Logic of
Computation. Springer-Verlag.
xGordon, M. J.
The Denotational Description of Programming
Languages: An Introduction. Springer-Verlag.
Gordon, Michael R., 1939-
xGordon, Michael R.
Conflict & Consensus in Labour's Foreign
Policy, 1914-1965. Stanford U Pr.
Gordon, Michael W.
xGordon, Michael W.
The Cuban Nationalizations: The Demise of
Foreign Private Property. W S Hein.
Gordon, Milton M. see Gordon, Milton Myron.
Gordon, Milton Myron, 1918-
xGordon, Milton M.
Assimilation in American Life: The Role of
Race, Religion & National Origins. Oxford U
Pr.
Human Nature, Class, & Ethnicity. Oxford U
Pr.
Gordon, Mitchell.
xGordon, M.
Sick Cities. Macmillan.
Gordon, Murray.
xGordon, Murray.
Conflict in the Persian Gulf. Facts on File.
Gordon, Myron.
xGordon, Myron.
Theme-Centered Interaction: An Original
Focus on Counseling & Education. Natl Educ
Pr.
Gordon, Myron J.
xGordon, Myron J.
Accounting: A Management Approach. Irwin.
The Cost of Capital to a Public Utility. Mich St
U Busn.
Gordon, Noah.
xGordon, Noah.
The Jerusalem Diamond. Random.
Gordon, Patricia.
xGordon, Patricia.
The Boy Jones. Gregg.
Gordon, Paul, 1918-
xGordon, Paul.
Principles of Phase Diagrams in Materials
Systems. McGraw.
Gordon, Pearl, 1927-
xGordon, Pearl S.
Simply Elegant: A Guide for Elegant but
Simple Entertaining. Simply Elegant.
Gordon, Pearl S. see Gordon, Pearl.
Gordon, Peter.
xGordon, Peter.
Philosophers As Educational Reformers: The
Influence of Idealism on British Educational
Thought & Practice, 1875-1925. Routledge &
Kegan.
Gordon, Philip.
xGordon, Philip.
The Availability of Contemporary American
Music for Performing Groups in High
Schools & Colleges. AMS Pr.
Gordon, R. A. see Gordon, Roderick Angus.
Gordon, R. L. see Gordon, Richard Laurence.
Gordon, Richard Laurence.
xGordon, R. L.

You'll Hear Me Laughing. T Y Crowell.
Gordon, Robert A. see Gordon, Robert Aaron.
Gordon, Robert Aaron.
xGordon, Robert A.
Economic Instability & Growth: The American
Record. Har-Row.
Gordon, Roderick Angus, 1911-
xGordon, R. A.
Anaesthesia & Resuscitation: A Manual for
Medical Students. U of Toronto Pr.
Gordon, Roderick D.
xGordon, Roderick D.
The World of Musical Sound. Kendall-Hunt.
Gordon, Ronald. see Gordon, Ronald J.
Gordon, Ronald J.
xGordon, Ronald.
Cardiovascular Physiology for
Anesthesiologists. C C Thomas.
Gordon, Roxy.
xGordon, Roxy L.
Some Things I Did. Encino Pr.
Gordon, Roxy L. see Gordon, Roxy.
Gordon, S. see Gordon, Saul.
Gordon, Sanford D.
xGordon, Sanford D.
Introductory Economics. Heath.
Gordon, Saul.
xGordon, S.
Gordon's Modern Annotated Forms of
Agreement. P-H.
Gordon, Sheila.
xGordon, Sheila.
A Monster in the Mailbox. Dutton.
Gordon, Shirley.
xGordon, Shirley.
The Boy Who Wanted a Family. Har-Row.
Crystal Is My Friend. Har-Row.
Crystal Is the New Girl. Har-Row.
Grandma Zoo. Har-Row.
Gordon, Sid. see Gordon, Sid W.
Gordon, Sid W.
xGordon, Sid.
How to Fish from Top to Bottom. Stackpole.
Gordon, Sol, 1923-
xGordon, Sol.
The Facts About VD for Today's Youth. John
Day.
Gordon, Stewart.
xGordon, Stewart.
Gunswift. Belmont-Tower.
Gordon, Suzanne, 1945-
xGordon, Suzanne.
Lonely in America. S&S.
Lonely in America. S&S.
Gordon, Taylor, 1893-
xGordon, Taylor.
Born to Be. U of Wash Pr.
Gordon, Theodore J.
xGordon, Theodore J.
Life-Extending Technologies: A Technology
Assessment. Pergamon.
Gordon, Thomas F. see Gordon, Thomas Francis.
Gordon, Thomas Francis, 1787-1860
xGordon, Thomas F.
History of Pennsylvania, from Its Discovery by
Europeans to the Declaration of
Independence in 1776. Reprint.
Gordon, Walter K.
xGordon, Walter K.
ed. Literature in Critical Perspectives: An
Anthology. P-H.
Gordon, Wendell C. see Gordon, Wendell Chaffee.
Gordon, Wendell Chaffee, 1916-
xGordon, Wendell C.
The Expropriation of Foreign Owned Property
in Mexico. Arno.
The Expropriation of Foreign-Owned Property
in Mexico. Greenwood.
Gordon, William, 1728-1807
xGordon, William.

History of the Rise, Progress, & Establishment
of the Independence of the United States of
America. Arno.
Gordon, William J. see Gordon, William J. J.
Gordon, William J. J.
xGordon, William J.
Synectics: The Development of Creative
Capacity. Macmillan.
Gordon, Yvonne.
xGordon, Yvonne.
Moment of Magic. Ace Bks.
Gordons, The.
xTheGordons.
Night After the Wedding. Doubleday.
Gordy, Walter, 1909-
xGordy, Walter.
Theory & Applications of Electron Spin
Resonance. Wiley.
Gore, Art, 1926-
xGore, Art.
Images of Yesterday. Crown.
Gore, Catherine.
xGore, Catherine.
Dalmatians. Arco.
Dalmatians. Palmetto Pub.
Gore, Daniel.
xGore, Daniel.
ed. Farewell to Alexandria: Solutions to Space,
Growth & Performance Problems of
Libraries. Greenwood.
Gore, George J.
xGore, George J.
The Academic-Consultant Connection.
Kendall-Hunt.
Gore, George W. see Gore, George William.
Gore, George William, 1901-
xGore, George W.
In-Service Professional Improvement of Negro
Public School Teachers in Tennessee. AMS
Pr.
Gore, H. see Gore, Harriet Margolis.
Gore, Harriet Margolis.
xGore, H.
What to Do When There's No One but You.
P-H.
Gore, Irene.
xGore, Irene.
Add Years to Your Life & Life to Your Years.
Stein & Day.
Gore, Marvin.
xGore, Marvin.
Computers & Data Processing. McGraw.
Elements of Systems Analysis for Business
Data Processing. Wm C Brown.
Gore, Thomas P. see Gore, Thomas Page.
Gore, Thomas Page, 1900-
xGore, Thomas P.
Gore's Forms for Tennessee Annotated.
Michie.
Gorecki, Jan.
xGorecki, Jan.
ed. Sociology & Jurisprudence of Leon
Petrazycki. U of Ill Pr.
A Theory of Criminal Justice. Columbia U Pr.
Goren, Charles H. see Goren, Charles Henry.
Goren, Charles Henry, 1901-
xGoren, Charles H.
Charles H. Goren's New Contract Bridge in a
Nutshell. Doubleday.
Goren's Modern Backgammon Complete.
Doubleday.
Play As You Learn Bridge. Doubleday.
Precision Bridge for Everyone. Doubleday.
Gorenstein, Shirley.
xGorenstein, Shirley.
North America. St Martin.
Prehispanic America. St Martin.
Gorer, Geoffrey.
xGorer, Geoffrey.

The Life & Ideas of the Marquis de Sade.
Greenwood.
Gorer, Richard.
xGorer, Richard.
The Growth of Gardens. Merrimack Bk Serv.
Goreux, Louis M., 1927-
xGoreux, Louis M.
Interdependence in Planning: Multilevel
Programming Studies of the Ivory Coast.
Johns Hopkins.
Gorey, Edward. see Gorey, Edward St. John.
Gorey, Edward St. John.
xGorey, Edward.
Amphigorey. Berkley Pub.
Amphigorey. Putnam.
The Awdrey-Gore Legacy. Dodd.
Dancing Cats & Neglected Murderesses.
Workman Pub.
Fletcher & Zenobia Save the Circus. Dodd.
Gorey Games. Troubador Pr.
The Loathsome Couple. Dodd.
Gorham, Melvin. see Gorham, Melvin Ezell.
Gorham, Melvin E. see Gorham, Melvin Ezell.
Gorham, Melvin Ezell, 1910-
xGorham, Melvin.
The Ring Cycle. Sovereign Pr.
xGorham, Melvin E.
Pagan Bible. Binford.
Goring, C. A. see Goring, Cleve A. I.
Goring, Cleve A. I.
xGoring, C. A.
ed. Organic Chemicals in the Soil
Environment. Dekker.
Gorlick. see Gorlick, Sheldon H.
Gorlick, Sheldon H.
xGorlick.
Now That You've Incorporated: A
Management Manual for Physicians. Van
Nos Reinhold.
Gorlin, R. V. see Gorlin, Robert J.
Gorlin, Richard.
xGorlin, Richard.
Coronary Artery Disease. Saunders.
Gorlin, Robert J.
xGorlin, R. V.
Syndromes of the Head & Neck. McGraw.
Gorman, B. S. see Gorman, Bernard S.
Gorman, Bernard S.
xGorman, B. S.
ed. The Personal Experience of Time. Plenum
Pub.
Gorman, D. J. see Gorman, Daniel J.
Gorman, Daniel J., 1930-
xGorman, D. J.
Free Vibration Analysis of Beams & Shafts.
Wiley.
Gorman, G. E.
xGorman, G. E.
ed. The South African Novel in English Since
1950: An Information & Resource Guide. G
K Hall.
Gorman, George. see Gorman, George Humphrey.
Gorman, George Humphrey.
xGorman, George.
The Society of Friends. Pergamon.
Gorman, James E., 1940-
xGorman, James E.
Simplified Guide to Construction Management
for Architects & Engineers. CBI Pub.
Gorman, Michael.
xGorman, Michael.
ed. Anglo-American Cataloguing Rules. ALA.
Gorman, Ralph.
xGorman, Ralph.
Last Hours of Jesus. Guild Bks.
Gorman, Robert.
xGorman, Robert.

Catholic Apologetical Literature in the United
States (1784-1858). AMS Pr.
Gorman, T. P.
xGorman, T. P.
Advanced Reading & Composition Skills: A
Workbook for Students of English. P-H.
Gorman, Tom.
xGorman, Tom.
Three & Two!. Berkley Pub.
Gorman, Walter. see Gorman, Walter P.
Gorman, Walter P.
xGorman, Walter.
Selling: Personality Persuasion Strategy.
Random.
Gormican, Annette.
xGormican, Annette.
Controlling Diabetes with Diet. C C Thomas.
Gormley, William T., 1950-
xGormley, William T.
Effects of Newspaper-Television
Cross-Ownership on News Homogeneity. U
NC Inst Res Soc Sci.
Gorney, Roderic, 1924-
xGorney, Roderic.
The Human Agenda. Guild of Tutors.
The Human Agenda. S&S.
Gornick, Vivian.
xGornick, Vivian.
Essays in Feminism. Har-Row.
Gornitz, Vivien.
xGornitz, Vivien.
ed. Geology of the Planet Mars. DH&R.
Gorodetzky, Charles. see Gorodetzky, Charles W.
Gorodetzky, Charles W.
xGorodetzky, Charles.
What You Should Know About Drugs.
HarBraceJ.
Gorodetzky, Nadejda, 1904-
xGorodetzky, Nadejda.
Humiliated Christ in Modern Russian Thought.
AMS Pr.
Gorog, Ralph De. see De Gorog, Ralph.
Gorostiza, Jose, 1901-
xGorostiza, Jose.
Death Without End. U of Tex Hum Res.
Gorovitz, Samuel.
xGorovitz, Samuel.
Philosophical Analysis: An Introduction to Its
Language & Techniques. Random.
Gorr, Alan.
xGorr, Alan.
ed. Problems in Todays Education. Mss Info.
Gorree, Georges.
xGorree, Georges.
Love Without Boundaries: Mother Teresa of
Calcutta. Our Sunday Visitor.
Gorrell, Robert. see Gorrell, Robert M.
Gorrell, Robert M.
xGorrell, Robert.
Modern English Handbook. P-H.
Gorshkov, S. G. see Gorshkov, Sergei Georgievich.
Gorshkov, Sergei. see Gorshkov, Sergei Georgievich.
Gorshkov, Sergei Georgievich, 1910-
xGorshkov, S. G.
Sea Power of the State. Pergamon.
xGorshkov, Sergei.
Sea Power of the State. Naval Inst Pr.
Gorski, Berni.
xGorski, Berni.
Beyond Limitations: The Creative Art of the
Mentally Retarded. C C Thomas.
Gorst, Sheila.
xGorst, Sheila.
Co-Operative Credit for Producers &
Consumers. Intl Pubns Serv.
Gorsuch, Edwin N.
xGorsuch, Edwin N.
The Future of Atlanta's Central City. Ga St U
Busn Pub.
Gorter, C. J. see Gorter, Cornelis Jacobus.

Gorter, Cornelis Jacobus, 1907-
　xGorter, C. J.
　　ed. Progress in Low Temperature Physics.
　　　Elsevier.
Gorth, William P.
　xGorth, William P.
　　Comprehensive Achievement Monitoring: A
　　　Criterion-Referenced Evaluation System.
　　　Educ Tech Pubns.
Gortner, H. F. see Gortner, Harold F.
Gortner, Harold F., 1940-
　xGortner, H. F.
　　Administration in the Public Sector. Wiley.
Gorton, Audrey A. see Gorton, Audrey Alley.
Gorton, Audrey Alley.
　xGorton, Audrey A.
　　Venison Book: How to Dress, Cut up & Cook
　　　Your Deer. Greene.
Gorton, Richard A.
　xGorton, Richard A.
　　School Administration & Supervision:
　　　Important Issues, Concepts & Case Studies.
　　　Wm C Brown.
Gorton, Ron.
　xGorton, Ron.
　　The Lawyers of Hell. Fell.
Gorvine, Beverly. see Gorvine, Beverly F.
Gorvine, Beverly F.
　xGorvine, Beverly.
　　ed. Maternal-Newborn Nursing: PreTest
　　　Self-Assessment & Review. McGraw-Pretest.
Gosch, Martin A.
　xGosch, Martin A.
　　The Last Testament of Lucky Luciano. Little.
Goschen, George J. see Goschen, George Joachim
　Goschen.
Goschen, George Joachim Goschen, Viscount, 1831-1907
　xGoschen, George J.
　　The Theory of the Foreign Exchanges. Arno.
Gosciewski, F. William.
　xGosciewski, F. William.
　　Effective Child Rearing: The Behaviorally
　　　Aware Parent. Human Sci Pr.
Goscinny. see Goscinny, Rene.
Goscinny, R. see Goscinny, Rene.
Goscinny, Rene.
　xGoscinny.
　　Asterix & Cleopatra. Charles River Bks.
　　Asterix the Gaul. Charles River Bks.
　　Asterix the Legionary. Charles River Bks.
　xGoscinny, R.
　　Asterix & Cleopatra. French & Eur.
　　Asterix the Gaul. French & Eur.
　　Asterix the Legionary. French & Eur.
　　Asterix y Cleopatra. French & Eur.
Gosden, P. H. see Gosden, P. H. J. H.
Gosden, P. H. J. H.
　xGosden, P. H.
　　Friendly Societies in England, 1815-1875.
　　　Kelley.
Gosfield, Alice.
　xGosfield, Alice.
　　PSRO's: The Law & the Health Consumer.
　　　Ballinger Pub.
Goshen, Charles E.
　xGoshen, Charles E.
　　Drinks, Drugs, & Do-Gooders. Free Pr.
　　Society & the Youthful Offender. C C Thomas.
Goshgarian, Gary.
　xGoshgarian, Gary.
　　ed. Exploring Language. Little.
Gosline, William A.
　xGosline, William A.
　　Functional Morphology & Classification of
　　　Teleostean Fishes. U Pr of Hawaii.
Gosling, J. C. see Gosling, Justin Cyril Bertrand.
Gosling, Justin Cyril Bertrand.
　xGosling, J. C.
　　Plato. Routledge & Kegan.
Gosling, William G. see Gosling, William Gilbert.

Gosling, William Gilbert, 1863-
　xGosling, William G.
　　Life of Sir Humphrey Gilbert, England's First
　　　Empire Builder. Greenwood.
Gosnell, Cullen B. see Gosnell, Cullen Bryant.
Gosnell, Cullen Bryant.
　xGosnell, Cullen B.
　　Fundamentals of American Government:
　　　National, State & Local. Greenwood.
Gosnell, Harold F. see Gosnell, Harold Foote.
Gosnell, Harold Foote.
　xGosnell, Harold F.
　　American Parties & Elections. Merrill.
　　Boss Platt & His New York Machine: A Study
　　　of the Political Leadership of Thomas C.
　　　Platt, Theodore Roosevelt, & Others. Ams
　　　Pr.
　　Democracy, the Threshold of Freedom.
　　　Greenwood.
　　Getting Out the Vote: An Experiment in the
　　　Stimulation of Voting. AMS Pr.
　　Getting Out the Vote: An Experiment in the
　　　Stimulation of Voting. Greenwood.
　　Grass Roots Politics: National Voting Behavior
　　　of Typical States. Russell.
　　Negro Politicians: The Rise of Negro Politics
　　　in Chicago. U of Chicago Pr.
　　Truman's Crises: A Political Biography of
　　　Harry S. Truman. Greenwood.
Gosney, E. S. see Gosney, Ezra Seymour.
Gosney, Ezra Seymour.
　xGosney, E. S.
　　Sterilization for Human Betterment. Arno.
Goss, Albert E.
　xGoss, Albert E.
　　Paired-Associates Learning: The Role of
　　　Meaningfulness, Similarity & Familiarization.
　　　Acad Pr.
Goss, Helen (Rocca).
　xGoss, Helen R.
　　The California White Cap Murders: An
　　　Episode in Vigilantism. Holmes.
Goss, Helen R. see Goss, Helen (Rocca).
Goss, John D. see Goss, John Dean.
Goss, John Dean.
　xGoss, John D.
　　History of Tariff Administration in the United
　　　States from Colonial Times to the McKinley
　　　Administrative Bill. AMS Pr.
Goss, Madeleine. see Goss, Madeleine (Binkley).
Goss, Madeleine (Binkley), 1892-
　xGoss, Madeleine.
　　Modern Music-Makers: Contemporary
　　　American Composers. Greenwood.
Goss, Michael.
　xGoss, Michael.
　　Compiled by Poltergeists: An Annotated
　　　Bibliography of Works in English, Circa
　　　1880-1975. Scarecrow.
Goss, R. O.
　xGoss, R. O.
　　ed. Advances in Maritime Economics.
　　　Cambridge U Pr.
　　Studies in Maritime Economics. Cambridge U
　　　Pr.
Goss, Richard J.
　xGoss, Richard J.
　　Adaptive Growth. Acad Pr.
　　Principles of Regeneration. Acad Pr.
Gossage, Loyce C.
　xGossage, Loyce C.
　　Business Mathematics: A College Course. SW
　　　Pub.
Gosse, E. see Gosse, Edmund William.
Gosse, Edmund. see Gosse, Edmund William.
Gosse, Edmund W. see Gosse, Edmund William.
Gosse, Edmund William, Sir, 1849-1928
　xGosse, E.
　　Aspects & Impressions. R West.
　xGosse, Edmund.

Aspects & Impressions. Arden Lib.
Books on the Table. R West.
English Odes. Folcroft.
From Shakespeare to Pope: An Inquiry into the
　Causes & Phenomena of the Rise of Classical
　Poetry in England. R West.
Gossip in a Library. R West.
Gray. R West.
History of Eighteenth Century Literature.
　Arno.
A History of Eighteenth Century Literature.
　Folcroft.
Life of William Congreve. Folcroft.
Life of William Congreve. Kennikat.
More Books on the Table. R West.
Northern Studies. Kennikat.
Northern Studies. R West.
Portraits & Sketches. Norwood Edns.
Questions at Issue. Arno.
Questions at Issue. Folcroft.
Silhouettes. R West.
Swinburne: An Essay Written in 1875 & Now
　First Printed. Folcroft.
　xGosse, Edmund W.
　　Aspects & Impressions. Arno.
　　Aspects & Impressions. Johnson Repr.
　　Aspects & Impressions. Scholarly.
　　Books on the Table. Arno.
　　Coventry Patmore. Greenwood.
　　Coventry Patmore. R West.
　　Coventry Patmore. Scholarly.
　　English Odes. Folcroft.
　　From Shakespeare to Pope: An Inquiry into the
　　　Causes & Phenomena of the Rise of Classical
　　　Poetry in England. Kraus Repr.
　　Gossip in a Library. Scholarly.
　　Gray. AMS Pr.
　　Leaves & Fruit. Arno.
　　Life of William Congreve. Somerset Pub.
　　More Books on the Table. Arno.
　　Portraits & Sketches. Arno.
　　Portraits & Sketches. Scholarly.
　　Raleigh. Folcroft.
　　Silhouettes. Arno.
　　Some Diversions of a Man of Letters. Arno.
　　Some Diversions of a Man of Letters. R West.
Gosse, Philip, 1879-1959
　xGosse, Philip.
　　History of Piracy. B Franklin.
　　The History of Piracy. Gale.
Gosselin, Louis L. see Gosselin, Louis Leon Theodore.
Gosselin, Louis Leon Theodore, 1857-1935
　xGosselin, Louis L.
　　Flight of Marie Antoinette. AMS Pr.
Gossen, Gary H.
　xGossen, Gary H.
　　Chamulas in the World of the Sun: Time &
　　　Space in a Maya Oral Tradition. Harvard U
　　　Pr.
Gossez, J. P., 1943-
　xGossez, J. P.
　　ed. Nonlinear Operators & the Calculus &
　　　Variations: Summer School Held in Bruxelles,
　　　8-19 Sept. 1975. Springer-Verlag.
Gostelow, Mary.
　xGostelow, Mary.
　　The Complete International Book of
　　　Embroidery. S&S.
　　Mary Gostelow's Embroidery Book. Dutton.
　　A World of Embroidery. Scribner.
Gosvami, O.
　xGosvami, O.
　　The Story of Indian Music: Its Growth &
　　　Synthesis. Scholarly.
Goswami, Amit.
　xGoswami, Amit.
　　The Concepts of Physics. Heath.
Goswami, B. C. see Goswami, Bhuvenesh Chandra.
Goswami, Bhuvenesh Chandra.
　xGoswami, B. C.

Textile Yarns: Technology, Structure &
Applications. Wiley.
Gothmann, W. see Gothmann, William H.
Gothmann, William H., 1937-
xGothmann, W.
Electronics: A Contemporary Approach. P-H.
Gotlieb, Phylkis (Bloom).
xGotlieb, Phyllis.
Sunburst. Berkley Pub.
Gotlieb, Phyllis. see Gotlieb, Phylkis (Bloom).
Goto, Toshio.
xGoto, Toshio.
Problems in Advanced Organic Chemistry.
Holden-Day.
Gotoff, Harold C.
xGotoff, Harold C.
Cicero's Elegant Style: An Analysis of the Pro
Archia. U of Ill Pr.
Gotshalk, D. W. see Gotshalk, Dilman Walter.
Gotshalk, Dilman W. see Gotshalk, Dilman Walter.
Gotshalk, Dilman Walter, 1901-
xGotshalk, D. W.
Patterns of Good & Evil: A Value Analysis. U
of Ill Pr.
xGotshalk, Dilman W.
Structure & Reality: A Study of First
Principles. Greenwood.
Gotshall, Daniel.
xGotshall, Daniel W.
Fishwatchers' Guide to the Inshore Fishes of
the Pacific Coast. Sea Chall.
Gotshall, Daniel W. see Gotshall, Daniel.
Gottcent, John H.
xGottcent, John H.
The Bible As Literature: A Selective
Bibliography. G K Hall.
Gottdiener, Mark.
xGottdiener, Mark.
Planned Sprawl: Private & Public Interests in
Suburbia. Sage.
Gottesfeld, Harry.
xGottesfeld, Harry.
Alternatives to Psychiatric Hospitalization.
Halsted Pr.
Strategies in Innovative Human Services
Programs. Human Sci Pr.
Gottesfeld, Mary.
xGottesfeld, Mary.
ed. Education for Clinical Social Work: A
Special Issue of Clinical Social Work Journal.
Human Sci Pr.
Profiles in Social Work. Human Sci Pr.
Gottesman, R. see Gottesman, Ronald.
Gottesman, Ronald.
xGottesman, R.
ed. Focus on Orson Welles. P-H.
xGottesman, Ronald.
Literary Manuscripts of Upton Sinclair. Ohio
St U Pr.
ed. The Norton Anthology of American
Literature. Norton.
Gottfried, Byron S., 1934-
xGottfried, Byron S.
Data Processing. Quantum Pubs.
Introduction to Optimization Theory. P-H.
Programming with Fortran IV. Quantum Pubs.
Gottfried, John.
xGottfried, John.
A Wine-Tasting Course: The Practical Way to
Know & Enjoy Wine. McKay.
xGottfried, Patricia.
jt. auth. A Wine-Tasting Course: The Practical
Way to Know & Enjoy Wine. McKay.
Gottfried, Martin.
xGottfried, Martin.
Broadway Musicals. Abrams.
Gottfried, Patricia. see Gottfried, John.
Gottfried, Paul.
xGottfried, Paul.

Conservative Millenarians: The Romantic
Experience in Bavaria. Fordham.
Gotthainer, Lew.
xGotthainer, Lew.
Collecting Post WW II Cars for Fun...& Profit.
TAB Bks.
Gottheil, Fred M.
xGottheil, Fred M.
Marx's Economic Predictions. Northwestern U
Pr.
Gottheil, Richard J. see Gottheil, Richard James Horatio.
Gottheil, Richard James Horatio.
xGottheil, Richard J.
ed. Fragments from the Cairo Genizah in the
Freer Collection. Johnson Repr.
Gottily, Doris R. see Gottily, Doris Rockwell.
Gottily, Doris Rockwell.
xGottily, Doris R.
Creative Dollmaking: From Papier Mache,
Cloth, Clothespins & Appleheads to Yarn,
Corn Cob, Bottle & Seashell Dolls. Century
Hse.
Gottlieb, Abraham Arthur, 1937-
xGottlieb, Arthur A.
ed. Developments in Lymphoid Cell Biology.
CRC Pr.
Gottlieb, Alan B. see Gottlieb, Alan M.
Gottlieb, Alan M.
xGottlieb, Alan B.
The Gun Owner's Political Action Manual.
Green Hill.
Gottlieb, Arthur A. see Gottlieb, Abraham Arthur.
Gottlieb, Dale.
xGottlieb, Dale.
Ontological Economy: Substitutional
Quantification & Mathematics. Oxford U Pr.
Gottlieb, Gidon.
xGottlieb, Gidon.
The Logic of Choice: An Investigation of the
Concepts of Rule & Rationality. Allen
Unwin.
Gottlieb, Gilbert, 1929-
xGottlieb, Gilbert.
Development of Species Identification in Birds:
An Inquiry into the Prenatal Determinants of
Perception. U of Chicago Pr.
Gottlieb, Irving. see Gottlieb, Irving M.
Gottlieb, Irving M.
xGottlieb, Irving.
Principles & Applications of Inverters &
Converters. Sams.
Switching Regulators & Power Supplies with
Practical Inverters & Converters. TAB Bks.
xGottlieb, Irving M.
Regulated Power Supplies. Sams.
Solid-State Power Electronics. Sams.
Gottlieb, Lois C.
xGottlieb, Lois C.
Rachel Crothers. Twayne.
Gottlieb, Manuel.
xGottlieb, Manuel.
Long Swings in Urban Development. Columbia
U Pr.
Long Swings in Urban Development. Natl Bur
Econ Res.
Gottlieb, Marvin. see Gottlieb, Marvin R.
Gottlieb, Marvin I.
xGottlieb, Marvin I.
ed. The Learning-Disabled Child. Grune.
Gottlieb, Marvin R.
xGottlieb, Marvin.
Oral Interpretation. McGraw.
Gottlieb, Naomi, 1925-
xGottlieb, Naomi.
ed. Alternative Social Services for Women.
Columbia U Pr.
Gottlieb, Stephen E.
xGottlieb, Stephen E.
Systematic Litigation Planning. BNA.
Gottman, John M. see Gottman, John Mordechai.

Gottman, John Mordechai.
xGottman, John M.
Marital Interaction: Experimental
Investigations. Acad Pr.
Gottmann, J. see Gottmann, Jean.
Gottmann, Jean.
xGottmann, J.
Megalopolis: The Urbanized Northeastern
Seaboard of the United States. Kraus Repr.
xGottmann, Jean.
ed. Centre & Periphery: Spatial Variation in
Politics. Sage.
The Significance of Territory. U Pr of Va.
Gottschalk, Alexander.
xGottschalk, Alexander.
Diagnostic Nuclear Medicine. Williams &
Wilkins.
Gottschalk, Elin T. see Gottschalk, Elin Toona.
Gottschalk, Elin Toona.
xGottschalk, Elin T.
In Search of Coffee Mountains.
Elsevier-Nelson.
Gottschalk, G. see Gottschalk, Gerhard.
Gottschalk, Gerhard.
xGottschalk, G.
Bacterial Metabolism. Springer-Verlag.
Gottschalk, Louis. see Gottschalk, Louis Reichenthal.
Gottschalk, Louis A.
xGottschalk, Louis.
ed. Pharmacokinetics of Psychoactive Drugs:
Further Studies. Spectrum Pub.
xGottschalk, Louis A.
ed. The Content Analysis of Verbal Behavior:
Further Studies. Halsted Pr.
The Measurement of Psychological States
Through the Content Analysis of Verbal
Behavior. U of Cal Pr
Gottschalk, Louis M. see Gottschalk, Louis Moreau.
Gottschalk, Louis Moreau.
xGottschalk, Louis M.
Notes of a Pianist. Da Capo.
Gottschalk, Louis Reichenthal.
xGottschalk, Louis.
Toward the French Revolution: Europe &
America in the Eighteenth-Century World.
Irvington.
xGottschalk, Louis M.
Understanding History: A Primer of Historical
Method. Knopf.
Gottsdanker, Robert.
xGottsdanker, Robert.
Experimenting in Psychology. P-H.
Gottsegen, Gloria B.
xGottsegen, Gloria B.
ed. Group Behavior: A Guide to Information
Sources. Gale.
Gottshall, F. H. see Gottshall, Franklin H.
Gottshall, Franklin H.
xGottshall, F. H.
How to Make Colonial Furniture. Glencoe.
xGottshall, Franklin H.
How to Make Colonial Furniture. Macmillan.
Masterpiece Furniture Making. Stackpole.
Wood Carving & Whittling for Everyone.
Scribner.
Wood Carving & Whittling Made Easy.
Macmillan.
Gottwald, Norman K. see Gottwald, Norman Karol.
Gottwald, Norman Karol, 1926-
xGottwald, Norman K.
The Tribes of Yahweh: A Sociology of the
Religion of Liberated Israel, 1250-1050 B.C..
Orbis Bks.
Goudey, Alice E., 1898-
xGoudey, Alice E.
Day We Saw the Sun Come Up. Scribner.
Goudge, Elizabeth, 1900-
xGoudge, Elizabeth.

A City of Bells. Coward.
Linnets & Valerians. Avon.
The Little White Horse. Gregg.
Pedlar's Pack. Arno.
Goudge, Thomas A. *see* Goudge, Thomas Anderson.
Goudge, Thomas Anderson, 1910-
xGoudge, Thomas A.
Ascent of Life: A Philosophical Study of the
Theory of Evolution. U of Toronto Pr.
Goudket, Michael.
xGoudket, Michael.
Audiovisual Primer. Tchrs Coll.
Goudsblom, Johan.
xGoudsblom, Johan.
Dutch Society. Phila Bk Co.
Goudy, Frederic W. *see* Goudy, Frederic William.
Goudy, Frederic William.
xGoudy, Frederic W.
Alphabet & Elements of Lettering. Peter Smith.
Typologia: Studies in Type Design & Type
Making with Comments on the Invention of
Typography, the First Types, Legibility &
Fine Printing. U of Cal Pr.
xGoudy, Frederick W.
Alphabet & Elements of Lettering. Dover.
Goudy, Frederick W. *see* Goudy, Frederic William.
Goudzwaard, B.
xGoudzwaard, Bob.
Capitalism & Progress: A Diagnosis of Western
Society. Eerdmans.
Capitalism & Progress: A Diagnosis of Western
Society. Radix Bks.
Goudzwaard, Bob. *see* Goudzwaard, B.
Gougaud, Henri.
xGougaud, Henri.
Egypt Observed. Oxford U Pr.
Gough, Aidan.
xGough, Aidan.
Standards Relating to Non-Criminal
Misbehavior. Ballinger Pub.
Gough, Barry M.
xGough, Barry M.
ed. Canada. P-H.
Gough, Chester R. *see* Gough, Chet.
Gough, Chet.
xGough, Chester R.
Systems Analysis in Libraries: A Question &
Answer Approach. K G Saur.
Systems Analysis in Libraries: A Question &
Answer Approach. Shoe String.
Gough, H. *see* Gough, Henry.
Gough, Henry, 1821-1906
xGough, H.
A Glossary of Terms Used in Heraldry.
Gordon Pr.
xGough, Henry.
Glossary of Terms Used in Heraldry. Gale.
Gough, Irene.
xGough, Irene.
Golden Lamb. Lerner Pubns.
Gough, John.
xGough, John.
Into Print. David & Charles.
Into Print. Hippocrene Bks.
Gough, John W. *see* Gough, John Wiedhofft.
Gough, John Wiedhofft.
xGough, John W.
The Social Contract: A Critical Study of Its
Development. Greenwood.
Gough, Vera.
xGough, Vera.
Planned Speaking & Your Career. Pergamon.
Goulart, Ron, 1933-
xGoulart, Ron.
After Things Fell Apart. Gregg.
The Chameleon Corps & Other Shape
Changers. Macmillan.
Cowboy Heaven. Doubleday.
Nemo. Berkley Pub.
Gould, Alan. *see* Gould, Alan David.

Gould, Alan David, 1949-
xGould, Alan.
Icelandic Solitaries. U of Queensland Pr.
Gould, Barry K.
xGould, Barry K.
Galactorrhea. C C Thomas.
Gould, Benjamin A. *see* Gould, Benjamin Apthorp.
Gould, Benjamin Apthorp, 1824-1896
xGould, Benjamin A.
Investigations in the Military &
Anthropological Statistics of American
Soldiers. Arno.
Gould, Bernard.
xGould, Bernard.
The Horseplayer's Guide to Picking Winners.
McKay.
Gould, Bruce G.
xGould, Bruce G.
The Dow Jones-Irwin Guide to Commodities
Trading. Dow Jones-Irwin.
Gould, Cecil. *see* Gould, Cecil Hilton Monk.
Gould, Cecil Hilton Monk, 1918-
xGould, Cecil.
The Paintings of Correggio. Cornell U Pr.
Gould, Clarence P. *see* Gould, Clarence Pembroke.
Gould, Clarence Pembroke, 1884-
xGould, Clarence P.
The Land System in Maryland, 1720-1765.
AMS Pr.
Land System in Maryland, 1720-1765. Arno.
Gould, Elaine.
xGould, Elaine.
Arts & Crafts for Physically & Mentally
Disabled: The How, What & Why of It. C C
Thomas.
Gould, Elizabeth P. *see* Gould, Elizabeth Porter.
Gould, Elizabeth Porter, 1848-1906
xGould, Elizabeth P.
Anne Gilchrist & Walt Whitman. Folcroft.
Anne Gilchrist & Walt Whitman. Norwood
Edns.
Gould, F. R. *see* Gould, Francis R.
Gould, Francis R.
xGould, F. R.
Specialty Papers. Noyes.
Gould, Frank W.
xGould, Frank W.
Grass Systematics. McGraw.
The Grasses of Texas. Tex A&M Univ Pr.
Gould, G. *see* Gould, Grahame Warwick.
Gould, Grahame Warwick.
xGould, G.
Bacterial Spore. Acad Pr.
Gould, Heywood.
xGould, Heywood.
Glitterburn. St Martin.
One Dead Debutante. Ballantine.
One Dead Debutante. St Martin.
Gould, James.
xGould, James.
Marketing Anthology. West Pub.
Gould, James A., 1922-
xGould, James A.
Classic Philosophical Questions. Merrill.
Love, Sex & Identity. Boyd & Fraser.
Gould, Jay R. *see* Gould, Jay Reid.
Gould, Jay Reid.
xGould, Jay R.
Opportunities in Technical Writing Today. Natl
Textbk.
Gould, Jean, 1909-
xGould, Jean.
Amy: The World of Amy Lowell & the Imagist
Movement. Dodd.
Story of Israel in Coins. Wilshire.
xGould, Maurice.

jt. auth. Story of Israel in Coins. Wilshire.
Gould, John, 1927-
xGould, John.
The Development of Plato's Ethics. Russell.
Gould, John. *see* Gould, John A.
Gould, John A., 1944-
xGould, John.
The Greenleaf Fires. Scribner.
Gould, John P., 1939-
xGould, John P.
Davis-Bacon Act: The Economics of Prevailing
Wage Laws. Am Enterprise.
Gould, Lawrence. *see* Gould, Lawrence A.
Gould, Lawrence A.
xGould, Lawrence.
ed. Vasodilator Therapy for Cardiac Disorders.
Futura Pub.
Gould, Leonard A., 1927-
xGould, Leonard A.
Chemical Process Control: Theory &
Applications. A-W.
Gould, Lewis L.
xGould, Lewis L.
ed. The Progressive Era. Syracuse U Pr.
Gould, Lois.
xGould, Lois.
Necessary Objects. Random.
Not Responsible for Personal Articles. Warner
Bks.
Such Good Friends. Dell.
Such Good Friends. Random.
Gould, Mary E. *see* Gould, Mary Earle.
Gould, Mary Earle.
xGould, Mary E.
Antique Tin & Tole Ware: Its History &
Romance. C E Tuttle.
Gould, Maurice. *see* Gould, Maurice M.
Gould, Maurice M.
xGould, Maurice.
Gould's Gold & Silver Guide to Coins. Fleet.
Gould, Nathaniel D. *see* Gould, Nathaniel Duren.
Gould, Nathaniel Duren, 1781-1864
xGould, Nathaniel D.
Church Music in America, Comprising Its
History & Its Peculiarities at Different
Periods. AMS Pr.
Gould, P. R. *see* Gould, Peter R.
Gould, Peter R.
xGould, P. R.
Spatial Diffusion. Assn Am Geographers.
Gould, R. A. *see* Gould, Richard A.
Gould, Richard A.
xGould, R. A.
Living Archaeology. Cambridge U Pr.
xGould, Richard A.
Archaeology of the Point St. George Site, &
Tolowa Prehistory. U of Cal Pr.
ed. Explorations in Ethnoarchaeology. U of
NM Pr.
Gould, Rosalind, 1912-
xGould, Rosalind.
Child Studies Through Fantasy:
Cognitive-Affective Patterns in Development.
Times Bks.
Gould, Rupert T. *see* Gould, Rupert Thomas.
Gould, Rupert Thomas, 1890-1948
xGould, Rupert T.
The Case for the Sea Serpent. Gale.
Oddities: A Book of Unexplained Facts. Univ
Bks.
Gould, Samuel B.
xGould, Samuel B.
ed. Explorations in Non-Traditional Study.
Jossey-Bass.
Gould, Shirley, 1917-
xGould, Shirley.

The Challenge of Achievement: Helping Your
  Child Succeed. Dutton.
How to Raise an Independent Child. St Martin.
Swimming the Shane Gould Way. Cornerstone.
Gould, Stephen J. see Gould, Stephen Jay.
Gould, Stephen Jay.
  xGould, Stephen J.
    Ever Since Darwin: Reflections in Natural
      History. Norton.
    Ontogeny & Phylogeny. Harvard U Pr.
Gould, Tony.
  xGould, Tony.
    In Limbo: The Story of Stanley's Rear Column.
      David & Charles.
Gould, Wilbur A., 1920-
  xGould, Wilbur A.
    Food Quality Assurance. AVI.
Gould, Zack.
  xGould, Zack.
    The Owner-Built Fireplace. Van Nos Reinhold.
Goulden, Clyde E.
  xGoulden, Clyde E.
    Systematics & Evolution of the Moinidae. Am
      Philos.
Goulder, M. D.
  xGoulder, Michael.
    ed. Incarnation & Myth: The Debate
      Continued. Eerdmans.
Goulder, Michael. see Goulder, M. D.
Goulding, Mary. see Goulding, Mary Mcclure.
Goulding, Mary McClure.
  xGoulding, Mary.
    Changing Lives Through Redecision Therapy.
      Brunner-Mazel.
Gouldman, Clyde W. see Gouldman, W. Clyde.
Gouldman, W. Clyde.
  xGouldman, Clyde W.
    Virginia Forms. Michie.
Gouldner, Alvin W. see Gouldner, Alvin Ward.
Gouldner, Alvin Ward, 1920-
  xGouldner, Alvin W.
    Coming Crisis of Western Sociology. Avon.
    The Coming Crisis of Western Sociology.
      Basic.
    The Dialectic of Ideology & Technology: The
      Origins, Grammar & Future of Ideology.
      Continuum.
    ed. Studies in Leadership: Leadership &
      Democratic Action. Russell.
    The Two Marxisms: Contradictions &
      Anomalies in the Development of Theory.
      Continuum.
Gouldner, Helen. see Gouldner, Helen P.
Gouldner, Helen P.
  xGouldner, Helen.
    Teacher's Pets, Troublemakers, & Nobodies:
      Black Children in Elementary School.
      Greenwood.
Goulet, Denis.
  xGoulet, Denis.
    Cruel Choice: A New Concept in the Theory
      of Development. Atheneum.
Goulooze, W. see Goulooze, William.
Goulooze, William, 1903-
  xGoulooze, W.
    Christian Worker's Handbook. Baker Bk.
Goult, R. J.
  xGoult, R. J.
    Applied Linear Algebra. Halsted Pr.
    Computational Methods in Linear Algebra.
      Halsted Pr.
Gounod, Charles. see Gounod, Charles Francois.
Gounod, Charles Francois, 1818-1893
  xGounod, Charles.
    Autobiographical Reminiscences: With Family
      Letters & Notes on Music. Da Capo.
Gourdie, Tom.
  xGourdie, Tom.

Calligraphic Styles. Taplinger.
Calligraphy for the Beginner. Taplinger.
Puffin Book of Lettering. Penguin.
Goure, Leon.
  xGoure, Leon.
    Convergence of Communism & Capitalism: The
      Soviet View. AISI.
    The Siege of Leningrad. Stanford U Pr.
    Soviet Penetration of Latin America. AISI.
Gourevitch, D. see Gourevitch, Doris-Jeanne.
Gourevitch, Doris-Jeanne.
  xGourevitch, D.
    Premiers Textes Litteraires. Wiley.
Gourfinkel, Nina, 1898-
  xGourfinkel, Nina.
    Lenin. Greenwood.
Gourlay, Logan.
  xGourlay, Logan.
    ed. Olivier. Stein & Day.
Gourley, G. Douglas. see Gourley, Gerald Douglas.
Gourley, Gerald Douglas, 1911-
  xGourley, G. Douglas.
    Effective Municipal Police Organization.
      Glencoe.
Gourmet Magazine. see Gourmet: the Magazine of Good
  Living.
Gourmet: the Magazine of Good Living.
  xGourmet Magazine.
    ed. The Gourmet Cookbook. Gourmet Bks.
    ed. Gourmet's France. Gourmet Bks.
    ed. Gourmet's Menu Cookbook. Gourmet Bks.
Gourou, Pierre, 1900-
  xGourou, Pierre.
    The Tropical World: Its Social & Economic
      Conditions & Its Future Status. Halsted Pr.
Gourvitch, Alexander.
  xGourvitch, Alexander.
    Survey of Economic Theory on Technological
      Change & Employment. Kelley.
Gouveia, W. A. see Gouveia, William A.
Gouveia, William A.
  xGouveia, W. A.
    ed. Clinical Pharmacy & Clinical
      Pharmacology: Proceedings of an
      International Symposium Held in Sept. 1975.
      Elsevier.
Gouw, T. H.
  xGouw, T. H.
    ed. Guide to Modern Methods of Instrumental
      Analysis. Wiley.
Gouy, Louis P. De. see De Gouy, Louis P.
Govan, Gilbert E. see Govan, Gilbert Eaton.
Govan, Gilbert Eaton.
  xGovan, Gilbert E.
    The Chattanooga Country, 1540-1976: From
      Tomahawks to TVA. U of Tenn Pr.
    A Different Valor, the Story of General Joseph
      E. Johnston, C.S.A.. Greenwood.
Goveia, Elsa V.
  xGoveia, Elsa V.
    Slave Society in the British Leeward Islands at
      the End of the Eighteenth Century.
      Greenwood.
Gover, Robert, 1929-
  xGover, Robert.
    Getting Pretty on the Table. Capra Pr.
**Governor's Conference on Crime, the Criminal and
  Society, Albany, 1935.**
  xGovernor's Conference on Crime, the Criminal &
    Society, Sep 30-Oct 3, 1935, New York.
    Proceedings. Arno.
Govoni, Laura E.
  xGovoni, Laura E.
    Drugs & Nursing Implications. ACC.
Govoni, Norman A. see Govoni, Norman A. P.
Govoni, Norman A. P.
  xGovoni, Norman A.
    Marketing Problems: Cases for Analysis. Grid
      Pub.
Govorchin, Gerald G. see Govorchin, Gerald Gilbert.

Govorchin, Gerald Gilbert.
  xGovorchin, Gerald G.
    Americans from Yugoslavia. R & E Res Assoc.
    Americans from Yugoslavia. Ragusan Pr.
    Americans from Yugoslavia. U Presses Fla.
Gow, Doris T.
  xGow, Doris T.
    Design & Development of Curricular Materials.
      U Ctr Intl St.
Gow, Gordon.
  xGow, Gordon.
    Hollywood in the Fifties. A S Barnes.
Gowan, Donald E.
  xGowan, Donald E.
    Bridge Between the Testaments: Reappraisal of
      Judaism from the Exile to the Birth of
      Christianity. Pickwick.
    Reclaiming the Old Testament for the Christian
      Pulpit. John Knox.
    The Triumph of Faith in Habakkuk. John
      Knox.
    When Man Becomes God: Humanism &
      Hybris in the Old Testament. Pickwick.
Gowan, John C. see Gowan, John Curtis.
Gowan, John Curtis.
  xGowan, John C.
    Academically Talented Student & Guidance.
      HM.
Gowans, Alan.
  xGowans, Alan.
    Images of American Living: Four Centuries of
      Architecture & Furniture As Cultural
      Expression. Har-Row.
Gowar, N. W.
  xGowar, Norman.
    An Invitation to Mathematics. Oxford U Pr.
Gowar, Norman. see Gowar, N. W.
Gowen, Herbert H. see Gowen, Herbert Henry.
Gowen, Herbert Henry, 1864-
  xGowen, Herbert H.
    History of Indian Literature from Vedic Times
      to the Present Day. Greenwood.
Gowen, James A.
  xGowen, James A.
    English Review Manual: A Program for
      Self-Instruction. McGraw.
    Progress in Writing: A Learning Program.
      McGraw.
Gower, H. D.
  xGower, H. D.
    The Camera As Historian. Arno.
Gower, Ronald C. see Gower, Ronald Charles
  Sutherland.
Gower, Ronald Charles Sutherland, Lord, 1845-1916
  xGower, Ronald C.
    Last Days of Marie Antoinette: An Historical
      Sketch. AMS Pr.
Gowing, Clara.
  xGowing, Clara.
    The Alcotts As I Knew Them. Folcroft.
    The Alcotts As I Knew Them. Norwood Edns.
Gowing, Lawrence.
  xGowing, Lawrence.
    Matisse. Oxford U Pr.
Gowing, Margaret. see Gowing, Margaret M.
Gowing, Margaret M.
  xGowing, Margaret.
    The Atomic Bomb. Butterworths.
Gowitzke, Barbara. see Gowitzke, Barbara A.
Gowitzke, Barbara A.
  xGowitzke, Barbara.
    Understanding the Scientific Bases of Human
      Movement. Williams & Wilkins.
Gowland, David.
  xGowland, David.
    Monetary Policy & Credit Control: The Uk
      Experience. Biblio Dist.
  xGowland, David H.
    ed. Modern Economic Analysis. Butterworths.
Gowland, David H. see Gowland, David.

Gowland, Peter.
    xGowland, Peter.
        Gowland's Guide to Glamour Photography.
            Crown.
Goy, Robert W.
    xGoy, Robert W.
        Sexual Differentiation of the Brain. MIT Pr.
Goyal, R. C. see Goyal, Ramesh Chandra.
Goyal, Ramesh Chandra, 1923-
    xGoyal, R. C.
        Problems in Personnel & Industrial Relations in
            India. Verry.
Goyder, Alice.
    xGoyder, Alice.
        illus. Christmas in Catland. T Y Crowell.
        illus. Party in Catland. T Y Crowell.
Goyen, William.
    xGoyen, William.
        The House of Breath. Random.
Goyette, Richert E.
    xGoyette, Richert E.
        Digestive & Hepatobiliary Pathology &
            Pathophysiology Case Studies. Med Exam.
        Renal, Genitourinary, & Breast Pathology &
            Pathophysiology Case Studies. Med Exam.
    xGoyette, Rickert E.
        Cardiopulmonary Pathology & Pathophysiology
            Case Studies. Med Exam.
Goyette, Rickert E. see Goyette, Richert E.
Goyvaerts, D. L.
    xGoyvaerts, D. L.
        Pref. by Present-Day Historical & Comparative
            Linguistics: An Introductory Guide to Theory
            & Method Part One General
            Background-Phonological Change.
            Humanities.
Grabar, Oleg.
    xGrabar, Oleg.
        The Alhambra. Harvard U Pr.
        The Formation of Islamic Art. Yale U Pr.
Grabau, Amadeus W. see Grabau, Amadeus William.
Grabau, Amadeus William, 1870-1946
    xGrabau, Amadeus W.
        Rhythm of the Ages. Krieger.
Grabeklis, Lita.
    xGrabeklis, Lita.
        Destiny's Darling. Raven Print.
Graber, G. S.
    xGraber, G. S.
        The History of the S. S.. Charter Bks.
Graber, Kay, 1938-
    xGraber, Kay.
        Compiled by Nebraska Pioneer Cookbook. U of
            Nebr Pr.
Graber, Richard.
    xGraber, Richard.
        A Little Breathing Room. Har-Row.
        Pay Your Respects. Har-Row.
Graber, T. M. see Graber, Touro M.
Graber, Touro M.
    xGraber, T. M.
        ed. Current Orthodontic Concepts &
            Techniques. Saunders.
        Orthodontics: Principles & Practice. Saunders.
        Removable Orthodontic Appliances. Saunders.
Grabes, H. see Grabes, Herbert.
Grabes, Herbert.
    xGrabes, H.
        Fictitious Biographies: Vladimir Nabokov's
            English Novels. Mouton.
Grabill, Joseph L.
    xGrabill, Joseph L.
        Protestant Diplomacy & the Near East:
            Missionary Influence in American Policy,
            1810-1927. U of Minn Pr.
Grabill, Paul.
    xGrabill, Paul.
        Youth's a Stuff Will Not Endure. Avon.
Grabiner, Sandy, 1939-
    xGrabiner, Sandy.

        Derivations & Automorphisms of Banach
            Algebras of Power Series. Am Math.
Grabo, Carl. see Grabo, Carl Henry.
Grabo, Carl A. see Grabo, Carl Henry.
Grabo, Carl Henry, 1881-
    xGrabo, Carl.
        Meaning of the Witch of Atlas. Russell.
    xGrabo, Carl A.
        Newton Among Poets: Shelley's Use of
            Science in Prometheus Unbound. Cooper Sq.
Grabo, Norman S.
    xGrabo, Norman S.
        Edward Taylor. Coll & U Pr.
        Edward Taylor. Twayne.
Graburn, Nelson H. see Graburn, Nelson H. H.
Graburn, Nelson H. H.
    xGraburn, Nelson H.
        ed. Ethnic & Tourist Arts: Cultural Expressions
            from the Fourth World. U of Cal Pr.
Grace, Clive.
    xGrace, Clive.
        Negotiating the Law: Social Work & Legal
            Services. Routledge & Kegan.
Grace, Evelyn, 1913-
    xGrace, Evelyn.
        Introduction to Fashion Merchandising. P-H.
Grace, Gerald. see Grace, Gerald Rupert.
Grace, Gerald Rupert.
    xGrace, Gerald.
        Teachers, Ideology & Control: A Study in
            Urban Education. Routledge & Kegan.
Grace, Harvey, 1874-1944
    xGrace, Harvey.
        Musician at Large. Arno.
Grace, John P. see Grace, John Patrick.
Grace, John Patrick, 1942-
    xGrace, John P.
        Hearing His Voice. Ave Maria.
Grace, Nancy.
    xGrace, Nancy.
        Earrings for Celia. Pantheon.
Grace, Robert A., 1938-
    xGrace, Robert A.
        Marine Outfall Systems: Planning, Design, &
            Construction. P-H.
Grace, Virginia, 1921-
    xGrace, Virginia R.
        Amphoras & the Ancient Wine Trade. Am Sch
            Athens.
Grace, Virginia R. see Grace, Virginia.
Grace, William J. see Grace, William Joseph.
Grace, William Joseph, 1910-
    xGrace, William J.
        Ideas in Milton. U of Notre Dame Pr.
Gracy, David B.
    xGracy, David B.
        Littlefield Lands: Colonization on the Texas
            Plains, 1912-1920. U of Tex Pr.
Grad, Andrew J. see Grad, Andrew Jonah.
Grad, Andrew Jonah, 1899-
    xGrad, Andrew J.
        Formosa Today: An Analysis of the Economic
            Development & Strategic Importance of
            Japan's Tropical Colony. AMS Pr.
        Modern Korea. Octagon.
Grad, Laurie B. see Grad, Laurie Burrows.
Grad, Laurie Burrows.
    xGrad, Laurie B.
        Dining In-Los Angeles. Peanut Butter.
Gradman, Barry, 1944-
    xGradman, Barry.
        Metamorphosis in Keats. NYU Pr.
Graduate Institute Of International Studies - Geneva. see
    Geneva. Graduate Institute of International Studies.
Grady, Michael.
    xGrady, Mike.
        Precalculus. Wadsworth Pub.
Grady, Michael. see Grady, Michael P.
Grady, Michael J.
    xGrady, Michael J.

        Evolution & Education. U Pr of Amer.
Grady, Michael P.
    xGrady, Michael.
        Education & the Brain. Phi Delta Kappa.
Grady, Mike. see Grady, Michael.
Grae, Ida.
    xGrae, Ida.
        Nature's Colors: Dyes from Plants. Macmillan.
        Nature's Colors: Dyes from Plants. Macmillan.
Graeber, Charlotte T. see Graeber, Charlotte Towner.
Graeber, Charlotte Towner.
    xGraeber, Charlotte T.
        Grey Cloud. Schol Bk Serv.
Graeber, Isacque.
    xGraeber, Isacque.
        Jews in a Gentile World: The Problem of
            Anti-Semitism. Greenwood.
Graebner, Norman. see Graebner, Norman A.
Graebner, Norman A.
    xGraebner, Norman.
        Nationalism & Communism in Asia: The
            American Response. Heath.
    xGraebner, Norman A.
        ed. Freedom in America: A 200-Year
            Perspective. Pa St U Pr.
        A History of the American People. McGraw.
        History of the United States. McGraw.
        ed. An Uncertain Tradition: American
            Secretaries of State in the Twentieth Century.
            Greenwood.
Graedel, T. E.
    xGraedel, T. E.
        Chemical Compounds in the Atmosphere. Acad
            Pr.
Graef, Hilda. see Graef, Hilda C.
Graef, Hilda C.
    xGraef, Hilda.
        Adult Christianity. Franciscan Herald.
Graeffe, Arnold D. see Graeffe, Arnold Didier.
Graeffe, Arnold Didier.
    xGraeffe, Arnold D.
        Creative Education in the Humanities. Arno.
Graendorf, Werner. see Graendorf, Werner C.
Graendorf, Werner C.
    xGraendorf, Werner.
        ed. An Introduction to Christian Camping.
            Moody.
Graetz, Heinrich. see Graetz, Heinrich Hirsch.
Graetz, Heinrich Hirsch, 1817-1891
    xGraetz, Heinrich.
        History of the Jews. Jewish Pubn.
        The Structure of Jewish History & Other
            Essays. Ktav.
Graetz, Richard P. see Graetz, Rick.
Graetz, Rick.
    xGraetz, Richard P.
        photos by Montana. Country Beautiful.
Graf, Calvin R.
    xGraf, Calvin R.
        Listen to Radio Energy, Light, & Sound. Sams.
        One Evening Electronic Projects. Bobbs.
Graf, Herbert, 1903-
    xGraf, Herbert.
        The Opera & Its Future in America. Kennikat.
        Opera for the People. Da Capo.
Graf, Max, 1873-
    xGraf, Max.
        From Beethoven to Shostakovich: The
            Psychology of the Composing Process.
            Greenwood.
        Legend of a Musical City. Greenwood.
        Modern Music: Composers & Music of Our
            Time. Greenwood.
Graf, Rudolf. see Graf, Rudolf F.
Graf, Rudolf F.
    xGraf, Rudolf.
        Build-It Book of Home Electronics. Sams.
        Build-It Book of Safety Electronics. Sams.
    xGraf, Rudolf F.

How It Works Illustrated: Every Day Devices
& Mechanisms. Har-Row.
Modern Dictionary of Electronics. Sams.
VNR Illustrated Guide to Power Tools. Van
Nos Reinhold.
xGraf, Rudolph F.
How It Works, Illustrated Everyday Devices &
Mechanisms. Van Nos Reinhold.
Graf, Rudolph F. see Graf, Rudolf F.
Graf, W. H. see Graf, Walter Hans.
Graf, Walter Hans, 1936-
xGraf, W. H.
Hydraulics of Sediment Transport. McGraw.
Graff, Gerald.
xGraff, Gerald.
Literature Against Itself: Literary Ideas in
Modern Society. U of Chicago Pr.
Graff, John R. see Graff, John Ronald.
Graff, John Ronald.
xGraff, John R.
Variety Is. Mojave Bks.
Graff, Mab.
xGraff, Mab.
Clangor in the Bell Tower. Accent Bks.
Graff, Richard A., 1944-
xGraff, Richard A.
Elements of Non-Linear Functional Analysis.
Am Math.
Graff, Stewart.
xGraff, Stewart.
The Story of World War II. Dutton.
Graff, Willem L. see Graff, Willem Laurens.
Graff, Willem Laurens, 1890-
xGraff, Willem L.
Rainer Maria Rilke: Creative Anguish of a
Modern Poet. Greenwood.
Grafton, Carol B. see Grafton, Carol Belanger.
Grafton, Carol Belanger.
xGrafton, Carol B.
Geometric Patchwork Patterns: Full-Size
Cut-Outs & Instructions for 12 Quilts. Dover.
ed. Pictorial Archive of Printer's Ornaments
from the Renaissance to the 20th Century.
Dover.
ed. Silhouettes: A Pictorial Archive of Varied
Illustrations. Dover.
Grafton, John.
xGrafton, John.
The American Revolution: A Picture
Sourcebook. Dover.
Graglia, Lino A.
xGraglia, Lino A.
Disaster by Decree: The Supreme Court
Decisions on Race & the Schools. Cornell U
Pr.
Graham, A. see Graham, Alan.
Graham, A. Richard. see Graham, Archie Richard.
Graham, Ada.
xGraham, Ada.
Bug Hunters. Delacorte.
Coyote Song. Delacorte.
Falcon Flight. Delacorte.
Let's Discover Birds in Our World. Western
Pub.
Let's Discover Changes Everywhere. Western
Pub.
Let's Discover the Floor of the Forest.
Western Pub.
jt. auth. Let's Discover Winter Woods.
Western Pub.
Puffin Island. Thorndike Pr.

Graham, Alan.
xGraham, A.
Vegetation & Vegetational History of Northern
Latin America. Elsevier.
Graham, Alexander, M.sc.
xGraham, Alexander.

Matrix Theory & Applications for Engineers &
Mathematicians. Halsted Pr.
Matrix Theory & Applications for Engineers &
Mathematicians. Wiley.
Graham, Alice H. see Graham, Alice Holderby.
Graham, Alice Holderby, 1913-
xGraham, Alice H.
Desert Ballet. Miller Bks.
Graham, Archie Richard, 1934-
xGraham, A. Richard.
An Introduction to Engineering Measurements.
P-H.
Graham, Ben.
xGraham, Ben S.
The Amazing Oversight: Total Participation for
Productivity. Am Mgmt.
Graham, Ben S. see Graham, Ben.
Graham, Benjamin, 1894-
xGraham, Benjamin.
The Intelligent Investor: A Book of Practical
Counsel. Har-Row.
Graham, Billy. see Graham, William Franklin.
Graham, Brenda K. see Graham, Brenda Knight.
Graham, Brenda Knight.
xGraham, Brenda K.
Stone Gables. Broadman.
Graham, C. C. see Graham, Colin C.
Graham, Carroll.
xGraham, Carroll.
Queer People. Popular Lib.
Graham, Colin C.
xGraham, C. C.
Essays in Commutative Harmonic Analysis.
Springer-Verlag.
Graham, Daniel O. see Graham, Daniel Orrin.
Graham, Daniel Orrin, 1925-
xGraham, Daniel O.
Shall America Be Defended?: Salt II & Beyond.
Arlington Hse.
Graham, David, 1927-
xGraham, David D.
The Practical Side of Reincarnation. P-H.
Graham, David D. see Graham, David.
Graham, Don. see Graham, Donald.
Graham, Donald, 1940-
xGraham, Don.
The Fiction of Frank Norris: The Aesthetic
Context. U of Mo Pr.
Graham, Edward H. see Graham, Edward Harrison.
Graham, Edward Harrison, 1902-
xGraham, Edward H.
Natural Principles of Land Use. Greenwood.
Graham, Ellen B. see Graham, Ellen Blume.
Graham, Ellen Blume, 1931-
xGraham, Ellen B.
The Growling Gourmet. S&S.

Graham, Frank.

xGraham, Frank.
The Adirondack Park: A Political History.
Knopf.
Great Hitters of the Major Leagues. Random.
Great No Hit Games of the Major Leagues.
Random.

Great Pennant Races of the Major Leagues.
Random.
Gulls: A Social History. Random.
Potomac: The Nation's River. Lippincott.
Since Silent Spring. Fawcett.
Graham, Frank D. see Graham, Frank Dunstone.
Graham, Frank Dunstone, 1890-1949
xGraham, Frank D.
Abolition of Unemployment. Kennikat.
Golden Avalanche. Arno.
Theory of International Values. Greenwood.
Graham, Gerald H.
xGraham, Gerald H.

Business: The Process of Enterprise. SRA.
Graham, Gerald S.
xGraham, Gerald S.
Secular Abyss: An Interpretation of History &
the Human Situation. Theos Pub Hse.
Graham, Gerald S. see Graham, Gerald Sandford.
Graham, Gerald Sandford, 1903-
xGraham, Gerald S.
The China Station: War & Diplomacy
1830-1860. Oxford U Pr.
A Concise History of the British Empire.
Thames Hudson.
Graham, H. see Graham, Hugh Davis.
Graham, H. D. see Graham, Horace Delbert.
Graham, Harry E. see Graham, Harry Edward.
Graham, Harry Edward.
xGraham, Harry E.
Paper Rebellion: Development & Upheaval in
Pulp & Paper Unionism. U of Iowa Pr.
Graham, Helga.
xGraham, Helga.
Arabian Time Machine. Holmes & Meier.
Graham, Horace Delbert, 1925-
xGraham, H. D.
Food Colloids. AVI.
Graham, Hugh D. see Graham, Hugh Davis.
Graham, Hugh Davis.
xGraham, H.
ed. Huey Long. P-H.
xGraham, Hugh D.
Crisis in Print: Desegregation & the Press in
Tennessee. Vanderbilt U Pr.
ed. Violence in America: Historical &
Comparative Perspectives. Sage.
Graham, Ilse, 1914-
xGraham, Ilse.
Goethe: Portrait of the Artist. De Gruyter.
Graham, J. D. see Graham, James David Provins.
Graham, James David Provins.
xGraham, J. D.
An Introduction to Human Pharmacology.
Oxford U Pr.
Graham, James H.
xGraham, James H.
ed. Dermal Pathology. Har-Row.
Graham, James W. see Graham, James Walter.
Graham, James Walter, 1906-
xGraham, James W.
Palaces of Crete. Princeton U Pr.
Graham, John, 1933-
xGraham, John.
Fast Reactor Safety. Acad Pr.
I Love You, Mouse. HarBraceJ.
I Love You, Mouse. HarBraceJ.
Graham, John F.
xGraham, John F.
Fiscal Adjustment & Economic Development:
A Case Study of Nova Scotia. U of Toronto
Pr.
Graham, John R. see Graham, John Remington.
Graham, John Remington, 1940-
xGraham, John R.
Constitutional History of the Military Draft.
Ross.
Graham, John W. see Graham, John William.
Graham, John William, 1859-1932
xGraham, John W.
Intro. by Conscription & Conscience: A
History, 1916-1919. Garland Pub.
Conscription & Conscience: A History
1916-1919. Kelley.
Graham, Jorie, 1951-
xGraham, Jorie.
Hybrids of Plants & Ghosts. Princeton U Pr.
Graham, Kennard C. see Graham, Kennard Codville.
Graham, Kennard Codville.
xGraham, Kennard C.

Industrial & Commercial Wiring. Am
Technical.
Graham, Kenneth R., 1943-
xGraham, Kenneth R.
Psychological Research: Controlled
Interpersonal Interaction. Brooks-Cole.
Graham, L. A.
xGraham, Lloyd A.
Ingenious Mathematical Problems & Methods.
Dover.
Surprise Attack in Mathematical Problems.
Dover.
Graham, L. R. *see* Graham, Loren R.
Graham, Lawrence S.
xGraham, Lawrence S.
Civil Service Reform in Brazil: Principles
Versus Practice. U of Tex Pr.
ed. Contemporary Portugal: The Revolution &
Its Antecedents. U of Tex Pr.
Graham, Lloyd A. *see* Graham, L. A.
Graham, Loren R.
xGraham, L. R.
Soviet Academy of Sciences & the Communist
Party, 1927-1932. Princeton U Pr.
Graham, Lorenz. *see* Graham, Lorenz B.
Graham, Lorenz B.
xGraham, Lorenz.
God Wash the World & Start Again. T Y
Crowell.
North Town. NAL.
Return to South Town. T Y Crowell.
South Town. NAL.
Graham, Lou.
xGraham, Lou.
Mastering Golf. Contemp Bks.
Graham, Malbone W. *see* Graham, Malbone Watson.
Graham, Malbone Watson, 1898-
xGraham, Malbone W.
American Diplomacy in the International
Community. Arno.
Graham, Malcolm, 1923-
xGraham, Malcolm.
Modern Elementary Mathematics. HarBraceJ.
Graham, Margaret. *see* Graham, Margaret (Collier).
Graham, Margaret (Collier), 1850-1910
xGraham, Margaret.
Stories of the Foot Hills. Arno.
Graham, Martha.
xGraham, Martha.
The Notebooks of Martha Graham. HarBraceJ.
Graham, Neill, 1941-
xGraham, Neill.
Artificial Intelligence. TAB Bks.
Introduction to Computer Science: A
Structured Approach. West Pub.
The Mind Tool: Computers & Their Impact on
Society. West Pub.
Graham, Otis L.
xGraham, Otis L.
Toward a Planned Society: From Roosevelt to
Nixon. Oxford U Pr.
Graham, P. C.
xGraham, P. C.
Simple Circuit Building. Hayden.
Graham, Patricia A. *see* Graham, Patricia Albjerg.
Graham, Patricia Albjerg.
xGraham, Patricia A.
Community & Class in American Education
1865-1918. Wiley.
Graham, Pearson.
xGraham, Pearson.
Managerial Economics. A-W.
Graham, Peter J.
xGraham, Peter J.
Planning & Delivering Leisure Services. Wm C
Brown.
Graham, R. *see* Graham, Richard.
Graham, R. B. *see* Graham, Robert Bontine
Cunninghame.

Graham, R. Cunninghame. *see* Graham, Robert Bontine
Cunninghame.
Graham, R. William, 1922-
xGraham, R. William.
Instant College. Branden.
Graham, Richard, 1934-
xGraham, R.
Britain & the Onset of Modernization in Brazil,
1850-1914. Cambridge U Pr.
xGraham, Richard.
Independence in Latin America. Knopf.
Graham, Richard. *see* Graham, Richard M.
Graham, Richard M.
xGraham, Richard.
Teaching Music to the Exceptional Child: A
Handbook for Mainstreaming. P-H.
xGraham, Richard M.
ed. Music for the Exceptional Child. Music Ed.
Graham, Robert.
xGraham, Robert.
Attar's Revenge. PB.
Iran: The Illusion of Power. St Martin.
Graham, Robert B. *see* Graham, Robert Bontine
Cunninghame.
Graham, Robert Bontine Cunninghame, 1852-1936
xGraham, R. B.
Jose Antonio Paez. Kennikat.
Pedro De Valdivia, Conqueror of Chile.
Greenwood.
The South American Sketches of R. B.
Cunninghame Graham. U of Okla Pr.
xGraham, R. Cunninghame.
Jose Antonio Paez. Cooper Sq.
Pedro De Valdivia, Conqueror of Chile.
Longwood Pr.
xGraham, Robert B.
Brought Forward. Arno.
Thirteen Stories. Arno.
Thirty Tales and Sketches. Arno.
Vanished Arcadia: Being Some Account of the
Jesuits in Paraguay. Haskell.
Graham, Robert M., 1929-
xGraham, Robert M.
Principles of Systems Programming. Wiley.
Graham, Robin L. *see* Graham, Robin Lee.
Graham, Robin Lee.
xGraham, Robin L.
jt. auth. The Boy Who Sailed Around the
World Alone. Western Pub.
Dove. Har-Row.
Dove. Bantam.
Graham, Rosemarie.
xGraham, R.
Officiating Soccer. Contemp Bks.
Graham, Samuel A. *see* Graham, Samuel Alexander.
Graham, Samuel Alexander.
xGraham, Samuel A.
Principles of Forest Entomology. McGraw.
Graham, Sheila. *see* Graham, Sheilah.
Graham, Sheilah.
xGraham, Sheila.
Confessions of a Hollywood Columnist.
Morrow.
Graham, Shirley.
xGraham, Shirley.
Dr. George Washington Carver: Scientist.
Messner.
Graham, Stephen, 1884-
xGraham, Stephen.
Alexander of Yugoslavia: The Story of the
King Who Was Murdered at Marseilles. Shoe
String.
Boris Godunof. Shoe String.
Great Russian Short Stories. Arden Lib.
ed. Great Russian Short Stories. Liveright.
Soul of John Brown. AMS Pr.
Graham, Susan.
xGraham, Susan.

Quick Simple Meals. Transatlantic.
Graham, Sylvester, 1794-1851
xGraham, Sylvester.
A Lecture to Young Men. Arno.
Graham, Victor E. *see* Graham, Victor Ernest.
Graham, Victor Ernest.
xGraham, Victor E.
The Royal Tour of France by Charles IX &
Catherine de' Medici: Festivals & Entries,
1564-6. U of Toronto Pr.
Graham, Virginia L.
xGraham, Virginia L.
A Book on Casino Gambling: Written by a
Mathematician and a Computer Expert. Van
Nos Reinhold.
Graham, W. *see* Graham, William.
Graham, W. S. *see* Graham, William Sydney.
Graham, Walter. *see* Graham, Walter James.
Graham, Walter J. *see* Graham, Walter James.
Graham, Walter James, 1885-
xGraham, Walter.
Tory Criticism in the Quarterly Review, 1809 -
1853. AMS Pr.
xGraham, Walter J.
English Literary Periodicals. Octagon.
Graham, William, 1839-1911
xGraham, W.
English Political Philosophy from Hobbes to-
Maine. Gordon Pr.
xGraham, William.
English Political Philosophy from Hobbes to
Maine. B Franklin.
Last Links with Byron, Shelley & Keats.
Folcroft.
Graham, William Franklin, 1918-
xGraham, Billy.
Angels: God's Secret Agents. G K Hall.
How to Be Born Again. Warner Bks.
How to Be Born Again. Word Bks.
My Answer. Doubleday.
My Answer. PB.
Graham, William Sydney, 1918-
xGraham, W. S.
Implements in Their Places. Merrimack Bk
Serv.
Graham, Winston.
xGraham, Winston.
The Merciless Ladies. Doubleday.
Merciless Ladies. G K Hall.
Graham-Jones, Oliver.
xGraham-Jones, Oliver.
First Catch Your Tiger. Taplinger.
Graham-White, Anthony.
xGraham-White, Anthony.
The Drama of Black Africa. French.
Grahame, Kenneth, 1859-1922
xGrahame, Kenneth.
Dream Days. Avon.
Dream Days. Garland Pub.
The Golden Age. Garland Pub.
Pagan Papers. Arno.
Reluctant Dragon. Holiday.
Grahn, Judy, 1940-
xGrahn, Judy.
The Work of a Common Woman. St Martin.
Grainger, Stuart E.
xGrainger, Stuart E.
Creative Ropecraft. Norton.
Grainger, Sylvia.
xGrainger, Sylvia.
How to Make Your Own Moccasins.
Lippincott.
illus. Leatherwork. Lippincott.
Gram, T. E. *see* Gram, Theodore E.
Gram, Theodore E.
xGram, T. E.
ed. Extrahepatic Metabolism of Drugs & Other
Foreign Compounds. Spectrum Pub.
Gramatky, H. *see* Gramatky, Hardie.

Gramatky, Hardie, 1907-
  xGramatky, H.
    illus. Little Toot on the Thames. Putnam.
  xGramatky, Hardie.
    illus. Little Toot on the Mississippi. Putnam.
    Little Toot on the Thames. Putnam.
Gramatky, Hardie. *see* Gramatky, Hardy.
Gramatky, Hardy.
  xGramatky, Hardie.
    Little Toot Through the Golden Gate. Putnam.
Grambs, Jean D. *see* Grambs, Jean Dresden.
Grambs, Jean Dresden.
  xGrambs, Jean D.
    Modern Methods in Secondary Education.
    HR&W.
Gramiak, Raymond.
  xGramiak, Raymond.
    Cardiac Ultrasound. Mosby.
Gramling, Roger M.
  xGramling, Roger M.
    A Ministry of Hope: Portrait of Arthur J.
    Moore. Upper Room.
Grammer, Norma R. *see* Grammer, Norma Rutledge.
Grammer, Norma Rutledge.
  xGrammer, Norma R.
    Marriage Record of Washington County,
    Tennessee, 1787-1840. Genealog Pub.
Gramophone Shop Inc. - New York. *see* Gramophone
  Shop, Inc., New York.
Gramophone Shop, Inc., New York.
  xGramophone Shop Inc. - New York.
    Gramophone Shop Encyclopedia of Recorded
    Music. Greenwood.
Grams, Ralph R. *see* Grams, Ralph Raymond.
Grams, Ralph Raymond.
  xGrams, Ralph R.
    Medical Information Systems: The Laboratory
    Module. Humana.
  xGrams, Ralph Raymond.
    Problem Solving, Systems Analysis, &
    Medicine. C C Thomas.
Gramsci, Antonio, 1891-1937
  xGramsci, Antonio.
    Letters from Prison. Har-Row.
Gran, Peter, 1941-
  xGran, Peter.
    Islamic Roots of Capitalism: Egypt, 1760-1840.
    U of Tex Pr.
Grana, Cesar.
  xGrana, Cesar.
    Fact & Symbol: Essays in the Sociology of Art
    & Literature. Oxford U Pr.
Grana, Janice.
  xGrana, Janice.
    ed. Images: Women in Transition. St Mary's.
  xGrana, Janice T.
    Images: Women in Transition. Upper Room.
Grana, Janice T. *see* Grana, Janice.
Granatstein, J. L.
  xGranatstein, J. L.
    Broken Promises: A History of Conscription in
    Canada. Oxford U Pr.
    Politics of Survival: The Conservative Party of
    Canada 1939-1945. U of Toronto Pr.
Granbeck, Marilyn.
  xGranbeck, Marilyn.
    Social Work Careers. Watts.
Granberg, Ron.
  xGranberg, Ron.
    Introduction to California Law Finding. Why
    Not.
Grancsay, Stephen V. *see* Grancsay, Stephen Vincent.
Grancsay, Stephen Vincent, 1897-
  xGrancsay, Stephen V.
    Master French Gunsmith's Designs from the
    XVII to the XIX Centuries. Arma Pr.
Grand, Yves Le. *see* Le Grand, Yves.
Grande, Hyppolite La. *see* La Grande, Hyppolite.
Grandgent, C. H. *see* Grandgent, Charles Hall.
Grandgent, Charles H. *see* Grandgent, Charles Hall.

Grandgent, Charles Hall.
  xGrandgent, C. H.
    ed. Companion to the Divine Comedy. Harvard
    U Pr.
  xGrandgent, Charles H.
    Dante. Folcroft.
    Dante Alighieri. Norwood Edns.
    Discourses on Dante. Russell.
    From Latin to Italian: An Historical Outline of
    the Phonology & Morphology of the Italian
    Language. Russell.
    Prunes & Prism: With Other Odds & Ends.
    Arno.
Grandine, Jonathan. *see* Grandine, Jonathan R.
Grandine, Jonathan R.
  xGrandine, Jonathan.
    Problem of Shape in the Prelude: The Conflict
    of Private & Public Speech. Harvard U Pr.
Grandy, Richard E.
  xGrandy, Richard E.
    Advanced Logic for Applications. Kluwer
    Boston.
    Theories & Observation in Science. P-H.
Grandy, Walter T., 1933-
  xGrandy, Walter T.
    Introduction to Electrodynamics & Radiation.
    Acad Pr.
Graneau, Peter.
  xGraneau, Peter.
    Underground Power Transmission: The
    Science, Technology, & Economics of High
    Voltage Cables. Wiley.
Granet, Irving.
  xGranet, Irving.
    Modern Materials Science. Reston.
    Strength of Materials for Engineering
    Technology. Reston.
    Thermodynamics & Heat Power. Reston.
Granet, Marcel, 1884-1940
  xGranet, Marcel.
    Chinese Civilization. AMS Pr.
    The Religion of the Chinese People. Har-Row.
Granfield, David.
  xGranfield, David.
    Abortion Decision. Doubleday.
Granfield, Patrick.
  xGranfield, Patrick.
    Ecclesial Cybernetics: A Study of Democracy
    in the Church. Macmillan.
    The Papacy in Transition. Doubleday.
Grange, McQuilkin De. *see* De Grange, McQuilkin.
Granger, Alfred H. *see* Granger, Alfred Hoyt.
Granger, Alfred Hoyt, 1867-1939
  xGranger, Alfred H.
    Charles Follen McKim: A Study of His Life &
    Work. AMS Pr.
    Charles Follen McKim: A Study of His Life &
    Work. Arno.
Granger, Bruce I. *see* Granger, Bruce Ingham.
Granger, Bruce Ingham.
  xGranger, Bruce I.
    American Essay Serials from Franklin to
    Irving. U of Tenn Pr.
    Political Satire in the American Revolution,
    1763-83. Russell.
Granger, C. W. *see* Granger, Clive William John.
Granger, Clive W. *see* Granger, Clive William John.
Granger, Clive William John.
  xGranger, C. W.
    ed. Forecasting Economic Time Series. Acad
    Pr.
    Forecasting in Business & Economics. Acad Pr.
  xGranger, Clive W.
    Predictability of Stock Market Prices.
    Lexington Bks.
Granger, Jean, 1907-
  xGranger, Jean.

    Mushroom Matings: The Best in Mushroom
    Cookery. Cragmont Pubns.
Granger, Peg.
  xGranger, Peggy.
    Everywoman's Guide to a New Image. Les
    Femmes Pub.
Granger, Peggy. *see* Granger, Peg.
Granick, David.
  xGranick, David.
    Enterprise Guidance in Eastern Europe: A
    Comparison of Four Socialist Economies.
    Princeton U Pr.
    The European Executive. Arno.
    Soviet Metal-Fabricating & Economic
    Development: Practice Versus Policy. U of
    Wis Pr.
Granit, Ragnar, 1900-
  xGranit, Ragnar.
    The Purposive Brain. MIT Pr.
Grannis, Gary E.
  xGrannis, Gary E.
    Modern Power Mechanics. Bobbs.
Granof, Michael H.
  xGranof, Michael H.
    Financial Accounting: Principles & Issues. P-H.
    How to Cost Your Labor Contract. BNA.
Granovetter, Mark S.
  xGranovetter, Mark S.
    Getting a Job: A Study of Contacts & Careers.
    Harvard U Pr.
Granqvist, H. *see* Granqvist, Hilma Natalia.
Granqvist, Hilma N. *see* Granqvist, Hilma Natalia.
Granqvist, Hilma Natalia, 1890-
  xGranqvist, H.
    Marriage Conditions in a Palestinian Village.
    Humanities.
  xGranqvist, Hilma N.
    Marriage Conditions in a Palestinian Village.
    AMS Pr.
Granrud, John E. *see* Granrud, John Edward.
Granrud, John Edward, 1895-
  xGranrud, John E.
    The Organization & Objectives of State
    Teachers' Associations. AMS Pr.
Grant, A. J. *see* Grant, Arthur James.
Grant, Alexander, Sir, Bart, 1826-1884
  xGrant, Alexander.
    Aristotle. R West.
Grant, Allan.
  xGrant, Allan.
    A Preface to Coleridge. Longman.
Grant, Anne. *see* Grant, Anne (MacVicar).
Grant, Anne (MacVicar).
  xGrant, Anne.
    Memoirs of an American Lady: With Sketches
    of Manners & Scenes in America As They
    Existed Previous to the Revolution; with
    Unpublished Letters & a Memoir of Mrs.
    Grant, by James Grant Wilson. Arno.
Grant, Arthur J. *see* Grant, Arthur James.
Grant, Arthur James, 1862-1948
  xGrant, A. J.
    ed. English Historians. Kennikat.
    English Historians. R West.
  xGrant, Arthur J.
    The French Monarchy (1483-1789). AMS Pr.
    Greece in the Age of Pericles. Cooper Sq.
    Huguenots. Shoe String.
Grant, Barbara M.
  xGrant, Barbara M.
    The Teacher Moves: An Analysis of
    Non-Verbal Activity. Tchrs Coll.
Grant, Barry K., 1947-
  xGrant, Barry K.
    ed. Film Genre: Theory & Criticism.
    Scarecrow.
Grant, Blanche C. *see* Grant, Blanche Chloe.
Grant, Blanche Chloe, 1874-1948
  xGrant, Blanche C.

The Taos Indians. Rio Grande.
Grant, Bruce, 1893-
  xGrant, Bruce.
    Encyclopedia of Rawhide & Leather Braiding.
      Cornell Maritime.
    Leather Braiding. Cornell Maritime.
Grant, C. L.
  xGrant, C. L.
    The Hour of the Oxrun Dead. Popular Lib.
Grant, C. L. *see* Grant, Charles L.
Grant, Carl A.
  xGrant, Carl A.
    Community Participation in Education. Allyn.
    ed. Multicultural Education: Commitments,
      Issues & Applications. Assn Supervision.
Grant, Charles.
  xGrant, Charles.
    Wargame Tactics. Hippocrene Bks.
Grant, Charles. *see* Grant, Charles L.
Grant, Charles L.
  xGrant, C. L.
    Ascension. Berkley Pub.
    The Sound of Midnight. Popular Lib.
  xGrant, Charles.
    The Last Call of Mourning. Popular Lib.
  xGrant, Charles L.
    The Last Call of Mourning. Doubleday.
    The Sound of Midnight. Doubleday.
Grant, Charles S., 1917-
  xGrant, Charles S.
    Democracy in the Connecticut Frontier Town
      of Kent. AMS Pr.
    Democracy in the Connecticut Frontier Town
      of Kent. Norton.
Grant, Cherri. *see* Grant, Cherry.
Grant, Cherry.
  xGrant, Cherri.
    Swingers Three. Holloway.
Grant, Clay.
  xGrant, Clay.
    Demon Samurai. Belmont-Tower.
Grant, Donald P.
  xGrant, Donald P.
    A Partially Annotated Bibliography on Space
      Planning Methods for Architecture &
      Physical Planners. Vance Biblios.
Grant, Douglas.
  xGrant, Douglas.
    Fortunate Slave: An Illustration of African
      Slavery in the Early Eighteenth Century.
      Oxford U Pr.
Grant, E. *see* Grant, Edward.
Grant, E. H. *see* Grant, Edward Hector.
Grant, Edward, 1926-
  xGrant, E.
    Physical Science in the Middle Ages.
      Cambridge U Pr.
  xGrant, Edward.
    A Source Book in Medieval Science. Harvard
      U Pr.
Grant, Edward Hector.
  xGrant, E. H.
    Dielectric Behaviour of Biological Molecules in
      Solution. Oxford U Pr.
Grant, Elliott M. *see* Grant, Elliott Mansfield.
Grant, Elliott Mansfield, 1895-1969
  xGrant, Elliott M.
    ed. Four French Plays of the Twentieth
      Century. Greenwood.
Grant, Eugene L. *see* Grant, Eugene Lodewick.
Grant, Eugene Lodewick.
  xGrant, Eugene L.
    Statistical Quality Control. McGraw.
    Statistical Quality Control. McGraw.
Grant, F. *see* Grant, Francis Richard Charles.
Grant, Francis Richard Charles.
  xGrant, F.

Life of Samuel Johnson. Arden Lib.
Life of Samuel Johnson. Kennikat.
Life of Samuel Johnson. R West.
Grant, Frederick C. *see* Grant, Frederick Clifton.
Grant, Frederick Clifton, 1891-1974
  xGrant, Frederick C.
    Ancient Judaism & the New Testament.
      Greenwood.
    ed. Ancient Roman Religion. Bobbs.
    The Economic Background of the Gospels.
      Russell.
Grant, Gerald.
  xGrant, Gerald.
    On Competence: A Critical Analysis of
      Competence-Based Reforms in Higher
      Education. Jossey-Bass.
    The Perpetual Dream: Reform & Experiment in
      the American College. U of Chicago Pr.
Grant, H. *see* Grant, Harvey.
Grant, H. Roger, 1943-
  xGrant, Roger H.
    Insurance Reform: Consumer Action in the
      Progressive Era. Iowa St U Pr.
Grant, Harvey.
  xGrant, H.
    Emergency Care. R J Brady.
Grant, Hiram E.
  xGrant, Hiram E.
    Engineering Drawing with Creative Design.
      McGraw.
Grant, Isabel F. *see* Grant, Isabel Frances.
Grant, Isabel Frances.
  xGrant, Isabel F.
    The Economic History of Scotland. AMS Pr.
    The Economic History of Scotland.
      Greenwood.
Grant, J. Jason.
  xGrant, J. Jason.
    The Square Jungle. Holloway.
Grant, Jan.
  xGrant, Jan.
    Our New Baby. Childrens.
Grant, Jim.
  xGrant, Jim.
    A Thief in the Night. Moody.
Grant, John.
  xGrant, John.
    ed. Aries I. David & Charles.
Grant, John. *see* Grant, John Alexander.
Grant, John Alexander.
  xGrant, John.
    Garden Design Illustrated. U of Wash Pr.
Grant, Karen A.
  xGrant, Karen A.
    Hummingbirds & Their Flowers. Columbia U
      Pr.
Grant, Madison, 1865-1937
  xGrant, Madison.
    The Conquest of a Continent. Noontide.
Grant, Marcia L. *see* Grant, Marcia Moeller.
Grant, Marcia Moeller.
  xGrant, Marcia L.
    Case Studies in Clinical Pharmacology. Davis
      Co.
Grant, Michael.
  xGrant, Michael.
    Civilizations of Europe. NAL.
    Cleopatra. S&S.
    History of Rome. Scribner.
    ed. Latin Literature: An Anthology. Penguin.
  xGrant, Micheal.
    Ancient History Atlas. Macmillan.
Grant, Micheal. *see* Grant, Michael.
Grant, Mildred B. *see* Grant, Mildred Bricker.
Grant, Mildred Bricker.
  xGrant, Mildred B.
    Compiled by Indexes to "The Competitor".
      Greenwood.
Grant, Murray.
  xGrant, Murray.

Handbook of Community Health. Lea &
  Febiger.
Grant, Myrna.
  xGrant, Myrna.
    Vanya. Creation Hse.
Grant, Neil.
  xGrant, Neil.
    Cathedrals. Watts.
    Guilds. Watts.
    The Industrial Revolution. Watts.
    The Partition of Palestine, 1947: Jewish
      Triumph, British Failure, Arab Disaster.
      Watts.
Grant, Nigel, 1932-
  xGrant, Nigel.
    Soviet Education. Penguin.
Grant, P. T. *see* Grant, Patrick Thomas.
Grant, Parks.
  xGrant, Parks.
    Music for Elementary Teachers. Irvington.
Grant, Patrick.
  xGrant, Patrick.
    Images & Ideas in Literature of the English
      Renaissance. U of Mass Pr.
    Six Modern Authors & Problems of Belief.
      B&N.
Grant, Patrick Thomas.
  xGrant, P. T.
    ed. Chemoreception in Marine Organisms.
      Acad Pr.
Grant, Peter H.
  xGrant, Peter H.
    Holistic Therapy: The Risk & Pay-Offs of
      Being Alive. Citadel Pr.
Grant, Philip.
  xGrant, Philip.
    Biology of Developing Systems. HR&W.
Grant, Richard B.
  xGrant, Richard B.
    The Goncourt Brothers. Twayne.
    Perilous Quest: Image, Myth & Prophecy in
      the Narratives of Victor Hugo. Duke.
    Theophile Gautier. Twayne.
Grant, Robert, 1852-1940
  xGrant, Robert.
    Face to Face. AMS Pr.
    The Law Breakers & Other Stories. Mss Info.
    The Law Breakers & Other Stories. Somerset
      Pub.
    The Orchid. Irvington.
Grant, Robert. *see* Grant, Robert McQueen.
Grant, Robert M. *see* Grant, Robert McQueen.
Grant, Robert McQueen, 1917-
  xGrant, Robert.
    A Historical Introduction to the New
      Testament. S&S.
  xGrant, Robert M.
    Earliest Lives of Jesus. Allenson.
    ed. Gnosticism: A Source Book of Heretical
      Writings from the Early Christian Period.
      AMS Pr.
    U-Boat Intelligence, 1914-1918. Shoe String.
Grant, Robert W.
  xGrant, Robert W.
    The Handbook of Civil War Patriotic
      Envelopes & Postal History. R W Grant.
Grant, Roderick, 1941-
  xGrant, Roderick.
    The Great Canal. Gordon-Cremonesi.
Grant, Roger H. *see* Grant, H. Roger.
Grant, Ulysses S. *see* Grant, Ulysses Simpson.
Grant, Ulysses Simpson.
  xGrant, Ulysses S.
    General Grant's Letters to a Friend,
      1861-1880. AMS Pr.
Grant, Verne.
  xGrant, Verne.

Genetics of Flowering Plants. Columbia U Pr.
Origin of Adaptations. Columbia U Pr.

Grant, Vernon W.
xGrant, Vernon W.
The Psychology of Sexual Emotion: The Basis of Selective Attraction. Greenwood.

Grant, Zalin.
xGrant, Zalin.
Survivors. Norton.

Grantham, Dewey W.
xGrantham, Dewey W.
Contemporary American History: The United States Since 1945. Am Hist Assn.
Democratic South. Norton.
Hoke Smith & the Politics of the New South. La State U Pr.
The Regional Imagination: The South & Recent American History. Vanderbilt U Pr.

Grantham, Donald J.
xGrantham, Donald J.
Fundamental Properties of AC Circuits. G S E Pubns.
Geometry for Science & Technology. G S E Pubns.
Grantham's FCC License Study Guide. G S E Pubns.
Mathematics for Basic Circuit Analysis. G S E Pubns.

Grantham, Rudolph E.
xGrantham, Rudolph E.
Lay Shepherding. Judson.

Grantz, Gerald J.
xGrantz, Gerald J.
Home Book of Taxidermy & Tanning. Stackpole.

Granville, Joseph E. see Granville, Joseph Ensign.

Granville, Joseph Ensign, 1923-
xGranville, Joseph E.
Granville's New Strategy of Daily Stock Market Timing for Maximum Profit. P-H.

Granville, Wilfred.
xGranville, Wilfred.
Theater Dictionary: British & American Terms in the Drama, Opera, and Ballet. Greenwood.

Granville-Barker, H. see Granville-Barker, Harley Granville.

Granville-Barker, Harley Granville, 1877-1946
xGranville-Barker, H.
Associating with Shakespeare. Folcroft.
From Henry V to Hamlet. Folcroft.

Graovac, A. see Graovac, Ante.

Graovac, Ante.
xGraovac, A.
Topological Approach to the Chemistry of Conjugated Molecules. Springer-Verlag.

Gras, Norman S. see Gras, Norman Scott Brien.

Gras, Norman Scott Brien, 1884-1956
xGras, Norman S.
Evolution of the English Corn Market from the Twelfth to the Eighteenth Century. Russell.
Industrial Evolution. Kelley.
Introduction to Economic History. Kelley.
The Massachusetts First National Bank of Boston, 1784-1934. Arno.

Grasha, Anthony. see Grasha, Anthony F.

Grasha, Anthony F.
xGrasha, Anthony.
Practical Applications of Psychology. Winthrop.
Psychology of Adjustment & Competence: An Applied Approach. Winthrop.

Grass, Geunter. see Grass, Gunter.
Grass, Guenter. see Grass, Gunter.

Grass, Gunter, 1927-
xGrass, Geunter.
The Flounder. Fawcett.
xGrass, Guenter.
Max: A Play. HarBraceJ.
xGrass, Gunter.

Cat & Mouse. NAL.
Dog Years. Fawcett.
The Flounder. HarBraceJ.
From the Diary of a Snail. HarBraceJ.
From the Diary of a Snail. HarBraceJ.
In the Egg & Other Poems. HarBraceJ.
tr. Inmarypraise. HarBraceJ.
Local Anaesthetic. Fawcett.
Local Anaesthetic. HarBraceJ.
Speak Out: Speeches, Open Letters, Commentaries. HarBraceJ.

Grasse, Pierre P. see Grasse, Pierre Paul.

Grasse, Pierre Paul, 1895-
xGrasse, Pierre P.
Evolution of Living Organisms: Evidence for a New Theory of Transformation. Acad Pr.

Grassi, Ernesto.
xGrassi, Ernesto.
Rhetoric As Philosophy: The Humanist Tradition. Pa St U Pr.

Grassi, Joseph A.
xGrassi, Joseph A.
Jesus As Teacher: A New Testament Guide to Learning the Way. St Mary's.

Grassi, Joseph R., 1915-
xGrassi, Joseph R.
Grassi Block Substitution Test for Measuring Organic Brain Pathology. C C Thomas.

Grassie, N. see Grassie, Norman.

Grassie, Norman.
xGrassie, N.
ed. Developments in Polymer Degradation. Burgess-Intl Ideas.

Grassman, Sven.
xGrassman, Sven.
ed. World Economic Order: Past & Prospects. St Martin.

Grassmuck, George. see Grassmuck, George L.

Grassmuck, George L.
xGrassmuck, George.
Reformed Administration in Lebanon. Ctr for NE & North African Stud.

Grasso, Domenico, 1917-
xGrasso, Domenico.
Proclaiming God's Message: A Study in the Theology of Preaching. U of Notre Dame Pr.

Grasty, William K.
xGrasty, William K.
Introduction to Basic Speech. Glencoe.

Grathwol, Robert P., 1939-
xGrathwol, Robert P.
Stresemann & the DNVP: Reconciliation or Revenge in German Foreign Policy, 1924-1928. Regents Pr Ks.

Gratsch, Edward J.
xGratsch, Edward J.
Where Peter Is: A Survey of Ecclesiology. Alba.

Grattan, C. Hartley. see Grattan, Clinton Hartley.
Grattan, Clinton H. see Grattan, Clinton Hartley.

Grattan, Clinton Hartley, 1902-
xGrattan, C. Hartley.
In Quest of Knowledge: A Historical Perspective on Adult Education. Arno.
xGrattan, Clinton H.
ed. Critique of Humanism: A Symposium. Arno.
xGrattan, Clinton Hartley.
Australian Literature. Folcroft.

Grattan, J. H. see Grattan, John Henry Grafton.

Grattan, John Henry Grafton.
xGrattan, J. H.
Anglo-Saxon Magic & Medicine. Folcroft.

Grattan, Thomas C. see Grattan, Thomas Colley.

Grattan, Thomas Colley, 1792-1864
xGrattan, Thomas C.
Civilized America. Johnson Repr.

Gratus, Jack.
xGratus, Jack.

The Great White Lie: Slavery, Emancipation & Changing Racial Attitudes. Monthly Rev.

Gratz, Rebecca, 1781-1869
xGratz, Rebecca.
Letters of Rebecca Gratz. Arno.

Gratzer, G. H. see Gratzer, George.

Gratzer, George, 1936-
xGratzer, G. H.
Lattice Theory: First Concepts & Distributive Lattices. W H Freeman.

Grau, Robert, 1858-1916
xGrau, Robert.
The Business Man in the Amusement World: A Volume of Progress in the Field of the Theatre. Ozer.
Stage in the Twentieth Century. Arno.

Grau, Shirley A. see Grau, Shirley Ann.

Grau, Shirley Ann.
xGrau, Shirley A.
Evidence of Love. Fawcett.
Evidence of Love. Knopf.

Graubard, Stephen R. see Graubard, Stephen Richards.

Graubard, Stephen Richards.
xGraubard, Stephen R.
ed. Generations. Norton.

Grauer, Robert T.
xGrauer, Robert T.
The Cobol Environment. P-H.

Grauert, H. see Grauert, Hans.

Grauert, Hans.
xGrauert, H.
Theory of Stein Spaces. Springer-Verlag.

Graulich, Paul.
xGraulich, Paul.
Guide to Foreign Legal Materials: Belgium, Luxembourg, Netherlands. Oceana.

Graunt, John, 1620-1674
xGraunt, John.
Natural & Political Observations Mentioned in a Following Index, & Made Upon the Bills of Mortality. Arno.

Graupe, Daniel.
xGraupe, Daniel.
Identification of Systems. Krieger.

Grautoff, F. H. see Grautoff, Ferdinand Heinrich.

Grautoff, Ferdinand Heinrich, 1871-1935
xGrautoff, F. H.
Banzai. Arno.

Gravanis, Michael B.
xGravanis, Michael B.
Specialty Board Review: Anatomic Pathology. Arco.

Gravelle, H. F. E. see Gravelle, Hugh.

Gravelle, Hugh.
xGravelle, H. F. E.
Microeconomics. Longman.

Graver, Lawrence, 1931-
xGraver, Lawrence.
Carson McCullers. U of Minn Pr.
Conrad's Short Fiction. U of Cal Pr.

Graves, Robert P. see Graves, Robert Perceval.

Graves, Algernon.
xGraves, Algernon.
Century of Loan Exhibitions, 1813-1912. B Franklin.
Dictionary of Artists Who Have Exhibited Works in the Principal London Exhibitions from 1760-1893. B Franklin.

Graves, Allen W. see Graves, Allen Willis.

Graves, Allen Willis, 1915-
xGraves, Allen W.
Principles of Administration for a Baptist Association. Broadman.

Graves, Charles B., 1926-
xGraves, Charles E.
When Tragedy Strikes. Moody.

Graves, Charles E. see Graves, Charles B.
Graves, Charles L. see Graves, Charles Larcom.

Graves, Charles Larcom, 1856-1944
xGraves, Charles L.

Life & Letters of Sir George Grove. Longwood
Pr.
Graves, Charles P. *see* Graves, Charles Parlin.
Graves, Charles Parlin, 1911-
xGraves, Charles P.
Fourth of July. Garrard.
Graves, Clay.
xGraves, Clay.
Hurry up, Christmas!. Garrard.
Graves, Douglas R.
xGraves, Douglas R.
Drawing a Likeness. Watson-Guptill.
Drawing Portraits. Watson-Guptill.
Figure Painting in Oil. Watson-Guptill.
Life Drawing in Charcoal. Watson-Guptill.
Graves, Frank P. *see* Graves, Frank Pierrepont.
Graves, Frank Pierrepont, 1869-1943
xGraves, Frank P.
ed. Great Educators of Three Centuries: Their
Work & Its Influence on Modern Education.
AMS Pr.
A History of Education Before the Middle
Ages. Gordon Pr.
A History of Education Before the Middle
Ages. Norwood Edns.
History of Education During the Middle Ages
& the Transition to Modern Times.
Greenwood.
A History of Education During the Middle
Ages & the Transition of Modern Times.
Norwood Edns.
A History of Education in Modern Times.
Gordon Pr.
A History of Education in Modern Times.
Norwood Edns.
Graves, Harvey W.
xGraves, Harvey W.
Nuclear Fuel Management. Wiley.
Graves, John C. *see* Graves, John Cowperthwaite.
Graves, John Cowperthwaite.
xGraves, John C.
Conceptual Foundations of Contemporary
Relativity Theory. MIT Pr.
Graves, Katharine B. *see* Graves, Katharine Bradford.
Graves, Katharine Bradford, 1897-
xGraves, Katharine B.
The Influence of Specialized Training on Tests
of General Intelligence. AMS Pr.
Graves, Lawrence L.
xGraves, Lawrence L.
ed. History of Lubbock. West Tex Mus.
Graves, Maitland E., 1902-
xGraves, Maitland E.
Art of Color & Design. McGraw.
Graves, Merle D. *see* Graves, Merle Dixon.
Graves, Merle Dixon, 1887-
xGraves, Merle D.
Bubblin's An' B'ilin's at the Center. Arno.
Graves, Nora C. *see* Graves, Nora Calhoun.
Graves, Nora Calhoun.
xGraves, Nora C.
Two Culture Theory in C. P. Snow's Novels. U
Pr of Miss.
Graves, Norman. *see* Graves, Norman John.
Graves, Norman John.
xGraves, Norman.
Curriculum Planning in Geography. Heinemann
Ed.
Graves, Richard. *see* Graves, Richard H.
Graves, Richard H.
xGraves, Richard.
Bushcraft: A Serious Guide to Survival &
Camping. Schocken.
Bushcraft: A Serious Guide to Survival &
Camping. Warner Bks.
Graves, Richard L.
xGraves, Richard L.

C. L. A. W.. Stein & Day.
Cobalt 60. Stein & Day.
The Platinum Bullet. Stein & Day.
Quicksilver. Stein & Day.
Graves, Richard L. *see* Graves, Richard Layton.
Graves, Richard Layton, 1931-
xGraves, Richard L.
Rhetoric & Composition: A Sourcebook for
Teachers. Hayden.
Graves, Richard P. *see* Graves, Richard Perceval.
Graves, Richard Perceval.
xGraves, Richard P.
Lawrence of Arabia & His World. Scribner.
Graves, Robert, 1895-
xGraves, Robert.
Good-Bye to All That. Doubleday.
Goodbye to All That. Octagon.
Greek Gods & Heroes. Doubleday.
The Greek Myths. Braziller.
Greek Myths. Penguin.
The More Deserving Cases: Eighteen Old
Poems for Reconsideration. Folcroft.
My Head, My Head. Haskell.
Occupation : Writer. Octagon.
On English Poetry: Being an Irregular
Approach to the Psychology of This Art from
Evidence Mainly Subjective. Haskell.
On English Poetry: Being an Irregular
Approach to the Psychology of This Art,
from Evidence Mainly Subjective. Somerset
Pub.
The Reader Over Your Shoulder: A Handbook
for Writers of English Prose. Random.
The White Goddess: A Historical Grammar of
Poetic Myth. FS&G.
The White Goddess: A Historical Grammar of
Poetic Myth. Octagon.
Graves, Robert P. *see* Graves, Robert Perceval.
Graves, Robert Perceval.
xGraves , Robert P.
Life of Sir William Rowan Hamilton. Chelsea
Pub.
xGraves, Robert P.
Life of Sir William Rowan Hamilton. Arno.
Graves, Robert W. *see* Graves, Robert Windham.
Graves, Robert Windham, Sir, 1858-
xGraves, Robert W.
Storm Centres of the Near East. AMS Pr.
Graves, Thornton S. *see* Graves, Thornton Shirley.
Graves, Thornton Shirley, 1883-
xGraves, Thornton S.
Court & the London Theatres During the
Reign of Elizabeth. Folcroft.
Court & the London Theatres During the
Reign of Elizabeth. Russell.
Graves, W. S. *see* Graves, William Sidney.
Graves, Wallace.
xGraves, Wallace.
From Word to Story. HarBraceJ.
Graves, William B. *see* Graves, William Brooke.
Graves, William Brooke, 1899-
xGraves, William B.
Public Administration in a Democratic Society.
Greenwood.
Graves, William H. *see* Graves, William Howard.
Graves, William Howard, 1940-
xGraves, William H.
On the Theory of Vector Measures. Am Math.
Graves, William S. *see* Graves, William Sidney.
Graves, William Sidney, 1865-1940
xGraves, W. S.
America's Siberian Adventure. Gordon Pr.
xGraves, William S.
America's Siberian Adventure, 1918-1920.
Arno.
Grawoig, Dennis E.
xGrawoig, Dennis E.

Decision Mathematics. McGraw.
Mathematics: A Foundation for Decisions.
A-W.
Gray, A. William.
xGray, A. William.
Applications of College Mathematics. Glencoe.
Mathematics for the College Student:
Elementary Concepts. Glencoe.
Gray, Alexander, Sir, 1882-
xGray, Alexander.
The Development of Economic Doctrine: An
Introductory Survey. AMS Pr.
Gray, Andrew, 1847-1925
xGray, Andrew.
Absolute Measurements in Electricity &
Magnetism. Dover.
Gray, Arthur, 1852-1940
xGray, Arthur.
Chapter in the Early Life of Shakespeare:
Polesworth in Arden. AMS Pr.
Gray, Arthur A. *see* Gray, Arthur Amos.
Gray, Arthur Amos, 1885-
xGray, Arthur A.
Men Who Built the West. Arno.
Gray, Asa, 1810-1888
xGray, Asa.
Letters of Asa Gray. B Franklin.
Gray, Basil, 1904-
xGray, Basil.
Persian Painting. Rizzoli Intl.
Gray, Benjamin K. *see* Gray, Benjamin Kirkman
Gray, Benjamin Kirkman , 1862-1907
xGray, Benjamin K.
History of English Philanthropy: From the
Dissolution of the Monasteries to the Taking
of the First Census. Biblio Dist.
Gray, Bettyanne.
xGray, Bettyanne.
Manya's Story. Lerner Pubns.
Gray, Bill.
xGray, Bill.
More Studio Tips for Artists & Graphic
Designers. Van Nos Reinhold.
Gray, Bradford H., 1942-
xGray, Bradford H.
Human Subjects in Medical Experimentation:
A Sociological Study of the Conduct &
Regulation of Clinical Research. Krieger.
Human Subjects in Medical Experimentation:
A Sociological Study of the Conduct &
Regulation of Clinical Research. Wiley.
Gray, Brayton.
xGray, Brayton.
Homotopy Theory: An Introduction to
Algebraic Topology. Acad Pr.
Gray, Cecil, 1895-1951
xGray, Cecil.
Contingencies & Other Essays. Arno.
Forty-Eight Preludes & Fugues of J. S. Bach.
Da Capo.
The Forty-Eight Preludes & Fugues of J. S.
Bach. Hyperion Conn.
The History of Music. Greenwood.
A History of Music. Routledge & Kegan.
Sibelius. Hyperion Conn.
Survey of Contemporary Music. Arno.
A Survey of Contemporary Music. Greenwood.
Gray, Charles G. *see* Gray, Charles Glass.
Gray, Charles Glass, b. 1820
xGray, Charles G.
Off at Sunrise: The Overland Journal of
Charles Glass Gray. Huntington Lib.
Gray, Charles H. *see* Gray, Charles Horace.
Gray, Charles Horace.
xGray, Charles H.
ed. Hormones in Blood. Acad Pr.
Gray, Colin S.
xGray, Colin S.

The Geopolitics of the Nuclear Era: Heartland,
Rimlands, & the Technological Revolution.
Crane-Russak Co.
The Soviet-American Arms Race. Lexington
Bks.
Gray, D. F. see Gray, David F.
Gray, Daniel S. see Gray, Daniel Savage.
Gray, Daniel Savage.
xGray, Daniel S.
Alabama: A Place, a People, a Point of View.
Kendall-Hunt.
Gray, David F., 1938-
xGray, D. F.
ed. Stellar Turbulence: Proceedings of
Colloquium 51 of the International
Astronomical Union, Held at the University
of Western Ontario, London, Ontario,
Canada, August 27-30, 1979. Springer-Verlag.
xGray, David F.
The Observation & Analysis of Stellar
Photospheres. Wiley.
Gray, Donald. see Gray, Donald P.
Gray, Donald P.
xGray, Donald.
Finding God Among Us. St Mary's.
xGray, Donald P.
Where Is Your God. Pflaum Pr.
Gray, Douglas.
xGray, Douglas.
Themes & Images in the Medieval English
Religious Lyric. Routledge & Kegan.
Gray, Duncan, 1892-1958
xGray, Duncan.
The Life & Work of Lord Byron. Folcroft.
Gray, E. G. see Gray, Edward George.
Gray, Eden.
xGray, Eden.
Complete Guide to the Tarot. Bantam.
Complete Guide to the Tarot. Crown.
Mastering the Tarot: Basic Lessons in an
Ancient Mystic Art. NAL.
Gray, Edmund R.
xGray, Edmund R.
ed. Business Policy & Strategy: Selected
Readings. Austin Pr.
Gray, Edward George, 1924-
xGray, E. G.
The Synapse. Carolina Biological.
Gray, Edwyn.
xGray, Edwyn.
Action Atlantic. Pinnacle Bks.
Gray, Eileen, 1922-
xGray, Eileen.
Everywoman's Guide to College. Les Femmes
Pub.
Gray, Elizabeth J. see Gray, Elizabeth Janet.
Gray, Elizabeth Janet.
xGray, Elizabeth J.
Adam of the Road. Viking Pr.
Gray, Francine D. see Gray, Francine Du Plessix.
Gray, Francine Du Plessix.
xGray, Francine D.
Lovers & Tyrants. PB.
xGray, Francine Du Plessix.
Lovers & Tyrants. S&S.
Gray, Francis C. see Gray, Francis Calley.
Gray, Francis Calley, 1790-1856
xGray, Francis C.
Prison Discipline in America. Patterson Smith.
Gray, G. see Gray, George E.
Gray, Genevieve. see Gray, Genevieve S.
Gray, Genevieve S.
xGray, Genevieve.

Break-In. EMC.
Ghost Story. Lothrop.
Hot Shot. EMC.
How Far, Felipe?. Har-Row.
Sore Loser. HM.
The Spiderweb Stone. EMC.
Stand-off. EMC.
Stray. EMC.
The Tall Singer. EMC.
Two Tickets to Memphis. EMC.
Varnell Roberts, Super-Pigeon. HM.
Gray, George. see Gray, George Robert.
Gray, George E.
xGray, G.
Public Transportation: Planning, Operations &
Management. P-H.
Gray, George Robert.
xGray, George.
Composition & Properties of Oil Well Drilling
Fluids. Gulf Pub.
Gray, H. J. see Gray, Harry Joshua.
Gray, H. L. see Gray, Henry L.
Gray, H. Peter.
xGray, H. Peter.
An Aggregate Theory of International
Payments Adjustment. Lexington Bks.
International Trade, Investment & Payments.
HM.
Gray, Harold.
xGray, Harold.
Little Orphan Annie & Little Orphan Annie in
Cosmic City. Dover.
illus. Little Orphan Annie in the Great
Depression. Dover.
Gray, Harry B.
xGray, Harry B.
Chemical Bonds: An Introduction to Atomic &
Molecular Structure. Benjamin-Cummings.
Gray, Harry Joshua, 1924-
xGray, H. J.
High Speed Digital Memories & Circuits. A W.
Gray, Henry L.
xGray, H. L.
The Generalized Jackknife Statistic. Dekker.
xGray, Henry L.
Probability for Practicing Engineers. CBI Pub.
Gray, Howard A. see Gray, Howard Aaron.
Gray, Howard Aaron, 1899-
xGray, Howard A.
Some Factors in the Undergraduate Careers of
Young College Students with Particular
Reference to Columbia & Barnard Colleges.
AMS Pr.
Gray, Ilse.
xGray, Ilse.
Designing & Making Dolls. Watson-Guptill.
Gray, J. see Gray, John.
Gray, J. A. see Gray, John Armstrong Muir.
Gray, Jack.
xGray, Jack.
Striker Schneiderman. U of Toronto Pr.
Gray, Jack C.
xGray, Jack C.
Accounting & Management Action. McGraw.
Gray, James, 1921-
xGray, James.
The American Civil Liberties Union of
Southern California & Imperial Valley
Agricultural Labor Disturbances,1930,1934. R
& E Res Assoc.
Edna St. Vincent Millay. U of Minn Pr.
Johnson's Sermons: A Study. Oxford U Pr.
Gray, James R.
xGray, James R.
Ranch Economics. Iowa St U Pr.
Gray, Jane.
xGray, Jane.
Medicine. David & Charles.
Gray, Jeffrey. see Gray, Jeffrey Alan.
Gray, Jeffrey A. see Gray, Jeffrey Alan.

Gray, Jeffrey Alan.
xGray, Jeffrey.
Psychology of Fear & Stress. McGraw.
xGray, Jeffrey A.
Ivan Pavlov. Viking Pr.
Gray, Jennifer.
xGray, Jennifer.
Canvas Work. Branford.
Gray, Jenny.
xGray, Jenny.
Teacher's Survival Guide. Pitman Learning.
Gray, Jeremy.
xGray, Jeremy.
Ideas of Space: Euclidean, Non-Euclidean &
Relativistic. Oxford U Pr.
Gray, Jerry. see Gray, Jerry L.
Gray, Jerry L.
xGray, Jerry.
Organizational Behavior: Concepts &
Applications. Merrill.
Readings in Organizational Behavior: Concepts
and Applications. Merrill.
xGray, Jerry L.
ed. The Glacier Project: Concepts &
Critiques-Selected Readings on the Glacier
Theories of Organization & Management.
Crane-Russak Co.
Gray, John, 1799-1883
xGray, J.
The Social System: A Treatise on the Principle
of Exchange. Kraus Repr.
xGray, John.
Lectures on the Nature & Use of Money.
Kelley.
Social System: A Treatise on the Principle of
Exchange. Kelley.
Gray, John Armstrong Muir.
xGray, J. A.
Man Against Disease: Preventive Medicine.
Oxford U Pr.
Gray, John E.
xGray, John E.
Energy Policy: Industry Perspectives. Ballinger
Pub.
Gray, John M. see Gray, John Morgan.
Gray, John Morgan.
xGray, John M.
Lord Selkirk of Red River. Mich St U Pr.
Gray, John S. see Gray, John Stephen.
Gray, John Stephen, 1910-
xGray, John S.
Centennial Campaign: The Sioux War of 1876.
Old Army.
Gray, John W. see Gray, John Wylie.
Gray, John Wylie.
xGray, John W.
Communication & Leadership. Natl Assn
Principals.
Gray, Joseph M. see Gray, Joseph M. M.
Gray, Joseph M. M., 1877-
xGray, Joseph M.
Prophets of the Soul. Arno.
Gray, L. C. see Gray, Lewis Cecil.
Gray, Laman A. see Gray, Laman Alexander.
Gray, Laman Alexander, 1908-
xGray, Laman A.
Endometrial Carcinoma & Its Treatment: The
Role of Irradiation, Extent of Surgery &
Approach to Chemotherapy. C C Thomas.
Vaginal Hysterectomy: Indications, Technique
& Complications. C C Thomas.
Gray, Lewis C. see Gray, Lewis Cecil.
Gray, Lewis Cecil, 1881-
xGray, L. C.
Farm Ownership & Tenancy. Arno.
xGray, Lewis C.

History of Agriculture in the Southern United
   States to 1860. Kelley.
History of Agriculture in the Southern United
   States to 1860. Peter Smith.
Gray, Madeline.
   xGray, Madeline.
      Changing Years: The Menopause Without Fear.
       NAL.
      Margaret Sanger: A Biography of the
       Champion of Birth Control. Marek.
Gray, Malcolm.
   xGray, Malcolm.
      The Highland Economy: 1750-1850.
       Greenwood.
Gray, Marlowe.
   xGray, Marlowe.
      The Lovers Guide to Sensuous Astrology.
       NAL.
Gray, Martin.
   xGray, Martin.
      For Those I Loved. Little.
      For Those I Loved.. NAL.
Gray, Michael H., 1946-
   xGray, Michael H.
      Beecham: A Centenary Discography. Holmes &
       Meier.
Gray, N. *see* Gray, Nicolette Mary (Binyon).
Gray, Nicholas S. *see* Gray, Nicholas Stuart.
Gray, Nicholas Stuart.
   xGray, Nicholas S.
      A Wind from Nowhere. Merrimack Bk Serv.
Gray, Nicolete.
   xGray, Nicolete.
      Nineteenth-Century Ornamented Type Faces.
       U of Cal Pr.
Gray, Nicolette Mary (Binyon).
   xGray, N.
      Lettering on Buildings. Krieger.
Gray, Nigel.
   xGray, Nigel.
      The Deserter. Har-Row.
      It'll All Come Out in the Wash. Har-Row.
Gray, Oscar S., 1926-
   xGray, Oscar S.
      Cases & Materials on Environmental Law.
       BNA.
Gray, Peter, 1908-
   xGray, Peter.
      Encyclopedia of Microscopy &
       Micro-Technique. Van Nos Reinhold.
      Handbook of Basic Microtechnique. McGraw.
      ed. Student Dictionary of Biology. Van Nos
       Reinhold.
Gray, R. *see* Gray, Ronald D.
Gray, Ralph.
   xGray, Ralph.
      Economic Development of the United States.
       Irwin.
Gray, Richard A.
   xGray, Richard A.
      Compiled by Guide to Book Review Citations:
       A Bibliography of Sources. Ohio St U Pr.
Gray, Richard B. *see* Gray, Richard Butler.
Gray, Richard Butler, 1922-
   xGray, Richard B.
      Jose Marti: Cuban Patriot. U Presses Fla.
Gray, Richard J.
   xGray, Richard J.
      The Literature of Memory: Modern Writers of
       the American South. Johns Hopkins.
Gray, Robert.
   xGray, Robert.
      A History of London. Taplinger.
Gray, Robert M.
   xGray, Robert M.
      The Church & the Older Person. Eerdmans.
      ed. Ergodic & Information Theory. Acad Pr.
Gray, Ronald D.
   xGray, R.

Brecht the Dramatist. Cambridge U Pr.
German Poetry: A Guide to Free Appreciation.
   Cambridge U Pr.
xGray, Ronald D.
   German Tradition in Literature. Cambridge U
   Pr.
Gray, Simon. *see* Gray, Simon James Holliday.
Gray, Simon James Holliday.
   xGray, Simon.
      Otherwise Engaged & Other Plays. Penguin.
      The Rear Column, Dog Days, & Other Plays.
       Penguin.
Gray, Stephen, 1941-
   xGray, Stephen.
      Southern African Literature: An Introduction.
       B&N.
Gray, Susan W. *see* Gray, Susan Walton.
Gray, Susan Walton, 1913-
   xGray, Susan W.
      Psychologist in the Schools. Irvington.
Gray, T. R. *see* Gray, Timothy R. G.
Gray, Thomas.
   xGray, Thomas.
      Correspondence of Thomas Gray. Oxford U Pr.
Gray, Timothy R. G.
   xGray, T. R.
      Soil Micro-Organisms. Longman.
Gray, Tony.
   xGray, Tony.
      Champions of Peace: The Story of Alfred
       Nobel, the Peace Prize, & the Laureates.
       Paddington.
      The Orange Order. Transatlantic.
Gray, Valeria B. *see* Gray, Valerie Bonita.
Gray, Valerie Bonita.
   xGray, Valeria B.
      Invisible Man's Literary Heritage: Benito
       Cereno & Moby Dick. Humanities.
Gray, Vanessa.
   xGray, Vanessa.
      The Lonely Earl. NAL.
Gray, Vera.
   xGray, Vera.
      Music, Movement & Mime for Children.
       Oxford U Pr.
Gray, Virginia.
   xGray, Virginia.
      Mud, Space and Spirit: Handmade Adobes.
       Capra Pr.
Gray, W. A. *see* Gray, William Alan.
Gray, Wanda.
   xGray, Wanda.
      Intro. by I Live Here Too. Humanics Ltd.
Gray, William A.
   xGray, William A.
      Learning by Doing: Developing Teaching
       Skills. A-W.
Gray, William Alan.
   xGray, W. A.
      Engineering Calculations in Radiative Heat
       Transfer. Pergamon.
Gray, William G.
   xGray, William G.
      Inner Traditions of Magic. Weiser.
      The Talking Tree. Weiser.
Gray, William R.
   xGray, William R.
      Pacific Crest Trail. Natl Geog.
Gray, William S.
   xGray, William S.
      Hotel & Motel Management & Operations.
       P-H.
Gray, William S. *see* Gray, William Scott.
Gray, William Scott, 1885-1960
   xGray, William S.
      On Their Own in Reading: How to Give
       Children Independence in Analyzing New
       Words. Scott F.
Gray, Wood, 1905-
   xGray, Wood.

Historian's Handbook: A Key to the Study &
   Writing of History. HM.
Graybill, Franklin A.
   xGraybill, Franklin A.
      Introduction to Linear Statistical Models.
       McGraw.
Graydon, Nell S.
   xGraydon, Nell S.
      Tales of Beaufort. Beaufort.
Grayson. *see* Grayson, Merrill.
Grayson, A. K. *see* Grayson, Albert Kirk.
Grayson, Albert Kirk.
   xGrayson, A. K.
      Assyrian & Babylonian Chronicles. J J
       Augustin.
      Babylonian Historical-Literary Texts. U of
       Toronto Pr.
Grayson, Benson L., 1932-
   xGrayson, Benson L.
      ed. The American Image of Russia, 1917-1977.
       Ungar.
Grayson, Benson L. *see* Grayson, Benson Lee.
Grayson, Benson Lee, 1932-
   xGrayson, Benson L.
      ed. The American Image of China. Ungar.
Grayson, C. Jackson. *see* Grayson, Charles Jackson.
Grayson, Cary T. *see* Grayson, Cary Travers.
Grayson, Cary Travers, 1878-1938
   xGrayson, Cary T.
      Woodrow Wilson: An Intimate Memoir.
       Potomac.
Grayson, Charles Jackson.
   xGrayson, C. Jackson.
      Decisions Under Uncertainty: Drilling
       Decisions by Oil & Gas Operators. Arno.
Grayson, Fred N.
   xGrayson, Fred N.
      Oysters. Messner.
Grayson, Harry, d. 1968
   xGrayson, Harry.
      They Played the Game: The Story of Baseball
       Greats. Arno.
Grayson, Henry.
   xGrayson, Henry.
      ed. Changing Approaches to the
       Psychotherapies. Halsted Pr.
Grayson, Merrill, 1919-
   xGrayson.
      Diseases of the Cornea. Mosby.
Grayson, Theodore J. *see* Grayson, Theodore Julius.
Grayson, Theodore Julius, 1880-
   xGrayson, Theodore J.
      Leaders & Periods of American Finance. Arno.
Grazda, Edward E.
   xGrazda, Edward E.
      Handbook of Applied Mathematics. Krieger.
Grazer, Frederick M.
   xGrazer, Frederick M.
      Body Image: A Surgical Perspective. Mosby.
Grazia, Alfred De. *see* De Grazia, Alfred.
Graziani, Vicenzo G. De. *see* De Graziani, Vincenzo G.
Graziano, Anthony M., 1932-
   xGraziano, Anthony M.
      Child Without Tomorrow. Pergamon.
Graziano, Frank, 1955-
   xGraziano, Frank.
      From Sheepshead, from Paumanok. Porch
       Pubns.
Greacen, Robert.
   xGreacen, Robert.
      Art of Noel Coward. Folcroft.
Grealy, Joseph I.
   xGrealy, Joseph I.
      School Crime & Violence: Problems &
       Solutions. F E Peters.
Grear, John W., 1937-
   xGrear, John W.

A Revision of the New World Species of
Rhynchosia(Leguminosae-Faboideae). NY
Botanical.
Greasybear, Charley J. *see* Greasybear, Charley John.
Greasybear, Charley John.
xGreasybear, Charley J.
Songs. Ahsahta Pr.
Great Britain - Admiralty. *see* Great Britain. Admiralty.
Great Britain - Colonial Office, London. *see* Great
Britain. Colonial Office.
Great Britain - Her Majesty's Stationery Office, London.
see Great Britain. Stationery Office.
Great Britain. Admiralty.
xGreat Britain - Admiralty.
Handbook of German East Africa. Negro U Pr.
Handbook of Portuguese Nyasaland. Negro U
Pr.
Great Britain, Census Office. *see* Great Britain. Office of
Population Censuses and Surveys.
Great Britain Court Of The Star Chamber. *see* Great
Britain. Court of Star Chamber.
Great Britain Gold & Silver Commission. *see* Great
Britain. Gold and Silver Commission.
Great Britain. Gold and Silver Commission.
xGreat Britain Gold & Silver Commission.
Monetary Problem: Gold & Silver. AMS Pr.
Great Britain. Historical Manuscripts Commission.
xGreat Britain. Historical Manuscripts
Commission. Report on Manuscripts in Various
Collections.
Manuscripts of Captain H. V. Knox (from Vol.
VI). Irvington.
Manuscripts of the Earl of Dartmouth.
Irvington.
Report of the Manuscripts of Mrs.
Stopford-Sackville of Drayton House,
Northamptonshire. Irvington.
Report on American Manuscripts in the Royal
Institution of Great Britain. Irvington.
Great Britain House Of Commons. *see* Great Britain.
Parliament. House of Commons.
Great Britain. House of Lords.
xGreat Britain House Of Lords - 1621.
Notes of the Debates in the House of Lords.
Johnson Repr.
xGreat Britain House Of Lords - 1624.
Notes of the Debates in the House of Lords.
Johnson Repr.
Great Britain. Board of Agriculture.
xGreat Britain Board of Agriculture.
Agriculture State of the Kingdom, 1816.
Kelley.
Great Britain. British Council.
xBritish Council.
British Scientific Documentation Services.
Longman.
ed. British Writers. Scribner.
xTheBritish Council.
Higher Education in the United Kingdom:
1980-1982. Longman.
Great Britain. Challenger Office.
xGreat Britain Challenger Office.
Report on the Scientific Results of the Voyage
of H. M. S. Challenger During the Years
1873-1876. Johnson Repr.
Great Britain. Colonial Office.
xGreat Britain - Colonial Office, London.
Catalogue of the Colonial Office Library,
London. G K Hall.
xGreat Britain Colonial Office.
Colonial Reports: Nyasaland 1955. Greenwood.
Great Britain. Colonial Office. Library.
xForeign & Commonwealth Office, London.
Catalogue of the Colonial Office Library: Third
Supplement. G K Hall.
**Great Britain. Commonwealth Relations Office. India
Office Library.**
xCommonwealth Relations Office - London.

Index of Post-Nineteen Thirty Seven European
Manuscript Accessions, India Office Library.
G K Hall.
Great Britain. Court of Star Chamber.
xGreat Britain Court Of The Star Chamber.
Reports of Cases in Courts of Star Chamber &
High Commission. Johnson Repr.
Great Britain. Foreign Office.
xBritish Foreign Office.
British Foreign Office : Russia Correspondence,
1914 - 1918: Indexes & Guides to the
Microfilm Collection. Scholarly Res Inc.
xGreat Britain Foreign Office.
British Documents of the Origin of the War
1898-1914. Johnson Repr.
Great Britain. Foreign Office. Historical Section.
xGreat Britain Foreign Office Historical Section.
British Possessions, 2: The Congo. Negro U Pr.
German African Possessions, Late. Negro U
Pr.
Spanish & Italian Possessions: Independent
States. Negro U Pr.
Great Britain House Of Lords - 1621. *see* Great Britain.
House of Lords.
Great Britain House Of Lords - 1624. *see* Great Britain.
House of Lords.
Great Britain Ministry Of Defence - London. *see* Great
Britain.Ministry of Defence.
Great Britain, Patent Office. *see* Great Britain.Patent
Office.
Great Britain Sovereigns. *see* Great Britain. Sovereigns,
Etc.
Great Britain.Ministry of Defence.
xGreat Britain Ministry Of Defence - London.
Author & Subject Catalogues of the Naval
Library, Ministry of Defence. G K Hall
**Great Britain. Office of Population Censuses and
Surveys.**
xGreat Britain, Census Office.
Abstract of the Answers & Returns: The
Census Report for 1801. Kelley.
Great Britain. Parliament.
xGreat Britain Parliament.
British West Indies at Westminster, 1789-1823.
Negro U Pr.
Proceedings & Debates of the British
Parliaments Respecting North America.
Kraus Repr.
Report of Select Committee on Aborigines.
Verry.
Sheffield Outrages: Report Presented to the
Trades Unions Commissioners. Kelley.
xParliamentary Debates, Great Britain.
Report from the Select Committee on the High
Price of Gold Bullion. Arno.
Great Britain. Parliament. House of Commons.
xGreat Britain House Of Commons.
Debates in the House of Commons in 1625.
Johnson Repr.
Parliamentary Debates in 1610. Johnson Repr.
xGreat Britain. Parliament. House of Commons.
Fifth Report from the Select Committee of the
House of Commons on the Affairs of the
East India Company. Kelley.
Report from the Select Committee to Whom
the Several Petitions Complaining of the
Distressed State of the Agriculture in the
United Kingdom Were Referred, 18 June
1821. Kelley.
Substance of the Debate in the House of
Commons, on the 15th of May, 1823. Negro
U Pr.
**Great Britain. Parliament. House of Commons. Select
Committee on Artisans and Machinery.**
xGreat Britain, Parliament, House of Commons,
Select Committee on Artizans & Machinery.

Six Reports from the Select Committee on
Artizans & Machinery, 23 February - 21 May
1824. Kelley.
Great Britain.Patent Office.
xGreat Britain, Patent Office.
Alphabetical Index of Patentees of Inventions
1617-1852. Kelley.
Patents for Inventions. Arno.
Great Britain. Poor Law Board.
xGreat Britain Poor Law Board.
Official Circulars of Public Documents &
Information. Kelley.
Great Britain. Poor Law Commissioners.
xGreat Britain Poor Law Commissioners.
Reports of Special Assistant Poor Law
Commissioners on the Employment of
Women & Children in Agriculture: Eighteen
Forty-Three. Kelly.
Great Britain. Public Record Office.
xBritish Government Public Record Office.
Still in British Hands: American Revolutionary
Documents in British Hands. Pendragon Hse.
xPublic Record Office Of Great Britain.
Guide to the Contents of the Public Record
Office. Kraus Repr.
**Great Britain. Royal Commission Upon the Duties of
the Metropolitan Police.**
xRoyal Commission Upon The Duties Of The
Metropolitan Police.
Minutes of Evidence of the Royal Commission
Upon the Duties of the Metropolitan Police.
Arno.
Great Britain. Schools Council.
xBritish Schools Council.
Project Technology Briefs. Heinemann Ed.
xSchools Council.
Basic Electrical & Electronic Construction
Methods. Heinemann Ed.
Mathematics Applicable: Algebra with
Applications. Heinemann Ed.
Mathematics Applicable: Polynomial Models.
Heinemann Ed.
Mathematics Applicable: Vector Models.
Heinemann Ed.
Simple Computer & Control Logic. Heinemann
Ed.
Great Britain. Schools Council. History 13-16 Project.
xSchools Council History 13-16 Project.
Arab-Israeli Conflict. Greenhaven.
The Rise of Communist China. Greenhaven.
xSchools Councils History 13-16 Project.
The Irish Question. Greenhaven.
Great Britain. Sovereigns, Etc.
xGreat Britain Sovereigns.
British Royal Proclamations Relating to
America, 1603-1783. B Franklin.
Great Britain. Stationery Office.
xGreat Britain - Her Majesty's Stationery Office,
London.
Catalogue of the Foreign Office Library,
1926-1968. G K Hall.
xStationery Office (Great Britain).
Annual Catalogues of British Official &
Parliamentary Publications 1894 to 1909.
Somersct Hse.
Great Britain. War Office. General Staff.
xGerman War Office.
Handbook of the German Army in War,
January 1917. Beekman Pubs.
xWar Office.
Dress Regulations for the Officers of the Army,
1900. C E Tuttle.
Great Northern Railroad. *see* Great Northern Railway.
Great Northern Railway.
xGreat Northern Railroad.
Dedication & Opening of the New Cascade
Tunnel. Shorey.
Great Plains Flora Assn. *see* Great Plains Flora
Association.

Great Plains Flora Association.
  xGreat Plains Flora Assn.
      Atlas of the Flora of the Great Plains. Iowa St
      U Pr.
Greater London Council.
  xGreater London Council.
      Historic Buildings in London. St Martin.
      Home Sweet Home. St Martin.
      Survey of London, Vol. 38: The Museum Area
      of South Kensington & Westminster.
      Humanities.
      Survey of London, Vol. 39: The Grosvenor
      Estate in Mayfair, Part. 1, General History.
      Humanities.
Greater London Council Department of Architecture &
  Civic Design. see Greater London Council. Dept. of
  Architecture and Civic Design.
**Greater London Council. Dept. of Architecture and Civic
  Design.**
  xGreater London Council Department of
      Architecture & Civic Design.
      Good Practice Details. Nichols Pub.
      Introduction to Housing Layout. Nichols Pub.
Greaves, A. A. see Greaves, Anthony A.
Greaves, Anthony A.
  xGreaves, A. A.
      Maurice Barres. Twayne.
Greaves, Bettina B. see Greaves, Bettina Bien.
Greaves, Bettina Bien.
  xGreaves, Bettina B.
      ed. Free Market Economics: A Basic Reader.
      Foun Econ Ed.
      Free Market Economics: A Syllabus. Foun
      Econ Ed.
Greaves, Margaret.
  xGreaves, Margaret.
      A Net to Catch the Wind. Har-Row.
Greaves, Percy L., 1906-
  xGreaves, Percy L.
      Understanding the Dollar Crisis. Western
      Islands.
Greaves, Richard L.
  xGreaves, Richard L.
      Compiled by An Annotated Bibliography of
      John Bunyan Studies. C E Barbour.
Grebanier, Bernard. see Grebanier, Bernard D. N.
Grebanier, Bernard D. N., 1903-
  xGrebanier, Bernard.
      Thornton Wilder. U of Minn Pr.
Grebanier, Joseph, 1912-
  xGrebanier, Joseph.
      Chinese Stoneware Glazes. Watson-Guptill.
Grebene, Alan B., 1939-
  xGrebene, Alan B.
      Analog Integrated Circuit Design. Krieger.
Grebinger, P. see Grebinger, Paul.
Grebinger, Paul.
  xGrebinger, P.
      Discovering Past Behavior: Experiments in the
      Archaeology of the American Southwest.
      Gordon.
Grech, Paul.
  xGrech, Paul.
      Hip Arthrography. Lippincott.
Greeley, A. M. see Greeley, Andrew M.
Greeley, Andrew. see Greeley, Andrew M.
Greeley, Andrew M., 1928-
  xGreeley, A. M.
      Ethnicity. Seabury.
  xGreeley, Andrew.
      Ethnic Drinking Subcultures. Praeger.
      Everything You Wanted to Know About the
      Catholic Church but Were Too Pious to Ask.
      Thomas More.
      Neighborhood. Continuum.
      ed. The Persistence of Religion. Seabury.
  xGreeley, Andrew M.

      The American Catholic: A Social Portrait.
      Basic.
      Afterword by Catholic Schools in a Declining
      Church. Andrews & McMeel.
      Changing Catholic College. NORC.
      The Communal Catholic: A Personal
      Manifesto. Seabury.
      Death in April. McGraw.
      The Denominational Society: A Sociological
      Approach to Religion in America. Scott F.
      The Devil, You Say: Man & His Personal
      Devils & Angels. Doubleday.
      Education of Catholic Americans. NORC.
      Ethnicity in the United States: A Preliminary
      Reconnaissance. Wiley.
      Everything You Wanted to Know About the
      Catholic Church but Were Too Pious to Ask.
      B&N.
      Friendship Game. Doubleday.
      The Great Mysteries: An Essential Catechism.
      Seabury.
      Love & Play. Seabury.
      The Mary Myth: On the Femininity of God.
      Seabury.
      The Sinai Myth. Doubleday.
      That Most Distressful Nation: The Taming of
      the American Irish. Times Bks.
Greely, Margaret.
  xGreely, Margaret.
      Arabian Exodus. J A Allen.
Green, A. E. see Green, Albert Edward.
Green, Alan G.
  xGreen, Alan G.
      Regional Aspects of Canada's Economic
      Growth. U of Toronto Pr.
Green, Albert E. see Green, Albert Edward.
Green, Albert Edward.
  xGreen, A. E.
      Reliability Technology. Wiley.
  xGreen, Albert E.
      Theoretical Elasticity. Oxford U Pr.
Green, Alex E. see Green, Alex Edward Samuel.
Green, Alex Edward Samuel.
  xGreen, Alex E.
      Atomic & Space Physics. A-W.
Green, Alexander, 1888-
  xGreen, Alexander.
      Dative of Agency: A Chapter of
      Indo-European Case-Syntax. AMS Pr.
Green, Andrew.
  xGreen, Andrew.
      Ghosts of the South East. David & Charles.
Green, Archie.
  xGreen, Archie.
      Only a Miner: Studies in Recorded
      Coal-Mining Songs. U of Ill Pr.
Green, Arthur, 1941-
  xGreen, Arthur.
      Tormented Master: A Life of Rabbi Nahman of
      Bratslav. U of Ala Pr.
Green, B. S. see Green, Bryan S. R.
Green, Ben K.
  xGreen, Ben K.
      Horse Tradin'. Knopf.
      Some More Horse Tradin'. Knopf.
Green, Benny, 1927-
  xGreen, Benny.
      The Reluctant Art: The Growth of Jazz. Arno.
Green, Bill, 1943-
  xGreen, Bill.
      The Dancing Was Lively: Fort Concho, Texas:
      a Social History, 1867 to 1882. Fort Concho.
Green, Bryan S. R.
  xGreen, B. S.
      An Introduction to Sociology. Pergamon.
Green, Carol.
  xGreen, Carol.
      Dressage Explained. Arco.
Green, Celia. see Green, Celia Elizabeth.

Green, Celia Elizabeth.
  xGreen, Celia.
      Apparitions. State Mutual Bk.
      Out-of-the-Body Experiences. State Mutual Bk.
Green, Christopher.
  xGreen, Christopher.
      Leger & the Avant-Garde. Yale U Pr.
      Negative Taxes & the Poverty Problem.
      Brookings.
Green, Clifford J.
  xGreen, Clifford J.
      The Sociality of Christ & Humanity: Dietrich
      Bonhoeffer's Early Theology, 1927-1933.
      Scholars Pr Ca.
Green, Constance (McLaughlin), 1897-
  xGreen, Constance M.
      The Church on Lafayette Square: A History of
      St. John's Church, Washington, D. C.
      1815-1970. Potomac.
Green, Constance M. see Green, Constance
  (McLaughlin).
Green, D. H. see Green, Dennis Howard.
Green, Dana S., 1925-
  xGreen, Dana S.
      ed. Chasms in the Americas. Friend Pr.
Green, David, 1942-
  xGreen, David.
      Containment of Latin America: A History of
      the Myths & Realities of the Good Neighbor
      Policy. Times Bks.
Green, David. see Green, David Burnet.
Green, David Burnet, 1929-
  xGreen, David.
      A Handbook of Pottery Glazes.
      Watson-Guptill.
      Pottery Glazes. Watson-Guptill.
      Understanding Pottery Glazes. Merrimack Bk
      Serv.
Green, David E. see Green, David Ezra.
Green, David Ezra.
  xGreen, David E.
      Energy & the Mitochondrion. Acad Pr.
Green, David M. see Green, David Marvin.
Green, David Marvin.
  xGreen, David M.
      Signal Detection Theory & Psychophysics.
      Krieger.
Green, Dennis Howard, 1922-
  xGreen, D. H.
      Irony in the Medieval Romance. Cambridge U
      Pr.
Green, Donald E. see Green, Donald Edward.
Green, Donald Edward, 1936-
  xGreen, Donald E.
      Fifty Years of Service to West Texas
      Agriculture: A History of Texas Tech
      University's College of Agricultural Sciences,
      1925-1975. Tex Tech Pr.
      Panhandle Pioneer: Henry C. Hitch, His
      Ranch, & His Family. U of Okla Pr.
Green, Douglass M. see Green, Douglass Marshall.
Green, Douglass Marshall, 1926-
  xGreen, Douglass M.
      Form in Tonal Music: An Introduction to
      Analysis. HR&W.
Green, Edith P. see Green, Edith Pinero.
Green, Edith Pinero.
  xGreen, Edith P.
      Sneaks. Dutton.
Green, Edward J., 1924-
  xGreen, Edward J.
      Psychology for Law Enforcement. Wiley.
Green, Edward Michael Bankers.
  xGreen, Michael.
      I Believe in the Holy Spirit. Eerdmans.
Green, Edward Michael Bankes.
  xGreen, Michael.
      Evangelism in the Early Church. Eerdmans.
Green, Elizabeth A. see Green, Elizabeth Alden.

Green, Elizabeth Alden, 1908-
  xGreen, Elizabeth A.
    Mary Lyon & Mount Holyoke: Opening the
      Gates. U Pr of New Eng.
Green, Eric F.
  xGreen, Eric F.
    Profitable Food & Beverage Management:
      Planning. Hayden.
    Profitable Food & Beverage Management:
      Operations. Hayden.
Green, Ernest J.
  xGreen, Ernest J.
    Birth Order, Parental Interest & Academic
      Achievement. R & E Res Assoc.
    Personal Relationships: An Approach to
      Marriage & Family. McGraw.
Green, Fitzhugh, 1917-
  xGreen, Fitzhugh.
    A Change in the Weather. Norton.
    Some Famous Sea Fights. Arno.
Green, Frederick C. see Green, Frederick Charles.
Green, Frederick Charles, 1891-1964
  xGreen, Frederick C.
    Eighteenth-Century France: Six Essays. Ungar.
    French Novelists from the Revolution to
      Proust. Ungar.
    Stendhal. Russell.
Green, G. D. see Green, George Dennis.
Green, G. H. see Green, George Herbert.
Green, George Dennis.
  xGreen, G. D.
    ed. Assessment & Performance of Implanted
      Cardiac Pacemakers. Butterworths.
Green, George Herbert.
  xGreen, G. H.
    Cervical & Nasopharyngeal Carcinoma. Mss
      Info.
Green, Gerald.
  xGreen, Gerald.
    The Artists of Terezin. Schocken.
    Cactus Pie: Ten Stories. HM.
    The Chains. Seaview Bks.
    The Healers. Berkley Pub.
    Holocaust. Brodart.
    The Lotus Eaters. Am Repr-Rivercity Pr.
    The Lotus Eaters. Berkley Pub.
    Tourist. Popular Lib.
Green, Gil. see Green, Gilbert.
Green, Gilbert.
  xGreen, Gil.
    Whats Happening to Labor. Intl Pub Co.
Green, Gion.
  xGreen, Gion.
    Introduction to Security. Butterworths.
Green, H. D.
  xGreen. H. D.
    Carving Realistic Birds: A Step-by-Step Manual
      with Full-Size Patterns. Dover.
    Carving Realistic Birds: A Step-by-Step Manual
      with Full-Size Patterns. Peter Smith.
Green, Hannah.
  xGreen, Hannah.
    I Never Promised You a Rose Garden.
      HR&W.
Green, Henrietta.
  xGreen, Henrietta.
    The Marinade Cookbook. Har-Row.
Green, Henry, 1905-
  xGreen, Henry.
    Doting. Kelley.
    Nothing. Kelley.
Green, Henry M. see Green, Henry Mackenzie.
Green, Henry Mackenzie, 1881-
  xGreen, Henry M.
    ed. Modern Australian Poetry. Granger Bk.
Green, I. see Green, Ivah.
Green, I. M.
  xGreen, I. M.

    The Re-Establishment of the Church of
      England, 1660-1663. Oxford U Pr.
Green, Ira.
  xGreen, Ira.
    ed. Mechanisms of Tumor Immunity. Wiley.
Green, Isaac.
  xGreen, Isaac.
    Housing for the Elderly: The Development &
      Design Process. Van Nos Reinhold.
Green, Ivah.
  xGreen, I.
    Where Is Duckling Three?. Oddo.
Green, J. R. see Green, John Robert.
Green, Jack.
  xGreen, Jack.
    ed. Geological Problems in Lunar & Planetary
      Research. Am Astronaut.
Green, James R.
  xGreen, James R.
    Boston's Workers: A Labor History. Boston
      Public Lib.
    Grass-Roots Socialism: Radical Movements in
      the Southwest, 1895-1943. La State U Pr.
Green, Jane.
  xGreen, Jane.
    Gift-Giver's Cookbook. S&S.
Green, Jerry F. see Green, Jerry Franklin.
Green, Jerry Franklin.
  xGreen, Jerry F.
    Mechanical Concepts in Cardiovascular &
      Pulmonary Physiology. Lea & Febiger.
Green, Joan L.
  xGreen, Joan L.
    Curriculum Evaluation: Theory & Practice,
      with a Case Study from Nursing Education.
      Springer Pub.
Green, John. see Green, John Willison.
Green, John A.
  xGreen, John A.
    Teacher-Made Tests. Har-Row.
Green, John A. see Green, John Alfred.
Green, John Alfred, 1867-
  xGreen, John A.
    Educational Ideas of Pestalozzi. Greenwood.
Green, John C.
  xGreen, John C.
    Stratigraphy & Structure of the Boundary
      Mountain Anticlinorium in the Errol
      Quadrangle, New Hampshire-Maine. Geol
      Soc.
Green, John H.
  xGreen, John H.
    Food Processing Waste Management. AVI.
Green, John H. see Green, John H Chase.
Green, John H Chase.
  xGreen, John H.
    Speak to Me. Odyssey Pr.
Green, John Herbert.
  xGreen, John H.
    An Introduction to Human Physiology. Oxford
      U Pr.
Green, John R. see Green, John Raymond.
Green, John Raymond, 1915-
  xGreen, John R.
    Medical History for Students. C C Thomas.
Green, John Robert.
  xGreen, J. R.
    Statistical Treatment of Experimental Data.
      Elsevier.
Green, John Willison, 1927-
  xGreen, John.
    Sasquatch: The Apes Among Us. Hancock Hse.
    Sasquatch: The Apes Among Us. Universe.
Green, Judith. see Green, Judith S.
Green, Judith S.
  xGreen, Judith.
    Review of Maternal Child Nursing. McGraw.
Green, Julien, 1900-
  xGreen, Julien.

    The Dark Journey. Greenwood.
    Memories of Evil Days. U Pr of Va.
    Memories of Happy Days. Greenwood.
Green, Karen.
  xGreen, Karen.
    The Great International Noodle Experience.
      Atheneum.
Green, Kathleen.
  xGreen, Kathleen.
    Leprechaun Tales. Lippincott.
Green, Landis K. see Green, Landis Knight.
Green, Landis Knight.
  xGreen, Landis K.
    The Astrologer's Manual. Arco.
Green, Lee.
  xGreen, Lee.
    Use Your Overhead. Victor Bks.
Green, Leon, 1888-
  xGreen, Leon.
    The Litigation Process in Tort Law. Michie.
    Rationale of Proximate Cause. Rothman.
Green, Leroy.
  xGreen, Leroy.
    Introduction to BASIC & FORTRAN: A
      Comparative Analysis. Univ Microfilms.
Green, Lewis, 1925-
  xGreen, Lewis.
    The Gold Hustlers. Alaska Northwest.
Green, Lewis W., 1932-
  xGreen, Lewis W.
    And Scatter the Proud. Blair.
Green, Lila.
  xGreen, Lila.
    Tales from Africa. Silver.
Green, M. see Green, Mino.
Green, M. C. see Green, Michael Clifford.
Green, Marguerite.
  xGreen, Marguerite.
    The National Civic Federation & the American
      Labor Movement. Greenwood.
Green, Mark. see Green, Mark J.
Green, Mark J.
  xGreen, Mark.
    ed. The Big Business Reader. Pilgrim NY.
    Who Runs Congress?. Viking Pr.
  xGreen, Mark J.
    The Other Government: The Unseen Power of
      Washington Lawyers. Norton.
    Who Runs Congress?. Bantam.
Green, Martin, 1928-
  xGreen, Martin.
    Dreams of Adventure, Deeds of Empire. Basic.
Green, Martin. see Green, Martin Burgess.
Green, Martin Burgess, 1927-
  xGreen, Martin.
    The Problem of Boston: Some Readings in
      Cultural History. Peter Smith.
Green, Martin I.
  xGreen, Martin I.
    A Sigh of Relief: The First-Aid Handbook for
      Childhood Emergencies. Bantam.
Green, Maurice B. see Green, Maurice Berkeley.
Green, Maurice Berkeley.
  xGreen, Maurice B.
    Chemicals for Crop Protection & Pest Control.
      Pergamon.
    Eating Oil: Energy Use in Food Production.
      Westview.
Green, Melinda.
  xGreen, Melinda.
    illus. Rachel's Recital. Little.
Green, Michael.
  xGreen, Michael.
    illus. A Hobbit's Travels: Being the Hitherto
      Unpublished Travel Sketches of Sam Gamgee
      with Space for Notes. Running Pr.
Green, Michael. see Green, Edward Michael Bankes.
Green, Michael Clifford.
  xGreen, M. C.

Space Age Puppets & Masks. Plays.
Green, Michael Frederick.
  xGreen, Michael.
    The Art of Coarse Cruising. Merrimack Bk
    Serv.
Green, Mino.
  xGreen, M.
    ed. Solid State Surface Science. Dekker.
  xGreen, Mino.
    ed. Solid State Surface Science. Dekker.
Green, Norma. *see* Green, Norma B.
Green, Norma B.
  xGreen, Norma.
    Retold by The Hole in the Dike. Schol Bk
    Serv.
    The Hole in the Dike. T Y Crowell.
Green, Norman B.
  xGreen, Norman B.
    Earthquake Resistant Building Design &
    Construction. Van Nos Reinhold.
Green Note Music Publications.
  xGreen Note Music Publications Staff.
    Country Rock Guitar. Green Note Music.
    Electric Blues Guitar. Green Note Music.
Green Note Music Publications Staff. *see* Green Note
  Music Publications.
Green, Otis H. *see* Green, Otis Howard.
Green, Otis Howard, 1898-
  xGreen, Otis H.
    Spain & the Western Tradition: The Castilian
    Mind in Literature from El Cid to Calderon.
    U of Wis Pr.
Green, Paul, 1894-
  xGreen, Paul.
    Home to My Valley. U of NC Pr.
Green, Percy B.
  xGreen, Percy B.
    History of Nursery Rhymes. Folcroft.
    History of Nursery Rhymes. Gale.
    A History of Nursery Rhymes. Gordon Pr.
Green, Peter.
  xGreen, Peter.
    The Parthenon. Newsweek.
Green, Philip, 1932-
  xGreen, Philip.
    Deadly Logic: The Theory of Nuclear
    Deterrence. Ohio St U Pr.
    Deadly Logic: The Theory of Nuclear
    Deterrence. Schocken.
Green, Phyllis.
  xGreen, Phyllis.
    The Empty Seat. Elsevier-Nelson.
    Gloomy Louie. A Whitman.
    Grandmother Orphan. Elsevier-Nelson.
    Ice River. A-W.
    A New Mother for Martha. Human Sci Pr.
    Nicky's Lopsided, Lumpy, but Delicious
    Orange. A-W.
Green, R. D. *see* Green, Robert D.
Green, R. L. *see* Green, Roger Lancelyn.
Green, Robert A. *see* Green, Robert Alan.
Green, Robert Alan.
  xGreen, Robert A.
    Marks of American Silversmiths,1650-1850. R
    a Green.
Green, Robert C.
  xGreen, Robert C.
    The Care & Management of the Sick &
    Incompetent Physician. C C Thomas.
Green, Robert D.
  xGreen, R. D.
    Hydrogen Bonding by C-H Groups. Halsted Pr.
Green, Robert T.
  xGreen, Robert T.
    The United States & World Trade: Changing
    Patterns & Dimensions. Praeger.
Green, Roger H.
  xGreen, Roger H.

South Slav Settlement in Western Washington:
  Perception & Choice. R & E Res Assoc.
South Slav Settlement in Western Washington:
  Perception & Choice. Ragusan Pr.
Green, Roger H. *see* Green, Roger Harrison.
Green, Roger Harrison, 1939-
  xGreen, Roger H.
    Sampling Design & Statistical Methods for
    Environmental Biologists. Wiley.
Green, Roger L. *see* Green, Roger Lancelyn.
Green, Roger Lancelyn.
  xGreen, R. L.
    The Tale of Thebes. Cambridge U Pr.
  xGreen, Roger L.
    C. S. Lewis: A Biography. HarBraceJ.
    C. S. Lewis: A Biography. HarBraceJ.
    ed. Century of Humorous Verse. Dutton.
    A Century of Humorous Verse 1850-1950.
    Arden Lib.
    Tales of Ancient Egypt. Penguin.
Green, Ronald M. *see* Green, Ronald Michael.
Green, Ronald Michael.
  xGreen, Ronald M.
    Religious Reason: The Rational & Moral Basis
    of Religious Belief. Oxford U Pr.
Green, Rose B. *see* Green, Rose Basile.
Green, Rose Basile, 1914-
  xGreen, Rose B.
    Primo Vino. A S Barnes.
Green, Stanley.
  xGreen, Stanley.
    The Broadway Musical: A Picture Quiz Book.
    Dover.
    Encyclopedia of the Musical Theatre. Da Capo.
    Encyclopedia of the Musical Theatre. Dodd.
    Kings of Jazz. A S Barnes.
    Starring Fred Astaire. Dodd.
    Starring Fred Astaire. Doubleday.
Green, T. F. *see* Green, Thomas F.
Green, T. H. *see* Green, Thomas Hill.
Green, Thad B.
  xGreen, Thaddeus B.
    The Decision Science Process. Petrocelli.
Green, Thaddeus B. *see* Green, Thad B.
Green, Thomas F.
  xGreen, T. F.
    Activities of Teaching. McGraw.
Green, Thomas H. *see* Green, Thomas Hill.
Green, Thomas Henry, 1932-
  xGreen, Thomas H.
    Opening to God: A Guide to Prayer. Ave
    Maria.
Green, Thomas Hill.
  xGreen, T. H.
    The Political Theory of T. H. Green: Selected
    Writings. AHM Pub.
  xGreen, Thomas H.
    Hume & Locke. Peter Smith.
    Prolegomena to Ethics. Kraus Repr.
    Works of Thomas Hill Green. AMS Pr.
    Works of Thomas Hill Green. Kraus Repr.
Green, Thomas J. *see* Green, Thomas Jefferson.
Green, Thomas Jefferson, 1801-1863
  xGreen, Thomas J.
    Journal of the Texian Expedition Against Mier.
    Arno.
Green, Thomas M. *see* Green, Thomas Marshall.
Green, Thomas Marshall, 1837-1904
  xGreen, Thomas M.
    Historic Families of Kentucky: With Special
    Reference to Stocks Immediately Derived
    from the Valley of Virginia. Genealog Pub.
    The Spanish Conspiracy: A Review of Early
    Spanish Movements in the South-West. Peter
    Smith.
Green Vale School. 9th Grade English Class, 1973.
  xGreenvale School, Ninth Grade English Class.
    Bulldozers, Loaders, & Spreaders. Doubleday.
Green, Wayne.
  xGreen, Wayne.

    ed. Fascinating World of Radio
    Communications. TAB Bks.
    Solid-State Projects for the Experimenter. TAB
    Bks.
Green, William.
  xGreen, William.
    The Aircraft of the World. Arno.
    Famous Bombers of the Second World War.
    Doubleday.
    Famous Fighters of the Second World War.
    Doubleday.
    The Jet Aircraft of the World. Arno.
    Observer's Basic Military Aircraft Directory.
    Warne.
Green, William S. *see* Green, William Scott.
Green, William Scott.
  xGreen, William S.
    Approaches to Ancient Judaism: Theory &
    Practice. Scholars Pr Ca.
Greenacre, Phyllis.
  xGreenacre, Phyllis.
    Swift & Carroll: A Psychoanalytic Study of
    Two Lives. Intl Univs Pr.
Greenan, Russell. *see* Greenan, Russell H.
Greenan, Russell H.
  xGreenan, Russell.
    Keepers. St Martin.
  xGreenan, Russell H.
    Bric-a-Brac Man. Random.
Greenaway, George W. *see* Greenaway, George William.
Greenaway, George William.
  xGreenaway, George W.
    Arnold of Brescia. AMS Pr.
Greenbaum, Edward I.
  xGreenbaum, Edward I.
    Radiographic Atlas of Colon Disease. Year Bk
    Med.
Greenbaum, Howard H.
  xGreenbaum, Howard H.
    Organizational Communication Abstracts,
    1974. Am Busn Comm Assn.
    Organizational Communication Abstracts '75.
    Am Busn Comm Assn.
Greenbaum, Joan M., 1942-
  xGreenbaum, Joan M.
    In the Name of Efficiency: Management
    Theory & Shopfloor Practice in Data
    Processing Work. Temple U Pr.
Greenbaum, S. *see* Greenbaum, Sidney.
Greenbaum, Sidney.
  xGreenbaum, S.
    Acceptability in Language. Mouton.
  xGreenbaum, Sidney.
    Studies in English Adverbial Usage. U of
    Miami Pr.
Greenbaum, W. *see* Greenbaum, William.
Greenbaum, William.
  xGreenbaum, W.
    Measuring Educational Progress: A Study of
    the National Assessment. McGraw.
Greenberg. *see* Greenberg, Lewis.
Greenberg, Allan.
  xGreenberg, Allan M.
    Standards Relating to Architecture of Facilities.
    Ballinger Pub.
Greenberg, Allan C. *see* Greenberg, Allan Carl.
Greenberg, Allan Carl, 1940-
  xGreenberg, Allan C.
    Artists & Revolution: Dada & the Bauhaus,
    1917-1925. Univ Microfilms.
Greenberg, Allan M. *see* Greenberg, Allan.
Greenberg, Alvin.
  xGreenberg, Alvin.
    The House of the Would-Be Gardener. SBD.
    In--Direction. Godine.
Greenberg, Arnold.
  xGreenberg, Arnold.
    Caracas Alive. Alive Pubns.
  xGreenberg, Arnold L.

Caracas Alive. Alive Pubns.
Greenberg, Arnold L. *see* Greenberg, Arnold.
Greenberg, Arthur.
　xGreenberg, Arthur.
　　Strained Organic Molecules. Acad Pr.
Greenberg, Barbara.
　xGreenberg, Barbara.
　　The Bravest Babysitter. Dial.
Greenberg, Barnett.
　xGreenberg, Barnett.
　　The Classification of Consumer Goods: An
　　　Empirical Study. Ga St U Busn Pub.
Greenberg, Bette, 1937-
　xGreenberg, Bette.
　　ed. How to Find Out in Psychiatry: A Guide
　　　to Sources of Mental Health Information.
　　　Pergamon.
Greenberg, Bruce. *see* Greenberg, Bruce C.
Greenberg, Bruce C.
　xGreenberg, Bruce.
　　Greenberg's Price Guide to Lionel Trains:
　　　1901-1942. Crown.
　xGreenberg, Bruce C.
　　Greenberg's Price Guide to Lionel Trains:
　　　1901-1942. Greenberg Pub Co.
　　ed. Greenberg's Repair & Operating Manual
　　　for Lionel Trains. Greenberg Pub Co.
　　Greenberg's Repair & Operating Manual for
　　　Lionel Trains. Van Nos Reinhold.
Greenberg, Calvin L.
　xGreenberg, Calvin L.
　　How to Become a Successful Store Leasing
　　　Broker. P-H.
　　Profit Opportunities in Real Estate
　　　Investments. P-H.
Greenberg, Carol A. *see* Greenberg, Carol Arnel.
Greenberg, Carol Arnel.
　xGreenberg, Carol A.
　　The Day Before Cookbook. Little.
Greenberg, Clement, 1909-
　xGreenberg, Clement.
　　Art & Culture: Critical Essays. Beacon Pr.
Greenberg, David F.
　xGreenberg, David F.
　　Corrections & Punishment. Sage.
　　Mathematical Criminology. Rutgers U Pr.
Greenberg, Douglas.
　xGreenberg, Douglas.
　　Crime & Law Enforcement in the Colony of
　　　New York, 1691-1776. Cornell U Pr.
Greenberg, Edward.
　xGreenberg, Edward.
　　Regulation, Market Prices, & Process
　　　Innovation: The Case of the Ammonia
　　　Industry. Westview.
Greenberg, Edward S., 1942-
　xGreenberg, Edward S.
　　The American Political System: A Radical
　　　Approach. Winthrop.
　　ed. Political Socialization. Lieber-Atherton.
　　Understanding Modern Government: The Rise
　　　& Decline of the American Political
　　　Economy. Wiley.
Greenberg, Emanuel M. *see* Greenberg, Emanuel Martin.
Greenberg, Emanuel Martin.
　xGreenberg, Emanuel M.
　　ed. Journey to Motherhood. St Martin.
Greenberg, Harold, 1928-
　xGreenberg, Harold.
　　Integer Programming. Acad Pr.
Greenberg, Harold I.
　xGreenberg, Harold I.
　　Poverty in Israel: Economic Realities & the
　　　Promise of Social Justice. Praeger.
Greenberg, Ira A., 1924-
　xGreenberg, Ira A.

　　ed. Group Hypnotherapy & Hypnodrama.
　　　Nelson-Hall.
　　Psychodrama & Audience Attitude Change.
　　　Behavioral Studies.
Greenberg, Jack, 1924-
　xGreenberg, Jack.
　　Race Relations & American Law. Columbia U
　　　Pr.
Greenberg, Jan.
　xGreenberg, Jan.
　　A Season In-Between. FS&G.
Greenberg, Jerrold S.
　xGreenberg, Jerrold S.
　　Student-Centered Health Instruction: A
　　　Humanistic Approach. A-W.
Greenberg, Jerry.
　xGreenberg, Jerry.
　　The Living Reef. Seahawk Pr.
Greenberg, Joanne.
　xGreenberg, Joanne.
　　Founder's Praise. Avon.
　　Founder's Praise. HR&W.
　　High Crimes & Misdemeanors. HR&W.
　　In This Sign. Avon.
　　In This Sign. HR&W.
　　Summering: A Book of Short Stories. HR&W.
Greenberg, L. M. *see* Greenberg, Lewis.
Greenberg, Leon.
　xGreenberg, Leon.
　　A Practical Guide to Productivity
　　　Measurement. BNA.
Greenberg, Lewis.
　xGreenberg.
　　Velikovsky & Establishment Science. Kronos
　　　Pr.
　xGreenberg, L. M.
　　jt. auth. Velikovsky & Establishment Science.
　　　Kronos Pr.
Greenberg, Linda.
　xGreenberg, Linda.
　　ed. Greenberg's Operating Instructions with
　　　Layout Plans for Lionel Trains. Greenberg
　　　Pub Co.
Greenberg, M. *see* Greenberg, Marvin.
Greenberg, Martin. *see* Greenberg, Martin Harry.
Greenberg, Martin H. *see* Greenberg, Martin Harry.
Greenberg, Martin Harry.
　xGreenberg, Martin.
　　Science Fiction of the Fifties. Avon.
　xGreenberg, Martin H.
　　ed. Dawn of Time: Prehistory Through Science
　　　Fiction. Elsevier-Nelson.
　　ed. Ray Bradbury. Taplinger.
Greenberg, Marvin.
　xGreenberg, M.
　　Music Handbook for the Elementary School.
　　　P-H.
　xGreenberg, Marvin.
　　Your Children Need Music: A Guide for
　　　Parents & Teachers of Young Children. P-H.
Greenberg, Marvin J.
　xGreenberg, Marvin J.
　　Euclidean & Non-Euclidean Geometries:
　　　Development & History. W H Freeman.
　　Lectures on Algebraic Topology.
　　　Benjamin-Cummings.
　　Lectures on Forms in Many Variables.
　　　Benjamin-Cummings.
Greenberg, Michael. *see* Greenberg, Michael R.
Greenberg, Michael D., 1935-
　xGreenberg, Michael D.
　　Foundations of Applied Mathematics. P-H.
Greenberg, Michael R.
　xGreenberg, Michael.

Environmental Impact Statements. Assn Am
　Geographers.
Local Population & Employment Projection
　Techniques. Ctr Urban Pol Res.
A Primer on Industrial Environmental Impact.
　Ctr Urban Pol Res.
Greenberg, Moshe.
　xGreenberg, Moshe.
　　Introduction to Hebrew. P-H.
　　Understanding Exodus. Behrman.
Greenberg, Pearl.
　xGreenberg, Pearl.
　　Art & Ideas for Young People. Van Nos
　　　Reinhold.
Greenberg, Polly.
　xGreenberg, Polly.
　　Oh Lord, I Wish I Was a Buzzard. Macmillan.
Greenberg, S. *see* Greenberg, Simon.
Greenberg, Selma. *see* Greenberg, Selma Betty.
Greenberg, Selma Betty.
　xGreenberg, Selma.
　　Right from the Start: A Guide to Nonsexist
　　　Child Rearing. HM.
Greenberg, Simon, 1901-
　xGreenberg, S.
　　The Ethical in the Jewish & American
　　　Heritage. Ktav.
Greenberg, Stanley.
　xGreenberg, Stanley.
　　GPSS Primer. Krieger.
Greenberg, Stanley B., 1945-
　xGreenberg, Stanley B.
　　Race & State in Capitalist Development:
　　　Comparative Perspectives. Yale U Pr.
Greenberger, Evelyn B. *see* Greenberger, Evelyn Barish.
Greenberger, Evelyn Barish.
　xGreenberger, Evelyn B.
　　Arthur Hugh Clough: Growth of a Poet's
　　　Mind. Harvard U Pr.
Greenberger, Martin.
　xGreenberger, Martin.
　　ed. Computers, Communications, & the Public
　　　Interest. Johns Hopkins.
Greenbie, Marjorie B. *see* Greenbie, Marjorie Latta
　Barstow.
Greenbie, Marjorie L. *see* Greenbie, Marjorie Latta
　(Barstow).
Greenbie, Marjorie Latta (Barstow), 1891-
　xGreenbie, Marjorie L.
　　In Quest of Contentment. Arno.
Greenbie, Marjorie Latta Barstow, 1891-
　xGreenbie, Marjorie B.
　　My Dear Lady: The Story of Anna Ella
　　　Carroll, the "Great Unrecognized Member of
　　　Lincoln's Cabinet". Arno.
Greenblatt, Bernard.
　xGreenblatt, Bernard.
　　Children on Campus: A Survey of
　　　Prekindergarten Programs at Institutions of
　　　Higher Learning in the United States. Day
　　　Care & Child Dev.
　　Responsibility for Child Care: The Changing
　　　Role of Family & State in Child
　　　Development.. Jossey-Bass.
Greenblatt, Edwin.
　xGreenblatt, Edwin.
　　Suddenly Single: A Survival Kit for the Single
　　　Man. Times Bks.
Greenblatt, Gordon M.
　xGreenblatt, Gordon M.
　　Cat Musculature. U of Chicago Pr.
Greenblatt, M. *see* Greenblatt, Milton.
Greenblatt, M. H.
　xGreenblatt, M. H.
　　Multiple Sclerosis & Me. C C Thomas.
Greenblatt, Milton.
　xGreenblatt, M.
　　ed. Poverty & Mental Health. Am Psychiatric.
　xGreenblatt, Milton.

ed. Alcoholism Problems in Women &
Children. Grune.
ed. Drugs in Combination with Other
Therapies. Grune.
Dynamics of Institutional Change: The
Hospital in Transition. U of Pittsburgh Pr.
From Custodial to Therapeutic Patient Care in
Mental Hospitals. Arno.
Psychopolitics. Grune.
Greenblatt, Robert B. *see* Greenblatt, Robert Benjamin.
Greenblatt, Robert Benjamin, 1906-
xGreenblatt, Robert B.
Geriatric Endocrinology. Raven.
ed. Induction of Ovulation. Lea & Febiger.
Greenblatt, Stanley.
xGreenblatt, Stanley.
Understand Computers Through Common
Sense. Cornerstone.
Greendyke, Robert M.
xGreendyke, Robert M.
Introduction to Blood Banking. Med Exam.
Greene, A. C.
xGreene, A. C.
A Christmas Tree. Encino Pr.
The Last Captive. Encino Pr.
A Personal Country. Tex A&M Univ Pr.
Greene, Bert, 1923-
xGreene, Bert.
Bert Greene's Kitchen Bouquets. Contemp Bks.
Pity the Poor Rich. Contemp Bks.
Greene, Bette.
xGreene, Bette.
Morning Is a Long Time Coming. Archway.
Morning Is a Long Time Coming. PB.
Morning Is a Long Time Coming. Dial.
Summer of My German Soldier. Dial.
Summer of My German Soldier. Bantam.
Greene, Bob.
xGreene, Bob.
Johnny Deadline Reporter: The Best of Bob
Greene. Nelson-Hall.
Greene, Carla.
xGreene, Carla.
Gregor Mendel. Dial.
How Man Began. Bobbs.
Let's Learn About Lighthouses. Harvey.
Manuel, Young Mexican-American. Lantern.
Soldiers & Sailors: What Do They Do.
Har-Row.
Trip to the Aquarium. Lantern.
Trip to the Zoo. Lantern.
Greene, Carol.
xGreene, Carol.
God's My Friend. Concordia.
xGreene, Carole.
The Super Snoops & the Missing Sleepers.
Childrens.
Greene, Carole. *see* Greene, Carol.
Greene, Constance C.
xGreene, Constance C.
The Ears of Louis. Viking Pr.
Getting Nowhere. Viking Pr.
Getting Nowhere. Dell.
A Girl Called Al. Dell.
A Girl Called Al. Viking Pr.
I & Sproggy. Viking Pr.
I Know You, Al. Dell.
I Know You, Al. Viking Pr.
Leo the Lioness. Viking Pr.
Your Old Pal, Al. Viking Pr.
Greene, David G.
xGreene, David G.
Steel & Economic Development: Capital
Output Ratios in Three Latin American Steel
Plants. Mich St U Busn.
Greene, David H. *see* Greene, David Herbert.
Greene, David Herbert, 1913-
xGreene, David H.

ed. An Anthology of Irish Literature. NYU Pr.
Greene, David L.
xGreene, David L.
The Oz Scrapbook. Random.
Greene, David L. *see* Greene, David Lee.
Greene, David Lee, 1938-
xGreene, David L.
Dentition of Meroitic X-Group, & Christian
Populations from Wadi Halfa, Sudan. AMS
Pr.
Greene, Donald A. *see* Greene, Donald Johnson.
Greene, Donald Johnson.
xGreene, Donald A.
The Politics of Samuel Johnson. Kennikat.
Greene, Edward H.
xGreene, Edward H.
The Law & Your Horse. Arco.
The Law & Your Horse. Wilshire.
Greene, Ellin.
xGreene, Ellin.
Compiled by Clever Cooks: A Concoction of
Stories, Charms, Recipes & Riddles. Lothrop.
ed. A Multimedia Approach to Children's
Literature: A Selective List of Films,
Filmstrips & Recordings Based on Children's
Books. ALA.
Greene, Eva.
xGreene, Eva.
Chance of a Lifetime: An Anthology for the
Ageless. Wheelwright.
Greene, Evarts B. *see* Greene, Evarts Boutell.
Greene, Evarts Boutell, 1870-1947
xGreene, Evarts B.
Religion & the State: The Making & Testing of
an American Tradition. AMS Pr.
Revolutionary Generation: 1763-1790. New
Viewpoints.
Greene, Felix.
xGreene, Felix.
Awakened China: The Country Americans
Don't Know. Greenwood.
Greene, Francis V. *see* Greene, Francis Vinton.
Greene, Francis Vinton, 1850-1921
xGreene, Francis V.
General Greene. Kennikat.
Greene, Fred.
xGreene, Fred.
Stresses in U.S. - Japanese Security Relations.
Brookings.
Greene, Gardiner G.
xGreene, Gardiner G.
How to Start & Manage Your Own Business.
NAL.
Greene, George W. *see* Greene, George Washington.
Greene, George Washington, 1811-1883
xGreene, George W.
Historical View of the American Revolution.
Kennikat.
Greene, Graham.
xGreene, Graham.

Brighton Rock. Penguin.
British Dramatists. Folcroft.
A Burnt-Out Case. Penguin.
The Comedians. Penguin.
The End of the Affair. PB.
The End of the Affair. Penguin.
England Made Me. PB.
The Honorary Consul. S&S.
The Honorary Consul. PB.
The Human Factor. Avon.
The Human Factor. G K Hall.
The Human Factor. S&S.
The Little Fire Engine. Doubleday.
Loser Takes All. Penguin.
Orient Express. PB.
Our Man in Havana. PB.
Our Man in Havana. Penguin.
The Portable Graham Greene. Penguin.
The Power & the Glory. Penguin.
The Quiet American. Penguin.
A Sort of Life. S&S.
A Sort of Life. S&S.
Third Man. PB.
The Third Man. S&S.
Greene, Hal.
xGreene, Hal.
Professional Modeling. Killy-Moon Pr.
Greene, Harry A. *see* Greene, Harry Andrew.
Greene, Harry Andrew.
xGreene, Harry A.
Developing Language Skills in the Elementary
Schools. Allyn.
Greene, Hugh.
xGreene, Hugh.
ed. The American Rivals of Sherlock Holmes.
Pantheon.
ed. The American Rivals of Sherlock Holmes.
Penguin.
ed. Cosmopolitan Crimes: The Foreign Rivals
of Sherlock Holmes. Penguin.
ed. The Further Rivals of Sherlock Holmes.
Penguin.
Greene, J. H. *see* Greene, James Harnsberger.
Greene, Jack P.
xGreene, Jack P.
Compiled by American Colonies in the
Eighteenth Century, 1689-1763. AHM Pub.
ed. Great Britain & the American Colonies,
1606-1763. U of SC Pr.
ed. Nature of Colony Constitutions: Two
Pamphlets on the Wilkes Fund Controversy
in South Carolina by Sir Egerton Leigh &
Arthur Lee. U of SC Pr.
Preachers & Politicians: Two Essays on the
Origins of the American Revolution. Am
Antiquarian.
Quest for Power: The Lower Houses of
Assembly in the Southern Royal Colonies,
1689-1776. Norton.
The Quest for Power: The Lower Houses of
Assembly in the Southern Royal Colonies
1689-1776. U of NC Pr.
ed. Reinterpretation of the American
Revolution: 1763-1789. Har-Row.
Greene, James.
xGreene, James.
Foreign Investment & Employment: An
Examination of Foreign Investments to Make
58 Products Overseas. Conference Bd.
Greene, James. *see* Greene, James Hoffman.
Greene, James H. *see* Greene, James Harnsberger.
Greene, James Harnsberger, 1915-
xGreene, J. H.
Production & Inventory Control Handbook.
McGraw.
xGreene, James H.
Production & Inventory Control: Systems &
Decisions. Irwin.
Greene, James Hoffman, 1927-
xGreene, James.

Organizing for Exporting. Conference Bd.
Greene, John C.
xGreene, John C.
Darwin & the Modern World View. La State U Pr.
Death of Adam: Evolution & Its Impact on Western Thought. Iowa St U Pr.
The Science of Minerals in the Age of Jefferson. Am Philos.
Greene, Joshua.
xGreene, Joshua.
Readings in Vedic Literature for Children. Bala Bks.
Greene, Laura.
xGreene, Laura.
I Am an Orthodox Jew. HR&W.
I Am Somebody. Childrens.
Greene, Laurence, 1906-1955
xGreene, Laurence.
America Goes to Press: The News of Yesterday. Arno.
Greene, Letha C.
xGreene, Letha C.
Long Live the Delta Queen. Hastings.
Greene, Lorenzo J. see Greene, Lorenzo Johnston.
Greene, Lorenzo Johnston, 1899-
xGreene, Lorenzo J.
Negro in Colonial New England. Atheneum.
Negro Wage Earner. AMS Pr.
Negro Wage Earner. Russell.
Greene, Lorne.
xGreene, Lorne.
The Lorne Greene Book of Remarkable Animals. S&S.
Greene, M. Louise. see Greene, Maria Louise.
Greene, Maria Louise.
xGreene, M. Louise.
Development of Religious Liberty in Connecticut. Arno.
Development of Religious Liberty in Connecticut. Da Capo.
Greene, Nathanael, 1935-
xGreene, Nathanael.
Crisis & Decline: The French Socialist Party in the Popular Front Era. Cornell U Pr.
Greene, Nicholas M.
xGreene, Nicholas M.
Key Words in Anesthesiology. Williams & Wilkins.
Greene, Orville.
xGreene, Orville.
The Practical Inventor's Handbook. McGraw.
Greene, Patrick.
xGreene, Patrick.
tr. Paris Observed. Oxford U Pr.
Greene, R. E. see Greene, Robert Everist.
Greene, Raymond, 1901-
xGreene, Raymond.
ed. Current Concepts in Migraine Research. Raven.
Greene, Richard, 1938-
xGreene, Richard.
Assuring Quality in Medical Care: The State of the Art. Ballinger Pub.
Greene, Richard L. see Greene, Richard Leighton.
Greene, Richard Leighton.
xGreene, Richard L.
ed. The Early English Carols. Oxford U Pr.
The Early English Carols. Scholarly.
Greene, Robert Everist.
xGreene, R. E.
Function Theory on Manifolds Which Possess a Pole. Springer-Verlag.
Greene, Robert W.
xGreene, Robert W.
Six French Poets of Our Time: A Critical & Historical Study. Princeton U Pr.
Greene, Ruth. see Greene, Ruth Altman.
Greene, Ruth Altman, 1896-
xGreene, Ruth.

Hsiang-Ya Journal. Shoe String.
Greene, Sarah P. see Greene, Sarah Pratt (McLean).
Greene, Sarah Pratt (McLean), 1856-1935
xGreene, Sarah P.
Some Other Folks. Arno.
Greene, Shep.
xGreene, Shep.
The Boy Who Drank Too Much. Dell.
The Boy Who Drank Too Much. Viking Pr.
Greene, Suzanne E. see Greene, Suzanne Ellery.
Greene, Suzanne Ellery.
xGreene, Suzanne E.
Books for Pleasure: Popular Fiction 1914-1945. Bowling Green Univ.
Greene, Theodore M. see Greene, Theodore Meyer.
Greene, Theodore Meyer, 1897-
xGreene, Theodore M.
The Arts & the Art of Criticism. Gordian.
Greene, Thomas M.
xGreene, Thomas M.
The Descent from Heaven: A Study in Epic Continuity. Yale U Pr.
Greene, Victor. see Greene, Victor R.
Greene, Victor R.
xGreene, Victor.
For God & Country: The Rise of Polish & Lithuanian Ethnic Consciousness in America, 1860-1910. State Hist Soc Wis.
Greene, Vivian.
xGreene, Vivian.
Chip, Oh Brother!. Watts.
Cleveland, the Disco King. Watts.
Oops! Odessa. Watts.
Rotunda Ate a Cookie. Watts.
Greene, Vivien.
xGreene, Vivien.
English Dolls' Houses of the Eighteenth & Nineteenth Centuries. Scribner.
Family Dolls' Houses. Branford.
Greene, Warwick, 1879-1929
xGreene, Warwick.
Letters of Warwick Greene, 1915-28. Arno.
Greene, William B. see Greene, William Batchelder.
Greene, William Batchelder, 1819-1878
xGreene, William B.
Mutual Banking. Gordon Pr.
Socialistic, Communistic, Mutualistic, & Financial Fragments. Hyperion Conn.
Greene, William C. see Greene, William Chase.
Greene, William Chase, 1890-
xGreene, William C.
The Achievement of Greece: (A Chapter in Human Experience). R West.
Greenewalt, C. H. see Greenewalt, Crawford Hallock.
Greenewalt, Crawford Hallock.
xGreenewalt, C. H.
Ritual Dinners in Early Historic Sardis. U of Cal Pr.
Greenfeld, Howard.
xGreenfeld, Howard.
Chanukah. HR&W.
Rosh Hashanah & Yom Kippur. HR&W.
Sumer Is Icumen in: Our Ever-Changing Language. Crown.
Greenfeld, Josh.
xGreenfeld, Josh.
A Child Called Noah: A Family Journey. HR&W.
A Place for Noah. HR&W.
Greenfield , Jeff. see Greenfield, Jeff.
Greenfield, Edward.
xGreenfield, Edward.
Penguin Cassette Guide. Penguin.
Penguin Stereo Record Guide. Penguin.
Greenfield, Eloise.
xGreenfield, Eloise.

Childtimes: A Three-Generation Memoir. T Y Crowell.
First Pink Light. T Y Crowell.
Grandmama's Joy. Philomel.
Mary McLeod Bethune. T Y Crowell.
Me & Neesie. T Y Crowell.
Paul Robeson. T Y Crowell.
Greenfield, Eric V. see Greenfield, Eric Viele.
Greenfield, Eric Viele, 1882-
xGreenfield, Eric V.
German Grammar. Har-Row.
Greenfield, George B.
xGreenfield, George B.
Radiology of Bone Diseases. Lippincott.
Greenfield, Irving. see Greenfield, Irving A.
Greenfield, Irving A.
xGreenfield, Irving.
High Terror. Popular Lib.
xGreenfield, Irving A.
Tagget. Arbor Hse.
Greenfield, Jeff.
xGreenfield , Jeff.
The World's Greatest Team: A Portrait of the Boston Celtics 1957-69. Random.
Greenfield, Kent R. see Greenfield, Kent Roberts.
Greenfield, Kent Roberts, 1893-1967
xGreenfield, Kent R.
American Strategy in World War II: A Reconsideration. Greenwood.
Economics & Liberalism in the Risorgimento: A Study of Nationalism in Lombardy, 1814-1848. Greenwood.
Historian & the Army. Kennikat.
Greenfield, Lazar J.
xGreenfield, Lazar J.
ed. Surgery in the Aged. Saunders.
Greenfield, Margaret.
xGreenfield, Margaret.
Meeting the Costs of Health Care: The Bay Area Experience & the National Issues. Inst Gov Stud Berk.
Greenfield, Robert.
xGreenfield, Robert.
Haymon's Crowd. Summit Bks.
Greenfield, Sidney M.
xGreenfield, Sidney M.
English Rustics in Black Skin: A Study of Modern Family Forms in a Pre-Industrialized Society. Coll & U Pr.
ed. Entrepreneurs in Cultural Context. U of NM Pr.
Greenfield, Stanely R.
xGreenfield, Stanley R.
ed. National Directory of Addresses & Telephone Numbers. Sterling.
Greenfield, Stanley B.
xGreenfield, Stanley B.
A Critical History of Old English Literature. NYU Pr.
Studies in Old English Literature in Honor of Arthur G. Brodeur. Russell.
Greenfield, Stanley R. see Greenfield, Stanely R.
Greengard, Paul, 1925-
xGreengard, Paul.
Cyclic Nucleotides, Phosphorylated Proteins, & Neuronal Function. Raven.
Greenhalgh, John.
xGreenhalgh, John.
Practitioner's Guide to School Business Management. Allyn.
Greenhalgh, Michael.
xGreenhalgh, Michael.
ed. Art in Society: Studies in Style, Culture & Aesthetics. St Martin.
The Classical Tradition in Art. Biblio Dist.
Greenhill, Basil.
xGreenhill, Basil.

Archaeology of the Boat: A New Introductory
Study. Columbia U Pr.
A Quayside Camera, 1845-1917. Columbia U
Pr.
Greenhill, Eleanor S.
xGreenhill, Eleanor S.
Dictionary of Art. Dell.
Greenhill, George, Sir, 1847-1927
xGreenhill, George.
Gyroscopic Theory. Chelsea Pub.
Greenhill, J. P. see Greenhill, Jacob Pearl.
Greenhill, Jacob Pearl, 1895-
xGreenhill, J. P.
Office Gynecology. Year Bk Med.
Greenhouse, Herbert B.
xGreenhouse, Herbert B.
The Astral Journey. Avon.
Greenhowe, Jean.
xGreenhowe, Jean.
Dolls in National & Folk Costume. Branford.
Making a Victorian Doll's House. David &
Charles.
Making a Victorian Dolls' House. Taplinger.
Greenhut, Melvin L.
xGreenhut, Melvin L.
A Theory of the Firm in Economic Space.
Austin Pr.
Greenidge, A. H. see Greenidge, Abel Hendy Jones.
Greenidge, Abel Hendy Jones, 1865-1906
xGreenidge, A. H.
Legal Procedure of Cicero's Time. Rothman.
Greening, Roy R.
xGreening, Roy R.
The Chest. Year Bk Med.
Greenlaw. see Greenlaw, Paul Stephen.
Greenlaw, Edwin. see Greenlaw, Edwin Almiron.
Greenlaw, Edwin Almiron, 1874-1931
xGreenlaw, Edwin.
An Outline of the Literature of the English
Renaissance. Folcroft.
Province of Literary History. Kennikat.
Greenlaw, Paul S. see Greenlaw, Paul Stephen.
Greenlaw, Paul Stephen.
xGreenlaw.
Modern Personnel Management. Dryden Pr.
xGreenlaw, Paul S.
Finansim: A Financial Management Simulation.
West Pub.
Greenlea, Denice.
xGreenlea, Denice.
The Ardent Suitor. Fawcett.
Greenleaf, Barbar K. see Greenleaf, Barbara Kaye.
Greenleaf, Barbara K. see Greenleaf, Barbara Kaye.
Greenleaf, Barbara Kaye.
xGreenleaf, Barbar K.
Help: A Handbook for Working Mothers.
Berkley Pub.
xGreenleaf, Barbara K.
America Fever: The Story of American
Immigration. NAL.
Help: A Handbook for Working Mothers. T Y
Crowell.
Greenleaf, E. see Greenleaf, Elizabeth.
Greenleaf, Elizabeth.
xGreenleaf, E.
Pricky, a Pet Porcupine. Oddo.
Greenleaf, Frederick P.
xGreenleaf, Frederick P.
Introduction to Complex Variables. HR&W.
Greenleaf, J. Cameron.
xGreenleaf, J. Cameron.
Excavations at Punta De Agua in the Santa
Cruz River Basin, Southeastern Arizona. U of
Ariz Pr.
Greenleaf, Nancy. see Greenleaf, Nancy P.
Greenleaf, Nancy P.
xGreenleaf, Nancy.
ed. The Politics of Self-Esteem. Nursing Res.
Greenleaf, Robert. see Greenleaf, Robert K.

Greenleaf, Robert K.
xGreenleaf, Robert.
Teacher As a Servant: A Parable. Paulist Pr.
Greenleaf, William, 1917-
xGreenleaf, William.
ed. American Economic Development Since
1860. U of SC Pr.
Greenlee, Douglas.
xGreenlee, Douglas.
Peirce's Concept of Sign. Mouton.
Greenlee, Herbert B.
xGreenlee, Herbert B.
Surgery of the Small & Large Intestine. Year
Bk Med.
Greenman, Emerson F. see Greenman, Emerson Frank.
Greenman, Emerson Frank, 1895-
xGreenman, Emerson F.
Old Birch Island Cemetery & the Early
Historic Trade Route: Georgian Bay, Ontario.
U Mich Mus Anthro.
Greenman, Russell L.
xGreenman, Russell L.
Personnel Administration & the Law. BNA.
Greeno, James G.
xGreeno, James G.
Associative Learning: A Cognitive Analysis.
P-H.
Greenough, Chester N. see Greenough, Chester Noyes.
Greenough, Chester Noyes.
xGreenough, Chester N.
Collected Studies. Arno.
Greenough, George B. see Greenough, George Bellas.
Greenough, George Bellas, 1778-1855
xGreenough, George B.
A Critical Examination of the First Principles
of Geology. Arno.
Greenough, William C. see Greenough, William Croan.
Greenough, William Croan.
xGreenough, William C.
Pension Plans & Public Policy. Columbia U Pr.
Greenslet, Ferris, 1875-1959
xGreenslet, Ferris.
Life of Thomas Bailey Aldrich. Kennikat.
The Life of Thomas Bailey Aldrich. R West.
Greensmith, J. T.
xGreensmith, J. T.
Petrology of the Sedimentary Rocks. Allen
Unwin.
Greenspan, Donald.
xGreenspan, Donald.
Discrete Models. A-W.
Discrete Numerical Methods in Physics &
Engineering. Acad Pr.
Greenspan, H. P. see Greenspan, Harvey Philip.
Greenspan, Harvey Philip.
xGreenspan, H. P.
Theory of Rotating Fluids. Cambridge U Pr.
Greenspan, Jay.
xGreenspan, Jay Seth.
Hebrew Calligraphy: A Step-by-Step Guide.
Schocken.
Greenspan, Jay Seth. see Greenspan, Jay.
Greenspan, Morris.
xGreenspan, Morris.
Soldier's Guide to the Laws of War. Pub Aff
Pr.
Greenspan, Nancy B.
xGreenspan, Nancy B.
Accent on Home Economics. Messner.
Greenstein, Fred I.
xGreenstein, Fred I.
Children & Politics. Yale U Pr.
Evolution of the Modern Presidency: A
Bibliographical Survey. Am Enterprise.
Personality & Politics: Problems of Evidence,
Inference, & Conceptualization. Norton.
Greenstein, Jesse L. see Greenstein, Jesse Leonard.
Greenstein, Jesse Leonard, 1909-
xGreenstein, Jesse L.

ed. Stellar Atmospheres. U of Chicago Pr.
Greenstein, Julius S. see Greenstein, Julius Sidney.
Greenstein, Julius Sidney, 1927-
xGreenstein, Julius S.
ed. Contemporary Readings in Biology. Mss
Info.
Greenstone, J. David.
xGreenstone, J. David.
Race & Authority in Urban Politics:
Community Participation & the War on
Poverty. Russell Sage.
Greenvale School, Ninth Grade English Class. see Green
Vale School. 9th Grade English Class, 1973.
Greenwald, Anthony G.
xGreenwald, Anthony G.
Psychological Foundations of Attitudes. Acad
Pr.
Greenwald, Bruce C. see Greenwald, Bruce C. N.
Greenwald, Bruce C. N., 1946-
xGreenwald, Bruce C.
Adverse Selection in the Labor Market.
Garland Pub.
Greenwald, Carol S. see Greenwald, Carol Schwartz.
Greenwald, Carol Schwartz.
xGreenwald, Carol S.
Group Power: Lobbying & Public Policy.
HR&W.
Greenwald, Dorothy.
xGreenwald, Dorothy.
Learning to Live with the Love of Your Life.
HarBraceJ.
Greenwald, Edward S.
xGreenwald, Edward S.
Cancer Chemotherapy. Med Exam.
Greenwald, Harold, 1910-
xGreenwald, Harold.
ed. Great Cases in Psychoanalysis. Aronson.
Greenwald, Howard P.
xGreenwald, Howard P.
Social Problems in Cancer Control. Ballinger
Pub.
Greenwald, Nancy.
xGreenwald, Nancy.
Lady Cat. Crown.
Greenwald, Sheila.
xGreenwald, Sheila.
illus. All the Way to Wit's End. Little.
illus. The Atrocious Two. HM.
It All Began with Jane Eyre: Or, the Secret
Life of Franny Dillman. Little.
Greenwalt, Emmett A.
xGreenwalt, Emmett A.
The Point Loma Community in California,
1897-1942: A Theosophical Experiment.
AMS Pr.
Greenway, James C. see Greenway, James Cowan.
Greenway, James Cowan, 1903-
xGreenway, James C.
Extinct & Vanishing Birds of the World.
Dover.
Extinct & Vanishing Birds of the World. Peter
Smith.
Greenway, John.
xGreenway, John.
American Folksongs of Protest. Octagon.
Literature Among the Primitives. Gale.
The Primitive Reader: An Anthology of Myths,
Tales, Songs, Riddles, & Proverbs of
Aboriginal Peoples Around the World. Gale.
Tales from the British Isles. Silver.
Tales from the United States. Silver.
Greenway, John L.
xGreenway, John L.
The Golden Horns: Mythic Imagination & the
Nordic Past. U of Ga Pr.
Greenwood. see Greenwood, Norman Neil.
Greenwood, Davydd J.
xGreenwood, Davydd J.

Nature, Culture, & Human History: A
Bio-Cultural Introduction to Anthropology.
Har-Row.
Greenwood, Donald T.
xGreenwood, Donald T.
ed. Principles of Dynamics. P-H.
Greenwood, Douglas C.
xGreenwood, Douglas C.
Engineering Data for Product Design.
McGraw.
ed. Mechanical Details for Product Design.
McGraw.
Greenwood, Ernest, 1910-
xGreenwood, Ernest.
Experimental Sociology: A Study in Method.
Octagon.
Greenwood, George. *see* Greenwood, Granville George.
Greenwood, Gordon E.
xGreenwood, Gordon E.
Problem Situations in Teaching. Har-Row.
Greenwood, Granville George, Sir, 1850-1928
xGreenwood, George.
Lee, Shakespeare & a Tertium Quid. Haskell.
Greenwood, Isaac J. *see* Greenwood, Isaac John.
Greenwood, Isaac John, 1833-1911
xGreenwood, Isaac J.
Circus, Its Origin & Growth Prior to 1835.
Hobby Hse.
Greenwood, James R.
xGreenwood, Jim.
Parachuting for Sport. TAB Bks.
Greenwood, James W.
xGreenwood, James W.
jt. auth. Managing Executive Stress: A Systems
Approach. Wiley.
Greenwood, Jim. *see* Greenwood, James R.
Greenwood, Leonard H. *see* Greenwood, Leonard Hugh
Graham.
Greenwood, Leonard Hugh Graham.
xGreenwood, Leonard H.
Aspects of Euripidean Tragedy. Russell.
Greenwood, Major, 1880-
xGreenwood, Major.
Some British Pioneers of Social Medicine.
Arno.
Greenwood, Ned H.
xGreenwood, Ned J.
Human Environments & Natural Systems.
Duxbury Pr.
Greenwood, Ned J. *see* Greenwood, Ned H.
Greenwood, Norman Neil.
xGreenwood.
Index of Vibrational Spectra of Inorganic &
Organometallic Compounds. Butterworths.
Greenwood, Peter R. *see* Greenwood, Peter W.
Greenwood, Peter W.
xGreenwood, Peter R.
Prosecution of Adult Felony Defendents: A
Policy Perspective. Lexington Bks.
xGreenwood, Peter W.
The Criminal Investigation Process. Heath.
The Criminal Investigation Process. Lexington
Bks.
Greenwood, Theresa.
xGreenwood, Theresa.
Gospel Graffiti. M Evans.
Greep, Roy O. *see* Greep, Roy Orval.
Greep, Roy Orval.
xGreep, Roy O.
Histology. McGraw.
Greer, Alan.
xGreer, Alan.
An Introduction to Lettering. Penguin.
Greer, Colin.
xGreer, Colin.
The Divided Society: The Ethnic Experience in
America. Basic.
Greer, David. *see* Greer, David Clive.
Greer, David Clive, 1937-
xGreer, David.

ed. Hamilton Harty: His Life & Music. Da
Capo.
Greer, Douglas F.
xGreer, Douglas F.
Industrial Organization & Public Policy.
Macmillan.
Greer, Edward.
xGreer, Edward.
Big Steel: Black Politics & Corporate Power in
Gary, Indiana. Monthly Rev.
Greer, Frances.
xGreer, Frances A.
Instant Notetaking. Intl Educ Systems.
Greer, Frances A. *see* Greer, Frances.
Greer, Gaylon E.
xGreer, Gaylon E.
The Real-Estate Investment Decision.
Lexington Bks.
The Real Estate Investor & the Federal Income
Tax. Wiley.
Greer, Germaine, 1939-
xGreer, Germaine.
The Female Eunuch. Bantam.
The Female Eunuch. McGraw.
Female Eunuch. McGraw.
Greer, L. F. *see* Greer, Lou.
Greer, Lou.
xGreer, L. F.
Your Personal Plumber. Plumbing Pubns.
Greer, Louise.
xGreer, Louise.
Browning & America. Greenwood.
Greer, Rebecca. *see* Greer, Rebecca E.
Greer, Rebecca E.
xGreer, Rebecca.
How to Live Rich When You're Not.
Ballantine.
Greer, Roger C.
xGreer, Roger C.
Illustration Index. Scarecrow.
Greer, Scott. *see* Greer, Scott A.
Greer, Scott A.
xGreer, Scott.
ed. Accountability in Urban Society: Public
Agencies Under Fire. Sage.
ed. Neighborhood & Ghetto: The Local Area
in Large Scale Society. Basic.
Greer, Thomas H.
xGreer, Thomas H.
American Social Reform Movements: Their
Pattern Since 1865. Greenwood.
A Brief History of Western Man. HarBraceJ.
Greer, Tom.
xGreer, Tom.
A Modern Daedalus. Arno.
Greer, Virginia.
xGreer, Virginia.
Emergency: The True Story of a Woman's
Faith & Service As an Emergency Room
Volunteer. Christian Herald.
Greet, Brian A.
xGreet, Brian A.
Broken Bread in a Broken World. Judson.
Greever, William S.
xGreever, William S.
Arid Domain. Arno.
Greg, Walter W. *see* Greg, Walter Wilson.
Greg, Walter Wilson.
xGreg, Walter W.

ed. Companion to Arber: Being a Calendar of
Documents in Edward Arber's Transcript of
the Registers of the Company of Stationers of
London, 1554-1640. Oxford U Pr.
List of English Plays Written Before 1643 &
Printed Before 1700. Haskell.
Principles of Emendation in Shakespeare.
Folcroft.
Principles of Emendation in Shakespeare.
Scholarly.
Gregg, Alan, M.D., 1890-1957
xGregg, Alan.
For Future Doctors. U of Chicago Pr.
Gregg, Davis W. *see* Gregg, Davis Weinert.
Gregg, Davis Weinert.
xGregg, Davis W.
ed. Life & Health Insurance Handbook. Irwin.
Gregg, Edward.
xGregg, Edward.
Queen Anne. Routledge & Kegan.
Gregg, James R., 1914-
xGregg, James R.
How to Communicate in Optometric Practice.
Chilton.
Gregg, John. *see* Gregg, John J.
Gregg, John J.
xGregg, John.
Best Loved Poems of the American West.
Doubleday.
Gregg, John R. *see* Gregg, John Robert.
Gregg, John Robert, 1867-1948
xGregg, John R.
Applied Secretarial Practice. McGraw.
Gregg Shorthand. McGraw.
Gregg Shorthand Manual, Simplified. McGraw.
Gregg Speed Building. McGraw.
Gregg, Josiah, 1806-1850
xGregg, Josiah.
Commerce of the Prairies. Peter Smith.
Commerce of the Prairies. U of Nebr Pr.
Commerce of the Prairies. U of Okla Pr.
Gregg, Pauline.
xGregg, Pauline.
Free-Born John: A Biography of John Lilburne.
Greenwood.
Gregg, Richard B. *see* Gregg, Richard Bartlett.
Gregg, Richard Bartlett, 1885-
xGregg, Richard B.
Power of Non-Violence. Attic Pr.
The Power of Nonviolence. Schocken.
Psychology & Strategy of Gandhi's Nonviolent
Resistance. Garland Pub.
Gregg, Robert D. *see* Gregg, Robert Danforth.
Gregg, Robert Danforth, 1901-
xGregg, Robert D.
The Influence of Border Troubles on Relations
Between the United States & Mexico,
1876-1910. AMS Pr.
xGregg, Robert S.
Influence of Border Troubles on Relations
Between the United States & Mexico,
1876-1910. Da Capo.
Gregg, Robert S. *see* Gregg, Robert Danforth.
Gregor, A. James.
xGregor, A. James.
Fascist Persuasion in Radical Politics.
Princeton U Pr.
Young Mussolini & the Intellectual Origins of
Fascism. U of Cal Pr.
Gregor, Arthur S.
xGregor, Arthur S.
How the World's First Cities Began. Dutton.
Gregor, Thomas.
xGregor, Thomas.
Mehinaku: The Drama of Daily Life in a
Brazilian Indian Village. U of Chicago Pr.
Gregor, Walter, 1827-1897
xGregor, Walter.

Counting Out Rhymes of Children. Folcroft.
Gregorian, Arthur T.
  xGregorian, Arthur T.
    Oriental Rugs & the Stories They Tell.
    Scribner.
Gregorian, Joyce. *see* Gregorian, Joyce Ballou.
Gregorian, Joyce B. *see* Gregorian, Joyce Ballou.
Gregorian, Joyce Ballou.
  xGregorian, Joyce.
    The Broken Citadel. Atheneum.
  xGregorian, Joyce B.
    Castledown. Atheneum.
Gregory. *see* Gregory, Isabella Augusta Persse.
Gregory, A. Charles. *see* Gregory, Augustus Charles.
Gregory, Allene.
  xGregory, Allene.
    The French Revolution & the English Novel.
    Folcroft.
    French Revolution & the English Novel.
    Haskell.
    French Revolution & the English Novel.
    Kennikat.

Gregory, Augustus Charles.

  xGregory, A. Charles.
    Journals of Australian Explorations.
    Greenwood.

Gregory, C. E. *see* Gregory, Cedric Errol.
Gregory, Cedric Errol.
  xGregory, C. E.
    Explosives for Australasian Engineers. U of
    Queensland.
    Explosives for North American Engineers.
    Trans Tech.
Gregory, Charles O. *see* Gregory, Charles Oscar.
Gregory, Charles Oscar.
  xGregory, Charles O.
    Labor & the Law. Norton.
Gregory, Derek, 1951-
  xGregory, Derek.
    Ideology, Science & Human Geography. St
    Martin.
Gregory, Diana.
  xGregory, Diana.
    Dairy Goats. Arco.
    I'm Boo, That's Who!. A-W.
    Owning a Horse: A Practical Guide. Har-Row.
Gregory, Dick.
  xGregory, Dick.
    Dick Gregory's Bible Tales, with Commentary.
    Stein & Day.
    Dick Gregory's Natural Diet for Folks Who
    Eat: Cookin' with Mother Nature. Har-Row.
    Dick Gregory's Natural Diet for Folks Who
    Eat: Cookin' with Mother Nature. Har-Row.
    Nigger: An Autobiography. Dutton.
    No More Lies: The Myth & the Reality of
    American History. Har-Row.

Gregory, Horace, 1898-
  xGregory, Horace.
    D. H. Lawrence: Pilgrim of the Apocalypse: A
    Critical Study. Grove.
    World of James McNeill Whistler. Arno.
Gregory, Howard.
  xGregory, Howard.
    Parachuting's Unforgettable Jumps. H Gregory.
Gregory, Hugo H.
  xGregory, Hugo H.
    ed. Learning Theory & Stuttering Therapy.
    Northwestern U Pr.
Gregory, Isabella A. *see* Gregory, Isabella Augusta
  Persse.
Gregory, Isabella Augusta (Persse), Lady, 1852-1932
  xGregory, Isabella A.

Our Irish Theatre: A Chapter of
    Autobiography. Oxford U Pr.
Gregory, Isabella Augusta Persse, Lady, 1852-1932
  xGregory.
    Gods & Fighting Men: The Story of the Tuatha
    De Danaan & of the Fianna of Ireland.
    Humanities.
  xGregory, Isabella A.
    Gods & Fighting Men: The Story of the Tuatha
    de Danaan & of the Fianna of Ireland.
    Oxford U Pr.
    Ideals in Ireland. AMS Pr.
Gregory, J. W. *see* Gregory, John Walter.
Gregory, John, 1724-1773
  xGregory, John.
    A Father's Legacy to His Daughters. Garland
    Pub.
    Legacy of the Stars. Nordon Pubns.
Gregory, John W. *see* Gregory, John Walter.
Gregory, John Walter, 1864-1932
  xGregory, J. W.
    ed. The Structure of Asia. Krieger.
  xGregory, John W.
    Foundation of British East Africa. Negro U Pr.
Gregory, Michael S.
  xGregory, Michael S.
    ed. Sociobiology & Human Nature: An
    Interdisciplinary Critique & Defense.
    Jossey-Bass.
Gregory, Mollie.
  xGregory, Mollie.
    Making Films Your Business. Schocken.
Gregory, Paul. *see* Gregory, Paul R.
Gregory, Paul R.
  xGregory, Paul.
    Comparative Economic Systems. HM.
  xGregory, Paul R.
    Soviet Economic Structure & Performance.
    Har-Row.
Gregory, Peter.
  xGregory, Peter.
    Industrial Wages in Chile. NY Sch Indus Rel.
Gregory, R. E. *see* Gregory, Robert Todd.
Gregory, R. L. *see* Gregory, Richard Langton.
Gregory, Richard L. *see* Gregory, Richard Langton.
Gregory, Richard Langton.
  xGregory, R. L.
    Concepts & Mechanisms of Perception.
    Scribner.
    Illusion in Nature & Art. Scribner.
  xGregory, Richard L.
    Intelligent Eye. McGraw.
Gregory, Robert Todd.
  xGregory, R. E.
    A Collection of Matrices for Testing
    Computational Algorithms. Krieger.
Gregory, Ross.
  xGregory, Ross.
    Origins of American Intervention in First
    World War. Norton.
Gregory, Ruth W. *see* Gregory, Ruth Wilhelme.
Gregory, Ruth Wilhelme.
  xGregory, Ruth W.
    Anniversaries & Holidays. ALA.
Gregory, Tappan, 1886-
  xGregory, Tappan.
    Nature Photography at Night. Denver Mus
    Natl Hist.
Gregory, Theodor E. *see* Gregory, Theodor Emanuel
  Gugenheim.
Gregory, Theodor Emanuel Gugenheim, Sir, 1890-
  xGregory, Theodor E.
    The Gold Standard & Its Future. Arno.
Gregory, Thomas W. *see* Gregory, Thomas West.
Gregory, Thomas West.
  xGregory, Thomas W.

Adolescence in Literature. Longman.
    ed. Juvenile Delinquency in Literature.
    Longman.
Gregory, Timothy E.
  xGregory, Timothy E.
    Vox Populi: Popular Opinion & Violence in the
    Religious Controversies of the Fifth Century
    A.D.. Ohio St U Pr.
Gregory, William, 1803-1858
  xGregory, William.
    Animal Magnetism: Or Mesmerism & Its
    Phenomena. Arno.
Gregson, Robert. *see* Gregson, Robert Anthony Mills.
Gregson, Robert Anthony Mills.
  xGregson, Robert.
    Psychometrics of Similarity. Acad Pr.
Greibach, S. A. *see* Greibach, Sheila.
Greibach, Sheila, 1939-
  xGreibach, S. A.
    Theory of Program Structures:
    Schemes,Semantics,Verification.
    Springer-Verlag.
Greider, Janice E.
  xGreider, Janice E.
    Law & the Life Insurance Contract. Irwin.
    Principles of Life Insurance. Irwin.
Greiff, Barrie S.
  xGreiff, Barrie S.
    Tradeoffs: Executive, Family & Organizational
    Life. NAL.
Greiff, Constance M.
  xGreiff, Constance M.
    Princeton Architecture: A Pictorial History of
    Town & Campus. Princeton U Pr.
Greig, John Y. *see* Greig, John Young Thomson.
Greig, John Young Thomson, 1891-
  xGreig, John Y.
    Psychology of Laughter & Comedy. Cooper Sq.
Greig, W. Smith. *see* Greig, William Smith.
Greig, William Smith, 1925-
  xGreig, W. Smith.
    Economics of Food Processing. AVI.
Greinacher, Norbert.
  xGreinacher, Norbert.
    The Poor & the Church. Seabury.
Greiner, Donald J.
  xGreiner, Donald J.
    ed. American Poets Since World War II. Gale.
    Comic Terror: The Novels of John Hawkes.
    Memphis St Univ.
Greinke, Eric. *see* Greinke, L. Eric.
Greinke, L. Eric.
  xGreinke, Eric.
    The Broken Lock: New & Selected Poems.
    Pilot Pr.
Greis, Noel.
  xGreis, Noel P.
    Oceans. Pendulum Pr.
Greis, Noel P. *see* Greis, Noel.
Greist. *see* Greist, John H.
Greist, John H.
  xGreist.
    Anti-Depressant Treatment: The Essentials.
    Williams & Wilkins.
Grele, Ronald J.
  xGrele, Ronald J.
    ed. Envelopes of Sound: Six Practitioners
    Discuss the Method, Theory & Practice of
    Oral History & Oral Testimony. Precedent
    Pub.
Grell, Rhoda F. *see* Grell, Rhoda Frank.
Grell, Rhoda Frank.
  xGrell, Rhoda F.
    ed. Mechanisms in Recombination. Plenum
    Pub.
Gremillion, Joseph. *see* Gremillion, Joseph B.
Gremillion, Joseph B.
  xGremillion, Joseph.

The Gospel of Peace & Justice: Catholic Social
Teaching Since Pope John. Orbis Bks.
Grendon, Felix, 1882-1965
xGrendon, Felix.
Anglo-Saxon Charms. Folcroft.
Grene, David.
xGrene, David.
Greek Political Theory: The Image of Man in
Thucydides & Plato. U of Chicago Pr.
Reality & the Heroic Pattern: Last Plays of
Ibsen, Shakespeare & Sophocles. U of
Chicago Pr.
Grene, Marjorie. *see* Grene, Marjorie (Glicksman).
Grene, Marjorie (Glicksman), 1910-
xGrene, Marjorie.
Introduction to Existentialism. U of Chicago
Pr.
A Portrait of Aristotle. U of Chicago Pr.
Grene, Nicholas.
xGrene, Nicholas.
Synge: A Critical Study of the Plays. Rowman.
Grenell, Zelotes.
xGrenell, Zelotes.
The Work of the Clerk. Judson.
Grenfell, Newell.
xGrenfell, Newell.
Switch on: Switch off: The Mass Media
Audiences of Malaysia. Oxford U Pr.
Grenfell, Russell.
xGrenfell, Russell.
Horatio Nelson: A Short Biography.
Greenwood.
Grennell, Dean A.
xGrennell, Dean A.
ABC's of Reloading. Follett.
ed. Law Enforcement Handgun Digest. Follett.
ed. Pistol & Revolver Digest. Follett.
Grennes, Thomas.
xGrennes, Thomas.
Economics of World Grain Trade. Praeger.
Grenville, John A. *see* Grenville, John Ashley Soames.
Grenville, John Ashley Soames.
xGrenville, John A.
Politics, Strategy & American Diplomacy:
Studies in Foreign Policy, 1873-1917. Yale U
Pr.
Gresham, Elizabeth, 1904-
xGresham, Elizabeth.
Poisoners' Base. Popular Lib.
Gresham, G. A. *see* Gresham, Geoffrey Austin.
Gresham, G. Austin. *see* Gresham, Geoffrey Austin.
Gresham, Geoffrey A. *see* Gresham, Geoffrey Austin.
Gresham, Geoffrey Austin.
xGresham, G. A.
Primate Atherosclerosis. S Karger.
Reversing Atherosclerosis. C C Thomas.
xGresham, G. Austin.
Color Atlas of Forensic Pathology. Year Bk
Med.
Post-Mortem Procedures: An Illustrated
Textbook. Year Bk Med.
xGresham, Geoffrey A.
Introduction to Comparative Pathology: A
Consideration of Some Reactions of Humans
& Animal Tissues to Injurious Agents. Acad
Pr.
Gresham, Matilda. *see* Gresham, Matilda (McGrain).
Gresham, Matilda (McGrain), b. 1839
xGresham, Matilda.
Life of Walter Quintin Gresham 1832-1895.
Arno.
Gress, James R.
xGress, James R.
ed. Curriculum: An Introduction to the Field.
McCutchan.
Gresser, Seymour.
xGresser, Seymour.
A Garland for Stephen. Olivant.
Gressitt, J. L. *see* Gressitt, J. Linsley.

Gressitt, J. Linsley.
xGressitt, J. L.
ed. Entomology of Antarctica. Am
Geophysical.
Gressley, Gene M., 1931-
xGressley, Gene M.
The Twentieth-Century American West: A
Potpourri. U of Mo Pr.
Grether, Ewald T. *see* Grether, Ewald Theophilus.
Grether, Ewald Theophilus, 1899-
xGrether, Ewald T.
Price Control Under Fair Trade Legislation.
Arno.
Greub, H. *see* Greub, Werner Hildbert.
Greub, W. *see* Greub, Werner Hildbert.
Greub, Werner Hildbert, 1925-
xGreub, H.
Linear Algebra. Springer-Verlag.
xGreub, W.
Multilinear Algebra. Springer-Verlag.
Greulach, Victor A.
xGreulach, Victor A.
Plant Function & Structure. Macmillan.
Plants: An Introduction to Modern Botany.
Wiley.
Greven, Philip. *see* Greven, Philip J.
Greven, Philip J.
xGreven, Philip.
The Protestant Temperament: Patterns of Child
Rearing, Religious Experience, & the Self in
Early America. NAL.
Grew, Eva. *see* Grew, Eva Mary (Instone).
Grew, Eva M. *see* Grew, Eva Mary (Instone).
Grew, Eva Mary (Instone).
xGrew, Eva.
Bach. Biblio Dist.
xGrew, Eva M.
Bach. Littlefield.
Grew, Joseph C. *see* Grew, Joseph Clark.
Grew, Joseph Clark, 1880-1965
xGrew, Joseph C.
Turbulent Era-a Diplomatic Record of Forty
Years, 1904-1945. Arno.
Grew, Raymond.
xGrew, Raymond.
Sterner Plan for Italian Unity: The Italian
National Society in the Risorgimento.
Princeton U Pr.
Grey, Aida.
xGrey, Aida.
The Aida Grey Beauty Book. Lippincott.
Grey, Alan L., 1919-
xGrey, Alan L.
ed. Class & Personality in Society.
Lieber-Atherton.
Grey, Anthony.
xGrey, Anthony.
The Bulgarian Exclusive. Dial.
The Chinese Assassin. HR&W.
Grey, Arnold.
xGrey, Arnold.
The Choice of Life: A New Perspective on
Human Nature and Inhuman Events. Emet
Bks.
Grey, Charles.
xGrey, Charles.
Pirates of the Eastern Seas 1618-1723: A Lurid
Page of History. Kennikat.
Grey, Charles E. *see* Grey, Henry George Grey, 3rd
Earl.
Grey, David L.
xGrey, David L.
Supreme Court & the News Media.
Northwestern U Pr.
Grey, Georgina.
xGrey, Georgina.
Turn of the Cards. Fawcett.
Grey, H. G. *see* Grey, Henry George Grey, 3rd Earl.
Grey, Henry George Grey, 3rd Earl, 1802-1894
xGrey, Charles E.

Colonial Policy of Lord John Russell's
Administration. Kelley.
xGrey, H. G.
Colonial Policy of Lord John Russell's
Administration. Kraus Repr.
Grey, Jerry.
xGrey, Jerry.
Enterprise. Morrow.
Enterprise. PB.
The Facts of Flight. Westminster.
The Race for Electric Power. Westminster.
Grey, Jonathan.
xGrey, Jonathan.
How to Get Out of Debt & Stay Out. Fortuna.
Grey, Michael.
xGrey, Michael.
Intro. by Pre-Columbian Art. St Martin.
Grey, Robert W. *see* Grey, Robert Waters.
Grey, Robert Waters.
xGrey, Robert W.
ed. White Trash: An Anthology of
Contemporary Southern Poets. New South
Co.
Grey, Zane, 1872-1939
xGrey, Zane.
Arizona Clan. PB.
Boulder Dam. PB.
The Call of the Canyon. PB.
Captives of the Desert. PB.
Code of the West. PB.
The Deer Stalker. PB.
Forlorn River. G K Hall.
Forlorn River. PB.
Horse Heaven Hill. PB.
The Last of the Plainsmen. Am Repr-Rivercity
Pr.
The Last Trail. Am Repr-Rivercity Pr.
The Lone Star Ranger. Am Repr-Rivercity Pr.
Lone Star Ranger. PB.
The Lost Wagon Train. PB.
Raiders of Spanish Peaks. PB.
Rainbow Trail. PB.
The Reef Girl. Ace Bks.
The Reef Girl. Har-Row.
The Rustlers of Pecos County. G K Hall.
Stranger from the Tonto. PB.
Sunset Pass. PB.
Twin Sombreros. PB.
Under the Tonto Rim. PB.
Valley of Wild Horses. G K Hall.
Valley of Wild Horses. PB.
Greygoose, Frank.
xGreygoose, Frank.
Chessmen. Arco.
Greyser, Stephen A.
xGreyser, Stephen A.
Cases in Advertising & Communications
Management. P-H.
Greytak, David.
xGreytak, David.
Municipal Output & Performance in New York
City. Lexington Bks.
Griaule, Marcel, 1898-1956
xGriaule, Marcel.
Conversations with Ogotemmeli: An
Introduction to Dogon Religious Ideas.
Oxford U Pr.
Gribbin, John. *see* Gribbin, John R.
Gribbin, John R.
xGribbin, John.
The Death of the Sun. Delacorte.
Our Changing Planet. T Y Crowell.
Timewarps. Delacorte.
Timewarps. Dell.
Weather Force: Climate & Its Impact on Our
World. Putnam.
White Holes: Cosmic Gushers in the Universe.
Delacorte.
Gribble, Francis H. *see* Gribble, Francis Henry.

Gribble, Francis Henry, 1862-1946
xGribble, Francis H.
George Sand & Her Lovers. Folcroft.
Gribbon, H. D.
xGribbon, H. D.
History of Water Power in Ulster. Kelley.
Gribov, Lev A. see Gribov, Lev Aleksandrovich.
Gribov, Lev Aleksandrovich.
xGribov, Lev A.
Intensity Theory for Infrared Spectra of
Polyatomic Molecules. Plenum Pub.
Grice-Hutchinson, Marjorie.
xGrice-Hutchinson, Marjorie.
Early Economic Thought in Spain. Allen
Unwin.
Grider, Edgar M., 1934-
xGrider, Edgar M.
Can I Make It One More Year?: Overcoming
the Hazards of the Ministry. John Knox.
Gridley, Marion E. see Gridley, Marion Eleanor.
Gridley, Marion Eleanor, 1906-
xGridley, Marion E.
Maria Tallchief. Dillon.
Gridley, Roy E.
xGridley, Roy E.
Browning. Routledge & Kegan.
Grieb, Kenneth J.
xGrieb, Kenneth J.
The Latin American Policy of Warren G.
Harding. Tex Christian.
Grieb, Lyndal, 1940-
xGrieb, Lyndal C.
The Operas of Gian Carlo Menotti, 1937-1972:
A Selective Bibliography. Scarecrow.
Grieb, Lyndal C. see Grieb, Lyndal.
Grieco, Michael H.
xGrieco, Michael H.
ed. Infections in the Abnormal Host. Yorke
Med.
Grieder, Jerome B.
xGrieder, Jerome B.
Hu Shih & the Chinese Renaissance: Liberalism
in the Chinese Revolution, 1917-1937.
Harvard U Pr.
Grieder, Terence.
xGrieder, Terence.
The Art & Archaeology of Pashash. U of Tex
Pr.
Grieder, Theodore, 1926-
xGrieder, Theodore.
Acquisitions: Where, What, & How - a Guide
to Orientation & Procedures for Students in
Librarianship, Librarians, & Academic
Faculty. Greenwood.
A Student's First Aid to Writing. Littlefield.
Grieger, Russell.
xGrieger, Russell.
Rational-Emotive Therapy: A Skills-Based
Approach. Van Nos Reinhold.
Griem, Hans R.
xGriem, Hans R.
Spectral Line Broadening by Plasmas. Acad Pr.
Griep, John A.
xGriep, John A.
ed. Clinical Uses of Frozen-Thawed Red Blood
Cells: Proceedings of a Symposium Held in
Indianapolis, April 29-30, 1976. A R Liss.
Grier, Mary C. see Grier, Mary Catharine.
Grier, Mary Catharine, 1907-
xGrier, Mary C.
ed. Oceanography of the North Pacific Ocean,
Bering Sea & Bering Strait. Greenwood.
Grierson, Herbert. see Grierson, Herbert John Clifford.
Grierson, Herbert J. see Grierson, Herbert John Clifford.
Grierson, Herbert John Clifford, Sir, 1866-1960
xGrierson, Herbert.
Carlyle & Hitler. Folcroft.
First Half of the Seventeenth Century. Folcroft.
Rhetoric & English Composition. R West.
xGrierson, Herbert J.

Background of English Literature, Classical &
Romantic, & Other Collected Essays &
Addresses. Core Collection.
The English Bible. Folcroft.
ed. Metaphysical Lyrics & Poems of the
Seventeenth Century: Donne to Butler.
Oxford U Pr.
ed. The Personal Note: Or First & Last Words
from Prefaces, Introductions, Dedications,
Epilogues. Greenwood.
Rhetoric & English Composition. Folcroft.
Grierson, Mary.
xGrierson, Mary.
Donald Francis Tovey: A Biography Based on
Letters. Greenwood.
Grierson, Philip.
xGrierson, Philip.
The Origins of Money. Humanities.
Gries, D. see Gries, David.
Gries, David, 1939-
xGries, D.
ed. Programming Methodology: A Collection of
Articles by Members of IFIP WG 2.3.
Springer-Verlag.
xGries, David.
Compiler Construction for Digital Computers.
Wiley.
Griesbach, C. B.
xGriesbach, G. B.
Historic Ornament: A Pictorial Archive; 900
Fine Examples from Ancient Egypt to 1800
Suitable for Reproduction. Peter Smith.
Griesbach, G. B. see Griesbach, C. B.
Griese, Arnold. see Griese, Arnold A.
Griese, Arnold A.
xGriese, Arnold.
At the Mouth of the Luckiest River. T Y
Crowell.
xGriese, Arnold A.
Do You Read Me?: Practical Approaches to
Teaching Reading Comprehension. Goodyear.
The Wind Is Not a River. T Y Crowell.
Griese, Bob.
xGriese, Bob.
Offensive Football. Atheneum.
Offensive Football. Atheneum.
Griesinger, F. K. see Griesinger, Frank K.
Griesinger, Frank K.
xGriesinger, F. K.
How to Cut Costs & Improve Service of Your
Telephone, Telex, TWX & Other
Telecommunications. McGraw.
Griesse, Rosalie.
xGriesse, Rosalie.
The Crooked Shall Be Made Straight. John
Knox.
Grieve, M. see Grieve, Maud.
Grieve, Maud.
xGrieve, M.
Culinary Herbs & Condiments. Dover.
Culinary Herbs & Condiments. Peter Smith.
Grieves, Foerest L. see Grieves, Forest L.
Grieves, Forest L., 1938-
xGrieves, Foerest L.
ed. Transnationalism in World Politics &
Business. Pergamon.
xGrieves, Forest L.
Conflict & Order: An Introduction to
International Relations. HM.
ed. Transnationalism in World Politics &
Business. Pergamon.
Griff, A. see Griff, Allan L.
Griff, Allan L.
xGriff, A.
Plastics Extrusion Technology. Krieger.
Griffel, William.
xGriffel, William.

Handbook of Formulas for Stress & Strain.
Ungar.
Plate Formulas. Ungar.
Griffen, Clyde.
xGriffen, Clyde.
Natives & Newcomers: The Ordering of
Opportunity in Mid-Nineteenth-Century
Poughkeepsie. Harvard U Pr.
Griffen, Elizabeth.
xGriffen, Elizabeth.
Dog's Book of Bugs. Atheneum.
Griffen, William B.
xGriffen, William B.
Culture Change & Shifting Populations in
Central Northern Mexico. U of Ariz Pr.
Indian Assimilation in the Franciscan Area of
Nueva Vizcaya. U of Ariz Pr.
Griffen, William L.
xGriffen, William L.
ed. Education for a Culture in Crisis. Mss Info.
Griffey, Carl H. see Griffey, Carl Hayes.
Griffey, Carl Hayes, 1879-
xGriffey, Carl H.
The History of Local School Control in the
State of New York. AMS Pr.
Griffin. see Griffin, Ivan H.
Griffin, Al.
xGriffin, Al.
How to Start & Operate a Day Care Home.
Contemp Bks.
Griffin, Alice Sylvia (Venezky), 1921-
xGriffin, Alice V.
Pageantry on the Shakespearean Stage. Coll &
U Pr.
Griffin, Alice V. see Griffin, Alice Sylvia (Venezky).
Griffin, Barbara. see Griffin, Barbara C.
Griffin, Barbara C.
xGriffin, Barbara.
A Successful Business of Your Own.
Sherbourne.
Griffin, Charles H.
xGriffin, Charles H.
Advanced Accounting. Irwin.
Griffin, Clare E. see Griffin, Clare Elmer.
Griffin, Clare Elmer, 1892-
xGriffin, Clare E.
The Free Society. Am Enterprise.
Griffin, D. M. see Griffin, David Michael.
Griffin, David, 1939-
xGriffin, David R.
God, Power, & Evil: A Process Theodicy.
Westminster.
Griffin, David Michael, 1929-
xGriffin, D. M.
Ecology of Soil Fungi. Syracuse U Pr.
Griffin, David R. see Griffin, David.
Griffin, Donald R. see Griffin, Donald Redfield.
Griffin, Donald Redfield, 1915-
xGriffin, Donald R.
Animal Structure & Function. HR&W.
Listening in the Dark: The Acoustic
Orientation of Bats & Men. Peter Smith.
The Question of Animal Awareness:
Evolutionary Continuity of Mental
Experience. Rockefeller.
Griffin, E. see Griffin, Ernest G.
Griffin, Edward M., 1937-
xGriffin, Edward M.
Jonathan Edwards. U of Minn Pr.
Griffin, Eldon, 1895-
xGriffin, Eldon.
Clippers & Consuls: American Consular &
Commercial Relations with Eastern Asia,
1845-1860. Chinese Materials.
Clippers & Consuls: American Consular &
Commercial Relations with Eastern Asia,
1854-1860.. Scholarly Res Inc.
Griffin, Ernest G., 1916-
xGriffin, E.

Eugene O'Neill: A Collection of Criticism.
McGraw.
Griffin, G. Edward.
xGriffin, G. Edward.
The Life & Words of Robert Welch, Founder
of the John Birch Society. Am Media.
World Without Cancer: The Story of Vitamin B
17. Am Media.
Griffin, G Edward.
xGriffin, G. Edward.
Fearful Master: A Second Look at the United
Nations. Western Islands.
Griffin, Gerald, 1803-1840
xGriffin, Gerald.
The Collegians. Garland Pub.
The Rivals & Tracy's Ambition. AMS Pr.
The Rivals & Tracy's Ambition. Garland Pub.
Tales of the Munster Festivals. Garland Pub.
Griffin, Glen C.
xGriffin, Glen C.
About You...& Other Important People.
Deseret Bk.
Not About Birds. Deseret Bk.
Griffin, I. H. see Griffin, Ivan H.
Griffin, Ivan H.
xGriffin.
Welding Processes. Delmar.
xGriffin, I. H.
Pipe Welding Techniques. Delmar.
xGriffin, Ivan H.
Basic Arc Welding. Delmar.
Pipe Welding Techniques. Van Nos Reinhold.
Welding Processes. Van Nos Reinhold.
Griffin, James.
xGriffin, James.
ed. Papua New Guinea Portraits: The
Expatriate Experience. Bks Australia.
Griffin, James B. see Griffin, James Bennett.
Griffin, James Bennett.
xGriffin, James B.
Burial Complexes of the Knight & Norton
Mounds in Illinois & Michigan. U Mich Mus
Anthro.
Griffin, James M.
xGriffin, James M.
Energy Conservation in the OECD: 1980 to
2000. Ballinger Pub.
Griffin, Jeff.
xGriffin, Jeff W.
Cold Weather Flying. TAB Bks.
Study Guide for the Airline Transport Pilot's
Written Exam. TAB Bks.
Griffin, Jeff W. see Griffin, Jeff.
Griffin, John H. see Griffin, John Howard.
Griffin, John Howard, 1920-
xGriffin, John H.
Church & the Black Man. Pflaum Pr.
Twelve Photographic Portraits. Unicorn Pr.
Griffin, John I. see Griffin, John Ignatius.
Griffin, John Ignatius, 1916-
xGriffin, John I.
Statistics Essential for Police Efficiency. C C
Thomas.
Strikes: A Study in Quantitative Economics.
AMS Pr.
Griffin, Joseph A. see Griffin, Joseph Aloysius.
Griffin, Joseph Aloysius, 1901-
xGriffin, Joseph A.
The Contribution of Belgium to the Catholic
Church in America (1523-1857). AMS Pr.
Griffin, Judith B. see Griffin, Judith Berry.
Griffin, Judith Berry.
xGriffin, Judith B.
Nat Turner. Coward.
Griffin, K. B. see Griffin, Keith B.
Griffin, Kathryn.
xGriffin, Kathryn.
Teaching Teens the Truth. Broadman.
Griffin, Keith. see Griffin, Keith B.

Griffin, Keith B.
xGriffin, K. B.
Planning Development. A-W.
xGriffin, Keith.
Land Concentration & Rural Poverty. Holmes
& Meier.
Griffin, Lepel H. see Griffin, Lepel Henry.
Griffin, Lepel Henry, Sir, 1840-1908
xGriffin, Lepel H.
The Great Republic. Arno.
Griffin, Margaret P. see Griffin, Margaret Pierce.
Griffin, Margaret Pierce.
xGriffin, Margaret P.
Practical Approach to Communicating in
Writing & Speech. Glencoe.
Griffin, Martin I. see Griffin, Martin Ignatius Joseph.
Griffin, Martin Ignatius Joseph, 1906-
xGriffin, Martin I.
Frank R. Stockton: A Critical Biography.
Kennikat.
Griffin, Nicholas.
xGriffin, Nicholas.
Relative Identity. Oxford U Pr.
Griffin, Robert, 1936-
xGriffin, Robert.
Clement Marot & the Inflections of Poetic
Voice. U of Cal Pr.
Coronation of the Poet: Joachim Du Bellay's
Debt to the Trivium. U of Cal Pr.
I Never Said I Didn't Love You. Paulist Pr.
In the Kingdom of the Lonely God. Paulist Pr.
Griffin, Roger. see Griffin, Roger C.
Griffin, Roger C.
xGriffin, Roger.
Principles of Package Development. AVI.
Griffin, Susan.
xGriffin, Susan.
Like the Iris of an Eye. Har-Row.
Woman & Nature: The Roaring Inside Her.
Har-Row.
Woman & Nature: The Roaring Inside Her.
Har-Row.
Griffin, William, 1935-
xGriffin, William.
Endtime: The Doomsday Catalog. Macmillan.
Griffin, William L. see Griffin, William Lloyd.
Griffin, William Lloyd.
xGriffin, William L.
Cross Fire. Valley Pubns.
ed. Quality American - Poetry - 1975 - 1976.
Valley Pubns.
Griffing, Marie F. see Griffing, Marie Fenton.
Griffing, Marie Fenton, 1925-
xGriffing, Marie F.
Fitness for the Working Woman. Contemp Bks.
Griffis, William E. see Griffis, William Elliot.
Griffis, William Elliot, 1843-1928
xGriffis, William E.
Corea, the Hermit Nation. AMS Pr.
Religions of Japan: From the Dawn of History
to the Era of Meiji. Arno.
Griffiss, James E., 1928-
xGriffiss, James E.
A Silent Path to God. Fortress.
Griffith, Arthur Leonard, 1920-
xGriffith, Leonard.
Gospel Characters: The Personalities Around
Jesus. Eerdmans.
Griffith, B. C. see Griffith, Benjamin Lease Crozer.
Griffith, Benjamin Lease Crozer, 1869-1900
xGriffith, B. C.
ed. Monologues & Novelties. Arno.
Griffith, Bob.
xGriffith, Bob.
Blue Water: A Guide to Self-Reliant Sailboat
Cruising. Sail Bks.
xGriffith, Robert.

Blue Water: A Guide to Self Reliant Sailboat
Cruising. Norton.
Griffith, Cyril E.
xGriffith, Cyril E.
The African Dream: Martin R. Delany & the
Emergence of Pan-African Thought. Pa St U
Pr.
Griffith, Dudley. see Griffith, Dudley David.
Griffith, Dudley David, 1882-
xGriffith, Dudley.
Origin of the Griselda Story. Folcroft.
The Origin of the Griselda Story. R West.
Griffith, Earle G. see Griffith, Earle Gordon.
Griffith, Earle Gordon.
xGriffith, Earle G.
The Pastor As God's Minister. Reg Baptist.
Griffith, Edward J.
xGriffith, Edward J.
ed. Environmental Phosphorus Handbook.
Krieger.
Griffith, Elizabeth. see Griffith, Elizabeth (Griffith).
Griffith, Elizabeth (Griffith), 1720?-1793
xGriffith, Elizabeth.
Morality of Shakespeare's Drama Illustrated.
Biblio Dist.
Morality of Shakespeare's Drama Illustrated.
Kelley.
Griffith, Ernest S. see Griffith, Ernest Stacey.
Griffith, Ernest Stacey, 1896-
xGriffith, Ernest S.
The American Presidency: The Dilemmas of
Shared Power and Divided Government.
NYU Pr.
Congress: Its Contemporary Role. NYU Pr.
Griffith, Frank B.
xGriffith, Frank B.
How to Live with a Horse. Arco.
Griffith, George see Griffith, George Chetwynd.
Griffith, George Chetwynd.
xGriffith, George.
A Honeymoon in Space. Arno.
The Mummy & Miss Nitocris: A Phantasy of
the Fourth Dimension. Arno.
Griffith, H. Winter. see Griffith, Henry Winter.
Griffith, Harry C.
xGriffith, Harry C.
Adventure in Discipleship. Zondervan.
Griffith, Helen.
xGriffith, Helen.
Dauntless in Mississippi: The Life of Sarah A.
Dickey. Zenger Pub.
Griffith, Henry Winter, 1926-
xGriffith, H. Winter.
Drug Information for Patients. Saunders.
Instructions for Patients. Saunders.
Griffith, J. A. see Griffith, John Aneurin Grey.
Griffith, J. S. see Griffith, John Stanley.
Griffith, Jerry.
xGriffith, Jerry.
Phonetic Context Drill Book. P-H.
Griffith, Jim N.
xGriffith, Jim N.
Stepping Stones. Broadman.
Sure You Can. Broadman.
Griffith, John Aneurin Grey.
xGriffith, J. A.
The Politics of the Judiciary. Humanities.
Griffith, John R.
xGriffith, John R.
Quantitative Techniques for Hospital Planning
& Control. Lexington Bks.
Griffith, John S. see Griffith, John Stanley.
Griffith, John Stanley.
xGriffith, J. S.
Mathematical Neurobiology: An Introduction
to the Mathematics of the Nervous System.
Acad Pr.
xGriffith, John S.

Theory of Transition-Metal Ions. Cambridge U Pr.

Griffith, Leonard. *see* Griffith, Arthur Leonard.

Griffith, Liddon R.
xGriffith, Liddon R.
Mugging: You Can Protect Yourself. P-H.

Griffith, Mark.
xGriffith, Mark.
The Authenticity of Prometheus Bound. Cambridge U Pr.

Griffith, Phillip A.
xGriffith, Phillip A.
Infinite Abelian Group Theory. U of Chicago Pr.

Griffith, Reginald H. *see* Griffith, Reginald Harvey.

Griffith, Reginald Harvey, 1873-1957
xGriffith, Reginald H.
Alexander Pope: A Bibliography. AMS Pr.

Griffith, Richard, 1912-
xGriffith, Richard.
The World of Robert Flaherty. Da Capo.
World of Robert Flaherty. Greenwood.

Griffith, Robert.
xGriffith, Robert W.
Politics of Fear: Joseph R. McCarthy & the Senate. Hayden.

Griffith, Robert. *see* Griffith, Bob.

Griffith, Robert W. *see* Griffith, Robert.

Griffith, Samuel B.
xGriffith, Samuel B.
Chinese People's Liberation Army. McGraw.

Griffith, William, 1766-1826
xGriffith, William.
Annual Law Register of the United States. Arno.

Griffith, William E.
xGriffith, William E.
The Ostpolitik of the Federal Republic of Germany. MIT Pr.
The World & the Great Power Triangles. MIT Pr.

Griffith, William H.
xGriffith, William H.
Confronting Death. Judson.

Griffiths, Bede, 1906-
xGriffiths, Bede.
Vedanta & Christian Faith. Dawn Horse Pr.

Griffiths, Brian.
xGriffiths, Brian.
Inflation: The Price of Prosperity. Holmes & Meier.

Griffiths, G. D. *see* Griffiths, Gordon Douglas.

Griffiths, Gordon Douglas.
xGriffiths, G. D.
Mattie: The Story of a Hedgehog. Delacorte.

Griffiths, H. B. *see* Griffiths, Hubert Brian.

Griffiths, Harry J.
xGriffiths, Harry J.
Contemporary Radiology: An Introduction to Imaging. Saunders.

Griffiths, Helen.
xGriffiths, Helen.
Grip, a Dog Story. Holiday.

Griffiths, Hubert Brian.
xGriffiths, H. B.
A Comprehensive Textbook of Classical Mathematics: A Contemporary Interpretation. Springer-Verlag.

Griffiths, J. F. *see* Griffiths, John F.

Griffiths, John, 1942-
xGriffiths, John.
The Crossword Finisher. St Martin.

Griffiths, John C.
xGriffiths, John C.
Clinical Enzymology. Masson Pub.

Griffiths, John F.
xGriffiths, J. F.
Climates of Africa. Elsevier.
xGriffiths, John F.

Applied Climatology: An Introduction. Oxford U Pr.

Griffiths, Julia.
xGriffiths, Julia.
ed. Autographs for Freedom. Arno.

Griffiths, M. *see* Griffiths, Mervyn.

Griffiths, Mary.
xGriffiths, Mary.
Introduction to Human Physiology. Macmillan.

Griffiths, Mervyn.
xGriffiths, M.
Echidnas. Pergamon.
xGriffiths, Mervyn.
The Biology of the Monotremes. Acad Pr.

Griffiths, Michael, 1928-
xGriffiths, Michael.
Grace-Gifts. Eerdmans.

Griffiths, Michael. *see* Griffiths, Michael C.

Griffiths, Michael C.
xGriffiths, Michael.
God's Forgetful Pilgrims: Recalling the Church to Its Reason for Being. Eerdmans.
xGriffiths, Michael C.
Give up Your Small Ambitions. Moody.

Griffiths, N. E. *see* Griffiths, Naomi Elizabeth Saundaus.

Griffiths, Naomi Elizabeth Saundaus.
xGriffiths, N. E.
Penelope's Web: Some Perceptions of Women in European & Canadian Society. Oxford U Pr.

Griffiths, Paul.
xGriffiths, Paul.
Concise History of Avant Garde Music: From Debussy to Boulez. Oxford U Pr.
A Guide to Electronic Music. Thames Hudson.

Griffiths, Percival. *see* Griffiths, Percival Joseph.

Griffiths, Percival Joseph, Sir, 1899-
xGriffiths, Percival.
Modern India. InterCulture.

Griffiths, Peter, 1944-
xGriffiths, Peter.
Final Approach. St Martin.

Griffiths, Phillip, 1938-
xGriffiths, Phillip.
Principles of Algebraic Geometry. Wiley.
xGriffiths, Phillip A.
Entire Holomorphic Mappings in One & Several Complex Variables. Princeton U Pr.

Griffiths, Phillip A. *see* Griffiths, Phillip.

Griffiths, Trevor.
xGriffiths, Trevor.
Comedians. Grove.

Griffiths, Walter G.
xGriffiths, Walter G.
The Kol Tribe of Central India. AMS Pr.

Grigarick, A. A. *see* Grigarick, Albert A.

Grigarick, Albert A.
xGrigarick, A. A.
Reichenbachia Found in the United States West of the Continental Divide (Coleoptera: Pselaphidae). U of Cal Pr.
xGrigarick, Albert A.
A Revision of Actium Casey & Actiastes Casey (Coleoptera: Pselaphidae). U of Cal Pr.

Grigg, Carolyn D. *see* Grigg, Carolyn Doub.

Grigg, Carolyn Doub.
xGrigg, Carolyn D.
Compiled by Music Translation Dictionary: An English-Czech-Danish-Dutch-French-German -Hungarian-Italian-Polish-Portuguese-Russian- Spanish-Swedish Vocabulary of Music. Greenwood.

Grigg, Richard W.
xGrigg, Richard W.
Hawaii's Precious Corals. Island Her.

Griggs, Earl L. *see* Griggs, Earl Leslie.

Griggs, Earl Leslie, 1899-
xGriggs, Earl L.

Coleridge Fille: A Biography of Sara Coleridge. Folcroft.
Thomas Clarkson: The Friend of Slaves. Negro U Pr.
Wordsworth & Coleridge: Studies in Honor of George McLean Harper. Russell.

Griggs, Edward H. *see* Griggs, Edward Howard.

Griggs, Edward Howard, 1868-1951
xGriggs, Edward H.
American Statesmen: An Interpretation of Our History & Heritage. Arno.
Goethe's Faust: A Handbook of Ten Lectures. Folcroft.
Great Leaders in Human Progress. Arno.

Griggs, John E.
xGriggs, John E.
Evaluating Marketing Change: An Application of Systems Theory. Mich St U Busn.

Griggs, Sutton E. *see* Griggs, Sutton Elbert.

Griggs, Sutton Elbert, 1872-
xGriggs, Sutton E.
Hindered Hand: Or, Reign of the Repressionist. Arno.
Imperium in Imperio. AMS Pr.
Imperium in Imperio. Arno.
Imperium in Imperio. Mnemosyne.

Griggs, Tamar.
xGriggs, Tamar.
There's a Sound in the Sea: A Child's-Eye View of the Whale. Scrimshaw Calif.

Grigsby, Gordon.
xGrigsby, Gordon.
Tornado Watch. Ohio St U Pr.

Grigsby, Joan S. *see* Grigsby, Joan Savell.

Grigsby, Joan Savell, 1891-1937
xGrigsby, Joan S.
Orchid Door: Ancient Korean Poems. Paragon.

Grigson. *see* Grigson, Jane.

Grigson, Geoffrey, 1905-
xGrigson, Geoffrey.
The Contrary View: Glimpses of Fudge & Gold. Rowman.
Intro. by & ed. The Faber Book of Epigrams & Epitaphs. Merrimack Bk Serv.
ed. Gambit Book of Popular Verse. Gambit.
A Master of Our Time: A Study of Wyndham Lewis. Folcroft.
More Shapes & Stories: A Book About Pictures. Vanguard.
ed. Penguin Book of Ballads. Penguin.

Grigson, Jane.
xGrigson.
Art of Charcuterie. Radio City.
xGrigson, Jane.
Food with the Famous. Atheneum.
Jane Grigson's Vegetable Book. Atheneum.

Grijpstra, B. G.
xGrijpstra, B. G.
Common Efforts in the Development of Rural Sarawak, Malaysia. Humanities.

Grilliot, Harold J.
xGrilliot, Harold J.
Introduction to Law & the Legal System. HM.

Grillo, John P.
xGrillo, John P.
Microcomputer Systems: An Applications Approach. Wm C Brown.

Grillo, Paul J. *see* Grillo, Paul Jacques.

Grillo, Paul Jacques.
xGrillo, Paul J.
Form, Function & Design. Dover.
Form, Function & Design. Peter Smith.

Grillo, Virgil.
xGrillo, Virgil.
Charles Dickens' Sketches by Boz: End in the Beginning. Colo Assoc.

Grillot, Gerald F. *see* Grillot, Gerald Francis.

Grillot, Gerald Francis, 1914-
xGrillot, Gerald F.

A Chemical Background for the Paramedical
Sciences. Har-Row.

Grillparzer, Franz, 1791-1872
xGrillparzer, Franz.
Poor Fiddler. Ungar.

Grim, Ralph E. *see* Grim, Ralph Early.

Grim, Ralph Early, 1902-
xGrim, Ralph E.
Clay Mineralogy. McGraw.

Grimal, Henri, 1910-
xGrimal, Henri.
Decolonization of the British, French, Dutch &
Belgian Empires: 1919-1963. Westview.

Grime, J. P. *see* Grime, John Philip.

Grime, John Philip.
xGrime, J. P.
Plant Strategies & Vegetation Processes. Wiley.

Grime, William E. *see* Grime, William Ed.

Grime, William Ed, 1940-
xGrime, William E.
Ethno-Botany of the Black Americans. Ref
Pubns.

Grimes, Alan P. *see* Grimes, Alan Pendleton.

Grimes, Alan Pendleton, 1919-
xGrimes, Alan P.
Democracy & the Amendments to the
Constitution. Lexington Bks.

Grimes, John M. *see* Grimes, John Maurice.

Grimes, John Maurice, 1885-
xGrimes, John M.
Institutional Care of Mental Patients in the
United States. Arno.

Grimes, Nikki.
xGrimes, Nikki.
Growin'. Dial.

Grimes, Orville. *see* Grimes, Orville F.

Grimes, Orville F., 1943-
xGrimes, Orville.
Housing for Low Income Urban Families:
Economics & Policy in the Developing
World. Johns Hopkins.

Grimes, Ronald L.
xGrimes, Ronald L.
Symbol & Conquest: Public Ritual & Drama in
Santa Fe, New Mexico. Cornell U Pr.

Grimes, Russell N., 1935-
xGrimes, Russell N.
Carboranes. Acad Pr.

Grimes, William A. *see* Grimes, William Alvan.

Grimes, William Alvan, 1911-
xGrimes, William A.
Criminal Law Outline. Natl Judicial Coll.

Grimke, Angelina E. *see* Grimke, Angelina Emily.

Grimke, Angelina Emily, 1805-1879
xGrimke, Angelina E.
Appeal to the Christian Women of the South.
Arno.
Letters to Catherine E. Beecher. Arno.

Grimke, Frederick.
xGrimke, Frederick.
Nature & Tendency of Free Institutions.
Harvard U Pr.

Grimke, Thomas S. *see* Grimke, Thomas Smith.

Grimke, Thomas Smith, 1786-1834
xGrimke, Thomas S.
Address on the Truth, Dignity, Power &
Beauty of the Principles of Peace, & on the
Unchristian Character & Influence of War &
the Warrior. Ozer.

Grimm. *see* Grimm, Jakob Ludwig Karl.

Grimm, Brothers. *see* Grimm, Jakob Ludwig Karl.

Grimm, Florence M. *see* Grimm, Florence Marie.

Grimm, Florence Marie.
xGrimm, Florence M.
Astronomical Lore in Chaucer. AMS Pr.

Grimm, H. *see* Grimm, Herman Friedrich.

Grimm, Harold J. *see* Grimm, Harold John.

Grimm, Harold John, 1901-
xGrimm, Harold J.

Lazarus Spengler: A Lay Leader of the
Reformation. Ohio St U Pr.
The Reformation. Am Hist Assn.
The Reformation Era: 1500-1650. Macmillan.

Grimm, Herman F. *see* Grimm, Herman Friedrich.

Grimm, Herman Friedrich, 1828-1901
xGrimm, H.
Life of Michaelangelo. Gordon Pr.
xGrimm, Herman F.
Life of Michael Angelo. Greenwood.
Life of Michael Angelo. Scholarly.

Grimm, Jacob. *see* Grimm, Jakob Ludwig Karl.

Grimm, Jakob Ludwig Karl.
xGrimm.
Grimm's Fairy Tales. Oxford U Pr.
xGrimm, Brothers.
Brave Little Tailor. Troll Assocs.
Bremen Town Musicians. Troll Assocs.
Twelve Dancing Princesses. Troll Assocs.
Wolf & the Seven Kids. Troll Assocs.
xGrimm, Jacob.
Grimms' Fairy Tales. Biblio Dist.

Grimm, Ruediger H. *see* Grimm, Ruediger Hermann.

Grimm, Ruediger Hermann, 1947-
xGrimm, Ruediger H.
Nietzsche's Theory of Knowledge. De Gruyter.

Grimm, Tom.
xGrimm, Tom.
The Basic Darkroom Book: A Complete Guide
to Processing & Printing Color &
Black-&-White Photographs. NAL.

Grimm, William. *see* Grimm, William Carey.

Grimm, William C. *see* Grimm, William Carey.

Grimm, William Carey, 1907-
xGrimm, William.
Indian Harvests. McGraw.
xGrimm, William C.
Book of Trees. Dutton.
Wondrous World of Seedless Plants. Bobbs.

Grimmelshausen, Hans Jacob Christoffel von, 1625-1676
xGrimmelshausen, Johann.
Simplicius Simplicissimus. Bobbs.

Grimmelshausen, Johann. *see* Grimmelshausen, Hans
Jacob Christoffel von.

Grimmer, Elsa H.
xGrimmer, Elsa H.
Wave Crest Ware: An Illustrated Guide to the
Victorian World of C. F. Monroe.
Wallace-Homestead.

Grimond, Joseph.
xGrimond, Joseph.
The Liberal Challenge. Greenwood.

Grimsditch, Herbert B. *see* Grimsditch, Herbert
Borthwick.

Grimsditch, Herbert Borthwick, 1898-
xGrimsditch, Herbert B.
Character & Environment in the Novels of
Thomas Hardy. Russell.
xGrimsditch, Herbert R.
Character & Environment in the Novels of
Thomas Hardy. Haskell.

Grimsditch, Herbert R. *see* Grimsditch, Herbert
Borthwick.

Grimshaw. *see* Grimshaw, William J.

Grimshaw, Beatrice. *see* Grimshaw, Beatrice Ethel.

Grimshaw, Beatrice Ethel.
xGrimshaw, Beatrice.
In the Strange South Seas. Arno.

Grimshaw, William J.
xGrimshaw.
Union Rule in the Schools: Big-City Politics in
Transformation. Lexington Bks.

Grimsley, Linda.
xGrimsley, Linda.
Guerrilla in the Kitchen. Condor Pub Co.

Grimwood, Ken.
xGrimwood, Ken.
Breakthrough. Ballantine.
Elise. Doubleday.

Grinder, J. T. *see* Grinder, John T.

Grinder, John T.
xGrinder, J. T.
Guide to Transformational Grammar: History,
Theory, Practice. HR&W.
xGrinder, John T.
On Deletion Phenomena in English. Mouton.

Grinder, Robert E.
xGrinder, Robert E.
Adolescence. Wiley.

Grindle, Merilee S. *see* Grindle, Merilee Serrill.

Grindle, Merilee Serrill.
xGrindle, Merilee S.
Bureaucrats, Politicians, & Peasants in Mexico:
A Case Study in Public Policy. U of Cal Pr.
ed. Politics & Policy Implementation in the
Third World. Princeton U Pr.

Grindley, Kit.
xGrindley, Kit.
Systematics: A New Approach to Systems
Analysis. Petrocelli.

Gringauz, Alex, 1934-
xGringauz, Alex.
Drugs: How They Act & Why. Mosby.

Grinich, Victor. *see* Grinich, Victor H.

Grinich, Victor H.
xGrinich, Victor.
Introduction to Integrated Circuits. McGraw.

Grinker, Roy R. *see* Grinker, Roy Richard.

Grinker, Roy Richard.
xGrinker, Roy R.
The Borderline Patient. Aronson.
Fifty Years in Psychiatry: A Living History. C
C Thomas.
Men Under Stress. Irvington.
Psychiatry in Broad Perspective. Human Sci Pr.
Psychosomatic Concepts. Aronson.
War Neuroses. Arno.

Grinnell, George B. *see* Grinnell, George Bird.

Grinnell, George Bird, 1849-1938
xGrinnell, George B.
By Cheyenne Campfires. U of Nebr Pr.
Cheyenne Indians, Their History & Ways of
Life. Cooper Sq.
Fighting Cheyennes. U of Okla Pr.
ed. Hunting & Conservation. Arno.
Last of the Buffalo. Arno.

Grinnell, Isabel H. *see* Grinnell, Isabel Hoopes.

Grinnell, Isabel Hoopes.
xGrinnell, Isabel H.
Greek Temples. Arno.

Grinnell, Joseph, 1877-1939
xGrinnell, Joseph.
Joseph Grinnell's Philosophy of Nature:
Selected Writings of a Western Naturalist.
Arno.

Grinnell-Milne, Duncan. *see* Grinnell-Milne, Duncan
William.

Grinnell-Milne, Duncan William.
xGrinnell-Milne, Duncan.
Wind in the Wires. Arno.

Grinsell, L. V. *see* Grinsell, Leslie V.

Grinsell, Leslie V.
xGrinsell, L. V.
The Ancient Burial-Mounds of England.
Greenwood.

Grinspoon, Lester.
xGrinspoon, Lester.
Cocaine: A Drug & Its Social Evolution. Basic.
Marihuana Reconsidered. Harvard U Pr.
Psychedelic Drugs Reconsidered. Basic.
The Speed Culture: Amphetamine Use &
Abuse in America. Harvard U Pr.

Grinstead, J. E.
xGrinstead, J. E.
Maverick Guns. Belmont-Tower.

Grinstein, Alexander.
xGrinstein, Alexander.

On Sigmund Freud's Dreams. Wayne St U Pr.
Sigmund Freud's Dreams. Intl Univs Pr.

Gripe, Maria.
xGripe, Maria.
Elvis & His Secret. Delacorte.
The Glassblower's Children. Delacorte.
The Green Coat. Delacorte.
Hugo & Josephine. Delacorte.
In the Time of the Bells. Delacorte.
The Night Daddy. Delacorte.

Gripp, Richard C.
xGripp, Richard C.
The Political System of Communism. Har-Row.

Gris, Henry.
xGris, Henry.
The New Soviet Psychic Discoveries. P-H.
The New Soviet Psychic Discoveries. Warner
Bks.

Grisar, Hartmann, 1845-1932
xGrisar, Hartmann.
History of Rome & the Popes in the Middle
Ages. AMS Pr.

Grisez, Germain. see Grisez, Germain Gabriel.

Grisez, Germain Gabriel.
xGrisez, Germain.
Life & Death with Liberty & Justice: A
Contribution to the Euthanasia Debate. U of
Notre Dame Pr.

Grisham, Noel.
xGrisham, Noel.
Tame the Restless Wind: The Life & Legends
of Sam Bass. Jenkins.

Grislis, Egil.
xGrislis, Egil.
Richard Hooker: A Selected Bibliography. C E
Barbour.

Grismer, R. L. see Grismer, Raymond Leonard.
Grismer, Raymond L. see Grismer, Raymond Leonard.

Grismer, Raymond Leonard, 1895-
xGrismer, R. L.
Cervantes: A Bibliography. Kraus Repr.
xGrismer, Raymond L.
Reference Index to Twelve Thousand Spanish
American Authors. B Franklin.

Grist, Donald H. see Grist, Donald Honey.

Grist, Donald Honey, 1891-
xGrist, Donald H.
Rice. Longman.

Griswold, Bert J. see Griswold, Bert Joseph.

Griswold, Bert Joseph.
xGriswold, Bert J.
ed. Fort Wayne, Gateway of the West,
1802-1813: Garrison Orderly Books, Indian
Agency Account Book. AMS Pr.

Griswold, Hattie. see Griswold, Hattie (Tyng).

Griswold, Hattie (Tyng), 1840-1909
xGriswold, Hattie.
Personal Sketches of Recent Authors. R West.

Griswold, Ralph E.

xGriswold, Ralph E.
Opportunities in Landscape Architecture. Natl
Textbk.

Griswold, Rufus. see Griswold, Rufus Wilmot.
Griswold, Rufus W. see Griswold, Rufus Wilmot.

Griswold, Rufus Wilmot, 1815-1857
xGriswold, Rufus.
The Prose Writers of America. Century
Bookbindery.
xGriswold, Rufus W.
ed. The Female Poets of America. Mss Info.
ed. The Female Poets of America. Somerset
Pub.
ed. The Prose Writers of America. Mss Info.
The Prose Writers of America. R West.

Griswold, Wesley S., 1909-
xGriswold, Wesley S.

The Night the Revolution Began: The Boston
Tea Party, 1773. Greene.

Griswold, Whit, 1944-
xGriswold, Whit.
Berkshire Trails for Walking & Ski Touring.
East Woods.

Griswold, William H. see Griswold, William McCrillis.

Griswold, William McCrillis, 1853-1899
xGriswold, William H.
Descriptive Lists of American, International,
Romantic & British Novels. B Franklin.

Grittner, Frank M.
xGrittner, Frank M.
Teaching Foreign Languages. Har-Row.

Groat, Dick.
xGroat, Dick.
Groat: I Hit & Ran. Moore Pub Co.

Grob, Gerald N., 1931-
xGrob, Gerald N.
Compiled by American Social History Before
1860. AHM Pub.
Edward Jarvis & the Medical World of
Nineteenth-Century America. U of Tenn Pr.
Workers & Utopia: A Study of Ideological
Conflict in the American Labor Movement,
1865-1900. Times Bks.

Grob, Mollie C.
xGrob, Mollie C.
Adolescent Patients in Transition: Impact &
Outcome of Psychiatric Hospitalization.
Human Sci Pr.

Grob, Robert L. see Grob, Robert Lee.

Grob, Robert Lee.
xGrob, Robert L.
ed. Chromatographic Analysis of the
Environment. Dekker.

Grobani, Anton.
xGrobani, Anton.
ed. Guide to Baseball Literature. Gale.
ed. Guide to Football Literature. Gale.

Grobler, N. J. see Grobler, Nicolaas Johannes.

Grobler, Nicolaas Johannes.
xGrobler, N. J.
Textbook of Clinical Anatomy. Elsevier.

Grobstein, Clifford, 1916-
xGrobstein, Clifford.
A Double Image of the Double Helix: The
Recombinant-DNA Debate. W H Freeman.
The Strategy of Life. W H Freeman.

Groch, Dick.
xGroch, Dick.
Mastering Baseball. Contemp Bks.

Groch, Judith.
xGroch, Judith.
Play the Bach, Dear!. Doubleday.

Grochla, Erwin.
xGrochla, Erwin.
ed. Information Systems & Organizational
Structure. De Gruyter.

Grodecki, Louis.
xGrodecki, Louis.
Gothic Architecture. Abrams.

Groden, Michael.
xGroden, Michael.
Ulysses in Progress. Princeton U Pr.

Groder, Martin G.
xGroder, Martin G.
Games People Play in Business. Boardroom.

Grodner, Murray.
xGrodner, Murray.
Comprehensive Catalog of Available Literature
for the Double Bass. Lemur.
ed. Concepts in String Playing: Reflections by
Artist-Teachers at the Indiana University
School of Music. Ind U Pr.

Groenjes, Kathleen.
xGroenjes, Kathleen.

Adrift in Space & Other Stories. Lerner Pubns.
Graduated Robot & Other Stories. Lerner
Pubns.
Journey to Another Star & Other Stories.
Lerner Pubns.

Groer, Maureen E.
xGroer, Maureen E.
Basic Pathophysiology: A Conceptual
Approach. Mosby.

Groetsch, C. W.
xGroetsch, C. W.
Generalized Inverses of Linear Operators:
Representation & Approximation. Dekker.

Grof, Stanislav.
xGrof, Stanislav.
The Human Encounter with Death. Dutton.
Realms of Human Unconscious: Observations
from LSD Research. Dutton.

Groff, Betty.
xGroff, Betty.
Good Earth & Country Cooking. Stackpole.

Groff, Warren F.
xGroff, Warren F.
Story Time: God's Story & Ours. Brethren.

Grogan, Denis. see Grogan, Denis Joseph.

Grogan, Denis Joseph.
xGrogan, Denis.
More Case Studies in Reference Work. Shoe
String.

Grogono, Peter.
xGrogono, Peter.
Programming in Pascal. A W.

Grohskopf, Bernice.
xGrohskopf, Bernice.
Blood & Roses. Atheneum.
Children in the Wind. Atheneum.
Notes on the Hauter Experiment: A Journey
Through the Inner World of Evelyn B.
Chestnut. Atheneum.

Grolier Club. see Grolier Club, New York.
Grolier Club - New York. see Grolier Club, New York.

Grolle, Carl G., 1933-
xGrolle, Carl G.
Complete Guide to Electrical & Electronic
Repairs. P-H.

Grolier Club, New York.
xGrolier Club.
Catalog of Original & Early Editions of Some
of the Poetical & Prose Works from Langland
to Prior. Saifer.
Grolier Seventy-Five, a Bibliographical
Retrospective to Celebrate the 75th
Anniversary of The Grolier Club. Grolier
Club.
xGrolier Club - New York.
Bibliographical Notes on One Hundred Books
Famous in English Literature. Kraus Repr.
One Hundred Books Famous in English
Literature with 100 Facsimiles of the
Title-Pages. Kraus Repr.
One Hundred Influential American Books
Printed Before 1900. Kraus Repr.

Grollenberg, Lucas. see Grollenberg, Lucas Hendricus.

Grollenberg, Lucas Hendricus, 1916-
xGrollenberg, Lucas.
Jesus. Westminster.
Paul. Westminster.

Grollman, Earl A.
xGrollman, Earl A.
Caring for Your Aged Parents. Beacon Pr.
ed. Concerning Death: A Practical Guide for
the Living. Beacon Pr.
ed. Explaining Death to Children. Beacon Pr.
Living - When a Loved One Has Died. Beacon
Pr.
Living Through Your Divorce. Beacon Pr.
When Your Loved One Is Dying. Beacon Pr.

Grollman, Sigmund.
xGrollman, Sigmund.

Human Body: Its Structure & Physiology.
   Macmillan.
Gromacki, Robert G. see Gromacki, Robert Glenn.
Gromacki, Robert Glenn.
   xGromacki, Robert G.
   Are These the Last Days?. Reg Baptist.
Grombach, John V.
   xGrombach, John V.
   The Great Liquidator. Doubleday.
Gronbeck, Bruce E.
   xGronbeck, Bruce E.
   The Articulate Person: A Guide to Everyday
      Public Speaking. Scott F.
Groneman, Chris. see Groneman, Chris Harold.
Groneman, Chris H. see Groneman, Chris Harold.
Groneman, Chris Harold.
   xGroneman, Chris.
   Leathercraft. Bennett Co.
   xGroneman, Chris H.
   General Industrial Education. McGraw.
   General Woodworking. McGraw.
   Getting Started in Drawing & Planning.
      McGraw.
   Getting Started in Electricity & Electronics.
      McGraw.
   Getting Started in Metalworking. McGraw.
   Getting Started in Woodworking. McGraw.
   Leather Tooling & Carving. Dover.
   Leather Tooling & Carving. Peter Smith.
Groner, Pat N.
   xGroner, Pat N.
   Cost Containment Through Employee
      Incentives Program. Aspen Systems.
Gronlund, Laurence, 1846-1897
   xGronlund, Laurence.
   Our Destiny: The Influence of Socialism on
      Morals & Religion; an Essay on Ethics.
      Hyperion Conn.
Gronlund, Norman E. see Gronlund, Norman Edward.
Gronlund, Norman Edward, 1920-
   xGronlund, Norman E.
   Constructing Achievement Tests. P-H.
   Determining Accountability for Classroom
      Instruction. Macmillan.
   Improving Marking & Reporting in Classroom
      Instruction. Macmillan.
   Individualizing Classroom Instruction.
      Macmillan.
   Measurement & Evaluation in Teaching.
      Macmillan.
   Preparing Criterion-Referenced Tests for
      Classroom Instruction. Macmillan.
Groom, A. J. see Groom, A. J. R.
Groom, A. J. R.
   xGroom, A. J.
   ed. Functionalism: Theory & Practice in
      International Relations. Crane-Russak Co.
Groom, Bernard, 1892-
   xGroom, Bernard.
   On the Diction of Tennyson, Browning &
      Arnold. Folcroft.
   On the Diction of Tennyson, Browning &
      Arnold. Shoe String.
Groome, Francis H. see Groome, Francis Hindes.
Groome, Francis Hindes.
   xGroome, Francis H.
   Edward Fitzgerald: an Aftermath: With
      Miscellanies in Verse & Prose. Arno.
   Gypsy Folk-Tales. Arno.
Groome, Harry. see Groome, Harry Connelly.
Groome, Harry Connelly, 1908-
   xGroome, Harry.
   Opportunities in Advertising Careers. Natl
      Textbk.
Groos, Karl, 1861-1946
   xGroos, Karl.
   Play of Animals. Arno.
   Play of Man. Arno.
Groot, Jan J. see Groot, Jan Jakob Maria de.

Groot, Jan Jakob Maria de, 1854-1921
   xGroot, Jan J.
   The Religion of the Chinese. Hyperion Conn.
Groot, Roy A. De. see De Groot, Roy A.
Groot, Roy De. see De Groot, Roy A.
Groover, Mikell, 1939-
   xGroover, Mikell P.
   Automation, Production Systems &
      Computer-Aided Manufacturing. P-H.
Groover, Mikell P. see Groover, Mikell.
Gropman, Donald.
   xGropman, Donald C.
   Say It Ain't So, Joe!: The Story of Shoeless
      Joe Jackson. Little.
Gropman, Donald C. see Gropman, Donald.
Gropper, George L. see Gropper, George Leonard.
Gropper, George Leonard.
   xGropper, George L.
   Diagnosis & Revision in the Development of
      Instructional Materials. Educ Tech Pubns.
   Instructional Strategies. Educ Tech Pubns.
Gropper, Rena C.
   xGropper, Rena C.
   Gypsies in the City: Culture Patterns &
      Survival. Darwin Pr.
Gros, Vonnie, 1935-
   xGros, Vonnie.
   Inside Field Hockey for Women. Contemp Bks.
Grosch, Audrey N., 1934-
   xGrosch, Audrey N.
   Minicomputers in Libraries. Knowledge Indus.
Grose, Francis, 1731?-1791
   xGrose, Francis.
   A Classical Dictionary of the Vulgar Tongue.
      Arno.
Grose, M. W.
   xGrose, M. W.
   Old English Literature. Rowman.
Groseclose, Elgin. see Groseclose, Elgin Earl.
Groseclose, Elgin Earl, 1899-
   xGroseclose, Elgin.
   The Kiowa. Cook.
Grosjean, Daniel.
   xGrosjean, Daniel.
   ed. Nitrogenous Air Pollutants: Chemical &
      Biological Implications. Ann Arbor Science.
Groslier, Bernard P. see Groslier, Bernard Philippe.
Groslier, Bernard Philippe.
   xGroslier, Bernard P.
   Indochina. Hippocrene Bks.
Grosman, Brian A.
   xGrosman, Brian A.
   Prosecutor: An Inquiry into the Exercise of
      Discretion. U of Toronto Pr.
Gross. see Gross, Ruth Belov.
Gross, Alan.
   xGross, Alan.
   Sometimes I Worry. Childrens.
   What If the Teacher Calls on Me?. Childrens.
Gross, Alan J.
   xGross, Alan J.
   Survival Distributions: Reliability Applications
      in the Biomedical Sciences. Wiley.
Gross, Anthony, 1905-
   xGross, Anthony.
   Etching, Engraving & Intaglio Printing. Oxford
      U Pr.
Gross, Arthur W. see Gross, Arthur William.
Gross, Arthur William, 1896-
   xGross, Arthur W.
   Concordia Bible Story Book. Concordia.
Gross, Barry R., 1936-
   xGross, Barry R.
   Discrimination in Reverse: Is Turn-About Fair
      Play?. NYU Pr.
   ed. Reverse Discrimination. Prometheus Bks.
Gross, Beatrice.
   xGross, Beatrice.

   ed. Radical School Reform. S&S.
   Teaching Under Pressure. Goodyear.
Gross, Bertram M. see Gross, Bertram Myron.
Gross, Bertram Myron, 1912-
   xGross, Bertram M.
   The Legislative Struggle: A Study in Social
      Combat. Greenwood.
   Organizations & Their Managing. Free Pr.
Gross, Charles W.
   xGross, Charles W.
   Business Forecasting. HM.
Gross, David C., 1923-
   xGross, David C.
   ed. Love Poems from the Hebrew. Doubleday.
   Pride of Our People: The Stories of One
      Hundred Outstanding Jewish Men & Women.
      Doubleday.
Gross, Donald.
   xGross, Donald.
   Fundamentals of Queueing Theory. Wiley.
Gross, E. L. see Gross, Eugene L.
Gross, Eugene L.
   xGross, E. L.
   Small Business Works!: How to Compete &
      Win in the Free Enterprise System. Am
      Mgmt.
Gross, Eugenie. see Gross, Eugenie Harris.
Gross, Eugenie Harris.
   xGross, Eugenie.
   The Soviet Union: A Guide for Travelers.
      Har-Row.
Gross, Feliks, 1906-
   xGross, Feliks.
   Ethnics in a Borderland: An Inquiry into the
      Nature of Ethnicity & Reduction of Ethnic
      Tensions in a One-Time Genocide Area.
      Greenwood.
   The Revolutionary Party: Essays in the
      Sociology of Politics. Greenwood.
   Seizure of Political Power in a Century of
      Revolutions. Greenwood.
   World Politics & Tension Areas. NYU Pr.
Gross, Gerald.
   xGross, Gerald.
   ed. Responsibility of the Press. S&S.
Gross, Grant M. see Gross, Meredith Grant.
Gross, Harvey. see Gross, Harvey Seymour.
Gross, Harvey Seymour, 1922-
   xGross, Harvey.
   Sound & Form in Modern Poetry: A Study of
      Prosody from Thomas Hardy to Robert
      Lowell. U of Mich Pr.
   Sound & Form in Modern Poetry: A Study of
      Prosody from Thomas Hardy to Robert
      Lowell. U of Mich Pr.
Gross, Herbert, 1936-
   xGross, Herbert.
   Quadratic Forms in Infinite Dimensional
      Vector Spaces. Birkhauser.
Gross, Hyman.
   xGross, Hyman.
   A Theory of Criminal Justice. Oxford U Pr.
Gross, Irma Hannah.
   xGross, Irman H.
   Management for Modern Families. P-H.
Gross, Irman H. see Gross, Irma Hannah.
Gross, J. see Gross, Jerome S.
Gross, Jan T. see Gross, Jan Tomasz.
Gross, Jan Tomasz.
   xGross, Jan T.
   Polish Society Under German Occupation: The
      Generalgouvernement 1939-1944, (a Foreign
      Word: the Strange Spelling). Princeton U Pr.
Gross, Jerome S.
   xGross, J.
   Encyclopedia of Real Estate Forms. P-H.
   xGross, Jerome S.

Concise Desk Guide to Real Estate Practice &
Procedure. P-H.

Gross, Joel.
xGross, Joel.
The Books of Rachel. NAL.
The Books of Rachel. Seaview Bks.

Gross, Jonathan L.
xGross, Jonathan L.
Fundamental Programming Concepts.
Har-Row.

Gross, Judith.
xGross, Judith.
Needlepoint Designs for Chair Covers. Van
Nos Reinhold.

Gross, L. see Gross, Ludwik.

Gross, Leo, 1903-
xGross, Leo.
The Future of the International Court of
Justice. Oceana.

Gross, Linda.
xGross, Linda.
Enterostomal Therapy: Developing Institutional
& Community Programs. Nursing Res.

Gross, Ludwik.
xGross, L.
Oncogenic Viruses. Pergamon.

Gross, Lynne S.
xGross, Lynne S.
See-Hear: Introduction to Broadcasting. Wm C
Brown.

Gross, M. see Gross, Maurice.
Gross, M. Grant. see Gross, Meredith Grant.

Gross, Malvern J.
xGross, Malvern J.
Financial & Accounting Guide for Nonprofit
Organizations. Ronald Pr.
Principles of Accounting & Financial Reporting
for Nonprofit Organizations. Wiley.

Gross, Martin. see Gross, Martin Arnold.
Gross, Martin A. see Gross, Martin Arnold.

Gross, Martin Arnold, 1934-
xGross, Martin.
The Nostalgia Quiz Book. NAL.
xGross, Martin A.
Nostalgia Quiz Book. NAL.

Gross, Mary P. see Gross, Mary Preston.

Gross, Mary Preston.
xGross, Mary P.
The Officers Family Social Guide. Beau Lac.

Gross, Maurice.
xGross, M.
Introduction to Formal Grammars.
Springer-Verlag.
xGross, Maurice.
Mathematical Models in Linguistics. P-H.

Gross, Meredith Grant, 1933-
xGross, Grant M.
Ocean World. Merrill.
xGross, M. Grant.
Oceanography. Merrill.
Oceanography: A View of the Earth. P-H.

Gross, Michael L.
xGross, Michael L.
ed. High Performance Mass Spectrometry:
Chemical Applications. Am Chemical.

Gross, Miriam.
xGross, Miriam.
ed. The World of George Orwell. S&S.

Gross, Neal. see Gross, Neal Crasilneck.

Gross, Neal Crasilneck.
xGross, Neal.
Implementing Organizational Innovations: A
Sociological Analysis of Planned Change in
Schools. Basic.

Gross, Paul. see Gross, Paul F.

Gross, Paul F.
xGross, Paul.
Systems Analysis & Design for Management.
Tech Pub.

Gross, R. W. see Gross, Rolf W. F.

Gross, Raphael H. see Gross, Raphael Henry.

Gross, Raphael Henry.
xGross, Raphael H.
ed. Century of the Catholic Essay. Arno.

Gross, Richard E.
xGross, Richard E.
ed. British Secondary Education: Overview &
Appraisal. Oxford U Pr.

Gross, Robert E. see Gross, Robert Edward.

Gross, Robert Edward, 1905-
xGross, Robert E.
Atlas of Children's Surgery. Saunders.

Gross, Rolf W. F.
xGross, R. W.
Handbook of Chemical Lasers. Wiley.

Gross, Ronald.
xGross, Ronald.
Diversity in Higher Education: Reform in the
Colleges. Phi Delta Kappa.
High School. S&S.
High School. S&S.
The Lifelong Learner. S&S.
ed. Open Poetry: Four Anthologies of
Expanded Poems. S&S.
Revolution in the Schools. HarBraceJ.

Gross, Ruth B. see Gross, Ruth Belov.

Gross, Ruth Belov.
xGross.
If You Were a Ballet Dancer. Schol Bk Serv.
xGross, Ruth B.
Alligators & Other Crocodilians. Schol Bk
Serv.
A Book About Your Skeleton. Hastings.
Dangerous Adventure!: Lindbergh's Famous
Flight. Walker & Co.
If You Were a Ballet Dancer. Dial.
Money, Money, Money. Schol Bk Serv.

Gross, S. see Gross, Sam.

Gross, Sam.
xGross, S.
I Am Blind & My Dog Is Dead. Avon.
I Am Blind & My Dog Is Dead. Dodd.

Gross, Seymour L. see Gross, Seymour Lee.

Gross, Seymour Lee.
xGross, Seymour L.
ed. Images of the Negro in American
Literature. U of Chicago Pr.

Gross, Stephen H.
xGross, Stephen H.
Legal & Business Aspects of the Magazine
Industry, 1979. PLI.

Gross, Theodore. see Gross, Theodore L.

Gross, Theodore L.
xGross, Theodore.
Albion W. Tourgee. Coll & U Pr.
xGross, Theodore L.
Albion W. Tourgee. Irvington.
America in Literature. Wiley.
Literature of American Jews. Free Pr..
Thomas Nelson Page. Coll & U Pr.

Gross, W. F. see Gross, William F.

Gross, William F.
xGross, W. F.
Applications Manual for Paint & Protective
Coatings: A Guide to Types of Coatings,
Methods of Surface Preparation & Hand
Application Techniques. McGraw.

Grossack, Irvin M. see Grossack, Irvin Millman.

Grossack, Irvin Millman, 1927-
xGrossack, Irvin M.
The International Economy & the National
Interest. Ind U Pr.

Grossack, Martin, Ph. D.
xGrossack, Martin.
Love, Sex & Self-Fulfillment: Keys to
Successful Living. NAL.

Grossbach, Robert, 1941-
xGrossbach, Robert.

Never Say Die: An Autonecrographical Novel.
Har-Row.

Grosser, Alfred, 1925-
xGrosser, Alfred.
French Foreign Policy Under de Gaulle.
Greenwood.

Grosser, Charles. see Grosser, Charles F.

Grosser, Charles F.
xGrosser, Charles.
ed. Nonprofessionals in the Human Services.
Jossey-Bass.

Grosser, Morton.
xGrosser, Morton.
Diesel, the Man & the Engine. Atheneum.
The Discovery of Neptune. Dover.

Grossinger, Richard, 1944-
xGrossinger, Richard.
The Continents. Black Sparrow.
Early Field Notes from the All-American
Revival Church. North Atlantic.
The Long Body of the Dream. North Atlantic.
Martian Homecoming at the All-American
Revival Church. North Atlantic.
Solar Journal Oecological Sections. Black
Sparrow.

Grossinger, Richard. see Grossinger, Richards.

Grossinger, Richards, 1944-
xGrossinger, Richard.
ed. Alchemy: Pre-Egyptian Legacy, Millennial
Promise. North Atlantic.

Grossman, A. Richard, 1933-
xGrossman, A. Richard.
Augmentation Mammoplasty. C C Thomas.

Grossman, Alvin.
xGrossman, Alvin.
Breeding Better Cocker Spaniels. Denlingers.

Grossman, Edith, 1936-
xGrossman, Edith.
The Antipoetry of Nicanor Parra. NYU Pr.

Grossman, Gregory.
xGrossman, Gregory.
Economic Systems. P-H.
ed. Money & Plan: Financial Aspects of East
European Economic Reforms. U of Cal Pr.

Grossman, Harold J.
xGrossman, Harold J.
Grossman's Guide to Wines, Beers, & Spirits.
Scribner.

Grossman, Herbert J.
xGrossman, Herbert J.
ed. Manual on Terminology & Classification in
Mental Retardation. Am Assn Mental.

Grossman, Howard R., 1934-
xGrossman, Howard R.
For Health's Sake: A Critical Analysis of
Medical Care in the United States. Pacific
Bks.

Grossman, I. see Grossman, Israel.

Grossman, Israel.
xGrossman, I.
Groups & Their Graphs. Math Assn.

Grossman, Jack. see Grossman, Jack H.

Grossman, Jack H., 1934-
xGrossman, Jack.
The Business of Living. Stein & Day.

Grossman, Joel B.
xGrossman, Joel B.
Constitutional Law & Judicial Policy-Making.
Wiley.
Lawyers & Judges: The ABA & the Politics of
Judicial Selection. Krieger.
Supplemental Cases for Constitutional Law &
Judicial Policy Making: 1975 Ed.. Wiley.

Grossman, Lawrence, 1945-
xGrossman, Lawrence.
The Democratic Party & the Negro: Northern
& National Politics, 1868-92. U of Ill Pr.

Grossman, Lee.
xGrossman, Lee.

The Change Agent. Am Mgmt.
Fat Paper: Diets for Trimming Paperwork.
McGraw.
Grossman, Leonid P. *see* Grossman, Leonid Petrovich.
Grossman, Leonid Petrovich, 1888-1965
xGrossman, Leonid P.
Confession of a Jew. Arno.
Grossman, Louis I. *see* Grossman, Louis Irwin.
Grossman, Louis Irwin.
xGrossman, Louis I.
Endodontic Practice. Lea & Febiger.
Grossman, Mary L. *see* Grossman, Mary Louise.
Grossman, Mary Louise.
xGrossman, Mary L.
Our Vanishing Wilderness. G&D.
Grossman, Michael.
xGrossman, Michael.
Non-Newtonian Calculus. Mathco.
Grossman, Mort, 1933-
xGrossman, Mort.
The Summer Ends Too Soon. Westminster.
Grossman, Richard. *see* Grossman, Richard Lee.
Grossman, Richard Lee.
xGrossman, Richard.
Energy, Jobs & the Economy. Carrier Pigeon.
Grossman, S. P. *see* Grossman, Sebastian Peter.
Grossman, Sebastian Peter.
xGrossman, S. P.
Essentials of Physiological Psychology. Wiley.
Grossman, Stanley. *see* Grossman, Stanley I.
Grossman, Stanley I.
xGrossman, Stanley.
Calculus. Acad Pr.
Elementary Linear Algebra. Wadsworth Pub.
Grossman, Vigdor.
xGrossman, Vigdor.
Employing Handicapped Persons: Meeting
EEO Obligations. BNA.
Grossman, William.
xGrossman, William.
ed. Cardiac Catheterization & Angiography.
Lea & Febiger.
Grossman, William L. *see* Grossman, William Leonard.
Grossman, William Leonard, 1906-
xGrossman, William L.
ed. Modern Brazilian Short Stories. U of Cal
Pr.
Grossmith, George.
xGrossmith, George.
Diary of a Nobody. Dutton.
Grossnickle, F. E. *see* Grossnickle, Foster Earl.
Grossnickle, Foster E. *see* Grossnickle, Foster Earl.
Grossnickle, Foster Earl, 1896-
xGrossnickle, F. E.
Discovering Meanings in Elementary School
Mathematics. HR&W.
xGrossnickle, Foster E.
Capital Outlay in Relation to a State's
Minimum Educational Program. AMS Pr.
Grossvogel, David I., 1925-
xGrossvogel, David I.
Four Playwrights & a Postscript: Brecht,
Ionesco, Beckett, Genet. Greenwood.
Limits of the Novel: Evolutions of a Form
from Chaucer to Robbe-Grillet. Cornell U Pr.
Mystery & Its Fictions: From Oedipus to
Agatha Christie. Johns Hopkins.
Grosswald, E. *see* Grosswald, Emil.
Grosswald, Emil.
xGrosswald, E.
Bessel Polynomials. Springer-Verlag.
Grosvenor, Charles.
xGrosvenor, Charles.
The Portraits of T.E. Lawrence. Otterden.
Grosvenor, Theodore P.
xGrosvenor, Theodore P.
Contemporary Contact Lens Practice. Prof
Press.
Grosvenor, William M. *see* Grosvenor, William Mason.

Grosvenor, William Mason, 1835-1900
xGrosvenor, William M.
American Securities: The Causes Influencing
Investment & Speculation & the Fluctuations
in Values, 1872 to 1885. Greenwood.
Grosz, George, 1893-1959
xGrosz, George.
Ecce Homo. Dover.
Grote, Caroline, 1863-
xGrote, Caroline.
Housing & Living Conditions of Women
Students in the Western Illinois State
Teachers College at Macomb - School Years
1926-1927, 1927-1928, & 1928-1929. AMS
Pr.
Grote, George, 1794-1871
xGrote, George.
Aristotle. Arno.
Grotewold, Andreas, 1927-
xGrotewold, Andreas.
The Regional Theory of World Trade. Ptolemy
Pr.
Groth, A. N. *see* Groth, A. Nicholas.
Groth, A. Nicholas.
xGroth, A. N.
Men Who Rape: The Psychology of the
Offender. Plenum Pub.
Groth, Alexander. *see* Groth, Alexander J.
Groth, Alexander J.
xGroth, Alexander.
Contemporary Politics: Europe. Winthrop.
Grothendieck, A. *see* Grothendieck, Alexandre.
Grothendieck, Alexander. *see* Grothendieck, Alexandre.
Grothendieck, Alexandre.
xGrothendieck, A.
Tame Fundamental Group of a Formal
Neighbourhood of a Divisor with Normal
Crossing on a Scheme. Springer-Verlag.
xGrothendieck, Alexander.
Produits Tensoriels Topologiques et Espaces
Nucleaires. Am Math.
Grotius, Hugo.
xGrotius, Hugo.
Prolegomena to the Law of War & Peace.
Bobbs.
Grotjahn, Martin.
xGrotjahn, Martin.
The Art & Technique of Analytic Group
Therapy. Aronson.
Grotpeter, John J.
xGrotpeter, John J.
Historical Dictionary of Swaziland. Scarecrow.
Historical Dictionary of Zambia. Scarecrow.
Grotz, George.
xGrotz, George.
Antique Restorer's Handbook: A Dictionary of
the Crafts & Materials Used in Restoring
Antiques & Works of Art. Doubleday.
Grounds, Roger.
xGrounds, Roger.
ed. The Complete Handbook of Pruning.
Macmillan.
The Natural Garden. Stein & Day.
Group for the Advancement of Psychiatry.
xGroup for the Advancement of Psychiatry.

Application of Psychiatric Insights to
Cross-Cultural Communication. Adv
Psychiatry.
Clinical Psychiatry: Problems of Treatment,
Research & Prevention. Aronson.
Death & Dying: Attitudes of Patient & Doctor.
Adv Psychiatry.
Diagnosis & Treatment in Child Psychiatry.
Aronson.
Factors Used to Increase the Susceptibility of
Individuals to Forceful Indoctrination;
Observations & Experiments. Adv Psychiatry.
Illustrative Strategies for Research on
Psychopathology in Mental Health. Adv
Psychiatry.
Joys & Sorrows of Parenthood. Scribner.
Medical Uses of Hypnosis. Adv Psychiatry.
Methods of Forceful Indoctrination;
Observations & Interviews. Adv Psychiatry.
Normal Adolescence: Its Dynamics & Impact.
Scribner.
Pavlovian Conditioning & American
Psychiatry. Adv Psychiatry.
Pharmacotherapy & Psychotherapy: Paradoxes,
Problems & Progress. Brunner-Mazel.
Psychological & Medical Aspects of the Use of
Nuclear Energy. Adv Psychiatry.
Psychopathological Disorders in Childhood:
Theoretical Considerations & a Proposed
Classification. Aronson.
Right to Abortion: A Psychiatric View.
Scribner.
The Right to Die: Decision & Decision
Makers. Aronson.
Some Considerations of Early Attempts in
Cooperation Between Religion & Psychiatry.
Adv Psychiatry.
Treatment of Families in Conflict: The Clinical
Study of Family Process. Aronson.
The VIP with Psychiatric Impairment. Scribner.
**Group for the Advancement of Psychiatry. Committee on
Psychiatry and Social Work.**
xGAP Committee on Psychiatry & Social Work.
The Welfare System & Mental Health. Adv
Psychiatry.
**Group for the Advancement of Psychiatry. Committee on
Adolescence.**
xGAP Committee on Adolescence.
Normal Adolescence: Its Dynamics & Impact.
Adv Psychiatry.
Power & Authority in Adolescence: The
Origins & Resolutions of Intergenerational
Conflict. Adv Psychiatry.
**Group for the Advancement of Psychiatry. Committee on
Aging.**
xGAP Committee on Aging.
Aged & Community Mental Health: A Guide
to Program Development. Adv Psychiatry.
The Right to Die: Decision & Decision
Makers. Adv Psychiatry.
Toward a Public Policy on Mental Health Care
of the Elderly. Adv Psychiatry.
**Group for the Advancement of Psychiatry. Committee on
Child Psychiatry.**
xGAP Committee on Child Psychiatry.
The Diagnostic Process in Child Psychiatry.
Adv Psychiatry.
From Diagnosis to Treatment: An Approach to
Treatment Planning for the Emotionally
Disturbed Child. Adv Psychiatry.
Psychopathological Disorders in Childhood:
Theoretical Considerations & a Proposed
Classification. Adv Psychiatry.
**Group for the Advancement of Psychiatry. Committee of
Governmental Agencies.**
xGAP Committee on Governmental Agencies.

Effect of the Method of Payment on Mental
Health Care Practice. Adv Psychiatry.
Preventive Psychiatry in the Armed Forces:
With Some Implications for Civilian Use.
Adv Psychiatry.
VIP with Psychiatric Impairment. Adv
Psychiatry.

**Group for the Advancement of Psychiatry. Committee on
International Relations.**
xGAP Committee on International Relations.
Psychiatrist & Public Issues. Adv Psychiatry.
Self-Involvement in the Middle East Conflict.
Adv Psychiatry.

**Group for the Advancement of Psychiatry. Committee on
Medical Education.**
xGAP Committee on Med. Education.
Education for Community Psychiatry. Adv
Psychiatry.
xGAP Committee on Medical Education.
Assessment of Sexual Function: A Guide to
Interviewing. Adv Psychiatry.
The Preclinical Teaching of Psychiatry. Adv
Psychiatry.

**Group for the Advancement of Psychiatry. Committee on
Mental Health Services.**
xGAP Committee on Mental Health Services.
Drug Misuse: a Psychiatric View of a Modern
Dilemma. Adv Psychiatry.
Nonpsychotic Alcoholic Patient & the Mental
Hospital. Adv Psychiatry.

**Group for the Advancement of Psychiatry. Committee on
Mental Retardation.**
xGAP Committee on Mental Retardation.
Basic Considerations in Mental Retardation: A
Preliminary Report. Adv Psychiatry.
Mental Retardation: A Family Crisis; the
Therapeutic Role of the Physician. Adv
Psychiatry.
Mild Mental Retardation: A Growing
Challenge to the Physician. Adv Psychiatry.

**Group for the Advancement of Psychiatry. Committee on
Preventive Psychiatry.**
xGAP Committee on Preventive Psychiatry.
Dimensions of Community Psychiatry. Adv
Psychiatry.
Humane Reproduction. Adv Psychiatry.
Problems of Estimating Changes in Frequency
of Mental Disorders. Adv Psychiatry.

**Group for the Advancement of Psychiatry. Committee on
Psychiatry and Religion.**
xGAP Committee on Psychiatry & Religion.
Mysticism: Spiritual Quest or Psychic Disorder.
Adv Psychiatry.
The Psychic Function of Religion in Mental
Illness & Health. Adv Psychiatry.

**Group for the Advancement of Psychiatry. Committee on
Psychiatry in Industry.**
xGAP Committee on Psychiatry in Industry.
What Price Compensation?. Adv Psychiatry.

**Group for the Advancement of Psychiatry. Committee on
Public Education.**
xGAP Committee on Public Education.
The Joys & Sorrows of Parenthood. Adv
Psychiatry.
Medical Practice & Psychiatry: The Impact of
Changing Demands. Adv Psychiatry.

**Group for the Advancement of Psychiatry. Committee on
Research.**
xGAP Committee on Research.
Pharmacotherapy & Psychotherapy: Paradoxes,
Problems & Progress. Adv Psychiatry.
Psychiatric Research & the Assessment of
Change. Adv Psychiatry.

**Group for the Advancement of Psychiatry. Committee on
Social Issues.**
xGAP Committee on Social Issues.

Psychiatric Aspects of School Desegregation.
Adv Psychiatry.
Psychiatric Aspects of the Prevention of
Nuclear War. Adv Psychiatry.

**Group for the Advancement of Psychiatry. Committee on
the College Student.**
xGAP Committee on the College Student.
A College Experience: The Focus for
Psychiatric Research. Adv Psychiatry.
Educated Woman: Prospects & Problems. Adv
Psychiatry.
Sex & the College Student. Adv Psychiatry.

**Group for the Advancement of Psychiatry. Committee on
the Family.**
xGAP Committee on Family.
Case History Method in the Study of Family
Process. Adv Psychiatry.
Field of Family Therapy. Adv Psychiatry.

**Group for the Advancement of Psychiatry. Committee on
the Family.**
xGAP Committee on the Family.
Integration & Conflict in Family Behavior. Adv
Psychiatry.

**Group for the Advancement of Psychiatry. Committee on
Therapeutic Care.**
xGAP Committee on Therapeutic Care.
Community Worker: A Response to Human
Need. Adv Psychiatry.
Crisis in Psychiatric Hospitalization. Adv
Psychiatry.
Toward Therapeutic Care: A Guide for Those
Who Work with the Mentally Ill. Adv
Psychiatry.

**Group for the Advancement of Psychiatry. Committee on
Therapy.**
xGAP Committee on Therapy.
Problems of Psychiatric Leadership. Adv
Psychiatry.
Psychotherapy & Its Financial Feasibility
Within the National Health Care System.
Adv Psychiatry.
Psychotherapy & the Dual Research Tradition.
Adv. Psychiatry.

Group of European Nutritionists.
xGroup of European Nutritionists, 10th Meeting,
Saltsjoebaden, 1971.
Complete Intravenous Nutrition. S Karger.
xGroup of European Nutritionists, 12th
Symposium, Cambridge, July 1973.
Gut & Nutrition: Proceedings. S Karger.
xSymposium of the Group of European
Nutritionists, 9th, Chianciano, 1970.
Assessment of Nutritional Status & Food
Consumption Surveys: Proceedings. S Karger.
Clinical Nutrition. S Karger.
Nutrition & Nervous System: Proceedings. S
Karger.
Nutrition & Technology of Foods for Growing
Humans: Proceedings. S Karger.
Group of European Nutritionists, 10th Meeting,
Saltsjoebaden, 1971. see Group of European
Nutritionists.
Group of European Nutritionists, 12th Symposium,
Cambridge, July 1973. see Group of European
Nutritionists.
Grousset, P. see Grousset, Paschal.
Grousset, Paschal, 1844-1909
xGrousset, P.
The Conquest of the Moon: A Story of the
Bayouda. Arno.
Grousset, Rene, 1885-1952
xGrousset, Rene.
In the Footsteps of the Buddha. Arno.
In the Footsteps of the Buddha. Chinese
Materials.
Grout, Donald J. see Grout, Donald Jay.
Grout, Donald Jay.
xGrout, Donald J.

History of Western Music. Norton.
Grout, Jack.
xGrout, Jack.
Let Me Teach You Golf As I Taught Jack
Nicklaus. Atheneum.
Grout, Phil, 1945-
xGrout, Phil.
illus. A Spell in Plains. Stemmer Hse.
Grove, A. T. see Grove, Alfred Thomas.
Grove, Alfred Thomas.
xGrove, A. T.
Africa. Oxford U Pr.
Rural Africa. Cambridge U Pr.
Grove, David C.
xGrove, David C.
The Olmec Paintings of Oxtotitlan Cave,
Guerrero, Mexico. Dumbarton Oaks.
Grove, Edward A.
xGrove, Edward A.
Introduction to Complex Variables. HM.
Grove, Fred.
xGrove, Fred.
The Buffalo Runners. Ace Bks.
Bush Track. Doubleday.
The Great Horse Race. Doubleday.
Grove, Frederick P. see Grove, Frederick Philip.
Grove, Frederick Philip, 1879-1948
xGrove, Frederick P.
The Letters of Frederick Philip Grove. U of
Toronto Pr.
Grove, Nancy.
xGrove, Nancy.
The Sculpture of Isamu Noguchi, 1924-1979: A
Catalogue. Garland Pub.
Grove, Pearce S., 1930-
xGrove, Pearce S.
ed. Nonprint Media in Academic Libraries.
ALA.
Grove, Richard.
xGrove, Richard.
The Cambridgeshire Coprolite Mining Rush.
Oleander Pr.
Grove, Theodore G.
xGrove, Theodore S.
Experiences in Interpersonal Communication.
P-H.
Grove, Theodore S. see Grove, Theodore G.
Grover, David H. see Grover, David Hubert.
Grover, David Hubert.
xGrover, David H.
Debaters & Dynamiters: The Story of the
Haywood Trial. Oreg St U Pr.
Grover, David S., 1939-
xGrover, David S.
The Piano: Its Story, from Zither to Grand.
Scribner.
Grover, Dorys C.
xGrover, Dorys C.
Vardis Fisher: The Novelist As Poet.
Revisionist Pr.
Grover, F. see Grover, Fred.
Grover, Fred.
xGrover, F.
Laboratory Organization & Management.
Butterworths.
Grover, Frederic J.
xGrover, Frederic J.
Drieu la Rochelle & the Fiction of Testimony.
U of Cal Pr.
Grover, Philip L.
xGrover, Philip L.
Chemical Carcinogens & DNA. CRC Pr.
Grover, Ray.
xGrover, Ray.
Art Glass Nouveau. C E Tuttle.
Carved & Decorated European Art Glass. C E
Tuttle.
Groves, Colin P.
xGroves, Colin P.

Horses, Asses & Zebras in the Wild. R Curtis
Bks.
Groves, Donald G.
xGroves, Donald G.
The Ocean World Encyclopedia. McGraw.
Groves, Ernest R. *see* Groves, Ernest Rutherford.
Groves, Ernest Rutherford.
xGroves, Ernest R.
American Marriage & Family Relationships.
Arno.
The American Woman: The Feminine Side of a
Masculine Civilization. Arno.
Groves, L. *see* Groves, Lilian.
Groves, Lilian, 1928-
xGroves, L.
ed. Physical Education for Special Needs.
Cambridge U Pr.
Groves, Philip M.
xGroves, Philip M.
An Introduction to Biological Psychology. Wm
C Brown.
Grow, Lynn M.
xGrow, Lynn M.
The Prose Style of Samuel Taylor Coleridge.
Humanities.
Grow, Michael.
xGrow, Michael.
Scholars' Guide to Washington, D.C., for Latin
American & Caribbean Studies. Smithsonian.
Grow, Thomas A., 1921-
xGrow, Thomas A.
Construction: A Guide for the Profession. P-H.
Groza, Mavis A. *see* Groza, Mavis Arthur.
Groza, Mavis Arthur.
xGroza, Mavis A.
Everywoman's Guide to Financial
Independence. Les Femmes Pub.
Groza, V. *see* Groza, Vivian Shaw.
Groza, Vivan S. *see* Groza, Vivian Shaw.
Groza, Vivian. *see* Groza, Vivian Shaw.
Groza, Vivian Shaw.
xGroza, V.
Modern Elementary Algebra for College
Students. HR&W.
xGroza, Vivan S.
Plane Trigonometry. HR&W.
xGroza, Vivian.
Precalculus Mathematics. Irvington.
Grozny, Yvonne.
xGrozny, Yvonne.
The Fables of Phonecius. Ann Arbor Bk.
Grubb, Davis, 1919-
xGrubb, Davis.
The Night of the Hunter. Penguin.
Twelve Tales of Suspense & the Supernatural.
Fawcett.
Grubb, Norman P. *see* Grubb, Norman Percy.
Grubb, Norman Percy, 1895-
xGrubb, Norman P.
Deep Things of God. Chr Lit.
Grubb, R. *see* Grubb, Rune.
Grubb, Reba D.
xGrubb, Reba D.
Designing Hospital Training Programs. C C
Thomas.
Operating Room Guidelines: An Illustrated
Manual. Mosby.
Planning Ambulatory Surgery Facilities.
Mosby.
Grubb, Rune.
xGrubb, R.
Genetic Markers of Human Immunoglobulins.
Springer-Verlag.
Human Anti-Human Gammaglobulins: Their
Specificity & Function. Pergamon.
Grubbs, Donald H., 1936-
xGrubbs, Donald H.

Cry from the Cotton: The Southern Tenant
Farmers' Union & the New Deal. U of NC
Pr.
Grubbs, H. A. *see* Grubbs, Henry Alexander.
Grubbs, Henry A. *see* Grubbs, Henry Alexander.
Grubbs, Henry Alexander.
xGrubbs, H. A.
Introduction a la Poesie Francaise. Wiley.
xGrubbs, Henry A.
Paul Valery. Irvington.
Grubbs, John W., 1927-
xGrubbs, John W.
ed. Current Thought in Musicology. U of Tex
Pr.
Grubbs, Robert. *see* Grubbs, Robert Lowell.
Grubbs, Robert L. *see* Grubbs, Robert Lowell.
Grubbs, Robert Lowell.
xGrubbs, Robert.
Gregg Shorthand for Colleges, Speed Building.
McGraw.
xGrubbs, Robert L.
Gregg Shorthand for Colleges, Speed Building.
McGraw.
Grube, Frank.
xGrube, Frank.
ed. The Big Book of Sailing: The Sailors, the
Ships, & the Sea. Barron.
Grube, Max, 1854-1934
xGrube, Max.
Story of Meininger. U of Miami Pr.
Grubel, Herbert G.
xGrubel, Herbert G.
Forward Exchange, Speculation, & the
International Flow of Capital. Stanford U Pr.
ed. World Monetary Reform: Plans & Issues.
Stanford U Pr.
Gruber, Alan R.
xGruber, Alan R.
Children in Foster Care: Destitute,
Neglected Betrayed. Human Sci Pr.
Gruber, C. *see* Gruber, Christian.
Gruber, Christian.
xGruber, C.
Group Analysis of Classical Lattice Systems.
Springer-Verlag.
Gruber, Frederick C. *see* Gruber, Frederick Charles.
Gruber, Frederick Charles, 1903-
xGruber, Frederick C.
ed. Education & the State. Greenwood.
Gruber, Gary R.
xGruber, Gary R.
Preparation for the Scholastic Aptitude Test
(SAT). Contemp Bks.
Gruber, Helmut, 1928-
xGruber, Helmut.
The Temptation of Adam. Everest Hse.
Gruber, Ira D.
xGruber, Ira D.
The Howe Brothers & the American
Revolution. Norton.
The Howe Brothers & the American
Revolution. U of NC Pr.
Gruber, Jacob W.
xGruber, Jacob W.
A Conscience in Conflict: The Life of St.
George Jackson Mivart. Greenwood.
Gruber, Josef, 1865-1925
xGruber, Josef.
ed. Czechoslovakia: A Survey of Economic &
Social Conditions. Arno.
Gruber, Kathleen M.
xGruber, Kathleen M.
The Fast Food Guide. Franklin Pr OH.
Gruber, Ruth, 1911-
xGruber, Ruth.
Raquela: A Woman of Israel. Coward.
Raquela: A Woman of Israel. NAL.
Gruber, Terry. *see* Gruber, Terry Deroy.
Gruber, Terry Deroy.
xGruber, Terry.

Working Cats. Lippincott.
Gruchy, Allan G. *see* Gruchy, Allan Garfield.
Gruchy, Allan Garfield, 1906-
xGruchy, Allan G.
Comparative Economic Systems: Competing
Ways to Stability, Growth & Welfare. HM.
Modern Economic Thought: The American
Contribution. Kelley.
Grudin, Louis, 1898-
xGrudin, Louis.
Tales & Poems. Horizon.
Grudin, Robert.
xGrudin, Robert.
Mighty Opposites: Shakespeare & Renaissance
Contrariety. U of Cal Pr.
Gruelle, John B.
xGruelle, Johnny.
More Raggedy Ann & Andy Stories. Bobbs.
ed. Raggedy Ann & Andy & Witchie Kissabye.
Bobbs.
Raggedy Ann & the Golden Ring. Dell.
Raggedy Ann & the Golden Ring. Bobbs.
Raggedy Ann & the Happy Meadow. Dell.
Raggedy Ann & the Happy Meadow. Bobbs.
Raggedy Ann & the Hobby Horse. Bobbs.
Raggedy Ann & the Wonderful Witch. Bobbs.
Raggedy Ann & the Wonderful Witch. Dell.
Raggedy Ann in the Deep, Deep Woods.
Bobbs.
Raggedy Ann in the Deep Deep Woods. Dell.
Gruelle, Johnny. *see* Gruelle, John B.
Gruen, Erich S.
xGruen, Erich S.
The Last Generation of the Roman Republic.
U of Cal Pr.
xGruen, Erich S.
Imperialism in the Roman Republic. Krieger.
Gruen, Erick S. *see* Gruen, Erich S.
Gruen, F. H. *see* Gruen, Fred Henry George.
Gruen, Fred Henry George.
xGruen, F. H.
ed. Surveys of Australian Economics. Allen
Unwin.
Gruen, John.
xGruen, John.
The Private World of Ballet. Penguin.
The Private World of Ballet. Viking Pr.
Gruenberg, K. W. *see* Gruenberg, Karl W.
Gruenberg, Karl W.
xGruenberg, K. W.
Linear Geometry. Springer-Verlag.
xGruenberg, Karl W.
Cohomological Topics in Group Theory.
Springer-Verlag.
Gruenberg, Sidonie (Matsner), 1881-
xGruenberg, Sidonie M.
Wonderful Story of How You Were Born.
Doubleday.
xGruenberg, Sidonie Matsner.
ed. Favorite Stories Old & New. Doubleday.
Gruenberg, Sidonie M. *see* Gruenberg, Sidonie (Matsner).
Gruenberg, Sidonie Matsner. *see* Gruenberg, Sidonie
(Matsner).
Gruenberger, F. J. *see* Gruenberger, Fred Joseph.
Gruenberger, Fred Joseph.
xGruenberger, F. J.
Problems for Computer Solution. Wiley.
Gruendemann, Barbara J.
xGruendemann, Barbara J.
The Surgical Patient: Behavioral Concepts for
the Operating Room Nurse. Mosby.
Gruerio, Anthony.
xGruerio, Anthony.
Painting with a Palette Knife. G&D.
Gruffydd, W. J. *see* Gruffydd, William John.
Gruffydd, William John, 1881-1954
xGruffydd, W. J.
Folklore & Myth in the Mabinogion. Folcroft.
Grugel, Lee E., 1940-
xGrugel, Lee E.

George Jacob Holyoake: A Study in the
Evolution of a Victorian Radical. Porcupine
Pr.
Gruhn, Isebill V.
xGruhn, Isebill V.
Regionalism Reconsidered: The Economic
Commission for Africa. Westview.
Gruhn, William T. see Gruhn, William Theodore.
Gruhn, William Theodore.
xGruhn, William T.
The Modern Junior High School. Wiley.
Gruman, Gerald J.
xGruman, Gerald J.
A History of Ideas About the Prolongation of
Life: The Evolution of Prolongevity
Hypotheses to 1800. Arno.
Grumbach, Doris.
xGrumbach, Doris.
Chamber Music. Dutton.
Chamber Music. Fawcett.
Grumbach, Jane.
xGrumbach, Jane.
Actors Guide to Scenes. Drama Bk.
More Actors Guide to Monologues. Drama Bk.
Grumbach, Melvin M.
xGrumbach, Melvin M.
ed. Control of the Onset of Puberty. Wiley.
Grummer, Arnold E., 1923-
xGrummer, Arnold E.
Paper by Kids. Dillon.
Grun, Paul.
xGrun, Paul.
Cytoplasmic Genetics and Evolution. Columbia
U Pr.
Grunbaum, Adolf.
xGrunbaum, Adolf.
Geometry & Chronometry in Philosophical
Perspective. U of Minn Pr.
Grunbaum, B. see Grunbaum, Branko.
Grunbaum, Branko.
xGrunbaum, B.
Arrangements & Spreads. Am Math.
Grundlehner, Philip, 1945-
xGrundlehner, Philip.
The Lyrical Bridge: Essays from Holderlin to
Benn. Fairleigh Dickinson.
Grundmann, E. see Grundmann, Ekkehard.
Grundmann, Ekkehard.
xGrundmann, E.
ed. Cancer Registry. Springer-Verlag.
Grundon, M. A. see Grundon, M. F.
Grundon, M. F.
xGrundon, M. A.
Organic Chemistry: An Introduction. Elsevier.
Grundt, Leonard, 1936-
xGrundt, Leonard.
Efficient Patterns for Adequate Library Service
in a Large City: A Survey of Boston. U of Ill
Lib Sci.
Grundy, Denis.
xGrundy, Denis.
Secular, Compulsory & Free: The Education
Act of 1872. Intl Schol Bk Serv.
Grundy, Joan.
xGrundy, Joan.
Hardy & the Sister Arts. B&N.
Grundy, Julia M. see Grundy, Julia Margaret Kunkle.
Grundy, Julia Margaret Kunkle, 1874-
xGrundy, Julia M.
Ten Days in the Light of 'Akka. Baha'i.
Grundy, Kenneth W.
xGrundy, Kenneth W.
Ideologies of Violence. Merrill.
Gruneberg, Michael M.
xGruneberg, Michael M.
ed. Aspects of Memory. Methuen Inc.
Grunelius, Elizabeth M.
xGrunelius, Elizabeth M.

Early Childhood Education & the Waldorf
School Plan. St George Bk Serv.
Gruner, Charles R.
xGruner, Charles R.
Speech Communication in Society. Allyn.
Understanding Laughter: The Workings of Wit
& Humor. Nelson-Hall.
Gruner, Mark.
xGruner, Mark.
Mark Gruner's Numbers of Life: An
Introduction to Numerology. Taplinger.
Grunfeld, Frederic V.
xGrunfeld, Frederic V.
Music. Newsweek.
Grunfeld, Joseph.
xGrunfeld, Joseph.
ed. Growth in a Finite World. Franklin Inst Pr.
Grunlan, Stephen A.
xGrunlan, Stephen A.
Cultural Anthropology: A Christian
Perspective. Zondervan.
Grunwald, Ernest.
xGrunwald, Ernest.
Megawatt Infrared Laser Chemistry. Wiley.
Grunwald, Joseph, 1920-
xGrunwald, Joseph.
Latin America & World Economy: A Changing
International Order. Sage.
Natural Resources in Latin American
Development. Johns Hopkins.
Grunwald, Kurt.
xGrunwald, Kurt.
Industrialization in the Middle East.
Greenwood.
Grunwald, Stefan.
xGrunwald, Stefan.
My Poetry, My Therapy. Donning Co.
Grupo Cubano de Investigaciones Economicas.
xCuban Economic Research Project, University of
Miami.
Labor Conditions in Communist Cuba. U of
Miami Pr.
Gruppe, Emil A., 1896-
xGruppe, Emile.
Gruppe on Painting: Direct Techniques in Oil.
Watson-Guptill.
Gruppe, Emile. see Gruppe, Emil A.
Gruppe, Henry.
xGruppe, Henry.
The Frigates. Time-Life.
Gruppe, Otto, 1851-1921
xGruppe, Otto.
Griechische Mythologie und
Religionsgeschichte. Arno.
Gruska, J. see Gruska, Jozef.
Gruska, Jozef.
xGruska, J.
ed. Mathematical Foundations of Computer
Science 1977: Proceedings, 6th Symposium,
Tatranska Lmnica, Sept. 5-9, 1977.
Springer-Verlag.
Grusky, Oscar.
xGrusky, Oscar.
ed. The Sociology of Organizations: Basic
Studies. Free Pr.
Gruson, Edward. see Gruson, Edward S.
Gruson, Edward S.
xGruson, Edward.
Words for Birds: A Lexicon of North
American Birds with Biographical Notes.
Times Bks.
Gruver, Bert. see Gruver, Elbert A.
Gruver, Elbert A.
xGruver, Bert.
The Stage Manager's Handbook. Drama Bk.
Gruver, Rebecca B. see Gruver, Rebecca Brooks.
Gruver, Rebecca Brooks.
xGruver, Rebecca B.

An American History. A-W.
An American History. A-W.
Gruver, Suzanne C. see Gruver, Suzanne Cary.
Gruver, Suzanne Cary.
xGruver, Suzanne C.
The Cape Cod Cook Book. Peter Smith.
The Cape Cod Cookbook. Dover.
Gruzanski, Charles V.
xGruzanski, Charles V.
Spike & Chain: Japanese Fighting Arts. C E
Tuttle.
Gruzinov, V. P. see Gruzinov, Vladimir Petrovich.
Gruzinov, Vladimir Petrovich.
xGruzinov, V. P.
The USSR's Management of Foreign Trade. M
E Sharpe.
Gryboski, Joyce.
xGryboski, Joyce.
Gastrointestinal Problems in the Infant.
Saunders.
Grylls, Glynn R. see Grylls, Rosalie Glynn.
Grylls, R. Glynn. see Grylls, Rosalie Glynn.
Grylls, Rosalie Glynn, 1905-
xGrylls, Glynn R.
Mary Shelley: A Biography. Folcroft.
xGrylls, R. Glynn.
Mary Shelley: A Biography. Haskell.
Grzegorczyk, A. see Grzegorczyk, Andrzej.
Grzegorczyk, Andrzej.
xGrzegorczyk, A.
An Outline of Mathematical Logic:
Fundamental Results & Notions Explained
with All Details. Kluwer Boston.
Grzesinski, Albert C. see Grzesinski, Albert Carl.
Grzesinski, Albert Carl, 1879-1947
xGrzesinski, Albert C.
Inside Germany. AMS Pr.
Grzybowski, Kazimierz.
xGrzybowski, Kazimierz.
ed. East-West Trade. Oceana.
Grzynkowicz, Wineva. see Grzynkowicz, Wineva
Montooth.
Grzynkowicz, Wineva M. see Grzynkowicz, Wineva
Montooth.
Grzynkowicz, Wineva Montooth.
xGrzynkowicz, Wineva.
Basic Education for Children with Learning
Disabilities. C C Thomas.
Meeting the Needs of Learning Disabled
Children in the Regular Class. C C Thomas.
xGrzynkowicz, Wineva M.
Teaching Inefficient Learners. C C Thomas.
Gschwend, N. see Gschwend, Norbert.
Gschwend, Norbert.
xGschwend, N.
Total Hip Prosthesis. Williams & Wilkins.
Guandolo, John.
xGuandolo, John.
Transportation Law. Wm C Brown.
Guannu, Joseph S. see Guannu, Joseph Saye.
Guannu, Joseph Saye.
xGuannu, Joseph S.
Compiled by The Inaugural Addresses of the
Presidents of Liberia: From Joseph Jenkins
Robert to William Richard Tolbert Jr., 1848
to 1976. Exposition.
Guard, David.
xGuard, David.
Deirdre: A Celtic Legend. Celestial Arts.
Guardians of the Poor. see Pennsylvania. Laws,
Statutes, Etc.
Guardini, Romano, 1885-
xGuardini, Romano.
Lord. Regnery-Gateway.
Guardino, Joseph R., 1939-
xGuardino, Joseph R.
Accounting, Legal & Tax Aspects of Corporate
Acquisitions. P-H.
Guardo, Carol, 1939-
xGuardo, Carol J.

The Adolescent As Individual: Issues & Insights. Har-Row.
Guardo, Carol J. *see* Guardo, Carol.
Guareschi, Giovanni, 1908-1968
　xGuareschi, Giovanni.
　　The Family Guareschi: Chronicles of the Past & Present. FS&G.
　　A Husband in Boarding School. FS&G.
　　My Home, Sweet Home. FS&G.
Guay, Terrie.
　xGuay, Terrie.
　　Avoid or Achieve Pregnancy Naturally. Emergence.
　　Creation of Life...Your Choice: Avoid or Achieve Pregnancy Naturally. Emergence.
Guazzo, Stefano, 1530-1593
　xGuazzo, Stefano.
　　Civile Conversation of M. Steeven Guazzo. AMS Pr.
Gubbins, John H. *see* Gubbins, John Harington.
Gubbins, John Harington, 1852-1929
　xGubbins, John H.
　　Progress of Japan, 1853-1871. AMS Pr.
Gubler, Brent H.
　xGubler, Brent H.
　　A Constitutional Analysis of the Criminal Jurisdiction & Procedural Guarantees of the American Indian. R & E Res Assoc.
Gubrium, Jaber F.
　xGubrium, Jaber F.
　　Living & Dying at Murray Manor. St Martin.
Gubser, Mary.
　xGubser, Mary.
　　Mary's Bread Basket & Soup Kettle. Morrow.
Gubser, Peter.
　xGubser, Peter.
　　Politics & Change in Al-Karak, Jordan: A Study of a Small Arab Town & Its District. Oxford U Pr.
Cudas, Fabian.
　xGudas, Fabian.
　　ed. Extrasensory Perception. Arno.
Gudde, Erwin G.
　xGudde, Erwin G.
　　California Gold Camps: A Geographical & Historical Dictionary of Camps, Towns, & Localities Where Gold Was Found & Mines, & of Wayside Stations & Trading Centers. U of Cal Pr.
Gudde, Erwin G. *see* Gudde, Erwin Gustav.
Gudde, Erwin Gustav, 1889-
　xGudde, Erwin G.
　　California Place Names: The Origin & Etymology of Current Geographical Names. U of Cal Pr.
Gudder, Stanley.
　xGudder, Stanley.
　　A Mathematical Journey. McGraw.
Gude, Mary L. *see* Gude, Mary Louise.
Gude, Mary Louise, 1939-
　xGude, Mary L.
　　Le Page Disgracie: The Text As Confession. Romance.
Gudehus, G.
　xGudehus, G.
　　Finite Elements in Geomechanics. Wiley.
Gudeman, Stephen.
　xGudeman, Stephen.
　　The Demise of a Rural Economy: From Subsistence to Capitalism in a Latin American Village. Routledge & Kegan.
Guder, Eileen. *see* Guder, Eileen L.
Guder, Eileen L.
　xGuder, Eileen.
　　Learn to Live with Style: Qualities of the Christian Life. Word Bks.
Guderian, Heinz, 1888-
　xGuderian, Heinz.

Panzer Leader. Ballantine.
　　Panzer Leader. Zenger Pub.
Guderian, R. *see* Guderian, Robert.
Guderian, Robert.
　xGuderian, R.
　　Air Pollution: Phytotoxicity of Acidic Gases & Its Significance in Air Pollution Control. Springer-Verlag.
Gudmundsson, J. *see* Gudmundsson, Jon.
Gudmundsson, Jon.
　xGudmundsson, J.
　　Jon Gudmundsson & His Natural History of Iceland. Kraus Repr.
Gudschinsky, Sarah C. *see* Gudschinsky, Sarah Caroline.
Gudschinsky, Sarah Caroline.
　xGudschinsky, Sarah C.
　　Literacy: The Growing Influence of Linguistics. Mouton.
Gudzii, Nikolai K. *see* Gudzii, Nikolai Kallinikovich.
Gudzii, Nikolai Kallinikovich, 1887-1965
　xGudzii, Nikolai K.
　　History of Early Russian Literature. Octagon.
Gudzinowicz, B. J. *see* Gudzinowicz, Benjamin J.
Gudzinowicz, Benjamin J.
　xGudzinowicz, B. J.
　　Fundamentals of Integrated Gc-Ms. Dekker.
　　Gas Chromatographic Analysis of Drugs & Pesticides. Dekker.
Gue, Ronald L.
　xGue, Ronald L.
　　Mathematical Methods in Operations Research. Macmillan.
Guedalla, Philip, 1889-1944
　xGuedalla, Philip.
　　The Duke. Greenwood.
Guedes, M. *see* Guedes, Michel.
Guedes, Michel.
　xGuedes, M.
　　Morphology of Seed Plants. Intl Schol Bk Serv.
　　Morphology of Seed Plants. Lubrecht & Cramer.
Guemple, D. L. *see* Guemple, D. Lee.
Guemple, D. Lee.
　xGuemple, D. L.
　　ed. Alliance in Eskimo Society. U of Wash Pr.
Guenter, Clarence A.
　xGuenter, Clarence A.
　　Clinical Aspects of Respiratory Physiology. Lippincott.
　　ed. Pulmonary Medicine. Lippincott.
Guenther, Herbert V.
　xGuenther, Herbert V.
　　Buddhist Philosophy in Theory & Practice. Shambhala Pubns.
　　ed. Life & Teaching of Naropa: Translated from the Original Tibetan with Philosophical Commentary Based on the Oral Transmission. Oxford U Pr.
　　The Tantric View of Life. Shambhala Pubns.
Guenther, William B.
　xGuenther, William B.
　　Chemical Equilibrium: A Practical Introduction for the Physical & Life Sciences. Plenum Pub.
Guenther, William C.
　xGuenther, William C.
　　Concepts of Statistical Inference. McGraw.
Guenthner. *see* Guenthner, Franz.
Guenthner, F. *see* Guenthner, Franz.
Guenthner, Franz.
　xGuenthner.
　　Studies in Formal Semantics: Intensionality, Temporality, Negation. Elsevier.
　xGuenthner, F.
　　ed. Formal Semantics & Pragmatics for Natural Languages. Kluwer Boston.
Guerard, A. L. *see* Guerard, Albert Leon.
Guerard, Albert. *see* Guerard, Albert Leon.
Guerard, Albert J. *see* Guerard, Albert Joseph.

Guerard, Albert Joseph, 1914-
　xGuerard, Albert J.
　　Andre Gide. Harvard U Pr.
　　Conrad the Novelist. Harvard U Pr.
　　The Triumph of the Novel: Dickens, Dostoevsky & Faulkner. Oxford U Pr.
Guerard, Albert L. *see* Guerard, Albert Leon.
Guerard, Albert Leon, 1880-1959
　xGuerard, A. L.
　　Literature & Society. Kraus Repr.
　xGuerard, Albert.
　　France: A Modern History. U of Mich Pr.
　xGuerard, Albert L.
　　Bottle in the Sea. Greenwood.
　　Literature & Society. Cooper Sq.
　　A Short History of the International Language Movement. Hyperion Conn.
Guerard, Michel, 1933-
　xGuerard, Michel.
　　Michel Guerard's Cuisine Gourmande. Morrow.
Guerber, H. A. *see* Guerber, Helene Adeline.
Guerber, Helene Adeline, d. 1929
　xGuerber, H. A.
　　Legends of the Middle Ages: Narrated with Special Reference to Literature & Art. Gordon Pr.
　　Stories of the Wagner Operas. Gordon Pr.
　　Stories of the Wagner Operas. Longwood Pr.
Guercio, E. *see* Guercio, Eugene.
Guercio, Eugene.
　xGuercio, E.
　　Reading Interpretation in Social Sciences, Natural Sciences, & Literature: Preparation & Review for the Reading Parts of the High School Equivalency Diploma Test. Arco.
Guercio, Francis M. *see* Guercio, Francis Michael.
Guercio, Francis Michael.
　xGuercio, Francis M.
　　ed. Anthology of Contemporary Italian Prose. Kennikat.
Guercio, Louis R. Del. *see* Del Guercio, Louis R.
Guerin, Daniel, 1904-
　xGuerin, Daniel.
　　Fascism & Big Business. Monad Pr.
Guerin, Wilfred L.
　xGuerin, Wilfred L.
　　A Handbook of Critical Approaches to Literature. Har-Row.
Guerinot, J. V. *see* Guerinot, Joseph V.
Guerinot, Joseph V.
　xGuerinot, J. V.
　　Pamphlet Attacks on Alexander Pope 1711-1744: A Descriptive Bibliography. NYU Pr.
Guerney, B. G. *see* Guerney, Bernard G.
Guerney, Bernard G., 1930-
　xGuerney, B. G.
　　Psychotherapeutic Agents: New Roles for Nonprofessionals, Parents & Teachers. Krieger.
　xGuerney, Bernard G.
　　Relationship Enhancement: Skill-Training Programs for Therapy, Problem Prevention, & Enrichment. Jossey-Bass.
Guernsey, Alfred H. *see* Guernsey, Alfred Hudson.
Guernsey, Alfred Hudson, 1824-1902
　xGuernsey, Alfred H.
　　Ralph Waldo Emerson. R West.
Guernsey, Dennis.
　xGuernsey, Dennis.
　　If I'm So Free, How Come I Feel Boxed in?. Word Bks.
　　Thoroughly Married. Word Bks.
Guerra, Cyvette.
　xGuerra, Cyvette.
　　The Joy Robbers. Impact Tenn.
Guerra, Frank.
　xGuerra, Frank.

ed. Emotional & Psychological Responses to
   Anesthesia & Surgery. Grune.
Guerry, Vincent.
   xGuerry, Vincent.
   Life with the Baoule. Three Continents.
Guertin, Richard L.
   xGuertin, Richard L.
   Introduction to Pl360 Programming.
   Wadsworth Pub.
Guertner, Beryl.
   xGuertner, Beryl.
   Cake Icing & Decorating for All Occasions.
   Taplinger.
Guest, Anthony.
   xGuest, Anthony.
   Art & the Camera. Arno.
Guest, Edgar A. *see* Guest, Edgar Albert.
Guest, Edgar Albert, 1881-1959
   xGuest, Edgar A.
   All in a Lifetime. Arno.
Guest, Edwin, 1800-1880
   xGuest, Edwin.
   History of English Rhythms. Haskell.
   A History of English Rhythms. R West.
Guest, Harry.
   xGuest, Harry.
   Arrangements. SBD.
   A House Against the Night. SBD.
Guest, Ivor. *see* Guest, Ivor Forbes.
Guest, Ivor Forbes.
   xGuest, Ivor.
   The Divine Virginia: A Biography of Virginia
   Zucchi. Dekker.
   Fanny Elssler. Columbia U Pr.
Guest, Judith.
   xGuest, Judith.
   Ordinary People. Ballantine.
   Ordinary People. Viking Pr.
Guest, R. *see* Guest, Robert H.
Guest, Robert H.
   xGuest, R.
   Organizational Change Through Effective
   Leadership. P-H.
Guetti, James L.
   xGuetti, James L.
   Word-Music: The Aesthetic Aspect of
   Narrative Fiction. Rutgers U Pr.
Guetzkow, Harold. *see* Guetzkow, Harold Steere.
Guetzkow, Harold Steere.
   xGuetzkow, Harold.
   ed. Simulation in Social & Administrative
   Science: Overviews & Case-Examples. P-H.
Guevara, E. Che. *see* Guevara, Ernesto.
Guevara, Ernesto, 1928-1967
   xGuevara, E. Che.
   Guerrilla Warfare. Random.
Guffey, George R. *see* Guffey, George Robert.
Guffey, George Robert.
   xGuffey, George R.
   ed. A Concordance to the English Poems of
   Andrew Marvell. U of NC Pr.
   Concordance to the Poetry of Thomas
   Traherne. U of Cal Pr.

Gugas, Chris, 1921-

   xGugas, Chris.
   The Silent Witness: A Polygraphist's Casebook.
   P-H.

Gugenheim, V. K. A. M.

   xGugenheim, V. K.
   On the Theory & Applications of Differential
   Torsion Products. Am Math.

Guggenheim, Marguerite.

   xGuggenheim, Peggy.

Out of This Century: Confessions of an Art
   Addict. Doubleday.
   Out of This Century: Confessions of an Art
   Addict. Universe.
Guggenheim, Peggy. *see* Guggenheim, Marguerite.
Guggenheimer, Elinor C.
   xGuggenheimer, Elinor C.
   Planning for Parks & Recreation Needs in
   Urban Areas. Cyrco Pr.
   Planning for Parks & Recreation Needs in
   Urban Areas. Irvington.
Guggenheimer, Eva H.
   xGuggenheimer, Eva H.
   Rhyme Effects & Rhyming Figures: A
   Comparative Study of Sound Repetitions in
   the Classics with Emphasis on Latin Poetry.
   Mouton.
Guggisberg, Frederick G. *see* Guggisberg, Frederick
   Gordon.
Guggisberg, Frederick Gordon.
   xGuggisberg, Frederick G.
   Future of the Negro: Some Chapters in the
   Development of a Race. Negro U Pr.
Gugliotta, Bobette.
   xGugliotta, Bobette.
   Nolle Smith, Cowboy, Engineer, Statesman.
   Dodd.
Guiart, Jean.
   xGuiart, Jean.
   The Arts of the South Pacific. Braziller.
Guiasu, S. *see* Guiasu, Silviu.
Guiasu, Silviu.
   xGuiasu, S.
   Coalition & Connection in Games. Pergamon.
   xGuiasu, Silviu.
   Information Theory with New Applications.
   McGraw.
Guichardet, A. *see* Guichardet, Alain.
Guichardet, Alain.
   xGuichardet, A.
   Special Topics in Topological Algebras.
   Gordon.
Guicharnaud, Jacques.
   xGuicharnaud, Jacques.
   Modern French Theatre: From Giraudoux to
   Genet. Yale U Pr.
Guideline Publishing Co. Staff. *see* Guidelines
   Publications.
Guidelines Publications.
   xGuideline Publishing Co. Staff.
   The California Retail Liquor Store. Guideline
   Pub.
Guidelines Subcommittee, SLA Networking Committee.
   see Special Libraries Associations. Networking
   Committee. Guidelines Subcommittee.
Guidepost Magazine. *see* Guideposts.
Guideposts.
   xGuidepost Magazine.
   ed. The Guideposts Treasury of Hope. Bantam.
Guidoni, Enrico, 1939-
   xGuidoni, Enrico.
   Primitive Architecture. Abrams.
Guie, H. Dean. *see* Guie, Heister Dean.
Guie, Heister Dean.
   xGuie, H. Dean.
   Bugles in the Valley: Garnett's Fort Simcoe.
   Oreg Hist Soc.
Guilbault, George. *see* Guilbault, George G.
Guilbault, George G.
   xGuilbault, George.
   Handbook of Enzymatic Methods of Analysis.
   Dekker.
Guild, Leo.
   xGuild, Leo.
   Street of Ho's. Holloway.
Guild, Nelson. *see* Guild, Nelson Prescott.
Guild, Nelson Prescott.
   xGuild, Nelson.

Introduction to Politics: Essays & Readings.
   Krieger.
Guild, Nicholas.
   xGuild, Nicholas.
   Old Acquaintance. Seaview Bks.
   Summer Soldier. BJ Pub Group.
Guild, Reuben A. *see* Guild, Reuben Aldridge.
Guild, Reuben Aldridge, 1822-1899
   xGuild, Reuben A.
   Early History of Brown University, Including
   the Life, Times, & Correspondence of
   President Manning, 1756-1791. Arno.
   The Librarian's Manual: A Treatise on
   Bibliography, Comprising a Select &
   Descriptive List of Bibliographical Works; to
   Which Are Added, Sketches of Public
   Libraries. Gale.
Guild, Vera P.
   xGuild, Vera P.
   Painting with Stitches: A Guide to Embroidery,
   Needlepoint, Crochet & Macrame. Davis
   Mass.
Guilday, Peter K. *see* Guilday, Peter Keenan.
Guilday, Peter Keenan, 1884-1947
   xGuilday, Peter K.
   History of the Councils of Baltimore,
   1791-1884. Arno.
Guilds, J. C. *see* Guilds, John Caldwell.
Guilds, John Caldwell, 1924-
   xGuilds, J. C.
   ed. Nineteenth Century Southern Fiction.
   Brown Bk.
Guiles, Fred L. *see* Guiles, Fred Lawrence.
Guiles, Fred Lawrence.
   xGuiles, Fred L.
   Tyrone Power: The Last Idol. Berkley Pub.
   Tyrone Power: The Last Idol. Doubleday.
Guilfoile, Elizabeth.
   xGuilfoile, Elizabeth.
   Nobody Listens to Andrew. Schol Bk Serv.
   Nobody Listens to Andrew. Follett.
   Valentine's Day. Garrard.
Guilford, Carol.
   xGuilford, Carol.
   The Easiest Cookbook. Lippincott.
Guilford, J. P. *see* Guilford, Joy Paul.
Guilford, Joy P. *see* Guilford, Joy Paul.
Guilford, Joy Paul.
   xGuilford, J. P.
   Cognitive Psychology with a Frame of
   Reference. EDITS Pubs.
   xGuilford, Joy P.
   Analysis of Intelligence. McGraw.
   Fundamental Statistics in Psychology &
   Education. McGraw.
   Nature of Human Intelligence. McGraw.
   Psychometric Methods. McGraw.
Guilfoyle, Ann.
   xGuilfoyle, Ann.
   The Peaceable Kingdom: A Loving Look at the
   Family of Animals. Macmillan.
Guilland, Antoine, 1861-
   xGuilland, Antoine.
   Modern Germany & Her Historians.
   Greenwood.
Guillaume, Paul, 1878-1962
   xGuillaume, Paul.
   Imitation in Children. U of Chicago Pr.
Guillebaud, Claude W. *see* Guillebaud, Claude William.
Guillebaud, Claude William, 1890-
   xGuillebaud, Claude W.
   Economic Recovery of Germany from 1933 to
   the Incorporation of Austria in March 1938.
   AMS Pr.
Guillemard, Francis H. *see* Guillemard, Francis Henry
   Hill.
Guillemard, Francis Henry Hill, 1852-1933
   xGuillemard, Francis H.

Life of Ferdinand Magellan & the First
Circumnavigation of the Globe. AMS Pr.
Guillemin, V.
xGuillemin, Victor.
Differential Topology. P-H.
Geometric Asymptotics. Am Math.
Guillemin, Victor.
xGuillemin, Victor.
Story of Quantum Mechanics. Scribner.
Guillemin, Victor. *see* Guillemin, V.
Guillen, Jorge.
xGuillen, Jorge.
Guillen on Guillen: The Poetry & the Poet.
Princeton U Pr.
Guillet, David.
xGuillet, David.
Agrarian Reform & Peasant Economy in
Southern Peru. U of Mo Pr.
Guillet, Edwin C. *see* Guillet, Edwin Clarence.
Guillet, Edwin Clarence, 1898-
xGuillet, Edwin C.
The Great Migration: The Atlantic Crossing by
Sailing-Ship Since 1770. Ozer.
Guillet, J. *see* Guillet, Jacques.
Guillet, Jacques.
xGuillet, J.
Religious Experience of Jesus & His Disciples.
Abbey.
xGuillet, Jacques.
A God Who Speaks. Paulist Pr.
Guillory, William A.
xGuillory, William A.
Introduction to Molecular Structure &
Spectroscopy. Allyn.
Guillot, Rene, 1900-
xGuillot, Rene.
Grishka & the Bear. Abelard.
Guimond, James.
xGuimond, James.
The Art of William Carlos Williams: A
Discovery & Possession of America. U of Ill
Pr.
Guin, Ursula K. Le. *see* Le Guin, Ursula K.
Guin, Ursula Le. *see* Le Guin, Ursula K.
Guinagh, Kevin, 1897-
xGuinagh, Kevin.
ed. Dictionary of Foreign Phrases &
Abbreviations. Wilson.
Inspired Amateurs. Arno.
Guinan, Edward.
xGuinan, Edward.
ed. Peace & Non-Violence: Basic Writings.
Paulist Pr.
Guinee, Kathleen K.
xGuinee, Kathleen K.
Professional Nurse: Orientation, Roles &
Responsibilities. Macmillan.
Guiney, David.
xGuiney, David.
The Dunlop Book of the Olympics. State
Mutual Bk.
Guion, Robert M.
xGuion, Robert M.
Personnel Testing. McGraw.
Guirdham, Arthur.
xGuirdham, Arthur.
Cathars & Reincarnation. Theos Pub Hse.
Guirma, Frederic.
xGuirma, Frederic.
tr. Princess of the Full Moon. Macmillan.
Guisewite, Cathy.
xGuisewite, Cathy.
The Cathy Chronicles. Andrews & McMeel.
Guitard, Lucien.
xGuitard, Lucien.
French Pronunciation Illustrated. Cambridge U
Pr.
Guitart, Jorge M., 1937-
xGuitart, Jorge M.

Markedness & a Cuban Dialect of Spanish.
Georgetown U Pr.
Guither, Harold D.
xGuither, Harold D.
The Food Lobbyists: Behind the Scenes of
Food & Agri-Politics. Lexington Bks.
Guizot, Francois. *see* Guizot, Francois Pierre Guillaume.
Guizot, Francois P. *see* Guizot, Francois Pierre
Guillaume.
Guizot, Francois Pierre Guillaume, 1787-1874
xGuizot, Francois.
Historical Essays & Lectures. U of Chicago Pr.
xGuizot, Francois P.
ed. Memoirs to Illustrate the History of My
Time. AMS Pr.
Gukiina, Peter. *see* Gukiina, Peter M.
Gukiina, Peter M.
xGukiina, Peter.
Uganda: A Case Study in African Political
Development. U of Notre Dame Pr.
Gulati, Bodh R., 1930-
xGulati, Bodh R.
College Mathematics with Applications to the
Business & Social Sciences. Har-Row.
Finite Mathematics: An Introduction.
Har-Row.
Gulcher, Coen.
xGulcher, Conrad.
Racing Techniques Explained. De Graff.
Gulcher, Conrad. *see* Gulcher, Coen.
Guldbeck, Per E. *see* Guldbeck, Per Ernst.
Guldbeck, Per Ernst.
xGuldbeck, Per E.
Care of Historical Collections: A Conservation
Handbook for the Nonspecialist. AASLH.
Gulezian. *see* Gulezian, R. C.
Gulezian, R. C.
xGulezian.
Elements of Business Statistics. Dryden Pr.
Statistics for Decision Making. Dryden Pr.
xGulezian, Ronald C.
Statistics for Decision Making. HR&W.
Gulezian, Ronald C. *see* Gulezian, R. C.
Gulf Coast History & Humanities Conference. *see* Gulf
Coast History and Humanities Conference, 2nd,
University of West Florida, 1970.
**Gulf Coast History and Humanities Conference, 1st,
University of West Florida, 1969.**
xGulf Coast History & Humanities Conference.
In Search of Gulf Coast Colonial History:
Proceedings. Historic Pensacola.
**Gulf Coast History and Humanities Conference, 2nd,
University of West Florida, 1970.**
xGulf Coast History & Humanities Conference.
Spain & Her Rivals on the Gulf Coast:
Proceedings. Historic Pensacola.
**Gulf Coast History and Humanities Conference, 3rd,
Pensacola, Fla., 1971.**
xGulf Coast History & Humanities Conference.
The Americanization of the Gulf Coast:
Proceedings. Historic Pensacola.
Guli, Francesca.
xGuli, Francesca.
I Sing of Summer. Golden Quill.
Gulick, Joh, 1924-
xGulick, John.
Tripoli: A Modern Arab City. Harvard U Pr.
Gulick, John, 1924-
xGulick, John.
Cherokees at the Crossroads. U NC Inst Res
Soc Sci.
Gulick, John. *see* Gulick, Joh.
Gulick, Sidney L. *see* Gulick, Sidney Lewis.
Gulick, Sidney Lewis, 1860-1945
xGulick, Sidney L.
American Democracy & Asiatic Citizenship.
Arno.
Gullahorn, Jeanne E.
xGullahorn, Jeanne E.

Psychology & Women: In Transition. Halsted
Pr.
Gulland, J. A.
xGulland, John A.
ed. Fish Population Dynamics. Wiley.
Gulland, John A. *see* Gulland, J. A.
Gullett, Henry, 1914-
xGullett, Henry J.
Not As a Duty Only: An Infantryman's War.
Intl Schol Bk Serv.
Gullett, Henry J. *see* Gullett, Henry.
Gullette, Margaret M. *see* Gullette, Margaret
Morganroth.
Gullette, Margaret Morganroth.
xGullette, Margaret M.
The Lost Bellybutton. Lollipop Power.
Gulley, Elsie E. *see* Gulley, Elsie Elizabeth.
Gulley, Elsie Elizabeth, 1889-
xGulley, Elsie E.
Joseph Chamberlain & English Social Politics.
Octagon.
Gulley, Kent.
xGulley, Kent.
ed. The Papers of Betty Gannett: Guide to a
Microfilm Edition. State Hist Soc Wis.
Gulliver, Ann W.
xGulliver, Ann W.
A Guide to Creative Filmmaking. Pendulum
Pr.
Gulliver, Lucile, 1882-
xGulliver, Lucile.
Louisa May Alcott, a Bibliography. B Franklin.
Gulliver, P. H.
xGulliver, Philip H.
Disputes & Negotiations: A Cross-Cultural
Perspective. Acad Pr.
Gulliver, Philip H. *see* Gulliver, P. H.
Gumbel, Emil J. *see* Gumbel, Emil Julius.
Gumbel, Emil Julius, 1891-
xGumbel, Emil J.
Statistics of Extremes. Columbia U Pr.
Gumbert, Edgar B.
xGumbert, Edgar B.
The Superschool & the Superstate: American
Education in the Twentieth Century,
1918-1970. Wiley.
Gumbiner, Joseph H. *see* Gumbiner, Joseph Henry.
Gumbiner, Joseph Henry, 1906-
xGumbiner, Joseph H.
Leaders of Our People. UAHC.
Gumerman, George J.
xGumerman, George J.
ed. Papers on the Archaeology of Black Mesa,
Arizona. S Ill U Pr.
Gummer, E. N. *see* Gummer, Ellis Norman.
Gummer, Ellis N. *see* Gummer, Ellis Norman.
Gummer, Ellis Norman.
xGummer, E. N.
Dickens' Works in Germany: 1837-1937.
Gordon Pr.
xGummer, Ellis N.
Dickens' Works in Germany, 1837-1937.
Octagon.
Gummere, Amelia (Mott), 1859-1937
xGummere, Amelia M.
Quaker: A Study in Costume. Arno.
Gummere, Amelia M. *see* Gummere, Amelia (Mott).
Gummere, Francis B. *see* Gummere, Francis Barton.
Gummere, Francis Barton, 1855-1919
xGummere, Francis B.
ed. Old English Ballads. Russell.
The Popular Ballad. Gordon Pr.
Popular Ballad. Peter Smith.
Popular Ballad. R West.
Gumowski, Igor.
xGumowski, Igor.
Optimization in Control Theory & Practice.
Cambridge U Pr.
Gump, Margaret.
xGump, Margaret.

Adalbert Stifter. Twayne.
Gumpert, Gary.
　xGumpert, Gary.
　　ed. Inter-Media: Interpersonal Communication
　　in a Media World. Oxford U Pr.
Gumpertz, Robert, 1925-
　xGumpertz, Robert.
　　Dream Notebook. SF Bk Co.
Gumplowicz, Ludwig, 1838-1909
　xGumplowicz, Ludwig.
　　The Outlines of Sociology. Arno.
　　Outlines of Sociology. Transaction Bks.
The Gun Digest.
　xTheEditors of Gun Digest.
　　Gun Digest's Book of Gun Accessories.
　　Follett.
Gun, Nerin E.
　xGun, Nerin E.
　　Day of the Americans. Fleet.
Gundersen, Roy M.
　xGundersen, Roy M.
　　Linearized Analysis of One-Dimensional
　　Magnetohydrodynamic Flows.
　　Springer-Verlag.
Gundersheimer, Werner L.
　xGundersheimer, Werner L.
　　Ferrara: The Style of a Renaissance Despotism.
　　Princeton U Pr.
Gunderson, E. K. *see* Gunderson, Ellsworth K. Eric.
Gunderson, Ellsworth K. Eric.
　xGunderson, E. K.
　　ed. Life Stress & Illness. C C Thomas.
Gunderson, John G.
　xGunderson, John G.
　　ed. Psychotherapy of Schizophrenia. Aronson.
Gunderson, Morley.
　xGunderson, Morley.
　　ed. Collective Bargaining in the Essential &
　　Public Service Sectors. U of Toronto Pr.
Gundry, Robert H. *see* Gundry, Robert Horton.
Gundry, Robert Horton.
　xGundry, Robert H.
　　Survey of the New Testament. Zondervan.
Gunkel, Hermann, 1862-1932
　xGunkel, Hermann.
　　Psalms: A Form-Critical Introduction. Fortress.
Gunn, A. V. *see* Gunn, Argyle Vernon.
Gunn, Angus M. *see* Gunn, Angus MacLeod.
Gunn, Angus MacLeod, 1920-
　xGunn, Angus M.
　　Habitat: Human Settlements in an Urban Age.
　　Pergamon.
Gunn, Argyle Vernon, 1919-
　xGunn, A. V.
　　How to Design Better Products for Less
　　Money. Halls of Ivy.
Gunn, Charles R.
　xGunn, Charles R.
　　World Guide to Tropical Drift Seeds & Fruits.
　　Times Bks.
Gunn, Clare A.
　xGunn, Clare A.
　　Tourism Planning. Crane-Russak Co.
Gunn, Drewey W. *see* Gunn, Drewey Wayne.
Gunn, Drewey Wayne, 1939-
　xGunn, Drewey W.
　　American & British Writers in Mexico:
　　1556-1970. U of Tex Pr.
Gunn, Elizabeth.
　xGunn, Elizabeth.
　　A Daring Coiffeur: Reflections on "War &
　　Peace" & "Anna Karenina". Rowman.
Gunn, Giles. *see* Gunn, Giles B.
Gunn, Giles B.
　xGunn, Giles.
　　The Interpretation of Otherness: Literature
　　Religion & the American Imagination.
　　Oxford U Pr.
Gunn, James. *see* Gunn, James Edward.

Gunn, James Edward, 1920-
　xGunn, James.
　　This Fortress World. Berkley Pub.
Gunn, John R.
　xGunn, John R.
　　Good Morning, Lord: Devotions on the Hope
　　of Glory. Baker Bk.
Gunn, Mary K. *see* Gunn, Mary Kemper.
Gunn, Mary Kemper.
　xGunn, Mary K.
　　Guide to Academic Protocol. Columbia U Pr.
Gunn, Peter.
　xGunn, Peter.
　　Burgundy: Landscape with Figures. Verry.
Gunn, Scout. *see* Gunn, Scout Lee.
Gunn, Scout Lee.
　xGunn, Scout.
　　Therapeutic Recreation Program Design:
　　Principles & Procedures. P-H.
Gunn, Thom.
　xGunn, Thom.
　　Positives. Merrimack Bk Serv.
　　Selected Poems. FS&G.
　　Selected Poems. Merrimack Bk Serv.
　　Selected Poems. U of Chicago Pr.
Gunn, Virginia.
　xGunn, Virginia S.
　　The Wayward Season. Doubleday.
Gunn, Virginia S. *see* Gunn, Virginia.
Gunnell, John.
　xGunnell, John G.
　　How to Convert-Restore Old Cars, Station
　　Wagons, Vans, Trucks & Buses into RVs.
　　TAB Bks.
Gunnell, John G.
　xGunnell, John G.
　　Political Theory: Tradition & Interpretation.
　　Winthrop.
Gunnell, John G. *see* Gunnell, John.
Gunnemann. *see* Gunnemann, Jon P.
Gunnemann, Jon P.
　xGunnemann.
　　The Moral Meaning of Revolution. Yale U Pr.
Gunnerson, James H.
　xGunnerson, James H.
　　The Fremont Culture: A Study in Culture
　　Dynamics on the Northern Anasazi Frontier.
　　Peabody Harvard.
Gunneweg, A. H. *see* Gunneweg, Antonius H. J.
Gunneweg, Antonius H. J.
　xGunneweg, A. H.
　　Understanding the Old Testament.
　　Westminster.
Gunning, B. E. S. *see* Gunning, Brian E. S.
Gunning, Brian E. S.
　xGunning, B. E.
　　ed. Intercellular Communication in Plants:
　　Studies on Plasmodesmata. Springer-Verlag.
　　Plant Cell Biology: An Ultrastructural
　　Approach. Crane-Russak Co.
Gunning, Dennis.
　xGunning, Dennis.
　　The Teaching of History. Biblio Dist.
Gunning, Monica.
　xGunning, Monica.
　　The Two Georges: Los Dos Jorges. Blaine
　　Ethridge.
Gunning, R. C. *see* Gunning, Robert Clifford.
Gunning, Robert C. *see* Gunning, Robert Clifford.
Gunning, Robert Clifford, 1931-
　xGunning, R. C.
　　Riemann Surfaces & Generalized Theta
　　Functions. Springer-Verlag.
　xGunning, Robert C.
　　Lectures on Modular Forms. Princeton U Pr.
　　Lectures on Vector Bundles Over Riemann
　　Surfaces. Princeton U Pr.
Gunningham, Neil.
　xGunningham, Neil.

Pollution, Social Interest & the Law. Rothman.
Gunnis, R. *see* Gunnis, Rupert.
Gunnis, Rupert.
　xGunnis, R.
　　Dictionary of British Sculptors 1660-1851.
　　Newbury Bks Inc.
Gunson, Niel, 1930-
　xGunson, Niel.
　　Messengers of Grace: Evangelical Missionaries
　　in the South Seas 1797-1860. Oxford U Pr.
Gunston, Bill.
　xGunston, Bill.
　　Early Supersonic Fighters of the West.
　　Scribner.
　　Submarines in Color. Arco.
Gunstone, F. D.
　xGunstone, F. D.
　　Guidebook to Stereochemistry. Longman.
Gunstream, Stanley E.
　xGunstream, Stanley E.
　　Explorations in Basic Biology. Burgess.
Gunter, Laurie M.
　xGunter, Laurie M.
　　Education for Gerontic Nursing. Springer Pub.
Guntharp, Matthew G.
　xGuntharp, Matthew G.
　　Learning the Fiddler's Ways. Pa St U Pr.
Gunther, Bernard.
　xGunther, Bernard.
　　How the West Is One. Macmillan.
Gunther, Hans. *see* Gunther, Hans F. K.
Gunther, Hans F. K., 1891-
　xGunther, Hans.
　　The Racial Elements of European History.
　　Gordon Pr.
Gunther, John, 1901-1970
　xGunther, John.
　　Death Be Not Proud. Har-Row.
　　Death Be Not Proud. Modern Lib.
　　Inside Asia. Greenwood.
　　Inside Europe Today. Har-Row.
　　Inside Latin America. Greenwood.
　　Inside Russia Today. Har-Row.
　　The Riddle of MacArthur: Japan, Korea, & the
　　Far East. Greenwood.
Gunther, Louise.
　xGunther, Louise.
　　Anna's Snow Day. Garrard.
　　Where Is Maria?. Garrard.
Gunton, Colin E.
　xGunton, Colin E.
　　Becoming & Being: The Doctrine of God in
　　Charles Hartshorne & Karl Barth. Oxford U
　　Pr.
Guntrip, Harry. *see* Guntrip, Henry James Samuel.
Guntrip, Henry James Samuel.
　xGuntrip, Harry.
　　Personality Structure & Human Interaction:
　　The Developing Synthesis of Psychodynamic
　　Theory. Intl Univs Pr.
　　Psychoanalytic Theory, Therapy, & the Self.
　　Basic.
Gunz, Frederick.
　xGunz, Frederick W.
　　ed. Leukemia. Grune.
Gunz, Frederick W. *see* Gunz, Frederick.
Gup, Benton. *see* Gup, Benton E.
Gup, Benton E.
　xGup, Benton.
　　Guide to Strategic Planning. McGraw.
　xGup, Benton E.
　　The Basics of Investing. Wiley.
　　Financial Intermediaries: An Introduction. HM.
Gupta, A. *see* Gupta, Alok K.
Gupta, Alok K.
　xGupta, A.
　　Petrology & Genesis of Leucite-Bearing Rocks.
　　Springer-Verlag.
Gupta, Brijen K. *see* Gupta, Brijen Kishore.

Gupta, Brijen Kishore, 1929-
xGupta, Brijen K.
India in English Fiction, 1800-1970: An
Annotated Bibliography. Scarecrow.
Gupta, D. C.
xGupta, D. C.
Indian Government & Politics. Advent Bk.
Indian Government & Politics. Intl Pubns Serv.
Gupta, Giri R. see Gupta, Giri Raj.
Gupta, Giri Raj.
xGupta, Giri R.
ed. Cohesion & Conflict in Modern India.
Carolina Acad Pr.
ed. Contemporary India: Some Sociological
Perspectives. Carolina Acad Pr.
Gupta, K. C.
xGupta, K. C.
Microstrip Lines & Slotlines. Artech Hse.
Gupta, M. M. see Gupta, Madan M.
Gupta, Madan M.
xGupta, M. M.
ed. Advances in Fuzzy Set Theory &
Applications. Elsevier.
Fuzzy Automata & Decision Processes.
Elsevier.
Gupta, Narain. see Gupta, Raj Narain.
Gupta, Partha S. see Gupta, Partha Sarathi.
Gupta, Partha Sarathi.
xGupta, Partha S.
Imperialism & the British Labour Movement
1914-1964. Holmes & Meier.
Gupta, R. L.
xGupta, R. L.
Politics of Commitment: A Study Based on the
Fifth General Elections in India. Verry.
Gupta, Raj Narain.
xGupta, Narain.
Oil in the Modern World. Hyperion Conn.
Gupta, S. N. see Gupta, Suraj N.
Gupta, Shanti C. see Gupta, Shanti Swarup.
Gupta, Shanti Swarup.
xGupta, Shanti C.
Multiple Decision Procedures: Theory &
Methodology of Selecting & Ranking
Populations. Wiley.
Gupta, Suraj N., 1924-
xGupta, S. N.
Quantum Electrodynamics. Gordon.
Gupta, U. L. see Gupta, Umrao Lal.
Gupta, Umrao Lal, 1931-
xGupta, U. L.
Working of Stock Exchanges in India. Verry.
Gupta, V. J. see Gupta, Vishwa Jit.
Gupta, Vishwa Jit, 1942-
xGupta, V. J.
Indian Palaeozoic Stratigraphy. College Mktg
Grp.
Guptill, Arthur L. see Guptill, Arthur Leighton.
Guptill, Arthur Leighton, 1891-1956
xGuptill, Arthur L.
Oil Painting Step-By-Step. Watson-Guptill.
Rendering in Pencil. Watson-Guptill.
Gupton, James A.
xGupton, James A.
Getting Down to Business with Your
Microcomputer. Sourcebooks CA.
Gupton, Oscar W.
xGupton, Oscar W.
Wildflowers of the Shenandoah Valley & Blue
Ridge Mountains. U Pr of Va.
Gurdjian, E. Stephen. see Gurdjian, Elisha Stephens.
Gurdjian, Elisha Stephens.
xGurdjian, E. Stephen.
Operative Neurosurgery. Krieger.
Gurdon, J. B.
xGurdon, J. B.
Control of Gene Expression in Animal
Development. Harvard U Pr.
Gurel, Lois M.
xGurel, Lois M.

Dimensions of Dress & Adornment: A Book of
Readings. Kendall-Hunt.
Gurevich, A. see Gurevich, Aleksandr Viktorovich.
Gurevich, Aleksandr Viktorovich.
xGurevich, A.
Nonlinear Phenomena in the Ionosphere.
Springer-Verlag.
Gurganus, George P.
xGurganus, George P.
ed. Guidelines for World Evangelism. Bibl Res
Pr.
Gurin, Gerald.
xGurin, Gerald.
Americans View Their Mental Health. Arno.
Gurko, Leo, 1914-
xGurko, Leo.
Thomas Wolfe: Beyond the Romantic Ego. T Y
Crowell.
Two Lives of Joseph Conrad. T Y Crowell.
Gurko, Miriam.
xGurko, Miriam.
Clarence Darrow. T Y Crowell.
Gurko, Vladimir I. see Gurko, Vladimir Iosifovich.
Gurko, Vladimir Iosifovich, 1863-1927
xGurko, Vladimir I.
Features & Figures of the Past: Government &
Opinion in the Reign of Nicholas Second.
Russell.
Gurland, A. R. see Gurland, Arcadius Rudolph Lang.
Gurland, Arcadius Rudolph Lang.
xGurland, A. R.
The Fate of Small Business in Nazi Germany.
Fertig.
Gurney, A. R. see Gurney, Albert Ramsdell.
Gurney, Albert Ramsdell, 1930-
xGurney, A. R.
Entertaining Strangers. Avon.
Gurney, Eric.
xGurney, Eric.
The Calculating Cat Returns. P-H.
The Calculating Cat Returns. P-H.
How to Live with a Calculating Cat. PB.
Gurney, Gene.
xGurney, Gene.
Agriculture Careers. Watts.
Americans into Orbit: The Story of Project
Mercury. Random.
The Colony of Maryland. Watts.
Five Down & Glory: A History of the
American Air Ace. Arno.
Space Technology Spinoffs. Watts.
ed. Test Pilots. Arno.
Test Pilots. Beachcomber Bks.
Gurney, Oliver R. see Gurney, Oliver Robert.
Gurney, Oliver Robert.
xGurney, Oliver R.
Some Aspects of Hittite Religion. Oxford U Pr.
Gurney, T. R. see Gurney, Timothy Russell.
Gurney, Timothy Russell.
xGurney, T. R.
Fatigue of Welded Structures. Cambridge U Pr.
Guroff. see Guroff, Gordon.
Guroff, Gordon, 1933-
xGuroff.
Molecular Neurobiology. Dekker.
Gurr, David, 1936-
xGurr, David.
Troika. Berkley Pub.
Troika. Methuen Inc.
Gurr, John E. see Gurr, John Edwin.
Gurr, John Edwin.
xGurr, John E.
Principle of Sufficient Reason in Some
Scholastic Systems, 1750-1900. Marquette.
Gurr, Robin.
xGurr, Robin.
Song Is a Mirror. Soccer.
Gurr, Ted R. see Gurr, Ted Robert.
Gurr, Ted Robert.
xGurr, Ted R.

The Politics of Crime & Conflict: A
Comparative History of Four Cities. Sage.
Gurtov, Melvin.
xGurtov, Melvin.
China & Southeast Asia--The Politics of
Survival: A Study of Foreign Policy
Interaction. Johns Hopkins.
Making Changes: The Politics of Self
Liberation. Harvest Moon.
Southeast Asia Tomorrow: Problems &
Prospects for U.S. Policy. Johns Hopkins.
Gurvitch, Georges, 1894-1965
xGurvitch, Georges.
Sociology of Law. Routledge & Kegan.
Gurwitsch, Aron.
xGurwitsch, Aron.
Phenomenology & the Theory of Science.
Northwestern U Pr.
Phenomenology & the Theory of Science. Univ
Microfilms.
Studies in Phenomenology & Psychology.
Northwestern U Pr.
Gusev, N. G. see Gusev, Nikolai Grigorevich.
Gusev, Nikolai Grigorevich.
xGusev, N. G.
Quantum Radiation of Radioactive Nuclides.
Pergamon.
Gusfield, Joseph R., 1923-
xGusfield, Joseph R.
Community: A Critical Response. Har-Row.
Symbolic Crusade: Status Politics & the
American Temperance Movement.
Greenwood.
Symbolic Crusade: Status Politics & the
American Temperance Movement. U of Ill
Pr.
Gusler, Wallace B.
xGusler, Wallace B.
Decorated Firearms, 1540-1870, from the
Collection of Clay P. Bedford. U Pr of Va.
Furniture of Williamsburg & Eastern Virginia,
1710-1790. VA Mus Fine Arts.
Gussman, Boris.
xGussman, Boris.
Out in the Mid-Day Sun. Greenwood.
Gussow, Don.
xGussow, Don.
Chaia Sonia: A Family's Odyssey - Russian
Style. Delacorte.
Gussow, Joan. see Gussow, Joan Dye.
Gussow, Joan Dye.
xGussow, Joan.
The Feeding Web: Issues in Nutritional
Ecology. Bull Pub.
Gussow, Mel.
xGussow, Mel.
Don't Say Yes Until I Finish Talking: A
Biography of Darryl F. Zanuck. PB.
Gust, Dodie.
xGust, Dodie.
Face to Face with Alcoholism. Hazelden.
Gustafson , W. Eric. see Gustafson, W. Eric.
Gustafson, Alrik, 1903-
xGustafson, Alrik.
History of Swedish Literature. Am
Scandinavian.
History of Swedish Literature. U of Minn Pr.
Gustafson, Dana. see Gustafson, Dana C.
Gustafson, Dana C.
xGustafson, Dana.
ed. Food from Afar. Grace Pub Co.
Gustafson, James.
xGustafson, James.
Bright Eyes Talks Crazy to Rembrandt.
Hanging Loose.
Gustafson, James M.
xGustafson, James M.

Christ & the Moral Life. U of Chicago Pr.
Christian Ethics & the Community. Pilgrim
NY.
Church As Moral Decision-Maker. Pilgrim NY.
ed. On Being Responsible: Issues in Personal
Ethics. Har-Row.
Protestant & Roman Catholic Ethics: Prospects
for Rapprochement. U of Chicago Pr.
Theology & Christian Ethics. Pilgrim NY.
Gustafson, Janie.
xGustafson, Janie.
Celibate Passion. Har-Row.
Gustafson, R. David. *see* Gustafson, Roy David.
Gustafson, Richard F.
xGustafson, Richard F.
The Imagination of Spring: The Poetry of
Afanasy Fet. Greenwood.
Gustafson, Robert J.
xGustafson, Robert J.
Fundamentals of Electricity for Agriculture.
AVI.
Gustafson, Roy David.
xGustafson, R. David.
College Algebra. Brooks-Cole.
Gustafson, W. Eric.
xGustafson , W. Eric.
ed. Pakistan & Bangladesh: Bibliographic
Essays in Social Science. South Asia Bks.
Gustafsson, Bo, 1931-
xGustafsson, Bo.
ed. Post-Industrial Society. St Martin.
Gustafsson, Lars, 1936-
xGustafsson, Lars.
Forays into Swedish Poetry. U of Tex Pr.
Gustason, Gerilee.
xGustason, Gerilee.
Signing Exact English. Modern Signs.
Signing Exact English. Modern Signs.
Gustavson, Carl G.
xGustavson, Carl G.
Preface to History. McGraw.
Gustavson, Frances. *see* Gustavson, Frances G.
Gustavson, Frances G.
xGustavson, Frances.
Problem Solving in Basic: A Modular
Approach. SRA.
Gustavson, Karl H. *see* Gustavson, Karl Helmer.
Gustavson, Karl Helmer.
xGustavson, Karl H.
Chemistry & Reactivity of Collagen. Acad Pr.

Gustely, Richard D.
xGustely, Richard D.
Municipal Public Employment & Public
Expenditure. Lexington Bks.

Gustorf, Frederick. *see* Gustorf, Frederick Julius.

Gustorf, Frederick Julius.
xGustorf, Frederick.
Uncorrupted Heart: Journal & Letters of
Frederick Julius Gustorf 1800-1845. U of Mo
Pr.

Guszak, Frank J.
xGuszak, Frank J.
Diagnostic Reading Instruction in the
Elementary School. Har-Row.

Gutas, Dimitri.

xGutas, Dimitri.
Greek Wisdom Literature in Arabic
Translation: A Study of the Graeco-Arabic
Gnomologia. Am Orient Soc.
Gutch, C. F.
xGutch, C. F.
Review of Hemodialysis for Nurses and
Dialysis Personnel. Mosby.
Gutcheon, Beth. *see* Gutcheon, Beth Richardson.

Gutcheon, Beth Richardson.
xGutcheon, Beth.
The Perfect Patchwork Primer. Penguin.
xGutcheon, Elizabeth.
The New Girls. Putnam.
Gutcheon, Elizabeth. *see* Gutcheon, Beth Richardson.
Gutcho, M.
xGutcho, M.
Dairy Products & Eggs: Recent Developments.
Noyes.
Edible Oils & Fats: Recent Developments.
Noyes.
xGutcho, M. H.
Fortified & Soft Drinks. Noyes.
Freeze Drying Processes for the Food Industry.
Noyes.
ed. Household & Industrial Fabric
Conditioners. Noyes.
Tampons & Other Catamenial Receptors.
Noyes.
Gutcho, M. H. *see* Gutcho, M.
Gutek, Gerald. *see* Gutek, Gerald Lee.
Gutek, Gerald L. *see* Gutek, Gerald Lee.
Gutek, Gerald Lee.
xGutek, Gerald.
Joseph Neef: The Americanization of
Pestalozzianism 1800-1840. U of Ala Pr.
xGutek, Gerald L.
Educational Theory of George S. Counts. Ohio
St U Pr.
Historical Introduction to American Education.
Har-Row.
A History of the Western Educational
Experience. Random.
Guterbock, Thomas M.
xGuterbock, Thomas M.
Machine Politics in Transition: Party &
Community in Chicago. U of Chicago Pr.
Guterman, Simeon L. *see* Guterman, Simeon Leonard.
Guterman, Simeon Leonard, 1907-
xGuterman, Simeon L.
Religious Toleration & Persecution in Ancient
Rome. Allenson.
Religious Toleration & Persecution in Ancient
Rome. Greenwood.
Gutfeld, Arnon.
xGutfeld, Arnon.
Montana's Agony: Years of War & Hysteria,
1917-1921. U Presses Fla.
Gutgesell, Howard P.
xGutgesell, Howard P.
Atlas of Pediatric Echocardiography. Har-Row.
Guth, Christine.
xGuth, Christine.
The Arts of Shinto. Weatherhill.
Guth, Hans P. *see* Guth, Hans Paul.
Guth, Hans Paul, 1926-
xGuth, Hans P.
American English Today. McGraw.
American English Today. McGraw.
Concise English Workbook. Wadsworth Pub.
The Uses of Language. McGraw.
Words & Ideas: A Handbook for College
Writing. Wadsworth Pub.
Guth, Phyllis.
xGuth, Phyllis.
Crafts for Kids. TAB Bks.
Gutheil, Emil. *see* Gutheil, Emil A.
Gutheil, Emil A.
xGutheil, Emil.
Handbook of Dream Analysis. Liveright.
Guthmundsson, Barthi.
xGuthmundsson, Barthi.
The Origin of the Icelanders. U of Nebr Pr.
Guthorn, Peter J.
xGuthorn, Peter J.

American Maps & Map Makers of the
Revolution. Freneau.
British Maps of the American Revolution.
Freneau.
Guthrie, A. B. *see* Guthrie, Alfred Bertram.
Guthrie, Al.
xGuthrie, Al.
Hospitality Route. A Guthrie.
Guthrie, Alfred Bertram, 1901-
xGuthrie, A. B.
The Last Valley. HM.
No Second Wind. HM.
The Way West. Larlin Corp.
The Way West. Bantam.
Guthrie, Andrew, 1915-
xGuthrie, Andrew.
Vacuum Technology. Wiley.
Guthrie, Anna M. *see* Guthrie, Anna M. B.
Guthrie, Anna M. B.
xGuthrie, Anna M.
Wordsworth & Tolstoi & Other Papers.
Folcroft.
Guthrie, David L.
xGuthrie, David L.
ed. A Solar Energy Bibliography. Info Transfer.
Guthrie, Edwin. *see* Guthrie, Edwin Ray.
Guthrie, Edwin R.
xGuthrie, Edwin R.
The Psychology of Human Conflict: The Clash
of Motives Within the Individual.
Greenwood.
Guthrie, Edwin Ray, 1886-1959
xGuthrie, Edwin.
The Psychology of Learning. Peter Smith.
Guthrie, Helen. *see* Guthrie, Helen Andrews.
Guthrie, Helen A. *see* Guthrie, Helen Andrews.
Guthrie, Helen Andrews.
xGuthrie, Helen.
Introductory Nutrition. Mosby.
xGuthrie, Helen A.
Programmed Nutrition. Mosby.
Guthrie, James. *see* Guthrie, James W.
Guthrie, James W.
xGuthrie, James.
Teachers & Politics. Phi Delta Kappa.
Guthrie, John T.
xGuthrie, John T.
Cognition, Curriculum & Comprehension. Intl
Reading.
Guthrie, Kenneth M., 1922-
xGuthrie, Kenneth M.
ed. Work Items for Construction Estimating.
Craftsman.
Guthrie, Ramon, 1896-
xGuthrie, Ramon.
Maximum Security Ward. FS&G.
Guthrie, Robert V.
xGuthrie, Robert V.
Even the Rat Was White: A Historical View of
Psychology. Har-Row.
Guthrie, Rufus K.
xGuthrie, Rufus K.
Food Sanitation. AVI.
Guthrie, Thomas A. *see* Guthrie, Thomas Anstey.
Guthrie, Thomas Anstey, 1856-1934
xGuthrie, Thomas A.
Talking Horse. Arno.
Guthrie, Tyrone, Sir, 1900-
xGuthrie, Tyrone.
In Various Directions: A View of the Theatre.
Greenwood.
Guthrie, W. D. *see* Guthrie, William Dameron.
Guthrie, W. K. *see* Guthrie, William Keith Chambers.
Guthrie, William D. *see* Guthrie, William Dameron.
Guthrie, William Dameron, 1859-1935
xGuthrie, W. D.
Lectures on the Fourteenth Article of
Amendment to the Constitution of the
United States. Da Capo.
xGuthrie, William D.

Lectures on the Fourteenth Article of
Amendment to the Constitution of the
United States. Johnson Repr.
Guthrie, William K. *see* Guthrie, William Keith
Chambers.
Guthrie, William Keith Chambers, 1906-
xGuthrie, W. K.
A History of Greek Philosophy. Cambridge U
Pr.
xGuthrie, William K.
Greeks & Their Gods. Beacon Pr.
Sophists. Cambridge U Pr.
Guthrie, Woody.
xGuthrie, Woody.
Born to Win. Macmillan.
Bound for Glory. Dutton.
Bound for Glory. NAL.
Gutierrez, Gustavo.
xGutierrez, Gustavo.
Liberation & Change. John Knox.
Gutierrez, Luis T.
xGutierrez, Luis T.
Ecosystem Succession: A General Hypothesis
& a Test Model of a Grassland. MIT Pr.
Gutman, Bill.
xGutman, Bill.
Famous Baseball Stars. Dodd.
Football Superstars of the '70s. Messner.
Gamebreakers of the NFL. Random.
Great Sports Feats of the 70's. Messner.
Modern Baseball Superstars. Dodd.
Modern Football Superstars. Dodd.
Modern Hockey Superstars. Dodd.
Modern Soccer Superstars. Dodd.
More Modern Baseball Superstars. Dodd.
More Modern Women Superstars. Dodd.
The Picture Life of Reggie Jackson. Avon.
Superstars of the Sports World. Messner.
Gutman, Herbert G. *see* Gutman, Herbert George.
Gutman, Herbert George, 1928-
xGutman, Herbert G.
Work Culture & Society in Industrializing
America: Essays in America's Working Class
& Social History. Random.
Gutman, Richard.
xGutman, Richard.
American Diner. Har-Row.
American Diner. Har-Row.
xGutman, Richard J.
John Wilkes Booth Himself. Hired Hand.
Gutman, Richard J. *see* Gutman, Richard.
Gutman, Robert.
xGutman, Robert.
ed. People & Buildings. Basic.
Gutman, Robert W.
xGutman, Robert W.
Richard Wagner: The Man, His Mind, & His
Music. HarBraceJ.
Gutman, Walter. *see* Gutman, Walter Knowlton.
Gutman, Walter Knowlton, 1903-
xGutman, Walter.
The Gutman Letter. Ultramarine Pub.
Gutmann, F. *see* Gutmann, Fredrick T.
Gutmann, Felix.
xGutmann, Felix.
Organic Semiconductors. Krieger.
Gutmann, Fredrick T., 1915-
xGutmann, F.
Metric Guide to Mechanical Design &
Drafting. Indus Pr.
Gutmann, Viktor.
xGutmann, Viktor.
Coordination Chemistry in Non-Aqueous
Solutions. Springer-Verlag.
The Donor-Acceptor Approach to Molecular
Interactions. Plenum Pub.
Gutnik, Martin. *see* Gutnik, Martin J.
Gutnik, Martin J.
xGutnik, Martin.

Energy: Its Past, Its Present, Its Future.
Childrens.
Gutsch, Kenneth U. *see* Gutsch, Kenneth Urial.
Gutsch, Kenneth Urial.
xGutsch, Kenneth U.
Guidance in Action: Ideas & Innovations for
School Counselors. P-H.
Insights into Human Development:
Commentaries. U Pr of Miss.
Nexus Psychotherapy: Between Humanism &
Behaviorism. C C Thomas.
Gutsche, C. David. *see* Gutsche, Carl David.
Gutsche, Carl David.
xGutsche, C. David.
Fundamentals of Organic Chemistry. P-H.
Guttchen, Robert S., 1926-1971
xGuttchen, Robert S.
Felix Adler. Twayne.
Guttenplan, Samuel. *see* Guttenplan, Samuel D.
Guttenplan, Samuel D.
xGuttenplan, Samuel.
ed. Mind & Language: Wolfson College
Lectures 1974. Oxford U Pr.
Guttentag, Marcia.
xGuttentag, Marcia.
Undoing Sex Stereotypes: Research &
Resources for Educators. McGraw.
Gutteridge, H. C. *see* Gutteridge, Harold Cooke.
Gutteridge, Harold Cooke.
xGutteridge, H. C.
The Law of Bankers' Commercial Credits. Intl
Pubns Serv.
Guttmacher, Alan F. *see* Guttmacher, Alan Frank.
Guttmacher, Alan Frank, 1898-
xGuttmacher, Alan F.
Pregnancy, Birth & Family Planning: A Guide
for Expectant Parents in the 1970s. Viking
Pr.
Guttman, Irwin.
xGuttman, T.
Statistical Tolerance Regions: Classical &
Bayesian. Hafner.
Guttman, Mel.
xGuttman, Mel.
A Comprehensive Guide to College & Career
Planning. Rosen Pr.
Guttman, Samuel. *see* Guttman, Samuel A.
Guttman, Samuel A.
xGuttman, Samuel.
ed. The Concordance to the Standard Edition
of the Complete Psychological Works of
Sigmund Freud. G K Hall.
Guttman, T. *see* Guttman, Irwin.
Guttmann, Allen.
xGuttmann, Allen.
From Ritual to Record: The Nature of Modern
Sports. Columbia U Pr.
Guttmann, R. *see* Guttmann, Ronald D.
Guttmann, Ronald D.
xGuttmann, R.
ed. Immunology. Krieger.
Guttridge, George H. *see* Guttridge, George Herbert.
Guttridge, George Herbert, 1898-
xGuttridge, George H.
English Whiggism & the American Revolution.
AMS Pr.
Gutwinski, W. *see* Gutwinski, Waldemar.
Gutwinski, Waldemar.
xGutwinski, W.
Cohesion in Literary Texts: A Study of Some
Grammatical & Lexical Features of English
Discourse. Mouton.
Gutwirth, Marcel. *see* Gutwirth, Marcel Marc.
Gutwirth, Marcel Marc, 1923-
xGutwirth, Marcel.
Stendhal. Twayne.
Gutzke, Manford. *see* Gutzke, Manford George.
Gutzke, Manford G. *see* Gutzke, Manford George.
Gutzke, Manford George.
xGutzke, Manford.

Plain Talk on Romans. Zondervan.
xGutzke, Manford G.
Plain Talk About Christian Words. Zondervan.
Plain Talk on Acts. Zondervan.
Plain Talk on Deuteronomy. Zondervan.
Plain Talk on Ephesians. Zondervan.
Plain Talk on Exodus. Zondervan.
Plain Talk on Genesis. Zondervan.
Plain Talk on Hebrews. Zondervan.
Plain Talk on Isaiah. Zondervan.
Plain Talk on James. Zondervan.
Plain Talk on John. Zondervan.
Plain Talk on Luke. Zondervan.
Plain Talk on Mark. Zondervan.
Plain Talk on Matthew. Zondervan.
Plain Talk on Peter & Jude. Zondervan.
Plain Talk on Revelation. Zondervan.
Plain Talk on Thessalonians. Zondervan.
Plain Talk on Timothy, Titus, & Philemon.
Zondervan.
Gutzke, Manfred George.
xGutzke, Manford G.
Plain Talk on the Epistles of John. Zondervan.
Guy, A. G. *see* Guy, Albert G.
Guy, Albert G.
xGuy, A. G.
Essentials of Materials Science. McGraw.
Guy, Francis S. *see* Guy, Francis Shaw.
Guy, Francis Shaw, 1906-
xGuy, Francis S.
Edmund Bailey O'Callaghan: A Study in
American Historiography (1797-1880). AMS
Pr.
Guy, Randor.
xGuy, Randor.
Indian Ribaldry. C E Tuttle.
Guy, Rosa.
xGuy, Rosa.
The Disappearance. Delacorte
Edith Jackson. Viking Pr.
The Friends. HR&W.
Guyau, Jean Marie, 1854-1888
xGuyau, M.
The Non-Religion of the Future: A Sociological
Study. Schocken.
Guyau, M. *see* Guyau, Jean Marie.
Guyer, Paul, 1948-
xGuyer, Paul.
Kant & the Claims of Taste. Harvard U Pr.
Guyler, Vivan V. *see* Guyler, Vivian Varney.
Guyler, Vivian Varney.
xGuyler, Vivan V.
Design in Nature. Davis Mass.
Guyol, N. B. *see* Guyol, Nathaniel B.
Guyol, Nathaniel B., 1908-
xGuyol, N. B.
The World Electric Power Industry. U of Cal
Pr.
Guyon, Rene, 1876-
xGuyon, Rene.
The Ethics of Sexual Acts. Octagon.
Guyot, Charles.
xGuyot, Charles.
The Legend of the City of Ys. U of Mass Pr.
Guyton, Arthur C.
xGuyton, Arthur C.
Textbook of Medical Physiology. Saunders.
Guyton, Arthur C. *see* Guyton, Arthur G.
Guyton, Arthur G.
xGuyton, Arthur C.
Physiology of the Human Body. Saunders.
Guze, Samuel B.
xGuze, Samuel B.
Criminality & Psychiatric Disorders. Oxford U
Pr.
Guzie, Tad. *see* Guzie, Tad W.
Guzie, Tad W.
xGuzie, Tad.
The Forgiveness of Sin. Thomas More.
Guzman, Martin L. *see* Guzman, Martin Luis.

Guzman, Martin Luis, 1887-
xGuzman, Martin L.
The Eagle & the Serpent. Peter Smith.
Guzman, Ralph C.
xGuzman, Ralph C.
The Political Socialization of the Mexican
American People. Arno.
Guzzwell, John.
xGuzzwell, John.
Modern Wooden Yacht Construction:
Cold-Molding Joinery, Fitting Out. Intl
Marine.
Trekka Round the World. De Graff.
Gwaltney, Francis I. see Gwaltney, Francis Irby.
Gwaltney, Francis Irby.
xGwaltney, Francis I.
Idols & Axle Grease. G K Hall.
Gwartney, James D.
xGwartney, James D.
Macroeconomics: Private & Public Choice.
Acad Pr.
Microeconomics: Private & Public Choice.
Acad Pr.
Gwatkin, H. M. see Gwatkin, Henry Melvill.
Gwatkin, Henry M. see Gwatkin, Henry Melvill.
Gwatkin, Henry Melvill, 1844-1916
xGwatkin, H. M.
Early Church History to A. D. 313. Gordon
Pr.
xGwatkin, Henry M.
The Arian Controversy. AMS Pr.
Early Church History to A.D. 313. AMS Pr.
Gwatkin, Ralph B. see Gwatkin, Ralph B. L.
Gwatkin, Ralph B. L.
xGwatkin, Ralph B.
Fertilization Mechanisms in Man & Mammals.
Plenum Pub.
Gwinner, Robert F.
xGwinner, Robert F.
Marketing: An Environmental Perspective.
West Pub.
Gwon, Pu G. see Gwon, Pu Gill.
Gwon, Pu Gill.
xGwon, Pu G.
Dynamic Art of Breaking. Wehman.
Gwyn, Julian.
xGwyn, Julian.
The Enterprising Admiral: The Personal
Fortune of Admiral Sir Peter Warren.
McGill-Queens U Pr.
Gwyn, William B.
xGwyn, William B.
Pref. by Democracy & the Cost of Politics in
Britain. Greenwood.
Gwynn, Denis. see Gwynn, Denis Rolleston.
Gwynn, Denis Rolleston, 1893-
xGwynn, Denis.
The Life of John Redmond. Arno.
Gwynn, Frederick. see Gwynn, Frederick Landis.
Gwynn, Frederick L. see Gwynn, Frederick Landis.
Gwynn, Frederick Landis.
xGwynn, Frederick.
Sturge Moore & the Life of Art. Folcroft.
xGwynn, Frederick L.
The Fiction of J. D. Salinger. U of Pittsburgh
Pr.
Gwynn, Stephen. see Gwynn, Stephen Lucius.
Gwynn, Stephen L. see Gwynn, Stephen Lucius.
Gwynn, Stephen Lucius, 1864-1950
xGwynn, Stephen.
Fond Opinions. Kennikat.
The Life of Horace Walpole. Arno.
Life of Horace Walpole. Haskell.
Life of Horace Walpole. R West.
The Life of Sir Walter Scott. R West.
The Masters of English Literature. R West.
Oliver Goldsmith. Folcroft.
Oliver Goldsmith. Haskell.
Thomas Moore. Folcroft.
xGwynn, Stephen L.

Fond Opinions. Arno.
Life of Horace Walpole. Kennikat.
Masters of English Literature. Arno.
Gwynne, Fred.
xGwynne, Fred.
illus. The Sixteen Hand Horse. Windmill Bks.
Gyarmati, I. see Gyarmati, Istvan.
Gyarmati, Istvan.
xGyarmati, I.
Non-Equilibrium Thermodynamics: Field
Theory & Variational Principles.
Springer-Verlag.
Gyepes, Michael T.
xGyepes, Michael T.
Cardiac Catheterization & Angiocardiography
in Severe Neonatal Heart Disease. C C
Thomas.
Gyftopoulos, E. P.
xGyftopoulos, Elias.
Potential Fuel Effectiveness in Industry.
Ballinger Pub.
Gyftopoulos, Elias. see Gyftopoulos, E. P.
Gyles, Mary F. see Gyles, Mary Francis.
Gyles, Mary Francis.
xGyles, Mary F.
ed. Laudatores Temporis Acti: Studies in
Memory of Wallace Everett Caldwell. U of
NC Pr.
Gymer, Roger G.
xGymer, Roger G.
Chemistry in the Natural World. Heath.
Gyorgy, Andrew, 1917-
xGyorgy, Andrew.
ed. Communism in Eastern Europe. Ind U Pr.
Governments of Danubian Europe. Greenwood.
ed. Innovation in Communist Systems.
Westview.
Gyorgyey, Clara.
xGyorgyey, Clara.
Ferenc Molnar. Twayne.
Gyulay, Jo-Eileen.
xGyulay, Jo-Eileen.
The Dying Child. McGraw.
Haac, Oscar A.
xHaac, Oscar A.
Actualite et Avenir: A Guide to France & to
French Conversation. P-H.
Marivaux. Twayne.
Haack, Susan.
xHaack, Susan.
Philosophy of Logics. Cambridge U Pr.
Haack, W. see Haack, Wolfgang.
Haack, Wolfgang.
xHaack, W.
Lectures on Partial & Pfaffian Differential
Equations. Pergamon.
Haag, Ernest Van Den. see Van den Haag, Ernest.
Haag, Leonard H.
xHaag, Leonard H.
Cash Management & Short Term Investments
for Colleges & Universities. Natl Assn Coll.
Haaga, John.
xHaaga, John.
Computed Tomography of Abdominal
Abnormalities. Mosby.
Haagensen, Cushman D. see Haagensen, Cushman Davis.
Haagensen, Cushman Davis, 1900-
xHaagensen, Cushman D.
Diseases of the Breast. Saunders.
Haagensen, Jan.
xHaagensen, Jan.
Like a Diamondback in the Trunk of a
Witness's Buick. Cleveland St Univ Poetry
Ctr.
Haan, C. T. see Haan, Charles Thomas.
Haan, Charles Thomas, 1941-
xHaan, C. T.
Statistical Methods in Hydrology. Iowa St U
Pr.
Haan, Martin De. see De Haan, Martin.

Haan, Martin R. De. see De Haan, Martin R.
Haan, Sheri D. see Haan, Sheri Dunham.
Haan, Sheri Dunham.
xHaan, Sheri D.
Good News for Children. Baker Bk.
Haar, Charles M. see Haar, Charles Monroe.
Haar, Charles Monroe, 1921-
xHaar, Charles M.
The End of Innocence: A Suburban Reader.
Scott F.
Housing the Poor in Suburbia: Public Policy at
the Grass Roots. Ballinger Pub.
Haar, Francis.
xHaar, Francis.
Artists of Hawaii. U Pr of Hawaii.
Haar, Jerry, 1947-
xHaar, Jerry.
The Politics of Higher Education in Brazil.
Praeger.
Haas, Ben.
xHaas, Ben.
Daisy Canfield. S&S.
The Foragers. PB.
Haas, Charlie.
xHaas, Charlie.
Over the Edge. Grove.
The Soul Hit. Har-Row.
Haas, David F.
xHaas, David F.
Interaction in the Thai Bureaucracy: Structure,
Culture, & Social Exchange. Westview.
Haas, Edward F.
xHaas, Edward F.
DeLesseps S. Morrison & the Image of
Reform: New Orleans Politics, 1946-1961. La
State U Pr.
Haas, Elsa De. see De Haas, Elsa.
Haas, Ernest B. see Haas, Ernst B.
Haas, Ernst, 1921-
xHaas, Ernst.
The Creation. Penguin.
Haas, Ernst B.
xHaas, Ernst B.
Dynamics of International Relations.
Greenwood.
xHaas, Ernst B.
Human Rights & International Action: The
Case of Freedom of Association. Stanford U
Pr.
The Obsolescence of Regional Integration
Theory. U of Cal Intl St.
Haas, Frederick C.
xHaas, Frederick C.
Living in a Metric America. Haas.
Haas, Harold M. see Haas, Harold Milburn.
Haas, Harold Milburn.
xHaas, Harold M.
Social & Economic Aspects of the Chain Store
Movement. Arno.
Haas, Irvin.
xHaas, Irvin.
America's Historic Inns & Taverns. Arco.
America's Historic Ships: Replicas &
Restorations. Arco.
Citadels, Ramparts, & Stockades: America's
Historic Forts. Everest Hse.
Haas, John J.
xHaas, John J.
Corporate Social Responsibilities in a Changing
Society. Gaus.
Haas, Kenneth. see Haas, Kenneth Brooks.
Haas, Kenneth Brooks, 1898-
xHaas, Kenneth.
Opportunities in Sales & Marketing Careers.
Natl Textbk.
Haas, Kurt.
xHaas, Kurt.

Abnormal Psychology. Van Nos Reinhold.
Growth Encounter: A Guide for Groups.
Nelson-Hall.
You Can Change Your Personality--& Your
Life. Nelson-Hall.
Haas, Mary. *see* Haas, Mary Rosamond.
Haas, Mary R. *see* Haas, Mary Rosamond.
Haas, Mary Rosamond, 1910-
xHaas, Mary.
Thai Reader. Spoken Lang Serv.
xHaas, Mary R.
Thai Vocabulary. Spoken Lang Serv.
Haas, Ralph.
xHaas, Ralph.
Pavement Management Systems. McGraw.
Haas, Raymond M.
xHaas, Raymond M.
Long-Range New Product Planning in
Business: A Conceptual Model. McClain.
Haas, Robert. *see* Haas, Robert Bartlett.
Haas, Robert B. *see* Haas, Robert Bartlett.
Haas, Robert Bartlett.
xHaas, Robert.
Muybridge: Man in Motion. U of Cal Pr.
xHaas, Robert B.
A Catalogue of the Published & Unpublished
Writings of Gertrude Stein - Exhibited in the
Yale University Library 22 February to 29
March 1941. Folcroft.
Haas, Robert F. *see* Haas, Robert W.
Haas, Robert W.
xHaas, Robert F.
Industrial Marketing Management. Van Nos
Reinhold.
Haase, John.
xHaase, John.
Big Red. Har-Row.
Haase, Rolf.
xHaase, Rolf.
Thermodynamics of Irreversible Processes.
A-W.
Habakkuk, H. J.
xHabakkuk, H. J.
Population Growth & Economic Development
Since 1750. Humanities.
Habbe, S. *see* Habbe, Stephen.
Habbe, Stephen, 1903-
xHabbe, S.
Personality Adjustments of Adolescent Boys
with Impaired Hearing. AMS Pr.
Habel, K. *see* Habel, Karl.
Habel, Karl.
xHabel, K.
ed. Fundamental Techniques in Virology. Acad
Pr.
Habel, Norman C.
xHabel, Norman C.
Literary Criticism of the Old Testament.
Fortress.
Habel, Robert E. *see* Habel, Robert Earl.
Habel, Robert Earl, 1918-
xHabel, Robert E.
Guide to the Dissection of Domestic
Ruminants. Habel.
Habenstreit, Barbara.
xHabenstreit, Barbara.
Changing America & the Supreme Court.
Messner.
Haber, Audrey.
xHaber, Audrey.
Fundamentals of Psychology. A-W.
General Statistics. A-W.
Haber, Edgar.
xHaber, Edgar.
ed. Antibodies in Human Diagnosis & Therapy.
Raven.
Haber, Eitan. *see* Haber, Eithan.
Haber, Eithan.
xHaber, Eitan.

Menahem Begin: The Legend & the Man.
Delacorte.
Haber, Francis C.
xHaber, Francis C.
The Age of the World: Moses to Darwin.
Greenwood.
Haber, Fred.
xHaber, Fred.
An Introduction to Information &
Communication Theory. A-W.
Haber, Heinz.
xHaber, Heinz.
Our Blue Planet: The Story of the Earth's
Evolution. Scribner.
Haber, Joyce.
xHaber, Joyce.
The Users. Delacorte.
The Users. Dell.
Haber, Judith.
xHaber, Judith.
Comprehensive Psychiatric Nursing. McGraw.
Haber, L. F. *see* Haber, Ludwig Fritz.
Haber, Louis.
xHaber, Louis.
Women Pioneers of Science. HarBraceJ.
Haber, Ludwig Fritz.
xHaber, L. F.
Chemical Industry During the Nineteenth
Century: A Study of the Economic Aspect of
Applied Chemistry in Europe & North
America. Oxford U Pr.
Chemical Industry, 1900-1930: International
Growth & Technological Change. Oxford U
Pr.
Haber, Paul.
xHaber, Paul.
Inside Handball. Contemp Bks.
Haber, Ralph. *see* Haber, Ralph Norman.
Haber, Ralph N. *see* Haber, Ralph Norman.
Haber, Ralph Norman.
xHaber, Ralph.
The Psychology of Visual Perception. HR&W.
xHaber, Ralph N.
Psychology of Visual Perception. HR&W.
Haber, Tom B. *see* Haber, Tom Burns.
Haber, Tom Burns, 1900-
xHaber, Tom B.
Comparative Study of the Beowulf & the
Aeneid. Phaeton.
Comparative Study of the Beowulf & the
Aeneid. R West.
Haber, William, 1899-
xHaber, William.
Industrial Relations in the Building Industry.
Arno.
Haberer, Joseph, 1929-
xHaberer, Joseph.
Politics & the Community of Science. Van Nos
Reinhold.
Haberlen, John.
xHaberlen, John.
Mastering Conducting Techniques. Mark
Foster Mus.
Haberler, Gottfried.
xHaberler, Gottfried.
Economic Growth & Stability: An Analysis of
Economic Change & Policies. Humanities.
Economic Growth & Stability: An Analysis of
Economic Change & Policies. Inst Humane.
Economic Growth & Stability: An Analysis of
Economic Change & Policies. Nash Pub.
The World Economy, Money, & the Great
Depression. Am Enterprise.
Haberler, Gottfried. *see* Haberler, Gottfried, 1900-.
Haberler, Gottfried, 1900-.
xHaberler, Gottfried.

Prosperity & Depression: A Theoretical
Analysis of Cyclical Movement. Atheneum.
Prosperity & Depression: A Theoretical
Analysis of Cyclical Movements. Harvard U
Pr.
Haberling, Wilhelm, 1871-1940
xHaberling, Wilhelm.
German Medicine. AMS Pr.
Haberman. *see* Haberman, Charles M.
Haberman, Charles M.
xHaberman.
Use of Digital Computers for Engineering
Applications. Merrill.
Haberman, Jacob.
xHaberman, Jacob.
Maimonides & Aquinas: A Contemporary
Appraisal. Ktav.
Haberman, Paul W.
xHaberman, Paul W.
Alcohol, Other Drugs & Violent Death. Oxford
U Pr.
Haberman, R. *see* Haberman, Richard.
Haberman, Richard, 1945-
xHaberman, R.
Mathematical Models: Mechanical Vibrations,
Population, Dynamics & Traffic Flow, An
Introduction to Applied Mathematics. P-H.
Haberman, Shelby J.
xHaberman, Shelby J.
The Analysis of Frequency Data. U of Chicago
Pr.
Haberman, William L.
xHaberman, William L.
Engineering Thermodynamics. Allyn.
Habermas, Jurgen.
xHabermas, Jurgen.
Communication & the Evolution of Society.
Beacon Pr.
Knowledge & Human Interests. Beacon Pr.
Legitimation Crisis. Beacon Pr.
Theory & Practice. Beacon Pr.
Toward a Rational Society: Student Protest,
Science, & Politics. Beacon Pr.
Habershon, Ada R. *see* Habershon, Ada Ruth.
Habershon, Ada Ruth, 1861-
xHabershon, Ada R.
Study of the Miracles. Kregel.
Habets, Alfred, 1839-1908
xHabets, Alfred.
Borodin & Liszt. AMS Pr.
Habib, I. S.
xHabib, I. S.
Engineering Analysis Methods. Lexington Bks.
Habig, Marion. *see* Habig, Marion Alphonse.
Habig, Marion A. *see* Habig, Marion Alphonse.
Habig, Marion Alphonse, 1901-
xHabig, Marion.
Franciscan Book of Saints. Franciscan Herald.
xHabig, Marion A.
In Journeyings Often: Franciscan Pioneers in
the Orient. Franciscan Inst.
Habraken, N. J.
xHabraken, N. John.
Variations: The Systematic Design of Supports.
MIT Pr.
Habraken, N. John. *see* Habraken, N. J.
Hacche, Graham.
xHacche, Graham.
The Theory of Economic Growth: An
Introduction. St Martin.
Hack, Michel, 1947-
xHack, Michel.
Decidability Questions for Petri Nets. Garland
Pub.
Hack, Roy K. *see* Hack, Roy Kenneth.
Hack, Roy Kenneth.
xHack, Roy K.
God in Greek Philosophy to the Time of
Socrates. B Franklin.
Hackel, Eduard. *see* Hackel, Eduardo.

Hackel, Eduardo.
  xHackel, Eduard.
    Monographia Festucarum Europaearum.
    Johnson Repr.
Hackensmith, Charles W. *see* Hackensmith, Charles
  William.
Hackensmith, Charles William, 1906-
  xHackensmith, Charles W.
    History of Physical Education. Har-Row.
Hacker. *see* Hacker, Diana.
Hacker, Andrew.
  xHacker, Andrew.
    ed. Corporation Take-Over. Arno.
    End of the American Era. Atheneum.
Hacker, Diana.
  xHacker.
    A Practical Guide for Writers. Winthrop.
Hacker, Frederick J.
  xHacker, Frederick J.
    Crusaders, Criminals, Crazies: Terror &
    Terrorism in Our Time. Norton.
Hacker, Leonard.
  xHacker, Leonard.
    Cinematic Design. Arno.
Hacker, Louis M. *see* Hacker, Louis Morton.
Hacker, Louis Morton, 1899-
  xHacker, Louis M.
    American Capitalism. Krieger.
    The Course of American Economic Growth &
    Development. Krieger.
    Proskauer, His Life & Times. U of Ala Pr.
Hacker, P. M. *see* Hacker, Peter Michael Stephan.
Hacker, Peter Michael Stephan.
  xHacker, P. M.
    Insight & Illusion: Wittgenstein on Philosophy
    & the Metaphysics of Experience. Oxford U
    Pr.
    Insight & Illusion: Wittgenstein on Philosophy
    & the Metaphysics of Experience. Oxford U
    Pr.
Hackett, Brian.
  xHackett, Brian.
    Planting Design. McGraw.
Hackett, Charles J.
  xHackett, Charles J.
    The Last Happy Hour. Manor Bks.
Hackett, Donald W., 1945-
  xHackett, Donald W.
    Franchising: The State of the Art. Am Mktg.
Hackett, Francis, 1883-1962
  xHackett, Francis.
    Francis the First. Greenwood.
    On American Books. Arden Lib.
    On American Books. Darby Bks.
    On Judging Books: In General & in Particular.
    Arno.
    On Judging Books: In General & in Particular.
    Norwood Edns.
Hackett, H. *see* Hackett, Herbert.
Hackett, Herbert.
  xHackett, H.
    Of Studies: Reading & Writing. McGraw.
Hackett, James H. *see* Hackett, James Henry.
Hackett, James Henry, 1800-1871
  xHackett, James H.
    Notes, Criticisms, & Correspondence Upon
    Shakespeare's Plays & Actors. Arno.
Hackett, John. *see* Hackett, John Winthrop.
Hackett, John Winthrop, Sir, 1910-
  xHackett, John.
    The Third World War: August 1985.
    Macmillan.
Hackett, L. C. *see* Hackett, Layne C.
Hackett, Laura. *see* Hackett, Laura L.
Hackett, Laura L.
  xHackett, Laura.
    Anatomy of Reading. Krieger.
Hackett, Layne C.
  xHackett, L. C.

    A Guide to Movement Exploration. Peek
    Pubns.
Hackett, Neil J.
  xHackett, Neil J.
    The World of Europe. Ind Sch Pr.
Hackett, Patricia.
  xHackett, Patricia.
    The Musical Classroom: Models, Skills, &
    Backgrounds for Elementary Teaching. P-H.
Hackett, Stuart C. *see* Hackett, Stuart Cornelius.
Hackett, Stuart Cornelius.
  xHackett, Stuart C.
    Oriental Philosophy: A Westerner's Guide to
    Eastern Thought. U of Wis Pr.
Hacking, Ian.
  xHacking, Ian.
    Concise Introduction to Logic. Random.
  xHacking, Ian M.
    Logic of Statistical Inference. Cambridge U Pr.
Hacking, Ian M. *see* Hacking, Ian.
Hackler, James C.
  xHackler, James C.
    The Prevention of Youthful Crime: The Great
    Stumble Forward. Methuen Inc.
Hackman, George G. *see* Hackman, George Gottlob.
Hackman, George Gottlob.
  xHackman, George G.
    Sumerian & Akkadian Administrative Texts:
    From Pre-Dynastic Times to the End of the
    Akkad Dynasty. AMS Pr.
Hackmann, Duane.
  xHackmann, Duane.
    Nebraska Subcounty Population Estimates. Bur
    Busn Res U Nebr.
Hackney, Harold.
  xHackney, Harold L.
    Counseling Strategies & Objectives. P-H.
Hackney, Harold L. *see* Hackney, Harold.
Hackney, Sheldon.
  xHackney, Sheldon.
    Populism to Progressivism in Alabama.
    Princeton U Pr.
Hackwood, Frederick W. *see* Hackwood, Frederick
  William.
Hackwood, Frederick William, 1851-
  xHackwood, Frederick W.
    Christ Lore: Being the Legends, Traditions,
    Myths, Symbols, Customs, & Superstitions of
    the Christian Church. Gale.
Hadas, Moses, 1900-
  xHadas, Moses.
    Ancilla to Classical Reading. Columbia U Pr.
    The Greek Ideal & Its Survival. Gannon.
    History of Greek Literature. Columbia U Pr.
    History of Latin Literature. Columbia U Pr.
    History of Rome from Its Origins to 529 A.D.
    Peter Smith.
    Imperial Rome. Silver.
    Imperial Rome. Time-Life.
Hadd, H. E. *see* Hadd, Harry E.
Hadd, Harry E.
  xHadd, H. E.
    Conjugates of Steroid Hormones. Acad Pr.
Hadd, John R.
  xHadd, John R.
    Evolution: Reconciling the Controversy.
    Kronos Pr.
Hadda, Janet.
  xHadda, Janet.
    Yankev Glatshteyn. Twayne.
Haddad, C. A.
  xHaddad, C. A.
    Operation Apricot. Har-Row.
Haddad, William W.
  xHaddad, William W.
    ed. Nationalism in a Non-National State: The
    Dissolution of the Ottoman Empire. Ohio St
    U Pr.
Haddad's Fine Arts.
  xHaddad's Fine Arts Inc.

    Through One's Eyes. Haddad's Fine Arts.
Haddad's Fine Arts Inc. *see* Haddad's Fine Arts.
Haddan, Eugene E.
  xHaddan, Eugene E.
    Evolving Instruction. Macmillan.
Haddelsey, Vincent.
  xHaddelsey, Vincent.
    Haddelsey's Horses. St Martin.
Hadden, James C. *see* Hadden, James Cuthbert.
Hadden, James Cuthbert, 1861-1914
  xHadden, James C.
    Chopin. AMS Pr.
Hadden, Jeffrey K.
  xHadden, Jeffrey K.
    Gathering Storm in the Churches. Doubleday.
    ed. Religion in Radical Transition. Transaction
    Bks.
Haddix, Cecille.
  xHaddix, Cecille.
    Who Speaks for Appalachia?. PB.
Haddle, Jan, 1950-
  xHaddle, Jan.
    The Complete Book of the Appaloosa. A S
    Barnes.
Haddon, Alfred C. *see* Haddon, Alfred Cort.
Haddon, Alfred Cort, 1855-1940
  xHaddon, Alfred C.
    The Decorative Art of British New Guinea: A
    Study in Papuan Ethnography. AMS Pr.
    Evolution in Art: As Illustrated by the Life
    Histories of Designs. AMS Pr.
    History of Anthropology. AMS Pr.
    History of Anthropology. Gordon Pr.
    The Study of Man. AMS Pr.
    The Wanderings of Peoples. AMS Pr.
Haddon, Kathleen.
  xHaddon, Kathleen.
    Artists in String: String Figures, Their Regional
    Distribution & Social Significance. AMS Pr.
Haddow, Anna.
  xHaddow, Anna.
    Political Science in American Colleges &
    Universities, 1630-1900. Octagon.
Haddox, John H. *see* Haddox, John Herbert.
Haddox, John Herbert, 1929-
  xHaddox, John H.
    Vasconcelos of Mexico: Philosopher & Prophet.
    U of Tex Pr.
Haden, Pat.
  xHaden, Pat.
    Pat Haden: My Rookie Season with Los
    Angeles Rams. Morrow.
Haders, Phyllis.
  xHaders, Phyllis.
    Sunshine & Shadow: The Amish & Their
    Quilts. Universe.
Hadfield, Charles. *see* Hadfield, Ellis Charles Raymond.
Hadfield, Ellis Charles Raymond.
  xHadfield, Charles.
    Canals of South & Southeast England. Kelley.
    The Canals of South Wales & the Border.
    David & Charles.
    Inland Waterways. David & Charles.
    William Jessop, Engineer. David & Charles.
Hadfield, James A. *see* Hadfield, James Arthur.
Hadfield, James Arthur.
  xHadfield, James A.
    ed. Psychology & Modern Problems. Arno.
Hadfield, P. *see* Hadfield, Percival.
Hadfield, Percival.
  xHadfield, P.
    Traits of Divine Kingship in Africa.
    Greenwood.
  xHadfield, Percival.
    Traits of Divine Kingship in Africa. Negro U
    Pr.
Hadfield, Robert L.
  xHadfield, Robert L.

Mutiny at Sea. E M Coleman Ent.

Hadgopoulos, Saralyn P.
xHadgopoulos, Saralyn P.
Imagination's Wine. Windy Row.

Hadidian, Allen, 1950-
xHadidian, Allen.
Successful Discipling. Moody.

Hadley, Arthur T. see Hadley, Arthur Twining.

Hadley, Arthur Twining, 1856-1930
xHadley, Arthur T.
Baccalaureate Addresses & Other Talks on
Kindred Themes. Arno.
Conflict Between Liberty & Equality. Arno.
Economic Problems of Democracy. Arno.
Economic Problems of Democracy. Kennikat.
Some Influences in Modern Philosophic
Thought. Kennikat.
Standards of Public Morality. Arno.

Hadley, George, 1930-
xHadley, George.
Linear Algebra. A-W.

Hadley, George. see Hadley, George F.

Hadley, George F., 1930-
xHadley, George.
Linear Programming. A-W.

Hadley, Lee A., M.D.
xHadley, Lee A.
Anatomico-Roentgenographic Studies of the
Spine. C C Thomas.

Hadley, Leila.
xHadley, Leila.
Fielding's Guide to Traveling with Children in
Europe. Fielding.

Hadley, Roger.
xHadley, Roger.
Across the Generations: Old People & Young
Volunteers. Allen Unwin.

Hadlock, Charles. see Hadlock, Charles Robert.

Hadlock, Charles Robert.
xHadlock, Charles.
Field Theory & Its Classical Problems. Math
Assn.

Hadlow, Leonard, 1908-
xHadlow, Leonard.
Climate, Vegetation & Man. Greenwood.
Climate, Vegetation & Man. Philos Lib.

Hadorn, E. see Hadorn, Ernst.

Hadorn, Ernst, 1902-
xHadorn, E.
Experimental Studies of Amphibian
Development. Springer-Verlag.

Hadow, Grace E. see Hadow, Grace Eleanor.

Hadow, Grace Eleanor, 1875-1940
xHadow, Grace E.
Chaucer & His Times. Arno.

Hadow, W. H. see Hadow, William Henry.

Hadow, William H. see Hadow, William Henry.

Hadow, William Henry, Sir, 1859-1937
xHadow, W. H.
Studies in Modern Music. Kennikat.
xHadow, William H.
Collected Essays. Arno.
Music. AMS Pr.
Sonata Form. AMS Pr.

Hadwiger, Don F. see Hadwiger, Don Frank.

Hadwiger, Don Frank, 1930-
xHadwiger, Don F.
Federal Wheat Commodity Programs. Iowa St
U Pr.

Hady, Maureen E.
xHady, Maureen E.
Asian-American Periodicals & Newspapers: A
Union List of Holdings in the Library of the
State Historical Society of Wisconsin & the
Libraries of the University of
Wisconsin-Madison. State Hist Soc Wis.

Hadzsits, George D. see Hadzsits, George Depue.

Hadzsits, George Depue, 1875-
xHadzsits, George D.

Lucretius & His Influence. Cooper Sq.

Haeckel, Ernst. see Haeckel, Ernst Heinrich Philipp
August.

Haeckel, Ernst Heinrich Philipp August, 1834-1919
xHaeckel, Ernst.
Art Forms in Nature. Dover.
Art Forms in Nature. Peter Smith.
The Riddle of the Universe, at the Close of the
Nineteenth Century. R West.

Haefner, George E. see Haefner, George Edward.

Haefner, George Edward, 1897-
xHaefner, George E.
Critical Estimate of the Educational Theories -
Practices of A. Bronson Alcott. Greenwood.

Haefner, Ralph, 1894-
xHaefner, Ralph.
Educational Significance of Left-Handedness.
AMS Pr.

Haeger, John. see Haeger, John D.

Haeger, John D.
xHaeger, John.
The Bosses. Forum Pr MO.

Haeger, John W. see Haeger, John Winthrop.

Haeger, John Winthrop.
xHaeger, John W.
ed. Crisis & Prosperity in Sung China. U of
Ariz Pr.

Haendel, Dan, 1950-
xHaendel, Dan.
The Process of Priority Formulation: U.S.
Foreign Policy in the Indo-Pakistani War of
1971. Westview.

Haeussler, Ernest F.
xHaeussler, Ernest F.
Introductory Mathematical Analysis for
Students of Business & Economics. Reston.

Hafen, Brent Q.
xHafen, Brent Q.
First Aid for Health Emergencies. West Pub.
Medicines & Drugs: Problems & Risks, Use &
Abuse. Lea & Febiger.

Hafen, LeRoy Reuben, 1893-
xHafen, LeRoy R.
Broken Hand: The Life of Thomas Fitzpatrick,
Mountain Man, Guide & Indian Agent. Old
West.
Colorado: The Story of a Western
Commonwealth. AMS Pr.
ed. Overland Routes to the Gold Fields, 1859:
From Contemporary Diaries. Porcupine Pr.

Hafen, LeRoy R. see Hafen, LeRoy Reuben.

Hafer, Charles R., 1938-
xHafer, Charles R.
Electronics Engineering for Professional
Engineer's Examinations. McGraw.

Hafer, W. Keith.
xHafer, W. Keith.
Advertising Writing. West Pub.

Hafez, E. S. see Hafez, E. S. E.

Hafez, E. S. E.
xHafez, E. S.
ed. Accessory Glands of the Male
Reproductive Tract. Ann Arbor Science.
ed. Animal Growth & Nutrition. Lea &
Febiger.
Human Reproduction: Conception &
Contraception. Har-Row.
ed. The Human Vagina. Elsevier.
ed. Hypothalamic Hormones. Ann Arbor
Science.

Hafley, James R. see Hafley, James Robert.

Hafley, James Robert, 1928-
xHafley, James R.
Glass Roof: Virginia Woolf As Novelist.
Russell.

Hafner, Lawrence E.
xHafner, Lawrence E.

Patterns of Teaching Reading in the
Elementary School. Macmillan.

Haft, Jabob I., 1937-
xHaft, Jacob I.
ed. Acute Myocardial Infarction & Coronary
Artery Disease. Futura Pub.

Haft, Jacob I.
xHaft, Jacob I.
Consultation with a Cardiologist: Coronary
Heart Disease & Heart Attacks:
Management. Nelson-Hall.
ed. Therapeutics, Hypertension & Aspects of
Echocardiography. Futura Pub.

Haft, Jacob I. see Haft, Jabob I.

Hagan, Kenneth J.
xHagan, Kenneth J.
American Gunboat Diplomacy & the Old
Navy. Greenwood.
ed. In Peace & War: Interpretations of
American Naval History, 1775-1978.
Greenwood.

Hagan, Patti.
xHagan, Patti.
The Road Runner's Guide to New York City.
Times Bks.

Hagan, William T. see Hagan, William Thomas.

Hagan, William Thomas.
xHagan, William T.
American Indians. U of Chicago Pr.
Indian Police & Judges: Experiments in
Acculturation & Control. U of Nebr Pr.

Hagar, Warren A.
xHagar, Warren A.
Cognitive Awareness and the LPM. Philos Lib.

Hagberg, Janet.
xHagberg, Janet.
Inventurers: Excursions in Life & Career
Renewal. A-W.

Hage, George S. see Hage, George Sigrud.

Hage, George Sigrud.
xHage, George S.
Newspapers on the Minnesota Frontier,
1849-1860. Minn Hist.

Hage, Jerald, 1932-
xHage, Jerald.
Theories of Organizations: Form, Process, &
Transformation. Wiley.

Hagedorn, P.
xHagedorn, P.
ed. Differential Games & Applications:
Proceedings of a Workshop, Enschede,
Netherlands, March 16-25,1977.
Springer-Verlag.

Hagedorn, R. see Hagedorn, Rolf.

Hagedorn, Rolf.
xHagedorn, R.
Relativistic Kinematics: A Guide to the
Kinematic Problems of High-Energy Physics.
Benjamin-Cummings.

Hagel, Bob.
xHagel, Bob.
Game Loads & Practical Ballistics for the
American Hunter. Knopf.

Hagelman, Charles W.
xHagelman, Charles W.
ed. Concordance to Byron's Don Juan. Cornell
U Pr.

Hageman, Howard G.
xHageman, Howard G.
Lily Among the Thorns. Reformed Church.

Hagen, Everett E. see Hagen, Everett Einar.

Hagen, Everett Einar, 1906-
xHagen, Everett E.
Economics of Development. Irwin.

Hagen, John D.
xHagen, John D.
What's Wrong with America. Our Sunday
Visitor.

Hagen, Lorinda.
xHagen, Lorinda.

Amy Jean. Belmont Tower.
Destiny & Desire. Nordon Pubns.
In Love & War. Nordon Pubns.
In the Eye of the Law. Belmont-Tower.
Letitia. Belmont-Tower.
Hagen, Mary.
xHagen, Mary.
Hiking Trails of Northern Colorado. Pruett.
Hagen, Oscar. *see* Hagen, Oskar Frank Leonard.
Hagen, Oskar Frank Leonard, 1888-
xHagen, Oscar.
Art Epochs & Their Leaders: A Survey of the
Genesis of Modern Art. Arno.
Hagen, Richard, 1935-
xHagen, Richard.
The Bio-Sexual Factor. Doubleday.
Hagen, Uta, 1919-
xHagen, Uta.
Love for Cooking. Macmillan.
Love for Cooking. Macmillan.
Respect for Acting. Macmillan.
Hagen, Victor W. Von. *see* Von Hagen, Victor W.
Hagen, Willis W.
xHagen, Willis W.
Digest of Business Law. West Pub.
Hagen-Ansert, Sandra L.
xHagen-Ansert, Sandra L.
Textbook of Diagnostic Ultrasonography.
Mosby.
Hagendorf, S. *see* Hagendorf, Stanley.
Hagendorf, Stanley.
xHagendorf, S.
Tax Guide for Buying & Selling & Business.
P-H.
xHagendorf, Stanley.
Tax Guide for Buying & Selling a Business.
P-H.
Tax Manual for Corporate Liquidations,
Redemptions, & Estate Planning
Recapitalizations. P-H.
Hagenmuller, Paul.
xHagenmuller, Paul.
ed. Preparative Methods in Solid State
Chemistry. Acad Pr.
ed. Solid Electrolytes: General Principles,
Characterization, Materials, Applications.
Acad Pr.
Hager, Lowell P.
xHager, Lowell P.
ed. Chemistry & Functions of Colicins. Acad
Pr.
Hager, W. E. *see* Hager, Walter Ellsworth.
Hager, Walter Ellsworth, 1896-
xHager, W. E.
Quest for Vocational Adjustment in the
Profession of Education. AMS Pr.
Hagerman, Paul S. *see* Hagerman, Paul Stirling.
Hagerman, Paul Stirling.
xHagerman, Paul S.
It's a Mad Mad World. Sterling.
Hagerstrand, Torsten.
xHagerstrand, Torsten.
Innovation Diffusion As a Spatial Process. U of
Chicago Pr.
Hagerty, Cornelius, 1885-
xHagerty, Cornelius.
The Problem of Evil. Chris Mass.
xHagerty, Cornelius J.
The Holy Trinity. Chris Mass.
Hagerty, Cornelius J. *see* Hagerty, Cornelius.
Hagerty, D. J.
xHagerty, D. Joseph.
Solid Waste Management. Van Nos Reinhold.
Hagerty, D. Joseph. *see* Hagerty, D. J.
Hagerty, Gilbert.
xHagerty, Gilbert.
Massacre at Fort Bull: The DeLery Expedition
Against Oneida Carry, 1756. Mowbray Co.
Hagerty, W. W. *see* Hagerty, William W.

Hagerty, William W.
xHagerty, W. W.
Engineering Mechanics. Krieger.
Haggai, John. *see* Haggai, John Edmund.
Haggai, John E. *see* Haggai, John Edmund.
Haggai, John Edmund.
xHaggai, John.
How to Win Over Loneliness. Nelson.
xHaggai, John E.
My Son Johnny. Tyndale.
Haggard, H. Rider. *see* Haggard, Henry Rider.
Haggard, Henry Rider.
xHaggard, H. Rider.
Ayesha: The Return of She. Am Repr-Rivercity
Pr.
Ayesha: The Return of She. Borgo Pr.
Ayesha: The Return of She. Dover.
Ayesha: The Return of She. Newcastle Pub.
The Spirit of Bambatse: A Romance. Borgo Pr.
Haggard, Howard W. *see* Haggard, Howard Wilcox.
Haggard, Howard Wilcox, 1891-1959
xHaggard, Howard W.
Doctor in History. Arno.
The Doctor in History. Elliots Bks.
The Doctor in History. R West.
Haggart, Sue A.
xHaggart, Sue A.
Program Budgeting for School District
Planning. Educ Tech Pubns.
Haggerty, Brian A.
xHaggerty, Brian A.
Out of the House of Slavery: On the Meaning
of the Ten Commandments. Paulist Pr.
Haggerty, Helen R. *see* Haggerty, Helen Ruth.
Haggerty, Helen Ruth, 1903-
xHaggerty, Helen R.
Certain Factors in the Professional Education
of Women Teachers of Physical Education.
AMS Pr.
Haggerty, James. *see* Haggerty, James J.
Haggerty, James J., 1920-
xHaggerty, James.
Aviation's Mr. Sam. Aero.
Haggett, P. *see* Haggett, Peter.
Haggett, Peter.
xHaggett, P.
Locational Analysis in Human Geography. St
Martin.
xHaggett, Peter.
Geography: A Modern Synthesis. Har-Row.
Locational Analysis in Human Geography.
Halsted Pr.
Hagglund, Bengt, 1920-
xHagglund, Bengt.
The Background of Luther's Doctrine of
Justification in Late Medieval Theology.
Fortress.
Hagin, F. G. *see* Hagin, Frank G.
Hagin, Frank G.
xHagin, F. G.
A First Course in Differential Equations. P-H.
Hagin, Kenneth. *see* Hagin, Kenneth E.
Hagin, Kenneth E., 1917-
xHagin, Kenneth.
I Believe in Visions. Revell.
Hagiwara, Sakutar O.
xHagiwara, Sakutaro.
Face at the Bottom of the World & Other
Poems. C E Tuttle.
Hagiwara, Sakutaro. *see* Hagiwara, Sakutar O.
Hagler, M. O.
xHagler, M. O.
An Introduction to Controlled Thermonuclear
Fusion. Lexington Bks.
Hagood, L. M. *see* Hagood, Lewis Marshall.
Hagood, Lewis M. *see* Hagood, Lewis Marshall.
Hagood, Lewis Marshall, 1853-1936
xHagood, L. M.

Colored Man in the Methodist Episcopal
Church. Arno.
xHagood, Lewis M.
Colored Man in the Methodist Episcopal
Church. Negro U Pr.
Hagopian, Mark N.
xHagopian, Mark N.
Regimes, Movements, & Ideologies: A
Comparative Introduction to Political
Science. Longman.
Hagstrom, Julie.
xHagstrom, Julie.
Games Babies Play: A Handbook of Games to
Play with Infants. A & W Pubs.
Hague, Harlan.
xHague, Harlan.
Road to California: The Search for a Southern
Overland Route, 1540-1848. A H Clark.
Hague, John A.
xHague, John A.
American Character & Culture in a Changing
World: Some Twentieth-Century
Perspectives. Greenwood.
Hahm, David E.
xHahm, David E.
The Origins of Stoic Cosmology. Ohio St U Pr.
Hahmann, Gail Von. *see* Von Hahmann, Gail.
Hahn, C. H. *see* Hahn, Carl Hugo Linsingen.
Hahn, Carl Hugo Linsingen.
xHahn, C. H.
Native Tribes of South West Africa. Biblio
Dist.
Hahn, Christine.
xHahn, Christine.
Amusement Park Machines. Raintree Pubs.
Hahn, Emily, 1905-
xHahn, Emily.
China to Me: A Partial Autobiography. Da
Capo.
Cooking of China. Time-Life.
Love Conquers Nothing: A Glandular History
of Civilization. Arno.
Once Upon a Pedestal. NAL.
Soong Sisters. Greenwood.
Hahn, F. E. *see* Hahn, Fred Ernest.
Hahn, Frank. *see* Hahn, Frank Horace.
Hahn, Frank Horace.
xHahn, Frank.
ed. Philosophy & Economic Theory. Oxford U
Pr.
Hahn, Fred Ernest, 1916-
xHahn, F. E.
ed. Mechanism of Action of Antibacterial
Agents. Springer-Verlag.
Hahn, H. George. *see* Hahn, Henry George.
Hahn, Harlan.
xHahn, Harlan.
ed. Urban Politics: Past, Present & Future.
Longman.
Hahn, Harriet.
xHahn, Harriet.
The Plantain Season. Norton.
Hahn, Henry George, 1942-
xHahn, H. George.
Henry Fielding: An Annotated Bibliography.
Scarecrow.
Hahn, J. *see* Hahn, Josef.
Hahn, James.
xHahn, James.

Aim for a Job in a Small Business Occupation.
Rosen Pr.
Aim for a Job in the Construction Industry.
Rosen Pr.
Aim for a Job in the Printing Trades. Rosen Pr.
Aim for a Job in the Telephone Company.
Rosen Pr.
Environmental Careers. Watts.
Franco Harris: The Quiet Ironman. EMC.
Hamsters, Gerbils, Guinea Pigs, Pet Mice &
Pet Rats. Avon.
Hamsters, Gerbils, Guinea Pigs, Pet Mice, &
Pet Rats. Watts.
Plastics. Watts.
Reggie Jackson: Slugger Supreme. EMC.

Hahn, John F.
xHahn, John F.
Psychology: The Basic Principles. Littlefield.

Hahn, Josef.
xHahn, J.
Structural Analysis of Beams & Slabs. Ungar.
Hahn, Julia L. see Hahn, Julia Letheld.
Hahn, Julia Letheld, 1891-1942
xHahn, Julia L.
Critical Evaluation of a Supervisory Program in
Kindergarten - Primary Grades. AMS Pr.

Hahn, Martin E.
xHahn, Martin E.
ed. Communicative Behavior & Evolution.
Acad Pr.
ed. Development & Evolution of Brain Size:
Behavioral Implications. Acad Pr.
Hahn, Mary D. see Hahn, Mary Downing.
Hahn, Mary Downing.
xHahn, Mary D.
The Sara Summer. HM.
Hahn, Peter. see Hahn, Peter A.
Hahn, Peter A.
xHahn, Peter.
Guide to the Literature for the Industrial
Microbiologist. IFI Plenum.
Hahn, Roger, 1932-
xHahn, Roger.
The Anatomy of a Scientific Institution: The
Paris Academy of Sciences, 1666-1803. U of
Cal Pr.
Hahn, Walter A.
xHahn, Walter A.
ed. Assessing the Future & Policy Planning.
Gordon.
Hahn, Walter F.
xHahn, Walter F.
ed. Atlantic Community in Crisis: A
Redefinition of the Transatlantic
Relationship. Pergamon.
Hahn, Werner G.
xHahn, Werner G.
The Politics of Soviet Agriculture: 1960-1970.
Johns Hopkins.
Hahner, June E. see Hahner, June Edith.
Hahner, June Edith, 1940-
xHahner, June E.
Civilian-Military Relations in Brazil,
1889-1898. U of SC Pr.
Haider, Carmen, 1906-
xHaider, Carmen.
Capital & Labor Under Fascism. AMS Pr.
Haifeez, Moonat.
xHaifeez, Moonat.
Reminiscent Singapore. Vantage.
Haig, Robert M. see Haig, Robert Murray.
Haig, Robert Murray, 1887-1957
xHaig, Robert M.

History of the General Property Tax in Illinois.
Johnson Repr.
Toward an Understanding of the Metropolis.
Arno.
Haig-Brown, Roderick L. see Haig-Brown, Roderick
Langmere Haig.
Haig-Brown, Roderick Langmere Haig, 1908-
xHaig-Brown, Roderick L.
Measure of the Year. Arno.
Haigh, A. E. see Haigh, Arthur Elam.
Haigh, Arthur Elam.
xHaigh, A. E.
The Attic Theatre: A Description of the Stage
& Theatre of the Athenians, & of the
Dramatic Performances at Athens. R West.
Haigh, C. see Haigh, Christopher.
Haigh, Christopher.
xHaigh, C.
Reformation & Resistance in Tudor Lancashire.
Cambridge U Pr.
Haigh, Gerald.
xHaigh, Gerald.
Reluctant Adolescent. Intl Pubns Serv.
Teaching Slow Learners. Transatlantic.
Haight, A. Lynn, 1936-
xHaight, A. Lynn.
The Soccer Coaching Guide. A S Barnes.
Haight, Amanda.
xHaight, Amanda.
Anna Akhmatova: A Poetic Pilgrimage. Oxford
U Pr.
Haight, Elizabeth H. see Haight, Elizabeth Hazelton.
Haight, Elizabeth Hazelton, 1872-
xHaight, Elizabeth H.
Apuleius & His Influence. Cooper Sq.
Apuleius & His Influence. Folcroft.
Haight, F. A. see Haight, Frank A.
Haight, Frank A.
xHaight, F. A.
Mathematical Theories of Traffic Flow. Acad
Pr.
Haight, Fulton.
xHaight, Fulton.
California Courtroom Evidence. Parker & Son.
Haight, Roger.
xHaight, Roger.
The Experience & Language of Grace. Paulist
Pr.
Haight, William.
xHaight, William.
Retail Advertising: Management & Technique.
Scott F.
Hail, William J. see Hail, William James.
Hail, William James, 1877-
xHail, William J.
Tseng Kuo-Fan & the Taiping Rebellion.
Paragon.
Haile, Berard, 1874-1961
xHaile, Berard.
Head & Face Masks in Navaho Ceremonialism.
AMS Pr.
Starlore Among the Navaho. Gannon.
A Stem Vocabulary of the Navaho Language.
AMS Pr.
Haile, H. G. see Haile, Harry Gerald.
Haile, Harry Gerald, 1931-
xHaile, H. G.
Artist in Chrysalis: A Biographical Study of
Goethe in Italy. U of Ill Pr.
Hailey, Arthur.
xHailey, Arthur.

Airport. Bantam.
Airport. Doubleday.
Final Diagnosis. Bantam.
Final Diagnosis. Doubleday.
Hotel. Bantam.
Hotel. Doubleday.
The Moneychangers. Bantam.
The Moneychangers. Doubleday.
Overload. Bantam.
Overload. Doubleday.
Wheels. Bantam.
Wheels. Doubleday.
Hailey, Homer, 1904-
xHailey, Homer.
Commentary on the Minor Prophets. Baker Bk.
Hailey, Sheila, 1927-
xHailey, Sheila.
I Married a Best Seller. Doubleday.
Hailman, Jack P. see Hailman, Jack Parker.
Hailman, Jack Parker, 1936-
xHailman, Jack P.
Optical Signals: Animal Communication &
Light. Ind U Pr.
Hailstones, Thomas J.
xHailstones, Thomas J.
Contemporary Economic Problems & Issues.
SW Pub.
Introduction to Managerial Economics. P-H.
Readings in Economics. SW Pub.
Haim, Andre, 1924-1969
xHaim, Andre.
Adolescent Suicide. Intl Univs Pr.
Haim, Sylvia G.
xHaim, Sylvia G.
ed. Arab Nationalism: An Anthology. U of Cal
Pr.
Haiman, John.
xHaiman, John.
Targets & Syntactic Change. Mouton.
Haimann, Theo.
xHaimann, Theo.
Supervisory Management for Health Care
Institutions. Cath Health.
Haimes, Leonard.
xHaimes, Leonard.
How to Triple Your Energy. NAL.
Haimes, Yacov Y.
xHaimes, Yacov Y.
Scientific, Technological & Institutional
Aspects of Water Resource Policy. Westview.
Haimo, Oscar.
xHaimo, Oscar.
Cocktail & Wine Digest: The Barmen's Bible.
Haimo.
Haimson, Leopold H.
xHaimson, Leopold H.
ed. The Politics of Rural Russia, 1905-1914.
Ind U Pr.
Hainaux, Rene.
xHainaux, Rene.
ed. Stage Design Throughout the World:
1970-1975. Theatre Arts.
Haine, Edgar A., 1908-
xHaine, Edgar A.
Seven Railroads. A S Barnes.
Haines, Brian.
xHaines, Brian.
Introduction to Quantitative Economics. Allen
Unwin.
Haines, C. Grove. see Haines, Charles Grove.
Haines, Charles G. see Haines, Charles Grove.
Haines, Charles Grove, 1906-
xHaines, C. Grove.
ed. European Integration. Johns Hopkins.
xHaines, Charles G.

ed. Africa Today. Greenwood.
The American Doctrine of Judicial Supremacy.
Boulevard.
The American Doctrine of Judicial Supremacy.
Da Capo.
Haines, Charles R. *see* Haines, Charles Reginald.
Haines, Charles Reginald.
xHaines, Charles R.
Christianity & Islam in Spain, A. D. 756-1031.
AMS Pr.
Haines, Charles W.
xHaines, Charles W.
Analysis for Engineers. West Pub.
Haines, Connie.
xHaines, Connie.
For Once in My Life. Warner Bks.
Haines, Gail K. *see* Haines, Gail Kay.
Haines, Gail Kay.
xHaines, Gail K.
Explosives. Morrow.
Fire. Morrow.
Natural & Synthetic Poisons. Morrow.
Haines, George, 1903-
xHaines, George.
German Influence Upon English Education and
Science, 1800-1866. Conn Coll Bkshp.
Haines, John. *see* Haines, John Meade.
Haines, John E., 1903-
xHaines, John E.
Automatic Control of Heating & Air
Conditioning. McGraw.
Haines, John M. *see* Haines, John Meade.
Haines, John Meade, 1924-
xHaines, John.
The Stone Harp. Columbia U Pr.
Twenty Poems. Unicorn Pr.
xHaines, John M.
In a Dusty Light. Graywolf.
Haines, M. *see* Haines, Magnus.
Haines, Magnus.
xHaines, M.
Gynaecological Pathology. Churchill.
Haines, Michael R.
xHaines, Michael R.
Economic-Demographic Interrelations in
Developing Agricultural Regions: A Case
Study of Prussian Upper Silesia, 1840-1914.
Arno.
Haines, R. G. *see* Haines, Robert G.
Haines, R. W. *see* Haines, Roger W.
Haines, R. Wheeler. *see* Haines, Richard Wheeler.
Haines, Richard F., 1937-
xHaines, Richard F.
Observing UFO's: An Investigative Handbook.
Nelson-Hall.
ed. UFO Phenomena & the Behavioral
Scientist. Scarecrow.
Haines, Richard Wheeler.
xHaines, R. Wheeler.
Handbook of Human Embryology. Churchill.
Haines, Robert G.
xHaines, R. G.
Food Preparation for Hotels, Restaurants, &
Cafeterias. Am Technical.
Haines, Roger W.
xHaines, R. W.
Control Systems for Heating, Ventilating & Air
Conditioning. Delmar.
xHaines, Roger W.
Control Systems for Heating, Ventilating, &
Air Conditioning. Van Nos Reinhold.
Haines, Walter W.
xHaines, Walter W.
Money, Prices & Policy. McGraw.
Haining, Peter.
xHaining, Peter.

ed. The Ancient Mysteries Reader. Doubleday.
ed. Circle of Witches: An Anthology of
Victorian Witchcraft Stories. Taplinger.
ed. Clans of Darkness: Scottish Stories of
Fantasy & Horror. Taplinger.
ed. The Ghost's Companion: A Haunting
Anthology. Taplinger.
Ghosts: The Illustrated History. Macmillan.
ed. Gothic Tales of Terror: Classic Horror
Stories from Great Britain, Europe & the
United States 1765-1840. Taplinger.
ed. Hollywood Nightmare: Tales of Fantasy &
Horror from the Film World. Taplinger.
ed. The Lucifer Society: Macabre Tales by
Great Modern Writers. Taplinger.
ed. Monster Makers: Creators & Creations of
Fantasy & Horror. Taplinger.
ed. The Shilling Shockers: Stories of Terror
from the Gothic Bluebooks. St Martin.
Hains, Thornton J. *see* Hains, Thornton Jenkins.
Hains, Thornton Jenkins, 1866-
xHains, Thornton J.
Strife of the Sea. Arno.
Hainsworth, Marguerite D. *see* Hainsworth, Marguerite
Dorothy.
Hainsworth, Marguerite Dorothy.
xHainsworth, Marguerite D.
Experiments in Animal Behaviour. HM.
Hair, D. S. *see* Hair, Donald S.
Hair, Donald S.
xHair, D. S.
Browning's Experiments with Genre. U of
Toronto Pr.
Hair, William I. *see* Hair, William Ivy.
Hair, William Ivy.
xHair, William I.
Bourbonism & Agrarian Protest: Louisiana
Politics, 1877-1900. La State U Pr.
Carnival of Fury: Robert Charles & the New
Orleans Race Riot of 1900. La State U Pr.
Hairston, Maxine.
xHairston, Maxine.
A Contemporary Rhetoric. HM.
xHairston, Maxine C.
George Sessions Perry: His Life & Works.
Jenkins.
Hairston, Maxine C. *see* Hairston, Maxine.
Haislip, John.
xHaislip, John.
Not Every Year. U of Wash Pr.
Haist, Grant.
xHaist, Grant.
Monobath Manual. Morgan.
Haithcox, John P. *see* Haithcox, John Patrick.
Haithcox, John Patrick, 1933-
xHaithcox, John P.
Communism & Nationalism in India: M. N.
Roy & Comintern Policy, 1920-1939.
Princeton U Pr.
Haitovsky, Yoel.
xHaitovsky, Yoel.
Forecasts with Quarterly Macroeconometric
Models. Natl Bur Econ Res.
Haiz, Danah.
xHaiz, Danah.
Jonah's Journey. Lerner Pubns.
Haj, Fareed.
xHaj, Fareed.
Disability in Antiquity. Philos Lib.
Hajdu, Steven I.
xHajdu, Steven I.
Cytopathology of Sarcomas & Other
Non-Epithelial Malignant Tumors. Saunders.
Pathology of Soft Tissue Tumors. Lea &
Febiger.
Hajducki, S. Maxwell.
xHajducki, S. Maxwell.
A Railway Atlas of Ireland. David & Charles.
Hajek, Jaroslav.
xHajek, Jaroslav.

Theory of Rank Tests. Acad Pr.
Hajek, Otomar.
xHajek, Otomar.
Dynamical Systems in the Plane. Acad Pr.
Pursuit Games: An Introduction to the Theory
& Applications of Differential Games of
Pursuit & Evasion. Acad Pr.
Hajek, P. *see* Hajek, Petr.
Hajek, Petr.
xHajek, P.
Mechanizing Hypothesis Formation:
Mathematical Foundations for a General
Theory. Springer-Verlag.
Hajos, A. *see* Hajos, Andor.
Hajos, Andor.
xHajos, A.
Complex Hydrides & Related Reducing Agents
in Organic Synthesis. Elsevier.
Hake, Gordon, 1809-1895
xHake, Thomas G.
Memoirs of Eighty Years. AMS Pr.
Hake, Thomas.
xHake, Thomas.
Life & Letters of Theodore Watts-Dunton.
Johnson Repr.
Hake, Thomas G. *see* Hake, Gordon.
Haken, H.
xHaken, H.
ed. Cooperative Phenomena. Springer-Verlag.
ed. Excitons at High Density. Springer-Verlag.
Hakim, Seymour.
xHakim, Seymour.
Substituting Memories. Poet Gal Pr.
Under Moon. Poet Gal Pr.
Hakkila, E. Arnold.
xHakkila, E. Arnold.
ed. Nuclear Safeguards Analysis:
Nondestructive & Analytical Chemical
Techniques. Am Chemical.
Hakluyt, Richard, 1552?-1616
xHakluyt, Richard.
Principal Navigations, Voyages, Traffiques &
Discoveries of the English Nation. AMS Pr.
Hakutani, Yoshinobu, 1935-
xHakutani, Yoshinobu.
Young Dreiser: A Critical Study. Fairleigh
Dickinson.
Halacy, D. S. *see* Halacy, Daniel Stephen.
Halacy, Dan. *see* Halacy, Daniel Stephen.
Halacy, Daniel Stephen, 1919-
xHalacy, D. S.

The Coming Age of Solar Energy. Avon.
The Coming Age of Solar Energy. Har-Row.
Earthquakes: A Natural History. Bobbs.
Feast & Famine. Macrae.
Geometry of Hunger. Har-Row.
On the Move: Man & Transportation. Macrae.
Surfer. Macmillan.
Survival in the World of Work. Scribner.
xHalacy, Dan.
How to Improve Your Memory. Watts.
Halanay, A.
xHalanay, A.
Differential Equations: Stability, Oscillations,
Time Lags. Acad Pr.
Halasz, Nicholas, 1895-
xHalasz, Nicholas.
Captain Dreyfus: The Story of Mass Hysteria.
S&S.
Halasz, Zoltan.
xHalasz, Zoltan.
ed. Hungary: A Guide with a Difference. Intl
Pubns Serv.
Halayya, M., 1921-
xHalayya, M.
Introduction to Political Science. Asia.
Halberg, Leland R.
xHalberg, Leland R.

Mathematics for Technicians with an
Introduction to Calculus. Wadsworth Pub.
Halberstam, David.
xHalberstam, David.
The Powers That Be. Dell.
The Powers That Be. Knopf.
Unfinished Odyssey of Robert Kennedy.
Random.
Halberstam, H. see Halberstam, Heini.
Halberstam, Heini.
xHalberstam, H.
Sieve Methods. Acad Pr.
Halberstam, Michael.
xHalberstam, Michael.
A Coronary Event. Popular Lib.
The Wanting of Levine. Berkley Pub.
Halbert, Sara.
xHalbert, Sara.
Call Me Counselor. Lippincott.
Halbfas, Hubert. see Halbfas, Hubertus.
Halbfas, Hubertus.
xHalbfas, Hubert.
Theory of Catechetics: Language & Experience
in Religious Education. Seabury.
Halbouty, Michel T. see Halbouty, Michel Thomas.
Halbouty, Michel Thomas, 1909-
xHalbouty, Michel T.
Salt Domes, Gulf Region, United States &
Mexico. Gulf Pub.
Halbritter, Kurt.
xHalbritter, Kurt.
Halbritter's Arms Through the Ages: An
Introduction to the Secret Weapons of
History. Penguin.
illus. Halbritter's Arms Through the Ages: An
Introduction to the Secret Weapons of
History. Viking Pr.
Halbwachs, Maurice, 1877-1945
xHalbwachs, Maurice.
The Causes of Suicide. Free Pr.
Halcrow, Harold G.
xHalcrow, Harold G.
Economics of Agriculture. McGraw.
Food Policy for America. McGraw.
Hald, A. see Hald, Anders.
Hald, Anders, 1913-
xHald, A.
Statistical Tables & Formulas. Wiley.
Haldane, A. R. see Haldane, Archibald Richard Burdon.
Haldane, Archibald Richard Burdon, 1900-
xHaldane, A. R.
By River, Stream & Loch: Thirty Years with a
Trout Rod. David & Charles.
Haldane, Bernard.
xHaldane, Bernard.
Career Satisfaction & Success: A Guide to Job
Freedom. Am Mgmt.
Haldane, Charlotte. see Haldane, Charlotte (Franken).
Haldane, Charlotte (Franken), 1894-1969
xHaldane, Charlotte.
Marcel Proust. Kennikat.
Haldane, Duncan.
xHaldane, Duncan.
Mamluk Painting. Intl Schol Bk Serv.
Haldane, Jean M.
xHaldane, Jean M.
Prescriptions for Parishes. Seabury.
Haldane, John B. see Haldane, John Burdon Sanderson.

Haldane, John Burdon Sanderson, 1892-1964

xHaldane, John B.
Marxist Philosophy & the Sciences. Arno.

Haldeman, H. R.
xHaldeman, H. R.
The Ends of Power. Dell.
The Ends of Power. G K Hall.
The Ends of Power. Times Bks.

Haldeman, Joe. see Haldeman, Joe W.
Haldeman, Joe W.
xHaldeman, Joe.
All My Sins Remembered. Avon.
All My Sins Remembered. St Martin.
The Forever War. Ballantine.
The Forever War. St Martin.
Infinite Dreams. Avon.
Infinite Dreams. St Martin.
ed. Study War No More: A Selection of
Alternatives. Avon.
ed. Study War No More: A Selection of
Alternatives. St Martin.
Haldeman, Linda.
xHaldeman, Linda.
The Lastborn of Elvinwood. Avon.
The Lastborn of Elvinwood. Doubleday.
Star of the Sea. Doubleday.
Halder, Animesh, 1942-
xHalder, Animesh.
India's Export Pattern: Analysis of Potential
Diversification. South Asia Bks.
Hale, Anita.
xHale, Anita.
People Sounds. Broadman.
Hale, Arlene.
xHale, Arlene.
Camp Nurse. Ace Bks.
Glimpse of Paradise. G K Hall.
Hungry Heart. Dell.
In Love's Own Fashion. NAL.
Legacy of Love. NAL.
Lovers Reunion. NAL.
One More Bridge to Cross. Little.
The Other Side of the World. G K Hall.
The Other Side of the World. Little.
The Stormy Sea of Love. NAL.
Hale, B. M. see Hale, Barbara M.
Hale, Barbara M.
xHale, B. M.
The Subject Bibliography of the Social Sciences
& Humanities. Pergamon.
Hale, Charles D.
xHale, Charles D.
Fundamentals of Police Administration.
Holbrook.
Personal Characteristics of Assaulted &
Non-Assaulted Officers. Univ OK Gov Res.
Hale, Douglas.
xHale, Douglas.
The Germans from Russia in Oklahoma. U of
Okla Pr.
Hale, Edward E. see Hale, Edward Everett.
Hale, Edward Everett, 1822-1909
xHale, Edward E.
Brick Moon, & Other Stories. Arno.
Crusoe in New York & Other Tales. Mss Info.
Franklin in France. B Franklin.
If, Yes, & Perhaps. Mss Info.
Letters on Irish Emigration. Arno.
Sybaris & Other Homes. Arno.
Hale, Francis J.
xHale, Francis J.
Introduction to Control System Analysis &
Design. P-H.
Hale, Frederick.
xHale, Frederick.
Trans-Atlantic Conservative Protestantism in
the Evangelical Free & Mission Covenant
Traditions. Arno.
Hale, G. A. see Hale, Gordon A.
Hale, Geoffrey.
xHale, Geoffrey.
A Doctor in Practice. Routledge & Kegan.
Hale, George E. see Hale, George Ellery.
Hale, George Ellery, 1868-1938
xHale, George E.

National Academies & the Progress of
Research. Arno.
Hale, Gordon A.
xHale, G. A.
Attention & Cognitive Development. Plenum
Pub.
Hale, J. K. see Hale, Jack K.
Hale, J. R. see Hale, John Rigby.
Hale, Jack. see Hale, Jack K.
Hale, Jack K.
xHale, J. K.
Theory of Functional Differential Equations.
Springer-Verlag.
xHale, Jack.
Class of Functional Equations of Neutral Type.
Am Math.
Ordinary Differential Equations. Wiley.
xHale, Jack K.
Ordinary Differential Equations. Krieger.
Hale, John.
xHale, John.
Lovers & Heretics. Dial.
Hale, John R. see Hale, John Rigby.
Hale, John Rigby, 1923-
xHale, J. R.
Florence & the Medici: The Pattern of Control.
Thames Hudson.
Renaissance Exploration. Norton.
ed. Renaissance Venice. Merrimack Bk Serv.
xHale, John R.
Age of Exploration. Silver.
Renaissance. Silver.
ed. Renaissance Venice. Rowman.
Hale, Julian. see Hale, Julian Anthony Stuart.
Hale, Julian Anthony Stuart, 1940-
xHale, Julian.
Radio Power: Propaganda & International
Broadcasting. Temple U Pr.
Hale, Katherine.
xHale, Katherine.
Affinity. Avon.
Hale, Leon.
xHale, Leon.
Addison. Doubleday.
Hale, Mason E.
xHale, Mason E.
How to Know the Lichens. Wm C Brown.
Hale, Matthew.
xHale, Matthew.
History of the Common Law of England. U of
Chicago Pr.
Human Science & Social Order: Hugo
Munsterberg & the Origins of Applied
Psychology. Temple U Pr.
Hale, Meredith S., 1927-
xHale, Meredith S.
ed. A Practical Approach to Arm Pain. C C
Thomas.
Hale, Nancy, 1908-
xHale, Nancy.
The Realities of Fiction: A Book About
Writing. Greenwood.
Hale, Nathan C. see Hale, Nathan Cabot.
Hale, Nathan Cabot.
xHale, Nathan C.
The Birth of a Family: The New Role of the
Father in Childbirth. Doubleday.
Hale, Oron J. see Hale, Oron James.
Hale, Oron James.
xHale, Oron J.
Captive Press in the Third Reich. Princeton U
Pr.
Hale, Philip L. see Hale, Philip Leslie.
Hale, Philip Leslie, 1865-1931
xHale, Philip L.
ed. Great Masters in Art. Arno.
Hale, R. see Hale, Rosemary.
Hale, Robert B. see Hale, Robert Beverly.
Hale, Robert Beverly.
xHale, Robert B.

Anatomy Lessons from the Great Masters. Watson-Guptill.
Drawing Lessons from the Great Masters. Watson-Guptill.
Hale, Rosemary.
 xHale, R.
  The Principles & Practice of Health Visiting. Pergamon.
Hale, Will T. see Hale, Will Taliaferro.
Hale, Will Taliaferro, 1880-
 xHale, Will T.
  Anne Bronte: Her Life & Writings. Arden Lib.
  Anne Bronte: Her Life & Writings. Folcroft.
Hale-White, William, Sir, 1857-1949
 xHale-White, William.
  Great Doctors of the Nineteenth Century. Arno.
Halecki, O. see Halecki, Oskar.
Halecki, Oscar. see Halecki, Oskar.
Halecki, Oskar, 1891-
 xHalecki, O.
  Borderlands of Western Civilization: A History of East Central Europe. Wiley.
 xHalecki, Oscar.
  A History of Poland. McKay.
Halen, Harry.
 xHalen, Harry.
  Handbook of Oriental Collections in Finland: Manuscripts, Xylographs, Inscriptions & Russian Minority Literature. Humanities.
Hales, John W. see Hales, John Wesley.
Hales, John Wesley, 1836-1914
 xHales, John W.
  Notes & Essays on Shakespeare. AMS Pr.
Halevy, Daniel, 1872-1962
 xHalevy, Daniel.
  The End of the Notables. Columbia U Pr.
Halevy, Ludovic, 1834-1908
 xHalevy, Ludovic.
  Parisian Points of View. Arno.
Haley, Albert W.
 xHaley, Albert W.
  tr. Beowulf. Branden.
Haley, Alex.
 xHaley, Alex.
  Roots. Dell.
  Roots. Doubleday.
  Roots. G K Hall.
Haley, Charles W.
 xHaley, Charles W.
  Theory of Financial Decisions. McGraw.
Haley, D. K. see Haley, David K.
Haley, David K., 1942-
 xHaley, D. K.
  Equational Compactness in Rings with Applications to the Theory of Topological Rings. Springer-Verlag.
Haley, Gail. see Haley, Gail E.
Haley, Gail E.
 xHaley, Gail.
  illus. The Green Man. Scribner.
  Noah's Ark. Atheneum.
  illus. The Post Office Cat. Scribner.
 xHaley, Gail E.
  Go Away, Stay Away. Scribner.
  illus. Noah's Ark. Atheneum.
Haley, Jay.
 xHaley, Jay.
  Leaving Home: The Therapy of Disturbed Young People. McGraw.
  Problem-Solving Therapy: New Strategies for Effective Family Therapy. Jossey-Bass.
  Strategies of Psychotherapy. Grune.
  Uncommon Therapy: The Psychiatric Techniques of Milton H. Erickson, M. D.. Norton.
Haley, Margaret.
 xHaley, Margaret.
  Gardener Mind. AMS Pr.
Haley, Marie. see Haley, Marie Philip.

Haley, Marie Philip, Sister, 1899-
 xHaley, Marie.
  Racine & the Art Poetique of Boileau. Octagon.
Haley, Neale.
 xHaley, Neale.
  Grooming Your Horse. A S Barnes.
  How to Have Fun with a Horse. Arco.
  Teach Yourself To Ride. A S Barnes.
  Understanding Your Horse: Equine Character & Psychology. A S Barnes.
Haley, P. Edward.
 xHaley, P. Edward.
  ed. Lebanon in Crisis: Participants & Issues. Syracuse U Pr.
  Revolution & Intervention: The Diplomacy of Taft & Wilson with Mexico, 1910-17. MIT Pr.
Halfacre, Gordon. see Halfacre, R. Gordon.
Halfacre, R. Gordon.
 xHalfacre, Gordon.
  Horticulture. McGraw.
Halfon, Efraim.
 xHalfon, Efraim.
  ed. Theoretical Systems Ecology: Advances & Case Studies. Acad Pr.
Halfpenny, William, fl. 1750
 xHalfpenny, William.
  Art of Sound Building. Arno.
Haliburton, Gordon. see Haliburton, Gordon Mackay.
Haliburton, Gordon M. see Haliburton, Gordon Mackay.
Haliburton, Gordon Mackay.
 xHaliburton, Gordon.
  Historical Dictionary of Lesotho. Scarecrow.
 xHaliburton, Gordon M.
  The Prophet Harris: A Study of an African Prophet & His Mass-Movement in the Ivory Coast & the Gold Coast, 1913-1915. Oxford U Pr.
Haliburton, Thomas C. see Haliburton, Thomas Chandler.
Haliburton, Thomas Chandler, 1796-1865
 xHaliburton, Thomas C.
  The Clockmaker. Irvington.
Halich, Wasyl.
 xHalich, Wasyl.
  Ukrainians in the United States. Arno.
Halifax, Edward F. see Halifax, Edward Frederick Lindley Wood.
Halifax, Edward Frederick Lindley Wood.
 xHalifax, Edward F.
  Speeches on Foreign Policy, 1934-1939. Arno.
Halifax, Joan.
 xHalifax, Joan.
  Shamanic Voices: A Survey of Visionary Narratives. Dutton.
Halkett, John G.
 xHalkett, John G.
  ed. This Powerful Rime: An Anthology of Ten Poets. Irvington.
Halkin, Hillel, 1939-
 xHalkin, Hillel.
  Letters to an American Jewish Friend: A Zionist's Polemic. Jewish Pubn.
Hall. see Hall, Carl W.
Hall , Marshall. see Hall, Marshall.
Hall, A. E. see Hall, Anthony E.
Hall, Adam.
 xHall, Adam.
  The Quiller Memorandum. BJ Pub Group.
Hall, Al.
 xHall, Al.
  ed. Complete Book of Vega. Petersen Pub.
Hall, Alfred Daniel, Sir, 1864-1942
 xHall, Daniel.
  The Frustration of Science. Arno.
Hall, Alice.
 xHall, Alice.
  Dairy Goats: Selecting, Fitting, Showing. Hall Pr.
Hall, Anna M. see Hall, Anna Maria Fielding.

Hall, Anna Maria. see Hall, Anna Maria Fielding.
Hall, Anna Maria Fielding, 1800-1881
 xHall, Anna M.
  Tales of Irish Life & Character. Arno.
 xHall, Anna Maria.
  Lights & Shadows of Irish Life. Garland Pub.
  Sketches of Irish Character. Garland Pub.
  Stories of the Irish Peasantry. Garland Pub.
 xHall, Anna-Maria.
  Tales of Irish Life & Character. Arno.
Hall, Anna-Maria. see Hall, Anna Maria Fielding.
Hall, Anthony E.
 xHall, A. E.
  ed. Agriculture in Semi-Arid Environments. Springer-Verlag.
Hall, Arethusa, 1802-1891
 xHall, Arethusa.
  ed. Life & Character of the Rev. Sylvester Judd. Kennikat.
Hall, Arthur C. see Hall, Arthur Cleveland.
Hall, Arthur Cleveland, 1865-1910
 xHall, Arthur C.
  Crime in Its Relations to Social Progress. AMS Pr.
Hall, B. K. see Hall, Brian Keith.
Hall, Ben M.
 xHall, Ben M.
  The Golden Age of the Movie Palace: The Best Remaining Seats. Potter.
Hall, Benjamin H. see Hall, Benjamin Homer.
Hall, Benjamin Homer, 1830-1893
 xHall, Benjamin H.
  Collection of College Words & Customs. Gale.
Hall, Brian. see Hall, Brian P.
Hall, Brian Keith, 1941-
 xHall, B. K.
  Chondrogenesis of the Somitic Mesoderm. Springer-Verlag.
Hall, Brian P.
 xHall, Brian.
  Value Clarification As Learning Process: A Handbook for Christian Educators. Paulist Pr.
Hall, C. M. see Hall, Constance Margaret.
Hall, C. Margaret. see Hall, Constance Margaret.
Hall, Calvin S. see Hall, Calvin Springer.
Hall, Calvin Springer.
 xHall, Calvin S.
  Dreams, Life & Literature: A Study of Franz Kafka. U of NC Pr.
  Meaning of Dreams. McGraw.
  A Primer of Freudian Psychology. NAL.
  A Primer of Freudian Psychology. Octagon.
  A Primer of Jungian Psychology. NAL.
  Primer of Jungian Psychology. Taplinger.
  Theories of Personality. Wiley.
Hall, Carl W.
 xHall.
  Dictionary of Drying. Dekker.
 xHall, Carl W.
  Drying of Milk & Milk Products. AVI.
  Encyclopedia of Food Engineering. AVI.
  Processing Equipment for Agricultural Products. AVI.
Hall, Carolyn V. see Hall, Carolyn Vosburg.
Hall, Carolyn Vosburg, 1927-
 xHall, Carolyn V.
  Sewing Machine Craft Book. Van Nos Reinhold.
Hall, Cecil E. see Hall, Cecil Edwin.
Hall, Cecil Edwin, 1912-
 xHall, Cecil E.
  Introduction to Electron Microscopy. McGraw.
Hall, Clarence W. see Hall, Clarence Wilbur.
Hall, Clarence Wilbur, 1902-
 xHall, Clarence W.
  Adventurers for God. Har-Row.
Hall, Claude H. see Hall, Claude Hampton.
Hall, Claude Hampton, 1922-
 xHall, Claude H.

Abel Parker Upshur: Conservative Virginian 1790-1844. State Hist Soc Wis.

Hall, Constance Margaret.
xHall, C. M.
Woman Unliberated: Difficulties & Limitations in Changing Self. Hemisphere Pub.
xHall, C. Margaret.
Bric-a-Brac. Antietam Pr.
Giving Birth. Antietam Pr.
Individual & Society: Basic Concepts. Antietam Pr.
Pearls. Antietam Pr.
xHall, Margaret.
Sociology of Pierre Joseph Proudhon, 1809-65. Philos Lib.

Hall, Courtney R. see Hall, Courtney Robert.

Hall, Courtney Robert, 1894-
xHall, Courtney R.
History of American Industrial Science. Arno.

Hall, Craig, 1950-
xHall, Craig.
The Real Estate Turnaround: Craig Hall's Investment Formula That Makes Millions. P-H.

Hall, D. see Hall, D. H.

Hall, D. G. see Hall, Daniel George Edward.

Hall, D. H.
xHall, D.
History of the Earth Sciences During the Scientific & Industrial Revolution with Special Emphasis on Physical Geosciences. Elsevier.

Hall, Dale M. see Hall, Darl Merideth.

Hall, Daniel. see Hall, Alfred Daniel.

Hall, Daniel G. see Hall, Daniel George Edward.

Hall, Daniel George Edward, 1891-
xHall, D. G.
A History of South East Asia. St Martin.
xHall, Daniel G.
Burma. AMS Pr.
History of South-East Asia. St Martin.

Hall, Darl Merideth, 1895-
xHall, Dale M.
Dynamics of Group Action. Interstate.

Hall, David, 1931-
xHall, David.
Geography & the Geography Teacher. Allen Unwin.

Hall, David. see Hall, David J.

Hall, David D.
xHall, David D.
The Faithful Shepherd: A History of the New England Ministry in the Seventeenth Century. Norton.
The Faithful Shepherd: A History of the New England Ministry in the Seventeenth Century. U of NC Pr.

Hall, David J.
xHall, David.
ed. Beyond Separation: Further Studies of Children in Hospital. Routledge & Kegan.

Hall, David L.
xHall, David L.
The Civilization of Experience: A Whiteheadian Theory of Culture. Fordham.

Hall, Don Alan.
xHall, Don Alan.
On Top of Oregon. Binford.

Hall, Donald, 1928-
xHall, Donald.
ed. Contemporary American Poetry. Penguin.
Ox-Cart Man. Viking Pr.
Riddle Rat. Warne.
String Too Short to Be Saved. G K Hall.
ed. A Writer's Reader. Little.
Writing Well. Little.

Hall, Donald E.
xHall, Donald E.

Musical Acoustics: An Introduction. Wadsworth Pub.

Hall, Donald R. see Hall, Donald Roots.

Hall, Donald Roots.
xHall, Donald R.
Cooperative Lobbying: The Power of Pressure. U of Ariz Pr.

Hall, Dorothy. see Hall, Dorothy Grame.

Hall, Dorothy Grame.
xHall, Dorothy.
Natural Health Book. Scribner.

Hall, Douglas J. see Hall, Douglas John.

Hall, Douglas John, 1928-
xHall, Douglas J.
Has the Church & a Future?. Westminster.
Lighten Our Darkness: Toward an Indigenous Theology of the Cross. Westminster.

Hall, Douglas K. see Hall, Douglas Kent.

Hall, Douglas Kent.
xHall, Douglas K.
Van People: The Great American Rainbow Boogie. T Y Crowell.

Hall, Douglas T., 1940-
xHall, Douglas T.
Careers in Organizations. Goodyear.
Experiences in Management & Organizational Behavior. Wiley.
Organizational Climates & Careers: The Work Lives of Priests. Acad Pr.

Hall, E. Raymond. see Hall, Eugene Raymond.

Hall, Edward T. see Hall, Edward Twitchell.

Hall, Edward Twitchell, 1914-
xHall, Edward T.
The Silent Language. Doubleday.
The Silent Language. Greenwood.

Hall, Edwin P. see Hall, Edwin Presley.

Hall, Edwin Presley.
xHall, Edwin P.
A Doctor Reminisces. Strode.

Hall, Elizabeth, 1929-
xHall, Elizabeth.
Possible Impossibilities: A Look at Parapsychology. HM.

Hall, Ennen R. see Hall, Ennen Reaves.

Hall, Ennen Reaves.
xHall, Ennen R.
Looking Inward, Looking Upward. Word Bks.

Hall, Eric D. see Hall, Eric J.

Hall, Eric J.
xHall, Eric D.
Radiobiology for the Radiologist. Har-Row.
xHall, Eric J.
Radiation & Life. Pergamon.

Hall, Eugene Raymond.
xHall, E. Raymond.
Mammals of North America. Wiley.

Hall, Evelyn B. see Hall, Evelyn Beatrice.

Hall, Evelyn Beatrice, 1868-1919
xHall, Evelyn B.
Life of Voltaire. R West.

Hall, F. H., 1926-
xHall, F. H.
In the Lamb White Days. PB.

Hall, F. M. see Hall, Frederick Michael.

Hall, Florence H. see Hall, Florence Marion (Howe).

Hall, Florence Marion (Howe), 1845-1922
xHall, Florence H.
The Story of the Battle Hymn of the Republic. Arno.

Hall, Francine. see Hall, Francine S.

Hall, Francine S.
xHall, Francine.
The Management of Affirmative Action. Goodyear.

Hall, Fred, A.M.I.P.H.E.
xHall, Fred.
Building Services & Equipment. Longman.

Hall, Frederic T. see Hall, Frederic Thomas.

Hall, Frederic Thomas, d. 1885
xHall, Frederic T.

The Pedigree of the Devil. Arno.

Hall, Frederick Michael.
xHall, F. M.
Introduction to Abstract Algebra. Cambridge U Pr.

Hall, Frederick W. see Hall, Frederick William.

Hall, Frederick William, 1863-1933
xHall, Frederick W.
Companion to Classical Texts. Arno.

Hall, G.
xHall, G.
ed. Modern Numerical Methods for Ordinary Differential Equations. Oxford U Pr.

Hall, (G. K.) and Company.
xG. K. Hall & Co.
Compiled by Cumulated Subject Index to Psychological Abstracts, 1927-1960. G K Hall.

Hall, G. Stanley. see Hall, Granville Stanley.

Hall, Gerald.
xHall, Gerald.
How to Completely Secure Your Home. TAB Bks.

Hall, Gertrude H.
xHall, Gertrude H.
Guide to Development of Protective Services for Older People. C C Thomas.

Hall, Granville Stanley.
xHall, G. Stanley.
Aspects of Child Life & Education. Arno.
Hints Toward a Select & Descriptive Bibliography of Education. Gale.
Life & Confessions of a Psychologist. Arno.

Hall, Gus.
xHall, Gus.
Imperialism Today: An Evaluation of Major Issues & Events of Our Time. Intl Pub Co.

Hall, H. E. see Hall, Henry Edgar.

Hall, Harry S.
xHall, Harry S.
Congressional Attitudes Toward Science & Scientists: A Study of Legislative Reactions to Atomic Energy & the Political Participation of Scientists. Arno.

Hall, Henry Edgar, 1928-
xHall, H. E.
Solid State Physics. Wiley.

Hall, Hubert, 1857-1944
xHall, Hubert.
Court Life Under the Plantagenets: Reign of Henry the Second. Arno.
Studies in English Official Historical Documents. B Franklin.

Hall, J. L. see Hall, John Lloyd.

Hall, Jacquelyn D. see Hall, Jacquelyn Dowd.

Hall, Jacquelyn Dowd.
xHall, Jacquelyn D.
Revolt Against Chivalry: Jessie Daniel Ames & the Women's Campaign Against Lynching. Columbia U Pr.

Hall, James, 1917-
xHall, James.
Dictionary of Subjects & Symbols in Art. Har-Row.
Memoir of the Public Services of William Henry Harrison, of Ohio. Arno.

Hall, James B.
xHall, James B.
Modern Culture & the Arts. McGraw.
The Realm of Fiction: 74 Short Stories. McGraw.

Hall, James H. see Hall, James Hust.

Hall, James Hust.
xHall, James H.
Art Song. U of Okla Pr.

Hall, James N. see Hall, James Norman.

Hall, James Norman, 1887-1951
xHall, James N.
Under a Thatched Roof. Arno.

Hall, James P. see Hall, James Patrick.

Hall, James Patrick, 1937-
    xHall, James P.
        Peacekeeping in America: A Developmental
            Study of American Law Enforcement:
            Philosophy & Systems. Kendall-Hunt.
Hall, James W. see Hall, James William.
Hall, James William, 1937-
    xHall, James W.
        ed. Forging the American Character. Krieger.
Hall, Jay C. see Hall, Jay Cameron.
Hall, Jay Cameron, 1915-
    xHall, Jay C.
        Inside the Crime Lab. P-H.
Hall, Jennie, 1875-1921
    xHall, Jennie.
        Buried Cities. Macmillan.
Hall, Jerome, 1901-
    xHall, Jerome.
        Comparative Law & Social Theory. La State U
            Pr.
Hall, Joan J. see Hall, Joan Joffe.
Hall, Joan Joffe.
    xHall, Joan J.
        The Rift Zone. Curbstone.
Hall, Joanne E.
    xHall, Joanne E.
        Distributive Nursing Practice: A Systems
            Approach to Community Health. Lippincott.
Hall, John F. see Hall, John Fry.
Hall, John Fry, 1919-
    xHall, John F.
        Classical Conditioning & Instrumental
            Learning: A Contemporary Approach.
            Lippincott.
Hall, John Lloyd.
    xHall, J. L.
        Cell Membranes & Ion Transport. Longman.
        Plant Cell Structure & Metabolism. Longman.
Hall, John W. see Hall, John Whitney.
Hall, John Whitney, 1916-
    xHall, John W.
        Government & Local Power in Japan, 500 to
            1700: A Study Based on the Bizen Province.
            Princeton U Pr.
        ed. Medieval Japan: Essays in Institutional
            History. Yale U Pr.
Hall, Katy.
    xHall, Katy.
        Nothing but Soup. Follett.
Hall, Kenneth, 1906-
    xHall, Kenneth.
        The Origins of the English-Speaking People.
            Vantage.
Hall, Kermit.
    xHall, Kermit L.
        The Politics of Justice: Lower Federal Judicial
            Selection & the Second Party System,
            1829-1861. U of Nebr Pr.
Hall, Kermit L. see Hall, Kermit.
Hall, Lawrence B., 1909-
    xHall, Lawrence B.
        ed. Planetary Quarantine: Principles, Methods
            & Problems. Gordon.
Hall, Leonard, 1899-
    xHall, Leonard.
        Stars Upstream: Life Along an Ozark River. U
            of Chicago Pr.
        Stars Upstream: Life Along an Ozark River. U
            of Mo Pr.
Hall, Lynn.
    xHall, Lynn.

Dragon Defiant. Follett.
Flash, Dog of Old Egypt. Garrard.
Flowers of Anger. Avon.
Flowers of Anger. Follett.
Gently Touch the Milkweed. Avon.
Horse Called Dragon. Follett.
The Mystery of the Lost & Found Hound.
    Garrard.
The Mystery of the Schoolhouse Dog. Garrard.
Ride a Wild Dream. Avon.
Riff, Remember. Avon.
Riff Remember. Follett.
The Shy Ones. Avon.
The Siege of Silent Henry. Avon.
The Siege of Silent Henry. Follett.
Sticks & Stones. Dell.
Sticks & Stones. Follett.
Stray. Avon.
Stray. Follett.
Troublemaker. Avon.
Troublemaker. Follett.
Hall, Malcolm.
    xHall, Malcolm.
        And Then the Mouse.... Schol Bk Serv.
        Caricatures. Coward.
        Derek Koogar Was a Star. Coward.
        Forecast. Coward.
Hall, Manly P. see Hall, Manly Palmer.
Hall, Manly Palmer, 1901-
    xHall, Manly P.
        Astrological Keywords. Littlefield.
        Astrological Keywords. Philos Res.
        Buddhism & Psychotherapy. Philos Res.
        Magic: A Treatise on Esoteric Ethics. Philos
            Res.
        Pathways of Philosophy. Philos Res.
        Psychoanalyzing the Twelve Zodiacal Types.
            Philos Res.
        The Spiritual Centers in Man. Philos Res.
Hall, Marcia B.
    xHall, Marcia B.
        Renovation & Counter-Reformation: Vasari &
            Duke Cosimo in Sta Maria Novella & Sta
            Croce 1565-1577. Oxford U Pr.
Hall, Margaret. see Hall, Constance Margaret.
Hall, Marie B. see Hall, Marie Bauer.
Hall, Marie Bauer.
    xHall, Marie B.
        The Christ Principle & True Christianity to Be.
            Veritas.
Hall, Marjory, 1908-
    xHall, Marjory.
        The April Ghost. Westminster.
        The Carved Wooden Ring. Westminster.
        The Gold-Lined Box. Westminster.
        The Other Girl. Westminster.
Hall, Mark W.
    xHall, Mark W.
        Broadcast Journalism: An Introduction to
            News Writing. Hastings.
Hall, Marshall, 1910-
    xHall , Marshall.
        The Theory of Groups. Chelsea Pub.
Hall, Mary A. see Hall, Mary Anne.
Hall, Mary Anne.
    xHall, Mary A.
        Linguistic Foundations for Reading. Merrill.
    xHall, MaryAnne.
        Reading & the Elementary School Child. Van
            Nos Reinhold.
        Teaching Reading As a Language Experience.
            Merrill.
Hall, MaryAnne. see Hall, Mary Anne.
Hall, Michael G. see Hall, Michael Garibaldi.
Hall, Michael Garibaldi.
    xHall, Michael G.

Edward Randolph & the American Colonies,
    1676-1703. Norton.
Edward Randolph & the American Colonies,
    1676-1703. U of NC Pr.
Hall, N. John.
    xHall, N. John.
        Trollope & His Illustrators. St Martin.
Hall, Nancy L. see Hall, Nancy Lee.
Hall, Nancy Lee.
    xHall, Nancy L.
        A True Story of a Drunken Mother. Daughters.
Hall, Nor.
    xHall, Nor.
        The Moon & the Virgin: Reflections on the
            Archetypal Feminine. Har-Row.
Hall, Norman.
    xHall, Norman.
        Botanists of the Eucalypts. Intl Schol Bk Serv.
Hall, Oakley. see Hall, Oakley M.
Hall, Oakley M.
    xHall, Oakley.
        The Bad Lands. Atheneum.
        The Bad Lands. Fawcett.
        Warlock. U of Nebr Pr.
Hall, Peter.
    xHall, Peter.
        The Containment of Urban England. Allen
            Unwin.
Hall, Peter. see Hall, Peter Geoffrey.
Hall, Peter Geoffrey.
    xHall, Peter.
        World Cities. McGraw.
Hall, Phoebe.
    xHall, Phoebe.
        Reforming the Welfare: The Politics of Change
            in the Personal Social Services. Heinemann
            Ed.
Hall, R. see Hall, Robert Anderson.
Hall, Richard. see Hall, Richard Seymour.
Hall, Richard H., 1934-
    xHall, Richard H.
        Occupations & the Social Structure. P-H.
    xHall, Richard S.
        Organizations: Structure & Process. P-H.
Hall, Richard S. see Hall, Richard H.
Hall, Richard Seymour, 1925-
    xHall, Richard.
        The High Price of Principles: Kaunda & the
            White South. Holmes & Meier.
        Lovers on the Nile: The Incredible African
            Journeys of Sam & Florence Baker. Random.
Hall, Robert. see Hall, Robert Tom.
Hall, Robert A. see Hall, Robert Anderson.
Hall, Robert Anderson, 1911-
    xHall, R.
        Proto-Romance Phonology. Elsevier.
    xHall, Robert A.
        Analytical Grammar of the Hungarian
            Language. Kraus Repr.
        Antonio Fogazzaro. Twayne.
        The Comic Style of P. G. Wodehouse. Shoe
            String.
        Descriptive Italian Grammar. Greenwood.
        External History of the Romance Languages.
            Elsevier.
        Hungarian Grammar. Kraus Repr.
        Melanesian Pidgin English: Grammar, Texts,
            Vocabulary. AMS Pr.
Hall, Robert B. see Hall, Robert Benjamin.
Hall, Robert Benjamin.
    xHall, Robert B.
        Anyone Can Prophesy. Episcopal Ctr.
        Anyone Can Prophesy. Seabury.
Hall, Robert Burnett.
    xHall, Robert B.
        Japanese Geography: A Guide to Japanese
            Reference & Research Materials. Greenwood.
Hall, Robert K. see Hall, Robert King.
Hall, Robert King, 1912-
    xHall, Robert K.

Education for a New Japan. Greenwood.
Hall, Robert L. see Hall, Robert Lee.
Hall, Robert Lee.
  xHall, Robert L.
    Exit Sherlock Holmes: The Great Detective's
    Final Days. Scribner.
    The King Edward Plot. McGraw.
Hall, Robert Lowe, Sir.
  xHall, Robert L.
    Economic System in a Socialist State. Russell.
Hall, Robert Tom.
  xHall, Robert.
    Moral Education in Theory & Practice.
    Prometheus Bks.
Hall, Rodney, 1935-
  xHall, Rodney.
    Black Bagatelles. U of Queensland Pr.
    Place Among People. U of Queensland Pr.
Hall, Rosalys. see Hall, Rosalys Haskell.
Hall, Rosalys Haskell.
  xHall, Rosalys.
    Bright & Shining Breadboard. Lothrop.
Hall, Steven.
  xHall, Steven.
    Down Came the Sun. Barlenmir.
Hall, Susan.
  xHall, Susan.
    Gentleman of Leisure: A Year in the Life of a
    Pimp. NAL.
Hall, Thadd E., 1936-
  xHall, Thadd E.
    France & the Eighteenth-Century Corsican
    Question. NYU Pr.
Hall, Thomas S. see Hall, Thomas Steele.
Hall, Thomas Steele, 1909-
  xHall, Thomas S.
    Source Book in Animal Biology. Harvard U Pr.
Hall, Thor, 1927-
  xHall, Thor.
    Anders Nygren. Word Bks.
Hall, Timothy C.
  xHall, Timothy C.
    Nucleic Acids in Plants. CRC Pr.
Hall, Tom, 1938-
  xHall, Tom.
    Total Sailing. A S Barnes.
Hall, Trevor H.
  xHall, Trevor H.
    Search for Harry Price. Biblio Dist.
Hall, Vivian A. see Hall, Vivian Anderson.
Hall, Vivian Anderson, 1932-
  xHall, Vivian A.
    Be My Guest. Moody.
Hall, Walter.
  xHall, Walter.
    Barnacle Parp's Chain Saw Guide. Rodale Pr
    Inc.
Hall, Walter P. see Hall, Walter Phelps.
Hall, Walter Phelps, 1884-1962
  xHall, Walter P.
    British Radicalism, 1791-1797. Octagon.
Hall, William C.
  xHall, William C.
    Wordsworth. Folcroft.
Hall, William J. see Hall, William John.
Hall, William John, 1939-
  xHall, William J.
    Pulmonary Disease Review. Arco.
Hall, William W.
  xHall, William W.
    General Sessions Court. Michie.
Hall-Quest, A. L. see Hall-Quest, Alfred Lawrence.
Hall-Quest, Alfred Lawrence, 1879-
  xHall-Quest, A. L.
    Professional Secondary Education in Teacher's
    Colleges. AMS Pr.
Hall-Smith, Patrick.
  xHall-Smith, Patrick.
    Dermatology. Grune.
Hallahan, D. see Hallahan, Daniel P.

Hallahan, Daniel P.
  xHallahan, D.
    Introduction to Learning Disabilities: The
    Psycho-Behavioral Approach. P-H.
  xHallahan, Daniel P.
    Exceptional Children: Introduction to Special
    Education. P-H.
Hallahan, William. see Hallahan, William H.
Hallahan, William H.
  xHallahan, William.
    Keeper of the Children. Morrow.
  xHallahan, William H.
    Keeper of the Children. Avon.
Hallam, A. see Hallam, Anthony.
Hallam, Anthony.
  xHallam, A.
    Atlas of Palaeobiogeography. Elsevier.
Hallam, Harry M. see Hallam, Harry Maurice.
Hallam, Harry Maurice.
  xHallam, Harry M.
    Saudi Arabia & the Economic & Political
    Control of the World. Inst Econ Pol.
Hallam, Jack.
  xHallam, Jack.
    Ghosts' Who's Who. David & Charles.
Hallberg, Edmond C.
  xHallberg, Edmund.
    The Gray Itch: The Male Metapause
    Syndrome. Warner Bks.
Hallberg, Edmund. see Hallberg, Edmond C.
Hallberg, Peter.
  xHallberg, Peter.
    Halldor Laxness. Irvington.
    Old Icelandic Poetry: Eddic Lay & Skaldic
    Verse. U of Nebr Pr.
Hallberg, Robert Von. see Von Hallberg, Robert.
Halle, Louis J. see Halle, Louis Joseph.
Halle, Louis Joseph, 1910-
  xHalle, Louis J.
    Cold War As History. Har-Row.
    Dream & Reality: Aspects of American Foreign
    Policy. Greenwood.
    Ideological Imagination. Times Bks.
    Men & Nations. Princeton U Pr.
    Out of Chaos. HM.
    The Society of Man. Greenwood.
    The Storm Petrel & the Owl of Athena.
    Princeton U Pr.
Halle, Morris.
  xHalle, Morris.
    ed. Linguistic Theory & Psychological Reality.
    MIT Pr.
    Sound Pattern of Russian: A Linguistic &
    Acoustical Investigation. Mouton.
Halleck, Seymour. see Halleck, Seymour L.
Halleck, Seymour L.
  xHalleck, Seymour.
    Politics of Therapy. Aronson.
    Psychiatric Aspects of Criminology. C C
    Thomas.
  xHalleck, Seymour L.
    Psychiatry & the Dilemmas of Crime: A Study
    of Causes, Punishment & Treatment. U of
    Cal Pr.
Hallenbeck, Cleve.
  xHallenbeck, Cleve.
    Legends of the Spanish Southwest. Gale.
Hallenbeck, Phyllis N. see Hallenbeck, Phyllis Newton.
Hallenbeck, Phyllis Newton, 1921-
  xHallenbeck, Phyllis N.
    Dogmatism & Visual Loss. Am Foun Blind.
Hallendorff, Carl J. see Hallendorff, Carl Jakob Herman.
Hallendorff, Carl Jakob Herman.
  xHallendorff, Carl J.
    History of Sweden. AMS Pr.
Haller, J. Alex. see Haller, J. Alexander.
Haller, J. Alexander.
  xHaller, J. Alex.

Surgical Emergencies in the Newborn. Lea &
    Febiger.
Haller, John S.
  xHaller, John S.
    Outcasts from Evolution: Scientific Attitudes of
    Racial Inferiority, 1859-1900. McGraw.
    Outcasts from Evolution: Scientific Attitudes of
    Racial Inferiority, 1859-1900. U of Ill Pr.
Haller, Jurgen.
  xHaller, Jurgen.
    Hormonal Contraception. Geron-X.
Haller, Margaret.
  xHaller, Margaret.
    Collecting Old Photographs. Arco.
Haller, Mark H. see Haller, Mark Hughlin.
Haller, Mark Hughlin, 1928-
  xHaller, Mark H.
    Eugenics: Hereditarian Attitudes in American
    Thought. Rutgers U Pr.
Haller, Raphael M.
  xHaller, Raphael M.
    Speech Pathology & Audiology in Medical
    Settings. Thieme-Stratton.
Haller, William, 1885-
  xHaller, William.
    Early Life of Robert Southey. Octagon.
    The Early Life of Robert Southey: 1774-1803.
    Norwood Edns.
    Liberty & Reformation in the Puritan
    Revolution. Columbia U Pr.
Hallett, Garth.
  xHallett, Garth.
    A Companion to Wittgenstein's Philosophical
    Investigations. Cornell U Pr.
Hallett, Kathryn, 1937-
  xHallett, Kathryn.
    A Guide for Single Parents: Transactional
    Analysis for People in Crisis. Celestial Arts.
Halley, Edmond, 1656-1742
  xHalley, Edmond.
    Correspondence & Papers of Edmond Halley.
    Arno.
Halley, Laurence.
  xHalley, Laurence.
    Simultaneous Equations. St Martin.
Hallgarten, F. L. see Hallgarten, S. F.
Hallgarten, Peter.
  xHallgarten, Peter.
    Spirits & Liqueurs. Merrimack Bk Serv.
Hallgarten, S. F.
  xHallgarten, F. L.
    Wines & Wine Gardens of Austria. Intl Pubns
    Serv.
Halliburton, David.
  xHalliburton, David.
    Edgar Allan Poe: A Phenomenological View.
    Princeton U Pr.
Halliburton, John H. see Halliburton, John Howard.
Halliburton, John Howard, 1954-
  xHalliburton, John H.
    Clarksville Architecture. J Halliburton.
Halliburton, R.
  xHalliburton, R.
    The Tulsa Race War of 1921. R & E Res
    Assoc.
Halliburton, Warren. see Halliburton, Warren J.
Halliburton, Warren J.
  xHalliburton, Warren.
    The Fighting Redtails: America's First Black
    Airmen. Silver.
Halliday, Anne.
  xHalliday, Anne.
    Decorating with Crochet. HM.
Halliday, Brett.
  xHalliday, Brett.
    Guilty As Hell. Dell.
Halliday, Carol.
  xHalliday, Carol.

Stimulating Environments for Children Who
Are Visually Impaired. C C Thomas.

Halliday, David.
xHalliday, David.
Fundamentals of Physics. Wiley.
Halliday, Frank E. see Halliday, Frank Ernest.

Halliday, Frank Ernest, 1903-
xHalliday, Frank E.
The Enjoyment of Shakespeare. Greenwood.

Halliday, Fred.
xHalliday, Fred.
Iran: Dictatorship & Development. Penguin.

Halliday, Jerry.
xHalliday, Jerry.
Spaced Out & Gathered in: A Sort of an
Autobiography of a Jesus Freak. Revell.

Halliday, Jon.
xHalliday, Jon.
ed. The Psychology of Gambling. Har-Row.
ed. The Psychology of Gambling. Peter Smith.
Halliday, Michael A. see Halliday, Michael Alexander
Kirkwood.

Halliday, Michael Alexander Kirkwood.
xHalliday, Michael A.
Explorations in the Functions of Language.
Elsevier.
Learning How to Mean: Explorations in the
Development of Language. Elsevier.

Halliday, Tim, 1945-
xHalliday, Tim.
Vanishing Birds: Their Natural History &
Conservation. HR&W.
Halliday, W. R. see Halliday, William Reginald.
Halliday, William. see Halliday, William Reginald.

Halliday, William R., 1926-
xHalliday, William R.
Depths of the Earth: Caves & Cavers of the
United States. Har-Row.
Halliday, William R. see Halliday, William Reginald.

Halliday, William Reginald, 1886-
xHalliday, W. R.
Pagan Background of Early Christianity.
Cooper Sq.
xHalliday, William.
Indo-European Folk-Tales & Greek Legend.
Folcroft.
xHalliday, William R.
Greek & Roman Folklore. Cooper Sq.
Hallie, Philip P. see Hallie, Philip Paul.

Hallie, Philip Paul.
xHallie, Philip P.
Lest Innocent Blood Be Shed: The Story of the
Village of Le Chambon & How Goodness
Happened There. Har-Row.
The Paradox of Cruelty. Columbia U Pr.
xHallie, Phillip.
Lest Innocent Blood Be Shed: The Story of the
Village of Le Chambon, & How Goodness
Happened There. Har-Row.
Hallie, Phillip. see Hallie, Philip Paul.
Hallinan, M. see Hallinan, Maureen T.

Hallinan, Maureen T.
xHallinan, M.
The Structure of Positive Sentiment. Elsevier.

Hallinan, P. K.
xHallinan, P. K.
I'm Glad to Be Me. Childrens.
illus. That's What a Friend Is. Childrens.
Where's Michael?. Childrens.
Halline, Allan G. see Halline, Allan Gates.

Halline, Allan Gates.
xHalline, Allan G.
ed. American Plays. AMS Pr.

Halling, J.
xHalling, J.
ed. Principles of Tribology. Scholium Intl.

Hallion, Richard.
xHallion, Richard P.

Legacy of Flight: The Guggenheim
Contribution to American Aviation. U of
Wash Pr.
Hallion, Richard P. see Hallion, Richard.

Hallissey, Robert C., 1941-
xHallissey, Robert C.
The Rajput Rebellion Against Aurangzeb: A
Study of the Mughal Empire in
Seventeenth-Century India. U of Mo Pr.

Halliwell, Leslie.
xHalliwell, Leslie.
Halliwell's Movie Quiz. Penguin.
Halliwell-Phillipps, James O. see Halliwell-Phillipps,
James Orchard.

Halliwell-Phillipps, James Orchard, 1820-1889
xHalliwell-Phillipps, James O.
Dictionary of Archaic & Provincial Words,
Obsolete Phrases, Proverbs, & Ancient
Customs, from the Fourteenth Century. AMS
Pr.
Dictionary of Archaic & Provincial Words,
Obsolete Phrases, Proverbs, & Ancient
Customs, from the Fourteenth Century. Gale.
ed. Dictionary of Archaic & Provincial Words,
Obsolete Phrases, Proverbs, & Ancient
Customs from the 14th Century. Johnson
Repr.
Illustrations of the Fairy Mythology of a
Midsummer Night's Dream. AMS Pr.
An Introduction to Shakespeare's Midsummer
Night's Dream. Folcroft.
Life of William Shakespeare. AMS Pr.
Memoranda on All's Well That Ends Well,
The Two Gentlemen of Verona, Much Ado
About Nothing & on Titus Andronicus. AMS
Pr.
Memoranda on Love's Labour's Lost, King
John, Othello, & Romeo & Juliet. AMS Pr.
Memoranda on Shakespeare's Comedy of
Measure for Measure. AMS Pr.
Memoranda on Shakespeare's Tragedy of
Troilus & Cressida. AMS Pr.
Memoranda on the Tragedy of Hamlet. AMS
Pr.
Observations on Some of the Manuscript
Emendations of the Text of Shakespeare.
AMS Pr.
Outlines of the Life of Shakespeare. AMS Pr.
ed. Thornton Romances: The Early English
Metrical Romances of Perceval, Isumbras,
Eglamour & Degravant. AMS Pr.
Hallman, E. S. see Hallman, Eugene S.

Hallman, Eugene S.
xHallman, E. S.
Broadcasting in Canada. Routledge & Kegan.

Hallman, Grady L.
xHallman, Grady L.
Surgical Treatment of Congenital Heart
Disease. Lea & Febiger.

Hallman, Howard W.
xHallman, Howard W.
Community-Based Employment Programs.
Johns Hopkins.
Neighborhood Government in a Metropolitan
Setting. Sage.
The Organization & Operation of
Neighborhood Councils: A Practical Guide.
Praeger.

Hallman, Ruth, 1929-
xHallman, Ruth.
Gimme Something, Mister!. Westminster.
I Gotta Be Free. Westminster.
Midnight Wheels. Westminster.
Secrets of a Silent Stranger. Westminster.

Hallmark, Clayton.
xHallmark, Clayton.

Computerist's Handy Databook-Dictionary.
TAB Bks.
Computerist's Handy Manual. TAB Bks.
Lasers, the Light Fantastic. TAB Bks.
Understanding & Using the Oscilloscope. TAB
Bks.
xHallmark, Clayton L.
How to Repair Old-Time Radios. TAB Bks.

Hallmark, Clayton L.
xHallmark, Clayton L.
The Master IC Cookbook. TAB Bks.
Hallmark, Clayton L. see Hallmark, Clayton.

Hallmark, Rufus E., 1943-
xHallmark, Rufus E.
The Genesis of Schumann's Dichterliebe: A
Source Study. Univ Microfilms.

Hallo, William W.
xHallo, William W.
The Ancient Near East: A History. HarBraceJ.
Hallock, Richard T. see Hallock, Richard Treadwell.

Hallock, Richard Treadwell, 1906-
xHallock, Richard T.
Persepolis Fortification Tablets. U of Chicago
Pr.

Halloran, Jack, 1931-
xHalloran, Jack.
Applied Human Relations: An Organizational
Approach. P-H.
Halloran, James D. see Halloran, James Dermot.

Halloran, James Dermot.
xHalloran, James D.
Attitude Formation & Change. Greenwood.
Hallowell, A. Irving. see Hallowell, Alfred Irving.

Hallowell, Alfred Irving, 1892-1974
xHallowell, A. Irving.
Contributions to Anthropology: Selected Papers
of A. Irving Hallowell. U of Chicago Pr.
Culture & Experience. U of Pa Pr.

Hallowell, Christopher.
xHallowell, Christopher L.
People of the Bayou: Cajun Life in Lost
America. Dutton.
Hallowell, Christopher L. see Hallowell, Christopher.
Hallowell, John H. see Hallowell, John Hamilton.

Hallowell, John Hamilton, 1913-
xHallowell, John H.
Moral Foundation of Democracy. U of Chicago
Pr.

Halls, W. D.
xHalls, W. D.
Maurice Maeterlinck: A Study of His Life &
Thought. Greenwood.

Hallstead, William F.
xHallstead, William F.
Conqueror of the Clouds. Elsevier-Nelson.
Ghost Plane of Blackwater. HarBraceJ.
Ghost Plane of Blackwater. HarBraceJ.
The Man Downstairs. Elsevier-Nelson.

Hallstein, Walter, 1901-
xHallstein, Walter.
Europe in the Making. Norton.
European Community: A New Path to Peaceful
Union. Asia.
Halm, George N. see Halm, George Nikolaus.

Halm, George Nikolaus, 1901-
xHalm, George N.
A Guide to International Monetary Reform.
Lexington Bks.
Halmos, P. R. see Halmos, Paul Richard.

Halmos, Paul.
xHalmos, Paul.
The Faith of the Counsellors: A Study in the
Theory & Practice of Social Case Work &
Psychotherapy. Schocken.
The Personal Service Society. Schocken.
Solitude & Privacy: A Study of Social Isolation,
Its Causes & Therapy. Greenwood.
Halmos, Paul R. see Halmos, Paul Richard.

Halmos, Paul Richard, 1914-
xHalmos, P. R.

A Hilbert Space Problem Book.
Springer-Verlag.
Lectures on Boolean Algebras. Springer-Verlag.
Measure Theory. Springer-Verlag.
xHalmos, Paul R.
Lectures on Ergodic Theory. Chelsea Pub.
Halper, Albert.
xHalper, Albert.
The Chute. AMS Pr.
The Little People. AMS Pr.
Halper, Emanuel B., 1933-
xHalper, Emanuel B.
The Wonderful World of Real Estate. Warren.
Halper, Emmanuel B. *see* Halper, Emanuel B.
Halper, Stefan A.
xHalper, Stefan A.
ed. Latin America: The Dynamics of Social
Change. St Martin.
Halperin, Don A.
xHalperin, Don A.
Ancient Synagogues of the Iberian Peninsula. U
Presses Fla.
Halperin, John, 1941-
xHalperin, John.
Egoism & Self Discovery in the Victorian
Novel: Studies in the Ordeal of Knowledge in
the Nineteenth Century. B Franklin.
ed. The Theory of the Novel: New Essays.
Oxford U Pr.
Halperin, Mark, 1940-
xHalperin, Mark.
Backroads. U of Pittsburgh Pr.
Halperin, Michael.
xHalperin, Michael.
Helping Maltreated Children: School &
Community Involvement. Mosby.
Halperin, Morton H.
xHalperin, Morton H.
Bureaucratic Politics & Foreign Policy.
Brookings.
Defense Strategies for the Seventies. Little.
The Lawless State: The Crimes of the U.S.
Intelligence Agencies. Penguin.
Limited War: An Essay on the Development of
the Theory & an Annotated Bibliography.
AMS Pr.
Limited War in the Nuclear Age. Greenwood.
Halperin, Rhoda.
xHalperin, Rhoda.
Peasant Livelihood: Studies in Economic
Anthropology & Cultural Ecology. St Martin.
Halperin-Donghi, T. *see* Halperin-Donghi, Tulio.
Halperin-Donghi, Tulio.
xHalperin-Donghi, T.
Politics, Economics & Society in Argentina in
the Revolutionary Period. Cambridge U Pr.
Halpern, Ben.
xHalpern, Ben.
Idea of the Jewish State. Harvard U Pr.
Halpern, Daniel, 1945-
xHalpern, Daniel.
ed. The American Poetry Anthology. Avon.
Street Fire. SBD.
Street Fire. Viking Pr.
Halpern, Frieda.
xHalpern, Frieda.
Full-Color Russian Folk Needlepoint Designs
Charted for Easy Use.. Dover.
Halpern, Harvey.
xHalpern, Harvey.
Adult Aphasia. Bobbs.
Halpern, Jay.
xHalpern, Jay.
The Jade Unicorn. Avon.
The Jade Unicorn. Macmillan.
Halpern, Joseph.
xHalpern, Joseph.

Critical Fictions: The Literary Criticism of
Jean-Paul Sartre. Yale U Pr.
Halpern, Leopold.
xHalpern, Leopold.
ed. On the Measurement of Cosmological
Variations of the Gravitational Constant.
Univ Microfilms.
Halpern, Manfred.
xHalpern, Manfred.
Politics of Social Change in the Middle East &
North Africa. Princeton U Pr.
Halpern, Paul G., 1937-
xHalpern, Paul G.
Mediterranean Naval Situation, 1908-1914.
Harvard U Pr.
Halpern, S. *see* Halpern, Siegmund.
Halpern, Siegmund, 1918-
xHalpern, S.
The Assurance Sciences: An Introduction to
Quality Control & Reliability. P-H.
Halpern, Stephen M. *see* Halpern, Stephen Mark.
Halpern, Stephen Mark.
xHalpern, Stephen M.
Looking Back: Modern America in Historical
Perspective. Rand.
Halpern, Susan.
xHalpern, Susan.
Drug Abuse & Your Company. Am Mgmt.
Halpern, Werner I.
xHalpern, Werner I.
Human Resources for Troubled Children.
Krieger.
Halpin, Daniel W.
xHalpin, Daniel W.
Design of Construction & Process Operations.
Wiley.
Halpine, Charles G. *see* Halpine, Charles Graham.
Halpine, Charles Graham, 1829-1868
xHalpine, Charles G.
Life & Adventures, Songs, Services, &
Speeches of Private Miles O'reilly. AMS Pr.
Halprin, Lawrence.
xHalprin, Lawrence.
Cities. MIT Pr.
Halsall, E. *see* Halsall, Elizabeth.
Halsall, Elizabeth.
xHalsall, E.
The Comprehensive School: Guidelines for the
Reorganization of Secondary Education.
Pergamon.
Halsband, Robert, 1914-
xHalsband, Robert.
Life of Lady Mary Wortley Montagu. Oxford
U Pr.
Lord Hervey, Eighteenth Century Courtier.
Oxford U Pr.
Halse, Albert O., 1910-
xHalse, Albert O.
The Use of Color in Interiors. McGraw.
Halsell, Grace.
xHalsell, Grace.
The Illegals. Stein & Day.
Soul Sister. Fawcett.
Halseth, James A.
xHalseth, James A.
ed. Northwest Mosaic: Minority Conflicts in
Pacific Northwest History. Pruett.
Halsey, A. H.
xHalsey, A. H.
British Academics. Harvard U Pr.
ed. Education, Economy, & Society: A Reader
in the Sociology of Education. Free Pr.
Halsey, Elizabeth, 1890-
xHalsey, Elizabeth.
Inquiry & Invention in Physical Education. Lea
& Febiger.
Halsey, Harlan. *see* Halsey, Harlan Page.
Halsey, Harlan Page, 1839?-1898
xHalsey, Harlan.

Flyaway Ned: The Old Detective's Pupil.
Arno.
Halsey, Henry R. *see* Halsey, Henry Rowland.
Halsey, Henry Rowland, 1885-
xHalsey, Henry R.
Borrowing Money for the Public Schools: A
Study of Borrowing Practices in the
Administration of Public Schools in Florida.
AMS Pr.
Halsey, Margaret, 1910-
xHalsey, Margaret.
No Laughing Matter: The Autobiography of a
WASP. Lippincott.
Halsey, Martha T.
xHalsey, Martha T.
Antonio Buero Vallejo. Twayne.
Halsey, Peggy L.
xHalsey, Peggy L.
ed. If You Want to Know Me: Reflections of
Life in Southern Africa. Friend Pr.
Halsey, Richard S., 1929-
xHalsey, Richard S.
Classical Music Recordings for Home &
Library. ALA.
Halsey, William M., 1945-
xHalsey, William M.
The Survival of American Innocence:
Catholicism in an Era of Disillusionment,
1920-1940. U of Notre Dame Pr.
Halstead, Beverly.
xHalstead, Beverly.
A Closer Look at Prehistoric Mammals. Watts.
A Closer Look at Prehistoric Reptiles. Watts.
A Closer Look at the Dawn of Life. Watts.
Halstead, Fred.
xHalstead, Fred.
Out Now!: A Participant's Account of the
American Movement Against the Vietnam
War. Monad Pr.
Halstead, John P.
xHalstead, John P.
Compiled by Modern European Imperialism: A
Bibliography of Books & Articles, 1815-1972.
G K Hall.
Halsted, Byron D. *see* Halsted, Byron David.
Halsted, Byron David, 1852-1918
xHalsted, Byron D.
ed. Barns, Sheds & Outbuildings. Dairy Goat.
ed. Barns, Sheds & Outbuildings. Greene.
Halter, Jon C.
xHalter, Jon C.
Their Backs to the Wall: Famous Last Stands.
Messner.
Halvorsen, Robert.
xHalvorsen, Robert.
Econometric Models of U.S. Energy Demand.
Lexington Bks.
Halvorson, Loren. *see* Halvorson, Loren E.
Halvorson, Loren E., 1927-
xHalvorson, Loren.
Peace on Earth Handbook. Augsburg.
Halvorson, Peter L.
xHalvorson, Peter L.
Atlas of Religious Change in America:
1952-1971. Glenmary Res Ctr.
Ham, Arthur W. *see* Ham, Arthur Worth.
Ham, Arthur Worth.
xHam, Arthur W.
Blood Cell Formation & the Cellular Basis of
Immune Responses. Lippincott.
Histology. Lippincott.
Histophysiology of Cartilage, Bone & Joints.
Lippincott.
Ham, Richard G.
xHam, Richard G.
Mechanisms of Development. Mosby.
Ham, Roswell G. *see* Ham, Roswell Gray.
Ham, Roswell Gray, 1891-
xHam, Roswell G.

Otway & Lee: Biography from a Baroque Age. Greenwood.

Hamachek, Don E.
xHamachek, Don E.
Human Dynamics in Psychology & Education: Selected Readings. Allyn.
Psychology in Teaching, Learning, & Growth. Allyn.

Hamacher, V. C.
xHamacher, V. C.
Computer Organization. McGraw.

Hamada, Hirosuke.
xHamada, Hirosuke.
Little Mouse Who Tarried. Schol Bk Serv.

Hamalainen, P. K. see Hamalainen, Pekka Kalevi.

Hamalainen, Pekka Kalevi.
xHamalainen, P. K.
In Time of Storm: Revolution, Civil War & the Ethnolinguistic Issue in Finland. State U NY Pr.

Hamalian, Leo.
xHamalian, Leo.
Burn After Reading. Ararat Pr.
ed. Grammar in Context. Putnam.
New Writing from the Middle East. NAL.
ed. New Writing from the Middle East. Ungar.
Rogues: Stories of Swindlers, Thieves, & Confidence Men. T Y Crowell.

Hamann, H. P. see Hamann, Henry Paul.

Hamann, Henry Paul.
xHamann, H. P.
A Popular Guide to New Testament Criticism. Concordia.

Hamberg, Daniel.
xHamberg, Daniel.
Economic Growth & Instability: A Study in the Problem of Capital Accumulation, Employment, & the Business Cycle. Greenwood.

Hambidge, Jay.
xHambidge, Jay.
Practical Applications of Dynamic Symmetry. Devin.

Hamblen, Abigail Ann.
xHamblen, Abigal A.
Ruth Suckow. Boise St Univ.

Hamblen, Abigal A. see Hamblen, Abigail Ann.

Hamblen, Emily S., 1864-
xHamblen, Emily S.
On the Minor Prophecies of William Blake. Haskell.
On the Minor Prophecies of William Blake. R West.

Hambleton, Robin.
xHambleton, Robin.
Policy Planning & Local Government. Allanheld.

Hamblett, Theora.
xHamblett, Theora.
Theora Hamblett Paintings. U Pr of Miss.

Hamblin, Dora J. see Hamblin, Dora Jane.

Hamblin, Dora Jane, 1920-
xHamblin, Dora J.
That Was the Life. Norton.
xHamblin, Dora Jane.
That Was the LIFE. Norton.

Hamblin, Douglas.
xHamblin, Douglas H.
The Teacher & Counselling. Biblio Dist.
The Teacher & Pastoral Care. Biblio Dist.

Hamblin, Douglas H. see Hamblin, Douglas.

Hamblin, F. D. see Hamblin, Frederick Douglas.

Hamblin, Frederick Douglas.
xHamblin, F. D.
Abridged Thermodynamic & Thermochemical Tables in S. I. Units. Pergamon.

Hamblin, Kenneth W. see Hamblin, William Kenneth.

Hamblin, R. L. see Hamblin, Robert Lee.

Hamblin, Robert. see Hamblin, Robert Lee.

Hamblin, Robert Lee, 1927-
xHamblin, R. L.
A Mathematical Theory of Social Change. Krieger.
xHamblin, Robert.
ed. The Humanization Processes: A Social, Behavioral Analysis of Children's Problems. Krieger.

Hamblin, Robert W.
xHamblin, Robert W.
Selections from the William Faulkner Collection of Louis Daniel Brodsky: A Descriptive Catalogue. U Pr of Va.

Hamblin, W. K. see Hamblin, William Kenneth.

Hamblin, W. Kenneth. see Hamblin, William Kenneth.

Hamblin, William Kenneth.
xHamblin, Kenneth W.
The Earth's Dynamic Systems: A Textbook Physical Geology. Burgess.
xHamblin, W. K.
The Earth's Dynamic Systems: A Textbook in Physical Geology. Burgess.
xHamblin, W. Kenneth.
Exercises in Physical Geology. Burgess.

Hamburg, C. Bruce.
xHamburg, C. Bruce.
Patent Fraud & Inequitable Conduct. Boardman.

Hamburg, David A.
xHamburg, David A.
The Great Apes. Benjamin-Cummings.

Hamburg, Morris, 1922-
xHamburg, Morris.
Basic Statistics: A Modern Approach. HarBraceJ.
Case Studies in Elementary School Administration. Tchrs Coll.
Library Planning & Decision-Making Systems. MIT Pr.

Hamburger, Henry, 1940-
xHamburger, Henry.
Games As Models of Social Phenomena. W H Freeman.

Hamburger, Jean.
xHamburger, Jean.
The Power & the Frailty: The Future of Medicine & the Future of Man. Macmillan.
Structure & Function of the Kidney. Saunders.

Hamburger, John, 1948-
xHamburger, John.
ed. Cross-Country Skiing Guide. Anderson World.

Hamburger, Marilyn G.
xHamburger, Marilyn G.
Collecting Figural Doorstops. A S Barnes.

Hamburger, Max.
xHamburger, Max.
Awakening of Western Legal Thought. Biblo.
Awakening of Western Legal Thought. Greenwood.

Hamburger, Robert.
xHamburger, Robert.
A Stranger in the House. Macmillan.
A Stranger in the House. Macmillan.

Hamburgh, Max, 1922-
xHamburgh, Max.
Theories of Differentiation. Univ Park.

Hamby, Robert I.
xHamby, Robert I.
Clinical-Anatomical Correlates in Coronary Artery Disease. Futura Pub.

Hameka, Hendrik F.
xHameka, Hendrik F.
Quantum Theory of the Chemical Bond. Hafner.

Hamel, Esther V. see Hamel, Esther Veramae (Knopp).

Hamel, Esther Veramae (Knopp), 1922-
xHamel, Esther V.

Encyclopedia of Judging & Exhibiting Floriculture & Flora-Artistry. Ponderosa.

Hamel, Henry G.
xHamel, Henry G.
Fiscal Years & Accounting Periods. Conference Bd.

Hamel, Peter M. see Hamel, Peter Michael.

Hamel, Peter Michael, 1947-
xHamel, Peter M.
Through Music to the Self: How to Appreciate & Experience Music Anew. Shambhala Pubns.

Hamer, Andrew. see Hamer, Andrew Marshall.

Hamer, Andrew Marshall.
xHamer, Andrew.
ed. Out of Cars - into Transit: Urban Transportation Planning Crisis. Ga St U Busn Pub.

Hamer, D. A. see Hamer, David Allan.

Hamer, D. W. see Hamer, Donald W.

Hamer, David Allan.
xHamer, D. A.
The Politics of Electoral Pressure: A Study in the History of Victorian Reform Agitation. Humanities.

Hamer, Donald W.
xHamer, D. W.
Thick Film Hybrid Microcircuit Technology. Wiley.

Hamer, Frank.
xHamer, Frank.
Potter's Dictionary of Materials & Techniques. Watson-Guptill.

Hamermesh, Morton, 1919-
xHamermesh, Morton.
Group Theory & Its Application to Physical Problems. A-W.

Hamerow, Theodore S.
xHamerow, Theodore S.
ed. Otto Von Bismarck: A Historical Assessment. Heath.
Restoration, Revolution, Reaction: Economics & Politics in Germany, 1815-1871. Princeton U Pr.

Hamerstrom, Frances, 1907-
xHamerstrom, Frances.
An Eagle to the Sky. Crossing Pr.

Hamerton, John L., 1929-
xHamerton, John L.
Human Cytogenetics. Acad Pr.

Hamerton, Philip G. see Hamerton, Philip Gilbert.

Hamerton, Philip Gilbert, 1834-1894
xHamerton, Philip G.
Intellectual Life. Arno.
Intellectual Life. C E Tuttle.
The Intellectual Life. Folcroft.
The Intellectual Life. R West.
Modern Frenchmen: Five Biographies. Arno.
Portfolio Papers. Arno.

Hamerton-Kelly, R. G.
xHamerton-Kelly, R. G.
Pre-existence, Wisdom & the Son of Man: A Study of the Idea of Pre-Existence in the New Testament. Cambridge U Pr.

Hamil, Fred C. see Hamil, Frederick Coyne.

Hamil, Frederick Coyne, 1903-
xHamil, Fred C.
The Valley of the Lower Thames, 1640-1850. U of Toronto Pr.

Hamil, James R.
xHamil, James R.
Farmland, USA. Lowell Pr.

Hamill, Ann D. see Hamill, Ann D'Onofrio.

Hamill, Ann D'Onofrio.
xHamill, Ann D.
Typing in Plain English. Pitman Learning.

Hamill, B. J. see Hamill, Bernard J.

Hamill, Bernard J.
xHamill, B. J.

Work Measurement in the Office: An MTM
    Systems Workbook. Intl Pubns Serv.
Hamill, Denis.
    xHamill, Denis.
        Stomping Ground. Delacorte.
Hamill, Edson T. see Hamill, T. Edson.
Hamill, Pete, 1935-
    xHamill, Peter.
        The Gift. Random.
Hamill, Peter. see Hamill, Pete.
Hamill, Peter V. see Hamill, Peter V. V.
Hamill, Peter V. V.
    xHamill, Peter V.
        Forced Vital Capacity of Children 6-11 Years,
           United States. Natl Ctr Health Stats.
Hamill, Sam.
    xHamill, Sam.
        The Calling Across Forever. Copper Canyon.
Hamill, T. Edson.
    xHamill, Edson T.
        The Child Killer. Nordon Pubns.
Hamilton. see Hamilton, William Roger.
Hamilton, A.
    xHamilton, A.
        Sources of the Religious Element in Flaubert's
           Salammbo. Kraus Repr.
Hamilton, Alan.
    xHamilton, Alan.
        Essential Edinburgh. Transatlantic.
Hamilton, Alexander.
    xHamilton, Alexander.
        Alexander Hamilton: A Biography in His Own
           Words. Har-Row.
        Gentleman's Progress: The Itinerarium of Dr.
           Alexander Hamilton, 1744. Greenwood.
        Industrial & Commercial Correspondence of
           Alexander Hamilton Anticipating His Report
           on Manufactures. Kelley.
        Letters of Pacificus & Helvidius. Scholl
           Facsimiles.
        Works of Alexander Hamilton. Haskell.
        The Works of Alexander Hamilton. Scholarly.
Hamilton, Angus, 1874-1913
    xHamilton, Angus.
        Somaliland. Negro U Pr.
Hamilton, Beth A.
    xHamilton, Beth A.
        Multitype Library Cooperation. Bowker.
Hamilton, Carl, 1914-
    xHamilton, Carl.
        In No Time at All. Iowa St U Pr.
Hamilton, Charles D. see Hamilton, Charles Daniel.
Hamilton, Charles Daniel, 1940-
    xHamilton, Charles D.
        Sparta's Bitter Victories: Politics & Diplomacy
           in the Corinthian War. Cornell U Pr.
Hamilton, Charles F. see Hamilton, Charles Franklin.
Hamilton, Charles Franklin, 1915-
    xHamilton, Charles F.
        As Bees in Honey Drown: Elbert Hubbard &
           the Roycrofters. A S Barnes.
        Photographing Nudes. P-H.
Hamilton, Cicely M. see Hamilton, Cicely Mary.
Hamilton, Cicely Mary, 1875-
    xHamilton, Cicely M.
        Marriage As a Trade. Gale.
Hamilton, Clarence G. see Hamilton, Clarence Grant.
Hamilton, Clarence Grant, 1865-1935
    xHamilton, Clarence G.
        Ornaments in Classical & Modern Music. AMS
           Pr.
        Touch & Expression in Piano Playing. AMS Pr.
Hamilton, Clayton M. see Hamilton, Clayton Meeker.
Hamilton, Clayton Meeker, 1881-1946
    xHamilton, Clayton M.
        Conversations on Contemporary Drama. Arno.
Hamilton, Cosmo.
    xHamilton, Cosmo.

People Worth Talking About. Arno.
People Worth Talking About. R West.
Hamilton, David.
    xHamilton, David.
        Diary of Sir David Hamilton. Oxford U Pr.
        jt. auth. Dreams of a Young Girl. Morrow.
        The Thames & Hudson Manual of
           Architectural Ceramics. Thames Hudson.
Hamilton, David. see Hamilton, David Boyce.
Hamilton, David Boyce, 1918-
    xHamilton, David.
        Evolutionary Economics: A Study of Change in
           Economic Thought. U of NM Pr.
         A Primer on the Economics of Poverty. Phila
           Bk Co.
Hamilton, David O. see Hamilton, David Osborne.
Hamilton, David Osborne.
    xHamilton, David O.
        Four Gardens. AMS Pr.
Hamilton, Donald.
    xHamilton, Donald.
        Ambushers. Fawcett.
        Death of a Citizen. Fawcett.
        The Devastators. Fawcett.
        The Menacers. Fawcett.
        Murderers' Row. Fawcett.
        The Ravagers. Fawcett.
        The Removers. Fawcett.
        Retaliators. Fawcett.
        The Silencers. Fawcett.
Hamilton, Dorothy.
    xHamilton, Dorothy.
        Anita's Choice. Herald Pr.
        Busboys at Big Bend. Herald Pr.
        The Castle. Herald Pr.
        Charco. Herald Pr.
        Christmas for Holly. Herald Pr.
        Cricket. Herald Pr.
        The Eagle. Herald Pr.
        Eric's Discovery. Herald Pr.
        The Gift of a Home. Herald Pr.
        Ken's Hideout. Herald Pr.
        Linda's Rain Tree. Herald Pr.
        Mari's Mountain. Herald Pr.
        The Quail. Herald Pr.
        Scamp & the Blizzard Boys. Herald Pr.
        Straight Mark. Herald Pr.
Hamilton, Dorothy M.
    xHamilton, Dorothy M.
        A Primer of Cooking. Ross Bks.
Hamilton, E. I.
    xHamilton, E. I.
        The Chemical Elements & Man:
           Measurements, Perspectives, Applications. C
           C Thomas.
Hamilton, E. I. see Hamilton, Eric Ishmael.
Hamilton, Earl J. see Hamilton, Earl Jefferson.
Hamilton, Earl Jefferson, 1899-
    xHamilton, Earl J.
        American Treasure & the Price Revolution in
           Spain, 1501-1650. Octagon.
        Money, Prices, & Wages in Valencia, Aragon &
           Navarre 1351-1500. Porcupine Pr.
Hamilton, Edith, 1867-1963
    xHamilton, Edith.
        Ever-Present Past. Norton.
        The Greek Way. Avon.
        Greek Way. Norton.
Hamilton, Edmond.
    xHamilton, Edmond.
        Doomstar. Belmont-Tower.
Hamilton, Edward Pierce.
    xHamilton, Edward Pierce.
        A History of Milton. U Pr. of New Eng.
Hamilton, Edwin L.
    xHamilton, Edwin L.
        Sunken Islands of the Mid-Pacific Mountains.
           Geol Soc.
Hamilton, Eleanor, 1909-
    xHamilton, Eleanor.

Partners in Love. A S Barnes.
Hamilton, Elizabeth, 1758-1816
    xHamilton, Elizabeth.
        The Cottagers of Glenburnie: A Tale for the
           Farmer's Ingle-Nook. Garland Pub.
        First Book of Caves. Watts.
        Letters Addressed to the Daughter of a
           Nobleman on the Formation of the Religious
           & the Moral Principle. Garland Pub.
        Memoirs of Modern Philosophers: A Novel.
           Garland Pub.
Hamilton, Eric Ishmael.
    xHamilton, E. I.
        Applied Geochronology. Acad Pr.
Hamilton, F. E. see Hamilton, F. E. Ian.
Hamilton, F. E. Ian.
    xHamilton, F. E.
        ed. Contemporary Industrialization: Spatial
           Analysis & Regional Analysis. Longman.
        ed. Spatial Analysis, Industry & the Industrial
           Environment-Progress in Research &
           Applications: Industrial Systems. Wiley.
        ed. Spatial Perspectives on Industrial
           Organization & Decision-Making. Wiley.
Hamilton, Frederic Rutherford, 1881-
    xHamilton, Frederick R.
        Fiscal Support of State Teachers Colleges.
           AMS Pr.
Hamilton, Frederick R. see Hamilton, Frederic
Rutherford.
Hamilton, Gail.
    xHamilton, Gail.
        Candle to the Devil. Atheneum.
Hamilton, Geneva.
    xHamilton, Geneva.
        Where the Highway Ends. Padre Prods.
Hamilton, George H. see Hamilton, George Heard.
Hamilton, George Heard.
    xHamilton, George H.
        Art and Architecture of Russia. Viking Pr.
        Painting & Sculpture in Europe: 1880-1940.
           Penguin.
        Painting & Sculpture in Europe, 1880-1940.
           Viking Pr.
Hamilton, George L. see Hamilton, George Livingstone.
Hamilton, George Livingstone, 1874-1940
    xHamilton, George L.
        Indebtedness of Chaucer's Troilus & Criseyde
           to Guido Delle Colonne's Historia Trojana.
           AMS Pr.
Hamilton, Gordon.
    xHamilton, Gordon.
        Principles of Social Case Recording. Columbia
           U Pr.
        Psychotherapy in Child Guidance. Columbia U
           Pr.
        Theory & Practice of Social Case Work.
           Columbia U Pr.
Hamilton, Henry, 1896-
    xHamilton, Henry.
        English Brass & Copper Industries to 1880.
           Biblio Dist.
        English Brass & Copper Industries to 1800.
           Kelley.
        Industrial Revolution in Scotland. Biblio Dist.
        Industrial Revolution in Scotland. Kelley.
Hamilton, Holman.
    xHamilton, Holman.
        White House Images & Realities. U Presses
           Fla.
Hamilton, J. R.
    xHamilton, J. R.
        Alexander the Great. U of Pittsburgh Pr.
Hamilton, J. Ronald. see Hamilton, James Roland.
Hamilton, James R.
    xHamilton, James R.
        Readings for an Introduction to Philosophy.
           Macmillan.
Hamilton, James Roland.
    xHamilton, J. Ronald.

Using Electricity. P-H.
Hamilton, Joan Lesley.
    xHamilton, Joan Lesley.
        The Lion & the Cross. Doubleday.
Hamilton, John A. *see* Hamilton, John Arnott.
Hamilton, John Arnott.
    xHamilton, John A.
        Byzantine Architecture & Decoration. Arno.
Hamilton, John Robert, 1908-
    xHamilton, Robert.
        Housman the Poet. Folcroft.
Hamilton, K. G. *see* Hamilton, Kenneth Gordon.
Hamilton, Kenneth.
    xHamilton, Kenneth.
        What's New in Religion?: A Critical Study of
        New Theology, New Morality and Secular
        Christianity. Attic Pr.
Hamilton, Kenneth G. *see* Hamilton, Kenneth Gordon.
Hamilton, Kenneth Gordon.
    xHamilton, K. G.
        ed. Studies in Recent Australian Novel. U of
        Queensland Pr.
    xHamilton, Kenneth G.
        The Two Harmonies: Poetry & Prose in the
        Seventeenth Century. Greenwood.
Hamilton, L. F. *see* Hamilton, Leicester Forsyth.
Hamilton, Leicester Forsyth.
    xHamilton, L. F.
        Calculations of Analytical Chemistry. McGraw.
Hamilton, M. N. *see* Hamilton, Mary (Neal).
Hamilton, Madelen C.
    xHamilton, Madelen C.
        Where the Thunderbirds Dwell. Moody.
Hamilton, Marshall L.
    xHamilton, Marshall L.
        Father's Influence on Children. Nelson-Hall.
Hamilton, Mary (Neal).
    xHamilton, M. N.
        Music in Eighteenth Century Spain. Da Capo.
Hamilton, Max.
    xHamilton, Max.
        Lectures on the Methodology of Clinical
        Research. Churchill.
Hamilton, Michael. *see* Hamilton, Michael Pollock.
Hamilton, Michael Pollock, 1927-
    xHamilton, Michael.
        ed. This Little Planet. Scribner.
Hamilton, Morse.
    xHamilton, Morse.
        My Name Is Emily. Greenwillow.
Hamilton, Nicholas. *see* Hamilton, Nicholas Esterhazy
    Stephen Armytage.
**Hamilton, Nicholas Esterhazy Stephen Armytage, d.
1915**
    xHamilton, Nicholas.
        Inquiry into the Genuineness of the Manuscript
        Corrections in Mr. J. Payne Collier's
        Annotated Shakespeare, Folio 1632. AMS Pr.
Hamilton, Otto T. *see* Hamilton, Otto Templar.
Hamilton, Otto Templar, 1883-
    xHamilton, Otto T.
        Courts & the Curriculum. AMS Pr.
Hamilton, Persis M. *see* Hamilton, Persis Mary.
Hamilton, Persis Mary.
    xHamilton, Persis M.
        Basic Maternity Nursing. Mosby.
Hamilton, Peter, 1917-
    xHamilton, Peter.
        Computer Security. Van Nos Reinhold.
Hamilton, Peter J. *see* Hamilton, Peter Joseph.
Hamilton, Peter Joseph, 1859-1927
    xHamilton, Peter J.
        Colonial Mobile. U of Ala Pr.
Hamilton, R. *see* Hamilton, Roger.
Hamilton, R. F. *see* Hamilton, Richard F.
Hamilton, R. J. *see* Hamilton, Richard John.
Hamilton, Richard F.
    xHamilton, R. F.
        Class & Politics in the United States. Wiley.
    xHamilton, Richard F.

Affluence & the French Worker in the Fourth
        Republic. Princeton U Pr.
Hamilton, Richard John.
    xHamilton, R. J.
        Introduction to High Performance Liquid
        Chromatography. Methuen Inc.
Hamilton, Robert, 1743-1829
    xHamilton, Robert.
        Progress of Society. Kelley.
Hamilton, Robert. *see* Hamilton, John Robert.
Hamilton, Roger, B.Sc.
    xHamilton, R.
        Electronics for Technicians. Oxford U Pr.
Hamilton, Rowland.
    xHamilton, Rowland.
        Money & Value: An Inquiry into the Means &
        Ends of Economic Production. Kelley.
Hamilton, T. H. *see* Hamilton, Terrell H.
Hamilton, T. M.
    xHamilton, T. M.
        Early Indian Trade Guns: 1625-1775. Mus
        Great Plains.
Hamilton, Terrell H.
    xHamilton, T. H.
        ed. Ontogeny of Receptors & Reproductive
        Hormone Action. Raven.
Hamilton, Tnomas, 1789-1842
    xHamilton, Thomas.
        Men & Manners in America. Johnson Repr.
        Men & Manners in America. Kelley.
        Men & Manners in America. Russell.
Hamilton, Vernon.
    xHamilton, Vernon.
        Human Stress & Cognition: An Information
        Processing Approach. Wiley.
Hamilton, Virginia.
    xHamilton, Virginia.
        Dustland. Greenwillow.
        The House of Dies Drear. Dell.
        House of Dies Drear. Macmillan.
        House of Dies Drear. Macmillan.
        Jahdu. Greenwillow.
        Paul Robeson: The Life & Times of a Free
        Black Man. Dell.
        Paul Robeson: The Life & Times of a Free
        Black Man. Har-Row.
        The Planet of Junior Brown. Dell.
        Planet of Junior Brown. Macmillan.
        Planet of Junior Brown. Macmillan.
Hamilton, W. H. *see* Hamilton, William Hamilton.
Hamilton, W. M. *see* Hamilton, William.
Hamilton, Wade.
    xHamilton, Wade.
        Gunsmoke. Nordon Pubns.
        Longhorn Brand. Belmont-Tower.
        Ride the Wild Country. Belmont-Tower.
Hamilton, Wallace, 1919-
    xHamilton, Wallace.
        David at Olivet. St Martin.
        Kevin. St Martin.
Hamilton, Walter, 1844-1899
    xHamilton, Walter.
        Aesthetic Movement in England. AMS Pr.
        The Aesthetic Movement in England. Folcroft.
Hamilton, Walton. *see* Hamilton, Walton Hale.
Hamilton, Walton H. *see* Hamilton, Walton Hale.
Hamilton, Walton Hale.
    xHamilton, Walton.
        Antitrust in Action. Da Capo.
        Price & Price Policies. Arno.
    xHamilton, Walton H.
        Control of Wages. Kelley.
        Industrial Policy & Institutionalism: Selected
        Essays. Kelley.
Hamilton, William, 1924-
    xHamilton, W. M.
        ed. Surgical Treatment of Endocrine Disorders.
        Butterworths.
    xHamilton, William.

Christian Man. Westminster.
        Money Should Be Fun. HM.
    xHamilton, William F.
        Electric Automobiles: Energy, Environmental
        & Economic Prospects for the Future.
        McGraw.
Hamilton, William F. *see* Hamilton, William.
Hamilton, William Hamilton, 1886-
    xHamilton, W. H.
        ed. Holyrood: A Garland of Modern Scots
        Poems. Arno.
Hamilton, William L.
    xHamilton, William L.
        A Social Experiment in Program
        Administration: The Housing Allowance
        Administrative Agency Experiment. Abt
        Assoc.
Hamilton, William P.
    xHamilton, William P.
        Decision Making in the Coronary Care Unit.
        Mosby.
Hamilton, William Roger.
    xHamilton.
        Larousse Guide to Minerals, Rocks & Fossils.
        Larousse.
Hamilton-Adams, C P.
    xHamilton-Adams, C. P.
        The Racing Schooner Westward. Van Nos
        Reinhold.
Hamilton-Head, Ian.
    xHamilton-Head, Ian.
        Leatherwork. Sterling.
Hamilton-Paterson, James.
    xHamilton-Paterson, James.
        House in the Waves. S G Phillips.
Hamizrachi, Joram. *see* Hamizrachi, Yoram.
Hamizrachi, Yoram.
    xHamizrachi, Joram.
        The Cedar & the Star. Elsevier-Nelson.
Hamley, Dennis.
    xHamley, Dennis.
        Pageants of Despair. S G Phillips.
Hamlin, A. D. *see* Hamlin, Alfred Dwight Foster.
Hamlin, Alfred Dwight Foster, 1855-1926
    xHamlin, A. D.
        A History of Ornament. Cooper Sq.
Hamlin, Anna M.
    xHamlin, Anna M.
        Father Was a Tenor. Exposition.
Hamlin, Charles H. *see* Hamlin, Charles Hughes.
Hamlin, Charles Hughes, 1907-
    xHamlin, Charles H.
        They Went Thataway. Genealog Pub.
Hamlin, Herbert M. *see* Hamlin, Herbert Menee.
Hamlin, Herbert Menee, 1894-
    xHamlin, Herbert M.
        Citizens' Committees in the Public Schools.
        Interstate.
Hamlin, Marie C. *see* Hamlin, Marie Caroline Watson.
Hamlin, Marie Caroline Watson.
    xHamlin, Marie C.
        Legends of Le Detroit. Gale.
Hamlin, Paul L. *see* Hamlin, Paul Mahlon.
Hamlin, Paul Mahlon.
    xHamlin, Paul L.
        Legal Education in Colonial New York. Da
        Capo.
Hamlin, Talbot. *see* Hamlin, Talbot Faulkner.
Hamlin, Talbot Faulkner, 1889-1956
    xHamlin, Talbot.
        Architecture, an Art for All Men. Greenwood.
        Architecture Through the Ages. Putnam.
        Some European Architectural Libraries: Their
        Methods, Equipment & Administration. AMS
        Pr.
Hamlyn, D. W., 1924-
    xHamlyn, D. W.

Experience & the Growth of Understanding.
Routledge & Kegan.
Hamlyn, D W, 1924-
xHamlyn, D. W.
Psychology of Perception: A Philosophical
Examination of Gestalt Theory & Derivative
Theories of Perception. Humanities.
Hamm, Charles. *see* Hamm, Charles E.
Hamm, Charles E.
xHamm, Charles.
Opera. Da Capo.
Yesterdays: Popular Song in America. Norton.
Hamm, Jack.
xHamm, Jack.
Cartooning the Head & Figure. G&D.
illus. How to Draw Animals. G&D.
Still Life Drawing & Painting. G&D.
Hamm, Marie R. *see* Hamm, Marie Roberson.
Hamm, Marie Roberson.
xHamm, Marie R.
Crockery Cookbook. Fawcett.
Gold Medal Blender Cookbook. Fawcett.
Gold Medal Fondue Cookbook. Fawcett.
Money-in-the-Bank Cookbook. Macmillan.
Hamm, Michael F.
xHamm, Michael F.
ed. The City in Russian History. U Pr of Ky.
Hammack, Edward O., 1942-
xHammack, Edward O.
Complete Book of Practical Astrology. P-H.
Hammaker, Paul M.
xHammaker, Paul M.
Plain Talk to Young Executives. Irwin.
Hammann, Louis J., 1929-
xHammann, Louis J.
The Puzzle of Religion: The Parts & the
Whole. U Pr of Amer.
Hammar, Russell A.
xHammar, Russell A.
Singing—An Extension of Speech. Scarecrow.
Hammarberg, Melvyn.
xHammarberg, Melvyn.
The Indiana Voter: The Historical Dynamics of
Party Allegiance During the 1870s. U of
Chicago Pr.
Hammarskjold, Dag, 1905-1961
xHammarskjold, Dag.
Markings. Knopf.
Markings. Merrimack Bk Serv.
Hammel, E. A. *see* Hammel, Eugene A.
Hammel, Eugene A.
xHammel, E. A.
The SOCSIM Demographic-Sociological
Microsimulation Program: Operating Manual.
U of Cal Intl St.
Hammel, H. T. *see* Hammel, Harold T.
Hammel, Harold T.
xHammel, H. T.
Osmosis & Tensile Solvent. Springer-Verlag.
Hammel, William M.
xHammel, William M.
ed. The Popular Arts in America: A Reader.
HarBraceJ.
Hammer, Carl, 1910-
xHammer, Carl.
Goethe & Rousseau: Resonances of the Mind
U Pr of Ky.
ed. Studies in German Literature. La State U
Pr.
Hammer, Eliot R.
xHammer, Eliot R.
Environmental Policy: A Sociological
Assessment of Abatement Alternatives.
Gordon Pr.
Hammer, Emanuel F. *see* Hammer, Emanuel Frederick.
Hammer, Emanuel Frederick.
xHammer, Emanuel F.
Clinical Application of Projective Drawings. C
C Thomas.
Hammer, L. Ivanescu. *see* Hammer, Peter L.

Hammer, Marian B. *see* Hammer, Marian Behan.
Hammer, Marian Behan, 1928-
xHammer, Marian B.
The Complete Handbook of How to Start &
Run a Money-Making Business in Your
Home. P-H.
Hammer, Max, 1930-
xHammer, Max.
ed. The Theory & Practice of Psychotherapy
with Specific Disorders. C C Thomas.
Hammer, Peter L.
xHammer, L. Ivanescu.
Boolean Methods in Operations Research &
Related Areas. Springer-Verlag.
Hammer, Signe.
xHammer, Signe.
Daughters & Mothers-Mothers & Daughters.
NAL.
Hammer, W. *see* Hammer, Willie.
Hammer, Willie.
xHammer, W.
Product Safety Management & Engineering.
P-H.
Hammerman, Donald R.
xHammerman, Donald R.
Teaching in the Outdoors. Burgess.
Hammerschmidt, William W., 1916-
xHammerschmidt, William W.
Whitehead's Philosophy of Time. Russell.
Hammersley, J. M. *see* Hammersley, John Michael.
Hammersley, John Michael.
xHammersley, J. M.
Monte Carlo Methods. Methuen Inc.
Hammerstein, Oscar.
xHammerstein, Oscar.
Songs of Oscar Hammerstein II. Schirmer Bks.
Hammerton, A. James.
xHammerton, A. James.
Emigrant Gentlewomen: Genteel Poverty &
Female Emigration, 1830-1914. Rowman.
Hammerton, John A. *see* Hammerton, John Alexander.
Hammerton, John Alexander, Sir, 1871-1949
xHammerton, John A.
Memories of Books & Places. Arno.
Hammerton, M.
xHammerton, Max.
Statistics for the Human Sciences. Longman.
Hammerton, Max. *see* Hammerton, M.
Hammes, John A.
xHammes, John A.
Humanistic Psychology: A Christian
Interpretation. Grune.
Hammett, Dashiell, 1894-1961
xHammett, Dashiell.
The Continental Op. Random.
The Continental Op. Random.
The Dain Curse. Random.
The Thin Man. Random.
Hammett, Evelyn A. *see* Hammett, Evelyn Allen.
Hammett, Evelyn Allen.
xHammett, Evelyn A.
I, Priscilla. Macmillan.
Hammett, Hugh B.
xHammett, Hugh B.
Hilary Abner Herbert: A Southerner Returns to
the Union. Am Philos.
Hammett, K. R. *see* Hammett, K. R. W.
Hammett, K. R. W.
xHammett, K. R.
Plant Propagation. Sterling.
Hammett, Ralph W. *see* Hammett, Ralph Warner.
Hammett, Ralph Warner.
xHammett, Ralph W.
Architecture in the United States: A Survey of
Architectural Styles Since 1776. Wiley.
Hammil, Carrie E.
xHammil, Carrie E.

The Celestial Journey & the Harmony of the
Spheres. Tex Christian.
Hammill, Donald D.
xHammill, Donald D.
ed. Educational Perspectives in Learning
Disabilities. Wiley.
Hamming, Edward, 1915-
xHamming, Edward.
The Port of Milwaukee. Augustana Coll.
Hamming, R. W. *see* Hamming, Richard Wesley.
Hamming, Richard W. *see* Hamming, Richard Wesley.
Hamming, Richard Wesley, 1915-
xHamming, R. W.
Digital Filters. P-H.
xHamming, Richard W.
Coding & Information Theory. P-H.
Hammond. *see* Hammond, Stephen M.
Hammond, Albert L. *see* Hammond, Albert Lanphier.
Hammond, Albert Lanphier, 1892-
xHammond, Albert L.
Ideas About Substance. Johns Hopkins.
Hammond, Bill.
xHammond, Bill.
How to Make Money in Advertising
Photography. Amphoto.
Hammond, Bray.
xHammond, Bray.
Sovereignty & an Empty Purse: Banks &
Politics in the Civil War. Princeton U Pr.
Hammond (C. S.) and Company, Inc.
xC. S. Hammond & Co.
The First Book Atlas. Watts.
xHammond, Inc.
Favorite Recipes from My Kitchen. Hammond
Inc.
The Hammond New Contemporary World
Atlas. Doubleday.
xHammond Inc. Editorial Staff.
Webster's Atlas With Zip Code Directory
Merriam.
xHammond Incorporated.
The Hammond Large Type World Atlas.
Hammond Inc.
Vacation Money Saver & Road Atlas.
Hammond Inc.
The Whole Earth Atlas. Hammond Inc.
xHammond Incorporated Editors.
Ambassador World Atlas. Hammond Inc.
Atlas Moderno Universal. Hammond Inc.
Atlas of United States History. Hammond Inc.
Atlas of World History. Hammond Inc.
Citation World Atlas. Hammond Inc.
Comparative World Atlas. Hammond Inc.
Headline World Atlas. Hammond Inc.
Historical Atlas. Hammond Inc.
History Atlas of Our Country. Hammond Inc.
Intermediate World Atlas. Hammond Inc.
International World Atlas. Hammond Inc.
Landmarks of Liberty. Hammond Inc.
Medallion World Atlas. Hammond Inc.
Pictorial Atlas of the Bible World. Hammond
Inc.
United States History Atlas. Hammond Inc.
World Atlas for Students. Hammond Inc.
xTheHammond Staff.
ed. The Easy to Read Book of Road Maps.
Hammond Inc.
Hammond, D. B.
xHammond, D. B.
Stories of Scientific Discovery. Arno.
Hammond, Dorothy. *see* Hammond, Dorothy M.
Hammond, Dorothy M.
xHammond, Dorothy.
Price Guide to Country Antiques & American
Primitives. T Y Crowell.
Hammond, George P. *see* Hammond, George Peter.
Hammond, George Peter, 1896-
xHammond, George P.
The Californian. J Howell.
Hammond, Inc. *see* Hammond (C. S.) and Company, Inc.

Hammond Inc. Editorial Staff. *see* Hammond (C. S.) and
    Company, Inc.
Hammond Incorporated. *see* Hammond (C. S.) and
    Company, Inc.
Hammond Incorporated Editors. *see* Hammond (C. S.)
    and Company, Inc.
Hammond, J. L. *see* Hammond, John Lawrence le
    Breton.
Hammond, James J.
    xHammond, James J.
        Woodworking Technology. McKnight.
Hammond, John H. *see* Hammond, John Hays.
Hammond, John Hays, 1855-1936
    xHammond, John H.
        The Autobiography of John Hays Hammond.
        Arno.
Hammond, John L. *see* Hammond, John Lawrence le
    Breton.
Hammond, John Lawrence le Breton, 1872-1949
    xHammond, J. L.
        Gladstone & the Irish Nation. Biblio Dist.
        Lord Shaftesbury. Biblio Dist.
        Lord Shaftesbury. Folcroft.
        Lord Shaftesbury. Shoe String.
    xHammond, John L.
        Gladstone & the Irish Nation. Greenwood.
        Lord Shaftesbury. Arno.
Hammond, Kenneth A.
    xHammond, Kenneth A.
        Sourcebook on the Environment: A Guide to
        the Literature. U of Chicago Pr.
Hammond, Mac. *see* Hammond, Macsawyer.
Hammond, Macsawyer, 1926-
    xHammond, Mac.
        Cold Turkey. Swallow.
Hammond, Mason, 1903-
    xHammond, Mason.
        Augustan Principate in Theory & Practice
        During the Julio-Claudian Period. Russell.
        The City in the Ancient World. Harvard U Pr.
Hammond, Nicholas G. *see* Hammond, Nicholas
    Geoffrey Lempriere.
Hammond, Nicholas Geoffrey Lempriere.
    xHammond, Nicholas G.
        History of Greece to 322 B. C.. Oxford U Pr.
Hammond, Otis G. *see* Hammond, Otis Grant.
Hammond, Otis Grant, 1869-1944
    xHammond, Otis G.
        Tories of New Hampshire in the War of the
        Revolution. Irvington.
Hammond, P. *see* Hammond, Phillip E.
Hammond, Paul Y.
    xHammond, Paul Y.
        Cold War & Detente: The American Foreign
        Policy Process Since 1945. HarBraceJ.
        Organizing for Defense: The American Military
        Establishment in the Twentieth Century.
        Greenwood.
Hammond, Peter B.
    xHammond, Peter B.
        Cultural & Social Anthropology: Introductory
        Readings in Ethnology. Macmillan.
        An Introduction to Cultural & Social
        Anthropology. Macmillan.
Hammond, Phillip E.
    xHammond, P.
        The Structure of Human Society. Heath.
Hammond, Reginald J. *see* Hammond, Reginald J. W.
Hammond, Reginald J. W.
    xHammond, Reginald J.
        ed. Complete Dorset & Wiltshire. Intl Pubns
        Serv.
        ed. Complete Wye Valley, Hereford &
        Worcester. Hippocrene Bks.
Hammond, Robert. *see* Hammond, Robert H.
Hammond, Robert H.
    xHammond, Robert.
        Introduction to Fortran IV. McGraw.
    xHammond, Robert H.

Engineering Graphics:
    Design-Analysis-Communication. Krieger.
Hammond, Sandra N. *see* Hammond, Sandra Noll.
Hammond, Sandra Noll.
    xHammond, Sandra N.
        Ballet Basics. Mayfield Pub.
Hammond, Stephen M.
    xHammond.
        Antibiotics & Antimicrobial Action. Univ Park.
Hammond, Thomas T. *see* Hammond, Thomas Taylor.
Hammond, Thomas Taylor.
    xHammond, Thomas T.
        ed. The Anatomy of Communist Takeovers.
        Yale U Pr.
        Lenin on Trade Unions & Revolution,
        1893-1917. Greenwood.
        ed. Soviet Foreign Relations & World
        Communism: A Selected, Annotated
        Bibliography. Princeton U Pr.
Hammond, Winifred G.
    xHammond, Winifred G.
        The Riddle of Teeth. Coward.
        The Story of Your Eye. Coward.
Hammonds, Michael.
    xHammonds, Michael.
        Incident on the Way to a Killing. BJ Pub
        Group.
Hammonds, T. M.
    xHammonds, T. M.
        The Commodity Futures Market from an
        Agricultural Producer's Point of View. Mss
        Info.
Hamner, Burks.
    xHamner, Burks.
        Great Recipes from Los Angeles: Favorite
        Dishes from the City's Leading Restaurants.
        J P Tarcher.
Hamner, Charles E.
    xHamner, Charles E.
        Sperm Capacitation. Mss Info.
Hamner, Earl.
    xHamner, Earl.
        Spencer's Mountain. Dell.
        Spencer's Mountain. Dial.
Hamner, Robert D.
    xHamner, Robert D.
        Critical Perspectives on V. S. Naipaul. Three
        Continents.
        V. S. Naipaul. Twayne.
Hamner, W. Clay.
    xHamner, W. Clay.
        ed. Contemporary Problems in Personnel.
        Wiley.
Hamnett, Brian R.
    xHamnett, Brian R.
        Politics & Trade in Southern Mexico,
        1750-1821. Cambridge U Pr.
Hamon, Augustin. *see* Hamon, Augustin Frederic.
Hamon, Augustin Frederic, 1862-
    xHamon, Augustin.
        The Twentieth Century Moliere: Bernard Shaw.
        Folcroft.
Hamori, Laszlo, 1911-
    xHamori, Laszlo.
        Dangerous Journey. HarBraceJ.
        Dangerous Journey. HarBraceJ.
Hamp, Pierre, 1876-
    xHamp, Pierre.
        People. Arno.
Hampden, John, 1898-
    xHampden, John.
        Francis Drake, Privateer: Contemporary
        Narratives & Documents. U of Ala Pr.
        House of Cats & Other Stories. FS&G.
Hampe, Johann C. *see* Hampe, Johann Christoph.
Hampe, Johann Christoph, 1913-
    xHampe, Johann C.

To Die Is Gain: The Experience of One's Own
        Death. John Knox.
Hampe, Karl, 1869-1936
    xHampe, Karl.
        Germany Under the Salian & Hohenstaufen
        Emperors. Rowman.
Hampel, Clifford. *see* Hampel, Clifford A.
Hampel, Clifford A.
    xHampel, Clifford.
        Glossary of Chemical Terms. Van Nos
        Reinhold.
    xHampel, Clifford A.
        ed. The Encyclopedia of Chemistry. Van Nos
        Reinhold.
Hampers, Constantine. *see* Hampers, Constantine L.
Hampers, Constantine L.
    xHampers, Constantine.
        Long-Term Hemodialysis: The Management of
        the Patient with Chronic Renal Failure.
        Grune.
Hampshire, S. *see* Hampshire, Stuart.
Hampshire, Stuart, 1914-
    xHampshire, S.
        Public & Private Morality. Cambridge U Pr.
    xHampshire, Stuart.
        Freedom of Mind & Other Essays. Princeton U
        Pr.
        Freedom of the Individual. Princeton U Pr.
        Spinoza. Penguin.
        Two Theories of Morality. Oxford U Pr.
Hampson, Norman.
    xHampson, Norman.
        Danton. Holmes & Meier.
        The Enlightenment. Penguin.
        The French Revolution: A Concise History.
        Scribner.
Hampton, Benjamin. *see* Hampton, Benjamin Bowles.
Hampton, Benjamin B. *see* Hampton, Benjamin Bowles.
Hampton, Benjamin Bowles, 1875-1932
    xHampton, Benjamin.
        History of the Movies. Gordon Pr.
    xHampton, Benjamin B.
        History of the American Film Industry from Its
        Beginnings to 1931. Dover.
        History of the American Film Industry from Its
        Beginnings to 1931. Peter Smith.
        History of the Movies. Arno.
Hampton, David R.
    xHampton, David R.
        Contemporary Management. McGraw.
        Contemporary Management. McGraw.
        Organizational Behavior & the Practice of
        Management. Scott F.
Hampton Institute. *see* Hampton Institute, Hampton, Va.
Hampton Institute, Hampton, Va.
    xHampton Institute.
        Religious Folk Songs of the Negro. AMS Pr.
    xHampton Institute, Virginia.
        A Classified Catalog of the Negro Collection in
        the Collis P. Huntington Library. Scholarly.
Hampton Institute, Virginia. *see* Hampton Institute,
    Hampton, Va.
Hampton, John J., 1942-
    xHampton, John J.
        Financial Decision Making: Concepts,
        Problems, & Cases. Reston.
Hampton, John R.
    xHampton, John R.
        The E C G Made Easy. Churchill.
Hampton, Mack W.
    xHampton, Mack W.
        Once There Were Three. Moody.
Hampton, Nora.
    xHampton, Nora.
        The Steadfast Heart. Fawcett.
Hampton, R. E. *see* Hampton, Robert E.
Hampton, Robert E.
    xHampton, R. E.

College Salesmanship. McGraw.

Hampton, Russell K., 1931-
  xHampton, Russell K.
    The Far Side of Despair: A Personal Account
      of Depression. Nelson-Hall.

Hampton, Ruth E.
  xHampton, Ruth E.
    ed. The Girl in the Wall. Moody.

Hampton, William.
  xHampton, William.
    Expert Motorcycling. Contemp Bks.
    Fell's Guide to Doubling the Performance of
      Your Car. Fell.

Hamre, Leif, 1914-
  xHamre, Leif.
    Operation Arctic. Atheneum

Hamsa, Bobbi.
  xHamsa, Bobbie.
    Your Pet Bear. Childrens.
    Your Pet Beaver. Childrens.
Hamsa, Bobbie. see Hamsa, Bobbi.

Hamscher, Albert N.
  xHamscher, Albert N.
    The Parlement of Paris After the Fronde,
      1653-1673. U of Pittsburgh Pr.

Hamsher, J. Herbert.
  xHamsher, J. Herbert.
    Psychology & Social Issues. Macmillan.

Hamshere, Cyril.
  xHamshere, Cyril.
    The British in the Caribbean. Harvard U Pr.
Hamson, Charles J. see Hamson, Charles John.

Hamson, Charles John.
  xHamson, Charles J.
    Executive Discretion & Judicial Control: An
      Aspect of the French Conseil D'Etat.
      Hyperion Conn
Hamsun, Knul. see Hamsun, Knut.

Hamsun, Knut.
  xHamsun, Knul.
    Hunger. Avon.
  xHamsun, Knut.
    Cultural Life of Modern America. Harvard U
      Pr.
    Hunger. FS&G.
    Pan: From Lieutenant Thomas Glahn's Papers.
      FS&G.
    Wayfarers. FS&G.

Han, Jaok.
  xHan, Jaok.
    ed. Cardiac Arrhythmias: A Symposium. C C
      Thomas.

Han, Seong S.
  xHan, Seong S.
    Cell Biology. McGraw.
    Human Microscopic Anatomy. McGraw.

Han, Sungjoo.
  xHan, Sungjoo.
    The Failure of Democracy in South Korea. U
      of Cal Pr.
Hanaburgh, David H. see Hanaburgh, David Henry.

Hanaburgh, David Henry, 1910-
  xHanaburgh, David H.
    Your Future in Forestry. Arco.
    Your Future in Forestry. Rosen Pr.

Hanack, Michael.
  xHanack, Michael.
    Conformation Theory. Acad Pr.

Hanagan, Eva.
  xHanagan, Eva.
    The Upas Tree. St Martin.

Hanagan, Michael P., 1947-
  xHanagan, Michael P.
    The Logic of Solidarity: Artisans & Industrial
      Workers in Three French Towns, 1871-1914.
      U of Ill Pr.
Hanami, T. A. see Hanami, Tadashi.

Hanami, Tadashi.
  xHanami, T. A.
    Labour Law & Industrial Relations in Japan.
      Kluwer Boston.
  xHanami, Tadashi.
    Labor Relations in Japan Today. Kodansha.
Hanan, J. J. see Hanan, Joe J.

Hanan, Joe J.
  xHanan, J. J.
    Greenhouse Management. Springer-Verlag.

Hanan, Mack.
  xHanan, Mack.
    Accelerated Growth Planning: Profit
      Improvement Strategies for Consumer,
      Industrial, & Service Business Game Plans.
      McGraw.
    Fast-Growth Management: How to Improve
      Profits with Entrepreneurial Stategies. Am
      Mgmt.
    Take-Charge Sales Management: Successful
      First-Year Strategies for the Newly
      Appointed Sales Manager. Am Mgmt.

Hanan, Patrick.
  xHanan, Patrick.
    The Chinese Short Story: Studies in Dating,
      Authorship, & Composition. Harvard U Pr.
Hanauer, Elsie. see Hanauer, Elsie V.

Hanauer, Elsie V.
  xHanauer, Elsie.
    Guns of the Wild West. A S Barnes.
  xHanauer, Elsie V.
    The Horse Owner's Concise Guide. Arco.
    Horse Owner's Concise Guide. Wilshire.
    No Foot-No Horse. Burgess.
Hanauer, James E. see Hanauer, James Edward.

Hanauer, James Edward, 1850-
  xHanauer, James E.
    Folk-Lore of the Holy Land: Moslem, Christian
      & Jewish. Folcroft.

Hanauer, Milton L.
  xHanauer, Milton L.
    Chess Made Simple. Doubleday.
Hanbury, H. G. see Hanbury, Harold Greville.

Hanbury, Harold Greville.
  xHanbury, H. G.
    English Courts of Law. Oxford U Pr.
Hance, Kenneth G. see Hance, Kenneth Gordon.

Hance, Kenneth Gordon.
  xHance, Kenneth G.
    Principles of Speaking. Wadsworth Pub.
Hance, William A. see Hance, William Adams.

Hance, William Adams, 1916-
  xHance, William A.
    The Geography of Modern Africa. Columbia U
      Pr.
    ed. Southern Africa & the United States.
      Columbia U Pr.

Hanckel, Frances.
  xHanckel, Frances.
    A Way of Love, a Way of Life: A Young
      Person's Introduction to What It Means to
      Be Gay. Lothrop.

Hancock, Alan, fl. 1965-
  xHancock, Alan.
    Planning for Educational Mass Media.
      Longman.
Hancock, Albert E. see Hancock, Albert Elmer.

Hancock, Albert Elmer, 1870-1915
  xHancock, Albert E.
    French Revolution & the English Poets: Study
      in Historical Criticism. Kennikat.
Hancock, Anson U. see Hancock, Anson Uriel.

Hancock, Anson Uriel.
  xHancock, Anson U.
    History of Chile. AMS Pr.
Hancock, F. D. see Hancock, Frances Dean.

Hancock, Frances Dean.
  xHancock, F. D.
    Susan Brown, Camp Counselor. Assoc Bk.
Hancock, Harold B. see Hancock, Harold Bell.

Hancock, Harold Bell, 1913-
  xHancock, Harold B.
    The Delaware Loyalists. Irvington.

Hancock, James.
  xHancock, James.
    The Herons of the World. Har-Row.
Hancock, Keith. see Hancock, William Keith.

Hancock, Lyn.
  xHancock, Lyn.
    Love Affair with a Cougar. Doubleday.
    There's a Raccoon in My Parka. Doubleday.
Hancock, M. A. see Hancock, Mary A.

Hancock, M. Donald.
  xHancock, M. Donald.
    The Bundeswehr & the National Peoples
      Army: A Comparative Study of German
      Civil-Military Polity. U of Denver Intl.
    ed. Politics in the Post Welfare State:
      Responses to the New Individualism.
      Columbia U Pr.

Hancock, Mary A.
  xHancock, M. A.
    Menace on the Mountain. Macrae.

Hancock, Maxine.
  xHancock, Maxine.
    Living on Less & Liking It More. Moody.
    Love, Honor & Be Free. Moody.
    People in Process: The Preschool Years. Revell.

Hancock, Niel.
  xHancock, Niel.
    Calix Stay. Popular Lib.
Hancock, Norman N. see Hancock, Norman Napoleon.

Hancock, Norman Napoleon.
  xHancock, Norman N.
    Matrix Analysis of Electrical Machinery.
      Pergamon.

Hancock, Ralph.
  xHancock, Ralph.
    Super Machines. Viking Pr.

Hancock, Roger N., 1929-
  xHancock, Roger N.
    Twentieth Century Ethics. Columbia U Pr.

Hancock, Sheila.
  xHancock, Sheila.
    Connections: Ideas for Writing. HarBraceJ.

Hancock, Sibyl.
  xHancock, Sibyl.
    Freaky Francie. P-H.
    Theodore Roosevelt. Putnam.

Hancock, William A.
  xHancock, William A.
    Executive's Guide to Business Law. McGraw.
Hancock, William K. see Hancock, William Keith.

Hancock, William Keith, Sir, 1898-
  xHancock, Keith.
    Professing History. Intl Schol Bk Serv.
  xHancock, William K.
    Country & Calling. Greenwood.
    Discovering Monaro: A Study of Man's Impact
      on His Environment. Cambridge U Pr.
    Ricasoli & the Risorgimento in Tuscany. Fertig.

Hand, A. J.
  xHand, A. J.
    Home Energy How to. Har-Row.

Hand, Jackson.
  xHand, Jackson.
    Home Guide to Solar Heating & Cooling.
      Har-Row.
    How to Do Your Own Painting & Wall
      Papering. Har-Row.
    How to Do Your Own Wood Finishing.
      Har-Row.

Hand, Robert.
  xHand, Robert.
    Planets in Transit: Life Cycles for Living. Para
      Res.

Handel, Bea.
  xHandel, Beatrice.

National Directory for the Performing
Arts-Educational. Wiley.
Handel, Beatrice. *see* Handel, Bea.
Handel, Gerald.
xHandel, Gerald.
ed. Psychosocial Interior of the Family: A
Sourcebook for the Study of Whole Families.
Aldine Pub.
Handel, Lawrence.
xHandel, Lawrence.
ed. College Confidential. Trident.
Handel, Leo A.
xHandel, Leo A.
Hollywood Looks at Its Audience: A Report of
Film Audience Research. Arno.
xHandel, Leo H.
Dog Named Duke: True Stories of German
Shepherds at Work with the Law. Lippincott.
Handel, Leo H. *see* Handel, Leo A.
Handford, Jack.
xHandford, Jack.
Professional Patternmaking for Designer's of
Women's Wear. Plycon Pr.
Handke, Peter.
xHandke, Peter.
Inner World of the Outerworld of the
Innerworld. Continuum.
The Left-Handed Woman. FS&G.
Nonsense & Happiness. Urizen Bks.
The Ride Across Lake Constance & Other
Plays. FS&G.
Handler, Andrew, 1935-
xHandler, Andrew.
tr. & ed. Ararat: A Collection of
Hungarian-Jewish Short Stories. Fairleigh
Dickinson.
tr. & ed. Rabbi Eizik: Hasidic Stories About
the Zaddik of Kallo. Fairleigh Dickinson.
Handler, Edward.
xHandler, Edward.
America & Europe in the Political Thought of
John Adams. Harvard U Pr.
Handler, Gabriel Y.
xHandler, Gabriel Y.
Location on Networks: Theory & Algorithms.
MIT Pr.
Handler, Jerome S.
xHandler, Jerome S.
Plantation Slavery in Barbados: An
Archaeological & Historical Investigation.
Harvard U Pr.
Handler, Joel. *see* Handler, Joel F.
Handler, Joel F.
xHandler, Joel.
Social Movements & the Legal System: A
Theory of Law Reform & Social Change.
Acad Pr.
xHandler, Joel F.
The Deserving Poor: A Study of Welfare
Administration. Acad Pr.
Protecting the Social Service Client: Legal &
Structural Controls on Official Discretion.
Acad Pr.
Handler, M. *see* Handler, Milton.
Handler, Milton, 1903-
xHandler, M.
Federal Trade Commission: A Fiftieth
Anniversary Symposium. Da Capo.
Handley, George D.
xHandley, George D.
Personality, Learning & Teaching. Routledge &
Kegan.
Handlin, David. *see* Handlin, David P.
Handlin, David P.
xHandlin, David.
The American Home: Architecture & Society,
1815-1915. Little.
Handlin, Oscar, 1915-
xHandlin, Oscar.

Al Smith & His America. Little.
Boston's Immigrants: A Study of
Acculturation. Harvard U Pr.
Chance or Destiny: Turning Points in
American History. Greenwood.
ed. Children of the Uprooted. Braziller.
Commonwealth: A Study of the Role of
Government in the American Economy,
Massachusetts, 1774-1861. Harvard U Pr.
Dimensions of Liberty. Atheneum.
Dimensions of Liberty. Harvard U Pr.
ed. Popular Sources of Political Authority:
Documents on the Massachusetts
Constitution of 1780. Harvard U Pr.
Statue of Liberty. Newsweek.
ed. This Was America: True Accounts of
People & Places, Manners & Customs, As
Recorded by European Travelers to the
Western Shore in the 18th, 19th & 20th
Centuries. Harvard U Pr.
Truth in History. Harvard U Pr.
Hands, A. R. *see* Hands, Arthur Robinson.
Hands, Arthur Robinson, 1924-
xHands, A. R.
Charities & Social Aid in Greece & Rome.
Cornell U Pr.
Handy, Charles. *see* Handy, Charles B.
Handy, Charles B.
xHandy, Charles.
Understanding Organizations. Penguin.
Handy, E. S. *see* Handy, Edward Smith Craighill.
Handy, Edward Smith Craighill.
xHandy, E. S.
The Polynesian Family System in Kau, Hawaii.
C E Tuttle.
Handy, Robert T.
xHandy, Robert T.
Christian America: Protestant Hopes &
Historical Realities. Oxford U Pr.
Christian America: Protestant Hopes &
Historical Realities. Oxford U Pr.
A History of the Churches in the United States
& Canada. Oxford U Pr.
A History of the Churches in the United States
& Canada. Oxford U Pr.
ed. Religion in the American Experience: The
Pluralistic Style. U of SC Pr.
Handy, Rollo.
xHandy, Rollo.
A Current Appraisal of the Behavioral
Sciences. Behavioral Mass.
Useful Procedures of Inquiry. Behavioral Mass.
Handy, William C. *see* Handy, William Christopher.
Handy, William Christopher, 1873-1958
xHandy, William C.
Negro Authors & Composers of the United
States. AMS Pr.
Handy, William J.
xHandy, William J.
Twentieth Century Criticism: The Major
Statements. Free Pr.
Haner, F. T. *see* Haner, Frederick Theodore.
Haner, Frederick Theodore.
xHaner, F. T.
Contemporary Management. Merrill.
Introduction to Business: Concepts & Careers.
Winthrop.
Haney, David.
xHaney, David.
Renewal Reminders. Broadman.
xHaney, David P.
The Idea of the Laity. Zondervan.
The Lord & His Laity. Broadman.
Haney, David P. *see* Haney, David.
Haney, J. D. *see* Haney, John Dearling.
Haney, John D. *see* Haney, John Dearling.
Haney, John Dearling.
xHaney, J. D.

Registration of City School Children: A
Consideration of the Subject of the City
School Census. AMS Pr.
xHaney, John D.
Lessing's Education of the Human Race. AMS
Pr.
Haney, John L. *see* Haney, John Louis.
Haney, John Louis, 1877-1960
xHaney, John L.
ed. Early Reviews of English Poets. B Franklin.
Early Reviews of English Poets. Folcroft.
German Influence on Samuel Taylor Coleridge.
Haskell.
Haney, Lewis H. *see* Haney, Lewis Henry.
Haney, Lewis Henry, 1882-1969
xHaney, Lewis H.
Business Organization & Combination. Arno.
Haney, Lynn.
xHaney, Lynn.
Perfect Balance: The Story of an Elite
Gymnast. Putnam.
Haney, Robert.
xHaney, Robert.
Woodstock Handmade Houses. Ballantine.
Haney, Robert W.
xHaney, Robert W.
Comstockery in America: Patterns of
Censorship & Control. Da Capo.
Hanff, Helene.
xHanff, Helene.
Apple of My Eye. Doubleday.
Butch Elects a Mayor. Schol Bk Serv.
The Duchess of Bloomsbury Street. Lippincott.
Hanfmann, George M. *see* Hanfmann, George Maxim
Anossov.
Hanfmann, George Maxim Anossov, 1911-
xHanfmann, George M.
From Croesus to Constantine: The Cities of
Western Asia Minor & Their Arts in Greek
& Roman Times. U of Mich Pr.
Letters from Sardis. Harvard U Pr.
Hanford, James H. *see* Hanford, James Holly.
Hanford, James Holly.
xHanford, James H.
Milton. AHM Pub.
ed. Restoration Reader. Kennikat.
Hanford, Lloyd. *see* Hanford, Lloyd D.
Hanford, Lloyd D.
xHanford, Lloyd.
Analysis & Management of Investment
Property. Inst Real Estate.
Hanft, Marshall.
xHanft, Marshall.
The Cape Forts: Guardians of the Columbia.
Oreg Hist Soc.
Hangen, Eva C. *see* Hangen, Eva Catherine.
Hangen, Eva Catherine.
xHangen, Eva C.
Concordance to the Complete Poetical Works
of Sir Thomas Wyatt. Johnson Repr.
Hanham, H. J.
xHanham, H. J.
Elections & Party Management: Politics in the
Time of Disraeli & Gladstone. Shoe String.
Hanhardt, Arthur M. *see* Hanhardt, Arthur Monroe.
Hanhardt, Arthur Monroe, 1932-
xHanhardt, Arthur M.
German Democratic Republic. Johns Hopkins.
Hanifi, M. Jamil. *see* Hanifi, Mohammed Jamil.
Hanifi, Mohammed Jamil.
xHanifi, M. Jamil.
Historical & Cultural Dictionary of
Afghanistan. Scarecrow.
Hanington, Edda.
xHanington, Edda.
How to Cope with Migraine Headaches.
Sterling.
Hanisch, Gertrude S.
xHanisch, Gertrude S.

Love Elegies of the Renaissance: Marot, Louise
Labe & Ronsard. Anma Libri.

Hanke, Lewis.
xHanke, Lewis.
Aristotle & the American Indians: A Study in
Race Prejudice in the Modern World. Ind U
Pr.

Hankey, Clyde T.
xHankey, Clyde T.
A Colorado Word Geography. U of Ala Pr.

Hankins, Frank H. *see* Hankins, Frank Hamilton.

Hankins, Frank Hamilton, 1877-
xHankins, Frank H.
Adolphe Quetelet As Statistician. AMS Pr.

Hankins, John E. *see* Hankins, John Erskine.

Hankins, John Erskine, 1905-
xHankins, John E.
Backgrounds of Shakespeare's Thought. Shoe
String.
Character of Hamlet. Arno.
Source & Meaning in Spenser's Allegory: A
Study of the Faerie Queene. Oxford U Pr.

Hankins, Norman E.
xHankins, Norman E.
How to Become the Person You Want to Be.
Nelson-Hall.
Psychology for Contemporary Education.
Merrill.

Hankins, Warren.
xHankins, Warren.
Introduction to Chemistry. Mosby.

Hankinson, John.
xHankinson, John.
Pituitary & Parapituitary Tumours. Saunders.

Hankinson, Ken.
xHankinson, Ken.
Rigging Small Sailboats. Glen-L Marine.

Hanks, David A.
xHanks, David A.
The Decorative Designs of Frank Lloyd
Wright. Dutton.

Hanks, Kurt.
xHanks, Kurt.
Design Yourself!. W Kaufmann.
Draw!: A Visual Approach to Thinking,
Learning & Communicating. W Kaufmann.

Hanks, R. J. *see* Hanks, Ronald J.

Hanks, Ronald J.
xHanks, R. J.
Applied Soil Physics: Soil Water &
Temperature Applications. Springer-Verlag.

Hanlan, Archie J.
xHanlan, Archie J.
Autobiography of Dying. Doubleday.

Hanley, Boniface.
xHanley, Boniface.
Ten Christians: By Their Deeds You Shall
Know Them. Ave Maria.

Hanley, D. E.
xHanley, D. E.
Guidance & the Needs of the Special Child.
HM.

Hanley, D. L. *see* Hanley, David L.

Hanley, David L.
xHanley, D. L.
Contemporary France: Politics & Society Since
1945. Routledge & Kegan.

Hanley, Elizabeth.
xHanley, Elizabeth.
Guilty As Charged. Belmont Tower.

Hanley, Hope.
xHanley, Hope.
The ABC's of Needlepoint. Scribner.
Hope Hanley's Patterns for Needlepoint.
Scribner.
Needlepoint. Scribner.

Hanley, James, 1901-
xHanley, James.

A Dream Journey. Horizon.
A Dream Journey. Popular Lib.

Hanley, Julian R.
xHanley, Julian R.
Legal Aspects of Criminal Evidence.
McCutchan.

Hanley, Mike.
xHanley, Mike.
Owyhee Trails: The West's Forgotten Corner.
Caxton.

Hanley, Susan B.
xHanley, Susan B.
Economic & Demographic Change in
Preindustrial Japan, 1600-1868. Princeton U
Pr.

Hanley, Theodore D.
xHanley, Theodore O.
Developing Vocal Skills. Irvington.

Hanley, Theodore O. *see* Hanley, Theodore D.

Hanley, Wayne.
xHanley, Wayne.
ed. The Energy Book: A Non-Technical
Approach to the Issues. Greene.
Natural History in America: From Mark
Catesby to Rachel Carson. Times Bks.

Hanlin, Richard T.
xHanlin, Richard T.
Atlas of Introductory Mycology. Hunter NC.

Hanlon, Emily.
xHanlon, Emily.
How a Horse Grew Hoarse on the Site Where
He Sighted a Bare Bear: A Tale of
Homonyms. Delacorte.
The Swing. Bradbury Pr.

Hanlon, John J. *see* Hanlon, John Joseph.

Hanlon, John Joseph.
xHanlon, John J.
Public Health: Administration & Practice.
Mosby.

Hanlon, Joseph. *see* Hanlon, Joseph F.

Hanlon, Joseph F.
xHanlon, Joseph.
ed. Packaging Marketplace: The Practical
Guide to Packaging Sources. Gale.

Hanly, Charles. *see* Hanly, Charles Mervyn Taylor.

Hanly, Charles Mervyn Taylor.
xHanly, Charles.
ed. Psychoanalysis & Philosophy. Intl Univs Pr.

Hanmer, Thomas, Sir, Bart, 1677-1746
xHanmer, Thomas.
Some Remarks on the Tragedy of Hamlet,
Prince of Denmark. AMS Pr.

Hann, C. M., 1953-
xHann, C. M.
Tazlar, A Village in Hungary. Cambridge U Pr.

Hann, Jacquie.
xHann, Jacquie.
illus. Crybaby. Schol Bk Serv.
Where's Mark?. Schol Bk Serv.

Hann, Roy W.
xHann, Roy W.
Fundamental Aspects of Water Quality
Management. Technomic.

Hann, Scott.
xHann, Scott.
Wire Art. Chilton.

Hanna, D. C. *see* Hanna, David C.

Hanna, David.
xHanna, David.
Angel. Nordon Pubns.
The Love Goddess. Belmont-Tower.
The Vacant Throne. Belmont Tower.

Hanna, David C.
xHanna, D. C.
Nonlinear Optics of Free Atoms & Molecules.
Springer-Verlag.

Hanna, Donald G.
xHanna, Donald G.

Guide to Primary Police Management
Concepts. C C Thomas.

Hanna, Faith M.
xHanna, Faith M.
An American Mission: The Role of the
American University of Beirut. Alphabet Pr.

Hanna, Judith Lynn. *see* Hanna, Judith Lynne.

Hanna, Judith Lynne.
xHanna, Judith Lynn.
To Dance Is Human: A Theory of Nonverbal
Communication. U of Tex Pr.

Hanna, M. G. *see* Hanna, Michael G.

Hanna, M. W. *see* Hanna, Melvin W.

Hanna, Mary. *see* Hanna, Mary T.

Hanna, Mary C. *see* Hanna, Mary Carr.

Hanna, Mary Carr.
xHanna, Mary C.
Cassie & Ike. Blair.

Hanna, Mary T., 1935-
xHanna, Mary.
Catholics & American Politics. Harvard U Pr.

Hanna, Melvin W.
xHanna, M. W.
Quantum Mechanics in Chemistry.
Benjamin-Cummings.
xHanna, Melvin W.
Foundation Studies in General Chemistry: A
Self-Study Guide. Benjamin-Cummings.

Hanna, Michael G., 1936-
xHanna, M. G.
ed. Contemporary Topics in Immunobiology.
Plenum Pub.

Hanna, Mike.
xHanna, Mike.
Lacrosse for Men & Women: Skills &
Strategies for the Athlete & Coach. Dutton.

Hanna, Nessim.
xHanna, Nessim.
Marketing Opportunities in Egypt: A Business
Guide. R & E Res Assoc.

Hanna, Patricia B. *see* Hanna, Patricia Brennan.

Hanna, Patricia Brennan, 1930-
xHanna, Patricia B.
People Make It Happen: The Possibilities of
Outreach in Every Phase of Public Library
Service. Scarecrow.

Hanna, T. H. *see* Hanna, Thomas H.

Hanna, Thomas, 1928-
xHanna, Thomas.
The Body of Life. Knopf.
The End of Tyranny: An Essay on the
Possibility of America. Freeperson.

Hanna, Thomas H.
xHanna, T. H.
Foundation Instrumentation. Trans Tech.

Hanna, Warren. *see* Hanna, Warren Leonard.

Hanna, Warren L. *see* Hanna, Warren Leonard.

Hanna, Warren Leonard, 1898-
xHanna, Warren.
Montana's Many Splendored Glacier Land.
Superior Pub.
xHanna, Warren L.
The Grizzlies of Glacier. Mountain Pr.
Lost Harbor: The Controversy Over Drake's
California Anchorage. U of Cal Pr.

Hanna, Willard A. *see* Hanna, Willard Anderson.

Hanna, Willard Anderson, 1911-
xHanna, Willard A.
Bali Profile: People, Events, Circumstances
1001-1976. Am U Field.
Indonesian Banda: Colonialism & Its Aftermath
in the Nutmeg Islands. Inst Study Human.

Hannah, Barbara.
xHannah, Barbara.
Striving Towards Wholeness. C G Jung Foun.

Hannah, Barry.
xHannah, Barry.
Airships. Dell.
Airships. Knopf.

Hannah, Charles J. *see* Hannah, Charles Jerry.

Hannah, Charles Jerry.
  xHannah, Charles J.
    Ashes to the Wind. Avon.
Hannah, H. W. *see* Hannah, Harold Winford.
Hannah, Harold Winford, 1911-
  xHannah, H. W.
    The Legal Base for Universities in Developing
      Countries. U of Ill Pr.
Hannah, Larry S. *see* Hannah, Larry Stanley.
Hannah, Larry Stanley.
  xHannah, Larry S.
    Comprehensive Framework for Instructional
      Objectives: A Guide to Systematic Planning
      & Evaluation. A-W.
Hannah, Leslie.
  xHannah, Leslie.
    Electricity Before Nationalisation: A Study of
      the Development of the Electricity Supply
      Industry in Britain to 1948. Johns Hopkins.
Hannam, Charles.
  xHannam, Charles.
    A Boy in That Situation: An Autobiography.
      Har-Row.
Hannan, Edward J. *see* Hannan, Edward James.
Hannan, Edward James, 1921-
  xHannan, Edward J.
    Multiple Time Series. Wiley.
Hannavy, John.
  xHannavy, John.
    Masters of Victorian Photography. Holmes &
      Meier.
Hannaway, Owen.
  xHannaway, Owen.
    The Chemists & the Word: The Didactic
      Origins of Chemistry. Johns Hopkins.
Hannay, Agnes, 1909-
  xHannay, Agnes.
    A Chronicle of Industry on the Mill River.
      Arno.
Hannay, D. *see* Hannay, David.
Hannay, David, 1853-1934
  xHannay, D.
    Life of Frederick Marryat. Haskell.
  xHannay, David.
    Diaz. Kennikat.
    The Later Renaissance. B Franklin.
    Later Renaissance. Folcroft.
    Life & Writings of Tobias George Smollett.
      Arno.
    Life of Frederick Marryat. R West.
    Life of Tobias George Smollett. Folcroft.
    Life of Tobias George Smollett. Kennikat.
Hannay, David R. *see* Hannay, David Rainsford.
Hannay, David Rainsford.
  xHannay, David R.
    The Symptom Iceberg: A Study of Community
      Health. Routledge & Kegan.
Hannay, James O. *see* Hannay, James Owen.
Hannay, James Owen, 1865-1950
  xHannay, James O.
    From Dublin to Chicago. Arno.
    Our Casualty & Other Stories. Arno.
Hannay, Margaret P., 1944-
  xHannay, Margaret P.
    ed. As Her Whimsey Took Her: Critical Essays
      on the Work of Dorothy L. Sayers. Kent St
      U Pr.
Hanne, John A. *see* Hanne, John Anthony.
Hanne, John Anthony.
  xHanne, John A.
    Prayer or Pretense?. Zondervan.
Hannebaum, Leroy G.
  xHannebaum, Leroy G.
    Landscape Operations: Management, Methods,
      & Materials. Reston.
Hannema, Philip A.
  xHannema, Philip A.

    Let's Have a Reunion!: A How-to-Do-It Guide
      for Your Class Reunion. Second Thoughts.
Hanneman, Gerhard J.
  xHanneman, Gerhard J.
    Communication & Behavior. A-W.
Hanneman, L. J. *see* Hanneman, Leonard John.
Hanneman, Leonard John.
  xHanneman, L. J.
    Modern Cake Decoration. Intl Ideas.
    Patisserie. Intl Pubns Serv.
Hannemann, Manfred, 1938-
  xHannemann, Manfred.
    The Diffusion of the Reformation in
      Southwestern Germany, 1518-1534. U
      Chicago Dept Geog.
Hannerz, Ulf.
  xHannerz, Ulf.
    Exploring the City: Inquiries Toward an Urban
      Anthropology. Columbia U Pr.
    Soulside: Inquiries into Ghetto Culture &
      Community. Columbia U Pr.
Hannibal, Edward.
  xHannibal, Edward.
    Blood Feud. Ballantine.
    Chocolate Days, Popsicle Weeks. NAL.
    Liberty Square Station. Putnam.
Hanniball, A. *see* Hanniball, August.
Hanniball, August, 1922-
  xHanniball, A.
    Aircraft, Engines & Airmen: A Selective
      Review of the Periodical Literature,
      1930-1969. Scarecrow.
Hannigan, Jane A.
  xHannigan, Jane A.
    Compiled by Media Center Facilities Design.
      ALA.
Hanning, Barbara R. *see* Hanning, Barbara Russano.
Hanning, Barbara Russano, 1940-
  xHanning, Barbara R.
    Of Poetry & Music's Power: Humanism & the
      Creation of the Opera. Univ Microfilms.
Hanning, Robert W.
  xHanning, Robert W.
    The Individual in Twelfth-Century Romance.
      Yale U Pr.
Hannon, Ezra.
  xHannon, Ezra.
    Doors. Stein & Day.
    Doors. Warner Bks.
Hannon, James. *see* Hannon, James J.
Hannon, James J.
  xHannon, James.
    Nasakenai: We Are Forsaken. Grossmont Pr.
Hannon, Jessie G. *see* Hannon, Jessie Gould.
Hannon, Jessie Gould.
  xHannon, Jessie G.
    Boston-Newton Company Venture: From
      Massachusetts to California in 1849. U of
      Nebr Pr.
Hannon, Ralph H.
  xHannon, Ralph H.
    Mathematics for Technical Careers. Merrill.
Hannon, Ruth.
  xHannon, Ruth.
    Children's Bible Stories from the Old
      Testament. Western Pub.
Hannon, Sharron.
  xHannon, Sharron.
    Working Woman's Beauty Book. Stein & Day.
Hannula, Reino.
  xHannula, Reino.
    Computers & Programming: A System 360-370
      Assembler Language Approach. HM.
Hannum, Alberta (Pierson), 1906-
  xHannum, Alberta P.
    Look Back with Love: A Recollection of the
      Blue Ridge. Vanguard.
Hannum, Alberta P. *see* Hannum, Alberta (Pierson).
Hanny, Diane.
  xHanny, Diane.

    Closer Than My Shadow. Logos.
Hanrahan, John.
  xHanrahan, John D.
    Lost Frontier: The Marketing of Alaska.
      Norton.
Hanrahan, John D. *see* Hanrahan, John.
Hanrieder, Wolfram F.
  xHanrieder, Wolfram F.
    ed. Arms Control & Security: Current Issues.
      Westview.
    ed. Words & Arms: A Dictionary of Security &
      Defense Terms with Supplementary Data.
      Westview.
Hansard Society for Parliamentary Government.
  xHansard Society for Parliamentary Government.
    The British People: Their Voice in Europe.
      Lexington Bks.
Hansburg, Henry. *see* Hansburg, Henry G.
Hansburg, Henry C., 1910-
  xHansburg, Henry G.
    Adolescent Separation Anxiety. Krieger.
Hansburg, Henry G., 1910-
  xHansburg, Henry.
    Experimental Study of the Effect of the Use of
      the Print Shop in the Improvement of
      Spelling, Reading, & Visual Perception. AMS
      Pr.
Hansburg, Henry G. *see* Hansburg, Henry C.
Hansch, Corwin. *see* Hansch, Corwin H.
Hansch, Corwin H.
  xHansch, Corwin.
    Substituent Constants for Correlation Analysis
      in Chemistry & Biology. Wiley.
Hansel, Tim.
  xHansel, Tim.
    When I Relax I Feel Guilty. Cook.
Hansell, Grant E., 1909-
  xHansell, Grant E.
    Filter Design & Evaluation. Van Nos Reinhold.
Hansell, Haywood S.
  xHansell, Haywood S.
    The Air Plan That Defeated Hitler. Arno.
Hansen, Alvin H. *see* Hansen, Alvin Harvey.
Hansen, Alvin Harvey, 1887-
  xHansen, Alvin H.
    The American Economy. Greenwood.
    Business Cycles & National Income. Norton.
    Fiscal Policy & Business Cycles. Greenwood.
    Postwar American Economy: Performance &
      Problems. Norton.
Hansen, Arthur G.
  xHansen, Arthur G.
    Fluid Mechanics. Wiley.
Hansen, B. *see* Hansen, Bent.
Hansen, B. E. *see* Hansen, Beatrice E.
Hansen, Barbara J. *see* Hansen, Barbara Joan.
Hansen, Barbara Joan.
  xHansen, Barbara J.
    Good Bread. Macmillan.
Hansen, Beatrice E.
  xHansen, B. E.
    Progressive Typewriting Speed Practice.
      McGraw.
Hansen, Bent, 1920-
  xHansen, B.
    Survey of General Equilibrium Systems.
      McGraw.
Hansen, Carl F.
  xHansen, Carl F.
    The Amidon Elementary School: A Successful
      Demonstration in Basic Education.
      Greenwood.
Hansen, Carla.
  xHansen, Carla.
    jt. auth. Barnaby Bear Builds a Boat. Random.
Hansen, David A.
  xHansen, David A.
    An Analysis of Police Concepts & Programs. C
      C Thomas.
Hansen, E. *see* Hansen, Edward.

Hansen, Edward.
xHansen, E.
Strain Facies. Springer-Verlag.
Hansen, Eldon.
xHansen, Eldon R.
Table of Series & Products. P-H.
Hansen, Eldon R. *see* Hansen, Eldon.
Hansen, Emmanuel.
xHansen, Emmanuel.
Frantz Fanon: Social & Political Thought. Ohio
St U Pr.
Hansen, Harry.
xHansen, Harry.
Longfellow's New England. Hastings.
Hansen, J. *see* Hansen, Jorn.
Hansen, J. P. *see* Hansen, Jean Pierre.
Hansen, James. *see* Hansen, James C.
Hansen, James C.
xHansen, James.
ed. Group Guidance & Counseling in the
Schools: Selected Readings. P-H.
xHansen, James C.
Appalachian Students & Guidance. HM.
Counseling Process & Procedures. Macmillan.
Counseling: Theory & Process. Allyn.
Group Counseling: Theory & Process. Rand.
Hansen, Jean Pierre.
xHansen, J. P.
The Theory of Simple Liquids. Acad Pr.
Hansen, Jorn.
xHansen, J.
Tables for Texture Analysis of Cubic Crystals.
Springer-Verlag.
Hansen, Joseph.
xHansen, Joseph.
Intro. by Dynamics of the Cuban Revolution:
The Trotskyist View. Path Pr Ny.
The Leninist Strategy of Party Building. The
Debate on Guerrilla Warfare in Latin
America. Path Pr NY.
Skinflick. HR&W.
Hansen, Joseph H. *see* Hansen, Joseph S.
Hansen, Joseph S.
xHansen, Joseph H.
How to Breed & Whelp Dogs. C C Thomas.
Hansen, Klaus J.
xHansen, Klaus J.
Quest for Empire: The Political Kingdom of
God & the Council of Fifty in Mormon
History. Mich St U Pr.
Quest for Empire: The Political Kingdom of
God & the Council of Fifty in Mormon
History. U of Nebr Pr.
Hansen, L. Taylor.
xHansen, L. Taylor.
Ancient Atlantic. Amherst Pr.
Hansen, Lorraine S. *see* Hansen, Lorraine Sundal.
Hansen, Lorraine Sundal.
xHansen, Lorraine S.
Career Guidance Practices in School &
Community. Am Personnel.
Hansen, Max.
xHansen, Max.
Constitution of Binary Alloys. McGraw.
Hansen, Niles M.
xHansen, Niles M.
France in the Modern World. Van Nos
Reinhold.
Improving Access to Economic Opportunity:
Nonmetropolitan Labor Markets in an Urban
Society. Ballinger Pub.
Location Preferences, Migration, & Regional
Growth: A Study of the South & Southwest
United States. Irvington.
Rural Poverty & the Urban Crisis: A Strategy
for Regional Development. Greenwood.
Hansen, R. C. *see* Hansen, Robert Clinton.
Hansen, R. Gaurth. *see* Hansen, Roger Gaurth.
Hansen, Robert Clinton.
xHansen, R. C.

ed. Significant Phased Array Papers. Artech
Hse.
Hansen, Roger D.
xHansen, Roger D.
Beyond the North-South Stalemate. McGraw.
The Politics of Mexican Development. Johns
Hopkins.
Hansen, Roger Gaurth.
xHansen, R. Gaurth.
Nutritional Quality Index of Foods. AVI.
Hansen-Krening, Nancy.
xHansen-Krening, Nancy.
Competency & Creativity in Language Arts: A
Multi-Ethnic Focus. A-W.
Hanser, Richard.
xHanser, Richard.
A Noble Treason: The Revolt of the Munich
Students Against Hitler. Putnam.
Hanslowe, Kurt L.
xHanslowe, Kurt L.
Procedures & Policies of the New York State
Labor Relations Board. NY Sch Indus Rel.
Hansome, Marius, 1887-
xHansome, Marius.
World Workers' Educational Movements, Their
Social Significance. AMS Pr.
Hanson. *see* Hanson, Charles E.
Hanson, Agnes O.
xHanson, Agnes O.
ed. Executive & Management Development for
Business & Government: A Guide to
Information Sources. Gale.
Hanson, Albert. *see* Hanson, Albert Henry.
Hanson, Albert Henry.
xHanson, Albert.
Parliament & Public Ownership. Greenwood.
Hanson, Arthur B., 1916-
xHanson, Arthur B.
Libel & Related Torts. Am Newspaper.
Hanson, Carl A.
xHanson, Carl A.
Dissertations on Iberian & Latin American
History. Whitston Pub.
Hanson, Charles E., 1917-
xHanson.
The Plains Rifle. Gun Room.
Hanson, D. *see* Hanson, Derek.
Hanson, Derek.
xHanson, D.
From College to Classroom: The Probationary
Year. Routledge & Kegan.
Hanson, Donald W.
xHanson, Donald W.
From Kingdom to Commonwealth: The
Development of Civic Consciousness in
English Political Thought. Harvard U Pr.
Hanson, E. Mark, 1938-
xHanson, Mark E.
Educational Administration & Organizational
Behavior. Allyn.
Hanson, Earl D.
xHanson, Earl D.
Animal Diversity. P-H.
The Origin & Early Evolution of Animals.
Columbia U Pr.
Hanson, Eric O.
xHanson, Eric O.
Catholic Politics in China & Korea. Orbis Bks.
Hanson, F. Allan, 1913-
xHanson, F. Allan.
Meaning in Culture. Routledge & Kegan
Hanson, Harold C. *see* Hanson, Harold Carsten.
Hanson, Harold Carsten, 1917-
xHanson, Harold C.
Giant Canada Goose. S Ill U Pr.
Hanson, Harry.
xHanson, Harry.
Canal People. David & Charles.
Hanson, Harvey, 1941-
xHanson, Harvey.

Game Time. Watts.
Hanson, Howard G. *see* Hanson, Howard Gordon.
Hanson, Howard Gordon.
xHanson, Howard G.
Future Coin or Climber & Other Poems. Blair.
Hanson, J. R. *see* Hanson, James Ralph.
Hanson, James Ralph.
xHanson, J. R.
Introduction to Steroid Chemistry. Pergamon.
Hanson, Joan.
xHanson, Joan.
illus. I Don't Like Timmy. Carolrhoda Bks.
I Won't Be Afraid. Carolrhoda Bks.
I'm Going to Run Away. Platt.
illus. Still More Antonyms: Together & Apart
& Other Words That Are As Different in
Meaning As Rise & Fall. Lerner Pubns.
illus. Still More Homonyms: Night & Knight &
Other Words That Sound the Same but Look
As Different As Ball & Bawl. Lerner Pubns.
Hanson, Joseph J. *see* Hanson, Joseph John.
Hanson, Joseph John.
xHanson, Joseph J.
Launching the Church School Year. Judson.
Hanson, June A. *see* Hanson, June Andrea.
Hanson, June Andrea.
xHanson, June A.
Summer of the Stallion. Macmillan.
Hanson, Kenneth. *see* Hanson, Kenneth O.
Hanson, Kenneth O., 1922-
xHanson, Kenneth.
The Uncorrected World. Columbia U Pr.
xHanson, Kenneth O.
Distance Anywhere. U of Wash Pr.
Hanson, L. P.
xHanson, L. P.
Commercial Processing of Fruits. Noyes.
Commercial Processing of Vegetables. Noyes.
Vegetable Protein Processing. Noyes.
Hanson, Laurence William.
xHanson, Lawrence W.
Contemporary Printed Sources for British &
Irish Economic History, 1701-1750.
Cambridge U Pr.
Hanson, Lawrence.
xHanson, Lawrence.
Life of S. T. Coleridge: The Early Years.
Russell.
Hanson, Lawrence W. *see* Hanson, Laurence William.
Hanson, Louise G.
xHanson, Louise G.
Beekeeping for Fun & Profit. McKay.
Hanson, Mark E. *see* Hanson, E. Mark.
Hanson, N. R. *see* Hanson, Norwood Russell.
Hanson, Norwood R. *see* Hanson, Norwood Russell.
Hanson, Norwood Russell.
xHanson, N. R.
Constellations & Conjectures. Kluwer Boston.
xHanson, Norwood R.
Perception & Discovery: An Introduction to
Scientific Inquiry. Freeman C.
Hanson, Paul D.
xHanson, Paul D.
The Dawn of the Apocalyptic: The Historical
& Sociological Roots of Jewish Apocalyptic
Eschatology. Fortress.
Dynamic Transcendence: The Correlation of
Confessional Heritage & Contemporory
Experience in a Biblical Model of Divine
Activity. Fortress
Hanson, Peggy. *see* Hanson, Peggy L.
Hanson, Peggy L.
xHanson, Peggy.
Operating Data Entry Systems. P-H.
Hanson, Philip.
xHanson, Philip.
Consumer in the Soviet Economy.
Northwestern U Pr.
Hanson, Richard. *see* Hanson, Richard A.

Hanson, Richard A.
  xHanson, Richard.
    Child Development: Concepts, Issues, &
      Readings. West Pub.
Hanson, Richard E. *see* Hanson, Richard Elmer.
Hanson, Richard Elmer, 1916-
  xHanson, Richard E.
    The Manager's Guide to Copying &
      Duplicating. McGraw.
Hanson, Richard S.
  xHanson, Richard S.
    The Future of the Great Planet Earth: What
      Does Biblical Prophecy Mean for You?.
      Augsburg.
Hanson, Simon G. *see* Hanson, Simon Gabriel.
Hanson, Simon Gabriel.
  xHanson, Simon G.
    Utopia in Uruguay: Chapters in the Economic
      History of Uruguay. Hyperion Conn.
Hanson, W. G.
  xHanson, William G.
    The Early Monastic Schools of Ireland, Their
      Missionaries, Saints & Scholars. B Franklin.
Hanson, Whittier L. *see* Hanson, Whittier Lorenz.
Hanson, Whittier Lorenz, 1879-
  xHanson, Whittier L.
    Costs of Compulsory Attendance Service in the
      State of New York & Some Factors Affecting
      the Cost. AMS Pr.
Hanson, William G. *see* Hanson, W. G.
Hanssen, Hans P. *see* Hanssen, Hans Peter.
Hanssen, Hans Peter, 1852-1936
  xHanssen, Hans P.
    Diary of a Dying Empire. Kennikat.
Hanssmann, Fred.
  xHanssmann, Fred.
    Operations Research Techniques for Capital
      Investment. Krieger.
Hantzschel, Walter.
  xHantzschel, Walter.
    Coprolites: An Annotated Bibliography. Geol
      Soc.
Hanzak, Jan.
  xHanzak, Jan.
    Encyclopedia of Animals. St Martin.
Hanzlicek, C. G., 1942-
  xHanzlicek, C. G.
    Stars: Poems. U of Mo Pr.
Hanzlik, Robert P.
  xHanzlik, Robert P.
    ed. Inorganic Aspects of Biological & Organic
      Chemistry. Acad Pr.
Hapgood, Charles H.
  xHapgood, Charles H.
    Maps of the Ancient Sea Kings: Evidence of
      Advanced Civilization in the Ice Age.
      Dutton.
Hapgood, David.
  xHapgood, David.
    Africa: From Independence to Tomorrow.
      Atheneum.
    The Average Man Fights Back. Condor Pub
      Co.
Hapgood, Fred.
  xHapgood, Fred.
    Why Males Exist: An Inquiry into the
      Evolution of Sex. Morrow.
    Why Males Exist: An Inquiry into the
      Evolution of Sex. NAL.
Hapgood, Hatchins. *see* Hapgood, Hutchins.
Hapgood, Hutchins, 1869-1944
  xHapgood, Hatchins.
    Types from City Streets. Mss Info.
  xHapgood, Hutchins.
    Autobiography of a Thief. Johnson Repr.
Hapgood, Marilyn.
  xHapgood, Marilyn.
    Supporting the Learning Teacher: A Source
      Book for Teacher Centers. Agathon.
Hapgood, Ruth. *see* Hapgood, Ruth K.

Hapgood, Ruth K.
  xHapgood, Ruth.
    First Horse: Basic Horse Care Illustrated.
      Chronicle Bks.
Happ, H. H., 1928-
  xHapp, H. H.
    Diakoptics & Networks. Acad Pr.
    Piecewise Methods & Applications to Power
      Systems. Wiley.
Happel, Margaret.
  xHappel, Margaret.
    Cool Cooking Cookbook. Butterick Pub.
    Desserts for Dieters. Butterick Pub.
    Dollar-Wise Recipes. Butterick Pub.
    Meals in a Hurry. Butterick Pub.
    Quick Dinner Menus. Butterick Pub.
    Something Special Cookbook. Butterick Pub.
Haq, B. U. *see* Haq, Bilal U.
Haq, Bilal U.
  xHaq, B. U.
    Introduction to Marine Micropaleontology.
      Elsevier.
Haque, Rizwanel. *see* Haque, Rizwanul.
Haque, Rizwanul.
  xHaque, Rizwanel.
    Environmental Dynamics of Pesticides. Plenum
      Pub.
Harada, Minoru, 1925-
  xHarada, Minoru.
    Meiji Western Painting. Weatherhill.
Haralambos, Michael.
  xHaralambos, Michael.
    Right on: From Blues to Soul in Black
      America. Da Capo.
Haran, Menahem.
  xHaran, Menahem.
    Temples & Temple Service in Ancient Israel:
      An Inquiry into the Character of Cult
      Phenomena & the Historical Setting of the
      Priestly School. Oxford U Pr.
Harari, Ehud.
  xHarari, Ehud.
    The Politics of Labor Legislation in Japan:
      National-International Interaction. U of Cal
      Pr.
Harari, Herbert.
  xHarari, Herbert.
    Psychology: Personal & Social Adjustment.
      Har-Row.
Harari, Josue V.
  xHarari, Josue V.
    Intro. by Textual Strategies: Perspectives in
      Post-Structuralist Criticism. Cornell U Pr.
Harary, Frank.
  xHarary, Frank.
    Graph Theory. A-W.
    Graphical Enumeration. Acad Pr.
    ed. Topics in Graph Theory. NY Acad Sci.
Harasymiw, Bohdan.
  xHarasymiw, Bohdan.
    ed. Education & the Mass Media in the Soviet
      Union & Eastern Europe. Praeger.
Haraszti, Miklos, 1945-
  xHaraszti, Miklos.
    A Worker in a Worker's State. Universe.
Haraszty, Eszter.
  xHaraszty, Eszter.
    Living with Flowers. Liveright.
    Needlepainting: A Garden of Stitches.
      Liveright.
Haraway, Donna J. *see* Haraway, Donna Jeanne.
Haraway, Donna Jeanne.
  xHaraway, Donna J.
    Crystals, Fabrics, & Fields: Metaphors of
      Organicism in the Twentieth-Century
      Developmental Biology. Yale U Pr.
Harbage, Alfred, 1901-
  xHarbage, Alfred.
    Thomas Killigrew, Cavalier Dramatist. Arno.
Harbaugh, John W. *see* Harbaugh, John Warvelle.

Harbaugh, John Warvelle.
  xHarbaugh, John W.
    Computer Simulation in Geology. Krieger.
    Probability Methods in Oil Exploration. Wiley.
Harbaugh, William H. *see* Harbaugh, William Henry.
Harbaugh, William Henry, 1920-
  xHarbaugh, William H.
    The Life & Times of Theodore Roosevelt.
      Oxford U Pr.
    Power & Responsibility: The Life & Times of
      Theodore Roosevelt. Octagon.
Harbeck, Charles T. *see* Harbeck, Charles Thomas.
Harbeck, Charles Thomas, 1850-
  xHarbeck, Charles T.
    Contribution to the Bibliography of the History
      of the United States Navy. B Franklin.
Harben, William N. *see* Harben, William Nathaniel.
Harben, William Nathaniel, 1858-1919
  xHarben, William N.
    Northern Georgia Sketches. Arno.
Harber, Jean R.
  xHarber, Jean R.
    Reading & the Black English Speaking Child:
      An Annotated Bibliography. Intl Reading.
Harberger, Arnold C.
  xHarberger, Arnold C.
    Taxation & Welfare. U of Chicago Pr.
    ed. The Taxation of Income from Capital.
      Brookings.
Harbers, Eberhard.
  xHarbers, Eberhard.
    Introduction to Nucleic Acids: Chemistry,
      Biochemistry & Functions. Van Nos
      Reinhold.
Harbert, Anita S., 1937-
  xHarbert, Anita S.
    Federal Grants-in-Aid: Maximizing Benefits to
      the States. Praeger.
Harbert, Earl N., 1934-
  xHarbert, Earl N.
    The Force So Much Closer Home: Henry
      Adams & the Adams Family. NYU Pr.
Harbert, Wilhelmina K.
  xHarbert, Wilhelmina K.
    Opening Doors Through Music: A Practical
      Guide for Teachers, Therapists, Students,
      Parents. C C Thomas.
Harbeson, John W. *see* Harbeson, John Willis.
Harbeson, John Willis, 1938-
  xHarbeson, John W.
    Nation-Building in Kenya: The Role of Land
      Reform. Northwestern U Pr.
Harbin, Calvin E. *see* Harbin, Calvin Edward.
Harbin, Calvin Edward, 1916-
  xHarbin, Calvin E.
    Teaching Power. Philos Lib.
Harbinson, W. H. *see* Harbinson, William Allen.
Harbinson, William Allen, 1941-
  xHarbinson, W. H.
    The Illustrated Elvis. Ace Bks.
Harbison, E. H. *see* Harbison, Elmore Harris.
Harbison, E. Harris. *see* Harbison, Elmore Harris.
Harbison, Elmore Harris, 1907-
  xHarbison, E. H.
    Christianity & History: Essays. Princeton U Pr.
  xHarbison, E. Harris.
    Age of Reformation. Cornell U Pr.
    The Christian Scholar in the Age of the
      Reformation. Porcupine Pr.
Harbison, Frederick H. *see* Harbison, Frederick Harris.
Harbison, Frederick Harris.
  xHarbison, Frederick H.
    Education, Manpower, & Economic Growth:
      Strategies of Human Resource Development.
      McGraw.
Harbison, Robert.
  xHarbison, Robert.

Deliberate Regression. Knopf.
Eccentric Spaces. Avon.
Eccentric Spaces. Knopf.
Harbold, Harry. see Harbold, Harry S.
Harbold, Harry S.
xHarbold, Harry.
Sanitary Engineering Problems & Calculations
for the Professional Engineer. Ann Arbor
Science.
Harborne, J. see Harborne, Jeffrey B.
Harborne, Jeffrey B.
xHarborne, J.
ed. The Flavonoids. Acad Pr.
xHarborne, Jeffrey B.
ed. Comparative Biochemistry of Flavonoids.
Acad Pr.
Harbottle, G.
xHarbottle, G.
ed. Chemical Effects of Nuclear
Transformations in Inorganic Systems.
Elsevier.
Harbottle, T. B. see Harbottle, Thomas Benfield.
Harbottle, Thomas. see Harbottle, Thomas Benfield.
Harbottle, Thomas B. see Harbottle, Thomas Benfield.
Harbottle, Thomas Benfield.
xHarbottle, T. B.
Dictionary of Battles. Gordon Pr.
xHarbottle, Thomas.
Dictionary of Battles. Beekman Pubs.
Dictionary of Battles. Stein & Day.
xHarbottle, Thomas B.
Dictionary of Battles. Gale.
Dictionary of Historical Allusions. Gale.
Harbrecht, P. P. see Harbrecht, Paul P.
Harbrecht, Paul P.
xHarbrecht, P. P.
Pension Funds & Economic Power. Kraus
Repr.
Harbuck, Don B.
xHarbuck, Don B.
Dynamics of Belief. Broadman.
Harburg, E. Y. see Harburg, Edgar Y.
Harburg, Edgar Y., 1896-
xHarburg, E. Y.
At This Point in Rhyme. Crown.
Harburn, G.
xHarburn, G.
Atlas of Optical Transforms. Cornell U Pr.
Harcourt, Freda.
xHarcourt, Freda.
Twentieth Century World History: A Select
Bibliography. B&N.
Harcourt, G. C. see Harcourt, Geoffrey Colin.
Harcourt, Geoffrey Colin.
xHarcourt, G. C.
Some Cambridge Controversies in the Theory
of Capital. Cambridge U Pr.
Harcourt, Palma.
xHarcourt, Palma.
Agents of Influence. Walker & Co.
At High Risk. Walker & Co.
Harcum, E. Rae. see Harcum, Eugene Rae.
Harcum, Eugene Rae, 1927-
xHarcum, E. Rae.
Psychology for Daily Living: Simple Guidance
in Human Relations for Parents, Teachers, &
Others. Nelson-Hall.
Harcus, A. W.
xHarcus, Alfred.
Arteries & Veins. Churchill.
Harcus, Alfred. see Harcus, A. W.
Hard, Miron E. see Hard, Miron Elisha.
Hard, Miron Elisha, 1845-1914
xHard, Miron E.
Mushrooms, Edible & Otherwise: Habitat &
Time of Growth. Peter Smith.
Hard, Roger, 1931-
xHard, Roger E.

Build Your Own Low-Cost Log Home. Garden
Way Pub.
Hard, Roger E. see Hard, Roger.
Hard, William, 1878-1962
xHard, William.
Raymond Robins' Own Story. Arno.
Hardaway. see Hardaway, John.
Hardaway, C. see Hardaway, M. Conrad.
Hardaway, Francine, 1941-
xHardaway, Francine.
Creative Rhetoric. P-H.
Hardaway, John.
xHardaway.
Thinking into Writing: The Basics & Beyond.
Winthrop.
Hardaway, M. Conrad, 1910-
xHardaway, C.
Central America by Recreation Vehicle.
Trail-R.
Hardee, Melvene D. see Hardee, Melvene Draheim.
Hardee, Melvene Draheim.
xHardee, Melvene D.
ed. Personnel Services in Education. U of
Chicago Pr.
Harden, John. see Harden, John William.
Harden, John William, 1903-
xHarden, John.
Tar Heel Ghosts. U of NC Pr.
Harden, Linda B. see Harden, Linda Burr.
Harden, Linda Burr.
xHarden, Linda B.
The LTR Money Book: The Personal Finance
Guide for Every Kind of Living Together
Relationship. Everest Hse.
Harden, Maximilian, 1861-1927
xHarden, Maximillian.
I Meet My Contemporaries. Arno.
Harden, Maximillian. see Harden, Maximilian.
Harden, William, 1844-1936
xHarden, William.
History of Savannah & South Georgia.
Cherokee.
Hardendorff, Jeanne B.
xHardendorff, Jeanne B.
Libraries & How to Use Them. Watts.
Harder, Helmut.
xHarder, Helmut.
Guide to Faith. Faith & Life.
Harder, Marvin A. see Harder, Marvin Andrew.
Harder, Marvin Andrew.
xHarder, Marvin A.
The Legislature As an Organization: A Study
of the Kansas Legislature. Regents Pr KS.
Hardesty, D. L. see Hardesty, Donald L.
Hardesty, Dan.
xHardesty, Dan.
The Louisiana Tigers: LSU Football. Strode.
Hardesty, Donald L., 1941-
xHardesty, D. L.
Ecological Anthropology. Wiley.
Hardgrave, Robert L.
xHardgrave, Robert L.
The Politics of Bilingual Education: A Study of
Four Southwest Texas Communities. Sterling
Swift.
Hardie, Frank.
xHardie, Frank.
The Abyssinian Crisis. Shoe String.
Hardie, Melissa.
xHardie, Melissa.
ed. Nursing Auxiliaries in Health Care. Biblio
Dist.
Hardigree, Peggy. see Hardigree, Peggy Ann.
Hardigree, Peggy A. see Hardigree, Peggy Ann.
Hardigree, Peggy Ann, 1945-
xHardigree, Peggy.
Working Outside: A Career &
Self-Employment Handbook. Crown.
xHardigree, Peggy A.

The Free Food Seafood Book. Stackpole.
Hardin, Charles M. see Hardin, Charles Meyer.
Hardin, Charles Meyer.
xHardin, Charles M.
Freedom in Agricultural Education. Arno.
Presidential Power & Accountability: Toward a
New Constitution. U of Chicago Pr.
Hardin, Garrett. see Hardin, Garrett James.
Hardin, Garrett James, 1915-
xHardin, Garrett.
Exploring New Ethics for Survival: The Voyage
of the Spaceship Beagle. Penguin.
Exploring New Ethics for Survival: The Voyage
of the Spaceship Beagle. Viking Pr.
The Limits of Altruism: An Ecologist's View of
Survival. Ind U Pr.
Nature & Man's Fate. NAL.
ed. Population, Evolution, & Birth Control: A
Collage of Controversial Ideas. W H
Freeman.
Stalking the Wild Taboo. W Kaufmann.
Hardin, James W. see Hardin, James Walker.
Hardin, James Walker.
xHardin, James W.
Human Poisoning from Native & Cultivated
Plants. Duke.
Hardin, Russell.
xHardin, Russell.
What We Go by. SBD.
Harding, Alfred, 1892-1969
xHarding, Alfred.
The Revolt of the Actors. Greenwood.
Harding, Anthony.
xHarding, Anthony.
The Arco Guide to Vintage Sports & Racing
Cars. Arco.
ed. Car Facts & Feats. Sterling.
Harding, D. E. see Harding, Douglas Edison.
Harding, Delma E.
xHarding, Delma E.
Creative Biology Teaching. Iowa St U Pr.
Harding, Douglas Edison, 1909-
xHarding, D. E.
The Hierarchy of Heaven & Earth: A New
Diagram of Man in the Universe. U Presses
Fla.
Harding, Frank J. see Harding, Frank James William.
Harding, Frank James William.
xHarding, Frank J.
Matthew Arnold, The Critic & France. Arden
Lib.
Matthew Arnold, the Critic & France..
Folcroft.
Harding, G. Lankester. see Harding, Gerald Lankester.
Harding, Gerald Lankester, 1901-
xHarding, G. Lankester.
An Index & Concordance of Pre-Islamic
Arabian Names & Inscriptions. U of Toronto
Pr.
Harding, Gunnar.
xHarding, Gunnar.
ed. Modern Swedish Poetry in Translation. U
of Minn Pr.
Harding, Jack, 1914-
xHarding, Jack.
Retail Selling Is Fun. Interstate.
Harding, James.
xHarding, James.
Massenet. St Martin.
The Pre-Raphaelites. Rizzoli Intl.
Harding, John J.
xHarding, John J.
Birding the Delaware Valley Region: A
Comprehensive Guide to Birdwatching in

Southeastern Pennsylvania, Central &

Southern New Jersey, & Northcentral

Delaware. Temple U Pr.

Harding, Laurence V.

xHarding, Laurence V.
The Dramatic Art of Ferdinand Raimund &
Johann Nestroy: A Critical Study. Mouton.

Harding, Lee. *see* Harding, Lee John.

Harding, Lee John, 1937-

xHarding, Lee.
Misplaced Persons. Har-Row.
Rooms of Paradise. St Martin.

Harding, M. Esther. *see* Harding, Mary Esther.

Harding, Mary.

xHarding, Mary.
Easy-Going Sewing. Van Nos Reinhold.

Harding, Mary Esther, 1888-1971

xHarding, M. Esther.
Psychic Energy: Its Source & Its
Transformation. Princeton U Pr.

Harding, Neil.

xHarding, Neil.
Lenin's Political Thought. St Martin.

Harding, Robert R., 1946-

xHarding, Robert R.
Anatomy of a Power Elite: The Provincial
Governors of Early Modern France. Yale U
Pr.

Harding, S. G. *see* Harding, Sandra G.
Harding, Samuel B. *see* Harding, Samuel Bannister.

Harding, Samuel Bannister, 1866-1927

xHarding, Samuel B.
Contest Over the Ratification of the Federal
Constitution in the State of Massachusetts.
Da Capo.

Harding, Sandra G.

xHarding, S. G.
Can Theories Be Refuted?: Essays on the
Duhem-Quine Thesis. Kluwer Boston.

Harding, T. D.

xHarding, T. D.
ed. The Games of the World Correspondence
Chess Championships. David & Charles.
The Italian Game. David & Charles.
Leningrad Dutch. David & Charles.

Harding, T. Swann. *see* Harding, Thomas Swann.

Harding, Thomas Swann, 1890-

xHarding, T. Swann.
The Popular Practice of Fraud. Arno.
Two Blades of Grass: A History of Scientific
Development in the U. S. Department of
Agriculture. Arno.

Harding, Valerie.

xHarding, Valerie.
Faces & Figures in Embroidery. Branford.

Harding, Walter. *see* Harding, Walter Roy.

Harding, Walter Roy.

xHarding, Walter.
The New Thoreau Handbook. NYU Pr.
A Thoreau Handbook. NYU Pr.

Hardingham, Martin.

xHardingham, Martin.
The Fabric Catalog. PB.

Hardison, O. B.

xHardison, O. B.
illus. Christian Rite & Christian Drama in the
Middle Ages: Essays in the Origin & Early
History of Modern Drama. Johns Hopkins.
Forms of Imagination: An Anthology of
Poetry, Fiction & Drama. P-H.
ed. Modern Continental Literary Criticism.
P-H.
Practical Rhetoric. P-H.
Toward Freedom & Dignity: The Humanities &
the Idea of Humanity. Johns Hopkins.

Hardison, Thomas B., 1922-

xHardison, Thomas B.

Fluid Mechanics for Technicians. Reston.

Hardison, Thomas B. *see* Hardison, Thomas D.

Hardison, Thomas D.

xHardison, Thomas B.
Introduction to Kinematics. Reston.

Hardisty, George.

xHardisty, George.
Successful Financial Planning. Revell.

Hardisty, Margaret.

xHardisty, Margaret.
Forever My Love. Harvest Hse.
jt. auth. Successful Financial Planning. Revell.

Hardman, Ann C. Leighton.

xHardman, Ann L.
A Guide to Feeding Horses & Ponies.
Merrimack Bk Serv.

Hardman, Ann L. *see* Hardman, Ann C. Leighton.

Hardman, Laurence.

xHardman, Laurence.
The Survivor's Guide to Leaving Home.
Celebration Pr.

Hardon, John A.

xHardon, John A.
Christianity in the Twentieth Century. Dghtrs
St Paul.
Holiness in the Church. Dghtrs St Paul.
Modern Catholic Dictionary. Doubleday.
Religions of the Orient: A Christian View.
Loyola.
Religious Life Today. Dghtrs St Paul.

Hardt, Anton.

xHardt, Anton.
Third Harvest of Souvenir Spoons. Greenwich
Pr.

Hardt, Hanno.

xHardt, Hanno.
Social Theories of the Press: Early German &
American Perspectives. Sage.

Hardt, Lorraine.

xHardt, Lorraine.
How to Make Money Writing Greeting Cards.
Fell.

Hardwick, Elizabeth.

xHardwick, Elizabeth.
Seduction & Betrayal: Women & Literature.
Random.
Seduction & Betrayal: Women & Literature.
Random.
Sleepless Nights. Random.
Sleepless Nights. Random.
A View of My Own: Essays in Literature &
Society. Octagon.

Hardwick, John Michael Drinkrow, 1924-

xHardwick, Michael.
Endings & Beginnings. G K Hall.
Literary Atlas & Gazetteer of the British Isles.
Gale.
On with the Dance. G K Hall.
Regency Royal. Coward.

Hardwick, Michael. *see* Hardwick, John Michael
Drinkrow.

Hardwick, Mollie.

xHardwick, Mollie.
The War to End Wars. G K Hall.
The World of Upstairs, Downstairs. HR&W.
The Years of Change. G K Hall.

Hardwick, Richard.

xHardwick, Richard.
Charles Richard Drew: Pioneer in Blood
Research. Scribner.

Hardy, Alan.

xHardy, Alan.
Queen Victoria Was Amused. Taplinger.

Hardy, Alan G.

xHardy, Alan G.
Practical Management of Spinal Injuries for
Nurses. Churchill.

Hardy, Alister. *see* Hardy, Alister Clavering.

Hardy, Alister Clavering, Sir.

xHardy, Alister.
Open Sea: Its Natural History. HM.

Hardy, Arthur S. *see* Hardy, Arthur Sherburne.

Hardy, Arthur Sherburne, 1847-1930

xHardy, Arthur S.
But Yet a Woman: A Novel. Arno.

Hardy, Barbara. *see* Hardy, Barbara Nathan.

Hardy, Barbara Nathan.

xHardy, Barbara.
The Advantage of Lyric: Essays on Feeling in
Poetry. Ind U Pr.
The Appropriate Form: An Essay on the
Novel. Northwestern U Pr.

Hardy, C. Colburn.

xHardy, C. Colburn.
ABC's of Investing Your Retirement Funds.
Med Economics.
Dun & Bradstreet's Guide to Your Investments
1981. Lippincott & Crowell.
Dun & Bradstreet's Guide to Your Investments
1980-1981. T Y Crowell.
Your Money & Your Life: How to Plan Your
Long-Range Financial Security. Am Mgmt.

Hardy, Charles O. *see* Hardy, Charles Oscar.

Hardy, Charles Oscar, 1884-1948

xHardy, Charles O.
Odd-Lot Trading on the New York Stock
Exchange. Arno.

Hardy, Dennis.

xHardy, Dennis.
Alternative Communities in Nineteenth
Century England. Longman.

Hardy, Edward J. *see* Hardy, Edward John.

Hardy, Edward John, 1849-1920

xHardy, Edward J.
Love Affairs of Some Famous Men. Arno.

Hardy, Eric.

xHardy, Eric.
The Naturalist in Lakeland. David & Charles.

Hardy, Ernest G. *see* Hardy, Ernest George.

Hardy, Ernest George, 1852-1925

xHardy, Ernest G.
The Catilinarian Conspiracy in Its Context: A
Re-Study of the Evidence. AMS Pr.

Hardy, Evelyn, 1902-

xHardy, Evelyn.
Thomas Hardy: A Critical Biography. Russell.

Hardy, F. Lane. *see* Hardy, Flournoy Lane.

Hardy, Florence E. *see* Hardy, Florence Emily.

Hardy, Florence Emily, 1881-1937

xHardy, Florence E.
Early Life of Thomas Hardy 1840-1891. R
West.
Early Life of Thomas Hardy: 1840-1891.
Scholarly.

Hardy, Flournoy Lane, 1928-

xHardy, F. Lane.
Finite Mathematics. Har-Row.
Precalculus Mathematics. Merrill.

Hardy, Forsyth.

xHardy, Forsyth.
John Grierson: A Documentary Biography.
Merrimack Bk Serv.

Hardy, G. H. *see* Hardy, Godfrey Harold.

Hardy, Godfrey H. *see* Hardy, Godfrey Harold.

Hardy, Godfrey Harold.

xHardy, G. H.
The General Theory of Dirichlet's Series.
Hafner.
xHardy, Godfrey H.
Mathematician's Apology. Cambridge U Pr.

Hardy, Gordon.

xHardy, Gordon.
Music Literature: A Workbook for Analysis.
Har-Row.

Hardy, J. P. *see* Hardy, John P.

Hardy, James D., 1918-

xHardy, James D.

ed. Critical Surgical Illness. Saunders.

Hardy, James K.
  xHardy, Jim.
    High Frequency Circuit Design. Reston.

Hardy, Janet B.
  xHardy, Janet B.
    The First Year of Life. Johns Hopkins.

Hardy, Jim. *see* Hardy, James K.

Hardy, John E. *see* Hardy, John Edward.

Hardy, John Edward.
  xHardy, John E.
    Curious Frame: Seven Poems in Text &
    Context. U of Notre Dame Pr.

Hardy, John P.
  xHardy, J. P.
    Samuel Johnson: A Critical Study. Routledge &
    Kegan.

Hardy, Malcolm.
  xHardy, Malcolm.
    Beginning Psychology. Holmes & Meier.

Hardy, Margaret E.
  xHardy, Margaret E.
    ed. Theoretical Foundations for Nursing. Mss
    Info.

Hardy, P. *see* Hardy, Peter.

Hardy, Peter, 1931-
  xHardy, P.
    Muslims of British India. Cambridge U Pr.
  xHardy, Peter.
    A Lifetime of Badgers. David & Charles.

Hardy, R. H. *see* Hardy, Richard Henry.

Hardy, Randall W.
  xHardy, Randall W.
    China's Oil Future: A Case of Modest
    Expectations. Westview.

Hardy, Richard E.
  xHardy, Richard E.
    ed. Applied Psychology in Law Enforcement &
    Corrections. C C Thomas.
    ed. Career Guidance for Young Women:
    Considerations in Planning Professional
    Careers. C C Thomas.
    ed. Climbing Ghetto Walls: Disadvantagement,
    Delinquency & Rehabilitation. C C Thomas.
    ed. Counseling & Rehabilitating the Cancer
    Patient. C C Thomas.
    ed. Creative Divorce Through Social &
    Psychological Approaches. C C Thomas.
    Drug Dependence & Rehabilitation
    Approaches. C C Thomas.
    ed. Drug Language & Lore. C C Thomas.
    ed. Educational & Psychosocial Aspects of
    Deafness. C C Thomas.
    ed. Fundamentals of Juvenile Criminal
    Behavior & Drug Abuse. C C Thomas.
    ed. Group Counseling & Therapy Techniques
    in Special Settings. C C Thomas.
    ed. Introduction to Correctional Rehabilitation.
    C C Thomas.
    ed. Organization & Administration of Service
    Programs for the Older American. C C
    Thomas.
    ed. Psychological & Vocational Rehabilitation
    of the Youthful Delinquent. C C Thomas.

Hardy, Richard Henry.
  xHardy, R. H.
    Accidents & Emergencies: A Practical
    Handbook for Personal Use. Oxford U Pr.

Hardy, Robin.
  xHardy, Robin.
    The Wicker Man. PB.

Hardy, Ronald.
  xHardy, Ronald.
    Rivers of Darkness. Putnam.

Hardy, Stella P. *see* Hardy, Stella Pickett.

Hardy, Stella Pickett, 1877-
  xHardy, Stella P.

Colonial Families of the Southern States of
America: A History and Genealogy of
Colonial Families Who Settled in the
Colonies Prior to the Revolution. Genealog
Pub.

Hardy, Thomas.
  xHardy, Thomas.
    The Collected Letters of Thomas Hardy,
    1840-1842. Oxford U Pr.
    The Complete Poems of Thomas Hardy.
    Macmillan.
    Far from the Madding Crowd. Har-Row.
    Far from the Madding Crowd. NAL.
    Far from the Madding Crowd. Penguin.
    Far from the Madding Crowd. St Martin.
    Far from the Madding Crowd. Airmont.
    Mayor of Casterbridge. NAL.
    The Mayor of Casterbridge. Norton.
    The Mayor of Casterbridge. Penguin.
    Mayor of Casterbridge. St Martin.
    Mayor of Casterbridge. HM.
    Mayor of Casterbridge. AMSCO Sch.
    Mayor of Casterbridge. Airmont.
    Mayor of Casterbridge. PB.
    The Old Clock. Folcroft.
    Our Exploits at West Poley. Folcroft.
    Our Exploits at West Poley. Oxford U Pr.
    A Pair of Blue Eyes. St Martin.
    The Return of the Native. Heinemann Ed.
    Return of the Native. Merrimack Bk Serv.
    The Return of the Native. NAL.
    Return of the Native. Norton.
    The Return of the Native. Penguin.
    The Return of the Native. St Martin.
    The Return of the Native. Pendulum Pr.
    Return of the Native. AMSCO Sch.
    Return of the Native. HM.
    Return of the Native. PB.
    Return of the Native. Airmont.
    The Thomas Hardy Omnibus. St Martin.
    Thomas Hardy's Chosen Poems. Ungar.
    Two on a Tower. St Martin.
    The Woodlanders. St Martin.

Hardy, Thomas J. *see* Hardy, Thomas John.

Hardy, Thomas John, 1868-
  xHardy, Thomas J.
    Books on the Shelf. Arno.

Hardy, W. G. *see* Hardy, William George.

Hardy, William George, 1896-
  xHardy, W. G.
    The Greek & Roman World. Schenkman.

Hardy, William J. *see* Hardy, William John.

Hardy, William John, 1857-1919
  xHardy, William J.
    Book-Plates. Arno.

Hardyck, Curtis D.
  xHardyck, Curtis D.
    Introduction to Statistics for the Behavioral
    Sciences. HR&W.

Hare, A. Paul. *see* Hare, Alexander Paul.

Hare, Alexander Paul.
  xHare, A. Paul.
    ed. Liberation Without Violence: A Third Party
    Approach. Rowman.

Hare, Cyril.
  xHare, Cyril.
    An English Murder. Har-Row.

Hare, David, 1947-
  xHare, David.
    Knuckle. Merrimack Bk Serv.

Hare, James R.
  xHare, James R.
    ed. Hiking the Appalachian Trail. Rodale Pr
    Inc.

Hare, Norma Q.
  xHare, Norma Q.
    Who Is Root Beer?. Garrard.
    Wish Upon a Birthday. Garrard.

Hare, Peter H.
  xHare, Peter H.

Causing, Perceiving & Believing: An
Examination of the Philosophy of C. J.
Ducasse. Kluwer Boston.

Hare, R. D. *see* Hare, Robert D.

Hare, R. M. *see* Hare, Richard Mervyn.

Hare, Richard.
  xHare, Richard.
    Maxim Gorky: Romantic Realist &
    Conservative Revolutionary. Greenwood.
    Portraits of Russian Personalities Between
    Reform & Revolution. Greenwood.

Hare, Richard M. *see* Hare, Richard Mervyn.

Hare, Richard Mervyn.
  xHare, R. M.
    Practical Inferences. U of Cal Pr.
  xHare, Richard M.
    Freedom & Reason. Oxford U Pr.

Hare, Robert D.
  xHare, R. D.
    Psychopathic Behaviour: Approaches to
    Research. Wiley.

Hare, Ronald.
  xHare, Ronald.
    Bacteriology & Immunity for Nurses. Churchill.

Hare, Van C. *see* Hare, Van Court.

Hare, Van Court.
  xHare, Van C.
    Introduction to Programming: A BASIC
    Approach. HarBraceJ.

Harel, D. *see* Harel, David.

Harel, David, 1950-
  xHarel, D.
    First-Order Dynamic Logic. Springer-Verlag.

Hareven, Shulamith.
  xHareven, Shulamith.
    City of Many Days. Popular Lib.

Hareven, Tamara K.
  xHareven, Tamara K.
    Amoskeag: Life & Work in an American
    Factory-City. Pantheon.
    ed. Family & Population in Nineteenth-Century
    America. Princeton U Pr.
    ed. Themes in the History of the Family. Am
    Antiquarian.

Harfield, Henry.
  xHarfield, Henry.
    Bank Credits & Acceptances. Ronald Pr.

Hargens, Alan R.
  xHargens, Alan R.
    Tissue Fluid Pressure & Composition. Williams
    & Wilkins.

Harger, Robert O.
  xHarger, Robert O.
    Optical Communication Theory. Acad Pr.

Hargest, George E.
  xHargest, George E.
    History of Letter Post Communication Between
    the United States & Europe 1845-1875.
    Quarterman.

Hargis, Charles. *see* Hargis, Charles H.

Hargis, Charles H.
  xHargis, Charles.
    English Syntax: An Outline for Clinicians &
    Teachers of Language Handicapped Children.
    C C Thomas.

Hargittai, I. *see* Hargittai, Istvan.

Hargittai, Istvan.
  xHargittai, I.
    Sulphone Molecular Structures: Conformation
    & Geometry from Electron Diffraction &
    Microwave Spectroscopy; Structural
    Variations. Springer-Verlag.

Hargrave, Leonie.
  xHargrave, Leonie.
    Clara Reeve. Ballantine.

Hargrave, Letitia (Mactavish).
  xHargrave, Letitia M.
    Letters of Letitia Hargrave. Greenwood.

Hargrave, Letitia M. *see* Hargrave, Letitia (Mactavish).

Hargreaves, David H.
xHargreaves, David H.
Deviance in Classrooms. Routledge & Kegan.
Hargreaves, Dorothy.
xHargreaves, Dorothy.
African Blossoms. Hargreaves.
African Trees. Hargreaves.
Tropical Blossoms of the Pacific. Hargreaves.
Tropical Trees of Hawaii. Hargreaves.
Tropical Trees of the Pacific. Hargreaves.
Hargreaves, G. R. *see* Hargreaves, George Ronald.
Hargreaves, George Ronald.
xHargreaves, G. R.
Psychiatry & the Public Health. Humanities.
Hargreaves, J. D. *see* Hargreaves, John D.
Hargreaves, J. H. *see* Hargreaves, John Keith.
Hargreaves, John. *see* Hargreaves, John Henry
Monsarrat.
Hargreaves, John D.
xHargreaves, J. D.
Prelude to the Partition of West Africa. St
Martin.
xHargreaves, John D.
The End of Colonial Rule in West Africa:
Essays in Contemporary History. B&N.
Hargreaves, John Henry Monsarrat, 1911-
xHargreaves, John.
A Guide to the Parables. Judson.
Hargreaves, John Keith, 1930-
xHargreaves, J. H.
The Upper Atmosphere & Solar-Terrestrial
Relations. Litton Educ Pub.
Hargreaves, Robert, 1933-
xHargreaves, Robert.
Superpower: A Portrait of America in the 70's.
St Martin.
Hargreaves-Mawdsley, W. N.
xHargreaves-Mawdsley, W. N.
Eighteenth-Century Spain, 1700-1788: A
Political, Diplomatic & Institutional History.
Rowman.
Oxford in the Age of John Locke. U of Okla
Pr.
Hargrove, Barbara. *see* Hargrove, Barbara W.
Hargrove, Barbara W.
xHargrove, Barbara.
The Sociology of Religion: Classical &
Contemporary Approaches. AHM Pub.
Hargrove, Erwin C.
xHargrove, Erwin C.
The Power of the Modern Presidency.
Random.
The Power of the Modern Presidency. Temple
U Pr.
The Presidency: A Question of Power. Little.
Presidential Leadership: Personality & Political
Style. Macmillan.
Hargrove, John, 1750-1839
xHargrove, John.
Compiled by The Weavers Draft Book &
Clothiers Assistant. Am Antiquarian.
Hargrove, Merwin M.
xHargrove, Merwin M.
Cases in Administrative Policies &
Contemporary Issues. Irwin.
Hargrove, Robert, 1947-
xHargrove, Robert.
Est: Making Life Work. Dell.
Harich-Schneider, Eta.
xHarich-Schneider, Eta.
A History of Japanese Music. Oxford U Pr.
Haried, Andrew A.
xHaried, Andrew A.
Advanced Accounting. Wiley.
Haring, Albert, 1901-
xHaring, Albert.
Retail Price Cutting & Its Control by
Manufacturers. Arno.
Haring, Bernard. *see* Haring, Bernhard.
Haring, Bernard C. Ss. R. *see* Haring, Bernhard.

Haring, Bernhard, 1912-
xHaring, Bernard.
Church on the Move. Alba.
The Ethics of Manipulation: Issues in
Medicine, Behavior Control & Genetics.
Seabury.
Toward a Christian Moral Theology. U of
Notre Dame Pr.
xHaring, Bernard C. Ss. R.
The Christian Existentialist: The Philosophy &
Theology of Self-Fulfillment in Modern
Society. NYU Pr.
Haring, C. H. *see* Haring, Clarence Henry.
Haring, Clarence H. *see* Haring, Clarence Henry.
Haring, Clarence Henry, 1885-1960
xHaring, C. H.
The Spanish Empire in America. Peter Smith.
xHaring, Clarence H.
South America Looks at the United States.
Arno.
Spanish Empire in America. HarBraceJ.
Haring, L. Lloyd.
xHaring, Lloyd.
Introduction to Scientific Geographic Research.
Wm C Brown.
Haring, Lloyd. *see* Haring, L. Lloyd.
Haring, Norris. *see* Haring, Norris Grover.
Haring, Norris G. *see* Haring, Norris Grover.
Haring, Norris Grover.
xHaring, Norris.
Attitudes of Educators Toward Exceptional
Children. Greenwood.
xHaring, Norris G.
ed. Improvement of Instruction. Spec Child.
Teaching Special Children. McGraw.
Harington, Donald.
xHarington, Donald.
Architecture of the Arkansas Ozarks: A Novel.
Little.
Harkabi, Y. *see* Harkabi, Yehoshafat.
Harkabi, Yehoshafat, 1921-
xHarkabi, Y.
Arab Attitudes to Israel. Biblio Dist.
The Palestinian Covenant & Its Meaning.
Biblio Dist.
xHarkabi, Yehoshafat.
Arab Attitudes to Israel. Transaction Bks.
Arab Strategies & Israel's Response. Free Pr.
Palestinians & Israel. Transaction Bks.
Harkavy, Robert E.
xHarkavy, Robert E.
The Arms Trade & International Systems.
Ballinger Pub.
Harker, Alfred, 1859-1939
xHarker, Alfred.
Natural History of Igneous Rocks. Hafner.
Harker, Herbert.
xHarker, Herbert.
Goldenrod. Random.
Turn Again Home. NAL.
Turn Again Home. Random.
Harker, W. John.
xHarker, W. John.
ed. Classroom Strategies for Secondary
Reading. Intl Reading.
Harkey, W. G. *see* Harkey, William George.
Harkey, William George.
xHarkey, W. G.
Appreciating the Nine Fine. Northwood Inst.
Harkins, Philip, 1912-
xHarkins, Philip.
Breakaway Back. Morrow.
Day of the Drag Race. Berkley Pub.
The Day of the Drag Race. Morrow.
Fight Like a Falcon. Morrow.
Game, Carol Canning. Morrow.
Harkins, William E. *see* Harkins, William Edward.
Harkins, William Edward.
xHarkins, William E.

Dictionary of Russian Literature. Greenwood.
Harkness, Charles A.
xHarkness, Charles A.
Career Counseling: Dreams & Reality. C C
Thomas.
Harkness, David J. *see* Harkness, David James.
Harkness, David James.
xHarkness, David J.
Lincoln's Favorite Poets. U of Tenn Pr.
Harkness, E. L. *see* Harkness, Edward L.
Harkness, Edward L.
xHarkness, E. L.
Solar Radiation Control in Buildings.
Burgess-Intl Ideas.
Harkness, Georgia E. *see* Harkness, Georgia Elma.
Harkness, Georgia Elma, 1891-1974
xHarkness, Georgia E.
The Sources of Western Morality: From
Primitive Society Through the Beginning of
Christianity. AMS Pr.
Harkness, R. *see* Harkness, Richard.
Harkness, Richard.
xHarkness, R.
OTC Handbook: What to Recommend & Why.
Med Economics.
Harkness, Sarah. *see* Harkness, Sarah P.
Harkness, Sarah P.
xHarkness, Sarah.
Building Without Barriers for the Disabled.
Watson-Guptill.
Harkonen, Helen B.
xHarkonen, Helen B.
Farms & Farmers in Art. Lerner Pubns.
Harlan, Jack R. *see* Harlan, Jack Rodney.
Harlan, Jack Rodney.
xHarlan, Jack R.
ed. Origins of African Plant Domestication.
Beresford Bk Serv.
Harlan, Louis R.
xHarlan, Louis R.
Booker T. Washington: The Making of a Black
Leader, 1856-1901. Oxford U Pr.
Booker T. Washington: The Making of a Black
Leader, 1856-1901. Oxford U Pr.
Harland, Henry, 1861-1905
xHarland, Henry.
Comedies & Errors. Arno.
Grey Roses. Arno.
Harland, John.
xHarland, John.
Brave New World: A Different Projection.
Sovereign Pr.
Harle, J. C. *see* Harle, James C.
Harle, James C.
xHarle, J. C.
Gupta Sculpture: Indian Sculpture of the
Fourth to the Sixth Centuries A.D.. Oxford
U Pr.
Harle, Philippe.
xHarle, Philippe.
Glenans Sailing Manual. De Graff.
Harle, Vilho.
xHarle, Vilho.
ed. Political Economy of Food. Renouf.
Harlem, O. K. *see* Harlem, Ole Kristian.
Harlem, Ole Kristian, 1917-
xHarlem, O. K.
Communication in Medicine: A Challenge to
the Profession. S Karger.
Harless, Marion.
xHarless, Marion.
Turtles: Perspectives & Research. Wiley.
Harleston, Rebekah M.
xHarleston, Rebekah M.
Administration of Government Documents
Collections. Libs Unl.
Harley, Brian.
xHarley, Brian.

Mate in Two Moves: The Two-Move Chess
Problem Made Easy. Dover.
Harley, George W. see Harley, George Way.
Harley, George Way, 1894-
xHarley, George W.
Masks As Agents of Social Control in
Northeast Liberia. Kraus Repr.
Harley, J. B. see Harley, John Brian.
Harley, John Brian.
xHarley, J. B.
Mapping the American Revolutionary War. U
of Chicago Pr.
Harley, John E. see Harley, John Eugene.
Harley, John Eugene, 1892-
xHarley, John E.
World-Wide Influences of the Cinema: A Study
of Official Censorship & the International
Cultural Aspects of Motion Pictures. Ozer.
Harley, Lewis R. see Harley, Lewis Reifsneider.
Harley, Lewis Reifsneider, 1866-
xHarley, Lewis R.
Francis Lieber: His Life & Political Philosophy.
AMS Pr.
Harley, M.
xHarley, M.
Priory of St. Bernard: An Old English Tale.
Arno.
Harley, Marjorie.
xHarley, Marjorie.
ed. The Analyst & the Adolescent at Work.
Times Bks.
Harley, Randall K.
xHarley, Randall K.
The Teaching of Braille Reading. C C Thomas.
Harley, Robinson D. see Harley, Robison Dooling.
Harley, Robison Dooling, 1911-
xHarley, Robinson D.
ed. Pediatric Ophthalmology. Saunders.
Harley, Timothy.
xHarley, Timothy.
Moon Lore. Beekman Pubs.
Moon Lore. Charles River Bks.
Moon Lore. C E Tuttle.
Harloe, Michael.
xHarloe, Michael.
Captive Cities: Studies in the Political
Economy of Cities & Regions. Wiley.
Harlow, Enid.
xHarlow, Enid.
Crashing. St Martin.
Harlow, Harry F. see Harlow, Harry Frederick.
Harlow, Harry Frederick.
xHarlow, Harry F.
The Human Model: Primate Perspectives.
Halsted Pr.
Learning to Love. Albion.
Learning to Love. Ballantine.
Psychology. Albion.
Harlow, Jan.
xHarlow, Jan.
The Good Age Cookbook: Recipes from the
Institute for Creative Aging. HM.
Harlow, Jules.
xHarlow, Jules.
Lessons from Our Living Past. Behrman.
Harlow, Lewis A.
xHarlow, Lewis A.
Covered Bridges Can Talk. Wake-Brook.
Harlow, Neal.
xHarlow, Neal.
Maps & Surveys of the Pueblo Lands of Los
Angeles. Dawsons.
Harlow, S. Ralph. see Harlow, Samuel Ralph.
Harlow, Samuel Ralph, 1885-
xHarlow, S. Ralph.
A Life After Death. Manor Bks.
Harlow, William M. see Harlow, William Morehouse.
Harlow, William Morehouse, 1900-
xHarlow, William M.

Art Forms from Plant Life. Dover.
Art Forms from Plant Life. Peter Smith.
Harm, Walter, 1925-
xHarm, Walter.
Biological Effects of Ultraviolet Radiation.
Cambridge U Pr.
Harman, Bob, 1918-
xHarman, Bob.
Use Your Head in Doubles. Scribner.
Use Your Head in Tennis. Kennikat.
Use Your Head in Tennis. Scribner.
Use Your Head in Tennis. T Y Crowell.
Harman, Earl W.
xHarman, Earl W.
Introduction to Mechanical Drawing. Allyn.
Harman, Edward G. see Harman, Edward George.
Harman, Edward George, 1862-1921
xHarman, Edward G.
Edmund Spenser & the Impersonations of
Francis Bacon. AMS Pr.
Gabriel Harvey & Thomas Nashe. Folcroft.
Impersonality of Shakespeare. Haskell.
Impersonality of Shakespeare. R West.
xHarman, Edwin G.
Edmund Spenser & the Impersonations of
Francis Bacon. R West.
Harman, Edwin G. see Harman, Edward George.
Harman, Eleanor.
xHarman, Eleanor.
ed. The Thesis & the Book. U of Toronto Pr.
Harman, G. S. see Harman, Grant Stewart.
Harman, Gilbert.
xHarman, Gilbert.
The Nature of Morality: An Introduction to
Ethics. Oxford U Pr.
ed. On Noam Chomsky: Critical Essays.
Doubleday.
xHarman, Gilbert H
Thought. Princeton U Pr.
Harman, Gilbert H. see Harman, Gilbert.
Harman, Grant Stewart.
xHarman, G. S.
ed. The Politics of Education: A Bibliographical
Guide. Crane-Russak Co.
Harman, Harry H. see Harman, Harry Horace.
Harman, Harry Horace, 1913-
xHarman, Harry H.
Modern Factor Analysis. U of Chicago Pr.
Harman, Thomas L.
xHarman, Thomas L.
Guide to the National Electrical Code. P-H.
Harman, Willis W.
xHarman, Willis W.
An Incomplete Guide to the Future. SF Bk Co.
Harmatta, J. see Harmatta, Janos.
Harmatta, Janos, 1917-
xHarmatta, J.
ed. Prolegomena to the Sources on the History
of Pre-Islamic Central Asia. Heyden.
Harmatz. see Harmatz, Morton G.
Harmatz, Morton G.
xHarmatz.
Abnormal Psychology. P-H.
Harmer, Ruth M. see Harmer, Ruth Mulvey.
Harmer, Ruth Mulvey.
xHarmer, Ruth M.
Unfit for Human Consumption. P-H.
Harmin, Merrill.
xHarmin, Merrill.
The Peaceable Classroom: Activities to Calm &
Free Student Energies. Winston Pr.
Harmon, A. J. see Harmon, Allen Jackson.
Harmon, Allen Jackson, 1926-
xHarmon, A. J.
Remodeling for Security. McGraw.
Harmon Foundation, Inc.
xHarmon Foundation, Inc.
Negro Artists. Arno.
Harmon, Glynn.
xHarmon, Glynn.

Human Memory & Knowledge: A Systems
Approach. Greenwood.
Harmon, Margaret.
xHarmon, Margaret.
The Engineering Medicine Man: The New
Pioneer. Westminster.
Ms. Engineer. Westminster.
Working with Words: Careers for Writers.
Westminster.
Harmon, Mont J. see Harmon, Mont Judd.
Harmon, Mont Judd.
xHarmon, Mont J.
Political Thought: From Plato to the Present.
McGraw.
Harmon, R. B. see Harmon, Robert Bartlett.
Harmon, Robert B. see Harmon, Robert Bartlett.
Harmon, Robert Bartlett.
xHarmon, R. B.
An Annotated Guide to the Works of Dorothy
L. Sayers. Garland Pub.
xHarmon, Robert B.
Developing the Library Collection in Political
Science. Scarecrow.
Political Science Bibliographies. Scarecrow.
Understanding Ernest Hemingway: A Study &
Research Guide. Scarecrow.
Harmon, Robert E.
xHarmon, Robert E.
ed. Chemistry & Biology of Nucleosides &
Nucleotides. Acad Pr.
Harmon, Ronald. see Harmon, Ronald M.
Harmon, Ronald M.
xHarmon, Ronald.
Brazil: A Working Bibliography in Literature,
Linguistics, Humanities & the Social
Sciences. ASU Lat Am St.
Harms, Alvin.
xHarms, Alvin.
Jose Maria de Heredia. Twayne.
Harms, Edward.
xHarms, Edward.
Introduction to APL & Computer
Programming. Wiley.
Harms, Ernest, 1895-
xHarms, Ernest.
ed. Pathogenesis of Nervous & Mental
Diseases in Children. Libra.
Understanding Mental Disorders in Childhood.
Interstate.
Harms, L. S. see Harms, Leroy Stanley.
Harms, Leroy Stanley.
xHarms, L. S.
ed. Right to Communicate: Collected Papers. U
Pr of Hawaii.
Harmsen, W. D. see Harmsen, William.
Harmsen, William.
xHarmsen, W. D.
Patterns & Sources of Navajo Weaving.
Harmsen.
Harmston, Floyd K.
xHarmston, Floyd K.
Application of an Input-Output Framework to
a Community Economic System. U of Mo Pr.
Harmsworth, Cecil. see Harmsworth, Cecil Bisshopp
Harmsworth.
**Harmsworth, Cecil Bisshopp Harmsworth, Baron,
1869-1948**
xHarmsworth, Cecil.
Immortals at First Hand. Folcroft.
Harnack, Curtis, 1927-
xHarnack, Curtis.
Limits of the Land. Doubleday.
Harnad, S. see Harnad, Stevan R.
Harnad, Stevan. see Harnad, Stevan R.
Harnad, Stevan R.
xHarnad, S.
ed. Lateralization in the Nervous System. Acad
Pr.
xHarnad, Stevan.

ed. Origins & Evolution of Language & Speech.
NY Acad Sci.

Harnan, Terry.
xHarnan, Terry.
African Rhythm-American Dance: A
Biography of Katherine Dunham. Knopf.

Harned, David B. *see* Harned, David Baily.

Harned, David Baily.
xHarned, David B.
Images for Self-Recognition: The Christian As
Player, Sufferer, Vandal. Seabury.

Harner, Michael.
xHarner, Michael.
Cannibal. Morrow.

Harner, Michael J.
xHarner, Michael J.
ed. Hallucinogens & Shamanism. Oxford U Pr.
ed. Hallucinogens & Shamanism. Oxford U Pr.

Harner, Nevin C. *see* Harner, Nevin Cowger.

Harner, Nevin Cowger, 1901-1951
xHarner, Nevin C.
Factors Related to Sunday School Growth &
Decline in the Eastern Synod of the
Reformed Church in the U. S.. AMS Pr.

Harner, Philip B.
xHarner, Philip B.
I Am of the Fourth Gospel: A Study in
Johannine Usage & Thought. Fortress.

Harnett, D. L. *see* Harnett, Donald L.

Harnett, Donald L.
xHarnett, D. L.
Introductory Statistical Analysis. A-W.
xHarnett, Donald L.
Introduction to Statistical Methods. A-W.
Introductory Statistical Analysis. A-W.

Harney, David M.
xHarney, David M.
Medical Malpractice. A Smith Co.

Harney, G. Julian. *see* Harney, George Julian.

Harney, George Julian.
xHarney, G. Julian.
ed. The Democratic Review of British &
Foreign Politics, History & Literature. Kelley.

Harney, Kenneth R., 1944-
xHarney, Kenneth R.
Beating Inflation with Real Estate. Random.

Harney, Martin P. *see* Harney, Martin Patrick.

Harney, Martin Patrick, 1896-
xHarney, Martin P.
Catholic Church Through the Ages. Dghtrs St
Paul.
Medieval Ties Between Italy & Ireland. Dghtrs
St Paul.

Harney, Robert F.
xHarney, Robert F.
Immigrants: A Portrait of the Urban
Experience, 1890-1930. Van Nos Reinhold.

Harney, William E. *see* Harney, William Edward.

Harney, William Edward.
xHarney, William E.
Yarns from an Aussie Bushcook. Cobbers.

Harnishfeger, Lloyd.
xHarnishfeger, Lloyd.
Prisoner of the Mound Builders. Lerner Pubns.
xHarnishfeger, Lloyd C.
A Collector's Guide to American Indian
Artifacts. Lerner Pubns.
Hunters of the Black Swamp. Lerner Pubns.

Harnishfeger, Lloyd C. *see* Harnishfeger, Lloyd.

Harnwell, G. P. *see* Harnwell, Gaylord Probasco.

Harnwell, Gaylord Probasco.
xHarnwell, G. P.
Experimental Atomic Physics. Krieger.

Haro, Michael S.
xHaro, Michael S.
Explorations in Personal Health. HM.

Harootunian, H. D. *see* Harootunian, Harry D.

Harootunian, Harry D., 1929-
xHarootunian, H. D.

Toward Restoration: The Growth of Political
Consciousness in Tokugawa Japan. U of Cal
Pr.

Harpending, Asbury.
xHarpending, Asbury.
Great Diamond Hoax & Other Stirring
Incidents in the Life of Asbury Harpending.
U of Okla Pr.

Harper, Anita.
xHarper, Anita.
How We Live. Har-Row.
How We Work. Har-Row.

Harper, Ann K.
xHarper, Ann K.
The Location of the United States Steel
Industry, 1879-1919. Arno.

Harper, Charles A.
xHarper, Charles A.
Handbook of Components for Electronics.
McGraw.
Handbook of Electronic Packaging. McGraw.
Handbook of Electronic Systems Design.
McGraw.

Harper, Charles A. *see* Harper, Charles Athiel.

Harper, Charles Athiel.
xHarper, Charles A.
Century of Public Teacher Education: The
Story of the State Teachers Colleges.
Greenwood.

Harper, Charlie, 1931-
xHarper, Charlie.
Introduction to Mathematical Physics. P-H.

Harper, D. T. *see* Harper, Donald T.

Harper, David.
xHarper, David.
The Patchwork Man. Dodd.
The Patchwork Man. G K Hall.

Harper, Donald T.
xHarper, D. T.
Paper Coatings. Noyes.

Harper, E. J.
xHarper, E. J.
Banker's Complete Letter Book. P-H.

Harper, Frances E. *see* Harper, Frances Ellen Watkins.

Harper, Frances Ellen Watkins, 1825-1911
xHarper, Frances E.
Idylls of the Bible. AMS Pr.

Harper, Frederick D.
xHarper, Frederick D.
Jogotherapy: Jogging As a Therapeutic
Strategy. Douglass Pubs.

Harper, G. Neil. *see* Harper, Goin Neil.

Harper, George M. *see* Harper, George Mclean.

Harper, George Mclean, 1863-1947
xHarper, George M.
Charles-Augustin Sainte-Beuve. Arno.
Literary Appreciations. Arno.
Masters of French Literature. Arno.
Spirit of Delight. Arno.

Harper, Goin Neil.
xHarper, G. Neil.
Computer Applications in Architecture &
Engineering. McGraw.

Harper, Harold A.
xHarper, Harold A.
Review of Physiological Chemistry. Lange.

Harper, Henry H. *see* Harper, Henry Howard.

Harper, Henry Howard, 1871-
xHarper, Henry H.
Byron's Malach Hamoves. Arden Lib.

Harper, Howard M.
xHarper, Howard M.
Desperate Faith: A Study of Bellow, Salinger,
Mailer, Baldwin, & Updike. U of NC Pr.

Harper, Howard V.
xHarper, Howard V.
Profiles of Protestant Saints. Fleet.

Harper, Ida H. *see* Harper, Ida Husted.

Harper, Ida Husted, 1851-1931
xHarper, Ida H.

ed. Life & Work of Susan B. Anthony. Arno.

Harper, J. Russell.
xHarper, J. Russell.
Krieghoff. U of Toronto Pr.
Painting in Canada: A History. U of Toronto
Pr.
A People's Art: Primitive, Naive, Provincial &
Folk Painting in Canada. U of Toronto Pr.

Harper, Joan.
xHarper, Joan.
I'm Still Me. Logos.

Harper, Maxwell J.
xHarper, Maxwell J.
How to Get the Job You Want After Forty.
Pilot Bks.

Harper, Michael S.
xHarper, Michael S.
ed. Chant of Saints: A Gathering of
Afro-American Literature, Art, &
Scholarship. U of Ill Pr.
History Is Your Own Heartbeat: Poems. U of
Ill Pr.
Images of Kin: New & Selected Poems. U of Ill
Pr.

Harper, Norman. *see* Harper, Norman Denholm.

Harper, Norman Denholm.
xHarper, Norman.
ed. Pacific Orbit: Australian-American
Relations Since 1942. Verry.

Harper, Ralph, 1915-
xHarper, Ralph.
The Existential Experience. Johns Hopkins.
The Path of Darkness. UPBS.
The World of the Thriller. Johns Hopkins.

Harper, Robert A. *see* Harper, Robert Allan.

Harper, Robert Allan.
xHarper, Robert A.
Psychoanalysis & Psychotherapy: 36 Systems.
Aronson.
Psychoanalysis & Psychotherapy: 36 Systems.
P-H.

Harper, Robert G. *see* Harper, Robert Gale.

Harper, Robert Gale.
xHarper, Robert G.
Nonverbal Communication: The State of the
Art. Wiley.

Harper, Robert J. *see* Harper, Robert James.

Harper, Robert James.
xHarper, Robert J.
ed. Reading & the Law. Intl Reading.

Harper, Wilhelmina.
xHarper, Wilhelmina.
ed. Gunniwolf. Dutton.

Harper, William A.
xHarper, William A.
Community, Junior, & Technical Colleges: A
Public Relations Sourcebook. Hemisphere
Pub.
xHarper, William C.
ed. Toward a New Politics. Mss Info.

Harper, William C. *see* Harper, William A.

Harper's Magazine.
xHarper's Magazine.
Gentlemen, Scholars & Scoundrels: A Treasury
of the Best of Harper's Magazine; from 1850
to the Present. Arno.

Harpole, C. H. *see* Harpole, Charles Henry.

Harpole, Charles Henry.
xHarpole, C. H.
Gradients of Depth in the Cinema Image.
Arno.

Harpool, Jack D.
xHarpool, Jack D.
Business Data Systems: A Practical Guide. Wm
C Brown.

Harr, Dorothy N. *see* Harr, Dorothy Nebel.

Harr, Dorothy Nebel.
xHarr, Dorothy N.

Eastern Shore by Coach-and-Four & Other
Stories. Cornell Maritime.
Harr, John E. see Harr, John Ensor.
Harr, John Ensor, 1926-
xHarr, John E.
Professional Diplomat. Princeton U Pr.
Harr, Milton E. see Harr, Milton Edward.
Harr, Milton Edward, 1925-
xHarr, Milton E.
Groundwater & Seepage. McGraw.
Mechanics of Particulate Media: A
Probabilistic Approach. McGraw.
Harraden, Beatrice, 1864-1936
xHarraden, Beatrice.
In Varying Moods. Arno.
Harragan, Betty L. see Harragan, Betty Lehan.
Harragan, Betty Lehan.
xHarragan, Betty L.
Games Mother Never Taught You: Corporate
Gamesmanship for Women. Warner Bks.
Harrah, Barbara K.
xHarrah, Barbara K.
Alternate Sources of Energy: A Bibliography of
Solar, Geothermal, Wind & Tidal Energy, &
Environmental Architecture. Scarecrow.
Funeral Service: A Bibliography of Literature
on Its Past, Present, & Future, the Various
Means of Disposition, & Memorialization.
Scarecrow.
Sports Books for Children: An Annotated
Bibliography. Scarecrow.
Harrah, Ezra C. see Harrah, Ezra Clarence.
Harrah, Ezra Clarence, 1889-
xHarrah, Ezra C.
North American Monostomes Primarily from
Fresh Water Hosts. Johnson Repr.
Harrah, Michael.
xHarrah, Michael.
First Offender. Philomel.
Harral, Stewart, 1906-
xHarral, Stewart.
When It's Laughter You're After. U of Okla
Pr.
Harrar, Ellwood Scott.
xHarrar, Elwood S.
Guide to Southern Trees. Dover.
Guide to Southern Trees. Peter Smith.
Harrar, Elwood S. see Harrar, Ellwood Scott.
Harre, R. see Harre, Romano.
Harre, Rom. see Harre, Romano.
Harre, Romano.
xHarre, R.
Matter & Method. Ridgeview.
xHarre, Rom.
Life Sentences: Aspects of the Social Role of
Language. Wiley.
ed. Personality. Rowman.
Principles of Scientific Thinking. U of Chicago
Pr.
ed. Problems of Scientific Revolution: Progress
& Obstacles to Progress in the Sciences, the
Herbert Spencer Lectures 1973. Oxford U Pr.
Social Being: A Theory for Social Psychology.
Littlefield.
Social Being: A Theory for Social Psychology.
Rowman.
xHarre, Romano.
Causal Powers: A Theory of Natural Necessity.
Rowman.
Harrell, Costen J. see Harrell, Costen Jordan.
Harrell, Costen Jordan, 1885-
xHarrell, Costen J.
Stewardship & the Tithe. Abingdon.
Harrell, David E. see Harrell, David Edwin.
Harrell, David Edwin.
xHarrell, David E.
White Sects & Black Men in the Recent South.
Vanderbilt U Pr.
Harrell, George T.
xHarrell, George T.

Planning Medical Center Facilities for
Education, Research, & Public Service. Pa St
U Pr.
Harrell, Isaac S. see Harrell, Isaac Samuel.
Harrell, Isaac Samuel.
xHarrell, Isaac S.
Loyalism in Virginia: Chapters in the Economic
History of the Revolution. AMS Pr.
Harrell, Jean. see Harrell, Jean Gabbert.
Harrell, Jean Gabbert.
xHarrell, Jean.
ed. Aesthetics in Twentieth-Century Poland:
Selected Essays. Bucknell U Pr.
Harrell, Monette R.
xHarrell, Monette R.
The Ham Book: A Comprehensive Guide to
Ham Cookery. Donning Co.
Harrell, Pat E. see Harrell, Pat Edwin.
Harrell, Pat Edwin.
xHarrell, Pat E.
Letter of Paul to the Philippians. Sweet.
Harrell, Ruth F. see Harrell, Ruth Flinn.
Harrell, Ruth Flinn, 1900-
xHarrell, Ruth F.
Effect of Added Thiamine on Learning. AMS
Pr.
Further Effects of Added Thiamin on Learning
& Other Processes. AMS Pr.
Harrell, Sara G. see Harrell, Sara Gordon.
Harrell, Sara Gordon.
xHarrell, Sara G.
Cottage by the Sea. Concordia.
John Ross. Dillon.
Harrell-Bond, Barbara E.
xHarrell-Bond, Barbara E.
Modern Marriage in Sierra Leone: A Study of
the Professional Group. Mouton.
Harrelson, Bud.
xHarrelson, Bud
How to Play Better Baseball. Atheneum.
How to Play Better Baseball. Atheneum.
Harrier, Richard. see Harrier, Richard C.
Harrier, Richard C.
xHarrier, Richard.
The Canon of Sir Thomas Wyatt's Poetry.
Harvard U Pr.
xHarrier, Richard C.
ed. An Anthology of Jacobean Drama. NYU
Pr.
Harries, J. T. see Harries, John Thomas.
Harries, John Thomas.
xHarries, J. T.
Essentials of Paediatric Gastroenterology.
Churchill.
Harries, K. D. see Harries, Keith D.
Harries, Karsten.
xHarries, Karsten.
Meaning of Modern Art: A Philosophical
Interpretation. Northwestern U Pr.
Harries, Keith D.
xHarries, K. D.
Crime & the Environment. C C Thomas.
xHarries, Keith D.
The Geography of Laws & Justice: Spatial
Perspectives on the Criminal Justice System.
Praeger.
Harries-Jones, Peter.
xHarries-Jones, Peter.
Freedom & Labour: Mobilization & Political
Control on the Zambian Copperbelt. St
Martin.
Harrigan, John J.
xHarrigan, John J.
Governing the Twin Cities Region: The
Metropolitan Council in Comparative
Perspective. U of Minn Pr.
Harrigan, Stephen, 1948-
xHarrigan, Stephen.
Aransas. Knopf.
Harriman, Averell. see Harriman, William Averell.

Harriman, John E.
xHarriman, John E.
ed. Theoretical Foundations of Electron Spin
Resonance. Acad Pr.
Harriman, Karl E. see Harriman, Karl Edwin.
Harriman, Karl Edwin, 1875-1935
xHarriman, Karl E.
Ann Arbor Tales. Arno.
Homebuilders. Arno.
Harriman, Margaret (Case).
xHarriman, Margaret C.
Take Them up Tenderly: A Collection of
Profiles. Arno.
Harriman, Margaret C. see Harriman, Margaret (Case).
Harriman, William Averell.
xHarriman, Averell.
Special Envoy to Churchill & Stalin 1941-1946.
Random.
Harrington, A. P. see Harrington, Anthony Patrick.
Harrington, Alan, 1919-
xHarrington, Alan.
The Immortalist. Celestial Arts.
Harrington, Anthony P. see Harrington, Anthony Patrick.
Harrington, Anthony Patrick.
xHarrington, A. P.
Defend Yourself with Kung Fu: A Practical
Guide. B&N.
xHarrington, Anthony P.
Every Boy's Judo. NAL.
Every Boy's Judo. Emerson.
Harrington, Bob, 1927-
xHarrington, Bob.
Bring Them in. Broadman.
God's Super Salesman. Broadman.
Harrington, Evans.
xHarrington, Evans.
ed. The South & Faulkner's Yoknapatawpha:
The Actual & the Apocryphal. U Pr of Miss
Harrington, Geri.
xHarrington, Geri.
The College Cookbook. Scribner.
Grow Your Own Chinese Vegetables.
Macmillan.
Grow Your Own Chinese Vegetables.
Macmillan.
The Wood-Burning Stove Book. Macmillan.
The Wood-Burning Stove Book. Macmillan.
The Woodburning Stove Book. Macmillan.
Harrington, H. D. see Harrington, Harold David.
Harrington, Harold David, 1903-
xHarrington, H. D.
Edible Native Plants of the Rocky Mountains.
U of NM Pr.
How to Identify Plants. Swallow.
Harrington, J. see Harrington, John.
Harrington, James.
xHarrington, James.
James Harrington's Oceana. Hyperion Conn.
Harrington, Joan. see Harrington, Joan Delong.
Harrington, Joan Delong.
xHarrington, Joan.
Patient Care in Renal Failure. Saunders.
Harrington, John, 1942-
xHarrington, J.
Rhetoric of Film. HR&W.
Harrington, Joseph, 1908-
xHarrington, Joseph.
Computer Integrated Manufacturing. Krieger.
Harrington, Karl P. see Harrington, Karl Pomeroy.
Harrington, Karl Pomeroy, 1861-1953
xHarrington, Karl P.
Catullus & His Influence. Cooper Sq.
Richard Alsop "A Hartford Wit". Columbia U
Pr.
Harrington, M. R. see Harrington, Mark Raymond.
Harrington, Mark R. see Harrington, Mark Raymond.
Harrington, Mark Raymond, 1882-
xHarrington, M. R.

The Indians of New Jersey: Dickon Among the
  Lenapes. Rutgers U Pr.
xHarrington, Mark R.
  Cuba Before Columbus. AMS Pr.
Harrington, Michael.
xHarrington, Michael.
  Accidental Century. Macmillan.
  Decade of Decision. S&S.
  The Lesser Evil?: The Left Debates the
    Democratic Party & Social Change. Path Pr
    NY.
  The Other America: Poverty in the United
    States. Macmillan.
  Socialism. Bantam.
  Twilight of Capitalism. S&S.
Harrington, Paul V.
xHarrington, Paul V.
  Parent & Child. Dghtrs St Paul.
Harrington, Richard, Photographer.
xHarrington, Richard.
  Richard Harrington's Antarctic. Alaska
    Northwest.
  Richard Harrington's Yukon. Alaska
    Northwest.
Harrington, Wilfrid J.
xHarrington, Wilfrid J.
  Explaining the Gospels. Paulist Pr.
Harriott, Peter.
xHarriott, Peter.
  Process Control. McGraw.
Harris. see Harris, Anthony B.
Harris, A. see Harris, Alan Edward.
Harris, Abram L. see Harris, Abram Lincoln.
Harris, Abram Lincoln, 1899-
xHarris, Abram L.
  Economics & Social Reform. Greenwood.
  The Negro As Capitalist: A Study of Banking
    & Business Among American Negroes. Peter
    Smith.
  Negro As Capitalist: Study of Banking and
    Business Among American Negroes. Negro U
    Pr.
Harris, Alan Edward.
xHarris, A.
  Argument. Cambridge U Pr.
Harris, Albert J. see Harris, Albert Josiah.
Harris, Albert Josiah.
xHarris, Albert J.
  How to Increase Reading Ability: A Guide to
    Developmental & Remedial Methods.
    Longman.
  How to Teach Reading: A Competency-Based
    Program. Longman.
Harris, Alexander, 1827-
xHarris, Alexander.
  Review of the Political Conflict in America,
    from the Commencement of the Anti-Slavery
    Agitation to the Close of Southern
    Reconstruction. Negro U Pr.
Harris, Andrea.
xHarris, Andrea.
  A Scream Away. Playboy Pbks.
Harris, Ann G.
xHarris, Ann G.
  Geology of National Parks. Kendall-Hunt.
Harris, Anthony. see Harris, Anthony B.
Harris, Anthony B.
xHarris.
  Overdrive: A Human Maintenance Manual.
    David & Charles.
xHarris, Anthony.
  Human Measurement. Heinemann Ed.
Harris, Arthur H.
xHarris.
  An Archaeological Survey of the Chuska
    Valley & the Chaco Plateau, New Mexico.
    Museum NM Pr.
Harris, B. F. see Harris, Bruce Fairgray.
Harris, Barbara.
xHarris, Barbara.

Let's Cook Microwave!. B Harris.
Harris, Barbara S.
xHarris, Barbara S.
  Who Is Julia?. Popular Lib.
Harris, Ben C. see Harris, Ben Charles.
Harris, Ben Charles.
xHarris, Ben C.
  Eat the Weeds. Barre.
  Eat the Weeds. Keats.
Harris, Ben M.
xHarris, Ben M.
  Personnel Administration in Education:
    Leadership for Instructional Improvement.
    Allyn.
  Supervisory Behavior in Education. P-H.
Harris, Bertha, 1937-
xHarris, Bertha.
  Lover. Daughters.
Harris, Bruce Fairgray, 1921-
xHarris, B. F.
  Comedy in European Literature. Folcroft.
Harris, Bryan.
xHarris, Bryan.
  Structure & Properties of Engineering
    Materials. Longman.
Harris, C. C. see Harris, Christopher Charles.
Harris, C. R. see Harris, Charles Reginald Schiller.
Harris, Carl V. see Harris, Carl Vernon.
Harris, Carl Vernon, 1937-
xHarris, Carl V.
  Political Power in Birmingham, 1871-1921. U
    of Tenn Pr.
Harris, Catherine.
xHarris, Catherine.
  Practical Pony Keeping. Arco.
Harris, Charles.
xHarris, Charles.
  The Proofs of Christianity. Gospel Pub.
Harris, Charles M.
xHarris, Charles M.
  Developmental Tasks Resource Guide for
    Elementary School Children. Scarecrow.
Harris, Charles Reginald Schiller, 1896-
xHarris, C. R.
  Germany's Foreign Indebtedness. Arno.
Harris, Charles S. see Harris, Charles Samuel.
Harris, Charles Samuel, 1938-
xHarris, Charles S.
  ed. Visual Coding & Adaptability. L Erlbaum
    Assocs.
Harris, Charles W.
xHarris, Charles W.
  The Cowboy: Six-Shooters, Songs, & Sex. U of
    Okla Pr.
Harris, Chauncy D. see Harris, Chauncy Dennison.
Harris, Chauncy Dennison, 1914-
xHarris, Chauncy D.
  Annotated World List of Selected Current
    Geographical Serials. U Chicago Dept Geog.
  Guide to Geographical Bibliographies &
    Reference Works on Russian or in the Soviet
    Union. U Chicago Dept Geog.
Harris, Christie.
xHarris, Christie.
  Let X Be Excitement. Atheneum.
  Mouse Woman & the Muddleheads.
    Atheneum.
  Once More Upon a Totem. Atheneum.
Harris, Christopher Charles.
xHarris, C. C.
  Readings in Kinship in Urban Society.
    Pergamon.
  The Sociological Enterprise: A Discussion of
    Fundamental Concepts. St Martin.
Harris, Clifford C., 1922-
xHarris, Clifford C.
  The Break Even Handbook: Techniques for
    Profit Planning & Control. P-H.
Harris, Curtis C., 1943-
xHarris.

Pathogenesis & Therapy of Lung Cancer.
    Dekker.
Harris, Cyril M.
xHarris, Cyril M.
  Dictionary of Architecture & Construction.
    McGraw.
  Historic Architecture Sourcebook. McGraw.
Harris, Dale B.
xHarris, Dale B.
  ed. The Concept of Development: An Issue in
    the Study of Human Behavior. U of Minn Pr.
Harris, Daniel C.
xHarris, Daniel C.
  Symmetry & Spectroscopy: An Introduction to
    Vibrational & Electronic Spectroscopy.
    Oxford U Pr.
Harris, David, 1946-
xHarris, David.
  I Shoulda Been Home Yesterday. Delacorte.
Harris, David. see Harris, David John.
Harris, David John.
xHarris, David.
  Socialist Origins in the United States:
    American Forerunners of Marx, 1817-1832.
    Humanities.
Harris, Delmer.
xHarris, Delmer.
  Multiple Defenses for Winning Basketball. P-H.
Harris, Donald J.
xHarris, Donald J.
  Capital Accumulation & Income Distribution.
    Stanford U Pr.
Harris, Dorothy J. see Harris, Dorothy Joan.
Harris, Dorothy Joan.
xHarris, Dorothy J.
  The House Mouse. Warne.
Harris, Douglas.
xHarris, Douglas.
  Structures in Topology. Am Math.
Harris, E. Edward. see Harris, Earl Edward.
Harris, Earl Edward, 1931-
xHarris, E. Edward.
  Marketing Research. McGraw.
Harris, Edward D. see Harris, Edward Day.
Harris, Edward Day, 1937-
xHarris, Edward D.
  ed. Rheumatoid Arthritis. Krieger.
Harris, Edward G.
xHarris, Edward G.
  Pedestrian Approach to Quantum Field
    Theory. Wiley.
Harris, Ernest E.
xHarris, Ernest E.
  ed. Music Education: A Guide to Information
    Sources. Gale.
Harris, Errol E.
xHarris, Errol E.
  Annihilation & Utopia: The Principles of
    International Politics. Humanities.

Harris, F. W. see Harris, Frank Wayne.

Harris, Frank, 1855-1931

xHarris, Frank.

  Montes the Matador. Irvington.

  My Life & Loves. Grove.

Harris, Frank Wayne.
xHarris, F. W.
  ed. Structure-Solubility Relationships in
    Polymers. Acad Pr.
Harris, Fred R., 1930-
xHarris, Fred R.
  America's Democracy: The Ideal & the
    Reality. Scott F.
  Potomac Fever. Norton.
Harris, George, 1844-1922
xHarris, George.
  Inequality & Progress. Arno.
Harris, George S. see Harris, George Sellers.

Harris, George Sellers, 1931-
   xHarris, George S.
      The Origins of Communism in Turkey. Hoover
        Inst Pr.
Harris, George W. see Harris, George Washington.
Harris, George Washington.
   xHarris, George W.
      Sut Lovingood's Yarns. Coll & U Pr.
Harris, Gertrude, 1914-
   xHarris, Gertrude.
      Pasta International. One Hund One Prods.
Harris, Gloria G.
   xHarris, Gloria G.
      ed. The Group Treatment of Human Problems:
        A Social Learning Approach. Grune.
Harris, Gordon. see Harris, Gordon L.
Harris, Gordon L.
   xHarris, Gordon.
      Apostle from Space. Logos.
Harris, Grace M. see Harris, Grace Mcadams.
Harris, Grace Mcadams.
   xHarris, Grace M.
      West to the Sunrise. Iowa St U Pr.
Harris, H. G. see Harris, Henry Gordon.
Harris, Harold A. see Harris, Harold Arthur.
Harris, Harold Arthur.
   xHarris, Harold A.
      Greek Athletes & Athletics. Greenwood.
Harris, Harry.
   xHarris, Harry.
      Prenatal Diagnosis & Selective Abortion.
        Harvard U Pr.
Harris, Helen.
   xHarris, Helen.
      Industrial Archaeology of Dartmoor. David &
        Charles.
      Industrial Archaeology of Dartmoor. Kelley.
Harris, Henry, 1925-
   xHarris, Henry
      ed. Scientific Models & Man. Oxford U Pr.
Harris, Henry G. see Harris, Henry Gordon.
Harris, Henry Gordon.
   xHarris, H. G.
      Advanced Watch & Clock Repair. Emerson.
      Advanced Watch & Clock Repair.
        Wallace-Homestead.
      Collecting & Identifying Old Clocks.
        Wallace-Homestead.
   xHarris, Henry G.
      Collecting & Identifying Old Clocks. Emerson.
Harris, Homer I. see Harris, Homer Irving.
Harris, Homer Irving, 1902-
   xHarris, Homer I.
      Family Estate Planning Guide. Lawyers Co-Op.
Harris, Howard.
   xHarris, Howard.
      An Annotated Bibliography on the
        Architectural Design Implications of
        Residential Homes for Old People. Vance
        Biblios.
Harris, Irving. see Harris, Irving D.
Harris, Irving D.
   xHarris, Irving.
      The Breeze of the Spirit: Sam Shoemaker & the
        Story of Faith-at-Work. Seabury.
Harris, J. Donald. see Harris, John Donald.
Harris, J. M. see Harris, James Michael.
Harris, J. Milton. see Harris, Joe Milton.
Harris, James. see Harris, James Wesley.
Harris, James E.
   xHarris, James E.
      ed. An X-Ray Atlas of the Royal Mummies. U
        of Chicago Pr.
Harris, James Michael.
   xHarris, J. M.
      Evolution of the Plio-Pleistocene African
        Suidae. Am Philos.
Harris, James R. see Harris, James Rendel.
Harris, James Rendel, 1852-1941
   xHarris, James R.

      Wordsworth's Lucy. Folcroft.
Harris, James Wesley.
   xHarris, James.
      Spanish Phonology. MIT Pr.
Harris, Jane A.
   xHarris, Jane A.
      Dance a While: Handbook of Folk, Square &
        Social Dance. Burgess.
Harris, Janet.
   xHarris, Janet.
      Astrology for Everyday Living. Wilshire.
      Crisis in Corrections: The Prison Problem.
        McGraw.
      Students in Revolt. McGraw.
      The Woman Who Created Frankenstein: A
        Portrait of Mary Shelley. Har-Row.
Harris, Joe Milton.
   xHarris, J. Milton.
      Fundamentals of Organic Reaction
        Mechanisms. Wiley.
Harris, Joel C. see Harris, Joel Chandler.
Harris, Joel Chandler, 1848-1908
   xHarris, Joel C.
      The Chronicles of Aunt Minervy Ann. MSS
        Info.
      Complete Tales of Uncle Remus. HM.
      Little Union Scout. Arno.
      On the Plantation: A Story of a Georgia Boy's
        Adventures During the War. U of Ga Pr.
      On the Wing of Occasions. Arno.
      On the Wing of Occasions. Folcroft.
      On the Wing of Occasions. Irvington.
      Plantation Pageants. Arno.
      Stories of Georgia. Cherokee.
      Stories of Georgia. Gale.
      Stories of Georgia. Reprint.
      Tales of the Home Folks in Peace & War.
        Arno.
      Uncle Remus. Schocken.
Harris, John, 1931-
   xHarris, John.
      A Catalogue of British Drawings for
        Architecture, Decoration, Sculpture &
        Landscape Gardening: 1550-1900, in
        American Collections. Irvington.
      A Century of New England News Photos.
        Globe Pequot.
      Endangered Predators. Doubleday.
Harris, John. see Harris, John Hobbis.
Harris, John B. see Harris, John Buchanan.
Harris, John Buchanan, 1940-
   xHarris, John B.
      ed. Muscular Dystrophy & Other Inherited
        Diseases of Skeletal Muscle in Animals. NY
        Acad Sci.
Harris, John Donald, 1914-
   xHarris, J. Donald.
      Anatomy & Physiology of the Peripheral
        Hearing Mechanism. Bobbs.
      Psychoacoustics. Bobbs.
      Psychoacoustics. Irvington.
Harris, John Harold, 1925-
   xHarris, John.
      The Radiology of Acute Cervical Spine
        Trauma. Williams & Wilkins.
Harris, John Hobbis, Sir, 1874-
   xHarris, John.
      Century of Emancipation. Kennikat.
Harris, John R. see Harris, John Raymond.
Harris, John Raymond.
   xHarris, John R.
      ed. Liverpool & Merseyside: Essays in the
        Economic & Social History of the Port & Its
        Hinterland. Biblio Dist.
Harris, John S.
   xHarris, John S.
      Government Patronage of the Arts in Great
        Britain. U of Chicago Pr.
Harris, John S. see Harris, John Sterling.

Harris, John Sterling.
   xHarris, John S.
      Barbed Wire. Brigham.
Harris, Jose.
   xHarris, Jose.
      Unemployment & Politics: A Study in English
        Social Policy 1886-1914. Oxford U Pr.
      William Beveridge: A Biography. Oxford U Pr.
Harris, Joseph P. see Harris, Joseph Pratt.
Harris, Joseph Pratt, 1896-
   xHarris, Joseph P.
      Advice & Consent of the Senate: A Study of
        the Confirmation of Appointments by the
        United States Senate. Greenwood.
      Congress & the Legislative Process. McGraw.
      Congressional Control of Administration.
        Greenwood.
Harris, Jules E.
   xHarris, Jules E.
      The Immunology of Malignant Disease. Mosby.
Harris, Julia C. see Harris, Julia Florida (Collier).
Harris, Julia Florida (Collier), 1875-
   xHarris, Julia C.
      Life & Letters of Joel Chandler Harris. AMS
        Pr.
      The Life & Letters of Joel Chandler Harris. R
        West.
Harris, Karyn J. see Harris, Karyn Jean.
Harris, Karyn Jean.
   xHarris, Karyn J.
      Costume Display Techniques. AASLH.
Harris, Katerina.
   xHarris, Katerina.
      Colloquial Greek. Routledge & Kegan.
Harris, Kathryn G. see Harris, Kathryn Gibbs.
Harris, Kathryn Gibbs.
   xHarris, Kathryn G.
      Robert Frost: Studies of the Poetry. G K Hall.
Harris, Kenneth Weldon.
   xHarris, W. Kenneth.
      Quality Control in the Hospital Discharge
        Survey. Natl Ctr Health Stats.
Harris, Kevin.
   xHarris, Kevin.
      Education & Knowledge: The Structured
        Misrepresentation of Reality. Routledge &
        Kegan.
Harris, L. M.
   xHarris, L. M.
      An Introduction to Deepwater Floating Drilling
        Operations. Pennwell Pub.
Harris, Leon. see Harris, Leon A.
Harris, Leon A.
   xHarris, Leon.
      Merchant Princes: An Intimate History of
        Jewish Families Who Built Great Department
        Stores. Har-Row.
Harris, Leonard, 1929-
   xHarris, Leonard.
      Don't Be No Hero. Popular Lib.
Harris, Lester. see Harris, Lester E.
Harris, Lester E.
   xHarris, Lester.
      The Frog-Eating Electric Light Bug. Southern
        Pub.
Harris, Lloyd J., 1947-
   xHarris, Lloyd J.
      The Book of Garlic. Panjandrum.
Harris, Lucien, 1899-
   xHarris, Lucien.
      Butterflies of Georgia. U of Okla Pr.
Harris, M. see Harris, Marvin.
Harris, M. A., 1908-
   xHarris, M. A.
      Negro History Tour of Manhattan. Greenwood.
Harris, Maria.
   xHarris, Maria.
      ed. Parish Religious Education. Paulist Pr.
Harris, Marie.
   xHarris, Marie.

Interstate. Slow Loris.
Raw Honey. Alicejamesbooks.
Harris, Marilyn.
xHarris, Marilyn.
The Eden Passion. Ballantine.
The Eden Passion. Putnam.
The Prince of Eden. Avon.
Prince of Eden. Putnam.
This Other Eden. Avon.
This Other Eden. Putnam.
The Women of Eden. Putnam.
Harris, Mark, 1922-
xHarris, Mark.
City of Discontent: An Interpretive Biography
of Vachel Lindsay, Being Also the Story of
Springfield, Illinois, USA. Octagon.
It Looked Like for Ever. McGraw.
Something About a Soldier. Ballantine.
xHarris, Mark C.
Index to Birthplaces of United Kingdom
Authors. G K Hall.
Harris, Mark C. see Harris, Mark.
Harris, Mark J. see Harris, Mark Jonathan.
Harris, Mark Jonathan, 1941-
xHarris, Mark J.
With a Wave of the Wand. Lothrop.
Harris, Markham, 1907-
xHarris, Markham.
tr. The Life of Meriasek: A Medieval Cornish
Miracle Play. Intl Schol Bk Serv.
Harris, Marshall D. see Harris, Marshall Dees.
Harris, Marshall Dees, 1903-
xHarris, Marshall D.
Origin of the Land Tenure System in the
United States. Greenwood.
Harris, Martin.
xHarris, Martin.
The Evolution of French Syntax: A
Comparative Approach. Longman.
Harris, Martin L.
xHarris, Martin L.
Introduction to Data Processing. Wiley.
Harris, Marvin, 1927-
xHarris, M.
Culture, People, Nature: An Introduction to
General Anthropology. Har-Row.
xHarris, Marvin.
Cows, Pigs, Wars, & Witches: The Riddles of
Culture. Random.
Cows, Pigs, Wars, & Witches: The Riddles of
Culture. Random.
Cultural Materialism: The Struggle for a
Science of Culture. Random.
Cultural Materialism: The Struggle for a
Science of Culture. Random.
Patterns of Race in the Americas. Greenwood.
Patterns of Race in the Americas. Norton.
Harris, Michael.
xHarris, Michael.
A Field Guide to the Birds of Galapagos.
Taplinger.
Heating with Wood. Citadel Pr.
Heating with Wood. Lyle Stuart.
Harris, Michael H.
xHarris, Michael H.
ed. American Library History: A Bibliography.
U of Tex Pr.
A Guide to Research in American Library
History. Scarecrow.
ed. Reader in American Library History.
IHS-PDS.
Harris, Miles F.
xHarris, Miles F.
Opportunities in Meteorology. Natl Textbk.
Harris, Morgan.
xHarris, Morgan.
How to Make News & Influence People. TAB
Bks.
Harris, N. D. see Harris, Norman Duncan Campany.

Harris, Neil, 1938-
xHarris, Neil.
Humbug: The Art of P. T. Barnum. Little.
Harris, Nigel.
xHarris, Nigel.
India--China: Underdevelopment & Revolution.
Carolina Acad Pr.
Harris, Norman. see Harris, Norman C.
Harris, Norman C.
xHarris, Norman.
Introductory Applied Physics. McGraw.
xHarris, Norman C.
Career Education in Colleges: A Guide for
Planning Two- & Four-Year Occupational
Programs. Jossey-Bass.
Introductory Applied Physics. McGraw.
Harris, Norman Duncan Campany.
xHarris, N. D.
Preparing Educational Materials. Biblio Dist.
Harris, O. Jeff.
xHarris, O. Jeff.
How to Manage People at Work: A Short
Course for Professionals. Wiley.
Harris, Patricia.
xHarris, Patricia.
Adlai: the Springfield Years. Aurora Pubs.
Harris, Paula, 1947-
xHarris, Paula.
Pisces. Creative Ed.
Harris, Philip R. see Harris, Phillip R.
Harris, Phillip R.
xHarris, Philip R.
Managing Cultural Differences. Gulf Pub.
Harris, R. Baine, 1927-
xHarris, R. Baine.
ed. Authority: A Philosophical Analysis. U of
Ala Pr.
ed. The Significance of Neoplatonism. State U
NY Pr.
Harris, R. C. see Harris, Robert John Cecil.
Harris, R. Cole. see Harris, Richard Colebrook.
Harris, Ralph W.
xHarris, Ralph W.
The Incomparable Story. Gospel Pub.
Harris, Richard, 1926-
xHarris, Richard.
Decision. Dutton.
Freedom Spent. Little.
Harris, Richard Colebrook.
xHarris, R. Cole.
Canada Before Confederation: A Study in
Historical Geography. Oxford U Pr.
Harris, Richard J.
xHarris, Richard J.
A Primer of Multivariate Statistics. Acad Pr.
Harris, Ricky.
xHarris, Ricky.
Choreography & Style for Ice Skaters. St
Martin.
Harris, Robert B. see Harris, Robert Blynn.
Harris, Robert Blynn, 1918-
xHarris, Robert B.
Precedence & Arrow Networking Techniques
for Construction. Wiley.
Harris, Robert J. see Harris, Robert John Cecil.
Harris, Robert John Cecil.
xHarris, R. C.
ed. What We Know About Cancer. Allen
Unwin.
xHarris, Robert J.
ed. Cellular Basis & Aetiology of Late Somatic
Effects of Ionizing Radiations: Proceedings.
Acad Pr.
Harris, Robert S. see Harris, Robert Samuel.
Harris, Robert Samuel.
xHarris, Robert S.

ed. Art & Science of Dental Caries Research.
Acad Pr.
ed. Feeding & Nutrition of Nonhuman
Primates. Acad Pr.
Harris, Robie H.
xHarris, Robie H.
Don't Forget to Come Back. Knopf.
Harris, Robin S. see Harris, Robin Sutton.
Harris, Robin Sutton, 1919-
xHarris, Robin S.
A History of Higher Education in Canada:
1663-1960. U of Toronto Pr.
Quiet Evolution: A Study of the Educational
System in Ontario. U of Toronto Pr.
Harris, Roger W. see Harris, Roger Williams.
Harris, Roger Williams.
xHarris, Roger W.
How to Keep on Smoking & Live. St Martin.
Harris, Rosemary.
xHarris, Rosemary.
Retold by Beauty & the Beast. Doubleday.
The Bright & Morning Star. Macmillan.
Double Snare. S&S.
Harris, Roy D.
xHarris, Roy D.
Computer Models in Operations Management:
A Computer-Augmented System. Har-Row.
Harris, Ruth.
xHarris, Ruth.
Decades. NAL.
Decades. S&S.
The Last Romantics. S&S.
The Rich & the Beautiful. S&S.
Harris, Ruth M. see Harris, Ruth Miriam.
Harris, Ruth Miriam, 1898-
xHarris, Ruth M.
Teachers' Social Knowledge & Its Relation to
Pupils' Responses: A Study of Four St. Louis
Negro Elementary Schools. AMS Pr.
Harris, Seymour E. see Harris, Seymour Edwin.
Harris, Seymour Edwin, 1897-
xHarris, Seymour E.
Assignats. AMS Pr.
ed. Economic Problems of Latin America.
Arno.
Economics of Harvard. McGraw.
Economics of Mobilization & Inflation.
Greenwood.
ed. Foreign Economic Policy for the United
States. Greenwood.
ed. Postwar Economic Problems. Arno.
xHarris, Seymoure E.
Exchange Depreciation. Arno.
Harris, Seymoure E. see Harris, Seymour Edwin.
Harris, Stacy.
xHarris, Stacy.
Comedians of Country Music. Lerner Pubns.
Harris, Stanley E. see Harris, Stanley Edwards.
Harris, Stanley Edwards.
xHarris, Stanley E.
Exploring the Land & Rocks of Southern
Illinois: A Geological Guide. S Ill U Pr.
Harris, Stephen. see Harris, Stephen L.
Harris, Stephen L., 1937-
xHarris, Stephen.
Fire & Ice: The Cascade Volcanoes.
Mountaineers.
xHarris, Stephen L.
Fire & Ice: The Cascade Volcanoes. Pacific
Search.
Harris, Stuart K. see Harris, Stuart Kimball.
Harris, Stuart Kimball.
xHarris, Stuart K.
Flora of Essex County, Massachusetts. Peabody
Mus Salem.
Harris, Susan.
xHarris, Susan.

Boats & Ships. Watts.
Creatures That Look Alike. Watts.
Helicopters. Watts.
Odd Animals. Watts.
Space. Watts.
Volcanoes. Watts.
The World Beneath the Sea. Watts.

Harris, Sydney J.
xHarris, Sydney J.
The Authentic Person: Dealing with Dilemma.
Argus Comm.
For the Time Being. HM.
Would You Believe,.... Argus Comm.
Harris, Thomas A. see Harris, Thomas Anthony.

Harris, Thomas Anthony, 1913-
xHarris, Thomas A.
I'm Ok-You're Ok: A Practical Guide to
Transactional Analysis. Har-Row.
Harris, Thomas L. see Harris, Thomas Lake.

Harris, Thomas Lake, 1823-1906
xHarris, Thomas L.
The New Republic: A Discourse of the
Prospects, Dangers, Duties & Safeties of the
Time. AMS Pr.

Harris, Timothy, 1946-
xHarris, Timothy.
Goodnight & Goodbye. Delacorte.
Goodnight & Goodbye. Dell.
Harris, W. E. see Harris, Walter Edgar.
Harris, W. Kenneth. see Harris, Kenneth Weldon.
Harris, W. S. see Harris, William Shuler.

Harris, W. Stuart, 1933-
xHarris, W. Stuart.
Dead Towns of Alabama. U of Ala Pr.
Harris, Walter. see Harris, Walter D.

Harris, Walter D.
xHarris, Walter.
The Growth of Latin American Cities. Ohio U
Pr.

Harris, Walter Edgar.
xHarris, W. E.
Programmed Temperature Gas
Chromatography. Krieger.

Harris, Warren G.
xHarris, Warren G.
Gable & Lombard. S&S.

Harris, Wendell V.
xHarris, Wendell V.
British Short Fiction in the Nineteenth
Century: A Literary & Bibliographic Guide.
Wayne St U Pr.
Harris, William C. see Harris, William Charles.

Harris, William Charles, 1933-
xHarris, William C.
The Day of the Carpetbagger: Republican
Reconstruction in Mississippi. La State U Pr.
Presidential Reconstruction in Mississippi. La
State U Pr.
Harris, William J. see Harris, William James.

Harris, William James.
xHarris, William J.
First Printed Translations into English of the
Great Foreign Classics. B Franklin.
First Printed Translations into English of the
Great Foreign Classics. Folcroft.
Harris, William L. see Harris, William Logan.

Harris, William Logan, Bp, 1817-1887
xHarris, William L.
Constitutional Powers of the General
Conference: With a Special Application to
the Subject of Slave Holding. Arno.

Harris, William Shuler, 1865-
xHarris, W. S.
Life in a Thousand Worlds. Arno.
Harris, William V. see Harris, William Vernon.

Harris, William Vernon.
xHarris, William V.
War & Imperialism in Republican Rome,
327-70 B.C.. Oxford U Pr.
Harris, Zellig. see Harris, Zellig Sabbettai.

Harris, Zellig S. see Harris, Zellig Sabbettai.

Harris, Zellig Sabbettai, 1909-
xHarris, Zellig.
Mathematical Structures of Language. Krieger.
xHarris, Zellig S.
Structural Linguistics. U of Chicago Pr.

Harris-Warren, H B.
xHarris-Warren, H. B.
Dive: The Story of an Atomic Submarine.
Har-Row.
Harrison, A. J. see Harrison, Anthony John.

Harrison, Albert A.
xHarrison, Albert A.
Individuals & Groups: Understanding Social
Behavior. Brooks-Cole.

Harrison, Andrew.
xHarrison, Andrew.
Making & Thinking: A Study of Intelligent
Activities. Hackett Pub.

Harrison, Anthony John, 1938-
xHarrison, A. J.
Economics & Land Use Planning. St Martin.
The Economics of Transport Appraisal. Halsted
Pr.

Harrison, Austin, 1873-1928
xHarrison, Austin.
Frederic Harrison: Thoughts & Memories.
AMS Pr.

Harrison, Bernard.
xHarrison, Bernard.
An Introduction to the Philosophy of
Language. St Martin.

Harrison, Betty D., 1928-
xHarrison, Betty D.
Dial-a-Skill: A Manual of Procedures for Team
Members of Special Education & Related
Services. Brigham.

Harrison, C William.
xHarrison, C. William.
First Book of Hiking. Watts.
Harrison, Charles R. see Harrison, Charles Richmond.

Harrison, Charles Richmond.
xHarrison, Charles R.
Ornamental Conifers. Hafner.
Harrison, Constance C. see Harrison, Constance Cary.

Harrison, Constance Cary, 1843-1920
xHarrison, Constance C.
The Anglomaniacs. Arno.

Harrison, Cynthia.
xHarrison, Cynthia E.
ed. Women in American History: A
Bibliography. ABC-Clio.
Harrison, Cynthia E. see Harrison, Cynthia.
Harrison, D. K. see Harrison, David Kent.

Harrison, David.
xHarrison, David.
Patterns in Biology. Halsted Pr.
Patterns in Biology. Krieger.
Problems in Genetics: With Notes & Examples.
A-W.
Who Pays for Clean Air: The Cost & Benefit
Distribution of Federal Automobile Emission
Standards. Ballinger Pub.
Harrison, David. see Harrison, David Lee.

Harrison, David Kent, 1931 -
xHarrison, D. K.
Finite & Infinite Primes for Rings & Fields.
Am Math.

Harrison, David Lee.
xHarrison, David.
The Boy with a Drum. Western Pub.
Harrison, Evelyn B. see Harrison, Evelyn Byrd.

Harrison, Evelyn Byrd.
xHarrison, Evelyn B.
Archaic & Archaistic Sculpture. Am Sch
Athens.
Harrison, Frank L. see Harrison, Frank Llewellyn.

Harrison, Frank Llewellyn.
xHarrison, Frank L.

Musicology. Greenwood.

Harrison, Fraser.
xHarrison, Fraser.
The Dark Angel: Aspects of Victorian
Sexuality. Universe.

Harrison, Frederic, 1831-1923
xHarrison, Frederic.
Autobiographic Memoirs. AMS Pr.
Autobiographic Memoirs. R West.
Byzantine History in the Early Middle Ages:
The Rede Lecture Delivered in Senate
House, Cambridge, June 12, 1900. Arno.
National & Social Problems. Arno.
On Society. Arno.
On Society. Norwood Edns.
Studies in Early Victorian Literature. Folcroft.

Harrison, Frederick, 1884-
xHarrison, Frederick.
Medieval Man & His Notions. Folcroft.
Old Brighton, Old Preston, Old Hove. Intl
Pubns Serv.
Harrison, Frederick. see Harrison, Frederick Williams.

Harrison, Frederick Williams.
xHarrison, Frederick.
ed. Aspects of Sponge Biology. Acad Pr.
Harrison, G. A. see Harrison, Geoffrey Ainsworth.
Harrison, G. B. see Harrison, George Bagshawe.

Harrison, Geoffrey Ainsworth.
xHarrison, G. A.
Human Biology: An Introduction to Human
Evolution, Variation, Growth, & Ecology.
Oxford U Pr.
ed. Population Structure & Human Variation.
Cambridge U Pr.
ed. The Structure of Human Populations.
Oxford U Pr.
Harrison, George. see Harrison, George H.
Harrison, George B. see Harrison, George Bagshawe.

Harrison, George Bagshawe, 1894-
xHarrison, G. B.
Profession of English. HarBraceJ.
The Story of Elizabethan Drama. Octagon.
xHarrison, George B.
ed. England in Shakespeare's Day. Arno.
England in Shakespeare's Day. Folcroft.
The Life & Death of Robert Devereux, Earl of
Essex. Folcroft.
Story of Elizabethan Drama. Folcroft.

Harrison, George H.
xHarrison, George.
Roger Tory Peterson's Dozen Birding Hot
Spots. S&S.
xHarrison, George H.
Backyard Bird Watcher. S&S.
Roger Tory Peterson's Dozen Birding Hot
Spots. S&S.
Harrison, George R. see Harrison, George Russell.

Harrison, George Russell, 1898-
xHarrison, George R.
First Book of Energy. Watts.

Harrison, Gilbert A.
xHarrison, Gilbert A.
ed. The Critic As Artist: Essays on Books
1920-1970. Liveright.
A Timeless Affair: The Life of Anita
McCormick Blaine. U of Chicago Pr.
Harrison, Grant V. see Harrison, Grant Von.

Harrison, Grant Von.
xHarrison, Grant V.
Structured Tutoring. Educ Tech Pubns.
Harrison, Grant Von. see Harrison, Grant V.

Harrison, H. B., 1930-
xHarrison, H. B.
Computer Methods in Structural Analysis. P-H.
Structural Analysis & Design: Some
Minicomputer Applications. Pergamon.

Harrison, Hal H.
xHarrison, Hal H.

World of the Snake. Lippincott.
Harrison, Harold E.
xHarrison, Harold E.
Disorders of Calcium & Phosphate Metabolism
in Childhood & Adolescence. Saunders.
Harrison, Harry.
xHarrison, Harry.
The Adventures of the Stainless Steel Rat.
Berkley Pub.
The California Iceberg. Walker & Co.
Captive Universe. Berkley Pub.
Make Room! Make Room!. Berkley Pub.
Make Room!, Make Room!. Gregg.
The Men from P.I.G. & R.O.B.O.T..
Atheneum.
Montezuma's Revenge. Manor Bks.
One Step from Earth. Macmillan.
Planet Story. A & W Pubs.
Skyfall. Atheneum.
Harrison, Henry S.
xHarrison, Henry S.
Houses: The Illustrated Guide to Construction,
Design & Systems. Realtors Natl.
Harrison, Howard L.
xHarrison, Howard L.
Introduction to Automatic Controls. Har-Row.
Harrison, Ian T.
xHarrison, Ian T.
Compendium of Organic Synthetic Methods.
Wiley.
Harrison, J. see Harrison, John R.
Harrison, J. A. see Harrison, James Albert.
Harrison, James, 1937-
xHarrison, Jim.
Farmer. Dell.
Legends of the Fall. Delacorte.
Legends of the Fall. Dell.
Letters to Yesenin. Sumac Mich.
Locations. Norton.
Plain Song. Norton.
Harrison, James Albert, 1848-1911
xHarrison, J. A.
Life of Edgar Allan Poe. Haskell.
Harrison, James C.
xHarrison, James C.
Care & Training of the Trotter & Pacer. US
Trotting.
Harrison, James P.
xHarrison, James P.
Communists & Chinese Peasant Rebellions: A
Study in the Rewriting of Chinese History.
Atheneum.
The Long March to Power: A History of the
Chinese Communist Party, 1971-72. HR&W.
Harrison, Jane. see Harrison, Jane Ellen.
Harrison, Jane E. see Harrison, Jane Ellen.
Harrison, Jane Ellen, 1850-1928
xHarrison, Jane.
Ancient Art & Ritual. Humanities.
Prolegomena to the Study of Greek Religion.
Humanities.
xHarrison, Jane E.
Alpha & Omega. AMS Pr.
Ancient Art & Ritual. Greenwood.
Prolegomena to the Study of Greek Religion.
Arno.
Harrison, Jim. see Harrison, James.
Harrison, John A. see Harrison, John Armstrong.
Harrison, John Armstrong.
xHarrison, John A.
The Chinese Empire. HarBraceJ.
The Founding of the Russian Empire in Asia &
America. U of Miami Pr.
Harrison, John B.
xHarrison, John B.
Good Food Naturally: How to Grow It, Cook
It, Keep It. Keats.
Harrison, John B. see Harrison, John Baugham.
Harrison, John Baugham.
xHarrison, John B.

A Short History of Western Civilization.
Knopf.
Harrison, John F. see Harrison, John Fletcher Clews.
Harrison, John Fletcher Clews.
xHarrison, John F.
The Second Coming: Popular Millenarianism
1780-1850. Rutgers U Pr.
ed. Utopianism & Education: Robert Owen &
the Owenites. Tchrs Coll.
Harrison, John R.
xHarrison, J.
The Library of Isaac Newton. Cambridge U Pr.
Harrison, Jonathan.
xHarrison, J.
Hume's Moral Epistemology. Oxford U Pr.
Harrison, Joseph.
xHarrison, Joseph.
An Economic History of Modern Spain.
Holmes & Meier.
Harrison, Julius. see Harrison, Julius Allen Greenway.
Harrison, Julius Allen Greenway, 1885-1963
xHarrison, Julius.
Brahms & His Four Symphonies. Da Capo.
Harrison, K. see Harrison, Kenneth.
Harrison, K. C. see Harrison, Kenneth Cecil.
Harrison, Kenneth.
xHarrison, K.
The Framework of Anglo-Saxon History to A.
D. 900. Cambridge U Pr.
Harrison, Kenneth Cecil.
xHarrison, K. C.
ed. Prospects for British Librarianship. Gaylord
Prof Pubns.
Harrison, Leonard H.
xHarrison, Leonard H.
How to Teach Police Subjects: Theory &
Practice. C C Thomas.
Harrison, Lowell. see Harrison, Lowell Hayes.
Harrison, Lowell H. see Harrison, Lowell Hayes.
Harrison, Lowell Hayes, 1922-
xHarrison, Lowell.
The Civil War in Kentucky. U Pr of Ky.
xHarrison, Lowell H.
George Rogers Clark & the War in the West.
U Pr of Ky.
Harrison, M. A. see Harrison, Michael A.
Harrison, M. John. see Harrison, Mike John.
Harrison, Margaret W. see Harrison, Margaret Wynne.
Harrison, Margaret Wynne.
xHarrison, Margaret W.
Angels Then & Now. Branch-Smith.
Harrison, Martin, 1930-
xHarrison, Martin.
ed. French Politics. Heath.
Harrison, Michael.
xHarrison, Michael.
In the Footsteps of Sherlock Holmes. Berkley
Pub.
Harrison, Michael A.
xHarrison, M. A.
Lectures on Linear Sequential Machines. Acad
Pr.
xHarrison, Michael A.
Introduction to Formal Language Theory.
A-W.
Harrison, Mike John.
xHarrison, M. John.
The Centauri Device. Bantam.
Harrison, Nancy S.
xHarrison, Nancy S.
Understanding Behavioral Research.
Wadsworth Pub.
Harrison, Paul M. see Harrison, Paul Mansfield.
Harrison, Paul Mansfield.
xHarrison, Paul M.
Authority & Power in the Free Church
Tradition: A Social Case Study of the
American Baptist Convention. S Ill U Pr.
Harrison, Paul R.
xHarrison, Paul R.

Analysis of Industrial Air Pollutants. Mss Info.
Harrison, Peter D.
xHarrison, Peter D.
ed. Pre-Hispanic Maya Agriculture. U of NM
Pr.
Harrison, R. J. see Harrison, Richard John.
Harrison, Richard John, 1920-
xHarrison, R. J.
Functional Anatomy of Marine Mammals.
Acad Pr.
Harrison, Richard M.
xHarrison, Richard M.
Animal Laparoscopy. Williams & Wilkins.
Harrison, Ross.
xHarrison, Ross.
On What There Must Be. Oxford U Pr.
Harrison, Ross G. see Harrison, Ross Granville.
Harrison, Ross Granville, 1870-1959
xHarrison, Ross G.
Organization & Development of the Embryo.
Yale U Pr.
Harrison, Sarah, 1942-
xHarrison, Sarah.
The Flowers of the Field. Coward.
Harrison, Saul I.
xHarrison, Saul I.
ed. Childhood Psychopathology: An Anthology
of Basic Readings. Intl Univs Pr.
Harrison, Shelley A.
xHarrison, Shelley A.
ed. Improving Instructional Productivity in
Higher Education. Educ Tech Pubns.
Harrison, Sidney.
xHarrison, Sidney.
Grand Piano. Merrimack Bk Serv.
Harrison, Stanley R.
xHarrison, Stanley R.
Edgar Fawcett. Twayne.
Harrison, Thomas P. see Harrison, Thomas Perrin.
Harrison, Thomas Perrin.
xHarrison, Thomas P.
ed. Pastoral Elegy: An Anthology. Octagon.
Harrison, W. Jerome. see Harrison, William Jerome.
Harrison, Walter A. see Harrison, Walter Ashley.
Harrison, Walter Ashley, 1930-
xHarrison, Walter A.
Solid State Theory. Dover.
Harrison, William, 1933-
xHarrison, William.
Africana. Morrow.
Colloquial Russian. Routledge & Kegan.
Harrison, William Jerome, 1845-1909
xHarrison, W. Jerome.
A History of Photography Written As a
Practical Guide & an Introduction to Its
Latest Developments. Arno.
Harriss, Joseph.
xHarriss, Joseph.
The Tallest Tower: Eiffel & the Belle Epoque.
HM.
Harriss, H. see Harrisse, Henry.
Harrisse, Henry, 1829-1910
xHarrisse, H.
Discovery of North America: A Critical
Documentary & Historic Investigation.
Heinman.
Harrisson, Thomas H. see Harrisson, Thomas Harnett.
Harrisson, Thomas Harnett.
xHarrisson, Thomas H.
Living Among Cannibals. AMS Pr.
Harrod, Roy. see Harrod, Roy Forbes.
Harrod, Roy F. see Harrod, Roy Forbes.
Harrod, Roy Forbes, Sir, 1900-
xHarrod, Roy.
The British Economy. Greenwood.
xHarrod, Roy F.

Life of John Maynard Keynes. Kelley.
Towards a Dynamic Economics: Some Recent
Developments of Economic Theory & Their
Application to Policy. Greenwood.
Harrold, Charles F. see Harrold, Charles Frederick.
Harrold, Charles Frederick, 1897-1948
xHarrold, Charles F.
Carlyle & German Thought, 1819-1834. AMS
Pr.
Harrold, Robert, 1951-
xHarrold, Robert.
Cassadaga: An Inside Look at the South's
Oldest Psychic Community with True
Experiences of People Who Have Been
There. Banyan Bks.
Harrold, William.
xHarrold, William E.
The Variance & the Unity: A Study of the
Complementary Poems of Robert Browning.
Ohio U Pr.
Harrold, William E. see Harrold, William.
Harron, Thomas. see Harron, Thomas J.
Harron, Thomas J.
xHarron, Thomas.
Law for Business Managers: The Regulatory
Environment. Holbrook.
Harrop, David.
xHarrop, David.
America's Paychecks: Who Makes What. Facts
on File.
Harrow, Anita J.
xHarrow, Anita J.
A Taxonomy of the Psychomotor Domain: A
Guide for Developing Behavioral Objectives.
Longman.
Harry, David P. see Harry, David Percival.
Harry, David Percival, 1893-
xHarry, David P.
Cost of Living of Teachers in the State of New
York. AMS Pr.
Harry, James W. see Harry, James Warner.
Harry, James Warner.
xHarry, James W.
The Maryland Constitution of 1851. AMS Pr.
Harryhausen, Ray.
xHarryhausen, Ray.
Film Fantasy Scrapbook. A S Barnes.
Harsch, Earnest. see Harsch, Ernest.
Harsch, Ernest.
xHarsch, Earnest.
Angola: The Hidden History of Washington's
War. Path Pr NY.
Harsent, David, 1942-
xHarsent, David.
Dreams of the Dead. Oxford U Pr.
Harsh, Philip W. see Harsh, Philip Whaley.
Harsh, Philip Whaley, 1905-
xHarsh, Philip W.
A Handbook of Classical Drama. Stanford U
Pr.
Harsh, Wayne.
xHarsh, Wayne.
Subjunctive in English. U of Ala Pr.
Harshaw, Ruth. see Harshaw, Ruth (Hetzel).
Harshaw, Ruth (Hetzel).
xHarshaw, Ruth.
In What Book. Macmillan.
Harshbarger, Ronald J., 1938-
xHarshbarger, Ronald J.
Business Mathematics. Har-Row.
Hart, A. Tindal. see Hart, Arthur Tindal.
Hart, Albert B. see Hart, Albert Bushnell.
Hart, Albert Bushnell, 1854-1943
xHart, Albert B.

Foundations of American Foreign Policy. Da
Capo.
How Our Grandfathers Lived. Gale.
Practical Essays on American Government.
Arno.
Southern South. Da Capo.
Southern South. Negro U Pr.
Hart, Archibald D.
xHart, Archibald D.
Feeling Free. Revell.
Hart, Arthur Tindal.
xHart, A. Tindal.
The Country Priest in English History. R West.
Hart, Basil H. Liddel. see Liddell Hart, Basil H.
Hart, Basil H. Liddell. see Liddell Hart, Basil H.
Hart, Beatrice O. see Hart, Beatrice Ostern.
Hart, Beatrice Ostern.
xHart, Beatrice O.
Teaching Reading to Deaf Children. Alexander
Graham.
Hart, Benjamin L. see Hart, Benjamin Leslie.
Hart, Benjamin Leslie.
xHart, Benjamin L.
Experimental Psychobiology: A Laboratory
Manual. W H Freeman.
Hart, Bernard, 1879-
xHart, Bernard.
Psychology of Insanity. Cambridge U Pr.
Hart, C. W.
xHart, C. W.
Pollution Ecology of Freshwater Invertebrates.
Acad Pr.
Hart, Carole.
xHart, Carole.
Delilah. Har-Row.
Hart, Clive.
xHart, Clive.
A Concordance to Finnegans Wake. Appel.
Hart, David M. see Hart, David Montgomery.
Hart, David Montgomery.
xHart, David M.
The Aith Waryaghar of the Moroccan Rif: An
Ethnography & History. U of Ariz Pr.
Hart, Donn V. see Hart, Donn Vorhis.
Hart, Donn Vorhis, 1918-
xHart, Donn V.
Compadrinazgo: Ritual Kinship in the
Philippines. N Ill U Pr.
Southeast Asian Birth Customs: Three Studies
in Human Reproduction. HRAFP.
Hart, Dorothy.
xHart, Dorothy.
Memoir by & ed. Thou Swell, Thou Witty: The
Life & Lyrics of Lorenz Hart. Har-Row.
Hart, Douglas. see Hart, Douglas A.
Hart, Douglas A.
xHart, Douglas.
Strategic Planning in London: The Rise & Fall
of the Primary Road Network. Pergamon.
Hart, E. K. see Hart, Eric Keith.
Hart, Edward, fl. 1969-
xHart, Edward.
The Hill Shepherd. David & Charles.
Pony Trekking. David & Charles.
Showing Livestock. David & Charles.
Hart, Edward L. see Hart, Edward Leroy.
Hart, Edward Leroy, 1916-
xHart, Edward L.
To Utah. Brigham.
Hart, Eric Keith.
xHart, E. K.
Directory of Philanthropic Trusts in Australia.
Verry.
Hart, Ernest H.
xHart, Ernest H.
Cocker Spaniel Handbook. TFH Pubns.
The Complete Guide to All Cats. Scribner.
How to Raise & Train a Pointer. TFH Pubns.
How to Train Your Dog. TFH Pubns.
Hart, F. L. see Hart, Frank Leslie.

Hart, Francis R. see Hart, Francis Russell.
Hart, Francis Russell, 1868-1938
xHart, Francis R.
Admirals of the Caribbean. Arno.
Hart, Frank Leslie.
xHart, F. L.
Modern Food Analysis. Springer-Verlag.
Hart, Freeman H. see Hart, Freeman Hansford.
Hart, Freeman Hansford, 1889-1965
xHart, Freeman H.
Valley of Virginia in the American Revolution,
1763-1789. Russell.
Hart, Gavin.
xHart, Gavin.
Human Sexual Behavior. Carolina Biological.
Hart, Gordon M.
xHart, Gordon M.
Values Clarification for Counselors: How
Counselors, Social Workers, Psychologists, &
Other Human Service Workers Can Use
Available Techniques. C C Thomas.
Hart, H. L. see Hart, Herbert Lionel Adolphus.
Hart, Harold.
xHart, Harold.
Organic Chemistry: A Short Course. HM.
Hart, Henry, 1903-
xHart, Henry.
A Relevant Memoir: The Story of the Equinox
Cooperative Press. Three Mtn Pr.
Hart, Henry C. see Hart, Henry Cowles.
Hart, Henry Cowles.
xHart, Henry C.
ed. Indira Ghandi's India: The Political System
Reappraised. Westview.
Hart, Henry H. see Hart, Henry Harper.
Hart, Henry Harper.
xHart, Henry H.
Conceptual Index to Psychoanalytic Technique
& Training. North River.
Hart, Henry Hersch, 1886-
xHart, Henry H.
Luis De Camoens & the Epic of the Lusiads. U
of Okla Pr.
Hart, Herbert L. see Hart, Herbert Lionel Adolphus.
Hart, Herbert Lionel Adolphus.
xHart, H. L.
Law, Liberty & Morality. Stanford U Pr.
xHart, Herbert L.
Punishment & Responsibility: Essays in the
Philosophy of Law. Oxford U Pr.
Hart, Ivor B. see Hart, Ivor Blashka.
Hart, Ivor Blashka, 1889-
xHart, Ivor B.
Great Engineers. Arno.
Great Physicists. Arno.
Hart, J. A.
xHart, J. A.
Books for the Retarded Reader. Verry.
Hart, James, 1896-1959
xHart, James.
Ordinance-Making Powers of the President of
the United States. AMS Pr.
Ordinance Making Powers of the President of
the United States. Da Capo.
Hart, James D. see Hart, James David.
Hart, James David, 1911-
xHart, James D.
A Companion to California. Oxford U Pr.
Popular Book: A History of America's Literary
Taste. Greenwood.
The Popular Book: A History of America's
Literary Taste. U of Cal Pr.
Hart, Jeffrey A.
xHart, Jeffrey A.
The Anglo-Icelandic Cod War of 1972-1973: A
Case Study of a Fishery Dispute. U of Cal
Intl St.
Hart, John, 1948-
xHart, John.

The Climbers. U of Pittsburgh Pr.
Hiking the Bigfoot Country: Exploring the
Wildlands of Northern California & Southern
Oregon. Sierra.
San Francisco's Wilderness Next Door.
Presidio Pr.
Social Work & Sexual Conduct. Routledge &
Kegan.
Hart, John E. see Hart, John Edward.
Hart, John Edward, 1917-
xHart, John E.
Albert Halper. Twayne.
Hart, John F., 1933-
xHart, John F.
Computer Approximations. Krieger.
Hart, John F. see Hart, John Fraser.
Hart, John Fraser.
xHart, John F.
The Look of the Land. P-H.
ed. Regions of the United States. Har-Row.
The South. Van Nos Reinhold.
Hart, John M. see Hart, John Mason.
Hart, John Mason, 1935-
xHart, John M.
Anarchism & the Mexican Working Class,
1860-1931. U of Tex Pr.
Hart, Johnny.
xHart, Johnny.
Back to B.C.. Fawcett.
Long Live the King!. Fawcett.
Hart, Joseph K. see Hart, Joseph Kinmont.
Hart, Joseph Kinmont, 1876-1949
xHart, Joseph K.
Education in the Humane Community.
Greenwood.
Hart, Laura K., 1938-
xHart, Laura K.
The Arithmetic of Dosages & Solutions: A
Programmed Presentation. Mosby.
Hart, Leslie A.
xHart, Leslie A.
How the Brain Works: A New Understanding
of Human Learning, Emotion & Thinking.
Basic.
Hart, Lois B. see Hart, Lois Borland.
Hart, Lois Borland.
xHart, Lois B.
A Conference & Workshop Planner's Manual.
Am Mgmt.
Hart, Madge A. see Hart, Madge Amelia.
Hart, Madge Amelia.
xHart, Madge A.
Utopias, Old & New. Folcroft.
Hart, Marion (Rice), 1891-
xHart, Marion R.
How to Navigate Today. Cornell Maritime.
Hart, Marion R. see Hart, Marion (Rice).
Hart, Norman A.
xHart, Norman A.
Industrial Advertising & Publicity. Halsted Pr.
Hart, Philip, 1914-
xHart, Philip.
Conductors: A New Generation. Scribner.
Hart, Robert.
xHart, Robert.
The I. G. in Peking: Letters of Robert Hart,
Chinese Maritime Customs, 1868-1907.
Harvard U Pr.
Hart, Roderick P.
xHart, Roderick P.
The Political Pulpit. Purdue.
Public Communication. Har-Row.
Hart, Roy H. see Hart, Roy Hanu.
Hart, Roy Hanu, 1929-
xHart, Roy H.
Bitter Grass: The Cruel Truth About
Marijuana. Psychoneurologia.
Hart, S. L.
xHart, S. L.

Lifetime of Love. Dghtrs St Paul.
Hart, Stuart L.
xHart, Stuart L.
Green Goals & Greenbacks: State-Level
Environmental Review Programs & Their
Associated Costs. Westview.
Hart, T. L. see Hart, Thomas L.
Hart, Thomas. see Hart, Thomas N.
Hart, Thomas L.
xHart, T. L.
Multi-Media Indexes, Lists, & Review Sources:
A Bibliographic Guide. Dekker.
xHart, Thomas L.
ed. Instruction in School Media Center Use.
ALA.
Hart, Thomas N.
xHart, Thomas.
Living Happily Everafter: Toward a Theology
of Christian Marriage. Paulist Pr.
Hart, W. E., Pseud
xHart, W. E.
Hitler's Generals. Arno.
Hart, Walter M. see Hart, Walter Morris.
Hart, Walter Morris, 1872-
xHart, Walter M.
Ballad & Epic: A Study in the Development of
the Narrative Art. Russell.
Reeve's Tale: A Comparative Study of
Chaucer's Narrative Art. Folcroft.
Hart, William L. see Hart, William le Roy.
Hart, William le Roy, 1892-
xHart, William L.
Calculus with Applications to Social & Life
Sciences. Burgess.
Calculus with Applications to Social & Life
Sciences. Page-Ficklin.
College Algebra & Trigonometry. Heath.
Mathematics of Investment. Heath.
Preparation for Calculus. Har-Row.
Hartbarger, Neil.
xHartbarger, Neil.
Your Career in Banking. Arco.
Your Career in Teaching. Arco.
Hartbauer, R. E.
xHartbauer, R. E.
Aural Habilitation: A Total Approach. C C
Thomas.
Counseling in Communicative Disorders. C C
Thomas.
Harte, Bret, 1836-1902
xHarte, Bret.
Ancestors of Peter Atherly & Other Tales.
Arno.
By Shore & Sedge. Arno.
Colonel Starbottle's Client & Some Other
People. Arno.
Condensed Novels. Arno.
Condensed Novels. Irvington.
Drift from Two Shores. Arno.
In a Hollow of the Hills. Irvington.
The Letters of Bret Harte. AMS Pr.
On the Frontier. Arno.
Openings in the Old Trail. Arno.
Stories in Light & Shadow. Arno.
Tales of the Argonauts & Other Sketches.
Arno.
Tales of Trail & Town. Arno.
Thankful Blossom, & Other Eastern Tales &
Sketches. Arno.
Under the Redwoods. Arno.
xHarte, Geoffrey B.
The Letters of Bret Harte. Sharon Hill.
Harte, Geoffrey B. see Harte, Bret.
Harte, Marjorie.
xHarte, Marjorie.
The Closing Web. Manor Bks.
Harte, Thomas. see Harte, Thomas Joseph.
Harte, Thomas Joseph, 1914-
xHarte, Thomas.

Papal Social Principles: A Guide & Digest.
Peter Smith.
Hartelius, Margaret A.
xHartelius, Margaret A.
The Chicken's Child. Doubleday.
The Chicken's Child. Schol Bk Serv.
Hartenberg, R. S. see Hartenberg, Richard Scheunemann.
Hartenberg, Richard Scheunemann.
xHartenberg, R. S.
ed. National Historic Mechanical Engineering
Landmarks. ASME.
Hartenstein, R. W. see Hartenstein, Reiner.
Hartenstein, Reiner.
xHartenstein, R. W.
Fundamentals of Structured Hardware Design:
A Design Language Approach at Register
Transfer Level. Elsevier.
Hartenstein, Roy.
xHartenstein, Roy.
Human Anatomy & Physiology: Principles &
Applications. Van Nos Reinhold.
Principles of Physiology. Van Nos Reinhold.
Harter, James. see Harter, James H.
Harter, James H.
xHarter, James.
Mathematics Applied to Electronics. Reston.
Harter, Jim.
xHarter, Jim.
ed. Food & Drink: A Pictorial Archive from
Nineteenth-Century Sources. Dover.
Harter, W. see Harter, Walter L.
Harter, Walter. see Harter, Walter L.
Harter, Walter L.
xHarter, W.
Osceola's Head & Other American Ghost
Stories. P-H.
xHarter, Walter.
Coal: The Rock That Burns. Elsevier-Nelson.
Hartford, Ellis F. see Hartford, Ellis Ford.
Hartford, Ellis Ford, 1905-
xHartford, Ellis F.
The Little White Schoolhouse. U Pr of Ky.
Hartford, Margaret E.
xHartford, Margaret E.
Groups in Social Work: Application of Small
Group Theory & Research to Social Work
Practice. Columbia U Pr.
Hartigan, J. A. see Hartigan, John A.
Hartigan, John A., 1937-
xHartigan, J. A.
Clustering Algorithms. Wiley.
Hartill, Rufus M. see Hartill, Rufus Mackay.
Hartill, Rufus Mackay, 1891-
xHartill, Rufus M.
Homogeneous Grouping As a Policy in the
Elementary Schools in New York City. AMS
Pr.
Hartjen, Clayton A., 1943-
xHartjen, Clayton A.
Crime & Criminalization. HR&W.
Crime & Criminalization. Krieger.
Hartkopf, Roy, 1914-
xHartkopf, Roy.
Math Without Tears. Emerson.
Hartl, Daniel L.
xHartl, Daniel L.
Our Uncertain Heritage: Genetics & Human
Diversity. Har-Row.
Principles of Population Genetics. Sinauer
Assoc.
Hartland, E. S. see Hartland, Edwin Sidney.
Hartland, E. Sidney. see Hartland, Edwin Sidney.
Hartland, Edwin S. see Hartland, Edwin Sidney.
Hartland, Edwin Sidney, 1848-1927
xHartland, E. S.
The Legend of Perseus: A Study of Tradition
in Story, Custom & Belief. Gordon Pr.
xHartland, E. Sidney.
Primitive Law. Kennikat.
xHartland, Edwin S.

Legend of Perseus: A Study of Tradition in
Story, Custom & Belief. AMS Pr.
Primitive Paternity: The Myth of Supernatural
Birth in Relation to the History of the
Family. Arno.

Hartland-Thunberg, Penelope.
xHartland-Thunberg, Penelope.
Botswana: An African Growth Economy.
Westview.

Hartle, D. G. *see* Hartle, Douglas G.

Hartle, Douglas G.
xHartle, D. G.
A Theory of the Expenditure Budgetary
Process. U of Toronto Pr.

Hartley, Al.
xHartley, Allan.
Come, Meet My Friend. Revell.

Hartley, Allan. *see* Hartley, Al.

Hartley, Eugene. *see* Hartley, Eugene Leonard.

Hartley, Eugene Leonard, 1912-
xHartley, Eugene.
Problems in Prejudice. Octagon.

Hartley, F. R.
xHartley, F. R.
Chemistry of Platinum & Palladium: With
Particular Reference to Complexes of the
Elements. Halsted Pr.
Solution Equilibria. Halsted Pr.

Hartley, Isaac S. *see* Hartley, Isaac Smithson.

Hartley, Isaac Smithson, 1830-1899
xHartley, Isaac S.
Memorial of Robert Milham Hartley. Arno.

Hartley, Joel, 1910-
xHartley, Joel.
First Aid without Panic. Popular Lib.

Hartley, Keith.
xHartley, Keith.
Problems of Economic Policy. Allen Unwin.

Hartley, Leslie P. *see* Hartley, Leslie Poles.

Hartley, Leslie Poles.
xHartley, Leslie P.
Hireling. Dufour.

Hartley, Livingston, 1900-
xHartley, Livingston.
Looking Forward: Trial & Triumph. Branden.

Hartley, Lodwick. *see* Hartley, Lodwick Charles.

Hartley, Lodwick Charles, 1906-
xHartley, Lodwick.
Plum Tree Lane. Sandlapper Store.

Hartley, Lucie K.
xHartley, Lucie K.
Maria Sanford, Pioneer Professor. Dillon.

Pauline Johnson. Dillon.

Hartley, Margaret L, 1909-
xHartley, Margaret L.
ed. The Southwest Review Reader. SMU Press.

Hartley, May L. *see* Hartley, May Laffan.

Hartley, May Laffan, Mrs.
xHartley, May L.
Hogan, M. P.. Garland Pub.

Hartley, Norman.
xHartley, Norman.
Quicksilver. Atheneum.

Hartley, P. J.
xHartley, P. J.
Introduction to BASIC: A Case Study
Approach. Intl Schol Bk Serv.

Hartley, R. F. *see* Hartley, Robert F.

Hartley, Rachel. *see* Hartley, Rachel M.

Hartley, Rachel M.
xHartley, Rachel.
The Story of Hamden: Land of the Sleeping
Giant. Shoe String.

Hartley, Robert. *see* Hartley, Robert E.

Hartley, Robert E.
xHartley, Robert.

Big Jim Thompson of Illinois. Rand.

Hartley, Robert F.
xHartley, R. F.
Marketing Fundamentals for Responsive
Management. Har-Row.
xHartley, Robert.
Marketing Fundamentals for Responsive
Management. Tech Pub.
xHartley, Robert F.
Marketing Mistakes. Grid Pub.
Retailing: Challenge & Opportunity. HM.
Sales Management. HM.

Hartley, Robert M. *see* Hartley, Robert Milham.

Hartley, Robert Milham, 1796-1881
xHartley, Robert M.
An Historical Scientific & Practical Essay on
Milk, As an Article of Human Sustenance:
Consideration of the Effects Consequent
Upon the Unnatural Methods of Producing It
for the Supply of Large Cities. Arno.

Hartley, Ronald V.
xHartley, Ronald V.
Operations Research: A Managerial Emphasis.
Goodyear.

Hartley, Ruth E. *see* Hartley, Ruth Edith.

Hartley, Ruth Edith.
xHartley, Ruth E.
Complete Book of Children's Play. T Y
Crowell.
Understanding Children's Play. Columbia U Pr.

Hartley, Shirley F. *see* Hartley, Shirley Foster.

Hartley, Shirley Foster.
xHartley, Shirley F.
Illegitimacy. U of Cal Pr.

Hartley, Thomas A. *see* Hartley, Thomas Allen.

Hartley, Thomas Allen, 1903-
xHartley, Thomas A.
Taxation of Decedents' Estates. P-H.

Hartley, W. C. *see* Hartley, W. C. F.

Hartley, W. C. F.
xHartley, W. C.
Cash Management: Planning, Forecasting,
Control. P-H.
An Introduction to Business Accounting for
Managers. Pergamon.
xHartley, W. C. F.
Introduction to Business Accounting for
Managers. Pergamon.

Hartley, William.
xHartley, William.
In the Beginning God: Jottings from Genesis.
Baker Bk.

Hartling, Peter.
xHartling, Peter.
Oma. Har-Row.

Hartman, Ann.
xHartman, Ann.
Finding Families: An Ecological Approach to
Family Assessment in Adoption. Sage.

Hartman, Bernard.
xHartman, Bernard.
Fundamentals of Television: Theory & Service.
Merrill.

Hartman, Chester. *see* Hartman, Chester W.

Hartman, Chester W.
xHartman, Chester.
Housing & Social Policy. P-H.

Hartman, Doug.
xHartman, Doug.
Guidebook to Discipleship. Harvest Hse.

Hartman, Edwin, 1941-
xHartman, Edwin.
Substance, Body, & Soul: Aristotelian
Investigations. Princeton U Pr.

Hartman, Geoffrey H.
xHartman, Geoffrey H.
The Fate of Reading & Other Essays. U of
Chicago Pr.

Hartman, Grietje.
xHartman, Grietje.

Popmooi: European Dolls to Make Yourself.
Chronicle Bks.

Hartman, J. Ted. *see* Hartman, James Ted.

Hartman, James Ted, 1925-
xHartman, J. Ted.
Fracture Management: A Practical Approach.
Lea & Febiger.

Hartman, Jane E.
xHartman, Jane E.
Animals That Live in Groups. Holiday.
Armadillos, Anteaters, & Sloths: How They
Live. Holiday.
Living Together in Nature: How Symbiosis
Works. Holiday.
Looking at Lizards. Holiday.

Hartman, John G. *see* Hartman, John Geoffrey.

Hartman, John Geoffrey, 1907-
xHartman, John G.
Development of American Social Comedy from
1787 to 1936. Octagon.
Development of American Social Comedy
1787-1963. Folcroft.

Hartman, John J.
xHartman, John J.
Methods for the Social Sciences: A Handbook
for Students & Non-Specialists. Greenwood.

Hartman, Mary. *see* Hartman, Mary S.

Hartman, Mary S.
xHartman, Mary.
ed. Clio's Consciousness Raised: New
Perspectives on the History of Women.
Har-Row.

Hartman, O. *see* Hartman, Olga.

Hartman, Olga, 1900-
xHartman, O.
ed. Polychaeta Errantia of Antarctica. Am
Geophysical.
ed. Polychaeta Myzostomidae & Sedentaria of
Antarctica. Am Geophysical.

Hartman, Rhondda E. *see* Hartman, Rhondda Evans.

Hartman, Rhondda Evans.
xHartman, Rhondda E.
Exercises for True Natural Childbirth.
Har-Row.

Hartman, Robert.
xHartman, Robert.
The Remainder Biscuit. Transatlantic.

Hartman, Robert W.
xHartman, Robert W.
ed. The Rewards of Public Service:
Compensating Top Federal Officials.
Brookings.

Hartman, Susan, 1952-
xHartman, Susan.
Dumb Show. U Presses Fla.

Hartmann, A. C. *see* Hartmann, Alfred C.

Hartmann, Alfred C., 1948-
xHartmann, A. C.
A Concurrent Pascal Compiler for
Minicomputers. Springer-Verlag.

Hartmann, Arthur.
xHartmann, Arthur.
Deafmutism & the Education of Deafmutes by
Lip-Reading & Articulation. Gordon Pr.

Hartmann, Edward G. *see* Hartmann, Edward George.

Hartmann, Edward George, 1912-
xHartmann, Edward G.
American Immigration. Lerner Pubns.
Americans from Wales. Octagon.

Hartmann, Ernest.
xHartmann, Ernest L.
The Functions of Sleep. Yale U Pr.

Hartmann, Ernest L. *see* Hartmann, Ernest.

Hartmann, Frederick H.
xHartmann, Frederick H.
Relations of Nations. Macmillan.

Hartmann, George W. *see* Hartmann, George Wilfried.

Hartmann, George Wilfried, 1904-
xHartmann, George W.

Gestalt Psychology: A Survey of Facts &
Principles. Greenwood.
Hartmann, Gregory K. see Hartmann, Gregory Kemenyi.
Hartmann, Gregory Kemenyi.
xHartmann, Gregory K.
Weapons That Wait: Mine Warfare in the U. S.
Navy. Naval Inst Pr.
Hartmann, H. F. see Hartmann, Hans F.
Hartmann, Hans F.
xHartmann, H. F.
Nature in the Balance. Taplinger.
Hartmann, Heinz.
xHartmann, Heinz.
Authority & Organization in German
Management. Greenwood.
Psychoanalysis & Moral Values. Intl Univs Pr.
Hartmann, Michael, 1944-
xHartmann, Michael.
The Hunted. St Martin.
Hartmann, Peter M.
xHartmann, Peter M.
ed. Guide to Hematologic Disorders. Grune.
Hartmann, Sadakichi, 1867-1944
xHartmann, Sadakichi.
Composition in Portraiture. Arno.
Conversations with Walt Whitman. Gordon Pr.
Conversations with Walt Whitman. Haskell.
Hartmann Von Aue. see Hartmann Von Aue, Th Cent.
Hartmann, William K.
xHartmann, William K.
Astronomy: The Cosmic Journey. Wadsworth
Pub.
Hartmann Von Aue, Th Cent.
xHartmann Von Aue.
Gregorius: A Medieval Oedipus Legend. AMS
Pr.
Hartnagel, Hans, 1934-
xHartnagel, Hans L.
Gunn-Effect Logic Devices. Heinemann Ed.
Hartnagel, Hans L. see Hartnagel, Hans.
Hartness, James, 1861-1934
xHartness, James.
The Human Factor in Works Management.
Hive Pub.
Hartney, Harold E. see Hartney, Harold Evans.
Hartney, Harold Evans, 1888-1945
xHartney, Harold E.
Up & at 'Em. Arno.
Hartnoll, Phyllis.
xHartnoll, Phyllis.
Concise History of the Theatre. Scribner.
Concise History of Theatre. Abrams.
ed. The Concise Oxford Companion to the
Theatre. Oxford U Pr.
ed. Oxford Companion to the Theatre. Oxford
U Pr.
Hartog, Howard, 1913-
xHartog, Howard.
ed. European Music in the Twentieth Century.
Greenwood.
Hartog, Jacob P. Den. see Den Hartog, Jacob P.
Hartog, Jan De, 1914-
xHartog, Jan De.
The Spiral Road. Queens Hse.
Hartrich, Edwin.
xHartrich, Edwin.
The Fourth & Richest Reich. Macmillan.
Hartshorn, Edward A.
xHartshorn, Edward A.
Handbook of Drug Interactions. Drug Intl
Pubns.
Hartshorn, Leon. see Hartshorn, Leon R.
Hartshorn, Leon R.
xHartshorn, Leon.
ed. Outstanding Stories by General Authorities.
Deseret Bk.
Remarkable Stories from the Lives of
Latter-Day Saint Women. Deseret Bk.
xHartshorn, Leon R.

Inspirational Missionary Stories. Deseret Bk.
Compiled by Inspiring Stories for Young
Latter-Day Saints. Deseret Bk.
Put on the Whole Armor of God. Deseret Bk.
Compiled by Remarkable Stories from the
Lives of Latter-Day Saint Women. Deseret
Bk.
Hartshorn, S. R.
xHartshorn, S. R.
Aliphatic Nucleophilic Substitution. Cambridge
U Pr.
Hartshorn, Truman A.
xHartshorn, Truman A.
Interpreting the City: Urban Geography. Wiley.
Hartshorne, Charles, 1897-
xHartshorne, Charles.
Anselm's Discovery: A Re-Examination of the
Ontological Proof for God's Existence. Open
Court.
Divine Relativity: A Social Conception of God.
Yale U Pr.
Hartshorne, Norman H. see Hartshorne, Norman Holt.
Hartshorne, Norman Holt.
xHartshorne, Norman H.
Practical Optical Crystallography. Elsevier.
Hartshorne, R. see Hartshorne, Robin.
Hartshorne, Richard, 1899-
xHartshorne, Richard.
The Nature of Geography: A Critical Survey of
Current Thought in the Light of the Past.
Greenwood.
Hartshorne, Robin.
xHartshorne, R.
Algebraic Geometry. Springer-Verlag.
Ample Subvarieties of Algebraic Varieties.
Springer-Verlag.
xHartshorne, Robin.
Foundations of Projective Geometry.
Benjamin-Cummings.
Hartshorne, Thomas L.
xHartshorne, Thomas L.
The Distorted Image: Changing Conceptions of
the American Character Since Turner.
Greenwood.
Hartstein, Jack.
xHartstein, Jack.
Questions & Answers on Contact Lens
Practice. Mosby.
Review of Refraction. Mosby.
Hartsuch, Paul J. see Hartsuch, Paul Jackson.
Hartsuch, Paul Jackson, 1902-
xHartsuch, Paul J.
Think Metric Now!: A Step-by-Step Guide to
Understanding & Applying the Metric
System. Penguin.
Hartt, Frederick.
xHartt, Frederick.
History of Italian Renaissance Art: Painting,
Sculpture, Architecture. Abrams.
Hartt, Julian N. see Hartt, Julian Norris.
Hartt, Julian Norris.
xHartt, Julian N.
Lost Image of Man. La State U Pr.
Theological Method & Imagination. Seabury.
Hartt, Rollin L. see Hartt, Rollin Lynde.
Hartt, Rollin Lynde, 1869-1946
xHartt, Rollin L.
The People at Play. Arno.
Hartung, Frank E., 1908-
xHartung, Frank E.
Crime, Law & Society. Wayne St U Pr.
Hartveit, Lars.
xHartveit, Lars.
The Art of Persuasion: A Study of Six Novels.
Universitet.
Hartwell, Herbert.
xHartwell, Herbert.

Theology of Karl Barth: An Introduction.
Biblio Dist.
Hartwick, Harry.
xHartwick, Harry.
Foreground of American Fiction. Gordian.
Hartwig, Daphne M. see Hartwig, Daphne Metaxas.
Hartwig, Daphne Metaxas.
xHartwig, Daphne M.
Make Your Own Groceries. Bobbs.
Hartwig, G. W. see Hartwig, Gerald W.
Hartwig, Gerald. see Hartwig, Gerald W.
Hartwig, Gerald W.
xHartwig, G. W.
The Student Africanist's Handbook: A Guide
to Resources. Halsted Pr.
xHartwig, Gerald.
The Art of Survival in East Africa: The Kerebe
& Long-Distance Trade, 1800-1895. Holmes
& Meier.
xHartwig, Gerald W.
The Student Africanist's Handbook: A Guide
to Resources. Schenkman.
Hartwig, Marie.
xHartwig, Marie D.
Camping Leadership: Counseling &
Programming. Mosby.
Hartwig, Marie D. see Hartwig, Marie.
Hartz, Louis, 1919-
xHartz, Louis.
Founding of New Societies: Studies in the
History of the United States, Latin America,
South Africa, Canada, & Australia.
HarBraceJ.
Liberal Tradition in America: An Interpretation
of American Political Thought Since the
Revolution. HarBraceJ.
Hartzler, Daniel D., 1941-
xHartzler, Daniel D.
Arms Makers of Maryland. Shumway.
Hartzler, F. E.
xHartzler, F. E.
The Retail Salesperson: A Programmed Text.
McGraw.
Harvard Advocate.
xHarvard Advocate.
Harvard Advocate Anthology. Arno.
Harvard African Expedition. see Harvard African
Expedition, 1926-1927.
Harvard African Expedition, 1926-1927.
xHarvard African Expedition.
African Republic of Liberia & the Belgian
Congo, Based on the Observations Made &
Material Collected During the Harvard
African Expediton, 1926-1927. Greenwood.
Harvard Business Review.
xHarvard Business Review Editors.
ed. Harvard Business Review - on
Management. Har-Row.
Harvard Business Reviews on Human
Relations. Har-Row.
Harvard Business Review Editors. see Harvard Business
Review.
Harvard Child Health Project.
xHarvard Child Health Project.
Harvard Child Health Project Report:
Developing a Better Health Care System for
Children. Ballinger Pub.
Harvard Child Health Project Report: Toward
a Primary Medical Care System Responsive
to Children's Needs. Ballinger Pub.
Harvard College Library. see Harvard University.
Library.
Harvard Committee. see Harvard University.
Harvard Educational Review. see Harvard Educational
Review (The).
Harvard Educational Review (The).
xHarvard Educational Review.

ed. Education & Life Chances. Harvard Educ
Rev.

ed. Education, Participation, & Power: Essays
in Theory & Practice. Harvard Educ Rev.

xHarvard Educational Review Editorial Board.
Stage Theories of Cognitive & Moral
Development: Criticisms & Application.
Harvard Educ Rev.

xHarvard Educational Review Staff.
Guidance, an Examination. Johnson Repr.

Harvard Educational Review Editorial Board. *see*
Harvard Educational Review (The).

Harvard Educational Review Staff. *see* Harvard
Educational Review (The).

Harvard Medical Library. *see* Boston Medical Library.

Harvard Student Agencies. *see* Harvard Student
Agencies, Cambridge, Massachusetts.

Harvard University - Dumbarton Oaks Research Library
And Collection - Washington D.C. *see* Harvard
University. Dumbarton Oaks Research Library and
Collection, Washington, D.C.

Harvard University - Graduate School Of Design. *see*
Harvard University. Graduate School of Design.

Harvard University Center for Italian Renaissance
Studies at Villa I Tatti (Florence, Italy). *see* Harvard
University. Villa I Tatti, Florence.

Harvard University Faculty Of Art. *see* Harvard
University. Faculty of Arts and Sciences.

Harvard University, Phillips Brooks House Association.
see Phillips Brooks House.

Harvard University Psychologists. *see* Harvard
University.

**Harvard-Smithsonian Conference on Stellar
Atmospheres, 3d, Cambridge, Massachusetts, 1968.**
xHarvard-Smithsonian Conference on Stellar
Atmosphere - 3rd.
Theory & Observations of Normal Stellar
Atmospheres: Proceedings. MIT Pr.

Harvard Student Agencies, Cambridge, Massachusetts.
xHarvard Student Agencies.
Let's Go, Britain & Ireland: The Budget Guide
1981 to 1982 Edition. Dutton.
Let's Go, Britain Nineteen Seventy-Nine to
Nineteen Eighty. Dutton.
Let's Go, Europe Nineteen Seventy-Nine to
Nineteen Eighty. Dutton.
Let's Go, Europe 1981-82. Dutton.
Let's Go, France Nineteen Seventy-Nine to
Nineteen Eighty. Dutton.
Let's Go France: The Budget Guide 1981 to
1982 Edition. Dutton.
Let's Go, Greece, Israel & Europe 1981-82.
Dutton.
Let's Go, Italy Nineteen Seventy-Nine to
Nineteen Eighty. Dutton.
Let's Go: Italy: The Budget Guide 1980-1981
Edition. Dutton.
Let's Go, Italy: The Budget Guide 1981 to
1982 Edition. Dutton.
Let's Go, USA 1981-82. Dutton.

Harvard University.
xHarvard Committee.
Graduate Study of Education. Harvard U Pr.
xHarvard University.
Catalog of the Farlow Reference Library of
Cryptogamic Botany. G K Hall.
Catalogue of the Harvard University Fine Arts
Library, the Fogg Art Museum. G K Hall.
Catalogue of the Library of the Graduate
School of Design, Harvard University: Third
Supplement. G K Hall.
Harvard Studies in Education. Johnson Repr.
Harvard Studies in English. Johnson Repr.
Harvard University Hymn Book. Harvard U Pr.
Kress Library of Business & Economics
Catalogue. Kelley.
xHarvard University Psychologists.

Harvard List of Books in Psychology. Harvard
U Pr.

Harvard University. Center for International Affairs.
xHarvard University, Center for International
Affairs.
Occasional Papers in International Affairs.
AMS Pr.

**Harvard University. Dumbarton Oaks Research Library
and Collection, Washington, D.C.**
xHarvard University - Dumbarton Oaks Research
Library And Collection - Washington D.C.
Dumbarton Oaks Papers. Johnson Repr.
xHarvard University Dumbarton Oaks Research
Library.
Dictionary Catalogue of the Byzantine
Collection of the Dumbarton Oaks Research
Library. G K Hall.

Harvard University. Faculty of Arts and Sciences.
xHarvard University Faculty Of Art.
Teaching of Economics. Johnson Repr.

**Harvard University. Graduate School of Business
Administration.**
xHarvard University, Graduate School of Business
Administration.
Author-Title Catalog of the Baker Library,
First Supplement. G K Hall.
Author-Title Catalogs of the Baker Library. G
K Hall.
Subject Catalog of the Baker Library. G K
Hall.
Subject Catalog of the Baker Library: First
Supplement. G K Hall.

Harvard University. Graduate School of Design.
xHarvard University - Graduate School Of Design.
Catalogue of the Library of the Graduate
School of Design. G K Hall.
Catalogue of the Library of the Graduate
School of Design, First Supplement. G K
Hall.
xHarvard University, Graduate School of Design.
Catalog of the Library of the Graduate School
of Design, Harvard University, 2nd Suppl. G
K Hall.

Harvard University. Gray Herbarium.
xHarvard University, Gray Herbarium.
Gray Herbarium Index. G K Hall.

Harvard University. Law School.
xHarvard University Law School.
Path of Law from 1967: Proceedings & Papers
at the Harvard Law School Convocation
Held on the 150th Anniversary of Its
Founding. Harvard U Pr.

Harvard University. Law School. Library.
xHarvard University Law School Library.
Preliminary Union List of Materials on Chinese
Law: With a List of Chinese Studies &
Translations of Foreign Law. Harvard U Pr.
Soviet Legal Bibliography: A Classified &
Annotated Listing of Books & Serials
Published in the Soviet Union Since 1917 As
Represented in the Collection of the Harvard
Law School Library As of January 1, 1965.
Harvard U Pr.
Writings on Soviet Law & Soviet International
Law: A Bibliography of Books & Articles
Published Since 1917 in Languages Other
Than East European. Harvard U Pr.

Harvard University. Library.
xHarvard College Library.
Kilgour Collection of Russian Literature,
1750-1920: With Notes on Early Books &
Manuscripts of the 16th & 17th Centuries.
Harvard U Pr.
xHarvard University Library.

African History & Literatures. Harvard U Pr.

Ancient Greek Literature. Harvard U Pr.

Ancient History: Classification Schedule
Author & Title Listing, Chronological Listing.
Harvard U Pr.

Archaeology. Harvard U Pr.

Canadian History & Literature: Classified,
Alphabetical & Chronological Listings.
Harvard U Pr.

Catalogue of English & American Chap-Books
& Broadside Ballads in Harvard College
Library. Gale.

Catalogue of Hebrew Books. Harvard U Pr.

Catalogue of Hebrew Books: Supplement I.
Harvard U Pr.

Celtic Literatures: Classification Schedule,
Classified Listing by Call Number,
Chronological Listing, Author & Title Listing.
Harvard U Pr.

China, Japan, & Korea: Classified, Alphabetical
& Chronological Listings. Harvard U Pr.

Classical Studies. Harvard U Pr.

Current Journals in the Sciences. Harvard U
Pr.

Education. Harvard U Pr.

English Literature: Classification Schedule,
Alphabetical Listing by Author or Title,
Chronological Listing. Harvard U Pr.

Finnish & Baltic History & Literatures:
Classification Schedule, Author & Title
Listing, Chronological Listing. Harvard U Pr.

French Literature: Classification Schedule,
Author & Title Listing, Chronological Listing.
Harvard U Pr.

General European & World History:
Classification Schedule, Author & Title
Listing, Chronological Listing. Harvard U Pr.

Geography & Anthropology. Harvard U Pr.

German Literature: Classification Schedule -
Author & Title Listing. Harvard U Pr.

Government: Classification Schedule, Author &
Title Listing, Chronological Listing. Harvard
U Pr.

Harvard College Library, Department of
Printing & Graphic Arts, Catalogue of Books
& Manuscripts: French 16th Century Books.
Harvard U Pr.

Harvard University Library Catalogue of
Arabic, Persian & Ottoman Turkish Bks.
Harvard U Pr.

Houghton Library, 1942-1967: A Selection of
Books & Manuscripts in Harvard Collections.
Harvard U Pr.

Hungarian History & Literature: Classification
Schedule, Author & Title Listing,
Chronological Listing. Harvard U Pr.

Italian History & Literature: Classification
Schedule - Author & Title Listing. Harvard U
Pr.

Judaica: Classification Schedule, Author & Title
Listing, Chronological Listing. Harvard U Pr.

Latin American Literature: Classification
Schedule, Classified Listing by Call Number,
Authors and Title Listing. Harvard U Pr.

Latin Literature. Harvard U Pr.

Literature, General & Comparative: Classified,
Alphabetical, & Chronological Listings.
Harvard U Pr.

Periodical Classes. Harvard U Pr.

Philosophy & Psychology: Classification
Schedule, Author & Title Listing,
Chronological Listing. Harvard U Pr.

Reference Collections Shelved in the Reading
Room & Acquisitions Department: Classified
& Alphabetical Listings. Harvard U Pr.

Slavic History & Literatures. Harvard U Pr.

Sociology: Classification Schedule, Author &
Title Listing, Chronological Listing. Harvard
U Pr.

Southern Asia: Classified, Alphabetical, &

Chronological Listings.. Harvard U Pr.
Spanish History & Literature: Classification
Schedule, Author & Title Listing,
Chronological Listing. Harvard U Pr.
Theodore Roosevelt Collection: Dictionary
Catalogue & Shelflist. Harvard U Pr.

Harvard University. Medical School.
xHarvard University Medical School.
Community Mental Health & Social
Psychology: A Reference Guide. Harvard U
Pr.

Harvard University. Museum of Comparative Zoology.
xHarvard University Museum of Comparative
Zoology.
Catalogue of the Library of the Museum of
Comparative Zoology, First Supplement. G K
Hall.
Catalogue of the Library of the Museum of
Comparative Zoology, Harvard University. G
K Hall.

Harvard University. Peabody Museum of Archaeology and Ethnology.
xHarvard University. Peabody Museum of
Archaeology & Ethnology.
Antiquities of the New World: Early
Explorations in Archaeology. AMS Pr.
Author & Subject Catalogues of the Library of
the Peabody Museum of Archaeology &
Ethnology, Second Supplement. G K Hall.
Russian Translation Series. AMS Pr.
xPeabody Museum of Archaeology & Ethnology.
Author & Subject Catalogues of the Library of
the Peabody Museum of Archaeology &
Ethnology: Fourth Supplement. G K Hall.

Harvard University. Villa I Tatti, Florence.
xHarvard University Center for Italian Renaissance
Studies at Villa I Tatti (Florence, Italy).
Catalogues of the Berenson Library of the
Harvard University Center for Italian
Renaissance Studies at Villa I Tatti, Florence,
Italy. G K Hall.

Harvard-Yenching Institute.
xHarvard-Yenching Institute.
Combined Indices to Shih Chi & the Notes of
P'ei Yin, Ssu-Ma Cheng, Chang Shou-Chieh,
& Takigawa Kametaro. Harvard U Pr.
Concordance to Chuang Tzu. Harvard U Pr.

Harven, Emile De. see De Harven, Emile.
Harvey. see Harvey, Abner McGehee.
Harvey, A. E. see Harvey, Anthony Ernest.
Harvey, Abner McGehee.
xHarvey.
The Principles & Practice of Medicine. ACC.
Harvey, Alexander, 1945-
xHarvey, Alexander.
Months & Seasons. Hollow Spring Pr.
Harvey, Anthony.
xHarvey, Anthony.
The World of the Dinosaurs. Lerner Pubns.
Harvey, Anthony Ernest.
xHarvey, A. E.
Something Overheard: An Invitation to the
New Testament. John Knox.
Harvey, Barbara. see Harvey, Barbara F.
Harvey, Barbara F.
xHarvey, Barbara.
Westminster Abbey & Its Estates in the Middle
Ages. Oxford U Pr.
Harvey, Bernard G.
xHarvey, Bernard G.
Introduction to Nuclear Physics & Chemistry.
P-H.
Harvey, Bill.
xHarvey, Bill.
Mind Magic. Irvington.
Harvey, Bruce. see Harvey, Norman Bruce.
Harvey, Carol D. see Harvey, Carol D. H.
Harvey, Carol D. H.
xHarvey, Carol D.

The Sunshine Widows: Adapting to Sudden
Bereavement. Lexington Bks.
Harvey, Chris.
xHarvey, Chris.
E Type: End of an Era. St Martin.
Healey: The Handsome Brute. St Martin.
The Jaguar XK. St Martin.
xHarvey, Christopher A.
Jaguars in Competition. Motorbooks Intl.
Harvey, Christopher A. see Harvey, Chris.
Harvey, Curtis E.
xHarvey, Curtis E.
The Economics of Kentucky Coal. U Pr of Ky.
Harvey, D. see Harvey, David.
Harvey, Daniel C. see Harvey, Daniel Cobb.
Harvey, Daniel Cobb, 1886-
xHarvey, Daniel C.
French Regime in Prince Edward Island. AMS
Pr.
Harvey, David.
xHarvey, D.
Society, the City & the Space-Economy of
Urbanism. Assn Am Geographers.
Harvey, Denis. see Harvey, Denis E.
Harvey, Denis E.
xHarvey, Denis.
The Gypsies: Waggon Time & After. David &
Charles.
Harvey, E. Newton. see Harvey, Edmund Newton.
Harvey, Edmund N. see Harvey, Edmund Newton.
Harvey, Edmund Newton, 1887-
xHarvey, E. Newton.
History of Luminescence from the Earliest
Times Until 1900. Am Philos.
xHarvey, Edmund N.
Living Light. Hafner.
Harvey, Edward B.
xHarvey, Edward B.
Industrial Society: Structures, Roles &
Relations. Dorsey.
Harvey, Geoffrey, 1943-
xHarvey, Geoffrey.
The Art of Anthony Trollope. St Martin.
Harvey, Geraldine, 1936-
xHarvey, Geraldine.
Child Psychology. Wiley.
Harvey, Godfrey E. see Harvey, Godfrey Eric.
Harvey, Godfrey Eric, 1889-
xHarvey, Godfrey E.
British Rule in Burma, 1824-1942. AMS Pr.
Harvey, Hildbrande Wolfe, 1887-
xHarvey, Hildbrande W.
Chemistry & Fertility of Sea Waters.
Cambridge U Pr.
Harvey, Hildbrande W. see Harvey, Hildbrande Wolfe.
Harvey, James.
xHarvey, James.
Convict Guns. Belmont-Tower.
Harvey, James C., 1925-
xHarvey, James C.
Civil Rights During the Kennedy
Administration. U Pr of Miss.
Harvey, Joan M.
xHarvey, Joan M.
Sources of Statistics. Shoe String.
ed. Statistics--Africa: Sources for Social,
Economic, & Market Research. Gale.
Statistics Africa: Sources for Social Economic
& Market Research. Intl Pubns Serv.
ed. Statistics-Europe: Sources for Social,
Economic & Market Research. Gale.

Harvey, John. see Harvey, John Hooper.

Harvey, John F. see Harvey, John Frederick.

Harvey, John Frederick, 1921-
xHarvey, John F.
ed. Church & Synagogue Libraries. Scarecrow.

ed. Comparative & International Library
Science. Scarecrow.
Harvey, John Hooper.
xHarvey, John.
Cathedrals of England & Wales. Hastings.
Harvey, John M. see Harvey, John Martin-.
Harvey, John Martin-, Sir, 1863-1944
xHarvey, John M.
Autobiography of Sir John Martin Harvey.
Johnson Repr.
Harvey, Jonathan.
xHarvey, Jonathan.
The Music of Stockhausen: An Introduction. U
of Cal Pr.
Harvey, Karen G.
xHarvey, Karen G.
Alexandria: A Pictorial History. Donning Co.
Harvey, Katherine A.
xHarvey, Katherine A.
The Lonaconing Journals: The Founding of a
Coal & Iron Community,1837-1840. Am
Philos.
Harvey, Norman Bruce.
xHarvey, Bruce.
Portfolio of New Zealand Birds. C E Tuttle.
Harvey, Paul, Sir, 1869-1948
xHarvey, Paul.
ed. Oxford Companion to Classical Literature.
Oxford U Pr.
Harvey, Ray F. see Harvey, Ray Forrest.
Harvey, Ray Forrest.
xHarvey, Ray F.
Politics of This War. Arno.
Harvey, Richard W., 1943-
xHarvey, Richard W.
Coaching Basketball's Multiple Set Zone
Offense. P-H.
Harvey, Robert, 1953-
xHarvey, Robert.
Portugal: Birth of a Democracy. St Martin.
Harvey, Roger.
xHarvey, Roger.
Building Pottery Equipment. Watson-Guptill.
Harvey, T.
xHarvey, T.
Railroads. Lerner Pubns.
Harvey, W. J.
xHarvey, William J.
Character & the Novel. Cornell U Pr.
Harvey, Warren.
xHarvey, Warren.
Dental Identification & Forensic Odontology.
Year Bk Med.
Harvey, William.
xHarvey, William.
Works. Johnson Repr.
Harvey, William B. see Harvey, William Burnet.
Harvey, William Burnet.
xHarvey, William B.
Law & Social Change in Ghana. Princeton U
Pr.
Harvey, William H. see Harvey, William Hope.
Harvey, William Hope, 1851-1936
xHarvey, William H.
Coin on Money, Trusts & Imperialism.
Hyperion Conn.
Coin's Financial School. Harvard U Pr.
Harvey, William J. see Harvey, W. J.
Harvey, William John, 1925-
xHarvey, William J.
The Art of George Eliot. Greenwood.
Harvey, Youngsook K. see Harvey, Youngsook Kim.
Harvey, Youngsook Kim.
xHarvey, Youngsook K.
Six Korean Women: The Socialization of
Shamans. West Pub.
Harvitt, Helene. see Harvitt, Helene Josephine.
Harvitt, Helene Josephine, 1884-
xHarvitt, Helene.

Eustorg De Beaulieu: A Disciple of Marot.
AMS Pr.
Harwell, Charles. *see* Harwell, Charles W.
Harwell, Charles W., 1934-
xHarwell, Charles.
ed. Disordered Personalities in Literature.
Longman.
Harwell, Edward M.
xHarwell, Edward M.
Meat Management & Operations. Lebhar
Friedman.
Personnel Management & Training. Lebhar
Friedman.
Harwell, R. B. *see* Harwell, Richard Barksdale.
Harwell, Richard B. *see* Harwell, Richard Barksdale.
Harwell, Richard Barksdale.
xHarwell, R. B.
Confederate Reader. McKay.
xHarwell, Richard B.
ed. Confederate Imprints in the University of
Georgia Libraries. U of Ga Pr.
More Confederate Imprints. U Pr of Va.
Harwit, Martin, 1931-
xHarwit, Martin.
Astrophysical Concepts. Wiley.
Hadamard Transform Optics. Acad Pr.
Harwood, B. *see* Harwood, Bruce M.
Harwood, Bruce. *see* Harwood, Bruce M.
Harwood, Bruce M., 1941-
xHarwood, B.
Real Estate: An Introduction to the Profession.
Reston.
xHarwood, Bruce.
Real Estate Principles. Reston.
Harwood, Don.
xHarwood, Don.
Everything You Always Wanted to Know
About Citizens Band Radio. VTR Pub.
Everything You Always Wanted to Know
About Portable Videotape Recording. VTR
Pub.
Harwood, Herbert H.
xHarwood, Herbert H.
Impossible Challenge: The Baltimore & Ohio
Railroad in Maryland. Barnard Roberts.
Harwood, Pearl A. *see* Harwood, Pearl Augusta.
Harwood, Pearl Augusta.
xHarwood, Pearl A.
Carnival with Mr. & Mrs. Bumba. Lerner
Pubns.
Climbing a Mountain with Mr. & Mrs. Bumba.
Lerner Pubns.
Long Vacation for Mr. & Mrs. Bumba. Lerner
Pubns.
Mrs. Moon & Her Friends. Lerner Pubns.
Mrs. Moon & the Dark Stairs. Lerner Pubns.
Mrs. Moon Goes Shopping. Lerner Pubns.
Mrs. Moon Takes a Drive. Lerner Pubns.
Mrs. Moon's Cement Hat. Lerner Pubns.
Mrs. Moon's Harbor Trip. Lerner Pubns.
Mrs. Moon's Picnic. Lerner Pubns.
Mrs. Moon's Polliwogs. Lerner Pubns.
Mrs. Moon's Rescue. Lerner Pubns.
Mrs. Moon's Story Hour. Lerner Pubns.
Thief Visits Mr. & Mrs. Bumba. Lerner Pubns.
Harwood, Richard R.
xHarwood, Richard R.
Small Farm Development: Understanding &
Improving Farming Systems in the Humid
Tropics. Westview.
Harwood, Robert F. *see* Harwood, Robert Frederick.
Harwood, Robert Frederick.
xHarwood, Robert F.
Entomology in Human & Animal Health.
Macmillan.
Harwood, Sharon, 1945-
xHarwood, Sharon E.
Rhetoric in the Tragedies of Corneille. Univ
Microfilms.
Harwood, Sharon E. *see* Harwood, Sharon.

Harzem, P.
xHarzem, P.
Conceptual Issues in Operant Psychology.
Wiley.
Harzfeld, Lois A., 1932-
xHarzfeld, Lois A.
Periodical Indexes in the Social Sciences &
Humanities: A Subject Guide. Scarecrow.
Hasan, Masood.
xHasan, Masood.
India's Trade Relations with Rupee Payments
Countries. Verry.
Hasan, Saiyid Z. *see* Zafar al-Hasan, Saiyid.
Hasbach, W. *see* Hasbach, Wilhelm.
Hasbach, Wilhelm.
xHasbach, W.
History of the English Agricultural Labourer.
Biblio Dist.
xHasbach, Wilhelm.
History of the English Agricultural Labourer.
Kelley.
Haschemeyer, Rudolph. *see* Haschemeyer, Rudy Harm.
Haschemeyer, Rudy Harm.
xHaschemeyer, Rudolph.
Proteins: A Guide to Study by Physical &
Chemical Methods. Wiley.
Hasdorff, Lawrence, 1929-
xHasdorff, Lawrence.
Gradient Optimization & Nonlinear Control.
Wiley.
Hasegawa, A. *see* Hasegawa, Akira.
Hasegawa, Akira, 1934-
xHasegawa, A.
Plasma Instabilities & Nonlinear Effects.
Springer-Verlag.
Hasegawa, Goro.
xHasegawa, Goro.
How to Win at Othello. HarBraceJ.
Hasegawa, Hideo, 1924-
xHasegawa, Hideo.
Ice Carving. Continental CA.
Hasegawa, Sam.
xHasegawa, Sam.
Stevie Wonder. Creative Ed.
Hasegawa, Seikan, 1945-
xHasegawa, Seikan.
The Cave of Poison Grass: Essays on the
Hannya Sutra. Great Ocean.
Hasel, Gerhard. *see* Hasel, Gerhard F.
Hasel, Gerhard F.
xHasel, Gerhard.
Jonah, Messenger of the Eleventh Hour. Pacific
Pr Pub Assn.
Haselfoot, A. J.
xHaselfoot, A. J.
Batsford Guide to the Industrial Archaeology
of South-East England. David & Charles.
Haselkorn, Avigdor.
xHaselkorn, Avigdor.
The Evolution of Soviet Security Strategy:
1965-1975. Crane-Russak Co.
Haseman, William D.
xHaseman, William D.
Introduction to Data Management. Irwin.
Hasenau, J. James, 1919-
xHasenau, J. James.
Build Your Own Home: A Guide for
Subcontracting the Easy Way a System to
Save Time & Money. Holland Hse Pr.
xHasenau, James J.
Gerbils: How to Buy, Breed, Raise & Train.
Arco.
Hasenau, James J. *see* Hasenau, J. James.
Hasenfeld, Yeheskel.
xHasenfeld, Yeheskel.
ed. Human Service Organizations: A Book of
Readings. U of Mich Pr.
Hasford, Gustav.
xHasford, Gustav.

The Short-Timers. Bantam.
The Short-Timers. Har-Row.
Hashimi, Rasool M. *see* Hashimi, Rasool M H.
Hashimi, Rasool M H, 1919-
xHashimi, Rasool M.
Studies in Functional Income Distribution.
Mich St U Busn.
Hashway, Robert M.
xHashway, Robert M.
Objective Mental Measurement: Individual &
Program Evaluation Using the Rasch Model.
Praeger.
Haskell, Charles M.
xHaskell, Charles M.
ed. Cancer Treatment. Saunders.
Haskell, Edward. *see* Haskell, Edward Froelich.
Haskell, Edward Froelich.
xHaskell, Edward.
ed. Full Circle: The Moral Force of Unified
Science. Gordon.
Haskell, Francis, 1928-
xHaskell, Francis.
Patrons & Painters: A Study in the Relations
Between Italian Art & Society in the Age of
the Baroque. Yale U Pr.
Haskell, Lendall L.
xHaskell, Lendall L.
Teaching Children Through Art in the Early
Childhood Years. Merrill.
Haskell, Martin R.
xHaskell, Martin R.
Crime & Delinquency. Rand.
Juvenile Delinquency. Rand.
Haskell, Molly.
xHaskell, Molly.
From Reverence to Rape: The Treatment of
Women in the Movies. Penguin.
Haskell, Richard E.
xHaskell, Richard E.
FORTRAN Programming Using Structured
Flowcharts. SRA.
Haskell, Simon H. *see* Haskell, Simon Hai.
Haskell, Simon Hai.
xHaskell, Simon H.
Arithmetical Disabilities in Cerebral Palsied
Children: Programmed Instruction - a
Remedial Approach. C C Thomas.
The Education of Motor & Neurologically
Handicapped Children. Halsted Pr.
Haskin, Gretchen.
xHaskin, Gretchen.
An Imperial Affair. Dial.
Haskins & Sells Government Services Group. *see* Haskins
and Sells. Government Services Group.
Haskins and Sells. Government Services Group.
xHaskins & Sells Government Services Group.
Implementing Effective Cash Management in
Local Government: A Practical Guide.
Municipal.
Haskins, C. H. *see* Haskins, Charles Homer.
Haskins, Charles H. *see* Haskins, Charles Homer.
Haskins, Charles Homer, 1870-1937
xHaskins, C. H.
The Normans in European History. Century
Bookbindery.
xHaskins, Charles H.
The Normans in European History. Arden Lib.
Normans in European History. Norton.
The Renaissance of the Twelfth Century.
Harvard U Pr.
Haskins, Charles W. *see* Haskins, Charles Waldo.
Haskins, Charles Waldo.
xHaskins, Charles W.
Business Education & Accountancy. Arno.
Haskins, George L. *see* Haskins, George Lee.
Haskins, George Lee, 1915-
xHaskins, George L.

The Growth of English Representative
    Government. A S Barnes.
Growth of English Representative Government.
    Peter Smith.
The Statute of York & the Interest of the
    Commons. Greenwood.
Haskins, Ida.
    xHaskins, Ida.
        Adventures on the Airboat Trail. E A
            Seemann.
Haskins, Ilma.
    xHaskins, Ilma.
        illus. Color Seems. Vanguard.
Haskins, James, 1941-
    xHaskins, James.
        Babe Ruth & Hank Aaron: The Home Run
            Kings. Lothrop.
        Creoles of Color of New Orleans. T Y Crowell.
        From Lew Alcindor to Kareem Abdul-Jabbar.
            Lothrop.
        The Life & Death of Martin Luther King, Jr..
            Lothrop.
        The Quiet Revolution: The Struggle for the
            Rights of Disabled Americans. T Y Crowell.
        Religions. Lippincott.
        The Story of Stevie Wonder. Dell.
        The Story of Stevie Wonder. Lothrop.
    xHaskins, James M.
        The Psychology of Black Language. B&N.
    xHaskins, James S.
        Pele: A Biography. Doubleday.
        Who Are the Handicapped?. Doubleday.
    xHaskins, Jim.
        The Cotton Club. Random.
        The Long Struggle: The Story of American
            Labor. Westminster.
        The Psychology of Black Language. Har-Row.
        Real Estate Careers. Watts.
Haskins, James M. *see* Haskins, James.
Haskins, James S. *see* Haskins, James.
Haskins, Jim. *see* Haskins, James.
Haskins, Ron.
    xHaskins, Ron.
        ed. Care & Education in Young Children in
            America: Policy, Politics & Social Science.
            Ablex Pub.
Haslam, Gerald. *see* Haslam, Gerald W.
Haslam, Gerald W.
    xHaslam, Gerald.
        California Heartland: Writing from the Great
            Central Valley. Capra Pr.
        Masks: A Novel. Old Adobe Pr.
        The Okies: Selected Stories. Peregrine Smith.
Haslam, M. T. *see* Haslam, Michael Trevor.
Haslam, Michael Trevor.
    xHaslam, M. T.
        Psychosexual Disorders: A Review. C C
            Thomas.
Haslam, Robert H. *see* Haslam, Robert H. A.
Haslam, Robert H. A.
    xHaslam, Robert H.
        ed. Medical Problems in the Classroom: The
            Teacher's Role in Diagnosis & Management.
            Univ Park.
Hasler, A. D. *see* Hasler, Arthur Davis.
Hasler, Arthur Davis.
    xHasler, A. D.
        ed. Coupling of Land & Water Systems.
            Springer-Verlag.
Hasler, Doris.
    xHasler, Doris.
        Personal, Home & Community Health.
            Macmillan.
        Practical Nurse & Today's Family. Macmillan.
Haslett, Harriet Holmes.
    xHaslett, Harriet Holmes.
        Dolores of the Sierra & Other One Act Plays.
            Core Collection.
Haslett, J. W., 1912-
    xHaslett, John W.

Business Systems Handbook: Strategies for
    Administrative Control. McGraw.
Haslett, John W. *see* Haslett, J. W.
Haslewood, G. A. *see* Haslewood, G. A. D.
Haslewood, G. A. D.
    xHaslewood, G. A.
        The Biological Importance of Bile Salts.
            Elsevier.
Hasling. *see* Hasling, John.
Hasling, J. *see* Hasling, John.
Hasling, John.
    xHasling.
        The Audience, the Message, the Speaker.
            McGraw.
    xHasling, J.
        Group Discussion & Decision Making.
            Har-Row.
Hasluck, F. W. *see* Hasluck, Frederick William.
Hasluck, Frederick William, 1878-1920
    xHasluck, F. W.
        Christianity & Islam Under the Sultans.
            Octagon.
Hasluck, Paul N. *see* Hasluck, Paul Nooneree.
Hasluck, Paul Nooneree, 1854-1931
    xHasluck, Paul N.
        Manual of Traditional Wood Carving. Dover.
Haspel, Eleanor C.
    xHaspel, Eleanor C.
        Marriage in Trouble: A Time of Decision.
            Nelson-Hall.
Hass. *see* Hass, Glen.
Hass, Glen.
    xHass.
        Curriculum Planning: A New Approach. Allyn.
Hass, Jerome E.
    xHass, Jerome E.
        Financing the Energy Industry. Ballinger Pub.
Hass, Robert.
    xHass, Robert.
        Field Guide. Yale U Pr.
        Praise. Ecco Pr.
Hassall, Arthur, 1853-1930
    xHassall, Arthur.
        Mazarin. Arno.
Hassan, Ihab. *see* Hassan, Ihab Habib.
Hassan, Ihab Habib, 1925-
    xHassan, Ihab.
        The Right Promethean Fire: Imagination,
            Science, & Cultural Change. U of Ill Pr.
Hassan, William E.
    xHassan, William E.
        Hospital Pharmacy. Lea & Febiger.
        Law for the Pharmacy Student. Lea & Febiger.
Hassani, N., 1938-
    xHassani, N.
        Ultrasound in Gynecology & Obstetrics.
            Springer-Verlag.
Hasse, Adelaide R. *see* Hasse, Adelaide Rosalia.
Hasse, Adelaide Rosalia, 1868-1953
    xHasse, Adelaide R.
        Index to United States Documents Relating to
            Foreign Affairs, 1828-1861. Kraus Repr.
Hassel, R. Chris. *see* Hassel, Rudolph Chris.
Hassel, Rudolph Chris, 1939-
    xHassel, R. Chris.
        Faith & Folly in Shakespeare's Romantic
            Comedies. U of Ga Pr.
        Renaissance Drama & the English Church
            Year. U of Nebr Pr.
Hasselberger, Francis. *see* Hasselberger, Francis X.
Hasselberger, Francis X.
    xHasselberger, Francis.
        Uses of Enzymes & Immobilized Enzymes.
            Nelson-Hall.
Hasselbrink, Gustav.
    xHasselbrink, Gustav.
        Alternative Analyses of Phonemic System in
            Central South-Lappish. Res Ctr Lang
            Semiotic.
Hassell, Michael P. *see* Hassell, Michael Patrick.

Hassell, Michael Patrick.
    xHassell, Michael P.
        The Dynamics of Arthropod Predator-Prey
            Systems. Princeton U Pr.
Hassenstein, B. *see* Hassenstein, Bernhard.
Hassenstein, Bernhard.
    xHassenstein, B.
        Information & Control in the Living Organism:
            An Elementary Introduction. Halsted Pr.
Hassett, James.
    xHassett, James.
        A Primer of Psychophysiology. W H Freeman.
Hassid, Patricia.
    xHassid, Patricia.
        A Textbook for Childbirth Educators.
            Har-Row.
Hassler, Jon.
    xHassler, Jon.
        Four Miles to Pinecone. Warne.
        Simon's Night. Atheneum.
        Staggerford. Atheneum.
Hassler, Kenneth. *see* Hassler, Kenneth Wayne.
Hassler, Kenneth Wayne.
    xHassler, Kenneth.
        Mark Twain, Dean of American Humorists.
            SamHar Pr.
Hassler, R. *see* Hassler, Rolf.
Hassler, Rolf.
    xHassler, R.
        Stereotaxis in Parkinson Syndrome.
            Springer-Verlag.
Hassler, Warren W.
    xHassler, Warren W.
        Commanders of the Army of the Potomac.
            Greenwood.
        Crisis at the Crossroads: The First Day at
            Gettysburg. U of Ala Pr.
        General George B. McClellan, Shield of the
            Union. Greenwood.
        The President As Commander-in-Chief. A-W.
Hassler, William W. *see* Hassler, William Woods.
Hassler, William Woods.
    xHassler, William W.
        Colonel John Pelham: Lee's Boy Artillerist. U
            of NC Pr.
Hassner. *see* Hassner, Pierre.
Hassner, Pierre.
    xHassner.
        Europe in the Age of Negotiation. Sage.
Hassouna, Hussein. *see* Hassouna, Hussein A.
Hassouna, Hussein A., 1937-
    xHassouna, Hussein.
        The League of Arab States & Regional
            Disputes: A Study of Middle East Conflicts.
            Oceana.
Hastenrath, S.
    xHastenrath, Stefan.
        The Climatic Atlas of the Indian Ocean. U of
            Wis Pr.
    xHastenrath, Stefan L.
        Climatic Atlas of the Tropical Atlantic &
            Eastern Pacific Oceans. U of Wis Pr.
Hastenrath, Stefan. *see* Hastenrath, S.
Hastenrath, Stefan L. *see* Hastenrath, S.
Hastie, John W.
    xHastie, John W.
        High Temperature Vapors: Science &
            Technology. Acad Pr.
Hastie, Reid.
    xHastie, Reid.
        ed. Person Memory: The Cognitive Basis of
            Social Perception. L Erlbaum Assocs.
Hastings, A. *see* Hastings, Adrian.
Hastings, Adrian.
    xHastings, A.
        A History of African Christianity: 1950-1975.
            Cambridge U Pr.
    xHastings, Adrian.

African Christianity. Seabury.
Church & Mission in Modern Africa. Fordham.
The Faces of God: Reflections on Church &
Society. Orbis Bks.

Hastings, Cecil, 1920-
xHastings, Cecil.
Approximations for Digital Computers.
Princeton U Pr.

Hastings, Donald W.
xHastings, Donald W.
A Doctor Speaks on Sexual Expression in
Marriage. Little.

Hastings, Glen E.
xHastings, Glen E.
The Primary Nurse Practitioner: A Multiple
Track Curriculum. Banyan Bks.

Hastings, James.
xHastings, James.
ed. Dictionary of the Bible. Scribner.

Hastings, Margaret.
xHastings, Margaret.
Court of Common Pleas in Fifteenth Century
England: A Study of Legal Administration &
Procedure. Shoe String.

Hastings, Max.
xHastings, Max.
Barricades in Belfast: The Fight for Civil Rights
in Northern Ireland. Taplinger.
Fire This Time: America's Year of Crisis.
Taplinger.

Hastings, Milo, 1884-1957
xHastings, Milo.
City of Endless Night. Hyperion Conn.
Hastings, Paul G. see Hastings, Paul Guiler.

Hastings, Paul Guiler, 1914-
xHastings, Paul G.
Introduction to Business. McGraw.
Personal Finance. McGraw.

Hastings, Phyllis.
xHastings, Phyllis.
House of the Twelve Caesars. Berkley Pub.

Hastings, Robert J.
xHastings, Robert J.
Christian Faith & Life. Broadman.

Hastings, Thomas, 1784-1872
xHastings, Thomas.
The History of Forty Choirs. AMS Pr.

Hastings, William M.
xHastings, William M.
How to Think About Social Problems: A
Primer for Citizens. Oxford U Pr.
Hastings, William T. see Hastings, William Thomson.

Hastings, William Thomson, 1881-
xHastings, William T.
Conrade Webb of Hampstead. Brown U Pr.

Hastorf, Albert H.
xHastorf, Albert H.
jt. auth. Person Perception. A-W.

Hasty, Ronald W.
xHasty, Ronald W.
Marketing. Har-Row.
Haswell. see Haswell, Chetwynd John Drake.

Haswell, Chetwynd John Drake, 1919-
xHaswell.
D-Day: Intelligence & Deception. Times Bks.
xHaswell, Jock.
Spies & Spymasters: A Concise History of
Intelligence. Thames Hudson.
Haswell, Jock. see Haswell, Chetwynd John Drake.

Hatada, Takashi, 1908-
xHatada, Takashi.
A History of Korea. ABC-Clio.

Hatch, Denison.
xHatch, Denison.
Cedarhurst Alley. Eriksson.
The Fingered City. Eriksson.
The Stork. BJ Pub Group.
The Stork. Morrow.

Hatch, Edwin, 1835-1889
xHatch, Edwin.
The Organization of the Early Christian
Churches: Eight Lectures Delivered Before
the University of Oxford in the Year 1880 on
the Foundation of the Late Rev. John
Bampton, M. A., Canon of Salisbury. B
Franklin.

Hatch, Elvin.
xHatch, Elvin.
Biography of a Small Town. Columbia U Pr.

Hatch, Elvin J.
xHatch, Elvin J.
Theories of Man & Culture. Columbia U Pr.

Hatch, Jane M.
xHatch, Jane M.
ed. American Book of Days. Wilson.
Hatch, Louis C. see Hatch, Louis Clinton.

Hatch, Louis Clinton, 1872-1931
xHatch, Louis C.
Administration of the American Revolutionary
Army. B Franklin.
History of the Vice-Presidency of the United
States. Greenwood.
Hatch, Raymond N. see Hatch, Raymond Norris.

Hatch, Raymond Norris.
xHatch, Raymond N.
ed. The Organization of Pupil Personnel
Programs-Issues & Practices. Mich St U Pr.

Hatch, Richard C.
xHatch, Richard C.
Experimental Chemistry. Van Nos Reinhold.

Hatch, Ronald B.
xHatch, Ronald B.
Crabbe's Arabesque: Social Drama in the
Poetry of George Crabbe. McGill-Queens U
Pr.
Hatcher, A. G. see Hatcher, Anna Granville.

Hatcher, Anna Granville, 1905-
xHatcher, A G
Reflexive Verbs, Latin, Old French, Modern
French. Johnson Repr.
Hatcher, Harlan H. see Hatcher, Harlan Henthone.

Hatcher, Harlan Henthone, 1898-
xHatcher, Harlan H.
Creating the Modern American Novel. Russell.

Hatcher, Hayes A., 1942-
xHatcher, Hayes A.
Correctional Casework & Counseling. P-H.
Hatcher, John B. see Hatcher, John Bell.

Hatcher, John Bell.
xHatcher, John B.
The Ceratopsia: Based on Preliminary Studies
by Othniel C. Marsh. Arno.
Hatcher, Mattie A. see Hatcher, Mattie Alice Austin.

Hatcher, Mattie Alice Austin.
xHatcher, Mattie A.
The Opening of Texas to Foreign Settlement,
1801-1821. Porcupine Pr.
Hatfield, Antoinette. see Hatfield, Antoninette
Kuzmanich.

Hatfield, Antoninette Kuzmanich.
xHatfield, Antoinette.
Food for Family & Friends. Word Bks.
Hatfield, David D. see Hatfield, David Daniel.

Hatfield, David Daniel, 1903-
xHatfield, David D.
The Dominguez Air Meet, 1910. Aviation.
Los Angeles Aeronautics, 1920-1929. Aviation.
Hatfield, Edwin F. see Hatfield, Edwin Francis.

Hatfield, Edwin Francis, 1807-1883
xHatfield, Edwin F.
Poets of the Church: A Series of Biographical
Sketches of Hymn-Writers, with Notes on
Their Hymns. Gale.

Hatfield, Henry Caraway, 1912-
xHatfield, Henry.
From "The Magic Mountain": Mann's Later
Masterpieces. Cornell U Pr.
Hatfield, Henry. see Hatfield, Henry Caraway.

Hatfield, Mark O., 1922-
xHatfield, Mark O.
Conflict & Conscience. Word Bks.

Hatfield, Philip M.
xHatfield, Phillip M.
Radiology of the Gallbladder & Bile Ducts.
Williams & Wilkins.
Hatfield, Phillip M. see Hatfield, Philip M.

Hatfield, Rab, 1937-
xHatfield, Rab.
Botticelli's Uffizi Adoration: A Study in
Pictorial Content. Princeton U Pr.

Hatfield, William E.
xHatfield, William E.
Problems in Structural Inorganic Chemistry.
Benjamin-Cummings.
Symmetry in Chemical Bonding & Structure.
Merrill.

Hathaway, Baxter, 1909-
xHathaway, Baxter.
The Age of Criticism: The Late Renaissance in
Italy. Greenwood.
Petulant Children. SBD.
Hathaway, Esse V. see Hathaway, Esse Virginia.

Hathaway, Esse Virginia, 1871-1939
xHathaway, Esse V.
Partners in Progress. Arno.

Hathaway, James, 1955-
xHathaway, James.
Foraging. SBD.

Hathaway, Jay.
xHathaway, Jay.
Children at Birth. Academy Pubns.

Hathaway, Lulu.
xHathaway, Lulu.
Partners in Teaching Older Children. Judson.

Hathaway, Nancy.
xHathaway, Nancy.
Halloween Crafts & Cookbook. Harvey.
Thanksgiving Crafts & Cookbook. Harvey.
Hathaway, Starke R. see Hathaway, Starke Rosecrans.

Hathaway, Starke Rosecrans.
xHathaway, Starke R.
Adolescent Personality & Behavior: MMPI
Patterns of Normal, Delinquent, Dropout &
Other Outcomes. U of Minn Pr.
Hathaway, William E. see Hathaway, William Ellison.

Hathaway, William Ellison.
xHathaway, William E.
Perinatal Coagulation. Grune.
Hathorn, Richmond Y. see Hathorn, Richmond Yancey.

Hathorn, Richmond Yancey, 1917-
xHathorn, Richmond Y.
Crowell's Handbook of Classical Drama. T Y
Crowell.

Hatlen, Theodore W.
xHatlen, Theodore W.
Drama: Principles & Plays. P-H.
Orientation to the Theatre. P-H.

Hatmon, Paul W.
xHatmon, Paul W.
Yesterday's Fire Engines. Lerner Pubns.

Hatry, Harry P.
xHatry, Harry P.
Practical Program Evaluation for State & Local
Government Officials. Urban Inst.

Hattaway, Herman.
xHattaway, Herman.
General Stephen D. Lee. U Pr of Miss.

Hatter, D. J.
xHatter, D. J.
Matrix Computer Methods of Vibration
Analysis. Halsted Pr.

Hattersley, Ralph.
xHattersley, Ralph.
Beginner's Guide to Color Photography.
Doubleday.
Hattery, Lowell H. see Hattery, Lowell Harold.

Hattery, Lowell Harold, 1916-
xHattery, Lowell H.

Executive Control & Data Processing.
Anderson Kramer.
Hatton. *see* Hatton, Corrine Loing.
Hatton, Austin L. *see* Hatton, Austin Linton.
Hatton, Austin Linton.
xHatton, Austin L.
A Calendar of Birds. Soccer.
Hatton, Corrine Loing.
xHatton.
Suicide: Assessment & Intervention. ACC.
Hatton, E. M.
xHatton, E. M.
The Tent Book. HM.
Hatton, Raymond R., 1932-
xHatton, Raymond R.
Bend in Central Oregon. Binford.
Hatton, Richard G. *see* Hatton, Richard George.
Hatton, Richard George, 1864-1926
xHatton, Richard G.
Figure Drawing. Dover.
Figure Drawing. Peter Smith.
Hattum, Roland J. Van. *see* Van Hattum, Rolland J.
Hattum, Rolland J. Van. *see* Van Hattum, Rolland J.
Hatvary, George E. *see* Hatvary, George Egon.
Hatvary, George Egon.
xHatvary, George E.
Horace Binney Wallace. Twayne.
Hatzfeld, Helmut A. *see* Hatzfeld, Helmut Anthony.
Hatzfeld, Helmut Anthony, 1892-
xHatzfeld, Helmut A.
A Critical Bibliography of the New Stylistics
Applied to the Romance Literatures,
1900-1952. Johnson Repr.
Literature Through Art: A New Approach to
French Literature.. U of NC Pr.
Hauberg, Clifford A.
xHauberg, Clifford A.
Puerto Rico & the Puerto Ricans. Hippocrene
Bks.
Puerto Rico & the Puerto Ricans. Twayne.
Haublein, Ernst, fl. 1971-
xHaublein, Ernst.
The Stanza. Methuen Inc.
Hauch, Edward F. *see* Hauch, Edward Franklin.
Hauch, Edward Franklin, 1879-
xHauch, Edward F.
Gottfried Keller As a Democratic Idealist.
AMS Pr.
Hauck, Paul. *see* Hauck, Paul A.
Hauck, Paul A.
xHauck, Paul.
Rational Management of Children. Libra.
xHauck, Paul A.
How to Do What You Want to Do: The Art of
Self Discipline. Westminster.
How to Stand up for Yourself. Westminster.
Marriage Is a Loving Business. Westminster.
Overcoming Depression. Westminster.
Overcoming Frustration & Anger. Westminster.
Overcoming Worry & Fear. Westminster.
Hauenstein. *see* Hauenstein, A. Dean.
Hauenstein, A. Dean.
xHauenstein.
World of Communications: Audiovisual Media.
McKnight.
Hauer, Mary. *see* Hauer, Mary G.
Hauer, Mary G.
xHauer, Mary.
Books, Libraries, & Research. Kendall-Hunt.
Hauerwas, Stanley, 1940-
xHauerwas, Stanley.
Character & the Christian Life: A Study in
Theological Ethics. Trinity U Pr.
Truthfulness & Tragedy: Further Investigations
in Christian Ethics. U of Notre Dame Pr.
Hauf, Harold D. *see* Hauf, Harold Dana.
Hauf, Harold Dana.
xHauf, Harold D.

Building Contracts for Design & Construction.
Wiley.
Hauff, Wilhelm, 1802-1827
xHauff, Wilhelm.
Tales. Arno.
Hauffe, Karl, 1913-
xHauffe, Karl.
Oxidation of Metals. Plenum Pub.
Haufrecht, Herbert, 1909-
xHaufrecht, Herbert.
Folk Songs in Settings by Master Composers.
Da Capo.
Haug, Edward J.
xHaug, Edward J.
Applied Optimal Design: Mechanical &
Structural Systems. Wiley.
Haug, F. M. *see* Haug, Finn-Mogens Smejda.
Haug, Finn-Mogens Smejda.
xHaug, F. M.
Sulphide Silver Pattern & Cytoarchitectonics of
Parahippocampal Areas in the Rat.
Springer-Verlag.
Haugaard, Erik C. *see* Haugaard, Erik Christian.
Haugaard, Erik Christian.
xHaugaard, Erik C.
Chase Me, Catch Nobody!. HM.
Cromwell's Boy. HM.
Hakon of Rogen's Saga. HM.
Hakon of Rogen's Saga. HM.
Little Fishes. HM.
Haugaard, Erik Christian. *see* Andersen, Hans Christian.
Haugen, Einar. *see* Haugen, Einar Ingvald.
Haugen, Einar Ingvald, 1906-
xHaugen, Einar.
Ibsen's Drama: Author to Audience. U of
Minn Pr.
Reading Norwegian. Spoken Lang Serv.
Haugh, James B. *see* Haugh, James Bertram.
Haugh, James Bertram.
xHaugh, James B.
Power & Influence in a Southern City:
Compared with the Classic Community
Power Studies of the Lynds, Hunter, Vidich
& Bensman, & Dahl. U Pr of Amer.
Haughey, Thomas Brace.
xHaughey, Tom B.
The Case of the Frozen Scream. Bethany Fell.
Haughey, Tom B. *see* Haughey, Thomas Brace.
Haughton, Claire S. *see* Haughton, Claire Shaver.
Haughton, Claire Shaver.
xHaughton, Claire S.
Green Immigrants: The Plants That
Transformed America. HarBraceJ.
Green Immigrants: The Plants That
Transformed America. HarBraceJ.
Haughton, Rosemary.
xHaughton, Rosemary.
Carpenter's Son. Macmillan.
The Drama of Salvation. Seabury.
On Trying to Be Human. Templegate.
Problems of Christian Marriage. Paulist Pr.
Tales from Eternity: The World of Fairytales &
the Spiritual Search. Continuum.
Haugland, Vern, 1908-
xHaugland, Vern.
The Eagle Squadrons: Yanks in the RAF
1940-1942. Ziff-Davis Pub.
Hauk, Minnie, 1852-1929
xHauk, Minnie.
Memories of a Singer. Arno.
Haukelid, Knut.
xHaukelid, Knut.
Attack on Telemark. Ballantine.
Haupt, Georges.
xHaupt, Georges.
Socialism & the Great War: The Collapse of
the Second International. Oxford U Pr.
Haupt, W. *see* Haupt, Wolfgang.
Haupt, Wolfgang.
xHaupt, W.

ed. Physiology of Movements. Springer-Verlag.
Hauptman, Tatjana.
xHauptman, Tatjana.
A Day in the Life of Petronella Pig. Mayflower
Bks.
Haurowitz, Felix, 1896-
xHaurowitz, Felix.
The Chemistry & Function of Proteins. Acad
Pr.
Hauser, Benjamin Gayelord.
xHauser, Gayelord.
Gayelord Hauser's New Treasury of Secrets.
Fawcett.
Look Younger, Live Longer. Fawcett.
Hauser, Gayelord. *see* Hauser, Benjamin Gayelord.
Hauser, Hillary.
xHauser, Hillary.
The Living World of the Reef. Walker & Co.
Hauser, M. M. *see* Hauser, Mark M.
Hauser, Mark M.
xHauser, M. M.
The Economics of Medical Care. Allen Unwin.
Hauser, Philip M. *see* Hauser, Philip Morris.
Hauser, Philip Morris, 1909-
xHauser, Philip M.
ed. World Population & Development:
Challenges & Prospects. Syracuse U Pr.
Hauser, Priscilla.
xHauser, Priscilla.
Priscilla Hauser Book of Tole & Decorative
Painting. Van Nos Reinhold.
Hauser, Ronald.
xHauser, Ronald.
Georg Buchner. Twayne.
Hauser, Thomas.
xHauser, Thomas.
The Execution of Charles Horman: An
American Sacrifice. HarBraceJ.
The Trial of Patrolman Thomas Shea. Viking
Pr.
Hauser, W. B. *see* Hauser, William B.
Hauser, William B.
xHauser, W. B.
Economic Institutional Change in Tokugawa
Japan: Osaka & the Kinai Cotton Trade.
Cambridge U Pr.
Hauser, William L.
xHauser, William L.
America's Army in Crisis: A Study in
Civil-Military Relations. Johns Hopkins.
Hausman, Gerald.
xHausman, Gerald.
Circle Meadow. Bookstore Pr.
Night Herding Song. Copper Canyon.
Hausman, Jim.
xHausman, Jim.
When I Was a Boy. Centennial.
xHausman, Tim.
When I Was a Boy. Cliffs.
Hausman, Ruth L.
xHausman, Ruth L.
Australia: Traditional Music in Its History.
Chris Mass.
Hausman, Tim. *see* Hausman, Jim.
Hausmann, Renee.
xHausmann, Renee.
Practical Rhetoric for College Writers.
Wadsworth Pub.
Hausner, H. H. *see* Hausner, Henry Herman.
Hausner, Henry Herman.
xHausner, H. H.
Fundamentals of Refractory Compounds.
Plenum Pub.
Hausner, Melvin.
xHausner, Melvin.
Lie Groups, Lie Algebras. Gordon.
Hausser, D. L. *see* Hausser, Doris L.
Hausser, Doris L.
xHausser, D. L.

Survey-Guided Development II: A Manual for
Consultants. Univ Assocs.

Haussig, H. W. *see* Haussig, Hans Wilhelm.

Haussig, Hans Wilhelm.
xHaussig, H. W.
tr. A History of Byzantine Civilization.
Humanities.

Haussman, Fay.
xHaussman, Fay.
Education in Brazil. Shoe String.

Hautala, Richard R.
xHautala, Richard R.
ed. Solar Energy: Chemical Conversion &
Storage. Humana.

Hautzig, Esther. *see* Hautzig, Esther (Rudomin).

Hautzig, Esther (Rudomin).
xHautzig, Esther.
At Home: A Visit in Four Languages.
Macmillan.
Endless Steppe: Growing up in Siberia. T Y
Crowell.
In the Park: An Excursion in Four Languages.
Macmillan.
Let's Make More Presents: Easy & Inexpensive
Gifts for Every Occasion. Macmillan.

Havard, C. W. *see* Havard, Cyril William Holmes.

Havard, Cyril William Holmes.
xHavard, C. W.
Lectures in Medicine. Green.

Havard, William C.
xHavard, William C.
ed. The Changing Politics of the South. La
State U Pr.

Havel, Vaclav.
xHavel, Vaclav.
The Memorandum. Grove.

Havelick, Franklin J.
xHavelick, Franklin J.
ed. Collective Bargaining: New Dimensions in
Labor Relations. Westview.

Haveliwala, Yoosuf A.
xHaveliwala, Yoosuf A.
Common Sense in Therapy: A Handbook for
the Mental Health Worker. Brunner Mazel.

Havelock, Eric A. *see* Havelock, Eric Alfred.

Havelock, Eric Alfred.
xHavelock, Eric A.
ed. Communication Arts in the Ancient World.
Hastings.
The Greek Concept of Justice: From Its
Shadow in Homer to Its Substance in Plato.
Harvard U Pr.

Havelock, Ronald G.
xHavelock, Ronald G.
The Change Agent's Guide to Innovation in
Education. Educ Tech Pubns.
Planning for Innovation Through Dissemination
& Utilization of Knowledge. U of Mich Soc
Res.

Havelock, T. H. *see* Havelock, Thomas Henry.

Havelock, Thomas Henry, Sir, 1877-
xHavelock, T. H.
The Propagation of Disturbances in Dispersive
Media. Hafner.

Haveman, Robert H.
xHaveman, Robert H.
ed. A Decade of Federal Antipoverty
Programs: Achievements, Failures & Lessons.
Acad Pr.
The Economics of the Public Sector. Wiley.
ed. Public Expenditure & Policy Analysis.
Rand.
Unemployment, Idle Capacity, & the
Evaluation of Public Expenditures: National
& Regional Analyses. Johns Hopkins.

Havemann, Ernest.
xHavemann, Ernest.
Age of Psychology. S&S.

Haven, Richard, 1924-
xHaven, Richard.

Patterns of Consciousness: An Essay on
Coleridge. U of Mass Pr.

Haven, Tom De. *see* De Haven, Tom.

Havener, William H.
xHavener, William H.
Ocular Pharmacology. Mosby.
Synopsis of Ophthalmology. Mosby.
xHavener, William Lh.
Do You Really Need Eye Surgery?. C C
Thomas.

Havener, William Lh. *see* Havener, William H.

Havens, Daniel F., 1931-
xHavens, Daniel F.
Columbian Muse of Comedy: The
Development of a Native Tradition in Early
American Social Comedy 1787-1845. S Ill U
Pr.

Havens, David.
xHavens, David.
The Woodburners Handbook. Harpswell Pr.

Havens, George R. *see* Havens, George Remington.

Havens, George Remington, 1890-
xHavens, George R.
Abbe Prevost & English Literature. Haskell.
Abbe Prevost & English Literature. Kraus
Repr.
The Age of Ideas: From Reaction to
Revolution in Eighteenth Century France.
Irvington.

Havens, Leston L.
xHavens, Leston L.
Approaches to the Mind: Movement of the
Psychiatric Schools from Sects Toward
Science. Little.

Havens, Munsen A. *see* Havens, Munson Aldrich.
Havens, Munson A. *see* Havens, Munson Aldrich.

Havens, Munson Aldrich, 1873-
xHavens, Munsen A.
Horace Walpole & the Strawberry Hill Press
1757-1789. Arden Lib.
xHavens, Munson A.
Horace Walpole & the Strawberry Hill Press.
Folcroft.

Havens, Murray C. *see* Havens, Murray Clark.

Havens, Murray Clark.
xHavens, Murray C.
Assassination & Terrorism: Their Modern
Dimensions. Sterling Swift.

Havens, Ronald A.
xHavens, Ronald A.
How to Train Humans: A Behavior
Modification Manual. Scholium Intl.

Havens, Thomas R. *see* Havens, Thomas R. H.

Havens, Thomas R. H.
xHavens, Thomas R.
Farm & Nation in Modern Japan: Agrarian
Nationalism, 1870-1940. Princeton U Pr.
Nishi Amane & Modern Japanese Thought.
Princeton U Pr.
Valley of Darkness: The Japanese People &
World War Two. Norton.

Haver, Ron.
xHaver, Ronald.
David O. Selznick's Hollywood. Knopf.

Haver, Ronald. *see* Haver, Ron.

Haverfield, Francis J. *see* Haverfield, Francis John.

Haverfield, Francis John.
xHaverfield, Francis J.
The Romanization of Roman Britain.
Greenwood.

Havers, J. *see* Havers, John Alan.

Havers, John Alan.
xHavers, J.
Handbook of Heavy Construction. McGraw.

Haverstock, Mary S. *see* Haverstock, Mary Sayre.

Haverstock, Mary Sayre.
xHaverstock, Mary S.
An American Bestiary. Abrams.

Havighurst, A. F. *see* Havighurst, Alfred F.

Havighurst, Alfred F.
xHavighurst, A. F.
Modern England: 1901-1970. Cambridge U Pr.
xHavighurst, Alfred F.
Britain in Transition: The Twentieth-Century.
U of Chicago Pr.

Havighurst, Clark C.
xHavighurst, Clark C.
ed. Medical Progress & the Law. Oceana.

Havighurst, Robert J. *see* Havighurst, Robert James.

Havighurst, Robert James, 1900-
xHavighurst, Robert J.
American Higher Education in the 1960's.
Greenwood.
American Indian & White Children: A
Sociopsychological Investigation. U of
Chicago Pr.
Developmental Tasks & Education. Longman.
Society & Education. Allyn.

Havighurst, Walter, 1901-
xHavighurst, Walter.
The Great Lakes Reader. Macmillan.
Masters of the Modern Short Story. Darby
Bks.
ed. Midwest & Great Plains. Fideler.
Proud Prisoner. Williamsburg.
xHavighurst, Walter E.
ed. Masters of the Modern Short Story.
HarBraceJ.

Havighurst, Walter E. *see* Havighurst, Walter.

Haviland, Diana.
xHaviland, Diana.
The Moreland Legacy. Bobbs.
The Moreland Legacy. Fawcett.
Passionate Pretenders. Fawcett.

Haviland, Henry F. *see* Haviland, Henry Field.

Haviland, Henry Field, 1919-
xHaviland, Henry F.
The Political Role of the General Assembly.
Greenwood.

Haviland, John B. *see* Haviland, John Beard.

Haviland, John Beard.
xHaviland, John B.
Gossip, Reputation, & Knowledge in
Zinacantan. U of Chicago Pr.

Haviland, R. P. *see* Haviland, Robert P.
Haviland, Robert. *see* Haviland, Robert P.

Haviland, Robert P.
xHaviland, R. P.
Build-It Book of Digital Electronic Timepieces.
TAB Bks.
xHaviland, Robert.
Build-It Book of Miniature Test &
Measurement Instruments. TAB Bks.
xHaviland, Robert P.
Engineering Reliability & Long Life Design.
Van Nos Reinhold.
How to Design, Build & Program Your Own
Working Computer System. TAB Bks.

Haviland, Virginia, 1911-
xHaviland, Virginia.
The Fairy Tale Treasury. Coward.
The Fairy Tale Treasury. Dell.
Favorite Fairy Tales Told in Czechoslovakia.
Little.
Favorite Fairy Tales Told in India. Little.
Favorite Fairy Tales Told in Italy. Little.
Favorite Fairy Tales Told in Japan. Little.
Favorite Fairy Tales Told in Scotland. Little.
Favorite Fairy Tales Told in Spain. Little.
Favorite Fairy Tales Told in Sweden. Little.
ed. North American Legends. Philomel.
xHaviland, Viriginia.
Children & Literature: Views & Reviews. Scott
F.

Haviland, Viriginia. *see* Haviland, Virginia.
Haviland, W. A. *see* Haviland, William A.

Haviland, William A.
xHaviland, W. A.

Anthropology. HR&W.
xHaviland, William A.
Cultural Anthropology. HR&W.
Human Evolution & Prehistory. HR&W.
Havlice, Patricia P. *see* Havlice, Patricia Pate.
Havlice, Patricia Pate.
xHavlice, Patricia P.
Index to American Author Bibliographies.
Scarecrow.
Index to Artistic Biography. Scarecrow.
Index to Literary Biography. Scarecrow.
Popular Song Index. Scarecrow.
Popular Song Index: First Supplement.
Scarecrow.
Havner, Vance, 1901-
xHavner, Vance.
Hope Thou in God. Revell.
In Times Like These. Revell.
Moments of Decision. Revell.
Pepper 'n Salt. Revell.
Though I Walk Through the Valley. Revell.
Havner, Vance. *see* Havner, Vance Houston.
Havner, Vance Houston, 1901-
xHavner, Vance.
Peace in the Valley. Revell.
Havoc, June.
xHavoc, June.
More Havoc. Har-Row.
Havran, Martin J.
xHavran, Martin J.
The Catholics in Caroline England. Stanford U
Pr.
Havrevold, Finn.
xHavrevold, Finn.
Undertow. Atheneum.
Havrilesky, Thomas M.
xHavrilesky, Thomas M.
ed. Current Perspectives in Banking:
Operations, Management, & Regulation.
AHM Pub.
Monetary Macroeconomics. AHM Pub.
Hawaii. University, Honolulu.
xUniversity of Hawaii, Honolulu.
Dictionary Catalog of the Hawaiian
Collection-Sinclair Library. G K Hall.
Hawaii. University, Honolulu. Dept. of Geography.
xDepartment of Geography, University of Hawaii.
Compiled by Atlas of Hawaii. U Pr of Hawaii.
Hawaii. University, Honolulu. Land Study Bureau.
xLand Study Bureau, Univ. of Hawaii.
Compensible Regulations: Their Potential for
Land Use & Development Control in Hawaii.
U Pr of Hawaii.
Kauai Lands Classified by Physical Qualities
for Urban Usage. U Pr of Hawaii.
Land Use & Productivity Data, State of
Hawaii, 1968. U Pr of Hawaii.
Land Use Classification & Determination of
Highest & Best Use of Hawaii's Agricultural
Lands. U Pr of Hawaii.
Maui Lands Classified by Physical Qualities for
Urban Usage. U Pr of Hawaii.
Molokai: Present & Potential Land Use. U Pr
of Hawaii.
Haward, R. N. *see* Haward, Robert Nobbs.
Haward, Robert Nobbs, 1914-
xHaward, R. N.
ed. Developments in Polymerisation.
Burgess-Intl Ideas.
Haweis, E. *see* Haweis, Mary Eliza Joy.
Haweis, H. R. *see* Haweis, Hugh Reginald.
Haweis, Hugh Reginald, 1839-1901
xHaweis, H. R.
American Humorists. Folcroft.
Haweis, Mary Eliza Joy, 1852-1898
xHaweis, E.
The Art of Decoration. Garland Pub.
Hawes, Adeline B. *see* Hawes, Adeline Belle.
Hawes, Adeline Belle, 1857-1932
xHawes, Adeline B.

Citizens of Long Ago: Essays on Life & Letters
in the Roman Empire. Arno.
Hawes, Bill, 1931-
xHawes, Bill.
The Puppet Book. Beta Bk.
Hawes, G. *see* Hawes, Gordon K.
Hawes, Gene R.
xHawes, Gene R.
How to Get the Money to Pay for College.
McKay.
Hawes, Gordon. *see* Hawes, Gordon K.
Hawes, Gordon K.
xHawes, G.
Atlas of Man & Religion. British Bk Ctr.
xHawes, Gordon.
Atlas of Man & Religion. Pergamon.
Hawes, H. W. *see* Hawes, Hubert William Richmond.
Hawes, Hubert William Richmond.
xHawes, H. W.
Planning the Primary School Curriculum in
Developing Countries. Unipub.
Hawes, Joseph. *see* Hawes, Joseph M.
Hawes, Joseph M.
xHawes, Joseph.
ed. Law & Order in American History.
Kennikat.
xHawes, Joseph M.
Children in Urban Society: Juvenile
Delinquency in Nineteenth-Century America.
Oxford U Pr.
Hawes, Judy.
xHawes, Judy.
Fireflies in the Night. T Y Crowell.
My Daddy Longlegs. T Y Crowell.
Hawes, William, 1931-
xHawes, William.
The Performer in Mass Media: In Media
Professions & in the Community. Hastings.
Hawk, Emory Q. *see* Hawk, Emory Quinter.
Hawk, Emory Quinter, 1892-
xHawk, Emory Q.
Economic History of the South. Greenwood.
Hawk, Grace E.
xHawk, Grace E.
Pembroke College in Brown University: The
First Seventy-Five Years, 1891-1966. Brown
U Pr.
Hawke, David F. *see* Hawke, David Freeman.
Hawke, David Freeman.
xHawke, David F.
Paine. Har-Row.
Hawke, G. *see* Hawke, Gary Richard.
Hawke, Gary Richard.
xHawke, G.
Economics for Historians. Cambridge U Pr.
Hawke, Sharryl.
xHawke, Sharryl.
One Child by Choice. P-H.
Hawker, Geoffrey. *see* Hawker, Geoffrey N.
Hawker, Geoffrey N.
xHawker, Geoffrey.
Politics & Policy in Australia. U of Queensland
Pr.
Hawkes, J. *see* Hawkes, Jacquetta Hopkins.
Hawkes, J. G. *see* Hawkes, John Gregory.
Hawkes, Jacquetta. *see* Hawkes, Jacquetta Hopkins.
Hawkes, Jacquetta Hopkins, 1910-
xHawkes, J.
Atlas of Ancient Archaeology. McGraw.
xHawkes, Jacquetta.
The Atlas of Early Man. St Martin.
Nothing But or Something More. U of Wash
Pr.
World of the Past. S&S.
Hawkes, John, 1925-
xHawkes, John.

Cannibal. New Directions.
Death, Sleep & the Traveler. New Directions.
Innocent Party: Four Short Plays. New
Directions.
Lime Twig. New Directions.
The Owl. New Directions.
Hawkes, John Gregory.
xHawkes, J. G.
ed. Conservation & Agriculture. Allanheld.
Hawkes, Ken.
xHawkes, Ken.
Sark. David & Charles.
Hawkes, P. W.
xHawkes, P. W.
ed. Computer Processing of Electron
Microscope Images. Springer-Verlag.
Hawkes, Terence.
xHawkes, Terence.
Structuralism & Semiotics. U of Cal Pr.
Hawkesworth, John.
xHawkesworth, John.
In My Lady's Chamber. G K Hall.
Upstairs Downstairs. Dell.
Upstairs Downstairs. G K Hall.
Hawkey, William S.
xHawkey, William S.
Living with Plants: A Book of Home
Decorating & Plant Care. Morrow.
Hawking, S. W.
xHawking, S. W.
ed. General Relativity: An Einstein Centenary
Survey. Cambridge U Pr.
Hawkins, Anthony H. *see* Hawkins, Anthony Hope.
Hawkins, Anthony Hope, Sir, 1863-1933
xHawkins, Anthony H.
Cut & a Kiss. Arno.
Dolly Dialogues. Arno.
Hawkins, Arthur.
xHawkins, Arthur.
The Architectural Cookbook. McGraw.
Hawkins, Brett. *see* Hawkins, Brett W.
Hawkins, Brett W.
xHawkins, Brett.
Ethnic Factor in American Politics. Merrill.
Politics & Urban Policies. Bobbs.
Hawkins, Christopher.
xHawkins, Christopher.
Adventures of Christopher Hawkins. Arno.
Hawkins, Clark A.
xHawkins, Clark A.
The Field Price Regulation of Natural Gas. U
Presses Fla.
Statistical Analysis: Applications to Business &
Economics. Har-Row.
Hawkins, Clifford. *see* Hawkins, Clifford J.
Hawkins, Clifford J.
xHawkins, Clifford.
Absolute Configuration of Metal Complexes.
Krieger.
Hawkins, Clifford W.
xHawkins, Clifford W.
Log of the Huia. Intl Pubns Serv.
Hawkins, Cora F. *see* Hawkins, Cora Frear.
Hawkins, Cora Frear, 1887-
xHawkins, Cora F.
Buggies, Blizzards, & Babies. Iowa St U Pr.
Hawkins, D. F. *see* Hawkins, Denis Frank.
Hawkins, Darnell F. *see* Hawkins, Darnell Felix.
Hawkins, Darnell Felix, 1941-
xHawkins, Darnell F.
Nonresponse in Detroit Area Study Surveys: A
Ten-Year Analysis. U NC Inst Res Soc Sci.
Hawkins, David, 1913-
xHawkins, David.
The Informed Vision: Essays on Learning &
Human Nature. Agathon.
Hawkins, David F.
xHawkins, David F.

Accounting for Leases. Finan Exec.
Corporate Financial Reporting: Text & Cases.
Irwin.
Hawkins, Denis Frank.
xHawkins, D. F.
Human Fertility Control: The Theory &
Practice. Butterworths.
Hawkins, Denis J. *see* Hawkins, Denis John Bernard.
Hawkins, Denis John Bernard, 1906-
xHawkins, Denis J.
The Essentials of Theism. Greenwood.
xHawkins, Dennis J.
Approach to Philosophy. Magi Bks.
Hawkins, Dennis J. *see* Hawkins, Denis John Bernard.
Hawkins, Desmond, 1908-
xHawkins, Desmond.
Avalon & Sedgemoor. David & Charles.
Thomas Hardy. Folcroft.
Hawkins, Freda.
xHawkins, Freda.
Canada & Immigration: Public Policy & Public
Concern. McGill-Queens U Pr.
Hawkins, Frederick. *see* Hawkins, Frederick William.
Hawkins, Frederick W. *see* Hawkins, Frederick William.
Hawkins, Frederick William, 1849-1900
xHawkins, Frederick.
Annals of the French Stage from Its Origin to
the Death of Racine. Scholarly.
French Stage in the Eighteenth Century.
Scholarly.
xHawkins, Frederick W.
Annals of the French Stage from Its Origin to
the Death of Racine. Greenwood.
Annals of the French Stage from Its Origin to
the Death of Racine. Haskell.
French Stage in the Eighteenth Century.
Greenwood.
French Stage in the Eighteenth Century.
Haskell.
Hawkins, Gary. *see* Hawkins, Karen.
Hawkins, Gordon, 1919-
xHawkins, Gordon.
The Prison: Policy & Practice. U of Chicago
Pr.
Hawkins, J. K. *see* Hawkins, Joseph K.
Hawkins, John N.
xHawkins, John N.
Teacher's Resource Handbook for Latin
American Studies: An Annotated
Bibliography of Curriculum Materials. UCLA
Lat Am Ctr.
Hawkins, Joseph, b. 1772
xHawkins, Joseph.
History of a Voyage to the Coast of Africa &
Travels into the Interior of That Country,
Etc.: 1796-1797. Biblio Dist.
A History of a Voyage to the Coast of Africa
& Travels into the Interior of That Country.
Metro Bks.
Hawkins, Joseph K.
xHawkins, J. K.
Circuit Design of Digital Computers. Krieger.
Hawkins, Karen.
xHawkins, Gary.
jt. auth. Bicycle Touring in Europe. Pantheon.
xHawkins, Karen.
Bicycle Touring in Europe. Pantheon.
Hawkins, Laurence F. *see* Hawkins, Laurence Faulkner.
Hawkins, Laurence Faulkner, 1902-
xHawkins, Laurence F.
Notescript. Har-Row.
Hawkins, Leslie V.
xHawkins, Leslie V.
Art Metal & Enameling. Bennett Co.
Hawkins, Mark.
xHawkins, Mark.
A Lion Under Her Bed. HR&W.
Hawkins, Reginald.
xHawkins, Reginald.

Production of Micro-Forms. Greenwood.
Hawkins, Richard.
xHawkins, Richard.
The Creation of Deviance: Interpersonal &
Organizational Determinants. Merrill.
Hawkins, Van, 1946-
xHawkins, Van R.
The Historic Triangle: An Illustrated History of
Jamestown, Williamsburg & Yorktown.
Donning Co.
Hawkins, Van R. *see* Hawkins, Van.
Hawkins, Walter E. *see* Hawkins, Walter Everette.
Hawkins, Walter Everette.
xHawkins, Walter E.
Chords & Discords. AMS Pr.
Hawkinson, John, 1912-
xHawkinson, John.
illus. A Ball of Clay. A Whitman.
Collect, Print & Paint from Nature. A
Whitman.
illus. Pastels Are Great. A Whitman.
jt. auth. Rhythms, Music & Instruments to
Make. A Whitman.
Hawkridge, Emma.
xHawkridge, Emma.
Indian Gods & Kings: The Story of a Living
Past. Arno.
Hawksworth, Henry.
xHawksworth, Henry.
The Five of Me: The Autobiography of a
Multiple Personality. PB.
Hawley, Amos H. *see* Hawley, Amos Henry.
Hawley, Amos Henry.
xHawley, Amos H.
Human Ecology: A Theory of Community
Structure. Wiley.
Societal Growth: Processes & Implications
Free Pr.
Hawley, C. E. *see* Hawley, Claude Edward.
Hawley, Cameron.
xHawley, Cameron.
Cash McCall. Queens Hse.
Hawley, Charles A. *see* Hawley, Charles Arthur.
Hawley, Charles Arthur, 1889-
xHawley, Charles A.
Critical Examination of the Peshitta Version of
the Book of Ezra. AMS Pr.
Hawley, Claude Edward.
xHawley, C. E.
ed. Administrative Questions & Political
Answers. Van Nos Reinhold.
Hawley, J. Richard.
xHawley, J. Richard.
ed. Experiencing-Living-Sharing Christ:
Sermons on the Evangelistic Life Style.
Judson.
Hawley, John T. *see* Hawley, John Theodore.
Hawley, John Theodore.
xHawley, John T.
Precious Metals & the Economic Future of
Mankind. Inst Econ Pol.
Hawley, Robert C.
xHawley, Robert C.
Building Motivation in the Classroom: A
Structured Approach to Improving Student
Achievement. ERA Pr.
Developing Human Potential: A Handbook of
Activities for Personal & Social Growth.
ERA Pr.
Hawley, Ruth.
xHawley, Ruth.
Omani Silver. Longman.
Hawley, W. D. *see* Hawley, Willis D.
Hawley, Walter A. *see* Hawley, Walter Augustus.
Hawley, Walter Augustus, 1863-1920
xHawley, Walter A.

Oriental Rugs Antique & Modern. Dover.
Oriental Rugs, Antique & Modern. Peter
Smith.
Hawley, Willis D.
xHawley, W. D.
Improving the Quality of Urban Management.
Sage.
Improving Urban Management. Sage.
Theoretical Perspectives on Urban Politics.
P-H.
Haworth, Josephine.
xHaworth, Josephine.
Riding from Scratch. St Martin.
Haworth, Lawrence.
xHaworth, Lawrence.
Good City. Ind U Pr.
Haworth, Mary R. *see* Haworth, Mary Robbins.
Haworth, Mary Robbins, 1911-
xHaworth, Mary R.
ed. Child Psychotherapy: Practice & Theory.
Basic.
Hawrylyshyn, Oli.
xHawrylyshyn, Oli.
Planning for Economic Development: The
Construction & Use of a Multisectoral Model
for Tunisia. Praeger.
Hawthorn, Audrey.
xHawthorn, Audrey.
Kwakiutl Art. U of Wash Pr.
Hawthorn, Geoffrey.
xHawthorn, Geoffrey.
ed. Population & Development. Biblio Dist.
Hawthorn, Jeremy.
xHawthorn, Jeremy.
Identity & Relationship: A Contribution to
Marxist Theory of Literary Criticism.
Norwood Edns.
Hawthorne, Julian, 1846-1934
xHawthorne, Julian.
Confessions & Criticisms. AMS Pr.
Confessions & Criticisms. Folcroft.
David Poindexter's Disappearance. Arno.
Nathaniel Hawthorne & His Wife: A
Biography. Shoe String.
One of Those Coincidences, & Ten Other
Stories. Arno.
Hawthorne, Mary E. *see* Hawthorne, Mary Elizabeth.
Hawthorne, Mary Elizabeth.
xHawthorne, Mary E.
Community Colleges & Primary Health Care:
A Study of Allied Health Education Report.
Am Assn Comm Jr Coll.
Hawthorne, Nathaniel.
xHawthorne, Nathaniel.

American Notebooks. Ohio St U Pr.
The House of Seven Gables. Brown Bk.
The House of Seven Gables. Dutton.
House of Seven Gables. WSP.
House of Seven Gables. HM.
House of Seven Gables. Regents Pub.
House of the Seven Gables. Macmillan.
The House of the Seven Gables. Ohio St U Pr.
House of the Seven Gables. NAL.
The House of the Seven Gables. Pendulum Pr.
House of the Seven Gables. Airmont.
House of the Seven Gables. Dodd.
The House of the Seven Gables.
  McDougal-Littell.
House of the Seven Gables. Norton.
House of the Seven Gables. PB.
House of the Seven Gables. AMSCO Sch.
Life of Franklin Pierce. Mss Info.
Life of Franklin Pierce. Somerset Pub.
Portable Hawthorne. Penguin.
The Portable Hawthorne. Viking Pr.
The Scarlet Letter. Abaris Bks.
The Scarlet Letter. Brown Bk.
Scarlet Letter. Dutton.
Scarlet Letter. Fleet.
The Scarlet Letter. G K Hall.
Scarlet Letter. HM.
Scarlet Letter. HR&W.
The Scarlet Letter. Modern Lib.
The Scarlet Letter. Norton.
The Scarlet Letter. Ohio St U Pr.
Scarlet Letter. NAL.
Scarlet Letter. Pendulum Pr.
The Scarlet Letter. Schol Bk Serv.
The Scarlet Letter. Bantam.
Scarlet Letter. Airmont.
Scarlet Letter. AMSCO Sch.
Scarlet Letter. Dodd.
Scarlet Letter. Har-Row.
Scarlet Letter. HM.
Scarlet Letter. Norton.
The Scarlet Letter. WSP.
Tales, Sketches, & Other Papers. Arno.
Tanglewood Tales. Biblio Dist.
Tanglewood Tales. G&D.
Tanglewood Tales. Airmont.
True Stories from History & Biography. Ohio
  St U Pr.
Twice-Told Tales. Ohio St U Pr.
Twice Told Tales. Airmont.
A Wonder Book. Biblio Dist.
Wonder Book. Airmont.
Wonder Book & Tanglewood Tales. Ohio St U
  Pr.
Hawthorne, W. R. see Hawthorne, William R.
Hawthorne, William R.
  xHawthorne, W. R.
  ed. Aerodynamics of Turbines & Compressors.
    Princeton U Pr.
Hawton, Hector, 1901-
  xHawton, Hector.
  Feast of Unreason. Greenwood.
Hawtrey, Ralph G. see Hawtrey, Ralph George.
Hawtrey, Ralph George, Sir, 1879-
  xHawtrey, Ralph G.
  Art of Central Banking. Biblio Dist.
  Art of Central Banking. Kelley.
  The Economic Problem. Hyperion Conn.
  The Gold Standard in Theory & Practice.
    Greenwood.
  Good & Bad Trade: An Inquiry into the
    Causes of Trade Fluctuations. Kelley.
Hax, A. see Hax, Arnoldo C.
Hax, Arnoldo C.
  xHax, A.
  Studies in Operations Management. Elsevier.
Haxby, J. A. see Haxby, James A.
Haxby, James A.
  xHaxby, J. A.

Coins of Canada. Western Pub.
Haxtun, Annie A. see Haxtun, Annie Arnoux.
Haxtun, Annie Arnoux.
  xHaxtun, Annie A.
  Signers of the Mayflower Compact. Genealog
    Pub.
Hay, Alex.
  xHay, Alex.
  The Mechanics of Golf. St Martin.
  Skills & Tactics of Golf. Arco.
Hay, Clarence. see Hay, Clarence L.
Hay, Clarence L.
  xHay, Clarence.
  The Maya & Their Neighbors: Essays on
    Middle American Anthropology &
    Archaeology. Peter Smith.
  xHay, Clarence L.
  ed. The Maya & Their Neighbors: Essays on
    Middle American Anthropology &
    Archaeology. Dover.

Hay, Denys.

  xHay, Denys.
  The Church in Italy in the Fifteenth Century.
    Cambridge U Pr.

  ed. The Renaissance Debate. Krieger.
Hay, Doddy.
  xHay, Doddy.
  Hit the Silk. S G Phillips.
Hay, Donald A.
  xHay, Donald A.
  Industrial Economics: Theory & Evidence.
    Oxford U Pr.
Hay, George.
  xHay, George.
  Architecture of Scotland. Routledge & Kegan.
  Two Essays on the Liberty of the Press. Da
    Capo.
Hay, George E. see Hay, George Edward.
Hay, George Edward, 1914-
  xHay, George E.
  Vector & Tensor Analysis. Dover.
Hay, Henrietta.
  xHay, Henrietta.
  Clay Pot Cooking. Greene.
Hay, J. M. see Hay, John Mckay.
Hay, J. R. see Hay, J. Roy.
Hay, J. Roy.
  xHay, J. R.
  The Development of the British Welfare State,
    1880-1975. St Martin.
Hay, James, 1838-1904
  xHay, James.
  Johnson: His Characteristics & Aphorisms.
    Folcroft.
  Swift: The Mystery of His Life & Love.
    Folcroft.
Hay, John, 1838-1905
  xHay, John.
  Addresses of John Hay. Arno.
  Castilian Days. AMS Pr.
  Castilian Days. R West.
  Castilian Days. Scholars Ref Lib.
  The Great Beach. Norton.
  The Run. Norton.
  The Run. G K Hall.
Hay, John Mckay.
  xHay, J. M.
  Reactive Free Radicals. Acad Pr.
Hay, Leon E. see Hay, Leon Edwards.
Hay, Leon Edwards.
  xHay, Leon E.
  Governmental Accounting. Irwin.
Hay, Roy.
  xHay, Roy.

The Color Dictionary of Flowers & Plants for
  Home & Garden. Crown.
  ed. Practical Gardening Encyclopedia. Van Nos
    Reinhold.
Hay, William W. see Hay, William Walter.
Hay, William Walter, 1908-
  xHay, William W.
  Railroad Engineering. Wiley.
Hayaishi, Osamu, 1920-
  xHayaishi, Osamu.
  ed. Oxygenases. Acad Pr.
Hayakawa, Masao, 1925-
  xHayakawa, Masao.
  The Garden Art of Japan. Weatherhill.
Hayakawa, S. see Hayakawa, Satio.
Hayakawa, S. I. see Hayakawa, Samuel Ichiye.
Hayakawa, Samuel I. see Hayakawa, Samuel Ichiye.
Hayakawa, Samuel Ichiye.
  xHayakawa, S. I.
  ed. Dimensions of Meaning. Bobbs.
  xHayakawa, Samuel I.
  Symbol, Status, & Personality. HarBraceJ.
Hayakawa, Satio, 1923-
  xHayakawa, S.
  Cosmic Ray Physics: Nuclear & Astrophysical
    Aspects. Krieger.
Hayami, Itaru, 1933-
  xHayami, Itaru.
  A Systematic Survey of the Mesozoic Bivalvia
    from Japan. Intl Schol Bk Serv.
  Systematic Survey of the Paleozoic & Mesozoic
    Gastropoda & Paleozoic Bivalvia from Japan.
    Intl Schol Bk Serv.
Hayami, y Ujir O.
  xHayami, Yujiro.
  Agricultural Development: An International
    Perspective. Johns Hopkins.
Hayami, Yujiro. see Hayami, y Ujir O.
Hayashi, Ry Oichi, 1918-
  xHayashi, Ryoichi.
  The Silk Road & the Shoso-in. Weatherhill.
Hayashi, Ryoichi. see Hayashi, Ry Oichi.
Hayashi, Taizo, 1922-
  xHayashi, Taizo.
  Guide to Japanese Taxes: 1975-76. Intl Pubns
    Serv.
  Guide to Japanese Taxes, 1978-79. Rothman.
Hayashi, Tetsumaro.
  xHayashi, Tetsumaro.
  An Index to Arthur Miller Criticism.
    Scarecrow.
  Steinbeck's Literary Dimension: A Guide to
    Comparative Studies. Scarecrow.
Hayashiya, Seizo.
  xHayashiya, Seizo.
  Chinese Ceramics from Japanese Collections:
    T'ang Through Ming Dynasties. Weatherhill.
Hayat, M. A., 1936-
  xHayat, M. A.
  Introduction to Biological Scanning Electron
    Microscopy. Univ Park.
  xHayat, M. Arif.
  Principles & Techniques of Electron
    Microscopy: Biological Applications. Van
    Nos Reinhold.
  Principles & Techniques of Scanning Electron
    Microscopy. Van Nos Reinhold.
Hayat, M. Arif. see Hayat, M. A.
Haycock, G. Sibley. see Haycock, George Sibley.
Haycock, George Sibley.
  xHaycock, G. Sibley.
  The Teaching of Speech. Alexander Graham.
Haycox, Ernest.
  xHaycox, Ernest.

Action by Night. NAL.
Adventurers. Am Repr-Rivercity Pr.
By Rope & Lead. Am Repr-Rivercity Pr.
Canyon Passage. Gregg.
Dead Man Range. G K Hall.
The Earthbreakers. Am Repr-Rivercity Pr.
The Earthbreakers. Gregg.
Guns up. Belmont-Tower.
The Last Rodeo. Am Repr-Rivercity Pr.
Rawhide Range. Am Repr-Rivercity Pr.
Return of a Fighter. G K Hall.
Return of a Fighter. NAL.
Whispering Range. Am Repr-Rivercity Pr.

Haycraft, John.
xHaycraft, John.
Introduction to English Language Teaching.
Longman.

Hayden, Alice H. see Hayden, Alice Hazel.

Hayden, Alice Hazel.
xHayden, Alice H.
Systematic Thinking About Education. Phi
Delta Kappa.

Hayden, Arthur, 1868-1946
xHayden, Arthur.
Chats on Old Sheffield Plate. Charles River
Bks.

Hayden Book Company.
xHayden Editorial Staff.
CBers' Five-Star, Ten-Pounder Wordbook (a
Guide to CB Land for Bear Hunters, Cadillac
Cowboys, & Foxy Ladies). Hayden.

Hayden, Donald E.
xHayden, Donald E.
ed. Classics in Composition. Philos Lib.
ed. Classics in Linguistics. Philos Lib.
ed. Classics in Semantics. Arno.

Hayden Editorial Staff. see Hayden Book Company.

Hayden, George A., 1939-
xHayden, George A.
tr. Crime & Punishment in Medieval Chinese
Drama: Three Judge Pao Plays of the Yuan
& Ming Dynasties. Harvard U Pr.

Hayden, J. M. see Hayden, James Michael.

Hayden, James Michael, 1934-
xHayden, J. M.
France & the Estates General of 1614.
Cambridge U Pr.

Hayden, Naura.
xHayden, Naura.
Isle of View. Arbor Hse.

Hayden, Nicky.
xHayden, Nicky.
Leather. Scribner.

Hayden, Robert. see Hayden, Robert Earl.

Hayden, Robert C.
xHayden, Robert C.
Nine Black American Doctors. A-W.

Hayden, Robert Earl.
xHayden, Robert.
Afro-American Literature: An Introduction.
HarBraceJ.
Angle of Ascent: New and Selected Poems.
Liveright.

Hayden, Torey L.
xHayden, Torey L.
One Child. Putnam.

Haydn, Hiram. see Haydn, Hiram Collins.

Haydn, Hiram C. see Haydn, Hiram Collins.

Haydn, Hiram Collins, 1907-
xHaydn, Hiram.
Words & Faces. HarBraceJ.
ed. A World of Great Stories. Crown.
xHaydn, Hiram C.
Counter-Renaissance. HarBraceJ.
The Counter-Renaissance. Peter Smith.

Hayek, F. A. see Hayek, Friedrich August Von.

Hayek, Friedrich A. see Hayek, Friedrich August Von.

Hayek, Friedrich August Von.
xHayek, F. A.

Individualism & Economic Order. Routledge &
Kegan.
Studies in Philosophy, Politics & Economics. U
of Chicago Pr.
xHayek, Friedrich A.
ed. Capitalism & the Historians. U of Chicago
Pr.
Constitution of Liberty. U of Chicago Pr.
Individualism & Economic Order. U of
Chicago Pr.
Monetary Nationalism & International
Stability. Kelley.

Hayes, Aden.
xHayes, Aden.
A Runner's Guide to Europe. Penguin.

Hayes, Alden C.
xHayes, Alden C.
The Four Churches of Pecos. U of NM Pr.

Hayes, Ann.
xHayes, Ann.
The Living & the Dead. Carnegie-Mellon.

Hayes, C. A. see Hayes, Charles A.

Hayes, Carlton J. see Hayes, Carlton Joseph Huntley.

Hayes, Carlton Joseph Huntley, 1882-1964
xHayes, Carlton J.
France: A Nation of Patriots. Octagon.
Generation of Materialism, 1871-1900.
Har-Row.
Historical Evolution of Modern Nationalism.
Russell.

Hayes, Charles A.
xHayes, C. A.
Derivation & Martingales. Springer-Verlag.
xHayes, Charles A.
Concepts of Real Analysis. Krieger.

Hayes, Charles R., 1919-
xHayes, Charles R.
The Dispersed City: The Case of Piedmont,
North Carolina. U Chicago Dept Geog.

Hayes, Charles W., d. 1905
xHayes, Charles W.
Galveston: History of the Island & the City.
Jenkins.

Hayes, Colin.
xHayes, Colin.
Complete Guide to Painting & Drawing.
Mayflower Bks.

Hayes, Denis, 1944-
xHayes, Denis.
Energy for Development: Third World Options.
Worldwatch Inst.
Energy: The Solar Prospect. Worldwatch Inst.
The Solar Energy Timetable. Worldwatch Inst.

Hayes, Dorsha.
xHayes, Dorsha.
Who Walk with the Earth. AMS Pr.

Hayes, E. see Hayes, Elvin.

Hayes, E. Kent. see Hayes, Kent.

Hayes, Edward J.
xHayes, Edward J.
Catholicism & Life. Our Sunday Visitor.
Catholicism & Reason. Our Sunday Visitor.

Hayes, Elvin.
xHayes, E.
They Call Me the Big E. P-H.

Hayes, Frederick O. see Hayes, Frederick O'R.

Hayes, Frederick O'R.
xHayes, Frederick O.
Productivity in Local Government. Lexington
Bks.

Hayes, Geoffrey.
xHayes, Geoffrey.
illus. Patrick Comes to Puttyville & Other
Stories. Har-Row.
illus. The Secret Inside. Har-Row.

Hayes, Gerald R. see Hayes, Gerald Ravenscourt.

Hayes, Gerald Ravenscourt, 1889-
xHayes, Gerald R.

King's Music: An Anthology. Hyperion Conn.
Musical Instruments & Their Music:
1500-1750. AMS Pr.

Hayes, Harold.
xHayes, Harold.
The Last Place on Earth. Stein & Day.

Hayes, Helen.
xHayes, Helen.
On Reflection: An Autobiography. M Evans.

Hayes, Helen Foreword by. see Kopperl, Bert.

Hayes, Irene.
xHayes, Irene.
What's Cooking in Kentucky. Hayes Bk Co.
What's Cooking in Kentucky. Lippincott.

Hayes, J. Y. see Hayes, James.

Hayes, James, 1930-
xHayes, J. Y.
Hong Kong Region, 1850-1911: Institutions &
Leadership in Town & Countryside. Shoe
String.

Hayes, James M., 1875-
xHayes, James M.
ed. In Praise of Nuns: An Anthology of Verse.
Arno.

Hayes, James T., 1923-
xHayes, James T.
Introduction to Natal Astrology. Univ Bks.

Hayes, John H. see Hayes, John Haralson.

Hayes, John Haralson, 1934-
xHayes, John H.
An Introduction to Old Testament Study.
Abingdon.
Understanding the Psalms. Judson.

Hayes, Julia.
xHayes, Julia.
French Cooking for the People Who Can't.
Atheneum.

Hayes, Kent.
xHayes, E. Kent.
Broken Promise. Putnam.

Hayes, Lilian.
xHayes, Lilian.
Thirtieth Piece of Silver. Arno.

Hayes, Louis D.
xHayes, Louis D.
Impact of U. S. Policy on the Kashmir
Conflict. U of Ariz Pr.

Hayes, Lynton R., 1943-
xHayes, Lynton R.
Energy, Economic Growth, & Regionalism in
the West. U of NM Pr.

Hayes, M. H. see Hayes, Matthew Horace.

Hayes, M. L. see Hayes, Margaret Louise.

Hayes, Margaret Louise, 1898-
xHayes, M. L.
Study of the Classroom Disturbances of Eighth
Grade Boys & Girls. AMS Pr.

Hayes, Matthew Horace, 1842-1904
xHayes, M. H.
Illustrated Horse Training. Wilshire.

Hayes, Michael.
xHayes, Michael.
The Dow Jones-Irwin Guide to Stock Market
Cycles. Dow Jones-Irwin.
Money: How to Get It, Keep It, & Make It
Grow. Am Mgmt.

Hayes, Patrick, 1948-
xHayes, Patrick.
Mathematical Methods in the Social &
Managerial Sciences. Wiley.

Hayes, Paul. see Hayes, Paul M.

Hayes, Paul M.
xHayes, Paul.
Fascism. Free Pr.
The Twentieth Century, 1880-1939. St Martin.

Hayes, R. B. see Hayes, Rutherford Birchard Pres. U. S.

Hayes, Ralph.
xHayes, Ralph.

By Passion Possessed. Belmont-Tower.
Dark Water. Belmont-Tower.
The Deadly Prey. Nordon Pubns.
Dragon's Fire. Nordon Pubns.
Forbidden Splendor. Nordon Pubns.
Golden Passion. Nordon Pubns.
Love's Dark Conquest. Belmont-Tower.

Hayes, Raphael.
  xHayes, Raphael.
    Adventuring. BJ Pub Group.

Hayes, Richard.
  xHayes, Richard.
    The Secret Army. Viking Pr.

Hayes, Rick S. see Hayes, Rick Stephan.

Hayes, Rick Stephan, 1946-
  xHayes, Rick S.
    Business Loans: A Guide to Money Sources &
    How to Approach Them Successfully. CBI
    Pub.
    Credit & Collections: A Practical Guide. CBI
    Pub.

Hayes, Robert M. see Hayes, Robert Mayo.

Hayes, Robert Mayo.
  xHayes, Robert M.
    Handbook of Data Processing for Libraries.
    Wiley.

Hayes, Roy.
  xHayes, Roy.
    The Hungarian Game. S&S.

Hayes, Rutherford Birchard, Pres. U. S.
  xHayes, R. B.
    Teach the Freeman: The Correspondence of
    Rutherford B. Hayes & the Slater Fund for
    Negro Education 1881-1887. Kraus Repr.

Hayes, Sheila.
  xHayes, Sheila.
    The Carousel Horse. Elsevier-Nelson.

Hayes, T. Wilson. see Hayes, Thomas Wilson.

Hayes, Thomas Wilson, 1940-
  xHayes, T. Wilson.
    Winstanley the Digger: A Literary Analysis of
    Radical Ideas in the English Revolution.
    Harvard U Pr.

Hayes, Tom, 1909-
  xHayes, Tom.
    How to Hunt the Whitetail Deer. A S Barnes.

Hayes, W. see Hayes, William.
Hayes, Wallace D. see Hayes, Wallace Dean.

Hayes, Wallace Dean.
  xHayes, Wallace D.
    Gasdynamic Discontinuities. Princeton U Pr.

Hayes, Wayland J. see Hayes, Wayland Jackson.

Hayes, Wayland Jackson, 1893-
  xHayes, Wayland J.
    Some Factors Influencing Participation in
    Voluntary School Group Activities: Case
    Study of One High School. AMS Pr.

Hayes, William.
  xHayes, W.
    ed. Crystals with the Fluorite Structure:
    Electronic, Vibrational & Defect Properties.
    Oxford U Pr.

Hayford, Casely.
  xHayford, Casely.
    Truth About the West African Land Question.
    Negro U Pr.

Hayford, Jack. see Hayford, Jack W.

Hayford, Jack W.
  xHayford, Jack.
    Prayer Is Invading the Impossible. Logos.

Hayhurst, G. see Hayhurst, George.

Hayhurst, George.
  xHayhurst, G.
    Mathematical Programming for Management &
    Business. Intl Ideas.

Haykin, D. J. see Haykin, David Judson.

Haykin, David Judson.
  xHaykin, D. J.

Subject Headings: A Practical Guide. Gordon
  Pr.

Haykin, S. see Haykin, S. S.

Haykin, S. S.
  xHaykin, S.
    ed. Nonlinear Methods of Spectral Analysis.
    Springer-Verlag.
  xHaykin, S. S.
    Active Network Theory. A-W.

Hayley, Thomas T. see Hayley, Thomas Theodore
  Steiger.

Hayley, Thomas Theodore Steiger, 1913-
  xHayley, Thomas T.
    Anatomy of Lango Religion & Groups. Negro
    U Pr.

Hayley, William.
  xHayley, William.
    The Life of Milton. Folcroft.
    Life of Milton. Schol Facsimiles.
    Two Dialogues: Containing a Comparative
    View of the Lives, Characters, & Writings of
    Philip, the Late Earl of Chesterfield, & Dr.
    Samuel Johnson. Schol Facsimiles.

Haymaker, Webb.
  xHaymaker, Webb.
    Founders of Neurology: One Hundred &
    Forty-Six Biographical Sketches by
    Eighty-Nine Authors. C C Thomas.
    Hypothalamus. C C Thomas.

Hayman, David.
  xHayman, David.
    ed. In the Wake of the "Wake". U of Wis Pr.

Hayman, John L.
  xHayman, John L.
    Evaluation in the Schools: A Human Process
    for Renewal. Brooks-Cole.

Hayman, Leroy.
  xHayman, Leroy.
    Thirteen Who Vanished: True Stories of
    Mysterious Disappearances. Messner.
    Up, up, & Away: All About Balloons, Blimps,
    & Dirigibles. Messner.

Hayman, Ronald, 1932-
  xHayman, Ronald.
    Arnold Wesker. Ungar.
    Arthur Miller. Ungar.
    De Sade: A Critical Biography. T Y Crowell.
    Edward Albee. Ungar.
    Eugene Ionesco. Ungar.
    How to Read a Play. Grove.
    Leavis. Rowman.

Haymes, Robert C., 1931-
  xHaymes, Robert C.
    Introduction to Space Science. Wiley.

Haynes, Betsy.
  xHaynes, Betsy.
    The Against-Taffy Sinclair Club.
    Elsevier-Nelson.
    Cowslip. Elsevier-Nelson.
    Spies on the Devil's Belt. Elsevier-Nelson.

Haynes, Brian. see Haynes, R. Brian.
Haynes, George E. see Haynes, George Edmund.

Haynes, George Edmund, 1880-1960
  xHaynes, George E.
    Negro at Work in New York City: A Study in
    Economic Progress. Arno.

Haynes, Glynn W., 1936-
  xHaynes, Glynn W.
    The American Paint Horse. U of Okla Pr.

Haynes, Judy L., 1947-
  xHaynes, Judy L.
    Organizing a Speech: A Programmed Guide.
    P-H.

Haynes, Michael D.
  xHaynes, Michael D.
    Haynes on Air Brush Taxidermy. Arco.

Haynes, R. Brian.
  xHaynes, Brian.
    Compliance in Health Care. Johns Hopkins.

Haynes, R. D. see Haynes, Roslynn D.

Haynes, Robert V.
  xHaynes, Robert V.
    The Natchez District & the American
    Revolution. U Pr of Miss.
    A Night of Violence: The Houston Riot of
    1917. La State U Pr.

Haynes, Roslynn D.
  xHaynes, R. D.
    H. G. Wells: Discoverer of the Future: The
    Influence of Science on His Thought. NYU
    Pr.

Haynes, Stephen N.
  xHaynes, Stephen N.
    Behavioral Assessment: Recent Advances in
    Methods, Concepts, & Applications.
    Jossey-Bass.
    Principles of Behavioral Assessment. Halsted
    Pr.

Haynes, W. Warren. see Haynes, William Warren.

Haynes, William D.
  xHaynes, William D.
    Stress Related Disorders in Policemen. R & E
    Res Assoc.

Haynes, William Warren.
  xHaynes, W. Warren.
    Pricing Decisions in Small Business.
    Greenwood.

Haynes, Williams, 1886-1960
  xHaynes, Williams.
    Southern Horizons. Arno.

Haynie, Paul, 1928-
  xHaynie, Paul J.
    Cabinetmaking. P-H.

Haynie, Paul J. see Haynie, Paul.
Hayreh, S. S. see Hayreh, Sohan Singh.

Hayreh, Sohan Singh, 1928-
  xHayreh, S. S.
    Anterior Ischemic Optic Neuropathy.
    Springer-Verlag.

Hays, Arthur Garfield, 1881-1954
  xHays, Arthur Garfield.
    Let Freedom Ring. Da Capo.

Hays, Daniel M.
  xHays, Daniel M.
    Biliary Atresia: The Japanese Experience.
    Harvard U Pr.

Hays, Hoffman R. see Hays, Hoffman Reynolds.

Hays, Hoffman Reynolds.
  xHays, Hoffman R.
    From Ape to Angel: An Informal History of
    Social Anthropology. Greenwood.

Hays, James D., 1926-
  xHays, James D.
    ed. Geological Investigations of the North
    Pacific. Geol Soc.
    Our Changing Climate. Atheneum.

Hays, Joyce. see Hays, Joyce Samhammer.
Hays, Joyce S. see Hays, Joyce Samhammer.

Hays, Joyce Samhammer.
  xHays, Joyce.
    An Apple a Day. A S Barnes.
  xHays, Joyce S.
    Interacting with Patients. Macmillan.

Hays, Lee.
  xHays, Lee.
    The Gamblers. Popular Lib.

Hays, Louise F. see Hays, Louise Frederick.

Hays, Louise Frederick, Mrs, 1881-
  xHays, Louise F.
    History of Macon County Georgia. Reprint.

Hays, Marion P. see Hays, Marion Prather.

Hays, Marion Prather.
  xHays, Marion P.
    Simple Talks for Special Days. Word Bks.

Hays, Mary, 1759 or 60-1843
  xHays, Mary.

Appeal to the Men of Great Britain on Behalf
of Women. Garland Pub.
Letters & Essays, Moral & Miscellaneous.
Garland Pub.
Memoirs of Emma Courtney. Garland Pub.
Hays, Robert. see Hays, Robert William.
Hays, Robert William, 1925-
xHays, Robert.
Principles of Technical Writing. A-W.
Hays, Samuel.
xHays, Samuel.
The Engineering Industries. Heinemann Ed.
Hays, Samuel P.
xHays, Samuel P.
Response to Industrialism. U of Chicago Pr.
Hays, Terence E.
xHays, Terence E.
Anthropology in the New Guinea Highlands:
An Annotated Bibliography. Garland Pub.
Hays, W. L. see Hays, William Lee.
Hays, William Lee, 1926-
xHays, W. L.
Statistics for the Social Sciences. HR&W.
Hays, Wilma P. see Hays, Wilma Pitchford.
Hays, Wilma Pitchford.
xHays, Wilma P.
Abe Lincoln's Birthday. Coward.
Christmas on the Mayflower. Coward.
The French Are Coming. Williamsburg.
Siege: The Story of St. Augustine in 1702.
Coward.
Hayslett, H T.
xHayslett, H. T.
Statistics Made Simple. Doubleday.
Hayt, Emanuel, 1899-
xHayt, Emanuel.
Medicolegal Aspects of Hospital Records.
Physicians Rec.
Hayt, William. see Hayt, William Hart.
Hayt, William H. see Hayt, William Hart.
Hayt, William Hart.
xHayt, William.
Engineering Circuit Analysis. McGraw.
xHayt, William H.
Engineering Circuit Analysis. McGraw.
Engineering Electromagnetics. McGraw.
Introduction to Electrical Engineering.
McGraw.
Hayter, Alethea.
xHayter, Alethea.
Opium & the Romantic Imagination. U of Cal
Pr.
Hayter, Earl W.
xHayter, Earl W.
Education in Transition: The History of
Northern Illinois University. N Ill U Pr.
Hayter, Stanley W. see Hayter, Stanley William.
Hayter, Stanley William, 1901-
xHayter, Stanley W.
About Prints. Oxford U Pr.
Hayter, Tony, 1938-
xHayter, Tony.
The Army & the Crowd in Mid-Georgian
England. Rowman.
Haythornthwaite, Philip. see Haythornthwaite, Philip J.
Haythornthwaite, Philip J.
xHaythornthwaite, Philip.
Weapons & Equipment of the Napoleonic
Wars. Sterling.
Hayward, Alan.
xHayward, Alan T.
Flowmeters: A Basic Guide & Source-Book for
Users. Halsted Pr.
Hayward, Alan T. see Hayward, Alan.
Hayward, Arthur L. see Hayward, Arthur Lawrence.
Hayward, Arthur Lawrence, 1885-
xHayward, Arthur L.

Days of Dickens: A Glance at Some Aspects of
Early Victorian Life in London. R West.
Days of Dickens: A Glance at Some Aspects of
Early Victorian Life in London. Shoe String.
Dickens Encyclopaedia: An Alphabetical
Dictionary of Reference to Every Character
& Place Mentioned in the Works of Fiction,
with Explanatory Notes on Obscure Allusions
& Phrases. Shoe String.
Hayward, Bill, 1942-
xHayward, Bill.
Cat People. Doubleday.
Cat People. Doubleday.
Hayward, Charles. see Hayward, Charles Harold.
Hayward, Charles H. see Hayward, Charles Harold.
Hayward, Charles Harold, 1898-
xHayward, Charles.
Antique Furniture Repairs. Scribner.
English Period Furniture. Scribner.
xHayward, Charles H.
Antique Furniture Designs. Scribner.
The Complete Book of Woodwork. Sterling.
ed. The Complete Handyman. Sterling.
Practical Veneering. Sterling.
Practical Woodwork. Sterling.
Practical Woodwork. Emerson.
Woodwork Joints: Kinds of Joints., How They
Are Cut, & Where Used. Sterling.
Hayward, Frank H. see Hayward, Frank Herbert.
Hayward, Frank Herbert, 1872-
xHayward, Frank H.
The Educational Ideas of Pestalozzi & Frobel.
Greenwood.
Hayward, Herman E. see Hayward, Herman Eliot.
Hayward, Herman Eliot, 1892-
xHayward, Herman E.
The Structure of Economic Plants. Lubrecht &
Cramer.
Hayward, J. see Hayward, Jack Ernest Shalom.
Hayward, J. F. see Hayward, John Forrest.
Hayward, Jack. see Hayward, Jack Ernest Shalom.
Hayward, Jack Ernest Shalom.
xHayward, J.
Planning in Europe. St Martin.
xHayward, Jack.
The One & Indivisible French Republic.
Norton.
ed. State & Society in Contemporary Europe.
St Martin.
Hayward, James R.
xHayward, James R.
Oral Surgery. C C Thomas.
Hayward, John, 1905-
xHayward, John.
ed. Oxford Book of Nineteenth-Century
English Verse. Oxford U Pr.
Teaching Soccer: Tactics, Skills & Drills of the
Most Popular Ball Game in the World. Per
Ardua.
Hayward, John Forrest, 1916-
xHayward, J. F.
The Courtauld Silver: An Introduction to the
Work of the Courtauld Family of
Goldsmiths.. Biblio Dist.
Hayward, Linda.
xHayward, Linda.
Letters, Sounds & Words: A Phonic
Dictionary. Platt.
Hayward, Robert.
xHayward, Robert.
The Brick Book. T Y Crowell.
Haywood, Carolyn, 1898-
xHaywood, Carolyn.

illus. Away Went the Balloons. Morrow.
illus. Back to School with Betsy. HarBraceJ.
illus. Back to School with Betsy. HarBraceJ.
illus. Betsy & Billy. HarBraceJ.
Betsy & Billy. HarBraceJ.
Betsy's Play School. Archway.
Betsy's Play School. Morrow.
A Christmas Fantasy. Morrow.
Eddie the Dog Holder. Archway.
illus. Eddie the Dog Holder. Morrow.
Eddie, the Dog Holder. PB.
illus. Eddie's Green Thumb. Morrow.
Eddie's Green Thumb. PB.
illus. Eddie's Happenings. Morrow.
Eddie's Menagerie. Archway.
Eddie's Menagerie. PB.
Eddie's Menagerie. Morrow.
illus. Ever-Ready Eddie. Morrow.
The King's Monster. Morrow.
A Valentine Fantasy. Morrow.
Haywood, Dixie.
xHaywood, Dixie.
The Contemporary Crazy Quilt Project Book.
Crown.
Haywood, Eliza. see Haywood, Eliza Fowler.
Haywood, Eliza Fowler, 1693?-1756
xHaywood, Eliza.
The History of Jemmy & Jenny Jessamy, 1753.
Garland Pub.
The History of Miss Betsy Thoughtless.
Garland Pub.
Memoirs of a Certain Island Adjacent to the
Kingdom of Utopia. Garland Pub.
xHaywood, Elizabeth.
Adventures of Eovaai, Princess of Ijaveo.
Garland Pub.
Haywood, Elizabeth. see Haywood, Eliza Fowler.
Haywood, H. L. see Haywood, Harry le Roy.
Haywood, Harry le Roy, 1886-1956
xHaywood, H. L.
ed. The Great Teachings of Masonry. Macoy
Pub.
ed. How to Become a Masonic Lodge Officer.
Macoy Pub.
Haywood, John, 1762-1826
xHaywood, John.
Civil & Political History of the State of
Tennessee from Its Earliest Settlement up to
the Year 1796 Including the Boundaries of
the State. Arno.
Haywood, R. W. see Haywood, Richard Wilson.
Haywood, Richard M. see Haywood, Richard Mansfield.
Haywood, Richard Mansfield, 1905-
xHaywood, Richard M.
The Myth of Rome's Fall. Greenwood.
Haywood, Richard Wilson.
xHaywood, R. W.
The Analysis of Engineering Cycles. Pergamon.
Hazan, Marcella.
xHazan, Marcella.
More Classic Italian Cooking. Knopf.
Hazard, Blanche E. see Hazard, Blanche Evans.
Hazard, Blanche Evans.
xHazard, Blanche E.
Organization of Boot & Shoe Industry in
Massachusetts Before 1875. Johnson Repr.
Organization of the Boot & Shoe Industry in
Massachusetts Before 1875. Kelley.
Hazard, Geoffrey C.
xHazard, Geoffrey C.
Ethics in the Practice of Law. Yale U Pr.
Hazard, John N. see Hazard, John Newbold.
Hazard, John Newbold.
xHazard, John N.

Communists & Their Law: A Search for the
Common Core of the Legal Systems of the
Marxian Socialist States. U of Chicago Pr.
Law & Social Change in the USSR. Hyperion
Conn.
Settling Disputes in Soviet Society: The
Formative Years of Legal Institutions.
Octagon.
Soviet System of Government. U of Chicago
Pr.

Hazard, Paul, 1878-1944
xHazard, Paul.
European Thought in the Eighteenth Century:
From Montesquieu to Lessing. Peter Smith.

Hazard, William R.
xHazard, William R.
Education & the Law: Cases & Materials on
Public Schools. Free Pr.

Hazari, Bharat R.
xHazari, Bharat R.
The Pure Theory of International Trade &
Distortions. Halsted Pr.

Hazari, Rabindra K. see Hazari, Rabindra Kishen.

Hazari, Rabindra Kishen.
xHazari, Rabindra K.
Structure of the Corporate Private Sector: A
Study of Concentration, Ownership &
Control. Asia.

Hazaz, Haim, 1898-1973
xHazaz, Haim.
Gates of Bronze. Jewish Pubn.

Hazel, Paul.
xHazel, Paul.
Yearwood. Little.

Hazelden. see Hazelden Foundation.

Hazelden Foundation.
xHazelden.
Profile of Hazelden Patients Discharged in
Nineteen Seventy-Seven. Hazelden.

Hazelhurst, Cameron, 1941-
xHazelhurst, Cameron.
ed. Australian Conservatism: Essays in
Twentieth Century Political History. Bks
Australia.

Hazell, Lester D. see Hazell, Lester Dessez.

Hazell, Lester Dessez.
xHazell, Lester D.
Commonsense Childbirth. Berkley Pub.

Hazelrigg, Charles T. see Hazelrigg, Charles Tabb.

Hazelrigg, Charles Tabb.
xHazelrigg, Charles T.
American Literary Pioneer: A Biographical
Study of James A. Hillhouse. Arden Lib.

Hazeltine, Cheryl.
xHazeltine, Cheryl.
The Central Texas Gardener. Tex A&M Univ
Pr.

Hazelton, Nika. see Hazelton, Nika Standen.
Hazelton, Nika S. see Hazelton, Nika Standen.

Hazelton, Nika Standen.
xHazelton, Nika.
American Home Cooking. Viking Pr.
Raggedy Ann & Andy's Cookbook. Bobbs.
The Regional Italian Kitchen. M Evans.
The Swiss Cookbook. Atheneum.
xHazelton, Nika S.
The Art of Cheese Cookery. Ross Bks.
Cooking of Germany. Time-Life.
Cooking of Germany. Silver.

Hazen, Barbara S. see Hazen, Barbara Shook.

Hazen, Barbara Shook.
xHazen, Barbara S.

Animal Manners. Western Pub.
The Gorilla Did It. Atheneum.
The Gorilla Did It. Atheneum.
Gorilla Wants to Be the Baby. Atheneum.
If It Weren't for Benjamin (I'd Always Get to
Lick the Icing Spoon). Human Sci Pr.
I'm Glad to Be Me. Childs World.
A Nose for Trouble. Western Pub.
Tight Times. Viking Pr.
What's Inside. Lion.
Where Do Bears Sleep. A-W.
World, World, What Can I Do?. Abingdon.

Hazen, Charles D. see Hazen, Charles Downer.

Hazen, Charles Downer, 1868-1941
xHazen, Charles D.
Alsace-Lorraine Under German Rule. Arno.

Hazen, Nancy.
xHazen, Nancy.
Grownups Cry Too: Los Adultos Tambien
Lloran. Lollipop Power.

Hazen, William E. see Hazen, William Eugene.

Hazen, William Eugene, 1925-
xHazen, William E.
Readings in Population & Community Ecology.
HR&W.

Hazleton, Jared E.
xHazleton, Jared E.
The Economics of the Sulphur Industry. Johns
Hopkins.

Hazlett, C. B.
xHazlett, C. B.
Primary Care Nursing: A Manual of Clinical
Skills. Davis Co.

Hazlitt, Henry, 1894-
xHazlitt, Henry.
ed. The Critics of Keynesian Economics.
Arlington Hse.
Economics in One Lesson. Arlington Hse.
The Inflation Crisis, & How to Resolve It.
Arlington Hse.
ed. Practical Program for America. Arno.

Hazlitt, W. C. see Hazlitt, William Carew.

Hazlitt, William, 1778-1830
xHazlitt, William.
The Fight. Folcroft.
Lectures on the English Comic Writers.
Dutton.
Lectures on the English Comic Writers.
Russell.
ed. Lectures on the English Poets. Russell.

Hazlitt, William C. see Hazlitt, William Carew.

Hazlitt, William Carew, 1834-1913
xHazlitt, W. C.
Gleanings in Old Garden Literature. Gordon
Pr.
Old Cookery Books & Ancient Cuisine.
Gordon Pr.
xHazlitt, William C.
ed. The English Drama & Stage Under the
Tudor & Stuart Princes, 1543-1664. B
Franklin.
Gleanings in Old Garden Literature. Gale.
Old Cookery Books & Ancient Cuisine. Gale.

Hazo, Samuel. see Hazo, Samuel John.

Hazo, Samuel John.
xHazo, Samuel.
Inscripts. Ohio U Pr.
Once for the Last Bandit: New & Previous
Poems. U of Pittsburgh Pr.
Quartered. U of Pittsburgh Pr.

Hazra, Tapan A.
xHazra, Tapan A.
ed. Recent Advances in Clinical Oncology:
Proceedings of a Conference Held in
Williamsburg, Va., 1977. A R Liss.

Hazzard, Mary E.
xHazzard, Mary E.

Critical Care Nursing. Med Exam.
Medical Surgical Nursing Review. Arco.

Hazzard, Shirley, 1931-
xHazzard, Shirley.
Defeat of an Ideal: A Study of the Self
Destruction of the United Nations. Little.
The Transit of Venus. Viking Pr.

Hazzledine, George D. see Hazzledine, George Douglas.

Hazzledine, George Douglas.
xHazzledine, George D.
White Man in Nigeria. Negro U Pr.

Heacox, Arthur. see Heacox, Arthur Edward.

Heacox, Arthur Edward, 1867-
xHeacox, Arthur.
Project Lessons in Orchestration. AMS Pr.

Heacox, Cecil E.
xHeacox, Cecil E.
The Education of an Outdoorsman. Winchester
Pr.
The Gallant Grouse: All About the Hunting &
Natural History of Old Ruff. McKay.

Head. see Head, Robert V.

Head, Constance.
xHead, Constance.
Ahaz. Broadman.
Imperial Twilight: The Palaiologos Dynasty &
the Decline of Byzantium. Nelson-Hall.

Head, Diane, 1945-
xHead, Diane.
A Precious Bit of Forever. Zondervan.

Head, George, Sir, 1782-1855
xHead, George.
Home Tour Through the Manufacturing
Districts of England in the Summer of 1835.
Biblio Dist.
Home Tour Through the Manufacturing
Districts of England in the Summer of 1835.
Kelley.

Head, George L., 1941-
xHead, George L.
Insurance to Value. Irwin.

Head, Gwen, 1940-
xHead, Gwen.
Special Effects. U of Pittsburgh Pr.
The Ten Thousandth Night. U of Pittsburgh Pr.

Head, John G.
xHead, John G.
Public Goods & Public Welfare. Duke.

Head, Matthew.
xHead, Matthew.
The Congo Venus. Garland Pub.

Head, Richard G.
xHead, Richard G.
Crisis Resolution: Presidential Decision Making
in the Mayaguez & Korean Confrontations.
Westview.

Head, Robert V.
xHead.
A Guide to Packaged Systems. Krieger.
xHead, Robert V.
Strategic Planning for Information Systems.
QED Info Sci.

Head, Sydney W.
xHead, Sydney W.
Pref. by & ed. Broadcasting in Africa: A
Continental Survey of Radio & Television.
Temple U Pr.

Head, W. S. see Head, Winfield Scott.

Head, Winfield Scott, 1909-1967
xHead, W. S.
The California Chaparral: An Elfin Forest.
Naturegraph.

Headey, Bruce. see Headey, Bruce W.

Headey, Bruce W.
xHeadey, Bruce.
British Cabinet Ministers: The Roles of
Politicians in Executive Office. Allen Unwin.

Heading, J. see Heading, John.

Heading, John.
xHeading, J.

Mathematical Methods in Science &
Engineering. Elsevier.
Headings, Philip. *see* Headings, Philip Ray.
Headings, Philip R. *see* Headings, Philip Ray.
Headings, Philip Ray, 1922-
xHeadings, Philip.
T. S. Eliot. Coll & U Pr.
xHeadings, Philip R.
T. S. Eliot. Twayne.
Headington, Bonnie J. *see* Headington, Bonnie Jay.
Headington, Bonnie Jay.
xHeadington, Bonnie J.
Communication in the Counseling Relationship.
Carroll Pr.
Headington, Christopher.
xHeadington, Christopher.
The History of Western Music. Schirmer Bks.
Headley, Robert K. *see* Headley, Robert Kirk.
Headley, Robert Kirk.
xHeadley, Robert K.
Cambodian-English Dictionary. Intl Schol Bk
Serv.
Headstrom, Birger Richard, 1902-
xHeadstrom, Richard.
Families of Flowering Plants. A S Barnes.
Lobsters, Crabs, Shrimps, & Their Relatives. A
S Barnes.
Nature in Miniature. Knopf.
Spiders of the United States. A S Barnes.
The Weird & the Beautiful. A S Barnes.
Headstrom, Richard. *see* Headstrom, Birger Richard.
Heady. *see* Heady, Ferrel.
Heady, Earl O. *see* Heady, Earl Orel.
Heady, Earl Orel, 1915-
xHeady, Earl O.
Agricultural Policy Under Economic
Development. Iowa St U Pr.
ed. Economic Models & Quantitative Methods
for Decisions & Planning in Agriculture. Iowa
St U Pr.
ed. Externalities in the Transformation of
Agriculture: Distribution of Benefits & Costs
from Development. Iowa St U Pr.
Future Farm Programs: Comparative Costs &
Consequences. Iowa St U Pr.
Spatial Sector Programming Models in
Agriculture. Iowa St U Pr.
Heady, Eleanor B.
xHeady, Eleanor B.
Brave Johnny O'Hare. Schol Bk Serv.
Heady, Ferrel.
xHeady.
Public Administration: A Comparative
Perspective. Dekker.
Heady, Harold F.
xHeady, Harold F.
Rangeland Management. McGraw.
Heafford, Philip. *see* Heafford, Phillip Ernest.
Heafford, Phillip Ernest.
xHeafford, Philip.
Math Entertainer. Emerson.
Heal, Ambrose, Sir, 1872-
xHeal, Ambrose.
The London Furniture Makers from the
Restoration to the Victorian Era: 1660-1840.
Peter Smith.
Heal, David W.
xHeal, David W.
The Steel Industry in Post War Britain. David
& Charles.
Heal, Felicity.
xHeal, Felicity.
Church & Society in England: Henry VIII to
James I. Shoe String.
Heald, M. A. *see* Heald, Mark A.
Heald, Mark A.
xHeald, M. A.
Plasma Diagnostics with Microwaves. Krieger.
Heald, Mark M. *see* Heald, Mark Mortimer.

Heald, Mark Mortimer, 1892-
xHeald, Mark M.
Free Society: An Evaluation of Contemporary
Democracy. Philos Lib.
Heald, Morrell.
xHeald, Morrell.
Culture & Diplomacy: The American
Experience. Greenwood.
Heald, Tim.
xHeald, Tim.
Just Desserts. Scribner.
Let Sleeping Dogs Die. Stein & Day.
Healey, James C. *see* Healey, James Christopher.
Healey, James Christopher, 1881-
xHealey, James C.
Foc's'le & Glory-Hole: A Study of the
Merchant Seaman & His Occupation.
Greenwood.
Healey, John B.
xHealey, John B.
Charismatic Renewal: Reflections of a Pastor.
Paulist Pr.
Healey, John H.
xHealey, John H.
Administrative Practices in Boys & Girls
Interscholastic Athletics. C C Thomas.
Healey, Larry.
xHealey, Larry.
The Claw of the Bear. Watts.
The Town Is on Fire. Watts.
Healey, Tim.
xHealey, Tim.
Adapted by The Life of Monkeys & Apes.
Silver.
Healey, William A. *see* Healey, William Albert.
Healey, William Albert.
xHealey, William A.
High School Basketball. Coaching, Managing,
Administering. Interstate.
Healy, Anthony.
xHealy, Anthony.
Australian Crustaceans in Colour. C E Tuttle.
Healy, C. *see* Healy, Charles C.
Healy, Charles C.
xHealy, C.
Career Counseling in the Community College.
C C Thomas.
xHealy, Charles C.
Career Counseling for Teachers & Counselors.
HM.
Healy, David. *see* Healy, David F.
Healy, David F.
xHealy, David.
Gunboat Diplomacy in the Wilson Era: The
U.S. Navy in Haiti, 1915-1916. U of Wis Pr.
Healy, G. P. A. *see* Healy, George Peter Alexander.
Healy, George Peter Alexander, 1813-1894
xHealy, G. P. A.
Reminiscences of a Portrait Painter. Da Capo.
Healy, George W.
xHealy, George W.
Lifetime on Deadline. Pelican.
Healy, Gerald B.
xHealy, Gerald B.
Laryngo-Tracheal Problems in the Pediatric
Patient. C C Thomas.
Healy, Mary E. *see* Healy, Mary Edward.
Healy, Mary Edward, Sister, 1906-
xHealy, Mary E.
Society & Social Change in the Writings of St.
Thomas, Ward, Sumner, & Cooley.
Greenwood.
Healy, R. J. *see* Healy, Richard J.
Healy, Richard J.
xHealy, R. J.
Design for Security. Wiley.
Healy, Timothy J.
xHealy, Timothy J.

Energy & Society. Boyd & Fraser.
Heaney, Seamus.
xHeaney, Seamus.
Door into the Dark. Merrimack Bk Serv.
Heaps, H. S.
xHeaps, H. S.
Introduction to Computer Languages. P-H.
Heaps, Willard A. *see* Heaps, Willard Allison.
Heaps, Willard Allison, 1908-
xHeaps, Willard A.
Psychic Phenomena. Elsevier-Nelson.
Superstition!. Elsevier-Nelson.
Taxation, U. S. A. HM.
Heard, Alexander.
xHeard, Alexander.
Costs of Democracy. U of NC Pr.
Southern Primaries & Elections 1920-1949.
Arno.
Heard, H. C. *see* Heard, Hugh Corey.
Heard, Hugh Corey, 1931-
xHeard, H. C.
ed. Flow and Fracture of Rocks. Am
Geophysical.
Heard, Isaac V. D., b. 1834
xHeard, Issac V.
History of the Sioux War & Massacres of 1862
& 1863. Kraus Repr.
Heard, Issac V. *see* Heard, Isaac V. D.
Heard, J. Norman. *see* Heard, Joseph Norman.
Heard, Joseph Norman, 1922-
xHeard, J. Norman.
Bookman's Guide to Americana. Scarecrow.
White into Red: A Study of the Assimilation of
White Persons Captured by Indians.
Scarecrow.
Heard, Niel.
xHeard, Niel.
How the Value Added Tax Can Boost Our
Economy. Pilot Bks.
Heard, William H. *see* Heard, William Henry.
Heard, William Henry, Bp, 1850-1937
xHeard, William H.
Bright Side of African Life. Negro U Pr.
Hearder, H. *see* Hearder, Harry.
Hearder, Harry.
xHearder, H.
Europe in the Nineteenth Century 1830-1880.
Longman.
Hearle, J. W. *see* Hearle, J. W. S.
Hearle, J. W. S.
xHearle, J. W.
Use of the Scanning Electron Microscope.
Pergamon.
Hearn, Charles R.
xHearn, Charles R.
The American Dream in the Great Depression.
Greenwood.
Hearn, Emily.
xHearn, Emily.
Stop It's a Birthday. Garrard.
TV Kangaroo. Garrard.
Hearn, Francis.
xHearn, Francis.
Domination, Legitimation, & Resistance: The
Incorporation of the Nineteenth-Century
English Working Class. Greenwood.
Hearn, Janice W.
xHearn, Janice W.
Making Friends, Keeping Friends. Doubleday.
Hearn, L. *see* Hearn, Lafcadio.
Hearn, Lafcadio, 1850-1904
xHearn, L.
Appreciations of Poetry. Kraus Repr.
xHearn, Lafcadio.

Appreciations of Poetry. Arno.
Books & Habits: From the Lectures of Lafcadio
Hearn. Folcroft.
Chita, a Memory of Last Island. AMS Pr.
Fantastics & Other Fancies. Arno.
Gleanings in Buddha-Fields: Studies of Hand &
Soul in the Far East. C E Tuttle.
Glimpses of Unfamiliar Japan. AMS Pr.
Glimpses of Unfamiliar Japan. C E Tuttle.
Glimpses of Unfamiliar Japan. Scholarly.
Japanese Fairy Tales. Core Collection.
Lectures on Shakespeare. Folcroft.
Life & Literature. Arno.
Life & Literature. Folcroft.
Occidental Gleanings: Sketches & Essays.
Arno.
Some Chinese Ghosts. Mss Info.
Some Chinese Ghosts. Somerset Pub.
Some Strange English Literary Figures of the
Eighteenth & Nineteenth Centuries. Arno.
Talks to Writers. Arno.
Two Years in the French West Indies.
Irvington.
Hearn, Setsu K. see Hearn, Setsu Koizumi.
Hearn, Setsu Koizumi.
xHearn, Setsu K.
Reminiscences of Lafcadio Hearn. Norwood
Edns.
Hearnden, Arthur.
xHearnden, Arthur.
Education, Culture & Politics in West
Germany. Pergamon.
Education in the Two Germanies. Westview.
Hearne, Betsy G. see Hearne, Betsy Gould.
Hearne, Betsy Gould.
xHearne, Betsy G.
Home. Atheneum.
South Star. Atheneum.
Hearnshaw, Fossey J. see Hearnshaw, Fossey John Cobb.
Hearnshaw, Fossey John Cobb, 1869-1946
xHearnshaw, Fossey J.
ed. Political Principles of Some Notable Prime
Ministers of the Nineteenth Century. Arno.
Some Great Political Idealists of the Christian
Era. Arno.
Hearnshaw, Leslie S. see Hearnshaw, Leslie Spencer.
Hearnshaw, Leslie Spencer.
xHearnshaw, Leslie S.
Cyril Burt, Psychologist. Cornell U Pr.
Hearon, Shelby, 1931-
xHearon, Shelby.
A Prince of a Fellow. PB.
Hearst, Eliot. see Hearst, Eliot Sanford.
Hearst, Eliot Sanford, 1932-
xHearst, Eliot.
ed. The First Century of Experimental
Psychology. Halsted Pr.
Hearst, John E.
xHearst, John E.
Contemporary Chemistry. W H Freeman.
Heartwell, Charles M.
xHeartwell, Charles M.
Syllabus of Complete Dentures. Lea & Febiger.
Heasley, Bernice E.
xHeasley, Bernice E.
Programmed Language & Speech Correction
Through Perceptual Activities. C C Thomas.
Programmed Lessons for Young
Language-Disabled Children: A Handbook for
Therapists, Educators & Parents. C C
Thomas.
Heasley, Jerry, 1949-
xHeasley, Jerry.
The Production Figure Book for U. S. Cars.
Motorbooks Intl.
Heaslip, George B., 1942-
xHeaslip, George B.
Environmental Data Handling. Wiley.
Heasman, Kathleen.
xHeasman, Kathleen.

Home, Family & Community. Allen Unwin.
Heath, Catherine.
xHeath, Catherine.
Lady on the Burning Deck. Taplinger.
Heath, Charles D. see Heath, Charles Dickinson.
Heath, Charles Dickinson, 1941-
xHeath, Charles D.
Your Future As a Legal Assistant. Rosen Pr.
Heath, Dwight B.
xHeath, Dwight D.
Historical Dictionary of Bolivia. Scarecrow.
Heath, Dwight D. see Heath, Dwight B.
Heath, E. G.
xHeath, E. G.
A History of Target Archery. A S Barnes.
Heath, E. G. see Heath, Ernest Gerald.
Heath, Edward.
xHeath, Edward.
Music: A Joy for Life. Mayflower Bks.
Heath, Ernest Gerald.
xHeath, E. G.
Archery: The Modern Approach. Merrimack
Bk Serv.
Heath, G. Louis.
xHeath, G. Louis.
The Hot Campus: The Politics That Impede
Change in the Technoversity. Scarecrow.
ed. Mutiny Does Not Happen Lightly: The
Literature of the American Resistance to the
Vietnam War. Scarecrow.
ed. Off the Pigs!: The History & Literature of
the Black Panther Party. Scarecrow.
Vandals in the Bomb Factory: The History &
Literature of the Students for a Democratic
Society. Scarecrow.
Heath, Helen T. see Heath, Helen Truesdell.
Heath, Helen Truesdell.
xHeath, Helen T.
ed. The Letters of Samuel Pepys & His Family
Circle. Greenwood.
Heath, Henry. see Heath, Henry B.
Heath, Henry B.
xHeath, Henry.
Flavor Technology: Profiles, Products,
Applications. AVI.
Heath, J. see Heath, Jeffrey.
Heath, Jeffrey.
xHeath, J.
Ngandi Grammar, Texts & Dictionary.
Humanities.
Heath, Jim F.
xHeath, Jim F.
Decade of Disillusionment: The
Kennedy-Johnson Years. Ind U Pr.
Heath, Mary E. see Heath, Mary Ellen.
Heath, Mary Ellen.
xHeath, Mary E.
Benjamin & Jon. Bethany Fell.
Benjamin & Jon. Jeremy Bks.
Heath, Maurice E.
xHeath, Maurice E.
Forages: The Science of Grassland Agriculture.
Iowa St U Pr.
Heath, Monica.
xHeath, Monica.
Duncraig. NAL.
Falconlough. NAL.
Marshwood. NAL.
Heath, Royal V. see Heath, Royal Vale.
Heath, Royal Vale.
xHeath, Royal V.
Mathemagic: Magic, Puzzles & Games with
Numbers. Dover.
Heath, Royton E.
xHeath, Royton E.
Miniature Shrubs. Barrie & Jenkins.
Heath, Thomas L. see Heath, Thomas Little.
Heath, Thomas Little, Sir, 1861-1940
xHeath, Thomas L.

Greek Astronomy. AMS Pr.
Heath-Stubbs, John. see Heath-Stubbs, John Francis
Alexander.
Heath-Stubbs, John Francis Alexander, 1918-
xHeath-Stubbs, John.
The Watchman's Flute. Persea Bks.
Heathcote, Niels H. see Heathcote, Niels Hugh De
Vaudrey.
Heathcote, Niels Hugh De Vaudrey.
xHeathcote, Niels H.
Nobel Prize Winners in Physics, 1901-1950.
Arno.
Heathcote, R. L.
xHeathcote, R. L.
Australia. Longman.
Heatherington, M. see Heatherington, Madelon E.
Heatherington, Madelon E.
xHeatherington, M.
How Language Works. Winthrop.
xHeatherington, Madelon E.
Outside-In. Scott F.
Heathfield, David. see Heathfield, David F.
Heathfield, David F.
xHeathfield, David.
ed. Perspectives on Inflation: Models &
Policies. Longman.
Heatley, A. J.
xHeatley, Alistair.
The Government of the Northern Territory. U
of Queensland Pr.
Heatley, Alistair. see Heatley, A. J.
Heaton, Alma.
xHeaton, Alma.
Fun Dance Rhythms. Brigham.
Heaton, Herbert, 1919-
xHeaton, Herbert.
Productivity in Service Organizations:
Organizing for People. McGraw.
Heaton, Israel C.
xHeaton, Israel C.
Planning for Social Recreation. HM.
Heaton, Peter, 1919-
xHeaton, Peter.
The Yachtsman's Vade Mecum. Dodd.
Heaton-Ward, W. Alan. see Heaton-Ward, William Alan.
Heaton-Ward, William Alan.
xHeaton-Ward, W. Alan.
Left Behind: A Study of Mental Handicap.
Biblio Dist.
Heatter, Basil.
xHeatter, Basil.
Devlin's Triangle. Pinnacle Bks.
Heatter, Maida.
xHeatter, Maida.
Maida Heatter's Book of Great Chocolate
Desserts. Knopf.
Heaven, Constance.
xHeaven, Constance.
The Fires of Glenlochy. NAL.
Heir to Kuragin. Coward.
Heir to Kuragin. NAL.
Heir to Kuragin. G K Hall.
Lord of Ravensley. Coward.
Lord of Ravensley. NAL.
The Queen & the Gypsy. Coward.
The Queen & the Gypsy. G K Hall.
The Queen & the Gypsy. NAL.
Heavener, U. S. A.
xHeavener, Ulysses S.
German New River Settlement - Virginia.
Genealog Pub.
Heavener, Ulysses S. see Heavener, U. S. A.
Heavilin, Jay.
xHeavilin, Jay.
Fear Rides High. Doubleday.
Heawood, Edward, 1863-1949
xHeawood, Edward.

History of Geographical Discovery in the
Seventeenth & Eighteenth Centuries.
Octagon.
Hebant, C. see Hebant, Charles.
Hebant, Charles.
xHebant, C.
The Conducting Tissues of Bryophytes.
Lubrecht & Cramer.
xHebant, Charles.
The Conducting Tissues of Bryophytes. Intl
Schol Bk Serv.
Hebard, Grace R. see Hebard, Grace Raymond.
Hebard, Grace Raymond.
xHebard, Grace R.
The Bozeman Trail: Historical Accounts of the
Blazing of the Overland Routes into the
Northwest & the Fights with Red Cloud's
Warriors. AMS Pr.
Hebb, D. O. see Hebb, Donald Olding.
Hebb, David.
xHebb, David.
The Complete Rally Book. Stein & Day.
Hebb, Donald Olding.
xHebb, D. O.
Essay on Mind. L Erlbaum Assocs.
Hebbard, William W. see Hebbard, William Wallace.
Hebbard, William Wallace.
xHebbard, William W.
The Night of Freedom. Arno.
Hebblethwaite, Peter.
xHebblethwaite, Peter.
The Year of Three Popes. Collins Pubs.
Hebden, John.
xHebden, John.
Pathways to Participation. Halsted Pr.
Hebel, J. William. see Hebel, John William.
Hebel, John William, 1891-1934
xHebel, J. William.
ed. Prose of the English Renaissance. Irvington.
Hebel, Rudolf.
xHebel, Rudolph.
Anatomy of the Laboratory Rat. Williams &
Wilkins.
Hebel, Rudolph. see Hebel, Rudolf.
Hebert, Ernest.
xHebert, Ernest.
The Dogs of March. Penguin.
The Dogs of March. Viking Pr.
Hebert, Jacques.
xHebert, Jacques.
Two Innocents in Red China. Oxford U Pr.
Hebly, J A.
xHebly, J. A.
Protestants in Russia. Eerdmans.
Hebrew Union College-Jewish Institute of Religion.
American Jewish Archives.
xAmerican Jewish Archives, Cincinnati.
Manuscript Catalog of the American Jewish
Archives. G K Hall.
Hecaen, Henri.
xHecaen, Henri.
Human Neuropsychology. Wiley.
Hechinger, Fred. see Hechinger, Fred M.
Hechinger, Fred M.
xHechinger, Fred.
Growing Up in America. McGraw.
Hecht, Ben, 1893-1964
xHecht, Ben.
Fantazius Mallare: A Mysterious Oath.
HarBraceJ.
Hecht, E. see Hecht, Eugene.
Hecht, Eugene.
xHecht, E.
Optics. A-W.
xHecht, Eugene.
Optics. McGraw.
Hecht, Helen.
xHecht, Helen.

Gifts in Good Taste. Atheneum.
Hecht, Leo.
xHecht, Leo.
USSR Today: Facts & Interpretations.
Scholasticus.
Hecht, Marie B.
xHecht, Marie B.
The Women, Yes!. Krieger.
Hecht, Matthew S.
xHecht, Matthew S.
Flow Analysis of Computer Programs. Elsevier.
Hecht, Miriam.
xHecht, Miriam.
Alternatives to College. Macmillan Info.
Hecht, Robert A.
xHecht, Robert A.
Joseph Brant, Iroquois Ally of the British.
SamHar Pr.
Hechtlinger, Adelaide.
xHechtlinger, Adelaide.
Simple Soupbook. Branden.
Hechtman, Herbert B.
xHechtman, Herbert B.
Acute Respiratory Failure: Etiology &
Treatment. CRC Pr.
Heck, Anne.
xHeck, Anne.
The Complete Kitchen. Oliver Pr.
Heck, Edward T.
xHeck, Edward T.
A Guide to Mental Health Services. U of
Pittsburgh Pr.
Heck, Shirley. see Heck, Shirley F.
Heck, Shirley F.
xHeck, Shirley.
All the Classroom Is a Stage: The Creative
Classroom Environment. Pergamon.
Heckart, Beverly.
xHeckart, Beverly.
From Bassermann to Bebel: The Grand Bloc's
Quest for Reform in the Kaiserreich,
1900-1914. Yale U Pr.
Heckelman, A. Joseph.
xHeckelman, A. Joseph.
American Volunteers & Israel's War of
Independence. Ktav.
Heckelmann, Charles N.
xHeckelmann, Charles N.
Bullet Law. Popular Lib.
Let the Guns Roar. Popular Lib.
The Rawhider. Popular Lib.
Hecker, Melvin.
xHecker, Melvin.
The Greeks in America: A Chronology & Fact
Book. Oceana.
Heckewelder, John. see Heckewelder, John Gottlieb
Ernestus.
Heckewelder, John Gottlieb Ernestus, 1743-1823
xHeckeweleder, John.
History, Manners, & Customs of the Indian
Nations Who Once Inhabited Pennsylvania &
the Neighboring States. Arno.
Heckman, Carol.
xHeckman, Carol.
ed. GeoRef Thesaurus & Guide to Indexing.
Am Geol.
Heckmann, I. L.
xHeckmann, I. L.
Human Relations in Management. SW Pub.
Heckner, Fritz.
xHeckner, Fritz.
Practical Microscopic Hematology: A Manual
for the Clinical Laboratory & Clinical
Practice. Urban & S.
Heckscher, August.
xHeckscher, August.
Open Spaces: The Life of American Cities.
Har-Row.
Heckscher, Eli F. see Heckscher, Eli Filip.

Heckscher, Eli Filip, 1879-1952
xHeckscher, Eli F.
Economic History of Sweden. Harvard U Pr.
Heclo, Hugh.
xHeclo, Hugh.
A Government of Strangers: Executive Politics
in Washington. Brookings.
Hector, M. L. see Hector, Marie Louise.
Hector, Marie Louise.
xHector, M. L.
EEG Recording. Butterworths.
Hedden, Jay. see Hedden, Jay W.
Hedden, Jay W.
xHedden, Jay.
Successful Shelves & Built-Ins. Structures Pub.
Heddens, James. see Heddens, James W.
Heddens, James W., 1925-
xHeddens, James.
Today's Mathematics. SRA.
Heden, Carl Goran.
xHeden, Carl-Coran.
ed. Automation in Microbiology &
Immunology. Krieger.
Heden, Carl-Coran. see Heden, Carl Goran.
Hedgecoe, John.
xHedgecoe, John.
The Art of Color Photography. S&S.
John Hedgecoe's Basic Photography Course.
S&S.
John Hedgecoe's Pocket Guide to Practical
Photography. S&S.
illus. Possessions. A & W Pubs.
Hedgepeth, William.
xHedgepeth, William B.
The Hog Book. Doubleday.
Hedgepeth, William B. see Hedgepeth, William.
Hedges, James B. see Hedges, James Blaine.
Hedges, James Blaine, 1894-1965
xHedges, James B.
Building the Canadian West: The Land &
Colonization Policies of the Canadian Pacific
Railway. Russell.
Hedges, William D.
xHedges, William D.
At What Age Should Children Enter First
Grade?: A Comprehensive Review of the
Research. Univ Microfilms.
Hedgpeth, Don.
xHedgpeth, Don.
Bettina: Portraying Life in Art. Northland.
Cowboy Artist: The Joe Beeler Story.
Northland.
Texas Breed: A Cowboy Anthology. Northland.
Hedgpeth, J. W. see Hedgpeth, Joel Walker.
Hedgpeth, Joel W. see Hedgpeth, Joel Walker.
Hedgpeth, Joel Walker, 1911-
xHedgpeth, J. W.
Animal Structure & Function. McGraw.
xHedgpeth, Joel W.
Introduction to Seashore Life of the San
Francisco Bay Region & the Coast of
Northern California. U of Cal Pr.
Hediger, H. see Hediger, Heini.
Hediger, Heini.
xHediger, H.
The Psychology & Behaviour of Animals in
Zoos & Circuses. Peter Smith.
Hedin, Sven. see Hedin, Sven Anders.
Hedin, Sven A. see Hedin, Sven Anders.
Hedin, Sven Anders, 1865-1952
xHedin, Sven.
Jehol, City of Emperors. Hyperion Conn.
xHedin, Sven A.
Across the Gobi Desert. Greenwood.
Overland to India. Greenwood.
Hedley, Arthur.
xHedley, Arthur.
Chopin. Biblio Dist.
Chopin. Littlefield.
Hedley, George P. see Hedley, George Percy.

Hedley, George Percy, 1899-
  xHedley, George P.
    The Superstitions of the Irreligious.
      Greenwood.
Hedley, R. H. see Hedley, Ronald Henderson.
Hedley, Ronald Henderson.
  xHedley, R. H.
    ed. Foraminifera. Acad Pr.
Hedrick, Addie M.
  xHedrick, Addie M.
    Cup of Stars. Golden Quill.
Hedrick, Basil C. see Hedrick, Basil Calvin.
Hedrick, Basil Calvin.
  xHedrick, Basil C.
    Historical Dictionary of Panama. Scarecrow.
Hedrick, Hannah. see Hedrick, Hannah Lucille.
Hedrick, Hannah Lucille, 1939-
  xHedrick, Hannah.
    Theo Van Doesburg, Propagandist &
      Practitioner of the Avant-Garde: Belletristic
      Activity in Holland, Germany & France,
      1909-1923. Univ Microfilms.
Hedrick, Ulysses P. see Hedrick, Ulysses Prentiss.
Hedrick, Ulysses Prentiss.
  xHedrick, Ulysses P.
    A History of Agriculture in the State of New
      York. Fenimore Bk.
Heeger, Gerald. see Heeger, Gerald A.
Heeger, Gerald A.
  xHeeger, Gerald.
    The Politics of Underdevelopment. St Martin.
Heenan, David A.
  xHeenan, David A.
    Multinational Organization Development. A-W.
Heepe, Evelyn.
  xHeepe, Evelyn.
    ed. Modern Danish Authors. Folcroft.
Heer, C. see Heer, Clarence.
Heer, Clarence, 1893-
  xHeer, C.
    Federal Aid & the Tax Problem. Arno.
Heer, David M.
  xHeer, David M.
    Society & Population. P-H.
Heer, Friedrich, 1916-
  xHeer, Friedrich.
    Challenge of Youth. U of Ala Pr.
Heer, John E.
  xHeer, John E.
    Environmental Assessments & Statements. Van
      Nos Reinhold.
Heeren, Arnold H. see Heeren, Arnold Hermann Ludwig.
Heeren, Arnold Hermann Ludwig, 1760-1842
  xHeeren, Arnold H.
    Historical Researches into the Politics,
      Intercourse, & Trade of the Carthaginians,
      Ethiopians & Egyptians. Negro U Pr.
Heermance, J. Noel.
  xHeermance, J. Noel.
    Charles W. Chesnutt: America's First Great
      Black Novelist. Shoe String.
Heers, J. see Heers, Jacques.
Heers, Jacques.
  xHeers, J.
    ed. Parties & Political Life in the Medieval
      West. Elsevier.
Heertje, Arnold, 1934-
  xHeertje, Arnold.
    Economics & Technical Change. Halsted Pr.
Heese, Fred.
  xHeese, Fred.
    Canoe Racing. Contemp Bks.
Heezen, B. C. see Heezen, Bruce C.
Heezen, Bruce C.
  xHeezen, B. C.
    Influence of Abyssal Circulation on
      Sedimentary Accumulations in Space &
      Time. Elsevier.
Hefele, Karl J. see Hefele, Karl Joseph Von.

Hefele, Karl Joseph Von, 1809-1893
  xHefele, Karl J.
    A History of the Councils of the Church from
      the Original Documents. AMS Pr.
Heffel, Leonard E.
  xHeffel, Leonard E.
    Opportunities in Osteopathic Medicine Today.
      Natl Textbk.
Heffern, Richard.
  xHeffern, Richard.
    The Complete Book of Ginseng. Celestial Arts.
Heffernan, Charles W.
  xHeffernan, Charles W.
    Teaching Children to Read Music. Irvington.
Heffernan, William, 1940-
  xHeffernan, Wwilliam.
    Broderick. Crown.
Heffernan, Wwilliam. see Heffernan, William.
Heffner, Elaine, 1926-
  xHeffner, Elaine.
    Mothering: The Emotional Experience of
      Motherhood After Freud & Feminism.
      Doubleday.
    Mothering: The Emotional Experience of
      Motherhood After Freud & Feminism.
      Doubleday.
Heffner, Richard D.
  xHeffner, Richard D.
    Documentary History of the United States.
      NAL.
Heffner, Roe-Merrill S. see Heffner, Roe-Merrill Secrist.
Heffner, Roe-Merrill Secrist.
  xHeffner, Roe-Merrill S.
    ed. Word-Index to the Texts of Steinmeyer Die
      Kleineren Althochdeutschen
      Sprachdenkmaler. U of Wis Pr.
Heffron, Dorris.
  xHeffron, Dorris.
    Nice Fire & Some Moonpennies. Atheneum.
Heffron, Floyd N. see Heffron, Floyd Nicholas.
Heffron, Floyd Nicholas, 1907-
  xHeffron, Floyd N.
    Evidence for the Patrolman. C C Thomas.
Heflebower, R. B. see Heflebower, Richard Brooks.
Heflebower, Richard Brooks, 1903-
  xHeflebower, R. B.
    Cooperatives & Mutuals in the Market System.
      U of Wis Pr.
Hefley, James. see Hefley, James C.
Hefley, James C.
  xHefley, James.
    The Church That Takes on Trouble. Cook.
    God Goes to High School. Word Bks.
    Prisoners of Hope. Chr Pubns.
  xHefley, James C.
    Get the Facts. Broadman.
Hefter, Richard.
  xHefter, Richard.
    ed. Hippo Jogs for Health. HR&W.
    illus. Lion Is Down in the Dumps. HR&W.
    illus. Moody Moose Buttons. HR&W.
    ed. No Kicks for Dog. HR&W.
    ed. Pig Thinks Pink. HR&W.
    illus. Stork Spills the Beans. HR&W.
    Turtle Throws a Tantrum. HR&W.
    Xerus Won't Allow It. HR&W.
Heftmann, E. see Heftmann, Erich.
Heftmann, Erich.
  xHeftmann, E.
    Chromatography of Steroids. Elsevier.
    Steroid Biochemistry. Acad Pr.
  xHeftmann, Erich.
    ed. Modern Methods of Steroid Analysis. Acad
      Pr.
Hegarty, E. see Hegarty, John.
Hegarty, E. see Hegarty, Edward J.
Hegarty, Edward J.
  xHegarty, E.
    How to Talk Your Way to the Top. P-H.
  xHegarty, Edward J.

    How to Run Better Meetings. Krieger.
    Humor & Eloquence in Public Speaking. P-H.
Hegarty, John.
  xHegarty.
    Calculus for the Management & Social
      Sciences. Allyn.
Hegarty, Walter.
  xHegarty, Walter.
    An Age for Fortunes. Coward.
Hegedus, Andras, 1922-
  xHegedus, Andras.
    Socialism & Bureaucracy. St Martin.
    Structure of Socialist Society. St Martin.
Hegedus, Louis S.
  xHegedus, Louis S.
    Compendium of Organic Synthetic Methods.
      Wiley.
Hegel, G. W. see Hegel, Georg Wilhelm Friedrich.
Hegel, Georg W. see Hegel, Georg Wilhelm Friedrich.
Hegel, Georg Wilhelm Friedrich.
  xHegel, G. W.
    The Difference Between the Fichtean &
      Schellingian Systems of Philosophy.
      Ridgeview.
  xHegel, Georg W.
    Reason in History: A General Introduction to
      the Philosophy of History. Bobbs.
Hegel, Richard, 1927-
  xHegel, Richard.
    Carriages from New Haven: New Haven's
      Nineteenth-Century Carriage Industry. Shoe
      String.
    Nineteenth Century Historians of New Haven.
      Shoe String.
Hegeland, Hugo.
  xHegeland, Hugo.
    Multiplier Theory. Kelley.
Hegeler, Inge.
  xHegeler, Inge.
    Living Is Loving. Stein & Day.
Hegemann, Werner.
  xHegemann, Werner.
    American Vitruvius: An Architects' Handbook
      of Civic Art. Arno.
Hegener, Karen C.
  xHegener, Karen C.
    ed. National College Databank. Peterson's
      Guides.
Heggen, Franz J.
  xHeggen, Franz J.
    Confession & the Service of Penance. U of
      Notre Dame Pr.
Heginbotham, Stanley J.
  xHeginbotham, Stanley J.
    Cultures in Conflict: The Four Faces of Indian
      Bureaucracy. Columbia U Pr.
Heglar, Mary S. see Heglar, Mary Schnall.
Heglar, Mary Schnall.
  xHeglar, Mary S.
    Grand Prix Champions. Norton.
Hegner, Robert W. see Hegner, Robert William.
Hegner, Robert William, 1880-1942
  xHegner, Robert W.
    Parade of the Animal Kingdom. Macmillan.
Hegwood, Mamie.
  xHegwood, Mamie.
    My Friend Fish. HR&W.
Hehn, Paul N.
  xHehn, Paul N.
    The German Struggle Against the Yugoslav
      Guerrillas in World War II. East Eur
      Quarterly.
Heiberg, Milton.
  xHeiberg, Milton.
    The Yashica Guide. Amphoto.
  xHeiberg, Milton J.
    The Olympus Guide. Amphoto.
Heiberg, Milton J. see Heiberg, Milton.
Heichelheim, Fritz M. see Heichelheim, Fritz Moritz.

Heichelheim, Fritz Moritz.
  xHeichelheim, Fritz M.
    History of the Roman People. P-H.
Heicklen, Julian.
  xHeicklen, Julian.
    ed. Atmospheric Chemistry. Acad Pr.
Heide, Florence. *see* Heide, Florence Parry.
Heide, Florence P. *see* Heide, Florence Parry.
Heide, Florence Parry.
  xHeide, Florence.
    That's What Friends Are For. Schol Bk Serv.
  xHeide, Florence P.
    Banana Twist. Holiday.
    Body in the Brillstone Garage. A Whitman.
    Brillstone Break-in. A Whitman.
    The Face at the Brillstone Window. A
      Whitman.
    Fear at Brillstone. A Whitman.
    Giants Are Very Brave People. Schol Bk Serv.
    God & Me. Concordia.
    Growing Anyway Up. Bantam.
    Growing Anyway Up. Lippincott.
    I Love Everypeople. Concordia.
    Mystery of the Forgotten Island. A Whitman.
    The Shrinking of Treehorn. Dell.
    The Shrinking of Treehorn. Holiday.
    Sound of Sunshine, Sound of Rain. Schol Bk
      Serv.
    When the Sad One Comes to Stay. Lippincott.
    Who Needs Me. Augsburg.
    Who Taught Me. Concordia.
Heide, Robert.
  xHeide, Robert.
    Dime Store Dream Parade: Popular Culture
      1925-1955. Dutton.
Heidegger, Martin, 1889-
  xHeidegger, Martin.
    Early Greek Thinking. Har Row.
    Identity & Difference. Har-Row.
    An Introduction to Metaphysics. Yale U Pr.
    Nietzsche. Adler.
    On Time & Being. Har-Row.
    The Question Concerning Technology & Other
      Essays. Garland Pub.
    The Question Concerning Technology & Other
      Essays. Har-Row.
Heidelberg Seminar in Nephrology.
  xHeidelberg Seminars in Nephrology, Heidelberg,
    September 1978.
    Pathophysiological Problems in Clinical
      Nephrology. S Karger.
Heidelberg Seminars in Nephrology, Heidelberg,
  September 1978. *see* Heidelberg Seminar in
  Nephrology.
Heiden, Konrad, 1901-1966
  xHeiden, Konrad.
    Hitler: A Biography. AMS Pr.
Heidenheimer, A. *see* Heidenheimer, Arnold J.
Heidenheimer, Arnold J.
  xHeidenheimer, A.
    Governments of Germany. Har-Row.
Heidenreich, Steve.
  xHeidenreich, Steve.
    Running Back. Dutton.
Heidensohn, Klaus.
  xHeidensohn, Klaus.
    ed. The Book of Money. McGraw.
Heidenstam, Oscar, 1911-
  xHeidenstam, Oscar.
    Fit at Forty & After. Emerson.
Heider, Karl G., 1935-
  xHeider, Karl G.
    Ethnographic Film. U of Tex Pr.
Heider, M. W. Von. *see* Von Heider, W. M.
Heidingsfield, Myron S. *see* Heidingsfield, Myron
  Samuel.
Heidingsfield, Myron Samuel.
  xHeidingsfield, Myron S.
    Marketing. Har-Row.
Heidt, E. U. *see* Heidt, Erhard U.

Heidt, Erhard U.
  xHeidt, E. U.
    Instructional Media & the Individual Learner:
      A Classification & Systems Appraisal.
      Nichols Pub.
Heifetz, Milton D.
  xHeifetz, Milton D.
    The Right to Die. Berkley Pub.
Height, Frank.
  xHeight, Frank.
    ed. Design for Passenger Transport. Pergamon.
Heighton, Elizabeth. *see* Heighton, Elizabeth J.
Heighton, Elizabeth J.
  xHeighton, Elizabeth.
    Advertising in the Broadcast Media.
      Wadsworth Pub.
Heijendort, Jean Van. *see* Van Heijenoort, Jean.
Heijenoort, Jean Van. *see* Van Heijenoort, Jean.
Heikoff, Joseph M. *see* Heikoff, Joseph Meyer.
Heikoff, Joseph Meyer, 1917-
  xHeikoff, Joseph M.
    Marine & Shoreland Resources Management.
      Ann Arbor Science.
Heilbron, Bertha L. *see* Heilbron, Bertha Lion.
Heilbron, Bertha Lion, 1895-
  xHeilbron, Bertha L.
    The Thirty-Second State: A Pictorial History of
      Minnesota. Minn Hist.
Heilbron, J. L.
  xHeilbron, John L.
    H. G. J. Moseley: The Life & Letters of an
      English Physicist, 1887-1915. U of Cal Pr.
Heilbron, John L. *see* Heilbron, J. L.
Heilbron, Louis H.
  xHeilbron, Louis H.
    The College & University Trustee. Jossey-Bass.
Heilbroner, R. *see* Heilbroner, Robert L.
Heilbroner, Robert L.
  xHeilbroner, R.
    Economic Problem. P-H.
  xHeilbroner, Robert L.
    The Economic Problem. P-H.
    ed. Economic Relevance: A Second Look.
      Goodyear.
    The Economic Transformation of America.
      HarBraceJ.
    Great Ascent: The Struggle for Economic
      Development in Our Time. Har-Row.
    An Inquiry into the Human Prospect. Norton.
    Limits of American Capitalism. Har-Row.
    The Making of Economic Society. P-H.
    Primer on Government Spending. Random.
    Understanding Macroeconomics. P-H.
    Understanding Microeconomics. P-H.
Heilbrun, Carolyn. *see* Heilbrun, Carolyn G.
Heilbrun, Carolyn G., 1926-
  xHeilbrun, Carolyn.
    Reinventing Womanhood. Norton.
    Toward a Recognition of Androgyny. Har
      Row.
  xHeilbrun, Carolyn G.
    Reinventing Womanhood. Norton.
Heilbrun, James.
  xHeilbrun, James.
    Real Estate Taxes & Urban Housing. Columbia
      U Pr.
Heilbut, Tony.
  xHeilbut, Tony.
    Gospel Sound: Good News & Bad Times. S&S.
Heilig, Matthias R.
  xHeilig, Matthias R.
    Conversations on the Styx. Philos Lib.
    Discussions on the Styx. Philos Lib.
Heiligenberg, W. *see* Heiligenberg, Walter.
Heiligenberg, Walter, 1938-
  xHeiligenberg, W.

    Principles of Electrolocation & Jamming
      Avoidance in Electric Fish: A
      Neuroethological Approach. Springer-Verlag.
Heilman, Arthur W.
  xHeilman, Arthur W.
    Principles & Practices of Teaching Reading.
      Merrill.
Heilman, Grant, 1919-
  xHeilman, Grant.
    Wheat Country. Greene.
Heilman, Kenneth M.
  xHeilman, Kenneth M.
    ed. Clinical Neuropsychology. Oxford U Pr.
Heilman, Robert B. *see* Heilman, Robert Bechtold.
Heilman, Robert Bechtold, 1906-
  xHeilman, Robert B.
    ed. Aspects of Democracy. Arno.
    The Iceman, the Arsonist, & the Troubled
      Agent: Tragedy & Melodrama on the Modern
      Stage. U of Wash Pr.
    This Great Stage: Image & Structure in King
      Lear. Greenwood.
Heilman, Samuel C.
  xHeilman, Samuel C.
    Synagogue Life: A Study in Symbolic
      Interaction. U of Chicago Pr.
Heilmann, Gerhard, 1859-
  xHeilmann, Gerhard.
    The Origin of Birds. Peter Smith.
Heilpern, John.
  xHeilpern, John.
    Conference of the Birds. Bobbs.
Heim, Karl, 1874-1958
  xHeim, Karl.
    Christian Faith & Natural Science. Peter Smith.
Heim, Pamela.
  xHeim, Pamela.
    The Art of Married Love. Harvest Hse.
Heim, Ralph D. *see* Heim, Ralph Daniel.
Heim, Ralph Daniel, 1895-
  xHeim, Ralph D.
    Reader's Companion to the Bible. Fortress.
Heimann, Jim.
  xHeimann, Jim.
    California Crazy: Roadside Vernacular
      Architecture. Chronicle Bks.
Heimanson, Rudolph.
  xHeimanson, Rudolph.
    Dictionary of Political Science & Law. Oceana.
Heimbeck, Raeburne S. *see* Heimbeck, Raeburne Seeley.
Heimbeck, Raeburne Seeley.
  xHeimbeck, Raeburne S.
    Theology & Meaning: A Critique of
      Metatheological Scepticism. Stanford U Pr.
Heimberg, Marilyn M. *see* Heimberg, Marilyn Markham.
Heimberg, Marilyn Markham.
  xHeimberg, Marilyn M.
    Discover Your Roots: A New, Easy Guide for
      Tracing Your Family Tree. Comm Creat.
Heimer, Ralph T.
  xHeimer, Ralph T.
    Strategies for Teaching Children Mathematics.
      A-W.
Heimler, Eugene.
  xHeimler, Eugene.
    Night of the Mist. Greenwood.
    The Storm (the Tragedy of Sinai). SBD.
Heimstra, Norman W.
  xHeimstra, Norman W.
    Injury Control in Traffic Safety. C C Thomas.
Hein, Eleanor C.
  xHein, Eleanor C.
    Communication in Nursing Practice. Little.
Hein, Leonard. *see* Hein, Leonard W.
Hein, Leonard W.
  xHein, Leonard.
    Quantitative Approach to Managerial
      Decisions. P-H.
  xHein, Leonard W.

The British Companies Acts & the Practice of
    Accountancy: 1844-1962. Arno.
Hein, Lucille. *see* Hein, Lucille E.
Hein, Lucille E.
    xHein, Lucille.
    From Sea to Shining Sea. Judson.
    xHein, Lucille E.
    I Can Make My Own Prayers. Judson.
Hein, Morris.
    xHein, Morris.
    College Chemistry: An Introduction to
        Inorganic, Organic & Biochemistry.
        Brooks-Cole.
    Foundations of College Chemistry. Dickenson.
Heinberg, John G. *see* Heinberg, John Gilbert.
Heinberg, John Gilbert, 1901-
    xHeinberg, John G.
    The Office of the Comptroller of the Currency:
        Its History, Activities & Organization. AMS
        Pr.
Heindel, Ned D.
    xHeindel, Ned D.
    ed. The Chemistry of Radiopharmaceuticals.
        Masson Pub.
Heine, Heinrich.
    xHeine, Heinrich.
    The Prose Writings of Heinrich Heine. Arno.
Heine, Helme.
    xHeine, Helme.
    The Pigs' Wedding. Atheneum.
Heineke, J. M. *see* Heineke, John M.
Heineke, John M., 1938-
    xHeineke, J. M.
    ed. Economic Models of Criminal Behavior.
        Elsevier.
Heineman, E. Richard. *see* Heineman, Ellis Richard.
Heineman, Ellis Richard.
    xHeineman, E. Richard.
    Plane Trigonometry. McGraw.
Heineman, John L., 1935-
    xHeineman, John L.
    Readings in European History: A Collection of
        Primary Sources, 1789 to the Present.
        Kendall-Hunt.
Heineman, John L. *see* Heineman, John Louis.
Heineman, John Louis, 1935-
    xHeineman, John L.
    Hitler's First Foreign Minister: Constantin
        Freiherr von Neurath. U of Cal Pr.
Heineman, Stephen S.
    xHeineman, Stephen S.
    Machine Tools: Processes & Applications.
        Har-Row.
Heinemann, Charles B. *see* Heinemann, Charles Brunk.
Heinemann, Charles Brunk, 1882-
    xHeinemann, Charles B.
    First Census of Kentucky, 1790. Genealog Pub.
Heinemann, Gisella.
    xHeinemann, Gisella.
    Cutting It. Dial.
Heinemann, Joseph.
    xHeinemann, Joseph.
    Prayer in the Talmud: Forms & Patterns. De
        Gruyter.
Heinemann, Larry.
    xHeinemann, Larry.
    Close Quarters. FS&G.
    Close Quarters. Popular Lib.
Heinesen, William, 1900-
    xHeinesen, William.
    The Lost Musicians. Am Scandinavian.
    The Lost Musicians. Hippocrene Bks.
    The Lost Musicians. Irvington.
Heinich, Robert.
    xHeinich, Robert.
    ed. Educating All Handicapped Children. Educ
        Tech Pubns.
Heinicke, Christoph M. *see* Heinicke, Christoph
    Matthew.

Heinicke, Christoph Matthew.
    xHeinicke, Christoph M.
    Brief Separations. Intl Univs Pr.
Heinisch, K. F. *see* Heinisch, Kurt Franz.
Heinisch, Kurt Franz.
    xHeinisch, K. F.
    Dictionary of Rubber. Halsted Pr.
Heinl, Robert D. *see* Heinl, Robert Debs.
Heinl, Robert Debs, 1916-
    xHeinl, Robert D.
    Handbook for Marine NCOs. Naval Inst Pr.
    Marine Officer's Guide. Naval Inst Pr.
Heinlein, Robert. *see* Heinlein, Robert Anson.
Heinlein, Robert A.
    xHeinlein, Robert A.
    Stranger in a Strange Land. Berkley Pub.
    Stranger in a Strange Land. Putnam.
Heinlein, Robert A. *see* Heinlein, Robert Anson.
Heinlein, Robert Anson, 1907-
    xHeinlein, Robert.
    The Green Hills of Earth. Amereon Ltd.
    The Menace from Earth. Amereon Ltd.
    xHeinlein, Robert A.
    Assignment in Eternity. NAL.
    Citizen of the Galaxy. Ballantine.
    Citizen of the Galaxy. Scribner.
    Day After Tomorrow. NAL.
    The Door into Summer. Gregg.
    Door into Summer. NAL.
    Farmer in the Sky. Ballantine.
    Glory Road. Berkley Pub.
    Glory Road. Gregg.
    The Green Hills of Earth. NAL.
    I Will Fear No Evil. Berkley Pub.
    Menace from Earth. NAL.
    Moon Is a Harsh Mistress. Berkley Pub.
    The Moon Is a Harsh Mistress. Putnam.
    The Notebooks of Lazarus Long. Putnam.
    Orphans of the Sky. Berkley Pub.
    Orphans of the Sky. Putnam.
    The Past Through Tomorrow: Future History
        Stories. Putnam.
    The Puppet Masters. Gregg.
    Puppet Masters. NAL.
    The Puppet Masters. NAL.
    The Star Beast. Ballantine.
    Star Beast. Scribner.
    Starman Jones. Ballantine.
    Starship Troopers. Berkley Pub.
    Time for the Stars. Ballantine.
    Time for the Stars. Scribner.
    Tunnel in the Sky. Ballantine.
Heinlein, W. E. *see* Heinlein, Walter E.
Heinlein, Walter E.
    xHeinlein, W. E.
    Active Filters for Integrated Circuits. Springer
        Verlag.
Heinmets, Ferdinand.
    xHeinmets, Ferdinand.
    Analysis of Normal & Abnormal Cell Growth:
        Model-System Formulations & Analog
        Computer Studies. Plenum Pub.
Heinonen, Janet.
    xHeinonen, Janet.
    Sports Illustrated Running for Women.
        Lippincott.
Heinonen, Tom.
    xHeinonen, Tom.
    All About Road Racing. Tafnews.
Heinrich, Bernd, 1940-
    xHeinrich, Bernd.
    Bumblebee Economics. Harvard U Pr.
Heinrich, Herbert W. *see* Heinrich, Herbert William.
Heinrich, Herbert William.
    xHeinrich, Herbert W.
    Industrial Accident Prevention. McGraw.
Heins, A. James.
    xHeins, A. James.

Constitutional Restrictions Against State Debt.
    U of Wis Pr.
Heins, C. P. *see* Heins, Conrad P.
Heins, Conrad P.
    xHeins, C. P.
    Applied Plate Theory for the Engineer.
        Lexington Bks.
Heins, Maurice, 1915-
    xHeins, Maurice.
    Complex Function Theory. Acad Pr.
Heinsheimer, Hans W.
    xHeinsheimer, Hans W.
    Menagerie in F Sharp. Greenwood.
Heinsohn, A. G., 1896-
    xHeinsohn, A. G.
    Cousin Mercedes & the White Russian.
        Western Islands.
Heinsohn, G. E. *see* Heinsohn, George E.
Heinsohn, George E.
    xHeinsohn, G. E.
    Ecology & Reproduction of the Tasmanian
        Bandicoots (Perameles gunni & Isodon
        obesulus). U of Cal Pr.
Heintz, Wulff D. *see* Heintz, Wulff Dieter.
Heintz, Wulff Dieter.
    xHeintz, Wulff D.
    Double Stars. Kluwer Boston.
Heintze, Carl.
    xHeintze, Carl.
    The Bottom of the Sea & Beyond.
        Elsevier-Nelson.
    Genetic Engineering: Man & Nature in
        Transition. Elsevier-Nelson.
Heintze, Ingeborg.
    xHeintze, Ingeborg.
    Organization of the Small Public Library.
        Unipub.
Heintzelman, Donald. *see* Heintzelman, Donald S.
Heintzelman, Donald S.
    xHeintzelman, Donald.
    Hawks & Owls of North America: A Complete
        Guide to North American Birds of Prey.
        Universe.
    xHeintzelman, Donald S.
    Autumn Hawk Flights: The Migrations in
        Eastern North America. Rutgers U Pr.
    A Guide to Eastern Hawk Watching. Pa St U
        Pr.
    A Manual for Bird Watching in the Americas.
        Universe.
    North American Ducks, Geese & Swans.
        Winchester Pr.
Heintzelman, Oliver Harry.
    xHeintzelman, Oliver K.
    World Regional Geography. P-H.
Heintzelman, Oliver K. *see* Heintzelman, Oliver Harry.
Heinz, E. *see* Heinz, Erich.
Heinz, Erich, 1912-
    xHeinz, E.
    Mechanics & Energetics of Biological
        Transport. Springer-Verlag.
Heinz, H. J. *see* Heinz, Hans Joachim.
Heinz, Hans Joachim.
    xHeinz, H. J.
    Namkwa: Life Among the Bushmen. HM.
Heinz, W. C. *see* Heinz, Wilfred Charles.
Heinz, Wilfred Charles, 1915-
    xHeinz, W. C.
    Once They Heard the Cheers. Doubleday.
Heinze, R. M. *see* Heinze, Rudolph W.
Heinze, Rudolph W.
    xHeinze, R. M.
    The Proclamations of Tudor Kings. Cambridge
        U Pr.
Heinzelman, Kurt.
    xHeinzelman, Kurt.
    The Economics of the Imagination. U of Mass
        Pr.
Heinzkill, Richard, 1933-
    xHeinzkill, Richard.

Film Criticism: An Index to Critics'
Anthologies. Scarecrow.

Heirich, Max.
xHeirich, Max.
The Spiral of Conflict: Berkeley, 1964.
Columbia U Pr.

Heiron, George.
xHeiron, George.
Steam's Indian Summer. Allen Unwin.

Heironimus , Terring W. *see* Heironimus, Terring W.

Heironimus, Terring W.
xHeironimus , Terring W.
Mechanical Artificial Ventilation: A Manual for
Students & Practitioners. C C Thomas.

Heise, David R.
xHeise, David R.
Causal Analysis. Wiley.

Heise, Eorge W. *see* Heise, George W.

Heise, George W.
xHeise, Eorge W.
The Primary Battery. Wiley.
xHeise, George W.
ed. The Primary Battery. Krieger.

Heisenfelt, Kathryn.
xHeisenfelt, Kathryn.
Pussycat in Business. Denison.

Heiser, Charles B. *see* Heiser, Charles Bixler.

Heiser, Charles Bixler, 1920-
xHeiser, Charles B.
The Gourd Book. U of Okla Pr.
The Sunflower. U of Okla Pr.

Heiserman, D. *see* Heiserman, David L.

Heiserman, D. L. *see* Heiserman, David L.

Heiserman, Dave.
xHeiserman, David L.
Radio Astronomy for the Amateur. TAB Bks.

Heiserman, David L., 1940-
xHeiserman, D.
Handbook of Digital IC Applications. P-H.
xHeiserman, D. L.
Handbook of Major Appliance
Trouble-Shooting & Repair. P-H.
xHeiserman, David L.
Build Your Own Working Robot. TAB Bks.
How to Build Your Own Self-Programming
Robot. TAB Bks.
How to Design & Build Your Own Custom TV
Games. TAB Bks.

Heiserman, David L. *see* Heiserman, Dave.

Heisey, John. *see* Heisey, John W.

Heisey, John W.
xHeisey, John.
ed. A Checklist of American Coverlet Weavers.
U Pr of Va.

Heisig, James W., 1944-
xHeisig, James W.
Imago Dei: A Study of C. G. Jung's
Psychology of Religion. Bucknell U Pr.

Heisler, Martin O.
xHeisler, Martin O.
ed. Ethnic Conflict in the World Today. Am
Acad Pol Soc Sci.

Heiss, Ann M.
xHeiss, Ann M.
Challenges to Graduate Schools. Jossey-Bass.

Heiss, Jerold.
xHeiss, Jerold.
The Case of the Black Family: A Sociological
Inquiry. Columbia U Pr.
ed. Family Roles & Interaction: An Anthology.
Rand.

Heisserer, A. J.
xHeisserer, A. J.
Alexander the Great & the Greeks: The
Epigraphic Evidence. U of Okla Pr.

Heit, Robert.
xHeit, Robert.
Day That Monday Ran Away. Lion.

Heitger, Lester E.
xHeitger, Lester E.

Managerial Accounting. McGraw.

Heitland, William E. *see* Heitland, William Emerton.

Heitland, William Emerton, 1847-1935
xHeitland, William E.
Agricola: A Study of Agriculture & Rustic Life
in the Greco-Roman World from the Point of
View of Labour. Greenwood.

Heitman, Francis B. *see* Heitman, Francis Bernard.

Heitman, Francis Bernard, 1838-1926
xHeitman, Francis B.
Historical Register of Officers of the
Continental Army During the War of the
Revolution, April 1775 to December 1783.
Genealog Pub.

Heitner, Joseph.
xHeitner, Joseph.
Automotive Mechanics: Principles & Practices.
Van Nos Reinhold.

Heitner, Robert R.
xHeitner, Robert R.
ed. Contemporary Novel in German: A
Symposium. U of Tex Pr.

Heitzman. *see* Heitzman, William R.

Heitzman, William R.
xHeitzman.
Statistics for Business & Economics. Allyn.

Heizer, Robert F. *see* Heizer, Robert Fleming.

Heizer, Robert Fleming.
xHeizer, Robert F.
ed. The California Indians: A Source Book. U
of Cal Pr.
ed. Federal Concern About Conditions of
California Indians 1853-1913: Eight
Documents. Ballena Pr.
The Natural World of the California Indians. U
of Cal Pr.
The Other Californians: Prejudice &
Discrimination Under Spain, Mexico, & the
United States to 1920. U of Cal Pr

Hejhal, Dennis A.
xHejhal, Dennis A.
Theta Functions, Kernel Functions, & Abelian
Integrals. Am Math.

Hekker, Terry.
xHekker, Terry.
Ever Since Adam & Eve. Fawcett.

Hekmat, Forough. *see* Hekmat, Forough-Es-Saltaneh.

Hekmat, Forough-Es-Saltaneh.
xHekmat, Forough.
Folk Tales of Ancient Persia. Caravan Bks.

Helander, Joel E. *see* Helander, Joel Eliot.

Helander, Joel Eliot.
xHelander, Joel E.
Noose & Collar: The Story of the Rockland
Murder, Madison, Connecticut. Helander.

Helbig, Ray.
xHelbig, W. Ray.
Let's Learn a Little Hawaiian. Hawaiian Serv.

Helbig, W. Ray. *see* Helbig, Ray.

Helbing, Terry.
xHelbing, Terry.
ed. Gay Theatre Alliance Directory of Gay
Plays. JH Pr.

Held, Gilbert.
xHeld, Gilbert.
Data Communication Components:
Characteristics, Operation, Applications.
Hayden.
Data Communications Procurement Manual.
McGraw.
Data Communications Procurement Manual.
McGraw.

Held, Julius S. *see* Held, Julius Samuel.

Held, Julius Samuel.
xHeld, Julius S.
The Oil Sketches of Peter Paul Rubens: A
Critical Catalogue. Princeton U Pr.

Held, R. E. *see* Held, Ray E.

Held, Ray E.
xHeld, R. E.

Public Libraries in California, 1849-1878. U of
Cal Pr.

Held, Ronald G.
xHeld, Ronald G.
Learning Together. Gospel Pub.

Held, Virginia.
xHeld, Virginia.
Property, Profits & Economic Justice.
Wadsworth Pub.

Heldman, D. R. *see* Heldman, Dennis R.

Heldman, Dan C.
xHeldman, Dan C.
Unions & Lobbying: The Representation
Function. Collectors Choice.

Heldman, Dennis R.
xHeldman, D. R.
Food Process Engineering. AVI.

Heldman, Gladys.
xHeldman, Gladys.
The Harmonetics Investigation. Crown.

Helen Vale Foundation.
xHelen Vale Foundation.
Is Your Sickness Real?: Mind-Made Disease.
Macmillan.

Helena, Ann.
xHelena, Ann.
The Lie. Raintree Pubs.

Helfaer, Philip M.
xHelfaer, Philip M.
The Psychology of Religious Doubt. Beacon Pr.

Helfant, Richard H.
xHelfant, Richard H.
A Clinical & Angiographic Approach to
Coronary Heart Disease. Davis Co.

Helfer, Ray E.
xHelfer, Ray E.
ed. Child Abuse & Neglect: The Family & the
Community. Ballinger Pub.

Helferich, William.
xHelferich, William.
All About Yogurt. P-H.

Helfet, Arthur J.
xHelfet, Arthur J.
Disorders of the Foot. Lippincott.
Disorders of the Knee. Lippincott.
Disorders of the Lumbar Spine. Lippincott.

Helfferich, Karl T. *see* Helfferich, Karl Theodor.

Helfferich, Karl Theodor.
xHelfferich, Karl T.
Money. Kelley.

Helfman, Elizabeth S.
xHelfman, Elizabeth S.
Apples, Apples, Apples. Elsevier-Nelson.
Maypoles & Wood Demons: The Meaning of
Trees. HM.
Our Fragile Earth. Lothrop.
Signs & Symbols Around the World. Lothrop.
Signs & Symbols of the Sun. HM.
Wheels, Scoops, & Buckets: How People Lift
Water for Their Fields. Lothrop.

Helfman, Harry. *see* Helfman, Harry Carmozin.

Helfman, Harry Carmozin.
xHelfman, Harry.
Strings on Your Fingers: How to Make String
Figures. Morrow.

Helfrich, Charles T.
xHelfrich, Charles T.
Silurian Conodonts from Wills Mountain
Anticline, Virginia, West Virginia, &
Maryland. Geol Soc.

Helgeson, Lloyd H.
xHelgeson, Lloyd H.
Total Pass Defense. P-H.

Helick, R. Martin.
xHelick, R. Martin.
The Complex Vision of Philo St. John. Regent
Graphic Serv.

Heline, Theodore.
xHeline, Theodore.

Dead Sea Scrolls. New Age.
Helitzer, Morrie.
xHelitzer, Morrie.
The Cold War. Watts.
Helke, Michael, 1943-
xHelke, Michael.
The Grammar of English Reflexives. Garland
Pub.
Hellberg, Hans-Eric.
xHellberg, Hans-Eric.
Grandpa's Maria. Morrow.
Helleberg, Marilyn M.
xHelleberg, Marilyn M.
Your Hearing Loss: How to Break the Sound
Barrier. Nelson-Hall.
Hellekson, Terry, 1938-
xHellekson, Terry.
Popular Fly Patterns. Peregrine Smith.
Hellen, J. A. see Hellen, John A.
Hellen, John A.
xHellen, J. A.
North Rhine-Westphalia. Oxford U Pr.
Heller, Agnes.
xHeller, Agnes.
Renaissance Man. Routledge & Kegan.
The Theory of Need in Marx. St Martin.
Heller, Beatrice.
xHeller, Beatrice.
Cooking Crystal Craft. Chilton.
Heller, Celia S. see Heller, Celia Stopnicka.
Heller, Celia Stopnicka.
xHeller, Celia S.
On the Edge of Destruction: Jews of Poland
Between the Two World Wars. Schocken.
Heller, David.
xHeller, David.
Vortex. Avon.
Heller, Denise L.
xHeller, Denise L.
An Analysis of Police Assailants in
Albuquerque. Univ OK Gov Res.
Heller, Erich, 1911-
xHeller, Erich.
The Artist's Journey into the Interior & Other
Essays. HarBraceJ.
Heller, Francis H. see Heller, Francis Howard.
Heller, Francis Howard.
xHeller, Francis H.
ed. The Truman White House: The
Administration of the Presidency, 1945-1953.
Regents Pr KS.
Heller, H. Robert. see Heller, Heinz Robert.
Heller, Heinz Robert.
xHeller, H. Robert.
The Economic System. Macmillan.
Heller, Jack, 1929-
xHeller, Jack.
Typing for the Physically Handicapped:
Methods & Keyboard Presentation Charts.
McGraw.
Heller, James E. see Heller, James Edward Isidore.
Heller, James Edward Isidore, 1906-1973
xHeller, James E.
Our Share of Morning. Greenwood.
Heller, Joseph.
xHeller, Joseph.
Good As Gold. S&S.
Good As Gold. PB.
Something Happened. Ballantine.
Something Happened. Knopf.
Heller, Jules.
xHeller, Jules.
Papermaking. Watson-Guptill.
Printmaking Today: A Studio Handbook.
HR&W.
Heller, Kenneth.
xHeller, Kenneth.
Psychology & Community Change. Dorsey.
Heller, L. G. see Heller, Louis G.

Heller, Linda.
xHeller, Linda.
Alexis & the Golden Ring. Macmillan.
illus. Lily at the Table. Macmillan.
Heller, Louie R. see Heller, Louie Regina.
Heller, Louie Regina, 1870-
xHeller, Louie R.
Early American Orations. Arno.
Heller, Louis G.
xHeller, L. G.
Communicational Analysis & Methodology for
Historians. NYU Pr.
Heller, Marjorie K.
xHeller, Marjorie K.
A Complete Course in Legal Secretarial
Practice. Monarch Pr.
Heller, Mark. see Heller, Mark F.
Heller, Mark F.
xHeller, Mark.
ed. The Illustrated Encyclopedia of Ice Skating.
Paddington.
ed. The Skier's Encyclopedia. Paddington.
Heller, Otto, 1863-1941
xHeller, Otto.
Studies in Modern German Literature. Arno.
Studies in Modern German Literature. Folcroft.
Heller, Peter, 1920-
xHeller, Peter.
Dialectics & Nihilism: Essays on Lessing,
Nietzsche, Mann & Kafka. U of Mass Pr.
Heller, Robert. see Heller, Robert Leo.
Heller, Robert Leo, 1919-
xHeller, Robert.
Earth Science. McGraw.
Heller, Robert W.
xHeller, Robert W.
ed. Child & the Articulated Curriculum.
Interstate.
Heller, Samuel, 1911-
xHeller, Samuel.
Automatic Control Basics: Designing &
Repairing Controllers Using Schematic
Diagrams. Datarule.
Heller, Saul.
xHeller, Saul.
Digital Computers Made Simple. AMECO.
Digital Computers Made Simple. Herman Pub.
Heller, Steven.
xHeller, Steven.
Compiled by Artists' Christmas Cards. A & W
Pubs.
Heller, Suzanne.
xHeller, Suzanne.
More Misery. Eriksson.
Heller, Walter. see Heller, Walter W.
Heller, Walter W.
xHeller, Walter.
Revenue Sharing & the City. AMS Pr.
xHeller, Walter W.
Revenue Sharing & the City. Johns Hopkins.
Heller, Wendy.
xHeller, Wendy.
Clementine & the Cage. Kalimat.
Heller, Wilfried.
xHeller, Wilfried.
Angular Scattering Functions for Spheroids.
Wayne St U Pr.
Hellerman, Herbert, 1927-
xHellerman, Herbert.
Digital Computer System Principles. McGraw.
Hellicar, Eileen.
xHellicar, Eileen.
Prime Ministers of Britain. David & Charles.
Hellie, Ann.
xHellie, Ann.
Brian & the Long, Long Scarf. Carolrhoda Bks.
Hellie, Richard.
xHellie, Richard.

Enserfment & Military Change in Muscovy. U
of Chicago Pr.
Helling, Rafael.
xHelling, Rafael.
Century of Trollope Criticism. Kennikat.
Hellinger, Douglas A.
xHellinger, Douglas A.
Unemployment & the Multinationals: A
Strategy for Technological Change in Latin
America. Kennikat.
Hellinger, Mark, 1903-1947
xHellinger, Mark.
Moon Over Broadway. Arno.
Helliwell, Robert A.
xHelliwell, Robert A.
Whistlers & Related Ionospheric Phenomena.
Stanford U Pr.
Hellman, Arthur D., 1942-
xHellman, Arthur D.
Laws Against Marijuana: The Price We Pay. U
of Ill Pr.
Hellman, Dorothy G. see Hellman, Dorothy Gurkin.
Hellman, Dorothy Gurkin.
xHellman, Dorothy G.
Let Go My Love. Bloch.
Hellman, Geoffrey T. see Hellman, Geoffrey Theodore.
Hellman, Geoffrey Theodore, 1907-
xHellman, Geoffrey T.
How to Disappear for an Hour. Arno.
Hellman, Hal. see Hellman, Harold.
Hellman, Harold, 1927-
xHellman, Hal.
The City in the World of the Future. M Evans.
Deadly Bugs & Killer Insects. M Evans.
Energy & Inertia. M Evans.
Energy in the World of the Future. M Evans.
The Lever & the Pulley. M Evans.
Population. Lippincott.
Hellman, Judith A. see Hellman, Judith Adler.
Hellman, Judith Adler.
xHellman, Judith A.
Mexico in Crisis. Holmes & Meier.
Hellman, Lillian, 1905-
xHellman, Lillian.
The Collected Plays. Little.
Maybe: A Story. Little.
Hellman, Robert.
xHellman, Robert.
tr. Fabliaux: Ribald Tales from the Old French.
Greenwood.
Hellman, Sam.
xHellman, Sam.
Low Bridge & Punk Pungs. Arno.
Hellmich, Eugene W. see Hellmich, Eugene William.
Hellmich, Eugene William, 1902-
xHellmich, Eugene W.
The Mathematics in Certain Elementary Social
Studies in Secondary Schools & Colleges.
AMS Pr.
Hellmuth, George A.
xHellmuth, George A.
ed. Prevention of Heart Attack: A Challenge to
the Health Professions. Univ Microfilms.
Hellmuth, Jerome.
xHellmuth, Jerome.
ed. Educational Therapy. Spec Child.
ed. Learning Disorders. Spec Child.
Hellriegel, Don.
xHellriegel, Don.
Organizational Behavior. West Pub.
Hellsing, Lennart.
xHellsing, Lennart.
The Wonderful Pumpkin. Atheneum.
Hellstrom, Ward, 1930-
xHellstrom, Ward.
On the Poems of Tennyson. U Presses Fla.
Hellwig, G. see Hellwig, Gunter.
Hellwig, Gunter, 1926-
xHellwig, G.

Differential Operators of Mathematical Physics: An Introduction. A-W.

Hellwig, Monika.
xHellwig, Monika.
The Eucharist & the Hunger of the World. Paulist Pr.
The Meaning of the Sacraments. Pflaum Pr.
xHellwig, Monika K.
What Are They Saying About Death & Christian Hope?. Paulist Pr.
Hellwig, Monika K. *see* Hellwig, Monika.

Helm, Frederick.
xHelm, Frederick.
ed. Cancer Dermatology. Lea & Febiger.

Helm, Mackinley, 1896-
xHelm, MacKinley.
Angel Mo' & Her Son, Roland Hayes. Greenwood.
Modern Mexican Painters. Arno.

Helm, Mary.
xHelm, Mary.
From Darkness to Light: The Story of Negro Progress. Negro U Pr.

Helm, Mike.
xHelm, Mike.
Eugene, Oregon: A Guide. Rainy Day Oreg.
Helm, P. J. *see* Helm, Peter J.

Helm, Peter J., 1916-
xHelm, P. J.
England Under the Yorkists & Tudors 1471 - 1603. Humanities.
Exploring Prehistoric England. Newbury Bks Inc.

Helm, Robert M.
xHelm, Robert M.
Gloomy Dean: The Thought of William Ralph Inge. Philos.
Helm, Sanford M. *see* Helm, Sanford Marion.

Helm, Sanford Marion, 1915-
xHelm, Sanford M.
Catalog of Chamber Music for Wind Instruments. Da Capo.

Helm, Thomas.
xHelm, Thomas.
Everglades: Florida Wonderland. Dodd.
Helm, W. *see* Helm, William Henry.
Helm, W. H. *see* Helm, William Henry.

Helm, William Henry, 1860-1936
xHelm, W.
Aspects of Balzac. Gordon Pr.
xHelm, W. H.
Aspects of Balzac. Haskell.

Helmer, John.
xHelmer, John.
The Deadly Simple Mechanics of Society. Continuum.

Helmericks, Harmon, 1917-
xHelmericks, Harmon.
Last of the Bush Pilots. Comstock Edns.
Last of the Bush Pilots. Knopf.
Helmes, Winifred G. *see* Helmes, Winifred Gertrude.

Helmes, Winifred Gertrude, 1913-
xHelmes, Winifred G.
ed. Notable Maryland Women. Cornell Maritime.

Helmholz, R. H.
xHelmholz, R. H.
Marriage Litigation in Medieval England. Cambridge U Pr.

Helmlinger, Trudy.
xHelmlinger, Trudy.
After You've Said Goodbye: How to Recover After Ending a Relationship. Schenkman.
After You've Said Goodbye: How to Recover After Ending a Relationship. Two Continents.
Helmore, Leonard M. *see* Helmore, Leonard Mervyn.

Helmore, Leonard Mervyn.
xHelmore, Leonard M.

Corrupt & Illegal Practices: A General Survey & a Case Study of an Election Petition. Humanities.
Helmreich, Ernst. *see* Helmreich, Ernst Christian.
Helmreich, Ernst C. *see* Helmreich, Ernst Christian.

Helmreich, Ernst Christian.
xHelmreich, Ernst.
The German Churches Under Hitler: Background, Struggle & Epilogue. Wayne St U Pr.
xHelmreich, Ernst C.
Diplomacy of the Balkan Wars, 1912-1913. Russell.
History at a Glance: A Chronological Chart of European Civilization. Barron.
ed. Hungary. Greenwood.
Religious Education in German Schools: An Historical Approach. Harvard U Pr.

Helmreich, Paul C.
xHelmreich, Paul C.
From Paris to Sevres: The Partition of the Ottoman Empire at the Peace Conference of 1919-1920. Ohio St U Pr.

Helmreich, William B.
xHelmreich, William B.
Compiled by Afro-Americans & Africa: Black Nationalism at the Crossroads. Greenwood.
Helmrich, Elsie W. *see* Helmrich, Elsie Winifred.

Helmrich, Elsie Winifred, 1886-
xHelmrich, Elsie W.
History of the Chorus in the German Drama. AMS Pr.
Helms, Donald. *see* Helms, Donald B.

Helms, Donald B.
xHelms, Donald.
Exploring Child Behavior. HR&W.
Helms, L. L. *see* Helms, Lester la Verne.

Helms, Lester la Verne, 1927-
xHelms, L. L.
Introduction to Potential Theory. Krieger.

Helms, Mary W.
xHelms, Mary W.
Ancient Panama: Chiefs in Search of Power. U of Tex Pr.
ed. Frontier Adaptations in Lower Central America. Inst Study Human.

Helms, Robert B.
xHelms, Robert B.
Natural Gas Regulation: An Evaluation of Fpc Price Controls. Am Enterprise.

Helms, Tom.
xHelms, Tom.
Against All Odds. T Y Crowell.
Against All Odds. Warner Bks.
Helper, Hinton R. *see* Helper, Hinton Rowan.

Helper, Hinton Rowan, 1829-1909
xHelper, Hinton R.
Compendium of the Impending Crisis of the South. Arno.

Helper, Rose.
xHelper, Rose.
Racial Policies & Practices of Real Estate Brokers. U of Minn Pr.

Helpern, Milton.
xHelpern, Milton.
Autopsy: The Memoirs of a Medical Detective. St Martin.

Helpman, Elhanan.
xHelpman, Elhanan.
A Theory of International Trade Under Uncertainty. Acad Pr.

Helprin, Ben.
xHelprin, Ben.
Photographic Self-Assignments. Petersen Pub.
Helps, E. A. *see* Helps, Edmund Arthur.

Helps, Edmund Arthur.
xHelps, E. A.
ed. Songs & Ballads from Over the Sea. Arno.
ed. Songs & Ballads of Greater Britain. Arno.
Helsel, Jay. *see* Helsel, Jay D.

Helsel, Jay D.
xHelsel, Jay.
Reading Engineering Drawings Through Conceptual Sketching. McGraw.
Helseth, Inga O. *see* Helseth, Inga Olla.

Helseth, Inga Olla, 1888-
xHelseth, Inga O.
Children's Thinking: A Study of the Thinking Done by a Group of Grade Children When Encouraged to Ask Questions About United States History. AMS Pr.

Helstrom, Jo.
xHelstrom, Jo.
Le Francais a Decouvrir. McGraw.
Helszajn, J. *see* Helszajn, Joseph.

Helszajn, Joseph.
xHelszajn, J.
Nonreciprocal Microwave Junctions & Circulators. Wiley.
Passive & Active Microwave Circuits. Wiley.
Helton, Floyd F. *see* Helton, Floyd Franklin.

Helton, Floyd Franklin, 1912-
xHelton, Floyd F.
Analytic Trigonometry. HR&W.
Heltzel, V. B. *see* Heltzel, Virgil Barney.

Heltzel, Virgil Barney, 1896-
xHeltzel, V. B.
Fair Rosamond: A Study of the Development of a Literary Theme. AMS Pr.

Helveston, Eugene M., 1934-
xHelveston, Eugene M.
Atlas of Strabismus Surgery. Mosby.

Helvey, T. C.
xHelvey, T. C.
Age of Information: An Interdisciplinary Survey of Cybernetics. Educ Tech Pubns.
Hembdt, Phil H. *see* Hembdt, Phil Harold.

Hembdt, Phil Harold.
xHembdt, Phil H.
Analysis of Prose Style. Folcroft.

Hembroff-Schleicher, Edythe.
xHembroff-Schleicher, Edythe.
Emily Carr: The Untold Story. Hancock Hse.

Hemdal, John F.
xHemdal, John F.
The Energy Center: New Alternative for Effective Energy Use. Ann Arbor Science.

Hemenway, David.
xHemenway, David.
Industrywide Voluntary Product Standards. Ballinger Pub.
Prices & Choices: Microeconomic Vignettes. Ballinger Pub.

Hemery, David.
xHemery, David.
Another Hurdle: The Making of an Olympic Champion. Taplinger.

Hemingway, Ernest, 1899-1961
xHemingway, Ernest.
Across the River & into the Trees. Scribner.
Collected Poems. Haskell.
The Collected Poems of Ernest Hemingway. Folcroft.
The Collected Poems of Ernest Hemingway. Gordon Pr.
Death in the Afternoon. Scribner.
Farewell to Arms. Scribner.
Farewell to Arms. Scribner.
For Whom the Bell Tolls. Scribner.
Green Hills of Africa. Scribner.
The Nick Adams Stories. Scribner.
The Nick Adams Stories. Bantam.
The Sun Also Rises. Intl Bk Ctr.
Sun Also Rises. Scribner.

Hemingway, Gregory, 1931-
xHemingway, Gregory H.
Papa: A Personal Memoir. HM.
Hemingway, Gregory H. *see* Hemingway, Gregory.

Hemingway, Joan.
xHemingway, Joan.

The Picnic Gourmet. Random.
The Picnic Gourmet. Random.

Hemingway, John.
xHemingway, John.
Conflict & Democracy: Studies in Trade Union Government. Oxford U Pr.

Hemingway, Mary. see Hemingway, Mary Welsh.

Hemingway, Mary M. see Hemingway, Mary Moon.

Hemingway, Mary Moon.
xHemingway, Mary M.
Food Processor Baking Magic. Hastings.

Hemingway, Mary W. see Hemingway, Mary Welsh.

Hemingway, Mary Welsh, 1908-
xHemingway, Mary.
How It Was. Ballantine.
xHemingway, Mary W.
How It Was. Knopf.

Hemleben, Sylvester J. see Hemleben, Sylvester John.

Hemleben, Sylvester John, 1902-
xHemleben, Sylvester J.
Plans for World Peace Through Six Centuries. Garland Pub.

Hemlow, Joyce.
xHemlow, Joyce.
A Catalogue of the Burney Family Correspondence, 1749-1878. McGill-Queen's U Pr.
Catalogue of the Burney Family Correspondence 1749-1878. NY Pub Lib.
History of Fanny Burney. Oxford U Pr.

Hemmer, William, 1936-
xHemmer, William J.
Arithmetic by Example. Heath.

Hemmer, William J. see Hemmer, William.

Hemming, John, 1935-
xHemming, John.
The Search for El Dorado. Dutton.

Hemminghaus, Edgar H. see Hemminghaus, Edgar Hugo.

Hemminghaus, Edgar Hugo, 1900-
xHemminghaus, Edgar H.
Mark Twain in Germany. AMS Pr.

Hemmings. see Hemmings, Gwynneth.

Hemmings, F. W. see Hemmings, Frederick William John.

Hemmings, Frederick William John.
xHemmings, F. W.
ed. The Age of Realism. Humanities.

Hemmings, Gwynneth.
xHemmings.
Biological Basis of Schizophrenia. Univ Park.

Hemon, Louis, 1880-1913
xHemon, Louis.
My Fair Lady. Arno.

Hemp, William. see Hemp, William H.

Hemp, William H.
xHemp, William.
If Ever You Go to Dublin Town. Devin.

Hempel, Arthur J.
xHempel, Arthur J.
Claim Your Inheritance. Circle Pr.

Hempel, Carl G. see Hempel, Carl Gustav.

Hempel, Carl Gustav, 1905-
xHempel, Carl G.
Fundamentals of Concept Formation in Empirical Science. U of Chicago Pr.

Hempel, George. see Hempel, George H.

Hempel, George H.
xHempel, George.
Financial Management of Financial Institutions. P-H.
xHempel, George H.
Bank Capital: Determining & Meeting Your Bank's Capital Needs. Bankers.

Hempenstall, Peter J.
xHempenstall, Peter J.
Pacific Islanders Under German Rule: A Study in the Meaning of Colonial Resistance. Bks Australia.

Hemphill, C. see Hemphill, Charles F.

Hemphill, Charles F.
xHemphill, C.
Modern Security Methods. P-H.
xHemphill, Charles F.
Criminal Procedure: The Administration of Justice. Goodyear.
Dictionary of Practical Law. P-H.

Hemphill, George.
xHemphill, George.
Allen Tate. U of Minn Pr.
A Mathematical Grammar of English. Mouton.

Hemphill, John K. see Hemphill, John Knox.

Hemphill, John Knox, 1919-
xHemphill, John K.
Group Dimensions: A Manual for Their Measurement. Ohio St U Admin Sci.

Hemphill, Paul, 1936-
xHemphill, Paul.
The Good Old Boys. S&S.

Hemphill, Phyllis D., 1919-
xHemphill, Phyllis D.
Business Communications with Writing Improvement Exercises. P-H.
Career English: Skill Development for Effective Communication. P-H.

Hempl, G. see Hempl, George.

Hempl, George, 1859-1921
xHempl, G.
Chaucer's Pronunciation & the Spelling of the Ellesmere MS. Folcroft.

Hemrich, G. see Hemrich, Gerald I.

Hemrich, Gerald I.
xHemrich, G.
Handbook of Jade. Gembooks.

Hemschemeyer, Judith.
xHemschemeyer, Judith.
I Remember the Room Was Filled with Light. Columbia U Pr.

Hemsing, Esther D.
xHemsing, Esther D.
ed. Children & Drugs. ACEI.

Henao, J. see Henao, Jesus Maria.

Henao, Jesus M. see Henao, Jesus Maria.

Henao, Jesus Maria.
xHenao, J.
History of Colombia. Gordon Pr.
xHenao, Jesus M.
History of Colombia. Greenwood.
History of Colombia. Kennikat.

Henault, Marie.
xHenault, Marie.
Stanley Kunitz. Twayne.

Henbest, Nigel.
xHenbest, Nigel.
The Exploding Universe. Macmillan.

Henche, H. R. see Henche, Hans-Rudolf.

Henche, Hans-Rudolf, 1940-
xHenche, H. R.
Arthroscopy of the Knee Joint. Springer-Verlag.

Hendee, W. R. see Hendee, William R.

Hendee, William R., 1938-
xHendee, W. R.
Radioactive Isotopes in Biological Research. Wiley.
Radiologic Physics, Equipment & Quality Control. Year Bk Med.

Hendel, Samuel, 1909-
xHendel, Samuel.
Charles Evans Hughes & the Supreme Court. Russell.
ed. The Politics of Confrontation. Irvington.

Hendershot, Carl H.
xHendershot, Carl H.
Compiled by Programmed Learning: A Bibliography of Programs & Presentation Devices. Hendershot.

Hendershott, Patric H.
xHendershott, Patric H.

Regulation & Reform of the Housing Finance System. Am Enterprise.

Henderson, A. see Henderson, Archibald.

Henderson, A. Corbin. see Henderson, Alice (Corbin).

Henderson, Alfred J. see Henderson, Alfred James.

Henderson, Alfred James, 1905-
xHenderson, Alfred J.
London & the National Government 1721-1742: A Study of City Politics & the Walpole Administration. Porcupine Pr.

Henderson, Algo D. see Henderson, Algo Donmyer.

Henderson, Algo Donmyer.
xHenderson, Algo D.
Higher Education in America: Problems, Priorities & Prospects. Jossey-Bass.

Henderson, Alice (Corbin), 1881-1949
xHenderson, A. Corbin.
Brothers of Light: The Penitentes of the Southwest. Gannon.

Henderson, Archibald, 1877-1963
xHenderson, A.
The Twenty-Seven Lines Upon the Cubic Surface. Hafner.
xHenderson, Archibald.
The Conquest of the Old Southwest: The Romantic Story of the Early Pioneers into Virginia, the Carolinas, Tennessee & Kentucky, 1740-1790. Reprint. Contemporary Immortals. Arno.
Mark Twain. Folcroft.
Mark Twain. Haskell.

Henderson, B.
xHenderson, B.
Defects in Crystalline Solids. Intl Schol Bk Serv.
Defects in the Alkaline Earth Oxides: With Applications to Radiation Damage & Catalysis. Halsted Pr.

Henderson, Bernard W. see Henderson, Bernard William.

Henderson, Bernard William, 1872-1929
xHenderson, Bernard W.
The Great War Between Athens & Sparta. Arno.

Henderson, Bill, 1941-
xHenderson, Bill.
ed. The Pushcart Prize: Best of the Small Presses. Pushcart Pr.

Henderson, Brian.
xHenderson, Brian.
Critique of Film Theory. Dutton.

Henderson, Bruce.
xHenderson, Bruce.
Ghetto Cops. Major Bks.

Henderson, Bruce. see Henderson, Bruce E.

Henderson, Bruce D.
xHenderson, Bruce D.
Henderson on Corporate Strategy. ABT Assoc.

Henderson, Bruce E.
xHenderson, Bruce.
The World's Great Detectives & Their Most Famous Cases. B&N.

Henderson, David, 1942-
xHenderson, David.
Jimi Hendrix: Voodoo Child of the Aquarian Age. Doubleday.

Henderson, David. see Henderson, David Kennedy.

Henderson, David Kennedy.
xHenderson, David.
Textbook of Psychiatry for Students & Practitioners. Oxford U Pr.

Henderson, Diane.
xHenderson, Diane.
Guide to Basic Reference Materials for Canadian Libraries. U of Toronto Pr.

Henderson, Dwight F., 1937-
xHenderson, Dwight F.
Courts for a New Nation. Pub Aff Pr.

Henderson, Edith G.
xHenderson, Edith G.

Foundations of English Administrative Law: Certiorari & Mandamus in the Seventeenth Century. Harvard U Pr.

Henderson, Elisha L. *see* Henderson, Elisha Lane.

Henderson, Elisha Lane, 1884-
  xHenderson, Elisha L.
  The Organization & Administration of Student Teaching in State Teachers Colleges. AMS Pr.

Henderson, Ellen C.
  xHenderson, Ellen C.
  Teaching Reading to Bilingual Children: A Step-by-Step Guide That Guarantees Reading Success. Exposition.

Henderson, Elliott B. *see* Henderson, Elliott Blaine.

Henderson, Elliott Blaine.
  xHenderson, Elliott B.
  The Soliloquy of Satan, & Other Poems. Arno.

Henderson, Ernest F. *see* Henderson, Ernest Flagg.

Henderson, Ernest Flagg, 1861-1928
  xHenderson, Ernest F.
  History of Germany in the Middle Ages. Haskell.

Henderson, Euan S.
  xHenderson, Euan S.
  Evaluation of in-Service Teacher Training. Biblio Dist.

Henderson, Francis M. *see* Henderson, Francis Martin.

Henderson, Francis Martin, 1921-
  xHenderson, Francis M.
  Open Channel Flow. Macmillan.

Henderson, G. *see* Henderson, George Surgeon.

Henderson, G. F. *see* Henderson, George Francis Robert.

Henderson, G. P. *see* Henderson, George Patrick.

Henderson, Gavin B. *see* Henderson, Gavin Burns.

Henderson, Gavin Burns, 1909-1945
  xHenderson, Gavin B.
  Crimean War Diplomacy, & Other Historical Essays. Russell.

Henderson, George, 1904-
  xHenderson, George.
  The Farming Ladder. Merrimack Bk Serv.
  Human Relations in the Military: Problems & Programs. Nelson Hall.
  A Religious Foundation of Human Relations: Beyond Games. U of Okla Pr.
  Understanding & Counseling Ethnic Minorities. C C Thomas.

Henderson, George. *see* Association for Supervision and Curriculum Development. Yearbook Committee.

Henderson, George David Smith, 1931-
  xHenderson, George.
  Gothic. Penguin.

Henderson, George Francis Robert.
  xHenderson, G. F.
  Stonewall Jackson & the American Civil War. Peter Smith.

Henderson, George Patrick.
  xHenderson, G. P.
  Revival of Greek Thought, 1620-1830. State U NY Pr.

Henderson, George Surgeon, Surgeon.
  xHenderson, G.
  The Popular Rhymes, Sayings, & Proverbs of the County of Berwick. Folcroft.

Henderson, Gordon G. *see* Henderson, Gordon Grant.

Henderson, Gordon Grant, 1931-
  xHenderson, Gordon G.
  An Introduction to Political Parties. Har-Row.

Henderson, Gregory.
  xHenderson, Gregory.
  Public Diplomacy & Political Change: Four Case Studies: Okinawa, Peru, Czechoslovakia, Guinea. Irvington.

Henderson, Harold G. *see* Henderson, Harold Gould.

Henderson, Harold Gould.
  xHenderson, Harold G.

The Bamboo Broom: An Introduction to Japanese Haiku. Folcroft.
  Haiku in English. C E Tuttle.

Henderson, Hazel.
  xHenderson, Hazel.
  Creating Alternative Futures: The End of Economics. Berkley Pub.

Henderson, Helen R. *see* Henderson, Helen Ruth.

Henderson, Helen Ruth, 1898-
  xHenderson, Helen R.
  A Curriculum Study in a Mountain District. AMS Pr.

Henderson, Hubert. *see* Henderson, Hubert Douglas.

Henderson, Hubert Douglas, Sir, 1890-1952
  xHenderson, Hubert.
  Supply & Demand. Cambridge U Pr.

Henderson, J. Frank. *see* Henderson, Joseph Franklin.

Henderson, J. L. *see* Henderson, James Lewis.

Henderson, J. Lloyd. *see* Henderson, James Lloyd.

Henderson, J. M. *see* Henderson, James Mitchell.

Henderson, J. Neil. *see* Henderson, James Neil.

Henderson, James, 1905-
  xHenderson, James.
  Frigates: An Account of the Lesser Warships of the Wars from 1793 - 1815. Dodd.
  Silver Collecting for Amateurs. Soccer.

Henderson, James A.
  xHenderson, James A.
  The Torts Process. Little.

Henderson, James Lewis, 1910-
  xHenderson, J. L.
  Education for World Understanding. Pergamon.

Henderson, James Lloyd.
  xHenderson, J. Lloyd.
  Fluid Milk Industry. AVI.

Henderson, James Mitchell.
  xHenderson, J. M.
  Microeconomic Theory: A Mathematical Approach. McGraw.

Henderson, James Neil.
  xHenderson, J. Neil.
  ed. Polymerization Reactors & Processes. Am Chemical.

Henderson, Jean G. *see* Henderson, Jean Glidden.

Henderson, Jean Glidden.
  xHenderson, Jean G.
  Ms. Goes to College. S Ill U Pr.

Henderson, Joe, 1943-
  xHenderson, Joe.
  ed. The Complete Marathoner. Anderson World.
  Long Slow Distance: The Humane Way to Train. Tafnews.
  Longrun Solution. Anderson World.
  Run Farther, Run Faster. Anderson World.

Henderson, John, 1943-
  xHenderson, John.
  Off the Beaten Path: Short Hikes in the White Mountains. Glen-Bartlett.

Henderson, John C. *see* Henderson, John Cleaves.

Henderson, John Cleaves.
  xHenderson, John C.
  Thomas Jefferson's Views on Public Education. AMS Pr.

Henderson, John W. *see* Henderson, John Warren.

Henderson, John Warren.
  xHenderson, John W.
  Orbital Tumors. Saunders.

Henderson, Joseph Franklin, 1933-
  xHenderson, J. Frank.
  Regulation of Purine Biosynthesis. Am Chemical.

Henderson, Joseph L. *see* Henderson, Joseph Lindsey.

Henderson, Joseph Lindsey, 1869-
  xHenderson, Joseph L.
  Admission to College by Certificate. AMS Pr.

Henderson, Lawrence J. *see* Henderson, Lawrence Joseph.

Henderson, Lawrence Joseph, 1878-1942
  xHenderson, Lawrence J.

Fitness of the Environment: An Inquiry into the Biological Significance of the Properties of Matter. Peter Smith.

Henderson, Lawrence W., 1921-
  xHenderson, Lawrence W.
  Angola: Five Centuries of Conflict. Cornell U Pr.

Henderson, Lois T.
  xHenderson, Lois T.
  Hagar: A Novel. Christian Herald.
  Lydia: A Novel. Christian Herald.

Henderson, Marjorie.
  xHenderson, Marjorie.
  Naturally Powered Old Time Toys: How to Make Sun Yachts, Sail Cars, a Monkey on a String, & Other Moving Toys. Lippincott.

Henderson, Nancy. *see* Henderson, Nancy Wallace.

Henderson, Nancy Wallace.
  xHenderson, Nancy.
  Celebrate America: A Baker's Dozen of Plays. Messner.
  Circle of Life: The Miccosukee Indian Way. Messner.

Henderson, P. D. *see* Henderson, Patrick David.

Henderson, Patrick David.
  xHenderson, P. D.
  India: The Energy Sector. Oxford U Pr.

Henderson, Peter, 1944-
  xHenderson, Peter.
  Functional Programming. P-H.

Henderson, Philip, 1906-
  xHenderson, Philip.
  Richard Coeur De Lion: A Biography. Greenwood.
  Swinburne: Portrait of a Poet. Macmillan.

Henderson, Richard, 1924-
  xHenderson, Richard.
  The Cruiser's Compendium: A Complete Guide to Coastal, Inland, & Gunkhole Cruising. Contemp Bks.
  East to the Azores: A Guide to Offshore Passage-Making. Intl Marine.

Henderson, Richard I., 1926-
  xHenderson, Richard I.
  Compensation Management: Rewarding Performance. Reston.
  The Operating Manager: An Integrative Approach. P-H.
  Performance Appraisal: Theory to Practice. Reston.

Henderson, Robert. *see* Henderson, Robert J.

Henderson, Robert J.
  xHenderson, Robert.
  Life in Bible Times. Rand.

Henderson, Robert W. *see* Henderson, Robert William.

Henderson, Robert William, 1888-
  xHenderson, Robert W.
  Ball, Bat & Bishop: The Origin of Ball Games. Gale.

Henderson, Ronald W.
  xHenderson, Ronald W.
  The Cultural Context of Childhood. Merrill.

Henderson, S. M. *see* Henderson, Silas Milton.

Henderson, S. T. *see* Henderson, Stanley Thomas.

Henderson, Scott D.
  xHenderson, Scott D.
  Pathology in Computed Tomography of the Brain. C C Thomas.

Henderson, Silas Milton.
  xHenderson, S. M.
  Agricultural Process Engineering. AVI.

Henderson, Stanley Thomas.
  xHenderson, S. T.
  Daylight & Its Spectrum. Halsted Pr.

Henderson, Stephen. *see* Henderson, Stephen Evangelist.

Henderson, Stephen Evangelist, 1925-
  xHenderson, Stephen.

ed. Understanding the New Black Poetry:
Black Speech & Black Music As Poetic
References. Morrow.
Henderson, T. F. *see* Henderson, Thomas Finlayson.
Henderson, Thomas A.
xHenderson, Thomas A.
Congressional Oversight of Executive Agencies:
A Study of the House Committee on
Government Operations. U Presses Fla.
Urban Policy Game: A Simulation of Urban
Politics. Wiley.
Henderson, Thomas F. *see* Henderson, Thomas
Finlayson.
Henderson, Thomas Finlayson, 1844-1923
xHenderson, T. F.
The Ballad in Literature. Folcroft.
xHenderson, Thomas F.
The Ballad in Literature. Arden Lib.
Henderson, Thomas M.
xHenderson, Thomas M.
Tammany Hall & the New Immigrants: The
Progressive Years. Arno.
Henderson, W. F.
xHenderson, W. F.
Looking at Australia. Lippincott.
Henderson, W. Guy.
xHenderson, W. Guy.
Passport to Missions. Broadman.
Henderson, W. J. *see* Henderson, William James.
Henderson, W. O. *see* Henderson, William Otto.
Henderson, William, 1922-
xHenderson, William D.
Why the Vietcong Fought: A Study of
Motivation & Control in a Modern Army in
Combat. Greenwood.
Henderson, William C. *see* Henderson, William Leroy.
Henderson, William D. *see* Henderson, William.
Henderson, William J. *see* Henderson, William James.
Henderson, William James, 1855-1937
xHenderson, W. J.
The Art of Singing. Da Capo.
xHenderson, William J.
Early History of Singing. AMS Pr.
Some Forerunners of Italian Opera. Arno.
Henderson, William Leroy.
xHenderson, William C.
The Public Economy: An Introduction to
Government Finance. Phila Bk Co.
Henderson, William Otto, 1904-
xHenderson, W. O.
Studies in German Colonial History. Biblio
Dist.
Henderson, Zenna.
xHenderson, Zenna.
The Anything Box. Avon.
Holding Wonder. Avon.
Hendin, David.
xHendin, David.
Collecting Coins. NAL.
Death As a Fact of Life. Warner Bks.
Genetic Connection. NAL.
The Life Givers. Morrow.
The World Almanac Whole Health Guide.
NAL.
Hendin, Herbert.
xHendin, Herbert.
Age of Sensation. McGraw.
The Age of Sensation. Norton.
Hendin, Josephine.
xHendin, Josephine.
World of Flannery O'Connor. Ind U Pr.
Hendon, William S. *see* Hendon, William Scott.
Hendon, William Scott, 1933-
xHendon, William S.
Analyzing an Art Museum. Praeger.
Economics for Urban Social Planning. U of
Utah Pr.
Hendren, S. R. *see* Hendren, Samuel Rivers.
Hendren, Samuel R. *see* Hendren, Samuel Rivers.

Hendren, Samuel Rivers, 1872-
xHendren, S. R.
Government & Religion of the Virginia Indians.
Johnson Repr.
xHendren, Samuel R.
Government & Religion of the Virginia Indians.
AMS Pr.
Hendrich, Paula.
xHendrich, Paula.
The Girl Who Slipped Through Time. Lothrop.
Who Says So?. G K Hall.
Who Says So?. Lothrop.
Hendrick. *see* Hendrick, Joanne.
Hendrick, Burton J. *see* Hendrick, Burton Jesse.
Hendrick, Burton Jesse.
xHendrick, Burton J.
Life & Letters of Walter H. Page. Scholarly.
Hendrick, Clyde.
xHendrick, Clyde.
Nature of Theory & Research in Social
Psychology. Acad Pr.
Hendrick, Irving G., 1936-
xHendrick, Irving G.
California Education: A Brief History. Boyd &
Fraser.
Hendrick, Ives, 1898-
xHendrick, Ives.
Psychiatry Education Today. Intl Univs Pr.
Hendrick, Joanne, 1928-
xHendrick.
The Whole Child: New Trends in Early
Education. Mosby.
Hendricks, David W.
xHendricks, David W.
ed. Environmental Design for Public Projects.
WRP.
Hendricks, Gary.
xHendricks, Gary.
Consumer Durables & Installment Debt: A
Study of American Households. U of Mich
Soc Res.
Hendricks, Gordon.
xHendricks, Gordon.
The Life & Work of Winslow Homer. Abrams.
Origins of the American Film. Arno.
Hendricks, Harryette. *see* Hendricks, Harryette S.
Hendricks, Harryette S.
xHendricks, Harryette.
How to Make Christmas Ornaments. Country
Beautiful.
Hendricks, J. Edwin. *see* Hendricks, James Edwin.
Hendricks, James Edwin, 1935-
xHendricks, J. Edwin.
Charles Thomson & the Making of a New
Nation, 1729-1824. Fairleigh Dickinson.
Hendricks, Jeanne. *see* Hendricks, Jeanne W.
Hendricks, Jeanne W.
xHendricks, Jeanne.
Afternoon. Nelson.
Hendricks, John. *see* Hendricks, Jon.
Hendricks, Jon.
xHendricks, John.
Aging in Mass Society: Myths & Realities.
Winthrop.
Hendricks, Rhoda. *see* Hendricks, Rhoda A.
Hendricks, Rhoda A.
xHendricks, Rhoda.
Intro. by Classical Gods & Heroes: Myths As
Told by Ancient Authors. Ungar.
xHendricks, Rhoda A.
tr. Classical Gods & Heroes: Myths As Told by
Ancient Authors. Ungar.
Intro. by & tr. Classical Gods & Heroes: Myths
As Told by the Ancient Authors. Morrow.
Hendricks, William. *see* Hendricks, William Cornelius.
Hendricks, William C.
xHendricks, William C.

Object Lessons from Sports & Games. Baker
Bk.
Hendricks, William Cornelius.
xHendricks, William.
Bible Jumble Word Puzzles. Zondervan.
Hendrickson, J. B. *see* Hendrickson, James Briggs.
Hendrickson, James B. *see* Hendrickson, James Briggs.
Hendrickson, James Briggs.
xHendrickson, J. B.
Organic Chemistry. McGraw.
xHendrickson, James B.
jt. auth. Organic Chemistry. McGraw.
Hendrickson, James M.
xHendrickson, James M.
Spice of Life. HarBraceJ.
Hendrickson, Robert, 1933-
xHendrickson, Robert.
The Great American Tomato Book: The One
Complete Guide to Growing & Using
Tomatoes Everywhere. Doubleday.
Hendrickson, Walter B.
xHendrickson, Walter B.
Who Really Invented the Rocket?. Putnam.
Hendrie, Robert A.
xHendrie, Robert A.
Granulated Fertilizers. Noyes.
Hendriksen, Eldon S.
xHendriksen, Eldon S.
Accounting Theory. Irwin.
Hendrix, Sue.
xHendrix, Sue.
Dwight D. Eisenhower. Creative Ed.
Hendrix, T. G. *see* Hendrix, Theresa Gail.
Hendrix, Theresa Gail.
xHendrix, T. G.
Mathematics for Auto Mechanics. Delmar.
Hendry, George S. *see* Hendry, George Stuart.
Hendry, George Stuart, 1904-
xHendry, George S.
Theology of Nature. Westminster.
Heneghan, Donald A.
xHeneghan, Donald A.
A Concordance to the Poems & Fragments of
Wilfred Owen. G K Hall.
Henely, Kandy N. *see* Henely, Kandy Norton.
Henely, Kandy Norton.
xHenely, Kandy N.
The Farmer's Daughter Cookbook. Fawcett.
Heneman, Herbert G. *see* Heneman, Herbert Gerhard.
Heneman, Herbert Gerhard.
xHeneman, Herbert G.
ed. Perspectives on Personnel - Human
Resource Management. Irwin.
Henerson, Marlene. *see* Henerson, Marlene E.
Henerson, Marlene E.
xHenerson, Marlene.
How to Measure Attitudes. Sage.
Henfrey, Colin.
xHenfrey, Colin.
ed. Chilean Voices: Activists Describe Their
Experiences of the Popular Unity Period.
Humanities.
Hengel, Martin.
xHengel, Martin.
Acts & the History of Earliest Christianity.
Fortress.
Christ & Power. Fortress.
Henglein, F. A. *see* Henglein, Friedrich August.
Henglein, Friedrich August, 1893-
xHenglein, F. A.
Chemical Technology. Pergamon.
Hengstebeck, R J.
xHengstebeck, Robert J.
Distillation: Principles & Design Procedures.
Krieger.
Hengstebeck, Robert J. *see* Hengstebeck, R J.
Henig, Stanley.
xHenig, Stanley.

ed. Political Parties in the European
Community. Allen Unwin.
Henige, David P.
xHenige, David P.
The Chronology of Oral Tradition: Quest for a
Chimera. Oxford U Pr.
Heninger, S. K.
xHeninger, S. K.
The Cosmographical Glass: Renaissance
Diagrams of the Universe. Huntington Lib.
ed. English Prose, Prose Fiction, & Criticism to
1660: A Guide to Information Sources. Gale.
Touches of Sweet Harmony: Pythagorean
Cosmology & Renaissance Poetics.
Huntington Lib.
Henion, Karl E.
xHenion, Karl E.
ed. The Conserver Society. Am Mktg.
Henisch, Bridget A. *see* Henisch, Bridget Ann.
Henisch, Bridget Ann.
xHenisch, Bridget A.
Medieval Armchair Travels. Carnation.
xHenisch, Bridget Ann.
Fast and Feast: Food in Medieval Society. Pa
St U Pr.
Henisch, Heinz K.
xHenisch, Heinz K.
Crystal Growth in Gels. Pa St U Pr.
Henissart, Paul.
xHenissart, Paul.
Margin of Error. S&S.
Narrow Exit. PB.
Henke, Emerson O.
xHenke, Emerson O.
Introduction to Nonprofit Organization
Accounting. Wadsworth Pub.
Henke, Thomas R.
xHenke, Thomas R.
How to Love...& Be Loved. Trans Traffic.
Henkel, Barbara O. *see* Henkel, Barbara Osborn.
Henkel, Barbara Osborn, 1921-
xHenkel, Barbara O.
Foundations of Health Science. Allyn.
Henkes, Robert.
xHenkes, Robert.
Eight American Women Painters. Gordon Pr.
Insights in Art & Education. Gordon Pr.
Henkin, Bill. *see* Henkin, William A.
Henkin, Harmon.
xHenkin, Harmon.
Complete Fisherman's Catalog: A Source Book
of Information About Tackle & Accessories.
Lippincott.
Crisscross. Dell.
Fly Tackle: A Guide to the Tools of the Trade.
Lippincott.
Henkin, Louis.
xHenkin, Louis.
Arms Control & Inspection in American Law.
Greenwood.
Foreign Affairs & the Constitution. Norton.
Henkin, Shepard.
xHenkin, Shepard.
Opportunities in Hotel & Motel Management.
Natl Txtbk.
Henkin, William A., 1944-
xHenkin, Bill.
The Rocky Horror Picture Show Book. Dutton.
Henle, Jane. *see* Henle, Jane Elizabeth.
Henle, Jane Elizabeth, 1913-
xHenle, Jane.
Greek Myths: A Vase Painter's Notebook. Ind
U Pr.
Henle, Mary.
xHenle, Mary.
ed. Historical Conceptions of Psychology.
Springer Pub.
Henley, B. M. *see* Henley, Martin.
Henley, Diana.
xHenley, Diana.

ASPCA Guide to Pet Care. Taplinger.
Henley, Gail.
xHenley, Gail.
Where the Cherries End up. Little.
Henley, Karyn.
xHenley, Karyn.
Hatch!. Carolrhoda Bks.
Henley, Martin.
xHenley, B. M.
Orienteering. Charles River Bks.
xHenley, Martin.
Orienteering. Sterling.
Orienteering. Sterling.
Henley, Pauline.
xHenley, Pauline.
Spenser in Ireland. Folcroft.
Spenser in Ireland. Russell.
Spenser in Ireland. Scholarly.
Henley, Thomas. *see* Henley, Thomas A.
Henley, Thomas A.
xHenley, Thomas.
Hiking Trails in the Northeast. Contemp Bks.
Henley, Wallace.
xHenley, Wallace.
White House Mystique. Pillar Bks.
Henn, Harry G.
xHenn, Harry G.
Copyright Primer. PLI.
Henn, R. *see* Henn, Rudolf.
Henn, Rudolf.
xHenn, R.
ed. Optimization & Operations Research:
Proceedings of a Workshop Held at the
University of Bonn, October 2-8, 1977.
Springer-Verlag.
Henn, Thomas R. *see* Henn, Thomas Rice.
Henn, Thomas Rice.
xHenn, Thomas R.
Last Essays. B&N.
Last Essays. Humanities.
Hennelly, Alfred T.
xHennelly, Alfred T.
Theologies in Conflict: The Challenge of Juan
Luis Segundo. Orbis Bks.
Henneman, J. B. *see* Henneman, John Bell.
Henneman, John Bell, 1935-
xHenneman, J. B.
The Medieval French Monarchy. Krieger.
Hennen, M. L. *see* Hennen, Malinda A.
Hennen, Malinda A.
xHennen, M. L.
Identifying Handicapped Children for Child
Development Programs. Humanics Ltd.
Hennessey, James.
xHennessey, James.
The Nomadic Handbook: A Guide to Moving
& to Finding & Adapting Your Next Home.
Pantheon.
Hennessy, Alistair.
xHennessy, Alistair.
The Frontier in Latin American History. U of
NM Pr.
Hennessy, Bernard C.
xHennessy, Bernard C.
Public Opinion. Duxbury Pr.
Hennessy, Madeleine.
xHennessy, Madeleine.
Pavor Nocturnus & Other Poems. Washout.
Hennessy, Max.
xHennessy, Max.
The Lion at Sea. Atheneum.
Hennie, Fred. *see* Hennie, Frederick C.
Hennie, Frederick C.
xHennie, Fred.
Introduction to Computability. A-W.
Hennig, Helen. *see* Hennig, Helen (Kohn).
Hennig, Helen (Kohn).
xHennig, Helen.

Great South Carolinians. Arno.
Hennig, Willi, 1913-
xHennig, Willi.
Phylogenetic Systematics. U of Ill Pr.
Henniker, Florence. *see* Henniker, Florence Ellen
Hungerford Milnes.
**Henniker, Florence Ellen Hungerford Milnes, Hon, d.
1923**
xHenniker, Florence.
In Scarlet & Grey. Garland Pub.
Henning, Alyson. *see* Henning, Alyson B.
Henning, Alyson B.
xHenning, Alyson.
A Guide to Hartford. Globe Pequot.
Henning, Charles. *see* Henning, Charles N.
Henning, Charles N.
xHenning, Charles.
Financial Markets & the Economy. P-H.
xHenning, Charles N.
Financial Markets & the Economy. P-H.
Henning, D. H. *see* Henning, Daniel H.
Henning, Daniel H.
xHenning, D. H.
Environmental Policy & Administration.
Elsevier.
Henning, Doug.
xHenning, Doug.
Houdini: His Legend & His Magic. Times Bks.
Houdini: His Legend & His Magic. Warner
Bks.
Henning, Edward B.
xHenning, Edward B.
Spirit of Surrealism. Ind U Pr.
Henning, Joel.
xHenning, Joel.
Holistic Running: Beyond the Threshold of
Fitness. Atheneum.
Holistic Running: Beyond the Threshold of
Fitness. NAL.
Henninger, Joseph. *see* Henninger, Joseph M.
Henninger, Joseph M., 1906-
xHenninger, Joseph.
Drawing of the Hand & Its Anatomy. Borden.
Hennings, Dorothy G. *see* Hennings, Dorothy Grant.
Hennings, Dorothy Grant.
xHennings, Dorothy G.
Communication in Action: Dynamic Teaching
of the Language Arts. Rand.
Hennock, E. P., 1926-
xHennock, E. P.
Fit & Proper Persons: Ideal & Reality in
Nineteenth-Century Urban Government.
McGill-Queens U Pr.
Henrey, Robert, Mrs, 1906-
xHenrey, Robert.
The Golden Visit. Biblio Dist.
Henri, Florette.
xHenri, Florette.
George Mason of Virginia. Macmillan.
Henrich, Edith. *see* Henrich, Edith (Dodd).
Henrich, Edith (Dodd), 1907-
xHenrich, Edith.
Person in the World. Poems. SMU Press.
Henrichsen, Margaret.
xHenrichsen, Margaret K.
Seven Steeples. Thorndike Pr.
Henrichsen, Margaret K. *see* Henrichsen, Margaret.
Henrichsen, Walter A.
xHenrichsen, Walter A.
Disciples Are Made-Not Born. Victor Bks.
A Layman's Guide to Interpreting the Bible.
NavPress.
A Layman's Guide to Interpreting the Bible.
Zondervan.
Henrici, Peter, 1923-
xHenrici, Peter.

Computational Analysis with the Hp 25 Pocket
Calculator. Wiley.
Discrete Variable Methods in Ordinary
Differential Equations. Wiley.
Henrickson, Robert L. see Henrickson, Robert Lee.
Henrickson, Robert Lee, 1920-
xHenrickson, Robert L.
Meat, Poultry & Seafood Technology. P-H.
Henriod, Lorraine.
xHenriod, Lorraine.
Ancestor Hunting. Messner.
Henrion, Pierre.
xHenrion, Pierre.
Gulliver's Secret. Arden Lib.
Henriques, E. Frank.
xHenriques, E. Frank.
The Signet Encyclopedia of Wine. NAL.
Henriques, Fernando.
xHenriques, Fernando.
Children of Conflict: A Study of Interracial Sex
& Marriage. Dutton.
Henriques, Ursula R. see Henriques, Ursula R. Q.
Henriques, Ursula R. Q.
xHenriques, Ursula R.
Before the Welfare State: Social Administration
in Early Industrial Britain. Longman.
Henriquez-Urena, Pedro, 1884-1946
xHenriquez-Urena, Pedro.
Literary Currents in Hispanic America. Russell.
Henry, Arthur, 1867-1934
xHenry, Arthur.
Nicholas Blood, Candidate. Arno.
Henry, Carl F. see Henry, Carl Ferdinand Howard.
Henry, Carl F. H. see Henry, Carl Ferdinand Howard.
Henry, Carl Ferdinand Howard.
xHenry, Carl F.
Evangelicals in Search of Identity. Word Bks.
ed. Horizons of Science: Christian Scholars
Speak Out. Har-Row.
xHenry, Carl F. H.
ed. Baker's Dictionary of Christian Ethics.
Baker Bk.
Henry, D. P. see Henry, Desmond Paul.
Henry, David D. see Henry, David Dodds.
Henry, David Dodds.
xHenry, David D.
Challenges Past, Challenges Present: An
Analysis of American Higher Education
Since 1930. Jossey-Bass.
Henry, Desmond Paul.
xHenry, D. P.
Commentary on 'De Grammatico': The
Historical-Logical Dimensions of a Dialogue
of St. Anselm's. Kluwer Boston.
Medieval Logic & Metaphysics: A Modern
Introduction. Humanities.
Henry, Franklin J.
xHenry, Franklin J.
The Experience of Discrimination: A Case
Study Approach. R & E Res Assoc.
Henry, George W. see Henry, George William.
Henry, George William, 1889-
xHenry, George W.
All the Sexes: A Study of Masculinity &
Femininity. Octagon.
Masculinity & Femininity. Macmillan.
Society & the Sex Variant. Macmillan.
Henry, Hugh F., 1916-
xHenry, Hugh F.
Fundamentals of Radiation Protection. Wiley.
Henry, J. P. see Henry, James Paget.
Henry, James Paget.
xHenry, J. P.
Stress, Health, & the Social Environment: A
Sociobiologic Approach to Medicine.
Springer Verlag.
Henry, John J. see Henry, John Joseph.
Henry, John Joseph, 1758-1811
xHenry, John J.

Account of Arnold's Campaign Against
Quebec. Arno.
Henry, Jules, 1904-
xHenry, Jules.
Culture Against Man. Random.
Pathways to Madness. Random.
Henry, Laurin L.
xHenry, Laurin L.
Presidential Transitions. Brookings.
Henry, Marguerite, 1902-
xHenry, Marguerite.
All About Horses. Random.
Brighty of the Grand Canyon. Rand.
Five O'Clock Charlie. Rand.
The Little Fellow. Rand.
Mustang, Wild Spirit of the West. Rand.
One Man's Horse. Rand.
White Stallion of Lipizza. Rand.
Henry, Mark.
xHenry, Mark.
A Patchwork Family. Broadman.
Henry, N. see Henry, Nicholas.
Henry, Nicholas, 1943-
xHenry, N.
Public Administration & Public Affairs. P-H.
xHenry, Nicholas.
Doing Public Administration: Exercises, Essays
& Cases. Allyn.
xHenry, Nicholas J.
Governing at the Grassroots: State & Local
Politics. P-H.
Henry, Nicholas J. see Henry, Nicholas.
Henry, Orville.
xHenry, Orville.
The Razorbacks: A Story of Arkansas Football.
Strode.
Henry, Patrick, 1939-
xHenry, Patrick.
New Directions in New Testament Study.
Westminster.
Henry, Patrick. see Henry, Patrick Mark.
Henry, Patrick Mark, 1928-
xHenry, Patrick.
Palladium Catalyzed Oxidation of
Hydrocarbons. Kluwer Boston.
Henry, Paul B.
xHenry, Paul B.
Politics for Evangelicals. Judson.
Henry, Rene A.
xHenry, Rene A.
How to Profitably Buy & Sell Land. Wiley.
Henry, Robert. see Henry, Robert Selph.
Henry, Robert M. see Henry, Robert Mitchell.
Henry, Robert Mitchell, 1873-1950
xHenry, Robert M.
Evolution of Sinn Fein. Arno.
Evolution of Sinn Fein. Kennikat.
Henry, Robert Selph, 1889-
xHenry, Robert.
The Story of Reconstruction. Peter Smith.
Henry, Sarah Ann.
xHenry, Sarah Ann.
The Little Book of Big Knock Knock Jokes.
Harvey.
Henry, Sheila E.
xHenry, Sheila E.
Cultural Persistence & Socio-Economic
Mobility: A Comparative Study of
Assimilation Among Armenians & Japanese
in Los Angeles. R & E Res Assoc.
Henry, William E. see Henry, William Earl.
Henry, William Earl.
xHenry, William E.
Public & Private Lives of Psychotherapists.
Jossey-Bass.
Henry, William S. see Henry, William Seaton.
Henry, William Seaton, 1816-1851
xHenry, William S.

Campaign Sketches of the War with Mexico.
Arno.
Henry, William W. see Henry, William Wirt.
Henry, William Wirt.
xHenry, William W.
Patrick Henry, Life Correspondence &
Speeches. B Franklin.
Henryson, Robert, 1430?-1506?
xHenryson, Robert.
Moral Fables of Robert Henryson. AMS Pr.
Henschel, George, Sir, 1850-1934
xHenschel, George.
Musings & Memories of a Musician. Da Capo.
Henschel, Stan.
xHenschel, Stan.
How to Raise & Train a Chesapeake Bay
Retriever. TFH Pubns.
How to Raise & Train a Coonhound. TFH
Pubns.
Hensel, Evelyn.
xHensel, Evelyn.
Purchasing Library Materials in Public &
School Libraries: A Study of Purchasing
Procedures & the Relationship Between
Libraries, Purchasing Agencies & Dealers.
ALA.
Hensel, Nancy B.
xHensel, Nancy H.
Evaluating Children's Development in
Creativity & Creative Drama. R & E Res
Assoc.
Hensel, Nancy H. see Hensel, Nancy B.
Henshaw, Richard, 1945-
xHenshaw, Richard.
The Encyclopedia of World Soccer. New
Republic.
Henshaw, Richard C.
xHenshaw, Richard C.
Concepts & Applications of Modern Decision
Models. Mich St U Busn.
Executive Game. Irwin.
Henshel, Anne-Marie, 1940-
xHenshel, Anne-Marie.
The Forgotten Ones: A Sociological Study of
Anglo & Chicano Retardates. U of Tex Pr.
Henshel, Richard L.
xHenshel, Richard L.
On the Future of Social Prediction. Bobbs.
Perception in Criminology. Columbia U Pr.
Hensley, J. Clark. see Hensley, John Clark.
Hensley, Joe L., 1926-
xHensley, Joe L.
Deliver Us to Evil. Condor Pub Co.
Hensley, John Clark, 1912-
xHensley, J. Clark.
Coping with Being Single Again. Broadman.
Henslin, James M.
xHenslin, James M.
ed. Introducing Sociology: Selected Readings.
Free Pr.
ed. Marriage & Family in a Changing Society.
Free Pr.
Social Problems in American Society. Allyn.
ed. Sociology of Sex: An Introductory Reader.
Schocken.
Henslow, George, 1835-1925
xHenslow, George.
Medical Works of the Fourteenth Century,
Together with a List of Plants Recorded in
Contemporary Writings, with Their
Identifications. B Franklin.
Hensman, C. R.
xHensman, C. R.
Rich Against Poor: The Reality of Aid.
Schenkman.
Henson, Clyde E.
xHenson, Clyde E.
Joseph Kirkland. Coll & U Pr.
Joseph Kirkland. Irvington.
Henson, H. H. see Henson, Herbert Hensley.

Henson, Herbert H. *see* Henson, Herbert Hensley.
Henson, Herbert Hensley, Bp. of Durham, 1863-1947
  xHenson, H. H.
    Byron. Haskell.
  xHenson, Herbert H.
    Byron. Folcroft.
    Puritanism in England. B Franklin.
Henson, Josiah, 1789-1883
  xHenson, Josiah.
    Father Henson's Story of His Own Life.
      Corinth Bks.
    Father Henson's Story of His Own Life.
      Corner Hse.
    Father Henson's Story of His Own Life. Metro
      Bks.
Henson, Kenneth T.
  xHenson, Kenneth T.
    Personalizing Teaching in the Elementary
      School. Merrill.
Henson, Matthew A. *see* Henson, Matthew Alexander.
Henson, Matthew Alexander, 1866-1955
  xHenson, Matthew A.
    Negro Explorer at the North Pole. Arno.
Henson, Ray D., 1924-
  xHenson, Ray D.
    Handbook on Secured Transactions Under the
      Uniform Commercial Code. West Pub.
Henstra, Friso.
  xHenstra, Friso.
    illus. Wait & See. A-W.
Henszey, Benjamin N.
  xHenszey, Benjamin N.
    Introduction to Basic Legal Principles.
      Kendall-Hunt.
Henthorn, William E.
  xHenthorn, William E.
    History of Korea. Free Pr.
Hentig, Hans Von, 1887-1974
  xHentig, Hans Von.
    The Criminal & His Victim: Studies in the
      Sociobiology of Crime. Schocken.
    The Criminal & His Victim: Studies in the
      Sociobiology of Crime. Shoe String.
Hentoff, Nat.
  xHentoff, Nat.
    Doctor Among the Addicts. Rand.
    The First Freedom: The Tumultuous History of
      Free Speech in America. Delacorte.
    I'm Really Dragged but Nothing Gets Me
      Down. Dell.
    I'm Really Dragged but Nothing Gets Me
      Down. S&S.
    In the Country of Ourselves. S&S.
Hentze, Carl.
  xHentze, Carl.
    Chinese Tomb Figures: A Study in the Beliefs
      & Folklore of Ancient China. AMS Pr.
Henzke, Lucile.
  xHenzke, Lucille.
    American Art Pottery. Nelson.
Henzke, Lucille. *see* Henzke, Lucile.
Hepburn, A. Barton. *see* Hepburn, Alonzo Barton.
Hepburn, Alonzo B. *see* Hepburn, Alonzo Barton.
Hepburn, Alonzo Barton, 1846-1922
  xHepburn, A. Barton.
    History of Currency in the United States.
      Kelley.
  xHepburn, Alonzo B.
    History of Coinage & Currency in the United
      States & the Perennial Contest for Sound
      Money. Greenwood.
Hepburn, H. R.
  xHepburn, H. R.
    ed. The Insect Integument. Elsevier.
Hepburn, J. *see* Hepburn, James C.
Hepburn, James C.
  xHepburn, J.
    The Art of Arnold Bennett. Haskell.
Hepburn, Ronald W.
  xHepburn, Ronald W.

    Christianity & Paradox: Critical Studies in
      Twentieth-Century Theology. Bobbs.
Hepler, Loren G.
  xHepler, Loren G.
    Principles of Chemistry. Macmillan.
Hepner, Harry W. *see* Hepner, Harry Walker.
Hepner, Harry Walker, 1893-
  xHepner, Harry W.
    Psychology Applied to Life & Work. P-H.
Heppenheimer, T. A., 1947-
  xHeppenheimer, T. A.
    Colonies in Space. Stackpole.
    Colonies in Space. Warner Bks.
    Toward Distant Suns. Stackpole.
Heppenstall, Margit S. *see* Heppenstall, Margit Strom.
Heppenstall, Margit Strom.
  xHeppenstall, Margit S.
    Deborah. Southern Pub.
Heppenstall, R. Bruce.
  xHeppenstall, R. Bruce.
    ed. Fracture Treatment & Healing. Saunders.
Heppenstall, Rayner, 1911-
  xHeppenstall, Raynor.
    The Connecting Door. Dufour.
Heppenstall, Raynor. *see* Heppenstall, Rayner.
Hepperle, Winifred L.
  xHepperle, Winifred L.
    ed. Women in Courts. Natl Ctr St Courts.
Hepple, Peter.
  xHepple, Peter.
    ed. Outlook for Natural Gas: A Quality Fuel.
      Halsted Pr.
Heptinstall, Robert H.
  xHeptinstall, Robert H.
    Pathology of the Kidney. Little.
Heptner, Angela M.
  xHeptner, Angelo M.
    Multivista Cultural. Allyn
Heptner, Angelo M. *see* Heptner, Angela M.
Hepworth, Cecil M.
  xHepworth, Cecil M.
    Animated Photography: The ABC of the
      Cinematograph. Arno.
Hepworth, George H. *see* Hepworth, George Hughes.
Hepworth, George Hughes, 1833-1902
  xHepworth, George H.
    The Whip, Hoe & Sword. Arno.
    The Whip, Hoe, & Sword. La State U Pr.
Hepworth, Martyn.
  xHepworth, Martyn.
    Amateur Drama: Production & Management.
      David & Charles.
Hepworth, N. P. *see* Hepworth, Noel Peers.
Hepworth, Noel Peers.
  xHepworth, N. P.
    Finance of Local Government. Allen Unwin.
Hepworth, T. C. *see* Hepworth, Thomas Cradock.
Hepworth, Thomas Cradock.
  xHepworth, T. C.
    Evening Work for Amateur Photographers.
      Arno.
Heradstveit, Daniel, 1940-
  xHeradstveit, Daniel.
    The Arab-Israeli Conflict: Psychological
      Obstacles to Peace. Universitet.
Heravi, Mehdi, 1940-
  xHeravi, Mehdi.
    ed. Concise Encyclopedia of the Middle East.
      Pub Aff Pr.
Herbart, Johann F. *see* Herbart, Johann Friedrich.
Herbart, Johann Friedrich, 1776-1841
  xHerbart, Johann F.
    Outlines of Educational Doctrine. Folcroft.
Herbel, Norman.
  xHerbel, Norman.
    The Complete Lhasa Apso. Howell Bk.
Herber, Bernard P.
  xHerber, Bernard P.

    Modern Public Finance. Irwin.
Herber, Harold L.
  xHerber, Harold L.
    ed. Developing Study Skills in Secondary
      Schools. Intl Reading.
    Teaching Reading in Content Areas. P-H.
Herber, Howard T. *see* Herber, Howard Tilghman.
Herber, Howard Tilghman, 1901-
  xHerber, Howard T.
    The Influence of the Public Works
      Administration on School Building
      Construction in New York State, 1933-1936.
      AMS Pr.
Herber, William.
  xHerber, William.
    Hold Saipan!. Nordon Pubns.
Herberg, Will.
  xHerberg, Will.
    Protestant-Catholic-Jew: An Essay in American
      Religious Sociology. Doubleday.
    Protestant, Catholic, Jew: An Essay in
      American Religious Sociology. Peter Smith.
Herberholz, Barbara. *see* Herberholz, Barbara J.
Herberholz, Barbara J.
  xHerberholz, Barbara.
    Early Childhood Art. Wm C Brown.
Herbers, John.
  xHerbers, John.
    No Thank You, Mr. President. Norton.
Herbert, Auberon. *see* Herbert, Auberon Edward William
  Molyneux.
Herbert, Auberon Edward William Molyneux.
  xHerbert, Auberon.
    The Right & Wrong of Compulsion by the
      State, & Other Essays. Liberty Fund.
Herbert, Charles, 1757-1808
  xHerbert, Charles.
    Relic of the Revolution. Arno.
Herbert, Cheryl.
  xHerbert, Cheryl.
    Night Chase. Southern Pub.
Herbert, David T.
  xHerbert, David T.
    ed. Social Problems & the City: Geographical
      Perspectives. Oxford U Pr.
Herbert, Edward H. *see* Herbert, Edward Herbert.
Herbert, Edward Herbert.
  xHerbert, Edward H.
    Autobiography of Edward, Lord Herbert of
      Cherbury. Greenwood.
Herbert, Eugenia W.
  xHerbert, Eugenia W.
    The Artist & Social Reform: France - Belgium,
      1885-1898. Arno.
Herbert, Frank.
  xHerbert, Frank.
    Children of Dune. Berkley Pub.
    Dune. Berkley Pub.
    Dune. Chilton.
    Dune Messiah. Berkley Pub.
    Dune Messiah. Putnam.
    Eyes of Heisenberg. Berkley Pub.
    The Jesus Incident. Berkley Pub.
Herbert, George.
  xHerbert, George.
    Works. Oxford U Pr.
Herbert, James.
  xHerbert, James.
    The Fluke. NAL.
    The Fog. NAL.
    The Survivor. NAL.
Herbert, Janice S. *see* Herbert, Janice Summers.
Herbert, Janice Summers.
  xHerbert, Janice S.

Affordable Oriental Rugs: The Buyer's Guide
to Rugs from China, India, Pakistan &
Romania. Macmillan.
Oriental Rugs: The Illustrated Guide.
Macmillan.
Herbert, John, 1926-
xHerbert, John.
Fortune & Men's Eyes. Grove.
Herbert, John A. see Herbert, John Alexander.
Herbert, John Alexander, 1862-
xHerbert, John A.
Illuminated Manuscripts. B Franklin.
Herbert, John D.
xHerbert, John D.
Urban Development in the Third World: Policy
Guidelines. Praeger.
Herbert, Leo, 1912-
xHerbert, Leo.
Auditing the Performance of Management. CBI
Pub.
Auditing the Performance of Management.
Lifetime Learn.
Herbert, R. T. see Herbert, Robert T.
Herbert, Robert T., 1928-
xHerbert, R. T.
Paradox & Identity in Theology. Cornell U Pr.
Herbert, Sid. see Herbert, Sydney.
Herbert, Susan.
xHerbert, Susan.
The Crepe Book. Owlswood Prods.
Herbert, Sydney.
xHerbert, Sid.
The Man in Hu-Man. Amherst Pr.
Herbert, Theodore T.
xHerbert, Theodore T.
Dimensions of Organizational Behavior.
Macmillan.
Management Education & Development: An
Annotated Resource Book. Greenwood.
Herbert, W. L.
xHerbert, W. L.
Marriage Counselling in the Community.
Pergamon.
Herberts, Peter.
xHerberts, Peter.
ed. The Control of the Upper-Extremity
Prostheses & Orthoses. C C Thomas.
**Herbette Symposium on Species Concept
Hymenomycetes, University of Lausanne, 1976.**
xSymposium Lausanne, Switzerland Aug. 16 to 20
1976.
Species Concept Hymenomycetes: Proceedings.
Lubrecht & Cramer.
Herbig, George H.
xHerbig, George H.
ed. Spectroscopic Astrophysics: An Assessment
of the Contributions of Otto Struve. U of Cal
Pr.
Herbin, Robert.
xHerbin, Robert.
Soccer the Way the Pros Play. Sterling.
Herbruck, Christine. see Herbruck, Christine Comstock.
Herbruck, Christine Comstock.
xHerbruck, Christine.
Breaking the Cycle of Child Abuse. Winston
Pr.
Herbst. see Herbst, Thomas.
Herbst, Alma.
xHerbst, Alma.
Negro in the Slaughtering & Meat-Packing
Industry in Chicago. Arno.
Herbst, Josephine, 1897-1969
xHerbst, Josephine.
The Executioner Waits. AMS Pr.
Money for Love. Arno.
Nothing Is Sacred. Arno.
Herbst, Jurgen.
xHerbst, Jurgen.

Compiled by The History of American
Education. AHM Pub.
Herbst, P. G.
xHerbst, P. G.
Alternatives to Hierarchies. Kluwer Boston.
Herbst, Thomas.
xHerbst.
Grimm's Grandchildren: Current Topics in
German Linguistics. Longman.
Hercules, Patricia R. see Hercules, Patricia Robertson.
Hercules, Patricia Robertson.
xHercules, Patricia R.
Pulmonary Restriction & Obstruction: A
Programmed Text. Year Bk Med.
Herd, David.
xHerd, David.
ed. Ancient & Modern Scottish Songs, Heroic
Ballads, Etc.. Rowman.
Herda, D. J., 1948-
xHerda, D. J.
Growing Trees Indoors. Nelson-Hall.
Roller Skating. Watts.
Vegetables in a Pot. Messner.
Herdan, G. see Herdan, Gustav.
Herdan, Gustav.
xHerdan, G.
Advanced Theory of Language As Choice &
Chance. Springer-Verlag.
Quantitative Linguistics. Shoe String.
Herdeck, Donald E., 1924-
xHerdeck, Donald E.
ed. African Authors: A Companion to Black
African Writing 1300-1973. Gale.
African Authors: A Companion to Black
African Writing, 1300-1973. Inscape Corp.
Herder, Johann G. Von. see Herder, Johann Gottfried
Von.
Herder, Johann Gottfried Von, 1744-1803
xHerder, Johann G. Von.
Spirit of Hebrew Poetry. Allenson.
Hereford, Carl F.
xHereford, Carl F.
Changing Parental Attitudes Through Group
Discussion. U of Tex Pr.
Heren, Louis.
xHeren, Louis.
China's Three Thousand Years: The Story of a
Great Civilisation. Macmillan.
Herfarth, C. see Herfarth, Christian.
Herfarth, Christian.
xHerfarth, C.
ed. Gastric Cancer. Springer-Verlag.
Herff, Ferdinand P. see Herff, Ferdinand Peter.
Herff, Ferdinand Peter, 1883-1965
xHerff, Ferdinand P.
The Doctors Herff: A Three-Generation
Memoir. Trinity U Pr.
Herfindal, Eric T.
xHerfindal, Eric T.
Clinical Pharmacy & Therapeutics. Williams &
Wilkins.
Herford, C. H. see Herford, Charles Harold.
Herford, Charles H. see Herford, Charles Harold.
Herford, Charles Harold, 1853-1931
xHerford, C. H.
Permanent Power of English Poetry. Folcroft.
xHerford, Charles H.
The Age of Wordsworth. Arno.
The Age of Wordsworth. Folcroft.
Wordsworth. AMS Pr.
Wordsworth. Folcroft.
Herford, Oliver, 1863-1935
xHerford, Oliver.
Child's Primer of Natural History. Dover.
More Animals. Dover.
Hergenhahn, B. R., 1934-
xHergenhahn, B. R.

An Introduction to the Theories of Personality.
P-H.
Hergesheimer, Joseph, 1880-1954
xHergesheimer, Joseph.
Swords & Roses. Arno.
Herhold, Robert M.
xHerhold, Robert M.
The Promise Beyond the Pain. Abingdon.
Hering, Ewald.
xHering, Ewald.
The Theory of Binocular Vision. Plenum Pub.
Heringer, H. J. see Heringer, Hans-Jurgen.
Heringer, Hans-Jurgen, 1939-
xHeringer, H. J.
Practical Semantics: A Study in the Rules of
Speech & Action. Mouton.
Herington, C. J.
xHerington, C. J.
Author of the Prometheus Bound. U of Tex Pr.
Herink, Richie.
xHerink, Richie.
ed. The Psychotherapy Handbook. NAL.
Heriot, Angus, 1927-
xHeriot, Angus.
The Castrati in Opera. Da Capo.
Herisko, Clarence.
xHerisko, Clarence.
How to Be an Entertainer. Key Bks.
Heritage Home Plans, Inc. see Heritage Homes Plan
Service.
Heritage Homes Plan Service.
xHeritage Home Plans, Inc.
Luxury Home Plans. HarBraceJ.
Heriteau, Jacqueline.
xHeriteau, Jacqueline.
The Complete Book of Beans. Dutton.
Easy Gardening Projects. Popular Lib.
Oriental Cooking the Fast Wok Way. Dutton.
Oriental Cooking the Fast Wok Way. NAL.
Preserving & Pickling: Putting Foods by in
Small Batches. Western Pub.
xHeriteau, Jacqueline.
ed. Budget Recipes. Winchester Pr.
Heriteau, Jacqueline. see Heriteau, Jacqueline.
Herivel, John.
xHerivel, John.
Joseph Fourier: The Man & the Physicist.
Oxford U Pr.
Herkimer, Allen G.
xHerkimer, Allen G.
Understanding Hospital Financial Management.
Aspen Systems.
Herkimer, Herbert, 1885-
xHerkimer, Herbert.
Cost Manual for Piping & Mechanical
Construction. Chem Pub.
Herkimer, L. R.
xHerkimer, L. R.
ed. The Complete Book of Cheerleading.
Doubleday.
Herklots, G. A. C. see Herklots, Geoffrey Alton Craig.
Herklots, Geoffrey Alton Craig.
xHerklots, G. A. C.
Vegetables in South-East Asia. Allen Unwin.
Herley, Richard, 1950-
xHerley, Richard.
The Stone Arrow. St Martin.
Herlick, Stanford D.
xHerlick, Stanford D.
California Workers' Compensation Law
Handbook. Parker & Son.
Herlihy, David.
xHerlihy, David.
ed. History of Feudalism. Humanities.
History of Feudalism. Walker & Co.
Herlihy, James L. see Herlihy, James Leo.
Herlihy, James Leo.
xHerlihy, James L.

All Fall Down. Avon.
Herlin, Hans, 1925-
 xHerlin, Hans.
  Commemorations. Ballantine.
  Which Way the Wind. Avon.
  Which Way the Wind. St Martin.
Herman. *see* Herman, Charlotte.
Herman, A. L.
 xHerman, A. L.
  Introduction to Indian Thought. P-H.
Herman, A. L. *see* Herman, Arthur L.
Herman, Arthur L.
 xHerman, A. L.
  The Problem of Evil & Indian Thought. Orient
   Bk Dist.
Herman, Charlotte.
 xHerman.
  Our Snowman Had Olive Eyes. Schol Bk Serv.
 xHerman, Charlotte.
  The Difference of Ari Stein. Har-Row.
  On the Way to the Movies. Dutton.
  Our Snowman Had Olive Eyes. Dutton.
  String Bean. O'Hara.
Herman, Daniel J.
 xHerman, Daniel J.
  The Philosophy of Henri Bergson. U Pr of
   Amer.
Herman, Donald L.
 xHerman, Donald L.
  Comintern in Mexico. Pub Aff Pr.
  The Communist Tide in Latin America: A
   Selected Treatment. U of Tex Hum Res.
Herman, E. *see* Herman, Emily.
Herman, Emily, 1876-1923
 xHerman, E.
  The Meaning & Value of Mysticism. Arno.
  The Meaning & Value of Mysticism. Gordon
   Pr.
Herman, F. *see* Herman, Frank.
Herman, Frank.
 xHerman, F.
  ed. Computational Methods for Large
   Molecules & Localized States in Solids.
   Plenum Pub.
Herman, Frederick Herman.
 xHerman, Frederick W.
  The Little Doctor. Sutter House.
Herman, Frederick W. *see* Herman, Frederick Herman.
Herman, G. *see* Herman, Gary.
Herman, Gary.
 xHerman, G.
  The Who. Macmillan.
  The Who. Macmillan.
Herman, Harriet.
 xHerman, Harriet.
  The Forest Princess. Over the Rainbow.
  Return of the Forest Princess. Over the
   Rainbow.
Herman, Jerry J. *see* Herman, Jerry John.
Herman, Jerry John, 1930-
 xHerman, Jerry J.
  Developing an Effective School Staff
   Evaluation Program. P-H.
  School Administrator's Accountability Manual:
   Tested Programs to Improve Your School's
   Effectiveness. P-H.
Herman, Lawrence.
 xHerman, Lawrence.
  The Right to Counsel in Misdemeanor Court.
   Ohio St U Pr.
Herman, Lewis. *see* Herman, Lewis Helmar.
Herman, Lewis Helmar, 1905-
 xHerman, Lewis.
  Practical Manual of Screen Playwriting for
   Theater & Television Films. NAL.
Herman, Linda.
 xHerman, Linda.

Corpus Delicti of Mystery Fiction: A Guide to
 the Body of the Case. Scarecrow.
Herman, Melvin.
 xHerman, Melvin.
  The Pursuit of Mental Health: For the
   Individual, the Community & the Nation.
   Macmillan.
Herman, Stephen A.
 xHerman, Stephen A.
  Natural Gas Users' Handbook. BNA.
Herman, Therese M., 1940-
 xHerman, Therese M.
  Creating Learning Environments: The
   Behavioral Approach to Education. Allyn.
Herman, Valentine.
 xHerman, Valentine.
  ed. Cabinet Studies: A Reader. St Martin.
  The European Parliament & the European
   Community. St Martin.
Herman, Victor.
 xHerman, Victor.
  Coming Out of the Ice: An Unexpected Life.
   HarBraceJ.
Herman, Wayne L.
 xHerman, Wayne L.
  Principal's Guide to Teacher Personnel
   Problems in the Elementary School. P-H.
Herman, William, 1926-
 xHerman, William.
  Reading, Writing, Rhetoric. HR&W.
  Troubleshooting: Basic Writing Skills. HR&W.
Hermann, Alice.
 xHermann, Alice.
  Early Child Care in Hungary. Gordon.
Hermann, Bernard.
 xHermann, Bernard.
  jt. auth. The Joy of Paris. Viking Pr.
Hermann, Henry R.
 xHermann, Henry R.
  ed. Social Insects. Acad Pr.
Hermann, Margaret G.
 xHermann, Margaret G.
  ed. A Psychological Examination of Political
   Leaders. Free Pr.
Hermann, Philip J.
 xHermann, Philip J.
  Do You Need a Lawyer?. P-H.
Hermann, Robert.
 xHermann, Robert.
  Algebraic & Geometric Structures in Current
   Algebra Theory. Mgmt Info Serv.
  Counsel for the Poor: Criminal Defense in
   Urban America. Lexington Bks.
  Fourier Analysis on Groups & Partial Wave
   Analysis. Benjamin-Cummings.
  Geometry, Physics & Systems. Dekker.
  Lie Algebras & Quantum Mechanics.
   Benjamin-Cummings.
  Lie Groups for Physicists. Benjamin-Cummings.
  Linear Systems Theory and Introductory
   Algebraic Geometry. Math Sci Pr.
  Spinors, Clifford, and Cayley Algebras. Math
   Sci Pr.
  Vector Bundles in Mathematical Physics.
   Benjamin-Cummings.
  Yang-Mills, Kaluza-Klein & the Einstein
   Program. Math Sci Pr.
Hermannsson, H. *see* Hermannsson, Halldor.
Hermannsson, Halldor, 1878-
 xHermannsson, H.
  The Northmen in America. Gordon Pr.
 xHermannsson, Halldor.

Ancient Laws of Norway & Iceland. Kraus
 Repr.
Cartography of Iceland. Kraus Repr.
Eggert Olafsson: A Biographical Sketch. Kraus
 Repr.
Icelandic Books of the Seventeenth Century.
 Kraus Repr.
Icelandic Books of the Sixteenth Century.
 Kraus Repr.
Illuminated Manuscripts of the Jonsbok. Kraus
 Repr.
Problem of Wineland. Kraus Repr.
Hermanson, Renee.
 xHermanson, Renee.
  Raspberry Kingdom. Upper Room.
Hermanson, Roger H.
 xHermanson, Roger H.
  Accounting for Human Assets. Mich St U
   Busn.
  Auditing Theory & Practice. Irwin.
Hermassi, Elbaki.
 xHermassi, Elbaki.
  Leadership & National Development in North
   Africa: A Comparative Study. U of Cal Pr.
Hermens, Ferdinand A. *see* Hermens, Ferdinand Aloys.
Hermens, Ferdinand Aloys, 1906-
 xHermens, Ferdinand A.
  Introduction to Modern Politics. U of Notre
   Dame Pr.
Hermeren, Goran, 1938-
 xHermeren, Goran.
  Influence in Art & Literature. Princeton U Pr.
Hermes, Hans.
 xHermes, Hans.
  Enumerability, Decidability, Computability: An
   Introduction to the Theory of Recursive
   Functions. Springer-Verlag.
  Introduction to Mathematical Logic.
   Springer-Verlag.
Hermes, Henry.
 xHermes, Henry.
  Functional Analysis & Time Optimal Control.
   Acad Pr.
Hermes, Patricia.
 xHermes, Patricia.
  What If They Knew. HarBraceJ.
Hernandez, Jose.
 xHernandez, Jose.
  Gaucho Martin Fierro. Gordon Pr.
  The Gaucho Martin Fierro. Schol Facsimiles.
Hernandez, Jose. *see* Hernandez, Jose Hernandez
 Pueyrredon.
Hernandez, Jose Alvarez. *see* Hernandez Alvarez, Jose.
Hernandez, Jose Hernandez Pueyrredon, 1834-1886
 xHernandez, Jose.
  Martin Fierro. State U NY Pr.
Hernandez Alvarez, Jose.
 xHernandez Alvarez, Jose.
  Return Migration to Puerto Rico. Greenwood.
Herndon, Angelo, 1913-
 xHerndon, Angelo.
  Let Me Live. Arno.
Herndon, Booton.
 xHerndon, Booton.
  Mary Pickford & Douglas Fairbanks: The Most
   Popular Couple the World Has Known.
   Norton.
  The Seventh Day: The Story of the Seventh
   Day Adventists. Greenwood.
Herndon, James, 1926-
 xHerndon, James.
  How to Survive in Your Native Land. S&S.
  How to Survive in Your Native Land. S&S.
Herndon, Jeanne H.
 xHerndon, Jeanne H.
  A Survey of Modern Grammars. HR&W.
Herndon, Marcia.
 xHerndon, Marcia.

Music As Culture. Norwood Edns.
Herner & Co. Staff. *see* Herner and Company,
    Washington, D.C.
Herner and Company, Washington, D.C.
    xHerner & Co. Staff.
        EIS Cumulative Nineteen Seventy-Seven. Info
            Resources.
Herner, Charles.
    xHerner, Charles.
        The Arizona Rough Riders. U of Ariz Pr.
Herner, Saul.
    xHerner, Saul.
        Compiled by Exhibits of Sources of Scientific
            & Technical Information. Info Resources.
Hernon, Peter.
    xHernon, Peter.
        Library & Library Related Publications: A
            Directory of Publishing Opportunities in
            Journals, Serials & Annuals. Libs Unl.
        Use of Government Publications by Social
            Scientists. Ablex Pub.
Herod, F. G. *see* Herod, Frederic George.
Herod, Frederic George.
    xHerod, F. G.
        The Gospels: A First Commentary. John Knox.
Herodotus.
    xHerodotus.
        Histories. Penguin.
        History of Herodotus. AMS Pr.
Herold, David E.
    xHerold, David E.
        The Assassination of President Lincoln & the
            Trial of the Conspirators: The Courtroom
            Testimony As Originally Compiled by Benn
            Pitman. Greenwood.
Herold, J. Christopher.
    xHerold, J. Christopher.
        Mistress to an Age: A Life of Madame De
            Stael. Crown.
        Mistress to an Age: A Life of Madame de
            Stael. Greenwood.
        The Swiss Without Halos. Greenwood.
Heron, Gayle A.
    xHeron, Gayle A.
        Twenty-Six Species of Oncaeidae (Copepoda:
            Cyclopoida) from the Southwest
            Pacific--Antarctic Area: Paper 2 in Biology of
            the Antarctic Seas IV. Am Geophysical.
Heron, Inez, 1935-
    xHeron, Inez.
        When Trees Were Green: The Story of Robin
            Heron. St Martin.
Heron-Allen, Edward, 1873-1956
    xHeron-Allen, Edward.
        The Strange Papers of Dr. Blayre. Arno.
Herpel, George. *see* Herpel, George Lloyd.
Herpel, George Lloyd.
    xHerpel, George.
        Specialty Advertising in Marketing. Dow
            Jones-Irwin.
Herr, Edwin L.
    xHerr, Edwin L.
        Decision-Making & Vocational Development.
            HM.
Herr, Ethel. *see* Herr, Ethel L.
Herr, Ethel L.
    xHerr, Ethel.
        Growing up Is a Family Affair. Moody.
Herr, John J.
    xHerr, John J.
        Counseling Elders & Their Families: Practical
            Techniques in Applied Gerontology. Springer
            Pub.
Herr, Michael.
    xHerr, Michael.
        Dispatches. Avon.
        Dispatches. Knopf.
Herr, Richard.
    xHerr, Richard.

Eighteenth-Century Revolution in Spain.
    Princeton U Pr.
An Historical Essay on Modern Spain. U of
    Cal Pr.
ed. Ideas in History: Essays Presented to Louis
    Gottschalk by His Former Students. Duke.
Spain. P-H.
Herr, Selma E.
    xHerr, Selma E.
        Diagnostic & Corrective Procedure in Teaching
            Reading. Lucas.
        Effective Reading for Adults. Wm C Brown.
Herrera, Barbara H. *see* Herrera, Barbara Hand.
Herrera, Barbara Hand.
    xHerrera, Barbara H.
        Funky. Pacific Pr Pub Assn.
Herreshoff, L. Francis. *see* Herreshoff, Lewis Francis.
Herreshoff, Lewis Francis, 1890-
    xHerreshoff, L. Francis.
        The Common Sense of Yacht Design.
            Caravan-Maritime.
Herrick, C. J. *see* Herrick, Charles Judson.
Herrick, C. N. *see* Herrick, Clyde N.
Herrick, Charles J. *see* Herrick, Charles Judson.
Herrick, Charles Judson.
    xHerrick, C. J.
        Brains of Rats & Men: A Survey of the Origin
            & Biological Significance of the Cerebral
            Cortex. Hafner.
    xHerrick, Charles J.
        Clarence Luther Herrick, Pioneer Naturalist,
            Teacher & Psychobiologist. Am Philos.
Herrick, Cheesman A. *see* Herrick, Cheesman Abiah.
Herrick, Cheesman Abiah, 1866-1956
    xHerrick, Cheesman A.
        White Servitude in Pennsylvania: Indentured &
            Redemption Labor in Colony &
            Commonwealth. Arno.
        White Servitude in Pennsylvania: Indentured &
            Redemption Labor in Colony &
            Commonwealth. Negro U Pr.
Herrick, Clyde N.
    xHerrick, C. N.
        Instruments & Measurements for Electronics.
            McGraw.
    xHerrick, Clyde N.
        Audio Systems. Reston.
        Oscilloscope Handbook. Reston.
        Survey of Electronics. Macmillan.
Herrick, E. C. *see* Herrick, Elbert C.
Herrick, Elbert C.
    xHerrick, E. C.
        Unit Process Guide to Organic Chemical
            Industries. Ann Arbor Science.
Herrick, James E.
    xHerrick, James E.
        Theory Building for Basic Institutional Change.
            R & E Res Assoc.
Herrick, Joy F.
    xHerrick, Joy F.
        Something's Got to Help - & Yoga Can. M
            Evans.
Herrick, Marvin T. *see* Herrick, Marvin Theodore.
Herrick, Marvin Theodore, 1899-
    xHerrick, Marvin T.
        Comic Theory in the Sixteenth Century. U of
            Ill Pr.
Herrick, Robert, 1868-1938
    xHerrick, Robert.
        Clark's Field. Mss Info.
        The Common Lot. Irvington.
        Common Lot. Johnson Repr.
        The Common Lot. Lighthouse Pr NY.
        Complete Poetry of Robert Herrick. Norton.
        Love's Dilemmas. Arno.
        The Master of the Inn. Irvington.
        The Master of the Inn. Lighthouse Pr NY.
        One Woman's Life. AMS Pr.
Herrick, Samuel, 1911-
    xHerrick, Samuel.

Astrodynamics. Van Nos Reinhold.
Herrick, Tracy G., 1933-
    xHerrick, Tracy G.
        Bank Analysts Handbook. Wiley.
Herrick, Virgil E.
    xHerrick, Virgil E.
        Strategies of Curriculum Development: The
            Works of Virgil E. Herrick. Greenwood.
Herrick, William, 1915-
    xHerrick, William.
        The Last to Die. Ultramarine Pub.
Herring, Clyde L. *see* Herring, Clyde Lee.
Herring, Clyde Lee.
    xHerring, Clyde L.
        If God Talked Out Loud. Broadman.
Herring, Edward P. *see* Herring, Edward Pendleton.
Herring, Edward Pendleton, 1903-
    xHerring, Edward P.
        Presidential Leadership: The Political Relations
            of Congress & the Chief Executive.
            Greenwood.
    xHerring, Pendleton.
        Group Representation Before Congress.
            Russell.
        Public Administration & the Public Interest.
            Russell.
Herring, Harriet L. *see* Herring, Harriet Laura.
Herring, Harriet Laura.
    xHerring, Harriet L.
        Passing of the Mill Village: Revolution in a
            Southern Institution. Greenwood.
Herring, James E.
    xHerring, James E.
        Teaching Library Skills in Schools. Humanities.
Herring, Pendleton. *see* Herring, Edward Pendleton.
Herring, R. J. *see* Herring, Richard.
Herring, Ralph. *see* Herring, Ralph A.
Herring, Ralph A.
    xHerring, Ralph.
        How to Understand the Bible. Broadman.
Herring, Reuben.
    xHerring, Reuben.
        Your Family Worship Guidebook. Broadman.
Herring, Richard.
    xHerring, R. J.
        National Monetary Policies & International
            Financial Markets. Elsevier.
Herrington, Donald. *see* Herrington, Donald E.
Herrington, Donald E.
    xHerrington, Donald.
        How to Read Schematic Diagrams. Sams.
Herriot, James.
    xHerriot, James.
        All Creatures Great & Small. G K Hall.
        All Creatures Great & Small. St Martin.
        All Things Bright & Beautiful. G K Hall.
        All Things Bright & Beautiful. St Martin.
        All Things Bright & Beautiful. Bantam.
        All Things Wise & Wonderful. G K Hall.
        All Things Wise & Wonderful. St Martin.
        All Things Wise & Wonderful. Bantam.
        Animals Tame & Wild. Sterling.
        If Only They Could Talk. G K Hall.
        James Herriot's Yorkshire. St Martin.
Herriott, Robert E.
    xHerriott, Robert E.
        ed. The Dynamics of Planned Educational
            Change: Case Studies & Analyses.
            McCutchan.
Herrman, Louis.
    xHerrman, Louis.
        A History of the Jews in South Africa from the
            Earliest Times to 1895. Greenwood.
Herrmann, Albert.
    xHerrmann, Albert.
        An Historical Atlas of China. Mouton.
Herrmann, Elisabeth Rutschi.
    xHerrmann, Elizabeth R.

ed. German Women Writers of the Twentieth Century. Pergamon.
Herrmann, Elizabeth R. *see* Herrmann, Elisabeth Rutschi.
Herrmann, Nina, 1943-
  xHerrmann, Nina.
    Go Out in Joy. John Knox.
Herrmann, Siegfried, 1926-
  xHerrmann, Siegfried.
    A History of Israel in the Old Testament Times. Fortress.
Herrnstein, Richard J.
  xHerrnstein, Richard J.
    ed. Source Book in the History of Psychology. Harvard U Pr.
Herron, Bill, 1943-
  xHerron, Bill.
    Rituals of Our Time. Carolina Wren.
Herron, Edward A. *see* Herron, Edward Albert.
Herron, Edward Albert, 1912-
  xHerron, Edward A.
    Cobra in the Sky: The Supersonic Transport. Macmillan.
Herron, Gaylord O. *see* Herron, Gaylord Oscar.
Herron, Gaylord Oscar.
  xHerron, Gaylord O.
    photos by Vagabond. Penumbra Projects.
Herron, George D. *see* Herron, George Davis.
Herron, George Davis, 1862-1925
  xHerron, George D.
    Christian Society. Johnson Repr.
Herron, Jeannine.
  xHerron, Jeannine.
    ed. Neuropsychology of Left-Handedness. Acad Pr.
Herron, Orley. *see* Herron, Orley R.
Herron, Orley R.
  xHerron, Orley.
    A Christian Executive in a Secular World. Nelson.
Herron, Shaun.
  xHerron, Shaun.
    Aladale. Summit Bks.
Herschberger, Ruth, 1917-
  xHerschberger, Ruth.
    Nature & Love Poems. Eakins.
Herschdoerfer, S. M.
  xHerschdoerfer, S. M.
    Quality Control in the Food Industry. Acad Pr.
Herschel, Sir William James, Bart, 1833-1917
  xHerschel, William J.
    The Origin of Fingerprinting. AMS Pr.
Herschel, William J. *see* Herschel, Sir William James.
Herschensohn, Bruce.
  xHerschensohn, Bruce.
    The Gods of Antenna. Arlington Hse.
Herschensohn, Wes, 1928-
  xHerschensohn, Wes.
    Resurrection in Cannes: The Making of the Picasso Summer. A S Barnes.
Herschy, R. W.
  xHerschy, R. W.
    Hydrometry: Principles & Practices. Wiley.
Hersen, Michael.
  xHersen, Michel.
    ed. Progress in Behavior Modification. Acad Pr.
Hersen, Michel. *see* Hersen, Michael.
Hersey, G. L. *see* Hersey, George L.
Hersey, George L.
  xHersey, G. L.
    Pythagorean Palaces: Magic & Architecture in the Italian Renaissance. Cornell U Pr.
  xHersey, George L.
    High Victorian Gothic: A Study in Associationism. Johns Hopkins.
Hersey, Jean, 1902-
  xHersey, Jean.
    Cooking with Herbs. Scribner.
Hersey, John.
  xHersey, John.

    The Child Buyer. Bantam.
    Child Buyer. Knopf.
    Marmot Drive. Knopf.
Hersey, John. *see* Hersey, John Richard.
Hersey, John Backett. *see* Hersey, John Brackett.
Hersey, John Brackett, 1913-
  xHersey, John Backett.
    ed. Deep-Sea Photography. Johns Hopkins.
Hersey, John R. *see* Hersey, John Richard.
Hersey, John Richard, 1914-
  xHersey, John.
    Hiroshima. Bantam.
    White Lotus. Knopf.
  xHersey, John R.
    Hiroshima. Knopf.
    Under the Eye of the Storm. Knopf.
Hersey, Mavo Dver, 1886-
  xHersey, Mayo D.
    Theory & Research in Lubrication: Foundations for Future Developments. Krieger.
Hersey, Mayo D. *see* Hersey, Mavo Dver.
Hersey, Paul.
  xHersey, Paul.
    Family Game: A Situational Approach to Effective Parenting. A-W.
Hersey, William D.
  xHersey, William D.
    How to Cash in on Your Hidden Memory Power. P-H.
Hersh, Burton.
  xHersh, Burton.
    The Education of Edward Kennedy: A Family Biography. Morrow.
    The Mellon Family: A Fortune in History. Morrow.
Hersh, Evan M.
  xHersh, Evan M.
    Immunotherapy of Cancer in Man: Scientific Basis & Current Status. C C Thomas.
Hersh, S. P. *see* Hersh, Stephen P.
Hersh, Stephen P.
  xHersh, S. P.
    The Executive Parent. Sovereign Bks.
Hershey, A. D. *see* Hershey, Alfred Day.
Hershey, Alfred Day, 1908-
  xHershey, A. D.
    ed. The Bacteriophage Lambda. Cold Spring Harbor.
Hershey, Daniel.
  xHershey, Daniel.
    Chemical Engineering in Medicine & Biology. Plenum Pub.
    Lifespan - & Factors Affecting It: Aging Theories in Gerontology. C C Thomas.
    A New Age-Scale for Humans. Lexington Bks.
Hershey Foods Corporation.
  xHershey Foods Corporation.
    Hershey's 1934 Cookbook. Western Pub.
Hershey, Nathan.
  xHershey, Nathan.
    Human Experimentation & the Law. Aspen Systems.
Hershey, Robert D.
  xHershey, Robert D.
    Advent Landmarks: From a Preacher's Notebook. Fortress.
Hershfield, David C.
  xHershfield, David C.
    The Multinational Union Challenges the Multinational Company. Conference Bd.
Hershhorn, Bernard. *see* Hershhorn, Bernard S.
Hershhorn, Bernard S.
  xHershhorn, Bernard.
    Active Years for Your Aging Dog. Dutton.
Hershko, Ch. *see* Hershko, Chaim.
Hershko, Chaim.
  xHershko, Ch.

    ed. Pathophysiology of Blood Disorders. S Karger.
Hershkovitz, Philip.
  xHershkovitz, Philip.
    Living New World Monkeys (Platyrrhini): With an Introduction to Primates. U of Chicago Pr.
Hershkowitz, Harry, 1886-
  xHershkowitz, Harry.
    Democratic Ideas in Turgenev's Works. AMS Pr.
Hershman, Jerome M.
  xHershman, Jerome M.
    ed. Endocrine Pathophysiology: A Patient Oriented Approach. Lea & Febiger.
    ed. Management of Endocrine Disorders. Lea & Febiger.
Hershon, Robert.
  xHershon, Robert.
    Grocery Lists. Crossing Pr.
    Little Red Wagon Painted Blue. Unicorn Pr.
    The Public Hug: New & Selected Poems. La State U Pr.
Hersk, Bernadette.
  xHersk, Bernadette.
    The ABC's of Batik. Chilton.
Hersker, Barry J.
  xHersker, Barry J.
    Purchasing Agent's Guide to the Naked Salesman. CBI Pub.
Herskovits, Melville J. *see* Herskovits, Melville Jean.
Herskovits, Melville Jean, 1895-1963
  xHerskovits, Melville J.
    Anthropometry of the American Negro. AMS Pr.
    Anthropometry of the American Negro. Haskell.
    Life in a Haitian Valley. Octagon.
    Suriname Folk-Lore. AMS Pr.
Herskowitz, Irwin H. *see* Herskowitz, Irwin Herman.
Herskowitz, Irwin Herman, 1920-
  xHerskowitz, Irwin H.
    The Elements of Genetics. Macmillan.
    Principles of Genetics. Macmillan.
Herspring, Dale R. *see* Herspring, Dale Roy.
Herspring, Dale Roy.
  xHerspring, Dale R.
    ed. Civil-Military Relations in Communist Systems. Westview.
Herst, Herman.
  xHerst, Herman.
    Fun & Profit in Stamp Collecting. Dutton.
Herstein, I. N.
  xHerstein, I. N.
    Matters Mathematical. Chelsea Pub.
    Noncommutative Rings. Math Assn.
    Notes from Ring-Theory Conference. Am Math.
    Topics in Ring Theory. U of Chicago Pr.
Hertz, Frederick. *see* Hertz, Friedrich Otto.
Hertz, Friedrich. *see* Hertz, Friedrich Otto.
Hertz, Friedrich Otto.
  xHertz, Frederick.
    The German Public Mind, in the Nineteenth Century: A Social History of German Political Sentiments, Aspirations & Ideas. Rowman.
  xHertz, Friedrich.
    Race & Civilization. Ktav.
Hertz, Geraldine.
  xHertz, Geraldine.
    Following Mary Today. Our Sunday Visitor.
    What's in It for Mothers?. Our Sunday Visitor.
Hertz, Hamilton.
  xHertz, Hamilton.
    How to Raise & Train a Standard Schnauzer. TFH Pubns.
Hertz, Louis H. *see* Hertz, Louis Heilbroner.
Hertz, Louis Heilbroner.
  xHertz, Louis H.

Essentials of Semi-Conductor Circuits. P-H.
Hess, Fred C.
  xHess, Fred C.
    Chemistry Made Simple. Doubleday.
Hess, Gary N. *see* Hess, Gary Newton.
Hess, Gary Newton.
  xHess, Gary N.
    An Historical Study of the Du Mont Television
      Network. Arno.
Hess, H. H. *see* Hess, Harry Hammond.
Hess, Hans, Art Curator.
  xHess, Hans.
    How Pictures Mean. Pantheon.
Hess, Harry Hammond, 1906-
  xHess, H. H.
    ed. Caribbean Geological Investigations. Geol
      Soc.
Hess, Irene.
  xHess, Irene.
    Probability Sampling of Hospitals & Patients.
      Health Admin Pr.
Hess, J. Daniel. *see* Hess, John Daniel.
Hess, Jeffrey A.
  xHess, Jeffrey A.
    Magic. Creative Ed.
    Skateboarding Skills. Creative Ed.
Hess, John Daniel, 1937-
  xHess, J. Daniel.
    Integrity: Let Your Yea Be Yea. Herald Pr.
Hess, John L.
  xHess, John L.
    The Taste of America. Penguin.
    Vanishing France. Times Bks.
Hess, Karen M., 1939-
  xHess, Karen M.
    Appreciating Literature: As You Read It.
      Wiley.
    Developing Reading Efficiency. Wiley.
Hess, Karl, 1923-
  xHess, Karl.
    Community Technology. Har-Row.
    Community Technology. Har-Row.
Hess, L. Y.
  xHess, L. Y.
    ed. Insulation Guide for Buildings & Industrial
      Processes. Noyes.
Hess, Lilo.
  xHess, Lilo.
    photos by The Curious Raccoons. Scribner.
    illus. Life Begins for Puppies. Scribner.
    Listen to Your Kitten Purr. Scribner.
    photos by A Pony to Love. Scribner.
    illus. A Puppy for You. Scribner.
Hess, Max W. *see* Hess, Max Walter.
Hess, Max Walter.
  xHess, Max W.
    Experimental Thymectomy, Possibilities &
      Limitations. Springer-Verlag.
Hess, Nancy R.
  xHess, Nancy R.
    The Home Buyer's Guide. P-H.
Hess, Norah.
  xHess, Norah.
    Caleb's Bride. Playboy Pbks.
    Hunter's Moon. Playboy Pbks.
Hess, Patricia. *see* Hess, Patricia A.
Hess, Patricia A.
  xHess, Patricia.
    Understanding the Aging Patient. R J Brady.
Hess, Robert. *see* Hess, Robert D.
Hess, Robert D.
  xHess, Robert.
    Teachers of Young Children. HM.
  xHess, Robert D.
    Teachers of Young Children. HM.
Hess, Robert P.
  xHess, Robert P.

Desk Book for Setting up the Closely - Held
    Corporation. Inst Busn Plan.
Hess, Seymour L.
  xHess, Seymour L.
    Introduction to Theoretical Meteorology.
      Krieger.
Hess, Stephen.
  xHess, Stephen.
    Organizing the Presidency. Brookings.
    The Presidential Campaign. Brookings.
    The Ungentlemanly Art: A History of
      American Political Cartoons. Macmillan.
Hess, Thom.
  xHess, Thom.
    A Dictionary of Puget Salish. U of Wash Pr.
Hess, Thomas B.
  xHess, Thomas B.
    Light in Art. Macmillan.
Hesse, Everett W. *see* Hesse, Everett Wesley.
Hesse, Everett Wesley, 1908-
  xHesse, Everett W.
    Calderon de la Barca. Twayne.
Hesse, Herman, 1877-1962
  xHesse, Hermann.
    Gertrude. FS&G.
Hesse, Herman. *see* Hesse, Hermann.
Hesse, Hermann, 1877-1962
  xHesse, Herman.
    Steppenwolf. Bantam.
  xHesse, Hermann.
    Autobiographical Writings. FS&G.
    Hours in the Garden & Other Poems. FS&G.
    My Belief: Essays on Life & Art. FS&G.
    Reflections. FS&G.
    Siddhartha. New Directions.
    Siddhartha. Bantam.
    Steppenwolf. HR&W.
    Steppenwolf. HR&W.
    Stories of Five Decades. FS&G.
    Tales of Student Life. FS&G.
Hesse, Hermann. *see* Hesse, Herman.
Hesse, Mary. *see* Hesse, Mary B.
Hesse, Mary B.
  xHesse, Mary.
    Structure of Scientific Inference. U of Cal Pr.
Hesse, Rick.
  xHesse, Rick.
    Applied Management Science. SRA.
Hesse, Walter H.
  xHesse, Walter H.
    Our Evolving Universe. Dickenson.
Hessel, Alfred.
  xHessel, Alfred.
    History of Libraries. Scarecrow.
Hesselgrave, David J.
  xHesselgrave, David J.
    Communicating Christ Cross-Culturally.
      Zondervan.
    ed. Dynamic Religious Movements: Case
      Studies of Rapidly Growing Religious
      Movement Around the World. Baker Bk.
Hesseltine, William B. *see* Hesseltine, William Best.
Hesseltine, William Best, 1902-1963
  xHesseltine, William B.
    Civil War Prisons: A Study in War Psychology.
      Ungar.
    Confederate Leaders in the New South.
      Greenwood.
    Lincoln's Plan of Reconstruction. Peter Smith.
    Lincoln's Plan of Reconstruction. Times Bks.
    Ulysses S. Grant: Politician. Ungar.
Hessen, Robert, 1936-
  xHessen, Robert.
    In Defense of the Corporation. Hoover Inst Pr.
    Steel Titan: The Life of Charles M. Schwab.
      Oxford U Pr.
Hession, Roy.
  xHession, Roy.

My Calvary Road. Chr Lit.
Hessler, Gene, 1928-
  xHessler, Gene.
    The Comprehensive Catalog of U.S. Paper
      Money. BNR Pr.
Hessler, Robert R. *see* Hessler, Robert Raymond.
Hessler, Robert Raymond, 1932-
  xHessler, Robert R.
    The Desmosomatidae (Isopoda: Asellota) of the
      Gay Head Bermuda Transect. U of Cal Pr.
Hestenes, David.
  xHestenes, David.
    Space-Time Algebra. Gordon.
Hestenes, M. *see* Hestenes, Magnus Rudolph.
Hestenes, Magnus R. *see* Hestenes, Magnus Rudolph.
Hestenes, Magnus Rudolph, 1906-
  xHestenes, M.
    Conjugate Direction Methods in Optimization.
      Springer-Verlag.
  xHestenes, Magnus R.
    Calculus of Variations & Optimal Control
      Theory. Krieger.
    Optimization Theory: The Finite Dimensional
      Case. Krieger.
Hester, Claudie F.
  xHester, Claudie F.
    Initiation a la Culture Francaise. Har-Row.
Hester, Donald D.
  xHester, Donald D.
    Bank Management & Portfolio Behavior. Yale
      U Pr.
Hester, James J.
  xHester, James J.
    Prehistoric Settlement Patterns in the Libyan
      Desert. AMS Pr.
Hester, T. R. *see* Hester, Thomas R.
Hester, Thomas R.
  xHester, T. R.
    Great Basin Atlatl Studies. Ballena Pr.
Heston, Charlton.
  xHeston, Charlton.
    The Actors Life: Journals, 1956-1976. Dutton.
Heston, Leonard L.
  xHeston, Leonard L.
    The Medical Casebook of Adolf Hitler: His
      Illnesses, Doctors & Drugs. Stein & Day.
Heth, Edward H. *see* Heth, Edward Harris.
Heth, Edward Harris.
  xHeth, Edward H.
    Wisconsin Country Cookbook & Journal.
      Tamarack Pr.
Hetherington, Duncan C. *see* Hetherington, Duncan
  Charteris.
Hetherington, Duncan Charteris, 1895-
  xHetherington, Duncan C.
    Comparative Studies on Certain Features of
      Nematodes & Their Significance. Johnson
      Repr.
Hetherington, Hugh W.
  xHetherington, Hugh W.
    Melville's Reviewers: British & American,
      1846-1891. Russell.
Hetherington, Penelope.
  xHetherington, Penelope.
    British Paternalism & Africa 1920-1940. Biblio
      Dist.
Hetrick, David L., 1927-
  xHetrick, David L.
    Dynamics of Nuclear Reactors. U of Chicago
      Pr.
Hettinger, Herman S. *see* Hettinger, Herman Strecker.
Hettinger, Herman Strecker, 1902-
  xHettinger, Herman S.
    Decade of Radio Advertising. Arno.
Hettinger, Richard F. *see* Hettinger, Richard Frederick.
Hettinger, Richard Frederick.
  xHettinger, Richard F.

How Will We Feed the Hungry Billions: Food
for Tomorrow's World. Messner.
Heyck, Thomas W. see Heyck, Thomas William.
Heyck, Thomas William, 1938-
xHeyck, Thomas W.
The Dimensions of British Radicalism: The
Case of Ireland, 1874-95. U of Ill Pr.
Heyd, Uriel.
xHeyd, Uriel.
Foundations of Turkish Nationalism: The Life
& Teachings of Ziya Gokalp. Hyperion Conn.
Studies in Old Ottoman Criminal Law. Oxford
U Pr.
Heyde, C. C.
xHeyde, C. C.
I. J. Bienayme: Statistical Theory Anticipated.
Springer-Verlag.
Heyden, Doris.
xHeyden, Doris.
Pre-Columbian Architecture of Mesoamerica.
Abrams.
Heydenreich, Ludwig. see Heydenreich, Ludwig
Heinrich.
Heydenreich, Ludwig H. see Heydenreich, Ludwig
Heinrich.
Heydenreich, Ludwig Heinrich.
xHeydenreich, Ludwig.
Architecture in Italy: 1400-1600. Viking Pr.
xHeydenreich, Ludwig H.
Leonardo: The Last Supper. Viking Pr.
Heydenryk, Henry.
xHeydenryk, Henry.
Right Frame: A Consideration of the Right &
Wrong Methods of Framing Pictures.
Heineman.
Heye, Jurgen B.
xHeye, Jurgen B.
A Sociolinguistic Investigation of
Multilingualism in the Canton of Ticino
Switzerland. Mouton.
Heyel, Carl, 1908-
xHeyel, Carl.
Computers, Office Machines, & the New
Information Technology. Macmillan.
ed. Encyclopedia of Management. Van Nos
Reinhold.
Foreman's Handbook. McGraw.
Handbook of Industrial Research Management.
Van Nos Reinhold.
ed. The VNR Concise Guide to Accounting &
Control. Van Nos Reinhold.
ed. The VNR Concise Guide to Financial
Management. Van Nos Reinhold.
ed. The VNR Concise Guide to Human
Resources Development. Van Nos Reinhold.
ed. The VNR Concise Guide to Industrial
Management. Van Nos Reinhold.
ed. VNR Concise Guide to Management
Decision Making. Van Nos Reinhold.
Heyen, William, 1940-
xHeyen, William.
The Swastika Poems. Vanguard.
Heyer, Georgette.
xHeyer, Georgette.

April Lady. Berkley Pub.
April Lady. Putnam.
Arabella. Putnam.
Charity Girl. Fawcett.
A Civil Contract. Berkley Pub.
A Civil Contract. Putnam.
Cousin Kate. Fawcett.
Friday's Child. Berkley Pub.
Friday's Child. Putnam.
The Grand Sophy. Putnam.
The Great Roxhythe. Buccaneer Bks.
Infamous Army. Fawcett.
The Masqueraders. Fawcett.
The Nonesuch. Fawcett.
The Reluctant Widow. Putnam.
The Talisman Ring. Fawcett.
These Old Shades. Fawcett.
Venetia. Berkley Pub.
Venetia. Putnam.
xHeyer, Georgette E.
The Reluctant Widow. Berkley Pub.
Heyer, Georgette E. see Heyer, Georgette.
Heyer, H. see Heyer, Herbert.
Heyer, Herbert.
xHeyer, H.
Probability Measures on Locally Compact
Groups. Springer-Verlag.
Heyer, R. see Heyer, Robert J.
Heyer, Robert.
xHeyer, Robert.
ed. Pentecostal Catholics. Paulist Pr.
Heyer, Robert. see Heyer, Robert J.
Heyer, Robert J.
xHeyer, R.
Aware Person in Today's Church. HR&W.
xHeyer, Robert.
Discovery in Prayer. Paulist Pr.
Heyerdahl, Thor.
xHeyerdahl, Thor.
Art of Easter Island. Doubleday.
Early Man & the Ocean: A Search for the
Beginnings of Navigation & Seaborne
Civilizations. Doubleday.
Early Man & the Ocean: A Search for the
Beginnings of Navigation & Seaborne
Civilizations. Random.
The RA Expeditions. NAL.
Heyl, Edgar. see Heyl, Edgar G.
Heyl, Edgar G.
xHeyl, Edgar.
I Didn't Know That: An Exhibition of First
Happenings in Maryland. Md Hist.
Heylbut, Rose.
xHeylbut, Rose.
Backstage at the Metropolitan Opera. Arno.
Heyman, Abigail.
xHeyman, Abigail.
Butcher, Baker, Cabinetmaker: Photographs of
Women at Work. T Y Crowell.
Heyman, Anita.
xHeyman, Anita.
Exit from Home. Crown.
Heyman, Jacques.
xHeyman, Jacques.
Coulomb's Memoir on Statics: An Essay in the
History of Civil Engineering. Cambridge U
Pr.
Heyman, Margaret M.
xHeyman, Margaret M.
Alcoholism Programs in Industry: The Patient's
View. Rutgers Ctr Alcohol.
Heyman, Mark.
xHeyman, Mark.
Places & Spaces: Environmental Psychology in
Education. Phi Delta Kappa.
Simulation Games for the Classroom. Phi Delta
Kappa.
Heymann, C. David. see Heymann, Clemens David.
Heymann, Clemens David, 1945-
xHeymann, C. David.

American Aristocracy: The Lives & Times of
James Russell, Amy, & Robert Lowell. Dodd.
Heymann, Frederick G. see Heymann, Frederick
Gotthold.
Heymann, Frederick Gotthold, 1900-
xHeymann, Frederick G.
Poland & Czechoslovakia. Greenwood.
Heymans, Margriet.
xHeymans, Margriet.
illus. Cats & Dolls. A-W.
Heyne. see Heyne, Carl J.
Heyne, Carl J.
xHeyne.
Art for Young America. Bennett Co.
Heyne, Paul. see Heyne, Paul T.
Heyne, Paul T.
xHeyne, Paul.
The Economic Way of Thinking. SRA.
Toward Understanding Macroeconomics. SRA.
xHeyne, Paul T.
Private Keepers of the Public Interest.
McGraw.
Toward Economic Understanding. SRA.
Heynen, James.
xHeynen, James.
The Man Who Kept Cigars in His Cap.
Graywolf.
xHeynen, Jim.
How the Sow Became a Goddess. Confluence
Pr.
Heynen, Jim. see Heynen, James.
Heyningen, Christina Van. see Van Heyningen, Christina.
Heyns, Barbara L. see Heyns, Barbara Lee.
Heyns, Barbara Lee.
xHeyns, Barbara L.
Summer Learning & the Effects of Schooling.
Acad Pr.
Heyting, A. see Heyting, Arend.
Heyting, Arend, 1898-
xHeyting, A.
Axiomatic Projective Geometry. Elsevier.
Heyward, Carter.
xHeyward, Carter.
A Priest Forever. Har-Row.
Heyward, Du Bose, 1885-1940
xHeyward, Du Bose.
Porgy. Larlin Corp.
Heyward, Edna Earl.
xHeyward, Edna Earle.
The Rehabilitation of the Severely Mentally
Retarded Trainable Child. Exposition.
Heyward, Edna Earle. see Heyward, Edna Earl.
Heywood, Arthur.
xHeywood, Arthur.
A First Program in Mathematics. Dickenson.
Heywood, Chester D. see Heywood, Chester Dodd.
Heywood, Chester Dodd, 1887-
xHeywood, Chester D.
Negro Combat Troops in the World War: The
Story of the 371st Infantry. AMS Pr.
Heywood, Christopher.
xHeywood, Christopher.
ed. Aspects of South African Literature.
Holmes & Meier.
Heywood, John.
xHeywood, John.
Assessment in Higher Education. Wiley.
Foreign Exchange & the Corporate Treasurer.
Am Mgmt.
Foreign Exchange & the Corporate Treasurer.
Transatlantic.
Play of the Weather. AMS Pr.
Spider & the Flie. B Franklin.
Heywood, Philip.
xHeywood, Philip.
Planning & Human Need. David & Charles.
Heywood, Thomas.
xHeywood, Thomas.

Fair Maid of the West, Parts I & II. U of Nebr
Pr.

Hiatt, Mary P., 1920-
xHiatt, Mary P.
Artful Balance: The Parallel Structures of Style.
Tchrs Coll.

Hibbard, Benjamin H. *see* Hibbard, Benjamin Horace.

Hibbard, Benjamin Horace, 1870-
xHibbard, Benjamin H.
History of the Public Land Policies. U of Wis
Pr.

Hibbard, George A. *see* Hibbard, George Abiah.

Hibbard, George Abiah, 1858-1928
xHibbard, George A.
Stories of the Railway. Arno.

Hibbard, Howard, 1928-
xHibbard, Howard.
Carlo Maderno & Roman Architecture,
1580-1630. Pa St U Pr.
Michelangelo: Painter, Sculptor, Architect.
Viking Pr.

Hibbard, Jack.
xHibbard, Jack.
Weaponless Defense: A Law Enforcement
Guide to Non-Violent Control. C C Thomas.

Hibben, Frank C. *see* Hibben, Frank Cummings.

Hibben, Frank Cummings, 1910-
xHibben, Frank C.
Lost Americans. Peter Smith.
Lost Americans. T Y Crowell.

Hibben, John G. *see* Hibben, John Grier.

Hibben, John Grier, 1861-1933
xHibben, John G.
Higher Patriotism. Arno.

Hibben, Paxton.
xHibben, Paxton.
Peerless Leader, William Jennings Bryan.
Russell.

Hibberd, R. G.
xHibberd, R. G.
Questions & Answers on Integrated Circuits.
Hayden.
xHibberd, Robert G.
Integrated Circuits: A Basic Course for
Engineers & Technicians. McGraw.
Solid-State Electronics: A Basic Course for
Engineers & Technicians. McGraw.

Hibberd, Robert G. *see* Hibberd, R. G.

Hibbert, Christopher, 1924-
xHibbert, Christopher.
The Court of St. James's: The Monarch at
Work from Victoria to Elizabeth II. Morrow.
Disraeli & His World. Scribner.
The Great Mutiny: India 1857. Viking Pr.
The House of Medici: Its Rise & Fall. Morrow.
House of Medici: Its Rise & Fall. Morrow.

Hibbert, F. Aidan. *see* Hibbert, Francis Aidan.

Hibbert, Francis Aidan, 1866-1933
xHibbert, F. Aidan.
Influence & Development of English Gilds.
Kelley.

Hibbett, Howard.
xHibbett, Howard.
Contemporary Japanese Literature: An
Anthology of Fiction, Film, & Other Writing
Since 1945. Knopf.
The Floating World in Japanese Fiction. Arno.
The Floating World in Japanese Fiction. C E
Tuttle.
xHibbett, Howard S.
Modern Japanese: A Basic Reader. Harvard U
Pr.

Hibbett, Howard S. *see* Hibbett, Howard.

Hibbitt, George W. *see* Hibbitt, George Whiting.

Hibbitt, George Whiting, 1895-
xHibbitt, George W.
How to Speak Effectively on All Occasions. R
West.

Hibbs, Douglas A., 1944-
xHibbs, Douglas A.

Mass Political Violence: A Cross-National
Causal Analysis. Krieger.

Hibdon, J. E. *see* Hibdon, James E.

Hibdon, James E.
xHibdon, J. E.
Price & Welfare Theory. McGraw.

Hichborn, Franklin, 1869-
xHichborn, Franklin.
System: As Uncovered by the San Francisco
Graft Prosecution. Patterson Smith.

Hichens, Robert. *see* Hichens, Robert Smythe.

Hichens, Robert S. *see* Hichens, Robert Smythe.

Hichens, Robert Smythe.
xHichens, Robert.
Green Carnation. U of Nebr Pr.
xHichens, Robert S.
An Imaginative Man. Garland Pub.
The Londoners: An Absurdity. Garland Pub.

Hick, John.
xHick, John.
Classical & Contemporary Readings in the
Philosophy of Religion. P-H.
xHick, John H.
Evil & the God of Love. Har-Row.
Existence of God. Macmillan.
ed. Many-Faced Argument: Recent Studies in
the Ontological Argument for the Existence
of God. Macmillan.

Hick, John H. *see* Hick, John.

Hicken, Victor, 1921-
xHicken, Victor.
The World Is Coming to an End: An Irreverent
Look at Modern Doomsayers. Arlington Hse.

Hickerson, Nancy P. *see* Hickerson, Nancy Parrott.

Hickerson, Nancy Parrott.
xHickerson, Nancy P.
Linguistic Anthropology. HR&W.

Hickey, Doralyn J., 1929-
xHickey, Doralyn J.
Problems in Organizing Library Collections.
Bowker.

Hickey, H. *see* Hickey, Henry V.

Hickey, Harry E.
xHickey, Harry E.
Public Fire Safety Organization: A Systems
Approach. Natl Fire Prot.

Hickey, Henry V.
xHickey, H.
Elements of Electronics. McGraw.
xHickey, Henry V.
Elements of Electronics. McGraw.

Hickey, Joseph E.
xHickey, Joseph E.
Toward a Just Correctional System:
Experiments in Implementing Democracy in
Prisons. Jossey-Bass.

Hickey, Joseph J. *see* Hickey, Joseph James.

Hickey, Joseph James, 1907-
xHickey, Joseph J.
A Guide to Bird Watching. Dover.
A Guide to Bird Watching. Peter Smith.

Hickey, Leo J.
xHickey, Leo J.
Stratigraphy & Paleobotany of the Golden
Valley Formation (Early Tertiary) of Western
North Dakota. Geol Soc.

Hickey, Michael.
xHickey, S. M.
Out of the Sky: A History of Airborne
Warfare. Scribner.

Hickey, S. M. *see* Hickey, Michael.

Hickey, Tom, 1939-
xHickey, Tom.
Health & Aging. Brooks-Cole.

Hickford, Jessie.
xHickford, Jessie.
I Never Walked Alone. St Martin.

Hickin, Norman E. *see* Hickin, Norman Ernest.

Hickin, Norman Ernest.
xHickin, Norman E.

Caddis Larvae: Larvae of the British
Trichoptera. Fairleigh Dickinson.

Hickle, Ruth.
xHickle, Ruth.
Bible Story Word Puzzles. Zondervan.

Hickler, Holly.
xHickler, Holly.
Creative Writing: From Thought to Action.
Allyn.

Hickman, Albert. *see* Hickman, William Albert.

Hickman, B. G. *see* Hickman, Bert G.

Hickman, Bert G.
xHickman, B. G.
An Annual Growth Model of the U. S.
Economy. Elsevier.

Hickman, Cleveland P. *see* Hickman, Cleveland
Pendleton.

Hickman, Cleveland Pendleton.
xHickman, Cleveland P.
jt. auth. Integrated Principles of Zoology.
Mosby.

Hickman, Gail M. *see* Hickman, Gail Morgan.

Hickman, Gail Morgan.
xHickman, Gail M.
The Films of George Pal. A S Barnes.

Hickman, Janet.
xHickman, Janet.
The Stones. Macmillan.
The Valley of the Shadow. Macmillan.

Hickman, Mae.
xHickman, Mae.
Care of the Wild Feathered & Furred: A Guide
to Wildlife Handling & Care. Unity Pr.

Hickman, Martha.
xHickman, Martha W.
I'm Moving. Abingdon.
Love Speaks Its Voice: The Sights & Sounds of
Life. Word Bks.

Hickman, Martha W. *see* Hickman, Martha.

Hickman, Martha Whitmore.
xHickman, Martha W.
My Friend William Moved Away. Abingdon.

Hickman, Martin. *see* Hickman, Martin B.

Hickman, Martin B.
xHickman, Martin.
Problems of American Foreign Policy. Glencoe.
xHickman, Martin B.
Problems in American Foreign Policy. Glencoe.

Hickman, William Albert, 1877-
xHickman, Albert.
Canadian Nights. Arno.

Hickok, Floyd, 1907-
xHickok, Floyd.
Your Energy Efficient Home: Improvements to
Save Utility Dollars. P-H.

Hickok, L. P. *see* Hickok, Laurens Perseus.

Hickok, Laurens Perseus, 1798-1888
xHickok, L. P.
Rational Psychology. Schol Facsimiles.

Hickok, Robert.
xHickok, Robert.
Exploring Music. A-W.

Hickrod, G. Alan.
xHickrod, G. Alan.
Increasing Social & Economic Inequalities
Among Suburban Schools. Interstate.

Hicks, Clifford B.
xHicks, Clifford B.
Alvin Fernald, Mayor for a Day. HR&W.
Alvin Fernald, Mayor for a Day. PB.
Alvin Fernald, Superweasel. HR&W.
Alvin's Secret Code. HR&W.
Alvin's Secret Code. Schol Bk Serv.

Hicks, David.
xHicks, David.
David Hicks on Living with Taste. Macmillan.
Living with Design. Morrow.

Hicks, David E.
xHicks, David E.

CB Radio Antennas. Sams.
CB Radio Operating Procedures. Sams.
Citizens Band Radio Handbook. Sams.
Hicks, Dorothy J.
xHicks, Dorothy J.
Patient Care Techniques. Bobbs.
Hicks, Ellis A.
xHicks, Ellis A.
Check List & Bibliography on the Occurrence
of Insects in Birds' Nests. Iowa St U Pr.
Hicks, Frederick C. see Hicks, Frederick Charles.
Hicks, Frederick Charles, 1875-
xHicks, Frederick C.
Men & Books Famous in the Law. Rothman.
Hicks, Granville, 1901-
xHicks, Granville.
Figures of Transition: A Study of British
Literature at the End of the Nineteenth
Century. Greenwood.
First to Awaken. Arno.
Literary Horizons: A Quarter Century of
American Fiction. NYU Pr.
Where We Came Out. Greenwood.
Hicks, Herbert G.
xHicks, Herbert G.
Dimensions of American Business. McGraw.
Hicks, J. L.
xHicks, J. L.
A Closer Look at Arctic Lands. Watts.
Hicks, Jim.
xHicks, Jim.
The Persians. Time-Life.
The Persians. Silver.
Hicks, John. see Hicks, John Richard.
Hicks, John D. see Hicks, John Donald.
Hicks, John Donald, 1890-
xHicks, John D.
The American Tradition. Greenwood.
Populist Revolt: A History of the Farmers'
Alliance & the People's Party. U of Nebr Pr.
Rehearsal for Disaster: The Boom & Collapse
of 1919-1920. U Presses Fla.
Hicks, John G.
xHicks, John G.
Welded Joint Design. Halsted Pr.
Hicks, John Harland.
xHicks, John.
ed. Revolution & Reaction: The Paris
Commune 1871. U of Mass Pr.
Hicks, John R. see Hicks, John Richard.
Hicks, John Richard, Sir, 1904-
xHicks, John.
Capital & Growth. Oxford U Pr.
Causality in Economics. Basic.
xHicks, John R.
Capital & Growth. Oxford U Pr.
Capital & Time: A Neo-Austrian Theory.
Oxford U Pr.
Contribution to the Theory of the Trade Cycle.
Oxford U Pr.
Theory of Wages. St Martin.
Hicks, Maynard.
xHicks, Maynard.
Where the Jobs Are: Communications.
Exposition.
Hicks, Philip E.
xHicks, Philip E.
ed. Introduction to Industrial Engineering &
Management Science. McGraw.
Hicks, R. D. see Hicks, Randolph D.
Hicks, Randolph D.
xHicks, R. D.
Undercover Operations & Persuasion. C C
Thomas.
Hicks, Ray R.
xHicks, Ray R.
Woody Plants of the Western Gulf Region.
Kendall-Hunt.
Hicks, Raymond L.
xHicks, Raymond L.

Pitching to Win. A S Barnes.
Hicks, Robert D. see Hicks, Robert Drew.
Hicks, Robert Drew, 1850-1929
xHicks, Robert D.
Stoic & Epicurean. Russell.
Hicks, Ronald G.
xHicks, Ronald G.
A Survey of Mass Communication. Pelican.
Hicks, Tyler G. see Hicks, Tyler Gregory.
Hicks, Tyler Gregory, 1921-
xHicks, Tyler G.
How to Borrow Your Way to a Great Fortune.
P-H.
How to Borrow Your Way to a Great Fortune.
P-H.
How to Build a Second Income Fortune in
Your Spare Time. P-H.
How to Make One Million Dollars in Real
Estate in Three Years Starting with No Cash.
P-H.
Pump Application Engineering. McGraw.
Pump Operation & Maintenance. McGraw.
ed. Standard Handbook of Engineering
Calculations. McGraw.
Successful Engineering Management: Modern
Techniques for Effective & Profitable
Direction of the Engineering Function.
McGraw.
Tyler Hicks Encyclopedia of Wealth-Building
Secrets. P-H.
Hicks, Ursula K. see Hicks, Ursula Kathleen (Webb).
Hicks, Ursula Kathleen (Webb), 1896-
xHicks, Ursula K.
Development Finance: Planning & Control.
Oxford U Pr.
Public Finance. Cambridge U Pr.
Hicks, Ursula Kathleen Webb, Lady, 1896-
xHicks, Ursula K.
Federalism: Failure & Success: A Comparative
Study. Oxford U Pr.
Hicks, Warren B.
xHicks, Warren B.
Developing Multi-Media Libraries. Bowker.
Hida, T. see Hida, Takeyuki.
Hida, Takeyuki, 1927-
xHida, T.
Brownian Motion. Springer-Verlag.
Hidayatullah, M., 1905-
xHidayatullah, M.
Democracy in India & the Judicial Process.
Asia.
South-West Africa Case. Asia.
Hiden, Martha (Woodroof), 1883-
xHiden, Martha W.
How Justice Grew - Virginia Counties: An
Abstract of Their Formation. U Pr of Va.
Hiden, Martha W. see Hiden, Martha (Woodroof).
Hiden, Mikael.
xHiden, Mikael.
The Ombudsman in Finland: The First Fifty
Years. Inst Gov Stud Berk.
Hidy, George M.
xHidy, George M.
The Character & Origins of Smog Aerosols: A
Digest of Results from the California Aerosol
Characterization Experiment (ACHEX).
Wiley.
Hidy, Muriel E.
xHidy, Muriel E.
George Peabody, Merchant & Financier:
1829-1854. Arno.
Hidy, Ralph W. see Hidy, Ralph Willard.
Hidy, Ralph Willard, 1905-
xHidy, Ralph W.
House of Baring in American Trade & Finance:
English Merchant Bankers at Work,
1763-1861. Russell.
Hieatt, A. Kent, 1921-
xHieatt, A. Kent.

Chaucer, Spenser, Milton: Mythopoeic
Continuities & Transformations.
McGill-Queens U Pr.
Hieatt, Constance. see Hieatt, Constance B.
Hieatt, Constance B.
xHieatt, Constance.
The Castle of Ladies. T Y Crowell.
Hiebert, D. Edmond.
xHiebert, D. Edmond.
First Timothy. Moody.
Hieger, I.
xHieger, I.
Carcinogenesis. Acad Pr.
Hiemstra, Roger.
xHiemstra, Roger.
The Educative Community: Linking the
Community, School & Family. Prof Educ
Pubn.
Lifelong Learning. Prof Educ Pubn.
Hiernaux, Jean.
xHiernaux, Jean.
The People of Africa. Scribner.
Hiers, Richard H.
xHiers, Richard H.
The Historical Jesus & the Kingdom of God:
Present & Future in the Message & Ministry
of Jesus. U Presses Fla.
Hiestand, Dale L.
xHiestand, Dale L.
Changing Careers After Thirty-Five: New
Horizons Through Professional & Graduate
Study. Columbia U Pr.
Discrimination in Employment: An Appraisal
of the Research. U of Mich Inst Labor.
Economic Growth & Employment
Opportunities for Minorities. Columbia U Pr.
Higashi, Sumiko.
xHigashi, Sumiko.
Virgins, Vamps & Flappers: The American
Silent Movie Heroine. Eden Woman.
Higbee, J. A. see Higbee, Jay Anders.
Higbee, Jay Anders, 1919-
xHigbee, J. A.
Development & Administration of the New
York State Law Against Discrimination. U of
Ala Pr.
Higbee, Kenneth L.
xHigbee, Kenneth L.
Influence: What It Is & How to Use It.
Brigham.
Higby, Chester P. see Higby, Chester Penn.
Higby, Chester Penn, 1885-
xHigby, Chester P.
Religious Policy of the Bavarian Government
During the Napoleonic Period. AMS Pr.
Higdon, Archie, 1905-
xHigdon, Archie.
Mechanics of Materials. Wiley.
Higdon, Hal.
xHigdon, Hal.
Fitness After Forty. Anderson World.
Horse That Played Center Field. Avon.
The Marathoners. Putnam.
On the Run from Dogs & People. Chicago
Review.
Higginbotham, James.
xHigginbotham, James B.
Focus Group Interviews: A Reader. Am Mktg.
Higginbotham, James B. see Higginbotham, James.
Higginbotham, Jay.
xHigginbotham, Jay.
The Pascagoula Indians. Rockwell.
Higginbotham, Virginia, 1935-
xHigginbotham, Virginia.
The Comic Spirit of Federico Garcia Lorca. U
of Tex Pr.
Luis Bunuel. Twayne.
Higgins, Afred. see Higgins, Alfred.
Higgins, Aidan, 1927-
xHiggins, Aidan.

Asylum & Other Stories. Riverrun Texas.

Higgins, Alfred, 1906-
xHiggins, Afred.
Common-Sense Guide to Refinishing Antiques.
T Y Crowell.

Higgins, Benjamin. *see* Higgins, Benjamin Howard.

Higgins, Benjamin Howard.
xHiggins, Benjamin.
Economic Development of a Small Planet.
Norton.

Higgins, David. *see* Higgins, David A.

Higgins, David A.
xHiggins, David.
Program Design & Construction. P-H.

Higgins, Dick.
xHiggins, Dick.
City with All the Angles: A Radio Play.
Printed Edns.

Higgins, Dick. *see* Higgins, Richard Carter.

Higgins, Don.
xHiggins, Don.
Catlin. St Martin.

Higgins, E. L. *see* Higgins, Earl Leroy.

Higgins, Earl Leroy.
xHiggins, E. L.
ed. The French Revolution As Told by
Contemporaries. Cooper Sq.

Higgins, F. R. *see* Higgins, Francis Roger.

Higgins, Francis Roger, 1940-
xHiggins, F. R.
The Pseudo-Cleft Construction in English.
Garland Pub.

Higgins, George M. *see* Higgins, George Marsh.

Higgins, George Marsh, 1890-
xHiggins, George M.
Nasal Organ in Amphibia. Johnson Repr.

Higgins, George V., 1939-
xHiggins, George V.
The Digger's Game. Popular Lib.
Dreamland. Ballantine.
Dreamland. Little.
Friends of Eddie Coyle. Knopf.
The Friends of Richard Nixon. Ballantine.
Kennedy for the Defense. Knopf.
A Year or So with Edgar. Berkley Pub.
A Year or So with Edgar. Har-Row.

Higgins, Godfrey, 1773-1833
xHiggins, Godfrey.
Celtic Druids. Philos Res.

Higgins, Ian.
xHiggins, Ian.
Francis Ponge. Humanities.

Higgins, J. C. *see* Higgins, James Craig.

Higgins, J. R. *see* Higgins, John Rowland.

Higgins, Jack.
xHiggins, Jack.
East of Desolation. Fawcett.
In the Hour Before Midnight. Fawcett.
A Prayer for the Dying. Fawcett.
Solo. Stein & Day.

Higgins, James C. *see* Higgins, James Craig.

Higgins, James Craig, 1856-
xHiggins, J. C.
Life of Robert Burns. R West.
xHiggins, James C.
Life of Robert Burns. AMS Pr.

Higgins, Joan.
xHiggins, Joan M.
The Poverty Business: Britain & America.
Biblio Dist.

Higgins, Joan M. *see* Higgins, Joan.

Higgins, John F. *see* Higgins, John H.

Higgins, John H.
xHiggins, John F.
Swimming & Diving. Arco.

Higgins, John J.
xHiggins, John J.
Thomas Merton on Prayer. Doubleday.

Higgins, John Rowland, 1935-
xHiggins, J. R.

Completeness & Basis Properties of Sets of
Special Functions. Cambridge U Pr.

Higgins, Joseph R.
xHiggins, Joseph R.
Human Movement: An Integrated Approach.
Mosby.

Higgins, L. R. *see* Higgins, Lindley R.

Higgins, Lindley R.
xHiggins, L. R.
Cost Reduction from A to Z. McGraw.
xHiggins, Lindley R.
Handbook of Construction Equipment
Maintenance. McGraw.

Higgins, R. *see* Higgins, Rosalyn.

Higgins, R. A. *see* Higgins, Raymond Aurelius.

Higgins, Raymond Aurelius.
xHiggins, R. A.
Properties of Engineering Materials. Krieger.

Higgins, Richard Carter.
xHiggins, Dick.
Legends & Fishnets. Ultramarine Pub.
Some Recent Snowflakes (& Other Things).
Printed Edns.

Higgins, Robert C.
xHiggins, Robert C.
Financial Management: Theory & Applications.
SRA.

Higgins, Rosalyn.
xHiggins, R.
Administration of United Kingdom Foreign
Policy Through the United Nations. Oceana.

Higginson, James J. *see* Higginson, James Jackson.

Higginson, James Jackson, 1884-
xHigginson, James J.
Spenser's Shepherd's Calendar in Relation to
Contemporary Affairs. Folcroft.

Higginson, M. Valliant.
xHigginson, Margaret V.
The Ambitious Woman's Guide to a Successful
Career. Am Mgmt.

Higginson, Margaret V. *see* Higginson, M. Valliant.

Higginson, Thomas W. *see* Higginson, Thomas
Wentworth.

Higginson, Thomas Wentworth, 1823-1911
xHigginson, Thomas W.
Army Life in a Black Regiment. Corner Hse.
Army Life in a Black Regiment. Macmillan.
Army Life in a Black Regiment: 1960. Mich St
U Pr.
Carlyle's Laugh, & Other Surprises. Arno.
Cheerful Yesterdays. Arno.
Cheerful Yesterdays. R West.
Contemporaries. R West.
Letters & Journals of Thomas Wentworth
Higginson, 1846-1906. Da Capo.
Letters & Journals of Thomas Wentworth
Higginson: 1846-1906. Negro U Pr.
Margaret Fuller Ossoli. Chelsea Hse.
Margaret Fuller Ossoli. Greenwood.
Margaret Fuller Ossoli. Haskell.
Margaret Fuller Ossoli. R West.
Part of a Man's Life. Kennikat.
Part of a Man's Life. R West.
Tales of the Enchanted Islands of the Atlantic.
Core Collection.

Higgs, David, 1939-
xHiggs, David.
Ultraroyalism in Toulouse: From Its Origins to
Revolution of 1830. Johns Hopkins.

Higgs, R. *see* Higgs, Robert.

Higgs, Robert.
xHiggs, R.
Competition & Coercion: Blacks in the
American Economy, 1865-1914. Cambridge
U Pr.
xHiggs, Robert.

Competition & Coercion: Blacks in the
American Economy, 1865 to 1914. U of
Chicago Pr.

High Fidelity.
xHigh Fidelity Editors.
High Fidelity's Silver Anniversary Treasury.
Wyeth Pr.
xHigh Fidelity Magazine.
The Recordings of Beethoven. Greenwood.

High Fidelity Editors. *see* High Fidelity.

High Fidelity Magazine. *see* High Fidelity.

High, Monique R. *see* High, Monique Raphel.

High, Monique Raphel.
xHigh, Monique R.
The Four Winds of Heaven. Delacorte.
The Four Winds of Heaven. Dell.

Higham, Charles, 1931-
xHigham, Charles.
The Adventures of Conan Doyle: The Life of
the Creator of Sherlock Holmes. Norton.
Celebrity Circus. Delacorte.
Earliest Farmers & the First Cities. Cambridge
U Pr.
Errol Flynn: The Untold Story. Doubleday.
The Films of Orson Welles. U of Cal Pr.
Life in the Old Stone Age. Cambridge U Pr.
Life in the Old Stone Age. Lerner Pubns.
Marlene. PB.
Marlene: The Life of Marlene Dietrich.
Norton.

Higham, Florence M. *see* Higham, Florence May Greir
Evans.

Higham, Florence May Greir Evans, 1896-
xHigham, Florence M.
Charles I: A Study. Folcroft.

Higham, Robin. *see* Higham, Robin D. S.

Higham, Robin D. S.
xHigham, Robin.
Britain's Imperial Air Routes, 1918 to 1939:
The Story of Britain's Overseas Airlines.
Shoe String.
ed. Flying Combat Aircraft of the
USAAF-USAF. Iowa St U Pr.
ed. Flying Combat Aircraft of USAAF-USAF.
Iowa St U Pr.

Highberger, Ruth.
xHighberger, Ruth.
Child Development for Day Care Workers.
HM.

Highet, Gilbert, 1906-
xHighet, Gilbert.
Anatomy of Satire. Princeton U Pr.
Art of Teaching. Random.
Explorations. Oxford U Pr.
People, Places, & Books. Oxford U Pr.
Poets in a Landscape. Greenwood.
Powers of Poetry. Oxford U Pr.
The Speeches in Vergil's Aeneid. Princeton U
Pr.

Highfield, Arnold R.
xHighfield, Arnold R.
The French Dialect of St. Thomas U.S. Virgin
Islands: A Descriptive Grammar with Texts
& Glossary. Karoma.

Highland, Esther H. *see* Highland, Esther Harris.

Highland, Esther Harris.
xHighland, Esther H.
Business Mathematics. Reston.

Highlights Editors. *see* Highlights for Children.

Highlights for Children.
xHighlights Editors.
Creative Craft Activities. Highlights.
ed. Crossword Puzzles. Highlights.
Holiday Handbooks of Crafts. Highlights.
Jokes from Highlights. Highlights.
Jumbo Holiday Handbook. Highlights.
Riddles from Highlights. Highlights.
Tricks & Teasers. Highlights.

Highnam, Kenneth C. *see* Highnam, Kenneth Charles.

Highnam, Kenneth Charles.
  xHighnam, Kenneth C.
    The Comparative Endocrinology of the
      Invertebrates. Univ Park.
Highsmith, Patricia, 1921-
  xHighsmith, Patricia.
    The Boy Who Followed Ripley. Lippincott &
      Crowell.
    Edith's Diary. PB.
    Edith's Diary. S&S.
    Strangers on a Train. Penguin.
Hight, Donald W.
  xHight, Donald W.
    A Concept of Limits. Dover.
Highton, N. B. see Highton, N. Berry.

Highton, N. Berry.

  xHighton, N. B.
    The Home Book of Vegetarian Cookery.
      Merrimack Bk Serv.

Highwater, Jamake.

  xHighwater, Jamake.
    Song from the Earth: American Indian
      Painting. NYGS.
    The Sun, He Dies. Lippincott & Crowell.

Higley, John.
  xHigley, John.
    Elites in Australia. Routledge & Kegan.
Higman, Bryan.
  xHigman, Bryan.
    Comparative Study of Programming Languages.
      Elsevier.
Hignett, Charles.
  xHignett, Charles.
    History of the Athenian Constitution to the
      End of the Fifth Century, B.C. Oxford U Pr.
Higonnet, Patrice L. see Higonnet, Patrice L. R.
Higonnet, Patrice L. R.
  xHigonnet, Patrice L.
    Pont-De-Montvert: Social Structure & Politics
      in a French Village 1700-1914. Harvard U
      Pr.
Higonnet-Schnopper, Janet.
  xHigonnet-Schnopper, Janet.
    tr. Tales from Atop a Russian Stove. A
      Whitman.
Higson, James D.
  xHigson, James D.
    Building & Remodeling for Energy Savings.
      Craftsman.
Higson, John W., 1924-
  xHigson, John W.
    A Historical Guide to Florence. Universe.
Hijiya, Yukihito.
  xHijiya, Yukihito.
    Ishikawa Takuboku. Twayne.
Hilado, Carlos J., 1933-
  xHilado, Carlos J.
    ed. Flammability Handbook for Plastics.
      Technomic.
    Flammability of Consumer Products.
      Technomic.
    Handbook of Flammability Regulations.
      Technomic.
    Oxygen Index of Materials. Technomic.
    Surface Flame Spread. Technomic.
Hilado, Carlos J. see Hilado, Carols J.
Hilado, Carols J., 1933-
  xHilado, Carlos J.
    Flammability of Cellulosic Materials.
      Technomic.
Hilaire. see Hilaire, Frank.
Hilaire, Frank.
  xHilaire.
    Traficante. St Martin.
  xHilaire, Frank.

    Thanatos. PB.
Hilberg, Raul, 1926-
  xHilberg, Raul.
    The Destruction of the European Jews.
      Octagon.
Hilberry, Conrad.
  xHilberry, Conrad.
    ed. Third Coast: Contemporary Michigan
      Poetry. Wayne St U Pr.
Hilberseimer, Ludwig.
  xHilberseimer, Ludwig.
    Contemporary Architecture: Its Roots &
      Trends. Theobald.
Hilbert, David, 1862-1943
  xHilbert, David.
    Geometry & the Imagination. Chelsea Pub.
    Principles of Mathematical Logic. Chelsea Pub.
Hilburn. see Hilburn, R. E.
Hilburn, May S. see Hilburn, May Stafford.
Hilburn, May Stafford.
  xHilburn, May S.
    Golden Tributes: Fraternal Ceremonies. Macoy
      Pub.
    One Hundred Short Prayers. Macoy Pub.
Hilburn, R. E., 1913-
  xHilburn.
    The Successful Electronics Servicing Business.
      P-H.
Hilde, Reuben.
  xHilde, Rueben.
    In the Manner of Jesus. Pacific Pr Pub Assn.
Hilde, Rueben. see Hilde, Reuben.
Hildebrand, Alice J. Von. see Von Hildebrand, Alice J.
Hildebrand, B. P.
  xHildebrand, B. P.
    An Introduction to Acoustical Holography.
      Plenum Pub.
  xHildebrand, B. Percy.
    An Introduction to Acoustical Holography.
      Plenum Pub.
Hildebrand, B. Percy. see Hildebrand, B. P.
Hildebrand, David K.
  xHildebrand, David K.
    Prediction Analysis of Cross Classifications.
      Wiley.
Hildebrand, Dietrich Von. see Von Hildebrand, Dietrich.
Hildebrand, Francis B. see Hildebrand, Francis Begnaud.
Hildebrand, Francis Begnaud.
  xHildebrand, Francis B.
    Advanced Calculus for Applications. P-H.
    Introduction to Numerical Analysis. McGraw.
Hildebrand, George H. see Hildebrand, George Herbert.
Hildebrand, George Herbert.
  xHildebrand, George H.
    Growth & Structure in the Economy of
      Modern Italy. Harvard U Pr.
Hildebrand, Grant, 1934-
  xHildebrand, Grant.
    Designing for Industry: The Architecture of
      Albert Kahn. MIT Pr.
Hildebrand, J. see Hildebrand, Jerzy.
Hildebrand, Jerzy.
  xHildebrand, J.
    ed. Lesions of the Nervous System in Cancer
      Patients. Raven.
Hildebrand, Klaus.
  xHildebrand, Klaus.
    The Foreign Policy of the Third Reich. U of
      Cal Pr.
Hildebrand, Milton, 1918-
  xHildebrand, Milton.
    Analysis of Vertebrate Structure. Wiley.
    Anatomical Preparations. U of Cal Pr.
Hildebrand, Verna.
  xHildebrand, Verna.
    Guiding Young Children. Macmillan.
    Introduction to Early Childhood Education.
      Macmillan.
Hildebrandt, Tim.
  xHildebrandt, Tim.

    jt. auth. How Do They Build It?. Platt.
Hildemann, W. H., 1927-
  xHildemann, William H.
    Immunogenetics. Holden-Day.
Hildemann, William H. see Hildemann, W. H.
Hildenbrand, W. see Hildenbrand, Werner.
Hildenbrand, Werner, 1936-
  xHildenbrand, W.
    Core & Equilibria of a Large Economy.
      Princeton U Pr.
Hildick, E. W.
  xHildick, E. W.
    Great Rabbit Rip-off. PB.
Hildick, E. W. see Hildick, Edmund Wallace.
Hildick, E. Wallace. see Hildick, Edmund Wallace.
Hildick, Edmund Wallace.
  xHildick, E. W.
    The Case of the Phantom Frog. Macmillan.
    The Case of the Secret Scribbler. Macmillan.
    The Case of the Treetop Treasure. Macmillan.
    A Cat Called Amnesia. Archway.
    A Cat Called Amnesia. D White.
    A Cat Called Amnesia. PB.
    Deadline for McGurk. Macmillan.
    Louie's Lot. D White.
    Louie's Ransom. Knopf.
    The Nose Knows. G&D.
  xHildick, E. Wallace.
    The Active-Enzyme Lemon-Freshened Junior
      High School Witch. Doubleday.
Hildick, Wallace.
  xHildick, Wallace.
    Word for Word: The Rewriting of Fiction.
      Norton.
Hildreth, Gertrude H. see Hildreth, Gertrude Howell.
Hildreth, Gertrude Howell.
  xHildreth, Gertrude H.
    Educating Gifted Children at Hunter College
      Elementary School. Greenwood.
Hildreth, Richard, 1807-1865
  xHildreth, Richard.
    Archy Moore, the White Slave: Or Memoirs of
      a Fugitive. Negro U Pr.
    Banks, Banking, & Paper Currencies.
      Greenwood.
    Despotism in America: An Inquiry into the
      Nature Results & Legal Basis of the
      Slaveholding System in the United States.
      Negro U Pr.
    History of the United States of America.
      Kelley.
    White Slave: Or, Memoirs of a Fugitive. Arno.
Hildt, John C. see Hildt, John Coffey.
Hildt, John Coffey, 1882-1938
  xHildt, John C.
    Early Diplomatic Negotiations of the United
      States with Russia. AMS Pr.
Hilen, Andrew. see Hilen, Andrew R.
Hilen, Andrew R., 1913-
  xHilen, Andrew.
    Longfellow & Scandinavia: A Study of the
      Poet's Relationship with the Northern
      Languages & Literature. Shoe String.
Hiler, Hilaire, 1898-1966
  xHiler, Hilaire.
    From Nudity to Raiment: An Introduction to
      the Study of Costume. Gordon Pr.
    The Painter's Pocket Book of Methods &
      Materials. Merrimack Bk Serv.
Hiles, David. see Hiles, David A.
Hiles, David A.
  xHiles, David.
    ed. Intraocular Lens Implants in Children.
      Grune.
Hilgard, E. R. see Hilgard, Ernest Ropiequet.
Hilgard, Ernest J. see Hilgard, Ernest Ropiequet.
Hilgard, Ernest R.
  xHilgard, Ernest R.
    Introduction to Psychology. HarBraceJ.
Hilgard, Ernest R. see Hilgard, Ernest Ropiequet.

Hilgard, Ernest Ropiequet, 1904-
  xHilgard, E. R.
    Hypnosis in the Relief of Pain. W Kaufmann.
  xHilgard, Ernest J.
    Theories of Learning. P-H.
  xHilgard, Ernest R.
    Divided Consciousness: Multiple Controls in
      Human Thought & Action. Wiley.
    Experience of Hypnosis. HarBraceJ.
    Hypnotic Susceptibility. HarBraceJ.
    Theories of Learning. P-H.

Hilgard, Josephine (Rohrs).
  xHilgard, Josephine R.
    Personality & Hypnosis: A Study of
      Imaginative Involvement. U of Chicago Pr.

Hilgard, Josephine R. see Hilgard, Josephine (Rohrs).

Hilgartner, Beth.
  xHilgartner, Beth.
    Great Gorilla Grins: An Abundance of Animal
      Alliterations. Little.
    A Necklace of Fallen Stars. Little.

Hilger, Inez.
  xHilger, Inez.
    Chippewa Child Life & Its Cultural
      Background. AMS Pr.
    Chippewa Child Life & Its Cultural
      Background. Scholarly.

Hilgers, Thomas. see Hilgers, Thomas W.
Hilgers, Thomas W.
  xHilgers, Thomas.
    ed. Abortion & Social Justice. Andrews &
      McMeel.

Hilgert, Raymond L.
  xHilgert, Raymond L.
    Cases & Policies in Human Resources
      Management. HM.

Hilhorst, J. G. see Hilhorst, Jozef Gijsbertus Maria.

Hilhorst, Jozef Gijsbertus Maria.
  xHilhorst, J. G.
    Monopolistic Competition, Technical Progress
      & Income Distribution. Gordon.

Hilken, Thomas J. see Hilken, Thomas John Norman.

Hilken, Thomas John Norman.
  xHilken, Thomas J.
    Engineering at Cambridge University,
      1783-1965. Cambridge U Pr.

Hilkey, Charles J. see Hilkey, Charles Joseph.

Hilkey, Charles Joseph, 1880-
  xHilkey, Charles J.
    Legal Development in Colonial Massachusetts,
      1630-1686. AMS Pr.
Hill & Knowlton Executives. see Hill and Knowlton, Inc.
Hill, Adrian. see Hill, Adrian Keith Graham.
Hill, Adrian Keith Graham, 1895-
  xHill, Adrian.
    Drawing & Painting Trees. Sterling.
Hill, Alice P. see Hill, Alice Polk.
Hill, Alice Polk, 1854-1921
  xHill, Alice P.
    Tales of the Colorado Pioneers. Rio Grande.
Hill and Knowlton, Inc.
  xHill & Knowlton Executives.
    Critical Issues in Public Relations. P-H.
Hill, Ann.
  xHill, Ann.
    The Sultanate of Oman: A Heritage. Longman.
Hill, Archibald A.
  xHill, Archibald A.
    Constituent & Pattern in Poetry. U of Tex Pr.
Hill, Archie.
  xHill, Archie.
    Closed World of Love. Avon.
    Closed World of Love. S&S.
Hill, Bennett D.
  xHill, Bennett D.

English Cistercian Monasteries & Their Patrons
  in the Twelfth Century. U of Ill Pr.
Hill, Brian. see Hill, Brian W.
Hill, Brian W.
  xHill, Brian.
    The Growth of Parliamentary Parties:
      1689-1742. Shoe String.
Hill, C. W. see Hill, Cuthbert William.
Hill, C. William. see Hill, Charles William.
Hill, Carol.
  xHill, Carol.
    Let's Fall in Love. Ballantine.
Hill, Carole E.
  xHill, Carole E.
    ed. Symbols & Society: Essays on Belief
      Systems in Action. U of Ga Pr.
Hill, Caroline (Miles), 1866-1951
  xHill, Caroline M.
    ed. The World's Great Religious Poetry.
      Greenwood.
Hill, Caroline M. see Hill, Caroline (Miles).
Hill, Charles E. see Hill, Charles Edward.
Hill, Charles Edward, 1881-1936
  xHill, Charles E.
    Leading American Treaties. AMS Pr.
Hill, Charles G., 1937-
  xHill, Charles G.
    An Introduction to Chemical Engineering
      Kinetics & Reactor Design. Wiley.
Hill, Charles William, 1940-
  xHill, C. William.
    The Political Theory of John Taylor of
      Caroline. Fairleigh Dickinson.
Hill, Christopher.
  xHill, Christopher.
    Century of Revolution, 1603-1714. Norton.
    Change & Continuity in Seventeenth-Century
      England. Harvard U Pr.
    Lenin & the Russian Revolution. Penguin.
Hill, Christopher. see Hill, John Edward Christopher.
Hill, Christopher T.
  xHill, Christopher T.
    ed. Federal Regulation & Chemical Innovation.
      Am Chemical.
    ed. Technological Innovation for a Dynamic
      Economy. Pergamon.
Hill, Claire C. see Hill, Claire Conley.
Hill, Claire Conley.
  xHill, Claire C.
    Problem Solving, Learning & Teaching: An
      Annotated Bibliography. Nichols Pub.
Hill, Claude.
  xHill, Claude.
    Drama of German Expressionism: A
      German-English Bibliography. AMS Pr.
Hill, Cuthbert William.
  xHill, C. W.
    Edwardian Scotland. Rowman.
Hill, D. A. see Hill, Douglas Arthur.
Hill, D. W. see Hill, Dennis Walter.
Hill, David, Rev.
  xHill, David.
    New Testament Prophecy. John Knox.
Hill, David. see Hill, David Campbell.
Hill, David Campbell.
  xHill, David.
    The Deadly Messiah. Avon.
Hill, David S., 1940-
  xHill, David S.
    Landlord & Tenant Law in a Nutshell. West
      Pub.
Hill, Deborah.
  xHill, Deborah.
    House of Kingsley Merrick. Coward.
    The House of Kingsley Merrick. NAL.
    This Is the House. NAL.
Hill, Dennis Walter.
  xHill, D. W.

Principles of Electronics in Medical Research.
  Butterworths.
Hill, Donald L. see Hill, Donald Lynch.
Hill, Donald Louis, 1914-
  xHill, Donald L.
    Richard Wilbur. Coll & U Pr.
Hill, Donald Lynch, 1937-
  xHill, Donald L.
    A Review of Cyclophosphamide. C C Thomas.
Hill, Donna.
  xHill, Donna.
    Ms Glee Was Waiting. Atheneum.
Hill, Dorothy M.
  xHill, Dorothy M.
    Mud, Sand & Water. Natl Assn Child Ed.
Hill, Douglas.
  xHill, Douglas.
    Supernatural. NAL.
Hill, Douglas. see Hill, Douglas Arthur.
Hill, Douglas Arthur, 1935-
  xHill, D. A.
    Northern Ireland. Cambridge U Pr.
  xHill, Douglas.
    Galactic Warlord. Atheneum.
Hill, E. see Hill, Edward.
Hill, Earle, 1941-
  xHill, Earle.
    Quietly Crush the Lizard. Vanguard.
Hill, Edward, 1938-
  xHill, E.
    A Comparative Study of Very Large Data
      Bases. Springer-Verlag.
Hill, Edward B. see Hill, Edward Burlingame.
Hill, Edward Burlingame, 1872-1960
  xHill, Edward B.
    Modern French Music. Da Capo.
    Modern French Music. Greenwood.
Hill, Edward E.
  xHill, Edward E.
    Office of Indian Affairs, 1824-1880: Historical
      Sketches. Clearwater Pub.
Hill, Eldon C. see Hill, Eldon Gleon.
Hill, Eldon Gleon, 1906-
  xHill, Eldon C.
    George Bernard Shaw. Twayne.
Hill, Elizabeth S. see Hill, Elizabeth Starr.
Hill, Elizabeth Starr.
  xHill, Elizabeth S.
    Ever-After Island. Dutton.
Hill, Evan.
  xHill, Evan.
    The Primary State: An Historical Guide to
      New Hampshire. Countryman.
Hill, Evelyn F.
  xHill, Evelyn F.
    The Holtzman Inkblot Technique: A Handbook
      for Clinical Application. Jossey-Bass.
Hill, Everett.
  xHill, Everett W.
    Orientation & Mobility Techniques: A Guide
      for the Practitioner. Am Foun Blind.
Hill, Everett W. see Hill, Everett.
Hill, Fiona.
  xHill, Fiona.
    The Autumn Rose. Berkley Pub.
    The Love Child. Berkley Pub.
    Love in a Major Key. Berkley Pub.
    The Practical Heart. Berkley Pub.
    Sweet's Folly. Berkley Pub.
    Sweet's Folly. Berkley Pub.
Hill, Frederick J. see Hill, Fredrick J.
Hill, Fredrick J.
  xHill, Frederick J.
    Digital Systems: Hardware Organization &
      Design. Wiley.
    Introduction to Switching Theory & Logical
      Design. Wiley.
Hill, G. F. see Hill, George Francis.
Hill, Geoffrey.
  xHill, Geoffrey.

Tenebrae. HM.

Hill, George E.
xHill, George E.
Guidance for Children in Elementary Schools.
Irvington.

Hill, George Francis, Sir, 1867-1948
xHill, G. F.
Historical Greek Coins. Ares.
Historical Roman Coins. Ares.
Imperial Persian Coinage. Obol Intl.

Hill, George J.
xHill, George J.
Leprosy in Five Young Men. Colo Assoc.
Outpatient Surgery. Saunders.

Hill, George R. see Hill, George Robert.

Hill, George Robert, 1943-
xHill, George R.
A Preliminary Checklist of Research on the
Classic Symphony & Concerto to the Time of
Beethoven (Excluding Haydn & Mozart).
Eur-Am Music.
A Thematic Catalog of the Instrumental Music
of Florian Leopold Gassmann. Eur-Am
Music.
A Thematic Locator for Mozart's Works, As
Listed in Koechel's Chronologisch
Thematisches Verzeichnis. Eur-Am Music.

Hill, Grace (Livingston), 1865-1947
xHill, Grace C.
A Girl to Come Home to. Am Repr-Rivercity
Pr.
xHill, Grace L.
All Through the Night. Am Repr-Rivercity Pr.
Bright Arrows. Am Repr-Rivercity Pr.
Bright Arrows. Bantam.
By Way of the Silverthorns. Am Repr-Rivercity
Pr.
The City of Fire. Am Repr-Rivercity Pr.
Crimson Mountain. Am Repr-Rivercity Pr.
Exit Betty. Am Repr-Rivercity Pr.
The Finding of Jasper Holt. Am Repr-Rivercity
Pr.
The Finding of Jasper Holt. Bantam.
Found Treasure. Am Repr-Rivercity Pr.
The Girl from Montana. Am Repr-Rivercity
Pr.
A Girl to Come Home to. Bantam.
The Honor Girl. Am Repr-Rivercity Pr.
The Honor Girl. Bantam.
Lo, Michael. Am Repr-Rivercity Pr.
Marigold. Am Repr-Rivercity Pr.
Not Under the Law. Am Repr-Rivercity Pr.
The Story of a Whim. Am Repr-Rivercity Pr.
xHill, Grace Livingston.
The Obsession of Victoria Gracen. Bantam.

Hill, Grace C. see Hill, Grace (Livingston).
Hill, Grace L. see Hill, Grace (Livingston).
Hill, Grace Livingston. see Hill, Grace (Livingston).

Hill, Graham L.
xHill, Graham L.
Ileostomy: Surgery, Physiology & Management.
Grune.

Hill, H. see Hill, Howard E.
Hill, Hamlin. see Hill, Hamlin Lewis.

Hill, Hamlin Lewis, 1931-
xHill, Hamlin.
Mark Twain: God's Fool. Har-Row.

Hill, Harold.
xHill, Harold.
How to Be a Winner. Logos.
How to Live Like a King's Kid. Logos.
Instant Answers for King's Kids in Training.
Logos.

Hill, Harry G.
xHill, Harry G.
Automotive Service & Repair Tools. Delmar.
Automotive Service & Repair Tools. Van Nos
Reinhold.

Hill, Helen.
xHill, Helen.

Straight on till Morning: Poems of the
Imaginary World. T Y Crowell.

Hill, Herbert, 1924-
xHill, Herbert.
ed. Anger, & Beyond: The Negro Writer in the
United States. Har-Row.
Citizen's Guide to Desegregation: A Study of
Social & Legal Change in American Life.
Greenwood.
ed. Soon, One Morning: New Writing by
American Negroes, 1940-1962. Knopf.
xHill, Herbet.
Citizen's Guide to Desegregation: A Study of
Social & Legal Change in American Life.
Negro U Pr.

Hill, Herbet. see Hill, Herbert.

Hill, Howard E.
xHill, H.
How to Think Like a Millionaire & Get Rich.
P-H.
xHill, Howard E.
Introduction to Lecithin. BJ Pub Group.
Nine Magic Secrets of Long Life. P-H.

Hill, Ivan.
xHill, Ivan.
ed. The Ethical Basis of Economic Freedom.
Am Viewpoint.
ed. The Ethical Basis of Economic Freedom.
Praeger.

Hill, J. C. see Hill, John Campbell.
Hill, James J. see Hill, James Jerome.

Hill, James Jerome, 1838-1916
xHill, James J.
Highways of Progress. Arno.

Hill, James N., 1934-
xHill, James N.
Broken K Pueblo, Prehistoric Social
Organization in the American Southwest. U
of Ariz Pr.
ed. Explanation of Prehistoric Change. U of
NM Pr.
ed. The Individual in Prehistory: Studies of
Variability in Style in Prehistoric
Technologies. Acad Pr.

Hill, James R. Foreword by. see Peckham, Elsie Maye.

Hill, Janet.
xHill, Janet.
Children Are People: The Librarian in the
Community. T Y Crowell.

Hill, Janet (McKenzie).
xHill, Janet M.
Cooking for Two. Little.

Hill, Janet M. see Hill, Janet (McKenzie).

Hill, Jeanne.
xHill, Jeanne.
Daily Breath. Word Bks.

Hill, Jim D. see Hill, Jim Dan.

Hill, Jim Dan.
xHill, Jim D.
The Civil War Sketchbook of Charles Ellery
Stedman, Surgeon, United States Navy.
Presidio Pr.

Hill, John. see Hill, John Walter.
Hill, John B. see Hill, John Benjamin.

Hill, John Benjamin.
xHill, John B.
Botany, a Textbook for Colleges. Krieger.

Hill, John Campbell, 1888-
xHill, J. C.
Teaching & the Unconscious Mind. Intl Univs
Pr.

Hill, John Edward Christopher, 1912-
xHill, Christopher.
Milton & the English Revolution. Penguin.
Milton & the English Revolution. Viking Pr.
Some Intellectual Consequences of the English
Revolution. U of Wis Pr.

Hill, John H.
xHill, John H.

Princess Malah. AMS Pr.

Hill, John L., 1923-
xHill, John L.
Texan's Guide to Consumer Protection. Gulf
Pub.

Hill, John S. see Hill, John Spencer.

Hill, John Spencer, 1943-
xHill, John S.
John Milton--Poet, Priest & Prophet: A Study
of Divine Vocation in Milton's Poetry &
Prose. Rowman.

Hill, John W. see Hill, John William.

Hill, John Walter, 1942-
xHill, John.
The Life & Works of Francesco Maria
Veracini. Univ Microfilms.

Hill, John William, 1933-
xHill, John W.
Chemistry & Life: An Introduction to General,
Organic, & Biological Chemistry. Burgess.
Chemistry for Changing Times. Burgess.

Hill, Joseph E.
xHill, Joseph E.
How Schools Can Apply Systems Analysis. Phi
Delta Kappa.

Hill, Justine.
xHill, Justine.
ed. Women Talking. Lyle Stuart.

Hill, Katherine E. see Hill, Katherine Elizabeth.

Hill, Katherine Elizabeth, 1912-
xHill, Katherine E.
Children's Contributions in Science
Discussions: A Consideration of Children's
Verbal Responses in Relation to Certain
Objectives for Science Instruction. AMS Pr.

Hill, Ken.
xHill, Ken.
The Four-Wheeled Morgan. Motorbooks Intl.

Hill, L. A. see Hill, Louise Alfreda.
Hill, L. F. see Hill, Lawrence Francis.
Hill, Lance. see Hill, R. Lance.
Hill, Lawrence F. see Hill, Lawrence Francis.

Hill, Lawrence Francis, 1890-
xHill, L. F.
Diplomatic Relations Between the United
States & Brazil. Gordon Pr.
xHill, Lawrence F.
Diplomatic Relations Between the United
States & Brazil. AMS Pr.
Diplomatic Relations Between the United
States & Brazil. Greenwood.
Diplomatic Relations Between the United
States & Brazil. Kraus Repr.
Diplomatic Relations Between the United
States & Brazil. Scholarly.

Hill, Leslie. see Hill, Leslie Alexander.

Hill, Leslie Alexander.
xHill, Leslie.
Free Composition Book. Oxford U Pr.

Hill, Lewis B.
xHill, Lewis B.
Psychotherapeutic Intervention in
Schizophrenia. U of Chicago Pr.

Hill, Lindsay. see Hill, Linsay.

Hill, Linsay.
xHill, Lindsay.
Avelaval. SBD.

Hill, Louis B. see Hill, Louise Biles.

Hill, Louise Alfreda.
xHill, L. A.
Tudors in French Drama. Johnson Repr.

Hill, Louise Biles, 1891-
xHill, Louis B.
Joseph E. Brown & the Confederacy.
Greenwood.

Hill, M. see Hill, Martin.

Hill, Marie, 1931-
xHill, Marie.

Gentleman Joe: The Story of Harness Driver
    Joe O'Brien. Arco.
Hill, Marnesba. *see* Hill, Marnesba D.
Hill, Marnesba D.
    xHill, Marnesba.
    Puerto Rican Authors: A Biobibliographic
        Handbook. Scarecrow.
Hill, Martin.
    xHill, M.
    Immunities & Privileges of International
        Officials: The Experience of the League of
        Nations. Kraus Repr.
Hill, Mary, 1923-
    xHill, Mary.
    Geology of the Sierra Nevada. U of Cal Pr.
Hill, Mary L. *see* Hill, Mary Lou.
Hill, Mary Lou.
    xHill, Mary L.
    My Dad's a Park Ranger. Childrens.
    My Dad's a Smokejumper. Childrens.
Hill, Matthew D. *see* Hill, Matthew Davenport.
Hill, Matthew Davenport, 1792-1872
    xHill, Matthew D.
    Suggestions for the Repression of Crime.
        Patterson Smith.
Hill, Michael. *see* Hill, Michael J.
Hill, Michael J.
    xHill, Michael.
    The State, Administration & the Individual.
        Rowman.
    xHill, Michael J.
    The Sociology of Public Administration.
        Crane-Russak Co.
Hill, N. B. *see* Hill, Norman Berkeley.
Hill, Napoleon, 1883-1970
    xHill, Napoleon.
    Grow Rich with Peace of Mind. Fawcett.
    Master-Key to Riches. Fawcett.
    Succeed & Grow Rich Through Persuasion.
        Fawcett.
    Success Through a Positive Mental Attitude.
        P-H.
    Success Through a Positive Mental Attitude.
        PB.
    Think & Grow Rich. Fawcett.
    Think & Grow Rich. Wehman.
    Think & Grow Rich. Wilshire.
Hill, Norman Berkeley.
    xHill, N. B.
    Introduction to Economics for Students of
        Agriculture. Pergamon.
Hill, Norman C., 1951-
    xHill, Norman C.
    Increasing Managerial Effectiveness: Keys to
        Management & Motivation. A-W.
Hill, Norman L. *see* Hill, Norman Llewellyn.
Hill, Norman Llewellyn, 1895-
    xHill, Norman L.
    Claims to Territory in International Law &
        Relations. Greenwood.
Hill, O Mary.
    xHill, O. Mary.
    Canada's Salesman to the World: The
        Department of Trade & Commerce.
        McGill-Queens U Pr.
Hill, Pamela.
    xHill, Pamela.
    Daneclere. Fawcett.
    Daneclere. St Martin.
    The Green Salamander. Fawcett.
    The Green Salamander. St Martin.
    Norah. Fawcett.
    Strangers' Forest. Fawcett.
    Stranger's Forest. St Martin.
Hill, Patricia K. *see* Hill, Patricia Kneas.
Hill, Patricia Kneas.
    xHill, Patricia K.

Oglethorpe Ladies & the Jacobite Conspiracies.
    Cherokee.
Hill, Paul.
    xHill, Paul.
    Dialogue with Photography. FS&G.
Hill, Paul J.
    xHill, Paul J.
    The Edible Sea. A S Barnes.
Hill, Percy H.
    xHill, Percy H.
    Making Decisions: A Multi-Disciplinary
        Introduction. A-W.
Hill, Peter, fl. 1976-
    xHill, Peter.
    The Enthusiast. HM.
    The Fanatics. Scribner.
    The Liars. HM.
Hill, Philip G.
    xHill, Philip G.
    Mechanics & Thermodynamics of Propulsion.
        A-W.
Hill, R. *see* Hill, Rodney.
Hill, R. Lance.
    xHill, Lance.
    The Evil That Men Do. Bantam.
Hill, R. R. *see* Hill, Roscoe R.
Hill, Ralph, 1900-1950
    xHill, Ralph.
    ed. The Concerto. Greenwood.
    ed. The Symphony. Scholarly.
Hill, Ralph N. *see* Hill, Ralph Nading.
Hill, Ralph Nading, 1917-
    xHill, Ralph N.
    ed. College on the Hill: A Dartmouth
        Chronicle. U Pr of New Eng.
    The Story of the Ticonderoga: A Chronicle of
        Steamboating. Shelburne.
Hill, Ray.
    xHill, Ray.
    Pro Basketball's Little Men. Random.
Hill, Reuben, 1912-
    xHill, Reuben.
    Families Under Stress: Adjustment to the
        Crises of War Separation & Reunion.
        Greenwood.
Hill, Richard B. *see* Hill, Rick.
Hill, Richard L. *see* Hill, Richard Leslie.
Hill, Richard Leslie.
    xHill, Richard L.
    Toryism & the People 1832-1846. Porcupine
        Pr.
Hill, Richard M.
    xHill, Richard M.
    Industrial Marketing. Irwin.
Hill, Rick.
    xHill, Richard B.
    Too Young to Die. Hill Pubns.
Hill, Robert.
    xHill, Robert.
    Stained Glass: Music for the Eye. U of Wash
        Pr.
Hill, Robert. *see* Hill, Robert Henry.
Hill, Robert G. *see* Hill, Robert Gardiner.
Hill, Robert Gardiner, 1811-1878
    xHill, Robert G.
    Total Abolition of Personal Restraint in the
        Treatment of the Insane. Arno.
Hill, Robert H. *see* Hill, Robert Henry.
Hill, Robert Henry, 1900-
    xHill, Robert.
    ed. Dictionary of Difficult Words. Philos Lib.
    xHill, Robert H.
    Dictionary of Difficult Words. NAL.
Hill, Robert W. *see* Hill, Robert White.
Hill, Robert White, 1919-
    xHill, Robert W.
    What the Moon Astronauts Do. John Day.
Hill, Rodney, 1921-
    xHill, R.

Principles of Dynamics. Pergamon.
Hill, Rolla B. *see* Hill, Rolla Bennett.
Hill, Rolla Bennett.
    xHill, Rolla B.
    ed. Principles of Pathobiology. Oxford U Pr.
Hill, Roscoe R.
    xHill, R. R.
    Descriptive Catalogue of Documents Relating
        to the History of the United States in the
        Papeles Procedentes De Cuba in the Archivo
        General De Indias at Seville. Kraus Repr.
Hill, Roy L.
    xHill, Roy L.
    ed. Rhetoric of Racial Revolt. Golden Bell.
Hill, Ruth Beebe.
    xHill, Ruth Beebe.
    Hanta Yo. Doubleday.
Hill, Ruth L. *see* Hill, Ruth Livingston.
Hill, Ruth Livingston.
    xHill, Ruth L.
    This Side of Tomorrow. Zondervan.
Hill, S R.
    xHill, S. R.
    The Distributive System. Pergamon.
Hill, Samuel S.
    xHill, Samuel S.
    Religion & the Solid South. Abingdon.
Hill, Susan, 1942-
    xHill, Susan.
    I'm the King of the Castle. Penguin.
Hill, Terrell L.
    xHill, Terrell L.
    Introduction to Statistical Thermodynamics.
        A-W.
    Thermodynamics for Chemists & Biologists.
        A-W.
Hill, Thomas A.
    xHill, Thomas A.
    Country Music. Watts.
    The Drum: An Introduction to the Instrument.
        Watts.
    The Guitar: An Introduction to the Instrument.
        Watts.
Hill, Thomas M. *see* Hill, Thomas Mason.
Hill, Thomas Mason.
    xHill, Thomas M.
    Institution Building in India: A Study of
        International Collaboration in Management
        Education. Harvard Busn.
Hill, Tom, 1922-
    xHill, Tom.
    Color for the Watercolor Painter.
        Watson-Guptill.
    The Watercolor Painter's Problem Book.
        Watson Guptill.
Hill, Victor E.
    xHill, Victor E.
    Groups, Representations, and Characters.
        Hafner.
Hill, W. F. *see* Hill, Winfred F.
Hill, W. M. *see* Hill, William Munro.
Hill, West T. *see* Hill, West Thompson.
Hill, West Thompson, 1915-
    xHill, West T.
    Theatre in Early Kentucky, 1790-1820. U Pr of
        Ky.
Hill, William Fawcett, 1918-
    xHill, W. F.
    Learning Thru Discussion. Sage.
Hill, William G. *see* Hill, William Gilliam.
Hill, William Gilliam.
    xHill, William G.
    Family Service Agencies & Mental Health
        Clinics: A Comparative Study. Family Serv.
Hill, William H. *see* Hill, William Henry.
Hill, William Henry.
    xHill, William H.

Antonio Stradivari, His Life & Work
(1644-1739). Dover.
A Brief History of the Printing Press in
Washington, Saratoga & Warren Counties,
State of New York: Together with a
Checklist of Their Publications Prior to 1825,
& a Selection of Books Relating Particularly
to This Vicinity. Harbor Hill Bks.
Hill, William Munro.
xHill, W. M.
Coarse Fishing for New Anglers. David &
Charles.
Hill, Winfred F.
xHill, W. F.
Learning: A Survey of Psychological
Interpretations. Har-Row.
Hill-Peters, Mary.
xHill-Peters, Mary.
Charlotte Perkins Gilman: The Making of a
Radical Feminist, 1860-1896. Temple U Pr.
Hillard, James M.
xHillard, James M.
Where to Find More: A Handbook to
Reference Service. Scarecrow.
Hillary, Edmund, Sir.
xHillary, Edmund.
From the Ocean to the Sky. Viking Pr.
Hillary, Louise.
xHillary, Louise.
High Time. Dutton.
Hillas, A. M.
xHillas, A. M.
Cosmic Rays. Pergamon.
Hillbrand, Percle V.
xHillbrand, Percle V.
Swedes in America. Lerner Pubns.
Hillcourt, William.
xHillcourt, William.
Norman Rockwell's World of Scouting.
Abrams.
Hille, Einar, 1894-
xHille, Einar.
Analysis. Krieger.
Analytic Function Theory. Chelsea Pub.
Einar Hille: Classical Analysis & Functional
Analysis: Selected Papers. MIT Pr.
Lectures on Ordinary Differential Equations.
A-W.
Ordinary Differential Equations in the
Complex Domain. Wiley.
Hilleboe, Guy L. see Hilleboe, Guy Leonard.
Hilleboe, Guy Leonard, 1897-
xHilleboe, Guy L.
Finding & Teaching Atypical Children. AMS
Pr.
Hillebrand, Harold N. see Hillebrand, Harold Newcomb.
Hillebrand, Harold Newcomb, 1887-1953
xHillebrand, Harold N.
Child Actors: A Chapter in Elizabethan Stage
History. Russell.
Edmund Kean. AMS Pr.
Hillebrand, W. F. see Hillebrand, William Francis.
Hillebrand, William Francis.
xHillebrand, W. F.
Applied Inorganic Analysis: With Special
Reference to the Analysis of Metals,
Minerals & Rocks. Krieger.
Hillegas, Howard C. see Hillegas, Howard Clemens.
Hillegas, Howard Clemens, 1872-1918
xHillegas, Howard C.
Oom Paul's People: A Narrative of the
British-Boer Troubles in South Africa. Negro
U Pr.
Hillegas, Mark R. see Hillegas, Mark Robert.
Hillegas, Mark Robert, 1926-
xHillegas, Mark R.

ed. Shadows of Imagination: The Fantasies of
C. S. Lewis, J. R. R. Tolkien, & Charles
Williams. S Ill U Pr.
Hillel, Daniel.
xHillel, Daniel.
Soil & Water: Physical Principles & Processes.
Acad Pr.
Hillel, Marc.
xHillel, Marc.
Of Pure Blood. McGraw.
Of Pure Blood. PB.
Hillenbrand, Martin J. see Hillenbrand, Martin Joseph.
Hillenbrand, Martin Joseph.
xHillenbrand, Martin J.
ed. The Future of Berlin. Allanheld.
Hiller, Catherine.
xHiller, Catherine.
Argentaybee & the Boonie. Coward.
Hiller, Doris.
xHiller, Doris.
Little Big Top. Childrens.
Hiller, Ernest T. see Hiller, Ernest Theodore.
Hiller, Ernest Theodore, 1883-
xHiller, Ernest T.
Nature & Basis of Social Order. Coll & U Pr.
The Strike: A Study in Collective Action.
Arno.
Hiller, Ferdinand, 1811-1885
xHiller, Ferdinand.
Mendelssohn: Letters & Recollections. Vienna
Hse.
Hiller, Joseph A. see Hiller, Joseph Anthony.
Hiller, Joseph Anthony.
xHiller, Joseph A.
Albrecht Von Eyb, Medieval Moralist. AMS
Pr.
Hiller, Lejaren A. see Hiller, Lejaren Arthur.
Hiller, Lejaren Arthur.
xHiller, Lejaren A.
Experimental Music: Composition with an
Electronic Computer. Greenwood.
Hillerbrand, Hans J. see Hillerbrand, Hans Joachim.
Hillerbrand, Hans Joachim.
xHillerbrand, Hans J.
Christendom Divided: The Protestant
Reformation. Westminster.
Men & Ideas in the Sixteenth Century. Rand.
ed. Protestant Reformation. Har-Row.
ed. The Reformation: A Narrative History
Related by Contemporary Observers &
Participants. Baker Bk.
Hillerich, Robert L., 1927-
xHillerich, Robert L.
Reading Fundamentals for Preschool and
Primary Children. Merrill.
A Writing Vocabulary of Elementary Children.
C C Thomas.
Hillerman, Tony.
xHillerman, Tony.
Dance Hall of the Dead. Avon.
Dance Hall of the Dead. Har-Row.
Listening Woman. Avon.
ed. The Spell of New Mexico. U of NM Pr.
Hillers, Delbert R.
xHillers, Delbert R.
Covenant: The History of a Biblical Idea. Johns
Hopkins.
Hillert, Margaret.
xHillert, Margaret.
The Baby Bunny. Follett.
Circus Fun. Follett.
Come Play with Me. Follett.
The Cookie House. Follett.
The Golden Goose. Follett.
Happy Easter, Dear Dragon. Follett.
Play Ball. Follett.
What Am I?. Follett.
What Is It?. Follett.
Hilles, F. W. see Hilles, Frederick Whiley.
Hilles, Frederick W. see Hilles, Frederick Whiley.

Hilles, Frederick Whiley, 1900-
xHilles, F. W.
ed. The Age of Johnson: Essays Presented to
Chauncey Brewster Tinker. AMS Pr.
xHilles, Frederick W.
Dr. Johnson Rebuked: A Hitherto Unrecorded
Incident in His Life As Revealed in a Letter
from Dr. Samuel Glasse. Folcroft.
Literary Career of Sir Joshua Reynolds. Shoe
String.
Hillgarth, J. N.
xHillgarth, J. N.
Ramon Lull & Lullism in Fourteenth-Century
France. Oxford U Pr.
Hillhouse, James Abraham, 1789-1841
xHillhouse, James T.
Dramas, Discourses & Other Pieces. Arno.
Hillhouse, James T. see Hillhouse, James Abraham.
Hillhouse, James Theodore, 1890-1956
xHillhouse, James T.
Grub-Street Journal. Arno.
Hilliard, David. see Hilliard, David Lockhart.
Hilliard, David Lockhart, 1941-
xHilliard, David.
God's Gentlemen: A History of the
Melanesian Mission, 1849-1942. U of
Queensland Pr.
Hilliard, Robert L.
xHilliard, Robert L.
ed. Radio Broadcasting: An Introduction to the
Sound Medium. Hastings.
Hillier, Frederick S.
xHillier, Frederick S.
Introduction to Operations Research.
Holden-Day.
Hilher, H. G. see Hillier, Harold G.
Hillier, Harold G.
xHillier, H. G.
Hillier's Manual of Trees & Shrubs. A S
Barnes.
Hillier, Norman G. see Hillier, Norman Gilbert.
Hillier, Norman Gilbert, 1903-
xHillier, Norman G.
The Life & Beauty of Your Hair. Devin.
Hilliker, Grant, 1921-
xHilliker, Grant.
The Politics of Reform in Peru: The Aprista &
Other Mass Parties of Latin America. Johns
Hopkins.
Hilling, John B.
xHilling, John B.
The Historic Architecture of Wales: An
Introduction. Verry.
Hillis, Don W.
xHillis, Don W.
Live Happily with Yourself. Victor Bks.
Hillis, Newell D. see Hillis, Newell Dwight.
Hillis, Newell Dwight, 1858-1929
xHillis, Newell D.
Great Men As Prophets of a New Era. Arno.
Great Men As Prophets of a New Era. R West.
Hillman, Abraham P.
xHillman, Abraham P.
First Undergraduate Course in Abstract
Algebra. Wadsworth Pub.
Hillman, Howard.
xHillman, Howard.
The Art of Winning Foundation Grants.
Vanguard.
The Art of Winning Government Grants.
Vanguard.
The Book of World Cuisines. Penguin.
Hillman, James.
xHillman, James.

The Dream & the Underworld. Har-Row.
The Dream & the Underworld. Har-Row.
Re-Visioning Psychology. Har-Row.
Re-Visioning Psychology. Har-Row.
Suicide & the Soul. Spring Pubns.
Hillman, Jimmye S., 1923-
  xHillman, Jimmye S.
    Nontariff Agricultural Trade Barriers. U of
      Nebr Pr.
Hillman, Ruth E. see Hillman, Ruth Estelyn.
Hillman, Ruth Estelyn, 1925-
  xHillman, Ruth E.
    Life Along the Fencerow. Herald Pr.
Hillquit, Morris, 1869-1933
  xHillquit, Morris.
    History of Socialism in the United States. Peter
      Smith.
    Loose Leaves from a Busy Life. Da Capo.
Hills, B. A. see Hills, Brian Andrew.
Hills, Brian Andrew.
  xHills, B. A.
    Decompression Sickness: The Biophysical Basis
      of Prevention & Treatment. Wiley.
    Gas Transfer in the Lung. Cambridge U Pr.
Hills, C. A. R.
  xHills, Car.
    The Rhine. Silver.
Hills, Car. see Hills, C. A. R.
Hills, Christopher. see Hills, Christopher B.
Hills, Christopher B.
  xHills, Christopher.
    Into Meditation Now: A Course in Direct
      Enlightenment. Univ of Trees.
Hills, John W. see Hills, John Waller.
Hills, John Waller, 1867-1938
  xHills, John W.
    History of Fly Fishing for Trout. Freshet Pr.
Hills, Lawrence D. see Hills, Lawrence Donegan.
Hills, Lawrence Donegan, 1911-
  xHills, Lawrence D.
    Comfrey: Fodder, Food & Remedy. Universe.
    Fertility Without Fertilizers: A Basic Approach
      to Organic Gardening. Universe.
    The Propagation of Alpines. Theophrastus.
Hills, Leon C. see Hills, Leon Clark.
Hills, Leon Clark, 1877-1968
  xHills, Leon C.
    History & Genealogy of the Mayflower
      Planters & First Comers to Ye Olde Colonie.
      Genealog Pub.
Hills, Patricia.
  xHills, Patricia.
    The Genre Painting of Eastman Johnson: The
      Sources & Development of His Styles &
      Themes. Garland Pub.
Hills, Philip James.
  xHills, Phillip J.
    Teaching & Learning As a Communication
      Process. Halsted Pr.
Hills, Phillip J. see Hills, Philip James.
Hills, Theo L.
  xHills, Theo L.
    Canada. Fideler.
Hills, William G., 1937-
  xHills, William G.
    Conducting the People's Business: The
      Framework & Functions of Public
      Administration. U of Okla Pr.
Hillstrom, Tom.
  xHillstrom, Tom.
    Coal. Morrow.
Hillway, Tyrus.
  xHillway, Tyrus.
    Herman Melville. Coll & U Pr.
    Herman Melville. G K Hall.
    Herman Melville. Twayne.
Hillyer, Robert. see Hillyer, Robert Silliman.
Hillyer, Robert Silliman, 1895-
  xHillyer, Robert.

First Principles of Verse. Writer.
Hils, Karl.
  xHils, Karl.
    Crafts for All: A Natural Approach to Crafts.
      Routledge & Kegan.
Hilsinger, Serena S. see Hilsinger, Serena Sue.
Hilsinger, Serena Sue, 1937-
  xHilsinger, Serena S.
    Foxes on the Hill. Gambit.
Hilsman, Roger.
  xHilsman, Roger.
    Politics of Policy Making in Defense & Foreign
      Affairs. Har-Row.
Hilson, J. C.
  xHilson, J. C.
    ed. Augustan Worlds: New Essays in
      Eighteenth Century Literature. B&N.
Hilsum, S. see Hilsum, Sidney.
Hilsum, Sidney.
  xHilsum, S.
    The Teacher's Day. Humanities.
  xHilsum, Sidney.
    The Teacher at Work. Humanities.
Hilt, Nancy E.
  xHilt, Nancy E.
    Manual of Orthopedics. Mosby.
    Pediatric Orthopedic Nursing. Mosby.
Hiltner, Seward, 1909-
  xHiltner, Seward.
    Theological Dynamics. Abingdon.
Hilton, Bruce.
  xHilton, Bruce.
    Delta Ministry. Macmillan.
Hilton, David, 1938-
  xHilton, David.
    Huladance. Crossing Pr.
Hilton, George W. see Hilton, George Woodman.
Hilton, George Woodman.
  xHilton, George W.
    The Great Lakes Car Ferries. Howell-North.
    Monon Route. Howell-North.
    The Northeast Railroad Problem. Am
      Enterprise.
Hilton, Jack.
  xHilton, Jack.
    Quest for Carp. Transatlantic.
Hilton, John B. see Hilton, John Buxton.
Hilton, John Buxton.
  xHilton, John B.
    The Anathema Stone. St Martin.
    Some Run Crooked. St Martin.
Hilton, P. see Hilton, Peter John.
Hilton, P. J. see Hilton, Peter John.
Hilton, Peter. see Hilton, Peter John.
Hilton, Peter J. see Hilton, Peter John.
Hilton, Peter John.
  xHilton, P.
    Homotopy Theory & Duality. Gordon.
  xHilton, P. J.
    Course in Homological Algebra.
      Springer-Verlag.
    Differential Calculus. Routledge & Kegan.
    ed. Localization in Group Theory & Homotopy
      Theory & Related Topics. Springer-Verlag.
    Partial Derivatives. Routledge & Kegan.
    ed. Studies in Modern Topology. Math Assn.
  xHilton, Peter.
    Lectures in Homological Algebra. Am Math.
  xHilton, Peter J.
    General Cohomology Theory & K. Theory.
      Cambridge U Pr.
    Introduction to Homotopy Theory. Cambridge
      U Pr.
Hilton, Ruth B.
  xHilton, Ruth B.
    An Index to Early Music in Selected
      Anthologies. Eur-Am Music.
Hilton, Suzanne.
  xHilton, Suzanne.

Getting There: Frontier Travel Without Power.
  Westminster.
How Do They Cope with It?. Westminster.
Who Do You Think You Are?: Digging for
  Your Family Roots. NAL.
Who Do You Think You Are?: Digging for
  Your Family Roots. Westminster.
Hilton, Thomas L. see Hilton, Thomas Leonard.
Hilton, Thomas Leonard.
  xHilton, Thomas L.
    Confronting the Future: A Conceptual
      Framework for Secondary School Career
      Guidance. College Bd.
Hilton, Timothy, 1941-
  xHilton, Timothy.
    Pre-Raphaelites. Abrams.
    Pre-Raphaelites. Oxford U Pr.
Hilton, W. S. see Hilton, William Samuel.
Hilton, William Samuel.
  xHilton, W. S.
    Industrial Relations in Construction. Pergamon.
Hilton-Simpson, Melville W. see Hilton-Simpson,
  Melville William.
Hilton-Simpson, Melville William, 1881-1938
  xHilton-Simpson, Melville W.
    Arab Medicine & Surgery: A Study of the
      Healing Art in Algeria. AMS Pr.
Hilts, Len. see Hilts, Leonard Finley.
Hilts, Leonard Finley.
  xHilts, Len.
    National Forest Guide. Rand.
    Popular Mechanics Complete Book of
      Furniture. Hearst Bks.
Hilts, Victor L.
  xHilts, Victor L.
    A Guide to Francis Galton's "English Men of
      Science". Am Philos.
Hiltz, Starr R. see Hiltz, Starr Roxanne.
Hiltz, Starr Roxanne.
  xHiltz, Starr R.
    Creating Community Services for Widows: A
      Pilot Project. Kennikat.
    Network Nation: Human Communication Via
      Computer. A-W.
Himadeh, Sa'id B. see Himadeh, Said B.
Himadeh, Said B., 1894-
  xHimadeh, Sa'id B.
    Economic Organization of Syria. AMS Pr.
    Monetary & Banking System of Syria. AMS Pr.
Himber, Jacob.
  xHimber, Jacob.
    The Complete Family Guide to Dental Health.
      McGraw.
Himelblau, Jack.
  xHimelblau, Jack.
    Alejandro O. Deustua: Philosophy in Defense
      of Man. U Presses Fla.
Himelstein, Morgan Y. see Himelstein, Morgan Yale.
Himelstein, Morgan Yale.
  xHimelstein, Morgan Y.
    Drama Was a Weapon: The Left-Wing Theatre
      in New York, 1929-1941. Greenwood.
Himes, Chester.
  xHimes, Chester.
    All Shot up. Chatham Bkseller.
    Cotton Comes to Harlem. Chatham Bkseller.
    The Crazy Kill. Chatham Bkseller.
Himes, Chester. see Himes, Chester B.
Himes, Chester B, 1909-
  xHimes, Chester.
    If He Hollers, Let Him Go. NAL.
    The Real Cool Killers. Chatham Bkseller.
    The Third Generation. Chatham Bkseller.
Himes, John A. see Himes, John Andrew.
Himes, John Andrew, 1848-1923
  xHimes, John A.
    A Study of Milton's Paradise Lost. Folcroft.
Himes, Joseph S.
  xHimes, Joseph S.

Conflict & Conflict Management. U of Ga Pr.

Himes, Norman E. see Himes, Norman Edwin.

Himes, Norman Edwin, 1899-1949
xHimes, Norman E.
Medical History of Contraception. Schocken.

Himes, Roger.
xHimes, Roger.
Counselor, State Your Case!. Accent Bks.

Himler, Ronald.
xHimler, Ronald.
jt. auth. Little Owl, Keeper of the Trees.
Har-Row.
illus. Wake Up, Jeremiah. Har-Row.

Himmah, Gael. see Himmah, Gael C.

Himmah, Gael C.
xHimmah, Gael.
The Listing Master. Gael Himmah.
Real Estate Listing Magic. Gael Himmah.
Real Estate Selling Magic. Gael Himmah.

Himmel, Richard.
xHimmel, Richard.
The Twenty-Third Web. Ballantine.
The Twenty-Third Web. Random.

Himmelberg, Robert F.
xHimmelberg, Robert F.
The Origins of the National Recovery
Administration: Business, Government & the
Antitrust Question, 1921-1933. Fordham.

Himmelblau, David M. see Himmelblau, David Mautner.

Himmelblau, David Mautner, 1923-
xHimmelblau, David M.
Applied Nonlinear Programming. McGraw.
Process Analysis by Statistical Methods. Wiley.

Himmelfarb, Gertrude.
xHimmelfarb, Gertrude.
Darwin & the Darwinian Revolution. Norton.
Darwin & the Darwinian Revolution. Peter
Smith.

Himstreet. see Himstreet, William C.

Himstreet, William C.
xHimstreet.
Business English in Communications. Pitman
Learning.

Himwich, Williamina (Armstrong), 1912-
xHimwich, Williamina A.
Developmental Neurobiology. C C Thomas.

Himwich, Williamina A. see Himwich, Williamina
(Armstrong).

Hinchey, F. A. see Hinchey, Fred A.

Hinchey, Fred A.
xHinchey, F. A.
Vectors & Tensors for Engineers & Scientists.
Halsted Pr.

Hinchey, Roy W.
xHinchey, Roy W.
Plain Talk About the Pastorate. Broadman.

Hinchliff, Susan M.
xHinchliff, Susan M.
ed. Teaching Clinical Nursing. Churchill.

Hinchliffe, A. P. see Hinchliffe, Arnold P.

Hinchliffe, Arnold P., 1930-
xHinchliffe, A. P.
The Absurd. Methuen Inc.
xHinchliffe, Arnold P.
British Theatre 1950-1970. Rowman.

Hinchman, Walter S. see Hinchman, Walter Swain.

Hinchman, Walter Swain, 1879-
xHinchman, Walter S.
Pedestrian Papers. Arno.

Hinckley, A. D. see Hinckley, Alden D.

Hinckley, Alden D.
xHinckley, A. D.
Renewable Resources in Our Future.
Pergamon.
xHinckley, Alden D.
Applied Ecology: A Nontechnical Approach.
Macmillan.

Hinckley, Barbara, 1937-
xHinckley, Barbara.

Coalitions & Time: Cross-Disciplinary Studies.
Sage.
Stability & Change in Congress. Har-Row.

Hind, C. L. see Hind, Charles Lewis.

Hind, Charles L. see Hind, Charles Lewis.

Hind, Charles Lewis, 1862-1927
xHind, C. L.
Authors & I. R West.
xHind, Charles L.
Authors & I. Arno.
More Authors & I. Arno.
Post Impressionists. Arno.

Hinde, R. A.
xHinde, R. A.
ed. Non-Verbal Communication. Cambridge U
Pr.

Hinde, Sidney L. see Hinde, Sidney Langford.

Hinde, Sidney Langford, 1863-1930
xHinde, Sidney L.
Fall of the Congo Arabs. Negro U Pr.

Hinde, Thomas, 1926-
xHinde, Thomas.
Our Father. Braziller.

Hindelang, Michael J.
xHindelang, Michael L.
Criminal Victimization in Eight American
Cities: A Descriptive Analysis of Common
Theft & Assault. Ballinger Pub.

Hindelang, Michael L. see Hindelang, Michael J.

Hindemith, Paul, 1895-
xHindemith, Paul.
A Composer's World: Horizons & Limitations.
Peter Smith.

Hinderer, K.
xHinderer, Karl.
Foundations of Non-Stationary Dynamic
Programming with Discrete Time Parameter.
Springer-Verlag.

Hinderer, Karl. see Hinderer, K.

Hindess, Barry.
xHindess, Barry.
Pre-Capitalist Modes of Production. Routledge
& Kegan.

Hindle, Brooke.
xHindle, Brooke.
ed. America's Wooden Age: Aspects of Its
Early Technology. Sleepy Hollow.
David Rittenhouse. Arno.
The Pursuit of Science in Revolutionary
America, 1735-1789. Norton.
Pursuit of Science in Revolutionary America,
1735-1789. U of NC Pr.

Hindle, G. B. see Hindle, Gordon Bradley.

Hindle, Gordon Bradley.
xHindle, G. B.
Provision for the Relief of the Poor in
Manchester, 1754-1826. Humanities.

Hindley, Geoffrey.
xHindley, Geoffrey.
England in the Age of Caxton. St Martin.
World Art Treasures. Mayflower Bks.

Hindley, Margaret Patricia.
xHindley, Patricia.
The Tangled Net: Basic Issues in Canadian
Communications. U of Wash Pr.

Hindley, Patricia. see Hindley, Margaret Patricia.

Hindman, James. see Hindman, James Thomas.

Hindman, James Thomas.
xHindman, James.
TV Acting: A Manual for Camera
Performance. Hastings.

Hindman, Juanita L. see Hindman, Juanita Lewis.

Hindman, Juanita Lewis.
xHindman, Juanita L.
Postpioneers. Branch-Smith.

Hindmarsh, Albert E. see Hindmarsh, Albert Edward.

Hindmarsh, Albert Edward.
xHindmarsh, Albert E.

Force in Peace: Force Short of War in
International Relations. Kennikat.

Hinds, Dudley. see Hinds, Dudley S.

Hinds, Dudley S.
xHinds, Dudley.
Winning at Zoning. McGraw.

Hinds, Marjorie M.
xHinds, Marjorie M.
How to Make Money Writing Short Articles &
Fillers. Fell.

Hindus, Maurice. see Hindus, Maurice Gerschon.

Hindus, Maurice Gerschon, 1891-1969
xHindus, Maurice.
Humanity Uprooted. Greenwood.

Hindus, Michael S. see Hindus, Michael Stephen.

Hindus, Michael Stephen, 1946-
xHindus, Michael S.
Prison & Plantation: Crime, Justice, &
Authority in Massachusetts & South
Carolina, 1767-1878. U of NC Pr.

Hindwood, Keith. see Hindwood, Keith Alfred.

Hindwood, Keith Alfred, 1904-
xHindwood, Keith.
Australian Birds in Colour. U Pr of Hawaii.

Hine, Al.
xHine, Al.
A Letter to Anywhere. HarBraceJ.
ed. This Land Is Mine: An Anthology of
American Verse. Lippincott.

Hine, Darlene C. see Hine, Darlene Clark.

Hine, Darlene Clark.
xHine, Darlene C.
Black Victory: The Rise & Fall of the White
Primary in Texas. Kraus Intl.

Hine, Frederick R., 1925-
xHine, Frederick R.
Introduction to Psychodynamics: A
Conflict Adaptational Approach. Duke.

Hine, Jack. see Hine, Jack Sylvester.

Hine, Jack Sylvester, 1923-
xHine, Jack.
Structural Effects on Equilibria in Organic
Chemistry. Krieger.

Hine, Maynard K. see Hine, Maynard Kiplinger.

Hine, Maynard Kiplinger, 1907-
xHine, Maynard K.
Review of Dentistry: Questions & Answers.
Mosby.

Hine, Reginald L. see Hine, Reginald Leslie.

Hine, Reginald Leslie, 1883-1949
xHine, Reginald L.
Charles Lamb & His Hertfordshire.
Greenwood.
Charles Lamb & His Hertfordshire. R West.

Hine, Robert V, 1921-
xHine, Robert V.
California's Utopian Colonies. Norton.

Hine, Virginia. see Hine, Virginia H.

Hine, Virginia H.
xHine, Virginia.
Last Letter to the Pebble People: Aldie Soars.
Unity Pr.

Hineline, Harris D. see Hineline, Harris Dale.

Hineline, Harris Dale, 1890-
xHineline, Harris D.
Forms & Their Use in Patent & Trade Mark
Practice in the United States & Canada.
Michie.

Hines, Donald M., 1931-
xHines, Donald M.
An Index of Archived Resources for a Folklife
& Cultural History of the Inland Pacific
Northwest Frontier. Univ Microfilms.

Hines, Jeanne.
xHines, Jeanne.
The Third Wife. Popular Lib.

Hines, Mary A. see Hines, Mary Alice.

Hines, Mary Alice.
xHines, Mary A.

Principles & Practices of Real Estate. Irwin.
Real Estate Finance. P-H.
Real Estate Investment. Macmillan.
Hines, Neal O.
xHines, Neal O.
Denny's Knoll: A History of the Metropolitan
Tract of the University of Washington. U of
Wash Pr.
Fish of Rare Breeding: Salmon & Trout of the
Donaldson Strains. Smithsonian.
Proving Ground: An Account of the
Radiobiological Studies in the Pacific,
1946-61. U of Wash Pr.
Hines, Thomas J., 1940-
xHines, Thomas J.
The Later Poetry of Wallace Stevens:
Phenomenological Parallels with Husserl &
Heidegger. Bucknell U Pr.
Hingley, Ronald.
xHingley, Ronald.
Russian Writers & Soviet Society, 1917-1978.
Random.
The Undiscovered Dostoyevsky. Greenwood.
Hingorani, R. C.
xHingorani, R. C.
Indian Extradition Law. Asia.
Hiniker, Paul J.
xHiniker, Paul J.
Revolutionary Ideology & Chinese Reality:
Dissonance Under Mao. Sage.
Hinkemeyer, M. Thomas. see Hinkemeyer, Michael T.
Hinkemeyer, Michael. see Hinkemeyer, Michael. T.
Hinkemeyer, Michael. T.
xHinkemeyer, Michael.
Harbinger. PB.
Hinkemeyer, Michael T.
xHinkemeyer, M. Thomas.
The Fields of Eden. PB.
xHinkemeyer, Michael T.
The Fields of Eden. Putnam.
Summer Solstice. Berkley Pub.
Hinkhouse, Fred J. see Hinkhouse, Fred Junkin.
Hinkhouse, Fred Junkin, 1895-
xHinkhouse, Fred J.
Preliminaries of the American Revolution As
Seen in the English Press, 1763-1775.
Octagon.
Hinkle, Charles L.
xHinkle, Charles L.
Marketing Dynamics: Decision & Control.
McGraw.
Hinkle, Dennis. see Hinkle, Dennis E.
Hinkle, Dennis E.
xHinkle, Dennis.
Applied Statistics for the Behavioral Sciences.
Rand.
Hinkle, J. Herbert.
xHinkle, J. Herbert.
Soul Winning in Black Churches. Baker Bk.
Hinkle, Joseph. see Hinkle, Joseph W.
Hinkle, Joseph W.
xHinkle, Joseph.
How to Minister to Families in Your Church.
Broadman.
Hinkle, Roscoe C.
xHinkle, Roscoe C.
Founding Theory of American Sociology
1881-1915. Routledge & Kegan.
Hinkle, Vernon.
xHinkle, Vernon.
Music to Murder by. Belmont-Tower.
Hinkley, Edyth.
xHinkley, Edyth.
Mazzini: The Story of a Great Italian. Arno.
Hinkley, James W.
xHinkley, James W.
The Book of Vampires. Watts.
Hinks, Roger. see Hinks, Roger Packman.
Hinks, Roger Packman.
xHinks, Roger.

Carolingian Art: A Study of Early Medieval
Painting & Sculpture in Western Europe. U
of Mich Pr.
Hinman, Albert G. see Hinman, Albert Greene.
Hinman, Albert Greene, 1894-
xHinman, Albert G.
Population Growth & Its Demands Upon Land
for Housing in Evanston, Illinois. Arno.
Hinman, Bob.
xHinman, Bob.
The Duck Hunter's Handbook. Follett.
The Duck Hunter's Handbook. Winchester Pr.
Hinman, Frank.
xHinman, Frank.
Hydrodynamics of Micturition. C C Thomas.
Impact of the New Physics. Philos Lib.
Hinnant, Charles H.
xHinnant, Charles H.
Thomas Hobbes. Twayne.
Thomas Hobbes: A Reference Guide. G K
Hall.
Hinnebusch, Paul.
xHinnebusch, Paul.
Community in the Lord. Ave Maria.
Friendship in the Lord. Ave Maria.
Jesus, the New Elijah. Servant.
Sword of Sorrow. Franciscan Herald.
Hinnebusch, William A.
xHinnebusch, William A.
The Dominicans: A Short History. Alba.
Hinnells, John R.
xHinnells, John R.
ed. Hinduism. Routledge & Kegan.
Hinrichs, Harley. see Hinrichs, Harley H.
Hinrichs, Harley H.
xHinrichs, Harley.
Program Budgeting & Benefit Cost Analysis:
Cases, Text & Readings. Goodyear.
Systematic Analysis: A Primer on Benefit-Cost
Analysis & Program Evaluation. Goodyear.
xHinrichs, Harley H.
A General Theory of Tax Structure Change
During Economic Development. Harvard
Law Intl Tax.
Hinrichs, John R.
xHinrichs, John R.
Practical Management for Productivity. Van
Nos Reinhold.
Hinshaw, H. Corwin. see Hinshaw, Horton Corwin.
Hinshaw, Horton Corwin.
xHinshaw, H. Corwin.
Diseases of the Chest. Saunders.
Hinshaw, Randall. see Hinshaw, Randall Weston.
Hinshaw, Randall Weston.
xHinshaw, Randall.
ed. Stagflation: An International Problem.
Dekker.
Hinshaw, Robert E., 1933-
xHinshaw, Robert E.
Panajachel: A Guatemalan Town in
Thirty-Year Perspective. U of Pittsburgh Pr.
Hinshelwood, Cyril N. see Hinshelwood, Cyril Norman.
Hinshelwood, Cyril Norman, 1897-
xHinshelwood, Cyril N.
Structure of Physical Chemistry. Oxford U Pr.
Hinsie, Leland E. see Hinsie, Leland Earl.
Hinsie, Leland Earl.
xHinsie, Leland E.
Psychiatric Dictionary. Oxford U Pr.
Hinsley, F. H. see Hinsley, Francis Harry.
Hinsley, Francis Harry, 1918-
xHinsley, F. H.
British Intelligence in the Second World War:
Its Influence on Strategy & Operations.
Cambridge U Pr.
Hinson, Dolores A.
xHinson, Dolores A.
A Quilter's Companion. Arco.
Hinson, E. Glenn.
xHinson, E. Glenn.

ed. Doubleday Devotional Classics. Doubleday.
ed. Doubleday Devotional Classics. Doubleday.
The Integrity of the Church. Broadman.
The Reaffirmation of Prayer. Broadman.
Hinson, Maurice.
xHinson, Maurice.
Guide to the Pianist's Repertoire. Ind U Pr.
Hintikka, Jaakko. see Hintikka, Kaarlo Jaakko Juhani.
Hintikka, Kaarlo Jaakko Juhani, 1929-
xHintikka, Jaakko.
Logic, Language-Games, & Information:
Kantian Themes in the Philosophy of Logic.
Oxford U Pr.
Hinton, Charles H. see Hinton, Charles Howard.
Hinton, Charles Howard, 1853-1907
xHinton, Charles H.
The Fourth Dimension. Arno.
Hinton, David B., 1950-
xHinton, David B.
The Films of Leni Riefenstahl. Scarecrow.
Hinton, Eugene M. see Hinton, Eugene Mark.
Hinton, Eugene Mark, 1896-
xHinton, Eugene M.
An Analytical Study of the Qualities of Style &
Rhetoric Found in English Compositions.
AMS Pr.
Hinton, H. C. see Hinton, Harold C.
Hinton, Harold C.
xHinton, H. C.
Introduction to Chinese Politics. HR&W.
xHinton, Harold C.
Introduction to Chinese Politics. Krieger.
ed. Major Topics on China & Japan: A
Handbook for Teachers. Greenwood.
The People's Republic of China: A Handbook.
Westview.
Hinton, James.
xHinton, James.
The First Shop Stewards' Movement. Allen
Unwin.
Hinton, John, 1926-
xHinton, John.
Dying. Gannon.
Dying. Penguin.
Hinton, Nigel.
xHinton, Nigel.
Collision Course. Dell.
Collision Course. Elsevier-Nelson.
Getting Free. Elsevier-Nelson.
Hinton, S. E.
xHinton, S. E.
The Outsiders. Dell.
Tex. Delacorte.
Tex. Dell.
That Was Then, This Is Now. Dell.
xHinton, Susie E.
Outsiders. Viking Pr.
That Was Then, This Is Now. Viking Pr.
Hinton, Susie E. see Hinton, S. E.
Hinton, Ted.
xHinton, Ted.
Ambush: The Real Story of Bonnie & Clyde.
Shoal Creek Pub.
Hinton, William.
xHinton, William.
Fanshen: A Documentary of Revolution in a
Chinese Village. Random.
Fanshen: A Documentary of Revolution in a
Chinese Village. Monthly Rev.
Hundred Day War: The Cultural Revolution at
Tsinghua University. Monthly Rev.
Turning Point in China: An Essay on the
Cultural Revolution. Monthly Rev.
Hintz, H. F. see Hintz, Harold Franklin.
Hintz, Harold Franklin, 1937-
xHintz, H. F.
Horses in the Movies. A S Barnes.
Hintz, Howard W. see Hintz, Howard William.
Hintz, Howard William, 1903-
xHintz, Howard W.

Quaker Influence in American Literature.
Greenwood.

Hintze, Naomi A.
xHintze, Naomi A.
The Psychic Realm: What Can You Believe?.
Random.

Hintze, Otto, 1861-1940
xHintze, Otto.
The Historical Essays of Otto Hintze. Oxford
U Pr.

Hintzman, Douglas L.
xHintzman, Douglas L.
The Psychology of Learning & Memory. W H
Freeman.

Hinz, Berthold.
xHinz, Berthold.
Art in the Third Reich. Pantheon.

Hinz, Earl. see Hinz, Earl R.

Hinz, Earl R.
xHinz, Earl.
Sail Before Sunset. McKay.
xHinz, Earl R.
Landfalls of Paradise: The Guide to Pacific
Islands. Western Marine Ent.

Hinze, J. O.
xHinze, J. O.
Turbulence. McGraw.

Hip Society.
xHip Society.
Hip Society: The Hip. Mosby.
Hip Society: The Hip Society. Mosby.

Hippchen, Leonard J. see Hippchen, Leonard Joseph.

Hippchen, Leonard Joseph, 1923-
xHippchen, Leonard J.
ed. Ecologic-Biochemical Approaches to
Treatment of Delinquents & Criminals. Van
Nos Reinhold.

Hippel, Arndt Von. see Von Hippel, Arndt.

Hippel, Ursula Von. see Von Hippel, Ursula.

Hippisley, J. H.
xHippisley, J. H.
Chapters on Early English Literature.
Kennikat.

Hipple, John.
xHipple, John.
The Counselor & Suicidal Crisis: Diagnosis &
Intervention. C C Thomas.

Hipple, Theodore W.
xHipple, Theodore W.
Crucial Issues in Contemporary Education.
Goodyear.
The Future of Education: 1975-2000.
Goodyear.
ed. The Worlds of Science Fiction. Allyn.

Hippler, Arthur E.
xHippler, Arthur E.
The Subarctic Athabascans: A Selected,
Annotated Bibliography. U Alaska Inst Res.

Hipsher, Edward E. see Hipsher, Edward Ellsworth.

Hipsher, Edward Ellsworth, 1871-1948
xHipsher, Edward E.
American Opera & Its Composers. Da Capo.

Hirai, Kiyoshi, 1929-
xHirai, Kiyoshi.
Feudal Architecture of Japan. Weatherhill.

Hirn, Yrjo, 1870-1952
xHirn, Yrjo.
The Origins of Art: A Psychological &
Sociological Inquiry. Arno.

Hiro, Dilip.
xHiro, Dilip.
Inside India Today. Monthly Rev.

Hirota, Naotaka, 1935-
xHirota, Naotaka.
Steam Locomotives of Japan. Kodansha.

Hirsch, Arthur H. see Hirsch, Arthur Henry.

Hirsch, Arthur Henry, 1878-
xHirsch, Arthur H.

Huguenots of Colonial South Carolina. Shoe
String.

Hirsch, Charles P. see Hirsch, Charles Sidney.

Hirsch, Charles S. see Hirsch, Charles Sidney.

Hirsch, Charles Sidney.
xHirsch, Charles P.
Handbook of Legal Medicine. Mosby.
xHirsch, Charles S.
jt. auth. Handbook of Legal Medicine. Mosby.

Hirsch, Charlotte T. see Hirsch, Charlotte Teller.

Hirsch, Charlotte Teller.
xHirsch, Charlotte T.
The Cage. AMS Pr.

Hirsch, Doris F.
xHirsch, Doris F.
Indoor Plants: Comprehensive Care & Culture.
Chilton.

Hirsch, E. D. see Hirsch, Eric Donald.

Hirsch, E. G.
xHirsch, E. G.
Copyright It Yourself. Whitehall Co.

Hirsch, Edwin W. see Hirsch, Edwin Walter.

Hirsch, Edwin Walter, 1892-
xHirsch, Edwin W.
Impotence & Frigidity. Wilshire.

Hirsch, Eric Donald.
xHirsch, E. D.
The Aims of Interpretation. U of Chicago Pr.
Innocence & Experience: An Introduction to
Blake. U of Chicago Pr.
Wordsworth & Schelling: A Typological Study
of Romanticism. Shoe String.

Hirsch, Foster.
xHirsch, Foster.
George Kelly. Twayne.
The Hollywood Epic. A S Barnes.
Laurence Olivier. Twayne.
A Portrait of the Artist: The Plays of
Tennessee Williams. Kennikat.

Hirsch, H. see Hirsch, Herbert.

Hirsch, Herbert.
xHirsch, H.
Poverty & Politicization: Political Socialization
in an American Sub-Culture. Free Pr.
xHirsch, Herbert.
Learning to Be Militant: Ethnic Identity & the
Development of Political Militance in a
Chicano Community. R & E Res Assoc.
The Right of the People: An Introduction to
American Politics. U Pr of Amer.

Hirsch, Jay.
xHirsch, Jay.
The Last American Convertibles. Macmillan.

Hirsch, Jerry A.
xHirsch, Jerry A.
Concepts in Theoretical Organic Chemistry.
Allyn.

Hirsch, John D.
xHirsch, John D.
The Complete Book of Car Maintenance &
Repair. Scribner.

Hirsch, Linda.
xHirsch, Linda.
The Sick Story. Hastings.

Hirsch, Morris.
xHirsch, Morris.
Differential Equations, Dynamical Systems &
Linear Algebra. Acad Pr.

Hirsch, Paul M. see Hirsch, Paul Morris.

Hirsch, Paul Morris.
xHirsch, Paul M.
Strategies for Communication Research. Sage.

Hirsch, Richard, 1912-
xHirsch, Richard.
Crimes That Shook the World. Arno.

Hirsch, Richard G.
xHirsch, Richard G.
There Shall Be No Poor. UAHC.

Hirsch, S. Carl.
xHirsch, S. Carl.

Guardians of Tomorrow: Pioneers in Ecology.
Viking Pr.
Living Community: A Venture into Ecology.
Viking Pr.
The Riddle of Racism. Viking Pr.
Stilts. Viking Pr.

Hirsch, Sampson R. see Hirsch, Samson Raphael.

Hirsch, Samson Raphael, 1808-1888
xHirsch, Sampson R.
From the Wisdom of Mishle. Feldheim.

Hirsch, Seev.
xHirsch, Seev.
Location of Industry & International
Competitiveness. Oxford U Pr.

Hirsch, Seymour C.
xHirsch, Seymour C.
BASIC Programming: Self-Taught. Reston.

Hirsch, Stuart M.
xHirsch, Stuart M.
Dental Assistants Examination Review. Arco.

Hirsch, Sylvia.
xHirsch, Sylvia.
Art of Table Setting & Flower Arrangement. T
Y Crowell.

Hirsch, Thomas L.
xHirsch, Thomas L.
More Puzzles for Pleasure & Leisure. Abelard.

Hirsch, W. Z. see Hirsch, Werner Zvi.

Hirsch, Werner Z. see Hirsch, Werner Zvi.

Hirsch, Werner Zvi, 1920-
xHirsch, W. Z.
Financing Public First-Level & Second-Level
Education in the U. S. A.. Unipub.
xHirsch, Werner Z.
Local Government Program Budgeting Theory
& Practice: With Special Reference to Los
Angeles. Praeger.
Program Budgeting for Primary & Secondary
Public Education: Current Status & Prospects
in Los Angeles. Irvington.

Hirschbach, Frank Donald.
xHirschbach, Frank Donald.
The Arrow & the Lyre: A Study of the Role of
Love in the Works of Thomas Mann.
Folcroft.

Hirschel, J. David.
xHirschel, Joseph D.
Fourth Amendment Rights. Lexington Bks.

Hirschel, Joseph D. see Hirschel, J. David.

Hirschfeld, Burt, 1923-
xHirschfeld, Burt.
Acapulco. Arbor Hse.
Generation of Victors. Arbor Hse.
Generation of Victors. PB.
Key West. Morrow.
Masters Affair. Arbor Hse.
The Master's Affair. PB.
Provincetown. Brodart.
Secrets. PB.
Secrets. S&S.

Hirschfeld, Herman, 1904-
xHirschfeld, Herman.
Understanding Your Allergy. Arco.

Hirschfeld, J. see Hirschfeld, Joram.

Hirschfeld, Joram.
xHirschfeld, J.
Forcing, Arithmetic, Division Rings.
Springer-Verlag.

Hirschfeld, Magnus, 1868-1935
xHirschfeld, Magnus.
Men & Women: The World Journey of a
Sexologist. AMS Pr.

Hirschfield, Robert S.
xHirschfield, Robert S.
ed. The Power of the Presidency: Concepts &
Controversy. Aldine Pub.

Hirschhorn, Bernard.
xHirschhorn, Bernard.

ed. Alfred Hitchcock Presents: The Master's Choice. Random.
Murder Racquet. Dell.

Hitchcock, Anthony.
xHitchcock, Anthony.
Country New England Antiques, Crafts, & Factory Outlets. B Franklin.

Hitchcock, Bert.
xHitchcock, Bert.
Richard Malcolm Johnston. G K Hall.
Richard Malcolm Johnston. Twayne.

Hitchcock, C. Leo. *see* Hitchcock, Charles Leo.

Hitchcock, Charles Leo.
xHitchcock, C. Leo.
Flora of the Pacific Northwest: An Illustrated Manual. U of Wash Pr.
Revision of the North American Species of Lathyrus. U of Wash Pr.

Hitchcock, Enos, 1745-1803
xHitchcock, Enos.
Memoirs of the Bloomsgrove Family. Irvington.

Hitchcock, Ethan A. *see* Hitchcock, Ethan Allen.

Hitchcock, Ethan Allen, 1798-1870
xHitchcock, Ethan A.
Alchemy & the Alchemists. Philos Res.
Remarks Upon Alchemy & the Alchemists. AMS Pr.

Hitchcock, H. Perry. *see* Hitchcock, Henry Perry.

Hitchcock, H. Wiley. *see* Hitchcock, Hugh Wiley.

Hitchcock, Henry Perry, 1921-
xHitchcock, H. Perry.
Orthodontics for Undergraduates. Lea & Febiger.

Hitchcock, Henry R. *see* Hitchcock, Henry Russell.

Hitchcock, Henry Russell, 1903-
xHitchcock, Henry R.
In the Nature of Materials: The Buildings of Frank Lloyd Wright 1887-1941. Da Capo.
Netherlandish Scroll & Gable of the Sixteenth & Early Seventeenth Centuries. NYU Pr.
xHitchcock, Henry-Russell.
Architecture: Nineteenth & Twentieth Centuries. Penguin.
Architecture of H. H. Richardson & His Times. MIT Pr.
Early Victorian Architecture in Britain. Da Capo.
In the Nature of Materials: The Buildings of Frank Lloyd Wright, 1887-1941. Da Capo.
Latin American Architecture Since 1945. Arno.
Modern Architecture: Romanticism & Reintegration. Hacker.
Rhode Island Architecture. Da Capo.

Hitchcock, Henry-Russell. *see* Hitchcock, Henry Russell.

Hitchcock, Hugh Wiley, 1923-
xHitchcock, H. Wiley.
Music in the United States: A Historical Introduction. P-H.

Hitchcock, James.
xHitchcock, James.
Catholicism & Modernity: Confrontation or Capitulation?. Seabury.

Hitchcock, John. *see* Hitchcock, John Thayer.

Hitchcock, John Thayer, 1917-
xHitchcock, John.
A Mountain Village in Nepal. HR&W.

Hitchcock, Mary J.
xHitchcock, Mary J.
Foodservice Systems Administration. Macmillan.

Hitchcock, Raymond.
xHitchcock, Raymond.
Attack the Lusitania!. St Martin.

Hitchcock, Roswell D. *see* Hitchcock, Roswell Dwight.

Hitchcock, Roswell Dwight.
xHitchcock, Roswell D.
The Life, Writings & Character of Edward Robinson. Arno.

Hitchcock, Susan T. *see* Hitchcock, Susan Tyler.

Hitchcock, Susan Tyler.
xHitchcock, Susan T.
Gather Ye Wild Things: A Forager's Year. Har-Row.

Hitchener, Elizabeth.
xHitchener, Elizabeth.
Letters of Elizabeth Hitchener to Percy Bysshe Shelley. Folcroft.

Hitching, Francis.
xHitching, Francis.
The Mysterious World: An Atlas of the Unexplained. HR&W.

Hitchins, Keith, 1931-
xHitchins, Keith.
Orthodoxy & Nationality: Andreiu Saguna & the Rumanians of Transylvania, 1846-1873. Harvard U Pr.

Hitchman, Janet.
xHitchman, Janet.
Such a Strange Lady: A Biography of Dorothy L. Sayers. Har-Row.

Hitchman, M. L.
xHitchman, Michael L.
Measurement of Dissolved Oxygen. Wiley.

Hitchman, Michael L. *see* Hitchman, M. L.

Hitchner, Dell G. *see* Hitchner, Dell Gillette.

Hitchner, Dell Gillette.
xHitchner, Dell G.
Modern Government. Har-Row.

Hite, James C., 1941-
xHite, James C.
The Economics of Environmental Quality. Am Enterprise.
Room & Situation: The Political Economy of Land-Use Policy. Nelson-Hall.

Hite, Jordan F.
xHite, Jordan F.
Readings, Cases, Materials in Canon Law: A Textbook for Ministerial Students. Liturgical Pr.

Hitselberger, Mary F. *see* Hitselberger, Mary Fitzhugh.

Hitselberger, Mary Fitzhugh.
xHitselberger, Mary F.
Bridge in Time: The Complete 1850 Census of Frederick County, Maryland. Monocacy.

Hitt, Frisco.
xHitt, Frisco.
A Coffin Full of Dreams. Intl Schol Bk Serv.

Hitt, Henry C.
xHitt, Henry C.
Old Chinese Snuff Bottles: Notes with a Catalogue of a Modest Collection. C E Tuttle.

Hitt, James E.
xHitt, James E.
Tennessee Smith. Dutton.

Hitt, Michael A.
xHitt, Michael A.
Effective Management. West Pub.

Hitt, Russell T.
xHitt, Russell T.
How Christians Grow. Oxford U Pr.

Hitti, Philip K. *see* Hitti, Philip Khuri.

Hitti, Philip Khuri, 1886-
xHitti, Philip K.
Origins of the Druze People & Religion, with Extracts from Their Sacred Writings. AMS Pr.
xHitti, Philp K.
Islam & the West: A Historical Cultural Survey. Krieger.

Hitti, Philp K. *see* Hitti, Philip Khuri.

Hittle, David R.
xHittle, David R.
Sourcebook for Chemistry & Physics. Macmillan.

Hittle, J. Michael, 1938-
xHittle, J. Michael.

The Service City: State & Townsmen in Russia, 1600-1800. Harvard U Pr.

Hittleman, Daniel R.
xHittleman, Daniel R.
Developmental Reading: A Psycholinguistic Perspective. Rand.

Hitz, Demi.
xHitz, Dimi.
illus. The Book of Moving Pictures. Pantheon.

Hitz, Dimi. *see* Hitz, Demi.

Hitz, Donna.
xHitz, Donna.
The Triangular Pattern of Life. Philos Lib.

Hively, Wells, 1931-
xHively, Wells.
ed. Domain-Referenced Testing. Educ Tech Pubn.

Hix, Charles.
xHix, Charles.
Dressing Right. St Martin.

Hix, Hubert. *see* Hix, Hubert E.

Hix, Hubert E.
xHix, Hubert.
God's Special Book. Concordia.

Hix, John, 1938-
xHix, John.
The Glass House. MIT Pr.

Hixon, Thomas J.
xHixon, Thomas J.
Introduction to Communication Disorders. P-H.

Hixson, Allie C. *see* Hixson, Allie Corbin.

Hixson, Allie Corbin.
xHixson, Allie C.
Edwin Muir: A Critical Study. Vantage.

Hixson, William B.
xHixson, William B.
Moorfield Storey & the Abolitionist Tradition. Oxford U Pr.

Hjelm, J. *see* Hjelm, Jerry.

Hjelm, Jerry, 1936-
xHjelm, J.
Thaddeus Jones & the Dragon. Oddo.

Hjelmfelt, A. T.
xHjelmfelt, A. T.
Hydrology for Engineers & Planners. Iowa St U Pr.

Hjelmslev, Louis, 1899-1965
xHjelmslev, Louis.
Resume of a Theory of Language. U of Wis Pr.

Hjelte, George.
xHjelte, George.
Administration of Public Recreation. Greenwood.
Public Administration of Recreational Services. Lea & Febiger.

Hjersman, Peter.
xHjersman, Peter.
Dome Notes. Bookpeople.
Light Growth. Bookpeople.

Hjert, Jeri.
xHjert, Jeri.
Loom Construction. Van Nos Reinhold.

Hjortsberg, William, 1941-
xHjortsberg, William.
Falling Angel. HarBraceJ.
Toro! Toro! Toro!. S&S.

Hlavac, Harry. *see* Hlavac, Harry F.

Hlavac, Harry F.
xHlavac, Harry.
The Foot Book: Advice for Athletes. Anderson World.

Hlawiczka, P. *see* Hlawiczka, Paul.

Hlawiczka, Paul.
xHlawiczka, P.
Introduction to Quantum Electronics. Acad Pr.

Hnatek, E. R. *see* Hnatek, Eugene R.

Hnatek, Eugene R.
xHnatek, E. R.

A User's Handbook of Integrated Circuits.
  Wiley.
xHnatek, Eugene R.
  Applications of Linear Integrated Circuits.
    Wiley.
  A User's Handbook of Semiconductor
    Memories. Wiley.
Ho, B. T. see Ho, Bang T.
Ho, Bang T.
  xHo, B. T.
    ed. Drug Discrimination & State Dependent
      Learning. Acad Pr.
Ho, Betty Y. see Ho, Betty Yu-Lin.
Ho, Betty Yu-Lin.
  xHo, Betty Y.
    How to Stay Healthy a Lifetime Without
      Medicines. Juvenescent.
    Living Function of Sleep, Life & Aging.
      Juvenescent.
    Origin of Variation of Races of Mankind & the
      Cause of Evolution. Juvenescent.
Ho, Ching-Ju, 1901-
  xHo, Ching-Ju.
    Personnel Studies of Scientists in the United
      States. AMS Pr.
Ho, H. C. Y.
  xHo, H. C. Y.
    The Fiscal System of Hong Kong. Biblio Dist.
Ho, Kan-Chih.
  xHo, Kan-Chih.
    A History of the Modern Chinese Revolution.
      AMS Pr.
    The History of the Modern Chinese
      Revolution. Gordon Pr.
Ho, Yhi-Min, 1934-
  xHo, Yhi-Min.
    Agricultural Development of Taiwan,
      1903-1960. Vanderbilt U Pr.
Hoadley, Frank T.
  xHoadley, Frank T.
    Baptists Who Dared. Judson.
Hoadley, Irene B. see Hoadley, Irene Braden.
Hoadley, Irene Braden.
  xHoadley, Irene B.
    ed. Quantitative Methods in Librarianship:
      Standards, Research, Management.
      Greenwood.
Hoag, Edwin.
  xHoag, Edwin.
    American Houses: Colonial, Classic,
      Contemporary. Lippincott.
    How Business Works. Bobbs.
Hoag, J. Marshall, 1912-
  xHoag, J. Marshall.
    Osteopathic Medicine. McGraw.
Hoagland, Edward.
  xHoagland, Edward.
    African Calliope: A Journey to the Sudan.
      Random.
    The Circle Home. Avon.
    Courage of Turtles. Random.
    The Edward Hoagland Reader. Random.
Hoagland, H. E. see Hoagland, Henry Elmer.
Hoagland, Henry E. see Hoagland, Henry Elmer.
Hoagland, Henry Elmer, 1886-
  xHoagland, H. E.
    Collective Bargaining in the Lithographic
      Industry. AMS Pr.
  xHoagland, Henry E.
    Real Estate Finance. Irwin.
Hoagland, Mahlon B.
  xHoagland, Mahlon B.
    The Roots of Life: A Layman's Guide to
      Genes, Evolution & the Ways of Cells. Avon.
    The Roots of Life: A Layman's Guide to
      Genes, Evolution, & the Ways of Cells. HM.
Hoar, W. S. see Hoar, William Stewart.
Hoar, William S. see Hoar, William Stewart.
Hoar, William Stewart.
  xHoar, W. S.

ed. Fish Physiology. Acad Pr.
xHoar, William S.
  General & Comparative Physiology. P-H.
Hoare, Dorothy M. see Hoare, Dorothy Mackenzie.
Hoare, Dorothy Mackenzie, 1901-
  xHoare, Dorothy M.
    Some Studies in the Modern Novel. Core
      Collection.
    Some Studies in the Modern Novel. Folcroft.
    Some Studies in the Modern Novel. Haskell.
    The Works of Morris & of Yeats in Relation to
      Early Saga Literature. Russell.
    Works of Morris & Yeats in Relation to Early
      Saga Literature. Folcroft.
Hoare, Frederick R. see Hoare, Frederick Russell.
Hoare, Frederick Russell, 1888-1951
  xHoare, Frederick R.
    Eight Decisive Books of Antiquity. Arno.
    Eight Decisive Books of Antiquity. R West.
Hoare, H. R. see Hoare, Henry Ronald.
Hoare, Henry Ronald.
  xHoare, H. R.
    Project Management Using Network Analysis.
      McGraw.
Hoban, Abrom.
  xHoban, Brom.
    illus. Jason & the Bees. Har-Row.
Hoban, Brom. see Hoban, Abrom.
Hoban, Lillian.
  xHoban, Lillian.
    Arthur's Christmas Cookies. Har-Row.
    illus. Arthur's Honey Bear. Har-Row.
    illus. Arthur's Pen Pal. Har-Row.
    illus. Arthur's Prize Reader. Har-Row.
    Harry's Song. Greenwillow.
    ed. Here Come Raccoons. HR&W.
    illus. Stick-in-the-Mud Turtle. Greenwillow.
    illus. The Sugar Snow Spring. Har-Row.
    Turtle Spring. Greenwillow.
Hoban, Russell.
  xHoban, Russell.
    Arthur's New Power. Dell.
    Arthur's New Power. T Y Crowell.
    A Baby Sister for Frances. Har-Row.
    Baby Sister for Frances. Har-Row.
    A Bargain for Frances. Har-Row.
    Bargain for Frances. Har-Row.
    Bread & Jam for Frances. Har-Row.
    Bread & Jam for Frances. Schol Bk Serv.
    Charlie the Tramp. Schol Bk Serv.
    Dinner at Alberta's. T Y Crowell.
    Egg Thoughts & Other Frances Songs.
      Har-Row.
    How Tom Beat Captain Najork & His Hired
      Sportsmen. Atheneum.
    How Tom Beat Captain Najork & His Hired
      Sportsmen. Atheneum.
    Letitia Rabbit's String Song. Coward.
    A Near Thing for Captain Najork. Atheneum.
    Nothing to Do. Har-Row.
    Sorely Trying Day. Har-Row.
    The Stone Doll of Sister Brute. Avon.
    Stone Doll of Sister Brute. Macmillan.
    Turtle Diary. Avon.
    Turtle Diary. Random.
    The Twenty-Elephant Restaurant. Atheneum.
    Ugly Bird. Macmillan.
Hoban, Tana.
  xHoban, Tana.

illus. Circles, Triangles & Squares. Macmillan.
illus. Count & See. Macmillan.
illus. Count & See. Macmillan.
Look Again. Macmillan.
photos by Over, Under & Through & Other
  Spatial Concepts. Macmillan.
Push Pull, Empty Full: A Book of Opposites.
  Macmillan.
illus. Push Pull, Empty Full: A Book of
  Opposites. Macmillan.
Where Is It?. Macmillan.
Hobbes, Thomas.
  xHobbes, Thomas.
    Dialogue Between a Philosopher & a Student
      of the Common Laws of England. U of
      Chicago Pr.
    Leviathan. Bobbs.
    Leviathan. Collins Pubs.
    Leviathan. Dutton.
    Leviathan. Penguin.
Hobbie, Barbara, 1946-
  xHobbie, Barbara.
    Oil Company Divestiture & the Press:
      Economic Vs. Journalistic Perceptions.
      Praeger.
Hobbie, Holly.
  xHobbie, Holly.
    illus. The Days of Holly Hobbie. Platt.
Hobbie, Margaret.
  xHobbie, Margaret.
    Compiled by Museums, Sites, & Collections of
      Germanic Culture in North America: An
      Annotated Directory of German Immigrant
      Culture in the United States & Canada.
      Greenwood.
Hobbs, Albert H. see Hobbs, Albert Hoyt.
Hobbs, Albert Hoyt, 1910-
  xHobbs, Albert H.
    Man Is Moral Choice. Arlington Hse.
Hobbs, B. E. see Hobbs, Bruce E.
Hobbs, Bruce E.
  xHobbs, B. E.
    An Outline of Structural Geology. Wiley.
Hobbs, Donald A.
  xHobbs, Donald A.
    Sociology & the Human Experience. Wiley.
Hobbs, Edward C.
  xHobbs, Edward C.
    ed. Stubborn Faith: Papers on Old Testament
      & Related Subjects Presented to Honor
      William Andrew Irwin. SMU Press.
Hobbs, Harry J.
  xHobbs, Harry J.
    Veneer Craft for Everyone. Scribner.
    Veneering Simplified. Scribner.
Hobbs, Herschel H.
  xHobbs, Herschel H.
    The Axioms of Religion. Broadman.
    Fundamentals of Our Faith. Broadman.
    A Layman's Handbook of Christian Doctrine.
      Broadman.
    Preacher Talk. Broadman.
Hobbs, Jack.
  xHobbs, Jack.
    Installing & Servicing Home Audio Systems.
      TAB Bks.
Hobbs, Laura.
  xHobbs, Laura.
    Cars. Watts.
Hobbs, Marvin.
  xHobbs, Marvin.
    Modern CB Radio Servicing. Hayden.
    Modern Communications Switching Systems.
      TAB Bks.
Hobbs, Michael.
  xHobbs, Michael.
    ed. Golf for the Connoisseur: A Golfing
      Anthology. David & Charles.
Hobbs, Peter V. see Hobbs, Peter Victor.

Hobbs, Peter Victor, 1936-
  xHobbs, Peter V.
    Ice Physics. Oxford U Pr.
Hobbs, Richard, 1931-
  xHobbs, Richard.
    The Myth of Victory: What Is Victory in War?.
      Westview.
Hobbs, Walter C.
  xHobbs, Walter C.
    ed. Government Regulation of Higher
      Education. Ballinger Pub.
Hobday, Victor C.
  xHobday, Victor C.
    Sparks at the Grassroots: Municipal
      Distribution of TVA Electricity in Tennessee.
      U of Tenn Pr.
Hobe, Laura.
  xHobe, Laura.
    Try God. Warner Bks.
Hobe, Phyllis.
  xHobe, Phyllis.
    The Meaning of Christmas. Holman.
    ed. The Meaning of Love. Holman.
    ed. Tapestries of Life. Holman.
Hoberman , Mary A. see Hoberman, Mary Ann.
Hoberman, Mary A. see Hoberman, Mary Ann.
Hoberman, Mary Ann.
  xHoberman , Mary A.
    I Like Old Clothes. Knopf.
  xHoberman, Mary A.
    Looking Book. Knopf.
  xHoberman, Mary Ann.
    Bugs: Poems. Viking Pr.
    A House Is a House for Me. Viking Pr.
Hobhouse, L. T. see Hobhouse, Leonard Trelawney.
Hobhouse, Leonard T. see Hobhouse, Leonard
  Trelawney.
Hobhouse, Leonard Trelawney, 1864-1929
  xHobhouse, L. T.
    Liberalism. Arden Lib.
    Liberalism. Oxford U Pr.
  xHobhouse, Leonard T.
    Development & Purpose: An Essay Towards a
      Philosophy of Evolution. Scholarly.
    Liberalism. Greenwood.
    The Material Culture & Social Institutions of
      the Simpler Peoples: An Essay in Correlation.
      Arno.
Hobsbaum, Philip.
  xHobsbaum, Philip.
    Coming Out Fighting. Dufour.
    A Reader's Guide to Charles Dickens. FS&G.
    Tradition & Experiment in English Poetry.
      Rowman.
Hobsbawm, Eric. see Hobsbawm, Eric J.
Hobsbawm, Eric J.
  xHobsbawm, Eric.
    The Age of Capital. Scribner.
Hobson, Andrew.
  xHobson, Andrew.
    Film Animation As a Hobby. Sterling.
Hobson, Anne.
  xHobson, Anne.
    In Old Alabama: Being the Chronicles of Miss
      Mouse, the Little Black Merchant. Arno.
Hobson, Arthur.
  xHobson, Arthur.
    Concepts in Statistical Mechanics. Gordon.
Hobson, Burton.
  xHobson, Burton.
    Coin Collecting As a Hobby. Cornerstone.
    Coins & Coin Collecting. Dover.
    Getting Started in Stamp Collecting. Sterling.
  xHobson, Burton H.
    Coin Collecting As a Hobby. Sterling.
Hobson, Burton H. see Hobson, Burton.
Hobson, E. W. see Hobson, Ernest William.
Hobson, Ernest W. see Hobson, Ernest William.
Hobson, Ernest William, 1856-1933
  xHobson, E. W.

    The Domain of Natural Science. Peter Smith.
  xHobson, Ernest W.
    The Domain of Natural Science. AMS Pr.
    The Domain of Natural Science. Dover.
Hobson, G. D. see Hobson, George Douglas.
Hobson, G. S.
  xHobson, G. S.
    Charge Transfer Devices. Halsted Pr.
    The Gunn Effect. Oxford U Pr.
Hobson, George Douglas.
  xHobson, G. D.
    ed. Developments in Petroleum Geology.
      Burgess-Intl Ideas.
Hobson, J. A. see Hobson, John Atkinson.
Hobson, John A. see Hobson, John Atkinson.
Hobson, John Atkinson, 1858-1940
  xHobson, J. A.
    Confessions of an Economic Heretic. Shoe
      String.
  xHobson, John A.
    The Crisis of Liberalism: New Issues of
      Democracy. Humanities.
    Economics of Distribution. Kelley.
    Incentives in the New Industrial Order.
      Hyperion Conn.
    Veblen. Kelley.
Hobson, Laura Keane Zametkin.
  xHobson, Laura Z.
    Over & Above. Doubleday.
Hobson, Laura Z. see Hobson, Laura Keane Zametkin.
Hobson, Lawrence B.
  xHobson, Lawrence B.
    Examination of the Patient: A Text for Nursing
      & Allied Health Personnel. McGraw.
Hobson, Phyllis.
  xHobson, Phyllis.
    Garden Way's Guide to Food Drying. Garden
      Way Pub.
    Home-Drying Vegetables, Fruits & Herbs.
      Garden Way Pub.
    Raising a Calf for Beef. Garden Way Pub.
    The Soybean Book: Growing & Using Nature's
      Miracle Protein. Garden Way Pub.
Hobson, R. L. see Hobson, Robert Lockhart.
Hobson, Robert L. see Hobson, Robert Lockhart.
Hobson, Robert Lockhart, 1872-1941
  xHobson, R. L.
    Chinese Pottery & Porcelain: An Account of
      the Potter's Art in China from Primitive
      Times to the Present Day. Peter Smith.
    The Wares of the Ming Dynasty. Dover.
  xHobson, Robert L.
    Wares of the Ming Dynasty. C E Tuttle.
Hobson, W. see Hobson, William.
Hobson, Wilder, 1906-1964
  xHobson, Wilder.
    American Jazz Music. Da Capo.
Hobson, William.
  xHobson, W.
    ed. The Theory & Practice of Public Health.
      Oxford U Pr.
  xHobson, William.
    ed. The Theory & Practice of Public Health.
      Oxford U Pr.
Hobst, Leos.
  xHobst, Leos.
    Anchoring in Rock. Elsevier.
Hoch, Edward D., 1930-
  xHoch, Edward D.
    The Thefts of Nick Velvet. Mysterious Pr.
Hoch, Frederic L., 1920-
  xHoch, Frederick L.
    Energy Transformations in Mammals:
      Regulatory Mechanisms. Saunders.
Hoch, Frederick L. see Hoch, Frederic L.
Hochachka, Peter W.
  xHochachka, Peter W.

    Living Without Oxygen: Closed & Open
      Systems in Hypoxia Tolerance. Harvard U
      Pr.
Hochberg, Bette.
  xHochberg, Bette.
    Handspinner's Handbook. B&B Hochberg.
    Spin Span Spun: Fact & Folklore for Spinners.
      B&B Hochberg.
Hochberg, Herbert. see Hochberg, Herbert Irving.
Hochberg, Herbert Irving, 1929-
  xHochberg, Herbert.
    Thought, Fact, & Reference: The Origins &
      Ontology of Logical Atomism. U of Minn Pr.
Hochberg, Julian. see Hochberg, Julian E.
Hochberg, Julian E.
  xHochberg, Julian.
    Perception. P-H.
Hochheimer, Wolfgang.
  xHochheimer, Wolfgang.
    The Psychotherapy of C. G. Jung. C G Jung
      Foun.
Hochhuth, Rolf.
  xHochhuth, Rolf.
    Deputy. Grove.
Hochman, Baruch, 1930-
  xHochman, Baruch.
    Another Ego: The Changing View of Self &
      Society in the Work of D. H. Lawrence. U of
      SC Pr.
Hochman, Louis.
  xHochman, Louis.
    Complete Archery Book. Arco.
    Hot Rod Handbook. Arco.
Hochman, Sandra.
  xHochman, Sandra.
    Endangered Species. Avon.
    Jogging: A Love Story. Putnam.
    Streamer Life Secrets for Writing Poems &
      Songs. P-H.
Hochman, Shel.
  xHochman, Shel.
    How to Save Money on Car Repairs. Dodd.
Hochman, Stanley.
  xHochman, Stanley.
    Yesterday & Today: A Dictionary of Recent
      American History. McGraw.
Hochschild, Arlie R. see Hochschild, Arlie Russell.
Hochschild, Arlie Russell, 1940-
  xHochschild, Arlie R.
    The Unexpected Community: Portrait of an
      Old Age Subculture. U of Cal Pr.
Hochschild, Harold K.
  xHochschild, Harold K.
    Adirondack Resort in the Nineteenth Century:
      Blue Mountain Lake, 1870-1900,
      Stagecoaches & Luxury Hotels. Syracuse U
      Pr.
    Life & Leisure in the Adirondack Backwoods.
      Syracuse U Pr.
    Lumberjacks & Rivermen in the Central
      Adirondacks, 1850-1950. Syracuse U Pr.
Hochstadt, Harry.
  xHochstadt, Harry.
    Differential Equations: A Modern Approach.
      Dover.
    Differential Equations: A Modern Approach.
      Peter Smith.
    Functions of Mathematical Physics. Wiley.
    Integral Equations. Wiley.
Hochstein, Peter.
  xHochstein, Peter.
    The Fatal Fetish. Berkley Pub.
Hochstein, Rolaine. see Hochstein, Rolaine A.
Hochstein, Rolaine A.
  xHochstein, Rolaine.
    Stepping Out: A Love Story. Norton.
Hochster, Melvin.
  xHochster, Melvin.

Topics in the Homological Theory of Modules
Over Commutative Rings. Am Math.
Hock, Ronald F., 1944-
xHock, Ronald F.
The Social Context of Paul's Ministry:
Tentmaking & Apostleship. Fortress.
Hocken, Sheila.
xHocken, Sheila.
Emma & I. Dutton.
Emma & I. NAL.
Hocker, Harold W., 1926-
xHocker, Harold W.
Introduction to Forest Biology. Wiley.
Hockett, Charles F. see Hockett, Charles Francis.
Hockett, Charles Francis.
xHockett, Charles F.
Course in Modern Linguistics. Macmillan.
Progressive Exercises in Chinese Pronunciation.
Far Eastern Pubns.
Hockett, Shirley O.
xHockett, Shirley O.
Developing Skills for the High School
Equivalency Examination (GED) in
Mathematics: In 17 Lessons. Barron.
Hockey, S. W.
xHockey, S. W.
Introduction to Calculus. Pergamon.
Hockin, T. see Hockin, Thomas A.
Hockin, Thomas A., 1938-
xHockin, T.
Apex of Power: The Prime Minister & Political
Leadership in Canada. P-H.
xHockin, Thomas A.
Government in Canada. Norton.
Hocking, David. see Hocking, David L.
Hocking, David L.
xHocking, David.
Be a Leader People Follow. Regal.
Hocking, G. D. see Hocking, George Drew D'Arcy.
Hocking, George Drew D'Arcy, 1897-
xHocking, G. D.
Study of the Tragoediae Sacrae of Father
Caussin, 1583-1651. Johnson Repr.
Hocking, William E. see Hocking, William Ernest.
Hocking, William Ernest, 1873-
xHocking, William E.
The Coming World Civilization. Greenwood.
Living Religions & a World Faith. AMS Pr.
Hockings, Paul.
xHockings, Paul.
ed. Principles of Visual Anthropology.
Beresford Bk Serv.
Hockley, Graham. see Hockley, Graham Charles.
Hockley, Graham C. see Hockley, Graham Charles.
Hockley, Graham Charles.
xHockley, Graham.
Public Finance: An Introduction. Routledge &
Kegan.
xHockley, Graham C.
Monetary Policy & Public Finance. Kelley.
Hockney, David.
xHockney, David.
David Hockney. Abrams.
Hocquenghem, Guy, 1946-
xHocquenghem, Guy.
Homosexual Desire. Schocken.
Hocutt, Max.
xHocutt, Max.
First Philosophy: An Introduction to
Philosophical Issues. Wadsworth Pub.
Hodann, Max, 1894-1946
xHodann, Max.
History of Modern Morals. AMS Pr.
Hodas, Daniel, 1927-
xHodas, Daniel.
The Business Career of Moses Taylor:
Merchant, Finance Capitalist, & Industrialist.
NYU Pr.
Hodder, B. W.
xHodder, B. W.

Africa Today: A Short Introduction to African
Affairs. Holmes & Meier.
Economic Development in the Tropics.
Methuen Inc.
Hodder, I. see Hodder, Ian.
Hodder, Ian.
xHodder, I.
Spatial Analysis in Archaeology. Cambridge U
Pr.
xHodder, Ian.
ed. The Spatial Organisation of Culture. U of
Pittsburgh Pr.
Hodder-Williams, Christopher, 1926-
xHodder-Williams, Christopher.
The Prayer Machine. St Martin.
Hodeir, Andre, 1921-
xHodeir, Andre.
Toward Jazz. Da Capo.
The Worlds of Jazz. Grove.
Hodel, Michael P.
xHodel, Michael P.
ed. Enter the Lion: A Posthumous Memoir of
Mycroft Holmes. Dutton.
Hodes, Barnet.
xHodes, Barnet.
The Law of Mobile Homes. BNA.
Hodes, R. see Hodes, Robert.
Hodes, Robert, 1915-1966
xHodes, R.
Aims & Methods of Scientific Research. Am
Inst Marxist.
Hodgart, Alan.
xHodgart, Alan.
The Economics of European Imperialism.
Norton.
Hodgart, Matthew. see Hodgart, Matthew John Caldwell.
Hodgart, Matthew J. see Hodgart, Matthew John
Caldwell.
Hodgart, Matthew John Caldwell.
xHodgart, Matthew.
James Joyce: A Student's Guide. Routledge &
Kegan.
xHodgart, Matthew J.
Ballads. Norton.
Hodge, A. A. see Hodge, Archibald Alexander.
Hodge, A. Trevor.
xHodge, A. Trevor.
Woodwork of Greek Roofs. Cambridge U Pr.
Hodge, Archibald Alexander, 1823-1886
xHodge, A. A.
Outlines of Theology. Zondervan.
Hodge, Bartow, 1920-
xHodge, Bartow.
Computers for Engineers: Introduction to
Computing Machines & Programming.
McGraw.
Hodge, Ben.
xHodge, Ben.
Football. Watts.
Hodge, Carleton T. see Hodge, Carleton Taylor.
Hodge, Carleton Taylor.
xHodge, Carleton T.
ed. Papers on the Manding. Res Ctr Lang
Semiotic.
Hodge, Francis.
xHodge, Francis.
Play Directing: Analysis, Communication &
Style. P-H.
Hodge, Frederick W. see Hodge, Frederick Webb.
Hodge, Frederick Webb, 1864-1956
xHodge, Frederick W.
ed. Handbook of American Indians North of
Mexico. Scholarly.
Hodge, James R.
xHodge, James R.
Practical Psychiatry for the Primary Physician.
Nelson Hall.
Hodge, Jane (Aiken).
xHodge, Jane A.

The Adventurers. Fawcett.
Greek Wedding. Fawcett.
Last Act. Coward.
Marry in Haste. Fawcett.
Maulever Hall. BJ Pub Group.
One Way to Venice. Fawcett.
Rebel Heiress. Fawcett.
Strangers in Company. Coward.
Strangers in Company. Fawcett.

Hodge, Jane A. see Hodge, Jane (Aiken).

Hodge, Jeannine G. see Hodge, Jeannine Goble.

Hodge, Jeannine Goble.
xHodge, Jeannine G.
History of Holliday, Texas. Nortex Pr.
Hodge, P. C. see Hodge, Philip Gibson.
Hodge, Paul W.
xHodge, Paul W.
Concepts of Contemporary Astronomy.
McGraw.
Hodge, Peggy H. see Hodge, Peggy Hickok.
Hodge, Peggy Hickok.
xHodge, Peggy H.
Tropical Gardening: A Handbook for the
Home Gardener. C E Tuttle.
Hodge, Philip G. see Hodge, Philip Gibson.
Hodge, Philip Gibson, 1920-
xHodge, P. C.
Continuum Mechanics: An Introductory Text
for Engineers. McGraw.
xHodge, Philip G.
Plastic Analysis of Structures. McGraw.
Hodge, R. I. see Hodge, Robert Ian Vere.
Hodge, Robert Ian Vere.
xHodge, R. I.
Foreshortened Time: Andrew Marvell &
Seventeenth Century Revolutions. Rowman.
Hodge, Robert P. see Hodge, Robert Parker.
Hodge, Robert Parker, 1938-
xHodge, Robert P.
Amphibians & Reptiles in Alaska, the Yukon &
Northwest Territories. Alaska Northwest.
Hodgen, Margaret T. see Hodgen, Margaret Trabue.
Hodgen, Margaret Trabue, 1890-
xHodgen, Margaret T.
The Doctrine of Survivals: A Chapter in the
History of Scientific Method in the Study of
Man. Folcroft.
Early Anthropology in the Sixteenth &
Seventeenth Centuries. U of Pa Pr.
Hodges. see Hodges, Glen A.
Hodges, C. Walter. see Hodges, Cyril Walter.
Hodges, Cyril W. see Hodges, Cyril Walter.
Hodges, Cyril Walter, 1909-
xHodges, C. Walter.
Plain Lane Christmas. Coward.
xHodges, Cyril W.
Globe Restored: A Study of the Elizabethan
Theatre. Norton.
The Globe Restored: A Study of the
Elizabethan Theatre. Somerset Pub.
Hodges, Donald C. see Hodges, Donald Clark.
Hodges, Donald Clark, 1923-
xHodges, Donald C.
The Latin American Revolution: Politics &
Strategy from Apro-Marxism to Guevarism.
Morrow.
Socialist Humanism: The Outcome of Classical
European Morality. Green.
Hodges, Elizabeth J. see Hodges, Elizabeth Jamison.
Hodges, Elizabeth Jamison.
xHodges, Elizabeth J.
Song for Gilgamesh. Atheneum.
Hodges, Glen A.
xHodges.
Lost Bear. Dutton.
Hodges, H. A. see Hodges, Herbert Arthur.
Hodges, Harold M.
xHodges, Harold M.

Conflict & Consensus: An Introduction to
Sociology. Har-Row.
Hodges, Herbert Arthur, 1905-
xHodges, H. A.
God Beyond Knowledge. B&N.
Hodges, Holli S. *see* Hodges, Hollis.
Hodges, Hollis.
xHodges, Holli S.
The Fabricator. Avon.
Hodges, Laurent.
xHodges, Laurent.
Environmental Pollution. HR&W.
Hodges, Lewis H.
xHodges, Lewis H.
Building Antique Doll House Furniture from
Scratch. TAB Bks.
How to Build Your Own Fine Doll Houses &
Furnishings. TAB Bks.
Hodges, Margaret.
xHodges, Margaret.
The Fire Bringer: A Paiute Indian Legend.
Little.
The High Riders. Scribner.
Hopkins of the Mayflower: Portrait of a
Dissenter. FS&G.
Persephone & the Springtime. Little.
Hodges, Melvin L.
xHodges, Melvin L.
The Indigenous Church. Gospel Pub.
A Theology of the Church & Its Mission: A
Pentecostal Perspective. Gospel Pub.
Hodges, Raymond G.
xHodges, Raymond W.
High School Equivalency Test Guide. Par Inc.
Hodges, Raymond W. *see* Hodges, Raymond G.
Hodges, Robert E. *see* Hodges, Robert Edgar.
Hodges, Robert Edgar, 1922-
xHodges, Robert E.
Nutrition in Medical Practice. Saunders.
Hodgetts. *see* Hodgetts, Richard M.
Hodgetts, Blake. *see* Hodgetts, Blake Christopher.
Hodgetts, Blake Christopher.
xHodgetts, Blake.
Dream of the Dinosaurs. Doubleday.
Hodgetts, J. E. *see* Hodgetts, John Edwin.
Hodgetts, John Edwin, 1917-
xHodgetts, J. E.
Canadian Public Service: A Physiology of
Government, 1867-1970. U of Toronto Pr.
Hodgetts, Richard M.
xHodgetts.
Organizational Behavior. Dryden Pr.
xHodgetts, Richard M.
Administrative Policy: Text & Cases in
Strategic Management. Wiley.
The Business Enterprise: Social Challenge,
Social Response. HR&W.
Introduction to Business. A-W.
Management: Theory, Process, & Practice.
HR&W.
Hodgkin, E. C.
xHodgkin, E. C.
The Arabs. Viking Pr.
Hodgkin, Robin. *see* Hodgkin, Robin A.
Hodgkin, Robin A.
xHodgkin, Robin.
Born Curious: New Perspectives in Educational
Theory. Wiley.
Hodgkin, Thomas, 1831-1913
xHodgkin, Thomas.
Charles the Great. Kennikat.
The History of England from the Earliest
Times to the Norman Conquest (to 1066).
AMS Pr.
History of England from the Earliest Times to
the Norman Conquest. Greenwood.
History of England from the Earliest Times to
the Norman Conquest, 1066. Kraus Repr.
Hodgkin, Thomas. *see* Hodgkin, Thomas Lionel.

Hodgkin, Thomas Lionel, 1910-
xHodgkin, Thomas.
ed. Nigerian Perspectives: An Historical
Anthology. Oxford U Pr.
Hodgkinson, Edie, 1959-
xHodgkinson, Edith.
Season's Edge. Hanging Loose.
Hodgkinson, Edith. *see* Hodgkinson, Edie.
Hodgkinson, Harold L.
xHodgkinson, Harold L.
ed. Identity Crisis in Higher Education.
Jossey-Bass.
ed. Power & Authority: Transformation of
Campus Governance. Jossey-Bass.
Hodgskin, Thomas, 1787-1869
xHodgskin, Thomas.
Natural & Artificial Right of Property
Contrasted. Kelley.
Hodgson, Geraldine E. *see* Hodgson, Geraldine Emma.
Hodgson, Geraldine Emma, 1865-1937
xHodgson, Geraldine E.
Criticism at a Venture. Folcroft.
Criticism at a Venture. Kennikat.
Criticism of a Venture. R West.
English Mystics. Folcroft.
English Mystics. Gordon Pr.
Hodgson, J. M. *see* Hodgson, John Michael.
Hodgson, Joan, 1913-
xHodgson, Joan.
Reincarnation Through the Zodiac. CRCS
Pubns WA.
Hodgson, John. *see* Hodgson, John Reed.
Hodgson, John H. *see* Hodgson, John Humphrey.
Hodgson, John Humphrey, 1913-
xHodgson, John H.
Earthquakes & Earth Structure. P-H.
Hodgson, John Michael.
xHodgson, J. M.
Soil Sampling & Soil Description. Oxford U Pr.
Hodgson, John Reed.
xHodgson, John.
Improvisation. Grove.
Hodgson, Julian.
xHodgson, Julian.
Music Titles in Translation: A Checklist of
Musical Compositions. Shoe String.
Hodgson, Louise.
xHodgson, Louise.
Geraldine Goes to a Restaurant. Denison.
Hodgson, Mary Anne.
xHodgson, Mary Anne.
Fast & Easy Needlepoint. Doubleday.
Hodgson, Moira.
xHodgson, Moira.
The Hot & Spicy Cookbook. McGraw.
Quintet: Five American Dance Companies.
Morrow.
xHodgson, Moria.
The Campus Cookbook. Bobbs.
Hodgson, Moria. *see* Hodgson, Moira.
Hodgson, P. E. *see* Hodgson, Peter Edward.
Hodgson, Peter Edward.
xHodgson, P. E.
Growth Points in Nuclear Physics. Pergamon.
Hodgson, Robert D. *see* Hodgson, Robert David.
Hodgson, Robert David.
xHodgson, Robert D.
Changing Map of Africa. Van Nos Reinhold.
Hodgson, Shadworth H. *see* Hodgson, Shadworth
Hollway.
Hodgson, Shadworth Hollway, 1832-1912
xHodgson, Shadworth H.
The Metaphysic of Experience. Garland Pub.
Hodgson, W. H. *see* Hodgson, William Hope.
Hodgson, William H. *see* Hodgson, William Hope.
Hodgson, William Hope, 1875-1918
xHodgson, W. H.
The Ghost Pirates. Lighthouse Pr NY.
House on the Borderland. Lighthouse Pr NY.
xHodgson, William H.

The Ghost Pirates. Hyperion-Conn.
The House on the Borderland. Hyperion Conn.
House on the Borderland. Manor Bks.
Hodnett, Edward, 1901-
xHodnett, Edward.
Francis Barlow: First Master of English Book
Illustration. U of Cal Pr.
Hodous, Lewis, 1872-
xHodous, Lewis.
Folkways in China. AMS Pr.
Folkways in China. Chinese Materials.
Hodson, Bernard A.
xHodson, Bernard A.
Modern Data Processing for Management: A
Basic Systems Approach. CBI Pub.
Hodson, C. J. *see* Hodson, Cecil John.
Hodson, Cecil John.
xHodson, C. J.
ed. Radiology & the Kidney: Some Present
Concepts. S Karger.
xHodson, John C.
ed. Reflux Nephropathy. Masson Pub.
Hodson, Geoffrey.
xHodson, Geoffrey.
The Christ Life from Nativity to Ascension.
Theos Pub Hse.
Meditations on the Occult Life. Theos Pub
Hse.
Hodson, H. V. *see* Hodson, Henry Vincent.
Hodson, Henry Vincent, 1906-
xHodson, H. V.
ed. The International Foundation Directory.
Gale.
Hodson, J. H. *see* Hodson, John Howard.
Hodson, John C. *see* Hodson, Cecil John.
Hodson, John Howard.
xHodson, J. H.
The Administration of Archives. Pergamon.
Hodson, W. A. *see* Hodson, William Alan.
Hodson, William Alan, 1935-
xHodson, W. A.
Development of the Lung. Dekker.
Hodupp, Shelley.
xHodupp, Shelley.
Compiled by Second Shopper's Guide to
Museum Stores. Universe.
Hoe, Susanna.
xHoe, Susanna.
God Save the Tsar. St Martin.
Hoebel, E. Adamson. *see* Hoebel, Edward Adamson.
Hoebel, Edward A. *see* Hoebel, Edward Adamson.
Hoebel, Edward Adamson.
xHoebel, E. Adamson.
Anthropology & the Human Experience.
McGraw.
Law of Primitive Man: A Study in
Comparative Legal Dynamics. Atheneum.
The Plains Indians: A Critical Bibliography. Ind
U Pr.
xHoebel, Edward A.
Cultural & Social Anthropology. McGraw.
Hoeber, Ralph. *see* Hoeber, Ralph Carl Louis.
Hoeber, Ralph Carl Louis.
xHoeber, Ralph.
Contemporary Business Law: Principles &
Cases. McGraw.
Hoefs, J. *see* Hoefs, Jochen.
Hoefs, Jochen.
xHoefs, J.
Stable Isotope Geochemistry. Springer-Verlag.
Hoehling, Adolph A.
xHoehling, Adolph A.
The Great War at Sea: A History of Naval
Action, 1914-18. Greenwood.
Hoehn, Robert G., 1937-
xHoehn, Robert G.

Playing Slow Pitch Softball. Sterling.

Hoehner, Harold W.
xHoehner, Harold W.
Chronological Aspects of the Life of Christ.
Zondervan.

Hoekema, Anthony A., 1913-
xHoekema, Anthony A.
The Bible & the Future. Eerdmans.
The Christian Looks at Himself. Eerdmans.
Holy Spirit Baptism. Eerdmans.

Hoeksema, Herman.
xHoeksema, Herman.
Reformed Dogmatics. Kregel.

Hoel, Paul. *see* Hoel, Paul Gerhard.

Hoel, Paul G. *see* Hoel, Paul Gerhard.

Hoel, Paul Gerhard, 1905-
xHoel, Paul.
Introduction to Probability Theory. HM.
Introduction to Statistical Theory. HM.
Introduction to Stochastic Processes. HM.
xHoel, Paul G.
Finite Mathematics & Calculus with
Applications to Business. Wiley.
Introduction to Mathematical Statistics. Wiley.

Hoel, Robert F.
xHoel, Robert F.
Marketing Now!. Scott F.

Hoenig, Stuart A.
xHoenig, Stuart A.
How to Build & Use Electronic Devices
Without Frustration, Panic, Mountains of
Money, or an Engineering Degree. Little.
Medical Instrumentation & Electrical Safety:
The View from the Nursing Station. Wiley.

Hoeniger, F. D. *see* Hoeniger, F. David.

Hoeniger, F. David.
xHoeniger, F. D.
Development of Natural History in Tudor
England. Folger Bks.
xHoeniger, J. F.
jt. auth. Development of Natural History in
Tudor England. Folger Bks.

Hoeniger, J. F. *see* Hoeniger, F. David.

Hoenigswald, H. M. *see* Hoenigswald, Henry M.

Hoenigswald, Henry M., 1915-
xHoenigswald, H. M.
Studies in Formal Historical Linguistics.
Kluwer Boston.

Hoepli, Nancy L.
xHoepli, Nancy L.
ed. The Aftermath of Colonialism. Wilson.
ed. Common Market. Wilson.

Hoerder, Dick. *see* Hoerder, Dirk.

Hoerder, Dirk.
xHoerder, Dick.
ed. Protest, Direct Action, Repression: Dissent
in American Society from Colonial Times to
the Present. K G Saur.
xHoerder, Dirk.
Crowd Action in Revolutionary Massachusetts,
1765-1780. Acad Pr.

Hoernes, G. *see* Hoernes, Gerhard E.

Hoernes, Gerhard E.
xHoernes, G.
Introduction to Boolean Algebra & Logic
Design: A Program for Self-Instruction.
McGraw.

Hoernle, Reinhold F. *see* Hoernle, Reinhold Friedrich
Alfred.

Hoernle, Reinhold Friedrich Alfred, 1880-1943
xHoernle, Reinhold F.
South African Native Policy & the Liberal
Spirit. Negro U Pr.
Studies in Philosophy. Arno.

Hoeschele, D. *see* Hoeschele, David F.

Hoeschele, David F.
xHoeschele, D.
Analog to Digital-Digital to Analog Conversion
Techniques. Wiley.

Hoesen, Karl Van. *see* Van Hoesen, Karl.

Hoesen, Walter H. Van. *see* Van Hoesen, Walter H.

Hoetink, H.
xHoetink, Harry.
Caribbean Race Relations: A Study of Two
Variants. Oxford U Pr.
Two Variants in Caribbean Race Relations: A
Contribution to the Sociology of Segmented
Societies. Oxford U Pr.

Hoetink, Harry. *see* Hoetink, H.

Hoetzsch, Otto, 1876-1946
xHoetzsch, Otto.
Evolution of Russia. HarBraceJ.

Hoexter, Corinne K.
xHoexter, Corinne K.
From Canton to California: The Epic of
Chinese Immigration. Schol Bk Serv.

Hofacker, Ursula A.
xHofacker, Ursula A.
Chemical Experimentation: An Integrated
Course in Inorganic, Analytical & Physical
Chemistry. W H Freeman.

Hofeditz, Calvin A.
xHofeditz, Calvin A.
Computers & Data Processing Made Simple.
Doubleday.

Hofer, Charles W.
xHofer, Charles W.
Strategy Formulation: Analytical Concepts.
West Pub.

Hofer, Jack. *see* Hofer, Jack L.

Hofer, Jack L.
xHofer, Jack.
Sexercise: How to Exercise Your Way to
Sexual Fitness. A & W Pubs.

Hofer, Philip, 1898-
xHofer, Philip.
Edward Lear As a Landscape Draughtsman.
Harvard U Pr.

Hoff, Arne.
xHoff, Arne.
Dutch Firearms. Biblio Dist.

Hoff, Carol.
xHoff, Carol.
Johnny Texas. Jenkins.

Hoff, Ebbe C. *see* Hoff, Ebbe Curtis.

Hoff, Ebbe Curtis, 1906-
xHoff, Ebbe C.
Alcoholism: The Hidden Addiction. Seabury.

Hoff, G. C. *see* Hoff, George C.

Hoff, George C.
xHoff, G. C.
ed. Chemical Polymer & Fiber Additives for
Low Maintenance Highways. Noyes.

Hoff, Lee A. *see* Hoff, Lee Ann.

Hoff, Lee Ann.
xHoff, Lee A.
People in Crisis: Understanding & Helping.
A-W.

Hoff, Nicholas J. *see* Hoff, Nicholas John.

Hoff, Nicholas John, 1906-
xHoff, Nicholas J.
Analysis of Structures: Based on the Minimal
Principles & the Principle of Virtual
Displacement. Wiley.

Hoff, Syd. *see* Hoff, Sydney.

Hoff, Sydney, 1912-
xHoff, Syd.

The Art of Cartooning. Stravon.
illus. Barkley. Har-Row.
tr. Danielito y el Dinosauro. Har-Row.
Danny & the Dinosaur. Har-Row.
illus. Danny & the Dinosaur. Har-Row.
illus. Gentleman Jim & the Great John L..
Coward.
illus. Henrietta, Circus Star. Garrard.
Henrietta Goes to the Fair. Garrard.
illus. Henrietta's Halloween. Garrard.
illus. Horse in Harry's Room. Har-Row.
illus. Jokes to Enjoy, Draw & Tell. Putnam.
Lengthy. Putnam.
Lengthy. Putnam.
illus. Merry Christmas, Henrietta!. Garrard.
illus. My Aunt Rosie. Har-Row.
When Will It Snow. Har-Row.
illus. Where's Prancer. Har-Row.

Hoff, Trygve J. *see* Hoff, Trygve J. B.

Hoff, Trygve J. B.
xHoff, Trygve J.
Economic Calculation in the Socialist Society.
Hyperion Conn.

Hoff, Ursula.
xHoff, Ursula.
National Gallery of Victoria. Transatlantic.

Hoffberg, Judith A.
xHoffberg, Judith A.
Directory of Art Libraries & Visual Resource
Collections in North America.
Neal-Schuman.

Hoffbrand, A. V.
xHoffbrand, A. V.
Recent Advances in Haematology. Churchill.

Hoffenberg, Jack.
xHoffenberg, Jack.
The Desperate Adversaries. Avon.

Hoffer, Abram.
xHoffer, Abram.
Hallucinogens. Acad Pr.
How to Live with Schizophrenia. Citadel Pr.
How to Live with Schizophrenia. Univ Bks.
Orthomolecular Nutrition: New Lifestyle for
Super Good Health. Keats.

Hoffer, Charles. *see* Hoffer, Charles R.

Hoffer, Charles R.
xHoffer, Charles.
A Concise Introduction to Music Listening.
Wadsworth Pub.
xHoffer, Charles R.
Teaching Music in the Secondary Schools.
Wadsworth Pub.
Understanding of Music. Wadsworth Pub.

Hoffer, Eric.
xHoffer, Eric.
Before the Sabbath. Har-Row.

Hoffer, Jay.
xHoffer, Jay.
The Complete Broadcast Sales Guide for
Stations, Reps & Ad Agencies. TAB Bks.
Organization & Operation of Broadcast
Stations. TAB Bks.
Radio Production Techniques. TAB Bks.

Hoffer, Jerry M.
xHoffer, Jerry M.
Geothermal Exploration of Western
Trans-Pecos Texas. Tex Western.

Hoffer, Paul B.
xHoffer, Paul B.
Gallium-67 Imaging. Wiley.

Hoffer, William.
xHoffer, William.
Saved!: The Story of the Andrea Doria--the
Greatest Sea Rescue in History. Bantam.
Saved!: The Story of the Andrea Doria-the
Greatest Sea Rescue in History. Summit Bks.

Hofferbert, Richard I., 1937-
xHofferbert, Richard I.
The Study of Public Policy. Bobbs.

Hoffman. *see* Hoffman, Virginia.

Hoffman, Abbie.
  xHoffman, Abbie.
    Revolution for the Hell of It. Dial.
Hoffman, Adeline M. *see* Hoffman, Adeline Mildred.
Hoffman, Adeline Mildred.
  xHoffman, Adeline M.
    Clothing for the Handicapped, the Aged &
      Other People with Special Needs. C C
      Thomas.
    Daily Needs & Interests of Older People. C C
      Thomas.
Hoffman, Alice.
  xHoffman, Alice.
    The Drowning Season. Dutton.
Hoffman, Charles F. *see* Hoffman, Charles Fenno.
Hoffman, Charles Fenno, 1806-1884
  xHoffman, Charles F.
    Greyslaer: A Romance of the Mohawk.
      Scholarly.
    Greyslaer: A Romance of the Mohawk.
      Somerset Pub.
Hoffman, Daniel, 1923-
  xHoffman, Daniel.
    Pref. by Form & Fable in American Fiction.
      Norton.
Hoffman, David, 1784-1854
  xHoffman, David.
    A Course of Legal Study, Addressed to
      Students & the Profession Generally. Arno.
Hoffman, Dona.
  xHoffman, Dona.
    My Children, All Children. Concordia.
    When You Are Close, God Is. Concordia.
Hoffman, E. *see* Hoffman, Edward G.
Hoffman, E. J. *see* Hoffman, Edward Jack.
Hoffman, Edward, 1945-
  xHoffman, Edward G.
    Jig & Fixture Design. Van Nos Reinhold.
Hoffman, Edward G.
  xHoffman, E.
    Practical Problems in Mathematics for
      Machinists. Delmar.
Hoffman, Edward G. *see* Hoffman, Edward.
Hoffman, Edward Jack, 1925-
  xHoffman, E. J.
    Azeotropic & Extractive Distillation. Krieger.
    Coal Conversion. Energon Co.
Hoffman, Elizabeth, 1921-
  xHoffman, Elizabeth P.
    This House Is Haunted!. Raintree Pubs.
Hoffman, Elizabeth P. *see* Hoffman, Elizabeth.
Hoffman, Erik P.
  xHoffman, Erik P.
    ed. The Conduct of Soviet Foreign Policy.
      Aldine Pub.
Hoffman, F. *see* Hoffman, Frank.
Hoffman, F. J. *see* Hoffman, Frederick John.
Hoffman, Frank.
  xHoffman, F.
    Accounting Fundamentals: A Gregg Text-Kit
      for Adult Education. McGraw.
Hoffman, Frederick J. *see* Hoffman, Frederick John.
Hoffman, Frederick John.
  xHoffman, F. J.
    Little Magazine: A History & a Bibliography.
      Kraus Repr.
  xHoffman, Frederick J.
    Art of Southern Fiction: A Study of Some
      Modern Novelists. S Ill U Pr.
    Conrad Aiken. Coll & U Pr.
    Freudianism & the Literary Mind. Greenwood.
    Gertrude Stein. U of Minn Pr.
Hoffman, Frederick L. *see* Hoffman, Frederick Ludwig.
Hoffman, Frederick Ludwig, 1865-1946
  xHoffman, Frederick L.
    Race Traits & Tendencies of the American
      Negro. AMS Pr.
Hoffman, George. *see* Hoffman, George Cleborn.
Hoffman, George Cleborn, 1916-
  xHoffman, George.

How to Inspect a House. Delacorte.
How to Inspect a House. Dell.
Hoffman, Greg, 1946-
  xHoffman, Greg.
    The Art of World Team Tennis. SF Bk Co.
    The Art of World Team Tennis. Stein & Day.
Hoffman, H. Wilbur.
  xHoffman, H. Wilbur.
    Sagas of Old Western Travel & Transport.
      Howell-North.
Hoffman, Herbert H.
  xHoffman, Herbert H.
    Alphanumeric Filing Rules for Business
      Documents. Headway Pubns.
    Descriptive Cataloging in a New Light:
      Polemical Chapters for Librarians. Headway
      Pubns.
Hoffman, Joan, 1942-
  xHoffman, Joan.
    Racial Discrimination & Economic
      Development. Lexington Bks.
Hoffman, John, 1944-
  xHoffman, John.
    Marxism & the Theory of Praxis: A Critique of
      Some New Versions of Old Fallacies. Intl
      Pub Co.
Hoffman, John C. *see* Hoffman, John Charles.
Hoffman, John Charles, 1931-
  xHoffman, John C.
    Ethical Confrontation in Counseling. U of
      Chicago Pr.
Hoffman, John P. *see* Hoffman, John Paul.
Hoffman, John Paul.
  xHoffman, John P.
    Introduction to Electronics for Technologists.
      HM.
Hoffman, Kenneth.
  xHoffman, Kenneth.
    Linear Algebra. P-H.
Hoffman, L. J. *see* Hoffman, Lance J.
Hoffman, L. Richard, 1930-
  xHoffman, L. Richard.
    Group Problem Solving Process: Studies of a
      Valence Model. Praeger.
Hoffman, Lance J.
  xHoffman, L. J.
    Security & Privacy in Computer Systems.
      Wiley.
  xHoffman, Lance J.
    Modern Methods for Computer Security &
      Privacy. P-H.
Hoffman, Laurence D.
  xHoffman, Laurence D.
    Mathematics with Applications. McGraw.
Hoffman, Lawrence A., 1942-
  xHoffman, Lawrence A.
    The Canonization of the Synagogue Service. U
      of Notre Dame Pr.
Hoffman, Lee.
  xHoffman, Lee.
    The Valdez Horses. Ace Bks.
Hoffman, Lois Norma Wladis.
  xHoffman, Lois W.
    Working Mothers: An Evaluative Review of
      the Consequences for Wife, Husband, &
      Child. Jossey-Bass.
Hoffman, Lois W. *see* Hoffman, Lois Norma Wladis.
Hoffman, M. David.
  xHoffman, M. David.
    ed. Leadership in a Changing World. Arno.
Hoffman, Mable.
  xHoffman, Mable.
    Crepe Cookery. Bantam.
    Crepe Cookery. H P Bks.
    Crockery Cookery. Bantam.
    Crockery Cookery. H P Bks.
Hoffman, Martin, 1935-
  xHoffman, Martin.

Gay World: Male Homosexuality & the Social
    Creation of Evil. Basic.
Hoffman, Moses N. *see* Hoffman, Moses Naphtali
  Hirsch.
Hoffman, Moses Naphtali Hirsch, 1903-
  xHoffman, Moses N.
    The Measurement of Bilingual Background.
      AMS Pr.
Hoffman, Nancy.
  xHoffman, Nancy.
    Intro. by & ed. Women Working: An
      Anthology of Stories & Poems. Feminist Pr.
Hoffman, Nancy J. *see* Hoffman, Nancy Jo.
Hoffman, Nancy Jo.
  xHoffman, Nancy J.
    Spenser's Pastorals: The Shepheardes Calender
      & "Colin Clout". Johns Hopkins.
Hoffman, Nicholas Von. *see* Von Hoffman, Nicholas.
Hoffman, P. *see* Hoffman, Peter.
Hoffman, Paul, 1934-
  xHoffman, Paul.
    Courthouse. Dutton.
    Lions in the Street: The Inside Story of the
      Great Wall Street Law Firms. NAL.
Hoffman, Peter.
  xHoffman, P.
    ed. Algebraic Topology: Proceedings,
      University of British Columbia, Vancouver,
      August 1977. Springer-Verlag.
Hoffman, Phyllis.
  xHoffman, Phyllis.
    Steffie & Me. Har-Row.
Hoffman, Richard, 1831-1909
  xHoffman, Richard.
    Some Musical Recollections of Fifty Years.
      Info Coord.
Hoffman, Richard L. *see* Hoffman, Richard Lester.
Hoffman, Richard Lester.
  xHoffman, Richard L.
    Ovid & the Canterbury Tales. U of Pa Pr.
Hoffman, Robert L. *see* Hoffman, Robert Louis.
Hoffman, Robert Louis, 1937-
  xHoffman, Robert L.
    ed. Anarchism. Lieber-Atherton.
    Revolutionary Justice: The Social & Political
      Theory of P.-J. Proudhon. U of Ill Pr.
Hoffman, Rosekrans.
  xHoffman, Rosekrans.
    illus. Anna Banana. Knopf.
Hoffman, Ross J. *see* Hoffman, Ross John Swartz.
Hoffman, Ross John Swartz, 1902-
  xHoffman, Ross J.
    The Marquis: A Study of Lord Rockingham,
      1730-1782. Fordham.
Hoffman, Virginia.
  xHoffman.
    Navajo Biographies. Navajo Curr.
  xHoffman, Virginia.
    Navajo Biographies. Navajo Curr.
Hoffman, Walter J. *see* Hoffman, Walter James.
Hoffman, Walter James, 1846-1899
  xHoffman, Walter J.
    The Menomini Indians. Johnson Repr.
Hoffman, William. *see* Hoffman, William S.
Hoffman, William S.
  xHoffman, William.
    The Stockholder. Lyle Stuart.
Hoffmann, Ann.
  xHoffmann, Ann.
    ed. Lives of the Tudor Age. B&N.
Hoffmann, Banesh, 1906-
  xHoffmann, Banesh.
    About Vectors. Dover.
Hoffmann, Charles, 1921-
  xHoffmann, Charles.

The Chinese Worker. State U NY Pr.
Depression of the Nineties: An Economic
History. Greenwood.
Work Incentive Practices & Policies in the
People's Republic of China, 1953-1965. State
U NY Pr.

Hoffmann, Charles G.
xHoffmann, Charles G.
Ford Madox Ford. Twayne.

Hoffmann, Donald.
xHoffmann, Donald.
The Architecture of John Wellborn Root. Johns
Hopkins.
Frank Lloyd Wright's Fallingwater: The House
& Its History. Dover.

Hoffmann, Helmut, 1912-
xHoffmann, Helmut.
The Religions of Tibet. Greenwood.

Hoffmann, Herbert, 1930-
xHoffmann, Herbert.
Collecting Greek Antiquities. Crown.
Greek Gold: Jewelry from the Age of
Alexander. Bklyn Mus.

Hoffmann, Laurence. see Hoffmann, Laurence D.

Hoffmann, Laurence D., 1943-
xHoffmann, Laurence.
Practical Calculus for the Social & Managerial
Sciences. McGraw.

Hoffmann, Oswald. see Hoffmann, Oswald C. J.

Hoffmann, Oswald C. J.
xHoffmann, Oswald.
God Is No Island. Concordia.

Hoffmann, Peter, 1930-
xHoffmann, Peter.
Hitler's Personal Security. MIT Pr.

Hoffmann, Stanley.
xHoffmann, Stanley.
Primacy or World Order: American Foreign
Policy Since the Cold War. McGraw.

Hoffmann, W. G. see Hoffmann, Walther G.

Hoffmann, Walther G, 1903-
xHoffmann, W. G.
Growth of Industrial Economies. Oceana.

Hoffmann, William S.
xHoffmann, William S.
Andrew Jackson & North Carolina Politics.
Peter Smith.

Hoffmeister, Donald F. see Hoffmeister, Donald
Frederick.

Hoffmeister, Donald Frederick.
xHoffmeister, Donald F.
Fieldbook of Illinois Mammals. Dover.
Fieldbook of Illinois Mammals. Peter Smith.

Hoffmeister, Karel.
xHoffmeister, Karel.
Antonin Dvorak. Greenwood.

Hoffsommer, Alan.
xHoffsommer, Alan.
Wood Carving Made Easy. TAB Bks.

Hoffstein, Robert. see Hoffstein, Robert M.

Hoffstein, Robert M.
xHoffstein, Robert.
The English Alphabet: An Inquiry into Its
Mystical Construction. Kaedmon.
xHoffstein, Robert M.
The English Alphabet: An Inquiry into Its
Mystical Construction. Kaedmon.

Hofheinz, Roy, 1935-
xHofheinz, Roy.
The Broken Wave: The Chinese Communist
Peasant Movement, 1922-1928. Harvard U
Pr.

Hofinger, Johannes.
xHofinger, Johannes.
Good News & Its Proclamation. U of Notre
Dame Pr.
Imparting the Christian Message. U of Notre
Dame Pr.

Hofman, David.
xHofman, David.

The Renewal of Civilization. Baha'i.

Hofman, Jaroslav.
xHofman, Jaroslav.
Ornamental Shrubs. Transatlantic.

Hofmann, Adele D.
xHofmann, Adele D.
The Hospitalized Adolescent: A Guide to
Managing the Ill & Injured Youth. Free Pr.

Hofmann, Charles, 1914-
xHofmann, Charles.
Sounds for Silents. Drama Bk.

Hofmann, K. H. see Hofmann, Karl Heinrich.

Hofmann, Karl Heinrich.
xHofmann, K. H.
Duality of Compact Semigroups & C-Bigebras.
Springer-Verlag.
General Character Theory for Partially
Ordered Sets & Lattices. Am Math.
The Pontryagin Duality of Compact
O-Dimensional Semilattices & Its
Applications. Springer-Verlag.

Hofmann, Ruth B.
xHofmann, Ruth B.
How to Build Special Furniture & Equipment
for Handicapped Children. C C Thomas.

Hofmann, W. see Hofmann, Wilhelm.

Hofmann, Werner, 1928-
xHofmann, Werner.
Gustav Klimt. NYGS.

Hofmann, Wilhelm, 1903-1965
xHofmann, W.
Lead & Lead Alloys: Properties & Technology.
Springer-Verlag.

Hofsinde, Robert.
xHofsinde, Robert.
illus. Indian Arts. Morrow.
illus. Indian Beadwork. Morrow.
illus. Indian Costumes. Morrow.
illus. Indian Music Makers. Morrow.
illus. Indian Picture Writing. Morrow.
illus. Indian Sign Language. Morrow.
illus. Indians on the Move. Morrow.

Hofstadter, Albert, 1910-
xHofstadter, Albert.
Agony & Epitaph: Man, His Art & His Poetry.
Braziller.
Truth & Art. Columbia U Pr.

Hofstadter, Douglas. see Hofstadter, Douglas R.

Hofstadter, Douglas R., 1945-
xHofstadter, Douglas.
Godel, Escher, Bach: An Eternal Golden Braid.
Basic.
xHofstadter, Douglas R.
Godel, Escher, Bach: An Eternal Golden Braid.
Random.

Hofstadter, Richard, 1916-
xHofstadter, Richard.
Academic Freedom in the Age of the College.
Columbia U Pr.
Age of Reform: From Bryan to F. D. R. Knopf.
The Age of Reform: From Bryan to F. D. R..
Random.
ed. American Violence: A Documentary
History. Random.
The Idea of a Party System: The Rise of
Legitimate Opposition in the United States,
1780-1840. U of Cal Pr.
ed. Progressive Movement 1900-1915. Peter
Smith.

Hofstein, Sadie.
xHofstein, Sadie.
Human Story: Facts on Birth, Growth &
Reproduction. Lothrop.

Hogan, Bernice.
xHogan, Bernice.
The Church Is a Who. Bethany Pr.

Hogan, Bernice. see Hogan, Benrice.

Hogan, Desmond.
xHogan, Desmond.

The Ikon Maker. Braziller.

Hogan, Elizabeth.
xHogan, Elizabeth.
Stevie's Day off. Broadman.

Hogan, Inez.
xHogan, Inez.
A Dog for Danny. Garrard.

Hogan, James P.
xHogan, James P.
The Genesis Machine. Ballantine.
Inherit the Stars. Ballantine.

Hogan, John J. see Hogan, John Joseph.

Hogan, John Joseph, Bp, 1829-1913
xHogan, John J.
On the Mission in Missouri, 1857-1868. Rio
Grande.

Hogan, Paula Z.
xHogan, Paula Z.
The Beaver. Raintree Pubs.
The Black Swan. Raintree Pubs.
The Butterfly. Raintree Pubs.
The Crocodile. Raintree Pubs.
The Dandelion. Raintree Pubs.
The Elephant. Raintree Pubs.
The Frog. Raintree Pubs.
The Gorilla. Raintree Pubs.
The Honeybee. Raintree Pubs.
The Hospital Scares Me. Raintree Child.
I Hate Boys - I Hate Girls. Raintree Child.
The Oak Tree. Raintree Pubs.
The Penguin. Raintree Pubs.
The Salmon. Raintree Pubs.
Sometimes I Don't Like School. Raintree
Child.
Sometimes I Get So Mad. Raintree Child.
The Tiger. Raintree Pubs.
The Whale. Raintree Pubs.
Will Dad Ever Move Back Home?. Raintree
Child.
The Wolf. Raintree Pubs.

Hogan, Ray, 1908-
xHogan, Ray.
The Doomsday Trail. Doubleday.
The Doomsday Trail. NAL.
The Glory Trail. Doubleday.
The Glory Trail. G K Hall.
The Glory Trail. NAL.
The Peace Keeper. Doubleday.
The Peace Keeper. G K Hall.
The Peace Keeper. NAL.
Pilgrim. Doubleday.
Pilgrim. NAL.
The Proving Gun. Doubleday.
The Raptors. Doubleday.
The Raptors. NAL.

Hogan, Robert. see Hogan, Robert Goode.

Hogan, Robert Goode, 1930-
xHogan, Robert.
ed. Dictionary of Irish Literature. Greenwood.

Hogan, Robert J.
xHogan, Robert J.
Stampede Canyon. Manor Bks.

Hogan, William T. see Hogan, William Thomas.

Hogan, William Thomas, 1919-
xHogan, William T.
An Economic History of the Iron & Steel
Industry in the United States. Lexington Bks.

Hogarth, Burne.
xHogarth, Burne.
Drawing Dynamic Hands. Watson-Guptill.
Drawing the Human Head. Watson-Guptill.
Dynamic Anatomy. Watson-Guptill.
Dynamic Figure Drawing. Watson-Guptill.
The Golden Age of Tarzan 1939-42. Chelsea
Hse.

Hogarth, C. A. see Hogarth, Cyril Alfred.

Hogarth, Cyril Alfred, 1924-
xHogarth, C. A.

Materials Used in Semiconductor Devices.
Krieger.
Hogarth, D. G. *see* Hogarth, David George.
Hogarth, David G. *see* Hogarth, David George.
Hogarth, David George, 1862-1927
xHogarth, D. G.
The Ancient East. Norwood Edns.
The Life of Charles M. Doughty. Scholarly.
xHogarth, David G.
Ancient East. Greenwood.
Arabia. Hyperion Conn.
Authority & Archaeology, Sacred & Profane:
Essays on the Relation of Monuments to
Biblical & Classical Literature. Arden Lib.
The Penetration of Arabia: A Record of the
Development of Western Knowledge
Concerning the Arabian Peninsula. Hyperion
Conn.
Hogarth, George, 1783-1870
xHogarth, George.
Musical History, Biography, & Criticism. Da
Capo.
Hogarth, Paul.
xHogarth, Paul.
America Observed. Potter.
Creative Ink Drawing. Watson-Guptill.
Creative Pencil Drawing. Watson-Guptill.
Hogarth, Peter. *see* Hogarth, Peter J.
Hogarth, Peter J.
xHogarth, Peter.
Dragons. Viking Pr.
Hogarth, Robin M.
xHogarth, Robin M.
Evaluating Management Education. Wiley.
Hogbin, H. Ian. *see* Hogbin, Herbert Ian.
Hogbin, Herbert Ian, 1904-
xHogbin, H. Ian.
Experiments in Civilization: The Effects of
European Culture on a Native Community of
the Solomon Islands. Schocken.
Hogbin, Stephen.
xHogbin, Stephen.
Wood Turning. Van Nos Reinhold.
Hoge, Dean R., 1937-
xHoge, Dean R.
Commitment on Campus: Changes in Religion
& Values Over Five Decades. Westminster.
Hoge, Tom.
xHoge, Tom.
Potato Cookery. Cornerstone.
Hogendorn, J. *see* Hogendorn, Jan S.
Hogendorn, Jan S.
xHogendorn, J.
Markets in the Modern Economy: An
Introduction to Microeconomics. Winthrop.
Hogg, A. H. *see* Hogg, Alexander Hubert Arthur.
Hogg, Alexander Hubert Arthur.
xHogg, A. H.
Surveying for Archaeologists & Other
Fieldworkers. St Martin.
Hogg, Anthony.
xHogg, Anthony.
Guide to Visiting Vineyards. Transatlantic.
Hogg, Clayton. *see* Hogg, Clayton L.
Hogg, Clayton L.
xHogg, Clayton.
Okinawa. Kodansha.
Hogg, Garry.
xHogg, Garry.
The English Country Inn. Hastings.
Facets of the English Scene. David & Charles.
Guide to English Country Houses. Arco.
Hogg, Ian. *see* Hogg, Ian V.
Hogg, Ian V.
xHogg, Ian.
Artillery. Ballantine.
Artillery. Scribner.
xHogg, Ian V.

Gas. Ballantine.
Hogg, James, 1770-1835
xHogg, James.
Domestic Manners of Sir Walter Scott. Arden
Lib.
Private Memoirs & Confessions of a Justified
Sinner. Norton.
Private Memoirs & Confessions of a Justified
Sinner. Oxford U Pr.
Hogg, John. *see* Hogg, John Mervyn.
Hogg, John Mervyn.
xHogg, John.
Success in Swimming. Transatlantic.
Hogg, Robert V.
xHogg, Robert V.
Introduction to Mathematical Statistics.
Macmillan.
Hogg, Thomas J. *see* Hogg, Thomas Jefferson.
Hogg, Thomas Jefferson, 1792-1862
xHogg, Thomas J.
Life of Percy Bysshe Shelley. Folcroft.
Life of Percy Bysshe Shelley. Scholarly.
Hoggart, Richard, 1918-
xHoggart, Richard.
An Idea & Its Servants: Unesco from Within.
Oxford U Pr.
On Culture & Communication. Oxford U Pr.
Hoggett, J. G.
xHoggett, J. G.
Nitration & Aromatic Reactivity. Cambridge U
Pr.
Hogins, J. Burl. *see* Hogins, James Burl.
Hogins, James B. *see* Hogins, James Burl.
Hogins, James Burl.
xHogins, J. Burl.
Reading for Insight: A Perceptual Approach to
College English. Glencoe.
The Structure of Writing. Heath.
xHogins, James B.
Contemporary Exposition. Har-Row.
Reading, Writing, & Rhetoric. SRA.
Theme & Rhetoric. SRA.
Hogner, Dorothy C. *see* Hogner, Dorothy Childs.
Hogner, Dorothy Childs.
xHogner, Dorothy C.
Endangered Plants. T Y Crowell.
Frogs & Polliwogs. T Y Crowell.
Sea Mammals. T Y Crowell.
Spiders. T Y Crowell.
Hogrefe, Pearl.
xHogrefe, Pearl.
Life & Times of Sir Thomas Elyot, Englishman.
Iowa St U Pr.
Tudor Women: Commoners & Queens. Iowa St
U Pr.
Hogrogian, Nonny.
xHogrogian, Nonny.
illus. Apples. Macmillan.
Carrot Cake. Greenwillow.
The Contest. Greenwillow.
Hogrogian, Rachel.
xHogrogian, Rachel.
Armenian Cookbook. Atheneum.
Hogue, Arthur. *see* Hogue, Arthur Reed.
Hogue, Arthur Reed, 1906-
xHogue, Arthur.
Origins of the Common Law. Shoe String.
Hogue, C. B. *see* Hogue, C. Bill.
Hogue, C. Bill.
xHogue, C. B.
I Want My Church to Grow. Broadman.
Love Leaves No Choice: Lifestyle Evangelism.
Word Bks.
Hoheisel, Guido, 1894-
xHoheisel, Guido.

Integral Equations. Ungar.
Hohenberg, John.
xHohenberg, John.
A Crisis for the American Press. Columbia U
Pr.
Foreign Correspondence: The Great Reporters
& Their Times. Columbia U Pr.
The Professional Journalist: A Guide to the
Practices & Principles of the News Media.
HR&W.
Hohfeld, Wesley N. *see* Hohfeld, Wesley Newcomb.
Hohfeld, Wesley Newcomb.
xHohfeld, Wesley N.
Fundamental Legal Conceptions, As Applied in
Judicial Reasoning. Greenwood.
Hohimer, Frank.
xHohimer, Frank.
The Home Invaders: Confessions of a Cat
Burglar. Chicago Review.
Hohlenberg, Johannes. *see* Hohlenberg, Johannes
Edouard.
Hohlenberg, Johannes Edouard, 1881-
xHohlenberg, Johannes.
Soren Kierkegaard. Octagon.
Hohlwein, Ludwig, 1874-
xHohlwein, Ludwig.
Hohlwein Posters in Full Color. Peter Smith.
Hohman, Elmo P. *see* Hohman, Elmo Paul.
Hohman, Elmo Paul, 1894-
xHohman, Elmo P.
American Whale Man: A Study of Life &
Labor in the Whaling Industry. Kelley.
Hohn, Max T.
xHohn, Max T.
ed. Stories in Verse. Odyssey Pr.
Hohne, Heinz, 1926-
xHohne, Heinz.
Canaris. Doubleday.
Hohns, H. Murray.
xHohns, H. Murray.
Preventing & Solving Construction Contract
Disputes. Van Nos Reinhold.
Hoig, Stan.
xHoig, Stan.
The Battle of the Washita: The Sheridan-Custer
Indian Campaign of 1867-1869. U of Nebr
Pr.
The Peace Chiefs of the Cheyennes. U of Okla
Pr.
Hoinville, Gerald.
xHoinville, Gerald.
Survey Research Practice. Heinemann Ed.
Hokanson, Nels. *see* Hokanson, Nels Magnus.
Hokanson, Nels Magnus, 1885-
xHokanson, Nels.
Swedish Immigrants in Lincoln's Time. Arno.
Hoke, H. *see* Hoke, Henry Reed.
Hoke, Helen, 1903-
xHoke, H.
Fleas. Watts.
xHoke, Helen.
ed. A Chilling Collection. Elsevier-Nelson.
Devils, Devils, Devils. Watts.
ed. Dragons, Dragons, Dragons. Watts.
Hoke's Jokes Cartoons & Funny Things. Watts.
Horrors, Horrors, Horrors. Watts.
Jokes & Fun. Watts.
Jokes, Giggles & Guffaws. Watts.
ed. Jokes, Jokes, Jokes. Watts.
Monsters, Monsters, Monsters. Watts.
More Riddles, Riddles, Riddles. Watts.
Owls. Watts.
Riddle Giggles. Watts.
Terrors, Terrors, Terrors. Watts.
Hoke, Henry Reed, 1894-
xHoke, H.
What You Should Know About Direct Mail.
Oceana.
Hoke, John, 1925-
xHoke, John.

Discovering the World of the Three-Toed
   Sloth. Watts.
Ecology. Watts.
Solar Energy. Watts.
Holaday, Perry W. see Holaday, Perry Ward.
Holaday, Perry Ward.
   xHoladay, Perry W.
   Getting Ideas from the Movies. Arno.
Holbeck, Elmer S. see Holbeck, Elmer Scott.
Holbeck, Elmer Scott, 1893-
   xHolbeck, Elmer S.
   An Analysis of the Activities & Potentialities
      for Achievement of the Parent-Teacher
      Association, with Recommendations. AMS
      Pr.
Holberg, Ludwig, Baron, 1684-1754
   xHolberg, Ludwig.
   A Journey to the World Underground, 1742.
      Garland Pub.
Holberg, Ruth (Langland).
   xHolberg, Ruth L.
   Luke & the Indians. Hastings.
Holberg, Ruth L. see Holberg, Ruth (Langland).
Holbert, E. Joe.
   xHolbert, Joe.
   Word Banquet & Party Book. Word Bks.
Holbert, Hayward J. see Holbert, Hayward Janes.
Holbert, Hayward Janes.
   xHolbert, Hayward J.
   A History of Professional Management in
      American Industry. Arno.
Holbert, Joe. see Holbert, E. Joe.
Holbert, Neil, 1931-
   xHolbert, Neil.
   Advertising Research. Am Mktg.
   Careers in Marketing. Am Mktg.
Holbert, Sue E.
   xHolbert, Sue E.
   History Tour of 50 Twin City Landmarks.
      Minn Hist.
Holbik, Karel.
   xHolbik, Karel.
   Industrialization & Employment in Puerto
      Rico, 1950-1972. U of Tex Busn Res.
Holborn, Hajo, 1902-1969
   xHolborn, Hajo.
   Ulrich Von Hutten & the German Reformation.
      Greenwood.
Holborn, Louise W. see Holborn, Louise Wilhelmine.
Holborn, Louise Wilhelmine.
   xHolborn, Louise W.
   Refugees: a Problem of Our Time: The Work
      of the United Nations High Commissioner
      for Refugees; 1951-1972. Scarecrow.
Holborn, Mark.
   xHolborn, Mark.
   The Ocean in the Sand: Japan-from Landscape
      to Garden. Shambhala Pubns.
Holbourne, David.
   xHolbourne, David.
   The Basic Book of Machine Knitting. Van Nos
      Reinhold.
Holbraad, Carsten.
   xHolbraad, Carsten.
   Superpowers & International Conflict. St
      Martin.
Holbrook, Clyde A.
   xHolbrook, Clyde A.
   The Ethics of Jonathan Edwards: Morality &
      Aesthetics. U of Mich Pr.
Holbrook, David.
   xHolbrook, David.
   Dylan Thomas: The Code of Night.
      Humanities.
   Lost Bearings in English Poetry. B&N.
   Quest for Love. U of Ala Pr.
   Sylvia Plath: Poetry & Existence. Humanities.
Holbrook, H. T.
   xHolbrook, H. T.

Etude Sur Pathelin. Kraus Repr.
Holbrook, Iola B. see Holbrook, Iola Belle.
Holbrook, Iola Belle, 1906-
   xHolbrook, Iola B.
   Eat Your Way to Health. De Vorss.
Holbrook, John.
   xHolbrook, John.
   A Closer Look at Elephants. Watts.
Holbrook, Richard T. see Holbrook, Richard Thayer.
Holbrook, Richard Thayer, 1870-
   xHolbrook, Richard T.
   Dante & the Animal Kingdom. AMS Pr.
Holbrook, Sabra.
   xHolbrook, Sabra.
   The French Founders of North America &
      Their Heritage. Atheneum.
   Growing up in France. Atheneum.
Holbrook, Steward. see Holbrook, Stewart.
Holbrook, Stewart.
   xHolbrook, Steward.
   America's Ethan Allen. HM.
Holbrook, Stewart H. see Holbrook, Stewart Hall.
Holbrook, Stewart Hall, 1893-1964
   xHolbrook, Stewart H.
   Ethan Allen. Binford.
Holbrook, Wallace W.
   xHolbrook, Wallace W.
   Contemporary Lamps. McKnight.
Holck, Frederick H., 1927-
   xHolck, Frederick H.
   ed. Death & Eastern Thought: Understanding
      Death in Eastern Religions & Philosophies.
      Abingdon.
Holcomb, J. D. see Holcomb, J. David.
Holcomb, J. David.
   xHolcomb, J. D.
   Improving Teaching in Medical Schools: A
      Practical Handbook. C C Thomas.
Holcomb Research Institute.
   xHolcomb Research Institute.
   Environmental Modeling & Decision Making:
      The United States Experience. Praeger.
Holcomb, W. P. see Holcomb, William Penn.
Holcomb, William P. see Holcomb, William Penn.
Holcomb, William Penn.
   xHolcomb, W. P.
   Pennsylvania Boroughs. Johnson Repr.
   xHolcomb, William P.
   Pennsylvania Boroughs. AMS Pr.
Holcombe, Arthur N. see Holcombe, Arthur Norman.
Holcombe, Arthur Norman, 1884-
   xHolcombe, Arthur N.
   The Chinese Revolution: A Phase in the
      Regeneration of a World Power. Fertig.
   Our More Perfect Union: From
      Eighteenth-Century Principles to
      Twentieth-Century Practice. Harvard U Pr.
   Strategy of Peace in a Changing World.
      Harvard U Pr.
Holcroft, M. H. see Holcroft, Montague Harry.
Holcroft, Montague Harry.
   xHolcroft, M. H.
   Old Invercargill. Intl Pubns Serv.
Holcroft, Thomas, 1745-1809
   xHolcroft, Thomas.
   Anna St. Ives. Oxford U Pr.
   Life of Thomas Holcroft. Arno.
   Memoirs of Bryan Perdue. Garland Pub.
   Theatrical Recorder. B Franklin.
Holdcroft, David.
   xHoldcroft, David.
   Words & Deeds: Problems of the Theory of
      Speech Acts. Oxford U Pr.
Holden, Alan.
   xHolden, Alan.
   Nature of Atoms. Oxford U Pr.
   The Nature of Solids. Columbia U Pr.
Holden, Anna.
   xHolden, Anna.

The Bus Stops Here: A Study of School
   Desegregation in Three Cities. Agathon.
Holden, Donald.
   xHolden, Donald.
   Whistler Landscapes & Seascapes.
      Watson-Guptill.
Holden, Edward S. see Holden, Edward Singleton.
Holden, Edward Singleton, 1846-1914
   xHolden, Edward S.
   A Primer of Heraldry for Americans. Gale.
Holden, George, 1926-
   xHolden, George.
   On Loving. Rosen Pr.
Holden, H. B. see Holden, Harold Benjamin.
Holden, Harold Benjamin.
   xHolden, H. B.
   Practical Cryosurgery. Year Bk Med.
Holden, John A. see Holden, John Allan.
Holden, John Allan.
   xHolden, John A.
   The Bookman's Glossary. R West.
Holden, Jonathan.
   xHolden, Jonathan.
   The Mark to Turn: A Reading of William
      Stafford's Poetry. Regents Pr KS.
Holden, Matthew, 1931-
   xHolden, Matthew.
   Varieties of Political Conservatism. Sage.
Holden, Philip.
   xHolden, Philip.
   Backblocks. Intl Pubns Serv.
   Hunter by Profession. Intl Pubns Serv.
Holden, Raymond. see Holden, Raymond Peckham.
Holden, Raymond Peckham, 1894-1972
   xHolden, Raymond.
   What So Proudly We Hailed. Countryman.
Holden, Stephen.
   xHolden, Stephen.
   Triple Platinum. Dell.
Holden, Ursula.
   xHolden, Ursula.
   Cloud Catchers. Methuen Inc.
   Fallen Angels. Methuen Inc.
Holden, Vincent F.
   xHolden, Vincent F.
   The Early Years of Isaac Thomas Hecker
      (1819-1844). AMS Pr.
Holden, William C. see Holden, William Curry.
Holden, William Curry, 1896-
   xHolden, William C.
   Studies of the Yaqui Indians of Sonora,
      Mexico. AMS Pr.
Holden, Willis S. see Holden, Willis Sprague.
Holden, Willis Sprague, 1909-
   xHolden, Willis S.
   Australia Goes to Press. Greenwood.
Holder, Angela R. see Holder, Angela Roddey.
Holder, Angela Roddey.
   xHolder, Angela R.
   Legal Issues in Pediatrics & Adolescent
      Medicine. Wiley.
   Meaning of the Constitution. Barron.
   Medical Malpractice Law. Wiley.
Holder, Glenn, 1906-
   xHolder, Glenn.
   Talking Totem Poles. Dodd.
Holder, Jack J.
   xHolder, Jack J.
   Corporate Support Programs to Institutions of
      Higher Learning. Interstate.
Holder, Judith.
   xHolder, Judith.
   Sweethearts & Valentines. A & W Pubs.
Holder, Leonard. see Holder, Leonard Irvin.
Holder, Leonard Irvin, 1923-
   xHolder, Leonard.
   Primer for Calculus. Wadsworth Pub.
Holder, Preston, 1907-
   xHolder, Preston.

The Hoe & the Horse on the Plains: A Study
of Cultural Development Among North
American Indians. U of Nebr Pr.
Holder, William G., 1937-
xHolder, William G.
Convair F-106 Delta Dart. Aero.
General Dynamics F-16. Aero.
Holder-Barell, Alexander.
xHolder-Barell, Alexander.
Development of Imagery & Its Functional
Significance in Henry James's Novels.
Haskell.
Holderness, B. A.
xHolderness, B. A.
Pre-Industrial England: Economy & Society
from 1500 to 1750. Rowman.
Holderness, Ginny W. see Holderness, Ginny Ward.
Holderness, Ginny Ward, 1946-
xHolderness, Ginny W.
The Exuberant Years: A Guide for Junior High
Leaders. John Knox.
Holdgate, M. W. see Holdgate, Martin W.
Holdgate, Martin W.
xHoldgate, M. W.
ed. Antarctic Ecology. Acad Pr.
A Perspective of Environmental Pollution.
Cambridge U Pr.
Holdren, Bob R.
xHoldren, Bob R.
Structure of a Retail Market & the Market
Behavior of Retail Units. Iowa St U Pr.
Holdridge, L. R. see Holdridge, Leslie R.
Holdridge, Leslie R., 1907-
xHoldridge, L. R.
Forest Environments in Tropical Life Zones: A
Pilot Study. Pergamon.
Holdstock, Robert.
xHoldstock, Robert.
Earthwind. PB.
Eye Among the Blind. NAL.
xHoldstock, Robert P.
Eye Among the Blind. Doubleday.
Holdstock, Robert P. see Holdstock, Robert.
Holdsworth, William S. see Holdsworth, William Searle.
Holdsworth, William Searle, Sir, 1871-1944
xHoldsworth, William S.
Charles Dickens As a Legal Historian. Haskell.
Historians of Anglo-American Law. Shoe
String.
Hole, Christina.
xHole, Christina.
British Folk Customs. Standing Orders.
English Traditional Customs. Rowman.
Hole, Francis D. see Hole, Francis Doan.
Hole, Francis Doan.
xHole, Francis D.
Soils of Wisconsin. U of Wis Pr.
Hole, Frank.
xHole, Frank.
Prehistoric Archeology: A Brief Introduction.
HR&W.
Prehistory & Human Ecology of the Deh
Luran Plain: An Early Village Sequence from
Khuzistan, Iran. U Mich Mus Anthro.
Hole, Hugh M. see Hole, Hugh Marshall.
Hole, Hugh Marshall, 1865-1941
xHole, Hugh M.
Passing of the Black Kings. Negro U Pr.
Hole, James.
xHole, James.
Light, More Light: On the Present State of
Education Amongst Working Classes. Biblio
Dist.
Hole, John. see Hole, John W.
Hole, John W.
xHole, John.
Human Anatomy & Physiology. Wm C Brown.
xHole, John W.
Human Anatomy & Physiology. Wm C Brown.
Hole, S. Reynolds. see Hole, Samuel Reynolds.

Hole, Samuel Reynolds, 1819-1904
xHole, S. Reynolds.
Little Tour in America. Arno.
Holeckova, E. see Holeckova, Ema.
Holeckova, Ema.
xHoleckova, E.
Aging in Cell & Tissue Culture. Plenum Pub.
Holeman, Jack R., 1929-
xHoleman, Jack R.
Condominium Management. P-H.
Holesovsky, Vaclav.
xHolesovsky, Vaclav.
Economic Systems: Analysis & Comparison.
McGraw.
Holiday.
xHoliday Editors.
ed. Holiday Guide to Britain. Random.
ed. Holiday Guide to Caribbean. Random.
ed. Holiday Guide to France. Random.
ed. Holiday Guide to Greece & the Aegean
Islands. Random.
ed. Holiday Guide to Hawaii. Random.
Holiday Guide to Ireland. Random.
ed. Holiday Guide to Israel. Random.
Holiday Guide to Italy. Random.
ed. Holiday Guide to London. Random.
ed. Holiday Guide to Mexico. Random.
ed. Holiday Guide to Paris. Random.
ed. Holiday Guide to Rome. Random.
ed. Holiday Guide to Scandinavia. Random.
ed. Holiday Guide to Spain. Random.
ed. Holiday Guide to West Germany. Random.
xHoliday Magazine Editors.
American Panorama, East of the Mississippi.
Arno.
Holiday Editors. see Holiday.
Holiday, Ensor.
xHoliday, Ensor.
Altair Design. Pantheon.
Altair Design 3. Pantheon.
Altair Design 4. Pantheon.
Holiday Magazine Editors. see Holiday.
Holiday, Mike.
xHoliday, Mike.
Bagtime. Popular Lib.
Holifield, E. Brooks.
xHolifield, E. Brooks.
The Covenant Sealed: The Development of
Puritan Sacramental Theology in Old & New
England, 1570-1720. Yale U Pr.
The Gentlemen Theologians: American
Theology in Southern Culture, 1795-1860.
Duke.
Holinshed, Raphael.
xHolinshed, Raphael.
Holinshed's Chronicles of England, Scotland &
Ireland. AMS Pr.
Holinshed's Chronicles: Richard I!, 1398-1400,
Henry IV & Henry V. Greenwood.
Holl, Adelaide.
xHoll, Adelaide.
Colors Are Nice. Western Pub.
Gus Gets the Message. Garrard.
If We Could Make Wishes. Garrard.
Let's Count. A-W.
The Little Viking. Western Pub.
The Long Birthday. Garrard.
Moon Mouse. Random.
One Kitten for Kim. A-W.
Remarkable Egg. Lothrop.
Small Bear Solves a Mystery. Garrard.
Sylvester, the Mouse with the Musical Ear.
Western Pub.
Holl, Adolf.
xHoll, Adolf.
Death & the Devil. Seabury.
Holl, Karl.
xHoll, Karl.
The Reconstruction of Morality. Augsburg.
Holladay, William L. see Holladay, William Lee.

Holladay, William Lee.
xHolladay, William L.
Architecture of Jeremiah, 1-20. Bucknell U Pr.
Hollaender, A. see Hollaender, Alexander.
Hollaender, Alexander, 1898-
xHollaender, A.
ed. Chemical Mutagens: Principles & Methods
for Their Detection. Plenum Pub.
xHollaender, Alexander.
ed. The Biosaline Concept: An Approach to
the Utilization of Underexploited Resources.
Plenum Pub.
ed. Genetic Engineering for Nitrogen Fixation.
Plenum Pub.
Holland, Allyne. see Holland, Allyne S.
Holland, Allyne S.
xHolland, Allyne.
Student Journalist & the Literary Magazine.
Rosen Pr.
Holland, Barbara.
xHolland, Barbara.
The Pony Problem. Schol Bk Serv.
The Pony Problem. Dutton.
Prisoners at the Kitchen Table. HM.
Holland, Barron.
xHolland, Barron.
Compiled by Popular Hinduism & Hindu
Mythology: An Annotated Bibliography.
Greenwood.
Holland, Brad, 1943-
xHolland, Brad.
The Human Scandals. T Y Crowell.
Holland, Cecelia, 1943-
xHolland, Cecelia.
Floating Worlds. Knopf.
Floating Worlds. PB.
Great Maria. Knopf.
xHolland, Cecilia.
Great Maria. Warner Bks.
Holland, Cecilia. see Holland, Cecelia.
Holland, Charles D. see Holland, Charles Donald.
Holland, Charles Donald.
xHolland, Charles D.
Fundamentals of Chemical Reaction
Engineering. P-H.
Holland, Claude V.
xHolland, Claude V.
More of Little Top Sail. Hol-Land Bks.
Tortugas Run. Hol-Land Bks.
Holland, Clifton L., 1939-
xHolland, Clifton L.
The Religious Dimension in Hispanic Los
Angeles: A Protestant Case Study. William
Carey Lib.
Holland, Clive, 1866-1959
xHolland, Clive.
Thomas Hardy's Wessex Scene. R West.
Holland, Dan. see Holland, Daniel John.
Holland, Daniel John.
xHolland, Dan.
The Trout Fisherman's Bible. Doubleday.
Holland, David.
xHolland, David.
If Jesus Came Back to Earth. Croydon.
Holland, Edwin C. see Holland, Edwin Clifford.
Holland, Edwin Clifford.
xHolland, Edwin C.
Refutation of the Calumnies Circulated Against
the Southern & Western States, Respecting
the Institution & Existence of Slavery Among
Them. Negro U Pr.
Holland, Ellen B. see Holland, Ellen Morland (Bowie).
Holland, Ellen Morland (Bowie).
xHolland, Ellen B.
Quiet, Please. Branch-Smith.
Holland, Ernest O. see Holland, Ernest Otto.
Holland, Ernest Otto, 1874-1950
xHolland, Ernest O.

Pennsylvania State Normal Schools & Public
School System. AMS Pr.
Holland, Francis R. *see* Holland, Francis Ross.
Holland, Francis Ross, 1927-
xHolland, Francis R.
America's Lighthouses: Their Illustrated
History Since 1716. Greene.
Holland, Frederic M. *see* Holland, Frederic May.
Holland, Frederic May, 1836-1908
xHolland, Frederic M.
Frederick Douglass: The Colored Orator.
Negro U Pr.
xHolland, Frederick.
Frederick Douglass: The Colored Orator.
Haskell.
Holland, Frederick. *see* Holland, Frederic May.
Holland, Heinrich D.
xHolland, Heinrich D.
The Chemistry of the Atmosphere & Oceans.
Wiley.
Holland, Henry. *see* Holland, Henry Scott.
Holland, Henry Scott.
xHolland, Henry.
Memoir of Madame Jenny Lind-Goldschmidt:
Her Early Art-Life & Dramatic Career
1820-1851. Longwood Pr.
Holland, Isabelle.
xHolland, Isabelle.
Alan & the Animal Kingdom. Dell.
Alan the Animal Kingdom. Lippincott.
Amanda's Choice. Lippincott.
Counterpoint. Rawson Wade.
Hitchhike. Dell.
Hitchhike. Lippincott.
Journey for Three. HM.
Now Is Not Too Late. Lothrop.
Of Love & Death & Other Journeys. Dell.
Of Love & Death & Other Journeys.
Lippincott.
Holland, James G. *see* Holland, James Gordon.
Holland, James Gordon.
xHolland, James G.
Analysis of Behavior in Planning Instruction.
A-W.
Holland, Janet.
xHolland, Janet.
Mathematical Sociology: A Selective
Annotated Bibliography. Schocken.
Holland, Joe.
xHolland, Joe.
The American Journey: A Theology in the
Americas Working Paper. IDOC.
Holland, John.
xHolland, John.
Come to France. Watts.
Holland, John H. *see* Holland, John Henry.
Holland, John Henry, 1929-
xHolland, John H.
Adaptation in Natural & Artificial Systems: An
Introductory Analysis with Applications to
Biology, Control & Artificial Intelligence. U
of Mich Pr.
Holland, Josiah G. *see* Holland, Josiah Gilbert.
Holland, Josiah Gilbert, 1819-1881
xHolland, Josiah G.
The Marble Prophecy, & Other Poems. Arno.
Holland, Joyce. *see* Holland, Joyce Flint.
Holland, Joyce F. *see* Holland, Joyce Flint.
Holland, Joyce Flint.
xHolland, Joyce.
Porter, the Pouting Pigeon. Denison.
xHolland, Joyce F.
Danny & the Old Pest. Denison.
Holland, L.
xHolland, L.
Vacuum Manual. Methuen Inc.
Holland, Louise A. *see* Holland, Louise Adams.
Holland, Louise Adams.
xHolland, Louise A.

Lucretius & the Transpadanes. Princeton U Pr.
Holland, Marion, 1908-
xHolland, Marion.
No Room for a Dog. Random.
Holland, Maurice.
xHolland, Maurice.
Architects of Aviation. Arno.
Holland, Morris K.
xHolland, Morris K.
Psychology: An Introduction to Human
Behavior. Heath.
Using Psychology: Principles of Behavior &
Your Life. Little.
Holland, Nina, 1934-
xHolland, Nina.
Inkle Loom Weaving. Watson-Guptill.
Holland, Norman N. *see* Holland, Norman Norwood.
Holland, Norman Norwood, 1927-
xHolland, Norman N.
The Dynamics of Literary Response. Norton.
Psychoanalysis & Shakespeare. Octagon.
Holland, Richard.
xHolland, Richard.
Design of Resonant Piezoelectric Devices. MIT
Pr.
Holland, Rupert S. *see* Holland, Rupert Sargent.
Holland, Rupert Sargent, 1878-1952
xHolland, Rupert S.
ed. Historic Poems & Ballads. Arno.
Holland, Ruth. *see* Holland, Ruth (Robins).
Holland, Ruth (Robins), 1924-
xHolland, Ruth.
Forgotten Minority: America's Tenant Farmers
& Migrant Workers. Macmillan.
Holland, Sheila.
xHolland, Sheila.
Dancing Hill. Playboy Pbks.
Holland Society of New York.
xTheHolland Society of New York.
Records of the Reformed Dutch Church of
Albany, New York, 1683-1809. Genealog
Pub.
Holland, Stuart.
xHolland, Stuart.
ed. Beyond Capitalist Planning. St Martin.
Capital Versus the Regions. St Martin.
The Regional Problem. St Martin.
Holland, T. *see* Holland, Tim.
Holland, Tim.
xHolland, T.
Backgammon for People Who Hate to Lose.
McKay.
Holland, Vicki. *see* Holland, Viki.
Holland, Viki.
xHolland, Vicki.
photos by How to Photograph Your World.
Scribner.
Holland, Vyvyan. *see* Holland, Vyvyan Beresford.
Holland, Vyvyan Beresford, 1886-1967
xHolland, Vyvyan.
Oscar Wilde & His World. Scribner.
Son of Oscar Wilde. Arden Lib.
Son of Oscar Wilde. Greenwood.
Son of Oscar Wilde. Norwood Edns.
Hollanda, Francisco De.
xHollanda, Francisco De.
Four Dialogues on Painting. Hyperion Conn.
Hollander, Carlton.
xHollander, Carlton.
How to Build a Sauna. Sterling.
Hollander, Edward. *see* Hollander, Edward D.
Hollander, Edward D.
xHollander, Edward.
The Future of Small Business. Arno.
Hollander, Edwin P. *see* Hollander, Edwin Paul.
Hollander, Edwin Paul.
xHollander, Edwin P.

ed. Classic Contributions to Social Psychology.
Oxford U Pr.
Leadership Dynamics: A Practical Guide to
Effective Relationships. Free Pr.
Hollander, Gayle D. *see* Hollander, Gayle Durham.
Hollander, Gayle Durham.
xHollander, Gayle D.
Soviet Political Indoctrination: Developments
in Mass Media & Propaganda Since Stalin.
Irvington.
Hollander, Jacob H. *see* Hollander, Jacob Harry.
Hollander, Jacob Harry, 1871-1940
xHollander, Jacob H.
The Abolition of Poverty. Arno.
Studies in American Trade Unionism. Arno.
ed. Studies in American Trade Unionism.
Kelley.
Hollander, John.
xHollander, John.
Spectral Emanations: New & Selected Poems.
Atheneum.
Hollander, Myles.
xHollander, Myles.
Nonparametric Statistical Methods. Wiley.
Hollander, Nicole.
xHollander, Nicole.
I'm in Training to Be Tall & Blonde. St
Martin.
Hollander, Patricia.
xHollander, Patricia A.
Legal Handbook for Educators. Westview.
Hollander, Patricia A. *see* Hollander, Patricia.
Hollander, Paul.
xHollander, Paul.
Soviet & American Society: A Comparison.
Oxford U Pr.
Soviet & American Society: A Comparison. U
of Chicago Pr.
Hollander, Samuel.
xHollander, Samuel.
Economics of Adam Smith. U of Toronto Pr.
The Economics of David Ricardo. U of
Toronto Pr.
Sources of Increased Efficiency: A Study of
DuPont Rayon Plants. MIT Pr.
Hollander, Stanley C., 1919-
xHollander, Stanley C.
Multinational Retailing. Mich St U Busn.
Hollander, Zander.
xHollander, Zander.
The Complete Handbook of Pro Basketball,
1981. NAL.
Great Moments in Pro Football. Random.
Illustrated Sports Record Book. NAL.
The Modern Encyclopedia of Basketball.
Doubleday.
More Strange but True Football Stories.
Random.
ed. The Pro Basketball Encyclopedia. Corwin.
ed. Strange But True Football Stories. Random.
xHollander, Zandes.
ed. Encyclopedia of Sports Talk. Corwin.
Hollander, Zandes. *see* Hollander, Zander.
Hollaran, Carolyn.
xHollaran, Carolyn.
Meet the Stars of Country Music. Aurora Pubs.
Hollaway, Ida N. *see* Hollaway, Ida Nelle.
Hollaway, Ida Nelle.
xHollaway, Ida N.
To Teach a Child. Broadman.
xHollaway, Ida Nelle.
Punching Holes in the Darkness. Broadman.
Hollaway, Stephen. *see* Hollaway, Steve.
Hollaway, Steve.
xHollaway, Stephen.
Working Things Out. Broadman.
Holle, F. *see* Holle, Fritz.
Holle, Fritz.
xHolle, F.

ed. Vagotomy: Latest Advances with Special
Reference to Gastric & Duodenal Ulcer
Disease. Springer-Verlag.
Hollen, Norma. *see* Hollen, Norma R.
Hollen, Norma R.
xHollen, Norma.
Pattern Making by the Flat Pattern Method.
Burgess.
Textiles. Macmillan.
xHollen, Norma R.
Pattern Making by the Flat Pattern Method.
Burgess.
Hollender, E. A.
xHollender, Edward A.
Humanity at the Crossroads. Philos Lib.
Hollender, Edward A. *see* Hollender, E. A.
Hollender, L. F.
xHollender, Louis F.
Highly Selective Vagotomy. Masson Pub.
Hollender, Louis F. *see* Hollender, L. F.
Holler, Frederick L.
xHoller, Frederick L.
The Information Sources of Political Science.
ABC-Clio.
Holler, Ronald F.
xHoller, Ronald F.
Human Services Technology. Mosby.
Holleran, Mary P. *see* Holleran, Mary Patricia.
Holleran, Mary Patricia, 1905-
xHolleran, Mary P.
Church & State in Guatemala. Octagon.
Holles, Robert. *see* Holles, Robert O.
Holles, Robert O.
xHolles, Robert.
Spawn. Berkley Pub.
Spawn. BJ Pub Group.
Spawn. Doubleday.
Holley, Donald, 1940-
xHolley, Donald.
Uncle Sam's Farmers: The New Deal
Communities in the Lower Mississippi Valley.
U of Ill Pr.
Holley, Horace, 1887-
xHolley, Horace.
Religion for Mankind. Baha'i.
Holley, I. B. *see* Holley, Irving Brinton.
Holley, Irving Brinton, 1919-
xHolley, I. B.
Ideas & Weapons: Exploitation of the Aerial
Weapon by the United States During World
War I. Shoe String.
Holley, Raymond.
xHolley, Raymond.
Religious Education & Religious
Understanding: An Introduction to the
Philosophy of Religious Education. Routledge
& Kegan.
Holley, Sallie.
xHolley, Sallie.
Life for Liberty: Anti-Slavery & Other Letters
of Sallie Holley. Negro U Pr.
Holley, W. *see* Holley, William C.
Holley, William C.
xHolley, W.
Plantation South. Da Capo.
xHolley, William C.
The Plantation South, 1934-7. Arno.
Holliday, Bob.
xHolliday, Bob.
Norton Story. Aztex.
Holliday, Carl, 1879-1936
xHolliday, Carl.
A History of Southern Literature. Gordon Pr.
History of Southern Literature. Kennikat.
Holliday, Laurel, 1946-
xHolliday, Laurel.
The Violent Sex: Male Psychobiology & the
Evolution of Consciousness. Bluestocking.
Holliday, Leslie.
xHolliday, Leslie.

ed. Composite Materials. Elsevier.
Holling, C. S.
xHolling, C. S.
ed. Adaptive Environmental Assessment &
Management. Wiley.
Hollingdale, R. J.
xHollingdale, R. J.
Thomas Mann: a Critical Study. Bucknell U Pr.
Hollings, Michael.
xHollings, Michael.
Living Priesthood. Our Sunday Visitor.
Hollingshead, Arthur D. *see* Hollingshead, Arthur Dack.
Hollingshead, Arthur Dack, 1894-
xHollingshead, Arthur D.
An Evaluation of the Use of Certain
Educational & Mental Measurements for
Purposes of Classification. AMS Pr.
Hollingsworth. *see* Hollingsworth, Abner Thomas.
Hollingsworth, Abner Thomas.
xHollingsworth.
Readings in Basic Management. Dryden Pr.
Hollingsworth, Buckner.
xHollingsworth, Buckner.
Gardening on Main Street. Rutgers U Pr.
Hollingsworth, J. Rogers. *see* Hollingsworth, Joseph
Rogers.
Hollingsworth, Joseph Rogers.
xHollingsworth, J. Rogers.
Dimensions in Urban History: Historical &
Social Science Perspectives. U of Wis Pr.
ed. Social Theory & Public Policy. Am Acad
Pol Soc Sci.
Whirligig of Politics: Democracy of Cleveland
& Bryan. U of Chicago Pr.
Hollingsworth, M. J. *see* Hollingsworth, Michael John.
Hollingsworth, Michael John.
xHollingsworth, M. J.
Principles & Processes of Biology. Methuen
Inc.
Hollingsworth, T. H. *see* Hollingsworth, Thomas Henry.
Hollingsworth, Thomas Henry.
xHollingsworth, T. H.
Historical Demography. Cornell U Pr.
Hollingworth, G. E. *see* Hollingworth, Gertrude Eleanor.
Hollingworth, Gertrude E. *see* Hollingworth, Gertrude
Eleanor.
Hollingworth, Gertrude Eleanor.
xHollingworth, G. E.
A Primer of Literary Criticism. Folcroft.
xHollingworth, Gertrude E.
A Primer of Literary Criticism. Arden Lib.
Hollingworth, Leta. *see* Hollingworth, Leta (Stetter).
Hollingworth, Leta (Stetter), 1886-1939
xHollingworth, Leta.
Functional Periodicity: Experimental Study of
the Mental & Motor Abilities of Women
During Menstruation. AMS Pr.
Psychology of Special Disability in Spelling.
AMS Pr.
Hollis, Christopher, 1902-
xHollis, Christopher.
Can Parliament Survive. Kennikat.
Dr. Johnson. R West.
Dr. Johnson: 1707-1784. Darby Bks.
Dryden. Folcroft.
Dryden. Haskell.
Hollis, Ernest V. *see* Hollis, Ernest Victor.
Hollis, Ernest Victor.
xHollis, Ernest V.
Social Work Education in the United States:
The Report of a Study Made for the National
Council on Social Work Education.
Greenwood.
Hollis, Harry.
xHollis, Harry.
ed. A Matter of Life & Death: Christian
Perspectives. Broadman.
Hollis, Jocelyn.
xHollis, Jocelyn.

Sex Songs. Am Poetry Pr.
Hollis, John H.
xHollis, John H.
ed. Developmental Deficiencies: A
Comparative Approach. Mss Info.
Hollis, John P. *see* Hollis, John Porter.
Hollis, John Porter, 1872-
xHollis, John P.
The Early Period of Reconstruction in South
Carolina. AMS Pr.
Hollis, Joseph. *see* Hollis, Joseph William.
Hollis, Joseph W. *see* Hollis, Joseph William.
Hollis, Joseph William.
xHollis, Joseph.
Psychological Report Writing: Theory &
Practice. Accel Devel.
xHollis, Joseph W.
Pupil Personnel Staff & Program Development
Using LORS Experiential Technique. Accel
Devel.
Hollis, L. Y. *see* Hollis, Loye Yvorne.
Hollis, Loye Yvorne.
xHollis, L. Y.
Acquiring Competencies to Teach Mathematics
in Elementary Schools. Prof Educ Pubn.
Hollis, Lucile Ussery.
xHollis, Lucille U.
Career Education & Business Education. HM.
Hollis, Lucille U. *see* Hollis, Lucile Ussery.
Hollis, Patricia.
xHollis, Patricia.
ed. Pressure from Without in Early Victorian
England. St Martin.
Hollister, C. Warren. *see* Hollister, Charles Warren.
Hollister, Charles Warren.
xHollister, C. Warren.
Medieval Europe: A Short History. Wiley.
Hollister, Herbert A.
xHollister, Herbert A.
Algebra & Trigonometry. Har-Row.
Hollister, Leo E.
xHollister, Leo E.
Clinical Pharmacology of Psychotherapeutic
Drugs. Churchill.
Clinical Use of Psychotherapeutic Drugs. C C
Thomas.
Hollister, Paul. *see* Hollister, Paul M.
Hollister, Paul M.
xHollister, Paul.
Paperweights: Flowers Which Clothe the
Meadows. Corning.
Hollmann, Clide. *see* Hollmann, Clide Anne.
Hollmann, Clide Anne.
xHollmann, Clide.
Pontiac, King of the Great Lakes. Hastings.
Hollo, Anselm.
xHollo, Anselm.
Finite Continued. Blue Wind.
Hollon, W. Eugene. *see* Hollon, William Eugene.
Hollon, William Eugene, 1913-
xHollon, W. Eugene.
The Great American Desert Then & Now. U
of Nebr Pr.
Southwest: Old & New. U of Nebr Pr.
Hollowak, Thomas L.
xHollowak, Thomas L.
Index to Marriages & Deaths in the
(Baltimore) Sun 1837-1850. Genealog Pub.
Index to Marriages in the (Baltimore) Sun,
1851-1860. Genealog Pub.
Holloway, Charles A.
xHolloway, Charles A.
Decision Making Under Uncertainty: Models &
Choices. P-H.
Holloway, John.
xHolloway, John.

Later English Broadside Ballads. Routledge & Kegan.

ed. Later English Broadside Ballads. U of Nebr Pr.

The Lion Hunt: A Pursuit of Poetry & Reality. Shoe String.

ed. State & Capital: A Marxist Debate. U of Tex Pr.

Holloway, John W. *see* Holloway, John Wesley.

Holloway, John Wesley.
xHolloway, John W.
From the Desert. AMS Pr.

Holloway, Joseph.
xHolloway, Joseph.
Joseph Holloway's Abbey Theatre: A Selection from His Unpublished Journal "Impressions of a Dublin Playgoer". S Ill U Pr.

Holloway, L. *see* Holloway, Louis G.

Holloway, Louis G.
xHolloway, L.
Full Time Gambler. Lyle Stuart.

Holloway, Marcella M. *see* Holloway, Marcella Marie.

Holloway, Marcella Marie, 1913-
xHolloway, Marcella M.
The Prosodic Theory of Gerard Manley Hopkins. Intl Schol Bk Serv.

Holloway, Maurice R.
xHolloway, Maurice R.
Introduction to Natural Theology. Irvington.

Holloway, Nancy M. *see* Holloway, Nancy Meyer.

Holloway, Nancy Meyer, 1947-
xHolloway, Nancy M.
Nursing the Critically Ill Adult. A-W.

Holloway, Richard.
xHolloway, Richard.
A New Heaven. Eerdmans.

Holloway, William J. *see* Holloway, William James.

Holloway, William James, 1873-
xHolloway, William J.
Participation in Curriculum Making As a Means of Supervision of Rural Schools. AMS Pr.

Hollwich, F. *see* Hollwich, Fritz.

Hollwich, Fritz, 1909-
xHollwich, F.
The Influence of Ocular Light Perception on Metabolism in Man & Animal. Springer-Verlag.

Holm, Anne, 1922-
xHolm, Anne.
North to Freedom. HarBraceJ.
xHolm, Anne S.
North to Freedom. HarBraceJ.

Holm, Anne S. *see* Holm, Anne.

Holm, Bill.
xHolm, Bill.
Edward S. Curtis in the Land of the War Canoes: A Pioneer Cinematographer in the Pacific Northwest. U of Wash Pr.
Northwest Coast Indian Art: An Analysis of Form. U of Wash Pr.

Holm, Don.
xHolm, Don.
Don Holm's Book of Food Drying, Pickling & Smoke Curing. Caxton.

Holm, H. H. *see* Holm, Hans Henrik.

Holm, Hans Henrik.
xHolm, H. H.
Abdominal Ultrasound. Univ Park.

Holm, Leroy. *see* Holm, Leroy G.

Holm, Leroy G.
xHolm, Leroy.
A Geographical Atlas of World Weeds. Wiley.
xHolm, LeRoy G.
The World's Worst Weeds: Distribution & Biology. U Pr of Hawaii.

Holm, Mayling M. *see* Holm, Mayling Mack.

Holm, Mayling Mack.
xHolm, Mayling M.

illus. A Forest Christmas. Har-Row.

Holm, Niels W.
xHolm, Niels W.
ed. Manual on Radiation Dosimetry. Dekker.

Holm, Richard. *see* Holm, Richard W.

Holm, Richard W.
xHolm, Richard.
Introduction to the Plant Sciences. McGraw.

Holman (A. J.) Company, Philadelphia.
xHolman Company.
Holman Bible Concordance. Holman.

Holman, B. L. *see* Holman, Bruce Leonard.

Holman, B. Leonard. *see* Holman, Bruce Leonard.

Holman, Bruce Leonard.
xHolman, B. L.
ed. Regional Pulmonary Function in Health & Disease. S Karger.
Regional Pulmonary Function in Health & Disease. Univ Park.
xHolman, B. Leonard.
ed. Principles of Cardiovascular Nuclear Medicine. Grune.

Holman, C. Hugh. *see* Holman, Clarence Hugh.

Holman, Clarence Hugh, 1914-
xHolman, C. Hugh.
The American Novel Through Henry James. AHM Pub.
A Handbook to Literature. Bobbs.
The Loneliness at the Core: Studies in Thomas Wolfe. La State U Pr.
Windows on the World: Essays on American Social Fiction. U of Tenn Pr.

Holman Company. *see* Holman (A. J.) Company, Philadelphia.

Holman, Felice.
xHolman, Felice.
At the Top of My Voice & Other Poems. Scribner.
The Drac: French Tales of Dragons & Demons. Scribner.
The Murderer. Scribner.
Professor Diggins' Dragons. Macmillan.

Holman, Jack. *see* Holman, Jack Phillip.

Holman, Jack P. *see* Holman, Jack Phillip.

Holman, Jack Phillip.
xHolman, Jack.
Thermodynamics. McGraw.
xHolman, Jack P.
Experimental Methods for Engineers. McGraw.
Thermodynamics. McGraw.

Holman, L. Bruce.
xHolman, L. Bruce.
Cinema Equipment You Can Build. Walnut Pr.

Holman, Michael.
xHolman, Michael.
Cats. Watts.

Holman, Robert.
xHolman, Robert.
Poverty: Explanations of Social Deprivation. St Martin.

Holman, Sona.
xHolman, Sona.
How to Lie About Your Age. Macmillan.

Holmberg, Bengt, 1942-
xHolmberg, Bengt.
Paul & Power: The Structure of Authority in the Primitive Church As Reflected in the Pauline Epistles. Fortress.

Holmberg, Borje.
xHolmberg, Borje.
Distance Education: A Survey & Bibliography. Nichols Pub.

Holmberg, Rita.
xHolmberg, Rita.
Farm Journal's Great Dishes from the Oven. S&S.

Holme, Charles, 1848-1923
xHolme, Charles.

ed. Art in Photography. Arno.

Holmelund, Paul, 1890-
xHolmelund, Paul.
Ride Gently - Ride Well. Arco.

Holmer, Paul L.
xHolmer, Paul L.
The Grammar of Faith. Har-Row.

Holmes, Arthur.
xHolmes, Arthur.
Holmes Principles of Physical Geology. Halsted Pr.

Holmes, Arthur F. *see* Holmes, Arthur Frank.

Holmes, Arthur Frank, 1924-
xHolmes, Arthur F.
All Truth Is God's Truth. Eerdmans.
The Idea of a Christian College. Eerdmans.

Holmes, Arthur W. *see* Holmes, Arthur Wellington.

Holmes, Arthur Wellington.
xHolmes, Arthur W.
Auditing: Standards & Procedures. Irwin.
Holmes & Moore Audit Case. Irwin.

Holmes, Bernham.
xHolmes, Burnham.
The World's First Baseball Game. Silver.

Holmes, Beth.
xHolmes, Beth.
The Whipping Boy. BJ Pub Group.

Holmes, Brian.
xHolmes, Brian.
ed. Educational Policy & the Mission Schools: Case Studies from the British Empire. Humanities.

Holmes, Burnham, 1942-
xHolmes, Burnham.
Basic Training: A Portrait of Today's Army. Schol Bk Serv.
The First Seeing Eye Dogs. Silver.

Holmes, Burnham. *see* Holmes, Bernham.

Holmes, C. *see* Holmes, Clive.

Holmes, C. Raymond, 1929-
xHolmes, C. Raymond.
Stranger in My Home. Southern Pub.

Holmes, Charles H. *see* Holmes, Charles Henry.

Holmes, Charles Henry, 1874-
xHolmes, Charles H.
Ethiopia, the Land of Promise: A Book with a Purpose. AMS Pr.

Holmes, Charles J. *see* Holmes, Charles John.

Holmes, Charles John, Sir, 1868-1936
xHolmes, Charles J.
Grammar of the Arts. AMS Pr.

Holmes, Charles M. *see* Holmes, Charles Mason.

Holmes, Charles Mason, 1923-
xHolmes, Charles M.
Aldous Huxley & the Way to Reality. Greenwood.

Holmes, Charles S. *see* Holmes, Charles Shiveley.

Holmes, Charles Shiveley.
xHolmes, Charles S.
The Clocks of Columbus: The Literary Career of James Thurber. Atheneum.

Holmes, Clive.
xHolmes, C.
The Eastern Association in the English Civil War. Cambridge U Pr.

Holmes, Colin, 1938-
xHolmes, Colin.
ed. Immigrants & Minorities in British Society. Allen Unwin.

Holmes, Deborah A. *see* Holmes, Deborah Aydt.

Holmes, Deborah Aydt, 1949-
xHolmes, Deborah A.
Survival Prayers for Young Mothers. John Knox.

Holmes, Donald J.
xHolmes, Donald J.
Adolescent in Psychotherapy. Little.

Holmes, Dwight O. *see* Holmes, Dwight Oliver Wendell.

Holmes, Dwight Oliver Wendell, 1877-
xHolmes, Dwight O.

Evolution of the Negro College. AMS Pr.
Evolution of the Negro College. Arno.

Holmes, Edward.
xHolmes, Edward.
Great Men of Science. Watts.
Horse & Pony Care in Pictures. Arco.
The Life of Mozart. Da Capo.
The Life of Mozart. Greenwood.
Ramble Among the Musicians of Germany. Da Capo.

Holmes, Efner T. see Holmes, Efner Tudor.

Holmes, Efner Tudor.
xHolmes, Efner T.
Amy's Goose. T Y Crowell.
Carrie's Gift. Philomel.
The Christmas Cat. T Y Crowell.

Holmes, Emma.
xHolmes, Emma.
The Diary of Miss Emma Holmes, 1861-1866. La State U Pr.

Holmes, Ernest. see Holmes, Ernest Shurtleff.

Holmes, Ernest Shurtleff.
xHolmes, Ernest.
This Thing Called Life. Dodd.

Holmes, F. see Holmes, Fred R.

Holmes, Fred R.
xHolmes, F.
Prejudice & Discrimination: Can We Eliminate Them. P-H.

Holmes, George, 1927-
xHolmes, George.
Dante. Hill & Wang.
The Good Parliament. Oxford U Pr.
Toward an Effective Pulpit Ministry. Gospel Pub.

Holmes, George. see Holmes, George Andrew.

Holmes, George Andrew.
xHolmes, George.
Later Middle Ages, 1272-1485. Norton.

Holmes, Isaac.
xHolmes, Isaac.
An Account of the United States of America. Arno.

Holmes, Jack E. see Holmes, Jack Ellsworth.

Holmes, Jack Ellsworth.
xHolmes, Jack E.
Politics in New Mexico. U of NM Pr.

Holmes, Jean. see Holmes, Marjorie Jean.

Holmes, John C. see Holmes, John Clellon.

Holmes, John Clellon, 1926-
xHolmes, John C.
Go. Appel.
Go. NAL.

Holmes, John H. see Holmes, John Haynes.

Holmes, John Haynes.
xHolmes, John H.
The Enduring Significance of Emerson's Divinity School Address. Folcroft.
Palestine To-Day & To-Morrow: A Gentile's Survey of Zionism. Arno.

Holmes, John W. see Holmes, John Wendell.

Holmes, John Wendell, 1910-
xHolmes, John W.
The Shaping of Peace: Canada & the Search for World Order 1943-57. U of Toronto Pr.

Holmes, L. P.
xHolmes, L. P.
Catch & Saddle. Popular Lib.

Holmes, L. P. see Holmes, Llewellyn Perry.

Holmes, Llewellyn Perry, 1895-
xHolmes, L. P.
Brandon's Empire. Popular Lib.
Delta Deputy. Popular Lib.
High Starlight. Popular Lib.
Hill Smoke. Popular Lib.
Somewhere They Die. Popular Lib.
Summer Range. Popular Lib.

Holmes, Lulu H. see Holmes, Lulu Haskell.

Holmes, Lulu Haskell, 1899-
xHolmes, Lulu H.

History of the Position of Dean of Women in a Selected Group of Co-Educational Colleges & Universities in the U. S.. AMS Pr.

Holmes, Malcolm H. see Holmes, Malcom Haughton.

Holmes, Malcom Haughton, 1906-
xHolmes, Malcolm.
Conducting an Amateur Orchestra. Harvard U Pr.

Holmes, Marjorie, 1910-
xHolmes, Marjorie.
Hold Me up a Little Longer, Lord. Doubleday.
Hold Me up a Little Longer, Lord. G K Hall.
How Can I Find You, God?. Bantam.
How Can I Find You, God?. Doubleday.
Lord, Let Me Love: A Marjorie Holmes Treasury. Doubleday.
Love & Laughter. Bantam.
Love & Laughter. Doubleday.
Love & Laughter. G K Hall.
Two from Galilee. Bantam.
Two from Galilee. Revell.
Who Am I God?. Bantam.
Who Am I, God. Doubleday.

Holmes, Marjorie Jean.
xHolmes, Jean.
The Australian Federal System. Allen Unwin.
The Government of Victoria. U of Queensland Pr.

Holmes, Mary J. see Holmes, Mary Jane (Hawes).

Holmes, Mary Jane (Hawes), 1828-1907
xHolmes, Mary J.
Lena Rivers. AMS Pr.
Lena Rivers. Scholarly.

Holmes, Monica. see Holmes, Monica Bychowski.

Holmes, Monica Bychowski.
xHolmes, Monica.
jt. auth. The Therapeutic Classroom. Aronson.

Holmes, Oliver W. see Holmes, Oliver Wendel.

Holmes, Oliver Wendel, 1809-1894
xHolmes, Oliver W.
Autocrat of the Breakfast-Table. Airmont.

Holmes, Oliver Wendell, 1841-1935
xHolmes, Oliver W.
The Common Law. Little.
The Guardian Angel. Arden Lib.
The Guardian Angel. Irvington.
Oliver Wendell Holmes: Representative Selections. AMS Pr.
Over the Teacups. Arden Lib.
Ralph Waldo Emerson. Gale.
Ralph Waldo Emerson. R West.

Holmes, Paul C.
xHolmes, Paul C.
The Touch of a Poet. Har-Row.

Holmes, R. B. see Holmes, Richard B.

Holmes, Reed M.
xHolmes, Reed M.
The Patriarchs. Herald Hse.

Holmes, Richard B.
xHolmes, R. B.
A Course on Optimization & Best Approximation. Springer-Verlag.
Geometric Functional Analysis & Its Applications. Springer-Verlag.

Holmes, Roy.
xHolmes, Roy.
Easy Magic: Good Tricks & How to Present Them. Har-Row.

Holmes, Thomas R. see Holmes, Thomas Rice Edward.

Holmes, Thomas Rice Edward, 1855-1933
xHolmes, Thomas R.
Ancient Britain & the Invasions of Julius Caesar. Arno.
The Architect of the Roman Empire. AMS Pr.
Caesar's Conquest of Gaul. AMS Pr.

Holmes, Tommy, 1903-
xHolmes, Tommy.
The Dodgers. Macmillan.

Holmes, Urban. see Holmes, Urban Tigner.

Holmes, Urban T. see Holmes, Urban Tigner.

Holmes, Urban Tigner, 1900-
xHolmes, Urban.
The Priest in Community: Exploring the Roots of Ministry. Seabury.
xHolmes, Urban T.
Chretien de Troyes. Irvington.

Holmes, W. H. see Holmes, William Henry.

Holmes, William Henry, 1846-1933
xHolmes, W. H.
Archaeological Studies Among the Ancient Cities of Mexico. Kraus Repr.

Holmes-Walker, W. A., 1926-
xHolmes-Walker, W. A.
Polymer Conversion. Halsted Pr.

Holmgren, Frederick, 1926-
xHolmgren, Frederick.
The God Who Cares: A Christian Looks at Judaism. John Knox.

Holmgren, John H.
xHolmgren, John H.
Purchasing for the Health Care Facility. C C Thomas.

Holmgren, Rod.
xHolmgren, Rod.
The Mass Media Book. P-H.

Holmquist, Eve.
xHolmquist, Eve.
The Giant Giraffe. Carolrhoda Bks.

Holoien, Martin O., 1928-
xHoloien, Martin O.
Computers & Their Societal Impact. Wiley.

Holoman, D. Kern, 1947-
xHoloman, D. Kern.
The Creative Process in the Autograph Musical Documents of Hector Berlioz, C. 1818-1840. Univ Microfilms.

Holorenshaw, Henry.
xHolorenshaw, Henry.
Levellers & the English Revolution. Fertig.

Holroyd, Sam V. see Holroyd, Samuel V.

Holroyd, Samuel V., 1931-
xHolroyd, Sam V.
ed. Clinical Pharmacology in Dental Practice. Mosby.

Holroyd, Stuart.
xHolroyd, Stuart.
PSI & the Consciousness Explosion. Taplinger.

Holscher, Harry H. see Holscher, Harry Heltman.

Holscher, Harry Heltman.
xHolscher, Harry H.
Simplified Statistical Analysis: Handbook of Methods, Examples & Tables. CBI Pub.

Holst, Alison.
xHolst, Alison.
More Food Without Fuss. Intl Pubns Serv.

Holst, Imogen, 1907-
xHolst, Imogen.
Bach. T Y Crowell.
Gustav Holst, a Biography. Oxford U Pr.
Music of Gustav Holst. Oxford U Pr.

Holst, Spencer.
xHolst, Spencer.
Spencer Holst Stories. Berkley Pub.
Spencer Holst Stories. Horizon.

Holsti, O. R. see Holsti, Ole R.

Holsti, Ole R.
xHolsti, O. R.
Content Analysis for the Social Sciences & Humanities. A-W.

Holstrum, Gary L.
xHolstrum, Gary L.
Operational Audits of Production Control. Inst Inter Aud.

Holt, Alfred H. see Holt, Alfred Hubbard.

Holt, Alfred Hubbard, 1897-
xHolt, Alfred H.
American Place Names. Gale.

Holt, Anne, 1899-
xHolt, Anne.

Life of Joseph Priestley. Greenwood.

Holt, Charles C.
xHolt, Charles C.
Unemployment-Inflation Dilemma: A
Manpower Solution. Urban Inst.

Holt, Claire.
xHolt, Claire.
Art in Indonesia: Continuities & Change.
Cornell U Pr.
ed. Culture & Politics in Indonesia. Cornell U
Pr.

Holt, D. B.
xHolt, D. B.
ed. Quantitative Scanning Electron
Microscopy. Acad Pr.

Holt, Edwin. *see* Holt, Edwin Bissell.
Holt, Edwin B. *see* Holt, Edwin Bissell.

Holt, Edwin Bissell, 1873-1946
xHolt, Edwin.
The Freudian Wish & Its Place in Ethics.
Sharon Hill.
xHolt, Edwin B.
Animal Drive & the Learning Process: An
Essay Toward Radical Empiricism. Octagon.
The Concept of Consciousness. Arno.
The Freudian Wish & Its Place in Ethics.
Johnson Repr.

Holt, Elizabeth Basye Gilmore.
xHolt, Elizabeth Gilmore.
ed. Triumph of Art for the Public: The
Emerging Role of Exhibitions & Critics.
Doubleday.

Holt, Elizabeth Gilmore. *see* Holt, Elizabeth Basye
Gilmore.

Holt, Fred C. *see* Holt, Fred D.

Holt, Fred D.
xHolt, Fred C.
The Pupil Personnel Team in the Elementary
School. HM.

Holt, Herbert, 1912-
xHolt, Herbert.
Free to Be Good or Bad. Har-Row.
Free to Be Good or Bad. M Evans.

Holt, J. *see* Holt, John.

Holt, John.
xHolt, J.
Attempte to Rescue That Aunciente, English
Poet & Playwrighte, Maister Williaume
Shakespere. AMS Pr.

Holt, John. *see* Holt, John Caldwell.
Holt, John B. *see* Holt, John Bradshaw.

Holt, John Bradshaw.
xHolt, John B.
German Agricultural Policy, 1918-1934: The
Development of a National Philosophy
Toward Agriculture in Postwar Germany.
Russell.

Holt, John Caldwell, 1923-
xHolt, John.
Freedom & Beyond. Dell.
Freedom & Beyond. Dell.
Underachieving School. Dell.
Underachieving School. Dell.

Holt, John D. *see* Holt, John Dominis.

Holt, John Dominis.
xHolt, John D.
On Being Hawaiian. Topgallant.

Holt, Marion P.
xHolt, Marion P.
The Contemporary Spanish Theater,
1949-1972. Twayne.
Jose Lopez Rubio. Twayne.

Holt, Mary Margaret.
xHolt, Mary Margaret.
Guide to Apartment House Management.
Exposition.

Holt, Maurice, 1931-
xHolt, Maurice.

The Common Curriculum: Its Structure & Style
in the Comprehensive School. Routledge &
Kegan.
Regenerating the Curriculum. Routledge &
Kegan.

Holt, Michael.
xHolt, Michael.
Maps, Tracks, & the Bridges of Konigsberg: A
Book About Networks. T Y Crowell.
Math Puzzles & Games. Walker & Co.

Holt, P. M. *see* Holt, Peter Malcolm.

Holt, Peter Malcolm.
xHolt, P. M.
ed. The Eastern Mediterranean Lands in the
Period of the Crusades. Intl Schol Bk Serv.

Holt, R. C. *see* Holt, Richard C.

Holt, Rackham.
xHolt, Rackham.
George Washington Carver: An American
Biography. Doubleday.

Holt, Richard C.
xHolt, R. C.
Programming Standard Pascal. Reston.

Holt, Robert. *see* Holt, Robert Lawrence.
Holt, Robert L. *see* Holt, Robert Lawrence.

Holt, Robert Lawrence.
xHolt, Robert.
Straight Teeth: Orthodontics & Dental Care for
Everyone. Morrow.
xHolt, Robert L.
Hemorrhoids: A Cure & Preventive. Morrow.
Hemorrhoids: A Cure & Preventive. Morrow.

Holt, Robert R.
xHolt, Robert R.
Assessing Personality. HarBraceJ.

Holt, Robert T.
xHolt, Robert T.
Radio Free Europe. U of Minn Pr.
Strategic Psychological Operations & American
Foreign Policy. U of Chicago Pr.

Holt, Sol. *see* Holt, Solomon.

Holt, Solomon.
xHolt, Sol.
Dictionary of American Government. Manor
Bks.

Holt, Thomas J., 1928-
xHolt, Thomas J.
Total Investing. Arlington Hse.
Total Investing. Popular Lib.

Holt, Victoria.
xHolt, Victoria.
Bride of Pendorric. Doubleday.
Curse of the Kings. Doubleday.
The Curse of the Kings. Fawcett.
The House of a Thousand Lanterns.
Doubleday.
The House of a Thousand Lanterns. Fawcett.
Legend of the Seventh Virgin. Doubleday.
Menfreya in the Morning. Doubleday.
Menfreya in the Morning. Fawcett.

Holt, William S. *see* Holt, William Stull.

Holt, William Stull, 1896-
xHolt, William S.
The Bureau of Public Roads: Its History,
Activities & Organization. AMS Pr.
The Federal Board for Vocational Education:
Its History, Activities & Organization. AMS
Pr.
The Federal Trade Commission: Its History,
Activities & Organization. AMS Pr.
The Office of the Chief of Engineers of the
Army: Its Non-Military History, Activities &
Organization. AMS Pr.

Holtby, Winifred, 1898-1935
xHoltby, Winifred.
Truth Is Not Sober. Arno.
Women in a Changing Civilization. Academy
Chi Ltd.

Holten, N. Gary.
xHolten, N. Gary.

The System of Criminal Justice. Little.

Holthaus, Gary, 1932-
xHolthaus, Gary.
Unexpected Manna. Copper Canyon.

Holtje, Adrienne.
xHoltje, Adrienne.
Cardcraft: Twenty-Two Techniques for Making
Your Own Greeting Card & Notepaper.
Chilton.

Holtje, Herbert.
xHoltje, Herbert.
How to Borrow Everything You Need to Build
a Great Personal Fortune. P-H.
xHoltje, Herbert F.
Parker Lifetime Treasury of Wealth-Building
Secrets. P-H.

Holtje, Herbert F. *see* Holtje, Herbert.
Holton, Gerald. *see* Holton, Gerald James.
Holton, Gerald J. *see* Holton, Gerald James.

Holton, Gerald James.
xHolton, Gerald.
ed. Limits of Scientific Inquiry. Norton.
xHolton, Gerald J.
Introduction to Concepts & Theories in
Physical Science. A-W.

Holton, Milne.
xHolton, Milne.
ed. Reading the Ashes: An Anthology of the
Poetry of Modern Macedonia. U of
Pittsburgh Pr.

Holtz, David.
xHoltz, David.
ed. Municipal Water Systems: The Challenge
for Urban Resource Management. Ind U Pr.

Holtz, William V.
xHoltz, William V.
Image & Immortality: A Study of Tristram
Shandy. Brown U Pr.

Holtzman, Wayne H.
xHoltzman, Wayne H.
Inkblot Perception & Personality: Holtzman
Inkblot Technique. U of Tex Pr.
Introduction to Psychology. Har-Row.
Personality Development in Two Cultures: A
Cross-Cultural Longitudinal Study of School
Children in Mexico & the United States. U of
Tex Pr.

Holub, Robert.
xHolub, Robert.
The Chemical Equilibrium of Gaseous Systems.
Kluwer Boston.

Holubnychy, Lydia.
xHolubnychy, Lydia.
Michael Borodin & the Chinese Revolution,
1923-1925. Univ Microfilms.

Holum, John R.
xHolum, John R.
Fundamentals of General, Organic, &
Biological Chemistry. Wiley.
Organic & Biological Chemistry. Wiley.
Organic Chemistry: A Brief Course. Wiley.
Principles of Physical, Organic, & Biological
Chemistry: An Introduction to the Molecular
Basis of Life. Wiley.

Holwerda, David E. *see* Holwerda, David Earl.

Holwerda, David Earl.
xHolwerda, David E.
ed. Exploring the Heritage of John Calvin.
Baker Bk.

Holy, Ladislav.
xHoly, Ladislav.
Neighbours & Kinsmen: A Study of the Berti
People of Darfur. St Martin.

Holy, R. A. *see* Holy, Russell Arthur.

Holy, Russell Arthur, 1898-
xHoly, R. A.
Relationship of City Planning to School Plant
Planning. AMS Pr.

Holy Transfiguration Monastery.
xHoly Transfiguration Monastery.

tr. Seraphim's Seraphim: The Life of Pelagia
   Ivanovna Serebrenikova, Fool for Christ's
   Sake of the Seraphim-Diveyevo Convent. St
   Nectarios.
Holyer, Ernie.
   xHolyer, Ernie.
   Sigi's Fire Helmet. Pacific Pr Pub Assn.
Holyoake, George J. *see* Holyoake, George Jacob.
Holyoake, George Jacob, 1817-1906
   xHolyoake, George J.
   The History of the Last Trial by Jury for
      Atheism in England. Arno.
Holz, Loretta.
   xHolz, Loretta.
   The How-to Book of International Dolls: A
      Comprehensive Guide to Making, Costuming
      & Collecting Dolls. Crown.
   illus. Teach Yourself Stitchery. Lothrop.
Holzenthaler, Jean.
   xHolzenthaler, Jean.
   My Feet Do. Dutton.
   My Hands Can. Dutton.
Holzer, Hans. *see* Holzer, Hans W.
Holzer, Hans W., 1920-
   xHolzer, Hans.
   Psychic Investigator. Manor Bks.
   Word Play. Strawberry Hill.
Holzer, Marc.
   xHolzer, Marc.
   Literature in Bureaucracy: Readings in
      Administrative Fiction. Avery Pub.
   Productivity in Public Organizations. Kennikat.
Holzknecht, Karl J. *see* Holzknecht, Karl Julius.
Holzknecht, Karl Julius.
   xHolzknecht, Karl J.
   Literary Patronage in the Middle Ages.
      Octagon.
Holzman, Franklyn D.
   xHolzman, Franklyn D.
   Foreign Trade Under Central Planning.
      Harvard U Pr.
Holzman, Philip S., 1922-
   xHolzman, Philip S.
   Psychoanalysis & Psychopathology. McGraw.
Holzman, Richard W.
   xHolzman, Richard W.
   Impact of Nature Photography. Amphoto.
Holzman, Robert S.
   xHolzman, Robert S.
   Adapt or Perish: The Life of General Roger A.
      Pryor, C. S. A. Shoe String.
   Dun & Bradstreet's Handbook of Executive
      Tax Management. T Y Crowell.
   Stormy Ben Butler. Octagon.
   A Survival Kit for Taxpayers: Staying on Good
      Terms with the I.R.S.. Macmillan.
Holzmann, R. T. *see* Holzmann, Richard T.
Holzmann, Richard I. *see* Holzmann, Richard T.
Holzmann, Richard T.
   xHolzmann, R. T.
   Chemical Rockets & Flame & Explosives
      Technology. Dekker.
   xHolzmann, Richard I.
   Production of the Boranes & Related Research.
      Acad Pr.
Homan, Helen. *see* Homan, Helen Mary (Walker).
Homan, Helen Mary (Walker), 1893-
   xHoman, Helen.
   By Post to the Apostles. Arno.
Homan, William E., 1919-
   xHoman, William E.
   Child Sense: A Guide to Loving Level-Headed
      Parenthood. Basic.
Homans, George C. *see* Homans, George Caspar.
Homans, George Caspar, 1910-
   xHomans, George C.

English Villagers of the Thirteenth Century.
   Norton.
The Human Group. HarBraceJ.
Nature of Social Science. HarBraceJ.
Homans, Isaac Smith, 1832-1879
   xHomans, J. Smith.
   ed. An Historical & Statistical Account of the
      Foreign Commerce of the United States.
      Arno.
Homans, J. Smith. *see* Homans, Isaac Smith.
Homans, Peter.
   xHomans, Peter.
   ed. Dialogue Between Theology & Psychology.
      U of Chicago Pr.
   Jung in Context: Modernity & the Making of a
      Psychology. U of Chicago Pr.
   Theology After Freud: An Interpretive Inquiry.
      Irvington.
Homberger, Conrad P.
   xHomberger, Conrad P.
   Foundation Course in German. Heath.
Homberger, Eric.
   xHomberger, Eric.
   The Art of the Real: Poetry in England &
      America Since 1939. Rowman.
Home Economics Ducation Association. *see* Home
   Economics Education Association.
Home Economics Education Association.
   xHome Economics Ducation Association.
   Test Item Construction in the Cognitive
      Domain. Home Econ Educ.
Home Planners, Inc. *see* Home Planners, Inc., Detroit.
Home Planners, Inc., Detroit.
   xHome Planners, Inc.
   One Eighty Five Homes: One Story Designs
      Over 2,000 Sq. Ft.. Home Planners.
   Two Hundred & Fifty Homes: One Story
      Designs Under 2,000 Square Feet. Home
      Planners
   Two Thirty Nine & a Half Two Story Homes.
      Home Planners.
   Two Twenty Three Homes: Vacation Homes.
      Home Planners.
Homer, Joel.
   xHomer, Joel.
   Jargon: How to Talk to Anyone About
      Anything. Times Bks.
Homer, Larona. *see* Homer, Larona C.
Homer, Larona C.
   xHomer, Larona.
   Blackbeard the Pirate & Other Stories of the
      Pine Barrens. Mid Atlantic.
Homer, Sidney, 1902-
   xHomer, Sidney.
   The Great American Bond Market: Selected
      Speeches of Sidney Homer. Dow Jones-Irwin.
   A History of Interest Rates. Rutgers U Pr.
Homer, William I. *see* Homer, William Innes.
Homer, William Innes.
   xHomer, William I.
   Seurat & the Science of Painting. MIT Pr.
Homerus.
   xHomerus.
   Homeric Hymns. Arno.
Homewood, Harry.
   xHomewood, Harry.
   Final Harbor. McGraw.
   A Matter of Size. O'Hara.
Homewood, Inez V.
   xHomewood, Inez V.
   Music in Further Education. Dufour.
Homo, Leon P. *see* Homo, Leon Pol.
Homo, Leon Pol, 1872-1957
   xHomo, Leon P.
   Primitive Italy & the Beginnings of Roman
      Imperialism. Greenwood.
Homola, S. *see* Homola, Samuel.
Homola, Samuel.
   xHomola, S.

Doctor Homola's Life Extender Health Guide:
   Secrets That Help You Live Longer. P-H.
Muscle Training for Athletes. P-H.
   xHomola, Samuel.
   Chiropractor's Treasury of Health Secrets. P-H.
   Doctor Homola's Fat-Disintegrator Diet. P-H.
   Doctor Homola's Natural Health Remedies.
      P-H.
   Secrets of Naturally Youthful Health &
      Vitality. P-H.
Homze, Edward L.
   xHomze, Edward L.
   Foreign Labor in Nazi Germany. Princeton U
      Pr.
Honadle, George.
   xHonadle, George.
   ed. International Development Administration:
      Implementation Analysis for Development
      Projects. Praeger.
Honda, Masaaki, 1914-
   xHonda, Masaaki.
   Suzuki Changed My Life. Summy.
Honderich, Ted.
   xHonderich, Ted.
   Political Violence. Cornell U Pr.
Hone, Elizabeth B.
   xHone, Elizabeth B.
   Teaching Elementary Science: A Sourcebook
      for Elementary Science. HarBraceJ.
Hone, Joseph M. *see* Hone, Joseph Maunsell.
Hone, Joseph Maunsell.
   xHone, Joseph M.
   The Life of George Moore. Greenwood.
Hone, Percy F. *see* Hone, Percy Frederick.
Hone, Percy Frederick.
   xHone, Percy F.
   Southern Rhodesia. Negro U Pr.
Hone, Philip, 1780-1851
   xHone, Philip.
   Diary of Philip Hone, 1828-1851. Kraus Repr.
Hone, Ralph E.
   xHone, Ralph E.
   Dorothy L. Sayers: A Literary Biography. Kent
      St U Pr..
Hone, William, 1780-1842
   xHone, William.
   Table Book. Gale.
   The Table Book. Gordon Pr.
Honeij, James A. *see* Honeij, James Albert.
Honeij, James Albert, 1880-
   xHoneij, James A.
   South-African Folk-Tales. AMS Pr.
   South-African Folk Tales. Negro U Pr.
Honesty, Henrene.
   xHonesty, Henrene.
   Essentials of Abdominal Ostomy Care. Springer
      Pub.
Honey, John C.
   xHoney, John C.
   Toward Strategies for Public Administration
      Development in Latin America. Syracuse U
      Pr.
Honey, Peter.
   xHoney, Peter.
   Face to Face: Business Communication for
      Results. P-H.
Honey, W. B. *see* Honey, William Bowyer.
Honey, William Bowyer.
   xHoney, W. B.
   Old English Porcelain: A Handbook for
      Collectors. Merrimack Bk Serv.

Honeycombe, Gordon.
   xHoneycombe, Gordon.
   Dragon Under the Hill. S&S.

Honeycutt. *see* Honeycutt, Roy Lee.

Honeycutt, Roy Lee.
   xHoneycutt.
   These Ten Words. Broadman.

Hosea & His Message. Broadman.
Honeywell, Roy J. *see* Honeywell, Roy John.
Honeywell, Roy John, 1886-
xHoneywell, Roy J.
Educational Work of Thomas Jefferson.
Russell.
Hong, Christopher C.
xHong, Christopher C.
Israel in Ancient Near Eastern Setting. Univ
Microfilms.
To Whom the Land of Palestine Belongs.
Exposition.
Hong, Edna. *see* Hong, Edna Hatlestad.
Hong, Edna Hatlestad, 1913-
xHong, Edna.
The Downward Ascent. Augsburg.
From This Good Ground. Augsburg.
The Gayety of Grace. Augsburg.
Hong, Wallace Y. *see* Hong, Wallace Yee.
Hong, Wallace Yee.
xHong, Wallace Y.
Chinese Cook Book. Crown.
Honig, Albert M.
xHonig, Albert M.
China Today: Sin or Virtue?. Exposition.
Honig, Alice S.
xHonig, Alice S.
Parent Involvement in Early Childhood
Education. Natl Assn Child Ed.
Honig, Donald.
xHonig, Donald.
Breaking In. Watts.
Coming Back. Watts.
An End of Innocence. Putnam.
Hurry Home. A-W.
In the Days of the Cowboy. Random.
The Journal of One Davey Wyatt. Watts.
The Last Great Season. S&S.
Marching Home. St Martin.
Honig, Edwin.
xHonig, Edwin.
Calderon & the Seizures of Honor. Harvard U
Pr.
Dark Conceit: The Making of Allegory. Brown
U Pr.
Four Springs. Swallow.
Honig, Mariana, 1940-
xHonig, Mariana.
Breads of the World: An Easy-to-Bake
Collection from 46 Countries. Chelsea Hse.
Honig, Werner K.
xHonig, Werner K.
ed. Animal Memory. Acad Pr.
ed. Operant Behavior: Areas of Research &
Application. P-H.
Honigfeld, G. *see* Honigfeld, Gilbert.
Honigfeld, Gilbert.
xHonigfeld, G.
Psychiatric Drugs: A Desk Reference. Acad Pr.
Honigmann, John J. *see* Honigmann, John Joseph.
Honigmann, John Joseph.
xHonigmann, John J.
Culture & Personality. Greenwood.
Understanding Culture. Greenwood.
Honjo, Eijiro, 1888-
xHonjo, Eijiro.
Economic Theory & History of Japan in the
Tokugawa Period. Russell.
Honore, Antony Maurice, 1921-
xHonore, Tony.
Sex Law in England. Shoe String.
Honore, Tony. *see* Honore, Antony Maurice.
Honour, Alan.
xHonour, Alan.
Tormented Genius: The Struggles of Vincent
Van Gogh. Morrow.
Honour, Hugh.
xHonour, Hugh.

Chinoiserie: The Vision of Cathay. Har-Row.
The Companion Guide to Venice. Scribner.
Neo-Classicism. Penguin.
Romanticism. Har-Row.
Honour, Walter W.
xHonour, Walter W.
Management of Local Pollution Control
Programs. Technomic.
Honti, G. D.
xHonti, G. D.
The Nitrogen Industry. Intl Pubns Serv.
Hoobler, Dorothy.
xHoobler, Dorothy.
An Album of World War I. Watts.
An Album of World War II. Watts.
Photographing the Frontier. Putnam.
Hood, Christopher C.
xHood, Christopher C.
The Limits of Administration. Wiley.
Hood, Donald W., 1918-
xHood, Donald W.
Impingement of Man on the Oceans. Krieger.
Hood, Gail H.
xHood, Gail H.
Medical-Surgical Nursing: Workbook for
Nurses. Mosby.
jt. auth. Total Patient Care: Foundations &
Practice. Mosby.
Hood, George J. *see* Hood, George Jussen.
Hood, George Jussen.
xHood, George J.
Geometry of Engineering Drawing. Krieger.
Hood, Graham, 1936-
xHood, Graham.
Charles Bridges & William Dering: Two
Virginia Painters, 1735-1750. U Pr of Va.
Hood, Leroy. *see* Hood, Leroy E.
Hood, Leroy E.
xHood, Leroy.
Immunology. Benjamin-Cummings.
Hood, M. *see* Hood, Mantle.
Hood, Mantle.
xHood, M.
Ethnomusicologist. McGraw.
Hood, Marguerite V. *see* Hood, Marguerite Vivian.
Hood, Marguerite Vivian.
xHood, Marguerite V.
Learning Music Through Rhythm. Greenwood.
Hood, Neil.
xHood, Neil.
The Economics of Multinational Enterprise.
Longman.
Hood, Peter, 1905-
xHood, Peter.
How Time Is Measured. Oxford U Pr.
Hood, Sinclair.
xHood, Sinclair.
The Arts in Prehistoric Greece. Penguin.
The Arts in Prehistoric Greece. Viking Pr.
Home of the Heroes: The Aegean Before the
Greeks. McGraw.
The Home of the Heroes: The Aegean Before
the Greeks. Transatlantic.
Hood, Stuart. *see* Hood, Stuart Clink.
Hood, Stuart Clink, 1915-
xHood, Stuart.
The Mass Media. Humanities.
Radio & Television. David & Charles.
Hood, Thomas.
xHood, Thomas.
The Letters of Thomas Hood. Octagon.
Hood, W. Edmund.
xHood, W. Edmund.
Practical Handbook of Stage Lighting & Sound.
TAB Bks.
Hoogenboom, Ari. *see* Hoogenboom, Ari Arthur.
Hoogenboom, Ari Arthur.
xHoogenboom, Ari.

ed. An Interdisciplinary Approach to American
History. P-H.
Outlawing the Spoils: A History of the Civil
Service Reform Movement, 1865-1883. U of
Ill Pr.
Hoogvelt, Ankie M. M.
xHoogvelt, Ankie M. M.
The Sociology of Developing Societies.
Humanities.
Hook, Andrew.
xHook, Andrew.
ed. Dos Passos: A Collection of Critical Essays.
P-H.
Hook, Diana F. *see* Hook, Diana Ffarington.
Hook, Diana Ffarington.
xHook, Diana F.
I Ching & Mankind. Routledge & Kegan.
I Ching & You. Dutton.
The I Ching & You. Routledge & Kegan.
Hook, Donal D.
xHook, Donal D.
ed. Plant Life in Anaerobic Environments. Ann
Arbor Science.
Hook, H. Phillip, 1932-
xHook, Phillip.
Who Art in Heaven. Zondervan.
Hook, J. N. *see* Hook, Julius Nicholas.
Hook, J. Nicholas. *see* Hook, Julius Nicholas.
Hook, Judith.
xHook, Judith.
The Baroque Age of England. Transatlantic.
Hook, Julius Nicholas, 1913-
xHook, J. N.
History of the English Language. Wiley.
Modern English Grammar for Teachers. Wiley.
The Teaching of High School English. Wiley.
xHook, J. Nicholas.
A Long Way Together: A Personal View of
NCTE's First Sixty-Seven Years. NCTE.
Hook, Martha.
xHook, Martha.
Little Ones Listen to God. Zondervan.
Little Ones Listen to God. Zondervan.
Hook, Peter Edwin.
xHook, Peter Edwin.
Compound Verb in Hindi. Ctr S&SE Asian.
Hook, Phillip. *see* Hook, H. Phillip.
Hook, Sidney, 1902-
xHook, Sidney.
ed. American Philosophers at Work: The
Philosophic Scene in the United States.
Greenwood.
Common Sense & the Fifth Amendment.
Constructive Action.
Education & the Taming of Power. Open
Court.
Education for Modern Man: A New
Perspective. Humanities.
From Hegel to Marx: Studies in the Intellectual
Development of Karl Marx. U of Mich Pr.
ed. The Idea of a Modern University.
Prometheus Bks.
Marx & the Marxists: The Ambiguous Legacy.
Van Nos Reinhold.
The Paradoxes of Freedom. U of Cal Pr.
Philosophy & Public Policy. S Ill U Pr.
Political Power & Personal Freedom: Critical
Studies in Democracy, Communism & Civil
Rights. Macmillan.
Religion in a Free Society. U of Nebr Pr.
Revolution Reform & Social Justice: Studies in
the Theory & Practice of Marxism. NYU Pr.
Hook, Theodore E. *see* Hook, Theodore Edward.
Hook, Theodore Edward.
xHook, Theodore E.
The Life & Remains of Theodore Edward
Hook. AMS Pr.
Hooke, Robert.
xHooke, Robert.

Hooke, S. H. *see* Hooke, Samuel Henry.

Hooke, Samuel H. *see* Hooke, Samuel Henry.

Hooke, Samuel Henry, 1874-

    xHooke, S. H.
        Babylonian & Assyrian Religion. U of Okla Pr
    xHooke, Samuel H.
        In the Beginning. Greenwood.
        The Siege Perilous: Essays in Biblical
          Anthropology & Kindred Subjects. Arno.

Hooker, Alan.

    xHooker, Alan.
        Vegetarian Gourmet Cookery. One Hund One
          Prods.

Hooker, C. A. *see* Hooker, Clifford Alan.

Hooker, Clifford A. *see* Hooker, Clifford Alan.

Hooker, Clifford Alan.

    xHooker, C. A.
        ed. Contemporary Research in the Foundations
          & Philosophy of Quantum Theory. Kluwer
          Boston.
    xHooker, Clifford A.
        ed. Physical Theory As Logico-Operational
          Structure. Kluwer Boston.

Hooker, D. *see* Hooker, Davenport.

Hooker, Davenport, 1887-

    xHooker, D.
        Prenatal Origin of Behavior. Hafner.

Hooker, J. D. *see* Hooker, Joseph Dalton.

Hooker, Jeremy, 1941-

    xHooker, Jeremy.
        Solent Shore. Persea Bks.

Hooker, Joseph Dalton, Sir.

    xHooker, J. D.
        The Botany of the Antartic Voyage of H. M
          Discovery Ships Erebus & Terror in the
          Years 1839-43. Lubrecht & Cramer.

Hooker, Kenneth W. *see* Hooker, Kenneth Ward.

Hooker, Kenneth Ward, 1908-

    xHooker, Kenneth W.
        Fortunes of Victor Hugo in England. AMS Pr.
        The Fortunes of Victor Hugo in England. R
          West.

Hooker, M. B.

    xHooker, M. B.
        A Concise Legal History of South-East Asia.
          Oxford U Pr.
        Legal Pluralism: An Introduction to Colonial &
          Neo - Colonial Laws. Oxford U Pr.

Hooker, Mildred P. *see* Hooker, Mildred Phelps (Stokes).

Hooker, Mildred Phelps (Stokes).

    xHooker, Mildred P.
        Camp Chronicles. Syracuse U Pr.

Hooker, Morna. *see* Hooker, Morna Dorothy.

Hooker, Morna Dorothy.

    xHooker, Morna.
        A Preface to Paul. Oxford U Pr.

Hooker, Richard.

    xHooker, Richard.
        MASH. PB.
        MASH Mania. Dodd.
        MASH Mania. PB.
        Of the Laws of Ecclesiastical Polity. Harvard U
          Pr.

Hooker, Richard J. *see* Hooker, Richard James.

Hooker, Richard James, 1913-

    xHooker, Richard J.
        ed. American Revolution: The Search for
          Meaning. Wiley.

Hooker, Ruth.

    xHooker, Ruth.
        The Kidnapping of Anna. A Whitman.
        The Pelican Mystery. A Whitman.

Hooker, Susan.

    xHooker, Susan.

        Caring for Elderly People: Understanding &
          Practical Help. Routledge & Kegan.

Hooker, Thomas, 1586-1647

    xHooker, Thomas.
        Application of Redemption, by the Effectual
          Work of the Word, & the Spirit of Christ, for
          the Bringing Home of Lost Sinners to God.
          Arno.
        Christian's Two Chiefe Lessons, Viz. Selfe
          Deniall, & Selfe Tryall. Arno.
        Thomas Hooker: Writings in England &
          Holland, 1626-1633. Harvard U Pr.

Hooker, W. J. *see* Hooker, William Jackson.

Hooker, William Jackson.

    xHooker, W. J.
        The Botany of Captain Beechey's Voyage.
          Lubrecht & Cramer.

Hooks, Janet Montgomery.

    xHooks, Janet W.
        Women's Occupations Through Seven
          Decades. Zenger Pub.

Hooks, Janet W. *see* Hooks, Janet Montgomery.

Hooks, William H.

    xHooks, William H.
        Crossing the Line. Knopf.
        Maria's Cave. Coward.

Hoole, Axalla J.

    xHoole, Axalla J.
        Patient Care Guidelines for Family Nurse
          Practitioners. Little.

Hoole, Daryl (Van Dam).

    xHoole, Daryl V.
        Art of Homemaking. Deseret Bk.
        Art of Teaching Children. Deseret Bk.

Hoole, Daryl V. *see* Hoole, Daryl (Van Dam).

Hoole, Francis W.

    xHoole, Francis W.
        Evaluation Research & Development Activities.
          Sage.
        Politics & Budgeting in the World Health
          Organization. Ind U Pr.

Hoole, K.

    xHoole, K.
        North Eastern Locomotive Sheds. David &
          Charles.

Hoole, W. Stanley. *see* Hoole, William Stanley.

Hoole, William S. *see* Hoole, William Stanley.

Hoole, William Stanley, 1903-

    xHoole, W. Stanley.
        According to Hoole: The Collected Essays &
          Tales of a Scholar-Librarian & Literary
          Maverick. U of Ala Pr.
    xHoole, William S.
        Alias Simon Suggs: The Life & Times of
          Johnson Jones Hooper. Greenwood.

Hooley, C., 1928-

    xHooley, C.
        Applications of Sieve Methods to the Theory
          of Numbers. Cambridge U Pr.

Hooley, James R.

    xHooley, James R.
        Hospital Dental Practice. Mosby.

Hooper, Finley. *see* Hooper, Finley Allison.

Hooper, Finley Allison, 1922-

    xHooper, Finley.
        Greek Realities: Life & Thought in Ancient
          Greece. Wayne St U Pr.

Hooper, Lucy H. *see* Hooper, Lucy Hamilton (Jones).

Hooper, Lucy Hamilton (Jones), 1835-1893

    xHooper, Lucy H.
        The Tsar's Window. Arno.

Hooper, Meredith.

    xHooper, Meredith.
        The Story of Australia. Taplinger.

Hooper, Paul F., 1938-

    xHooper, Paul F.

        Elusive Destiny: The Internationalist
          Movement in Modern Hawaii. U Pr of
          Hawaii.

Hooper, Walter.

    xHooper, Walter.
        Past Watchful Dragons: The Narnian
          Chronicles of C. S. Lewis. Macmillan.

Hoopes, Ann.

    xHoopes, Ann.
        Eye Power. Knopf.

Hoopes, David.

    xHoopes, David T.
        Alaska in Haiku. C E Tuttle.

Hoopes, David S.

    xHoopes, David S.
        ed. Intercultural Sourcebook: Cross-Cultural
          Training Methodologies. Intercult Pr.

Hoopes, David T. *see* Hoopes, David.

Hoopes, Donelson F.

    xHoopes, Donelson F.
        Childe Hassam. Watson-Guptill.

Hoopes, Ned. *see* Hoopes, Ned E.

Hoopes, Ned E.

    xHoopes, Ned.
        Who Am I: Essays on the Alienated. Dell.

Hoopes, Penrose R. *see* Hoopes, Penrose Robinson.

Hoopes, Penrose Robinson, 1892-

    xHoopes, Penrose R.
        Connecticut Clockmakers of the Eighteenth
          Century. C E Tuttle.
        Connecticut Clockmakers of the Eighteenth
          Century. New Eng Pub.
        Connecticut Clockmakers of the Eighteenth
          Century. Peter Smith.

Hoopes, Roy, 1922-

    xHoopes, Roy.
        Political Campaigning. Watts.
        Primaries & Conventions. Watts.

Hoopes, Townsend, 1922-

    xHoopes, Townsend.
        The Limits of Intervention: An Inside Account
          of How the Johnson Policy of Escalation Was
          Reversed in Vietnam. Longman.

Hoople, Cheryl G.

    xHoople, Cheryl G.
        As I Saw It: Women Who Lived the American
          Adventure. Dial.

Hoops, Richard A.

    xHoops, Richard A.
        Speech Science: Acoustics in Speech. C C
          Thomas.

Hoorweg, J. C.

    xHoorweg, J. C.
        Protein-Energy Malnutrition & Intellectual
          Abilities: A Study of Teenage Ugandan
          Children. Mouton.
    xHoorweg, Jan.
        Evaluation of Nutrition Education in Africa:
          Community Research in Uganda, 1971-1972.
          Mouton.

Hoorweg, Jan. *see* Hoorweg, J. C.

Hoose, William Van. *see* Van Hoose, William H.

Hooten, William J.

    xHooten, William J.
        Fifty-Two Years a Newsman. Tex Western.

Hootkins, Hirsch.

    xHootkins, Hirsch.
        Spanish Through Reading. Wahr.

Hooton, Earnest A. *see* Hooton, Earnest Albert.

Hooton, Earnest Albert, 1887-1954

    xHooton, Earnest A.
        Apes, Men & Morons. Arno.
        Apes, Men & Morons. R West.
        Survey in Seating. Greenwood.

Hoover, C. B. *see* Hoover, Calvin Bryce.

Hoover, Calvin Bryce, 1897-

    xHoover, C. B.

The Economy, Liberty, & the State. Kraus Repr.

Hoover, Clark H. *see* Hoover, Herbert Clark.

Hoover, Dwight W., 1926-
 xHoover, Dwight W.
  ed. Cities. Bowker.
  Teacher's Guide to American Urban History. Times Bks.
  ed. Understanding Negro History. New Viewpoints.

Hoover, Glenn E.
 xHoover, Glenn E.
  ed. Twentieth Century Economic Thought. Arno.

Hoover, H. M.
 xHoover, H. M.
  The Delikon. Avon.
  The Delikon. Viking Pr.
  The Lost Star. Avon.
  The Lost Star. Viking Pr.
  The Rains of Eridan. Avon.
  The Rains of Eridan. Viking Pr.
  Return to Earth. Viking Pr.

Hoover, Helen.
 xHoover, Helen.
  Animals at My Doorstep. Schol Bk Serv.
  Animals Near & Far. Schol Bk Serv.
  Gift of the Deer. Knopf.
  Great Wolf & the Good Woodsman. Schol Bk Serv.
  Place in the Woods. Knopf.
 xHoover, Helene.
  The Long-Shadowed Forest. Norton.

Hoover, Helene. *see* Hoover, Helen.

Hoover, Helene M.
 xHoover, Helene M.
  Concepts & Methodologies in the Family: An Instructor's Resource Handbook. Allyn.

Hoover, Herbert Clark, Pres. U.s, 1874-1964
 xHoover, Clark H.
  American Individualism. Garland Pub.

Hoover, Herbert T.
 xHoover, Herbert T.
  The Sioux: A Critical Bibliography. Ind U Pr.

Hoover Institution Staff. *see* Stanford University. Hoover Institution on War, Revolution and Peace.

Hoover, Kenneth. *see* Hoover, Kenneth H.

Hoover, Kenneth H.
 xHoover, Kenneth.
  A Handbook for Elementary School Teachers. Allyn.
 xHoover, Kenneth H.
  Professional Teacher's Handbook: A Guide for Improving Instruction in Today's Middle & Secondary Schools. Allyn.

Hoover, Kenneth R., 1940-
 xHoover, Kenneth R.
  A Politics of Identity: Liberation & the Natural Community. U of Ill Pr.

Hoover, Larry T.
 xHoover, Larry T.
  Guidelines for Criminal Justice Programs in Community & Junior Colleges. Am Assn Comm Jr Coll.

Hoover, Norman K. *see* Hoover, Norman Kurtz.

Hoover, Norman Kurtz, 1913-
 xHoover, Norman K.
  Approved Practices in Beautifying the Home Grounds. Interstate.

Hoover, Robert F., 1913-1970
 xHoover, Robert F.
  The Vascular Plants of San Luis Obispo County, California. U of Cal Pr.

Hoover, Thomas, 1941-
 xHoover, Thomas.

The Zen Experience. NAL.

Hooykaas, C. *see* Hooykaas, Christiaan.

Hooykaas, Christiaan, 1902-
 xHooykaas, C.
  A Balinese Temple Festival. Kluwer Boston.

Hooykaas, R. *see* Hooykaas, Reijer.

Hooykaas, Reijer, 1906-
 xHooykaas, R.
  Religion & the Rise of Modern Science. Eerdmans.

Hopcroft, John E.
 xHopcroft, John E.
  Introduction to Automata Theory, Languages, & Computation. A-W.

Hope, A. D. *see* Hope, Alec Derwent.

Hope, A. Guy.
 xHope, A. Guy.
  Symbols of the Nations. Pub Aff Pr.

Hope, Alec D. *see* Hope, Alec Derwent.

Hope, Alec Derwent, 1907-
 xHope, A. D.
  Cave & the Spring: Essays on Poetry. U of Chicago Pr.
 xHope, Alec D.
  The New Cratylus: Notes on the Craft of Poetry. Oxford U Pr.

Hope, C. E. *see* Hope, C. E. G.

Hope, C. E. G.
 xHope, C. E.
  The Horseman's Manual. Scribner.

Hope, Charles Evelyn Graham.
 xHope, C. E.
  Horse Riding. Soccer.

Hope, Kempe R.
 xHope, Kempe R.
  Development Policy in Guyana: Planning, Finance, & Administration. Westview.
  The Post War Planning Experience in Guyana. ASU Lat Am St.

Hope, Laura L. *see* Hope, Laura Lee.

Hope, Laura Lee.
 xHope, Laura L.
  The Bobbsey Twins in a TV Mystery Show. G&D.

Hope, Penelope.
 xHope, Penelope.
  Long Ago Is Far Away: Accounts of the Early Exploration & Settlement of the Papuan Gulf Area. Bks Australia.

Hope, Quentin M. *see* Hope, Quentin Manning.

Hope, Quentin Manning.
 xHope, Quentin M.
  Reading French for Comprehension. Macmillan.

Hope, Richard O.
 xHope, Richard O.
  Racial Strife in the U. S. Military: Toward the Elimination of Discrimination. Praeger.

Hope, T. E.
 xHope, T. E.
  Lexical Borrowing in the Romance Languages: A Critical Study of Italianisms in French & Gallicisms in Italian from 1100 to 1900. NYU Pr.

Hope, Thomas, 1770?-1831
 xHope, Thomas.
  Household Furniture & Interior Decoration: Classic Style Book of the Regency Period. Dover.
  Household Furniture & Interior Decoration: Classic Style Book of the Regency Period. Peter Smith.

Hope-Simpson, Jacynth.
 xHope-Simpson, Jacynth.
  Who Knows?: Twelve Unsolved Mysteries. Elsevier-Nelson.

Hopeman, Richard. *see* Hopeman, Richard J.

Hopeman, Richard J.
 xHopeman, Richard.

Production: Concepts, Analysis & Control. Merrill.
  Systems Analysis & Operations Management. Merrill.

Hopewell, Donald.
 xHopewell, Donald.
  Enduring Brontes. Folcroft.
  The Enduring Brontes. R West.

Hopf, Alice L. *see* Hopf, Alice Lightner.

Hopf, Alice Lightner, 1904-
 xHopf, Alice L.
  Animal & Plant Life Spans. Holiday.
  Biography of a Snowy Owl. Putnam.
  Nature's Pretenders. Putnam.
  Pigs Wild & Tame. Holiday.

Hopf, Carl. *see* Hopf, Carl Hermann Friedrich Johann.

Hopf, Carl Hermann Friedrich Johann, 1832-1873
 xHopf, Carl.
  Geschichte Griechenlands Vom Beginn Des Mittelalters Bis Auf Unsere Neure Zeit, 395-1821. B Franklin.

Hopf, Eberhard, 1902-
 xHopf, F.
  Mathematical Problems of Radiative Equilibrium. Hafner.

Hopf, F. *see* Hopf, Eberhard.

Hopf, Harry A. *see* Hopf, Harry Arthur.

Hopf, Harry Arthur, 1882-1949
 xHopf, Harry A.
  Papers on Management. Hive Pub.

Hopf, Peter S., 1929-
 xHopf, Peter S.
  Handbook of Building Security Planning & Design. McGraw.

Hopfe, Lewis M.
 xHopfe, Lewis M.
  Religions of the World. Glencoe.

Hopfinger, A. J.
 xHopfinger, A. J.
  Conformational Properties of Macromolecules. Acad Pr.

Hopkin, D. *see* Hopkin, David.

Hopkin, David.
 xHopkin, D.
  Automata. Elsevier.

Hopkin, John A.
 xHopkin, John A.
  Financial Management in Agriculture. Interstate.

Hopkins, A. G. *see* Hopkins, Anthony G.

Hopkins, Annette B. *see* Hopkins, Annette Brown.

Hopkins, Annette Brown, 1879-
 xHopkins, Annette B.
  Father of the Brontes. Greenwood.

Hopkins, Anthony G.
 xHopkins, A. G.
  An Economic History of West Africa. Columbia U Pr.
 xHopkins, Anthony G.
  An Economic History of West Africa. Columbia U Pr.

Hopkins, Arthur J. *see* Hopkins, Arthur John.

Hopkins, Arthur John, 1864-1939
 xHopkins, Arthur J.
  Alchemy Child of Greek Philosophy. AMS Pr.

Hopkins, Bruce R.
 xHopkins, Bruce R.
  The Law of Tax-Exempt Organizations. Ronald Pr.
  The Law of Tax-Exempt Organizations. Wiley.

Hopkins, Charles D.
 xHopkins, Charles D.

Classroom Measurement & Evaluation.
Peacock Pubs.
Classroom Testing: Administration, Scoring &
Score Interpretation. Peacock Pubs.
Classroom Testing: Construction. Peacock
Pubs.
Describing Data Statistically. Merrill.
Hopkins, David S.
xHopkins, David S.
Options in New-Product Organization.
Conference Bd.
Hopkins, E. Washburn. *see* Hopkins, Edward Washburn.
Hopkins, Edward W. *see* Hopkins, Edward Washburn.
Hopkins, Edward Washburn, 1857-1932
xHopkins, E. Washburn.
Ethics of India. Kennikat.
xHopkins, Edward W.
The Great Epic of India: Its Character &
Origin. Intl Pubns Serv.
Origin & Evolution of Religion. Cooper Sq.
Hopkins, Ernest M. *see* Hopkins, Ernest Martin.
Hopkins, Ernest Martin, 1877-
xHopkins, Ernest M.
This Our Purpose. U Pr of New Eng.
Hopkins, George E.
xHopkins, George E.
Airline Pilots: A Study in Elite Unionization.
Harvard U Pr.
Hopkins, J. F. *see* Hopkins, John F.
Hopkins, Jack. *see* Hopkins, Jack W.
Hopkins, Jack W.
xHopkins, Jack.
Latin America in World Affairs: The Politics of
Inequality. Barron.
xHopkins, Jack W.
Government Executive of Modern Peru. U
Presses Fla.
Hopkins, James T.
xHopkins, James T.
Fifty Years of Citrus: The Florida Citrus
Exchange, 1909-1959. U Presses Fla.
Hopkins, Jasper.
xHopkins, Jasper.
A Companion to the Study of St. Anselm. U of
Minn Pr.
A Concise Introduction to the Philosophy of
Nicholas of Cusa. U of Minn Pr.
Hopkins, Jeanne.
xHopkins, Jeanne.
ed. Glossary of Astronomy & Astrophysics. U
of Chicago Pr.
Hopkins, John A. *see* Hopkins, John Abel.
Hopkins, John Abel.
xHopkins, John A.
Farm Records & Accounting. Iowa St U Pr.
Hopkins, John F.
xHopkins, J. F.
McEckr'n. St Martin.
Hopkins, Kenneth.
xHopkins, Kenneth.
Portraits in Satire. Scholarly.
Hopkins, Lee B. *see* Hopkins, Lee Bennett.
Hopkins, Lee Bennett.
xHopkins, Lee B.

The Best of Book Bonanza. HR&W.
ed. Easter Buds Are Springing: Poems for
Easter. HarBraceJ.
Go to Bed!: A Book of Bedtime Poems. Knopf.
ed. Good Morning to You, Valentine.
HarBraceJ.
I Loved Rose Ann. Knopf.
Important Dates in Afro-American History.
Watts.
ed. Me: A Book of Poems. HM.
ed. Merely Players: An Anthology of Life
Poems. Elsevier-Nelson.
Monsters, Ghoulies, & Creepy Creatures. A
Whitman.
ed. My Mane Catches the Wind: Poems About
Horses. HarBraceJ.
xHopkins, Lee Bennett.
Do You Know What Day Tomorrow Is?: A
Teacher's Almanac. Schol Bk Serv.
Hopkins, Livingston.
xHopkins, Livingston.
Comic History of the United States. Arno.
Hopkins, Mansell H.
xHopkins, Mansell H.
Introduction to Electrical Engineering. Wiley.
Hopkins, Marjorie.
xHopkins, Marjorie.
A Gift for Tolum. Schol Bk Serv.
Hopkins, Pauline E. *see* Hopkins, Pauline Elizabeth.
Hopkins, Pauline Elizabeth.
xHopkins, Pauline E.
Contending Forces: A Romance Illustrative of
Negro Life North & South. AMS Pr.
Hopkins, Prynce. *see* Hopkins, Pryns.
Hopkins, Pryns, 1885-
xHopkins, Prynce.
Orientation, Socialization, & Individuation.
Asia.
Hopkins, R. Thurston. *see* Hopkins, Robert Thurston.
Hopkins, Raymond F.
xHopkins, Raymond F.
ed. Food, Politics, & Agricultural Development:
Case Studies in Public Policy of Rural
Modernization. Westview.
ed. The Global Political Economy of Food. U
of Wis Pr.
Hopkins, Robert H. *see* Hopkins, Robert Hazen.
Hopkins, Robert Hazen, 1930-
xHopkins, Robert H.
The True Genius of Oliver Goldsmith. Johns
Hopkins.
Hopkins, Robert Thurston, 1884-1915
xHopkins, R. Thurston.
Oscar Wilde. Folcroft.
Hopkins, S. J. *see* Hopkins, Sidney John.
Hopkins, Samuel, 1721-1803
xHopkins, Samuel.
Historical Memoirs, Relating to the Housatonic
Indians. Johnson Repr.
Hopkins, Sidney John.
xHopkins, S. J.
Drugs & Pharmacology for Nurses. Churchill.
Hopkins, Steven, 1953-
xHopkins, Steven.
The Leaving. Mudborn.
Hopkins, Terence K.
xHopkins, Terence K.
ed. Processes of the World-System. Sage.
Hopkins, Vincent C. *see* Hopkins, Vincent Charles.
Hopkins, Vincent Charles, 1912-
xHopkins, Vincent C.
Dred Scott's Case. Atheneum.
Dred Scott's Case. Russell.
Hopkins, William F. *see* Hopkins, William Foster.
Hopkins, William Foster.
xHopkins, William F.
Murder Is My Business. Landfall Pr.
Hopkins, William J. *see* Hopkins, William John.
Hopkins, William John, 1863-1926
xHopkins, William J.

Clammer. Arno.
Hopkinson, Cecil.
xHopkinson, Cecil.
Dictionary of Parisian Music Publishers
(1700-1950). Da Capo.
Hopkinson, Francis, 1737-1791
xHopkinson, Francis.
Pretty Story. Arno.
Hopkinson, Leslie W. *see* Hopkinson, Leslie White.
Hopkinson, Leslie White.
xHopkinson, Leslie W.
Greek Leaders. Arno.
Hopkinson, Shirley L. *see* Hopkinson, Shirley Lois.
Hopkinson, Shirley Lois.
xHopkinson, Shirley L.
Descriptive Cataloging of Library Materials.
Claremont House.
Hopp, Ralph H. *see* Hopp, Ralph Harvey.
Hopp, Ralph Harvey, 1915-
xHopp, Ralph H.
Enjoying the Active Life After Fifty. Stone
Wall Pr.
Hoppe, Donald J.
xHoppe, Donald J.
How to Invest in Gold Coins. Arco.
How to Invest in Gold Coins. Arlington Hse.
Hoppe, Elisabeth.
xHoppe, Elisabeth.
Carding, Spinning, Dyeing: An Introduction to
the Traditional Wool & Flax Crafts. Van Nos
Reinhold.
Hoppe, H. *see* Hoppe, Heinrich.
Hoppe, Heinrich.
xHoppe, H.
Whittling & Wood Carving. Sterling.
Hoppe, Joanne.
xHoppe, Joanne.
April Spell. Warne.
The Lesson Is Murder. HarBraceJ.
Hoppe, Willie, 1887-1959
xHoppe, Willie.
Thirty Years of Billiards. Dover.
Hopper, Arthur F.
xHopper, Arthur F.
Foundations of Animal Development. Oxford
U Pr.
Hopper, C. Edmund.
xHopper, C. Edmund.
Sex Education for Physically Handicapped
Youth. C C Thomas.
Hopper, Earl.
xHopper, Earl.
Readings in the Theory of Educational
Systems. Humanities.
Hopper, Nancy J.
xHopper, Nancy J.
Secrets. Elsevier-Nelson.
Hopper, R. J. *see* Hopper, Robert John.
Hopper, Robert.
xHopper, Robert.
Communication Concepts & Skills. Har-Row.
Human Message Systems. Har-Row.
Hopper, Robert John, 1910-
xHopper, R. J.
Trade & Industry in Classical Greece. Thames
Hudson.
Hopper, Vincent F. *see* Hopper, Vincent Foster.
Hopper, Vincent Foster.
xHopper, Vincent F.
Essentials of English. Barron.
Medieval Number Symbolism: Its Sources,
Meaning & Influence on Thought &
Expression. Cooper Sq.
Hoppin, Richard H.
xHoppin, Richard H.
Medieval Music. Norton.
Hopson, Rex C.
xHopson, Rex C.

Adobe: A Comprehensive Bibliography.
Lightning Tree.
Hopson, William.
xHopson, William.
Apache Kill. Bouregy.
Cry Viva!. Belmont-Tower.
Gringo Bandit. Manor Bks.
The Gringo Bandit. Nordon Pubns.
Gunfighters Pay. Bouregy.
Gunfighter's Pay. Nordon Pubns.
Gunfire at Salt Fork. Nordon Pubns.
The Last Apaches. Bouregy.
Trouble Rides Tall. Belmont-Tower.
Hopson, William L.
xHopson, William L.
The Laughing Vaquero. Belmont-Tower.
Hopwood, Henry V., 1866-1919
xHopwood, Henry V.
Living Pictures: Their History,
Photo-Production & Practical Working. Arno.
Hora, H. see Hora, Heinrich.
Hora, Heinrich, 1931-
xHora, H.
Nonlinear Plasma Dynamics at Laser
Irradiation. Springer-Verlag.
Hora, Thomas.
xHora, Thomas.
Dialogues in Metapsychiatry. Seabury.
Existential Metapsychiatry. Seabury.
Horadam, A. F.
xHoradam, A. F.
Outline Course of Pure Mathematics.
Pergamon.
Horak, M. see Horak, Milan.
Horak, Milan.
xHorak, M.
Interpretation & Processing of Vibrational
Spectra. Wiley.
Horan, James D. see Horan, James David.
Horan, James David, 1914-
xHoran, James D.
The Desperate Years: A Pictorial History of
the Thirties. Crown.
Horan, James F.
xHoran, James F.
Experiments in Metropolitan Government.
Praeger.
Horan, John J., 1945-
xHoran, John J.
Counseling for Effective Decision Making: A
Cognitive-Behavioral Perspective. Duxbury
Pr.
Horan, Kenneth. see Horan, Kenneth (O'Donnell).
Horan, Kenneth (O'Donnell), 1890-
xHoran, Kenneth.
ed. Parnassus En Route: An Anthology of
Poems About Places, Not People, on the
European Continent. Arno.
Horatius Flaccus, Q. see Horatius Flaccus, Quintus.
Horatius Flaccus, Quintus.
xHoratius Flaccus, Q.
The Works of Horace. AMS Pr.
xHoratius Flaccus, Quintus.
Horace His Arte of Poetrie, Pistles, & Satyrs
Englished (1567). Schol Facsimiles.
Horchler, Gabriel F. see Horchler, Gabriel Francis.
Horchler, Gabriel Francis, 1944-
xHorchler, Gabriel F.
Compiled by Hungarian Economic Reforms: A
Selective, Partially Annotated Bibliography.
Am Hungarian Foun.
Hord, Fred.
xHord, Fred.
After H(Ours). Third World.
Horder, Mervyn. see Horder, Mervyn Horder.
Horder, Mervyn Horder.
xHorder, Mervyn.

ed. On Christmas Day: First Carols to Play &
Sing. Macmillan.
Hordern, William.
xHordern, William.
Living by Grace. Westminster.
xHordern, William E.
Layman's Guide to Protestant Theology.
Macmillan.
Hordern, William E. see Hordern, William.
Hordeski, Michael.
xHordeski, Michael F.
Microprocessor Cookbook. TAB Bks.
Hordeski, Michael F. see Hordeski, Michael.
Hore, B. D. see Hore, Brian D.
Hore, Brian D.
xHore, B. D.
Alcohol Dependence. Butterworths.
Horecky, Paul L. see Horecky, Paul Louis.
Horecky, Paul Louis.
xHorecky, Paul L.
ed. East Central & Southeast Europe: A
Handbook of Library & Archival Resources
in North America. ABC-Clio.
Libraries & Bibliographic Centers in the Soviet
Union. Ind U Pr.
Southeastern Europe: A Guide to Basic
Publications. U of Chicago Pr.
Horejsi, Charles R.
xHorejsi, Charles R.
Foster Family Care: A Handbook for Social
Workers, Allied Professionals, & Concerned
Citizens. C C Thomas.
Horemis, George.
xHoremis, George.
Medical-Surgical Nursing Examination Review.
Arco.
xHoremis, Goerge.
Comprehensive Medical Boards Examination
Review. Arco.
Horemis, Goerge. see Horemis, George.
Horgan, J. J. see Horgan, John J.
Horgan, John J.
xHorgan, J. J.
Criminal Investigation. McGraw.
Horgan, Paul, 1903-
xHorgan, Paul.
Approaches to Writing. FS&G.
Citizen of New Salem. FS&G.
Conquistadors in North American History.
FS&G.
A Distant Trumpet. FS&G.
Everything to Live For. FS&G.
The Peach Stone: Stories from Four Decades.
FS&G.
Songs After Lincoln. FS&G.
The Thin Mountain Air. FS&G.
Whitewater. Warner Bks.
Whitewater. FS&G.
Hori, Ichir O, 1910-
xHori, Ichiro.
Folk Religion in Japan: Continuity & Change.
U of Chicago Pr.
Hori, Ichiro. see Hori, Ichir O.
Horigan, James E.
xHorigan, James E.
Chance or Design?. Philos Lib.
Horikawa, K. see Horikawa, Kiyoshi.
Horikawa, Kiyoshi.
xHorikawa, K.
Coastal Engineering: An Introduction to Ocean
Engineering. Halsted Pr.
Horizon.
xHorizon Magazine.
ed. A Horizon Guide: Great Historic Places of
Europe. Am Heritage.
xHorizon Magazine Editors.
Great Historic Places of Europe: A Horizon
Guide. S&S.
Horizon Magazine. see Horizon.
Horizon Magazine Editors. see Horizon.

Horkheimer, Max, 1895-1973
xHorkheimer, Max.
Dawn & Decline: Notes 1926-1931 &
1950-1969. Continuum.
Dialectic of Enlightenment. Continuum.
Horler, A. see Horler, A. R.
Horler, A. R.
xHorler, A.
Progress in Clinical Medicine. Churchill.
Horlick, Allan S. see Horlick, Allan Stanley.
Horlick, Allan Stanley, 1941-
xHorlick, Allan S.
Country Boys & Merchant Princes: The Social
Control of Young Men in New York.
Bucknell U Pr.
Hormachea, Carroll R.
xHormachea, Carroll R.
Sourcebook in Criminalistics. Reston.
Hormander, L. see Hormander, Lars.
Hormander, Lars.
xHormander, L.
An Introduction to Complex Analysis in
Several Variables. Elsevier.
xHormander, Lars.
ed. Seminar on Singularities of Solutions of
Linear Partial Differential Equations.
Princeton U Pr.
Horn, Andras.
xHorn, Andras.
Byron's Don Juan & the Eighteenth Century
English Novel. Folcroft.
Horn, Bob.
xHorn, Bob.
Swimming Techniques in Pictures. G&D.
Horn, Carl E. Van. see Van Horn, Carl E.
Horn, David.
xHorn, David.
Hadron Physics at Very High Energies.
Benjamin-Cummings.
Horn, David J.
xHorn, David J.
Biology of Insects. HR&W.
Horn, Delton T.
xHorn, Delton T.
Electronic Music Synthesizers. TAB Bks.
Horn, Ernest, 1882-1967
xHorn, Ernest.
Distribution of Opportunity for Participation
Among the Various Pupils in Classroom
Recitations. AMS Pr.
Horn, Francis H.
xHorn, Francis H.
Challenge & Perspective in Higher Education.
S Ill U Pr.
ed. Go Forth, Be Strong: Advice & Reflections
from Commencement Speakers. S Ill U Pr.
Horn, George F.
xHorn, George F.
Contemporary Posters: Design & Techniques.
Davis Mass.
Crafts for Today's Schools. Davis Mass.
The Crayon, a Versatile Medium for Creative
Expression. Davis Mass.
Texture: A Design Element. Davis Mass.
Horn, Harold R.
xHorn, Harold R.
Practical Considerations for Successful Crown
and Bridge Therapy: Biologic Considerations-
Psychologic Considerations-Preventive
Factors. Saunders.
Horn, Henry S., 1941-
xHorn, Henry S.
Adaptive Geometry of Trees. Princeton U Pr.
Horn, James Van. see Van Horn, James.
Horn, Joshua S.
xHorn, Joshua S.
Away with All Pests: An English Surgeon in
People's China, 1954-1969. Monthly Rev.
Horn, Maurice.
xHorn, Maurice.

Comics of the American West. Follett.
Comics of the American West. Winchester Pr.
ed. The World Encyclopedia of Comics. Avon.
The World Encyclopedia of Comics. Bowker.
ed. The World Encyclopedia of Comics.
Chelsea Hse.

Horn, Pamela.
xHorn, Pamela.
Education in Rural England, 1800-1914. St
Martin.

Horn, Robert A.
xHorn, Robert A.
Groups & the Constitution. AMS Pr.

Horn, Robert E.
xHorn, Robert E.
ed. The Guide to Simulations-Games for
Education & Training. Sage.

Horn, Ronald C.
xHorn, Ronald C.
Subrogation in Insurance Theory & Practice.
Irwin.

Horn, Stanley F. *see* Horn, Stanley Fitzgerald.

Horn, Stanley Fitzgerald, 1889-
xHorn, Stanley F.
Army of Tennessee. U of Okla Pr.
Decisive Battle of Nashville. U of Tenn Pr.

Horn, Tom, 1860-1903
xHorn, Tom.
The Life of Tom Horn, Government Scout &
Interpreter. Rio Grande.

Horn, Vivian.
xHorn, Vivian.
Composition Steps. Newbury Hse.

Hornabrook, R. W.
xHornabrook, R. W.
Topics in Tropical Neurology. Davis Co.

Hornaday, William T. *see* Hornaday, William Temple.

Hornaday, William Temple, 1854-1937
xHornaday, William T.
Thirty Years War for Wild Life. Arno.

Hornback, Ned B.
xHornback, Ned B.
Self-Assessment of Current Knowledge in
Therapeutic Radiology. Med Exam.

Hornbeck, Stanley K. *see* Hornbeck, Stanley Kuhl.

Hornbeck, Stanley Kuhl, 1883-1966
xHornbeck, Stanley K.
Contemporary Politics in the Far East. Arno.

Hornblow, Leonora.
xHornblow, Leonora.
Fish Do the Strangest Things. Random.
Insects Do the Strangest Things. Random.
Prehistoric Monsters Did the Strangest Things.
Random.

Hornbostel, Caleb.
xHornbostel, Caleb.
Materials & Methods for Contemporary
Construction. P-H.

Hornby, A. S. *see* Hornby, Albert Sydney.
Hornby, Albert S. *see* Hornby, Albert Sydney.

Hornby, Albert Sydney.
xHornby, A. S.
Guide to Patterns & Usage in English. Oxford
U Pr.
Oxford Advanced Learner's Dictionary of
Current English. Oxford U Pr.
xHornby, Albert S.
ed. English-Reader's Dictionary. Oxford U Pr.

Horne. *see* Horne, Douglas Favel.

Horne, Alistair.
xHorne, Alistair.
The Price of Glory: Verdun 1916. Penguin.
A Savage War of Peace: Algeria, 1954-1962.
Penguin.
A Savage War of Peace: Algeria 1954-1962.
Viking Pr.

Horne, Caroline.
xHorne, Caroline.

Crochet: Pretty & Practical. Transatlantic.
Fashion Crochet. Hearthside.

Horne, D. F. *see* Horne, Douglas Favel.

Horne, Douglas Favel, 1915-
xHorne.
Optical Production Technology. Heyden.
xHorne, D. F.
Lens Mechanism Technology. Crane-Russak
Co.

Horne, Herman H. *see* Horne, Herman Harrell.

Horne, Herman Harrell.
xHorne, Herman H.
The Democratic Philosophy of Education:
Companion to Dewey's Democracy and
Education; Exposition and Comment.
Greenwood.

Horne, James C. Van. *see* Van Horne, James C.
Horne, Michael R. *see* Horne, Michael Rex.

Horne, Michael Rex.
xHorne, Michael R.
Plastic Theory of Structures. MIT Pr.

Horne, R. A. *see* Horne, Ralph Albert.

Horne, Ralph Albert, 1929-
xHorne, R. A.
The Chemistry of Our Environment. Wiley.
Marine Chemistry: The Structure of Water &
the Chemistry of the Hydrosphere. Wiley.

Horne, Shirley.
xHorne, Shirley.
An Hour to the Stone Age. Moody.

Horne, Thomas A.
xHorne, Thomas A.
The Social Thought of Bernard Mandeville:
Virtue & Commerce in Early Eighteenth
Century England. Columbia U Pr.

Hornemann, Grace V.
xHornemann, Grace V.
Basic Nursing Procedures. Delmar.

Horner, Harlan H. *see* Horner, Harlan Hoyt.

Horner, Harlan Hoyt, 1878-
xHorner, Harlan H.
Lincoln & Greeley. Greenwood.

Horner, John, 1911-
xHorner, John.
Studies in Industrial Democracy. Verry.

Horner, John. *see* Horner, John Leonard.

Horner, John Leonard, 1926-
xHorner, John.
Special Cataloguing: With Particular Reference
to Music, Films, Maps, Serials & the
Multi-Media Computerized Catalog. Shoe
String.

Horner, Lance.
xHorner, Lance.
Golden Stud. Fawcett.
The Street of the Sun. Fawcett.

Horner, Thomas Marland, 1927-
xHorner, Tom.
Jonathan Loved David: Homosexuality in
Biblical Times. Westminster.

Horner, Tom.
xHorner, Tom.
Take Them Round, Please: The Art of Judging
Dogs. David & Charles.

Horner, Tom. *see* Horner, Thomas Marland.

Horney, Karen, M.d, 1885-1952
xHorney, Karen.
ed. Are You Considering Psychoanalysis?.
Norton.
Feminine Psychology. Norton.

Horngren, Charles T.
xHorngren, Charles T.
CPA Problems & Approaches to Solutions.
P-H.

Hornik, Edith L. *see* Hornik, Edith Lynn.

Hornik, Edith Lynn.
xHornik, Edith L.

The Drinking Woman. Follett.
The Drinking Woman. Follett.

Hornsby, Ken.
xHornsby, Ken.
Is That the Library Speaking?. St Martin.

Hornsby, Roger A.
xHornsby, Roger A.
Patterns of Action in the Aeneid: An
Interpretation of Vergil's Epic Similes. U of
Iowa Pr.
Reading Latin Poetry. U of Okla Pr.

Hornsey. *see* Hornsey, Edward.

Hornsey, Edward.
xHornsey.
Mechanics of Materials: An Individualized
Approach. HM.

Hornstein, Harvey. *see* Hornstein, Harvey A.

Hornstein, Harvey A, 1938-
xHornstein, Harvey.
Cruelty & Kindness: A New Look at
Aggression & Altruism. P-H.

Hornung, Clarence P. *see* Hornung, Clarence Pearson.

Hornung, Clarence Pearson.
xHornung, Clarence P.
Allover Patterns for Designers & Craftsmen.
Dover.
Allover Patterns for Designers & Craftsmen.
Peter Smith.
Old-Fashioned Christmas in Illustration &
Decoration. Dover.
ed. An Old-Fashioned Christmas in Illustration
& Decoration. Peter Smith.

Hornung, E. W. *see* Hornung, Ernest William.
Hornung, Ernest W. *see* Hornung, Ernest William.

Hornung, Ernest William, 1866-1921
xHornung, E. W.
Raffles. Penguin.
xHornung, Ernest W.
Amateur Cracksman. Arno.
Stingaree. Arno.
xHornung, W.
Raffles. Lighthouse Pr NY.

Hornung, W. *see* Hornung, Ernest William.

Hornung, William J.
xHornung, William J.
Architectural Drafting. P-H.
Builder's Vestpocket Reference Book. P-H.

Horodniceanu, Michael.
xHorodniceanu, Michael.
Transportation-System Safety. Lexington Bks.

Horonjeff, Robert.
xHoronjeff, Robert.
Planning & Design of Airports. McGraw.

Horos, Carol V.
xHoros, Carol V.
Vaginal Health. Tobey Pub.

Horosz, William.
xHorosz, William.
The Crisis of Responsibility: Man As the
Source of Accountability. U of Okla Pr.
The Promise & Peril of Human Purpose: The
New Relevance of Purpose & Existence.
Green.

Horovitz, J. *see* Horovitz, Joseph.

Horovitz, Jacques, 1947-
xHorovitz, Jacques H.
Top Management Control in Europe. St
Martin.

Horovitz, Jacques H. *see* Horovitz, Jacques.

Horovitz, Joseph.
xHorovitz, J.
Law & Logic: A Critical Account of Legal
Argument. Springer-Verlag.

Horowitz. *see* Horowitz, Mardi Jon.

Horowitz, Dan.
xHorowitz, Dan.
Origins of the Israeli Polity: Palestine Under
the Mandate. U of Chicago Pr.

Horowitz, David, 1899-
xHorowitz, David.

Above the Pacific. Aero.

Horvath, Allan.
xHorvath, Allan.
How to Create Photographic Special Effects. H
P Bks.

Horvath, Joan.
xHorvath, Joan.
Filmmaking for Beginners. Cornerstone.
Filmmaking for Beginners. Elsevier-Nelson.

Horvath, Violet M.
xHorvath, Violet M.
Andre Malraux: The Human Adventure. NYU
Pr.

Horvitz, P. see Horvitz, Paul M.

Horvitz, Paul M.
xHorvitz, P.
Monetary Policy & the Financial System. P-H.

Horvitz, Simeon L.
xHorvitz, Simeon L.
Legal Protection for Today's Consumer.
Kendall-Hunt.

Horward, Donald D.
xHorward, Donald D.
The French Revolution & Napoleon Collection
at Florida State University: A Bibliographical
Guide. Friends Fla St.

Horwath, Ernest B.
xHorwath, Ernest B.
Hotel Accounting. Wiley.

Horwill, H. W. see Horwill, Herbert William.

Horwill, Herbert William, 1864-1952
xHorwill, H. W.
An Anglo-American Interpreter: A Vocabulary
& Phrase Book. Folcroft.

Horwitz, Eliner L. see Horwitz, Elinor Lander.

Horwitz, Elinor. see Horwitz, Elinor Lander.

Horwitz, Elinor L. see Horwitz, Elinor Lander.

Horwitz, Elinor Lander.
xHorwitz, Eliner L.
The Strange Story of the Frog Who Became a
Prince. Dell.
xHorwitz, Elinor.
Soothsayer's Handbook: A Guide to Bad Signs
& Good Vibrations. Lippincott.
xHorwitz, Elinor L.
Capital Punishment, U. S. A.. Lippincott.
Communes in America: The Place Just Right.
Lippincott.
Contemporary American Folk Artists.
Lippincott.
When the Sky Is Like Lace. Lippincott.

Horwitz, Henry.
xHorwitz, Henry.
Parliament, Policy & Politics in the Reign of
William III. U Delaware Pr.

Horwitz, James.
xHorwitz, James.
They Went Thataway. Ballantine.

Horwitz, Julius, 1920-
xHorwitz, Julius.
The Married Lovers. Dial.
The Married Lovers. Popular Lib.
Natural Enemies. Ballantine.

Horwitz, Orville.
xHorwitz, Orville.
ed. Index of Suspicion in Treatable Diseases.
Lea & Febiger.

Horwitz, Richard, 1949-
xHorwitz, Richard.
Anthropology Toward History: Culture &
Work in a 19th-Century Maine Town.
Columbia U Pr.

Horwitz, Robert H.
xHorwitz, Robert H.
Moral Foundations of the American Republic.
U Pr of Va.

Horwitz, Tem.
xHorwitz, Tem.

Arts Administration: How to Set up & Run a
Successful Nonprofit Arts Organization.
Chicago Review.
The Runner's Guide to Chicago & the Suburbs.
Chicago Review.

Hosek, William R.
xHosek, William R.
Monetary Theory, Policy & Financial Markets.
McGraw.

Hoselitz, Bert F.
xHoselitz, Bert F.
ed. A Reader's Guide to the Social Sciences.
Free Pr.

Hoselitz, Bert F. see Hoselitz, Berthold Frank.

Hoselitz, Berthold F. see Hoselitz, Berthold Frank.

Hoselitz, Berthold Frank.
xHoselitz, Bert F.
ed. Progress of Underdeveloped Areas. U of
Chicago Pr.
ed. Theories of Economic Growth. Free Pr.
xHoselitz, Berthold F.
ed. Economics & the Idea of Mankind.
Columbia U Pr.

Hosford, Ray E.
xHosford, Ray E.
ed. The Crumbling Walls: Treatment &
Counseling of Prisoners. U of Ill Pr.

Hoshizaki, Barbara J. see Hoshizaki, Barbara Joe.

Hoshizaki, Barbara Joe.
xHoshizaki, Barbara J.
Fern Growers Manual. Knopf.

Hosie, Dorothea. see Hosie, Dorothea Soothill.

Hosie, Dorothea Soothill, Lady, 1885-
xHosie, Dorothea.
Two Gentlemen of China: An Intimate
Description of the Private Life of Two
Patrician Chinese Families. Hyperion Conn.

Hosking, Eric. see Hosking, Eric John.

Hosking, Eric John.
xHosking, Eric.
A Passion for Birds: Fifty Years of
Photographing Wildlife. Coward.

Hosking, Geoffrey. see Hosking, Geoffrey A.

Hosking, Geoffrey A.
xHosking, Geoffrey.
Beyond Socialist Realism. Holmes & Meier.

Hoskins, Halford L. see Hoskins, Halford Lancaster.

Hoskins, Halford Lancaster, 1891-
xHoskins, Halford L.
European Imperialism in Africa. Russell.

Hoskins, Katherine B.
xHoskins, Katherine B.
Anderson County. Memphis St Univ.

Hoskins, R. F.
xHoskins, R. F.
Generalised Functions. Halsted Pr.

Hoskins, Robert, 1933-
xHoskins, Robert.
To Escape the Stars. Ballantine.

Hoskins, Robert L.
xHoskins, Robert L.
Black Administrators in Higher Education:
Conditions & Perceptions. Praeger.

Hoskins, William G. see Hoskins, William George.

Hoskins, William George, 1908-
xHoskins, William G.
Devon & Its People. Kelley.

Hoskot, S. S.
xHoskot, S. S.
T. S. Eliot: His Mind & Personality. Llanerch
Bks.

Hosmer, H. L. see Hosmer, Hezekiah L.

Hosmer, Hezekiah L.
xHosmer, H. L.
Adela, the Octoroon. Arno.

Hosmer, Larue T.
xHosmer, Larue T.

Entrepreneurial Function: Text & Cases on
Smaller Firms. P-H.

Hosmer, Stephen T.
xHosmer, Stephen T.
The Fall of South Vietnam: Statements by
Vietnamese Military & Civilian Leaders.
Crane-Russak Co.

Hosmer, William.
xHosmer, William.
Higher Law, in Its Relations to Civil
Government: With Particular Reference to
Slavery, & the Fugitive Slave Law. Arno.

Hosokawa, B. see Hosokawa, Bill.

Hosokawa, Bill.
xHosokawa, B.
Thirty-Five Years in the Frying Pan. McGraw.

Hospers, John, 1918-
xHospers, John.
ed. Artistic Expression. Irvington.
Introduction to Philosophical Analysis. P-H.

Hospital Financial Management Association.
xHospital Financial Management Association.
Cost Effectiveness Notebook. Hospital Finan.
Departmental Method Handbook. Hospital
Finan.

Hospital Research & Educational Trust of the AHA. see
Hospital Research and Educational Trust.

Hospital Research and Educational Trust.
xHospital Research & Educational Trust of the
AHA.
Administracion De Salas. R J Brady.
Being a Food Service Worker. R J Brady.
Being a Housekeeping Aide. R J Brady.
Being a Nursing Aide. R J Brady.
Being a Ward Clerk. R J Brady.
Caring for Children in the Hospital. R J Brady.
Enfermera Auxiliar (Nursing Aide). R J Brady.
Servicio De Alimentacion (Food Service
Worker). R J Brady.
Training the Food Service Worker. R J Brady.
Training the Housekeeping Aide. R J Brady.
Training the Nursing Aide. R J Brady.
Training the Ward Clerk. R J Brady.

Hossain, Kamal.
xHossain, Kamal.
ed. Legal Aspects of the New International
Economic Order. Nichols Pub.

Hossaini, Ali A.
xHossaini, Ali A.
Medical Technology Examination Review.
Arco.

Hostetler, John. see Hostetler, John Andrew.

Hostetler, John A. see Hostetler, John Andrew.

Hostetler, John Andrew, 1918-
xHostetler, John.
The Hutterites in North America. HR&W.
xHostetler, John A.
Amish Life. Herald Pr.
Amish Society. Johns Hopkins.
Children in Amish Society: Socialization &
Community Education. HR&W.
Communitarian Societies. HR&W.
Hutterite Society. Johns Hopkins.

Hostetler, Marian.
xHostetler, Marian.
African Adventure. Herald Pr.
Journey to Jerusalem. Herald Pr.
Secret in the City. Herald Pr.

Hostetter, G. H., 1939-
xHostetter, Gene H.
Fundamentals of Network Analysis. Har-Row.

Hostetter, Gene H. see Hostetter, G. H.

Hostrop, Richard. see Hostrop, Richard W.

Hostrop, Richard W.
xHostrop, Richard.
ed. Accountability for Educational Results.
Shoe String.
xHostrop, Richard W.

Education Inside the Library Media Center.
Shoe String.
ed. Foundations of Futurology in Education.
ETC Pubns.

Hot Rod Magazine.
xHot Rod Magazine Editorial Staff.
Big Book of Kit Cars. Petersen Pub.
xHot Rod Magazine Editors.
ed. Engine Swapping. Petersen Pub.

Hot Rod Magazine Editorial Staff. *see* Hot Rod
Magazine.

Hot Rod Magazine Editors. *see* Hot Rod Magazine.

Hotchin, J. *see* Hotchin, John.

Hotchin, John.
xHotchin, J.
Persistent & Slow Virus Infections. S Karger.

Hotchkiss, Jeanette.
xHotchkiss, Jeanette K.
African-Asian Reading Guide for Children &
Young Adults. Scarecrow.
American Historical Fiction & Biography for
Children & Young People. Scarecrow.
European Historical Fiction & Biography for
Children & Young People. Scarecrow.

Hotchkiss, Jeanette K. *see* Hotchkiss, Jeanette.

Hotchkiss, John F.
xHotchkiss, John F.
Cut Glass Handbook & Price Guide. Dutton.
Cut Glass Handbook & Price Guide. Hotchkiss
House.
Cut Glass Handbook & Price Guide.
Wallace-Homestead.
Hummel Art. Wallace-Homestead.

Hotchkiss, Neil.
xHotchkiss, Neil.
Common Marsh Underwater &
Floating-Leaved Plants of the United States
& Canada. Dover.
Common Marsh, Underwater &
Floating-Leaved Plants of the United States
& Canada. Peter Smith.

Hotchner, A. E.
xHotchner, A. E.
Looking for Miracles: A Memoir About
Loving. Har-Row.
Sophia Living & Loving: Her Own Story.
Morrow.

Hotchner, Katherine F. *see* Hotchner, Katherine
Feingold.

Hotchner, Katherine Feingold.
xHotchner, Katherine F.
The Green Hopper. Mediaworks.

Hotman, Francois.
xHotman, Francois.
Franco-Gallia. Gordon Pr.

Hotson, Leslie, 1897-
xHotson, Leslie.
I, William Shakespeare Do Appoint Thomas
Russell, Esquire. Arno.
I, William Shakespeare Do Appoint Thomas
Russell, Esquire. R West.

Hotta, Susumu, 1918-
xHotta, Susumu.
Dengue & Related Hemorrhagic Diseases.
Green.

Hotten, John C. *see* Hotten, John Camden.

Hotten, John Camden, 1832-1873
xHotten, John C.
Abyssinia & Its People: Or, Life in the Land of
Prester John. Negro U Pr.
The Original Lists of Persons of Quality:
Emigrants, Religious Exiles, Political Rebels,
Serving Men Sold for a Term of Years,
Apprentices...and Others Who Went from
Great Britian to the American Plantations,
1600-1700. Genealog Pub.

Hotton, Peter.
xHotton, Peter.
So You Want to Fix up an Old House. Little.

Hotz, Henry G. *see* Hotz, Henry Gustave.

Hotz, Henry Gustave, 1880-1972
xHotz, Henry G.
First Year Algebra Scales. AMS Pr.

Houart, Victor.
xHouart, Victor.
Buttons: A Collector's Guide. Scribner.

Houck, Carter.
xHouck, Carter.
American Quilts & How to Make Them.
Scribner.
The Boat Buff's Book of Embroidery:
Needlepoint, Crewel, Applique. Scribner.
ed. White Work: Techniques & 180 Designs.
Dover.

Houck, J. C. *see* Houck, John C.

Houck, John. *see* Houck, John W.

Houck, John C., 1931-
xHouck, J. C.
Chalones. Elsevier.

Houck, John W.
xHouck, John.
Outdoor Advertising: History & Regulation. U
of Notre Dame Pr.

Houck, Louis, 1840-1925
xHouck, Louis.
History of Missouri from the Earliest
Explorations & Settlements Until the
Admission of the State into the Union. Arno.

Houck, Margaret. *see* Houck, Margaret Evah.

Houck, Margaret Evah, 1890-
xHouck, Margaret.
Sources of the Roman de Brut of Wace.
Folcroft.

Hougan, Jim.
xHougan, Jim.
Decadence: Radical Nostalgia, Narcissism, &
Decline in the Seventies. Morrow.

Hougen, Richard T. *see* Hougen, Richard Torgor.

Hougen, Richard Torgor, 1912-
xHougen, Richard T.
Cooking with Hougen. Abingdon.
Look No Further. Abingdon.

Hough, C. A. *see* Hough, C. A. M.

Hough, C. A. M.
xHough, C. A.
ed. Developments in Sweeteners. Burgess-Intl
Ideas.

Hough, Charlotte. *see* Hough, Charlotte Woodyatt.

Hough, Charlotte Woodyatt, 1924-
xHough, Charlotte.
The Bassington Murder. St Martin.

Hough, Douglas E.
xHough, Douglas E.
The Market for Human Blood. Lexington Bks.

Hough, Franklin B. *see* Hough, Franklin Benjamin.

Hough, Franklin Benjamin, 1822-1885
xHough, Franklin B.
American Biographical Notes, Being Short
Notices of Deceased Persons. Harbor Hill
Bks.
The Siege of Savannah, by the Combined
American & French Forces, Under the
Command of Gen. Lincoln & the Count
dEstaing, in the Autumn of 1779. Reprint.

Hough, Graham. *see* Hough, Graham Goulden.

Hough, Graham G. *see* Hough, Graham Goulden.

Hough, Graham Goulden, 1908-
xHough, Graham.
The Last Romantics. B&N.
Reflections on a Literary Revolution. Intl Schol
Bk Serv.
xHough, Graham G.
Image & Experience: Studies in Literary
Revolution. Greenwood.
The Last Romantics. AMS Pr.

Hough, Henry B. *see* Hough, Henry Beetle.

Hough, Henry Beetle, 1896-
xHough, Henry B.

Soundings at Sea Level. HM.
Thoreau of Walden: The Man & His Eventful
Life. Shoe String.

Hough, Jack L. *see* Hough, Jack Luin.

Hough, Jack Luin, 1909-
xHough, Jack L.
Geology of the Great Lakes. U of Ill Pr.

Hough, Jerry F., 1935-
xHough, Jerry F.
Soviet Prefects: The Local Party Organs in
Industrial Decision-Making. Harvard U Pr.
The Soviet Union & Social Science Theory.
Harvard U Pr.

Hough, Lindy, 1944-
xHough, Lindy.
Psyche. North Atlantic.

Hough, Richard. *see* Hough, Richard Alexander.

Hough, Richard Alexander, 1922-
xHough, Richard.
The Fight of the Few. Morrow.
History of the World's Motorcycles. Har-Row.
History of the World's Racing Cars. Har-Row.
The Last Voyage of Captain James Cook.
Morrow.
The Potemkin Mutiny. Greenwood.
Wings Against the Sky. Morrow.

Hough, Robert L. *see* Hough, Robert Lee.

Hough, Robert Lee.
xHough, Robert L.
Quiet Rebel: William Dean Howells As Social
Commentator. Shoe String.

Hough, Romeyn B. *see* Hough, Romeyn Beck.

Hough, Romeyn Beck, 1857-1924
xHough, Romeyn B.
Hough's Encyclopedia of American Woods.
Speller.

Hougham, Paul. *see* Hougham, Paul C.

Hougham, Paul C, 1914-
xHougham, Paul.
The Encyclopedia of Archery. A S Barnes.

Houghteling, James L. *see* Houghteling, James Lawrence.

Houghteling, James Lawrence, 1920-
xHoughteling, James L.
Dynamics of Law. HarBraceJ.

Houghton, Bernard.
xHoughton, Bernard.
ed. Computer Based Information Retrieval
Systems. Shoe String.
Mechanical Engineering: The Sources of
Information. Shoe String.
ed. Standardization for Documentation. Shoe
String.

Houghton, Bryan, 1911-
xHoughton, Bryan.
Mitre & Crook. Arlington Hse.
Mitre & Crook. Tan Bks Pubs.

Houghton, D. Hobart.
xHoughton, D. Hobart.
ed. Source Material on South African
Economy: 1860-1970. Oxford U Pr.
ed. Source Material on the South African
Economy, 1860-1870. Oxford U Pr.

Houghton, Eric.
xHoughton, Eric.
The Mouse & the Magician. Andre Deutsch.

Houghton, Leighton.
xHoughton, Leighton.
Guide to the British Cathedrals. Transatlantic.

Houghton, Neal D. *see* Houghton, Nealie Doyle.

Houghton, Nealie Doyle, 1895-
xHoughton, Neal D.
ed. Struggle Against History: U. S. Foreign
Policy in an Age of Revolution. S&S.

Houk, C. C. *see* Houk, Clifford C.

Houk, Clifford C.
xHouk, C. C.
Chemistry: Concepts & Problems. Wiley.

Houk, Nancy, 1940-
xHouk, Nancy.

Michigan Catalogue of Two-Dimensional
Spectral Types for the HD Stars. Univ
Microfilms.
Houlden, J. L. *see* Houlden, James Leslie.
Houlden, James Leslie.
xHoulden, J. L.
ed. Paul's Letters from Prison: Philippians,
Colossians, Philemon & Ephesians.
Westminster.
Houle, Cyril O. *see* Houle, Cyril Orvin.
Houle, Cyril Orvin, 1913-
xHoule, Cyril O.
The Design of Education. Jossey-Bass.
The External Degree. Jossey-Bass.
Houlgate, Deke.
xHoulgate, Deke.
The Handbook of High Performance Driving.
Dodd.
Houlgate, Laurence. *see* Houlgate, Laurence D.
Houlgate, Laurence D.
xHoulgate, Laurence.
The Child & the State: A Normative Theory of
Juvenile Rights. Johns Hopkins.
Hoult, Thomas F. *see* Hoult, Thomas Ford.
Hoult, Thomas Ford.
xHoult, Thomas F.
Dictionary of Modern Sociology. Littlefield.
Dictionary of Modern Sociology. Rowman.
Sociology for a New Day. Random.
Houpt, C. Theodore. *see* Houpt, Charles Theodore.
Houpt, Charles Theodore, 1912-
xHoupt, C. Theodore.
Mark Akenside: A Biographical & Critical
Study. Russell.
Houpt, Jeffrey L.
xHoupt, Jeffrey L.
The Importance of Mental Health Services to
General Health Care. Ballinger Pub.
Hourani, George F. *see* Hourani, George Fadlo.
Hourani, George Fadlo.
xHourani, George F.
Arab Seafaring in the Indian Ocean in Ancient
& Early Medieval Times. Octagon.
Ethical Value. Greenwood.
Hourwich, Isaac A. *see* Hourwich, Isaac Aaronovich.
Hourwich, Isaac Aaronovich, 1860-1924
xHourwich, Isaac A.
Economics of the Russian Village. AMS Pr.
Immigration & Labor. AMS Pr.
Immigration & Labor: The Economic Aspects
of European Immigration to the United
States. Arno.
House. *see* House, Clifford R.
House & Garden. *see* House and Garden.
House & Garden Editors. *see* House and Garden.
House and Garden.
xHouse & Garden.
House & Garden's Twenty Six Easy Little
Gardens. Penguin.
ed. Twentieth Century Decorating Architecture
& Gardens. HR&W.
xHouse & Garden Editors.
ed. The Art of Carving. S&S.
ed. House & Garden's Book of Remodeling.
Viking Pr.
House & Garden's New Cookbook. S&S.
These Simple Things. S&S.
xHouse And Garden Editors.
Art of Carving. S&S.
House And Garden Editors. *see* House and Garden.
House, Arthur H.
xHouse, Arthur H.
The U.N. in the Congo: The Political &
Civilian Efforts. U Pr of Amer.
House, Charles.
xHouse, Charles.
World at Christmas. Glencoe.
House, Charles Van. *see* Van House, Charles.
House, Clifford R.
xHouse.

Reference Manual for Office Personnel. SW
Pub.
House, Ernest R.
xHouse, Ernest R.
The Politics of Educational Innovation.
McCutchan.
Survival in the Classroom: Negotiating with
Kids, Colleagues & Bosses. Allyn.
House, Floyd N. *see* House, Floyd Nelson.
House, Floyd Nelson, 1893-
xHouse, Floyd N.
Development of Sociology. Greenwood.
House, J. D.
xHouse, J. D.
Contemporary Entrepreneurs: The Sociology of
Residential Real Estate Agents. Greenwood.
House, Jack, 1906-
xHouse, Jack.
Portrait of the Clyde. Intl Pubns Serv.
House, Kay S. *see* House, Kay Seymour.
House, Kay Seymour.
xHouse, Kay S.
Cooper's Americans. Ohio St U Pr.
House, Peter W. *see* House, Peter William.
House, Peter William.
xHouse, Peter W.
The Future Indefinite: Decision-Making in a
Transition Economy. Lexington Bks.
Getting It off the Shelf: A Methodology for
Implementing Federal Research. Westview.
Planning & Conservation: The Emergence of
the Frugal Society. Praeger.
House, Robert W. *see* House, Robert William.
House, Robert William, 1920-
xHouse, Robert W.
Administration in Music Education. P-H.
House, William C.
xHouse, William C.
ed. Business Simulation for Decision Making.
Petrocelli.
ed. Data Base Management. Van Nos
Reinhold.
Interactive Decision Oriented Data Base
Systems. Van Nos Reinhold.
Household, Geoffrey.
xHousehold, Geoffrey.
Arabesque. Intl Pubns Serv.
Dance of the Dwarfs. Penguin.
Dance of the Dwarfs. State Mutual Bk.
The Europe That Was. St Martin.
Hostage London: The Diary of Julian Despard.
Little.
The Last Two Weeks of Georges Rivac. Little.
The Last Two Weeks of Georges Rivac.
Penguin.
The Last Two Weeks of Georges Rivac. G K
Hall.
The Sending. Little.
Household, Humphrey.
xHousehold, Humphrey W.
Thames & Severn Canal. Kelley.
Household, Humphrey W. *see* Household, Humphrey.
Householder, A. S. *see* Householder, Alston Scott.
Householder, Alston S. *see* Householder, Alston Scott.
Householder, Alston Scott.
xHouseholder, A. S.
Lectures on Numerical Algebra. Math Assn.
xHouseholder, Alston S.
The Theory of Matrices in Numerical Analysis.
Dover.
Houselander, Caryll. *see* Houselander, Frances Caryll.
Houselander, Frances Caryll.
xHouselander, Caryll.
Guilt. Gordian.
Houseman, Gerald. *see* Houseman, Gerald L.
Houseman, Gerald L.
xHouseman, Gerald.
G. D. H. Cole. G K Hall.
xHouseman, Gerald L.

G. D. H. Cole. Twayne.
The Right of Mobility. Kennikat.
Houseman, John.
xHouseman, John.
Front & Center. S&S.
Houser, Norman W.
xHouser, Norman W.
Drugs: Facts on Their Use & Abuse. Lothrop.
Houser, Roy.
xHouser, Roy.
Catalogue of Chamber Music for Woodwind
Instruments. Da Capo.
Housing & Urban Development Dept. *see* United States.
Dept. of Housing and Urban Development.
Housley, Trevor, 1941-
xHousley, Trevor.
Data Communications & Teleprocessing
Systems. P-H.
Housman, John E.
xHousman, John E.
ed. British Popular Ballads. Arno.
Housman, Laurence, 1865-1959
xHousman, Laurence.
All-Fellows & the Cloak of Friendship. Arno.
House of Joy. Arno.
Little Plays of St. Francis: A Dramatic Cycle
from the Life & Legend of St. Francis of
Assisi. Core Collection.
Odd Pairs: A Book of Tales. Arno.
Houston, David F. *see* Houston, David Franklin.
Houston, David Franklin, 1866-1940
xHouston, David F.
A Critical Study of Nullification in South
Carolina. Peter Smith.
Critical Study of Nullification in South
Carolina. Russell.
Houston, James. *see* Houston, James A.
Houston, James A, 1921-
xHouston, James.
Ghost Fox. Avon.
Ghost Fox. HarBraceJ.
illus. Ghost Paddle: A Northwest Coast Indian
Tale. HarBraceJ.
River Runners: A Tale of Hardship & Bravery.
Atheneum.
illus. & ed. Songs of the Dream People: Chants
& Images from the Indians & Eskimos of
North America. Atheneum.
Spirit Wrestler. HarBraceJ.
The White Archer: An Eskimo Legend.
HarBraceJ.
The White Archer: An Eskimo Legend.
HarBraceJ.
White Dawn: A Eskimo Saga. HarBraceJ.
xHouston, James A.
illus. Eagle Mask: A West Coast Indian Tale.
HarBraceJ.
Houston, James D.
xHouston, James D.
Continental Drift. Berkley Pub.
Continental Drift. Knopf.
Houston, James Macintosh.
xHouston, James.
I Believe in the Creator. Eerdmans.
Houston, John A. *see* Houston, John Albert.
Houston, John Albert, 1914-
xHouston, John A.
Latin America in the United Nations.
Greenwood.
Houston, John P.
xHouston, John P.
Fundamentals of Learning. Acad Pr.
Invitation to Psychology. Acad Pr.
Houston, John P. *see* Houston, John Porter.
Houston, John Porter.
xHouston, John P.

Demonic Imagination: Style & Theme in
French Romantic Poetry. La State U Pr.
The Design of Rimbaud's Poetry. Greenwood.
Fictional Technique in France, 1802-1927: An
Introduction. La State U Pr.
Houston, Martha L. *see* Houston, Martha Lou.
Houston, Martha Lou.
xHouston, Martha L.
Indexes to the County Wills of South Carolina.
Genealog Pub.
Houston, Mary G. *see* Houston, Mary Galway.
Houston, Mary Galway, 1871-
xHouston, Mary G.
Ancient Greek, Roman & Byzantine Costume
& Decoration. B&N.
Houston, Robert.
xHouston, Robert.
Monday, Tuesday, Wednesday. Avon.
Houston, Robert W. *see* Houston, W. Robert.
Houston, Susan H. *see* Houston, Susan Hilary.
Houston, Susan Hilary, 1943-
xHouston, Susan H.
A Survey of Psycholinguistics. Mouton.
Houston, W. J. *see* Houston, W. J. B.
Houston, W. J. B.
xHouston, W. J.
Orthodontic Diagnosis. Year Bk Med.
Houston, W. Robert.
xHouston, Robert W.
Exploring Competency Based Education.
McCutchan.
Houten, Franklyn B. Van. *see* Van Houten, Franklyn B.
Houten, Ron Van. *see* Van Houten, Ron.
Houthakker, Hendrik S.
xHouthakker, Hendrik S.
Economic Policy for the Farm Sector. Am
Enterprise.
Houwink, R. *see* Houwink, Roelof.
Houwink, Roelof, 1897-
xHouwink, R.
ed. Odd Book of Data. Elsevier.
Hovanec, Helene, 1941-
xHovanec, Helene.
A Puzzler's Paradise: From the Garden of
Eden to the Computer Age. Paddington.
Hovanessian, S. A. *see* Hovanessian, Shahen A.
Hovanessian, Shahen A., 1931-
xHovanessian, S. A.
Computational Mathematics in Engineering.
Lexington Bks.
Digital Computer Methods in Engineering.
McGraw.
Hovda, Robert. *see* Hovda, Robert W.
Hovda, Robert W.
xHovda, Robert.
Strong, Loving & Wise: Presiding in Liturgy.
Liturgical Conf.
Hovde, Louise.
xHovde, Louise.
Compiled by The Cradle Book of Verse: An
Anthology of Baby Poetry. Arno.
ed. The Cradle Book of Verse: An Anthology
of Baby Poetry. Granger Bk.
Hove, M. A. Van. *see* Van Hove, M. A.
Hovell, Mark.
xHovell, Mark.
Chartist Movement. Kelley.
Hovet, Thomas.
xHovet, Thomas.
Africa in the United Nations. Northwestern U
Pr.
Hovey, Richard, 1864-1900
xHovey, Richard.
Along the Trail. AMS Pr.
How, Walter W. *see* How, Walter Wybergh.
How, Walter Wybergh.
xHow, Walter W.
ed. Commentary on Herodotus. Oxford U Pr.
Howar, Barbara.
xHowar, Barbara.

Laughing All the Way. Fawcett.
Howard, Alan, 1934-
xHoward, Alan.
Ain't No Big Thing: Coping Strategies in a
Hawaiian-American Community. U Pr of
Hawaii.
Learning to Be Rotuman: Enculturation in the
South Pacific. Tchrs Coll.
Howard, Albert, Sir, 1873-1947
xHoward, Albert.
The Soil & Health: A Study of Organic
Agriculture. Schocken.
Howard, Arthur D. *see* Howard, Arthur David.
Howard, Arthur David, 1906-
xHoward, Arthur D.
Evolution of the Landscape of the San
Francisco Bay Region. U of Cal Pr.
Geology in Environmental Planning. McGraw.
Howard, C. *see* Howard, Charles Gerard.
Howard, C. Jerial. *see* Howard, C. Jeriel.
Howard, C. Jeriel.
xHoward, C.
Contact: A Textbook in Applied
Communications. P-H.
xHoward, C. Jerial.
Contact: A Textbook in Applied
Communications. P-H.
Howard, Charles Gerard.
xHoward, C.
Law, Its Nature, Functions & Limits. P-H.
Howard, Christopher.
xHoward, Christopher.
Britain & the Casus Belli 1822-1902: A Study
of Britain's International Position from
Canning to Salisbury. Humanities.
Howard, Clark.
xHoward, Clark.
The Hunters. BJ Pub Group.
The Hunters. Dial.
Six Against the Rock. BJ Pub Group.
Six Against the Rock. Dial.
Howard, Clive.
xHoward, Clive.
Goose from Scarsdale. Lyle Stuart.
Howard, Constance.
xHoward, Constance.
Inspiration for Embroidery. Branford.
Textile Crafts. Scribner.
Howard, Daniel F. *see* Howard, Daniel Francis.
Howard, Daniel Francis.
xHoward, Daniel F.
ed. The Modern Tradition: An Anthology of
Short Stories. Little.
Howard, David, 1948-
xHoward, David.
Perspectives. SF Center Vis Stud.
illus. Realities. SF Center Vis Stud.
Howard, David. *see* Howard, David M.
Howard, David H.
xHoward, David H.
The Disequilibrium Model in a Controlled
Economy. Lexington Bks.
Howard, David M.
xHoward, David.
By the Power of the Holy Spirit. Inter-Varsity.
xHoward, David M.
How Come, God?: Reflections from Job About
God & Puzzled Man. Holman.
Student Power in World Missions.
Inter-Varsity.
Howard, David S. *see* Howard, David Sanctuary.
Howard, David Sanctuary.
xHoward, David S.
China for the West: Chinese Porcelain & Other
Decorative Arts for Export Illustrated from
the Mottahedeh Collection. Biblio Dist.
Howard, Delton T. *see* Howard, Delton Thomas.
Howard, Delton Thomas, 1883-
xHoward, Delton T.

Analytical Syllogistics: A Pragmatic
Interpretation of the Aristotelian Logic. AMS
Pr.
Howard, Dick, 1943-
xHoward, Dick.
The Development of the Marxian Dialectic. S
Ill U Pr.
The Marxian Legacy. Urizen Bks.
Howard, Donald R. *see* Howard, Donald Roy.
Howard, Donald Roy.
xHoward, Donald R.
ed. Critical Studies of Sir Gawain & the Green
Knight. U of Notre Dame Pr.
The Idea of the Canterbury Tales. U of Cal Pr.
Howard, Dorothy, 1912-
xHoward, Dorothy.
No Longer Alone. Cook.
Howard, Edward, d. 1841
xHoward, Edward.
Rattlin the Reefer. Oxford U Pr.
Howard, Edward N.
xHoward, Edward N.
Local Power & the Community Library. ALA.
Howard, Edwin J. *see* Howard, Edwin Johnston.
Howard, Edwin Johnston, 1901-
xHoward, Edwin J.
Geoffrey Chaucer. St Martin.
Geoffrey Chaucer. Twayne.
Howard, Elizabeth.
xHoward, Elizabeth.
Out of Step with the Dancers. Morrow.
Howard, Eugene R.
xHoward, Eugene R.
How School Administrators Make Things
Happen. P-H.
Howard, Frederick T. *see* Howard, Frederick Thomas.
Howard, Frederick Thomas, 1909-
xHoward, Frederick T.
Complexity of Mental Processes in Science
Testing. AMS Pr.
Howard, George.
xHoward, George.
How We Find Out About the Sea.
Transatlantic.
Howard, George E. *see* Howard, George Elliott.
Howard, George Elliott, 1849-1928
xHoward, George E.
Preliminaries of the Revolution, 1763-1775.
AMS Pr.
Howard, George P.
xHoward, George P.
ed. Airport Economic Planning. MIT Pr.
Howard, Harry N. *see* Howard, Harry Nicholas.
Howard, Harry Nicholas, 1902-
xHoward, Harry N.
Turkey, the Straits & U. S. Policy. Johns
Hopkins.
Howard, Helen A. *see* Howard, Helen Addison.
Howard, Helen Addison.
xHoward, Helen A.
American Frontier Tales. Mountain Pr.
American Indian Poetry. Twayne.
Howard, Homer, 1897-
xHoward, Homer.
Mathematics Teachers' Views on Certain
Issues in the Teaching of Mathematics. AMS
Pr.
Howard, J. Grant.
xHoward, J. Grant.
Trauma of Transparency: A Biblical Approach
to Inter-Personal Communication.
Multnomah.
Howard, J. Woodford.
xHoward, J. Woodford.
Courts of Appeals in the Federal Judicial
System: A Study of the Second, Fifth, &
District of Columbia. Princeton U Pr.
Howard, Jan.
xHoward, Jan.

ed. Humanizing Health Care. Wiley.
Howard, Jane.
  xHoward, Jane.
    Families. Berkley Pub.
    Families. S&S.
Howard, Jean G.
  xHoward, Jean G.
    illus. Half a Cage. Tidal Pr.
    illus. Of Mice & Mice. Tidal Pr.
Howard, John A.
  xHoward, John A.
    Marketing: Executive & Buyer Behavior.
      Columbia U Pr.
Howard, John K. *see* Howard, John Kenneth.
Howard, John Kenneth.
  xHoward, John K.
    Distribution & Relative Abundance of Billfishes
      (Istiophoridae) of the Pacific Ocean. U
      Miami Marine.
Howard, John R., 1933-
  xHoward, John R.
    ed. An Overview of International Studies. Mss
      Info.
    ed. Urban Black Politics. Am Acad Pol Soc
      Sci.
Howard, John T. *see* Howard, John Tasker.
Howard, John Tasker.
  xHoward, John T.
    Modern Music: A Popular Guide to Greater
      Musical Enjoyment. Greenwood.
Howard, John Trasker, 1890-
  xHoward, John T.
    Stephen Foster: America's Troubadour. Peter
      Smith.
    Stephen Foster: America's Troubadour. T Y
      Crowell.
Howard, Joyce.
  xHoward, Joyce.
    New Tole & Folk Art Designs: Painting
      Techniques & Patterns. Chilton.
Howard, Katherine.
  xHoward, Katherine.
    Max, the Nosey Bear. Western Pub.
Howard, L. V. *see* Howard, Lawrence Vaughan.
Howard, Lawrence Vaughan, 1900-
  xHoward, L. V.
    Civil Service Development in Louisiana. Tulane
      Stud Pol.
Howard, Linda.
  xHoward, Linda.
    Expecting Miracles. Putnam.
    Sons for King Yah. Logos.
Howard, Linden.
  xHoward, Linden.
    Foxglove Country. St Martin.
Howard, Marion, 1936-
  xHoward, Marion.
    Only Human: Teenage Pregnancy &
      Parenthood. Continuum.
Howard, Marshall C.
  xHoward, Marshall C.
    Legal Aspects of Marketing. McGraw.
Howard, Maureen, 1930-
  xHoward, Maureen.
    Before My Time. Little.
    Before My Time. Penguin.
    Before My Time. Popular Lib.
    Facts of Life. Little.
    Facts of Life. Penguin.
Howard, Michael. *see* Howard, Michael Eliot.
Howard, Michael C. *see* Howard, Michael Charles.
Howard, Michael Charles, 1945-
  xHoward, Michael C.
    Modern Theories of Income Distribution. St
      Martin.
Howard, Michael E. *see* Howard, Michael Eliot.
Howard, Michael Eliot, 1922-
  xHoward, Michael.

ed. Restraints on War: Studies in the
    Limitation of Armed Conflict. Oxford U Pr.
  xHoward, Michael E.
    Soldiers & Governments: Nine Studies in
      Civil-Military Relations. Greenwood.
Howard, Patricia.
  xHoward, Patricia.
    Gluck & the Birth of Modern Opera. St
      Martin.
    The Operas of Benjamin Britten: An
      Introduction. Greenwood.
Howard, Patsy C.
  xHoward, Patsy C.
    Theses in American Literature, 1896-1971.
      Pierian.
Howard, Perry H.
  xHoward, Perry H.
    Political Tendencies in Louisiana. La State U
      Pr.
Howard, Philip, 1933-
  xHoward, Philip.
    London's River. St Martin.
    Weasel Words. Oxford U Pr.
Howard, Rhoda.
  xHoward, Rhoda.
    Colonialism & Underdevelopment in Ghana.
      Holmes & Meier.
Howard, Robert E.
  xHoward, Robert E.
    Almuric. Berkley Pub.
    The Last Ride. Berkley Pub.
    Marchers of Valhalla. Berkley Pub.
    Marchers of Valhalla. D M Grant.
Howard, Robert E. *see* Howard, Robert Ervin.
Howard, Robert Ervin.
  xHoward, Robert E.
    Red Nails. Berkley Pub.
    Son of the White Wolf. Berkley Pub.
    Swords of Shahrazar. Berkley Pub.
Howard, Robert W. *see* Howard, Robert West.
Howard, Robert West, 1908-
  xHoward, Robert W.
    ed. This Is the South. Arno.
Howard, Roger, 1938-
  xHoward, Roger.
    Contemporary Chinese Theatre. Heinemann
      Ed.
    Mao Tse Tung & the Chinese People. Monthly
      Rev.
Howard, Ronald A.
  xHoward, Ronald A.
    Dynamic Probabilistic Systems. Wiley.
Howard, Ronnalie R. *see* Howard, Ronnalie Roper.
Howard, Ronnalie Roper.
  xHoward, Ronnalie R.
    The Dark Glass: Vision & Technique in the
      Poetry of Dante Gabriel Rossetti. Ohio U Pr.
Howard, Sam.
  xHoward, Sam.
    Communications Machines. Raintree Child.
Howard, Seymour, 1928-
  xHoward, Seymour.
    The Lansdowne Herakles. J P Getty Mus.
Howard, Thomas.
  xHoward, Thomas.
    Hallowed Be This House. Shaw Pubs.
Howard University Libraries, Washington, D.C. *see*
  Howard University, Washington, D.C. Library.
Howard University, Washington, D.C. Library.
  xHoward University Libraries, Washington, D.C.
    Dictionary Catalog of the Arthur B. Spingarn
      Collection of Negro Authors. G K Hall.
    Dictionary Catalog of the Jesse E. Moorland
      Collection of Negro Life & History. G K
      Hall.
Howard, Vechel.
  xHoward, Vechel.
    Tall in the West. Fawcett.
Howard, Vernon. *see* Howard, Vernon Linwood.

Howard, Vernon Linwood.
  xHoward, Vernon.
    Pantomimes, Charades & Skits. Sterling.
    Pathways to Perfect Living. Stein & Day.
    The Power of Your Supermind. De Vorss.
    Psycho-Pictography: The New Way to Use the
      Miracle Power of Your Mind. P-H.
Howard W. Sams Editorial Staff. *see* Sams (Howard W.)
  and Company, Inc., Indianapolis.
Howard W. Sams Engineering Staff. *see* Sams (Howard
  W.) and Company, Inc., Indianapolis. Engineering
  Staff.
Howard, William W.
  xHoward, William W.
    Atlas of Operative Dentistry. Mosby.
    Dental Practice Planning. Mosby.
Howard-Williams, Jeremy, 1922-
  xHoward-Williams, Jeremy.
    The Care & Repair of Sails. Norton.
    The Care & Repair of Sails. Sail Bks.
    Racing Dinghy Sails. Times Bks.
Howards, Melvin.
  xHowards, Melvin.
    Reading Diagnosis & Instruction: An
      Integrated Approach. Reston.
Howarth, David. *see* Howarth, David Armine.
Howarth, David Armine.
  xHowarth, David.
    The Dreadnoughts. Time-Life.
  xHowarth, David P.
    The Dreadnoughts. Silver.
Howarth, David P. *see* Howarth, David Armine.
Howarth, O. W. *see* Howarth, Oliver.
Howarth, Oliver.
  xHowarth, O. W.
    Theory of Spectroscopy: Elementary
      Introduction. Halsted Pr.
Howarth, P. *see* Howarth, Patrick.
Howarth, Patrick.
  xHowarth, P.
    When the Riviera Was Ours. Routledge &
      Kegan.
Howarth, R. G. *see* Howarth, Robert Guy.
Howarth, Robert Guy, 1906-
  xHowarth, R. G.
    Literary Particles. Kennikat.
Howarth, T. *see* Howarth, Thomas.
Howarth, Thomas, 1914-
  xHowarth, T.
    Charles Rennie Mackintosh & the Modern
      Movement. Routledge & Kegan.
  xHowarth, Thomas.
    Charles Rennie Mackintosh & the Modern
      Movement. Garland Pub.
Howarth, W. D. *see* Howarth, William Driver.
Howarth, William Driver.
  xHowarth, W. D.
    ed. Comic Drama: The European Heritage. St
      Martin.
Howarth, William L., 1940-
  xHowarth, William L.
    The Literary Manuscripts of Henry David
      Thoreau. Ohio St U Pr.
Howat, G. M. *see* Howat, Gerald Malcolm David.
Howat, Gerald Malcolm David.
  xHowat, G. M.
    Stuart & Cromwellian Foreign Policy. St
      Martin.
Howat, Henry T.
  xHowat, Henry T.
    ed. The Exocrine Pancreas. Saunders.
Howat, John K.
  xHowat, John K.
    The Hudson River & Its Painters. Penguin.
Howatch, Susan.
  xHowatch, Susan.

Call in the Night. Fawcett.
Cashelmara. Fawcett.
Cashelmara. S&S.
The Dark Shore. Fawcett.
Devil on Lammas Night. Fawcett.
Penmarric. Fawcett.
The Rich Are Different. Fawcett.
The Rich Are Different. S&S.
Sins of the Fathers. S&S.
A Susan Howatch Treasury. Stein & Day.

Howatson, A. M.
xHowatson, A. M.
An Introduction to Gas Discharges. Pergamon.

Howay, Frederic William.
xHoway, Frederic William.
A List of Trading Vessels in the Maritime Fur Trade, 1785-1825. Limestone Pr.

Howe, Carrol. see Howe, Carrol B.

Howe, Carrol B., 1910-
xHowe, Carrol.
Ancient Modocs of California & Oregon. Binford.
xHowe, Carrol B.
Ancient Tribes of the Klamath Country. Binford.

Howe, Charles W.
xHowe, Charles W.
Inland Waterway Transportation: Studies in Public & Private Management & Investment Decisions. Johns Hopkins.
Interbasin Transfers of Water: Economic Issues & Impacts. Johns Hopkins.
Natural Resource Economics: Issues Analysis & Policy. Wiley.

Howe, Christopher.
xHowe, Christopher.
China's Economy: A Basic Guide. Basic.

Howe, Daniel W. see Howe, Daniel Walker.

Howe, Daniel Walker.
xHowe, Daniel W.
The Political Culture of the American Whigs. U of Chicago Pr.

Howe, Deborah.
xHowe, Deborah.
Bunnicula: A Rabbit-Tale of Mystery. Avon.
Bunnicula: A Rabbit Tale of Mystery. Atheneum.
Teddy Bear's Scrapbook. Atheneum.

Howe, E. D. see Howe, Everett Dumser.

Howe, Eunice D.
xHowe, Eunice D.
The Hospital of Santo Spirito & Pope Sixtus IV. Garland Pub.

Howe, Everett Dumser, 1903-
xHowe, E. D.
Fundamentals of Water Desalination. Dekker.

Howe, Fanny.
xHowe, Fanny.
Holy Smoke. Fiction Coll.
The White Slave. Avon.

Howe, Florence.
xHowe, Florence.
ed. No More Masks: An Anthology of Poems by Women. Doubleday.

Howe, Frederic. see Howe, Frederic Clemson.
Howe, Frederic C. see Howe, Frederic Clemson.

Howe, Frederic Clemson, 1867-1940
xHowe, Frederic.
Confessions of a Monopolist. Alpine Ent.
xHowe, Frederic C.
Confessions of a Monopolist. Irvington.
Privilege & Democracy in America. Arno.

Howe, George.
xHowe, George.
Handbook of Classical Mythology. Gale.

Howe, Harlan.
xHowe, Harlan.
Stripline Circuit Design. Artech Hse.

Howe, Helen.
xHowe, Helen.

The Success. Queens Hse.
Howe, Henry F. see Howe, Henry Forbush.

Howe, Henry Forbush, 1905-
xHowe, Henry F.
Prologue to New England. Kennikat.

Howe, Henry V. see Howe, Henry Van Wagenen.

Howe, Henry Van Wagenen, 1896-
xHowe, Henry V.
Ostracod Taxonomy. La State U Pr.

Howe, I. see Howe, Irving.

Howe, Irving.
xHowe, I.
Literature of America. McGraw.
The UAW & Walter Reuther. Da Capo.
xHowe, Irving.
ed. Ashes Out of Hope: Fiction by Soviet-Yiddish Writers. Schocken.
Celebrations & Attacks: Thirty Years of Literary & Cultural Commentary. Horizon.
ed. Classics of Modern Fiction: Ten Short Novels. HarBraceJ.
Decline of the New. HarBraceJ.
Decline of the New. Horizon.
ed. Essential Works of Socialism. Yale U Pr.
ed. Fiction As Experience: An Anthology. HarBraceJ.
How We Lived: A Documentary History of Immigrant Jews in America, 1880-1930. Marek.
ed. The Idea of the Modern in Literature & the Arts. Horizon.
Leon Trotsky. Penguin.
Leon Trotsky. Viking Pr.
ed. Literature As Experience: An Anthology. HarBraceJ.
Politics & the Novel. Arno.
Politics & the Novel. Horizon.
Steady Work: Essays in the Politics of Democratic Radicalism 1953-1966. HarBraceJ.
Thomas Hardy. Macmillan.
World of Our Fathers. HarBraceJ.
World of Our Fathers. PB.
World of Our Fathers. S&S.
ed. The World of the Blue-Collar Worker. Times Bks.

Howe, James, 1935-
xHowe, James R.
Marlowe, Tamburlaine, & Magic. Ohio U Pr.

Howe, James R. see Howe, James Robert.

Howe, James Robert, 1943-
xHowe, James R.
Patient Care in Neurosurgery. Little.

Howe, John.
xHowe, John.
Choosing the Right Dog: A Buyer's Guide to All 121 Breeds. Har-Row.

Howe, Joseph W. see Howe, Joseph William.

Howe, Joseph William, 1843-1890
xHowe, Joseph W.
Excessive Venery, Masturbation & Continence. Arno.

Howe, Julia. see Howe, Julia (Ward).

Howe, Julia (Ward), 1819-1910
xHowe, Julia.
Trip to Cuba. Negro U Pr.
xHowe, Julia W.
Margaret Fuller - Marchesa Ossoli. Greenwood.

Howe, Julia W. see Howe, Julia (Ward).

Howe, K. R.
xHowe, K. R.
The Loyalty Islands: History of Culture Contacts, 1840-1900. U Pr of Hawaii.

Howe, M. see Howe, Mark De Wolfe.
Howe, M. De Wolfe. see Howe, Mark Antony De Wolfe.
Howe, M. DeWolfe. see Howe, Mark Antony De Wolfe.
Howe, Mark A. see Howe, Mark Anthony De Wolfe.

Howe, Mark Anthony De Wolfe, 1864-1960
xHowe, Mark A.

ed. Later Years of the Saturday Club, 1870-1920. Arno.

Howe, Mark Antony De Wolfe, 1864-1960
xHowe, M.
Memories of a Hostess. R West.
xHowe, M. De Wolfe.
The Boston Symphony Orchestra: 1881-1931. Da Capo.
Boston the Place & the People. Norwood Edns.
Life & Letters of George Bancroft. Kennikat.
xHowe, M. DeWolfe.
Holmes of the Breakfast-Table. Appel.
xHowe, Mark A.
Venture in Remembrance. Greenwood.
xHowe, Mark D.
The Life & Letters of George Bancroft. Da Capo.

Howe, Mark D. see Howe, Mark Antony De Wolfe.

Howe, Mark De Wolfe.
xHowe, M.
ed. Readings in American Legal History. Da Capo.
xHowe, Mark D.
Garden & the Wilderness: Religion & Government in American Constitutional History. U of Chicago Pr.

Howe, Michael. see Howe, Michael J. A.
Howe, Michael J. see Howe, Michael J. A.

Howe, Michael J. A., 1940-
xHowe, Michael.
Learning in Infants & Young Children. Stanford U Pr.
xHowe, Michael J.
The Psychology of Human Learning. Har-Row.
Understanding School Learning: A New Look at Educational Psychology. Har-Row.
xHowe, Michael J. A.
Adult Learning: Psychological Research & Applications. Wiley.

Howe, Paul S. see Howe, Paul Sturtevant.

Howe, Paul Sturtevant.
xHowe, Paul S.
Mayflower Pilgrim Descendants in Cape May County, New Jersey. Genealog Pub.

Howe, Percival. see Howe, Percival Presland.
Howe, Percival P. see Howe, Percival Presland.

Howe, Percival Presland, 1886-1944
xHowe, Percival.
The Life of William Hazlitt. Greenwood.
xHowe, Percival P.
ed. Dramatic Portraits. Kennikat.

Howe, Reuel L, 1905-
xHowe, Reuel L.
Creative Years. Seabury.
Survival Plus. Seabury.

Howe, Robin.
xHowe, Robin.
Rice Cooking. Transatlantic.

Howe, Samuel G. see Howe, Samuel Gridley.

Howe, Samuel Gridley.
xHowe, Samuel G.
On the Causes of Idiocy. Arno.

Howe, W. W. see Howe, William Wirt.
Howe, Will D. see Howe, Will David.

Howe, Will David, 1873-1946
xHowe, Will D.
Charles Lamb & His Friends. Greenwood.

Howe, William W. see Howe, William Wirt.

Howe, William Wirt, 1833-1909
xHowe, W. W.
Municipal History of New Orleans. Johnson Repr.
xHowe, William W.
Municipal History of New Orleans. AMS Pr.

Howe, Winifred E. see Howe, Winifred Eva.

Howe, Winifred Eva, 1876-
xHowe, Winifred E.

A History of the Metropolitan Museum of Art:
    With a Chapter on the Early Institutions of
    Art in New York. Arno.
Howell, A. Ferrers. see Howell, Alan George Ferrers.
Howell, Alan George Ferrers, 1855-
    xHowell, A. Ferrers.
    Dante, His Life & Work. Kennikat.
Howell, Benjamin F. see Howell, Benjamin Franklin.
Howell, Benjamin Franklin, 1917-
    xHowell, Benjamin F.
    Introduction to Geophysics. Krieger.
Howell, Clinton. see Howell, Clinton Talmage.
Howell, Clinton Talmage, 1913-
    xHowell, Clinton.
    Joyous Journey. Nelson.
Howell, Cotton.
    xHowell, Cotton.
    How to Write a Will. Johnson Colo.
Howell, D. see Howell, Derek.
Howell, Daisy.
    xHowell, Daisy.
    Activities for Teaching Mathematics to Low
        Achievers. U Pr of Miss.
Howell, David, 1945-
    xHowell, David.
    British Social Democracy: A Study in
        Development & Decay. St Martin.
Howell, Derek.
    xHowell, D.
    Your Solar Energy Home: Including Wind &
        Methane Applications. Pergamon.
Howell, F. Clark. see Howell, Francis Clark.
Howell, Francis Clark.
    xHowell, F. Clark.
    Early Man. Silver.
    Early Man. Silver.
Howell, Harry D.
    xHowell, Harry D.
    Strange Negro Stories of the Old Deep South.
        Arno.
Howell, James E. see Howell, James Edwin.
Howell, James Edwin.
    xHowell, James E.
    Mathematical Analysis for Business Decisions.
        Irwin.
Howell, John C.
    xHowell, John C.
    Equality & Submission in Marriage. Broadman.
Howell, John T. see Howell, John Thomas.
Howell, John Thomas, 1903-
    xHowell, John T.
    Marin Flora: Manual of the Flowering Plants &
        Ferns of Marin County, California. U of Cal
        Pr.
Howell, Leon.
    xHowell, Leon.
    Asia, Oil Politics & the Energy Crisis: The
        Haves & the Have-Nots. IDOC.
Howell, M. G. see Howell, M Gertrude.
Howell, M Gertrude.
    xHowell, M. G.
    Formula Index to NMR Literature Data. IFI
        Plenum.
Howell, Robert G.
    xHowell, Robert G.
    Discipline in the Classroom: Solving the
        Teaching Puzzle. Reston.
Howell, Robert L. see Howell, Robert Lee.
Howell, Robert Lee.
    xHowell, Robert L.
    Fish for My People. Morehouse.
Howell, Roger.
    xHowell, Roger.
    Cromwell. Little.
    The Origins of the English Revolution. Forum
        Pr MO.
Howell, Sarah, 1929-
    xHowell, Sarah.

Creative Crafts for Self Expression. Broadman.
Howell, Thomas.
    xHowell, Thomas.
    Avant-Garde Flute: A Handbook for
        Composers & Flutists. U of Cal Pr.
Howell, Thomas R.
    xHowell, Thomas R.
    Breeding Biology of the Gray Gull, Larus
        Modestus. U of Cal Pr.
Howell, Wilbur S. see Howell, Wilbur Samuel.
Howell, Wilbur Samuel, 1904-
    xHowell, Wilbur S.
    Eighteenth-Century British Logic & Rhetoric.
        Princeton U Pr.
Howell, William B. see Howell, William Boyman.
Howell, William Boyman, 1873-
    xHowell, William B.
    Medicine in Canada. AMS Pr.
Howell, William C. see Howell, William Carl.
Howell, William Carl.
    xHowell, William C.
    Essentials of Industrial & Organizational
        Psychology. Dorsey.
Howell, William S. see Howell, William Smiley.
Howell, William Smiley.
    xHowell, William S.
    Presentational Speaking for Business & the
        Professions. Har-Row.
Howell-Koehler, Nancy.
    xHowell-Koehler, Nancy.
    Photo Art Processes. Davis Mass.
    Soft Jewelry: Design Techniques & Materials.
        P-H.
    Soft Jewelry: Design, Techniques, Materials.
        Prndlc Whirr.
Howells, Coral A. see Howells, Coral Ann.
Howells, Coral Ann.
    xHowells, Coral A.
    Love, Mystery & Misery: Feeling in Gothic
        Fiction. Humanities.
Howells, John G.
    xHowells, John G.
    Principles of Family Psychiatry.
        Brunner-Mazel.
    ed. World History of Psychiatry.
        Brunner-Mazel.
Howells, Roscoe.
    xHowells, Roscoe.
    Heronsmill. St Martin.
Howells, W. D. see Howells, William Dean.
Howells, W. W. see Howells, William White.
Howells, William.
    xHowells, William.
    Cambrian Superstitions, Comprising Ghosts,
        Omens, Witchcraft, & Traditions. Folcroft.
Howells, William. see Howells, William White.
Howells, William D. see Howells, William Dean.
Howells, William Dean, 1837-1920
    xHowells, W. D.
    Altrurian Romances. Ind U Pr.
    April Hopes. Ind U Pr.
    Chance Acquaintance. Ind U Pr.
    Indian Summer. Ind U Pr.
    The Leatherwood God. Ind U Pr.
    A Modern Instance. Ind U Pr.
    A Pair of Patient Lovers. Arden Lib.
    The Quality of Mercy. Ind U Pr.
    The Son of Royal Langbrith. Ind U Pr.
    Their Wedding Journey. Ind U Pr.
    xHowells, William D.

Annie Kilburn. Folcroft.
Boy's Town, Described for Harper's Young
    People. Greenwood.
Chance Acquaintance. Folcroft.
Chance Acquaintance. Greenwood.
A Chance Acquaintance. Irvington.
Chance Acquaintance. Scholarly.
Doctor Breen's Practice: A Novel. Folcroft.
A Foregone Conclusion. Irvington.
A Foregone Conclusion. Scholarly.
Imaginary Interviews. Folcroft.
Imaginary Interviews. Greenwood.
Impressions & Experiences. Arno.
Leatherwood God. AMS Pr.
Leatherwood God. Folcroft.
Leatherwood God. Scholarly.
Life & Letters of William Dean Howells.
    Scholarly.
Life in Letters of William Dean Howells.
    Russell.
Literary Friends & Acquaintance: A Personal
    Retrospect of American Authorship. Folcroft.
Literary Friends & Acquaintance: A Personal
    Retrospect of American Authorship.
    Greenwood.
Modern Instance. HM.
Modern Italian Poets: Essays & Versions.
    Russell.
Pair of Patient Lovers. Arno.
Pair of Patient Lovers. Folcroft.
Quality of Mercy. Folcroft.
Quality of Mercy. Scholarly.
Questionable Shapes. Arno.
Questionable Shapes. Folcroft.
Suburban Sketches. Arno.
Suburban Sketches. Folcroft.
Their Wedding Journey. Queens Hse.
Undiscovered Country. Folcroft.
Undiscovered Country. Scholarly.
Venetian Life. AMS Pr.
Venetian Life. Folcroft.
xHowells, William Dean.
    In After Days: Thoughts on Future Life. Arno.
Howells, William White.
    xHowells, W. W.
    Craniometry & Multivariate Analysis. Peabody
        Harvard.
    xHowells, William.
    Evolution of the Genus Homo.
        Benjamin-Cummings.
    ed. Ideas on Human Evolution: Selected
        Essays, 1949-1961. Atheneum.
Hower, Ralph M. see Hower, Ralph Merle.
Hower, Ralph Merle, 1903-1973
    xHower, Ralph M.
    The History of an Advertising Agency. Arno.
Hower, Rolland O.
    xHower, Rolland O.
    Freeze-Drying Biological Specimens: A
        Laboratory Manual. Smithsonian.
Howes, Barbara.
    xHowes, Barbara.
    A Private Signal: Poems New & Selected.
        Columbia U Pr.
Howes, C.
    xHowes, C.
    Practical Upholstery. Sterling.
Howes, F. A. see Howes, Frederick A.
Howes, F. N. see Howes, Frank Norman.
Howes, Frank. see Howes, Frank Stewart.
Howes, Frank Norman.
    xHowes, F. N.
    Dictionary of Useful & Everyday Plants &
        Their Common Names. Cambridge U Pr.
Howes, Frank Stewart, 1891-
    xHowes, Frank.

The Music of Ralph Vaughan Williams.
Greenwood.
The Music of William Walton. Oxford U Pr.
Howes, Frederick A., 1948-
xHowes, F. A.
Boundary-Interior Layer Interactions in
Nonlinear Singular Perturbation Theory. Am
Math.
Howes, M. J.
xHowes, M. J.
ed. Variable Impedance Devices. Wiley.
Howes, V. M. *see* Howes, Virgil M.
Howes, Virgil M.
xHowes, V. M.
Informal Teaching in the Open Classroom.
Macmillan.
xHowes, Virgil M.
Individualizing Instruction in Science &
Mathematics: Selected Readings on
Programs, Practices, & Uses of Technology.
Macmillan.
Howgate, George W. *see* Howgate, George Washburne.
Howgate, George Washburne, 1903-1950
xHowgate, George W.
George Santayana. Russell.
Howie, J. G. *see* Howie, John Garvie Robertson.
Howie, J. M. *see* Howie, John Mackintosh.
Howie, John.
xHowie, John.
ed. Contemporary Studies in Philosophical
Idealism. C Stark.
Howie, John Garvie Robertson.
xHowie, J. G.
Research in General Practice. Biblio Dist.
Howie, John Mackintosh.
xHowie, J. M.
ed. An Introduction to Semigroup Theory.
Acad Pr.
Howie, John Marshall.
xHowie, J. M.
Acoustical Studies of Mandarin Vowels &
Tones. Cambridge U Pr.
Howington, Nolan. *see* Howington, Nolan P.
Howington, Nolan P.
xHowington, Nolan.
Growing Disciples Through Preaching.
Broadman.
Howitt, Mary (Botham).
xHowitt, Mary B.
Mary Howitt: An Autobiography. AMS Pr.
Howitt, Mary B. *see* Howitt, Mary (Botham).
Howitt, William, 1792-1879
xHowitt, William.
Colonization & Christianity: A Popular History
of the Treatment of the Natives by the
Europeans in All Their Colonies. Negro U
Pr.
Homes & Haunts of the Most Eminent British
Poets. Folcroft.
Homes & Haunts of the Most Eminent British
Poets. Johnson Repr.
Woodburn Grange. Garland Pub.
Howl, Barbara.
xHowl, Barbara.
Simplified Physics for Radiology Students. C C
Thomas.
Howland, John L.
xHowland, John L.
Cell Physiology. Macmillan.
A Mathematical Approach to Biology. Heath.
Howland, Richard H. *see* Howland, Richard Hubbard.
Howland, Richard Hubbard.
xHowland, Richard H.
Greek Lamps & Their Survivals. Am Sch
Athens.
Howlett, Charles F.
xHowlett, Charles F.

Troubled Philosopher: John Dewey & the
Struggle for World Peace. Kennikat.
Howlett, John, 1940-
xHowlett, John.
The Christmas Spy. HarBraceJ.
Howley, Joan.
xHowley, Joan.
Journey to Self-Discovery: A Valuing
Workbook. Winston Pr.
Howorth, Peter, 1944-
xHoworth, Peter C.
The Abalone Book. Naturegraph.
Howorth, Peter C. *see* Howorth, Peter.
Howse, Derek.
xHowse, Derek.
Greenwich Time & the Discovery of the
Longitude. Oxford U Pr.
Howson, Gerald.
xHowson, Gerald.
Burgoyne of Saratoga: A Biography. Times Bks.
Howson, Susan, 1945-
xHowson, Susan.
Domestic Monetary Management in Britain,
1919-38. Cambridge U Pr.
Hoxha, Enver, 1908-
xHoxha, Enver.
Imperialism & the Revolution. World View
Pubns.
Hoy, Don R.
xHoy, Don R.
Essentials of Geography & Development:
Concepts & Processes. Macmillan.
Hoy, Peter C.
xHoy, Peter C.
Checklist of Writings About Edwin Muir.
Whitston Pub.
Hoy, Ray.
xHoy, Ray.
Ford Vans: 1969-1979 Shop Manual. Clymer
Pubns.
Honda 125-200cc Twins, 1964-1977: Service,
Repair, Performance. Clymer Pubns.
Honda 250 & 350cc Twins, 1964-1974:
Service-Repair-Performance. Clymer Pubns.
Honda 250 & 360cc Twins, 1974-1977:
Service-Repair-Performance. Clymer Pubns.
Opel Service Repair Handbook: All Models,
1966-1977. Clymer Pubns.
Subaru Service Repair Handbook: All Models,
1972-1977. Clymer Pubns.
Suzuki Service-Repair Handbook 125-500cc
Twins: 1964-1976. Clymer Pubns.
Hoy, Wayne K.
xHoy, Wayne K.
Educational Administration: Theory, Research,
& Practice. Random.
Hoyaux, M. F. *see* Hoyaux, Max Florian.
Hoyaux, Max Florian, 1919-
xHoyaux, M. F.
Arc Physics. Springer-Verlag.
Hoye, Robert E.
xHoye, Robert E.
ed. Index to Computer Based Learning. Educ
Tech Pubns.
Hoyenga, Katharine B. *see* Hoyenga, Katharine Blick.
Hoyenga, Katharine Blick.
xHoyenga, Katharine B.
The Question of Sex Differences:
Psychological, Cultural, & Biological Issues.
Little.
Hoyland, John S. *see* Hoyland, John Somervell.
Hoyland, John Somervell, 1887-
xHoyland, John S.
Indian Crisis: The Background. Arno.
Hoyle, B. S.
xHoyle, Brian S.
Spatial Aspects of Development. Wiley.
Hoyle, Brian S. *see* Hoyle, B. S.
Hoyle, Fred.
xHoyle, Fred.

Action at a Distance in Physics & Cosmology.
W H Freeman.
Andromeda Breakthrough. Har-Row.
Astronomy & Cosmology: A Modern Course.
W H Freeman.
Commonsense in Nuclear Energy. W H
Freeman.
The Cosmogony of the Solar System. Enslow
Pubs.
Diseases from Space. Har-Row.
Fifth Planet. Har-Row.
Frontiers of Astronomy. Har-Row.
Highlights in Astronomy. W H Freeman.
The Incandescent Ones. Har-Row.
Nature of the Universe. Har-Row.
October the First Is Too Late. Har-Row.
Of Men & Galaxies. U of Wash Pr.
On Stonehenge. W H Freeman.
Hoyle, L. *see* Hoyle, Leslie.
Hoyle, Leslie.
xHoyle, L.
Influenza Viruses. Springer-Verlag.
Hoyle, Robert J.
xHoyle, Robert J.
Wood Technology in the Design of Structures.
Mountain Pr.
Hoyt, Edwin C. *see* Hoyt, Edwin Chase.
Hoyt, Edwin Chase, 1916-
xHoyt, Edwin C.
National Policy & International Law: Case
Studies from American Canal Policy. U of
Denver Intl.
Hoyt, Edwin P. *see* Hoyt, Edwin Palmer.
Hoyt, Edwin Palmer.
xHoyt, Edwin P.
American Attitude: The Story of the Making of
Foreign Policy in the United States. Abelard.
Asians in the West. Elsevier-Nelson.
Franklin Pierce: The Fourteenth President of
the United States. Abelard.
The Improper Bostonian: Dr. Oliver Wendell
Holmes. Morrow.
The Men of the Gambier Bay. Eriksson.
The Mutiny on the Globe. Random.
Storm Over the Gilberts: War in the Central
Pacific: 1943. Van Nos Reinhold.
William O. Douglas: A Biography. Eriksson.
Hoyt, Elizabeth E. *see* Hoyt, Elizabeth Ellis.
Hoyt, Elizabeth Ellis, 1893-
xHoyt, Elizabeth E.
The Consumption of Wealth. Arno.
Hoyt, George C. *see* Hoyt, George Calvin.
Hoyt, George Calvin.
xHoyt, George C.
A Study of Retirement Problems. R & E Res
Assoc.
Hoyt, Herman A. *see* Hoyt, Herman Arthur.
Hoyt, Herman Arthur, 1909-
xHoyt, Herman A.
The End Times. BMH Bks.
End Times. Moody.
Hoyt, K. *see* Hoyt, Kendall K.
Hoyt, Kendall K.
xHoyt, K.
Drunk Before Noon: The Behind-the-Scenes
Story of the Washington Press Corps. P-H.
Hoyt, Kenneth B.
xHoyt, Kenneth B.
Career Education & the Elementary School
Teacher. Olympus Pub Co.
Career Education in the High School. Olympus
Pub Co.
Hoyt, Murray.
xHoyt, Murray.
Creative Retirement: Planning the Best Years
Yet. Garden Way Pub.
Hoyt, Olga.
xHoyt, Olga.

American Indians Today. Abelard.
Demons, Devils & Djinn. Abelard.
Exorcism. Watts.
xHoyt, Olga G.
Freedom of the News Media. HM.
Hoyt, Olga G. see Hoyt, Olga.
Hoyt, Patricia.
xHoyt, Patricia.
How to Get Started When You Dont Know
Where to Begin. HarBraceJ.
Hoyt, Robert G.
xHoyt, Robert G.
Martin Luther King, Jr.. Country Beautiful.
Hoyt, Robert S. see Hoyt, Robert Stuart.
Hoyt, Robert Stuart.
xHoyt, Robert S.
Europe in the Middle Ages. HarBraceJ.
Hoyt, William G. see Hoyt, William Graves.
Hoyt, William Graves.
xHoyt, William G.
Planets X & Pluto. U of Ariz Pr.
Hozumi, Nobushige, 1855-1926
xHozumi, Nobushige.
Ancestor-Worship & Japanese Law. Arno.
Hraba, Joseph.
xHraba, Joseph.
American Ethnicity. Peacock Pubs.
Hrbacek, Karel.
xHrbacek, Karel.
Introduction to Set Theory. Dekker.
Hrbkova, Sarka B., 1878-
xHrbkova, Sarka B.
ed. Czechoslovak Stories. AMS Pr.
tr. Czechoslovak Stories. Arno.
Hrdlicka, Ales, 1869-1943
xHrdlicka, Ales.
The Anthropology of Kodiak Island. AMS Pr.
Old Americans: A Physiological Profile. Arno.
Practical Anthropometry. AMS Pr.
Hrebiniak, Lawrence G
xHrebiniak, Lawrence G.
Complex Organizations. West Pub.
Hren, John J.
xHren, John J.
ed. Field-Ion Microscopy. Plenum Pub.
ed. Introduction to Analytical Electron
Microscopy. Plenum Pub.

Hsia, Chih-Tsing, 1921-
xHsia, Chih-Tsing.
ed. Twentieth Century Chinese Stories.
Columbia U Pr.

Hsia, Linda.
xHsia, Linda.
Speak Chinese: Supplementary Materials. Far
Eastern Pubns.
Hsia, Ronald.
xHsia, Ronald.
Industrialisation Employment & Income
Distribution: A Case Study of Hong Kong.
Biblio Dist.
Hsia, Tao-T'Ai.
xHsia, Tao-Tai.
China's Language Reforms. Far Eastern Pubns.
Hsia, Tao-Tai. see Hsia, Tao-T'Ai.
Hsia, Tien C.
xHsia, Tien C.
System Identification: Least Squares Method.
Lexington Bks.

Hsia, Tsi-An, 1916-1965

xHsia, Tsi-An.
Gate of Darkness: Studies on the Leftist
Literary Movement in China. U of Wash Pr.

Hsia, Y. Edward. see Hsia, Yujen Edward.

Hsia, Yujen Edward, 1931-
xHsia, Y. Edward.

ed. Counseling in Genetics. A R Liss.
Hsiang, W. Y. see Hsiang, Wu Yi.
Hsiang, Wu Yi, 1937-
xHsiang, W. Y.
Cohomology Theory of Topological
Transformation Groups. Springer-Verlag.
Hsiao, David K.
xHsiao, David K.
Computer Security. Acad Pr.
Hsiao, Ellen.
xHsiao, Ellen.
illus. A Chinese Year. M Evans.
Hsiao, Gene T.
xHsiao, Gene T.
Foreign Trade of China: Policy, Law, &
Practice. U of Cal Pr.
Hsiao, H. S. see Hsiao, Henry S.
Hsiao, Henry S.
xHsiao, H. S.
Attraction of Moths to Light & to Infrared
Radiation. San Francisco Pr.
Hsiao, Katharine Huang.
xHsiao, Katherine H.
Money & Monetary Policy in Communist
China. Columbia U Pr.
Hsiao, Katherine H. see Hsiao, Katharine Huang.
Hsiao, Kung-Chuan, 1897-
xHsiao, Kung-Chuan.
A Modern China & a New World: K'ang
Yu-Wei, Reformer & Utopian, 1858-1927. U
of Wash Pr.
Hsiao, Tso-Liang, 1910-
xHsiao, Tso-Liang.
Power Relations Within the Chinese
Communist Movement, 1930-34: A Study of
Documents. U of Wash Pr.
Hsie, Abraham W.
xHsie, Abraham W.
ed. Mammalian Cell Mutagenesis: The
Maturation of Test Systems. Cold Spring
Harbor.
Hsieh, Alice L. see Hsieh, Alice Langley.
Hsieh, Alice Langley.
xHsieh, Alice L.
Communist China's Strategy in Nuclear Era.
Greenwood.
Hsieh, Chiao-Min, 1921-
xHsieh, Chiao-Min.
Atlas of China. McGraw.
Hsieh, J. S. see Hsieh, Jui Sheng.
Hsieh, Jui Sheng, 1921-
xHsieh, J. S.
Principles of Thermodynamics. McGraw.
Hsieh, Pao C. see Hsieh, Pao Chao.
Hsieh, Pao Chao, 1896-
xHsieh, Pao C.
Government of China, 1644-1911. Octagon.
xHsieh, Pao Chao.
The Government of China: 1644-1911. AMS
Pr.
Hsieh, Winston.
xHsieh, Winston.
Chinese Historiography on the Revolution of
1911: A Critical Survey & a Selected
Bibliography. Hoover Inst Pr.
Hsiung, James C. see Hsiung, James Chieh.
Hsiung, James Chieh, 1935-
xHsiung, James C.
ed. The Logic of "Maoism": Critiques &
Explication. Praeger.
xHsiung, James Chieh.
Law & Policy in China's Foreign Relations: A
Study of Attitudes & Practices. Columbia U
Pr.
Hsiung, Wenchin Y. see Hsiung, Wenchin Yu.
Hsiung, Wenchin Yu.
xHsiung, Wenchin Y.

Chinese Cooking for American Kitchens.
Aurora Pubs.
Hsu, Cho-Yun.
xHsu, Cho-yun.
Han Agriculture: The Formation of the Early
Chinese Agrarian Economy. U of Wash Pr.
Hsu, Donald K.
xHsu, Donald K.
Spectral Atlas of Nitrogen Dioxide: 5530a to
6480a. Acad Pr.
Hsu, Dorothy.
xHsu, Dorothy.
Mending. Cook.
Hsu, Francis L. see Hsu, Francis L. K.
Hsu, Francis L. K.
xHsu, Francis L.
Under the Ancestors' Shadow: Kinship,
Personality & Social Mobility in China.
Stanford U Pr.
Hsu, J. C. see Hsu, Jay C.
Hsu, Jay C.
xHsu, J. C.
Modern Control Principles & Applications.
McGraw.
Hsu, Kai-Yu, 1922-
xHsu, Kai-Yu.
The Chinese Literary Scene: A Writer's Visit
to the People's Republic. Random.
tr. & ed. Twentieth Century Chinese Poetry:
An Anthology. Cornell U Pr.
Hsu, Mongton C. see Hsu, Mongton Chih.
Hsu, Mongton Chih, 1885-
xHsu, Mongton C.
Railway Problems in China. AMS Pr.
Hsu, T. C.
xHsu, T. C.
Atlas of Mammalian Chromosomes.
Springer-Verlag.
Human & Mammalian Cytogenetics: A
Historical Perspective. Springer-Verlag.
Hsu, T. H. see Hsu, Tah-Hsiung.
Hsu, Tah-Hsiung.
xHsu, T. H.
Endocrinology Review. Arco.
Hsueh, Chun-Tu, 1922-
xHsueh, Chun-Tu.
ed. Dimensions of China's Foreign Relations.
Praeger.
ed. Revolutionary Leaders of Modern China.
Oxford U Pr.
Hsun-Tzu.
xHsun-Tzu.
The Works of Hsuntze. AMS Pr.
Htin Aung, U.
xHtin Aung, U.
Folk Elements in Burmese Buddhism.
Greenwood.
Hu, C. T. see Hu, Chang-Tu.
Hu, Chang-Tu, 1920-
xHu, C. T.
ed. Chinese Education Under Communism.
Tchrs Coll.
Hu, H. see Hu, Hsun.
Hu, Hsun.
xHu, H.
ed. The Nature & Behavior of Grain
Boundaries. Plenum Pub.
Hu, John Y. see Hu, John Y. H.
Hu, John Y. H., 1936-
xHu, John Y.
Ts'Ao Yu. Twayne.
Hu, S. T. see Hu, Sze-Tsen.
Hu, Shih, 1891-1962
xHu, Shih.
The Development of the Logical Method in
Ancient China. Krishna Pr.
Hu, Sze-Tsen, 1914-
xHu, S. T.
Homotopy Theory. Acad Pr.
xHu, Sze-Tsen.

Mathematical Theory of Switching Circuits &
Automata. U of Cal Pr.
Theory of Retracts. Wayne St U Pr.
Hu, T. C. see Hu, Te Chiang.
Hu, Te Chiang, 1930-
xHu, T. C.
Integer Programming & Network Flows. A-W.
Hu, Y. S.
xHu, Y. S.
Impact of U. S. Investment in Europe: A Case
Study of the Automotive & Computer
Industries. Irvington.
Hua, Lo-Keng, 1911-
xHua, Lo-Keng.
Additive Theory of Prime Numbers. Am Math.
Huang, Bob.
xHuang, Bob.
Teaching Your Child Tennis. Contemp Bks.
Huang, David S., 1930-
xHuang, David S.
Regression & Econometric Methods. Krieger.
Huang, Kee-Chang, 1917-
xHuang, Kee-Chang.
Outline of Pharmacology. C C Thomas.
Huang, Mab.
xHuang, Mab.
Intellectual Ferment for Political Reforms in
Taiwan, 1971-1973. U of Mich Ctr Chinese.
Huang, Parker P. see Huang, Po-Fei.
Huang, Paul. see Huang, Paul C.
Huang, Paul C.
xHuang, Paul.
The Illustrated Step-by-Step Chinese
Cookbook. S&S.
xHuang, Paul C.
Illustrated Step-by-Step Beginner's Cookbook.
Schol Bk Serv.
Huang, Pei, 1928-
xHuang, Pei.
Autocracy at Work: A Study of the
Yung-cheng Period, 1723-1735. Ind U Pr.
Huang, Po-Fei, 1914-
xHuang, Parker P.
Cantonese Dictionary: Cantonese-English,
English-Cantonese. Yale U Pr.
Twenty Lectures on Chinese Culture: An
Intermediary Chinese Textbook. Yale U Pr.
xHuang, Po-Fei.
Cantonese Sounds & Tones. Far Eastern Pubns.
Speak Cantonese. Far Eastern Pubns.
Huang, T. S. see Huang, Thomas S.
Huang, Thomas S.
xHuang, T. S.
ed. Picture Processing & Digital Filtering.
Springer-Verlag.
Huard, P. see Huard, Pierre.
Huard, Pierre.
xHuard, P.
ed. Point-to-Set Maps & Mathematical
Programming. Elsevier.
Huard, Pierre. see Huard, Pierre Alphonse.
Huard, Pierre A. see Huard, Pierre Alphonse.
Huard, Pierre Alphonse.
xHuard, Pierre.
Oriental Methods of Mental & Physical
Fitness: The Complete Book of Meditation,
Kinesitherapy & Martial Arts in China, India
& Japan. T Y Crowell.
xHuard, Pierre A.
Connaissance du Viet-Nam. AMS Pr.
Huart, Clement. see Huart, Clement Imbault.
Huart, Clement Imbault, 1854-1926
xHuart, Clement.
Ancient Persia & Iranian Civilization. Gordon
Pr.
Ancient Persia & Iranian Civilization.
Routledge & Kegan.
Hubala, Erich, 1920-
xHubala, Erich.

Baroque & Rococo Art. Universe.
Hubank, Roger.
xHubank, Roger.
North Wall. Avon.
North Wall. Viking Pr.
Hubbard, Bela, 1814-1896
xHubbard, Bela.
Memorials of a Half-Century in Michigan &
the Lake Region. Gale.
Hubbard, Benjamin J. see Hubbard, Benjamin Jerome.
Hubbard, Benjamin Jerome.
xHubbard, Benjamin J.
The Matthean Redaction of a Primitive
Apostolic Commissioning: An Exegesis of
Matthew 28: 16-20. Scholars Pr Ca.
Hubbard, Charles W. see Hubbard, Charles William.
Hubbard, Charles William.
xHubbard, Charles W.
Family Planning Education. Mosby.
Hubbard, David A. see Hubbard, David Allan.
Hubbard, David Allan.
xHubbard, David A.
The Book of James: Wisdom That Works.
Word Bks.
Galatians: Gospel of Freedom. Word Bks.
How to Face Your Fears. Holman.
More Psalms for All Seasons. Eerdmans.
Strange Heroes. Holman.
Thessalonians: Life That's Radically Christian.
Word Bks.
Hubbard, Don. see Hubbard, Donald.
Hubbard, Donald, 1926-
xHubbard, Don.
The Complete Book of Inflatable Boats.
Western Marine Ent.
Hubbard, Earl.
xHubbard, Earl.
The Creative Intention. Interbk Inc.
Hubbard, Ethel D. see Hubbard, Ethel Daniels.
Hubbard, Ethel Daniels.
xHubbard, Ethel D.
Ann of Ava. Arno.
Hubbard, George, 1859-
xHubbard, George.
On the Site of the Globe Playhouse of
Shakespeare. Folcroft.
Hubbard, Harlan.
xHubbard, Harlan.
illus. Payne Hollow: Life on the Fringe of
Society. T Y Crowell.
Hubbard, John I., 1930-
xHubbard, John I.
ed. The Peripheral Nervous System. Plenum
Pub.
Hubbard, John P. see Hubbard, John Perry.
Hubbard, John Perry, 1903-
xHubbard, John P.
Measuring Medical Education: The Tests & the
Experience of the National Board of Medical
Examiners. Lea & Febiger.
Hubbard, Joshua C.
xHubbard, Joshua C.
Creation of Income by Taxation. Greenwood.
Hubbard, L. Ron. see Hubbard, la Fayette Ronald.
Hubbard, la Fayette Ronald, 1911-
xHubbard, L. Ron.
Dianetics, the Original Thesis. Church Scient
NY.
Dianetics Today. Pubns Organization.
Final Blackout. Garland Pub.
The Problems of Work: Scientology Applied to
the Work-a-Day World. Pubns Organization.
Return to Tomorrow. Garland Pub.
Hubbard, P. M. see Hubbard, Philip Maitland.
Hubbard, Philip Maitland, 1910-
xHubbard, P. M.
The Quiet River. Doubleday.
Hubbard, Preston J.
xHubbard, Preston J.

Origins of the TVA: The Muscle Shoals
Controversy, 1920-1932. Norton.
Hubbard, R. H. see Hubbard, Robert Hamilton.
Hubbard, Robert Hamilton, 1916-
xHubbard, R. H.
Rideau Hall: An Illustrated History of
Government House, Ottawa, from Victorian
Times to the Present Day. McGill-Queens U
Pr.
Hubbard, Theodora. see Hubbard, Theodora Kimball.
Hubbard, Theodora Kimball.
xHubbard, Theodora.
Our Cities to-Day & to-Morrow; A Survey of
Planning & Zoning Progress in the United
States. Arno.
Hubbell, Jay B. see Hubbell, Jay Broadus.
Hubbell, Jay Broadus, 1885-
xHubbell, Jay B.
ed. American Life in Literature. Arno.
South & Southwest: Literary Essays and
Reminiscences. Duke.
South in American Literature , 1607-1900.
Duke.
Hubbell, Lindley W. see Hubbell, Lindley Williams.
Hubbell, Lindley Williams, 1901-
xHubbell, Lindley W.
Dark Pavilion. AMS Pr.
Lectures on Shakespeare. AMS Pr.
Hubbell, Ned.
xHubbell, Ned.
Adventures of Creighton Holmes. Popular Lib.
Hubbert, William T.
xHubbert, William T.
ed. Diseases Transmitted from Animals to
Man. C C Thomas.
Hubbs, Carl L. see Hubbs, Carl Leavitt.
Hubbs, Carl Leavitt.
xHubbs, Carl L.
Fishes of the Great Lakes Region. U of Mich
Pr.
xHubbs, D. L.
External & Internal Characters, Horizontal &
Vertical Distribution, Luminescence, & Food
of the Dwarf Pelagic Shark, Euproomicrus
bispinatus. U of Cal Pr.
Hubbs, D. L. see Hubbs, Carl Leavitt.
Huber, Alfred, 1918-
xHuber, Alfred.
Eye Signs and Symptoms in Brain Tumors.
Mosby.
Huber, Evelyn.
xHuber, Evelyn M.
Enlist, Train, Support Church Leaders. Judson.
Huber, Evelyn M. see Huber, Evelyn.
Huber, George. see Huber, George P.
Huber, George P.
xHuber, George.
Managerial Decision Making. Scott F.
Huber, Jack T.
xHuber, Jack T.
Goals & Behavior in Psychotherapy &
Counseling: Readings & Questions. Merrill.
Huber, Joan.
xHuber, Joan.
Income & Ideology: An Analysis of the
American Political Formula. Free Pr.
Huber, Joan E.
xHuber, John E.
ed. Kline Guide to the Paper Industry. Kline.
Huber, John E. see Huber, Joan E.
Huber, Miriam (Blanton), 1889-
xHuber, Miriam B.
The Influence of Intelligence Upon Children's
Reading Interests. AMS Pr.
Huber, Miriam B. see Huber, Miriam (Blanton).
Huber, Rina, 1928-
xHuber, Rina.

From Pasta to Pavlova: A Comparative Study
of Italian Settlers in Sydney & Griffith. U of
Queensland Pr.

Huberman, A. M.
xHuberman, A. M.
Understanding Change in Education. Unipub.

Huberman, Leo.
xHuberman, Leo.
Introduction to Socialism. Monthly Rev.
Socialism in Cuba. Monthly Rev.

Hubert, Karen M.
xHubert, Karen M.
Teaching & Writing Popular Fiction: Horror,
Adventure, Mystery & Romance in the
American Classroom. Tchrs & Writers Coll.

Hubert, Margaret.
xHubert, Margaret.
One-Piece Knits That Fit: How to Knit &
Crochet One-Piece Garments. Van Nos
Reinhold.
Weekend Knitting Projects. Van Nos Reinhold.

Hubmann, Franz, 1914-
xHubmann, Franz.
Habsburg Empire: The World of the
Austro-Hungarian Monarchy in Original
Photographs 1840-1916. Open Court.

Huby, Pamela. see Huby, Pamela M.

Huby, Pamela M.
xHuby, Pamela.
Plato & Modern Morality. Humanities.

Huch, Ricarda. see Huch, Ricarda Octavia.

Huch, Ricarda Octavia, 1864-1947
xHuch, Ricarda.
Der Letzte Sommer. Norton.

Huch, Ronald K.
xHuch, Ronald K.
The Radical Lord Radnor: The Public Life of
Viscount Folkestone, Third Earl of Radnor,
1779-1869. U of Minn Pr.

Huck, Arthur.
xHuck, Arthur.
Chinese in Australia. Intl Pubns Serv.

Huck, Charlotte S.
xHuck, Charlotte S.
Children's Literature in the Elementary School.
HR&W.

Huck, Gabe.
xHuck, Gabe.
A Book of Family Prayer. Seabury.

Huck, Schuyler W.
xHuck, Schuyler W.
Reading Statistics & Research. Har-Row.
Rival Hypotheses: Alternative Interpretations
of Data Based Conclusions. Har-Row.

Huckabay, Loucine M. see Huckabay, Loucine M.
Daderian.

Huckabay, Loucine M. Daderian, 1939-
xHuckabay, Loucine M.
The Conditions of Learning & Instruction in
Nursing: Modularized. Mosby.

Hucker, Charles O.
xHucker, Charles O.
The Censorial System of Ming China. Stanford
U Pr.
China: A Critical Bibliography. U of Ariz Pr.
China's Imperial Past: An Introduction to
Chinese History & Culture. Stanford U Pr.
Some Approaches to China's Past. Am Hist
Assn.
Two Studies on Ming History. U of Mich Ctr
Chinese.

Huckett, H. C. see Huckett, Hugh C.

Huckett, Hugh C.
xHuckett, H. C.
The Anthomyiidae of California, Exclusive of
Subfamily Scatophaginae (Diptera). U of Cal
Pr.

Huckins, Wesley. see Huckins, Wesley C.

Huckins, Wesley C.
xHuckins, Wesley.

Ethical & Legal Considerations in Guidance.
HM.

Huckleberry, E. B. see Huckleberry, E. R.

Huckleberry, E. R., 1894-
xHuckleberry, E. B.
How to Make Your Own Wooden Jewelry.
TAB Bks.

Huckshorn, Robert J. see Huckshorn, Robert Jack.

Huckshorn, Robert Jack, 1928-
xHuckshorn, Robert J.
Party Leadership in the States. U of Mass Pr.
The Politics of Defeat: Campaigning for
Congress. U of Mass Pr.

Hudak, Joseph.
xHudak, Joseph.
Trees for Every Purpose. McGraw.

Huddart, Henry.
xHuddart, Henry.
Comparative Structure & Function of Muscle.
Pergamon.

Huddle, David, 1942-
xHuddle, David.
A Dream with No Stump Roots in It: Stories.
U of Mo Pr.
Paper Boy. U of Pittsburgh Pr.

Huddleston, Joe D., 1937-
xHuddleston, Joe D.
Colonial Riflemen in the American Revolution.
Shumway.

Huddleston, Lee E. see Huddleston, Lee Eldridge.

Huddleston, Lee Eldridge.
xHuddleston, Lee E.
Origins of the American Indians: European
Concepts, 1492-1729. U of Tex Pr.

Huddleston, Rodney. see Huddleston, Rodney D.

Huddleston, Rodney D.
xHuddleston, Rodney.
An Introduction to English Transformational
Syntax. Longman.

Huddleston, Sisley, 1883-1952
xHuddleston, Sisley.
A History of France. Folcroft.
A History of France. Norwood Edns.
Popular Diplomacy & War. Devin.

Huddleston, Trevor. see Huddleston, Trevor Ernest
Urban.

Huddleston, Trevor Ernest Urban, 1913-
xHuddleston, Trevor.
Naught for Your Comfort. Collins Pubs.

Huddy, Delia.
xHuddy, Delia.
Time Piper. Greenwillow.

Hudec, Robert E.
xHudec, Robert E.
The GATT Legal System & World Trade
Diplomacy. Praeger.

Huden, John C. see Huden, John Charles.

Huden, John Charles, 1899-
xHuden, John C.
Indian Place Names of New England. Mus Am
Ind.

Hudenburg, Roy.
xHudenburg, Roy.
Planning the Community Hospital. Krieger.

Hudgins, Bryce B. see Hudgins, Bryce Byrne.

Hudgins, Bryce Byrne, 1929-
xHudgins, Bryce B.
Learning & Thinking: A Primer for Teachers.
Peacock Pubs.

Hudlicky, Milos.
xHudlicky, Milos.
Organic Fluorine Chemistry. Plenum Pub.

Hudlow, Emily E. see Hudlow, Emily Ellison.

Hudlow, Emily Ellison.
xHudlow, Emily E.
Alabaster Chambers. NAL.
Alabaster Chambers. St Martin.

Hudnut, Joseph, 1886-1968
xHudnut, Joseph.

Architecture & the Spirit of Man. Greenwood.

Hudnut, Robert K.
xHudnut, Robert K.
The Bootstrap Fallacy: What the Self-Help
Books Don't Tell You. Collins Pubs.
Church Growth Is Not the Point. Har-Row.

Hudoba, Michael.
xHudoba, Michael.
The Artifact Hunter's Handbook. Contemp
Bks.

Hudson, A. B. see Hudson, Alfred B.
Hudson, Alfred. see Hudson, Alfred B.

Hudson, Alfred B.
xHudson, A. B.
Padju Epat: The Ma'anyan of Indonesian
Borneo. Irvington.
xHudson, Alfred.
Barito Isolects of Borneo: A Classification
Based on Comparative Reconstruction &
Lexicostatistics. Cornell SE Asia.

Hudson, Anne, 1938-
xHudson, Anne.
ed. Selections from English Wycliffite Writings.
Cambridge U Pr.

Hudson, Arthur P. see Hudson, Arthur Palmer.

Hudson, Arthur Palmer, 1892-
xHudson, Arthur P.
Folklore Keeps the Past Alive. U of Ga Pr.
ed. Humor of the Old Deep South. Kennikat.

Hudson, Bess.
xHudson, Bess.
Windows to Nature. U Pr of Idaho.

Hudson, C. N. see Hudson, Christopher N.
Hudson, Charles. see Hudson, Charles M.

Hudson, Charles M.
xHudson, Charles.
The Southeastern Indians. U of Tenn Pr.
xHudson, Charles M.
ed. Black Drink: A Native American Tea. U of
Ga Pr.
Catawba Nation. U of Ga Pr.
ed. Four Centuries of Southern Indians. U of
Ga Pr.

Hudson, Christopher N.
xHudson, C. N.
The Female Reproductive System. Churchill.

Hudson, D. F.
xHudson, D. F.
Teach Yourself Bengali. McKay.

Hudson, Derek.
xHudson, Derek.
Lewis Carroll. Folcroft.
Lewis Carroll. Greenwood.
Lewis Carroll. R West.
Lewis Carroll: An Illustrated Biography. NAL.
Lewis Carroll: An Illustrated Biography. Potter.

Hudson, Fred S. see Hudson, Fred Stansfield.

Hudson, Fred Stansfield.
xHudson, Fred S.
North America. Intl Pubns Serv.

Hudson, Frederic, 1819-1875
xHudson, Frederic.
Journalism in the United States from 1690 to
1872. Haskell.

Hudson, G. F. see Hudson, Geoffrey Francis.

Hudson, Geoffrey Francis, 1903-
xHudson, G. F.
ed. Reform & Revolution in Asia. St Martin.

Hudson, Gladys W.
xHudson, Gladys W.
Paradise Lost: A Concordance. Gale.

Hudson Institute.
xHudson Institute.
The U. K. in 1980: The Hudson Report.
Halsted Pr.

Hudson, J. see Hudson, Joyce A.
Hudson, James W. see Hudson, James William.

Hudson, James William.
xHudson, James W.

History of Adult Education. Kelley.
Hudson, Jeffery.
xHudson, Jeffery.
A Case of Need. NAL.
Hudson, Joyce A.
xHudson, J.
The Core of Walmatjari Grammar. Humanities.
Hudson, K. see Hudson, Kenneth.
Hudson, Kenneth.
xHudson, K.
World Industrial Archaeology. Cambridge U
Pr.
xHudson, Kenneth.
Air Travel: A Social History. Rowman.
The Archaeology of Industry. Scribner.
The Businessman in Public. Halsted Pr.
Directory of World Museums. Columbia U Pr.
Directory of World Museums. Facts on File.
Guide to the Industrial Archaeology of Europe.
Fairleigh Dickinson.
Industrial Archaeology: A New Introduction.
Humanities.
Industrial Archaeology: An Introduction.
Dufour.
Hudson, Leslie.
xHudson, Leslie.
Practical Immunology. Mosby.
Hudson, Manley O. see Hudson, Manley Ottmer.
Hudson, Manley Ottmer, 1886-
xHudson, Manley O.
The Permanent Court of International Justice,
1920-1942: A Treatise. Arno.
Permanent Court of International Justice,
1920-1942: A Treatise. Garland Pub.
Hudson, Michael C.
xHudson, Michael C.
Arab Politics: The Search for Legitimacy. Yale
U Pr.
Hudson, Nigel R. L.
xHudson, R. L.
Money & Exchange Dealing in International
Banking. Halsted Pr.
Hudson, Nora E. see Hudson, Nora Eileen.
Hudson, Nora Eileen, 1902-
xHudson, Nora E.
Ultra-Royalism & the French Restoration.
Octagon.
Hudson, Norman.
xHudson, Norman.
Soil Conservation. Cornell U Pr.
xHudson, Norman W.
Soil Conservation. David & Charles.
Hudson, Norman. see Hudson, William Norman.
Hudson, Norman W. see Hudson, Norman.
Hudson, R. A.
xHudson, Richard A.
Arguments for a Non-Transformational
Grammar. U of Chicago Pr.
Hudson, R. L. see Hudson, Nigel R. L.
Hudson, Richard A. see Hudson, R. A.
Hudson, Richard D.
xHudson, Richard D.
Infrared System Engineering. Wiley.
Hudson River Sloop Restoration, Inc.
xHudson River Sloop Restoration, Inc.
Hudson River Sloops. Morgan.
Hudson, Roy L., 1906-
xHudson, Roy L.
The Pruning Handbook. P-H.
Hudson, Thomson. see Hudson, Thomson Jay.
Hudson, Thomson J. see Hudson, Thomson Jay.
Hudson, Thomson Jay, 1834-1903
xHudson, Thomson.
Law of Psychic Phenomena. Weiser.
xHudson, Thomson J.
Frwd. by Law of Psychic Phenomena.
Hudson-Cohan.
Hudson, W. D. see Hudson, William Donald.
Hudson, W. H. see Hudson, William Henry.

Hudson, William Donald.
xHudson, W. D.
Modern Moral Philosophy. St Martin.
Reason & Right: A Critical Examination of
Richard Price's Moral Philosophy. Freeman
C.
Hudson, William H. see Hudson, William Henry.
Hudson, William Henry, 1841-1922
xHudson, W. H.
Idle Days in Patagonia. Creative Arts.
Tales of the Pampas. Creative Arts.
xHudson, William H.
Adventures Among Birds. AMS Pr.
Adventures Among Birds. Folcroft.
Afoot in England. AMS Pr.
Afoot in England. Folcroft.
British Birds. AMS Pr.
Crystal Age. AMS Pr.
Crystal Age. Folcroft.
Dead Man's Plack, an Old Thorn &
Miscellanea. AMS Pr.
Dead Man's Plack An Old Thorn &
Miscellanea. Folcroft.
Gray & His Poetry. AMS Pr.
Gray & His Poetry. Folcroft.
Green Mansions. AMS Pr.
Green Mansions. Airmont.
Green Mansions. AMSCO Sch.
Hampshire Days. AMS Pr.
Hampshire Days. Folcroft.
Hind in Richmond Park. AMS Pr.
Hind in Richmond Park. Folcroft.
Idle Days in Patagonia. AMS Pr.
Johnson & Goldsmith & Their Poetry. AMS
Pr.
Johnson & Goldsmith & Their Poetry. Arden
Lib.
Johnson & Goldsmith & Their Poetry. Folcroft.
Lowell & His Poetry. AMS Pr.
Lowell & His Poetry. Folcroft.
Naturalist in La Plata. AMS Pr.
Nature in Downland. AMS Pr.
Quiet Corner in a Library. Arno.
Quiet Corner in a Library. Folcroft.
Whittier & His Poetry. AMS Pr.
Whittier & His Poetry. Arden Lib.
Whittier & His Poetry. Folcroft.
Wordsworth & His Poetry. AMS Pr.
Wordsworth & His Poetry. Folcroft.
Wordsworth & His Poetry. Kennikat.
Hudson, William Norman.
xHudson, Norman.
Antiques Illustrated & Priced. A S Barnes.
Hudson, Wilson M. see Hudson, Wilson Mathis.
Hudson, Wilson Mathis, 1907-
xHudson, Wilson M.
Andy Adams: His Life & Writings. SMU Press.
Intro. by & ed. Diamond Bessie & the
Shepherds. Encino Pr.
ed. The Sunny Slopes of Long Ago. SMU
Press.
Hudson, Winthrop S. see Hudson, Winthrop Still.
Hudson, Winthrop Still, 1911-
xHudson, Winthrop S.
American Protestantism. U of Chicago Pr.
Baptist Convictions. Judson.
Baptists in Transition. Judson.
The Great Tradition of the American
Churches. Peter Smith.
Nationalism & Religion in America: Concepts
of American Identity & Mission. Peter Smith.
Huebener, Theodore.
xHuebener, Theodore.

Audio-Visual Techniques in Teaching Foreign
Languages: A Practical Handbook. NYU Pr.
How to Teach Foreign Languages Effectively.
NYU Pr.
Opportunities in Foreign Language Careers.
Natl Textbk.
Huebner, Kenneth H., 1942-
xHuebner, Kenneth H.
Finite Element Method for Engineers. Wiley.
Huebner, S. S. see Huebner, Solomon Stephen.
Huebner, Solomon Stephen.
xHuebner, S. S.
Life Insurance. P-H.
Hueffer, Francis, 1845-1889
xHueffer, Francis.
Half a Century of Music in England
1837-1887: Essays Towards a History.
Longwood Pr.
Hueffer, Oliver M. see Hueffer, Oliver Madox.
Hueffer, Oliver Madox, 1877-1931
xHueffer, Oliver M.
The Book of Witches. Rowman.
Huegel, F. J. see Huegel, Frederick Julius.
Huegel, Frederick Julius, 1889-
xHuegel, F. J.
Cross Through the Scriptures. Bethany Fell.
Forever Triumphant. Bethany Fell.
Reigning with Christ. Bethany Fell.
Huelsenbeck, Richard, 1892-1974
xHuelsenbeck, Richard.
Memoirs of a Dada Drummer. Viking Pr.
Huelsman, Lawrence P.
xHuelsman, Lawrence P.
Introduction to the Theory & Design of Active
Filters. McGraw.
Theory & Design of Active RC Circuits.
McGraw.
Hueper, W. C. see Hueper, Wilhelm C.
Hueper, Wilhelm C., 1894-
xHueper, W. C.
Occupational & Environmental Cancers of the
Respiratory System. Springer-Verlag.
Huertas-Jourda, Jose.
xHuertas-Jourda, Jose.
Existentialism of Miguel De Unamuno. U
Presses Fla.
Huestis, Douglas W.
xHuestis, Douglas W.
Practical Blood Transfusion. Little.
Hueston, J. T.
xHueston, J. T.
ed. Dupuytren's Disease. Grune.
Huet, Michel.
xHuet, Michel.
The Dance, Art, & Ritual of Africa. Pantheon.
Huettig, Mae D. see Huettig, Mae Dena.
Huettig, Mae Dena, 1911-
xHuettig, Mae D.
Economic Control of the Motion Picture
Industry: A Study in Industrial Organization.
Ozer.

Hufbauer, G. see Hufbauer, G. C.
Hufbauer, G. C.
xHufbauer, G.
Overseas Manufacturing Investment & the
Balance of Payments. Arno.
Hufeland, Christoph W. see Hufeland, Christoph
Wilhelm.
Hufeland, Christoph Wilhelm.
xHufeland, Christoph W.
Art of Prolonging Life. Arno.
Huff, Darrell.
xHuff, Darrell.
How to Take a Chance. Norton.
How to Work with Concrete & Masonry.
Har-Row.
Huff, Doug, 1943-
xHuff, Doug.

Sports in West Virginia: A Pictorial History.
Donning Co.
Huff, Robert, 1924-
xHuff, Robert.
The Ventriloquist: New & Selected Poems. U
Pr of Va.
Huff, T. E.
xHuff, Tom.
Marabelle. Bantam.
xHuff, Tom E.
Marabelle. St Martin.
Huff, Theodore.
xHuff, Theodore.
Charlie Chaplin. Arno.
Huff, Tom. *see* Huff, T. E.
Huff, Tom E. *see* Huff, T. E.
Huff, Vivian.
xHuff, Vivian.
Let's Make Paper Dolls. Har-Row.
Let's Make Paper Dolls. Har-Row.
Huffaker, C. B.
xHuffaker, C. B.
ed. Theory & Practice of Biological Control.
Acad Pr.
xHuffaker, Carl B.
ed. New Technology of Pest Control. Wiley.
Huffaker, Carl B. *see* Huffaker, C. B.
Huffaker, Clair.
xHuffaker, Clair.
Badge for a Gunfighter. PB.
Clair Huffaker's Profiles of the American West.
PB.
Cowboy. PB.
The Cowboy & the Cossack. PB.
The Cowboy & the Cossack. Trident.
Guns from Thunder Mountain. PB.
Guns of Rio Conchos. PB.
Posse from Hell. PB.
Huffman, Edna K.
xHuffman, Edna K.
Medical Record Management. Physicians Rec.
Medical Records in Nursing Homes. Physicians
Rec.
Huffman, Franklin E.
xHuffman, Franklin E.
Cambodian Literary Reader & Glossary. Yale
U Pr.
English-Khmer Dictionary. Yale U Pr.
Huffman, H. *see* Huffman, Harry.
Huffman, Harry.
xHuffman, H.
Mathematics for Business Careers. McGraw.
Huffman, James L., 1941-
xHuffman, James L.
Politics of the Meiji Press: The Life of Fukuchi
Gen'ichiro. U Pr of Hawaii.
Huffman, Jim.
xHuffman, Jim.
Personal Computing. Reston.
Huffman, John.
xHuffman, John A.
Growing Toward Wholeness. Word Bks.
Huffman, John A.
xHuffman, John A.
Liberating Limits: A Fresh Look at the Ten
Commandments. Word Bks.
Huffman, John A. *see* Huffman, John.
Huffmon, Herbert B. *see* Huffmon, Herbert Bardwell.
Huffmon, Herbert Bardwell.
xHuffmon, Herbert B.
Amorite Personal Names in the Mari Texts: A
Structural and Lexical Study. Johns Hopkins.
Hufford, Susan.
xHufford, Susan.
Melody of Malice. Popular Lib.
Hufner, S.
xHufner, S.

Optical Spectra of Transparent Rare Earth
Compounds. Acad Pr.
Hufton, Olwen H.
xHufton, Olwen H.
The Poor of Eighteenth-Century France
1750-1789. Oxford U Pr.
Hug, William E.
xHug, William E.
Instructional Design & the Media Program.
ALA.
Hugard, Jean.
xHugard, Jean.
Encyclopedia of Card Tricks. Dover.
Encyclopedia of Card Tricks. Merrimack Bk
Serv.
Encyclopedia of Card Tricks. Wehman.
Huggett, Frank E. *see* Huggett, Frank Edward.
Huggett, Frank Edward.
xHuggett, Frank E.
Life Below Stairs: Domestic Servants in
England from Victorian Times. Scribner.
Huggett, Richard.
xHuggett, Richard.
Supernatural on Stage: Ghosts & Superstitions
of the Theatre. Taplinger.
Huggins, Charles, 1901-
xHuggins, Charles B.
Experimental Leukemia & Mammary Cancer:
Induction, Prevention, Cure. U of Chicago
Pr.
Huggins, Charles B. *see* Huggins, Charles.
Huggins, Nathan I. *see* Huggins, Nathan Irvin.
Huggins, Nathan Irvin, 1927-
xHuggins, Nathan I.
Black Odyssey: The Afro-American Ordeal in
Slavery. Pantheon.
Black Odyssey: The Afro-American Ordeal in
Slavery. Random.
Protestants Against Poverty: Boston's
Charities, 1870-1900. Greenwood.
Slave & Citizen: The Life of Frederick
Douglass. Little.
Huggins, William H.
xHuggins, William H.
Iconic Communication: An Annotated
Bibliography. Johns Hopkins.
Hugh-Jones, Stephen.
xHugh-Jones, Stephens.
Amazonian Indians. Watts.
Hugh-Jones, Stephens. *see* Hugh-Jones, Stephen.
Hughes, A. *see* Hughes, Alan Hugo.
Hughes, A. Stuart. *see* Hughes, Henry Stuart.
Hughes, Alan Hugo.
xHughes, A.
Psychology & the Political Experience.
Cambridge U Pr.
Hughes, Allison.
xHughes, Allison.
Love Honor & Frustration. Zondervan.
Hughes, Andrew.
xHughes, Andrew.
Medieval Music: The Sixth Liberal Art. U of
Toronto Pr.
Hughes, Ann.
xHughes, Ann J.
Linear Programming: An Emphasis on
Decision Making. A-W.
Hughes, Ann J. *see* Hughes, Ann.
Hughes, Anselm, 1889-
xHughes, Dom A.
Compiled by Liturgical Terms for Music
Students: A Dictionary. Scholarly.
Hughes, Arthur J.
xHughes, Arthur J.
American Government. Glencoe.
Hughes, Barry, 1945-
xHughes, Barry B.

World Modeling: The Mesarovic-Pestel World
Model in the Context of Its Contemporaries.
Lexington Bks.
Hughes, Barry B. *see* Hughes, Barry.
Hughes, Catherine A.
xHughes, Catherine A.
ed. Economic Education: A Guide to
Information Sources. Gale.
Hughes, Charles E. *see* Hughes, Charles Evans.
Hughes, Charles Evans.
xHughes, Charles E.
The Autobiographical Notes of Charles Evans
Hughes. Harvard U Pr.
Conditions of Progress in Democratic
Government. Arno.
Our Relations to the Nations of the Western
Hemisphere. Johnson Repr.
Hughes, Charles W. *see* Hughes, Charles William.
Hughes, Charles William, 1900-
xHughes, Charles W.
Human Side of Music. Da Capo.
Hughes, Clarence.
xHughes, Clarence.
Some Basics for Boards of Education. C
Hughes.
Hughes, Clarence R.
xHughes, Clarence R.
ed. Collective Negotiations in Higher
Education: A Reader. Blackburn Coll.
Hughes, D. R. *see* Hughes, Daniel R.
Hughes, D. T. *see* Hughes, David Treharne Dillon.
Hughes, Daniel R.
xHughes, D. R.
Projective Planes. Springer-Verlag.
Hughes, David. *see* Hughes, David W.
Hughes, David Treharne Dillon.
xHughes, D. T.
Tropical Health Science. Cambridge U Pr.
Hughes, David W.
xHughes, David.
The Star of Bethlehem: An Astronomer's
Confirmation. PB.
The Star of Bethlehem: An Astronomer's
Confirmation. Walker & Co.
Hughes, Dean, 1943-
xHughes, Dean T.
Under the Same Stars. Deseret Bk.
Hughes, Dean T. *see* Hughes, Dean.
Hughes, Dom A. *see* Hughes, Anselm.
Hughes, Dorothy.
xHughes, Dorothy.
Illustrations of Chaucer's England. Arden Lib.
Illustrations of Chaucer's England. Folcroft.
Hughes, Dorothy. *see* Hughes, Dorothy Berry.
Hughes, Dorothy Berry, 1910-
xHughes, Dorothy.
Great Victory Mosaic: Poems. U of Mo Pr.
Hughes, E. R. *see* Hughes, Ernest Richard.
Hughes, Edward, 1899-
xHughes, Edward.
Studies in Administration & Finance,
1558-1825: With Special Reference to the
History of Salt Taxation in England.
Porcupine Pr.
Hughes, Edward F. X.
xHughes, Edward F. X.
Hospital Cost Containment Programs: A Policy
Analysis. Ballinger Pub.
Hughes, Emmet J. *see* Hughes, Emmet John.
Hughes, Emmet John, 1920-
xHughes, Emmet J.
Church & the Liberal Society. U of Notre
Dame Pr.
Ordeal of Power: A Political Memoir of the
Eisenhower Years. Atheneum.
Hughes, Eric. *see* Hughes, Eric Lester.
Hughes, Eric Lester, 1923-
xHughes, Eric.

ed. Gymnastics for Girls: A Competitive
  Approach for Teacher & Coach. Wiley.
Hughes, Ernest R. *see* Hughes, Ernest Richard.
Hughes, Ernest Richard, 1883-1956
  xHughes, E. R.
    The Great Learning & The Mean-in-Action.
    AMS Pr.
  xHughes, Ernest R.
    ed. China, Body & Soul. Arno.
    Two Chinese Poets: Vignettes of Han Life &
    Thought. Greenwood.
Hughes, Evan.
  xHughes, Evan.
    Banking. David & Charles.
Hughes, Everett C. *see* Hughes, Everett Cherrington.
Hughes, Everett Cherrington, 1897-
  xHughes, Everett C.
    French Canada in Transition. U of Chicago Pr.
Hughes, G. Bernard. *see* Hughes, George Bernard.
Hughes, G. David. *see* Hughes, George David.
Hughes, G. M. *see* Hughes, George Morgan.
Hughes, George B. *see* Hughes, George Bernard.
Hughes, George Bernard, 1896-
  xHughes, G. Bernard.
    The Country Life Collector's Pocket Book.
    Transatlantic.
  xHughes, George B.
    Living Crafts. Arno.
Hughes, George David.
  xHughes, G. David.
    Demand Analysis for Marketing Decisions.
    Irwin.
    Marketing Management: A Planning Approach.
    A-W.
Hughes, George M. *see* Hughes, George Morgan.
Hughes, George Morgan.
  xHughes, G. M.
    ed. Respiration of Amphibious Vertebrates.
    Acad Pr.
  xHughes, George M.
    Comparative Physiology of Vertebrate
    Respiration. Harvard U Pr.
Hughes, Gerard W.
  xHughes, Gerard W.
    In Search of a Way: Two Journeys of
    Discovery. Doubleday.
Hughes, Gervase.
  xHughes, Gervase.
    Composers of Operetta. Greenwood.
    The Music of Arthur Sullivan. Greenwood.
Hughes, Glenn, 1894-
  xHughes, Glenn.
    History of the American Theatre, 1700-1950.
    French.
    Imagism & Imagists: A Study in Modern
    Poetry. Biblo.
Hughes, Glyn T. *see* Hughes, Glyn Tegai.
Hughes, Glyn Tegai.
  xHughes, Glyn T.
    Romantic German Literature. Holmes & Meier.
Hughes, Gordon.
  xHughes, Gordon.
    Radiation Chemistry. Oxford U Pr.
Hughes, Graham. *see* Hughes, Graham Beynon John.
Hughes, Graham Beynon John.
  xHughes, Graham.
    ed. Law, Reason, & Justice: Essays in Legal
    Philosophy. NYU Pr.
Hughes, Griffith, fl. 1750
  xHughes, Griffith.
    Natural History of Barbados. Arno.
Hughes, H. Stuart. *see* Hughes, Henry Stuart.
Hughes, Harold K. *see* Hughes, Harold Kenneth.
Hughes, Harold Kenneth, 1911-
  xHughes, Harold K.
    A Dictionary of Abbreviations in Medicine &
    the Health Sciences. Lexington Bks.
Hughes, Helen.
  xHughes, Helen.

ed. Foreign Investment & Industrialisation in
  Singapore. U of Wis Pr.
Hughes, Helen M. *see* Hughes, Helen MacGill.
Hughes, Helen MacGill.
  xHughes, Helen M.
    Inquiries in Sociology. Allyn.
Hughes, Henry S. *see* Hughes, Henry Stuart.
Hughes, Henry Stuart, 1916-
  xHughes, A. Stuart.
    Contemporary Europe: A History. P-H.
  xHughes, H. Stuart.
    Consciousness & Society: The Reorientation of
    European Social Throught, 1890-1930.
    Octagon.
    Consciousness & Society: The Reorientation of
    European Social Thought 1890-1930.
    Random.
    Contemporary Europe: A History. P-H.
    History As Art & As Science: Twin Vistas on
    the Past. U of Chicago Pr.
    United States & Italy. Harvard U Pr.
  xHughes, Henry S.
    Oswald Spengler: A Critical Estimate.
    Greenwood.
Hughes, Herbert L. *see* Hughes, Herbert Leland.
Hughes, Herbert Leland.
  xHughes, Herbert L.
    Theory & Practice in Henry James. Folcroft.
Hughes, J.
  xHughes, J.
    ed. Centrally Acting Peptides. Univ Park.
Hughes, J. *see* Hughes, Joan Kirkby.
Hughes, J. Donald.
  xHughes, J. Donald.
    Ecology in Ancient Civilizations. U of NM Pr.
Hughes, J. R. *see* Hughes, Jonathan R. T.
Hughes, J. Trevor. *see* Hughes, John Trevor.
Hughes, James G. *see* Hughes, James Gilliam.
Hughes, James Gilliam, 1910-
  xHughes, James G.
    Synopsis of Pediatrics. Mosby.
Hughes, James L. *see* Hughes, James Laughlin.
Hughes, James Laughlin, 1846-1935
  xHughes, James L.
    Dickens As an Educator. Haskell.
    Dickens As an Educator. R West.
Hughes, James M. *see* Hughes, James Monroe.
Hughes, James Monroe.
  xHughes, James M.
    Education in America. Har-Row.
Hughes, Jim, 1918-
  xHughes, Jim.
    Uncle Sam, Super Cop: A Satirical View of
    American History. Lawrence Hill.
Hughes, Joan. *see* Hughes, Joan Kirkby.
Hughes, Joan Kirkby.
  xHughes, J.
    A Structured Approach to Programming. P-H.
  xHughes, Joan.
    Programming the IBM 1130. Wiley.
Hughes, John M. *see* Hughes, John Milton Charles.
Hughes, John Milton Charles, 1923-
  xHughes, John M.
    Negro Novelist: A Discussion of the Writings
    of American Negro Novelists, 1940-1950.
    Arno.
Hughes, John Trevor.
  xHughes, J. Trevor.
    Pathology of Muscle. Saunders.
Hughes, Jonathan R. *see* Hughes, Jonathan R. T.
Hughes, Jonathan R. T.
  xHughes, J. R.
    Industrialization & Economic History: Theses
    & Conjectures. McGraw.
  xHughes, Jonathan R.
    The Governmental Habit: Economic Controls
    from Colonial Times to the Present. Basic.
Hughes, Langston, 1902-
  xHughes, Langston.

First Book of Africa. Watts.
The First Book of Jazz. Watts.
I Wonder As I Wander: An Autobiographical
  Journey. Hill & Wang.
Not Without Laughter. Macmillan.
Simple's Uncle Sam. Hill & Wang.
Something in Common & Other Stories. Hill &
  Wang.
Hughes, Larry. *see* Hughes, Larry W.
Hughes, Larry W.
  xHughes, Larry.
    Desegregating America's Schools. Longman.
  xHughes, Larry W.
    The Secondary Principal's Handbook: A Guide
    to Executive Action. Allyn.
Hughes, Leo, 1908-
  xHughes, Leo.
    A Century of English Farce. Greenwood.
    Drama's Patrons: A Study of the
    Eighteenth-Century London Audience. U of
    Tex Pr.
Hughes, Lynn.
  xHughes, Lynn.
    ed. Owls. Workman Pub.
Hughes, M. L. *see* Hughes, Marion L.
Hughes, M. N. *see* Hughes, Martin Neville.
Hughes, Marion L.
  xHughes, M. L.
    Decision Tables. McGraw.
Hughes, Martin Neville.
  xHughes, M. N.
    The Inorganic Chemistry of Biological
    Processes. Wiley.
Hughes, Megan.
  xHughes, Megan.
    Givers & Takers. Nordon Pubns.
Hughes, Melvin C. *see* Hughes, Melvin Clyde.
Hughes, Melvin Clyde.
  xHughes, Melvin C.
    County Government in Georgia. Greenwood.
Hughes, Meredydd.
  xHughes, Meredydd.
    ed. Administering Education: International
    Challenge. Humanities.
Hughes, Merritt Y. *see* Hughes, Merritt Yerkes.
Hughes, Merritt Yerkes.
  xHughes, Merritt Y.
    ed. A Variorum Commentary on the Poems of
    John Milton. Columbia U Pr.
Hughes, Monica.
  xHughes, Monica.
    Crisis on Conshelf Ten. Atheneum.
Hughes, Philip, 1895-
  xHughes, Philip.
    Popular History of the Catholic Church.
    Macmillan.
Hughes, R. D. *see* Hughes, Richard D.
Hughes, Ray H.
  xHughes, Ray H.
    The Order of Future Events. Pathway Pr.
Hughes, Richard.
  xHughes, Richard.
    The Tranquilizing of America: Pill-Popping &
    the American Way of Life. HarBraceJ.
Hughes, Richard. *see* Hughes, Richard Arthur Warren.
Hughes, Richard Arthur Warren, 1900-
  xHughes, Richard.
    Fox in the Attic. Har-Row.
    Gertrude's Child. Quist.
    A High Wind in Jamaica. Har-Row.
Hughes, Richard D., 1931-
  xHughes, R. D.
    Living Insects. Taplinger.
Hughes, Richard S.
  xHughes, Richard S.
    Logarithmic Video Amplifiers. Artech Hse.
Hughes, Richard V.
  xHughes, Richard V.

Oil Property Valuation. Krieger.
Hughes, Rupert, 1872-1956
xHughes, Rupert.
Souls for Sale. Garland Pub.
Hughes, Samuel C. *see* Hughes, Samuel Carlyle.
Hughes, Samuel Carlyle.
xHughes, Samuel C.
Pre-Victorian Drama in Dublin. B Franklin.
Hughes, Shirley.
xHughes, Shirley.
David & Dog. P-H.
illus. George the Babysitter. P-H.
Moving Molly. P-H.
Hughes, Stella.
xHughes, Stella.
Chuck Wagon Cookin'. U of Ariz Pr.
Hughes, Ted.
xHughes, Ted.
Cave Birds: An Alchemical Cave Drama.
Viking Pr.
Crow: From the Life & Songs of the Crow.
Har-Row.
Moortown. Har-Row.
Hughes, Thomas, 1854-1934
xHughes, Thomas.
Indian Chiefs of Southern Minnesota. Ross.
Hughes, Thomas. *see* Hughes, Thomas Mears.
Hughes, Thomas A. *see* Hughes, Thomas Aloysius.
Hughes, Thomas Aloysius, 1849-1939
xHughes, Thomas A.
Loyola & the Educational System of the
Jesuits. Gordon Pr.
Hughes, Thomas Mears.
xHughes, Thomas.
Casebook for Special Education & Elementary
Education. Interstate.
Hughes, Thomas P. *see* Hughes, Thomas Patrick.
Hughes, Thomas Patrick, 1838-1911
xHughes, Thomas P.
Dictionary of Islam: Being a Cyclopaedia of the
Doctrines, Rites, Ceremonies, & Customs,
Together with the Technical & Theological
Terms, of the Muhannadan Religion.
Humanities.
Hughes, Tom.
xHughes, Tom.
Chemistry: Ideas to Interpret Your Changing
Environment. Dickenson.
Hughes, Trevor J. *see* Hughes, Trevor Jones.
Hughes, Trevor Jones.
xHughes, Trevor J.
The Economic Development of Communist
China, 1949-1960. Greenwood.
Hughes, W. H. *see* Hughes, William Howard.
Hughes, William, 1936-
xHughes, William.
Aspects of Biophysics. Wiley.
Hughes, William F. *see* Hughes, William Frank.
Hughes, William Frank, 1930-
xHughes, William F.
Introduction to Viscous Flow. McGraw.
Hughes, William Howard.
xHughes, W. H.
Concise Antibiotic Treatment. Butterworths.
Hughes-Stanton, Penelope.
xHughes-Stanton, Penelope.
See Inside an Ancient Chinese Town. Watts.
Hughlett, Lloyd J.
xHughlett, Lloyd J.
ed. Industrialization of Latin America.
Greenwood.
Hughson, S. C. *see* Hughson, Shirley Carter.
Hughson, Shirley C. *see* Hughson, Shirley Carter.
Hughson, Shirley Carter, 1867-1949
xHughson, S. C.
Carolina Pirates & Colonial Commerce:
1670-1740. Johnson Repr.
xHughson, Shirley C.

The Carolina Pirates & Colonial Commerce,
1670-1740. AMS Pr.
Carolina Pirates & Colonial Commerce,
1670-1740. Reprint.
Hughston, L. *see* Hughston, L. P.
Hughston, L. P., 1951-
xHughston, L.
Twistors & Particles. Springer-Verlag.
Hugins, Walter. *see* Hugins, Walter Edward.
Hugins, Walter Edward, 1925-
xHugins, Walter.
ed. The Reform Impulse, 1825-1850. U of SC
Pr.
Hugo, Grant.
xHugo, Grant.
Appearance & Reality in International
Relations. Columbia U Pr.
Hugo, I. S. *see* Hugo, I. St. J.
Hugo, I. St. J.
xHugo, I. S.
Marketing & the Computer. Pergamon.
Hugo, Richard. *see* Hugo, Richard F.
Hugo, Richard F.
xHugo, Richard.
The Right Madness of Skye: Poems. Norton.
What Thou Lovest Well, Remains American:
Poems. Norton.
Hugo, Victor. *see* Hugo, Victor Marie.
Hugo, Victor Marie.
xHugo, Victor.
The Hunchback of Notre Dame. Dutton.
The Hunchback of Notre Dame. Intl Bk Ctr.
Hunchback of Notre Dame. NAL.
The Hunchback of Notre Dame. Pendulum Pr.
The Hunchback of Notre Dame. Bantam.
Hunchback of Notre Dame. Dodd.
Hunchback of Notre-Dame. Airmont.
Les Miserables. Fawcett.
Miserables. French & Eur.
Les Miserables. Intl Bk Ctr.
Les Miserables. Larousse.
Les Miserables. Penguin.
Les Miserables. Dodd.
Les Miserables. AMSCO Sch.
Les Miserables. PB.
Notre-Dame of Paris. Penguin.
Hugo, W. B. *see* Hugo, William Barry.
Hugo, William Barry.
xHugo, W. B.
ed. Inhibition & Destruction of the Microbial
Cell. Acad Pr.
Hugot, E. *see* Hugot, Emile.
Hugot, Emile.
xHugot, E.
Handbook of Cane Sugar Engineering. Elsevier.
Huheey, James E.
xHuheey, James E.
Amphibians & Reptiles of Great Smoky
Mountains National Park. U of Tenn Pr.
Inorganic Chemistry: Principles of Structure &
Reactivity. Har-Row.
Huhn, A. P. *see* Huhn, Andras P.
Huhn, Andras P.
xHuhn, A. P.
Lattice Theory. Elsevier.
Huhn, Dieter.
xHuhn, Dieter.
ed. Fine Structure of Blood & Bone Marrow:
An Introduction to Electron Microscopic
Hematology. Hafner.
Hui, Y. H. *see* Hui, Yiu H.
Hui, Yiu H.
xHui, Y. H.
United States Food Laws, Regulations &
Standards. Wiley.
Huidekoper, Virginia.
xHuidekoper, Virginia.
Early Days in Jackson Hole. Colo Assoc.
Huie, William B. *see* Huie, William Bradford.

Huie, William Bradford, 1910-
xHuie, William B.
It's Me O Lord. Nelson.
Huijing, F.
xHuijing, F.
ed. Protein Phosphorylation in Control
Mechanisms. Acad Pr.
Huitson, Alan.
xHuitson, Alan.
Analysis of Variance. Hafner.
Huitt, Ralph K.
xHuitt, Ralph K.
Congress: Two Decades of Analysis.
Greenwood.
Huizer, Gerrit.
xHuizer, Gerrit.
ed. The Politics of Anthropology: From
Colonialism & Sexism Toward a View from
Below. Mouton.
Huizinga, Jehan. *see* Huizinga, Johan.
Huizinga, Johan, 1872-1945
xHuizinga, Jehan.
Homo Ludens: A Study of the Play Element in
Culture. Routledge & Kegan.
xHuizinga, Johan.
Homo Ludens: A Study of the Play Element in
Culture. Beacon Pr.
Hujar, Peter, 1934-
xHujar, Peter.
Portraits in Life & Death. Da Capo.
Hulan, Richard.
xHulan, Richard.
A Guide to the Reading and Study of Historic
Site Archaeology. Mus Anthro Mo.
Hulbert, Homer B. *see* Hulbert, Homer Bezaleel.
Hulbert, Homer Bezaleel.
xHulbert, Homer B.
History of Korea. Humanities.
Hulbert, James R. *see* Hulbert, James Root.
Hulbert, James Root, 1884-
xHulbert, James R.
Chaucer's Official Life. Phaeton.
Hulbert, Terry C.
xHulbert, Terry C.
World Missions Today. Evang Tchr.
Hulke, Malcolm.
xHulke, Malcolm.
ed. The Encyclopedia of Alternative Medicine
& Self-Help. Schocken.
Hull. *see* Hull, Edna Mayne.
Hull, Anthony H.
xHull, Anthony H.
Charles III & the Revival of Spain. U Pr of
Amer.
Hull, Arthur E. *see* Hull, Arthur Eaglefield.
Hull, Arthur Eaglefield, 1876-1928
xHull, Arthur E.
ed. Dictionary of Modern Music & Musicians.
AMS Pr.
ed. A Dictionary of Modern Music &
Musicians. Scholarly.
Hull, Clark L. *see* Hull, Clark Leonard.
Hull, Clark Leonard, 1884-1952
xHull, Clark L.
Essentials of Behavior. Elliots Bks.
Essentials of Behavior. Greenwood.
Hypnosis & Suggestibility: An Experimental
Approach. Irvington.
Mathematico-Deductive Theory of Rote
Learning: A Study in Scientific Methodology.
Greenwood.
Hull, Clinton. *see* Hull, Clinton R.
Hull, Clinton R.
xHull, Clinton.
How to Build Recreation Vehicles. Trail-R.
Hull, David S. *see* Hull, David Stewart.
Hull, David Stewart.
xHull, David S.

Film in the Third Reich: A Study of the
German Cinema, 1933-1945. U of Cal Pr.

Hull, Derek.
xHull, Derek.
Introduction to Dislocations. Pergamon.

Hull, Edna Mayne.
xHull.
Planets for Sale. G&D.

Hull, Eleanor, 1860-1935
xHull, Eleanor.
Folklore of the British Isles. Folcroft.
Text Book of Irish Literature. AMS Pr.

Hull, Eleanor. *see* Hull, Eleanor Means.

Hull, Eleanor Means.
xHull, Eleanor.
Women Who Carried the Good News. Judson.

Hull, Katharine.
xHull, Katharine.
Far Distant Oxus. Macmillan.

Hull, R. *see* Hull, Richard W.

Hull, Raymond, 1919-
xHull, Raymond.
How to Get What You Want. Dutton.
Successful Public Speaking. Arco.
Vancouver's Past. U of Wash Pr.

Hull, Richard W.
xHull, R.
Modern Africa: Change & Continuity. P-H.
xHull, Richard W.
African Cities & Towns Before the European
Conquest. Norton.

Hull, Robert, 1931-
xHull, Robert.
September Champions: The Story of America's
Air Racing Pioneers. Stackpole.

Hull, Roger. *see* Hull, Roger H.

Hull, Roger H.
xHull, Roger.
Law & Vietnam. Oceana.

Hull, W. Frank. *see* Hull, William Frank.

Hull, W. I. *see* Hull, William Isaac.

Hull, William Frank, 1941-
xHull, W. Frank.
Foreign Students in the United States of
America: Coping Behavior Within the
Educational Environment. Praeger.

Hull, William I. *see* Hull, William Isaac.

Hull, William Isaac, 1868-1939
xHull, W. I.
Two Hague Conferences & Their Contributions
to International Law. Kraus Repr.
xHull, William I.
Preparedness: The American Versus the
Military Programme. Garland Pub.
The Two Hague Conferences & Their
Contributions to International Law. Arden
Lib.
Two Hague Conferences & Their Contributions
to International Law. Garland Pub.

Hulliung, Mark.
xHulliung, Mark.
Montesquieu & the Old Regime. U of Cal Pr.

Hulme, F. E. *see* Hulme, Frederick Edward.

Hulme, F. Edward. *see* Hulme, Frederick Edward.

Hulme, Frederick E. *see* Hulme, Frederick Edward.

Hulme, Frederick Edward, 1841-1909
xHulme, F. E.
History, Principles & Practice of Symbolism in
Christian Art. Gordon Pr.
xHulme, F. Edward.
History, Principles, & Practice of Symbolism in
Christian Art. Gale.
xHulme, Frederick E.
History, Principles & Practice of Heraldry.
Haskell.

Hulme, Hilda M.
xHulme, Hilda M.

Explorations in Shakespeare's Language: Some
Problems of Word Meaning in the Dramatic
Text. Longman.

Hulme, T. E. *see* Hulme, Thomas Ernest.

Hulme, Thomas Ernest, 1883-1917
xHulme, T. E.
Further Speculations. U of Nebr Pr.
Notes on Language & Style. Folcroft.
Notes on Language & Style. Haskell.

Hulme, William. *see* Hulme, William Edward.

Hulme, William E. *see* Hulme, William Edward.

Hulme, William Edward, 1920-
xHulme, William.
Living with Myself. Augsburg.
When I Don't Like Myself. Popular Lib.
xHulme, William E.
Am I Losing My Faith?. Fortress.
Building a Christian Marriage. Augsburg.
The Fire of Little Jim: Power for Growth from
the Letter of James. Abingdon.
Let the Spirit in: Practicing Christian
Devotional Meditation. Abingdon.
Two Ways of Caring: A Biblical Design for
Balanced Ministry. Augsburg.
When Two Become One: Reflections for the
Newly Married. Augsburg.

Hulse. *see* Hulse, Stewart H.

Hulse, Frederick. *see* Hulse, Frederick Seymour.

Hulse, Frederick Seymour, 1906-
xHulse, Frederick.
Human Species: An Introduction to Physical
Anthropology. Random.

Hulse, James W.
xHulse, James W.
The Forming of the Communist International.
Stanford U Pr.
Nevada Adventure: A History. U of Nev Pr.

Hulse, Stewart H.
xHulse.
The Psychology of Learning. McGraw.
xHulse, Stewart H.
ed. Cognitive Processes in Animal Behavior.
Halsted Pr.
The Psychology of Learning. McGraw.

Hulten, Eric, 1894-
xHulten, Eric.
Flora of Alaska & Neighboring Territories: A
Manual of the Vascular Plants. Stanford U
Pr.

Hulteng, John L.
xHulteng, John L.
Fourth Estate: An Informal Appraisal of the
News & Opinion Media. Har-Row.
The News Media: What Makes Them Tick?.
P-H.

Hultgren, Arland J.
xHultgren, Arland J.
Jesus & His Adversaries: The Form & Function
of the Conflict Stories in the Synoptic
Tradition. Augsburg.

Hultgren, T. *see* Hultgren, Thor.

Hultgren, Thor, 1902-
xHultgren, T.
Cost, Prices, & Profits: Their Cyclical
Relations. Natl Bur Econ Res.

Hultkrantz, Ake.
xHultkrantz, Ake.
The Religions of the American Indians. U of
Cal Pr.

Hultman, G. Eric.
xHultman, G. Eric.
Trees, Shrubs & Flowers of the Midwest.
Contemp Bks.

Human Relations Area Files, Inc.
xHuman Relations Area Files Inc.
North Borneo, Brunei, Sarawak (British
Borneo). Greenwood.

Human Resources Network.
xHuman Resources Network.

Handbook of Corporate Social Responsibility:
The Profiles of Involvement. Chilton.
How to Get Money for: Arts & Humanities,
Drug & Alcohol Abuse, Health. Chilton.
How to Get Money for: Conservation &
Community Development. Chilton.
How to Get Money for: Education, Fellowships
& Scholarships. Chilton.
How to Get Money for Youth, the Elderly, the
Handicapped, Women & Civil Liberties.
Chilton.
User's Guide to Funding Resources. Chilton.

Human Resources Planning Institute.
xHuman Resources Planning Institute, Seattle,
Washington.
A Forecast of Industrial & Occupational
Employment in Alaska. U Alaska Inst Res.
A Forecast of Industrial & Occupational
Employment in Alaska. U of Wash Pr.

Human Resources Research Organisation.
xHuman Resources Research Organization.
Academic Computing Directory: A Search for
Exemplary Institutions Using Computers for
Learning & Teaching. Human Resources.

Human Resources Research Organization. *see* Human
Resources Research Organisation.

Humane Society of the United States.
xHumane Society of the United States.
Careers: Working with Animals. Acropolis.

Humason, Gretchen L.
xHumason, Gretchen L.
Animal Tissue Techniques. W H Freeman.

Humayun Kabir, 1906-1969
xHumayun Kabir.
Compiled by Green & Gold: Stories & Poems
from Bengal. Greenwood.

Humber, James M.
xHumber, James M.
ed. Biomedical Ethics & the Law. Plenum Pub.

Humbert, Jack. *see* Humbert, Jack T.

Humbert, Jack T.
xHumbert, Jack.
Petroleum Marketing. McGraw.

Humble, John W. *see* Humble, John William.

Humble, John William.
xHumble, John W.
How to Manage by Objectives. Am Mgmt.

Humble, R. *see* Humble, Richard.

Humble, Richard.
xHumble, R.
The Explorers. Time-Life.
xHumble, Richard.
The Explorers. Silver.

Humble, S.
xHumble, S.
Introduction to Particle Production in Hadron
Physics. Acad Pr.

Humboldt, Alexander.
xHumboldt, Alexander Von.
Personal Narrative of Travels to the
Equinoctial Regions of America During the
Years 1799-1804. Arno.

Humboldt, Alexander Von. *see* Humboldt, Alexander.

Hume, Alexander, 1560?-1609
xHume, Alexander.
Hymns & Sacred Songs. AMS Pr.
Hymns & Sacred Songs. Johnson Repr.

Hume, Audrey Noel. *see* Noel Hume, Audrey.

Hume, Beryl.
xHume, Beryl.
An Introduction to Probability & Statistics. Intl
Schol Bk Serv.

Hume, David, 1711-1776
xHume, David.

An Enquiry Concerning Human
Understanding: Letter from a Gentleman to
His Friend in Edinburgh. Hackett Pub.
History of England: From the Invasion of
Julius Caesar to the Revolution of 1688. U of
Chicago Pr.
Inquiry Concerning the Principles of Morals:
With a Supplement, a Dialogue. Bobbs.
The Natural History of Religion. Stanford U
Pr.
Treatise of Human Nature. Collins Pubs.
Treatise of Human Nature. Dutton.
A Treatise of Human Nature. Oxford U Pr.
A Treatise on Human Nature. AMS Pr.
Hume, Edward H. see Hume, Edward Hicks.
Hume, Edward Hicks, 1876-1957
xHume, Edward H.
The Chinese Way in Medicine. Hyperion
Conn.
Hume, George, 1836-
xHume, George.
Thirty-Five Years in Russia. Arno.
Hume, Ivor Noel. see Noel Hume, Ivor.
Hume, John R.
xHume, John R.
Beardmore: The History of a Scottish Industrial
Giant. Heinemann Ed.
Hume, Kathryn, 1945-
xHume, Kathryn.
The Owl & the Nightingale: The Poem & Its
Critics. U of Toronto Pr.
Hume, Martin. see Hume, Martin Andrew Sharp.
Hume, Martin A. see Hume, Martin Andrew Sharp.
Hume, Martin Andrew Sharp, 1847-1910
xHume, Martin.
Spanish Influence on English Literature.
Folcroft.
xHume, Martin A.
Great Lord Burghley: A Study in Elizabethan
Statecraft. Haskell.
Hume, Michael.
xHume, Michael.
Venous Thrombosis & Pulmonary Embolism.
Harvard U Pr.
Hume, Robert D.
xHume, Robert D.
The Development of English Drama in the
Late Seventeenth Century. Oxford U Pr.
Dryden's Criticism. Cornell U Pr.
Humes, James C.
xHumes, James C.
Instant Eloquence: A Lazy Man's Guide to
Public Speaking. Har-Row.
Speaker's Treasury of Anecdotes About the
Famous. Har-Row.
Humes, Thomas W. see Humes, Thomas William.
Humes, Thomas William, 1815-1892
xHumes, Thomas W.
The Loyal Mountaineers of Tennessee. Reprint.
Humez, Alexander.
xHumez, Alexander.
Latin for People: Latina Pro Populo. Little.
xHumez, Nicholas.
jt. auth. Latin for People: Latina Pro Populo.
Little.
Humez, Nicholas. see Humez, Alexander.
Huminik, John.
xHuminik, John F.
High Temperature Inorganic Coatings. Van
Nos Reinhold.
Huminik, John F. see Huminik, John.
Hummel. see Hummel, Paul Matthew.
Hummel, Charles E.
xHummel, Charles E.
Fire in the Fireplace: Contemporary
Charismatic Renewal. Inter-Varsity.
Hummel, Dean L.
xHummel, Dean L.

The Counselor & Military Service
Opportunities. HM.
How to Help Your Child Plan a Career.
Acropolis.
How to Help Your Child Plan a Career.
Garrett Pk.
Hummel, Paul Matthew.
xHummel.
Mathematics of Finance. McGraw.
Hummel, Ralph P.
xHummel, Ralph P.
The Bureaucratic Experience. St Martin.
Politics for Human Beings. Duxbury Pr.
Hummel, Ray O. see Hummel, Ray Orvin.
Hummel, Ray Orvin.
xHummel, Ray O.
Southeastern Broadsides Before 1877: A
Bibliography. U Pr of Va.
ed. Southeastern Broadsides Before 1877: A
Bibliography. VA State Lib.
Hummer, Patricia M., 1946-
xHummer, Patricia M.
The Decade of Elusive Promise: Professional
Women in the United States, 1920-1930.
Univ Microfilms.
Humphrey, Clifford C.
xHumphrey, Clifford C.
What's Ecology?. Hubbard Sci.
Humphrey, David C., 1937-
xHumphrey, David C.
From King's College to Columbia, 1746-1800.
Columbia U Pr.
Humphrey, Edward F. see Humphrey, Edward Frank.
Humphrey, Edward Frank, 1878-
xHumphrey, Edward F.
Nationalism & Religion in America, 1774-1789.
Russell.
Humphrey, Grace, 1882-
xHumphrey, Grace.
Stories of the World's Holidays. Dynamic
Learn Corp.
Stories of the World's Holidays. Folcroft.
Stories of the World's Holidays. Gale.
Humphrey, Henry, 1930-
xHumphrey, Henry.
The Farm. Doubleday.
Sailing the High Seas. McKay.
photos by What's Inside?. S&S.
Humphrey, Hubert H. see Humphrey, Hubert Horatio.
Humphrey, Hubert Horatio, 1911-
xHumphrey, Hubert H.
Education of a Public Man: My Life & Politics.
Doubleday.
Political Philosophy of the New Deal. La State
U Pr.
Humphrey, J. H. see Humphrey, James Harry.
Humphrey, James H. see Humphrey, James Harry.
Humphrey, James Harry, 1911-
xHumphrey, J. H.
Teaching Slow Learners Through Active
Games. C C Thomas.
xHumphrey, James H.
Education of Children Through Motor
Activity. C C Thomas.
Improving Learning Ability Through
Compensatory Physical Education. C C
Thomas.
Physical Education As a Career: A Text for the
Introductory Course. C C Thomas.
Teaching Elementary School Science Through
Motor Learning. C C Thomas.
Humphrey, John A.
xHumphrey, John A.
Administration of Justice: Law Enforcement
Courts & Corrections. Human Sci Pr.
Humphrey, Marylou.
xHumphrey, Marylou.
Cheerleading & Song Leading. C E Tuttle.
Humphrey, Michael.
xHumphrey, Michael.

Hostage Seekers: A Study of Childless &
Adopting Couples. Humanities.
Humphrey, Richard D.
xHumphrey, Richard D.
Georges Sorel-Prophet Without Honor: A
Study in Anti-intellectualism. Octagon.
Humphrey, Richard V.
xHumphrey, Richard V.
Building Fiberglass Ship Models from Scratch.
TAB Bks.
Humphrey, Robert E.
xHumphrey, Robert E.
Children of Fantasy: The First Rebels of
Greenwich Village. Wiley.
Humphrey, Robert R. see Humphrey, Robert Regester.
Humphrey, Robert Regester, 1904-
xHumphrey, Robert R.
Range Ecology. Wiley.
Humphrey, S. D. see Humphrey, Samuel D.
Humphrey, Samuel D.
xHumphrey, S. D.
American Hand Book of the Daguerreotype.
Arno.
Humphrey, William.
xHumphrey, William.
Ah, Wilderness: The Frontier in American
Literature. Tex Western.
Farther off from Heaven. Knopf.
Home from the Hill. Knopf.
My Moby Dick. Doubleday.
My Moby Dick. Penguin.
The Spawning Run. Delacorte.
Humphreys, Alice L. see Humphreys, Alice Lee.
Humphreys, Alice Lee.
xHumphreys, Alice L.
Angels in Pinafores. John Knox.
Humphreys, Christmas, 1901-
xHumphreys, Christmas.
Both Sides of the Circle: The Autobiography of
Christmas Humphreys. Allen Unwin.
Exploring Buddhism. Theos Pub Hse.
A Popular Dictionary of Buddhism. Rowman.
ed. The Wisdom of Buddhism. Humanities.
Humphreys, Clarence B. see Humphreys, Clarence Blake.
Humphreys, Clarence Blake.
xHumphreys, Clarence B.
The Southern New Hebrides: An Ethnological
Record. AMS Pr.
Humphreys, David, 1689-1740
xHumphreys, David.
Historical Account of the Incorporated Society
for the Propagation of the Gospel in Foreign
Parts - to the Year 1728. Arno.
Humphreys, Fisher.
xHumphreys, Fisher.
The Death of Christ. Broadman.
Speaking in Tongues. Insight Pr.
Humphreys, Gertrude.
xHumphreys, Gertrude.
Adventures in Good Living. McClain.
Humphreys, J. Anthony. see Humphreys, Joseph
Anthony.
Humphreys, J. E. see Humphreys, James Edward.
Humphreys, J. R. see Humphreys, John R.
Humphreys, James E.
xHumphreys, J. E.
Introduction to Lie Algebras & Representation
Theory. Springer-Verlag.
Linear Algebraic Groups. Springer-Verlag.
Ordinary & Modular Representations of
Chevalley Groups. Springer-Verlag.
Humphreys, James Edward.
xHumphreys, J. E.
Algebraic Groups & Modular Lie Algebras. Am
Math.
Humphreys, John R., 1918-
xHumphreys, J. R.

Subway to Samarkand. Berkley Pub.
Subway to Samarkand. Doubleday.
Subway to Samarkand. G K Hall.
Humphreys, Joseph Anthony.
xHumphreys, J. Anthony.
Guidance Services. SRA.
Humphreys, Laud.
xHumphreys, Laud.
Out of the Closets: The Sociology of
Homosexual Liberation. P-H.
Humphreys, R. Stephen.
xHumphreys, R. Stephen.
From Saladin to the Mongols: The Ayyubids of
Damascus, 1193-1260. State U NY Pr.
Humphreys, Robert A. see Humphreys, Robert Arthur.
Humphreys, Robert Arthur, 1907-
xHumphreys, Robert A.
Latin American History: A Guide to the
Literature in English. Greenwood.
xHumphreys, Robin A.
The Evolution of Modern Latin America.
Cooper Sq.
Humphreys, Robin A. see Humphreys, Robert Arthur.
Humphreys, S. C. see Humphreys, Sarah C.
Humphreys, Sarah C.
xHumphreys, S. C.
Anthropology & the Greeks. Routledge &
Kegan.
Humphreys, W. Lee.
xHumphreys, W. Lee.
Crisis & Story: Introduction to the Old
Testament. Mayfield Pub.
Humphreys, Willard C.
xHumphreys, Willard C.
Anomalies & Scientific Theories. Freeman C.
Humphries, Adelaide.
xHumphries, Adelaide.
Clinic Nurse. Assoc Bk.
Navy Nurse. Assoc Bk.
Humphries, Jackie.
xHumphries, Jackie.
All the Things You Aren't...Yet. Word Bks.
Humphries, Russell J.
xHumphries, Russell J.
Stop Stuttering, Stop Stammering, Stop
Stumbling. Sterling.
Huncke, Herbert E., 1915-
xHuncke, Herbert E.
The Evening Sun Turned Crimson. Cherry
Valley.
Hundhausen, A. J., 1936-
xHundhausen, A. J.
Coronal Expansion & Solar Wind.
Springer-Verlag.
Hundley, D. R. see Hundley, Daniel Robinson.
Hundley, Daniel R. see Hundley, Daniel Robinson.
Hundley, Daniel Robinson, 1832-1899
xHundley, D. R.
Social Relations in Our Southern States. Arno.
xHundley, Daniel R.
Social Relations in Our Southern States. La
State U Pr.
Hundley, Norris.
xHundley, Norris.
Dividing the Waters: A Century of Controversy
Between the United States & Mexico. U of
Cal Pr.
Huneker, James G. see Huneker, James Gibbons.
Huneker, James Gibbons, 1857-1921
xHuneker, James G.

Chopin: Man & His Music. Dover.
Chopin: The Man & His Music. Scholarly.
Egoists, a Book of Supermen: Stendhal,
Baudelaire, Flaubert, Anatole France,
Huysmans, Barres, Nietzsche, Blake, Ibsen,
Stirner, & Ernest Hello. AMS Pr.
Franz Liszt. AMS Pr.
Melomaniacs. AMS Pr.
Melomaniacs. Gordon Pr.
Intro. by Old Fogy, His Musical Opinions &
Grotesques. Hyperion Conn.
Promenades of an Impressionist. Arno.
Unicorns. AMS Pr.
**Hungarian Bioflavonoid Symposium, 4th, Keszthely,
Hungary, 1973.**
xHungarian Bioflavonoid Symposium, 4th,
Hungary, 1973.
Topics in Flavonoid Chemistry & Biochemistry:
Proceedings. Elsevier.
Hungerford, Edward, 1875-1948
xHungerford, Edward.
Men & Iron: The History of New York
Central. Arno.
The Story of Public Utilities. Arno.
The Story of the Baltimore & Ohio Railroad,
1827-1927. Arno.
Hungerford, H. B. see Hungerford, Herbert Barker.
Hungerford, Harold.
xHungerford, Harold.
English Linguistics: An Introductory Reader.
Scott F.
Hungerford, Herbert Barker, 1883-
xHungerford, H. B.
The Corixidae of the Western Hemisphere
(Hemiptera). Entomological Repr.
Hungerford, Mary J. see Hungerford, Mary Jane.
Hungerford, Mary Jane.
xHungerford, Mary J.
Childbirth Education. C C Thomas.
Hunker, Henry L.
xHunker, Henry L.
Industrial Evolution of Columbus, Ohio. Ohio
St U Admin Sci.
Hunkins, Dalton R.
xHunkins, Dalton R.
Mathematics: Tools & Models. A-W.
Hunkins, Francis P., 1938-
xHunkins, Francis P.
Review of Research in Social Studies
Education: 1970-1975. Coun Soc Studies.
Review of Research in Social Studies
Education: 1970-1975. Soc Sci Ed.
Hunnicutt, Benjamin H. see Hunnicutt, Benjamin Harris.
Hunnicutt, Benjamin Harris, 1886-
xHunnicutt, Benjamin H.
Brazil, World Frontier. Greenwood.
Hunnicutt, R. P., 1926-
xHunnicutt, R. P.
Sherman: A History of the American Medium
Tank. Presidio Pr.
Hunsberger, Bruce, 1937-
xHunsberger, Bruce.
Railroad Street. Lyle Stuart.
Hunsicker, L. M. see Hunsicker, Lilian May.
Hunsicker, Lilian May, 1872-
xHunsicker, L. M.
Study of the Relationship Between Rate &
Ability. AMS Pr.
Hunt, Abby C. see Hunt, Abby Campbell.
Hunt, Abby Campbell.
xHunt, Abby C.
The World of Books for Children: A Parents
Guide. Sovereign Bks.
Hunt, Agnes, 1876-1923
xHunt, Agnes.
Provincial Committees of Safety of the
American Revolution. Haskell.
Hunt, Alan.
xHunt, Alan.

The Sociological Movement in Law. Temple U
Pr.
Hunt, Alfred.
xHunt, Alfred L.
Corporate Cash Management: Including
Electronic Funds Transfer. Am Mgmt.
Hunt, Alfred L. see Hunt, Alfred.
Hunt, Bernice. see Hunt, Bernice Kohn.
Hunt, Bernice K. see Hunt, Bernice Kohn.
Hunt, Bernice Kohn.
xHunt, Bernice.
Great Bread!: The Easiest Possible Way to
Make Almost 100 Kinds. Viking Pr.
Prime Time: A Guide to the Pleasures &
Opportunities of the New Middleage. Stein &
Day.
xHunt, Bernice K.
Apples: A Bushel of Fun & Facts. Enslow
Pubs.
Marriage. HR&W.
The Whatchamacallit Book. Putnam.
Hunt, Bishop C. see Hunt, Bishop Carleton.
Hunt, Bishop Carleton.
xHunt, Bishop C.
Development of the Business Corporation in
England, 1800-1867. Russell.
Hunt, Cecil, 1902-
xHunt, Cecil.
A Dictionary of Word Makers: Pen Pictures of
the People Behind Our Language. Folcroft.
Hunt, Charles B. see Hunt, Charles Butler.
Hunt, Charles Butler, 1906-
xHunt, Charles B.
Death Valley: Geology, Ecology, Archaeology.
U of Cal Pr.
Natural Regions of the United States &
Canada. W H Freeman.
Hunt, Chester L.
xHunt, Chester L.
Ethnic Dynamics: Patterns of Intergroup
Relations in Various Societies. Learning
Pubns.
Hunt, Clay.
xHunt, Clay.
Lycidas & the Italian Critics. Yale U Pr.
Hunt, Dennis D.
xHunt, Dennis D.
Common Sense Industrial Relations. David &
Charles.
Employment Dismissal Without Fear. David &
Charles.
Hunt, Derald D.
xHunt, Derald D.
California Criminal Law Manual. Burgess.
Hunt, Donnell.
xHunt, Donnell R.
Farm Machinery Mechanisms. Iowa St U Pr.
Hunt, Donnell R. see Hunt, Donnell.
Hunt, E. H. see Hunt, Edward H.
Hunt, E. Howard. see Hunt, Howard.
Hunt, E. K.
xHunt, E. K.
Economics: An Introduction to Traditional &
Radical Views. Har-Row.
History of Economic Thought: A Critical
Perspective. Wadsworth Pub.
Property & Prophets: The Evolution of
Economic Institutions & Ideologies.
Har-Row.
Hunt, Earl B.
xHunt, Earl B.
Artificial Intelligence. Acad Pr.
Hunt, Earl W.
xHunt, Earl W.
The Living Wilderness. Lerner Pubns.
Hunt, Edward H.
xHunt, E. H.
Regional Wage Variations in Britain 1850-1914.
Oxford U Pr.
Hunt, Effie H. see Hunt, Effie Harder.

Hunt, Effie Harder.
  xHunt, Effie H.
    How to Have a Perfect Wedding. Fell.
Hunt, Erling M. *see* Hunt, Erling Messer.
Hunt, Erling Messer, 1901-
  xHunt, Erling M.
    American Precedents in Australian Federation.
    AMS Pr.
Hunt, Everett N. *see* Hunt, Everett Nichols.
Hunt, Everett Nichols.
  xHunt, Everett N.
    Protestant Pioneers in Korea. Orbis Bks.
Hunt, Frederick V.
  xHunt, Frederick V.
    Origins in Acoustics: The Science of Sound
    from Antiquity to the Age of Newton. Yale
    U Pr.
Hunt, G. N. *see* Hunt, Geoffrey.
Hunt, Gaillard, 1862-1924
  xHunt, Gaillard.
    Life in America One Hundred Years Ago.
    Corner Hse.
    Life in America One Hundred Years Ago.
    Gale.
    Life of James Madison. Russell.
Hunt, Gary T.
  xHunt, Gary T.
    Communication Skills in the Organization.
    P-H.
Hunt, Geoffrey.
  xHunt, G. N.
    About the New English Bible. Cambridge U Pr.
Hunt, Gladys. *see* Hunt, Gladys M.
Hunt, Gladys M.
  xHunt, Gladys.
    Honey for a Child's Heart. Zondervan.
    MS Means Myself. Zondervan.
Hunt, Henry T. *see* Hunt, Henry Thomas.
Hunt, Henry Thomas, 1878
  xHunt, Henry T.
    Case of Thomas J. Mooney & Warren K.
    Billings. Da Capo.
Hunt, Herbert J. *see* Hunt, Herbert James.
Hunt, Herbert James.
  xHunt, Herbert J.
    Balzac's Comedie Humaine. Humanities.
Hunt, Howard, 1918-
  xHunt, E. Howard.
    The Hargrave Deception. Stein & Day.
Hunt, Hugh, 1911-
  xHunt, Hugh.
    The Live Theatre: An Introduction to the
    History & Practice of the Stage. Greenwood.
Hunt, Ignatius, 1920-
  xHunt, Ignatius.
    Understanding the Bible. Andrews & McMeel.
Hunt, Inez.
  xHunt, Inez.
    Lightning in His Hand: The Life Story of
    Nikola Tesla. Heinman.
Hunt, Irene.
  xHunt, Irene.
    Across Five Aprils. G&D.
    Across Five Aprils. Follett.
    No Promises in the Wind. G&D.
Hunt, J. M. *see* Hunt, Joseph McVicker.
Hunt, J. McVicker. *see* Hunt, Joseph McVicker.
Hunt, J. William. *see* Hunt, John William.
Hunt, James, 1833-1869
  xHunt, James.
    Stammering & Stuttering: Their Nature &
    Treatment. Hafner.
Hunt, James G.
  xHunt, James G.
    ed. Crosscurrents in Leadership. S Ill U Pr.
    Leadership Frontiers. Kent St U Pr.
Hunt, James W.
  xHunt, James W.

    Employer's Guide to Labor Relations. BNA.
Hunt, John, 1827-ca. 1908
  xHunt, John.
    Pantheism & Christianity. Kennikat.
Hunt, John D. *see* Hunt, John Dixon.
Hunt, John Dixon.
  xHunt, John D.
    Andrew Marvell: His Life & Writings. Cornell
    U Pr.
    The Pre-Raphaelite Imagination, 1848-1900. U
    of Nebr Pr.
Hunt, John M. *see* Hunt, John Meacham.
Hunt, John Meacham.
  xHunt, John M.
    Petroleum Geochemistry & Geology. W H
    Freeman.
Hunt, John William, 1930-
  xHunt, J. William.
    Forms of Glory: Structure & Sense in Virgil's
    'Aeneid'. S Ill U Pr.
Hunt, Joseph McVicker, 1906-
  xHunt, J. M.
    Intelligence & Experience. Wiley.
  xHunt, J. McVicker.
    The Challenge of Incompetence & Poverty:
    Papers on the Role of Early Education. U of
    Ill Pr.
Hunt, June.
  xHunt, June.
    Above All Else. Revell.
Hunt, K. H. *see* Hunt, Kenneth H.
Hunt, Kari.
  xHunt, Kari.
    Masks & Mask Makers. Abingdon.
Hunt, Kenneth H.
  xHunt, K. H.
    Kinematic Geometry of Mechanisms. Oxford U
    Pr.
Hunt, Lacy H.
  xHunt, Lacy H.
    Dynamics of Forecasting Financial Cycles:
    Theory, Technique & Implementation. Jai Pr.
Hunt, Leigh, 1784-1859
  xHunt, Leigh.
    Leigh Hunt's Dramatic Criticism. Octagon.
    Literary Criticism. Octagon.
    Musical Evenings: Or Selections, Vocal &
    Instrumental. U of Mo Pr.
    Prefaces by Leigh Hunt, Mainly to His
    Periodicals. Kennikat.
    Tales. Folcroft.
Hunt, Lesley.
  xHunt, Lesley.
    Inside Tennis for Women. Contemp Bks.
Hunt, Lyall. *see* Hunt, Lyall J.
Hunt, Lyall J.
  xHunt, Lyall.
    ed. Westralian Portraits. Intl Schol Bk Serv.
Hunt, Lynn A. *see* Hunt, Lynn Avery.
Hunt, Lynn Avery.
  xHunt, Lynn A.
    Revolution & Urban Politics in Provincial
    France: Troyes & Reims, 1786-1790. Stanford
    U Pr.
Hunt, M. Briggs.
  xHunt, M. Briggs.
    Greco-Roman Wrestling. Athletic.
Hunt, Mary L. *see* Hunt, Mary Leland.
Hunt, Mary Leland.
  xHunt, Mary L.
    Thomas Dekker: A Study. Arden Lib.
Hunt, Maurice P.
  xHunt, Maurice P.
    Foundations of Education: Social & Cultural
    Perspectives. HR&W.
Hunt, Morton.
  xHunt, Morton.

    The Divorce Experience. NAL.
    Gay: What You Should Know About
    Homosexuality. PB.
    Gay: What You Should Know About
    Homosexuality. FS&G.
Hunt, Morton. *see* Hunt, Morton M.
Hunt, Morton M., 1920-
  xHunt, Morton.
    What Is a Man? What Is a Woman?. FS&G.
Hunt, Pauline.
  xHunt, Pauline.
    Gender & Class Consciousness. Holmes &
    Meier.
Hunt, Reginald.
  xHunt, Reginald.
    Extemporization for Music Students. Oxford U
    Pr.
    A First Harmony Book. Greenwood.
Hunt, Richard A.
  xHunt, Richard A.
    Creative Marriage. Allyn.
Hunt, Robert.
  xHunt, Robert.
    ed. Ethical Issues in Modern Medicine.
    Mayfield Pub.
    The Normandy Campaign. Hippocrene Bks.
Hunt, Robert. *see* Hunt, Robert Cushman.
Hunt, Robert Cushman.
  xHunt, Robert.
    ed. Personalities & Cultures: Readings in
    Psychological Anthropology. U of Tex Pr.
Hunt, Robert L. *see* Hunt, Robert Lee.
Hunt, Robert Lee.
  xHunt, Robert L.
    Farm Management in the South. Interstate.
Hunt, Robert S.
  xHunt, Robert S.
    Law & Locomotives: The Impact of the
    Railroad on Wisconsin Law in the
    Nineteenth Century. State Hist Soc Wis.
Hunt, Roberta.
  xHunt, Roberta.
    Obstacles to Interstate Adoption. Child
    Welfare.
Hunt, Rockwell D. *see* Hunt, Rockwell Dennis.
Hunt, Rockwell Dennis, 1868-
  xHunt, Rockwell D.
    The Genesis of California's First Constitution
    (1846-49). AMS Pr.
    Genesis of California's First Constitution:
    1846-49. Johnson Repr.
Hunt, S. *see* Hunt, Stephen.
Hunt, S. E. *see* Hunt, Stanely Ernest.
Hunt, Sarah E. *see* Hunt, Sarah Ethridge.
Hunt, Sarah Ethridge.
  xHunt, Sarah E.
    Games & Sports the World Around. Ronald Pr.
Hunt, Shelby D.
  xHunt, Shelby D.
    Marketing Theory: Conceptual Foundations of
    Research in Marketing. Grid Pub.
Hunt, Stanely Ernest.
  xHunt, S. E.
    Fission, Fusion, & the Energy Crisis.
    Pergamon.
Hunt, Stephen.
  xHunt, S.
    Polysaccharide-Protein Complexes in
    Invertebrates. Acad Pr.
Hunt, Thomas K.
  xHunt, Thomas K.
    ed. Fundamentals of Wound Management.
    ACC.
Hunt, V. Daniel.
  xHunt, V. Daniel.
    Energy Dictionary. Van Nos Reinhold.
Hunt, Violet, 1866-1942
  xHunt, Violet.
    More Tales of the Uneasy. Folcroft.
Hunt, W. Ben. *see* Hunt, Walter Bernard.

Hunt, Walter Bernard, 1888-1970
xHunt, W. Ben.
How to Build & Furnish a Log Cabin: The
Easy-Natural Way Using Only 12 Hand
Tools & the Woods Around You. Macmillan.
Indian Silversmithing. Macmillan.
Hunt, William, 1934-
xHunt, William.
Of the Map That Changes. Swallow.
Hunter. *see* Hunter, William.
Hunter, Alan.
xHunter, Alan.
Gently in the Highlands. Macmillan.
Gently Through the Woods. Macmillan.
Gently with the Innocents. Macmillan.
Gently with the Ladies. Macmillan.
Gently with the Painters. Macmillan.
Hunter, Albert.
xHunter, Albert.
Symbolic Communities: The Persistence &
Change of Chicago's Local Communities. U
of Chicago Pr.
Hunter, Alex.
xHunter, Alex.
Competition & the Law. Kelley.
Hunter, Archibald M. *see* Hunter, Archibald Macbride.
Hunter, Archibald Macbride.
xHunter, Archibald M.
According to John: The New Look at the
Fourth Gospel. Westminster.
Gleanings from the New Testament.
Westminster.
Gospel According to St. Paul. Westminster.
Introducing the New Testament. Westminster.
The Parables Then & Now. Westminster.
A Pattern for Life: An Exposition of the
Sermon on the Mount. Westminster.
The Work & Words of Jesus. Westminster.
Hunter, Beatrice T. *see* Hunter, Beatrice Trum.
Hunter, Beatrice Trum.
xHunter, Beatrice T.
Beatrice Trum Hunter's Additives Book. Keats.
The Great Nutrition Robbery. Scribner.
The Natural Foods Cookbook. BJ Pub Group.
Natural Foods Cookbook. S&S.
Natural Foods Cookbook. S&S.
Intro. by Prize-Winning Recipes from the
Golden Harvest Kitchens. Keats.
Hunter, Ben.
xHunter, Ben.
The Baja Feeling. Brasch & Brasch.
Hunter, Beverly.
xHunter, Beverly.
Learning Alternatives in U. S. Education:
Where Student & Computer Meet. Educ
Tech Pubns.
Hunter, Brian.
xHunter, Brian.
Soviet-Yugoslav Relations, 1948-1972: A
Bibliography of Soviet, Western & Yugoslav
Comment & Analysis. Garland Pub.
Hunter, C. Bruce.
xHunter, C. Bruce.
A Guide to Ancient Maya Ruins. U of Okla
Pr.
A Guide to Ancient Mexican Ruins. U of Okla
Pr.
Hunter, Charles.
xHunter, Charles.
How to Make Your Marriage Exciting. Hunter
Bks.
Hunter, David E.
xHunter, David E.
Anthropology: Contemporary Perspectives.
Little.
ed. Readings in Physical Anthropology &
Archaeology. Har-Row.
Hunter, Donald, 1898-
xHunter, Donald.

The Diseases of Occupations. Little.
Hunter, Edith F. *see* Hunter, Edith Fisher.
Hunter, Edith Fisher.
xHunter, Edith F.
Sue Ellen. HM.
Hunter, Eileen.
xHunter, Eileen.
Tales of Waybeyond. Andre Deutsch.
Hunter, Evan, 1926-
xHunter, Evan.
Come Winter. NAL.
Last Summer. NAL.
Me & Mr. Stenner. Dell.
Me & Mr. Stenner. Lippincott.
Streets of Gold. Random.
Hunter, Floyd.
xHunter, Floyd.
Community Organization: Action & Inaction.
Greenwood.
Community Power Succession: Atlanta's Policy
Makers Revisited. U of NC Pr.
Hunter, Frances. *see* Hunter, Frances Gardner.
Hunter, Frances Gardner, 1916-
xHunter, Frances.
Hot Line to Heaven. Hunter Bks.
Hunter, Frederick W. *see* Hunter, Frederick William.
Hunter, Frederick William, 1865-1919
xHunter, Frederick W.
Stiegel Glass. Dover.
Stiegel Glass. Peter Smith.
Hunter, G. K.
xHunter, G. K.
Dramatic Identities & Cultural Tradition:
Studies in Shakespeare & His
Contemporaries. B&N.
Hunter, George. *see* Hunter, George G.
Hunter, George G.
xHunter, George.
The Contagious Congregation: Frontiers in
Evangelism & Church Growth. Abingdon.
Hunter, George W. *see* Hunter, George William.
Hunter, George William.
xHunter, George W.
Tropical Medicine. Saunders.
Hunter, Gordon C.
xHunter, Gordon C.
Grace Abounding. Abingdon.
Hunter, Guy.
xHunter, Guy.
Education for a Developing Region: A Study in
East Africa. Greenwood.
Hunter, Holland.
xHunter, Holland.
ed. The Future of the Soviet Economy:
1978-1985. Westview.
Hunter, Ilene.
xHunter, Ilene.
Simple Folk Instruments to Make & Play. S&S.
Simple Folk Instruments to Make & to Play.
S&S.
Hunter, J. A. *see* Hunter, James Alston Hope.
Hunter, J. Paul, 1934-
xHunter, J. Paul.
Occasional Form: Henry Fielding & the Chains
of Circumstance. Johns Hopkins.
The Reluctant Pilgrim: Defoe's Emblematic
Method & Quest for Form in Robinson
Crusoe. Johns Hopkins.
Hunter, Jack. *see* Hunter, Jack D.
Hunter, Jack D.
xHunter, Jack.
Spies, Inc.. Baronet.
xHunter, Jack D.
The Blood Order. Bantam.
The Blood Order. Times Bks.
Hunter, James Alston Hope.
xHunter, J. A.

Challenging Mathematical Teasers. Dover.
Fun with Figures. Dover.
Mathematical Brain-Teasers. Dover.
Mathematical Diversions. Dover.
Hunter, James M.
xHunter, James M.
Rehabilitation of the Hand. Mosby.
Hunter, James T., 1923-
xHunter, James T.
Our Second Revolution. Caxton.
Hunter, Jim, 1939-
xHunter, Jim.
The Gamecocks: South Carolina Football.
Strode.
A Man Against the Mountain. Cook.
Hunter, Joan.
xHunter, Joan.
Under the Raging Moon. PB.
Hunter, John.
xHunter, John.
Impact. Chr Lit.
Hunter, John D. *see* Hunter, John Dunn.
Hunter, John Dunn, 1798?-1827
xHunter, John D.
Memoirs of a Captivity Among the Indians of
North America, from Childhood to the Age
of Nineteen. Johnson Repr.
Hunter, John E. *see* Hunter, John Edward.
Hunter, John Edward, 1909-
xHunter, John E.
Finding the Living Christ in the Psalms.
Zondervan.
World in Rebellion. Beta Bk.
Hunter, Joseph, 1783-1861
xHunter, Joseph.
South Yorkshire. Rowman.
Hunter, Julius. *see* Hunter, Julius K.
Hunter, Julius K.
xHunter, Julius.
Absurd Alphabedtime Stories. Bethany Pr.
Hunter, Kim.
xHunter, Kim.
Loose in the Kitchen. Double M Pr.
Hunter, Kristin.
xHunter, Kristin.
Boss Cat. Avon.
Boss Cat. Scribner.
Soul Brothers & Sister Lou. Avon.
Soul Brothers & Sister Lou. Scribner.
The Survivors. Scribner.
Hunter, Laurence Colvin.
xHunter, Lawrence C.
Economics of Wages & Labour. Kelley.
Hunter, Lawrence C. *see* Hunter, Laurence Colvin.
Hunter, Lynette.
xHunter, Lynette.
G. K. Chesterton: Explorations in Allegory. St
Martin.
Hunter, Mac.
xHunter, Mac.
Golf for Beginners. G&D.
Hunter, Margaret K.
xHunter, Margaret K.
The Indoor Garden: Design, Construction &
Furnishing. Wiley.
Hunter, Mary V. *see* Hunter, Mary Vann.
Hunter, Mary Vann.
xHunter, Mary V.
Sassafras. NAL.
Hunter, Mollie.
xHunter, Mollie.
A Stranger Came Ashore. Har-Row.
A Stranger Came Ashore. Har-Row.
Hunter, Richard S. *see* Hunter, Richard Sewall.
Hunter, Richard Sewall, 1909-
xHunter, Richard S.
The Measurement of Appearance. Wiley.
Hunter, Rixie.
xHunter, Rixie.

Checkerboard Corridor. Blair.
Hunter, Robert.
   xHunter, Robert.
      To Save a Whale: The Voyages of Greenpeace.
         Chronicle Bks.
Hunter, Robert E. *see* Hunter, Robert Edwards.
Hunter, Robert Edwards, 1940-
   xHunter, Robert E.
      Security in Europe. Ind U Pr.
Hunter, Robert S., 1919-
   xHunter, Robert S.
      Federal Trial Handbook. Lawyers Co-Op.
Hunter, Ronald P., 1938-
   xHunter, Ronald P.
      Automated Process Control Systems: Concepts
         & Hardware. P-H.
Hunter, Sam.
   xHunter, Sam.
      Art in Business: The Philip Morris Story.
         Abrams.
      Chryssa. Abrams.
Hunter, Stanley A. *see* Hunter, Stanley Armstrong.
Hunter, Stanley Armstrong, 1888-
   xHunter, Stanley A.
      ed. Music & Religion. AMS Pr.
Hunter, Stephen, 1946-
   xHunter, Stephen.
      The Master Sniper. Morrow.
Hunter, Steve.
   xHunter, Steven.
      Home Inspection Workbook. Hammond Inc.
Hunter, Steven. *see* Hunter, Steve.
Hunter, William.
   xHunter.
      Hunter's Lectures of Anatomy. Elsevier.
Hunter, William. *see* Hunter, William L.
Hunter, William B. *see* Hunter, William Bridges.
Hunter, William Bridges.
   xHunter, William B.
      Bright Essence: Studies in Milton's Theology.
         U of Utah Pr.
Hunter, William L.
   xHunter, William.
      Master Handbook of Digital Logic
         Applications. TAB Bks.
   xHunter, William L.
      Modern Amateur Radio License Study Guide
         for Novice, Technician & General Class
         Exams. TAB Bks.
Hunter, William W. *see* Hunter, William Wilson.
Hunter, William Wilson, Sir, 1840-1900
   xHunter, William W.
      Annals of Rural Bengal. Johnson Repr.
      History of British India. AMS Pr.
      History of British India. Intl Pubns Serv.
      Indian Empire: Its Peoples, History &
         Products. AMS Pr.
Hunting, Gardner.
   xHunting, Gardner.
      Working with God. Unity Bks.
Hunting, Robert.
   xHunting, Robert.
      Jonathan Swift. Twayne.
Hunting, Warren B. *see* Hunting, Warren Belnap.
Hunting, Warren Belnap, 1888-1918
   xHunting, Warren B.
      The Obligation of Contracts Clause of the
         United States Constitution. AMS Pr.
      The Obligation of Contracts Clause of the
         United States Constitution. Greenwood.
Huntington, Archer M. *see* Huntington, Archer Milton.
Huntington, Archer Milton, 1870-
   xHuntington, Archer M.
      Collected Verse. Hispanic Soc.
      The Torch Bearers. Hispanic Soc.
      Turning Pages. Hispanic Soc.
Huntington, Ellsworth, 1876-1947
   xHuntington, Ellsworth.

Civilization & Climate. Quality Lib.
Civilization & Climate. Shoe String.
Climatic Changes: Their Nature & Causes.
   AMS Pr.
The Climatic Factor As Illustrated in Arid
   America. AMS Pr.
World-Power & Evolution. Arno.
Huntington, Harriet E.
   xHuntington, Harriet E.
      Let's Look at Dogs. Doubleday.
      Let's Look at Reptiles. Doubleday.
Huntington, John F.
   xHuntington, John F.
      Computer-Assisted Instruction Using BASIC.
         Educ Tech Pubns.
Huntington, Lee. *see* Huntington, Lee Pennock.
Huntington, Lee Pennock.
   xHuntington, Lee.
      Simple Shelters. Coward.
Huntington, R. T. *see* Huntington, Roy Theodore.
Huntington, Roy Theodore, 1916-
   xHuntington, R. T.
      Hall's Breechloaders: John H. Hall's Invention
         & Development of a Breechloading Rifle with
         Precision-Made Interchangeable Parts, & Its
         Introduction into the United States Service.
         Shumway.
Huntington, Samuel P.
   xHuntington, Samuel P.
      Common Defense: Strategic Programs in
         National Politics. Columbia U Pr.
      No Easy Choice: Political Participation in
         Developing Countries. Harvard U Pr.
      Soldier & the State: The Theory & Politics of
         Civil Military Relations. Harvard U Pr.
Huntington, Virginia. *see* Huntington, Virginia Ethel
   (Haist).
Huntington, Virginia Ethel (Haist) 1889-
   xHuntington, Virginia.
      Celebrations. Golden Quill.
Huntington, William R. *see* Huntington, William Reed.
Huntington, William Reed, 1838-1909
   xHuntington, William R.
      Sonnets & a Dream. Arno.
Huntley, Chet, 1911-
   xHuntley, Chet.
      Generous Years: Remembrances of a Frontier
         Boyhood. Random.
Huntley, Frank L. *see* Huntley, Frank Livingstone.
Huntley, Frank Livingstone, 1902-
   xHuntley, Frank L.
      Bishop Joseph Hall (1574-1656): A
         Biographical & Critical Study. Rowman.
      On Dryden's "Essay of Dramatic Poesy". Shoe
         String.
Huntley, H. Robert.
   xHuntley, H. Robert.
      Alien Protagonist of Ford Madox Ford. U of
         NC Pr.
Huntley, James L., 1914-
   xHuntley, James L.
      Ferryboats in Idaho. Caxton.
Huntley, James R. *see* Huntley, James Robert.
Huntley, James Robert.
   xHuntley, James R.
      Uniting the Democracies: Institutions of the
         Emerging Atlantic-Pacific System. NYU Pr.
Huntley, John, 1921-
   xHuntley, John.
      British Film Music. Arno.
Hunton, Addie. *see* Hunton, Addie D. (Waite).
Hunton, Addie D. (Waite).
   xHunton, Addie.
      Two Colored Women with the American
         Expeditionary Forces. AMS Pr.
Huntoon, Emery.
   xHuntoon, Emery.
      Intercept & Board. Binford.
Huntress, Keith. *see* Huntress, Keith Gibson.

Huntress, Keith Gibson, 1913-
   xHuntress, Keith.
      ed. Narratives of Shipwrecks & Disasters,
         1586-1860. Iowa St U Pr.
Huntsberger. *see* Huntsberger, David V.
Huntsberger, David V.
   xHuntsberger.
      Statistical Inference for Management &
         Economics. Allyn.
Huntsberger, Paul E.
   xHuntsberger, Paul E.
      Highland Mosaic: A Critical Anthology of
         Ethiopian Literature in English. Ohio U Ctr
         Intl.
Huppe, Bernard F. *see* Huppe, Bernard Felix.
Huppe, Bernard Felix, 1911-
   xHuppe, Bernard F.
      Doctrine & Poetry: Augustine's Influence on
         Old English Poetry. State U NY Pr.
      Reading of the Canterbury Tales. State U NY
         Pr.
Huppert, George, 1934-
   xHuppert, George.
      The Idea of Perfect History: Historical
         Erudition & Historical Philosophy in
         Renaissance France. U of Ill Pr.
Huppes, T.
   xHuppes, T.
      ed. Economics & Sociology: Towards an
         Integration. Kluwer Boston.
Hur, Robin.
   xHur, Robin.
      Food Reform: Our Desperate Need. Heidelberg
         Pubs.
Hurd, Clement. *see* Hurd, Edith Thacher.
Hurd, Colin M.
   xHurd, Colin M.
      Hall Effect in Metals & Alloys. Plenum Pub.
Hurd, Edith T. *see* Hurd, Edith Thacher.
Hurd, Edith Thacher.
   xHurd, Clement.
      illus. Hurry Hurry. Har-Row.
      illus. No Funny Business. Har-Row.
      illus. Stop Stop. Har-Row.
      illus. Stop Stop. Schol Bk Serv.
      illus. Under the Lemon Tree. Little.
   xHurd, Edith T.
      The Black Dog Who Went into the Woods.
         Har-Row.
      Catfish. Penguin.
      Christmas Eve. Har-Row.
      Come & Have Fun. Har-Row.
      Come with Me to Nursery School. Coward.
      Dinosaur My Darling. Har-Row.
      Hurry Hurry. Har-Row.
      Johnny Lion's Bad Day. Har-Row.
      Johnny Lion's Rubber Boots. Har-Row.
      Last One Home Is a Green Pig. Har-Row.
      Look for a Bird. Har-Row.
      No Funny Business. Har-Row.
      Starfish. T Y Crowell.
      Stop Stop. Har-Row.
      Stop Stop. Schol Bk Serv.
      Under the Lemon Tree. Little.
      White Horse. Har-Row.
Hurd, Florence.
   xHurd, Florence.
      Legacy. Avon.
      Night Wind at Northriding. NAL.
Hurd, Geoffrey.
   xHurd, Geoffrey.
      Human Societies: An Introduction to
         Sociology. Routledge & Kegan.
Hurd, Henry M. *see* Hurd, Henry Mills.
Hurd, Henry Mills, 1843-1927
   xHurd, Henry M.
      ed. The Institutional Care of the Insane in the
         United States & Canada. Arno.
Hurd, John C. *see* Hurd, John Codman.

Hurd, John Codman, 1816-1892
xHurd, John C.
Law of Freedom & Bondage in the United
States. Negro U Pr.
Hurd, M. K. see Hurd, Mary Krumboltz.
Hurd, Mary Krumboltz.
xHurd, M. K.
Formwork for Concrete. ACI.
Hurd, Michael.
xHurd, Michael.
The Ordeal of Ivor Gurney. Oxford U Pr.
Hurd, Paul D. see Hurd, Paul David.
Hurd, Paul David.
xHurd, Paul D.
A Classification of the Squash & Gourd Bees
Peponapis & Xenoglossa (Hymenoptera:
Apoidea). U of Cal Pr.
Hurd, Richard, Bp. of Worcester, 1720-1808
xHurd, Richard.
Hurd's Letters on Chivalry & Romance, with
the Third Elizabethan Dialogue. AMS Pr.
Works. AMS Pr.
Hurd, Richard M. see Hurd, Richard Melancthon.
Hurd, Richard Melancthon, 1865-1941
xHurd, Richard M.
Principles of City Land Values. Arno.
Hurd, Thacher.
xHurd, Thacher.
The Quiet Evening. Greenwillow.
Hurdle, J. Frank, 1927-
xHurdle, J. Frank.
A Country Doctor's Common Sense Health
Manual. P-H.
Doctor Hurdle's Program to Retain
Youthfulness. P-H.
Low Blood Sugar: A Doctor's Guide to Its
Effective Control. P-H.
Low Blood Sugar: A Doctor's Guide to Its
Effective Control. P-H.
Hurdy, John M. see Hurdy, John Major.
Hurdy, John Major.
xHurdy, John M.
jt. auth. Two Years Before the Mast. Pitman
Learning.
Hurewicz, Witold.
xHurewicz, Witold.
Dimension Theory. Princeton U Pr.
Hurewitz, J. C., 1914-
xHurewitz, J. C.
The Persian Gulf: After Iran's Revolution.
Foreign Policy.
Hurewitz, J. C. see Hurewitz, Jacob Coleman.
Hurewitz, Jacob C. see Hurewitz, Jacob Coleman.
Hurewitz, Jacob Coleman, 1914-
xHurewitz, J. C.
The Struggle for Palestine. Schocken.
xHurewitz, Jacob C.
Struggle for Palestine. Greenwood.
Hurford, J. R. see Hurford, James R.
Hurford, James R.
xHurford, J. R.
The Linguistic Theory of Numerals. Cambridge
U Pr.
Hurgronje, Christiaan Snouck, 1857-1936
xHurgronje, Christian S.
Mohammedanism: Lectures in Its Origin, Its
Religious & Political Growth, & Its Present
State. Hyperion Conn.
Hurgronje, Christian S. see Hurgronje, Christiaan Snouck.
Hurh, Won M. see Hurh, Won Moo.
Hurh, Won Moo.
xHurh, Won M.
Comparative Study of Korean Immigrants in
the United States: A Typological Approach.
R & E Res Assoc.
Hurlburt, Allen, 1910-
xHurlburt, Allen.

Publication Design: A Guide to Page Layout,
Typography, Format & Style. Van Nos
Reinhold.
Hurlburt, Regina.
xHurlburt, Regina.
Left-Handed Crochet. Van Nos Reinhold.
Left-Handed Knitting. Van Nos Reinhold.
Left-Handed Needlepoint. Van Nos Reinhold.
Hurlburt, Sarah, 1925-
xHurlburt, Sarah.
The Mussel Cookbook. Harvard U Pr.
Hurlbut, Jesse L. see Hurlbut, Jesse Lyman.
Hurlbut, Jesse Lyman, 1843-1930
xHurlbut, Jesse L.
Story of the Christian Church. Zondervan.
Hurlbut, Phillip R.
xHurlbut, Phillip R.
Jeraboam & the Amazing Spaghetti Mountain.
Entertainment Factory.
Hurley. see Hurley, Gale E.
Hurley, Cynthia G.
xHurley, Cynthia G.
Teach Yourself to Ride a Horse: A Complete
Illustrated Guide from Beginner to Advanced
Lessons. P-H.
Hurley, F. Jack. see Hurley, Forrest Jack.
Hurley, Forrest Jack.
xHurley, F. Jack.
Portrait of a Decade: Roy Stryker & the
Development of Documentary Photography
in the Thirties. Da Capo.
Portrait of a Decade: Roy Stryker & the
Development of Documentary Photography
in the Thirties. La State U Pr.
Hurley, Gale E., 1932-
xHurley.
Personal Money Management: A Consumer
Guide. P-H.
Hurley, George.
xHurley, George.
Ocean City: A Pictorial History. Donning Co.
Hurley, James P.
xHurley, James P.
Principles of Physics. HM.
Hurley, Lucille. see Hurley, Lucille S.
Hurley, Lucille S.
xHurley, Lucille.
Developmental Nutrition. P-H.
Hurley, Neil. see Hurley, Neil P.
Hurley, Neil P.
xHurley, Neil.
The Reel Revolution: A Film Primer on
Liberation. Orbis Bks.
Hurley, Patrick M., 1912-
xHurley, Patrick M.
How Old Is the Earth. Doubleday.
How Old Is the Earth?. Greenwood.
Hurley, Wilfred G. see Hurley, Wilfred Geoffrey.
Hurley, Wilfred Geoffrey, 1895-
xHurley, Wilfred G.
Catholic Devotional Life. Dghtrs St Paul.
Hurlimann, Martin, 1897-
xHurlimann, Martin.
France. Viking Pr.
India. Intl Bk Dist.
Hurlimann, Ruth.
xHurlimann, Ruth.
The Proud White Cat. Morrow.
Hurll, Estelle M. see Hurll, Estelle May.
Hurll, Estelle May, 1863-1924
xHurll, Estelle M.
Life of Our Lord in Art: With Some Account
of the Artistic Treatment of the Life of St.
John the Baptist. Gale.
Hurlock, Elizabeth B. see Hurlock, Elizabeth Bergner.
Hurlock, Elizabeth Bergner, 1898-
xHurlock, Elizabeth B.

Adolescent Development. McGraw.
Child Growth & Development. McGraw.
Child Growth & Development. McGraw.
Developmental Psychology. McGraw.
Developmental Psychology: A Life-Span
Approach. McGraw.
Personality Development. McGraw.
The Psychology of Dress: An Analysis of
Fashion & Its Motive. Arno.
Hurman, Ann.
xHurman, Ann.
A Charter for Choice: A Study of Options
Schemes. Humanities.
Hurmence, Belinda.
xHurmence, Belinda.
Tough Tiffany. Doubleday.
Hurn, Christopher J., 1938-
xHurn, Christopher J.
The Limits & Possibilities of Schooling: An
Introduction to the Sociology of Education.
Allyn.
Hurry, Jamieson B. see Hurry, Jamieson Boyd.
Hurry, Jamieson Boyd, 1857-1930
xHurry, Jamieson B.
Imhotep, the Vizier & Physician of King Zoser
& Afterwards the Egyptian God of Medicine.
AMS Pr.
xHurry, Jamison B.
Poverty & Its Vicious Circles. Arno.
Hurry, Jamison B. see Hurry, Jamieson Boyd.
Hursh, Robert D.
xHursh, Robert D.
American Law of Products Liability. Lawyers
Co-Op.
Hurst, Charles. see Hurst, Charles E.
Hurst, Charles E.
xHurst, Charles.
The Anatomy of Social Inequality. Mosby.
Hurst, G. Cameron, 1941-
xHurst, G. Cameron.
Insei: Abdicated Sovereigns in the Politics of
Late Heian Japan, 1086-1185. Columbia U
Pr.
Hurst, Gloria, 1928-
xHurst, Gloria.
No Valley Too Deep. Moody.
Hurst, J. M.
xHurst, J. M.
Profit Magic of Stock Transaction Timing. P-H.
Hurst, J. Willard. see Hurst, James Willard.
Hurst, J. Willis. see Hurst, John Willis.
Hurst, James B. see Hurst, James Willard.
Hurst, James W. see Hurst, James Willard.
Hurst, James Willard, 1910-
xHurst, J. Willard.
Law & the Conditions of Freedom in the
Nineteenth-Century United States. U of Wis
Pr.
xHurst, James B.
Law & Social Order in the United States.
Cornell U Pr.
xHurst, James W.
The Growth of American Law: The Law
Makers. Little.
Law of Treason in the United States: Collected
Essays. Greenwood.
Hurst, John Willis.
xHurst, J. Willis.
Introduction to Electrocardiography. McGraw.
ed. The Problem Oriented System. Williams &
Wilkins.
Hurst, Richard M. see Hurst, Richard Maurice.
Hurst, Richard Maurice, 1938-
xHurst, Richard M.
Republic Studios: Between Poverty Row & the
Majors. Scarecrow.
Hurst, Walter E.
xHurst, Walter E.

How to Be a Music Publisher. Borden.
How to Be a Music Publisher. Seven Arts.
The Record Industry Book. Seven Arts.

Hurstfield, Joel.
xHurstfield, Joel.
Freedom, Corruption, & Government in
Elizabethan England. Harvard U Pr.
The Historian As Moralist: Reflections on the
Study of Tudor England. Humanities.
Queen's Wards: Wardship & Marriage Under
Elizabeth I. Biblio Dist.
ed. The Reformation Crisis. Har-Row.
Hurston, Zora N. *see* Hurston, Zora Neale.

Hurston, Zora Neale.
xHurston, Zora N.
Dust Tracks on a Road: An Autobiography.
Arno.
I Love Myself When I Am Laughing...& Then
Again When I Am Looking Mean &
Impressive. Feminist Pr.
Jonah's Gourd Vine. Lippincott.
Mules & Men. Ind U Pr.
Mules & Men. Negro U Pr.
Their Eyes Were Watching God: A Novel.
Negro U Pr.

Hurt, H. Thomas.
xHurt, H. Thomas.
Communication in the Classroom. A-W.
Hurt, J. *see* Hurt, James.

Hurt, James, 1934-
xHurt, J.
Focus on Film & Theatre. P-H.

Hurt, Marcia, 1953-
xHurt, Marcia.
Inside Basketball for Women. Contemp Bks.

Hurt, William C., 1922-
xHurt, William C.
Periodontics in General Practice. C C Thomas.

Hurter, Bill.
xHurter, Bill.
Sports Photography. Petersen Pub.

Hurtik, Emil.
xHurtik, Emil.
In Phase: Sentence, Structure, Style. Har-Row.
Insight: A Rhetoric Reader. Har-Row.
ed. Insight: A Rhetoric Reader. Lippincott.
ed. Introduction to Short Fiction & Criticism.
Wiley.
Hurtt, Waller. *see* Hurtt, Waller A.

Hurtt, Waller A.
xHurtt, Waller.
Posse Comitatus. Ashley Bks.

Hurwitz, Abraham B.
xHurwitz, Abraham B.
Games to Improve Your Child's English. S&S.
Games to Improve Your Child's English. S&S.
More Number Games: Mathematics Made
Easy Through Play. T Y Crowell.

Hurwitz, Al.
xHurwitz, Al.
Programs of Promise: Art in the Schools.
HarBraceJ.

Hurwitz, Emanuel.
xHurwitz, Emanuel.
ed. Challenges to Education: Readings for
Analysis of Major Issues. Har-Row.
Hurwitz, Howard L. *see* Hurwitz, Howard Lawrence.

Hurwitz, Howard Lawrence.
xHurwitz, Howard L.
Theodore Roosevelt & Labor in New York
State, 1880-1900. AMS Pr.

Hurwitz, Johanna.
xHurwitz, Johanna.

Aldo Applesauce. Morrow.
Busybody Nora. Morrow.
Busybody Nora. Morrow.
The Law of Gravity. Morrow.
Much Ado About Aldo. Morrow.
New Neighbors for Nora. Morrow.
Nora & Mrs. Mind Your Own Business. Dell.
Nora & Mrs. Mind-Your-Own-Business.
Morrow.
Once I Was a Plum Tree. Morrow.

Hurwitz, Ken.
xHurwitz, Ken.
Marching Nowhere. Norton.

Hurwitz, Leon.
xHurwitz, Leon.
ed. Contemporary Perspectives on European
Integration: Attitudes, Nongovernmental
Behavior & Collective Decision Making.
Greenwood.

Hurwood, B. J.
xHurwood, B. J.
Assault on Bordeaux. Nordon Pubns.

Hurwood, Bernhardt J.
xHurwood, Bernhardt J.
Passport to the Supernatural: An Occult
Compendium from All Ages & Many Lands.
Taplinger.
xHurwood, Richardt J.
Burt Reynolds. Music Sales.

Hurwood, David L.
xHurwood, David L.
Sales Forecasting. Conference Bd.
Hurwood, Richardt J. *see* Hurwood, Bernhardt J.

Hus, Alain.
xHus, Alain.
The Etruscans. Greenwood.
Husain, Abrar. *see* Husain, Sheikh Abrar.
Husain, Itra. *see* Husain, Itrat.

Husain, Itrat.
xHusain, Itra.
Dogmatic & Mystical Theology of John Donne.
Folcroft.
xHusain, Itrat.
Dogmatic & Mystical Theology of John Donne.
Greenwood.

Husain, Sheikh Abrar, 1931-
xHusain, Abrar.
Marriage Customs Among Muslims in India: A
Sociological Study of the Shia Marriage
Customs. Verry.
Husain, T. *see* Husain, Taqdir.

Husain, Taqdir.
xHusain, T.
Barrelledness in Topological & Ordered Vector
Spaces. Springer-Verlag.
ed. Topology & Maps. Plenum Pub.
xHusain, Taqdir.
The Open Mapping & Closed Graph Theorems
in Topological Vector Spaces. Krieger.

Husain, Zakir.
xHusain, Zakir.
Dynamic University. Asia.

Husband, Joseph, 1885-1938
xHusband, Joseph.
The Story of the Pullman Car. Arno.
Story of the Pullman Car. Black Letter.
Husband, William H. *see* Husband, William Hollow.

Husband, William Hollow.
xHusband, William H.
Modern Corporation Finance. Irwin.
Huse, Charles P. *see* Huse, Charles Phillips.

Huse, Charles Phillips.
xHuse, Charles P.
Financial History of Boston from May 1, 1822
to January 31, 1909. Russell.

Huse, Edgar F.
xHuse, Edgar F.

The Modern Manager. West Pub.
Organization Development & Change. West
Pub.

Huseman, Richard C.
xHuseman, Richard C.
Readings in Interpersonal & Organizational
Communication. Holbrook.
Readings in Organizational Behavior:
Dimensions of Management Actions. Allyn.
Husemoller, D. *see* Husemoller, Dale.

Husemoller, Dale.
xHusemoller, D.
Fibre Bundles. Springer-Verlag.
Huser, H. J. *see* Huser, Hans-Jurg.

Huser, Hans-Jurg.
xHuser, H. J.
Atlas of Comparative Primate Hematology.
Acad Pr.

Husik, Isaac, 1876-1939
xHusik, Isaac.
History of Mediaeval Jewish Philosophy.
Atheneum.

Huskisson, E. C.
xHuskisson, E. C.
Joint Disease-All the Arthropathies. Year Bk
Med.

Huson, Paul.
xHuson, Paul.
The Coffee Table Book of Witchcraft &
Demonology. Berkley Pub.
How to Test & Develop Your ESP. Stein &
Day.
Huss, Sally M. *see* Huss, Sally Moore.

Huss, Sally Moore.
xHuss, Sally M.
How to Play Power Tennis with Ease.
HarBraceJ.

Hussein, Mahmoud,
xHussein, Mahmoud.
Class Conflict in Egypt, 1945-1970. Monthly
Rev.
Husselman, Elinor. *see* Husselman, Elinor Mullett.

Husselman, Elinor Mullett.
xHusselman, Elinor.
Karanis Excavations of the University of
Michigan in Egypt, 1928-1935: Topography
& Architecture. Univ Microfilm.

Husserl, Edmund, 1859-1938
xHusserl, Edmund.
Crisis of European Sciences & Transcendental
Phenomenology: An Introduction to
Phenomenological Philosophy. Northwestern
U Pr.

Hussey, Anne, 1934-
xHussey, Anne.
Baddeck & Other Poems. Columbia U Pr.
Hussey, D. E. *see* Hussey, David E.
Hussey, David. *see* Hussey, David E.

Hussey, David E.
xHussey, D. E.
Introducing Corporate Planning. Pergamon.
xHussey, David.
Corporate Planning: The Human Factor.
Pergamon.
Inflation & Business Policy. Longman.
xHussey, David E.
Introducing Corporate Planning. Pergamon.

Hussey, Dyneley, 1893-
xHussey, Dyneley.
Some Composers of Opera. Arno.

Hussey, Edward.
xHussey, Edward.
The Presocratics. Biblio Dist.
The Presocratics. Scribner.

Hussey, Harry.
xHussey, Harry.
Venerable Ancestor: The Life & Times of Tz'u
Hsi, 1835-1908, Empress of China.
Greenwood.
Hussey, Jane S. *see* Hussey, Jane Strickland.

Hussey, Jane Strickland.
xHussey, Jane S.
Some Useful Plants of Early New England.
Channing Bks.
Hussey, John A.
xHussey, John A.
Champoeg, Place of Transition: A Disputed
History. Oreg Hist Soc.
Hussey, Lois J. *see* Hussey, Lois Jackson.
Hussey, Lois Jackson.
xHussey, Lois J.
Collecting Cocoons. T Y Crowell.
Collecting for the City Naturalist. T Y Crowell.
Collecting Small Fossils. T Y Crowell.
Hussey, Maurice.
xHussey, Maurice.
Introduction to Chaucer. Cambridge U Pr.
The World of Shakespeare & His
Contemporaries: A Visual Approach.
Heinemann Ed.
Hussey, Roland Dennis.
xHussey, Roland Dennis.
The Caracas Company, 1728-1784: Study in
the History of Spanish Monopolistic Trade.
Arno.
Husted, Darrell.
xHusted, Darrell.
Miss Cordelia Harling. Popular Lib.
Husted, Helen. *see* Husted, Helen McLanahan.
Husted, Helen McLanahan, 1901-
xHusted, Helen.
ed. Love Poems of Six Centuries. Arno.
Huston, Fred.
xHuston, Fred.
Those S. O. B.'s at Tarryall & Other Tales of
the Rockies. Nortex Pr.
Huston, Ted L.
xHuston, Theodore.
ed. Foundations of Interpersonal Attraction.
Acad Pr.
Huston, Theodore. *see* Huston, Ted L.
Hustvedt, S. B. *see* Hustvedt, Sigurd Bernhard.
Hustvedt, Sigurd Bernhard, 1882-1954
xHustvedt, S. B.
Ballad Criticism in Scandinavia & Great Britain
During the Eighteenth Century. Kraus Repr.
Hutchcroft, Vera.
xHutchcroft, Vera.
Nature Stories for Children. Baker Bk.
Object Lessons for Church Groups. Baker Bk.
Hutchens, Alice S.
xHutchens, Alice S.
The Gift of Little Things. Caxton.
Hutchens, John K., 1905-
xHutchens, John K.
ed. The Gambler's Bedside Book. Taplinger.
Hutcheson, Ernest.
xHutcheson, Ernest.
Literature of the Piano: A Guide for Amateur
& Student. Knopf.
Hutcheson, Francis.
xHutcheson, Francis.
Illustrations on the Moral Sense. Harvard U Pr.
Hutcheson, J. D. *see* Hutcheson, John D.
Hutcheson, John D.
xHutcheson, J. D.
Racial Attitudes in Atlanta. Ctr Res Soc Chg.
xHutcheson, John D.
Citizen Groups in Local Politics: A
Bibliographic Review. ABC-Clio.
Hutchings, Arthur, 1906-
xHutchings, Arthur.
Church Music in the Nineteenth Century.
Greenwood.
Delius. Greenwood.
xHutchings, Arthur J.
The Baroque Concerto. Scribner.
Hutchings, Arthur J. *see* Hutchings, Arthur.
Hutchings, D. *see* Hutchings, Donald William.

Hutchings, Donald William.
xHutchings, D.
ed. Late Seventeenth Century Scientists.
Pergamon.
Hutchings, Margaret.
xHutchings, Margaret.
Nature's Toyshop. Transatlantic.
Hutchings, Raymond.
xHutchings, Raymond.
Soviet Economic Development. Biblio Dist.
Soviet Science, Technology, Design: Interaction
& Convergence. Oxford U Pr.
Hutchings, Tony.
xHutchings, Tony.
illus. Silly Dinosaurs. Rand.
Things That Go Word Book. Rand.
Hutchins, Bobbie.
xHutchins, Bobbie.
Child Nutrition & Health. McGraw.
Hutchins, Carleen M. *see* Hutchins, Carleen Maley.
Hutchins, Carleen Maley.
xHutchins, Carleen M.
Who Will Drown the Sound?. Coward.
Hutchins, Pat, 1942-
xHutchins, Pat.
illus. Changes, Changes. Macmillan.
illus. Changes, Changes. Macmillan.
illus. Clocks & More Clocks. Macmillan.
Don't Forget the Bacon!. Penguin.
Don't Forget the Bacon!. Greenwillow.
Follow That Bus!. Greenwillow.
illus. Good-Night Owl. Macmillan.
Good-Night, Owl!. Macmillan.
The House That Sailed Away. Greenwillow.
One-Eyed Jake. Greenwillow.
illus. The Silver Christmas Tree. Macmillan.
illus. Surprise Party. Macmillan.
illus. Surprise Party. Macmillan.
The Tale of Thomas Mead. Greenwillow.
Hutchins, R. E. *see* Hutchins, Ross E.
Hutchins, R. M. *see* Hutchins, Robert Maynard.
Hutchins, Robert M. *see* Hutchins, Robert Maynard.
Hutchins, Robert Maynard, 1899-
xHutchins, R. M.
The Higher Learning in America. Yale U Pr.
xHutchins, Robert M.
The Conflict in Education in a Democratic
Society. Greenwood.
The Higher Learning in America. AMS Pr.
The Higher Learning in America. Greenwood.
ed. The Humanities Today. Arno.
No Friendly Voice. Greenwood.
Hutchins, Ross E.
xHutchins, R. E.
illus. World of Dragonflies & Damselflies.
Dodd.
xHutchins, Ross E.
Amazing Seeds. Dodd.
The Bug Clan. Dodd.
Grasshoppers & Their Kin. Dodd.
ed. Insects. P-H.
Nature Invented It First. Dodd.
World of Dragonflies & Damselflies. Dodd.
Hutchins, Thomas.
xHutchins, Thomas.
Historical Narrative & Topographical
Description of Louisiana & West Florida. U
Presses Fla.
Hutchinson, Bruce, 1901-
xHutchinson, Bruce.
The Struggle for the Border. Arno.
Hutchinson, Duane.
xHutchinson, Duane.
Exon, Biography of a Governor. Foun Bks.
Hutchinson, E. C. *see* Hutchinson, Edward C.
Hutchinson, Edward C.
xHutchinson, E. C.
Strokes: Natural History, Pathology & Surgical
Treatment. Saunders.
Hutchinson, Edward P. *see* Hutchinson, Edward Prince.

Hutchinson, Edward Prince.
xHutchinson, Edward P.
Immigrants & Their Children: 1850-1950.
Russell.
Hutchinson, Eliot D. *see* Hutchinson, Eliot Dole.
Hutchinson, Eliot Dole.
xHutchinson, Eliot D.
Rhymes for Our Times. Windy Row.
Hutchinson, G. E. *see* Hutchinson, George Evelyn.
Hutchinson, G. Evelyn. *see* Hutchinson, George Evelyn.
Hutchinson, George Evelyn, 1903-
xHutchinson, G. E.
Some Continental European Aberrations of
Abraxas Grossulariata Linn, Lepidoptera:
With a Note on the Theoretical Significance
of the Variation Observed in the Species.
Shoe String.
xHutchinson, G. Evelyn.
Ecological Theater & the Evolutionary Play.
Yale U Pr.
An Introduction to Population Ecology. Yale U
Pr.
Hutchinson, Harry D.
xHutchinson, Harry D.
Economics & Social Goals: An Introduction.
SRA.
Hutchinson, Helene. *see* Hutchinson, Helene D.
Hutchinson, Helene D.
xHutchinson, Helene.
Hutchinson Guide to Writing Research Papers.
Glencoe.
xHutchinson, Helene D.
Horizons: Readings & Communication
Activities for Vocational-Technical Students.
Glencoe.
Hutchinson, Henry N. *see* Hutchinson, Henry Neville.
Hutchinson, Henry Neville, 1856-1927
xHutchinson, Henry N.
Marriage Customs in Many Lands. Gale.
Hutchinson, Horace G. *see* Hutchinson, Horace Gordon.
Hutchinson, Horace Gordon, 1859-1932
xHutchinson, Horace G.
Portraits of the Eighties. Folcroft.
xHutchinson, Horatio.
Portraits of the Eighties. Arno.
Hutchinson, Horatio. *see* Hutchinson, Horace Gordon.
Hutchinson, James H. *see* Hutchinson, James Holmes.
Hutchinson, James Holmes, Md.
xHutchinson, James H.
Practical Paediatric Problems. Year Bk Med.
Hutchinson, John, 1884-
xHutchinson, John.
British Wild Flowers. Fairleigh Dickinson.
Hutchinson, Lois. *see* Hutchinson, Lois Irene.
Hutchinson, Lois Irene.
xHutchinson, Lois.
Standard Handbook for Secretaries. McGraw.
Hutchinson, Lucille.
xHutchinson, Lucille.
The Centennial History of North Tarrytown. T
Hutchinson.
Hutchinson, Lucy. *see* Hutchinson, Lucy (Apsley).
Hutchinson, Lucy (Apsley), b. 1620
xHutchinson, Lucy.
Memoirs of the Life of Colonel Hutchinson.
Dutton.
Hutchinson, Martha C. *see* Hutchinson, Martha
Crenshaw.
Hutchinson, Martha Crenshaw.
xHutchinson, Martha C.
Revolutionary Terrorism: The FLN in Algeria,
1954-1962. Hoover Inst Pr.
Hutchinson, Peter.
xHutchinson, Peter.
Evolution Explained. David & Charles.
Hutchinson, Warner.
xHutchinson, Warner.
The Oral Roberts Scrapbook. G&D.
Hutchinson, Warner. *see* Hutchinson, Warner A.

Hutchinson, Warner A.
xHutchinson, Warner.
New York!. Newbury Hse.
Hutchinson, William H. *see* Hutchinson, William Henry.
Hutchinson, William Henry, 1910-
xHutchinson, William H.
The World, the Work, & the West of W. H. D.
Koerner. U of Okla Pr.
Hutchinson, William T. *see* Hutchinson, William Thomas.
Hutchinson, William Thomas, 1895-
xHutchinson, William T.
The Bounty Lands of the American Revolution
in Ohio. Arno.
Hutchison, Frances.
xHutchison, Frances.
Gardening for Beginners. Macmillan.
Hutchison, Howard.
xHutchison, Howard.
The Complete Handbook of Sewing Machine
Repair. TAB Bks.
Hutchison, John A. *see* Hutchison, John Alexander.
Hutchison, John Alexander, 1912-
xHutchison, John A.
Living Options in World Philosophy. U Pr of
Hawaii.
Paths of Faith. McGraw.
Hutchison, Keith.
xHutchison, Keith.
Decline & Fall of British Capitalism. Shoe
String.
Hutchison, Polly A., 1939-
xHutchison, Polly A.
Oh, King, Live Forever!. Beta Bk.
Hutchison, Sidney C.
xHutchison, Sidney C.
History of the Royal Academy 1768-1968.
Taplinger.
Hutchison, Terence W. *see* Hutchison, Terence Wilmot.
Hutchison, Terence Wilmot.
xHutchison, Terence W.
A Review of Economic Doctrines, 1870-1929.
Greenwood.
Significance & Basic Postulates of Economic
Theory. Kelley.
Huth, Angela, 1938-
xHuth, Angela.
Infidelities. Potter.
Huth, Hans, 1892-
xHuth, Hans.
Nature & the American: Three Centuries of
Changing Attitudes. U of Nebr Pr.
Huth, Mark W.
xHuth, Mark W.
Introduction to Construction. Delmar.
Hutheesing, Gunottam Purushottam.
xHutheesing, Raja.
ed. The Great Peace: An Asian's Candid
Report on Red China. Da Capo.
Hutheesing, Raja. *see* Hutheesing, Gunottam
Purushottam.
Huthmacher, J Joseph.
xHuthmacher, J. Joseph.
Massachusetts People & Politics, 1919-1933.
Atheneum.
Hutka, Ed.
xHutka, Ed F.
Boom or Busted: Family Dollars & Sense.
Logos.
Hutka, Ed F. *see* Hutka, Ed.
Hutschnecker, Arnold A.
xHutschnecker, Arnold A.
The Drive for Power. M Evans.
Hutson, A. B. *see* Hutson, A. B. A.
Hutson, A. B. A.
xHutson, A. B.
The Navigator's Art. Transatlantic.
Hutson, James H.
xHutson, James H.

Pennsylvania Politics, 1746-1770: The
Movement for Royal Government & Its
Consequences. Princeton U Pr.
Hutson, Joan.
xHutson, Joan.
A Hunger for Wholeness. Ave Maria.
Hutson, Percival W., 1891-
xHutson, Percival W.
Guidance Function in Education. Irvington.
Hutt, Frederick B., 1897-
xHutt, Frederick B.
Genetics for Dog Breeders. W H Freeman.
Hutt, Frederick B. *see* Hutt, Frederick Bruce.
Hutt, Frederick Bruce, 1897-
xHutt, Frederick B.
Animal Genetics. Wiley.
Genetic Resistance to Disease in Domestic
Animals. Comstock.
Hutt, Max L.
xHutt, Max L.
Atlas for the Hutt Adaptation of the
Bender-Gestalt Test. Grune.
The Mentally Retarded Child: Development,
Training, & Education. Allyn.
Hutt, S. J. *see* Hutt, Sidney John.
Hutt, Sidney John.
xHutt, S. J.
Direct Observation & Measurement of
Behavior. C C Thomas.
ed. Early Human Development. Oxford U Pr.
Hutt, W. H. *see* Hutt, William Harold.
Hutt, William Harold, 1899-
xHutt, W. H.
The Keynesian Episode: A Reassessment.
Liberty Fund.
A Rehabilitation of Say's Law. Ohio U Pr.
Huttar, Leora W.
xHuttar, Leora W.
Church Time for Preschoolers. Accent Bks.
Hutten, Ernest H. *see* Hutten, Ernest Hirchlaff Name
Orig. Ernst Hirchlaff.
**Hutten, Ernest Hirchlaff Name Orig. Ernst Hirchlaff,
1908-**
xHutten, Ernest H.
The Origins of Science: An Inquiry into the
Foundations of Western Thought.
Greenwood.
Huttenback, Robert A.
xHuttenback, Robert A.
The British Imperial Experience. Greenwood.
Racism & Empire: White Settlers & Colored
Immigrants in the British Self-Governing
Colonies, 1830-1910. Cornell U Pr.
Hutter, Heribert.
xHutter, Heribert.
Styles in Art: An Historical Survey. Universe.
Huttl, Willy.
xHuttl, Willy.
Antoninus Pius. Arno.
Huttman, Elizabeth D.
xHuttman, Elizabeth D.
Housing & Social Services for the Elderly:
Social Policy Trends. Praeger.
Hutton, Darryl.
xHutton, Darryl.
Ventriloquism: How to Put on an Act, Use the
Power of Suggestion, Write a Clever
Accompanying Patter, & Make Your Own
Dummy. Sterling.
Hutton, Edward, 1875-
xHutton, Edward.
Catholicism & English Literature. Folcroft.
Hutton, Geoffrey. *see* Hutton, Geoffrey William.
Hutton, Geoffrey William, 1909-
xHutton, Geoffrey.
Adam Lindsay Gordon: The Man & the Myth.
Merrimack Bk Serv.
Hutton, Harold.
xHutton, Harold.

Vigilante Days: Frontier Justice Along the
Niobrara. Swallow.
Hutton, John, 1933-
xHutton, John.
Building & Construction in Australia. Intl
Pubns Serv.
Hutton, John. *see* Hutton, John P.
Hutton, John H. *see* Hutton, John Henry.
Hutton, John Henry, 1885-
xHutton, John H.
Caste in India: Its Nature, Function, & Origins.
Oxford U Pr.
Hutton, John P.
xHutton, John.
The Mystery of Wealth: Political Economy, Its
Development & Impact on World Events.
Halsted Pr.
Hutton, Laurence, 1843-1904
xHutton, Laurence.
ed. Occasional Addresses. B Franklin.
xHutton, Lawrence.
Curiosities of the American Stage. Johnson
Repr.
Curiosities of the American Stage. Scholarly.
Hutton, Lawrence. *see* Hutton, Laurence.
Hutton, Maurice, 1856-1940
xHutton, Maurice.
Greek Point of View. Kennikat.
Many Minds. Arno.
Hutton, Richard.
xHutton, Richard.
Bio-Revolution: DNA & the Ethics of
Man-Made Life. NAL.
Hutton, Richard H. *see* Hutton, Richard Holt.
Hutton, Richard Holt.
xHutton, Richard H.
Brief Literary Criticisms. Kennikat.
Cardinal Newman. AMS Pr.
Cardinal Newman. Darby Bks.
Hutton, Samuel W. *see* Hutton, Samuel Ward.
Hutton, Samuel Ward, 1886-
xHutton, Samuel W.
Dedication Services. Baker Bk.
Hutton, Warwick.
xHutton, Warwick.
Noah & the Great Flood. Atheneum.
The Sleeping Beauty. Atheneum.
Hutton, William, 1723-1815
xHutton, William.
An History of Birmingham. Rowman.
Hutzinger, O.
xHutzinger, O.
Chemistry of PCB's. CRC Pr.
Huus, Helen, 1913-
xHuus, Helen.
The Education of Children & Youth in
Norway. Greenwood.
Huxford, Folks, 1893-
xHuxford, Folks.
The History of Brooks County Georgia.
Reprint.
Huxford, Sharon.
xHuxford, Sharon.
The Collector's Encyclopedia of Brush McCoy
Pottery. Collector Bks.
Collector's Encyclopedia of McCoy Pottery.
Collector Bks.
The Collector's Encyclopedia of Roseville
Pottery. Collector Bks.
Collector's Encyclopedia of Weller Pottery.
Collector Bks.
Huxhold, Harry N.
xHuxhold, Harry N.
ed. Adventures with God. Concordia.
Power for the Church in the Midst of Chaos.
Concordia.
Huxley, Aldous.
xHuxley, Aldous.

After Many a Summer Dies the Swan.
  Har-Row.
After Many a Summer Dies the Swan. Queens
  Hse.
Ape & Essence. Har-Row.
Crome Yellow. Har-Row.
Huxley, Aldous. see Huxley, Aldous Leonard.
Huxley, Aldous L. see Huxley, Aldous Leonard.
Huxley, Aldous Leonard, 1894-1963
  xHuxley, Aldous.
  Art of Seeing. Madrona Pubs.
  Brave New World. Har-Row.
  Brave New World. Har-Row.
  Ends & Means: An Inquiry into the Nature of
    Ideals & into the Methods Employed for
    Their Realization. Greenwood.
  Eyeless in Gaza. Har-Row.
  Eyeless in Gaza. Queens Hse.
  Letters of Aldous Huxley. Har-Row.
  Perennial Philosophy. Har-Row.
  xHuxley, Aldous L.
  Along the Road: Notes & Essays of a Tourist.
    Arno.
  Do What You Will: Essays. Arno.
  On Art & Artists. Kraus Repr.
  Perennial Philosophy. Arno.
  Themes & Variations. Arno.
Huxley, Alyson.
  xHuxley, Alyson.
  Huxley's House of Plants. Paddington.
Huxley, Anthony. see Huxley, Anthony Julian.
Huxley, Anthony Julian, 1920-
  xHuxley, Anthony.
  An Illustrated History of Gardening.
    Paddington.
  Plant & Planet. Penguin.
  Plant & Planet. Viking Pr.
Huxley, Elspeth. see Huxley, Elspeth Joscelin Grant.
Huxley, Elspeth Joscelin (Grant), 1907-
  xHuxley, Elspeth.
  The Sorcerer's Apprentice: A Journey Through
    East Africa. Greenwood.
Huxley, Elspeth Joscelin Grant, 1907-
  xHuxley, Elspeth.
  Four Guineas: A Journey Through West
    Africa. Greenwood.
Huxley, Francis.
  xHuxley, Francis.
  The Dragon: Nature of Spirit, Spirit of Nature.
    Macmillan.
  The Raven & the Writing Desk. Har-Row.
Huxley, Frederick C. see Huxley, Frederick Charles.
Huxley, Frederick Charles.
  xHuxley, Frederick C.
  Wasita in a Lebanese Context: Social Exchange
    among Villagers & Outsiders. U Mich Mus
    Anthro.
Huxley, G. L. see Huxley, George Leonard.
Huxley, George Leonard.
  xHuxley, G. L.
  The Early Ionians. Biblio Dist.
  Early Ionians. Humanities.
Huxley, Julian. see Huxley, Julian Sorell.
Huxley, Julian S. see Huxley, Julian Sorell.
Huxley, Julian Sorell, Sir, 1887-
  xHuxley, Julian.
  Ants. Arden Lib.
  Memories. Har-Row.
  Problems of Relative Growth. Dover.
  Problems of Relative Growth. Peter Smith.
  xHuxley, Julian S.
  Africa View. Greenwood.
  Ants. AMS Pr.
  Democracy Marches. Arno.
  On Living in a Revolution. Arno.
  Religion Without Revelation. Greenwood.
Huxley, Laura. see Huxley, Laura Archera.
Huxley, Laura Archera.
  xHuxley, Laura.

This Timeless Moment: A Personal View of
  Aldous Huxley. Celestial Arts.
Huxley, T. H. see Huxley, Thomas Henry.
Huxley, Thomas H. see Huxley, Thomas Henry.
Huxley, Thomas Henry, 1825-1895
  xHuxley, T. H.
  The Crayfish: An Introduction to the Study of
    Zoology. MIT Pr.
  xHuxley, Thomas H.
  Collected Essays. Greenwood.
  Critiques & Addresses. Arno.
  Evolution & Ethics, & Other Essays. Scholarly.
  Touchstone for Ethics, 1893-1943. Arno.
Huxley-Blythe, Peter J.
  xHuxley-Blythe, Peter J.
  East Came West. Caxton.
Huyck, Peter. see Huyck, Peter H.
Huyck, Peter H.
  xHuyck, Peter.
  Design & Memory: Computer Programming in
    the 20th Century. McGraw.
Huygen, Wil.
  xHuygen, Wil.
  Gnomes. Abrams.
  Gnomes. Bantam.
Huyghe, Rene.
  xHuyghe, Rene.
  Gauguin. Crown.
  Van Gogh. Barron.
  Van Gogh. Crown.
Huyser, Earl S., 1927-
  xHuyser, Earl S.
  General College Chemistry. Heath.
Huysmans, J. K. see Huysmans, Joris Karl.
Huysmans, Joris K. see Huysmans, Joris Karl.
Huysmans, Joris Karl, 1848-1907
  xHuysmans, J. K.
  Against the Grain. Peter Smith.
  xHuysmans, Joris K.
  Against the Grain. Dover.
  The Oblate. Fertig.
Hvidt, Kristian.
  xHvidt, Kristian.
  Flight to America: The Social Background of
    300,000 Danish Emigrants. Acad Pr.
Hwang, C. L. see Hwang, Ching Lai.
Hwang, Ching Lai.
  xHwang, C. L.
  Multiple Objective Decision Making-Methods
    & Applications: A State-of-the-Art Survey.
    Springer-Verlag.
Hwang, Kai.
  xHwang, Kai.
  Computer Arithmetic: Principles, Architecture
    & Design. Wiley.
Hy, Ronn J.
  xHy, Ronn J.
  Using the Computer in the Social Sciences: A
    Nontechnical Approach. Elsevier.
Hyams, Dennis.
  xHyams, Dennis.
  The Care of the Aged. Technomic.
Hyams, Edward. see Hyams, Edward S.
Hyams, Edward S.
  xHyams, Edward.
  Animals in the Service of Man. Lippincott.
  Soil & Civilization. Har-Row.
Hyams, Joe.
  xHyams, Joe.
  Zen in the Martial Arts. J P Tarcher.
  Zen in the Martial Arts. St Martin.
Hyams, Joe. see Hyams, Joseph.
Hyams, Joseph.
  xHyams, Joe.
  The Pool. Popular Lib.
  The Pool. Seaview Bks.
Hyamson, Albert M. see Hyamson, Albert Montefiore.
Hyamson, Albert Montefiore, 1875-1954
  xHyamson, Albert M.

Intro. by & ed. The British Consulate in
  Jerusalem in Relation to the Jews of
  Palestine, 1838-1914. AMS Pr.
Dictionary of English Phrases: Phraseological
  Allusions, Catchwords, Stereotyped Modes of
  Speech & Metaphors, Nicknames, Sobriquets,
  Derivations from Personal Names. Gale.
Palestine: A Policy. Hyperion Conn.
Palestine under the Mandate, 1920-1948.
  Greenwood.
Hyatt, Ada. see Hyatt, Ada V.
Hyatt, Ada V., 1896-
  xHyatt, Ada.
  The Place of Oral Reading in the School
    Program: Its History & Development from
    1880-1941. AMS Pr.
Hyatt, Carole.
  xHyatt, Carole.
  The Woman's Selling Game: How to Sell
    Yourself -- and Anything Else. M Evans.
Hyatt, E. C. see Hyatt, Edwin Charles.
Hyatt, Edwin Charles.
  xHyatt, E. C.
  Respirators & Protective Clothing. Unipub.
Hyatt, Herman R.
  xHyatt, Herman R.
  Introduction to Technical Mathematics: A
    Calculator Approach. Wiley.
  Modern College Algebra. Scott F.
Hyatt, Jessica.
  xHyatt, Jessica.
  Summer Share. Belmont Tower.
Hyatt, Richard, 1944-
  xHyatt, Richard.
  The Carters of Plains. Strode.
  Chinese Herbal Medicine: Ancient Art &
    Modern Science. Schocken.
Hyde. see Hyde, Margaret Oldroyd.
Hyde, Albert C.
  xHyde, Albert C.
  ed. Program Evaluation in the Public Sector.
    Praeger.
Hyde, Arthur M. see Hyde, Arthur May.
Hyde, Arthur May, 1864-
  xHyde, Arthur M.
  A Diplomatic History of Bulgaria, 1870-1886.
    Greenwood.
Hyde, Christopher S.
  xHyde, Christopher S.
  The Complete Book of Rock Tumbling.
    Chilton.
Hyde, Douglas, Pres. Irish Free State, 1860-1949
  xHyde, Douglas.
  A Literary History of Ireland from Earliest
    Times to the Present Day. Longwood Pr.
  The Story of Early Gaelic Literature. Folcroft.
  The Story of Early Gaelic Literature.
    Longwood Pr.
Hyde, Floy. see Hyde, Floy (Salls).
Hyde, Floy (Salls).
  xHyde, Floy.
  Protestant Leadership Education Schools. AMS
    Pr.
Hyde, George E., 1882-
  xHyde, George E.
  Indians of the High Plains: From the
    Prehistoric Period to the Coming of
    Europeans. U of Okla Pr.
  Indians of the Woodlands: From Prehistoric
    Times to 1725. U of Okla Pr.
  The Pawnee Indians. U of Okla Pr.
Hyde, Georgie. see Hyde, Georgie D. M.
Hyde, Georgie D. M.
  xHyde, Georgie.
  Education in Modern Egypt: Ideals & Realities.
    Routledge & Kegan.
Hyde, Gordon. see Hyde, Gordon M.
Hyde, Gordon M.
  xHyde, Gordon.

Rags to Righteousness. Pacific Pr Pub Assn.
Hyde, H. Montgomery. *see* Hyde, Harford Montgomery.
Hyde, Harford M. *see* Hyde, Harford Montgomery.
Hyde, Harford Montgomery, 1907-
xHyde, H. Montgomery.
A Solitary in the Ranks: Lawrence of Arabia
As Airman & Private Soldier. Atheneum.
xHyde, Harford M.
Oscar Wilde: The Aftermath. Greenwood.
xHyde, Montgomery.
Oscar Wilde: A Biography. FS&G.
Hyde, Janet. *see* Hyde, Janet Shibley.
Hyde, Janet Shibley.
xHyde, Janet.
Understanding Human Sexuality. McGraw.
Hyde, Lawrence, 1894-
xHyde, Lawrence.
Prospects of Humanism. Arno.
Prospects of Humanism. Greenwood.
Prospects of Humanism. Kennikat.
Prospects of Humanism. R West.
Hyde, Margaret O. *see* Hyde, Margaret Oldroyd.
Hyde, Margaret Oldroyd, 1917-
xHyde.
Crime & Justice in Our Time. Watts.
xHyde, Margaret O.
Brainwashing & Other Forms of Mind Control.
McGraw.
Fears & Phobias. McGraw.
Hotline. McGraw.
My Friend Wants to Run Away. McGraw.
Psychology in Action. McGraw.
Speak Out on Rape. McGraw.
Suicide: The Hidden Epidemic. Watts.
Where Speed Is King. McGraw.
Hyde, Mary. *see* Hyde, Mary Morley (Crapo).
Hyde, Mary Morley (Crapo).
xHyde, Mary.
The Impossible Friendship: Boswell & Mrs.
Thrale. Harvard U Pr.
Hyde, Melvin W. *see* Hyde, Melvin Watson.
Hyde, Melvin Watson, 1905-
xHyde, Melvin W.
Standards for Publicity Programs in State
Supported Colleges & Universities Derived
from the Institutions Responsibility for
Reporting to Its Constituents. AMS Pr.
Hyde, Montgomery. *see* Hyde, Harford Montgomery.
Hyde, R. M. *see* Hyde, Richard M.
Hyde, Richard M.
xHyde, R. M.
Immunology. Reston.
Hyde, Stuart W. *see* Hyde, Stuart Wallace.
Hyde, Stuart Wallace, 1923-
xHyde, Stuart W.
Television & Radio Announcing. HM.
Hyde, Walter W. *see* Hyde, Walter Woodburn.
Hyde, Walter Woodburn, 1871-1966
xHyde, Walter W.
Greek Religion & Its Survivals. Cooper Sq.
Paganism to Christianity in the Roman Empire.
Octagon.
Hyde, Wayne.
xHyde, Wayne.
Men Behind the Astronauts. Dodd.
Hyder, Clyde K. *see* Hyder, Clyde Kenneth.
Hyder, Clyde Kenneth, 1902-
xHyder, Clyde K.
Swinburne's Literary Career & Fame. AMS Pr.
Hyder, O. Quentin, 1930-
xHyder, O. Quentin.
Shape up. Revell.
Hyink, Bernard L.
xHyink, Bernard L.
Politics & Government in California. Har-Row.
Hyland, Ann.
xHyland, Ann.
Endurance Riding. Lippincott.
Endurance Riding. Wilshire.
Hylander, Clarence J. *see* Hylander, Clarence John.

Hylander, Clarence John, 1897-
xHylander, Clarence J.
Animals in Fur. Macmillan.
Hylkema, Randall.
xHylkema, Randall.
Rudebarbs. Bks in Focus.
Hyltin, Tom M.
xHyltin, Tom M.
Digital Electronic Watch. Van Nos Reinhold.
Hyma, Albert.
xHyma, Albert.
Streams of Civilization. CLP Pubs.
Hyman, Allen.
xHyman, Allen.
ed. Advertising & Free Speech. Lexington Bks.
Hyman, Dick, 1904-
xHyman, Dick.
Lest Ill Luck Befall Thee: Superstitions of the
Great & Small. Greene.
Hyman, Harold M. *see* Hyman, Harold Melvin.
Hyman, Harold Melvin, 1924-
xHyman, Harold M.
A More Perfect Union: The Impact of the Civil
War & Reconstruction on the Constitution.
HM.
ed. The Radical Republicans & Reconstruction,
1861-1870. Irvington.
Soldiers & Spruce: Origins of the Loyal Legion
of Loggers & Lumbermen. U Cal LA Indus
Rel.
Hyman, Harold T. *see* Hyman, Harold Thomas.
Hyman, Harold Thomas, 1894-
xHyman, Harold T.
Differential Diagnosis: An Integrated
Handbook. Lippincott.
Hyman, Herbert H. *see* Hyman, Herbert Hiram.
Hyman, Herbert Hiram.
xHyman, Herbert H.
Education's Lasting Influence on Values. U of
Chicago Pr.
The Enduring Effects of Education. U of
Chicago Pr.
Political Socialization: A Study in the
Psychology of Political Behavior. Free Pr.
ed. Readings in Reference Group Theory &
Research. Free Pr.
Hyman, Herbert Hyman.
xHyman, Herbert H.
ed. Noble Gas Compounds. U of Chicago Pr.
Hyman, Irwin.
xHyman, Irwin A.
ed. Corporal Punishment in American
Education: Readings in History, Practice, &
Alternatives. Temple U Pr.
Hyman, Irwin A. *see* Hyman, Irwin.
Hyman, Isabelle.
xHyman, Isabelle.
Fifteenth Century Florentine Studies: The
Palazzo Medici & a Ledger for the Church of
San Lorenzo. Garland Pub.
Hyman, Lawrence. *see* Hyman, Lawrence William.
Hyman, Lawrence William, 1919-
xHyman, Lawrence.
The Quarrel Within: Art & Morality in
Milton's Poetry. Kennikat.
Hyman, Mac.
xHyman, Mac.
Love Boy: The Letters of Mac Hyman. La
State U Pr.
No Time for Sergeants. Random.
Hyman, Ray.
xHyman, Ray.
Nature of Psychological Inquiry. P-H.
Hyman, Richard J. *see* Hyman, Richard Joseph.
Hyman, Richard Joseph.
xHyman, Richard J.
Analytical Access: History, Resources, Needs.
Queens Coll Pr.
Hyman, Ronald T.
xHyman, Ronald T.

Paper, Pencils, Pennies: Games for Learning &
Having Fun. P-H.
Simulation Gaming for Values Education: The
Prisoner's Dilemma. U Pr of Amer.
Strategic Questioning. P-H.
Hyman, Sidney.
xHyman, Sidney.
The American President. Greenwood.
The Aspen Idea. U of Okla Pr.
Lives of William Benton. U of Chicago Pr.
Hyman, Stanley E. *see* Hyman, Stanley Edgar.
Hyman, Stanley Edgar, 1919-1970
xHyman, Stanley E.
Nathanael West. U of Minn Pr.
Standards: A Chronicle of Books for Our Time.
Horizon.
Hyman, Virginia R., 1929-
xHyman, Virginia R.
Ethical Perspective in the Novels of Thomas
Hardy. Kennikat.
Hymes, Dell. *see* Hymes, Dell H.
Hymes, Dell H.
xHymes, Dell.
Foundations in Sociolinguistics: An
Ethnographic Approach. U of Pa Pr.
ed. Reinventing Anthropology. Random.
Hymes, James L., 1913-
xHymes, James L.
Behavior & Misbehavior: A Teacher's Guide to
Action. Greenwood.
A Child Development Point of View.
Greenwood.
Early Childhood Education: An Introduction to
the Profession. Natl Assn Child Ed.
Teaching the Child Under Six. Merrill.
Hymoff, Edward.
xHymoff, Edward
Jdg Van Dusen International Tribunal Inquiry
for Peace. Heineman.
Hymovich, Debra. *see* Hymovich, Debra P.
Hymovich, Debra P.
xHymovich, Debra.
Family Health Care. McGraw.
Hynd, Noel.
xHynd, Noel.
Revenge. Dial.
The Sandler Inquiry. Dell.
The Sandler Inquiry. Dial.
Hynding, Alan, 1938-
xHynding, Alan A.
California Historymakers. Kendall-Hunt.
Hynding, Alan A. *see* Hynding, Alan.
Hyndman, Michael.
xHyndman, Michael.
Schools & Schooling in England & Wales
(1800-1977): A Documentary History.
Har-Row.
Hynds, Ernest C.
xHynds, Ernest C.
Antebellum Athens & Clarke County Georgia.
U of Ga Pr.
Hyne, Charles J. *see* Hyne, Charles John Cutcliffe
Wright.
Hyne, Charles John Cutcliffe Wright, 1866-1944
xHyne, Charles J.
Atoms of Empire. Arno.
Hynek, J. Allen. *see* Hynek, Joseph Allen.

Hynek, Joseph Allen, 1910-
xHynek, J. Allen.
The UFO Experience: A Scientific Inquiry.
Contemp Bks.
Hyneman, Charles. *see* Hyneman, Charles Shang.
Hyneman, Charles S. *see* Hyneman, Charles Shang.
Hyneman, Charles Shang, 1900-
xHyneman, Charles.
Bureaucracy in a Democracy. AMS Pr.
xHyneman, Charles S.

The First American Neutrality: A Study of the
American Understanding of Neutral
Obligations During the Years 1792 to 1815.
Porcupine Pr.
The Supreme Court on Trial. Greenwood.
Voting in Indiana: A Century of Persistence &
Change. Ind U Pr.

Hynes, Richard O.
xHynes, Richard O.
ed. Surfaces of Normal & Malignant Cells.
Wiley.
Hynes, Samuel. *see* Hynes, Samuel Lynn.

Hynes, Samuel Lynn.
xHynes, Samuel.
Pattern of Hardy's Poetry. U of NC Pr.

Hyppolite, Jean.
xHyppolite, Jean.
Genesis & Structure of Hegel's Phenomenology
of Spirit. Northwestern U Pr.
Hyslop, Beatrice F. *see* Hyslop, Beatrice Fry.

Hyslop, Beatrice Fry, 1899-
xHyslop, Beatrice F.
French Nationalism in 1789 According to the
General Cahiers. Octagon.

Hyslop, Marjorie R.
xHyslop, Marjorie R.
A Brief Guide to Sources of Metals
Information. Info Resources.
Hyslop, Theo. B. *see* Hyslop, Theophilus Bulkeley.
Hyslop, Theophilus B. *see* Hyslop, Theophilus Bulkeley.

Hyslop, Theophilus Bulkeley, 1863-1933
xHyslop, Theo. B.
The Great Abnormals. Arden Lib.
xHyslop, Theophilus B.
Great Abnormals. Gale.
Hytier. *see* Hytier, Jean.

Hytier, Jean.
xHytier.
Questions de Litterature: Etudes Valeryennes
et Autres. French & Eur.
xHytier, Jean.
Andre Gide. Ungar.
I. A. U. Symposium No. 58, Canberra, Australia, 12-15
August 1973. *see* International Astronomical Union.
I. A. U Symposium No. 61, Perth, Western Australia,
13-17 August, 1973. *see* International Astronomical
Union.
I. A. U. Symposium No. 65, Torun, Poland, 5-8
September 1973. *see* International Astronomical
Union.

I Ching.
xI Ching.
I Ching: The Book of Changes. Peter Smith.
I. O. T. T. S. Group. *see* International Oil Tanker
Terminal Safety Group.

Iacovetta, R. G.
xIacovetta, Ronald.
ed. Critical Issues in Criminal Justice. Carolina
Acad Pr.
Iacovetta, Ronald. *see* Iacovetta, R. G.

Iacovo, James S.
xIacovo, James S.
A Comprehensive Guide to United States
Commemorative Coins. Ivy Pr.
Ianni, Francis A. *see* Ianni, Francis A. J.

Ianni, Francis A. J.
xIanni, Francis A.
A Family Business: Kinship & Social Control in
Organized Crime. Russell Sage.

Ianni, Octavio.
xIanni, Octavio.
Crisis in Brazil. Columbia U Pr.
Iannone, N. *see* Iannone, N. F.

Iannone, N. F.
xIannone, N.

Supervision of Police Personnel. P-H.
xIannone, N. F.
Principles of Police Patrol. McGraw.
Iarrobino, Anthony. *see* Iarrobino, Anthony A.

Iarrobino, Anthony A., 1943-
xIarrobino, Anthony.
Punctual Hilbert Schemes. Am Math.

Iatrides, John O.
xIatrides, John O.
Revolt in Athens: The Greek Communist
"Second Round," 1944-1945. Princeton U Pr.
IAU Symposium, 62nd, Warsaw, Poland, 5-8 September
1973. *see* International Astronomical Union.

Ibadan, Nigeria. University. Library.
xIbadan University Library -(Ibadan - Nigeria).
Africana Catalogue of the Ibadan University
Library. G K Hall.

Ibadan University Library -(Ibadan - Nigeria). *see* Ibadan,
Nigeria. University. Library.
Ibele, Oscar. *see* Ibele, Oscar H.

Ibele, Oscar H.
xIbele, Oscar.
Political Science: An Introduction. Har-Row.

Ibele, Warren E.
xIbele, Warren E.
ed. Modern Developments in Heat Transfer.
Acad Pr.
Iberall, A. S. *see* Iberall, Arthur S.

Iberall, Arthur S.
xIberall, A. S.
Toward a General Science of Viable Systems.
McGraw.

Ibingira, G. S. K.
xIbingira, Grace S.
African Upheavals Since Independence.
Westview.
Ibingira, Grace S. *see* Ibingira, G. S. K.
Ibragimov, I. A. *see* Ibragimov, Ildar Abdulovich.

Ibragimov, Ildar Abdulovich.
xIbragimov, I. A.
Gaussian Random Processes. Springer-Verlag.
Ibrahim, I. *see* Ibrahim, Ibrahim B.

Ibrahim, Ibrahim B.
xIbrahim, I.
Readings in Managerial Economics. Pergamon.
Ibrahim, M. Z. *see* Ibrahim, Mohamed Z. M.

Ibrahim, Mohamed Z. M.
xIbrahim, M. Z.
Glycogen & Its Related Enzymes of
Metabolism in the Central Nervous System.
Springer-Verlag.

Ibsen, Henrik.
xIbsen, Henrik.
Correspondence of Henrik Ibsen. Haskell.
From Ibsen's Workshop: Notes Scenarios &
Drafts of the Modern Plays. Da Capo.
Speeches & New Letters. Haskell.

Ibsen, Sigurd, 1859-1930
xIbsen, Sigurd.
Human Quintessence. Arno.

Ice Skating Institute of America.
xIce Skating Institute of America Staff.
Olympic Alpine Skiing. Childrens.
Olympic Bobsledding. Childrens.
Olympic Figure Skating. Childrens.
Olympic Ice Hockey. Childrens.
Olympic Nordic Skiing. Childrens.
Olympic Speed Skating. Childrens.

Ice Skating Institute of America Staff. *see* Ice Skating
Institute of America.
Icenhower, Joseph B. *see* Icenhower, Joseph Bryan.

Icenhower, Joseph Bryan.
xIcenhower, Joseph B.
First Book of the Antarctic. Watts.
Panay Incident, December 12, 1937: The
Sinking of an American Gunboat Worsens U.
S. - Japanese Relations. Watts.

Ichikawa, Satomi.
xIchikawa, Satomi.
illus. A Child's Book of Seasons. Schol Bk
Serv.
Friends. Schol Bk Serv.
From Morn to Midnight. T Y Crowell.
illus. Sun Through Small Leaves: Poems of
Spring. Philomel.
illus. Suzanne & Nicholas in the Garden.
Watts.
Under the Cherry Tree. Philomel.

Ichioka, Yuji.
xIchioka, Yuji.
Compiled by A Buried Past: An Annotated
Bibliography of the Japanese American
Research Project Collection. U of Cal Pr.

**Ichthyological Symposium on Genetics and Mutagenesis,
Neuherberg, Germany, 1972.**
xSymposium on Icthygenetics, 1st.
Genetics & Mutagenesis of Fish: Proceedings.
Springer-Verlag.
Ickes, Harold L. *see* Ickes, Harold le Claire.

Ickes, Harold le Claire, 1874-1952
xIckes, Harold L.
Fightin' Oil. Hyperion Conn.

Ickis, Marguerite, 1897-
xIckis, Marguerite.
The Standard Book of Quilt-Making &
Collecting. Peter Smith.
Standard Book of Quiltmaking & Collecting.
Dover.
Icks, Robert J. *see* Icks, Robert Joseph.

Icks, Robert Joseph, 1899-
xIcks, Robert J.
Tanks & Armored Vehicles, 1900-1945. Paladin
Ent.
Tanks & Armored Vehicles 1900-1945.
Sycamore Island.

**ICN-UCLA Symposium on Neurobiology, Squaw Valley,
California, 1976.**
xIcn-Ucla Symposium on Neurobiology, Squaw
Valley, Cal., Mar. 1976.
Cellular Neurobiology: Proceedings. A R Liss.
I.C.S.S.D. *see* International Committee for Social Science
Information and Documentation.

Idaikkadar, N. M.
xIdaikkadar, N. M.
Agricultural Statistics: A Handbook for
Developing Countries. Pergamon.
Idleman, H. K. *see* Idleman, Hillis K.

Idleman, Hillis K., 1910-
xIdleman, H. K.
Housing, Furniture & Appliances. McGraw.
Understanding the Marketplace. McGraw.

Idler, D. R.
xIdler, David R.
ed. Steroids in Nonmammalian Vertebrates.
Acad Pr.
Idler, David R. *see* Idler, D. R.

Idung, Of Prufening.
xIdung.
Cistercians & Cluniacs: The Case for Citeaux.
Cistercian Pubns.
Idyll, C. P. *see* Idyll, Clarence P.

Illinois Crime Survey. Patterson Smith.

Illinois Conference on Medical Information Systems, 1st, University of Illinois, 1974.
  xFirst Illinois Conference on Medical Information Systems, October 1974, Urbana, IL.
    First Illinois Conference on Medical Information Systems: Proceedings. Instru Soc.

Illinois Junior High School Principal Association.
  xIllinois Junior High School Principals' Association.
    Go Where the Action Is: Teach in Junior High. Interstate.

Illinois. University at Urbana-Champaign. Library.
  xUniversity of Illinois at Urbana-Champaign - Library.
    Catalog of the Rare Book Room. G K Hall.
    Mereness Calendar: Federal Documents on the Upper Mississippi Valley, 1780-1890. G K Hall.

Illinois University. Davis Lecture Committee.
  xDavis Lecture Committee.
    Essays in the History of Medicine, in Honor of David J. Davis. U of Ill Pr.

Illinois. University. Department of English.
  xUniversity Of Illinois - English Dept.
    Studies by Members of the English Department, University of Illinois, in Memory of John Jay Parry. Arno.

Ilowite, Sheldon. see Ilowite, Sheldon A.

Ilowite, Sheldon A.
  xIlowite, Sheldon.
    Hockey Defenseman. Hastings.
    Penalty Killer: A Hockey Story. Hastings.

Imagerie Pellerin, Epinal, France.
  xEpinal.
    Antique Paper Dolls: The Edwardian Era. Dover.

Imai, Hideki.
  xImai, Hideki.
    ed. Geological Studies of the Mineral Deposits in Japan & East Asia. Intl Schol Bk Serv.

Imai, Ry Ukichi.
  xImai, Ryukichi.
    Nuclear Energy & Nuclear Proliferation: Japanese & American Views. Westview.

Imai, Ryukichi. see Imai, Ry Ukichi.

Imam, Zafar.
  xImam, Zafar.
    ed. Muslims in India. South Asia Bks.

Imber, Walter.
  xImber, Walter.
    Sweden. J J Binns.

Imbrie, John.
  xImbrie, John.
    Ice Ages: Solving the Mystery. Enslow Pubs.

Imfeld, Al, 1935-
  xImfeld, Al.
    China As a Model of Development. Orbis Bks.

Imlah, Albert H. see Imlah, Albert Henry.

Imlah, Albert Henry, 1901-
  xImlah, Albert H.
    Economic Elements in the Pax Britannica: Studies in British Foreign Trade in the 19th Century. Russell.

Imlay, Gilbert, 1754?-1828?
  xImlay, Gilbert.
    Topographical Description of the Western Territory of North America. Johnson Repr.
    Topographical Description of the Western Territory of North America. Kelley.

Immegart, Glenn L.
  xImmegart, Glenn L.
    An Introduction to Systems for the Educational Administrator. A-W.
    ed. Problem-Finding in Educational Administration: Trends in Research & Theory. Lexington Bks.

Immel, Mary B. see Immel, Mary Blair.

Immel, Mary Blair.
  xImmel, Mary B.

River of Wind. Aurora Pubs.
  xImmel, Mary Blair.
    Call up the Thunder. Bethany Pr.

Immigration Information Bureau. see Immigration Information Bureau, Inc.

Immigration Information Bureau, Inc.
  xImmigration Information Bureau.
    Directory Relating to Record of Arrival of Passenger Steamships at the Ports of N. Y., Phila., Boston & Baltimore, 1904 to 1926. R & E Res Assoc.

Immler, Robert.
  xImmler, Robert.
    Bicycling in Hawaii. Wilderness.

Immroth, J. Philip. see Immroth, John Phillip.

Immroth, John Phillip.
  xImmroth, J. Philip.
    Library Cataloging: A Guide for a Basic Course. Scarecrow.

Imms, A. D. see Imms, Augustus Daniel.

Imms, Augustus Daniel.
  xImms, A. D.
    Imms' General Textbook of Entomology. Methuen Inc.

Impe, Jack Van. see Van Impe, Jack.

Imperato, Pascal J. see Imperato, Pascal James.

Imperato, Pascal James.
  xImperato, Pascal J.
    African Folk Medicine: Practices & Beliefs of the Bambara & Other Peoples. York Pr.
    ed. Historical Dictionary of Mali. Scarecrow.
    Medical Detective. Marek.

Imperial Society of Teachers of Dancing, Incorporated.
  xImperial Society of Teachers of Dancing.
    Sequence Dancing. British Bk Ctr.
    Teach Yourself Dancing. McKay.

Imundo, Louis V.
  xImundo, Louis V.
    The Effective Supervisor's Handbook. Am Mgmt.

Imwinkelried, Edward J.
  xImwinkelried, Edward J.
    Criminal Evidence. West Pub.

Inayat, Taj, 1943-
  xInayat, Taj.
    The Crystal Chalice: Spiritual Themes for Women. Sufi Order Pubns.

Inbar, Michael.
  xInbar, Michael.
    Simulation & Gaming in Social Science. Free Pr.

Incani, Albert G.
  xIncani, Albert G.
    Coordinated Activity Programs for the Aged: A How-to-Do-It Manual. Am Hospital.

Ince, Edward L. see Ince, Edward Lindsay.

Ince, Edward Lindsay, 1891-1941
  xInce, Edward L.
    Ordinary Differential Equations. Dover.

Ince, Laurence P.
  xInce, Lawrence P.
    Behavioral Psychology in Rehabilitation Medicine: Clinical Application. Williams & Wilkins.

Ince, Lawrence P. see Ince, Laurence P.

Ince, Richard B. see Ince, Richard Basil.

Ince, Richard Basil, 1881-
  xInce, Richard B.
    At the Sign of Sagittarius. Arno.
    Calverley & Some Cambridge Wits of the Nineteenth Century. Folcroft.

Inch, Morris A., 1925-
  xInch, Morris A.
    The Evangelical Challenge. Westminster.

Inciardi, James A.
  xInciardi, James A.

Careers in Crime. Rand.
    Crime & the Criminal Justice Process. Kendall-Hunt.
    Historical Approaches to Crime: Research Strategies & Issues. Sage.
    Legal & Illicit Drug Use: Acute Reactions of Emergency Room Populations. Praeger.
    ed. Violent Crime: Historical & Contemporary Issues. Sage.

Incropera, Frank P.
  xIncropera, Frank P.
    Introduction to Molecular Structure & Thermodynamics. Wiley.

Inden, Ronald B.
  xInden, Ronald B.
    Marriage & Rank in Bengali Culture: A History of Caste & Clan in Middle-Period Bengal. U of Cal Pr.

India. Famine Inquiry Commission.
  xFamine Inquiry Commission of India.
    Report on Bengal. Arno.

India. Hemp Drugs Commission, 1893-1894.
  xIndia. Hemp Drugs Commission, 1893-1894.
    Report. Johnson Repr.

India Office Library.
  xCommonwealth Relations Office - London.
    Catalogue of European Printed Books, India Office Library. G K Hall.

Indian Council for Cultural Relations.
  xIndian Council For Cultural Relations.
    Studies in Asian History: Proceedings of the Asian History Congress 1961. Asia.

Indian Council of Social Science Research.
  xIndian Council of Social Science Research, New Delhi.
    A Survey of Research in Geography. Intl Pubns Serv.

Indian Council of World Affairs.
  xIndian Council on World Affairs.
    India & the United Nations. Greenwood.

Indian Council on World Affairs. see Indian Council of World Affairs.

Indiana. Laws, Statues, etc.
  xPublisher's Editorial Staff.
    Indiana Banking & Related Laws. Michie.

Indiana Public School Study Council.
  xIndiana Public School Study Council.
    Exploring Junior High School Guidance. Interstate.

Indiana. University.
  xIndiana University.
    The Arts of Thailand: A Handbook of the Architecture, Sculpture, & Painting of Thailand. Greenwood.
    General Biology Laboratory Manual. Kendall-Hunt.

Indiana. University. Archives of Traditional Music.
  xIndiana University, Folklore Institute, Archives of Traditional Music.
    Catalog of the Archives of Traditional Music. G K Hall.

Indiana. University. Department of Government.
  xIndiana University Dept. of Government.
    Toward the Comparative Study of Public Administration. Greenwood.

Indiana University Dept. of Government. see Indiana. University. Department of Government.

Indiana University, Folklore Institute, Archives of Traditional Music. see Indiana. University. Archives of Traditional Music.

Indiana. University. Institute for Sex Research.
  xIndiana University, Institute for Sex Research.

Compiled by If I Had My Ministry to Live
   Over, I Would.... Broadman.
Ingle, Stephen.
   xIngle, Stephen.
      Socialist Thought in Imaginative Literature.
      Rowman.
Inglefield, Eric.
   xInglefield, Eric.
      Flags. Arco.
Inglehart, Ronald.
   xInglehart, Ronald.
      The Silent Revolution: Changing Values &
      Political Styles Among Western Publics.
      Princeton U Pr.
Ingleton, Roy D.
   xIngleton, Roy D.
      Police of the World. Scribner.
Inglett, G. E.
   xInglett, G. E.
      ed. Tropical Foods: Chemistry & Nutrition.
      Acad Pr.
   xInglett, George.
      ed. Dietary Fibers: Chemistry & Nutrition.
      Acad Pr.
Inglett, George. *see* Inglett, G. E.
Inglett, George E.
   xInglett, George E.
      ed. Fabricated Foods. AVI.
Inglis, Amirah.
   xInglis, Amirah.
      The White Women's Protection Ordinance:
      Sexual Anxiety & Politics in Papua,
      1920-1934. St Martin.
Inglis, Brian, 1916-
   xInglis, Brian.
      The Forbidden Game: A Social History of
      Drugs. Scribner.
      The Freedom of the Press in Ireland,
      1784-1841. Greenwood.
      Men of Conscience. Macmillan.
Inglis, David R. *see* Inglis, David Rittenhouse.
Inglis, David Rittenhouse, 1905-
   xInglis, David R.
      Wind Power & Other Energy Options. U of
      Mich Pr.
Inglis, J. K. *see* Inglis, John Kenneth.
Inglis, John Kenneth.
   xInglis, J. K.
      A Textbook of Human Biology. Pergamon.
Ingman, Nicholas.
   xIngman, Nicholas.
      The Story of Music. Taplinger.
Ingmanson, Dale.
   xIngmanson, Dale E.
      Oceanography: An Introduction. Wadsworth
      Pub.
Ingmanson, Dale E. *see* Ingmanson, Dale.
Ingold. *see* Ingold, Cecil Terence.
Ingold, C. K. *see* Ingold, Christopher Kelk.
Ingold, Cecil Terence.
   xIngold.
      The Biology of Mucor & Its Allies. Univ Park.
Ingold, Christopher Kelk, 1893-
   xIngold, C. K.
      Structure & Mechanism in Organic Chemistry.
      Cornell U Pr.
Ingraham, Barton. *see* Ingraham, Barton L.
Ingraham, Barton L.
   xIngraham, Barton.
      Political Crime in Europe: A Comparative
      Study of France, Germany, & England. U of
      Cal Pr.
Ingraham, Joseph H. *see* Ingraham, Joseph Holt.
Ingraham, Joseph Holt, 1809-1860
   xIngraham, Joseph H.
      South-West. Negro U Pr.
Ingraham, Mark H. *see* Ingraham, Mark Hoyt.
Ingraham, Mark Hoyt, 1896-
   xIngraham, Mark H.

Charles Sumner Slichter: The Golden Vector.
   U of Wis Pr.
Outer Fringe: Faculty Benefits Other Than
   Annuities & Insurance. U of Wis Pr.
Ingram, Arthur.
   xIngram, Arthur.
      Fire Engines in Color. Sterling.
      ed. Trucks of the World Highways. Sterling.
Ingram, Barbara K. *see* Ingram, Barbara Kilroy.
Ingram, Barbara Kilroy.
   xIngram, Barbara K.
      The Workshop Approach to Classroom Interest
      Centers: A Teacher's Handbook of Learning
      Games & Activities. P-H.
Ingram, C. Fred. *see* Ingram, Culpepper Fred.
Ingram, Culpepper Fred.
   xIngram, C. Fred.
      ed. Beadland to Barrow: A History of Barrow
      County, Georgia from the Earliest Days to
      the Present. Cherokee.
Ingram, D. *see* Ingram, Derek.
Ingram, D. J. *see* Ingram, David John Edward.
Ingram, Dave.
   xIngram, Dave.
      The Complete Handbook of Slow Scan TV.
      TAB Bks.
Ingram, David John Edward.
   xIngram, D. J.
      Radiation & Quantum Physics. Oxford U Pr.
      Spectroscopy at Radio & Microwave
      Frequencies. Plenum Pub.
Ingram, Derek.
   xIngram, D.
      The Commonwealth at Work. Pergamon.
Ingram, Edward.
   xIngram, Edward.
      The Beginning of the Great Game in Asia
      1828-1834. Oxford U Pr.
Ingram, Eleanor M. *see* Ingram, Eleanor Marie.
Ingram, Eleanor Marie, 1886-1921
   xIngram, Eleanor M.
      The Thing from the Lake. Arno.
Ingram, G. K. *see* Ingram, Gregory K.
Ingram, Grace.
   xIngram, Grace.
      Gilded Spurs. Fawcett.
      Gilded Spurs. Stein & Day.
Ingram, Gregory K.
   xIngram, G. K.
      Detroit Prototype of the NBER Urban
      Simulation Model. Natl Bur Econ Res.
Ingram, Helen. *see* Ingram, Helen M.
Ingram, Helen M.
   xIngram, Helen.
      ed. Why Policies Succeed or Fail. Sage.
Ingram, I. M. *see* Ingram, Ian Malcolm.
Ingram, Ian Malcolm.
   xIngram, I. M.
      Notes on Psychiatry. Churchill.
Ingram, J. B. *see* Ingram, James B.
Ingram, James B.
   xIngram, J. B.
      Curriculum Integration & Lifelong Education.
      Pergamon.
Ingram, John H. *see* Ingram, John Henry.
Ingram, John Henry, 1842-1916
   xIngram, John H.
      Chatterton & His Poetry. AMS Pr.
      Chatterton & His Poetry. Folcroft.
      Chatterton & His Poetry. R West.
      Marlowe & His Poetry. AMS Pr.
      Marlowe & His Poetry. Arden Lib.
      Marlowe & His Poetry. Folcroft.
Ingram, John K. *see* Ingram, John Kells.
Ingram, John Kells, 1823-1907
   xIngram, John K.
      History of Political Economy. Kelley.
Ingram, Kenneth, 1882-
   xIngram, Kenneth.

History of the Cold War. Philos Lib.
Ingram, Tom.
   xIngram, Tom.
      Garranane. Bradbury Pr.
Ingram, W. *see* Ingram, Walter Robinson.
Ingram, Walter Robinson, 1905-
   xIngram, W.
      A Review of Anatomical Neurology. Univ
      Park.
Ingram, William.
   xIngram, William.
      A London Life in the Brazen Age: Francis
      Langley, 1548-1602. Harvard U Pr.
Ingrao, Charles W.
   xIngrao, Charles W.
      In Quest & Crisis: Emperor Joseph I & the
      Habsburg Monarchy,. Purdue.
Ingwersen, Faith.
   xIngwersen, Faith.
      Martin A. Hansen. Twayne.
Ingwersen, Ulla.
   xIngwersen, Ulla.
      Respiratory Physical Therapy & Pulmonary
      Care. Wiley.
Ingzel, Marjorie.
   xIngzel, Marjorie.
      ed. Table Graces for the Family. Nelson.
Inhaber, Herbert, 1941-
   xInhaber, Herbert.
      Environmental Indices. Wiley.
      Physics of the Environment. Ann Arbor
      Science.
Inhelder, Barbel.
   xInhelder, Barbel.
      Learning & the Development of Cognition.
      Harvard U Pr.
Inkeles, Alex.
   xInkeles, Alex.
      ed. Annual Review of Sociology. Annual
      Reviews.
      Public Opinion in Soviet Russia: A Study in
      Mass Persuasion. Harvard U Pr.
Inkeles, Gordon.
   xInkeles, Gordon.
      The Art of Sensual Massage. S&S.
      The New Massage: Total Body Conditioning
      for People Who Exercise. Putnam.
Inkiow, Dimiter.
   xInkiow, Dimiter.
      Me & Clara & Casimir the Cat. Pantheon.
      Me & Clara & Snuffy the Dog. Pantheon.
      Me & My Sister Clara. Pantheon.
Inlow, Edgar B. *see* Inlow, Edgar Burke.
Inlow, Edgar Burke, 1915-
   xInlow, Edgar B.
      The Patent Grant. AMS Pr.
Inman, Billie A. *see* Inman, Billie Andrew.
Inman, Billie Andrew.
   xInman, Billie A.
      Aspects of Composition. HarBraceJ.
Inman, Fred W.
   xInman, Fred W.
      Contemporary Physics. Macmillan.
Inman, Marianne.
   xInman, Marianne.
      Foreign Languages, English As a Second &
      Foreign Language, & the U. S. Multinational
      Corporation. Ctr Appl Ling.
Inman, Nancy A. *see* Inman, Nancy Aldrich.
Inman, Nancy Aldrich.
   xInman, Nancy A.
      Tropical Flower Arranging: A Practical Guide.
      C E Tuttle.
Inman, Thomas, 1820-1876
   xInman, Thomas.
      Ancient Pagan & Modern Christian Symbolism.
      Longwood Pr.
Inman, Verne T. *see* Inman, Verne Thompson.
Inman, Verne Thompson, 1905-
   xInman, Verne T.

The Joints of the Ankle. Williams & Wilkins.

Innaurato, Albert, 1947-
  xInnaurato, Albert.
    Ulysses in Traction. Dramatists Play.

Innes, Brian.
  xInnes, Brian.
    Horoscopes: How to Draw & Interpret Them.
      Arco.
    The Tarot: How to Use & Interpret the Cards.
      Arco.

Innes, C. D.
  xInnes, Christopher.
    Modern German Drama: A Study in Form.
      Cambridge U Pr.

Innes, Catherine L. see Innes, Catherine Lynette.

Innes, Catherine Lynette.
  xInnes, Catherine L.
    ed. Critical Perspectives on Chinua Achebe.
      Three Continents.

Innes, Christopher. see Innes, C. D.

Innes, G. S.
  xInnes, G. S.
    ed. The Production & Hazards of a Hyperbaric
      Oxygen Environment: Proceedings.
      Pergamon.

Innes, Hammond.
  xInnes, Hammond.
    Campbell's Kingdom. Ballantine.
    The Doomed Oasis. Ballantine.
    The Last Voyage: Captain Cook's Lost Diary.
      Knopf.
    Levkas Man. Ballantine.
    Levkas Man. Knopf.
    North Star. Ballantine.
    North Star. Knopf.

Innes, Lowell.
  xInnes, Lowell.
    Pittsburgh Glass, 1797-1891: A History &
      Guide for Collectors. HM.

Innes, Michael.
  xInnes, Michael.
    Appleby's End. Ballantine.

Inness, George, 1854-1926
  xInness, George.
    Life, Art, & Letters of George Inness. Da
      Capo.

Innis, G. S. see Innis, George S.

Innis, George S., 1937-
  xInnis, G. S.
    ed. Grassland Simulation Model.
      Springer-Verlag.
    ed. Systems Analysis of Ecosystems. Intl
      Co-Op.

Innis, Harold A. see Innis, Harold Adams.

Innis, Harold Adams, 1894-1952
  xInnis, Harold A.
    The Cod Fisheries: A History of an
      International Economy. U of Toronto Pr.
    Fur Trade in Canada: An Introduction to
      Canadian Economic History. U of Toronto
      Pr.
    History of the Canadian Pacific Railway. U of
      Toronto Pr.
    The Press: A Neglected Factor in the
      Economic History of the Twentieth Century.
      AMS Pr.

Innocent, C. F. see Innocent, Charles Frederick.

Innocent, Charles Frederick.
  xInnocent, C. F.
    The Development of English Building
      Construction (1916). David & Charles.

Inokuma, Isao.
  xInokuma, Isao.
    Best Judo. Kodansha.

Inoue, Yasushi, 1907-
  xInoue, Yasushi.

Counterfeiter & Other Stories. C E Tuttle.
    Journey Beyond Samarkand. Kodansha.
    Lou-Lan & Other Stories. Kodansha.

Inouye, Carol.
  xInouye, Carol.
    Naturecraft. Doubleday.

Inouye, Masayori.
  xInouye, Masayori.
    Bacterial Outer Membranes: Biogenesis &
      Functions. Wiley.

Inrig, Gary.
  xInrig, Gary.
    ed. Hearts of Iron, Feet of Clay. Moody.

Insdorf, Annette.
  xInsdorf, Annette.
    Pref. by Francois Truffaut. Morrow.
    Francois Truffaut. Twayne.

Insdorf, Cecile.
  xInsdorf, Cecile.
    Montaigne & Feminism. U of NC Pr.

Insel, Paul M.
  xInsel, Paul M.
    Core Concepts in Health. Mayfield Pub.

Inselberg, H. see Inselberg, Henry S.

Inselberg, Henry S.
  xInselberg, H.
    How to Build a More Lucrative Accounting
      Practice. P-H.

Insingel, Mark.
  xInsingel, Mark.
    Reflections. Red Dust.

Inskeep, R. R.
  xInskeep, R. R.
    The Peopling of Southern Africa. B&N.

Insler, Vaclav.
  xInsler, Vaclav.
    Practical Obstetrics & Gynecology: Manual of
      Selected Procedures & Treatments. S Karger.

Inst. of Real Estate Management. see Institute of Real
  Estate Management.

Institut du Petrole Francaise. see Institut francais du
  petrole.

Institut Francais De Pertrole. see Institut francais du
  petrole.

Institut francais du petrole.
  xInstitut du Petrole Francaise.
    ed. Drilling Data Handbook. Gulf Pub.
  xInstitut Francais De Pertrole.
    Manual of Economic Analysis of Chemical
      Processes. McGraw.

Institut National De la Statistique et Des Etudes
  Economiques. see France. Institut National De la
  Statistique et Des Etudes Economiques.

Institute for Architecture & Urban Studies. see Institute
  for Architecture and Urban Studies.

Institute for Architecture and Urban Studies.
  xInstitute for Architecture & Urban Studies.
    Oppositions 4: Oppositions: a Forum for Ideas
      & Criticism in Architecture. Wittenborn.

Institute for Business Planning, Inc.
  xInstitute for Business Planning Research &
    Editorial Staff.
    Business & Financial Tables Desk Book. Inst
      Busn Plan.

Institute for Business Planning Research & Editorial
  Staff. see Institute for Business Planning, Inc.

Institute for Contemporary Curriculum Development.
  xInstitute for Contemporary Curriculum
    Development.
    Develop Number Skills (Three). Cambridge Bk.
    Discover Mathematics (Five). Cambridge Bk.
    Explore Mathematics (Four). Cambridge Bk.
    Learn About Numbers (One). Cambridge Bk.
    Succeed with Mathematics. Cambridge Bk.
    Think Mathematics. Cambridge Bk.
    Urban Studies-the City: Promise & Problem.
      Cambridge Bk.
    Work with Numbers (Two). Cambridge Bk.
  xTheInstitute for Contemporary Curriculum
    Development.

Achieve with Mathematics. Cambridge Bk.

Institute for Paralegal Training.
  xInstitute for Paralegal Training.
    Introduction to Estates & Trusts. West Pub.
  xTheInstitute for Paralegal Training.
    Introduction to Real Estate Law. West Pub.

Institute for Propaganda Analysis. see Institute for
  Propaganda Analysis, Inc., New York.

Institute for Propaganda Analysis, Inc., New York.
  xInstitute for Propaganda Analysis.
    Propaganda Analysis. Gordon Pr.

Institute for Religious & Social Studies. see Institute for
  Religious and Social Studies. Jewish Theological
  Seminary of America.

**Institute for Religious and Social Studies. Jewish
  Theological Seminary of America.**
  xInstitute for Religious & Social Studies.
    Communication of Ideas. Cooper Sq.
    Hour of Insight. Arno.
    Integrity & Compromise: Problems of Public &
      Private Conscience. Arno.
    Labor's Relation to Church & Community: A
      Series of Addresses. Arno.
    New Horizons in Creative Thinking.
      Greenwood.

Institute for Sex Research. see Indiana. University.
  Institute for Sex Research.

Institute for Tax Assessors. see Institute for Tax
  Assessors, University of Texas.

Institute for Tax Assessors, University of Texas.
  xInstitute for Tax Assessors.
    Proceedings. LBJ Sch Public Affairs.

Institute for the History of Art, Florence.
  Kunsthistorischen Institut - Florence. see
  Kunsthistorischer Institut, Florence, Italy.

Institute of Advanced Legal Studies, University of
  London. see London. University. Institute of
  Advanced Legal Studies.

Institute of Criminology, University of Cambridge,
  England. see Cambridge. University. Institute of
  Criminology.

Institute of Electrical & Electronics Engineers, Inc. see
  Institute of Electrical and Electronics Engineers.

Institute of Electrical and Electronics Engineers.
  xIEEE.
    IEEE-Arinc Standard Atlas Syntax. Wiley.
  xInstitute of Electrical & Electronics Engineers,
    Inc.
    IEEE Recommended Practice for Emergency
      & Standby Power Systems. Wiley.
    IEEE: Recommended Practice for Protection &
      Coordination of Industrial & Commercial
      Power Systems. Wiley.
    IEEE Standard Dictionary of Electrical &
      Electronics Terms. Wiley.

Institute of Environmental Sciences.
  xInstitute of Environmental Sciences 22nd Annual
    Technical Meeting, Philadelphia.
    Bridging the Gap.... Between an Understanding
      of the Physics & the Engineering
      Applications: Proceedings. Inst Environ Sci.
    Energy & the Environment: Proceedings. Inst
      Environ Sci.
    Environmental Evolution: Proceedings. Inst
      Environ Sci.
    Environmental Progress in Science &
      Education: Proceedings. Inst Environ Sci.
    Environmental Technology 76: Proceedings.
      Inst Environ Sci.
    Living in Our Environment: Proceedings. Inst
      Environ Sci.
    Man in His Environment: Proceedings. Inst
      Environ Sci.
    New Horizons: Proceedings. Inst Environ Sci.
    Realism in Environmental Testing & Control:
      Proceedings. Inst Environ Sci.

Institute of Graphic Designers, San Francisco.
  xTheInstitute of Graphic Designers.

Graphic Design, San Francisco. Chronicle Bks.

Institute of High Fidelity.
xTheInstitute of High Fidelity.
Official Guide to High Fidelity. Sams.
Institute of Historical Studies. *see* Institute of Historical Studies, Calcutta.

Institute of Historical Studies, Calcutta.
xInstitute of Historical Studies.
Modern Bengal: A Socio-Economic Survey. Intl Pubns Serv.

Institute of Internal Auditors.
xBoard of Regents of IIA.
Certified Internal Auditor Examination--May 1979: Questions & Suggested Solutions. Inst Inter Aud.
xInstitute of Internal Auditors.
Bibliography of Internal Auditing: Nineteen Fifty to Nineteen Sixty-Eight. Inst Inter Aud.
Certified Internal Auditor Examination Personal Review Course. Inst Inter Aud.
One-Day Seminar on Contract Audits: Digest of Controls & Tests & Audit Questionnaire & Survey Guide. Inst Inter Aud.
xInstitute of Internal Auditors, Inc.
Compendium: Questions & Suggested Solutions, Certified Internal Auditor Examinations, 1976 Through 1979. Inst Inter Aud.
How to Save Fourteen Million, Five Hundred Thousand Dollars Through Internal Auditing. Inst Inter Aud.
Survey of Internal Auditing: 1979. Inst Inter Aud.

Institute of Internal Auditors, Inc. *see* Institute of Internal Auditors.

Institute of Labor & Industrial Relations. *see* Institute of Labor and Industrial Relations (University of Michigan-Wayne State University).

Institute of Labor and Industrial Relations (University of Michigan-Wayne State University).
xInstitute of Labor & Industrial Relations.
Document & Reference Text: 1971 Supplement. U of Mich Inst Labor.
xInstitute Of Labor And Industrial Relations.
Document & Reference Text: An Index to Minority Group Employment Information. U of Mich Inst Labor.

Institute Of Laboratory Animal Research. *see* National Research Council. Institute of Laboratory Animal Resources.

Institute Of Laboratory Animal Resources. *see* National Research Council. Institute of Laboratory Animal Resources.

Institute of Latin American Studies. *see* Texas. University. Institute of Latin American Studies.

Institute of Medicine.
xInstitute of Medicine.
Assessing Quality in Health Care. Natl Acad Pr.
Assessment of Medical Care for Children. Natl Acad Pr.
Beyond Malpractice: Compensation for Medical Injuries. Natl Acad Pr.
Controlling the Supply of Hospital Beds. Natl Acad Pr.
Controls on Health Care. Natl Acad Pr.
Ethics of Health Care. Natl Acad Pr.
A Manpower Policy for Primary Health Care. Natl Acad Pr.
Pharmaceuticals for Developing Countries. Natl Acad Pr.
A Strategy for Evaluating Health Services. Natl Acad Pr.

Institute of Modern Languages.
xInstitute of Modern Languages.
Basic Electricity. Inst Mod Lang.
xInstitute Of Modern Languages.
Contemporary Spoken English. Har-Row.
Institute Of Modern Languages Inc. *see* Institute of Modern Languages.

Institute of Pacific Relations.
xInstitute of Pacific Relations.
Agrarian China: Selected Source Materials from Chinese Authors. AMS Pr.
Economic Trends & Problems in the Early Republican Period: 1931. Garland Pub.
Industrial Japan. AMS Pr.
Institute of Pacific Relations: A Selection of Monographs. AMS Pr.
Institute Of Pacific Relations Conference - 1st - 4th. *see* Institute of Pacific Relations, 1st Conference, Honolulu, 1925.

Institute of Pacific Relations, 1st Conference, Honolulu, 1925.
xInstitute Of Pacific Relations Conference - 1st - 4th.
Proceedings. Greenwood.

Institute of Personnel Management.
xInstitute of Personnel Management.
IPM Bibliography: Part Three, Education Training & Development. Intl Pubns Serv.
Staff Status for All. Intl Pubns Serv.

Institute of Personnel Management. National Committee on Employee Relations.
xInstitute of Personnel Management's National Committee on Employee Relations.
Trade Union Recognition. Intl Pubns Serv.
Institute of Personnel Management's National Committee on Employee Relations. *see* Institute of Personnel Management. National Committee on Employee Relations.

Institute of Petroleum. *see* Institute of Petroleum, London.

Institute of Petroleum, London.
xInstitute of Petroleum.
Mechanical Systems for the Recovery of Oil Spilled on Water. Intl Ideas.

Institute of Petroleum, London. Oil Pollution Analysis Committee.
xInstitute of Petroleum Oil Pollution Analysis Committee, London.
Marine Pollution by Oil. Intl Ideas.
Institute of Petroleum Oil Pollution Analysis Committee, London. *see* Institute of Petroleum, London. Oil Pollution Analysis Committee.

Institute of Real Estate Management.
xInst. of Real Estate Management.
Expense Analysis: Condominiums, Cooperatives, and Planned Unit Developments. Inst Real Estate.
Income-Expense Analysis: Apartments. Inst Real Estate.
xInstitute of Real Estate Management Staff.
How To Write an Operations Manual: A Guide for Apartment Management. Inst Real Estate.

Institute of Traffic Engineers.
xInstitute of Traffic Engineers.
Transportation & Traffic Engineering Handbook. P-H.

Institute of World Affairs.
xInstitute of World Affairs.
Problems of the Peace: Proceedings. Arno.

Institution of Electrical Engineers.
xInstitution of Electrical Engineers.
Conference on Power Thyristors & Their Applications. Intl Pubns Serv.
Institution Of Metallurgists. *see* Institution of Metallurgists, London.

Institution of Metallurgists, London.
xInstitution Of Metallurgists.
Progress in Metallurgical Technology. Gordon.
The Structure of Metals: A Modern Conception. Gordon.

Instrument Society of America.
xInstrument Society Of America.
Dynamic Response Testing of Process Control Instrumentation Standard. Instru Soc.
Int'l Workshop on Appropriate Tech., Delft Univ. of Technology, Sept. 4-7, 1979. *see* Manning, Sidney A.

Intel Marketing Communications.
xIntel Marketing Communications.
The Eighty Eighty-Eighty Eighty-Five Microprocessor Book. Wiley.
xIntel Marketing Corporations.
The Semiconductor Memory Book. Wiley.
Intel Marketing Corporations. *see* Intel Marketing Communications.

Inter- American Statistical Institute. *see* Inter-American Statistical Institute.

Inter-American Commission of Women.
xInteramerican Commission of Women.
Final Act of the Eighteenth Assembly. OAS.
Inter-American Commission on Human Rights. *see* Inter-American Institute on Human Rights.

Inter-American Conference on Intellectual Interchange, University of Texas, 1943.
xInter-American Conference on Intellectual Interchange, 1943, University of Texas.
Proceedings. Arno.

Inter-American Institute of International Legal Studies.
xInter-American Institute of International Legal Studies.
ed. Instruments of Economic Integration in Latin America & in the Caribbean. Oceana.
Instruments Relating to the Economic Integration of Latin America. Oceana.
Inter-American System: Its Development & Strengthening. Oceana.

Inter-American Institute on Human Rights.
xInter-American Commission on Human Rights.
American Declaration of the Rights & Duties of Man. OAS.
Organization of American States & Human Rights 1960-1967. OAS.
Report on the Situation of Human Rights in Chile, Third. OAS.

Inter-American Juridical Committee.
xInter-American Juridical Committee.
Charter of the OAS & Inter-American Treaty of Reciprocal Assistance. OAS.

Inter-American Statistical Institute.
xInter- American Statistical Institute.
Bibliography of Selected Statistical Sources of the American Nations: A Guide to the Principal Statistical Materials of the 22 American Nations, Including Data, Analyses, Methodology, & Laws & Organization of Statistical Agencies. Blaine Ethridge.
Interamerican Commission of Women. *see* Inter-American Commission of Women.
Interchurch World Movement, Commission of Inquiry. *see* Interchurch World Movement of North America. Commission of Inquiry.

Interchurch World Movement of North America. Commission of Inquiry.
xInterchurch World Movement, Commission of Inquiry.
Public Opinion & the Steel Strike. Da Capo.
Interdisciplinary Conference, Ann Arbor, March 1973. *see* Conference on the Formal Aspects of Cognitive Processes, Ann Arbor, Michigan, 1973.

Interdisciplinary Research Committee, University of Wisconsin, 1961.
xInterdisciplinary Research Conference - 1961.
Physiological Correlates of Psychological Disorder: Proceedings. U of Wis Pr.
Interdisciplinary Research Conference - 1961. *see* Interdisciplinary Research Committee, University of Wisconsin, 1961.
Interdisciplinary Symposium Held at Odense University, Denmark, 1974. *see* Interdisciplinary Symposium on the Measurement of Oxygen, Odense University, 1974.

Interdisciplinary Symposium on the Measurement of Oxygen, Odense University, 1974.
xInterdisciplinary Symposium Held at Odense University, Denmark, 1974.
Measurement of Oxygen: Proceedings. Elsevier.
Intergovernmental Group Oilseeds, Oils, & Fats, 10th

A Handbook of Kidney Nomenclature &
Nosology. Little.

**International Committee for Social Science Information
and Documentation.**
xI.C.S.S.D.
International Bibliography of the Social
Sciences: Sociology, 1978. Methuen Inc.
xInternational Committee for Social Science
Information & Documentation.
International Bibliography of Political Science
1976. Intl Pubns Serv.

**International Conference of Agricultural Economists,
13th, University of Sydney, 1967.**
xInternational Conference Of Agricultural
Economists - 13th - University Of Sydney -
Sydney - New South Wales - Australia - 21 To
30 Aug. 1967.
Economist & Farm People in a Rapidly
Changing Word. Oxford U Pr.

**International Conference on Atherosclerosis, Milan,
November, 1977.**
xInternational Conference on Atherosclerosis,
Milan, November 1977.
Proceedings. Raven.

**International Conference on Automation in
Warehousing, University of Nottingham, 1975.**
xInternational Conference on Automation in
Warehousing, 1st, Univ. of Nottingham, England,
April 1975.
Proceedings. Scholium Intl.

**International Conference on Computing Methods in
Optimization Problems, 2nd, San Remo, Italy, 1968.**
xInternational Conference on Computing Methods
in Optimization Problems - 2nd San Remo, Italy
- 1968.
Proceedings. Springer-Verlag.

**International Conference on Cyclic Nucleotides, 3rd,
New Orleans, 1977.**
xInternational Conference on Cyclic Nucleotide,
3rd, New Orleans, la., July 1977.
Advances in Cyclic Nucleotide Research:
Proceedings. Raven.

**International Conference on Drag Reduction,
Cambridge, Eng. 1974.**
xFirst International Conference on Drag
Reduction.
Proceedings. BHRA Fluid.

**International Conference on Environmental
Carcinogenesis,amsterdam, 1979.**
xInternational Conference on Environmental
Carcinogensis, Amsterdam, May 1979.
Environmental Carcinogenesis. Occurrence
Risk Evaluation & Mechanisms: Proceedings.
Elsevier.

**International Conference on Equine Infectious Diseases,
2d, Paris, 1969.**
xInternational Conference on Equine Infectious
Diseases, 2nd, Paris, 1969.
Equine Infectious Diseases II: Proceedings. S
Karger.

**International Conference on Equine Infectious Diseases,
3d, Paris, 1972.**
xInternational Conference on Equine Infectious
Diseases, 3rd.
Equine Infectious Diseases III: Proceedings. S
Karger.

**International Conference on Fluid Sealing, 7th,
University of Nottingham, 1975.**
xSeventh International Conference on Fluid
Sealing.
Proceedings. BHRA Fluid.

**International Conference on Gastrointestinal Cancer, Tel
Aviv, 1977.**
xInternational Conference on Gastrointestinal
Cancer, Tel Aviv, Israel, November 1977.
Abstracts. S Karger.

International Conference on General Inequalities.
xInternational Conference on General Inequalities,
1st, Mathematical Research Institute
Oberwolfach, May 1976.

Proceedings. Renouf.

**International Conference on High Energy Collisions,
5th, Stony Brook, N.Y., 1973.**
xAIP Conference.
High Energy Collisions-1973: Proceedings. Am
Inst Physics.

**International Conference on Hot Electrons in Semi
Conductors, Denton, Texas, 1977.**
xInternational Conference on Hot Electrons in
Semiconductors, Denton, TX, 6-8 Jul. 1977.
Hot Electrons in Semiconductors. Pergamon.

**International Conference on Housing Planning
Financing and Construction in North Central, South
American, and Caribbean Countries, Miami Beach,
1977.**
xInternational Conference on Housing, Planning,
Financing, Construction, 2-7 December, 1979,
Miami Beach, Florida.
Housing As Human Habitat: Proceedings.
Pergamon.

**International Conference on Hydraulics, Pneumatics and
Fluidics in Control and Automation, Toronto,
Ontario, 1976.**
xInternational Conference on Hydraulics,
Pneumatics & Fluidics in Control & Automation.
Proceedings. BHRA Fluid.

**International Conference on Hyperbaric Medicine, 3rd,
Durham, North Carolina, 1965.**
xInternational Conference On Hyperbaric
Medicine - 3rd - Durham - N. C. - 1965.
Proceedings. Natl Acad Pr.

**International Conference on Intra-Uterine
Contraception, 3rd, Cairo, 1974.**
xInternational Conference on Intrauterine
Contraception, 3rd, Cairo, 1974.
Analysis of Intrauterine Contraception:
Proceedings. Elsevier.
International Conference on Intrauterine Contraception,
3rd, Cairo, 1974. *see* International Conference on
Intra-Uterine Contraception, 3rd, Cairo, 1974.

**International Conference on Leukemia-Lymphoma,
University of Michigan, 1967.**
xInternational Conference on
Leukemia-Lymphoma.
Proceedings. Lea & Febiger.

**International Conference on Light Scattering in Solids,
3rd, Campinas, Brazil, 1975.**
xInternational Conference on Light Scattering in
Solids, 3rd.
Proceedings. Halsted Pr.

**International Conference on Light Scattering Spectra of
Solids, New York University, 1968.**
xInternational Conference on Light Scattering
Spectra of Solids, New York University, New
York, 1968.
Proceedings. Springer-Verlag.
International Conference on Man &
Computer-1st-Bordeaux-1970. *see* International
Conference on Man and Computer, Ist, Bordeaux,
1970.

**International Conference on Man and Computer, Ist,
Bordeaux, 1970.**
xInternational Conference on Man &
Computer-1st-Bordeaux-1970.
Man & Computer: Proceedings. S Karger.

**International Conference on Mechanisms of Salivary
Secretion and Their Regulation, 2nd, Birmingham,
Alabama, 1966.**
xInternational Conference On Mechanisms Of
Salivary Secretion And Their Regulation - 2nd -
Birmingham - Ala. - 1966.
Secretory Mechanisms of Salivary Glands.
Acad Pr.

**International Conference on Military Trials, London,
1945.**
xInternational Conference on Military Trials,
London, 1945.

Report of Robert H. Jackson, U.S.
Representative to the International
Conference on Military Trials, London, 1945.
AMS Pr.

**International Conference on Morphogenesis and
Malformations, 1st, Airlie House, 1974.**
xInternational Conference on Morphogenesis &
Malformation, 1st, Airlie House, Va., June 1974.
Morphogenesis & Malformation of Face &
Brain. A R Liss.

**International Conference on Neutrino Physics and
Astrophysics, 4th, Downington, Pa, 1974.**
xAIP Conference, Philadelphia 1974.
Neutrinos-1974: Proceedings. Am Inst Physics.

**International Conference on Nucleon Structure,
Stanford, California, 1963.**
xInternational Conference On Nucleon Structure -
Stanford University - 1963.
Nucleon Structure: Proceedings. Stanford U Pr.

**International Conference on Nuclidic Masses. 2d,
Vienna, 1963.**
xInternational Conference On Nuclidic Masses -
2nd - Vienna - 1963.
Proceedings. Springer-Verlag.

**International Conference on Number Theory, Moscow,
1971.**
xSteklov Institute of Mathematics, Academy of
Sciences, U S S R, Vol. 132.
International Conference on Number Theory:
Proceedings. Am Math.

**International Conference on Numerical Methods in
Fluid Dynamics, 4th, University of Colorado, 1974.**
xInternational Conference on Numerical Methods
in Fluid Dynamics, 4th, University of Colorado,
June 24-28, 1974.
Meningiomas Diagnostic & Therapeutic
Problems: Proceeding. Springer-Verlag.

**International Conference on Numerical Methods in
Fluid Dynamics,5th, Twente University of
Technology, 1976.**
xFifth Intl. Conference on Numerical Methods in
Fluid Dynamics.
Proceedings. Springer-Verlag.

**International Conference on Plant Growth Substances,
7th, Canberra, 1970.**
xInternational Conference on Plant Growth
Substances, 7th, Canberra, 1970.
Plant Growth Substances, 1970: Proceedings.
Springer-Verlag.

**International Conference on Polymer Processing,
Massachussetts Institute of Technology, 1977.**
xInternational Conference on Polymer Processing.
Science & Technology of Polymer Processing:
Proceedings. MIT Pr.

**International Conference on Pressure Vessel
Technology, San Antonio, 1973.**
xInternational Conference on Pressure Vessel
Technology, San Antonio, 2nd 1973.
Discussions, Pt. III. ASME.

**International Conference on Probability in Banach
Spaces, 1st, Oberwolfach, Germany, 1975.**
xInternational Conference on Probability in Banach
Spaces, First, Oberwolfach, July 20-26, 1975.
Probability in Banach Spaces: Proceedings.
Springer-Verlag.

**International Conference on Reactor Shielding, 5th,
Knoxville, Tennessee, 1977.**
xInternational Conference on Reactor Shielding,
5th.
Nuclear Reactor Shielding: Proceedings. Sci Pr.

**International Conference on Red Cell Metabolism and
Function, 3d, University of Michigan, 1974.**
xInternational Conference on Red Cell Metabolism
& Function, 3rd, Ann Arbor, Michigan, Oct.,
1974.
Erythrocyte Structure & Function: Proceedings.
A R Liss.

**International Conference on Selenodesy and Lunar
Topography, 2d, Manchester, England, 1966.**
xInternational Conference on Selenodesy & Lunar

Topograph,2nd,University of Manchester,England
May 30-June 4,1966.
Measure of the Moon: Proceedings. Kluwer
Boston.

**International Conference on Silicon Carbide, 3d, Miami
Beach, Fla. 1973.**
xConference on Silicon Carbide, 3rd, 1973.
Silicon Carbide: Proceedings. U of SC Pr.

**International Conference on Social Welfare, 18, San
Juan, Puerto Rico, 1976.**
xInternational Conference on Social Welfare, 18th,
San Juan, P.R.
International Council of Social Welfare: The
Struggle for Equal Opportunity: Proceedings.
Columbia U Pr.

**International Conference on Structure and Excitations
of Amorphous Solids, Williamsburg, Va., 1976.**
xAIP International Conf., Williamsburg, 1976.
Structure & Excitation of Amorphous Solids:
Proceedings. Am Inst Physics.

**International Conference on Super Novae, Lecce, Italy,
1973.**
xTheInternational Conference on Supernovae; May
7-11, 1973, Lecce, Italy.
Supernovae & Supernova Remnants:
Proceedings. Kluwer Boston.

International Conference on Tay-Sachs Disease -
Screening & Prevention, 1st, Palm Springs, Calif., Dec.
1975. *see* International Conference on Taysachs
Disease:, Screening and Prevention, 1st, Palm Springs,
California, 1975.

**International Conference on Taysachs Disease:,
Screening and Prevention, 1st, Palm Springs,
California, 1975.**
xInternational Conference on Tay-Sachs Disease -
Screening & Prevention, 1st, Palm Springs, Calif.,
Dec. 1975.
Tay-Sachs Disease - Screening & Prevention:
Papers. A R Liss.

**International Conference on Tetrahedrally Bonded
Amorphous Semiconductors, Yorktown Heights, N.Y.,
1974.**
xAIP Conference, Yorktown Heights.
Tetrahedrally Bonded Amorphous
Semiconductors: Proceedings. Am Inst
Physics.

**International Conference on the Biogenesis of
Mitochondria, Rosa Marina, Italy, 1973.**
xConference, Rosa Marni, Italy, June 1973.
The Biogenesis of Mitochondria:
Transcriptional,Translational & Genetic
Aspects, Proceedings. Acad Pr.

**International Conference on the Mediterranean Monk
Seal.**
xInternational Conference on the Mediterranean
Monk Seal, 1st, Rhodes, Greece, 1978.
The Mediterranean Monk Seal: Proceedings.
Pergamon.

International Conference on the Neurohypophysics.
xInternational Conference on the
Neurohypophysis, Key Biscayne, Fla., November
1976.
Proceedings. S Karger.

**International Conference on the Nuclear Optical Model,
Florida State University, 1959.**
xInternational Conference On The Nuclear Optical
Model.
Proceedings. U Presses Fla.

**International Conference on the Origin of Life, 4th,
Barcelona, 1973.**
xTheFourth International Conference on the Origin
of Life, 1973, Invited Papers & Contributed
Papers.
Cosmochemical Evolution & the Origins of
Life. Kluwer Boston.

**International Conference on the Physics of Electronic
and Atomic Collision, 9th, Seattle, 1975.**
xInternational Conference on the Physics of
Electronic & Atomic Collisions, No. 9.

Proceedings. U of Wash Pr.

**International Conference on the Theory of Groups,
Australian National University, 1965.**
xInternational Conference On Theory Of Groups -
Australian National University - 1965.
Theory of Groups. Gordon.

**International Conference on the Theory of Groups, 2d,
Australian National University, 1973.**
xInternational Conference on the Theory of
Groups, 2nd.
Proceedings. Springer-Verlag.

**International Conference on the Unity of the Sciences,
2d, Tokyo, 1973.**
xInternational Conference on the Unity of the
Sciences, 2nd, Tokyo, Nov. 18-21, 1973.
Modern Science & Moral Values: Proceedings.
ICF Pr.

**International Conference on the Unity of the Sciences,
3d, London, 1974.**
xInternational Conference on the Unity of the
Sciences, 3rd, London, Nov. 21-24 1974.
Science & Absolute Values: Proceedings. ICF
Pr.

**International Conference on the Unity of the Sciences,
4th, New York, 1975.**
xInternational Conference on the Unity of the
Sciences, 4th, New York, Nov. 27-30, 1975.
The Centrality of Science & Absolute Values:
Proceedings. ICF Pr.

**International Conference on the Use of Computers in
Radiation Therapy, 5th, Dartmouth College, 1974.**
xInternational Conference on the Use of
Computers in Radiation Therapy, Fifth,
Dartmouth College, 18-23 August 1974.
Computer Applications in Radiation Oncology:
Proceedings. U Pr of New Eng.

International Conference On Theory Of Groups -
Australian National University - 1965. *see*
International Conference on the Theory of Groups,
Australian National University, 1965.

**International Conference on Transfer of Water
Resources Knowledge, 1st, Colorado State University,
Fort Collins, 1972.**
xInternational Conference on Transfer of Water
Resources Knowledge. 1st, Colorado State Univ.,
Sep. 14-16, 1972.
Transfer of Water Resources Knowledge:
Proceedings. WRP.

**International Conference on Tropical Oceanography,
Miami Beach, Florida, 1965.**
xInternational Conference on Tropical
Oceanography, November 17-24, 1965, Miami
Beach, Florida.
Proceedings. U Miami Marine.

**International Conference on World Educational
Problems, Poughkeepsie, New York, 1961.**
xInternational Conference On World Educational
Problems.
Education in World Perspective. Arno.

**International Congress for Analytical Psychology, 5th,
London, 1971.**
xInternational Congress for Analytical Psychology,
5th.
Success & Failure in Analysis: Proceedings. C
G Jung Foun.

**International Congress for Hypnosis and Psychosomatic
Medicine, Paris, 1965.**
xInternational Congress for Hypnosis &
Psychosomatic Medicine, Paris, 1965.
Proceedings. Springer-Verlag.

**International Congress for Microbiology, 8th, Montreal,
1962.**
xInternational Congress for Microbiology,
Montreal, 8th, 1962.
Recent Progress in Microbiology. U of Toronto
Pr.

International Congress for Stereology.
xInternational Congress For Stereology - 2nd -
Chicago - 1967.

Proceedings. Springer-Verlag.

International Congress for Virology, 2d, Budapest, 1971.
xInternational Congress for Virology, 2nd,
Budapest, 1971.
Virology Two: Proceedings. S Karger.

**International Congress of Americanists, 29th, New York,
1949.**
xInternational Congress of Americanists - 29th.
Acculturation in the Americas. Cooper Sq.
Civilizations of Ancient America. Cooper Sq.
Indian Tribes of Aboriginal America. Cooper
Sq.

International Congress of Atomic Absorption & Atomic
Fluorescence Spectometry, 3rd. *see* International
Congress of Atomic Fluorescence Spectrometry, 3d,
Paris, 1971.

**International Congress of Atomic Fluorescence
Spectrometry, 3d, Paris, 1971.**
xInternational Congress of Atomic Absorption &
Atomic Fluorescence Spectometry, 3rd.
Proceedings. Halsted Pr.

**International Congress of Chemotherapy, 6th, Tokyo,
1969.**
xInternational Congress On Chemotherapy- 6th.
Progress in Antimicrobial & Anticancer
Chemotherapy: Proceedings. Univ Park.

**International Congress of Criminology, 6th, Madrid,
1970.**
xInternational Congress on Criminology, 6th,
Madrid, 1970.
Criminological Research Trends in Western
Germany: German Reports. Springer-Verlag.

**International Congress of Cybernetics and Systems,
University of Oxford, 1972.**
xEuropean Meeting, Vienna, 1972.
Advances in Cybernetics & Systems Research:
Proceedings. Hemisphere Pub.

International Congress of Ecology, 1st, the Hague, 1974.
xInternational Congress of Ecology, 1st, the
Hague, Netherlands, Sept. 1974.
Proceedings. Unipub.
Unifying Concept in Ecology: Proceedings.
Unipub.

**International Congress of Electroencephalography and
Clinical Neurophysiology, 6th, Vienna, 1965.**
xInternational Congress of Electroencephalography
and Clinical Neurophysiology, 6th - Vienna,
1967.
Recent Advances in Clinical Neurophysiology.
Elsevier.

**International Congress of Hedrologicum Conlegium, 3d,
Universtat Erlangen-Nurnberg, 1968.**
xInternational Congress of Hedrologicum
Conlegium, 3rd, Erlangen-Nuremberg Germany,
1968.
Progress in Proctology: Proceedings.
Springer-Verlag.

**International Congress of Internal Medicine, 12th, Tel
Aviv, 1974.**
xInternational Congress of Internal Medicine, 12th,
Tel Aviv, 1974.
Frontiers of Internal Medicine 1974:
Proceedings. S Karger.

International Congress of Nutrition, 9th, Mexico, 1972.
xInternational Congress of Nutrition, Mexico, Sept.
1972.
Proceedings. S Karger.

International Congress of Pediatric Dermatology.
xCongress of Pediatric Dermatology, 2nd, Mexico
City, October 20-23, 1976.
Pediatric Dermatology & Internal Medicine:
Internal Medicine & External Medicine,
Proceedings. S Karger.

**International Congress of Primatology, 5th, Nagoya,
Japan, 1974.**
xInternational Congress of Primatology, 5th,
Nagoya, Japan, August 21-24, 1974.

Contemporary Primatology: Proceedings. S Karger.

International Congress of Protozoology, 5th. *see* Delaware. Laws, Statutes. Etc.

International Congress of Psychosomatic Medicine in Obstetrics and Gynaecology, 3rd, London, 1971.

xInternational Congress of Psychosomatic Medicine in Obstetrics & Gynecology, 3rd, London, 1971.

Psychosomatic Medicine in Obstetrics & Gynecology: Proceedings. S Karger.

International Congress of Psychotherapy, 9th, Oslo, 1973.

xInternational Congress of Psychotherapy, 9th, Oslo, June 1973.

What Is Psychotherapy?: Proceedings. S Karger.

International Congress of Schools of Social Work, 17th, Nairobi, 1974.

xIntl Congress of Schools of Social Work, 17th, Nairobi, Kenya, July 1974.

Education for Social Change, Human Development & National Progress: Proceedings. Intl Assn Schools.

International Congress On Chemotherapy- 6th. *see* International Congress of Chemotherapy, 6th, Tokyo, 1969.

International Congress on Child Abuse and Neglect. 2nd, London, September 1978.

xInternaional Congress on Child Abuse & Neglect, 2nd, London, September 1978.

Selected Papers. Pergamon.

International Congress on Criminology, 6th, Madrid, 1970. *see* International Congress of Criminology, 6th, Madrid, 1970.

International Congress on Medicinal Plant Research, 1st, University of Munich, 1976.

xInternational Congress on Medicinal Plant Research, Section A, University of Munich, Germany, September 6-10, 1976.

New Natural Products & Plant Drugs with Pharmacological, Biological or Therapeutical Activity: Proceedings. Springer-Verlag.

International Congress on Pharmacology, 5th, San Francisco, 1972.

xInternational Congress on Pharmacology, 5th, San Francisco, 1972.

The Pharmacology of Thermoregulation: Proceedings of a Satellite Symposium. S Karger.

International Congress on Quantum Chemistry, 1st, Menton, 1973.

xFirst International Congress of Quantum Chemistry, Menton, France, July 4-10, 1973.

The World of Quantum Chemistry: Proceedings. Kluwer Boston.

International Congress on X-Ray Optics and Microanalysis, 5th, Tubingen, 1968.

xInternational Congress on X-Ray Optics & Microanalysis, 5th, 1968.

Proceedings. Springer-Verlag.

International Convocation in Immunology, 2nd, Buffalo, 1970. *see* International Convocation on Immunology, 2d, Buffalo, N.Y., 1970.

International Convocation on Immunology, 2d, Buffalo, N.Y., 1970.

xInternational Convocation in Immunology, 2nd, Buffalo, 1970.

Cellular Interactions in the Immune Response. S Karger.

International Convocation on Immunology, 3d, Buffalo, N.Y., 1972.

xInternational Convocation on Immunology, 3rd, Buffalo, 1972.

Specific Receptors of Antibodies, Antigens & Cells: Proceedings. S Karger.

International Convocation on Immunology, 4th, Buffalo, N.Y., 1974.

xInternational Convocation on Immunology, 4th, Buffalo, Jun 1974.

The Immune System & Infectious Diseases: Proceedings. S Karger.

International Co-Operative Alliance.

xInternational Co-Operative Alliance.

ed. Bibliographie cooperative internationale. AMS Pr.

International Council for Philosophy and Humanistic Studies.

xInternational Council for Philosophy & Humanistic Studies.

Marx & Contemporary Scientific Thought. Mouton.

The Third Reich. Fertig.

International Council for the Quality of Working Life.

xInternational Council for the Quality of Working Life.

Working on the Quality of Working Life. Kluwer Boston.

International Council of Scientific Unions. Committee on Data for Science and Technology.

xCommittee On Data For Science And Technology Of The International Council Of Scientific Unions.

International Compendium of Numerical Data Projects. Springer-Verlag.

International Council of Scientific Unions. Committee on Space Research.

xCommittee on Space Research, Seattle, Wash.

Space Research: Proceedings. Intl Pubns Serv.

International Council of Scientific Unions. Committee on Space Research, 11th Plenary Meeting, Tokyo, 1968.

xC O S P A R, 11th Plenary Meeting, Tokyo, 1968.

Life Sciences & Space Research: Proceedings. Humanities.

International Council of Scientific Unions. Committee on Space Research, 12th Plenary Meeting, Prague, 1969.

xC O S P A R, 12th Meeting, Prague, 1969.

Life Sciences & Space Research: Proceedings. Humanities.

International Council on Health, Physical Education and Recreation.

xInternational Council on Health, Physical Education & Recreation.

ICHPER Book of Worldwide Games & Dances. AAHPER.

International Council on Social Welfare.

xInternational Council on Social Welfare.

Development & Participation: Operational Implications for Social Welfare. Columbia U Pr.

International Cyclotron Conference, 6th, Vancouver, B.C.1972.

xAIP Conference, Univ. of British Columbia, Vancouver, 1972.

Cyclotrons 1972: Proceedings. Am Inst Physics.

International Dance Teachers' Association.

xIntl. Dance Teachers Assn.

Compiled by Ballroom Dancing for Beginners & Bronze Medalists. Soccer.

International Economic Association.

xInternational Economic Association.

Theory of Interest Rates: Proceedings. St Martin.

Theory of Wage Determination: Proceedings. St Martin.

International Economic Studies Institute.

xInternational Economic Studies Institute.

Raw Materials & Foreign Policy. Westview.

International Federation for Documentation.

xInternational Federation for Documentation.

Directories of Science Information Sources: International Bibliography. Intl Pubns Serv.

Scientific Conference Papers & Proceedings: Contents, Influence, Value, Availability. Unipub.

International Federation of Operation Research Societies.

xIFORS International Conference on Operational Research, 7th, Japan, 1975.

Operational Research '75: Proceedings. Elsevier.

International Film & Television Council (IFTC). *see* International Film and Television Council.

International Film and Television Council.

xInternational Film & Television Council (IFTC).

Cinematographic Institutions. Unipub.

International Fire Service Training Association.

xIFSTA Committee.

Essentials of Fire Fighting, IFSTA 200. Intl Fire Serv.

Fire Apparatus Practices. Intl Fire Serv.

Fire Apparatus Practices: 106. Intl Fire Serv.

The Fire Department Company Officer. Intl Fire Serv.

Fire Department Facilities, Planning & Procedures: 302. Intl Fire Serv.

The Fire Department Officer: 301. Intl Fire Serv.

Fire Prevention & Inspection, IFSTA 110. Intl Fire Serv.

Fire Service Ground Ladder Practices: 102. Intl Fire Serv.

Fire Service Instructor Training: 303. Intl Fire Serv.

Fire Service Orientation & Indoctrination: 202. Intl Fire Serv.

Fire Service Practices for Volunteer Fire Departments: I 201. Intl Fire Serv.

Fire Service Rescue & Protective Breathing Practices: 108. Intl Fire Serv.

Fire Service Training Programs: 203. Intl Fire Serv.

Fire Stream Practices. Intl Fire Serv.

Fire Stream Practices: 105. Intl Fire Serv.

Fire Ventilation Practices. Intl Fire Serv.

Fire Ventilation Practices: 107. Intl Fire Serv.

Firefighters Occupational Safety: 209. Intl Fire Serv.

Forcible Entry, Rope & Portable Extinguisher Practices. Intl Fire Serv.

Fundamental Principles of Mathematics Applied to the Fire Service: 401. Intl Fire Serv.

Fundamental Principles of Science Applied to the Fire Service: 402. Intl Fire Serv.

Ground Cover Fire Fighting Practices: 207. Intl Fire Serv.

Photography for the Fire Service: IFSTA 204. Intl Fire Serv.

Private Fire Protection & Detection Systems. Intl Fire Serv.

Records & Reports for the Fire Service. Intl Fire Serv.

Self-Instruction for IFSTA 200: Essentials of Fire Fighting. Intl Fire Serv.

Water Supplies for Fire Protection. Intl Fire Serv.

xIFSTA Committee Members.

Fire Hose Practices: 103. Intl Fire Serv.

Fire Problems in High Rise Buildings: 304. Intl Fire Serv.

International Gas Bearing Symposium, 6th, University of Southampton, 1974.

xSixth International Gas Bearing Symposium. Proceedings. BHRA Fluid.

International Geographical Congress, 22d, Montreal, 1972.

xInternational Geographical Congress, 22nd, Canada.

International Geography 1972: Papers. U of
Toronto Pr.

**International Geographical Union. Commission on
Quantitative Geography.**
xIgu Commission on Quantitative Geography,
Meeting, 1972.
Proceedings. McGill-Queens U Pr.

**International Geographical Union, Urbanization in
Europe.**
xEuropean Regional Conference of the
International Geographical Union, Budapest.
Urbanization in Europe: Proceedings. Intl
Pubns Serv.

International Glaucoma Symposium, Nara, Japan, 1978.
xInternational Glaucoma Symposium, Nara, Japan,
May 7-11, 1978.
Glaucoma Update: Proceedings.
Springer-Verlag.

**International IFIP Conference on Very Large Data
Bases.**
xIFIP Working Conference.
Very Large Data Bases: Proceedings. Elsevier.

International Information Center.
xInternational Irrigation Information Center, Bet
Dagan, Israel.
ed. Irrigation Equipment Manufacturers
Directory. Pergamon.

International Institute for Educational Planning.
xInternational Institute for Educational Planning.
Planning the Development of Univeristies - 4.
Unipub.

**International Institute for Environment and
Development.**
xInternational Institute for Environment &
Development (I.I.E.D.)
Human Settlements, an Annotated
Bibliography. Pergamon.
United Nations Conference on Human
Settlements, Vancouver, B. C., 1976: Human
Settlements, National Reports: Summaries &
Reference Guides. Pergamon.

International Institute for Strategic Studies.
xInternational Institute for Strategic Studies.
ed. The Military Balance, Nineteen
Seventy-Nine to Nineteen Eighty. Westview.
The Military Balance, 1975-1976. Westview.
The Military Balance, 1977-1978. Westview.
The Military Balance: 1978-1979. Westview.
ed. Stragetic Survey Nineteen Seventy-Eight.
Westview.
Strategic Survey 1975. Westview.
Strategic Survey 1976. Westview.

International Institute for Temporary Work.
xInternational Institute for Temporary Work.
Temporary Work in Modern Society. Kluwer
Boston.

**International Institute for the Unification of Private
Law.**
xInternational Institute for the Unification of
Private Law.
Digest of Legal Activities of International
Organizations & Other Institutions. Oceana.
New Directions in International Trade Law:
Acts & Proceedings of the Second
International Congress on Private Law.
Oceana.
Uniform Law Cases, 1959-1970. Oceana.

International Institute of Refrigeration.
xInternational Institute of Refrigeration.

Heat Transfer - Current Application of Air
Conditioning. Pergamon.
Low Temperatures & Electric Power.
Pergamon.
The New International Dictionary of
Refrigeration in English, French, Russian,
German, Italian, Spanish, & Norwegian.
Pergamon.
Progress in Refrigeration Science &
Technology, 11th Conference. Pergamon.

International Irrigation Information Center, Bet Dagan,
Israel. *see* International Information Center.

International Isa Power Instrumentation Symposium.
xPower Instrumentation Symposium, May 22-25,
1977, New Orleans.
Instrumentation in the Power Industry:
Proceedings. Instru Soc.

**International IUPAC Congress of Pesticide Chemistry, 2d,
Tel Aviv, 1971.**
xInternational IUPAC Congress-2nd.
Pesticide Chemistry: Proceedings. Gordon.

International IUPAC Congress-2nd. *see* International
Iupac Congress of Pesticide Chemistry, 2d, Tel Aviv,
1971.

**International Kant Congress, 3d, University of
Rochester, 1970.**
xInternational Kant Congress, 3rd, University of
Rochester, 1970.
Proceedings. Kluwer Boston.
xThird International Kant Congress.
Kant's Theory of Knowledge: Selected Papers.
Kluwer Boston.

International Kant Congress, 3rd, University of
Rochester, 1970. *see* International Kant Congress, 3d,
University of Rochester, 1970.

International Labour Office.
xInternational Labour Office.
Employment, Growth, & Basic Needs: A
One-World Problem. Praeger.
Family Living Studies: A Symposium.
Greenwood.
Man in His Working Environment. Intl Labour
Office.
New Forms of Work Organisation: German
Democratic Republic, India, Italy, USSR,
Economic Costs & Benefits. Intl Labour
Office.
Tasks to Jobs: Developing a Modular System
of Training for Hotel Occupations. Intl.
Labour Office.
xInternational Labour Office, Geneva.

Audiovisual, Draughting, Office, Reproduction
& Other Ancillary Equipment & Supplies:
Equipment Planning Guide for Vocational &
Technical Trading & Education Programmes.
Intl Labour Office.
Building Work: A Compendium of
Occupational Safety & Health. Intl Labour
Office.
Children at Work. Intl Labour Office.
Employment & Basic Needs in Portugal. Intl
Labour Office.
Employment: Outlook & Insights. A Collection
of Essays on Industrialised Market-Economy
Countries. Intl Labour Office.
Guide to Health & Hygiene in Agricultural
Work. Intl Labour Office.
Guidelines for the Development of
Employment & Manpower Information
Programmes in Developing Countries: A
Practical Manual. Intl Labour Office.
Labour Market Information in Asia: Present
Issues & Tasks for the Future. Report on
Two Workshops Conducted with the Support
of the Federal Republic of Germany. Intl
Labour Office.
Migrant Workers. Intl Labour Office.
Optimisation of the Working Environment:
New Trends. Intl Labour Office.
Profiles of Rural Poverty. Intl Labour Office.
Technical Guide, Nineteen Eighty: Consumer
Prices. Descriptions of Series Published in the
Bulletin of Labour Statistics. Intl Labour
Office.
Ten Years of Training: Developments in
France, Federal Republic of Germany &
United Kingdom, 1968-1978. Intl Labour
Office.
World Employment Programme, Seventh
Progress Report on Income Distribution &
Employment: A Progress Report on WEP
Research Undertaken Within the Framework
of the Income Distribution & Employment
Programme. Intl Labour Office.
Year Book of Labour Statistics,1979. Intl
Labour Office.

International Labor Organization.
xInternational Labour Organization.
Encyclopedia of Occupational Health.
McGraw.

International Labour Office, Geneva. *see* International
Labour Office.

International Labour Organization. *see* International
Labor Organization.

**International Magnus Huss Symposium, 1st, Stockholm,
Sweden, 1976.**
xInternational Magnus Huss Symposium, First,
Sweden, 1976.
Recent Advances in the Study of Alcoholism:
Proceedings. Elsevier.

**International Mathematical Conference, University of
Maryland, 1970.**
xInternational Mathematical Conference, College
Park, 1970.
Several Complex Variables 1: Proceedings.
Springer-Verlag.
Several Complex Variables 2: Proceedings.
Springer-Verlag.

**International Meeting on the Use of Computers in
Radiology, Brussels, 1969.**
xInternational Meeting on the Use of Computers in
Radiology, Brussels, 1969.
Computers in Radiology: Proceedings. S
Karger.

**International Mineral Processing Congress, 7th, New
York, 1964.**
xInternational Mineral Processing Congress - 7th -
1964.
Proceedings. Gordon.

International Missionary Council - Department of Social
& Economic Research & Council. *see* International

Missionary Council. Department of Social and
Economic Research and Counsel.

**International Missionary Council. Department of Social
and Economic Research and Counsel.**
xInternational Missionary Council - Department of
Social & Economic Research & Council.
Modern Industry & the African. Kelley.

International Monetary Fund.
xInternational Monetary Fund.
Government Finance Statistics Yearbook. Intl
Monetary.
xMembers of the Staff of the International
Monetary Fund.
The Monetary Approach to the Balance of
Payments: A Collection of Research Papers.
Intl Monetary.

**International Museum of Photography at George
Eastman House.**
xInternational Museum of Photography at George
Eastman House.
British Masters of the Albumen Print: A
Selection of Mid-Nineteenth Century
Victorian Photography. U of Chicago Pr.
Lewis Wickes Hine's Interpretative
Photography: The Six Early Projects. U of
Chicago Pr.

International Oil Tanker Terminal Safety Group.
xI. O. T. T. S. Group.
International Oil Tanker & Terminal Safety
Guide. Halsted Pr.

International Organization of Citrus Virologists, 2d.
xInternational Organization of Citrus Virologists,
2nd Conference.
Proceedings. U Presses Fla.

**International Pediatric Urological Seminar,
Philadelphia, 1976.**
xInternational Pediatric Urological Seminar, Phila.,
Pa., Apr. 1976.
Urinary System Malformations in Children:
Proceedings. A R Liss.

International Penal and Prison Commission.
xInternational Penal and Prison Commission.
Children's Courts in the United States. AMS
Pr.

**International Pigment Cell Conference. 4th, Houston,
Tex., 1957.**
xConference On The Biology Of Normal And
A-Typical Pigment Cell Growth - 4th - Houston
- Texas - 1957.
Pigment Cell Biology: Proceedings. Acad Pr.

International Pigment Cell Conference, 6th, Sofia, 1965.
xInternational Pigment Cell Conference - 6th.
Structure & Control of the Melanocyte:
Proceedings. Springer-Verlag.

**International Pigment Cell Conference, 8th, Sydney,
1972.**
xInternational Pigment Cell Conference, 8th,
Sydney, March, 1972.
Mechanisms in Pigmentation: Proceedings. S
Karger.

International Planned Parenthood Federation.
xInternational Planned Parenthood Federation.
Family Planning Handbook for Doctors. Intl
Pubns Serv.
Family Planning Handbook for Midwives &
Nurses. Intl Pubns Serv.
Population Seventy: Family Planning & Social
Change. Intl Pubns Serv.
Systemic Contraception. Intl Pubns Serv.

**International Porphyrin Meeting, 1st, Freiburg I.B.,
1975.**
xInternational Porphyrin Meeting, 1st, Freiburg,
Germany, May, 1975.
Porphyrin in Human Diseases: Proceedings. S
Karger.

International Press Institute.
xInternational Press Institute.

The Flow of the News. Arno.

International Protoplast Symposium.
xInternational Protoplast Symposium, 5th, July
1979, Szeged, Hungary.
Advances in Protoplast Research: Proceedings.
Pergamon.

International Radio & Television Society. see
International Radio and Television Society.

International Radio and Television Society.
xInternational Radio & Television Society.
Broadcasting: The Critical Challenges.
Hastings.

**International Research Conference of Proteinase
Inhibitors, 2nd, Grosse Ledder, 1973.**
xBayer Symposium, 5th - Proteinase Conference,
2nd, Cologne, Germany, 1973.
Proteinase Inhibitors: Proceedings.
Springer-Verlag.

**International Research Society for Children's
Literature.**
xFourth Symposium of the International Research
Society for Children's Literature, Held at the
University of Exeter, September 9-12, 1978.
Responses to Children's Literature:
Proceedings. K G Saur.

**International Sawmill Seminar, 2d, Jonkoping, Sweden,
1975.**
xInternational Sawmill Seminar, 2nd, Jonkopins,
Sweden June 1975.
Nordic & North American Sawmill
Techniques: Proceedings. Miller Freeman.

International Sawmill Seminar, 2nd, Jonkopins, Sweden
June 1975. see International Sawmill Seminar, 2d,
Jonkoping, Sweden, 1975.

International School on Electro & Photonuclear
Reactions, First Course, Erice, June 2-17, 1976. see
International School on Electro and Photonuclear
Reactions, Erice, Italy, 1976.

**International School on Electro and Photonuclear
Reactions, Erice, Italy, 1976.**
xInternational School on Electro & Photonuclear
Reactions, First Course, Erice, June 2-17, 1976.
International School on Electro & Photonuclear
Reactions I: Proceedings. Springer-Verlag.

International Seminar on Approval & Gathering Plans in
Large & Medium Size Academic Libraries, 3rd. see
International Seminar on Approval and Gathering
Plans in Large and Medium Size Academic Libraries,
3d, West Palm Beach, Fla., 1971.

**International Seminar on Approval and Gathering Plans
in Large and Medium Size Academic Libraries, 3d,
West Palm Beach, Fla., 1971.**
xInternational Seminar on Approval & Gathering
Plans in Large & Medium Size Academic
Libraries, 3rd.
Economics of Approval Plans: Proceedings.
Greenwood.

**International Seminar on Biomechanics, 3d, Rome,
1971.**
xInternational Seminar on Biomechanics, 3rd,
Rome, 1971.
Biomechanics 3: Proceedings. S Karger.

**International Seminar on Reproductive Physiology and
Sexual Endocrinology, 2d, Brussels, 1968.**
xInternational Seminar on Reproductive Physiology
& Sexual Endrocrinology, 2nd, Brussels, 1968.
Ovo-Implantation, Human Gonadotropines &
Prolactin. S Karger.

**International Seminar on Reproductive Physiology and
Sexual Endocrinology, 3d, Brussels, 1970.**
xInternational Seminar on Reproductive Physiology
& Sexual Endocrinology, 3rd, Brussels, 1970.
Basic Actions of Sex Steroids on Target
Organs: Proceedings. S Karger.

**International Seminar on Reproductive Physiology and
Sexual Endocrinology, 4th, Brussels, 1972.**
xInternational Seminar on Reproductive Physiology
& Sexual Endocrinology, 4th, Brussels, May
1972.

Hormones & Antagonists: Proceedings. S
Karger.

**International Seminar on Reproductive Physiology and
Sexual Endocrinology, 5th, Brussels, Belgium, 1975.**
xInternational Seminar on Reproductive Physiology
& Sexual Endocrinology, 5th, Brussels, May,
1975.
Sperm Action: Proceedings. S Karger.

**International Seminar on Reproductive Physiology and
Sexual Endocrinology, 6th, Brussels, 1976.**
xInternational Seminar on Reproductive Physiology
& Sexual Endocrinology, 6th, Brussels,
May-June, 1976.
Clinical Reproductive Neuroendocrinology:
Proceedings. S Karger.

**International Seminar on Trends in Mathematical
Modelling, Venice, 1971.**
xInternational Seminar on Trends in Mathematical
Modelling, Venice, Dec. 1971.
Proceedings. Springer-Verlag.

**International Seminar on Vocational Rehabilitation for
Mentally Retarded Persons.**
xInternational Seminar on Vocational
Rehabilitation for Mentally Retarded Persons,
2nd.
Proceedings. Am Assn Mental.

**International Shock Tube Symposium, 7th, University of
Toronto, 1969.**
xInternational Shock Tube Symposium - 7th.
Shock Tubes: Proceedings. U of Toronto Pr.

**International Shock Tube Symposium, 9th, Stanford
University, 1973.**
xInternational Shock Tube Symposium, 9th,
Stanford Univ., 1973.
Recent Developments in Shock Tube Research:
Proceedings. Stanford U Pr.

International Society for Cell Biology.
xInternational Society For Cell Biology.
Cellular Dynamics of the Neuron. Acad Pr.
Control Mechanisms in the Expression of
Cellular Phenotypes. Acad Pr.
Cytogenetics of Cells in Culture. Acad Pr.
Differentiation & Immunology. Acad Pr.
Formation & Fate of Cell Organelles. Acad Pr.
Intracellular Transport. Acad Pr.
Use of Radioautography in Investigating
Protein Synthesis. Acad Pr.

**International Society for the Study of Behavioral
Development.**
xSymposium of the International Society for the
Study of Behavioral Development, University of
Nijmegen, the Netherlands, July, 1971.
Determinants of Behavioral Development.
Acad Pr.

International Society of Psychoneuroendocrinology.
xConference of the Int. Society for
Psychoneuroendocrinology, Mieken, Sep, 1973.
Psychoneuroendocrinology: Proceedings. S
Karger.
xSymposium of the International Society of
Psychoneuroendocrinology Visgrad, Hungary,
Dec. 1975.
Celular & Molecular Bases of Neuroendoctrine
Processes: Proceedings. Intl Pubns Serv.

International Solar Energy Society.
xInternational Solar Energy Society.
International Solar Energy Congress:
Proceedings Held May 28 to June 1,1979,
Atlanta, Georgia. Pergamon.

**International Spring School on Crystal Growth, 2d, Fuji
View Hotel, 1974.**
xInternational Spring School on Crystal Growth,
2nd, Japan, 1974.
Crystal Growth & Characterization:
Proceedings. Elsevier.

International Studies Conference, 10th, Paris, 1937.
xInternational Studies Conference, 10th.

International Workshop on Dynamic Aspects of
Cerebral Edema, 3rd, Montreal, Quebec, 1976.
   xDynamic Aspects of Cerebral Edema
     International Workshop, 3rd, Montreal June
     25-9, 1976.
      Dynamics of Brain Edema: Proceedings.
      Springer-Verlag.
International Workshop on HBS Antigen Subtypes, 1st,
Paris, April 1975. see International Workshop on Thr
Hbs Antigen Subtypes, Centre National De
Transfusion Sanguine, 1975.
International Workshop on Human Gene Mapping, 3rd,
Baltimore, 1975.
   xBaltimore Conference, 1975.
     Human Gene Mapping 3: Proceedings. S
     Karger.
International Workshop on Morphogenesis and
Malformation.
   xInternational Workshop on Morphogenesis &
     Malformation, 4th, Grand Canyon, Ariz., 1977.
     Morphogenesis & Malformation of the
     Cardiovascular System: Proceedings. A R
     Liss.
International Workshop on The Hbs Antigen Subtypes,
Centre National De Transfusion Sanguine, 1975.
   xInternational Workshop on HBS Antigen
     Subtypes, 1st, Paris, April 1975.
     HBS Antigen Subtypes: Proceedings. S Karger.
International Workshop, Zurich, September 15-17, 1976.
see International Workshop on Behavioral Effects of
Nicotine, Zurich, 1976.
Internationale Universitatswochen Fuer Kernphysik der
Karl-Franzens-Universitat Graz, 14th, Schladming,
Austria, 1975.
   xFourteen International Universitaetswochen Fuer
     Kernphysik 1975 der Karlfranzens-Universitaet at
     Schladming.
     Electromagnetic Interactions & Field Theory:
     Proceedings. Springer-Verlag.
Intl City Management Assn. see International City
Management Association.
Intl Congress of Schools of Social Work, 17th, Nairobi,
Kenya, July 1974. see International Congress of
Schools of Social Work, 17th, Nairobi, 1974.
Intl. Dance Teachers Assn. see International Dance
Teachers' Association.
Intl. Summer Inst. on Theoretical Physics, Bonn, 1974.
see International Summer Institute on Theoretical
Physics, 6th, Bonn, 1974.
Intravaia, Lawrence. see Intravaia, Lawrence J.
Intravaia, Lawrence J.
   xIntravaia, Lawrence.
     Building a Superior School Band Library. P-H.
Intriligator, Michael D.
   xIntriligator, Michael D.
     Econometric Models, Techniques &
     Applications. P-H.
     Mathematical Optimization & Economic
     Theory. P-H.
Iocolano, Mark.
   xIocolano, Mark.
     Nikon FM & FE. Amphoto.
Ionesco, Eugene.
   xIonesco, Eugene.
     Fragments of a Journal. Grove.
Ionescu, Ghita.
   xIonescu, Ghita.
     Communism in Rumania, 1944-1962.
     Greenwood.
Ionescu Tulcea, A.
   xIonescu Tulcea, A.
     Topics in the Theory of Lifting.
     Springer-Verlag.
   xIonescu Tulcea, C.
     jt. auth. Topics in the Theory of Lifting.
     Springer-Verlag.
Ionescu Tulcea, C. see Ionescu Tulcea, A.
Ionin, B. I.
   xIonin, B. I.

NMR Spectroscopy in Organic Chemistry.
Plenum Pub.
Iordan, Iorgu, 1888-
   xIordan, Iorgu.
     Introduction to Romance Linguistics, Its
     Schools & Scholars. Greenwood.
Iorio, James.
   xIorio, James.
     Fifth Season. Golden Quill.
     Silence Interrupted. Golden Quill.
Iosifescu, Marius.
   xIosifescu, Marius.
     Random Processes & Learning.
     Springer-Verlag.
Iowa Child Welfare Research Station, State University of
Iowa. see Iowa. University. Child Welfare Research
Station.
Iowa. Home Economics Association.
   xIowa Home Economics Association.
     Unit Method of Clothing Construction. Iowa St
     U Pr.
Iowa. State Department of Health.
   xDietary Consultants of the Iowa State
     Department of Health.
     Simplified Diet Manual Study Guide. Iowa St
     U Pr.
Iowa. State Historical Society.
   xIowa State Historical Society.
     Documentary Material Relating to the History
     of Iowa. AMS Pr.
Iowa State University - Center For Agricultural And
Economic Development. see Iowa. State University of
Science and Technology, Ames. Center for
Agricultural and Economic Development.
Iowa State University Center for Agricultural and
Economic Development. see Iowa. State University of
Science and Technology, Ames. Center for
Agricultural and Economic Development.
Iowa State University of Science & Technology Center
for Agricultural & Economic Adjustment. see Iowa.
State University of Science and Technology, Ames.
Center for Agricultural and Economic Development.
Iowa. State University of Science and Technology,
Ames. Center for Agricultural and Economic
Development.
   xIowa State University - Center For Agricultural
     And Economic Development.
     Adjustments in Agriculture - a National
     Basebook. Iowa St U Pr.
     Alternatives for Balancing World Food
     Production & Needs. Iowa St U Pr.
     Economic Development of Agriculture. Iowa St
     U Pr.
     Family Mobility in Our Dynamic Society. Iowa
     St U Pr.
     Farm Goals in Conflict. Iowa St U Pr.
     Farmers in the Market Economy. Iowa St U
     Pr.
     Food Goals, Future Structural Changes &
     Agricultural Policy: A National Basebook.
     Iowa St U Pr.
     Research & Education for Regional & Area
     Development. Iowa St U Pr.
   xIowa State University Center for Agricultural and
     Economic Development.
     North American Common Market. Iowa St U
     Pr.
   xIowa State University of Science & Technology
     Center for Agricultural & Economic Adjustment.
     Labor Mobility & Population in Agriculture.
     Greenwood.
   xIowa State University-Center For Agricultural
     And Economic Development.
     Our Changing Rural Society. Iowa St U Pr.
Iowa State University-Center For Agricultural And
Economic Development. see Iowa. State University of
Science and Technology, Ames. Center for
Agricultural and Economic Development.

Iowa. University. Child Welfare Research Station.
   xIowa Child Welfare Research Station, State
     University of Iowa.
     Fortieth Anniversary of the Iowa Child Welfare
     Research Station, 1917-1957. Kraus Repr.
Iowa. University Hospitals. Dept. of Nutrition.
   xUniversity of Iowa Hospitals & Clinic Staff.
     Recent Advances in Therapeutic Diets. Iowa St
     U Pr.
Iparraguirre, Ignacio.
   xIparraguirre, Ignacio.
     Contemporary Trends in Studies on the
     Constitutions of the Society of Jesus:
     Annotated Bibliographical Orientations. Inst
     Jesuit.
Ipcar, Dahlov. see Ipcar, Dahlov Zorach.
Ipcar, Dahlov Zorach, 1917-
   xIpcar, Dahlov.
     illus. Bug City. Holiday.
     A Dark Horn Blowing. Penguin.
     A Dark Horn Blowing. Viking Pr.
Ipcar, Dahloy.
   xIpcar, Dahlov.
     illus. Bright Barnyard. Knopf.
Ippolito, D. S. see Ippolito, Dennis S.
Ippolito, Dennis S.
   xIppolito, D. S.
     The Budget & National Politics. W H Freeman.
     Public Opinion & Responsible Democracy.
     P-H.
   xIppolito, Dennis S.
     Political Parties: Interest Groups & Public
     Policy: Group Influence in American Politics.
     P-H.
Ipswitch, Elaine.
   xIpswitch, Elaine.
     Scott Was Here. Delacorte.
Iqbal, Afzal.
   xIqbal, Afzal.
     The Prophet's Diplomacy: The Art of
     Negotiation As Conceived & Developed by
     the Prophet of Islam. C Stark.
Irby, William B., 1913-
   xIrby, William B.
     ed. Current Advances in Oral Surgery. Mosby.
     ed. Facial Trauma & Concomitant Problems -
     Evaluation & Treatment. Mosby.
     Facial Trauma & Concomitant Problems:
     Evaluation & Treatment. Mosby.
Iredale, O. see Iredale, Queenie.
Iredale, Queenie.
   xIredale, O.
     Thomas Traherne. Folcroft.
   xR. D. Cortina Company.
     Conversational French in Twenty Lessons.
     Har-Row.
Ireland, Bernard.
   xIreland, Bernard.
     Warships of the World: Escort Vessels.
     Scribner.
Ireland, David.
   xIreland, David.
     Letters to an Unborn Child. Har-Row.
Ireland, Gordon, 1880-
   xIreland, Gordon.
     Boundaries, Possessions & Conflicts in Central
     & North America & the Caribbean. Octagon.
Ireland, Norma (Olin).
   xIreland, Norma O.
     Index to Full-Length Plays: 1944-1964. Faxon.
     An Index to Skits & Stunts. Faxon.
Ireland, Norma O. see Ireland, Norma (Olin).
Ireland, Norma Olin, 1907-
   xIreland, Norma O.
     The Pamphlet File in School, College & Public
     Libraries. Faxon.
Ireland, Patrick J. see Ireland, Patrick John.
Ireland, Patrick John.
   xIreland, Patrick J.

Drawing & Designing Children's & Teenage
Fashions. Halsted Pr.
Drawing & Designing Menswear. Halsted Pr.
Ireland, Robert M.
xIreland, Robert M.
The County Courts in Antebellum Kentucky. U
Pr of Ky.
The County in Kentucky History. U Pr of Ky.
Little Kingdoms: The Counties of Kentucky,
1850-1891. U Pr of Ky.
Ireland, Thomas R., 1942-
xIreland, Thomas R.
Monetarism: How the Financial Crisis Can
Help You Make Money in the Stock Market.
Arlington Hse.
Iremonger, Valentin.
xIremonger, Valentin.
Horan's Field & Other Reservations.
Humanities.
Ireson, Amy G.
xIreson, Amy G.
Cooking for One or Two-or More. HM.
Foods for One or Two--or More. HM.
Ireson, Barbara.
xIreson, Barbara.
ed. April Witch & Other Strange Tales.
Scribner.
The Barnes Book of Nursery Verse. A S
Barnes.
Cottage Crafts. Transatlantic.
Ireson, W. Grant. see Ireson, William Grant.
Ireson, William Grant.
xIreson, W. Grant.
ed. Handbook of Industrial Engineering &
Management. P-H.
Ireys, Alice R. see Ireys, Alice Recknagel.
Ireys, Alice Recknagel.
xIreys, Alice R.
How to Plan & Plant Your Own Property.
Morrow.
Ircys, Katharine.
xIreys, Katharine.
Encyclopedia of Canvas Embroidery Stitch
Patterns. T Y Crowell.
Finishing & Mounting Your Needlepoint
Pieces. T Y Crowell.
Irgolic, K. see Irgolic, Kurt J.
Irgolic, Kurt J.
xIrgolic, K.
Organic Chemistry of Tellurium. Gordon.
Iribarne, J. V. see Iribarne, Julio Victor.
Iribarne, Julio Victor.
xIribarne, J. V.
Atmospheric Thermodynamics. Kluwer Boston.
Irion, Clyde.
xIrion, Clyde.
Profit & Loss of Dying. De Vorss.
Irion, Paul E.
xIrion, Paul E.
The Funeral: Vestige or Value?. Arno.
Irion, Ruth H. see Irion, Ruth Hershey.
Irion, Ruth Hershey.
xIrion, Ruth H.
The Christmas Cookie Tree. Westminster.
Irish, Donald P. see Irish, Donald Paul.
Irish, Donald Paul.
xIrish, Donald P.
ed. Multinational Corporations in Latin
America: Private Rights & Public
Responsibilities. Ohio U Ctr Intl.
Irish, Jerry A., 1936-
xIrish, Jerry A.
A Boy Thirteen: Reflections on Death.
Westminster.
Irish, Marian D. see Irish, Marian Doris.
Irish, Marian Doris.
xIrish, Marian D.
The Politics of American Democracy. P-H.
xIrish, Marion D.

Introduction to Comparative Politics: Thirteen
Nation States. P-H.
Politics of American Democracy. P-H.
Irish, Marion D. see Irish, Marian Doris.
Irish, Richard K.
xIrish, Richard K.
Go Hire Yourself an Employer. Doubleday.
Irish, Wynot R.
xIrish, Wynot R.
ed. The Modern American Muse: A Complete
Bibliography of American Verse, 1900-1925.
Ultramarine Pub.
Iriye, Adira. see Iriye, Akira.
Iriye, Akira.
xIriye, Adira.
The World of Asia. Forum Pr MO.
xIriye, Akira.
Across the Pacific: An Inner History of
American-East Asian Relations. HarBraceJ.
After Imperialism: The Search for a New
Order in the Far East, 1921-1931. Atheneum.
ed. The Chinese & the Japanese: Essays in
Political & Cultural Interactions. Princeton U
Pr.
Irizarry, Estelle.
xIrizarry, Estelle.
Francisco Ayala. Twayne.
Irland, Lloyd C.
xIrland, Lloyd C.
Wilderness Economics & Policy. Lexington
Bks.
Irmscher, W. F. see Irmscher, William F.
Irmscher, William F.
xIrmscher, W. F.
The Holt Guide to English: A Contemporary
Handbook of Rhetoric, Language &
Literature. HR&W.
xIrmscher, William F.
Teaching Expository Writing. HR&W.
Iroh, Eddie.
xIroh, Eddie.
Toads of War. Heinemann Ed.
Ironmonger, Elizabeth. see Ironmonger, Elizabeth
(Hogg).
Ironmonger, Elizabeth (Hogg), 1891-
xIronmonger, Elizabeth.
Hogg Family of York & Gloucester Counties,
Va.. Va Bk.
Irons, Bruce.
xIrons, Bruce.
Techniques of Finite Elements. Halsted Pr.
Irons, Patricia. see Irons, Patricia Duggan.
Irons, Patricia Duggan.
xIrons, Patricia.
Psychotropic Drugs & Nursing Intervention.
McGraw.
Ironside, H. A. see Ironside, Henry Allan.
Ironside, Henry Allan, 1876-1951
xIronside, H. A.
Holiness: The False & the True. Loizeaux.
Irschick, Eugene F.
xIrschick, Eugene F.
Politics & Social Conflict in South India: The
Non-Brahman Movement & Tamil
Separatism, 1916-1929. U of Cal Pr.
Irvin, George.
xIrvin, George.
Modern Cost-Benefit Methods: An
Introduction to Financial, Economic & Social
Appraisal of Development Projects. B&N.
Irvin, Helen D. see Irvin, Helen Deiss.
Irvin, Helen Deiss.
xIrvin, Helen D.
Women in Kentucky. U Pr of Ky.
Irvine, Betty J. see Irvine, Betty Jo.
Irvine, Betty Jo.
xIrvine, Betty J.

Slide Libraries: A Guide for Academic
Institutions, Museums, & Special Collections.
Libs Unl.
Irvine, J. M. see Irvine, John Maxwell.
Irvine, John Maxwell.
xIrvine, J. M.
Neutron Stars. Oxford U Pr.
Irvine, R. R.
xIrvine, R. R.
Horizontal Hold. Popular Lib.
Irvine, S. H.
xIrvine, S. H.
ed. Cultural Adaptation Within Modern Africa.
Tchrs Coll.
Human Behavior in Africa: A Bibliography of
Psychological & Related Writings.
Greenwood.
Irvine, William, 1840-1911
xIrvine, William.
Army of the Indian Moghuls: Its Organization
& Administration. Verry.
Irvine, William D., 1944-
xIrvine, William D.
French Conservatism in Crisis: The Republican
Federation of France in the 1930s. La State
U Pr.
Irving, Brian.
xIrving, Brian.
Guyana: A Composite Monograph. Inter Am U
Pr.
Irving, David. see Irving, David John Cawdell.
Irving, David John Cawdell, 1938-
xIrving, David.
Hitler's War. Viking Pr.
Irving, Edward.
xIrving, Edward.
Paleomagnetism & Its Application to
Geological & Geophysical Problems. Krieger.
Irving, Hancock.
xIrving, Hancock.
Money Begets Money: A Guide to Personal
Finance. Money Digest.
Irving, Henry, Sir, 1838-1905
xIrving, Henry.
Drama: Addresses. Arno.
Irving, John, 1942-
xIrving, John.
The World According to Garp. Dutton.

The World According to Garp. PB.

Irving, John B. see Irving, John Beaufain.
Irving, John Beaufain, 1800-1881
xIrving, John B.
The South Carolina Jockey Club. Reprint.
Irving, L. see Irving, Laurence.
Irving, Laurence, 1895-
xIrving, L.
Arctic Life of Birds & Mammals Including
Man. Springer-Verlag.

Irving, Robert M. see Irving, Robert Mccardle.

Irving, Robert McCardle, 1930-

xIrving, Robert M.

Readings in Canadian Geography. HR&W.
Irving, Theodore, 1809-1880
xIrving, Theodore.
Conquest of Florida Under Hernando De Soto.
Island Pr.
Irving, Washington.

xIrving, Washington.

Adventures of Captain Bonneville. Binford.
The Adventures of Captain Bonneville.
    Twayne.
Astoria. Binford.
Astoria. Gordon Pr.
Bracebridge Hall. AMS Pr.
Bracebridge Hall. Sleepy Hollow.
A History of New York. Coll & U Pr.
A History of New York from the Beginning of
    the World to the End of the Dutch Dynasty.
    Somerset Pub.
Journal of Washington Irving, 1823-1824. Shoe
    String.
The Legend of Sleepy Hollow. Andor Pub.
Letters from Sunnyside & Spain. Arden Lib.
Letters from Sunnyside & Spain. Elliots Bks.
Letters from Sunnyside & Spain. Folcroft.
The Life & Voyages of Christopher Columbus.
    AMS Pr.
Life of George Washington. Sleepy Hollow.
Old Christmas. Mayflower Bks.
Old Christmas. Sleepy Hollow.
Rip Van Winkle & the Legend of Sleepy
    Hollow. Mayflower Bks.
Rip Van Winkle & the Legend of Sleepy
    Hollow. Macmillan.
Rip Van Winkle & the Legend of Sleepy
    Hollow. Sleepy Hollow.
Spanish Papers. Core Collection.
Tales of a Traveller. Arno.
The Wit & Whimsy of Washington Irving.
    Sleepy Hollow.
    ed. Wolfert's Roost. Twayne.
Works. Scholarly.
Irving, William H. see Irving, William Henry.
Irving, William Henry.
    xIrving, William H.
    The Providence of Wit in English Letter
        Writers. Octagon.
Irwin, Ann.
    xIrwin, Ann.
    Moon of the Red Strawberry. Aurora Pubs.
Irwin, Francis W. see Irwin, Francis William.
Irwin, Francis William.
    xIrwin, Francis W.
    Intentional Behavior & Motivation: A
        Cognitive Theory. Lippincott.
Irwin, Godfrey.
    xIrwin, Godfrey.
    American Tramp & Underworld Slang. Gale.
Irwin, Graham W.
    xIrwin, Graham W.
    ed. Africans Abroad: A Documentary History
        of the Black Diaspora in Asia, Latin
        America, and the Caribbean in the Age of
        Slavery. Columbia U Pr.
Irwin, H. J. see Irwin, Harvey J.
Irwin, Hadley.
    xIrwin, Hadley.
    Bring to a Boil & Separate. Atheneum.
    The Lilith Summer. Feminist Pr.
Irwin, Harvey J.
    xIrwin, H. J.
    PSI & the Mind: An Information Processing
        Approach. Scarecrow.
Irwin, Inez H. see Irwin, Inez Haynes.
Irwin, Inez Haynes, 1873-1970
    xIrwin, Inez H.
    Angels & Amazons: A Hundred Years of
        American Women. Arno.
    Angels & Amazons: A Hundred Years of
        American Women. Norwood Edns.
Irwin, J. see Irwin, John V.
Irwin, J. David.
    xIrwin, J. David.
    Industrial Noise & Vibration Control. P-H.
Irwin, James R. see Irwin, James Ross.
Irwin, James Ross, 1918-
    xIrwin, James R.

A Ghetto Principal Speaks Out: A Decade of
    Crisis in Urban Public Schools. Wayne St U
    Pr.
Irwin, John, 1929-
    xIrwin, John.
    Felon. P-H.
Irwin, John. see Irwin, John L.
Irwin, John L., 1942-
    xIrwin, John.
    Modern Britain: An Introduction. Allen Unwin.
    Modern Britain: An Introduction. Shoe String.
Irwin, John V.
    xIrwin, J.
    Principles of Childhood Language Disabilities.
        P-H.
Irwin, Kevin W.
    xIrwin, Kevin W.
    A Celebrant's Guide to the New Sacramentary:
        A Cycle. Pueblo Pub Co.
Irwin, Leonard B. see Irwin, Leonard Bertram.
Irwin, Leonard Bertram, 1904-
    xIrwin, Leonard B.
    Pacific Railways & Nationalism in the
        Canadian American Northwest, 1845-1873.
        Greenwood.
Irwin, Mabel M. see Irwin, Mabel MacCoy.
Irwin, Mabel MacCoy.
    xIrwin, Mabel M.
    Whitman, the Poet-Liberator of Woman.
        Folcroft.
Irwin, Mary.
    xIrwin, Mary.
    The Moon Is Not Enough. Zondervan.
Irwin, Mary L. see Irwin, Mary Leslie.
Irwin, Mary Leslie.
    xIrwin, Mary L.
    Anthony Trollope: A Bibliography. B. Franklin.
Irwin, Michael.
    xIrwin, Michael.
    Picturing: Description & Illusion in the
        Nineteenth Century Novel. Allen Unwin.
Irwin, Orvis C., 1891-
    xIrwin, Orvis C.
    Communication Variables of Cerebral Palsied &
        Mentally Retarded Children. C C Thomas.
Irwin, Richard G. see Irwin, Richard Gregg.
Irwin, Richard Gregg, 1909-
    xIrwin, Richard G.
    Evolution of a Chinese Novel: Shui-Hu-Chuan.
        Harvard U Pr.
Irwin, Robert, 1941-
    xIrwin, Robert.
    How to Buy a Home at a Reasonable Price.
        McGraw.
    How to Buy & Sell Real Estate for Financial
        Security. McGraw.
    Protect Yourself in Real Estate. McGraw.
    The Real Estate Agent's & Investor's Tax
        Book. McGraw.
Irwin, Ruth (Beckey).
    xIrwin, Ruth B.
    Speech & Hearing Therapy. Stanwix.
Irwin, Ruth B. see Irwin, Ruth (Beckey).
Irwin, Stevens.
    xIrwin, Stevens.
    Dictionary of Pipe Organ Stops. Schirmer Bks.
Irwin, Terence.
    xIrwin, Terence.
    Plato's Moral Theory: The Early & Middle
        Dialogues. Oxford U Pr.
Irwin, W. R. see Irwin, William Robert.
Irwin, Wallace, 1876-1959
    xIrwin, Wallace.
    Letters of a Japanese Schoolboy. Irvington.
    Seed of the Sun. Arno.
Irwin, Will. see Irwin, William Henry.
Irwin, William H. see Irwin, William Henry.
Irwin, William Henry, 1873-1948
    xIrwin, Will.

House That Shadows Built. Arno.
    xIrwin, William H.
    Propaganda & the News: Or, What Makes You
        Think So. Johnson Repr.
Irwin, William Robert, 1915-
    xIrwin, W. R.
    The Game of the Impossible: A Rhetoric of
        Fantasy. U of Ill Pr.
Isaac, Glynn. see Isaac, Glynn L.
Isaac, Glynn L.
    xIsaac, Glynn.
    Intro. by Human Ancestors: Readings from
        Scientific American. W H Freeman.
    xIsaac, Glynn L.
    Olorgesailie: Archeological Studies of a Middle
        Pleistocene Lake Basin in Kenya. U of
        Chicago Pr.
Isaac, Godfrey.
    xIsaac, Godfrey.
    I'll See You in Court. Contemp Bks.
Isaac, Paul E.
    xIsaac, Paul E.
    Prohibition & Politics: Turbulent Decades in
        Tennessee, 1885-1920. U of Tenn Pr.
Isaacs, A. D. see Isaacs, Anthony Donald.
Isaacs, Abram S. see Isaacs, Abram Samuel.
Isaacs, Abram Samuel, 1852-1920
    xIsaacs, Abram S.
    Stories from the Rabbis. Arno.
    Stories from the Rabbis. Darby Bks.
    Stories from the Rabbis. Havertown Bks.
Isaacs, Anthony Donald.
    xIsaacs, A. D.
    Studies in Geriatric Psychiatry. Wiley.
Isaacs, Edith J. see Isaacs, Edith Juliet (Rich).
Isaacs, Edith Juliet (Rich), 1878-1956
    xIsaacs, Edith J.
    ed. Theatre: Essays on the Arts of the Theatre.
        Arno.
Isaacs, Elizabeth, 1917-
    xIsaacs, Elizabeth.
    An Introduction to the Poetry of Yvor Winters.
        Swallow.
Isaacs, Elizabeth. see Isaacs, Emily Elizabeth.
Isaacs, Emily Elizabeth, 1917-
    xIsaacs, Elizabeth.
    Introduction to Robert Frost. Haskell.
Isaacs, Harold R. see Isaacs, Harold Robert.
Isaacs, Harold Robert, 1910-
    xIsaacs, Harold R.
    Power & Identity: Tribalism in World Politics.
        Foreign Policy.
Isaacs, J. see Isaacs, Jacob.
Isaacs, Jacob, 1896-
    xIsaacs, J.
    Production & Stage Management at the
        Blackfriars Theatre. Folcroft.
    xIsaacs, Jacob.
    Background of Modern Poetry. Dutton.
Isaacs, Jorge, 1837-1895
    xIsaacs, Jorge.
    Maria: A South American Romance. Gordon
        Pr.
Isaacs, Ken.
    xIsaacs, Ken.
    How to Build Your Own Living Structures.
        Crown.
Isaacs, Nathan, 1895-1966
    xIsaacs, Nathan.
    Brief Introduction to Piaget. Agathon.
    A Brief Introduction to Piaget. Schocken.
Isaacs, Neil. see Isaacs, Neil S.
Isaacs, Neil D. see Isaacs, Neil David.
Isaacs, Neil David, 1931-
    xIsaacs, Neil D.
    Structural Principles in Old English Poetry. U
        of Tenn Pr.
Isaacs, Neil S., 1934-
    xIsaacs, Neil.

Reactive Intermediates in Organic Chemistry.
Wiley.
Isaacs, Susan, 1943-
xIsaacs, Susan.
Compromising Positions. Times Bks.
The Inner Parent: Raising Ourselves, Raising
Our Children. HarBraceJ.
Isaacs, Susan. *see* Isaacs, Susan Sutherland Fairhurst.
Isaacs, Susan Sutherland Fairhurst, 1885-1948
xIsaacs, Susan.
Troubles of Children & Parents. Schocken.
Isaacson, Ben.
xIsaacson, Ben.
Dictionary of the Jewish Religion. Bantam.
Dictionary of the Jewish Religion. SBS Pub.
Isaacson, Eugene.
xIsaacson, Eugene.
The Analysis of Numerical Methods. Wiley.
Isaacson, Knight.
xIsaacson, Knight.
The Store. Walker & Co.
Isaacson, Lee E.
xIsaacson, Lee E.
Career Information in Counseling & Teaching.
Allyn.
Isaacson, Robert L. *see* Isaacson, Robert Lee.
Isaacson, Robert Lee.
xIsaacson, Robert L.
The Limbic System. Plenum Pub.
Isaak. *see* Isaak, Robert A.
Isaak, Robert. *see* Isaak, Robert A.
Isaak, Robert A.
xIsaak.
Individuals & World Politics. Duxbury Pr.
xIsaak, Robert.
jt. auth. Politics for Human Beings. Duxbury
Pr.
xIsaak, Robert A.
American Democracy & World Power. St
Martin.
Individuals & World Politics. Duxbury Pr.
Isabella Stewart Gardner Museum. *see* Isabella Stewart
Gardner Museum, Boston.
Isabella Stewart Gardner Museum, Boston.
xIsabella Stewart Gardner Museum.
A Selection of Paintings, Drawings &
Watercolors. U of Chicago Pr.
Isachenko, A. G. *see* Isachenko, Anatolii Grigorevich.
Isachenko, Anatolii Grigorevich.
xIsachenko, A. G.
Principles of Landscape Science &
Physical-Geographic Regionalization. Intl
Schol Bk Serv.
Isadora, Rachel.
xIsadora, Rachel.
illus. Ben's Trumpet. Greenwillow.
My Ballet Class. Greenwillow.
illus. The Potters' Kitchen. Greenwillow.
Isard, W. *see* Isard, Walter.
Isard, Walter.
xIsard, W.
Spatial Dynamics & Optimal Space-Time
Development. Elsevier.
xIsard, Walter.
Introduction to Regional Science. P-H.
Regional Input-Output Study: Recollections,
Reflections & Diverse Notes on the
Philadelphia Experience. MIT Pr.
Iscoe, Ira.
xIscoe, Ira.
ed. Community Psychology in Transition:
Proceedings of the National Conference on
Training in Community Psychology. Halsted
Pr.
Iselin, Marc.
xIselin, Marc.
Atlas of Hand Surgery. McGraw.
Isely, M. D. *see* Isely, Malcolm D.
Isely, Malcolm D.
xIsely, M. D.

Arkansas Valley Interurban. Interurban.
Iseminger, Gary.
xIseminger, Gary.
Introduction to Deductive Logic. Irvington.
ed. Logic & Philosophy: Selected Readings.
Irvington.
Isenbart, Hans-Heinrich.
xIsenbart, Hans-Heinrich.
A Foal Is Born. Putnam.
Isenberg, Anita.
xIsenberg, Anita.
How to Work in Stained Glass. Chilton.
Stained Glass Lamps: Construction & Design.
Chilton.
Isenberg, Irwin.
xIsenberg, Irwin.
ed. The Arab World. Wilson.
ed. The Death Penalty. Wilson.
ed. Ferment in Eastern Europe. Wilson.
ed. France Under De Gaulle. Wilson.
ed. The Nations of the Indian Subcontinent.
Wilson.
ed. Outlook for Western Europe. Wilson.
ed. South America: Problems & Prospects.
Wilson.
Isenhour, Thomas L.
xIsenhour, Thomas L.
Introduction to Computer Programming for
Chemists: Fortran. Allyn.
Iser, Wolfgang.
xIser, Wolfgang.
The Act of Reading: A Theory of Aesthetic
Response. Johns Hopkins.
The Implied Reader: Patterns of
Communication in Prose Fiction from
Bunyan to Beckett. Johns Hopkins.
Ish-Kishor, S. *see* Ish-Kishor, Sulamith.
Ish-Kishor, Sulamith.
xIsh-Kishor, S.
A Boy of Old Prague. Schol Bk Serv.
xIsh-Kishor, Sulamith.
Boy of Old Prague. Pantheon.
Our Eddie. Pantheon.
Our Eddie. Random.
Pathways Through the Jewish Holidays. Ktav.
Isham, C. J.
xIsham, C. J.
ed. Quantum Gravity: An Oxford Symposium.
Oxford U Pr.
Isham, Giles S., d. 1864
xIsham, Giles S.
Guide to California & the Mines. Ye Galleon.
Isham, Linda.
xIsham, Linda.
On Behalf of Children. Judson.
Isham, N. M. *see* Isham, Norman Morrison.
Isham, Norman M. *see* Isham, Norman Morrison.
Isham, Norman Morrison.
xIsham, N. M.
Early Connecticut Houses: Historical &
Architectural Study. Peter Smith.
xIsham, Norman M.
Early Connecticut Houses: An Historical &
Architectural Study. Dover.
Ishee, John. *see* Ishee, John A.
Ishee, John A.
xIshee, John.
From Here to Maturity. Broadman.
Isherwood, Christopher, 1904-
xIsherwood, Christopher.

Approach to Vedanta. Vedanta Pr.
Intro. by Berlin Stories. Bentley.
Christopher & His Kind. Avon.
Christopher & His Kind. FS&G.
Down There on a Visit. Avon.
A Meeting by the River. Avon.
The Memorial: Portrait of a Family. Avon.
Prater Violet. Avon.
Ramakrishna & His Disciples. S&S.
Ramakrishna & His Disciples. Vedanta Pr.
ed. Vedanta for Modern Man. NAL.
The World in the Evening. Avon.
Ishida, M. *see* Ishida, Makoto.
Ishida, Makoto, 1932-
xIshida, M.
The Genus Fields of Algebraic Number Fields.
Springer-Verlag.
Ishiguro, Hide.
xIshiguro, Hide.
Leibniz's Philosophy of Logic & Language.
Cornell U Pr.
Ishii, T. Koryu. *see* Ishii, Thomas Koryu.
Ishii, Thomas Koryu, 1927-
xIshii, T. Koryu.
Maser & Laser Engineering. Krieger.
Ishikawa, Akira, 1934-
xIshikawa, Akira.
Corporate Planning & Control Model Systems.
NYU Pr.
Ishikawa, T. *see* Ishikawa, Tadashi.
Ishikawa, Tadashi.
xIshikawa, T.
Imperial Villas of Kyoto. Kodansha.
Ishwaran, K. *see* Ishwaran, Karigoudar.
Ishwaran, Karigoudar.
xIshwaran, K.
ed. Change & Continuity in India's Villages.
Columbia U Pr.
Isichei, Elizabeth. *see* Isichei, Elizabeth Allo.
Isichei, Elizabeth Allo.
xIsichei, Elizabeth.
A History of the Igbo People. St Martin.
History of West Africa Since 1800. Holmes &
Meier.
Igbo Worlds: An Anthology of Oral Histories
& Historical Descriptions. Inst Study Human.
Isihara, A. *see* Isihara, Akira.
Isihara, Akira.
xIsihara, A.
Statistical Physics. Acad Pr.
Iskandar, Marwan.
xIskandar, Marwan.
The Arab Oil Question. Intl Schol Bk Serv..
Islam, A. Aminul. *see* Islam, A. K. M. Aminul.
Islam, A. K. M. Aminul.
xIslam, A. Aminul.
Victorious Victims: Political Transformation in
a Traditional Society. Schenkman.
Islam, Nural. *see* Islam, Nurul.
Islam, Nurul.
xIslam, Nural.
Development Strategy of Bangladesh.
Pergamon.
Isler, Charlotte.
xIsler, Charlotte.
Workbook for the Nurses' Aide. Springer Pub.
Isler, Hansruedi.
xIsler, Hansruedi.
Thomas Willis, 1621-1675: Doctor & Scientist.
Hafner.
Isles, Keith S. *see* Isles, Keith Sydney.
Isles, Keith Sydney.
xIsles, Keith S.
An Economic Survey of Northern Ireland.
Greenwood.
Ismael, Tareq Y.
xIsmael, Tareq Y.
Arab Left. Syracuse U Pr.
Isman, Warren E.
xIsman, Warren E.

Fire Service Pumps & Hydraulics. Delmar.
Ismay, Hastings Lionel Ismay, Baron, 1887-1965
xIsmay, Lord.
The Memoirs of General Lord Ismay.
Greenwood.
Ismay, Lord. *see* Ismay, Hastings Lionel Ismay.
Isocrates.
xIsocrates.
Ad Demonicum et Panegyricus. Arno.
Cyprian Orations. Arno.
Isogai, Hiroshi.
xIsogai, Hiroshi.
Marketplaces of the World. Kodansha.
Ison, Terence G. *see* Ison, Terence George.
Ison, Terence George.
xIson, Terence G.
Credit Marketing & Consumer Protection.
Biblio Dist.
Israel, Benjamin. *see* Israel, Benjamin L.
Israel, Benjamin L.
xIsrael, Benjamin.
How to Prepare for the Professional &
Administrative Career Examination (PACE).
McGraw.
Israel, Charles E.
xIsrael, Charles E.
Five Ships West: The Story of Magellan.
Macmillan.
Israel, Elaine.
xIsrael, Elaine.
The Hungry World. Messner.
Israel, J. I. *see* Israel, Jonathan Irvine.
Israel, Joachim.
xIsrael, Joachim.
Alienation from Marx to Modern Sociology: A
Macrosociological Analysis. Humanities.
The Language of Dialectics & Dialectics of
Language. Humanities.
Israel, John.
xIsrael, John.
Student Nationalism in China, 1927-1937.
Stanford U Pr.
Israel, Jonathan Irvine.
xIsrael, J. I.
Race, Class & Politics in Colonial Mexico,
1610-1665. Oxford U Pr.
Israel, Lee.
xIsrael, Lee.
Kilgallen. Delacorte.
Israel, Lucien.
xIsrael, Lucien.
Conquering Cancer. Random.
Conquering Cancer. Random.
Israel, Peter, fl. 1967-
xIsrael, Peter.
Hush Money. Avon.
The Stiff Upper Lip. Avon.
The Stiff Upper Lip. T Y Crowell.
Israel, Richard J.
xIsrael, Richard J.
Jewish Identity Games: A How to Do It Book.
B'nai B'rith-Hillel.
Israels, M. C. *see* Israels, M. C. G.
Israels, M. C. G.
xIsraels, M. C.
Atlas of Bone-Marrow Pathology. Grune.
xIsraels, M. G.
Haematological Aspects of Systemic Disease.
Saunders.
Israels, M. G. *see* Israels, M. C. G.
Issari, M. Ali. *see* Issari, Mohammad Ali.
Issari, Mohammad Ali.
xIssari, M. Ali.
What Is Cinema Verite?. Scarecrow.
Issawi. *see* Issawi, Charles Philip.
Issawi, Charles Philip.
xIssawi.
Oil, the Middle East & the World. Sage.
Issler, Anne (Roller), 1892-
xIssler, Anne R.

Our Mountain Hermitage: Silverado & Robert
Louis Stevenson. R West.
Issler, Anne R. *see* Issler, Anne (Roller).
Istanbul Summer School of Theoretical Physics, 1962.
xIstanbul Summer School Of Theoretical Physics -
1962.
Group Theoretical Concepts & Methods in
Elementary Particle Physics. Gordon.
Istvan, Donald F.
xIstvan, Donald F.
Accounting Principles. HarBraceJ.
Iten, Richard J. Van. *see* Van Iten, Richard J.
Itkis, U.
xItkis, U.
Control Systems of Variable Structure. Halsted
Pr.
Ito, Robert.
xIto, Robert.
Mastering Women's Gymnastics. Contemp
Bks.
Ito, Yohei, 1923-
xIto, Yohei.
ed. Viruses & Human Cancer. S Karger.
Ittaman, K. P.
xIttaman, K. P.
Amini Islanders: Social Structure & Change.
South Asia Bks.
Ittelson, W. *see* Ittelson, William H.
Ittelson, William H.
xIttelson, W.
Introduction to Environmental Psychology.
HR&W.
Itzkowitz, David C.
xItzkowitz, David C.
Peculiar Privilege: A Social History of English
Fox-Hunting 1753-1885. Humanities.
Itzkowitz, Norman.
xItzkowitz, Norman.
Ottoman Empire & Islamic Tradition. U of
Chicago Pr.
**Iutam-Symposium on Instability of Continuous Systems,
Herrenalb, Germany, 1969.**
xSymposium Herrenalb - Germany - September
8-12 1969.
Instability of Continuous Systems.
Springer-Verlag.
**Iutam on the Generalized Continuum and the Continuum
Theory of Dislocations with Applications,
Freudenstadt, Germany and Stuttgart, 1967.**
xSymposium On The Generalized Cosserat
Continuum And The Continuum Theory Of
Dislocations With Applications - Freudenstadt
And Stuttgart - 1967.
Mechanics of Generalized Continua:
Proceedings. Springer-Verlag.
Ivancevich, John M.
xIvancevich, John M.
Business in a Dynamic Environment. West
Pub.
Organizational Behavior & Performance.
Goodyear.
ed. Readings in Organizational Behavior &
Performance. Goodyear.
Ivanoff, Pierre, 1924-
xIvanoff, Pierre.
Maya. G&D.
Ivanov, Vsevolod V. *see* Ivanov, Vsevolod
Viacheslavovich.
Ivanov, Vsevolod Viacheslavovich, 1895-1963
xIvanov, Vsevolod V.
The Adventures of a Fakir. Hyperion Conn.
Ivask, Ivar.
xIvask, Ivar.
World Literature Since 1945: Critical Surveys
of the Contemporary Literature of Europe &
the Americas. Ungar.
Ivens, Dorothy.
xIvens, Dorothy.

Glorious Stew. Har-Row.
Ivens, Joris, 1898-
xIvens, Joris.
Camera & I. Intl Pub Co.
Ivens, W. G. *see* Ivens, Walter George.
Ivens, Walter G. *see* Ivens, Walter George.
Ivens, Walter George, 1871-
xIvens, W. G.
Melanesians of the South-East Solomon
Islands. Arno.
xIvens, Walter G.
A Dictionary of the Language of Bugotu, Santa
Isabel Island, Solomon Islands. AMS Pr.
Ivers, Larry E.
xIvers, Larry E.
British Drums on the Southern Frontier: The
Military Colonization of Georgia, 1733-1749.
U of NC Pr.
Iversen, B. *see* Iversen, Birger.
Iversen, Birger.
xIversen, B.
Generic Local Structure of the Morphisms in
Commutative Algebra. Springer-Verlag.
Linear Determinants with Applications to
Picard Scheme of a Family of Algebraic
Groups. Springer-Verlag.
Iversen, Carl, 1899-
xIversen, Carl.
Aspects of the Theory of International Capital
Movements. Kelley.
Iversen, Gudmund. *see* Iversen, Gudmund R.
Iversen, Gudmund R.
xIversen, Gudmund.
Analysis of Variance. Sage.
xIversen, Gudmund R.
Statistics for Sociology. Wm C Brown.
Iversen, John O. *see* Iversen, John Orville.
Iversen, John Orville.
xIversen, John O.
Love in Escrow. Pacific Pr Pub Assn.
Iverson, Eric.
xIverson, Eric.
Wereblood. Belmont-Tower.
Iverson, Genie.
xIverson, Genie.
Louis Armstrong. T Y Crowell.
Iverson, Noel.
xIverson, Noel.
Germania, U.S.A.: Social Change in New Ulm,
Minnesota. U of Minn Pr.
Iverson, Peter.
xIverson, Peter.
The Navajos: A Critical Bibliography. Ind U
Pr.
Iverstine, Joe C.
xIverstine, Joe C.
Cases in Production & Operations
Management. Merrill.
Ives, David J.
xIves, David J.
The Crescent Hills Prehistoric Quarrying Area.
Mus Anthro Mo.
Ives, Edward D.
xIves, Edward D.
The Tape-Recorded Interview: A Manual for
Field Workers in Folklore & Oral History. U
of Tenn Pr.
Ives, Howard C. *see* Ives, Howard Colby.
Ives, Howard Chapin, 1878-
xIves, Howard C.
Natural Trigonometric Functions to Seven
Decimal Places for Every Ten Seconds of
Arc. Wiley.
Ives, Howard Colby.
xIves, Howard C.
Portals to Freedom. Baha'i.
Ives, John.
xIves, John.

Fear in a Handful of Dust. BJ Pub Group.
Ives, Josephine P.
  xIves, Josephine P.
    Word Identification Techniques. Rand.
Ives, Margaret C.
  xIves, Margaret C.
    Enlightenment & National Revival: Patterns of
    Interplay & Paradox in Late 18th Century
    Hungary. Univ Microfilms.
Ives, Suzy.
  xIves, Suzy.
    Creating Children's Costumes from Paper &
    Card. Taplinger.
    Ideas for Patchwork. Branford.
    Patterns for Patchwork Quilts & Cushions.
    Branford.
Ivey, Donald.
  xIvey, Donald.
    Sound Pleasure: A Prelude to Active Listening.
    Schirmer Bks.
Ivimey, John W. *see* Ivimey, John William.
Ivimey, John William.
  xIvimey, John W.
    Complete Version of Ye Three Blind Mice.
    Warne.
Ivimy, John, 1911-
  xIvimy, John.
    The Sphinx & the Megaliths. Har-Row.
Ivin, K. J. *see* Ivin, Kenneth John.
Ivin, Kenneth John.
  xIvin, K. J.
    ed. Structural Studies of Macromolecules by
    Spectroscopic Methods. Wiley.
Ivins, David, 1928-
  xIvins, David.
    The Complete Book of Woodburning Stoves.
    Sterling.
Ivins, William M. *see* Ivins, William Mills.
Ivins, William Mills, 1881-1961
  xIvins, William M.
    Art & Geometry: A Study in Space Intuitions.
    Gannon.
    On the Rationalization of Sight: With an
    Examination of Three Renaissance Texts on
    Perspective to Which Is Appended "De
    Artificiali Perspectiva" by Viator (Pelerin).
    Da Capo.
    Prints & Visual Communication. Da Capo.
    Prints & Visual Communication. MIT Pr.
Ivker, Barry, 1941-
  xIvker, Barry.
    An Anthology & Analysis of 17th & 18th
    Century French Libertine Fiction. Univ
    Microfilms.
Iwamoto, Kaoru, 1902-
  xIwamoto, Kaoru.
    Go for Beginners. Pantheon.
Iwamura, Susan. *see* Iwamura, Susan Grohs.
Iwamura, Susan Grohs.
  xIwamura, Susan.
    The Verbal Games of Pre-School Children. St
    Martin.
Iwanska, Alicja.
  xIwanska, Alicja.
    Purgatory & Utopia: A Mazahua Indian Village
    of Mexico. Schenkman.
    The Truths of Others: An Essay on Nativistic
    Intellectuals in Mexico. Schenkman.
Iwasaki, C. *see* Iwasaki, Chihiro.
Iwasaki, Chihiro, 1918-
  xIwasaki, C.
    What's Fun Without a Friend. McGraw.
Iwasaki, y Oji, 1928-
  xIwasaki, Yoji.
    ed. Cadaveric Renal Transplantation.
    Igaku-Shoin.
Iwasaki, Yoji. *see* Iwasaki, y Oji.
Iwasawa, Kenkichi.
  xIwasawa, Kenkichi.

Lectures on p-Adic L-Functions. Princeton U
    Pr.
Iwatsuki, Zennoske. *see* Iwatsuki, Zennosuke.
Iwatsuki, Zennosuke.
  xIwatsuki, Zennoske.
    Bryological Herbaria: A Guide to the
    Bryological Herbaria of the World. Intl Schol
    Bk Serv.
Iyanaga, Shokichi. *see* Nihon Sugakkai.
Iyer, Raghavan. *see* Iyer, Raghavan Narasimhan.
Iyer, Raghavan N. *see* Iyer, Raghavan Narasimhan.
Iyer, Raghavan Narasimhan.
  xIyer, Raghavan.
    Moral & Political Thought of Mahatma
    Gandhi. Oxford U Pr.
  xIyer, Raghavan N.
    The Moral & Political Thought of Mahatma
    Gandhi. Oxford U Pr.
Izard, C. E. *see* Izard, Carroll E.
Izard, Carroll E.
  xIzard, C. E.
    ed. Human Emotions. Plenum Pub.
Izard, Ralph S.
  xIzard, Ralph S.
    Fundamentals of News Reporting.
    Kendall-Hunt.
Izatt, Reed M. *see* Izatt, Reed Mcneil.
Izatt, Reed Mcneil.
  xIzatt, Reed M.
    Progress in Macrocyclic Chemistry. Wiley.
    ed. Synthetic Multidentate Macrocyclic
    Compounds. Acad Pr.
Izenberg, G. N. *see* Izenberg, Gerald N.
Izenberg, Gerald N., 1939-
  xIzenberg, G. N.
    The Existentialist Critique of Freud: The Crisis
    of Autonomy. Princeton U Pr.
Izenour, G. C. *see* Izenour, George C.
Izenour, George C.
  xIzenour, G. C.
    Theater Design. McGraw.
Izikowitz, Karl G. *see* Izikowitz, Karl Gustav.
Izikowitz, Karl Gustav, 1903-
  xIzikowitz, Karl G.
    Lamet: Hill Peasants in French Indochina.
    AMS Pr.
Izmidlian, Georges.
  xIzmidlian, Georges.
    Oriental Rugs & Carpets Today. Hippocrene
    Bks.
Izraeli, D. *see* Izraeli, Dov.
Izraeli, Dov.
  xIzraeli, D.
    Societal Marketing Boards. Halsted Pr.
Izzo, Herbert J.
  xIzzo, Herbert J.
    Tuscan & Etruscan: The Problem of Linguistic
    Substratum Influence in Central Italy. U of
    Toronto Pr.
J. J. Keller & Asociates, Inc. *see* Keller (J.J.) and
    Associates.
J. J. Keller & Assoc. *see* Keller (J.J.) and Associates.
J. J. Keller & Associates, Inc. *see* Keller (J.J.) and
    Associates.
J. K. Lasser Institute. *see* Lasser (J.K.) Tax Institute,
    New York.
J. K. Lasser Tax Institute. *see* Lasser (J.K.) Tax Institute,
    New York.
Jabati, S. A., 1929-
  xJabati, S. A.
    Agriculture in Sierra Leone. Vantage.
Jabay, Earl.
  xJabay, Earl.
    God-Players. Zondervan.
    Precisely How to Take Care of Your Self.
    Logos.
Jabbour, J. T.
  xJabbour, J. T.

    ed. Pediatric Neurology Handbook. Med Exam.
Jabenis, Elaine.
  xJabenis, Elaine.
    The Fashion Director: What She Does & How
    to Be One. Wiley.
Jaber, Kamel S. Abu. *see* Abu Jaber, Kamel S.
Jaber, William.
  xJaber, William.
    Exploring the Sun. Messner.
    Whatever Happened to the Dinosaurs?.
    Messner.
Jabes, Jak.
  xJabes, Jak.
    Individual Processes in Organizationa
    Behavior. AHM Pub.
Jabine, William.
  xJabine, William.
    Case Histories in Construction Law: A Guide
    for Architects, Engineers, Contractors,
    Builders. CBI Pub.
Jablonski, Edward.
  xJablonski, Edward.
    The Gershwin Years. Doubleday.
Jablonski, Ramona, 1939-
  xJablonski, Ramona.
    Traditional Designs of Armenia & the Near
    East to Color. Stemmer Hse.
Jachimowicz, Elizabeth.
  xJachimowicz, Elizabeth.
    Eight Chicago Women & Their Fashions,
    1860-1929. Chicago Hist.
Jack, Adolphus A. *see* Jack, Adolphus Alfred.
Jack, Adolphus Alfred, 1868-1945
  xJack, Adolphus A.
    Thackeray: A Study. Kennikat.
Jack, Alex, 1945-
  xJack, Alex.
    Dragonbrood. Kanthaka.
Jack, Ian. *see* Jack, Ian Robert James.
Jack, Ian Robert James
  xJack, Ian.
    Browning's Major Poetry. Oxford U Pr.
    English Literature, 1815-1832. Oxford U Pr.
Jack, James W. *see* Jack, James William.
Jack, James William.
  xJack, James W.
    Daybreak in Livingstonia: The Story of the
    Livingstonia Mission, British Central Africa.
    Negro U Pr.
Jack, Nancy.
  xJack, Nancy.
    The Complete Pack Provisioning Book.
    Contemp Bks.
Jack, R. I.
  xJack, R. Ian.
    Medieval Wales. Cornell U Pr.
Jack, R. Ian. *see* Jack, R. I.
Jack, Robert L. *see* Jack, Robert Logan.
Jack, Robert Logan, 1845-1921
  xJack, Robert L.
    Back Blocks of China: A Narrative of
    Experiences Among the Chinese, Sifans,
    Lolos, Tibetans, Shans & Kachins, Between
    Shanghai & the Irrawadi. Greenwood.
Jack, Theodore H. *see* Jack, Theodore Henley.
Jack, Theodore Henley, 1881-
  xJack, Theodore H.
    Sectionalism & Party Politics in Alabama,
    1819-1842. Reprint.
Jacka, Jerry D.
  xJacka, Jerry D.
    Indian Jewelry of the Prehistoric Southwest. U
    of Ariz Pr.
Jackel, Eberhard.
  xJackel, Eberhard.
    Hitler's Weltanschauung: A Blueprint for
    Power. Columbia U Pr.
Jackendoff, Nathaniel, 1919-
  xJackendoff, Nathaniel.

Group Counseling: Dynamic Possibilities for
  Small Groups. Pilgrim NY.
The Many Faces of Grief. Abingdon.
When Someone Dies. Fortress.
Jackson, Edward A. Mather. *see* Mather Jackson,
  Edward A.
Jackson, Eileen.
  xJackson, Eileen.
  Autumn Lace. Fawcett.
  Autumn Lace. G K Hall.
  Autumn Lace. Walker & Co.
  Castle in the Rock. Walker & Co.
  Lord Rivington's Lady. G K Hall.
  Lord Rivington's Lady. NAL.

Jackson, Elizabeth R.
  xJackson, Elizabeth R.
  Worlds Apart: Structural Parallels in Poetry of
    Paul Valery, Saint-John Perse, Benjamin
    Peret & Rene Char. Mouton.
Jackson, Ellen. *see* Jackson, Ellen Pauline.

Jackson, Ellen Pauline.
  xJackson, Ellen.
  Subject Guide to Major United States
    Government Publications. ALA.

Jackson, Emily, 1861-
  xJackson, Emily.
  The History of Hand Made Lace: Dealing with
    the Origin of Lace, the Growth of the Great
    Lace Centres, Etc.. Gale.

Jackson, Eugene.
  xJackson, Eugene.
  French Made Simple. Doubleday.
  German Made Simple. Doubleday.
  Spanish Made Simple. Doubleday.
Jackson, F. *see* Jackson, Frank.

Jackson, Francis. *see* Jackson, Francis Leslie.
Jackson, Francis Leslie.
  xJackson, Francis.
  Life on Mars. Norton.

Jackson, Frank, 1943-
  xJackson, F.
  Perception: A Representative Theory.
    Cambridge U Pr.

Jackson, Franklin C., 1917-
  xJackson, Franklin C.
  Echoes from the Sandhills. Word Serv.
Jackson, Gabriel.
  xJackson, Gabriel.
  ed. The Spanish Civil War. New Viewpoints.
  Spanish Republic & the Civil War, 1931-1939.
    Princeton U Pr.
Jackson, Geoffrey, Sir, 1915-
  xJackson, Geoffrey.
  Surviving the Long Night: An Autobiographical
    Account of a Political Kidnapping. Vanguard.
Jackson, George D.
  xJackson, George D.
  Comintern & Peasant in East Europe,
    1919-1930. Columbia U Pr.
Jackson, George L. *see* Jackson, George Leroy.
Jackson, George Leroy, 1876-
  xJackson, George L.
  Development of School Support in Colonial
    Massachusetts. AMS Pr.
  Development of School Support in Colonial
    Massachusetts. Arno.
Jackson, George S. *see* Jackson, George Stuyvesant.
Jackson, George Stuyvesant.
  xJackson, George S.
  Early Songs of Uncle Sam. Branden.
  Hamlet: Scene by Scene. Branden.
Jackson, Giles B.
  xJackson, Giles B.
  Industrial History of the Negro Race of the
    United States. Arno.
Jackson, Gordon.
  xJackson, Gordon.

The British Whaling Trade. Shoe String.
Jackson, Gordon E.
  xJackson, Gordon E.
  How to Stay Union Free. Management Pr.
Jackson, Guida.
  xJackson, Guida.
  Passing Through. S&S.
Jackson, H. *see* Jackson, Henry.
Jackson, H. D. *see* Jackson, H. David.
Jackson, H. David, 1935-
  xJackson, H. D.
  Building Model Airplanes from Scratch. TAB
    Bks.
Jackson, H. W. *see* Jackson, Herbert W.
Jackson, Harry, 1924-
  xJackson, Harry.
  Lost Wax Bronze Casting: A Photographic
    Essay on This Antique & Venerable Art. Van
    Nos Reinhold.
Jackson, Harvey H.
  xJackson, Harvey H.
  Lachlan McIntosh & the Politics of
    Revolutionary Georgia. U of Ga Pr.
Jackson, Helen Hunt. *see* Jackson, Helen Maria Fiske
  Hunt.
Jackson, Helen Maria Fiske Hunt, 1831-1885
  xJackson, Helen Hunt.
  Nelly's Silver Mine: A Story of Colorado Life.
    Garland Pub.
Jackson, Henry, 1839-1921
  xJackson, H.
  About Edwin Drood. Folcroft.
  About Edwin Drood. Haskell.
  xJackson, Henry.
  About Edwin Drood. Arden Lib.
Jackson, Henry F.
  xJackson, Henry F.
  The FLN in Algeria: Party Development in a
    Revolutionary Society. Greenwood.
Jackson, Herbert L., 1921-
  xJackson, Herbert L.
  Mathematics of Radiology & Nuclear
    Medicine. Green.
Jackson, Herbert W.
  xJackson, H. W.
  Introduction to Electric Circuits. P-H.
  xJackson, Herbert W.
  Introduction to Electric Circuits. P-H.
Jackson, Holbrook, 1874-1948
  xJackson, Holbrook.
  The Anatomy of Bibliomania. AMS Pr.
  The Anatomy of Bibliomania. Octagon.
  Dreamers of Dreams: The Rise & Fall of 19th
    Century Idealism. Folcroft.
  Dreamers of Dreams: The Rise & Fall of 19th
    Century Idealism. Scholarly.
  Great English Novelists. Arno.
  Great English Novelists. R West.
  Printing of Books. Arno.
Jackson, Howard.
  xJackson, Howard.
  Analyzing English: An Introduction to
    Descriptive Linguistics. Pergamon.
Jackson, Ian J. *see* Jackson, Ian Joseph.
Jackson, Ian Joseph.
  xJackson, Ian J.
  Climate, Water and Agriculture in the Tropics.
    Longman.
Jackson, Irene V.
  xJackson, Irene V.
  Compiled by Afro-American Religious Music:
    A Bibliography & a Catalogue of Gospel
    Music. Greenwood.
Jackson, J. *see* Jackson, John Harold.
Jackson, J. B. *see* Jackson, John Brinckerhoff.
Jackson, J. D. *see* Jackson, John David.
Jackson, J. H. *see* Jackson, Joseph Harrison.
Jackson, J. Hampden. *see* Jackson, John Hampden.
Jackson, J. Howard. *see* Jackson, James Howard.

Jackson, Jacqueline.
  xJackson, Jacqueline.
  illus. The Ghost Boat. Little.
  The Taste of Spruce Gum. Little.
Jackson, Jacquelyne J. *see* Jackson, Jacquelyne Johnson.
Jackson, Jacquelyne Johnson.
  xJackson, Jacquelyne J.
  Minorities & Aging. Wadsworth Pub.
Jackson, James. *see* Jackson, James E.
Jackson, James E.
  xJackson, James.
  Revolutionary Tracings. Intl Pub Co.
Jackson, James Howard.
  xJackson, J. Howard.
  Word Power for Effective Writing. Bobbs.
Jackson, James J., 1926-
  xJackson, James J.
  Steam Boiler Operation: Principles & Practice.
    P-H.
Jackson, Jane.
  xJackson, Jane.
  Adapted by The New American Pocket
    Medical Dictionary. Churchill.
Jackson, Jane F. *see* Jackson, Jane Flannery.
Jackson, Jane Flannery.
  xJackson, Jane F.
  Infant Culture. NAL.
  Infant Culture. T Y Crowell.
Jackson, Jesse.
  xJackson, Jesse.
  Charley Starts from Scratch. Dell.
Jackson, John A. *see* Jackson, John Archer.
Jackson, John Archer.
  xJackson, John A.
  ed. Professions & Professionalization.
    Cambridge U Pr.
Jackson, John B. *see* Jackson, John Brinckerhoff.
Jackson, John Brinckerhoff, 1909-
  xJackson, J. B.
  The Necessity for Ruins & Other Topics. U of
    Mass Pr.
  xJackson, John B.
  American Space: The Centennial Years,
    1865-1876. Norton.
Jackson, John David, 1925-
  xJackson, J. D.
  Classical Electrodynamics. Wiley.
Jackson, John G.
  xJackson, John G.
  Introduction to African Civilizations. Negro U
    Pr.
Jackson, John H. *see* Jackson, John Hampden.
Jackson, John Hampden, 1907-
  xJackson, J. Hampden.
  England Since the Industrial Revolution,
    1815-1848. Greenwood.
  xJackson, John H.
  Clemenceau & The Third Republic. Hyperion
    Conn.
  Estonia. Greenwood.
  The World in the Postwar Decade: 1945-1955.
    Arno.
Jackson, John Harold.
  xJackson, J.
  Organization Theory: A Macro-Perspective for
    Management. P-H.
  xJackson, John H.
  Successful Supervision. P-H.
Jackson, John N.
  xJackson, John N.
  Surveys for Town & Country Planning.
    Greenwood.
Jackson, John W.
  xJackson, John W.
  With the British Army in Philadelphia,
    1777-1778. Presidio Pr.
Jackson, Jon A.
  xJackson, Jon A.

The Blind Pig. Random.
The Diehard. Random.
Jackson, Joseph F. see Jackson, Joseph Francis.
Jackson, Joseph Francis.
xJackson, Joseph F.
Louise Colet et Ses Amis Litteraires. AMS Pr.
Jackson, Joseph Harrison, 1900-
xJackson, J. H.
Unholy Shadows & Freedom's Holy Light.
Townsend Pr.
Jackson, Judith.
xJackson, Judith.
Man & the Automobile. McGraw.
Jackson, K. C. see Jackson, Kern C.
Jackson, K. F. see Jackson, Keith F.
Jackson, Karl D.
xJackson, Karl D.
ed. Political Power & Communications in
Indonesia. U of Cal Pr.
Traditional Authority, Islam, & Rebellion: A
Study of Indonesian Political Behavior. U of
Cal Pr.
Jackson, Keith F.
xJackson, K. F.
The Art of Solving Problems. St Martin.
Jackson, Kern C., 1920-
xJackson, K. C.
Textbook of Lithology. McGraw.
Jackson, Laird G.
xJackson, Laird G.
Clinical Genetics: A Sourcebook for Physicians.
Wiley.
Jackson, Laura R. see Jackson, Laura Riding.
Jackson, Laura Riding.
xJackson, Laura R.
A Survey of Modernist Poetry. Folcroft.
Jackson, Louise A.
xJackson, Louise A.
Grandpa Had a Windmill, Grandma Had a
Churn. Schol Bk Serv.
Over on the River. Lothrop.
Jackson, Luther P. see Jackson, Luther Porter.
Jackson, Luther Porter, 1892-1950
xJackson, Luther P.
Free Negro Labor & Property Holding in
Virginia, 1830-1860. Atheneum.
Free Negro Labor & Property Holding in
Virginia, 1830-1860. Russell.
Jackson, M. A.
xJackson, M. A.
Principles of Program Design. Acad Pr.
Jackson, M. Katherine, 1875-
xJackson, M. Katherine.
Outlines of the Literary History of Colonial
Pennsylvania. AMS Pr.
Jackson, Michael, 1942-
xJackson, Michael.
The Pocket Bartender's Guide. S&S.
Jackson, Michael P. see Jackson, Michael Peart.
Jackson, Michael Peart.
xJackson, Michael P.
Financial Aid Through Social Work. Routledge
& Kegan.
Industrial Relations: A Textbook. Biblio Dist.
Jackson, Neil.
xJackson, Neil.
Pref. by Civil Engineering Materials. Scholium
Intl.
Jackson, O. T.
xJackson, O. T.
Aftermath. Nordon Pubns.
Jackson, Percival E., 1891-
xJackson, Percival E.
Dissent in the Supreme Court: A Chronology.
U of Okla Pr.
Jackson, Philip C., 1949-
xJackson, Philip C.
Introduction to Artificial Intelligence. Van Nos
Reinhold.
Jackson, Philip W. see Jackson, Philip Wesley.

Jackson, Philip Wesley, 1928-
xJackson, Philip W.
Life in Classrooms. HR&W.
The Teacher & the Machine. U of Pittsburgh
Pr.
Jackson, R. J. see Jackson, Robert John Victor.
Jackson, Reggie.
xJackson, Reggie.
Inside Hitting. Contemp Bks.
Jackson, Richard, 1948-
xJackson, Richard.
Holistic Massage. Sterling.
Jackson, Richard H., 1941-
xJackson, Richard H.
ed. The Mormon Role in the Settlement of the
West. Brigham.
Jackson, Richard L., 1937-
xJackson, Richard L.
Black Writers in Latin America. U of NM Pr.
Jackson, Robert, 1941-
xJackson, Robert.
Air War Over Korea. Scribner.
Bomber!. St Martin.
Dunkirk. Playboy Pbks.
Dunkirk. St Martin.
Fighter Pilots of World War I. St Martin.
Fighter Pilots of World War II.
Belmont-Tower.
Fighter Pilots of World War II. St Martin.
Morphological Dermatology: A Study of the
Living Gross Pathology of the Skin. C C
Thomas.
Jackson, Robert. see Jackson, Robert Victor.
Jackson, Robert H. see Jackson, Robert Houghwout.
Jackson, Robert Houghwout, 1892-1954
xJackson, Robert H.
The Struggle for Judicial Supremacy: A Study
of a Crisis in American Power Politics.
Octagon.
Jackson, Robert John Victor.
xJackson, R. J.
Canonical Differential Operators &
Lower-Order Symbols. Am Math.
Jackson, Robert L. see Jackson, Robert Louis.
Jackson, Robert Louis.
xJackson, Robert L.
ed. Chekhov: A Collection of Critical Essays.
P-H.
Dostoevsky's Quest for Form: A Study of His
Philosophy of Art. Physsardt.
Jackson, Robert Victor.
xJackson, Robert.
South Asian Crisis - India, Pakistan, &
Bangladesh: A Political & Historical Analysis
of the 1971 War. Praeger.
Jackson, Robert W.
xJackson, Robert W.
ed. Arthroscopy of the Knee. Grune.
Jackson, Robert W. see Jackson, Robert Wyse.
Jackson, Robert Wyse.
xJackson, Robert W.
Oliver Goldsmith: Essays Towards an
Interpretation. Arno.
Jackson, Ronald. see Jackson, Ronald W.
Jackson, Ronald W., 1946-
xJackson, Ronald.
China Clipper. Everest Hse.
Jackson, Ruth.
xJackson , Ruth.
The Cervical Syndrome. C C Thomas.
Jackson, Samuel M. see Jackson, Samuel Macauley.
Jackson, Samuel Macauley.
xJackson, Samuel M.
Huldreich Zwingli, the Reformer of German
Switzerland. Scholarly.
Jackson, Samuel T. see Jackson, Samuel Trevena.
Jackson, Samuel Trevena, 1869-
xJackson, Samuel T.

Lincoln's Use of the Bible. Folcroft.
Jackson, Sheila.
xJackson, Sheila.
Costumes for the Stage: A Complete Handbook
for Every Kind of Play. Dutton.
Jackson, Shirley, 1920-
xJackson, Shirley.
Life Among the Savages. Popular Lib.
The Lottery. Popular Lib.
Raising Demons. Popular Lib.
The Sundial. Popular Lib.
Jackson, Stanley, 1910-
xJackson, Stanley.
Guy De Maupassant. Folcroft.
Inside Monte Carlo. Stein & Day.
Jackson, Terence G. see Jackson, Terrence G.
Jackson, Terrence G.
xJackson, Terence G.
Postwar Monetary Reform in Severely
Damaged Economies: Its Role in Recovery
from Nuclear Attack. Mgmt Info Serv.
Jackson, Thomas G. see Jackson, Thomas Graham.
Jackson, Thomas Graham, Sir, Bart, 1835-1924
xJackson, Thomas G.
Architecture. Arno.
Gothic Architecture in France, England &
Italy. Hacker.
Gothic Architecture in France, England &
Italy. Somerset Pub.
Renaissance of Roman Architecture. Hacker.
Jackson, Thomas H.
xJackson, Thomas H.
Early Poetry of Ezra Pound. Harvard U Pr.
Jackson, W. P.
xJackson, W. P.
Building Layout. Craftsman.
Jackson, W. T. see Jackson, William Thomas Hobdell.
Jackson, W. Turrentine. see Jackson, William Turrentine.
Jackson, Wallace, 1930-
xJackson, Wallace.
The Probable & the Marvelous: Blake,
Wordsworth, & the Eighteenth-Century
Critical Tradition. U of Ga Pr.
Jackson, Wes.
xJackson, Wes.
Man & the Environment. Wm C Brown.
Jackson, William Eric.
xJackson, William Eric.
The Structure of Local Government in England
& Wales. Greenwood.
Jackson, William T. see Jackson, William Thomas
Hobdell.
Jackson, William Thomas Hobdell, 1915-
xJackson, W. T.
ed. The Interpretation of Medieval Lyric
Poetry. Columbia U Pr.
xJackson, William T.
Literature of the Middle Ages. Columbia U Pr.
Medieval Literature: A History & a Guide.
Macmillan.
Jackson, William Turrentine, 1915-
xJackson, W. Turrentine.
Wagon Roads West: A Study of Federal Road
Surveys and Construction in the
Trans-Mississippi West, 1846-1869. U of
Nebr Pr.
Jaco, E. Gartly.
xJaco, E. Gartly.
ed. Patients, Physicians, & Illness: A
Sourcebook in Behavioral Science & Health.
Free Pr.
Jacob, Alphons.
xJacob, Alphons.
Clinical Cardiac Roentgen Diagnosis. Green.
Jacob, Dorothy.
xJacob, Dorothy.
Cures & Curses. Taplinger.
Jacob, Ernest. see Jacob, Ernest Fraser.
Jacob, Ernest Fraser, 1894-
xJacob, Ernest.

The Renaissance. Folcroft.

Jacob, Francois, 1920-
xJacob, Francois.
The Logic of Life: A History of Heredity.
Random.
xJacob, Francoise.
The Logic of Life: A History of Heredity.
Pantheon.
Jacob, Francoise. see Jacob, Francois.
Jacob, Gale S. see Jacob, Gale Sypher.

Jacob, Gale Sypher.
xJacob, Gale S.
Independent Reading Grades One Through
Three: An Annotated Bibliography with
Reading Levels. Brodart.
Jacob, H. see Jacob, Herbert.
Jacob, Heinrich E. see Jacob, Heinrich Eduard.

Jacob, Heinrich Eduard, 1889-1967
xJacob, Heinrich E.
Felix Mendelssohn & His Times. Greenwood.
Jacob, Helen P. see Jacob, Helen Pierce.

Jacob, Helen Pierce.
xJacob, Helen P.
The Diary of the Strawbridge Place. Atheneum.
Garland for Gandhi. Parnassus.

Jacob, Herbert, 1933-
xJacob, H.
Crime & Justice in Urban America. P-H.
xJacob, Herbert.
ed. Politics in the American States: A
Comparative Analysis. Little.
ed. The Potential for Reform of Criminal
Justice. Sage.
Jacob, M. see Jacob, Maurice.

Jacob, Margaret C., 1943-
xJacob, Margaret C.
The Newtonians & the English Revolution,
1689-1720. Cornell U Pr.

Jacob, Maurice.
xJacob, M.
Gauge Theories & Neutrino Physics. Elsevier.
Jacob, Naomi. see Jacob, Naomi Ellington.

Jacob, Naomi Ellington.
xJacob, Naomi.
Opera in Italy. Arno.

Jacob, Philip E.
xJacob, Philip E.
Changing Values in College: An Exploratory
Study of the Impact of College Teaching.
Greenwood.

Jacob, William, 1762?-1851
xJacob, William.
Historical Inquiry into the Production &
Consumption of the Precious Metals. Kelley.

Jacobi, Carl, 1908-
xJacobi, Carl.
Disclosures in Scarlet. Arkham.

Jacobi, Charles A.
xJacobi, Charles A.
Textbook of Anatomy & Physiology in
Radiologic Technology. Mosby.
Textbook of Radiologic Technology. Mosby.
Jacobi, Jolande. see Jacobi, Jolande Szekacs.

Jacobi, Jolande Szekacs, 1890-
xJacobi, Jolande.
Masks of the Soul. Eerdmans.

Jacobini, H. B.
xJacobini, H. B.
A Study of the Philosophy of International
Law As Seen in Works of Latin American
Writers. Hyperion Conn.

Jacobs, Allan B.
xJacobs, Allan B.
Making City Planning Work. Planners Pr.
Jacobs, Betty E. see Jacobs, Betty E. M.

Jacobs, Betty E. M.
xJacobs, Betty E.

Growing Herbs & Plants for Dyeing. Select
Bks.
Profitable Herb Growing at Home. Garden
Way Pub.
Jacobs, C. L. see Jacobs, Charles Louis.

Jacobs, Charles Louis, 1879-
xJacobs, C. L.
Relation of the Teacher's Education to Her
Effectiveness. AMS Pr.

Jacobs, Charles M.
xJacobs, Charles M.
Measuring the Quality of Patient Care: The
Rationale for Outcome Audit. Ballinger Pub.

Jacobs, David, 1939-
xJacobs, David.
An American Conscience: Woodrow Wilson's
Search for World Peace. Har-Row.
Architecture. Newsweek.
Chaplin, the Movies & Charlie. Har-Row.
Jacobs, David M. see Jacobs, David Michael.

Jacobs, David Michael, 1942-
xJacobs, David M.
UFO Controversy in America. Ind U Pr.

Jacobs, Diane.
xJacobs, Diane.
Hollywood Renaissance. A S Barnes.
Hollywood Renaissance. Dell.

Jacobs, Donald M.
xJacobs, Donald M.
Antebellum Black Newspapers: Indices to New
York Freedom's Journal (1827-1829), Rights
of All (1829) The Weekly Advocate (1837) &
The Colored American (1837-1841).
Greenwood.

Jacobs, Donald T.
xJacobs, Donald T.
Ride & Tie: The Challenge of Running &
Riding. Anderson World.

Jacobs, Dorri.
xJacobs, Dorri.
Priorities: How to Stay Young & Keep
Growing. Watts.

Jacobs, Eric.
xJacobs, Eric.
European Trade Unionism. Holmes & Meier.

Jacobs, Everett M.
xJacobs, Everett M.
ed. The Organization of Agriculture in the
Soviet Union & Eastern Europe. Allanheld.
Jacobs, Flora G. see Jacobs, Flora Gill.

Jacobs, Flora Gill.
xJacobs, Flora G.
Dolls' Houses in America: Historic
Preservation in Miniature. Scribner.

Jacobs, Francine.
xJacobs, Francine.
Africa's Flamingo Lake. Morrow.
The Freshwater Eel. Morrow.
The Legs of the Moon. Coward.
Sounds in the Sea. Morrow.

Jacobs, Francis Geoffrey.
xJacobs, G. F.
European Law & the Individual. Elsevier.

Jacobs, Frank.
xJacobs, Frank.
Alvin Steadfast on Vernacular Island.
Taplinger.
Jacobs, G. F. see Jacobs, Francis Geoffrey.
Jacobs, Gabriel. see Jacobs, Gabriel H. L.

Jacobs, Gabriel H. L.
xJacobs, Gabriel.
When Children Think: Using Journals to
Encourage Creative Thinking. Tchrs Coll.
Jacobs, George W. see Jacobs, George Wayne.

Jacobs, George Wayne.
xJacobs, George W.
How to Get Along in Portugal & Spain. S&S.
Jacobs, H. Barry. see Jacobs, Harvey Barry.

Jacobs, Harold R.
xJacobs, Harold R.

Elementary Algebra. W H Freeman.
Geometry. W H Freeman.

Jacobs, Harriet (Brent), 1818-1896
xJacobs, Harriet B.
Incidents in the Life of a Slave Girl. AMS Pr.
Incidents in the Life of a Slave Girl. Arno.
Jacobs, Harriet B. see Jacobs, Harriet (Brent).

Jacobs, Harvey Barry.
xJacobs, H. Barry.
The Spectre of Malpractice. Nationwide Pr.
Jacobs, Helen H. see Jacobs, Helen Hull.

Jacobs, Helen Hull.
xJacobs, Helen H.
Famous Modern American Women Athletes.
Dodd.

Jacobs, Henry E.
xJacobs, Henry E.
An Annotated Bibliography of Shakespearean
Burlesques, Parodies & Travesties. Garland
Pub.
Jacobs, Henry E. see Jacobs, Henry Eyster.

Jacobs, Henry Eyster, 1844-1932
xJacobs, Henry E.
Martin Luther, the Hero of the Reformation.
AMS Pr.
Jacobs, Herbert. see Jacobs, Herbert Austin.

Jacobs, Herbert Austin.
xJacobs, Herbert.
A Practical Guide for the Beginning Farmer.
Dover.

Jacobs, Howard.
xJacobs, Howard.
Charlie the Mole & Other Droll Souls. Pelican.
Jacobs, J. see Jacobs, Joseph.
Jacobs, J. A. see Jacobs, John Arthur.
Jacobs, J. Vernon. see Jacobs, James Vernon.

Jacobs, Jack.
xJacobs, Jack.
The Films of Norma Shearer. A S Barnes.
The Films of Norma Shearer. Citadel Pr.

Jacobs, Jack A.
xJacobs, J. A.
A Textbook on Geonomy. Halsted Pr.

Jacobs, James B.
xJacobs, James B.
Guard Unions & the Future of the Prisons. NY
Sch Indus Rel.

Jacobs, James Vernon, 1898-
xJacobs, J. Vernon.
Pref. by How to Speak & Pray in Public.
Standard Pub.

Jacobs, Jane, 1916-
xJacobs, Jane.
Death & Life of Great American Cities.
Random.
Economy of Cities. Random.
Economy of Cities. Random.

Jacobs, Jay.
xJacobs, Jay.
Color Encyclopedia of World Art. Crown.
Winning the Restaurant Game. McGraw.

Jacobs, Joan.
xJacobs, Joan.
Feelings: Where They Come from & How to
Handle Them. Tyndale.

Jacobs, John.
xJacobs, John.
Practical Golf. Times Bks.
Quick Cures for Weekend Golfers. S&S.

Jacobs, John Arthur, 1916-
xJacobs, J. A.
The Earth's Core. Acad Pr.
Geomagnetic Micropulsations. Springer-Verlag.
Jacobs, John K. see Jacobs, John Kedzie.

Jacobs, John Kedzie, 1918-
xJacobs, John K.
Against All Odds. Macmillan.

Jacobs, Joseph, 1854-1916
xJacobs, J.

Celtic Fairy Tales. Peter Smith.
English Fairy Tales. Peter Smith.
More Celtic Fairy Tales. Peter Smith.
xJacobs, Joseph.
Celtic Fairy Tales. Gordon Pr.
Celtic Fairy Tales. Dover.
Coo-My-Dove, My Dear. Atheneum.
English Fairy Tales. Dover.
English Fairy Tales. Merrimack Bk Serv.
Indian Fairy Tales. Gordon Pr.
Indian Fairy Tales. Peter Smith.
Indian Fairy Tales. Dover.
ed. Indian Fairy Tales. Core Collection.
Johnny Cake. Putnam.
More Celtic Fairy Tales. Gordon Pr.
More Celtic Fairy Tales. Dover.
Jacobs, Julius.
xJacobs, Julius.
Bronx Cheer: A Memoir. Lib Res.
Jacobs, Konrad, 1928-
xJacobs, Konrad.
Measure & Integral. Acad Pr.
Jacobs, Lawrence.
xJacobs, Lawrence.
Computerized Tomography of the Orbit &
Sella Turcica. Raven.
Jacobs, Leland B. see Jacobs, Leland Blair.
Jacobs, Leland Blair.
xJacobs, Leland B.
April Fool!. Garrard.
ed. Funny Bone Ticklers in Verse & Rhyme.
Garrard.
I Don't I Do. Garrard.
ed. Read-It-Yourself Storybook. Western Pub.
ed. Using Literature with Young Children.
Tchrs Coll.
What Would You Do?. Garrard.
Jacobs, Lewis.
xJacobs, Lewis.
The Documentary Tradition. Norton.
Jacobs, Linda.
xJacobs, Linda.
Arthur Ashe: Alone in the Crowd. EMC.
A Candle, a Feather, a Wooden Spoon. EMC.
Cathy Rigby: On the Beam. EMC.
Checkmate, Julie. EMC.
Chris Evert, Tennis Pro. EMC.
Everyone's Watching Tammy. EMC.
Laura Baugh: Golf's Golden Girl. EMC.
Lee Elder: The Daring Dream. EMC.
Mary Decker: Speed Records & Spaghetti.
EMC.
Natalie Cole: Star Child. EMC.
Jacobs, Lou.
xJacobs, Lou.
Amphoto Guide to Lighting. Amphoto.
Amphoto Guide to Selling Photographs: Rates
& Rights. Amphoto.
Expressive Photography. Goodyear.
How to Take Great Pictures with Your SLR. H
P Bks.
Instant Photography. Lothrop.
Olympus OM Camera Manual. Amphoto.
Jacobs, Louis.
xJacobs, Louis.
Hasidic Prayer. Schocken.
Theology in the Responsa. Routledge & Kegan.
Jacobs, M. H. see Jacobs, Merkel Henry.
Jacobs, Marcia.
xJacobs, Marcia.
The Excuse Book. Price Stern.
Jacobs, Melville, 1902-
xJacobs, Melville.
Content & Style of an Oral Literature:
Clackamas Chinook Myths & Tales. U of
Chicago Pr.
Northwest Sahaptin Texts. AMS Pr.
Jacobs, Merkel Henry, 1884-
xJacobs, M. H.

Diffusion Processes. Springer-Verlag.
Jacobs, Michael.
xJacobs, Michael.
Mythological Painting. Mayflower Bks.
Jacobs, Milton C., 1901-
xJacobs, Milton C.
Outline of Theatre Law. Greenwood.
Jacobs, Morris B. see Jacobs, Morris Boris.
Jacobs, Morris Boris, 1905-1965
xJacobs, Morris B.
Chemical Analysis of Foods & Food Products.
Krieger.
Jacobs, Muriel.
xJacobs, Muriel.
Antiquing in New Jersey & Bucks County,
Pennsylvania. Rutgers U Pr.
Jacobs, O. L. see Jacobs, O. L. R.
Jacobs, O. L. R.
xJacobs, O. L.
Introduction to Control Theory. Oxford U Pr.
Jacobs, P. see Jacobs, Philip.
Jacobs, Paul.
xJacobs, Paul.
Prelude to Riot: A View of Urban America
from the Bottom. Random.
Jacobs, Peter A.
xJacobs, Peter A.
Carboniogenic Activity of Zeolites. Elsevier.
Jacobs, Philip.
xJacobs, P.
Atlas of Hand Radiographs. Univ Park.
Jacobs, Roderick A.
xJacobs, Roderick A.
Readings in English Transformational
Grammar. Georgetown U Pr.
Jacobs, Sheldon.
xJacobs, Sheldon.
Put Money in Your Pocket: The Art of
Selecting No-Load Mutual Funds for
Maximum Gains. S&S.
Jacobs, Sidney.
xJacobs, Sidney.
The Right to a Decent House. Routledge &
Kegan.
Jacobs, Suzanne E.
xJacobs, Suzanne E.
The College Writer's Handbook. Wiley.
Jacobs, Sylvester.
xJacobs, Sylvester.
photos by Portrait of a Shelter. Inter-Varsity.
Jacobs, W. W. see Jacobs, William Wymark.
Jacobs, Wilbur R.
xJacobs, Wilbur R.
Turner, Bolton, & Webb: Three Historians of
the American Frontier. U of Wash Pr.
Jacobs, William. see Jacobs, William J.
Jacobs, William J.
xJacobs, William.
The Pastor & the Patient: An Informal Guide
to New Directions in Medical Ethics. Paulist
Pr.
Jacobs, William P. see Jacobs, William Paul.
Jacobs, William Paul, 1919-
xJacobs, William P.
Plant Hormones & Plant Development.
Cambridge U Pr.
Jacobs, William W. see Jacobs, William Wymark.
Jacobs, William Wymark, 1863-1943
xJacobs, W. W.
Cargoes. Branden.
xJacobs, William W.
Captains All. Arno.
Light Freights. Arno.
Many Cargoes. Arno.
More Cargoes. Arno.
Jacobs, Zeney. see Jacobs, Zeney P.
Jacobs, Zeney P.
xJacobs, Zeney.

Communicating with the Computer:
Introductory Experiences, Basic. Allyn.
Jacobsen, C. see Jacobsen, C. G.
Jacobsen, C. G.
xJacobsen, C.
Soviet Strategy-Soviet Foreign Policy: Military
Considerations Affecting Soviet
Policy-Making. Humanities.
Jacobsen, C. J. see Jacobsen, Carl G.
Jacobsen, Carl G.
xJacobsen, C. J.
Soviet Strategic Initiatives: Challenge &
Response. Praeger.
Jacobsen, Charles W.
xJacobsen, Charles W.
Check Points on How to Buy Oriental Rugs. C
E Tuttle.
Jacobsen, Einar W. see Jacobsen, Einar William.
Jacobsen, Einar William, 1893-
xJacobsen, Einar W.
Educational Opportunities Provided for
Post-Graduate Students in Public High
Schools. AMS Pr.
Jacobsen, Thorkild, 1904-
xJacobsen, Thorkild.
Sumerian King List. U of Chicago Pr.
Toward the Image of Tammuz & Other Essays
on Mesopotamian History & Culture.
Harvard U Pr.
Jacobsohn, Gary J., 1946-
xJacobsohn, Gary J.
Pragmatism, Statesmanship, & the Supreme
Court. Cornell U Pr.
Jacobson, Angeline, 1910-
xJacobson, Angeline.
Contemporary Native American Literature: A
Selected & Partially Annotated Bibliography.
Scarecrow.
Jacobson, Arthur. see Jacobson, Arthur Clarence.
Jacobson, Arthur C. see Jacobson, Arthur Clarence.
Jacobson, Arthur Clarence, 1872-
xJacobson, Arthur.
Genius: Some Revaluations. R West.
xJacobson, Arthur C.
Genius: Some Revaluations. Kennikat.
Jacobson, Bernard.
xJacobson, Bernard.
Conductors on Conducting. Columbia Pub.
The Music of Johannes Brahms. Fairleigh
Dickinson.
Jacobson, Bertil.
xJacobson, Bertil.
Medicine & Clinical Engineering. P-H.
Jacobson, D. H. see Jacobson, David H.
Jacobson, Dan.
xJacobson, Dan.
The Confessions of Josef Baisz. Har-Row.
Jacobson, Daniel.
xJacobson, Daniel.
The Gatherers. Watts.
Jacobson, David H.
xJacobson, D. H.
Extensions of Linear-Quadratic Control,
Optimization & Matrix Theory. Acad Pr.
Jacobson, Edith.
xJacobson, Edith.
Depression: Comparative Studies of Normal,
Neurotic & Psychotic Conditions. Intl Univs
Pr.
Psychotic Conflict & Reality. Intl Univs Pr.
Jacobson, Edmund, 1888-
xJacobson, Edmund.
Progressive Relaxation: A Physiological &
Clinical Investigation of Muscular States &
Their Significance in Psychology & Medical
Practice. U of Chicago Pr.
Jacobson, Gary C.
xJacobson, Gary C.
Money in Congressional Elections. Yale U Pr.
Jacobson, Harold K. see Jacobson, Harold Karan.

Jacobson, Harold Karan.
xJacobson, Harold K.
America's Foreign Policy. Phila Bk Co.
Networks of Interdependence: International
Organizations & the Global Political System.
Knopf.
Jacobson, Helen.
xJacobson, Helen.
First Book of Letter Writing. Watts.
Jacobson, Howard, 1940-
xJacobson, Howard.
Ovid's Heroides. Princeton U Pr.
Jacobson, Howard B. see Jacobson, Howard Boone.
Jacobson, Howard Boone.
xJacobson, Howard B.
ed. Automation & Society. Greenwood.
ed. Mass Communications Dictionary: A
Reference Work of Common Terminologies
for Press, Print, Broadcast, Film, Advertising
& Communications Research. Greenwood.
Jacobson, Marcus, 1930-
xJacobson, Marcus.
Developmental Neurobiology. Plenum Pub.
Jacobson, Martin, 1919-
xJacobson, Martin.
Insect Sex Pheromones. Acad Pr.
Insecticides of the Future. Dekker.
ed. Naturally Occurring Insecticides. Dekker.
Jacobson, Michael F.
xJacobson, Michael F.
Eater's Digest: The Consumer's Factbook of
Food Additives. Doubleday.
Jacobson, Morris. see Jacobson, Morris K.
Jacobson, Morris K.
xJacobson, Morris.
Wonders of Jellyfish. Dodd.
Wonders of Sponges. Dodd.
xJacobson, Morris K.
Wonders of Snails & Slugs. Dodd.
Wonders of Starfish. Dodd.
Wonders of the World of Shells Sea Land &
Fresh Water. Dodd.
Jacobson, Myrtle S.
xJacobson, Myrtle S.
Night & Day: The Interaction Between an
Academic Institution & Its Evening College.
Scarecrow.
Jacobson, N. see Jacobson, Nathan.
Jacobson, Nathan, 1910-
xJacobson, N.
Exceptional Lie Algebras. Dekker.
Lectures in Abstract Algebra. Springer-Verlag.
xJacobson, Nathan.
Structure & Representations of Jordan
Algebras. Am Math.
Structure of Rings. Am Math.
Jacobson, Neil S.
xJacobson, Neil S.
Marital Therapy: Strategies Based on Social
Learning & Behavior Exchange Principles.
Brunner Mazel.
Jacobson, Nolan P. see Jacobson, Nolan Pliny.
Jacobson, Nolan Pliny.
xJacobson, Nolan P.
Buddhism: The Religion of Analysis. S Ill U Pr.
Jacobson, Norman.
xJacobson, Norman.
Pride & Solace: The Functions & Limits of
Political Theory. U of Cal Pr.
Jacobson, Patricia.
xJacobson, Patricia.
A Horse Around the House. Crown.
Jacobson, Phyllis C.
xJacobson, Phyllis C.
Fundamental Skills in Physical Education.
Brigham.
Jacobson, Sally.
xJacobson, Sally.

ed. The Dance Horizons Travel Guide to Six of
the World's Dance Capitals: New York,
Washington, London, Paris, Leningrad &
Moscow.. Dance Horiz.
Jacobson, Sheldon A., 1903-
xJacobson, Sheldon A.
Comparative Pathology of the Tumors of Bone.
C C Thomas.
Jacobson, Sven.
xJacobson, Sven.
On the Use, Meaning & Syntax of English
Preverbal Adverbs. Humanities.
Jacobson, Walter O.
xJacobson, Walter O.
Compliance with Occupational Safety & Health
Act: State Programs for State & Local
Agencies in the United States. Intl Personnel
Mgmt.
Jacobson, Willard. see Jacobson, Willard J.
Jacobson, Willard J.
xJacobson, Willard.
Science for Children: A Book for Teachers.
P-H.
xJacobson, Willard J.
Population Education: A Knowledge Base.
Tchrs Coll.
Jacobsson, Erin E.
xJacobsson, Erin E.
A Life for Sound Money: Per Jacobsson-His
Biography. Oxford U Pr.
Jacobstein, J Myron.
xJacobstein, J. Myron.
Law Books in Print. Glanville.
ed. Law Books in Print, 1965. Glanville.
Jacobus, Charles. see Jacobus, Charles J.
Jacobus, Charles J.
xJacobus, Charles.
Texas Real Estate Law. Reston.
Jacobus, Donald L. see Jacobus, Donald Lines.
Jacobus, Donald Lines, 1887-
xJacobus, Donald L.
Genealogy As Pastime & Profession. Genealog
Pub.
Hale, House & Related Families Mainly of the
Connecticut River Valley. Genealog Pub.
History & Genealogy of the Families of Old
Fairfield. Genealog Pub.
Jacobus, Lee. see Jacobus, Lee A.
Jacobus, Lee A.
xJacobus, Lee.
Developing College Reading. HarBraceJ.
xJacobus, Lee A.
The Paragraph & Essay Book. HarBraceJ.
Sudden Apprehension: Aspects of Knowledge
in Paradise Lost. Mouton.
Jacobus de Vitriaco.
xJacobus De Vitriaco.
Exempla, or Illustrative Stories from the
Sermones Vulgares of Jacques De Vitry. B
Franklin.
Jacoby, Erich H, 1903-
xJacoby, Erich H.
Agrarian Unrest in Southeast Asia. Greenwood.
Jacoby, Felix, 1876-1959
xJacoby, Felix.
Apollodors Chronik: Eine Sammlung der
Fragmente. Arno.
Atthis: The Local Chronicles of Ancient
Athens. Arno.
Jacoby, G. Polly. see Jacoby, Gertrude Polly.
Jacoby, Gertrude Polly.
xJacoby, G. Polly.
Preparing for a Home Economics Career.
McGraw.
Jacoby, Henry.
xJacoby, Henry.
The Bureaucratization of the World. U of Cal
Pr.
Jacoby, Henry D.
xJacoby, Henry D.

Analysis of Investment in Electric Power.
Arno.
Clearing the Air: Federal Policy on Automotive
Emissions Control. Ballinger Pub.
Jacoby, Hilla.
xJacoby, Hilla.
photos by The Land of Israel. Thames Hudson.
Jacoby, J. H. see Jacoby, Jacob H.
Jacoby, Jacob.
xJacoby, Jacob.
Brand Loyalty: Measurement & Management.
Wiley.
Jacoby, Jacob H.
xJacoby, J. H.
ed. Serotonin Neurotoxins. NY Acad Sci.
Jacoby, Joan E.
xJacoby, Joan E.
The American Prosecutor: A Search for
Identity. Lexington Bks.
Jacoby, John E.
xJacoby, John E.
Two Mystic Communities in America.
Hyperion Conn.
Jacoby, Neil H. see Jacoby, Neil Herman.
Jacoby, Neil Herman, 1909-
xJacoby, Neil H.
Corporate Power & Social Responsibility: A
Blueprint for the Future. Free Pr.
Multinational Oil: A Study in Industrial
Dynamics. Macmillan.
The Polluters: Industry or Government.
Transatlantic.
Jacoby, Oswald.
xJacoby, Oswald.
The Backgammon Book. Bantam.
Backgammon Book. Penguin.
Penny Ante & up. Doubleday.
Jacoby, Samuel L. see Jacoby, Samuel L. S.
Jacoby, Samuel L. S.
xJacoby, Samuel L.
Mathematical Modeling with Computers. P H.
Jacoby, Sidney B. see Jacoby, Sidney Bernhard.
Jacoby, Sidney Bernhard, 1908-
xJacoby, Sidney B.
Ohio Civil Practice: A Guide to Civil Practice
in Ohio Under the Rules of Civil Procedure.
Banks-Baldwin.
Jacoby, Stephen M.
xJacoby, Stephen M.
Architectural Sculpture in New York City.
Dover.
Architectural Sculpture in New York City.
Peter Smith.
Jacoby, Susan.
xJacoby, Susan.
Inside Soviet Schools. Hill & Wang.
Inside Soviet Schools. Schocken.
The Possible She. Ballantine.
The Possible She. FS&G.
Jacot, Michael.
xJacot, Michael.
Last Butterfly. Ballantine.
Jacoway, Elizabeth, 1944-
xJacoway, Elizabeth.
Yankee Missionaries in the South: The Penn
School Experiment. La State U Pr.
Jacquard, A. see Jacquard, Albert.
Jacquard, Albert.
xJacquard, A.
The Genetic Structure of Populations.
Springer-Verlag.
Jacquemin, A. P. see Jacquemin, Alex.
Jacquemin, Alex.
xJacquemin, A. P.
ed. Welfare Aspects of Industrial Markets.
Kluwer Boston.
Jacques, Reginald, 1894-
xJacques, Reginald.
ed. Oxford S-A-B Song Book. Oxford U Pr.
Jacquet, H. see Jacquet, Herve.

Jacquet, Herve.
  xJacquet, H.
    Automorphic Forms on GL 2. Springer-Verlag.
Jacquier, Henri, 1907-
  xJacquier, Henri.
    Piracy in the Pacific: The Story of the
    Notorious Rorique Brothers. Dodd.
Jaczewski, J. see Jaczewski, Jerzy.
Jaczewski, Jerzy.
  xJaczewski, J.
    Logical Systems for Industrial Applications.
    Elsevier.
Jaedicke, Robert K.
  xJaedicke, Robert K.
    Accounting Flows: Income, Funds & Cash.
    P-H.
Jaeger, C. see Jaeger, Charles.
Jaeger, Charles, 1901-
  xJaeger, C.
    Rock Mechanics & Engineering. Cambridge U
    Pr.
Jaeger, Charles De. see De Jaeger, Charles.
Jaeger, Edmund C. see Jaeger, Edmund Carroll.
Jaeger, Edmund Carroll, 1887-
  xJaeger, Edmund C.
    The California Deserts. Stanford U Pr.
    Desert Wild Flowers. Stanford U Pr.
    Desert Wildlife. Stanford U Pr.
Jaeger, Ellsworth.
  xJaeger, Ellsworth.
    Nature Crafts. Macmillan.
Jaeger, J. C. see Jaeger, John Conrad.
Jaeger, John Conrad, 1907-
  xJaeger, J. C.
    An Introduction to Applied Mathematics.
    Oxford U Pr.
Jaeger, Murial. see Jaeger, Muriel.
Jaeger, Muriel.
  xJaeger, Murial.
    Adventures in Living, from Cato to George
    Sand. Arno.
Jaeger, Richard M.
  xJaeger, Richard M.
    ed. Minimum Competency Achievement
    Testing: Motives, Models, Measures &
    Consequences. McCutchan.
Jaensch, Dean.
  xJaensch, Dean.
    The Government of South Australia. U of
    Queensland Pr.
Jaffa, Harry V.
  xJaffa, Harry V.
    The Conditions of Freedom: Essays in Political
    Philosophy. Johns Hopkins.
    Thomism & Aristotelianism: A Study of the
    Commentary by Thomas Aquinas on the
    Nicomachean Ethics. Greenwood.
Jaffa, Herbert C.
  xJaffa, Herbert C.
    ed. Modern Australian Poetry: A Guide to
    Information Sources. Gale.
Jaffe. see Jaffe, Eugene D.
Jaffe, Adrian. see Jaffe, Adrian H.
Jaffe, Adrian H.
  xJaffe, Adrian.
    Process of Kafka's Trial. Mich St U Pr.
Jaffe, Austin J.
  xJaffe.
    Property Management in Real Estate
    Investment Decision-Making. Lexington Bks.
Jaffe, Bernard, 1896-
  xJaffe, Bernard.
    Men of Science in America: The Story of
    American Science Told Through the Lives &
    Achievements of Twenty Outstanding Men
    from Earliest Colonial Times to the Present
    Day. Arno.
    Michelson & the Speed of Light. Greenwood.
Jaffe, Dan.
  xJaffe, Dan.

    ed. Frontier Literature: Images of the American
    West. McGraw.
Jaffe, Dennis T.
  xJaffe, Dennis T.
    Healing from Within. Knopf.
Jaffe, Eugene D.
  xJaffe.
    Barron's How to Prepare for the Graduate
    Management Admission Test (GMAT).
    Barron.
Jaffe, Grace M. see Jaffe, Grace Mary Spurway.
Jaffe, Grace Mary Spurway.
  xJaffe, Grace M.
    Years of Grace. Iroquois Hse.
Jaffe, H. H. see Jaffe, Hans H.
Jaffe, Hans H.
  xJaffe, H. H.
    Symmetry in Chemistry. Krieger.
Jaffe, Harold.
  xJaffe, Harold.
    Mole's Pity. Braziller.
    Mole's Pity. Fiction Coll.
Jaffe, Hilda. see Jaffe, Hilde.
Jaffe, Hilde.
  xJaffe, Hilda.
    Children's Wear Design. Fairchild.
  xJaffe, Hilde.
    Draping for Fashion Design. Reston.
Jaffe, Irma. see Jaffe, Irma B.
Jaffe, Irma B.
  xJaffe, Irma.
    The Sculpture of Leonard Baskin. Viking Pr.
Jaffe, Leonard.
  xJaffe, Leonard.
    The Pitzel Holiday Book. Ktav.
Jaffe, Louis L. see Jaffe, Louis Leventhal.
Jaffe, Louis Leventhal.
  xJaffe, Louis L.
    Administrative Law: Cases & Materials. Little.
Jaffe, Norman S., 1924-
  xJaffe.
    Cataract Surgery & Its Complications. Mosby.
  xJaffe, Norman S.
    Pseudophakos. Mosby.
Jaffe, Rona.
  xJaffe, Rona.
    The Last Chance. S&S.
Jaffe, Sandra S. see Jaffe, Sandra Sohn.
Jaffe, Sandra Sohn.
  xJaffe, Sandra S.
    Becoming Parents: Preparing for the Emotional
    Changes of First-Time Parenthood.
    Atheneum.
Jaffe, Sherril, 1945-
  xJaffe, Sherril.
    This Flower Only Blooms Every Hundred
    Years. Black Sparrow.
Jaffin, David, 1937-
  xJaffin, David.
    As One. SBD.
    Space of. Elizabeth Pr.
Jagannath, S., 1953-
  xJagannath, S.
    Calculator Programs for the Hydrocarbon
    Processing Industries. Gulf Pub.
Jagchid, Sechin.
  xJagchid, Sechin.
    Mongolia's Culture & Society. Westview.
Jagendorf, M. A. see Jagendorf, Moritz Adolph.
Jagendorf, Moritz A. see Jagendorf, Moritz Adolph.
Jagendorf, Moritz Adolph.
  xJagendorf, M. A.
    One-Act Plays for Young Folks. Core
    Collection.
    Stories & Lore of the Zodiac. Vanguard.
  xJagendorf, Moritz A.
    Tales from the First Americans. Silver.
    Tales of Mystery. Silver.
  xJagendorf, Mortiz.

    Gypsies' Fiddle & Other Gypsy Tales.
    Vanguard.
Jagendorf, Mortiz. see Jagendorf, Moritz Adolph.
Jagerskiold, Stig. see Jagerskiold, Stig Axel Fridolf.
Jagerskiold, Stig Axel Fridolf, 1911-
  xJagerskiold, Stig.
    Collective Bargaining Rights of State Officials
    in Sweden. U of Mich Inst Labor.
Jagger, Brenda, 1936-
  xJagger, Brenda.
    Verity. Doubleday.
Jagoda, Robert.
  xJagoda, Robert.
    A Friend in Deed. Norton.
Jaguaribe, Helio.
  xJaguaribe, Helio.
    Economic & Political Development: A
    Theoretical Approach & a Brazilian Case
    Study. Harvard U Pr.
Jahn, Mike.
  xJahn, Mike.
    How to Make a Hit Record. Bradbury Pr.
    The Quark Maneuver. Ballantine.
    Switch. Berkley Pub.
Jahn, Otto, 1813-1869
  xJahn, Otto.
    Life of Mozart. Cooper Sq.
Jahn, Theodore L. see Jahn, Theodore Louis.
Jahn, Theodore Louis.
  xJahn, Theodore L.
    How to Know the Protozoa. Wm C Brown.
Jahoda, Gerald.
  xJahoda, Gerald.
    The Librarian & Reference Queries: A
    Systematic Approach. Acad Pr.
Jahoda, Gustav.
  xJahoda, Gustav.
    The Psychology of Superstition. Aronson.
    Psychology of Superstition. Penguin.
Jahoda, Marie.
  xJahoda, Marie.
    Freud & the Dilemmas of Psychology. Basic.
    Race Relations & Mental Health. Unipub.
Jahss, Melvin.
  xJahss, Melvin.
    Inro & Other Miniature Forms of Japanese
    Lacquer Art. C E Tuttle.
Jain, Chaman L.
  xJain, Chaman L.
    An Introduction to Direct Marketing. Am
    Mgmt.
Jain, D. see Jain, Devaki.
Jain, D. C.
  xJain, D. C.
    Parliamentary Privileges Under the Indian
    Constitution. Verry.
Jain, Devaki, 1933-
  xJain, D.
    ed. Indian Women. Heinman.
  xJain, Devaki.
    Indian Women. InterCulture.
Jain, H. C. see Jain, Hem Chandra.
Jain, Hem C. see Jain, Hem Chand.
Jain, Hem Chand, 1928-
  xJain, Hem C.
    ed. Worker Participation: Success & Problems.
    Praeger.
Jain, Hem Chandra, 1933-
  xJain, H. C.
    Law Library Administration & Reference. Intl
    Pubns Serv.
Jain, J. P. see Jain, Jagdish P.
Jain, Jagdish P., 1930-
  xJain, J. P.
    China, Pakistan & Bangladesh. South Asia Bks.
    Soviet Policy Towards Pakistan & Bangladesh.
    South Asia Bks.
Jain, Jyoti Prasad.
  xJain, J. P.

Religion & Culture of the Jains. South Asia
Bks.
Jain, M. K. *see* Jain, Mahinder Kumar.
Jain, Mahendra K.
xJain, Mahendra K.
Introduction to Biological Membranes. Wiley.
Jain, Mahinder Kumar, 1932-
xJain, M. K.
Numerical Solution of Differential Equations.
Halsted Pr.
Jain, R. K. *see* Jain, Ravinder Kumar.
Jain, Ranbir S. *see* Jain, Ranbir Singh.
Jain, Ranbir Singh.
xJain, Ranbir S.
Growth & Development of Governor-General's
Executive Council, 1858-1919. Verry.
Jain, Ravinder K. *see* Jain, Ravinder Kumar.
Jain, Ravinder Kumar.
xJain, R. K.
Environmental Impact Analysis: A New
Dimension in Decision Making. Van Nos
Reinhold.
xJain, Ravinder K.
Environmental Impact Analysis: A New
Dimension in Decision Making. Van Nos
Reinhold.
Jain, Ravindra K.
xJain, Ravindra K.
South Indians on the Plantation Frontier in
Malaya. Yale U Pr.
ed. Text & Context: The Social Anthropology
of Tradition. Inst Study Human.
Jain, Subhash C.
xJain, Subhash C.
Cases in Marketing Management. Grid Pub.
Jaini, Padmanabh S.
xJaini, Padmanabh S.
The Jaina Path of Purification. U of Cal Pr.
Jairazbhoy, R. A. *see* Jairazbhoy, Rafique Ali.
Jairazbhoy, Rafique Ali, 1925-
xJairazbhoy, R. A.
Ancient Egyptians & Chinese in America.
Rowman.
Jaiswal, N. K.
xJaiswal, N. K.
Priority Queues. Acad Pr.
Jakes, John.
xJakes, John.
On Wheels. Warner Bks.
Jakes, John. *see* Jakes, John W.
Jakes, John W., 1932-
xJakes, John.
The Bastard. BJ Pub Group.
The Furies. BJ Pub Group.
The Rebels. BJ Pub Group.
Secrets of Stardeep. NAL.
The Seekers. BJ Pub Group.
The Titans. BJ Pub Group.
The Warriors. BJ Pub Group.
Jaki, Stanley L.
xJaki, Stanley L.
Brain, Mind & Computers. Regnery-Gateway.
The Origin of Science & the Science of Its
Origin. Regnery-Gateway.
The Paradox of Olbers' Paradox: A Case
History of Scientific Thought. N Watson.
Planets & Planetarians: A History of Theories
of the Origin of Planetary Systems. Halsted
Pr.
Relevance of Physics. U of Chicago Pr.
Jakle, John A.
xJakle, John A.
Images of the Ohio Valley: A Historical
Geography of Travel. Oxford U Pr.
Jakobson, Roman.
xJakobson, Roman.

Preliminaries to Speech Analysis: The
Distinctive Features & Their Correlates. MIT
Pr.
The Sound Shape of Language. Ind U Pr.
Yeats' "Sorrow of Love" Through the Years.
Humanities.
Jakubowski, Patricia.
xJakubowski, Patricia.
The Assertive Option: Your Rights &
Responsibilities. Res Press.
Jalee, Pierre.
xJalee, Pierre.
Imperialism in the Seventies. Okpaku
Communications.
Jallade, Jean Pierre.
xJallade, Jean-Pierre.
Public Expenditures on Education & Income
Distribution in Colombia. Johns Hopkins.
Jallade, Jean-Pierre. *see* Jallade, Jean Pierre.
Jamaica Assembly - 1795-1796. *see* Jamaica. Assembly,
1795-1796.
Jamaica. Assembly, 1795-1796.
xJamaica Assembly - 1795-1796.
Proceedings: In Regard to the Maroon
Negroes. Negro U Pr.
Jambro, D. *see* Jambro, Donald J.
Jambro, Donald J., 1940-
xJambro, D.
Manufacturing Processes: Plastics. P-H.
James. *see* James, John A.
James, A.
xJames, A.
Biological Indicators of Water Quality. Wiley.
ed. Mathematical Models in Water Pollution
Control. Wiley.
James, A. Everette. *see* James, Alton Everette.
James, Allston.
xJames, Allston.
Attic Light. Capra Pr.
James, Alton Everette.
xJames, A. Everette.
Pediatric Nuclear Medicine. Saunders.
James, Anthony.
xJames, Antony.
Capital Punishment. Belmont-Tower.
James, Antony. *see* James, Anthony.
James, Arthur E. *see* James, Arthur Edwin.
James, Arthur Edwin, 1897-
xJames, Arthur E.
Chester County Clocks & Their Makers.
Schiffer.
James, Arthur M.
xJames, Arthur M.
A Dictionary of Thermodynamics. Halsted Pr.
James, Bessie (Rowland), 1895-
xJames, Bessie R.
Anne Royall's U. S. A.. Rutgers U Pr.
James, Bessie R. *see* James, Bessie (Rowland).
James, Brian R., 1936-
xJames, Brian R.
Homogeneous Hydrogenation. Wiley.
James, C. D. *see* James, Cecil David.
James, C. L. *see* James, Cyril Lionel Robert.
James, C. L. R. *see* James, Cyril Lionel Robert.
James, Cecil David.
xJames, C. D.
Twentieth Century French Reader. Pergamon.
James, Charles F. *see* James, Charles Fenton.
James, Charles Fenton, 1844-1902
xJames, Charles F.
Documentary History of the Struggle for
Religious Liberty in Virginia. Da Capo.
James, Coy H. *see* James, Coy Hilton.
James, Coy Hilton.
xJames, Coy H.
Silas Deane, Patriot or Traitor. Mich St U Pr.
James, Cyril Lionel Robert, 1901-
xJames, C. L.

Mariners, Renegades & Castaways: The Story
of Herman Melville & the World We Live in.
Norwood Edns.
xJames, C. L. R.
Nkrumah & the Ghana Revolution. Lawrence
Hill.
James, D. E.
xJames, D. E.
Student's Guide to Efficient Study. Pergamon.
James, D. E. *see* James, David Edward.
James, D. G. *see* James, David Gwilym.
James, Dan.
xJames, Dan.
Gunsmoke Mesa. Bouregy.
James, David.
xJames, David.
Better Boxing. Intl Pubns Serv.
Better Boxing. Soccer.
Driving to Here. Applezaba.
James, David Edward.
xJames, D. E.
Introduction to Quantitative Methods in
Economics. Wiley.
James, David G. *see* James, David Gwilym.
James, David Gwilym, 1905-1968
xJames, D. G.
Byron & Shelley. Folcroft.
The Life of Reason (Hobbes, Locke,
Bolingbroke). Dynamic Learn Corp.
Wordsworth & Tennyson. Folcroft.
xJames, David G.
Wordsworth & Tennyson. Haskell.
James, Dilmus. *see* James, Dilmus D.
James, Dilmus D.
xJames, Dilmus.
Used Machinery & Economic Development.
Mich St U Busn.
James, Don.
xJames, Don.
Butte's Memory Book. Caxton.
James, Don L.
xJames, Don L.
Retailing Today: An Introduction. HarBraceJ.
James, Dorothy. *see* James, Dorothy Buckton.
James, Dorothy B. *see* James, Dorothy Buckton.
James, Dorothy Buckton, 1937-
xJames, Dorothy.
Poverty, Politics & Change. P-H.
xJames, Dorothy B.
ed. Analyzing Poverty Policy. Lexington Bks.
The Contemporary Presidency. Pegasus.
James, E. O.
xJames, Edwin O.
Christian Myth & Ritual: A Historical Study.
Peter Smith.
James, Edwin O. *see* James, E. O.
James, Edgar C.
xJames, Edgar C.
Arabs, Oil, & Energy. Moody.
James, Edward T.
xJames, Edward T.
ed. Notable American Women, 1607-1950: A
Biographical Dictionary. Harvard U Pr.
James, Edwin O. *see* James, E. O.
James, Elizabeth.
xJames, Elizabeth.
How to Grow a Hundred Dollars. Lothrop.
How to Keep a Secret: Writing & Talking in
Code. Lothrop.
The Simple Facts of Simple Machines.
Lothrop.
Understanding Money. Raintree Pubs.
James, Fleming, 1904-
xJames, Fleming.
Civil Procedure. Little.
James Ford Bell Library, University of Minnesota. *see*
Minnesota. University. Library. James Ford Bell
Collection.
James, G. D. *see* James, Gordon Douglas.
James, George W. *see* James, George Wharton.

James, George Wharton, 1858-1923
xJames, George W.
Indian Blankets & Their Makers. Dover.
Indian Blankets & Their Makers. Rio Grande.
The Old Franciscan Missions of California.
Longwood Pr.
James, Gordon Douglas, 1945-
xJames, G. D.
The Representation Theory of the Symmetric
Groups. Springer-Verlag.
James, Grace.
xJames, Grace.

Japanese Fairy Tales. Mayflower Bks.
James, Harry C. *see* James, Harry Clebourne.

James, Harry Clebourne, 1896-
xJames, Harry C.

Pages From Hopi History. U of Ariz Pr.
James, Henry, 1843-1916

xJames, Henry.
The Ambassadors. Dutton.
Ambassadors. Har-Row.
Ambassadors. Kelley.
Ambassadors. NAL.
The Ambassadors. Penguin.
Ambassadors. HM.
Ambassadors. Norton.
Ambassadors. Airmont.
American. HR&W.
American. Kelley.
American. NAL.
American. HM.
American. Airmont.
American Scene. Ind U Pr.
The Aspern Papers & Other Stories. Penguin.
Awkward Age. Kelley.
Awkward Age. Norton.
Awkward Age. Penguin.
Bostonians. Modern Lib.
The Bostonians. NAL.
The Bostonians. Penguin.
Bundle of Letters. Folcroft.
A Bundle of Letters. R West.
Charles W. Eliot, President of Harvard
University. AMS Pr.
The Europeans. Penguin.
The Europeans. Queens Hse.
The Europeans: A Facsimile of the Manuscript.
Fertig.
French Poets & Novelists. Arno.
French Poets & Novelists. Folcroft.
French Poets & Novelists. Gordon Pr.
French Poets & Novelists. R West.
Golden Bowl. Kelley.
The Golden Bowl. Penguin.
The Golden Bowl. Popular Lib.
Henry James & H. G. Wells: A Record of
Their Friendship, Their Debate on the Art of
Fiction, & Their Quarrel. Greenwood.
Henry James & Robert Louis Stevenson: A
Record of Friendship & Criticism. Hyperion
Conn.
The House of Fiction: Essays on the Novel.
Greenwood.
Letters. Octagon.
The Letters of Henry James: 1883-1895.
Harvard U Pr.
Literary Reviews & Essays, on American,
English & French Literature. AMS Pr.
Literary Reviews & Essays on American,
English, & French Literature. Coll & U Pr.
Little Tour in France. AMS Pr.
Little Tour in France. Folcroft.
A Little Tour in France. Gordon Pr.
A Little Tour in France. Scholarly.
A London Life. Grove.
Master Eustace. Arno.
Master Eustace. Folcroft.
Notes & Reviews. Arno.

The Other House. Arno.
The Other House. Queens Hse.
Partial Portraits. Folcroft.
Partial Portraits. Greenwood.
Partial Portraits. Haskell.
Partial Portraits. U of Mich Pr.
Portable Henry James. Penguin.
Portrait of a Lady. Kelley.
Portrait of a Lady. Modern Lib.
Portrait of a Lady. NAL.
Portrait of a Lady. Oxford U Pr.
The Portrait of a Lady. Penguin.
Portrait of a Lady. HM.
The Portrait of a Lady. Regents Pub.
Portrait of a Lady. Airmont.
Portraits of Places. Arno.
Princess Casamassima. Kelley.
Princess Casamassima. Peter Smith.
The Princess Casamassima. T Y Crowell.
Real Thing, & Other Tales. Arno.
Real Thing & Other Tales. Folcroft.
The Reverberator. Grove.
Soft Side. Arno.
Soft Side. Folcroft.
The Speech & Manners of American Women.
Lancaster Hse Pr.
Watch & Ward. Grove.
James, Hunter.
xJames, Hunter.
The Quiet People of the Land: A Story of the
North Carolina Moravians in Revolutionary
Times. U of NC Pr.
James, I. M. *see* James, Ioan Mackenzie.
James, Ioan Mackenzie, 1928-
xJames, I. M.
The Topology of Stiefel Manifolds. Cambridge
U Pr.
James, Ivor.
xJames, Ivor.
The Source of "the Ancient Mariner". Folcroft.
James, J. A. *see* James, James Alton.
James, James A. *see* James, James Alton.
James, James Alton, 1864-1962
xJames, J. A.
Constitution & Admission of Iowa into the
Union. Johnson Repr.
English Institutions & the American Indian.
Johnson Repr.
xJames, James A.
Constitution & Admission of Iowa into the
Union. AMS Pr.
English Institutions & the American Indian.
AMS Pr.
Life of George Rogers Clark. AMS Pr.
Life of George Rogers Clark. Greenwood.
Life of George Rogers Clark. Scholarly.
James, John, 1913-
xJames, John.
Flowers When You Want Them: A Grower's
Guide to Out-of-Season Bloom. Dutton.
History of the Worsted Manufacture in
England. Biblio Dist.
James, John A., 1946-
xJames.
Renal Disease in Childhood. Mosby.
xJames, John A.
Money & Capital Markets in Postbellum
America. Princeton U Pr.
James, Joseph B. *see* James, Joseph Bliss.
James, Joseph Bliss, 1912-
xJames, Joseph B.
Framing of the Fourteenth Amendment. Peter
Smith.
Framing of the Fourteenth Amendment. U of
Ill Pr.
James, L. *see* James, Leonard Frank.
James, L. D. *see* James, Leonard Douglas.
James, Leigh.
xJames, Leigh.

The Capitol Hill Affair. Manor Bks.
James, Leigh. *see* James, Robert Leigh.
James, Leonard Douglas.
xJames, L. D.
Economics of Water Resources Planning.
McGraw.
James, Leonard F. *see* James, Leonard Frank.
James, Leonard Frank.
xJames, L.
How to Prepare for the College Board
Achievement Test: European History &
World Cultures. Barron.
xJames, Leonard F.
Following the Frontier: American
Transportation in the Nineteenth Century.
HarBraceJ.
James, Margaret.
xJames, Margaret.
A Voice in the Darkness. St Martin.
A Voice in the Darkness. G K Hall.
James, Marquis, 1891-1955
xJames, Marquis.
Andrew Jackson: The Border Captain. Peter
Smith.
The Raven: A Biography of Sam Houston.
Larlin Corp.
James, Michael.
xJames, Michael.
Dizzy Gillespie. A S Barnes.
James, Montague R. *see* James, Montague Rhodes.
James, Montague Rhodes, 1862-1936
xJames, Montague R.
The Five Jars. Arno.
Ghost-Stories of an Antiquary. Arno.
Ghost Stories of an Antiquary. Dover.
Ghost Stories of an Antiquary. Peter Smith.
More Ghost Stories of an Antiquary. Arno.
Thin Ghost, & Others. Arno.
James, Muriel.
xJames, Muriel.
Born to Win: Transactional Analysis with
Gestalt Experiments. A-W.
Marriage Is for Loving. A-W.
James, Naomi, Dame.
xJames, Naomi.
Alone Around the World. Coward.
James, Otis.
xJames, Otis.
Dolly Parton. Music Sales.
James, P. D.
xJames, P. D.
Cover Her Face. Popular Lib.
Cover Her Face. G K Hall.
Death of an Expert Witness. G K Hall.
Death of an Expert Witness. Popular Lib.
Innocent Blood. Scribner.
A Mind to Murder. Popular Lib.
A Mind to Murder. G K Hall.
James, Peter N., 1940-
xJames, Peter N.
Soviet Conquest from Space. Arlington Hse.
James, Preston E. *see* James, Preston Everett.
James, Preston Everett.
xJames, Preston E.
One World Divided: A Geographer Looks at
the Modern World. Wiley.
James, Rebecca.
xJames, Rebecca.
The House Is Dark. Popular Lib.
Tomorrow Is Mine. Doubleday.
James, Rebecca. *see* James, Rebecca Salsbury.
James, Rebecca Salsbury.
xJames, Rebecca.
Storm's End. Popular Lib.
James, Richard.
xJames, Richard.

Study Guide to the Multiple Choice
Examinations for Third & Second Mates.
Cornell Maritime.
James, Robert Leigh, 1918-
xJames, Leigh.
The Caliph Intrigue. Dodd.
James, Robert R. see James, Robert Rhodes.
James, Robert Rhodes, 1933-
xJames, Robert R.
The British Revolution 1880-1939. Knopf.
James, Sidney V. see James, Sydney V.
James, Stewart.
xJames, Stewart.
ed. Abbott's Encyclopedia of Rope Tricks for
Magicians. Dover.
Abbott's Encyclopedia of Rope Tricks for
Magicians. Peter Smith.
James, Stuart, 1926-
xJames, Stuart.
The Complete Beginner's Guide to Judo.
Doubleday.
James, Sydney C.
xJames, Sydney C.
Farm Accounting & Business Analysis. Iowa St
U Pr.
James, Sydney V.
xJames, Sidney V.
Colonial Rhode Island: A History. Kraus Intl.
xJames, Sydney V.
People Among Peoples: Quaker Benevolence in
Eighteenth Century America. Harvard U Pr.
James, T. H. see James, Thomas Howard.
James, Thomas Howard.
xJames, T. H.
ed. Theory of the Photographic Process.
Macmillan.
James, Thomas N.
xJames, Thomas N.
Anatomy of the Coronary Arteries. Har-Row.
James, Tony.
xJames, Tony.
The Grabbers. Nordon Pubns.
James, Vivian H. see James, Vivian Hector Thomas.
James, Vivian Hector Thomas.
xJames, Vivian H.
ed. The Adrenal Gland. Raven.
James, William.
xJames, William.
Collected Essays & Reviews. Russell.
The Meaning of Truth: A Sequel to
Pragmatism. Harvard U Pr.
Meaning of Truth: A Sequel to Pragmatism. U
of Mich Pr.
Memories & Studies. Folcroft.
Memories & Studies. Greenwood.
Memories & Studies. Scholarly.
On Some of Life's Ideals. Folcroft.
Pragmatism. Hackett Pub.
Pragmatism. NAL.
Principles of Psychology. Dover.
Principles of Psychology. Peter Smith.
Some Problems of Philosophy. Harvard U Pr.
Some Problems of Philosophy: A Beginning of
an Introduction to Philosophy. Greenwood.
The Varieties of Religious Experience.
Doubleday.
Varieties of Religious Experience. Macmillan.
Varieties of Religious Experience. Modern Lib.
Varieties of Religious Experience. NAL.
James, William M.
xJames, William M.
The Death Train. Pinnacle Bks.
First Death. Pinnacle Bks.
Sonora Slaughter. Pinnacle Bks.
James, William M. see James, William Milburne.
James, William Milburne, Sir, 1881-
xJames, William M.
British Navy in Adversity: A Study of the War
of American Independence. Russell.
James, Wilma R. see James, Wilma Roberts.

James, Wilma Roberts.
xJames, Wilma R.
Propagate Your Own Plants. Naturegraph.
Jameson, Anna Brownell (Murphy), 1794-1860
xJameson, Anna M.
Memoirs of the Loves of the Poets:
Biographical Sketches of Women Celebrated
in Ancient & Modern Poetry. Arno.
Jameson, Anna M. see Jameson, Anna Brownell
(Murphy).
Jameson, Cynthia.
xJameson, Cynthia.
Catofy the Clever. Coward.
The Clay Pot Boy. Coward.
A Day with Whisker Wickles. Coward.
The Flying Shoes. Schol Bk Serv.
One for the Price of Two. Schol Bk Serv.
Jameson, D. L. see Jameson, David L.
Jameson, David L.
xJameson, D. L.
Genetics of Speciation. Acad Pr.
Jameson, Edwin. see Jameson, Edwin Milton.
Jameson, Edwin M. see Jameson, Edwin Milton.
Jameson, Edwin Milton, 1902-
xJameson, Edwin.
Gynecology & Obstetrics. Hafner.
xJameson, Edwin M.
Gynecology & Obstetrics. AMS Pr.
Jameson, Fredric.
xJameson, Fredric.
Fables of Aggression: Wyndham Lewis, the
Modernist As Fascist. U of Cal Pr.
Marxism & Form: Twentieth-Century
Dialectical Theories of Literature. Princeton
U Pr.
The Prison-House of Language: A Critical
Account of Structuralism & Russian
Formalism. Princeton U Pr.
Jameson, G. J. see Jameson, Graham James Oscar.
Jameson, Graham James Oscar.
xJameson, G. J.
Ordered Linear Spaces. Springer-Verlag.
Topology & Normed Spaces. Methuen Inc.
Jameson, J. Franklin. see Jameson, John Franklin.
Jameson, James S. see Jameson, James Sligo.
Jameson, James Sligo, 1856-1888
xJameson, James S.
Story of the Rear Column of the Emin Pasha
Relief Expedition. Negro U Pr.
Jameson, John F. see Jameson, John Franklin.
Jameson, John Franklin.
xJameson, J. Franklin.
Dictionary of United States History:
Alphabetical, Chronological, Statistical. Gale.
The History of Historical Writing in America.
Gordon Pr.
The History of Historical Writing in America.
Irvington.
xJameson, John F.
History of Historical Writing in America.
Greenwood.
ed. Privateering & Piracy in the Colonial
Period. Kelley.
Jameson, Kay C. see Jameson, Kay Charles.
Jameson, Kay Charles.
xJameson, Kay C.
The Influence of the United States Court of
Appeals for the District of Columbia on
Federal Policy in Broadcasting Regulation:
1929-1971. Arno.
Jameson, Kenneth.
xJameson, Kenneth P.
ed. Directions in Economic Development. U of
Notre Dame Pr.
Jameson, Kenneth P. see Jameson, Kenneth.
Jameson, Storm, 1897
xJameson, Storm.

The Captain's Wife. Berkley Pub.
Love in Winter. Berkley Pub.
The Lovely Ship. Berkley Pub.
Jameson, Thomas.
xJameson, Thomas.
Essays on the Changes of the Human Body at
Its Different Ages. Arno.
Jamet, F. see Jamet, Francis.
Jamet, Francis.
xJamet, F.
Flash Radiography. Elsevier.
Jamieson, B. G. see Jamieson, B. G. M.
Jamieson, B. G. M.
xJamieson, B. G.
Tropical Plant Types. Pergamon.
Jamieson, Madolyn.
xJamieson, Madolyn.
Life Shine. Valkyrie Pr.
Jamieson, Pat.
xJamieson, Pat.
A Topsy-Turvy Tale. Western Pub.
Jamieson, Robert.
xJamieson, Robert.
Burns in His Youth, & How He Grew to Be a
Poet; Burns in His Maturity, & How He
Spent It. Folcroft.
Jamison, Andrew.
xJamison, Andrew.
Steam-Powered Automobile: An Answer to Air
Pollution. Ind U Pr.
Jamison, Dean.
xJamison, Dean.
Radio for Education & Development. Sage.
Jamison, Philip, 1925-
xJamison, Philip.
Capturing Nature in Watercolor.
Watson-Guptill.
Jamison, Ronald D.
xJamison, Ronald D.
Modern College Algebra & Trigonometry: With
Applications. HarBraceJ.
Jamison, Ted. see Jamison, Ted R.
Jamison, Ted R.
xJamison, Ted.
George Monck & the Restoration: Victor
Without Bloodshed. Tex Christian.
Jamison, William A. see Jamison, William Alexander.
Jamison, William Alexander.
xJamison, William A.
Arnold & the Romantics. Folcroft.
Jampol, Hyman.
xJampol, Hyman.
The Weekend Athlete's Way to a Pain Free
Monday. J P Tarcher.
Jampolsky, Gerald G., 1925-
xJampolsky, Gerald G.
Love Is Letting Go of Fear. Celestial Arts.
Janaro, R. P. see Janaro, Richard Paul.
Janaro, Richard P. see Janaro, Richard Paul.
Janaro, Richard Paul.
xJanaro, R. P.
Human Worth. HR&W.
xJanaro, Richard P.
The Art of Being Human: The Humanities As
a Technique for Living. Har-Row.
Jancel, R. see Jancel, Raymond.
Jancel, Raymond.
xJancel, R.
Foundations of Classical & Quantum Statistical
Mechanics. Pergamon.
Jancura, Elise G., 1938-
xJancura, Elise G.
Audit & Control of Computer Systems. Van
Nos Reinhold.
Janda, Kenneth.
xJanda, Kenneth.
Data Processing: Applications to Political
Research. Northwestern U Pr.
Jandt, Fred E.
xJandt, Fred E.

The Process of Interpersonal Communication.
     Har-Row.
Jane, Lionel C. *see* Jane, Lionel Cecil.
Jane, Lionel Cecil, 1879-1932
     xJane, Lionel C.
     Liberty & Despotism in Spanish America.
          Cooper Sq.
Janes, E. C. *see* Janes, Edward C.
Janes, Edward C.
     xJanes, E. C.
     A Boy & His Gun. A S Barnes.
     The First Book of Camping. Watts.
Janet, Pierre, 1859-1947
     xJanet, Pierre.
     Principles of Psychotherapy. Arno.
     xJanet, Pierre M.
     Psychological Healing: A Historical & Clinical
          Study. Arno.
Janet, Pierre M. *see* Janet, Pierre.
Janeway, Elizabeth.
     xJaneway, Elizabeth.
     Powers of the Weak. Knopf.
Janger, Allen R.
     xJanger, Allen R.
     Corporate Organization Structures: Service
          Companies. Conference Bd.
     The Personnel Function: Changing Objectives
          & Organization. Conference Bd.
Janick, Jules.
     xJanick, Jules.
     Advances in Fruit Breeding. Purdue.
     Horticultural Science. W H Freeman.
     Plant Science: An Introduction to World
          Crops. W H Freeman.
Janifer, Laurence. *see* Janifer, Laurence M.
Janifer, Laurence M.
     xJanifer, Laurence.
     Survivor. Ace Bks.
Janik, Carolyn.
     xJanik, Carolyn.
     The House Hunt Game: A Guide to Winning.
          Macmillan.
     Selling Your Home: A Guide to Getting the
          Best Price with or Without a Broker.
          Macmillan.
Janis, Irving L. *see* Janis, Irving Lester.
Janis, Irving Lester.
     xJanis, Irving L.
     Decision Making: A Psychological Analysis of
          Conflict, Choice & Commitment. Free Pr.
     Stress & Frustration. HarBraceJ.
Janis, J. Harold. *see* Janis, Jack Harold.
Janis, Jack Harold, 1910-
     xJanis, J. Harold.
     Business Writing. Har-Row.
Janis, Sidney, 1897-
     xJanis, Sidney.
     Abstract & Surrealist Art in America. Arno.
Janitch, Valerie.
     xJanitch, Valerie.
     Country Collage. Chilton.
     Dolls in Miniature. Chilton.
     Paper Flowers. Chilton.
Jank, Margaret, 1939-
     xJank, Margaret.
     Culture Shock. Moody.
Janke, Rolf.
     xJanke, Rolf.
     Architectural Models. Architectural.
     Architectural Models. Hastings.
Jankelevitch, Vladimir.
     xJankelevitch, Vladimir.
     Ravel. Greenwood.
Jankowsky, Kurt R.
     xJankowsky, Kurt R.
     The Neogrammarians: A Re-Evaluation of
          Their Place in the Development of Linguistic
          Science. Mouton.
Jannersten, Eric.
     xJannersten, Eric.

Precision Bridge. Scribner.
Janney, Samuel M. *see* Janney, Samuel Macpherson.
Janney, Samuel Macpherson, 1801-1880
     xJanney, Samuel M.
     The Life of William Penn: With Selections
          from His Correspondence & Autobiography.
          Arno.
Jannis, C. Paul.
     xJannis, C. Paul.
     Managing & Accounting for Inventories:
          Control, Income Recognition, & Tax
          Strategy. Wiley.
Jannott, Paul F.
     xJannott, Paul F.
     The Effective Bank Supervisor: How to
          Develop Management Skills. Bankers.
Janouch, Gustav.
     xJanouch, Gustav.
     Conversations with Kafka. New Directions.
Janov, Arthur.
     xJanov, Arthur.
     The Feeling Child. S&S.
     Feeling Child. S&S.
     Primal Man: The New Consciousness. T Y
          Crowell.
Janower, Murray L.
     xJanower, Murray L.
     Administration of a Radiology Department:
          Hints for Day-to-Day Operation. C C
          Thomas.
Janowitz, Morris.
     xJanowitz, Morris.
     ed. Community Political Systems. Greenwood.
     The Community Press in an Urban Setting. U
          of Chicago Pr.
     Institution Building in Urban Education.
          Russell Sage.
     Institution Building in Urban Education. U of
          Chicago Pr.
     The Last Half Century: Societal Change &
          Politics in America. U of Chicago Pr.
     Professional Soldier: A Social & Political
          Portrait. Free Pr.
Janowitz, Phyllis.
     xJanowitz, Phyllis.
     Rites of Strangers. U Pr of Va.
Jansen, C. J. *see* Jansen, Clifford J.
Jansen, Clifford J.
     xJansen, C. J.
     Readings in the Sociology of Migration.
          Pergamon.
Jansen, F. J. *see* Jansen, Frederik Julius Billeskov.
Jansen, Frederik Julius Billeskov, 1907-
     xJansen, F. J.
     Ludvig Holberg. Twayne.
Jansen, John.
     xJansen, John.
     The Love Diet: The Way to Permanent Weight
          Control. Macmillan.
Jansen, John F. *see* Jansen, John Frederick.
Jansen, John Frederick.
     xJansen, John F.
     The Resurrection of Jesus Christ in New
          Testament Theology. Westminster.
Jansen, Robert B., 1922-
     xJansen, Robert B.
     The ABC's of Bureaucracy. Nelson-Hall.
Jansky, Jeannette. *see* Jansky, Jeannette Jefferson.
Jansky, Jeannette Jefferson.
     xJansky, Jeannette.
     Preventing Reading Failure: Prediction,
          Diagnosis, Intervention. Har-Row.
Jansky, L. *see* Jansky, Ladislav.
Jansky, Ladislav.
     xJansky, L.
     Regulation of Depressed Metabolism &
          Thermogenesis. C C Thomas.
Janson, Florence E. *see* Janson, Florence Edith.
Janson, Florence Edith.
     xJanson, Florence E.

Background of Swedish Immigration,
          1840-1930. Arno.
Janson, H. *see* Janson, Horst Woldemar.
Janson, H. W. *see* Janson, Horst Woldemar.
Janson, Horst Woldemar.
     xJanson, H.
     History of Art & Music. P-H.
     xJanson, H. W.
     A Basic History of Art. P-H.
     xJanson, W.
     History of Art & Music. Abrams.
Janson, Lone E.
     xJanson, Lone E.
     The Copper Spike. Alaska Northwest.
Janson, Robert L., 1931-
     xJanson, Robert L.
     Production Control Desk Book. P-H.
Janson, W. *see* Janson, Horst Woldemar.
Janssen, Arlo T.
     xJanssen, Arlo T.
     International Stories: A Conversation Reader to
          Improve Your English. P-H.
Janssen, Johannes, 1829-1891
     xJanssen, Johannes.
     History of the German People at the Close of
          the Middle Ages. AMS Pr.
Janssen, L. P. *see* Janssen, Leon P. B. M.
Janssen, Leon P. B. M.
     xJanssen, L. P.
     Twin Screw Extrusion. Elsevier.
Janssen-Jurreit, Marielouise, 1941-
     xJanssen-Jurreit, Marielouise.
     Sexism: The Male Monopoly on History &
          Thought. FS&G.
Jansson, Tove.
     xJansson, Tove.
     Finn Family Moomintroll. Avon.
     Moominpappa at Sea. Avon.
     Sun City. Avon.
Jantsch, Erich.
     xJantsch, Erich.
     Design for Evolution: Self-Organization &
          Planning in the Life of Human Systems.
          Braziller.
Jantscher, Gerald R.
     xJantscher, Gerald R.
     Bread Upon the Waters: Federal Aids to the
          Maritime Industries. Brookings.
Jantz, Harold. *see* Jantz, Harold Stein.
Jantz, Harold S. *see* Jantz, Harold Stein.
Jantz, Harold Stein, 1907-
     xJantz, Harold.
     The Form of Faust: The Work of Art & Its
          Intrinsic Structures. Johns Hopkins.
     xJantz, Harold S.
     The First Century of New England Verse.
          Folcroft.
     The First Century of New England Verse.
          Norwood Edns.
Jantzen, Steven, 1941-
     xJantzen, Steven.
     Hooray for Peace: Hurrah for War: The United
          States During World War I. NAL.
Janusz, Gerald J.
     xJanusz, Gerald J.
     Algebraic Number Fields. Acad Pr.
Janvier, Jeannine.
     xJanvier, Jeannine.
     Fantastic Fish You Can Make. Sterling.
Janvier, T. A. *see* Janvier, Thomas Allibone.
Janvier, Thomas A. *see* Janvier, Thomas Allibone.
Janvier, Thomas Allibone, 1849-1913
     xJanvier, T. A.
     In Old New York. Gordon Pr.
     xJanvier, Thomas A.

The Aztec Treasure-House. Irvington.
Color Studies. Mss Info.
Color Studies. Somerset Pub.
Dutch Founding of New York. Friedman.
In Old New York. Mss Info.
Stories of Old New Spain. Mss Info.
Stories of Old New Spain. Somerset Pub.

Janzen, John M.
xJanzen, John M.
The Quest for Therapy in Lower Zaire. U of Cal Pr.

Japan - United States Seminar on Ordinary Differential & Functional Equations, Kyoto, 1971. *see* Japan-United States Seminar on Ordinary Differential and Functional Equations, Kyoto, 1971.

Japan External Trade Organization & Press International, Ltd. (Tokyo). *see* Nihon Boeki Shinkokai.

Japan-U. S. Seminar, Tokyo, 1973. *see* Japan-United States Seminar on Significance of Defects Inwelded Structures, Tokyo, 1973.

Japan-United States Conference on Libraries and Information Science in Higher Education, 3rd, Kyoto, 1975.
xJapan-U.S. Conference on Libraries & Information Science in Higher Education, 3rd, Kyoto, Japan, Oct. 28-31, 1975.
Japanese & U.S. Research Libraries at the Turning Point: Proceedings. Scarecrow.

Japan-United States Seminar on Ordinary Differential and Functional Equations, Kyoto, 1971.
xJapan - United States Seminar on Ordinary Differential & Functional Equations, Kyoto, 1971.
Proceedings. Springer-Verlag.

Japan-United States Seminar on Significance of Defects Inwelded Structures, Tokyo, 1973.
xJapan-U. S. Seminar, Tokyo, 1973.
Significance of Defects in Welded Structures: Proceedings. Intl Schol Bk Serv.

Japan-U.S. Conference on Libraries & Information Science in Higher Education, 3rd, Kyoto, Japan, Oct. 28-31, 1975. *see* Japan-United States Conference on Libraries and Information Science in Higher Education, 3rd, Kyoto, 1975.

Japan-USSR Symposium on Probability Theory, 3rd, Tashkent, 1975.
xJapan-USSR Symposium on Probablity Theory, 3rd.
Proceedings. Springer-Verlag.

Japan-USSR Symposium on Probablity Theory, 3rd. *see* Japan-Ussr Symposium on Probability Theory, 3rd, Tashkent, 1975.

Japp, Alexander H. *see* Japp, Alexander Hay.

Japp, Alexander Hay, 1839-1905
xJapp, Alexander H.
Thoreau: His Life & Aims. Folcroft.

Jaques Catell Press.
xJaques Catell Press.

ed. American Art Directory 1980. Bowker.
ed. American Book Trade Directory 1978-1979. Bowker.
ed. American Book Trade Directory 1979. Bowker.
ed. American Book Trade Directory 1980. Bowker.
ed. American Library Directory. Bowker.
ed. American Library Directory 1979. Bowker.
ed. American Library Directory 1980. Bowker.
American Men & Women of Science, Cumulative Index. Bowker.
ed. American Society of Composers, Authors & Publishers Biographical Dictionary. Bowker.
ed. Association of Executive Recruiting Consultants. Bowker.
ed. Biographical Directory of the American Academy of Pediatrics. Bowker.
ed. Biographical Directory of the American College of Physicians 1979. Bowker.
ed. Biographical Directory of the American Public Health Association. Bowker.
ed. Energy Research Programs Directory. Bowker.
ed. Industrial Research Laboratories of the U. S.. Bowker.
Compiled by Leaders in Education. Bowker.
ed. The Librarians Phone Book 1981. Bowker.
ed. Library Journal Book Review, 1979. Bowker.
ed. Who's Who in American Art 1980. Bowker.
Compiled by Who's Who in American Politics. Bowker.
ed. Who's Who in American Politics 1978-1980. Bowker.
xJaques Cattell Press for the APA.
ed. Biographical Directory of the American Psychiatric Association. Bowker.

Jaques Cattell Press. *see* Jaques Catell Press.
Jaques Cattell Press for the APA. *see* Jaques Catell Press.
Jaques, E. *see* Jaques, Elliott.

Jaques, Elliott.
xJaques, E.
Measurement of Responsibility: A Study of Work, Payment & Individual Capacity. Halsted Pr.

Jaques, Faith.
xJaques, Faith.
illus. Tilly's House. Atheneum.

Jaquish, M. P. *see* Jaquish, Michael P.

Jaquish, Michael P.
xJaquish, M. P.
Personal Resume Preparation. Wiley.

Jaray, Cornell.
xJaray, Cornell.
ed. Historic Chronicles of New Amsterdam, Colonial New York & Early Long Island, First & Second Series. Friedman.

Jarcho, Saul.
xJarcho, Saul.
ed. Medicine & Health Care. Arno.

Jarchow, Merrill E., 1910-
xJarchow, Merrill E.
Earth Brought Forth: A History of Minnesota Agriculture to 1855. Johnson Repr.

Jarde, Auguste. *see* Jarde, Auguste Francois Victor.

Jarde, Auguste Francois Victor.
xJarde, Auguste.
Formation of the Greek People. Cooper Sq.

Jardim, Anne.
xJardim, Anne.
First Henry Ford: A Study in Personality & Business Leadership. MIT Pr.

Jardin, Rosamond. *see* Du Jardin, Rosamond.
Jardin, Rosamond Du. *see* Du Jardin, Rosamond.

Jardine, Lisa.
xJardine, Lisa.
Francis Bacon: Discovery & the Art of Discourse. Cambridge U Pr.

Jardine, N. *see* Jardine, Nicholas.

Jardine, Nicholas.
xJardine, N.
Mathematical Taxonomy. Wiley.

Jaremko, Matt E.
xJaremko, Matt E.
Cognitive-Behavioral Reflections on Some Dimensions of Personality. U Pr of Amer.

Jares, Joe. *see* Jares, Joseph Frank.

Jares, Joseph Frank, 1937-
xJares, Joe.
illus. Whatever Happened to Gorgeous George. G&D.

Jarman, A. O. *see* Jarman, Alfred Owen Hughes.

Jarman, Alfred Owen Hughes.
xJarman, A. O.
ed. A Guide to Welsh Literature. Humanities.

Jarman, Catherine.
xJarman, Cathy.
Atlas of Animal Migration. T Y Crowell.

Jarman, Cathy. *see* Jarman, Catherine.

Jarman, Christopher.
xJarman, Christopher.
Fun with Pens. Taplinger.
Teach Your Children Woodwork. Sterling.

Jarman, Douglas.
xJarman, Douglas.
The Music of Alban Berg. U of Cal Pr.

Jarman, Lytton P.
xJarman, Lytton P.
The Bullnose & Flatnose Morris. David & Charles.

Jarman, Mark.
xJarman, Mark.
North Sea. Cleveland St Univ Poetry Ctr.

Jarman, Rosemary H. *see* Jarman, Rosemary Hawley.

Jarman, Rosemary Hawley.
xJarman, Rosemary H.
Crispin's Day: The Glory of Agincourt. Little.
Crown & Candlelight. Little.
Crown in Candlelight. Popular Lib.

Jarman, Rufus.
xJarman, Rufus.
Energy Merchant. Rosen Pr.

Jarman, T. L. *see* Jarman, Thomas Leckie.

Jarman, Thomas Leckie.
xJarman, T. L.
Democracy & World Conflict, 1868-1965: A History of Modern Britain. Humanities.
Socialism in Britain: From the Industrial Revolution to the Present Day. Taplinger.

Jarnow, J. A. *see* Jarnow, Jeannette A.

Jarnow, Jeannette A.
xJarnow, J. A.
Inside the Fashion Business: Text & Readings. Textile Bk.
xJarnow, Jeannette A.
Inside the Fashion Business: Text & Readings. Wiley.

Jarnow, Jill.
xJarnow, Jill.
The Complete Book of Pillow Stitchery. S&S.
The Patchwork Point of View. S&S.

Jarolimek, John.
xJarolimek, John.
Teaching & Learning in the Elementary School. Macmillan.

Jarrard, Leonard E.
xJarrard, Leonard E.
ed. Cognitive Processes of Nonhuman Primates. Acad Pr.

Jarrell, Randall, 1914-1965
xJarrell, Randall.

The Complete Poems. FS&G.
Poetry & the Age. FS&G.
Poetry & the Age. Octagon.
Poetry & the Age. Ecco Pr.
The Third Book of Criticism. FS&G.
Jarrell, Steve.
xJarrell, Steve.
Working Out with Weights. Arco.
Jarrett, Emmett.
xJarrett, Emmett.
God's Body. Hanging Loose.
Jarrett, Fred.
xJarrett, Fred.
Stamps of British North America. Quarterman.
Jarrett, H. R. see Jarrett, Harold Reginald.
Jarrett, Harold Reginald.
xJarrett, H. R.
Africa. Intl Pubns Serv.
Jarrett, James L. see Jarrett, James Louis.
Jarrett, James Louis, 1917-
xJarrett, James L.
The Humanities & Humanistic Education.
A-W.
Jarrod, Keith.
xJarrod, Keith.
Night Riders. Dell.
The Night Riders. Doubleday.
Jarry, Madeleine.
xJarry, Madeleine.
Period Needlepoint for Antique Furniture.
Morrow.
Jarvenpa, Aili.
xJarvenpa, Aili.
Half Immersed & Other Poems. North Star.
Jarves, J. J. see Jarves, James Jackson.
Jarves, James Jackson, 1818-1888
xJarves, J. J.
Glimpse at the Art of Japan. Saifer.
Jarvi, Edith. see Jarvi, Edith T.
Jarvi, Edith T.
xJarvi, Edith.
ed. Canadian Selection: Books & Periodicals for
Libraries. U of Toronto Pr.
Jarvie, I. C. see Jarvie, Ian C.
Jarvie, Ian C.
xJarvie, I. C.
Functionalism. Burgess.
Jarvik. see Jarvik, Murray E.
Jarvik, Murray E.
xJarvik.
Psychopharmacology in the Practice of
Medicine. ACC.
Jarvis. see Jarvis, Howard.
Jarvis, Ana C.
xJarvis, Ana C.
Career Education & Foreign Languages. HM.
Continuemos: Curso Intermedio De Espanol.
Heath.
Jarvis, D. C. see Jarvis, Deforest Clinton.
Jarvis, Deforest Clinton, M.D.
xJarvis, D. C.
Arthritis & Folk Medicine. Fawcett.
Folk Medicine. Fawcett.
Jarvis, Gilbert A.
xJarvis, Gilbert A.
The Challenge of Communication. Natl Textbk.
Responding to New Realities. Natl Textbk.
Jarvis, Howard.
xJarvis.
I'm Mad As Hell. Berkley Pub.
xJarvis, Howard.
I'm Mad As Hell. Times Bks.
Jarzebski, Z. M. see Jarzebski, Zdzisaw.
Jarzebski, Zdzisaw.
xJarzebski, Z. M.
Oxide Semiconductors. Pergamon.
Jaschek, Carlos.
xJaschek, Carlos.

ed. The Compilation, Critical Evaluation &
Distribution of Stellar Data. Kluwer Boston.
Jasen, David A.
xJasen, David A.
Rags & Ragtime: A Musical History.
Continuum.
Jasentuliyana, Nandasiri.
xJasentuliyana, Nandasiri.
Manual on Space Law. Oceana.
Jasmin, Sylvia.
xJasmin, Sylvia.
Behavioral Concepts & the Nursing Process.
Mosby.
Jason, Stuart.
xJason, Stuart.
Mayday Over Manhattan. Pinnacle Bks.
Jaspers, K. see Jaspers, Karl.
Jaspers, Karl, 1883-1969
xJaspers, K.
General Psychopathology. State Mutual Bk.
xJaspers, Karl.
Anaximander, Heraclitus, Parmenides, Plotinus,
Lao-Tzu, Nagarjuna. HarBraceJ.
Anselm & Nicholas of Cusa. HarBraceJ.
Future of Mankind. U of Chicago Pr.
General Psychopathology. U of Chicago Pr.
The Nature of Psychotherapy: A Critical
Appraisal. U of Chicago Pr.
The Origin & Goal of History. Greenwood.
Perennial Scope of Philosophy. Shoe String.
The Question of German Guilt. Greenwood.
Reason & Anti-Reason in Our Time. Shoe
String.
Spinoza. HarBraceJ.
Jaspersohn, William.
xJaspersohn, William.
A Day in the Life of a Veterinarian. Little.
How the Forest Grew. Greenwillow.
Jassem, Kate.
xJassem, Kate.
Chief Joseph, Leader of Destiny. Troll Assocs.
Jassey, William.
xJassey, William.
Spanish Grammar with Ease. Arc Bks.
Jastram, Roy W., 1915-
xJastram, Roy W.
The Golden Constant: The English &
American Experience, 1560-1976. Wiley.
Jastrow, Joseph, 1863-1944
xJastrow, Joseph.
ed. Story of Human Error. Arno.
Jastrow, Morris, 1861-1921
xJastrow, Morris.
Aspects of Religious Belief & Practice in
Babylonia & Assyria. Arno.
Jastrow, Robert.
xJastrow, Robert.
Astronomy: Fundamentals & Frontiers. Wiley.
God & the Astronomers. Norton.
Jastrzebski, Zbigniew D.
xJastrzebski, Zbigniew D.
The Nature & Properties of Engineering
Materials. Wiley.
The Nature & Properties of Engineering
Materials: SI Version. Wiley.
Jaswon, M. A. see Jaswon, Maurice Aaron.
Jaswon, Maurice Aaron.
xJaswon, M. A.
Integral Equation Methods in Potential Theory
& Elastostatics. Acad Pr.
Jaszi, Oscar. see Jaszi, Oszkar.
Jaszi, Oszkar, 1875-1957
xJaszi, Oscar.
Dissolution of the Habsburg Monarchy. U of
Chicago Pr.
Revolution & Counter-Revolution in Hungary.
Fertig.
Jategaonkar, A. V.
xJategaonkar, A. V.

Left Principal Ideal Rings. Springer-Verlag.
Jauncey, James. see Jauncey, James H.
Jauncey, James H.
xJauncey, James.
One-on-One Evangelism. Moody.
Jaures, Jean. see Jaures, Jean Leon.
Jaures, Jean Leon, 1859-1914
xJaures, Jean.
Histoire Socialiste De la Revolution Francaise.
AMS Pr.
Javadpour, Nasser.
xJavadpour, Nasser.
Principles & Management of Urologic Cancer.
Williams & Wilkins.
Javarek, Vera.
xJavarek, Vera.
Teach Yourself Serbo-Croat. McKay.
Javits, Jacob K. see Javits, Jacob Koppell.
Javits, Jacob Koppell.
xJavits, Jacob K.
The Defense Sector & the American Economy.
NYU Pr.
Javitz, Alex E. see Javitz, Alexander E.
Javitz, Alexander E.
xJavitz, Alex E.
ed. Materials Science & Technology for Design
Engineers. Hayden.
Javor, George. see Javor, George T.
Javor, George T., 1940-
xJavor, George.
Once Upon a Molecule. Southern Pub.
Jawetz, Ernest.
xJawetz, Ernest.
Review of Medical Microbiology. Lange.
Jaworski, Leon.
xJaworski, Leon.
After Fifteen Years. Gulf Pub.
Confession & Avoidance: A Memoir.
Doubleday.
Jay, Bill.
xJay, Bill.
Negative-Positive: A Philosophy of
Photography. Kendall-Hunt.
Jay, Carroll E.
xJay, Carroll E.
Gretchen, I Am. Avon.
Jay, John.
xJay, John.
Correspondence & Public Papers of John Jay,
1763-1781. B Franklin.
Jay, Karla.
xJay, Karla.
Lavender Culture. BJ Pub Group.
Jay, Martin, 1944-
xJay, Martin.
The Dialectical Imagination: A History of the
Frankfurt School & the Institute of Social
Research, 1923-1950. Little.
Jay, Ricky.
xJay, Ricky.
Cards As Weapons. Images Graphiques.
Jay, William, 1789-1858
xJay, William.
Review of the Causes & Consequences of the
Mexican War. Arno.
Jayakanthan, D., 1934-
xJayakanthan, D.
A Literary Man's Political Experiences:
Tamilnadu Politics Since 1946. South Asia
Bks.
Jayaram, R.
xJayaram, R.
Mass Spectrometry: Theory & Applications.
Plenum Pub.
Jayaratne, Srinika.
xJayaratne, Srinika.
Empirical Clinical Practice. Columbia U Pr.
Jayatilaka, Ayal De S.
xJayatilaka, Ayal De S.

Fracture of Engineering Brittle Materials.
Burgess-Intl Ideas.
Jayewardene, C. H. see Jayewardene, C. H. S.
Jayewardene, C. H. S., 1927-
xJayewardene, C. H.
Penalty of Death: The Canadian Experiment.
Lexington Bks.
Jayne, Benjamin A.
xJayne, Benjamin A.
ed. Theory & Design of Wood & Fiber
Composite Materials. Syracuse U Pr.
Jayne, Walter A. see Jayne, Walter Addison.
Jayne, Walter Addison, 1853-1929
xJayne, Walter A.
The Healing Gods of Ancient Civilizations.
AMS Pr.
Healing Gods of Ancient Civilizations. Elliots
Bks.
Jaynes, Julian.
xJaynes, Julian.
The Origin of Consciousness in the Breakdown
of the Bicameral Mind. HM.
Jayson, Malcolm.
xJayson, Malcolm.
ed. The Lumbar Spine & Back Pain. Grune.
xJayson, Malcolm I.
Understanding Arthritis & Rheumatism: A
Complete Guide to the Problems &
Treatment. Pantheon.
Jayson, Malcolm I. see Jayson, Malcolm.
Jazbi, B. see Jazbi, Basharat.
Jazbi, Basharat, 1932-
xJazbi, B.
ed. Pediatric Otorhinolaryngology. S Karger.
Jazwinski, A. H. see Jazwinski, Andrew H.
Jazwinski, Andrew H.
xJazwinski, A. H.
Stochastic Processes & Filtering Theory. Acad
Pr.
Jeal, Tim.
xJeal, Tim.
A Marriage of Convenience. S&S.
Jean, Marcel.
xJean, Marcel.
ed. The Autobiography of Surrealism. Viking
Pr.
Jean-Aubry, G. see Jean-Aubry, Georges.
Jean-Aubry, Georges, 1882-1950
xJean-Aubry, G.
Joseph Conrad in the Congo. Haskell.
Jeans, D. N. see Jeans, Dennis Norman.
Jeans, Dennis Norman.
xJeans, D. N.
Australia: A Geography. St Martin.
Jebb, Marjorie.
xJebb, Marjorie.
Tuscan Heritage. Verry.
Jech, Thomas. see Jech, Thomas J.
Jech, Thomas J.
xJech, Thomas.
Set Theory. Acad Pr.
Jedamus, Paul.
xJedamus, Paul.
Business Decision Theory. McGraw.
Jedin, Hubert.
xJedin, Hubert.
Handbook of Church History. Seabury.
Jedlicka, Allen D.
xJedlicka, Allen D.
Organization for Rural Development: Risk
Taking & Appropriate Technology. Praeger.
Jedrysek, Eleonora.
xJedrysek, Eleonora.
Psychoeducational Evaluation of the Preschool
Child: A Manual Utilizing the Haeussermann
Approach. Grune.
Jeejeebhoy, Khursheed N.
xJeejeebhoy, Khursheed N.

Gastrointestinal Diseases: Focus on Clinical
Diagnosis. Med Exam.
Jeep, Elizabeth.
xJeep, Elizabeth.
Classroom Creativity: An Idea Book for
Religion Teachers. Seabury.
Jeevar, Peter.
xJeevar, Peter.
Dovecots of Cambridgeshire. Oleander Pr.
Jeffares, A. Norman. see Jeffares, Alexander Norman.
Jeffares, Alexander Norman.
xJeffares, A. Norman.
The Circus Animals: Essays on W. B. Yeats.
Stanford U Pr.
A Commentary on the Collected Plays of W.
B. Yeats. Stanford U Pr.
A Commentary on the Collected Poems of W.
B. Yeats. Stanford U Pr.
Jeffares, Bo.
xJeffares, Bo.
The Artist in Nineteenth Century English
Fiction. Humanities.
Landscape Painting. Mayflower Bks.
Jefferies, Richard, 1848-1887
xJefferies, Richard.
The Gamekeeper at Home & the Amateur
Poacher. Oxford U Pr.
Wood Magic. Okpaku Communications.
Jefferis, Barbara.
xJefferis, Barbara.
The Tall One. Morrow.
Jeffers, H. Paul. see Jeffers, Harry Paul.
Jeffers, Harry Paul, 1934-
xJeffers, H. Paul.
The Adventure of the Stalwart Companions:
Heretofore Unpublished Letters & Papers
Concerning a Singular Collaboration Between
Theodore Roosevelt & Sherlock Holmes.
Edited & Annotated by H. Paul Jeffers.
Har-Row.
Jeffers, Janet.
xJeffers, Janet.
Look, Now Hear This: Combined Auditory
Training & Speechreading Instruction. C C
Thomas.
Speechreading (Lipreading). C C Thomas.
Jeffers, Robert J.
xJeffers, Robert J.
Principles & Methods for Historical Linguistics.
MIT Pr.
Jeffers, Susan.
xJeffers, Susan.
illus. All the Pretty Horses. Macmillan.
All the Pretty Horses. Schol Bk Serv.
Jeffers, William R.
xJeffers, William R.
Selling Yourself: The Way to a Better Job.
P-H.
Jefferson, Bernard L. see Jefferson, Bernard Levi.
Jefferson, Bernard Levi, 1887-1939
xJefferson, Bernard L.
Chaucer - the Consolation of Philosophy of
Boethius. Haskell.
Chaucer & the Consolation of Philosophy of
Boethius. Gordian.
Jefferson, George, Writer on Librarianship.
xJefferson, George.
Library Cooperation. Westview.
Jefferson, James W.
xJefferson, James W.
Primer of Lithium Therapy. Williams &
Wilkins.
Jefferson, Joseph, 1829-1905
xJefferson, Joseph.
Autobiography. Harvard U Pr.
Jefferson, Mark S. see Jefferson, Mark Sylvester William.
Jefferson, Mark Sylvester William, 1863-1949
xJefferson, Mark S.

Peopling the Argentine Pampa. Kennikat.
Jefferson, Thomas, Pres. U. S. 1743-1826
xJefferson, Thomas.
Calendar of the Correspondence of Thomas
Jefferson. B Franklin.
Correspondence of Jefferson & Du Pont de
Nemours. B Franklin.
Crusade Against Ignorance: Thomas Jefferson
on Education. Tchrs Coll.
Democracy. Greenwood.
The Portable Thomas Jefferson. Penguin.
Thomas Jefferson: A Biography in His Own
Words. Har-Row.
Jeffery, C. R. see Jeffery, Clarence Ray.
Jeffery, Clarence Ray.
xJeffery, C. R.
ed. Biology & Crime. Sage.
Crime Prevention Through Environmental
Design. Sage.
Jeffery, J. see Jeffery, Jonathan.
Jeffery, Jonathan, 1935-
xJeffery, J.
ed. Dehydrogenases Requiring Nicotinamide
Coenzymes. Birkhauser.
Jeffery, P. G. see Jeffery, Paul Geoffrey.
Jeffery, Paul Geoffrey.
xJeffery, P. G.
Chemical Methods of Rock Analysis.
Pergamon.
Jefferys, James B. see Jefferys, James Bavington.
Jefferys, James Bavington.
xJefferys, James B.
Story of the Engineers, 1800-1845. Johnson
Repr.
Jeffrey. see Jeffrey, D. Balfour.
Jeffrey, Adi-Kent T. see Jeffrey, Adi-Kent Thomas.
Jeffrey, Adi-Kent Thomas.
xJeffrey, Adi-Kent T.
Across the Land from Ghost to Ghost. New
Hope.
More Ghosts in the Valley. New Hope.
They Dared the Devil's Triangle. Warner Bks.
Jeffrey, D. Balfour.
xJeffrey.
Take It off & Keep It off: A Behavioral
Program for Weight Loss & Healthy Living.
P-H.
Jeffrey, David L., 1941-
xJeffrey, David L.
The Early English Lyric & Franciscan
Spirituality. U of Nebr Pr.
Jeffrey, Ernie.
xJeffrey, Ernie.
Armwrestling: How to Become a Champion. M
Sheldon Pub.
Jeffrey, Hugh C. see Jeffrey, Hugh Crozier.
Jeffrey, Hugh Crozier.
xJeffrey, Hugh C.
Atlas of Medical Helminthology &
Protozoology. Churchill.
Jeffrey, Julie R. see Jeffrey, Julie Roy.
Jeffrey, Julie Roy.
xJeffrey, Julie R.
Education for Children of the Poor: A Study of
the Origins & Implementation of the
Elementary & Secondary Education Act of
1965. Ohio St U Pr.
Frontier Women: The Trans-Mississippi West
1840-1880. Hill & Wang.
Jeffrey, Lloyd N.
xJeffrey, Lloyd N.
Thomas Hood. Twayne.
Jeffrey, Robin.
xJeffrey, Robin.

Decline of Nayar Dominance: Society &
Politics in Travancore 1847-1908. Holmes &
Meier.
ed. People, Princes & Paramount Power:
Society & Politics in the Indian Princely
States. Oxford U Pr.
Jeffrey, Sara.
xJeffrey, Sara.
Who Lives Here?. Dandelion Pr.
Jeffreys, A. E. *see* Jeffreys, Alan E.
Jeffreys, Alan E.
xJeffreys, A. E.
ed. The Art of the Librarian: A Collection of
Original Papers from the Library of the
University of Newcastle Upon Tyne.
Routledge & Kegan.
Jeffreys, Eurig.
xJeffreys, T. E.
Disorders of the Cervical Spine. Butterworths.
Jeffreys, Harold, Sir, 1891-
xJeffreys, Harold.
Cartesian Tensors. Cambridge U Pr.
Jeffreys, John.
xJeffreys, John.
Perennials for Cutting. Merrimack Bk Serv.
Jeffreys, T. E. *see* Jeffreys, Eurig.
Jeffries. *see* Jeffries, Vincent.
Jeffries, Derwin J.
xJeffries, Derwin J.
Lesson Planning & Lesson Teaching. Home &
Sch.
Jeffries, John W., 1942-
xJeffries, John W.
Testing the Roosevelt Coalition: Connecticut
Society & Politics in the Era of World War
II. U of Tenn Pr.
Jeffries, Joseph M. *see* Jeffries, Joseph Mary Nagle.
Jeffries, Joseph Mary Nagle, 1880-
xJeffries, Joseph M.
Palestine: The Reality. Hyperion Conn.
Jeffries, Roderic.
xJeffries, Roderic.
Against Time!. Har-Row.
Murder Begets Murder. St Martin.
Patrol Car. Har-Row.
Troubled Deaths. St Martin.
Jeffries, Vincent.
xJeffries.
Social Stratification: A Multiple Hierarchy
Approach. Allyn.
Jeffs, A. J. *see* Jeffs, Anthony J.
Jeffs, Angela.
xJeffs, Angela.
ed. Creative Crafts. Sterling.
Jeffs, Anthony J.
xJeffs, A. J.
Young People & the Youth Service. Routledge
& Kegan.
Jefimenko, Oleg D.
xJefimenko, Oleg D.
How to Entertain with Your Pocket Calculator:
Pastimes, Diversions, Games & Magic Tricks.
Electret Sci.
Jefkins, F. W. *see* Jefkins, Frank William.
Jefkins, Frank.
xJefkins, Frank.
Planned Press & Public Relations. Intl Ideas.
Jefkins, Frank William.
xJefkins, F. W.
Marketing & PR Media Planning. Pergamon.
Jegen, Mary E. *see* Jegen, Mary Evelyn.
Jegen, Mary Evelyn.
xJegen, Mary E.
ed. The Earth Is the Lord's: Essays on
Stewardship. Paulist Pr.
Jehlen, Myra.
xJehlen, Myra.

Class & Character in Faulkner's South. Citadel
Pr.
Class & Character in Faulkners South.
Columbia U Pr.
Jekyll, Gertrude, 1843-1932
xJekyll, Gertrude.
Old English Household Life: Some Account of
Cottage Objects & Country Folk. Rowman.
Jelavich, Barbara. *see* Jelavich, Barbara (Brightfield).
Jelavich, Barbara (Brightfield).
xJelavich, Barbara.
The Habsburg Empire in European Affairs,
1814-1918. Shoe String.
Jelavich, Charles.
xJelavich, Charles.
ed. The Balkans in Transition: Essays on the
Development of Balkan Life & Politics Since
the Eighteenth Century. Shoe String.
The Establishment of the Balkan National
States, 1804-1920. U of Wash Pr.
Tsarist Russia & Balkan Nationalism: Russian
Influence in International Affairs of Bulgaria
& Serbia, 1879-1886. Greenwood.
Jelen, F. C.
xJelen, F. C.
Cost & Optimization Engineering. McGraw.
Jelinek, Estelle C.
xJelinek, Estelle C.
ed. Women's Autobiography: Essays in
Criticism. Ind U Pr.
Jelinek, Mariann.
xJelinek, Mariann.
Institutionalizing Innovation: A Study of
Organizational Learning Systems. Praeger.
Jell, George C. *see* Jell, George Clarence.
Jell, George Clarence.
xJell, George C.
Master Builders of Opera. Arno.
Jellema, William W.
xJellema, William W.
ed. Efficient College Management. Jossey-Bass.
Jelliffe, D. B.
xJelliffe, D. B.
Infant Nutrition in the Subtropics & Tropics.
World Health.
Jellinek, E. M. *see* Jellinek, Elvin Morton.
Jellinek, Elvin Morton, 1890-1963
xJellinek, E. M.
The Disease Concept of Alcoholism. Coll & U
Pr.
Disease Concept of Alcoholism. Hillhouse.
Jellinek, Frank, 1908-
xJellinek, Frank.
The Civil War in Spain. Fertig.
Jellinek, Georg, 1851-1911
xJellinek, Georg.
The Declaration of the Rights of Man & of
Citizens: A Contribution to Modern
Constitutional History. Hyperion Conn.
Jellinek, J. Stephan. *see* Jellinek, Joseph Stephan.
Jellinek, Joseph Stephan.
xJellinek, J. Stephan.
The Use of Fragrance in Consumer Products.
Wiley.
xJellinek, S.
Formulation & Function of Cosmetics. Wiley.
Jellinek, S. *see* Jellinek, Joseph Stephan.
Jellison, Charles A. *see* Jellison, Charles Albert.
Jellison, Charles Albert.
xJellison, Charles A.
Fessenden of Maine, Civil War Senator.
Syracuse U Pr.
Jellison, Jerald M., 1942-
xJellison, Jerald M.
I'm Sorry - I Didn't Mean to - & Other Lies
We Love to Tell. Chatham Sq.
Jellison, Phyllis G. *see* Jellison, Phyllis Gift.
Jellison, Phyllis Gift.
xJellison, Phyllis G.

The Colonial Dollhouse. Van Nos Reinhold.
The Remember When Dollhouse. Van Nos
Reinhold.
Jen, Eva L. *see* Jen, Eva Lee.
Jen, Eva Lee.
xJen, Eva L.
Chinese Cooking in the American Kitchen.
Kodansha.
Jen Min Jih Pao, Peking.
xJen Min Jih Pao, Peking.
The Historical Experience of the Dictatorship
of the Proletariat. AMS Pr.
Jencks, Charles.
xJencks, Charles.
Le Corbusier & the Tragic View of
Architecture. Harvard U Pr.
Modern Movements in Architecture.
Doubleday.
Jencks, Christopher.
xJencks, Christopher.
The Academic Revolution. U of Chicago Pr.
Inequality: A Reassessment of the Effect of
Family & Schooling in America. Har-Row.
Who Gets Ahead?: The Determinants of
Economic Success in America. Basic.
Jencks, William P., 1927-
xJencks, William P.
Catalysis in Chemistry & Enzymology.
McGraw.
Jenkins, Alan, 1914-
xJenkins, Alan.
The Forties. Universe.
The Thirties. Stein & Day.
Jenkins, Annibel.
xJenkins, Annibel.
Nicholas Rowe. Twayne.
Jenkins, Brian. *see* Jenkins, Brian A.
Jenkins, Brian A.
xJenkins, Brian.
Britain & the War for the Union.
McGill-Queens U Pr.
Fenians & Anglo-American Relations During
Reconstruction. Cornell U Pr.
Jenkins, C. Francis. *see* Jenkins, Charles Francis.
Jenkins, Charles Francis, 1869-1934
xJenkins, C. Francis.
Animated Pictures. Arno.
Jenkins, Claude, 1877-1959
xJenkins, Claude.
The Monastic Chronicler & the Early School of
St. Albans: A Lecture. Folcroft.
Jenkins, Clive.
xJenkins, Clive.
Power at the Top: A Critical Survey of the
Nationalized Industries. Greenwood.
White-Collar Unionism: The Rebellious
Salariat. Routledge & Kegan.
Jenkins, D. T. *see* Jenkins, David T.
Jenkins, Dan.
xJenkins, Dan.
Dead Solid Perfect. Atheneum.
Dead Solid Perfect. Warner Bks.
Limo. Atheneum.
Limo. PB.
Jenkins, David R. *see* Jenkins, David Ross.
Jenkins, David Ross, 1913-
xJenkins, David R.
Growth & Decline of Agricultural Villages.
AMS Pr.
Jenkins, David T.
xJenkins, D. T.
Taxonomic & Nomenclatural Study of the
Genus Amanita Section Amanita for North
America. Lubrecht & Cramer.
xJenkins, David T.
A Taxonomic & Nomenclatural Study of the
Genus Amanita Section Amanita for North
America. Intl Schol Bk Serv.
Jenkins, E. N. *see* Jenkins, Eric Neil.
Jenkins, Edward S. *see* Jenkins, Edward Stanley.

Jenkins, Edward Stanley.
  xJenkins, Edward S.
    Teach Yourself French Grammar. McKay.
Jenkins, Elizabeth, 1907-
  xJenkins, Elizabeth.
    Harriet. Penguin.
    The Princes in the Tower. Coward.
Jenkins, Eric Neil.
  xJenkins, E. N.
    Radioactivity: A Science in Its Historical &
    Social Context. Crane-Russak Co.
Jenkins, F. H.
  xJenkins, Foster H.
    Journal of a Voyage to San Francisco: 1849.
    CSUN.
Jenkins, Farish A., 1940-
  xJenkins, Farish A.
    ed. Primate Locomotion. Acad Pr.
Jenkins, Ferguson.
  xJenkins, Ferguson.
    Inside Pitching. Contemp Bks.
Jenkins, Foster H. see Jenkins, F. H.
Jenkins, Francis A. see Jenkins, Francis Arthur.
Jenkins, Francis Arthur.
  xJenkins, Francis A.
    Fundamentals of Optics. McGraw.
Jenkins, Geoffrey.
  xJenkins, Jeffrey.
    Twist of Sand. Watts.
Jenkins, Geraint H.
  xJenkins, Geraint H.
    Literature, Religion & Society in Wales,
    1660-1730. Verry.
Jenkins, Gladys G. see Jenkins, Gladys Gardner.
Jenkins, Gladys Gardner.
  xJenkins, Gladys G.
    These Are Your Children. Scott F.
Jenkins, Gwilym M.
  xJenkins, Gwilym M.
    Spectral Analysis & Its Applications.
    Holden-Day.
Jenkins, Hal.
  xJenkins, Hal.
    A Valley Renewed: The History of the
    Muskingum Watershed Conservancy District.
    Kent St U Pr.
Jenkins, Harold.
  xJenkins, Harold.
    Edward Benlowes (1602-1676): Biography of a
    Minor Poet. R West.
Jenkins, Hester D. see Jenkins, Hester Donaldson.
Jenkins, Hester Donaldson, 1869-1941
  xJenkins, Hester D.
    Ibrahim Pasha: Grand Vizir of Suleiman the
    Magnificent. AMS Pr.
Jenkins, Hugh.
  xJenkins, Hugh.
    The Culture Gap: An Experience of
    Government & the Arts. Merrimack Bk Serv.
Jenkins, J. Geraint. see Jenkins, John Geraint.
Jenkins, Jeffrey. see Jenkins, Geoffrey.
Jenkins, John B.
  xJenkins, John B.
    Genetics. HM.
Jenkins, John Geraint.
  xJenkins, J. Geraint.
    ed. The Wool Textile Industry in Great Britain.
    Routledge & Kegan.
Jenkins, John H.
  xJenkins, John H.
    Works of Genius: A Catalogue & a
    Commentary. Jenkins.
Jenkins, John H. see Jenkins, John Holmes.
Jenkins, John Holmes.
  xJenkins, John H.
    Audubon & Other Capers: Confessions of a
    Texas Bookmaker. Jenkins.
Jenkins, Jordan.
  xJenkins, Jordan.

    Learning About Love. Childrens.
Jenkins, Lulu M. see Jenkins, Lulu Marie.
Jenkins, Lulu Marie, 1897-
  xJenkins, Lulu M.
    A Comparative Study of Motor Achievements
    of Children of Five, Six & Seven Years of
    Age. AMS Pr.
Jenkins, Marie M., 1909-
  xJenkins, Marie M.
    Animals Without Parents. Holiday.
    The Curious Mollusks. Holiday.
    Deer, Moose, Elk, & Their Family. Holiday.
    Goats, Sheep, & How They Live. Holiday.
Jenkins, Myra E. see Jenkins, Myra Ellen.
Jenkins, Myra Ellen.
  xJenkins, Myra E.
    A Brief History of New Mexico. U of NM Pr.
    Navajo Activities Affecting the Acoma-Laguna
    Area, 1746-1910. Clearwater Pub.
Jenkins, Peggy D. see Jenkins, Peggy Davison.
Jenkins, Peggy Davison.
  xJenkins, Peggy D.
    The Magic of Puppetry: A Guide for Those
    Working with Young Children. P-H.
Jenkins, Peter, 1951-
  xJenkins, Peter.
    A Walk Across America. Fawcett.
    A Walk Across America. Morrow.
Jenkins, R. see Jenkins, Ronald.
Jenkins, Reese.
  xJenkins, Reese V.
    Images & Enterprise: Technology & the
    American Photographic Industry, 1839-1925.
    Johns Hopkins.
Jenkins, Reese V. see Jenkins, Reese.
Jenkins, Rhys O. see Jenkins, Rhys Owen.
Jenkins, Rhys Owen, 1948-
  xJenkins, Rhys O.
    Dependent Industrialization in Latin America:
    The Automotive Industry in Argentina, Chile,
    & Mexico. Praeger.
Jenkins, Richard L. see Jenkins, Richard Leos.
Jenkins, Richard Leos.
  xJenkins, Richard L.
    ed. Understanding Disturbed Children:
    Professional Insights into Their Psychiatric &
    Developmental Problems. Spec Child.
Jenkins, Robin, 1912-
  xJenkins, Robin.
    Fergus Lamont. Taplinger.
Jenkins, Ronald.
  xJenkins, R.
    Practical X-Ray Spectrometry. Springer-Verlag.
Jenkins, Shirley.
  xJenkins, Shirley.
    Comparative Recreation Needs & Services in
    New York Neighborhoods. Comm Coun
    Great NY.
    Filial Deprivation & Foster Care. Columbia U
    Pr.
    Paths to Child Placement: Family Situations
    Prior to Foster Care. Comm Coun Great NY.
Jenkins, Thomas W.
  xJenkins, Thomas W.
    Functional Mammalian Neuroanatomy: With
    Emphasis on the Dog and Cat, Including an
    Atlas of the Central Nervous System of the
    Dog. Lea & Febiger.
Jenkinson, Denis.
  xJenkinson, Denis.
    Racing Driver: The Theory & Practice of Fast
    Driving. Bentley.
  xJenkinson, Dennis.
    Batsford Guide to Racing Cars. David &
    Charles.
Jenkinson, Dennis. see Jenkinson, Denis.
Jenkinson, Edward B.
  xJenkinson, Edward B.

    ed. Books for Teachers of English: An
    Annotated Bibliography. Ind U Pr.
    Censors in the Classroom: The Mind Benders.
    S Ill U Pr.
    ed. On Teaching Literature: Essays for
    Secondary School Teachers. Ind U Pr.
    ed. Teaching Literature in Grades Seven
    Through Nine. Ind U Pr.
Jenkinson, Hilary, Sir.
  xJenkinson, Hilary.
    Later Court Hands in England from the
    Fifteenth to the Seventeenth Century. Ungar.
Jenkinson, Thomas B.
  xJenkinson, Thomas B.
    Amazulu: The Zulus, Their Past History,
    Manners, Customs & Language. Negro U Pr.
Jenks, Chris.
  xJenks, Chris.
    ed. Rationality, Education & the Social
    Organization of Knowledge. Routledge &
    Kegan.
Jenks, Jeremiah W. see Jenks, Jeremiah Whipple.
Jenks, Jeremiah Whipple.
  xJenks, Jeremiah W.
    The Trust Problem. Arno.
Jenks, Leland H. see Jenks, Leland Hamilton.
Jenks, Leland Hamilton, 1892-
  xJenks, Leland H.
    Our Cuban Colony: A Study in Sugar. Arno.
    Our Cuban Colony: A Study in Sugar.
    Scholarly.
Jenks, Tudor, 1857-1922
  xJenks, Tudor.
    In the Days of Chaucer. Folcroft.
    In the Days of Milton. AMS Pr.
    In the Days of Scott. Folcroft.
Jenks, William A. see Jenks, William Alexander.
Jenks, William Alexander, 1918-
  xJenks, William A.
    The Austrian Electoral Reform of 1907.
    Octagon.
    Francis Joseph & the Italians: 1849-1859. U Pr
    of Va.
Jenkyns, Richard.
  xJenkyns, Richard.
    The Victorians & Ancient Greece. Harvard U
    Pr.
Jenner, Bruce.
  xJenner, Bruce.
    Bruce Jenner's Guide to the Olympics.
    Andrews & McMeel.
    The Olympics & Me. Doubleday.
Jenner, Chrystie, 1950-
  xJenner, Chrystie.
    I Am Chrystie. Les Femmes Pub.
Jenner, Heather.
  xJenner, Heather.
    Marriages Are Made on Earth. David &
    Charles.
Jenner, Philip N.
  xJenner, Philip N.
    Southeast Asian Literatures in Translation: A
    Preliminary Bibliography. U Pr of Hawaii.
Jenner, W. J. see Jenner, William John Francis.
Jenner, William John Francis.
  xJenner, W. J.
    tr. & ed. Modern Chinese Stories. Oxford U
    Pr.
Jenness, Aylette.
  xJenness, Aylette.
    Along the Niger River: An African Way of
    Life. T Y Crowell.
    A Life of Their Own: An Indian Family in
    Latin America. T Y Crowell.
Jenness, Diamond, 1886-
  xJenness, Diamond.

The Indians of Canada. U of Toronto Pr.
Life of the Copper Eskimos. Johnson Repr.
Northern D'Entrecasteaux. Johnson Repr.
People of the Twilight. U of Chicago Pr.

Jennett, Bryan.
xJennett, Bryan.
A Introduction to Neurosurgery. Year Bk Med.

Jennett, Sean.
xJennett, Sean.
Cork & Kerry. Hippocrene Bks.

Jenney, Charles.
xJenney, Charles.
First Year Latin. Allyn.
First Year Latin. Allyn.
Second Year Latin. Allyn.

Jennings, Alan.
xJennings, Alan.
Matrix Computation for Engineers & Scientists. Wiley.

Jennings, B. R. see Jennings, Barry Randall.

Jennings, Barry Randall.
xJennings, B. R.
Atoms in Contact. Oxford U Pr.

Jennings, Burgess H. see Jennings, Burgess Hill.

Jennings, Burgess Hill.
xJennings, Burgess H.
Interactions of Man & His Environment. Plenum Pub.
The Thermal Environment: Conditioning & Control. Har-Row.

Jennings, Dana C. see Jennings, Dana Close.

Jennings, Dana Close.
xJennings, Dana C.
Days of Steam & Glory. North Plains.

Jennings, David H. see Jennings, David Harry.

Jennings, David Harry.
xJennings, David H.
Integration of Activity in the Higher Plant. Cambridge U Pr.

Jennings, Don.
xJennings, Don.
Light from Many Candles. Wallace-Homestead.

Jennings, Elizabeth, 1926-
xJennings, Elizabeth.
Animals Arrival. Dufour.

Jennings, Eugene E. see Jennings, Eugene Emerson.

Jennings, Eugene Emerson, 1926-
xJennings, Eugene E.
Executive in Crisis. McGraw.
Executive in Crisis. Mich St U Busn.

Jennings, Gary.
xJennings, Gary.
The Earth Book. Lippincott.
March of the Demons. Follett.
March of the Demons. Follett.
Sow the Seeds of Hemp. Norton.

Jennings, Gordon.
xJennings, Gordon.
Motorcycles. P-H.

Jennings, Hilda, 1894-
xJennings, Hilda.
Societies in the Making: A Study of Development & Redevelopment Within a Country Borough. Humanities.

Jennings, Ivor. see Jennings, William Ivor.

Jennings, Jerry. see Jennings, Jerry E.

Jennings, Jerry E.
xJennings, Jerry.
ed. The Northeast. Fideler.
xJennings, Jerry E.
China. Fideler.
ed. Great Americans & Great Ideas. Fideler.
Inquiring About Freedom: Civil Rights & Individual Responsibilities. Fideler.
A Pictorial Story of Our Country. Fideler.
The South. Fideler.
ed. The United States. Fideler.

Jennings, Jesse D. see Jennings, Jesse David.

Jennings, Jesse David, 1909-
xJennings, Jesse D.

ed. Ancient Native Americans. W H Freeman.
Prehistory of North America. McGraw.
xJennings, Jessie D.
ed. The Prehistory of Polynesia. Harvard U Pr.

Jennings, Jessie D. see Jennings, Jesse David.

Jennings, Paul F. see Jennings, Paul Francis.

Jennings, Paul Francis, 1918-
xJennings, Paul F.
Oodles of Oddlies. Greenwood.

Jennings, Richard.
xJennings, Richard.
Natural Elements of Political Economy. Kelley.

Jennings, Robert K.
xJennings, Robert K.
Protistan Kingdom: Protists & Viruses. Van Nos Reinhold.

Jennings, Vivien. see Jennings, Vivien.

Jennings, Vivien, 1934-
xJennings, Vivian.
Valiant Woman: At the Heart of Reconciliation. Alba.

Jennings, Walter, 1922-
xJennings, Walter.
ed. Gas Chromatography with Glass Capillary Columns. Acad Pr.

Jennings, William I. see Jennings, William Ivor.

Jennings, William Ivor, Sir, 1903-1965
xJennings, Ivor.
Cabinet Government. Cambridge U Pr.
xJennings, William I.
The British Commonwealth of Nations. Greenwood.
Constitutional Problems in Pakistan. Greenwood.
Problems of the New Commonwealth. Duke.

Jennison, George.
xJennison, George.
Noah's Cargo: Some Curious Chapters of Natural History. Arno.

Jennison, R. C. see Jennison, Roger Clifton.

Jennison, Roger Clifton.
xJennison, R. C.
Introduction to Radio Astronomy. Philos Lib.

Jens, Arlene Johnson.
xJens, Arlene Johnson.
I Am the Lord Thy Sex: An Interpretation of Genesis & Exodus. Exposition.

Jensen. see Jensen, David.

Jensen, Albert C.
xJensen, Albert C.
Wildlife of the Oceans. Abrams.

Jensen, Alfred.
xJensen, Alfred.
Applied Strength of Materials. McGraw.
xJensen, Alfred E.
Applied Engineering Mechanics. McGraw.

Jensen, Alfred E. see Jensen, Alfred.

Jensen, Ann. see Jensen, Ann (Oden).

Jensen, Ann (Oden).
xJensen, Ann.
Franz Anton Mesmer: Physician Extraordinaire. Garrett-Helix.

Jensen, Arthur R. see Jensen, Arthur Robert.

Jensen, Arthur Robert.
xJensen, Arthur R.
Bias in Mental Testing. Free Pr.
Educability & Group Differences. Har-Row.

Jensen, Bernard, 1905-
xJensen, Bernard.
World Keys to Health & Long Life. Bi World Indus.

Jensen, C. H. see Jensen, Cecil Howard.

Jensen, Cecil Howard.
xJensen, C. H.
Interpreting Engineering Drawings. Delmar.

Jensen, Clayne R.
xJensen, Clayne R.

Leisure & Recreation: Introduction & Overview. Lea & Febiger.
Measurement in Physical Education & Athletics. Macmillan.
Outdoor Recreation in America: Trends, Problems, & Opportunities. Burgess.
Scientific Basis of Athletic Conditioning. Lea & Febiger.

Jensen, Daniel. see Jensen, Daniel L.

Jensen, Daniel L.
xJensen, Daniel.
Advanced Accounting & the Rule-Making Agencies. Grid Pub.

Jensen, David, 1926-
xJensen.
Principles of Physiology. ACC.

Jensen, David E.
xJensen, David E.
Minerals of New York State. Ward Pr.

Jensen, De Lamar, 1925-
xJensen, DeLamar.
Diplomacy & Dogmatism: Bernardino De Mendoza & the French Catholic League. Harvard U Pr.

Jensen, DeLamar. see Jensen, De Lamar.

Jensen, Dwight W. see Jensen, Dwight William.

Jensen, Dwight William.
xJensen, Dwight W.
Discovering Idaho, a History. Caxton.

Jensen, Erik, 1906-
xJensen, Erik.
The Iban & Their Religion. Oxford U Pr.

Jensen, F. B. see Jensen, Finn B.

Jensen, Finn B.
xJensen, F. B.
ed. Readings in International Economic Relations. Wiley.

Jensen, G. see Jensen, Gary.

Jensen, Gary, 1941-
xJensen, G.
Higher Order Contact of Submanifolds of Homogeneous Spaces. Springer-Verlag.

Jensen, H. James.
xJensen, H. James.
Glossary of John Dryden's Critical Terms. U of Minn Pr.

Jensen, J. T. see Jensen, Jens Trygve.

Jensen, Jens Trygve.
xJensen, J. T.
College General Chemistry. Merrill.

Jensen, Larry C.
xJensen, Larry C.
Feelings: Helping Children Understand Emotions. Brigham.
Responsibility & Morality: Helping Children Become Responsible & Morally Mature. Brigham.
That's Not Fair!: Helping Children Make Moral Decisions. Brigham.

Jensen, Laura, 1948-
xJensen, Laura.
Bad Boats. Ecco Pr.

Jensen, M. L. see Jensen, Mead Leroy.

Jensen, Malcolm C.
xJensen, Malcolm C.
Francisco Coronado. Watts.
Leif Erikson the Lucky. Watts.

Jensen, Margaret. see Jensen, Margaret Duncan.

Jensen, Margaret Duncan.
xJensen, Margaret.
Handbook of Maternity Care: A Guide for Nursing Practice. Mosby.
Maternity Care: The Nurse & the Family. Mosby.

Jensen, Mary E.
xJensen, Mary E.
Women of the Bible Tell Their Stories. Augsburg.

Jensen, Mead Leroy.
xJensen, M. L.

Economic Mineral Deposits. Wiley.
Jensen, Merill. *see* Jensen, Merrill.
Jensen, Merrill.
　xJensen, Merill.
　　Articles of Confederation: An Interpretation of
　　the Social Constitutional History of the
　　American Revolution, 1774-1781. U of Wis
　　Pr.
　xJensen, Merrill.
　　The American Revolution Within America.
　　NYU Pr.
　　ed. A Documentary History of the First
　　Federal Elections. U of Wis Pr.
　　The Making of the American Constitution.
　　Krieger.
Jensen, Paul M.
　xJensen, Paul M.
　　Boris Karloff & His Films. A S Barnes.
　　The Cinema of Fritz Lang. A S Barnes.
Jensen, R. *see* Jensen, Randall W.
Jensen, R. C. *see* Jensen, Rodney Charles.
Jensen, R. W. *see* Jensen, Randall W.
Jensen, Randall W.
　xJensen, R.
　　Software Engineering. P-H.
　xJensen, R. W.
　　IBM Electronic Circuit Analysis Program:
　　Techniques & Applications. P-H.
Jensen, Richard A.
　xJensen, Richard A.
　　Telling the Story: Variety & Imagination in
　　Preaching. Augsburg.
　　Touched by the Spirit: One Man's Struggle to
　　Understand His Experience of the Holy
　　Spirit. Augsburg.
Jensen, Rodney Charles.
　xJensen, R. C.
　　Regional Economic Planning: Generation of
　　Regional Input-Output Analysis. Biblio Dist.
Jensen, Rolf.
　xJensen, Rolf.
　　Cities of Vision. Burgess-Intl Ideas.
Jensen, Ronald J., 1939-
　xJensen, Ronald J.
　　The Alaska Purchase & Russian-American
　　Relations. U of Wash Pr.
Jensen, Ronald W.
　xJensen, Ronald W.
　　Sell Your Home " by Owner " & Save the
　　Commission. Warner Bks.
Jensen, Rosalie.
　xJensen, Rosalie.
　　Exploring Mathematical Concepts & Skills in
　　the Elementary School. Merrill.
Jensen, Rue.
　xJensen, Rue.
　　Diseases of Feedlot Cattle. Lea & Febiger.
Jensen, Sheila R.
　xJensen, Shelia R.
　　ed. Poemscapes. M O Pub Co.
　　ed. Threshold. M O Pub Co.
Jensen, Shelia R. *see* Jensen, Sheila R.
Jensen, Vernon H.
　xJensen, Vernon H.
　　Decasualization & Modernization of Dock
　　Work in London. NY Sch Indus Rel.
　　Lumber & Labor. Arno.
Jensen, Virginia A. *see* Jensen, Virginia Allen.
Jensen, Virginia Allen.
　xJensen, Virginia A.
　　What's That?. Philomel.
Jensen, William A.
　xJensen, William A.
　　Biology. Wadsworth Pub.
　　Plant Cell. Wadsworth Pub.
Jensen, William B.
　xJensen, William B.

The Lewis Acid-Base Concepts: An Overview.
　Wiley.
Jenson, Andrew, 1850-1941
　xJenson, Andrew.
　　History of the Scandinavian Mission. Arno.
Jentz, Barry C.
　xJentz, Barry C.
　　Leadership & Learning: Personal Change in a
　　Professional Setting. McGraw.
Jentz, Gaylord A.
　xJentz, Gaylord A.
　　Texas Uniform Commercial Code: Practical
　　Aspects on Secured Transactions. U of Tex
　　Busn Res.
Jenyns, Roger Soame, 1904-
　xJenyns, Soame.
　　A Background to Chinese Painting. Schocken.
Jenyns, Soame. *see* Jenyns, Roger Soame.
Jeppesen, Knud, 1892-
　xJeppesen, Knud.
　　Style of Palestrina & the Dissonance. Dover.
Jeppson, J. O.
　xJeppson, J. O.
　　The Last Immortal. HM.
Jeppson, Roland W.
　xJeppson, Roland W.
　　Analysis of Flow in Pipe Networks. Ann Arbor
　　Science.
Jepsen, Stanley M.
　xJepsen, Stanley M.
　　The Coach Horse: Servant with Style. A S
　　Barnes.
　　The Gentle Giants: The Story of Draft Horses.
　　Arco.
Jepson, Joanne H.
　xJepson, Joanne H.
　　Hematologic Problems in Renal Disease. A-W.
Jepson, Willis L. *see* Jepson, Willis Linn.
Jepson, Willis Linn, 1867-
　xJepson, Willis L.
　　A Manual of the Flowering Plants of
　　California. U of Cal Pr.
Jepson, Winston. *see* Jepson, Winston F.
Jepson, Winston F.
　xJepson, Winston.
　　Plan of Salvation. Hawkes Pub Inc.
Jeremiah, James T.
　xJeremiah, James T.
　　The Importance of Inspiration. Reg Baptist.
Jeremiah, Maryalyce, 1943-
　xJeremiah, Maryalyce.
　　Coaching Basketball: Ten Winning Concepts.
　　Wiley.
Jeremias, Joachim, 1900-
　xJeremias, Joachim.
　　Parables of Jesus. Scribner.
　　The Prayers of Jesus. Fortress.
　　Problem of the Historical Jesus. Fortress.
Jeresaty, Robert M.
　xJeresaty, Robert M.
　　Mitral Valve Prolapse. Raven.
Jerge, Charles R.
　xJerge, Charles R.
　　ed. Group Practice & the Future of Dental
　　Care. Lea & Febiger.
Jerison, Harry J.
　xJerison, Harry J.
　　Evolution of the Brain & Intelligence. Acad Pr.
Jeritza, Maria, 1887-
　xJeritza, Maria.
　　Sunlight & Song: A Singer's Life. Arno.
Jerlov, N. G. *see* Jerlov, Nils Gunnar.
Jerlov, Nils Gunnar, 1909-
　xJerlov, N. G.
　　Marine Optics. Elsevier.
Jern, Helen Z.
　xJern, Helen Z.
　　Hormone Therapy of the Menopause & Aging.
　　C C Thomas.
Jernberg, Ann M. *see* Jernberg, Ann Marshak.

Jernberg, Ann Marshak, 1928-
　xJernberg, Ann M.
　　Theraplay: A New Treatment Using Structured
　　Play for Problem Children & Their Families.
　　Jossey-Bass.
Jerome, Carl.
　xJerome, Carl.
　　The Complete Chicken. Random.
Jerome, Jerome K. *see* Jerome, Jerome Klapka.
Jerome, Jerome Klapka, 1859-1927
　xJerome, Jerome K.
　　Observations of Henry. Arno.
Jerome, Judson.
　xJerome, Judson.
　　I Never Saw. A Whitman.
　　The Poet & the Poem. Writers Digest.
　　Thirty Years of Poetry: Collected Poems:
　　1949-1979. Cedar Rock.
Jerome, Lawrence E.
　xJerome, Lawrence E.
　　Astrology Disproved. Prometheus Bks.
Jerrehian, Aram, 1934-
　xJerrehian, Aram K.
　　Oriental Rug Primer: Buying & Understanding
　　New Oriental Rugs. Running Pr.
Jerrehian, Aram K. *see* Jerrehian, Aram.
Jerrett, Robert.
　xJerrett, Robert.
　　Public Works, Government Spending & Job
　　Creation: The Job Opportunities Program.
　　Praeger.
Jerrold, Blanchard, 1826-1884
　xJerrold, Blanchard.
　　Life of Gustave Dore. Gale.
Jerrold, Clare A. *see* Jerrold, Clare Armstrong
　(Bridgman).
Jerrold, Clare Armstrong (Bridgman), 1861-
　xJerrold, Clare A.
　　Story of Dorothy Jordan. Arno.
Jerrold, Walter C. *see* Jerrold, Walter Copeland
Jerrold, Walter Copeland.
　xJerrold, Walter C.
　　Century of Parody & Imitation. Gale.
　　A Century of Parody & Imitation. Gordon Pr.
　　A Descriptive Index to Shakespeare's
　　Characters, in Shakespeare's Words. Gale.
　　George Meredith: An Essay Towards
　　Appreciation. Folcroft.
Jersild, Arthur T. *see* Jersild, Arthur Thomas.
Jersild, Arthur Thomas, 1902-
　xJersild, Arthur T.
　　Child Psychology. P-H.
　　In Search of Self: An Exploration of the Role
　　of the School in Promoting
　　Self-Understanding. Tchrs Coll.
　　Psychology of Adolescence. Macmillan.
　　When Teachers Face Themselves. Tchrs Coll.
Jersild, P. T. *see* Jersild, Paul T.
Jersild, Paul T.
　xJersild, P. T.
　　Moral Issues & Christian Response. HR&W.
**Jerusalem Ideological Conference, Hebrew University,
　1957.**
　xJerusalem Ideological Conference Hebrew
　　University.
　　Proceedings, World Zionist Organization.
　　Greenwood.
**Jerusalem Symposium on Quantum Chemistry and
　Biochemistry, 8th, 1975.**
　xSymposium on Quantum, Chemistry, &
　　Biochemistry, 8th, Jerusalem, April 1975.
　　Environmental Effects on Molecular Structure
　　& Properties: Proceedings. Kluwer Boston.
Jervell, Jacob.
　xJervell, Jacob.
　　Luke & the People of God: A New Look at
　　Luke-Acts. Augsburg.
Jervey, Phyllis.
　xJervey, Phyllis.

Rice & Spice: Rice Recipes from East to West.
C E Tuttle.

Jervis, Robert.
xJervis, Robert.
Logic of Images in International Relations.
Princeton U Pr.
Perception & Misperception in International
Politics. Princeton U Pr.

Jeschke, Susan.
xJeschke, Susan.
illus. Angela & Bear. HR&W.
Sidney. HR&W.
illus. Tamar & the Tiger. HR&W.

Jespersen, James.
xJespersen, James.
Time & Clocks for the Space Age. Atheneum.

Jespersen, Otto, 1860-1943
xJespersen, Otto.
Essentials of English Grammar. U of Ala Pr.
Language: Its Nature, Development & Origin.
Allen Unwin.
Language: Its Nature, Development & Origin.
Longwood Pr.

Jespersen, Robert C.
xJespersen, Robert C.
Using German. Har-Row.

Jesse, Fryniwyd T. *see* Jesse, Fryniwyd Tennyson.

Jesse, Fryniwyd Tennyson.
xJesse, Fryniwyd T.
Many Latitudes. Arno.
The Story of Burma. AMS Pr.

Jesse, John, 1915-
xJesse, John.
Strength, Power & Muscular Endurance for
Runners & Hurdlers. Athletic.

Jessee, Jill. *see* Jessee, Jill Eva.

Jessee, Jill Eva, 1906-
xJessee, Jill.
Perfume Album. Krieger.

Jessel, Camilla.
xJessel, Camilla.
illus. Life at the Royal Ballet School. Methuen
Inc.
photos by Manuela Lives in Portugal. Hastings.

Jessel, Levic.
xJessel, Levic.
The Ethnic Process: An Evolutionary Concept
of Languages & Peoples. Mouton.

Jessen, Raymond J. *see* Jessen, Raymond James.

Jessen, Raymond James, 1910-
xJessen, Raymond J.
Statistical Survey Techniques. Wiley.

Jesser, David L.
xJesser, David L.
Career Education: A Priority of the Chief State
School Officers. Olympus Pub Co.

Jessopp, Augustus, 1823-1914
xJessopp, Augustus.
The Coming of the Friars & Other Historic
Essays. Arno.
Studies by a Recluse in Cloister, Town, &
Country. B Franklin.

Jessor, Richard.
xJessor, Richard.
Society, Personality & Deviant Behavior: A
Study of a Tri-Ethnic Community. Krieger.

Jessup, Claudia.
xJessup, Claudia.
The Woman's Guide to Starting a Business.
HR&W.

Jessup, Cortland.
xJessup, Cortland.
Actor's Guide to Breaking into TV
Commercials. Pilot Bks.

Jessup, Frank W.
xJessup, Frank W.
Historical & Cultural Influences Upon the
Development of Residential Centers for
Continuing Education. Syracuse U Cont Ed.

Jessup, Paul. *see* Jessup, Paul F.

Jessup, Paul F.
xJessup, Paul.
Returns in Over-the-Counter Stock Markets. U
of Minn Pr.
xJessup, Paul F.
Competing for Stock Market Profits. Wiley.
Modern Bank Management. West Pub.
Modern Bank Management: A Casebook. West
Pub.
Theory & Practice of Nonpar Banking.
Northwestern U Pr.

Jessup, Philip C. *see* Jessup, Philip Caryl.

Jessup, Philip Caryl, 1897-
xJessup, Philip C.
Price of International Justice. Columbia U Pr.

Jessup, Ronald. *see* Jessup, Ronald Frederick.

Jessup, Ronald Frederick, 1906-
xJessup, Ronald.
Anglo-Saxon Jewellery. Intl Pubns Serv.

Jester, Pat.
xJester, Pat.
Brunch Cookery. H P Bks.
Burger Cookery. H P Bks.

Jeter, J. W.
xJeter, K. W.
Morlock Night. DAW Bks.

Jeter, Jacky.
xJeter, Jacky.
The Cat & the Fiddler. Schol Bk Serv.

Jeter, Jeremiah B. *see* Jeter, Jeremiah Bell.

Jeter, Jeremiah Bell, 1802-1880
xJeter, Jeremiah B.
Recollections of a Long Life. Arno.

Jeter, K. W. *see* Jeter, J. W.

Jetzinger, Franz.
xJetzinger, Franz.
Hitler's Youth. Greenwood.

Jeune, Paul, 1951-
xJeune, Paul.
The Whale Who Wouldn't Die: The True Story
of "Miracle". Follett.

Jevons, Frank B. *see* Jevons, Frank Byron.

Jevons, Frank Byron, 1858-
xJevons, Frank B.
Comparative Religion.. Folcroft.

Jevons, H. Stanley. *see* Jevons, Herbert Stanley.

Jevons, Herbert Stanley, 1875-1955
xJevons, H. Stanley.
British Coal Trade. Kelley.

Jevons, W. Stanley. *see* Jevons, William Stanley.

Jevons, William S. *see* Jevons, William Stanley.

Jevons, William Stanley, 1835-1882
xJevons, W. Stanley.
Pure Logic & Other Minor Works. B Franklin.
xJevons, William S.
Theory of Political Economy. Kelley.

Jewel, John, Bp. of Salisbury, 1522-1571
xJewel, John.
An Apology of the Church of England. Folger
Bks.

Jewell, Derek.
xJewell, Derek.
Duke: A Portrait of Duke Ellington. Norton.

Jewell, Don, 1921-
xJewell, Don.
Public Assembly Facilities: Planning &
Management. Wiley.

Jewell, Frank.
xJewell, Frank.
Annotated Bibliography of Chicago History.
Chicago Hist.

Jewell, Malcolm E. *see* Jewell, Malcolm Edwin.

Jewell, Malcolm Edwin.
xJewell, Malcolm E.
The Legislative Process in the United States.
Random.
Legislative Representation in the Contemporary
South. Duke.

Jewell, Nancy.
xJewell, Nancy.

Bus Ride. Har-Row.
Calf, Goodnight. Har-Row.
Cheer up, Pig. Har-Row.
The Family Under the Moon. Har-Row.
Try & Catch Me. Har-Row.

Jewett, Claudia L., 1939-
xJewett, Claudia L.
Adopting the Older Child. Harvard Common
Pr.

Jewett, Don L.
xJewett, Don L.
Nerve Repair & Regeneration: Its Clinical &
Experimental Basis. Mosoy.

Jewett, Robert.
xJewett, Robert.
The American Monomyth. Doubleday.
A Chronology of Paul's Life. Fortress.
Jesus Against the Rapture: Seven Unexpected
Prophecies. Westminster.

Jewett, Sarah O. *see* Jewett, Sarah Orne.

Jewett, Sarah Orne, 1849-1909
xJewett, Sarah O.
Country By-Ways. Arden Lib.
Country By-Ways. Arno.
A Country Doctor. Mss Info.
The Country of the Pointed Firs. Arden Lib.
The Country of the Pointed Firs. Avon.
Country of the Pointed Firs. Watts.
Deephaven. Lighthouse Pr NY.
Life of Nancy. Arno.
Old Friends & New. Arno.
Queen's Twin, & Other Stories. Arno.
The Queen's Twin & Other Stories. Mss Info.
Strangers & Wayfarers. Mss Info.
Tales of New England. Arno.

Jewish Agency for Israel. *see* Jewish Agency for Isreal.

Jewish Agency for Isreal.
xJewish Agency for Israel.
Memorandum Submitted to the Palestine Royal
Commission on Behalf of the Jewish Agency
for Palestine. Greenwood.

Jewish Frontier.
xJewish Frontier (Periodical).
Anthology, Nineteen Thirty-Four to Nineteen
Forty-Four. Arno.

Jewish Frontier (Periodical). *see* Jewish Frontier.

Jewish Publication Society of America.
xJewish Publication Society of America.
ed. The Eternal Light. Bloch.

Jewkes, John, 1902-
xJewkes, John.
Public & Private Enterprise. U of Chicago Pr.

Jewkes, Wilfred T. *see* Jewkes, Wilfred Thomas.

Jewkes, Wilfred Thomas, 1928-
xJewkes, Wilfred T.
Act Division in Elizabethan & Jacobean Plays,
1583-1616. AMS Pr.

Jha, Akhileshwar.
xJha, Akhileshwar.
Sexual Designs in Indian Culture. Humanities.
Sexual Designs in Indian Culture. Intl Pubns
Serv.

Jha, D. N. *see* Jha, Dwijendra Narayan.

Jha, Dwijendra Narayan.
xJha, D. N.
Revenue System in Post-Maurya & Gupta
Times. Verry.

Jha, Manoranjan.
xJha, Manoranjan.
Civil Disobedience & After: The American
Reaction to Political Developments in India
During 1930-1935. Intl Pubns Serv.

Jha, P. *see* Jha, Parameshwar.

Jha, Parameshwar.
xJha, P.
Political Representation in India. South Asia
Bks.

Jhabvala, Ruth P. *see* Jhabvala, Ruth Prawer.

Jhabvala, Ruth Prawer, 1927-
xJhabvala, Ruth P.

The Householder. Norton.
How I Became a Holy Mother & Other Stories. Har-Row.

Jick, Leon A.
xJick, Leon A.
The Americanization of the Synagogue, 1820-1870. U Pr of New Eng.

Jiggins, Janice.
xJiggins, Janice.
Caste & Family in the Politics of the Sinhalese. Cambridge U Pr.

Jilling, Michael, 1937-
xJilling, Michael.
Foreign Exchange Risk Management in U. S. Multinational Corporations.. Univ Microfilms.

Jimenez, Nilda.
xJimenez, Nilda.
Compiled by The Bible & the Poetry of Christina Rossetti: A Concordance. Greenwood.

Jimenez-Fajardo, Salvador.
xJimenez-Fajardo, Salvador.
Claude Simon. Twayne.
Luis Cernuda. Twayne.

Jipson, W. see Jipson, Wayne R.

Jipson, Wayne R.
xJipson, W.
High School Vocal Music Program. P-H.

Jirasek, Alois, 1851-1930
xJirasek, Alois.
Gaudeamus Igitur. Greenwood.

Jirasek, Jan E. see Jirasek, Jan Evangelista.

Jirasek, Jan Evangelista.
xJirasek, Jan E.
Development of the Genital System & Male Pseudohermaphroditism. Johns Hopkins.

Jiriczek, Otto L. see Jiriczek, Otto Luitpold.

Jiriczek, Otto Luitpold, 1867-1941
xJiriczek, Otto L.
Northern Hero Legends. Folcroft.

Jirsch, D. W. see Jirsch, Dennis W.

Jirsch, Dennis W.
xJirsch, D. W.
ed. Immunological Engineering. Univ Park.

JK Lasser Tax Inst. see Lasser (J.K.) Tax Institute, New York.

Joachim, H. Henry. see Joachim, Harold Henry.

Joachim, Harold H. see Joachim, Harold Henry.

Joachim, Harold Henry.
xJoachim, H. Henry.
Nature of Truth: An Essay. Greenwood.
xJoachim, Harold H.
Descartes's Rules for the Direction of the Mind. Greenwood.

Joad, C. E. see Joad, Cyril Edwin Mitchinson.

Joad, Cyril E. see Joad, Cyril Edwin Mitchinson.

Joad, Cyril Edwin Mitchinson, 1891-1953
xJoad, C. E.
Guide to Philosophy. Gannon.
xJoad, Cyril E.
Guide to Philosophy. Dover.
Guide to the Philosophy of Morals & Politics. Greenwood.
The Present & Future of Religion. Greenwood.
Return to Philosophy: Being a Defence of Reason, an Affirmation of Values & a Plea for Philosophy. AMS Pr.

Joan, Polly.
xJoan, Polly.
Guide to Women's Publishing. Dustbooks.

Job, John. see Job, John B.

Job, John B.
xJob, John.
Job Speaks to Us Today. John Knox.

Jobb, Jamie.
xJobb, Jamie.

The Complete Book of Community Gardening. Morrow.
The Night Sky Book: An Everyday Guide to Every Night. Little.

Jobson, Hamilton.
xJobson, Hamilton.
To Die a Little. St Martin.

Jobson, John.
xJobson, John.
The Complete Book of Practical Camping. Follett.
The Complete Book of Practical Camping. Winchester Pr.

Joe, Eugene B. see Joe, Eugene Baatsoslanii.

Joe, Eugene Baatsoslanii.
xJoe, Eugene B.
Navajo Sandpainting Art. Treasure Chest.

Joel, C. A. see Joel, Charles Akiba.

Joel, Charles Akiba.
xJoel, C. A.
ed. Fertility Disturbances in Men & Women: A Textbook with Special Reference to Etiology, Diagnosis & Treatment. S Karger.

Joel, Lucille A.
xJoel, Lucille A.
Psychiatric Nursing: Theory & Application. McGraw.

Joel, Shirley.
xJoel, Shirley.
Fairchild's Book of Window Display. Fairchild.

Joels, Merrill E.
xJoels, Merrill E.
How to Get into Show Business. Hastings.

Joerns, Consuelo.
xJoerns, Consuelo.
illus. The Foggy Rescue. Schol Bk Serv.
The Forgotten Bear. Schol Bk Serv.
illus. The Lost & Found House. Schol Bk Serv.

Joesten, Melvin D.
xJoesten, Melvin D.
Hydrogen Bonding. Dekker.

Joffe. see Joffe, Anatole.

Joffe, Anatole.
xJoffe.
Branching Processes. Dekker.

Joffe, Carole E.
xJoffe, Carole E.
Friendly Intruders: Childcare Professionals & Family Life. U of Cal Pr.

Joffe, Ellis.
xJoffe, Ellis.
Party & Army: Professionalism & Political Control in the Chinese Officer Corps, 1949-1964. Harvard U Pr.

Joffe, Irwin L.
xJoffe, Irwin L.
Reading Skills for Successful Living. Wadsworth Pub.

Joffo, Joseph.
xJoffo, Joseph.
A Bag of Marbles. G K Hall.
A Bag of Marbles. HM.

Johann Gottfried Herder Institute.
xJohann Gottfried Herder-Instituts, Marburg, Lahn.
Alphabetischer Katalog der Bibliothek. G K Hall.

Johann Gottfried Herder-Instituts, Marburg, Lahn. see Johann Gottfried Herder Institute.

Johann, Robert O.
xJohann, Robert O.
ed. Freedom & Value. Fordham.
Pragmatic Meaning of God. Marquette.

Johannesen, Richard I. see Johannesen, Richard L.

Johannesen, Richard L.
xJohannesen, Richard I.
ed. Contemporary Theories of Rhetoric: Selected Readings. Har-Row.

Johannides, David F.
xJohannides, David F.

Cost Containment Through Systems Engineering: A Guide for Hospitals. Aspen Systems.

Johannsen, Albert, 1874-
xJohannsen, Albert.
House of Beadle & Adams & Its Dime & Nickel Novels: The Story of Vanished Literature Vol. 3. Supplement. U of Okla Pr.

Johannsen, Nicholas A. see Johannsen, Nicolas August Ludwig Jacob.

Johannsen, Nicolas August Ludwig Jacob, 1844-
xJohannsen, Nicholas A.
Neglected Point in Connection with Crises. Kelley.

Johannsen, Robert W.
xJohannsen, Robert W.
Frontier Politics on the Eve of the Civil War. U of Wash Pr.

Johannsen, Robert W. see Johannsen, Robert Walter.

Johannsen, Robert Walter, 1925-
xJohannsen, Robert W.
Stephen A. Douglas. Oxford U Pr.

Johansen, Bruce.
xJohansen, Bruce.
Wasi'chu: The Continuing Indian Wars. Monthly Rev.

Johansen, Erling.
xJohansen, Erling.
ed. Continuing Evaluation of the Use of Fluorides. Westview.

Johansen, L. see Johansen, Leif.

Johansen, Leif.
xJohansen, L.
Public Economics. Elsevier.

Johansen, Robert C.
xJohansen, Robert C.
Toward a Dependable Peace: A Proposal for an Appropriate Security System. Inst World Order.

Johansson, Bertil.
xJohansson, Bertil.
The Adapter Adapted: A Study of Sir John Vanbrugh's Comedy the Mistake, Its Predecessors & Successors. Humanities.

Johansson, Stig, 1939-
xJohansson, Stig.
Some Aspects of the Vocabulary of Learned & Scientific English. Humanities.
Studies of Error Gravity: Native Reactions to Errors Produced by Swedish Learners of English. Humanities.

Johar, Surinder S. see Johar, Surinder Singh.

Johar, Surinder Singh.
xJohar, Surinder S.
Sikh Gurus & Their Shrines. Verry.

John, Augustus E. see John, Augustus Edwin.

John, Augustus Edwin.
xJohn, Augustus E.
Augustus John. AMS Pr.

John, B. see John, Bernard.

John, Bernard.
xJohn, B.
Chromosome Complement. Springer-Verlag.
Chromosome Cycle. Springer-Verlag.
Meiotic System. Springer-Verlag.
xJohn, Bernard.
Chromosome Hierarchy: An Introduction to the Biology of the Chromosome. Oxford U Pr.

John, Brian.
xJohn, Brian.
Supreme Fictions: Studies in the Work of William Blake, Thomas Carlyle, W. B. Yeats & D. H. Lawrence. McGill-Queens U Pr.

John, Brian. see John, Brian Stephen.

John, Brian Stephen.
xJohn, Brian.
Pembrokeshire. David & Charles.

John Carter Brown Library. see Brown University. John Carter Brown Library.

John Crerar Library. *see* John Crerar Library, Chicago.

John Crerar Library - Chicago. *see* John Crerar Library, Chicago.

John Crerar Library, Chicago.
 xJohn Crerar Library.
  Catalogue of French Economic Documents from the Sixteenth, Seventeenth & Eighteenth Centuries. B Franklin.
  List of Bibliographies on Special Subjects. B Franklin.
  List of Books on the History of Industry & the Industrial Arts. Gale.
  List of Books on the History of Science. Kraus Repr.
 xJohn Crerar Library - Chicago.
  Author-Title Catalog. G K Hall.
  Classified Subject Catalog. G K Hall.
 xJohn Dewey Society.
  Yearbook (Second): Educational Freedom & Democracy. Greenwood.

John Dewey Society. *see* John Crerar Library, Chicago.

John, Dewitt, 1915-
 xJohn, DeWitt.
  The Christian Science Way of Life. Chr Science.

John E. Fogarty International Center for Advanced Study in the Health Sciences.
 xJohn E. Fogarty International Center for Advanced Study in the Health Sciences.
  tr. The Barefoot Doctor's Manual: The American Translation of the Official Chinese Paramedical Manual. Running Pr.

John, E. Roy. *see* John, Erwin Roy.

John, Edith.
 xJohn, Edith.
  Creative Stitches. Dover.
  Creative Stitches. Peter Smith.
  Experimental Embroidery. Branford.

John, Elizabeth A. H. *see* John, Elizabeth Ann Harper.

John, Elizabeth Ann Harper, 1928-
 xJohn, Elizabeth A. H.
  Storms Brewed in Other Men's Worlds: The Confrontation of Indians, Spanish, & French in the Southwest, 1540-1795. Tex A&M Univ Pr.

John, Erwin Roy.
 xJohn, E. Roy.
  Mechanisms of Memory. Acad Pr.

John, F. *see* John, Fritz.

John, Fritz, 1910-
 xJohn, F.
  Lectures on Advanced Numerical Analysis. Gordon.
  Partial Differential Equations. Springer-Verlag.
 xJohn, Fritz.
  Partial Differential Equations. Am Math.

John, Helen. *see* John, Helen James.

John, Helen James.
 xJohn, Helen.
  Thomist Spectrum. Fordham.

John Hopkins University, Department of International Health. *see* Johns Hopkins University. Department of International Health.

John, J. *see* John, James E. A.

John, James E. *see* John, James E. A.

John, James E. A., 1933-
 xJohn, J.
  Introduction to Fluid Mechanics. P-H.
 xJohn, James E.
  Gas Dynamics. Allyn.

John, Laurie.
 xJohn, Laurie.
  ed. Cosmology Now. Taplinger.

John, P. V. *see* John, Perukattu Verkey.

John, Perukattu Verkey.
 xJohn, P. V.

Some Aspects of the Structure of the Indian Agricultural Economy, 1947-48 to 1961-62. Asia.

John of Salisbury.
 xJohn Of Salisbury.
  Policraticus: The Statesman's Book. Ungar.

John Stephenson Co. *see* John Stephenson Company.

John Stephenson Company.
 xJohn Stephenson Co.
  Electric Railway Cars & Trucks, 1905. Glenwood.

Johnk, Carl T. *see* Johnk, Carl Theodore Adolf.

Johnk, Carl Theodore Adolf, 1919-
 xJohnk, Carl T.
  Engineering Electromagnetic Fields & Waves. Wiley.

Johns, Albert C. *see* Johns, Albert Cameron.

Johns, Albert Cameron.
 xJohns, Albert C.
  American Politics in Transition. Kendall-Hunt.
  Nevada Politics. Kendall-Hunt.

Johns, Donnell F.
 xJohns, Donnell F.
  Clinical Management of Neurogenic Communicative Disorders. Little.

Johns, E. A. *see* Johns, Edward Alistair.

Johns, Edward Alistair.
 xJohns, E. A.
  The Social Structure of Modern Britain. Pergamon.
  The Sociology of Organizational Change. Pergamon.

Johns, Eric.
 xJohns, Eric.
  Dames of the Theatre. Arlington Hse.

Johns Hopkins Hospital, Baltimore. Nutrition Dept.
 xNutrition Department, Johns Hopkins Hospital.
  Manual of Applied Nutrition. Johns Hopkins.

Johns Hopkins University.
 xJohns Hopkins University.
  Herbert B. Adams: Tributes of Friends. AMS Pr.
  State Aid to Higher Education: A Series of Addresses Delivered at Johns Hopkins University. AMS Pr.
  Studies in Historical & Political Science, 1882-1965. AMS Pr.

Johns Hopkins University - History Of Ideas Club. *see* Johns Hopkins University. History of Ideas Club.

Johns Hopkins University. Department of International Health.
 xJohn Hopkins University, Department of International Health.
  The Functional Analysis of Health Needs & Services. Asia.

Johns Hopkins University. History of Ideas Club.
 xJohns Hopkins University - History Of Ideas Club.
  Studies in Intellectual History. Greenwood.

Johns, Jerry L.
 xJohns, Jerry L.
  ed. Assessing Reading Behavior: Informal Reading Inventories. Intl Reading.

Johns, Marjorie P., 1922-
 xJohns, Marjorie P.
  Drug Therapy & Nursing Care. Macmillan.

Johns, P. B.
 xJohns, P. B.
  Communication Systems Analysis. Van Nos Reinhold.

Johns, Roe L. *see* Johns, Roe Lyell.

Johns, Roe Lyell.
 xJohns, Roe L.
  The Economics & Financing of Education: A Systems Approach. P-H.

Johns, W. F. *see* Johns, William Francis.

Johns, William Francis, 1930-
 xJohns, W. F.

Steroids. Butterworths.

Johnsen, Jan.
 xJohnsen, Jan.
  Gardening Without Soil. Lippincott.

Johnsgard, Paul A.
 xJohnsgard, Paul A.
  Birds of the Great Plains: Breeding Species & Their Distribution. U of Nebr Pr.
  Grouse & Quails of North America. U of Nebr Pr.
  A Guide to North American Waterfowl. Ind U Pr.
  North American Game Birds of Upland & Shoreline. U of Nebr Pr.
  Song of the North Wind: A Story of the Snow Goose. U of Nebr Pr.

Johnson. *see* Johnson, Stanley W.

Johnson & Johnson. *see* Johnson and Johnson, Inc.

Johnson & Johnson Baby Products Company. *see* Johnson and Johnson, Inc.

Johnson, A. H. *see* Johnson, Arthur Henry.

Johnson, A. M. *see* Johnson, Arvid M.

Johnson, A. S.
 xJohnson, A. S.
  Marketing & Financial Control. Pergamon.

Johnson, Abby A. *see* Johnson, Abby Arthur.

Johnson, Abby Arthur.
 xJohnson, Abby A.
  Propaganda & Aesthetics: The Literary Politics of Afro-American Magazines in the Twentieth Century. U of Mass Pr.

Johnson, Adelaide M. *see* Johnson, Adelaide Margaret.

Johnson, Adelaide Margaret.
 xJohnson, Adelaide M.
  Experience, Affect & Behavior: Psychoanalytic Explorations of Doctor Adelaide McFayden Johnson. U of Chicago Pr.

Johnson, Alan, 1935-
 xJohnson, Alan.
  Driving in Competition. Norton.

Johnson, Allen, 1870-1931
 xJohnson, Allen.
  Stephen A. Douglas: A Study in American Politics. Da Capo.

Johnson, Allen W.
 xJohnson, Allen W.
  Quantification in Cultural Anthropology: An Introduction to Research Design. Stanford U Pr.

Johnson, Alvin D.
 xJohnson, Alvin D.
  Celebrating Your Church Anniversary. Judson.
  The Work of the Usher. Judson.

Johnson, Alvin S. *see* Johnson, Alvin Saunders.

Johnson, Alvin Saunders, 1874-
 xJohnson, Alvin S.
  Introduction to Economics. Kennikat.

Johnson, Amandus, 1877-
 xJohnson, Amandus.
  Swedish Settlements on the Delaware: Their History & Relation to the Indians, Dutch & English, 1638-1664. B Franklin.
  Swedish Settlements on the Delaware 1638-1664. Genealog Pub.

Johnson, Anabel. *see* Johnson, Annabell.

Johnson and Johnson, Inc.
 xJohnson & Johnson.
  Your Toddler. Macmillan.
 xJohnson & Johnson Baby Products Company.
  The First Wondrous Year: You & Your Baby. Macmillan.

Johnson, Andrew.
 xJohnson, Andrew.
  Speeches of Andrew Johnson, President of the United States. B Franklin.

Johnson, Ann D. *see* Johnson, Ann Donegan.

Johnson, Ann Donegan.
 xJohnson, Ann D.

The Value of Caring: The Story of Eleanor
Roosevelt. Value Comm.
The Value of Determination: The Story of
Helen Keller. Value Comm.
The Value of Fairness: The Story of Nellie Bly.
Value Comm.
Value of Foresight: The Story of Thomas
Jefferson. Value Comm.
The Value of Friendship: The Story of Jane
Addams. Value Comm.
The Value of Helping: The Story of Harriet
Tubman. Value Comm.
The Value of Love: The Story of Johnny
Appleseed. Value Comm.
The Value of Respect: The Story of Abraham
Lincoln. Value Comm.
The Value of Responsibility: The Story of
Ralph Bunche. Value Comm.
The Value of Truth & Trust: The Story of
Cochise. Value Comm.
Johnson, Annabel. see Johnson, Annabell.
Johnson, Annabell.
xJohnson, Anabel.
Count Me Gone. S&S.
xJohnson, Annabell.
Golden Touch. Har-Row.
The Grizzly. Schol Bk Serv.
The Grizzly. Har-Row.
The Grizzly. Har-Row.
Johnson, Arno H.
xJohnson, Arno H.
The American Market of the Future. NYU Pr.
Johnson, Arnold. see Johnson, Arnold Harvey.
Johnson, Arnold Harvey.
xJohnson, Arnold.
ed. Encyclopedia of Food Technology. AVI.
Johnson, Arthur Henry, 1845-1927
xJohnson, A. H.
The Disappearance of the Small Landowner.
Gordon Pr.
The Disappearance of the Small Landowner
Kelly.
Johnson, Arthur M. see Johnson, Arthur Menzies.
Johnson, Arthur Menzies, 1921-
xJohnson, Arthur M.
ed. The American Economy: An Historical
Introduction to the Problem's of the 1970's.
Free Pr.
Johnson, Arvid M.
xJohnson, A. M.
Styles of Folding: Mechanics & Mechanisms of
Folding of Natural Elastic Materials. Elsevier.
Johnson, Aubrey R. see Johnson, Aubrey Rodway.
Johnson, Aubrey Rodway.
xJohnson, Aubrey R.
The Cultic Prophet & Israel's Psalmody. Verry.
Johnson, Audrey.
xJohnson, Audrey.
Dressing Dolls. Branford.
Furnishing Dolls' Houses. Branford.
How to Repair & Dress Old Dolls. Branford.
Johnson, Audrey P.
xJohnson, Audrey P.
Hush, Winifred Is Dead. Bouregy.
Johnson, B. E. see Johnson, Barry Edward.
Johnson, B. L. see Johnson, Basil Leonard Clyde.
Johnson, Barbara. see Johnson, Barbara E.
Johnson, Barbara E.
xJohnson, Barbara.
Where Does a Mother Go to Resign?. Bethany
Fell.
Johnson, Barbara F. see Johnson, Barbara Ferry.
Johnson, Barbara Ferry.
xJohnson, Barbara F.
Delta Blood. Avon.
Homeward Winds the River. Avon.
Tara's Song. Avon.
Johnson, Barry Edward, 1937-
xJohnson, B. E.

Cohomology in Banach Algebras. Am Math.
Johnson, Barry L.
xJohnson, Barry L.
Practical Measurements for Evaluation in
Physical Education. Burgess.
Johnson, Basil Leonard Clyde.
xJohnson, B. L.
Pakistan. Heinemann Ed.
Johnson, Ben. see Johnson, Ben E.
Johnson, Ben A.
xJohnson, Ben E.
Learn to Rapid-Write. Sams.
Johnson, Ben C. see Johnson, Ben Campbell.
Johnson, Ben Campbell.
xJohnson, Ben C.
Matthew & Mark: A Relational Paraphrase.
Word Bks.
Johnson, Ben E.
xJohnson, Ben.
What Was That Verse Again?: Memory
Improvement Methods for the Christian
Worker. Quill Pubns.
xJohnson, Ben E.
How to Rapid Read, Naturally. Quill Pubns.
Learn to Rapid-Read. Sams.
Rapid Reading Naturally: What It Is, How to
Teach It. Quill Pubns.
Johnson, Ben E. see Johnson, Ben A.
Johnson, Bervin A. see Johnson, Bervin M.
Johnson, Bervin M.
xJohnson, Bervin A.
Opportunities in Photography Careers. Natl
Textbk.
Johnson, Broderick H.
xJohnson, Broderick H.
ed. Stories of Traditional Navajo Life &
Culture. Navajo Coll Pr.
Johnson, Bruce, 1933-
xJohnson, Bruce.
Conrad's Models of Mind. U of Minn Pr.
Johnson, Bruce L.
xJohnson, Bruce L.
Chinese Wand Exercise. Morrow.
Chinese Wand Exercise. Morrow.
Johnson, Burges, 1877-
xJohnson, Burges.
As I Was Saying. Arno.
ed. Little Book of Necessary Nonsense. Arno.
Little Book of Necessary Nonsense. R West.
Professor at Bay. Arno.
Johnson, C. see Johnson, Carol L.
Johnson, C. D. see Johnson, Colin D.
Johnson, C. Douglas.
xJohnson, C. Douglas.
Formal Aspects of Phonological Description.
Mouton.
Johnson, C. G. see Johnson, Cecil George.
Johnson, C. L. see Johnson, Clarence L.
Johnson, C. W. see Johnson, Warner C.
Johnson, Carl. see Johnson, Carl Thomas.
Johnson, Carl G.
xJohnson, Carl G.
Preaching Truths for Perilous Times. Baker Bk.
Johnson, Carl M.
xJohnson, Carl M.
Common Native Trees of Utah. Utah St U Pr.
Johnson, Carl Thomas.
xJohnson, Carl.
Success in Athletics. Transatlantic.
Johnson, Carol L.
xJohnson, C.
Practical Arithmetic: The Third "R". P-H.
Johnson, Carroll B.
xJohnson, Carroll B.
Inside Guzman De Alfarache. U of Cal Pr.
Matias de los Reyes & the Craft of Fiction. U
of Cal Pr.
Johnson, Cecil, 1900-
xJohnson, Cecil.

British West Florida, 1763-1783. Shoe String.
Johnson, Cecil George.
xJohnson, C. G.
Insect Migration. Carolina Biological.
Johnson, Chalmers. see Johnson, Chalmers A.
Johnson, Chalmers A.
xJohnson, Chalmers.
Autopsy on People's War. U of Cal Pr.
Japan's Public Policy Companies. Am
Enterprise.
Revolution & the Social System. Hoover Inst
Pr.
Revolutionary Change. Little.
xJohnson, Chalmers A.
Peasant Nationalism & Communist Power: The
Emergence of Revolutionary China,
1937-1945. Stanford U Pr.
Johnson, Charles B. see Johnson, Charles Bertram.
Johnson, Charles Bertram.
xJohnson, Charles B.
Songs of My People. Arno.
Johnson, Charles F. see Johnson, Charles Frederick.
Johnson, Charles Frederick, 1836-1931
xJohnson, Charles F.
Forms of English Poetry. Folcroft.
Forms of English Poetry. Norwood Edns.
Johnson, Charles S. see Johnson, Charles Spurgeon.
Johnson, Charles Spurgeon.
xJohnson, Charles S.
ed. Education & the Cultural Process: Papers
Presented at Symposium Commemorating the
Seventy-Fifth Anniversary of the Founding of
Fisk University, April 29-May 4, 1941.
Negro U Pr.
Negro College Graduate. Negro U Pr.
Johnson, Christopher, 1931-
xJohnson, Christopher.
Anatomy of U.K. Finance 1970-75. Longman.
Johnson, Christopher H.
xJohnson, Christopher H.
Utopian Communism in France: Cabet & the
Icarians 1839-1851. Cornell U Pr.
Johnson, Clarence L, 1922-
xJohnson, C. L.
Analog Computer Techniques. McGraw.
Johnson, Claudius O. see Johnson, Claudius Osborne.
Johnson, Claudius Osborne, 1894-
xJohnson, Claudius O.
Borah of Idaho. U of Wash Pr.
Johnson, Clifford, 1932-
xJohnson, C.
Introduction to Natural Selection. Univ Park.
Johnson, Clive, 1930-
xJohnson, Clive.
ed. Vedanta: An Anthology of Hindu Scripture,
Commentary, & Poetry. Weiser.
Johnson, Colin D.
xJohnson, C. D.
The Hammett Equation. Cambridge U Pr.
Johnson, Corinne B.
xJohnson, Corinne B.
Love & Sex & Growing up. Lippincott.
xJohnson, Corinne Benson.
Love & Sex & Growing up. Bantam.
Johnson, Corinne Benson. see Johnson, Corinne B.
Johnson, Curt. see Johnson, Curtis L.
Johnson, Curtis D., 1939-
xJohnson, Curtis D.
Process Control Instrumentation Technology.
Wiley.
Johnson, Curtis L, 1928-
xJohnson, Curt.
Nobody's Perfect. Carpenter Pr.
Johnson, Curtiss. see Johnson, Curtiss S.
Johnson, Curtiss S.
xJohnson, Curtiss.
Raymond E. Baldwin, Connecticut Statesman.
Globe Pequot.
Johnson, D. A. see Johnson, David Arthur.
Johnson, D. D. see Johnson, Dale D.

Johnson, D. E. *see* Johnson, David E.
Johnson, D. G. *see* Johnson, David George.
Johnson, D. Gale. *see* Johnson, David Gale.
Johnson, D. L.
    xJohnson, David.
       Presentations of Groups. Cambridge U Pr.
Johnson, Dale. *see* Johnson, Dale L.
Johnson, Dale D.
    xJohnson, D. D.
       Teaching Reading Vocabulary. HR&W.
Johnson, Dale L.
    xJohnson, Dale.
       The Sociology of Change & Reaction in Latin
        America. Bobbs.
Johnson, Daniel. *see* Johnson, Daniel E.
Johnson, Daniel E.
    xJohnson, Daniel.
       Building with Buses. Baker Bk.
Johnson, Daphne.
    xJohnson, Daphne.
       ed. Secondary Schools & the Welfare Network.
        Allen Unwin.
Johnson, Dave, 1931-
    xJohnson, Dave.
       The Success Principle. Harvest Hse.
Johnson, David, 1906-
    xJohnson, David.
       Home Decorating. David & Charles.
Johnson, David. *see* Johnson, D. L.
Johnson, David Arthur.
    xJohnson, D. A.
       Some Thermodynamic Aspects of Inorganic
        Chemistry. Cambridge U Pr.
Johnson, David E.
    xJohnson, D. E.
       Rapid Practical Designs of Active Filters.
        Wiley.
    xJohnson, David E.
       Digital Circuits & Microcomputers. P-H.
       A Handbook of Active Filters. P-H.
       Introduction to Filter Theory. P-H.
Johnson, David Gale, 1916-
    xJohnson, D. Gale.
       Forward Prices for Agriculture. Arno.
       The Sugar Program: Large Costs & Small
        Benefits. Am Enterprise.
Johnson, David George.
    xJohnson, D. G.
       Medieval Chinese Oligarchy. Westview.
Johnson, David R. *see* Johnson, David Ralph.
Johnson, David Ralph, 1942-
    xJohnson, David R.
       Policing the Urban Underworld: The Impact of
        Crime on the Development of the American
        Police, 1800-1887. Temple U Pr.
Johnson, David W., 1940-
    xJohnson, David W.
       ed. Contemporary Social Psychology.
        Lippincott.
       Educational Psychology. P-H.
       Human Relations & Your Career: A Guide to
        Interpersonal Skills. P-H.
       Joining Together: Group Theory & Group
        Skills. P-H.
       Learning Together & Alone: Cooperation,
        Competition, & Individualization. P-H.
Johnson, Denis, 1949-
    xJohnson, Denis.
       Inner Weather. Graywolf.
Johnson, Diane, 1943-
    xJohnson, Diane.
       Lying Low. Knopf.
       Lying Low. PB.
    xJohnson, Diane C.
       American Art Nouveau. Abrams.
Johnson, Diane C. *see* Johnson, Diane.
Johnson, Don, 1940 (may 19)-
    xJohnson, Don.

       Inside Bowling. Contemp Bks.
       Protean Body: A Rolfer's View of Human
        Flexibility. Har-Row.
Johnson, Donald C. *see* Johnson, Donald Clay.
Johnson, Donald Clay, 1940-
    xJohnson, Donald C.
       Index to Southeast Asian Journals, 1960-1974:
        A Guide to Articles, Book Reviews &
        Composite Works. G K Hall.
Johnson, Donald M. *see* Johnson, Donald Mcewen.
Johnson, Donald Mcewen, 1909-
    xJohnson, Donald M.
       Psychology of Thought & Judgment.
        Greenwood.
Johnson, Donald R., 1930-
    xJohnson, Donald R.
       The Study of Raptor Populations. U Pr of
        Idaho.
Johnson, Donna K. *see* Johnson, Donna Kay.
Johnson, Donna Kay.
    xJohnson, Donna K.
       illus. Brighteyes. HR&W.
Johnson, Donovan A.
    xJohnson, Donovan A.
       Guidelines for Teaching Mathematics.
        Wadsworth Pub.
Johnson, Doris. *see* Johnson, Doris J.
Johnson, Doris J.
    xJohnson, Doris.
       ed. Learning Disabilities-Educational Principles
        & Practices. Grune.
Johnson, Dorothea, 1929-
    xJohnson, Dorothea.
       Entertaining & Etiquette for Today. Acropolis.
Johnson, Dorothy E.
    xJohnson, Dorothy E.
       Barriers & Hazards in Counseling. HM.
       Expanding & Modifying Guidance Programs.
        HM.
Johnson, Dorothy M.
    xJohnson, Dorothy M.
       All the Buffalo Returning. Dodd.
       Buffalo Woman. Dodd.
       Greece: Wonderland of the Past & Present.
        Dodd.
       Indian Country. Gregg.
Johnson, Douglas W. *see* Johnson, Douglas Wilson.
Johnson, Douglas Wilson, 1878-1944
    xJohnson, Douglas W.
       Origin of Submarine Canyons: A Critical
        Review of Hypotheses. Hafner.
       Stream Sculpture on the Atlantic Slope: A
        Study in the Evolution of Appalachian
        Rivers. Hafner.
Johnson, E. A. *see* Johnson, Edgar Augustus Jerome.
Johnson, E. A. J. *see* Johnson, Edgar Augustus Jerome.
Johnson, E. Pauline. *see* Johnson, Emily Pauline.
Johnson, E. R. *see* Johnson, Emory Richard.
Johnson, Earl.
    xJohnson, Earl.
       Outside the Courts: A Survey of Diversion
        Alternatives in Civil Cases. Natl Ctr St
        Courts.
Johnson, Edgar A. *see* Johnson, Edgar Augustus Jerome.
Johnson, Edgar Augustus Jerome, 1900-1972
    xJohnson, E. A.
       Organization of Space in Developing Countries.
        Harvard U Pr.
    xJohnson, E. A. J.
       ed. The Dimensions of Diplomacy. Johns
        Hopkins.
       The Foundations of American Economic
        Freedom: Government & Enterprise in the
        Age of Washington. U of Minn Pr.
    xJohnson, Edgar A.
       Predecessors of Adam Smith: The Growth of
        British Economic Thought. Kelley.
Johnson, Edith L. *see* Johnson, Edith Line.
Johnson, Edith Line, 1911-
    xJohnson, Edith L.

       Secrets of Top Money Extra Income. P-H.
Johnson, Edward A. *see* Johnson, Edward Augustus.
Johnson, Edward Augustus, 1860-1944
    xJohnson, Edward A.
       Light Ahead for the Negro. AMS Pr.
Johnson, Edward D.
    xJohnson, Edward D.
       The First Folio of Shakespeare. Folcroft.
Johnson, Edward R.
    xJohnson, Edward R.
       Organization Development for Academic
        Libraries: An Evaluation of the Management
        Review & Analysis Program. Greenwood.
Johnson, Elden.
    xJohnson, Elden.
       The Arvilla Complex. Minn Hist.
       Prehistoric Peoples of Minnesota. Minn Hist.
Johnson, Eldon L. *see* Johnson, Eldon Lee.
Johnson, Eldon Lee.
    xJohnson, Eldon L.
       From Riot to Reason. U of Ill Pr.
Johnson, Ellen H.
    xJohnson, Ellen H.
       Modern Art & the Object: A Century of
        Changing Attitudes. Har-Row.
Johnson, Elmer C., 1898-
    xJohnson, Elmer C.
       Survey of American Law. Exposition.
Johnson, Elmer D.
    xJohnson, Elmer D.
       History of Libraries in the Western World.
        Scarecrow.
Johnson, Elmer H. *see* Johnson, Elmer Hubert.
Johnson, Elmer Hubert.
    xJohnson, Elmer H.
       Crime, Correction, & Society. Dorsey.
Johnson, Elvin R.
    xJohnson, Elvin R.
       Park Resources for Recreation. Merrill.
Johnson, Emily Pauline, 1861-1913
    xJohnson, E. Pauline.
       Legends of Vancouver. R West.
Johnson, Emory R. *see* Johnson, Emory Richard.
Johnson, Emory Richard.
    xJohnson, E. R.
       History of Domestic & Foreign Commerce of
        the United States. Kraus Repr.
    xJohnson, Emory R.
       History of Domestic & Foreign Commerce in
        the United States. B Franklin.
Johnson, Eric W.
    xJohnson, Eric W.
       Love & Sex in Plain Language. Lippincott.
       Love & Sex in Plain Language. Bantam.
       Stories in Perspective. Hayden.
Johnson, Ernest N. *see* Johnson, Ernest W.
Johnson, Ernest W.
    xJohnson, Ernest N.
       Practical Electromyography. Williams &
        Wilkins.
Johnson, Everett A.
    xJohnson, Everett A.
       Contemporary Hospital Trusteeship. Teach'em.
Johnson, Everett R., 1915-
    xJohnson, Everett R.
       Radiation-Induced Decomposition of Inorganic
        Molecular Ions. Gordon.
Johnson, F. N.
    xJohnson, F. N.
       Lithium Research & Therapy. Acad Pr.
Johnson, F. Roy. *see* Johnson, Frank Roy.
Johnson, Falk S., 1913-
    xJohnson, Falk S.
       Improving Your Spelling. HR&W.
Johnson, Fenton, 1888-1958
    xJohnson, Fenton.
       Songs of the Soil. AMS Pr.
       Tales of Darkest America. Arno.
Johnson, Ferne.
    xJohnson, Ferne.

ed. Start Early for an Early Start: You & the
Young Child. ALA.
Johnson, Frank H. *see* Johnson, Frank Harris.
Johnson, Frank Harris.
xJohnson, Frank H.
The Theory of Rate Processes in Biology &
Medicine. Wiley.
Johnson, Frank Roy, 1911-
xJohnson, F. Roy.
How & Why Stories in Carolina Folklore.
Johnson NC.
The Peanut Story. Johnson NC.
Supernaturals Among Carolina Folk & Their
Neighbors. Johnson NC.
Johnson, Franklin, 1875-
xJohnson, Franklin.
The Development of State Legislation
Concerning the Free Negro. Greenwood.
Johnson, Franklyn. *see* Johnson, Franklyn Arthur.
Johnson, Franklyn Arthur, 1921-
xJohnson, Franklyn.
Defence by Ministry. Holmes & Meier.
Johnson, Fred, 1908-
xJohnson, Fred.
The Foxes. Natl Wildlife.
Turtles & Tortoises. Natl Wildlife.
Johnson, Fred H.
xJohnson, Fred H.
The Anatomy of Hallucinations. Nelson-Hall.
Johnson, Frederick, 1904-
xJohnson, Frederick.
ed. Man in Northeastern North America. AMS
Pr.
Johnson, G. Orville. *see* Johnson, George Orville.
Johnson, G. Timothy.
xJohnson, T. C.
Doctor!: What You Should Know About
Health Care Before You Call a Physician.
McGraw.
Johnson, Gaylord.
xJohnson, Gaylord.
Hunting with the Microscope. Arco.
Johnson, George Orville.
xJohnson, G. Orville.
Learning Performance of Retarded & Normal
Children. Greenwood.
Johnson, Georgia. *see* Johnson, Georgia Douglas Camp.
Johnson, Georgia B. *see* Johnson, Georgia Borg.
Johnson, Georgia Borg, 1883-
xJohnson, Georgia B.
Organization of the Required Physical
Education for Women in State Universities.
AMS Pr.
Johnson, Georgia D. *see* Johnson, Georgia Douglas
Camp.
Johnson, Georgia Douglas Camp, 1886-1966
xJohnson, Georgia.
An Autumn Love Cycle. Arno.
xJohnson, Georgia D.
Bronze: A Book of Verse. AMS Pr.
Johnson, Gerald W. *see* Johnson, Gerald White.
Johnson, Gerald White, 1890-
xJohnson, Gerald W.
America-Watching: Perspectives in the Course
of an Incredible Century. Stemmer Hse.
The Cabinet. Morrow.
The Congress. Morrow.
The Lunatic Fringe. Greenwood.
Our English Heritage. Greenwood.
The Presidency. Morrow.
The Supreme Court. Morrow.
Johnson, Glen, 1907-
xJohnson, Glen.
Some Ethical Implications of a Naturalistic
Philosophy of Education. AMS Pr.
Johnson, Glen R.
xJohnson, Glen R.
Army Staff Officer's Guide. Gulf Pub.
Johnson, Glenn L.
xJohnson, Glenn L.

ed. The Overproduction Trap in U. S.
Agriculture: A Study of Resource Allocation
from World War I to the Late 1960's. Johns
Hopkins.
Johnson, Gus.
xJohnson, Gus.
F.D.N.Y.: The Fire Buff's Handbook of the
New York Fire Department. Western Islands.
Johnson, H. Earle. *see* Johnson, Harold Earle.
Johnson, H. Eugene.
xJohnson, H. Eugene.
The Christian Church Plea. Standard Pub.
Johnson, H. Wayne.
xJohnson, H. Wayne.
Preschool Test Descriptions: Test Matrix &
Correlated Test Descriptors. C C Thomas.
Johnson, H. Webster. *see* Johnson, Herbert Webster.
Johnson, Halvard, 1936-
xJohnson, Halvard.
Dance of the Red Swan. SBD.
Johnson, Hannah L. *see* Johnson, Hannah Lyons.
Johnson, Hannah Lyons.
xJohnson, Hannah L.
From Apple Seed to Applesauce. Lothrop.
From Seed to Jack-O-Lantern. Lothrop.
From Seed to Salad. Lothrop.
Let's Bake Bread. Lothrop.
Let's Make Soup. Lothrop.
Johnson, Harold E. *see* Johnson, Harold Edgar.
Johnson, Harold Earle.
xJohnson, H. Earle.
Musical Interludes in Boston, 1795-1830. AMS
Pr.
Symphony Hall, Boston. Da Capo.
Johnson, Harold Edgar, 1915-
xJohnson, Harold E.
Jean Sibelius. Greenwood.
Johnson, Harold L.
xJohnson, Harold L.
Disclosure of Corporate Social Performance:
Survey, Evaluation, & Prospects. Praeger.
Johnson, Harold V.
xJohnson, Harold V.
General-Industrial Machine Shop. Bennett Co.
Johnson, Harrison.
xJohnson, Harrison.
Johnson's History of Nebraska. Arno.
Johnson, Harry A. *see* Johnson, Harry Alleyn.
Johnson, Harry Alleyn.
xJohnson, Harry A.
ed. Ethnic American Minorities: A Guide to
Media & Materials. Bowker.
Johnson, Harry G. *see* Johnson, Harry Gordon.
Johnson, Harry Gordon, 1923-
xJohnson, Harry G.
Aspects of the Theory of Tariffs. Allen Unwin.
Aspects of the Theory of Tariffs. Harvard U
Pr.
Further Essays in Monetary Economics.
Harvard U Pr.
On Economics & Society. U of Chicago Pr.
Selected Essays in Monetary Economics. Allen
Unwin.
Two-Sector Model of General Equilibrium.
Beresford Bk Serv.
World Economy at the Crossroads: A Survey
of Current Problems of Money, Trade &
Economic Development. Oxford U Pr.
Johnson, Helgi.
xJohnson, Helgi.
ed. The Megatectonics of Continents &
Oceans. Rutgers U Pr.
Johnson, Henry C.
xJohnson, Henry C.
Teachers for the Prairie: The University of
Illinois & the Schools, 1868-1945. U of Ill Pr.
Johnson, Henry S. *see* Johnson, Henry Sioux.
Johnson, Henry Sioux.
xJohnson, Henry S.

ed. Educating the Mexican American. Judson.
Johnson, Herbert A. *see* Johnson, Herbert Alan.
Johnson, Herbert Alan.
xJohnson, Herbert A.
The Law Merchant & Negotiable Instruments
in Colonial New York 1664-1730. Loyola.
Johnson, Herbert Webster.
xJohnson, H. Webster.
Administrative Office Management. A-W.
Creative Selling. SW Pub.
Johnson, Hervey.
xJohnson, Hervey.
Tending the Talking Wire: A Buck Soldier's
View of Indian Country, 1863-1866. U of
Utah Pr.
Johnson, Hewlett, 1874-1966
xJohnson, Hewlett.
China's New Creative Age. Greenwood.
Soviet Russia Since the War. Greenwood.
Johnson, Hildegard B. *see* Johnson, Hildegard Binder.
Johnson, Hildegard Binder.
xJohnson, Hildegard B.
Carta Marina: World Geography in Strassburg,
1525. Greenwood.
Order Upon the Land: The U. S. Rectangular
Land Survey & the Upper Mississippi
Country. Oxford U Pr.
Johnson, Hubert C.
xJohnson, Hubert C.
Frederick the Great & His Officials. Yale U Pr.
Johnson, Ira.
xJohnson, Ira D.
Glenway Wescott: The Paradox of Voice.
Kennikat.
Johnson, Ira D. *see* Johnson, Ira.
Johnson, J. *see* Johnson, William.
Johnson, J. C. *see* Johnson, Jeanne Colbert.
Johnson, J. D. *see* Johnson, Joan D.
Johnson, J. Douglas, 1918-
xJohnson, J. Douglas.
Advertising Today. SRA.
Johnson, J. G.
xJohnson, J. G.
Great Basin Lower Devonian Brachiopoda.
Geol Soc.
Pridolian & Early Gedinnian Age Brachiopods
from the Roberts Mountains Formation of
Central Nevada. U of Cal Pr.
Johnson, J. R. *see* Johnson, Johnny Ray.
Johnson, J. T. *see* Johnson, John Theodore.
Johnson, James. *see* Johnson, James Leonard.
Johnson, James A.
xJohnson, James A.
Group Therapy: A Practical Approach.
McGraw.
Johnson, James A. *see* Johnson, James Allen.
Johnson, James Allen, 1932-
xJohnson, James A.
Introduction to the Foundations of American
Education. Allyn.
Johnson, James F. *see* Johnson, James Francis.
Johnson, James Francis.
xJohnson, James F.
Applied Mathematics. Glencoe.
Renovated Waste Water: An Alternative
Source of Municipal Water Supply in the
United States. U Chicago Dept Geog.
Johnson, James G. *see* Johnson, James Gibson.
Johnson, James Gibson, 1871-1957
xJohnson, James G.
Southern Fiction Prior to 1860: An Attempt at
First-Hand Bibliography. Johnson Repr.
Johnson, James L. *see* Johnson, James Leonard.
Johnson, James Leonard, 1927-
xJohnson, James.
Loneliness Is Not Forever. Moody.
xJohnson, James L.

Coming Back: One Man's Journey to the Edge
of Eternity & Spiritual Rediscovery.
Springhouse.

Johnson, James P., 1937-
xJohnson, James P.
A New Deal for Soft Coal: The Attempted
Revitalization of the Bituminous Coal
Industry Under the New Deal. Arno.
The Politics of Soft Coal: The Bituminous
Industry from World War I Through the New
Deal. U of Ill Pr.
Johnson, James T. see Johnson, James Turner.

Johnson, James Turner.
xJohnson, James T.
Ideology Reason, & the Limitation of War:
Religious & Secular Concepts, 1200-1740.
Princeton U Pr.
Johnson, James W. see Johnson, James Weldon.

Johnson, James Weldon, 1871-1938
xJohnson, James W.
The Autobiography of an Ex-Coloured Man.
Arden Lib.
Autobiography of an Ex-Coloured Man. Hill &
Wang.
Autobiography of an Ex-Coloured Man. Knopf.
Fifty Years & Other Poems. AMS Pr.
Negro Americans, What Now. AMS Pr.
Negro Americans, What Now?. Da Capo.

Johnson, James William, 1927-
xJohnson, James W.
The Formation of English Neo-Classical
Thought. Greenwood.
Prose in Practice: A Rhetorical Reader.
HarBraceJ.

Johnson, Jan.
xJohnson, Jan.
The Angel of the Prison: A Story About
Elizabeth Fry. Winston Pr.
Brother Francis: A Story About Saint Francis
of Assisi. Winston Pr.

Johnson, Janet H.
xJohnson, Janet H.
The Demotic Verbal System. Oriental Inst.

Johnson, Jeanne Colbert, 1920-
xJohnson, J. C.
Emulsifiers & Emulsifying Techniques. Noyes.
Industrial Enzymes: Recent Advances. Noyes.
Specialized Sugars for the Food Industry.
Noyes.

Johnson, Jerah, 1931-
xJohnson, Jerah.
Africa & the West. Krieger.
Age of Recovery: The Fifteenth Century.
Cornell U Pr.

Johnson, Joan D.
xJohnson, J. D.
Workbook for Tests & Measurements in
Physical Education. Peek Pubns.

Johnson, Joe, 1933-
xJohnson, Joe.
Compiled by A Field of Diamonds. Broadman.
xJohnson, Joseph S.
Precious Promises. Broadman.
Johnson, Joe. see Johnson, Joe Donald.

Johnson, Joe Donald.
xJohnson, Joe.
Hot. Telephone Bks.

Johnson, John, 1829-1907
xJohnson, John.
The Defense of Charleston Harbor: Including
Fort Sumter & the Adjacent Islands,
1863-1865. Arno.
Johnson, John E. see Johnson, John Emil.

Johnson, John Emil, 1929-
xJohnson, John E.
illus. My First Book of Things. Random.

Johnson, John J.
xJohnson, John J.

ed. Continuity & Change in Latin America.
Stanford U Pr.
Latin America in Caricature. U of Tex Pr.

Johnson, John M.
xJohnson, John M.
ed. Crime at the Top: Deviance in Business &
the Professions. Har-Row.
Doing Field Research. Free Pr.

Johnson, John Theodore, 1881-
xJohnson, J. T.
Relative Merits of Three Methods of
Subtraction: An Experimental Comparison of
the Decomposition Method of Subtraction
with the Equal Additions Method & the
Austrian Method. AMS Pr.
Johnson, John W. see Johnson, John Warren.

Johnson, John Warren, 1929-
xJohnson, John W.
Political Christians: A Guide for Christians in
Public Service. Augsburg.

Johnson, Johnni.
xJohnson, Johnni.
The Gift of Belonging. Broadman.

Johnson, Johnny Ray.
xJohnson, J. R.
Linear Systems Analysis. Wiley.
Johnson, Joseph A. see Johnson, Joseph Andrew.

Johnson, Joseph Andrew, 1914-
xJohnson, Joseph A.
The Soul of the Black Preacher. Pilgrim NY.
Johnson, Joseph S. see Johnson, Joe.

Johnson, Josephine.
xJohnson, Josephine.
Florence Farr: Bernard Shaw's "New Woman".
Rowman.
Johnson, Josephine. see Johnson, Josephine Winslow.
Johnson, Josephine W. see Johnson, Josephine Winslow.

Johnson, Josephine Winslow, 1910-
xJohnson, Josephine.
Inland Island. S&S.
xJohnson, Josephine W.
Inland Island. S&S.
Jordanstown: A Novel. AMS Pr.

Johnson, Joyce, 1935-
xJohnson, Joyce.
Bad Connections. PB.

Johnson, Julian.
xJohnson, Julian.
Surgery of the Chest. Year Bk Med.

Johnson, Karl R.
xJohnson, Karl R.
The Written Spirit: Thematic & Rhetorical
Structure in Wordsworth's the Prelude.
Humanities.

Johnson, Keith.
xJohnson, Keith.
Life's Priorities. Zoe Pubns.

Johnson, Ken.
xJohnson, Ken.
The Ancient Magic of the Pyramids. PB.
Johnson, Kenneth. see Johnson, Kenneth F.

Johnson, Kenneth A.
xJohnson, Kenneth A.
Public Order Criminal Behavior & Criminal
Laws: The Question of Legal
Decriminalization. R & E Res Assoc.

Johnson, Kenneth F.
xJohnson, Kenneth.
Mexican Democracy: A Critical View. Praeger.

Johnson, Kenneth G.
xJohnson, Kenneth G.
General Semantics: An Outline Survey. Intl
Gen Semantics.
Nothing Never Happens: Exercises to Trigger
Group Discussion & Promote Self-Discovery
with Selected Readings. Glencoe.

Johnson, Kenneth Jeffrey, 1942-
xJohnson.

Numerical Methods in Chemistry. Dekker.

Johnson, Kenneth R.
xJohnson, Kenneth.
Teaching the Culturally Disadvantaged: A
Rational Approach. SRA.
Johnson, L. see Johnson, Lincoln F.
Johnson, L. Murphy. see Johnson, Richard E.

Johnson, Lanny L.
xJohnson, Lanny L.
The Comprehensive Arthroscopic Examination
of the Knee. Mosby.
Johnson, Lee A. see Johnson, Lee Ann.

Johnson, Lee Ann.
xJohnson, Lee A.
Mary Hallock Foote. Twayne.
Mary Hallock Foote. Twayne.
Johnson, Lee H. see Johnson, Lee Harnie.

Johnson, Lee Harnie, 1909-
xJohnson, Lee H.
Nomography & Empirical Equations. Krieger.

Johnson, Lemuel.
xJohnson, Lemuel.
Highlife for Caliban. Ardis Pubs.

Johnson, Leonard R., 1942-
xJohnson, Leonard R.
Gastrointestinal Physiology. Mosby.

Johnson, Lincoln F.
xJohnson, L.
The Film: Space, Time, Light & Sound.
HR&W.
Johnson, Lionel. see Johnson, Lionel Pigot.
Johnson, Lionel P. see Johnson, Lionel Pigot.

Johnson, Lionel Pigot, 1867-1902
xJohnson, L.
Post Liminium: Essays & Critical Papers. R
West.
xJohnson, Lionel.
Art of Thomas Hardy. Haskell.
Reviews & Critical Papers. R West.
xJohnson, Lionel P.
Poetical Works of Lionel Johnson. AMS Pr.
Post Liminium: Essays & Critical Papers. Arno.
Reviews & Critical Papers. Arno.
Johnson, Lois W. see Johnson, Lois Walfrid.

Johnson, Lois Walfrid.
xJohnson, Lois W.
Either Way, I Win: A Guide for Growth in the
Power of Prayer. Augsburg.
Gift in My Arms: Thoughts for New Mothers.
Augsburg.

Johnson, Lynwood A.
xJohnson, Lynwood A.
Operations Research in Production Planning,
Scheduling, & Inventory Control. Wiley.
Johnson, M. see Johnson, Marcia K.

Johnson, M. Clemens, 1921-
xJohnson, M. Clemens.
Review of Research Methods in Education.
Rand.

Johnson, M. H.
xJohnson, M. H.
ed. Development in Mammals. Elsevier.
xJohnson, Martin H.
ed. Development in Mammals. Elsevier.

Johnson, Mae M.
xJohnson, Mae M.
Problem Solving in Nursing Practice. Wm C
Brown.

Johnson, Marcia K.
xJohnson, M.
Statistics: Tool of the Behavioral Sciences. P-H.

Johnson, Margaret.
xJohnson, Margaret.
Home Before Dark. Zondervan.

Johnson, Margo.
xJohnson, Margo.
The Psychology Teacher's Resource Book. Am
Psychol.

Johnson, Marian S.
xJohnson, Marian S.

Promoting Your Church Library. Augsburg.
Johnson, Marion.
xJohnson, Marion.
Derbyshire Village Schools in the Nineteenth Century. Kelley.
Johnson, Marion. *see* Johnson, Marion Lee.
Johnson, Marion Lee, 1937-
xJohnson, Marion.
Functional Administration in Physical & Health Education. HM.
Johnson, Marjorie.
xJohnson, Marjorie.
Songs from an Island. Golden Quill.
Johnson, Martin H. *see* Johnson, M. H.
Johnson, Mary, 1952-
xJohnson, Mary.
Tub Farming: Grow Vegetables Anywhere in Containers. Garden Way Pub.
Johnson, Mary E. *see* Johnson, Mary Elizabeth.
Johnson, Mary Elizabeth, 1944-
xJohnson, Mary E.
Country Quilt Patterns. Oxmoor Hse.
Rugs: Designs, Patterns, Projects. Oxmoor Hse.
Johnson, Merle A. *see* Johnson, Merle Allison.
Johnson, Merle Allison.
xJohnson, Merle A.
How to Be Happy in the Non Electric Church. Abingdon.
Johnson, Michael L.
xJohnson, Michael L.
Holistic Technology. Libra.
Johnson, Michael P., 1941-
xJohnson, Michael P.
Toward a Patriarchal Republic: The Secession of Georgia. La State U Pr.
Johnson, Mildred D.
xJohnson, Mildred D.
Problem Solving & Chemical Calculations. HarBraceJ.
Johnson, Mildred M. *see* Johnson, Mildred Mckenzie.
Johnson, Mildred Mckenzie.
xJohnson, Mildred M.
Lost Flamingos. Golden Quill.
Johnson, Moulton K.
xJohnson, Moulton K.
The Hand Atlas. C C Thomas.
The Hand Book. C C Thomas.
Johnson, Nancy A. *see* Johnson, Nancy Ainsworth.
Johnson, Nancy Ainsworth, 1942-
xJohnson, Nancy A.
Current Topics in Language: Introductory Readings. Winthrop.
Johnson, Nancy R.
xJohnson, Nancy R.
The Political Economic, & Labor Climate in Peru. Indus Res Unit-Wharton.
Johnson, Nevil.
xJohnson, Nevil.
Government in the Federal Republic of Germany: The Executive at Work. Pergamon.
In Search of the Constitution: Reflections on State & Society in Britain. Pergamon.
Parliament & Administration: The Estimates Committee, 1964-65. Kelley.
Johnson, Nicholas, 1934-
xJohnson, Nicholas.
How to Talk Back to Your Television Set. Little.
Johnson, Nora.
xJohnson, Nora.
Flashback: Nora Johnson on Nunnally Johnson. Doubleday.
Johnson, Norman H. *see* Johnson, Norman Henry.
Johnson, Norman Henry.
xJohnson, Norman H.
The Complete Kitten & Cat Book. Har-Row.
Johnson, Oakley C., 1890-
xJohnson, Oakley C.

Marxism in United States History Before the Russian Revolution, 1876-1917. Humanities.
Johnson, Ole S. *see* Johnson, Ole Simon.
Johnson, Ole Simon, 1917-
xJohnson, Ole S.
Industrial Store: Its History, Operations & Economic Significance. Va Bk.
Johnson, Olive.
xJohnson, Olive.
Catering for One. Intl Pubns Serv.
Johnson, Oliver A.
xJohnson, Oliver A.
Skepticism & Cognitivism: A Study in the Foundations of Knowledge. U of Cal Pr.
Johnson, Owen. *see* Johnson, Owen Mcmahon.
Johnson, Owen Mcmahon, 1878-1952
xJohnson, Owen.
Lawrenceville Stories. S&S.
Stover at Yale. Macmillan.
Johnson, P. S.
xJohnson, P. S.
The Economics of Invention & Innovation: With a Case Study of the Development of the Hovercraft. Biblio Dist.
Johnson, Palmer O. *see* Johnson, Palmer Oliver.
Johnson, Palmer Oliver.
xJohnson, Palmer O.
The National Youth Administration. Arno.
Johnson, Pamela H. *see* Johnson, Pamela Hansford.
Johnson, Pamela Hansford, 1912-
xJohnson, Pamela H.
The Good Husband. Scribner.
The Good Husband. G K Hall.
The Good Listener. G K Hall.
Johnson, Paul, 1928-
xJohnson, Paul.
The Civilization of Ancient Egypt. Atheneum.
Civilizations of the Holy Land. Atheneum.
Enemies of Society. Atheneum.
A History of Christianity. Atheneum.
Johnson, Paul. *see* Johnson, Paul Cornelius.
Johnson, Paul B. 1918-
xJohnson, Paul B.
From Sticks & Stones: Personal Adventures in Mathematics. SRA.
Johnson, Paul C., 1910-
xJohnson, Paul C.
California. Kodansha.
Grand Canyon. Kodansha.
Johnson, Paul C. *see* Johnson, Paul Christian.
Johnson, Paul Christian, 1928-
xJohnson, Paul C.
Peripheral Circulation. Wiley.
Johnson, Paul Cornelius, 1904-
xJohnson, Paul.
Farm Inventions in the Making of America. Wallace-Homestead.
Farm Power in the Making of America. Wallace-Homestead.
Johnson, Peter.
xJohnson, Peter.
Ocean Racing & Offshore Yachts. Dodd.
ed. Offshore Manual International. Dodd.
Johnson, Philip C. *see* Johnson, Philip Cortelyou.
Johnson, Philip Cortelyou.
xJohnson, Philip C.
Architecture: 1949 to 1965. HR&W.
Johnson, Philip L.
xJohnson, Philip L.
ed. Remote Sensing in Ecology. U of Ga Pr.
Johnson, Philip M., 1930-
xJohnson, Philip M.
How to Maximize Your Advertising Investment. CBI Pub.
Johnson, R. *see* Johnson, Roger A.
Johnson, R. Brimley. *see* Johnson, Reginald Brimley.
Johnson, R. E. *see* Johnson, Richard Eaton.
Johnson, R. M. *see* Johnson, Ronald Mark.
Johnson, R. P. *see* Johnson, Robert Proctor.
Johnson, R. W. *see* Johnson, Richard William.

Johnson, R. Winifred. *see* Johnson, R. Winifred Heyward.
Johnson, R. Winifred Heyward.
xJohnson, R. Winifred.
Introduction to Nursing Care. McGraw.
Johnson, Ralph W. *see* Johnson, Ralph Whitney.
Johnson, Ralph Whitney.
xJohnson, Ralph W.
Cleaning Up Europe's Waters: Economics, Management, Policies. Praeger.
Johnson, Ray C.
xJohnson, Ray C.
Mechanical Design Synthesis: Creative Design & Optimization. Krieger.
Optimum Design of Mechanical Elements. Wiley.
Johnson, Reginald B. *see* Johnson, Reginald Brimley.
Johnson, Reginald Brimley, 1867-1932
xJohnson, R. Brimley.
English Letter Writers. Folcroft.
English Letter Writers. Quaker City.
ed. Leigh Hunt. Haskell.
Leigh Hunt. R West.
xJohnson, Reginald B.
English Letter Writers. R West.
Johnson, Rex. *see* Johnson, Rex E.
Johnson, Rex E.
xJohnson, Rex.
At Home with Sex. Victor Bks.
Johnson, Richard, 1947-
xJohnson, Richard.
The French Communist Party Versus the Students: Revolutionary Politics in May-June 1968. Yale U Pr.
Johnson, Richard A. *see* Johnson, Richard Arvid.
Johnson, Richard Abraham, 1910-
xJohnson, Richard A.
Administration of United States Foreign Policy. U of Tex Pr.
Johnson, Richard Arvid.
xJohnson, Richard A.
Production & Operations Management: A systems Concept. HM.
Theory & Management of Systems. McGraw.
Johnson, Richard B. *see* Johnson, Richard Buhmann.
Johnson, Richard Buhmann.
xJohnson, Richard B.
ed. The Bank Director. SMU Press.
Johnson, Richard E.
xJohnson, L. Murphy.
College Algebra. Scott F.
xJohnson, Richard E.
Calculus with Analytic Geometry. Allyn.
College Algebra. Benjamin-Cummings.
Johnson, Richard Eaton, 1929-
xJohnson, R. E.
Existential Man: The Challenge of Psychotherapy. Pergamon.
Johnson, Richard M.
xJohnson, Richard M.
Dynamics of Compliance: Supreme Court Decision-Making from a New Perspective. Northwestern U Pr.
Johnson, Richard William.
xJohnson, R. W.
How Long Will South Africa Survive?. Oxford U Pr.
Johnson, Rita B.
xJohnson, Rita B.
Toward Individualized Learning: A Developer's Guide to Self-Instruction. A-W.
Johnson, Robbin S.
xJohnson, Robbin S.
More's Utopia, Ideal & Illusion. Yale U Pr.
Johnson, Robert, 1948-
xJohnson, Robert.
Culture & Crisis in Confinement. Lexington Bks.
Johnson, Robert. *see* Johnson, Robert Russell.
Johnson, Robert C. *see* Johnson, Robert Clyde.

Johnson, Robert Clyde.
  xJohnson, Robert C.
    The Meaning of Christ. Westminster.
Johnson, Robert G.
  xJohnson, Robert G.
    The Appraisal Interview Guide. Am Mgmt.
Johnson, Robert K.
  xJohnson, Robert K.
    Francis Ford Coppola. Twayne.
Johnson, Robert L. *see* Johnson, Robert Lynn.
Johnson, Robert Lee, 1919-
  xJohnson, Robert L.
    Letter of Paul to the Galatians. Sweet.
Johnson, Robert Lynn, 1929-
  xJohnson, Robert L.
    Men Who Work & Explore Under the Sea.
    Denison.
Johnson, Robert O. *see* Johnson, Robert Owen.
Johnson, Robert Owen.
  xJohnson, Robert O.
    An Index to Profiles in the New Yorker.
    Scarecrow.
Johnson, Robert Proctor, 1924-
  xJohnson, R. P.
    Chief Joseph. Dillon.
    Osceola. Dillon.
Johnson, Robert Russell, 1939-
  xJohnson, Robert.
    Elementary Statistics. Duxbury Pr.
  xJohnson, Siskin.
    Elementary Statistics for Business. Duxbury Pr.
Johnson, Robert W. *see* Johnson, Robert Willard.
Johnson, Robert Willard.
  xJohnson, Robert W.
    Financial Management. Allyn.
Johnson, Rodney D.
  xJohnson, Rodney D.
    Quantitative Techniques for Business
    Decisions. P-H.
Johnson, Roger A.
  xJohnson, R.
    Critical Issues in Modern Religion. P-H.
Johnson, Roger N.
  xJohnson, Roger N.
    Aggression in Man & Animals. HR&W.
Johnson, Ron, 1937-
  xJohnson, Ron.
    The Early Sculpture of Picasso, 1901-1914.
    Garland Pub.
    Understanding the Film. Amphoto.
Johnson, Ronald C. *see* Johnson, Ronald Conant.
Johnson, Ronald Conant, 1930-
  xJohnson, Ronald C.
    George Gascoigne. Twayne.
Johnson, Ronald Mark.
  xJohnson, R. M.
    The Determination of Organic Peroxides.
    Pergamon.
Johnson, Ross H.
  xJohnson, Ross H.
    Quantitative Methods for Management. HM.
Johnson, Rossall. *see* Johnson, Rossall James.
Johnson, Rossall James.
  xJohnson, Rossall.
    Business Environment in an Emerging Nation:
    Profiles of Indonesian Economy.
    Northwestern U Pr.
Johnson, Rossiter, 1840-1931
  xJohnson, Rossiter.
    ed. A Dictionary of Biographies of Authors
    Represented in the Authors Digest Series:
    With a Supplemental List of Later Titles & a
    Supplementary Biographical Section. Gale.
    ed. A Dictionary of Famous Names in Fiction,
    Drama, Poetry, History & Art. Gale.
    The Twentieth Century Biographical Dictionary
    of Notable Americans. Gordon Pr.
Johnson, Ruth.
  xJohnson, Ruth.

    What to Do till the Garbageman Arrives: A
    Miser's Craft Manual. Vanguard.
Johnson, Ryerson. *see* Johnson, Walter Ryerson.
Johnson, S. J. *see* Johnson, Stanley W.
Johnson, S. Lawrence. *see* Johnson, Samuel Lawrence.
Johnson, Samuel.
  xJohnson, Samuel.
    Doctor Johnson's Prayers. Folcroft.
    The History of the Yorubas: From the Earliest
    Times to the Beginning of the British
    Protectorate. Intl Pubns Serv.
    The History of the Yorubas: From the Earliest
    Times to the Beginning of the British
    Protectorate. Routledge & Kegan.
    Johnson's Proposals for Printing Bibliotheca
    Harleiana 1742. Folcroft.
    Journey to the Western Islands of Scotland.
    Yale U Pr.
    Lives of English Poets. Dutton.
    Lives of the English Poets. Adler.
    Lives of the English Poets. Octagon.
    Lives of the English Poets. Oxford U Pr.
    Rambler. Yale U Pr.
    Samuel Johnson on Literature. Ungar.
    Selected Letters of Samuel Johnson. AMS Pr.
    Wit & Wisdom of Samuel Johnson. Norwood
    Edns.
Johnson, Samuel A.
  xJohnson, Samuel A.
    Essentials of Comparative Government. Barron.
Johnson, Samuel Lawrence.
  xJohnson, S. Lawrence.
    Captain Ducky & Other Children's Sermons.
    Abingdon.
Johnson, Sandy.
  xJohnson, Sandy.
    The Cuppi. Dell.
Johnson, Sarah B. *see* Johnson, Sarah Barclay.
Johnson, Sarah Barclay, 1837-1885
  xJohnson, Sarah B.
    Hadji in Syria: Three Years in Jerusalem. Arno.
Johnson, Sheila K.
  xJohnson, Sheila K.
    American Attitudes Toward Japan, 1941-1975.
    Am Enterprise.
    Idle Haven: Community Building Among the
    Working-Class Retired. U of Cal Pr.
Johnson, Shirley A.
  xJohnson, Shirley A.
    ed. Circulating Platelet. Acad Pr.
Johnson, Sidney M.
  xJohnson, Sidney M.
    Design of Foundations for Buildings. McGraw.
    Deterioration, Maintenance & Repair of
    Structures. Krieger.
Johnson, Siskin. *see* Johnson, Robert Russell.
Johnson, Spencer.
  xJohnson, Spencer.

    The Value of Believing in Yourself: The Story
    of Louis Pasteur. Value Comm.
    The Value of Courage: The Story of Jackie
    Robinson. Value Comm.
    The Value of Curiosity: The Story of
    Christopher Columbus. Value Comm.
    The Value of Dedication: The Story of Albert
    Schweitzer. Value Comm.
    The Value of Fantasy: The Story of Hans
    Christian Andersen. Value Comm.
    The Value of Honesty: The Story of Confucius.
    Value Comm.
    The Value of Humor: The Story of Will
    Rogers. Value Comm.
    The Value of Imagination: The Story of Charles
    Dickens. Value Comm.
    The Value of Kindness: The Story of Elizabeth
    Fry. Value Comm.
    The Value of Patience: The Story of the Wright
    Brothers. Value Comm.
    The Value of Saving: The Story of Benjamin
    Franklin. Value Comm.
    The Value of Sharing: The Story of the Mayo
    Brothers. Value Comm.
    The Value of Understanding: The Story of
    Margaret Mead. Value Comm.
Johnson, Stanley. *see* Johnson, Stanley Lewis.
Johnson, Stanley Lewis.
  xJohnson, Stanley.
    ed. Play & the Reader. P-H.
Johnson, Stanley W., 1928-
  xJohnson, Stanley.
    Learning Disabilities. Allyn.
  xJohnson, S. J.
    The Freshman's Friend. Barron.
  xJohnson, Stanley W.
    Arithmetic & Learning Disabilities: Guidelines
    for Identification & Remediation. Allyn.
Johnson, Stephanie. *see* Johnson, Stephanie L.
Johnson, Stephanie L.
  xJohnson, Stephanie.
    The Best of the Berkshires. Globe Pequot.
Johnson, Stephen. *see* Johnson, Stephen M.
Johnson, Stephen M.
  xJohnson, Stephen.
    First Person Singular: Living the Good Life
    Alone. NAL.
  xJohnson, Stephen M.
    First Person Singular: Living the Good Life
    Alone. Lippincott.
Johnson, Steven L.
  xJohnson, Steven L.
    Guide to American Indian Documents in the
    Congressional Serial Set: 1817-1899.
    Clearwater Pub.
Johnson, Stuart E.
  xJohnson, Stuart E.
    The Military Equation in Northeast Asia.
    Brookings.
Johnson, Susan M.
  xJohnson, Susan M.
    Seized by Love. Playboy Pbks.
Johnson, Suzanne H. *see* Johnson, Suzanne Hall.
Johnson, Suzanne Hall.
  xJohnson, Suzanne H.
    High-Risk Parenting: Nursing Assessment &
    Strategies for the Family at Risk. Lippincott.
Johnson, Sylvia A.
  xJohnson, Sylvia A.
    Animals of the Grasslands. Lerner Pubns.
    Animals of the Polar Regions. Lerner Pubns.
    Animals of the Temperate Forests. Lerner
    Pubns.
    Animals of the Tropical Forests. Lerner Pubns.
    Downy the Duckling. Carolrhoda Bks.
    The Lions of Africa. Carolrhoda Bks.
    Penelope the Tortoise. Carolrhoda Bks.
    Penny and Pete the Lambs. Carolrhoda Bks.
Johnson, T. C. *see* Johnson, G. Timothy.
Johnson, Terence J. *see* Johnson, Terence James.

Johnson, Terence James.
xJohnson, Terence J.
Professions & Power. Humanities.
Johnson, Thomas, 1948-
xJohnson, Thomas.
The Ice Futures. Copper Canyon.
Johnson, Thomas A.
xJohnson, Thomas A.
Dollar Power. Pendulum Pr.
Johnson, Thomas F. see Johnson, Thomas Frank.
Johnson, Thomas Frank.
xJohnson, Thomas F.
Renewing America's Cities. Greenwood.
Johnson, Thomas H. see Johnson, Thomas Herbert.
Johnson, Thomas Herbert.
xJohnson, Thomas H.
Oxford Companion to American History.
Oxford U Pr.
Printed Writings of Jonathan Edwards
1703-1758: A Bibliography. B Franklin.
Johnson, Thomas P. see Johnson, Thomas Perry.
Johnson, Thomas Perry, 1922-
xJohnson, Thomas P.
When Nature Runs Wild. Creative Ed.
Johnson, Trevor.
xJohnson, Trevor.
Thomas Hardy. Arco.
Johnson, Uwe, 1934-
xJohnson, Uwe.
Speculations About Jakob. HarBraceJ.
Third Book About Achim. HarBraceJ.
Johnson, V. Webster. see Johnson, Vernon Webster.
Johnson, Vernon E.
xJohnson, Vernon E.
I'll Quit Tomorrow. Har-Row.
Johnson, Vernon Webster.
xJohnson, V. Webster.
Land Problems & Policies. Arno.
Johnson, Vicki M.
xJohnson, Vicki M.
Step-by-Step Learning Guide for Older
Retarded Children. Syracuse U Pr.
A Step-by-Step Learning Guide for Retarded
Infants & Children. Syracuse U Pr.
Johnson, Virginia W. see Johnson, Virginia Weisel.
Johnson, Virginia Weisel.
xJohnson, Virginia W.
Distance Riding from Start to Finish. HM.
Johnson, W. B. see Johnson, William B.
Johnson, W. Branch. see Johnson, William Branch.
Johnson, W. C. see Johnson, William Clarence.
Johnson, W. H. see Johnson, Willis Hugh.
Johnson, W. R.
xJohnson, W. R.
Darkness Visible: A Study of Vergil's Aeneid.
U of Cal Pr.
Johnson, Wallace J. see Johnson, Wallace J. S.
Johnson, Wallace J. S., 1913-
xJohnson, Wallace J.
The Uncommon Man in American Business.
Devin.
Johnson, Walter. see Johnson, Walter Livezey.
Johnson, Walter Gilbert, 1905-
xJohnson, Walter.
August Strindberg. Twayne.
Strindberg & the Historical Drama. U of Wash
Pr.
Johnson, Walter Livezey.
xJohnson, Walter.
Readings in Economic Development. SW Pub.
Johnson, Walter Ryerson.
xJohnson, Ryerson.
Let's Walk up the Wall. Schol Bk Serv.
Johnson, Walter S. see Johnson, Walter Seely.
Johnson, Walter Seely, 1880-
xJohnson, Walter S.
Maxims of the Civil Law: Essays in the
Evolution of Law. W W Gaunt.
Johnson, Warner C.
xJohnson, C. W.

Basic Psychotherapeutics: A Programmed Text.
Spectrum Pub.
Johnson, Warren. see Johnson, Warren A.
Johnson, Warren A.
xJohnson, Warren.
Muddling Toward Frugality. Sierra.
xJohnson, Warren A.
Muddling Toward Frugality. Shambhala Pubns.
Public Parks on Private Land in England &
Wales. Johns Hopkins.
Johnson, Warren R. see Johnson, Warren Russell.
Johnson, Warren Russell.
xJohnson, Warren R.
Human Sexual Behavior & Sex Education:
With Historical, Moral, Legal, Linguistic, &
Cultural Perspectives. Lea & Febiger.
Johnson, Wayne L., 1942-
xJohnson, Wayne L.
Ray Bradbury. Ungar.
Johnson, Wendell, 1906-
xJohnson, Wendell.
Stuttering & What You Can Do About It.
Wilshire.
xJohnson, Wendell.
Stuttering & What You Can Do About It.
Interstate.
Johnson, Wendell S. see Johnson, Wendell Stacy.
Johnson, Wendell Stacy, 1927-
xJohnson, Wendell S.
Living in Sin: The Victorian Sexual Revolution.
Nelson-Hall.
Johnson, Wilbur V.
xJohnson, Wilbur V.
Careers in Physics. B'nai B'rith Car.
Johnson, William.
xJohnson, J.
Engineering Plasticity. Van Nos Reinhold.
Johnson, William A. see Johnson, William Arthur.
Johnson, William Arthur, 1936-
xJohnson, William A.
Steel Industry of India. Harvard U Pr.
Johnson, William B., 1944-
xJohnson, W. B.
Symmetric Structures in Banach Spaces. Am
Math.
Johnson, William B. see Johnson, William Branch.
Johnson, William Branch, 1893-
xJohnson, W. Branch.
Industrial Archaeology of Hertfordshire.
Kelley.
xJohnson, William B.
Folktales of Provence. Folcroft.
Johnson, William C.
xJohnson, William C.
ed. Child Development & Learning. Mss Info.
ed. The Learner, the Learning Process, the
School. Mss Info.
Johnson, William Clarence.
xJohnson, W. C.
Milton Criticism: A Subject Index. Dawson
Pub.
Johnson, William O. see Johnson, William Oscar.
Johnson, William Oscar.
xJohnson, William O.
Zero Factor. PB.
Johnson, William P. see Johnson, William Percival.
Johnson, William Percival, 1854-1928
xJohnson, William P.
My African Reminiscences, 1875-1895. Negro
U Pr.
Johnson, William W. see Johnson, William Weber.
Johnson, William Weber, 1909-
xJohnson, William W.
Cortes. Little.
Kelly Blue. Tex A&M Univ Pr.
Kelly Blue. U of Nebr Pr.
The Story of Sea Otters. Random.
Johnson, Willis, 1938-
xJohnson, Willis.

The Year of the Longley. Penobscot Bay.
Johnson, Willis Hugh, 1902-
xJohnson, W. H.
Principles of Zoology. HR&W.
Johnson, Willoughby. see Johnson, Willoughby H.
Johnson, Willoughby H.
xJohnson, Willoughby.
College Reading & College Writing. Scott F.
Johnson-Davies, D. see Johnson-Davies, Denys.
Johnson-Davies, Denys.
xJohnson-Davies, D.
tr. Modern Arabic Short Stories. Three
Continents.
xJohnson-Davies, Denys.
ed. Modern Arabic Short Stories. Three
Continents.
Johnson-Laird, P. N. see Johnson-Laird, Philip Nicholas.
Johnson-Laird, Philip Nicholas.
xJohnson-Laird, P. N.
ed. Thinking: Readings in Cognitive Science.
Cambridge U Pr.
Johnsrude, Irwin S.
xJohnsrude, Irwin S.
A Practical Approach to Angiography. Little.
Johnsson, William. see Johnsson, William G.
Johnsson, William G., 1934-
xJohnsson, William.
Religion in Overalls. Southern Pub.
Johnston, A. P.
xJohnston, A. P.
ed. Planning Perspectives for Education. Mss
Info.
Johnston, Alexander.
xJohnston, Alexander.
ed. American Orations: Studies in American
Political History. Arno.
Connecticut: A Study of a
Commonwealth-Democracy. AMS Pr.
Johnston, Alexandra F.
xJohnston, Alexandra F.
ed. York. U of Toronto Pr.
Johnston, Alva.
xJohnston, Alva.
The Great Goldwyn. Arno.
Johnston, Arnold.
xJohnston, Arnold.
Of Earth & Darkness: The Novels of William
Golding. U of Mo Pr.
Johnston, Arthur. see Johnston, Arthur P.
Johnston, Arthur P.
xJohnston, Arthur.
The Battle for World Evangelism. Tyndale.
World Evangelism & the Word of God.
Bethany Fell.
Johnston, Basil.
xJohnston, Basil H.
Ojibway Heritage. Columbia U Pr.
Johnston, Basil H. see Johnston, Basil.
Johnston, Brian, 1932-
xJohnston, Brian.
To the Third Empire: Ibsen's Early Drama. U
of Minn Pr.
Johnston, Bruce F.
xJohnston, Bruce F.
Agriculture & Structural Transformation:
Economic Strategies in Late-Developing
Countries. Oxford U Pr.
The Staple Food Economies of Western
Tropical Africa. Stanford U Pr.
Johnston, Carol L. see Johnston, Carol Lee.
Johnston, Carol Lee.
xJohnston, Carol L.
Intermediate Algebra. Wadsworth Pub.
Johnston, Charles M. see Johnston, Charles Murray.
Johnston, Charles Murray, 1926-
xJohnston, Charles M.

Valley of the Six Nations: A Collection of
  Documents on the Indian Lands of the
  Grand River. U of Toronto Pr.
Johnston, Colin.
  xJohnston, Colin.
    Glasgow Stations. David & Charles.
Johnston, Dorothy F.
  xJohnston, Dorothy F.
    Total Patient Care: Foundations & Practice.
      Mosby.
Johnston, Dorothy G. *see* Johnston, Dorothy Grunbock.
Johnston, Dorothy Grunbock.
  xJohnston, Dorothy G.
    Pounding Hooves. Cook.
Johnston, Eliza G. *see* Johnston, Eliza Griffin.
Johnston, Eliza Griffin, 1821-1896
  xJohnston, Eliza G.
    Texas Wild Flowers. Shoal Creek Pub.
Johnston, Elizabeth B. *see* Johnston, Elizabeth Bryant.
Johnston, Elizabeth Bryant, 1833-1907
  xJohnston, Elizabeth B.
    The Days That Are No More. Arno.
Johnston, F. C.
  xJohnston, F. C.
    The Complete Oil Painter. St Martin.
Johnston, Frederick S.
  xJohnston, Frederick S.
    Logic of Relationship. Philos Lib.
Johnston, George A. *see* Johnston, George Alexander.
Johnston, George Alexander.
  xJohnston, George A.
    Development of Berkeley's Philosophy. Russell.
Johnston, Gerald S.
  xJohnston, Gerald S.
    ed. Breast Cancer Diagnosis. Plenum Pub.
Johnston, Grahame.
  xJohnston, Grahame.
    ed. The Australian Pocket Oxford Dictionary.
      Oxford U Pr.
Johnston, Harold W. *see* Johnston, Harold Whetstone.
Johnston, Harold Whetstone, 1859-1912
  xJohnston, Harold W.
    Private Life of the Romans. Arno.
    The Private Life of the Romans. Cooper Sq.
Johnston, Harry H. *see* Johnston, Harry Hamilton.
Johnston, Harry Hamilton, Sir, 1858-1927
  xJohnston, Harry H.
    A Comparative Study of the Bantu &
      Semi-Bantu Languages. AMS Pr.
    History of the Colonization of Africa by Alien
      Races. Cooper Sq.
    Liberia. Negro U Pr.
    Little Life Stories. Arno.
    Negro in the New World. Johnson Repr.
Johnston, Hiram.
  xJohnston, Hiram.
    The Learning Center Ideabook: Activities for
      the Elementary & Middle Grades. Allyn.
Johnston, J. Phillips. *see* Johnston, J. Phillips L.
Johnston, J. Phillips L.
  xJohnston, J. Phillips.
    Success in Small Business Is a Laughing
      Matter. Moore Pub Co.
Johnston, James H. *see* Johnston, James Hugo.
Johnston, James Hugo, 1891-
  xJohnston, James H.
    Race Relations in Virginia & Miscegenation in
      the South: 1776-1860. U of Mass Pr.
Johnston, James P.
  xJohnston, James P.
    A Hundred Years Eating: Food, Drink, & the
      Daily Diet in Britain Since the Late
      Nineteenth Century. McGill-Queens U Pr.
Johnston, Jennifer, 1930-
  xJohnston, Jennifer.

The Old Jest. Doubleday.
    The Old Jest. G K Hall.
    Shadows on Our Skin. Avon.
    Shadows on Our Skin. Doubleday.
Johnston, Jill.
  xJohnston, Jill.
    Gullibles Travels. Music Sales.
    Lesbian Nation: The Feminist Solution. S&S.
Johnston, Johanna.
  xJohnston, Johanna.
    Connecticut Colony. Macmillan.
    Edie Changes Her Mind. Putnam.
    The Fabulous Fox: An Anthology of Fact &
      Fiction. Dodd.
    The Indians & the Strangers. Dodd.
    Speak up, Edie!. Putnam.
    Special Bravery. Dodd.
    Sugarplum. Knopf.
Johnston, John, 1923-
  xJohnston, John.
    Econometric Methods. McGraw.
Johnston, Martin.
  xJohnston, Martin.
    The Sea-Cucumber. U of Queensland Pr.
Johnston, Mary.
  xJohnston, Mary.
    The Long Roll. Folcroft.
Johnston, Mary G. *see* Johnston, Mary Grace.
Johnston, Mary Grace, 1899-
  xJohnston, Mary G.
    Paper Sculpture. Davis Mass.
Johnston, Mary H. *see* Johnston, Mary Hollis.
Johnston, Mary Hollis.
  xJohnston, Mary H.
    Assessing Schizophrenic Thinking: A Clinical &
      Research Instrument for Measuring Thought
      Disorder. Jossey-Bass.
Johnston, Mary T. *see* Johnston, Mary Tabb.
Johnston, Mary Tabb.
  xJohnston, Mary T.
    Amelia Gayle Gorgas: A Biography. U of Ala
      Pr.
Johnston, Moira, 1934-
  xJohnston, Moira.
    The Last Nine Minutes: The Story of Flight
      981. Avon.
Johnston, Norma.
  xJohnston, Norma.
    Glory in the Flower. Atheneum.
    If You Love Me, Let Me Go. Atheneum.
    A Mustard Seed of Magic. Atheneum.
    Of Time & of Seasons. Atheneum.
    Pride of Lions. Atheneum.
    Strangers Dark & Gold. Atheneum.
    A Striving After Wind. Atheneum.
    The Swallows Song. Atheneum.
Johnston, Norman. *see* Johnston, Norman Bruce.
Johnston, Norman Bruce, 1921-
  xJohnston, Norman.
    The Human Cage: A Brief History of Prison
      Architecture. Walker & Co.
    Sociology of Punishment & Correction. Wiley.
Johnston, P. *see* Johnston, Patricia Veicht.
Johnston, Patricia Veicht.
  xJohnston, P.
    Nerve Membranes: A Study of the Biological &
      Chemical Aspects of Neuron Glia
      Relationships. Pergamon.
Johnston, Priscilla.
  xJohnston, Priscilla.
    Seattle's Super Shopper. Writing.
Johnston, R. J. *see* Johnston, Ronald John.
Johnston, Ray E. *see* Johnston, Ray Edward.
Johnston, Ray Edward.
  xJohnston, Ray E.
    ed. The Politics of Division, Partition, &
      Unification. Praeger.
Johnston, Richard M. *see* Johnston, Richard Malcolm.
Johnston, Richard Malcolm.
  xJohnston, Richard M.

Life of Alexander H. Stephens. Arno.
    Primes & Their Neighbors: Ten Tales of
      Middle Georgia. Arno.
Johnston, Robert B.
  xJohnston, Robert B.
    ed. Development Disorders: Assessment,
      Treatment, Education. Univ Park.
Johnston, Robert F. *see* Johnston, Robert Franklin.
Johnston, Robert Franklin.
  xJohnston, Robert F.
    ed. Pulmonary Care. Grune.
Johnston, Robert K., 1945-
  xJohnston, Robert K.
    Evangelicals at an Impasse: Biblical Authority
      in Practice. John Knox.
Johnston, Ron.
  xJohnston, Ron.
    ed. Directing Technology: Policies for
      Promotion & Control. St Martin.
Johnston, Ronald John.
  xJohnston, R. J.
    Multivariate Statistical Analysis in Geography:
      A Primer of the General Linear Model.
      Longman.
Johnston, Russ.
  xJohnston, Russ.
    God Can Make It Happen. Victor Bks.
Johnston, Ruth M.
  xJohnston, Ruth M.
    ed. Industrial Color Technology. Am Chemical.
Johnston, Thomas C. *see* Johnston, Thomas Crawford.
Johnston, Thomas Crawford.
  xJohnston, Thomas C.
    Did the Phoenicians Discover America?. St
      Thomas.
Johnston, Tony.
  xJohnston, Tony.
    The Adventures of Mole & Troll. Putnam.
    Four Scary Stories. Putnam.
    Four Scary Stories. Putnam.
    Happy Birthday, Mole & Troll. Putnam.
    Little Mouse Nibbling. Putnam.
    Night Noises & Other Mole & Troll Stories.
      Putnam.
Johnston, Trude.
  xJohnston, Trude.
    Home Book of Viennese Cookery. Merrimack
      Bk Serv.
Johnston, Velda.
  xJohnston, Velda.
    Deveron Hall. Dodd.
    Deveron Hall. NAL.
    The Frenchman. Dodd.
    The Frenchman. NAL.
    The People from the Sea. Bantam.
    The People from the Sea. Dodd.
    A Presence in an Empty Room. Dodd.
    The Silver Dolphin. Bantam.
    The Silver Dolphin. Dodd.
    The Silver Dolphin. G K Hall.
Johnston, Verna. *see* Johnston, Verna R.
Johnston, Verna R.
  xJohnston, Verna.
    Sierra Nevada. HM.
Johnston, Wiliam. *see* Johnston, William.
Johnston, William, 1925-
  xJohnston, Wiliam.
    The Inner Eye of Love: Mysticism & Religion.
      Har-Row.
  xJohnston, William.
    Christian Zen. Har Row.
    Echoes of a Summer. Ballantine.
    Silent Music: The Science of Meditation.
      Har-Row.
Johnston, William G. *see* Johnston, William Graham.
Johnston, William Graham, 1828-1913
  xJohnston, William G.
    Experiences of a Forty-Niner. Arno.
Johnston, William M, 1936-
  xJohnston, William M.

The Austrian Mind: An Intellectual & Social History. U of Cal Pr.

Johnston, William W.
xJohnston, William W.
Diagnostic Respiratory Cytopathology. Masson Pub.

Johnstone, D. Bruce. *see* Johnstone, Donald Bruce.

Johnstone, Donald Bruce.
xJohnstone, D. Bruce.
Vegetable Gardening Basics. Burgess.

Johnstone, Henry W.
xJohnstone, Henry W.
Problem of the Self. Pa St U Pr.

Johnstone, Ian. *see* Johnstone, Ian H.

Johnstone, Ian H.
xJohnstone, Ian.
Learning Music with the Recorder & Other Classroom Instruments. P-H.

Johnstone, Kenneth, 1909-
xJohnstone, Kenneth.
The Aquatic Explorers: A History of the Fisheries Research Board of Canada. U of Toronto Pr.

Johnstone, Margaret.
xJohnstone, Margaret.
The Stroke Patient: Principles of Rehabilitation. Churchill.

Johnstone, Mildred T.
xJohnstone, Mildred T.
Brother Wolf. Center Pubns.

Johnstone, P. T.
xJohnstone, P. T.
Topos Theory. Acad Pr.

Johnstone, Parker L. *see* Johnstone, Parker Lochiel.

Johnstone, Parker Lochiel.
xJohnstone, Parker L.
Life, Death, & Hereafter. Theoscience Found.

Johnstone, Paul.
xJohnstone, Paul.
The Seacraft of Prehistory. Harvard U Pr.

Johnstone, R. A. *see* Johnstone, Robert Alexander Walker.

Johnstone, Robert Alexander Walker.
xJohnstone, R. A.
Mass Spectrometry for Organic Chemists. Cambridge U Pr.

Johnstone, Ronald L.
xJohnstone, Ronald L.
Religion & Society in Interaction: The Sociology of Religion. P-H.

Johnstone, Sandy.
xJohnstone, Sandy.
Enemy in the Sky: My 1940 Diary. Presidio Pr.

Joiner, Charles A. *see* Joiner, Charles Adrian.

Joiner, Charles Adrian, 1932-
xJoiner, Charles A.
The Politics of Massacre: Political Processes in South Vietnam. Temple U Pr.

Joiner, Charles W.
xJoiner, Charles W.
Civil Justice & the Jury. Greenwood.

Joiner, Elizabeth. *see* Joiner, Elizabeth G.

Joiner, Elizabeth G.
xJoiner, Elizabeth.
ed. Developing Communication Skills: General Considerations & Specific Techniques. Newbury Hse.
xJoiner, Elizabeth G.
First-Year French. HR&W.

Joiner, Lee M.
xJoiner, Lee M.
Identifying Children with Special Needs: A Practical Guide to Developmental Screening. Learning Pubns.

Joiner, William A., 1868-
xJoiner, William A.
Compiled by A Half Century of Freedom of the Negro in Ohio. Arno.

Joint ASME - IEEE Railroad Conference, Pittsburgh,

Pa., April, 1974. *see* Joint Asme-Ieee-Aar Railroad Conference.

Joint ASME-IEEE-AAR Railroad Conference.
xJoint ASME - IEEE Railroad Conference, Pittsburgh, Pa., April, 1974.
Rail Transportation, 1974: Proceedings. ASME.

Joint Association of Classical Teachers.
xJoint Association of Classical Teachers.
Greek Vocabulary. Cambridge U Pr.
Reading Greek: Grammar, Vocabulary & Exercises. Cambridge U Pr.

Joint Association of Classical Teachers. Greek Project.
xJoint Association of Classical Teachers-Greek Course.
The Intellectual Revolution: Selections from Euripides, Thucydides & Plato. Cambridge U Pr.
A World of Heroes: Selections from Homer, Herodotus & Sophocles. Cambridge U Pr.

Joint Bank-Fund Library (Washington, D. C.). *see* Washington, D.C. Joint Library of the International Monetary Fund and the International Bank for Reconstruction and Development.

Joint Bank-Fund Library, Washington, D. C. *see* Washington, D.C. Joint Library of the International Monetary Fund and the International Bank for Reconstruction and Development.

Joint Center for Political Studies.
xJoint Center for Political Studies.
Profiles of Black Negroes in America. Johnson Chi.

Joint Commission on Mental Health of Children.
xJoint Commission on Mental Health of Children.
Adolescence: A Report. Har-Row.
Mental Health from Infancy Through Adolescence. Har-Row.

Joint Commission on Mental Illness and Health.
xJoint Commission on Mental Illness & Health.
Action for Mental Health. Arno.

Joint Committee of the American Bar Association and the American Medical Association on Narcotic Drugs.
xJoint Committee of the American Bar Association & the American Medical Association on Narcotic Drugs.
Drug Addiction: Crime or Disease?: Proceedings. Ind U Pr.
xJoint Committee on Slavic Studies.
Continuity & Change in Russian & Soviet Thought. Russell.

Joint Committee on Slavic Studies. *see* Joint Committee of the American Bar Association and the American Medical Association on Narcotic Drugs.

Joint Council on Economic Education.
xJoint Council On Economic Education.
Business & the Public Interest. McGraw.
Introduction to Economics & Business Enterprise. McGraw.

Joint FAO-IAEA Division of Atomic Energy in Food and Agriculture.
xJoint FAO-IAEA Division of Atomic Energy in Food & Agriculture, Vienna, December 2-6, 1974.
Tracer Techniques for Plant Breeding: Proceedings. Unipub.

Joint FAO-IAEA-WHO Expert Committee on the Technical Basis for Legislation on Irradiated Food.
xJoint FAO-IAEA-WHO Expert Committee, Rome, 1964.
Technical Basis for Legislation on Irradiated Food: A Report. World Health.

Joint FAO-WHO Expert Committee on Food Additives.
xFAO - WHO Joint Expert Committee on Food Additives.

Evaluation of Mercury, Lead, Cadmium & Food Additives Amaranth, Diethylpyrocarbonate, & Octyl Gallate. World Health.
Review of the Technological Efficiency of Some Antioxidants & Synergists. World Health.
Specifications for the Identity & Purity of Some Enzymes & Certain Other Substances. World Health.
Toxicological Evaluation of Some Enzymes, Modified Starches & Certain Other Substances. World Health.
xFAO Conference, 10th Session, Rome, 1959. Report. Unipub.
xFAO Conference, 11th Session, Rome, 1961. Report. Unipub.
xFAO Conference, 12th Session, Rome, 1963. Report. Unipub.
xFAO Conference, 13th Session, Rome, 1965. Report. Unipub.
xFAO Conference, 14th Session, Rome, 1967. Report. Unipub.
xFAO-WHO Expert Committee on Food Additives. Rome, 1974, 18th.
Evaluation of Certain Food Additives: Report. World Health.
Evaluation of Certain Food Additives & the Contaminants Mercury, Lead, & Cadmium: Report. World Health.
Evaluation of Certain Food Additives; Some Food Colours, Thickening Agents, Smoke Condensates & Certain Other Substances: Report. World Health.
Evaluation of Food Additives. Some Enzymes, Modified Starches & Certain Other Substances; Toxicological Evaluations & Specifications & a Review of the Technological Efficacy of Some Antioxidants: Report. World Health.
Evaluation of Food Additives: Specifications for the Identity & Purity of Food Additives & Their Toxocological Evaluation: Some Extraction Solvents & Certain Other Substances & a Review of the Technological Efficacy of Some Antimicrobial Agent: Report. World Health.
Toxicological Evaluation of Certain Food Additives with a Review of General Principles & of Specifications: Report. World Health.

Joint FAO-WHO Expert Committee on Nutrition.
xFAO-WHO Expert Committee on Nutrition, Rome, 1974, 9th.
Food & Nutrition Strategies in National Development: Report. World Health.
xFAO-WHO Joint Committee Expert Committee on Nutrition, 8th.
Proceedings. World Health.

Joint Organizing Committe,Eleventh Session. *see* Global Atmospheric Research Programme Joint Organizing Committee.

Joint Tax Program OAS IDB. *see* Joint Tax Program of the Organization of American States and the Inter-American Development Bank.

Joint Tax Program of the Organization of American States and the Inter-American Development Bank.
xJoint Tax Program OAS IDB.
Tax Systems of Latin America: Honduras & Nicaragua. OAS.

Joint Unit for Planning Research.
xJoint Unit for Planning Research.
The University in an Urban Environment. Sage.

Joint WHO-IABS, Geneva, 1976. *see* Joint Who-Iabs Symposium on the Standardization of Cell Substrates for the Production of Virus Vaccines, Geneva, Switzerland, 1976.

Joint Who-Iabs Symposium on the Standardization of Cell Substrates for the Production of Virus Vaccines, Geneva, Switzerland, 1976.
    xJoint WHO-IABS, Geneva, 1976.
      Standardization of Cell Substrates for the Production of Virus Vaccines: Proceedings. S Karger.

Jokai, Mor.
    xJokai, Mor.
      Tales from Jokai. Arno.

Jokl, Ernst.
    xJokl, Ernst.
      The Clinical Physiology of Physical Fitness & Rehabilitation. C C Thomas.

Joll, Gary. *see* Joll, Gary Douglas E.
Joll, Gary Douglas E.
    xJoll, Gary.
      To Alaska to Hunt. Intl Pubns Serv.

Joll, James.
    xJoll, James.
      The Anarchists. Harvard U Pr.
      Antonio Gramsci. Penguin.
      Antonio Gramsci. Viking Pr.

Jolles, Isaac.
    xJolles, Isaac.
      Clinical Approach to Training the Educable Mentally Retarded: A Handbook. Western Psych.

Jolles, P. *see* Jolles, Pierre.
Jolles, Pierre.
    xJolles, P.
      Chemical & Biological Basis of Adjuvants. Springer-Verlag.

Jollie, Malcolm.
    xJollie, Malcolm.
      Chordate Morphology. Krieger.

Jolliff, James V.
    xJolliff, James V.
      Naval Engineer's Guide. Naval Inst Pr.

Jolliffe, F. R. *see* Jolliffe, Flavia R.
Jolliffe, Flavia R.
    xJolliffe, F. R.
      Commonsense Statistics for Economists & Others. Routledge & Kegan.

Jolly, Alison.
    xJolly, Alison.
      The Evolution of Primate Behavior. Macmillan.
      Lemur Behavior: A Madagascar Field Study. U of Chicago Pr.

Jolly, Clifford. *see* Jolly, Clifford J.
Jolly, Clifford J.
    xJolly, Clifford.
      ed. Early Hominids of Africa. St Martin.

Jolly, Constance.
    xJolly, Constance.
      When You Teach English As a Second Language. Book-Lab.

Jolly, Erin.
    xJolly, Erin.
      Flowers of Stone. Golden Quill.

Jolly, Hugh.
    xJolly, Hugh.
      Diseases of Children. Mosby.

Jolly, P. W.
    xJolly, P. W.
      The Organic Chemistry of Nickel. Acad Pr.

Jolly, W. *see* Jolly, William L.
Jolly, W. L. *see* Jolly, William L.
Jolly, William L.
    xJolly, W.
      Synthesis & Characterization of Inorganic Compounds. P-H.
    xJolly, W. L.
      The Principles of Inorganic Chemistry. McGraw.

Jolson, Marvin A.
    xJolson, Marvin A.

      Contemporary Readings in Sales Management. Van Nos Reinhold.

Jomini, Henri, Baron, 1779-1869
    xJomini, Henri.
      Art of War. Greenwood.

Jonas, Doris.
    xJonas, Doris.
      Other Senses, Other Worlds. Stein & Day.

Jonas, Frank H.
    xJonas, Frank H.
      ed. Politics in the American West. U of Utah Pr.

Jonas, Hans, 1903-
    xJonas, Hans.
      Gnostic Religion: The Message of the Alien God & the Beginnings of Christianity. Peter Smith.

Jonas, Ilsedore B.
    xJonas, Ilsedore B.
      Thomas Mann & Italy. U of Ala Pr.

Jonas, Leah, 1907-
    xJonas, Leah.
      The Divine Science: The Aesthetic of Some Representative Seventeenth-Century English Poets. Octagon.

Jonas, Paul, 1922-
    xJonas, Paul.
      Taxation of Multinationals in Communist Countries. Praeger.

Jonas, Steven.
    xJonas, Steven.
      Quality Control of Ambulatory Care: A Task for Health Departments. Springer Pub.

Jonchay, Yvan du. *see* Du Jonchay, Yvan.
Jones. *see* Jones, Vernon F.
Jones, A. H. *see* Jones, Arnold Hugh Martin.
Jones, A. J. *see* Jones, Antony John.
Jones, a M.
    xJones, A. M.
      Studies in African Music. Oxford U Pr.
Jones, A. R. *see* Jones, Alick Rowe.
Jones, A. V. *see* Jones, Alister Vallance.
Jones, A. W. *see* Jones, Arthur W.
Jones, Adam L. *see* Jones, Adam Leroy.
Jones, Adam Leroy, 1873-1934
    xJones, Adam L.
      Early American Philosophers. Ungar.

Jones, Adrienne.
    xJones, Adrienne.
      The Beckoner. Har-Row.

Jones, Alan W., 1940-
    xJones, Alan W.
      Journey into Christ. Seabury.

Jones, Alice H. *see* Jones, Alice Hanson.
Jones, Alice Hanson, 1904-
    xJones, Alice H.
      American Colonial Wealth: Documents & Methods. Arno.
      Wealth of a Nation to Be: The American Colonies on the Eve of the Revolution. Columbia U Pr.

Jones, Alick R. *see* Jones, Alick Rowe.
Jones, Alick Rowe.
    xJones, A. R.
      The Ciliates. Humanities.
    xJones, Alick R.
      The Ciliates. St Martin.

Jones, Alister Vallance.
    xJones, A. V.
      Aurora. Kluwer Boston.

Jones, Allen.
    xJones, Allen.
      World Protein Resources. Halsted Pr.

Jones, Allen Richard.
    xJones, Alun R.
      The Life & Opinions of T. E. Hulme. AMS Pr.
Jones, Alun R. *see* Jones, Allen Richard.
Jones, Andrew, 1921-
    xJones, Andrew.

      Flight Seaward. Morrow.

Jones, Ann, 1938-
    xJones, Ann.
      Uncle Tom's Campus. S&S.

Jones, Annabel.
    xJones, Annabel.
      The Radiant Dove. Fawcett.

Jones, Anne.
    xJones, Anne.
      Counselling Adolescents in School. Nichols Pub.

Jones, Anson, 1798-1858
    xJones, Anson.
      Memoranda & Official Correspondence Relating to the Republic of Texas, Its History & Annexation. Arno.

Jones, Anthony S.
    xJones, Anthony S.
      Strategies for Teaching. Scarecrow.

Jones, Antony John.
    xJones, A. J.
      Game Theory: Mathematical Models of Conflict. Halsted Pr.
Jones, Arnold H. *see* Jones, Arnold Hugh Martin.
Jones, Arnold Hugh Martin, 1904-1970
    xJones, A. H.
      Augustus. Norton.
      ed. History of Rome Through the Fifth Century. Walker & Co.
      ed. Prosopography of the Later Roman Empire. Cambridge U Pr.
    xJones, Arnold H.
      History of Abyssinia. Negro U Pr.

Jones, Arthur, 1936-
    xJones, Arthur.
      Decline of Capital. T Y Crowell.
Jones, Arthur F. *see* Jones, Arthur Frederick.
Jones, Arthur Frederick, 1945-
    xJones, Arthur F.
      The Art of Paul Sawyier. U Pr of Ky.
Jones, Arthur J. *see* Jones, Arthur Julius.
Jones, Arthur Julius, 1871-
    xJones, A. J.
      Principles of Guidance. McGraw.
    xJones, Arthur J.
      Principles of Guidance. Norwood Edns.

Jones, Arthur W.
    xJones, A. W.
      Introduction to Parasitology. A-W.

Jones, Aubrey.
    xJones, Aubrey.
      Mathematical Astronomy with a Pocket Calculator. Halsted Pr.
Jones, B. M. *see* Jones, Benjamin Maelor.
Jones, Benjamin Maelor.
    xJones, B. M.
      Henry Fielding, Novelist & Magistrate. R West.
Jones, Bernard E. *see* Jones, Bernard Edward.
Jones, Bernard Edward, 1879-
    xJones, Bernard E.
      ed. Cassell's Cyclopaedia of Photography.. Arno.

Jones, Bryan D.
    xJones, Bryan D.
      Service Delivery in the City: Citizen Demand & Bureaucratic Rules. Longman.
Jones, Burton W. *see* Jones, Burton Wadsworth.
Jones, Burton Wadsworth, 1902-
    xJones, Burton W.
      An Introduction to Modern Algebra. Macmillan.
      Linear Algebra. Holden-Day.
Jones, C. C. *see* Jones, Charles Colcock.
Jones, C. M. *see* Jones, Clarence Medlycott.
Jones, Carolyn, 1933-
    xJones, Carolyn.
      Twice Upon a Time. Trident.
Jones, Charles, 1939-
    xJones, Charles.

Introduction to Middle English. Irvington.
Jones, Charles C. see Jones, Charles Colcock.
Jones, Charles Colcock, 1831-1893
xJones, C. C.
Religious Instruction of the Negroes in the
United States. Kraus Repr.
xJones, Charles C.
Antiquities of the Southern Indians Particularly
of the Georgia Tribes. AMS Pr.
Antiquities of the Southern Indians,
Particularly of the Georgia Tribes. Reprint.
Dead Towns of Georgia. Cherokee.
History of Georgia. Reprint.
Religious Instruction of the Negroes in the
United States. Arno.
Religious Instruction of the Negroes in the
United States. Negro U Pr.
Jones, Charles E. see Jones, Charles Edwin.
Jones, Charles Edward, 1927-
xJones, Charles E.
Life Is Tremendous. Tyndale.
Jones, Charles Edwin, 1932-
xJones, Charles E.
Guide to the Study of the Holiness Movement.
Scarecrow.
Perfectionist Persuasion: The Holiness
Movement & American Methodism,
1867-1936. Scarecrow.
Jones, Charles O.
xJones, Charles O.
Clean Air: The Policies & Politics of Pollution
Control. U of Pittsburgh Pr.
Public Policy Making in a Federal System.
Sage.
Jones, Cheslyn. see Jones, Cheslyn Peter Montague.
Jones, Cheslyn Peter Montague.
xJones, Cheslyn.
ed. The Study of Liturgy. Oxford U Pr.
Jones, Chester L. see Jones, Chester Lloyd.
Jones, Chester Lloyd, 1881-1941
xJones, Chester L.
Caribbean Backgrounds & Prospects. Kennikat.
Caribbean Interests of the United States. Arno.
Caribbean Interests of the United States.
Gordon Pr.
Caribbean Since 1900. Russell.
Costa Rica & Civilization in the Caribbean.
Gordon Pr.
Guatemala Past & Present. Gordon Pr.
Readings on Parties & Elections in the United
States. Negro U Pr.
Jones, Chris, 1939-
xJones, Chris.
Climbing in North America. U of Cal Pr.
Jones, Claire.
xJones, Claire.
The Chinese in America. Lerner Pubns.
Jones, Clarence Medlycott, 1912-
xJones, C. M.
Improving Your Tennis: Strokes & Techniques.
Transatlantic.
Starting Tennis. Barron.
Starting Tennis. Transatlantic.
Jones, Claudella A. see Jones, Claudella Archambeault.
Jones, Claudella Archambeault.
xJones, Claudella A.
Procedures for Nursing the Burned Patient.
Natl Inst Burn.
Jones, Clinton R.
xJones, Clinton R.
Homosexuality & Counseling. Fortress.
Understanding Gay Relatives & Friends.
Seabury.
Jones, Colin.
xJones, Colin.
ed. Urban Deprivation & the Inner City. Biblio
Dist.
Jones, Cordelia.
xJones, Cordelia.

Cat Called Camouflage. S G Phillips.
Jones, D. F.
xJones, D. F.
Colossus. Berkley Pub.
Colossus & the Crab. Berkley Pub.
Jones, D. G. see Jones, David Gareth.
Jones, D. S. see Jones, Douglas Samuel.
Jones, Daisy M. see Jones, Daisy Marvel.
Jones, Daisy Marvel, 1906-
xJones, Daisy M.
Curriculum Targets in the Elementary School.
P-H.
Jones, Dan B. see Jones, Dan Burne.
Jones, Dan Burne.
xJones, Dan B.
The Prints of Rockwell Kent: A Catalogue
Raisonne. U of Chicago Pr.
Jones, Dave, 1927-
xJones, Dave.
Practical Western Training. Arco.
Jones, David, 1736-1820
xJones, David.
Journal of Two Visits Made to Some Nations
of Indians on the West Side of the River
Ohio in the Years 1772 & 1773 by the Rev.
David Jones, Minister of Gospel at Freehold,
New Jersey. Arno.
A Journal of Two Visits Made to Some
Nations of Indians on the West Side of the
River Ohio, in the Years 1772 & 1773. Ye
Galleon.
Jones, David. see Jones, David Michael.
Jones, David A. see Jones, David Arthur.
Jones, David Arthur, 1946-
xJones, David A.
Crime & Criminal Responsibility. Nelson-Hall.
Crime Without Punishment. Lexington Bks.
ed. The Sociology of Correctional
Management. Mss Info.
Jones, David Gareth.
xJones, D. G.
Some Current Concepts of Synaptic
Organization. Springer-Verlag.
Jones, David L. see Jones, David Lewis.
Jones, David Lewis.
xJones, David L.
Books in English on the Soviet Union,
1917-73: A Bibliography. Garland Pub.
Jones, David Michael.
xJones, David.
The Dying Gaul & Other Writings. Merrimack
Bk Serv.
Jones, Dewitt.
xJones, DeWitt.
illus. & ed. What the Road Passes by. Graphic
Arts Ctr.
Jones, Diana W. see Jones, Diana Wynne.
Jones, Diana Wynne.
xJones, Diana W.
Cart & Cwidder. Atheneum.
Charmed Life. Greenwillow.
Charmed Life. PB.
Dogsbody. Dell.
Dogsbody. Greenwillow.
The Magicians of Caprona. Greenwillow.
Power of Three. Greenwillow.
The Spellcoats. Atheneum.
The Spellcoats. PB.
Jones, Diane.
xJones, Diane.
When You Least Expect Love. Bouregy.
Jones, Donald G.
xJones, Donald G.
The Sectional Crisis & Northern Methodism: A
Study in Piety, Political Ethics & Civil
Religion. Scarecrow.
Jones, Doris A. see Jones, Doris Arthur.
Jones, Doris Arthur, 1888-
xJones, Doris A.

Life & Letters of Henry Arthur Jones.
Scholarly.
Jones, Dorothy. see Jones, Dorothy A.
Jones, Dorothy A.
xJones, Dorothy.
Medical Surgical Nursing: A Conceptual
Approach. McGraw.
Jones, Douglas. see Jones, Douglas C.
Jones, Douglas C.
xJones, Douglas.
Arrest Sitting Bull. Warner Bks.
xJones, Douglas C.
Arrest Sitting Bull. G K Hall.
The Court-Martial of George Armstrong
Custer. Warner Bks.
A Creek Called Wounded Knee. Scribner.
A Creek Called Wounded Knee. Warner Bks.
Winding Stair. HR&W.
Jones, Douglas G.
xJones, D. G.
Butterfly on Rock: A Study of Themes &
Images in Canadian Literature. U of Toronto
Pr.
Jones, Douglas Samuel.
xJones, D. S.
Elementary Information Theory. Oxford U Pr.
Methods in Electromagnetic Wave Propagation.
Oxford U Pr.
Jones, E. J. see Jones, Ernest James Henry.
Jones, E. L. see Jones, Eric L.
Jones, E. Stanley. see Jones, Eli Stanley.
Jones, E. Terrence. see Jones, Endsley Terrence.
Jones, Edgar D. see Jones, Edgar De Witt.
Jones, Edgar De Witt, 1876-1956
xJones, Edgar D.
Lincoln & the Preachers. Arno.
Jones, Edna D.
xJones, Edna D.
ed. Patriotic Pieces from the Great War.
Granger Bk.
Jones, Edward A. see Jones, Edward Alfred.
Jones, Edward Alfred, 1872-1943
xJones, Edward A.
Loyalists of Massachusetts: Their Memorials,
Petitions & Claims. Genealog Pub.
Jones, Edward D. see Jones, Edward David.
Jones, Edward David, 1870-1944
xJones, Edward D.
Economic Crises. Hyperion Conn.
Jones, Edward E. see Jones, Edward Ellsworth.
Jones, Edward Ellsworth.
xJones, Edward E.
Foundations of Social Psychology. Krieger.
Jones, Eli Stanley, 1884-
xJones, E. Stanley.
Christian Maturity. Abingdon.
Conversion. Abingdon.
The Divine Yes. Abingdon.
Divine Yes. Pillar Bks.
Growing Spiritually. Abingdon.
How to Be a Transformed Person. Abingdon.
A Song of Ascents: A Spiritual Autobiography.
Abingdon.
The Word Became Flesh. Abingdon.
Jones, Elizabeth. see Jones, Elizabeth G.
Jones, Elizabeth G.
xJones, Elizabeth.
ed. Ranger Rick's Surprise Book. Natl Wildlife.
Jones, Elwyn.
xJones, Elwyn.
Barlow Exposed. St Martin.
Jones, Emrys.
xJones, Emrys.
An Introduction to Social Geography. Oxford
U Pr.
The Origins of Shakespeare. Oxford U Pr.
ed. Readings in Social Geography. Oxford U
Pr.
Jones, Endsley Terrence, 1941-
xJones, E. Terrence.

Conducting Political Research. Har-Row.
Jones, Eric L.
xJones, E. L.
Agriculture & the Industrial Revolution.
Halsted Pr.
Jones, Erin B. *see* Jones, Erin Bain.
Jones, Erin Bain.
xJones, Erin B.
Earth Satellite Telecommunications Systems &
International Law. U of Tex Hum Res.
Law of the Sea: Oceanic Resources. SMU
Press.
Jones, Ernest, 1879-1958
xJones, Ernest.
Hamlet & Oedipus. Norton.
Jones, Ernest James Henry.
xJones, E. J.
Production Engineering: Jig & Tool Design.
Transatlantic.
Jones, Eugene. *see* Jones, Eugene W.
Jones, Eugene W.
xJones, Eugene.
Practicing Texas Politics. HM.
xJones, Eugene W.
Practicing Texas Politics. HM.
Jones, Eva.
xJones, Eva.
Evalore. Fawcett.
Evalore. Lippincott.
Jones, Evan, 1915-
xJones, Evan.
ed. A Food Lover's Companion. Har-Row.
Recognitions. Bks Australia.
The World of Cheese. Knopf.
Jones, Evelyn G.
xJones, Evelyn G.
Living in Safety & Health. Lippincott.
Jones, Ezra E. *see* Jones, Ezra Earl.
Jones, Ezra Earl.
xJones, Ezra E.
Strategies for New Churches. Har-Row.
Jones, F. Avery. *see* Jones, Francis Avery.
Jones, F. C. *see* Jones, Francis Clifford.
Jones, F. R. *see* Jones, Frederick Robertson.
Jones, F. W. *see* Jones, Frederic Wood.
Jones, Francis Avery.
xJones, F. Avery.
ed. Peptic Ulcer Healing: Recent Studies on
Carbenoxolone. Univ Park.
Jones, Francis Clifford.
xJones, F. C.
Extraterritoriality in Japan & the Diplomatic
Relations Resulting in Its Abolition, Eighteen
Fifty-Three to Eighteen Ninety-Nine. Elliots
Bks.
The Far East: A Concise History. Pergamon.
Jones, Frank P. *see* Jones, Frank Pierce.
Jones, Frank Pierce.
xJones, Frank P.
Body Awareness in Action: A Study of the
Alexander Technique. Schocken.
Jones, Franklin, 1921-
xJones, Franklin.
Painting Nature: Solving Landscape Problems.
North Light Pub.
Jones, Fred M. *see* Jones, Fred Mitchell.
Jones, Fred Mitchell, 1905-
xJones, Fred M.
Introduction to Marketing Management.
Irvington.
Jones, Fred R. *see* Jones, Fred Rufus.
Jones, Fred Rufus, 1893-
xJones, Fred R.
Farm Gas Engines & Tractors. McGraw.
Jones, Frederic W. *see* Jones, Frederic Wood.
Jones, Frederic Wood, 1879-
xJones, F. W.
Arboreal Man. Hafner.
xJones, Frederic W.

Arboreal Man. AMS Pr.
Jones, Frederick R. *see* Jones, Frederick Robertson.
Jones, Frederick Robertson, 1872-1941
xJones, F. R.
History of Taxation in Connecticut: 1636-1776.
Johnson Repr.
xJones, Frederick R.
History of Taxation in Connecticut
(1636-1776). AMS Pr.
Jones, G. *see* Jones, Gareth E.
Jones, G. P. *see* Jones, Genevieve Priscilla.
Jones, Galen, 1896-
xJones, Galen.
Extra-Curricular Activities in Relation to the
Curriculum. AMS Pr.
Jones, Gareth. *see* Jones, Gareth H.
Jones, Gareth E.
xJones, G.
Vegetation Productivity. Longman.
Jones, Gareth H.
xJones, Gareth.
Anglo-American Trends in Restitution. Kluwer
Boston.
xJones, Gareth H.
History of the Law of Charity, 1532-1827.
Cambridge U Pr.
Jones, Garth N.
xJones, Garth N.
ed. Planning, Development, & Change: A
Bibliography on Development
Administration. U Pr of Hawaii.
Jones, Gavin. *see* Jones, Gavin W.
Jones, Gavin W.
xJones, Gavin.
Population Growth & Educational Planning in
Developing Nations. Halsted Pr.
xJones, Gavin W.
The Economic Effect of Declining Fertility in
Less Developed Countries. Population Coun.
Jones, Gayl.
xJones, Gayle.
Corregidora. Random.
Jones, Gayle. *see* Jones, Gayl.
Jones, Genesius.
xJones, Genesius.
Approach to the Purpose: A Study of the
Poetry of T. S. Eliot. Greenwood.
Jones, Genevieve Priscilla.
xJones, G. P.
Easy-to-Make Dolls with Nineteenth-Century
Costumes. Dover.
Jones, George F. *see* Jones, George Fenwick.
Jones, George Fenwick, 1916-
xJones, George F.
Honor in German Literature. AMS Pr.
Oswald Von Wolkenstein. Twayne.
Jones, George H. *see* Jones, George Hilton.
Jones, George Hilton.
xJones, George H.
Charles Middleton: The Life & Times of a
Restoration Politician. U of Chicago Pr.
Jones, George T. *see* Jones, George Thaddeus.
Jones, George Thaddeus.
xJones, George T.
Music Theory. Har-Row.
Jones, Gerre L., 1926-
xJones, Gerre L.
How to Market Professional Design Services.
McGraw.
How to Prepare Professional Design Brochures.
McGraw.
Jones, Gladys V.
xJones, Gladys V.
The Greek Love Mysteries. New Age.
Jones, Grace. *see* Jones, Grace A.
Jones, Grace A.
xJones, Grace.
The Political Structure. Longman.
Jones, Gwyn, 1907-
xJones, Gwyn.

A History of the Vikings. Oxford U Pr.
ed. The Oxford Book of Welsh Verse in
English. Oxford U Pr.
Jones, H. *see* Jones, Harry.
Jones, H. Bradley.
xJones, H. Bradley.
Professional & Executive Corporations. PLI.
Jones, Harold, 1904-
xJones, Harold.
There & Back Again. Atheneum.
Jones, Harold W. *see* Jones, Harold Whitmore.
Jones, Harold Whitmore.
xJones, Harold W.
ed. Anti-Achitophel: Three Verse Replies to
Absalom & Achitophel by John Dryden.
Schol Facsimiles.
Jones, Harry.
xJones, H.
Theory of Brillouin Zones & Electronic States
in Crystals. Elsevier.
xJones, Henry.
Forecasting Technology for Planning Decisions.
Petrocelli.
Jones, Harry S. *see* Jones, Harry Stuart Vedder.
Jones, Harry Stuart Vedder, 1878-1942
xJones, Harry S.
Spenser's Defense of Lord Grey. AMS Pr.
Spenser's Defense of Lord Grey. Johnson
Repr.
Jones, Harry W. *see* Jones, Harry Willmer.
Jones, Harry Willmer.
xJones, Harry W.
ed. Law & the Social Role of Science.
Rockefeller.
Jones, Henry, Sir, 1852-1922
xJones, Henry.
The Immortality of the Soul in the Poems of
Tennyson & Browning. Folcroft.
Jones, Henry. *see* Jones, Harry.
Jones, Henry A. *see* Jones, Henry Arthur.
Jones, Henry Arthur, 1851-1929
xJones, Henry A.
The Case of Rebellious Susan: A Comedy in
Three Acts. Folcroft.
Jones, Henry John Franklin.
xJones, John.
On Aristotle & Greek Tragedy. Stanford U Pr.
Jones, Hettie.
xJones, Hettie.
How to Eat Your ABC's: A Book About
Vitamins. Schol Bk Serv.
I Hate to Talk About Your Mother. Delacorte.
Jones, Hiram A. *see* Jones, Hiram Arthur.
Jones, Hiram Arthur, 1899-1945
xJones, Hiram A.
The Administration of Health & Physical
Education in New York State. AMS Pr.
Jones, Howard.
xJones, Howard.
Open Prisons. Routledge & Kegan.
ed. Towards a New Social Work. Routledge &
Kegan.
Jones, Howard M. *see* Jones, Howard Mumford.
Jones, Howard Mumford, 1892-
xJones, Howard M.
America & French Culture, 1750-1848.
Greenwood.
The Bright Medusa. Greenwood.
The Declaration of Independence: Two Essays.
Am Antiquarian.
Education & World Tragedy. Greenwood.
Howard Mumford Jones: An Autobiography. U
of Wis Pr.
Literature of Virginia in the Seventeenth
Century. U Pr of Va.
Pursuit of Happiness. Cornell U Pr.
Reflections on Learning. Arno.
Revolution & Romanticism. Harvard U Pr.
xJones, Howard Mumford.

ed. The Many Voices of Boston: A Historical Anthology, 1630-1975. Little.
Jones, Hywel. see Jones, Hywel G.
Jones, Hywel G.
xJones, Hywel.
Introduction to Modern Theories of Economic Growth. McGraw.
Jones, I. S. see Jones, Ian Shore.
Jones, Ian Shore.
xJones, I. S.
The Effect of Vehicle Characteristics on Road Accidents. Pergamon.
Jones, Idwal, 1890-
xJones, Idwal.
China Boy. Arno.
Jones, Ilion T. see Jones, Ilion Tingal.
Jones, Ilion Tingal, 1889-
xJones, Ilion T.
Principles & Practice of Preaching. Abingdon.
Jones, Ira S. see Jones, Ira Snow.
Jones, Ira Snow.
xJones, Ira S.
ed. Diseases of the Orbit. Har-Row.
Jones, J. see Jones, J. Harry.
Jones, J. D.
xJones, J. D.
The Gospel of Grace. Baker Bk.
Jones, J. Harry, 1930-
xJones, J.
Private Army. Macmillan.
Jones, J. Morgan.
xJones, J. Morgan.
Introduction to Decision Theory. Irwin.
Jones, Jack C. see Jones, Jack Colvard.
Jones, Jack Colvard.
xJones, Jack C.
The Circulatory System of Insects. C C Thomas.
Jones, James, 1921-
xJones, James.
From Here to Eternity. Delacorte.
From Here to Eternity. Dell.
Go to the Widowmaker. Dell.
The Pistol. Dell.
Some Came Running. Dell.
Thin Red Line. Scribner.
A Touch of Danger. Popular Lib.
Whistle. Delacorte.
Whistle. Dell.
Jones, James. see Jones, James E.
Jones, James E.
xJones, James.
Meeting Management: A Professional Approach. Bayard Pubns.
Jones, James Gay.
xJones, James Gay.
Appalachian Ghost Stories & Other Tales. McClain.
Jones, James L. see Jones, James Land.
Jones, James Land.
xJones, James L.
Adam's Dream: Mythic Consciousness in Keats & Yeats. U of Ga Pr.
Jones, James M.
xJones, James M.
Prejudice & Racism. A-W.
Jones, James S. see Jones, James Sawyer.
Jones, James Sawyer, 1861-
xJones, James S.
Life of Andrew Johnson, Seventeenth President of the United States. AMS Pr.
Jones, Jane L. see Jones, Jane Louise.
Jones, Jane Louise, 1889-1946
xJones, Jane L.
A Personnel Study of Women Deans in Colleges & Universities. AMS Pr.
Jones, Jesse H. see Jones, Jesse Holman.
Jones, Jesse Holman.
xJones, Jesse H.

Fifty Billion Dollars: My Thirteen Years with the RFC (1932-1945). Da Capo.
Jones, Jo.
xJones, Jo.
illus. Paintings & Drawings of the Gypsies of Granada. Gale.
Jones, John, 1729-1791
xJones, John.
Plain Concise Practical Remarks, on the Treatment of Wounds & Fractures. Arno.
Wonders of the Stereoscope. Knopf.
Jones, John. see Jones, Henry John Franklin.
Jones, John Bush.
xJones, John Bush.
Readings in Descriptive Bibliography. Kent St U Pr.
Jones, John L.
xJones, John L.
Crafts from the Countryside. David & Charles.
Jones, John P. see Jones, John Paul.
Jones, John Paul, 1912-
xJones, John P.
Gathering & Writing the News: A Reporter's Complete Guide to Techniques & Ethics of News Reporting. Nelson-Hall.
Plain of Dura & Other Poems. Chris Mass.
Jones, John W. see Jones, John Walter.
Jones, John Walter, 1892-
xJones, John W.
Historical Introduction to the Theory of Law. Greenwood.
Historical Introduction to the Theory of Law. Kelley.
Historical Introduction to the Theory of Law. Rothman.
Jones, Jonathan H.
xJones, Jonathan H.
A Condensed History of the Apache & Comanche Indian Tribes. Garland Pub.
Jones, Joseph, 1727-1805
xJones, Joseph.
Letters of Joseph Jones of Virginia 1777-1787. Arno.
Jones, Joseph. see Jones, Joseph Jay.
Jones, Joseph Jay, 1908-
xJones, Joseph.
ed. Image of Australia. U of Tex Pr.
Radical Cousins: Nineteenth Century American & Australian Writers. U of Queensland Pr.
Jones, Joseph R. see Jones, Joseph Ramon.
Jones, Joseph Ramon, 1935-
xJones, Joseph R.
Antonio De Guevara. Twayne.
Jones, Joshua H. see Jones, Joshua Henry.
Jones, Joshua Henry.
xJones, Joshua H.
By Sanction of Law. AMS Pr.
Jones, Judith P.
xJones, Judith P.
Thomas More. G K Hall.
Thomas More. Twayne.
Jones, Kathleen, 1922-
xJones, Kathleen.
A History of the Mental Health Services. Routledge & Kegan.
Opening the Door: A Study of New Policies for the Mentally Handicapped. Routledge & Kegan.
Jones, Kathy.
xJones, Kathy.
Learning to Live in the Country. State Mutual Bk.
Jones, Ken D.
xJones, Ken D.
Character People. A S Barnes.
Jones, Kenneth L. see Jones, Kenneth Lamar.
Jones, Kenneth Lamar.
xJones, Kenneth L.

Dimensions: A Changing Concept of Health. Har-Row.
Disease. Har-Row.
Drugs & Alcohol. Har-Row.
Human Body. Har-Row.
Human Sexuality. Har-Row.
Principles of Health Science. Har-Row.
Jones, L. L. see Jones, Leonard Leslie.
Jones, L. R. see Jones, Lewis Ralph.
Jones, Langdon, 1942-
xJones, Langdon.
The Eye of the Lens. Macmillan.
Jones, Larry.
xJones, Larry.
How to Make It to Friday. Harvest Hse.
Jones, Leon, 1936-
xJones, Leon.
From Brown to Boston: Desegregation in Education -- 1954-1974. Scarecrow.
Jones, Leonard Leslie.
xJones, L. L.
Ultimate Load Analysis of Reinforced & Prestressed Concrete Structures. Ungar.
Jones, Lewis.
xJones, Lewis.
Adapted by Darkness by the River & Other Stories. Newbury Hse.
Adapted by Portraits of Americans. Newbury Hse.
ed. The Tiger with the Bright Blue Eyes & Other Stories. Newbury Hse.
Jones, Lewis P.
xJones, Lewis P.
South Carolina - Synoptic History for Laymen. Sandlapper Store.
Jones, Lewis Ralph.
xJones, L. R.
The Handbook of Vermont Shrubs & Woody Vines. C E Tuttle.
Jones Library. see Jones Library, Incorporated, Amherst, Mass.
Jones Library, Incorporated, Amherst, Mass.
xJones Library.
Emily Dickinson. Folcroft.
Jones, Lincoln D.
xJones, Lincoln D.
Electrical Engineering License Review. Eng Pr.
Jones, Lloyd, 1811-1886
xJones, Lloyd.
Life, Times & Labours of Robert Owen. AMS Pr.
Jones, Lloyd M. see Jones, Lloyd Meredith.
Jones, Lloyd Meredith, 1900-1948
xJones, Lloyd M.
Factorial Analysis of Ability in Fundamental Motor Skills. AMS Pr.
Jones, Lois S. see Jones, Lois Swan.
Jones, Lois Swan.
xJones, Lois S.
Art Research Methods & Resources: A Guide to Finding Art Information. Kendall-Hunt.
Jones, Lorella M.
xJones, Lorella M.
An Introduction to Mathematical Methods of Physics. Benjamin-Cummings.
Jones, Louis C. see Jones, Louis Clark.
Jones, Louis Clark.
xJones, Louis C.
ed. Growing up in the Cooper Country: Boyhood Recollections of the New York Frontier. Syracuse U Pr.
Things That Go Bump in the Night. Hill & Wang.
Jones, Louis T. see Jones, Louis Thomas.
Jones, Louis Thomas.
xJones, Louis T.
Aboriginal American Oratory: The Tradition of Eloquence Among the Indian of the United States. Southwest Mus.
Jones, M. J. see Jones, M. J. B.

Jones, M. J. B.
    xJones, M. J.
        A Guide to Metrication. Pergamon.
Jones, M. S. see Jones, Mary S.
Jones, Madison, 1925-
    xJones, Madison.
        Passage Through Gehenna. La State U Pr.
Jones, Maitland.
    xJones, Maitland.
        ed. Carbenes. Krieger.
Jones, Maldwyn A. see Jones, Maldwyn Allen.
Jones, Maldwyn Allen.
    xJones, Maldwyn A.
        American Immigration. U of Chicago Pr.
Jones, Marc E. see Jones, Marc Edmund.
Jones, Marc Edmund, 1888-
    xJones, Marc E.
        The Guide to Horoscope Interpretation. Great
            Eastern.
        Guide to Horoscope Interpretation. Theos Pub
            Hse.
        How to Learn Astrology. Great Eastern.
        How to Learn Astrology. Shambhala Pubns.
        The Marc Edmund Jones 500. ASI Pubs Inc.
        Occult Philosophy: An Introduction, the Major
            Concepts & a Glossary. Shambhala Pubns.
    xJones, Marc-Edmund.
        How to Learn Astrology. Random.
Jones, Marc-Edmund. see Jones, Marc Edmund.
Jones, Margaret J. see Jones, Margaret Jean.
Jones, Margaret Jean.
    xJones, Margaret J.
        The World in My Mirror. Abingdon.
Jones, Margo.
    xJones, Margo.
        Theatre-In-The-Round. Greenwood.
Jones, Mark M. see Jones, Mark Martin.
Jones, Mark Martin, 1928-
    xJones, Mark M.
        Chemistry, Man & Society. HR&W.
Jones, Mary S.
    xJones, M. S.
        ed. An Approach to Occupational Therapy.
            Butterworths.
Jones, Maxwell.
    xJones, Maxwell.
        Maturation of the Therapeutic Community: An
            Organic Approach to Health & Mental
            Health. Human Sci Pr.
Jones, Mervyn.
    xJones, Mervyn.
        Lord Richard's Passion. Popular Lib.
        Twilight of the Day. PB.
        Twilight of the Day. S&S.
Jones, Morris V. see Jones, Morris Val.
Jones, Morris Val.
    xJones, Morris V.
        Speech & Language Problems: An Overview. C
            C Thomas.
Jones, N. D. see Jones, Neil D.
Jones, Neil D.
    xJones, N. D.
        TEMPO: A Unified Treatment of Binding
            Time & Parameter Passing Concepts in
            Programming Languages. Springer-Verlag.
Jones, Neil R.
    xJones, Neil R.
        Planet of the Double Sun. Garland Pub.
Jones, Neville, fl. 1926-
    xJones, Neville.
        Stone Age in Rhodesia. Negro U Pr.
Jones, O. Garfield. see Jones, Ossie Garfield.
Jones, Ossie Garfield.
    xJones, O. Garfield.
        Parliamentary Procedure at a Glance: Group
            Leadership Manual for Chairmanship & Floor
            Leadership. Irvington.
Jones, P. Mansell. see Jones, Percy Mansell.
Jones, Page H. see Jones, Page Helm.

Jones, Page Helm.
    xJones, Page H.
        Evolution of a Valley: The Androscoggin Story.
            Phoenix Pub.
Jones, Pamela.
    xJones, Pamela.
        Under the City Streets. HR&W.
Jones, Paul V. see Jones, Paul Van Brunt.
Jones, Paul Van Brunt, 1882-
    xJones, Paul V.
        Household of a Tudor Nobleman. Johnson
            Repr.
Jones, Penelope.
    xJones, Penelope.
        I Didn't Want to Be Nice. Bradbury Pr.
Jones, Percy M. see Jones, Percy Mansell.
Jones, Percy Mansell.
    xJones, P. Mansell.
        How They Educated Jones. Verry.
    xJones, Percy M.
        The Assault on French Literature & Other
            Essays. Greenwood.
        French Introspectives, from Montaigne to
            Andre Gide. Greenwood.
Jones, Peter, 1934-
    xJones, Peter.
        Basic Cabinet Making. Reston.
        Electrical Repairs Made Easy. Butterick Pub.
        How to Cut Heating & Cooling Costs.
            Butterick Pub.
        Indoor Home Repairs Made Easy. Butterick
            Pub.
        Outdoor Home Repairs Made Easy. Butterick
            Pub.
        Plan & Build More Storage Space. Butterick
            Pub.
        Plumbing Without a Plumber. Butterick Pub.
        Rebel in the Night. Dial.
Jones, Philip. see Jones, Phillip.
Jones, Phillip.
    xJones, Philip.
        Cooking Over Wood. Sterling.
Jones, Phyllis M. see Jones, Phyllis Maud.
Jones, Phyllis Maud.
    xJones, Phyllis M.
        Modern English Short Stories. Darby Bks.
        ed. Modern English Short Stories. Scholarly.
Jones, R. A. see Jones, Richard Alan.
Jones, R. G. see Jones, Robert Gerallt.
Jones, R. K. see Jones, R. Kenneth.
Jones, R. Kenneth.
    xJones, R. K.
        Sociology in Medicine. Halsted Pr.
Jones, R. M. see Jones, Richard Michael.
Jones, R. T. see Jones, Robert Tudor.
Jones, R. V. H. see Jones, Robert Vernon Holmes.
Jones, R. W. see Jones, Ronald Winthrop.
Jones, Ray G.
    xJones, Ray G.
        The Development of Georgia's Tufted Textile
            Industry. Ga St U Busn Pub.
        Essentials of Finance. P-H.
Jones, Raymond P.
    xJones, Raymond P.
        Framing, Sheathing & Insulation. Van Nos
            Reinhold.
Jones, Reginald L. see Jones, Reginald Lanier.
Jones, Reginald Lanier, 1931-
    xJones, Reginald L.
        Black Psychology. Har-Row.
        Problems & Issues in the Education of
            Exceptional Children. HM.
Jones, Richard, 1855-1923
    xJones, Richard.
        Growth of the Idylls of the King. AMS Pr.
        The Growth of the Idylls of the King. Gordon
            Pr.
        Supply in a Market Economy. Allen Unwin.
Jones, Richard. see Jones, Richard Matthew.

Jones, Richard Alan.
    xJones, R. A.
        The Chemistry of Pyrroles. Acad Pr.
        Introduction to Gas-Liquid Chromatography.
            Acad Pr.
Jones, Richard Arnold Yardley, 1936-
    xJones, R. A.
        Physical & Mechanistic Organic Chemistry.
            Cambridge U Pr.
Jones, Richard E. see Jones, Richard Elfyn.
Jones, Richard Elfyn.
    xJones, Richard E.
        David Wynne. Verry.
Jones, Richard F. see Jones, Richard Foster.
Jones, Richard Foster, 1886-
    xJones, Richard F.
        Ancients & Moderns: A Study of the Rise of
            the Scientific Movement in Seventeenth
            Century England. Peter Smith.
        The Triumph of the English Language: A
            Survey of Opinions Concerning the
            Vernacular from the Introduction of Printing
            to the Restoration. Stanford U Pr.
Jones, Richard M. see Jones, Richard Matthew.
Jones, Richard Matthew, 1925-
    xJones, Richard.
        The Dream Poet. G K Hall.
    xJones, Richard M.
        The Dream Poet. Schenkman.
        Fantasy & Feeling in Education. NYU Pr.
Jones, Richard Michael, 1937-
    xJones, R. M.
        Application of the Geometrical Theory of
            Diffraction to Terrestrial LF Radio Wave
            Propagation. Springer-Verlag.
Jones, Richard O.
    xJones, Richard O.
        Colorado Real Estate: An Introduction to the
            Profession. Reston.
Jones, Robert. see Jones, Robert Francis.
Jones, Robert A. see Jones, Robert Alun.
Jones, Robert Alun.
    xJones, Robert A.
        ed. Research in Sociology of Knowledge,
            Sciences & Art. Jai Pr.
Jones, Robert F. see Jones, Robert Francis.
Jones, Robert Francis, 1935-
    xJones, Robert.
        George Washington. Twayne.
    xJones, Robert F.
        ed. The Formation of the Constitution. Krieger.
Jones, Robert Gerallt.
    xJones, R. G.
        T. H. Parry-Williams. Verry.
Jones, Robert H. see Jones, Robert Huhn.
Jones, Robert Huhn, 1927-
    xJones, Robert H.
        Disrupted Decades: The Civil War &
            Reconstruction Years. Krieger.
Jones, Robert K. see Jones, Robert Kenneth.
Jones, Robert Kenneth, 1926-
    xJones, Robert K.
        The Shudder Pulps: A History of the Weird
            Menace Magazines of the 1930's. NAL.
Jones, Robert L. see Jones, Robert Leslie.
Jones, Robert Leslie.
    xJones, Robert L.
        History of Agriculture in Ontario 1613-1880. U
            of Toronto Pr.
Jones, Robert M., 1939-
    xJones, Robert M.
        Mechanics of Composite Materials. McGraw.
Jones, Robert O. see Jones, Robert Owen.
Jones, Robert Owen, 1928-
    xJones, Robert O.
        Theory of Thought Processes. Philos Lib.
Jones, Robert Tudor.
    xJones, R. T.

George Eliot. Cambridge U Pr.
Jones, Robert Vernon Holmes.
xJones, R. V. H.
Running a Practice. Biblio Dist.
Jones, Rochelle.
xJones, Rochelle.
The Big Switch: New Careers, New Lives After 35. McGraw.
The Other Generation: The New Power of Older People. P-H.
The Private World of Congress. Free Pr.
Jones, Ron, 1941-
xJones, Ron.
The Christmas Coat. Island CA.
Jones, Ronald Winthrop, 1931-
xJones, R. W.
International Trade: Essays in Theory. Elsevier.
Jones, Roy E.
xJones, Roy E.
Principles of Foreign Policy: The Civil State in Its World Setting. St Martin.
Jones, Rufus, 1915-
xJones, Rufus.
If I Were in My Thirties. Nelson.
Jones, Rufus M. see Jones, Rufus Matthew.
Jones, Rufus Matthew, 1863-1948
xJones, Rufus M.
The Flowering of Mysticism: The Friends of God in the Fourteenth Century. Hafner.
The Later Periods of Quakerism. Greenwood.
Studies in Mystical Religion. Russell.
Jones, Samuel A. see Jones, Samuel Arthur.
Jones, Samuel Arthur, 1834-1912
xJones, Samuel A.
Thoreau: A Glimpse. Haskell.
Jones, Sandy.
xJones, Sandy.
Good Things for Babies. HM.
Learning for Little Kids: Parents' Sourcebook for the Years 3 to 8. IIM.
Jones, Schuyler, 1930-
xJones, Schuyler.
Men of Influence in Nuristan: A Study of Social Control & Dispute Settlement in Waigal Valley, Afghanistan. Acad Pr.
Jones, Sonia.
xJones, Sonia.
Spanish One. D Van Nostrand.
Jones, Stan, 1943-
xJones, Stan.
Jones Complete Bar Guide. Bar Guide.
Jones, Stanley.
xJones, Stanley.
Lithography for Artists. Oxford U Pr.
Jones, Stanley E.
xJones, Stanley E.
The Dynamics of Discussion: Communication in Small Groups. Har-Row.
Jones, Stephen.
xJones, Stephen.
Backwaters. Norton.
Turpin. Macmillan.
Jones, Susan L.
xJones, Susan L.
Family Therapy: A Comparison of Approaches. R J Brady.
Jones, T. Gwynn. see Jones, Thomas Gwynn.
Jones, Ted. see Jones, Theodore A.
Jones, Thatcher C., 1888-
xJones, Thatcher C.
Clearings & Collections: Foreign & Domestic. AMS Pr.
Jones, Theodore A.
xJones, Ted.
The Dogwatch. Norton.
xJones, Theodore A.

Challenge '77: Newport & the America's Cup. Norton.
Learn to Sail. Rand.
Jones, Theodoric.
xJones, Theodoric.
ed. Great Story Poems. Lion.
Jones, Thomas B. see Jones, Thomas Brooks.
Jones, Thomas Brooks.
xJones, Thomas B.
Munich: A Tale of Two Myths. Dorrance.
Jones, Thomas Burton, 1927-
xJones, Thomas B.
A Franchising Guide for Blacks. Pilot Bks.
Jones, Thomas E. see Jones, Thomas Elsa.
Jones, Thomas Elsa, 1888-
xJones, Thomas E.
photos by Light on the Horizon: The Quaker Pilgrimage of Tom Jones. Friends United.
Jones, Thomas G. see Jones, Thomas Gwynn.
Jones, Thomas Gwynn, 1871-1949
xJones, T. Gwynn.
Welsh Folklore & Folk-Custom. Rowman.
xJones, Thomas G.
Welsh Folklore & Folk Custom. Folcroft.
Welsh Folklore & Folk-Custom. R West.
Jones, Thomas H., 1926-
xJones, Thomas H.
Furniture Fix & Finish Guide. Reston.
Jones, Thomas J. see Jones, Thomas Jesse.
Jones, Thomas Jesse, 1873-1950
xJones, Thomas J.
Sociology of a New York City Block. AMS Pr.
Jones, Thora B. see Jones, Thora Burnley.
Jones, Thora Burnley.
xJones, Thora B.
Neo-Classical Dramatic Criticism: 1560-1771. Cambridge U Pr.
Jones, Tom, 1941-
xJones, Tom.
No Prisoners. Scrimshaw Calif.
Jones, Tom B. see Jones, Tom Bard.
Jones, Tom Bard, 1909-
xJones, Tom B.
The Figure of the Earth. Coronado Pr.
The Silver-Plated Age. Coronado Pr.
South America Rediscovered. Greenwood.
ed. Sumerian Problem. Krieger.
Jones, Tristan, 1924-
xJones, Tristan.
Ice!. Andrews & McMeel.
The Incredible Voyage: A Personal Odyssey. Andrews & McMeel.
Saga of a Wayward Sailor. Andrews & McMeel.
Jones, Ulysses S.
xJones, Ulysses S.
Fertilizers & Soil Fertility. Reston.
Jones, V. see Jones, Victor.
Jones, Vernon A. see Jones, Vernon Augustus.
Jones, Vernon Augustus, 1897-
xJones, Vernon A.
Effect of Age & Experience on Tests of Intelligence. AMS Pr.
Jones, Vernon F., 1945-
xJones.
Adolescents with Behavior Problems: Strategies for Teaching, Counseling & Parent Involvement. Allyn.
xJones, Vernon F.
Adolescents with Behavior Problems: Strategies for Teaching, Counseling & Parent Involvement. Allyn.
Jones, Victor.
xJones, V.
Love in a London Flat. Lyle Stuart.
xJones, Victor.
Monument of Terror. Lyle Stuart.
Jones, Virgil C. see Jones, Virgil Carrington.
Jones, Virgil Carrington, 1906-
xJones, Virgil C.

Gray Ghosts & Rebel Raiders. Mockingbird Bks.
Jones, W. J.
xJones, W. J.
The Foundations of English Bankruptcy: Statutes & Commissions in the Early Modern Period. Am Philos.
Jones, W. M. see Jones, William Melville.
Jones, Weimar.
xJones, Weimar.
My Affair with a Weekly. Blair.
Jones, Wilbur D. see Jones, Wilbur Devereux.
Jones, Wilbur Devereux.
xJones, Wilbur D.
Peelites, 1846-1857. Ohio St U Pr.
Jones, William, 1871-1909
xJones, William.
Fox Texts. AMS Pr.
History & Mystery of Precious Stones. Gale.
History & Mystery of Precious Stones. Gordon Pr.
Compiled by Ojibwa Texts. AMS Pr.
Jones, William I.
xJones, William I.
Planning & Economic Policy: Socialist Mali & Her Neighbors. Three Continents.
Jones, William J. see Jones, William Jervis.
Jones, William Jervis, 1941-
xJones, William J.
Lexicon of French Borrowings in the German Vocabulary. De Gruyter.
Jones, William L.
xJones, William L.
Uncovering Up: A Guide to Excellence in School Public Relations. ETC Pubns.
Jones, William M.
xJones, William M.
Survival: A Manual on Manipulating. Am Mgmt.
Survival: A Manual on Manipulating. P-H
Jones, William M. see Jones, William Mckendrey.
Jones, William Mckendrey.
xJones, William M.
ed. The Present State of Scholarship in Sixteenth-Century Literature. U of Mo Pr.
Speaking up in Church. Broadman.
Jones, William Melville.
xJones, W. M.
ed. Chief Justice John Marshall: A Reappraisal. Da Capo.
Jones, William O.
xJones, William O.
Marketing Staple Food Crops in Tropical Africa. Cornell U Pr.
Jones, William S. see Jones, William Sidney Handley.
Jones, William Sidney Handley, 1884-
xJones, William S.
The Priest & the Siren, & Other Literary Studies. Folcroft.
Jones, Willis K. see Jones, Willis Knapp.
Jones, Willis Knapp, 1895-
xJones, Willis K.
tr. Men & Angels: Three South American Comedies. S Ill U Pr.
Jones-Baker, Doris.
xJones-Baker, Doris.
The Folklore of Hertfordshire. Rowman.
Jong, Dola De. see De Jong, Dola.
Jong, Erica.
xJong, Erica.
At the Edge of the Body. HR&W.
Half-Lives. HR&W.
Jong, Gerald F. De. see De Jong, Gerald F.
Jong, Kees A. De. see De Jong, Kees A.
Jong, Rudolph H. De. see De Jong, Rudolph H.
Jong, W. De. see De Jong, W.
Jonge, Alex De. see De Jonge, Alex.
Jonge, Alfred R. De. see De Jonge, Alfred R.
Jongeward, Dorothy.
xJongeward, Dorothy.

Affirmative Action for Women: A Practical
    Guide for Women & Management. A-W.
Choosing Success: Transactional Analysis on
    the Job. Wiley.
Jonsen, George.
    xJonsen, George.
    Favorite Tales of Monsters & Trolls. Random.
Jonson. *see* Jonson, Ben.
Jonson, Ben, 1573-1637
    xJonson.
    The Alchemist. Norton.
    xJonson, Ben.
    The Alchemist. Arden Lib.
    Alchemist. Barron.
    Alchemist. Cambridge U Pr.
    The Alchemist. Methuen Inc.
    The Alchemist. Yale U Pr.
    The Alchemist. AHM Pub.
    Catiline. U of Nebr Pr.
    The Complete Masques. Yale U Pr.
    Gypsies Metamorphosed. Kraus Repr.
    xJonson, Benjamin.
    The Alchemist. Walter J Johnson.
Jonson, Benjamin. *see* Jonson, Ben.
Jonson, G. C. *see* Jonson, George Charles Ashton.
Jonson, George Charles Ashton, 1861-
    xJonson, G. C.
    Handbook to Chopin's Works. Longwood Pr.
Jonsson, B. *see* Jonsson, Bjarni.
Jonsson, Bjarni, 1920-
    xJonsson, B.
    Topics in Universal Algebra. Springer-Verlag.
Joos, Martin.
    xJoos, Martin.
    English Verb: Form & Meanings. U of Wis Pr.
Joost, Nicholas.
    xJoost, Nicholas.
    D. H. Lawrence & "The Dial". S Ill U Pr.
Joplin, B. *see* Joplin, Bruce.
Joplin, Bruce.
    xJoplin, B.
    Effective Accounting Reports. P-H.
Joralemon, Ira B. *see* Joralemon, Ira Beaman.
Joralemon, Ira Beaman, 1884-1975
    xJoralemon, Ira B.
    Adventure Beacons. Soc Mining Eng.
Jordan. *see* Jordan, Peter C.
Jordan, A. C.
    xJordan, A. C.
    Retold by Tales from Southern Africa. U of
    Cal Pr.
Jordan, Arthur M. *see* Jordan, Arthur Melville.
Jordan, Arthur Melville, 1888-
    xJordan, Arthur M.
    Children's Interests in Reading. AMS Pr.
Jordan, Bill.
    xJordan, Bill.
    Freedom & the Welfare State. Routledge &
    Kegan.
Jordan, Bill. *see* Jordan, William.
Jordan, Brigitte.
    xJordan, Brigitte.
    Birth in Four Cultures: A Cross-Cultural
    Investigation of Childbirth in Yucatan,
    Holland, Sweden & the United States. Eden
    Women.
Jordan, Clarence.
    xJordan, Clarence.
    Cotton Patch Version of Hebrews & the
    General Epistles. Follett.
    Cotton Patch Version of Paul's Epistles.
    Follett.
Jordan, D. W. *see* Jordan, Dominic William.
Jordan, Dale R.
    xJordan, Dale R.
    Dyslexia in the Classroom. Merrill.
Jordan, Daniel C.
    xJordan, Daniel C.

The Meaning of Deepening: Gaining a Clearer
    Apprehension of the Purpose of God for
    Man. Baha'i.
Jordan Dataquest. *see* Jordan Dataquest Ltd.
Jordan Dataquest Ltd.
    xJordan Dataquest.
    ed. Britain's Top One Thousand Private
    Companies 1979. State Mutual Bk.
    xJordon Dataquest.
    Britain's Quoted Industrial Companies
    Nineteen Seventy-Nine. State Mutual Bk.
    ed. Britain's Top One Thousand Foreign
    Owned Companies 1979. State Mutual Bk.
    Scotland's Top Five Hundred Companies -
    1979. State Mutual Bk.
Jordan, David C.
    xJordan, David C.
    Spain, the Monarchy & the Atlantic
    Community. Inst Foreign Policy Anal.
Jordan, David P., 1939-
    xJordan, David P.
    Gibbon & His Roman Empire. U of Ill Pr.
Jordan, David S. *see* Jordan, David Starr.
Jordan, David Starr, 1851-1931
    xJordan, David S.
    Imperial Democracy. Garland Pub.
Jordan, Dominic William.
    xJordan, D. W.
    Nonlinear Ordinary Differential Equations.
    Oxford U Pr.
Jordan, Donald A., 1936-
    xJordan, Donald A.
    The Northern Expedition: China's National
    Revolution of 1926-1928. U Pr of Hawaii.
Jordan, Donald G.
    xJordan, Donald G.
    Chemical Process Development. Krieger.
Jordan, Donaldson.
    xJordan, Donaldson.
    Europe & the American Civil War. Octagon.
Jordan, Elizabeth G. *see* Jordan, Elizabeth Garver.
Jordan, Elizabeth Garver, 1867-1947
    xJordan, Elizabeth G.
    Tales of Destiny. Arno.
    Tales of the City Room. Arno.
    Tales of the Cloister. Arno.
Jordan, Emil L. *see* Jordan, Emil Leopold.
Jordan, Emil Leopold.
    xJordan, Emil L.
    Animal Atlas of the World. Hammond Inc.
Jordan, Frank.
    xJordan, Frank.
    ed. The English Romantic Poets: A Review of
    Research & Criticism. Modern Lang.
Jordan, Gilbert J. *see* Jordan, Gilbert John.
Jordan, Gilbert John, 1902-
    xJordan, Gilbert J.
    Yesterday in the Texas Hill Country. Tex
    A&M Univ Pr.
Jordan, Grace. *see* Jordan, Grace (Edgington).
Jordan, Grace (Edgington).
    xJordan, Grace.
    Home Below Hell's Canyon. U of Nebr Pr.
Jordan, Hope D. *see* Jordan, Hope Dahle.
Jordan, Hope Dahle.
    xJordan, Hope D.
    Stranger in Their Midst. Lothrop.
    Talk About the Tarchers. Lothrop.
Jordan, Jerry M. *see* Jordan, Jerry Marshall.
Jordan, Jerry Marshall.
    xJordan, Jerry M.
    The Brown Bag: A Bag Full of Sermons for
    Children. Pilgrim NY.
Jordan, Joseph A.
    xJordan, Joseph A.
    ed. The Cervix. Saunders.
Jordan, June, 1936-
    xJordan, June.

Dry Victories. Avon.
Fannie Lou Hamer. T Y Crowell.
His Own Where. Dell.
His Own Where. T Y Crowell.
Who Look at Me. T Y Crowell.
Jordan, June B.
    xJordan, June B.
    ed. Early Childhood Education for Exceptional
    Children: A Handbook of Ideas & Exemplary
    Practices. Coun Exc Child.
Jordan, Leah E. *see* Jordan, Leah Elizabeth.
Jordan, Leah Elizabeth, 1912-
    xJordan, Leah E.
    The Fundamentals of Emerson's Literary
    Criticism. Folcroft.
Jordan, Lewis G. *see* Jordan, Lewis Garnett.
Jordan, Lewis Garnett, 1854?-
    xJordan, Lewis G.
    Up the Ladder in Foreign Missions. Arno.
Jordan, Mildred. *see* Jordan, Mildred A.
Jordan, Mildred A., 1901-
    xJordan, Mildred.
    The Distelfink Country of the Pennsylvania
    Dutch. Crown.
Jordan, Pat.
    xJordan, Pat.
    Chase the Game. Dodd.
    The Suitors of Spring. Dodd.
Jordan, Patricia, 1922-
    xJordan, Patricia.
    District Nurse. St Martin.
Jordan, Payton.
    xJordan, Payton.
    Champions in the Making: Quality Training for
    Track & Field. P-H.
Jordan, Peter C.
    xJordan.
    Chemical Kinetics & Transport. Plenum Pub.
Jordan, Philip D. *see* Jordan, Philip Dillon.
Jordan, Philip Dillon, 1903-
    xJordan, Philip D.
    Frontier Law & Order: Ten Essays. U of Nebr
    Pr.
    The People's Health: A History of Public
    Health in Minnesota to 1948. Minn Hist.
Jordan, Robert P. *see* Jordan, Robert Paul.
Jordan, Robert Paul.
    xJordan, Robert P.
    The Civil War. Natl Geog.
Jordan, Robin.
    xJordan, Robin.
    Speak Out, My Heart. Naiad Pr.
Jordan, Ruth.
    xJordan, Ruth.
    George Sand: A Biographical Portrait.
    Taplinger.
    Nocturne: A Life of Chopin. Taplinger.
    Sophie Dorothea. Braziller.
Jordan, S. C. *see* Jordan, Stephan Christopher.
Jordan, Stephan Christopher.
    xJordan, S. C.
    A Synopsis of Cardiology. Year Bk Med.
Jordan, Terry G.
    xJordan, Terry G.
    German Seed in Texas Soil: Immigrant Farmers
    in Nineteenth Century Texas. U of Tex Pr.
    The Human Mosaic: A Thematic Introduction
    to Cultural Geography. Har-Row.
Jordan, Thomas E. *see* Jordan, Thomas Edward.
Jordan, Thomas Edward.
    xJordan, Thomas E.
    Development in the Preschool Years: Birth to
    Age Five. Acad Pr.
Jordan, Thomas H.
    xJordan, Thomas H.
    The Theatrical Craftsmanship of Richard
    Brinsley Sheridan's 'School for Scandal'.
    Revisionist Pr.
Jordan, Tom.
    xJordan, Tom.

Pre!. Tafnews.

Jordan, Weymouth T. *see* Jordan, Weymouth Tyree.

Jordan, Weymouth Tyree, 1912-
xJordan, Weymouth T.
Hugh Davis & His Alabama Plantation.
Greenwood.

Jordan, Wilbur Kitchener, 1902-
xJordan, William K.
The Charities of London, 1480-1660: The
Aspirations & the Achievements of the Urban
Society. Shoe String.

Jordan, William, 1941-
xJordan, Bill.
Helping in Social Work. Routledge & Kegan.
Paupers: The Making of the New Claiming
Class. Routledge & Kegan.

Jordan, William A.
xJordan, William A.
Airline Regulation in America: Effects &
Imperfections. Greenwood.

Jordan, William K. *see* Jordan, Wilbur Kitchener.

Jordan, William S.
xJordan, William S.
Community Medicine in the United Kingdom:
Medical Education & an Emerging Specialty
Within the Reorganized National Health
Service. Springer Pub.

Jordan, Winthorp D. *see* Jordan, Winthrop D.

Jordan, Winthrop. *see* Jordan, Winthrop D.

Jordan, Winthrop D.
xJordan, Winthorp D.
White Over Black: American Attitudes Toward
the Negro, 1550-1812. Norton.
xJordan, Winthrop.
White Man's Burden: Historical Origins of
Racism in the United States. Oxford U Pr.
xJordan, Winthrop D.
White Man's Burden: Historical Origins of
Racism in the United States. Oxford U Pr.
White Over Black: American Attitudes Toward
the Negro, 1550-1812. U of NC Pr.

Jorden, E. H. *see* Jorden, Eleanor Harz.

Jorden, Eleanor H. *see* Jorden, Eleanor Harz.

Jorden, Eleanor Harz.
xJorden, E. H.
Syntax of Modern Colloquial Japanese. Kraus
Repr.
xJorden, Eleanor H.
Reading Japanese. Yale U Pr.

Jordon Dataquest. *see* Jordan Dataquest Ltd.

Joreskog, K. G.
xJoreskog, Karl G.
Advances in Factor Analysis & Structural
Equation Models. Abt Assoc.

Joreskog, Karl G. *see* Joreskog, K. G.

Jorge, Antonio, 1931-
xJorge, Antonio.
Competition, Cooperation, Efficiency & Social
Organization. Fairleigh Dickinson.

Jorgensen, Caryl D. *see* Jorgensen, Caryl Dow.

Jorgensen, Caryl Dow.
xJorgensen, Caryl D.
The ABC's of Diabetes. Crown.

Jorgensen, Eric.
xJorgensen, Eric.

Chevette Service Repair Handbook: All Models
1976-1978. Clymer Pubns.
Fix Your Bicycle: All Speeds, All Major
Makes, Simplified, Step by Step. Clymer
Pubns.
ed. Honda 125-200cc Twins, 1964-1977:
Service, Repair, Performance. Clymer Pubns.
ed. Honda 250 & 350cc Twins, 1964-1974:
Service-Repair-Performance. Clymer Pubns.
ed. Honda 250 & 360cc Twins, 1974-1977:
Service-Repair-Performance. Clymer Pubns.
Porsche Service-Repair Handbook: 911 & 912
Series, 1965-1978. Clymer Pubns.
Powerboat Maintenance. Clymer Pubns.

Jorgensen, Jorgen, 1894-
xJorgensen, Jorgen.
Development of Logical Empiricism. Johnson
Repr.

Jorgensen, Joseph G., 1934-
xJorgensen, Joseph G.
Native Americans & Energy Development.
Anthropology Res.
The Sun Dance Religion: Power for the
Powerless. U of Chicago Pr.

Jorgensen, Neil.
xJorgensen, Neil.
A Guide to New England's Landscape. Globe
Pequot.
Sierra Club Naturalist's Guide to Southern
New England. Sierra.

Jorgensen, Niels B. *see* Jorgensen, Niels Bjorn.

Jorgensen, Niels Bjorn.
xJorgensen, Niels B.
Sedation, Local & General Anesthesia in
Dentistry. Lea & Febiger.

Jorgensen, Paul A.
xJorgensen, Paul A.
Our Naked Frailties: Sensational Art &
Meaning in Macbeth. U of Cal Pr.

Jorgensen, Poul.
xJorgensen, Poul.
Dressing Flies for Fresh & Salt Water. Freshet
Pr.
Modern Fly Dressings for the Practical Angler.
Winchester Pr.

Jorgensen, William L.
xJorgensen, William L.
The Organic Chemist's Book of Orbitals. Acad
Pr.

Jorgenson, D. W. *see* Jorgenson, Dale Weldeau.

Jorgenson, Dale Weldeau.
xJorgenson, D. W.
Optimal Replacement Policy. Elsevier.

Jorgenson, Theodore, 1894-
xJorgenson, Theodore.
History of Norwegian Literature. Haskell.
Norwegian Literature in Medieval & Early
Modern Times. Greenwood.

Jorns, Auguste.
xJorns, Auguste.
Quakers As Pioneers in Social Work. Kennikat.
Quakers As Pioneers in Social Work. Patterson
Smith.

Jorow, Marie.
xJorow, Marie.
The Central Service Technician at Work.
Springer Pub.

Jorrin, Miguel.
xJorrin, Miguel.
Latin-American Political Thought & Ideology.
U of NC Pr.

Joscelyn, Archie, 1899-
xJoscelyn, Archie.
Gunman. Bouregy.
Lost River Canyon. Bouregy.
Ride to Blizzard. Bouregy.

Jose, Arthur. *see* Jose, Arthur Wilberforce.

Jose, Arthur Wilberforce, 1863-1934
xJose, Arthur.

Builders & Pioneers of Australia. Arno.

Jose, F. Sionil. *see* Jose, Francisco Sionil.

Jose, Francisco Sionil.
xJose, F. Sionil.
ed. Asian P. E. N. Anthology. Taplinger.

Josefowitz, Natash. *see* Josefowitz, Natasha.

Josefowitz, Natasha.
xJosefowitz, Natash.
Paths to Power: A Working Woman's Guide
from First Job to Top Executive. A-W.

Joselyn, Robert W.
xJoselyn, Robert W.
Designing the Marketing Research Project. Van
Nos Reinhold.

Joseph, Alexander.
xJoseph, Alexander.
Teaching High School Science: A Source Book
for the Physical Sciences. HarBraceJ.

Joseph, Alice.
xJoseph, Alice.
Chamorros & Carolinians of Saipan: Personality
Studies. Greenwood.

Joseph, Andre.
xJoseph, Andre.
Intelligence, IQ & Race: When, How & Why
They Became Associated. R & E Res Assoc.

Joseph, Arthur, 1886-1956
xJoseph, Arthur.
Dark Metropolis. AMS Pr.

Joseph, Bertram. *see* Joseph, Bertram Leon.

Joseph, Bertram L. *see* Joseph, Bertram Leon.

Joseph, Bertram Leon.
xJoseph, Bertram.
Acting Shakespeare. Theatre Arts.
xJoseph, Bertram L.
Conscience & the King: A Study of Hamlet.
Somerset Pub.
xJoseph, Bertram.
Elizabethan Acting. Octagon.

Joseph, Bertram. *see* Joseph, Bertram Leon.

Joseph, Horace W. *see* Joseph, Horace William Brindley.

Joseph, Horace William Brindley, 1867-1943
xJoseph, Horace W.
Lectures on the Philosophy of Leibniz.
Greenwood.

Joseph, Joan.
xJoseph, Joan.
Folk Toys Around the World & How to Make
Them. US Comm UNICEF.
Folk Toys Around the World & How to Make
Them. Schol Bk Serv.

Joseph, Marie.
xJoseph, Marie.
One Step at a Time: Living with Arthritis. St
Martin.

Joseph, Marjory L.
xJoseph, Marjory L.
Essentials of Textiles. HR&W.

Joseph, Michael, 1897-1958
xJoseph, Michael.
How to Write a Short Story. Folcroft.

Joseph, N. R. *see* Joseph, Norman R.

Joseph, Norman R.
xJoseph, N. R.
Comparative Physical Biology. S Karger.

Joseph, O. L. *see* Joseph, Oscar Loos.

Joseph, Oscar L. *see* Joseph, Oscar Loos.

Joseph, Oscar Loos.
xJoseph, O. L.
The Influence of the English Bible Upon the
English Language & Upon English &
American Literature. Gordon Pr.
xJoseph, Oscar L.
The Influence of the English Bible Upon the
English Language & Upon English &
American Literature. Folcroft.

Joseph, R. F. *see* Joseph, Robert F.

Joseph, Richard A.
xJoseph, Richard A.

Radical Nationalism in Cameroun: Social
Origins of the U.P.C. Rebellion. Oxford U Pr.

Joseph, Robert F.
xJoseph, R. F.
Odile. Ballantine.

Joseph, Ronald S.
xJoseph, Ronald S.
The Power. Warner Bks.

Joseph, Samuel, 1881-
xJoseph, Samuel.
History of the Baron DeHirsch Fund: The
Americanization of the Jewish Immigrant.
Kelley.

Joseph, Stephen.
xJoseph, Stephen.
Theatre in the Round. Taplinger.

Joseph, Stephen C.
xJoseph, Stephen C.
Worldwide Overview of Health & Disease.
Springer Pub.

Joseph, Stephen M., 1938-
xJoseph, Stephen M.
ed. The Me Nobody Knows: Children's Voices
from the Ghetto. Avon.

Josephs, Lewis S., 1943-
xJosephs, Lewis S.
Palauan Reference Grammar. U Pr of Hawaii.

Josephson, Elmer A.
xJosephson, Elmer A.
God's Key to Health & Happiness. Revell.

Josephson, Hannah. see Josephson, Hannah (Geffen).

Josephson, Hannah (Geffen).
xJosephson, Hannah.
Golden Threads: New England's Mill Girls &
Magnates. Russell.

Josephson, Matthew, 1899-
xJosephson, Matthew.
Portrait of the Artist As American. Octagon.

Josephy, Alvin M., 1915-
xJosephy, Alvin M.
Indian Heritage of America. Bantam.
Indian Heritage of America. Knopf.
The Nez Perce Indians & the Opening of the
Northwest. U of Nebr Pr.
On the Hill: A History of the American,
Congress. S&S.

Josey, E. J.
xJosey, E. J.
ed. Handbook of Black Librarianship. Libs Unl.
ed. Information Society: Issues & Answers.
Oryx Pr.
Opportunities for Minorities in Librarianship.
Scarecrow.

Joshi, A. W.
xJoshi, A. W.
Matrices & Tensors in Physics. Halsted Pr.

Joshi, Baburao.
xJoshi, Baburao.
Understanding Indian Music. Greenwood.

Joshi, Heather.
xJoshi, Heather.
Abidjan: Urban Development & Employment
in the Ivory Coast. Intl Labour Office.

Joshi, P. S. see Joshi, Pranshankar Someshwar.

Joshi, Pranshankar Someshwar, 1897-
xJoshi, P. S.
The Tyranny of Colour: A Study of the Indian
Problem in South Africa. Kennikat.

Joshua, Wynfred.
xJoshua, Wynfred.
Arms for the Third World: Soviet Military Aid
Diplomacy. Johns Hopkins.

Josipovici, Gabriel, 1940-
xJosipovici, Gabriel.
World & the Book: A Study of Modern
Fiction. Stanford U Pr.

Joske, W D, 1928-
xJoske, W. D.
Material Objects. St Martin.

Joslin, E. C. see Joslin, Edward C.

Joslin, Edward C.
xJoslin, E. C.
The Standard Catalogue of British Orders,
Decorations & Medals. S J Durst.

Joslin, Edward O.
xJoslin, Edward O.
Analysis Design & Selection of Computer
Systems. College Readings.
Software for Computer Systems. College
Readings.

Joslin, Sesyle.
xJoslin, Sesyle.
The Gentle Savages. Atheneum.
illus. Last Summer's Smugglers. HarBraceJ.

Joslin, Theodore G. see Joslin, Theodore Goldsmith.

Joslin, Theodore Goldsmith, 1890-1944
xJoslin, Theodore G.
Hoover off the Record. Arno.

Joslyn-Scherer, Marcia S.
xJoslyn-Scherer, Marcia S.
Communication in the Human Services: A
Guide to Therapeutic Journalism. Sage.

Jospe, Michael.
xJospe, Michael L.
The Placebo Effect in Healing. Lexington Bks.

Jospe, Michael L. see Jospe, Michael.

Joss, E. E.
xJoss, E. E.
Growth Hormone Deficiency in Childhood:
Evaluation of Diagnostic Procedures. S
Karger.

Josselyn, Irene M. see Josselyn, Irene Milliken.

Josselyn, Irene Milliken, 1904-1978
xJosselyn, Irene M.
Psychosocial Development of Children. Family
Serv.

Jossua, J. P. see Jossua, Jean-Pierre.

Jossua, Jean-Pierre.
xJossua, J. P.
Doing Theology in New Places. Crossroad NY.

Jost, Francois.
xJost, Francois.
Introduction to Comparative Literature.
Pegasus.

Joubert, Laurent, 1529-1583
xJoubert, Laurent.
Treatise on Laughter. U of Ala Pr.

Joudry, Patricia, 1921-
xJoudry, Patricia.
And the Children Played. Tundra Bks.

Jouejati, R.
xJouejati, Rafic.
Quest for Total Peace: The Political Thought of
Roger Martin Du Gard. Biblio Dist.

Jouejati, Rafic. see Jouejati, R.

Joughin, Jean T.
xJoughin, Jean T.
Paris Commune in French Politics, 1871-1880:
The History of the Amnesty of 1880. Russell.

Joukowsky, Martha.
xJoukowsky, Martha.
A Complete Manual of Field Archaeology:
Tools & Techniques of Field Work for
Archaeologists. P-H.

Joule, J. A. see Joule, John Arthur.

Joule, John Arthur.
xJoule, J. A.
Heterocyclic Chemistry. Van Nos Reinhold.

Jourard, Sidney M.
xJourard, Sidney M.
Disclosing Man to Himself. Van Nos Reinhold.
Healthy Personality: An Approach from the
Viewpoint of Humanistic Psychology.
Macmillan.
Self Disclosure: An Experimental Analysis of
the Transparent Self. Krieger.

Jourdain, Eleanor F. see Jourdain, Eleanor Frances.

Jourdain, Eleanor Frances, 1863-1924
xJourdain, Eleanor F.

The Drama in Europe in Theory & Practice.
Haskell.
Dramatic Theory & Practice in France
1690-1808. Arno.

Jourdain, Rose, 1931-
xJourdain, Rose.
Those the Sun Has Loved. Ballantine.

Jousseaume, Andre.
xJousseaume, Andre.
Progressive Dressage. J A Allen.

Jovanovic, Uros J. see Jovanovic, Uros Jovan.

Jovanovic, Uros Jovan.
xJovanovic, Uros J.
Psychomotor Epilepsy: A Polydimensional
Study. C C Thomas.

Jovanovich, William.
xJovanovich, William.
Madmen Must. Har-Row.

Jowett, C. E. see Jowett, Charles Eric.

Jowett, Charles Eric.
xJowett, C. E.
The Engineering of Microelectronic Thin &
Thick Films. Intl Schol Bk Serv.

Jowett, Garth.
xJowett, Garth.
Film: The Democratic Art. Little.

Jowett, J. H, 1864-1923
xJowett, John H.
Eagle Life & Other Studies in the Old
Testament. Baker Bk.

Jowett, John H. see Jowett, J. H.

Jowitt, Kenneth.
xJowitt, Kenneth.
The Leninist Response to National
Dependency. U of Cal Intl St.
Revolutionary Breakthroughs & National
Development: The Case of Romania,
1944-1965. U of Cal Pr.

Joy, Donald M. see Joy, Donald Marvin.

Joy, Donald Marvin.
xJoy, Donald M.
Meaningful Learning in the Church. Light &
Life.

Joy, O. Maurice.
xJoy, O. Maurice.
Introduction to Financial Management. Irwin.

Joy, W. Brugh. see Joy, William Brugh.

Joy, William. see Joy, William Leonard.

Joy, William Brugh, 1939-
xJoy, W. Brugh.
Joy's Way: A Map for the Transformational
Journey & an Introduction to the Potentials
for Healing with Body Energies. St Martin.

Joy, William Leonard, 1902-
xJoy, William.
Intro. by The Aviators. Soccer.

Joyce, Bruce. see Joyce, Bruce R.

Joyce, Bruce R.
xJoyce, Bruce.
Models of Teaching. P-H.
xJoyce, Bruce R.
Creating the School: An Introduction to
Education. Little.
Models of Teaching. P-H.
Selecting Learning Experiences: Linking
Theory & Practice. Assn Supervision.

Joyce, George H. see Joyce, George Hayward.

Joyce, George Hayward, 1864-1943
xJoyce, George H.
Principles of Natural Theology. AMS Pr.

Joyce, James, 1882-1941
xJoyce, James.

Collected Poems. Penguin.
Dubliners. Modern Lib.
Dubliners. Penguin.
Finnegan's Wake. Penguin.
Finnegans Wake. Viking Pr.
A Portrait of the Artist As a Young Man.
Penguin.
Portrait of the Artist As a Young Man. Viking
Pr.
Stephen Hero. New Directions.
Ulysses. Modern Lib.
Ulysses. Random.
Ulysses. Random.
Ulysses: A Facsimile of the Manuscript.
Octagon.
Joyce, James A. *see* Joyce, James Avery.
Joyce, James Avery.
xJoyce, James A.
The New Politics of Human Rights. St Martin.
World Labour Rights & Their Protection. St
Martin.
World Population: Basic Documents. Oceana.
Joyce, John A. *see* Joyce, John Alexander.
Joyce, John Alexander, 1842-1915
xJoyce, John A.
Edgar Allan Poe. Folcroft.
Joyce, Michael.
xJoyce, Michael.
Edward Gibbon. R West.
My Friend H. John Cam Hobhouse, Baron
Broughton of Broughton De Gyfford.
Century Bookbindery.
Joyce, Patrick W. *see* Joyce, Patrick Weston.
Joyce, Patrick Weston, 1827-1914
xJoyce, Patrick W.
English As We Speak It in Ireland. Gale.
Joyce, Robert.
xJoyce, Robert.
The Esthetic Animal: Man, the Art-Created
Art Creator. Exposition.
Joyce, Robert. *see* Joyce, Robert E.
Joyce, Robert E.
xJoyce, Robert.
Let Us Be Born: The Inhumanity of Abortion.
Franciscan Herald.
Joyce, Walter.
xJoyce, Walter.
The Propaganda Gap. Greenwood.
Joyce, William L. *see* Joyce, William Leonard.
Joyce, William Leonard.
xJoyce, William L.
Editors & Ethnicity: A History of the
Irish-American Press, 1848-1883. Arno.
Joyce, William W.
xJoyce, William W.
Teaching Social Studies in the Elementary &
Middle Schools. HR&W.
Joyes, Claire.
xJoyes, Claire.
Monet at Giverny. Mayflower Bks.
Joyner, Claude R.
xJoyner, Claude R.
Ultrasound in the Diagnosis of
Cardiovascular-Pulmonary Disease. Year Bk
Med.
Joyner, Conrad.
xJoyner, Conrad.
American Politician. U of Ariz Pr.
Holman Versus Hughes: Extension of
Australian Commonwealth Powers. U Presses
Fla.
Joyner, Nancy C. *see* Joyner, Nancy Carol.
Joyner, Nancy Carol.
xJoyner, Nancy C.
ed. Edwin Arlington Robinson: A Reference
Guide. G K Hall.
Joyner, Nancy D. *see* Joyner, Nancy Douglas.
Joyner, Nancy Douglas, 1945-
xJoyner, Nancy D.

Aerial Hijacking As an International Crime.
Oceana.
Joyner, Nina G. *see* Joyner, Nina Glenn.
Joyner, Nina Glenn.
xJoyner, Nina G.
Dollhouse Construction & Restoration. Chilton.
Furniture Refinishing at Home. Chilton.
Joynes, St. Leger.
xJoynes, St. Leger M.
Insiders' Guide to New Orleans. Insiders Pub.
Joynes, St. Leger M. *see* Joynes, St. Leger.
Joynson, R. B. *see* Joynson, Robert Billington.
Joynson, Robert Billington.
xJoynson, R. B.
Psychology & Common Sense. Routledge &
Kegan.
Joynt, C. B.
xJoynt, Carey B.
Theory & Reality in World Politics. U of
Pittsburgh Pr.
Joynt, Carey B. *see* Joynt, C. B.
Jubb, K. V. *see* Jubb, K. V. F.
Jubb, K. V. F.
xJubb, K. V.
Pathology of Domestic Animals. Acad Pr.
Jubenville, Alan.
xJubenville, Alan.
Outdoor Recreation Management. HR&W.
Jubiz, William.
xJubiz, William.
Endocrinology: A Logical Approach for
Clinicians. McGraw.
Jucius, Michael J. *see* Jucius, Michael James.
Jucius, Michael James, 1907-
xJucius, Michael J.
Personnel Management. Irwin.
Jud, G. Donald.
xJud, Gustav D.
Inflation & the Use of Indexing in Developing
Countries. Praeger.
Jud, Gustav D. *see* Jud, G. Donald.
Juda, Lawrence
xJuda, Lawrence.
Ocean Space Rights: Developing U.S. Policy.
Praeger.
Judd, Charles H. *see* Judd, Charles Hubbard.
Judd, Charles Hubbard, 1873-1946
xJudd, Charles H.
The Psychology of Social Institutions. Arno.
Judd, Deane B. *see* Judd, Deane Brewster.
Judd, Deane Brewster.
xJudd, Deane B.
Color in Business, Science, & Industry. Wiley.
Judd, Denis, 1938-
xJudd, Denis.
Adventures of Long John Silver. Avon.
The Adventures of Long John Silver. St
Martin.
Eclipse of Kings: European Monarchies in the
Twentieth Century. Stein & Day.
Return to Treasure Island. St Martin.
Judd, Dennis R.
xJudd, Dennis R.
The Politics of American Cities: Private Power
& Public Policy. Little.
The Politics of Urban Planning: The East St.
Louis Experience. U of Ill Pr.
Judd, Frances K.
xJudd, Frances K.
The Double Disguise. Bantam.
The Double Disguise. Lamplight Pub.
In the Sunken Garden. Bantam.
In the Sunken Garden. Lamplight Pub.
Judd, Gerrit P. *see* Judd, Gerrit Parmele.
Judd, Gerrit Parmele, 1915-
xJudd, Gerrit P.
History of Civilization. Macmillan.
Horace Walpole's Memoirs. Coll & U Pr.
xJudd, Gerrit Parmele.

Members of Parliament, 1734-1832. Shoe
String.
Judd, H. S. *see* Judd, H. Stanley.
Judd, H. Stanley.
xJudd, H. S.
The California Weight Loss Program. PB.
xJudd, H. Stanley.
Think Rich. Delacorte.
xJudd, Stanley H.
Think Rich. Dell.
Judd, Jacob.
xJudd, Jacob.
ed. Aspects of Early New York Society &
Politics. Sleepy Hollow.
ed. Correspondence of the Van Cortlandt
Family of Cortlandt Manor, 1800-1814.
Sleepy Hollow.
Judd, Lawrence M.
xJudd, Lawrence M.
Lawrence M. Judd & Hawaii: An
Autobiography. C E Tuttle.
Judd, Neil M. *see* Judd, Neil Merton.
Judd, Neil Merton, 1887-
xJudd, Neil M.
Bureau of American Ethnology: A Partial
History. U of Okla Pr.
Judd, Stanley H. *see* Judd, H. Stanley.
Judd, W. W. *see* Judd, William Wallace.
Judd, Wallace.
xJudd, Wallace.
Dogfight & More Games Calculators Play.
Warner Bks.
Judd, Walter F.
xJudd, Walter F.
Let Us Go: The Narrative of Kamehameha II,
King of the Hawaiian Islands, 1819-1824.
Topgallant.
Judd, Wayne, 1941-
xJudd, Wayne.
How to Wait for Jesus. Southern Pub.
Kissing, Hugging, &.... Southern Pub.
Judd, William Wallace.
xJudd, W. W.
ed. Naturalist's Guide to Ontario. U of
Toronto Pr.
Judelle, Beatrice.
xJudelle, Beatrice.
The Branch Managers' Manual. Natl Ret
Merch.
Judge. *see* Judge, Vira H.
Judge, Arthur W. *see* Judge, Arthur William.
Judge, Arthur William, 1887-
xJudge, Arthur W.
Car Maintenance & Repair. Bentley.
Modern Electrical Equipment for Automobiles.
Bentley.
Judge, Clark S., 1948-
xJudge, Clark S.
The Best, Worst, Least & Most: The U. S.
Book of Rankings. HarBraceJ.
Judge, Ken.
xJudge, Ken.
Rationing Social Services: A Study of Resource
Allocation in the Personal Social Services.
Heinemann Ed.
Judge, Roy.
xJudge, Roy.
The Jack-in-the-Green: A May Day Custom.
Rowman.
Judge, Vira H., 1917-
xJudge.
Home Work: The Stay at-Home Money Book.
Deseret Bk.
Judge, W. James. *see* Judge, William James.
Judge, William James.
xJudge, W. James.
The PaleoIndian Occupation of the Central Rio
Grande Valley in New Mexico. U of NM Pr.
Judisch, Douglas.
xJudisch, Douglas.

An Evaluation of Claims to the Charismatic
Gifts. Baker Bk.

Judkins, Winthrop.
xJudkins, Winthrop.
Fluctuant Representation in Synthetic Cubism:
Picasso, Braque, Gris, 1910-1920. Garland
Pub.

Judson, Alexander C. see Judson, Alexander Corbin.

Judson, Alexander Corbin, 1883-
xJudson, Alexander C.
Sidney's Appearance: A Study in Elizabethan
Portraiture. Arno.
Spenser in Southern Ireland. Folcroft.

Judson, David M.
xJudson, David M.
Ghar Parau. Macmillan.

Judson, Harry P. see Judson, Harry Pratt.

Judson, Harry Pratt, 1849-1927
xJudson, Harry P.
Caesar's Army: A Study of the Military Art of
the Romans in the Last Days of the
Republic. Biblo.

Judson, Horace F. see Judson, Horace Freeland.

Judson, Horace Freeland.
xJudson, Horace F.
The Search for Solutions. HR&W.

Juel, Donald.
xJuel, Donald.
An Introduction to New Testament Literature.
Abingdon.

Juergens, George.
xJuergens, George.
Joseph Pulitzer & the New York World.
Princeton U Pr.

Juergenson, E. M. see Juergenson, Elwood M.
Juergenson, Edward M. see Juergenson, Elwood M.

Juergenson, Elwood M.
xJuergenson, E. M.
Handbook of Livestock Equipment. Interstate.
xJuergenson, Edward M.
ed. Approved Practices in Beef Cattle
Production. Interstate.
xJuergenson, Elwood M.
Approved Practices in Dairying. Interstate.
Approved Practices in Sheep Production.
Interstate.

Juffe, Mel.
xJuffe, Mel.
Flash. Viking Pr.

Jugenheimer, Donald W.
xJugenheimer, Donald W.
Advertising Media. Grid Pub.
Basic Advertising. Grid Pub.

Jugenheimer, Robert W.
xJugenheimer, Robert W.
Corn: Improvement, Seed Production, & Uses.
Wiley.

Juglar, Clement.
xJuglar, Clement.
Brief History of Panics & Their Periodical
Occurrence in the United States. Kelley.
Des Crises Commerciales et De Leur Retour
Periodique En France, En Angleterre et Aux
Etats-Unis. B Franklin.

Juilland, Alphonse. see Juilland, Alphonse G.

Juilland, Alphonse G.
xJuilland, Alphonse.
The Linguistic Concept of Word: Analytic
Bibliography. Mouton.

Juilliard School of Music - New York. see Juilliard
School of Music, New York.

Juilliard School of Music, New York.
xJuilliard School of Music - New York.
Juilliard Report on Teaching the Literature &
Materials of Music. Greenwood.

Jukes, Andrew. see Jukes, Andrew John.

Jukes, Andrew John, 1815-1901
xJukes, Andrew.

Law of the Offerings. Kregel.

Julesz, Bela.
xJulesz, Bela.
Foundations of Cyclopean Perception. U of
Chicago Pr.

Julg, A. see Julg, Andre.

Julg, Andre, 1926-
xJulg, A.
Crystals As Giant Molecules. Springer-Verlag.

Julian, D. G. see Julian, Desmond Gareth.
Julian, Desmond G. see Julian, Desmond Gareth.

Julian, Desmond Gareth.
xJulian, D. G.
Cardiology. Macmillan.
xJulian, Desmond G.
Angina Pectoris. Churchill.

Julian, George W. see Julian, George Washington.

Julian, George Washington, 1817-1899
xJulian, George W.
Political Recollections, 1840 to 1872. Negro U
Pr.
Political Recollections 1840-1872. Arno.
Speeches on Political Questions, 1850-1868.
Negro U Pr.

Julian, Joseph.
xJulian, Joseph.
Social Problems. P-H.

Julich, Louise. see Julich, Louise Milam.

Julich, Louise Milam.
xJulich, Louise.
Roster of Revolutionary Soldiers & Patriots in
Alabama. Parchment Pr.

Julien, Robert M.
xJulien, Robert M.
A Primer of Drug Action. W H Freeman.

Julty, Sam.
xJulty, Sam.
How Your Car Works. Har-Row.

July, Robert W. see July, Robert William.

July, Robert William.
xJuly, Robert W.
A History of the African People. Scribner.
A History of the African People. Scribner.

Jumikis, Alfred R. see Jumikis, Alfreds R.

Jumikis, Alfreds R.
xJumikis, Alfred R.
Thermal Geotechnics. Rutgers U Pr.

Jump, John D. see Jump, John Davies.

Jump, John Davies, 1913-
xJump, John D.
Byron. Routledge & Kegan.
Matthew Arnold. Folcroft.
The Ode. Methuen Inc.

Jumper, S. see Jumper, Sidney R.

Jumper, Sidney R.
xJumper, S.
Economic Growth & Disparities: A World
View. P-H.

Juneau, Patricia S.
xJuneau, Patricia S.
Fundamentals of Nursing Care. Macmillan.
Medical-Surgical Nursing. Macmillan.

Junell, Joseph S.
xJunell, Joseph S.
Matters of Feeling: Values Education
Reconsidered. Phi Delta Kappa.

Jung, Anees.
xJung, Anees.
When a Place Becomes a Person. Advent Bk.
When a Place Becomes a Person. Intl Bk Dist.

Jung, C. G. see Jung, Carl Gustav.
Jung, C. J. see Jung, Carl Gustav.
Jung, Carl G. see Jung, Carl Gustav.

Jung, Carl Gustav, 1875-1961
xJung, C. G.

Analytical Psychology, Its Theory & Practice:
The Tavistock Lectures, 1935. Pantheon.
Psychological Types. Princeton U Pr.
Psychology & the Occult. Princeton U Pr.
The Undiscovered Self. Little.
The Undiscovered Self. NAL.
xJung, C. J.
Ulysses: A Monologue. Haskell.
xJung, Carl G.
Answer to Job. Princeton U Pr.
Dreams. Princeton U Pr.
Modern Man in Search of a Soul. HarBraceJ.
Portable Jung. Penguin.
The Portable Jung. Viking Pr.
Psyche & Symbol: A Selection from the
Writings of C. G. Jung. Doubleday.
The Psychoanalytic Years. Princeton U Pr.
Psychology & Education. Princeton U Pr.
Psychology & Religion. Yale U Pr.
Psychology of Dementia Praecox. Johnson
Repr.
The Psychology of Dementia Praecox.
Princeton U Pr.
Psychology of the Transference. Princeton U
Pr.
Synchronicity: An Acausal Connecting
Principle. Princeton U Pr.

Jung, Hwa Y. see Jung, Hwa Yol.

Jung, Hwa Yol.
xJung, Hwa Y.
Crisis of Political Understanding: A
Phenomenological Perspective in the Conduct
of Political Inquiry. Duquesne.

Jung, John.
xJung, John.
Contemporary Psychology Experiments:
Adaptations for Laboratory. Wiley.

Jung, Leo, 1892-
xJung, Leo.
Fallen Angels in Jewish & Christian &
Mohammedan Literature. Ktav.
Love & Life. Philos Lib.

Jung, Walter. see Jung, Walter G.

Jung, Walter G.
xJung, Walter.
IC Timer Cookbook. Sams.
xJung, Walter G.
IC Op-Amp Cookbook. Sams.

Junge, C. E. see Junge, Christian E.

Junge, Christian E.
xJunge, C. E.
Air Chemistry & Radioactivity. Acad Pr.

Junge, Douglas.
xJunge, Douglas.
Nerve & Muscle Excitation. Sinauer Assoc.

Jungermann, Eric, 1923-
xJungermann, Eric.
ed. Cationic Surfactants. Dekker.

Jungk, Robert, 1913-
xJungk, Robert.
Brighter Than a Thousand Suns: A Personal
History of the Atomic Scientists. HarBraceJ.
China & the West: Mankind Evolving.
Humanities.
The New Tyranny: How Nuclear Power
Enslaves Us. G&D.
The New Tyranny: How Nuclear Power
Enslaves Us. Warner Bks.

Jungmann, Josef. see Jungmann, Josef Andreas.

Jungmann, Josef Andreas, 1889-1975
xJungmann, Josef.
Christian Prayer Through the Centuries. Paulist
Pr.

Junior League Fayetteville, N. C. see Junior Service
League of Fayetteville.

Junior League of New Orleans.
xJunior League of New Orleans.
The Plantation Cookbook. Doubleday.

Junior League of San Francisco.
xJunior League of San Francisco.

San Francisco a la Carte: A Cookbook.
Doubleday.
Junior League of Shreveport.
xJunior League of Shreveport, Inc.
A Cook's Tour of Shreveport. Jr League
Shreveport.
Revel. Jr League Shreveport.
Junior League of Shreveport, Inc. *see* Junior League of
Shreveport.
Junior League of Spartanburg.
xJunior League of Spartanburg (S. C.), Inc.
The Cooking Kit. Jr League Spartanburg.
Junior League of Spartanburg (S. C.), Inc. *see* Junior
League of Spartanburg.
Junior League of the City of New York.
xJunior League of the City of New York.
New York Entertains. Doubleday.
Junior League of the City of Washington.
xJunior League of Washington.
The City of Washington: An Illustrated
History. Knopf.
Junior League of the Palm Beaches.
xJunior League of the Palm Beaches, Inc.
Palm Beach Entertains: Then & Now. Coward.
Junior League of the Palm Beaches, Inc. *see* Junior
League of the Palm Beaches.
Junior League of Washington. *see* Junior League of the
City of Washington.
Junior Service League of Fayetteville.
xJunior League Fayetteville, N. C.
The Carolina Collection. Wimmer Bks.
Juniper, Dean F. *see* Juniper, Dean Francis.
Juniper, Dean Francis.
xJuniper, Dean F.
Decision-Making for Schools & Colleges.
Pergamon.
Junker, Bill.
xJunker, Bill.
Freedom Bound. Broadman.
Junkins, Donald, 1931-
xJunkins, Donald.
ed. The Contemporary World Poets.
HarBraceJ.
Crossing by Ferry: Poems New & Selected. U
of Mass Pr.
Junod, Henri P. *see* Junod, Henri Philippe.
Junod, Henri Philippe, 1897-
xJunod, Henri P.
Bantu Heritage. Negro U Pr.
Junod, Violaine I.
xJunod, Violaine I.
ed. The Handbook of Africa. NYU Pr.
Jupo, Frank.
xJupo, Frank.
illus. Christmas Here, There & Everywhere.
Dodd.
Juran, Joseph M.
xJuran, Joseph M.
Quality Control Handbook. McGraw.
Quality Planning & Analysis: From Product
Development Through Use. McGraw.
Quality Planning & Analysis: From Product
Development Through Usage. McGraw.
Jurgensen, Barbara.
xJurgensen, Barbara.
How to Live Better on Less: A Guide for
Waste Watchers. Augsburg.
A Polluter's Garden of Verses. Keats.
The Prophets Speak Again: A Brief
Introduction to Old Testament Prophecy.
Augsburg.
Juris, Hervey A.
xJuris, Hervey A.
ed. The Shrinking Perimeter: Unionism &
Labor Relations in the Manufacturing Sector.
Lexington Bks.
Jurji, Edward J.
xJurji, Edward J.

ed. Great Religions of the Modern World.
Princeton U Pr.
Jurmain, Suzanne.
xJurmain, Suzanne.
From Trunk to Tail: Elephants Legendary &
Real. HarBraceJ.
Jurs, Peter C.
xJurs, Peter C.
Chemical Applications of Pattern Recognition.
Wiley.
Jusserand, J. J. *see* Jusserand, Jean Adrien Antoine Jules.
Jusserand, Jean Adrien Antoine Jules, 1855-1932
xJusserand, J. J.
English Essays from a French Pen. Century
Bookbindery.
xJusserand, Jean J.
English Essays from a French Pen. AMS Pr.
English Novel in the Time of Shakespeare.
AMS Pr.
Literary History of the English People. Arno.
Literary History of the English People. R West.
Jusserand, Jean J. *see* Jusserand, Jean Adrien Antoine
Jules.
Just, Ward. *see* Just, Ward S.
Just, Ward S.
xJust, Ward.
Honor, Power, Riches, Fame, & the Love of
Women. Dutton.
Juster, F. Thomas. *see* Juster, Francis Thomas.
Juster, Francis Thomas.
xJuster, F. Thomas.
ed. Education, Income & Human Behavior.
Natl Bur Econ Res.
Juster, Norton, 1929-
xJuster, Norton.
The Dot & the Line: A Romance in Lower
Mathematics. Random.
Justice, Blair.
xJustice, Blair.
The Abusing Family. Human Sci Pr.
The Broken Taboo: Sex in the Family. Human
Sci Pr.
Justice, Donald. *see* Justice, Donald Rodney.
Justice, Donald Rodney, 1925-
xJustice, Donald.
Selected Poems. Atheneum.
The Summer Anniversaries. Columbia U Pr.
Justice, Jennifer. *see* Justice, Jennifer L.
Justice, Jennifer L.
xJustice, Jennifer.
The Tiger. Watts.
Justice, William M.
xJustice, William M.
Our Visited Planet. Word Serv.
Justin, Jules J.
xJustin, Jules J.
How to Manage with a Union. Van Nos
Reinhold.
Justman, Joseph, 1909-
xJustman, Joseph.
Theories of Secondary Education in the United
States. AMS Pr.
Justus, May, 1898-
xJustus, May.
Eben & the Rattlesnake. Garrard.
Surprise for Perky Pup. Garrard.
xJustus, May T.
Complete Peddler's Pack: Games, Songs,
Rhymes, & Riddles from Mountain Folklore.
U of Tenn Pr.
Justus, May T. *see* Justus, May.
Juszli, Frank L.
xJuszli, Frank L.
Elementary Technical Mathematics. P-H.
Elementary Technical Mathematics with
Calculus. P-H.
Juurmaa, Jyrki.
xJuurmaa, Jyrki.

Ability Structure & Loss of Vision. Am Foun
Blind.
Juviler, Peter H.
xJuviler, Peter H.
Revolutionary Law & Order: Politics & Social
Change in the USSR. Free Pr.
Juvinall, Robert C.
xJuvinall, Robert C.
Engineering Considerations of Stress, Strain, &
Strength. McGraw.
Kaam, Adrian L. Van. *see* Van Kaam, Adrian L.
Kaam, Adrian van. *see* Van Kaam, Adrian.
Kaatz, Evelyn.
xKaatz, Evelyn.
Race Car Driver. Little.
Kaayk, J.
xKaayk, Jan.
Education, Estrangement & Adjustment: A
Study Among Pupils & School Leavers in
Bukumbi, a Rural Community in Tanzania:
Change & Continuity in Africa. Mouton.
Kaayk, Jan. *see* Kaayk, J.
Kabaservice, Thomas P.
xKabaservice, Thomas P.
Applied Microelectronics. West Pub.
Kabbe, Fred.
xKabbe, Frederick.
Chemistry, Energy, & Human Ecology. HM.
Kabbe, Frederick. *see* Kabbe, Fred.
Kabdebo, Thomas.
xKabdebo, Thomas.
Diplomat in Exile: Francis Pulszky's Political
Activities in England, 1849-1860. East Eur
Quarterly.
Kabir, P. K.
xKabir, P. K.
ed. Development of Weak Interaction Theory.
Gordon.
Kabler, Ciel D. *see* Kabler, Ciel Dunne.
Kabler, Ciel Dunne.
xKabler, Ciel D.
Telecommunications & the Church. Multi
Media.
Kabrisky, Matthew.
xKabrisky, Matthew.
A Proposed Model for Visual Information
Processing in the Human Brain. U of Ill Pr.
Kac, Michael B.
xKac, Michael B.
Corepresentation of Grammatical Structure. U
of Minn Pr.
Kachru, Braj B.
xKachru, Braji B.
ed. Aspects of Sociolinguistics in South Asia.
Mouton.
Kachru, Braji B. *see* Kachru, Braj B.
Kacmarek, Robert M.
xKacmarek, Robert M.
The Essentials of Respiratory Therapy. Year
Bk Med.
Kaczkowski, Henry.
xKaczkowski, Henry.
Counseling & Psychology in Elementary
Schools. C C Thomas.
Kadalie, Clements, 1896-1951
xKadalie, Clements.
My Life & the I. C. U.: The Autobiography of
a Black Trade Unionist in South Africa.
Biblio Dist.
My Life & the I. C. U.: The Autobiography of
a Black Trade Unionist in South Africa.
Humanities.
Kadanoff, L. P. *see* Kadanoff, Leo P.
Kadanoff, Leo P.
xKadanoff, L. P.

Quantum Statistical Mechanics: Green's
Function Methods in Equilibrium &
Non-Equilibrium Problems.
Benjamin-Cummings.
Kadans, Joseph M.
xKadans, Joseph N.
Encyclopedia of Fruits, Vegetables, Nuts &
Seeds for Healthful Living. P-H.
Encyclopedia of Fruits, Vegetables, Nuts &
Seeds for Healthful Living. P-H.
Kadans, Joseph N. *see* Kadans, Joseph M.
Kadar, Bela, 1934-
xKadar, Bela.
Problems of Economic Growth in Latin
America. St Martin.
Kadel, Thomas E.
xKadel, Thomas E.
ed. Growth in Ministry. Fortress.
Kadel, William H.
xKadel, William H.
Prayers for Every Need. John Knox.
Kadesch, Robert R. *see* Kadesch, Robert Rudstone.
Kadesch, Robert Rudstone.
xKadesch, Robert R.
Math Menagerie. Har-Row.
Kadic, Ante.
xKadic, Ante.
Contemporary Serbian Literature. Mouton.
Kadish, Mortimer R. *see* Kadish, Mortimer Raymond.
Kadish, Mortimer Raymond.
xKadish, Mortimer R.
Discretion to Disobey: A Study of Lawful
Departures from Legal Rules. Stanford U Pr.
Kado, Clarence I.
xKado, Clarence I.
Principles & Techniques in Plant Virology. Van
Nos Reinhold.
Kadon, Ann.
xKadon, Ann.
Successful Public Relations Techniques.
Modern Schls.
Kadowaki, J. K. *see* Kadowaki, Kakichi.
Kadowaki, Kakichi, 1926-
xKadowaki, J. K.
Zen & the Bible: A Priest's Experience.
Routledge & Kegan.
Kadt, Emanuel De. *see* De Kadt, Emanuel.
Kaduck, John. *see* Kaduck, John M.
Kaduck, John M.
xKaduck, John.
World War II German Collectibles: Illustrated
Price Guide. Wallace-Homestead.
Kadushin, Alfred.
xKadushin, Alfred.
Adopting Older Children. Columbia U Pr.
Child Welfare Services. Macmillan.
The Social Work Interview. Columbia U Pr.
Supervision in Social Work. Columbia U Pr.
Kadushin, Max, 1895-
xKadushin, Max.
Rabbinic Mind. Bloch.
Worship & Ethics: A Study in Rabbinic
Judaism. Bloch.
Worship & Ethics: A Study in Rabbinic
Judaism. Greenwood.
Kael, Pauline.
xKael, Pauline.
Deeper into Movies. Little.
I Lost It at the Movies. Little.
Reeling. Little.
Reeling. Warner Bks.
When the Lights Go Down. HR&W.
Kaempfer, Engelbert.
xKaempfer, Englebert.
History of Japan: Together with a Description
of the Kingdom of Siam, 1690-92. AMS Pr.
Kaempfer, Englebert. *see* Kaempfer, Engelbert.
Kaempffer, F. A.
xKaempffer, F. A.

Concepts in Quantum Mechanics. Acad Pr.
Kaempffert, Waldemar. *see* Kaempffert, Waldemar
Bernhard.
Kaempffert, Waldemar B. *see* Kaempffert, Waldemar
Bernhard.
Kaempffert, Waldemar Bernhard, 1877-1956
xKaempffert, Waldemar.
A Popular History of American Invention. R
West.
xKaempffert, Waldemar B.
ed. A Popular History of American Invention.
AMS Pr.
Kaeppler, Adrienne L. *see* Kaeppler, Adrienne Lois.
Kaeppler, Adrienne Lois.
xKaeppler, Adrienne L.
ed. Cook Voyage Artifacts in Leningrad, Berne
& Florence Museums. Bishop Mus.
ed. Cook Voyage Artifacts in Leningrad, Berne,
& Florence Museums. U of Wash Pr.
Kaestle, C. F. *see* Kaestle, Carl F.
Kaestle, Carl F.
xKaestle, C. F.
Education & Social Change in Nineteenth
Century Massachusetts. Cambridge U Pr.
xKaestle, Carl F.
Joseph Lancaster & the Monitorial School
Movement: A Documentary History. Tchrs
Coll.
Kaestner, Dorothy.
xKaestner, Dorothy.
Bargello Antics. Scribner.
Designs for Needlepoint & Latch Hook Rugs.
Scribner.
Four Way Bargello. Scribner.
Needlepoint Bargello. Scribner.
Kafka, Francis J.
xKafka, Francis J.
Hand Decoration of Fabrics. Peter Smith.
How to Clothbind a Paperback Book: A
Step-by-Step Guide for Beginners. Dover.
Linoleum Block Printing. Dover.
Linoleum Block Printing. Peter Smith.
Kafka, Franz, 1883-1924
xKafka, Franz.
Castle. Knopf.
Castle. Modern Lib.
The Castle. Random.
The Castle. Schocken.
The Complete Stories. Schocken.
The Great Wall of China: Stories &
Reflections. Schocken.
I Am a Memory Come Alive: Autobiographical
Writings. Schocken.
Letter to His Father: Brief an Den Vater.
Schocken.
Letters to Felice. Schocken.
Letters to Friends, Family, & Editors.
Schocken.
Letters to Milena. Schocken.
Kagan, D. *see* Kagan, Donald.
Kagan, Donald.
xKagan, D.
Problems in Ancient History. Macmillan.
xKagan, Donald.
The Archidamian War. Cornell U Pr.
Problems in Ancient History. Macmillan.
The Western Heritage. Macmillan.
Kagan, Henri.
xKagan, Henri.
Organic Stereochemistry. Halsted Pr.
Kagan, Jerome.
xKagan, Jerome.

Infancy: Its Place in Human Development.
Harvard U Pr.
Personality Development. HarBraceJ.
Psychology: An Introduction. HarBraceJ.
Psychology & Education: An Introduction.
HarBraceJ.
Understanding Children: Behavior, Motives, &
Thought. HarBraceJ.
Kagan, Richard L., 1943-
xKagan, Richard L.
Students & Society in Early Modern Spain.
Johns Hopkins.
Kagan-Kans, Eva.
xKagan-Kans, Eva.
Hamlet & Don Quixote: Turgenev's
Ambivalent Vision. Mouton.
Kaganoff, Benzion C.
xKaganoff, Benzion C.
A Dictionary of Jewish Names & Their
History. Schocken.
Kagawa, Toyohiko, 1888-1960
xKagawa, Toyohiko.
Meditations. Greenwood.
Kagel, Sam.
xKagel, Sam.
Anatomy of a Labor Arbitration. BNA.
Kagen, Sergius.
xKagen, Sergius.
On Studying Singing. Dover.
Kagiwada, H. *see* Kagiwada, Harriet H.
Kagiwada, Harriet H.
xKagiwada, H.
Integral Equations via Imbedding Methods.
A-W.
xKagiwada, Harriet H.
Multiple Scattering Processes: Inverse &
Direct. A-W.
Kagle, Stephen. *see* Kagle, Steven E.
Kagle, Steven E.
xKagle, Stephen.
American Diary Literature. Twayne.
Kagler, S. H. *see* Kagler, Siegfried Hermann.
Kagler, Siegfried Hermann.
xKagler, S. H.
Spectroscopic & Chromatographic Analysis of
Mineral Oil. Halsted Pr.
Kagwa, A. *see* Kagwa, Apolo.
Kagwa, Apolo.
xKagwa, A.
Customs of the Baganda. AMS Pr.
Kagy, Frederick D.
xKagy, Frederick D.
Graphic Arts. Goodheart.
Kahan, Arcadius.
xKahan, Arcadius.
Industrial Labor in the USSR. Pergamon.
Kahan, Ellen H. *see* Kahan, Ellen House.
Kahan, Ellen House.
xKahan, Ellen H.
Cooking Activities for the Retarded Child.
Abingdon.
Kahan, Jerome H.
xKahan, Jerome H.
Security in the Nuclear Age: Developing U.S.
Strategic Arms Policy. Brookings.
Kahan, Stuart.
xKahan, Stuart.
Do I Really Need a Lawyer?. Chilton.
The Expectant Father's Survival Kit. Monarch
Pr.
Expectant Father's Survival Kit. Sovereign Bks.
For Divorced Fathers Only. Monarch Pr.
For Divorced Fathers Only. Sovereign Bks.
Kahane, Howard, 1928-
xKahane, Howard.

Logic & Contemporary Rhetoric. Wadsworth Pub.

Logic & Contemporary Rhetoric: The Use of Reason in Everyday Life. Wadsworth Pub.

Kahaner, Larry.
xKahaner, Larry.
Audio & Video Interference Cures. Hayden.

Kahin, George M. see Kahin, George McTurnan.

Kahin, George McTurnan.
xKahin, George M.
Asian-African Conference, Bandung, Indonesia, April 1955. Kennikat.

Kahl, Guenter. see Kahl, Gunter.

Kahl, Gunter, 1936-
xKahl, Guenter.
Biochemistry of Wounded Plant Tissues. De Gruyter.

Kahl, Joseph A. see Kahl, Joseph Alan.

Kahl, Joseph Alan, 1923-
xKahl, Joseph A.
The Measurement of Modernism: A Study of Values in Brazil & Mexico. U of Tex Pr.

Kahl, M. P.
xKahl, M. P.
Wonders of Storks. Dodd.

Kahl, Virginia.
xKahl, Virginia.
illus. Giants, Indeed!. Scribner.
illus. Gunhilde & the Halloween Spell. Scribner.
illus. How Do You Hide a Monster. Scribner.
illus. How Many Dragons Are Behind the Door ?. Scribner.

Kahlbaum, K. L., 1828-1899
xKahlbaum, K. L.
Catatonia. Johns Hopkins.

Kahler, Erich, 1885-
xKahler, Erich.
The Disintegration of Form in the Arts. Braziller.
The Germans. Princeton U Pr.
Out of the Labyrinth: Essays in Clarification. Braziller.
Rallying Idea. Unicorn Pr.

Kahmen, Volker, 1939-
xKahmen, Volker.
Art History of Photography. Viking Pr.

Kahn, Alfred J., 1919-
xKahn, Alfred J.
Neighborhood Information Centers: A Study & Some Proposals. Univ Bk Serv.
Not for the Poor Alone: European Social Services. Temple U Pr.
Planning Community Services for Children in Trouble. Columbia U Pr.
Social Policy & Social Services. Random.
Theory & Practice of Social Planning. Russell Sage.

Kahn, C. H. see Kahn, Charles Harry.

Kahn, Charles H. see Kahn, Charles Harry.

Kahn, Charles Harry, 1921-
xKahn, C. H.
Business & Professional Income Under Personal Income Tax. Princeton U Pr.
xKahn, Charles H.
Money Makes Sense. Pitman Learning.
Using Dollars & Sense. Pitman Learning.

Kahn, David, 1930-
xKahn, David.
Hitler's Spies: German Military Intelligence in World War II. Macmillan.

Kahn, Deborah.
xKahn, Deborah.
ed. The Handspun Project Book. Select Bks.

Kahn, Donald W., 1935-
xKahn, Donald W.
Topology: An Introduction to the Point-Set & Algebraic Areas. Krieger.

Kahn, Douglas A.
xKahn, Douglas A.

Corporate Taxation & Taxation of Partnerships & Partners. West Pub.

Kahn, E. J. see Kahn, Ely Jacques.

Kahn, Edgar A.
xKahn, Edgar A.
Journal of a Neurosurgeon. C C Thomas.

Kahn, Ely J. see Kahn, Ely Jacques.

Kahn, Ely Jacques, 1916-
xKahn, E. J.
About the New Yorker & Me: A Sentimental Journal. Putnam.
Far-Flung & Footloose: Pieces from the New Yorker 1937-1978. Putnam.
Georgia from Rabun Gap to Tybee Light. Cherokee.
xKahn, Ely J.
Who, Me?. Arno.

Kahn, F. see Kahn, Frank J.

Kahn, Frank J.
xKahn, F.
ed. Documents of American Broadcasting. P-H.

Kahn, Gilbert.
xKahn, Gilbert.
Progressive Filing. McGraw.
Progressive Filing. McGraw.

Kahn, Harold L.
xKahn, Harold L.
Monarchy in the Emperor's Eyes: Image & Reality in the Ch'ien-Lung Reign. Harvard U Pr.

Kahn, Herman.
xKahn, Herman.
The Japanese Challenge: The Success & Failure of Economic Success. Morrow.
The Japanese Challenge: The Success & Failure of Economic Success. T Y Crowell.
On Thermonuclear War. Greenwood.

Kahn, Itzchock.
xKahn, Yitzhak.
Portraits of Yiddish Writers. Vantage.

Kahn, J. H. see Kahn, Jack H.

Kahn, Jack. see Kahn, Jack H.

Kahn, Jack H.
xKahn, J. H.
Human Growth & the Development of Personality. Pergamon.
xKahn, Jack.
Human Growth & the Development of Personality. Pergamon.

Kahn, Joan.
xKahn, Joan.
ed. Some Things Dark & Dangerous. Avon.
ed. Some Things Fierce & Fatal. Avon.
ed. Some Things Strange & Sinister. Avon.
ed. Some Things Strange & Sinister. Har-Row.

Kahn, Judd, 1940-
xKahn, Judd.
Imperial San Francisco: Politics & Planning in an American City, 1897-1906. U of Nebr Pr.

Kahn, Kathy.
xKahn, Kathy.
Hillbilly Women. Avon.

Kahn, Lothar.
xKahn, Lothar.
Conversational German One. D Van Nostrand.
Insight & Action: The Life & Work of Lion Feuchtwanger. Fairleigh Dickinson.

Kahn, Margaret.
xKahn, Margaret.
Children of the Jinn: In Search of the Kurds & Their Country. Seaview Bks.
Children of the Jinn: In Search of the Kurds & Their Country. Wideview Bks.

Kahn, Mark.
xKahn, Mark.
Day I Died. Intl Pubns Serv.

Kahn, Morton C. see Kahn, Morton Charles.

Kahn, Morton Charles, 1894-
xKahn, Morton C.

Djuka, the Bush Negroes of Dutch Guiana. AMS Pr.

Kahn, Paul, 1916-
xKahn, Paul.
How to Open Your Classroom: A Systems Approach to Open Education. Innovative Ed.
A Practical Guide to Performance-Based Instruction: How to Develop the Skills of Attaining Classroom Objectives. Innovative Ed.
A Practical Guide to Positive Reinforcement: How to Develop the Skills of Behavior Modification in the Classroom. Innovative Ed.
A Practical Guide to Teaching in Four Dimensions: How to Develop the Skills of Reaching the Whole Child. Innovative Ed.
What to Teach in the Open Classroom: Developing an Integrated Curriculum Based on Environmental Themes. Innovative Ed.

Kahn, R. L. see Kahn, Robert Louis.

Kahn, Robert. see Kahn, Robert Leon.

Kahn, Robert Leon.
xKahn, Robert.
Power Skills in Science II. McGraw.

Kahn, Robert Louis.
xKahn, R. L.
Dynamics of Interviewing: Theory, Technique & Cases. Wiley.

Kahn, Roger.
xKahn, Roger.
Boys of Summer. Har-Row.
The Boys of Summer. NAL.

Kahn, Ruth E.
xKahn, Ruth E.
My Daddy ABC's. Denison.

Kahn, Samuel, 1898-
xKahn, Samuel.
Anxieties, Phobias & Fears. Philos Lib.
Child Guidance. Philos Lib.
Psychodrama Explained. Philos Lib.

Kahn, Sanders A.
xKahn, Sanders A.
Real Estate Appraisal & Investment. Wiley.

Kahn, Sholem J. see Kahn, Sholom Jacob.

Kahn, Sholom J. see Kahn, Sholom Jacob.

Kahn, Sholom Jacob, 1918-
xKahn, Sholem J.
ed. Whole Loaf: Stories from Israel. Vanguard.
xKahn, Sholom J.
Mark Twain's Mysterious Stranger: A Study of the Manuscript Texts. U of Mo Pr.

Kahn, Yitzhak. see Kahn, Itzchock.

Kahn-Freund, Otto, Sir, 1900-
xKahn-Freund, Otto.
Labour Relations: Heritage & Adjustment. Oxford U Pr.
A Source-Book on French Law: System, Methods, Outlines of Contract. Oxford U Pr.

Kaho, Elizabeth. see Kaho, Elizabeth Ellen.

Kaho, Elizabeth Ellen, 1907-
xKaho, Elizabeth.
Analysis of the Study of Music Literature in Selected American Colleges. AMS Pr.

Kahr, Madlyn M. see Kahr, Madlyn Millner.

Kahr, Madlyn Millner.
xKahr, Madlyn M.
Velazquez: The Art of Painting. Har-Row.

Kahrl, W. see Kahrl, William L.

Kahrl, William L.
xKahrl, W.
Introduction to Modern Food & Beverage Service. P-H.
xKahrl, William L.

Advanced Modern Food & Beverage Service. P-H.

Modern Food Service Planning. Lebhar Friedman.

Planning & Operating a Successful Food Service Operation. Lebhar Friedman.

Kail, Robert, 1950-
xKail, Robert.
The Development of Memory in Children. W H Freeman.
Swastika. Belmont-Tower.

Kailath, Thomas.
xKailath, Thomas.
Linear Systems. P-H.

Kaimann, R. A. *see* Kaimann, Richard A.

Kaimann, Richard A.
xKaimann, R. A.
Structured Information Files. Wiley.

Kain, John F.
xKain, John F.
Housing Markets & Racial Discrimination: A Microeconomic Analysis. Natl Bur Econ Res.

Kain, Richard M. *see* Kain, Richard Morgan.

Kain, Richard Morgan, 1908-
xKain, Richard M.
Susan L. Mitchell. Bucknell U Pr.

Kains, E. G. *see* Kains, Maurice Grenville.

Kains, M. G. *see* Kains, Maurice Grenville.

Kains, Maurice Grenville, 1868-1946
xKains, E. G.
The Original Victory Garden Book. Stein & Day.
xKains, M. G.
Gardening for Young People. Stein & Day.

Kaiser. *see* Kaiser, Dale E.

Kaiser, Arthur. *see* Kaiser, Artur.

Kaiser, Artur, 1943-
xKaiser, Arthur.
Questioning Techniques. Hunter Hse.
xKaiser, Artur.
Questioning Techniques. Hunter Hse.

Kaiser, Charles.
xKaiser, Charles.
Tourism Planning & Development. CBI Pub.

Kaiser, Dale E.
xKaiser.
Responsibilities of the School Business Administrator in Small School Districts. Assn Sch Busn.

Kaiser, E. T. *see* Kaiser, Emil Thomas.

Kaiser, Edgar P.
xKaiser, Edgar P.
How to Respond to the Latter Day Saints. Concordia.

Kaiser, Emil Thomas.
xKaiser, E. T.
Radical Ions. Krieger.

Kaiser, Hans E. *see* Kaiser, Hans Elmar.

Kaiser, Hans Elmar, 1928-
xKaiser, Hans E.
Neoplasms - Comparative Pathology of Growth in Animals, Plants & Man. Williams & Wilkins.

Kaiser, Harvey H., 1936-
xKaiser, Harvey H.
The Building of Cities: Development & Conflict. Cornell U Pr.

Kaiser, Karl, 1934-
xKaiser, Karl.
Europe & the United States: The Future of the Relationship. Columbia Bks.

Kaiser, Richard.
xKaiser, Richard L.
The Mending Heart. Harvest Hse.

Kaiser, Richard L. *see* Kaiser, Richard.

Kaiser, Robert. *see* Kaiser, Robert G.

Kaiser, Robert G., 1943-
xKaiser, Robert.
Russia from the Inside. Dutton.
xKaiser, Robert G.

Cold Winter, Cold War. Stein & Day.

Kaiser, Rolf, 1909-
xKaiser, Rolf.
ed. Medieval English: An Old English & Middle English Anthology. Scholarly.

Kaiser, W.
xKaiser, W.
ed. Two-Way Cable Television: Experiences with Pilot Projects in North America, Japan, & Europe. Proceedings of a Symposium Held in Munich, Germany, April 27-29, 1977. Springer-Verlag.

Kaiser, Walter. *see* Kaiser, Walter Jacob.

Kaiser, Walter C.
xKaiser, Walter C.
Classical Evangelical Essays in Old Testament Interpretation. Baker Bk.
Ecclesiastes: Total Life. Moody.

Kaiser, Walter Jacob.
xKaiser, Walter.
Praisers of Folly: Erasmus, Rabelais, Shakespeare. Harvard U Pr.

Kaissling, B. *see* Kaissling, Brigitte.

Kaissling, Brigitte.
xKaissling, B.
Structural Analysis of the Rabbit Kidney. Springer-Verlag.

Kajima, Morinosuke.
xKajima, Morinosuke.
Modern Japan's Foreign Policy. C E Tuttle.

Kakalik, James. *see* Kakalik, James S.

Kakalik, James S.
xKakalik, James.
The Private Police: Security & Danger. Crane-Russak Co.

Kakhun. *see* Kakhun, Sok.

Kakhun, Sok, 13th cent.
xKakhun.
Lives of Eminent Korean Monks: The Haedong Kosung Chon. Harvard U Pr.

Kakkar, N. K.
xKakkar, N. K.
Workers' Education in India. Verry.

Kakonen, Ulla, 1945-
xKakonen, Ulla.
Natural Cooking the Finnish Way. Times Bks.

Kakonis, Thomas E.
xKakonis, Tom E.
A Practical Guide to Police Report Writing. McGraw.

Kakonis, Tom E. *see* Kakonis, Thomas E.

Kalafatich. *see* Kalafatich, Audrey J.

Kalafatich, Audrey J.
xKalafatich.
Approaches to the Care of Adolescents. ACC.
xKalafatich, Audrey J.
Maternal & Child Health: A Handbook for Nurses. Littlefield.

Kalakaua. *see* Kalakaua, David.

Kalakaua, David, King of Hawaii, 1836-1891
xKalakaua.
The Legends & Myths of Hawaii: The Fables & Folk-Lore of a Strange People. C E Tuttle.

Kalakian, Leonard H.
xKalakian, Leonard H.
Introduction to Physical Education: A Humanistic Perspective. Allyn.

Kalan, Robert.
xKalan, Robert.
Blue Sea. Greenwillow.
Rain. Greenwillow.

Kalat, James W.
xKalat, James W.
ed. Foundations of Experimental Psychology. Mss Info.

Kalb, Jonah.
xKalb, Jonah.

The Easy Baseball Book. HM.
The Easy Hockey Book. HM.
The Goof That Won the Pennant. HM.
How to Play Baseball Better Than You Did Last Season. Macmillan.

Kalbag, R. M.
xKalbag, R. M.
Cerebral Venous Thrombosis: With Special Reference to Primary Aseptic Thrombosis. Oxford U Pr.

Kaldis, E.
xKaldis, E.
ed. Current Topics in Materials Science. Elsevier.

Kaldor, Mary.
xKaldor, Mary.
The Disintegrating West. Hill & Wang.

Kaldor, Nicholas, 1908-
xKaldor, Nicholas.
An Expenditure Tax. Greenwood.
Further Essays on Economic Theory. Holmes & Meier.
Strategic Factors in Economic Development. NY Sch Indus Rel.

Kaldy, Gyula, 1838-1901
xKaldy, Gyula.
History of Hungarian Music. Haskell.
History of Hungarian Music. Scholarly.

Kalechofsky, Roberta.
xKalechofsky, Roberta.
George Orwell. Ungar.
Orestes in Progress. Micah Pubns.
Stephen's Passion. Micah Pubns.

Kalectaca, Milo.
xKalectaca, Milo.
Lessons in Hopi. U of Ariz Pr.

Kalet, Beth.
xKalet, Beth.
Kris Kristofferson. Music Sales.

Kalich, Robert. *see* Kalich, Robert Allen.

Kalich, Robert Allen, 1937-
xKalich, Robert.
The Handicapper. Crown.
The Handicapper. Urizen Bks.

Kalin, Martin G.
xKalin, Martin G.
The Utopian Flight from Unhappiness: Freud Against Marx on Social Progress. Littlefield.
The Utopian Flight from Unhappiness: Freud Against Marx on Social Progress. Nelson-Hall.

Kalina, Sigmund.
xKalina, Sigmund.
The House That Nature Built. Lothrop.
How to Make a Dinosaur. Lothrop.
How to Sharpen Your Study Skills. Lothrop.

Kalinsky, G. *see* Kalinsky, George.

Kalinsky, George.
xKalinsky, G.
Take It All. Macmillan.

Kalir, Joseph.
xKalir, Joseph.
Introduction of Judaism. U Pr of Amer.

Kalisch, Beatrice J., 1943-
xKalisch, Beatrice J.
Child Abuse & Neglect: An Annotated Bibliography. Greenwood.

Kalisch, Philip A. *see* Kalisch, Philip Arthur.

Kalisch, Philip Arthur.
xKalisch, Philip A.
The Advance of American Nursing. Little.

Kalish, Richard A.
xKalish, Richard A.
Guide to Effective Study. Brooks-Cole.
The Later Years: Social Applications of Gerontology. Brooks-Cole.
The Psychology of Human Behavior. Brooks-Cole.

Kaliski, Burton S.
xKaliski, Burton S.

Business Mathematics. HarBraceJ.

Kalkman, Marion E.
xKalkman, Markian E.
New Dimensions in Mental Health-Psychiatric Nursing. McGraw.
Kalkman, Markian E. *see* Kalkman, Marion E.
Kall, P. *see* Kall, Peter.
Kall, Peter.
xKall, P.
Stochastic Linear Programming. Springer-Verlag.
Kalla-Bishop, P. M.
xKalla-Bishop, P. M.
Mediterranean Island Railways. Kelley.
Kallard, T. *see* Kallard, Thomas.
Kallard, Thomas.
xKallard, T.
Laser Art & Optical Transforms. Optosonic Pr.
xKallard, Thomas.
ed. Liquid Crystal Devices. Optosonic Pr.
Kallas, Aino. *see* Kallas, Aino (Krohn).
Kallas, Aino (Krohn), 1878-1956
xKallas, Aino.
The White Ship: Estonian Tales. Folcroft.
xKallas, Aino J.
White Ship: Estonian Tales. Arno.
Kallas, Aino J. *see* Kallas, Aino (Krohn).
Kallas, James. *see* Kallas, James G.
Kallas, James G.
xKallas, James.
Layman's Introduction to Christian Thought. Westminster.
Story of Paul. Augsburg.
Kallay, Miklos, 1887-
xKallay, Miklos.
Hungarian Premier: A Personal Account of a Nation's Struggle in the Second World War. Greenwood.
Kallberg, Sture.
xKallberg, Sture.
Off the Middle Way: Report from a Swedish Village. Irvington
Kallen, Horace M. *see* Kallen, Horace Meyer.
Kallen, Horace Meyer, 1882-
xKallen, Horace M.
Creativity, Imagination, Logic: Meditations for the Eleventh Hour. Gordon.
Cultural Pluralism & the American Idea: An Essay in Social Philosophy. U of Pa Pr.
The Decline & Rise of the Consumer: A Philosophy of Consumer Cooperation. Arno.
Frontiers of Hope. Arno.
Patterns of Progress. Arno.
A Study of Liberty. Greenwood.
Toward a Philosophy of the Seas. U Pr of Va.
Kallen, Lucille.
xKallen, Lucille.
Introducing C. B. Greenfield. Ballantine.
Introducing C. B. Greenfield. Crown.
Kallenbach, Joseph E. *see* Kallenbach, Joseph Ernest.
Kallenbach, Joseph Ernest, 1903-
xKallenbach, Joseph E.
Federal Cooperation with the States Under the Commerce Clause. Greenwood.
Kallenberg, Olav.
xKallenberg, Olav.
Random Measures. Adler.
Kallich, Martin, 1918-
xKallich, Martin.
The Other End of the Egg: Religious Satire in "Gulliver's Travels". NYU Pr.
Psychological Milieu of Lytton Strachey. Coll & U Pr.
Kallman, Chester, 1921-
xKallman, Chester.
Absent & Present. Columbia U Pr.
Kalmanoff, Alan.
xKalmanoff, Alan.

Criminal Justice: Enforcement & Administration. Little.
Kalmanson, Kenneth.
xKalmanson, Kenneth.
Calculus: A Practical Approach. Worth.
Kalmar, Roberta.
xKalmar, Roberta.
Abortion: The Emotional Implications. Kendall-Hunt.
Child Abuse: Perspectives on Diagnosis, Treatment & Prevention. Kendall-Hunt.
Kalnein, Wend G. *see* Kalnein, Wend Graf.
Kalnein, Wend Graf.
xKalnein, Wend G.
Art & Architecture of the Eighteenth Century in France. Viking Pr.
Kalodner, Howard I.
xKalodner, Howard I.
ed. Limits of Justice: Courts' Role in School Desegregation. Ballinger Pub.
Kalokerinos, Archie.
xKalokerinos, Archie.
Australian Precious Opal. Arco.
Kalovstian, V. M. Der. *see* Der Kaloustian, V. M.
Kals, W. S.
xKals, W. S.
The Stargazer's Bible. Doubleday.
xKals, William S.
The Riddle of the Winds. Doubleday.
Kals, William S. *see* Kals, W. S.
Kalsner, Stanley, 1936-
xKalsner, Stanley.
Trends in Autonomic Pharmacology. Urban & S.
Kalstone, David.
xKalstone, David.
Five Temperaments: Elizabeth Bishop, Robert Lowell, James Merrill, Adrienne Rich, John Ashbery. Oxford U Pr.
Kalstone, Shirlee.
xKalstone, Shirlee.
The Complete Poodle Clipping & Grooming Book. Howell Bk.
First Aid for Dogs. Arco.
Kaltenbach, H. *see* Kaltenbach, Henry J.
Kaltenbach, Henry J.
xKaltenbach, H.
Master Guide to the Successful Handling of Condemnation Valuation. P-H.
Kaltenbach, M. *see* Kaltenbach, Martin.
Kaltenbach, Martin.
xKaltenbach, M.
ed. Cardiomyopathy & Myocardial Biopsy. Springer-Verlag.
Exercise Testing of Cardiac Patients. Williams & Wilkins.
Kalter, Joanmarie.
xKalter, Joanmarie.
Actors on Acting: Performing in Theatre & Film Today. Sterling.
Kalter, Robert J. *see* Kalter, Robert John.
Kalter, Robert John.
xKalter, Robert J.
ed. Energy Supply & Government Policy. Cornell U Pr.
Kaluger. *see* Kaluger, George.
Kaluger, George.
xKaluger.
Profiles in Human Development. Mosby.
xKaluger, George.
Human Development: The Span of Life. Mosby.
Reading & Learning Disabilities. Merrill.
Kalupahana, David J., 1933-
xKalupahana, David J.
Buddhist Philosophy: A Historical Analysis. U Pr of Hawaii.
Kalven, Harry. *see* Kalven, Harry Jr.
Kalven, Harry Jr.
xKalven, Harry.

Negro & the First Amendment. U of Chicago Pr.
Kalvoda, Robert.
xKalvoda, Robert.
Operational Amplifiers in Chemical Instrumentation. Halsted Pr.
Kalyanam, N. P., 1927-
xKalyanam, N. P.
Common Insects of India. Asia.
Kamada, Annelise.
xKamada, Annelise.
A Love So Bold. Warner Bks.
Kamakau, S. M. *see* Kamakau, Samuel Manaiakalani.
Kamakau, Samuel Manaiakalani, 1815-1876
xKamakau, S. M.
The Works of the People of Old: Na Hana A Ka Po'e Kahiko. Bishop Mus.
Kamal, K. L.
xKamal, K. L.
Democratic Politics in India. Verry.
Kamarck, Andrew M.
xKamarck, Andrew M.
The Tropics & Economic Development: A Provocative Inquiry into the Poverty of Nations. Johns Hopkins.
Kamath, M. V., 1921-
xKamath, M. V.
Philosophy of Death & Dying. Himalayan Intl Inst.
Kamath, S. H., 1932-
xKamath, S. H.
Clinical Biochemistry for Medical Technologists. Little.
Kamber, F. *see* Kamber, Franz.
Kamber, Franz.
xKamber, F.
Flat Manifolds. Springer-Verlag.
Kamen, Henry. *see* Kamen, Henry Arthur Francis.
Kamen, Henry Arthur Francis.
xKamen, Henry.
Spanish Inquisition. NAL.
Kamen, Ira, 1918-
xKamen, Ira.
Questions & Answers About Pay TV. Sams.
Kamen, Martin D. *see* Kamen, Martin David.
Kamen, Martin David, 1913-
xKamen, Martin D.
Primary Processes in Photosynthesis. Acad Pr.
Kamen-Kaye, Dorothy. *see* Kamen-Kaye, Dorothy Allers.
Kamen-Kaye, Dorothy Allers.
xKamen-Kaye, Dorothy.
Venezuelan Folkways: Twentieth-Century Survivals of Folk Beliefs, Customs, and Traditions of Caracas and the Venezuelan Countryside. Blaine Ethridge.
Kamenetsky, Ihor, 1927-
xKamenetsky, Ihor.
Nationalism and Human Rights: Processes of Modernization in the USSR. Libs Unl.
Kamenka, Eugene.
xKamenka, Eugene.
ed. Bureaucracy: The Career of a Concept. St Martin.
The Ethical Foundations of Marxism. Routledge & Kegan.
ed. Human Rights. St Martin.
ed. Law & Society: The Crisis in Legal Ideals. St Martin.
Kamenkovich, J. M. *see* Kamenkovich, Vladimir Moiseevich.
Kamenkovich, Vladimir Moiseevich.
xKamenkovich, J. M.
Fundamentals of Ocean Dynamics. Elsevier.
Kamerschen, David R.
xKamerschen, David R.
Economics. Cliffs.
Kamhi, D. J.
xKamhi, D. J.

Modern Hebrew: An Introductory Course. Oxford U Pr.

Kamien, Roger.
xKamien, Roger.
ed. Norton Scores: An Anthology for Listening. Norton.

Kamieniecki, Sheldon.
xKamieniecki, Sheldon.
Public Representation in Environmental Policymaking: The Case of Water Quality Management. Westview.

Kamil, Alan C.
xKamil, Alan C.
Mastering Psychology: A Guide to Brown-Herrnstein's Psychology. Little.

Kamil, Jill.
xKamil, Jill.
The Ancient Egyptians: How They Lived & Worked. Dufour.

Kamimoto, Hideo.
xKamimoto, Hideo.
Complete Guitar Repair. Music Sales.

Kaminetzky, Harold A.
xKaminetzky, Harold A.
ed. New Techniques & Concepts in Maternal & Fetal Medicine. Van Nos Reinhold.

Kaminkow, Marion. *see* Kaminkow, Marion J.

Kaminkow, Marion J.
xKaminkow, Marion.
ed. Mariners of the American Revolution. C E Tuttle.

Kamins, Barry.
xKamins, Barry.
The Social Studies Student Investigates the Criminal Justice System. Rosen Pr.

Kamins, James.
xKamins, James.
The Cookout Conspiracy. Ashley Bks.

Kaminski, Gerald.
xKaminski, Gerald.
Cassette Piece. Holmgangers.

Kaminskii, A. *see* Kaminskii, Aleksandr Aleksandrovich.

Kaminskii, Aleksandr Aleksandrovich.
xKaminskii, A.
Laser Crystals: Physics & Properties. Springer-Verlag.

Kaminsky, Alice R., 1923-
xKaminsky, Alice R.
Chaucer's "Troilus & Criseyde" & the Critics. Ohio U Pr.
George Henry Lewes As Literary Critic. Syracuse U Pr.

Kaminsky, Howard, 1924-
xKaminsky, Howard.
A History of the Hussite Revolution. U of Cal Pr.

Kaminsky, J. *see* Kaminsky, Jack.

Kaminsky, Jack.
xKaminsky, J.
Logic: A Philosophical Introduction. A-W.

Kaminsky, Laura J.
xKaminsky, Laura J.
ed. Nonprofit Repertory Theatre in North America, 1958-1975: A Bibliography & Indexes to the Playbill Collection of the Theatre Communications Group. Greenwood.

Kaminsky, Manfred.
xKaminsky, Manfred.
Atomic & Ionic Impact Phenomena on Metal Surfaces. Springer-Verlag.

Kaminsky, Marc, 1943-
xKaminsky, Marc.
What's Inside You It Shines Out of You. Horizon.

Kaminsky, Stuart. *see* Kaminsky, Stuart M.

Kaminsky, Stuart M.
xKaminsky, Stuart.

Bullet for a Star. BJ Pub Group.
Bullet for a Star. St Martin.
Coop. St Martin.
The Howard Hughes Affair. Charter Bks.
The Howard Hughes Affair. St Martin.
Murder on the Yellow Brick Road. Penguin.
Murder on the Yellow Brick Road. St Martin.
You Bet Your Life. St Martin.
xKaminsky, Stuart M.
ed. Ingmar Bergman: Essays in Criticism. Oxford U Pr.

Kamisar, Yale.
xKamisar, Yale.
Modern Criminal Procedure: Cases, Comments & Questions. West Pub.

Kamke, E. *see* Kamke, Erich.

Kamke, Erich, 1890-
xKamke, E.
Theory of Sets. Dover.

Kamman, Madelaine M.
xKamman, Madeleine.
When French Women Cook: A Gastronomic Memoir. Atheneum.

Kamman, Madeleine.
xKamman, Madeleine.
Dinner Against the Clock. Atheneum.

Kamman, Madeleine. *see* Kamman, Madelaine M.

Kamman, William F. *see* Kamman, William Frederic.

Kamman, William Frederic, 1885-
xKamman, William F.
Socialism in German American Literature. Hyperion Conn.

Kammash, Terry.
xKammash, Terry.
Fusion Reactor Physics: Principles & Technology. Ann Arbor Science.

Kammen, Michael. *see* Kammen, Michael G.

Kammen, Michael G.
xKammen, Michael.
The Past Before Us: Contemporary Historical Writing in the United States. Cornell U Pr.

Kammerer, Gladys M. *see* Kammerer, Gladys Marie.

Kammerer, Gladys Marie.
xKammerer, Gladys M.
British & American Child Welfare Services: A Comparative Study in Administration. Wayne St U Pr.

Kamoroff, Bernard.
xKamoroff, Bernard.
Small Time Operator: How to Start Your Own Small Business, Keep Your Books, Pay Your Taxes, & Stay Out of Trouble. Bell Springs Pub.

Kamp, Peter Van De. *see* Van De Kamp, Peter.

Kampe, Livia.
xKampe, Livia.
How to Learn Spanish the Easy Way. U Pr of Amer.

Kampelman, Max M., 1920-
xKampelman, Max M.
Communist Party vs the Cio: A Study in Power Politics. Arno.

Kampen, Irene.
xKampen, Irene.
Fear Without Childbirth. Lippincott.

Kampf, Avram.
xKampf, Avram.
Contemporary Synagogue Art: Developments in the United States, 1945-1965. UAHC.

Kampf, Louis.
xKampf, Louis.
On Modernism: The Prospects for Literature & Freedom. MIT Pr.

Kampffmeyer, Paul, 1864-
xKampffmeyer, Paul.
Changes in the Theory & Tactics of the German Social Democracy. AMS Pr.

Kampmann, Lothar.
xKampmann, Lothar.

Creating with Colored Paper. Van Nos Reinhold.

Kamrany, Nake M.
xKamrany, Nake M.
Economic Issues for the Eighties. Johns Hopkins.

Kan, Diana.
xKan, Diana.
The How & Why of Chinese Painting. Van Nos Reinhold.

Kan, Johnny.
xKan, Johnny.
Eight Immortal Flavors. Cal Living Bks.

Kanahele, George S.
xKanahele, George S.
ed. Hawaiian Music & Musicians: An Illustrated History. U Pr of Hawaii.

Kanawati, Naguib.
xKanawati, Naguib.
The Egyptian Administration in the Old Kingdom: Evidence on Its Economic Decline. Intl Schol Bk Serv.

Kanazawa, Hiroshi, 1935-
xKanazawa, Hiroshi.
Japanese Ink Painting: Early Zen Masterpieces. Kodansha.

Kandel, Abraham.
xKandel, Abraham.
Fuzzy Switching & Automata: Theory & Applications. Crane-Russak Co.

Kandel, Denise B. *see* Kandel, Denise Bystryn.

Kandel, Denise Bystryn.
xKandel, Denise B.
ed. Longitudinal Research on Drug Use: Empirical Findings & Methodological Issues. Halsted Pr.

Kandel, Eric R.
xKandel, Eric R.
Cellular Basis of Behavior: An Introduction to Behavioral Neurobiology. W H Freeman.

Kandel, I. L. *see* Kandel, Isaac Leon.

Kandel, Isaac L. *see* Kandel, Isaac Leon.

Kandel, Isaac Leon, 1881-
xKandel, I. L.
Cult of Uncertainty. Arno.
Examinations & Their Substitutes in the United States. Arno.
ed. Twenty-Five Years of American Education. Arno.
xKandel, Isaac L.
Comparative Education. Greenwood.
xKandel, Issac L.
The Impact of the War Upon American Education. Greenwood.

Kandel, Issac L. *see* Kandel, Isaac Leon.

Kandel, Robert S.
xKandel, Robert S.
Earth & Cosmos. Pergamon.

Kandinsky, Wassily, 1866-1944
xKandinsky, Wassily.
Concerning the Spiritual in Art. Dover.
Concerning the Spiritual in Art. Peter Smith.
Point & Line to Plane. Dover.

Kando, Thomas M., 1941-
xKando, Thomas M.
Leisure & Popular Culture in Transition. Mosby.

Kane, Basil G.
xKane, Basil G.
How to Play Soccer. G&D.

Kane, G. R.
xKane, G. R.
Instant Navigation. Aztex.

Kane, George.
xKane, George.
Middle English Literature: A Critical Study of the Romances, the Religious Lyrics, "Piers Plowman". Greenwood.

Kane, H. Victor.
xKane, H. Victor.

Devotions for Dieters. Judson.
Devotions for Dieters. Revell.
Kane, Henry.
xKane, Henry.
Laughter in the Alehouse. Penguin.
Tripoli Documents. PB.
The Tripoli Documents. S&S.
Kane, J. E. see Kane, John Edward.
Kane, Jack.
xKane, Jack.
Buzzard Bait. Bouregy.
Kane, John Edward.
xKane, J. E.
ed. Psychological Aspects of Physical
Education & Sport. Routledge & Kegan.
Kane, Joseph N. see Kane, Joseph Nathan.
Kane, Joseph Nathan.
xKane, Joseph N.
Nicknames & Sobriquets of U. S. Cities, States,
& Counties. Scarecrow.
Kane, Lawrence.
xKane, Lawrence.
Die Laughing. Doubleday.
Kane, Lucile M.
xKane, Lucile M.
Guide to the Care & Administration of
Manuscripts. AASLH.
Kane, Mary K. see Kane, Mary Kay.
Kane, Mary Kay.
xKane, Mary K.
Civil Procedure in a Nutshell. West Pub.
Kane, Philip F.
xKane, Philip F.
Characterization of Semiconductor Materials.
McGraw.
Kane, Robert M.
xKane, Robert M.
Air Transportation. Kendall Hunt.
Kane, Robert S.
xKane, Robert S.
Africa A to Z. Doubleday.
London A to Z. Doubleday.
Kane, Thomas A. see Kane, Thomas Aloysius.
Kane, Thomas Aloysius, 1915-
xKane, Thomas A.
Who Controls Me?: A Psychotheological
Reflection. Exposition.
Kane, Thomas S.
xKane, Thomas S.
Writing Prose: Techniques & Purposes. Oxford
U Pr.
Kane, William Everett.
xKane, William Everett.
Civil Strife in Latin America: A Legal History
of U.S. Involvement. Johns Hopkins.
Kaneko, Akimoto. see Kaneko, Akitomo.
Kaneko, Akitomo.
xKaneko, Akimoto.
Olympic Gymnastics. Sterling.
xKaneko, Akitomo.
Olympic Gymnastics. Sterling.
Kanes, Martin.
xKanes, Martin.
Balzac's Comedy of Words. Princeton U Pr.
Kanet, Roger E., 1936-
xKanet, Roger E.
Soviet & East European Foreign Policy: A
Bibliography of English- & Russian-Language
Publications 1967-1971. ABC-Clio.
ed. The Soviet Union & the Developing
Nations. Johns Hopkins.
Kanetzke, Howard W.
xKanetzke, Howard W.
Story of Cars. Raintree Child.
Kaneyuki, S. see Kaneyuki, Soji.
Kaneyuki, Soji, 1936-
xKaneyuki, S.

Homogeneous Bounded Domains & Siegel
Domains. Springer-Verlag.
Kanfer, Frederick H.
xKanfer, Frederick H.
ed. Helping People Change: A Textbook of
Methods. Pergamon.
Learning Foundations of Behavior Therapy.
Wiley.
Kanfer, Stefan.
xKanfer, Stefan.
The Eighth Sin. Berkley Pub.
Kang, Shin T. see Kang, Shin Theke.
Kang, Shin Theke.
xKang, Shin T.
Sumerian Economic Texts from the Drehem
Archive. U of Ill Pr.
Sumerian Economic Texts from the Umma
Archive. U of Ill Pr.
Kang, Tai S.
xKang, Tai S.
ed. Nationalism & the Crises of Ethnic
Minorities in Asia. Greenwood.
Kang, Thomas H. see Kang, Thomas Hosuck.
Kang, Thomas Hosuck.
xKang, Thomas H.
The Chinese Mind in the Making. Human Dev
East.
Kangro, Hans.
xKangro, Hans.
Early History of Planck's Radiation Law.
Crane-Russak Co.
Kanin, Garson, 1912-
xKanin, Garson.
Moviola. S&S.
Kaniuk, Yoram.
xKaniuk, Yoram.
The Story of Aunt Shlomzion, the Great.
Har-Row.
Kanizsa, Gaetano.
xKanizsa, Gaetano.
Organization in Vision: Essays on Gestalt
Perception. Praeger.
Kann, Eduard, 1880-1962
xKann, Edward.
The Currencies of China: An Investigation of
Silver & Gold Transactions Affecting China,
with a Section on Copper. AMS Pr.
Kann, Edward. see Kann, Eduard.
Kann, Mark E.
xKann, Mark E.
Thinking About Politics: Two Political
Sciences. West Pub.
Kann, Robert A., 1906-
xKann, Robert A.
The Habsburg Empire: A Study in Integration
& Disintegration. Octagon.
A History of the Habsburg Empire, 1526-1918.
U of Cal Pr.
The Problem of Restoration: A Study in
Comparative Political History. U of Cal Pr.
Kann, Stan.
xKann, Stan.
The Totaled Handyman. J P Tarcher.
The Totaled Handyman. St Martin.
Kannan, D.
xKannan, D.
ed. An Introduction to Stochastic Processes.
Elsevier.
Kanne, Edward A., 1943-
xKanne, Edward A.
Fresh Food for Nicosia. U Chicago Dept Geog.
Kannenstine, Louis F., 1938-
xKannenstine, Louis F.
The Art of Djuna Barnes: Duality &
Damnation. NYU Pr.
Kanner, L. see Kanner, Leo.
Kanner, Leo, 1894-
xKanner, L.

A History of the Care & Study of the Mentally
Retarded. C C Thomas.
xKanner, Leo.
Child Psychiatry. C C Thomas.
Child Psychiatry. Darby Bks.
Kansas City Star.
xTheKansas City Star Staff.
William Rockhill Nelson: A Story of a Man, a
Newspaper, & a City. Beekman Pubs.
Kansas State Historical Society.
xKansas State Historical Society Staff.
Kansas: The Thirty-Fourth Star. Kansas St
Hist.
Kansas State Historical Society Staff. see Kansas State
Historical Society.
Kansas. University.
xKansas University.
Studies in Honor of Albert Morey Sturtevant.
Greenwood.
Kansas. University. Dept. of English.
xUniversity Of Kansas - Department Of English.
Studies in English in Honor of Raphael
Dorman O'leary & Seldon Lincoln
Whitcomb. Kansas Univ. Humanistic Studies.
Arno.
Kant, Immanuel.
xKant, Immanuel.
Critique of Judgment. Hafner.
Critique of Practical Reason. Bobbs.
Critique of Practical Reason & Other Writings
in Moral Philosophy. Garland Pub.
Critique of Pure Reason. Doubleday.
Critique of Pure Reason. Dutton.
Critique of Pure Reason. St Martin.
Kant's Inaugural Dissertation & Early Writings
on Space. Hyperion Conn.
Lectures on Ethics. Peter Smith.
Lectures on Philosophical Theology. Cornell U
Pr.
Logic. Bobbs
On History. Bobbs.
Prolegomena to Any Future Metaphysics That
Will Be Able to Come Forward As Science.
Hackett Pub.
Kantar, Edwin. see Kantar, Edwin B.
Kantar, Edwin B, 1932-
xKantar, Edwin.
Introduction to Defender's Play. Wilshire.
xKantar, Edwin B.
Introduction to Declarer's Play. P-H.
Kanter, Arnold.
xKanter, Arnold.
Defense Politics: A Budgetary Perspective. U
of Chicago Pr.
Kanter, Rosabeth M. see Kanter, Rosabeth Moss.
Kanter, Rosabeth Moss.
xKanter, Rosabeth M.
Commitment & Community: Communes &
Utopias in Sociological Perspective. Harvard
U Pr.
Men & Women of the Corporation. Basic.
A Tale of "O": On Being Different in an
Organization. Har-Row.
Work & Family in the United States: A Critical
Review & Agenda for Research & Policy.
Russell Sage.
Kantor, David.
xKantor, David.
Inside the Family. Har-Row.
Kantor, Frederick W.
xKantor, Frederick W.
Information Mechanics. Wiley.
Kantor, Harry.
xKantor, Harry.
Ideology & Program of the Peruvian Aprista
Movement. Octagon.
Kantor, J. R. see Kantor, Jacob Robert.
Kantor, Jacob Robert, 1888-
xKantor, J. R.

The Logic of Modern Science. Principia Pr.
Psychological Linguistics. Principia Pr.
Kantor, MacKinlay, 1904-
xKantor, MacKinlay.
Gettysburg. Random.
Hamilton County. Macmillan.
Lee & Grant at Appomattox. Random.
Valley Forge. Ballantine.
Valley Forge. M Evans.
xKantor, MacKinley.
Andersonville. NAL.
Andersonville. T Y Crowell.
Kantor, MacKinley. *see* Kantor, MacKinlay.
Kantor, Seth.
xKantor, Seth.
Who Was Jack Ruby?. Everest Hse.
Kantorovich, L. V. *see* Kantorovich, Leonid Vital'Evich.
Kantorovich, Leonid Vital'Evich.
xKantorovich, L. V.
Tables for the Numerical Solution of Boundary
Value Problems of the Theory of Harmonic
Functions. Ungar.
Kantorowicz, Herman. *see* Kantorowicz, Hermann.
Kantorowicz, Hermann.
xKantorowicz, Herman.
The Definition of Law. Octagon.
Kantowitz, Barry H.
xKantowitz, Barry H.
Experimental Psychology: Understanding
Psychological Research. Rand.
Kantrowitz, Arnie, 1940-
xKantrowitz, Arnie.
Under the Rainbow: Growing up Gay. Morrow.
Under the Rainbow: Growing up Gay. PB.
Kantrowitz, Joanne S. *see* Kantrowitz, Joanne Spencer.
Kantrowitz, Joanne Spencer, 1931-
xKantrowitz, Joanne S.
Dramatic Allegory: Lindsay's "Ane Satyre of
the Thrie Estaitis". U of Nebr Pr.
Kantrowitz, Martin P.
xKantrowitz, Martin P.
Que Paso?: An English-Spanish Guide for
Medical Personnel. U of NM Pr.
Kantrowitz, Mildred.
xKantrowitz, Mildred.
Good-Bye Kitchen. Schol Bk Serv.
Kantrowitz, P. *see* Kantrowitz, Philip.
Kantrowitz, Philip.
xKantrowitz, P.
Electronic Measurements. P-H.
Kantrowitz, Walter. *see* Kantrowitz, Walter L.
Kantrowitz, Walter L.
xKantrowitz, Walter.
How to Be Your Own Lawyer (Sometimes).
Putnam.
Kanwar, M. A. *see* Kanwar, Mahfooz A.
Kanwar, Mahfooz A.
xKanwar, M. A.
ed. Sociology of Family: An Interdisciplinary
Approach. Shoe String.
Kany, Charles E. *see* Kany, Charles Emil.
Kany, Charles Emil, 1895-
xKany, Charles E.
Life & Manners in Madrid, 1750-1800. AMS
Pr.
Kanza, Thomas. *see* Kanza, Thomas R.
Kanza, Thomas R.
xKanza, Thomas.
Evolution & Revolution in Africa. Schenkman.
Kapadia, K. M. *see* Kapadia, Kanailal Motilal.
Kapadia, Kanailal Motilal.
xKapadia, K. M.
Marriage & Family in India. Oxford U Pr.
Kapany, N. S.
xKapany, N. S.
Optical Waveguides. Acad Pr.
Kapelle, William E.
xKapelle, William E.

The Norman Conquest of the North: The
Region & Its Transformation, 1000-1135. U
of NC Pr.
Kapelner, Alan.
xKapelner, Alan.
All the Naked Heroes. Braziller.
Kapetanovic, Alojzije.
xKapetanovic, Alojzije.
Croatian Cuisine. Assoc Bk Pubs Guidance.
Kapfer, Philip G.
xKapfer, Philip G.
Inquiry ILPs: Individualized Learning Plans for
Life-Based Inquiry. Educ Tech Pubns.
ed. Learning Packages in American Education.
Educ Tech Pubns.
Preparing & Using Individualized Learning
Packages for Ungraded, Continuous Progress
Education. Educ Tech Pubns.
Project ILPs: Individualized Learning Plans for
Life-Based Projects. Educ Tech Pubns.
Kaplan. *see* Kaplan, William A.
Kaplan, Abraham.
xKaplan, Abraham.
In Pursuit of Wisdom: The Scope of
Philosophy. Glencoe.
ed. Individuality & the New Society. U of
Wash Pr.
Kaplan, Abraham D. *see* Kaplan, Abraham David
Hannath.
Kaplan, Abraham David Hannath, 1893-
xKaplan, Abraham D.
Big Enterprise in a Competitive System.
Greenwood.
Pricing in Big Business: A Case Approach.
Greenwood.
Small Business: Its Place & Problems. Arno.
Kaplan, Alex.
xKaplan, Alex.
Clinical Chemistry: Interpretation &
Techniques. Lea & Febiger.
Kaplan, Allan, 1932-
xKaplan, Allan.
Paper Airplane. Ultramarine Pub.
Kaplan, Arnold R.
xKaplan, Arnold R.
Human Behavior Genetics. C C Thomas.
Kaplan, Aryeh.
xKaplan, Aryeh.
Meditation & the Bible. Weiser.
Kaplan, Barbara.
xKaplan, Barbara.
Home Furnishings. Bobbs.
Kaplan, Bert, 1919-
xKaplan, Bert.
ed. The Inner World of Mental Illness: A
Series of First Person Accounts of What It
Was Like. Har-Row.
Kaplan, Berton H.
xKaplan, Berton H.
Family & Health: An Epidemiological
Approach. U NC Inst Res Soc Sci.
ed. Further Explorations in Social Psychiatry.
Basic.
Kaplan, Charles, 1919-
xKaplan, Charles.
ed. Criticism: The Major Statements. St
Martin.
Kaplan, David G. *see* Kaplan, David Gordon.
Kaplan, David Gordon, 1908-
xKaplan, David G.
World of Furs. Fairchild.
Kaplan, Don.
xKaplan, Don.
Video in the Classroom. Knowledge Indus.
Kaplan, Donald M.
xKaplan, Donald M.
Domesday Dictionary. S&S.
Kaplan, Edgar.
xKaplan, Edgar.

Competitive Bidding in Modern Bridge. Fleet.
Competitive Bidding in Modern Bridge.
Wilshire.
Kaplan, Eugene H.
xKaplan, Eugene H.
Drugs Don't Take People, People Take Drugs.
Lyle Stuart.
Kaplan, Eugene J.
xKaplan, Eugene J.
Evidence: A Law Enforcement Officer's Guide.
C C Thomas.
Kaplan, Fred, 1937-
xKaplan, Fred.
Dickens & Mesmerism: The Hidden Springs of
Fiction. Princeton U Pr.
Kaplan, Frederic M.
xKaplan, Fredric M.
ed. Encyclopedia of China Today. Har-Row.
Kaplan, Fredric M. *see* Kaplan, Frederic M.
Kaplan, H. Roy.
xKaplan, H. Roy.
Lottery Winners: How They Won & How
Winning Changed Their Lives. Har-Row.
Kaplan, Harold, 1916-
xKaplan, Harold.
Democratic Humanism & American Literature.
U of Chicago Pr.
Kaplan, Harold I.
xKaplan, Harold I.
Comprehensive Group Psychotherapy. Williams
& Wilkins.
Kaplan, Harold M. *see* Kaplan, Harold Morris.
Kaplan, Harold Morris, 1908-
xKaplan, Harold M.
Anatomy & Physiology of Speech. McGraw.
Kaplan, Helen S. *see* Kaplan, Helen Singer.
Kaplan, Helen Singer, 1929-
xKaplan, Helen S.
The Illustrated Manual of Sex Therapy. Times
Bks.
Kaplan, Henry S.
xKaplan, Henry S.
ed. Cancer in China. A R Liss.
Hodgkin's Disease. Harvard U Pr.
Kaplan, Herbert H.
xKaplan, Herbert H.
First Partition of Poland. AMS Pr.
Kaplan, Howard.
xKaplan, Howard.
The Damascus Cover. Fawcett.
Kaplan, Isaac R.
xKaplan, Isaac R.
ed. Natural Gases in Marine Sediments.
Plenum Pub.
Kaplan, Jane.
xKaplan, Jane R.
A Woman's Conflict: The Special Relationship
Between Women & Food. P-H.
Kaplan, Jane R. *see* Kaplan, Jane.
Kaplan, Janice.
xKaplan, Janice.
Women & Sports. Avon.
Women & Sports. Viking Pr.
Kaplan, Joanna.
xKaplan, Johanna.
Other People's Lives. Knopf.
Kaplan, Johanna. *see* Kaplan, Joanna.
Kaplan, Lawrence.
xKaplan, Lawrence.
Politics & Religion during the English
Revolution: The Scots & the Long Parliament
1643-1645. NYU Pr.
Kaplan, Lawrence J. *see* Kaplan, Lawrence Jay.
Kaplan, Lawrence Jay.
xKaplan, Lawrence J.
An Economic Analysis of Crime: Selected
Readings. C C Thomas.
Kaplan, Lawrence S.
xKaplan, Lawrence S.

Jefferson & France: An Essay on Politics &
Political Ideas. Greenwood.
Kaplan, Louis, 1909-
xKaplan, Louis.
ed. Reader in Library Services & the
Computer. IHS-PDS.
Kaplan, M. L. *see* Kaplan, Marvin L.
Kaplan, Marion. *see* Kaplan, Marion A.
Kaplan, Marion A.
xKaplan, Marion.
The Jewish Feminist Movement in Germany:
The Campaigns of the Judischer Frauenbund,
1904-1938. Greenwood.
Kaplan, Marshall. *see* Kaplan, Marshall H.
Kaplan, Marshall H.
xKaplan, Marshall.
Space Shuttle: America's Wings to the Future.
Aero.
Kaplan, Martin F.
xKaplan, Martin F.
ed. Readings for Social Psychology. Mss Info.
Kaplan, Marvin L., 1926-
xKaplan, M. L.
The Structural Approach in Psychological
Testing. Pergamon.
Kaplan, Melvin J. *see* Kaplan, Melvin James.
Kaplan, Melvin James.
xKaplan, Melvin J.
How to Get Your Creditors off Your Back
Without Losing Your Shirt. Contemp Bks.
Kaplan, Michael H.
xKaplan, Michael H.
ed. Community Education Perspectives:
Selections from the Community Education
Journal. Pendell Pub.
Kaplan, Mordecai M. *see* Kaplan, Mordecai Menahem.
Kaplan, Mordecai Menahem, 1881-
xKaplan, Mordecai M.
Religion of Ethical Nationhood: Judaism's
Contribution to World Peace. Macmillan.
Kaplan, Morton A.
xKaplan, Morton A.
Alienation & Identification. Free Pr.
The Life and Death of the Cold War: Selected
Studies in Postwar Statecraft. Nelson-Hall.
On Historical & Political Knowing: An Inquiry
into Some Problems of Universal Law &
Human Freedom. U of Chicago Pr.
Towards Professionalism in International
Theory: Macrosystems Analysis. Free Pr.
Kaplan, Norman M., 1931-
xKaplan, Norman M.
Clinical Hypertension. Williams & Wilkins.
Kaplan, Oscar J.
xKaplan, Oscar J.
ed. Psychopathology of Aging. Acad Pr.
Kaplan, Richard.
xKaplan, Richard.
Great Linebackers of the NFL. Random.
Kaplan, Robert B.
xKaplan, Robert B.
ed. On the Scope of Applied Linguistics.
Newbury Hse.
Kaplan, Robert S.
xKaplan, Robert S.
Financial Crisis in the Social Security System.
Am Enterprise.
Indexing Social Security: An Analysis of the
Issues. Am Enterprise.
Kaplan, S. A. *see* Kaplan, Samuil Aronovich.
Kaplan, S. L. *see* Kaplan, Steven L.
Kaplan, Samuel, 1935-
xKaplan, Samuel.
The Dream Deferred: People, Politics, &
Planning in Suburbia. Continuum.
The Dream Deferred: People, Politics, &
Planning in Suburbia. Random.
Kaplan, Samuil Aronovich.
xKaplan, S. A.

Plasma Astrophysics. Pergamon.
Kaplan, Sandra. *see* Kaplan, Sandra Nina.
Kaplan, Sandra Nina.
xKaplan, Sandra.
The Teacher's Choice: Ideas & Activities for
Teaching, Basic Skills. Goodyear.
Kaplan, Steven L.
xKaplan, S. L.
Bread, Politics & Political Economy in the
Reign of Louis XV. Kluwer Boston.
Kaplan, Stuart R.
xKaplan, Stuart R.
The Encyclopedia of Tarot. US Games Syst.
Kaplan, Sydney J. *see* Kaplan, Sydney Janet.
Kaplan, Sydney Janet, 1939-
xKaplan, Sydney J.
Feminine Consciousness in the Modern British
Novel. U of Ill Pr.
Kaplan, Wilfred, 1915-
xKaplan, Wilfred.
Advanced Calculus. A-W.
Operational Methods for Linear Systems. A-W.
Ordinary Differential Equations. A-W.
Kaplan, William A.
xKaplan.
The Student Scientist Explores Energy & Fuels.
Rosen Pr.
Kaplansky, Irving, 1917-
xKaplansky, Irving.
Fields & Rings. U of Chicago Pr.
Lie Algebras & Locally Compact Groups. U of
Chicago Pr.
Linear Algebra & Geometry: A Second Course.
Chelsea Pub.
Kapleau, Philip, 1912-
xKapleau, Philip.
The Three Pillars of Zen: Teaching, Practice,
Enlightenment. Doubleday.
Zen: Dawn in the West. Doubleday.
xKapleau, Roshi P.
Zen: Dawn in the West. Doubleday.
Kapleau, Roshi P. *see* Kapleau, Philip.
Kaplin, William A.
xKaplin, William A.
The Law of Higher Education: Legal
Implications of Administrative Decision
Making. Jossey-Bass.
Kaplinsky, Raphael.
xKaplinsky, Raphael.
ed. Readings on the Multinational Corporation
in Kenya. Oxford U Pr.
Kaploun, Uri.
xKaploun, Uri.
ed. The Synagogue. Jewish Pubn.
Kaplow, Robert.
xKaplow, Robert.
Two in the City. HM.
Kapner, Harold R.
xKapner, Harold R.
Not for Illegal Aliens Only: How to Get a
Green Card. Golden Door.
Kapoor, A. *see* Kapoor, Ashok.
Kapoor, Ashok, 1940-
xKapoor, A.
ed. Asian Business & Environment in
Transition: Selected Readings & Essays.
Darwin Pr.
xKapoor, Ashok.
Planning for International Business
Negotiations. Ballinger Pub.
Kapp, Ardeth G. *see* Kapp, Ardeth Greene.
Kapp, Ardeth Greene, 1931-
xKapp, Ardeth G.
The Gentle Touch. Deseret Bk.
Kapp, Colin.
xKapp, Colin.
The Chaos Weapon. Ballantine.
The Survival Game. Ballantine.
Kapp, Ernst, 1888-
xKapp, Ernst.

Greek Foundations of Traditional Logic. AMS
Pr.
Kapp, Helen.
xKapp, Helen.
Enjoying Pictures. Routledge & Kegan.
Kapp, Kenneth M.
xKapp, Kenneth M.
Completely O-Simple Semigroups: An Abstract
Treatment of the Lattice of Congruences.
Benjamin-Cummings.
Kapp, Ronald O.
xKapp, Ronald O.
How to Know Pollen & Spores. Wm C Brown.
Kappelman, Murray, 1931-
xKappelman, Murray.
Raising the Only Child. NAL.
Kappos, Demetrios. *see* Kappos, Demetrios Andreou.
Kappos, Demetrios Andreou, 1904-
xKappos, Demetrios.
Probability Algebras & Stochastic Spaces. Acad
Pr.
Kapral, Frank. *see* Kapral, Frank S.
Kapral, Frank S.
xKapral, Frank.
Illustrated Guide to Championship Football.
P-H.
Kaprielian, Walter.
xKaprielian, Walter.
The Captain's Cookbook. HR&W.
Kaps, Helen K. *see* Kaps, Helen Karen.
Kaps, Helen Karen, 1940-
xKaps, Helen K.
Moral Perspective in La Princesse De Cleves.
U of Oreg Bks.
Kapungu, Leonard. *see* Kapungu, Leonard T.
Kapungu, Leonard T.
xKapungu, Leonard.
Rhodesia: The Struggle for Freedom. Orbis
Bks.
Kapur, Ashde. *see* Kapur, Ashok.
Kapur, Ashok.
xKapur, Ashde.
International Nuclear Proliferation: Multilateral
Diplomacy & Regional Aspects. Praeger.
xKapur, Ashok.
India's Nuclear Option: Atomic Diplomacy &
Decision Making. Praeger.
Kapur, Gopal K.
xKapur, Gopal K.
IBM 360 Assembler Language Programming.
Wiley.
Programming in Standard COBOL. SRA.
Kapur, K. C. *see* Kapur, Kailash Chander.
Kapur, Kailash Chander.
xKapur, K. C.
Reliability in Engineering Design. Wiley.
Kapustin, Harry.
xKapustin, Harry.
Crowd Your Luck on Death. Arno.
Karabel, Jerome.
xKarabel, Jerome.
ed. Power & Ideology in Education. Oxford U
Pr.
Karan, Pradyumna P. *see* Karan, Pradyumna Prasad.
Karan, Pradyumna Prasad.
xKaran, Pradyumna P.
The Changing Face of Tibet: The Impact of
Chinese Communist Ideology on the
Landscape. U Pr of Ky.
Karant-Nunn, Susan C.
xKarant-Nunn, Susan C.
Luther's Pastors: The Reformation in the
Ernestine Countryside. Am Philos.
Karaoglan, Aida.
xKaraoglan, Aida.
A Gourmet's Delight: Selected Recipes from
the Haute Cuisine of the Arab World.
Caravan Bks.
Karas, Nicholas. *see* Karas, Nick.

Karas, Nick.
xKaras, Nicholas.
Complete Book of the Striped Bass. Follett.
Karaska, Gerald J.
xKaraska, Gerald J.
ed. Locational Analysis for Manufacturing: A Selection of Readings. MIT Pr.
Karassik, Igor J., 1911-
xKarassik, Igor J.
Pump Handbook. McGraw.
Karasu, Toksoz B.
xKarasu, Toksoz B.
ed. Psychotherapeutics in Medicine. Grune.
Karcher, Carolyn L., 1945-
xKarcher, Carolyn L.
Shadow Over the Promised Land: Slavery, Race, & Violence in Melville's America. La State U Pr.
Karczmar, A. G. *see* Karczmar, Alexander George.
Karczmar, Alexander George.
xKarczmar, A. G.
Anticholinesterase Agents. Pergamon.
ed. Brain & Human Behavior. Springer-Verlag.
Kardiner, A. *see* Kardiner, Abram.
Kardiner, Abram.
xKardiner, A.
Mark of Oppression: Explorations in the Personality of the American Negro. Peter Smith.
My Analysis with Freud: Reminiscences. Norton.
xKardiner, Abram.
Mark of Oppression: Explorations in the Personality of the American Negro. NAL.
Kardos, L. *see* Kardos, Lajos.
Kardos, Lajos.
xKardos, L.
ed. Problems of Information Processing & Perceptual Organization. Heyden.
xKardos, Lajos.
ed. Problems of Information Processing & Perceptual Organization. Intl Pubns Serv.
Kare, Morley R. *see* Kare, Morley Richard.
Kare, Morley Richard.
xKare, Morley R.
ed. The Chemical Senses & Nutrition. Acad Pr.
Karel, Leonard, 1912-
xKarel, Leonard.
Dried Flowers from Antiquity to the Present: A History & Practical Guide to Flower Drying. Scarecrow.
Dried Grasses, Grains, Gourds, Pods & Cones. Scarecrow.
Karen, Ruth.
xKaren, Ruth.
illus. Feathered Serpent: The Rise & Fall of the Aztecs. Schol Bk Serv.
Questionable Practices. Har-Row.
Karff, Samuel E.
xKarff, Samuel E.
Agada: The Language of Jewish Faith. Ktav.
Karfunkel, Thomas.
xKarfunkel, Thomas.
The Jewish Seat: Antisemitism & the Appointment of Jews to the Supreme Court. Exposition.
Karger, Barry L.
xKarger, Barry L.
Introduction to Separation Science. Wiley.
Karger, Delmar W.
xKarger, Delmar W.
How to Choose a Career. Watts.
Karginov, German.
xKarginov, German.
Rodchenko. Thames Hudson.
Kariara, J. *see* Kariara, Jonathan.
Kariara, Jonathan.
xKariara, J.

ed. An Introduction to East African Poetry. Oxford U Pr.
Kariel, Henry S.
xKariel, Henry S.
The Decline of American Pluralism. Stanford U Pr.
ed. Frontiers of Democratic Theory. Random.
Kariel, Herbert G.
xKariel, Herbert G.
Explorations in Social Geography. A-W.
Karim, S. M. *see* Karim, Sultan M. M.
Karim, Sultan M. M.
xKarim, S. M.
Prostaglandins & Reproduction. Univ Park.
Karimi, A. M. *see* Karimi, Amir Massoud.
Karimi, Amir Massoud.
xKarimi, A. M.
Toward a Definition of American Film Noir (1941-1949). Arno.
Karimi-Hakkak, Ahmad.
xKarimi-Hakkak, Ahmad.
tr. The Anthology of Modern Persian Poetry. Westview.
Karioki, James N.
xKarioki, James N.
Tanzania's Human Revolution. Pa St U Pr.
Kariuki, Josiah M. *see* Kariuki, Josiah Mwangi.
Kariuki, Josiah Mwangi, 1929-
xKariuki, Josiah M.
Mau Mau Detainee: The Account by a Kenya African of His Experiences in Detention Camps 1953-1960. Oxford U Pr.
Karkainen, Paul A.
xKarkainen, Paul A.
Narnia Explored. Revell.
Karkoschka, Erhard.
xKarkoschka, Erhard.
Notation in New Music: A Critical Guide to Interpretation & Realisation. Eur-Am Music.
Karl, Barry. *see* Karl, Barry Dean.
Karl, Barry D. *see* Karl, Barry Dean.
Karl, Barry Dean.
xKarl, Barry.
Executive Reorganization & Reform in the New Deal: The Genesis of Administrative Management, 1900-1939. U of Chicago Pr.
xKarl, Barry D.
Charles E. Merriam & the Study of Politics. U of Chicago Pr.
Karl, Frederick. *see* Karl, Frederick Robert.
Karl, Frederick R. *see* Karl, Frederick Robert.
Karl, Frederick Robert, 1927-
xKarl, Frederick.
C. P. Snow: The Politics of Conscience. S Ill U Pr.
ed. Existential Imagination. Fawcett.
xKarl, Frederick R.
Joseph Conrad: The Three Lives. FS&G.
A Reader's Guide to Great Twentieth-Century English Novels. Octagon.
Reader's Guide to the Contemporary English Novel. FS&G.
A Reader's Guide to the Contemporary English Novel. Octagon.
A Reader's Guide to the Nineteenth Century British Novel. Octagon.
Karl, Jean.
xKarl, Jean E.
The Turning Place: Stories of a Future Past. Dutton.
Karl, Jean E. *see* Karl, Jean.
Karlekar, Bhalchandra V.
xKarlekar, Bhalchandra V.
Engineering Heat Transfer. West Pub.
Karlen, Delmar.
xKarlen, Delmar.
Civil Litigation. Michie.
Karlgren, Bernhard, 1889-
xKarlgren, Bernhard.

Analytic Dictionary of Chinese and Sino-Japanese. Chinese Materials.
Analytic Dictionary of Chinese & Sino-Japanese. Peter Smith.
Karlin, Arthur.
xKarlin, Arthur.
ed. Neuronal Information Transfer. Acad Pr.
Karlin, Muriel. *see* Karlin, Muriel Schoenbrun.
Karlin, Muriel S. *see* Karlin, Muriel Schoenbrun.
Karlin, Muriel Schoenbrun.
xKarlin, Muriel.
Discipline & the Disruptive Child: A Practical Guide for Elementary School Teachers. P-H.
Successful Methods for Teaching the Slow Learner. P-H.
xKarlin, Muriel S.
An Administrator's Guide to a Practical Career Education Program. P-H.
Classroom Activities Desk Book for Fun & Learning. P-H.
Experiential Learning: An Effective Teaching Program for Elementary Schools. P-H.
Solving Your Career Mystery. Rosen Pr.
Karlin, Nurit.
xKarlin, Nurit.
No Comment. Scribner.
Karlin, Robert.
xKarlin, Robert.
Teaching Elementary Reading: Principles & Strategies. HarBraceJ.
Teaching Reading in High School: Improving Reading in Content Areas. Bobbs.
Karlin, Samuel, 1923-
xKarlin, Samuel.
A First Course in Stochastic Processes. Acad Pr.
Geometry of Moment Spaces. Am Math.
Karling, J. S. *see* Karling, John Sidney.
Karling, John Sidney, 1898-
xKarling, J. S.
Synchytrium. Acad Pr.
Karlins, Marvin.
xKarlins, Marvin.
ed. Psychology & Society: Readings for General Psychology. Wiley.
Karlson, P. *see* Karlson, Peter.
Karlson, Peter, 1918-
xKarlson, P.
Introduction to Modern Biochemistry. Acad Pr.
Karlsson, John L. *see* Karlsson, Jon L.
Karlsson, Jon L.
xKarlsson, John L.
Inheritance of Creative Intelligence. Nelson-Hall.
Karman, Theodore Von. *see* Von Karman, Theodore.
Karmas, E. *see* Karmas, Endel.
Karmas, Endel.
xKarmas, E.
Fresh Meat Technology. Noyes.
Processed Meat Technology. Noyes.
Karnani, Chetan, 1936-
xKarnani, Chetan.
Nirad C. Chaudhuri. Twayne.
Karnes, Frances.
xKarnes, Frances A.
Handbook of Instructional Resources & References for Teaching the Gifted. Allyn.
Karnes, Frances A. *see* Karnes, Frances.
Karnes, Merle B., 1916-
xKarnes, Merle B.
Creative Art for Learning. Coun Exc Child.
Culturally Disadvantaged Student & Guidance. HM.
Early Childhood. Coun Exc Child.
Karnes, Thomas. *see* Karnes, Thomas L.
Karnes, Thomas L.
xKarnes, Thomas.

Tropical Enterprise: Standard Fruit &
Steamship Company in Latin America. La
State U Pr.
xKarnes, Thomas L.
Readings in the Latin American Policy of the
United States. U of Ariz Pr.
Karnopp, B. H.
xKarnopp, Bruce H.
Introduction to Dynamics. A-W.
Karnopp, Bruce H. see Karnopp, B. H.
Karnopp, Dean.
xKarnopp, Dean C.
System Dynamics: A Unified Approach. Wiley.
Karnopp, Dean C. see Karnopp, Dean.
Karnow, Stanley.
xKarnow, Stanley.
Mao & China: From Revolution to Revolution.
Viking Pr.
Karo, Nancy.
xKaro, Nancy.
Adventure in Dying. Moody.
Karol, K. S.
xKarol, K. S.
China: The Other Communism. Hill & Wang.
Guerrillas in Power: The Course of the Cuban
Revolution. Hill & Wang.
Karolevitz, Robert. see Karolevitz, Robert F.
Karolevitz, Robert F.
xKarolevitz, Robert.
Everything's Green but My Thumb. North
Plains.
xKarolevitz, Robert F.
Challenge: The South Dakota Story. Brevet Pr.
Where Your Heart Is: The Story of Harvey
Dunn, Artist. North Plains.
Karp, Abraham J.
xKarp, Abraham J.
Golden Door to America: The Jewish
Immigrant Experience. Penguin.
Karp, David A. see Karp, David Allen.
Karp, David Allen.
xKarp, David A.
Symbols, Selves, & Society: Understanding
Interaction. Har-Row.
Karp, Gerald.
xKarp, Gerald.
Cell Biology. McGraw.
Karp, Harry. see Karp, Harry R.
Karp, Harry R., 1922-
xKarp, Harry.
Practical Applications of Data
Communications: A User's Guide. McGraw.
Karp, Ivan.
xKarp, Ivan.
Fields of Change Among the Iteso of Kenya.
Routledge & Kegan.
Karp, Laurence. see Karp, Laurence E.
Karp, Laurence E.
xKarp, Laurence.
The Hospital: The View from Bellevue. Charter
Bks.
Karp, Lila.
xKarp, Lila.
Queen Is in the Garbage. Vanguard.
Karp, Naomi J.
xKarp, Naomi J.
Nothing Rhymes with April. HarBraceJ.
The Turning Point. HarBraceJ.
Karp, Robert E.
xKarp, Robert E.
Cross Cultural Considerations of Marketing &
Consumer Behavior. Mss Info.
Karp, Theodore.
xKarp, Theodore.
Dictionary of Music. Dell.
Karp, Walter.
xKarp, Walter.

The Politics of War: The Story of Two Wars
Which Altered Forever the Political Life of
the American Republic (1890-1920).
Har-Row.
The Politics of War: The Story of Two Wars
Which Altered Forever the Political Life of
the American Republic (1890-1920).
Har-Row.
Karpat, K. H. see Karpat, Kemal H.
Karpat, Kemal H.
xKarpat, K. H.
The Gecekondu: Rural Migration &
Urbanization in Turkey. Cambridge U Pr.
Karpf, Fay B. see Karpf, Fay Berger.
Karpf, Fay Berger.
xKarpf, Fay B.
American Social Psychology: Its Origins,
Development, & European Background.
Irvington.
American Social Psychology: Its Origins,
Development & European Background.
Russell.
Psychology & Psychotherapy of Otto Rank: An
Historical & Comparative Introduction.
Greenwood.
Karpin, Fred L.
xKarpin, Fred L.
Bridge Strategy at Trick One. Dover.
Psychological Strategy in Contract Bridge: The
Techniques of Deception & Harassment in
Bidding & Play. Dover.
Karpinski, Leszek M.
xKarpinski, Leszek M.
The Religious Life of Man: Guide to Basic
Literature. Scarecrow.
Karpinski, Louis C. see Karpinski, Louis Charles.
Karpinski, Louis Charles, 1878-1956
xKarpinski, Louis C.
History of Arithmetic. Russell.
Karplus, M. see Karplus, Martin.
Karplus, Martin.
xKarplus, M.
Atoms & Molecules: An Introduction for
Students of Physical Chemistry.
Benjamin-Cummings.
Karpman, Benjamin, 1886-
xKarpman, Benjamin.
Alcoholic Woman. Assoc Bk.
Karpman, V. I. see Karpman, Vladimir Iosifovich.
Karpman, Vladimir Iosifovich.
xKarpman, V. I.
Non-Linear Waves in Dispersive Media.
Pergamon.
Karpov, Anatolii Evgenevich.
xKarpov, Anatoly.
Anatoly Karpov: Chess Is My Life. Pergamon.
Karpov, Anatoly. see Karpov, Anatolii Evgenevich.
Karpova, S. see Karpova, Sofia Nikolaevna.
Karpova, Sofia Nikolaevna.
xKarpova, S.
The Realization of the Verbal Composition of
Speech by Preschool Children. Mouton.
Karr, Clarence.
xKarr, Clarence.
ed. Analytical Methods for Coal & Coal
Products. Acad Pr.
ed. Infrared & Raman Spectroscopy of Lunar &
Terrestrial Minerals. Acad Pr.
Karras, A. L.
xKarras, A. L.
North to Cree Lake. Trident.
Karras, Alex.
xKarras, Alex.
Alex Karras: My Life in Football, Television, &
Movies. Doubleday.
Even Big Guys Cry. NAL.
Karras, U.
xKarras, U.

Cutting and Pasting of Manifolds: SK-Groups.
Publish or Perish.
Karrass, Chester L. see Karrass, Chester Louis.
Karrass, Chester Louis.
xKarrass, Chester L.
Give & Take: The Complete Guide to
Negotiating Strategies & Tactics. T Y
Crowell.
Karreman, George, 1920-
xKarreman, George.
ed. Cooperative Phenomena in Biology.
Pergamon.
Karren, Keith J.
xKarren, Keith J.
God's Special Children: Helping the
Handicapped Achieve. Horizon Utah.
Karrer, Rathe.
xKarrer, Rathe.
Developmental Psychophysiology of Mental
Retardation: Concepts & Studies. C C
Thomas.
Karris, Robert J.
xKarris, Robert J.
What Are They Saying About Luke & Acts?: A
Theology of the Faithful God. Paulist Pr.
Karsch, Robert. see Karsch, Robert Frederick.
Karsch, Robert Frederick, 1909-
xKarsch, Robert.
The Government of Missouri. Lucas.
Karselis, Terence.
xKarselis, Terence.
Descriptive Medical Electronics &
Instrumentation. C B Slack.
Karst, K. L. see Karst, Kenneth L.
Karst, Kenneth L.
xKarst, K. L.
Evolution of Law in the Barrios of Caracas.
UCLA Lat Am Ctr.
Karsten, Peter.
xKarsten, Peter.
Law, Soldiers, & Combat. Greenwood.
ed. The Military in America: From the
Colonial Era to the Present. Free Pr.
Patriot-Heroes in England & America: Political
Symbolism & Changing Values Over Three
Centuries. U of Wis Pr.
Soldiers & Society: The Effects of Military
Service & War on American Life.
Greenwood.
Karstorp, Lennart.
xKarstorp, Lennart.
May I Have a Word with You, Lord?: Prayers
When You Are Ill. Collins Pubs.
Kart, Cary S. see Kart, Cary Steven.
Kart, Cary Steven.
xKart, Cary S.
ed. Aging in America: Readings in Social
Gerontology. Alfred Pub.
Kartesz, John T.
xKartesz, John T.
Synonymized Checklist of the Vascular Flora
of the United States, Canada, & Greenland.
U of NC Pr.
Karteszi, F. see Karteszi, Ferenc.
Karteszi, Ferenc.
xKarteszi, F.
Introduction to Finite Geometries. Elsevier.
Kartiganer, Donald M., 1937-
xKartiganer, Donald M.
The Fragile Thread: The Meaning of Form in
Faulkner's Novels. U of Mass Pr.
Kartman, Ben.
xKartman, Ben.
ed. Disaster. Arno.
Karugire, Samwiri R. see Karugire, Samwiri Rubaraza.
Karugire, Samwiri Rubaraza.
xKarugire, Samwiri R.

A History of the Kingdom of Nkore in Western Uganda to 1896. Oxford U Pr.

Karush, Aaron.
xKarush, Aaron.
Psychotherapy in Chronic Ulcerative Colitis. Saunders.

Karush, William.
xKarush, William.
Crescent Dictionary of Mathematics. Macmillan.

Kasahara, Hiroshi.
xKasahara, Hiroshi.
North Pacific Fisheries Management. AMS Pr.

Kasahara, Shigeru.
xKasahara, Shigeru.
Coaching Techniques for Free-Style & Greco-Roman Wrestling. P-H.

Kasaian, John J.
xKasaian, John J.
The Pocket Dictionary of Legal Words. Doubleday.

Kasak, Nikolai, 1917-
xKasak, Nikoli.
Art of Kasak. October.

Kasak, Nikoli. see Kasak, Nikolai.

Kasas, E. Gy. see Kasas, Ernest Gy.

Kasas, Ernest Gy.
xKasas, E. Gy.
Professional Hungarian Artists Outside Hungary. Hungarian Rev.

Kasavana, Michael L., 1947-
xKasavana, Michael L.
Hotel Information Systems: A Contemporary Approach to Front Office Procedures. CBI Pub.

Kaschube, Dorothea V.
xKaschube, Dorothea V.
ed. Crow Texts. Univ Microfilms.

Kase, Kenneth R.
xKase, Kenneth R.
Concepts of Radiation Dosimetry. Pergamon.

Kase, Ronald J.
xKase, Ronald J.
ed. The Human Services. AMS Pr.

Kase, Toshikazu, 1903-
xKase, Toshikazu.
Journey to the Missouri. Shoe String.

Kaser, David, 1921-
xKaser, David.
Directory of the Book & Printing Industries in Ante-Bellum Nashville. NY Pub Lib.

Kash, Don E.
xKash, Don E.
Our Energy Future: The Role of Research, Development, & Demonstration in Reaching a National Consensus on Energy Supply. U of Okla Pr.

Kasha, Al.
xKasha, Al.
If They Ask You, You Can Write a Song. S&S.

Kashgarian, Michael.
xKashgarian, Michael.
The Endocrine Glands. Krieger.

Kashner, Sam.
xKashner, Samuel.
Driving at Night. Hanging Loose.

Kashner, Samuel. see Kashner, Sam.

Kashyap, Subhash. see Kashyap, Subhash C.

Kashyap, Subhash C.
xKashyap, Subhash.
Tryst with Freedom: A Pictorial Saga. Intl Pubns Serv.

Kasinsky, Renee G.
xKasinsky, Renee G.
Refugees from Militarism: Draft-Age Americans in Canada. Littlefield.
Refugees from Militarism: Draft-Age Americans in Canada. Transaction Bks.

Kasirsky, Gilbert.
xKasirsky, Gilbert.

Vasectomy, Manhood & Sex. Springer Pub.

Kaslas, Bronis J., 1910-
xKaslas, Bronis J.
The Baltic Nations: The Quest for Regional Integration & Political Liberty. Euramerica Pr.

Kasle, Myron J.
xKasle, Myron J.
An Atlas of Dental Radiographic Anatomy. Saunders.

Kasler, F.
xKasler, F.
Quantitative Analysis by NMR Spectroscopy. Acad Pr.

Kasper, Walter.
xKasper, Walter.
Theology of Christian Marriage. Crossroad NY.

Kasperski, Victoria. see Kasperski, Victoria R.

Kasperski, Victoria R.
xKasperski, Victoria.
How to Make Cut Flowers Last. Morrow.

Kasperson, Roger E.
xKasperson, Roger K.
ed. Structure of Political Geography. Aldine Pub.

Kasperson, Roger K. see Kasperson, Roger E.

Kasriel, Robert H.
xKasriel, Robert H.
Undergraduate Topology. Krieger.

Kass, Alvin.
xKass, Alvin.
Politics in New York State, 1800-1830. Syracuse U Pr.

Kass, Judith M.
xKass, Judith M.
The Films of Montgomery Clift. Citadel Pr.

Kass, Lawrence.
xKass, Lawrence.
Bone Marrow Interpretation. Lippincott.
Monocytes, Monocytosis & Monocytic Leukemia. C C Thomas.
Pernicious Anemia. Saunders.
Preleukemic Disorders. C C Thomas.
Refractory Anemia. C C Thomas.

Kassay, John, 1919-
xKassay, John.
The Book of Shaker Furniture. U of Mass Pr.

Kassil, Lev. see Kassil, Lev Abramovich.

Kassil, Lev Abramovich, 1905-
xKassil, Lev.
Brother of the Hero. Braziller.

Kassler, Jamie C. see Kassler, Jamie Croy.

Kassler, Jamie Croy.
xKassler, Jamie C.
The Science of Music in Britain, 1714-1830: A Catalogue of Writings, Lectures & Inventions. Garland Pub.

Kasson, John F., 1944-
xKasson, John F.
Amusing the Million: Coney Island at the Turn of the Century. Hill & Wang.
Civilizing the Machine: Technology & Republican Values in America 1776-1900. Penguin.

Kassorla, Irene.
xKassorla, Irene.
Putting It All Together. Warner Bks.

Kassouf, Sheen T.
xKassouf, Sheen T.
Evaluation of Convertible Securities. Analytic Invest.

Kast, Fremont. see Kast, Fremont Ellsworth.

Kast, Fremont E. see Kast, Fremont Ellsworth.

Kast, Fremont Ellsworth.
xKast, Fremont.
Organization & Management: A Systems & Contingency Approach. McGraw.
xKast, Fremont E.

Contingency Views of Organization & Management. SRA.

Kastein, Shulamith.
xKastein, Shulamith.
Raising the Young Blind Child: A Guide for Parents & Educators. Human Sci Pr.

Kastenbaum, Robert.
xKastenbaum, Robert.
Between Life & Death. Springer Pub.
Humans Developing: A Lifespan Perspective. Allyn.
Psychology of Death. Springer Pub.

Kastens, Merritt L.
xKastens, Merritt L.
Long Range Planning for Your Business: An Operating Manual. Am Mgmt.

Kaster, Lewis R.
xKaster, Lewis R.
ed. Sale-Leasebacks: Economics, Tax Aspects, & Lease Terms. PLI.

Kastl, Albert J.
xKastl, Albert J.
Journey Back: Escaping the Drug Trap. Nelson-Hall.

Kastner, Erich, 1899-
xKastner, Erich.
Little Man. Knopf.
The Little Man. Avon.

Kastner, Joseph.
xKastner, Joseph.
A Species of Eternity. Dutton.
A Species of Eternity. Knopf.

Kastner, L. E. see Kastner, Leon Emile.

Kastner, Leon E. see Kastner, Leon Emile.

Kastner, Leon Emile.
xKastner, L. E.
A History of French Versification. Folcroft.
xKastner, Leon E.
A History of French Versification. R West.

Kaston, B. J. see Kaston, Benjamin Julian.

Kaston, Benjamin Julian, 1906-
xKaston, B. J.
How to Know the Spiders. Wm C Brown.

Kastor, Frank S., 1933-
xKastor, Frank S.
Giles & Phineas Fletcher. Twayne.

Kasuya, Yoshi, 1894-
xKasuya, Yoshi.
Comparative Study of the Secondary Education of Girls in England, Germany & the United States, with a Consideration of the Secondary Education of Girls in Japan. AMS Pr.

Katare, Shyam S. see Katare, Shyam Sunder.

Katare, Shyam Sunder, 1937-
xKatare, Shyam S.
Patterns of Dacoity in India: A Case Study of Madhya Pradesh. Verry.

Katch, Frank I.
xKatch, Frank I.
Getting in Shape: An Optimum Approach to Fitness & Weight Control. HM.

Katchadourian, Herant. see Katchadourian, Herant A.

Katchadourian, Herant A.
xKatchadourian, Herant.
Biological Aspects of Human Sexuality. HR&W.
Fundamentals of Human Sexuality. HR&W.
Human Sexuality: Sense & Nonsense. Norton.
xKatchadourian, Herant A.
Fundamentals of Human Sexuality. Krieger.
ed. Human Sexuality: A Comparative & Developmental Perspective. U of Cal Pr.

Katchalsky, Aharon.
xKatchalsky, Aharon.
Nonequilibrium Thermodynamics in Biophysics. Harvard U Pr.

Katchen, Carole, 1944-
xKatchen, Carole.
Promoting & Selling Your Art. Watson-Guptill.

Katcher, Philip. see Katcher, Philip R. N.

Katcher, Philip R. N.
xKatcher, Philip.
Armies of the American Wars, 1753-1815.
Hastings.
Kateb, George.
xKateb, George.
Utopia & Its Enemies. Schocken.
Katen, Thomas E. see Katen, Thomas Ellis.
Katen, Thomas Ellis.
xKaten, Thomas E.
Doing Philosophy. P-H.
Kates, Don B., 1941-
xKates, Don B.
Restricting Handguns: The Liberal Skeptics
Speak Out. North River.
Kates, George. see Kates, George Norbert.
Kates, George N. see Kates, George Norbert.
Kates, George Norbert.
xKates, George.
Chinese Household Furniture. Dover.
xKates, George N.
Chinese Household Furniture. Peter Smith.
Kates, Morris.
xKates, Morris.
ed. Membrane Fluidity: Biophysical Techniques
& Cellular Regulation. Humana.
Kates, Robert W. see Kates, Robert William.
Kates, Robert William.
xKates, Robert W.
Industrial Flood Losses: Damage Estimation in
the Lehigh Valley. U Chicago Dept Geog.
Kato, Junzo.
xKato, Junzo.
Hormone Receptors in the Brain. Mss Info.
Kato, Tomomi, 1926-
xKato, Tomomi.
ed. Concordance to the Works of Sir Thomas
Malory. Intl Schol Bk Serv.
Katon, J. E.
xKaton, J. E.
ed. Organic Semiconducting Polymers. Dekker.
Katona, Anna.
xKatona, Anna B.
Mihaly Vitez Csokonai. Twayne.
Katona, Anna B. see Katona, Anna.
Katona, George.
xKatona, George.
Consumer Response to Income Increases.
Greenwood.
The Powerful Consumer: Psychological Studies
of the American Economy. Greenwood.
Psychological Economics. Elsevier.
Katope, Christopher. see Katope, Christopher George.
Katope, Christopher George.
xKatope, Christopher.
Rhetoric of Revolution. Macmillan.
Katritzky, Alan R.
xKatritzky, Alan R.
ed. Principles of Heterocyclic Chemistry. Acad
Pr.
Katsaris, Kenneth. see Katsaris, W. Ken.
Katsaris, W. Ken, 1943-
xKatsaris, Kenneth.
ed. Evidence & Procedure in the
Administration of Justice. Wiley.
Katsh, Abraham I. see Katsh, Abraham Isaac.
Katsh, Abraham Isaac, 1908-
xKatsh, Abraham I.
ed. Bar Mitzvah Illustrated. Shengold.
Katsushika, Hokusai.
xKatsushika, Hokusai.
Drawings of Hokusai. Borden.
Kattan, Naim, 1928-
xKattan, Naim.
Farewell, Babylon. Taplinger.
Katz, Abraham, 1926-
xKatz, Abraham.

The Politics of Economic Reform in the Soviet
Union. Irvington.
Katz, Alfred, 1938-
xKatz, Alfred.
Government & Politics in Contemporary Israel,
1948 to Present. U Pr of Amer.
Katz, Bill.
xKatz, Bill.
A Guide to Magazine & Serial Agents. Bowker.
Katz, Bobbi.
xKatz, Bobbi.
Nothing but a Dog. Feminist Pr.
Katz, Carol. see Katz, Carol G.
Katz, Carol G.
xKatz, Carol.
The Berry Cookbook. Butterick Pub.
Katz, D. L. see Katz, Donald La Verne.
Katz, Daniel.
xKatz, Daniel.
Bureaucratic Encounters: A Pilot Study in the
Evaluation of Government Services. U of
Mich Soc Res.
Katz, David, 1884-1953
xKatz, David.
Psychological Atlas. Greenwood.
World of Colour. Johnson Repr.
Katz, Donald La Verne, 1907-
xKatz, D. L.
Engineering Concepts & Perspectives. Krieger.
Katz, Elaine S.
xKatz, Elaine S.
Folklore for the Time of Your Life. Oxmoor
Hse.
Katz, Elias, 1912-
xKatz, Elias.
The Retarded Adult in the Community. C C
Thomas.
Katz, Elihu.
xKatz, Elihu.
Broadcasting in the Third World: Promise &
Performance. Harvard U Pr
Personal Influence: The Part Played by People
in the Flow of Mass Communications. Free
Pr.
The Secularization of Leisure: Culture &
Communication in Israel. Harvard U Pr.
Katz, Evelyn.
xKatz, Evelyn.
Some Factors Affecting Resumption of
Interrupted Activities by Preschool Children.
Greenwood.
Katz, Fred. see Katz, Fred E.
Katz, Fred E.
xKatz, Fred.
Structuralism in Sociology: An Approach to
Knowledge. State U NY Pr.
xKatz, Fred E.
Autonomy & Organization: The Limits of
Social Control. Phila Bk Co.
Contemporary Sociological Theory. Phila Bk
Co.
Katz, Harry S.
xKatz, Harry S.
Handbook of Fillers & Reinforcements for
Plastics. Van Nos Reinhold.
Katz, Herbert. see Katz, Herbert M.
Katz, Herbert M.
xKatz, Herbert.
Love & Marriage. Arbor Hse.
xKatz, Herbert M.
Nicolette. Arbor Hse.
Nicolette. Berkley Pub.
Katz, Howard S.
xKatz, Howard S.
The Paper Aristocracy. Bks in Focus.
The Warmongers. Bks in Focus.
Katz, J. see Katz, Joseph.
Katz, Jack, 1927-
xKatz, Jack.

The First Kingdom. PB.
The Handbook of Clinical Audiology. Williams
& Wilkins.
Katz, Jacob, 1904-
xKatz, Jacob.
Exclusiveness & Tolerance: Studies in
Jewish-Gentile Relations in Medieval &
Modern Times. Greenwood.
Out of the Ghetto: The Social Background of
Jewish Emancipation, 1770-1870. Harvard U
Pr.
Out of the Ghetto: The Social Background of
Jewish Emancipation, 1770-1870. Schocken.
Katz, James E. see Katz, James Everett.
Katz, James Everett.
xKatz, James E.
Presidential Politics & Science Policy. Praeger.
Katz, Jane B.
xKatz, Jane B.
ed. I Am the Fire of Time: The Voices of
Native American Women. Dutton.
ed. Let Me Be a Free Man: A Documentary
History of Indian Resistance. Lerner Pubns.
Katz, Jay.
xKatz, Jay.
Psychoanalysis, Psychiatry & Law. Free Pr.
Katz, Jerrold J.
xKatz, Jerrold J.
Problem of Induction & Its Solution. U of
Chicago Pr.
Propositional Structure & Illocutionary Force:
A Study of the Contribution of Sentence
Meaning to Speech Acts. Harvard U Pr.
Katz, Jerry.
xKatz, Jerry.
Liberating Learning: A Manual for
Individualized Educational Reform. Morgan.
Katz, Jonathan.
xKatz, Jonathan.
Coming Out: A Documentary Play About Gay
Life & Liberation in the U S A. Arno.
Katz, Jordan.
xKatz, Jordon.
ed. Anesthesia & Uncommon Diseases:
Pathophysiologic & Clinical Correlations.
Saunders.
Katz, Jordon. see Katz, Jordan.
Katz, Joseph, 1920-
xKatz, J.
Society, Schools & Progress in Canada.
Pergamon.
xKatz, Joseph.
Dreams Are Your Truest Friends. PB.
Dreams Are Your Truest Friends. S&S.
No Time for Youth: Growth & Constraint in
College Students. Jossey-Bass.
Intro. by & ed. Stephen Crane in Transition:
Centenary Essays. N Ill U Pr.
Katz, Judy H., 1950-
xKatz, Judy H.
White Awareness: A Handbook for
Anti-Racism Training. U of Okla Pr.
Katz, Kev. see Katz, Zev.
Katz, Lilian.
xKatz, Lilian G.
Ethical Behavior in Early Childhood
Education. Natl Assn Child Ed.
Talks with Teachers: Reflections on Early
Childhood Education. Natl Assn Child Ed.
Katz, Lilian G. see Katz, Lilian.
Katz, Marjorie P.
xKatz, Marjorie P.
Fingerprint Owls & Other Fantasies. M Evans.
Pegs to Hang Ideas on: A Book of Quotations.
M Evans.
Katz, Menke, 1906-
xKatz, Menke.
Burning Village. The Smith.
Katz, Michael B.
xKatz, Michael B.

The Weight. Herald Pr.
Kauffmann, Stanley, 1916-
  xKauffmann, Stanley.
    Before My Eyes: Film Criticism & Comment.
      Har-Row.
    Figures of Light: Film Criticism & Comment.
      Har-Row.
Kaufman, Alan S.
  xKaufman, Alan S.
    ed. Clinical Evaluation of Young Children with
      the McCarthy Scales. Grune.
    Intelligent Testing with the WISC-R. Wiley.
Kaufman, Andrew L.
  xKaufman, Andrew L.
    Problems in Professional Responsibility. Little.
Kaufman, Barry. see Kaufman, Barry Neil.
Kaufman, Barry N. see Kaufman, Barry Neil.
Kaufman, Barry Neil.
  xKaufman, Barry.
    Giant Steps. Fawcett.
  xKaufman, Barry N.
    Giant Steps. Coward.
    Son-Rise. Har-Row.
    Son-Rise. Warner Bks.
Kaufman, Bob.
  xKaufman, Bob.
    Golden Sardine. City Lights.
Kaufman, Burton I. see Kaufman, Burton Ira.
Kaufman, Burton Ira.
  xKaufman, Burton I.
    The Oil Cartel Case: A Documentary Study of
      Antitrust Activity in the Cold War Era.
      Greenwood.
Kaufman, Charles.
  xKaufman, Charles.
    The Frog & the Beanpole. Lothrop.
Kaufman, Charles N.
  xKaufman, Charles N.
    The History of the Keller Manufacturing
      Company. Arno.
Kaufman, Edmond G. see Kaufman, Edmund George.
Kaufman, Edmund George.
  xKaufman, Edmond G.
    Living Creatively. Faith & Life.
Kaufman, Edward. see Kaufman, Edward L.
Kaufman, Edward L.
  xKaufman, Edward.
    The Market for Executive Talent. McGraw.
Kaufman, Fredrich.
  xKaufman, Fredrick.
    The African Roots of Jazz. Alfred Pub.
Kaufman, Fredrick. see Kaufman, Fredrich.
Kaufman, George. see Kaufman, George G.
Kaufman, George G.
  xKaufman, George.
    Money, the Financial System & the Economy.
      Rand.
  xKaufman, George G.
    Money & the Financial System: Fundamentals.
      Rand.
Kaufman, Gordon D.
  xKaufman, Gordon D.
    God the Problem. Harvard U Pr.
    Relativism, Knowledge & Faith. U of Chicago
      Pr.
    Systematic Theology: A Historicist Perspective.
      Scribner.
Kaufman, H. G. see Kaufman, Harold G.
Kaufman, Harold G.
  xKaufman, H. G.
    Career Management: A Guide to Combating
      Obsolescence. Wiley.
Kaufman, Herbert, 1922-
  xKaufman, Herbert.
    Administrative Feedback: Monitoring
      Subordinates' Behavior. Brookings.
    Are Government Organizations Immortal?.
      Brookings.
Kaufman, Herman S.
  xKaufman, Herman S.

    ed. Introduction to Polymer Science &
      Technology: An SPE Textbook. Wiley.
Kaufman, Howard K. see Kaufman, Howard Keva.
Kaufman, Howard Keva.
  xKaufman, Howard K.
    Bangkhuad: A Community Study in Thailand.
      C E Tuttle.
Kaufman, Jacob J. see Kaufman, Jacob Joseph.
Kaufman, Jacob Joseph.
  xKaufman, Jacob J.
    Collective Bargaining in the Railroad Industry.
      Russell.
Kaufman, Leon.
  xKaufman, Leon.
    Medical Applications of Fluorescent Excitation
      Analysis. CRC Pr.
Kaufman, Lloyd.
  xKaufman, Lloyd.
    Perception: The World Transformed. Oxford U
      Pr.
    Sight & Mind: An Introduction to Visual
      Perception. Oxford U Pr.
Kaufman, Louis, 1922-
  xKaufman, Louis.
    Essentials of Advertising. HarBraceJ.
Kaufman, M. Ralph. see Kaufman, Moses Ralph.
Kaufman, Martin, 1941-
  xKaufman, Martin.
    American Medical Education: The Formative
      Years, 1765-1910. Greenwood.
    Homeopathy in America: The Rise & Fall of a
      Medical Heresy. Johns Hopkins.
    The University of Vermont College of
      Medicine. U Pr of New Eng.
Kaufman, Milton.
  xKaufman, Milton.
    Radio Operator's License Q & A Manual.
      Hayden.
Kaufman, Moses Ralph, 1900-
  xKaufman, M. Ralph.
    ed. Psychiatric Unit in a General Hospital: Its
      Current & Future Role. Intl Univs Pr.
Kaufman, P. J. see Kaufman, Perry J.
Kaufman, Paul.
  xKaufman, Paul.
    Community Library: A Chapter in English
      Social History. Am Philos.
    Double-Exposure. Barlenmir.
Kaufman, Perry J.
  xKaufman, P. J.
    Commodity Trading Systems & Methods.
      Wiley.
    Technical Analysis in Commodities. Wiley.
Kaufman, Peter B.
  xKaufman, Peter B.
    ed. Plants, People, & Environment. Macmillan.
Kaufman, Roger. see Kaufman, Roger A.
Kaufman, Roger A.
  xKaufman, Roger.
    Identifying & Solving Problems: A System
      Approach. Univ Assocs.
    Needs Assessment: Concept & Application.
      Educ Tech Pubns.
Kaufman, Sherwin A.
  xKaufman, Sherwin A.
    From a Gynecologist's Notebook: Questions
      Women Ask. Stein & Day.
Kaufman, Shirley.
  xKaufman, Shirley.
    From One Life to Another. U of Pittsburgh Pr.
    Gold Country. U of Pittsburgh Pr.
Kaufman, Stanley. see Kaufman, Stanley L.
Kaufman, Stanley L.
  xKaufman, Stanley.
    Practical & Legal Manual for the Investor.
      Oceana.
Kaufman, Stephen A.
  xKaufman, Stephen A.

    The Akkadian Influences on Aramaic. U of
      Chicago Pr.
Kaufman, Theodore N.
  xKaufman, Theodore N.
    Germany Must Perish. Gordon Pr.
Kaufman, Wallace.
  xKaufman, Wallace.
    The Beaches Are Moving: The Drowning of
      America's Shoreline. Doubleday.
Kaufman, William E.
  xKaufman, William E.
    Contemporary Jewish Philosophies. Behrman.
Kaufman, William I. see Kaufman, William Irving.
Kaufman, William Irving, 1922-
  xKaufman, William I.
    ed. Great Television Plays. Dell.
    The Peanut Butter Cookbook. S&S.
    Sugar-Free Cookbook. Doubleday.
Kaufmann, A. see Kaufmann, Arnold.
Kaufmann, Arnold.
  xKaufmann, A.
    Graphs, Dynamic Programming & Finite
      Games. Acad Pr.
  xKaufmann, Arnold.
    Introduction to Operations Research. Acad Pr.
Kaufmann, Arthur C.
  xKaufmann, Arthur C.
    Combating Shoplifting. Natl Ret Merch.
Kaufmann, Dale W. see Kaufmann, Dale Wilmer.
Kaufmann, Dale Wilmer, 1893-
  xKaufmann, Dale W.
    ed. Sodium Chloride: The Production &
      Properties of Salt & Brine. Am Chemical.
Kaufmann, David, 1852-1899
  xKaufmann, David.
    Studien uber Salomon Ibn Gabirol. Arno.
Kaufmann, Emil, 1891-1953
  xKaufmann, Emil.
    Architecture in the Age of Reason: Baroque &
      Post-Baroque in England, Italy & France.
      Dover.
    Architecture in the Age of Reason: Baroque &
      Post-Baroque in England, Italy & France.
      Shoe String.
Kaufmann, Fritz, 1891-
  xKaufmann, Fritz.
    Thomas Mann: The World As Will &
      Representation. Cooper Sq.
Kaufmann, Harry.
  xKaufmann, Harry.
    The Psychology of Slimming Down & Feeling
      Great. Plantagenet Pr.
Kaufmann, Helen (Loeb).
  xKaufmann, Helen L.
    From Jehovah to Jazz: Music in America from
      Psalmody to the Present Day. Arno.
Kaufmann, Helen L. see Kaufmann, Helen (Loeb).
Kaufmann, John.
  xKaufmann, John.
    illus. Chimney Swift. Morrow.
    illus. Fish Hawk. Morrow.
    illus. Fly It: Making & Flying Your Own Kites,
      Boomerangs, Helicopters, Hang Gliders &
      Hand-Launched Gliders. Doubleday.
    illus. Flying Hand-Launched Gliders. Morrow.
    Insect Travelers. Morrow.
    illus. Little Dinosaurs & Early Birds. T Y
      Crowell.
    Streamlined. T Y Crowell.
Kaufmann, P. see Kaufmann, Peter.
Kaufmann, Paul, 1928-
  xKaufmann, Paul.
    Paddling the Gate. Mara.
Kaufmann, Peter.
  xKaufmann, P.
    The Guinea-Pig Placenta. Springer-Verlag.
Kaufmann, Thomas D. see Kaufmann, Thomas Dacosta.
Kaufmann, Thomas Dacosta.
  xKaufmann, Thomas D.

Variations on the Imperial Theme: Studies in
Ceremonial Art & Collecting in the Age of
Maximilian II & Rudolf II. Garland Pub.
Kaufmann, Walter, 1907-
xKaufmann, Walter.
The Ragas of South India: A Catalogue of
Scalar Material. Ind U Pr.
Kaufmann, Walter. see Kaufmann, Walter Arnold.
Kaufmann, Walter A. see Kaufmann, Walter Arnold.
Kaufmann, Walter Arnold.
xKaufmann, Walter.
The Faith of a Heretic. NAL.
From Shakespeare to Existentialism. Arno.
ed. & tr. & ed. Twenty-Five German Poets: A
Bilingual Collection. Norton.
xKaufmann, Walter A.
ed. Existentialism from Dostoevsky to Sartre.
Peter Smith.
Kaufmann, Walter H.
xKaufmann, Walter H.
Monarchism in the Weimar Republic. Octagon.
Kaufmann, William J.
xKaufmann, William J.
Black Holes & Warped Spacetime. Bantam.
Black Holes & Warped Spacetime. W H
Freeman.
Galaxies & Quasars. W H Freeman.
Planets & Moons. W H Freeman.
Relativity & Cosmology. Har-Row.
Stars & Nebulas. W H Freeman.
Kaul, Donald.
xKaul, Donald.
The End of the World As We Know It &
Other Entertainments. Image & Idea.
Kaulla, Rudolf, 1872-
xKaulla, Rudolph.
Theory of the Just Price: A Historical &
Critical Study of the Problem of Economic
Value. Hyperion Conn.
Kaulla, Rudolph. see Kaulla, Rudolf.
Kaumeyer, Richard A.
xKaumeyer, Richard A.
Planning & Using Skills Inventory Systems.
Van Nos Reinhold.
Kaun, Alexander S. see Kaun, Alexander Samuel.
Kaun, Alexander Samuel, 1889-1944
xKaun, Alexander S.
Leonid Andreyev, a Critical Study. AMS Pr.
Maxim Gorky & His Russia. Arno.
Kauper, Paul G.
xKauper, Paul G.
Civil Liberties & the Constitution. Greenwood.
The Higher Law & the Rights of Man in a
Revolutionary Society. Am Enterprise.
Religion & the Constitution. La State U Pr.
Kausch, H. H.
xKausch, H. H.
Polymer Fracture. Springer-Verlag.
Kaushall, Philip.
xKaushall, Phillip.
The Growing Years: A Study Guide for the
Televised Course. McGraw.
Kaushall, Phillip. see Kaushall, Philip.
Kaushik, Devendra.
xKaushik, Devendra.
Indian Ocean: Towards a Peace Zone. Intl Bk
Dist.
Kaushik, R. P., 1926-
xKaushik, R. P.
Organic Alchemy. Journey Pubns.
Kausler, Donald H.
xKausler, Donald H.
Psychology of Verbal Learning & Memory.
Acad Pr.
Kauss, Theodore.
xKauss, Theodore.
Leaders Live with Crises. Phi Delta Kappa.
Kautsky, John H., 1922-
xKautsky, John H.

Communism & the Politics of Development:
Persistent Myths & Changing Behavior.
Krieger.
Kautsky, Karl, 1854-1938
xKautsky, Karl.
Are the Jews a Race?. Greenwood.
Communism in Central Europe at the Time of
the Reformation. Gordon Pr.
Communism in Central Europe in the Time of
the Reformation. Kelley.
Social Democracy Versus Communism.
Hyperion Conn.
Kautzky, Ted. see Kautzky, Theodore.
Kautzky, Theodore, 1896-1953
xKautzky, Ted.
The Ted Kautzky Pencil Book. Van Nos
Reinhold.
Kauvar, Gerald B.
xKauvar, Gerald B.
Intro. by & ed. Nineteenth Century English
Verse Drama. Fairleigh Dickinson.
Other Poetry of Keats. Fairleigh Dickinson.
Kauzmann, W. see Kauzmann, Walter.
Kauzmann, Walter, 1916-
xKauzmann, W.
Quantum Chemistry: An Introduction. Acad
Pr.
Kavaler, Lucy.
xKavaler, Lucy.
Artificial World Around Us. John Day.
Astors: An American Legend. Dodd.
Cold Against Disease. John Day.
Dangerous Air. John Day.
The Dangers of Noise. T Y Crowell.
Life Battles Cold. John Day.
Wonders of Fungi. John Day.
Kavan, Anna.
xKavan, Anna.
Ice. Popular Lib.
Kavanagh, Aidan.
xKavanagh, Aidan.
The Shape of Baptism: The Rite of Christian
Initiation. Pueblo Pub Co.
Kavanagh, Frederick, 1908-
xKavanagh, Frederick.
ed. Analytical Microbiology. Acad Pr.
Kavanagh, Herminie T. see Kavanagh, Herminie
Templeton.
Kavanagh, Herminie Templeton.
xKavanagh, Herminie T.
Ashes of Old Wishes, & Other Darby O'Gill
Tales. Arno.
Kavanagh, James F.
xKavanagh, James F.
Speech & Language in the Laboratory, School
& Clinic. MIT Pr.
Kavanagh, P. J. see Kavanagh, Patrick Joseph Gregory.
Kavanagh, Patrick.
xKavanagh, Patrick.
Collected Poems. Devin.
Collected Poems. Norton.
Kavanagh, Patrick Joseph Gregory, 1931-
xKavanagh, P. J.
The Irish Captain. Doubleday.
Kavanagh, Paul.
xKavanagh, Paul.
Triumph of Evil. PB.
Kavanagh, Peter.
xKavanagh, Peter.
Garden of the Golden Apples: A Bibliography
of Patrick Kavanagh. Kavanagh.
Kavanaugh, Dorriet.
xKavanaugh, Dorriet.
ed. Listen to Us: The Children's Express
Report. Workman Pub.
Kavanaugh, James. see Kavanaugh, James J.
Kavanaugh, James J.
xKavanaugh, James.

Celebrate the Sun. Dutton.
Kavanaugh, John, 1912-
xKavanaugh, John.
ed. Quaker Approach to Contemporary
Problems. Greenwood.
Kavanaugh, Robert.
xKavanaugh, Robert.
Grim Generation. Trident.
Kavasch, Barrie.
xKavasch, Barrie.
Native Harvests: Recipes & Botanicals of the
American Indian. Random.
Native Harvests: Recipes & Botanicals of the
American Indian. Random.
Kavena, Juanita. see Kavena, Juanita Tiger.
Kavena, Juanita Tiger.
xKavena, Juanita.
Hopi Cookery. U of Ariz Pr.
Kavenagh, W. Keith.
xKavenagh, W. Keith.
ed. Foundations of Colonial America: A
Documentary History. Chelsea Hse.
Kavner, Richard.
xKavner, Richard.
Total Vision. A & W Pubs.
xKavner, Richard S.
Total Vision. A & W Pubs.
Kavner, Richard S. see Kavner, Richard.
Kavolis, Vytautas. see Kavolis, Vytautas Martynas.
Kavolis, Vytautas Martynas, 1930-
xKavolis, Vytautas.
History on Art's Side: Social Dynamics in
Artistic Efflorescences. Cornell U Pr.
Kawabata, Yasunari, 1899-1972
xKawabata, Yasunari.
The Master of Go. Berkley Pub.
Kawai, Tatsuo, 1889-
xKawai, Tatsuo.
The Goal of Japanese Expansion. Greenwood.
Kawakami, Kiyoshi K. see Kawakami, Kiyoshi Karl.
Kawakami, Kiyoshi Karl, 1875-1949
xKawakami, Kiyoshi K.
The Real Japanese Question. Arno.
Kawakami, Toyo S.
xKawakami, Toyo S.
Acronyms in Education & the Behavioral
Sciences. ALA.
Kawakita, Michiaki, 1914-
xKawakita, Michiaki.
Modern Currents in Japanese Art. Weatherhill.
Kawashima, Masaaki.
xKawashima, Masaaki.
Fundamentals of Men's Fashion Design: A
Guide to Tailored Clothes. Fairchild.
Kawata, Tatsuo, 1911-
xKawata, Tatsuo.
Fourier Analysis in Probability Theory. Acad
Pr.
Kawharu, Ian H. see Kawharu, Ian Hugh.
Kawharu, Ian Hugh.
xKawharu, Ian H.
Maori Land Tenure: Studies of a Changing
Institution. Oxford U Pr.
Kawi, A. A. see Kawi, Ali A.
Kawi, Ali A.
xKawi, A. A.
Prenatal & Paranatal Factors in the
Development of Childhood Reading
Disorders. Kraus Repr.
Kawin, Bruce F., 1945-
xKawin, Bruce F.
Faulkner & Film. Ungar.
Kay, A. William.
xKay, William.
Moral Education: A Sociological Study of the
Influence of Society, Home & School. Shoe
String.
Kay, Alan.
xKay, Alan.

Creative Art Through Photography. Branford.

Kay, Barbara A.
xKay, Barbara A.
Probation & Parole. C C Thomas.

Kay, Beatrice.
xKay, Beatrice.
Victory in the Voting Booth. ETC Pubns.

Kay, David.
xKay, David.
Poultry Keeping for Beginners. David & Charles.

Kay, David A.
xKay, David A.
ed. The Changing United Nations: Options for the United States. Praeger.

Kay, Dorothea.
xKay, Dorothea.
Embroidered Samplers. Scribner.

Kay, E. *see* Kay, Emil.

Kay, E. Alison, 1928-
xKay, E. Alison.
ed. Natural History of the Hawaiian Islands: Selected Readings. U Pr of Hawaii.

Kay, Emil.
xKay, E.
A Mathematical Model for Handling in a Warehouse. Pergamon.

Kay, F. George. *see* Kay, Frederick George.

Kay, Frederick George, 1911-
xKay, F. George.
London. Rand.

Kay, G. B.
xKay, Geoffrey.
The Economic Theory of the Working Class. St Martin.

Kay, Geoffrey. *see* Kay, G. B.

Kay, George Marshall.
xKay, Marshall.
ed. Stratigraphy & Life History. Wiley.

Kay, Helen, Pseud.
xKay, Helen.
Apes. Macmillan.
A Day in the Life of a Baby Gibbon. Abelard.
A Pony for the Winter. Schol Bk Serv.

Kay, J. A. *see* Kay, John Alexander.

Kay, James T. De. *see* De Kay, James T.

Kay, Jane G.
xKay, Jane G.
Crafts for the Very Disabled & Handicapped: For All Ages. C C Thomas.

Kay, John Alexander.
xKay, J. A.
The British Tax System. Oxford U Pr.

Kay, John L.
xKay, John L.
Pennsylvania Postal History. Quarterman.

Kay, Mara.
xKay, Mara.
In Face of Danger. Crown.

Kay, Margarita. *see* Kay, Margarita Artschwager.

Kay, Margarita Artschwager.
xKay, Margarita.
Southwestern Medical Dictionary: Spanish-English & English-Spanish. U of Ariz Pr.

Kay, Marshall. *see* Kay, George Marshall.

Kay, Michele.
xKay, Michele.
Doing Business in Hong Kong. Barron.

Kay, Neil M.
xKay, Neil M.
The Innovating Firm: A Behavioral Theory of Corporate R & D. St Martin.

Kay, Norman.
xKay, Norman.
Complete Book of Duplicate Bridge. Har-Row.
The Complete Book of Duplicate Bridge. Putnam.

Kay, Ormonde De. *see* De Kay, Ormonde.

Kay, Richard, 1931-
xKay, Richard.
Dante's Swift & Strong: Essays on "Inferno XV". Regents Pr KS.

Kay, Ruth C. Mc. *see* McKay, Ruth C.

Kay, William. *see* Kay, A. William.

Kay-Robinson, Denys.
xKay-Robinson, Denys.
The First Mrs. Thomas Hardy. St Martin.

Kay-Shuttleworth, J. P. *see* Kay-Shuttleworth, James Phillips.

Kay-Shuttleworth, James P. *see* Kay-Shuttleworth, James Phillips.

Kay-Shuttleworth, James Phillips, Sir, Bart, 1804-1877
xKay-Shuttleworth, J. P.
The Moral & Physical Condition of the Working Classes Employed in the Cotton Manufacture in Manchester. Biblio Dist.
xKay-Shuttleworth, James P.
Memorandum on Popular Education. Kelley.

Kayal, Philip M.
xKayal, Philip M.
The Syrian-Lebanese in America. Twayne.

Kayden, Xandra.
xKayden, Xandra.
Campaign Organization. Heath.

Kaye, D. *see* Kaye, Donald.

Kaye, Donald.
xKaye, D.
Infective Endocarditis. Univ Park.

Kaye, Evelyn, 1937-
xKaye, Evelyn.
Crosscurrents: Children, Families, & Religion. Potter.

Kaye, G. *see* Kaye, Geoffrey.

Kaye, Geoffrey.
xKaye, G.
Tables of Co-efficients for the Analysis of Triple Angular Correlations of Gamma-Rays from Aligned Nuclei. Pergamon.

Kaye, Geraldine
xKaye, Geraldine.
Good-Bye Ruby Red. Childrens.

Kaye, M. M. *see* Kaye, Mary Margaret.

Kaye, Marvin.
xKaye, Marvin.
The Incredible Umbrella. Dell.
The Incredible Umbrella. Doubleday.
Masters of Solitude. Avon.
Masters of Solitude. Doubleday.
My Brother, the Druggist. Doubleday.
The Stein & Day Handbook of Magic. Stein & Day.

Kaye, Mary Margaret, 1911-
xKaye, M. M.
The Far Pavilions. Bantam.
The Far Pavilions. St Martin.
Shadow of the Moon. Bantam.
The Shadow of the Moon. St Martin.

Kaye, Percy L. *see* Kaye, Percy Lewis.

Kaye, Percy Lewis.
xKaye, Percy L.
The Colonial Executive Prior to the Restoration. AMS Pr.
The Colonial Executive Prior to the Restoration. Johnson Repr.

Kaye, Robert.
xKaye, Robert.
ed. Core Textbook of Pediatrics. Lippincott.

Kaye, Sidney, 1912-
xKaye, Sidney.
Handbook of Emergency Toxicology: A Guide for the Identification, Diagnosis, & Treatment of Poisoning. C C Thomas.

Kaye-Smith, Sheila, 1887-1956
xKaye-Smith, Sheila.
Quartet in Heaven. Arno.

Kayira, Legson.
xKayira, Legsons.

Looming Shadow. Macmillan.

Kayira, Legsons. *see* Kayira, Legson.

Kaylin, Walter.
xKaylin, Walter.
The Power Forward. Atheneum.

Kaynor, Richard S.
xKaynor, Richard S.
Industrial Development: A Practical Handbook for Planning & Implementing Development Programs. Irvington.

Kays, William M. *see* Kays, William Morrow.

Kays, William Morrow.
xKays, William M.
Convective Heat & Mass Transfer. McGraw.
Convective Heat & Mass Transfer. McGraw.

Kaysen, Carl.
xKaysen, Carl.
Higher Learning, the Universities & the Public. Princeton U Pr.

Kayser, Elmer L. *see* Kayser, Elmer Louis.

Kayser, Elmer Louis, 1896-
xKayser, Elmer L.
Grand Social Enterprise: A Study of Jeremy Bentham in His Relation to Liberal Nationalism. AMS Pr.

Kaysing, Bill. *see* Kaysing, William.

Kaysing, William.
xKaysing, Bill.
Fell's Beginner's Guide to Motorcycling. Fell.

Kayton, Myron.
xKayton, Myron.
Avionics Navigation Systems. Wiley.

Kaywaykla, James.
xKaywaykla, James.
Narrated by In the Days of Victorio: Recollections of a Warm Springs Apache. U of Ariz Pr.

Kazami, Takehide, 1914-
xKazami, Takehide.
Himalayas: A Journey to Nepal. Kodansha.

Kazamias, Andreas M.
xKazamias, Andreas M.
Education & the Quest for Modernity in Turkey. U of Chicago Pr.

Kazan, Elia.
xKazan, Elia.
Acts of Love. Knopf.
Acts of Love. Warner Bks.
America, America. Stein & Day.
The Understudy. Stein & Day.
The Understudy. Warner Bks.

Kazanas, H. *see* Kazanas, H. C.

Kazanas, H. C.
xKazanas, H.
Manufacturing Processes: Metals. P-H.
xKazanas, H. C.
Properties & Uses of Ferrous & Nonferrous Metals. Prakken.

Kazarian, E. A. *see* Kazarian, Edward A.

Kazarian, Edward A.
xKazarian, E. A.
Food Service Facilities Planning. AVI.
xKazarian, Edward A.
Work Analysis & Design for Hotels, Restaurants & Institutions. AVI.

Kazdin, Alan E.
xKazdin, Alan E.
Evaluation of Behavior Therapy: Issues, Evidence, & Research Strategies. Ballinger Pub.
Evaluation of Behavior Therapy: Issues, Evidence & Research Strategies. U of Nebr Pr.
New Perspectives in Abnormal Psychology. Oxford U Pr.
Research Design in Clinical Psychology. Har-Row.

Kazeck, Melvin E.
xKazeck, Melvin E.

North Dakota: A Human & Economic
Geography. N Dak Inst.
Kazin, Alfred, 1915-
xKazin, Alfred.
Bright Book of Life: American Novelists &
Storytellers from Hemingway to Mailer.
Little.
The Inmost Leaf: A Selection of Essays.
Greenwood.
New York Jew. Knopf.
New York Jew. Random.
Open Form: Essays for Our Time. HarBraceJ.
Starting Out in the Thirties. Random.
Kaziro, Y. see Kaziro, Yoshito.
Kaziro, Yoshito.
xKaziro, Y.
ed. Protein Synthesis. Univ Park.
Kazmann, Raphael G. see Kazmann, Raphael Gabriel.
Kazmann, Raphael Gabriel.
xKazmann, Raphael G.
Modern Hydrology. Har-Row.
Kazmier, Leonard J.
xKazmier, Leonard J.
Basic Statistics for Business & Economics.
McGraw.
Kazziha, Walid.
xKazziha, Walid.
Revolutionary Transformation in the Arab
World: Habash & His Comrades from
Nationalism to Marxism. St Martin.
xKazziha, Walid W.
Palestine in the Arab Dilemma. B&N.
Kazziha, Walid W. see Kazziha, Walid.
Keach, Benjamin, 1640-1704
xKeach, Benjamin.
Preaching from the Types & Metaphors of the
Bible. Kregel.
Keach, Richard L.
xKeach, Richard L.
God's Spirit in the Church. Judson.
Purple Pulpit. Judson.
Kealy, J. Kevin.
xKealy, J. Kevin.
Diagnostic Radiology of the Dog & Cat.
Saunders.
Kealy, John P.
xKealy, John P.
The Early Church & Africa: A School
Certificate Course Based on the East African
Syllabus for Christian Religious Education.
Oxford U Pr.
Kean, B. H. see Kean, Benjamin Harrison.
Kean, Benjamin Harrison.
xKean, B. H.
ed. Tropical Medicine & Parasitology: Classic
Investigations. Cornell U Pr.
Keane, Augustus H. see Keane, Augustus Henry.
Keane, Augustus Henry, 1833-1912
xKeane, Augustus H.
Gold of Ophir, Whence Brought & by Whom.
Negro U Pr.
Keane, Christopher.
xKeane, Christopher.
The Crossing. Arbor Hse.
The Tour. Stein & Day.
Keane, Claire (Brackman).
xKeane, Claire B.
Essentials of Nursing: A Medical Surgical Text
for Practical Nurses. Saunders.
Keane, Claire B. see Keane, Claire (Brackman).
Keane, Patrick J.
xKeane, Patrick J.
A Wild Civility: Interactions in the Poetry &
Thought of Robert Graves. U of Mo Pr.
Keane, Susan. see Keane, Susan M.
Keane, Susan M.
xKeane, Susan.

Image & Theme: Studies in Modern French
Fiction - Bernanos, Malraux, Sarraute, Gide,
Martin Du Gard. Harvard U Pr.
Kearney, G. E. see Kearney, George E.
Kearney, George E.
xKearney, G. E.
ed. Aboriginal Cognition: Retrospect &
Prospect. Humanities.
Kearney, James.
xKearney, James.
Prime Time. Nordon Pubns.
Kearney, Robert N.
xKearney, Robert N.
ed. Politics & Modernization in South &
Southeast Asia. Halsted Pr.
ed. Politics & Modernization in South &
Southeast Asia. Schenkman.
The Politics of Ceylon (Sri Lanka). Cornell U
Pr.
Kearns, George.
xKearns, George.
Guide to Ezra Pound's Selected Cantos.
Rutgers U Pr.
ed. Literature of the World. McGraw.
Kearny, Jillian.
xKearny, Jullian.
Agent of Love. Warner Bks.
Kearny, Jullian. see Kearny, Jillian.
Kearny, Mary Ann.
xKearny, Mary Ann.
Life, Liberty & the Pursuit of Happiness.
Newbury Hse.
Kearsley, Richard B.
xKearsley, Richard B.
ed. Infants at Risk: Assessment of Cognitive
Functioning. Halsted Pr.
Keast, Allen.
xKeast, Allen.
ed. Migrant Birds in the Neotropics: Ecology,
Behavior, Distribution & Conservation.
Smithsonian.
Keast, Laury.
xKeast, Laury.
The Abortion Controversy. SamHar Pr.
Keat, Donald B.
xKeat, Donald B.
Fundamentals of Child Counseling. HM.
Keates, J. S.
xKeates, J. S.
Cartographic Design & Production. Halsted Pr.
Keating, Bern.
xKeating, Bern.
Famous American Cowboys. Rand.
Keating, Charles J.
xKeating, Charles J.
The Leadership Book. Paulist Pr.
Keating, H. R. F. see Keating, Henry Reymond
Fitzwalter.
Keating, Henry.
xKeating, Henry.
Murder by Death. Warner Bks.
Keating, Henry Reymond Fitzwalter, 1926-
xKeating, H. R. F.
Inspector Ghote Draws a Line. Doubleday.
Keating, J. F. see Keating, John Fitzstephen.
Keating, John Fitzstephen, 1850-1911
xKeating, J. F.
Agape & the Eucharist in the Early Church:
Studies in the History of Christian Love
Feasts. AMS Pr.
Keating, L. Clark. see Keating, Louis Clark.
Keating, Lawrence A, 1903-
xKeating, Lawrence A.
Fleet Admiral: The Story of William F. Halsey.
Westminster.
Keating, Louis Clark, 1907-
xKeating, L. Clark.
Audubon: The Kentucky Years. U Pr of Ky.
Keating, P. J.
xKeating, P. J.

The Working Classes in Victorian Fiction.
Routledge & Kegan.
Keatley, Lu.
xKeatley, Lu.
Automobiles. Specialty Bks.
Keaton, Diane.
xKeaton, Diane.
Reservations. Knopf.
Keats, Ezra. see Keats, Ezra Jack.
Keats, Ezra J. see Keats, Ezra Jack.
Keats, Ezra Jack.
xKeats, Ezra.
illus. The Trip. Greenwillow.
xKeats, Ezra J.
illus. Dreams. Macmillan.
illus. Dreams. Macmillan.
illus. Goggles. Macmillan.
illus. Goggles. Macmillan.
illus. Letter to Amy. Har-Row.
Louie. Greenwillow.
Louie. Schol Bk Serv.
illus. Louie's Search. Schol Bk Serv.
illus. Maggie & the Pirate. Schol Bk Serv.
Pssst Doggie. Watts.
The Trip. Schol Bk Serv.
illus. Whistle for Willie. Penguin.
illus. Whistle for Willie. Viking Pr.
Keats, John.
xKeats, John.
Complete Works of John Keats. AMS Pr.
Letters of John Keats. Oxford U Pr.
Letters of John Keats, 1814-1821. Harvard U
Pr.
Poems of John Keats. T Y Crowell.
Keats-Shelley Memorial House, Rome. see Keats-Shelley
Memorial, Rome.
Keats-Shelley Memorial, Rome.
xKeats-Shelley Memorial House, Rome.
Catalog of Books & Manuscripts at the
Keats-Shelley Memorial House in Rome. G K
Hall.
Keats, Sidney.
xKeats, Sidney.
Cerebral Palsy. C C Thomas.
Operative Orthopedics in Cerebral Palsy. C C
Thomas.
Keats, Theodore E.
xKeats, Theodore E.
Atlas of Normal Developmental Roentgen
Anatomy. Year Bk Med.
Keaveney, Sydney S. see Keaveney, Sydney Starr.
Keaveney, Sydney Starr.
xKeaveney, Sydney S.
American Painting: A Guide to Information
Sources. Gale.
Keay, F. see Keay, Frederick.
Keay, Frederick.
xKeay, F.
Marketing & Sales Forecasting. Pergamon.
Marketing Through Measurement. Pergamon.
Keay, John.
xKeay, John.
The Gilgit Game: The Explorers of the
Western Himalayas, 1865-1895. Shoe String.
Kebabian, Paul B.
xKebabian, Paul B.
American Woodworking Tools. NYGS.
Kebart, Richard C.
xKebart, Richard C.
ed. Self-Assessment of Current Knowledge in
Radiologic Technology. Med Exam.
Kebbel, Thomas E. see Kebbel, Thomas Edward.
Kebbel, Thomas Edward, 1827-
xKebbel, Thomas E.
Life of George Crabbe. Kennikat.
Life of George Crabbe. R West.
Keck, Leander E.
xKeck, Leander E.

Paul & His Letters. Fortress.
　　ed. Studies in Luke-Acts. Fortress.
Keckhut, John.
　　xKeckhut, John.
　　　　The Dublin Pawn. Norton.
Kecskemeti, P. *see* Kecskemeti, Paul.
Kecskemeti, Paul.
　　xKecskemeti, P.
　　　　Insurgency As a Strategic Problem. Paladin
　　　　　　Ent.
　　xKecskemeti, Paul.
　　　　Strategic Surrender: The Politics of Victory &
　　　　　　Defeat. Stanford U Pr.
　　　　The Unexpected Revolution: Social Forces in
　　　　　　the Hungarian Uprising. Stanford U Pr.
Keddie, Kenneth M. *see* Keddie, Kenneth M. G.
Keddie, Kenneth M. G.
　　xKeddie, Kenneth M.
　　　　Action with the Elderly: A Handbook for
　　　　　　Relatives & Friends. Pergamon.
Keddie, William, 1809-1877
　　xKeddie, William.
　　　　ed. Cyclopaedia of Literary & Scientific
　　　　　　Anecdote: Illustrative of the Characters,
　　　　　　Habits, & Conversation of Men of Letters &
　　　　　　Science. Gale.
Kedourie, Elie.
　　xKedourie, Elie.
　　　　Afghani & Abduh: An Essay on Religious
　　　　　　Unbelief & Political Activism in Modern
　　　　　　Islam. Humanities.
　　　　Afghani & Abduh: Essay on Religious Unbelief
　　　　　　& Political Activism in Modern Islam. Biblio
　　　　　　Dist.
　　　　Arabic Political Memoirs & Other Studies.
　　　　　　Biblio Dist.
　　　　Chatham House Version & Other
　　　　　　Middle-Eastern Studies. Biblio Dist.
　　　　Islam in the Modern World & Other Studies.
　　　　　　New Republic.
　　　　ed. Nationalism in Asia & Africa. NAL.
Kee, Alistair, 1937-
　　xKee, Alistair.
　　　　ed. A Reader in Political Theology.
　　　　　　Westminster.
Kee, Howard C. *see* Kee, Howard Clark.
Kee, Howard Clark.
　　xKee, Howard C.
　　　　Christian Origins in Sociological Perspective:
　　　　　　Methods & Resources. Westminster.
　　　　Christianity. Argus Comm.
　　　　Community of the New Age: Studies in Mark's
　　　　　　Gospel. Westminster.
　　　　The Origins of Christianity: Sources &
　　　　　　Documents. P-H.
　　　　Understanding the New Testament. P-H.
Keech, Scott.
　　xKeech, Scott.
　　　　Ciphered. Har-Row.
Keedy, M. L. *see* Keedy, Mervin Laverne.
Keedy, Mervin L. *see* Keedy, Mervin Laverne.
Keedy, Mervin Laverne.
　　xKeedy, M. L.
　　　　Exploring Modern Mathematics. HR&W.
　　　　Exploring Modern Mathematics. HR&W.
　　xKeedy, Mervin L.
　　　　Arithmetic. A-W.
　　　　College Algebra: A Functions Approach. A-W.
　　　　Fundamental Algebra & Trigonometry. A-W.
　　　　Fundamental College Algebra. A-W.
　　　　Geometry: A Modern Introduction. A-W.
　　　　Introductory Algebra. A-W.
Keefe, Carolyn.
　　xKeefe, Carolyn.
　　　　Freedom for Me & Other Human Creatures.
　　　　　　Word Bks.
Keefe, Francis J.
　　xKeefe, Francis J.

A Practical Guide to Behavioral Assessment.
　　　　Springer Pub.
Keefe, John. *see* Keefe, John E.
Keefe, John E.
　　xKeefe, John.
　　　　Coping with the Interview. Rosen Pr.
　　xKeefe, John E.
　　　　Aim for a Job As Electronic Technician. Rosen
　　　　　　Pr.
Keefe, Robert, 1938-
　　xKeefe, Robert.
　　　　Charlotte Bronte's World of Death. U of Tex
　　　　　　Pr.
Keefe, William J.
　　xKeefe, William J.
　　　　Congress & the American People. P-H.
Keegan, John, 1934-
　　xKeegan, John.
　　　　The Face of Battle. Viking Pr.
　　　　Who Was Who in World War II. T Y Crowell.
Keegan, Marcia.
　　xKeegan, Marcia.
　　　　photos by The Taos Indians & Their Sacred
　　　　　　Blue Lake. Messner.
Keegan, Warren J.
　　xKeegan, Warren J.
　　　　Multinational Marketing Management. P-H.
Keehn, J. D.
　　xKeehn, J. D.
　　　　The Origins of Madness: The Psychopathology
　　　　　　of Animal Life. Pergamon.
Keel, Bennie C., 1934-
　　xKeel, Bennie C.
　　　　Cherokee Archaeology: A Study of the
　　　　　　Appalachian Summit. U of Tenn Pr.
Keele, Reba L.
　　xKeele, Reba L.
　　　　Let's Talk: Adults & Children Sharing
　　　　　　Feelings. Brigham.
Keeler, Clyde E. *see* Keeler, Clyde Edgar.
Keeler, Clyde Edgar, 1900-
　　xKeeler, Clyde E.
　　　　Cuna Indian Art: The Culture & Craft of
　　　　　　Panama's San Blas Islanders. Exposition.
Keeler, Harriet L. *see* Keeler, Harriet Louise.
Keeler, Harriet Louise, 1846-1921
　　xKeeler, Harriet L.
　　　　Our Northern Shrubs, & How to Identify
　　　　　　Them. Peter Smith.
Keeler, Laura, Mother.
　　xKeeler, Laura.
　　　　Geoffrey of Monmouth & the Late Latin
　　　　　　Chroniclers. Folcroft.
　　　　Geoffrey of Monmouth & the Late Latin
　　　　　　Chroniclers, 1300-1500. Arden Lib.
Keeler, Mary J. *see* Keeler, Mary Jerome.
Keeler, Mary Jerome, 1895-
　　xKeeler, Mary J.
　　　　Catholic Literary France from Verlaine to the
　　　　　　Present Time. Arno.
Keeley, Lawrence H.
　　xKeeley, Lawrence H.
　　　　Experimental Determination of Stone Tool
　　　　　　Uses: A Microwear Analysis. U of Chicago
　　　　　　Pr.
Keeley, Michael C.
　　xKeeley, Michael C.
　　　　ed. Population, Public Policy, & Economic
　　　　　　Development. Praeger.
Keeley, Steve.
　　xKeeley, Steve.
　　　　The Complete Book of Racquetball. Follett.
Keeling, B. Lewis. *see* Keeling, Billy Lewis.
Keeling, Billy Lewis.
　　xKeeling, B. Lewis.
　　　　Payroll Records & Accounting. SW Pub.
Keeling, Jill A. *see* Keeling, Jill Annette.
Keeling, Jill Annette.
　　xKeeling, Jill A.

The Old English Sheepdog. Arco.
The Old English Sheepdog. Palmetto Pub.
Keeling, S. V. *see* Keeling, Stanley Victor.
Keeling, Stanley V. *see* Keeling, Stanley Victor.
Keeling, Stanley Victor.
　　xKeeling, S. V.
　　　　Descartes. Oxford U Pr.
　　xKeeling, Stanley V.
　　　　Descartes. Greenwood.
Keely, Charles B.
　　xKeely, Charles B.
　　　　U. S. Immigration: A Policy Analysis.
　　　　　　Population Coun.
Keen, A. Myra. *see* Keen, Angeline Myra.
Keen, Angeline Myra.
　　xKeen, A. Myra.
　　　　Marine Molluscan Genera of Western North
　　　　　　America: An Illustrated Key. Stanford U Pr.
Keen, Benjamin, 1913-
　　xKeen, Benjamin.
　　　　The Aztec Image in Western Thought. Rutgers
　　　　　　U Pr.
　　　　David Curtis De Forest & the Revolution of
　　　　　　Buenos Aires. Greenwood.
　　　　David Curtis Deforest & the Revolution of
　　　　　　Buenos Aires. Elliots Bks.
　　　　ed. Latin American Civilization. HM.
　　　　A Short History of Latin America. HM.
Keen, C. P. *see* Keen, Clifford P.
Keen, Clifford P.
　　xKeen, C. P.
　　　　Championship Wrestling. Wehman.
　　xKeen, Clifford P.
　　　　Championship Wrestling. Arco.
Keen, E. *see* Keen, Ernest.
Keen, Ernest, 1937-
　　xKeen, E.
　　　　Primer in Phenomenological Psychology.
　　　　　　HR&W.
Keen, Harry.
　　xKeen, Harry.
　　　　Triumphs of Medicine. Merrimack Bk Serv.
Keen, M. J. *see* Keen, Michael John.
Keen, Martin L.
　　xKeen, Martin L.
　　　　Be a Rockhound. Messner.
　　　　Lightning & Thunder. Messner.
　　　　The World Beneath Our Feet: The Story of
　　　　　　Soil. Messner.
Keen, Maurice. *see* Keen, Maurice Hugh.
Keen, Maurice Hugh.
　　xKeen, Maurice.
　　　　Pelican History of Medieval Europe. Penguin.
Keen, Michael John, 1935-
　　xKeen, M. J.
　　　　An Introduction to Marine Geology.
　　　　　　Pergamon.
Keen, Sam.
　　xKeen, Sam.
　　　　Apology for Wonder. Har-Row.
　　　　Gabriel Marcel. John Knox.
　　　　What to Do When You're Bored & Blue.
　　　　　　Wyden.
Keenan, Brigid, 1939-
　　xKeenan, Brigid.
　　　　The Women We Wanted to Look Like. St
　　　　　　Martin.
Keenan, Charles W. *see* Keenan, Charles William.
Keenan, Charles William.
　　xKeenan, Charles W.
　　　　General College Chemistry. Har-Row.
Keenan, Henry F. *see* Keenan, Henry Francis.
Keenan, Henry Francis, 1850-
　　xKeenan, Henry F.
　　　　Money-Makers: A Social Parable. Johnson
　　　　　　Repr.
Keenan, Jeremy, 1945-
　　xKeenan, Jeremy.
　　　　The Tuareg: People of Ahaggar. St Martin.
Keenan, Joseph H. *see* Keenan, Joseph Henry.

Keenan, Joseph Henry.
xKeenan, Joseph H.
Gas Tables: Thermodynamic Properties of Air
Products of Combustion & Component Gases
Compressible Flow Functions Including
Those of Ascher H. Shapiro & Gilbert M.
Edelman.. Wiley.
Steam Tables: Thermodynamic Properties of
Water Including Vapor, Liquid, & Solid
Phases. Wiley.
Thermodynamics. MIT Pr.
Keenan, Philip C. see Keenan, Philip Childs.
Keenan, Philip Childs.
xKeenan, Philip C.
An Atlas of Spectra of the Cooler Stars: Types
G, K, M, S, & C. Ohio St U Pr.
Keene, Betsey D.
xKeene, Betsey D.
History of Bourne, 1622-1937. W S Sullwold.
Keene, Carolyn, Pseud.
xKeene, Carolyn.
Bungalow Mystery. G&D.
The Clue in the Crossword Cipher. G&D.
The Double Jinx Mystery. G&D.
The Flying Saucer Mystery. Wanderer Bks.
Ghost of Blackwood Hall. G&D.
Moonstone Castle Mystery. G&D.
Mystery of Crocodile Island. G&D.
Password to Larkspur Lane. G&D.
Quest of the Missing Map. G&D.
The Riddle of the Frozen Fountain. G&D.
The Sierra Gold Mystery. G&D.
Sign of the Twisted Candles. G&D.
Spider Sapphire Mystery. G&D.
Strange Message in the Parchment. G&D.
The Thirteenth Pearl. G&D.
The Witch's Omen. G&D.
Keene, Dennis, 1934-
xKeene, Dennis.
Yokomitsu Riichi, Modernist. Columbia U Pr.
Keene, Donald.
xKeene, Donald.
Bunraku: The Art of the Japanese Puppet
Theatre. Kodansha.
ed. Modern Japanese Literature: An
Anthology. Grove.
Some Japanese Portraits. Kodansha.
ed. Twenty Plays of the No Theatre. Columbia
U Pr.
World Within Walls: Japanese Literature of the
Pre-Modern Era 1600-1867. Grove.
Keene, Donald. see Keene, Donald Lawrence.
Keene, Donald Lawrence.
xKeene, Donald.
Modern Japanese Novels & the West. U Pr of
Va.
Keene, G. B. see Keene, Geoffrey Bourton.
Keene, Geoffrey Bourton.
xKeene, G. B.
First-Order Functional Calculus. Routledge &
Kegan.
Keene, Judy, 1943-
xKeene, Judy.
Travel Light Handbook. Contemp Bks.
Keene, Milton H. see Keene, Milton Henry.
Keene, Milton Henry, 1912-
xKeene, Milton H.
Patterns for Mature Living. Abingdon.
Keene, R. D. see Keene, Raymond D.
Keene, Raymond. see Keene, Raymond D.
Keene, Raymond D.
xKeene, R. D.
The Chess Combination from Philidor to
Karpov. Pergamon.
How to Play the King's Indian, Saemisch
Variation. Hippocrene Bks.
Learn from the Grandmasters. David &
Charles.
xKeene, Raymond.

Korchnoi vs Spassky: Chess Crisis. Allen
Unwin.
ed. Learn from the Grandmasters. McKay.
World Chess Championship: Korchnoi Vs
Karpov. S&S.
Keene, Roland.
xKeene, Roland.
ed. Money, Marbles, or Chalk: Student
Financial Support in Higher Education. S Ill
U Pr.
Keene, Tom.
xKeene, Tom.
Spyship. Marek.
Keenen, George.
xKeenen, George.
Preposterous Week. Dial.
Keener, Frederick M., 1937-
xKeener, Frederick M.
English Dialogues of the Dead: A Critical
History, an Anthology & a Check List.
Columbia U Pr.
Keenleyside, T. A. see Keenleyside, Terence A.
Keenleyside, Terence A.
xKeenleyside, T. A.
The Common Touch. Doubleday.
Keep, Austin B. see Keep, Austin Baxter.
Keep, Austin Baxter, 1875-1932
xKeep, Austin B.
The Library in Colonial New York. B Franklin.
The Library in Colonial New York. Gordon Pr.
Keeran, Roger, 1944-
xKeeran, Roger.
Communist Party & the Auto Workers Unions.
Ind U Pr.
Keers, John H.
xKeers, John H.
How to Make Liqueurs at Home. Manor Bks.
Kees, Beverly.
xKees, Beverly.
ed. Fondue on the Menu. Western Pub.
Wonderful Ways with Chicken. Greene.
Kees, Weldon, 1914-1955?
xKees, Weldon.
The Collected Poems of Weldon Kees. U of
Nebr Pr.
Keese, William L. see Keese, William Linn.
Keese, William Linn, 1835-1904
xKeese, William L.
Group of Comedians. B Franklin.
Keesing, Felix M. see Keesing, Felix Maxwell.
Keesing, Felix Maxwell, 1902-1961
xKeesing, Felix M.
Culture Change: An Analysis & Bibliography of
Anthropological Sources to 1952. Octagon.
The South Seas in the Modern World.
Octagon.
Keeslar, Oreon. see Keeslar, Oreon Pierre.
Keeslar, Oreon Pierre, 1907-
xKeeslar, Oreon.
Financial Aids for Higher Education: 80 to 81
Catalog. Wm C Brown.
Keeton, G. W. see Keeton, George Williams.
Keeton, George W. see Keeton, George Williams.
Keeton, George Williams.
xKeeton, G. W.
ed. British Industry & European Law.
Rothman.
xKeeton, George W.
The Development of Extraterritoriality in
China. Fertig.
English Law: The Judicial Contribution. David
& Charles.
Keeton, William R., 1947-
xKeeton, William R.
Equilibrium Credit Rationing. Garland Pub.
Keeton, William T.
xKeeton, William T.
Biological Science. Norton.
Kefauver, Estes.
xKefauver, Estes.

Crime in America. Greenwood.
Twentieth Century Congress. Greenwood.
Kefeli, V. I. see Kefeli, Valentin Ilich.
Kefeli, Valentin Ilich.
xKefeli, V. I.
Natural Plant Growth Inhibitors &
Phytohormones. Kluwer Boston.
Kegan, Frank R.
xKegan, Frank R.
I Ching Primer: An Introduction to Relevant.
Process Perspective Upon the Occult in
General & the Flux Tome. Aries Pr.
Kegley, Charles W.
xKegley, Charles W.
ed. Challenges to America: United States
Foreign Policy in the 1980's. Sage.
Kehler, Dorothea.
xKehler, Dorothea.
Problems in Literary Research: A Guide to
Selected Reference Works. Scarecrow.
Kehler, P. L., 1936-
xKehler, P. L.
The Lower Zuni Sequence in the Southwestern
United States. SMU Press.
Kehoe, M. see Kehoe, Monika.
Kehoe, Monika.
xKehoe, M.
ed. Applied Linguistics: A Survey for Language
Teachers. Macmillan.
Kehr, Eckart, 1902-1933
xKehr, Eckart.
Economic Interest, Militarism, & Foreign
Policy: Essays on German History. U of Cal
Pr.
Keightley, David N.
xKeightley, David N.
Sources of Shang History: The Oracle-Bone
Inscriptions of Bronze Age China. U of Cal
Pr.
Keighton, Robert L.
xKeighton, Robert L.
One Nation: An American Government Text
with Readings. Heath.
Keil, E. C.
xKeil, E. C.
Performance Appraisal & the Manager. Lebhar
Friedman.
Keil, Francis C. see Keil, Frank C.
Keil, Frank C., 1952-
xKeil, Francis C.
Semantic & Conceptual Development: An
Ontological Perspective. Harvard U Pr.
Keil, Sally V. see Keil, Sally Van Wagenen.
Keil, Sally Van Wagenen.
xKeil, Sally V.
Those Wonderful Women in Their Flying
Machines: The Unknown Heroines of World
War II. Rawson Wade.
Keiler, Manfred. see Keiler, Manfred L.
Keiler, Manfred L, 1908-
xKeiler, Manfred.
The Art in Teaching Art. U of Nebr Pr.
Keiley, Jarvis.
xKeiley, Jarvis.
Edgar Allan Poe: A Probe. Folcroft.
Keilin, David, 1887-1963
xKeilin, David.
History of Cell Respiration & Cytochrome.
Cambridge U Pr.
Keilson, J. see Keilson, Julian.
Keilson, Julian.
xKeilson, J.
Markov Chain Models - Rarity &
Exponentiality. Springer-Verlag.
xKeilson, Julian.
Green's Function Methods in Probability
Theory. Hafner.
Keily. see Keily, Helen J.
Keily, Danile, 1921-
xKeily, Danile.

Programmed Basic Chemistry for Allied Health
Students. Mosby.

Keily, Helen J.
xKeily.
How to Find & Apply for a Job. SW Pub.

Keim, Albert.
xKeim, Albert.
Charles Dickens. Folcroft.
Charles Dickens. R West.
Honore De Balzac. Haskell.

Keim, Albert N.
xKeim, Albert N.
ed. Compulsory Education & the Amish: The
Right Not to Be Modern. Beacon Pr.

Keim, Charles J.
xKeim, Charles J.
Alaska Game Trails with a Master Guide.
Alaska Northwest.

Keim, Hugo A.
xKeim, Hugo A.
The Adolescent Spine. Grune.

Keim, Willard D.
xKeim, Willard D.
The Korean Peasant at the Crossroads: A
Study of Attitudes. West Wash Univ.

Keiper, Ralph L.
xKeiper, Ralph L.
The Power of Biblical Thinking. Revell.

Keir, David L. *see* Keir, David Lindsay.

Keir, David Lindsay, Sir, 1895-
xKeir, David L.
Constitutional History of Modern Britain Since
1485. Norton.

Keir, Jack C. *see* Keir, Jack Cutler.

Keir, Jack Cutler.
xKeir, Jack C.
Life Insurance Sales Management Handbook.
P-H.

Keirstead, Phillip. *see* Keirstead, Phillip O.

Keirstead, Phillip D. *see* Keirstead, Phillip O.

Keirstead, Phillip O.
xKeirstead, Phillip.
Journalist's Notebook of Live Radio-TV News.
TAB Bks.
xKeirstead, Phillip D.
All-News Radio. TAB Bks.

Keiser, Albert, 1887-1959
xKeiser, Albert.
The Indian in American Literature. Gordon Pr.
Indian in American Literature. Octagon.

Keiser, B. J. *see* Keiser, Bernhard.

Keiser, Bernhard, 1928-
xKeiser, B. J.
Principles of Electromagnetic Compatibility.
Artech Hse.

Keiser, Clarence E. *see* Keiser, Clarence Elwood.

Keiser, Clarence Elwood.
xKeiser, Clarence E.
Neo-Sumerian Account Texts from Drehem.
Yale U Pr.

Keiser, John H., 1936-
xKeiser, John H.
Building for the Centuries: Illinois, 1865-1898.
U of Ill Pr.

Keisler, H. Jerome.
xKeisler, H. Jerome.
Foundations of Infinitesimal Calculus. Prindle.

Keister, D. C. *see* Keister, Douglas Carlyle.

Keister, Douglas Carlyle.
xKeister, D. C.
Food & Beverage Control. P-H.

Keitel, Wilhelm.
xKeitel, Wilhelm.
In the Service of the Reich. Stein & Day.

Keith. *see* Keith, Alec D.

Keith, A. B. *see* Keith, Arthur Berriedale.

Keith, Alec D.
xKeith.

The Aqueous Cytoplasm. Dekker.

Keith, Alexander, 1895-
xKeith, Alexander.
Burns & Folk-Song. Arden Lib.
Burns & Folk-Song. Folcroft.
Burns & Folk-Song. Norwood Edns.

Keith, Arthur B. *see* Keith, Arthur Berriedale.

Keith, Arthur Berriedale, 1879-1944
xKeith, A. B.
Buddhist Philosophy in India & Ceylon.
Krishna Pr.
Indian Logic & Atomism: An Exposition of the
Nyaya & Vaicesika Systems. Krishna Pr.
The Religion & Philosophy of the Veda &
Upanishads. Orient Bk Dist.
xKeith, Arthur B.
Indian Logic & Atomism: An Exposition of the
Nyaya & Vaicesika Systems. Greenwood.
The Religion & Philosophy of the Veda &
Upanishads. Greenwood.
Intro. by Speeches & Documents on the British
Dominions, 1918-1931: From
Self-Government to National Sovereignty.
AMS Pr.
Speeches & Documents on the British
Dominions, 1918-1931: From
Self-Government to National Sovereignty.
Greenwood.

Keith, C. Gregory. *see* Keith, Cyril Gregory.

Keith, Cyril Gregory.
xKeith, C. Gregory.
Genetics & Ophthalmology. Churchill.

Keith, Harold.
xKeith, Harold.
Go, Red, Go. Elsevier-Nelson.
The Obstinate Land. T Y Crowell.
Rifles for Watie. T Y Crowell.
Susy's Scoundrel. T Y Crowell.

Keith, J. A. *see* Keith, John Alexander Hull.

Keith, John Alexander Hull.
xKeith, J. A.
The Nation & the Schools. Arno.

Keith, L. A. *see* Keith, Lyman A.

Keith, Lawrence H.
xKeith, Lawrence H.
Identification & Analysis of Organic Pollutants
in Water. Ann Arbor Science.

Keith, Louis.
xKeith, Louis.
Sexually Transmitted Diseases. Irvington.

Keith, Lyman A.
xKeith, L. A.
Introduction to Business Enterprise. McGraw.

Keith, Nathaniel S. *see* Keith, Nathaniel Schnieder.

Keith, Nathaniel Schnieder, 1906-1973
xKeith, Nathaniel S.
Politics & the Housing Crisis Since 1930.
Universe.

Keith, Robert G.
xKeith, Robert G.
ed. Haciendas & Plantations in Latin American
History. Holmes & Meier.

Keith, Robert W.
xKeith, Robert W.
Audiology for the Physician. Williams &
Wilkins.

Keith-Lucas, Alan.
xKeith-Lucas, Alan.
Giving & Taking Help. U of NC Pr.
Group Child Care As a Family Service. U of
NC Pr.

Keithley, Erwin. *see* Keithley, Erwin M.

Keithley, Erwin M.
xKeithley, Erwin.
English for Modern Business. Irwin.

Keithley, George, 1935-
xKeithley, George.

The Donner Party. Braziller.
Song in a Strange Land. Braziller.

Keitner, Wendy, 1948-
xKeitner, Wendy.
Ralph Gustafson. Twayne.

Kekes, John.
xKekes, John.
The Nature of Philosophy. Rowman.

Kelalis, Panayotis P.
xKelalis, Panayotis P.
ed. Clinical Pediatric Urology. Saunders.

Kelber, Werner H.
xKelber, Werner H.
Mark's Story of Jesus. Fortress.
ed. The Passion in Mark: Studies on Mark
14-16. Fortress.

Kelbley, Charles A.
xKelbley, Charles A.
ed. The Value of Justice: Essays on the Theory
& Practice of Social Virtue. Fordham.

Kelchner, Georgia D. *see* Kelchner, Georgia Dunham.

Kelchner, Georgia Dunham.
xKelchner, Georgia D.
Dreams in Old Norse Literature & Their
Affinities in Folklore. Folcroft.

Kelcy, Raymond C., 1916-
xKelcy, Raymond C.
Letters of Paul to the Thessalonians. Sweet.

Kelder, D. *see* Kelder, Diane.

Kelder, Diane.
xKelder, D.
Rembrandt. McGraw.
xKelder, Diane.
Aspects of "Official" Painting & Philosophic
Art, 1789-1799. Garland Pub.
Great Masters of French Impressionism.
Artabras.
Great Masters of French Impressionism.
Crown.

Kelder, James.
xKelder, James.
How to Open a Swiss Bank Account. T Y
Crowell.

Keleher, James F. *see* Keleher, James Francis.

Keleher, James Francis, 1903-
xKeleher, James F.
Disputed Questions in Philosophy. Philos Lib.

Kelejian, Harry H.
xKelejian, Harry H.
Introduction to Econometrics: Principles &
Applications. Har-Row.

Keleman, Stanley.
xKeleman, Stanley.
Living Your Dying. Random.

Kelemen, Pal.
xKelemen, Pal.
Baroque & Rococo in Latin America. Dover.
Baroque & Rococo in Latin America. Peter
Smith.
Vanishing Art of the Americas. Walker & Co.

Kelen, Betty.
xKelen, Betty.
Muhammad: The Messenger of God.
Elsevier-Nelson.
Muhammad: The Messenger of God. PB.

Keleti. *see* Keleti, T.

Keleti, T.
xKeleti.
Mathematical Models of Metabolic Regulation.
Heyden.
xKeleti, Tamas.
ed. Mathematical Models of Metabolic
Regulation. Intl Pubns Serv.

Keleti, Tamas. *see* Keleti, T.

Kelidar, Abbas.
xKelidar, Abbas.
ed. Integration of Modern Iraq. St Martin.

Kell, Carl L.
xKell, Carl L.

Fundamentals of Effective Group
Communication. Macmillan.
Kellar, Elizabeth K., 1948-
xKellar, Elizabeth K.
ed. Managing with Less. Intl City Mgt.
Kellaway, Peter.
xKellaway, Peter.
ed. Quantitative Analytic Studies in Epilepsy.
Raven.
Kelleam, Joseph E.
xKelleam, Joseph E.
When the Red King Woke. Bouregy.
Kelleher, Stephen J. *see* Kelleher, Stephen Joseph.
Kelleher, Stephen Joseph, 1915-
xKelleher, Stephen J.
Divorce & Remarriage for Catholics.
Doubleday.
Kellejian, Robert.
xKellejian, Robert.
Applied Electronic Communication: Circuits,
Systems, Transmission. SRA.
Keller, A. G. *see* Keller, Albert Galloway.
Keller, Albert G. *see* Keller, Albert Galloway.
Keller, Albert Galloway, 1874-1956
xKeller, A. G.
Starting-Points in Social Science. Greenwood.
xKeller, Albert G.
Societal Evolution: A Study of the
Evolutionary Basis of the Science of Society.
Elliots Bks.
Starting Points in Social Science. Elliots Bks.
Keller, Allan.
xKeller, Allan.
Life Along the Hudson. Sleepy Hollow.
Keller, Beverly.
xKeller, Beverly.
Don't Throw Another One, Dover. Coward.
Keller, C. *see* Keller, Charles.
Keller, Charles.
xKeller, C.
Laugh Lines. P-H.
Still Going Bananas. P-H.
xKeller, Charles.
Ballpoint Bananas & Other Jokes for Kids.
P-H.
Compiled by Daffynitions. P-H.
Giggle Puss: Pet Jokes for Kids. P-H.
Laughing: A Historical Selection of American
Humor. P-H.
Llama Beans. P-H.
Compiled by More Ballpoint Bananas. P-H.
Punch Lines. P-H.
Keller, Charles E.
xKeller, Charles E.
Indiana Birds & Their Haunts: A Checklist &
Finding Guide. Ind U Pr.
Keller, Charles M.
xKeller, Charles M.
Montagu Cave in Prehistory: A Descriptive
Analysis. U of Cal Pr.
Keller, David H. *see* Keller, David Henry.
Keller, David Henry, 1880-1963
xKeller, David H.
The Devil & the Doctor. Arno.
Life Everlasting, & Other Tales of Science,
Fantasy & Horror. Hyperion Conn.
Keller, Dean H.
xKeller, Dean H.
Index to Plays in Periodicals. Scarecrow.
Keller, Edward. *see* Keller, Edward A.
Keller, Edward A.
xKeller, Edward.
Environmental Geology. Merrill.
Keller, Franklin J. *see* Keller, Franklin Jefferson.
Keller, Franklin Jefferson, 1887-
xKeller, Franklin J.

Comprehensive High School. Greenwood.
Double-Purpose High School: Closing the Gap
Between Vocational & Academic Preparation.
Greenwood.
Keller, Fred S. *see* Keller, Fred Simmons.
Keller, Fred Simmons, 1899-
xKeller, Fred S.
The Definition of Psychology. P-H.
Principles of Psychology: A Systematic Text in
the Science of Behavior. Irvington.
Summers & Sabbaticals: Selected Papers on
Psychology & Education. Res Press.
Keller, Gary D.
xKeller, Gary D.
Spanish Here & Now. HarBraceJ.
Keller, Gottfried, 1819-1890
xKeller, Gottfried.
People of Seldwyla & Seven Legends. Arno.
Keller, H. H. *see* Keller, Hans Heinrich.
Keller, Hans Heinrich, 1922-
xKeller, H. H.
Differential Calculus in Locally Convex Spaces.
Springer-Verlag.
Keller, Helen, 1880-1968
xKeller, Helen.
Story of My Life. Dell.
Story of My Life. Macmillan.
The Story of My Life. Pendulum Pr.
Story of My Life. Doubleday.
The Story of My Life. Schol Bk Serv.
Story of My Life. Airmont.
Keller, Helen R. *see* Keller, Helen Rex.
Keller, Helen Rex.
xKeller, Helen R.
Reader's Digest of Books. Macmillan.
Keller, Howard H.
xKeller, Howard H.
German Root Lexicon. U of Miami Pr.
A German Word Family Dictionary: Together
with English Equivalents. U of Cal Pr.
Keller (J.J.) and Associates.
xJ. J. Keller & Asociates, Inc.
Emergency & Trip Permit Handbook. J J
Keller.
xJ. J. Keller & Assoc.
Hazardous Materials Shipments. J J Keller.
xJ. J. Keller & Associates, Inc.
Driver's Guide to Low Underpasses. J J Keller.
Driver's Pocket Guide to Hazardous Materials.
J J Keller.
Federal Motor Carrier Safety Regulations
Handbook. J J Keller.
xKeller, J. J., & Assocs., Inc.
Fleet Safety Compliance Manual. J J Keller.
Freight Claims Manual. J J Keller.
Freight Security Manual. J J Keller.
Occupational Exposure Guide. J J Keller.
Toxic Substances Control Guide. J J Keller.
Keller, J. J., & Assocs., Inc. *see* Keller (J.J.) and
Associates.
Keller, James G. *see* Keller, James Gregory.
Keller, James Gregory.
xKeller, James G.
Men of Maryknoll. Arno.
Keller, John E., 1924-
xKeller, John E.
Drinking Problem. Fortress.
Keller, John E. *see* Keller, John Esten.
Keller, John Esten.
xKeller, John E.
Alfonso X, el Sabio. Irvington.
Gonzalo de Berceo. Twayne.
Keller, Julius.
xKeller, Julius.
From Riva Ridge to Riva. Vantage.
Keller, Karl, 1933-
xKeller, Karl.

The Only Kangaroo Among the Beauty: Emily
Dickinson & America. Johns Hopkins.
Keller, Morton.
xKeller, Morton.
Affairs of State: Public Life in Late Nineteenth
Century America. Harvard U Pr.
The Art & Politics of Thomas Nast. Oxford U
Pr.
Life Insurance Enterprise, 1885-1910: A Study
in the Limits of Corporate Power. Harvard U
Pr.
Keller, P. R. *see* Keller, Peter R.
Keller, Paul F. *see* Keller, Paull F.
Keller, Paull F.
xKeller, Paul F.
Studies in Lutheran Doctrine. Concordia.
Keller, Peter R.
xKeller, P. R.
Membrane Technology & Industrial Separation
Techniques. Noyes.
Keller, Philip. *see* Keller, Weldon Phillip.
Keller, Phillip. *see* Keller, Weldon Phillip.
Keller, R. E. *see* Keller, Rudolf Ernst.
Keller, Rudolf Ernst.
xKeller, R. E.
The German Language. Humanities.
Keller, W. Philip. *see* Keller, Weldon Phillip.
Keller, W. Phillip. *see* Keller, Weldon Phillip.
Keller, Walter D. *see* Keller, Walter David.
Keller, Walter David, 1900-
xKeller, Walter D.
Chemistry in Introductory Geology. Lucas.
Keller, Weldon Phillip, 1920-
xKeller, Philip.
A Shepherd Looks at the Good Shepherd &
His Sheep. Zondervan.
xKeller, Phillip.
A Gardener Looks at the Fruits of the Spirit.
Word Bks.
xKeller, W. Philip.
Layman Looks at the Lord's Prayer. Moody.
xKeller, W. Phillip.
A Layman Looks at the Lord's Prayer. World
Wide Pubs.
Still Waters. Revell.
Keller, Werner.
xKeller, Werner.
Diaspora: The Post-Biblical History of the
Jews. HarBraceJ.
The Etruscans. Knopf.
Kellerman, Henry.
xKellerman, Henry.
Group Psychotherapy & Personality:
Intersecting Structures. Grune.
Kellett, E. E. *see* Kellett, Ernest Edward.
Kellett, Ernest Edward, 1864-1950
xKellett, E. E.
The Appreciation of Literature. Folcroft.
Fashion in Literature: A Study of Changing
Taste. Folcroft.
Literary Quotation & Allusion. Folcroft.
Literary Quotation & Allusion. Kennikat.
Whirligig of Taste.. Folcroft.
Kelley, Alice H.
xKelley, Alice H.
Birds of Southeastern Michigan &
Southwestern Ontario. Cranbrook.
Kelley, Allen C.
xKelley, Allen C.
Dualistic Economic Development: Theory &
History. U of Chicago Pr.
Lessons from Japanese Development: An
Analytical Economic History. U of Chicago
Pr.
Kelley, C. F. *see* Kelley, Carl Franklin.
Kelley, Carl Franklin, 1914-
xKelley, C. F.

Meister Eckhart on Divine Knowledge. Yale U
  Pr.
Kelley, Colleen.
  xKelley, Colleen.
    Assertion Training: A Facilitator's Guide. Univ
      Assocs.
Kelley, Cornelia P. *see* Kelley, Cornelia Pulsifer.
Kelley, Cornelia Pulsifer, 1897-
  xKelley, Cornelia P.
    The Early Development of Henry James. U of
      Ill Pr.
Kelley, David H.
  xKelley, David H.
    Deciphering the Maya Script. U of Tex Pr.
Kelley, Donald R., 1943-
  xKelley, Donald R.
    ed. The Energy Crisis & the Environment: An
      International Perspective. Praeger.
    Foundations of Modern Historical Scholarship:
      Language, Law & History in the French
      Renaissance. Columbia U Pr.
    Francois Hotman: A Revolutionary's Ordeal.
      Princeton U Pr.
    ed. Soviet Politics in the Brezhnev Era.
      Praeger.
Kelley, Earl C. *see* Kelley, Earl Clarence.
Kelley, Earl Clarence.
  xKelley, Earl C.
    Education & the Nature of Man. Greenwood.
Kelley, Edith S. *see* Kelley, Edith Summers.
Kelley, Edith Summers.
  xKelley, Edith S.
    The Devil's Hand: A Novel. S Ill U Pr.
Kelley, Edward N.
  xKelley, Edward N.
    Practical Apartment Management. Inst Real
      Estate.
Kelley, Eugene J.
  xKelley, Eugene J.
    Marketing Planning & Competitive Strategy.
      P-H.
Kelley, Florence, 1859-1932
  xKelley, Florence.
    Some Ethical Gains Through Legislation. Arno.
Kelley, Frances.
  xKelley, Frances.
    Better Than I Was. Nelson.
Kelley, Harold. *see* Kelley, Harold Howard.
Kelley, Harold H.
  xKelley, Harold H.
    Personal Relationships: Their Structures &
      Processes. Halsted Pr.
Kelley, Harold Howard, 1926-
  xKelley, Harold.
    In Search of Your Family Tree. St Martin.
Kelley, J. L. *see* Kelley, John L.
Kelley, John L.
  xKelley, J. L.
    General Topology. Springer-Verlag.
Kelley, Kitty.
  xKelley, Kitty.
    Glamour Spas. PB.
    Jackie Oh!. Ballantine.
    Jackie Oh!. Lyle Stuart.
Kelley, Lee.
  xKelley, Lee.
    How to Build a Street Rod. Petersen Pub.
Kelley, Leo P.
  xKelley, Leo P.
    Dead Moon. Pitman Learning.
    Night of Fire & Blood. Childrens.
    Star Gold. Childrens.
    ed. The Supernatural in Fiction. McGraw.
Kelley, Maurice, 1903-
  xKelley, Maurice.
    This Great Argument: A Study of Milton's De
      Doctrina Christiana As a Gloss Upon
      Paradise Lost. Somerset Pub.
Kelley, Michael R., 1940-
  xKelley, Michael R.

Flamboyant Drama: A Study of "the Castle of
  Perseverance," "Mankind," & "Wisdom". S Ill
  U Pr.
Kelley, N. Edmund.
  xKelley, N. Edmund.
    The Contemporary Ecology of Arroyo Hondo,
      New Mexico. Schol Am Res.
Kelley, Patrick.
  xKelley, Patrick.
    Building Safe Driving Skills. Pitman Learning.
Kelley, Philip.
  xKelley, Philip.
    ed. The Brownings Correspondence: A
      Checklist. Browning Inst.
Kelley, Ramon.
  xKelley, Ramon.
    Ramon Kelley Paints Portraits & Figures.
      Watson-Guptill.
Kelley, Robert. *see* Kelley, Robert Lee.
Kelley, Robert K.
  xKelley, Robert K.
    Courtship, Marriage, & the Family. HarBraceJ.
    Guidebook for Marriage & the Family.
      HarBraceJ.
Kelley, Robert Lee, 1948-
  xKelley, Robert.
    Introduction to Communication.
      Benjamin-Cummings.
Kelley, Robert Lloyd, 1925-
  xKelley, Robert.
    The Sounds of Controversy: Crucial Arguments
      in the American Past. P-H.
Kelley, Sally.
  xKelley, Sally.
    Trouble with Explosives. Bradbury Pr.
Kelley, Shirley D. *see* Kelley, Shirley Dyckes.
Kelley, Shirley Dyckes.
  xKelley, Shirley D.
    Love Is Not for Cowards: The Autobiography
      of Shirley Dyckes Kelley. P-H.
Kelley, Stanley.
  xKelley, Stanley.
    Professional Public Relations & Political Power.
      Johns Hopkins.
Kelley, Victor. *see* Kelley, Victor E.
Kelley, Victor E., 1935-
  xKelley, Victor.
    How to Get into the Business of Photography.
      ETC Pubns.
Kelley, William, 1929-
  xKelley, William.
    Tyree Legend. S&S.
Kelley, William D. *see* Kelley, William Darrah.
Kelley, William Darrah, 1814-1890
  xKelley, William D.
    Speeches, Addresses & Letters on Industrial &
      Financial Questions. Greenwood.
Kelley, William M. *see* Kelley, William Melvin.
Kelley, William Melvin, 1937-
  xKelley, William M.
    Dancers on the Shore. Chatham Bkseller.
    Drop of Patience. Chatham Bkseller.
    Dunfords Travels Every Wheres. Ultramarine
      Pub.
  xKelley, William Melvin.
    Different Drummer. Doubleday.
Kelley, Win, 1923-
  xKelley, Win.
    Breaking the Barriers in Public Speaking.
      Kendall-Hunt.
Kelling, Furn.
  xKelling, Furn F.
    Prayer Is.... Broadman.
Kelling, Furn F. *see* Kelling, Furn.
Kelling, George W.
  xKelling, George W.
    Blind Mazes: A Study of Love. Nelson-Hall.
Kellison, Stephen G.
  xKellison, Stephen G.

Theory of Interest. Irwin.
Kellman, M. C.
  xKellman, Martin C.
    Plant Geography. Methuen Inc.
    Plant Geography. St Martin.
Kellman, Martin C. *see* Kellman, M. C.
Kellman, Steven G., 1947-
  xKellman, Steven G.
    The Self-Begetting Novel. Columbia U Pr.
Kellner, Bruce.
  xKellner, Bruce.
    Compiled by A Bibliography of the Work of
      Carl Van Vechten. Greenwood.
Kellner, Esther.
  xKellner, Esther.
    Animals Come to My House: A Story Guide to
      the Care of Small Wild Animals. Putnam.
Kellner, Leon, 1859-1928
  xKellner, Leon.
    Historical Outlines of English Syntax. Gordon
      Pr.
    Historical Outlines of English Syntax.
      Norwood Edns.
    Restoring Shakespeare: A Critical Analysis of
      the Misreadings in Shakespeare's Works.
      Biblo.
    Restoring Shakespeare: A Critical Analysis of
      the Misreadings in Shakespeare's Works. R
      West.
Kellner, Menachem M. *see* Kellner, Menachem Marc.
Kellner, Menachem Marc, 1946-
  xKellner, Menachem M.
    ed. Contemporary Jewish Ethics. Hebrew Pub.
Kellogg, Carolyn J. *see* Kellogg, Carolyn Jo.
Kellogg, Carolyn Jo.
  xKellogg, Carolyn J.
    ed. Current Perspectives in Oncologic Nursing.
      Mosby.
Kellogg, Charlotte. *see* Kellogg, Charlotte (Hoffman).
Kellogg, Charlotte (Hoffman).
  xKellogg, Charlotte.
    Paderewski. Viking Pr.
Kellogg, Clara L. *see* Kellogg, Clara Louise.
Kellogg, Clara Louise, 1842-1916
  xKellogg, Clara L.
    Memoirs of an American Prima Donna. Da
      Capo.
Kellogg, J. H. *see* Kellogg, John Harvey.
Kellogg, John Harvey, 1852-1943
  xKellogg, J. H.
    Plain Facts for Old & Young. Numarc Bk
      Corp.
Kellogg, Louise P. *see* Kellogg, Louise Phelps.
Kellogg, Louise Phelps, d. 1942
  xKellogg, Louise P.
    ed. Early Narratives of the Northwest,
      1634-1699. B&N.
    French Regime in Wisconsin & the Northwest.
      Cooper Sq.
Kellogg, Marion S.
  xKellogg, Marion S.
    Putting Management Theories to Work. Gulf
      Pub.
    Putting Management Theories to Work. P-H.
    Talking with Employees: A Guide for
      Managers. Gulf Pub.
Kellogg, Marjorie.
  xKellogg, Marjorie.
    Like the Lion's Tooth. NAL.
Kellogg, O. D. *see* Kellogg, Oliver Dimon.
Kellogg, Oliver D. *see* Kellogg, Oliver Dimon.
Kellogg, Oliver Dimon, 1878-
  xKellogg, O. D.
    Foundations of Potential Theory.
      Springer-Verlag.
    Foundations of Potential Theory. Ungar.
  xKellogg, Oliver D.
    Foundations of Potential Theory. Dover.
Kellogg, Paul U. *see* Kellogg, Paul Underwood.

Kellogg, Paul Underwood, 1879-1958
xKellogg, Paul U.
    ed. The Pittsburgh District Civic Frontage.
    Arno.
Kellogg, Rhoda, 1898-
xKellogg, Rhoda.
    Analyzing Children's Art. Mayfield Pub.
Kellogg, Robert H.
xKellogg, Robert H.
    Life & Death in Rebel Prisons. Arno.
Kellogg, Steven.
xKellogg, Steven.
    illus. Can I Keep Him. Dial.
    Can I Keep Him?. Dial.
    Much Bigger Than Martin. Dial.
    illus. Much Bigger Than Martin. Dial.
    illus. The Orchard Cat. Dial.
    illus. There Was an Old Woman. Schol Bk
    Serv.
    illus. Won't Somebody Play with Me?. Dial.
    Won't Somebody Play with Me?. Dial.
Kellogg, Walter G. *see* Kellogg, Walter Guest.
Kellogg, Walter Guest, 1877-1956
xKellogg, Walter G.
    Conscientious Objector. Da Capo.
Kellogg, Winthrop N. *see* Kellogg, Winthrop Niles.
Kellogg, Winthrop Niles, 1898-
xKellogg, Winthrop N.
    Porpoises & Sonar. U of Chicago Pr.
Kellow, H. A. *see* Kellow, Henry Arthur.
Kellow, Henry A. *see* Kellow, Henry Arthur.
Kellow, Henry Arthur.
xKellow, H. A.
    Burns & His Poetry. Folcroft.
    Burns & His Poetry. Kennikat.
xKellow, Henry A.
    Burns & His Poetry. AMS Pr.
Kells, Joe. *see* Kells, Joseph.
Kells, Joseph.
xKells, Joe.
    Advanced Driver. David & Charles.
Kellum, David F.
xKellum, David F.
    American History Through Conflicting
    Interpretations. Tchrs Coll.
Kelly, A. *see* Kelly, Anthony.
Kelly, A. K.
xKelly, Alex K.
    Economics: Principles & Practice. Littlefield.
Kelly, A. V. *see* Kelly, Albert Victor.
Kelly, Albert Victor.
xKelly, A. V.
    Case Studies in Mixed Ability Teaching.
    Har-Row.
Kelly, Alex K. *see* Kelly, A. K.
Kelly, Anthony.
xKelly, A.
    ed. Strengthening Methods in Crystals. Halsted
    Pr.
    Strong Solids. Oxford U Pr.
xKelly, Anthony.
    Crystallography & Crystal Defects. A-W.
    Wondering About God. Liguori Pubns.
Kelly, Chuck.
xKelly, Chuck.
    Supercock. Holloway.
Kelly, Dave.
xKelly, Dave.
    Instructions for Viewing a Solar Eclipse.
    Columbia U Pr.
Kelly, Desmond.
xKelly, Desmond.
    Anxiety & Emotions: Physiological Basis &
    Treatment. C C Thomas.
Kelly, E. Lowell. *see* Kelly, Everett Lowell.
Kelly, Edward. *see* Kelly, Edward James.
Kelly, Edward James, 1920-
xKelly, Edward.

    Parent-Teacher Interaction: A Special
    Educational Perspective. Spec Child.
Kelly, Eric P. *see* Kelly, Eric Philbrook.
Kelly, Eric Philbrook, 1884-1960
xKelly, Eric P.
    The Trumpeter of Krakow. Macmillan.
    Trumpeter of Krakow. Macmillan.
Kelly, Eugene, 1941-
xKelly, Eugene.
    Max Scheler. Twayne.
Kelly, Everett L. *see* Kelly, Everett Lowell.
Kelly, Everett Lowell, 1905-
xKelly, E. Lowell.
    Assessment of Human Characteristics.
    Brooks-Cole.
xKelly, Everett L.
    Prediction of Performance in Clinical
    Psychology. Greenwood.
Kelly, Frank K., 1914-
xKelly, Frank K.
    Starship Invincible: Science Fiction Stories of
    the 30's. Capra Pr.
Kelly, G. V. *see* Kelly, George V.
Kelly, Gary. *see* Kelly, Gary F.
Kelly, Gary F.
xKelly, Gary.
    Learning About Sex: The Contemporary Guide
    for Young Adults. Barron.
xKelly, Gary F.
    Good Sex: A Healthy Man's Guide to Sexual
    Fulfillment. HarBraceJ.
    Good Sex: The Healthy Man's Guide to Sexual
    Fulfillment. NAL.
Kelly, George A. *see* Kelly, George Anthony.
Kelly, George Alexander, 1905-1967
xKelly, George A.
    Theory of Personality: The Psychology of
    Personal Constructs. Norton.
Kelly, George Anthony, 1916-
xKelly, George A.
    The Catholic Church & the American Poor.
    Alba.
    The Political Struggle of Active Homosexuals
    to Gain Social Acceptance. Franciscan
    Herald.
    Sacrament of the Eucharist in Our Time.
    Dghtrs St Paul.
    ed. The Teaching Church in Our Time. Dghtrs
    St Paul.
Kelly, George V.
xKelly, G. V.
    The Old Gray Mayors of Denver. Pruett.
Kelly, Harold C. *see* Kelly, Harold Caleb.
Kelly, Harold Caleb.
xKelly, Harold C.
    Clock Repairing As a Hobby. Follett.
    Improving Your Clock Repairing Skills. Follett.
Kelly, Henry A. *see* Kelly, Henry Ansgar.
Kelly, Henry Ansgar, 1934-
xKelly, Henry A.
    Divine Providence in the England of
    Shakespeare's Histories. Harvard U Pr.
    Love & Marriage in the Age of Chaucer.
    Cornell U Pr.
Kelly, Isabel. *see* Kelly, Isabel Truesdell.
Kelly, Isabel T. *see* Kelly, Isabel Truesdell.
Kelly, Isabel Truesdell.
xKelly, Isabel.
    The Hodges Ruin: A Hohokam Community in
    the Tucson Basin. U of Ariz Pr.
xKelly, Isabel T.
    Southern Paiute Ethnography. Johnson Repr.
Kelly, Isabella.
xKelly, Isabella.
    The Abbey of St. Asaph: A Novel. Arno.
Kelly, J. *see* Kelly, Joe.
Kelly, J. C. *see* Kelly, James Chester.
Kelly, J. F.
xKelly, J. F.

    Pony Riding. Soccer.
Kelly, J. Frederick. *see* Kelly, John Frederick.
Kelly, J. Thomas.
xKelly, J. Thomas.
    Thorns on the Tudor Rose: Monks, Rogues,
    Vagabonds, & Sturdy Beggars. U Pr of Miss.
Kelly, Jack.
xKelly, Jack.
    The Unexpected Peace. Belmont-Tower.
    Unexpected Peace. Gambit.
Kelly, Jain.
xKelly, Jain.
    Nude: Theory. Lustrum Pr.
Kelly, James Chester.
xKelly, J. C.
    Clinician's Handbook for Auditory Training.
    Alexander Graham.
Kelly, James E.
xKelly, James E.
    The Dam Builders. A-W.
    Tunnel Builders. A-W.
Kelly, James G.
xKelly, James G.
    ed. Adolescent Boys in High School: A
    Psychological Study of Coping & Adaption.
    Halsted Pr.
Kelly, Jim.
xKelly, Jim.
    Neighbors. Glencoe.
Kelly, Joe.
xKelly, J.
    How Managers Manage. P-H.
Kelly, John, 1921-
xKelly, John.
    The Wooden Wolf. Dutton.
Kelly, John E. *see* Kelly, John Eoghan.
Kelly, John Eoghan, 1893-
xKelly, John E.
    Pedro De Alvarado, Conquistador. Kennikat.
Kelly, John F. *see* Kelly, John Frederick.
Kelly, John Frederick, 1888-1947
xKelly, J. Frederick.
    Early Domestic Architecture of Connecticut.
    Dover.
xKelly, John F.
    Early Domestic Architecture of Connecticut.
    Peter Smith.
Kelly, John M. *see* Kelly, John Maurice.
Kelly, John Maurice.
xKelly, John M.
    Fundamental Rights in the Irish Law &
    Constitution. Oceana.
Kelly, John R.
xKelly, John R.
    Pedro Prado. Twayne.
Kelly, Joseph F.
xKelly, Joseph F.
    Computerized Management Information
    Systems. Macmillan.
Kelly, Joseph G.
xKelly, Joseph G.
    Come Aside & Rest Awhile: A Book of Family
    Prayer. Paulist Pr.
Kelly, Karin.
xKelly, Karin.
    Careers with the Circus. Lerner Pubns.
    Carpentry. Lerner Pubns.
    Doll Houses. Lerner Pubns.
    Let's Bake Cookies!. Lerner Pubns.
    Soup's On. Lerner Pubns.
Kelly, L. G. *see* Kelly, Louis G.
Kelly, Leo J.
xKelly, Leo J.
    ed. A Dictionary of Exceptional Children. Mss
    Info.
Kelly, Lou.
xKelly, Lou.

From Dialogue to Discourse: An Open
Approach to Competence & Creativity. Scott
F.

Kelly, Louis G.
xKelly, L. G.
The True Interpreter: A History of Translation
Theory & Practice in the West. St Martin.

Kelly, M. see Kelly, Marty.

Kelly, Marty.
xKelly, M.
The House on the Deer Track Trail. McGraw.

Kelly, Mary Ann.
xKelly, Mary Ann.
My Old Kentucky Home, Good night.
Exposition.

Kelly, Mary G. see Kelly, Mary Gilbert.

Kelly, Mary Gilbert, Sister, 1894-
xKelly, Mary G.
Catholic Immigrant Colonization Projects in
the United States, 1815-1860. Ozer.

Kelly, Michael.
xKelly, Michael.
Reminiscences. Oxford U Pr.
Reminiscences of Michael Kelly of the King's
Theatre & Theatre Royal Drury Lane 2 Vols.
Da Capo.

Kelly, Orville E., 1930-
xKelly, Orville E.
Until Tomorrow Comes. Everest Hse.

Kelly, P. T. see Kelly, Patricia T.

Kelly, Patricia T., 1942-
xKelly, P. T.
Dealing with Dilemma: A Manual for Genetic
Counselors. Springer-Verlag.

Kelly, Paul J. see Kelly, Paul Joseph.

Kelly, Paul Joseph.
xKelly, Paul J.
Geometry & Convexity: A Study in
Mathematical Methods. Wiley.

Kelly, Raymond C. see Kelly, Raymond Case.

Kelly, Raymond Case.
xKelly, Raymond C.
Etoro Social Structure. A Study in Structural
Contradiction. U of Mich Pr.

Kelly, Reine C. see Kelly, Reine Cardaillac.

Kelly, Reine Cardaillac.
xKelly, Reine C.
Expressions Idiomatiques en Francais Vivant.
HarBraceJ.

Kelly, Richard. see Kelly, Richard Michael.

Kelly, Richard M. see Kelly, Richard Michael.

Kelly, Richard Michael, 1937-
xKelly, Richard.
Lewis Carroll. Twayne.
xKelly, Richard M.
Douglas Jerrold. Twayne.

Kelly, Rita M. see Kelly, Rita Mae.

Kelly, Rita Mae.
xKelly, Rita M.
Community Control of Economic
Development: The Boards of Directors of
Community Development Corporations.
Praeger.

Kelly, Rob R. see Kelly, Rob Roy.

Kelly, Rob Roy.
xKelly, Rob R.
ed. Wood Type Alphabets: 100 Fonts. Peter
Smith.

Kelly, Robert, 1935-
xKelly, Robert.
The Book of Persephone. Treacle.
Cities. Frontier Press Calif.
The Loom. Black Sparrow.
Theme & Variations: A Study of Linear Twelve
Tone Composition. U of Ill Pr.

Kelly, Thomas, 1929-
xKelly, Thomas.
A History of Argos to 500 B.C.. U of Minn Pr.

Kelly, Thomas. see Kelly, Thomas Raymond.

Kelly, Thomas Raymond, 1893-1941
xKelly, Thomas.
The Eternal Promise. Friends United.

Kelly, Walt.
xKelly, Walt.
Gone Pogo. Gregg.
I Go Pogo. Gregg.
I Go Pogo. S&S.
Impollutable Pogo. S&S.
The Incompleat Pogo. Gregg.
Incompleat Pogo. S&S.
Pot Luck Pogo. S&S.
Potluck Pogo. Gregg.
Uncle Pogo So-So Stories. Gregg.
Uncle Pogo So-So Stories. S&S.

Kelly, Walter K. see Kelly, Walter Keating.

Kelly, Walter Keating.
xKelly, Walter K.
A Collection of the Proverbs of All Nations,
Compared, Explained & Illustrated. Folcroft.

Kelman, G. R. see Kelman, George Richard.

Kelman, George Richard.
xKelman, G. R.
Applied Cardiovascular Physiology.
Butterworths.

Kelman, John, 1864-1929
xKelman, John.
Among Famous Books. Arno.
Among Famous Books. R West.

Kelsall, Charles.
xKelsall, Charles.
Horae Viaticae. Schol Facsimiles.

Kelsall, R. K. see Kelsall, Roger Keith.

Kelsall, Roger Keith, 1910-
xKelsall, R. K.
Population. Humanities.
Population. Longman.

Kelsen, Hans, 1881-
xKelsen, Hans.
Peace Through Law. Garland Pub.
Pure Theory of Law. U of Cal Pr.

Kelsey, Carl, 1870-1953
xKelsey, Carl.
The Negro Farmer. AMS Pr.

Kelsey, David H.
xKelsey, David H.
Uses of Scripture in Recent Theology. Fortress.

Kelsey, H. W. see Kelsey, Hugh Walter.

Kelsey, Hugh Walter.
xKelsey, H. W.
Advanced Play at Bridge. Merrimack Bk Serv.
The Tough Game. Merrimack Bk Serv.

Kelsey, Lorne.
xKelsey, Lorne.
Eye to the Future. Stanwix.

Kelsey, Morton. see Kelsey, Morton T.

Kelsey, Morton T.
xKelsey, Morton.
Afterlife: The Other Side of Dying. Paulist Pr.
xKelsey, Morton T.
God, Dreams & Revelation: A Christian
Interpretation of Dreams. Augsburg.
The Other Side of Silence: A Guide to
Christian Meditation. Paulist Pr.

Kelso, James L. see Kelso, James Leon.

Kelso, James Leon, 1892-
xKelso, James L.
An Archaeologist Follows the Apostle Paul.
Word Bks.
An Archaeologist Looks at the Gospels. Word
Bks.

Kelso, Louis O.
xKelso, Louis O.
The Capitalist Manifesto. Greenwood.

Kelso, Robert W. see Kelso, Robert Wilson.

Kelso, Robert Wilson, 1880-
xKelso, Robert W.

History of Public Poor Relief in Massachusetts:
1620-1920. Patterson Smith.

Kelso, Ruth, 1885-
xKelso, Ruth.
Doctrine for the Lady of the Renaissance. U of
Ill Pr.

Kelso, William A. see Kelso, William Alton.

Kelso, William Alton.
xKelso, William A.
American Democratic Theory: Pluralism & Its
Critics. Greenwood.

Kelso, William M.
xKelso, William M.
Captain Jones's Wormslow: A Historical,
Archaeological, & Architectural Study of an
Eighteenth-Century Plantation Site Near
Savannah, Georgia. U of Ga Pr.

Kelting, Herman.
xKelting, Herman.
Real Estate Investments. Grid Pub.

Keltner, Autumn.
xKeltner, Autumn.
English for Adult Competency. P-H.

Keltner, Chester W.
xKeltner, Chester W.
How to Make Money in Commodities. Keltner.

Keltner, John W.
xKeltner, John W.
Group Discussion Processes. Greenwood.

Kelton, Elmer.
xKelton, Elmer.
The Day the Cowboys Quit. Ace Bks.

Kelton, Nancy.
xKelton, Nancy.
Rebel Slave. Raintree Pubs.

Kelty, Mary G. see Kelty, Mary Gertrude.

Kelty, Mary Gertrude, 1890-
xKelty, Mary G.
Teaching American History in the Middle
Grades of the Elementary School. Norwood
Edns.

Kelty, Matthew.
xKelty, Matthew.
Flute Solo: Reflections of a Trappist Hermit.
Andrews & McMeel.
Flute Solo: Reflections of a Trappist Hermit.
Doubleday.

Kelvin, Norman.
xKelvin, Norman.
E. M. Forster. S Ill U Pr.
A Troubled Eden: Nature & Society in the
Works of George Meredith. Stanford U Pr.

Kelway, Christine.
xKelway, Christine.
Gardening on Sandy Soil in North Temperate
Areas. Dover.
Gardening on Sandy Soil in North Temperate
Areas. Peter Smith.

Kemball, Robin.
xKemball, Robin.
Alexander Blok: A Study in Rhythm & Metre.
Mouton.

Kemble, Frances A. see Kemble, Frances Anne.

Kemble, Frances Anne.
xKemble, Frances A.
Journal of a Residence on a Georgian
Plantation in 1838-1839. Metro Bks.
Journal of a Residence on a Georgian
Plantation in 1838-1839. NAL.
Notes Upon Some of Shakespeare's Plays.
AMS Pr.
Notes Upon Some of Shakespeare's Plays. R
West.

Kemelman, Harry.
xKemelman, Harry.

ed. Dispatches, with Related Documents, of
Milanese Ambassadors in France &
Burgundy, 1450-1483. Ohio U Pr.
Richard the Third. Allen Unwin.
Richard the Third. Norton.
Kendall, Philip C.
xKendall, Philip C.
ed. Cognitive Behavioral Interventions: Theory,
Research & Procedures. Acad Pr.
Kendall, Robert.
xKendall, Robert.
White Teacher in a Black School. Devin.
Kendall, T. Robert. *see* Kendall, Thomas Robert.
Kendall, Thomas Robert.
xKendall, T. Robert.
The Pacific Equatorial Countercurrent. Intl Ctr
Environment.
Kendeigh, S. Charles. *see* Kendeigh, Samuel Charles.
Kendeigh, Samuel Charles, 1904-
xKendeigh, S. Charles.
Ecology with Special Reference to Animals &
Man. P-H.
Invertebrate Populations of the Deciduous
Forest: Fluctuations & Relations to Weather.
U of Ill Pr.
Kender, Joseph P.
xKender, Joseph P.
ed. Reading & the Exceptional Child.
Interstate.
ed. Teaching Reading: The Growing Diversity.
Interstate.
Kendig, Edwin L.
xKendig, Edwin L.
ed. Disorders of the Respiratory Tract in
Children. Saunders.
Kendle, John. *see* Kendle, John Edward.
Kendle, John Edward.
xKendle, John.
John Bracken: A Political Biography. U of
Toronto Pr.
Kendon, Adam.
xKendon, Adam
ed. Organization of Behavior in Face-to-Face
Interaction. Beresford Bk Serv.
Kendrick, Benjamin B. *see* Kendrick, Benjamin Burks.
Kendrick, Benjamin Burks.
xKendrick, Benjamin B.
South Looks at Its Past. Russell.
Kendrick, David A.
xKendrick, David A.
The Planning of Industrial Investment
Programs: A Methodology. Johns Hopkins.
Programming Investment in the Process
Industries: An Approach to Sectoral
Planning. MIT Pr.
Kendrick, F. *see* Kendrick, Frank J.
Kendrick, Frank J., 1928-
xKendrick, F.
Strategies for Political Participation. Winthrop.
Kendrick, John. *see* Kendrick, John W.
Kendrick, John W.
xKendrick, John.
Understanding Productivity: An Introduction to
the Dynamics of Productivity Change. Johns
Hopkins.
xKendrick, John W.
The Formation & Stocks of Total Capital. Natl
Bur Econ Res.
Productivity in the United States: Trends &
Cycles. Johns Hopkins.
Productivity Trends in the United States. Arno.
Kendrick, Thomas D. *see* Kendrick, Thomas Downing.
Kendrick, Thomas Downing, Sir.
xKendrick, Thomas D.
History of the Vikings. Biblio Dist.
Kendrick, V. Ben.
xKendrick, V. Ben.

Buried Alive for Christ & Other Missionary
Stories. Reg Baptist.
Kendrick, Walter M.
xKendrick, Walter M.
The Novel Machine: The Theory & Fiction of
Anthony Trollope. Johns Hopkins.
Keneally, Thomas.
xKeneally, Thomas.
Gossip from the Forest. HarBraceJ.
Passenger. HarBraceJ.
Kenen, Peter B.
xKenen, Peter B.
British Monetary Policy & the Balance of
Payments, 1951-1957. Harvard U Pr.
ed. The Open Economy: Essays on
International Trade & Finance. Columbia U
Pr.
Kenez, Peter.
xKenez, Peter.
Civil War in South Russia, 1918: The First
Year of the Volunteer Army. U of Cal Pr.
Kenfield, John F.
xKenfield, John F.
Teaching & Coaching Tennis. Wm C Brown.
Kenilworth, Walter W. *see* Kenilworth, Walter Winston.
Kenilworth, Walter Winston.
xKenilworth, Walter W.
A Study of Oscar Wilde. Haskell.
Kenin, Richard.
xKenin, Richard.
Return to Albion: Americans in England
1760-1940. HR&W.
Keniston, Kenneth.
xKeniston, Kenneth.
All Our Children: The American Family Under
Pressure. HarBraceJ.
The Uncommitted: Alienated Youth in
American Society. Dell.
Uncommitted: Alienated Youth in American
Society. HarBraceJ.
Kenkel, J. L. *see* Kenkel, James L.
Kenkel, James L.
xKenkel, J. L.
Dynamic Linear Economic Models. Gordon.
Kenkel, William F.
xKenkel, William F.
The Family in Perspective. Goodyear.
Society in Action: Introduction to Sociology.
Har-Row.
Kenmare, Dallas, Pseud.
xKenmare, Dallas.
The Browning Love-Story. Folcroft.
Ever a Fighter: A Modern Approach to the
Work of Robert Browning. R West.
The Future of Poetry. Arden Lib.
Future of Poetry. Folcroft.
The Future of Poetry. Porter.
Love the Unknown. Transatlantic.
The Nature of Genius. Greenwood.
The Nature of Genius. R West.
Kennan, George, 1845-1924
xKennan, George.
Campaigning in Cuba. Kennikat.
Siberia & the Exile System. Russell.
xKennan, George F.
Siberia & the Exile System. U of Chicago Pr.
Kennan, George F. *see* Kennan, George Frost.
Kennan, George Frost, 1904-
xKennan, George F.

The Cloud of Danger: Current Realities of
American Foreign Policy. Little.
The Decline of Bismarck's European Order:
Franco-Russian Relations, 1875-1890.
Princeton U Pr.
From Prague After Munich: Diplomatic Papers,
1938-1939. Princeton U Pr.
Marquis De Custine & His Russia in 1839.
Princeton U Pr.
Realities of American Foreign Policy. Norton.
Soviet Foreign Policy: 1917-1941. Greenwood.
Soviet Foreign Policy: 1917-1941. Krieger.
Kennard, Howard P. *see* Kennard, Howard Percy.
Kennard, Howard Percy, d. 1915
xKennard, Howard P.
The Russian Peasant. AMS Pr.
Kennard, Joseph S. *see* Kennard, Joseph Spencer.
Kennard, Joseph Spencer, 1859-1944
xKennard, Joseph S.
Masks & Marionettes. Kennikat.
Kenneally, James J. *see* Kenneally, James Joseph.
Kenneally, James Joseph, 1929-
xKenneally, James J.
Women & American Trade Unions. Eden
Women.
Kennedy, A. C. *see* Kennedy, Arthur Colville.
Kennedy, Adam.
xKennedy, Adam.
Love Song. NAL.
Kennedy, Alan.
xKennedy, Alan.
Meaning & Signs in Fiction. St Martin.
Kennedy, Arthur Colville.
xKennedy, A. C.
Essentials of Medicine & Surgery for Dental
Students. Churchill.
Kennedy, Arthur G. *see* Kennedy, Arthur Garfield.
Kennedy, Arthur Garfield.
xKennedy, Arthur G.
A Concise Bibliography for Students of
English. Stanford U Pr.
Current English: A Study of Present-Day
Usages & Tendencies, Including
Pronunciation, Spelling, Grammatical
Practice, Word-Coining, & the Shifting of
Meanings. Greenwood.
Kennedy, Beatrice B. *see* Kennedy, Beatrice Burton.
Kennedy, Beatrice Burton.
xKennedy, Beatrice B.
Deep Within. Dorrance.
Kennedy, Brian. *see* Kennedy, Brian Ernest.
Kennedy, Brian Ernest, 1942-
xKennedy, Brian.
Silver, Sin & Sixpenny Ale: A Social History of
Broken Hill 1883-1921. Intl Schol Bk Serv.
Kennedy, Bruce M., 1929-
xKennedy, Bruce M.
Community Journalism: A Way of Life. Iowa
St U Pr.
Kennedy, C. R. *see* Kennedy, Clive Russell.
Kennedy, Carol.
xKennedy, Carol.
ed. Buying Antiques in Europe: What to Buy
and Where. Bowker.
Kennedy, Charles W. *see* Kennedy, Charles William.
Kennedy, Charles William, 1882-
xKennedy, Charles W.
ed. Anthology of Old English Poetry. Oxford
U Pr.
The Earliest English Poetry: A Critical Survey
of the Poetry Written Before the Norman
Conquest with Illustrative Translations.
Rowman.
Kennedy, Clive Russell, 1941-
xKennedy, C. R.

Ecological Animal Parasitology. Halsted Pr.
ed. Ecological Aspects of Parasitology.
Elsevier.
Kennedy, D. James. *see* Kennedy, Dennis James.
Kennedy, Dennis James, 1930-
xKennedy, D. James.
Truths That Transform. Revell.
xKennedy, James.
Evangelism Explosion. Tyndale.
Kennedy, Diana.
xKennedy, Diana.
The Cuisines of Mexico. Har-Row.
Recipes from the Regional Cooks of Mexico.
Har-Row.
The Tortilla Book. Har-Row.
Kennedy, Donald. *see* Kennedy, Donald, 1931.
Kennedy, Donald, 1931.
xKennedy, Donald.
Intro. by From Cell to Organism: Readings
from Scientific American. W H Freeman.
Kennedy, E. *see* Kennedy, Eugene C.
Kennedy, Eddie C. *see* Kennedy, Eddie Clifton.
Kennedy, Eddie Clifton.
xKennedy, Eddie C.
Classroom Approaches to Remedial Reading.
Peacock Pubs.
Kennedy, Edward D.
xKennedy, Edward D.
Dividends to Pay. Kelley.
Kennedy, Edward G. *see* Kennedy, Edward Guthrie.
Kennedy, Edward Guthrie, 1849-1932
xKennedy, Edward G.
The Etched Work of Whistler. A Wofsy Fine
Arts.
Compiled by The Etched Work of Whistler. Da
Capo.
Kennedy, Eugene. *see* Kennedy, Eugene C.
Kennedy, Eugene C.
xKennedy, E.
The Trouble Book. Cornerstone.
xKennedy, Eugene.
Free to Be Human. Cornerstone.
Free to Be Human. Thomas More.
On Becoming a Counselor: A Basic Guide for
Non-Professional Counselors. Continuum.
On Becoming a Counselor: A Basic Guide for
Non-Professional Counselors. Seabury.
The Trouble Book. Thomas More.
Kennedy, Gavin.
xKennedy, Gavin.
Burden Sharing in NATO. Holmes & Meier.
The Death of Captain Cook. Biblio Dist.
Kennedy, George.
xKennedy, George.
Art of Persuasion in Greece. Princeton U Pr.
Kennedy, George A. *see* Kennedy, George Alexander.
Kennedy, George Alexander, 1928-
xKennedy, George A.
Classical Rhetoric & Its Christian & Secular
Tradition from Ancient to Modern Times. U
of NC Pr.
Kennedy, Harold J.
xKennedy, Harold J.
No Pickle, No Performance: An Irreverent
Theatrical Excursion from Tallulah to
Travolta. Doubleday.
Kennedy, Helen, 1941-
xKennedy, Helen.
Systematics & Pollination of the "Closed
Flowered" Species of Calathea
(Mar-Antaceae). U of Cal Pr.
Kennedy, James. *see* Kennedy, James R.
Kennedy, James R.
xKennedy, James.
Library Research Guide to Religion &
Theology: Illustrated Search Strategy &
Sources. Pierian.
Kennedy, John, fl. 1870-1914
xKennedy, John.

Stem Dictionary of the English Language.
Gale.
A Stem Dictionary of the English Language. R
West.
Kennedy, John F. *see* Kennedy, John Fitzgerald.
Kennedy, John Fitzgerald, Pres. U.S. 1917-1963
xKennedy, John F.
Nation of Immigrants. Har-Row.
Profiles in Courage. Har-Row.
Profiles in Courage. Har-Row.
Kennedy, John G.
xKennedy, John G.
ed. Nubian Ceremonial Life: Studies in Islamic
Syncretism & Cultural Change. U of Cal Pr.
Kennedy, John H. *see* Kennedy, John Hines.
Kennedy, John Harold, 1898-
xKennedy, John H.
Thomas Dongan, Governor of New York
(1682-1688). AMS Pr.
Kennedy, John Hines.
xKennedy, John H.
ed. Cardiovascular Surgery, 1972. Am Heart.
ed. Cardiovascular Surgery 1973. Am Heart.
ed. Cardiovascular Surgery, 1974. Am Heart.
Kennedy, John M. *see* Kennedy, John Mcfarland.
Kennedy, John McFarland.
xKennedy, John M.
English Literature, 1880-1905. Folcroft.
Kennedy, John P. *see* Kennedy, John Pendleton.
Kennedy, John Pendleton, 1795-1870
xKennedy, John P.
Quodlibet. Irvington.
Swallow Barn: Or, a Sojourn in the Old
Dominion. Somerset Pub.
Kennedy, K. T.
xKennedy, K. T.
Piano Action Repairs & Maintenance. A S
Barnes.
Kennedy, Keith.
xKennedy, Keith.
Film Making in Creative Teaching.
Watson-Guptill.
Kennedy, Kenneth A. *see* Kennedy, Kenneth A. R.
Kennedy, Kenneth A. R.
xKennedy, Kenneth A.
Human Variation in Space & Time. Wm C
Brown.
Kennedy, Larry.
xKennedy, Larry W.
Down with Anxiety. Broadman.
Kennedy, Larry W. *see* Kennedy, Larry.
Kennedy, Leonard. *see* Kennedy, Leonard M.
Kennedy, Leonard M.
xKennedy, Leonard.
Games for Individualizing Mathematics
Learning. Merrill.
xKennedy, Leonard M.
Experiences for Teaching Children
Mathematics. Wadsworth Pub.
Guiding Children to Mathematical Discovery.
Wadsworth Pub.
Kennedy, M. Thomas. *see* Kennedy, Thomas.
Kennedy, Malcolm D. *see* Kennedy, Malcolm Duncan.
Kennedy, Malcolm Duncan, 1895-
xKennedy, Malcolm D.
The Estrangement of Great Britain & Japan,
1917-1935. U of Cal Pr.
Kennedy, Margaret, 1896-1967
xKennedy, Margaret.
The Outlaws on Parnassus. Arden Lib.
Outlaws on Parnassus. Arno.
Kennedy, Mark.
xKennedy, Mark.
The Pecking Order. AMS Pr.
Kennedy, Mary.
xKennedy, Mary.

Bourrichon. Gotham.
Kennedy, Michael, 1926-
xKennedy, Michael.
Richard Strauss. Biblio Dist.
Kennedy, Monty.
xKennedy, Monty.
Checkering & Carving of Gunstocks. Stackpole.
Kennedy, Patrick, 1801-1873
xKennedy, Patrick.
The Bardic Stories of Ireland. Folcroft.
The Fireside Stories of Ireland. Folcroft.
Legendary Fictions of the Irish Celts. Arno.
Legendary Fictions of the Irish Celts. Gale.
Kennedy, Paul M., 1945-
xKennedy, Paul M.
ed. The War Plans of the Great Powers. Allen
Unwin.
Kennedy, Peter, 1943-
xKennedy, Peter.
A Guide to Econometrics. MIT Pr.
xKennedy, Peter E.
Macroeconomics. Allyn.
Kennedy, Peter E. *see* Kennedy, Peter.
Kennedy, Philip. *see* Kennedy, Philip D.
Kennedy, Philip D.
xKennedy, Philip.
Understanding Television. Sams.
Kennedy, R. F. *see* Kennedy, John Fitzgerald.
Kennedy, Raymond, 1906-1950
xKennedy, Raymond.
Ageless Indies. Greenwood.
Kennedy, Richard, 1910-
xKennedy, Richard.
A Boy at the Hogarth Press. Penguin.
The Contests at Cowlick. Little.
Inside My Feet: The Story of a Giant.
Har-Row.
The Leprechaun's Story. Dutton.
The Lost Kingdom of Karnica. Sierra.
Lost Kingdom of Karnica. Scribner.
The Mouse God. Little.
Oliver Hyde's Dishcloth Concert. Little.
The Porcelain Man. Little.
Kennedy, Robert, 1938-
xKennedy, Robert.
Bodybuilding for Women. Emerson.
Shape up!: The New Unisex Body Building.
Fell.
Kennedy, Robert F., 1925-1968
xKennedy, Robert F.
Frwd. by Profiles in Courage. Har-Row.
Thirteen Days: A Memoir of the Cuban Missile
Crisis. Norton.
Thirteen Days: A Memoir of the Cuban Missile
Crisis. Watts.
Kennedy, Robert M.
xKennedy, Robert M.
German Campaign in Poland (1939). Zenger
Pub.
Kennedy, Robert W. *see* Kennedy, Robert Woods.
Kennedy, Robert Woods.
xKennedy, Robert W.
The House & the Art of Its Design. Krieger.
Kennedy, Sheila.
xKennedy, Sheila.
Working Family's Kitchen Guide. One Hund
One Prods.
Kennedy, Susan E. *see* Kennedy, Susan Estabrook.
Kennedy, Susan Estabrook.
xKennedy, Susan E.
The Banking Crisis of 1933. U Pr of Ky.
If All We Did Was to Weep at Home: A
History of White Working-Class Women in
America. Ind U Pr.
Kennedy, Theodore. *see* Kennedy, Theodore R.
Kennedy, Theodore R., 1936-
xKennedy, Theodore.

You Gotta Deal with It: Black Family
Relations in a Southern Community. Oxford
U Pr.
xKennedy, Theodore R.
You Gotta Deal with It: Black Family
Relations in a Southern Community. Oxford
U Pr.
Kennedy, Thomas, 1930-
xKennedy, M. Thomas.
European Labor Relations: Text & Cases.
Lexington Bks.
xKennedy, Thomas L.
The Arms of Kiangnan: Modernization in the
Chinese Ordnance Industry 1860-1895.
Westview.
Kennedy, Thomas C., 1932-
xKennedy, Thomas C.
Charles A. Beard & American Foreign Policy.
U Presses Fla.
Kennedy, Thomas L. see Kennedy, Thomas.
Kennedy, Tom.
xKennedy, Tom.
An Examination of Questionable Payments &
Practices. Praeger.
Kennedy, W. see Kennedy, William Jo.
Kennedy, William, 1928-
xKennedy, William.
Legs. Warner Bks.
Texas: The Rise, Progress, & Prospects of the
Republic of Texas. Kelley.
Kennedy, William F. see Kennedy, William Francis.
Kennedy, William Francis.
xKennedy, William F.
Humanist Versus Economist: The Economic
Thought of Samuel Taylor Coleridge.
Greenwood.
Kennedy, William J. see Kennedy, William Jerald.
Kennedy, William Jerald, 1932-
xKennedy, William J.
Adventures in Anthropology: A Reader in
Physical Anthropology. West Pub.
Kennedy, William Jo.
xKennedy, W.
ed Statistical Computing. Dekker.
Kennedy, William John, 1942-
xKennedy, William J.
Rhetorical Norms in Renaissance Literature.
Yale U Pr.
Kennedy, William S. see Kennedy, William Sloane.
Kennedy, William Sloane, 1850-1929
xKennedy, William S.
Oliver Wendell Holmes: Poet, Litterateur,
Scientist. Folcroft.
Kennedy, X. J.
xKennedy, X. J.
An Introduction to Fiction. Little.
Introduction to Poetry. Little.
Literature: An Introduction to Fiction, Poetry
& Drama. Little.
One Winter Night in August & Other
Nonsense Jingles. Atheneum.
Kenneke, Larry. see Kenneke, Larry J.
Kenneke, Larry J.
xKenneke, Larry.
Career Development Activities. Bobbs.
Kennelly, Brendan.
xKennelly, Brendan.
The Crooked Cross. Irish Bk Ctr.
Kenner, Charles L.
xKenner, Charles L.
History of New Mexican-Plains Indian
Relations. U of Okla Pr.
Kenner, Hugh.
xKenner, Hugh.
Bucky: A Guided Tour of Buckminster Fuller.
Morrow.
Geodesic Math & How to Use It. U of Cal Pr.
The Pound Era. U of Cal Pr.
A Reader's Guide to Samuel Beckett. FS&G.
Kennerly, David H. see Kennerly, David Hume.

Kennerly, David Hume, 1947-
xKennerly, David H.
Shooter. Newsweek.
Kenneson, Claude.
xKenneson, Claude.
A Cellist's Guide to the New Approach.
Exposition.
Kennet, Andrea.
xKennet, Andrea.
Beautiful Pittsburgh. Beautiful Am.
Kennett, Lee.
xKennett, Lee.
French Armies in the Seven Years' War: A
Study in Military Organization &
Administration. Duke.
Kennett, Lee. see Kennett, Lee B.
Kennett, Lee B.
xKennett, Lee.
The French Forces in America: 1780-1783.
Greenwood.
The Gun in America: The Origins of a
National Dilemma. Greenwood.
Kenneway, Eric.
xKenneway, Eric.
Folding Faces: Making Portraits in Paper.
Paddington.
Kenney, Charles L. see Kenney, Charles Lamb.
Kenney, Charles Lamb, 1821-1881
xKenney, Charles L.
A Memoir of Michael William Balfe. Da Capo.
Kenney, E. J.
xKenney, E. J.
The Classical Text: Aspects of Editing in the
Age of the Printed Book. U of Cal Pr.
Kenney, George B. see Kenney, George Brian.
Kenney, George Brian, 1951-
xKenney, George B.
An Analysis of the Energy Efficiency &
Economic Viability of Expanded Magnesium
Utilization. Garland Pub.
Kenney, Henry. see Kenney, W. Henry.
Kenney, John P. see Kenney, John Paul.
Kenney, John Paul.
xKenney, John P.
Principles of Investigation. West Pub.
Kenney, Sylvia W.
xKenney, Sylvia W.
Walter Frye & the Contenance Angloise. Da
Capo.
Kenney, W. Henry, 1918-
xKenney, Henry.
Path Through Teilhard's Phenomenon. Pflaum
Pr.
Kenney, W. Howland. see Kenney, William Howland.
Kenney, William Howland.
xKenney, W. Howland.
Laughter in the Wilderness: Early American
Humor to 1783. Kent St U Pr.
Kennick, W. E.
xKennick, W. E.
ed. Art & Philosophy: Readings in Aesthetics.
St Martin.
Kennon, Noel F.
xKennon, Noel F.
Patterns in Crystals. Wiley.
Kenny, A. J. see Kenny, Anthony John Patrick.
Kenny, Anthony.
xKenny, Anthony.
Action Emotion & Will. Humanities.
Kenny, Anthony. see Kenny, Anthony John Patrick.
Kenny, Anthony John Patrick.
xKenny, A. J.
Aristotle's Theory of the Will. Yale U Pr.
xKenny, Anthony.

ed. Aquinas: A Collection of Critical Essays. U
of Notre Dame Pr.
The Aristotelian Ethics: A Study of the
Relationship Between the Eudemian &
Nichomachean Ethics of Aristotle. Oxford U
Pr.
The Five Ways: St. Thomas Aquinas' Proofs of
God's Existence. U of Notre Dame Pr.
Kenny, David A., 1946-
xKenny, David A.
Correlation & Causality. Wiley.
Kenny, Herbert A.
xKenny, Herbert A.
Literary Dublin: A History. Taplinger.
Kenny, John B.
xKenny, John B.
Ceramic Design. Chilton.
The Complete Book of Pottery Making.
Chilton.
Kenny, Michael.
xKenny, Michael.
A Spanish Tapestry: Town & Country in
Castile. Peter Smith.
Kenny, Michael F.
xKenny, Michael F.
Concrete Estimating Handbook. Van Nos
Reinhold.
Masonry Estimating Handbook. Van Nos
Reinhold.
Kenny, T. see Kenny, Thomas.
Kenny, Terence.
xKenny, Terence.
The Political Thought of John Henry Newman.
Greenwood.
Kenny, Thomas.
xKenny, T.
Life & Genius of Shakespeare. AMS Pr.
Life & Genius of Shakespeare. R West.
Kenny, Vincent. see Kenny, Vincent S.
Kenny, Vincent S.
xKenny, Vincent.
Paul Green. Irvington.
Kenoyer, Natlee.
xKenoyer, Natlee.
Gymkhana Games. Wilshire.
Kenrick, Tony, 1935-
xKenrick, Tony.
The Chicago Girl. Berkley Pub.
The Nightime Guy. Morrow.
The Nightime Guy. NAL.
Kenschaft, Patricia C.
xKenschaft, Patricia C.
Linear Mathematics: A Practical Approach.
Worth.
Kenseth, Arnold.
xKenseth, Arnold.
Prayers for Worship Leaders. Fortress.
Kenstowicz, Michael. see Kenstowicz, Michael J.
Kenstowicz, Michael J.
xKenstowicz, Michael.
Generative Phonology: Description & Theory.
Acad Pr.
Kent. see Kent, Allen.
Kent, A. see Kent, Allen.
Kent, Alexander.
xKent, Alexander.

Command a King's Ship. Berkley Pub.
Command a King's Ship. Berkley Pub.
Command a King's Ship. Putnam.
In Gallant Company. Berkley Pub.
In Gallant Company. Putnam.
The Inshore Squadron. Putnam.
Passage to Mutiny. Berkley Pub.
Passage to Mutiny. BJ Pub Group.
Passage to Mutiny. Putnam.
Richard Bolitho--Midshipman. Putnam.
Signal - Close Action!. Berkley Pub.
Signal--Close Action!. Putnam.
To Glory We Steer. Berkley Pub.
Kent, Allen.
xKent.
Encyclopedia of Library & Information
Science. Dekker.
Use of Library Materials: University of
Pittsburgh Study. Dekker.
xKent, A.
ed. Encyclopedia of Library & Information
Science. Dekker.
xKent, Allen.
ed. Encyclopedia of Library & Information
Science. Dekker.
Information Analysis & Retrieval. Wiley.
Kent, B. *see* Kent, Bessie.
Kent, Bessie.
xKent, B.
Social Work Supervision in Practice. Pergamon.
Kent, Christopher, 1940-
xKent, Christopher.
Brains & Numbers: Elitism, Comtism, &
Democracy in Mid-Victorian England. U of
Toronto Pr.
Kent, David L. *see* Kent, David Lee.
Kent, David Lee.
xKent, David L.
Massachusetts Supplement for Modern Real
Estate Practice. Real Estate Ed Co.
Kent, Druzilla C. *see* Kent, Druzilla Crary.
Kent, Druzilla Crary, 1890-
xKent, Druzilla C.
Study of the Results of Planning for Home
Economics Education in the Southern States
As Organized Under the National Acts for
Vocational Education. AMS Pr.
Kent, Elizabeth. *see* Kent, Elizabeth Eaton.
Kent, Elizabeth E. *see* Kent, Elizabeth Eaton.
Kent, Elizabeth Eaton.
xKent, Elizabeth.
Goldsmith & His Booksellers. Folcroft.
xKent, Elizabeth E.
Goldsmith & His Booksellers. Arden Lib.
Goldsmith & His Booksellers. Kelley.
Kent, Fortune.
xKent, Fortune.
The House at Canterbury. PB.
Kent, Frank R. *see* Kent, Frank Richardson.
Kent, Frank Richardson, 1877-
xKent, Frank R.
The Great Game of Politics: An Effort to
Present the Elementary Human Facts About
Politics, Politicians, & Political Machines.
Arno.
The Story of Maryland Politics: An Outline
History of the Big Political Battles of the
State from 1864 to 1910, with Sketches &
Incidents of the Men & Measures That
Figured As Factors, & the Names of Most of
Those Who Held Office in That Period. Gale.
Kent, Fraser.
xKent, Fraser.
Nothing to Fear: Coping with Phobias. B&N.
Kent, George, 1939-
xKent, George.
Effects of Threats. Ohio St U Pr.
Kent, George. *see* Kent, George Cantine.
Kent, George C. *see* Kent, George Cantine.

Kent, George Cantine, 1914-
xKent, George.
Anatomy of the Vertebrates: A Laboratory
Guide. Mosby.
xKent, George C.
Comparative Anatomy of the Vertebrates.
Mosby.
Kent, Homer A.
xKent, Homer A.
Light in the Darkness: Studies in the Gospel of
John. BMH Bks.
Kent, Homer A. *see* Kent, Homer Austin.
Kent, Homer Austin, 1926-
xKent, Homer A.
The Pastor & His Work. BMH Bks.
Kent, Ian.
xKent, Ian.
I Amness: The Discovery of the Self Beyond
the Ego. Bobbs.
Kent, J. *see* Kent, James.
Kent, J. P. *see* Kent, John Philip Cozens.
Kent, Jack, 1920-
xKent, Jack.
illus. Christmas Pinata. Schol Bk Serv.
Clotilda. Random.
illus. The Egg Book. Macmillan.
illus. Grown-up Day. Schol Bk Serv.
Hoddy Doddy. Greenwillow.
illus. Jack Kent's Hokus Pokus Bedtime Book.
Random.
illus. More Fables of Aesop. Schol Bk Serv.
illus. Mrs. Mooley. Western Pub.
illus. Piggy Bank Gonzales. Parents.
illus. Socks for Supper. Parents.
Supermarket Magic. Random.
Kent, James, 1763-1847
xKent, J.
Commentaries on American Law. Da Capo.
Kent, John Philip Cozens.
xKent, J. P.
Roman Coins. Abrams.
Kent, P. *see* Kent, Patricia.
Kent, P. W. *see* Kent, Paul Welberry.
Kent, Patricia.
xKent, P.
American Woman & Alcohol. HR&W.
Kent, Paul Welberry.
xKent, P. W.
ed. Membrane Mediated Information. Elsevier.
Kent, R. C.
xKent, Randolph C.
ed. Study & Teaching of International
Relations: A Perspective on Mid-Career
Education. Nichols Pub.
Kent, R. K. *see* Kent, Raymond K.
Kent, Randolph C. *see* Kent, R. C.
Kent, Raymond K.
xKent, R. K.
Early Kingdoms in Madagascar: 1500-1700.
Krieger.
xKent, Raymond K.
From Madagascar to the Malagasy Republic.
Greenwood.
Kent, Robert W. *see* Kent, Robert Warren.
Kent, Robert Warren.
xKent, Robert W.
How to Get Rich in Real Estate. P-H.
Kent, Rockwell. *see* Kent, Rookwell.
Kent, Rookwell, 1882-
xKent, Rockwell.
Greenland Journal. Astor-Honor.
Kent, Rosalind.
xKent, Rosalind.
Reading the Russian Language: A Guide for
Librarians & Other Professionals. Dekker.
Kent, Thomas H.
xKent, Thomas H.

General Pathology: A Programmed Text. Little.
Introduction to Human Disease. ACC.
Kent, William, 1884-
xKent, William.
London for Americans. Arden Lib.
London for Americans. Century Bookbindery.
London for Dickens Lovers. Haskell.
London for Dickens Lovers. R West.
Memoirs & Letters of James Kent. Da Capo.
Kentish, Thomas.
xKentish, Thomas.
The Pyrotechnists Treasury: The Complete Art
of Firework-Making. Paladin Ent.
Kenton, Edna, 1876-1954
xKenton, Edna.
Simon Kenton, His Life & Period, 1755-1836.
Arno.
Kenton, Warren.
xKenton, Warren.
Stage Properties & How to Make Them.
Drama Bk.
Stage Properties & How to Make Them.
Soccer.
Kentsmith, David K.
xKentsmith, David K.
Treating Sexual Problems in Medical Practice.
Arco.
Kentucky. Adjutant-General's Office.
xKentucky Adjutant-General's Office.
Kentucky Soldiers of the War of 1812.
Genealog Pub.
Kenworthy, L. *see* Kenworthy, Leslie.
Kenworthy, Leonard S. *see* Kenworthy, Leonard Stout.
Kenworthy, Leonard Stout.
xKenworthy, Leonard S.
Free & Inexpensive Materials on World Affairs.
Tchrs Coll.
Sixteen Quaker Leaders Speak. Friends United.
The Story of Rice. Messner.
Studying Africa in Elementary & Secondary
Schools. Tchrs Coll.
Studying South America in Elementary &
Secondary Schools. Tchrs Coll.
Studying the U.S.S.R. in Elementary &
Secondary Schools. Tchrs Coll.
Kenworthy, Leslie.
xKenworthy, L.
ed. Chemicals in Ships. Intl Schol Bk Serv.
Kenyatta, Jomo.
xKenyatta, Jomo.
Facing Mount Kenya: The Tribal Life of
Gikuyu. AMS Pr.
Kenyon, Carl.
xKenyon, Carl.
How to Avoid Rip-Offs at the Dentist.
Sovereign Bks.
Kenyon, Cecelia M.
xKenyon, Cecelia M.
ed. The Antifederalists. Bobbs.
Kenyon, Charles F. *see* Kenyon, Charles Frederick.
Kenyon, Charles Frederick, 1879-1926
xKenyon, Charles F.
Tales of a Cruel Country. Arno.
Kenyon, Don J.
xKenyon, Don J.
The Glory of Grace: Romans. Chr Pubns.
Kenyon, Frederic G. *see* Kenyon, Frederic George.
Kenyon, Frederic George, Sir, 1863-1952
xKenyon, Frederic G.
The Bible & Modern Scholarship. Arden Lib.
The Bible & Modern Scholarship. Greenwood.
Books & Readers in Ancient Greece & Rome.
Ares.
Books & Readers in Ancient Greece & Rome.
Folcroft.
Kenyon, J. R. *see* Kenyon, John Philipps.
Kenyon, John Philipps, 1927-
xKenyon, J. R.

Stuart England. Penguin.
Stuart England. St Martin.
Kenyon, John S. *see* Kenyon, John Samuel.
Kenyon, John Samuel, 1874-
xKenyon, John S.
American Pronunciation. Wahr.
Kenyon, Kathleen. *see* Kenyon, Kathleen Mary.
Kenyon, Kathleen Mary, Dame.
xKenyon, Kathleen.
The Bible & Recent Archaeology. John Knox.
Kenyon, Keith.
xKenyon, Keith.
Pressure Points: Do It Yourself Acupuncture
Without Needles. Arco.
Keohane, Nannerl O., 1940-
xKeohane, Nannerl O.
Philosophy & the State in France: The
Renaissance to the Enlightenment. Princeton
U Pr.
Keohane, Robert O. *see* Keohane, Robert Owen.
Keohane, Robert Owen.
xKeohane, Robert O.
Power & Interdependence: World Politics in
Transition. Little.
Keough, Carol.
xKeough, Carol.
Water Fit to Drink. Rodale Pr Inc.
Keough, G. Arthur, 1909-
xKeough, G. Arthur.
Infinitely Happy. Southern Pub.
Keough, William F.
xKeough, William F.
Declining Enrollments: A New Dilemma for
Educators. Phi Delta Kappa.
Keown, Ian.
xKeown, Ian M.
Lover's Guide to America. Macmillan.
Lovers' Guide to America. Macmillan.
Lovers' Guide to the Caribbean & Mexico.
Macmillan.
Keown, Ian M. *see* Keown, Ian.
Keown, R.
xKeown, R.
An Introduction to Group Representation
Theory. Acad Pr.
Kepes, Gyorgy, 1906-
xKepes, Gyorgy.
ed. Arts of the Environment. Braziller.
ed. The Nature & Art of Motion. Braziller.
Kepes, Juliet.
xKepes, Juliet.
illus. Frogs Merry. Pantheon.
Kephart, William M.
xKephart, William M.
Extraordinary Groups: The Sociology of
Unconventional Life-Styles. St Martin.
Kepner, Charles D. *see* Kepner, Charles David.
Kepner, Charles David.
xKepner, Charles D.
Banana Empire: A Case Study of Economic
Imperialism. Russell.
Keppel, Charlotte.
xKeppel, Charlotte.
I Could Be Good to You. St Martin.
Keppel, Frederick P. *see* Keppel, Frederick Paul.
Keppel, Frederick Paul, 1875-1943
xKeppel, Frederick P.
Education for Adults, & Other Essays. Arno.
Keppel, Geoffrey.
xKeppel, Geoffrey.
Design & Analysis. A Researcher's Handbook.
P-H.
Introduction to Design & Analysis: A Student's
Handbook. W H Freeman.
Keppler, C. F. *see* Keppler, Carl F.
Keppler, Carl F.
xKeppler, C. F.
The Literature of the Second Self. U of Ariz
Pr.
Ker, Neil R. *see* Ker, Neil Ripley.

Ker, Neil Ripley.
xKer, Neil R.
ed. Medieval Manuscripts in British Libraries.
Oxford U Pr.
Ker, W. P. *see* Ker, William Paton.
Ker, William P. *see* Ker, William Paton.
Ker, William Paton, 1855-1923
xKer, W. P.
History of Ballads. Porter.
xKer, William P.
Art of Poetry: Seven Lectures, 1920-1922.
Arno.
Art of Poetry: Seven Lectures 1920-1922.
Folcroft.
Collected Essays. Arno.
Collected Essays of W. P. Ker. Russell.
The Dark Ages. Greenwood.
The Dark Ages. Hyperion Conn.
On Modern Literature: Lectures & Addresses.
Folcroft.
On Modern Literature: Lectures & Addresses.
Scholarly.
On the History of the Ballads. Folcroft.
Kerber, August.
xKerber, August.
ed. Quotable Quotes on Education. Wayne St
U Pr.
Kerber, Linda K.
xKerber, Linda K.
Federalists in Dissent: Imagery & Ideology in
Jeffersonian America. Cornell U Pr.
Kerby, Joe K. *see* Kerby, Joe Kent.
Kerby, Joe Kent.
xKerby, Joe K.
Essentials of Marketing Management. SW Pub.
Kerenskii, A. F. *see* Kerenskii, Aleksandr Fedorovich.
Kerenskii, Aleksandr Fedorovich, 1881-1970
xKerenskii, A. F.
The Crucifixion of Liberty. Kraus Repr.
Kerensky, Oleg, 1930-
xKerensky, Oleg.
The New British Drama: Fourteen Playwrights
Since Osborne & Pinter. Taplinger.
Kerenyi, C. *see* Kerenyi, Karoly.
Kerenyi, Karoly, 1897-1973
xKerenyi, C.
The Heroes of the Greeks. Thames Hudson.
xKerenyi, Karoly.
The Religion of the Greeks & Romans.
Greenwood.
Keresztesi, Michael.
xKeresztesi, Michael.
ed. German American History & Life: A Guide
to Information Sources. Gale.
Kerfoot, John Barrett, 1865-1927
xKerfoot, John Barrett.
American Pewter. Gale.
Kerimov, Liatif Gusein Ogly, 1906-
xKerimov, Lyatif.
Folk Designs from the Caucasus for Weaving &
Needlework. Dover.
Folk Designs from the Caucasus for Weaving &
Needlework. Peter Smith.
Kerimov, Lyatif. *see* Kerimov, Liatif Gusein Ogly.
Kerin. *see* Kerin, Roger A.
Kerin, Roger A.
xKerin.
Perspectives on Strategic Marketing
Management. Allyn.
xKerin, Roger A.
Strategic Marketing Problems: Cases &
Comments. Allyn.
Kerkut, G. A.
xKerkut, G. A.
ed. Progress in Neurobiology. Pergamon.
Kerkvliet, Benedict J.
xKerkvliet, Benedict J.

The Huk Rebellion: A Study of Peasant Revolt
in the Philippines. U of Cal Pr.
Kerle, Arthur G.
xKerle, Arthur G.
Whispering Trees: A Tale of Michigamaw.
North Star.
Kerlin, Robert T. *see* Kerlin, Robert Thomas.
Kerlin, Robert Thomas, 1866-1950
xKerlin, Robert T.
Contemporary Poetry of the Negro. Arno.
Theocritus in English Literature. Folcroft.
Kerlin, T. W.
xKerlin, T. W.
Frequency Response Testing in Nuclear
Reactors. Acad Pr.
Kerlinger, F. N. *see* Kerlinger, Frederick Nichols.
Kerlinger, Frederick Nichols.
xKerlinger, F. N.
Multiple Regression in Behavioral Research.
HR&W.
Kerman, Cynthia E. *see* Kerman, Cynthia Earl.
Kerman, Cynthia Earl.
xKerman, Cynthia E.
Creative Tension: The Life & Thought of
Kenneth Boulding. U of Mich Pr.
Kerman, Joseph, 1924-
xKerman, Joseph.
The Beethoven Quartets. Norton.
Listen. Worth.
Kermode, F. *see* Kermode, John Frank.
Kermode, Frank.
xKermode, Frank.
Intro. by & ed. English Pastoral Poetry: From
the Beginnings to Marvell. Norton.
Kermode, Frank. *see* Kermode, John Frank.
Kermode, John Frank.
xKermode, F.
Wallace Stevens. Chips.
xKermode, Frank.
The Genesis of Secrecy: On the Interpretation
of Narrative. Harvard U Pr.
ed. The Living Milton: Essays by Various
Hands. Routledge & Kegan.
ed. Oxford Reader: Varieties of Contemporary
Discourse. Oxford U Pr.
Kern, Alfred A. *see* Kern, Alfred Allan.
Kern, Alfred Allan, 1879-
xKern, Alfred A.
Ancestry of Chaucer. Folcroft.
Kern, Barbara.
xKern, Barbara.
The Owner Built Homestead. Scribner.
Kern, Frank D. *see* Kern, Frank Dunn.
Kern, Frank Dunn, 1883-
xKern, Frank D.
A Revised Taxonomic Account of
Gymnosporangium. Pa St U Pr.
Kern, Jean B.
xKern, Jean B.
Dramatic Satire in the Age of Walpole,
1720-1750. Iowa St U Pr.
Kern, John Philip, 1939-
xKern, John Philip.
Early Pliocene Marine Climate Environment of
the Eastern Ventura Basin, Southern
California. U of Cal Pr.
Kern, Ken.
xKern, Ken.
Owner-Builder & the Code: Politics of Building
Your Home. Scribner.
The Owner-Built Home. Scribner.
Kern, Marna E. *see* Kern, Marna Elyea.
Kern, Marna Elyea.
xKern, Marna E.
The Complete Book of Handcrafted Paper.
Coward.
An Introduction to Breadcraft. HM.
Kern, Mary M. *see* Kern, Mary Margaret.
Kern, Mary Margaret, 1906-
xKern, Mary M.

Be a Better Parent. Westminster.

Kern, Raymond.
xKern, Raymond.
Thermodynamics for Geologists. Freeman C.

Kern, Robert, 1934-
xKern, Robert W.
Liberals, Reformers, & Caciques in Restoration
Spain, 1875-1909. U of NM Pr.
Kern, Robert W. *see* Kern, Robert.

Kern, Stephen.
xKern, Stephen.
Anatomy & Destiny: A Cultural History of the
Human Body. Bobbs.

Kernaghan, Salvinija G.
xKernaghan, Salvinija G.
ed. Delivery of Health Care in Urban
Underserved Areas. Am Hospital.

Kernahan, Coulson, 1858-1943
xKernahan, Coulson.
In Good Company: Some Personal
Recollections of Swinburne, Lord Roberts,
Watts-Dunton, Oscar Wilde, Edward
Whymper S. J. Stone, & Stephen Phillips.
Arno.

Kernan, Alvin B.
xKernan, Alvin B.
ed. Character & Conflict: An Introduction to
Drama. HarBraceJ.
ed. Classics of the Modern Theater: Realism &
After. HarBraceJ.
The Playwright As Magician: Shakespeare's
Image of the Poet in the English Public
Theater. Yale U Pr.
Kernan, D. *see* Kernan, Doris.

Kernan, Doris.
xKernan, D.
Steps to English. McGraw.
Steps to English. McGraw.
xKernan, Doris.
Steps to English. McGraw.
Steps to English. McGraw.

Kernan, Roderick P.
xKernan, Roderick P.
Cell Potassium. Wiley.

Kernan, Thomas P.
xKernan, Thomas P.
The Future of Peace. Philos Lib.
Kernberg, Otto. *see* Kernberg, Otto F.

Kernberg, Otto F., 1928-
xKernberg, Otto.
Borderline Conditions & Pathological
Narcissism. Aronson.

Kernek, Sterling J.
xKernek, Sterling J.
Distractions of Peace During War: The Lloyd
George Government's Reactions to Woodrow
Wilson, December 1916 - November 1918.
Am Philos.
Kerner, H. T. *see* Kerner, Henry T.

Kerner, Henry T.
xKerner, H. T.
Foam Control Agents. Noyes.

Kernighan, Brian W.
xKernighan, Brian W.
The C Programming Language. P-H.
Software Tools. A-W.

Kernochan, Sarah.
xKernochan, Sarah.
Dry Hustle. Berkley Pub.
Kernodle, George R. *see* Kernodle, George Riley.

Kernodle, George Riley, 1907-
xKernodle, George R.
From Art to Theatre: Form & Convention in
the Renaissance. U of Chicago Pr.
Kerns, Frances C. *see* Kerns, Frances Casey.

Kerns, Frances Casey.
xKerns, Frances C.

Cana & Wine. Warner Bks.
A Cold Wild Wind. Avon.
This Land Is Mine. Warner Bks.

Kerns, Phil.
xKerns, Phil.
Peoples Temple, Peoples Tomb. Logos.

Kerns, Robert.
xKerns, Robert L.
Photojournalism: Photography with a Purpose.
P-H.
Kerns, Robert L. *see* Kerns, Robert.

Kerouac, Jack. *see* Kerouac, John.

Kerouac, John, 1922-
xKerouac, Jack.
Dharma Bums. NAL.
Dharma Bums. Penguin.
On the Road. NAL.
On the Road. Penguin.
On the Road. Viking Pr.
The Subterraneans. Ballantine.
Subterraneans. Grove.

Kerper, Hazel B. *see* Kerper, Hazel R.

Kerper, Hazel R.
xKerper, Hazel B.
Introduction to the Criminal Justice System.
West Pub.
Kerr, Alex. *see* Kerr, Alexander McBride.

Kerr, Alexander McBride.
xKerr, Alex.
Australia's North-West. Intl Schol Bk Serv.
Kerr, C. B. *see* Kerr, Charles Baldwin.

Kerr, Charles Baldwin, 1932-
xKerr, C. B.
The Etiology of Inherited Disorders. Mss Info.
Kerr, Clarence W. *see* Kerr, Clarence Ware.

Kerr, Clarence Ware, 1893-
xKerr, Clarence W.
Love: Familystyle: How to Have a Happy
Home. Good News.

Kerr, Clark, 1911-
xKerr, Clark.
The Uses of the University. Harvard U Pr.
ed. Work in America: The Decade Ahead. Van
Nos Reinhold.

Kerr, Don.
xKerr, Don.
The New England Vegetable Garden. Peregrine
Pr.

Kerr, Donald A.
xKerr, Donald A.
Oral Diagnosis. Mosby.
Oral Pathology: An Introduction to General &
Oral Pathology for Hygienists. Lea &
Febiger.

Kerr, Donald R.
xKerr, Donald R.
Basic Mathematics: Arithmetic with an
Introduction to Algebra. McGraw.
Elementary Algebra. McGraw.
Kerr, Elizabeth M. *see* Kerr, Elizabeth Margaret.

Kerr, Elizabeth Margaret.
xKerr, Elizabeth M.
Aspects of American English. HarBraceJ.
William Faulkner's Gothic Domain. Kennikat.
Kerr, George. *see* Kerr, George H.

Kerr, George H., 1911-
xKerr, George.
Formosa Betrayed. Da Capo.
xKerr, George H.
Formosa: Licensed Revolution & the Home
Rule Movement, 1895-1945. U Pr of Hawaii.

Kerr, Graham.
xKerr, Graham.
The Complete Galloping Gourmet Cookbook.
G&D.

Kerr, Howard.
xKerr, Howard.

Mediums, & Spirit-Rappers, & Roaring
Radicals: Spiritualism in American Literature,
1850-1900. U of Ill Pr.
Kerr, Hugh. *see* Kerr, Hugh Thomson.
Kerr, Hugh T. *see* Kerr, Hugh Thomson.

Kerr, Hugh Thomson, 1909-
xKerr, Hugh.
Protestantism. Barron.
xKerr, Hugh T.
ed. Readings in Christian Thought. Abingdon.
ed. Sons of the Prophets: Leaders in
Protestantism from Princeton Seminary.
Princeton U Pr.

Kerr, James Lennox, 1899-
xKerr, Lennox.
Back Door Guest. Arno.
Kerr, Jean. *see* Kerr, Jean Collins.

Kerr, Jean Collins.
xKerr, Jean.
How I Got to Be Perfect. Doubleday.
How I Got to Be Perfect. Fawcett.
How I Got to Be Perfect. G K Hall.

Kerr, Jennifer.
xKerr, Jennifer.
Honolulu Underground Gourmet. S&S.
Kerr, John G. *see* Kerr, John Graham.

Kerr, John Graham, Sir, 1869-
xKerr, John G.
Naturalist in the Gran Chaco. Greenwood.

Kerr, John R.
xKerr, John R.
Marketing: An Environmental Approach. P-H.

Kerr, Judith.
xKerr, Judith.
The Other Way Round. Coward.
When Hitler Stole Pink Rabbit. Dell.
illus. When Hitler Stole Pink Rabbit. Coward.
illus. When Willy Went to the Wedding. Schol
Bk Serv.
Kerr, Lennox. *see* Kerr, James Lennox.

Kerr, Lois.
xKerr, Lois.
How to Get the Most Out of Your Cruise to
Alaska. Madrona Pubs.

Kerr, M. E.
xKerr, M. E.
Dinky Hocker Shoots Smack. Dell.
Dinky Hocker Shoots Smack. Har-Row.
Gentlehands. Har-Row.
Gentlehands. Bantam.
If I Love You, Am I Trapped Forever?. Dell.
If I Love You, Am I Trapped Forever?.
Har-Row.
I'll Love You When You're More Like Me.
Dell.
I'll Love You When You're More Like Me.
Har-Row.
Love Is a Missing Person. Har-Row.
Love Is a Missing Person. Dell.
The Son of Someone Famous. Har-Row.
Kerr, Norm. *see* Kerr, Norman.

Kerr, Norman, 1930-
xKerr, Norm.
Technique of Photographic Lighting. Amphoto.
Kerr, Paul E. *see* Kerr, Paul Francis.

Kerr, Paul Francis.
xKerr, Paul E.
Optical Mineralogy. McGraw.

Kerr, Robert, 1899-
xKerr, Robert.
Dark Lady. Stein & Day.
The Stuart Legacy. Stein & Day.
Kerr, Stanley E. *see* Kerr, Stanley Elphinstone.

Kerr, Stanley Elphinstone.
xKerr, Stanley E.
The Lions of Marash: Personal Experiences
with American Near East Relief, 1919-1922.
State U NY Pr.

Kerr, Steven, 1941-
xKerr, Steven.

ed. Organizational Behavior. Grid Pub.
Kerr, Walter, 1913-
  xKerr, Walter.
    How Not to Write a Play. Writer.
    Journey to the Center of the Theater. Knopf.
    The Silent Clowns. Knopf.
    Thirty Plays Hath November: Pain & Pleasure
      in the Contemporary Theater. S&S.
Kerr, Walter. *see* Kerr, Walter Boardman.
Kerr, Walter Boardman, 1911-
  xKerr, Walter.
    The Secret of Stalingrad. Playboy Pbks.
Kerr, Wilfred B. *see* Kerr, Wilfred Brenton.
Kerr, Wilfred Brenton, 1896-1950
  xKerr, Wilfred B.
    Maritime Provinces of British North America
      & the American Revolution. Russell.
Kerr, William F.
  xKerr, William F.
    ed. God: What Is He Like. Tyndale.
Kerr, William H. *see* Kerr, William Henry.
Kerr, William Henry, 1855-
  xKerr, William H.
    Farmers' Union & Federation Advocate &
      Guide. Arno.
Kerrane, Kevin.
  xKerrane, Kevin.
    Baseball Diamonds: Tales, Traces Visions &
      Voodoo from a Native American Rite.
      Doubleday.
Kerridge, Eric.
  xKerridge, Eric.
    Agricultural Revolution. Kelley.
Kerrigan, Anthony.
  xKerrigan, Anthony.
    At the Front Door of the Atlantic. Dufour.
Kerrigan, H. D. *see* Kerrigan, Harry D.
Kerrigan, Harry D.
  xKerrigan, H. D.
    Fund Accounting. McGraw.
Kerrigan, William, 1943-
  xKerrigan, William.
    The Prophetic Milton. U Pr of Va.
Kerrigan, William J.
  xKerrigan, William J.
    Reading for the Point. HarBraceJ.
    Writing to the Point: Six Basic Steps.
      HarBraceJ.
Kerrod, Robin.
  xKerrod, Robin.
    The Challenge of Space. Lerner Pubns.
    Mission Outer Space. Lerner Pubns.
    The Mysterious Universe. Lerner Pubns.
    Race for the Moon. Lerner Pubns.
    See Inside a Space Station. Watts.
    Stars & Planets. Arco.
Kerschner, Paul.
  xKerschner, Paul A.
    ed. Advocacy & Age: Issues, Experiences,
      Strategies. USC Andrus Geron.
Kerschner, Paul A. *see* Kerschner, Paul.
Kersey, Harry A., 1935-
  xKersey, Harry A.
    Pelts, Plumes & Hides: White Traders Among
      the Seminole Indians, 1870-1930. U Presses
      Fla.
Kershaw, Andrew.
  xKershaw, Andrew.
    Modern Combat Aircraft & Insignia. Arco.
Kershaw, Joseph A. *see* Kershaw, Joseph Alexander.
Kershaw, Joseph Alexander, 1913-
  xKershaw, Joseph A.
    Government Against Poverty. Brookings.
Kershner, R. B. *see* Kershner, Richard.
Kershner, Richard.
  xKershner, R. B.
    The Anatomy of Mathematics. Wiley.
Kershner, William K.
  xKershner, William K.

Advanced Pilot's Flight Manual. Iowa St U Pr.
Flight Instructor's Manual. Iowa St U Pr.
Kerslake, D. M. *see* Kerslake, D. Mck.
Kerslake, D. Mck.
  xKerslake, D. M.
    The Stress of Hot Environments. Cambridge U
      Pr.
Kersley, Leo.
  xKersley, Leo.
    A Dictionary of Ballet Terms. Da Capo.
Kersten, Dorothy B.
  xKersten, Dorothy B.
    Classifying Church or Synagogue Library
      Materials. CSLA.
    Subject Headings for Church or Synagogue
      Libraries. CSLA.
Kersten, H. *see* Kersten, Helga.
Kersten, Helga.
  xKersten, H.
    Inhibitors of Nucleic Acid Synthesis:
      Biophysical & Biochemical Aspects.
      Springer-Verlag.
Kertesz, Andre.
  xKertesz, Andre.
    Andre Kertesz: Sixty Years of Photography.
      Penguin.
    Distortions. Knopf.
    Of New York. Knopf.
Kertesz, Andrew.
  xKertesz, Andrew.
    Aphasia & Associated Disorders: Taxonomy,
      Localization & Recovery. Grune.
Kertesz, G. A.
  xKertesz, G. A.
    ed. Documents in the Political History of the
      European Continent, 1815-1939. Oxford U
      Pr.
Kertesz, Louise, 1939-
  xKertesz, Louise.
    The Poetic Vision of Muriel Rukeyser. La State
      U Pr.
Kertesz, Stephan D. *see* Kertesz, Stephen Denis.
Kertesz, Stephen D. *see* Kertesz, Stephen Denis.
Kertesz, Stephen Denis, 1904-
  xKertesz, Stephan D.
    ed. American Diplomacy in a New Era. Arno.
  xKertesz, Stephen D.
    Diplomacy in a Changing World. Greenwood.
    ed. East Central Europe & the World:
      Developments in the Post-Stalin Era. U of
      Notre Dame Pr.
    ed. Task of Universities in a Changing World.
      U of Notre Dame Pr.
Kertz, George J.
  xKertz, George J.
    The Nature & Application of Mathematics.
      Goodyear.
Kertzer, Morris N. *see* Kertzer, Morris Norman.
Kertzer, Morris Norman, 1910-
  xKertzer, Morris N.
    Intro. by Tell Me, Rabbi. Bloch.
    Tell Me, Rabbi. Macmillan.
Kerwin, Jerome G. *see* Kerwin, Jerome Gregory.
Kerwin, Jerome Gregory, 1896-
  xKerwin, Jerome G.
    Federal Water-Power Legislation. AMS Pr.
Kerzner, Harold.
  xKerzner, Harold.
    Project Management: A Systems Approach to
      Planning, Scheduling & Controlling. Van Nos
      Reinhold.
    Project Management for Bankers. Van Nos
      Reinhold.
Kesey, Ken.
  xKesey, Ken.
    One Flew Over the Cuckoo's Nest. NAL.
    One Flew Over the Cuckoo's Nest. Penguin.
    One Flew Over the Cuckoo's Nest. Viking Pr.
Keshishian, Douglas. *see* Keshishian, Douglas T.

Keshishian, Douglas T.
  xKeshishian, Douglas.
    How to Keep Well While Traveling in the
      Tropics. Dennis-Landman.
Kesler, Jackson.
  xKesler, Jackson.
    ed. Theatrical Costume: A Guide to
      Information Sources. Gale.
Kesler, Jay.
  xKesler, Jay.
    Growing Places. Revell.
    I Never Promised You a Disneyland. Word
      Bks.
    Outside Disneyland: Practical Christianity for
      Real-Life Hassles. Word Bks.
Kespohl, Ruth C. *see* Kespohl, Ruth Carwell.
Kespohl, Ruth Carwell.
  xKespohl, Ruth C.
    Geometry Problems My Students Have
      Written. NCTM.
Kess, Sidney.
  xKess, Sidney.
    A Practical Guide to Tax Planning. BNA.
Kessel. *see* Kessel, Joseph.
Kessel, Barney.
  xKessel, Barney.
    The Guitar. Criterion Mus.
Kessel, I. *see* Kessel, Israel.
Kessel, Israel.
  xKessel, I.
    The Essentials of Paediatrics for Nurses.
      Churchill.
Kessel, Joseph, 1898-
  xKessel.
    Le Lion. EMC.
  xKessel, Joseph.
    The Road Back: A Report on Alcoholics
      Anonymous. Greenwood.
Kessel, Richard G.
  xKessel, Richard G.
    Tissues & Organs: A Text-Atlas of Scanning
      Electron Microscopy. W H Freeman.
Kessell, John L.
  xKessell, John L.
    Friars, Soldiers & Reformers: Hispanic Arizona
      & the Sonora Mission Frontier, 1767-1856. U
      of Ariz Pr.
    The Missions of New Mexico Since 1776. U of
      NM Pr.
Kesselman, Arthur.
  xKesselman, Arthur.
    The Social Studies Student Investigates Foreign
      Policy. Rosen Pr.
Kesselman, Judi R.
  xKesselman, Judi R.
    Stopping Out: A Guide to Leaving College &
      Getting Back In. M Evans.
    Vans. Dandelion Pr.
Kesselman, Steven.
  xKesselman, Steven.
    The Modernization of American Reform:
      Structures & Perceptions. Garland Pub.
Kessen, W. *see* Kessen, William.
Kessen, William.
  xKessen, W.
    The Child. Wiley.
Kessler. *see* Kessler, Ethel.
Kessler, Edward, 1927-
  xKessler, Edward.
    Coleridge's Metaphors of Being. Princeton U
      Pr.
Kessler, Ethel.
  xKessler.
    What's Inside the Box?. Schol Bk Serv.
  xKessler, Ethel.
    Our Tooth Story: A Tale of Twenty Teeth.
      Dodd.

Kessler, Evelyn S.
xKessler, Evelyn S.
Anthropology: The Humanizing Process. Allyn.
Kessler, Harry. *see* Kessler, Harry Klemens Ulrich.
Kessler, Harry Klemens Ulrich, Graf Von, 1868-1937
xKessler, Harry.
Germany & Europe. Kennikat.
Kessler, Jane W.
xKessler, Jane W.
Psychopathology of Childhood. P-H.
Kessler, Jascha. *see* Kessler, Jascha Frederick.
Kessler, Jascha Frederick, 1929-
xKessler, Jascha.
In Memory of the Future. Kayak.
Whatever Love Declares. Plantin Pr.
Kessler, Julia. *see* Kessler, Julia Braun.
Kessler, Julia Braun.
xKessler, Julia.
Getting Even with Getting Old. Nelson-Hall.
Kessler, Leonard. *see* Kessler, Ethel.
Kessler, Leonard P.
xKessler, Leonard.
Do You Have Any Carrots?. Garrard.
illus. The Forgetful Pirate. Garrard.
illus. Hey Diddle Diddle. Garrard.
Hickory Dickory Dock. Garrard.
illus. Last One in Is a Rotten Egg. Har-Row.
Mixed-up Mother Goose. Garrard.
The Mother Goose Game. Garrard.
illus. & jt. auth. Our Tooth Story: A Tale of
Twenty Teeth. Dodd.
illus. The Pirates' Adventure on Spooky Island.
Garrard.
illus. Riddles That Rhyme for Halloween Time.
Garrard.
The Silly Mother Hubbard. Garrard.
illus. Tale of Two Bicycles: Safety on Your
Bike. Lothrop.
Tricks for Treats on Halloween. Garrard.
Kessler, Seymour.
xKessler, Seymour.
ed. Genetic Counseling: Psychological
Dimensions. Acad Pr.
Kessler, Sheila.
xKessler, Sheila.
The American Way of Divorce: Prescriptions
for Change. Nelson-Hall.
Kessopulos, Gust.
xKessopulos, Gust.
Dog Obedience Training. A S Barnes.
Dog Obedience Training. Wilshire.
Dog Ownership & Responsibility. A S Barnes.
Kester, Howard, 1904-
xKester, Howard.
Revolt Among the Sharecroppers. Arno.
Kesterson, David B., 1938-
xKesterson, David B.
ed. Critics on Mark Twain. U of Miami Pr.
Kestin, Joseph.
xKestin, Joseph.
Course in Statistical Thermodynamics. Acad
Pr.
Kesting, R. E. *see* Kesting, Robert E.
Kesting, Robert E., 1933-
xKesting, R. E.
Synthetic Polymeric Membranes. McGraw.
Kestner, Joseph A.
xKestner, Joseph A.
The Spatiality of the Novel. Wayne St U Pr.
Ketcham, Charles B.
xKetcham, Charles B.
Federico Fellini: The Search for a New
Mythology. Paulist Pr.
A Theology of Encounter: The Ontological
Ground for a New Christology. Pa St U Pr.
Ketcham, Hank.
xKetcham, Hank.

Dennis the Menace Rides Again. Fawcett.
Dennis the Menace: Teacher's Threat. Fawcett.
Someone's in the Kitchen with Dennis.
Fawcett.
Ketcham, Ralph. *see* Ketcham, Ralph Louis.
Ketcham, Ralph Louis, 1927-
xKetcham, Ralph.
From Colony to Country: The Revolution in
American Thought, 1750-1820. Macmillan.
Ketchum, William C., 1931-
xKetchum, William C.
American Basketry & Woodenware: A
Collector's Guide. Macmillan.
The Catalog of American Antiques. Larousse.
Catalog of American Collectibles. Mayflower
Bks.
Hooked Rugs: A Historical Collector's Guide -
How to Make Your Own. HarBraceJ.
Ketels, Hank. *see* Ketels, Henry.
Ketels, Henry.
xKetels, Hank.
Sports Illustrated Scuba Diving. Lippincott.
Keto, David B.
xKeto, David B.
Law & Offshore Oil Development: The North
Sea Experience. Praeger.
Kettani, M. Ali.
xKettani, M. Ali.
Direct Energy Conversion. A-W.
Kettelkamp, Larry.
xKettelkamp, Larry.
Astrology, Wisdom of the Stars. Morrow.
illus. Dreams. Morrow.
illus. Hypnosis: the Wakeful Sleep. Morrow.
Lasers, the Miracle Light. Morrow.
illus. Religions East & West. Morrow.
illus. Song, Speech & Ventriloquism. Morrow.
illus. Spinning Tops. Morrow.
Kettell, Samuel, 1800-1855
xKettell, Samuel.
ed. Specimens of American Poetry with Critical
& Biographical Notices. Arno.
Ketter, Robert. *see* Ketter, Robert L.
Ketter, Robert L.
xKetter, Robert.
Structural Analysis & Design. McGraw.
xKetter, Robert L.
Modern Methods of Engineering Computation.
McGraw.
Ketterer, David.
xKetterer, David.
The Rationale of Deception in Poe. La State U
Pr.
Kettle, Arnold.
xKettle, Arnold.
Shakespeare in a Changing World: Essays. R
West.
Kettler, Ellen L.
xKettler, Ellen L.
Historic Preservation Law: An Annotated
Bibliography. Preservation Pr.
Keucher, William F.
xKeucher, William F.
Good News People in Action. Judson.
Keul, J. *see* Keul, Joseph.
Keul, Joseph.
xKeul, J.
Energy Metabolism of Human Muscle. Univ
Park.
Kevan, Larry.
xKevan, Larry.
Time Domain Electron Spin Resonance. Wiley.
Keve, Paul W.
xKeve, Paul W.
Imaginative Programming in Probation &
Parole. U of Minn Pr.
Prison Life & Human Worth. U of Minn Pr.
Kevles, Bettyann.
xKevles, Bettyann.

Thinking Gorillas: Testing & Teaching the
Greatest Ape. Dutton.
Kevles, Daniel J.
xKevles, Daniel J.
The Physicists: The History of a Scientific
Community in Modern America. Random.
Kevorkian, George.
xKevorkian, George.
Business Mathematics. Merrill.
Kevorkian, Jack.
xKevorkian, Jack.
Slimmeriks & the Demi-Diet. Penumbra Inc.
Kew Chromosome Conference, Kew, England, 1976.
xProceedings of the Kew Chromosome Conference
- Jodrell Laboratory, England.
Current Chromosome Research. Elsevier.
Kew, Clinton J.
xKew, Clinton J.
jt. auth. Therapist Responds. Philos Lib.
Key, Alexander.
xKey, Alexander.
The Case of the Vanishing Boy. Archway.
Case of the Vanishing Boy. PB.
The Incredible Tide. Westminster.
Return from Witch Mountain. Westminster.
Return from Witch Mountain. Archway.
Return from Witchmountain. PB.
The Sword of Aradel. Westminster.
Key, Ellen. *see* Key, Ellen Karolina Sofia.
Key, Ellen Karolina Sofia.
xKey, Ellen.
The Century of the Child. Arno.
Love & Marriage. Hacker.
The Renaissance of Motherhood. Hacker.
Key, Francis S. *see* Key, Francis Scott.
Key, Francis Scott.
xKey, Francis S.
Star-Spangled Banner. T Y Crowell.
Key, James . *see* Key, James D.
Key, James D.
xKey, James .
The Week-End Athletes' Guide to Sports
Medicine: Lower Body. Anna Pub.
Key, Marcus M.
xKey, Marcus M.
ed. Pulmonary Reactions to Coal Dust: A
Review of the U. S. Experience. Acad Pr.
Key, Mary R. *see* Key, Mary Ritchie.
Key, Mary Ritchie.
xKey, Mary R.
Nonverbal Communication: A Research Guide
& Bibliography. Scarecrow.
Paralanguage & Kinesics: Nonverbal
Communication with a Bibliography.
Scarecrow.
Key, Maude D.
xKey, Maude D.
Grandmother's Amazing Housekeeping Secrets.
Buck Hill.
Key, Pierre V. R. *see* Key, Pierre Van Rensselaer.
Key, Pierre Van Rensselaer.
xKey, Pierre V. R.
Enrico Caruso: A Biography. Vienna Hse.
Key, Wilson B. *see* Key, Wilson Bryan.
Key, Wilson Bryan, 1925-
xKey, Wilson B.
Media Sexploitation. P-H.
Media Sexploitation. NAL.
Keyan, Rostam.
xKeyan, Rostam.
The Evolution of Language. Philos Lib.
Poetics. Philos Lib.
Keyarts, Eugene.
xKeyarts, Gene.
Sixty Selected Short Walks in Connecticut.
Globe Pequot.
Keyarts, Gene. *see* Keyarts, Eugene.

Keyes, Charles Don.
xKeyes, D. D.
Four Types of Value Destruction: A Search for the Good Through an Ethical Analysis of Everyday Experience. U Pr of Amer.
Keyes, Charles F.
xKeyes, Charles F.
ed. Ethnic Adaptation & Identity: The Karen on the Thai Frontier with Burma. Inst Study Human.
Keyes, Charles H. *see* Keyes, Charles Henry.
Keyes, Charles Henry, 1858-1925
xKeyes, Charles H.
Progress Through the Grades of City Schools: A Study of Acceleration & Arrest. AMS Pr.
Keyes, D. D. *see* Keyes, Charles Don.
Keyes, Daniel.
xKeyes, Daniel.
Flowers for Algernon. AMSCO Sch.
Flowers for Algernon. HarBraceJ.
Flowers for Algernon. Bantam.
Keyes, Elizabeth.
xKeyes, Elizabeth.
What's Eating You?. De Vorss.
Keyes, Fenton.
xKeyes, Fenton.
Aim for a Job in the Allied Health Field. Rosen Pr.
Opportunities in Psychiatry. Natl Textbk.
Your Future in a Paramedic Career. Rosen Pr.
Keyes, Frances P. *see* Keyes, Frances Parkinson.
Keyes, Frances Parkinson (Wheeler), 1885-
xKeyes, Frances P.
The Explorer. Fawcett.
Fielding's Folly. PB.
Great Tradition. PB.
Honor Bright. PB.
Parts Unknown. PB.
Keyes, G. L. *see* Keyes, Gordon Lincoln.
Keyes, Gordon Lincoln.
xKeyes, G. L.
Christian Faith & the Interpretation of History: A Study of St. Augustine's Philosophy of History. U of Nebr Pr.
Keyes, John H.
xKeyes, John H.
Consumer Handbook of Solar Energy for the United States & Canada. Morgan.
Keyes, John W. *see* Keyes, John Wesley.
Keyes, John Wesley, 1940-
xKeyes, John W.
ed. CRC Manual of Nuclear Medicine Procedures. CRC Pr.
Keyes, Ken. *see* Keyes, Kenneth S.
Keyes, Kenneth S.
xKeyes, Ken.
A Conscious Person's Guide to Relationships. Living Love.
Loving Your Body. Living Love.
xKeyes, Kenneth S.
How to Develop Your Thinking Ability. McGraw.
Keyes, King.
xKeyes, King.
Master Guide to Preparing Your Natal Horoscope. P-H.
Keyes, Langley C. *see* Keyes, Langley Carleton.
Keyes, Langley Carleton.
xKeyes, Langley C.
Boston Rehabilitation Program: An Independent Analysis. Harvard U Pr.
Keyes, Margaret F. *see* Keyes, Margaret Frings.
Keyes, Margaret Frings, 1929-
xKeyes, Margaret F.
Staying Married. Les Femmes Pub.
Keyes, Paul T., 1936-
xKeyes, Paul T.

Pastoral Presence & the Diocesan Priest. Affirmation.
Keyes, R. J. *see* Keyes, Robert J.
Keyes, Ralph.
xKeyes, Ralph.
The Height of Your Life. Little.
Keyes, Robert J., 1927-
xKeyes, R. J.
ed. Optical & Infrared Detectors. Springer-Verlag.
Keyes, W. Noel.
xKeyes, W. Noel.
Government Contracts in a Nutshell. West Pub.
Keyfitz, Nathan, 1913-
xKeyfitz, Nathan.
Applied Mathematical Demography. Wiley.
World Population: An Analysis of Vital Data. U of Chicago Pr.
Keylor, William R., 1944-
xKeylor, William R.
Academy & Community: The Foundation of the French Historical Profession. Harvard U Pr.
Jacques Bainville & the Renaissance of Royalist History in Twentieth Century France. La State U Pr.
Keymer, John.
xKeymer, John.
Original Papers Regarding Trade in England & Abroad. Kelley.
Keynes, John M. *see* Keynes, John Maynard.
Keynes, John Maynard, 1883-1946
xKeynes, John M.
General Theory of Employment, Interest & Money. HarBraceJ.
General Theory of Employment, Interest & Money. HarBraceJ.
Indian Currency & Finance. B Franklin.
A Treatise on Probability. AMS Pr.
Keynes, M. *see* Keynes, Milo.
Keynes, Milo.
xKeynes, M.
ed. Essays on John Maynard Keynes. Cambridge U Pr.
xKeynes, Milo.
ed. Essays on John Maynard Keynes. Cambridge U Pr.
Keys, Alice M. *see* Keys, Alice Mapelsden.
Keys, Alice Mapelsden.
xKeys, Alice M.
Cadwallader Colden: A Representative Eighteenth Century Official. AMS Pr.
Keys, Ivor. *see* Keys, Ivor Christopher Barfield.
Keys, Ivor Christopher Barfield.
xKeys, Ivor.
Brahms Chamber Music. U of Wash Pr.
Keys, Kerry S. *see* Keys, Kerry Shawn.
Keys, Kerry Shawn, 1946-
xKeys, Kerry S.
Loose Leaves Fall: Selected Poems. Pine Pr.
Keys, Noel, 1893-
xKeys, Noel.
The Improvement of Measurement Through Cumulative Testing: An Empirical Study of Two Hundred Elementary School Children Over a Period of Four Years. AMS Pr.
Keys, Thomas E. *see* Keys, Thomas Edward.
Keys, Thomas Edward, 1908-
xKeys, Thomas E.
The History of Surgical Anesthesia. Krieger.
Keyser, J. W. *see* Keyser, James William.
Keyser, James William.
xKeyser, J. W.
Human Plasma Proteins: Their Investigation in Pathological Conditions. Wiley.
Keyser, S. Jay. *see* Keyser, Samuel Jay.
Keyser, Samuel Jay, 1935-
xKeyser, S. Jay.

Recent Transformational Studies in European Languages. MIT Pr.
Keysor, Charles W.
xKeysor, Charles W.
Come Clean. Victor Bks.
Keyssar, Alexander.
xKeyssar, Alexander.
Melville's Israel Potter: Reflections on the American Dream. Harvard U Pr.
Keyssar, Helene.
xKeyssar, Helene.
The Curtain & the Veil: Strategies in Black Drama. B Franklin.
Kezdi, A. *see* Kezdi, Arpad.
Kezdi, Arpad.
xKezdi, A.
Stabilized Earth Roads. Elsevier.
Kezer, Glenn.
xKezer, Glenn.
The Queen Is Dead. BJ Pub Group.
Khachaturian, Narbey.
xKhachaturian, Narbey.
Prestressed Concrete. McGraw.
Khadduri, Majid, 1909-
xKhadduri, Majid.
Arab Contemporaries: The Role of Personalities in Politics. Johns Hopkins.
Modern Libya: A Study in Political Development. Johns Hopkins.
Political Trends in the Arab World: The Role of Ideas & Ideals in Politics. Johns Hopkins.
Socialist Iraq: A Study in Iraqi Politics Since 1968. Mid East Inst.
Khalakdina, M. *see* Khalakdina, Margaret.
Khalakdina, Margaret.
xKhalakdina, M.
Early Child Care in India. Gordon.
Khalifa, Ali M. *see* Khalifa, Ali Mohammed.
Khalifa, Ali Mohammed.
xKhalifa, Ali M.
The United Arab Emirates: Unity in Fragmentation. Westview.
Khambata, A. J. *see* Khambata, Adi J.
Khambata, Adi J.
xKhambata, A. J.
Introduction to Large Scale Integration. Krieger.
Khan, Ahsan Raza, 1939-
xKhan, Ahsan R.
Chieftains in the Mughal-Empire During the Reign of Akbar. Intl Pubns Serv.
Khan, Aman U.
xKhan, Aman U.
Psychiatric Emergencies in Pediatrics. Year Bk Med.
Khan, Asham R. *see* Khan, Ahsan Raza.
Khan, Azizur R. *see* Khan, Azizur Rahman.
Khan, Azizur Rahman.
xKhan, Azizur R.
Collective Agriculture & Rural Development in Soviet Central Asia. St Martin.
Khan, M. A. *see* Khan, Mohammed Abdul Quddus.
Khan, M. Masud. *see* Khan, M. Masud R.
Khan, M. Masud R.
xKhan, M. Masud.
The Privacy of the Self: Papers on Psychoanalytic Theory & Technique. Intl Univs Pr.
Khan, Mahmood H. *see* Khan, Mahmood Hasan.
Khan, Mahmood Hasan.
xKhan, Mahmood H.
The Economics of the Green Revolution in Pakistan. Praeger.
Khan, Mohammed Abdul Quddus.
xKhan, M. A.
ed. Survival in Toxic Environments. Acad Pr.
Khan, Moinuz Z. *see* Khan, Moinuz Zafar.
Khan, Moinuz Zafar.
xKhan, Moinuz Z.

The Economic Benefits from Four Employment
& Training Programs. Garland Pub.
Kiefer, Warren, 1929-
xKiefer, Warren.
The Pontius Pilate Papers. BJ Pub Group.
The Pontius Pilate Papers. Har-Row.
Kieffer, George H., 1930-
xKieffer, George H.
Bioethics: A Textbook of Issues. A-W.
Kieffer, Richard J.
xKieffer, Richard J.
Applying Microeconomic Principles: A Student
Guide to Analyzing Economic News.
Har-Row.
Kieffer, Stephen A.
xKieffer, Stephen A.
Atlas of Cross-Sectional Anatomy: Computed
Tomography, Ultrasound, Radiography, Gross
Anatomy. Har-Row.
Kieffer, William F. see Kieffer, William Franklin.
Kieffer, William Franklin, 1915-
xKieffer, William F.
Chemistry Today. Har-Row.
Kiell, Norman.
xKiell, Norman.
The Adolescent Through Fiction: A
Psychological Approach. Intl Univs Pr.
ed. Psychiatry & Psychology in the Visual Arts
& Aesthetics: A Bibliography. U of Wis Pr.
ed. The Psychology of Obesity: Dynamics &
Treatment. C C Thomas.
Varieties of Sexual Experience: Psychosexuality
in Literature. Intl Univs Pr.
Kiell, Paul J.
xKiell, Paul J.
The Complete Guide to Physical Fitness.
Follett.
Kielland, Alexander L. see Kielland, Alexander Lange.
Kielland, Alexander Lange, 1849-1906
xKielland, Alexander L.
Tales of Two Countries. Arno.
Kiely, Dennis K., 1913-
xKiely, Dennis K.
Essentials of Music for New Musicians. P-H.
Kiemel, Ann.
xKiemel, Ann.
I'm Celebrating. Revell.
I'm Out to Change My World. Impact Tenn.
I'm Out to Change My World. PB.
Yes. Tyndale.
Kiemen, Mathias C. see Kiemen, Mathias Charles.
Kiemen, Mathias Charles, 1917-
xKiemen, Mathias C.
The Indian Policy of Portugal in the Amazon
Region, 1614-1693. Octagon.
Kiene, Paul F.
xKiene, Paul F.
The Tabernacle of God in the Wilderness of
Sinai. Zondervan.
Kienel, Paul A.
xKienel, Paul A.
What This Country Needs. Beta Bk.
Kienholz, Philip.
xKienholz, Philip.
The Third Rib Knife. N Dak Inst.
Kienzle, William. see Kienzle, William X.
Kienzle, William X.
xKienzle, William.
The Rosary Murders. Andrews & McMeel.
The Rosary Murders. Bantam.
Kierkegaard, Soren. see Kierkegaard, Sren Aabye.
Kierkegaard, Sren Aabye.
xKierkegaard, Soren.
The Sickness Unto Death: A Christian
Psychological Exposition for Upbuilding &
Awakening. Princeton U Pr.
Kiernan, Chris. see Kiernan, Chris C.
Kiernan, Chris C.
xKiernan, Chris.

Behaviour Assessment Battery. Humanities.
Kiernan, E. V. see Kiernan, E. Victor Gordon.
Kiernan, E. Victor Gordon.
xKiernan, E. V.
British Diplomacy in China, 1880-1885.
Octagon.
Kiernan, R. H. see Kiernan, Reginald Hugh.
Kiernan, Reginald H. see Kiernan, Reginald Hugh.
Kiernan, Reginald Hugh, 1900-
xKiernan, R. H.
Baden-Powell. Argosy.
xKiernan, Reginald H.
Lawrence of Arabia. Folcroft.
Lawrence of Arabia. R West.
Kiernan, Thomas.
xKiernan, Thomas.
The Arabs: Their History, Aims & Challenge to
the Industrialized World. Little.
The Intricate Music: A Biography of John
Steinbeck. Little.
The Secretariat Factor: The Story of a
Multi-Million Dollar Breeding Industry.
Doubleday.
Kiers, Luc.
xKiers, Luc.
The American Steel Industry: Problems,
Challenges, Perspectives. Westview.
Kierulff, Herbert E.
xKierulff, Herbert E.
The Economics of Decision: A Practical
Decision System for Business &
Management. Kennikat.
Kies, Cosette.
xKies, Cosette.
Problems in Library Public Relations. Bowker.
Kieselhorst, Daniel C.
xKieselhorst, Daniel C.
A Theoretical Perspective of Violence Against
Police. Univ OK Gov Res.
Kiesler, Charles A.
xKiesler, Charles A.
Attitude Change: A Critical Analysis of
Theoretical Approaches. Wiley.
ed. Conformity. A-W.
Psychology & National Health Insurance: A
Source Book. Am Psychol.
Psychology of Commitment: Experiments
Linking Behavior to Belief. Acad Pr.
Kiesler, Donald J.
xKiesler, Donald J.
The Process of Psychotherapy: Empirical
Foundations & Systems of Analysis.
Beresford Bk Serv.
Kiesler, Sara B., 1940-
xKiesler, Sara B.
Interpersonal Processes in Groups &
Organizations. AHM Pub.

Kiesling, Christopher.

xKiesling, Christopher.

Any News of God?. Pflaum Pr.

Celibacy, Prayer & Friendship: A

Making-Sense-Out-of-Life Approach. Alba.

Kiesselbach, T. A. see Kiesselbach, Theodore Alexander.
Kiesselbach, Theodore Alexander.
xKiesselbach, T. A.
The Structure & Reproduction of Corn. U of
Nebr Pr.
Kiessling, Elmer C. see Kiessling, Elmer Carl.
Kiessling, Elmer Carl, 1895-
xKiessling, Elmer C.
Early Sermons of Luther & Their Relation to
the Pre-Reformation Sermon. AMS Pr.
Kiessling, Nicolas.
xKiessling, Nicolas.
The Incubus in English Literature: Provenance
& Progeny. Wash St U Pr.
Kietzman, Mitchell. see Kietzman, Mitchell L.

Kietzman, Mitchell L.
xKietzman, Mitchell.
ed. Experimental Approaches to
Psychopathology. Acad Pr.
Kiev, Ari.
xKiev, Ari.
The Courage to Live. T Y Crowell.
A Strategy for Daily Living. Free Pr.
A Strategy for Handling Executive Stress.
Nelson-Hall.
A Strategy for Success. Macmillan.
Suicidal Patient: Recognition & Management.
Nelson-Hall.
Kiewiet, Cornelis W. De. see De Kiewiet, Cornelis W.
Kifer, R. S. see Kifer, Russell Stanley.
Kifer, Russell Stanley.
xKifer, R. S.
Farming Hazards in the Drought Area. Da
Capo.
Kigin, Denis J. see Kigin, Denis John.
Kigin, Denis John, 1923-
xKigin, Denis J.
Teacher Liability in School-Shop Accidents.
Prakken.
Kihl, Young W., 1932-
xKihl, Young W.
Conflict Issues & International Civil Aviation
Decisions: Three Cases. U of Denver Intl.
Kihlman, B. A. see Kihlman, Bengt A.
Kihlman, Bengt A.
xKihlman, B. A.
Caffeine & Chromosomes. Elsevier.
Kihlstrom, April L. see Kihlstrom, April Lynn.
Kihlstrom, April Lynn.
xKihlstrom, April L.
Paris Summer. Bouregy.
Kihlstrom, John F.
xKihlstrom, John F.
ed. Functional Disorders of Memory. Halsted
Pr
Kijima, T. see Kijima, Takashi.
Kijima, Takashi.
xKijima, T.
The Orchid. Mayflower Bks.
Kijowski, J.
xKijowski, J.
A Symplectic Framework for Field Theories.
Springer-Verlag.
Kilbourne, Edwin D.
xKilbourne, Edwin D.
ed. The Influenza Viruses & Influenza. Acad
Pr.
Kilbourne, Fannie, 1890-
xKilbourne, Fannie.
Horton Twins. Arno.
Kilbride, Ann. see Kilbride, Ann T.
Kilbride, Ann T.
xKilbride, Ann.
The Complete Book on Disco & Ballroom
Dancing. Hwong Pub.
Kilbride-Jones, H. E.
xKilbride-Jones, H. E.
Celtic Craftsmanship in Bronze. St Martin.
Kilburn, Nicholas, 1843-1923
xKilburn, Nicholas.
The Story of Chamber Music. Longwood Pr.
Kilburn, Robert E.
xKilburn, Robert E.
jt. auth. Exploring Life Science. Allyn.
Kilby, Clyde. see Kilby, Clyde S.
Kilby, Clyde S.
xKilby, Clyde.
Images of Salvation in the Fiction of C. S.
Lewis. Shaw Pubs.
xKilby, Clyde S.
Christian World of C. S. Lewis. Eerdmans.
Kildahl, John P.
xKildahl, John P.

Psychology of Speaking in Tongues. Har-Row.
Kiley, Dan.
　　xKiley, Dan.
　　　Nobody Said It Would Be Easy: Raising
　　　　Responsible Kids -- and Keeping Them Out
　　　　of Trouble. Har-Row.
Kiley, Denise, 1948-
　　xKiley, Denise.
　　　Biggest Machines. Raintree Child.
Kilgore, Dan. see Kilgore, Daniel Edmond.
Kilgore, Daniel Edmond, 1921-
　　xKilgore, Dan.
　　　How Did Davy Die?. Tex A&M Univ Pr.
Kilgore, James C.
　　xKilgore, James C.
　　　Until I Met You. Sharaqua.
Kilgore, James E.
　　xKilgore, James E.
　　　Try Marriage Before Divorce. Word Bks.
Kilgore, W. J. see Kilgore, William Jackson.
Kilgore, William A. see Kilgore, William Arlow.
Kilgore, William Arlow, 1903-
　　xKilgore, William A.
　　　Identification of Ability to Apply Principles of
　　　　Physics. AMS Pr.
Kilgore, William Jackson, 1917-
　　xKilgore, W. J.
　　　An Introductory Logic. HR&W.
Kilgour, Raymond L. see Kilgour, Raymond Lincoln.
Kilgour, Raymond Lincoln.
　　xKilgour, Raymond L.
　　　The Decline of Chivalry, As Shown in the
　　　　French Literature of the Late Middle Ages.
　　　　Peter Smith.
Kilian, Crawford.
　　xKilian, Crawford.
　　　The Empire of Time. Ballantine.
　　　Wonders, Inc.. HM.
Kilian, Michael.
　　xKilian, Michael.
　　　Who Runs Chicago?. St Martin.
Kilian, Sabbas. see Kilian, Sabbas J.
Kilian, Sabbas J, 1916-
　　xKilian, Sabbas.
　　　Theological Models for the Parish. Alba.
Kilinski, Kenneth. see Kilinski, Kenneth K.
Kilinski, Kenneth K.
　　xKilinski, Kenneth.
　　　Organization & Leadership in the Local
　　　　Church. Zondervan.
Killam, G. D.
　　xKillam, G. D.
　　　ed. African Writers on African Writing.
　　　　Northwestern U Pr.
Killanin. see Killanin, Michael Morris.
Killanin, Lord. see Killanin, Michael Morris.
Killanin, Michael Morris.
　　xKillanin.
　　　The Olympic Games 1980: Moscow & Lake
　　　　Placid. Macmillan.
　　xKillanin, Lord.
　　　ed. The Olympic Games: 80 Years of People,
　　　　Events & Records. Macmillan.
Killeen. see Killeen, Jacqueline.
Killeen, Jacqueline.
　　xKilleen.
　　　The Whole World Cookbook. Bennett Co.
Killeffer, David H. see Killeffer, David Herbert.
Killeffer, David Herbert, 1895-
　　xKilleffer, David H.
　　　Chemical Engineering. Am Chemical.
　　　How Did You Think of That: An Introduction
　　　　to the Scientific Method. Am Chemical.
Killey, H. C. see Killey, Homer Charles.
Killey, Homer Charles.
　　xKilley, H. C.
　　　The Prevention of Complications in Dental
　　　　Surgery. Churchill.
Killgallon, James. see Killgallon, James J.

Killgallon, James J.
　　xKillgallon, James.
　　　Life in Christ. ACTA Found.
Killham, John.
　　xKillham, John.
　　　ed. Critical Essays on the Poetry of Tennyson.
　　　　Routledge & Kegan.
Killian, Ray A.
　　xKillian, Ray A.
　　　Human Resource Management: An ROI
　　　　Approach. Am Mgmt.
　　　Managers Must Lead!. Am Mgmt.
Killigrew, John W.
　　xKilligrew, John W.
　　　The Impact of the Great Depression on the
　　　　Army. Garland Pub.
Killingbeck, J.
　　xKillingbeck, J.
　　　Mathematical Techniques & Physical
　　　　Applications. Acad Pr.
Killinger, George G. see Killinger, George Glenn.
Killinger, George Glenn.
　　xKillinger, George G.
　　　Penology: The Evolution of Corrections in
　　　　America. West Pub.
Killinger, John.
　　xKillinger, John.
　　　All You Lonely People - All You Lovely
　　　　People. Word Bks.
　　　Bread for the Wilderness - Wine for the
　　　　Journey: The Miracle of Prayer &
　　　　Meditation. Word Bks.
　　　His Power in You. Doubleday.
Killion, Ronald G.
　　xKillion, Ronald G.
　　　Georgia & the Revolution. Cherokee.
Killip, Margaret.
　　xKillip, Margaret.
　　　The Folklore of the Isle of Man. Rowman.
Killough, Hugh B. see Killough, Hugh Baxter.
Killough, Hugh Baxter.
　　xKillough, Hugh B.
　　　Raw Materials of Industrialism. Kennikat.
Killy, Jean Claude.
　　xKilly, Jean-Claude.
　　　Comeback. Macmillan.
Killy, Jean-Claude. see Killy, Jean Claude.
Kilmarx, R. A. see Kilmarx, Robert A.
Kilmarx, Robert A.
　　xKilmarx, R. A.
　　　History of Soviet Air Power. Intl Pubns Serv.
Kilmer, Aline M. see Kilmer, Aline Murray.
Kilmer, Aline Murray, 1888-1941
　　xKilmer, Aline M.
　　　Hunting a Hair Shirt: And Other Spiritual
　　　　Adventures. Arno.
Kilmister, C. W. see Kilmister, Clive William.
Kilmister, Clive William.
　　xKilmister, C. W.
　　　Special Theory of Relativity. Pergamon.
Kilner, Mary Ann, 1753-1831
　　xKilner, Mary J.
　　　Memoirs of a Peg-Top. Garland Pub.
Kilner, Mary J. see Kilner, Mary Ann.
Kilner, W. J. see Kilner, Walter John.
Kilner, Walter J. see Kilner, Walter John.
Kilner, Walter John.
　　xKilner, W. J.
　　　The Aura. Weiser.
　　xKilner, Walter J.
　　　The Human Aura. Citadel Pr.
Kiloh, L. G.
　　xKiloh, L. G.
　　　Clinical Electroencephalography. Butterworths.
Kilpatrick, Alexander. see Kilpatrick, Alexander.
Kilpatrick, Alexander.
　　xKilpatrick.
　　　Practical Dental Anaesthesia. Churchill.
Kilpatrick, Cathy.
　　xKilpatrick, Cathy.

Giraffes. Raintree Pubs.
Tigers. Raintree Pubs.
Kilpatrick, Christopher H.
　　xKilpatrick, Christopher H.
　　　Kirkmouse. EPM Pubns.
Kilpatrick, Franklin P. see Kilpatrick, Franklin Peirce.
Kilpatrick, Franklin Peirce, 1920-
　　xKilpatrick, Franklin P.
　　　Source Book of a Study of Occupational Values
　　　　& the Image of the Federal Service.
　　　　Brookings.
Kilpatrick, Harold. see Kilpatrick, Harold C.
Kilpatrick, Harold C.
　　xKilpatrick, Harold.
　　　Functional Dental Assisting. Saunders.
　　xKilpatrick, Harold C.
　　　Work Simplification in Dental Practice:
　　　　Applied Time & Motion Studies. Saunders.
Kilpatrick, James J. see Kilpatrick, James Jackson.
Kilpatrick, James Jackson, 1920-
　　xKilpatrick, James J.
　　　The Foxes' Union: And Other Stretchers, Tall
　　　　Tales & Discursive Reminiscences of Happy
　　　　Years in Scrabble, Virginia. EPM Pubns.
Kilpatrick, S. see Kilpatrick, S. James.
Kilpatrick, S. James, 1931-
　　xKilpatrick, S.
　　　Statistical Principles in Health Care
　　　　Information. Univ Park.
Kilpatrick, Thomas L.
　　xKilpatrick, Thomas L.
　　　Illinois! Illinois!: An Annotated Bibliography of
　　　　Fiction. Scarecrow.
Kilpatrick, William, 1940-
　　xKilpatrick, William K.
　　　Identity & Intimacy. Delacorte.
　　　Identity & Intimacy. Dell.
Kilpatrick, William H. see Kilpatrick, William Heard.
Kilpatrick, William Heard, 1871-1965
　　xKilpatrick, William H.
　　　ed. Educational Frontier. Arno.
　　　ed. Intercultural Attitudes in the Making:
　　　　Parents, Youth Leaders & Teachers at Work.
　　　　Arno.
　　　Montessori System Examined. Arno.
Kilpatrick, William K. see Kilpatrick, William.
Kilpi, Eeva.
　　xKilpi, Eeva.
　　　Tamara. PB.
　　xKilpi, Eeva.
　　　Tamara. Delacorte.
Kilpi, Eeva. see Kilpi, Eeva.
Kilroy, James.
　　xKilroy, James.
　　　The Playboy Riots. Humanities.
Kilroy-Silk, Robert.
　　xKilroy-Silk, Robert.
　　　Socialism Since Marx. Taplinger.
Kim, C. I. see Kim, Chong Ik Eugene.
Kim, Chaiho.
　　xKim, Chaiho.
　　　Quantitative Analysis for Managerial Decisions.
　　　　A-W.
Kim, Chong Ik Eugene.
　　xKim, C. I.
　　　An Introduction to Asian Politics. P-H.
Kim, Chong-Hak.
　　xKim, Jeong-Hak.
　　　The Prehistory of Korea. U Pr of Hawaii.
Kim, Choong H. see Kim, Choong Han.
Kim, Choong Han, 1923-
　　xKim, Choong H.
　　　Books by Mail: A Handbook for Libraries.
　　　　Greenwood.
Kim, Choong S. see Kim, Choong Soon.
Kim, Choong Soon, 1938-
　　xKim, Choong S.

An Asian Anthropologist in the South: Field
Experiences with Blacks, Indians, & Whites.
U of Tenn Pr.

Kim, Ilpyong J., 1931-
xKim, Ilpyong J.
Communist Politics in North Korea. Praeger.

Kim, Jae-On.
xKim, Jae-On.
Introduction to Factor Analysis: What It Is &
How to Do It. Sage.

Kim, Jeong-Hak. see Kim, Chong-Hak.

Kim, Joungwon A. see Kim, Joungwon Alexander.

Kim, Joungwon Alexander.
xKim, Joungwon A.
Divided Korea: The Politics of Development,
1945-1972. Harvard U Pr.

Kim, Key-Hiuk.
xKim, Key-Hiuk.
The Last Phase of the East Asian World Order:
Korea, Japan, & the Chinese Empire,
1860-1882. U of Cal Pr.

Kim, Kwang S. see Kim, Kwang Suk.

Kim, Kwang Suk.
xKim, Kwang S.
Growth & Structural Transformation. Harvard
U Pr.

Kim, Samuel.
xKim, Samuel.
The American POW's. Branden.

Kim, Samuel S., 1935-
xKim, Samuel S.
China, the United Nations, & World Order.
Princeton U Pr.

Kim, Se-Jin, 1933-
xKim, Se-Jin.
Politics of Military Revolution in Korea. U of
NC Pr.

Kim, Suk H.
xKim, Suk H.
An Introduction to International Financial
Management. U Pr of Amer.

Kim, Young C.
xKim, Young C.
ed. The Future of the Korean Peninsula.
Praeger.

Kim, Young H. see Kim, Young Hum.

Kim, Young Hum.
xKim, Young H.
ed. East Asia's Turbulent Century: With
American Diplomatic Documents. Irvington.

Kimball, Arthur G.
xKimball, Arthur G.
Crisis in Identity & Contemporary Japanese
Novels. C E Tuttle.

Kimball, Bonnie-Jean.
xKimball, Bonnie-Jean.
Alcoholic Woman's Mad, Mad World of
Denial & Mind Games. Hazelden.

Kimball, David.
xKimball, David.
Market Hunter. Dillon.

Kimball, Elsa P. see Kimball, Elsa Peverly.

Kimball, Elsa Peverly, 1889-
xKimball, Elsa P.
Sociology & Education: An Analysis of the
Theories of Spencer & Ward. AMS Pr.

Kimball, Gertrude S. see Kimball, Gertrude Selwyn.

Kimball, Gertrude Selwyn, 1863-1910
xKimball, Gertrude S.
Providence in Colonial Times. Da Capo.

Kimball, John W.
xKimball, John W.
Cell Biology. A-W.

Kimball, Kathleen.
xKimball, Kathleen M.
Big Foot, Little Foot. West Village.

Kimball, Kathleen M. see Kimball, Kathleen.

Kimball, Linda A. see Kimball, Linda Amy.

Kimball, Linda Amy.
xKimball, Linda A.

Borneo Medicine: The Healing Art of
Indigenous Brunei Malay Medicine. Univ
Microfilms.

Kimball, Lorenzo K.
xKimball, Lorenzo K.
The Changing Pattern of Political Power in
Iraq, 1958-1971. Speller.

Kimball, Marie. see Kimball, Marie Goebel.

Kimball, Marie Goebel, 1889-1955
xKimball, Marie.
Thomas Jefferson's Cook Book. U Pr of Va.

Kimball, P. see Kimball, Penn.

Kimball, Penn.
xKimball, P.
The Disconnected. Columbia U Pr.

Kimball, Robert.
xKimball, Robert.
Reminiscing with Sissle & Blake. Viking Pr.
xKimball, Robert E.
The Gershwins. Atheneum.

Kimball, Robert E. see Kimball, Robert.

Kimball, Sidney F. see Kimball, Sidney Fiske.

Kimball, Sidney Fiske.
xKimball, Sidney F.
A History of Architecture. Greenwood.

Kimball, Spencer. see Kimball, Spencer L.

Kimball, Spencer L.
xKimball, Spencer.
Insurance & Public Policy: A Study in the
Legal Implementation of Social & Economic
Public Policy, Based on Wisconsin Records,
1835-1959. U of Wis Pr.

Kimball, Spencer W., 1895-
xKimball, Spencer W.
Marriage. Deseret Bk.

Kimball, Stanley B. see Kimball, Stanley Buchholz.

Kimball, Stanley Buchholz.
xKimball, Stanley B.
The Austro-Slav Revival: A Study of
Nineteenth-Century Literary Foundations.
Am Philos.

Kimball, Warren F.
xKimball, Warren F.
Franklin D. Roosevelt & the World Crisis,
1937-1945. Heath.

Kimball, Warren Y. see Kimball, Warren Young.

Kimball, Warren Young.
xKimball, Warren Y.
Fire Service Communications for Fire Attack.
Natl Fire Prot.

Kimball, Yeffe.
xKimball, Yeffe.
Art of American Indian Cooking. Doubleday.

Kimbark, E. W. see Kimbark, Edward Wilson.

Kimbark, Edward Wilson, 1902-
xKimbark, E. W.
Direct Current Transmission. Wiley.
Power System Stability. Wiley.

Kimber, Edward, 1719-1769
xKimber, Edward.
The History of the Life & Adventures of Mr.
Anderson. Garland Pub.

Kimber, Richard.
xKimber, Richard.
ed. Campaigning for the Environment.
Routledge & Kegan.

Kimber, Richard T.
xKimber, Richard T.
Automation in Libraries. Pergamon.

Kimberly, Robert C.
xKimberly, Robert C.
Problems of Recurrent Hernia. C C Thomas.

Kimble, Daniel Porter.
xKimble, Daniel Porter.
Psychology As a Biological Science. Goodyear.

Kimble, George H. see Kimble, George Herbert Tinley.

Kimble, George Herbert Tinley, 1908-
xKimble, George H.

Geography in the Middle Ages. Russell.

Kimble, Gerald W.
xKimble, Gerald W.
Information and Computer Science. Irvington.

Kimble, Gregory. see Kimble, Gregory A.

Kimble, Gregory A.
xKimble, Gregory.
How to Use (& Misuse) Statistics. P-H.
xKimble, Gregory A.
Principles of General Psychology. Wiley.

Kimbrell, Grady.
xKimbrell, Grady.
Strategies for Implementing Work Experience
Programs. McKnight.
Succeeding in the World of Work. McKnight.

Kimbro, Harriet.
xKimbro, Harriet.
Tamotzu in Haiku. Sunstone Pr.

Kimbrough, Katheryn.
xKimbrough, Katheryn.
Evelyn, the Ambitious. Popular Lib.
Margaret, the Faithful. Popular Lib.
Patricia the Beautiful. Popular Lib.
Yvonne, the Confident. Popular Lib.

Kimishima, Hisako.
xKimishima, Hisako.
Lum Fu & the Golden Mountain. Schol Bk
Serv.

Kimizuka, Sumako.
xKimizuka, Sumako.
Teaching English to Japanese. Tail Feather.

Kimmel, Arthur S.
xKimmel, Arthur S.
ed. A Critical Edition of the Old Provencal
Epic "Daurel et Beton". U of NC Pr.

Kimmel, Douglas C.
xKimmel, Douglas C.
Adulthood & Aging: An Interdisciplinary
Developmental View. Wiley.

Kimmel, Eric. see Kimmel, Eric A.

Kimmel, Eric A.
xKimmel, Eric.
Why Worry?. Pantheon.
xKimmel, Eric A.
Nicanor's Gate. Jewish Pubn.

Kimmel, H. D.
xKimmel, H. D.
ed. Experimental Psychopathology: Recent
Research & Theory. Acad Pr.
ed. The Orienting Reflex in Humans: An
International Conference Sponsored by the
Scientific Affairs of the North Atlantic
Treaty Organization. Halsted Pr.

Kimmel, Jo, 1931-
xKimmel, Jo.
Steps to Prayer Power. Abingdon.
Steps to Prayer Power. Pillar Bks.

Kimmens, Andrew. see Kimmens, Andrew C.

Kimmens, Andrew C.
xKimmens, Andrew.
ed. Tales of Hashish. Morrow.
ed. Tales of the Ginseng. Morrow.

Kimmey, John L. see Kimmey, John Lansing.

Kimmey, John Lansing, 1922-
xKimmey, John L.
Experience & Expression: Reading &
Responding to Short Fiction. Scott F.

Kimmich, Christoph M.
xKimmich, Christoph M.
Germany & the League of Nations. U of
Chicago Pr.

Kimmich, Flora, 1939-
xKimmich, Flora.
Sonnets of Catharina von Greiffenberg:
Methods of Composition. U of NC Pr.

Kimpel, Ben. see Kimpel, Benjamin Franklin.

Kimpel, Benjamin Franklin.
xKimpel, Ben.

Principles of Moral Philosophy. Philos Lib.

Kimsey, Larry R.
xKimsey, Larry R.
Referring the Psychiatric Patient: A Guide for the Physician. C C Thomas.

Kimura, Ken-Ichi. see Kimura, Ken'Ichi.

Kimura, Ken'Ichi, 1933-
xKimura, Ken-Ichi.
Scientific Basis of Air Conditioning. Burgess-Intl Ideas.

Kimura, Motoo.
xKimura, Motoo.
Theoretical Aspects of Population Genetics. Princeton U Pr.

Kimura, Yasuko.
xKimura, Yasuko.
Fergus. McGraw.
Fergus & the Snow Deer. McGraw.

Kinard, Malvina. see Kinard, Malvina C.

Kinard, Malvina C.
xKinard, Malvina.
Loaves & Fishes: Foods from Bible Times. Keats.

Kinariwala, B. see Kinariwala, B. K.

Kinariwala, B. K.
xKinariwala, B.
Linear Circuits & Computation. Krieger.

Kincade, William H.
xKincade, William H.
ed. Negotiating Security: An Arms Control Reader. Carnegie Endow.

Kincaid, Dennis, 1905-1937
xKincaid, Dennis.
British Social Life in India, 1608-1937. Kennikat.
British Social Life in India 1608-1937. Routledge & Kegan.

Kincaid, Joseph J.
xKincaid, Joseph J.
Cristobal de Villalon. Twayne.

Kincaid, Stephanie.
xKincaid, Stephanie.
Highland Love Song. Dell.

Kinch, Sam.
xKinch, Sam.
Allan Shivers: The Pied Piper of Texas Politics. Shoal Creek Pub.
Texas Under a Cloud. Jenkins.

Kinder, Chuck.
xKinder, Chuck.
The Silver Ghost. HarBraceJ.

Kinder, Faye.
xKinder, Faye.
Meal Management. Macmillan.

Kinder, J. A.
xKinder, J. A.
ed. Decision Making in Public Education. Mesa Pubns.

Kinder, James S. see Kinder, James Screngo.

Kinder, James Screngo, 1895-
xKinder, James S.
Using Instructional Media. D Van Nostrand.

Kinderlehrer, David.
xKinderlehrer, David.
An Introduction to Variational Inequalities & Their Applications. Acad Pr.

Kinderlehrer, Jane.
xKinderlehrer, Jane.
How to Feel Younger, Longer. Rodale Pr Inc.

Kindleberger, Charles H. see Kindleberger, Charles Poor.

Kindleberger, Charles P. see Kindleberger, Charles Poor.

Kindleberger, Charles Poor, 1910-
xKindleberger, Charles H.
Economic Development. McGraw.
xKindleberger, Charles P.

American Business Abroad: Six Lectures on Direct Investment. Yale U Pr.
The Dollar Shortage. Arno.
Europe & the Dollar. MIT Pr.
The World in Depression, 1929-1939. U of Cal Pr.

Kindon, Thomas.
xKindon, Thomas.
Murder in the Moor. Garland Pub.

Kindred, Alton R., 1922-
xKindred, Alton R.
Data Systems & Management: An Introduction to Systems Analysis & Design. P-H.
Introduction to Computers. P-H.

Kindred, Wendy.
xKindred, Wendy.
illus. Lucky Wilma. Dial.

Kindregan, Charles P.
xKindregan, Charles P.
Quality of Life: Reflections on the Moral Values of American Law. Macmillan.

Kindrick, Robert L.
xKindrick, Robert L.
Robert Henryson. Twayne.

Kindsfather, William. see Kindsfather, William L.

Kindsfather, William L.
xKindsfather, William.
Today's Business World. Parr Pub.

King, A. D. see King, Anthony D.

King, A. Thomas. see King, Alvin Thomas.

King, Alexander, 1900-
xKing, Alexander.
Rich Man, Poor Man, Freud & Fruit: Advice to Amorous Ladies. S&S.

King, Alexander H. see King, Alexander Hyatt.

King, Alexander Hyatt.
xKing, Alexander H.
Chamber Music. Greenwood.

King, Alice G. see King, Alice Gore.

King, Alice Gore.
xKing, Alice G.
Data Processing Explained. Coun Career Plan.

King, Alvin Thomas.
xKing, A. Thomas.
Property Taxes, Amenities, & Residential Land Values. Ballinger Pub.

King, Alvy L., 1932-
xKing, Alvy L.
Louis T. Wigfall: Southern Fire-Eater. La State U Pr.

King, Anthony. see King, Anthony Stephen.

King, Anthony D.
xKing, A. D.
Colonial Urban Development: Culture, Social Power & Environment. Routledge & Kegan.

King, Anthony Stephen.
xKing, Anthony.
Britain Says Yes: The 1975 Referendum on the Common Market. Am Enterprise.

King, Barry G. see King, Barry Griffith.

King, Barry Griffith.
xKing, Barry G.
Human Anatomy & Physiology. Saunders.

King, Bart.
xKing, Bart.
How to Raise & Train a Gordon Setter. TFH Pubns.

King, Benjamin B.
xKing, Benjamin B.
Notes on the Mechanics of Growth & Debt. Johns Hopkins.

King, Blanche (Black) Busey.
xKing, Blanche B.
Under Your Feet: The Story of the American Mound Builders. Arno.

King, Blanche B. see King, Blanche (Black) Busey.

King, Bolton, 1860-
xKing, Bolton.

A History of Italian Unity: Being a Political History of Italy from 1814 to 1871. Russell.

King, Bruce. see King, Bruce Alvin.

King, Bruce Alvin.
xKing, Bruce.
Intro. by & ed. Introduction to Nigerian Literature. Holmes & Meier.
ed. Literatures of the World in English. Routledge & Kegan.
Marvell's Allegorical Poetry. Oleander Pr.
West Indian Literature. Shoe String.

King, Bucky.
xKing, Bucky.
Ecclesiastical Crafts. Van Nos Reinhold.

King, C. Daly. see King, Charles Daly.

King, C. J. see King, Cary Judson.

King, C. Judson. see King, Cary Judson.

King, Cary Judson, 1934-
xKing, C. J.
Separation Processes. McGraw.
xKing, C. Judson.
Intro. by Separation Processes. McGraw.

King, Cecil, 1881-1942
xKing, Cecil.
Atlantic Charter. Arno.

King, Charles, 1844-1933
xKing, Charles.
Campaigning with Crook. U of Okla Pr.
ed. Colonel's Christmas Dinner, & Other Stories. Arno.

King, Charles D.
xKing, Charles D.
Models of Industrial Democracy: Consultation, Co-Determination & Workers Management. Mouton.

King, Charles Daly, 1895-1963
xKing, C. Daly.
The Curious Mr. Tarrant. Dover.

King, Charles L.
xKing, Charles L.
Ramon J. Sender: An Annotated Bibliography, 1928-1974. Scarecrow.

King, Clive.
xKing, Clive.
Me & My Million. T Y Crowell.
Stig of the Dump. Penguin.

King, Clyde S.
xKing, Clyde S.
Compiled by Psychic & Religious Phenomena Limited: A Bibliographical Index. Greenwood.

King, Constance E. see King, Constance Eileen.

King, Constance Eileen.
xKing, Constance E.
Antique Toys & Dolls. Rizzoli Intl.
The Collector's History of Dolls. St Martin.

King, Cynthia.
xKing, Cynthia.
Beggars & Choosers. Viking Pr.

King, David, 1914-
xKing, David.
The Fiddler. Doubleday.
Rage on the Range. Doubleday.

King, David S., 1927-
xKing, David S.
No Church Is an Island. Pilgrim NY.

King, Donald B. see King, Donald Barnett.

King, Donald Barnett.
xKing, Donald B.
Consumer Protection Experiments in Sweden. Rothman.

King, Donald W. see King, Donald Ward.

King, Donald Ward.
xKing, Donald W.
The Evaluation of Information Services & Products. Info Resources.

King, Donald West.
xKing, Donald W.

Survey of Pathology: With Color Microfiche,
Illustrations, & Instructional Objectives.
Oxford U Pr.
King, Duane H.
xKing, Duane H.
ed. The Cherokee Indian Nation: A Troubled
History. U of Tenn Pr.
King, E. J. *see* King, Edmund James.
King, Edmund. *see* King, Edmund James.
King, Edmund J. *see* King, Edmund James.
King, Edmund James, 1914-
xKing, E. J.
Education & Social Change. Pergamon.
The Teacher & the Needs of Society in
Evolution. Pergamon.
xKing, Edmund.
ed. Post-Compulsory Education: A New
Analysis in Western Europe. Sage.
xKing, Edmund J.
Comparative Studies & Educational Decision.
Bobbs.
Comparative Studies and Educational Decision.
Irvington.
King, Edward, 1848-1896
xKing, Edward.
Great South. Arno.
Great South. B Franklin.
The Great South. La State U Pr.
King, Edward T. *see* King, Edward Thorp.
King, Edward Thorp, 1895-
xKing, Edward T.
Genealogy of Some Early Families in Grant &
Pleasant Districts, Preston County, West
Virginia. Genealog Pub.
King, Edwin J. *see* King, Edwin James.
King, Edwin James, Sir, 1887-1952
xKing, Edwin J.
The Grand Priory of the Order of the Hospital
of St. John of Jerusalem in England: A Short
History. AMS Pr.
King, Elbert A.
xKing, Elbert A.
Space Geology: An Introduction. Wiley.
King, Elizabeth C., 1941-
xKing, Elizabeth C.
Classroom Evaluation Strategies. Mosby.
King, Eunice M.
xKing, Eunice M.
Illustrated Manual of Nursing Techniques.
Lippincott.
King, F. P.
xKing, Frank P.
ed. Oceania & Beyond: Essays on the Pacific
Since 1945. Greenwood.
King, Florence.
xKing, Florence.
Southern Ladies & Gentlemen. Bantam.
King, Francis P. *see* King, Francis Paul.
King, Francis Paul.
xKing, Francis P.
Benefit Plans in Higher Education. Columbia U
Pr.
King, Frank, 1936-
xKing, Frank.
Night Vision. Marek.
King, Frank H. *see* King, Frank H. H.
King, Frank H. H.
xKing, Frank H.
Money & Monetary Policy in China,
1845-1895. Harvard U Pr.
King, Frank P. *see* King, F. P.
King, Georgiana G. *see* King, Georgiana Goddard.
King, Georgiana Goddard, 1871-1939
xKing, Georgiana G.
A Brief Account of the Military Orders in
Spain. AMS Pr.
King, Gordon J. *see* King, Gordon John.
King, Gordon John.
xKing, Gordon J.

The Audio Handbook. Transatlantic.
Master Hi-Fi Installation. Hayden.
Radio & Audio Servicing Handbook. Hayden.
Radio, Television & Audio Test Instruments.
Hayden.
King, Grace. *see* King, Grace Elizabeth.
King, Grace E. *see* King, Grace Elizabeth.
King, Grace Elizabeth, 1852-1932
xKing, Grace.
Grace King of New Orleans: A Selection of
Her Writings. La State U Pr.
Memories of a Southern Woman of Letters.
Arno.
xKing, Grace E.
Balcony Stories. Irvington.
Monsieur Motte. Arno.
Tales of a Time & Place. AMS Pr.
Tales of a Time & Place. Mss Info.
Tales of a Time & Place. Somerset Pub.
King, Graham, 1930-
xKing, Graham.
Garden of Zola: Emile Zola & His Novels for
English Readers. B&N.
King, Harold, 1945 (feb. 27)-
xKing, Harold.
Closing Ceremonies. Coward.
Closing Ceremonies. PB.
The Taskmaster. Coward.
The Taskmaster. PB.
King, Helen. *see* King, Helen Hayes.
King, Helen Hayes.
xKing, Helen.
Soul of Christmas. Johnson Chi.
King, Henry, 1842-1915
xKing, Henry.
American Journalism. Arno.
King, Henry C.
xKing, Henry C.
Geared to the Stars: The Evolution of
Planetariums, Orreries & Astronomical
Clocks. U of Toronto Pr.
The History of the Telescope. Dover.
King, Homer W.
xKing, Homer W.
Pulitzer's Prize Editor: A Biography of John A.
Cockerill, 1845-1896. Duke.
King, Horace M., 1918-
xKing, Horace M.
A Clear Introduction to Business Mathematics.
Dickenson.
King, Hugh.
xKing, Hugh.
Eve de Paris. Berkley Pub.
King, Irving H.
xKing, Irving H.
George Washington's Coast Guard: Origins of
the U. S. Revenue Cutter Service, 1789-1801.
Naval Inst Pr.
King, J. Estelle. *see* King, Junie Estelle Stewart.
King, J. O. *see* King, John Oliver Letts.
King, J. R. *see* King, John Russell.
King, James C. *see* King, James Cornelius.
King, James Cornelius.
xKing, James C.
A Program Verifier. Mgmt Info Serv.
King, James M. *see* King, James Marcus.
King, James Marcus, 1839-1907
xKing, James M.
Facing the Twentieth Century. Arno.
King, Jere C. *see* King, Jere Clemens.
King, Jere Clemens.
xKing, Jere C.
ed. The First World War. Walker & Co.
Foch Versus Clemenceau: France & German
Dismemberment, 1918-1919. Harvard U Pr.
Generals & Politicians: Conflict Between
France's High Command, Parliament, &
Government, 1914-1918. Greenwood.
King, Jerome B.
xKing, Jerome B.

Law V. Order: Legal Process & Free Speech in
Contemporary France. Shoe String.
King, Joe M. *see* King, Joe Madison.
King, Joe Madison, 1923-
xKing, Joe M.
A History of South Carolina Baptists. Church
History.
King, John H. *see* King, John Harry.
King, John Harry.
xKing, John H.
Atlas of Ophthalmic Surgery. Lippincott.
King, John L. *see* King, John Lafayette.
King, John Lafayette, 1917-
xKing, John L.
Human Behavior & Wall Street. Swallow.
King, John M. *see* King, John Mark.
King, John Mark, 1829-1899
xKing, John M.
Critical Study of In Memoriam. Haskell.
King, John O.
xKing, John O.
Joseph Stephen Cullinan: A Study of
Leadership in the Texas Petroleum Industry,
1897-1937. Vanderbilt U Pr.
King, John Oliver Letts.
xKing, J. O.
An Introduction to Animal Husbandry. Halsted
Pr.
King, John Russell.
xKing, J. R.
Production Planning & Control: An
Introduction to Quantitative Methods.
Pergamon.
King, Joseph L.
xKing, Joseph L.
History of the San Francisco Stock &
Exchange Board. Arno.
King, Joyce.
xKing, Joyce.
Imagine That!: Illustrated Poems & Creative
Learning Experiences. Goodyear.
King, Judith.
xKing, Judith.
The Greatest Gift Guide Ever. Variety Pr.
King, Junie E. *see* King, Junie Estelle Stewart.
King, Junie Estelle Stewart.
xKing, J. Estelle.
Abstracts of Wills, Inventories, &
Administration Accounts of Loudon County,
Virginia, 1757-1800. Genealog Pub.
xKing, Junie E.
Abstracts of Wills, Inventories &
Administrations Accounts of Fredrick
County, Virginia. Va Bk.
King, K. *see* King, Kenneth E.
King, Kenneth E., 1940-
xKing, K.
Introductory Algebra & Related Topics for
Technicians. P-H.
King, Kimball.
xKing, Kimball.
Ten Modern Irish Playwrights: A
Comprehensive Annotated Bibliography.
Garland Pub.
King, Larry L.
xKing, Larry L.
Of Outlaws, Con Men, Whores, Politicians &
Other Artists. Viking Pr.
King, Leonard W. *see* King, Leonard William.
King, Leonard William, 1869-1919
xKing, Leonard W.
Babylonian Religion & Mythology. AMS Pr.
Babylonian Religion & Mythology. Longwood
Pr.
History of Sumer & Akkad: An Account of the
Early Races of Babylonia from Prehistoric
Times to the Foundation of the Babylonian
Monarchy. Greenwood.
King, Leslie J.
xKing, Leslie J.

Cities, Space & Behavior: The Elements of
    Urban Geography. P-H.
King, Lester S. *see* King, Lester Snow.
King, Lester Snow, 1908-
    xKing, Lester S.
    Growth of Medical Thought. U of Chicago Pr.
    Medical World of the Eighteenth Century.
        Krieger.
    Why Not Say It Clearly: A Guide to Scientific
        Writing. Little.
King, Loretta.
    xKing, Loretta M.
    The Purple Sea Horse & Other Stories.
        Woodland.
King, Loretta M. *see* King, Loretta.
King, Luella M. *see* King, Luella Myrtle.
King, Luella Myrtle, 1887-
    xKing, Luella M.
    Learning & Applying Spelling Rules in Grades
        Three to Eight. AMS Pr.
King, M. A. *see* King, Mervyn A.
King, Mark.
    xKing, Mark.
    For We Are: Toward Understanding Your
        Personal Potential. A-W.
King, Martha. *see* King, Martha L.
King, Martha L.
    xKing, Martha.
    Informal Learning. Phi Delta Kappa.
King, Martin L. *see* King, Martin Luther.
King, Martin Luther.
    xKing, Martin L.
    Strength to Love. Collins Pubs.
    Trumpet of Conscience. Har-Row.
King, Mary E. *see* King, Mary Elizabeth.
King, Mary Elizabeth.
    xKing, Mary E.
    ed. Art & Environment in Native America. Tex
        Tech Pr.
King, Maurice. *see* King, Maurice Henry.
King, Maurice Henry.
    xKing, Maurice.
    A Medical Laboratory for Developing
        Countries. Oxford U Pr.
    Primary Child Care: A Manual for Health
        Workers. Oxford U Pr.
King, Maxwell C.
    xKing, Maxwell C.
    President-Trustee Relationships: Meeting the
        Challenge of Leadership. Am Assn Comm Jr
        Coll.
King, Mervyn A.
    xKing, M. A.
    Public Policy & the Corporation. Methuen Inc.
King, Nancy, 1936-
    xKing, Nancy.
    Giving Form to Feeling. Drama Bk.
King, Ouida M., 1942-
    xKing, Ouida M.
    Care of the Cardiac Surgical Patient. Mosby.
King, P. D.
    xKing, P. D.
    Law & Society in the Visigothic Kingdom.
        Cambridge U Pr.
King, P. E. *see* King, Philip Ernest.
King, Paul T.
    xKing, Paul T.
    Ego Psychology in Counseling. HM.
King, Philip Burke, 1903-
    xKing, Phillip B.
    The Evolution of North America. Princeton U
        Pr.
King, Philip Ernest.
    xKing, P. E.
    Pycnogonids. St Martin.
King, Phillip B. *see* King, Philip Burke.
King, Preston. *see* King, Preston T.
King, Preston T., 1936-
    xKing, Preston.

ed. Study of Politics: A Collection of Inaugural
    Lectures. Biblio Dist.
King, R. *see* King, Roger John Benjamin.
King, R. D. *see* King, Richard D.
King, Rachel H. *see* King, Rachel Hadley.
King, Rachel Hadley, 1904-
    xKing, Rachel H.
    Creation of Death & Life. Philos Lib.
    Omission of the Holy Spirit from Reinhold
        Niebuhr's Theology. Philos Lib.
King, Rella R.
    xKing, Rella R.
    Diagnostic Assessment & Counseling
        Techniques for Speech Pathologists &
        Audiologists. Stanwix.
King, Rev. R. Edwin Foreword by. *see* Salter, John R.
King, Richard. *see* King, Richard Ashe.
King, Richard A. *see* King, Richard Ashe.
King, Richard Ashe, 1839-1932
    xKing, Richard.
    Swift in Ireland. Folcroft.
    xKing, Richard A.
    Swift in Ireland. Haskell.
King, Richard D.
    xKing, R. D.
    ed. Developments in Food Analysis
        Techniques. Burgess-Intl Ideas.
King, Richard H.
    xKing, Richard H.
    A Southern Renaissance: The Cultural
        Awakening of the American South,
        1930-1915. Oxford U Pr.
King, Richard L.
    xKing, Richard L.
    Airport Noise Pollution: A Bibliography of Its
        Effects on People & Property. Scarecrow.
King, Robert B.
    xKing, Robert B.
    Ferguson's Castle: A Dream Remembered.
        Exposition.
King, Robert C.
    xKing, Robert C.
    A Dictionary of Genetics. Oxford U Pr.
    Genetics. Oxford U Pr.
    Ovarian Development in Drosophila
        Melanogaster. Acad Pr.
King, Robert G.
    xKing, Robert G.
    Forms of Public Address. Bobbs.
    Improving Articulation & Voice. Macmillan.
King, Robert R.
    xKing, Robert R.
    ed. Eastern Europe's Uncertain Future: A
        Selection of Radio Free Europe Research
        Reports. Praeger.
King, Robert W. *see* King, Robert Wylie.
King, Robert Wylie.
    xKing, Robert W.
    England from Wordsworth to Dickens.
        Folcroft.
King, Roger John Benjamin.
    xKing, R.
    Steroid-Cell Interactions. Univ Park.
King, Roma A. *see* King, Roma Alvah.
King, Roma Alvah, 1914-
    xKing, Roma A.
    The Focusing Artifice: The Poetry of Robert
        Browning. Ohio U Pr.
King, Ronald, 1934-
    xKing, Ronald.
    All Things Bright & Beautiful?: A Sociological
        Study of Infants' Classrooms. Wiley.
    Botanical Illustration. Potter.
    Education. Longman.
King, Ronold W. *see* King, Ronold Wyeth Percival.
King, Ronold Wyeth Percival, 1905-
    xKing, Ronold W.
    Tables of Antenna Characteristics. IFI Plenum.
King, Roy D.
    xKing, R. D.

A Taste of Prison: Custodial Conditions for
    Trial & Remand Prisoners. Routledge &
    Kegan.
King, Rufus, 1917-
    xKing, Rufus.
    The Drug Hang-up: America's Fifty Year
        Folly. C C Thomas.
King, Serge V.
    xKing, Serge V.
    Pyramid Energy Handbook. Warner Bks.
King, Stanley G.
    xKing, Stanley G.
    An Estate Planning Questionnaire. Lawyers &
        Judges.
King, Stephen, 1947-
    xKing, Stephen.
    The Dead Zone. NAL.
    The Dead Zone. Viking Pr.
    Night Shift. Doubleday.
    The Stand. Doubleday.
    The Stand. NAL.
    Stephen King's Danse Macabre. Everest Hse.
King, Thomas F.
    xKing, Thomas F.
    Anthropology in Historic Preservation: Caring
        for Culture's Clutter. Acad Pr.
King, Tom, 1929-
    xKing, Tom.
    On High Pinnacles & Snow: Mountain Climbs
        & Hikes, Past & Present. A S Barnes.
King, Wilfrid.
    xKing, Wilfrid.
    Matthew Arnold As a Poet. Folcroft.
King, William L.
    xKing, William L.
    The Newspaper Press of Charleston, S. C..
        Folcroft.
    Newspaper Press of Charleston, S.C. Arno.
King, William L. *see* King, William Lyon Mackenzie.
King, William Lyon Mackenzie, 1874-1950
    xKing, William L.
    Canada & the Fight for Freedom. Arno.
King, William R. *see* King, William Richard.
King, William Richard, 1938-
    xKing, William R.
    Marketing Management Information Systems.
        Van Nos Reinhold.
    ed. Marketing Scientific & Technical
        Information. Westview.
    Quantitative Analysis for Marketing
        Management. McGraw.
    Strategic Planning & Policy. Van Nos
        Reinhold.
King-Hall, Stephen.
    xKing-Hall, Stephen.
    German Parliaments: A Study of the
        Development of Representative Institutions in
        Germany. Hyperion Conn.
King-Stoops, Joyce.
    xKing-Stoops, Joyce B.
    The Child Wants to Learn: Elementary
        Teaching Methods. Little.
King-Stoops, Joyce B. *see* King-Stoops, Joyce.
Kingdon, Donald R. *see* Kingdon, Donald Ralph.
Kingdon, Donald Ralph.
    xKingdon, Donald R.
    Matrix Organization: Managing Information
        Technologies. Methuen Inc.
Kingdon, John W.
    xKingdon, John W.
    Candidates for Office: Beliefs & Strategies.
        Peter Smith.
Kingdon, Jonathan.
    xKingdon, Jonathan.
    East African Mammals: An Atlas of Evolution
        in Africa. Acad Pr.
Kingery, W. D.
    xKingery, W. D.

Introduction to Ceramics. Wiley.

Kinget, G. Marian, 1910-
xKinget, G. Marian.
On Being Human: A Systematic View.
HarBraceJ.

Kinghorn, Harriet, 1933-
xKinghorn, Harriet.
Classroom & Workshop-Tested Games,
Puzzles, & Activities for the Elementary
School. P-H.

Kinghorn, Kenneth C.
xKinghorn, Kenneth C.
Christ Can Make You Fully Human. Abingdon.
Dynamic Discipleship. Baker Bk.
Fresh Wind of the Spirit. Abingdon.
Gifts of the Spirit. Abingdon.

Kingma, Jacobus. see Kingma, Jacobus Theodorus.

Kingma, Jacobus Theodorus.
xKingma, Jacobus.
The Geological Structure of New Zealand.
Krieger.

Kingman, Daniel.
xKingman, Daniel.
American Music: A Panorama. Schirmer Bks.

Kingman, Lee.
xKingman, Lee.
Break a Leg Betsy Maybe. Dell.
Break a Leg Betsy Maybe. HM.
Georgina & the Dragon. HM.
Georgina & the Dragon. Archway.
ed. The Illustrator's Notebook. Horn Bk.
ed. Illustrators of Children's Books: 1957-1966.
Horn Bk.
ed. Illustrators of Children's Books: 1967-1976.
Horn Bk.

Kingman, Russ.
xKingman, Russ.
Pictorial Life of Jack London. Crown.

Kings Co., N.Y. Grand Jury.
xNew York, Kings Country, Grand Jury.
A Presentment Concerning the Enforcement of
the City of New York of the Laws Against
Gambling by the Grand Jury for the
Additional Extraordinary Special & Trial
Term. Arno.

Kings, John, 1923-
xKings, John.
In Search of Centennial: Journey with James
A. Michener. Random.

Kingsbury, A. A. see Kingsbury, Arthur A.

Kingsbury, Arthur A.
xKingsbury, A. A.
Introduction to Security & Crime Prevention
Surveys. C C Thomas.

Kingsbury, Jack D. see Kingsbury, Jack Dean.

Kingsbury, Jack Dean.
xKingsbury, Jack D.
Matthew: Structure, Christology, Kingdom.
Fortress.

Kingsbury, John M. see Kingsbury, John Merriam.

Kingsbury, John Merriam, 1928-
xKingsbury, John M.
Deadly Harvest: A Guide to Common
Poisonous Plants. HR&W.

Kingsbury, Susan M. see Kingsbury, Susan Myra.

Kingsbury, Susan Myra.
xKingsbury, Susan M.
Factory, Family & Woman in the Soviet
Union. AMS Pr.
Newspapers & the News: An Objective
Measurement of Ethical & Unethical
Behavior by Representative Newspapers.
Johnson Repr.

Kingscote, Georgiana. see Kingscote, Georgiana Wolff.
Kingscote, Georgiana H. see Kingscote, Georgiana Wolff.

Kingscote, Georgiana Wolff, d. 1908
xKingscote, Georgiana.
Tales of the Sun: Folklore of Southern India.
AMS Pr.
xKingscote, Georgiana H.

Compiled by Tales of the Sun: Folklore of
Southern India. Arno.

Kingsford, Charles L. see Kingsford, Charles Lethbridge.

Kingsford, Charles Lethbridge, 1862-1926
xKingsford, Charles L.
Chronicles of London. Rowman.
Prejudice & Promise in Fifteenth Century
England. Biblio Dist.

Kingsley, B. see Kingsley, Benedict.

Kingsley, Benedict.
xKingsley, B.
Advances in Non-Invasive Diagnostic
Cardiology. C B Slack.

Kingsley, Charles, 1819-1875
xKingsley, Charles.
Alton Locke: Tailor & Poet. Folcroft.
Charles Kingsley, His Letters & Memories of
His Life. Sharon Hill.
The Heroes. Biblio Dist.
The Heroes. Mayflower Bks.
Heroes. Macmillan.

Kingsley, Emily P. see Kingsley, Emily Perl.

Kingsley, Emily Perl.
xKingsley, Emily P.
Cookie Monster's Storybook. Random.

Kingsley, Linda K. see Kingsley, Linda Kurtz.

Kingsley, Linda Kurtz.
xKingsley, Linda K.
Teaching Art to the Deaf. Gordon Pr.

Kingsley-Smith, Terence.
xKingsley-Smith, Terence.
The Forsaken. PB.

Kingston, J. M. see Kingston, J Maurice.

Kingston, J Maurice.
xKingston, J. M.
Mathematics for Teachers of the Middle
Grades. Krieger.

Kingston, Jeremy.
xKingston, Jeremy.
Arts & Artists. Facts on File.

Kingston, Maxine H. see Kingston, Maxine Hong.

Kingston, Maxine Hong.
xKingston, Maxine H.
China Men. Knopf.

Kingston, R. H. see Kingston, Robert Hildreth.

Kingston, Robert Hildreth, 1928-
xKingston, R. H.
Detection of Optical & Infrared Radiation.
Springer-Verlag.

Kinietz, W. Vernon. see Kinietz, William Vernon.

Kinietz, William Vernon.
xKinietz, W. Vernon.
Indians of the Western Great Lakes,
1615-1760. U of Mich Pr.

Kinkade, Robert G.
xKinkade, Robert G.
ed. Thesaurus of Psychological Index Terms.
Am Psychol.

Kinkead, Eugene, 1906-
xKinkead, Eugene.
A Concrete Look at Nature: Central Park (&
Other) Glimpses. Times Bks.

Kinkle, Roger D., 1916-
xKinkle, Roger D.
The Complete Encyclopedia of Popular Music
& Jazz 1900-1950. Arlington Hse.

Kinlein, M. Lucille.
xKinlein, M. Lucille.
Independent Nursing Practice with Clients.
Lippincott.

Kinley, David, 1861-1944
xKinley, David.
History, Organization & Influence of the
Independent Treasury of the United States.
Greenwood.
Use of Credit Instruments in Payments in the
United States. Kelley.

Kinloch, George R. see Kinloch, George Richie.

Kinloch, George Richie, 1796?-1877
xKinloch, George R.

ed. Ancient Scottish Ballads Recovered from
Tradition & Never Before Published. AMS
Pr.

Kinloch, Graham C. see Kinloch, Graham Charles.

Kinloch, Graham Charles.
xKinloch, Graham C.
The Dynamics of Race Relations: A
Sociological Analysis. McGraw.
Sociological Theory: Its Development & Major
Paradigms. McGraw.
The Sociology of Minority Group Relations.
P-H.

Kinmond, William.
xKinmond, William.
The First Book of Communist China. Watts.

Kinnaird, John. see Kinnaird, John William.

Kinnaird, John William, 1924-
xKinnaird, John.
William Hazlitt, Critic of Power. Columbia U
Pr.

Kinnane, Adrian.
xKinnane, Adrian.
Policing. Nelson-Hall.

Kinnard, Douglas.
xKinnard, Douglas.
President Eisenhower & Strategy Management:
A Study in Defense Politics. U Pr of Ky.

Kinne, Russ.
xKinne, Russ.
The Complete Book of Nature Photography.
Amphoto.

Kinne, Willard A. see Kinne, Willard Austin.

Kinne, Willard Austin, 1892-
xKinne, Willard A.
Revivals & Importations of French Comedies
in England, 1749-1800. AMS Pr.

Kinne, Wisner P. see Kinne, Wisner Payne.

Kinne, Wisner Payne.
xKinne, Wisner P.
George Pierce Baker & the American Theatre.
Greenwood.

Kinnear, Thomas C.
xKinnear, Thomas C.
Marketing Research: An Applied Approach.
McGraw.

Kinney, Arthur F., 1933-
xKinney, Arthur F.
Dorothy Parker. G K Hall.
Dorothy Parker. Twayne.
Faulkner's Narrative Poetics: Style As Vision.
U of Mass Pr.

Kinney, Cle.
xKinney, Cle.
Don't Move--Improve!: Hundreds of Ways to
Make a Good House Better. T Y Crowell.

Kinney, J. P. see Kinney, Jay P.

Kinney, Jay P., 1875-
xKinney, J. P.
A Continent Lost - a Civilization Won: Indian
Land Tenure in America. Arno.
A Continent Lost, a Civilization Won: Indian
Land Tenure in America. Octagon.

Kinney, Jean.
xKinney, Jean.
Loosening the Grip: A Handbook of Alcohol
Information. Mosby.

Kinney, Jean. see Kinney, Jean Brown.

Kinney, Jean Brown.
xKinney, Jean.
How to Find & Finance a Great Country
Place. P-H.
How to Make 19 Kinds of American Folk Art
from Masks to TV Commercials. Atheneum.

Kinney, Peter.
xKinney, Peter.
The Early Sculpture of Bartolomeo Ammanati.
Garland Pub.

Kinney, William P.
xKinney, William P.

The Monetary Maze: Gold, the International
Monetary System, & the Emerging World
Economy. Kendall-Hunt.
Kinnison, William A.
xKinnison, William A.
Building Sullivant's Pyramid: An
Administrative History of the Ohio State
University, 1870-1907. Ohio St U Pr.
Kinross, John.
xKinross, John.
The Battlefields of Britain. Hippocrene Bks.
Kinsbourne, M. see Kinsbourne, Marcel.
Kinsbourne, Marcel.
xKinsbourne, M.
ed. Asymmetrical Function of the Brain.
Cambridge U Pr.
xKinsbourne, Marcel.
Children's Learning & Attention Problems.
Little.
Kinsbruner, Jay.
xKinsbruner, Jay.
The Spanish-American Independence
Movement. Krieger.
Kinsella, William E.
xKinsella, William E.
Leadership in Isolation: FDR & the Origins of
the Second World War. Schenkman.
Kinser, Charleen.
xKinser, Charleen.
illus. Outdoor Art for Kids. Follett.
Kinsey, Miriam.
xKinsey, Miriam.
Contemporary Netsuke. C E Tuttle.
Kinsler, F. Ross.
xKinsler, F. Ross.
The Extension Movement in Theological
Education: A Call to the Renewal of the
Ministry. William Carey Lib.
Kinsler, Lawrence E.
xKinsler, Lawrence E.
Fundamentals of Acoustics. Wiley.
Kinsley, Herbert. see Kinsley, Herbert M.
Kinsley, Herbert M.
xKinsley, Herbert.
One Hundred Recipes for the Chafing Dish.
Arno.
Kinslow, R. see Kinslow, Ray.
Kinslow, Ray.
xKinslow, R.
ed. High-Velocity Impact Phenomena. Acad Pr.
Kinsman, Robert.
xKinsman, Robert.
Your New Swiss Bank Book. Dow Jones-Irwin.
Kinsman, Robert S.
xKinsman, Robert S.
Darker Vision of the Renaissance: Beyond the
Fields of Reason. U of Cal Pr.
Kinsolving, William.
xKinsolving, William.
Born with the Century. Putnam.
Kinton, Ronald.
xKinton, Ronald.
The Theory of Catering. Intl Ideas.
Kintsch, W. see Kintsch, Walter.
Kintsch, Walter, 1932-
xKintsch, W.
Memory & Cognition. Wiley.
Kintzer, Frederick C.
xKintzer, Frederick C.
The Multi-Institution Junior College District.
Am Assn Comm Jr Coll.
Kinzel, Robert K.
xKinzel, Robert K.
Retirement: Creating Promise Out of Threat.
Am Mgmt.
Kinzer, Nora S. see Kinzer, Nora Scott.
Kinzer, Nora Scott.
xKinzer, Nora S.

Put Down & Ripped off: The American
Woman & the Beauty Cult. T Y Crowell.
xKinzer, Nora Scott.
Stress & the American Woman. Doubleday.
Kinzey, Vera G.
xKinzey, Vera G.
Mastering Ten-Key Calculators: Electronic &
Mechanical. HarBraceJ.
Kip, Arthur F.
xKip, Arthur F.
Fundamentals of Electricity & Magnetism.
McGraw.
Kipling, Rudyard, 1865-1936
xKipling, Rudyard.
American Notes. Arno.
Captains Courageous. NAL.
Captains Courageous. Pendulum Pr.
Captains Courageous. Airmont.
Captains Courageous. Schol Bk Serv.
Captains Courageous. AMSCO Sch.
Collected Works of Rudyard Kipling. AMS Pr.
Day's Work. Arno.
Favorite Just So Stories. G&D.
Favorite Just So Stories. G&D.
Mulvaney Stories. Arno.
The Seven Seas. Longwood Pr.
Soldier Stories. Arno.
The Two Jungle Books. Arno.
Kipnis, David.
xKipnis, David.
Character Structure & Impulsiveness. Acad Pr.
The Powerholders. U of Chicago Pr.
Kipnis, Ira.
xKipnis, Ira.
American Socialist Movement, 1897-1912.
Greenwood.
Kipnis, Lynne.
xKipnis, Lynne.
You Can't Catch Diabetes from a Friend. Triad
Pub FL.
Kippax, Janet.
xKippax, Janet.
The Gypsy. Zondervan.
Kippley, John F.
xKippley, John F.
The Art of Natural Family Planning. Couple to
Couple.
Kippley, Sheila.
xKippley, Sheila.
Breast-Feeding & Natural Child Spacing: The
Ecology of Natural Mothering. Har-Row.
Breast-Feeding & Natural Child Spacing: The
Ecology of Natural Mothering. Penguin.
Kiraly, Bela. see Kiraly, Bela K.
Kiraly, Bela K.
xKiraly, Bela.
ed. East Central European Perceptions of Early
America. Humanities.
xKiraly, Bela K.
The Hungarian Revolution of 1956 in
Retrospect. East Eur Quarterly.
Kiralyfalvi, Bela, 1937-
xKiralyfalvi, Bela.
The Aesthetics of Gyorgy Lukacs. Princeton U
Pr.
Kirban, Doreen.
xKirban, Doreen.
Stranger in Tomorrow's Land. Kirban.
Kirban, Salem.
xKirban, Salem.

Christian Science. Kirban.
Church Promotion Handbook. Kirban.
The Getting Back to Nature Diet. Keats.
The Getting Back to Nature Diet. Kirban.
Guide to Survival. Kirban.
How to Eat Your Way Back to Vibrant Health.
Kirban.
How to Keep Healthy & Happy by Fasting.
Kirban.
How to Live Above & Beyond Your
Circumstances. Kirban.
How to Live Above and Beyond Your
Circumstances. Tyndale.
I Predict. Kirban.
Questions Frequently Asked Me on Prophecy.
Kirban.
Kirby, Anthony J. see Kirby, Anthony John.
Kirby, Anthony John.
xKirby, Anthony J.
The Organic Chemistry of Phosphorus.
Elsevier.
Kirby, D. A. see Kirby, David Anthony.
Kirby, D. G.
xKirby, D. G.
Finland in the Twentieth Century: A History &
an Interpretation. U of Minn Pr.
Kirby, David. see Kirby, David K.
Kirby, David Anthony.
xKirby, D. A.
Slum Housing & Residential Renewal: The
Case in Urban Britain. Longman.
Kirby, David K.
xKirby, David.
Grace King. Twayne.
Kirby, Jack T. see Kirby, Jack Temple.
Kirby, Jack Temple.
xKirby, Jack T.
Darkness at the Dawning: Race & Reform in
the Progressive South. Lippincott.
Media-Made Dixie: The South in the American
Imagination. La State U Pr.
Kirby, John B., 1938-
xKirby, John B.
Black Americans in the Roosevelt Era:
Liberalism & Race. U of Tenn Pr.
Kirby, Jonell. see Kirby, Jonell H.
Kirby, Jonell H.
xKirby, Jonell.
Second Marriage. Accel Devel.
Kirby, Mary, 1908-
xKirby, Mary.
Designing on the Loom. Select Bks.
Kirby, Michael.
xKirby, Michael.
Futurist Performance. Dutton.
Kirby, Morrie.
xKirby, Morrie.
Real Estate Model Letter Desk Book. P-H.
Kirby, P. A.
xKirby, P. A.
Design for Structural Stability. Halsted Pr.
Kirby, Ronald F.
xKirby, Ronald F.
Para-Transit: Neglected Options for Urban
Mobility. Urban Inst.
Kirby, Thomas J. see Kirby, Thomas Joseph.
Kirby, Thomas Joseph, 1877-
xKirby, Thomas J.
Practice in the Case of School Children. AMS
Pr.
Kircher, Harry B.
xKircher, Harry B.
Diddledee Dog, the Dirt Digger. Interstate.
Kirchhoff, Frederick, 1942-
xKirchhoff, Frederick.
William Morris. Twayne.
Kirchmayer, Leon K.
xKirchmayer, Leon K.

Economic Operation of Power Systems. Wiley.

Kirchner, Glenn.
xKirchner, Glenn.
Introduction to Movement Education. Wm C Brown.

Kirchner, Walther.
xKirchner, Walther.
History of Russia. Har-Row.

Kirilov, Nikolai.
xKirilov, Nikolai.
ed. Introduction to Modern Bulgarian Literature: An Anthology of Short Stories. Irvington.

Kirk, Albert.
xKirk, Albert.
Commentary on the Gospel of Matthew. Paulist Pr.

Kirk, Barbara.
xKirk, Barbara.
Grandpa, Me & Our House in the Tree. Macmillan.

Kirk, Clare H. *see* Kirk, Hyland Clare.

Kirk, D. *see* Kirk, Donald E.

Kirk, Daniel F.
xKirk, Daniel F.
Charles Dodgson, Semeiotician. U Presses Fla.

Kirk, David, 1934-
xKirk, David L.
Biology Today. Random.

Kirk, David L. *see* Kirk, David.

Kirk, Donald E., 1937-
xKirk, D.
Optimal Control Theory: An Introduction. P-H.

Kirk, Eugene P., 1943-
xKirk, Eugene P.
Menippean Satire: An Annotated Catalogue of Texts & Criticism. Garland Pub.

Kirk, Francis G. *see* Kirk, Frank G.

Kirk, Frank G., 1933-
xKirk, Francis G.
Total System Development for Information Systems. Wiley.

Kirk, Franklin W. *see* Kirk, Franklyn W.

Kirk, Franklyn W.
xKirk, Franklin W.
Instrumentation. Am Technical.

Kirk, Gordon W.
xKirk, Gordon W.
The Promise of American Life: Social Mobility in a Nineteenth-Century Immigrant Community, Holland, Michigan. Am Philos.

Kirk, Hyland Clare, 1846-1917
xKirk, Clare H.
When Age Grows Young. Arno.

Kirk, Irina.
xKirk, Irina.
Profiles in Russian Resistance. Times Bks.

Kirk, J. Andrew.
xKirk, J. Andrew.
Liberation Theology: An Evangelical View from the Third World. John Knox.

Kirk, James A.
xKirk, James A.
Stories of the Hindus: An Introduction Through Texts & Interpretations. Macmillan.

Kirk, Jerry.
xKirk, Jerry R.
The Homosexual Crisis in the Mainline Church: A Presbyterian Minister Speaks Out. Nelson.

Kirk, Jerry R. *see* Kirk, Jerry.

Kirk, John.
xKirk, John.
How to Manage Your Money. Benjamin Co.

Kirk, John E., 1919-
xKirk, John E.
How to Build a Fortune Investing in Land. P-H.

Kirk, John T.
xKirk, John T.

The Impecunious Collector's Guide to American Antiques. Knopf.

Kirk, P. L. *see* Kirk, Paul Leland.

Kirk, Paul L. *see* Kirk, Paul Leland.

Kirk, Paul Leland.
xKirk, P. L.
Fire Investigation: Including Fire-Related Phenomena: Arson, Explosion, Asphyxiation. Wiley.
xKirk, Paul L.
Crime Investigation. Wiley.

Kirk, R. L. *see* Kirk, Robert L.

Kirk, R. M. *see* Kirk, Raymond Maurice.

Kirk, Raymond Maurice.
xKirk, R. M.
General Surgical Operations. Churchill.

Kirk, Robert L.
xKirk, R. L.
ed. The Origin of the Australians. Humanities.

Kirk, Russell.
xKirk, Russell.
The American Cause. Greenwood.
Lord of the Hollow Dark. St Martin.
The Princess of All Lands. Arkham.
Program for Conservatives. Constructive Action.

Kirk, Ruth.
xKirk, Ruth.
Badlands. Badlands Natl Hist.
illus. David, Young Chief of the Quileutes: An American Indian Today. HarBraceJ.
Desert: The American Southwest. HM.
Exploring Death Valley. Stanford U Pr.
Exploring Mount Rainier. U of Wash Pr.
Exploring Washington Archaeology. U of Wash Pr.
Sigemi: A Japanese Village Girl. HarBraceJ.

Kirk, Samuel A. *see* Kirk, Samuel Alexander.

Kirk, Samuel Alexander, 1904-
xKirk, Samuel A.
Educating Exceptional Children. HM.
Psycholinguistic Learning Disabilities: Diagnosis & Remediation. U of Ill Pr.
Teaching Reading to Slow & Disabled Learners. HM.

Kirk, Susan. *see* Kirk, Susan Lauxman.

Kirk, Susan Lauxman.
xKirk, Susan.
The Architecture of St. Charles Avenue. Pelican.

Kirk, William, 1880-
xKirk, William.
National Labor Federations in the United States. AMS Pr.

Kirk, Winifred D.
xKirk, Winifred D.
Aids & Precautions in Administering the Illinois Test of Psycholinguistic Abilities. U of Ill Pr.

Kirkbride, Alec, Sir, 1897-
xKirkbride, Alec.
From the Wings: Amman Memoirs, 1947-1951. Biblio Dist.

Kirkbride, Ronald. *see* Kirkbride, Ronald De Levingston.

Kirkbride, Ronald De Levingston, 1912-
xKirkbride, Ronald.
Song of the Undersea. Astor-Honor.

Kirkbride, Thomas S. *see* Kirkbride, Thomas Story.

Kirkbride, Thomas Story, 1809-1883
xKirkbride, Thomas S.
On the Construction, Organization, & General Arrangements of Hospitals for the Insane. Arno.

Kirkby, John, 1705-1754
xKirkby, John.

The Capacity & Extent of Human Understanding, Exemplified in the Extraordinary Case of Automathes. Garland Pub.

Kirkby, M. J.
xKirkby, M. J.
ed. Hillslope Hydrology. Wiley.

Kirke, Henry, 1842- 1925
xKirke, Henry.
Twenty-Five Years in British Guiana. Negro U Pr.

Kirkemo, Ronald B.
xKirkemo, Ronald B.
An Introduction to International Law. Littlefield.
An Introduction to International Law. Nelson-Hall.

Kirkendale, George A. *see* Kirkendale, George Alderson.

Kirkendale, George Alderson.
xKirkendale, George A.
Analytical Methods for Materials Investigation. Gordon.

Kirkendale, Warren.
xKirkendale, Warren.
tr. Fugue & Fugato in Rococo & Classical Chamber Music. Duke.

Kirkendall, Don R.
xKirkendall, Don R.
Measurement & Evaluation for Physical Educators. Wm C Brown.

Kirkendall, Lester A.
xKirkendall, Lester A.
Student's Guide to Marriage-Family Life Literature: An Aid to Individualized Study & Instruction. Wm C Brown.

Kirkendall, Richard S. *see* Kirkendall, Richard Stewart.

Kirkendall, Richard Stewart, 1928-
xKirkendall, Richard S.
A Global Power: America Since the Age of Roosevelt. Knopf.
ed. The Truman Period As a Research Field. U of Mo Pr.

Kirker, Harold.
xKirker, Harold.
The Architecture of Charles Bulfinch. Harvard U Pr.

Kirkham, Don.
xKirkham, Don.
Advanced Soil Physics. Wiley.

Kirkham, E. Bruce. *see* Kirkham, Edwin Bruce.

Kirkham, Edwin Bruce, 1938-
xKirkham, E. Bruce.
The Building of Uncle Tom's Cabin. U of Tenn Pr.
Indices to American Literary Annuals & Gift Books. Res Pubns Conn.

Kirkham, George.
xKirkham, George.
Signal Zero. Ballantine.
xKirkham, George L.
Introduction to Law Enforcement. Har-Row.

Kirkham, George L. *see* Kirkham, George.

Kirkland, Edward C. *see* Kirkland, Edward Chase.

Kirkland, Edward Chase.
xKirkland, Edward C.
Charles Francis Adams, Jr., 1835-1915: The Patrician at Bay. Harvard U Pr.
Dream & Thought in the Business Community, 1860-1900. Cornell U Pr.
Dream & Thought in the Business Community, 1860-1900. New Viewpoints.
History of American Economic Life. Irvington.
Men, Cities & Transportation: A Study in New England History, 1820-1900. Russell.

Kirkland, James W.
xKirkland, James W.
Fiction: The Narrative Art. P-H.

Kirkland, Joseph, 1830-1894
xKirkland, Joseph.

The Captain of Company K. Irvington.
Kirkland, Turner.
 xKirkland, Turner.
  Southern Derringers of the Mississippi Valley.
   Pioneer Pr.
Kirkley, Donald H.
 xKirkley, Donald H.
  A Descriptive Study of the Network Television
   Western During the Seasons 1955-56 to
   1962-63. Arno.
Kirkley, George. *see* Kirkley, George W.
Kirkley, George W.
 xKirkley, George.
  ed. Manual of Weighttraining. Soccer.
Kirklin, John W., 1917-
 xKirklin, John W.
  ed. Advances in Cardiovascular Surgery.
   Grune.
Kirkman, Patrick. *see* Kirkman, Patrick R. A.
Kirkman, Patrick R. *see* Kirkman, Patrick R. A.
Kirkman, Patrick R. A.
 xKirkman, Patrick.
  Modern Credit Management: A Study of the
   Management of Trade Credit Under
   Inflationary Conditions. Allen Unwin.
 xKirkman, Patrick R.
  Accounting Under Inflationary Conditions.
   Allen Unwin.
  Modern Credit Management: A Study of the
   Management of Trade Credit Under
   Inflationary Conditions. Allen Unwin.
Kirkpatrick, Charles A. *see* Kirkpatrick, Charles
 Atkinson.
Kirkpatrick, Charles Atkinson.
 xKirkpatrick, Charles A.
  Business. SRA.
Kirkpatrick, Clifford, 1898-
 xKirkpatrick, Clifford.
  Intelligence & Immigration. Arno.
Kirkpatrick, D. L.
 xKirkpatrick, D. L.
  ed. Twentieth-Century Children's Writers. St
   Martin.
Kirkpatrick, Donald L.
 xKirkpatrick, Donald L.
  A Practical Guide for Supervisory Training &
   Development. A-W.
Kirkpatrick, Doris.
 xKirkpatrick, Doris.
  Honey in the Rock. Elsevier-Nelson.
Kirkpatrick, Ellis L. *see* Kirkpatrick, Ellis Lore.
Kirkpatrick, Ellis Lore, 1884-
 xKirkpatrick, Ellis L.
  Farmer's Standard of Living. Arno.
Kirkpatrick, Frederick. *see* Kirkpatrick, Frederick
 Alexander.
Kirkpatrick, Frederick Alexander, 1861-1953
 xKirkpatrick, Frederick.
  History of the Argentine Republic. AMS Pr.
Kirkpatrick, Inez E., 1900-
 xKirkpatrick, Inez E.
  Stagecoach Trails in Iowa. J-B Pubs.
Kirkpatrick, Ivone, Sir.
 xKirkpatrick, Ivone.
  Mussolini, a Study in Power. Greenwood.
Kirkpatrick, Jeane. *see* Kirkpatrick, Jeane J.
Kirkpatrick, Jeane J.
 xKirkpatrick, Jeane.
  Political Woman. Basic.
Kirkpatrick, Rena K.
 xKirkpatrick, Rena K.

Look at Flowers. Raintree Child.
Look at Insects. Raintree Child.
Look at Leaves. Raintree Child.
Look at Magnets. Raintree Child.
Look at Pond Life. Raintree Child.
Look at Rainbow Colors. Raintree Child.
Look at Seeds & Weeds. Raintree Child.
Look at Shore Life. Raintree Child.
Look at Trees. Raintree Child.
Look at Weather. Raintree Child.
Kirkpatrick, Samual A. *see* Kirkpatrick, Samuel A.
Kirkpatrick, Samuel A.
 xKirkpatrick, Samual A.
  Sources of Organizational & Personal Power in
   the U.S. Senate: A Test of Alternative
   Models. Univ OK Gov Res.
 xKirkpatrick, Samuel A.
  Legislative Role Structures, Power Bases &
   Behavior Patterns: An Empirical Examination
   of the U. S. Senate. Univ OK Gov Res.
  The Oklahoma Voter: Politics, Elections, &
   Political Parties in the Sooner State. U of
   Okla Pr.
  Quantitative Analysis of Political Data. Merrill.
Kirkup, James.
 xKirkup, James.
  ed. Modern Japanese Poetry. U of Queensland
   Pr.
Kirkwood, G. M. *see* Kirkwood, Gordon MacDonald.
Kirkwood, Gordon MacDonald, 1916-
 xKirkwood, G. M.
  Early Greek Monody: The History of a Poetic
   Type. Cornell U Pr.
Kirkwood, James. *see* Kirkwood, Jim.
Kirkwood, Jim.
 xKirkwood, James.
  There Must Be a Pony. Avon.
Kirkwood, John G. *see* Kirkwood, John Gamble.
Kirkwood, John Gamble.
 xKirkwood, John G.
  Proteins. Gordon.
  Theory of Liquids. Gordon.
  Theory of Solutions. Gordon.
Kirkwood, Kenneth P. *see* Kirkwood, Kenneth Porter.
Kirkwood, Kenneth Porter, 1899-
 xKirkwood, Kenneth P.
  Renaissance in Japan: A Cultural Survey of the
   Seventeenth Century. C E Tuttle.
Kirkwood, Robert.
 xKirkwood, Robert.
  Journal & Order Book of Captain Robert
   Kirkwood of the Delaware Regiment of the
   Continental Line. Kennikat.
Kirmse, Wolfgang.
 xKirmse, Wolfgang.
  Carbene Chemistry. Acad Pr.
Kirn, Arthur G.
 xKirn, Arthur G.
  Life Work Planning. McGraw.
Kirp, David L.
 xKirp, David L.
  Doing Good by Doing Little: Race &
   Schooling in Britain. U of Cal Pr.
Kirpalani, V.
 xKirpalani, V.
  ed. Marketing Effectiveness: Insights from
   Accounting & Finance: An Annotated
   Bibliography. Am Mktg.
Kirsch, Arthur C.
 xKirsch, Arthur C.
  Dryden's Heroic Drama. Gordian.
Kirsch, Jonathan.
 xKirsch, Jonathan.
  Lovers in a Winter Circle. NAL.
Kirsch, Robert. *see* Kirsch, Robert R.
Kirsch, Robert R., 1922-
 xKirsch, Robert.

Lives, Works & Transformations: A Quarter
 Century of Book Reviews & Essays. Capra
 Pr.
Kirschen, Etienne S. *see* Kirschen, Etienne Sadi.
Kirschen, Etienne Sadi.
 xKirschen, Etienne S.
  Financial Integration in Western Europe.
   Columbia U Pr.
Kirschenbaum, Howard.
 xKirschenbaum, Howard.
  Advanced Value Clarification. Univ Assocs.
  Developing Support Groups: A Manual for
   Facilitators & Participants. Univ Assocs.
  On Becoming Carl Rogers. Delacorte.
Kirschner, Allen.
 xKirschner, Allen.
  ed. Journalism: Readings in the Mass Media.
   Odyssey Pr.
Kirschner, Don S.
 xKirschner, Don S.
  City & Country: Rural Responses to
   Urbanization in the 1920's. Greenwood.
Kirschner, Stephen M.
 xKirschner, Stephen M.
  The Rule Book. Doubleday.
Kirshenbaum, Gerald S.
 xKirshenbaum, Gerald S.
  Polymer Science Study Guide. Gordon.
Kirshner, Joseph M.
 xKirshner, Joseph M.
  Fluid Amplifiers. McGraw.
Kirsner, Joseph B. *see* Kirsner, Joseph Barnett.
Kirsner, Joseph Barnett.
 xKirsner, Joseph B.
  Inflammatory Bowel Disease. Lea & Febiger.
Kirst, Michael W.
 xKirst, Michael W.
  Politics of Education at the Local, State &
   Federal Levels. McCutchan.
Kirstein, Lincoln, 1907-
 xKirstein, Lincoln.
  Dance: A Short History of Classic Theatrical
   Dancing. Dance Horiz.
  Flesh Is Heir: An Historical Romance. S Ill U
   Pr.
  Nijinsky Dancing. Knopf.
Kirstein, Peter N.
 xKirstein, Peter N.
  Anglo Over Bracero: A History of the Mexican
   Worker in the United States from Roosevelt
   to Nixon. R & E Res Assoc.
Kirtley, Donald D.
 xKirtley, Donald D.
  The Psychology of Blindness. Nelson-Hall.
Kirvan, John J.
 xKirvan, John J.
  Restless Believers. Paulist Pr.
Kirwan, C. A. *see* Kirwan, Christopher.
Kirwan, Christopher.
 xKirwan, C. A.
  Logic & Argument. NYU Pr.
Kirwan, Richard, 1733-1812
 xKirwan, Richard.
  Geological Essays. Arno.
Kirwin, Gerald J.
 xKirwin, Gerald J.
  Basic Circuit Analysis. HM.
Kirzner, Israel M.
 xKirzner, Israel M.
  Competition & Entrepreneurship. U of Chicago
   Pr.
  The Economic Point of View: An Essay in the
   History of Economic Thought. Inst Humane.
  Perception, Opportunity & Profit: Studies in
   the Theory of Entrepreneurship. U of
   Chicago Pr.
Kis, Danilo, 1935-
 xKis, Danilo.

Garden, Ashes. HarBraceJ.
Garden, Ashes. HarBraceJ.
Kisch, Herbert, 1924-
xKisch, Herbert.
Prussian Mercantilism & the Rise of the
Krefeld Silk Industry: Variations Upon an
Eighteenth-Century Theme. Am Philos.
Kiselev, A. I.
xKiselev, A. I.
Ordinary Differential Equations. Ungar.
Kiselev, A. V. see Kiselev, Andrei Vladimirovich.
Kiselev, Andrei Vladimirovich.
xKiselev, A. V.
Gas-Adsorption Chromatography. Plenum Pub.
Infrared Spectra of Surface Compounds.
Halsted Pr.
Kiser, George C.
xKiser, George C.
ed. Mexican Workers in the United States:
Historical & Political Perspectives. U of NM
Pr.
Kish, George, 1914-
xKish, George.
ed. A Source Book in Geography. Harvard U
Pr.
Kish, Joseph L.
xKish, Joseph L.
Business Forms: Design & Control. Ronald Pr.
Kish, Leslie, 1910-
xKish, Leslie.
Survey Sampling. Wiley.
Kishi, Nami.
xKishi, Nami.
Ogre & His Bride. Schol Bk Serv.
Kishlansky, Mark A.
xKishlansky, Mark A.
The Rise of the New Model Army. Cambridge
U Pr.
Kisker, George W.
xKisker, George W.
The Disorganized Personality. McGraw.
ed. World Tension: The Psychopathology of
International Relations. Greenwood.
Kissam, Philip, 1896-
xKissam, Philip.
Surveying for Civil Engineers. McGraw.
Surveying: Instruments & Methods for Surveys
of Limited Extent. McGraw.
Kissane, John M.
xKissane, John M.
Pathology of Infancy & Childhood. Mosby.
Kissel, Irwin R.
xKissel, Irwin R.
How to Handle Claims & Returns: A Manual
for Manufacturers & Retailers. McGraw.
Kissin, S. F.
xKissin, S. F.
Farewell to Revolution: Marxist Philosophy &
the Modern World. St Martin.
Kissinger, Henry. see Kissinger, Henry Alfred.
Kissinger, Henry A. see Kissinger, Henry Alfred.

Kissinger, Henry Alfred.
xKissinger, Henry.
The White House Years. Little.
xKissinger, Henry A.
American Foreign Policy. Norton.
A World Restored: Metternich, Castlereagh &
the Problems of Peace, 1812-1822. HM.
Kister, Kenneth F., 1935-
xKister, Kenneth F.
ed. Dictionary Buying Guide: A Consumer
Guide to General English-Language
Wordbooks in Print. Bowker.
ed. Encyclopedia Buying Guide: A Consumer
Guide to General Encyclopedias in Print.
Bowker.
Kistler, Mary.
xKistler, Mary.

The Jarrah Tree. Popular Lib.
A Stranger at My Door. Doubleday.
Kistner, Robert W.
xKistner, Robert W.
Atlas of Infertility Surgery. Little.
Gynecology: Principles & Practice. Year Bk
Med.
Kitagawa, Evelyn M. see Kitagawa, Evelyn Mae.
Kitagawa, Evelyn Mae.
xKitagawa, Evelyn M.
Differential Mortality in the United States: A
Study in Socio-Economic Epidemiology.
Harvard U Pr.
Kitagawa, Joseph M. see Kitagawa, Joseph Mitsuo.
Kitagawa, Joseph Mitsuo.
xKitagawa, Joseph M.
ed. History of Religions: Essays on the
Problem of Understanding. U of Chicago Pr.
Religions of the East. Westminster.
Kitagawa, M. see Kitagawa, Masayasu.
Kitagawa, Masayasu.
xKitagawa, M.
ed. Cancer Immunology: Immune Surveillance
& Specific Recognition of Tumor Antigen.
Univ Park.
Kitamura, M. see Kitamura, Masatoshi.
Kitamura, Masatoshi, 1926-
xKitamura, M.
Tables of the Characteristic Functions of the
Eclipse & Related Delta-Functions for
Solution of Light Curves of Eclipsing Binary
Systems. Univ Park.
Kitano, Harry H. see Kitano, Harry H. L.
Kitano, Harry H. L.
xKitano, Harry H.
Race Relations. P-H.
Kitao, Timothy K.
xKitao, Timothy K.
Circle & Oval in the Square of Saint Peter's:
Bernini's Art of Planning. NYU Pr.
Kitay, P. M. see Kitay, Philip Morton.
Kitay, Philip Morton, 1911-
xKitay, P. M.
Radicalism & Conservatism Toward
Conventional Religion: A Psychological
Study Based on a Group of Jewish College
Students. AMS Pr.
Kitay, William, 1918-
xKitay, William.
Understanding Arthritis. Monarch Pr.
Kitchel, Denison.
xKitchel, Denison.
The Truth About the Panama Canal. Arlington
Hse.
Kitchell, Frank M.
xKitchell, Frank M.
Opportunities in Optometry. Natl Textbk.
Kitchen, Kenneth A. see Kitchen, Kenneth Anderson.
Kitchen, Kenneth Anderson.
xKitchen, Kenneth A.
Ancient Orient & Old Testament. Inter-Varsity.
Kitchen, Martin.
xKitchen, Martin.
The Silent Dictatorship: The Politics of the
German High Command Under Hindenburg
& Ludendorff, 1916-1918. Holmes & Meier.
Kitchen, Paddy.
xKitchen, Paddy.
Gerard Manley Hopkins. Atheneum.
Kitchens, James A.
xKitchens, James A.
Individuals in Society: A Modern Introduction
to Sociology. Merrill.
Kitchin, Frances.
xKitchin, Frances.
Cook Out. David & Charles.
Granny's Cookery Book. David & Charles.
Kitchin, George, 1892-1935
xKitchin, George.

Prisoner of the Ogpu. Arno.
Kitching, J. B. see Kitching, Jessie Beatrice.
Kitching, Jessie Beatrice.
xKitching, J. B.
Trout Fishing in North America: Where &
When. Oak Leaf.
Kitson, Charles H. see Kitson, Charles Herbert.
Kitson, Charles Herbert, 1874-1944
xKitson, Charles H.
The Art of Counterpoint. Da Capo.
Contrapuntal Harmony for Beginners.
Greenwood.
Kitson, Frank.
xKitson, Frank.
Bunch of Five. Merrimack Bk Serv.
Kittel, Charles.
xKittel, Charles.
Introduction to Solid State Physics. Wiley.
Quantum Theory of Solids. Wiley.
Thermal Physics. W H Freeman.
Kittel, Rudolf, 1853-1929
xKittel, Rudolf.
Great Men & Movements in Israel. Ktav.
Kittler, Glenn D.
xKittler, Glenn D.
Edgar Cayce on the Dead Sea Scrolls. Warner
Bks.
Kitto, Humphrey D. see Kitto, Humphrey Davy Findley.
Kitto, Humphrey Davy Findley.
xKitto, Humphrey D.
Greeks. Penguin.
Kitton, Frederic G. see Kitton, Frederic George.
Kitton, Frederic George, 1856-1904
xKitton, Frederic G.
The Dickens Country. Norwood Edns.
Kittredge, George L. see Kittredge, George Lyman.
Kittredge, George Lyman.
xKittredge, George L.
Advanced English Grammar, with Exercises.
AMS Pr.
Chaucer & His Poetry. Harvard U Pr.
Chaucer & Some of His Friends. Folcroft.
Chaucer & Some of His Friends. Gordon Pr.
Date of Chaucer's Troilus & Other Chaucer
Matters. Russell.
Observations on the Language of Chaucer's
Troilus. Gordon Pr.
Observations on the Language of Chaucer's
Troilus. Russell.
Kittredge, Henry C. see Kittredge, Henry Crocker.
Kittredge, Henry Crocker, 1890-
xKittredge, Henry C.
Mooncussers of Cape Cod. Shoe String.
Kittredge, William.
xKittredge, William.
ed. Stories into Film. Har-Row.
Kittrie, Nicholas N.
xKittrie, Nicholas N.
ed. Legality, Morality, & Ethics in Criminal
Justice. Praeger.
ed. Medicine, Law & Public Policy. AMS Pr.
The Right to be Different: Deviance &
Enforced Therapy. Johns Hopkins.
Kittross, John M., 1929-
xKittross, John M.
Television Frequency Allocation Policy in the
United States. Arno.
Kitts, David B.
xKitts, David B.
The Structure of Geology. SMU Press.
Kitts, Eustace J. see Kitts, Eustace John.
Kitts, Eustace John.
xKitts, Eustace J.
Pope John Twenty-Third & Master John Hus
of Bohemia. AMS Pr.
Kitzinger, Ernst, 1912-
xKitzinger, Ernst.

The Art of Byzantium & the Medieval West:
Selected Studies. Ind U Pr.
Byzantine Art in the Making: Main Lines of
Stylistic Development in Mediterranean Art,
3rd-7th Century. Harvard U Pr.

Kitzinger, Sheila.
xKitzinger, Sheila.
Birth at Home. Oxford U Pr.
Education & Counseling for Childbirth.
Schocken.
The Experience of Childbirth. Penguin.
The Experience of Childbirth. Taplinger.
Giving Birth: The Parents' Emotions in
Childbirth. Schocken.
Giving Birth: The Parents' Emotions in
Childbirth. Taplinger.
Women As Mothers. Random.

Kiuchi, Shinz O.
xKiuchi, Shinzo.
ed. Geography in Japan. Intl Schol Bk Serv.
Kiuchi, Shinzo. see Kiuchi, Shinz O.

Kivenson, Gilbert.
xKivenson, Gilbert.
The Art & Science of Inventing. Van Nos
Reinhold.

Kivett, Marvin F.
xKivett, Marvin F.
Woodland Sites in Nebraska. Nebraska Hist.

Kiwanuka, M. S. M. Semakula.
xKiwanuka, S.
History of Buganda from the Foundation of the
Kingdom to 1900. Holmes & Meier.
Kiwanuka, S. see Kiwanuka, M. S. M. Semakula.

Kiyosaki, Wayne S.
xKiyosaki, Wayne S.
North Korea's Foreign Relations: The Politics
of Accomodation, 1945-75. Praeger.

Kiyota, Minoru.
xKiyota, Minoru.
Mahayana Buddhist Meditation: Theory &
Practice. U Pr of Hawaii.

Kizilos, Tolly.
xKizilos, Tolly.
Dwarf's Legacy. Ashley Bks.
Kizziar, Janet. see Kizziar, Janet W.

Kizziar, Janet W.
xKizziar, Janet.
Search for Acceptance: The Adolescent &
Self-Esteem. Nelson-Hall.

Kjeldsen, Kitty.
xKjeldsen, Kitty.
Women's Gymnastics. Allyn.

Kjelgaard, James Arthur, 1910-1959
xKjelgaard, Jim.
Boomerang Hunter. Avon.
Desert Dog. Bantam.
Stormy. Bantam.
xKjelgaard, Jim A.
Explorations of Pere Marquette. Random.
Kjelgaard, Jim. see Kjelgaard, James Arthur.
Kjelgaard, Jim A. see Kjelgaard, James Arthur.

Kjellberg, Ernst.
xKjellberg, Ernst.
Greek & Roman Art: 3000 B.C. to A.D. 550. T
Y Crowell.

Kjellmer, Goran.
xKjellmer, Goran.
Did the Pearl Poet Write Pearl?. Humanities.

Kjervik, Diane K.
xKjervik, Diane K.
ed. Women in Stress: A Nursing Perspective.
ACC.

Klaasen, Ruth.
xKlaasen, Ruth.
How Green Is My Mountain. Inter-Varsity.
Klaeser, Barbara M. see Klaeser, Barbara Macknick.

Klaeser, Barbara Macknick.
xKlaeser, Barbara M.

Reading Improvement: A Complete Course for
Increasing Speed and Comprehension.
Nelson-Hall.

Klaf, A. Albert.
xKlaf, A. Albert.
Arithmetic Refresher for Practical Men. Dover.

Klafs, Carl E.
xKlafs, Carl E.
The Female Athlete: A Coach's Guide to
Conditioning & Training. Mosby.

Klagsbrun, Francine.
xKlagsbrun, Francine.
Read About the Sanitation Man. Watts.
Story of Moses. Watts.

Klah, Hasteen.
xKlah, Hasteen.
Navajo Creation Myth: The Story of
Emergence. AMS Pr.

Klaiber, Jeffrey L.
xKlaiber, Jeffrey L.
Religion & Revolution in Peru, 1824-1976. U
of Notre Dame Pr.

Klainer, Albert S.
xKlainer, Albert S.
Agents of Bacterial Disease. Har-Row.

Klainer, Jo-Ann.
xKlainer, Jo-Ann.
The Judas Gene. Marek.

Klaits, Barrie.
xKlaits, Barrie.
When You Find a Rock: A Field Guide.
Macmillan.
Klambauer, G. see Klambauer, Gabriel.
Klambauer, G. see Klambauer, Gabriel.

Klambauer, Gabriel.
xKlambauer.
Problems & Propositions in Analysis. Dekker.
xKlambauer, G.
Real Analysis. Elsevier.

Klamkin, Charles.
xKlamkin, Charles.
Railroadiana: The Collectors Guide to Railroad
Memorabilia. T Y Crowell.

Klamkin, Marian.
xKlamkin, Marian.
The Carnival Glass Collector's Price Guide.
Dutton.
The Collector's Guide to Carnival Glass.
Dutton.
Marine Antiques. Dodd.

Klammer, Enno.
xKlammer, Enno.
Paragraph Sense: A Basic Rhetoric. HarBraceJ.

Klang, Daniel M.
xKlang, Daniel M.
Tax Reform in Eighteenth-Century Lombardy.
East Eur Quarterly.

Klann, Margaret L.
xKlann, Margaret L.
Target Archery. A-W.
Klapp, Orrin E. see Klapp, Orrin Edgar.

Klapp, Orrin Edgar, 1915-
xKlapp, Orrin E.
Currents of Unrest: An Introduction to
Collective Behavior. Irvington.
Symbolic Leaders: Public Dramas & Public
Men. Irvington.
Klapper, C. F. see Klapper, Charles Frederick.
Klapper, Charles F. see Klapper, Charles Frederick.

Klapper, Charles Frederick.
xKlapper, C. F.
London's Lost Railways. Routledge & Kegan.
xKlapper, Charles F.
Golden Age of Buses. Routledge & Kegan.

Klapper, Gilbert.
xKlapper, Gilbert.

Silurian-Lower Devonian Conodont Sequence
in the Roberts Mountains Formation of
Central Nevada. U of Cal Pr.

Klapper, Joseph T.
xKlapper, Joseph T.
Effects of Mass Communication. Free Pr.

Klapper, Marvin.
xKlapper, Marvin.
Textile Glossary. Fairchild.

Klappert, Peter.
xKlappert, Peter.
Lugging Vegetables to Nantucket. Yale U Pr.
Klare, George R. see Klare, George Roger.

Klare, George Roger, 1922-
xKlare, George R.
Measurement of Readability. Iowa St U Pr.

Klare, Hugh J.
xKlare, Hugh J.
Anatomy of Prison. Greenwood.

Klarman, Herbert E.
xKlarman, Herbert E.
Economics of Health. Columbia U Pr.

Klasek, Charles B.
xKlasek, Charles B.
Instructional Media in the Modern School.
Prof Educ Pubn.

Klasne, William, 1933-
xKlasne, William.
Street Cops. P-H.

Klasner, Lily.
xKlasner, Lily.
My Girlhood Among Outlaws. U of Ariz Pr.

Klass, Donald W.
xKlass, Donald W.
ed. Current Practice of Clinical
Electroencephalography. Raven.

Klass, Michael W.
xKlass, Michael W.
Regulation & Entry: Energy, Communications,
& Banking. Mich St U Busn.

Klass, Morton.
xKlass, Morton.
Caste: The Emergence of the South Asian
Social System. Inst Study Human.
From Field to Factory: Community Structure
& Industrialization in West Bengal. Inst
Study Human.
Klass, Philip. see Klass, Philip J.

Klass, Philip J.
xKlass, Philip.
UFO's Explained. Random.
xKlass, Philip J.
UFO's Identified. Random.
Klassen, Peter J. see Klassen, Peter James.

Klassen, Peter James.
xKlassen, Peter J.
Europe in the Reformation. P-H.

Klatt, Lawrence A.
xKlatt, Lawrence A.
Human Resources Management: A Behavioral
Systems Approach. Irwin.

Klatzky, Roberta L.
xKlatzky, Roberta L.
Human Memory: Structures & Processes. W H
Freeman.

Klauder, Francis J.
xKlauder, Francis J.
Aspects of the Thought of Teilhard De
Chardin. Chris Mass.
Klaurens, M. K. see Klaurens, Mary K.
Klaurens, Mary. see Klaurens, Mary K.

Klaurens, Mary K.
xKlaurens, M. K.
Economics of Marketing. McGraw.
xKlaurens, Mary.
The Economics of Marketing. McGraw.

Klaus, Billie J.
xKlaus, Billie J.

Protocols Handbook for Nurse Practitioners.
Wiley.
Klausmeier, Herbert J. *see* Klausmeier, Herbert John.
Klausmeier, Herbert John.
  xKlausmeier, Herbert J.
    Cognitive Development of Children & Youth:
    A Longitudinal Study. Acad Pr.
    Individually Guided Education in Elementary
    & Middle Schools: A Handbook for
    Implementors & College Instructors. A-W.
Klausner, Joseph, 1874-1958
  xKlausner, Joseph.
    A History of Modern Hebrew Literature,
    1785-1930. Greenwood.
Klawiter, Randolph J.
  xKlawiter, Randolph J.
    Stefan Zweig: A Bibliography. U of NC Pr.
Klayer, Connie.
  xKlayer, Connie.
    Circus Time!: How to Put On Your Own
    Show. Lothrop.
Klebba, A. Joan.
  xKlebba, Joan.
    Comparability of Mortality Statistics for the
    Seventh & Eighth Revisions of the
    International Classification of Diseases: U.S..
    Natl Ctr Health Stats.
Klebba, Joan. *see* Klebba, A. Joan.
Kleberger, Ilse.
  xKleberger, Ilse.
    Grandmother Oma. Atheneum.
Klee, Paul.
  xKlee, Paul.
    The Diaries of Paul Klee, 1898-1918. U of Cal
    Pr.
    Paul Klee. Abrams.
Kleeberg, Gordon S. *see* Kleeberg, Gordon Saul Philip.
Kleeberg, Gordon Saul Philip, 1883-
  xKleeberg, Gordon S.
    Formation of the Republican Party As a
    National Political Organization. D Franklin
Kleeberg, Irene C. *see* Kleeberg, Irene Cumming.
Kleeberg, Irene Cumming.
  xKleeberg, Irene C.
    ed. The Butterick Fabric Handbook: A
    Consumer's Guide to Fabrics for Clothing &
    Home Furnishings. Butterick Pub.
    The Butterick Home Decorating Handbook: A
    Consumer's Guide to Selecting, Purchasing &
    Caring for Home Furnishings. Butterick Pub.
    Going to Camp. Watts.
Kleeman, Elayne J.
  xKleeman, Elayne J.
    How to Turn a Passion for Food into Profit.
    Rawson Wade.
Kleemeier, Robert W. *see* Kleemeier, Robert Watson.
Kleemeier, Robert Watson, 1915-
  xKleemeier, Robert W.
    Aging & Leisure. Arno.
Kleene, S. C. *see* Kleene, Stephen Cole.
Kleene, Stephen. *see* Kleene, Stephen Cole.
Kleene, Stephen Cole, 1909-
  xKleene, S. C.
    Introduction to Metamathematics. Elsevier.
  xKleene, Stephen.
    Mathematical Logic. Wiley.
Klees, Fredric.
  xKlees, Fredric.
    Pennsylvania Dutch. Macmillan.
Klehr, Harvey.
  xKlehr, Harvey E.
    Communist Cadre: The Social Background of
    the American Communist Party Elite.
    Hoover Inst Pr.
Klehr, Harvey E. *see* Klehr, Harvey.
Kleijnen, J. P. *see* Kleijnen, Jacobus Petrus Catharinus.
Kleijnen, Jacobus Petrus Catharinus.
  xKleijnen, J. P.

Statistical Techniques in Simulation. Dekker.
Kleiler, Frank M., 1914-
  xKleiler, Frank M.
    Can We Afford Early Retirement?. Johns
    Hopkins.
Klein, Aaron E.
  xKlein, Aaron E.
    Mind Trips: The Story of
    Consciousness-Raising Movements.
    Doubleday.
    Science & the Supernatural: A Scientific
    Overview of the Occult. Doubleday.
Klein, Alan F.
  xKlein, Alan F.
    Effective Groupwork: An Introduction to
    Principle & Method. Follett.
    The Professional Child-Care Worker: A Guide
    to Skills, Knowledge, Techniques &
    Attitudes. Follett.
Klein, Burton H.
  xKlein, Burton H.
    Dynamic Economics. Harvard U Pr.
Klein, Camille, 1882-
  xKlein, Camille.
    Professional Cook: His Training, Duties, &
    Rewards. Helios.
Klein, Carole.
  xKlein, Carole.
    Aline. Har-Row.
    How It Feels to Be a Child. Har-Row.
Klein, Charlotte.
  xKlein, Charlotte.
    Anti-Judaism in Christian Theology. Fortress.
Klein, D. C. *see* Klein, Donald C.
Klein, D. F. *see* Klein, Donald F.
Klein, Dave.
  xKlein, Dave.
    The Game of Their Lives. Random.
    The Game of Their Lives. NAL
    Great Infielders of the Major Leagues.
    Random.
    On the Way up: What It's Like in the Minor
    Leagues. Messner.
    Stars of the Major Leagues. Random.
Klein, David, 1880-
  xKlein, David.
    The Living Shakespeare. Cyrco Pr.
    Living Shakespeare. Irvington.
    More for Your Money: A Young Person's
    Guide to Earning, Saving & Spending.
    Penguin.
Klein, Dennis A.
  xKlein, Dennis A.
    Peter Shaffer. Twayne.
Klein, Donald. *see* Klein, Donald F.
Klein, Donald C.
  xKlein, D. C.
    Community Dynamics & Mental Health.
    Wiley.
  xKlein, Donald J.
    Developing Human Services in New
    Communities. Human Sci Pr.
Klein, Donald F.
  xKlein, D. F.
    ed. Progress in Psychiatric Drug Treatment.
    Brunner-Mazel.
  xKlein, Donald.
    ed. Psychology of the Planned Community:
    The New Town Experience. Human Sci Pr.
  xKlein, Donald F.
    Diagnosis & Drug Treatment of Psychiatric
    Disorders: Adults & Children. Williams &
    Wilkins.
Klein, Donald J. *see* Klein, Donald C.
Klein, Ernest.
  xKlein, Ernest.

Comprehensive Etymological Dictionary of the
    English Language. Elsevier.
Klein, Ernst E., 1916-1979
  xKlein, Ernst E.
    My Dialogue with Death. Judson.
Klein, Fannie J.
  xKlein, Fannie J.
    The Administration of Justice in the Courts: A
    Selected Annotated Bibliography. Oceana.
Klein, G. *see* Klein, Gerrit.
Klein, Georg, 1925-
  xKlein, George.
    ed. Viral Oncology. Raven.
Klein, George. *see* Klein, Georg.
  xKlein, George S.
Klein, George S. *see* Klein, George Stuart.
Klein, George Stuart, 1917-
    Perception, Motives & Personality. Phila Bk
    Co.
    Psychoanalytic Theory: An Exploration of
    Essentials. Intl Univs Pr.
Klein, Gerda (Weissmann), 1924-
  xKlein, Gerda W.
    All But My Life. Hill & Wang.
Klein, Gerda W. *see* Klein, Gerda (Weissmann).
Klein, Gerrit.
  xKlein, G.
    Precision Electronics. Springer-Verlag.
Klein, H. Arthur.
  xKlein, H. Arthur.
    Surf-Riding. Lippincott.
Klein, Henry, 1951-
  xKlein, Henry.
    Through Ferrengi Eyes: The Diary of a Peace
    Corps Volunteer in Ethiopia, 1974-1976.
    Exposition.
Klein, Herbert S.
  xKlein, Herbert S.
    Parties & Political Change in Bolivia
    1880-1952. Cambridge U Pr.
Klein, Herman. *see* Klein, Hermann.
Klein, Hermann, 1856-1934
  xKlein, Herman.
    Great Women-Singers of My Time. Arno.
    The Reign of Patti. Arno.
    The Reign of Patti. Da Capo.
    Unmusical New York: A Brief Criticism of
    Triumphs, Failures, & Abuses. Da Capo.
  xKlein, Hermann.
    Thirty Years of Musical Life in London. Da
    Capo.
Klein, Hilary D. *see* Klein, Hilary Dole.
Klein, Hilary Dole, 1945-
  xKlein, Hilary D.
    ed. Craft Digest. Follett.
Klein, Holger. *see* Klein, Holger Michael.
Klein, Holger Michael, 1938-
  xKlein, Holger.
    ed. The First World War in Fiction: A
    Collection of Critical Essays. B&N.
Klein, Howard. *see* Klein, Howard J.
Klein, Howard J., 1935-
  xKlein, Howard.
    Other People's Business: A Primer on
    Management Consultants. Van Nos Reinhold.
  xKlein, Howard J.
    Fad Money: How to Make Money from Fads,
    Crazes, & Trends. Watts.
Klein, I. *see* Klein, Isaac.
Klein, Irving. *see* Klein, Irving J.
Klein, Irving J.
  xKlein, Irving.
    Constitutional Law for Criminal Justice
    Professionals. Duxbury Pr.
Klein, Isaac.
  xKlein, I.

A Guide to Jewish Religious Practice. Ktav.
xKlein, Isaac.
   Responsa & Halakhic Studies. Ktav.
Klein, Jacob, 1899-
xKlein, Jacob.
   Commentary on Plato's Meno. U of NC Pr.
Klein, Jerome E.
xKlein, Jerome S.
   Great Shops of Europe. Natl Ret Merch.
Klein, Jerome S. *see* Klein, Jerome E.
Klein, Joel.
xKlein, Joel.
   Psychology Encounters Judaism. Philos Lib.
Klein, John F.
xKlein, John F.
   Check-Forgers. Lexington Bks.
Klein, John J., 1929-
xKlein, John J.
   Money & the Economy. HarBraceJ.
Klein, L. *see* Klein, Lewis.
Klein, Lawrence R. *see* Klein, Lawrence Robert.
Klein, Lawrence Robert.
xKlein, Lawrence R.
   ed. Econometric Model Performance:
   Comparative Simulation Studies of the U. S.
   Economy. U of Pa Pr.
   ed. An Introduction to Econometric
   Forecasting & Forecasting Models. Lexington
   Bks.
   An Introduction to Econometrics. Greenwood.
Klein, Leonore.
xKlein, Leonore.
   Only One Ant. Hastings.
Klein, Lewis.
xKlein, L.
   Dispersion Relations & the Abstract Approach
   to Field Theory. Gordon.
Klein, M. Frances.
xKlein, M. Francis.
   About Learning Materials. Assn Supervision.
Klein, M. Francis. *see* Klein, M. Frances.
Klein, M. L. *see* Klein, Mike L.
Klein, Marcus.
xKlein, Marcus.
   After Alienation: American Novels in
   Mid-Century. U of Chicago Pr.
Klein, Margaret C.
xKlein, Margaret C.
   Tombstone Inscriptions of Orange County,
   Virginia. Genealog Pub.
Klein, Martin A.
xKlein, Martin A.
   ed. Peasants in Africa: Historical &
   Comparative Perspectives. Sage.
Klein, Marvin L.
xKlein, Marvin L.
   Talk in the Language Arts Classroom. NCTE.
Klein, Maury.
xKlein, Maury.
   Great Richmond Terminal: A Study of
   Businessmen & Business Strategy. U Pr of
   Va.
   History of the Louisville & Nashville Railroad.
   Macmillan.
Klein, Melanie.
xKlein, Melanie.
   Psychoanalysis of Children. Delacorte.
   The Psychoanalysis of Children. Dell.
Klein, Mike L.
xKlein, M. L.
   ed. Rare Gas Solids. Acad Pr.
Klein, Miles V., 1933-
xKlein, Miles V.
   Optics. Wiley.
Klein, Milton M. *see* Klein, Milton Martin.
Klein, Milton Martin, 1917-
xKlein, Milton M.

Politics of Diversity: Essays in the History of
   Colonial New York. Kennikat.
Klein, Mina C.
xKlein, Mina C.
   Hitler's Hang-Ups: An Adventure in Insight.
   Dutton.
Klein, Norma.
xKlein, Norma.
   Blue Trees, Red Sky. Pantheon.
   Coming to Life. NAL.
   Confessions of an Only Child. Dell.
   Confessions of an Only Child. Pantheon.
   Girls Can Be Anything. Dutton.
   Girls Turn Wives. S&S.
   Give Me One Good Reason. Avon.
   If I Had My Way. Pantheon.
   Taking Sides. Avon.
   Taking Sides. Pantheon.
   Tomboy. Archway.
   Tomboy. PB.
   Tomboy. Schol Bk Serv.
   Visiting Pamela. Dial.
Klein, Paul.
xKlein, Paul.
   Inside the TV Business. Sterling.
Klein, Philip, 1889-
xKlein, Philip.
   From Philanthropy to Social Welfare: An
   American Cultural Perspective. Jossey-Bass.
Klein, Philip A.
xKlein, Philip A.
   Business Cycles in the Postwar World: Some
   Reflections on Recent Research. Am
   Enterprise.
Klein, Philip S. *see* Klein, Philip Shriver.
Klein, Philip Shriver.
xKlein, Philip S.
   A History of Pennsylvania. Pa St U Pr.
   Pennsylvania Politics, 1817-1832: A Game
   Without Rules. Porcupine Pr.
   President James Buchanan: A Biography. Pa St
   U Pr.
Klein, Randolph S. *see* Klein, Randolph Shipley.
Klein, Randolph Shipley.
xKlein, Randolph S.
   Portrait of an Early American Family: The
   Shippens of Pennsylvania Across Five
   Generations. U of Pa Pr.
Klein, Richard G.
xKlein, Richard G.
   Ice-Age Hunters of the Ukraine. U of Chicago
   Pr.
Klein, Richard M.
xKlein, Richard M.
   The Green World: An Introduction to Plants &
   People. Har-Row.
Klein, Robert, 1918-1967
xKlein, Robert.
   Form and Meaning: Essays on the Renaissance
   & Modern Art. Viking Pr.
Klein, Robert A.
xKlein, Robert A.
   Sovereign Equality among States: The History
   of an Idea. U of Toronto Pr.
Klein, Stuart M.
xKlein, Stuart M.
   Understanding Organizational Behavior. Kent
   Pub Co.
   Workers Under Stress: The Impact of Work
   Pressure on Group Cohesion. U Pr of Ky.
Kleinau, Marion. *see* Kleinau, Marion L.
Kleinau, Marion L.
xKleinau, Marion.
   Theatres for Literature. Alfred Pub.
Kleinbaum. *see* Kleinbaum, David G.
Kleinbaum, David G.
xKleinbaum.

Applied Regression Analysis & Other
   Multivariable Methods. Duxbury Pr.
Kleinberg, Harry.
xKleinberg, Harry.
   How You Can Learn to Live with Computers.
   Lippincott.
   How You Can Learn to Live with Computers.
   Penguin.
Kleinberg, Seymour, 1933-
xKleinberg, Seymour.
   ed. The Other Persuasion: An Anthology of
   Short Fiction About Gay Men & Women.
   Random.
Kleinberger, A. F. *see* Kleinberger, Aharon Fritz.
Kleinberger, Aharon Fritz, 1920-
xKleinberger, A. F.
   Society, Schools & Progress in Israel.
   Pergamon.
Kleiner, Fred S.
xKleiner, Fred S.
   Greek & Roman Coins in the Athenian Agora.
   Am Sch Athens.
Kleinfeld, Judith.
xKleinfeld, Judith.
   Village High Schools: Some Educational
   Strategies to Help Meet Developmental
   Needs of Rural Youth. U Alaska Inst Res.
xKleinfeld, Judith S.
   Eskimo School on the Andreafsky: A Study of
   Effective Bicultural Education. Praeger.
Kleinfeld, Judith S. *see* Kleinfeld, Judith.
Kleinke, C. *see* Kleinke, Chris L.
Kleinke, Chris L.
xKleinke, C.
   First Impressions: The Psychology of
   Encountering Others. P-H.
Kleinmuntz, Benjamin.
xKleinmuntz, Benjamin.
   Essentials of Abnormal Psychology. Har-Row.
   Personality Measurement: An Introduction.
   Krieger.
Kleinpoppen, H. *see* Kleinpoppen, Hans.
Kleinpoppen, Hans.
xKleinpoppen, H.
   ed. Coherence & Correlation in Atomic
   Collisions. Plenum Pub.
Kleist, Heinrich. *see* Kleist, Heinrich Von.
Kleist, Heinrich Von, 1777-1811
xKleist, Heinrich.
   Broken Jug. Ungar.
   Marquise of O-& Other Stories.. Ungar.
xKleist, Heinrich von.
   The Marquise of O & Other Stories. Penguin.
Klejment, Anne.
xKlejment, Anne.
   The Berrigans: A Bibliography of Published
   Works by Daniel, Philip, & Elizabeth
   Berrigan. Garland Pub.
Klem, Kaye W. *see* Klem, Kaye Wilson.
Klem, Kaye Wilson.
xKlem, Kaye W.
   Defiant Desire. Fawcett.
Klema, Ernest D.
xKlema, Ernest D.
   Public Regulation of Site Selection for Nuclear
   Power Plants: Present Procedures & Reform
   Proposals, an Annotated Bibliography. Johns
   Hopkins.
Klement, Frank L.
xKlement, Frank L.
   The Copperheads in the Middle West. Peter
   Smith.
Klemer, D. J.
xKlemer, D. J.
   ed. Chinese Love Poems. Doubleday.
Klemer, Richard H.
xKlemer, Richard H.

ed. Counseling in Marital & Sexual Problems:
A Physician's Handbook. Krieger.
Teaching About Family Relationships. Burgess.
Klemke, E. D., 1926-
xKlemke, E. D.
Reflections & Perspectives: Essays in
Philosophy. Mouton.
Klemm, W. R. *see* Klemm, William Robert.
Klemm, William Robert, 1934-
xKlemm, W. R.
Animal Electroencephalography. Acad Pr.
Applied Electronics for Veterinary Medicine &
Animal Physiology. C C Thomas.
Klemp, Egon.
xKlemp, Egon.
Compiled by America in Maps Dating from
1500 to 1856. Holmes & Meier.
Klenck, Robert H., 1921-
xKlenck, Robert H.
Words Fitly Spoken: Reflections & Prayers.
Dembner Bks.
Klenk, Robert W.
xKlenk, Robert W.
Practice of Social Work. Wadsworth Pub.
Kleper, Michael L.
xKleper, Michael L.
How to Build a Basic Typesetting System.
Graph Arts Res RIT.
How to Build a Basic Typesetting System.
Graphic Dimensions.
Klepko, V.
xKlepko, V.
A Practical Handbook on Stress in Russian.
Dover.
Kleppner, Daniel.
xKleppner, Daniel.
An Introduction to Mechanics. McGraw.
Kleppner, Otto, 1899-
xKleppner, Otto.
Advertising Procedure. P-H.
ed. Exploring Advertising. P-H.
Kleppner, Paul.
xKleppner, Paul.
The Third Electoral System, 1853-1892:
Parties, Voters, & Political Cultures. U of NC
Pr.
Klerer, M. *see* Klerer, Melvin.
Klerer, Melvin.
xKlerer, M.
Digital Computer User's Handbook. McGraw.
Kletter, G., 1942-
xKletter, G.
The Extra-Intracranial Bypass Operation for
Prevention & Treatment of Stroke.
Springer-Verlag.
Kletzing, Henry F.
xKletzing, Henry F.
Progress of a Race: Or the Remarkable
Advancement of the Afro-American from the
Bondage of Slavery, Ignorance & Poverty to
the Freedom of Citizenship, Intelligence
Affluence, Honor & Trust. Negro U Pr.
Kleven, Arthur.
xKleven, Arthur.
Memoirs of a Smoking Jacket. Assoc Bk.
Klibanoff, Susan.
xKlibanoff, Susan.
Let's Talk About Adoption. Little.
Klibbe, Lawrence H. *see* Klibbe, Lawrence Hadfield.
Klibbe, Lawrence Hadfield, 1923-
xKlibbe, Lawrence H.
Fernan Caballero. Twayne.
Klieman, Aaron S.
xKlieman, Aaron S.
Soviet Russia & the Middle East. Johns
Hopkins.
Kliever, Lonnie. *see* Kliever, Lonnie D.
Kliever, Lonnie D.
xKliever, Lonnie.

H. Richard Niebuhr. Word Bks.
Kliewer, Evelyn.
xKliewer, Evelyn.
Freedom from Fat. Revell.
Please, God, Help Me Get Well in Your Spare
Time. Bethany Fell.
Kliewer, Warren, 1931-
xKliewer, Warren.
Liturgies, Games, Farewells. Golden Quill.
Moralities & Miracles. Golden Quill.
Kliger, Samuel.
xKliger, Samuel.
The Goths in England: A Study in Seventeenth
& Eighteenth Century Thought. Octagon.
Kligerman, Jack, 1938-
xKligerman, Jack.
A Fancy for Pigeons. Dutton.
Klika, Thom.
xKlika, Thom.
Rainbows. St Martin.
Klima, Edward. *see* Klima, Edward S.
Klima, Edward S.
xKlima, Edward.
The Signs of Language. Harvard U Pr.
Klima, George J.
xKlima, George J.
Multi-Media & Human Perception. New
Meridian Pr.
Kliman, Ann S.
xKliman, Ann S.
Intro. by Crisis: Psychological First Aid for
Recovery & Growth. HR&W.
Kliman, Bernard.
xKliman, Bernard.
What You Should Know About Medical Lab
Tests. T Y Crowell.
Kliman, Gilbert.
xKliman, Gilbert.
Psychological Emergencies of Childhood.
Grune.
Klimley, April.
xKlimley, April.
Here Is Your Career: Banking, Money &
Finance. Putnam.
Klimowicz, Barbara.
xKlimowicz, Barbara.
When Shoes Eat Socks. Abingdon.
Klimsch, Karl, 1812-1890
xKlimsch, Karl.
Florid Victorian Ornament. Dover.
Klimt, Gustav, 1862-1918
xKlimt, Gustav.
One Hundred Drawings. Dover.
Kline, Draza.
xKline, Draza.
Foster Care of Children: Nurture & Treatment.
Columbia U Pr.
Kline, F. Gerald.
xKline, F. Gerald.
ed. Current Perspectives in Mass
Communication Research. Sage.
Kline, George L. *see* Kline, George Louis.
Kline, George Louis, 1921-
xKline, George L.
Religious & Anti-Religious Thought in Russia.
U of Chicago Pr.
Kline, Lloyd W.
xKline, Lloyd W.
Education & the Personal Quest. Merrill.
Kline, Meredith G.
xKline, Meredith G.
The Structure of Biblical Authority. Eerdmans.
Kline, Milton V.
xKline, Milton V.

Obesity: Etiology, Treatment, & Management.
C C Thomas.
Kline, Morris, 1908-
xKline, Morris.
Calculus: An Intuitive & Physical Approach.
Wiley.
Electromagnetic Theory & Geometrical Optics.
Krieger.
Mathematical Thought from Ancient to
Modern Times. Oxford U Pr.
Mathematics: A Cultural Approach. A-W.
Intro. by Mathematics: An Introduction to Its
Spirit & Use: Readings from Scientific
American. W H Freeman.
Mathematics for Liberal Arts. A-W.
Mathematics in Western Culture. Oxford U Pr.
Mathematics in Western Culture. Oxford U Pr.
Kline, Nathan. *see* Kline, Nathan S.
Kline, Nathan S.
xKline, Nathan.
From Sad to Glad: Kline on Depression.
Ballantine.
xKline, Nathan S.
ed. Factors in Depression. Raven.
Kline, Raymond M., 1929-
xKline, Raymond M.
Digital Computer Design. P-H.
Kline, Thomas J. *see* Kline, Thomas Jefferson.
Kline, Thomas Jefferson, 1942-
xKline, Thomas J.
Andre Malraux & the Metamorphosis of
Death. Columbia U Pr.
Klineberg, Otto.
xKlineberg, Otto.
At a Foreign University: An International
Study of Adaptation & Coping. Praeger.
Negro Intelligence & Selective Migration.
Greenwood.
Race Differences. Greenwood.
Race Differences. Norwood Edns.
Students, Values, & Politics: A Cross-Cultural
Comparison. Free Pr.
Klinefelter, Walter, 1899-
xKlinefelter, Walter.
Lewis Evans & His Maps. Am Philos.
Kling, Blair B.
xKling, Blair B.
ed. The Age of Partnership: Europeans in Asia
Before Dominion. U Pr of Hawaii.
Partner in Empire: Dwarkanath Tagore & the
Age of Enterprise in Eastern India. U of Cal
Pr.
Kling, Samuel G., 1910-
xKling, Samuel G.
The Complete Guide to Everyday Law. BJ Pub
Group.
Klingaman, David C.
xKlingaman, David C.
Colonial Virginia's Coastwise & Grain Trade.
Arno.
Klingberg, Frank J. *see* Klingberg, Frank Joseph.
Klingberg, Frank Joseph, 1883-
xKlingberg, Frank J.
Anglican Humanitarianism in Colonial New
York. Arno.
Anti-Slavery Movement in England: A Study
in English Humanitarianism. Shoe String.
An Appraisal of the Negro in Colonial South
Carolina: A Study in Americanization.
Porcupine Pr.
Klingberg, Frank W. *see* Klingberg, Frank Wysor.
Klingberg, Frank Wysor.
xKlingberg, Frank W.
The Southern Claims Commission. Octagon.
Klinge, Gunther.
xKlinge, Gunther.
Drifting with the Moon. C E Tuttle.
Klingele, William E., 1944-
xKlingele, William E.

Teaching in Middle Schools. Allyn.
Klingenberg. see Klingenberg, Wilhelm.
Klingenberg, W. see Klingenberg, Wilhelm.
Klingenberg, Wilhelm, 1924-
xKlingenberg.
Lectures on Closed Geodesics. Springer-Verlag.
xKlingenberg, W.
A Course in Differential Geometry.
Springer-Verlag.
Klingender, F. D. see Klingender, Francis Donald.
Klingender, Francis D. see Klingender, Francis Donald.
Klingender, Francis Donald.
xKlingender, F. D.
Money Behind the Screen. Arno.
xKlingender, Francis D.
Animals in Art & Thought to the End of the
Middle Ages. MIT Pr.
Art & the Industrial Revolution. Kelley.
Klingener, David.
xKlingener, David.
Laboratory Anatomy of the Mink. Wm C
Brown.
Klinger, Eric, 1933-
xKlinger, Eric.
Meaning & Void: Inner Experience & the
Incentives in People's Lives. U of Minn Pr.
Klinger, Georgette.
xKlinger, Georgette.
Georgette Klinger's Skincare. Morrow.
Klinghoffer, Arthur J. see Klinghoffer, Arthur Jay.
Klinghoffer, Arthur Jay, 1941-
xKlinghoffer, Arthur J.
Soviet Perspectives on African Socialism.
Fairleigh Dickinson.
The Soviet Union & International Oil Politics.
Columbia U Pr.
Klingman, Peter D., 1945-
xKlingman, Peter D.
Josiah Walls: Florida's Black Congressman of
Reconstruction. U Presses Fla.
Klingner, Donald. see Klingner, Donald E.
Klingner, Donald E.
xKlingner, Donald.
Public Personnel Management: Contexts &
Strategies. P-H.
xKlingner, Donald E.
The Job-Seeker's Guide: A Workbook for
Improving Your Career Situation. Human Sci
Pr.
Klink, William.
xKlink, William.
Maxwell Anderson & S. N. Behrman: A
Reference Guide. G K Hall.
xKlink, William R.
S.N. Behrman: The Major Plays. Humanities.
Klink, William R. see Klink, William.

Klinkowitz, Jerome.

xKlinkowitz, Jerome.

Donald Barthelme: A Comprehensive
Bibliography & an Annotated Secondary
Checklist. Shoe String.

The Life of Fiction. U of Ill Pr.
Literary Disruptions: The Making of a
Post-Contemporary American Fiction. U of
Ill Pr.

Klinzing, Dennis. see Klinzing, Dennis R.

Klinzing, Dennis R.

xKlinzing, Dennis.
The Hospitalized Child: Communication
Techniques for Health Personnel. P-H.

Kliot, Jules.
xKliot, Jules.

ed. Tatting: Designs from Victorian Lace Craft.
Lacis Pubns.
Klir, George J.
xKlir, J.
Synthesis of Switching Circuits. Gordon.
Klir, J. see Klir, George J.
Klise, Eugene S. see Klise, Eugene Storm.
Klise, Eugene Storm, 1908-
xKlise, Eugene S.
Money & Banking. SW Pub.
Klise, Thomas S.
xKlise, Thomas S.
The Last Western. Argus Comm.
Klobuchar, Jim.
xKlobuchar, Jim.
Tarkenton. Har-Row.
Klock, Frank.
xKlock, Frank.
Apes & Husbands. Borden.
Klockars, Carl B.
xKlockars, Carl B.
The Professional Fence. Free Pr.
Klocker, Harry R.
xKlocker, Harry R.
ed. Thomism & Modern Thought. Irvington.
Kloe, Donald R.
xKloe, Donald R.
Understanding the Spanish Subjunctive. Moore
Pub Co.
Kloefkorn, William.
xKloefkorn, William.
Ludi Jr.. Pentagram.
Uncertain the Final Run to Winter. Windflower
Pr.
Kloman, Erasmus H.
xKloman, Erasmus H.
ed. Cases in Accountability: The Work of the
Gao. Westview.
Klonoski, James R. see Klonoski, James Richard.
Klonoski, James Richard.
xKlonoski, James R.
ed. The Politics of Local Justice. Little.
Klooster, Fred H.
xKlooster, Fred H.
Quests for the Historical Jesus. Baker Bk.
Klopf, Donald W. see Klopf, Donald William.
Klopf, Donald William.
xKlopf, Donald W.
Academic Debate: Practicing Argumentative
Theory. Morton Pub.
Klopfer, Peter H.
xKlopfer, Peter H.
An Introduction to Animal Behavior:
Ethology's First Century. P-H.
Klopman, Gilles, 1933-
xKlopman, Gilles.
ed. Chemical Reactivity & Reaction Paths.
Wiley.
Kloppenburg, Bonaventura, 1919-
xKloppenburg, Bonaventure.
Pastoral Practice & the Paranormal. Franciscan
Herald.
Kloppenburg, Bonaventure. see Kloppenburg,
Bonaventura.
Klopper, A. I. see Klopper, Arnold.
Klopper, Arnold.
xKlopper, A. I.
ed. Placental Proteins. Springer-Verlag.
xKlopper, Arnold.
ed. Plasma Hormone Assays in Evaluation of
Fetal Wellbeing. Churchill.
Klose, Kevin.
xKlose, Kevin.
The Typhoon Shipments. Norton.
Kloss. see Kloss, Robert Marsh.
Kloss, Hans.
xKloss, Hans.
Application of Structural Steel Design. Ungar.
Kloss, Heinz.
xKloss, Heinz.

The American Bilingual Tradition. Newbury
Hse.
Kloss, Jethro.
xKloss, Jethro.
Back to Eden Cookbook. Woodbridge Pr.
Kloss, Robert Marsh.
xKloss.
Sociology-with a Human Face: Sociology As If
People Mattered. Mosby.
Klots, Alexander B. see Klots, Alexander Barrett.
Klots, Alexander Barrett, 1903-
xKlots, Alexander B.
A Field Guide to the Butterflies of North
America, East of the Great Plains. HM.
Klotsche, E. H. see Klotsche, Ernest Heinrich.
Klotsche, Ernest Heinrich.
xKlotsche, E. H.
History of Christian Doctrine. Baker Bk.
Klotter, John C.
xKlotter, John C.
Criminal Evidence for Police. Anderson Pub
Co.
Criminal Justice Instructional Techniques. C C
Thomas.
Klotz, Hans, 1900-
xKlotz, Hans.
Organ Handbook. Concordia.
Klotz, Irving M. see Klotz, Irving Myron.
Klotz, Irving Myron, 1916-
xKlotz, Irving M.
Energy Changes in Biochemical Reactions.
Acad Pr.
Klotz, John W. see Klotz, John William.
Klotz, John William.
xKlotz, John W.
Genes, Genesis & Evolution. Concordia.
Klotz, Leo J. see Klotz, Leo Joseph.
Klotz, Leo Joseph, 1895-
xKlotz, Leo J.
Color Handbook of Citrus Diseases. Ag Sci
Pubns.
Klotz, Marvin.
xKlotz, Marvin.
ed. The Experience of Fiction. St Martin.
Klotz, Suzanne.
xKlotz, Suzanne.
Everything's the Same. Illuminati.
Klubertanz, George P. see Klubertanz, George Peter.
Klubertanz, George Peter.
xKlubertanz, George P.
Being & God: Introduction to the Philosophy
of Being & to Natural Theology. Irvington.
Kluckhohn, Florence. see Kluckhohn, Florence
(Rockwood).
Kluckhohn, Florence (Rockwood).
xKluckhohn, Florence.
Variations in Value Orientations. Greenwood.
Klug, Ron.
xKlug, Ron.
Lord I've Been Thinking: Prayer Thoughts for
High School Boys. Augsburg.
Kluge, Arnold G.
xKluge, Arnold G.
Chordate Structure & Function. Macmillan.
Kluge, Eike-Henner W.
xKluge, Eike-Henner W.
The Practice of Death. Yale U Pr.
Kluge, M. see Kluge, Manfred.
Kluge, Manfred.
xKluge, M.
Crassulacean Acid Metabolism: Analysis of an
Ecological Adaptation. Springer-Verlag.
Kluger, Marilyn.
xKluger, Marilyn.
Preserving Summer's Bounty. M Evans.
Kluger, Richard.
xKluger, Richard.

Simple Justice: The History of Brown v. Board
of Education & Black America's Struggle for
Equality. Knopf.
Simple Justice: The History of Brown V. Board
of Education & Black America's Struggle for
Equality. Random.
Star Witness. Doubleday.
Klugh, Henry E. see Klugh, Henry Elicker.
Klugh, Henry Elicker.
xKlugh, Henry E.
Statistics: The Essentials for Research. Wiley.
Kluver, Heinrich, 1897-
xKluver, Heinrich.
An Experimental Study of the Eidetic Type.
Arno.
Klyver, F. H. see Klyver, Faye Huntington.
Klyver, Faye Huntington, 1893-
xKlyver, F. H.
Supervision of Student-Teachers in Religious
Education. AMS Pr.
Kmit, Ann.
xKmit, Ann.
Ukrainian Embroidery. Van Nos Reinhold.
Kmoch, Hans.
xKmoch, Hans.
Pawn Power in Chess. McKay.
Knab, Linda Z.
xKnab, Linda Z.
The Day Is Waiting. Viking Pr.
Knaggs, John R., 1934-
xKnaggs, John R.
The Bugles Are Silent: A Novel of the Texas
Revolution. Shoal Creek Pub.
Knap, Jerome. see Knap, Jerome J.
Knap, Jerome J.
xKnap, Jerome.
The Digest Book of Hunting Dogs. Follett.
Getting Hooked on Fishing: An Angler's
Handbook. Scribner.
Knaplund, Paul, 1885-
xKnaplund, Paul.
Britain: Commonwealth & Empire, 1901-1955.
Greenwood.
Knapman, C. E. see Knapman, C. E. H.
Knapman, C. E. H.
xKnapman, C. E.
ed. Developments in Chromatography.
Burgess-Intl Ideas.
Knapp, B. J. see Knapp, Brian J.
Knapp, Bettina. see Knapp, Bettina Liebowitz.
Knapp, Bettina L. see Knapp, Bettina Liebowitz.
Knapp, Bettina Liebowitz, 1926-
xKnapp, Bettina.
French Novelists Speak Out. Whitston Pub.
xKnapp, Bettina L.
Anais Nin. Ungar.
Georges Duhamel. Twayne.
Maurice Maeterlinck. Twayne.
The Prometheus Syndrome. Whitston Pub.
Knapp, Brian J.
xKnapp, B. J.
Elements of Geographical Hydrology. Allen
Unwin.
Soil Processes. Allen Unwin.
Knapp, Clyde. see Knapp, Clyde Guy.
Knapp, Clyde Guy.
xKnapp, Clyde.
Teaching Physical Education in Secondary
Schools: A Textbook on Instructional
Methods. McGraw.
Knapp, Daniel R.
xKnapp, Daniel R.
Handbook of Analytical Derivatization
Reactions. Wiley.
Knapp, James F.
xKnapp, James F.
Ezra Pound. Twayne.
Knapp, Joseph G. see Knapp, Joseph Grant.
Knapp, Joseph Grant, 1900-
xKnapp, Joseph G.

Edwin G. Nourse-Economist for the People.
Interstate.
Knapp, Justina, Sister, 1863-
xKnapp, Justina.
Christian Symbols & How to Use Them. Gale.
Knapp, Mark L.
xKnapp, Mark L.
Essentials of Nonverbal Communication.
HR&W.
Nonverbal Communication in Human
Interaction. HR&W.
Knapp, Mary.
xKnapp, Mary.
One Potato, Two Potato: The Secret Education
of American Children. Norton.
Knapp, P. see Knapp, Peggy Ann.
Knapp, Peggy Ann.
xKnapp, P.
The Style of John Wyclif's English Sermons.
Mouton.
Knapp, Ron.
xKnapp, Ron.
Tutankhamun & the Mysteries of Ancient
Egypt. Messner.
Knapp, Wilfrid.
xKnapp, Wilfrid F.
History of War & Peace, 1939-1965. Oxford U
Pr.
Knapp, Wilfrid F. see Knapp, Wilfrid.
Knappen, Marshall M. see Knappen, Marshall Mason.
Knappen, Marshall Mason, 1901-
xKnappen, Marshall M.
Constitutional & Legal History of England.
Shoe String.
Knappert, Jan.
xKnappert, Jan.
tr. & ed. An Anthology of Swahili Love
Poetry. U of Cal Pr.
Bantu Myths & Other Tales. Humanities.
Knapton, Ernest J. see Knapton, Ernest John.
Knapton, Ernest John.
xKnapton, Ernest J.
Revolutionary & Imperial France: 1750-1815.
Scribner.
Knapton, James.
xKnapton, James.
Teaching a Literature-Centered English
Program. Phila Bk Co.
Knaupp, Jonathan.
xKnaupp, Jonathan.
Patterns & Systems of Elementary
Mathematics. HM.
Knaus, William. see Knaus, William J.
Knaus, William J.
xKnaus, William.
Do It Now: How to Stop Procrastinating. P-H.
Knauth, Percy.
xKnauth, Percy.
The North Woods. Time-Life.
The North Woods. Silver.
Wind on My Wings. TAB Bks.
Kneass, Jack.
xKneass, Jack.
How to Buy Recreational Vehicles. Trail-R.
Knebel, Fletcher.
xKnebel, Fletcher.
Dark Horse. PB.
Dave Sulkin Cares!. Doubleday.
Knecht, Charles D.
xKnecht, Charles D.
Fundamental Techniques in Veterinary Surgery.
Saunders.
Knecht, Kenneth.
xKnecht, Kenneth.
Designing & Maintaining the CATV & Small
TV Studio. TAB Bks.
Knee, Stuart E.
xKnee, Stuart E.

The Concept of Zionist Dissent in the
American Mind 1917-1941. Speller.
Kneeland, George J. see Kneeland, George Jackson.
Kneeland, George Jackson.
xKneeland, George J.
Commercialized Prostitution in New York
City. Patterson Smith.
Kneer, Marian E.
xKneer, Marian E.
Softball: Slow & Fast Pitch. Wm C Brown.
Kneer, Warren G.
xKneer, Warren G.
Great Britain & the Caribbean: 1901-1913: a
Study in Anglo-American Relations. Mich St
U Pr.
Kneese, Allen V.
xKneese, Allen V.
Economics & the Environment. Penguin.
Kneider, A. P. see Kneider, Albert P.
Kneider, Albert P., 1937-
xKneider, A. P.
Mathematics of Merchandising. P-H.
xKneider, Albert P.
Mathematics of Merchandising. P-H.
Kneiling, John G.
xKneiling, John G.
Integral Train Systems. Kalmbach.
Kneisl, Carol R. see Kneisl, Carol Ren.
Kneisl, Carol Ren.
xKneisl, Carol R.
Current Perspectives in Psychiatric Nursing:
Issues & Trends. Mosby.
Kneller, George F.
xKneller, George F.
Educational Anthropology: An Introduction.
Krieger.
Educational Anthropology: An Introduction.
Wiley.
Kneller, George F. see Kneller, George Frederick.
Kneller, George Frederick.
xKneller, George F.
The Education of the Mexican Nation.
Octagon.
Existentialism & Education. Wiley.
ed. Foundations of Education. Wiley.
Knepper, William E.
xKnepper, William E.
Liability of Corporate Officers & Directors. A
Smith Co.
Ohio Eminent Domain Practice. A Smith Co.
Knerr, Michael E.
xKnerr, Michael E.
Heavy Weather. Belmont-Tower.
Knetsch, Jack L. see Knetsch, Jack Louis.
Knetsch, Jack Louis, 1933-
xKnetsch, Jack L.
ed. Outdoor Recreation and Water Resources
Planning. Am Geophysical.
Knewstubb, P. F. see Knewstubb, Peter Francis.
Knewstubb, Peter Francis.
xKnewstubb, P. F.
Mass Spectrometry & Ion-Molecule Reactions.
Cambridge U Pr.
Knezevich, Stephen. see Knezevich, Stephen J.
Knezevich, Stephen J.
xKnezevich, Stephen.
Administration of Public Education. Har-Row.
Knickerbocker, William. see Knickerbocker, William
Skinkle.
Knickerbocker, William S. see Knickerbocker, William
Skinkle.
Knickerbocker, William Skinkle, 1892-
xKnickerbocker, William.
ed. Twentieth Century English. Arno.
xKnickerbocker, William S.
Creative Oxford, Its Influence in Victorian
Literature. Folcroft.
Knickmeyer, Steve, 1944-
xKnickmeyer, Steve.

Cranmer. Random.
Straight. Random.

Knies, Earl A.
xKnies, Earl A.
The Art of Charlotte Bronte. Ohio U Pr.

Kniffen, Fred B. see Kniffen, Fred Bowerman.

Kniffen, Fred Bowerman, 1900-
xKniffen, Fred B.
Louisiana: Its Land & People. La State U Pr.

Knight. see Knight, Sarah Kemble.

Knight, Alanna.
xKnight, Alanna.
The White Rose. Nordon Pubns.

Knight, Arthur.
xKnight, Arthur.
The Liveliest Art: A Panoramic History of the
Movies. Macmillan.

Knight, Bernard.
xKnight, Bernard.
Legal Aspects of Medical Practice. Churchill.

Knight, Bruce W. see Knight, Bruce Winton.

Knight, Bruce Winton.
xKnight, Bruce W.
How to Run a War. Arno.

Knight, C. A. see Knight, Claude Arthur.

Knight, Cecil B.
xKnight, Cecil B.
Pentecostal Worship. Pathway Pr.

Knight, Charles W.
xKnight, Charles W.
Secrets of Green Thumb Gardening. Fell.

Knight, Claude Arthur, 1914-
xKnight, C. A.
Chemistry of Viruses. Springer-Verlag.

Knight, Damon. see Knight, Damon Francis.

Knight, Damon Francis, 1922-
xKnight, Damon.
ed. One Hundred Years of Science Fiction.
S&S.
ed. Perchance to Dream. Manor Bks.
ed. Turning Points: Essays on the Art of
Science Fiction. Har-Row.
ed. Western Classics from the Great Pulps.
B&N.

Knight, David. see Knight, David C.

Knight, David B.
xKnight, David B.
A Capital for Canada: Conflict & Compromise
in the Nineteenth Century. U Chicago Dept
Geog.

Knight, David C.
xKnight, David.
Let's Find Out About Sound. Watts.
xKnight, David C.
Comets. Watts.
Dinosaur Days. McGraw.
Galaxies, Islands in Space. Morrow.
Let's Find Out About Earth. Watts.
Let's Find Out About Mars. Watts.
Let's Find Out About the Ocean. Watts.
Let's Find Out About Weather. Watts.
The Moons of Our Solar System. Morrow.
Those Mysterious UFO's: The Story of
Unidentified Flying Objects. Parents.

Knight, Douglas. see Knight, Douglas M.

Knight, Douglas M., 1921-
xKnight, Douglas.
Pope & the Heroic Tradition: A Critical Study
of His Iliad. Shoe String.

Knight, Edgar W. see Knight, Edgar Wallace.

Knight, Edgar Wallace, 1885-1953
xKnight, Edgar W.

Education in the United States. Greenwood.
The Influence of Reconstruction on Education
in the South. AMS Pr.
Influence of Reconstruction on Education in
the South. Arno.
Public School Education in North Carolina.
Negro U Pr.

Knight, Eric.
xKnight, Eric.
This Above All. Queens Hse.

Knight, Eric. see Knight, Eric Mowbray.

Knight, Eric Mowbray.
xKnight, Eric.
Lassie Come Home. Dell.
Lassie Come-Home. HR&W.
Lassie Come Home. Dell.

Knight, Everett. see Knight, Everett W.

Knight, Everett W.
xKnight, Everett.
A Theory of the Classical Novel. Routledge &
Kegan.

Knight, F. B. see Knight, Frederic Butterfield.

Knight, Frank H. see Knight, Frank Hyneman.

Knight, Frank Hyneman.
xKnight, Frank H.
The Economic Order & Religion. Greenwood.
On the History & Method of Economics:
Selected Essays. U of Chicago Pr.

Knight, Franklin W.
xKnight, Franklin W.
The African Dimension in Latin American
Societies. Macmillan.

Knight, Frederic Butterfield, 1891-1948
xKnight, F. B.
Qualities Related to Success in Teaching. AMS
Pr.

Knight, G. Wilson. see Knight, George Wilson.

Knight, George A. see Knight, George Angus Fulton.

Knight, George Angus Fulton, 1909-
xKnight, George A.
Theology As Narration: A Commentary of the
Book Exodus. Eerdmans.

Knight, George W.
xKnight, George W.
Compiled By Church Bulletin Bits. Baker Bk.

Knight, George W. see Knight, George Wilson.

Knight, George Wilson, 1897-
xKnight, G. Wilson.
Lord Byron's Marriage: The Evidence of
Asterisks. Routledge & Kegan.
xKnight, George W.
The Burning Oracle: Studies in the Poetry of
Action. AMS Pr.
Byron's Dramatic Prose. Folcroft.
Chariot of Wrath. Arden Lib.

Knight, Grant C. see Knight, Grant Cochran.

Knight, Grant Cochran, 1893-1956
xKnight, Grant C.
American Literature & Culture. Cooper Sq.
American Literature & Culture. R West.
Strenuous Age in American Literature. Cooper
Sq.

Knight, H. Gary. see Knight, Herbert Gary.

Knight, Hardwicke.
xKnight, Hardwicke.
ed. Dunedin Then. Intl Pubns Serv.

Knight, Henry, Sir, 1886-
xKnight, Henry.
Food Administration in India, 1939-47.
Stanford U Pr.

Knight, Herbert Gary.
xKnight, H. Gary.
ed. Ocean Thermal Energy Conversion: Legal,
Political & Institutional Aspects. Lexington
Bks.

Knight, Hilary.
xKnight, Hilary.
illus. Where's Wallace. Har-Row.

Knight, J. W. see Knight, James Wilfred.

Knight, Jacqueline E.
xKnight, Jacqueline E.
The Hunter's Game Cookbook. Winchester Pr.

Knight, James M.
xKnight, James M.
The Juvenile Courts Functions & Relevant
Theory. R & E Res Assoc.

Knight, James T. see Knight, James Thomson.

Knight, James Thomson, 1942-1970
xKnight, James T.
Commutative Algebra. Cambridge U Pr.

Knight, James Wilfred.
xKnight, J. W.
The Starch Industry. Pergamon.

Knight, Joseph, 1829-1907
xKnight, Joseph.
Life of Dante Gabriel Rossetti. Arno.
Life of Dante Gabriel Rossetti. Kennikat.
Theatrical Notes. Arno.

Knight, Kenneth.
xKnight, Kenneth.
Matrix Management. Petrocelli.
Organizations: An Information Systems
Perspective. Wadsworth Pub.

Knight, Kenneth. see Knight, Kenneth W.

Knight, Kenneth W.
xKnight, Kenneth.
Formulating Government Budgets: Aspects of
Australian & North American Experience. U
of Queensland Pr.

Knight, Max.
xKnight, Max.
Return to the Alps. Friends Earth.
xKnight, Maxwell E.
The German Executive, 1890-1933. Fertig.

Knight, Maxwell E. see Knight, Max.

Knight, Melvin M. see Knight, Melvin Moses.

Knight, Melvin Moses, 1887-
xKnight, Melvin M.
Americans in Santo Domingo. Arno.

Knight, Michael.
xKnight, Michael.
Adapted by In Chains to Louisiana: Solomon
Northup's Story. Dutton.

Knight, Oliver.
xKnight, Oliver.
Life & Manners in the Frontier Army. U of
Okla Pr.

Knight, Richard A. see Knight, Richard Alden.

Knight, Richard Alden.
xKnight, Richard A.
Boys' Book of Gun Handling. Putnam.

Knight, Robert E. see Knight, Robert Edward Lee.

Knight, Robert Edward Lee.
xKnight, Robert E.
Industrial Relations in the San Francisco Bay
Area, 1900-1918. U of Cal Pr.

Knight, Sarah. see Knight, Sarah Kemble.

Knight, Sarah K. see Knight, Sarah Kemble.

Knight, Sarah Kemble, 1666-1727
xKnight.
Journal of Madam Knight. Peter Smith.
xKnight, Sarah.
The Journal of Madam Knight. Scholarly.
xKnight, Sarah K.
The Journal of Madam Knight. Godine.

Knight, Thomas J., 1937-
xKnight, Thomas J.
Latin America Comes of Age. Scarecrow.

Knight, U. G. see Knight, Upton George.

Knight, Upton George.
xKnight, U. G.
Power Systems Engineering & Mathematics.
Pergamon.

Knight, William. see Knight, William Angus.

Knight, William A. see Knight, William Angus.

Knight, William Angus.
xKnight, William.

Hume. Kennikat.
Hume. R West.
xKnight, William A.
The English Lake District As Interpreted in
the Poems of Wordsworth. Folcroft.
Knightley, Phillip.
xKnightley, Phillip.
Lawrence of Arabia. Elsevier-Nelson.
Knights, L. C. *see* Knights, Lionel Charles.
Knights, Lionel C. *see* Knights, Lionel Charles.
Knights, Lionel Charles, 1906-
xKnights, L. C.
Explorations: Essays in Criticism Mainly on
the Literature of the Seventeenth Century.
Arden Lib.
Explorations: Essays in Criticism Mainly on
the Literature of the Seventeenth Century.
NYU Pr.
xKnights, Lionel C.
Explorations: Essays in Criticism, Mainly on
the Literature of the Seventeenth Century.
Greenwood.
Knights, Peter R.
xKnights, Peter R.
The Plain People of Boston, 1830-1860: A
Study in City Growth. Oxford U Pr.
Knill, J. L.
xKnill, J. L.
ed. Industrial Geology. Oxford U Pr.
Knipping, Mark. *see* Knipping, Mark H.
Knipping, Mark H.
xKnipping, Mark.
Finns in Wisconsin. State Hist Soc Wis.
Knirk, Frederick G.
xKnirk, Frederick G.
Designing Productive Learning Environments.
Educ Tech Pubns.
Kniseley, S. Philip.
xKniseley, S. Philip.
Masses of Francesco Soriano: A Style-Critical
Study. U Presses Fla.
Knister, Raymond
xKnister, Raymond.
ed. Canadian Short Stories. Arno.
Knobel, Edward.
xKnobel, Edward.
Identify Trees & Shrubs by Their Leaves: A
Guide to Trees & Shrubs Native to the
Northeast. Peter Smith.
Knoben, James E.
xKnoben, James E.
Handbook of Clinical Drug Data. Drug Intl
Pubns.
Knobler, Nathan.
xKnobler, Nathan.
The Visual Dialogue. HR&W.
Knobloch, Hilda.
xKnobloch, Hilda.
Developmental Questionnaire for Infants Forty
Weeks of Age: An Evaluation. Kraus Repr.
Knobloch, Irving W. *see* Knobloch, Irving William.
Knobloch, Irving William, 1907-
xKnobloch, Irving W.
A Check List of Crosses in the Gramineae.
Lubrecht & Cramer.
ed. Readings in Biological Science. Irvington.
Knoch, A. E. *see* Knoch, Adolf E.
Knoch, Adolf E.
xKnoch, A. E.
Concordant Commentary on the New
Testament. Concordant.
Knodel, John E.
xKnodel, John E.
Decline of Fertility in Germany, 1871-1939.
Princeton U Pr.
Knodt, Kenneth S., 1940-
xKnodt, Kenneth S.
ed. Pursuing the American Dream. P-H.
Knoefel, Peter K. *see* Knoefel, Peter Klerner.

Knoefel, Peter Klerner, 1906-
xKnoefel, Peter K.
Absorption, Distribution, Transformation &
Excretion of Drugs. C C Thomas.
Knoell, Dorothy. *see* Knoell, Dorothy M.
Knoell, Dorothy M.
xKnoell, Dorothy.
Planning Colleges for the Community.
Jossey-Bass.
Knoepfle, John.
xKnoepfle, John.
Songs for Gail Guidry's Guitar. SBD.
Knoepfle, Rudolph J.
xKnoepfle, Rudolph J.
ed. Practice, a Pool of Teaching Experience.
Loyola.
Knoepflmacher, U. C.
xKnoepflmacher, U. C.
ed. Nature & the Victorian Imagination. U of
Cal Pr.
Religious Humanism & the Victorian Novel:
George Eliot, Walter Pater, & Samuel Butler.
Princeton U Pr.
Knoeppel, C. E. *see* Knoeppel, Charles Edward.
Knoeppel, Charles Edward, 1881-1936
xKnoeppel, C. E.
Installing Efficiency Methods. Hive Pub..
Organization & Administration. Hive Pub.
Knofel, Dietbert.
xKnofel, Dietbert.
Corrosion of Building Materials. Van Nos
Reinhold.
Knoles, George H. *see* Knoles, George Harmon.
Knoles, George Harmon.
xKnoles, George H.
ed. Crisis of the Union, 1860-1861. La State U
Pr.
The Presidential Campaign & Election of 1892.
AMS Pr.
Knoles, Jere J. *see* Knoles, Jere M.
Knoles, Jere M.
xKnoles, Jere J.
Individual Retirement Accounts Handbook.
Inst Busn Plan.
Knoll, J. *see* Knoll, Jozsef.
Knoll, Jozsef.
xKnoll, J.
Theory of Active Reflexes: Analysis of Some
Fundamental Mechanisms of Higher Nervous
Activity. Hafner.
Knoll, Robert E.
xKnoll, Robert E.
Christopher Marlowe. Twayne.
Knollenberg, Bernhard, 1892-
xKnollenberg, Bernhard.
George Washington: The Virginia Period
1732-1775. Duke.
Growth of the American Revolution
1766-1775. Free Pr.
Knop, A. *see* Knop, Andre.
Knop, Andre.
xKnop, A.
Chemistry & Application of Phenolic Resins.
Springer-Verlag.
Knopf, Irwin J.
xKnopf, Irwin J.
Childhood Psychopathology: A Developmental
Approach. P-H.
Knopf, Mildred O., 1895-
xKnopf, Mildred O.
Cook, My Darling Daughter. Knopf.
Perfect Hostess Cook Book. Knopf.
Knopf, Olga, 1888-
xKnopf, Olga.
Successful Aging. G K Hall.
Knopf, S. Adolphus. *see* Knopf, Sigard Adolphus.
Knopf, Sigard Adolphus, 1857-1940
xKnopf, S. Adolphus.

Tuberculosis As a Disease of the Masses &
How to Combat It. Arno.
Knopfmacher. *see* Knopfmacher, John.
Knopfmacher, J. *see* Knopfmacher, John.
Knopfmacher, John.
xKnopfmacher.
Analytic Arithmetic of Algebraic Function
Fields. Dekker.
xKnopfmacher, J.
Abstract Analytic Number Theory. Elsevier.
Knopke, Harold J.
xKnopke, Harry J.
Approaches to Teaching in the Health
Sciences. A-W.
Knopke, Harry J. *see* Knopke, Harold J.
Knopoff, L. *see* Knopoff, Leon.
Knopoff, Leon.
xKnopoff, L.
ed. The Crust & Upper Mantle of the Pacific
Area. Am Geophysical.
Knorr, Klaus. *see* Knorr, Klaus Eugen.
Knorr, Klaus Eugen, 1911-
xKnorr, Klaus.
ed. Historical Dimensions of National Security
Problems. Regents Pr KS.
On the Uses of Military Power in the Nuclear
Age. Princeton U Pr.
Knorr, L. C. *see* Knorr, Louis Carl.
Knorr, Louis Carl, 1914-
xKnorr, L. C.
Citrus Diseases & Disorders: An Alphabetized
Compendium with Particular Reference to
Florida. U Presses Fla.
Knott, Margaret.
xKnott, Margaret.
Proprioceptive Neuromuscular Facilitation:
Patterns & Techniques. Har-Row.
Knott, Russell.
xKnott, Russell.
Reflections. Plymon Pr.
Knott, Widnell D. *see* Knott, Widnell Dimsdale.
Knott, Widnell Dimsdale, 1893-
xKnott, Widnell D.
The Influence of Tax-Leeway on Educational
Adaptability: A Study of the Relationship of
Residual or Potential Economic Ability,
Expressed As Tax-Leeway, to Educational
Adaptations in the State of New York. AMS
Pr.
Knotts, Howard.
xKnotts, Howard.
The Lost Christmas. HarBraceJ.
illus. The Lost Christmas. HarBraceJ.
Knotts, Ulysses S.
xKnotts, Ulysses S.
Management Science for Management
Decisions. Allyn.
Knowler, L. A. *see* Knowler, Lloyd A.
Knowler, Lloyd A.
xKnowler, L. A.
Quality Control by Statistical Methods.
McGraw.
Knowles, Asa S. *see* Knowles, Asa Smallidge.
Knowles, Asa Smallidge, 1909-
xKnowles, Asa S.
Handbook of Cooperative Education.
Jossey-Bass.
Knowles, D. *see* Knowles, David.
Knowles, David, 1896-
xKnowles, D.
Christian Monasticism. McGraw.
xKnowles, David.
Evolution of Medieval Thought. Random.
Medieval Religious Houses in England &
Wales. St. Martin.
Thomas Becket. Stanford U Pr.
Knowles, Edmond.
xKnowles, Edmond.

Dynamics of the Family Unit. E & E
  Enterprise.
Knowles, Helen. *see* Knowles, Helen K.
Knowles, Helen K.
  xKnowles, Helen.
  How to Succeed in Fund Raising Today.
    Wheelwright.
Knowles, Henry P.
  xKnowles, Henry P.
  Personality & Leadership Behavior. A-W.
Knowles, James H. *see* Knowles, James Hinton.
Knowles, James Hinton.
  xKnowles, James H.
  Folk-Tales of Kashmir. Arno.
Knowles, John, 1926-
  xKnowles, John.
  A Vein of Riches. Little.
Knowles, Leo.
  xKnowles, Leo.
  Candidates for Sainthood. Carillon Bks.
  Saints Who Spoke English. Carillon Bks.
Knowles, Lilian Charlotte Anne (Tomn), 1870-1926
  xKnowles, Lillian C.
  Industrial & Commercial Revolutions in Great
    Britain During the Nineteenth Century.
    Kelley.
Knowles, Lillian C. *see* Knowles, Lilian Charlotte Anne
  (Tomn).
Knowles, Malcolm S. *see* Knowles, Malcolm Shepherd.
Knowles, Malcolm Shepherd, 1913-
  xKnowles, Malcolm S.
  The Adult Learner: A Neglected Species. Gulf
    Pub.
Knowles, R.
  xKnowles, R.
  North America in Maps: Topographical Map
    Studies of Canada and the USA. Longman.
Knowles, Ralph L.
  xKnowles, Ralph L.
  Energy & Form: An Ecological Approach to
    Urban Growth. MIT Pr.
Knowles, Tillie M. *see* Knowles, Tillie M. S.
Knowles, Tillie M. S.
  xKnowles, Tillie M.
  Sue & Mindy Find a New Friend. Moore Pub
    Co.
Knowlson, T. Sharper. *see* Knowlson, Thomas Sharper.
Knowlson, Thomas S. *see* Knowlson, Thomas Sharper.
Knowlson, Thomas Sharper.
  xKnowlson, T. Sharper.
  The Origins of Popular Superstitions &
    Customs. Newcastle Pub.
  xKnowlson, Thomas S.
  Origins of Popular Superstitions & Customs.
    Gale.
Knowlton, Derrick.
  xKnowlton, Derrick.
  The Naturalist in Central Southern England:
    Hampshire, Berkshire, Wiltshire, Dorset &
    Somerset. David & Charles.
  The Naturalist in Scotland. David & Charles.
  Naturalist in the Hebrides. David & Charles.
Knowlton, Helen M. *see* Knowlton, Helen Mary.
Knowlton, Helen Mary, 1832-1918
  xKnowlton, Helen M.
  Art-Life of William Morris Hunt. Arno.
Knowlton, Mary A. *see* Knowlton, Mary Arthur.
Knowlton, Mary Arthur.
  xKnowlton, Mary A.
  The Influence of Richard Rolle & of Julian of
    Norwich on the Middle English Lyrics.
    Mouton.
Knox. *see* Knox, R. Bruce.
Knox, Albert.
  xKnox, Albert.
  Cloth. Watts.
Knox, Bill, 1928-
  xKnox, Bill.

Live Bait. Doubleday.
Knox, David, 1943-
  xKnox, David.
  Exploring Marriage & the Family. Scott F.
  xKnox, David R.
  Portrait of Aphasia. Wayne St U Pr.
Knox, David R. *see* Knox, David.
Knox, E. V. *see* Knox, Edmund George Valpy.
Knox, Edmund George Valpy, 1881-
  xKnox, E. V.
  The Mechanism of Satire. Folcroft.
Knox, Franklyn G., 1937-
  xKnox, Franklyn G.
  ed. Textbook of Renal Pathophysiology.
    Har-Row.
Knox, George.
  xKnox, George.
  Critical Moments: Kenneth Burke's Categories
    & Critiques. U of Wash Pr.
Knox, George A. *see* Knox, George Albert.
Knox, George Albert.
  xKnox, George A.
  Dos Passos & the Revolting Playwrights.
    Folcroft.
Knox, Maxine.
  xKnox, Maxine.
  Making the Most of the Monterey Peninsula &
    Big Sur. Presidio Pr.
Knox, Norman D. *see* Knox, Norman Davis.
Knox, Norman Davis.
  xKnox, Norman D.
  The Word Irony & Its Context: 1500-1755.
    Duke.
Knox, R. A. *see* Knox, Ronald Arbuthnott.
Knox, R. Bruce.
  xKnox.
  Pollen Allergy. Univ Park.
Knox, Richard.
  xKnox, Richard.
  Experiments in Astronomy for Amateurs. St
    Martin.
  xKnox, Richard A.
  Experiments in Astronomy for Amateurs. St
    Martin.
Knox, Richard A. *see* Knox, Richard.
Knox, Robert.
  xKnox, Robert.
  Ancient China. Watts.
  Great Artists & Great Anatomists: A
    Biographical & Philosophical Study. AMS Pr.
Knox, Robert S. *see* Knox, Robert Seiple.
Knox, Robert Seiple, 1931-
  xKnox, Robert S.
  Theory of Excitons. Acad Pr.
Knox, Ronald Arbuthnott, 1888-1957
  xKnox, R. A.
  On English Translation. Folcroft.
Knox, Vera H.
  xKnox, Vera H.
  ed. Public Finance Information Sources. Gale.
Knudsen, Estelle H. *see* Knudsen, Estelle Hagen.
Knudsen, Estelle Hagen.
  xKnudsen, Estelle H.
  Children's Art Education. Bennett Co.
Knudsen, James G. *see* Knudsen, James George.
Knudsen, James George.
  xKnudsen, James G.
  Fluid Dynamics & Heat Transfer. Krieger.
Knudsen, Jens W.
  xKnudsen, Jens W.
  Collecting & Preserving Plants & Animals.
    Har-Row.
Knudsen, Johannes, 1902-
  xKnudsen, Johannes.
  The Formation of the Lutheran Church in
    America. Fortress.
Knudson, Douglas M.
  xKnudson, Douglas M.

Outdoor Recreation. Macmillan.
Knudson, Harry R.
  xKnudson, Harry R.
  Organizational Behavior: A Management
    Approach. Winthrop.
Knudson, R. R. *see* Knudson, R. Rozanne.
Knudson, R. Rozanne, 1932-
  xKnudson, R. R.
  Rinehart Lifts. FS&G.
  Zanbanger. Dell.
  Zanbanger. Har-Row.
Knudson, Richard L.
  xKnudson, Richard L.
  Classic Sports Cars. Lerner Pubns.
  Land Speed Record-Breakers. Lerner Pubns.
Knudson, S. J.
  xKnudson, S. J.
  Culture in Retrospect: An Introduction to
    Archaeology. Rand.
Knuth, Donald E.
  xKnuth, Donald E.
  TEX & METAFONT: New Directions in
    Typesetting. Digital Pr.
Knuti, Leo L. *see* Knuti, Leo Leonard.
Knuti, Leo Leonard.
  xKnuti, Leo L.
  Profitable Soil Management. P-H.
Knutson, D. *see* Knutson, Donald.
Knutson, Donald.
  xKnutson, D.
  Algebraic Spaces. Springer-Verlag.
Knutson, Donald C.
  xKnutson, Donald C.
  ed. Homosexuality & the Law. Haworth Pr.
Ko, Won, 1925-
  xKo, Won.
  Buddhist Elements in Dada: A Comparison of
    Tristan Tzara, Takahashi Shinkichi & Their
    Fellow Poets. NYU Pr.
Kobald, Karl.
  xKobald, Karl.
  Franz Schubert & His Times. Kennikat.
Kobayashi, Albert S., 1924-
  xKobayashi, Albert S.
  ed. Experimental Techniques in Fracture
    Mechanics. Iowa St U Pr.
Kobayashi, Hisashi.
  xKobayashi, Hisashi.
  Modeling & Analysis: An Introduction to
    System Performance Evaluation
    Methodology. A-W.
Kobayashi, Shoshichi, 1932-
  xKobayashi, Shoshichi.
  Hyperbolic Manifolds & Holomorphic
    Mappings. Dekker.
Kobayashi, Teruo.
  xKobayashi, Teruo.
  Anglo-Norwegian Fisheries Case of 1951 & the
    Changing Law of the Territorial Sea. U
    Presses Fla.
Kobayashi, Tetsuya, 1926-
  xKobayashi, Tetsuya.
  Society, Schools & Progress in Japan.
    Pergamon.
Kobayashi, Tetsuya. *see* Kobayashi, Tetsuya.
Kobayashi, Toshiji.
  xKobayashi, Toshiji.
  ed. Clinical Ultrasound of the Breast. Plenum
    Pub.
Kobetz, Richard W.
  xKobetz, Richard W.
  Target Terrorism: Providing Protective
    Services. Intl Assn Chiefs Police.
Kobishchanov, Iurii Mikhailovich.
  xKobishchanov, Yuri M.
  Axum. Pa St U Pr.
Kobishchanov, Yuri M. *see* Kobishchanov, Iurii
  Mikhailovich.
Koblas, John J., 1942-
  xKoblas, John J.

F. Scott Fitzgerald in Minnesota: His Homes &
    Haunts. Minn Hist.
Kobler, Frank J., 1915-
    xKobler, Frank J.
        Casebook in Psychopathology. Alba.
Kobler, John.
    xKobler, John.
        Damned in Paradise: A Life of John
            Barrymore. Atheneum.
Koblik, Steven.
    xKoblik, Steven.
        tr. & ed. Sweden's Development from Poverty
            to Affluence, 1750-1970. U of Minn Pr.
Koblitz, H. *see* Koblitz, Neal.
Koblitz, Neal, 1948-
    xKoblitz, H.
        P-Adic Numbers, P-Adic Analysis &
            Zeta-Functions. Springer-Verlag.
Kobrak, Peter.
    xKobrak, Peter.
        Private Assumption of Public Responsibilities:
            The Role of American Business in Urban
            Manpower Programs. Irvington.
Kobre, Kenneth, 1946-
    xKobre, Kenneth.
        Photojournalism: The Professionals' Approach.
            Van Nos Reinhold.
Kobre, Sidney, 1907-
    xKobre, Sidney.
        The Development of the Colonial Newspaper.
            Peter Smith.
        Foundations of American Journalism.
            Greenwood.
        Press & Contemporary Affairs. Greenwood.
Kobrin, Frances E.
    xKobrin, Frances E.
        The Ethnic Factor in Family Structure &
            Mobility. Ballinger Pub.
Kobryn, A. P.
    xKobryn, A. P.
        Poseidon's Shadow. Dell.
        Poseidon's Shadow. Rawson Wade.
Kocan, Peter. *see* Kocan, Peter Raymond.
Kocan, Peter Raymond, 1947-
    xKocan, Peter.
        The Other Side of the Fence. U of Queensland
            Pr.
Kocanda, S. *see* Kocanda, Stanisaw.
Kocanda, Stanisaw.
    xKocanda, S.
        Fatigue Failure of Metals. Sijthoff &
            Noordhoff.
Koch, Adrienne, 1912-
    xKoch, Adrienne.
        Power, Morals & the Founding Fathers: Essays
            in the Interpretation of the American
            Enlightenment. Cornell U Pr.
Koch, Albert C. *see* Koch, Albrecht Karl.
Koch, Albrecht Karl.
    xKoch, Albert C.
        Journey Through a Part of the United States of
            North America in the Years 1844-1846. S Ill
            U Pr.
Koch, Carl.
    xKoch, Carl.
        Strategies for Teaching the Composition
            Process. NCTE.
Koch, Charlotte.
    xKoch, Charlotte.
        Florence Nightingale. Dandelion Pr.
Koch, Christopher, 1932-
    xKoch, Christopher.
        The Year of Living Dangerously. St Martin.
Koch, Donald.
    xKoch, Donald.
        Chilton's Complete Guide to Motorcycles &
            Motorcycling. Chilton.
Koch, E. *see* Koch, Erhard.
Koch, Erhard.
    xKoch, E.

ed. Non-Isothermal Reaction Analysis. Acad
    Pr.
Koch, Eric, 1919-
    xKoch, Eric.
        The Last Thing You'd Want to Know. Tundra
            Bks.
Koch, H. *see* Koch, H. William.
Koch, H. L. *see* Koch, Helen Lois.
Koch, H. W. *see* Koch, Hannsjoachim W.
Koch, H. William, 1925-
    xKoch, H.
        How to Multiply Top Executive Effectiveness.
            P-H.
Koch, Hannsjoachim W.
    xKoch, H. W.
        A History of Prussia. Longman.
Koch, Harry W. *see* Koch, Harry Walter.
Koch, Harry Walter, 1909-
    xKoch, Harry W.
        California Wills & Probate. Ken Bks.
        Probation & Parole Examinations. Ken-Bks.
        Social Welfare Examinations. Ken-Bks.
Koch, Helen L. *see* Koch, Helen Lois.
Koch, Helen Lois, 1895-
    xKoch, H. L.
        Relation of Certain Formal Attributes of
            Siblings to Attitudes Held Toward Each
            Other and Toward Their Parents. Kraus
            Repr.
    xKoch, Helen L.
        Twins & Twin Relations. U of Chicago Pr.
Koch, James V., 1942-
    xKoch, James V.
        Industrial Organization & Prices. P-H.
Koch, Jarosla. *see* Koch, Jaroslav.
Koch, Jaroslav, fl. 1959-
    xKoch, Jarosla.
        Total Baby Development. PB.
Koch, Jean E.
    xKoch, Jean E.
        Industrial Archeology: An Introductory
            Bibliography. Vance Biblios.
Koch, John, 1050-1954
    xKoch, John.
        The Chronology of Chaucer's Writings.
            Folcroft.
Koch, Kenneth, 1925-
    xKoch, Kenneth.
        A Change of Hearts: Plays, Films, & Other
            Dramatic Works, 1951-1971. Random.
        The Duplications. Random.
        I Never Told Anybody...: Teaching Poetry
            Writing in a Nursing Home. Random.
        I Never Told Anybody: Teaching Poetry
            Writing in a Nursing Home. Random.
Koch, Kurt E.
    xKoch, Kurt E.
        Demonology, Past & Present. Kregel.
        Devil's Alphabet. Kregel.
        Revival Fires in Canada. Kregel.
        Strife of Tongues. Kregel.
        World Without Chance. Kregel.
Koch, Margaret.
    xKoch, Margaret.
        The Walk Around Santa Cruz Book: A Look at
            the City's Architectural Treasures. Western
            Tanager.
Koch, R. C. *see* Koch, Robert C.
Koch, Raymond.
    xKoch, Raymond.
        Educational Commune: The Story of
            Commonwealth College. Schocken.
Koch, Robert, 1918-
    xKoch, Robert.
        Louis C. Tiffany's Art Glass. Crown.
Koch, Robert C, 1927-
    xKoch, R. C.
        Activation Analysis Handbook. Acad Pr.
Koch, Tankred, 1908-
    xKoch, Tankred.

Anatomy of the Chicken & Domestic Birds.
    Univ Microfilms.
Koch, Theodore W. *see* Koch, Theodore Wesley.
Koch, Theodore Wesley, 1871-1941
    xKoch, Theodore W.
        ed. Tales for Bibliophiles. Arno.
Kochan, Lionel.
    xKochan, Lionel.
        Acton on History. Kennikat.
        Acton on History. R West.
Kochan, Miriam.
    xKochan, Miriam.
        Catherine the Great. St Martin.
    xKochan, Miriam L.
        The Last Days of Imperial Russia: 1910-1917.
            Macmillan.
Kochan, Miriam L. *see* Kochan, Miriam.
Kochanek, Stanley A.
    xKochanek, Stanley A.
        Business & Politics in India. U of Cal Pr.
Kochen, Manfred.
    xKochen, Manfred.
        ed. Information for Action: From Knowledge
            to Wisdom. Acad Pr.
        ed. Information for the Community. ALA.
        Integrative Mechanisms in Literature Growth.
            Greenwood.
        Principles of Information Retrieval. Wiley.
Kochenburger, Ralph J.
    xKochenburger, Ralph J.
        Computers in Modern Society. Wiley.
Kochetkov, N. K. *see* Kochetkov, Nikolai
    Konstantinovich.
Kochetkov, Nikolai Konstantinovich.
    xKochetkov, N. K.
        ed. Organic Chemistry of Nucleic Acids.
            Plenum Pub.
        ed. Radiation Chemistry of Carbohydrates.
            Pergamon.
Kochevar, Deloise E., 1930
    xKochevar, Deloise E.
        Individualized Remedial Reading Techniques
            for the Classroom Teacher. P-H.
Kochhar, A. K.
    xKochhar, A. K.
        Development of Computer-Based Production
            Systems. Halsted Pr.
        Development of Computer-Based Production
            Systems. Wiley.
Kochi, Jay K.
    xKochi, Jay K.
        ed. Free Radicals. Wiley.
Kochiss, John. *see* Kochiss, John M.
Kochiss, John M.
    xKochiss, John.
        Oystering from New York to Boston. Mystic
            Seaport.
Kochman, Thomas.
    xKochman, Thomas E.
        ed. Rappin' & Stylin' Out: Communication in
            Urban Black America. U of Ill Pr.
Kochman, Thomas E. *see* Kochman, Thomas.
Kocinski, J. *see* Kocinski, Jerzy.
Kocinski, Jerzy.
    xKocinski, J.
        Critical Scattering Theory: An Introduction.
            Elsevier.
Kock, Winston E.
    xKock, Winston E.
        Engineering Applications of Lasers &
            Holography. Plenum Pub.
    xKock, Winton E.
        Radar, Sonar & Holography: An Introduction.
            Acad Pr.
Kock, Winton E. *see* Kock, Winston E.
Kockelmans, J. A. *see* Kockelmans, Joseph J.
Kockelmans, Joseph J., 1923-
    xKockelmans, J. A.

Martin Heidegger: A First Introduction to His
   Philosophy. Duquesne.
xKockelmans, Joseph J.
   ed. Interdisciplinarity & Higher Education. Pa
      St U Pr.
   ed. On Heidegger & Language. Northwestern
      U Pr.
Kocsis, Miklos.
   xKocsis, Miklos.
      High Speed Silicon Planar-Epitaxial Switching
         Diodes. Halsted Pr.
Koda-Kimble, Mary Anne.
   xKoda-Kimble, Mary Anne.
      ed. Applied Therapeutics for Clinical
         Pharmacists. Applied Therapeutics.
Kodak. *see* Eastman Kodak Company.
Kodak Limited. *see* Kodak Ltd.
Kodak Ltd.
   xKodak Limited.
      Price List of General Photographic Apparatus
         & Materials. Arno.
Kodell, Jerome.
   xKodell, Jerome.
      Responding to the Word: A Biblical
         Spirituality. Alba.
Kodera, Takashi J. *see* Kodera, Takashi James.
Kodera, Takashi James, 1945-
   xKodera, Takashi J.
      tr. Dogen's Formative Years in China:
         Historical Study & Annotated Translation of
         the Hokyo-ki. Great Eastern.
Kodjak, Andrej, 1926-
   xKodjak, Andrej.
      Alexander Solzhenitsyn. Twayne.
Koedt, Anne.
   xKoedt, Anne.
      ed. Radical Feminism. Times Bks.
Koegler, Horst.
   xKoegler, Horst.
      The Concise Oxford Dictionary of Ballet.
         Oxford U Pr.
Koehler, J. K. *see* Koehler, James K.
Koehler, James K.
   xKoehler, J. K.
      ed. Advanced Techniques in Biological
         Electron Microscopy. Springer-Verlag.
      Advanced Techniques in Biological Electron
         Microscopy 2. Springer-Verlag.
Koehler, Jerry W.
   xKoehler, Jerry W.
      Organizational Communication: Behavioral
         Perspectives. HR&W.
Koehler, Stanley.
   xKoehler, Stanley.
      The Fact of Fall: Poems. U of Mass Pr.
Koehler, W. R. *see* Koehler, Wilhelm Reinhold Walter.
Koehler, Wilhelm Reinhold Walter, 1884-1959
   xKoehler, W. R.
      ed. Medieval Studies in Memory of A.
         Kingsley Porter. Arno.
Koehler, William R.
   xKoehler, William R.
      The Wonderful World of Disney Animals.
         Howell Bk.
Koehn, Michael F.
   xKoehn, Michael F.
      Bankruptcy Risk in Financial Depository
         Intermediaries: Assessing Regulatory Effects.
         Lexington Bks.
Koehn, Peter. *see* Koehn, Peter H.
Koehn, Peter H.
   xKoehn, Peter.
      Afocha: A Link Between Community &
         Administration in Harar Ethiopia. Maxwell
         Schl Citizen.
Koelle, Sigismund W. *see* Koelle, Sigismund Wilhelm.
Koelle, Sigismund Wilhelm.
   xKoelle, Sigismund W.

African Native Literature: Or, Proverbs, Tales,
   Fables & Historical Fragments in the Kanuri
   or Bornu Language. Arno.
Koen, Ross Y.
   xKoen, Ross Y.
      China Lobby in American Politics. Har-Row.
      The China Lobby in American Politics.
         Octagon.
Koenig, Allen E.
   xKoenig, Allen E.
      ed. Broadcasting & Bargaining: Labor Relations
         in Radio & Television. U of Wis Pr.
      ed. Farther Vision: Educational Television
         Today. U of Wis Pr.
Koenig, Alma J. *see* Koenig, Alma Johanna.
Koenig, Alma Johanna, 1887?-1942
   xKoenig, Alma J.
      Gudrun. Lothrop.
Koenig, Gloria K.
   xKoenig, Gloria K.
      Patent Invalidity: A Statistical & Substantive
         Analysis. Boardman.
Koenig, John, 1938-
   xKoenig, John.
      Jews & Christians in Dialogue: New Testament
         Foundations. Westminster.
Koenig, Laird.
   xKoenig, Laird.
      The Neighbor. Avon.
Koenig, Louis W. *see* Koenig, Louis William.
Koenig, Louis William, 1916-
   xKoenig, Louis W.
      The Chief Executive. HarBraceJ.
      Toward a Democracy: A Brief Introduction to
         American Government. HarBraceJ.
Koenig, Samuel.
   xKoenig, Samuel.
      Sociology: An Introduction to the Science of
         Society. Har-Row.
Koenig, Thomas.
   xKoenig, Thomas R.
      ed. An Introduction to Ethics: A Philosophical
         Orientation. Mss Info.
Koenig, Thomas R. *see* Koenig, Thomas.
Koenigil, Mark.
   xKoenigil, Mark.
      Bachelor's Travel Log. Speller.
Koenigsberg, Richard A.
   xKoenigsberg, Richard A.
      Hitler's Ideology: A Study in Psychoanalytic
         Sociology. Lib Soc Sci.
      The Psychoanalysis of Racism, Revolution &
         Nationalism. Lib Soc Sci.
Koenigsberger, Dorothy.
   xKoenigsberger, Dorothy.
      Renaissance Man & Creative Thinking: A
         History of Concepts of Harmony 1400-1700.
         Humanities.
Koenker, Robert H.
   xKoenker, Robert H.
      Simplified Statistics for Students in Education
         & Psychology. Littlefield.
Koepke. *see* Koepke, John A.
Koepke, John A., 1929-
   xKoepke.
      Guide to Clinical Laboratory Diagnosis. ACC.
Koepp, D. W. *see* Koepp, Donald W.
Koepp, Donald W., 1929-
   xKoepp, D. W.
      Public Library Government: Seven Case
         Studies. U of Cal Pr.
Koeppe, Clarence E. *see* Koeppe, Clarence Eugene.
Koeppe, Clarence Eugene.
   xKoeppe, Clarence E.
      Weather & Climate. Krieger.
      Weather & Climate. McGraw.
Koerner, James. *see* Koerner, James D.
Koerner, James D.
   xKoerner, James.

Hoffer's America. Open Court.
Koerper, Philip J., 1907-
   xKoerper, Phillip J.
      How to Talk Your Way to Success in Selling.
         P-H.
Koerper, Phillip J. *see* Koerper, Philip J.
Koertge, Ronald.
   xKoertge, Ronald.
      The Boogeyman. Norton.
Koestenbaum, Peter, 1928-
   xKoestenbaum, Peter.
      Managing Anxiety. Celestial Arts.
Koestler, A. *see* Koestler, Arthur.
Koestler, Arthur, 1905-
   xKoestler, A.
      Darkness at Noon. Macmillan.
   xKoestler, Arthur.
      Arrow in the Blue. Macmillan.
      The Case of the Midwife Toad. Random.
      The Case of the Midwife Toad. Random.
      Darkness at Noon. Bantam.
      Janus: A Summing Up. Random.
Koetting, Michael.
   xKoetting, Michael.
      Nursing-Home Organization & Efficiency:
         Profit Versus Non Profit. Lexington Bks.
Kofas, Jon V.
   xKofas, Jon V.
      International & Domestic Politics in Greece
         During the Crimean War. East Eur
         Quarterly.
Kofele-Kale, Ndiva.
   xKofele-Kale, Ndiva.
      ed. An African Experiment in Nation Building:
         The Bilingual Cameroon Republic. Westview.
Koff, Richard. *see* Koff, Richard M.
Koff, Richard M.
   xKoff, Richard.
      Home Computers: A Manual of Possibilities.
         HarBraceJ.
   xKoff, Richard M.
      How Does It Work. NAL.
Koffka, Kurt, 1886-1941
   xKoffka, Kurt.
      Principles of Gestalt Psychology. HarBraceJ.
Koffman, Elliot B.
   xKoffman, Elliot B.
      Problem Solving & Structured Programming in
         BASIC.. A-W.
Kofmehl, Kenneth. *see* Kofmehl, Kenneth Theodore.
Kofmehl, Kenneth Theodore.
   xKofmehl, Kenneth.
      Professional Staffs of Congress. Purdue.
Kofoid, C. A. *see* Kofoid, Charles Atwood.
Kofoid, Charles Atwood, 1865-1947
   xKofoid, C. A.
      The Plankton of the Illinois River 1894-1899.
         Intl Schol Bk Serv.
      The Plankton of the Illinois River, 1894-99.
         Lubrecht & Cramer.
Kofsky, Frank.
   xKofsky, Frank.
      Lenny Bruce: The Comedian As Social Critic
         & Secular Moralist. Monad Pr.
Kofstad, Per.
   xKofstad, Per.
      Nonstoichiometry, Diffusion, & Electrical
         Conductivity in Binarymetal Oxides. Krieger.
Kogan, Benjamin A.
   xKogan, Benjamin A.
      Human Sexual Expression. HarBraceJ.
      Readings in Health Science. HarBraceJ.
Kogan, Josef.
   xKogan, Josef.
      Crane Design: Theory & Calculations of
         Reliability. Halsted Pr.
Kogan, Leonard S.
   xKogan, Leonard S.

Indicators of Child Health & Welfare:
Development of the DIPOV Index. Columbia
U Pr.
Kogan, M. *see* Kogan, Marcos.
Kogan, M. N. *see* Kogan, Mikhail Naumovich.
Kogan, Marcos.
xKogan, M.
ed. Sampling Methods in Soybean Entomology.
Springer-Verlag.
Kogan, Maurice.
xKogan, Maurice.
Educational Policy-Making: A Study of Interest
Groups & Parliament. Allen Unwin.
Educational Policy-Making: A Study of Interest
Groups & Parliament. Shoe String.
Kogan, Mikhail Naumovich.
xKogan, M. N.
Rarefied Gas Dynamics. Plenum Pub.
Kogbetliantz, E. G. *see* Kogbetliantz, Ervand George.
Kogbetliantz, Ervand George, 1888-
xKogbetliantz, E. G.
Handbook of First Complex Prime Numbers.
Gordon.
Kogos, Fred.
xKogos, Fred.
Instant Yiddish. Citadel Pr.
Kohak, Erazim. *see* Kohak, Erazim V.
Kohak, Erazim V.
xKohak, Erazim.
Idea & Experience: Edmund Husserl's Project
of Phenomenology in Ideas I. U of Chicago
Pr.
Kohanski, Alexander. *see* Kohanski, Alexander Sissel.
Kohanski, Alexander Sissel, 1902-
xKohanski, Alexander.
Analytical Interpretation of Martin Buber's 'I
& Thou'. Barron.
Kohavi, Zvi.
xKohavi, Zvi.
Switching & Finite Automata Theory.
McGraw.
Kohen-Raz, R. *see* Kohen-Raz, Reuven.
Kohen-Raz, Reuven.
xKohen-Raz, R.
Psychobiological Aspects of Cognitive Growth.
Acad Pr.
Kohl, Arthur L.
xKohl, Arthur L.
Gas Purification. Gulf Pub.
Kohl, Benjamin G.
xKohl, Benjamin G.
The Earthly Republic: Italian Humanists on
Government & Society. U of Pa Pr.
Kohl, Herbert. *see* Kohl, Herbert R.
Kohl, Herbert R.
xKohl, Herbert.
Golden Boy As Anthony Cool: A Photoessay
on Naming & Graffiti. Dial.
On Teaching. Schocken.
xKohl, Herbert R.
The Age of Complexity. Greenwood.
On Teaching. Bantam.
Kohl, Marguerite.
xKohl, Marguerite.
Jokes for Children. Hill & Wang.
Kohl, Marvin.
xKohl, Marvin.
ed. Infanticide & the Value of Life. Prometheus
Bks.
Kohl, Sam.
xKohl, Sam.
All Breed Dog Grooming Guide. Arco.
Kohl, Wilfrid L.
xKohl, Wilfrid L.
French Nuclear Diplomacy. Princeton U Pr.
Kohler, Carl. *see* Kohler, Karl.
Kohler, Eric L. *see* Kohler, Eric Louis.
Kohler, Eric Louis, 1892-
xKohler, Eric L.

Dictionary for Accountants. P-H.
Kohler, Foy D.
xKohler, Foy D.
Soviet Strategy for the Seventies: From Cold
War to Peaceful Coexistence. AISI.
The Soviet Union & the October 1973 Middle
East War: Implications for Detente. AISI.
ed. The Soviet Union: Yesterday, Today,
Tomorrow: A Colloquy of American
Long-Timers in Moscow. AISI.
Kohler, Heinz.
xKohler, Heinz.
Economics & Urban Problems. Heath.
Kohler, Julilly H. *see* Kohler, Julilly House.
Kohler, Julilly House.
xKohler, Julilly H.
Plants & Flowers to Decorate Your Home.
Western Pub.
Kohler, Karl.
xKohler, Carl.
History of Costume. Dover.
History of Costume. Peter Smith.
Kohler, Kaufmann.
xKohler, Kaufmann.
The Origins of the Synagogue & the Church.
Arno.
Kohler, Wolfgang.
xKohler, Wolfgang.
Dynamics in Psychology. Liveright.
The Place of Value in a World of Facts.
Liveright.
Task of Gestalt Psychology. Princeton U Pr.
Kohli, S. S. *see* Kohli, Surindar Singh.
Kohli, Suresh.
xKohli, Suresh.
ed. Corruption in India. Intl Pubns Serv.
Kohli, Surindar Singh, 1920-
xKohli, S. S.
A Critical Study of Adi Granth, Being a
Comprehensive & Scientific Study of Guru
Granth Sahib, the Scripture of the Sikhs.
Verry.
Kohlmann, Willie.
xKohlmann, Willie.
No Trains on Sunday: A Boyhood
Reminiscence. Taplinger.
Kohlmeier, Louis M., 1926-
xKohlmeier, Louis M.
The Regulators: Watchdog Agencies & the
Public Interest. Har-Row.
Kohlmeyer, Jan.
xKohlmeyer, Jan.
Marine Mycology: The Higher Fungi. Acad Pr.
Kohlrausch, Frederick. *see* Kohlrausch, Friedrich.
Kohlrausch, Friedrich, 1780-1865
xKohlrausch, Frederick.
A History of Germany: From the Earliest
Period to the Present Time. Scholarly.
xKohlrausch, Friedrich.
History of Germany: From the Earliest Period
to the Present Time. AMS Pr.
Kohlstedt, Sally G. *see* Kohlstedt, Sally Gregory.
Kohlstedt, Sally Gregory, 1943-
xKohlstedt, Sally G.
The Formation of the American Scientific
Community: The American Association for
the Advancement of Science, 1848-1860. U
of Ill Pr.
Kohn, August, 1868-1930
xKohn, August.
The Cotton Mills of South Carolina. Reprint.
Kohn, Barry.
xKohn, Barry.
Barry & Alice: Portrait of a Bisexual Marriage.
P-H.
Kohn, Bernice.
xKohn, Bernice.

Light. Dandelion Pr.
Look-It-up Book of Transportation. Random.
The Organic Living Book. Penguin.
The Organic Living Book. Viking Pr.
Raccoons. P-H.
Kohn, Connie.
xKohn, Connie.
An Animal Counting Book. Dandelion Pr.
Kohn, H. *see* Kohn, Hans.
Kohn, Hans, 1891-
xKohn, H.
Nationalism & Realism: 1852-1879. Peter
Smith.
Nationalism: Its Meaning & History. Peter
Smith.
xKohn, Hans.
The Age of Nationalism: The First Era of
Global History. Greenwood.
American Nationalism: An Interpretative
Essay. Greenwood.
History of Nationalism in the East. Scholarly.
Living in a World Revolution: My Encounters
with History. S&S.
Nationalism & Imperialism in the Hither East.
Fertig.
Nationalism & Liberty: The Swiss Example.
Greenwood.
Nationalism & Realism: 1852-1879. Krieger.
Nationalism: Its Meaning & History. Van Nos
Reinhold.
Not by Arms Alone: Essays on Our Time.
Arno.
Reflections on Modern History: The Historian
& Human Responsibility. Greenwood.
Kohn, Melvin L., 1928-
xKohn, Melvin L.
Class & Conformity: A Study in Values. U of
Chicago Pr.
Kohn, Mervin.
xKohn, Mervin.
Dynamic Managing: Principles, Process,
Practice. Benjamin-Cummings.
Kohn, Michael.
xKohn, Michael.
The Dandelion Book of Nursery Games.
Dandelion Pr.
Kohn, Richard H.
xKohn, Richard H.
Eagle & Sword: The Federalists & the Creation
of the Military Establishment in America,
1783-1802. Free Pr.
Kohn, Robert E.
xKohn, Robert E.
Air Pollution Control: A Welfare-Economic
Interpretation. Lexington Bks.
A Linear Programming Model for Air Pollution
Control. MIT Pr.
Kohn, Robert R. *see* Kohn, Robert Rothenberg.
Kohn, Robert Rothenberg, 1925-
xKohn, Robert R.
Principles of Mammalian Aging. P-H.
Kohn, Walter S. *see* Kohn, Walter S. G.
Kohn, Walter S. G.
xKohn, Walter S.
Governments & Politics of the
German-Speaking Countries. Nelson-Hall.
Women in National Legislatures: A
Comparative Study of Six Countries. Praeger.
Kohnke, Helmut, 1901-
xKohnke, Helmut.
Soil Physics. McGraw.
Kohnke, Mary.
xKohnke, Mary F.
The Case for Consultation in Nursing: Designs
for Professional Practice. Wiley.
Kohnke, Mary F. *see* Kohnke, Mary.
Kohnstamm, Max, 1914-
xKohnstamm, Max.

European Community & Its Role in the World.
U of Mo Pr.
Kohonen, T. *see* Kohonen, Teuvo.
Kohonen, Teuvo.
xKohonen, T.
Associative Memory: A System-Theoretical
Approach. Springer-Verlag.
Content-Addressable Memories.
Springer-Verlag.
xKohonen, Tuevo.
Digital Circuits & Devices. P-H.
Kohonen, Tuevo. *see* Kohonen, Teuvo.
Kohout, Frank J.
xKohout, Frank J.
Statistics for Social Scientists: A Coordinated
Learning System. Wiley.
Kohout, Karen.
xKohout, Karen.
Alaska Natives in Higher Education. U Alaska
Inst Res.
Alaska Natives in Higher Education. U of
Wash Pr.
Kohr, Leopold, 1909-
xKohr, Leopold.
The Breakdown of Nations. Dutton.
The Overdeveloped Nations: The Diseconomies
of Scale. Schocken.
Kohr, Louise H. *see* Kohr, Louise Hannah.
Kohr, Louise Hannah.
xKohr, Louise H.
Fragrance of Geraniums. Douglas-West.
Kohs, Ellis B., 1916-
xKohs, Ellis B.
Musical Composition: Projects in Ways &
Means. Scarecrow.
Koht, Halvdan, 1873-1965
xKoht, Halvdan.
American Spirit in Europe: A Survey of
Transatlantic Influences. Octagon.
Life of Ibsen. Arno.
Kohut, Heinz.
xKohut, Heinz.
The Restoration of the Self. Intl Univs Pr.
Kohut, Nester C.
xKohut, Nester C.
Divorce for the Unbroken Marriage. Am
Family.
Koile, Earl.
xKoile, Earl.
Listening As a Way of Becoming. Word Bks.
Koistinen, Paul A. *see* Koistinen, Paul A. C.
Koistinen, Paul A. C.
xKoistinen, Paul A.
The Hammer & the Sword. Arno.
xKoistinen, Paul A. C.
The Military-Industrial Complex: A Historical
Perspective. Praeger.
Kojecky, Roger.
xKojecky, Roger.
T. S. Eliot's Social Criticism. FS&G.
Koke, Richard J.
xKoke, Richard J.
Accomplice in Treason: Joshua Hett Smith &
the Arnold Conspiracy. U Pr of Va.
Kokkedee, J. J. *see* Kokkedee, J. J. J.
Kokkedee, J. J. J.
xKokkedee, J. J.
Quark Model. Benjamin-Cummings.
Kolaja, Jiri T. *see* Kolaja, Jiri Thomas.
Kolaja, Jiri Thomas, 1919-
xKolaja, Jiri T.
Social System & Time & Space: An
Introduction to the Theory of Recurrent
Behavior. Greenwood.
Kolakowski, Leszek.
xKolakowski, Leszek.

Husserl & the Search for Certitude. Yale U Pr.
Main Currents of Marxism: Its Rise, Growth &
Dissolution. Oxford U Pr.
Kolarz, Walter.
xKolarz, Walter.
Peoples of the Soviet Far East. Shoe String.
Kolasa, Blair J. *see* Kolasa, Blair John.
Kolasa, Blair John, 1926-
xKolasa, Blair J.
Responsibility in Business: Issues & Problems.
P-H.
Kolattukudy, P. E.
xKolattukudy, P. E.
ed. Chemistry & Biochemistry of Natural
Waxes. Elsevier.
Kolb, David A.
xKolb, David A.
Organizational Psychology: A Book of
Readings. P-H.
Kolb, Eugene J., 1917-
xKolb, Eugene J.
A Framework for Political Analysis. P-H.
Kolb, Glen L., 1914-
xKolb, Glen L.
Democracy & Dictatorship in Venezuela,
1945-1958. Shoe String.
Kolb, Harold H.
xKolb, Harold H.
A Field Guide to the Study of American
Literature. U Pr of Va.
Illusion of Life: American Realism As a
Literary Form. U Pr of Va.
Kolb, John.
xKolb, John.
Product Safety & Liability: A Desk Reference.
McGraw.
Kolb, Lawrence C. *see* Kolb, Lawrence Coleman.
Kolb, Lawrence Coleman, 1911-
xKolb, Lawrence C.
Modern Clinical Psychiatry. Saunders.
Kolb, Patricia A. *see* Kolb, Patricia Anne.
Kolb, Patricia Anne.
xKolb, Patricia A.
H.I.T.: A Manual for the Classification, Filing,
& Retrieval of Palmprints. C C Thomas.
Kolber, Alan. *see* Kolber, Alan R.
Kolber, Alan R.
xKolber, Alan.
Mechanism & Regulation of DNA Replication.
Plenum Pub.
Kolchin, Valentin F. *see* Kolchin, Valentin Fedorovich.
Kolchin, Valentin Fedorovich.
xKolchin, Valentin F.
Random Allocations. Halsted Pr.
Kolde, Endel. *see* Kolde, Endel Jakob.
Kolde, Endel Jakob, 1917-
xKolde, Endel.
The Pacific Quest: The Concept & Scope of an
Oceanic Community. Lexington Bks.
Koldovsky, P. *see* Koldovsky, Pavel.
Koldovsky, Pavel.
xKoldovsky, P.
Tumor Specific Transplantation Antigen.
Springer-Verlag.
Kolenda, Konstantin.
xKolenda, Konstantin.
Religion Without God. Prometheus Bks.
Kolers, P. A. *see* Kolers, Paul A.
Kolers, Paul A.
xKolers, P. A.
ed. Processing of Visible Language. Plenum
Pub.
xKolers, Paul A.
Aspects of Motion Perception. Pergamon.
Kolesnik, Walter B. *see* Kolesnik, Walter Bernard.
Kolesnik, Walter Bernard, 1923-
xKolesnik, Walter B.
Educational Psychology. McGraw.
Kolevzon, Edward R.
xKolevzon, Edward R.

The Afro-Asian World: A Cultural
Understanding. Allyn.
Kolin, Michael J.
xKolin, Michael J.
The Custom Bicycle: Buying, Setting Up &
Riding the Quality Bicycle. Rodale Pr Inc.
Kolin, Philip C.
xKolin, Philip C.
Professional Writing for Nurses in Education,
Practice & Research. Mosby.
Kolinski, Charles J.
xKolinski, Charles J.
Independence or Death: Story of the
Paraguayan War. U Presses Fla.
Koliopoulos, John S.
xKoliopoulos, John S.
Greece & the British Connection, 1935-1941.
Oxford U Pr.
Kolitz, Zvi, 1913-
xKolitz, Zvi.
Survival for What. Philos Lib.
Kolko, Gabriel.
xKolko, Gabriel.
Railroads & Regulation, 1877-1916.
Greenwood.
Railroads & Regulation, 1877-1916. Norton.
The Triumph of Conservatism: A
Reinterpretation of American History,
1900-1916. Free Pr.
Kolko, Joyce.
xKolko, Joyce.
America & the Crisis of World Capitalism.
Beacon Pr.
Kolkowicz, Roman.
xKolkowicz, Roman.
The Soviet Union & Arms Control: A
Superpower Dilemma. Johns Hopkins.
Kollaritsch, Felix P.
xKollaritsch, Felix P.
Analysis & Terminology of Financial Statement
Items for Highway-Heavy Contractors. Ohio
St U Admin Sci.
Operating & Financial Ratios of Ohio Highway
Contractors. Ohio St U Admin Sci.
Kollat, D. T. *see* Kollat, David T.
Kollat, David T.
xKollat, D. T.
Strategic Marketing. HR&W.
Kollbrunner, C. F. *see* Kollbrunner, Curt Friedrich.
Kollbrunner, Curt Friedrich.
xKollbrunner, C. F.
Torsion in Structures: An Engineering
Approach. Springer-Verlag.
Koller, John M.
xKoller, John M.
Oriental Philosophies. Scribner.
Koller, Marvin. *see* Koller, Marvin R.
Koller, Marvin R.
xKoller, Marvin.
Families: A Multigenerational Approach.
McGraw.
xKoller, Marvin R.
Sociology of Childhood. P-H.
Koller, Peo C. *see* Koller, Peo Charles.
Koller, Peo Charles.
xKoller, Peo C.
Chromosomes & Genes: The Biological Basis of
Heredity. Norton.
Kollmann, W. *see* Kollmann, Wolfgang.
Kollmann, Wolfgang, 1942-
xKollmann, W.
ed. Computational Fluid Dynamics.
Hemisphere Pub.
xKollmann, Wolfgang.

ed. Computational Fluid Dynamics.
Hemisphere Pub.
ed. Prediction Methods for Turbulent Flows.
Hemisphere Pub.
Kollontai, Aleksandra M. *see* Kollontai, Aleksandra
Mikhailovna.
Kollontai, Aleksandra Mikhailovna, 1872-1952
xKollontai, Aleksandra M.
Great Love. Arno.
Kolman, Bernard.
xKolman, Bernard.
Elementary Linear Programming with
Applications. Acad Pr.
Introductory Linear Algebra with Applications.
Macmillan.
Kolnai, Aurel.
xKolnai, Aurel.
Ethics, Value, & Reality: Selected Papers of
Aurel Kolnai. Hackett Pub.
Kolodin, Irving, 1908-
xKolodin, Irving.
Orchestral Music. Greenwood.
Kolodny, Annette, 1941-
xKolodny, Annette.
The Lay of the Land: Metaphor As Experience
& History in American Life & Letters. U of
NC Pr.
Kolodny, Ralph. *see* Kolodny, Ralph L.
Kolodny, Ralph L., 1923-
xKolodny, Ralph.
Peer-Oriented Group Work for the Physically
Handicapped Child. Charles River Bks.
Kolodny, Robert C.
xKolodny, Robert C.
Textbook of Sexual Medicine. Little.
Kolodziej, Edward A.
xKolodziej, Edward A.
French International Policy Under de Gaulle &
Pompidou: The Politics of Grandeur. Cornell
U Pr.
Uncommon Defense & Congress, 1945-1963.
Ohio St U Pr.
Kolosimo, P. *see* Kolosimo, Peter.
Kolosimo, Peter.
xKolosimo, P.
Not of This World. Univ Bks.
Kolpas, Norman.
xKolpas, Norman.
The Chocolate Lover's Companion. Music
Sales.
Kolsky, H.
xKolsky, H.
Stress Waves in Solids. Dover.
Kolson, Clifford J.
xKolson, Clifford J.
Clinical Aspects of Remedial Reading. C C
Thomas.
Kolstad, Arthur, 1896-
xKolstad, Arthur.
Study of Opinions of Some International
Problems As Related to Certain Experience
& Background Factors. AMS Pr.
Kolstad, C. Kenneth.
xKolstad, C. Kenneth.
Rapid Electrical Estimating & Pricing: A
Handy, Quick Method of Directly
Determining the Selling Prices of Electrical
Construction Work. McGraw.
Kolstad, P. *see* Kolstad, Per.
Kolstad, Per.
xKolstad, P.
Atlas of Colposcopy. Univ Park.
Kolstoe, Oliver P.
xKolstoe, Oliver P.

College Professoring: Or, Through Academia
with Gun & Camera. S Ill U Pr.
High School Work-Study Program for Mentally
Subnormal Students. S Ill U Pr.
Teaching Educable Mentally Retarded
Children. HR&W.
Kolthoff, Isaak M. *see* Kolthoff, Izaak Maurits.
Kolthoff, Izaak Maurits, 1894-
xKolthoff, Isaak M.
Quantitative Chemical Analysis. Macmillan.
Kolton, M. *see* Kolton, Marilyn.
Kolton, Marilyn.
xKolton, M.
Innovative Approaches to Youth Services.
Stash.
Kolve, V. A.
xKolve, V. A.
Play Called Corpus Christi. Stanford U Pr.
Kolyer, John.
xKolyer, John.
Drawings & Sculpture. Branden.
Neptune Taming a Seahorse. Branden.
Odin's Other Eye. Branden.
xKolyer, John M.
Ares & the Dove. Branden.
Kolyer, John M. *see* Kolyer, John.
Komaiko, Jean.
xKomaiko, Jean.
Around Lake Michigan. HM.
Doing the Dunes. Dunes.
Komar, Arthur J.
xKomar, Arthur J.
Music & Human Experience. Schirmer Bks.
Komar, John J., 1944-
xKomar, John J.
The Great Escape from Your Dead-End Job.
Follett.
The Interview Game: Winning Strategies for
the Job Seeker. Follett.
Komarovsky, Mirra, 1906-
xKomarovsky, Mirra.
Dilemmas of Masculinity: A Study of College
Youth. Norton.
ed. Sociology & Public Policy: The Case of
Presidential Commissions. Elsevier.
Unemployed Man & His Family. Octagon.
Komendant, August E.
xKomendant, August E.
Contemporary Concrete Structures. Krieger.
Komjathy, Anthony T. *see* Komjathy, Anthony Tihamer.
Komjathy, Anthony Tihamer.
xKomjathy, Anthony T.
German Minorities & the Third Reich: Ethnic
Germans of East Central Europe Between the
Wars. Holmes & Meier.
Komkov, V. *see* Komkov, Vadim.
Komkov, Vadim.
xKomkov, V.
Optimal Control Theory for the Damping of
Vibrations of Simple Elastic Systems.
Springer-Verlag.
Komlev, N. G. *see* Komlev, Nikolai Georgievich.
Komlev, Nikolai Georgievich.
xKomlev, N. G.
Components of the Content Structure of the
Word. Mouton.
Kommers, Donald P.
xKommers, Donald P.
ed. Human Rights & American Foreign Policy.
U of Notre Dame Pr.
Kommunisticheskaia Partiia. *see* Kommunisticheskaia
Partiia Sovetskogo Soiuza.
Kommunisticheskaia Partiia Sovetskogo Soiuza.
xKommunisticheskaia Partiia.
Program of the Communist Party of the Soviet
Union. Greenwood.
Komoda, Beverly.
xKomoda, Beverly.
illus. Simon's Soup. Parents.
Kompa, K. L. *see* Kompa, Karl L.

Kompa, Karl L.
xKompa, K. L.
Chemical Lasers. Springer-Verlag.
Kon, Abraham. *see* Kon, Abraham Israel.
Kon, Abraham Israel.
xKon, Abraham.
Prayer. Bloch.
Koncelik, Joseph A.
xKoncelik, Joseph A.
Designing the Open Nursing Home. DH&R.
Konczacki, Z. A. *see* Konczacki, Zbigniew A.
Konczacki, Zbigniew A.
xKonczacki, Z. A.
The Economics of Pastoralism: A Case Study
of Sub-Saharan Africa. Biblio Dist.
xKonczacki, Zbigniew A.
Public Finance & Economic Development of
Natal, 1893-1910. Duke.
Kone, Eugene H.
xKone, Eugene H.
ed. The Greatest Adventure: Basic Research
That Shapes Our Lives. Rockefeller.
Konecky, Edith.
xKonecky, Edith.
Allegra Maud Goldman. Dell.
Konecsni, Johnemery.
xKonecsni, Johnemery.
A Post-Kantian Anthropology. U Pr of Amer.
Konefsky, Samuel J. *see* Konefsky, Samuel Joseph.
Konefsky, Samuel Joseph, 1915-
xKonefsky, Samuel J.
Chief Justice Stone & the Supreme Court.
Hafner.
Koneman, Elmer. *see* Koneman, Elmer W.
Koneman, Elmer W., 1932-
xKoneman, Elmer.
Color Atlas & Textbook of Diagnostic
Microbiology. Lippincott.
xKoneman, Elmer W.
Practical Laboratory Mycology. Williams &
Wilkins.
Practical Laboratory Parasitology. Krieger.
Kong, B. *see* Kong, Bucksam.
Kong, Bucksam.
xKong, B.
Hung Gar Kung-Fu. Wehman.
Konig, David T. *see* Konig, David Thomas.
Konig, David Thomas, 1947-
xKonig, David T.
Law & Society in Puritan Massachusetts: Essex
County, 1629-1692. U of NC Pr.
Konig, E.
xKonig, E.
Ligand Field Energy Diagrams. Plenum Pub.
Magnetic Diagrams for Transition Metal Ions.
Plenum Pub.
Konig, Hans-Jost.
xKonig, Hans-Jost.
Geheime Mission. EMC.
Konig, Rene, 1906-
xKonig, Rene.
The Community. Schocken.
Konigsburg, E. L.
xKonigsburg, E. L.

About the B'nai Bagels. Atheneum.
illus. About the B'nai Bagels. Atheneum.
The Dragon in the Ghetto Caper. Atheneum.
Father's Arcane Daughter. Atheneum.
Father's Arcane Daughter. Atheneum.
From the Mixed-up Files of Mrs. Basil E.
    Frankweiler. Dell.
illus. From the Mixed-Up Files of Mrs. Basil E.
    Frankweiler. Atheneum.
From the Mixed-up Files of Mrs. Basil E.
    Frankweiler. Atheneum.
A Proud Taste for Scarlet & Miniver.
    Atheneum.
illus. A Proud Taste for Scarlet & Miniver.
    Atheneum.
The Second Mrs. Giaconda. Atheneum.
The Second Mrs. Giaconda. Atheneum.
Throwing Shadows. Atheneum.

Konigsmark, Bruce W.
    xKonigsmark, Bruce W.
    Genetic & Metabolic Deafness. Saunders.
Konikow, Robert B.
    xKonikow, Robert B.
    Communications for the Safety Professional.
        Natl Safety Coun.
Koning, Hans, 1921-
    xKoning, Hans.
    A New Yorker in Egypt. G K Hall.
Konishi, Masatoshi, 1938-
    xKonishi, Masatoshi.
    Afghanistan. Kodansha.
Konkel, Mary H. *see* Konkel, Mary Hugolina.
Konkel, Mary Hugolina, Sister, 1907-
    xKonkel, Mary H.
    Rene Fernandat, Poet & Critic. AMS Pr.
Konkle, Burton A. *see* Konkle, Burton Alva.
Konkle, Burton Alva.
    xKonkle, Burton A.
    Standard History of the Medical Profession of
        Philadelphia. AMS Pr.
Konner, Alfred.
    xKonner, Alfred.
    Clever Coot. Carolrhoda Bks.
Konnyu, Leslie, 1914-
    xKonnyu, Leslie.
    Collected Poems. Hungarian Rev.
Konold. *see* Konold, William G.
Konold, William G.
    xKonold.
    What Every Engineer Should Know About
        Patents. Dekker.
Konolige, Frederica. *see* Konolige, Kit.
Konolige, Kit.
    xKonolige, Frederica.
    jt. auth. The Power of Their Glory: America's
        Ruling Class: the Episcopalians. Wyden.
    xKonolige, Kit.
    The Power of Their Glory: America's Ruling
        Class: the Episcopalians. Wyden.
Kononenko, Konstantyn, 1889-
    xKononenko, Konstantyn.
    Ukraine & Russia: A History of the Economic
        Relations Between Ukraine &
        Russia,1654-1917. Marquette.
Konopacki, Steven A.
    xKonopacki, Steven A.
    The Descent into Words: Jakob Bohme's
        Transcendental Linguistics. Karoma.
Konopka, G. *see* Konopka, Gisela.
Konopka, Gisela.
    xKonopka, G.
    Adolescent Girl in Conflict. P-H.
Konorski, Jerry. *see* Konorski, Jerzy.
Konorski, Jerzy.
    xKonorski, Jerry.
    Integrative Activity of the Brain: An
        Interdisciplinary Approach. U of Chicago Pr.
Konrad, Evelyn.
    xKonrad, Evelyn.

Indiscretions. Dell.
Indiscretions. Dial.
Konrad, George. *see* Konrad, Gyorgy.
Konrad, Gyorgy.
    xKonrad, George.
    The Case Worker. HarBraceJ.
    The Case Worker. HarBraceJ.
    The Intellectuals on the Road to Class Power.
        HarBraceJ.
Konrad, Patricia. *see* Konrad, Patricia N.
Konrad, Patricia N.
    xKonrad, Patricia.
    Pediatric Oncology. Med Exam.
Konrad, Roselinde.
    xKonrad, Roselinde.
    Essentials of German Grammar in Review.
        Har-Row.
    Reviewing German Grammar & Building
        Vocabulary. Har-Row.
Konstans, Constantine.
    xKonstans, Constantine.
    Effects of Data Processing Service Bureaus on
        the Practice of Public Accounting. Mich St U
        Busn.
Kontos, Alkis.
    xKontos, Alkis.
    ed. Domination. U of Toronto Pr.
Konvitz, Josef W.
    xKonvitz, Josef W.
    Cities & the Sea: Port City Planning in Early
        Modern Europe. Johns Hopkins.
Konvitz, Milton R. *see* Konvitz, Milton Ridvas.
Konvitz, Milton Ridvas, 1908-
    xKonvitz, Milton R.
    Civil Rights in Immigration. Greenwood.
    The Constitution & Civil Rights. Octagon.
    Expanding Liberties: Freedom's Gains in
        Postwar America. Greenwood.
    Fundamental Liberties of a Free People:
        Religion, Speech, Press Assembly.
        Greenwood.
    Judaism & the American Idea. Cornell U Pr.
    Judaism & the American Idea. Schocken.
    On the Nature of Value: The Philosophy of
        Samuel Alexander. Johnson Repr.
Konz, Stephan. *see* Konz, Stephan A.
Konz, Stephan A.
    xKonz, Stephan.
    Work Design. Grid Pub.
Konzo, Seichi.
    xKonzo, Seichi.
    Opportunities in Mechanical Engineering. Natl
        Textbk.
Koo, Vi K. *see* Koo, Vi Kyuin Wellington.
Koo, Vi Kyuin Wellington, 1888-
    xKoo, Vi K.
    Status of Aliens in China. AMS Pr.
Koo, Wellington.
    xKoo, Wellington.
    No Feast Lasts Forever. Times Bks.
Koob, Derry D.
    xKoob, Derry D.
    The Nature of Life. A-W.
Koocher, Gerald P.
    xKoocher, Gerald P.
    ed. Children's Rights & the Mental Health
        Professions. Wiley.
Kooi, E.
    xKooi, E.
    Surface Properties of Oxidized Silicon.
        Springer-Verlag.
Kooi, Kenneth A.
    xKooi, Kenneth A.
    Visual Evoked Potentials in Central Disorders
        of the Visual System. Har-Row.
Kooijman, S.
    xKooijman, Simon.
    Tapa in Polynesia. Bishop Mus.
Kooijman, Simon. *see* Kooijman, S.

Koolhaas, Rem.
    xKoolhaas, Rem.
    Delirious New York: A Retroactive Manifesto
        for Manhattan. Oxford U Pr.
Koontz, Dean.
    xKoontz, Dean R.
    Whispers. Putnam.
    Writing Popular Fiction. Writers Digest.
Koontz, Dean R. *see* Koontz, Dean.
Koontz, Harold, 1908-
    xKoontz, Harold.
    Essentials of Management. McGraw.
    A Practical Introduction to Business. Irwin.
    xKoontz, Harold D.
    Appraising Managers As Managers. McGraw.
Koontz, Harold D. *see* Koontz, Harold.
Koop, Albert J. *see* Koop, Albert James.
Koop, Albert James, 1877-1945
    xKoop, Albert J.
    Early Chinese Bronzes. Hacker.
Koop, C. Everett.
    xKoop, C. Everett.
    The Right to Live: the Right to Die. Tyndale.
Koopman, Barbara G. Foreword by. *see* Eden, Jerome.
Koopman, Bernard O. *see* Koopman, Bernard Osgood.
Koopman, Bernard Osgood, 1900-
    xKoopman, Bernard O.
    Search & Screening: General Principles with
        Historical Applications. Pergamon.
Koopman, Elizabeth. *see* Koopman, Elizabeth J.
Koopman, Elizabeth J.
    xKoopman, Elizabeth.
    Talking Together. Behaviordelia.
Koopman, Leroy.
    xKoopman, LeRoy.
    Beauty Care for the Feet. Zondervan.
Koopmans, L. H. *see* Koopmans, Lambert Herman.
Koopmans, Lambert Herman, 1930-
    xKoopmans, L. H.
    The Spectral Analysis of Time Series. Acad Pr.
Koos, Earl L. *see* Koos, Earl Lomon.
Koos, Earl Lomon, 1905-1960
    xKoos, Earl L.
    Families in Trouble. Russell.
Kooser, Ted.
    xKooser, Ted.
    Hatcher. Windflower Pr.
    Sure Signs: New & Selected Poems. U of
        Pittsburgh Pr.
Koosis, Donald J.
    xKoosis, Donald J.
    Business Statistics. Wiley.
    Probability. Wiley.
    Statistics. Wiley.
Kopaczynski, Germain.
    xKopaczynski, Germain.
    Linguistic Ramifications of the
        Essence-Existence Debate. U Pr of Amer.
Kopal, Z. *see* Kopal, Zdenek.
Kopal, Zdenek, 1914-
    xKopal, Z.
    The Moon in the Post-Apollo Era. Kluwer
        Boston.
    xKopal, Zdenek.
    Figures of Equilibrium of Celestial Bodies:
        With Emphasis on Problems of Motion of
        Artificial Satellites. U of Wis Pr.
    Language of the Stars: A Discourse on the
        Theory of the Light Changes of Eclipsing
        Variables. Kluwer Boston.
    The Solar System. Oxford U Pr.
Kopan, Andrew. *see* Kopan, Andrew T.
Kopan, Andrew T.
    xKopan, Andrew.
    Rethinking Educational Equality. McCutchan.
Kopell, Harvey P.
    xKopell, Harvey P.
    Peripheral Entrapment Neuropathies. Krieger.
Kopell, Sandra.
    xKopell, Sandra.

Spelling Mazes. G&D.

Kopf, Alfred W.
xKopf, Alfred W.
Atlas of Tumors of the Skin. Saunders.
Malignant Melanoma. Masson Pub.

Kopf, David.
xKopf, David.
The Brahmo Samaj & the Shaping of the
Modern Indian Mind. Princeton U Pr.
The Indian World. Forum Pr MO.

Kopmeyer, M. R.
xKopmeyer, M. R.
How to Get Whatever You Want. Success
Found.
How You Can Get Richer Quicker. Success
Found.

Kopp, C. B. see Kopp, Claire B.

Kopp, Claire B.
xKopp, C. B.
ed. Becoming Female: Perspectives on
Development. Plenum Pub.

Kopp, Ernestine.
xKopp, Ernestine.
How to Draft Basic Patterns. Fairchild.

Kopp, O. W. see Kopp, Oswald W.

Kopp, Oswald W.
xKopp, O. W.
Personalized Curriculum Through Excellence in
Leadership. Interstate.

Kopp, Richard D. see Kopp, Richard L.

Kopp, Richard L., 1934-
xKopp, Richard D.
Readings in French Literature. HM.
xKopp, Richard L.
Marcel Proust As a Social Critic. Fairleigh
Dickinson.

Kopp, Ruth. see Kopp, Ruth Lewshenia.

Kopp, Ruth Lewshenia.
xKopp, Ruth.
Encounter with Terminal Illness. Zondervan.

Kopp, Sheldon B., 1929-
xKopp, Sheldon B.
Guru: Metaphors from a Psychotherapist. Sci &
Behavior.

Kopp, W. LaMarr. see Kopp, William Lamarr.

Kopp, William LaMarr.
xKopp, W. LaMarr.
German Literature in the United States,
1945-1960. U of NC Pr.

Kopperl, Bert.
xKopperl, Bert.
With Two Wheels & a Camera. Exposition.

Koppett, Leonard.
xKoppett, Leonard.
All About Baseball. Times Bks.

Korb, Johann G. see Korb, Johann Georg.

Korb, Johann Georg.
xKorb, Johann G.
Diary of an Austrian Secretary of Legation at
the Court of Czar Peter the Great. Da Capo.

Korb, Lawrence J., 1939-
xKorb, Lawrence J.
The Fall & Rise of the Pentagon: American
Defense Policies in the 1970s. Greenwood.
The Price of Preparedness: The FY 1978-1982
Defense Program. Am Enterprise.

Korbel, Josef.
xKorbel, Josef.
Communist Subversion of Czechoslovakia,
1938-1948: The Failure of Coexistence.
Princeton U Pr.
Detente in Europe: Real or Imaginary.
Princeton U Pr.

Korchnoi, Viktor, 1931-
xKorchnoi, Viktor.
Chess Is My Life: Autobiography & Games.
Arco.

Korda, Michael, 1933-
xKorda, Michael.

Charmed Lives: A Family Romance. Random.
Power: How to Get It, How to Use It.
Ballantine.
Power: How to Get It, How to Use It.
Random.
Success. Ballantine.
Success!. Random.

Korea Stamp Society.
xKorea Stamp Society.
Philatelic Handbook for Korea, 1884-1905.
Collectors.

Kordel, Lelord.
xKordel, Lelord.
The Easy, Low-Cost Way to Total Beauty.
Putnam.
Eat & Grow Younger. Manor Bks.
Secrets for Staying Slim. NAL.

Korein, Julius.
xKorein, Julius.
ed. Brain Death: Interrelated Medical & Social
Issues. NY Acad Sci.

Koren, Edward.
xKoren, Edward.
Do You Want to Talk About It?. Pantheon.

Koren, Elizabeth. see Koren, Else Elisabeth Hysing.

Koren, Else Elisabeth Hysing, 1832-1918
xKoren, Elizabeth.
The Diary of Elisabeth Koren: 1853-1855.
Arno.

Koren, Henry J.
xKoren, Henry J.
Marx & the Authentic Man: A First
Introduction to the Philosophy of Karl Marx.
Humanities.

Koren, Herman.
xKoren, Herman.
Environmental Health & Safety. Pergamon.

Korey, William, 1922-
xKorey, William.
The Soviet Cage: Anti-Semitism in Russia.
Viking Pr.

Korfhage, Robert R.
xKorfhage, Robert R.
Discrete Computational Structures. Acad Pr.

Korfker, Dena.
xKorfker, Dena.
Good Morning, Lord: Devotions for Children.
Baker Bk.

Korg, Jacob.
xKorg, Jacob.
Dylan Thomas. Twayne.
George Gissing: A Critical Biography. U of
Wash Pr.

Korim, Andrew S.
xKorim, Andrew S.
Government Careers & the Community
College. Am Assn Comm Jr Coll.

Korin. see Korin, Basil P.

Korin, Basil P.
xKorin.
Introduction to Statistical Methods. Winthrop.

Korkisch, J. see Korkisch, Johann.

Korkisch, Johann.
xKorkisch, J.
Modern Methods for the Separation of Rarer
Metal Ions. Pergamon.

Korkunov, Nikolai. see Korkunov, Nikolai Mikhailovich.
Korkunov, Nikolai M. see Korkunov, Nikolai
Mikhailovich.

Korkunov, Nikolai Mikhailovich.
xKorkunov, Nikolai.
General Theory of Law. Rothman.
xKorkunov, Nikolai M.
General Theory of Law. Kelley.

Korliras, Panayotis G.
xKorliras, Panayotis G.
Modern Macroeconomics: Major Contributions
to Contemporary Thought. Har-Row.

Korman, Abraham. see Korman, Abraham K.

Korman, Abraham K.
xKorman, Abraham.
Career Success - Personal Failure. P-H.
Organizational Behavior. P-H.
xKorman, Abraham K.
The Psychology of Motivation. P-H.
xKorman, Rhoda.
jt. auth. Career Success - Personal Failure. P-H.
Korman, Rhoda. see Korman, Abraham K.
Kormondy, Edward J. see Kormondy, Edward John.

Kormondy, Edward John, 1926-
xKormondy, Edward J.
Concepts of Ecology. P-H.
Introduction to Genetics: A Program for
Self-Instruction. Krieger.

Korn, Berton W. see Korn, Bertram Wallace.

Korn, Bertram Wallace.
xKorn, Berton W.
Early Jews of New Orleans. KTAV.

Korn, Charlotte.
xKorn, Charlotte.
A Real Estate Agent's Guide to Successful
Sales & Listings. Reston.

Korn, Granino A. see Korn, Granino Arthur.

Korn, Granino Arthur.
xKorn, Granino A.
Digital Continuous System Simulation. P-H.

Korn, N. see Korn, Noel.

Korn, Noel.
xKorn, N.
Human Evolution: Readings for Physical
Anthropology. HR&W.

Korn, Richard.
xKorn, Richard.
Orchestral Accents. Arno.

Korn, Walter.
xKorn, Walter.
Modern Chess Openings. McKay.

Kornberg, Allan.
xKornberg, Allan.
Influence in Parliament; Canada. Duke.

Kornberg, Arthur, 1910-
xKornberg, Arthur.
DNA Replication. W H Freeman.
DNA Synthesis. W H Freeman.

Kornblum, Allan, 1949-
xKornblum, Allan.
Awkward Song. Toothpaste.

Kornblum, Allan N.
xKornblum, Allan N.
The Moral Hazards: Police Strategies for
Honesty & Ethical Behavior. Lexington Bks.

Kornbluth, Alfred. see Kornbluth, Alfred W.

Kornbluth, Alfred W.
xKornbluth, Alfred.
First Aid for Boaters. Crown.

Kornbluth, C. M.
xKornbluth, C. M.
The Syndic. Avon.

Kornegay, Francis A.
xKornegay, Francis A.
Equal Employment: Mandate & Challenge.
Vantage.

Korner, Ija N. see Korner, Ija Nome.

Korner, Ija Nome, 1914-
xKorner, Ija N.
Experimental Investigation of Some Aspects of
the Problem of Repression: Repressive
Forgetting. AMS Pr.

Korner, S. see Korner, Stephan.
Korner, Stepan. see Korner, Stephan.

Korner, Stephan.
xKorner, S.
Experience & Conduct: A Philosophical
Enquiry into Practical Thinking. Cambridge
U Pr.
xKorner, Stepan.
ed. Practical Reason. Yale U Pr.

Kornfeld, Alfred D.
xKornfeld, Alfred D.

ed. Readings in Psychopathology. Mss Info.
Kornfield, Jack, 1945-
  xKornfield, Jack.
    Living Buddhist Masters. Unity Pr.
Korngold, Ralph, 1886-
  xKorngold, Ralph.
    Citizen Toussaint. Greenwood.
Kornhauser, Arthur. *see* Kornhauser, Arthur William.
Kornhauser, Arthur William.
  xKornhauser, Arthur.
    ed. Industrial Conflict. Arno.
Kornhauser, William.
  xKornhauser, William.
    Politics of Mass Society. Free Pr.
Kornweibel, Theodore.
  xKornweibel, Theodore.
    No Crystal Stair: Black Life & the Messenger,
    1917-1928. Greenwood.
Korol, Alexander G.
  xKorol, Alexander G.
    Soviet Education for Science & Technology.
    Greenwood.
Korolenko, Vladimir. *see* Korolenko, Vladimir
Galaktionovich.
Korolenko, Vladimir Galaktionovich, 1853-1921
  xKorolenko, Vladimir.
    In a Strange Land. Greenwood.
Korolkovas, Andrejus.
  xKorolkovas, Andrejus.
    Essentials of Medicinal Chemistry. Wiley.
    Essentials of Molecular Pharmacology:
    Background for Drug Design. Wiley.
Korones. *see* Korones, Sheldon B.
Korones, Sheldon B.
  xKorones.
    High Risk Newborn Infants: The Basis for
    Intensive Nursing Care. Mosby.
Koropeckyj, I. S.
  xKoropeckyj, I. S.
    ed. The Ukraine Within the USSR: An
    Economic Balance Sheet. Praeger.
Korpalski, Adam.
  xKorpalski, Adam.
    The Gunnery 1850-1975: A Documentary
    History of Private Education in America. A
    Korpalski.
Korpas, J. *see* Korpas, Juraj.
Korpas, Juraj.
  xKorpas, J.
    Cough & Other Respiratory Reflexes. S Karger.
Korpi, Walter.
  xKorpi, Walter.
    The Working Class in Welfare Capitalism:
    Work, Unions & Politics in Sweden.
    Routledge & Kegan.
Korr, H., 1941-
  xKorr, H.
    Proliferation of Different Cell Types in the
    Brain. Springer-Verlag.
Kors, Alan C.
  xKors, Alan C.
    D'holbach's Coterie: An Enlightenment in
    Paris. Princeton U Pr.
Korsch, Karl, 1889-1961
  xKorsch, Karl.
    Marxism & Philosophy. Monthly Rev.
Korschelt, O.
  xKorschelt, O.
    Theory & Practice of Go. C E Tuttle.
Korschunow, Irina.
  xKorschunow, Irina.
    Who Killed Christopher?. Philomel.
Kort, Wolfgang, 1939-
  xKort, Wolfgang.
    Alfred Doblin. Twayne.
Korth, Eugene H.
  xKorth, Eugene H.
    Spanish Policy in Colonial Chile: The Struggle
    for Social Justice, 1535-1700. Stanford U Pr.
Korting, Gunter W. *see* Korting, Gunter Waldemar.

Korting, Gunter Waldemar.
  xKorting, Gunter W.
    Differential Diagnosis in Dermatology.
    Saunders.
Kosa, John.
  xKosa, John.
    The Home of the Learned Man: A Symposium
    on the Immigrant Scholar in America. Coll &
    U Pr.
    ed. Poverty & Health: A Sociological Analysis.
    Harvard U Pr.
    Two Generations of Soviet Man: A Study in
    the Psychology of Communism. Lib Soc Sci.
Kosary, Dominic G. *see* Kosary, Domokos G.
Kosary, Domokos G.
  xKosary, Dominic G.
    History of Hungary. Arno.
Kosciuszko Foundation. *see* Kosciuszko Foundation, New
York.
Kosciuszko Foundation, New York.
  xKosciuszko Foundation.
    Kosciuszko Foundation English-Polish,
    Polish-English Dictionary. Scribner.
Koshy, K. T.
  xKoshy, K. T.
    Revision Notes on Psychiatry. Lippincott.
Kosikowski, Frank V.
  xKosikowski, Frank V.
    Cheese & Fermented Milk Foods. F V
    Kosikowski.
Kosinski, Jerzy. *see* Kosinski, Jerzy N.
Kosinski, Jerzy N., 1933-
  xKosinski, Jerzy.
    Passion Play. Bantam.
    Passion Play. St Martin.
    Steps. Bantam.
  xKosinski, Jerzy N.
    Steps. Random.
Koskoff, David E., 1939-
  xKoskoff, David E.
    The Mellons: The Chronicle of America's
    Richest Family. T Y Crowell.
Koslow, Lawrence. *see* Koslow, Lawrence E.
Koslow, Lawrence E.
  xKoslow, Lawrence.
    ed. The Future of Mexico. ASU Lat Am St.
Kosnar, Carl J., 1938-
  xKosnar, Carl J.
    How to Sell Your Home Without a Real Estate
    Broker. McGraw.
Kosnik, Anthony.
  xKosnik, Anthony.
    Human Sexuality: New Directions in American
    Catholic Thought. Paulist Pr.
Kosok, Paul, 1896-1959
  xKosok, Paul.
    Modern Germany: A Study of Conflicting
    Loyalties. Russell.
Kosolapoff, G. M. *see* Kosolapoff, Gennady M.
Kosolapoff, Gennady M.
  xKosolapoff, G. M.
    Organic Phosphorus Compounds. Krieger.
    ed. Organic Phosphorus Compounds. Wiley.
Kosoy, Ted.
  xKosoy, Ted.
    A Budget Guide to California & the Pacific
    Coast States. St Martin.
    Kosoy's Travel Guide to Canada. Acropolis.
    Kosoy's Travel Guide to Europe. Acropolis.
    Kosoy's Travel Guide to Florida & the South.
    Acropolis.
Koss, Leopold G.
  xKoss, Leopold G.
    Diagnostic Cytology & It's Histopathologic
    Bases. Lippincott.
Koss, Stephen. *see* Koss, Stephen E.
Koss, Stephen E.
  xKoss, Stephen.

Asquith. St Martin.
    Nonconformity in Modern British Politics.
    Shoe String.
    The Pro-Boers: The Anatomy of an Anti-War
    Movement. U of Chicago Pr.
Kossen, Stan, 1931-
  xKossen, Stan.
    Human Side of Organizations. Har-Row.
Kossmann, E. H. *see* Kossmann, Ernst Heinrich.
Kossmann, Ernst Heinrich.
  xKossmann, E. H.
    ed. Texts Concerning the Revolt of the
    Netherlands. Cambridge U Pr.
Kost, Mary Lu.
  xKost, Mary Lu.
    Success or Failure Begins in the Early School
    Years. C C Thomas.
Kostecki, M. M.
  xKostecki, M. M.
    East-West Trade & the GATT System. St
    Martin.
Kostelanetz, Richard.
  xKostelanetz, Richard.
    ed. Assembling Assembling. Assembling Pr.
    ed. Esthetics Contemporary. Prometheus Bks.
    ed. Imaged Words & Worded Images. RK
    Edns.
    Master Minds: Portraits of Contemporary
    American Artists & Intellectuals. Macmillan.
    ed. On Contemporary Literature: An
    Anthology of Critical Essays on the Major
    Movements & Writings of Contemporary
    Literature. Arno.
    Portraits from Memory. RK Edns.
    ed. Twenties in the Sixties: Previously
    Uncollected Critical Essays. Greenwood.
    ed. Visual Literature Criticism: A New
    Collection. S Ill U Pr.
Kosten, L. *see* Kosten, Leendert.
Kosten, Leendert.
  xKosten, L.
    Stochastic Theory of Service Systems.
    Pergamon.
Koster, G. F.
  xKoster, George F.
    Space Groups & Their Representations. Acad
    Pr.
Koster, George F. *see* Koster, G. F.
Koster, R. M., 1934-
  xKoster, R. M.
    Mandragon. Morrow.
    Mandragon. Morrow.
Kosters, Marvin H.
  xKosters, Marvin H.
    Controls & Inflation: The Economic
    Stabilization Program in Retrospect. Am
    Enterprise.
Kostich, Dragos. *see* Kostich, Dragos D.
Kostich, Dragos D.
  xKostich, Dragos.
    George Morrison. Dillon.
Kostiner, Edward.
  xKostiner, Edward.
    Fundamentals of Chemistry. HarBraceJ.
Kostis, Nicholas.
  xKostis, Nicholas.
    The Exorcism of Sex & Death in Julien
    Green's Novels. Mouton.
Kostka, Edmund. *see* Kostka, Edmund K.
Kostka, Edmund K.
  xKostka, Edmund.
    Glimpses of Germanic-Slavic Relations from
    Pushkin to Heinrich Mann. Bucknell U Pr.
Kostka, Matthew.
  xKostka, Matthew.
    Climb to the Top. Doubleday.
Kostman, Samuel.
  xKostman, Samuel.

Twentieth Century Women of Achievement.
Rosen Pr.
Kostof, Spiro. *see* Kostof, Spiro K.
Kostof, Spiro K.
xKostof, Spiro.
ed. The Architect: Chapters in the History of
the Profession. Oxford U Pr.
Kostopoulos, George K., 1939-
xKostopoulos, George K.
Digital Engineering. Wiley.
Kostyu, Frank A.
xKostyu, Frank A.
How to Spark a Marriage When the Kids
Leave Home. Pilgrim NY.
Koszarowski, Tadeusz.
xKoszarowski, Tadeusz.
Cancer Surgery. Urban & S.
Koszarski, Diane K. *see* Koszarski, Diane Kaiser.
Koszarski, Diane Kaiser.
xKoszarski, Diane K.
The Complete Films of William S. Hart: A
Pictorial Record. Dover.
Koszarski, Richard.
xKoszarski, Richard.
ed. Hollywood Directors: 1914-1940. Oxford U
Pr.
ed. Hollywood Directors, 1914-1940. Oxford U
Pr.
ed. Hollywood Directors, 1941-1976. Oxford U
Pr.
ed. Hollywood Directors, 1941-1976. Oxford U
Pr.
Kotas, Richard.
xKotas, Richard.
Management Accounting for Hotels &
Restaurants. Hayden.
Kotelchuck, David.
xKotelchuck, David.
ed. Prognosis Negative: Crisis in the Health
Care System. Random.
Kotelnikov, V. A.
xKotelnikov, Vladimir A
Theory of Optimum Noise Immunity. Dover.
Kotelnikov, Vladimir A. *see* Kotelnikov, V. A.
Koteskey, Ronald L., 1942-
xKoteskey, Ronald L.
Psychology from a Christian Perspective.
Abingdon.
Kothari, R. *see* Kothari, Rajni.
Kothari, Rajni.
xKothari, R.
Caste in Indian Politics. Gordon.
xKothari, Rajni.
ed. Caste in Indian Politics. Humanities.
xKothari, Ranji.
Democratic Polity & Social Change in India:
Crisis & Opportunities. South Asia Bks.
Kothari, Ranji. *see* Kothari, Rajni.
Kotinsky, Ruth.
xKotinsky, Ruth.
Community Programs for Mental Health:
Theory, Practice, Evaluation. Harvard U Pr.
Kotler, Milton.
xKotler, Milton.
Neighborhood Government: The Local
Foundations of Political Life. Bobbs.
Kotler, Philip.
xKotler, Philip.
Marketing Management: Analysis, Planning &
Control. P-H.
Readings in Marketing Management. P-H.
xKotler, Phillip.
Marketing for Non-Profit Organizations. P-H.
Marketing Management: Analysis, Planning &
Control. P-H.
Kotler, Phillip. *see* Kotler, Philip.
Kotov, A. *see* Kotov, Aleksandr Aleksandrovich.
Kotov, Aleksandr Aleksandrovich.
xKotov, A.

The Soviet School of Chess. Dover.
Kotre, John. *see* Kotre, John N.
Kotre, John N.
xKotre, John.
Simple Gifts: The Lives of Pat & Patty
Crowley. Andrews & McMeel.
Kots, Iakov Mikhailovich.
xKots, Ya. M.
Organization of Voluntary Movement:
Neurophysiological Mechanisms. Plenum
Pub.
Kots, Ya. M. *see* Kots, Iakov Mikhailovich.
Kotschevar, Lendal H. *see* Kotschevar, Lendal Henry.
Kotschevar, Lendal Henry, 1908-
xKotschevar, Lendal H.
Quantity Food Purchasing. Wiley.
Standards Principles & Techniques in Quantity
Food Production. CBI Pub.
Kotsonis, H. *see* Kotsonis, Helen Hoch.
Kotsonis, Helen Hoch.
xKotsonis, H.
Modern Lesson Plans in Environmental
Science. P-H.
Kottak, Conrad P. *see* Kottak, Conrad Phillip.
Kottak, Conrad Phillip.
xKottak, Conrad P.
Cultural Anthropology. Random.
Kotter, John P., 1947-
xKotter, John P.
Organizational Dynamics: Diagnosis &
Intervention. A-W.
Power in Management. Am Mgmt.
Kottick, Edward. *see* Kottick, Edward L.
Kottick, Edward L.
xKottick, Edward.
The Collegium: A Handbook. October.
Kottke, Frank. *see* Kottke, Frank Joseph.
Kottke, Frank Joseph, 1913-
xKottke, Frank.
The Promotion of Price Competition Where
Sellers Are Few. Lexington Bks.
Kottler, Dorothy.
xKottler, Dorothy.
I Really Like Myself. Aurora Pubs.
Kottlowski, Frank E. *see* Kottlowski, Frank Edward.
Kottlowski, Frank Edward.
xKottlowski, Frank E.
Coal Resources of the Americas: Selected
Papers. Geol Soc.
Kottmeyer, William, 1910-
xKottmeyer, William A.
Teacher's Guide for Remedial Reading.
McGraw.
Kottmeyer, William A. *see* Kottmeyer, William.
Kottow, Michael H.
xKottow, Michael H.
Anterior Segment Fluorescein Angiography.
Williams & Wilkins.
Kotyk, Arnost.
xKotyk, Arnost.
Cell Membrane Transport: Principles &
Techniques. Plenum Pub.
Kotz, David M.
xKotz, David M.
Bank Control of Large Corporations in the
United States. U of Cal Pr.
Kotz, Nick.
xKotz, Nick.
A Passion for Equality: George Wiley & the
Movement. Norton.
Kotze, D. A.
xKotze, D. A.
African Politics in South Africa: Parties &
Issues. St Martin.
Kotzwinkle, William.
xKotzwinkle, William.

The Ants Who Took Away Time. Doubleday.
Doctor Rat. Knopf.
Dream of Dark Harbor. Doubleday.
The Fan Man. Avon.
Fata Morgana. Knopf.
The Leopard's Tooth. Avon.
The Leopard's Tooth. HM.
The Nap Master. HarBraceJ.
Night Book. Avon.
Nightbook. Avon.
The Supreme, Superb, Exalted & Delightful,
One & Only Magic Building. FS&G.
Koubourlis, Demetrius J.
xKoubourlis, Demetrius J.
ed. A Concordance to the Poems of Osip
Mandelstam. Cornell U pr.
Koulomzin, Sophie.
xKoulomzin, Sophie.
Our Church & Our Children. St Vladimirs.
Kounin, Jacob S. *see* Kounin, Jacob Sebatian.
Kounin, Jacob Sebatian, 1912-
xKounin, Jacob S.
Discipline & Group Management in
Classrooms. Krieger.
Kounovsky, Nicholas. *see* Kounovsky, Nicholas Alexis.
Kounovsky, Nicholas Alexis, 1913-
xKounovsky, Nicholas.
Instant Fitness: How to Stay Fit & Healthy in
Six Minutes a Day. Putnam.
Kourdakov, Sergei, 1951-1973
xKourdakov, Sergei.
Persecutor. Revell.
Kourvetaris, George A.
xKourvetaris, George A.
ed. World Perspectives in the Sociology of the
Military. Transaction Bks.
Koury, Michael J.
xKoury, Michael J.
ed. Custer Centennial Observance. Old Army.
Kousoulas, D. George. *see* Kousoulas, Dimitrios George.
Kousoulas, Dimitrios George, 1923-
nKousoulas, D. George.
Modern Greece: Profile of a Nation. Scribner.
On Government & Politics. Duxbury Pr.
Kousourou, Gabriel.
xKousourou, Gabriel.
An Introduction to Technical Mathematics
with Computing. Petrocelli.
Koutsoyiannis, A.
xKoutsoyiannis, A.
Modern Microeconomics. St Martin.
Theory of Econometrics: An Introductory
Exposition of Econometric Methods. B&N.
Kouwenhoven, John A. *see* Kouwenhoven, John Atlee.
Kouwenhoven, John Atlee.
xKouwenhoven, John A.
Columbia Historical Portrait of New York: An
Essay in Graphic History. Har-Row.
Kovacs, T.
xKovacs, T.
Principles of X-Ray Metallurgy. Plenum Pub.
Kovaleff, Theodore P. *see* Kovaleff, Theodore Philip.
Kovaleff, Theodore Philip, 1943-
xKovaleff, Theodore P.
Business & Government During the
Eisenhower Administration: A Study of the
Anti-Trust Policy of the Anti-Trust Division
of the Justice Department. Ohio U Pr.
Kovalevskii, Maksim Maksimovich, 1851-1916
xKovalevskii, Maxime.
Modern Customs & Ancient Laws of Russia:
Being the Ilchester Lectures 1889-90. B
Franklin.
Kovalevskii, Maxime. *see* Kovalevskii, Maksim
Maksimovich.
Kovaly, John. *see* Kovaly, John J.
Kovaly, John J., 1928-
xKovaly, John.
ed. Synthetic Aperture Radar. Artech Hse.
Kovar, Lillian C. *see* Kovar, Lillian Cohen.

Kovar, Lillian Cohen, 1918-
 xKovar, Lillian C.
  Wasted Lives: Children in Mental Hospitals &
  Their Families. Halsted Pr.
Kovash, Emily.
 xKovash, Emily.
  How to Have Fun Making Cards. Creative Ed.
Kovda, Viktor. see Kovda, Viktor Abramovich.
Kovda, Viktor Abramovich.
 xKovda, Viktor.
  Land Aridization & Drought Control.
  Westview.
Kovel, Joel, 1936-
 xKovel, Joel.
  A Complete Guide to Therapy: From
  Psychoanalysis to Behavior Modification.
  Pantheon.
Kovel, Ralph M.
 xKovel, Ralph M.
  Dictionary of Marks: Pottery & Porcelain.
  Crown.
Kovesi, Julius.
 xKovesi, Julius.
  Moral Notions. Humanities.
Kovic, Ron.
 xKovic, Ron.
  Born on the Fourth of July. McGraw.
Kovner, Abba.
 xKovner, Abba.
  A Canopy in the Desert: Selected Poems. U of
  Pittsburgh Pr.
Kovrig, Bennett.
 xKovrig, Bennett.
  The Hungarian People's Republic. Johns
  Hopkins.
Kowal, J. M. see Kowal, Jan M.
Kowal, Jan M.
 xKowal, J. M.
  Agricultural Ecology of Savanna: A Study of
  West Africa. Oxford U Pr.
Kowalski, Cash.
 xKowalski, Cash.
  The Impact of College on Persisting &
  Non-Persisting Students. Philos Lib.
Kowalski, Gene.
 xKowalski, Gene.
  How to Eat Cheap but Good. Popular Lib.
Kowalsky, Hans J. see Kowalsky, Hans Joachim.
Kowalsky, Hans Joachim, 1921-
 xKowalsky, Hans J.
  Topological Spaces. Acad Pr.
Kowet, Don.
 xKowet, Don.
  Pele. Atheneum.
Kowet, Donald K. see Kowet, Donald Kalinda.
Kowet, Donald Kalinda.
 xKowet, Donald K.
  Land, Labour Migration & Politics in Southern
  Africa: Botswana, Lesotho & Swaziland.
  Holmes & Meier.
Kownslar, A. O. see Kownslar, Allan O.
Kownslar, Allan O.
 xKownslar, A. O.
  Inquiring About American History: Studies in
  History & Political Science. HR&W.
 xKownslar, Allan O.
  American Government. McGraw.
  ed. Teaching American History: The Quest for
  Relevancy. Coun Soc Studies.
Kowtaluk, Helen.
 xKowtaluk, Helen.
  Discovering Food. Bennett Co.
  Food for Today. Bennett Co.
Koyre, Alexander, 1892-
 xKoyre, Alexander.
  Newtonian Studies. U of Chicago Pr.
 xKoyre, Alexandre.
  From the Closed World to the Infinite
  Universe. Johns Hopkins.
Koyre, Alexandre. see Koyre, Alexander.

Koza, Russell C.
 xKoza, Russell C.
  Mathematical & Operations Research
  Techniques in Health Administration. Colo
  Assoc.
Kozee, William C. see Kozee, William Carlos.
Kozee, William Carlos.
 xKozee, William C.
  Early Families of Eastern & Southeastern
  Kentucky & Their Descendants. Genealog
  Pub.
Kozelka, Paul.
 xKozelka, Paul.
  A Glossary to the Plays of Bernard Shaw.
  Folcroft.
Kozicki, Henry, 1924-
 xKozicki, Henry.
  Tennyson & Clio: History in the Major Poems.
  Johns Hopkins.
Kozicki, Richard J.
 xKozicki, Richard J.
  ed. South & Southeast Asia: Doctoral
  Dissertations & Masters' Theses Completed
  at the University of Cal. at Berkeley,
  1906-1973. Cellar.
Kozloff, Charles.
 xKozloff, Charles.
  Ondine. St Martin.
Kozloff, Eugene N.
 xKozloff, Eugene N.
  Plants & Animals of the Pacific Northwest: An
  Illustrated Guide to the Natural History of
  Western Oregon, Washington, & British
  Columbia. U of Wash Pr.
Kozloff, Martin A.
 xKozloff, Martin A.
  A Program for Families of Children with
  Learning & Behavior Problems. Wiley.
  Reaching the Autistic Child: A Parent Training
  Program. Res Press.
Kozloff, Max.
 xKozloff, Max.
  Renderings: Critical Essays on a Century of
  Modern Art. S&S.
Kozlovsky, Daniel G., 1937-
 xKozlovsky, Daniel G.
  ed. An Ecological & Evolutionary Ethic. P-H.
Kozlowski, T. T. see Kozlowski, Theodore Thomas.
Kozlowski, Theodore T. see Kozlowski, Theodore
 Thomas.
Kozlowski, Theodore Thomas.
 xKozlowski, T. T.
  ed. Fire & Ecosystems. Acad Pr.
  Growth & Development of Trees. Acad Pr.
 xKozlowski, Theodore T.
  Tree Growth & Environmental Stresses. U of
  Wash Pr.
Kozma, Robert B.
 xKozma, Robert B.
  Instructional Techniques in Higher Education.
  Educ Tech Pubns.
Kozol, Jonathan.
 xKozol, Jonathan.
  Death at an Early Age: The Destruction of the
  Hearts & Minds of Negro Children in the
  Boston Public Schools. HM.
Kozoll, Charles E.
 xKozoll, Charles E.
  Response to Need: A Case Study of Adult
  Education Graduate Program Development in
  the Southeast. Syracuse U Cont Ed.
Kozuszek, Jane E. see Kozuszek, Jane Eyerly.
Kozuszek, Jane Eyerly.
 xKozuszek, Jane E.
  Hygiene. Watts.
Kraay, Colin. see Kraay, Colin M.
Kraay, Colin M.
 xKraay, Colin.
  Archaic & Classical Greek Coins. U of Cal Pr.
Krabbe, G. see Krabbe, Gregers.

Krabbe, Gregers.
 xKrabbe, G.
  Operational Calculus. Springer-Verlag.
 xKrabbe, Gregors.
  Operational Calculus. Plenum Pub.
Krabbe, Gregors. see Krabbe, Gregers.
Krabbe, Hugo, 1857-1936
 xKrabbe, Hugo.
  The Modern Idea of the State. Hyperion Conn.
Krabs, W. see Krabs, Werner.
Krabs, Werner, 1934-
 xKrabs, W.
  Optimization & Approximation. Wiley.
Kracauer, Siegfreid. see Kracauer, Siegfried.
Kracauer, Siegfried, 1889-
 xKracauer, Siegfreid.
  From Caligari to Hitler: A Psychological
  History of the German Film. Princeton U Pr.
 xKracauer, Siegfried.
  Theory of Film: The Redemption of Physical
  Reality. Oxford U Pr.
Kracke, Don.
 xKracke, Don.
  How to Turn Your Idea into a Million Dollars.
  Doubleday.
  How to Turn Your Idea into a Million Dollars.
  NAL.
Kracke, Waud H.
 xKracke, Waud H.
  Force & Persuasion: Leadership in an
  Amazonian Society. U of Chicago Pr.
Kracum, Vincent D.
 xKracum, Vincent D.
  Respiratory Therapy Examination Review
  Book. Med Exam.
Krader, Lawrence.
 xKrader, Lawrence.
  The Asiatic Mode of Production: Sources
  Development & Critique in the Writings of
  Karl Marx. Humanities.
  Dialectic of Civil Society. Humanities.
  Peoples of Central Asia. Res Ctr Lang
  Semiotic.
Kraegel, Janet M.
 xKraegel, Janet M.
  Patient Care Systems. Lippincott.
Kraeling, C. H. see Kraeling, Carl Hermann.
Kraeling, Carl Hermann, 1897-1966
 xKraeling, C. H.
  The Synagogue. Ktav.
Kraemer, Kenneth L.
 xKraemer, Kenneth L.
  The Municipal Information Systems Directory.
  Lexington Bks.
Kraemer, Richard. see Kraemer, Richard H.
Kraemer, Richard H.
 xKraemer, Richard.
  Essentials of Texas Politics. West Pub.
  Texas Politics. West Pub.
 xKraemer, Richard H.
  Politics in Texas. West Pub.
  Understanding Texas Politics. West Pub.
Kraepelin, Emil, 1856-1926
 xKraepelin, Emil.
  Dementia Praecox & Paraphrenia. Krieger.
Kraeuchi, Ruth.
 xKraeuchi, Ruth.
  The New Cocker Spaniel. Howell Bk.
Kraf, Elaine.
 xKraf, Elaine.
  Find Him. Fiction Coll.
Kraft, Barbara, 1939-
 xKraft, Barbara.
  The Restless Spirit: Journal of a Gemini. Les
  Femmes Pub.
Kraft, Barbara S.
 xKraft, Barbara S.

The Peace Ship: Henry Ford's Pacifist
Adventure in the First World War.
Macmillan.
Kraft, Betsy H. *see* Kraft, Betsy Harvey.
Kraft, Betsy Harvey.
xKraft, Betsy H.
Careers in the Energy Industry. Watts.
Coal. Watts.
Oil & Natural Gas. Watts.
Kraft, Charles H.
xKraft, Charles H.
ed. Readings in Dynamic Indigeneity. William
Carey Lib.
Kraft Foods. *see* Kraft Foods Company.
Kraft Foods Company.
xKraft Foods.
Complete Cheese Cookbook. Benjamin Co.
Good Food Ideas from Kraft Cheese
Cookbook. Benjamin Co.
The Kraft Cookbook. Benjamin Co..
Kraft, George D.
xKraft, George D.
Mini-Microcomputer Hardware Design. P-H.
Kraft, Ken.
xKraft, Ken.
Exotic Vegetables: How to Grow & Cook
Them. Walker & Co.
Grow Your Own Dwarf Fruit Trees.
Cornerstone.
Mastering Wrestling. Contemp Bks.
Kraft Kitchens.
xKraft Kitchens.
The Parkay Margarine Cookbook. Benjamin
Co.
Salads from Beginning to Endive. Benjamin Co.
Travel Your Taste with Kraft Foodservice:
International Recipes from the World of
Foodservice. CBI Pub.
Kraft, Melvin D.
xKraft, Melvin D.
ed. Using Experts in Civil Cases. PLI.
Kraft, Stephanie.
yKraft, Stephanie.
No Castles on Main Street: American Authors
& Their Homes. Penguin.
No Castles on Main Street: American Authors
& Their Homes. Rand.
Kraft, William. *see* Kraft, William F.
Kraft, William F., 1938-
xKraft, William.
Sexual Dimensions of the Celibate Life.
Andrews & McMeel.
xKraft, William F.
Normal Modes of Madness: Hurdles in the
Path to Growth. Alba.
A Psychology of Nothingness. Westminster.
Kragten, J.
xKragten, J.
Atlas of Metal-Ligand Equilibria in Aqueous
Solution. Halsted Pr.
Krahl, Maurice E. *see* Krahl, Maurice Edward.
Krahl, Maurice Edward, 1908-
xKrahl, Maurice E.
Action of Insulin on Cells. Acad Pr.
Krahn, Fernando.
xKrahn, Fernando.
illus. April Fools. Dutton.
Catch That Cat!. Dutton.
illus. The Family Minus. Schol Bk Serv.
illus. The Family Minus's Summer House.
Parents.
A Funny Friend from Heaven. Lippincott.
illus. How Santa Claus Had a Long & Difficult
Journey Delivering His Presents. Delacorte.
illus. How Santa Claus Had a Long & Difficult
Journey Delivering His Presents. Delacorte.
illus. Little Love Story. Lippincott.
Krailsheimer, A. J.
xKrailsheimer, A. J.

Armand-Jean De Rance, Abbot of la Trappe:
His Influence in the Cloister & the World.
Oxford U Pr.
Kraines, Oscar, 1916-
xKraines, Oscar.
The Impossible Dilemma: Who Is a Jew in the
State of Israel?. Bloch.
The World & Ideas of Ernst Freund: The
Search for General Principles of Legistlation
& Administrative Law. U of Ala Pr.
Krainin, Harold L.
xKrainin, Harold L.
What You Should Know About Operating
Your Business As a Corporation. Oceana.
Kraitchik, Maurice, 1882-
xKraitchik, Maurice.
Mathematical Recreations. Dover.
Krajewski, Wadysaw.
xKrajewski, Wladislaw.
Correspondence Principle & Growth of
Science. Kluwer Boston.
Krajewski, Wladislaw. *see* Krajewski, Wadysaw.
Krakow, Kenneth K.
xKrakow, Kenneth K.
Georgia Place Names. Winship Pr.
Kral, Martin A.
xKral, Martin A.
Thou Shalt Not. Libra.
Kraljic, Frances.
xKraljic, Frances.
Croatian & Migration to & from the United
States, 1900-1914. Ragusan Pr.
Croatian Migration to & from the United
States, 1900-1914. Ragusan Pr.
Krall, A. M. *see* Krall, Allan M.
Krall, Allan M.
xKrall, A. M.
Linear Methods of Applied Analysis. A-W.
Krall, Leo P.
xKrall, Leo P.
ed. Joslin Diabetes Manual. Lea & Febiger.
Krall, N. A.
xKrall, Nicholas A.
Principles of Plasma Physics. McGraw.
Krall, Nicholas A. *see* Krall, N. A.
Kramer, Aaron, 1921-
xKramer, Aaron.
ed. On Freedom's Side: An Anthology of
American Poems of Protest. Macmillan.
Kramer, Amihud.
xKramer, Amihud.
Food & the Consumer. AVI.
Kramer, Charles, 1915-
xKramer, Charles.
Medical Malpractice. PLI.
Kramer, Dale, 1936-
xKramer, Dale.
ed. Critical Approaches to the Fiction of
Thomas Hardy. B&N.
Kramer, Edith.
xKramer, Edith.
Childhood & Art Therapy: Notes on Theory &
Application. Schocken.
Kramer, Fred A., 1941-
xKramer, Fred A.
Contemporary Approaches to Public Budgeting.
Winthrop.
Dynamics of Public Bureaucracy: An
Introduction to Public Administration.
Winthrop.
Kramer, Hilton.
xKramer, Hilton.
The Age of the Avant-Garde: An Art
Chronicle of 1956-1972. FS&G.
Kramer, J. J. *see* Kramer, Jack.
Kramer, Jack, 1927-
xKramer, J. J.
The Last of the Grand Hotels. Van Nos
Reinhold.
xKramer, Jack.

Bromeliads: Colorful House Plants. Van Nos
Reinhold.
Cacti As Decorative Plants. Scribner.
The Complete Book of Terrarium Gardening.
Scribner.
Drip System Watering for Bigger & Better
Plants. Norton.
Flowering House Plants Month by Month.
Cornerstone.
Fold-Away Furniture. Cornerstone.
Gardening & Home Landscaping Guide. Arco.
Gardens Under Glass: The Miniature
Greenhouse in a Bottle, Bowl or Dish. S&S.
How to Play Your Best Tennis All the Time.
Atheneum.
Human Anatomy & Figure Drawing: The
Integration of Structure & Form. Van Nos
Reinhold.
The Indoor Gardener's First Aid Book. S&S.
The Indoor Gardener's How-to-Build-It Book.
S&S.
The Indoor Gardener's How-to-Build-It Book.
S&S.
The Log House Book. NAL.
The Old-Fashioned Cutting Garden: Growing
Flowers for Pleasure & Profit. Macmillan.
Orchids: Flowers of Romance & Mystery.
Abrams.
Outdoor Garden Build-It Book. Scribner.
Painting on Glass. Van Nos Reinhold.
The Pineapple Top Grower's Handbook. P-H.
Plant Hobbies: A Beginner's Book of
Gardening Projects, Principles & Pleasures.
Philomel.
Plant Sculptures: Making Miniature Indoor
Topiaries. Morrow.
Plants That Grow on Air. S&S.
Plants Under Lights. S&S.
Starting from Seed. Ballantine.
Kramer, Jane.
xKramer, Jane.
Honor to the Bride Like the Pigeon That
Guards Its Grain Under the Clove Tree.
FS&G.
The Last Cowboy. Har-Row.
The Last Cowboy. PB.
Unsettling Europe. Random.
Kramer, Janice.
xKramer, Janice.
Christmas ABC Book. Concordia.
Kramer, Jerry, 1936-
xKramer, Jerry.
Instant Replay: The Green Bay Diary of Jerry
Kramer. NAL.
Lombardi: Winning Is the Only Thing. T Y
Crowell.
Kramer, Joel, 1937-
xKramer, Joel.
The Passionate Mind: A Manual for Living
Creatively with One's Self. Celestial Arts.
Kramer, Justin.
xKramer, Justin.
Cast in America. J Kramer.
Cast in America. Piper.
Kramer, Klaas, 1916-
xKramer, Klaas.
Teaching Elementary School Mathematics.
Allyn.
Kramer, Magdalene E., 1898-
xKramer, Magdalene E.
Dramatic Tournaments in the Secondary
Schools. AMS Pr.
Kramer, Marlene.
xKramer, Marlene.
Path to Biculturalism. Nursing Res.
Kramer, Martin. *see* Kramer, Martin S.
Kramer, Martin S.
xKramer, Martin.

Political Islam. Sage.

Kramer, Mary.
xKramer, Mary.
Illustrated Guide to Foreign & Fancy Foods.
Plycon Pr.

Kramer, Mary E. see Kramer, Mary Eleanor.

Kramer, Mary Eleanor.
xKramer, Mary E.
One Thousand Literary Questions & Answers.
Folcroft.

Kramer, Paul J. see Kramer, Paul Jackson.

Kramer, Paul Jackson.
xKramer, Paul J.
Physiology of Woody Plants. Acad Pr.
Plant & Soil Water Relationships: A Modern
Synthesis. McGraw.

Kramer, Ralph M.
xKramer, Ralph M.
ed. Readings in Community Organization
Practice. P-H.

Kramer, Reuben.
xKramer, Reuben.
Art of Reuben Kramer. Walters Art.

Kramer, Samuel N. see Kramer, Samuel Noah.

Kramer, Samuel Noah.
xKramer, Samuel N.
Cradle of Civilization. Time-Life.
Cradle of Civilization. Silver.
From the Poetry of Sumer: Creation,
Glorification, Adoration. U of Cal Pr.
Sumerians: Their History, Culture & Character.
U of Chicago Pr.

Kramer, Stella, 1870-1936
xKramer, Stella.
English Craft Gilds & the Government: An
Examination of the Accepted Theory
Regarding the Decay of the Craft Guilds.
AMS Pr.

Kramer, Steven P. see Kramer, Steven Philip.

Kramer, Steven Philip.
xKramer, Steven P.
Abel Gance. Twayne.

Kramers, H. A. see Kramers, Hendrik Anthony.

Kramers, Hendrik Anthony, 1894-1952
xKramers, H. A.
Quantum Mechanics. Peter Smith.

Kramlich, W. E.
xKramlich, W. E.
Processed Meats. AVI.

Krammer, Arnold, 1941-
xKrammer, Arnold.
Nazi Prisoners of War in America. Stein &
Day.

Kramnick, Isaac.
xKramnick, Isaac.
Age of Ideology: Political Thought 1750 to the
Present. P-H.
ed. Is Britain Dying?: Perspectives on the
Current Crisis. Cornell U Pr.
Rage of Edmund Burke: Portrait of an
Ambivalent Conservative. Basic.

Kramrisch, Stella.
xKramrisch, Stella.
Indian Sculpture in the Philadelphia Museum
of Art. U of Pa Pr.

Kramsky, J. see Kramsky, Jiri.

Kramsky, Jiri.
xKramsky, J.
Papers in General Linguistics. Mouton.
xKramsky, Jiri.
The Article & the Concept of Definiteness in
Language. Mouton.

Krane, Robert J.
xKrane, Robert J.
ed. Clinical Neuro-Urology. Little.

Krane, Ronald E.
xKrane, Ronald E.

International Labor Migration in Europe.
Praeger.

Kranes, David.
xKranes, David.
Hunters in the Snow: A Collection of Short
Stories. U of Utah Pr.

Krannich, Ronald L.
xKrannich, Ronald L.
Mayors & Managers in Thailand: The Struggle
for Political Life in Administrative Settings.
Ohio U Ctr Intl.

Krant, Melvin J.
xKrant, Melvin J.
Dying & Dignity: The Meaning & Control of a
Personal Death. C C Thomas.

Krantz, David L.
xKrantz, David L.
Radical Career Change: Life Beyond Work.
Free Pr.

Krantz, G. W.
xKrantz, Gerald W.
Manual of Acarology. Oreg St U Bkstrs.

Krantz, Gerald W. see Krantz, G. W.

Krantz, Hazel.
xKrantz, Hazel.
Freestyle for Michael. Vanguard.

Krantz, John C. see Krantz, John Christian.

Krantz, John Christian, 1899-
xKrantz, John C.
Historical Medical Classics Involving New
Drugs. Krieger.

Krantz, Judith.
xKrantz, Judith.
Princess Daisy. Crown.

Krantz, Sheldon, 1938-
xKrantz, Sheldon.
Police Policymaking: The Boston Experience.
Lexington Bks.

Krantzler, Mel.
xKrantzler, Mel.
Creative Divorce: A New Opportunity for
Personal Growth. M Evans.
Learning to Love Again. T Y Crowell.

Kranyik, R. see Kranyik, Robert D.

Kranyik, Robert D.
xKranyik, R.
Stimulating Creative Learning in the
Elementary School: A Sourcebook of
Activities. P-H.

Kranz, Harry.
xKranz, Harry.
The Participatory Bureaucracy: Women &
Minorities in a More Representative Public
Service. Lexington Bks.

Kranz, Henry B., 1895-1964
xKranz, Henry B.
ed. Abraham Lincoln: A New Portrait. Arno.

Kranz, J. see Kranz, Jurgen.

Kranz, Jurgen.
xKranz, J.
ed. Diseases, Pests & Weeds in Tropical Crops.
Wiley.

Kranz, Sheldon.
xKranz, Sheldon.
The H Persuasion: How Persons Have
Permanently Changed from Homosexuality
Through the Study of Aesthetic Realism with
Eli Siegel. Definition.

Kranzberg, Melvin.
xKranzberg, Melvin.
ed. Ethics in an Age of Pervasive Technology.
Westview.
Siege of Paris: 1870-1871; a Political & Social
History. Greenwood.

Kranzler, David, 1930-
xKranzler, David.

My Jewish Roots: A Practical Guide to Tracing
& Recording Your Genealogy & Family
History. Hermon.

Krapesh, Patti.
xKrapesh, Patti.
Adapted by A Tale of Two Cities. Raintree
Pubs.

Krapf, Ludwig, 1810-1881
xKrapf, Ludwig.
ed. Dictionary of the Suahili Language. Negro
U Pr.

Krapp, George P. see Krapp, George Philip.

Krapp, George Philip, 1872-1934
xKrapp, George P.
English Language in America. Ungar.
Pronunciation of Standard English in America.
AMS Pr.

Krar, S. F. see Krar, Stephen F.

Krar, Stephen F.
xKrar, S. F.
Drilling Technology. Delmar.
Grinding Technology. Delmar.
Turning Technology: Engine & Turret Lathes.
Delmar.

Krashinsky, M. see Krashinsky, Michael.

Krashinsky, Michael, 1947-
xKrashinsky, M.
Day Care & Public Policy in Ontario. U of
Toronto Pr.

Krasilovsky, Phyllis.
xKrasilovsky, Phyllis.
The Man Who Tried to Save Time. Doubleday.
The Shy Little Girl. HM.
Susan Sometimes. Macmillan.

Krasinski, Zygmunt, Hrabia, 1812-1859
xKrasinski, Zygmunt.
The Un-Divine Comedy. Greenwood.

Kraska, Edie.
xKraska, Edie.
Toys & Tales from Grandmother's Attic. HM.

Kraske, Robert.
xKraske, Robert.
America the Beautiful: Stories of Patriotic
Songs. Garrard.
Daredevils Do Amazing Things. Random.
Magicians Do Amazing Things. Random.
The Statue of Liberty Comes to America.
Garrard.
The Story of the Dictionary. HarBraceJ.

Krasner, Leonard, 1924-
xKrasner, Leonard.
ed. Environmental Design & Human Behavior:
A Psychology of the Individual in Society.
Pergamon.

Krasnow, Erwin G.
xKrasnow, Erwin G.
The Politics of Broadcast Regulation. St
Martin.

Kratcoski, P. see Kratcoski, Peter C.

Kratcoski, Peter C.
xKratcoski, P.
Juvenile Delinquency. P-H.
xKratcoski, Peter C.
Criminal Justice in America: Process & Issues.
Scott F.

Kratochvil, Paul.
xKratochvil, Paul.
Chinese Language Today: Features of an
Emerging Standard. Humanities.

Kratovil, Robert, 1910-
xKratovil, Robert.
Modern Mortgage Law & Practice. P-H.
Real Estate Law. P-H.

Kratoville, Betty L. see Kratoville, Betty Lou.

Kratoville, Betty Lou.
xKratoville, Betty L.
Listen, My Children, & You Shall Hear.
Interstate.
xKratoville, Betty Lou.

Listen, My Children, & You Shall Hear.
Interstate.

Kratzenstein, Marilou, 1937-
xKratzenstein, Marilou.
Survey of Organ Literature & Editions. Iowa St
U Pr.

Kraus, Barbara.
xKraus, Barbara.
Calories & Carbohydrates. NAL.

Kraus, C. Norman. see Kraus, Clyde Norman.

Kraus, Clyde Norman.
xKraus, C. Norman.
ed. Evangelicalism & Anabaptism. Herald Pr.

Kraus, David.
xKraus, David.
Concepts in Modern Biology. Cambridge Bk.

Kraus, David H.
xKraus, David H.
National Science Information Systems: A
Guide to Science Information Systems in
Bulgaria, Czechoslovakia, Hungary, Poland,
Rumania, & Yugoslavia. MIT Pr.

Kraus, Elizabeth M.
xKraus, Elizabeth M.
The Metaphysics of Experience: A Companion
to Whitehead's "Process & Reality. Fordham.

Kraus, Ernest A.
xKraus, Ernest A.
Pathways Back to the Community. Springer
Pub.

Kraus, Gerhard.
xKraus, Gerhard.
Homo Sapiens in Decline: A Reappraisal of
Natural Selection. Humanities.

Kraus, H. P. see Kraus, Hans Peter.

Kraus, Hans, 1905-
xKraus, Hans.
Clinical Treatment of Back & Neck Pain.
McGraw.

Kraus, Hans Peter, 1907-
xKraus, H. P.
A Rare Book Saga: The Autobiography of H.
P. Kraus. Putnam.

Kraus, Henry, 1905-
xKraus, Henry.
Gold Was the Mortar: The Economics of
Cathedral Building. Routledge & Kegan.

Kraus, John D. see Kraus, John Daniel.

Kraus, John Daniel, 1910-
xKraus, John D.
Radio Astronomy. McGraw.

Kraus, Karl.
xKraus, Karl.
The Last Days of Mankind: A Tragedy in Five
Acts. Ungar.
No Compromise: Selected Writings of Karl
Kraus. Ungar.

Kraus, Laurence G.
xKraus, Laurence G.
Illegitimate Power: The History of the Secret
Ballot We Lack Today - Its Acceptance in
Our Country's Early Years - Its Present-Day
Power to Reform Congress, the Conventions
& the Parties. Rovi.

Kraus, Michael.
xKraus, Michael.
Atlantic Civilization: Eighteenth-Century
Origins. Cornell U Pr.
Immigration, the American Mosaic: From
Pilgrims to Modern Refugees. Krieger.
Immigration, The American Mosaic: From
Pilgrims to Modern Refugees. Van Nos
Reinhold.
The North Atlantic Civilization. Peter Smith.

Kraus, Michelle. see Kraus, Michelle P.

Kraus, Michelle P., 1953-
xKraus, Michelle.

Allen Ginsberg: An Annotated Bibliography,
1699-1977. Scarecrow.

Kraus, Rene, 1902-
xKraus, Rene.
Men Around Churchill. Arno.

Kraus, Richard. see Kraus, Richard A.

Kraus, Richard A.
xKraus, Richard.
A Cotton & Cotton Goods in China. Garland
Pub.

Kraus, Richard G.
xKraus, Richard.
A History of the Dance in Art & Education.
P-H.
xKraus, Richard G.
Creative Administration in Recreation & Parks.
Mosby.
Folk Dancing: A Guide for Schools, Colleges,
& Recreation Groups. Macmillan.
Social Recreation: A Group Dynamics
Approach. Mosby.

Kraus, Robert.
xKraus, Robert.
Another Mouse to Feed. Windmill Bks.
Boris Bad Enough. Windmill Bks.
illus. How Spider Saved Halloween. Schol Bk
Serv.
The Littlest Rabbit. Schol Bk Serv.
illus. Trouble with Spider. Har-Row.

Kraus, Sidney.
xKraus, Sidney.
The Effects of Mass Communication on
Political Behavior. Pa St U Pr.
ed. The Great Debates:
Background-Perspective-Effects. Peter Smith.

Kraus, W. Keith.
xKraus, W. Keith.
Murder, Mischief, & Mayhem: A Process for
Creative Research Papers. NCTE.

Krause, Chester L.
xKrause, Chester L.
Guidebook of Franklin Mint Issues: 1980.
Krause Pubns.
Standard Catalog of World Coins. Krause
Pubns.
Standard Catalog of World Coins: 1981. Krause
Pubns.

Krause, E. see Krause, Eugene F.

Krause, Elliot A. see Krause, Elliott A.

Krause, Elliott. see Krause, Elliott A.

Krause, Elliott A.
xKrause, Elliot A.
Power & Illness: The Political Sociology of
Health & Medical Care. Elsevier.
xKrause, Elliott.
Why Study Sociology?. Random.

Krause, Eugene F., 1937-
xKrause, E.
Taxicab Geometry. A-W.
xKrause, Eugene F.
Mathematics for Elementary Teachers. P-H.

Krause, F.
xKrause, F.
Mean-Field Magnetohydrodynamics &
Dynamo Theory. Pergamon.

Krause, Fred, 1941-
xKrause, Frederick J.
Liturgy in Parish Life: A Study of Worship &
the Celebrating Community. Alba.

Krause, Frederick J. see Krause, Fred.

Krause, Gail.
xKrause, Gail.
The Encyclopedia of Duncan Glass.
Exposition.

Krause, J. V. see Krause, Jerome V.

Krause, Jerome V.
xKrause, J. V.

The Mechanical Foundations of Human
Motion: A Programmed Text. Mosby.

Krause, Lawrence B.
xKrause, Lawrence B.
ed. Common Market: Progress & Controversy.
Peter Smith.
ed. Economic Interaction in the Pacific Basin.
Brookings.
European Economic Integration & the United
States. Brookings.

Krause, Marie V.
xKrause, Marie V.
Food, Nutrition & Diet Therapy. Saunders.

Krause, Sydney J. see Krause, Sydney Joseph.

Krause, Sydney Joseph.
xKrause, Sydney J.
Mark Twain As Critic. Johns Hopkins.

Krause, W. see Krause, Werner.

Krause, Walter.
xKrause, Walter.
Latin America & Economic Integration:
Regional Planning for Development. U of
Iowa Pr.

Krause, Werner, Dr. Rer. Nat.
xKrause, W.
ed. Application of Vegetation Science to
Grassland Husbandry. Kluwer Boston.

Krause, William H.
xKrause, William H.
How to Get Started As a Manufacturers'
Representative. Am Mgmt.
How to Hire & Motivate Manufacturers'
Representatives. Am Mgmt.

Kraushaar, Otto F.
xKraushaar, Otto F.
Private Schools: From the Puritans to the
Present. Phi Delta Kappa.

Kraushopf, Konrad B. see Krauskopf, Konrad Bates.

Krauskopf, Konrad Bates.
xKrauskopf, Konrad B.
Fundamentals of Physical Science. McGraw.
Introduction to Geochemistry. McGraw.
The Physical Universe. McGraw.
The Third Planet: An Invitation to Geology.
Freeman C.

Krauss, Bob.
xKrauss, Bob.
Grove Farm Plantation: The Biography of a
Hawaiian Sugar Plantation. Pacific Bks.

Krauss, Irving.
xKrauss, Irving.
Stratification, Class & Conflict. Free Pr.

Krauss, L. see Krauss, Leonard I.

Krauss, Leonard I.
xKrauss, L.
Administering & Controlling the Company
Data Processing Function. P-H.
xKrauss, Leonard I.
Computer-Based Management Information
Systems. Am Mgmt.
Computer Fraud & Countermeasures. P-H.

Krauss, Melvyn B.
xKrauss, Melvyn B.
ed. The Economics of Integration: A Book of
Readings. Allen Unwin.

Krauss, P. H. see Krauss, Peter H.

Krauss, Peter H.
xKrauss, P. H.
Global Subdirect Products. Am Math.

Krauss, Rosalind E.
xKrauss, Rosalind E.
Passages in Modern Sculpture. Viking Pr.

Krauss, Ruth.
xKrauss, Ruth.

Backward Day. Har-Row.
Carrot Seed. Har-Row.
The Carrot Seed. Schol Bk Serv.
Hole Is to Dig: A First Book of First
    Definitions. Har-Row.
I'll Be You - You Be Me. Bookstore Pr.
I'll Be You & You Be Me. Har-Row.
Little Boat Lighter Than a Cork. Magic Circle
    Pr.
Somebody Spilled the Sky. Greenwillow.
There's a Little Ambiguity Over There Among
    the Bluebells & Other Theater Poems.
    Ultramarine Pub.
illus. This Breast Gothic. Bookstore Pr.
Krausse, Alexis. *see* Krausse, Alexis Sidney.
Krausse, Alexis Sidney, 1859-1904
    xKrausse, Alexis.
    Russia in Asia: A Record & Study 1558-1899.
        Humanities.
Krausz, A. S.
    xKrausz, A. S.
    Deformation Kinetics. Wiley.
Krausz, Ernest.
    xKrausz, Ernest.
    ed. Studies of Israeli Society. Transaction Bks.
Krausz, Michael.
    xKrausz, Michael.
    ed. Critical Essays on the Philosophy of R. G.
        Collingwood. Oxford U Pr.
Kraut, Benny.
    xKraut, Benny.
    From Reform Judaism to Ethical Culture: The
        Religious Evolution of Felix Adler. Ktav.
Kraut, Edgar A.
    xKraut, Edgar A.
    Fundamentals of Mathematical Physics.
        Krieger.
Krautheimer, R. *see* Krautheimer, Richard.
Krautheimer, Richard, 1897-
    xKrautheimer, R.
    Lorenzo Ghiberti. Princeton U Pr.
    xKrautheimer, Richard.
    Early Christian & Byzantine Architecture.
        Penguin.
Krautkramer, J. *see* Krautkramer, Josef.
Krautkramer, Josef.
    xKrautkramer, J.
    Ultrasonic Testing of Materials.
        Springer-Verlag.
Kravis, Irving B.
    xKravis, Irving B.
    Price Competitiveness in World Trade. Natl
        Bur Econ Res.
    A System of International Comparisons of
        Gross Product & Purchasing Power. Johns
        Hopkins.
Kravitz, Jerome.
    xKravitz, Jerome H.
    ed. The Future Is Now: Readings in
        Introductory Psychology. Peacock Pubs.
Kravitz, Jerome H. *see* Kravitz, Jerome.
Krawitt, Laura P.
    xKrawitt, Laura P.
    Practical Low Protein Cookery. C C Thomas.
Krawitz, Henry.
    xKrawitz, Henry.
    A Post-Symbolist Bibliography. Scarecrow.
Kraybill, Donald B.
    xKraybill, Donald B.
    Our Star-Spangled Faith. Herald Pr.
Kraybill, H. F. *see* Kraybill, Herman Fink.
Kraybill, Herman Fink.
    xKraybill, H. F.
    ed. Aquatic Pollutants & Biologic Effects with
        Emphasis on Neoplasia. NY Acad Sci.
Krcma, Vaclav.
    xKrcma, Vaclav.

Identification & Registration of Firearms. C C
    Thomas.
Krebs, Carl.
    xKrebs, Carl.
    Dittersdorfiana. Da Capo.
Krebs, Charles J.
    xKrebs, Charles J.
    Ecology: The Experimental Analysis of
        Distribution & Abundance. Har-Row.
Krebs, Dennis.
    xKrebs, Dennis.
    ed. Readings in Social Psychology:
        Contemporary Perspectives. Har-Row.
Krech, David.
    xKrech, David.
    Psychology: A Basic Course. Knopf.
    ed. Theoretical Models & Personality Theory.
        Greenwood.
Krech, Richard.
    xKrech, Richard.
    The Incompleat Works of Richard Krech:
        Poems 1966-74. Litmus.
Kreck, Lothar A.
    xKreck, Lothar A.
    ed. Dimensions of Hospitality Management:
        (an Industry Performance in Seven Acts).
        CBI Pub.
Kreeft, Peter.
    xKreeft, Peter J.
    Love Is Stronger Than Death. Har-Row.
Kreeft, Peter J. *see* Kreeft, Peter.
Kreh, Bernard L. *see* Kreh, Lefty.
Kreh, Lefty.
    xKreh, Bernard L.
    Fly Fishing in Salt Water. Crown.
    xKreh, Lefty.
    Fly Casting with Lefty Kreh. Lippincott.
    Practical Fishing Knots. Crown.
Kreh, R. T.
    xKreh, Richard T.
    Advanced Masonry Skills. Delmar.
    Advanced Masonry Skills. Van Nos Reinhold.
    Masonry Skills. Delmar.
    Masonry Skills. Van Nos Reinhold.
    Safety for Masons. Delmar.
Kreh, Richard T. *see* Kreh, R. T.
Krehbiel, Edward Benjamin, 1878-
    xKrehbiel, Edward K.
    Nationalism, War & Society. Garland Pub.
Krehbiel, Edward K. *see* Krehbiel, Edward Benjamin.
Krehbiel, Henry E. *see* Krehbiel, Henry Edward.
Krehbiel, Henry Edward, 1854-1923
    xKrehbiel, Henry E.
    Afro-American Folksongs: A Study in Racial &
        National Music. Longwood Pr.
    Afro-American Folksongs: A Study in Racial &
        National Music. Ungar.
    Chapters of Opera: Being Historical & Critical
        Observations & Records Concerning the
        Lyric Drama in New York from Its Earliest
        Days Down to the Present Time. Hyperion
        Conn.
    How to Listen to Music: Hints & Suggestions
        to Untaught Lovers of the Art. Arden Lib.
    How to Listen to Music: (Hints & Suggestions
        to Untaught Lovers of the Art). Norwood
        Edns.
    More Chapters of Opera: Being Historical &
        Critical Observations & Records Concerning
        the Lyric Drama in New York from
        1908-1918. Hyperion Conn.
    Notes on the Cultivation of Choral Music &
        the Oratorio Society of New York. AMS Pr.
Kreidberg, Marjorie.
    xKreidberg, Marjorie.
    Food on the Frontier: Minnesota Cooking from
        1850 to 1900, with Selected Recipes. Minn
        Hist.
Kreidberg, Marvin A.
    xKreidberg, Marvin A.

History of Military Mobilization in the United
    States Army: 1775-1945. Greenwood.
Kreider, Alan, 1941-
    xKreider, Alan.
    English Chantries: The Road to Dissolution.
        Harvard U Pr.
Kreider, Barbara.
    xKreider, Barbara A.
    Index to Children's Plays in Collections.
        Scarecrow.
Kreider, Barbara A. *see* Kreider, Barbara.
Kreider, Donald L.
    xKreider, Donald L.
    Introduction to Linear Analysis. A-W.
Kreider, Paul V. *see* Kreider, Paul Vernon.
Kreider, Paul Vernon, 1892-
    xKreider, Paul V.
    Repetition in Shakespeare's Plays. Octagon.
Kreidl, John.
    xKreidl, John F.
    Nicholas Ray. Twayne.
Kreidl, John F. *see* Kreidl, John.
Kreigh, Helen Z.
    xKreigh, Helen Z.
    Psychiatric & Mental Health Nursing:
        Commitment to Care & Concern. Reston.
Kreilkamp, Thomas, 1941-
    xKreilkamp, Thomas.
    The Corrosion of the Self: Society's Effects on
        People. NYU Pr.
Kreimer, G. S. *see* Kreimer, Gersh Semkhovich.
Kreimer, Gersh Semkhovich.
    xKreimer, G. S.
    Strength of Hard Alloys. Plenum Pub.
Krein, David F.
    xKrein, David F.
    Last Palmerston Government: Foreign Policy,
        Domestic Politics, & the Genesis of "Splendid
        Isolation". Iowa St U Pr.
Krein, Mike.
    xKrein, Mike.
    Learn to Swim. Rand.
Krein, S. G. *see* Krein, Selim Grigorevich.
Krein, Selim Grigorevich.
    xKrein, S. G.
    Linear Differential Equations in Banach Space.
        Am Math.
Kreindler, A. *see* Kreindler, Arthur.
Kreindler, Arthur.
    xKreindler, A.
    Experimental Epilepsy. Elsevier.
Kreinin, Mordechai E. *see* Kreinin, Mordechai Elihau.
Kreinin, Mordechai Elihau, 1930-
    xKreinin, Mordechai E.
    Alternative Commercial Policies: Their Effect
        on the American Economy. Mich St U Busn.
    International Economics: A Policy Approach.
        HarBraceJ.
Kreisberg, Luisa.
    xKreisberg, Luisa.
    Local Government & the Arts. Am Council
        Arts.
Kreith, Frank.
    xKreith, Frank.
    Economics of Solar Energy & Conservation
        Systems. CRC Pr.
    Principles of Heat Transfer. Har-Row.
    Principles of Solar Engineering. McGraw.
Kreith, K. *see* Kreith, Kurt.
Kreith, Kurt.
    xKreith, K.
    Oscillation Theory. Springer-Verlag.
Kreitler, Hans.
    xKreitler, Hans.
    Cognitive Orientation & Behavior. Springer
        Pub.
    Psychology of the Arts. Duke.
    xKreitler, Shulamith.

jt. auth. Cognitive Orientation & Behavior. Springer Pub.
jt. auth. Psychology of the Arts. Duke.
Kreitler, Shulamith. *see* Kreitler, Hans.
Kreitman, Norman.
xKreitman, Norman.
ed. Parasuicide. Wiley.
Kreke, Cynthia A. *see* Kreke, Cynthia Adele.
Kreke, Cynthia Adele, 1948-
xKreke, Cynthia A.
Glad & Sorry Seasons. Beta Bk.
Krem, Viju.
xKrem, Viju.
How to Become a Successful Model. Arco.
Kremen, Kathryn R., 1943-
xKremen, Kathryn R.
The Imagination of the Resurrection: The Poetic Continuity of a Religious Motif in Donne, Blake, & Yeats. Bucknell U Pr.
Krementz, Jill.
xKrementz, Jill.
A Very Young Circus Flyer. Knopf.
A Very Young Skater. Knopf.
Kremer, J. *see* Kremer, James N.
Kremer, James N.
xKremer, J.
A Coastal Marine Ecosystem: Simulation & Analysis. Springer-Verlag.
Kremer, William F.
xKremer, William F.
The Doctors' Metabolic Diet. Avon.
Kremkau, Frederich W. *see* Kremkau, Frederich W.
Kremkau, Frederich W.
xKremkau, Frederich W.
Diagnostic Ultrasound: Physical Principles & Exercises. Grune.
Kren, George. *see* Kren, George M.
Kren, George M.
xKren, George.
ed. Varieties of Psychohistory. Springer Pub.
xKren, George M.
Holocaust & the Crisis of Human Behavior. Holmes & Meier.
Krenek, Ernst, 1900-
xKrenek, Ernst.
Horizons Circled: Reflections on My Music. U of Cal Pr.
Krenkel, Roy G., 1918-
xKrenkel, Roy G.
Cities & Scenes from the Ancient World. Owlswick Pr.
Krenov, James.
xKrenov, James.
A Cabinetmaker's Notebook. Van Nos Reinhold.
Fine Art of Cabinetmaking. Van Nos Reinhold.
The Impractical Cabinetmaker. Van Nos Reinhold.
Krensky. *see* Krensky, Stephen.
Krensky, Stephen.
xKrensky.
The Dragon Circle. Schol Bk Serv.
xKrensky, Stephen.
Castles in the Air & Other Tales. Atheneum.
The Dragon Circle. Atheneum.
The Perils of Putney. Atheneum.
A Troll in Passing. Atheneum.
Woodland Crossings. Atheneum.
Krentz, Edgar.
xKrentz, Edgar.
The Historical-Critical Method. Fortress.
Krenz, Jerrold H., 1934-
xKrenz, Jerrold H.
Energy: Conversion & Utilization. Allyn.
Krenz, Nancy.
xKrenz, Nancy.
Southwestern Arts & Crafts Projects. Sunstone Pr.
Krepel, Wayne J.
xKrepel, Wayne J.

Education & Education-Related Serials: A Directory. Libs Unl.
Kreps, Juanita M. *see* Kreps, Juanita Morris.
Kreps, Juanita Morris.
xKreps, Juanita M.
Lifetime Allocation of Work & Income: Essays in the Economics of Aging. Duke.
Kresge (S.S.) Company.
xKresge's.
Kresge's Katalog of 5 Cent & 10 Cent Merchandise. Random.
Kresge's. *see* Kresge (S.S.) Company.
Kreslins, Janis A.
xKreslins, Janis A.
ed. Foreign Affairs Bibliography: 1962-1972. Bowker.
Kress, George.
xKress, George J.
Marketing Research. Reston.
Kress, George J. *see* Kress, George.
Kress, Gunther. *see* Kress, Gunther R.
Kress, Gunther R.
xKress, Gunther.
Language As Ideology. Routledge & Kegan.
Kressel, H. *see* Kressel, Henry.
Kressel, Henry.
xKressel, H.
ed. Characterization of Epitaxial Semiconductor Films. Elsevier.
ed. Semiconductor Devices for Optical Communication. Springer-Verlag.
Kresser, T. O. *see* Kresser, Theodore O. J.
Kresser, Theodore O. J.
xKresser, T. O.
Polyolefin Plastics. Van Nos Reinhold.
Kretchmer, Norman.
xKretchmer, Norman.
Intro. by Human Nutrition: Readings from Scientific American. W H Freeman.
Kreter, L. *see* Kreter, Leo.
Kreter, Leo, 1933-
xKreter, L.
Sight & Sound: A Manual of Aural Musicianship. P-H.
Kretschmer, Ernst, 1888-1964
xKretschmer, Ernst.
Hysteria, Reflex, & Instinct. Greenwood.
Kreuger, Bob.
xKreuger, Bob.
The Wild Mustangs. McKay.
Kreuger, Miles.
xKreuger, Miles.
ed. Souvenir Programs of Twelve Classic Movies: 1927-1941. Dover.
Kreusler, Abraham A.
xKreusler, Abraham A.
Contemporary Education & Moral Upbringing in the Soviet Union. Univ Microfilms.
Kreutler, Patricia. *see* Kreutler, Patricia A.
Kreutler, Patricia A.
xKreutler, Patricia.
Nutrition in Perspective. P-H.
Kreuzer, James R.
xKreuzer, James R.
Literature for Composition. HR&W.
Krey, August C. *see* Krey, August Charles.
Krey, August Charles, 1887-
xKrey, August C.
History & the Social Web: A Collection of Essays. U of Minn Pr.
Krey, Isabelle A.
xKrey, Isabelle A.
Principles & Techniques of Effective Business Communication: A Text-Workbook. HarBraceJ.
Kreyche, Robert J, 1920-
xKreyche, Robert J.
Logic for Undergraduates. HR&W.
Kreyling, Michael, 1948-
xKreyling, Michael.

Eudora Welty's Achievement of Order. La State U Pr.
Kribbs, Jayne K.
xKribbs, Jayne K.
ed. An Annotated Bibliography of American Literary Periodicals, 1741-1850. G K Hall.
Krich, Aron M., 1916-
xKrich, Aron M.
Homosexuals: As Seen by Themselves & Thirty Authorities. Citadel Pr.
Krichmar, Albert.
xKrichmar, Albert.
The Women's Rights Movement in the United States 1848-1970: A Bibliography & Sourcebook. Scarecrow.
Krick, Edward V.
xKrick, Edward V.
An Introduction to Engineering & Engineering Design. Wiley.
Introduction to Engineering: Methods, Concepts & Issues. Wiley.
Modern Engineering: A Short Course for Professionals. Wiley.
Krickus, Richard.
xKrickus, Richard.
Pursuing the American Dream: White Ethnics & the New Populism. Ind U Pr.
Krieg, Arthur F., 1930-
xKrieg, Arthur F.
Clinical Laboratory Computerization. Univ Park.
Krieg, Carl E.
xKrieg, Carl E.
What to Believe?: The Questions of Christian Faith. Fortress.
Kriegel, Annie.
xKriegel, Annie.
Eurocommunism: A New Kind of Communism?. Hoover Inst Pr.
The French Communists: Profile of a People. U of Chicago Pr.
Kriegel, Leonard, 1933-
xKriegel, Leonard.
Edmund Wilson. S Ill U Pr.
Of Men & Manhood. Dutton.
Krieger, David. *see* Krieger, David L.
Krieger, David L.
xKrieger, David.
illus. Letters & Words. A-W.
Krieger, Dolores.
xKrieger, Dolores.
The Therapeutic Touch: How to Use Your Hands to Help or to Heal. P-H.
Krieger, Elliot.
xKrieger, Elliot.
A Marxist Study of Shakespeare's Comedies. B&N.
Krieger, Laura B. *see* Krieger, Laura Bertha Maria.
Krieger, Laura Bertha Maria, 1902-
xKrieger, Laura B.
Prediction of Success in Professional Courses for Teachers. AMS Pr.
Krieger, Leonard.
xKrieger, Leonard.
Ranke: The Meaning of History. U of Chicago Pr.
Krieger, Morris, 1924-
xKrieger, Morris.
Homeowner's Encyclopedia of House Construction. McGraw.
Structured Microprocessor Programming. Yourdon.
Krieger, Murray, 1923-
xKrieger, Murray.

Classic Vision: The Retreat from Extremity in
Modern Literature. Johns Hopkins.
ed. Directions for Criticism: Structuralism & Its
Alternatives. U of Wis Pr.
The Play & Place of Criticism. Johns Hopkins.
Poetic Presence & Illusion: Essays in Critical
History & Theory. Johns Hopkins.
Theory of Criticism: A Tradition & Its System.
Johns Hopkins.
Krier, James E.
xKrier, James E.
Pollution & Policy: A Case Essay on California
& Federal Experience with Motor Vehicle
Air Pollution, 1940-1975. U of Cal Pr.
Kriesberg, Louis.
xKriesberg, Louis.
Mothers in Poverty: A Study of Fatherless
Families. Greenwood.
Social Inequality. P-H.
Sociology of Social Conflicts. P-H.
Krill, Donald F.
xKrill, Donald F.
Existential Social Work. Free Pr.
Krimm, Gerald.
xKrimm, Gerald.
A Copperplate Manual: An Introduction to
Writing with the Pointed Pen. Taplinger.
Krinitzsky, E. L.
xKrinitzsky, E. L.
Loess Deposits of Mississippi. Geol Soc.
Radiography in the Earth Sciences & Soil
Mechanics. Plenum Pub.
Krinsky, Fred, 1924-
xKrinsky, Fred.
ed. Democracy & Complexity: Who Governs
the Governors. Glencoe.
ed. Politics of Religion in America. Glencoe.
Kripke, Saul A., 1940-
xKripke, Saul A.
Naming & Necessity. Harvard U Pr.
Krippendorff, K. *see* Krippendorff, Klaus.
Krippendorff, Klaus.
xKrippendorff, K.
Communication & Control in Society. Gordon.
Krippner, Stanley.
xKrippner, Stanley.
ed. LSD in the Eighties. Unity Pr.
The Realms of Healing. Celestial Arts.
Kris, Ernst, 1900-
xKris, Ernst.
Psychoanalytic Explorations in Art. Intl Univs
Pr.
Krisberg, Barry.
xKrisberg, Barry A.
The Gang & the Community. R & E Res
Assoc.
Krisberg, Barry A. *see* Krisberg, Barry.
Krisch, Henry.
xKrisch, Henry.
German Politics Under Soviet Occupation.
Columbia U Pr.
Krishan, R. *see* Krishan, Ram.
Krishan, Ram, 1919-
xKrishan, R.
Agricultural Demonstration & Extension
Communication. Asia.
Krishef, Robert K.
xKrishef, Robert K.
Dolly Parton. Lerner Pubns.
Grand Ole Opry. Lerner Pubns.
Indianapolis 500. Lerner Pubns.
Introducing of Country Music. Lerner Pubns.
Loretta Lynn. Lerner Pubns.
More New Breed Stars. Lerner Pubns.
Our Remarkable Feet. Lerner Pubns.
Krishnamurti, J. *see* Krishnamurti, Jiddu.
Krishnamurti, Jiddu, 1895-
xKrishnamurti, J.

The Awakening of Intelligence. Avon.
Exploration into Insight. Har-Row.
Meditations. Har-Row.
The Wholeness of Life. Har-Row.
xKrishnamurti, Jiddu.
Education & the Significance of Life. Har-Row.
The First & Last Freedom. Har-Row.
Freedom from the Known. Har-Row.
The Impossible Question. Har-Row.
Life Ahead. Har-Row.
Only Revolution. Har-Row.
The Only Revolution. Har-Row.
Think on These Things. Har-Row.
Krishnan, S. S.
xKrishnan, S. S.
An Introduction to Modern Criminal
Investigation: With Basic Laboratory
Techniques. C C Thomas.
Krishnaswami, P. *see* Krishnaswami, P. R.
Krishnaswami, P. R., 1893-
xKrishnaswami, P.
In Thackeray's Workshop. Arden Lib.
xKrishnaswami, P. R.
In Thackeray's Workshop. Folcroft.
Krishnaswami, S.
xKrishnaswami, S.
Musical Instruments of India. InterCulture.
Krislov, Samuel.
xKrislov, Samuel.
ed. Compliance & the Law: A
Multi-Disciplinary Approach. Sage.
Negro in Federal Employment: The Quest for
Equal Opportunity. U of Minn Pr.
Krisman, Sue.
xKrisman, Sue.
The Thursby People. St Martin.
Krispyn, Egbert.
xKrispyn, Egbert.
Anti-Nazi Writers in Exile. U of Ga Pr.
Style & Society in German Literary
Expressionism. U Presses Fla.
Kristeller, Paul O. *see* Kristeller, Paul Oskar.
Kristeller, Paul Oskar.
xKristeller, Paul O.
ed. Catalogus Translationum et
Commentariorum: Mediaeval & Renaissance
Latin Translations & Commentaries,
Annotated Lists & Guides. Intl Schol Bk
Serv.
Eight Philosophers of the Italian Renaissance.
Stanford U Pr.
Renaissance Thought & Its Sources. Columbia
U Pr.
Renaissance Thought: The Classic, Scholastic &
Humanistic Strains. Peter Smith.
Kristensen, Thorkil, 1899-
xKristensen, Thorkil.
The Economic World Balance. Greenwood.
Kristeva, Julia, 1941-
xKristeva, Julia.
About Chinese Women. Urizen Bks.
Kristol, Irving.
xKristol, Irving.
America's Continuing Revolution: An Act of
Conservation. Am Enterprise.
Two Cheers for Capitalism. Basic.
Two Cheers for Capitalism. NAL.
Kritoboulos, 15th cent
xKritoboulos.
History of Mehmed the Conqueror.
Greenwood.
Kritzeck, James.
xKritzeck, James.
ed. Anthology of Islamic Literature: From the
Rise of Islam to Modern Times. NAL.
Kritzman, Ellen. *see* Kritzman, Ellen B.
Kritzman, Ellen B.
xKritzman, Ellen.

Little Mammals of the Pacific Northwest.
Pacific Search.
Krivoglaz, M. A. *see* Krivoglaz, Mikhail Aleksandrovich.
Krivoglaz, Mikhail Aleksandrovich.
xKrivoglaz, M. A.
Theory of X-Ray & Thermal Neutron
Scattering by Real Crystals. Plenum Pub.
Kriyananda, Swami.
xKriyananda, Swami.
The Path: Autobiography of a Western Yogi.
Ananda.
Kriyananda, Swami. *see* Kriyananda.
Krmpotic, Vesna, 1932-
xKrmpotic, Vesna.
Eyes of Eternity: A Spiritual Autobiography.
HarBraceJ.
Kroack, Lou.
xKroack, Lou.
Collecting & Building Model Trucks. TAB Bks.
Kroc, Ray.
xKroc, Ray.
Grinding It Out: The Making of McDonald's.
Berkley Pub.
Grinding It Out: The Making of McDonald's.
Contemp Bks.
Kroch, Anthony S.
xKroch, Anthony S.
The Semantics of Scope in English. Garland
Pub.
Krochalis, Jeanne.
xKrochalis, Jeanne.
ed. The World of Piers Plowman. U of Pa Pr.
Krochmal, Arnold.
xKrochmal, Arnold.
Caribbean Cooking. Times Bks.
The Complete Illustrated Book of Dyes from
Natural Sources. Doubleday.
Krochmal, Connie.
xKrochmal, Connie.
jt. auth. Caribbean Cooking. Times Bks.
jt. auth. The Complete Illustrated Book of
Dyes from Natural Sources. Doubleday.
Kroeber, A. L. *see* Kroeber, Alfred Louis.
Kroeber, Alfred. *see* Kroeber, Alfred Louis.
Kroeber, Alfred L. *see* Kroeber, Alfred Louis.
Kroeber, Alfred Louis, 1876-1960
xKroeber, A. L.
Cultural & Natural Areas of Native North
America. Kraus Repr.
Yurok Myths. U of Cal Pr.
xKroeber, Alfred.
Peoples of the Philippines. Greenwood.
xKroeber, Alfred L.
Anthropology: Biology & Race. HarBraceJ.
Anthropology: Culture Patterns & Processes.
HarBraceJ.
The Arapaho. Ye Galleon.
Nature of Culture. U of Chicago Pr.
Style & Civilizations. Greenwood.
Kroeber, Donald. *see* Kroeber, Donald W.
Kroeber, Donald W.
xKroeber, Donald.
The Manager's Guide to Statistics &
Quantitative Methods. McGraw.
Kroeber, Frederick V., 1904-
xKroeber, Frederick V.
Public Swimming Pools: A Manual of
Operation. A S Barnes.
Kroeber, Karl, 1926-
xKroeber, Karl.
Artifice of Reality: Poetic Style in Wordsworth,
Foscolo, Keats, & Leopardi. U of Wis Pr.
ed. Images of Romanticism: Verbal & Visual
Affinities. Yale U Pr.
Kroeber, Theodora.
xKroeber, Theodora.
Green Christmas. Parnassus.
Kroeker, Marvin E., 1928-
xKroeker, Marvin E.

Great Plains Command: William B. Hazen in the Frontier West. U of Okla Pr.

Kroes, William H.
xKroes, William H.
Society's Victim -- the Policeman: An Analysis of Job Stress in Policing. C C Thomas.

Kroger, F. A. *see* Kroger, Ferdinand Anne.

Kroger, Ferdinand Anne.
xKroger, F. A.
The Chemistry of Imperfect Crystals. Elsevier.

Kroger, William S.
xKroger, William S.
Childbirth with Hypnosis. Wilshire.
Clinical & Experimental Hypnosis in Medicine, Dentistry, & Psychology. Lippincott.
Hypnosis & Behavior Modification: Imagery Conditioning. Lippincott.

Krogh, August, 1874-1949
xKrogh, August.
Osmotic Regulation in Aquatic Animals. Dover.
Osmotic Regulation in Aquatic Animals. Peter Smith.

Krogman, W. M. *see* Krogman, Wilton Marion.

Krogman, Wilton M. *see* Krogman, Wilton Marion.

Krogman, Wilton Marion, 1903-
xKrogman, W. M.
Child Growth. U of Mich Pr.
xKrogman, Wilton M.
Human Skeleton in Forensic Medicine. C C Thomas.

Krohn, Ernst C. *see* Krohn, Ernst Christopher.

Krohn, Ernst Christopher, 1888-
xKrohn, Ernst C.
Music Publishing in the Middle Western States Before the Civil War. Info Coord.

Krohn, Lawrence H.
xKrohn, Lawrence H.
High-Resolution Electrocardiography: A Superior Diagnostic Modality. C C Thomas.

Krohn, Marvin D.
xKrohn, Marvin D.
ed. Crime, Law, & Sanctions: Theoretical Perspectives. Sage.

Krol, John C. *see* Krol, John Joseph.

Krol, John Joseph, 1910-
xKrol, John C.
God-the Cornerstone of Our Life. Dghtrs St Paul.

Krolick, Robert S.
xKrolick, Robert S.
Administrator's Manual for Plastics Education. Bobbs.

Kroll. *see* Kroll, Steven.

Kroll, Jarrett.
xKroll, Jarrett.
Cruising the Inland Waterways of Europe. Har-Row.

Kroll, John H.
xKroll, John H.
Athenian Bronze Allotment Plates. Harvard U Pr.

Kroll, Stanley.
xKroll, Stanley.
The Commodity Futures Market Guide. Har-Row.

Kroll, Steven.
xKroll.
Fat Magic. Schol Bk Serv.
xKroll, Steven.

Amanda & the Giggling Ghost. Holiday.
The Candy Witch. Holiday.
Fat Magic. Holiday.
If I Could Be My Grandmother. Pantheon.
Monster Birthday. Holiday.
Space Cats. Holiday.
T. J. Folger. Thief. Holiday.
That Makes Me Mad!. Pantheon.
The Tyrannosaurus Game. Holiday.

Kroman, Henry S.
xKroman, Henry S.
ed. Theory & Application of Gas Chromatography in Industry & Medicine. Grune.

Kroman, Vera.
xKroman, Vera.
How to Raise & Train a Samoyed. TFH Pubns.

Kromer, Helen.
xKromer, Helen.
Communes & Communitarians in America. Viking Pr.

Kromer, Ralph E. *see* Kromer, Ralph Eugene.

Kromer, Ralph Eugene.
xKromer, Ralph E.
Asymptotic Properties of the Autoregressive Spectral Estimator. Mgmt Info Serv.

Kronemeyer, Robert.
xKronemeyer, Robert.
Overcoming Homosexuality. Macmillan.

Kronenberger, Louis, 1904-
xKronenberger, Louis.
ed. Atlantic Brief Lives: A Biographical Companion to the Arts. Little.
The Last Word: Portraits of Fourteen Master Aphorists. Macmillan.
Oscar Wilde. Little.

Kronenthal, Richard L.
xKronenthal, Richard L.
ed. Polymers in Medicine & Surgery. Plenum Pub.

Kroner, Richard, 1884-
xKroner, Richard.
Culture & Faith. U of Chicago Pr.
The Primacy of Faith. AMS Pr.

Kronick, David A., 1917-
xKronick, David A.
History of Scientific & Technical Periodicals: The Origins & Development of the Scientific & Technical Press, 1665-1790. Scarecrow.

Kronovet, Esther.
xKronovet, Esther.
ed. In Pursuit of Awareness: The College Student in the Modern World. Irvington.

Kronstein, Heinrich. *see* Kronstein, Heinrich David.

Kronstein, Heinrich David.
xKronstein, Heinrich.
The Law of International Cartels. Cornell U Pr.

Krook, Dorothea.
xKrook, Dorothea.
Ordeal of Consciousness in Henry James. Cambridge U Pr.

Krooss, Herman E. *see* Krooss, Herman Edward.

Krooss, Herman Edward.
xKrooss, Herman E.
American Business History. P-H.
History of Financial Intermediaries. Phila Bk Co.

Kropotkin, P. A. *see* Kropotkin, Petr Alekseevich.

Kropotkin, Peter. *see* Kropotkin, Petr Alekseevich.

Kropotkin, Petr A. *see* Kropotkin, Petr Alekseevich.

Kropotkin, Petr Alekseevich, Kniaz', 1842-1921
xKropotkin, P. A.
Conquest of Bread. Kraus Repr.
xKropotkin, Peter.

Conquest of Bread. Arno.
The Conquest of Bread. NYU Pr.
The Great French Revolution. Schocken.
In Russian & French Prisons. Schocken.
Memoirs of a Revolutionist. Dover.
Memoirs of a Revolutionist. Peter Smith.
Mutual Aid: A Factor of Evolution. NYU Pr.
xKropotkin, Petr A.
Ideals & Realities in Russian Literature. Greenwood.
xKropotkin, Petra.
Ideals & Realities in Russian Literature. R West.

Kropotkin, Petra. *see* Kropotkin, Petr Alekseevich.

Kropp, Lloyd.
xKropp, Lloyd.
The Drift. Nordon Pubns.
One Hundred Times to China. Doubleday.

Krosby, H. Peter.
xKrosby, H. Peter.
Finland, Germany & the Soviet Union, 1940-1941: The Petsamo Dispute. U of Wis Pr.

Krotee, March L.
xKrotee, March L.
The Theory & Practice of Physical Activity. Kendall-Hunt.

Kroth, Jerome A.
xKroth, Jerome A.
Child Sexual Abuse: Analysis of a Family Therapy Approach. C C Thomas.
Counseling Psychology & Guidance: An Overview in Outline. C C Thomas.
Programmed Primer in Learning Disabilities. C C Thomas.

Kroth, Roger L.
xKroth, Roger L.
Getting Schools Involved with Parents. Coun Exc Child.

Krotkov, Iurii, 1917-
xKrotkov, Yuri.
The Nobel Prize. S&S.
The Red Monarch: Scenes from the Life of Stalin. Norton.

Krotkov, Yuri. *see* Krotkov, Iurii.

Krovetz, J. *see* Krovetz, L. Jerome.

Krovetz, L. Jerome.
xKrovetz, J.
Handbook of Pediatric Cardiology. Univ Park.

Krstic, R. V. *see* Krstic, Radivoj V.

Krstic, Radivoj V., 1935-
xKrstic, R. V.
Ultrastructure of the Mammalian Cell: An Atlas. Springer-Verlag.

Krueger, Elizabeth A.
xKrueger, Elizabeth A.
Hypodermic Injection: A Programed Unit. Tchrs Coll.

Krueger, Judith. *see* Krueger, Judith Amerkan.

Krueger, Judith Amerkan.
xKrueger, Judith.
Endocrine Problems in Nursing: A Physiologic Approach. Mosby.

Krueger, Robert G.
xKrueger, Robert G.
Introduction to Microbiology. Macmillan.

Krueger, Walter, 1881-
xKrueger, Walter.
From Down Under to Nippon: The Story of Sixth Army in World War II. Zenger Pub.

Kruer, A. C.
xKruer, A. C.
They Also Speak. Broadman.

Krug, Mark. *see* Krug, Mark M.

Krug, Mark M., 1915-
xKrug, Mark.
The Melting of the Ethnics: Education of the Immigrants, 1880-1914. Phi Delta Kappa.

Krug, Samuel E.
xKrug, Samuel E.

ed. Psychological Assessment in Medicine. Inst Personality & Ability.
Kruger, A. N. *see* Kruger, Arthur N.
Kruger, Arthur N.
xKruger, A. N.
Modern Debate: Its Logic & Strategy. McGraw.
xKruger, Arthur N.
Argumentation & Debate: A Classified Bibliography. Scarecrow.
Kruger, Daniel H.
xKruger, Daniel H.
Collective Bargaining in the Public Service. Phila Bk Co.
Kruger, Paul, 1925-
xKruger, Paul.
Principles of Activation Analysis. Wiley.
Krugers, J.
xKrugers, Jan.
ed. Instrumentation in Applied Nuclear Chemistry. Plenum Pub.
Krugers, Jan. *see* Krugers, J.
Kruglak, Theodore E. *see* Kruglak, Theodore Eduard.
Kruglak, Theodore Eduard.
xKruglak, Theodore E.
The Two Faces of TASS. Greenwood.
Krugman, Saul.
xKrugman, Saul.
Infectious Diseases of Children. Mosby.
Kruk, Zofia.
xKruk, Zofia.
The Taste of Hope. Merrimack Bk Serv.
Krulik, Stephen.
xKrulik, Stephen.
The Civil Service Examination Handbook. NAL.
Teaching Secondary School Mathematics. HR&W.
Krumbacher, Karl, 1856-1909
xKrumbacher, Karl.
Geschichte der Byzantinischen Litteratur: Von Justinian Bis Zum Ende Des Ostromischen Reiches. B Franklin.
Krumbein, William C. *see* Krumbein, William Christian.
Krumbein, William Christian, 1902-
xKrumbein, William C.
Stratigraphy & Sedimentation. W H Freeman.
Krumbhaar, E. B. *see* Krumbhaar, Edward Bell.
Krumbhaar, Edward B. *see* Krumbhaar, Edward Bell.
Krumbhaar, Edward Bell, M.d, 1882-
xKrumbhaar, E. B.
Pathology. Hafner.
xKrumbhaar, Edward B.
Pathology. AMS Pr.
Krumboltz, J. D. *see* Krumboltz, John D.
Krumboltz, John D.
xKrumboltz, J. D.
Counseling Methods. HR&W.
Krumgold, Joseph, 1908-
xKrumgold, Joseph.
Onion John. Apollo Eds.
Onion John. T Y Crowell.
Krumhansl, Bernice.
xKrumhansl, Bernice.
Opportunities in Physical Therapy. Natl Textbk.
Krump, John.
xKrump, John.
Hope for the Future?: Youth & the Church. Thomas More.
Krumpelmann, John T, 1892-
xKrumpelmann, John T.
Southern Scholars in Goethe's Germany. U of NC Pr.
Krupa, S. V. *see* Krupa, Sagar V.
Krupa, Sagar V.
xKrupa, S. V.
ed. Ecology of Root Pathogens. Elsevier.
Krupa, Viktor.
xKrupa, Viktor.

Polynesian Languages: A Survey of Research. Mouton.
Krupat, Edward.
xKrupat, Edward.
Psychology Is Social: Readings & Conversations in Social Psychology. Scott F.
Krupinski, Jerzy.
xKrupinski, Jerzy.
The Family in Australia: Social, Demographic & Psychological Aspects. Pergamon.
Krupp, Nate.
xKrupp, Nate.
The Omega Generation?. New Leaf.
Kruse. *see* Kruse, Louise C.
Kruse, Alexander Z., 1890-
xKruse, Alexander Z.
How to Draw & Paint. Har-Row.
Kruse, Arthur H., 1928-
xKruse, Arthur H.
Localization & Iteration of Axiomatic Set Theory. Wayne St U Pr.
Kruse Classic Auction Co. *see* Kruse Classic Auction Company.
Kruse Classic Auction Company.
xKruse Classic Auction Co.
The Kruse Professional Price Guide to Collector Cars. Hse of Collectibles.
Official Price Guide to Collector Cars. Hse of Collectibles.
xKruse Classic Auction Company, Inc.
The Kruse Professional Price Guide to Collector Cars. Wallace-Homestead.
Kruse Classic Auction Company, Inc. *see* Kruse Classic Auction Company.
Kruse, Frederik V. *see* Kruse, Frederik Vinding.
Kruse, Frederik Vinding, 1880-1963
xKruse, Frederik V.
The Foundation of Human Thought: The Problem of Science & Ethics. Greenwood.
Kruse, Louise C.
xKruse.
Cancer: Pathophysiology Etiology, Management: Selected Readings. Mosby.
Kruse, Paul J. *see* Kruse, Paul Jehu.
Kruse, Paul Jehu, 1883-
xKruse, Paul J.
The Overlapping of Attainments in Certain Sixth, Seventh & Eighth Grades. AMS Pr.
Krushkal, Samuel L. *see* Krushkal, Samuil Leibovich.
Krushkal, Samuil Leibovich.
xKrushkal, Samuel L.
Quasiconformal Mappings & Riemann Surfaces. Halsted Pr.
Krusich, Walter S.
xKrusich, Walter S.
Drugs: It Can't Happen to Me!. Accent Bks.
Krusz, Dorie.
xKrusz, Dorie.
Building Miniature Houses & Furniture. Arco.
Krutch, Joseph W. *see* Krutch, Joseph Wood.
Krutch, Joseph Wood, 1893-
xKrutch, Joseph W.
Comedy & Conscience After the Restoration. Columbia U Pr.
Comedy & Conscience After the Restoration. Russell.
Desert Year. Penguin.
Intro. by Grand Canyon. Luce.
Grand Canyon. Morrow.
Grand Canyon: Today & All Its Yesterdays. Peter Smith.
Human Nature & the Human Condition. Greenwood.
Measure of Man: On Freedom, Human Values, Survival & the Modern Temper. Peter Smith.
Krutchkoff, R. G. *see* Krutchkoff, Richard G.
Krutchkoff, Richard G., 1933-
xKrutchkoff, R. G.

Probability & Statistical Inference. Gordon.
Krutilla, John V.
xKrutilla, John V.
The Columbia River Treaty: The Economics of an International River Basin Development. Johns Hopkins.
Krutz, Ronald L., 1938-
xKrutz, Ronald L.
Microprocessors & Logic Design. Wiley.
Krutza, William J.
xKrutza, William J.
Devotionals for Modern Men. Baker Bk.
Dynamic Devotionals for Men. Baker Bk.
Facing the Issues. Baker Bk.
Graduate's Guide to Success. Baker Bk.
Kruuk, Hans.
xKruuk, Hans.
Hyaena. Oxford U Pr.
Kruus, Peeter, 1939-
xKruus, Peeter.
Liquids & Solutions: Structure & Dynamics. Dekker.
Krylov. *see* Krylov, Konstantin Arkadevich.
Krylov, Konstantin Arkadevich.
xKrylov.
The Soviet Economy: How It Really Works. Lexington Bks.
Krylov, Nikolai S. *see* Krylov, Nikolai Sergeevich.
Krylov, Nikolai Sergeevich, 1917-1947
xKrylov, Nikolai S.
Works on the Foundations of Statistical Physics. Princeton U Pr.
Krymov, Iurii S. *see* Krymov, Iurii Solomonovich.
Krymov, Iurii Solomonovich, 1908-1941
xKrymov, Iurii S.
Tanker Derbent. Hyperion Conn.
Krypton, Constantine, Pseud.
xKrypton, Constantine.
Northern Sea Route & the Economy of the Soviet North. Greenwood.
Krystal, Henry.
xKrystal, Henry.
ed. Massive Psychic Trauma. Intl Univs Pr.
Kryter, Karl D.
xKryter, Karl D.
Effects of Noise on Man. Acad Pr.
Krythe, Maymie R. *see* Krythe, Maymie Richardson.
Krythe, Maymie Richardson.
xKrythe, Maymie R.
All About Christmas. Har-Row.
What So Proudly We Hail: All About Our American Flag, Monuments & Symbols. Har-Row.
Krzyz, J. G. *see* Krzyz, Jan G.
Krzyz, Jan G.
xKrzyz, J. G.
Problems in Complex Variable Theory. Elsevier.
Kshirsagar, A. M. *see* Kshirsagar, Anant M.
Kshirsagar, Anant M.
xKshirsagar, A. M.
Multivariate Analysis. Dekker.
Kubala, T. S. *see* Kubala, Thomas S.
Kubala, Thomas S.
xKubala, T. S.
Circuit Concepts: Direct & Alternating Current. Delmar.
xKubala, Thomas S.
Circuit Concepts: Direct & Alternating Current. Van Nos Reinhold.
Kubalkova, V.
xKubalkova, V.
Marxism-Leninism & the Theory of International Relations. Routledge & Kegan.
Kubat, Daniel.
xKubat, Daniel.
ed. The Politics of Migration Policies: The First World in the 1970's. Ctr Migration.
Kubie, Lawrence S. *see* Kubie, Lawrence Schlesinger.

Kubie, Lawrence Schlesinger, 1896-
 xKubie, Lawrence S.
  Practical & Theoretical Aspects of
   Psychoanalysis. Intl Univs Pr.
Kubilius, Jonas.
 xKubilius, Jonas.
  Probabilistic Methods in the Theory of
   Numbers. Am Math.
Kubler, George, 1912-
 xKubler, George.
  Aspects of Classic Maya Rulership on Two
   Inscribed Vessels. Dumbarton Oaks.
  Portuguese Plain Architecture: Between Spices
   & Diamonds, 1521-1706. Columbia U Pr.
  Religious Architecture of New Mexico: In the
   Colonial Period & Since the American
   Occupation. U of NM Pr.
  Studies in Classic Maya Iconography. Shoe
   String.
Kubler-Ross, E. see Kubler-Ross, Elisabeth.
Kubler-Ross, Elisabeth.
 xKubler-Ross, E.
  Questions & Answers on Death & Dying.
   Macmillan.
 xKubler-Ross, Elisabeth.
  ed. Death: The Final Stage of Growth. P-H.
  Questions & Answers on Death & Dying.
   Macmillan.
Kublin, Hyman.
 xKublin, Hyman.
  China: Selected Readings. HM.
  India. HM.
Kubly, Herbert.
 xKubly, Herbert.
  Easter in Sicily. S&S.
Kubly, Vincent. see Kubly, Vincent F.
Kubly, Vincent F.
 xKubly, Vincent.
  The Louisiana Capitol: Its Art & Architecture.
   Pelican.
Kubo, Sakae, 1926-
 xKubo, Sakae.
  Acquitted!: Message from the Cross. Pacific Pr
   Pub Assn.
  God Meets Man: A Theology of the Sabbath &
   the Second Advent. Southern Pub.
Kubota, Akira.
 xKubota, Akira.
  Higher Civil Servants in Post-War Japan: Their
   Social Origins, Educational Background, &
   Career Patterns. Princeton U Pr.
Kucera, Clair L.
 xKucera, Clair L.
  The Challenge of Ecology. Mosby.
  Grasses of Missouri. U of Mo Pr.
Kucers, A.
 xKucers, A.
  The Use of Antibiotics: A Comprehensive
   Review with Clinical Emphasis. Lippincott.
Kucherov, Samuel.
 xKucherov, Samuel.
  Courts, Lawyers, & Trials Under the Last
   Three Tsars. Greenwood.
Kuchler, A. W. see Kuchler, August Wilhelm.
Kuchler, August Wilhelm, 1907-
 xKuchler, A. W.
  Vegetation Mapping. Wiley.
Kuchler, Frances W. see Kuchler, Frances W. H.
Kuchler, Frances W. H.
 xKuchler, Frances W.
  Law of Engagement & Marriage. Oceana.
Kuchler, Robert J. see Kuchler, Robert Joseph.
Kuchler, Robert Joseph, 1928-
 xKuchler, Robert J.
  ed. Animal Cell Culture & Virology. Acad Pr.
Kuck, David J.
 xKuck, David J.

  The Structure of Computers & Computations.
   Wiley.
Kuczkir, Mary.
 xKuczkir, Mary.
  My Dish Towel Flies at Half-Mast. Ballantine.
Kuczkowski, Joseph E.
 xKuczkowski, Joseph E.
  Abstract Algebra: A First Look. Dekker.
Kuczynski, Robert R. see Kuczynski, Robert Rene.
Kuczynski, Robert Rene, 1876-1947
 xKuczynski, Robert R.
  Demographic Survey of the British Colonial
   Empire. Kelley.
Kuder, Frederic. see Kuder, George Frederic.
Kuder, George Frederic, 1903-
 xKuder, Frederic.
  Activity Interests & Occupational Choice.
   SRA.
Kudo, Richard R. see Kudo, Richard Roksabro.
Kudo, Richard Roksabro, 1886-
 xKudo, Richard R.
  Protozoology. C C Thomas.
Kudrle, Robert T.
 xKudrle, Robert T.
  Agricultural Tractors: A World Industry Study.
   Ballinger Pub.
Kudrna, Dennis A., 1945-
 xKudrna, Dennis A.
  Purchasing Manager's Decision Handbook.
   CBI Pub.
Kuebler, Roy R. see Kuebler, Roy Raymond.
Kuebler, Roy Raymond.
 xKuebler, Roy R.
  Statistics: A Beginning. Wiley.
Kuehl, Joan.
 xKuehl, Joan.
  Secrets of Looking & Feeling Your Best.
   Macmillan.
Kuehl, Warren F, 1924-
 xKuehl, Warren F.
  Dissertations in History: An Index to
   Dissertations Completed in History
   Departments of the United States &
   Canadian Universities, 1837-1960. U Pr of
   Ky.
  Hamilton Holt: Journalist, Internationalist,
   Educator. U Presses Fla.
Kuehn, Douglas.
 xKuehn, Douglas.
  Takeovers & the Theory of the Firm: An
   Empirical Analysis for the United Kingdom
   1957-69. Holmes & Meier.
Kuehn, Richard A.
 xKuehn, Richard A.
  Cost-Effective Telecommunications. Am Mgmt.
Kuehn, Robert E., 1932-
 xKuehn, Robert E.
  ed. Aldous Huxley: A Collection of Critical
   Essays. P-H.
Kuehne, Robert S.
 xKuehne, Robert S.
  Business Systems Factomatic: A Portfolio of
   Successful Forms, Reports, Records, &
   Procedures. P-H.
Kuehnemann, Ursula.
 xKuehnemann, Ursula.
  Textile Printing & Painting Made Easy.
   Taplinger.
Kuehni, Rolf G.
 xKuehni, Rolf G.
  Computer Colorant Formulation. Lexington
   Bks.
Kuenen, Abraham, 1828-1891
 xKuenen, Abraham.
  National Religions & Universal Religions. AMS
   Pr.
Kuenne, Robert. see Kuenne, Robert E.
Kuenne, Robert E.
 xKuenne, Robert.

  Eugen von Bohm-Bawerk. Columbia U Pr.
 xKuenne, Robert E.
  Theory of General Economic Equilibrium.
   Princeton U Pr.
Kuenning, Larry.
 xKuenning, Larry.
  Exiles in Babylon. Pubs of Truth.
Kuester. see Kuester, James L.
Kuester, James L.
 xKuester.
  Optimization Techniques with Fortran.
   McGraw.
Kuethe, Arnold M. see Kuethe, Arnold Martin.
Kuethe, Arnold Martin.
 xKuethe, Arnold M.
  Foundations of Aerodynamics: Bases of
   Aerodynamic Design. Wiley.
Kuffel. see Kuffel, E.
Kuffel, E.
 xKuffel.
  High Voltage Engineering. Pergamon.
Kuffler, Stephen W.
 xKuffler, Stephen W.
  From Neuron to Brain: A Cellular Approach to
   the Function of the Nervous System. Sinauer
   Assoc.
Kugel, Yerachmiel.
 xKugel, Yerachmiel.
  Ethical Perspectives on Business & Society.
   Lexington Bks.
Kugelmass, I. Newton. see Kugelmass, Isaac Newton.
Kugelmass, Isaac Newton, 1896-
 xKugelmass, I. Newton.
  Autistic Child. C C Thomas.
Kuhlman, Kath. see Kuhlman, Kathryn.
Kuhlman, Kathryn.
 xKuhlman, Kath.
  I Believe in Miracles. Pillar Bks.
 xKuhlman, Kathryn.
  Captain LeVrier Believes in Miracles. Bethany
   Fell.
  Glimpse into Glory. Logos.
  How Big Is God?. Bethany Fell.
  I Believe in Miracles. BJ Pub Group.
  I Believe in Miracles. Revell.
  Nothing Is Impossible with God. Pillar Bks.
  Standing Tall. Bethany Fell.
Kuhlmann, William D. see Kuhlmann, William Daniel.
Kuhlmann, William Daniel, 1896-
 xKuhlmann, William D.
  Teacher Absence & Leave Regulations: Some
   Basic Facts & Principles Related to
   Temporary Absence of Teachers for Use in
   Formulating Valid Absence Regulations.
   AMS Pr.
Kuhn, A. see Kuhn, A. T.
Kuhn, A. T.
 xKuhn, A.
  ed. Industrial Electrochemical Processes.
   Elsevier.
Kuhn, Alfred, 1914-
 xKuhn, Alfred.
  The Logic of Social Systems: A Unified,
   Deductive, System-Based Approach to Social
   Science. Jossey-Bass.
Kuhn, Barbara, 1937-
 xKuhn, Barbara.
  The Whole Lay Ministry Catalog. Seabury.
Kuhn, Bob.
 xKuhn, Bob.
  The Animal Art of Bob Kuhn: A Lifetime of
   Drawing & Painting. North Light Pub.
Kuhn, Charles L. see Kuhn, Charles Louis.
Kuhn, Charles Louis.
 xKuhn, Charles L.
  German & Netherlandish Sculpture, 1280-1800:
   The Harvard Collections. Harvard U Pr.
Kuhn, Effie G. see Kuhn, Effie Georgine.
Kuhn, Effie Georgine, 1891-
 xKuhn, Effie G.

The Pronunciation of Vowel Sounds: An
Evaluation of Practice Material for College
Freshmen. AMS Pr.
Kuhn, Ferdinand.
xKuhn, Ferdinand.
Story of the Secret Service. Random.
Kuhn, G. see Kuhn, Gerald.
Kuhn, Gerald.
xKuhn, G.
Guide to Illinois Real Estate License
Preparation. P-H.
Kuhn, Howard A.
xKuhn, Howard A.
ed. Powder Metallurgy Processing: New
Techniques & Analyses. Acad Pr.
Kuhn, Isobel.
xKuhn, Isobel.
In the Arena. OMF Bks.
Stones of Fire. OMF Bks.
Kuhn, Margaret E.
xKuhn, Margaret E.
Get Out There & Do Something About
Injustice. Friend Pr.
Kuhn, Thomas S.
xKuhn, Thomas S.
Black-Body Theory & the Quantum
Discontinuity, 1894-1912. Oxford U Pr.
Copernican Revolution: Planetary Astronomy
in the Development of Western Thought.
Harvard U Pr.
The Essential Tension: Selected Studies in
Scientific Tradition & Change. U of Chicago
Pr.
Structure of Scientific Revolutions. U of
Chicago Pr.
Kuhn, William E. see Kuhn, William Ernest.
Kuhn, William Ernest, 1922-
xKuhn, William E.
Evolution of Economic Thought. SW Pub.
Kuhne, Cecil, 1952-
xKuhne, Cecil.
River Rafting. Anderson World.
Kuhne, Robert J.
xKuhne, Robert J.
Co-Determination in Business: Workers
Representatives in the Boardroom. Praeger.
Kuhnert-Brandstatter, M. see Kuhnert-Brandstatter,
Maria.
Kuhnert-Brandstatter, Maria, 1919-
xKuhnert-Brandstatter, M.
Thermomicroscopy in the Analysis of
Pharmaceuticals. Pergamon.
Kuhns, Levi O. see Kuhns, Levi Oscar.
Kuhns, Levi Oscar, 1856-1929
xKuhns, Levi O.
German & Swiss Settlements of Colonial
Pennsylvania. AMS Pr.
Kuhns, Maude (Pinney), 1889-
xKuhns, Maude P.
The "Mary & John": A Story of the Founding
of Dorchester, Massachusetts, 1630. C E
Tuttle.
Kuhns, Maude P. see Kuhns, Maude (Pinney).
Kuhns, Richard. see Kuhns, Richard Francis.
Kuhns, Richard Francis, 1924-
xKuhns, Richard.
The House, the City & the Judge: The Growth
of Moral Awareness in the Oresteia.
Irvington.
Kuhns, William.
xKuhns, William.
Exploring the Film. Pflaum-Standard.
Kuhr, Ronald J.
xKuhr, Ronald J.
Carbamate Insecticides: Chemistry,
Biochemistry & Toxicology. CRC Pr.
Kuida, H. see Kuida, Hiroshi.
Kuida, Hiroshi.
xKuida, H.

Fundamental Principles of Circulation
Physiology for Physicians. Elsevier.
Kuiper, B. K. see Kuiper, Barend Klaas.
Kuiper, Barend Klaas, 1877-
xKuiper, B. K.
The Church in History. Eerdmans.
Kuiper, Gerard P. see Kuiper, Gerard Peter.
Kuiper, Gerard Peter, 1905-
xKuiper, Gerard P.
ed. Earth As a Planet. U of Chicago Pr.
Kuiper, N. H. see Kuiper, Nicolaas Hendrik.
Kuiper, Nicolaas Hendrik.
xKuiper, N. H.
Linear Algebra & Geometry. Elsevier.
Kuipers, L. see Kuipers, Lauwerens.
Kuipers, Lauwerens.
xKuipers, L.
Handbook of Mathematics. Pergamon.
Kujoth, Jean. see Kujoth, Jean Spealman.
Kujoth, Jean S. see Kujoth, Jean Spealman.
Kujoth, Jean Spealman.
xKujoth, Jean.
Boys' & Girls' Book of Clubs & Organizations.
P-H.
xKujoth, Jean S.
Subject Guide to Humor: Anecdotes, Facetiae
& Satire from 365 Periodicals, 1968-74.
Scarecrow.
ed. Teacher & School Discipline. Scarecrow.
Kukarkin, B. V.
xKukarkin, B. V.
ed. Pulsating Stars. Halsted Pr.
Kuklick, Bruce, 1941-
xKuklick, Bruce.
American Policy & the Division of Germany:
The Clash with Russia Over Reparations.
Cornell U Pr.
Kuklick, Henrika.
xKuklick, Henrika.
The Imperial Bureaucrat: The Colonial
Administrative Service in the Gold
Coast,1920-1939. Hoover Inst Pr.
Kulaev, I. S. see Kulaev, Igor Stepanovich.
Kulaev, Igor Stepanovich.
xKulaev, I. S.
The Biochemistry of Inorganic Polyphosphates.
Wiley.
Kulash, Damian.
xKulash, Damian J.
Parking Taxes for Congestion Relief: A Survey
of Related Experience. Urban Inst.
Kulash, Damian J. see Kulash, Damian.
Kulasiewicz, Frank, 1930-
xKulasiewicz, Frank.
Glassblowing. Watson-Guptill.
Kulhanek, O. see Kulhanek, Ota.
Kulhanek, Ota.
xKulhanek, O.
Introduction to Digital Filtering in Geophysics.
Elsevier.
Kulik, William R. see Kulik, William T.
Kulik, William T.
xKulik, William R.
Faces of Authority. Scott F.
Kulish, Mykola. see Kulish, Mykola Hurovych.
Kulish, Mykola Hurovych, 1892-1937
xKulish, Mykola.
Sonata Pathetique. Ukrainian Acad.
Kullak, Adolf, 1823-1862
xKullak, Adolf.
The Aesthetics of Pianoforte-Playing. Da Capo.
Kulp, C. A. see Kulp, Clarence Arthur.
Kulp, Clarence Arthur.
xKulp, C. A.
Casualty Insurance. Ronald Pr.
Casualty Insurance. Wiley.
Kulshrestha, Chirantan, 1946-
xKulshrestha, Chirantan.

Saul Bellow: The Problem of Affirmation.
Humanities.
Saul Bellow: The Problem of Affirmation.
Orient Bk Dist.
Kultermann, Udo.
xKultermann, Udo.
Trova. Abrams.
Kumar, Baldev.
xKumar, Baldev.
The Early Kusanas. Verry.
Kumar, Girija. see Kumar, Girja.
Kumar, Girja, 1925-
xKumar, Girija.
Theory of Cataloguing. Intl Bk Dist.
Theory of Cataloguing. Intl Pubns Serv.
xKumar, Girja.
Politics, International Relations & Law: Scope,
Methodology & Classification. Asia.
Theory of Cataloguing. Advent Bk.
Kumar, N. see Kumar, Narinder.
Kumar, Narinder.
xKumar, N.
Trisul Ski Expedition. Advent Bk.
Kumar, Ravinder.
xKumar, Ravinder.
India & the Persian Gulf Region, 1858-1907: A
Study in British Imperial Policy. Asia.
Kumar, S. see Kumar, Sudhir.
Kumar, Shiv K. see Kumar, Shiv Kumar.
Kumar, Shiv Kumar, 1921-
xKumar, Shiv K.
Bergson & the Stream of Consciousness Novel.
Greenwood.
Bergson & the Stream of Consciousness Novel.
NYU Pr.
ed. British Romantic Poets: Recent
Revaluations. NYU Pr.
Kumar, Sudhir.
xKumar, S.
ed. Perinatal Medicine: Clinical & Biochemical
Aspects of the Evaluation, Diagnosis &
Management of the Fetus & Newborn.
Pergamon.
xKumar, Sudhir.
Biochemistry of the Brain. Pergamon.
Kumbula, Tendayi J.
xKumbula, Tendayi J.
Education & Social Control in Southern
Rhodesia. R & E Res Assoc.
Kumin, Libby.
xKumin, Libby.
Aphasia. Cliffs.
Kumin, Maxine. see Kumin, Maxine W.
Kumin, Maxine W.
xKumin, Maxine.
House, Bridge, Fountain, Gate. Penguin.
House, Bridge, Fountain, Gate. Viking Pr.
The Nightmare Factory. Har-Row.
To Make a Prairie: Essays on Poets, Poetry, &
Country Living. U of Mich Pr.
Kummel, Bernhard, 1919-
xKummel, Bernhard.
ed. Status of Invertebrate Paleontology, 1953.
Arno.
Kummel, P. see Kummel, Peter.
Kummel, Peter, 1932-
xKummel, P.
Formalization of Natural Languages.
Springer-Verlag.
Kummer, Hans, Writer on Comparative Psychology.
xKummer, Hans.
Primate Societies: Group Techniques of
Ecological Adaptations. AHM Pub.
Kundera, Milan.
xKundera, Milan.
The Farewell Party. Knopf.
The Farewell Party. Penguin.
Laughable Loves. Penguin.
Life Is Elsewhere. Knopf.
Kundu, Mukul R. see Kundu, Mukul Ranjan.

Kundu, Mukul Ranjan, 1930-
xKundu, Mukul R.
Solar Radio Astronomy. Krieger.
Kune, Gabriel A.
xKune, Gabriel A.
Current Practice of Biliary Surgery. Little.
Kunffy, Charles De. see De Kunffy, Charles.
Kung, David.
xKung, David.
Contemporary Artist in Japan. U Pr of Hawaii.
Kung, Hans.
xKung, Hans.
The Church. Doubleday.
The Church-Maintained in Truth: A
Theological Meditation. Seabury.
Freud & the Problem of God. Yale U Pr.
Future of Ecumenism. Paulist Pr.
On Being a Christian. Doubleday.
On Being a Christian. PB.
Papal Ministry in the Church. Seabury.
ed. Post-Ecumenical Christianity. Seabury.
Signposts for the Future. Doubleday.
Kuniansky, Harry R. see Kuniansky, Harry Richard.
Kuniansky, Harry Richard.
xKuniansky, Harry R.
New Cases in Managerial Finance. Har-Row.
Kuniczak, W. S., 1930-
xKuniczak, W. S.
The March. Doubleday.
Kuniholm, Bruce R. see Kuniholm, Bruce Robellet.
Kuniholm, Bruce Robellet, 1942-
xKuniholm, Bruce R.
The Origins of the Cold War in the Near East:
Great Power Conflict and Diplomacy in Iran,
Turkey, and Greece. Princeton U Pr.
Kunii, Daiz O.
xKunii, Daizo.
Fluidization Engineering. Krieger.
Kunii, Daizo see Kunii, Daiz O.
Kunin, Calvin M.
xKunin, Calvin M.
Detection, Prevention & Management of
Urinary Tract Infections. Lea & Febiger.
Kunkel, Fritz.
xKunkel, Fritz.
Creation Continues. Word Bks.
Kunkel, Guenther. see Kunkel, Gunther.
Kunkel, Gunther.
xKunkel, Guenther.
The Vegetation of Hormoz, Qeshm &
Neighbouring Islands (Southern Persian Gulf
Area). Intl Schol Bk Serv.
Kunkel, Wolfgang, 1902-
xKunkel, Wolfgang.
An Introduction to Roman Legal &
Constitutional History. Oxford U Pr.
Kunnes, Richard.
xKunnes, Richard.
The American Heroin Empire: Power, Profits
& Politics. Dodd.
Kuno, Susumu, 1933-
xKuno, Susumu.
The Structure of the Japanese Language. MIT
Pr.
Kunrathy, Cecile.
xKunrathy, Cecile.
Impudent Foreigner. Soccer.
Kunreuther, Howard.
xKunreuther, Howard.
Disaster Insurance Protection: Public Policy
Lessons. Wiley.
Kuns, Ray F. see Kuns, Ray Forest.
Kuns, Ray Forest, 1887-
xKuns, Ray F.
Automotive Essentials. Glencoe.
Kunst, David.
xKunst, David.

The Man Who Walked Around the World: A
True Story. Morrow.
Kunsthistorischer Institut, Florence, Italy.
xInstitute for the History of Art, Florence.
Kunsthistorischen Institut - Florence.
Katalog Des Kunsthistorischen Instituts in
Florenz, (Catalogue of the Institute for the
History of Art, Florence). G K Hall.
Kunstler, James Howard.
xKunstler, James Howard.
The Wampanaki Tales: A Novel. Doubleday.
Kunstler, William M. see Kunstler, William Moses.
Kunstler, William Moses, 1919-
xKunstler, William M.
And Justice for All. Oceana.
First Degree. Oceana.
Kuntscher, Gerhard.
xKuntscher, Gerhard.
Practice of Intramedullary Nailing. C C
Thomas.
Kuntz, J. Kenneth. see Kuntz, John Kenneth.
Kuntz, John Kenneth.
xKuntz, J. Kenneth.
The People of Ancient Israel: An Introduction
to the Old Testament Literature, History &
Thought. Har-Row.
Kuntz, Kenneth A.
xKuntz, Kenneth A.
The Congregation As Church. Bethany Pr.
Kuntz, Walter N., 1910-
xKuntz, Walter N.
Modern Corporate Management: New
Approaches to Financial Control, Operations,
Customer Development & Equity Sources.
P-H.
Kuntzleman, Charles T.
xKuntzleman, Charles T.
The Complete Book of Walking. G K Hall.
Rating the Exercises. Penguin.
Kunz, C. see Kunz, Christof.
Kunz, Christof.
xKunz, C.
ed. Synchrotron Radiation: Techniques &
Applications. Springer-Verlag.
Kunz, Josef L. see Kunz, Josef Laurenz.
Kunz, Josef Laurenz, 1890-
xKunz, Josef L.
Changing Law of Nations: Essays on
International Law. Ohio St U Pr.
Latin-American Philosophy of Law in the
Twentieth Century. Oceana.
Kunz, Virginia (Brainard).
xKunz, Virginia B.
French in America. Lerner Pubns.
Germans in America. Lerner Pubns.
Kunz, Virginia B. see Kunz, Virginia (Brainard).
Kunze, Reiner, 1933-
xKunze, Reiner.
The Wonderful Years. Braziller.
Kuo, Benjamin C., 1930-
xKuo, Benjamin C.
Automatic Control Systems. P-H.
Linear Networks & Systems. Krieger.
Kuo, Franklin F.
xKuo, Franklin F.
System Analysis by Digital Computer. Krieger.
Kuo, P. C. see Kuo, Pin-Chia.
Kuo, Pin-Chia.
xKuo, P. C.
A Critical Study of the First Anglo-Chinese
War with Documents. Chinese Materials.
Kuo, Shan S. see Kuo, Shan Sun.
Kuo, Shan Sun, 1922-
xKuo, Shan S.
Computer Applications of Numerical Methods.
A-W.
Kuong, Javier. F.
xKuong, Javier F.
Applied Nomography. Gulf Pub.
Kup, A. P. see Kup, Alexander Peter.

Kup, Alexander Peter.
xKup, A. P.
Sierra Leone: A Concise History. St Martin.
Kup, Karl.
xKup, Karl.
Christmas Story in Medieval & Renaissance
Manuscripts from the Spencer Collection, the
New York Public Library. NY Pub Lib.
Kupchella, Charles E.
xKupchella, Charles E.
Sights & Sounds: The Very Special Senses.
Bobbs.
Kupcinet, Sue.
xKupcinet, Sue.
The Chicago Gourmet. S&S.
Kuper, Adam.
xKuper, Adam.
Anthropologists & Anthropology: The British
School 1922-1972. Universe.
Changing Jamaica. Routledge & Kegan.
Kuper, C. G. see Kuper, Charles Goethe.
Kuper, Charles Goethe.
xKuper, C. G.
Relativity & Gravitation. Gordon.
Kuper, Hilda.
xKuper, Hilda.
Indian People in Natal. Greenwood.
xKuper, Hilder.
Swazi: A South African Kingdom. HR&W.
Kuper, Hilder. see Kuper, Hilda.
Kuper, Iurii.
xKuper, Yuri.
Holy Fools in Moscow. Times Bks.
Kuper, Jack.
xKuper, Jack.
Child of the Holocaust. NAL.
Kuper, Jessica.
xKuper, Jessica.
ed. The Anthropologists' Cookbook. Universe.
Kuper, L. see Kuper, Leo.
Kuper, Leo.
xKuper, L.
Passive Resistance in South Africa. Kraus Repr.
xKuper, Leo.
African Bourgeoisie: Race, Class, & Politics in
South Africa. Yale U Pr.
Race, Class & Power: Ideology &
Revolutionary Change in Plural Societies.
Beresford Bk Serv.
Kuper, Yuri. see Kuper, Iurii.
Kuperman, A. see Kuperman, Israel B.
Kuperman, Israel B.
xKuperman, A.
Approximate Linear Algebraic Equations. Van
Nos Reinhold.
Kupferberg, Herbert.
xKupferberg, Herbert.
Opera. Newsweek.
Tanglewood. McGraw.
Kupferberg, Tuli.
xKupferberg, Tuli.
Listen to the Mocking Bird: Satiric Songs to
Tunes You Know. Times Change.
Kupferer, Harriet J.
xKupferer, Harriet J.
Culture, Society & Guidance. HM.
Kupferle, Mary L.
xKupferle, Mary L.
God Never Fails. Unity Bks.
Kupinsky, Stanley.
xKupinsky, Stanley.
ed. The Fertility of Working Women: A
Synthesis of International Research. Praeger.
Kupper, Mike.
xKupper, Mike.
Racing to Indy. Raintree Pubs.
Kupperman, Karen O. see Kupperman, Karen Ordahl.
Kupperman, Karen Ordahl, 1939-
xKupperman, Karen O.

Settling with the Indians: The Meeting of
English & Indian Cultures in America,
1580-1640. Rowman.
Kupperman, Robert. see Kupperman, Robert H.
Kupperman, Robert H.
xKupperman, Robert.
Terrorism: Threat, Reality, Response. Hoover
Inst Pr.
Kuprin, Aleksandr I. see Kuprin, Aleksandr Ivanovich.
Kuprin, Aleksandr Ivanovich, 1870-1938
xKuprin, Aleksandr I.
The Duel. Hyperion Conn.
Kupsinel, Penelope E. see Kupsinel, Penelope Easton.
Kupsinel, Penelope Easton.
xKupsinel, Penelope E.
Home Economics Careers. Interstate.
Kuralt, Charles, 1934-
xKuralt, Charles.
Dateline America. HarBraceJ.
Kuramoto, Ford H.
xKuramoto, Ford H.
A History of the Shonien, 1914-1972: An
Account of a Program of Institutional Care of
Japanese Children in Los Angeles. R & E
Res Assoc.
Kuranov, V.
xKuranov, Victor.
ed. The Trans-Siberian Express. Sphinx Pr.
Kuranov, Victor. see Kuranov, V.
Kurath, Gertrude P. see Kurath, Gertrude Prokosch.
Kurath, Gertrude Prokosch.
xKurath, Gertrude P.
Music & Dance of the Tewa Pueblos. Museum
NM Pr.
Kurath, Hans, 1891-
xKurath, Hans.
ed. Linguistic Atlas of New England. AMS Pr.
Pronunciation of English in the Atlantic States:
Based Upon the Collections of the Linguistic
Atlas of the Eastern United States. U of
Mich Pr.
Word Geography of the Eastern United States.
U of Mich Pr.
Kuratowski, K. see Kuratowski, Kazimierz.
Kuratowski, Kazimierz, 1896-
xKuratowski, K.
Introduction to Calculus. Pergamon.
Introduction to Set Theory & Topology.
Pergamon.
Kurelek, William, 1927-
xKurelek, William.
The Last of the Arctic. Pagurian.
illus. Lumberjack. HM.
A Prairie Boys Summer. HM.
illus. A Prairie Boy's Winter. HM.
Kurien, C. T.
xKurien, C. T.
Theoretical Approach to the Indian Economy.
Asia.
Kurilecz, Margaret.
xKurilecz, Margaret.
A Remarkable Half-Dozen: Reading & Writing
in English As a Second Language. Har-Row.
Kurland, Albert A. see Kurland, Albert Alexander.
Kurland, Albert Alexander.
xKurland, Albert A.
Psychiatric Aspects of Opiate Dependence.
CRC Pr.
Kurland, Gerald, 1942-
xKurland, Gerald.

The Cold War: 1945-63. SamHar Pr.
The Conflict in Vietnam. SamHar Pr.
The Creation of Bangla Desh. SamHar Pr.
The Gulf of Tonkin Incidents. SamHar Pr.
The Hiroshima Atomic Bomb Blast. SamHar
Pr.
Lindbergh Flies the Atlantic. SamHar Pr.
The My Lai Massacre. SamHar Pr.
The Supreme Court Under Warren. SamHar Pr.
Thomas Edison, Father of Electricity & Master
Inventor of Our Modern Age. SamHar Pr.
Kurland, Howard D.
xKurland, Howard D.
Quick Headache Relief Without Drugs: How to
Relieve Your Headache in Seconds: a
Physician's Do-It-Yourself Technique.
Morrow.
Kurland, Michael.
xKurland, Michael.
The Last President. Morrow.
Princes of Earth. Elsevier-Nelson.
Kurland, Philip B.
xKurland, Philip B.
Free Speech & Association: The Supreme
Court & the First Amendment. U of Chicago
Pr.
Politics, the Constitution & the Warren Court.
U of Chicago Pr.
Religion & the Law: Of Church & State & the
Supreme Court. U of Chicago Pr.
Kurman, George.
xKurman, George.
Development of Written Estonian. Res Ctr
Lang Semiotic.
Kurmit, A. A. see Kurmit, Avgust Avgustovich.
Kurmit, Avgust Avgustovich.
xKurmit, A. A.
Information-Lossless Automata of Finite Order.
Halsted Pr.
Kuroda, S. Y. see Kuroda, S. Y.
Kuroda, S.Y.
xKuroda, S. Y.
Generative Grammatical Studies in the
Japanese Language. Garland Pub.
Kuropas, Myron. see Kuropas, Myron B.
Kuropas, Myron B.
xKuropas, Myron.
Ukrainians in America. Lerner Pubns.
Kurosh, A. G.
xKurosh, Alexander G.
Lectures on General Algebra. Chelsea Pub.
Kurosh, Alexander G. see Kurosh, a G.
Kurosumi, Kazumasa.
xKurosumi, Kazumasa.
Intro. by Functional Morphology of Endocrine
Glands: An Atlas of Electron Micrographs.
Igaku-Shoin.
Kurpius, DeWayne. see Kurpius, Dewayne J.
Kurpius, DeWayne J.
xKurpius, DeWayne.
Learning: Making Learning Environments
More Effective. Accel Devel.
xKurpius, DeWayne J.
ed. Supervision of Applied Training: A
Comparative Review. Greenwood.
Kurrik, Maire J. see Kurrik, Maire Jaanus.
Kurrik, Maire Jaanus.
xKurrik, Maire J.
Literature & Negation. Columbia U Pr.
xKurrik, Marie.
Georg Trakl. Columbia U Pr.
Kurrik, Marie. see Kurrik, Maire Jaanus.
Kursunoglu, Behram.
xKursunoglu, Berham.
ed. On the Path of Albert Einstein. Plenum
Pub.
Kursunoglu, Berham. see Kursunoglu, Behram.
Kurten, Bjorn.
xKurten, Bjorn.

The Age of Mammals. Columbia U Pr.
Pleistocene Mammals of North America.
Columbia U Pr.
xKurten, Bjory.
The Cave Bear Story.: Life & Death of a
Vanished Animal. Columbia U Pr.
Kurten, Bjory. see Kurten, Bjorn.
Kurten, Nancy.
xKurten, Nancy.
Needlepoint in Miniature. Scribner.
Kurth, Rudolf, 1917-
xKurth, Rudolf.
Dimensional Analysis & Group Theory in
Astrophysics. Pergamon.
Kurtis, Wilma.
xKurtis, Wilma.
Prairie Recipes & Kitchen Antiques.
Wallace-Homestead.
Kurtsin, I. T. see Kurtsin, Ivan Terentevich.
Kurtsin, Ivan Terentevich.
xKurtsin, I. T.
Theoretical Principles of Psychosomatic
Medicine. Halsted Pr.
Kurtz, A. K. see Kurtz, Albert Kenneth.
Kurtz, Albert Kenneth.
xKurtz, A. K.
Statistical Methods in Education & Psychology.
Springer-Verlag.
Kurtz, Benjamin P. see Kurtz, Benjamin Putnam.
Kurtz, Benjamin Putnam, 1878-1950
xKurtz, Benjamin P.
Pursuit of Death: A Study of Shelley's Poetry.
Octagon.
Kurtz, David L.
xKurtz, David L.
Professional Selling. Business Pubns.
Kurtz, Donald V.
xKurtz, Donald V.
The Politics of a Poverty Habitat. Ballinger
Pub.
Kurtz, Donna C.
xKurtz, Donna C.
Athenian White Lekythoi: Patterns & Painters.
Oxford U Pr.
Greek Burial Customs. Cornell U Pr.
Kurtz, Edwin B. see Kurtz, Edwin Bernard.
Kurtz, Edwin Bernard.
xKurtz, Edwin B.
The Lineman's & Cableman's Handbook.
McGraw.
Kurtz, Ernest.
xKurtz, Ernest.
Not-God: A History of Alcoholics Anonymous.
Hazelden.
Kurtz, Henry I. see Kurtz, Henry Ira.
Kurtz, Henry Ira.
xKurtz, Henry I.
Captain John Smith. Watts.
Kurtz, Katherine.
xKurtz, Katherine.
Camber of Culdi. Ballantine.
Saint Camber. Ballantine.
Kurtz, L. P. see Kurtz, Leonard Paul.
Kurtz, Laura S.
xKurtz, Laura S.
Historical Dictionary of Tanzania. Scarecrow.
Kurtz, Leonard Paul, 1892-
xKurtz, L. P.
The Dance of Death & the Macabre Spirit in
European Literature. Gordon Pr.
Kurtz, Max, 1920-
xKurtz, Max.
Comprehensive Structural Design Guide.
McGraw.
Engineering Economics for Professional
Engineers' Examinations. McGraw.
Structural Engineering for Professional
Engineer's Examination. McGraw.
Kurtz, Paul. see Kurtz, Paul W.

Kurtz, Paul W., 1925-
xKurtz, Paul.
Exuberance: A Philosophy of Happiness. Prometheus Bks.
The Fullness of Life. Prometheus Bks.
ed. Moral Problems in Contemporary Society: Essays in Humanistic Ethics. Prometheus Bks.
Kurtz, V. Ray. see Kurtz, Vernon Ray.
Kurtz, Vernon Ray.
xKurtz, V. Ray.
Teaching Metric Awareness. Mosby.
Kurtzman, Joel.
xKurtzman, Joel.
No More Dying: The Conquest of Aging & Extension of Human Life. Dell.
Kurtzman, Neil A.
xKurtzman, Neil A.
Pathophysiology of the Kidney. C C Thomas.
Kuryla, William C.
xKuryla, William C.
ed. Flame Retardancy of Polymeric Materials. Dekker.
Kurz, Harry, 1889-
xKurz, Harry.
European Characters in French Drama of the Eighteenth Century. AMS Pr.
European Characters in French Drama of the Eighteenth Century. R West.
Kurz, Paul K. see Kurz, Paul Konrad.
Kurz, Paul Konrad.
xKurz, Paul K.
On Modern German Literature. U of Ala Pr.
Kurz, Ron.
xKurz, Ron.
Lethal Gas. M Evans.
Kurzman, Dan.
xKurzman, Dan.
The Race for Rome. Pinnacle Bks.
Kurzweil, Edith.
xKurzweil, Edith.
The Age of Structuralism: Levi-Strauss to Foucault. Columbia U Pr.
Kusche, Larry. see Kusche, Lawrence David.
Kusche, Lawrence David.
xKusche, Larry.
Shape Up Your Hips & Thighs. Macmillan.
Kuschinsky, G. see Kuschinsky, Gustav.
Kuschinsky, Gustav.
xKuschinsky, G.
Textbook of Pharmacology. Acad Pr.
Kuschpeta, O.
xKuschpeta, O.
Banking & Credit System of the USSR. Kluwer Boston.
Kushev, V. V. see Kushev, Vladislav Valerianovich.
Kushev, Vladislav Valerianovich.
xKushev, V. V.
Mechanisms of Genetic Recombination. Plenum Pub.
Kushner, Gilbert.
xKushner, Gilbert.
Immigrants From India in Israel: Planned Change in an Administered Community. U of Ariz Pr.
Kushner, H. J. see Kushner, Harld Joseph.
Kushner, Harold Joseph.
xKushner, H. J.
Stochastic Approximation Methods for Constrained & Unconstrained Systems. Springer-Verlag.
Kushner, Harold S.
xKushner, Harold S.
When Children Ask About God. Schocken.
Kushner, Harvey W.
xKushner, Harvey W.
Understanding Basic Statistics. Holden-Day.
Kushner, Howard I.
xKushner, Howard I.

Conflict on the Northwest Coast: American-Russian Rivalry in the Pacific Northwest, 1790-1867. Greenwood.
Kushner, R. E. see Kushner, Rose (Estrin).
Kushner, Rose (Estrin), 1907-
xKushner, R. E.
Relationship Between Content of an Adult Intelligence Test & Intelligence Test Score As a Function of Age. AMS Pr.
Kushner, Sam, 1914-
xKushner, Sam.
Long Road to Delano. Intl Pub Co.
Kusin, Vladimir V.
xKusin, Vladimir V.
Intellectual Origins of the Prague Spring: The Development of Reformist Ideas in Czechoslovakia, 1958-1967. Cambridge U Pr.
Kuskin, Karla.
xKuskin, Karla.
A Boy Had a Mother Who Bought Him a Hat. HM.
illus. In the Flaky Frosty Morning. Har-Row.
illus. Near the Window Tree: Poems & Notes. Har-Row.
A Space Story. Har-Row.
illus. Which Horse Is William. Har-Row.
Kusko, Alexander, 1921-
xKusko, Alexander.
Solid-State DC Motor Drives. MIT Pr.
Kusmer, Kenneth L., 1945-
xKusmer, Kenneth L.
A Ghetto Takes Shape: Black Cleveland, 1870-1930. U of Ill Pr.
Kuspit, Donald B. see Kuspit, Donald Burton.
Kuspit, Donald Burton.
xKuspit, Donald B.
Clement Greenberg, Art Critic. U of Wis Pr.
Kussin, Louis.
xKussin, Louis.
How to Prepare Your College Application. Arco.
Kutcher, Arthur.
xKutcher, Arthur.
Looking at London: Illustrated Walks Through a Changing City. Thames Hudson.
Kutie, Rita.
xKutie, Rita.
The WP Book. Wiley.
Kutler, Stanley I.
xKutler, Stanley I.
ed. Looking for America: The People's History. Norton.
Privilege & Creative Destruction: The Charles River Bridge Case. Norton.
ed. The Supreme Court & the Constitution: Readings in American Constitutional History. Norton.
Kutner, Luis, 1908-
xKutner, Luis.
Intelligent Woman's Guide to Future Security. Dodd.
Kutscher, A. see Kutscher, Austin H.
Kutscher, Austin H.
xKutscher, A.
ed. Religion & Bereavement: Counsel for the Physician, Advice for the Bereaved. H S Pub Corp.
xKutscher, Austin H.
Death & Bereavement. C C Thomas.
Oral Care of the Aging & Dying Patient. C C Thomas.
Kutt. see Kutt, Henn.
Kutt, Henn.
xKutt.
Clinical Neuropharmacology. Churchill.
Kuttner, Henry.
xKuttner, Henry.

Destination Infinity. Garland Pub.
Mutant. Garland Pub.
Kuttner, Robert E.
xKuttner, Robert E.
ed. Race & Modern Science: A Collection of Essays by Biologists, Anthropologists, Sociologists, & Psychologists. Soc Sci Pr.
Kuttruff, H. see Kuttruff, Heinrich.
Kuttruff, Heinrich.
xKuttruff, H.
Room Acoustics. Halsted Pr.
xKuttruff, K. H.
Room Acoustics. Burgess-Intl Ideas.
Kuttruff, K. H. see Kuttruff, Heinrich.
Kutty, A. R. see Kutty, Abdul Rahman.
Kutty, Abdul Rahman.
xKutty, A. R.
Marriage & Kinship in an Island Society. Intl Pubns Serv.
Kuvshinoff, B. W.
xKuvshinoff, B. W.
ed. Fire Sciences Dictionary. Wiley.
Kuwana, Ted. see Kuwana, Theodore.
Kuwana, Theodore.
xKuwana, Ted.
ed. Physical Methods in Modern Chemical Analysis. Acad Pr.
xKuwana, Theodore.
ed. Physical Methods in Modern Chemical Analysis. Acad Pr.
Kuwayama, George.
xKuwayama, George.
Ancient Ritual Bronzes of China. LA Co Art Mus.
Contemporary Japanese Prints. LA Co Art Mus.
Kuykendall, Jack L.
xKuykendall, Jack L.
Community Police Administration. Nelson-Hall.
Kuyvenhoven, A.
xKuyvenhoven, Arie.
Planning with the Semi Input-Output Method. Kluwer Boston.
Kuyvenhoven, Arie. see Kuyvenhoven, A.
Kuzawa, M. Grace. see Kuzawa, Mary Grace.
Kuzawa, Mary Grace.
xKuzawa, M. Grace.
Modern Mathematics: The Genesis of a School in Poland. Coll & U Pr.
Kuzma, Kay.
xKuzma, Kay.
Prime Time Parenting. Rawson Wade.
Kuzmanovic, B.
xKuzmanovic, B. O.
Steel Design for Structural Engineers. P-H.
Kuzmanovic, B. O. see Kuzmanovic, B.
Kuznets, Simon. see Kuznets, Simon Smith.
Kuznets, Simon Smith, 1901-
xKuznets, Simon.
Capital in the American Economy: Its Formation & Financing. Arno.
Cyclical Fluctuations: Retail & Wholesale Trade, United States, 1919-1925. Hyperion Conn.

Growth, Population, & Income Distribution: Selected Essays. Norton.

Modern Economic Growth: Rate, Structure & Spread. Yale U Pr.

National Income: A Summary of Findings. Arno.

National Income & Capital Formation, 1919-1935: A Preliminary Report. Arno.
National Product in Wartime. Arno.
National Product Since 1869. Arno.

Kuznetsov, Eduard.
  xKuznetsov, Edward.
    Prison Diaries. Stein & Day.
Kuznetsov, Edward. *see* Kuznetsov, Eduard.
Kuzvart, M. *see* Kuzvart, Milos.
Kuzvart, Milos.
  xKuzvart, M.
    Prospecting & Exploration for Mineral Deposits. Elsevier.
Kvaraceus, William C. *see* Kvaraceus, William Clement.
Kvaraceus, William Clement.
  xKvaraceus, William C.
    Prevention & Control of Delinquency: The School Counselor's Role. HM.
Kverneland, Knut O., 1937-
  xKverneland, Knut O.
    World Metric Standards for Engineering. Indus Pr.
Kwak, N. K., 1932-
  xKwak, N. K.
    Mathematical Programming with Business Applications. McGraw.
  xKwak, No Kyoon.
    Quantitative Models for Business Decisions. Duxbury Pr.
Kwak, No Kyoon. *see* Kwak, N. K.
Kwakernaak, Huibert.
  xKwakernaak, Huibert.
    Linear Optimal Control Systems. Wiley.
Kwavnick, David.
  xKwavnick, David.
    Organized Labour & Pressure Politics: The Canadian Labour Congress 1956-1968. McGill-Queens U Pr.
Kwawer, Jay S.
  xKwawer, Jay S.
    ed. Borderline Phenomena & the Rorschach Test. Intl Univs Pr.
Kwiat, Joseph J.
  xKwiat, Joseph J.
    ed. Studies in American Culture: Dominant Ideas & Images. Johnson Repr.
Kwiatkowska, Hanna Y. *see* Kwiatkowska, Hanna Yaxa.
Kwiatkowska, Hanna Yaxa.
  xKwiatkowska, Hanna Y.
    Family Therapy & Evaluation Through Art. C C Thomas.
Kwitko, Marvin L.
  xKwitko, Marvin L.
    Pseudophakia: Current Trends & Concepts. Williams & Wilkins.
    Surgery of the Infant Eye. ACC.
Kwitny, Jonathan.
  xKwitny, Jonathan.
    Fountain Pen Conspiracy. Knopf.
    The Mullendore Murder Case. FS&G.
Kwitz, Mary. *see* Kwitz, Mary Deball.
Kwitz, Mary D. *see* Kwitz, Mary Deball.
Kwitz, Mary Deball.
  xKwitz, Mary.
    Rabbits' Search for a Little House. Crown.
  xKwitz, Mary D.
    Little Chick's Story. Har-Row.
Kwolek, Constance.
  xKwolek, Constance.
    Loner. Doubleday.
Kwong, Julia.
  xKwong, Julia.

Chinese Education in Transition: Prelude to the Cultural Revolution. McGill-Queens U Pr.

Kybett, Harry.
  xKybett, Harry.
    The Complete Handbook of Videocassette Recorders. TAB Bks.
    Electronics. Wiley.
Kyburg, Henry E. *see* Kyburg, Henry Ely.
Kyburg, Henry Ely, 1928-
  xKyburg, Henry E.
    The Logical Foundations of Statistical Inference. Kluwer Boston.
Kyd, Stewart, d. 1811
  xKyd, Stewart.
    A Treatise on the Law of Corporations. Garland Pub.
Kyd, Thomas.
  xKyd, Thomas.
    The Spanish Tragedy. AHM Pub.
Kydd, Rachael.
  xKydd, Rachael.
    Long Distance Riding Explained. Arco.
Kyger, Joanne.
  xKyger, Joanne.
    The Wonderful Focus of You. Z Pr.
Kyle, Duncan.
  xKyle, Duncan.
    Black Camelot. St Martin.
    Green River High. St Martin.
    Whiteout. Avon.
Kyle, James.
  xKyle, James.
    Crohn's Disease. Intl Ideas.
Kyle, John F., 1943-
  xKyle, John F.
    The Balance of Payments in a Monetary Economy. Princeton U Pr.
Kyle, Melvin G. *see* Kyle, Melvin Grove.
Kyle, Melvin Grove, 1858-1933
  xKyle, Melvin G.
    Explorations at Sodom: Story of Ancient Sodom in the Light of Modern Research. Arno.
Kyle, Peggy.
  xKyle, Peggy.
    My Heart Must Sing. Windy Row.
Kyle, Robert A.
  xKyle, Robert A.
    The Monoclonal Gammopathies: Multiple Myeloma & Related Plasma-Cell Disorders. C C Thomas.
Kyne, Peter B. *see* Kyne, Peter Bernard.
Kyne, Peter Bernard, 1880-
  xKyne, Peter B.
    The Pride of Palomar. Arno.
Kyner, James H. *see* Kyner, James Henry.
Kyner, James Henry.
  xKyner, James H.
    End of Track. U of Nebr Pr.
Kynerd, Thomas E.
  xKynerd, Thomas E.
    Administrative Reorganization of Mississippi Government: A Study in Politics. U Pr of Miss.
Kyper, Frank, 1940-
  xKyper, Frank.
    The Railroad That Came Out at Night: A Book of Railroading in & Around Boston. Greene.
Kyrala, A.
  xKyrala, A.
    Applied Functions of a Complex Variable. Wiley.
Kyrk, Hazel, 1888-
  xKyrk, Hazel.
    The Family in the American Economy. U of Chicago Pr.
    A Theory of Consumption. Arno.
Kysar, Robert.
  xKysar, Robert.

The Fourth Evangelist & His Gospel: An Examination of Contemporary Scholarship. Augsburg.

Kyselka, Will.
  xKyselka, Will.
    North Star to Southern Cross. U Pr of Hawaii.
Kyte, Barbara. *see* Kyte, Barbara Kanerva.
Kyte, Barbara Kanerva.
  xKyte, Barbara.
    Quick Breads. Nitty Gritty.
Kytle, Ray.
  xKytle, Ray.
    Clear Thinking for Composition. Random.
Kyvig, David. *see* Kyvig, David E.
Kyvig, David E.
  xKyvig, David.
    Your Family History: A Handbook for Research & Writing. AHM Pub.
  xKyvig, David E.
    Repealing National Prohibition. U of Chicago Pr.

L'Abate, Luciano.
  xL'Abate, Luciano.
    How to Avoid Divorce. John Knox.
    Understanding & Helping the Individual in the Family. Grune.
L'Amour. *see* L'Amour, Louis.
L'Amour, Louis.
  xL'Amour.
    Fair Blows the Wind. G K Hall.
  xL'Amour, Louis.
    Brionne. Bantam.
    The Burning Hills. Bantam.
    Callaghen. Bantam.
    Callaghen. G K Hall.
    Catlow. Bantam.
    Chancy. Bantam.
    Crossfire Trail. Fawcett.
    Crossfire Trail. Gregg.
    Dark Canyon. Bantam.
    Day Breakers. Bantam.
    The Daybreakers. G K Hall.
    Down the Long Hills. Bantam.
    Fair Blows the Wind. Bantam.
    Fair Blows the Wind. Dutton.
    Fair Blows the Wind. G K Hall.
    Fallon. Bantam.
    The Ferguson Rifle. Bantam.
    The First Fast Draw. Bantam.
    Flint. Bantam.
    Hondo. Fawcett.
    Hondo. Gregg.
    The Iron Marshall. Bantam.
    The Iron Marshall. G K Hall.
    Iron Marshall. G K Hall.
    Matagorda. Bantam.
    Over on the Dry Side. Bantam.
    The Quick & the Dead. Bantam.
    Radigan. Bantam.
    Ride the Dark Trail. Bantam.
    Silver Canyon. Bantam.
    Taggart. Bantam.
    Tall Stranger. Fawcett.
    Where the Long Grass Blows. Bantam.
    Where the Long Grass Blows. G K Hall.
L'Engle, Madeleine.
  xL'Engle, Madeleine.

Arm of the Starfish. FS&G.
A Circle of Quiet. FS&G.
Dance in the Desert. FS&G.
Dragons in the Waters. FS&G.
Everyday Prayers. Morehouse.
Moon by Night. FS&G.
The Other Side of the Sun. FS&G.
Prelude. Vanguard.
A Ring of Endless Light. FS&G.
ed. Spirit & Light: Essays in Historical
Theology. Seabury.
A Swiftly Tilting Planet. Dell.
A Swiftly Tilting Planet. FS&G.
xL'Engle, Madelene.
Meet the Austins. Vanguard.
xL'Engle, Madeline.
The Arm of the Starfish. Dell.
The Summer of the Great Grandmother.
FS&G.
L'Engle, Madelene. *see* L'Engle, Madeleine.
L'Engle, Madeline. *see* L'Engle, Madeleine.
La Barre, Weston, 1911-
xLa Barre, Weston.
Human Animal. U of Chicago Pr.
They Shall Take up Serpents: Psychology of
the Southern Snake-Handling Cult. Schocken.
La Belle, Jenijoy, 1943-
xLa Belle, Jenijoy.
The Echoing Wood of Theodore Roethke.
Princeton U Pr.
La Belle, Thomas J.
xLa Belle, Thomas J.
ed. Educational Alternatives in Latin America:
Social Change & Social Stratification. UCLA
Lat Am Ctr.
La Carrubba, Joseph.
xLa Carrubba, Joseph.
How to Buy, Install, & Maintain Your Own
Telephone Equipment. Almar.
La. Dis. Judges. *see* Louisiana District Judges
Association.
La Du, B. N. *see* La Du, Bert N.
La Du, Bert N.
xLa Du, B. N.
ed. Fundamentals of Drug Metabolism & Drug
Disposition. Krieger.
La Farge, John, 1835-1910
xLa Farge, John.
Artist's Letters from Japan. Da Capo.
Great Masters. Arno.
La Farge, Oliver, 1901-1963
xLa Farge, Oliver.
Eagle in the Egg. Arno.
The Enemy Gods. U of NM Pr.
La Farge, Phyllis.
xLa Farge, Phyllis.
Abby Takes Over. Dell.
Abby Takes Over. Lippincott.
A Christmas Adventure. HR&W.
Granny's Fish Story. Schol Bk Serv.
La Farge, W. E. *see* La Farge, W. E. R.
La Farge, W. E. R., 1930-
xLa Farge, W. E.
The Changing & Unchanging Harvest.
Heartwork Pr.
La Follette, Suzanne.
xLa Follette, Suzanne.
Concerning Women. Arno.
La Fontaine, J. S. *see* La Fontaine, Jean Sybil.
La Fontaine, Jean De.
xLa Fontaine, Jean De.
La Fontaine: Selected Fables. Viking Pr.
La Fontaine, Jean Sybil.
xLa Fontaine, J. S.
City Politics: A Study of Leopoldville, 1962-63.
Cambridge U Pr.
La Force, J. Clayburn. *see* La Force, James Clayburn.
La Force, James Clayburn.
xLa Force, J. Clayburn.

The Development of the Spanish Textile
Industry, 1750-1800. U of Cal Pr.
La Fountaine, George.
xLa Fountaine, George.
Two Minute Warning. Fawcett.
La Grande, Hyppolite.
xLa Grande, Hyppolite.
The Deceit of the New Economics. Am
Classical Coll Pr.
La Guardia Community College.
xLaguardia Community College, Social Science
Faculty.
Work & Society: An Introduction to the Social
Sciences. Kendall-Hunt.
La Guma, Alex.
xLa Guma, Alex.
Time of the Butcherbird. Heinemann Ed.
La, Mare, Walter De. *see* De La Mare, Walter.
La Monica, Elaine L. *see* La Monica, Elaine Lynne.
La Monica, Elaine Lynne, 1944-
xLa Monica, Elaine L.
The Nursing Process: A Humanistic Approach.
A-W.
La Monte, Robert R. *see* La Monte, Robert Rives.
La Monte, Robert Rives.
xLa Monte, Robert R.
Men Versus the Man: A Correspondence
Between Robert Rives La Monte, Socialist &
H. L. Mencken, Individualist. Arno.
La Motte, Ellen N. *see* La Motte, Ellen Newbold.
La Motte, Ellen Newbold, 1873-1961
xLa Motte, Ellen N.
Civilization: Tales of the Orient. Arno.
La Mure, Pierre.
xLa Mure, Pierre.
The Private Life of Mona Lisa. Little.
La Palombara, Joseph G.
xLa Palombara, Joseph G.
Initiative & Referendum in Oregon 1938-1948.
Oreg St U Pr.
La Piana, Angelina.
xLa Piana, Angelina.
Dante's American Pilgrimage: A Historical
Survey of Dante Studies in the United States,
Eighteen Hundred to Nineteen Forty-Four.
Elliots Bks.
La Plante, John. *see* La Plante, John D.
La Plante, John D.
xLa Plante, John.
Asian Art. Wm C Brown.
La Queriere, Yves De.
xLa Queriere, Yves de.
Celine et les mots: Etude stylistique des effets
de mots dans le Voyage au bout de la nuit. U
Pr of Ky.
La, Roche, Mazo De. *see* De La Roche, Mazo.
La Tourrette, Jacqueline, 1926-
xLa Tourrette, Jacqueline.
The Pompeii Scroll. Delacorte.
Shadows in Umbria. Putnam.
La Violette, Forrest E. *see* La Violette, Forrest
Emmanuel.
La Violette, Forrest Emmanuel, 1904-
xLa Violette, Forrest E.
Struggle for Survival: Indian Cultures & the
Protestant Ethic in British Columbia. U of
Toronto Pr.
Laan, Thomas F. Van. *see* Van Laan, Thomas F.
Labalme, Patricia H.
xLabalme, Patricial H.
ed. Beyond Their Sex: Learned Women of the
European Past. NYU Pr.
Labalme, Patricial H. *see* Labalme, Patricia H.
Laban. *see* Laban, Rudolf Von.
Laban, Rudolf. *see* Laban, Rudolf Von.
Laban, Rudolf Von.
xLaban.
Modern Educational Dance. Plays.
xLaban, Rudolf.

Mastery of Movement. Plays.
Labaree, Benjamin W. *see* Labaree, Benjamin Woods.
Labaree, Benjamin Woods.
xLabaree, Benjamin W.
The Boston Tea Party. NE U Pr.
Boston Tea Party. Oxford U Pr.
Colonial Massachusetts: A History. Kraus Intl.
Patriots & Partisans: The Merchants of
Newburyport, 1764-1815. Norton.
LaBarge, L. *see* Labarge, Lura.
LaBarge, Lura.
xLaBarge, L.
Crate Craft: Easy-to-Make Furniture &
Accessories You Can Build Quickly &
Inexpensively. Butterick Pub.
Labarge, Margaret W. *see* Labarge, Margaret Wade.
Labarge, Margaret Wade.
xLabarge, Margaret W.
Simon De Montfort. Greenwood.
Labastille, Anne.
xLabastille, Anne.
Assignment Wildlife. Dutton.
White-Tailed Deer. Natl Wildlife.
Woodswoman. Dutton.
Labatut, Jean.
xLabatut, Jean.
ed. Highways in Our National Life: A
Symposium. Arno.
Labby, David.
xLabby, David.
The Demystification of Yap: Dialectics of
Culture on a Micronesian Island. U of
Chicago Pr.
Labedz, Leopold.
xLabedz, Leopold.
ed. Solzhenitsyn: A Documentary Record.
Har-Row.
Labor Law Group. *see* Labor Law Group Trust.
Labor Law Group Trust.
xLabor Law Group.
Labor Relations & Social Problems, a Course
Book: Collective Bargaining in Private
Employment. BNA.
Labor Research Assn. *see* Labor Research Association.
Labor Research Associates. *see* Labor Research
Association.
Labor Research Association.
xLabor Research Assn.
Labor Fact Book, Vol. 1. Oriole Edns.
Labor Fact Book, Vol. 2. Oriole Edns.
Labor Fact Book, Vol. 3. Oriole Edns.
Labor Fact Book, Vol. 4. Oriole Edns.
Labor Fact Book, Vol. 5. Oriole Edns.
xLabor Research Associates.
Labor Fact Book. Oriole Edns.
Labor Facts Book. Oriole Edns.
Laborit, Henri, 1914-
xLaborit, Henri.
Decoding the Human Message. St Martin.
Labossiere, Eileen.
xLaBossiere, Eileen.
Histological Processing for the Neural Sciences.
C C Thomas.
Labov, William.
xLabov, William.
Sociolinguistic Patterns. U of Pa Pr.
Study of Nonstandard English. NCTE.
Labrie, Ross.
xLabrie, Ross.
The Art of Thomas Merton. Tex Christian.
Howard Nemerov. Twayne.
Labuta, J. *see* Labuta, Joseph A.
Labuta, Joseph A.
xLabuta, J.
Guide to Accountability in Music Instruction.
P-H.
xLabuta, Joseph A.

Teaching Musicianship in the High School
Band. P-H.

Labuza, T. P.
xLabuza, T. P.
Food for Thought. AVI.
xLabuza, Theodore P.
Contemporary Nutrition Controversies. West
Pub.
Food & Your Well-Being. West Pub.
Labuza, Theodore P. *see* Labuza, T. P.
Labys, Walter. *see* Labys, Walter C.
Labys, Walter C., 1937-
xLabys, Walter.
Speculation, Hedging, & Commodity Price
Forecasts. Lexington Bks.
xLabys, Walter C.
ed. Quantitative Models of Commodity
Markets. Ballinger Pub.
Lacan, Jacques, 1901-
xLacan, Jacques.
The Four Fundamental Concepts of
Psycho-Analysis. Norton.
LaCapra, Dominick, 1939-
xLaCapra, Dominick.
A Preface to Sartre. Cornell U Pr.
Lace, O. Jessie.
xLace, O. Jessie.
Understanding the New Testament. Cambridge
U Pr.
Understanding the Old Testament. Cambridge
U Pr.
Lacey, A. R. *see* Lacey, Alan Robert.
Lacey, Alan Robert.
xLacey, A. R.
A Dictionary of Philosophy. Routledge &
Kegan.
A Dictionary of Philosophy. Scribner.
Lacey, Charlotte A. *see* Lacey, Charlotte Alvord.
Lacey, Charlotte Alvord.
xLacey, Charlotte A.
Historical Story of Southport, Connecticut.
Modern Bks.
Lacey, Douglas R. *see* Lacey, Douglas Raymond.
Lacey, Douglas Raymond, 1913-
xLacey, Douglas R.
Dissent & Parliamentary Politics in England
1661-1689: A Study in the Perpetuation &
Tempering of Parliamentarianism. Rutgers U
Pr.
Lacey, John L.
xLacey, John L.
How to Do Woodcarving. Arco.
Lacey, R. *see* Lacey, Robert E.
Lacey, Robert.
xLacey, Robert.
Queens of the North Atlantic. Stein & Day.
Lacey, Robert E.
xLacey, R.
ed. Industrial Processing with Membranes.
Krieger.
Lacey, W. K. *see* Lacey, Walter Kirkpatrick.
Lacey, Walter Kirkpatrick.
xLacey, W. K.
Cicero & the End of the Roman Republic.
B&N.
Lach, Donald F. *see* Lach, Donald Frederick.
Lach, Donald Frederick, 1917-
xLach, Donald F.
China in the Eyes of Europe: The Sixteenth
Century. U of Chicago Pr.
India in the Eyes of Europe: The Sixteenth
Century. U of Chicago Pr.
Southeast Asia in the Eyes of Europe: The
Sixteenth Century. U of Chicago Pr.
LaChapelle, E. R. *see* Lachapelle, Edward R.
LaChapelle, Edward R.
xLaChapelle, E. R.
ABC of Avalanche Safety. Mountaineers.
xLaChapelle, Edward R.

Field Guide to Snow Crystals. U of Wash Pr.
Lachenbruch, David.
xLachenbruch, David.
Video Cassette Recorders: The Complete Home
Guide. Everest Hse.
Lachenbruch, Peter A.
xLachenbruch, Peter A.
Discriminant Analysis. Hafner.
Lacher, Mortimer J.
xLacher, Mortimer J.
ed. Hodgkin's Disease. Wiley.
Lachman, Ernest, 1901-
xLachman, Ernest.
Case Studies in Anatomy. Oxford U Pr.
Lachman, Janet L. *see* Lachman, Roy.
Lachman, Leon.
xLachman, Leon.
ed. The Theory & Practice of Industrial
Pharmacy. Lea & Febiger.
Lachman, Roy.
xLachman, Janet L.
jt. auth. Cognitive Psychology & Information
Processing: An Introduction. Halsted Pr.
xLachman, Roy.
Cognitive Psychology & Information
Processing: An Introduction. Halsted Pr.
Lachmann, Ludwig M.
xLachmann, Ludwig M.
Capital & Its Structure. Inst Humane.
Capital, Expectations, & the Market Process:
Essays on the Theory of the Market
Economy. Inst Humane.
Lachs, Samuel T. *see* Lachs, Samuel Tobias.
Lachs, Samuel Tobias.
xLachs, Samuel T.
Judaism. Argus Comm.
Lack, Leon C. *see* Lack, Leon Colburn.
Lack, Leon Colburn.
xLack, Leon C.
Selective Attention & the Control of Binocular
Rivalry. Mouton.
Lackey, Larry. *see* Lackey, Larry A.
Lackey, Larry A., 1940-
xLackey, Larry.
How to Start a Small Business. Exposition.
Lackington, James, 1746-1815
xLackington, James.
Memoirs of the Forty Five First Years of the
Life of James Lackington. Kelley.
Lackner, Stephan.
xLackner, Stephen.
Max Beckmann. Abrams.
Lackner, Stephen. *see* Lackner, Stephan.
LaCore, Kathleen.
xLaCore, Kathleen.
The Return to Natural Foods Cookery. P-H.
LaCoursiere, Roy. *see* Lacoursiere, Roy B.
Lacoursiere, Roy B.
xLaCoursiere, Roy.
The Life Cycle of Groups: Group
Developmental Stage Theory. Human Sci Pr.
Lacouture, Jean.
xLacouture, Jean.
Andre Malraux. Pantheon.
LaCroix, W. L. *see* Lacroix, Wilfred Lawrence.
LaCroix, Wilfred Lawrence, 1933-
xLaCroix, W. L.
Meaning & Reason in Ethics. U Pr of Amer.
Lacy, Creighton.
xLacy, Creighton.
Coming Home-To China. Westminster.
Frank Mason North: His Social & Ecumenical
Mission. Abingdon.
xLacy, Creighton B.
The Word-Carrying Giant: The Growth of the
American Bible Society. William Carey Lib.
Lacy, Creighton B. *see* Lacy, Creighton.
Lacy, Dan. *see* Lacy, Dan Mabry.
Lacy, Dan Mabry, 1914-
xLacy, Dan.

The Abolitionists. McGraw.
Freedom & Communications. U of Ill Pr.
The Lost Colony. Watts.
Lacy, Ed. *see* Lacy, Edward A.
Lacy, Edward A., 1935-
xLacy, Ed.
Handbook of Electronic Safety Procedures.
P-H.
xLacy, Edward A.
How to Cut Your Electric Bill & Install Your
Own Emergency Power System. TAB Bks.
Lacy, Gene M.
xLacy, Gene M.
Organizing & Developing the High School
Orchestra. P-H.
Lacy, Joseph R.
xLacy, Joseph R.
Infantile Spasms. Raven.
Lacy, Leslie. *see* Lacy, Leslie Alexander.
Lacy, Leslie A. *see* Lacy, Leslie Alexander.
Lacy, Leslie Alexander.
xLacy, Leslie.
Native Daughter. Macmillan.
xLacy, Leslie A.
Cheer the Lonesome Traveler: The Life of W.
E. B. Du Bois. Dial.
Lacy, Mary L. *see* Lacy, Mary Lou.
Lacy, Mary Lou.
xLacy, Mary L.
And God Wants People. John Knox.
Ladany, S. P. *see* Ladany, Shaul P.
Ladany, Shaul P.
xLadany, S. P.
ed. Optimal Strategies in Sports. Elsevier.
Ladas, Stephen. *see* Ladas, Stephen Pericles.
Ladas, Stephen Pericles, 1898-
xLadas, Stephen.
Patents, Trademarks, & Related Rights:
National & International Protection. Harvard
U Pr.
Ladbury, Ann.
xLadbury, Ann.
Dressmaking with Basic Patterns. David &
Charles.
Ladd. *see* Ladd, Marcus Frederick Charles.
Ladd, D. Robert, 1947-
xLadd, D. Robert.
Structure of Intonational Meaning: Evidence
from English. Ind U Pr.
Ladd, Everett C. *see* Ladd, Everett Carll.
Ladd, Everett Carll.
xLadd, Everett C.
Ideology in America: Change & Response in a
City, a Suburb & a Small Town. Cornell U
Pr.
Ideology in America: Change & Response in a
City, a Suburb, & a Small Town. Norton.
Negro Political Leadership in the South.
Atheneum.
Negro Political Leadership in the South.
Cornell U Pr.
Where Have All the Voters Gone?: The
Fracturing of America's Political Parties.
Norton.
Ladd, George E. *see* Ladd, George Eldon.
Ladd, George Eldon, 1911-
xLadd, George E.
The Presence of the Future: The Eschatology
of Biblical Realism. Eerdmans.
A Theology of the New Testament. Eerdmans.
Ladd, J. D.
xLadd, J. D.
Assault from the Sea 1939-1945: The Craft, the
Landings, the Men. Hippocrene Bks.
Ladd, John, 1917-
xLadd, John.
ed. Ethical Issues Relating to Life & Death.
Oxford U Pr.
Ladd, M. F. *see* Ladd, Marcus Frederick Charles.

Ladd, Marcus Frederick Charles.
  xLadd.
    ed. Structure Determination by X-Ray
      Crystallography. Plenum Pub.
  xLadd, M. F.
    Structure & Bonding in Solid State Chemistry.
      Halsted Pr.
    ed. Structure Determination by X-Ray
      Crystallography. Plenum Pub.
    ed. Theory & Practice of Direct Methods in
      Crystallography. Plenum Pub.
Ladd, Margaret R. *see* Ladd, Margaret Rhoads.
Ladd, Margaret Rhoads, 1899-
  xLadd, Margaret R.
    The Relation of Social, Economic, & Personal
      Characteristics to Reading Ability. AMS Pr.
Ladd, William, 1778-1841
  xLadd, William.
    On the Duty of Females to Promote the Cause
      of Peace. Gordon Pr.
Ladefoged, Peter.
  xLadefoged, Peter.
    A Course in Phonetics. HarBraceJ.
    Preliminaries to Linguistic Phonetics. U of
      Chicago Pr.
Laden, Alice.
  xLaden, Alice.
    The George Bernard Shaw Vegetarian
      Cookbook. BJ Pub Group.
Ladenburg, Thomas J.
  xLadenburg, Thomas J.
    Prosperity & Depression Decades. Hayden.
Ladendorf, Janice M.
  xLadendorf, Janice M.
    Practical Dressage for Amateur Trainers. A S
      Barnes.
Ladenson, Alex.
  xLadenson, Alex.
    American Library Laws. ALA.
Lader, Lawrence.
  xLader, Lawrence.
    Abortion. Beacon Pr.
    Abortion. Bobbs.
    Power on the Left: American Radical
      Movements Since 1946. Norton.
Lader, Malcolm. *see* Lader, Malcolm Harold.
Lader, Malcolm Harold.
  xLader, Malcolm.
    Psychophysiology of Mental Illness. Routledge
      & Kegan.
Ladies Home Journal. *see* Ladies' Home Journal.
Ladies Home Journal Editors. *see* Ladies' Home Journal.
Ladies' Home Journal.
  xLadies Home Journal.
    America's Twelve Great Women Leaders
      During the Past Hundred Years As Chosen
      by the Women of America. Arno.
  xLadies Home Journal Editors.
    Creative Sewing. Van Nos Reinhold.
    Knitting. Van Nos Reinhold.
Ladley, Barbara.
  xLadley, Barbara.
    Money & Finance: Sources of Print &
      Nonprint Materials. Neal-Schuman.
Ladley, Betty A.
  xLadley, Betty A.
    Office Procedures for the Dental Team. Mosby.
Ladner, Joyce. *see* Ladner, Joyce A.
Ladner, Joyce A.
  xLadner, Joyce.
    ed. The Death of White Sociology. Random.
    Mixed Families: Adopting Across Racial
      Boundaries. Doubleday.
  xLadner, Joyce A.
    ed. The Death of White Sociology. Random.
Lado, Robert, 1915-
  xLado, Robert.

    Linguistics Across Cultures: Applied Linguistics
      for Language Teachers. U of Mich Pr.
LaDou, Joseph.
  xLaDou, Joseph.
    Medicine & Money: Physicians As
      Businessmen. Ballinger Pub.
Ladusaw, William A., 1952-
  xLadusaw, William A.
    Polarity Sensitivity As Inherent Scope
      Relations. Garland Pub.
Laetsch, Watson M.
  xLaetsch, Watson M.
    Plants: Basic Concepts in Botany. Little.
Laeuchli, Samuel.
  xLaeuchli, Samuel.
    Power & Sexuality: The Emergence of Canon
      Law at the Synod of Elvira. Temple U Pr.
LaFara, Robert L.
  xLaFara, Robert L.
    Computer Methods for Science & Engineering.
      Hayden.
Lafaye, Jacques.
  xLafaye, Jacques.
    Quetzalcoatl & Guadalupe: The Formation of
      Mexican National Consciousness, 1531-1813.
      U of Chicago Pr.
LaFayette, Kenneth D.
  xLaFayette, Kenneth D.
    Flaming Brands: Fifty Years of Iron Making in
      the Upper Peninsula of Michigan, 1848-1898.
      Northern Mich.
LaFeber, Walter.
  xLaFeber, Walter.
    America, Russia & the Cold War, 1945-1980.
      Wiley.
    America, Russia & the Cold War, 1945-75.
      Wiley.
    The American Century: A History of the
      United States Since the 1890's. Wiley.
Laffal, Julius.
  xLaffal, Julius.
    Concept Dictionary of English. Gallery Pr.
    A Concept Dictionary of English. Halsted Pr.
Laffer, Arthur B.
  xLaffer, Arthur B.
    The Economics of the Tax Revolt: A Reader.
      HarBraceJ.
    Private Short-Term Capital Flows. Dekker.
Lafferty, J. M. *see* Lafferty, James Martin.
Lafferty, James Martin.
  xLafferty, J. M.
    ed. Vacuum Arcs: Theory & Application.
      Wiley.
Lafferty, R. A.
  xLafferty, R. A.
    The Devil Is Dead. Gregg.
    Funnyfingers & Cabrito. Pendragon Oregon.
    Horns on Their Heads. Pendragon Oregon.
    In the Wake of Man: A Science Fiction Triad.
      Bobbs.
    Past Master. Ace Bks.
    Past Master. Garland Pub.
    The Reefs of Earth. Berkley Pub.
    Strange Doings. Scribner.
Lafferty, Theodore T. *see* Lafferty, Theodore Thomas.
Lafferty, Theodore Thomas, 1901-1970
  xLafferty, Theodore T.
    Nature & Values: Pragmatic Essays in
      Metaphysics. U of SC Pr.
Laffey, James. *see* Laffey, James L.
Laffey, James L., 1934-
  xLaffey, James.
    ed. Reading in the Content Areas. Intl
      Reading.
Laffin, John.
  xLaffin, John.
    Codes & Ciphers: Secret Writing Through the
      Ages. Abelard.
Laffont, J. J. *see* Laffont, Jean Jacques.

Laffont, Jean Jacques.
  xLaffont, J. J.
    ed. Aggregation & Revelation of Preferences.
      Elsevier.
  xLaffont, Jean-Jacques.
    Essays in the Economics of Uncertainty.
      Harvard U Pr.
Laffont, Jean-Jacques. *see* Laffont, Jean Jacques.
Lafitte, Paul, 1915-
  xLafitte, Paul.
    The Person in Psychology: Reality or
      Abstraction. Humanities.
    Person in Psychology: Reality or Abstraction?.
      Philos Lib.
LaFontaine, Gary J.
  xLaFontaine, Gary J.
    Challenge of the Trout. Mountain Pr.
Laforgue, Rene.
  xLaforgue, Rene.
    The Defeat of Baudelaire: A Psycho-Analytical
      Study of the Neurosis of Charles Baudelaire.
      Folcroft.
Lafourcade, Georges.
  xLafourcade, Georges.
    Arnold Bennett: A Study. AMS Pr.
    Arnold Bennett: A Study. Haskell.
    Swinburne: A Literary Biography. Folcroft.
    Swinburne: A Literary Biography. Norwood
      Edns.
LaFrance, Arthur B.
  xLaFrance, Arthur B.
    Welfare Law: Structure & Entitlement in a
      Nutshell. West Pub.
LaFrance, Marston.
  xLaFrance, Marston.
    Reading of Stephen Crane. Oxford U Pr.
Lagal, Roy.
  xLagal, Roy.
    Detector Owner's Field Manual. Ram Pub.
    Gold Panning Is Easy. Ram Pub.
Lage, Gerald Luge. *see* Lage, Gerald M.
Lage, Gerald M.
  xLage, G.
    The Price System & Resource Allocation: A
      Book of Problems. HR&W.
Lagemann, Ellen C. *see* Lagemann, Ellen Condliffe.
Lagemann, Ellen Condliffe, 1945-
  xLagemann, Ellen C.
    A Generation of Women: Education in the
      Lives of Progressive Reformers. Harvard U
      Pr.
Lagercrantz, Rose.
  xLagercrantz, Rose.
    Tulla's Summer. HarBraceJ.
Lagercrantz, Sture.
  xLagercrantz, Sture.
    Contribution to the Ethnography of Africa.
      Greenwood.
    Contribution to the Ethnography of Africa.
      Negro U Pr.
Lagerkvist, Par. *see* Lagerkvist, Par Fabian.
Lagerkvist, Par Fabian, 1891-
  xLagerkvist, Par.
    Barabbas. Random.
    Evening Land: Aftonland. Wayne St U Pr.
    The Marriage Feast. Hill & Wang.
Lagerlof, Karl E. *see* Lagerlof, Karl Erik.
Lagerlof, Karl Erik.
  xLagerlof, Karl E.
    ed. Modern Swedish Prose in Translation. U of
      Minn Pr.
Lagerlof, Selma. *see* Lagerlof, Selma Ottiliana Lovisa.
Lagerlof, Selma Ottiliana Lovisa, 1858-1940
  xLagerlof, Selma.
    Marbacka. Gale.
Lagler, Karl F. *see* Lagler, Karl Frank.
Lagler, Karl Frank, 1912-
  xLagler, Karl F.
    Ichthyology. Wiley.
Lago, G. *see* Lago, Gladwyn Vaile.

Lago, Gladwyn Vaile.
    xLago, G.
        Circuit & System Theory. Wiley.
Lago, Mary M.
    xLago, Mary M.
        Rabindranath Tagore. Twayne.
Lagowski, J. J.
    xLagowski, J. J.
        ed. Chemistry of Non-Aqueous Solvents. Acad
        Pr.
        Modern Inorganic Chemistry. Dekker.
Laguardia Community College, Social Science Faculty.
    see La Guardia Community College.
Laguardia, Robert.
    xLaguardia, Robert.
        Monty: A Biography of Montgomery Clift.
        Arbor Hse.
        The Wonderful World of TV Soap Operas.
        Ballantine.
Laguerre, Michel S.
    xLaguerre, Michel S.
        Voodoo Heritage. Sage.
LaGumina, Salvatore J. *see* Lagumina, Salvatore John.
LaGumina, Salvatore John, 1928-
    xLaGumina, Salvatore J.
        An Album of the Italian American. Watts.
        ed. The Immigrants Speak: The Italian
        Americans Tell Their Story. Ctr Migration.
Laguna, Frederica De. *see* De Laguna, Frederica.
Laha, R. G.
    xLaha, R. G.
        Probability Theory. Wiley.
LaHaye, Beverly.
    xLaHaye, Beverly.
        The Spirit-Controlled Woman. Harvest Hse.
LaHaye, Tim. *see* Lahaye, Tim F.
LaHaye, Tim F.
    xLaHaye, Tim.
        How to Study the Bible for Yourself. Harvest
        Hse.
        How to Win Over Depression. Bantam.
        How to Win Over Depression. Zondervan.
        Spirit Controlled Family Living. Revell.
        Spirit-Controlled Temperament. Tyndale.
    xLaHaye, Tim F.
        The Ark on Ararat. CLP Pubs.
Lahee, Henry. *see* Lahee, Henry Charles.
Lahee, Henry C. *see* Lahee, Henry Charles.
Lahee, Henry Charles, 1856-1953
    xLahee, Henry.
        Famous Violinists of Today & Yesterday. Dunn
        & Webster.
    xLahee, Henry C.
        Famous Singers of Today & Yesterday.
        Longwood Pr.
        Famous Violinists of Today & Yesterday.
        Longwood Pr.
        Grand Opera in America. AMS Pr.
        Grand Opera in America. Arno.
Lahey, Benjamin B.
    xLahey, Benjamin B.
        ed. Behavior Therapy with Hyperactive &
        Learning Disabled Children. Oxford U Pr.
        Maladaptive Behavior: An Introduction to
        Abnormal Psychology. Scott F.
Lahey, Benjamin B. *see* Lahey, Benjamin G.
Lahey, Benjamin G.
    xLahey, Benjamin B.
        Psychology & Instruction: A Practical
        Approach to Educational Psychology. Scott
        F.
Lahey, G. F. *see* Lahey, Gerald F.
Lahey, Gerald F.
    xLahey, G. F.
        Gerard Manley Hopkins. Gordon Pr.
        Gerard Manley Hopkins. Haskell.
        Gerard Manley Hopkins. Octagon.
Lahey, James F. *see* Lahey, James Frederick.
Lahey, James Frederick, 1921-
    xLahey, James F.

Atlas of Five-Day Normal Sea-Level Pressure
    Charts for the Northern Hemisphere. U of
    Wis Pr.
Lahey, Margaret, 1932-
    xLahey, Margaret.
        ed. Readings in Childhood Language Disorders.
        Wiley.
Lahey, R. T. *see* Lahey, Richard T.
Lahey, Richard T.
    xLahey, R. T.
        The Thermal Hydraulics of a Boiling Water
        Nuclear Reactor. Am Nuclear Soc.
Lahr, John, 1941-
    xLahr, John.
        Prick up Your Ears: The Biography of Joe
        Orton. Knopf.
Lahue, Kalton C.
    xLahue, Kalton C.
        Photo Retouching & Restoration. Petersen Pub.
        World of Laughter: The Motion Picture
        Comedy Short 1910-1930. U of Okla Pr.
Lai, T. C. *see* Lai, Tien-Chang.
Lai, Tien-Chang.
    xLai, T. C.
        Ch'i Pai-shih. U of Wash Pr.
        Chinese Calligraphy: An Introduction. U of
        Wash Pr.
Lai, W. M. *see* Lai, W. Michael.
Lai, W. Michael.
    xLai, W. M.
        Introduction to Continuum Mechanics.
        Pergamon.
Laidlaw, Harry H. *see* Laidlaw, Harry Hyde.
Laidlaw, Harry Hyde, 1907-
    xLaidlaw, Harry H.
        Contemporary Queen Rearing. Dadant & Sons.
        Queen Rearing. U of Cal Pr.
Laidlaw, John P. *see* Laidlaw, John Patrick.
Laidlaw, John Patrick.
    xLaidlaw, John P.
        A Textbook of Epilepsy. Churchill.
Laidlaw, Robert A.
    xLaidlaw, Robert A.
        The Reason Why. Zondervan.
Laidlaw, W. G. *see* Laidlaw, William George.
Laidlaw, William George, 1936-
    xLaidlaw, W. G.
        Introduction to Quantum Concepts in
        Spectroscopy. Krieger.
Laidler, D. *see* Laidler, David E. W.
Laidler, David. *see* Laidler, David E. W.
Laidler, David E. W.
    xLaidler, D.
        Inflation & Labour Markets. U of Toronto Pr.
    xLaidler, David.
        Introduction to Microeconomics. Basic.
Laidler, Harry W. *see* Laidler, Harry Wellington.
Laidler, Harry Wellington, 1884-
    xLaidler, Harry W.
        Boycotts & the Labor Struggle: Economic &
        Legal Aspects. Russell.
Laidler, Keith J. *see* Laidler, Keith James.
Laidler, Keith James, 1916-
    xLaidler, Keith J.
        Theories of Chemical Reaction Rates. Krieger.
Laidman, Hugh.
    xLaidman, Hugh.
        Animals: How to Draw Them. Dutton.
        The Complete Book of Drawing & Painting.
        Penguin.
        The Complete Book of Drawing & Painting.
        Viking Pr.
        Figures-Faces: A Sketcher's Handbook. Viking
        Pr.
Laiken, Deidre S.
    xLaiken, Deidre S.
        Listen to Me, I'm Angry. Lothrop.
Laine, Annabel.
    xLaine, Annabel.

        The Reluctant Heiress. Avon.
        The Reluctant Heiress. Doubleday.
Laine, S. *see* Laine, Steven.
Laine, Steven.
    xLaine, S.
        Promotion in Food Service. McGraw.
Laing, Alexander. *see* Laing, Alexander Kinnan.
Laing, Alexander Kinnan, 1903-
    xLaing, Alexander.
        Brant Point: Poems. U Pr of New Eng.
Laing, Bertram M. *see* Laing, Bertram Mitchell.
Laing, Bertram Mitchell.
    xLaing, Bertram M.
        David Hume. Russell.
Laing, Frederick.
    xLaing, Frederick.
        Tales from Scandinavia. Silver.
Laing, Gordon. *see* Laing, Gordon Jennings.
Laing, Gordon Jennings, 1869-1945
    xLaing, Gordon.
        Survivals of Roman Religion. Cooper Sq.
Laing, Jeanie M.
    xLaing, Jeanie M.
        Notes on Superstition & Folk Lore. Folcroft.
        Notes on Superstition & Folk Lore. R West.
Laing, Jennifer.
    xLaing, Jenniger.
        Finding Roman Britain. David & Charles.
Laing, Jenniger. *see* Laing, Jennifer.
Laing, Lloyd. *see* Laing, Lloyd Robert.
Laing, Lloyd Robert.
    xLaing, Lloyd.
        Anglo-Saxon England. Scribner.
        Celtic Britain. Scribner.
        Orkney & Shetland: An Archaeological Guide.
        David & Charles.
Laing, R. D. *see* Laing, Ronald David.
Laing, Ronald D. *see* Laing, Ronald David.
Laing, Ronald David.
    xLaing, R. D.
        Conversations with Adam & Natasha.
        Pantheon.
        Divided Self. Pantheon.
        The Facts of Life: An Essay in Feelings, Facts
        & Fantasy. Pantheon.
        The Politics of Experience. Ballantine.
        The Politics of the Family & Other Essays.
        Random.
    xLaing, Ronald D.
        Divided Self. Penguin.
Laiou-Thomadakis, A. D. *see* Laiou-Thomadakis,
    Angeliki E.
Laiou-Thomadakis, Angeliki E.
    xLaiou-Thomadakis, A. D.
        Peasant Society in the Late Byzantine Empire:
        A Social & Demographic Study. Princeton U
        Pr.
Laird, Carobeth, 1895-
    xLaird, Carobeth.
        Limbo. Chandler & Sharp.
Laird, Charles. *see* Laird, Charlton Grant.
Laird, Charlton. *see* Laird, Charlton Grant.
Laird, Charlton G. *see* Laird, Charlton Grant.
Laird, Charlton Grant.
    xLaird, Charles.
        Modern English Reader. P-H.
    xLaird, Charlton.
        Reading About Language. HarBraceJ.
    xLaird, Charlton G.
        ed. World Through Literature. Arno.
Laird, Donald A. *see* Laird, Donald Anderson.
Laird, Donald Anderson.
    xLaird, Donald A.
        Psychology: Human Relations & Motivation.
        McGraw.
Laird, Dugan.
    xLaird, Dugan.
        Approaches to Training & Development. A-W.
Laird, Jean. *see* Laird, Jean E.

Laird, Jean E.
　xLaird, Jean.
　　The Homemaker's Book of Time & Money
　　　Savers. Greene.
Laird, John, 1887-1946
　xLaird, John.
　　Enquiry into Moral Notions. AMS Pr.
　　Hume's Philosophy of Human Nature. Shoe
　　　String.
　　The Idea of the Soul. Arden Lib.
　　Idea of the Soul. Arno.
　　Idea of Value. Kelley.
　　On Human Freedom. Humanities.
Laird, Melvin. *see* Laird, Melvin R.
Laird, Melvin R.
　xLaird, Melvin.
　　The Nixon Doctrine. Am Enterprise.
Laird, Roy. *see* Laird, Roy D.
Laird, Roy D.
　xLaird, Roy.
　　ed. Future of Agriculture in the Soviet Union
　　　& Eastern Europe: The 1976-1980 Five-Year
　　　Plans. Westview.
Laird, W. David, 1937-
　xLaird, W. David.
　　Hopi Bibliography: Comprehensive &
　　　Annotated. U of Ariz Pr.
Laistner, M. L. *see* Laistner, Max Ludwig Wolfram.
Laistner, Max L. *see* Laistner, Max Ludwig Wolfram.
Laistner, Max Ludwig Wolfram, 1890-
　xLaistner, M. L.
　　The Greater Roman Historians. U of Cal Pr.
　xLaistner, Max L.
　　Greek Economics. AMS Pr.
Laitin, David D.
　xLaitin, David D.
　　Politics, Language, & Thought: The Somali
　　　Experience. U of Chicago Pr.
Laitman, Leon.
　xLaitman, Leon.
　　Tunisia Today: Crisis in North Africa.
　　　Greenwood.
Lajpat Rai, Lala, 1865-1928
　xLajpat Rai, Lala.
　　Unhappy India. AMS Pr.
Lajtha, A. *see* Lajtha, Abel.
Lajtha, Abel.
　xLajtha, A.
　　ed. Brain Barrier Systems. Elsevier.
　xLajtha, Abel.
　　ed. Protein Metabolism of the Nervous System.
　　　Plenum Pub.
Lake, Alice, 1916-
　xLake, Alice.
　　Our Own Years: What Women Over 35 Should
　　　Know About Themselves. Random.
Lake, Anthony.
　xLake, Anthony.
　　ed. The Legacy of Vietnam: The War,
　　　American Society, & the Future of American
　　　Foreign Policy. NYU Pr.
Lake, Dale. *see* Lake, Dale G.
Lake, Dale G.
　xLake, Dale.
　　Perceiving & Behaving. Tchrs Coll.
　xLake, Dale G.
　　ed. Measuring Human Behavior: Tools for the
　　　Assessment of Social Functioning. Tchrs Coll.
Lake, Frances.
　xLake, Frances.
　　Mathematics As a Second Language. A-W.
Lake, James A.
　xLake, James A.
　　Law & Mineral Wealth: The Legal Profile of
　　　the Wisconsin Mining Industry. U of Wis Pr.
Lakein, Alan.
　xLakein, Alan.

　　How to Get Control of Your Time & Your
　　　Life. McKay.
　　How to Get Control of Your Time & Your
　　　Life. NAL.
Lakela, Olga.
　xLakela, Olga.
　　Flora of Northeastern Minnesota. U of Minn
　　　Pr.
　　Plants of the Tampa Bay Area. Banyan Bks.
Laki, Koloman, 1909-
　xLaki, Kolomon.
　　ed. Contractile Proteins & Muscle. Dekker.
Laki, Kolomon. *see* Laki, Koloman.
Lakier, Aleksandr B. *see* Lakier, Aleksandr Borisovich.
Lakier, Aleksandr Borisovich.
　xLakier, Aleksandr B.
　　A Russian Looks at America: The Journey of
　　　Aleksandr Borisovich Lakier in 1857. U of
　　　Chicago Pr.
Laklan, Carli.
　xLaklan, Carli.
　　Golden Girls: True Stories of Olympic Women
　　　Stars. McGraw.
Lakoff, George.
　xLakoff, George.
　　Metaphors We Live by. U of Chicago Pr.
Lakshmanan, M. S.
　xLakshmanan, M. S.
　　Economic Development in India. College Mktg
　　　Grp.
Lakshmikantham, V.
　xLakshmikantham, V.
　　ed. Nonlinear Systems & Applications: An
　　　International Conference. Acad Pr.
Lal, Basant K. *see* Lal, Basant Kumar.
Lal, Basant Kumar.
　xLal, Basant K.
　　Contemporary Indian Philosophy. Orient Bk
　　　Dist.
　　Contemporary Indian Philosophy. South Asia
　　　Bks.
Lal, K. S. *see* Lal, Kishori Saran.
Lal, Kishori Saran, 1920-
　xLal, K. S.
　　Growth of Muslim Population in Medieval
　　　India (A.D. 1000-1800). Intl Pubns Serv.
Lal, R.
　xLal, R.
　　ed. Soil Physical Properties & Crop Production
　　　in the Tropics. Wiley.
Lal, R. B. *see* Lal, Rajendra Behari.
Lal, Rajendra Behari.
　xLal, R. B.
　　Art of Working. Asia.
Laliberte, Elizabeth. *see* Laliberte, Elizabeth B.
Laliberte, Elizabeth B.
　xLaliberte, Elizabeth.
　　ed. Nursing Care of Children: PreTest
　　　Self-Assessment & Review. McGraw-Pretest.
Lall, Arthur. *see* Lall, Arthur Samuel.
Lall, Arthur Samuel, 1911-
　xLall, Arthur.
　　How Communist China Negotiates. Columbia
　　　U Pr.
Lall, Bernard. *see* Lall, Bernard M.
Lall, Bernard M.
　xLall, Bernard.
　　Marijuana--Friend or Foe?. Southern Pub.
Lallement, Gerard, 1935-
　xLallement, Gerard.
　　Semigroups & Combinatorial Applications.
　　　Wiley.
LaLonde, Bernard J.
　xLaLonde, Bernard J.
　　Differentials in Supermarket Drawing Power.
　　　Mich St U Busn.
Lam, T. Y., 1942-
　xLam, T. Y.

　　The Algebraic Theory of Quadratic Forms.
　　　Benjamin-Cummings.
Lam, W. *see* Lam, William M. C.
Lam, William M. C.
　xLam, W.
　　Perception & Lighting As Formgivers for
　　　Architecture. McGraw.
Lamantia, Philip, 1927
　xLamantia, Philip.
　　Touch of the Marvelous. Four Seasons Foun.
　　Touch of the Marvelous. SBD.
Lamar, Curt.
　xLamar, Curt.
　　ed. History of Rosedale, Mississippi,
　　　1876-1976. Reprint.
Lamar, Howard R. *see* Lamar, Howard Roberts.
Lamar, Howard Roberts.
　xLamar, Howard R.
　　ed. The Reader's Encyclopedia of the
　　　American West. T Y Crowell.
Lamar, Nedra N. *see* Lamar, Nedra Newkirk.
Lamar, Nedra Newkirk.
　xLamar, Nedra N.
　　How to Speak the Written Word: A Guide to
　　　Effective Public Reading. Revell.
Lamarck, Jean B. *see* Lamarck, Jean Baptiste Pierre
　　Antoine De Monet De.
**Lamarck, Jean Baptiste Pierre Antoine De Monet De,
1744-1829**
　xLamarck, Jean B.
　　Hydrogeology. U of Ill Pr.
Lamarsh, J. R. *see* Lamarsh, John R.
Lamarsh, John R.
　xLamarsh, J. R.
　　Introduction to Nuclear Reactor Theory. A-W.
　xLamarsh, John R.
　　Introduction to Nuclear Engineering. A-W.
Lamartine, Alphonse M. *see* Lamartine, Alphonse Marie
　　Louis De.
Lamartine, Alphonse Marie Louis De, 1790-1869
　xLamartine, Alphonse M.
　　History of the French Revolution of 1848.
　　　AMS Pr.
Lamb. *see* Lamb, Karl A.
Lamb, Berton L.
　xLamb, Berton L.
　　ed. Water Quality Administration: A Focus on
　　　Section 208. Ann Arbor Science.
Lamb, Caroline. *see* Lamb, Caroline Ponsonby.
Lamb, Caroline P. *see* Lamb, Caroline Ponsonby.
Lamb, Caroline Ponsonby, Lady, 1785-1828
　xLamb, Caroline.
　　Glenarvon. Schol Facsimiles.
　xLamb, Caroline P.
　　Glenarvon. AMS Pr.
Lamb, Charles.
　xLamb, Charles.
　　Charles Lamb: Prose & Poetry. Greenwood.
　　Life, Letters & Writings of Charles Lamb.
　　　Arno.
　　Specimens of English Dramatic Poets Who
　　　Lived About the Time of Shakespeare.
　　　Johnson Repr.
　　Works of Charles & Mary Lamb. AMS Pr.
　　The Works of Charles & Mary Lamb.
　　　Scholarly.
Lamb, Curt.
　xLamb, Curt.
　　Homestyles. St Martin.
Lamb, Dana S. *see* Lamb, Dana Storrs.
Lamb, Dana Storrs, 1901-
　xLamb, Dana S.
　　Beneath the Rising Mist. Stone Wall Pr.
Lamb, David.
　xLamb, David.

Language & Perception in Hegel &
 Wittgenstein. Moretus Pr.
Language & Perception in Hegel &
 Wittgenstein. St Martin.
Lamb, Doris.
 xLamb, Doris.
 Psychotherapy with Adolescent Girls.
  Jossey-Bass.
Lamb, Edgar.
 xLamb, Edgar.
 Popular Exotic Cacti in Color. Macmillan.
Lamb, Edward.
 xLamb, Edward.
 The Sharing Society. Lyle Stuart.
Lamb, G. H. *see* Lamb, George H.
Lamb, Geoffrey. *see* Lamb, Geoffrey Frederick.
Lamb, Geoffrey Frederick.
 xLamb, Geoffrey.
 Card Tricks. Elsevier-Nelson.
 Illustrated Magic Dictionary. Elsevier-Nelson.
 Pencil & Paper Tricks. Elsevier-Nelson.
 Table Tricks. Elsevier-Nelson.
Lamb, George H.
 xLamb, G. H.
 Underground Coal Gasification. Noyes.
Lamb, Gordon H.
 xLamb, Gordon H.
 Choral Techniques. Wm C Brown.
Lamb, H. Richard, 1929-
 xLamb, H. Richard.
 Rehabilitation in Community Mental Health.
  Jossey-Bass.
Lamb, Harold, 1892-1962
 xLamb, Harold.
 Marching Sands. Hyperion Conn.
Lamb, Hugh.
 xLamb, Hugh.
 ed. Return from the Grave. Taplinger.
 ed. The Taste of Fear: Thirteen Eerie Tales of
  Horror. Taplinger.
Lamb, I. Mackenzie. *see* Lamb, Ivan Mackenzie.
Lamb, Ivan Mackenzie.
 xLamb, I. Mackenzie.
 ed. Index Nominum Lichenum: Inter Annos
  1932 et 1960 divulgatorum. Wiley.
Lamb, Jackie.
 xLamb, Jackie.
 Parent Education & Elementary Counseling.
  Human Sci Pr.
Lamb, Karl A.
 xLamb.
 The People, Maybe. Duxbury Pr.
 xLamb, Karl A.
 As Orange Goes: Twelve California Families &
  the Future of American Politics. Norton.
Lamb, Lawrence E.
 xLamb, Lawrence E.
 Stay Youthful & Fit: A Doctor's Guide.
  Har-Row.
Lamb, Lynton.
 xLamb, Lynton.
 Materials & Methods of Painting. Oxford U Pr.
Lamb, M. W. *see* Lamb, Mina Marie (Wolf).
Lamb, Margaret, 1936-
 xLamb, Margaret.
 Antony & Cleopatra on the English Stage.
  Fairleigh Dickinson.
 Colorado High Country. Swallow.
Lamb, Michael E.
 xLamb, Michael E.
 ed. Social Interaction Analysis: Methodological
  Issues. U of Wis Pr.
Lamb, Mina Marie (Wolf).
 xLamb, M. W.
 Meaning of Human Nutrition. Pergamon.
Lamb, Norman.
 xLamb, Norman.
 Guide to Teaching Strings. Wm C Brown.
Lamb, Pose.
 xLamb, Pose.

Linguistics in Proper Perspective. Merrill.
 xLamb, Pose M.
 Reading: Foundations & Instructional
  Strategies. Wadsworth Pub.
Lamb, Pose M. *see* Lamb, Pose.
Lamb, Roger, 1756-1830
 xLamb, Roger.
 Original & Authentic Journal of Occurrences
  During the Late American War. Arno.
Lamb, Ruth (Stanton).
 xLamb, Ruth S.
 Latin America: Sites & Insights. Creative Pr.
 Latin America: Sites & Insights. Ocelot Pr.
Lamb, Ruth D. *see* Lamb, Ruth Deforest.
Lamb, Ruth Deforest.
 xLamb, Ruth D.
 American Chamber of Horrors: The Truth
  About Food & Drugs. Arno.
Lamb, Ruth S. *see* Lamb, Ruth (Stanton).
Lamb, Sidney. *see* Lamb, Sydney H.
Lamb, Sydney H.
 xLamb, Sidney.
 Mathematical Games, Puzzles & Fallacies.
  Arco.
Lamb, Sydney M.
 xLamb, Sydney M.
 An Outline of Stratificational Grammar.
  Georgetown U Pr.
Lamb, Ted.
 xLamb, Ted.
 The Bait Book: Fresh Water & Sea Angling.
  David & Charles.
Lamb, Tony.
 xLamb, Tony.
 Planning for Your Retirement. Penguin.
 The Retirement Threat. G K Hall.
Lamb, Walter, 1950-
 xLamb, Walter.
 Always Begin Where You Are: Themes in
  Poetry & Song. McGraw.
Lamb, Warren.
 xLamb, Warren.
 Body Code: The Meaning in Movement.
  Routledge & Kegan.
Lamballe, Nathaniel.
 xLamballe, Nathaniel.
 Art Secrets Artists Follow in Their Search for
  Greatness. Am Classical College Pr.
Lambdin, Bill.
 xLambdin, William.
 Doublespeak Dictionary. Pinnacle Bks.
Lambdin, Thomas O. *see* Lambdin, Thomas Oden.
Lambdin, Thomas Oden.
 xLambdin, Thomas O.
 An Introduction to Biblical Hebrew. Scribner.
Lambdin, William. *see* Lambdin, Bill.
Lambe, T. William.
 xLambe, T. William.
 Soil Mechanics. Wiley.
 Soil Mechanics, SI Version. Wiley.
Lamberg-Karlovsky, C. C.
 xLamberg-Karlovsky, C. C.
 Ancient Civilizations: The Near East &
  Mesoamerica. Benjamin-Cummings.
Lambert, Clark, 1931-
 xLambert, Clark.
 Field Sales Performance Appraisal. Wiley.
Lambert, David.
 xLambert, David.
 Dinosaurs. Crown.
Lambert, Dennis.
 xLambert, Dennis.
 Producing Hit Records. Schirmer Bks.
Lambert, Edward C.
 xLambert, Edward C.
 Modern Medical Mistakes. Ind U Pr.
Lambert, Eloise.
 xLambert, Eloise.

Our Names, Where They Came from & What
 They Mean. Lothrop.
Lambert, G. E. *see* Lambert, George Edmund.
Lambert, George Edmund.
 xLambert, G. E.
 Duke Ellington. A S Barnes.
 Johnny Dodds. A S Barnes.
Lambert, H. M. *see* Lambert, Hester Marjorie.
Lambert, Hazel.
 xLambert, Hazel.
 As the Colors Change. Windy Row.
Lambert, Herbert H., 1929-
 xLambert, Herbert H.
 Getting Inside the Bible. Bethany Pr.
Lambert, Hester Marjorie.
 xLambert, H. M.
 Gujarati Language Course. Cambridge U Pr.
Lambert, Isaac E., 1890-
 xLambert, Isaac E.
 The Public Accepts: Stories Behind Famous
  Trade-Marks, Names, & Slogans. Arno.
Lambert, J. D. *see* Lambert, James Dewe.
Lambert, James Dewe.
 xLambert, J. D.
 Vibrational & Rotational Relaxation in Gases.
  Oxford U Pr.
Lambert, Johann H. *see* Lambert, Johann Heinrich.
Lambert, Johann Heinrich, 1728-1777
 xLambert, Johann H.
 Cosmological Letters on the Arrangement of
  the World-Edifice. N Watson.
Lambert, John Denholm, 1932-
 xLambert, J. D.
 Computational Methods in Ordinary
  Differential Equations. Wiley.
Lambert, Joseph B.
 xLambert, Joseph B.
 Organic Structural Analysis. Macmillan.
 Physical Organic Chemistry Through Solved
  Problems. Holden-Day.
Lambert, Karel, 1928-
 xLambert, Karel.
 ed. Logical Way of Doing Things. Yale U Pr.
 The Nature of Argument. Macmillan.
Lambert, M. B.
 xLambert, M. B.
 Volcanoes. U of Wash Pr.
Lambert, Malcolm.
 xLambert, Malcolm.
 Medieval Heresy: Popular Movements from
  Bogomil to Hus. Holmes & Meier.
Lambert, Marjorie F.
 xLambert, Marjorie F.
 Survey & Excavation of Caves in Hidalgo
  County, New Mexico. Museum NM Pr.
Lambert, Mark.
 xLambert, Mark.
 Fossils. Arco.
Lambert, Nadine M.
 xLambert, Nadine M.
 The Educationally Retarded Child:
  Comprehensive Assessment & Planning for
  Slow Learners & the Educable Mentally
  Retarded. Grune.
Lambert, Neal. *see* Lambert, Neal E.
Lambert, Neal E., 1934-
 xLambert, Neal.
 George Frederick Ruxton. Boise St Univ.
Lambert, O. C. *see* Lambert, Orlando Clayton.
Lambert, Orlando Clayton, 1890-
 xLambert, O. C.
 Catholicism Against Itself. Lambert Bk.
Lambert, Regina.
 xLambert, Regina.
 Valerie's Wilderness Adventure. Moody.
Lambert, Samuel W. *see* Lambert, Samuel Waldron.
Lambert, Samuel Waldron, 1859-1942
 xLambert, Samuel W.

When Mr. Pickwick Went Fishing. Haskell.
Lambert, Terence.
xLambert, Terence.
Lambert's Birds of Shore & Estuary. Scribner.
Lambert, Vickie A.
xLambert, Vickie A.
The Impact of Physical Illness & Related
Mental Health Concepts. P-H.
Lambert, W. G.
xLambert, Wilfred G.
Babylonian Wisdom Literature. Oxford U Pr.
Lambert, Wallace E.
xLambert, Wallace E.
Child Rearing Values: A Cross National Study.
Praeger.
Lambert, Wilfred G. see Lambert, W. G.
Lamberth, John.
xLamberth, John.
Personality: An Introduction. Random.
Social Psychology. Macmillan.
Lamberton, Donald M. see Lamberton, Donald McLean.
Lamberton, Donald McLean.
xLamberton, Donald M.
ed. The Information Revolution. Am Acad Pol
Soc Sci.
Theory of Profit. Kelley.
Lambeth, James.
xLambeth, James.
Solar Designing: 1977. Lambeth.
Lambley, Hanne.
xLambley, Hanne.
The Home Book of German Cookery.
Merrimack Bk Serv.
Lambray, Maureen.
xLambray, Maureen.
The American Film Directors. Macmillan.
Lambright, W. Henry, 1939-
xLambright, W. Henry.
Governing Science & Technology. Oxford U
Pr.
Lambro, Donald.
xLambro, Donald.
The Conscience of a Young Conservative.
Arlington Hse.
Fat City: How Washington Wastes Your Taxes.
Regnery-Gateway.
The Federal Rathole. Arlington Hse.
Lambton, Lucinda.
xLambton, Lucinda.
Temples of Convenience. St Martin.
Lamer, Mirko, 1907-
xLamer, Mirko.
The World Fertilizer Economy. Stanford U Pr.
Lamere, Bernard.
xLamere, Bernard.
Guide to Home Air Conditioners &
Refrigeration Equipment. Hayden.
Lamerton, Richard.
xLamerton, Richard.
Care of the Dying. Technomic.
Lamm, Joyce.
xLamm, Joyce.
Let's Talk About the Metric System. Jonathan
David.
Lamm, Martin, 1880-1950
xLamm, Martin.
August Strindberg. Arno.
Modern Drama. Folcroft.
Modern Drama. R West.
Lamm, Maurice.
xLamm, Maurice.
The Jewish Way in Love & Marriage.
Har-Row.
Lamm, Michael, 1936-
xLamm, Michael.
The Fabulous Firebird. Lamm-Morada.
Lamm, Zvi.
xLamm, Zvi.

Conflicting Theories of Instruction: Conceptual
Dimensions. McCutchan.
Lammers, William W.
xLammers, William W.
Presidential Politics: Patterns & Prospects.
Har-Row.
Lamming, George, 1927-
xLamming, George.
In the Castle of My Skin. Macmillan.
Lammond, D.
xLammond, D.
Carlyle. Folcroft.
Lamola, Angelo. see Lamola, Angelo A.
Lamola, Angelo A.
xLamola, Angelo.
ed. Creation & Detection of the Excited State.
Dekker.
Lamon, William E.
xLamon, William E.
ed. Learning & the Nature of Mathematics.
SRA.
Lamont, Barbara.
xLamont, Barbara.
City People. Macmillan.
Lamont, Corliss, 1902-
xLamont, Corliss.
Humanist Funeral Service. Prometheus Bks.
Remembering John Masefield. Fairleigh
Dickinson.
Lamont, W. D. see Lamont, William Dawson.
Lamont, William. see Lamont, William M.
Lamont, William D. see Lamont, William Dawson.
Lamont, William Dawson.
xLamont, W. D.
Value Judgement. Philos Lib.
xLamont, William D.
Introduction to Green's Moral Philosophy.
Hyperion Conn.
The Value Judgement. Greenwood.
Lamont, William M.
xLamont, William.
ed. Politics, Religion & Literature in the
Seventeenth Century. Rowman.
Lamoreaux, Marcia.
xLamoreaux, Marcia.
Outdoor Gear You Can Make Yourself.
Stackpole.
Lamoureux, Richard E.
xLamoureux, Richard E.
Alberti's Church of San Sebastiano in Mantua.
Garland Pub.
Lampadius, W. A. see Lampadius, Wilhelm Adolf.
Lampadius, Wilhelm Adolf.
xLampadius, W. A.
Life of Felix Mendelssohn Bartholdy.
Longwood Pr.
Lampen, Dorothy, 1904-
xLampen, Dorothy.
Economic & Social Aspects of Federal
Reclamation. AMS Pr.
Economic & Social Aspects of Federal
Reclamation. Arno.
Lampen, Nevada.
xLampen, Nevada.
Fat-Free Recipes. Merrimack Bk Serv.
Lampert, E. see Lampert, Evgenii.
Lampert, Evgenii, 1913-
xLampert, E.
Sons Against Fathers: Studies in Russian
Radicalism & Revolution. Oxford U Pr.
Lampert, Harry.
xLampert, Harry.
The Fun Way to Learn Serious Bridge.
Cornerstone.
Lampert, Nicholas.
xLampert, Nicholas.
The Technical Intelligentsia & the Soviet State.
Holmes & Meier.
Lamperti, J. see Lamperti, John.

Lamperti, John.
xLamperti, J.
Stochastic Processes: A Survey of the
Mathematical Theory. Springer-Verlag.
xLamperti, John.
Probability: A Survey of the Mathematical
Theory. Benjamin-Cummings.
Lampkin, Richard H. see Lampkin, Richard Henry.
Lampkin, Richard Henry, 1911-
xLampkin, Richard H.
Variability in Recognizing Scientific Inquiry:
An Analysis of High School Science
Textbooks. AMS Pr.
Lampl, Paul.
xLampl, Paul.
Cities & Planning in the Ancient Near East.
Braziller.
Lampl-De Groot, Jeanne.
xLampl-de Groot, Jeanne.
Development of the Mind: Psychoanalytic
Papers on Clinical & Theoretical Problems.
Intl Univs Pr.
Lampley, J. Brad, 1935-
xLampley, J. Brad.
How to Go from Rags to Riches Fast with
Sound Real Estate Investments. P-H.
Lampman, Evelyn S. see Lampman, Evelyn Sibley.
Lampman, Evelyn Sibley.
xLampman, Evelyn S.
Bargain Bride. Atheneum.
Go Up the Road. G K Hall.
Go up the Road. Atheneum.
The Potlatch Family. Atheneum.
Rattlesnake Cave. Atheneum.
Three Knocks on the Wall. Atheneum.
White Captives. Atheneum.
Lampman, Linda.
xLampman, Linda.
Oregon for All Seasons. Writing.
The Portland Guidebook. Writing
Lamppa, William R., 1928-
xLamppa, William R.
In Familiar Fields with Old Friends. Branden.
Lamprecht, Sterling P. see Lamprecht, Sterling Power.
Lamprecht, Sterling Power, 1890-
xLamprecht, Sterling P.
Nature & History. Shoe String.
Our Philosophical Traditions: A Brief History
of Philosophy in Western Civilization.
Irvington.
Lampton. see Lampton, Chris.
Lampton, Chris.
xLampton.
Black Holes & Other Secrets of the Universe.
Watts.
xLampton, Chris.
Gateway to Limbo. Doubleday.
Lampton, David M.
xLampton, David M.
The Politics of Medicine in China: The Policy
Process, 1949-1977. Westview.
Lamsa, George M. see Lamsa, George Mamishisho.
Lamsa, George Mamishisho, 1893-
xLamsa, George M.
And the Scroll Opened. De Vorss.
Idioms in the Bible Explained: A Key to the
Holy Scriptures. Holman.
Lamson, Amy.
xLamson, Amy.
Guide for the Beginning Therapist:
Relationship Between Diagnosis &
Treatment. Human Sci Pr.
Lamson, David R. see Lamson, David Rich.
Lamson, David Rich, 1806-1886
xLamson, David R.
Two Years Experience Among the Shakers.
AMS Pr.
Lamson, Edna E. see Lamson, Edna Emma.
Lamson, Edna Emma, 1883-
xLamson, Edna E.

A Study of Young Gifted Children in Senior
High School. AMS Pr.

Lamson, Peggy.
xLamson, Peggy.
The Glorious Failure: Black Congressman
Robert Brown Elliott & the Reconstruction in
South Carolina. Norton.
In the Vanguard: Six American Women in
Public Life. HM.

Lamy, Peter P.
xLamy, Peter P.
Prescribing for the Elderly. PSG Pub.

Lana, Robert E., 1932-
xLana, Robert E.
Assumptions of Social Psychology. Irvington.

Lancaster. see Lancaster, Clay.

Lancaster, Arnold.
xLancaster, Arnold.
Nursing & Midwifery Sourcebook. Allen
Unwin.

Lancaster, Bruce.
xLancaster, Bruce.
Bright to the Wanderer. Am Repr-Rivercity Pr.
Guns of Burgoyne. Am Repr-Rivercity Pr.
Trumpet to Arms. Amereon Ltd.
Trumpet to Arms. Pinnacle Bks.
Venture in the East. Amereon Ltd.

Lancaster, Clay.
xLancaster.
Prospect Park Handbook. LIU Univ.

Lancaster, Don. see Lancaster, Donald E.

Lancaster, Donald E.
xLancaster, Don.
Active-Filter Cookbook. Sams.
The Incredible Secret Money Machine. Sams.
TV Typewriter Cookbook. Sams.
xLancaster, Donald E.
TTL Cookbook. Sams.

Lancaster, F. W. see Lancaster, Frederick Wilfrid.

Lancaster, Fidelity.
xLancaster, Fidelity.
The Bedouin. Watts.

Lancaster, Frederick Wilfrid.
xLancaster, F. W.
Information Retrieval on-Line. Wiley.
Information Retrieval Systems: Characteristics,
Testing & Evaluation. Wiley.

Lancaster, G. T.
xLancaster, G. T.
Programming in COBOL. Pergamon.

Lancaster, Graham.
xLancaster, Graham.
The Nuclear Letters. Atheneum.

Lancaster, H. O. see Lancaster, Henry Oliver.

Lancaster, Henry C. see Lancaster, Henry Carrington.

Lancaster, Henry Carrington, 1882-1954
xLancaster, Henry C.
Adventures of a Literary Historian: A
Collection of His Writings Presented to H. C.
Lancaster by His Former Students & Other
Friends in Anticipation of His Sixtieth
Birthday November 10, 1942. Arno.
Sunset: A History of Parisian Drama in the
Last Years of Louis XIV, 1701-1715.
Greenwood.

Lancaster, Henry Oliver, 1913-
xLancaster, H. O.
An Introduction to Medical Statistics. Wiley.

Lancaster, J. B. see Lancaster, Jane Beckman.

Lancaster, Jane Beckman, 1935-
xLancaster, J. B.
Primate Behavior & the Emergence of Human
Culture. HR&W.

Lancaster, Janet.
xLancaster, Janet.
Developments in Early Childhood Education.
Humanities.

Lancaster, Jeanette, 1944-
xLancaster, Jeanette.

Adult Psychiatric Nursing. Med Exam.

Lancaster, John.
xLancaster, John.
The Spirit-Filled Church. Gospel Pub.

Lancaster, John H. see Lancaster, John Herrold.

Lancaster, John Herrold, 1898-
xLancaster, John H.
The Use of the Library by Student Teachers:
Some Factors Related to the Use of the
Library by Student Teachers in Thirty-One
Colleges in the Area of the North Central
Association. AMS Pr.

Lancaster, Lane W., 1892-
xLancaster, Lane W.
Government in Rural America. Greenwood.

Lancaster, Larry E.
xLancaster, Larry E.
The Patient with End Stage Renal Disease.
Wiley.

Lancaster, Lydia.
xLancaster, Lydia.
Stolen Rapture. Warner Bks.

Lancaster, Osbert, 1908-
xLancaster, Osbert.
Classical Landscape with Figures. Transatlantic.

Lancaster, Otis C. see Lancaster, Otis E.

Lancaster, Otis E.
xLancaster, Otis C.
Effective Teaching & Learning. Gordon.

Lancaster, Peter.
xLancaster, Peter.
Mathematics: Models of the Real World. P-H.

Lancaster, Robert A. see Lancaster, Robert Alexander.

Lancaster, Robert Alexander, 1862-1940
xLancaster, Robert A.
Historic Virginia Homes & Churches. Reprint.

Lance, Algie L.
xLance, Algie L.
Introduction to Microwave Theory &
Measurements. McGraw.

Lance, Kathryn.
xLance, Kathryn.
Getting Strong: A Woman's Guide to Realizing
Her Physical Potential. Bantam.
Getting Strong: A Woman's Guide to Realizing
Her Physical Potential. Bobbs.
A Woman's Guide to Spectator Sports. A & W
Pubs.

Lance, Labelle.
xLance, LaBelle D.
This Too Shall Pass. Christian Herald.

Lance, LaBelle D. see Lance, Labelle.

Lanciani, Rodolfo. see Lanciani, Rodolfo Amedeo.

Lanciani, Rodolfo Amedeo, 1847-1929
xLanciani, Rodolfo.
Ancient & Modern Rome. Cooper Sq.
Pagan & Christian Rome. Arno.
Ruins & Excavations of Ancient Rome. Arno.

Lancour, Gene.
xLancour, Gene.
The Globes of Llarum. Doubleday.
The Man-Eaters of Cascalon. Doubleday.
Sword for the Empire. Doubleday.

Lanczos, C. see Lanczos, Cornelius.

Lanczos, Cornelius, 1893-
xLanczos, C.
Discourse on Fourier Series. Hafner.
xLanczos, Cornelius.
Variational Principles of Mechanics. U of
Toronto Pr.

Land, Barbara.
xLand, Barbara.
Evolution of a Scientist: The Two Worlds of
Theodosius Dobzhansky. T Y Crowell.

Land, Betty E. see Land, Betty Ewing.

Land, Betty Ewing.
xLand, Betty E.
The Art of Grandparentry. Georgetown Pr.

Land, Lois R. see Land, Lois Rhea.

Land, Lois Rhea.
xLand, Lois R.
Music in Today's Classroom: Creating,
Listening, Performing. HarBraceJ.

Land Planning Committee, U.S. National Resources
Board. see United States. National Resources Board.
Land Planning Committee.

Land Study Bureau, Univ. of Hawaii. see Hawaii.
University, Honolulu. Land Study Bureau.

Land Tenure Center. see Wisconsin. University-Madison.
Land Tenure Center.

Land Tenure Center, University of Wisconsin - Madison.
see Wisconsin. University-Madison. Land Tenure
Center.

Landa, L. N. see Landa, Lev Nakhmanovich.

Landa, Lev Nakhmanovich.
xLanda, L. N.
Instructional Regulation & Control:
Cybernetics, Algorithmization & Heuristics in
Education. Educ Tech Pubn.

Landa, Louis A.
xLanda, Louis A.
ed. Jonathan Swift: A List of Critical Studies
Published from 1895 to 1945. Octagon.

Landau, Abraham.
xLandau, Abraham.
Intelligence Anxiety & Pleasure. Philos Lib.

Landau, Barbara R. see Landau, Barbara Ruth.

Landau, Barbara Ruth, 1923-
xLandau, Barbara R.
Essential Human Anatomy & Physiology. Scott
F.

Landau, E. D. see Landau, Elliott D.

Landau, Elaine.
xLandau, Elaine.
Occult Visions: A Mystical Gaze into the
Future. Messner.

Landau, Elliot. see Landau, Elliott D.

Landau, Elliott D.
xLandau, E. D.
The Teaching Experience: An Introduction to
Education Through Literature. P-H.
xLandau, Elliot.
The Exceptional Child Through Literature.
P-H.
xLandau, Elliott D.
Family Within Your Walls. Horizon Utah.

Landau, Jacob M.
xLandau, Jacob M.
Arabs in Israel: A Political Study. Oxford U Pr.
Parliaments & Parties in Egypt. Hyperion
Conn.
A Word Count of Modern Arabic Prose.
Spoken Lang Serv.

Landau, L. D. see Landau, Lev Davidovich.

Landau, Lev Davidovich.
xLandau, L. D.
Lectures on Nuclear Theory. Plenum Pub.

Landau, Sidney. see Landau, Sidney I.

Landau, Sidney I.
xLandau, Sidney.
ed. Doubleday Roget's Thesaurus in Dictionary
Form. Doubleday.

Landau, Suzanne.
xLandau, Suzanne.
The Landau Strategy: How Working Women
Win Top Jobs. Potter.

Landay, Jerry M.
xLanday, Jerry M.
Dome of the Rock. Newsweek.

Lande, Carl H. see Lande, Carl Herman.

Lande, Carl Herman.
xLande, Carl H.
Southern Tagalog Voting, 1943-1963: Political
Behavior in a Philippine Region. Cellar.

Lande, Nathaniel.
xLande, Nathaniel.

The Emotional Maintenance Manual. Rawson
Wade.
Stages: Understanding How You Make Your
Moral Decisions. Har-Row.
Landeau, Jean Francois, 1944-
xLandeau, Jean-Francois.
Strategies of U. S. Independent Oil Companies
Abroad. Univ Microfilms.
Landeau, Jean-Francois. *see* Landeau, Jean Francois.
Landecker, Manfred.
xLandecker, Manfred.
The President & Public Opinion: Leadership in
Foreign Affairs. Pub Aff Pr.
Landecker, Mildred N.
xLandecker, Mildred N.
Creative Music Theory. Allyn.
Landeira, Ricardo. *see* Landeira, Ricardo L.
Landeira, Ricardo L.
xLandeira, Ricardo.
Ramiro De Maeztu. Twayne.
Landels, J. G.
xLandels, John.
Engineering in the Ancient World. U of Cal Pr.
Landels, John. *see* Landels, J. G.
Lander, Arthur B.
xLander, Arthur B.
A Guide to the Backpacking & Day Hiking
Trails of Kentucky. Thomas Pr.
Lander, Ernest M. *see* Lander, Ernest McPherson.
Lander, Ernest McPherson.
xLander, Ernest M.
Reluctant Imperialists: Calhoun, the South
Carolinians, & the Mexican War. La State U
Pr.
Textile Industry in Antebellum South Carolina.
La State U Pr.
Lander, J. R. *see* Lander, Jack Robert.
Lander, Jack Robert.
xLander, J. R.
Crown & Nobility, 1450-1509. McGill-Queens
U Pr.
Lander, Louise.
xLander, Louise.
Defective Medicine: Risk, Anger, & the
Malpractice Crisis. FS&G.
Lander, Mary K. *see* Lander, Mary Katherine (Gloth).
Lander, Mary Katherine (Gloth).
xLander, Mary K.
Index in Xenophontis Memorabilia. Johnson
Repr.
Landero, Victor.
xLandero, Victor.
The Victor: The Victor Landero Story. Revell.
Landers, Ann.
xLanders, Ann.
Ann Landers Speaks Out. Fawcett.
Landers, Gunnard.
xLanders, Gunnard.
The Hunting Shack. Arbor Hse.
The Hunting Shack. Dell.
Landers, Thomas J.
xLanders, Thomas J.
Essentials of School Management. HR&W.
Landes, David S.
xLandes, David S.
Unbound Prometheus: Technological Change &
Industrial Development in Western Europe
from 1750 to the Present. Cambridge U Pr.
Landes, George M.
xLandes, George M.
Student's Vocabulary of Biblical Hebrew:
Listed According to Frequency & Cognate.
Scribner.
Landes, Ruth, 1908-
xLandes, Ruth.
Ojibwa Sociology. AMS Pr.
Ojibwa Woman. AMS Pr.
Ojibwa Woman. Norton.
Landesman, Alter E. *see* Landesman, Alter F.

Landesman, Alter F.
xLandesman, Alter E.
Brownsville: The Birth, Development & Passing
of a Jewish Community in New York. Bloch.
Landesman, Bill.
xLandesman, Bill.
How to Care for Your Older Dog. Fell.
How to Train Your Dog in Six Weeks. Fell.
Landesman, Charles.
xLandesman, Charles.
Discourse & Its Presuppositions. Yale U Pr.
Landgrebe, John A.
xLandgrebe, John A.
Theory & Practice in the Organic Laboratory.
Heath.
Landis. *see* Landis, Judson T.
Landis, Arthur. *see* Landis, Arthur H.
Landis, Arthur H.
xLandis, Arthur.
World Called Camelot. DAW Bks.
Landis, Benson Y. *see* Landis, Benson Young.
Landis, Benson Young, 1897-
xLandis, Benson Y.
Outline of the Bible: Book by Book. Har-Row.
Professional Codes: A Sociological Analysis to
Determine Applications to the Educational
Profession. AMS Pr.
Landis, James D. *see* Landis, James David.
Landis, James David.
xLandis, James D.
The Sisters Impossible. Knopf.
Landis, James M. *see* Landis, James McCauley.
Landis, James McCauley, 1899-
xLandis, James M.
The Administrative Process. Greenwood.
Landis, John L.
xLandis, John L.
The Mechanics of Patent Claim Drafting. PLI.
Patents, Copyright, Trademarks, & Trade
Secrets for Corporate Counsel & General
Practitioners. PLI.
Landis, Joseph C.
xLandis, Joseph C.
ed. The Great Jewish Plays. Avon.
tr. & ed. The Great Jewish Plays. Horizon.
Landis, Judson R.
xLandis, Judson R.
Sociology: Concepts & Characteristics.
Wadsworth Pub.
Landis, Judson T.
xLandis.
Building a Successful Marriage. P-H.
Landkof, N. S. *see* Landkof, Naum Samoilovich.
Landkof, Naum Samoilovich.
xLandkof, N. S.
Foundations of Modern Potential Theory.
Springer-Verlag.
Landmann, Michael, 1913-
xLandmann, Michael.
Alienatory Reason. Univ Microfilms.
De Homine: Man in the Mirror of His
Thought. Univ Microfilms.
Reform of the Hebrew Alphabet. Univ
Microfilms.
Landolfi, Tammaso. *see* Landolfi, Tommaso.
Landolfi, Tommaso, 1908-
xLandolfi, Tammaso.
Cancerqueen & Other Stories. Dial.
Landolt, A. M. *see* Landolt, Alex M.
Landolt, Alex M., 1935-
xLandolt, A. M.
Ultrastructure of Human Sella Tumors:
Correlations of Clinical Findings &
Morphology. Springer-Verlag.
Landon, Charles E. *see* Landon, Charles Edward.
Landon, Charles Edward.
xLandon, Charles E.
North Carolina State Ports Authority. Duke.
Landon, D. H. *see* Landon, David Neil.

Landon, David Neil.
xLandon, D. H.
ed. The Peripheral Nerve. Methuen Inc.
Landon, Harold R.
xLandon, Harold R.
ed. Reinhold Niebuhr: A Prophetic Voice in
Our Time. Arno.
Landon, Kenneth P. *see* Landon, Kenneth Perry.
Landon, Kenneth Perry.
xLandon, Kenneth P.
The Chinese in Thailand. Russell.
Siam in Transition: A Brief Survey of Cultural
Trends in the Five Years Since the
Revolution of 1932. Greenwood.
Landon, Mary T. *see* Landon, Mary Taylor.
Landon, Mary Taylor.
xLandon, Mary T.
American Crewel Work. Macmillan.
American Crewel Work. Macmillan.
Landon, Michael.
xLandon, Michael.
Triumph of the Lawyers: Their Role in English
Politics, 1678-1689. U of Ala Pr.
xLandon, Michael deL.
The Honor & Dignity of the Profession: A
History of the Mississippi State Bar,
1906-1976. U Pr of Miss.
Landon, Michael deL. *see* Landon, Michael.
Landon, Richard G.
xLandon, Richard G.
Book Selling & Book Buying: Aspects of the
Nineteenth-Century British & North
American Book Trade. ALA.
ed. Book Selling & Book Buying: Aspects of
the Nineteenth Century British & North
American Book Trade. K G Saur.
Landor, Edward W. *see* Landor, Edward Wilson.
Landor, Edward Wilson, d. 1878
xLandor, Edward W.
The Bushman, or Life in a New Country.
Johnson Repr.
Landor, Walter S. *see* Landor, Walter Savage.
Landor, Walter Savage.
xLandor, Walter S.
The Complete Works of Walter Savage Landor.
AMS Pr.
Landor As Critic. U of Nebr Pr.
Landorf, Joyce.
xLandorf, Joyce.
Fragrance of Beauty. Victor Bks.
His Stubborn Love. Zondervan.
I Came to Love You Late. Revell.
Let's Have a Banquet. Zondervan.
The Richest Lady in Town. Zondervan.
Landow, George P.
xLandow, George P.
ed. Approaches to Victorian Autobiography.
Ohio U Pr.
Landphair, H. C. *see* Landphair, Harlow C.
Landphair, Harlow C.
xLandphair, H. C.
Landscape Architecture Construction. Elsevier.
Landreau, Anthony N.
xLandreau, Anthony N.
From the Bosporus to Samarkand: Flat-Woven
Rugs. Textile Mus.
Landreth, Catherine.
xLandreth, Catherine.
Preschool Learning & Teaching. Har-Row.
Landreth, Harry.
xLandreth, Harry H.
History of Economic Theory: Scope, Method &
Content. HM.
Landreth, Harry H. *see* Landreth, Harry.
Landru, H. C.
xLandru, H. C.
The Blue Parka Man: Alaskan Gold Rush
Bandit. Dodd.
Landry, Hilton.
xLandry, Hilton.

A Concordance to the Poems of Hart Crane.
   Scarecrow.
Landsberg, H. E. see Landsberg, Helmut.
Landsberg, Helmut, 1906-
   xLandsberg, H. E.
   ed. Advances in Geophysics. Acad Pr.
Landsberg, Peter T. see Landsberg, Peter Theodore.
Landsberg, Peter Theodore.
   xLandsberg, Peter T.
   Mathematical Cosmology: An Introduction.
      Oxford U Pr.
   Thermodynamics & Statistical Mechanics.
      Oxford U Pr.
Landsberger, Henry A.
   xLandsberger, Henry A.
   ed. Church & Social Change in Latin America.
      U of Notre Dame Pr.
   ed. Latin American Peasant Movements.
      Cornell U Pr.
Landsburg, Alan.
   xLandsburg, Alan.
   Secrets of the Bermuda Triangle. Warner Bks.
Landscape Architecture Dept. Of The Univ. Of Georgia.
   see Georgia. University. Department of Landscape
      Architecture.
Landshoff, P. V. see Landshoff, Peter.
Landshoff, Peter.
   xLandshoff, P. V.
   Simple Quantum Physics. Cambridge U Pr.
Landshoff, Ursula.
   xLandshoff, Ursula.
   illus. Okay, Good Dog. Har-Row.
Landsmeer, Johan M. see Landsmeer, Johan M. F.
Landsmeer, Johan M. F.
   xLandsmeer, Johan M.
   Atlas of Anatomy of the Hand. Churchill.
Landtman, Gunnar, 1878-1940
   xLandtman, Gunnar.
   The Origin of the Inequality of the Social
      Classes. AMS Pr.
   Origin of the Inequality of the Social Classes.
      Greenwood.
Landvater, Dorothy, 1927-
   xLandvater, Dorothy.
   David: A Mother's Story of Her Son's
      Recovery from Coma & Brain Damage. PB.
Landy, Alice S.
   xLandy, Alice S.
   To Read a Poem. Heath.
Landy, David.
   xLandy, David.
   Tropical Childhood: Cultural Transmission &
      Learning in a Rural Puerto Rico Village.
      Gannon.
Landy, Eugene E.
   xLandy, Eugene E.
   The Underground Dictionary. S&S.
Landy, Frank J.
   xLandy, Frank J.
   Psychology of Work Behavior. Dorsey.
Landy, Jacob.
   xLandy, Jacob.
   Architecture of Minard Lafever. Columbia U
      Pr.
Landy, Marc. see Landy, Marc Karnis.
Landy, Marc Karnis.
   xLandy, Marc.
   ed. Environmental Impact Statement Glossary:
      A Reference Source for EIS Writers,
      Reviewers & Citizens. IFI Plenum.
   xLandy, Marc Karnis.
   The Politics of Environmental Reform:
      Controlling Kentucky Strip Mining. Johns
      Hopkins.
Lane, Alfred H.
   xLane, Alfred H.
   Gifts & Exchange Manual. Greenwood.
Lane, Ann J., 1932-
   xLane, Ann J.

The Brownsville Affair: National Crisis & Black
   Reaction. Kennikat.
   ed. The Debate Over Slavery: Stanley Elkins &
      His Critics. U of Ill Pr.
Lane, Arthur E., 1937-
   xLane, Arthur E.
   An Adequate Response: The War Poetry of
      Wilfred Owen & Siegfried Sassoon. Wayne St
      U Pr.
Lane, Barbara M. see Lane, Barbara Miller.
Lane, Barbara Miller.
   xLane, Barbara M.
   Architecture & Politics in Germany,
      1918-1945. Harvard U Pr.
   tr. Nazi Ideology Before 1933: A
      Documentation. U of Tex Pr.
Lane, Christel.
   xLane, Christel.
   Christian Religion in the Soviet Union: A
      Sociological Study. State U NY Pr.
Lane, David. see Lane, David Stuart.
Lane, David Stuart.
   xLane, David.
   Politics & Society in the U.S.S.R. NYU Pr.
   The Socialist Industrial State: Towards a
      Political Sociology of State Socialism. Allen
      Unwin.
   The Soviet Industrial Worker: Social Class,
      Education & Control. St Martin.
Lane, Donald. see Lane, Donald John.
Lane, Donald John.
   xLane, Donald.
   Asthma: The Facts. Oxford U Pr.
Lane, Edward W. see Lane, Edward William.
Lane, Edward William, 1801-1876
   xLane, Edward W.
   An Account of the Manners & Customs of the
      Modern Egyptians. Peter Smith.
Lane, Frank W. see Lane, Frank Walter.
Lane, Frank Walter.
   xLane, Frank W.
   Nature Parade. Sheridan.
Lane, Frederic C. see Lane, Frederic Chapin.
Lane, Frederic Chapin, 1900-
   xLane, Frederic C.
   Profits from Power: Readings in Protection
      Rent & Violence-Controlling Enterprises.
      State U NY Pr.
   Venetian Ships & Shipbuilders of the
      Renaissance. Greenwood.
Lane, Frederick S., 1942-
   xLane, Frederick S.
   Current Issues in Public Administration. St
      Martin.
Lane, Gary.
   xLane, Gary.
   A Concordance to the Poems of Dylan
      Thomas. Scarecrow.
   A Concordance to the Poems of Hart Crane.
      Haskell.
   A Concordance to the Poems of Marianne
      Moore. Haskell.
   A Concordance to the Poems of Theodore
      Roethke. Scarecrow.
   I Am: A Study of E. E. Cummings' Poems.
      Regents Pr Ks.
   Sylvia Plath: A Bibliography. Scarecrow.
   ed. Sylvia Plath: New Views on the Poetry.
      Johns Hopkins.
Lane, George M. see Lane, George Martin.
Lane, George Martin, 1823-1897
   xLane, George M.
   Latin Grammar for Schools & Colleges. AMS
      Pr.
   Latin Grammar for Schools & Colleges.
      Greenwood.
   Latin Grammar for Schools & Colleges.
      Scholarly.
Lane, H. Richard H. see Lane, Harold Richard.

Lane, Harold Richard.
   xLane, H. Richard H.
   Late Mississippian & Early Pennsylvanian
      Conodonts, Arkansas & Oklahoma. Geol Soc.
Lane, J. S. see Lane, John S.
Lane, James B., 1942-
   xLane, James B.
   City of the Century: A History of Gary,
      Indiana. Ind U Pr.
Lane, James W. see Lane, James Warren.
Lane, James Warren, 1898-
   xLane, James W.
   Masters in Modern Art. Arno.
Lane, Jane.
   xLane, Jane.
   How to Make Play Places & Secret Hidy
      Holes. Doubleday.
Lane, John R.
   xLane, John R.
   Stuart Davis: Art & Art Theory. Bklyn Mus.
Lane, John S.
   xLane, J. S.
   On Optimal Population Paths. Springer-Verlag.
Lane, Lee.
   xLane, Lee.
   I Gathered the Bright Days: A Courageous
      Woman's Story of Her Family, Struggles, &
      Triumphs. Dial.
Lane, Leonard C.
   xLane, Leonard C.
   Simplified Radiotelephone License Course.
      Hayden.
Lane, Maggie.
   xLane, Maggie.
   Chinese Rugs Designed for Needlepoint.
      Scribner.
   Maggie Lane's Book of Beads. Scribner.
   More Needlepoint by Design. Scribner.
Lane, Marc J.
   xLane, Marc J.
   The Doctor's Lawyer: A Legal Handbook for
      Doctors. C C Thomas.
   Legal Handbook for Small Business. Am
      Mgmt.
Lane, Margaret.
   xLane, Margaret.
   The Magic Years of Beatrix Potter. Warne.
Lane, Mark.
   xLane, Mark.
   The Strongest Poison. Dutton.
Lane, Mary B.
   xLane, Mary B.
   Pref. by Education for Parenting. Natl Assn
      Child Ed.
Lane, Mary T. see Lane, Mary Turner.
Lane, Mary Turner.
   xLane, Mary T.
   A Structure for Population Education: Goals,
      Generalizations, & Behavioral Objectives.
      Carolina Pop Ctr.
Lane, Michael, fl. 1970-
   xLane, Michael.
   Books & Publishers: Commerce Against
      Culture in Postwar Britain. Lexington Bks.
Lane, N. Gary.
   xLane, N. Gary.
   Life of the Past. Merrill.
Lane, Patrick.
   xLane, Patrick.
   Poems New & Selected. Oxford U Pr.
Lane, Peter.
   xLane, Peter.
   The Industrial Revolution: The Birth of the
      Modern Age. B&N.
   The Stuart Age. David & Charles.
   Tudor England. David & Charles.
   What Rock Is All About. Messner.
Lane, Richard. see Lane, Richard Douglas.
Lane, Richard Douglas, 1926-
   xLane, Richard.

Images from the Floating World: The Japanese
Print, Including an Illustrated Dictionary of
Ukiyo-e. Putnam.
Lane, Robert.
xLane, Robert.
Analytical Transport Planning. Halsted Pr.
Analytical Transport Planning. Intl Pubns Serv.
Lane, Robert E. *see* Lane, Robert Edwards.
Lane, Robert Edwards.
xLane, Robert E.
Public Opinion. P-H.
Lane, Roger.
xLane, Roger.
Violent Death in the City: Suicide, Accident, &
Murder in Nineteenth-Century Philadelphia.
Harvard U Pr.
Lane, Ronald L.
xLane, Ronald L.
Rudder's Rangers. Ranger Assocs.
Lane, Rose (Wilder), 1887-1968
xLane, Rose W.
Discovery of Freedom: Man's Struggle Against
Authority. Arno.
Lane, Rose W. *see* Lane, Rose (Wilder).
Lane, Tamar, 1895-
xLane, Tamar.
What's Wrong with the Movies?. Ozer.
Lane, Theodore. *see* Lane, Theodore R.
Lane, Theodore R.
xLane, Theodore.
Life, the Individual, the Species. Mosby.
Lane, Thomas A., 1906-
xLane, Thomas A.
Cry Peace: The Kennedy Years. Guild Bks.
Lane, Wheaton J. *see* Lane, Wheaton Joshua.
Lane, Wheaton Joshua, 1902-
xLane, Wheaton J.
Commodore Vanderbilt: An Epic of the Steam
Age. Johnson Repr.
Lane, Winthrop D. *see* Lane, Winthrop David.
Lane, Winthrop David, 1887-1962
xLane, Winthrop D.
Civil War in West Virginia. Arno.
Lane, Yoti.
xLane, Yoti.
Psychology of the Actor. Greenwood.
Lane-Poole, Stanley, 1854-1931
xLane-Poole, Stanley.
The Life of the Right Honourable Stratford
Canning, Viscount Stratford de Redcliffe.
AMS Pr.
Laney, William R.
xLaney, William R.
ed. Maxillofacial Prosthetics. PSG Pub.
Lanfear, Vincent W. *see* Lanfear, Vincent Wesley.
Lanfear, Vincent Wesley, 1894-
xLanfear, Vincent W.
Business Fluctuations & the American Labor
Movement, 1915-1922. AMS Pr.
Lanford, H. W.
xLanford, H. W.
System Management: Planning & Control.
Kennikat.
Lanfrey, Pierre, 1828-1877
xLanfrey, Pierre.
History of Napoleon First. AMS Pr.
Lang. *see* Lang, Laszlo.
Lang, A. *see* Lang, Andrew.
Lang, Aldon S. *see* Lang, Aldon Socrates.
Lang, Aldon Socrates.
xLang, Aldon S.
Financial History of the Public Lands in Texas.
Arno.
Lang, Andres. *see* Lang, Andrew.
Lang, Andrew, 1844-1912
xLang, A.
Books & Bookmen. Gordon Pr.
xLang, Andres.
The Puzzle of Dicken's Last Plot. Arden Lib.
xLang, Andrew.

Adventures Among Books. Arno.
Adventures Among Books. Folcroft.
Alfred Tennyson. AMS Pr.
Alfred Tennyson. Arden Lib.
Alfred Tennyson. Folcroft.
Books & Bookmen. AMS Pr.
Books & Bookmen. Arden Lib.
Books & Bookmen. Folcroft.
The Brown Fairy Book. Peter Smith.
ed. Brown Fairy Book. Dover.
ed. Crimson Fairy Book. Dover.
The Crimson Fairy Book. Peter Smith.
Custom & Myth. AMS Pr.
Custom & Myth. Charles River Bks.
Disentanglers. AMS Pr.
ed. The Green Fairy Book. Peter Smith.
Green Fairy Book. Airmont.
ed. Green Fairy Book. Dover.
Green Fairy Book. Viking Pr.
Homer & His Age. AMS Pr.
Homer & the Epic. AMS Pr.
Letters on Literature. AMS Pr.
Letters on Literature. Folcroft.
Letters to Dead Authors. AMS Pr.
Letters to Dead Authors. Arden Lib.
Letters to Dead Authors. Folcroft.
Life & Letters of John Gibson Lockhart. AMS
Pr.
The Lilac Fairy Book. Peter Smith.
ed. Lilac Fairy Book. Dover.
Mark of Cain. AMS Pr.
Modern Mythology. AMS Pr.
The Orange Fairy Book. Peter Smith.
ed. Orange Fairy Book. Dover.
The Puzzle of Dicken's Last Plot. Folcroft.
ed. The Story of Robin Hood, & Other Tales of
Adventure & Battle. Schocken.
Valet's Tragedy & Other Studies. AMS Pr.
World of Homer. AMS Pr.
Lang, Andy, 1909-
xLang, Andy.
Andy Lang's Remodeling Handbook.
Hammond Inc.
Lang, Berel.
xLang, Berel.
Art & Inquiry. Wayne St U Pr.
ed. Marxism & Art: Writings in Aesthetics &
Criticism. Longman.
Lang, Brad.
xLang, Brad.
The Perdition Express. Nordon Pubns.
Lang, Cecil Y.
xLang, Cecil Y.
The Pre-Raphaelites & Their Circle. U of
Chicago Pr.
Lang, D. *see* Lang, Daniel.
Lang, Daniel.
xLang, D.
Casualties of War. McGraw.
Lang, David C.
xLang, David C.
Orchids of Britain: A Field Guide. Oxford U
Pr.
Lang, David M. *see* Lang, David Marshall.
Lang, David Marshall.
xLang, David M.
A Modern History of Soviet Georgia.
Greenwood.
Lang, Edgar A. *see* Lang, Edgar Anthony.
Lang, Edgar Anthony, 1896-
xLang, Edgar A.
Ludwig Tieck's Early Concept of Catholic
Clergy & Church. AMS Pr.
Lang, Edith M. *see* Lang, Edith Mae.
Lang, Edith Mae, 1944-
xLang, Edith M.

The Effects of Net Interregional Migration on
Agricultural Income Growth: The United
States, 1850-1860. Arno.
Lang, Gerald S.
xLang, Gerald S.
The Practice-Oriented Medical Record. Aspen
Systems.
Lang, James.
xLang, James.
Conquest & Commerce: Spain & England in
the Americas. Acad Pr.
Portuguese Brazil: The King's Plantation. Acad
Pr.
Lang, K. R. *see* Lang, Kenneth R.
Lang, Kenneth R.
xLang, K. R.
Astrophysical Formulae: A Compendium for
the Physicist & Astrophysicist.
Springer-Verlag.
xLang, Kenneth R.
ed. A Source Book in Astronomy &
Astrophysics, 1900-1975. Harvard U Pr.
Lang, Kurt.
xLang, Kurt.
Politics & Television. Times Bks.
Lang, L. *see* Lang, Laszlo.
Lang, Larry. *see* Lang, Larry R.
Lang, Larry R.
xLang, Larry.
Strategy for Personal Finance. McGraw.
Lang, Laszlo.
xLang.
Absorption Spectra in the Ultraviolet & Visible
Region. Krieger.
xLang, L.
ed. Absorption Spectra in the Ultraviolet &
Visible Region. Krieger.
Lang, Lothar.
xLang, Lothar.
Expressionist Book Illustration in Germany,
1907-1927. NYGS.
Lang, Mabel. *see* Lang, Mabel L.
Lang, Mabel L., 1917-
xLang, Mabel.
Socrates in the Agora. Am Sch Athens.
Lang, Maud.
xLang, Maud.
The Moon Tree. NAL.
Lang, Meredith.
xLang, Meredith.
Defender of the Faith: The High Court of
Mississippi, 1817-1875. U Pr of Miss.
Lang, Nancy M.
xLang, Nancy M.
Getting Started in Plastics. Macmillan.
Lang, Ossian H. *see* Lang, Ossian Herbert.
Lang, Ossian Herbert, 1865-1945
xLang, Ossian H.
ed. Educational Creeds of the Nineteenth
Century. Arno.
Lang, Othmar F. *see* Lang, Othmar Franz.
Lang, Othmar Franz, 1921-
xLang, Othmar F.
If You Are Silenced, I Will Speak for You.
Philomel.
Lang, Paul V. *see* Lang, V. Paul.
Lang, S. *see* Lang, Serge.
Lang, Serge, 1927-
xLang, S.
Introduction to Modular Forms.
Springer-Verlag.
xLang, Serge.
Calculus of Several Variables. A-W.
First Course in Calculus. A-W.
xLang, Serge A.

Introduction to Algebraic Geometry. A-W.
Introduction to Diophantine Approximations.
    A-W.
Introduction to Linear Algebra. A-W.
Linear Algebra. A-W.
Lang, Serge A. *see* Lang, Serge.
Lang, Sidney B.
    xLang, Sidney B.
        Sourcebook of Pyroelectricity. Gordon.
Lang, V. Paul.
    xLang, Paul V.
        Basics of Air Conditioning. Van Nos Reinhold.
    xLang, V. Paul.
        Principles of Air Conditioning. Delmar.
Lang, Varley. *see* Lang, Varley Howe.
Lang, Varley Howe, 1912-
    xLang, Varley.
        Follow the Water. Blair.
Langa, Harry.
    xLanga, Harry.
        Relative Analgesia in Dental Practice:
            Inhalation Analgesia & Sedation with Nitrous
            Oxide. Saunders.
Langacker, Ronald W.
    xLangacker, Ronald W.
        Fundamentals of Linguistic Analysis.
            HarBraceJ.
Langan, John, 1942-
    xLangan, John.
        English Skills. McGraw.
        Reading & Study Skills. McGraw.
        Sentence Skills: A Workbook for Writers.
            McGraw.
Langbaine, Gerard, 1656-1692
    xLangbaine, Gerard.
        Account of the English Dramatick Poets. B
            Franklin.
        An Account of the English Dramatick Poets.
            Garland Pub.
Langbein, D.
    xLangbein, D.
        Theory of Van der Waals Attraction.
            Springer-Verlag.
Langbein, Laura I. *see* Langbein, Laura Irwin.
Langbein, Laura Irwin.
    xLangbein, Laura I.
        Ecological Inference. Sage.
Langdon, Danny G.
    xLangdon, Danny G.
        The Adjunct Study Guide. Educ Tech Pubns.
        The Audio-Workbook. Educ Tech Pubns.
        The Construct Lesson Plan: Improving Group
            Instruction. Educ Tech Pubns.
        Interactive Instructional Designs for
            Individualized Learning. Educ Tech Pubns.
Langdon, Ida.
    xLangdon, Ida.
        Materials for a Study of Spenser's Theory of
            Fine Art. Folcroft.
Lange, Arthur J.
    xLange, Arthur J.
        Responsible Assertive Behavior:
            Cognitive-Behavioral Procedures for Trainers.
            Res Press.
Lange, Dale L.
    xLange, Dale L.
        Testing in Foreign Languages, ESL, & Bilingual
            Education, 1966-1979: A Select, Annotated
            ERIC Bibliography. Ctr Appl Ling.
Lange, Dorothea.
    xLange, Dorothea.
        photos by Dorothea Lange Looks at the
            American Country Woman. Amon Carter.
Lange, Harald.
    xLange, Harald.
        The Horse Today - and Tomorrow?. Arco.
Lange, John, 1931-
    xLange, John.

Cognitivity Paradox: An Inquiry Concerning
    the Claims of Philosophy. Princeton U Pr.
Lange, Joseph.
    xLange, Joseph.
        Called to Service. Paulist Pr.
Lange, Julian E.
    xLange, Julian E.
        The Construction Industry: Balance-Wheel of
            the Economy. Lexington Bks.
Lange, Oliver.
    xLange, Oliver.
        Next of Kin. Seaview Bks.
Lange, Oscar R. *see* Lange, Oscar Richard.
Lange, Oscar Richard, 1904-1965
    xLange, Oscar R.
        Price Flexibility & Employment. Greenwood.
    xLange, Oskar.
        Theory of Reproduction & Accumulation.
            Pergamon.
Lange, Oskar. *see* Lange, Oscar Richard.
Lange, Peter. *see* Lange, Peter Michael.
Lange, Peter Michael.
    xLange, Peter.
        ed. Italy in Transition: Conflict & Consensus.
            Biblio Dist.
Lange-Seidl, Annemarie.
    xLange-Seidl, Annemarie.
        Approaches to Theories for Nonverbal Signs.
            Humanities.
Langefors, Borje.
    xLangefors, Borje.
        Information & Data in Systems. Van Nos
            Reinhold.
Langellier, Alice.
    xLangellier, Alice.
        Chez Les Francais. HR&W.
Langendoen, D. Terence.
    xLangendoen, D. Terence.
        Essentials of English Grammar. HR&W.
        Study of Syntax: The
            Generative-Transformational Approach to the
            Structure of American English. HR&W.
Langer, Arthur W.
    xLanger, Arthur W.
        ed. Polyamine-Chelated Alkali Metal
            Compounds. Am Chemical.
Langer, Jonas.
    xLanger, Jonas.
        Theories of Development. HR&W.
Langer, Lawrence L.
    xLanger, Lawrence L.
        The Holocaust & the Literary Imagination.
            Yale U Pr.
Langer, Paul F. *see* Langer, Paul Fritz.
Langer, Paul Fritz.
    xLanger, Paul F.
        North Vietnam & the Pathet Lao: Partners in
            the Struggle for Laos. Harvard U Pr.
Langer, Richard W.
    xLanger, Richard W.
        After Dinner Gardening Book. Macmillan.
        Grow It: The Beginners Complete
            in-Harmony-with-Nature Small Farm
            Guide-from Vegetable & Grain Growing to
            Livestock Care. Dutton.
Langer, Steven.
    xLanger, Steven.
        ed. Available Pay Survey Reports: An
            Annotated Bibliography. Abbott Langer
            Assocs.
Langer, Susanne K. *see* Langer, Susanne Katherina
    (Knauth).
Langer, Susanne Katherina (Knauth), 1895-
    xLanger, Susanne K.
        Introduction to Symbolic Logic. Dover.
Langer, Thomas E.
    xLanger, Thomas E.
        Christian Marriage: A Guide for Young People.
            Glencoe.
Langer, William L. *see* Langer, William Leonard.

Langer, William Leonard.
    xLanger, William L.
        The Challenge to Isolation: The World Crisis of
            1937-1940 & American Foreign Policy. Peter
            Smith.
        European Alliances and Alignments,
            1871-1890. Greenwood.
        In & Out of the Ivory Tower: The
            Autobiography of William L. Langer. N
            Watson.
        The Undeclared War 1940-1941. Peter Smith.
Langfeld, Herbert S. *see* Langfeld, Herbert Sidney.
Langfeld, Herbert Sidney, 1879-
    xLangfeld, Herbert S.
        Aesthetic Attitude. Kennikat.
Langford, Alec J., 1926-
    xLangford, Alec J.
        Meditations & Devotions for Adults. Abingdon.
Langford, C. H. *see* Langford, Cooper Harold.
Langford, Carl T.
    xLangford, Carl T.
        Hizzoner the Mayor. Chateau Pub.
Langford, Cooper H. *see* Langford, Cooper Harold.
Langford, Cooper Harold.
    xLangford, C. H.
        Ligand Substitution Processes.
            Benjamin-Cummings.
    xLangford, Cooper H.
        The Development of Chemical Principles.
            A-W.
Langford, Gerald, 1911-
    xLangford, Gerald.
        ed. Faulkner's Revision of Absalom, Absalom:
            A Collation of the Manuscript & the
            Published Book. U of Tex Pr.
        ed. Faulkner's Revision of "Sanctuary": A
            Collation of the Unrevised Galleys & the
            Published Book. U of Tex Pr.
Langford, J. A. *see* Langford, John Alfred.
Langford, John Alfred, 1823-1903
    xLangford, J. A.
        Prison Books & Their Authors. Gordon Pr.
Langford, Louise M.
    xLangford, Louise M.
        Guidance of the Young Child. Wiley.
Langford, Michael. *see* Langford, Michael John.
Langford, Michael John, 1933-
    xLangford, Michael.
        The Instant Picture Camera Handbook. Knopf.
        Starting Photography. Hastings.
        The Step-by-Step Guide to Photography.
            Knopf.
Langford, Nathaniel P. *see* Langford, Nathaniel Pitt.
Langford, Nathaniel Pitt, 1832-1911
    xLangford, Nathaniel P.
        Discovery of Yellowstone Park: Journal of the
            Washburn Expedition to the Yellowstone &
            Firehole Rivers in the Year 1870. U of Nebr
            Pr.
Langford, Norman F, 1914-
    xLangford, Norman F.
        Barriers to Belief. Westminster.
Langford, P.
    xLangford, Paul.
        The Eighteenth Century 1688-1815. St Martin.
Langford, Paul. *see* Langford, P.
Langford, Thomas A.
    xLangford, Thomas A.
        Christian Wholeness. Upper Room.
Langhaar, Henry L. *see* Langhaar, Henry Louis.
Langhaar, Henry Louis, 1909-
    xLanghaar, Henry L.
        Dimensional Analysis & Theory of Models.
            Krieger.
        Energy Methods in Applied Mechanics. Wiley.
Langhans, Robert W., 1929-
    xLanghans, Robert W.

ed. A Growth Chamber Manual:
  Environmental Control for Plants. Cornell U
  Pr.
Langholm, Odd. *see* Langholm, Odd Inge.
Langholm, Odd Inge, 1928-
  xLangholm, Odd.
  Price & Value in the Aristotelian Tradition: A
    Study in Scholastic Economics. Universitet.
Langier, Jose D. *see* Langier, Jose David.
Langier, Jose David.
  xLangier, Jose D.
  Economical & Nutritional Diets Using Scarce
    Resources. Mich St U Busn.
Langlais, Robert P.
  xLanglais, Robert P.
  Advanced Oral Radiographic Interpretation.
    Saunders.
Langland, Olaf E.
  xLangland, Olaf E.
  Textbook of Dental Radiography. C C Thomas.
Langland, William.
  xLangland, William.
  Piers Plowman. Oxford U Pr.
Langlands, R. P. *see* Langlands, Robert P.
Langlands, Robert P., 1936-
  xLanglands, R. P.
  On the Functional Equations Satisfied by
    Eisenstein Series. Springer-Verlag.
  xLanglands, Robert P.
  Euler Products. Yale U Pr.
Langley, Bill C. *see* Langley, Billy C.
Langley, Billy. *see* Langley, Billy C.
Langley, Billy C., 1931-
  xLangley, Bill C.
  Refrigeration & Air Conditioning. Reston.
  xLangley, Billy.
  Air Conditioning & Refrigeration
    Trouble-Shooting Handbook. Reston.
  xLangley, Billy C.
  Comfort Heating. Reston.
Langley, Bob.
  xLangley, Bob.
  Traverse of the Gods. Morrow.
Langley, Bob. *see* Langley, Robert.
Langley, Kathleen M.
  xLangley, Kathleen M.
  Industrialization of Iraq. Harvard U Pr.
Langley, L. L. *see* Langley, Leroy Lester.
Langley, Lee, 1932-
  xLangley, Lee.
  From the Broken Tree. Dell.
  From the Broken Tree. Dutton.
Langley, Lee. *see* Langley, Leroy Lester.
Langley, Leroy L. *see* Langley, Leroy Lester.
Langley, Leroy Lester.
  xLangley, L. L.
  ed. Contraception. Acad Pr.
  Dynamic Anatomy & Physiology. McGraw.
  xLangley, Lee.
  Structure & Function of the Human Body: An
    Introduction to Anatomy & Physiology.
    Burgess.
  xLangley, Leroy L.
  Homeostasis. Van Nos Reinhold.
Langley, Lester D.
  xLangley, Lester D.
  Struggle for the American Mediterranean:
    United States-European Rivalry in the
    Gulf-Caribbean, 1776-1904. U of Ga Pr.
  The United States & the Caribbean, 1900-1970.
    U of Ga Pr.
Langley, Michael, 1933-
  xLangley, Michael.
  Inchon Landing: MacArthur's Last Triumph.
    Times Bks.
Langley, Myrtle.
  xLangley, Myrtle S.
  The Nandi of Kenya: Life Crisis Rituals in a
    Period of Change. St Martin.
Langley, Myrtle S. *see* Langley, Myrtle.

Langley, Noel, 1911-
  xLangley, Noel.
  Dream of Dragon Flies. Macmillan.
  Edgar Cayce on Reincarnation. Warner Bks.
Langley, Robert.
  xLangley, Bob.
  Death Stalk. Doubleday.
  Death Stalk. Penguin.
  War of the Running Fox. Scribner.
Langley, Russell.
  xLangley, Russell.
  Practical Statistics Simply Explained. Peter
    Smith.
  xLangley, Russell A.
  Practical Statistics Simply Explained. Dover.
Langley, Russell A. *see* Langley, Russell.
Langley, Stephen.
  xLangley, Stephen.
  Producers on Producing. Drama Bk.
  Theatre Management in America; Principle &
    Practice: Producing for the Commercial
    Stock, Resident, College, & Community
    Theatre. Drama Bk.
Langlois, Charles V. *see* Langlois, Charles Victor.
Langlois, Charles Victor.
  xLanglois, Charles V.
  Introduction to the Study of History.
    Greenwood.
Langlois, Walter G.
  xLanglois, Walter G.
  ed. The Persistent Voice: Essays on Hellenism
    in French Literature Since the 18th Century
    In Honor of Henri M. Peyre. NYU Pr.
Langman, Jan.
  xLangman, Jan.
  Atlas of Medical Anatomy. Saunders.
Langmeier, J. *see* Langmeier, Josef.
Langmeier, Josef.
  xLangmeier, J.
  Psychological Deprivation in Childhood.
    Halsted Pr.
  Psychological Deprivation in Childhood.
    Krieger.
Langmore, Diane.
  xLangmore, Diane.
  Tamate - a King: James Chalmers in New
    Guinea, 1877-1901. Intl Schol Bk Serv.
Langnas, I. A. *see* Langnas, Isaac A.
Langnas, Isaac A.
  xLangnas, I. A.
  ed. Concise Dictionary of Literature. Philos
    Lib.
Langnas, Isaac A. *see* Langnas, Izaak Abram.
Langnas, Izaak Abram, 1911-
  xLangnas, I. A.
  ed. Dictionary of Discoveries. Philos Lib.
  xLangnas, Isaac A.
  Dictionary of Discoveries. Greenwood.
Langner, Nola.
  xLangner, Nola.
  Dusty. Coward.
  illus. Freddy My Grandfather. Schol Bk Serv.
  illus. Go & Shut the Door. Dial.
Langness, Lewis L.
  xLangness, Lewis L.
  Other Fields, Other Grasshoppers: Readings in
    Cultural Anthropology. Har-Row.
Lango, John. *see* Lango, John W.
Lango, John W.
  xLango, John.
  Whitehead's Ontology. State U NY Pr.
Langone, John, 1929-
  xLangone, John.

Bombed, Buzzed, Smashed, or...Sober. Avon.
Death Is a Noun: A View of the End of Life.
  Little.
Goodbye to Bedlam: Understanding Mental
  Illness & Retardation. Little.
Life at the Bottom: The People of Antarctica.
  Little.
Long Life: What We Know & Are Learning
  About the Aging Process. Little.
Langridge, D. W. *see* Langridge, Derek Wilton.
Langridge, Derek Wilton.
  xLangridge, D. W.
  Classification & Indexing in the Humanities.
    Butterworths.
Langs, Robert.
  xLangs, Robert J.
  The Therapeutic Interaction. Aronson.
Langs, Robert J. *see* Langs, Robert.
Langsam, Walter C. *see* Langsam, Walter Consuelo.
Langsam, Walter Consuelo.
  xLangsam, Walter C.
  Cincinnati in Color. Hastings.
  ed. Documents & Readings in the History of
    Europe Since 1918. Kraus Repr.
  ed. Historic Documents of World War II.
    Greenwood.
Langsdale, Richard.
  xLangsdale, Richard.
  Getting Ready for Living Together. Fortress.
Langseth-Christensen, Lillian.
  xLangseth-Christensen, Lillian.
  Holiday Cook. Lion.
Langsjoen, Arne. *see* Langsjoen, Arne Nels.
Langsjoen, Arne Nels, 1919-
  xLangsjoen, Arne.
  Exercises in General, Organic, & Biological
    Chemistry. Burgess.
Langsner, Drew.
  xLangsner, Drew.
  Country Woodcraft. Rodale Pr Inc.
Langstaff, Anne L.
  xLangstaff, Anne L.
  Contingency Management. Merrill.
Langstaff, John. *see* Langstaff, John M.
Langstaff, John M.
  xLangstaff, John.
  Golden Vanity. HarBraceJ.
  Over in the Meadow. HarBraceJ.
  Over in the Meadow. HarBraceJ.
  The Two Magicians. Atheneum.
Langstaff, Nancy.
  xLangstaff, Nancy.
  Exploring with Clay. ACEI.
Langston, John M. *see* Langston, John Mercer.
Langston, John Mercer, 1829-1897
  xLangston, John M.
  From the Virginia Plantation to the National
    Capitol. Arno.
Langton, Daniel J.
  xLangton, Daniel J.
  Querencia: Poems. U of Mo Pr.
Langton, Jane.
  xLangton, Jane.
  Astonishing Stereoscope. Har-Row.
  The Boyhood of Grace Jones. Har-Row.
  The Boyhood of Grace Jones. Har-Row.
  Dark Nantucket Noon. Har-Row.
  Diamond in the Window. Har-Row.
  The Diamond in the Window. Har-Row.
  The Memorial Hall Murder. Har-Row.
  The Memorial Hall Murder. Penguin.
  Paper Chains. Har-Row.
  Swing in the Summerhouse. Har-Row.
Langton, Kenneth P., 1933-
  xLangton, Kenneth P.
  Political Participation & Learning. Chris Mass.
  Political Socialization. Oxford U Pr.
Langton, N. H. *see* Langton, Norman Harry.
Langton, Norman Harry.
  xLangton, N. H.

The Space Environment. Intl Pubns Serv.
Langville, Alan R., 1947-
  xLangville, Alan R.
    Compiled By Modern World Rulers: A
      Chronology. Scarecrow.
Langway, Chester C., 1929-
  xLangway, Chester C.
    Stratigraphic Analysis of a Deep Ice Core from
      Greenland. Geol Soc.
Langworth, Richard M.
  xLangworth, Richard M.
    Chrysler & Imperial: The Postwar Years.
      Motorbooks Intl.
    Studebaker: The Postwar Years. Motorbooks
      Intl.
Lanham, Richard A.
  xLanham, Richard A.
    Revising Prose. Scribner.
    Style: An Anti-Textbook. Yale U Pr.
Lanham, Url N. *see* Lanham, Urless Norton.
Lanham, Urless Norton, 1918-
  xLanham, Url N.
    The Fishes. Columbia U Pr.
    The Insects. Columbia U Pr.
    Origins of Modern Biology. Columbia U Pr.
Lanier, Sidney, 1842-1881
  xLanier, Sidney.
    Music & Poetry: Essays Upon Some Aspects &
      Interrelations of the Two Arts. Greenwood.
    The Science of English Verse. Folcroft.
    The Science of English Verse. Norwood Edns.
Laning. *see* Laning, Edward.
Laning, Edward, 1906-
  xLaning.
    Perspective for Artists. G&D.
  xLaning, Edward.
    Act of Drawing. McGraw.
Lanjalley, Paul.
  xLanjalley, Paul.
    Histoire De la Revolution Du 18 Mars. AMS
      Pr.
Lankester, Edwin R. *see* Lankester, Edwin Ray.
Lankester, Edwin Ray, Sir, 1847-1929
  xLankester, Edwin R.
    Diversions of a Naturalist. Arno.
    Great & Small Things. Arno.
    Secrets of Earth & Sea. Arno.
Lankevich, George. *see* Lankevich, George J.
Lankevich, George J., 1939-
  xLankevich, George.
    Atlanta: A Chronological & Documentary
      History. Oceana.
  xLankevich, George J.
    The World & West: Readings in Contemporary
      History. Avery Pub.
Lankford, Philip M.
  xLankford, Philip M.
    Regional Incomes in the United States
      1929-1967: Level, Distribution, Stability &
      Growth. U Chicago Dept Geog.
Lankford, T. Randall, 1942-
  xLankford, T. Randall.
    Integrated Science for Health Students. Reston.
Lanksch, W. *see* Lanksch, Wolfgang.
Lanksch, Wolfgang.
  xLanksch, W.
    ed. Cranial Computerized Tomography.
      Springer-Verlag.
Lanners, E. *see* Lanners, Edi.
Lanners, Edi.
  xLanners, E.
    Illusions. HR&W.
Lannie, Vincent. *see* Lannie, Vincent P.
Lannie, Vincent P.
  xLannie, Vincent.
    Public Money & Parochial Education: Bishop
      Hughes, Governor Seward & the New York
      School Controversy. U of Notre Dame Pr.
Lanning, Jean.
  xLanning, Jean.

The Great Dane. Arco.
Great Danes. Arco.
Lanning, John T. *see* Lanning, John Tate.
Lanning, John Tate, 1902-
  xLanning, John T.
    Spanish Missions of Georgia. Scholarly.
Lannon, John M.
  xLannon, John M.
    Technical Writing. Little.
Lannoy, Richard.
  xLannoy, Richard.
    Speaking Tree: A Study of Indian Culture &
      Society. Oxford U Pr.
    The Speaking Tree: A Study of Indian Culture
      & Society. Oxford U Pr.
Lanphear, Roger G., 1936-
  xLanphear, Roger G.
    Freedom from Crime Through the TM Sidhi
      Program. Nellen Pub.
Lansdale, David B.
  xLansdale, David B.
    The Vital Signs of Effective Packaging
      Management. Am Mgmt.
Lansdale, Nina.
  xLansdale, Nina.
    The White Island. Arbor Hse.
Lansdown, Brenda.
  xLansdown, Brenda.
    Teaching Elementary Science Through
      Investigation & Colloquium. HarBraceJ.
Lansing, John B.
  xLansing, John B.
    Planned Residential Environments. U of Mich
      Soc Res.
Lansing, Kenneth. *see* Lansing, Kenneth Melvin.
Lansing, Kenneth Melvin, 1925-
  xLansing, Kenneth.
    Art, Artists & Art Education. Kendall Hunt.
Lansing, Marion F. *see* Lansing, Marion Florence.
Lansing, Marion Florence, 1883-
  xLansing, Marion F.
    Liberators & Heroes of Mexico & Central
      America. Arno.
    Liberators & Heroes of South America. Arno.
Lansing, Robert, 1864-1928
  xLansing, Robert.
    Peace Negotiations: A Personal Narrative.
      Greenwood.
Lansky, Lester L.
  xLansky, Lester L.
    Pediatric Neurology: A Practitioner's Guide.
      Med Exam.
Lansley, Stewart.
  xLansley, Stewart.
    Housing & Public Policy. Biblio Dist.
Lantero, Erminie H. *see* Lantero, Erminie Huntress.
Lantero, Erminie Huntress.
  xLantero, Erminie H.
    Feminine Aspects of Divinity. Pendle Hill.
Lantis, David W.
  xLantis, David W.
    California: Land of Contrast. Kendall-Hunt.
Lantz, Herman R.
  xLantz, Herman R.
    Community in Search of Itself: A Case History
      of Cairo, Illinois. S Ill U Pr.
    People of Coal Town. S Ill U Pr.
Lantz, K. A.
  xLantz, Kenneth.
    Nikoly Leskov. Twayne.
Lantz, Kenneth. *see* Lantz, K. A.
Lantzeff, George V.
  xLantzeff, George V.
    Eastward to Empire: Exploration & Conquest
      on the Russian Open Frontier, to 1750.
      McGill-Queens U Pr.
Lanyon, R. I. *see* Lanyon, Richard I.
Lanyon, Richard I.
  xLanyon, R. I.

Personality Assessment. Wiley.
Lanyon, Walter C. *see* Lanyon, Walter Clemow.
Lanyon, Walter Clemow, 1887-
  xLanyon, Walter C.
    And It Was Told of a Certain Potter. Arno.
Lanz, Kurt, 1919-
  xLanz, Kurt.
    Around the World with Chemistry. McGraw.
Lanzerotti, L. J. *see* Lanzerotti, Louis J.
Lanzerotti, Louis J.
  xLanzerotti, L. J.
    ed. Upper Atmosphere Research in Antarctica.
      Am Geophysical.
Lanzkowsky, Philip.
  xLanzkowsky, Philip.
    Pediatric Hematology-Oncology: A Treatise for
      the Clinician. McGraw.
LaPage, Geoffrey.
  xLaPage, Geoffrey.
    Animals Parasitic in Man. Peter Smith.
Lapalombara, Lyda E.
  xLapalombara, Lydia.
    An Introduction to Grammar: Traditional,
      Structural, Transformational. Winthrop.
Lapalombara, Lydia. *see* Lapalombara, Lyda E.
Lapati, Americo D.
  xLapati, Americo D.
    Orestes A. Brownson. Coll & U Pr.
LaPatra, J. W. *see* LaPatra, Jack W.
LaPatra, Jack. *see* LaPatra, Jack W.
LaPatra, Jack W., 1927-
  xLaPatra, J. W.
    Public Welfare Systems. C C Thomas.
  xLaPatra, Jack.
    Analyzing the Criminal Justice System.
      Lexington Bks.
  xLapatra, Jack W.
    Applying the Systems Approach to Urban
      Development. DH&R.
Lapchick, Richard E. *see* Lapchick, Richard Edward.
Lapchick, Richard Edward.
  xLapchick, Richard E.
    The Politics of Race & International Sport: The
      Case of South Africa. Greenwood.
Lapham, Lewis H.
  xLapham, Lewis H.
    Fortune's Child. Doubleday.
Lapide, Phinn E., 1922-
  xLapide, Pinchas.
    Israelis, Jews, & Jesus. Doubleday.
Lapide, Pinchas. *see* Lapide, Phinn E.
Lapides, Jack.
  xLapides, Jack.
    Fundamentals of Urology. Saunders.
Lapidus, Jacqueline.
  xLapidus, Jacqueline.
    Ready to Survive. Hanging Loose.
Lapidus, L. *see* Lapidus, Leon.
Lapidus, Leon.
  xLapidus, L.
    Digital Computation for Chemical Engineers.
      McGraw.
Lapidus, Morris.
  xLapidus, Morris.
    An Architecture of Joy. E A Seemann.
LaPiere, Richard T. *see* LaPiere, Richard Tracy.
LaPiere, Richard Tracy, 1899-
  xLaPiere, Richard T.
    The Freudian Ethic. Greenwood.
Lapin, Howard S.
  xLapin, Howard S.
    Structuring the Journey to Work. U of Pa Pr.
Lapin, Lawrence. *see* Lapin, Lawrence L.
Lapin, Lawrence L.
  xLapin, Lawrence.
    Pref. by Statistics: Meaning & Method.
      HarBraceJ.
  xLapin, Lawrence L.

Management Science for Business Decisions.
HarBraceJ.
Statistics for Modern Business Decisions.
HarBraceJ.

Lapine, Jennifer.
xLapine, Jennifer.
My First Hebrew Alphabet Book. Bloch.
Lapiner, Alan. *see* Lapiner, Alan C.
Lapiner, Alan C.
xLapiner, Alan.
Pre-Columbian Art of South America. Abrams.
Lapis, Karoly.
xLapis, Karoly.
ed. Liver Carcinogenesis. Hemisphere Pub.
LaPlace, Jean, S.J.
xLaPlace, Jean.
Preparing for Spiritual Direction. Franciscan
Herald.
Laplace, John.
xLaplace, John.
Health. P-H.
Laplanche, Jean.
xLaplanche, Jean.
Life & Death in Psychoanalysis. Johns
Hopkins.
Laplante, Jerry C.
xLaplante, Jerry C.
Plastic Furniture for the Home Craftsman.
Sterling.
LaPlante, Mary C. *see* Laplante, Mary Cosma.
LaPlante, Mary Cosma.
xLaPlante, Mary C.
Come to the Holy Table. Our Sunday Visitor.
Lapointe, Francois.
xLapointe, Francois H.
Gabriel Marcel & His Critics: An International
Bibliography (1935-1976). Garland Pub.
Compiled by Ludwig Wittgenstein: A
Comprehensive Bibliography. Greenwood.
Maurice Merleau-Ponty & His Critics: An
International Bibliography (1942-1976)
Including a Bibliography of His Writings.
Garland Pub.
Lapointe, Francois H. *see* Lapointe, Francois.
Lapolla, Garibaldi M. *see* Lapolla, Garibaldi Marto.
Lapolla, Garibaldi Marto, 1888-1954
xLapolla, Garibaldi M.
The Fire in the Flesh. Arno.
The Grand Gennaro. Arno.
Laponce, J. A.
xLaponce, Jean A.
ed. Experimentation & Simulation in Political
Science. U of Toronto Pr.
Laponce, Jean A. *see* Laponce, J. A.
Laporte, Leo F.
xLaporte, Leo F.
Ancient Environments. P-H.
Intro. by Evolution & the Fossil Record:
Readings from Scientific American. W H
Freeman.
Laporte, Valerie.
xLaPorte, Valerie.
ed. Reform & Regulation of Long Term Care.
Praeger.
Lapow, Harry.
xLapow, Harry.
Coney Island Beach People. Dover.
Coney Island Beach People. Peter Smith.
Lapp, Carolyn.
xLapp, Carolyn.
Dentists' Tools. Lerner Pubns.
Lapp, Diane.
xLapp, Diane.
Teaching & Learning: Philosophical,
Psychological, Curricular Applications.
Macmillan.
Lapp, Eleanor J.
xLapp, Eleanor J.

Duane, the Collector. A-W.
In the Morning Mist. A Whitman.
Lapp, John. *see* Lapp, John Allen.
Lapp, John A. *see* Lapp, John Allen.
Lapp, John Allen.
xLapp, John.
Dream for America. Pillar Bks.
xLapp, John A.
A Dream for America. Herald Pr.
The Mennonite Church in India: 1897-1962.
Herald Pr.
Lapp, John C., 1917-
xLapp, John C.
Aspects of Racinian Tragedy. U of Toronto Pr.
Esthetics of Negligence: La Fontaine's Contes.
Cambridge U Pr.
Lapp, Ralph E. *see* Lapp, Ralph Eugene.
Lapp, Ralph Eugene.
xLapp, Ralph E.
Matter. Silver.
The Radiation Controversy. Reddy Comm.
Lapp, Rudolph M.
xLapp, Rudolph M.
Afro-Americans in California. Boyd & Fraser.
Lappe, Frances M. *see* Lappe, Frances Moore.
Lappe, Frances Moore.
xLappe, Frances M.
Diet for a Small Planet. Ballantine.
Great Meatless Meals. Ballantine.
World Hunger: Ten Myths. Inst Food &
Develop.
xLappe, Francis M.
Food First: Beyond the Myth of Scarcity. HM.
Lappe, Francis M. *see* Lappe, Frances Moore.
Lappenberg, J. M. *see* Lappenberg, Johann Martin.
Lappenberg, Johann Martin, 1794-1865
xLappenberg, J. M.
History of England Under the Anglo-Saxon
Kings. Kennikat.
Laprade, William T. *see* Laprade, William Thomas.
Laprade, William Thomas, 1883-
xLaprade, William T.
Public Opinion & Politics in Eighteenth
Century England to the Fall of Walpole.
Greenwood.
Public Opinion & Politics in Eighteenth
Century England to the Fall of Walpole.
Octagon.
LaPray, Margaret.
xLaPray, Margaret H.
On-the-Spot Reading Diagnosis File. Ctr Appl
Res.
LaPray, Margaret H. *see* Lapray, Margaret.
Lapsanski, Duane V.
xLapsanski, Duane V.
The First Franciscans & the Gospel. Franciscan
Herald.
Lapsley, Susan.
xLapsley, Susan.
I Am Adopted. Bradbury Pr.
Lapwood, E. R.
xLapwood, E. R.
Ordinary Differential Equations. Pergamon.
LaQue, Francis L. *see* LaQue, Francis Laurence.
LaQue, Francis Laurence, 1904-
xLaQue, Francis L.
Marine Corrosion: Causes & Prevention. Wiley.
Laqueur, Walter. *see* Laqueur, Walter Ze'Ev.
Laqueur, Walter Ze'ev, 1921-
xLaqueur, Walter.
A Continent Astray: Europe, 1970-1978.
Oxford U Pr.

Guerrilla: A Historical & Critical Study. Little.
The Guerrilla Reader: A Historical Anthology.
NAL.
ed. The Guerrilla Reader: A Historical
Anthology. Temple U Pr.
Historians in Politics. Sage.
A History of Zionism. HR&W.

A History of Zionism. Schocken.

ed. The Human Rights Reader. NAL.
ed. Human Rights Reader. Temple U Pr.
ed. Literature & Politics in the Twentieth
Century. Gannon.
Neo-Isolationism & the World of the Seventies.
Sage.

The Political Psychology of Appeasement:
Finlandization & Other Unpopular Essays on
World Affairs. Transaction Bks.

Struggle for the Middle East: The Soviet Union
& the Middle East 1958-1968. Macmillan.
Lara, Jesus.
xLara, Jesus.
Quechua Peoples Poetry. Curbstone.
Laracy, Hugh. *see* Laracy, Hugh M.
Laracy, Hugh M.
xLaracy, Hugh.
Marists & Melanesians: A History of Catholic
Missions in the Solomon Islands. U Pr of
Hawaii.
Laramore, Darryl, 1928-
xLaramore, Darryl.
Careers: A Guide for Parents & Counselors.
Brigham.
Larbalestrier, Deborah. *see* Larbalestrier, Deborah E.
Larbalestrier, Deborah E., 1934-
xLarbalestrier, Deborah.
Paralegal Practice & Procedure: A Practical
Guide for the Legal Assistant. P-H.
Larcher, Jean, 1947-
xLarcher, Jean.
Fantastic Alphabets. Dover.
Optical & Geometrical Allover Patterns: 70
Original Drawings. Dover.
Larcher, W. *see* Larcher, Walter.
Larcher, Walter, 1929-
xLarcher, W.
Physiological Plant Ecology. Springer-Verlag.
Larcom, Lucy, 1824-1893
xLarcom, Lucy.
An Idyl of Work. Greenwood.
Larcombe, Sam, 1940-
xLarcombe, Sam.
First Poems. Lightning Tree.
Larden, Ida C. *see* Larden, Ida Claire.
Larden, Ida Claire.
xLarden, Ida C.
The Off-Wheel Pottery Book. Scribner.
Lardner, Rex.
xLardner, Rex.
Complete Beginner's Guide to Tennis.
Doubleday.
Finding & Exploiting Your Opponents
Weaknesses. Doubleday.
The Fine Art of Tennis Hustling. Dutton.
Tactics in Women's Singles, Doubles & Mixed
Doubles. Doubleday.
Lardy, Nicholas R.
xLardy, Nicholas R.
ed. Chinese Economic Planning: Translations
from Chi-hua ching-chi. M E Sharpe.
Lareuse, Jean.
xLareuse, Jean.
Devils in the Castle. Scribner.
Larew, Walter B., 1904-
xLarew, Walter B.
Automatic Transmissions. Chilton.
Fluid Clutches & Torque Converters. Chilton.
Larg, David. *see* Larg, David Glass.
Larg, David Glass.
xLarg, David.
Giuseppe Garibaldi: A Biography. Kennikat.
Largay, James A.
xLargay, James A.

Accounting for Changing Prices: Replacement Cost & General Price Level Adjustments. Wiley.

Large, Brian.
xLarge, Brian.
Martinu. Holmes & Meier.

Largen, Velda L.
xLargen, Velda L.
Guide to Good Food. Goodheart.

Largent, Edward J.
xLargent, Edward J.
Fluorosis: The Health Aspects of Fluorine Compounds. Ohio St U Pr.

Larimer, Sarah L. *see* Larimer, Sarah Luse.

Larimer, Sarah Luse.
xLarimer, Sarah L.
The Capture & Escape: Or, Life Among the Sioux. Garland Pub.

Larkey, Patrick D., 1943-
xLarkey, Patrick D.
Evaluating Public Programs: The Impact of General Revenue-Sharing on Municipal Government. Princeton U Pr.

Larkin, David.
xLarkin, David.
ed. Christmas Book. Scribner.
ed. Innocent Art. Ballantine.

Larkin, Emmet. *see* Larkin, Emmet J.

Larkin, Emmet J., 1927-
xLarkin, Emmet.
Intro. by The Historical Dimensions of Irish Catholicism. Arno.
The Making of the Roman Catholic Church in Ireland, 1850-1860. U of NC Pr.
The Roman Catholic Church in Ireland & the Fall of Parnell, 1888-1891. U of NC Pr.

Larkin, Henry, 1820-1899
xLarkin, Henry.
Carlyle & the Open Secret of His Life. Haskell.
Carlyle & the Open Secret of His Life. R West.

Larkin, James. *see* Larkin, James J.

Larkin, James J.
xLarkin, James.
Vehicle Leasing As I See It. Atcom.

Larkin, Peter A. *see* Larkin, Peter Anthony.

Larkin, Peter Anthony.
xLarkin, Peter A.
Freshwater Pollution, Canadian Style. McGill-Queens U Pr.

Larkin, Philip.
xLarkin, Philip.
High Windows. FS&G.
ed. The Oxford Book of Twentieth Century English Verse. Oxford U Pr.

Larkin, Ralph W., 1940-
xLarkin, Ralph W.
Suburban Youth in Cultural Crisis. Oxford U Pr.

Larkin, Rochelle.
xLarkin, Rochelle.
Torches of Desire. NAL.

Larmie, W. *see* Larmie, Walter E.

Larmie, Walter E., 1920-
xLarmie, W.
Flower Arranging: Basics to Advanced Design. P-H.

Larmore, Lewis.
xLarmore, Lewis.
Introduction to Photographic Principles. Dover.
Introduction to Photographic Principles. Peter Smith.

Larmour, Peter J.
xLarmour, Peter J.
The French Radical Party in the 1930's. Stanford U Pr.

Larn, Richard.
xLarn, Richard.
Devon Shipwrecks. David & Charles.

Larned, Joseph N. *see* Larned, Josephus Nelson.

Larned, Josephus N. *see* Larned, Josephus Nelson.

Larned, Josephus Nelson, 1836-1913
xLarned, Joseph N.
Life & Work of William Pryor Letchworth, Student & Minister of Public Benevolence. Patterson Smith.
xLarned, Josephus N.
Books, Culture & Character. Arno.

Larner, Gerald.
xLarner, Gerald.
The Glasgow Style. Taplinger.

Larner, John, 1930-
xLarner, John.
Lords of Romagna: Romagnol Society & the Origins of the Signorie. Cornell U Pr.

Larney, Judith.
xLarney, Judith.
Restoring Ceramics. Watson-Guptill.

LaRoe, Marlene S. *see* Laroe, Marlene Shelton.

LaRoe, Marlene Shelton.
xLaRoe, Marlene S.
How Not to Ruin a Perfectly Good Marriage. Follett.

Larone, Davise H. *see* Larone, Davise Honig.

Larone, Davise Honig, 1939-
xLarone, Davise H.
Medically Important Fungi: A Guide to Identification. Har-Row.

LaRosa, Linda J.
xLaRosa, Linda J.
The Random Factor. BJ Pub Group.
The Random Factor. Doubleday.

LaRossa, Ralph.
xLaRossa, Ralph.
Conflict & Power in Marriage: Expecting the First Child. Sage.

LaRouche, Lyndon H.
xLaRouche, Lyndon H.
The Case of Walter Lippmann: A Presidential Strategy. Campaigner.
The Power of Reason: A Kind of an Autobiography. New Benjamin.
The Power of Reason: A Kind of Autobiography. New Benjamin.

Laroui, Abdallah, 1933-
xLaroui, Abdallah.
The Crisis of the Arab Intellectual: Traditionalism or Historicism. U of Cal Pr.
The History of the Maghrib: An Interpretive Essay. Princeton U Pr.

Larrabeiti, Michael De. *see* De Larrabeiti, Michael.

Larranaga, Robert D.
xLarranaga, Robert D.
Pirates & Buccaneers. Lerner Pubns.

Larrea, Jean-Jacques.
xLarrea, Jean-Jacques.
The Diary of a Paper Boy. Putnam.

Larrick, Nancy.
xLarrick, Nancy.
ed. Green Is Like a Meadow of Grass: An Anthology of Children's Pleasure in Poetry. Garrard.
ed. More Poetry for Holidays. Garrard.
ed. On City Streets: An Anthology of Poetry. M Evans.
A Parent's Guide to Children's Reading. Doubleday.
ed. Somebody Turned on a Tap in These Kids: Poetry & Young People Today. Delacorte.

Larrieu, Jean, 1927-
xLarrieu, V.
Principles of Linear Algebra. Gordon.

Larrieu, V. *see* Larrieu, Jean.

Larroche, Jeanne C. *see* Larroche, Jeanne-Claudie.

Larroche, Jeanne-Claudie.
xLarroche, Jeanne C.
Developmental Pathology of the Neonate. Elsevier.

Larsen, Earnest.
xLarsen, Earnest.

How to Understand & Overcome Depression. Liguori Pubns.
Something Wonderful Is Happening. Paulist Pr.
Will Religion Make Sense to Your Child. Liguori Pubns.

Larsen, G. *see* Larsen, Gunnar.

Larsen, Gunnar.
xLarsen, G.
ed. Diagenesis in Sediments & Sedimentary Rocks. Elsevier.

Larsen, Hanna A. *see* Larsen, Hanna Astrup.

Larsen, Hanna Astrup, 1873-1945
xLarsen, Hanna A.
ed. Sweden's Best Stories: An Introduction to Swedish Fiction. Arno.

Larsen, Hanne, 1942-
xLarsen, Hanne.
Don't Forget Tom. T Y Crowell.

Larsen, Judith L. *see* Larsen, Judith Labelle.

Larsen, Judith Labelle.
xLarsen, Judith L.
The Patchwork Quilt Design & Coloring Book. Butterick Pub.

Larsen, Knud S.
xLarsen, Knud S.
Aggression: Myths & Models. Nelson-Hall.

Larsen, Lawrence H.
xLarsen, Lawrence H.
The President Wore Spats: A Biography of Glenn Frank. State Hist Soc Wis.

Larsen, M. D. *see* Larsen, Max D.

Larsen, Max D.
xLarsen, M. D.
Essentials of Precalculus Mathematics. A-W.
Introduction to Modern Algebraic Concepts. A-W.
xLarsen, Max D.
Essentials of Elementary School Mathematics. Acad Pr.
Multiplicative Theory of Ideals. Acad Pr.

Larsen, Nella.
xLarsen, Nella.
Passing. Arno.
Passing. Macmillan.
Passing. Negro U Pr.
Quicksand. Negro U Pr.

Larsen, Norma C. *see* Larsen, Norma Clark.

Larsen, Norma Clark.
xLarsen, Norma C.
His Everlasting Love: Stories of the Father's Help to His Children. Horizon Utah.

Larsen, Peter.
xLarsen, Peter.
Boy of Bolivia. Dodd.
Boy of Dahomey. Dodd.
illus. Boy of Nepal. Dodd.

Larsen, Richard J.
xLarsen, Richard J.
Statistics for the Allied Health Sciences. Merrill.

Larsen-Freeman, Diane.
xLarsen-Freeman, Diane.
ed. Discourse Analysis in Second Language Research. Newbury Hse.

Larsgaard, Mary, 1946-
xLarsgaard, Mary.
Map Librarianship: An Introduction. Libs Unl.

Larson, A. *see* Larson, Arthur.

Larson, Agnes M. *see* Larson, Agnes Mathilda.

Larson, Agnes Mathilda, 1892-1967
xLarson, Agnes M.
History of the White Pine Industry in Minnesota. Arno.

Larson, Allan L.
xLarson, Allan L.

Comparative Political Analysis. Nelson-Hall.
Larson, Arthur.
xLarson, A.
Sovereignty Within the Law. Oceana.
Larson, Arthur. *see* Larson, Arthur Lewis.
Larson, Arthur D.
xLarson, Arthur D.
Civil-Military Relations & Militarism: A
Classified Bibliography Covering the United
States & Other Nations of the World with
Introductory Notes. KSU.
ed. National Security Affairs: A Guide to
Information Sources. Gale.
Larson, Arthur Lewis.
xLarson, Arthur.
When Nations Disagree: A Handbook on Peace
Through Law. La State U Pr.
Larson, Bruce.
xLarson, Bruce.
Ask Me to Dance. Word Bks.
Dare to Live Now. Zondervan.
The Meaning & Mystery of Being Human.
Word Bks.
No Longer Strangers. Word Bks.
One & Only You. Pillar Bks.
The One & Only You. Word Bks.
Thirty Days to a New You. Zondervan.
Larson, Bruce L.
xLarson, Bruce L.
Lindbergh of Minnesota: A Political Biography.
HarBraceJ.
Larson, Carl F. *see* Larson, Carl F. W.
Larson, Carl F. W., 1939-
xLarson, Carl F.
Compiled by American Regional Theatre
History to 1900: A Bibliography. Scarecrow.
Larson, Carroll B. *see* Larson, Carroll Bernard.
Larson, Carroll Bernard.
xLarson, Carroll B.
Orthopedic Nursing. Mosby.
Larson, Charles R.
xLarson, Charles R.
American Indian Fiction. U of NM Pr.
Larson, Charles U.
xLarson, Charles U.
Communication: Everyday Encounters.
Wadsworth Pub.
Larson, Clinton F.
xLarson, Clinton F.
Counterpoint: A Book of Poems. Brigham.
Larson, Dewey B.
xLarson, Dewey B.
Nothing but Motion. North Pacific.
Larson, Donald R., 1935-
xLarson, Donald R.
The Honor Plays of Lope De Vega. Harvard U
Pr.
Larson, E. Dixon.
xLarson, E. Dixon.
Colt Tips. Pioneer Pr.
Larson, E. Richard.
xLarson, E. Richard.
The Rights of Racial Minorities. Avon.
Larson, Emil. *see* Larson, Emil Leonard.
Larson, Emil L. *see* Larson, Emil Leonard.
Larson, Emil Leonard, 1888-
xLarson, Emil.
Arizona School Law. U of Ariz Pr.
xLarson, Emil L.
One-Room & Consolidated Schools of
Connecticut: A Comparative Study of
Teachers, Costs & Holding Power. AMS Pr.
Larson, Esther E. *see* Larson, Esther Elisabeth.
Larson, Esther Elisabeth.
xLarson, Esther E.
Swedish Commentators on America 1638-1865:
An Annotated List of Selected Manuscript &
Printed Materials. NY Pub Lib.
Larson, Gustave O. *see* Larson, Gustive Olof.

Larson, Gustive Olof, 1897-
xLarson, Gustave O.
Prelude to the Kingdom: Mormon Desert
Conquest, a Chapter in American
Cooperative Experience. Greenwood.
Larson, Harold J., 1934-
xLarson, Harold J.
Introduction to Probability Theory & Statistical
Inference. Wiley.
Statistics: An Introduction. Wiley.
Larson, Henrietta M. *see* Larson, Henrietta Melia.
Larson, Henrietta Melia.
xLarson, Henrietta M.
Guide to Business History: Materials for the
Study of American Business History &
Suggestions for Their Use. Canner.
History of Humble Oil & Refining Company: A
Study in Industrial Growth. Arno.
Wheat Market & the Farmer in Minnesota,
1858-1900. AMS Pr.
Larson, James L.
xLarson, James L.
Reason & Experience: The Representation of
Natural Order in the Work of Carl von
Linne. U of Cal Pr.
Larson, James S.
xLarson, James S.
Why Government Programs Fail: Improving
Policy Implementation. Praeger.
Larson, Jeanne.
xLarson, Jeanne.
The Vegetable Protein & Vegetarian Cookbook.
Arc Bks.
Larson, Judith. *see* Larson, Judith F.
Larson, Judith F.
xLarson, Judith.
Guide to Rapid Reading. Knopf.
Larson, Katherine A.
xLarson, Katherine A.
Let's Make Something with Shapes & Colors.
Burgess.
Larson, Keith A.
xLarson, Keith A.
Compiled by Public Relations, the Edward L.
Bernayses & the American Scene: A
Bibliography. Faxon.
Larson, Knut, 1903-
xLarson, Knut.
Rugs & Carpets of the Orient. Warne.
Larson, Martin. *see* Larson, Martin Alfred.
Larson, Martin A. *see* Larson, Martin Alfred.
Larson, Martin Alfred, 1897-
xLarson, Martin.
How You Can Save Money on Your Taxes
This Year. Liberty Lobby.
xLarson, Martin A.
Church Wealth & Business Income. Philos Lib.
The Continuing Tax Rebellion: What Millions
of Americans Are Doing to Restore
Constitutional Government. Devin.
When Parochial Schools Close: A Study in
Educational Financing. Luce.
Larson, Mildred. *see* Larson, Mildred L.
Larson, Mildred L.
xLarson, Mildred.
The Functions of Reported Speech in
Discourse. Summer Inst Ling.
Larson, Milton E.
xLarson, Milton E.
Teaching Related Subjects in Trade &
Industrial & Technical Education. Merrill.
Larson, Muriel.
xLarson, Muriel.
Joy Every Morning. Moody.
Larson, Orvin. *see* Larson, Orvin Prentiss.
Larson, Orvin Prentiss.
xLarson, Orvin.
When It's Your Turn to Speak. Har-Row.
Larson, Peggy. *see* Larson, Peggy Pickering.
Larson, Peggy P. *see* Larson, Peggy Pickering.

Larson, Peggy Pickering.
xLarson, Peggy.
Sierra Club Naturalist's Guide to the Deserts
of the Southwest. Sierra.
xLarson, Peggy P.
All About Ants. T Y Crowell.
Larson, Richard L. *see* Larson, Richard Leslie.
Larson, Richard Leslie, 1929-
xLarson, Richard L.
ed. Children & Writing in the Elementary
School: Theories & Techniques. Oxford U Pr.
Larson, Roland E.
xLarson, Roland E.
Calculus with Analytic Geometry. Heath.
Larson, Thomas B.
xLarson, Thomas B.
Soviet-American Rivalry. Norton.
Larson, William H. *see* Larson, William Herbert.
Larson, William Herbert.
xLarson, William H.
ed. Seven Great Detective Stories. Western
Pub.
Larssen, A. K.
xLarssen, A. K.
The ABC's of Fo'c'sle Living. Madrona Pubs.
Larsson, Carl. *see* Larsson, Carl Olof.
Larsson, Carl Olof.
xLarsson, Carl.
A Family. Putnam.
A Home. Putnam.
Lart, Charles E. *see* Lart, Charles Edmund.
Lart, Charles Edmund.
xLart, Charles E.
Huguenot Pedigrees. Genealog Pub.
Larteguy, Jean, 1920-
xLarteguy, Jean.
The Face of War: Reflections on Men &
Combat. Bobbs.
Lartigue, Jacques Henri.
xLartigue, Jacques-Henri
My Photography Book. Barron.
Lartigue, Jacques-Henri. *see* Lartigue, Jacques Henri.
Larue, Gerald A.
xLarue, Gerald A.
Ancient Myth & Modern Man. P-H.
Laruffa, A. L. *see* Laruffa, Anthony L.
Laruffa, Anthony L., 1933-
xLaruffa, A. L.
ed. City & Peasant: A Study in Sociocultural
Dynamics. NY Acad Sci.
Lary, N. M.
xLary, N. M.
Dostoevsky & Dickens: A Study of Literary
Influence. Routledge & Kegan.
Las Vergnas, Raymond, 1902-
xLas Vergnas, Raymond.
Chesterton, Belloc, Baring. Folcroft.
Lasagna, Louis.
xLasagna, Louis.
ed. Clinical Pharmacology. Pergamon.
ed. Controversies in Therapeutics. Saunders.
ed. Patient Compliance. Futura Pub.
The VD Epidemic: How It Started, Where It's
Going, & What to Do About It. Temple U
Pr.
Lasansky, Mauricio.
xLasansky, Mauricio.
Nazi Drawings. U of Iowa Pr.
Lasater, Alice E.
xLasater, Alice E.
Spain to England: A Comparative Study of
Arabic, European, & English Literature of the
Middle Ages. U Pr of Miss.
Lasby, Clarence. *see* Lasby, Clarence G.
Lasby, Clarence G., 1933-
xLasby, Clarence.
Project Paperclip: German Scientists & the
Cold War. Atheneum.
Lascari, Andre D.
xLascari, Andre D.

Leukemia in Childhood. C C Thomas.
Lascelles, Edward C. *see* Lascelles, Edward Charles
  Ponsonby.
Lascelles, Edward Charles Ponsonby, 1884-
  xLascelles, Edward C.
    Granville Sharp & the Freedom of Slaves in
     England. Negro U Pr.
Lasdon, Leon S., 1939-
  xLasdon, Leon S.
    Optimization Theory for Large Systems.
     Macmillan.
Laseau, Paul, 1937-
  xLaseau, Paul.
    Graphic Thinking for Architects & Designers.
     Van Nos Reinhold.
Laseron, Charles F. *see* Laseron, Charles Francis.
Laseron, Charles Francis.
  xLaseron, Charles F.
    Ancient Australia: The Story of Its Past
     Geography & Life. Taplinger.
Lash, Nicholas.
  xLash, Nicholas.
    Acts of the Apostles. Glencoe.
Lasher, H. L.
  xLasher, H. L.
    Cop Out. Belmont-Tower.
Lashley, Dolores. *see* Lashley, Dolores C.
Lashley, Dolores C.
  xLashley, Dolores.
    Legacy of Beauty. State Ptg.
Lasker, Bruno, 1880-1965
  xLasker, Bruno.
    Human Bondage in Southeast Asia.
     Greenwood.
    Peoples of Southeast Asia. AMS Pr.
    Propaganda from China & Japan: A Case Study
     in Propaganda Analysis. AMS Pr.
    Race Attitudes in Children. Greenwood.
Lasker, David.
  xLasker, David.
    The Boy Who Loved Music. Viking Pr.
Lasker, Edward, 1885-
  xLasker, Edward.
    Adventure of Chess. Dover.
    Chess for Fun & Chess for Blood. Dover.
    Chess Secrets I Learned from the Masters.
     Dover.
    Chess Strategy. Dover.
    Common Sense in Chess. McKay.
    Modern Chess Strategy. McKay.
Lasker, Emanuel, 1868-1941
  xLasker, Emanuel.
    Common Sense in Chess. Dover.
Lasker, Joe.
  xLasker, Joe.
    illus. Lentil Soup. A Whitman.
    ed. Nick Joins in. A Whitman.
    The Strange Voyage of Neptune's Car. Viking
     Pr.
    illus. Tales of a Seadog Family. Viking Pr.
    Tales of a Seadog Family. Penguin.
Laski, Harold J. *see* Laski, Harold Joseph.
Laski, Harold Joseph, 1893-1950
  xLaski, Harold J.
    Authority in the Modern State. Shoe String.
    Communism. Biblio Dist.
    Communism. Kelley.
    Democracy in Crisis. AMS Pr.
    Liberty in the Modern State. Kelley.
    Political Thought in England from Locke to
     Bentham. Greenwood.
    Reflections on the Revolution of Our Time.
     Biblio Dist.
    Studies in Law & Politics. Arno.
    Studies in Law & Politics. Greenwood.
    Studies in Law & Politics. Shoe String.
Laski, Marghanita, 1915-
  xLaski, Marghanita.

George Eliot & Her World. Scribner.
Laskin, Daniel M.
  xLaskin, Daniel M.
    Oral & Maxillofacial Surgery. Mosby.
Laskin, Joyce. *see* Laskin, Joyce Novis.
Laskin, Joyce Novis.
  xLaskin, Joyce.
    Arts & Crafts Activities Desk Book. P-H.
Lasko, Keith A. *see* Lasko, Keith Alan.
Lasko, Keith Alan.
  xLasko, Keith A.
    The Great Billion-Dollar Medical Swindle.
     Bobbs.
Lasko, Peter.
  xLasko, Peter.
    Ars Sacra: 800-1200. Viking Pr.
Lasky, Jesse. *see* Lasky, Jesse Lenard.
Lasky, Jesse Lenard.
  xLasky, Jesse.
    Love Scene: The Story of Laurence Olivier &
     Vivien Leigh. T Y Crowell.
Lasky, Kathryn.
  xLasky, Kathryn.
    I Have Four Names for My Grandfather.
     Little.
    My Island Grandma. Warne.
    Tall Ships. Scribner.
    Tugboats Never Sleep. Little.
Laslett, Peter.
  xLaslett, Peter.
    ed. Bastardy & Its Comparative History:
     Studies in the History of Illegitimacy &
     Martial Nonconformism. Harvard U Pr.
Lasley, John F. *see* Lasley, John Foster.
Lasley, John Foster, 1913-
  xLasley, John F.
    Genetics of Livestock Improvement. P-H.
Lasnik, Robert S.
  xLasnik, Robert S.
    A Parent's Guide to Adoption. Sterling.
Lasry, George.
  xLasry, George.
    Valuing Common Stock: The Power of
     Prudence. Am Mgmt.
Lass, Abraham H. *see* Lass, Abraham Harold.
Lass, Abraham Harold, 1907-
  xLass, Abraham H.
    How to Prepare for College. PB.
    How to Prepare for College. D White.
Lass, Norman J.
  xLass, Norman J.
    ed. Experimental Phonetics. Mss Info.
Lass, Roger.
  xLass, Roger.
    ed. Approaches to English Historical
     Linguistics: An Anthology. Irvington.
Lass, William E.
  xLass, William E.
    A History of Steamboating on the Upper
     Missouri River. U of Nebr Pr.
Lassen, Niels A.
  xLassen, Niels A.
    Tracer Kinetic Methods in Medical Physiology.
     Raven.
Lasser (J.K.) Tax Institute, New York.
  xJ. K. Lasser Institute.
    J. K. Lasser's Your Income Tax: 1979 Edition.
     S&S.
  xJ. K. Lasser Tax Institute.
    Financial Planning for Your Family.
     Cornerstone.
  xJK Lasser Tax Inst.
    How to Avoid a Tax Audit. Cornerstone.
  xLasser Institute.

Investing for Your Future. S&S.
    J. K. Lasser's Managing Your Family Finances.
     S&S.
    Learn How You Can Invest or Retire in
     Mexico. S&S.
    Your Income Tax 1976. S&S.
  xLasser Tax Institute.
    J. K. Lasser's Your Income Tax: 1978 Edition.
     S&S.
Lasser Institute. *see* Lasser (J.K.) Tax Institute, New
  York.
Lasser, Jacob K. *see* Lasser, Jacob Kay.
Lasser, Jacob Kay.
  xLasser, Jacob K.
    Business Management Handbook. McGraw.
    ed. Handbook of Auditing Methods.
     Greenwood.
    ed. Handbook of Cost Accounting Methods.
     Greenwood.
    How to Run a Small Business. McGraw.
Lasser Tax Institute. *see* Lasser (J.K.) Tax Institute, New
  York.
Lasser, Terese.
  xLasser, Terese.
    Reach to Recovery. S&S.
Lassey, William R.
  xLassey, William R.
    ed. Leadership & Social Change. Univ Assocs.
    Planning in Rural Environments. McGraw.
Lassiter, Barbara Babcock.
  xLassiter, Barbara Babcock.
    American Wilderness: The Hudson River
     School of Painting. Doubleday.
Lassiter, Luther.
  xLassiter, Luther.
    Modern Guide to Pocket Billiards. Fleet.
Lassiter, Perry.
  xLassiter, Perry.
    Once Saved...Always Saved. Broadman.
Lassiter, Roy L. *see* Lassiter, Roy Leland.
Lassiter, Roy Leland, 1927-
  xLassiter, Roy L.
    Association of Income & Educational
     Achievement. U Presses Fla.
Lassner, Jacob.
  xLassner, Jacob.
    The Shaping of 'Abbasid Rule. Princeton U Pr.
    Topography of Baghdad in the Early Middle
     Ages: Text & Studies. Wayne St U Pr.
Lasson, Frans.
  xLasson, Frans.
    The Life & Destiny of Isak Dinesen. U of
     Chicago Pr.
Lasson, Kenneth.
  xLasson, Kenneth.
    Private Lives of Public Servants. Ind U Pr.
Lasson, Nelson B. *see* Lasson, Nelson Bernard.
Lasson, Nelson Bernard, 1908-
  xLasson, Nelson B.
    The History & Development of the Fourth
     Amendment to the United States
     Constitution. AMS Pr.
    History & Development of the Fourth
     Amendment to the United States
     Constitution. Da Capo.
Lasson, Robert.
  xLasson, Robert.
    Glue It Yourself: Woodworking Without Nails.
     Dutton.
Lasswell, H. D. *see* Lasswell, Harold Dwight.
Lasswell, Harold D. *see* Lasswell, Harold Dwight.
Lasswell, Harold Dwight, 1902-
  xLasswell, H. D.
    A Pre-View of Policy Sciences. Elsevier.
  xLasswell, Harold D.

Future of Political Science. Greenwood.
National Security & Individual Freedom. Da
Capo.
Politics: Who Gets What, When & How. Peter
Smith.
Power & Personality. Greenwood.
Power & Personality. Norton.
Power & Society: A Framework for Political
Inquiry. Yale U Pr.
ed. Propaganda & Promotional Activities: An
Annotated Bibliography. U of Chicago Pr.
Psychopathology & Politics. U of Chicago Pr.
ed. Values & Development: Appraising Asian
Experience. MIT Pr.
Lasswell, Marcia. *see* Lasswell, Marcia E.
Lasswell, Marcia E.
xLasswell, Marcia.
The Styles of Loving: Why You Love the Way
You Do. Doubleday.
Lasswell, Thomas E.
xLasswell, Thomas E.
Life in Society: Readings in Sociology. Scott F.
Last, J. A. *see* Last, Jerold A.
Last, Jack.
xLast, Jack.
Everyday Law Made Simple. Doubleday.
Last, Jerold A.
xLast, J. A.
ed. Protein Biosynthesis in Bacterial Systems.
Dekker.
ed. Protein Biosynthesis in Nonbacterial
Systems. Dekker.
Last, Murray.
xLast, Murray.
Sokoto Caliphate. Humanities.
Last, R J.
xLast, R. J.
Anatomy: Regional & Applied. Churchill.
Laster, Clay.
xLaster, Clay.
Beginner's Handbook of Amateur Radio. Sams.
Laszlo, Ernest. *see* Laszlo, Ervin.
Laszlo, Ervin.
xLaszlo, Ernest.
Goals for Mankind: A Report to the Club of
Rome on the New Horizons of Global
Community. NAL.
xLaszlo, Ervin.
A Strategy for the Future: The Systems
Approach to World Order. Braziller.
ed. The United States, Canada & the New
International Economic Order. Pergamon.
Laszlo, Ivan J., 1924-
xLaszlo, Ivan J.
Choice. Libra.
Latane, Henry A.
xLatane, Henry A.
Security Analysis & Portfolio Management.
Wiley.
Latane, John H. *see* Latane, John Holladay.
Latane, John Holladay, 1869-1932
xLatane, John H.
America As a World Power, 1897-1907.
Scholarly.
Early Relations Between Maryland & Virginia.
Johnson Repr.
Latham, A. J. *see* Latham, A. J. H.
Latham, A. J. H.
xLatham, A. J.
The International Economy & the Undeveloped
World, 1865-1914. Rowman.
Latham, Earl.
xLatham, Earl.
ed. Meaning of McCarthyism. Heath.
Politics of Railroad Coordination, 1933-1936.
Harvard U Pr.
Latham, Edward.
xLatham, Edward.

Famous Sayings & Their Authors: A Collection
of Historical Sayings in English, French,
German, Greek, Italian, & Latin. Gale.
Latham, Frank B. *see* Latham, Frank Brown.
Latham, Frank Brown, 1910-
xLatham, Frank B.
Dred Scott Decision, March 6, 1857: Slavery &
the Supreme Court's Self-Inflicted Wound.
Watts.
Lincoln & the Emancipation Proclamation,
January 1, 1863: The Document That Turned
the Civil War into a Fight for Freedom.
Watts.
Panic of 1893: A Time of Strikes, Riots, Hobo
Camps, Coxey's Army, Starvation, Withering
Droughts & Fears of Revolution. Watts.
Latham, Helen C.
xLatham, Helen C.
Pediatric Nursing. Mosby.
Latham, Jean L. *see* Latham, Jean Lee.
Latham, Jean Lee.
xLatham, Jean L.
Anchor's Aweigh: The Story of David Glasgow
Farragut. Har-Row.
Story of Eli Whitney. Har-Row.
This Dear-Bought Land. Har-Row.
What Tabbit the Rabbit Found. Garrard.
Latham, Judy.
xLatham, Judy.
Women in the Bible: Helpful Friends.
Broadman.
Latham, Michael. *see* Latham, Michael C.
Latham, Michael C.
xLatham, Michael.
Planning & Evaluation of Applied Nutrition
Programmes. Unipub.
Latham, R. G. *see* Latham, Robert Gordon.
Latham, Richard T. *see* Latham, Richard Thomas Edwin.
Latham, Richard Thomas Edwin.
xLatham, Richard T.
Law & the Commonwealth. Greenwood.
Latham, Robert G. *see* Latham, Robert Gordon.
Latham, Robert Gordon, 1812-1888
xLatham, R. G.
Two Dissertations on the Hamlet of Saxo
Grammaticus & of Shakespear. AMS Pr.
xLatham, Robert G.
The Ethnology of the British Colonies &
Dependencies. AMS Pr.
Latham, Roger M. *see* Latham, Roger Marion.
Latham, Roger Marion.
xLatham, Roger M.
The Complete Book of the Wild Turkey.
Stackpole.
Latham, Sid. *see* Latham, Sidney.
Latham, Sidney.
xLatham, Sid.
Camera Afield. Stackpole.
Great Sporting Posters of the Golden Age.
Stackpole.
Leathercraft. Follett.
Leathercraft. Winchester Pr.
Latham, William R.
xLatham, William R.
Locational Behavior in Manufacturing
Industries. Kluwer Boston.
Lathen, Emma, Pseud.
xLathen, Emma.
Accounting for Murder. PB.
By Hook or by Crook. PB.
Murder Against the Grain. PB.
Murder to Go. PB.
Murder to Go. S&S.
Murder Without Icing. PB.
Murder Without Icing. S&S.
A Place for Murder. PB.
Sweet & Low. S&S.
Lathi, Bhagwandas P. *see* Lathi, Bhagwandas Pannalal.
Lathi, Bhagwandas P. *see* Lathi, Bhagwandas Pannalal.

Lathi, Bhagwandas Pannalal.
xLathi, Bhagawandas P.
Signals, Systems & Communication. Wiley.
xLathi, Bhagwandas P.
Communication Systems. Wiley.
Lathrop, Dorothy P. *see* Lathrop, Dorothy Pulis.
Lathrop, Dorothy Pulis, 1891-
xLathrop, Dorothy P.
illus. Let Them Live. Macmillan.
Lathrop, Elise. *see* Lathrop, Elise L.
Lathrop, Elise L.
xLathrop, Elise.
Where Shakespeare Set His Stage. Haskell.
xLathrop, Elise L.
Early American Inns & Taverns. Arno.
Lathrop, Henry B. *see* Lathrop, Henry Burrowes.
Lathrop, Henry Burrowes, 1867-1936
xLathrop, Henry B.
Art of the Novelist. Folcroft.
Lathrop, R. *see* Lathrop, Rose (Hawthorne).
Lathrop, Richard.
xLathrop, Richard.
The Job Market. Garrett Pk.
Lathrop, Rose (Hawthorne), 1851-1926
xLathrop, R.
Memories of Hawthorne. Gordon Pr.
xLathrop, Rose H.
Memories of Hawthorne. AMS Pr.
Memories of Hawthorne. Folcroft.
Lathrop, Rose H. *see* Lathrop, Rose (Hawthorne).
Lathrop, William A. *see* Lathrop, William Addison.
Lathrop, William Addison.
xLathrop, William A.
Little Stories from the Screen. Garland Pub.
Latimer, Elizabeth (Wormeley), 1822-1904
xLatimer, Elizabeth W.
Europe in Africa in the Nineteenth Century.
Negro U Pr.
Europe in Africa in the Nineteenth Century.
Norwood Edns.
Latimer, Elizabeth W. *see* Latimer, Elizabeth
(Wormeley).
Latimer, Patricia.
xLatimer, Patricia.
Sonoma-Mendocino Wine Tour. Vin Image.
Latin American Economic Institute.
xLatin American Economic Institute.
Economic Defense of the Western Hemisphere.
Arno.
Latin American School Of Physics - University Of
Mexico - 1965. *see* Latin American School of Physics,
University of Mexico, 1965.
**Latin American School of Physics, University of
Mexico, 1965.**
xLatin American School Of Physics - University
Of Mexico - 1965.
Many-Body Problems & Other Selected Topics
in Theoretical Physics. Gordon.
**Latin American Symposium on Mathematical Logic, 3d,
State University of Campinas, 1976.**
xLatin American Symposium on Mathematical
Logic, 3rd.
Non-Classical Logics, Model Theory &
Computability: Proceedings. Elsevier.
Latin, Howard A.
xLatin, Howard A.
Privacy: A Selected Bibliography & Topical
Index of Social Science Materials. Rothman.
Latner, Richard B.
xLatner, Richard B.
The Presidency of Andrew Jackson: White
House Politics, 1829-1837. U of Ga Pr.
Laton, Anita D. *see* Laton, Anita Duncan Elizabeth.
Laton, Anita Duncan Elizabeth, 1895-
xLaton, Anita D.

The Psychology of Learning Applied to Health
   Education Through Biology: An Experimental
   Application of Psychology in the Junior High
   School. AMS Pr.
Latorre Cabal, Hugo.
   xLatorre Cabal, Hugo.
   The Revolution of the Latin American Church.
      U of Okla Pr.
Latortue, Regine.
   xLatortue, Regine.
   tr. Les Cenelles: A Collection of Poems by
      Creole Writers of the Early Nineteenth
      Century. G K Hall.
Latour, Bruno.
   xLatour, Bruno.
   Laboratory Life: The Social Construction of
      Scientific Facts. Sage.
Latourelle, Rene.
   xLatourelle, Rene.
   Finding Jesus Through the Gospels: History &
      Hermeneutics. Alba.
Latourette, Kenneth S. *see* Latourette, Kenneth Scott.
Latourette, Kenneth Scott, 1884-
   xLatourette, Kenneth S.
   A History of Christian Missions in China.
      Chinese Materials.
   History of Christian Missions in China. Russell.
Latta, John.
   xLatta, John.
   Rubbing Torsos. SBD.

Lattimore, Eleanor F. *see* Lattimore, Eleanor Frances.

Lattimore, Eleanor Frances.
   xLattimore, Eleanor F.

   Adam's Key. Morrow.

   illus. The Bus Trip. Morrow.

   illus. The Girl on the Deer. Morrow.

   illus. More About Little Pear. Morrow.

   Proudfoot's Way. Morrow.
   The Taming of Tiger. Morrow.
Lattimore, Eleanor H. *see* Lattimore, Eleanor Holgate.
Lattimore, Eleanor Holgate, 1895-1970
   xLattimore, Eleanor H.

   Turkestan Reunion. AMS Pr.
Lattimore, Owen.
   xLattimore, Owen.
   China: A Short History. AMS Pr.
   Desert Road to Turkestan. AMS Pr.
   High Tartary. AMS Pr.
   Mongol Journeys. AMS Pr.
   Ordeal by Slander. Greenwood.
   Solution in Asia. AMS Pr.
Lattimore, Richmond. *see* Lattimore, Richmond
   Alexander.
Lattimore, Richmond Alexander, 1906-
   xLattimore, Richmond.
   tr. The Four Gospels & Revelation. FS&G.
   Story Patterns in Greek Tragedy. U of Mich
      Pr.
Lattimore, Steven.
   xLattimore, Steven.
   The Marine Thiasos in Greek Sculpture. UCLA
      Arch.
Lattin, Gerald W.
   xLattin, Gerald W.
   Modern Hotel & Motel Management. W H
      Freeman.
Latzko, Adolf A. *see* Latzko, Adolf Andreas.
Latzko, Adolf Andreas, 1876-
   xLatzko, Adolf A.
   Men in War. Arno.
Latzko, D. G. *see* Latzko, D. G. H.
Latzko, D. G. H.
   xLatzko, D. G.
   ed. Post-Yield Fracture Mechanics. Intl Ideas.
Lau, Theodora. *see* Lau, Theodore.
Lau, Theodore.
   xLau, Theodora.

The Handbook of Chinese Horoscopes.
   Har-Row.
   Handbook of Chinese Horoscopes. Har-Row.
Laub, Bryna.
   xLaub, Bryna.
   ed. The Official Soap Opera Annual.
      Ballantine.
Laub, Julian M. *see* Laub, Julian Martin.
Laub, Julian Martin.
   xLaub, Julian M.
   The College & Community Development: A
      Socioeconomic Analysis for Urban &
      Regional Growth. Irvington.
Laubenfels, David J. De. *see* De Laubenfels, David J.
Laubenfels, Jean.
   xLaubenfels, Jean M.
   The Gifted Student: An Annotated
      Bibliography. Greenwood.
Laubenfels, Jean M. *see* Laubenfels, Jean.
Laubengayer, Albert W. *see* Laubengayer, Albert
   Washington.
Laubengayer, Albert Washington.
   xLaubengayer, Albert W.
   Experiments & Problems in General Chemistry.
      HR&W.
Lauber, Patricia.
   xLauber, Patricia.

   Friendly Dolphins. Random.

   Great Whales. Garrard.

   Life on a Giant Cactus. Garrard.

   Look-It-Up Book of Stars and Planets.
      Random.
   Surprising Kangaroos & Other Pouched
      Mammals. Random.
   Tapping Earth's Heat. Garrard.
   This Restless. Earth. Random.
   What's Hatching Out of That Egg?. Crown.
   Who Needs Alligators?. Garrard.

Laubin, Reginald.

   xLaubin, Reginald.
   American Indian Archery. U of Okla Pr.

   Indian Dances of North America: Their

   Importance to Indian Life. U of Okla Pr.
   The Indian Tipi: Its History, Construction, &
      Use. U of Okla Pr.

Laubscher, G. G. *see* Laubscher, Gustav George.
Laubscher, Gustav George, 1883-1918

   xLaubscher, G. G.
   Syntactical Causes of Case Reduction in Old

   French. Kraus Repr.

Lauck, W. Jett. *see* Lauck, William Jett.
Lauck, William Jett.

   xLauck, W. Jett.

   Conditions of Labor in American Industries.

   Arno.

Laud, William, Abp. of Canterbury, 1573-1645
   xLaud, William.

   The Works of the Most Reverend Father in

   God, William Laud, D. D.. AMS Pr.

Lauda, Niki, 1949-
   xLauda, Niki.

   The Art & Science of Grand Prix Driving.

   Motorbooks Intl.
Laudal, O. A. *see* Laudal, Olav Arnfinn.
Laudal, Olav Arnfinn.

   Formal Moduli of Algebraic Structures.
      Springer-Verlag.
Laude, Jean.
   xLaude, Jean.

   The Arts of Black Africa. U of Cal Pr.
Lauder, Phyllis.
   xLauder, Phyllis.
   The Siamese Cat. David & Charles.
   The Siamese Cat. Scribner.
Lauder, Robert E.
   xLauder, Robert E.
   Loneliness Is for Loving. Ave Maria.
Lauderdale, Beverly.
   xLauderdale, Beverly.
   Ten Women & God. A S Barnes.
Lauderdale, Pat.
   xLauderdale, Pat.
   ed. Political Analysis of Deviance. U of Minn
      Pr.
Laudet, M.
   xLaudet, M.
   ed. Medical Data Processing. Crane-Russak Co.
Laudicina, R. *see* Laudicina, Robert.
Laudicina, Robert.
   xLaudicina, R.
   A Legal Perspective for Student Personnel
      Administrators. C C Thomas.
Laudon, Kenneth C., 1944-
   xLaudon, Kenneth C.
   Communications Technology & Democratic
      Participation. Praeger.
Lauenstein, Milton C.
   xLauenstein, Milton C.
   Building & Operating an Effective Board of
      Directors. Am Mgmt.
Lauer, A. R. *see* Lauer, Alvhh Ray.
Lauer, Alvhh Ray.
   xLauer, A. R.
   The Psychology of Driving: Factors of Traffic
      Enforcement. C C Thomas.
Lauer, David A.
   xLauer, David A.
   Design Basics. HR&W.
Lauer, Paul E. *see* Lauer, Paul Erasmus.
Lauer, Paul Erasmus.
   xLauer, Paul E.
   Church & State in New England. AMS Pr.
   Church & State in New England. Johnson
      Repr.
Lauer, Pierre, 1931-
   xLauer, Pierre.
   The Suns of Badarane. Morrow.
Lauer, Quentin.
   xLauer, Quentin.
   A Reading of Hegel's Phenomenology of Spirit.
      Fordham.
   The Triumph of Subjectivity: An Introduction
      to Transcendental Phenomenology. Fordham.
Lauerhass, Ludwig.
   xLauerhass, Ludwig.
   Library Resources on Latin America: Research
      Guide & Bibliographic Introduction. UCLA
      Lat Am Ctr.
Laufer, Arthur C.
   xLaufer, Arthur C.
   Operations Management. SW Pub.
Laufer, Berthold, 1874-1934
   xLaufer, Berthold.
   The Decorative Art of the Amur Tribes. AMS
      Pr.
Laufer, Henry B.
   xLaufer, Henry B.
   Normal Two-Dimensional Singularities.
      Princeton U Pr.
Lauffer, Armand.
   xLauffer, Armand.
   Doing Continuing Education & Staff
      Development. McGraw.
   Grantsmanship. Sage.
   Practice of Continuing Education in the
      Human Services. McGraw.
   Understanding Your Social Agency. Sage.
Laufman, Alan K.
   xLaufman, Alan K.

The Law of Medical Malpractice in Texas: A
Primer for the Medical Community. U of Tex
Pr.

Laufman, Dudley.
xLaufman, Dudley.
An Orchard & a Garden. Bauhan.

Laughlin, Florence.
xLaughlin, Florence.
Little Leftover Witch. Macmillan.
Little Leftover Witch. Macmillan.

Laughlin, James L. *see* Laughlin, James Laurence.

Laughlin, James Laurence, 1850-1933
xLaughlin, James L.
History of Bimetallism in the United States.
Greenwood.

Laughlin, Mildred.
xLaughlin, Mildred.
Reading for Young People: The Great Plains.
ALA.

Laughlin, W. *see* Laughlin, William H.

Laughlin, William H.
xLaughlin, W.
Laughlin's Fact Finder: People, Places, Things
& Events. P-H.

Laumann, Edward O.
xLaumann, Edward O.
Prestige & Association in an Urban
Community: An Analysis of an Urban
Stratification System. Bobbs.
Prestige & Association in an Urban
Community: An Analysis of an Urban
Stratification System. Irvington.

Laumer, Frank.
xLaumer, Frank.
Massacre!. U Presses Fla.

Laumer, Keith, 1925-
xLaumer, Keith.
Dinosaur Beach. DAW Bks.
Dinosaur Beach. Scribner.
How to Design & Build Flying Models.
Har-Row.
Retief & the Warlords. PB.
Retief of the CDT. PB.
Retief's War. PB.
The Ultimax Man. St Martin.
Worlds of the Imperium. Berkley Pub.

Launay, A. J. *see* Launay, Andre Joseph.

Launay, Andre Joseph.
xLaunay, A. J.
Dictionary of Contemporaries. Branden.
ed. Dictionary of Contemporaries. Philos Lib.

Laune, Paul.
xLaune, Paul.
America's Quarter Horses. Doubleday.

Launitz-Schurer, Leopold. *see* Launitz-Schurer, Leopold
S.

Launitz-Schurer, Leopold S., 1942-
xLaunitz-Schurer, Leopold.
Loyal Whigs & Revolutionaries: The Making of
the Revolution in New York, 1765-1776.
NYU Pr.

Laurance, Alice.
xLaurance, Alice.
ed. Cassandra Rising. Doubleday.

Laurance, Mike.
xLaurance, Mike.
The Canon Guide. Amphoto.

Laurance Urdang Associates. *see* Laurence Urdang
Associates.

Lauren, Jena.
xLauren, Jena.
Disco!. Price Stern.

Lauren, Paul G. *see* Lauren, Paul Gordon.

Lauren, Paul Gordon.
xLauren, Paul G.

Diplomacy: New Approaches in History,
Theory, & Policy. Free Pr.
Diplomats & Bureaucrats: The First
Institutional Responses to Twentieth-Century
Diplomacy in France & Germany. Hoover
Inst Pr.

Laurence, D. R. *see* Laurence, Desmond Roger.

Laurence, Desmond Roger.
xLaurence, D. R.
Clinical Pharmacology. Churchill.
ed. Evaluation of Drug Activities:
Pharmacometrics. Acad Pr.

Laurence, Jeanne.
xLaurence, Jeanne.
An Album of Alaskan Wildflowers. Superior
Pub.

Laurence, Margaret.
xLaurence, Margaret.
The Diviners. Bantam.

Laurence, Theodor.
xLaurence, Theodor.
The Parker Lifetime Treasury of Mystic &
Occult Powers. P-H.

Laurence Urdang Associates.
xLaurance Urdang Associates.
ed. Lives of the Stuart Age: 1603-1714. B&N.
xLaurence Urdang Associates.
Lives of the Georgian Age: 1714-1837. B&N.

Laurence, William. *see* Laurence, William Leonard.
Laurence, William L. *see* Laurence, William Leonard.

Laurence, William Leonard, 1888-
xLaurence, William.
Men & Atoms: The Discovery, the Uses & the
Future of Atomic Energy. S&S.
xLaurence, William L.
Dawn Over Zero: The Story of the Atomic
Bomb. Greenwood.

Laurendeau, Monique.
xLaurendeau, Monique.
Development of the Concept of Space in the
Child. Intl Univs Pr.

Laurens, John, 1754-1782
xLaurens, John.
Army Correspondence of Colonel John Laurens
in the Years 1777-1778. Arno.

Laurenson, Diana.
xLaurenson, Diana T.
The Sociology of Literature. Schocken.

Laurenson, Diana T. *see* Laurenson, Diana.

Laurent, Bob.
xLaurent, Bob.
A World of Differents. Revell.

Laurent, Pierre-Henri.
xLaurent, Pierre-Henri.
ed. The European Community After Twenty
Years. Am Acad Pol Soc Sci.

Laurentin, Rene.
xLaurentin, Rene.
Catholic Pentecostalism. Doubleday.

Laures, John, 1891-
xLaures, John.
Catholic Church in Japan: A Short History.
Greenwood.

Lauria, Marie.
xLauria, Marie.
How to Be a Good Secretary. B&N.

Laurie, A. P. *see* Laurie, Arthur Pillans.
Laurie, Arthur P. *see* Laurie, Arthur Pillans.

Laurie, Arthur Pillans, 1861-1949
xLaurie, A. P.
The Painter's Methods & Materials. Peter
Smith.
xLaurie, Arthur P.
Painter's Methods & Materials. Dover.

Laurie, David, 1833-1897
xLaurie, David.
Reminiscences of a Fiddle Dealer. Virtuoso.

Laurie, Edward J.
xLaurie, Edward J.

Computers, Automation, & Society. Irwin.

Laurie, Michael.
xLaurie, Michael.
An Introduction to Landscape Architecture.
Elsevier.

Laurie, Rona.
xLaurie, Rona.
Pref. by & ed. One Hundred Speeches from the
Theater. Macmillan.

Laurie, S. S. *see* Laurie, Simon Somerville.
Laurie, Simon S. *see* Laurie, Simon Somerville.

Laurie, Simon Somerville, 1829-1909
xLaurie, S. S.
Historical Survey of Pre-Christian Education.
Norwood Edns.
xLaurie, Simon S.
Historical Survey of Pre-Christian Education.
AMS Pr.
Historical Survey of Pre-Christian Education.
Scholarly.

Lauriers, Austin M. Des. *see* Des Lauriers, Austin M.

Laurin, Anne.
xLaurin, Anne.
Little Things. Atheneum.

Laurin, Robert B., 1927-
xLaurin, Robert B.
Contemporary Old Testament Theologians.
Judson.
The Layman's Introduction to the Old
Testament. Judson.

Laurita, Raymond E.
xLaurita, Raymond E.
Reading, Writing & Creativity. Spec Child.

Lauritsen, John.
xLauritsen, John.
Early Homosexual Rights Movement
(1864-1935). Times Change.

Lauritzen, Peter.
xLauritzen, Peter.
Palaces of Venice. Viking Pr.
Venice: A Thousand Years of Culture &
Civilization. Atheneum.

Lauritzen, Tryntje.
xLauritzen, Tryntje.
Painted Rock Creatures. Lerner Pubns.

Lauritzen, Tryntje. *see* Lauritzen, Trynitje.

Laursen, Dan.
xLaursen, Dan.
Quarternary Shells Collected by the Fifth
Thule Expedition 1921-24. AMS Pr.

Laursen, Harold I.
xLaursen, Harold I.
Structural Analysis. McGraw.

Laury, Jean R. *see* Laury, Jean Ray.

Laury, Jean Ray.
xLaury, Jean R.
Doll Making: A Creative Approach. Van Nos
Reinhold.

Lauterbach, Albert. *see* Lauterbach, Albert T.

Lauterbach, Albert T., 1904-
xLauterbach, Albert.
Psychological Challenges to Modernization.
Elsevier.

Lauterbach, Ann, 1942-
xLauterbach, Ann.
Many Times, But Then. U of Tex Pr.

Lauterbach, Jacob Z. *see* Lauterbach, Jacob Zallel.

Lauterbach, Jacob Zallel, 1873-1942
xLauterbach, Jacob Z.
Rabbinic Essays. Ktav.
Studies in Jewish Law, Custom & Folklore.
Ktav.

Lauterbach, William. *see* Lauterbach, William August.
Lauterbach, William A. *see* Lauterbach, William August.

Lauterbach, William August, 1903-
xLauterbach, William.
My Refuge & Strength. Concordia.
xLauterbach, William A.

Through Cloud & Sunshine. Concordia.
Lauterer, Jock.
xLauterer, Jock.
Wouldn't Take Nothin' for My Journey Now.
U of NC Pr.
Lauterpacht, Hersch. *see* Lauterpacht, Hersh.
Lauterpacht, Hersh, Sir, 1897-1960
xLauterpacht, Hersch.
Function of Law in the International
Community. Garland Pub.
xLauterpacht, Hersh.
Function of Law in the International
Community. Shoe String.
Lauther, Olive C. *see* Lauther, Olive Chapman.
Lauther, Olive Chapman.
xLauther, Olive C.
The Lonesome Road. Wake-Brook.
Laux, Dorothy.
xLaux, Dorothy.
Did I Do That. Broadman.
Laux, James M. *see* Laux, James Michael.
Laux, James Michael, 1927-
xLaux, James M.
In First Gear: The French Automobile Industry
to 1914. McGill-Queens U Pr.
Laval, Pierre, 1883-1945
xLaval, Pierre.
The Diary of Pierre Laval. AMS Pr.
Lavan, Spencer.
xLavan, Spencer.
The Ahmadiyah Movement: A History &
Perspective. South Asia Bks.
Lavatelli, Celia S. *see* Lavatelli, Celia Stendler.
Lavatelli, Celia Stendler.
xLavatelli, Celia S.
Readings in Child Behavior & Development.
HarBraceJ.
Lavater, J. C. *see* Lavater, Johann Caspar.
Lavater, Johann Caspar, 1741-1801
xLavater, J. C.
Aphorisms on Man. Schol Facsimiles.
Lave, Charles A.
xLave, Charles A.
An Introduction to Models in the Social
Sciences. Har-Row.
Lavelle, C. L. *see* Lavelle, Christopher Lawrence
Bannerman.
Lavelle, Christopher L. *see* Lavelle, Christopher
Lawrence Bannerman.
Lavelle, Christopher Lawrence Bannerman.
xLavelle, C. L.
Evolutionary Changes to the Primate Skull &
Dentition. C C Thomas.
xLavelle, Christopher L.
Clinical Pathology of the Oral Mucosa.
Har-Row.
Lavelle, Doris.
xLavelle, Doris.
Latin & American Dances. Soccer.
Lavender, Abraham D.
xLavender, Abraham D.
ed. A Coat of Many Colors: Jewish
Subcommunities in the United States.
Greenwood.
Lavender, David. *see* Lavender, David Sievert.
Lavender, David Sievert, 1910-
xLavender, David.
The Fist in the Wilderness. U of NM Pr.
Land of Giants: The Drive to the Pacific
Northwest, 1750-1950. U of Nebr Pr.
One Man's West. U of Nebr Pr.
Lavender, William.
xLavender, William.
Chinaberry. BJ Pub Group.
Laver, F. J. M.
xLaver, Murray.
Computers & Social Change. Cambridge U Pr.
Laver, James, 1899-
xLaver, James.

Concise History of Costume & Fashion.
Scribner.
Laver, Murray.
xLaver, Murray.
Computers, Communications, & Society.
Oxford U Pr.
Laver, Murray. *see* Laver, F. J. M.
Laverack, M. S.
xLaverack, M. S.
ed. Essential Invertebrate Zoology. Halsted Pr.
Laverdiere, Eugene.
xLaverdiere, Eugene.
Acts of the Apostles. Franciscan Herald.
Laverriere, Sophie.
xLaverriere, Sophie.
Fun with Photography. Watts.
Lavers, Norman.
xLavers, Norman.
Mark Harris. Twayne.
Laverty, F. *see* Laverty, Frank T.
Laverty, Frank T.
xLaverty, F.
O.K. Way to Slim: Weight Control Through
Transactional Analysis. P-H.
xLaverty, Frank T.
The O.K. Way to Slim: Weight Control
Through Transactional Analysis. Grove.
The O.K. Way to Slim: Weight Control
Through Transactional Analysis. Grove.
Laviera, Tato.
xLaviera, Tato.
La Carreta Made a U-Turn. Arte Publico.
Lavigne, John R.
xLavigne, John R.
An Introduction to Paper Industry
Instrumentation. Miller Freeman.
Lavin, Margaret M. *see* Lavin, Margaret Masland.
Lavin, Margaret Masland.
xLavin, Margaret M.
Charlie. Golden Quill.
Lavin, Paul.
xLavin, Paul.
Anecdotes to Develop Social & Self Awareness
with Elementary School Children. Pendell
Pub.
Lavine, Sigmund. *see* Lavine, Sigmund A.
Lavine, Sigmund A.
xLavine, Sigmund.
Wonders of Terrariums. Dodd.
Wonders of the Owl World. Dodd.
xLavine, Sigmund A.
Famous American Architects. Dodd.
Famous Merchants. Dodd.
The Ghosts the Indians Feared. Dodd.
The Houses the Indians Built. Dodd.
Indian Corn & Other Gifts. Dodd.
Wonders of Camels. Dodd.
Wonders of Donkeys. Dodd.
Wonders of Elephants. Dodd.
Wonders of Goats. Dodd.
Wonders of Herbs. Dodd.
Wonders of Marsupials. Dodd.
Wonders of Ponies. Dodd.
Wonders of the Bat World. Dodd.
Wonders of the Bison World. Dodd.
Wonders of the Eagle World. Dodd.
Wonders of the Fly World. Dodd.
Wonders of the Hawk World. Dodd.
Wonders of the World of Horses. Dodd.
Lavington, F. *see* Lavington, Frederick.
Lavington, Frederick.
xLavington, F.
English Capital Market. Biblio Dist.
xLavington, Frederick.
English Capital Market. Kelley.
Lavrenev, Boris A. *see* Lavrenev, Boris Andreevich.
Lavrenev, Boris Andreevich, 1891-1959
xLavrenev, Boris A.

The Forty-First. Hyperion-Conn.
Lavrin, Asuncion.
xLavrin, Asuncion.
ed. Latin American Women: Historical
Perspectives. Greenwood.
Lavrin, Janko, 1887-
xLavrin, Janko.
Dostoevsky: A Study. Russell.
ed. A First Series of Representative Russian
Stories, Pushkin to Gorky. Greenwood.
Gogol. Haskell.
Goncharov. Russell.
Lermontov. Humanities.
Pushkin & Russian Literature. Russell.
Studies in European Literature. Kennikat.
Law, David B.
xLaw, David B.
Atlas of Pedodontics. Saunders.
Law, Donald.
xLaw, Donald.
Astrology, Palmistry, & Dreams. Littlefield.
The Concise Herbal Encyclopedia. St Martin.
Law Enforcement Assistance Administration. *see* United
States. Law Enforcement Assistance Administration.
Law, Hugh A. *see* Law, Hugh Alexander.
Law, Hugh Alexander, 1872-1943
xLaw, Hugh A.
Anglo-Irish Literature. Folcroft.
Law, Janice.
xLaw, Janice.
The Shadow of the Palms. HM.
Under Orion. HM.
Law Librarian's Society of the District of Columbia. *see*
Law Librarians' Society of Washington, D.C.
Law Librarians' Society of Washington, D.C.
xLaw Librarian's Society of the District of
Columbia.
Compiled by Union List of Legislative
Histories: 47th Congress, 1881 - 92nd
Congress, 1972. Rothman.
Law, Marie H. *see* Law, Marie Hamilton.
Law, Marie Hamilton, 1884-
xLaw, Marie H.
English Familiar Essay in the Early Nineteenth
Century: The Elements Old & New Which
Went into Its Making, As Exemplified in the
Writings of Hunt, Hazlitt & Lamb. Russell.
Law, R. G. *see* Law, Reed G.
Law, Reed G.

xLaw, R. G.
jt. auth. From Reason to Romanticism. Haskell.
Law, Sylvia. *see* Law, Sylvia A.
Law, Sylvia A.
xLaw, Sylvia.
Pain & Profit: The Politics of Malpractice.
Har-Row.
Law, Virginia. *see* Law, Virginia W.
Law, Virginia W.
xLaw, Virginia.
As Far As I Can Step. Word Bks.
Lawall, Gilbert.
xLawall, Gilbert W.
Theocritus' Coan Pastorals: A Poetry Book.
Harvard U Pr.
Lawall, Gilbert W. *see* Lawall, Gilbert.
Lawani, S. M.
xLawani, S. M.
Farming Systems in Africa: A Working
Bibliography, 1930-1978. G K Hall.
Lawder, Douglas.
xLawder, Douglas.
Trolling: Poems by. Little.
Lawder, Standish D.
xLawder, Standish D.
The Cubist Cinema. NYU Pr.
Lawes, Lewis E. *see* Lawes, Lewis Edward.

Lawes, Lewis Edward, 1883-1947
    xLawes, Lewis E.
        Twenty Thousand Years in Sing Sing. Arno.
Lawes, William G. see Lawes, William George.
Lawes, William George, 1839-1907
    xLawes, William G.
        Grammar & Vocabulary of Language Spoken
        by Motu Tribe (New Guinea). AMS Pr.
Lawhead, Terry.
    xLawhead, Terry.
        The Ferry Story. Pacific Search.
Lawler, Ann.
    xLawler, Ann.
        The Substitute. Schol Bk Serv.
Lawler, Edward E.
    xLawler, Edward E.
        Information & Control in Organizations.
        Goodyear.
Lawler, James. see Lawler, James M.
Lawler, James M., 1940-
    xLawler, James.
        IQ, Heritability & Racism. Intl Pub Co.
Lawler, James R.
    xLawler, James R.
        ed. Anthology of French Poetry. Oxford U Pr.
        Rene Char: The Myth & the Poem. Princeton
        U Pr.
Lawler, Justus G. see Lawler, Justus George.
Lawler, Justus George.
    xLawler, Justus G.
        Celestial Pantomime: Poetic Structures of
        Transcendence. Yale U Pr.
Lawler, Lillian B. see Lawler, Lillian Beatrice.
Lawler, Lillian Beatrice, 1898-
    xLawler, Lillian B.
        The Dance of the Ancient Greek Theatre. U of
        Iowa Pr.
Lawler, Marcella R.
    xLawler, Marcella R.
        ed. Strategies for Planned Curricular
        Innovation. Tchrs Coll.
Lawler, Pat.
    xLawler, Pat.
        My Brother's Place. Pantheon.
Lawler, Sylvia. see Lawler, Sylvia D.
Lawler, Sylvia D.
    xLawler, Sylvia.
        Human Blood Groups & Inheritance. St
        Martin.
Lawless, David J.
    xLawless, David J.
        Organizational Behavior: The Psychology of
        Effective Management. P-H.
Lawless, Joann A., 1949-
    xLawless, Joann A.
        Strange Stories of Life. Raintree Pubs.
Lawless, Paul.
    xLawless, Paul.
        Urban Deprivation & Government Initiative.
        Merrimack Bk Serv.
Lawlis, G. Frank.
    xLawlis, G. Frank.
        Multivariate Approaches for the Behavioral
        Sciences: A Brief Text. Tex Tech Pr.
Lawlis, Merritt E, 1918-
    xLawlis, Merritt E.
        Apology for the Middle Class: The Dramatic
        Novels of Thomas Deloney. AMS Pr.
Lawlor, Steven. see Lawlor, Steven C.
Lawlor, Steven C.
    xLawlor, Steven.
        BASIC. Wadsworth Pub.
    xLawlor, Steven C.
        Business Mathematics. Har-Row.
Lawn, B. R.
    xLawn, B. R.
        Fracture of Brittle Solids. Cambridge U Pr.
Lawrence, A. A. see Lawrence, Andrew A.
Lawrence, A. W. see Lawrence, Arnold Walter.

Lawrence, Andrew A.
    xLawrence, A. A.
        Natural Gums for Edible Purposes. Noyes.
Lawrence, Anthony G.
    xLawrence, Anthony G.
        Pricing & Planning in the U. S. Natural Gas
        Industry: An Econometric & Programming
        Study. Arno.
Lawrence, Arnold Walter, 1900-
    xLawrence, A. W.
        Greek Architecture. Viking Pr.
Lawrence, Barbara, 1925-
    xLawrence, Barbara.
        Fisherman's Wharf Cookbook. Nitty Gritty.
Lawrence, Berta, 1906-
    xLawrence, Berta.
        Somerset Legends. David & Charles.
Lawrence, Clifford H. see Lawrence, Clifford Hugh.
Lawrence, Clifford Hugh.
    xLawrence, Clifford H.
        ed. English Church & the Papacy in the
        Middle Ages. Fordham.
Lawrence, D. H. see Lawrence, David Herbert.
Lawrence, David E.
    xLawrence, David E.
        The Natural Lean. Mojave Bks.
Lawrence, David H. see Lawrence, David Herbert.
Lawrence, David Herbert, 1885-1930
    xLawrence, D. H.
        Aaron's Rod. Penguin.
        Apocalypse. Penguin.
        The Centaur Letters. U of Tex Hum Res.
        Complete Poems of D. H. Lawrence. Penguin.
        David: A Play. Haskell.
        Four Short Novels. Penguin.
        Last Poems. Haskell.
        Last Poems. Scholarly.
        Letters to Thomas & Adele Seltzer. Black
        Sparrow.
        Lost Girl. Penguin.
        Portable D. H. Lawrence. Penguin.
        The Rainbow. Penguin.
        Sons & Lovers. Aurora Pubs.
        Sons & Lovers. Penguin.
        Sons & Lovers. Viking Pr.
        ed. Sons & Lovers: A Facsimile of the
        Manuscript. U of Cal Pr.
        Studies in Classic American Literature.
        Penguin.
        Twilight in Italy. Viking Pr.
    xLawrence, David H.
        Lovely Lady. Arno.
        Modern Lover. Arno.
        The Prussian Officer, & Other Stories. Arno.
        Sons & Lovers. Modern Lib.
        The Tales of D. H. Lawrence. Scholarly.
Lawrence, Douglas H.
    xLawrence, Douglas H.
        Deterrents & Reinforcement: The Psychology
        of Insufficient Reward. Stanford U Pr.
Lawrence, Edgar D.
    xLawrence, Edgar D.
        Ministering to the Silent Minority. Gospel Pub.
        Sign Language Made Simple. Gospel Pub.
Lawrence, G. R. see Lawrence, George Richard Peter.
Lawrence, George H. see Lawrence, George Hill
Mathewson.
Lawrence, George Hill Mathewson, 1910-
    xLawrence, George H.
        Taxonomy of Vascular Plants. Macmillan.
Lawrence, George Richard Peter.
    xLawrence, G. R.
        Randstad, Holland. Oxford U Pr.
Lawrence, Glenn.
    xLawrence, Glenn.
        Condemnation: Your Rights When the
        Government Acquires Your Property.
        Oceana.
Lawrence, Herbert.
    xLawrence, Herbert.

        The Life & Adventures of Common Sense,
        1769. Garland Pub.
Lawrence, Ian.
    xLawrence, Ian.
        Music & the Teacher. Beekman Pubs.
Lawrence, J. Dennis.
    xLawrence, J. Dennis.
        Catalog of Special Plane Curves. Dover.
Lawrence, J. F. see Lawrence, James F.
Lawrence, J. S. see Lawrence, John Stewart.
Lawrence, James F.
    xLawrence, J. F.
        Chemical Derivatization in Liquid
        Chromatography. Elsevier.
Lawrence, Jerome, 1915-
    xLawrence, Jerome.
        Inherit the Wind. Bantam.
Lawrence, John, 1933-
    xLawrence, John.
        Giant of Grabbist. D White.
        A History of Russia. NAL.
        Rabbit & Pork Rhyming Talk. T Y Crowell.
    xLawrence, John T.
        History of Russia. NAL.
Lawrence, John. see Lawrence, John Waldemar.
Lawrence, John R.
    xLawrence, John R.
        Polyester Resins. Krieger.
Lawrence, John S. see Lawrence, John Shelton.
Lawrence, John Shelton.
    xLawrence, John S.
        ed. Fair Use & Free Inquiry: Copyright Law &
        the New Media. Ablex Pub.
Lawrence, John Stewart.
    xLawrence, J. S.
        Rheumatism in Populations. Intl Ideas.
Lawrence, John T. see Lawrence, John.
Lawrence, John Waldemar, 1907-
    xLawrence, John.
        Soviet Russia. D White.
Lawrence, Judith.
    xLawrence, Judith.
        Goat for Carlo. Garrard.
Lawrence Livermore Laboratory.
    xLawrence Livermore Laboratory.
        Design Guide for Shallow Solar Ponds. Solar
        Energy Info.
Lawrence, Louise.
    xLawrence, Louise.
        Cat Call. Har-Row.
        Sing & Scatter Daisies. Har-Row.
        Star Lord. PB.
        Star Lord. Har-Row.
Lawrence, Louise D. see Lawrence, Louise de Kiriline.
Lawrence, Louise de Kiriline, 1894-
    xLawrence, Louise D.
        Another Winter, Another Spring: A Love
        Remembered. McGraw.
Lawrence, Lynda.
    xLawrence, Lynda.
        The Un-Marriage Manual: How to Live
        Together Without a License. Major Bks.
Lawrence, Marjorie Kahl.
    xLawrence, Marjorie Kahl.
        Fairy Smoke: Children's Poems. Exposition.
Lawrence, Mary (Chipman).
    xLawrence, Mary C.
        Captain's Best Mate: The Journal of Mary
        Chipman Lawrence on the Whaler Addison,
        1856-1860. Brown U Pr.
Lawrence, Mary C. see Lawrence, Mary (Chipman).
Lawrence, Mary S.
    xLawrence, Mary S.
        Reading, Thinking, Writing: A Text for
        Students of English As a Second Language.
        U of Mich Pr.
Lawrence, Michael. see Lawrence, Mike.
Lawrence, Mike.
    xLawrence, Michael.

How to Read Your Opponent's Cards: The
Bridge Experts' Way to Locate Missing High
Cards. P-H.

Lawrence, Mildred.
xLawrence, Mildred.
Forever & Always. HarBraceJ.
No Slipper for Cinderella. HarBraceJ.
Once at the Weary Why. HarBraceJ.
Touchmark. HarBraceJ.

Lawrence, P. A.
xLawrence, P. A.
Insect Development. Halsted Pr.

Lawrence, P. Scott.
xLawrence, P. Scott.
ed. Readings in Abnormal Psychology. Mss
Info.

Lawrence, Paul, 1941-
xLawrence, Paul.
Hiking the Teton Backcountry. Sierra.
How to Repair Solid-State Imports. TAB Bks.

Lawrence, Paul R.
xLawrence, Paul R.
Developing Organizations: Diagnosis & Action.
A-W.
Organization & Environment: Managing
Differentiation & Integration. Harvard Busn.
Organization & Environment: Managing
Differentiation & Integration. Irwin.

Lawrence, Peter. see Lawrence, Peter A.

Lawrence, Peter A.
xLawrence, Peter.
Managers & Management in West Germany. St
Martin.

Lawrence, R. D., 1921-
xLawrence, R. D.
The North Runner. HR&W.
Paddy: A Naturalist's Story of an Orphan
Beaver. Knopf.
Secret Go the Wolves. HR&W.

Lawrence, Ralph R. see Lawrence, Ralph Restieaux.

Lawrence, Ralph Restieaux, 1873-
xLawrence, Ralph R.
Principles of Alternating-Current Machinery.
McGraw.

Lawrence, Robert, 1912-
xLawrence, Robert.
The World of Opera. Greenwood.

Lawrence, Robert. see Lawrence, Robert M.

Lawrence, Robert M.
xLawrence, Robert.
New Dimensions to Energy Policy. Lexington
Bks.
xLawrence, Robert M.
ed. International Energy Policy. Lexington Bks.

Lawrence, T. E. see Lawrence, Thomas Edward.

Lawrence, Thomas E. see Lawrence, Thomas Edward.

Lawrence, Thomas Edward, 1888-1935
xLawrence, T. E.
Evolution of a Revolt: Early Postwar Writings
of T. E. Lawrence. Pa St U Pr.
xLawrence, Thomas E.
T. E. Lawrence to His Biographers, Robert
Graves & Liddell Hart. Greenwood.

Lawrence, W. G. see Lawrence, Willis Grant.

Lawrence, W. Gordon.
xLawrence, W. Gordon.
Exploring Individual & Organizational
Boundaries: A Tavistock Open Systems
Approach. Wiley.

Lawrence, Walter.
xLawrence, Walter.
Cancer Management. Grune.

Lawrence, William J. see Lawrence, William John.

Lawrence, William John, 1862-1940
xLawrence, William J.
Pre-Restoration Stage Studies. Arno.

Lawrence, William W. see Lawrence, William Witherle.

Lawrence, William Witherle, 1876-1958
xLawrence, William W.

Medieval Story & the Beginnings of the Social
Ideals of English-Speaking People. Ungar.

Lawrence, Willis Grant, 1916-
xLawrence, W. G.
Ceramic Science for the Potter. Chilton.

Lawrenson, Helen.
xLawrenson, Helen.
Stranger at the Party: A Memoir. Random.
Whistling Girl. Doubleday.

Lawrie, R. A. see Lawrie, Ralston Andrew.

Lawrie, Ralston Andrew.
xLawrie, R. A.
Meat Science. Pergamon.

Lawrie, W. H. see Lawrie, William H.

Lawrie, William H.
xLawrie, W. H.
All Fur Flies & How to Dress Them. A S
Barnes.

Laws, G. Malcolm. see Laws, George Malcolm.

Laws, George Malcolm.
xLaws, G. Malcolm.
The British Literary Ballad: A Study in Poetic
Imitation. S Ill U Pr.
Native American Balladry: A Descriptive
Study & a Bibliographical Syllabus. U of Tex
Pr.

Laws, Gertrude, 1886-
xLaws, Gertrude.
Parent-Child Relationships: A Study of the
Attitudes & Practices of Parents Concerning
Social Adjustment of Children. AMS Pr.

Laws, J. L. see Laws, Judith Long.

Laws, Judith Long.
xLaws, J. L.
The Second X: Sex Role & Social Role.
Elsevier.

Lawson, Alan.
xLawson, Alan.
Patrick White. Oxford U Pr.

Lawson, Alexander S.
xLawson, Alexander S.
Printing Types: An Introduction. Beacon Pr.

Lawson, Andrew.
xLawson, Andrew.
Discover Unexpected London. Two Continents.

Lawson, Charles L.
xLawson, Charles L.
Solving Least Squares Problems. P-H.

Lawson, Don.
xLawson, Don.
Democracy. Watts.
Education Careers. Watts.
F D R's New Deal. T Y Crowell.

Lawson, Frederick H. see Lawson, Frederick Henry.

Lawson, Frederick Henry.
xLawson, Frederick H.
A Common Lawyer Looks at the Civil Law:
Five Lectures Delivered at the University of
Michigan, November 16, 17, 18, 19, and 20,
1953. Greenwood.

Lawson, Harry O.
xLawson, Harry O.
Personnel Administration in the Courts.
Westview.

Lawson, J. H. see Lawson, James H.

Lawson, James.
xLawson, James.
The Girl Watcher. Warner Bks.

Lawson, James G. see Lawson, James Gilchrist.

Lawson, James Gilchrist, 1874-1946
xLawson, James G.
The World's Best Loved Poems. Arden Lib.
ed. World's Best Loved Poems. Har-Row.

Lawson, James H.
xLawson, J. H.
A Synopsis of Fevers & Their Treatment. Year
Bk Med.

Lawson, Joan.
xLawson, Joan.

Ballet Stories. Mayflower Bks.
The Story of Ballet. Taplinger.

Lawson, John, 1712-1759
xLawson, John.
Lectures Concerning Oratory. S Ill U Pr.

Lawson, Kay.
xLawson, Kay.
The Comparative Study of Political Parties. St
Martin.

Lawson, Laurie L.
xLawson, Laurie L.
The Diatom Flora of the Provo River Utah, U.
S. A.. Intl Schol Bk Serv.

Lawson, McEwan.
xLawson, McEwan.
Master John Milton of the Citie of London.
Folcroft.

Lawson, Merlin P., 1941-
xLawson, Merlin P.
The Climate of the Great American Desert:
Reconstruction of the Climate of Western
Interior United States, 1800-1850. U of Nebr
Pr.
Climatic Atlas of Nebraska. U of Nebr Pr.

Lawson, Richard H.
xLawson, Richard H.
Edith Wharton. Ungar.

Lawson, Robert, 1892-1957
xLawson, Robert.
Rabbit Hill. Penguin.
illus. Rabbit Hill. Viking Pr.
illus. The Tough Winter. Penguin.
illus. The Tough Winter. Viking Pr.

Lawson, Ted. see Lawson, Ted W.

Lawson, Ted W., 1917-
xLawson, Ted.
Thirty Seconds Over Tokyo. Random.

Lawson, Todd S. see Lawson, Todd S. J.

Lawson, Todd S. J.
xLawson, Todd S.
Patriotic Poems of Amerikkka. SF Arts &
Letters.

Lawson, Tom E.
xLawson, Tom E.
Formative Instructional Product Evaluation:
Instruments & Strategies. Educ Tech Pubns.

Lawson-Wood, D. see Lawson-Wood, Denis.

Lawson-Wood, Denis.

xLawson-Wood, D.

Acupuncture Handbook. State Mutual Bk.
Acupuncture Handbook. Weiser.

xLawson-Wood, Denis.
Acupuncture Handbook. Intl Pubns Serv.

Lawther, John D. see Lawther, John Dobson.

Lawther, John Dobson, 1899-
xLawther, John D.
The Learning & Performance of Physical Skills.
P-H.

Lawton, Denis.
xLawton, Denis.
Theory & Practice of Curriculum Studies.
Routledge & Kegan.

Lawton, E. P. see Lawton, Edward P.

Lawton, Edward P.
xLawton, E. P.
The South & the Nation. Island Pr.

Lawton, Harold W. see Lawton, Harold Walter.

Lawton, Harold Walter.
xLawton, Harold W.
ed. Handbook of French Renaissance Dramatic
Theory. Greenwood.

Lawton, M. Powell. see Lawton, Mortimer Powell.

Lawton, Mortimer Powell.
xLawton, M. Powell.

Environment & Aging. Brooks-Cole.
Planning & Managing Housing for the Elderly.
Wiley.
Lawton, Philip.
xLawton, Philip.
Living Philosophy. Har-Row.
Lawton, Richard.
xLawton, Richard.
ed. The Census & Social Structure: An
Interpretative Guide to Nineteenth-Century
Censuses for England & Wales. Biblio Dist.
Lawton, W. C. see Lawton, William Cranston.
Lawton, William Cranston, 1853-1941
xLawton, W. C.
Successors of Homer. Cooper Sq.
Lawyers Co-Op Editorial Staff. see Lawyers
Co-Operative Publishing Company.
Lawyers Co-Operative Publishing Company.
xLawyers Co-Op Editorial Staff.
Medical Malpractice: ALR 20 Cases &
Annotations. Lawyers Co-Op.
Modern Bankruptcy Manual: Law & Practice
with Forms. Lawyers Co-Op.
xLawyers Co-Operative Publishing Company Staff.
Decisions of the United States Supreme Court:
1963-64, 1964-65, 1965-66, 1966-67,
1967-68, 1968-69, 1969-70, 1970-71,
1971-72, 1972-73, 1973-74, 1974-75,
1975-76. Lawyers Co-Op.
Lax, Melvin. see Lax, Melvin J.
Lax, Melvin J.
xLax, Melvin.
Symmetry Principles in Solid State &
Molecular Physics. Wiley.
Lax, Peter. see Lax, Peter D.
Lax, Peter D.
xLax, Peter.
Calculus with Applications & Computing.
Springer-Verlag.
Laxalt, Robert, 1921-
xLaxalt, Robert.
Sweet Promised Land. Har-Row.
Lay, Beirne.
xLay, Beirne.
Twelve O'Clock High!. Arno.
Twelve O'Clock High. Dodd.
Lay, S. Houston.
xLay, S. Houston.
Law Relating to Activities of Man in Space. U
of Chicago Pr.
Laybourne, Kit.
xLaybourne, Kit.
The Animation Book. Crown.
Laycock, Frank, 1922-
xLaycock, Frank.
Gifted Children. Scott F.
Laycock, George.
xLaycock, George.
Autumn of the Eagle. Scribner.
Caves. Schol Bk Serv.
Complete Beginner's Guide to Photography.
Doubleday.
Deer Hunter's Bible. Doubleday.
Does Your Pet Have a Sixth Sense. Doubleday.
Hunting with Bow & Arrow. Arco.
People & Other Mammals. Doubleday.
The Sign of the Flying Goose: The Story of the
National Wildlife Refuges. Peter Smith.
Strange Monsters & Great Searches.
Doubleday.
Layde, Durward C.
xLayde, Durwood C.
Introduction to Qualitative Analysis. Allyn.
Layde, Durwood C. see Layde, Durward C.
Laye, Camara, 1928-
xLaye, Camara.
The Dark Child. FS&G.
illus. Dream of Africa. Macmillan.
Layman, Emma M. see Layman, Emma McCloy.

Layman, Emma McCloy, 1910-
xLayman, Emma M.
Buddhism in America. Nelson-Hall.
Layman, Gil.
xLayman, Gil.
I Can Play, I Will Play. Bookworld Comm.
Layman, R. D., 1928-
xLayman, R. D.
To Ascend from a Floating Base: Shipboard
Aeronautics & Aviation, 1783-1914. Fairleigh
Dickinson.
Layton, Bentley.
xLayton, Bentley.
The Gnostic Treatise on Resurrection from
Nag Hammadi. Scholars Pr Ca.
Layton, R. B. see Layton, Reber B.
Layton, Reber B.
xLayton, R. B.
The Purple Martin. Nature Bks Pubs.
Laz, Medard.
xLaz, Medard.
Lift up My Spirit, Lord. Paulist Pr.
Lazar, Irwin.
xLazar, Irwin.
Electrical Systems Analysis & Design for
Industrial Plants. McGraw.
Lazar, May, 1887-
xLazar, May.
Reading Interests, Activities, & Opportunities
of Bright, Average, & Dull Children. AMS
Pr.
Lazar, Stephen H.
xLazar, Stephen H.
Barron's Guide to Financial Aid for Medical
Students. Barron.
Lazard, Naomi.
xLazard, Naomi.
Ordinances. Ardis Pubs.
Lazare, Aaron.
xLazare, Aaron.
Outpatient Psychiatry: Diagnosis & Treatment.
Williams & Wilkins.
Lazarev, Nikolai I. see Lazarev, Nikolai Ivanovich.
Lazarev, Nikolai Ivanovich, 1907-
xLazarev, Nikolai I.
Dyshormonal Tumors: The Theory of
Prophylaxis & Treatment. Plenum Pub.
Lazarev, V. G. see Lazarev, Vladimir Georgievich.
Lazarev, Vladimir Georgievich.
xLazarev, V. G.
ed. Synthesis of Digital Automata. Plenum Pub.
Lazarnick, George, 1913-
xLazarnick, George.
The Signature Book of Netsuke, Inro & Ojime
Artists in Photographs. Reed Pubs.
Lazaro, Timothy. see Lazaro, Timothy R.
Lazaro, Timothy R.
xLazaro, Timothy.
Urban Hydrology: A Multidisciplinary
Perspective. Ann Arbor Science.
Lazaron, Hilda. see Lazaron, Hilda R.
Lazaron, Hilda R., 1895-
xLazaron, Hilda.
Gabriel Marcel the Dramatist. Humanities.
Lazarov, Conner. see Lazarov, Connor.
Lazarov, Connor.
xLazarov, Conner.
Complex Actions of Lie Groups. Am Math.
Lazarre, Jane.
xLazarre, Jane.
On Loving Men. Dial.
Lazarsfeld, Paul F. see Lazarsfeld, Paul Felix.
Lazarsfeld, Paul Felix.
xLazarsfeld, Paul F.

An Introduction to Applied Sociology. Elsevier.
ed. Mathematical Thinking in the Social
Sciences. Russell.
The People's Choice: How the Voter Makes up
His Mind in a Presidential Campaign.
Columbia U Pr.
Lazarus, Arnold. see Lazarus, Arnold A.
Lazarus, Arnold A.
xLazarus, Arnold.
I Can If I Want to. Warner Bks.
Multimodal Behavior Therapy. Springer Pub.
xLazarus, Arnold A.
Clinical Behavior Therapy. Brunner-Mazel.
Lazarus, Arnold L. see Lazarus, Arnold Leslie.
Lazarus, Arnold Leslie.
xLazarus, Arnold L.
ed. The Indiana Experience: An Anthology.
Ind U Pr.
Lazarus, Emma, 1849-1887
xLazarus, Emma.
Admetus. Irvington.
Songs of a Semite. Irvington.
Lazarus, Gerald. see Lazarus, Gerald S.
Lazarus, Gerald S.
xLazarus, Gerald.
Diagnosis of Skin Disease. Davis Co.
Lazarus, Herbert M. see Lazarus, Herbert R.
Lazarus, Herbert R.
xLazarus, Herbert M.
How to Get Your Money's Worth Out of
Psychiatry. Sherbourne.
xLazarus, Herbert R.
How to Get Your Money's Worth Out of
Psychiatry. Sherbourne.
Lazarus, Joseph.
xLazarus, Joseph.
In Praise of the King Without a Face. The
Smith.
Lazarus, Josephine, 1846-1910
xLazarus, Josephine.
Spirit of Judaism. Arno.
Lazarus, Julius.
xLazarus, Julius.
Martha's Vineyard in Color. Hastings.
Lazarus, Keo F. see Lazarus, Keo Felker.
Lazarus, Keo Felker.
xLazarus, Keo F.
illus. A Totem for Ti-Jacques. Waveland Pr.
Lazarus, Lois.
xLazarus, Lois.
Country Is My Music!. Messner.
Lazarus, Mell, 1927-
xLazarus, Mell.
The Momma Treasury. Andrews & McMeel.
Lazarus, Richard. see Lazarus, Richard S.
Lazarus, Richard S.
xLazarus, Richard.
Patterns of Adjustment. McGraw.
xLazarus, Richard S.
Personality. P-H.
Lazarus, Simon.
xLazarus, Simon.
The Genteel Populists. McGraw.
Lazdina, Tereza B. see Lazdina, Tereza Budina.
Lazdina, Tereza Budina.
xLazdina, Tereza B.
Teach Yourself Latvian. McKay.
Lazebnik, Edith.
xLaZebnik, Edith.
Such a Life. G K Hall.
Such a Life. Morrow.
Lazell, James D.
xLazell, James D.
This Broken Archipelago: Cape Cod & the
Islands, Amphibians & Reptiles. Times Bks.
Lazenby, J. F. see Lazenby, John Francis.
Lazenby, John Francis.
xLazenby, J. F.

Hannibal's War: A Military History of the
Second Punic War. Intl Schol Bk Serv.
Lazenby, Walter.
xLazenby, Walter.
Arthur Wing Pinero. Twayne.
Lazer, Robert I.
xLazer, Robert I.
Appraising Managerial Performance: Current
Practices & Future Directions. Conference
Bd.
Lazere, M. R. *see* Lazere, Monroe R.
Lazere, Monroe R.
xLazere, M. R.
Commercial Financing. Wiley.
xLazere, Monroe R.
ed. Commercial Financing. Ronald Pr.
Lazerson, Marvin.
xLazerson, Marvin.
ed. American Education & Vocationalism: A
Documentary History 1870-1970. Tchrs Coll.
Origins of the Urban School: Public Education
in Massachusetts, 1870-1915. Harvard U Pr.
Lazes, Peter.
xLazes, Peter.
ed. The Handbook of Health Education. Aspen
Systems.
Lazzari, Eugene P.
xLazzari, Eugene P.
ed. Dental Biochemistry. Lea & Febiger.
Lazzarino, Graziana.
xLazzarino, Graziana.
Prego!: An Invitation to Italian. Random.
Lazzaro, Victor.
xLazzaro, Victor.
Systems & Procedures: A Handbook for
Business & Industry. P-H.
LBJ School of Public Affairs. *see* Lyndon B. Johnson
School of Public Affairs.
LDA-Symposium Copenhagen, 1975. *see*
Lda-Symposium, Technical University of Denmark,
1975.
**Lda-Symposium, Technical University of Denmark,
1975.**
xLDA-Symposium Copenhagen, 1975.
The Accuracy of Flow Measurements by Laser
Doppler Methods: Proceedings. Hemisphere
Pub.
Le Bar, Lois E. *see* Le Bar, Lois Emogene.
Le Bar, Lois Emogene, 1907-
xLe Bar, Lois E.
Education That Is Christian. Revell.
Focus on People in Church Education. Revell.
Le Berrurier, Diane O.
xLe Berrurier, Diane O.
The Pictorial Sources of Mythological &
Scientific Illustrations in Hrabanus Maurus'
De rerum naturis. Garland Pub.
Le Bon, Gustave, 1841-1931
xLe Bon, Gustave.
The Psychology of Peoples. Arno.
Le Breton, Anna L. *see* Le Breton, Anna Letitia Aikin.
Le Breton, Anna Letitia Aikin, 1808-1885
xLe Breton, Anna L.
Memoir of Mrs. Barbauld, Including Letters &
Notices of Her Family & Friends. AMS Pr.
Le Breton, Preston P.
xLe Breton, Preston P.
Dynamic World of Education for Business:
Issues, Trends, Forecasts. SW Pub.
Le Brocquy, Sybil.
xLe Brocquy, Sybil.
Swift's Most Valuable Friend. Dufour.
Le Cain, Errol.
xLe Cain, Errol.
illus. The White Cat. Bradbury Pr.
Le Carre, John.
xLe Carre, John.

Call for the Dead. Bantam.
Call for the Dead. Popular Lib.
The Honourable Schoolboy. Bantam.
The Honourable Schoolboy. G K Hall.
The Honourable Schoolboy. Knopf.
The Looking Glass War. Coward.
A Murder of Quality. Bantam.
A Murder of Quality. Popular Lib.
Smiley's People. Bantam.
Smiley's People. G K Hall.
Smiley's People. Knopf.
The Spy Who Came in from the Cold. Bantam.
The Spy Who Came in from the Cold. Coward.
Le Cato, Nathaniel J. *see* Le Cato, Nathaniel James
Walter.
Le Cato, Nathaniel James Walter, 1835-
xLe Cato, Nathaniel J.
The Curse of Caste. Arno.
Le Clercq, Chretien.
xLe Clercq, Chretien.
First Establishment of the Faith in New
France. AMS Pr.
Le Conte, Joseph, 1823-1901
xLe Conte, Joseph.
Race Problem in the South. Arno.
Le Corbeiller, Philippe, 1891-
xLe Corbeiller, Philippe E.
Matrix Analysis of Electric Networks. Johnson
Repr.
Le Corbeiller, Philippe E. *see* Le Corbeiller, Philippe.
Le Fanu, J. S. *see* Le Fanu, Joseph Sheridan.
Le Fanu, J. Sheridan. *see* Le Fanu, Joseph Sheridan.
Le Fanu, Joseph S. *see* Le Fanu, Joseph Sheridan.
Le Fanu, Joseph Sheridan, 1814-1873
xLe Fanu, J. S.
Ghost Stories & Mysteries. Dover.
xLe Fanu, J. Sheridan.
The Purcell Papers. Arkham.
xLe Fanu, Joseph S.
Checkmate. Arno.
Chronicles of Golden Friars. Arno.
The Evil Guest. Arno.
Ghost Stories & Tales of Mystery. Arno.
Guy Deverell. Arno.
In a Glass Darkly. Arno.
The Purcell Papers. AMS Pr.
Uncle Silas: A Tale of Bartram-Haugh. Arno.
Le Gall, A. *see* Le Gall, Andre.
Le Gall, Andre, 1904-
xLe Gall, A.
Present Problems in the Democratization of
Secondary & Higher Education. Unipub.
Le Gallienne, Richard, 1866-1947
xLe Gallienne, Richard.
Attitudes & Avowals with Some Retrospective
Reviews. Arno.
Le Gallienne Book of American Verse. R West.
Le Gentil, Pierre.
xLe Gentil, Pierre.
Chanson De Roland. Harvard U Pr.
Le Grand, Yves, 1908-
xLe Grand, Yves.
Form & Space Vision. Ind U Pr.
Le Guin, Ursula. *see* Le Guin, Ursula K.
Le Guin, Ursula K., 1929-
xLe Guin, Ursula.
Leese Webster. Atheneum.
xLe Guin, Ursula K.

The Beginning Place. Har-Row.
The Farthest Shore. Atheneum.
The Farthest Shore. Bantam.
From Elfland to Poughkeepsie. Pendragon
Oregon.
ed. Interfaces. Ace Bks.
The Language of the Night: Essays on Fantasy
& Science Fiction. Putnam.
The Language of the Night: Essays on Fantasy
& Science Fiction. Putnam.
The Left Hand of Darkness. Har-Row.
Orsinian Tales. Har-Row.
Planet of Exile. Ace Bks.
Planet of Exile. Garland Pub.
Planet of Exile. Har-Row.
The Word for World Is Forest. Berkley Pub.
Le Massena, C.E.
xLe Massena, Clarence E.
Galli-Curci's Life of Song. Monitor.
Le Massena, Clarence E. *see* Le Massena, C.E.
Le Mee, Katharine W.
xLe Mee, Katherine W.
A Metrical Study of Five Lais of Marie De
France. Mouton.
Le Mee, Katharine W. *see* Le Mee, Katharine W.
Le Noble, William J. *see* Le Noble, William Jacobus.
Le Noble, William Jacobus, 1928
xLe Noble, William J.
Highlights of Organic Chemistry: An Advanced
Textbook. Dekker.
Le Paillot, Jean.
xLe Paillot, Jean.
Caroline & the King's Hunt. Schol Bk Serv.
Caroline at the King's Ball. Schol Bk Serv.
Le Patourel, John. *see* Le Patourel, John Herbert.
Le Patourel, John Herbert.
xLe Patourel, John.
The Norman Empire. Oxford U Pr.
Le Porrier, Herbert.
xLe Porrier, Herbert.
The Doctor from Cordova: A Biographical
Novel About the Great Philosopher
Maimonides. Doubleday.
Le Queux, William, 1864-1927
xLe Queux, William.
The Great White Queen: A Tale of Treasure &
Treason. Arno.
Le Rossignol, James E. *see* Le Rossignol, James Edward.
Le Rossignol, James Edward, 1866-
xLe Rossignol, James E.
Backgrounds to Communist Thought. Peter
Smith.
Le Roy, Alexander. *see* Le Roy, Alexandre.
Le Roy, Alexandre, Abp, 1854-1938
xLe Roy, Alexander.
Religion of the Primitives. Negro U Pr.
Le Roy, Gaylord C.
xLe Roy, Gaylord C.
Perplexed Prophets: Six Nineteenth Century
British Authors. Greenwood.
Le Sage, Alain R. *see* Le Sage, Alain Rene.
Le Sage, Alain Rene, 1668-1747
xLe Sage, Alain R.
The History & Adventures of Gil Blas of
Santillane. Garland Pub.
Le Sage, Laurent, 1913-
xLe Sage, Laurent.
Rhumb Line of Symbolism: French Poets from
Sainte-Beuve to Valery, Presentation &
Selected Texts. Pa St U Pr.
Le Senne, Rene.
xLe Senne, Rene.
Obstacle & Value. Northwestern U Pr.
Le Strange, Richard.
xLe Strange, Richard.
Complete Descriptive Guide to British
Monumental Brasses. Transatlantic.
A History of Herbal Plants. Arco.
Le Sueur, Meridel.
xLe Sueur, Meridel.

Conquistadores. Watts.
The Girl. West End.
Le Tord, Bijou.
xLe Tord, Bijou.
illus. The Generous Cow. Schol Bk Serv.
illus. Nice & cozy. Schol Bk Serv.
illus. A Perfect Place to Be. Schol Bk Serv.
Picking & Weaving. Schol Bk Serv.
Le Vine, Victor T.
xLe Vine, Victor T.
Cameroon Federal Republic. Cornell U Pr.
The Cameroons from Mandate to
Independence. Greenwood.
Historical Dictionary of Cameroon. Scarecrow.
Le Winn, Edward B. *see* Le Winn, Edward Bernard.
Le Winn, Edward Bernard, 1904-
xLe Winn, Edward B.
Human Neurological Organization. C C
Thomas.
Le-Tan, Pierre.
xLe-Tan, Pierre.
illus. The Afternoon Cat. Pantheon.
illus. Happy Birthday Oliver!. Random.
illus. Timothy's Dream Book. FS&G.
Lea, H. *see* Lea, Hermann.
Lea, Henry C. *see* Lea, Henry Charles.
Lea, Henry Charles.
xLea, Henry C.
The Duel & the Oath. U of Pa Pr.
History of Auricular Confession & Indulgences
in the Latin Church. Greenwood.
A History of the Inquisition in the Middle
Ages. Gordon Pr.
History of the Inquisition of the Middle Ages.
Russell.
The Ordeal. U of Pa Pr.
Torture. U of Pa Pr.
Lea, Hermann.
xLea, H.
Thomas Hardy's Wessex. Gordon Pr.
xLea, Hermann.
Thomas Hardy's Wessex. Arden Lib.
Thomas Hardy's Wessex.. Folcroft.
Lea, K. J.
xLea, K. J.
Geography of Scotland. David & Charles.
Lea, Tom, 1907-
xLea, Tom.
The Wonderful Country. Gregg.
Lea, W. *see* Lea, Wayne A.
Lea, Wayne A.
xLea, W.
Trends in Speech Recognition. P-H.
Leab, Daniel. *see* Leab, Daniel J.
Leab, Daniel J.
xLeab, Daniel.
From Sambo to Superspade: The Black
Experience in Motion Pictures. HM.
Leacacos, John P.
xLeacacos, John P.
Fires in the in-Basket: The ABC's of the State
Department. Greenwood.
Leach, Arthur F. *see* Leach, Arthur Francis.
Leach, Arthur Francis, 1851-1915
xLeach, Arthur F.
English Schools at the Reformation, 1546-1548.
Russell.
Leach, Bernard. *see* Leach, Bernard Howell.
Leach, Bernard Howell.
xLeach, Bernard.
Hamada, Potter. Kodansha.
Leach, Christopher.
xLeach, Christopher.
The Great Book Raid. Warne.
Meeting Miss Hannah. Warne.
Leach, D. *see* Leach, Donald P.
Leach, Donald P.
xLeach, D.
Mathematics for Electronics. Reston.
Leach, Douglas E. *see* Leach, Douglas Edward.

Leach, Douglas Edward, 1920-
xLeach, Douglas E.
Flintlock & Tomahawk: New England in King
Philip's War. Norton.
The Northern Colonial Frontier, 1607-1763. U
of NM Pr.
Leach, E. R. *see* Leach, Edmund Ronald.
Leach, Edmund R. *see* Leach, Edmund Ronald.
Leach, Edmund Ronald.
xLeach, E. R.
Political Systems of Highland Burma: A Study
of Kachin Social Structure. Humanities.
Rethinking Anthropology. Humanities.
xLeach, Edmund R.
Aspects of Caste in South India, Ceylon &
North West Pakistan. Cambridge U Pr.
Dialectic in Practical Religion. Cambridge U
Pr.
Leach, H. G. *see* Leach, Henry Goddard.
Leach, Henry G. *see* Leach, Henry Goddard.
Leach, Henry Goddard, 1880-1970
xLeach, H. G.
Angevin Britain & Scandinavia. Kraus Repr.
xLeach, Henry G.
ed. Pageant of Old Scandinavia. Arno.
Leach, John.
xLeach, John.
The Gift of Winter. P-H.
Pompey the Great. Rowman.
Leach, Joseph.
xLeach, Joseph.
Bright Particular Star: The Life & Times of
Charlotte Cushman. Yale U Pr.
What Then Is the American This New Woman.
Tex Western.
Leach, Josiah G. *see* Leach, Josiah Granville.
Leach, Josiah Granville, 1842-1922
xLeach, Josiah G.
The History of the Girard National Bank of
Philadelphia, 1832-1902. Greenwood.
Leach, MacEdward, 1896-
xLeach, MacEdward.
ed. Ballad Book. A S Barnes.
Leach, Maria.
xLeach, Maria.
The Lion Sneezed: Folktales & Myths of the
Cat. T Y Crowell.
The Luck Book. Dell.
Noodles, Nitwits & Numskulls. Dell.
Riddle Me, Riddle Me, Ree. Penguin.
Riddle Me, Riddle Me, Ree. Viking Pr.
Leach, Michael, 1940-
xLeach, Michael.
Don't Call Me Orphan!. Westminster.
Leach, R. *see* Leach, Robert.
Leach, Richard H.
xLeach, Richard H.
ed. Contemporary Canada. Duke.
Dimensions of State & Urban Policy Making.
Macmillan.
Leach, Robert.
xLeach, R.
ed. Folk Music in School. Cambridge U Pr.
Musical Thesaurus: A Dictionary of Musical
Language. Newbury Bks Inc.
Leach, Robert J.
xLeach, Robert J.
Women Ministers: A Quaker Contribution.
Pendle Hill.
Leach, W. Barton. *see* Leach, Walter Barton.
Leach, Walter Barton, 1900-
xLeach, W. Barton.
Cases & Text on the Law of Wills. Little.
Handbook of Massachusetts Evidence. Little.
Leacock, Eleanor B. *see* Leacock, Eleanor Burke.
Leacock, Eleanor Burke, 1922-
xLeacock, Eleanor B.

ed. Culture of Poverty: A Critique. S&S.
ed. North American Indians in Historical
Perspective. Random.
Leacock, Stephen. *see* Leacock, Stephen Butler.
Leacock, Stephen B. *see* Leacock, Stephen Butler.
Leacock, Stephen Butler, 1869-1944
xLeacock, Stephen.
Mark Twain. Haskell.
xLeacock, Stephen B.
Literary Lapses. Arno.
Sunshine Sketches of a Little Town. Arno.
Leacroft, Helen.
xLeacroft, Helen.
The Buildings of Ancient Egypt. A-W.
The Buildings of Ancient Greece. A-W.
The Buildings of Ancient Man. A-W.
Leacroft, Richard.
xLeacroft, Richard.
The Development of the English Playhouse.
Cornell U Pr.
Leadbeater, Charles W. *see* Leadbeater, Charles Webster.
Leadbeater, Charles Webster, 1847-1934
xLeadbeater, Charles W.
The Inner Life. Theos Pub Hse.
Leader, Mary.
xLeader, Mary.
Salem's Children. Coward.
Leader, Ninon A. *see* Leader, Ninon A. M.
Leader, Ninon A. M.
xLeader, Ninon A.
Hungarian Classical Ballads & Their Folklore.
Cambridge U Pr.
Leader, Robert W., 1919-
xLeader, Robert W.
Diseases of Latent & Slow Growth Viruses.
Mss Info.
Leaf, Alexander.
xLeaf, Alexander.
Renal Pathophysiology. Oxford U Pr.
ed. Renal Pathophysiology - Recent Advances.
Raven.
Leaf, David.
xLeaf, David.
The Beach Boys & the California Myth. G&D.
Leaf, Munro.
xLeaf, Munro.
Noodle. Schol Bk Serv.
Story of Ferdinand. Penguin.
The Story of Ferdinand. Viking Pr.
illus. Turnabout. Lippincott.
Leaf, Murray J.
xLeaf, Murray J.
Information & Behavior in a Sikh Village:
Social Organization Reconsidered. U of Cal
Pr.
Man, Mind, & Science: A History of
Anthropology. Columbia U Pr.
Leaf, Ruth.
xLeaf, Ruth.
Intaglio Printmaking Techniques.
Watson-Guptill.
Leaf, VaDonna. *see* Leaf, VaDonna Jean.
Leaf, VaDonna Jean.
xLeaf, VaDonna.
Robbie & the Stolen Minibike. Creation Hse.
League for Industrial Democracy.
xLeague for Industrial Democracy.
Industrial Democracy. Greenwood.
League for Social Reconstruction.
xLeague for Social Reconstruction.
Social Planning for Canada. U of Toronto Pr.
League of Nations.
xLeague of Nations.
European Conference on Rural Life. AMS Pr.
Taxation of Foreign & National Enterprises.
Oceana.
League of Women Voters Education Fund. *see* League of
Women Voters of the United States. Education Fund.
League of Women Voters of Massachusetts.
xLeague Of Women Voters Of Massachusetts.

Massachusetts State Government. Harvard U
Pr.

League of Women Voters of New Jersey.
xLeague of Women Voters of New Jersey.
New Jersey: Spotlight on Government. Rutgers
U Pr.

League of Women Voters of Pennsylvania.
xLeague of Women Voters of Pennsylvania.
Key to the Keystone State: Pennsylvania.
LWVPA.
Land Use. LWVPA.

League of Women Voters of the United States.
xLeague of Women Voters of the United States.
The Politics of Trade. LWV US.
Who Should Elect the President. LWV US.

**League of Women Voters of the United States.
Education Fund.**
xLeague of Women Voters Education Fund.
Achieving "Due Responsibility": Perspectives
on the American Presidency. LWV US.
Campaigning for Fair School Finance: Cases in
Point. LWV US.
Choosing the President. LWV US.
Choosing the President. Nelson.
Choosing the President: 1980 Edition. LWV
US.
Energy Dilemmas: An Overview of U. S.
Energy Problems & Issues. LWV US.
Energy Options: Examining Sources &
Defining Government's Role. LWV US.
The Growth of Judicial Power: Perspectives on
"the Least Dangerous Branch". LWV US.
Indian Country. LWV US.
Know Your Community. LWV US.
Our "Compound Republic": Perspectives on
American Federalism. LWV US.
Past As Prologue: Present Perspectives. LWV
US.
Perspectives on Congress: Performance &
Prospects. LWV US.
Reduce: Targets, Means & Impacts of Source
Reduction. LWV US.
Supercity, Hometown U. S. A.: Prospects for
Two-Tier Government. LWV US.
What Ever Happened to Open Housing: A
Handbook for Fair Housing Monitors. LWV
US.
You & Your National Government. LWV US.
xLeague Of Women Voters Of The United States
Education Fund.
Big Water Fight: Citizen Action. Greene.

Leahey, Thomas H. see Leahey, Thomas Hardy.
Leahey, Thomas Hardy.
xLeahey, Thomas H.
A History of Psychology. P-H.

Leahy, D. G.
xLeahy, D. G.
Novitas Mundi: Perception of the History of
Being. NYU Pr.

Leahy, Irene M.
xLeahy, Irene M.
The Nurse & Radiotherapy: A Manual for
Daily Care. Mosby.

Leahy, James.
xLeahy, James.
The Cinema of Joseph Losey. A S Barnes.

Leahy, Syrell R. see Leahy, Syrell Rogovin.
Leahy, Syrell Rogovin.
xLeahy, Syrell R.
Circle of Love. Putnam.

Leake, Jane A. see Leake, Jane Acomb.
Leake, Jane Acomb.
xLeake, Jane A.
Geats of Beowulf: A Study in the Geographical
Mythology of the Middle Ages. U of Wis Pr.

Leake, Lucy D.
xLeake, Lucy D.
Comparative Histology: An Introduction to the
Microscopic Structure of Animals. Acad Pr.

Leakey, C. L. see Leakey, C. L. A.

Leakey, C. L. A.
xLeakey, C. L.
ed. Food Crops of the Lowland Tropics.
Oxford U Pr.

Leakey, L. S. see Leakey, Louis Seymour Bazett.
Leakey, Louis S. see Leakey, Louis Seymour Bazett.
Leakey, Louis Seymour Bazett.
xLeakey, L. S.
Adam's Ancestors: The Evolution of Man &
His Culture. Har-Row.
xLeakey, Louis S.
Stone Age Africa: An Outline of Prehistory in
Africa. Negro U Pr.
White African: An Early Autobiography.
Schenkman.

Leakey, Richard. see Leakey, Richard E.
Leakey, Richard E.
xLeakey, Richard.
Origins: What New Discoveries Reveal About
the Emergence of Our Species & Its Possible
Future. Dutton.
xLeakey, Richard E.
People of the Lake: Mankind & Its Beginnings.
Doubleday.

Leaman, David R., 1947-
xLeaman, David R.
Making Decisions: A Guide for Couples.
Herald Pr.

Leamer, Edward E.
xLeamer, Edward E.
ed. Quantitative International Economics.
Aldine Pub.
Specification Searches: Ad Hoc Inference with
Nonexperimental Data. Wiley.

Leamer, Robert B.
xLeamer, Robert B.
Bottoms up Cookery. Fathom Ents.

Leaming. see Leaming, Marj P.
Leaming, Marj P.
xLeaming.
Administrative Office Management: A Practical
Approach. Wm C Brown.

Leamy, Edmund, 1848-1904
xLeamy, Edmund.
Fairy Minstrel of Glenmalure & Other Stories
for Children. Core Collection.
Golden Spears & Other Fairy Tales. Core
Collection.

Lean, Arthur E. see Lean, Arthur Edward.
Lean, Arthur Edward, 1909-
xLean, Arthur E.
And Merely Teach: Irreverent Essays on the
Mythology of Education. S Ill U Pr.

Lean, Geoffrey, 1947-
xLean, Geoffrey.
Rich World, Poor World. Allen Unwin.

Leander, Ed.
xLeander, Ed.
What's the Big Idea?. Quist.

Lear, Edward.
xLear, Edward.
The Courtship of the Yonghy-Bonghy-Bo & the
New Vestments. Viking Pr.
Four Little Children Who Went Around the
World. Macmillan.
The Owl & the Pussy Cat. Atheneum.
The Owl & the Pussycat. Little.

Lear, Jonathan.
xLear, Jonathan.
Aristotle & Logical Theory. Cambridge U Pr.

Lear, Martha W. see Lear, Martha Weinman.
Lear, Martha Weinman.
xLear, Martha W.
Heartsounds. S&S.

Lear, Roma.
xLear, Roma.
Play Helps: Toys & Activities for Handicapped
Children. Intl Ideas.

Learmouth, John.
xLearmouth, John.

Soccer Fundamentals: Basic Techniques &
Training for Beginning Players. St Martin.
Swimming for Fitness & Fun. David & Charles.

Learn, C. R.
xLearn, C. R.
ed. Backpacker's Digest. Follett.
Bowhunter's Digest. Follett.

Learned, Edmund P. see Learned, Edmund Philip.
Learned, Edmund Philip.
xLearned, Edmund P.
Organization Theory & Policy: Notes for
Analysis. Irwin.

Learned, Henry B. see Learned, Henry Barrett.
Learned, Henry Barrett, 1868-1931
xLearned, Henry B.
The President's Cabinet: Studies in the Origin,
Formation & Structure of an American
Institution. B Franklin.

Learned, William S. see Learned, William Setchel.
Learned, William Setchel, 1876-1950
xLearned, William S.
Quality of the Educational Process in the
United States & Europe. Arno.

Learning Institute of North Carolina.
xLearning Institute of North Carolina.
Who Cares for Children?: A Survey of Child
Care Services in North Carolina. Learning
Inst NC.

Learning Technology Inc. see Learning Technology
Incorporated.
Learning Technology Incorporated.
xLearning Technology Inc.
ed. Basic Spelling Skills: A Program for
Self-Instruction. McGraw.
ed. Library Skills: A Program for
Self-Instruction. McGraw.
ed. Paragraph Patterns: A Program for
Self-Instruction. McGraw.
ed. Writing Skills One: A Program for
Self-Instruction. McGraw.
ed. Writing Skills Two: A Program for
Self-Instruction. McGraw.
xLearning Technology Incorporated.
Basic Spelling Skills. McGraw.

Leary, Lewis. see Leary, Lewis Gaston.
Leary, Lewis Gaston, 1906-
xLeary, Lewis.
Articles on American Literature: 1900-1950.
Duke.
ed. Articles on American Literature:
1950-1967. Duke.
Compiled by Articles on American Literature,
1968-1975. Duke.
Norman Douglas. Columbia U Pr.
Ralph Waldo Emerson: An Interpretive Essay.
Twayne.
Soundings: Some Early American Writers. U of
Ga Pr.
Southern Excursions: Essays on Mark Twain &
Others. La State U Pr.

Leary, Timothy. see Leary, Timothy Francis.
Leary, Timothy Francis, 1920-
xLeary, Timothy.
The Game of Life. Peace Pr.

Leary, William G. see Leary, William Gordon.
Leary, William Gordon.
xLeary, William G.
Thought & Statement. HarBraceJ.

Leary, William M. see Leary, William Matthew.
Leary, William Matthew, 1934-
xLeary, William M.
The Dragon's Wings: The China National
Aviation Corporation & the Development of
Commercial Aviation in China. U of Ga Pr.

Lease, Benjamin.
xLease, Benjamin.
That Wild Fellow John Neal & the American
Literary Revolution. U of Chicago Pr.

Leasor, James.
xLeasor, James.

Boarding Party. HM.
Leatham, Aubrey.
xLeatham, Aubrey.
Auscultation of the Heart &
Phonocardiography. Churchill.
Leather, Edwin.
xLeather, Edwin.
The Mozart Score. Doubleday.
Leather, John.
xLeather, John.
Colin Archer & the Seaworthy Double-Ender.
Intl Marine.
A Panorama of Gaff Rig. Naval Inst Pr.
Leatherbarrow, Margaret. *see* Leatherbarrow, Margaret F.
Leatherbarrow, Margaret F.
xLeatherbarrow, Margaret.
Gold in the Grass. Rateavers.
Leathers. *see* Leathers, Dale G.
Leathers, Dale G., 1938-
xLeathers.
Orientations to Researching Communication.
SRA.
Leaton, E. H.
xLeaton, E. H.
Vectors. Allen Unwin.
Leavell, Byrd S. *see* Leavell, Byrd Stuart.
Leavell, Byrd Stuart.
xLeavell, Byrd S.
Fundamentals of Clinical Hematology.
Saunders.
Leavell, Landrum P.
xLeavell, Landrum P.
Angels, Angels, Angels. Broadman.
God's Spirit in You. Broadman.
Twelve Who Followed Jesus. Broadman.
Leavell, Robert N.
xLeavell, Robert N.
Cases & Materials on Equitable Remedies &
Restitution. West Pub.
Leavens, Evelyn.
xLeavens, Evelyn.
Boswell's Life of Boswell. S&S.
Leaver, R. H.
xLeaver, R. H.
Analysis & Presentation of Experimental
Results. Halsted Pr.
Leaver, Robin A.
xLeaver, Robin A.
Catherine Winkworth: The Influence of Her
Translations on English Hymnody. Univ
Microfilms.
Leavis, F. R. *see* Leavis, Frank Raymond.
Leavis, Frank R. *see* Leavis, Frank Raymond.
Leavis, Frank Raymond, 1895-
xLeavis, F. R.
The Common Pursuit. NYU Pr.
D. H. Lawrence. Haskell.
Dickens the Novelist. Rutgers U Pr.
The Living Principle: English As a Discipline
of Thought. Oxford U Pr.
Thought, Words & Creativity: Art & Thought
in Lawrence. Oxford U Pr.
xLeavis, Frank R.
Culture & Environment: The Training of
Critical Awareness. Greenwood.
D. H. Lawrence. Folcroft.
For Continuity. Arno.
For Continuity. Folcroft.
Revaluation: Tradition & Development in
English Poetry. Greenwood.
xLeavis, Q. D.
jt. auth. Dickens the Novelist. Rutgers U Pr.
Leavis, Q. D. *see* Leavis, Queenie Dorothy.
Leavis, Queenie Dorothy.
xLeavis, Q. D.
Fiction & the Reading Public. Folcroft.
Leavitt, Alga E.
xLeavitt, Alga W.

ed. Stories & Poems from the Old North State.
Arno.
Leavitt, Alga W. *see* Leavitt, Alga E.
Leavitt, G. S. *see* Leavitt, Glenn Sheffield.
Leavitt, Glenn Sheffield.
xLeavitt, G. S.
Oral-Aural Communications (OAC): A
Teacher's Manual. C C Thomas.
Leavitt, Guy P.
xLeavitt, Guy P.
Teach with Success. Standard Pub.
Leavitt, Harold. *see* Leavitt, Harold J.
Leavitt, Harold J.
xLeavitt, Harold.
ed. Organizations of the Future: Interaction
with the External Environment. Praeger.
xLeavitt, Harold J.
The Organizational World. HarBraceJ.
ed. Readings in Managerial Psychology. U of
Chicago Pr.
Leavitt, John F.
xLeavitt, John F.
illus. The Charles W. Morgan. Mystic Seaport.
Leavitt, Judith W. *see* Leavitt, Judith Walzer.
Leavitt, Judith Walzer.
xLeavitt, Judith W.
ed. Sickness & Health in America: Readings in
the History of Medicine & Public Health. U
of Wis Pr.
Leavitt, Richard F.
xLeavitt, Richard F.
The World of Tennessee Williams. Putnam.
Leavitt, Ruby R. *see* Leavitt, Ruby Rohrlich.
Leavitt, Ruby Rohrlich.
xLeavitt, Ruby R.
The Puerto Ricans: Culture Change &
Language Deviance. U of Ariz Pr.
Leavitt, Ruth.
xLeavitt, Ruth.
ed. Artist & Computer. Creative Comp.
ed. Artist & Computer. Crown.
Leavitt, Teddy C. *see* Leavitt, Teddy C. J.
Leavitt, Teddy C. J.
xLeavitt, Teddy C.
Limits & Continuity. McGraw.
Leavitt, Thomas W.
xLeavitt, Thomas W.
ed. The Hollingworth Letters: Technical
Change in the Textile Industry, 1826-1837.
Merrimack Vall Textile.
Leavy, Herbert T.
xLeavy, Herbert T.
Successful Small Farms: Building Plans &
Methods. Structures Pub.
Leavy, Morton L.
xLeavy, Morton L.
Law of Adoption. Oceana.
Lebaron, Dean.
xLeBaron, Dean.
The Ins and Outs of Institutional Investing.
Nelson-Hall.
Lebeaux, Richard, 1946-
xLebeaux, Richard.
Young Man Thoreau. Har-Row.
Young Man Thoreau. U of Mass Pr.
Lebeck, Anne.
xLebeck, Anne.
Oresteia: A Study in Language & Structure.
Harvard U Pr.
Lebedev, N. N. *see* Lebedev, Nikolai Nikolaevich.
Lebedev, Nikolai Nikolaevich.
xLebedev, N. N.
Special Functions & Their Applications. Dover.
Worked Problems in Applied Mathematics.
Dover.
Lebenthal, Emanuel.
xLebenthal, Emanuel.
ed. Digestive Diseases in Children. Grune.
Lebergott, Stanley.
xLebergott, Stanley.

The American Economy: Income, Wealth, &
Want. Princeton U Pr.
Lebesgue, Henri. *see* Lebesgue, Henri Leon.
Lebesgue, Henri Leon, 1875-1941
xLebesgue, Henri.
Lecons sur L'integration et la Recherche des
Fonctions Primitives. Chelsea Pub.
Lebhar, Godfrey M. *see* Lebhar, Godfrey Montague.
Lebhar, Godfrey Montague, 1882-
xLebhar, Godfrey M.
Chain Stores in America: 1859-1962. Lebhar
Friedman.
Leblanc. *see* Leblanc, Lawrence J.
LeBlanc, Dudley J.
xLeBlanc, J. Dudley.
The Acadian Miracle. Claitors.
Leblanc, Hughes. *see* Leblanc, Hugues.
Leblanc, Hugues, 1924-
xLeblanc, Hughes.
Existence, Truth, & Provability. State U NY
Pr.
LeBlanc, J. Dudley. *see* LeBlanc, Dudley J.
LeBlanc, Joyce Y. *see* LeBlanc, Joyce Yeldell.
LeBlanc, Joyce Yeldell.
xLeBlanc, Joyce Y.
Pelican Guide to Gardens of Louisiana.
Pelican.
Leblanc, Lawrence J.
xLeblanc.
The OAS & the Promotion & Protection of
Human Rights. Kluwer Boston.
Leblanc, Maurice, 1864-1941
xLeblanc, Maurice.
The Eight Strokes of the Clock. Hyperion
Conn.
The Exploits of Arsene Lupin. Arno.
Lebo, Fern.
xLebo, Fran.
The Elegance with Ease Cookbook. Hammond
Inc.
Lebo, Fran. *see* Lebo, Fern.
Leboeuf, Michael.
xLeBoeuf, Michael.
Working Smart: How to Accomplish More in
Half the Time. Warner Bks.
Lebon, J. H. *see* Lebon, J H G.
Lebon, J H G.
xLebon, J. H.
Introduction to Human Geography.
Humanities.
Lebow, Richard N. *see* Lebow, Richard Ned.
Lebow, Richard Ned.
xLebow, Richard N.
White Britain & Black Ireland: The Influence
of Stereotypes on Colonial Policy. Inst Study
Human.
Lebowitz, Alan.
xLebowitz, Alan.
Progress into Silence: A Study of Melville's
Heroes. Ind U Pr.
Lebowitz, Naomi.
xLebowitz, Naomi.
Humanism & the Absurd in the Modern Novel.
Northwestern U Pr.
The Imagination of Loving: Henry James's
Legacy to the Novel. Wayne St U Pr.
Leboyer, Frederick.
xLeboyer, Frederick.
Inner Beauty, Inner Light. Knopf.
Lebra, William P.
xLebra, William P.
ed. Culture-Bound Syndromes,
Ethno-Psychiatry, & Alternate Therapies. U
Pr of Hawaii.
Okinawan Religion: Belief, Ritual, & Social
Structure. U Pr of Hawaii.
Lechford, Thomas.
xLechford, Thomas.

Plain Dealing: Or News from New England.
Johnson Repr.

Lechler, Doris.
xLechler, Doris.
A Collector's Guide to Children's Glass
Dishes. Nelson.

Lechner, Alan. *see* Lechner, Alan B.

Lechner, Alan B.
xLechner, Alan.
Street Games: Inside Stories of the Wall Street
Hustle. Har-Row.

Lecht, Charles P. *see* Lecht, Charles Philip.

Lecht, Charles Philip.
xLecht, Charles P.
The Waves of Change: A Techno-Economic
Analysis of the Data Processing Industry.
Advanced Computer.

Lecht, Leonard A. *see* Lecht, Leonard Abe.

Lecht, Leonard Abe, 1920-
xLecht, Leonard A.
Experience Under Railway Labor Legislation.
AMS Pr.

Leckart, Bruce.
xLeckart, Bruce.
Up from Boredom, Down from Fear. Marek.

Lecker, Sidney.
xLecker, Sidney.
Family Ties: How to Love the Bonds & Leave
the Bondage. Wyden.
Money Personality. S&S.

Leckie, Robert.
xLeckie, Robert.
The World Turned Upside Down: The Story of
the American Revolution. Putnam.

Lecky, W. E. *see* Lecky, William Edward Hartpole.
Lecky, William. *see* Lecky, William Edward Hartpole.
Lecky, William E. *see* Lecky, William Edward Hartpole.

Lecky, William Edward Hartpole, 1838-1903
xLecky, W. E.
A History of Ireland in the Eighteenth
Century. U of Chicago Pr.
xLecky, William.
Historical & Political Essays. Arno.
xLecky, William E.
Historical & Political Essays. Folcroft.
History of England in the Eighteenth Century.
AMS Pr.
History of Ireland in the Eighteenth Century.
AMS Pr.
xLecky, Wm. Edward.
Leaders of Public Opinion in Ireland. Da Capo.
Lecky, Wm. Edward. *see* Lecky, William Edward
Hartpole.

Leclerc, Eloi.
xLeclerc, Eloi.
Exile & Tenderness. Franciscan Herald.
People of God in the Night. Franciscan Herald.

Leclerc, J. C.
xLeclerc, J. C.
Cell Surface Alteration As a Result of
Malignant Transformation, No. 1. Mss Info.

Leclercq, Jean, 1911-
xLeclercq, Jean.
Aspects of Monasticism. Cistercian Pubns.
Monks & Love in Twelfth-Century France:
Psycho-Historical Essays. Oxford U Pr.

Lecomber, Brian.
xLecomber, Brian.
Talk Down. Berkley Pub.
Talk Down. Coward.
Turn Killer. PB.
Turn Killer. S&S.

Lecomber, J. R. C.
xLecomber, Richard.
Economics of Natural Resources. Halsted Pr.
Lecomber, Richard. *see* Lecomber, J. R. C.

Lecourt, Dominique.
xLecourt, Dominique.

Proletarian Science?: The Case of Lysenko.
Schocken.

Ledbetter, Gordon.
xLedbetter, Gordon T.
The Great Irish Tenor. Scribner.
Ledbetter, Gordon T. *see* Ledbetter, Gordon.

Ledbetter, Jack W.
xLedbetter, Jack W.
Texas Family Law. U of Tex Busn Res.

Ledbetter, Rosanna, 1932-
xLedbetter, Rosanna.
A History of the Malthusian League,
1877-1927. Ohio St U Pr.

Leddy, Tracy, 1940-
xLeddy, Tracy.
The Song of Everything & Other Stories. Sant
Bani Ash.

Ledeen, Michael A. *see* Ledeen, Michael Arthur.

Ledeen, Michael Arthur, 1941-
xLedeen, Michael A.
The First Duce: D'Annunzio at Fiume. Johns
Hopkins.

Leder, Lawrence. *see* Leder, Lawrence H.

Leder, Lawrence H.
xLeder, Lawrence.
Liberty & Authority: Early American Political
Ideology, 1689-1763. Norton.
xLeder, Lawrence H.
Dimensions of Change: Problems & Issues of
American Colonial History. Burgess.
Liberty & Authority: Early American Political
Ideology, 1689-1763. Times Bks.
ed. Meaning of the American Revolution. New
Viewpoints.

Lederer, C. Michael. *see* Lederer, Charles Michael.

Lederer, Charles Michael.
xLederer, C. Michael.
Table of Isotopes. Wiley.

Lederer, Chloe.
xLederer, Chloe.
Down the Hill of the Sea. Lothrop.

Lederer, Katherine.
xLederer, Katherine.
Lillian Hellman. Twayne.

Lederer, Katrin.
xLederer, Katrin.
ed. Human Needs: A Contribution to the
Current Debate. Oelgeschlager.

Lederer, Muriel.
xLederer, Muriel.
The Guide to Career Education. Times Bks.
Lederer, W. *see* Lederer, William J.

Lederer, William J.
xLederer, W.
Ugly American. Fawcett.
xLederer, William J.
Complete Cross-Country Skiing & Ski Touring.
Norton.
The Deceptive American. Norton.
Nation of Sheep. Norton.
Our Own Worst Enemy. Norton.

Lederer, Wolfgang.
xLederer, Wolfgang.
Dragons, Delinquents & Destiny: An Essay on
Positive Superego Functions. Intl Univs Pr.
The Fear of Women. Grune.
Fear of Women. HarBraceJ.

Lederman, Minna.
xLederman, Minna.
ed. Stravinsky in the Theatre. Da Capo.
Ledermann, W. *see* Ledermann, Walter.

Ledermann, Walter, 1911-
xLedermann, W.
Introduction to Group Characters. Cambridge
U Pr.
xLedermann, Walter.
Integral Calculus. Routledge & Kegan.
Multiple Integrals. Routledge & Kegan.

Ledgard, Henry F.
xLedgard, Henry F.

Pascal with Style: Programming Proverbs.
Hayden.
Programming Proverbs. Hayden.
Programming Proverbs for FORTRAN
Programmers. Hayden.

Ledger, William J., 1932-
xLedger, William J.
Infection in the Female. Lea & Febiger.

Ledin, George.
xLedin, George.
The Programmer's Book of Rules. CBI Pub.
The Programmer's Book of Rules. Lifetime
Learn.
A Structured Approach to Essential Basic.
Boyd & Fraser.
A Structured Approach to General BASIC.
Boyd & Fraser.

Ledl, Arthur. *see* Ledl, Artur.

Ledl, Artur.
xLedl, Arthur.
Studien Zur Alteren Athenischen
Verfassungsgeschichte. Arno.

Lednicer, Daniel.
xLednicer, Daniel.
The Organic Chemistry of Drug Synthesis.
Wiley.

Ledogar, Robert J.
xLedogar, Robert J.
Hungry for Profits: U. S. Food & Drug
Multinationals in Latin America. IDOC.

Ledson, Sidney.
xLedson, Sidney.
Teach Your Child to Read in 60 Days. Norton.

Leduc, Violette, 1907-1972
xLeduc, Violette.
The Taxi. FS&G.

Lee, A. G. *see* Lee, Anthony Gordon.

Lee, A. James.
xLee, A. James.
Employment, Unemployment & Health
Insurance: Behavioral & Descriptive Analysis
of Health Insurance Loss Due to
Unemployment. Abt Assoc.

Lee, A. Collingwood.
xLee, A. Collingwood.
Decameron: Its Sources & Analogues. Haskell.

Lee, Albert.
xLee, Albert.
How to Profit from Your Arts & Crafts.
McKay.
How to Save Money Through Group Buying.
Stein & Day.
The Total Couple. Cornerstone.
The Total Couple. Lorenz Pr.

Lee, Alec M.
xLee, Alec M.
Applied Queueing Theory. St Martin.

Lee, Alfred M. *see* Lee, Alfred McClung.

Lee, Alfred McClung, 1906-
xLee, Alfred M.
The Daily Newspaper in America: The
Evolution of a Social Instrument. Octagon.
ed. Principles of Sociology. Har-Row.
Sociology for Whom?. Oxford U Pr.
xLee, Alfred McClung.
Multivalent Man. Braziller.

Lee, Alvin A., 1930-
xLee, Alvin A.
The Guest Hall of Eden: Four Essays on the
Design of Old English Poetry. Yale U Pr.

Lee, Amy.
xLee, Amy.

Call Him a Man: The Story of Hazzard Parks.
Friend Pr.
Lee, Anthony Gordon.
xLee, A. G.
Chemistry of Thallium. Burgess-Intl Ideas.
Lee, Asher.
xLee, Asher.
ed. The Soviet Air & Rocket Forces.
Greenwood.
Lee, Benjamin.
xLee, Benjamin.
It Can't Be Helped. FS&G.
Lee, Betsy, 1949-
xLee, Betsy.
Charles Eastman. Dillon.
Lee, Beverly.
xLee, Beverly.
Easy Way to Chinese Cooking. NAL.
Lee, Beverly. *see* Lee, Beverly Haskell.
Lee, Beverly Haskell.
xLee, Beverly.
The Secret of Van Rink's Cellar. Lerner Pubns.
Lee, Bradford A.
xLee, Bradford A.
Britain & the Sino-Japanese War, 1937-1939: A
Study in the Dilemmas of British Decline.
Stanford U Pr.
Lee, Brian.
xLee, Brian.
Theory & Personality: The Significance of T. S.
Eliot's Criticism. Humanities.
Lee, Bruce.
xLee, Bruce.
Bruce Lee's Fighting Method. Ohara Pubns.
Bruce Lee's Fighting Method. Wehman.
Bruce Lee's Fighting Method: Basic Training.
Ohara Pubns.
Tao of Jeet Kune Do. Ohara Pubns.
Lee, C. H. *see* Lee, Clive Howard.
Lee, Catherine. *see* Lee, Catherine Macaulay.
Lee, Catherine Macaulay.
xLee, Catherine.
The Growth & Development of Children.
Longman.
Lee, Chae-Jin, 1936-
xLee, Chae-Jin.
Communist China's Policy Toward Laos: A
Case Study, 1954-67. Paragon.
Lee, Charles R. *see* Lee, Charles Robert.
Lee, Charles Robert.
xLee, Charles R.
The Confederate Constitutions. Greenwood.
Lee, Charlotte E. *see* Lee, Charlotte I.
Lee, Charlotte I.
xLee, Charlotte E.
Oral Reading of the Scriptures. HM.
Lee, Chung Nim.
xLee, Chung-Nim.
On the Groups JO(G). Am Math.
Lee, Chung-Nim. *see* Lee, Chung Nim.
Lee, Clive Howard.
xLee, C. H.
The Quantitative Approach to Economic
History. St Martin.
Lee, David, 1944-
xLee, David.
Cocaine Consumer's Handbook. And-or Pr.
Lee, David D., 1948-
xLee, David D.
Tennessee in Turmoil: Politics in the Volunteer
State, 1920-1932. Memphis St Univ.
Lee, Dennis.
xLee, Dennis.
Alligator Pie. HM.
A Consumer's & Layman's Guide to
Psychotherapy & Counseling: Everything
About Headshrinking Without Getting
Psyched Out. Calif Books.
Lee, Dick.
xLee, Dick.

Operation Julie. St Martin.
Lee, Don C. *see* Lee, Don Chang.
Lee, Don Chang.
xLee, Don C.
Acculturation of Korean Residents in Georgia.
R & E Res Assoc.
Lee, Don L.
xLee, Don L.
Think Black. Broadside.
Lee, Donald G., 1935-
xLee, Donald G.
Oxidation of Organic Compounds by
Permanganate Ion & Hexavalent Chromium.
Open Court.
Lee, Dorothy S. *see* Lee, Dorothy Sara.
Lee, Dorothy Sara.
xLee, Dorothy S.
Native North American Music & Oral Data: A
Catalogue of Sound Recordings, 1893-1976.
Ind U Pr.
Lee, Dorris M. *see* Lee, Dorris May (Potter).
Lee, Dorris May (Potter), 1905-
xLee, Dorris M.
The Importance of Reading for Achieving in
Grades Four, Five, & Six. AMS Pr.
Learning to Read Through Experience. P-H.
Lee, Douglas A.
xLee, Douglas A.
The Works of Christoph Nichelmann: A
Thematic Index. Info Coord.
Lee, Douglas H. *see* Lee, Douglas Harry Kedgwin.
Lee, Douglas Harry Kedgwin, 1905-
xLee, Douglas H.
Climate & Economic Development in the
Tropics. Greenwood.
ed. Environmental Factors in Respiratory
Disease. Acad Pr.
ed. Multiple Factors in the Causation of
Environmentally Induced Disease. Acad Pr.
Lee, E. B. *see* Lee, Ernest Bruce.
Lee, E. C. *see* Lee, Eric Cuthbert Bernard
Lee, E. Lawrence. *see* Lee, Enoch Lawrence.
Lee, E. M. *see* Lee, Ernest Markham.
Lee, Eddie. *see* Lee, Eddie H.
Lee, Eddie H.
xLee, Eddie.
Journey into Nowhere. Branden.
Lee, Elisa T.
xLee, Elisa T.
Statistical Methods for Survival Data Analysis.
Lifetime Learn.
Lee, Eloise R.
xLee, Eloise R.
Concepts in Basic Nursing: A Modular
Approach. Saunders.
Lee, Elsie.
xLee, Elsie.
A Prior Betrothal. Arbor Hse.
Lee, Enoch Lawrence, 1912-
xLee, E. Lawrence.
Indian Wars in North Carolina, 1663-1763. NC
Archives.
Lee, Eric Cuthbert Bernard.
xLee, E. C.
Safety & Survival at Sea. Norton.
xLee, Kenneth.
jt. auth. Safety & Survival at Sea. Norton.
Lee, Ernest Bruce.
xLee, E. B.
Foundations of Optimal Control Theory. Wiley.
Lee, Ernest M. *see* Lee, Ernest Markham.
Lee, Ernest Markham, 1874-
xLee, E. M.
The Story of Opera. Gordon Pr.
The Story of Symphony. Gordon Pr.
xLee, Ernest M.
Brahms, the Man & His Music. AMS Pr.
Story of Opera. Gale.
Story of Symphony. Gale.
Lee, Essie. *see* Lee, Essie E.

Lee, Essie E.
xLee, Essie.
Careers in the Health Field. Messner.
xLee, Essie E.
Alcohol & You. Messner.
Marriage & Families. Messner.
Women in Congress. Messner.
Lee, Eugene C.
xLee, Eugene C.
ed. The Challenge of California: Text &
Readings. Little.
The Politics of Nonpartisanship: A Study of
California City Elections. U of Cal Pr.
Lee, Francis. *see* Lee, Francis Nigel.
Lee, Francis N. *see* Lee, Francis Nigel.
Lee, Francis Nigel.
xLee, Francis.
Origin & Destiny of Man. Presby & Reformed.
xLee, Francis N.
A Christian Introduction to the History of
Philosophy. Presby & Reformed.
Lee, Fred, 1927-
xLee, Fred.
The Computer Book. Artech Hse.
Lee, Frederic S. *see* Lee, Frederic Schiller.
Lee, Frederic Schiller, 1859-1939
xLee, Frederic S.
The Human Machine & Industrial Efficiency.
Hive Pub.
Lee, Gary.
xLee, Gary.
Chinese Vegetarian Cookbook. Nitty Gritty.
Lee, Georgia.
xLee, Georgia.
jt. auth. An Uncommon Guide to San Luis
Obispo County, California. Padre Prods.
Lee, Gordon C. *see* Lee, Gordon Canfield.
Lee, Gordon Canfield, 1916-
xLee, Gordon C.
The Struggle for Federal Aid, First Phase: A
History of the Attempts to Obtain Federal
Aid for the Common Schools. AMS Pr.
Lee, H. A. *see* Lee, Harry Andre.
Lee, H. B. *see* Lee, Howard Burton.
Lee, Hannah F. *see* Lee, Hannah Farnham (Sawyer).
Lee, Hannah Farnham (Sawyer), 1780-1865
xLee, Hannah F.
The Huguenots in France & America.
Genealog Pub.
Memoir of Pierre Toussaint, Born a Slave in St.
Domingo. Negro U Pr.
Lee, Harold B., 1899-
xLee, Harold B.
Stand Ye in Holy Places. Deseret Bk.
Lee, Harold N. *see* Lee, Harold Newton.
Lee, Harold Newton, 1899-
xLee, Harold N.
Perception & Aesthetic Value. Johnson Repr.
Percepts, Concepts & Theoretic Knowledge: A
Study in Epistemology. Memphis St Univ.
Lee, Harry, 1907-
xLee, Harry.
Race Horse Handicapping. Cornerstone.
Lee, Harry Andre.
xLee, H. A.
ed. Parenteral Nutrition in Acute Metabolic
Illness. Acad Pr.
Lee, Helen B. *see* Lee, Helen Bourne Joy.
Lee, Helen Bourne Joy, 1896-
xLee, Helen B.
Bourne Genealogy. Globe Pequot.
Lee, Helen C.
xLee, Helen C.
A Humanistic Approach to Teaching
Secondary School English. Merrill.
Lee, Helen Jackson.
xLee, Helen Jackson.
Nigger in the Window. Doubleday.
Lee, Hong Y. *see* Lee, Hong Yung.

Lee, Hong Yung, 1939-
xLee, Hong Y.
The Politics of the Chinese Cultural
Revolution: A Case Study. U of Cal Pr.

Lee, Howard Burton, 1879-
xLee, H. B.
Lost Tales of Appalachia. McClain.

Lee, Ian K. *see* Lee, Ian Kenneth.

Lee, Ian Kenneth.
xLee, Ian K.
ed. Soil Mechanics-New Horizons. Elsevier.

Lee, Ida J. *see* Lee, Ida Johnson.

Lee, Ida Johnson.
xLee, Ida J.
Abstracts Lancaster County Virginia Wills:
1653-1800. Genealog Pub.

Lee, Irving J., 1909-1955
xLee, Irving J.
Language Habits in Human Affairs: An
Introduction to General Semantics.
Greenwood.

Lee, Isaiah. *see* Lee, Isaiah C.

Lee, Isaiah C.
xLee, Isaiah.
Medical Care in a Mexican American
Community. Hwong Pub.

Lee, J. W.
xLee, J. W.
Preaching from Genesis: The Perfecting of the
Believer's Faith. Baker Bk.

Lee, James Michael.
xLee, James Michael.
The Flow of Religious Instruction: A
Social-Science Approach. Religious Educ.
ed. The Religious Education We Need: Toward
the Renewal of Christian Education.
Religious Educ.

Lee, Jasper S.
xLee, Jasper S.
Commercial Catfish Farming. Interstate.
Working in Agricultural Industry. McGraw.

Lee, Jennifer M.
xLee, Jennifer M.
Aids to Physiotherapy. Churchill.

Lee, Jo Anne.
xLee, Jo Anne.
First Hunger. Christopher's Bks.

Lee, Joanna.
xLee, Joanna.
I Want to Keep My Baby. NAL.

Lee, John, 1931-
xLee, John.
Lago. Doubleday.
The Ninth Man. Dell.
ed. Pitman's Dictionary of Industrial
Administration: A Comprehensive
Encyclopedia of the Organization,
Administration, & Management of Modern
Industry. Arno.
The Thirteenth Hour. Dell.
The Thirteenth Hour. Doubleday.

Lee, John A. *see* Lee, John A. N.

Lee, John A. N.
xLee, John A.
The Anatomy of a Compiler. D Van Nostrand.

Lee, John E. *see* Lee, John Francis.

Lee, John F. *see* Lee, John Francis.

Lee, John Francis.
xLee, John E.
Thermodynamics: An Introductory Text for
Engineering Students. A-W.
xLee, John F.
Statistical Thermodynamics. A-W.

Lee, John H. *see* Lee, John Hancock.

Lee, John Hancock.
xLee, John H.
The Origin & Progress of the American Party
in Politics: Embracing a Complete History of
the Philadelphia Riots in May & July, 1844.
Arno.

Lee, John M., 1907-
xLee, John M.
Counter-Clockwise. AMS Pr.

Lee, John R.
xLee, John R.
Teaching Social Studies in the Elementary
School. Free Pr.
Teaching Social Studies in the Secondary
School. Free Pr.

Lee, Joseph R., 1922-
xLee, Joseph R.
Advanced Calculus with Linear Analysis. Acad
Pr.

Lee, Josephine, 1921-
xLee, Josephine.
The Fabulous Manticora. John Day.

Lee, Judy.
xLee, Judy.
Save Me: A Young Woman's Journey Through
Schizophrenia to Health. Doubleday.

Lee, Julius.
xLee, Julius.
Essential Endocrinology. Oxford U Pr.

Lee, Jung Y. *see* Lee, Jung Young.

Lee, Jung Young.
xLee, Jung Y.
A Child Sacrifice in the Public School. Far
Eastern Cult.
Cosmic Religion. Har-Row.
Cosmic Religion. Philos Lib.
The Theology of Change: A Christian Concept
of God in an Eastern Perspective. Orbis Bks.

Lee, K. Francis.
xLee, K. Francis.
Neuroradiology of Sellar & Juxtasellar Lesions.
C C Thomas.

Lee, Kai N.
xLee, Kai N.
Electric Power & the Future of the Pacific
Northwest. U of Wash Pr.

Lee, Kaiman.
xLee, Kaiman.
Air Pollution: Its Effect on the Urban Man &
His Adaptive Strategies. Environ Design.
The Buyer's Book of Solar Water Heaters.
Environ Design.
Computer Aided Space Planning. Environ
Design.
Computer-Generated Perspective Drawings.
Environ Design.
Encyclopedia of Energy-Efficient Building
Design: 391 Practical Case Studies. Environ
Design.
Energy Conservation & Building Codes: The
Legislative & Planning Processes. Environ
Design.
Energy-Oriented Computer Programs for the
Design & Monitoring of Buildings. Environ
Design.
Environmental Design Evaluation: A Matrix
Method. Environ Design.
Evaluation of Computer Graphic Terminals.
Environ Design.
Integrated Municipal Information System.
Environ Design.
Interactive Computer Graphics in Architecture.
Environ Design.
Kaiman's Encyclopedia of Energy Topics.
Environ Design.
Performance Specification of Computer Aided
Environmental Design. Environ Design.

Lee, Karen.
xLee, Karen.
Chinese Cooking for the American Kitchen.
Atheneum.

Lee, Kay.
xLee, Kay.
The Illuminated Book of Days. Putnam.
xLee, Marshall.
jt. auth. The Illuminated Book of Days.
Putnam.

Lee, Keat Jin, 1940-
xLee, Keat-Jin.
ed. Essential Otolaryngology: A Board
Preparation & Concise Reference. Med
Exam.

Lee, Keat-Jin. *see* Lee, Keat Jin.

Lee, Kenneth. *see* Lee, Eric Cuthbert Bernard.

Lee, L. L. *see* Lee, Lawrence L.

Lee, La juana W. *see* Lee, Lajuana Williams.

Lee, Lajuana Williams.
xLee, LaJuana W.
Business Communication. Rand.

Lee, Laura L. *see* Lee, Laura Louise.

Lee, Laura Louise.
xLee, Laura L.
Developmental Sentence Analysis: A
Grammatical Assessment Procedure for
Speech & Language Clinicians. Northwestern
U Pr.
Interactive Language Development Teaching:
The Clinical Presentation of Grammatical
Structure. Northwestern U Pr.

Lee, Laurel.
xLee, Laurel.
Signs of Spring. Dutton.

Lee, Laurie.
xLee, Laurie.
As I Walked Out One Midsummer Morning.
Penguin.

Lee, Lawrence.
xLee, Lawrence.
The Appreciation of Stained Glass. Oxford U
Pr.

Lee, Lawrence B. *see* Lee, Lawrence Bacon.

Lee, Lawrence Bacon, 1917-
xLee, Lawrence B.
Kansas & the Homestead Act: 1862-1905.
Arno.
Reclaiming the American West: An
Historiography & Guide. ABC-Clio.

Lee, Lawrence L.
xLee, L. L.
Virginia Sorensen. Boise St Univ.

Lee, Lee C.
xLee, Lee C.
Personality Development in Childhood.
Brooks-Cole.

Lee, Linda.
xLee, Linda.
Bruce Lee: The Man Only I Knew. Warner
Bks.
One by One. PB.
One by One. S&S.

Lee, M. R. *see* Lee, Michael Radcliffe.

Lee, Mabel.
xLee, Mabel.
Fundamentals of Body Mechanics &
Conditioning: An Illustrated Teaching
Manual. Greenwood.
Memories of a Bloomer Girl. AAHPER.

Lee, Marjorie.
xLee, Marjorie.
Eye of Summer. S&S.

Lee, Marshall, 1921-
xLee, Marshall.
ed. Bookmaking: The Illustrated Guide to
Design, Production, Editing. Bowker.

Lee, Marshall. *see* Lee, Kay.

Lee, Meredith, 1945-
xLee, Meredith.

Studies in Goethe's Lyric Cycles. U of NC Pr.

Lee, Michael Radcliffe.
xLee, M. R.
Renin & Hypertension: A Modern Synthesis.
Krieger.

Lee, Mildred.
xLee, Mildred.
Fog. Dell.
Fog. HM.
Sycamore Year. NAL.
Sycamore Year. Lothrop.

Lee, Moon H.
xLee, Moon H.
Purchasing Power Parity. Dekker.

Lee, Nathaniel.
xLee, Nathaniel.
Lucius Junius Brutus. U of Nebr Pr.

Lee, Norma.
xLee, Norma.
Chewing Gum. P-H.

Lee, P. A. see Lee, Peter A.

Lee, Pao-Chen, 1907-
xLee, Pao-Chen.
Read About China. Far Eastern Pubns.

Lee, Peter A., 1926-
xLee, P. A.
ed. Optical & Electrical Properties. Kluwer
Boston.

Lee, Peter H., 1929-
xLee, Peter H.
ed. Flowers of Fire: Twentieth Century Korean
Stories. U Pr of Hawaii.

Lee, Philip R.
xLee, Phillip R.
Primary Care in a Specialized World. Ballinger
Pub.

Lee, Phillip R. see Lee, Philip R.

Lee, R. see Lee, Robert D.

Lee, R. Alton.
xLee, R. Alton.
A History of Regulatory Taxation. U Pr of Ky.

Lee, R. D. see Lee, Robert D.

Lee, R. G. see Lee, Robert Greene.

Lee, R. S. see Lee, Roy Stuart.

Lee, Ralph. see Lee, Ralph L.

Lee, Ralph L.
xLee, Ralph.
Modern Caravanning. Soccer.

Lee, Reginald.
xLee, Reginald.
Building Maintenance Management. Beekman
Pubs.
Building Maintenance Management. Renouf.

Lee, Richard, 1926-
xLee, Richard.
Forest Microclimatology. Columbia U Pr.

Lee, Richard B.
xLee, Richard B.
The Kung San: Men, Women, & Work in a
Foraging Society. Cambridge U Pr.

Lee, Richard W. see Lee, Richard Wilfon.

Lee, Richard Wilfon.
xLee, Richard W.
Politics & the Press. Acropolis.

Lee, Robert A.
xLee, Robert A.
Alistair MacLean: The Key Is Fear. Borgo Pr.
Orwell's Fiction. Irvington.
Orwell's Fiction. U of Notre Dame Pr.

Lee, Robert C.
xLee, Robert C.
Once Upon Another Time. Elsevier-Nelson.

Lee, Robert D.
xLee, Robert D.
Public Personnel Systems. Univ Park.
xLee, R. D.
ed. Public Budgeting Systems. Univ Park.

Lee, Robert E. see Lee, Robert E. A.

Lee, Robert E. A.
xLee, Robert E.

The Joy of Bach. Augsburg.

Lee, Robert Earl, 1906-
xLee, Robert E.
North Carolina Family Law. Michie.

Lee, Robert Edson, 1921-
xLee, Robert E.
The Dialogues of Lewis & Clark: A Narrative
Poem. Colo Assoc.

Lee, Robert G. see Lee, Robert Greene.

Lee, Robert Greene, 1886-
xLee, R. G.
Grapes from Gospel Vines. Broadman.
xLee, Robert G.
Payday Everyday. Broadman.

Lee, Ronald R.
xLee, Ronald R.
Clergy & Clients: The Practice of Pastoral
Psychotherapy. Seabury.

Lee, Roy Stuart.
xLee, R. S.
Psychology & Worship. Philos Lib.

Lee, Ruth M., 1913-
xLee, Ruth M.
Orientation to Health Services. Bobbs.

Lee, Ruth W. see Lee, Ruth Webb.

Lee, Ruth Webb.
xLee, Ruth W.
Antique Fakes & Reproductions. Lee Pubns.
Early American Pressed Glass. Lee Pubns.
Handbook of Early American Pressed Glass
Patterns. Lee Pubns.
A History of Valentines. Lee Pubns.
Nineteenth Century Art Glass. Lee Pubns.
Price Guide to Pattern Glass. Lee Pubns.

Lee, S. C.
xLee, S. C.
Full Time Player. Strode.
Young Bear: The Legend of Bear Bryant's
Boyhood. Strode.

Lee, S. D. see Lee, Si Duk.

Lee, Sammy.
xLee, Sammy.
Diving. Atheneum.

Lee, Samuel C., 1937-
xLee, Samuel C.
Digital Circuits & Logic Design. P-H.

Lee, Sang M.
xLee, Sang M.
Introduction to Decision Science. Van Nos
Reinhold.
Linear Optimization for Management. Van Nos
Reinhold.
ed. Personnel Management: A Computer Based
System. Petrocelli.

Lee, Sherman E.
xLee, Sherman E.
Chinese Landscape Painting. Har-Row.
Chinese Landscape Painting. Ind U Pr.
History of Far Eastern Art. Abrams.
A History of Far Eastern Art. P-H.

Lee, Si Duk.
xLee, S. D.
Assessing Toxic Effects of Environmental
Pollutants. Ann Arbor Science.
ed. Nitrogen Oxides & Their Effects on Health.
Ann Arbor Science.

Lee, Sidney, Sir, 1859-1926
xLee, Sidney.

Great Englishmen of the Sixteenth Century.
Arden Lib.
Great Englishmen of the Sixteenth Century.
Arno.
Great Englishmen of the Sixteenth Century.
Kennikat.
Great Englishmen of the Sixteenth Century. R
West.
A Life of William Shakespeare. Peter Smith.
Life of William Shakespeare. R West.
Life of William Shakespeare. Scholarly.
Principles of Biography. Folcroft.
Stratford-On-Avon from the Earliest Times to
the Death of Shakespeare. Arno.
Stratford-on-Avon from the Earliest Times to
the Death of Shakespeare. R West.

Lee, Soo Ann. see Lee, Soon Ann.

Lee, Soon Ann, 1939-
xLee, Soo Ann.
Industrialization in Singapore. Longman.

Lee, Sophia.
xLee, Sophia.
ed. Canterbury Tales. AMS Pr.

Lee, Stan.
xLee, Stan.
The Amazing Spiderman. PB.
Bring on the Bad Guys. S&S.
Captain America. PB.
Captain America. S&S.
Dr. Strange. S&S.
The Fantastic Four. S&S.
How to Draw Comics the Marvel Way. S&S.
The Incredible Hulk. PB.
Marvel's Greatest Superhero Battles. S&S.
Origins of Marvel Comics. S&S.
The Silver Surfer. S&S.
Son of Origins of Marvel Comics. S&S.
The Superhero Women. S&S.

Lee, Stephen J.
xLee, Stephen J.
Aspects of European History, 1494-1789.
Methuen Inc.

Lee, Steven J. see Lee, Steven James.

Lee, Steven James.
xLee, Steven J.
Buyer's Handbook for Cooperatives &
Condominiums. Van Nos Reinhold.
Women's Handbook of Independent Financial
Management. Van Nos Reinhold.

Lee, Sul H.
xLee, Sul H.
Emerging Trends in Library Organization:
What Influences Change. Pierian.
ed. Library Budgeting: Critical Challenges for
the Future. Pierian.

Lee, Susan.
xLee, Susan.
Inexpensive Wine: A Guide to Best Buys.
NAL.
Inexpensive Wine: A Guide to Best Buys.
Times Bks.

Lee, Susan D. see Lee, Susan.

Lee, Susan P. see Lee, Susan.

Lee, Tanith.
xLee, Tanith.

Companions on the Road. Bantam.
Companions on the Road. St Martin.
Death's Master. DAW Bks.
Dont Bite the Sun. DAW Bks.
East of Midnight. St Martin.
Quest for the White Witch. DAW Bks.
Storm Lord. DAW Bks.
Lee, Thomas A. *see* Lee, Thomas Alexander.
Lee, Thomas Alexander.
xLee, Thomas A.
Income & Value Measurement: Theory &
Practice. Univ Park.
Lee, Tong H. *see* Lee, Tong Hun.
Lee, Tong Hun.
xLee, Tong H.
Regional & Interregional Intersectoral Flow
Analysis: The Method & an Application to
the Tennessee Economy. U of Tenn Pr.
Lee, Trevor.
xLee, Trevor R.
Race & Residence: The Concentration &
Dispersal of Immigrants in London. Oxford
U Pr.
Lee, Trevor R. *see* Lee, Trevor.
Lee, Umphrey, 1893-1958
xLee, Umphrey.
Our Fathers & Us: The Heritage of the
Methodists. SMU Press.
Lee, Victor.
xLee, Victor.
Language Development. Halsted Pr.
Lee, W. Melville. *see* Lee, William Lauriston Melville.
Lee, W. R. *see* Lee, W. Robert.
Lee, W. Robert.
xLee, W. R.
European Demography & Economic Growth.
St Martin.
Population Growth, Economic Development &
Social Change in Bavaria: 1750-1850. Arno.
Lee, Warren F.
xLee, Warren F.
Agricultural Finance. Iowa St U Pr.
Lee, Wayne, 1935-
xLee, Wayne.
Experimental Design & Analysis. W H
Freeman.
Formulating & Reaching Goals. Res Press.
Lee, Wayne. *see* Lee, Wayne C.
Lee, Wayne C.
xLee, Wayne.
The Violent Man. Ace Bks.
xLee, Wayne C.
Law of the Lawless. Ace Bks.
Lee, William.
xLee, William.
Letters of William Lee, 1766-1783. Arno.
Lee, William Lauriston Melville, 1865-
xLee, W. Melville.
History of Police in England. Patterson Smith.
Lee, William T. *see* Lee, William Thomas.
Lee, William Thomas, 1926-
xLee, William T.
The Estimation of Soviet Defense
Expenditures, 1955-75: An Unconventional
Approach. Praeger.
Lee, William W. L.
xLee, William W. L.
Decisions in Marine Mining: The Role of
Preferences & Tradeoffs. Ballinger Pub.
Lee, Yur-Bok, 1934-
xLee, Yur-Bok.
Diplomatic Relations Between the United
States & Korea 1866-1887. Humanities.
Lee-Warner, William, Sir, 1846-1914
xLee-Warner, William.
Native States of India. AMS Pr.
Leebron, Elizabeth.
xLeebron, Elizabeth.

Walt Disney: A Guide to References &
Resources. G K Hall.
Leech, C. *see* Leech, Clifford.
Leech, Clifford.
xLeech, C.
ed. Marlowe: A Collection of Critical Essays.
P-H.
xLeech, Clifford.
Twelfth Night & Shakespearian Comedy. U of
Toronto Pr.
Leech, Daniel D. *see* Leech, Daniel D. Tompkins.
Leech, Daniel D. Tompkins, 1810-1869
xLeech, Daniel D.
The Post Office Department of the United
States of America. Arno.
Leech, Geoffrey.
xLeech, Geoffrey.
A Communicative Grammar of English.
Longman.
Leech, Harper.
xLeech, Harper.
Armour & His Times. Arno.
Leech, Jay, 1931-
xLeech, Jay.
How to Care for Your Horse. A S Barnes.
Leech, Kenneth.
xLeech, Kenneth.
Drugs for Young People: Their Use & Misuse.
Pergamon.
Soul Friend: The Practice of Christian
Spirituality. Har-Row.
Leech, Margaret, 1893-
xLeech, Margaret.
In the Days of McKinley. Greenwood.
Reveille in Washington, 1860-1865.
Greenwood.
Leed, Theodore W.
xLeed, Theodore W.
Food Merchandising: Principles & Practices.
Lebhar Friedman.
Leeds, Barry H.
xLeeds, Barry H.
The Structured Vision of Norman Mailer. NYU
Pr.
Leeds, E. Thurlow. *see* Leeds, Edward Thurlow.
Leeds, Edward Thurlow, 1877-1955
xLeeds, E. Thurlow.
Archaeology of the Anglo-Saxon Settlements.
Oxford U Pr.
Leeds, Eng. University. Institute of Education.
xLeeds University Institute of Education.
Objectives of Teacher Education. Humanities.
Teacher Education: The Teacher's Point of
View. Humanities.
Leeds, Morton.
xLeeds, Morton.
The Paranormal & the Normal: A Historical,
Philosophical & Theoretical Perspective.
Scarecrow.
Leeds University Institute of Education. *see* Leeds, Eng.
University. Institute of Education.
Leedy, Jack J., 1921-
xLeedy, Jack J.
ed. Compensation in Psychiatric Disability &
Rehabilitation. C C Thomas.
Leedy, Paul D.
xLeedy, Paul D.
Read with Speed & Precision. McGraw.
Leefeldt, Christine.
xLeefeldt, Christine.
The Art of Friendship. Berkley Pub.
The Art of Friendship. Pantheon.
Leeg, Elizabeth.
xLeeg, Elizabeth.
Container Farming. Major Bks.
Leek, Sybil.
xLeek, Sybil.

The Complete Art of Witchcraft. NAL.
Moon Signs. Berkley Pub.
Moon Signs. Berkley Pub.
The Night Voyagers: You & Your Dreams.
Ballantine.
Reincarnation: The Second Chance. Stein &
Day.
Star Speak: Your Body Language from the
Stars. Arbor Hse.
The Story of Faith Healing. Macmillan.
Sybil Leek Book of Fortune Telling.
Macmillan.
Leekley, Dorothy.
xLeekley, Dorothy.
Archaeological Excavations in Southern
Greece. Noyes.
Leeman, Wayne A.
xLeeman, Wayne A.
Centralized & Decentralized Economic
Systems: The Soviet-Type Economy, Market
Socialism, & Capitalism. Rand.
Leeming, Joseph, 1897-1968
xLeeming, Joseph.
Brave Ships of England & America. Arno.
First Book of Chess. Watts.
Fun with Shells. Lippincott.
Leen, Daniel, 1947-
xLeen, Daniel.
The Freighthopper's Manual for North
America. Capra Pr.
Leen, Jason.
xLeen, Jason.
The Death of the Prophet. Naturegraph.
Leen, Nina, 1909-
xLeen, Nina.
Cats. HR&W.
Images of Sound. Norton.
Love, Sunrise & Elevated Apes. Norton.
ed. Taking Pictures. HR&W.
Taking Pictures. Avon.
What Kind of a Dog Is That?. Norton.
Leenhardt, Maurice, 1878-1954
xLeenhardt, Maurice.
Do Kamo: Person & Myth in the Melanesian
World. U of Chicago Pr.
Leeper, Alexander W. *see* Leeper, Alexander Wigram
Allen.
Leeper, Alexander Wigram Allen.
xLeeper, Alexander W.
A History of Medieval Austria. AMS Pr.
Leeper, Geoffrey W. *see* Leeper, Geoffrey Winthrop.
Leeper, Geoffrey Winthrop, 1903-
xLeeper, Geoffrey W.
Introduction to Soil Science. Intl Schol Bk
Serv.
Leeper, Sarah H. *see* Leeper, Sarah Hammond.
Leeper, Sarah Hammond.
xLeeper, Sarah H.
Good Schools for Young Children. Macmillan.
Leer, Norman.
xLeer, Norman.
Limited Hero in the Novels of Ford Madox
Ford. Mich St U Pr.
Lees, Carlton B.
xLees, Carlton B.
New Budget Landscaping. HR&W.
Lees, Francis N. *see* Lees, Francis Noel.
Lees, Francis Noel.
xLees, Francis N.
Gerard Manley Hopkins. Columbia U Pr.
Lees, John D. *see* Lees, John David.
Lees, John David.
xLees, John D.
Committees in Legislatures: A Comparative
Analysis. Duke.
Political System of the United States.
Humanities.
Lees, Lynn.
xLees, Lynn H.

Exiles of Erin: Irish Migrants in Victorian
London. Cornell U Pr.
Lees, Lynn H. *see* Lees, Lynn.
Lees, Ray.
　xLees, Ray.
　　Politics & Social Work. Routledge & Kegan.
Lees, Susan. *see* Lees, Susan H.
Lees, Susan H.
　xLees, Susan.
　　Sociopolitical Aspects of Canal Irrigation in the
　　Valley of Oaxaca. U Mich Mus Anthro.
Lees-Smith, Hastings B. *see* Lees-Smith, Hastings
Bertrand.
Lees-Smith, Hastings Bertrand, 1878-1941
　xLees-Smith, Hastings B.
　　ed. The Encyclopaedia of the Labour
　　Movement. Gale.
Leese, Elizabeth, 1937-
　xLeese, Elizabeth.
　　Costume Design in the Movies. Ungar.
Leesley, Michael E., 1942-
　xLeesley, Michael E.
　　Freshman Chemical Engineering. Gulf Pub.
Leeson, C. Roland. *see* Leeson, Thomas Sydney.
Leeson, Marjorie.
　xLeeson, Marjorie.
　　Basic Concepts in Data Processing. Wm C
　　Brown.
　　Computer Operations: Procedures &
　　Management. SRA.
Leeson, R. A. *see* Leeson, Robert Arthur.
Leeson, Robert.
　xLeeson, Robert.
　　Silver's Revenge. Philomel.
Leeson, Robert Arthur.
　xLeeson, R. A.
　　Travelling Brothers: The Six Centuries' Road
　　from Craft Fellowship to Trade Unionism.
　　Allen Unwin.
Leeson, Thomas Sydney.
　xLeeson, C. Roland.
　　A Brief Atlas of Histology. Saunders
Leet, Don R.
　xLeet, Don R.
　　Economics: Concepts, Themes & Applications.
　　Wadsworth Pub.
Leet, Lewis D. *see* Leet, Lewis Don.
Leet, Lewis Don.
　xLeet, Lewis D.
　　ed. World of Geology. McGraw.
　xLeet, Louis D.
　　Earth Waves. Johnson Repr.
Leet, Louis D. *see* Leet, Lewis Don.
Leeton, Will C.
　xLeeton, Will C.
　　David & Goliath. Dandelion Pr.
　　The Tower of Babel. Dandelion Pr.
Leeuw, Adele De. *see* De Leeuw, Adele.
Leeuw, Frank De. *see* De Leeuw, Frank.
Leeuwen, Jean Van. *see* Van Leeuwen, Jean.
Leeuwenberg, E. L. *see* Leeuwenberg, Emanuel Laurens
Jan.
Leeuwenberg, Emanuel Laurens Jan.
　xLeeuwenberg, E. L.
　　Formal Theories of Visual Perception. Wiley.
Leevy, Carroll M. *see* Leevy, Carroll Moton.
Leevy, Carroll Moton.
　xLeevy, Carroll M.
　　Liver Regeneration in Man. C C Thomas.
Lefcoe, George.
　xLefcoe, George.
　　An Introduction to American Land Law: Cases
　　& Materials. Michie.
　　Land Development in Crowded Places: Lessons
　　from Abroad. Conservation Foun.
Lefcourt, Robert, 1939-
　xLefcourt, Robert.

ed. Law Against the People: Essays to
Demystify Law, Order & the Courts.
Random.
LeFeber, Larry. *see* Lefeber, Larry A.
Lefeber, Larry A.
　xLefeber, Larry.
　　Building a Young Adult Ministry. Judson.
Lefeber, Louis.
　xLefeber, Louis.
　　Location & Regional Planning. Intl Pubns Serv.
Lefebvre, Adrian.
　xLefebvre, Adrian.
　　The New Frontiers of Interior Decoration.
　　Gloucester Art.
Lefever, Ernest W.
　xLefever, Ernest W.
　　Nuclear Arms in the Third World: U. S. Policy
　　Dilemma. Brookings.
　　Spear & Scepter: Army, Police, & Politics in
　　Tropical Africa. Brookings.
Lefever, R. A. *see* Lefever, Robert A.
Lefever, Robert A.
　xLefever, R. A.
　　ed. Aspects of Crystal Growth. Dekker.
Lefevere, Andre.
　xLefevere, Andre.
　　Translating Literature: The German Tradition
　　from Luther to Rosenzweig. Humanities.
Lefevre, Adam, 1950-
　xLeFevre, Adam.
　　Everything All at Once. Columbia U Pr.
Lefevre, Carl A.
　xLefevre, Carl A.
　　Linguistics & the Teaching of Reading.
　　McGraw.
　　Linguistics, English & the Language Arts.
　　Tchrs Coll.
Lefevre, Gregg.
　xLeFevre, Gregg.
　　Creating with Sheet Plastic. Sterling.
LeFevre, Perry. *see* Lefevre, Perry D.
LeFevre, Perry D.
　xLeFevre, Perry.
　　Understandings of Man. Westminster.
　xLeFevre, Perry D.
　　ed. Conflict in a Voluntary Association: A Case
　　Study of a Classic Suburban Church Fight.
　　Exploration Pr.
Leff, Arthur A.
　xLeff, Arthur A.
　　Swindling & Selling: The Spanish Prisoner &
　　Other Bargains. Free Pr.
Leff, Gordon.
　xLeff, Gordon.
　　The Dissolution of the Medieval Outlook: An
　　Essay on Intellectual & Spiritual Change in
　　the Fourteenth Century. NYU Pr.
　　History & Social Theory. U of Ala Pr.
　　Tyranny of Concepts: A Critique of Marxism.
　　U of Ala Pr.
Leff, Herbert L., 1944-
　xLeff, Herbert L.
　　Experience, Environment & Human Potentials.
　　Oxford U Pr.
Leffingwell, Albert, 1845-1916
　xLeffingwell, Albert.
　　Illegitimacy & the Influence of Seasons Upon
　　Conduct: Two Studies in Demography. Arno.
Leffland, Ella.
　xLeffland, Ella.
　　Rumors of Peace. Har-Row.
　　Rumors of Peace. Popular Lib.
Leffler, G. L. *see* Leffler, George Leland.
Leffler, George Leland, 1899-
　xLeffler, G. L.
　　The Stock Market. Ronald Pr.
　　The Stock Market. Wiley.
Leffler, Melvyn P., 1945-
　xLeffler, Melvyn P.

The Elusive Quest: America's Pursuit of
European Stability & French Security,
1919-1933. U of NC Pr.
Leffler, William L.
　xLeffler, William L.
　　Petroleum Refining for the Non-Technical
　　Person. Pennwell Pub.
Lefkovits, Ivan.
　xLefkovits, Ivan.
　　ed. Immunological Methods. Acad Pr.
Lefkowitz, Bernard.
　xLefkowitz, Bernard.
　　Breaktime: Living Without Work in a
　　Nine-to-Five World. Penguin.
Lefkowitz, Jerome.
　xLefkowitz, Jerome.
　　Public Employee Unionism in Israel. U of
　　Mich Inst Labor.
Lefkowitz, Lester.
　xLefkowitz, Lester.
　　The Manual of Close-up Photography.
　　Amphoto.
Leflar, Robert A. *see* Leflar, Robert Allen.
Leflar, Robert Allen, 1901-
　xLeflar, Robert A.
　　American Conflicts Law. Michie.
Lefler, Hugh T. *see* Lefler, Hugh Talmage.
Lefler, Hugh Talmage.
　xLefler, Hugh T.
　　Colonial North Carolina: A History. Kraus Intl.
Lefort, Rafael.
　xLefort, Rafael.
　　The Teachers of Gurdjieff. Weiser.
Lefrak, Edward. *see* Lefrak, Edward A.
Lefrak, Edward A.
　xLefrak, Edward.
　　Cardiac Valve Prostheses. ACC.
Lefrancois, Guy R.
　xLefrancois, Guy R.
　　Of Children: An Introduction to Child
　　Development. Wadsworth Pub.
　　Psychology. Wadsworth Pub.
　　Psychology for Teaching: A Bear Sometimes
　　Faces the Front. Wadsworth Pub.
Lefschetz, S. *see* Lefschetz, Solomon.
Lefschetz, Solomon.
　xLefschetz, S.
　　Contributions to the Theory of Nonlinear
　　Oscillations. Kraus Repr.
　　Topics in Topology. Kraus Repr.
　xLefschetz, Solomon.
　　ed. Contributions to the Theory of Nonlinear
　　Oscillations. Princeton U Pr.
　　Differential Equations: Geometric Theory.
　　Dover.
Lefton, Lester A., 1946-
　xLefton, Lester A.
　　Psychology. Allyn.
Leftwich, A. W.
　xLeftwich, A. W.
　　A Dictionary of Zoology. Crane-Russak Co.
Leftwich, Richard H.
　xLeftwich, Richard H.
　　A Basic Framework for Economics. Business
　　Pubns.
　　Economics of Social Issues. Business Pubns.
Legendre, A. F. *see* Legendre, Aime Francois.
Legendre, Aime Francois, 1867-
　xLegendre, A. F.
　　Modern Chinese Civilization. Arno.
　　Modern Chinese Civilization. Chinese
　　Materials.
Legendre, Sidney J. *see* Legendre, Sidney Jennings.
Legendre, Sidney Jennings, 1903-1948
　xLegendre, Sidney J.
　　Okovango, Desert River. Greenwood.
Leger, Fernand, 1881-1955
　xLeger, Fernand.
　　Functions of Painting. Viking Pr.
Leger, Jacques N. *see* Leger, Jacques Nicolas.

Leger, Jacques Nicolas, 1859-
xLeger, Jacques N.
Haiti, Her History & Her Detractors. Negro U
Pr.

Leger, Robert G.
xLeger, Robert G.
The Sociology of Corrections: A Book of
Readings. Wiley.

Legeza, Ireneus Laszlo.
xLegeza, Laszlo.
Tao Magic: The Chinese Art of the Occult.
Pantheon.

Legeza, Laszlo. *see* Legeza, Ireneus Laszlo.
Legg, L. Wickham. *see* Legg, Leopold George Wickham.

Legg, Leopold George Wickham, 1877-
xLegg, L. Wickham.
Matthew Prior: A Study of His Public Career
& Correspondence. Octagon.

Leggatt, Alexander.
xLeggatt, Alexander.
Citizen Comedy in the Age of Shakespeare. U
of Toronto Pr.

Legge, John D. *see* Legge, John David.

Legge, John David.
xLegge, John D.
Britain in Fiji 1858-1880. Verry.

Legge, K. *see* Legge, Karen.

Legge, Karen.
xLegge, K.
Designing Organisations for Satisfaction &
Efficiency. Renouf.
Designing Organisations for Satisfaction &
Efficiency. Renouf.

Legge, Mary Dominica.
xLegge, Mary Dominica.
Anglo-Norman Literature & Its Background.
Greenwood.

Legget, Robert F. *see* Legget, Robert Ferguson.

Legget, Robert Ferguson.
xLegget, Robert F.
Cities & Geology. McGraw.
Ottawa Waterway: Gateway to a Continent. U
of Toronto Pr.
Rideau Waterway. U of Toronto Pr.

Leggett, B. J. *see* Leggett, Bobby Joe.

Leggett, Bobby Joe, 1938-
xLeggett, B. J.
Housman's Land of Lost Content: A Critical
Study of "A Shropshire Lad". U of Tenn Pr.

Leggett, G. *see* Leggett, Glenn H.

Leggett, Glenn H.
xLeggett, G.
Twelve Poets. HR&W.

Leggett, John, 1917-
xLeggett, John.
Gulliver House. HM.

Leggett, John. *see* Leggett, John C.

Leggett, John C.
xLeggett, John.
Race, Class & Political Consciousness.
Schenkman.

Leggett, S. *see* Leggett, Stanton F.

Leggett, Stanton F.
xLeggett, S.
Planning Flexible Learning Places. McGraw.

Leggett, Trevor.
xLeggett, Trevor.
The Chapter of the Self. Routledge & Kegan.

Leggett, William, 1801-1839
xLeggett, William.
Collection of the Political Writings of William
Leggett. Arno.

Legh-Jones, Alison. *see* Legh-Jones, Allison.

Legh-Jones, Allison.
xLegh-Jones, Alison.
My Sister Angie. St Martin.

Legman, Gershon, 1917-
xLegman, Gershon.

Horn Book: Studies in Erotic Folklore &
Bibliography. Univ Bks.
Love & Death: A Study in Censorship. Hacker.

Legouis, Emile. *see* Legouis, Emile Hyacinthe.

Legouis, Emile Hyacinthe, 1861-1937
xLegouis, Emile.
Bacchic Element in Shakespeare's Plays.
Folcroft.
Wordsworth in a New Light. Folcroft.

Legouis, Pierre, 1891-
xLegouis, Pierre.
Donne the Craftsman: An Essay Upon the
Structure of the Songs & Sonnets. Russell.

Legouix, Susan.
xLegouix, Susan.
Botticelli. Two Continents.

Legrenzi, Giovanni.
xLegrenzi, Giovanni.
Totila. Garland Pub.

Legros, Lucien. *see* Legros, Lucien Alphonse.

Legros, Lucien Alphonse.
xLegros, Lucien.
Typographical Printing-Surfaces: The
Technology & Mechanism of Their
Production. Garland Pub.

Leguin, Ursula K.
xLeGuin, Ursula K.
City of Illusions. Garland Pub.
City of Illusions. Har-Row.

Legum, Colin.
xLegum, Colin.
Conflict in the Horn of Africa. Holmes &
Meier.
Congo Disaster. Peter Smith.
Horn of Africa in Continuing Crisis. Holmes &
Meier.
Southern Africa: Year of the Whirlwind.
Holmes & Meier.

Legvold, Robert.
xLegvold, Robert.
Soviet Policy in West Africa. Harvard U Pr.

Lehan, Richard D. *see* Lehan, Richard Daniel.

Lehan, Richard Daniel, 1930-
xLehan, Richard D.
F. Scott Fitzgerald & the Craft of Fiction. S Ill
U Pr.

Lehane, B. *see* Lehane, Brendan.

Lehane, Brendan.
xLehane, B.
Dublin. Silver.
Dublin. Time-Life.

Lehane, Stephen.
xLehane, Stephen.
The Creative Child: How to Encourage the
Natural Creativity of Your Pre-Schooler.
P-H.

Lehiste, Ilse.
xLehiste, Ilse.
ed. Readings in Acoustic Phonetics. MIT Pr.
Suprasegmentals. MIT Pr.

Lehman, Chester K. *see* Lehman, Chester Kindig.

Lehman, Chester Kindig, 1893-
xLehman, Chester K.
Holy Spirit & the Holy Life. Herald Pr.

Lehman, David, 1948-
xLehman, David.
ed. Beyond Amazement: New Essays on John
Ashbery. Cornell U Pr.

Lehman, Edna. *see* Lehman, Edna S.

Lehman, Edna S.
xLehman, Edna.
Talking to Children About Sex. Har-Row.

Lehman, Edward R. *see* Lehman, Edward Richard.

Lehman, Edward Richard.
xLehman, Edward R.

Profits, Profitability, & the Oil Industry. Arno.

Lehman, Edward W.
xLehman, Edward W.
Political Society: A Macrosociology of Politics.
Columbia U Pr.

Lehman, Ernest, 1915-
xLehman, Ernest.
The French Atlantic Affair. Warner Bks.

Lehman, Godfrey.
xLehman, Godfrey.
What You Need to Know for Jury Duty.
Contemp Bks.

Lehman, Harold D., 1921-
xLehman, Harold D.
In Praise of Leisure. Herald Pr.

Lehman, J. P. *see* Lehman, Jean Pierre.

Lehman, James H.
xLehman, James H.
The Old Brethren. Brethren.

Lehman, Jean Pierre.
xLehman, J. P.
The Proofs of Evolution. Gordon-Cremonesi.

Lehman, John. *see* Lehman, John F.

Lehman, John F.
xLehman, John.
The Executive, Congress, & Foreign Policy:
Studies of the Nixon Administration. Praeger.

Lehman, Paul E. *see* Lehman, Paul Evan.

Lehman, Paul Evan.
xLehman, Paul E.
Bandit in Black. Belmont-Tower.
Gun-Whipped. Belmont-Tower.
Tough Texan. Nordon Pubns.
xLehman, Paul Evan.
Vultures on Horseback. Nordon Pubns.

Lehman, Richard S.
xLehman, Richard S.
Computer Simulation & Modeling: An
Introduction. Halsted Pr.

Lehman, Wallace B.
xLehman, Wallace B.
The Clubfoot. Lippincott.

Lehmann. *see* Lehmann, Erich Leo.

Lehmann, A. David.
xLehmann, David.
ed. Development Theory: Four Critical Studies.
Biblio Dist.

Lehmann, A. G. *see* Lehmann, Andrew George.

Lehmann, Andrew George.
xLehmann, A. G.
The Symbolist Aesthetic in France, 1885-1895.
Biblio Dist.
xLehmann, Arthur G.
The Symbolist Aesthetic in France, 1885-1895.
Folcroft.

Lehmann, Arthur G. *see* Lehmann, Andrew George.

Lehmann, Christian.
xLehmann, Christian.
Interaction of Radiation with Solids &
Elementary Defect Production. Elsevier.

Lehmann, David.
xLehmann, David.
ed. Peasants, Landlords & Governments:
Agrarian Reform in the Third World. Holmes
& Meier.

Lehmann, David. *see* Lehmann, A. David.

Lehmann, Donald R.
xLehmann, Donald R.
Market Research & Analysis. Irwin.

Lehmann, E. L. *see* Lehmann, Erich Leo.

Lehmann, Erich Leo.
xLehmann.
Nonparametrics: Statistical Methods Based on
Ranks. McGraw.
xLehmann, E. L.
Nonparametrics: Statistical Methods Based on
Ranks. Holden-Day.

Lehmann, Geoffrey, 1940-
xLehmann, Geoffrey.

Australian Primitive Painters. U of Queensland
 Pr.
Lehmann, H. see Lehmann, Hermann.
Lehmann, Hermann.
 xLehmann, H.
  ed. Human Haemoglobin Variants & Their
   Characteristics. Elsevier.
Lehmann, Irvin J.
 xLehmann, Irvin J.
  Educational Research: Readings in Focus.
   HR&W.
Lehmann, Johannes, 1929-
 xLehmann, Johannes.
  The Hittites: People of a Thousand Gods.
   Viking Pr.
Lehmann, John, 1907-
 xLehmann, John.
  Edward Lear & His World. Scribner.
  Open Night. Arno.
  Thrown to the Woolfs. HR&W.
Lehmann, L. H. see Lehmann, Leo Herbert.
Lehmann, Leo Herbert, 1895-
 xLehmann, L. H.
  Out of the Labyrinth. Gospel Advocate.
Lehmann, Liza, 1862-1918
 xLehmann, Liza.
  The Life of Liza Lehmann. Da Capo.
Lehmann, Paul L. see Lehmann, Paul Louis.
Lehmann, Paul Louis, 1906-
 xLehmann, Paul L.
  Ethics in a Christian Context. Greenwood.
  Ethics in a Christian Context. Har-Row.
Lehmann, R. P. see Lehmann, Ruth.
Lehmann, Rosamond, 1903-
 xLehmann, Rosamond.
  The Ballad & the Source. HarBraceJ.
  Dusty Answer. HarBraceJ.
  The Echoing Grove. HarBraceJ.
Lehmann, Ruth.
 xLehmann, R. P.
  An Introduction to Old Irish. Modern Lang.
Lehmann, Walter.
 xLehmann, Walter.
  The Art of Old Peru. Hacker.
Lehmann, Walter J., 1926-
 xLehmann, Walter J.
  Atomic & Molecular Structure: The
   Development of Our Concepts. Wiley.
Lehmann, Winfred P. see Lehmann, Winfred Philipp.
Lehmann, Winfred Philipp, 1916-
 xLehmann, Winfred P.
  Development of Germanic Verse Form.
   Gordian.
  ed. Directions for Historical Linguistics: A
   Symposium. U of Tex Pr.
  Historical Linguistics: An Introduction.
   HR&W.
  Proto-Indo-European Syntax. U of Tex Pr.
  ed. Syntactic Typology: Studies in the
   Phenomenology of Language. U of Tex Pr.
 xLehmann, Winifred P.
  Descriptive Linguistics: An Introduction.
   Random.
Lehmann, Winifred P. see Lehmann, Winfred Philipp.
Lehmann-Haupt, Hellmut, 1903-
 xLehmann-Haupt, Hellmut.
  Art Under a Dictatorship. Octagon.
  The Book of Trades in the Iconography of
   Social Typology. Boston Public Lib.
Lehmberg, S. E. see Lehmberg, Stanford E.
Lehmberg, Stanford E.
 xLehmberg, S. E.
  The Later Parliaments of Henry VIII,
   1536-1547. Cambridge U Pr.
Lehmkuhl, Dennis M.
 xLehmkuhl, Dennis M.
  How to Know the Aquatic Insects. Wm C
   Brown.
Lehnartz, Klaus.
 xLehnartz, Klaus.

New York in the Sixties. Dover.
Lehne, Richard.
 xLehne, Richard.
  The Quest for Justice: The Politics of School
   Finance Reform. Longman.
Lehner, Ernst, 1895-
 xLehner, Ernst.
  Alphabets & Ornaments. Dover.
  Alphabets & Ornaments. Peter Smith.
  Devils, Demons, Death, & Damnation. Peter
   Smith.
  Symbols, Signs & Signets. Dover.
  Symbols, Signs & Signets. Peter Smith.
Lehner, Joseph, 1912-
 xLehner, Joseph.
  Discontinuous Groups & Automorphic
   Functions. Am Math.
Lehner, Mark.
 xLehner, Mark.
  The Egyptian Heritage: Based on the Edgar
   Cayce Readings. ARE Pr.
Lehner, Philip. see Lehner, Philip N.
Lehner, Philip N., 1940-
 xLehner, Philip.
  The Handbook of Ethological Methods.
   Garland Pub.
Lehnert, Bruce E.
 xLehnert, Bruce E.
  The Pharmacology of Respiratory Care. Mosby.
Lehnert, Wendy G.
 xLehnert, Wendy G.
  The Process of Question Answering: A
   Computer Simulation of Cognition. Halsted
   Pr.
Lehnus, Donald J., 1934-
 xLehnus, Donald J.
  How to Determine Author & Title Entries
   According to AACR: An Interpretive Guide
   with Card Examples. Oceana.
  Signaturas Libristicas: Normas Para Su
   Aplicacion En Bibliotecas De Habla. U of PR
   Pr.
Lehrer, Keith, comp
 xLehrer, Keith.
  ed. Freedom & Determinism. Humanities.
Lehrer, Robert N.
 xLehrer, Robert N.
  Work Simplification: Creative Thinking About
   Work Problems. P-H.
Lehrer, Steven.
 xLehrer, Steven.
  Alternative Treatments for Cancer.
   Nelson-Hall.
  Explorers of the Body. Doubleday.
Lehrling, George.
 xLehrling, George.
  Machinist: Basic Skill Development. Am
   Technical.
Lehrman, Irving.
 xLehrman, Irving.
  In the Name of God. Bloch.
Lehrman, Nat.
 xLehrman, Nat.
  Masters & Johnson Explained. Playboy Pbks.
Lehrman, Neil.
 xLehrman, Neil.
  Perdut. Dryad Pr.
Lehrman, Robert. see Lehrman, Robert L.
Lehrman, Robert L.
 xLehrman, Robert.
  Doing Time: A Look at Crime & Prisons.
   Hastings.
  Doing Time: A Look at Crime & Prisons.
   Hastings.
Lehrs, Max.
 xLehrs, Max.
  Late Gothic Engravings of Germany & the
   Netherlands: 682 Copperplates from the
   Kritischer Katalog. Peter Smith.
Lehto, O. see Lehto, Olli.

Lehto, Olli.
 xLehto, O.
  Quasiconformal Mappings in the Plane.
   Springer-Verlag.
Leib, Amos P. see Leib, Amos Patten.
Leib, Amos Patten.
 xLeib, Amos P.
  Hawaiian Legends in English: An Annotated
   Bibliography. U Pr of Hawaii.
  The Many Islands of Polynesia. Scribner.
Leibee, Howard C. see Leibee, Howard Clinton.
Leibee, Howard Clinton, 1905-
 xLeibee, Howard C.
  Tort Liability for Injuries to Pupils. Campus.
Leibenstein, Harvey.
 xLeibenstein, Harvey.
  General X-Efficiency Theory & Economic
   Development. Oxford U Pr.
  Inflation, Income Distribution & X-Efficiency
   Theory: A Study Prepared for the
   International Labour Office Within the
   Framework of the World Employment
   Programme. B&N.
Leiber, Fritz.
 xLeiber, Fritz.
  Conjure Wife. Ace Bks.
  Conjure Wife. Gregg.
  Gather, Darkness!. Ballantine.
  Our Lady of Darkness. Berkley Pub.
  Pail of Air. Amereon Ltd.
  The Silver Eggheads. Ballantine.
  Swords Against Death. Ace Bks.
  Swords Against Death. Gregg.
  Swords Against Wizardry. Ace Bks.
  Swords Against Wizardry. Gregg.
  Swords & Deviltry. Ace Bks.
  Swords & Deviltry. Gregg.
  Swords & Ice Magic. Ace Bks.
  Swords & Ice Magic. Gregg.
  Swords in the Mist. Ace Bks.
  Swords in the Mist. Gregg.
  The Swords of Lankhmar. Ace Bks.
  The Swords of Lankhmar. Gregg.
  The Worlds of Fritz Leiber. Ace Bks.
  The Worlds of Fritz Leiber. Gregg.
Leibniz, Gottfried W. see Leibniz, Gottfried Wilhelm.
Leibniz, Gottfried Wilhelm.
 xLeibniz, Gottfried W.
  Discourse on the Natural Theology of the
   Chinese. U Pr of Hawaii.
Leibovich, Sidney.
 xLeibovich, Sidney.
  ed. Nonlinear Waves. Cornell U Pr.
Leibowitz, Alan.
 xLeibowitz, Alan.
  The Record Collector's Handbook. Everest
   Hse.
Leibowitz, Arnold H.
 xLeibowitz, Arnold H.
  Colonial Emancipation in the Pacific and the
   Caribbean: A Legal and Political Analysis.
   Praeger.
Leibrecht, Walter.
 xLeibrecht, Walter.
  Religion & Culture: Essays in Honor of Paul
   Tillich. Arno.
Leiby, Adrian C. see Leiby, Adrian Coulter.
Leiby, Adrian Coulter.
 xLeiby, Adrian C.
  The Revolutionary War in the Hackensack
   Valley: The Jersey Dutch & Neutral Ground,
   1775 - 1783. Rutgers U Pr.
Leiby, James.
 xLeiby, James.
  Charity & Correction in New Jersey: A History
   of State Welfare Institutions. Rutgers U Pr.
  A History of Social Welfare & Social Work in
   the United States, 1815-1972. Columbia U
   Pr.
 xLeiby, James R.

Carroll Wright & Labor Reform: The Origin of
Labor Statistics. Harvard U Pr.
Leiby, James R. *see* Leiby, James.
Leicester, Henry M. *see* Leicester, Henry Marshall.
Leicester, Henry Marshall, 1906-
xLeicester, Henry M.
Development of Biochemical Concepts from
Ancient to Modern Times. Harvard U Pr.
Historical Background of Chemistry. Dover.
The Historical Background of Chemistry. Peter
Smith.
Leicht, Kathleen F.
xLeicht, Kathleen F.
Understanding Yourself. Watts.
Leichtentritt, Hugo, 1874-1951
xLeichtentritt, Hugo.
Music, History, & Ideas. Harvard U Pr.
Leichter, Hope. *see* Leichter, Hope Jensen.
Leichter, Hope Jensen.
xLeichter, Hope.
Families & Communities As Educators. Tchrs
Coll.
Leider, Robert, 1929-
xLeider, Robert.
Don't Miss Out: The Ambitious Student's
Guide to Scholarships & Loans, 1980-1982.
Octameron Assocs.
Leideritz, Paula M.
xLeideritz, Paula M.
Key to the Study of East European Law.
Kluwer Boston.
Leiderman, P. Herbert.
xLeiderman, P. Herbert.
ed. Culture & Infancy: Variations in the
Human Experience. Acad Pr.
Leidheiser, Henry.
xLeidheiser, Henry.
The Corrosion of Copper, Tin, & Their Alloys.
Krieger.
Leidig, Paul, 1894-
xLeidig, Paul.
Franzosische Lehnworter und
Lehnbedeutungen Im Englischen Des 18.
Jahrhunderts. Johnson Repr.
Leiding, Harriette K. *see* Leiding, Harriette Kershaw.
Leiding, Harriette Kershaw, 1878-
xLeiding, Harriette K.
Historic Houses of South Carolina. Reprint.
Leiding, Oscar.
xLeiding, Oscar.
A Layman's Guide to Successful Publicity:
1979. Ayer Pr.
Leif, Irving P., 1947-
xLeif, Irving P.
Community Power & Decision Making: An
International Handbook. Scarecrow.
Leifchild, J. R. *see* Leifchild, John R.
Leifchild, John R., 1815-
xLeifchild, J. R.
Our Coal & Our Coal-Pits. Kelley.
Leifer, Glora. *see* Leifer, Gloria.
Leifer, Gloria.
xLeifer, Glora.
Principles & Techniques in Pediatric Nursing.
Saunders.
Leifer, Michael.
xLeifer, Michael.
The Foreign Relations of the New States.
Longman.
Leifer, Ronald, 1932-
xLeifer, Ronald.
In the Name of Mental Health: Social
Functions of Psychiatry. Aronson.
Leifson, Einar, 1902-
xLeifson, Einar.
Atlas of Bacterial Flagellation. Acad Pr.
Leigh, Bill.
xLeigh, Bill.
The Far Side of Fear. Viking Pr.
Leigh, D. *see* Leigh, Duane E.

Leigh, Dorian.
xLeigh, Dorian.
The Girl Who Had Everything: The Story of
the Fire & Ice Girl. Doubleday.
Leigh, Duane E.
xLeigh, D.
An Analysis of the Determinants of
Occupational Upgrading. Acad Pr.
Leigh, Hoyle.
xLeigh, Hoyle.
The Patient: Biological, Psychological, & Social
Dimensions of Medical Practice. Plenum Pub.
Leigh, Norman.
xLeigh, Norman.
Thirteen Against the Bank. Penguin.
Leigh, Oliver.
xLeigh, Oliver.
Edgar Allan Poe: The Man, The Master, The
Martyr. Arden Lib.
Edgar Allan Poe: The Man, the Master, the
Martyr. Folcroft.
Leigh, Petra.
xLeigh, Petra.
Garnet. Warner Bks.
Rosewood. PB.
Leigh, Roberta.
xLeigh, Roberta.
Night of Love. Fawcett.
Leigh, Susannah.
xLeigh, Susannah.
Glynda. NAL.
Leighton, George R. *see* Leighton, George Ross.
Leighton, George Ross, 1902-1966
xLeighton, George R.
Five Cities: The Story of Their Youth & Old
Age. Arno.
Leighton, Jack R.
xLeighton, Jack R.
Progressive Weight Training. Wiley.
Leighton, Lee.
xLeighton, Lee.
Gut Shot. Ballantine.
Leighton, Margaret. *see* Leighton, Margaret (Carver).
Leighton, Margaret (Carver).
xLeighton, Margaret.
Journey for a Princess. FS&G.
Other Island. FS&G.
Leighton, Paul J.
xLeighton, Paul J.
Delta Mind Dynamics. P-H.
Leighton, Ralph.
xLeighton, Ralph.
How to Count Sheep Without Falling Asleep.
P-H.
Leighton, Robert, Abp. of Glasgow, 1611-1684
xLeighton, Robert.
Commentary on First Peter. Kregel.
Leighton, Robert B.
xLeighton, Robert B.
Principles of Modern Physics. McGraw.
Leighton, Walter, 1907-
xLeighton, Walter.
First Course in Ordinary Differential
Equations. Wadsworth Pub.
Leighton, Walter L. *see* Leighton, Walter Leatherbee.
Leighton, Walter Leatherbee, 1876-
xLeighton, Walter L.
French Philosophers - New England
Transcendentalism. Greenwood.
Leighty, James C. *see* Leighty, Jim.
Leighty, Jim.
xLeighty, James C.
How to Develop a Strong High School Kicking
Game. P-H.
Leijonhufvud, Axel.
xLeijonhufvud, Axel.

On Keynesian Economics & the Economics of
Keynes: A Study in Monetary Theory.
Oxford U Pr.
Leik, Robert K.
xLeik, Robert K.
Mathematical Sociology. P-H.
Leiman, Sid Z.
xLeiman, Sid Z.
The Canonization of Hebrew Scripture: The
Talmudic & Midrashic Evidence. Shoe String.
Leimanis, E. *see* Leimanis, Eugene.
Leimanis, Eugene.
xLeimanis, E.
General Problem of the Motion of Coupled
Rigid Bodies About a Fixed Point.
Springer-Verlag.
Leimbach, Patricia P. *see* Leimbach, Patricia Penton.
Leimbach, Patricia Penton, 1927-
xLeimbach, Patricia P.
All My Meadows. P-H.
Lein, Charles F., 1928-
xLein, Charles F.
How Farmers Can Beat the Tax Ripoff.
Arlington Hse.
Leinbach, L. Carl.
xLeinbach, L. Carl.
Calculus with the Computer: A Laboratory
Manual. P-H.
Leiner, Katherine.
xLeiner, Katherine.
Ask Me What My Mother Does. Watts.
Leiner, Marvin.
xLeiner, Marvin.
Children Are the Revolution: Day Care in
Cuba. Penguin.
Children of the Cities: Education of the
Powerless. NAL.
Leinfellner, W. *see* Leinfellner, Werner.
Leinfellner, Werner.
xLeinfellner, W.
Developments in the Methodology of Social
Science. Kluwer Boston.
Leinsdorf, Erich, 1912-
xLeinsdorf, Erich.
Cadenza: A Musical Career. HM.
Leinwand, Gerald.
xLeinwand, Gerald.
ed. The Future. PB.
ed. Governing the City. PB.
ed. Prisons. PB.
Leinwoll, Stanley.
xLeinwoll, Stanley.
Candles & Candlecrafting. Scribner.
From Spark to Satellite: A History of Radio
Communication. Scribner.
Plasticrafts. S&S.
Leipold, L. E. *see* Leipold, L. Edmond.
Leipold, L. Edmond, 1902-
xLeipold, L. E.
Come Along to Saudi Arabia. Denison.
Folk Tales of England. Denison.
Folk Tales of Germany. Denison.
Leisenring, James. *see* Leisenring, James E.
Leisenring, James E.
xLeisenring, James.
Art of Tying the Wet Fly & Fishing the
Flymph. Crown.
Leiser, Burton M.
xLeiser, Burton M.
Liberty, Justice, & Morals: Contemporary
Value Conflicts. Macmillan.
Leiser, Eric.
xLeiser, Eric.
The Complete Book of Fly Tying. Knopf.
Leiser, Erwin, 1923-
xLeiser, Erwin.
Nazi Cinema. Macmillan.
Nazi Cinema. Macmillan.
Leiser, Joseph.
xLeiser, Joseph.

American Judaism: The Religion & Religious
Institutions of the Jewish People in the
United States. Greenwood.

Leiserson, Alcira.
xLeiserson, Alcira.
Notes on the Process of Industrialization in
Argentina, Chile, & Peru. U of Cal Intl St.

Leiserson, Avery, 1913-
xLeiserson, Avery.
Administrative Regulation: A Study in
Representation of Interests. U of Chicago Pr.
Leiserson, William M. see Leiserson, William Morris.

Leiserson, William Morris, 1883-1957
xLeiserson, William M.
Adjusting Immigrant & Industry. Arno.
Leish, Kenneth. see Leish, Kenneth W.

Leish, Kenneth W.
xLeish, Kenneth.
The White House. Newsweek.

Leiss, William, 1939-
xLeiss, William.
The Domination of Nature. Beacon Pr.
The Domination of Nature. Braziller.
Ecology Versus Politics in Canada. U of
Toronto Pr.
The Limits to Satisfaction: An Essay on the
Problem of Needs & Commodities. U of
Toronto Pr.

Leister, Mary.
xLeister, Mary.
Flying Fur, Fin & Scale: Strange Animals That
Swoop and Soar. Stemmer Hse.

Leisy, Ernest E, 1887-
xLeisy, Ernest E.
American Historical Novel. Folcroft.
American Historical Novel. U of Okla Pr.

Leitch, Alexander, 1900-
xLeitch, Alexander.
A Princeton Companion. Princeton U Pr.

Leitch, Cynthia J.
xLeitch, Cynthia J.
Primary Care. Davis Co.

Leitch, Susan M.
xLeitch, Susan M.
A Child Learns to Speak: A Guide for Parents
& Teachers of Preschool Children. C C
Thomas.

Leite, Elizabeth, 1946-

xLeite, Elizabeth.
Simply Beautiful: Living with the Earth in
Mind. Naturegraph.

Leite, Evelyn.

xLeite, Evelyn.
To Be Somebody. Hazelden.
Leitenberg, H. see Leitenberg, Harold.

Leitenberg, Harold.
xLeitenberg, H.
Handbook of Behavior Modification &
Behavior Therapy. P-H.

Leitenberg, Milton.
xLeitenberg, Milton.
ed. Great Power Intervention in the Middle
East. Pergamon.
Leiter, Robert D. see Leiter, Robert David.

Leiter, Robert David.
xLeiter, Robert D.
ed. Economics of Public Choice. Cyrco Pr.
ed. Economics of Public Choice. Irvington.
ed. Economics of Resources. Irvington.
Foreman in Industrial Relations. AMS Pr.
Modern Economics. Har-Row.
The Musicians & Petrillo. Octagon.

Leiter, Samuel L.
xLeiter, Samuel L.

The Art of Kabuki: Famous Plays in
Performance. U of Cal Pr.
Kabuki Encyclopedia: An English-Language
Adaptation of Kabuki Jiten. Greenwood.
Leites, N. see Leites, Nathan Constantin.
Leites, Nathan. see Leites, Nathan Constantin.

Leites, Nathan Constantin, 1912-
xLeites, N.
Psychopolitical Analysis: Selected Writings of
Nathan Leites. Halsted Pr.
xLeites, Nathan.
Depression & Masochism: An Account of
Mechanisms. Norton.
Interpreting Transference. Norton.

Leith, James A.
xLeith, James A.
Idea of Art as Propaganda in France,
1750-1799: A Study in the History of Ideas.
U of Toronto Pr.

Leith, John H.
xLeith, John H.
Assembly at Westminster: Reformed Theology
in the Making. John Knox.
ed. Creeds of the Churches: A Reader in
Christian Doctrine from the Bible to the
Present. John Knox.

Leithold, Louis.
xLeithold, Louis.
College Algebra. Macmillan.
Essentials of Calculus for Business &
Economics. Har-Row.
Intermediate Algebra for College Students.
Macmillan.
Leitmann, G. see Leitmann, George.

Leitmann, George.
xLeitmann, G.
ed. Multicriteria Decision Making.
Springer-Verlag.

Leitner, Isabella.
xLeitner, Isabella.
Fragments of Isabella: A Memoir of Auschwitz.
T Y Crowell.

Leive, Loretta.
xLeive, Loretta.
ed. Bacterial Membranes & Walls. Dekker.

Lejeune, Anthony.
xLejeune, Anthony.
The Gentlemen's Clubs of London. Mayflower
Bks.

Lekachman, Robert.
xLekachman, Robert.
The Age of Keynes. McGraw.
Economists at Bay: Why the Experts Will
Never Solve Your Problems. McGraw.
A History of Economic Ideas. McGraw.
Inflation: The Permanent Problem of Boom &
Bust. Random.
ed. National Policy for Economic Welfare at
Home & Abroad. Russell.
Lekai, Louis J. see Lekai, Louis Julius.

Lekai, Louis Julius, 1916-
xLekai, Louis J.
The Cistercians: Ideals & Reality. Kent St. U
Pr.
Lekhnitskii, S. G. see Lekhnitskii, Sergei Georgievich.

Lekhnitskii, Sergei Georgievich.
xLekhnitskii, S. G.
Anisotropic Plates. Gordon.
Leland, Abby P. see Leland, Abby Porter.

Leland, Abby Porter, 1879-1950
xLeland, Abby P.
The Educational Theory & Practice of T. H.
Green. AMS Pr.
Leland, Charles G. see Leland, Charles Godfrey.

Leland, Charles Godfrey, 1824-1903
xLeland, Charles G.

Gypsy Sorcery & Fortune-Telling. Peter Smith.
Meister Karl's Sketch-Book. Irvington.
Memoirs. Gale.

Leland, Henry.
xLeland, Henry.
ed. Abnormal Behavior: A Guide to
Information Sources. Gale.
Leland, Ottilie. see Leland, Ottilie M.

Leland, Ottilie M.
xLeland, Ottilie.
Master of Precision: Henry M. Leland.
Greenwood.

Leland, Thomas.
xLeland, Thomas.
Longsword, Earl of Salisbury: An Historical
Romance. Arno.
Leland, W. G. see Leland, Waldo Gifford.

Leland, Waldo Gifford, 1879-
xLeland, W. G.
Guide to Materials for American History in the
Libraries & Archives of Paris. Kraus Repr.

Lele, Uma J.
xLele, Uma J.
Food Grain Marketing in India: Private
Performance & Public Policy. Cornell U Pr.

Lely, James A.
xLely, James A.
Aquarius. Creative Ed.
Libra. Creative Ed.

Lelyveld, David, 1941-
xLelyveld, David.
Aligarh's First Generation: Muslim Solidarity
in British India. Princeton U Pr.

Lem, Stanislaw.
xLem, Stanislaw.
A Perfect Vacuum. HarBraceJ.
Return from the Stars. HarBraceJ.
Solaris. Berkley Pub.
Star Diaries. Avon.
The Star Diaries. Continuum.
Tales of Pirx the Pilot. HarBraceJ.

Lem, Stanislaw.
xLem, Stanislaw.
Memoirs Found in a Bathtub. Avon.
Memoirs Found in a Bathtub. Continuum.
Lem, Stanislaw. see Lem, Stanisaw.

Lemaitre, George D.
xLeMaitre, George D.
The Patient in Surgery: A Guide for Nurses.
Saunders.
Lemaitre, Georges E. see Lemaitre, Georges Edouard.

Lemaitre, Georges Edouard, 1898-1972
xLemaitre, Georges E.
From Cubism to Surrealism in French
Literature. Greenwood.

Lemaitre, Jules, 1853-1914
xLeMaitre, Jules.
Literary Impressions. Darby Bks.
Literary Impressions. Kennikat.
Literary Impressions. R West.
On the Margins of Old Books. Arno.
Theatrical Impressions. Kennikat.
xLemaitre, Julius.
Theatrical Impressions. R West.
Lemaitre, Julius. see Lemaitre, Jules.

Leman, Bonnie.
xLeman, Bonnie.
Quick & Easy Quilting. Hearthside.
Quick & Easy Quilting. Moon Over Mntn.

Leman, Christopher.
xLeman, Christopher.
The Collapse of Welfare Reform: Political
Institutions, Policy & the Poor in Canada &
the United States. MIT Pr.

Leman, Kevin.
xLeman, Kevin.
Parenthood Without Hassles - well almost.
Harvest Hse.
Leman, Walter M. see Leman, Walter Moore.

Leman, Walter Moore, b. 1810
    xLeman, Walter M.
        Memories of an Old Actor. Scholarly.
Lemarchand, Elizabeth.
    xLemarchand, Elizabeth.
        Suddenly While Gardening. Walker & Co.
Lemarchand, Rene.
    xLemarchand, Rene.
        African Kingships in Perspective: Political
        Change & Modernization in Monarchical
        Settings. Biblio Dist.
Lemaster, J. R., 1934-
    xLeMaster, J. R.
        Jesse Stuart: A Reference Guide. G K Hall.
Lemasters, E. E.
    xLeMasters, E. E.
        Parents in Modern America. Dorsey.
Lemay, Harding.
    xLemay, Harding.
        Inside, Looking Out: A Personal Memoir.
        Har-Row.
Lemay, J. Leo. see Lemay, Joseph A. Leo.
Lemay, Joseph A. Leo, 1935-
    xLemay, J. Leo.
        A Calendar of American Poetry in the Colonial
        Newspapers & Magazines & in the Major
        English Magazines Through 1765. Am
        Antiquarian.
        Men of Letters in Colonial Maryland. U of
        Tenn Pr.
Lemberg. see Lemberg, Louis.
Lemberg, Louis.
    xLemberg.
        Vectorcardiography: A Programmed
        Introduction. ACC.
Lembo, John M.
    xLembo, John M.
        The Counseling Process: A
        Cognitive-Behavioral Approach. Libra.
        When Learning Happens. Schocken.
Lembourn, Hans J. see Lembourn, Hans Jrgen.
Lembourn, Hans Jrgen, 1923-
    xLembourn, Hans J.
        Diary of a Lover of Marilyn Monroe. Arbor
        Hse.
Lemelin, Maurice.
    xLemelin, Maurice.
        The Public Service Alliance of Canada: A Look
        at a Union in the Public Sector. U Cal LA
        Indus Rel.
Lemelin, Robert, 1934-
    xLemelin, Robert.
        Pathway to the National Character, 1830-1861.
        Kennikat.
Lemert, Charles. see Lemert, Charles C.
Lemert, Charles C., 1937-
    xLemert, Charles.
        Sociology & the Twilight of Man:
        Homocentrism & Discourse in Sociological
        Theory. S Ill U Pr.
    xLemert, Charles C.
        Sociology & the Twilight of Man:
        Homocentrism & Discourse in Sociological
        Theory. S Ill U Pr.
Lemesurier, Peter.
    xLemesurier, Peter.
        Gospel of the Stars: A Celebration of the
        Mystery of the Zodiac. St Martin.
        The Great Pyramid Decoded. Avon.
Lemire, Robert.
    xLemire, Robert A.
        Creative Land Development: Bridge to the
        Future. HM.
Lemire, Robert A. see Lemire, Robert.
Lemire, Ronald J.
    xLemire, Ronald J.
        Anencephaly. Raven.
        Normal & Abnormal Development of the
        Human Nervous System. Har-Row.
Lemke, Bernhard C. see Lemke, Bernhard Carl.

Lemke, Bernhard Carl.
    xLemke, Bernhard C.
        Administrative Control & Executive Action.
        Merrill.
Lemke, Elmer.
    xLemke, Elmer.
        Principles of Psychological Measurement.
        Rand.
Lemke, Horst.
    xLemke, Horst.
        Ride with Me Through ABC. Scroll Pr.
Lemke, P. A. see Lemke, Paul A.
Lemke, Paul A., 1937-
    xLemke, P. A.
        Viruses & Plasmids in Fungi. Dekker.
Lemlech, Johanna.
    xLemlech, Johanna K.
        Classroom Management. Har-Row.
Lemlech, Johanna K. see Lemlech, Johanna.
Lemlich, Robert.
    xLemlich, Robert.
        Adsorptive Bubble Separation Techniques.
        Acad Pr.
Lemmel, Maurice.
    xLemmel, Maurice.
        Gambling Nevada Style. Doubleday.
Lemmerz, A. H. see Lemmerz, August Heinrich.
Lemmerz, August Heinrich.
    xLemmerz, A. H.
        Examples Illustrating the Use of Frank Leads.
        S Karger.
Lemmon, Ed.
    xLemmon, Ed.
        Boss Cowman: The Recollections of Ed
        Lemmon, 1857-1946. U of Nebr Pr.
Lemmon, Sarah M. see Lemmon, Sarah McCulloh.
Lemmon, Sarah McCulloh.
    xLemmon, Sarah M.
        Frustrated Patriots: North Carolina & the War
        of 1812. U of NC Pr.
        North Carolina's Role in the First World War.
        NC Archives.
        Parson Pettigrew of the "Old Church":
        1744-1807. U of NC Pr.
Lemoine, Suzanne.
    xLeMoine, Suzanne.
        Dieting Out in Seattle: Restaurant Feasts, Facts
        & Tips for the Slender Gourmet. Writing.
Lemon, Lee T.
    xLemon, Lee T.
        ed. Approaches to Literature. Oxford U Pr.
Lemon, Richard.
    xLemon, Richard.
        Troubled American. S&S.
Lemond, Alan.
    xLemond, Alan.
        Bravo Baryshnikov. G&D.
Lemons, Frank W., 1901-
    xLemons, Frank W.
        Perennial Pentecost. Pathway Pr.
        Profiles of Faith. Pathway Pr.
Lemons, Wayne.
    xLemons, Wayne.
        How to Repair Home & Auto Air
        Conditioners. TAB Bks.
        Learn Electronics Through Troubleshooting.
        Bobbs.
Lemos, Ramon M., 1927-
    xLemos, Ramon M.
        Hobbes & Locke: Power & Consent. U of Ga
        Pr.
Lemp, Helena B.
    xLemp, Helena B.
        Manual for the Organization of Scientific
        Congresses. S Karger.
Lenanton, Carola M. see Lenanton, Carola Mary Anima
    (Oman).
Lenanton, Carola Mary Anima (Oman), 1897-
    xLenanton, Carola M.

Nelson. Greenwood.
Lenarcic, R. J.
    xLenarcic, R. J.
        As Long As the Grass Shall Grow. Mss Info.
Lenard, Philipp. see Lenard, Philipp Eduard Anton.
Lenard, Philipp Eduard Anton, 1862-1947
    xLenard, Philipp.
        Great Men of Science: A History of Scientific
        Progress. Darby Bks.
Lenburg, Carrie B.
    xLenburg, Carrie B.
        Open Learning & Career Mobility in Nursing.
        Mosby.
Lenchner, George.
    xLenchner, George.
        The Overhead Projector in the Mathematics
        Classroom. NCTM.
Lenczowski, George.
    xLenczowski, George.
        The Middle East in World Affairs. Cornell U
        Pr.
        Oil & State in the Middle East. Cornell U Pr.
        Soviet Advances in the Middle East. Am
        Enterprise.
Lendt, David. see Lendt, David L.
Lendt, David L.
    xLendt, David.
        ed. The Publicity Process. Iowa St U Pr.
    xLendt, David L.
        Ding: The Life of Jay Norwood Darling. Iowa
        St U Pr.
Leng, Shao Chuan.
    xLeng, Snao-Chuan.
        ed. Law in Chinese Foreign Policy: Communist
        China & Selected Problems of International
        Law. Oceana.
Leng, Snao-Chuan. see Leng, Shao Chuan.
Lengermann. see Lengermann, Patricia M.
Lengermann, Patricia M.
    xLengermann.
        Definitions of Sociology: Historical Approach.
        Merrill.
Lengstrand, Rolf.
    xLengstrand, Rolf.
        Horse Astray in Stockholm. Lerner Pubns.
Lengyel, Cornel. see Lengyel, Cornel Adam.
Lengyel, Cornel Adam.
    xLengyel, Cornel.
        Four Dozen Songs. Blue Oak.
        Four Dozen Songs. Dragons Teeth.
        The Master Plan. Dragons Teeth.
        Presidents of the United States. Western Pub.
Lengyel, Emil, 1895-
    xLengyel, Emil.
        Asoka the Great: India's Royal Missionary.
        Watts.
        The Colony of New Hampshire. Watts.
        The Colony of Pennsylvania. Watts.
        Egypt's Role in World Affairs. Pub Aff Pr.
        Modern Egypt. Watts.
        The Oil Countries of the Middle East. Watts.
        Pakistan & Bangladesh. Watts.
        Siberia. Watts.
Lengyel, Jozsef.
    xLengyel, Jozsef.
        Confrontation. Citadel Pr.
Lenhoff, Howard M.
    xLenhoff, Howard M.
        ed. Experimental Coelenterate Biology. U Pr of
        Hawaii.
Lenihan, John.
    xLenihan, John.
        Human Engineering: The Body Re-Examined.
        Braziller.
Lenin, V. I. see Lenin, Vladimir Ilich.
Lenin, Vladimir I. see Lenin, Vladimir Ilich.
Lenin, Vladimir Ilich, 1870-1924
    xLenin, V. I.
        Lenin on the Jewish Question. Intl Pub Co.
    xLenin, Vladimir I.

Letters of Lenin. Hyperion Conn.
The Right of Nations to Self Determination:
Selected Writings. Greenwood.

Leningrad. Publichnaia Biblioteka.
xBibliotheque Imperiale Publique De St.
Petersbourg.
Catalogue De la Section Des Russica: Ecrits
Sur la Russie En Langues Etrangere. Da
Capo.

Lenk, John. *see* Lenk, John D.

Lenk, John D.
xLenk, John.
Handbook of Logic Circuits. Reston.
xLenk, John D.
Handbook of Basic Electronic Troubleshooting.
P-H.
Handbook of Controls & Instrumentation. P-H.
Handbook of Electronic Charts, Graphs &
Tables. P-H.
Handbook of Electronic Components &
Circuits. P-H.
Handbook of Electronic Test Equipment. P-H.
Handbook of Integrated Circuits: For Engineers
& Technicians. Reston.
Handbook of Microprocessors, Microcomputers
& Minicomputers. P-H.
Handbook of Practical Microcomputer
Troubleshooting. Reston.
Logic Designer's Manual. Reston.

Lenk, R.
xLenk, R.
Brownian Motion & Spin Relaxation. Elsevier.

Lenk, R. S., 1921-
xLenk, R. S.
Polymer Rheology. Intl Ideas.

Lenman, Bruce.
xLenman, Bruce.
An Economic History of Modern Scotland,
1660-1976. Shoe String.

Lenman, J. A. *see* Lenman, J. A. R.

Lenman, J. A. R.
xLenman, J. A.
Clinical Electromyography. Lippincott.

Lennarz, William J.
xLennarz, William J.
ed. The Biochemistry of Glycoproteins &
Proteoglycans. Plenum Pub.

Lennon, John J.
xLennon, John J.
A Comparative Study of the Patterns of
Acculturation of Selected Puerto Rican
Protestant & Roman Catholic Families in an
Urban Metropolitan Area. R & E Res Assoc.

Lennox, Charlotte. *see* Lennox, Charlotte Ramsay.

Lennox, Charlotte Ramsay, 1720-1804
xLennox, Charlotte.
Sophia. Garland Pub.

Lenoir, William B. *see* Lenoir, William Ballard.

Lenoir, William Ballard, 1847-
xLenoir, William B.
History of Sweetwater Valley, Tennessee.
Regional.

Lenowitz, Harris.
xLenowitz, Harris.
ed. Origins: Creation Texts from the Ancient
Mediterranean - a Chrestomathy. AMS Pr.

Lenrow, Gerald. *see* Lenrow, Gerald I.

Lenrow, Gerald I.
xLenrow, Gerald.
Federal Income Taxation of Insurance
Companies. Wiley.
xLenrow, Gerald I.
Federal Income Taxation of Insurance
Companies. Ronald Pr.

Lens, Sidney.
xLens, Sidney.

The Day Before Doomsday: An Anatomy of
the Nuclear Arms Race. Beacon Pr.
The Promise & Pitfalls of Revolution. Pilgrim
NY.
Unrepentant Radical: An American Activist's
Account of Five Turbulent Decades. Beacon
Pr.

Lensen, George A. *see* Lensen, George Alexander.

Lensen, George Alexander, 1923-
xLensen, George A.
The Damned Inheritance: The Soviet Union &
the Manchurian Crises, 1924-1935.
Diplomatic Fla.
The Strange Neutrality: Soviet - Japanese
Relations During the Second World War,
1941-1945. Diplomatic Fla.

Lenski, Gerhard E. *see* Lenski, Gerhard Emmanuel.

Lenski, Gerhard Emmanuel.
xLenski, Gerhard E.
Human Societies: An Introduction to
Macrosociology. McGraw.
Power & Privilege: A Theory of Social
Stratification. McGraw.
The Religious Factor: A Sociological Study of
Religion's Impact on Politics, Economics, &
Family Life. Greenwood.

Lenski, Lois, 1893-
xLenski, Lois.
illus. Little Auto. Walck.
illus. Prairie School. Dell.

Lenson, David, 1945-
xLenson, David.
Achilles' Choice: Examples of Modern
Tragedy. Princeton U Pr.
Ride the Shadow. SBD.

Lent, Deane.
xLent, Deane.
Analysis & Design of Mechanisms. P-H.

Lent, George E. *see* Lent, George Eidt.

Lent, George Eidt, 1912-
xLent, George E.
Impact of the Undistributed Profits Tax,
1936-37. AMS Pr.

Lent, John A.
xLent, John A.
ed. The Asian Newspapers Reluctant
Revolution. Iowa St U Pr.

Lent, Max.
xLent, Max.
Photography Galleries & Selected Museums: A
Survey & International Directory. Garlic Pr.

Lent, William T.
xLent, William T.
Speed Sketching. Doubleday.

Lentfoehr, Therese, 1902-
xLentfoehr, Therese.
Words & Silence: On the Poetry of Thomas
Merton. New Directions.

Lenthall, Patricia R. *see* Lenthall, Patricia Riley.

Lenthall, Patricia Riley.
xLenthall, Patricia R.
Carlotta & the Scientist. Lollipop Power.

Lento, Robert, 1933-
xLento, Robert.
Woodworking: Tools, Fabrication, Design, &
Manufacturing. P-H.

Lenton, H. T.
xLenton, H. T.
German Warships of the Second World War.
Arco.

Lentricchia, Frank.
xLentricchia, Frank.
After the New Criticism. U of Chicago Pr.

Lentz, Donald A.
xLentz, Donald A.
Gamelan Music of Java & Bali: An Artistic
Anomaly Complementary to Primary Tonal
Theoretical Systems. U of Nebr Pr.

Lentz, Theodore F. *see* Lentz, Theodore Ferdinand.

Lentz, Theodore Ferdinand, 1888-
xLentz, Theodore F.
An Experimental Method for the Discovery &
Development of Tests of Character. AMS Pr.

Lentz, Thomas L.
xLentz, Thomas L.
Primitive Nervous Systems. Yale U Pr.

Lenz, Frederick, 1950-
xLenz, Frederick.
Lifetimes: True Accounts of Reincarnation.
Bobbs.

Lenz, Robert W.
xLenz, Robert W.
Organic Chemistry of Synthetic High
Polymers. Wiley.

Lenz, Siegfried, 1926-
xLenz, Siegfried.
An Exemplary Life. Hill & Wang.
German Lesson. Hill & Wang.
xLenz, Sigfried.
Survivor. Hill & Wang.

Lenz, Sigfried. *see* Lenz, Siegfried.

Lenz, Widukind.
xLenz, Widukind.
Medical Genetics. U of Chicago Pr.

Leokum, Arkady.
xLeokum, Arkady.
The Curious Book: Fascinating Facts About
People, Places & Things. Sterling.
Where Words Were Born. Corwin.

Leon, Daniel De. *see* De Leon, Daniel.

Leon, Dennis.
xLeon, Dennis.
Paul Harris. Abrams.

Leon, Derrick, 1908-1944
xLeon, Derrick.
Introduction to Proust, His Life, His Circle, &
His Work. Folcroft.

Leon, George, 1914-
xLeon, George.
How to Use AF & RF Signal Generators. TAB
Bks.

Leon, M. *see* Leon, Melvin.

Leon, Melvin, 1936-
xLeon, M.
Particle Physics: An Introduction. Acad Pr.

Leon-Portilla, Miguel.
xLeon-Portilla, Miguel.
Aztec Thought & Culture: A Study of the
Ancient Nahuatl Mind. U of Okla Pr.

Leonard, David K.
xLeonard, David K.
Reaching the Peasant Farmer: Organization
Theory & Practice in Kenya. U of Chicago
Pr.

Leonard, Donna.
xLeonard, Donna.
Lord, I'm Listening. Victor Bks.

Leonard, Edson. *see* Leonard, J. Edson.

Leonard, Ellis P.
xLeonard, Ellis P.
Fundamentals of Small Animal Surgery.
Saunders.
Orthopedic Surgery of the Dog & Cat.
Saunders.

Leonard, Elmore.
xLeonard, Elmore.
Hombre. Ballantine.
Swag. Delacorte.

Leonard, Fred E. *see* Leonard, Fred Eugene.

Leonard, Fred Eugene.
xLeonard, Fred E.
A Guide to the History of Physical Education.
Greenwood.

Leonard, George. *see* Leonard, George Burr.
Leonard, George B. *see* Leonard, George Burr.

Leonard, George Burr, 1923-
xLeonard, George.

The Silent Pulse: A Search for the Perfect
Rhythm That Exists in Each of Us. Dutton.
xLeonard, George B.
Education & Ecstasy. Dell.
Leonard, George H.
xLeonard, George H.
Somebody Else Is on the Moon. PB.
Leonard, H. Jeffrey.
xLeonard, H. Jeffrey.
ed. Business & Environment: Toward Common
Ground. Conservation Foun.
Leonard, H. S. *see* Leonard, Henry Siggins.
Leonard, Henry Siggins, 1905-1967
xLeonard, H. S.
Principles of Reasoning: An Introduction to
Logic, Methodology & the Theory of Signs.
Peter Smith.
Leonard, Ira M.
xLeonard, Ira M.
American Nativism. Van Nos Reinhold.
Leonard, Irving A. *see* Leonard, Irving Albert.
Leonard, Irving Albert, 1896-
xLeonard, Irving A.
Baroque Times in Old Mexico:
Seventeenth-Century Persons, Places, &
Practices. U of Mich Pr.
Colonial Travelers in Latin America. Phila Bk
Co.
Leonard, J. Edson.
xLeonard, Edson.
Feather in the Breeze. Freshet Pr.
Leonard, John.
xLeonard, John.
Private Lives in the Imperial City. Ballantine.
Private Lives in the Imperial City. Knopf.
Leonard, John P. *see* Leonard, John Paul.
Leonard, John Paul, 1901-
xLeonard, John P.
The Use of Practice Exercises in the Teaching
of Capitalization & Punctuation. AMS Pr.
Leonard, Jonathan. *see* Leonard, Jonathan Norton.
Leonard, Jonathan N. *see* Leonard, Jonathan Norton.
Leonard, Jonathan Norton.
xLeonard, Jonathan.
Atlantic Beaches. Silver.
xLeonard, Jonathan N.
Atlantic Beaches. Time-Life.
The First Farmers. Time-Life.
The First Farmers. Silver.
Leonard, Karen I. *see* Leonard, Karen Isaksen.
Leonard, Karen Isaksen.
xLeonard, Karen I.
Social History of an Indian Caste: The
Kayasths of Hyderabad. U of Cal Pr.
Leonard, Lawrence E.
xLeonard, Lawrence E.
Centralized Book Processing: A Feasibility
Study Based on Colorado Academic
Libraries. Scarecrow.
Leonard, Lee.
xLeonard, Lee.
I Miss You When You're Here. Stein & Day.
Leonard, Phyllis. *see* Leonard, Phyllis G.
Leonard, Phyllis G.
xLeonard, Phyllis.
Tarnished Angel. Coward.
Leonard, Richard A. *see* Leonard, Richard Anthony.
Leonard, Richard Anthony.
xLeonard, Richard A.
A History of Russian Music. Greenwood.
Leonard, Thomas C., 1944-
xLeonard, Thomas C.
Above the Battle: War-Making in America
from Appomattox to Versailles. Oxford U Pr.
Leonard, V. A. *see* Leonard, Vivian Anderson.
Leonard, Vivian Anderson.
xLeonard, V. A.

Criminal Investigation & Identification. C C
Thomas.
Fundamentals of Law Enforcement: Problems
& Issues. West Pub.
Leonard, William E. *see* Leonard, William Ellery.
Leonard, William Ellery, 1876-1944
xLeonard, William E.
Byron & Byronism in America. Gordian.
Leonard, William F.
xLeonard, William F.
Electronic Structure & Transport Properties of
Crystals. Krieger.
Leonard, William N. *see* Leonard, William Norris.
Leonard, William Norris, 1912-
xLeonard, William N.
Railroad Consolidation Under the
Transportation Act of 1920. AMS Pr.
The Leonardo Scholars.
xTheLeonardo Scholars.
Resources & Decisions. Duxbury Pr.
Leonards, G. A.
xLeonards, G. A.
ed. Foundation Engineering. McGraw.
Leone, Charles A.
xLeone, Charles A.
Fetal Pig Manual. Burgess.
Leone, Gene.
xLeone, Gene.
Leone's Italian Cookbook. Har-Row.
Leone, Mark P.
xLeone, Mark P.
Roots of Modern Mormonism. Harvard U Pr.
Leone, Nicholas C.
xLeone, Nicholas C.
Cruising Sailors Medical Guide. McKay.
The Farmer's & Rancher's Medical Guide.
McKay.
Leong, James, 1924-
xLeong, James.
Low Calorie Chinese Gourmet Cookbook.
Corwin.
The Low Calorie Chinese Gourmet Cookbook.
Pinnacle Bks.
Leonhard, Charles.
xLeonhard, Charles.
Foundations & Principles of Music Education.
McGraw.
Leonhard, Karl.
xLeonhard, Karl.
The Classification of Endogenous Psychoses.
Halsted Pr.
Leonhard, Wolfgang.
xLeonhard, Wolfgang.
Eurocommunism: Challenge for East & West.
HR&W.
Leonidas, Prof., Pseud.
xLeonidas.
Secrets of Stage Hypnotism. Borgo Pr.
xLeonidas, Professor.
Secrets of Stage Hypnotism. Newcastle Pub.
Leonidas, Professor. *see* Leonidas.
Leonov, Leonid M. *see* Leonov, Leonid Maksimovich.
Leonov, Leonid Maksimovich, 1899-
xLeonov, Leonid M.
Soviet River. Hyperion Conn.
Leontief, Wassily. *see* Leontief, Wassily W.
Leontief, Wassily W.
xLeontief, Wassily.
The Future of the World Economy: A United
Nations Study. Oxford U Pr.
xLeontief, Wassily W.
Input-Output Economics. Oxford U Pr.
The Structure of American Economy,
1919-1939: An Empirical Application of
Equilibrium Analysis. M E Sharpe.
Leopold, A. *see* Leopold, Aldo Carl.
Leopold, A. Starker. *see* Leopold, Aldo Starker.
Leopold, Aldo Carl.
xLeopold, A.

Plant Growth & Development. McGraw.
Leopold, Aldo Starker, 1913-
xLeopold, A. Starker.
The California Quail. U of Cal Pr.
Leopold, Christopher.
xLeopold, Christopher.
Casablack. Doubleday.
Leopold, George R.
xLeopold, George R.
Fundamentals of Abdominal & Pelvic
Ultrasonography. Saunders.
Leopold, John A., 1937-
xLeopold, John A.
Alfred Hugenberg: The Radical Nationalist
Campaign Against the Weimar Republic.
Yale U Pr.
Leopold, Richard W. *see* Leopold, Richard William.
Leopold, Richard William.
xLeopold, Richard W.
Growth of American Foreign Policy: A
History. Knopf.
Lepage, Jane W. *see* Lepage, Jane Weiner.
Lepage, Jane Weiner, 1931-
xLepage, Jane W.
Women Composers, Conductors & Musicians
of the Twentieth Century: Selected
Biographies. Scarecrow.
Lepeltier, Robert.
xLepeltier, Robert.
The Restorer's Handbook of Drawings &
Prints. Van Nos Reinhold.
Lepetit Colloquium, 4th, Cocoyoc, Mexico, 1972.
xFourth Lepetit Colloquium Held in Cocoyoc,
Mex., Nov., 1972.
Possible Episomes in Eukaryotes: Proceedings.
Elsevier.
Lepetit Colloquium, 5th, Madrid, 1974.
xLepetit Colloquium, 5th, November 1974.
The Immunological Basis of Connective Tissue
Disorders: Proceedings. Elsevier.
Lepetit Colloquium, 5th, November 1974. *see* Lepetit
Colloquium, 5th, Madrid, 1974.
Lepley, Ray, 1903-
xLepley, Ray.
Dependability in Philosophy of Education.
AMS Pr.
Lepp, Henry.
xLepp, Henry.
Identifying & Collecting Rocks & Minerals. A
S Barnes.
Lepp, Ignace, 1909-
xLepp, Ignace.
Atheism in Our Time. Macmillan.
Death & Its Mysteries. Macmillan.
Lepper, F. A.
xLepper, F. A.
Trajan's Parthian War. Greenwood.
Leptin, Gert.
xLeptin, Gert.
Economic Reform in East German Industry.
Oxford U Pr.
Lequeux, James.
xLequeux, James.
Structure & Evolution of Galaxies. Gordon.
Leranbaum, Miriam.
xLeranbaum, Miriam.
Alexander Pope's Opus Magnum, 1729-1744.
Oxford U Pr.
Lerch, Constance.
xLerch, Constance.
Maternity Nursing. Mosby.
Lerche, Charles O.
xLerche, Charles O.
America in World Affairs. Greenwood.
Lere, John C., 1945-
xLere, John C.
Pricing Techniques for the Financial Executive.
Krieger.
Leridon, Henri.
xLeridon, Henri.

Human Fertility: The Basic Components. U of
   Chicago Pr.
Lerman, A. *see* Lerman, Abraham.
Lerman, Abraham.
   xLerman, A.
   Geochemical Processes: Water & Sediment
      Environments. Wiley.
Lerman, Eleanor, 1952-
   xLerman, Eleanor.
   Armed Love. Columbia U Pr.
Lerman, Paul.
   xLerman, Paul.
   Community Treatment & Social Control: A
      Critical Analysis of Juvenile Correctional
      Policy. U of Chicago Pr.
Lerman, Rhoda.
   xLerman, Rhoda.
   Call Me Ishtar. HR&W.
   Eleanor: A Novel. HR&W.
   The Girl That He Marries. PB.
Lerman, Sidney.
   xLerman, Sidney.
   ed. Radiant Energy & the Eye. Macmillan.
Lerner, A. Ya. *see* Lerner, Aleksandr Iakovlevich.
Lerner, Aaron B. *see* Lerner, Aaron Bunsen.
Lerner, Aaron Bunsen.
   xLerner, Aaron B.
   Einstein & Newton: A Comparison of the Two
      Greatest Scientists. Lerner Pubns.
Lerner, Abba P. *see* Lerner, Abba Ptachya.
Lerner, Abba Ptachya.
   xLerner, Abba P.
   The Economics of Efficiency & Growth:
      Lessons from Israel & the West Bank.
      Ballinger Pub.
   Economics of Employment. Greenwood.
   Essays in Economic Analysis. Hyperion Conn.
Lerner, Aleksandr Iakovlevich.
   xLerner, A. Ya.
   Fundamentals of Cybernetics. Plenum Pub.
Lerner, Carol.
   xLerner, Carol.
   illus. Flowers of a Woodland Spring. Morrow.
   illus. On the Forest Edge. Morrow.
Lerner, Daniel.
   xLerner, Daniel.
   ed. Communication Research: A Half-Century
      Appraisal. U Pr of Hawaii.
   ed. Human Meaning of the Social Sciences.
      Peter Smith.
   ed. Propaganda in War & Crisis. Arno.
   Psychological Warfare Against Nazi Germany:
      The Sykewar Campaign D-Day to VE-Day.
      MIT Pr.
Lerner, Eric.
   xLerner, Eric.
   Journey of Insight Meditation: A Personal
      Experience of the Buddha's Way. Schocken.
Lerner, Gerda, 1920-
   xLerner, Gerda.
   The Majority Finds Its Past: Placing Women in
      History. Oxford U Pr.
Lerner, I. Michael. *see* Lerner, Isadore Michael.
Lerner, Isadore Michael, 1910-
   xLerner, I. Michael.
   The Genetic Basis of Selection. Greenwood.
   Genetic Homeostasis. Dover.
   Genetic Homeostasis. Peter Smith.
Lerner, Joseph.
   xLerner, Joseph.
   A Review of Amino Acid Transport Processes
      in Animal Cells & Tissues. U Maine Orono.
Lerner, Laurence.
   xLerner, Laurence.
   A.R.T.H.U.R.: The Life & Opinions of a
      Digital Computer. U of Mass Pr.
   Love & Marriage: Literature & Its Social
      Context. St Martin.
Lerner, Marguerite R. *see* Lerner, Marguerite Rush.

Lerner, Marguerite Rush.
   xLerner, Marguerite R.
   Color & People: The Story of Pigmentation.
      Lerner Pubns.
   Dear Little Mumps Child. Lerner Pubns.
   Doctors' Tools. Lerner Pubns.
   Twins: The Story of Twins. Lerner Pubns.
   Where Do You Come From: The Story of
      Evolution. Lerner Pubns.
Lerner, Mark.
   xLerner, Mark.
   Careers in a Restaurant. Lerner Pubns.
   Careers in a Supermarket. Lerner Pubns.
   Careers in Beauty & Grooming. Lerner Pubns.
   Careers in Hotels & Motels. Lerner Pubns.
   Careers in Toy Making. Lerner Pubns.
   Careers in Trucking. Lerner Pubns.
   Careers with a Newspaper. Lerner Pubns.
Lerner, Max, 1902-
   xLerner, Max.
   Actions & Passions: Notes on the Multiple
      Revolution of Our Time. Kennikat.
   Ideas for the Ice Age: Studies in a
      Revolutionary Era. Greenwood.
   Values in Education: Notes Toward a Values
      Philosophy. Phi Delta Kappa.
Lerner, Michael. *see* Lerner, Michael G.
Lerner, Michael G.
   xLerner, Michael.
   Maupassant. Braziller.
   xLerner, Michael G.
   Edouard Rod (1857-1910): A Portrait of the
      Novelist & His Times. Mouton.
Lerner, Peter M. *see* Lerner, Peter Morris.
Lerner, Peter Morris.
   xLerner, Peter M.
   Famous Chess Players. Lerner Pubns.
Lerner, Ralph.
   xLerner, Ralph.
   ed. Medieval Political Philosophy: A
      Sourcebook. Cornell U Pr.
Lerner, Richard M.
   xLerner, Richard M.
   ed. Child Influences on Marital & Family
      Interaction: A Life-Span Perspectives. Acad
      Pr.
Lerner, Robert E.
   xLerner, Robert E.
   Age of Adversity: The Fourteenth Century.
      Cornell U Pr.
Lerner, Sharon.
   xLerner, Sharon.
   illus. Who Will Wake up Spring?. Lerner
      Pubns.
Leroux, Gaston, 1868-1927
   xLeroux, Gaston.
   The Bride of the Sun. Arno.
Leroy, Dave, 1920-
   xLeRoy, David.
   The Outdoorsman's Guide to Government
      Surplus. Contemp Bks.
LeRoy, David. *see* Leroy, Dave.
Leroy, Douglas.
   xLeroy, Douglas.
   I Didn't Know That. Pathway Pr.
LeRoy, G. C. *see* Leroy, Gaylord C.
Leroy, Gaylord C.
   xLeRoy, G. C.
   tr. Preserve & Create: Essays in Marxist
      Literary Criticism. Am Inst Marxist.
   xLeRoy, Gaylord C.
   ed. Preserve & Create: Essays in Marxist
      Literary Criticism. Humanities.
Leroy, Gen.
   xLeRoy, Gen.
   Bridget. Har-Row.
   Cold Feet. Har-Row.
   Hotheads. Har-Row.
Lerup, Lars.
   xLerup, Lars.

Building the Unfinished: Architecture &
   Human Action. Sage.
Lesea, Austin.
   xLesea, Austin.
   Microprocessor Interfacing Techniques. Sybex.
Lesh, Terry.
   xLesh, Terry.
   Meditation for Young People. Lothrop.
LeShan, Lawrence. *see* Leshan, Lawrence L.
Leshan, Lawrence L., 1920-
   xLeShan, Lawrence.
   How to Meditate: A Guide to Self-Discovery.
      Bantam.
   How to Meditate: A Guide to Self-Discovery.
      Little.
   The Medium, the Mystic & the Physicist:
      Toward a General Theory of the Paranormal.
      Viking Pr.
Leshin, George.
   xLeshin, George.
   Speech for the Hearing-Impaired Child. U of
      Ariz Pr.
Leshner, Marty.
   xLeshner, Marty.
   Trouble-Free Travel: What to Know Before
      You Go. Watts.
Lesiak, Michaeline.
   xLesiak, Michaeline.
   Art of Fine Lettering: Basic Skills &
      Techniques. U of Notre Dame Pr.
Lesikar, Raymond V. *see* Lesikar, Raymond Vincent.
Lesikar, Raymond Vincent.
   xLesikar, Raymond V.
   Basic Business Communication. Irwin.
   Business Communication: Theory &
      Application. Irwin.
   How to Write a Report Your Boss Will Read &
      Remember. Dow Jones-Irwin.
Lesko, Barbara S.
   xLesko, Barbara S.
   Remarkable Women of Ancient Egypt. B C
      Scribe.
Leskov, Nikolai S. *see* Leskov, Nikolai Semenovich.
Leskov, Nikolai Semenovich, 1831-1895
   xLeskov, Nikolai S.
   The Cathedral Folk. Greenwood.
   The Cathedral Folk. Hyperion Conn.
Lesky, Albin, 1896-
   xLesky, Albin.
   History of Greek Literature. T Y Crowell.
   Thalatta: Der Weg der Griechen Zum Meer.
      Arno.
Lesky, Albin. *see* Lesky, Albin, 1896-.
Lesky, Albin, 1896-.
   xLesky, Albin.
   Greek Tragedy. B&N.
Leslau, Wolf.
   xLeslau, Wolf.
   Etymological Dictionary of Harari. U of Cal
      Pr.
Lesley, Cole.
   xLesley, Cole.
   The Life of Noel Coward. Penguin.
   Noel Coward & His Friends. Morrow.
Lesley, Robert W. *see* Lesley, Robert Whitman.
Lesley, Robert Whitman, 1853-
   xLesley, Robert W.
   History of the Portland Cement Industry in the
      United States. Arno.
Leslie, Charles. *see* Leslie, Charles M.
Leslie, Charles M., 1923-
   xLeslie, Charles.
   ed. Asian Medical Systems: A Comparative
      Study. U of Cal Pr.
Leslie, D. C. *see* Leslie, David Clement.
Leslie, David Clement, 1924-
   xLeslie, D. C.

Developments in the Theory of Turbulence.
Oxford U Pr.
Leslie, Donald, 1922-
xLeslie, Donald D.
The Survival of the Chinese Jews: The Jewish
Community of Kaifeng. Humanities.
Leslie, Donald D. *see* Leslie, Donald.
Leslie, Douglas. *see* Leslie, Douglas L.
Leslie, Douglas L., 1942-
xLeslie, Douglas.
Cases & Materials on Labor Law: Process &
Policy. Little.
xLeslie, Douglas L.
Labor Law in a Nutshell. West Pub.
Leslie, Gerald R.
xLeslie, Gerald R.
The Family in Social Context. Oxford U Pr.
Introductory Sociology: Order & Change in
Society. Oxford U Pr.
Marriage in a Changing World. Wiley.
Leslie, John, 1940-
xLeslie, John.
Value & Existence. Rowman.
Leslie, John. F.
xLeslie, John F.
Core Mathematics. Scott F.
Leslie, Josephine.
xLeslie, Josephine.
The Devil & Mrs. Devine. PB.
Leslie, L. *see* Leslie, Louis A.
Leslie, Louis A.
xLeslie, L.
Gregg Shorthand for Colleges, Transcription.
McGraw.
xLeslie, Louis A.
College Dictation for Transcription. McGraw.
Gregg Shorthand for Colleges. McGraw.
Gregg Shorthand for Colleges, Transcription.
McGraw.
Gregg Transcription. McGraw.

Leslie, Noel.
xLeslie, Noel.
Three Plays. Core Collection.

Leslie, R. F.
xLeslie, R. F.
Reform & Insurrection in Russian Poland,
1856-1865. Greenwood.

Leslie, Robert C. *see* Leslie, Robert Campbell.

Leslie, Robert Campbell.
xLeslie, Robert C.
Sustaining Intimacy: Christian Faith &
Wholeness in Marriage. Abingdon.

Leslie, Robert F. *see* Leslie, Robert Franklin.

Leslie, Robert Franklin.
xLeslie, Robert F.
In the Shadow of a Rainbow: The True Story
of a Friendship Between Man & Wolf.
Norton.
In the Shadow of a Rainbow: The True Story
of a Friendship Between Man & Wolf. NAL.
xLeslie, Robert L.
Miracle at Square Top Mountain. Dutton.

Leslie, Robert L. *see* Leslie, Robert Franklin.

Leslie, Sarah.
xLeslie, Sarah.
Who Invented It & What Makes It Work.
Platt.
Leslie, Shane, Sir Bart, 1885-
xLeslie, Shane.
Men Were Different: Five Studies in Late
Victorian Biography. Arno.
Leslie-Melville, Betty.
xLeslie-Melville, Betty.
Raising Daisy Rothschild. S&S.
Raising Daisy Rothschild. Warner Bks.

Lesly, Philip, 1918-
xLesly, Philip.
How We Discommunicate. Am Mgmt.
Lesly's Public Relations Handbook. P-H.
Lesly's Public Relations Handbook. P-H.
Lesniak, Rose, 1955-
xLesniak, Rose.
Young Anger. Toothpaste.
Lesnoff-Caravaglia, Gari.
xLesnoff-Caravaglia, Gari.
Health Care of the Elderly: Strategies for
Prevention & Intervention. Human Sci Pr.
Lessa, William A. *see* Lessa, William Armand.
Lessa, William Armand.
xLessa, William A.
Drake's Island of Thieves: Ethnological
Sleuthing. U Pr of Hawaii.
Reader in Comparative Religion: An
Anthropological Approach. Har-Row.
Ulithi: A Micronesian Design for Living.
HR&W.
Lessem, Alan P. *see* Lessem, Alan Philip.
Lessem, Alan Philip.
xLessem, Alan P.
Music & Text in the Works of Arnold
Schoenberg: The Critical Years, 1908-1922.
Univ Microfilms.
Lesser, Gerald S.
xLesser, Gerald S.
Children & Television: Lessons from Sesame
Street. Random.
Lesser, Michael.
xLesser, Michael.
Nutrition & Vitamin Therapy. Grove.
Lesser, R. *see* Lesser, Ruth.
Lesser, R. H.
xLesser, R. H.
Indian Mosaic. InterCulture.
Lesser, Ruth.
xLesser, R.
Linguistic Investigations of Aphasia. Elsevier.
Lessing, Doris.
xLessing, Doris.
The Habit of Loving. NAL.
The Habit of Loving. Popular Lib.
Habit of Loving. T Y Crowell.
Proper Marriage: A Complete Novel from
Doris Lessing's Masterwork, Children of
Violence. NAL.
Lessing, Doris. *see* Lessing, Doris May.
Lessing, Doris May, 1919-
xLessing, Doris.
Briefing for a Descent into Hell. Bantam.
Briefing for a Descent into Hell. Knopf.
Going Home. Popular Lib.
The Golden Notebook. Bantam.
Golden Notebook. S&S.
The Grass Is Singing. NAL.
The Grass Is Singing. Popular Lib.
In Pursuit of the English. Beekman Pubs.
In Pursuit of the English. Popular Lib.
The Memoirs of a Survivor. Bantam.
The Memoirs of a Survivor. Knopf.
Particularly Cats. NAL.
Particularly Cats. S&S.
Stories. Knopf.
Stories. Random.
The Summer Before the Dark. Knopf.
Lessing, Erich.
xLessing, Erich.
Adventures of Ulysses: Homer's Epic in
Pictures. Dodd.
Lessing, Gotthold E. *see* Lessing, Gotthold Ephraim.
Lessing, Gotthold Ephraim.
xLessing, Gotthold E.
Nathan the Wise. Ungar.
Nathan the Wise. Barron.
Lessing, Otto E. *see* Lessing, Otto Eduard.
Lessing, Otto Eduard, 1875-
xLessing, Otto E.

Masters in Modern German Literature. Arno.
Lessner, Erwin C. *see* Lessner, Erwin Christian.
Lessner, Erwin Christian, 1898-1959
xLessner, Erwin C.
The Danube: The Dramatic History of the
Great River & the People Touched by Its
Flow. Greenwood.
Lester, Anthony.
xLester, Anthony.
Race & Law in Great Britain. Harvard U Pr.
Lester, David.
xLester, David.
Crime of Passion: Murder & the Murderer.
Nelson-Hall.
Crisis Intervention & Counseling by Telephone.
C C Thomas.
Gambling Today. C C Thomas.
ed. Suicide: A Guide to Information Sources.
Gale.
Lester, G. A.
xLester, G. A.
The Anglo Saxons: How They Lived &
Worked. Dufour.
Lester, Helen.
xLester, Helen.
illus. Cora Copycat. Dutton.
Lester, James D.
xLester, James D.
Writing Research Papers: A Complete Guide.
Scott F.
Lester, John A. *see* Lester, John Ashby.
Lester, John Ashby, 1915-
xLester, John A.
Journey Through Despair, 1880-1914:
Transformations in British Literary Culture.
Princeton U Pr.
Lester, Julius.
xLester, Julius.
All Is Well. Morrow.
Long Journey Home: Stories from Black
History. Dial.
Revolutionary Notes. Grove.
Two Love Stories. Dial.
Who I Am. Dial.
Lester, Lee.
xLester, Lee.
The Absolute Beginners Book of House Plants.
Citadel Pr.
Lester, Malcolm.
xLester, Malcom.
Anthony Merry Redivivus: A Reappraisal of
the British Minister to the United States,
1803-6. U Pr of Va.
Lester, Malcom. *see* Lester, Malcolm.
Lester, Margaret D.
xLester, Margaret D.
Brigham Street. Utah St Hist Soc.
Lester, Richard A. *see* Lester, Richard Allen.
Lester, Richard Allen.
xLester, Richard A.
As Unions Mature: An Analysis of the
Evolution of American Unionism. Princeton
U Pr.
Reasoning About Discrimination: The Analysis
of Professional & Executive Work in Federal
Antibias Programs. Princeton U Pr.
Lester, Richard I., 1930-
xLester, Richard I.
Confederate Finance & Purchasing in Great
Britain. U Pr of Va.
Lester, Robert C.
xLester, Robert C.
Theravada Buddhism in Southeast Asia. U of
Mich Pr.
Lester, Ronald H.
xLester, Ronald H.
Quality Control for Profit. Indus Pr.
Lesthaeghe, Ron J.
xLesthaeghe, Ron J.

The Decline of Belgian Fertility: 1890-1970.
Princeton U Pr.
Lesy, Michael, 1945-
xLesy, Michael.
Real Life: Louisville in the Twenties. Pantheon.
Letcher Lyle, Katie. *see* Lyle, Katie Letcher.
Lethaby, William. *see* Lethaby, William Richard.
Lethaby, William Richard, 1857-1931
xLethaby, William.
Architecture, Mysticism & Myth. Braziller.
Lethbridge, Henry J.
xLethbridge, Henry J.
Hong Kong: Stability & Change: A Collection
of Essays. Oxford U Pr.
Lethbridge, T. C. *see* Lethbridge, Thomas Charles.
Lethbridge, Thomas Charles.
xLethbridge, T. C.
The Power of the Pendulum. Routledge &
Kegan.
Letiche, John M, 1918-
xLetiche, John M.
Balance of Payments & Economic Growth.
Kelley.
Letis, Theodore P.
xLetis, Theodore P.
Martin Luther & Charismatic Ecumenism.
Reformation Res.
Letkemann, Peter, 1935-
xLetkemann, Peter.
Crime As Work. P-H.
Letokhov, V. S.
xLetokhov, V. S.
Nonlinear Laser Spectroscopy. Springer-Verlag.
Letourneau, Richard.
xLeTourneau, Richard H.
Success Without Compromise. Victor Bks.
LeTourneau, Richard H. *see* Letourneau, Richard.
Lett, Monica. *see* Lett, Monica R.
Lett, Monica R., 1942-
xLett, Monica.
Rent Control Concepts, Realities &
Mechanisms. Ctr Urban Pol Res.
Lettieri, Dan J.
xLettieri, Dan J.
ed. Drugs & Suicide: When Other Coping
Strategies Fail. Sage.
Letts, Mary.
xLetts, Mary.
Al Capone. St Martin.
Letwin, William.
xLetwin, William.
ed. A Documentary History of American
Economic Policy Since 1789. Norton.
The Origins of Scientific Economics.
Greenwood.
Leuba, James H. *see* Leuba, James Henry.
Leuba, James Henry, 1868-1946
xLeuba, James H.
Psychological Study of Religion: Its Origin,
Function, & Future. AMS Pr.
Leuchtenburg, William. *see* Leuchtenburg, William
Edward.
Leuchtenburg, William E. *see* Leuchtenburg, William
Edward.
Leuchtenburg, William Edward, 1922-
xLeuchtenburg, William.
Franklin D. Roosevelt & the New Deal,
1932-1940. Har-Row.
xLeuchtenburg, William E.
Flood Control Politics: The Connecticut River
Valley Problem, 1927-1950. Da Capo.
Franklin D. Roosevelt & the New Deal,
1932-1940. Har-Row.
A Troubled Feast: American Society Since
1945. Little.
ed. The Unfinished Century: America Since
1900. Little.
Leucocyte Conference, 9th, Williamsburg, Va., 1974.
xLeukocyte Culture Conference, 9th.

Immune Recognition: Proceedings. Acad Pr.
Leukel, Francis.
xLeukel, Francis.
Introduction to Physiological Psychology.
Mosby.
xLeukel, Francis P.
Essentials of Physiological Psychology. Mosby.
Leukel, Francis P. *see* Leukel, Francis.
Leukocyte Culture Conference, 9th. *see* Leucocyte
Conference, 9th, Williamsburg, Va., 1974.
Leung, Mai.
xLeung, Mai.
The Classic Chinese Cook Book. Har-Row.
Leupold, H. C. *see* Leupold, Herbert Carl.
Leupold, Herbert C. *see* Leupold, Herbert Carl.
Leupold, Herbert Carl, 1892-
xLeupold, H. C.
Exposition of Isaiah. Baker Bk.
xLeupold, Herbert C.
Exposition of Genesis. Baker Bk.
Leupp, Francis E. *see* Leupp, Francis Ellington.
Leupp, Francis Ellington, 1849-1918
xLeupp, Francis E.
In Red Man's Land: A Study of the American
Indian. Rio Grande.
Indian & His Problem. Arno.
The Indian & His Problem. Johnson Repr.
Leutenegger, Ralph R.
xLeutenegger, Ralph R.
Patient Care & Rehabilitation of
Communication-Impaired Adults. C C
Thomas.
Sounds of American English: An Introduction
to Phonetics. Scott F.
Leutze, James R., 1935-
xLeutze, James R.
Bargaining for Supremacy: Anglo-American
Naval Collaboration, 1937-1941. U of NC Pr.
Leuzinger, Elsy.
xLeuzinger, Elsy.
The Art of Black Africa. Rizzoli Intl.
Lev, Baruch.
xLev, Baruch.
Financial Statement Analysis: A New
Approach. P-H.
Levan, Susan, 1947-
xLevan, Susan.
The Vegetable Parade. Street Fiction.
Levantrosser, William F.
xLevantrosser, William F.
Congress & the Citizen-Soldier: Legislative
Policy-Making for the Federal Armed Forces
Reserve. Ohio St U Pr.
Levarie, Norma.
xLevarie, Norma.
Art & History of Books. Heineman.
Levasseur, Alain A.
xLevasseur, Alain A.
The Civil Code of the Ivory Coast. Michie.
Levcik, Friedrich.
xLevcik, Friedrich.
Industrial Cooperation Between East & West.
M E Sharpe.
Leve, Charles. *see* Leve, Chuck.
Leve, Chuck.
xLeve, Charles.
Inside Racquetball. Contemp Bks.
Leve, Robert.
xLeve, Robert.
Childhood: The Study of Development.
Random.
Levelt, W. J. *see* Levelt, Willem J. M.
Levelt, Willem J. M.
xLevelt, W. J.
Studies in the Perception of Language. Wiley.
Leven, Charles L.
xLeven, Charles L.

Analytical Framework for Regional
Development Policy. MIT Pr.
ed. The Mature Metropolis. Lexington Bks.
Leven, Jeremy.
xLeven, Jeremy.
Creator. Coward.
Levendosky, Charles.
xLevendosky, Charles.
Perimeters. Columbia U Pr.
Levene. *see* Levene, John R.
Levene, Donald L.
xLevene, Donald L.
ed. Chest Pain: An Integrated Diagnostic
Approach. Lea & Febiger.
Levene, G. M. *see* Levene, Gerald Max.
Levene, Gerald Max.
xLevene, G. M.
Color Atlas of Dermatology. Year Bk Med.
Levene, John R.
xLevene.
Clinical Refraction & Visual Science.
Butterworths.
Levens, A. S. *see* Levens, Alexander Sander.
Levens, Alexander. *see* Levens, Alexander Sander.
Levens, Alexander Sander, 1900-
xLevens, A. S.
Graphical Methods in Research. Krieger.
xLevens, Alexander.
Graphics in Engineering Design. Wiley.
Levenson, Alvin. *see* Levenson, Alvin J.
Levenson, Alvin J.
xLevenson, Alvin.
ed. The Neuropsychiatric Side Effects of Drugs
in the Elderly. Raven.
Levenson, Dorothy.
xLevenson, Dorothy.
First Book of the Civil War. Watts.
Homesteaders & Indians. Watts.
Levenson, J. R. *see* Levenson, Joseph Richmond.
Levenson, Jordan.
xLevenson, Jordon.
Retail Fruit Species: Your Shopper's Guide to
Their Best Varieties. Levenson Pr.
Levenson, Jordon. *see* Levenson, Jordan.
Levenson, Joseph R. *see* Levenson, Joseph Richmond.
Levenson, Joseph Richmond, 1920-1969
xLevenson, J. R.
Modern China: An Interpretive Anthology.
Macmillan.
xLevenson, Joseph R.
Confucian China & Its Modern Fate: A
Trilogy. U of Cal Pr.
Levenson, Sam. *see* Levenson, Samuel.
Levenson, Samuel, 1911-
xLevenson, Sam.
Everything but Money. PB.
Everything but Money. S&S.
In One Era & Out the Other. G K Hall.
In One Era & Out the Other. PB.
In One Era & Out the Other. S&S.
You Don't Have to Be in Who's Who to
Know What's What. PB.
You Don't Have to Be in Who's Who to
Know What's What. S&S.
You Don't Have to Be in Who's Who to
Know What's What. G K Hall.
Levenspiel, Octave.
xLevenspiel, Octave.
Chemical Reaction Engineering. Wiley.
Leventhal, F. M., 1938-
xLeventhal, F. M.
Respectable Radical: George Howell &
Victorian Working Class Politics. Harvard U
Pr.
Leventhal, Herbert, 1941-
xLeventhal, Herbert.

In the Shadow of the Enlightenment:
Occultism & Renaissance Science in
Eighteenth-Century America. NYU Pr.
Leventhal, Lance A., 1945-
xLeventhal, Lance A.
Introduction to Microprocessors: Software,
Hardware, Programming. P-H.
Leventhal, Ruth.
xLeventhal, Ruth.
Medical Parasitology: A Self-Instructional Text.
Davis Co.
LeVeque, W. J. *see* LeVeque, William Judson.
LeVeque, William J. *see* LeVeque, William Judson.
LeVeque, William Judson.
xLeVeque, W. J.
ed. Studies in Number Theory. Math Assn.
xLeVeque, William J.
Fundamentals of Number Theory. A-W.
Lever, Christopher, 1932-
xLever, Christopher.
The Naturalized Animals of the British Isles.
Merrimack Bk Serv.
Lever, J. W. *see* Lever, Julius Walter.
Lever, Julius Walter.
xLever, J. W.
Sonnets of the English Renaissance.
Humanities.
Lever, Walter F.
xLever, Walter F.
ed. Dermatomyositis & Polymyositis. Mss Info.
Histopathology of the Skin. Lippincott.
Lever, William E. *see* Lever, William Edward.
Lever, William Edward.
xLever, William E.
How to Obtain Money for College: A
Complete Guide to Sources of Financial Aid
for Education. Arco.
Leverant, Robert.
xLeverant, Robert.
On the Transmission of Photography. Images
Pr.
Leverenz, David.
xLeverenz, David.
The Language of Puritan Feeling: An
Exploration in Literature, Psychology, &
Social History. Rutgers U Pr.
Leverenz, Humboldt W.
xLeverenz, Humboldt W.
An Introduction to Luminescence of Solids.
Peter Smith.
Leverich, Kathleen.
xLeverich, Kathleen.
The Hungry Fox & the Foxy Duck. Parents.
Levering, Ralph B.
xLevering, Ralph B.
The Public & American Foreign Policy,
1918-1978. Morrow.
Levering, Robert, 1944-
xLevering, Robert.
Beating the Used Car Hustle. Chronicle Bks.
Levernier, James.
xLevernier, James.
Compiled by The Indians & Their Captives.
Greenwood.
xLevernier, James A.
ed. Souldiery Spiritualized: Seven Sermons
Preached Before the Artillery Companies of
New England, 1674-1774. Schol Facsimiles.
Levernier, James A. *see* Levernier, James.
Leverton, Garrett H. *see* Leverton, Garrett Hasty.
Leverton, Garrett Hasty, 1896-1949
xLeverton, Garrett H.
The Production of Later Nineteenth Century
American Drama: A Basis for Teaching.
AMS Pr.
Leverton, Ruth M.
xLeverton, Ruth M.
Food Becomes You. Iowa St U Pr.
Levertov, Denise, 1923-
xLevertov, Denise.

The Freeing of the Dust. New Directions.
Life in the Forest. New Directions.
Leveson, I. *see* Leveson, Irving.
Leveson, Irving.
xLeveson, I.
ed. Quantitative Explorations in Drug Abuse
Policy. Spectrum Pub.
Levesque, Jacques.
xLevesque, Jacques.
The USSR & the Cuban Revolution: Soviet
Ideological & Strategical Perspectives,
1959-77. Praeger.
Leveton, Eva.
xLeveton, Eva.
Psychodrama for the Timid Clinician. Springer
Pub.
Levey, Gerald S.
xLevey, Gerald S.
Hormone Receptor Interaction: Molecular
Aspects. Dekker.
Levey, Marc B.
xLevey, Marc B.
Photography: Buying. Choosing. Using.
Amphoto.
Photography: Composition, Color. Display.
Amphoto.
Levey, Michael.
xLevey, Michael.
The Case of Walter Pater. Thames Hudson.
A Concise History of Painting: From Giotto to
Cezanne. Oxford U Pr.
Durer. Norton.
High Renaissance. Penguin.
A History of Western Art. Oxford U Pr.
Life & Death of Mozart. Stein & Day.
Painting at Court. NYU Pr.
The World of Ottoman Art. Scribner.
Levi, Arrigo, 1926-
xLevi, Arrigo.
Journey Among the Economists. Open Court.
Levi, Edward H. *see* Levi, Edward Hirsch.
Levi, Edward Hirsch, 1911-
xLevi, Edward H.
Introduction to Legal Reasoning. U of Chicago
Pr.
Levi, Isaac, 1930-
xLevi, Isaac.
The Enterprise of Knowledge: An Essay on
Knowledge, Credal Probability, & Chance.
MIT Pr.
Gambling with Truth: An Essay on Induction
& the Aims of Science. MIT Pr.
Levi, Leo, 1926-
xLevi, Leo.
Applied Optics: A Guide to Optical System
Design. Wiley.
Levi, Margaret.
xLevi, Margaret.
Bureaucratic Insurgency: The Case of Police
Unions. Lexington Bks.
Levi, Mario A. *see* Levi, Mario Attilio.
Levi, Mario Attilio.
xLevi, Mario A.
Political Power in the Ancient World.
Greenwood.
Levi, Peter.
xLevi, Peter.
Collected Poems 1955-1975. SBD.
Levi, Primo.
xLevi, Primo.
Survival in Auschwitz: The Nazi Assault on
Humanity. Macmillan.
Levi, Werner, 1912-
xLevi, Werner.
Australia's Outlook on Asia. Greenwood.
Contemporary International Law: A Concise
Introduction. Westview.
Levi-Strauss, Claude.
xLevi-Strauss, Claude.

From Honey to Ashes. Octagon.
Myth & Meaning. Schocken.
The Origin of Table Manners. Har-Row.
The Origin of Table Manners. Har-Row.
The Raw & the Cooked. Octagon.
Totemism. Beacon Pr.
Tristes Tropiques. Adler.
Tristes-Tropiques. Atheneum.
Leviant, Curt.
xLeviant, Curt.
The Yemenite Girl. Avon.
Levich, Richard M.
xLevich, Richard M.
ed. Exchange Risk & Exposure: Current
Developments in International Financial
Management. Lexington Bks.
Levie, Albert.
xLevie, Albert.
The Meat Handbook. AVI.
Levin, Alfred.
xLevin, Alfred.
The Third Duma, Election & Profile. Shoe
String.
Levin, Beatrice.
xLevin, Beatrice S.
Women & Medicine. Scarecrow.
Levin, Beatrice S. *see* Levin, Beatrice.
Levin, Betsy.
xLevin, Betsy.
ed. The Courts, Social Science, & School
Desegregation. Transaction Bks.
Levin, Betty.
xLevin, Betty.
The Forespoken. Macmillan.
A Griffon's Nest. Macmillan.
Landfall. Atheneum.
The Sword of Culann. Macmillan.
Levin, Daniel L.
xLevin, Daniel L.
A Practical Guide to Pediatric Intensive Care.
Mosby.
Levin, David, 1924-
xLevin, David.
Cotton Mather: The Young Life of the Lord's
Remembrancer, 1663-1703. Harvard U Pr.
Levin, Edward.
xLevin, Edward.
Levin's Laws: Tactics for Winning Without
Intimidation. M Evans.
Levin, Gail.
xLevin, Gail.
Edward Hopper As Illustrator. Norton.
Synchromism & American Color Abstraction,
1910-1925. Braziller.
Levin, Gerald.
xLevin, Gerald.
ed. Prose Models. HarBraceJ.
Levin, Gerald. *see* Levin, Gerald Henry.
Levin, Gerald Henry, 1929-
xLevin, Gerald.
ed. Short Essays: Models for Composition.
HarBraceJ.
Sigmund Freud. Twayne.
Styles for Writing: A Brief Rhetoric.
HarBraceJ.
Levin, Gilbert.
xLevin, Gilbert.
The Dynamics of Human Service Delivery.
Ballinger Pub.
The Persistent Poppy: A Computer-Aided
Search for Heroin Policy. Ballinger Pub.
Levin, Harold L. *see* Levin, Harold Leonard.
Levin, Harold Leonard, 1929-
xLevin, Harold L.
Life Through Time. Wm C Brown.
Levin, Harry, 1912-
xLevin, Harry.

Contexts of Criticism. Atheneum.
The Eye-Voice Span. MIT Pr.
Grounds for Comparison. Harvard U Pr.
Question of Hamlet. Oxford U Pr.
Question of Hamlet. Oxford U Pr.
Refractions: Essays in Comparative Literature.
 Oxford U Pr.
 ed. Veins of Humor. Harvard U Pr.
Levin, Harry. *see* Levin, Harry Tuchman.
Levin, Harry Tuchman.
 xLevin, Harry.
 Overreacher: A Study of Christopher Marlowe.
  Peter Smith.
Levin, Ira.
 xLevin, Ira.
 The Boys from Brazil. Dell.
 The Boys from Brazil. Random.
 Rosemary's Baby. Dell.
 Rosemary's Baby. Random.
 The Stepford Wives. Random.
Levin, J. R. *see* Levin, Joel R.
Levin, Jack, 1941-
 xLevin, Jack.
 The Functions of Prejudice. Har-Row.
 Starting Sociology. Har-Row.
Levin, Jane W. *see* Levin, Jane Whitbread.
Levin, Jane Whitbread.
 xLevin, Jane W.
 Bringing up Puppies: A Child's Book of Dog
  Breeding & Care. HarBraceJ.
Levin, Joel R.
 xLevin, J. R.
 ed. Cognitive Learning in Children: Theories &
  Strategies. Acad Pr.
 xLevin, Joel R.
 Learner Differences: Diagnosis & Prescription.
  HR&W.
Levin, Kenneth, 1944-
 xLevin, Kenneth.
 Freud's Early Psychology of the Neuroses: A
  Historical Perspective. U of Pittsburgh Pr.
Levin, Kristine C. *see* Levin, Kristine Cox.
Levin, Kristine Cox, 1944-
 xLevin, Kristine C.
 Silent Wings: A Handbook for Building Paper
  Airplanes & Balsa Gliders. Pruett.
Levin, Malinda. *see* Levin, Malinda Jo.
Levin, Malinda Jo.
 xLevin, Malinda.
 Psychology: A Biographical Approach.
  McGraw.
Levin, Marlin.
 xLevin, Marlin.
 Balm in Gilead: The Story of Hadassah.
  Schocken.
Levin, Martin.
 xLevin, Martin.
 ed. Hollywood & the Great Fan Magazines.
  Arbor Hse.
 ed. How to Get from January Through
  December in Powerboating. Har-Row.
 ed. Love Stories. Popular Lib.
 ed. Love Stories. Times Bks.
 What's Happening to Your Inheritance: A
  Guide to What You Can Do About
  Psychological, Legal & Financial Hazards.
  Times Bks.
Levin, Marvin E.
 xLevin, Marvin E.
 The Diabetic Foot. Mosby.
Levin, Melvin R., 1924-
 xLevin, Melvin R.
 Community & Regional Planning: Issues in
  Public Policy. Praeger.
Levin, Meyer, 1905-
 xLevin, Meyer.

Eva: A Novel of the Holocaust. Behrman.
The Harvest. S&S.
Story of the Jewish Way of Life. Behrman.
Levin, Michael E.
 xLevin, Michael E.
 Metaphysics & the Mind-Body Problem.
  Oxford U Pr.
Levin, Milton.
 xLevin, Milton.
 Noel Coward. Twayne.
Levin, Murray B. *see* Levin, Murray Burton.
Levin, Murray Burton.
 xLevin, Murray B.
 Edward Kennedy: The Myth of Leadership.
  HM.
Levin, N. Gordon. *see* Levin, Norman Gordon.
Levin, Nora.
 xLevin, Nora.
 The Holocaust: The Destruction of European
  Jewry, 1933-1945. Schocken.
 While Messiah Tarried: Jewish Socialist
  Movements, 1871-1917. Schocken.
Levin, Norman Gordon.
 xLevin, N. Gordon.
 Woodrow Wilson & World Politics: America's
  Response to War & Revolution. Oxford U Pr.
Levin, Richard. *see* Levin, Richard Louis.
Levin, Richard I.
 xLevin, Richard I.
 Statistics for Management. P-H.
Levin, Richard Louis, 1922-
 xLevin, Richard.
 Multiple Plot in English Renaissance Drama. U
  of Chicago Pr.
 New Readings Vs. Old Plays: Recent Trends in
  the Reinterpretation of English Renaissance
  Drama. U of Chicago Pr.
Levin, Richard M.
 xLevin, Richard M.
 ed. Pediatric Anesthesia Handbook. Med
  Exam.
 Pediatric Respiratory Intensive Care Handbook.
  Med Exam.
Levin, Saul.
 xLevin, Saul.
 Indo-European & Semitic Languages: An
  Exploration of Structural Similarities Related
  to Accent, Chiefly in Greek, Sanskrit, &
  Hebrew. State U NY Pr.
 The Linear B Decipherment Controversy
  Re-examined. State U NY Pr.
Levin, Shmarya, 1867-1935
 xLevin, Shmarya.
 The Arena. Arno.
Levinas, Emmanuel.
 xLevinas, Emmanuel.
 The Theory of Intuition in Husserl's
  Phenomenology. Northwestern U Pr.
Levine. *see* Levine, Mark Lee.
Levine, Andrew, 1944-
 xLevine, Andrew.
 The Politics of Autonomy: A Kantian Reading
  of Rousseau's "Social Contract". U of Mass
  Pr.
Levine, Arnold J.
 xLevine, Arnold J.
 Alienation in the Metropolis. R & E Res
  Assoc.
Levine, Arthur.
 xLevine, Arthur E.
 Reform of Undergraduate Education.
  Jossey-Bass.
Levine, Arthur E. *see* Levine, Arthur.
Levine, Baroch. *see* Levine, Baruch.
Levine, Baruch.
 xLevine, Baroch.
 Group Psychotherapy: Practice &
  Development. P-H.
Levine, Bernard, 1934-
 xLevine, Bernard.

The Dissolving Image: Spiritual-Esthetic
 Development of W. B. Yeats. Wayne St U
 Pr.
Levine, Betty K.
 xLevine, Betty K.
 Hawk High. Atheneum.
Levine, Daniel, 1934-
 xLevine, Daniel.
 Varieties of Reform Thought. Greenwood.
Levine, Daniel H.
 xLevine, Daniel H.
 ed. Churches & Politics in Latin America.
  Sage.
 Conflict & Political Change in Venezuela.
  Princeton U Pr.
Levine, David, 1926-
 xLevine, David.
 The Arts of David Levine. Knopf.
Levine, David P., 1948-
 xLevine, David P.
 Economic Studies: Contributions to the
  Critique of Economic Theory. Routledge &
  Kegan.
Levine, Donald N. *see* Levine, Donald Nathan.
Levine, Donald Nathan, 1931-
 xLevine, Donald N.
 Greater Ethiopia: The Evolution of a
  Multiethnic Society. U of Chicago Pr.
Levine, Elaine S. *see* Levine, Elaine Sue.
Levine, Elaine Sue.
 xLevine, Elaine S.
 Ethnic Esteem Among Anglo, Black, &
  Chicano Children. R & E Res Assoc.
Levine, Erwin L.
 xLevine, Erwin L.
 An Introduction to American Government.
  Macmillan.
Levine, Faye.
 xLevine, Faye.
 Solomon & Sheba. Marek.
Levine, Frederick S.
 xLevine, Frederick S.
 The Apocalyptic Vision: The Art of Franz
  Marc As German Expressionism. Har-Row.
Levine, Gemma.
 xLevine, Gemma.
 illus. With Henry Moore: The Artist at Work.
  Times Bks.
Levine, George. *see* Levine, George Lewis.
Levine, George Lewis.
 xLevine, George.
 Art of Victorian Prose. Oxford U Pr.
 Boundaries of Fiction: Carlyle, Macaulay,
  Newman. Princeton U Pr.
 ed. The Endurance of Frankenstein: Essays on
  Mary Shelley's Novel. U of Cal Pr.
Levine, Gustav.
 xLevine, Gustav.
 Mathematical Model Techniques for Learning
  Theories. Acad Pr.
Levine, Harvey A.
 xLevine, Harvey A.
 National Transportation Policy: A Study of
  Studies. Lexington Bks.
Levine, Harvey R.
 xLevine, Harvey R.
 Legal Dimensions of Drug Abuse in the United
  States. C C Thomas.
Levine, Herbert J. *see* Levine, Herbert Jerome.
Levine, Herbert Jerome, 1928-
 xLevine, Herbert J.
 ed. Clinical Cardiovascular Physiology. Grune.
Levine, Herbert M.
 xLevine, Herbert M.
 An American Guide to British Social Science
  Resources. Scarecrow.
 Point-Counterpoint: Readings in American
  Government. Scott F.
Levine, I. E. *see* Levine, Israel E.

Levine, Ira N., 1937-
   xLevine, Ira N.
      Quantum Chemistry. Allyn.
Levine, Isaac D. see Levine, Isaac Don.
Levine, Isaac Don, 1892-
   xLevine, Isaac D.
      The Mind of an Assassin. Greenwood.
Levine, Israel.
   xLevine, Israel.
      Francis Bacon: 1561-1626. Kennikat.
Levine, Israel E.
   xLevine, I. E.
      The Many Faces of Slavery. Messner.
Levine, James. see Levine, James A.
Levine, James A.
   xLevine, James.
      Who Will Raise the Children?: New Options
         for Fathers (Mothers). Lippincott.
Levine, Jerome, 1934-
   xLevine, Jerome.
      ed. Contemporary Standards for the
         Pharmacotherapy of Mental Disorders.
         Futura Pub.
Levine, Joseph M.
   xLevine, Joseph M.
      Dr. Woodward's Shield: History, Science, &
         Satire in Augustan England. U of Cal Pr.
Levine, Larry.
   xLevine, Larry.
      The Treasure. Fawcett.
Levine, Lawrence W.
   xLevine, Lawrence W.
      ed. The National Temper: Readings in
         American History. HarBraceJ.
Levine, Lois.
   xLevine, Lois.
      Delicious Diet Cookbook: The Sensible Way to
         Slim. Macmillan.
      The Fine Restaurants of Connecticut. Globe
         Pequot.
      Lois Levine's Vegetable Favorites. Western
         Pub.
Levine, Louis, 1921-
   xLevine, Louis.
      Biology of the Gene. Mosby.
Levine, Mark L. see Levine, Mark Lee.
Levine, Mark Lee.
   xLevine.
      Realtors' Liability. Wiley.
   xLevine, Mark L.
      Real Estate Fundamentals. West Pub.
      Realtors' Liability. Ronald Pr.
Levine, Martin P.
   xLevine, Martin P.
      Gay Men: The Sociology of Male
         Homosexuality. Har-Row.
      ed. Gay Men: The Sociology of Male
         Homosexuality. Har-Row.
Levine, Marvin J., 1928-
   xLevine, Marvin J.
      Public Manager's Guide to Union
         Representation. Intl Personnel Mgmt.
      Public Sector Labor Relations. West Pub.
Levine, Maurice, 1902-
   xLevine, Maurice.
      Psychiatry & Ethics. Braziller.
Levine, Melvin D.
   xLevine, Melvin D.
      Pediatric Approach to Learning Disorders.
         Wiley.
Levine, Milton I. see Levine, Milton Isra.
Levine, Milton Isra.
   xLevine, Milton I.
      Parent's Encyclopedia of Infancy, Childhood,
         & Adolescence. Har-Row.
Levine, Morris E., 1914-
   xLevine, Morris E.

      Digital Theory & Practice Using Integrated
         Circuits. P-H.
Levine, Mortimer.
   xLevine, Mortimer.
      The Early Elizabethan Succession Question,
         1558-1568. Stanford U Pr.
Levine, Naomi.
   xLevine, Naomi.
      ed. Poor Jews: An American Awakening.
         Transaction Bks.
Levine, Nathan.
   xLevine, Nathan.
      Typing for Everyone. Arco.
Levine, Norman D.
   xLevine, Norman D.
      Nematode Parasites of Domestic Animals & of
         Man. Burgess.
      Protozoan Parasites of Domestic Animals & of
         Man. Burgess.
      Textbook of Veterinary Parasitology. Burgess.
Levine, Philip, 1928-
   xLevine, Philip.
      Ashes: Poems New & Old. Atheneum.
Levine, Phyllis.
   xLevine, Phyllis.
      Delinquency Proneness: A Comparison of
         Delinquent Tendencies in Minors Under
         Court Supervision. R & E Res Assoc.
Levine, Raphael D.
   xLevine, Raphael D.
      Quantum Mechanics of Molecular Rate
         Processes. Oxford U Pr.
Levine, Robert M.
   xLevine, Robert M.
      Historical Dictionary of Brazil. Scarecrow.
      Pernambuco in the Brazilian Federation,
         1889-1937. Stanford U Pr.
Levine, Robert P. see Levine, Robert Paul.
Levine, Robert Paul, 1926-
   xLevine, Robert P.
      Genetics. HR&W.
Levine, Samuel.
   xLevine, Samuel.
      Programmed Introduction to Research.
         Wadsworth Pub.
Levine, Samuel P.
   xLevine, Samuel P.
      Ham--Kosher Style!. S P Levine.
Levine, Sarah.
   xLeVine, Sarah.
      Mothers & Wives: Gusii Women of East
         Africa. U of Chicago Pr.
Levine, Seymour.
   xLevine, Seymour.
      Hormones & Behavior. Acad Pr.
Levine, Sol, 1914-
   xLevine, Sol.
      Mathematics Handbook. Rosen Pr.
Levine, Solomon B. see Levine, Solomon Bernard.
Levine, Solomon Bernard.
   xLevine, Solomon B.
      Human Resources in Japanese Industrial
         Development. Princeton U Pr.
Levine, Stephen.
   xLevine, Stephen.
      A Gradual Awakening. Doubleday.
Levine, Steven Z.
   xLevine, Steven Z.
      Monet & His Critics. Garland Pub.
Levine, Stuart.
   xLevine, Stuart.
      American Indian Today. Everett-Edwards.
      ed. American Indian Today. Penguin.
Levine, Talya.
   xLevine, Talya.
      Chronic Cholecystitis: Its Pathology & the Role
         of Vascular Factors in Its Pathogenesis.
         Halsted Pr.
Levinger, George. see Levinger, George Klaus.

Levinger, George Klaus.
   xLevinger, George.
      ed. Close Relationships: Perspectives on the
         Meaning of Intimacy. U of Mass Pr.
Levinger, Lee J. see Levinger, Lee Joseph.
Levinger, Lee Joseph, 1890-1966
   xLevinger, Lee J.
      Anti-Semitism in the United States: It's
         History & Causes. Greenwood.
Levins, Richard.
   xLevins, Richard.
      Evolution in Changing Environments: Some
         Theoretical Explorations. Princeton U Pr.
Levinsohn, Stephen.
   xLevinsohn, Stephen H.
      The Inga Language. Mouton.
Levinsohn, Stephen H. see Levinsohn, Stephen.
Levinsohn, Sylvia A.
   xLevinsohn, Sylvia A.
      Current Crostics. Times Bks.
Levinson, A. A. see Levinson, Alfred Abraham.
Levinson, Alfred Abraham, 1927-
   xLevinson, A. A.
      Introduction to Exploration Geochemistry.
         Applied Pub.
Levinson, Alfred L. see Levinson, Alfred Linden.
Levinson, Alfred Linden, 1933-
   xLevinson, Alfred L.
      Energy & Materials in Three Sectors of the
         Economy: A Dynamic Model with
         Technological Change As an Endogenous
         Variable. Garland Pub.
Levinson, Charles, 1920-
   xLevinson, Charles.
      Vodka Cola. Gordon-Cremonesi.
Levinson, Harold M. see Levinson, Harold Myer.
Levinson, Harold Myer, 1919-
   xLevinson, Harold M.
      Collective Bargaining by British Local
         Authority Employees. U of Mich Inst Labor.
      Collective Bargaining by Public Employees in
         Sweden. U of Mich Inst Labor.
      Determining Forces in Collective Wage
         Bargaining. Krieger.
Levinson, Harry.
   xLevinson, Harry.
      Exceptional Executive: A Psychological
         Conception. Harvard U Pr.
      Executive Stress. NAL.
      The Great Jackass Fallacy. Harvard Busn.
      Organizational Diagnosis. Harvard U Pr.
Levinson, Irving J.
   xLevinson, Irving J.
      Introduction to Mechanics. P-H.
      Mechanics of Materials. P-H.
Levinson, Jay C. see Levinson, Jay Conrad.
Levinson, Jay Conrad.
   xLevinson, Jay C.
      Earning Money Without a Job. HR&W.
Levinson, Jerome.
   xLevinson, Jerome.
      The Alliance That Lost Its Way: A Critical
         Report on the Alliance for Progress. Times
         Bks.
Levinson, L. L. see Levinson, Leonard Louis.
Levinson, Leonard L. see Levinson, Leonard Louis.
Levinson, Leonard Louis, 1904-
   xLevinson, L. L.
      The Complete Book of Pickles and Relishes.
         NAL.
   xLevinson, Leonard L.
      The Eating Rich Cookbook. Stein & Day.
      Left-Handed Dictionary. Macmillan.
Levinson, Norman.
   xLevinson, Norman.
      Complex Variables. Holden-Day.
Levinson, Ronald B. see Levinson, Ronald Bartlett.
Levinson, Ronald Bartlett, 1896-
   xLevinson, Ronald B.

In Defense of Plato. Russell.

Levinson, Samuel A. *see* Levinson, Samuel Azor.

Levinson, Samuel Azor.
    xLevinson, Samuel A.
      Clinical Laboratory Diagnosis. Lea & Febiger.

Levinthal, Charles F., 1945-
    xLevinthal, Charles F.
      The Physiological Approach in Psychology.
      P-H.

Levis, Donald J., 1936-
    xLevis, Donald J.
      ed. Learning Approaches to Therapeutic
      Behavior Change. Beresford Bk Serv.

Levison, Andrew.
    xLevison, Andrew.
      The Full Employment Alternative. Coward.
      The Working Class Majority. Penguin.

Levit, Martin.
    xLevit, Martin.
      ed. Curriculum. U of Ill Pr.

Levitan, B. M. *see* Levitan, Boris Moiseevich.

Levitan, Boris Moiseevich.
    xLevitan, B. M.
      Introduction to Spectral Theory: Selfadjoint
      Ordinary Differential Operators. Am Math.

Levitan, E. L. *see* Levitan, Eli L.

Levitan, Eli L.
    xLevitan, E. L.
      Alphabetical Guide to Motion Picture,
      Television & Videotape Production. McGraw.
    xLevitan, Eli L.
      Handbook of Animation Techniques. Van Nos
      Reinhold.

Levitan, Lois.
    xLevitan, Lois.
      Improve Your Gardening with Backyard
      Research. Rodale Pr Inc.

Levitan, Max.
    xLevitan, Max.
      Textbook of Human Genetics. Oxford U Pr.

Levitan, Sar A.
    xLevitan, Sar A.
      Antipoverty Work & Training Efforts: Goals &
      Reality. U of Mich Inst Labor.
      Child Care & ABC's Too. Johns Hopkins.
      Federal Aid to Depressed Areas: An
      Evaluation of the Area Redevelopment
      Administration. Johns Hopkins.
      ed. The Federal Social Dollar in Its Own Back
      Yard. BNA.
      The Great Society's Poor Law: A New
      Approach to Poverty. Johns Hopkins.
      Human Resources & Labor Markets: Labor &
      Manpower in the American Economy.
      Har-Row.
      Programs in Aid of the Poor. Johns Hopkins.
      The Promise of Greatness. Harvard U Pr.
      Still a Dream: The Changing Status of Blacks
      Since 1960. Harvard U Pr.
      Work & Welfare Go Together. Johns Hopkins.

Levitas, G. B. *see* Levitas, Gloria B.

Levitas, Gloria B.
    xLevitas, G. B.
      ed. The World of Psychology. Braziller.
    xLevitas, Gloria B.
      ed. Culture & Consciousness: Perspectives in
      the Social Sciences. Braziller.

Levitas, Maurice.
    xLevitas, Maurice.
      Marxist Perspectives in the Sociology of
      Education. Routledge & Kegan.

Levith, Murray J.
    xLevith, Murray J.
      What's in Shakespeare's Names. Shoe String.

Levitin, Sonia.
    xLevitin, Sonia.

Journey to America. Atheneum.
The Mark of Conte. Atheneum.
The Mark of Conte. Atheneum.
Nobody Stole the Pie. HarBraceJ.
Nobody Stole the Pie. HarBraceJ.
Reigning Cats & Dogs. Atheneum.
A Sound to Remember. HarBraceJ.

Levitine, George.
    xLevitine, George.
      The Dawn of Bohemianism: The Barbu
      Rebellion & Primitivism in Neoclassical
      France. Pa St U Pr.
      Girodet-Trioson: An Iconographical Study.
      Garland Pub.

Leviton, Roberta, 1939
    xLeviton, Roberta.
      The Jewish Low-Cholesterol Cookbook.
      Eriksson.
      The Jewish Low Cholesterol Cookbook. NAL.

Levitt, Albert P.
    xLevitt, Albert P.
      Whisker Technology. Krieger.

Levitt Bernstein Associates.
    xLevitt Bernstein Associates.
      Supervisor's Guide to Rehabilitation &
      Conversation. Nichols Pub.

Levitt, Eleanor.
    xLevitt, Eleanor.
      Natural Food Cookery. Dover.

Levitt, Eugene E.
    xLevitt, Eugene E.
      The Psychology of Anxiety. L Erlbaum Assocs.

Levitt, J. *see* Levitt, Jacob.

Levitt, Jacob, 1911-
    xLevitt, J.
      Responses of Plants to Environmental Stresses.
      Acad Pr.

Levitt, Kari.
    xLevitt, Kari.
      Silent Surrender: The Multinational
      Corporation in Canada. St Martin.

Levitt, Morton, 1920-
    xLevitt, Morton.
      Freud & Dewey on the Nature of Man.
      Greenwood.
      A Tissue of Lies: Nixon Vs. Hiss. McGraw.

Levitt, Paul M.
    xLevitt, Paul M.
      The Cancer Reference Book: Direct & Clear
      Answers to Everyone's Questions. Facts on
      File.
      The Cancer Reference Book: Direct & Clear
      Answers to Everyone's Questions.
      Paddington.

Levitt, Theodore, 1925-
    xLevitt, Theodore.
      Marketing for Business Growth. McGraw.
      Third Sector: New Tactics for a Responsive
      Society. Am Mgmt.

Levitt, Zola.
    xLevitt, Zola.
      Christ in the Country Club. Herald Pr.
      Meshumed!. Moody.
      The Underground Church of Jerusalem.
      Nelson.

Levitzki, A. *see* Levitzki, Alexander.

Levitzki, Alexander, 1940-
    xLevitzki, A.
      Quantitative Aspects of Allosteric Mechanisms.
      Springer-Verlag.

Levorsen, A. I. *see* Levorsen, Arville Irving.

Levorsen, Arville Irving, 1894-
    xLevorsen, A. I.
      Geology of Petroleum. W H Freeman.

Levoy, Myron.
    xLevoy, Myron.

Alan & Naomi. Dell.
Alan & Naomi. Har-Row.
Penny Tunes & Princesses. Har-Row.

Levoy, Robert P.
    xLevoy, Robert P.
      Successful Professional Practice. P-H.

Levring, Tore.
    xLevring, Tore.
      Marine Algae: A Survey of Research &
      Utilization. De Gruyter.

Levsen, K. *see* Levsen, Karsten.

Levsen, Karsten.
    xLevsen, K.
      Fundamental Aspects of Organic Mass
      Spectrometry. Verlag Chemie.

Levtzion, Nehemia.
    xLevtzion, Nehemia.
      ed. Conversion to Islam. Holmes & Meier.

Levy, Amy, 1861-1889
    xLevy, Amy.
      Reuben Sachs: A Sketch. AMS Pr.

Levy, B. M. *see* Levy, Barnet M.

Levy, Babette M. *see* Levy, Babette May.

Levy, Babette May, 1907-
    xLevy, Babette M.
      Cotton Mather. G K Hall.
      Cotton Mather. Twayne.
      Preaching in the First Half Century of New
      England History. Russell.

Levy, Barnet M.
    xLevy, B. M.
      The Marmoset Periodontium in Health &
      Disease. S Karger.

Levy, Bernard Henri.
    xLevy, Bernard-Henri.
      Barbarism with a Human Face. Har-Row.
      Barbarism with a Human Face. Har-Row.

Levy, Bernard S.
    xLevy, Bernard S.
      ed. Developments in the Early Renaissance.
      State U NY Pr.

Levy, Bernard-Henri. *see* Levy, Bernard Henri.

Levy, Charles. *see* Levy, Charles S.

Levy, Charles S., 1919-
    xLevy, Charles.
      Social Work Ethics. Human Sci Pr.

Levy, D. *see* Levy, David.

Levy, D. Lawrence.
    xLevy, D. Lawrence.
      The Potomac Conspiracy. Major Bks.

Levy, Daniel C.
    xLevy, Daniel C.
      University & Government in Mexico:
      Autonomy in a Authoritarian System.
      Praeger.

Levy, Darline G. *see* Levy, Darline Gay.

Levy, Darline Gay, 1939-
    xLevy, Darline G.
      The Ideas & Careers of Simon-Nicolas-Henri
      Linguet: A Study in Eighteenth-Century
      French Politics. U of Ill Pr.

Levy, David.
    xLevy, D.
      Gods of Foxcroft. Arbor Hse.

Levy, David. *see* Levy, David N. L.

Levy, David M. *see* Levy, David Mordecai M. D.

Levy, David Mordecai M. D., M.d
    xLevy, David M.
      Maternal Overprotection. Norton.

Levy, David N. L.
    xLevy, David.
      Benko Counter Gambit. David & Charles.
      An Opening Repertoire for the Attacking
      Player. David & Charles.
      An Opening Repertoire for the Attacking
      Player. Van Nos Reinhold.
      Sicilian Dragon. David & Charles.
    xLevy, David N. L.

ed. Learn Chess from the World Champions.
Pergamon.

Levy, Edward.
xLevy, Edward.
Came a Spider. Arbor Hse.
Came a Spider. Berkley Pub.

Levy, Elizabeth.
xLevy, Elizabeth.
Doctors for the People: Profiles of Six Who
Serve. Knopf.
Frankenstein Moved in on the Fourth Floor.
Har-Row.
Lawyers for the People: A New Breed of
Defenders & Their Work. Knopf.
Lizzie Lies a Lot. Dell.
Lizzie Lies a Lot. Delacorte.
Nice Little Girls. Delacorte.
Something Queer on Vacation. Delacorte.
Struggle & Lose, Struggle & Win: The United
Mine Workers Union. Schol Bk Serv.
The Tryouts. Schol Bk Serv.

Levy, Felice D.
xLevy, Felicia.
Obituaries on File. Facts on File.

Levy, Felicia. *see* Levy, Felice D.

Levy, Francis A. *see* Levy, Francis Alain.

Levy, Francis Alain, 1940-
xLevy, Francis A.
ed. Intercalated Layered Materials. Kluwer
Boston.

Levy, Gerald.
xLevy, Gerald.
Ghetto School: Class Warfare in an Elementary
School. Pegasus.

Levy, Gertrude R. *see* Levy, Gertrude Rachel.

Levy, Gertrude Rachel, 1883-
xLevy, Gertrude R.
The Sword from the Rock: An Investigation
into the Origins of Epic Literature & the
Development of the Hero. Greenwood.
The Sword from the Rock: Investigation into
the Origins of Epic Literature &
Development of the Hero. Gordon Pr.

Levy, H. *see* Levy, Haim.

Levy, Haim.
xLevy, H.
Capital Investment & Financial Decisions. P-H.

Levy, Harry L. *see* Levy, Harry Louis.

Levy, Harry Louis, 1906-
xLevy, Harry L.
Latin Reader for Colleges. U of Chicago Pr.

Levy, Hermann, 1881-1949
xLevy, Hermann.
Economic Liberalism. Hyperion Conn.
Monopolies, Cartels & Trusts in British
Industry. Kelley.
Monopoly & Competition: A Study in English
Industrial Organisation. Arno.

Levy, Howard S. *see* Levy, Howard Seymour.

Levy, Howard Seymour, 1923-
xLevy, Howard S.
tr. China's Dirtiest Trickster: Folklore About
Hsu Wen-ch'ang (1521-1593). Langstaff-Levy
Ent.

Levy, Jacques E.
xLevy, Jacques E.
Cesar Chavez: Autobiography of La Causa.
Norton.

Levy, Joseph, 1942-
xLevy, Joseph.
Play Behavior. Wiley.
Punched Card Data Processing. McGraw.

Levy, Julien.
xLevy, Julien.
Surrealism. Arno.

Levy, Kurt L.
xLevy, Kurt L.
Tomas Carrasquilla. Twayne.

Levy, Leo.
xLevy, Leo.

The Ecology of Mental Disorder. Human Sci
Pr.

Levy, Leon.
xLevy, Leon.
The Consumer in the Marketplace. Pitman
Learning.

Levy, Leon S.
xLevy, Leon S.
Discrete Structures of Computer Science.
Wiley.

Levy, Leonard W. *see* Levy, Leonard Williams.

Levy, Leonard Williams, 1923-
xLevy, Leonard W.
Law of the Commonwealth & Chief Justice
Shaw. Kelley.
Law of the Commonwealth & Chief Justice
Shaw. Rothman.
Origins of the Fifth Amendment: The Right
Against Self-Incrimination. Oxford U Pr.
Supreme Court Under Earl Warren. New
Viewpoints.

Levy, Lester S.
xLevy, Lester S.
Flashes of Merriment: A Century of Humorous
Songs in America 1805-1905. U of Okla Pr.
Give Me Yesterday: American History in Song,
1890-1920. U of Okla Pr.

Levy, M. *see* Levy, Maurice.

Levy, Maurice.
xLevy, M.
ed. New Developments in Quantum Field
Theory & Statistical Mechanics. Plenum Pub.

Levy, Paul, 1941-
xLevy, Paul.
Moore: G. E. Moore & the Cambridge
Apostles. HR&W.

Levy, R. *see* Levy, Ronald B.

Levy, Raphael, 1900-
xLevy, Raphael.
The Astrological Works of Abraham Ibn Ezra:
A Literary & Linguistic Study. Johnson Repr.
Contribution a la Lexicographie Francaise
Selon D'anciens Textes D'origies Juive.
Ultramarine Pub.

Levy, Reuben.
xLevy, Reuben.
A Baghdad Chronicle. Porcupine Pr.
An Introduction to Persian Literature.
Columbia U Pr.
Persian Literature: An Introduction.
Greenwood.

Levy, Reynold.
xLevy, Reynold.
Nearing the Crossroads: Contending
Approaches to Contemporary American
Foreign Policy. Free Pr.

Levy, Richard S.
xLevy, Richard S.
The Downfall of the Anti-Semitic Political
Parties in Imperial Germany. Yale U Pr.

Levy, Robert I. *see* Levy, Robert Isaac.

Levy, Robert Isaac, 1924-
xLevy, Robert I.
Tahitians: Mind & Experience in the Society
Islands. U of Chicago Pr.

Levy, Robert S.
xLevy, Robert S.
Directory of State & Federal Funds for
Business Development. Pilot Bks.

Levy, Ronald B., 1911-
xLevy, R.
I Can Only Touch You Now. P-H.

Levy, Sidney.
xLevy, Sidney.
Plastics Product Design Engineering
Handbook. Van Nos Reinhold.

Levy, Sidney J.
xLevy, Sidney J.

Marketing, Society, & Conflict. P-H.

Levy, Tedd.
xLevy, Tedd.
A Guidebook for Teaching United States
History: Earliest Times to the Civil War.
Allyn.

Levy-Bruhl, Lucien, 1857-1939
xLevy-Bruhl, Lucien.
History of Modern Philosophy in France. B
Franklin.
How Natives Think. Arno.
Notebooks on Primitive Mentality. Har-Row.
Primitive Mentality. AMS Pr.

Lew, Julian D. *see* Lew, Julian D. M.

Lew, Julian D. M.
xLew, Julian D.
International Commercial Arbitration: A
Selected Bibliography. Oceana.

Lew, Linda.
xLew, Linda.
Peking Table-Top Cooking. Gala Bks.

Lewald, H. Ernest. *see* Lewald, Herald Ernest.

Lewald, Herald Ernest.
xLewald, H. Ernest.
ed. The Cry of Home: Cultural Nationalism &
the Modern Writer. Lib Soc Sci.
ed. The Cry of Home: Cultural Nationalism &
the Modern Writer. U of Tenn Pr.
Eduardo Mallea. Twayne.

Lewallen, Joyce.
xLewallen, Joyce.
Galaxy of Games & Activities for the
Kindergarten. P-H.

Lewalski, Barbara K. *see* Lewalski, Barbara Kiefer.

Lewalski, Barbara Kiefer, 1931-
xLewalski, Barbara K.
Donne's Anniversaries & the Poetry of Praise:
The Creation of a Symbolic Mode. Princeton
U Pr.
Protestant Poetics & the Seventeenth-Century
Religious Lyric. Princeton U Pr.

Lewanski, Richard C.
xLewanski, Richard C.
ed. Guide to Polish Libraries & Archives. East
Eur Quarterly.

Lewanski, Richard C. *see* Lewanski, Richard Casimir.

Lewanski, Richard Casimir, 1918-
xLewanski, Richard C.
ed. Subject Collections in European Libraries.
Bowker.

LeWarne, Charles P. *see* Lewarne, Charles Pierce.

Lewarne, Charles Pierce, 1930-
xLeWarne, Charles P.
Utopias on Puget Sound, 1885-1915. U of
Wash Pr.

Lewellen, John. *see* Lewellen, John Bryan.

Lewellen, John Bryan, 1910-
xLewellen, John.
Understanding Electronics: From Vacuum Tube
to Thinking Machine. T Y Crowell.

Lewellen, T. C.
xLewellen, Theodore C.
Peasants in Transition: The Changing Economy
of the Peruvian Aymara: a General Systems
Approach. Westview.

Lewellen, Theodore C. *see* Lewellen, T. C.

Lewellen, Wilbur G.
xLewellen, Wilbur G.
Executive Compensation in Large Industrial
Corporations. Natl Bur Econ Res.

Lewery, A. J. *see* Lewery, Antony John.

Lewery, Antony John.
xLewery, A. J.
Narrow Boat Painting: A History &
Description of the English Narrow Boats'
Traditional Paintwork. David & Charles.

Lewes, George H. *see* Lewes, George Henry.

Lewes, George Henry, 1817-1878
xLewes, George H.

On Actors & the Art of Acting. Greenwood.
Principles of Success in Literature. Folcroft.
Ranthorpe. Ohio U Pr.

Lewi, Bee.
xLewi, Bee.
Fritz, the Too-Long Dog. Garrard.
A Holiday for August. Garrard.

Lewi, Grant, 1902-1951
xLewi, Grant.
Astrology for the Millions. Bantam.
Astrology for the Millions. Llewellyn Pubns.

Lewin, Bertram D. see Lewin, Bertram David.

Lewin, Bertram David, 1896-
xLewin, Bertram D.
Dreams & the Uses of Regression. Intl Univs
Pr.
The Image & the Past. Intl Univs Pr.

Lewin, David.
xLewin, David.
Public Sector Labor Relations: Analysis &
Readings. T Horton & Dghts.

Lewin, Douglas.
xLewin, Douglas.
Computer Aided Design of Digital Systems.
Crane-Russak Co.
Logical Design of Switching Circuits. Elsevier.

Lewin, Kurt, 1890-1947
xLewin, Kurt.
Principles of Topological Psychology. Johnson
Repr.

Lewin, Leif, 1941-
xLewin, Leif.
Governing Trade Unions in Sweden. Harvard
U Pr.

Lewin, Michael. see Lewin, Michael Z.

Lewin, Michael Z.
xLewin, Michael.
The Silent Salesman. Berkley Pub.
The Silent Salesman. Knopf.
xLewin, Michael Z.
Ask the Right Question. Berkley Pub.
The Enemies Within. Berkley Pub.
Night Cover. Berkley Pub.
Night Cover. Knopf.
The Way We Die Now. Berkley Pub.

Lewin, Miriam, 1931-
xLewin, Miriam.
Understanding Psychological Research: The
Student Researcher's Handbook. Wiley.

Lewin, Moshe.
xLewin, Moshe.
Lenin's Last Struggle. Monthly Rev.

Lewin, Ralph A.
xLewin, Ralph A.
The Genetics of Algae. U of Cal Pr.

Lewin, Ronald.
xLewin, Ronald.
Churchill As War Lord. Stein & Day.
The Life & Death of the Afrika Korps. Times
Bks.

Lewin, Sherry.
xLewin, Sherry.
Displacement of Water & Its Control of
Biochemical Reactions. Acad Pr.

Lewin, Stephen.
xLewin, Stephen.
ed. Crime & Its Prevention. Wilson.
ed. Nation's Health. Wilson.

Lewin, Thomas J., 1944-
xLewin, Thomas J.
Asante Before the British: The Prempean
Years, 1875-1900. Regents Pr KS.

Lewin, Walter.
xLewin, Walter.
Nathaniel Hawthorne. Folcroft.

Lewinska, Pelagia.
xLewinska, Pelagia.
Twenty Months in Auschwitz. Lyle Stuart.

Lewinski, Jan S. see Lewinski, Jan Stanislaw.

Lewinski, Jan Stanislaw, 1885-1930
xLewinski, Jan S.
Money, Credit & Prices. Hyperion Conn.

Lewinsohn, P. see Lewinsohn, Peter M.

Lewinsohn, Peter M.
xLewinsohn, P.
Control Your Depression. P-H.

Lewinsohn, Richard, 1894-
xLewinsohn, Richard.
Profits of War Through the Ages. Garland Pub.

Lewinson, Paul, 1900-
xLewinson, Paul.
Race, Class, & Party: A History of Negro
Suffrage & White Politics in the South.
Russell.

Lewis, Adele. see Lewis, Adele Beatrice.

Lewis, Adele Beatrice, 1927-
xLewis, Adele.
How to Write Better Resumes. Barron.

Lewis, Albert B. see Lewis, Albert Buell.

Lewis, Albert Buell, 1867-
xLewis, Albert B.
Melanesian Shell Money in Field Museum
Collections. Kraus Repr.

Lewis, Albert L.
xLewis, Albert L.
Automobiles of the World. S&S.

Lewis, Alexander D. see Lewis, Alexander Dodge.

Lewis, Alexander Dodge.
xLewis, Alexander D.
Gas Power Dynamics. Krieger.

Lewis, Alfred Allan.
xLewis, Alfred Allan.
Male: His Body, His Sex. Doubleday.

Lewis, Alfred H. see Lewis, Alfred Henry.

Lewis, Alfred Henry, 1857-1914
xLewis, Alfred H.
Apaches of New York. Arno.

Lewis, Alfred J.
xLewis, Alfred J.
Using Law Books. Kendall-Hunt.

Lewis, Allan.
xLewis, Allan.
American Plays & Playwrights of the
Contemporary Theatre. Crown.

Lewis, Allen.
xLewis, Allen.
This Date in Philadelphia Phillies History.
Stein & Day.

Lewis, Alvin G.
xLewis, Alvin G.
Teach Me, Lord: Devotions on Basic Christian
Teachings. Augsburg.

Lewis, Ann C.
xLewis, Ann C.
Four Concepts: An English Workbook. Krieger.

Lewis, Anthony, 1927-
xLewis, Anthony.
Clarence Earl Gideon & the Supreme Court.
Random.
Gideon's Trumpet. Random.
Gideon's Trumpet. Random.

Lewis, Archibald R. see Lewis, Archibald Ross.

Lewis, Archibald Ross, 1914-
xLewis, Archibald R.
Naval Power & Trade in the Mediterranean:
A.D. 500-1100. Johnson Repr.
The Northern Seas: Shipping & Commerce in
Northern Europe, A. D. 300-1100. Octagon.

Lewis, Arthur H., 1906-
xLewis, Arthur H.
Children's Party. Trident.
xLewis, Authur H.
Carnival. Trident.

Lewis, Arthur O. see Lewis, Arthur Orcutt.

Lewis, Arthur Orcutt.
xLewis, Arthur O.
ed. Of Men & Machines. Dutton.

Lewis, Aubrey. see Lewis, Aubrey Julian.

Lewis, Aubrey Julian.
xLewis, Aubrey.
The Later Papers of Sir Aubrey Lewis. Oxford
U Pr.

Lewis, Authur H. see Lewis, Arthur H.

Lewis, B. T. see Lewis, Bernard T.

Lewis, Bernard.
xLewis, Bernard.
Arabs in History. Har-Row.
The Assassins: A Radical Sect in Islam.
Octagon.
History - Remembered, Recovered, Invented.
Princeton U Pr.
Population & Revenue in the Towns of
Palestine in the Sixteenth Century. Princeton
U Pr.
Race & Color in Islam. Octagon.

Lewis, Bernard T.
xLewis, B. T.
Facilities & Plant Engineering Handbook.
McGraw.

Lewis, Bruce.
xLewis, Bruce.
Meet the Computer. Dodd.
What Is a Laser?. Dodd.

Lewis, C. P. see Lewis, Christopher Peter.

Lewis, C. S. see Lewis, Clive Staples.

Lewis, Canella.
xLewis, Canella.
The Music of Aquarius. Berkley Pub.

Lewis, Carola. see Lewis, Carola Regester.

Lewis, Carola Regester.
xLewis, Carola.
Ramblings. McClain.

Lewis, Cecil, 1898-
xLewis, Cecil.
Farewell to Wings. Arno.

Lewis, Charles B. see Lewis, Charles Bertrand.

Lewis, Charles Bertrand, 1842-1924
xLewis, Charles B.
Brother Gardner's Lime Kiln Club. Irvington.

Lewis, Charles L. see Lewis, Charles Lee.

Lewis, Charles Lee, 1886-
xLewis, Charles L.
Books of the Sea: An Introduction to Nautical
Literature. Greenwood.
Matthew Fontaine Maury, the Pathfinder of
the Seas. AMS Pr.

Lewis, Charlton M. see Lewis, Charlton Miner.

Lewis, Charlton Miner, 1866-1923
xLewis, Charlton M.
Genesis of Hamlet. Kennikat.

Lewis, Christine.
xLewis, Christine.
The Food Choice Jungle. Merrimack Bk Serv.

Lewis, Christopher Peter.
xLewis, C. P.
The Great Steam Trek. Mayflower Bks.

Lewis, Clarence I. see Lewis, Clarence Irving.

Lewis, Clarence Irving, 1883-
xLewis, Clarence I.
Analysis of Knowledge & Valuation. Open
Court.
Symbolic Logic. Dover.
Values & Imperatives: Studies in Ethics.
Stanford U Pr.

Lewis, Claudia. see Lewis, Claudia Louise.

Lewis, Claudia Louise.
xLewis, Claudia.
Indian Families of the Northwest Coast: The
Impact of Change. U of Chicago Pr.
Up & Down the River: Boat Poems. Har-Row.

Lewis, Cleona.
xLewis, Cleona.
America's Stake in International Investments.
Arno.

Lewis, Clive S. see Lewis, Clive Staples.

Lewis, Clive Staples, 1898-1963
xLewis, C. S.

Case for Christianity. Macmillan.
Christian Reflections. Eerdmans.
Chronicles of Narnia. Macmillan.
The Dark Tower & Other Stories. HarBraceJ.
The Dark Tower & Other Stories. HarBraceJ.
Four Loves. HarBraceJ.
Great Divorce. Macmillan.
A Grief Observed. Bantam.
A Grief Observed. Merrimack Bk Serv.
Grief Observed. Seabury.
Hamlet: The Prince or the Poem. Folcroft.
Last Battle. Macmillan.
Last Battle. Macmillan.
Letters to an American Lady. Eerdmans.
Letters to Malcolm: Chiefly on Prayer.
   HarBraceJ.
Narrative Poems. HarBraceJ.
Out of the Silent Planet. Macmillan.
Out of the Silent Planet. Macmillan.
Problem of Pain. Macmillan.
Silver Chair. Macmillan.
Silver Chair. Macmillan.
Spenser's Images of Life. Cambridge U Pr.
Studies in Medieval & Renaissance Literature.
   Cambridge U Pr.
Surprised by Joy: The Shape of My Early Life.
   HarBraceJ.
Till We Have Faces: A Myth Retold.
   HarBraceJ.
The World's Last Night & Other Essays.
   HarBraceJ.
xLewis, Clive S.
   Allegory of Love: A Study of Medieval
      Tradition. Oxford U Pr.
   Experiment in Criticism. Cambridge U Pr.
   Four Loves. HarBraceJ.
   Narrative Poems. HarBraceJ.
   Rehabilitations & Other Essays. Arno.
   Rehabilitations & Other Essays. Folcroft.
   Rehabilitations & Other Essays. Somerset Pub.
   Selected Literary Essays. Cambridge U Pr.
   Surprised by Joy: The Shape of My Early Life.
      HarBraceJ.
   Till We Have Faces: A Myth Retold.
      HarBraceJ.
Lewis, D. G.
   xLewis, D. G.
      Assessment in Education. Halsted Pr.
Lewis, Darrell R.
   xLewis, Darrell R.
      ed. Academic Rewards in Higher Education.
         Ballinger Pub.
Lewis, David. see Lewis, David Neville.
Lewis, David L.
   xLewis, David L.
      District of Columbia: A Bicentennial History.
         Norton.
Lewis, David L. see Lewis, David Lanier.
Lewis, David Lanier, 1927-
   xLewis, David L.
      The Public Image of Henry Ford: An American
         Folk Hero & His Company. Wayne St U Pr.
Lewis, David Neville, 1922-
   xLewis, David.
      Growth of Cities. Halsted Pr.
Lewis, Diane, 1944-
   xLewis, Diane.
      The Maple Harvest Cookbook. Stein & Day.
Lewis, Dio, 1823-1886
   xLewis, Dio.
      Our Girls. Arno.
Lewis, Dominic B. see Lewis, Dominic Bevan Wyndham.
Lewis, Dominic Bevan Wyndham, 1894-1969
   xLewis, Dominic B.
      James Boswell, a Short Life. Greenwood.
      ed. The Stuffed Owl: An Anthology of Bad
         Verse. AMS Pr.
Lewis, Dorothy O. see Lewis, Dorothy Otnow.
Lewis, Dorothy Otnow.
   xLewis, Dorothy O.

Delinquency & Psychopathology. Grune.
Lewis, Douglas, 1938-
   xLewis, Douglas.
      The Late Baroque Churches of Venice. Garland
         Pub.
Lewis, E. Glyn.
   xLewis, E. Glyn.
      Bilingualism & Bilingual Education: A
         Comparative Study. U of NM Pr.
      Multilingualism in the Soviet Union: Aspects of
         Language Policy & Its Implementation.
         Mouton.
Lewis, Edward R. see Lewis, Edward Rieman.
Lewis, Edward Rieman, 1886-
   xLewis, Edward R.
      History of American Political Thought from
         the Civil War to the World War. Octagon.
Lewis, Edward W. see Lewis, Edward Williams.
Lewis, Edward Williams, 1899-
   xLewis, Edward W.
      Comes the Revolution. Arbor Hse.
Lewis, Edwin H. see Lewis, Edwin Herbert.
Lewis, Edwin Henderson.
   xLewis, Edwin H.
      Marketing Channels: Structure & Strategy.
         McGraw.
Lewis, Edwin Herbert, 1866-1938
   xLewis, Edwin H.
      History of the English Paragraph. AMS Pr.
      The History of the English Paragraph. Gordon
         Pr.
Lewis, Ernest L.
   xLewis, Ernest L.
      The Use of Contrast Coefficients: Supplement
         to McNeil, Kelly, & McNeil, "Testing
         Research Hypotheses Using Multiple Linear
         Regression". S Ill U Pr.
Lewis, Evelyn L.
   xLewis, Evelyn L.
      Housing Decisions. Goodheart.
Lewis, Ewart. see Lewis, Ewart Kellogg.
Lewis, Ewart Kellogg.
   xLewis, Ewart.
      Medieval Political Ideas. Cooper Sq.
Lewis, Faye C. see Lewis, Faye Cashatt.
Lewis, Faye Cashatt.
   xLewis, Faye C.
      Nothing to Make a Shadow. Iowa St U Pr.
Lewis, Felice F. see Lewis, Felice Flanery.
Lewis, Felice Flanery.
   xLewis, Felice F.
      Literature, Obscenity, & Law. S Ill U Pr.
Lewis, Finlay.
   xLewis, Finlay.
      Mondale: Portrait of an American Politician.
         Har-Row.
Lewis, Frederick P.
   xLewis, Frederick P.
      The Dilemma in the Congressional Power to
         Enforce the Fourteenth Amendment. U Pr of
         Amer.
Lewis, G. L. see Lewis, Geoffrey L.
Lewis, Garland K.
   xLewis, Garland K.
      Nurse-Patient Communication. Wm C Brown.
Lewis, Geoffrey. see Lewis, Geoffrey B.
Lewis, Geoffrey B.
   xLewis, Geoffrey.
      Quantitative Methods in Economics. Intl Schol
         Bk Serv.
Lewis, Geoffrey L.
   xLewis, G. L.
      Teach Yourself Turkish. McKay.
   xLewis, Geoffrey L.
      Turkish Grammar. Oxford U Pr.
Lewis, George C. see Lewis, George Cornewall.
Lewis, George Cornewall.
   xLewis, George C.

Remarks on the Use & Abuse of Some Political
   Terms. U of Mo Pr.
Lewis, George E. see Lewis, George Elmer.
Lewis, George Elmer.
   xLewis, George E.
      The Indiana Company, 1763-1798: A Study in
         Eighteenth Century Frontier Land
         Speculation & Business Venture. Arno.
Lewis, George H.
   xLewis, George H.
      Side-Saddle on the Golden Calf: Social
         Structure & Popular Culture in America.
         Goodyear.
Lewis, Gerald E.
   xLewis, Gerald E.
      My Big Buck: Outdoor Stories of Maine.
         Thorndike Pr.
Lewis, Gilbert N. see Lewis, Gilbert Newton.
Lewis, Gilbert Newton, 1875-1946
   xLewis, Gilbert N.
      Anatomy of Science. Arno.
Lewis, Gordon. see Lewis, Gordon K.
Lewis, Gordon K.
   xLewis, Gordon.
      Notes on the Puerto Rican Revolution: An
         Essay on American Dominance & Caribbean
         Resistance. Monthly Rev.
   xLewis, Gordon K.
      Growth of the Modern West Indies. Monthly
         Rev.
      Notes on the Puerto Rican Revolution: An
         Essay on American Dominance & Caribbean
         Resistance. Monthly Rev.
      Puerto Rico: Freedom & Power in the
         Caribbean. Monthly Rev.
Lewis, Gordon R. see Lewis, Gordon Russell.
Lewis, Gordon Russell, 1926-
   xLewis, Gordon R.
      Confronting the Cults. Presby & Reformed.
      Decide for Yourself: A Theological Workbook.
         Inter-Varsity.
Lewis, Gwynne.
   xLewis, Gwynne.
      The Second Vendee: The Continuity of
         Counter-Revolution in the Department of the
         Gard 1789-1815. Oxford U Pr.
Lewis, H. D. see Lewis, Hywel David.
Lewis, H. Gordon. see Lewis, Herschell Gordon.
Lewis, H. Spencer. see Lewis, Harve Spencer.
Lewis, Harry R.
   xLewis, Harry R.
      Unsolvable Classes of Quantificational
         Formulas. A-W.
Lewis, Harve Spencer, 1883-1939
   xLewis, H. Spencer.
      Symbolic Prophecy of the Great Pyramid.
         AMORC.
Lewis, Harvey S.
   xLewis, Harvey S.
      Commercial Banking in Mississippi, 1940-1975.
         U MS Bus Econ.
Lewis, Helen B.
   xLewis, Helen Block.
      Psychic War in Men & Women. NYU Pr.
Lewis, Helen Block. see Lewis, Helen B.
Lewis, Henry, 1819-1904
   xLewis, Henry.
      Valley of the Mississippi Illustrated. Minn Hist.
Lewis, Herbert S.
   xLewis, Herbert S.
      Galla Monarchy: Jimma Abba Jifar, Ethiopia,
         1830-1932. U of Wis Pr.
Lewis, Herschell Gordon, 1926-
   xLewis, H. Gordon.
      How to Make Your Advertising Twice As
         Effective at Half the Cost. Nelson-Hall.
Lewis, Hilda S. see Lewis, Hilda Stoessiger.
Lewis, Hilda Stoessiger.
   xLewis, Hilda S.

Deprived Children: The Mersham Experiment; a Social & Clinical Study. Greenwood.

Lewis, Howard P., 1902-
xLewis, Howard P.
The History & the Physical Examination. ACC.

Lewis, Hywel David.
xLewis, H. D.
Our Experience of God. Collins Pubs.

Lewis, I. M.
xLewis, I. M.
Ecstatic Religion: An Anthropological Study of Spirit Possession & Shamanism. Penguin.

Lewis, Ida B. see Lewis, Ida Belle.

Lewis, Ida Belle, 1887-
xLewis, Ida B.
The Education of Girls in China. AMS Pr.
The Education of Girls in China. Chinese Materials.

Lewis, J. G.
xLewis, J. G.
Christopher Marlowe: Outlines of His Life & Works. Folcroft.

Lewis, J. G. see Lewis, Jerome Gerald.
Lewis, J. M. see Lewis, Jerry M.
Lewis, J. Parry. see Lewis, John Parry.
Lewis, J. R. see Lewis, John Royston.
Lewis, J. W. see Lewis, John Wilson.
Lewis, Jack. see Lewis, Jack P.

Lewis, Jack P., 1924-
xLewis, Jack.
ed. Archer's Digest. Follett.

Lewis, Jack R., 1911-
xLewis, Jack R.
Architects & Engineers Office Practice Guide. P-H.

Lewis, James, 1930-
xLewis, James.
Administering the Individualized Instruction Program. P-H
Appraising Teacher Performance. P-H.
Differentiating the Teaching Staff. P-H.

Lewis, James B.
xLewis, James B.
The Estate Tax. PLI.

Lewis, James C., 1936-
xLewis, James C.
The World of the Wild Turkey. Lippincott.

Lewis, James K., 1929-
xLewis, James K.
Religious Life of Fugitive Slaves & Rise of the Coloured Baptist Churches, 1820-1865, in What Is Now Ontario. Arno.

Lewis, James R.
xLewis, James R.
Yoga for Couples. Autumn Pr.

Lewis, Janet, 1899-
xLewis, Janet.
Ghost of Monsieur Scarron. Swallow.

Lewis, Jerome Gerald.
xLewis, J. G.
Therapeutics. PSG Pub.

Lewis, Jerry D.
xLewis, Jerry D.
ed. Great Baseball Stories. G&D.

Lewis, Jerry M., 1924-
xLewis, J. M.
No Single Thread: Psychological Health in Family Systems. Brunner-Mazel.

Lewis, Jesse W. see Lewis, Jesse Walter.

Lewis, Jesse Walter, 1937-
xLewis, Jesse W.
The Strategic Balance in the Mediterranean. Am Enterprise.

Lewis, John.
xLewis, John.

ed. Christianity & the Social Revolution. Arno.
Marxism & the Irrationalists. Greenwood.
Marxism & the Open Mind. Greenwood.
Marxism & the Open Mind. Transaction Bks.
Religions of the World Made Simple. Doubleday.

Lewis, John. see Lewis, John Noel Claude.

Lewis, John Noel Claude, 1912-
xLewis, John.
Repair of Wooden Boats. David & Charles.
Typography: Design & Practice. Taplinger.

Lewis, John P. see Lewis, John Prior.

Lewis, John Parry, 1927-
xLewis, J. Parry.
Introduction to Mathematics for Students of Economics. St Martin.

Lewis, John Prior.
xLewis, John P.
Business Conditions Analysis. McGraw.
Quiet Crisis in India: Economic Development & American Policy. Greenwood.

Lewis, John R. see Lewis, John Rodney.

Lewis, John Ransom.
xLewis, John R.
Atlas of Aesthetic Plastic Surgery. Little.

Lewis, John Roberts, 1895-
xLewis, John R.
First Year College Chemistry. Har-Row.

Lewis, John Rodney, 1949-
xLewis, John R.
Uncertain Judgment: A Bibliography of War Crimes Trials. ABC-Clio.

Lewis, John Royston.
xLewis, J. R.
Cases for Discussion. Pergamon.

Lewis, John W. see Lewis, John Wilson.

Lewis, John Wilson.
xLewis, J. W.
ed. Party Leadership & Revolutionary Power in China. Cambridge U Pr.
xLewis, John W.
ed. The City in Communist China. Stanford U Pr.
Leadership in Communist China. Greenwood.

Lewis, Joseph, 1889-
xLewis, Joseph.
Atheism & Other Addresses. Arno.

Lewis, Judith A.
xLewis, Judith A.
Community Counseling: A Human Services Approach. Wiley.

Lewis, L. J. see Lewis, Leonard John.

Lewis, Lancelot S., 1926-
xLewis, Lancelot S.
The West Indian in Panama: Black Labor in Panama, 1850-1914. U Pr of Amer.

Lewis, Laurel J.
xLewis, Laurel J.
Linear Systems Analysis. McGraw.

Lewis, Laurie.
xLewis, Laurie.
photos by The Concerts. A & W Pubs.

Lewis, LaVerne W. see Lewis, Luverne Wolff.
Lewis, Leonard J. see Lewis, Leonard John.

Lewis, Leonard John.
xLewis, L. J.
Society, Schools & Progress in Nigeria. Pergamon.
xLewis, Leonard J.
Education & Political Independence in Africa, & Other Essays. Greenwood.

Lewis, Linda.
xLewis, Linda.
The Ultimate Dessert Book. Random.

Lewis, Lloyd, 1891-1949
xLewis, Lloyd.
Captain Sam Grant. Little.

Lewis, Lucia. see Lewis, Lucia Z.

Lewis, Lucia Z.
xLewis, Lucia.

The First Book of Microbes. Watts.

Lewis, Lucile.
xLewis, Lucile.
Planning Patient Care. Wm C Brown.

Lewis, Luverne W. see Lewis, Luverne Wolff.

Lewis, Luverne Wolff.
xLewis, LaVerne W.
Fundamental Skills in Patient Care. Lippincott.
xLewis, Luverne W.
Fundamental Skills in Patient Care. Lippincott.
Lippincott's State Board Examination Review for Nurses. Lippincott.

Lewis, Lynne G.
xLewis, Lynne G.
Drayton Hall: Preliminary Archaeological Investigations at a Low Country Plantation. U Pr of Va.

Lewis, M. see Lewis, Michael.

Lewis, Margie M.
xLewis, Margie M.
The Hurting Parent. Zondervan.

Lewis, Marvin, 1923-1971
xLewis, Marvin.
Martha & the Doctor: A Frontier Family in Central Nevada. U of Nev Pr.

Lewis, Meriwether.
xLewis, Meriwether.
Journals of Lewis & Clark. HM.

Lewis, Michael.
xLewis, M.
ed. The Child & Its Family. Plenum Pub.
ed. The Development of Affect. Plenum Pub.
xLewis, Michael.
The Culture of Inequality. NAL.
The Culture of Inequality. U of Mass Pr.
ed. Interaction, Conversation, & the Development of Language. Wiley
Social Cognition & the Acquisition of Self. Plenum Pub.

Lewis, Morris M. see Lewis, Morris Michael.

Lewis, Morris Michael.
xLewis, Morris M.
Infant Speech: A Study of the Beginnings of Language. Arno.

Lewis, Naomi.
xLewis, Naomi.
The Butterfly Collector. P-H.
Adapted by The Snow Queen. Scroll Pr.

Lewis, Norman, 1912-
xLewis, Norman.
Correct Spelling Made Easy. Dell.
How to Read Better & Faster. Har-Row.
How to Read Better & Faster. T Y Crowell.
Naples '44. Pantheon.
Power with Words. T Y Crowell.

Lewis, Oscar, 1914-
xLewis, Oscar.
Death in the Sanchez Family. Random.
Death in the Sanchez Family. Random.
High Sierra Country. Greenwood.

Lewis, P. see Lewis, P. J.

Lewis, P. J.
xLewis, P.
Therapeutic Problems in Pregnancy. Univ Park.

Lewis, Paul. see Lewis, Paul David.

Lewis, Paul David.
xLewis, Paul.
The Human Body. Bantam.

Lewis, Paul G.
xLewis, Paul G.
ed. The Practice of Comparative Politics: A Reader. Longman.

Lewis, Paul M.
xLewis, Paul M.

Beautiful America. Beautiful Am.
Beautiful California Coast. Beautiful Am.
Beautiful California Desert. Beautiful Am.
Beautiful California Mountains. Beautiful Am.
Beautiful Florida. Beautiful Am.
Beautiful Pennsylvania. Beautiful Am.
Beautiful Utah Country. Beautiful Am.
Beauty of California. Beautiful Am.
Lewis, Paula G. see Lewis, Paula Gilbert.

Lewis, Paula Gilbert.
    xLewis, Paula G.
    The Aesthetics of Stephane Mallarme in
        Relation to His Public. Fairleigh Dickinson.

Lewis, Peter, 1938-
    xLewis, Peter.
    Maps & Statistics. Methuen Inc.

Lewis, Peter W.
    xLewis, Peter W.
    The Supreme Court & the Criminal Process:
        Cases & Comments. Saunders.

Lewis, Philip M.
    xLewis, Philip M.
    Compiler Design Theory. A-W.

Lewis, Phillip V.
    xLewis, Phillip V.
    Business Report Writing. Grid Pub.
    Organizational Communication: The Essence of
        Effective Management. Grid Pub.
Lewis, R. see Lewis, Robert.

Lewis, Rhys.
    xLewis, Rhys.
    Engineering Quantities & Systems of Units.
        Halsted Pr.

Lewis, Richard, 1935-
    xLewis, Richard.
    In a Spring Garden. Dial.
    ed. In a Spring Garden. Dial.
    ed. Muse of the Round Sky: Lyric Poetry of
        Ancient Greece. S&S.
    The Park. S&S.
    ed. Still Waters of the Air: Poems by Three
        Modern Spanish Poets. Dial.
Lewis, Richard A. see Lewis, Richard Albert.

Lewis, Richard Albert.
    xLewis, Richard A.
    Edwin Chadwick & the Public Health
        Movement 1832-1854. Kelley.

Lewis, Richard J.
    xLewis, Richard J.
    Logistical Information System for Marketing
        Analysis. SW Pub.

Lewis, Robert.
    xLewis, R.
    ed. Computers in the Life Sciences:
        Applications in Research & Education. Biblio
        Dist.
Lewis, Robert. see Lewis, Robert A.

Lewis, Robert A.
    xLewis, Robert.
    Science & Industrialization in USSR. Holmes &
        Meier.
    xLewis, Robert A.
    Nationality & Population Change in Russia &
        the USSR: An Evaluation of Census Data,
        1897-1970. Praeger.
    Population Redistribution in the USSR: Its
        Impact on Society 1897-1977. Praeger.

Lewis, Robert T.
    xLewis, Robert T.
    Taking Chances: The Psychology of Losing &
        How to Profit from It. HM.
Lewis, Robin J. see Lewis, Robin Jared.

Lewis, Robin Jared.
    xLewis, Robin J.
    E. M. Forster's Passages to India. Columbia U
        Pr.

Lewis, Roy, 1933-
    xLewis, Roy.

Nothing but Foxes. St Martin.
An Uncertain Sound. St Martin.
Lewis, Roy H. see Lewis, Roy Harley.

Lewis, Roy Harley.
    xLewis, Roy H.
    Antiquarian Books: An Insider's Account.
        Arco.
Lewis, S. M. see Lewis, Shirley Mitchell.
Lewis, Samella. see Lewis, Samella S.

Lewis, Samella S.
    xLewis, Samella.
    Art: African-American. HarBraceJ.
Lewis, Sasha G. see Lewis, Sasha Gregory.

Lewis, Sasha Gregory.
    xLewis, Sasha G.
    Slave Trade Today: American Exploitation of
        Illegal Aliens. Beacon Pr.
    Sunday's Women: A Report on Lesbian Life
        Today. Beacon Pr.

Lewis, Shari.
    xLewis, Shari.
    Folding Paper Puppets. Stein & Day.
    Folding Paper Toys. Stein & Day.
    How Kids Can Really Make Money. HR&W.
    Impossible--Unless You Know How. HR&W.
    Magic Show in a Book. HR&W.
    Spooky Stuff. HR&W.
    Things Kids Collect. HR&W.
    Toy Store-in-a-Book. HR&W.

Lewis, Shirley Mitchell.
    xLewis, S. M.
    Dyserythropoiesis. Acad Pr.

Lewis, Sinclair, 1885-1951
    xLewis, Sinclair.
    Arrowsmith. NAL.
    Arrowsmith. HarBraceJ.
    Dodsworth. NAL.
    Free Air. Scholarly.
    Gideon Planish. Manor Bks.
    The God-Seeker. Manor Bks.
    World So Wide. Manor Bks.

Lewis, Stephen, 1949-
    xLewis, Stephen.
    How's It Made?: A Photo Tour of Seven Small
        Factories. Greenwillow.

Lewis, Stephen R.
    xLewis, Stephen R.
    Economic Policy & Industrial Growth in
        Pakistan. MIT Pr.

Lewis, Steven, 1946-
    xLewis, Steven.
    Exits off a Toll Road. Pentagram.
Lewis, T. G. see Lewis, Theodore Gyle.

Lewis, T. M.
    xLewis, T. M.
    North Sea Oil & Scotland's Economic
        Prospects. Biblio Dist.
Lewis, Taylor B. see Lewis, Taylor Biggs.

Lewis, Taylor Biggs.
    xLewis, Taylor B.
    Christmas in Williamsburg. HR&W.
    Christmas in Williamsburg. Williamsburg.
Lewis, Theodore. see Lewis, Theodore Gyle.
Lewis, Theodore G. see Lewis, Theodore Gyle.

Lewis, Theodore Gyle.
    xLewis, T. G.
    Software Engineering for Micros: The
        Electrifying Streamlined Blueprint Speedcode
        Method. Hayden.
    xLewis, Theodore.
    Computer Principles of Modeling & Simulation.
        HM.
    xLewis, Theodore G.
    Applying Data Structures. HM.
    Distribution Sampling for Computer
        Simulation. Lexington Bks.

Lewis, Thomas E.
    xLewis, Thomas E.

Instructions for Dental Patients. Saunders.

Lewis, Thomas P.
    xLewis, Thomas P.
    Clipper Ship. Har-Row.
    Hill of Fire. Har-Row.
Lewis, Virginia S. see Lewis, Virginia Stolpe.

Lewis, Virginia Stolpe.
    xLewis, Virginia S.
    Comparative Clothing Construction
        Techniques. Burgess.
Lewis, W. see Lewis, W. Gary.
Lewis, W. Arthur. see Lewis, William Arthur.
Lewis, W. Arthur. see Lewis, William Arthur.
Lewis, W. David. see Lewis, Walter David.

Lewis, W. Frank.
    xLewis, W. Frank.
    Utilization of Short-Stay Hospitals: Summary of
        Non-Medical Statistics, U.S., 1971. Natl Ctr
        Health Stats.

Lewis, W. Gary, 1941-
    xLewis, W.
    Engine Service. P-H.

Lewis, Walter David.
    xLewis, W. David.
    Delta: The History of an Airline. U of Ga Pr.
Lewis, Walter H. see Lewis, Walter Hepworth.

Lewis, Walter Hepworth.
    xLewis, Walter H.
    Ecology Field Glossary: A Naturalist's
        Vocabulary. Greenwood.
    Medical Botany: Plants Affecting Man's
        Health. Wiley.

Lewis, Wilfred.
    xLewis, Wilfred.
    ed. Budget Concepts for Economic Analysis.
        Brookings.
    Federal Fiscal Policy in the Postwar
        Recessions. Brookings.
    Federal Fiscal Policy in the Postwar
        Recessions. Greenwood.

Lewis, William Arthur, 1915-
    xLewis, W. Arthur.
    The Theory of Economic Growth. Allen
        Unwin.
    xLewis, W. Arthur.
    Economic Survey 1919-1939. Allen Unwin.
    The Evolution of the International Economic
        Order. Princeton U Pr.
    Growth & Fluctuations 1870-1913. Allen
        Unwin.
Lewis, Willie N. see Lewis, Willie Newbury.

Lewis, Willie Newbury.
    xLewis, Willie N.
    Tapadero: The Making of a Cowboy. U of Tex
        Pr.
Lewis, Wilmarth S. see Lewis, Wilmarth Sheldon.

Lewis, Wilmarth Sheldon, 1895-
    xLewis, Wilmarth S.
    Horace Walpole. Natl Gallery Art.

Lewis, Wyndham, 1882-1957
    xLewis, Wyndham.
    America & Cosmic Man. Kennikat.
    America, I Presume. Haskell.
    The Art of Being Ruled. Haskell.
    Doom of Youth. Haskell.
    Filibusters in Barbary. Haskell.
    Hitler. Gordon Pr.
    The Hitler Cult. Gordon Pr.
    Men Without Art. Russell.
    Paleface: The Philosophy of the Melting Pot.
        Haskell.
    Revenge for Love. Regnery-Gateway.

Lewisohn, Ludwig, 1882-1955
    xLewisohn, Ludwig.
    Anniversary. Greenwood.
    The Island Within. Arno.
    The Island Within. Behrman.
Lewisohn, Sam A. see Lewisohn, Sam Adolph.

Lewisohn, Sam Adolph, 1884-
    xLewisohn, Sam A.

Painters & Personality: A Collector's View of Modern Art. Arno.

Lewittes, M. see Lewittes, Mendell.

Lewittes, Mendell.
xLewittes, M.
Religious Foundations of the Jewish State: The Concept & Practice of Jewish Statehood from Biblical Times to the Modern State of Israel. Ktav.

Lewontin, R. C. see Lewontin, Richard C.

Lewontin, Richard C., 1929-
xLewontin, R. C.
The Genetic Basis of Evolutionary Change. Columbia U Pr.

Lewy, Arieh.
xLewy, Arieh.
ed. Handbook of Curriculum Evaluation. Longman.

Lewy, Guenter, 1923-
xLewy, Guenter.
America in Vietnam. Oxford U Pr.
America in Vietnam. Oxford U Pr.
Religion & Revolution. Oxford U Pr.

Lexau, Joan. see Lexau, Joan M.

Lexau, Joan M.
xLexau, Joan.
Archimedes Takes a Bath. T Y Crowell.
I'll Tell on You. Dutton.
The Spider Makes a Web. Hastings.
xLexau, Joan M.
Crocodile & Hen. Har-Row.
House So Big. Har-Row.
I Hate Red Rover. Dutton.
I Should Have Stayed in Bed. Har-Row.
Me Day. Dial.
Olaf Is Late. Dial.
Olaf Reads. Dial.
The Spider Makes a Web. Schol Bk Serv.
Striped Ice Cream. Lippincott.
Striped Ice Cream. Schol Bk Serv.
T for Tommy. Garrard.
That's Just Fine & Who-O-O Did It. Garrard.

Ley, Alice C. see Ley, Alice Chetwynd.

Ley, Alice Chetwynd.
xLey, Alice C.
The Clandestine Betrothal. Ballantine.
The Master & the Maiden. Ballantine.

Ley, David.
xLey, David.
ed. Humanistic Geography: Prospects & Problems. Maaroufa Pr.

Ley, Mary.
xLey, Mary.
ed. Journey from Ignorant Ridge: Stories & Pictures of Texas Schools in the 1800's. Tex Congr Parent & Teach.

Ley, Sandra J., 1949-
xLey, Sandra J.
Foodservice Refrigeration. CBI Pub.

Ley, Willy, 1906-
xLey, Willy.
Our Work in Space. Macmillan.

Leyburn, James G. see Leyburn, James Graham.

Leyburn, James Graham.
xLeyburn, James G.
The Haitian People. Greenwood.

Leyden, D. E. see Leyden, Donald E.

Leyden, Donald E.
xLeyden, D. E.
Analytical Applications of NMR. Wiley.

Leyden, Michael B.
xLeyden, Michael B.
Career Education & Physical Sciences. HM.

Leydenfrost, Robert. see Leydenfrost, Robert J.

Leydenfrost, Robert J., 1925-
xLeydenfrost, Robert.
illus. Other Side of the Mountain. Macmillan.

Leyendekkers, J. V.
xLeyendekkers, J. V.
Thermodynamics of Seawater As a Multicomponent Electrolyte Solution. Dekker.

Leyh, Elizabeth.
xLeyh, Elizabeth.
Children Make Sculpture. Van Nos Reinhold.

Leymarie, Jean.
xLeymarie, Jean.
Van Gogh. Rizzoli Intl.
Zao Wou-Ki. Rizzoli Intl.

Leynse, James P.
xLeynse, James P.
Freedom's Gateway. Creative Pr.
Twain Shall Meet. Creative Pr.

Leypoldt, Martha M.
xLeypoldt, Martha M.
Learning Is Change. Judson.

Leys, Colin.
xLeys, Colin.
Underdevelopment in Kenya: The Political Economy of Neo-Colonialism, 1964-71. U of Cal Pr.

Leys, Norman M. see Leys, Norman Maclean.

Leys, Norman Maclean.
xLeys, Norman M.
Colour Bar in East Africa. Negro U Pr.

Leyser, K. J. see Leyser, Karl.

Leyser, Karl.
xLeyser, K. J.
Rule & Conflict in an Early Medieval Society: Ottonian Saxony. Ind U Pr.

Leyshon, Glynn. see Leyshon, Glynn A.

Leyshon, Glynn A., 1929-
xLeyshon, Glynn.
Programmed Functional Anatomy. Mosby.

Lezama Lima, Jos E.
xLezama Lima, Jose.
Paradiso. FS&G.

Lezama Lima, Jose. see Lezama Lima, Jos E.

Lezer, Leon R.
xLezer, Leon R.
Community Medicine: Organization & Application of Principles. Vantage.

Lezra, Giggy.
xLezra, Giggy.
Mechido, Aziza, & Ahmed. Atheneum.

Li. see Li, David Hsiang-Fu.

Li, Anthony C, 1920-
xLi, Anthony C.
The History of Privately Controlled Higher Education in the Republic of China. Greenwood.

Li, C. see Li, Ching-Chiin.

Li, Ching-Chiin.
xLi, C.
Introduction to Experimental Statistics. McGraw.

Li, David H. see Li, David Hsiang-Fu.

Li, David Hsiang-Fu, 1928-
xLi.
Accounting for Management Analysis. Merrill.
xLi, David H.
Accounting-Computers-Management Information Systems. McGraw.

Li, Dun J. see Li, Dun Jen.

Li, Dun Jen, 1920-
xLi, Dun J.
Ageless Chinese: A History. Scribner.
ed. Modern China: From Mandarin to Commissar. Scribner.

Li, Fang-Kuei.
xLi, Fang-Kuei.
A Handbook of Comparative Tai. U Pr of Hawaii.

Li, H. Y.
xLi, H. Y.
ed. I Ching Games of Duke Tan of Chou & C. C. T'ung. Cadleon Pr.

Li, Hsueh Jei.
xLi, Hsueh Jei.
ed. Chromatin & Chromosome Structure. Acad Pr.

Li, Hui-Lin, 1911-
xLi, Hui-Lin.
Woody Flora of Taiwan. Livingston.

Li, Jui.
xLi, Jui.
The Early Revolutionary Activities of Comrade Mao Tse-Tung. M E Sharpe.

Li, Peter S.
xLi, Peter S.
Occupational Mobility & Kinship Assistance: A Study of Chinese Immigrants in Chicago. R & E Res Assoc.

Li, T'ien-i.
xLi, Tien-Yi.
Woodrow Wilson's China Policy. Octagon.

Li, Tien-Yi, 1915-
xLi, Tien-Yi.
Chinese Fiction: A Bibliography of Books & Articles in Chinese & English. Far Eastern Pubns.

Li, Tien-Yi. see Li, T'ien-I.

Li, Tze-chung, 1927-
xLi, Tze-chung.
Social Science Reference Sources: A Practical Guide. Greenwood.

Li, Victor H.
xLi, Victor H.
ed. Law & Politics in China's Foreign Trade. U of Wash Pr.

Li, Wen-Hsiung.
xLi, Wen-Hsiung.
Principles of Fluid Mechanics. A-W.

Lial, Margaret L.
xLial, Margaret L.
Algebra & Trigonometry. Scott F.
Beginning Algebra. Scott F.
College Algebra. Scott F.
Finite Mathematics: With Applications in Business, Biology, & Behavioral Sciences. Scott F.
Mathematics & Calculus with Applications. Scott F.

Liang, Daniel S.
xLiang, Daniel S.
Facts About Aging. C C Thomas.

Liao, S. see Liao, Samuel Y.

Liao, Samuel Y.
xLiao, S.
Microwave Devices & Circuits. P-H.

Libbey, James K.
xLibbey, James K.
Alexander Gumberg & Soviet-American Relations, 1917-1933. U Pr of Ky.
Dear Alben: Mr. Barkley of Kentucky. U Pr of Ky.

Libby, Bill.
xLibby, Bill.
Bud Harrelson: Super Shortstop. Putnam.
Goliath: The Wilt Chamberlain Story. Dodd.
Great Stanley Cup Playoffs. Random.
Life in the Pit: The Deacon Jones Story. Doubleday.
Nolan Ryan: Fireballer. Putnam.
The Reggie Jackson Story. Lothrop.
Star Quarterbacks of the NFL. Random.
Star Running Backs of the NFL. Random.
Superdrivers: Three Auto Racing Champions. Garrard.

Libby, Hugo L.
xLibby, Hugo L.
Introduction to Electromagnetic Nondestructive Test Methods. Krieger.

Libby, L. M.
xLibby, Leona M.
The Uranium People. Crane-Russak Co.
The Uranium People. Scribner.

Libby, Leona M. see Libby, L. M.

Libby, M. S. see Libby, Margaret (Sherwood).

Libby, Margaret (Sherwood), 1898-
xLibby, M. S.
The Attitude of Voltaire to Magic & the
Sciences. Gordon Pr.
xLibby, Margaret S.
Attitude of Voltaire to Magic & the Sciences.
AMS Pr.
Libby, Margaret S. *see* Libby, Margaret (Sherwood).
Libby, O. G. *see* Libby, Orin Grant.
Libby, Orin Grant, 1864-1952
xLibby, O. G.
ed. The Arikara Narrative of the Campaign
Against the Hostile Dakotas, June 1876: The
Custer Battle at the Little Big Horn. Rio
Grande.
Libby, Roger W.
xLibby, Roger W.
Marriage & Alternatives: Exploring Intimate
Relationships. Scott F.
Libby, William C. *see* Libby, William Charles.
Libby, William Charles.
xLibby, William C.
Color & the Structural Sense. P-H.
Liben, Lynn S.
xLiben, Lynn S.
ed. Deaf Children: Developmental Perspectives.
Acad Pr.
Liberace, 1919-
xLiberace.
The Things I Love. G&D.
Liberman, Robert P. *see* Liberman, Robert Paul.
Liberman, Robert Paul.
xLiberman, Robert P.
Personal Effectiveness: Guiding People to
Assert Themselves & Improve Their Social
Skills. Res Press.
Liberman, Simon I. *see* Liberman, Simon Isaevich.
Liberman, Simon Isaevich, 1881-
xLiberman, Simon I.
Building Lenin's Russia. Hyperion-Conn.
Libes, S.
xLibes, Sol.
Repairing Transistor Radios. Hayden.
Libes, Sol.
xLibes, Sol.
Fundamentals & Applications of Digital Logic
Circuits. Hayden.
Libes, Sol. *see* Libes, S.
Libien, Lois.
xLibien, Lois.
Paint It Yourself: The Complete Indoor
House-Painting Book. Morrow.
Super-Economy House Cleaning. Morrow.
Super-Economy House-Cleaning. Popular Lib.
Libin, Arthur D., 1947-
xLibin, Arthur D.
ed. ASI Tables of Diurnal Planetary Motion.
ASI Pubs Inc.
Liblit, Jerome.
xLiblit, Jerome.
Housing the Cooperative Way: Selected
Readings. Cyrco Pr.
Libman, Gary.
xLibman, Gary.
Bjorn Borg. Creative Ed.
Reggie Jackson. Creative Ed.
Library Association.
xLibrary Association.
ed. British Technology Index: Annual Volume
1977. Intl Pubns Serv.
xLibrary Association (London).
ed. British Humanities Index 1978. Intl Pubns
Serv.
xLibrary Association, London.
ed. British Technology Index: Annual Volume
1978. Intl Pubns Serv.
Library Association (London). *see* Library Association.
Library Association, London. *see* Library Association.
Library Association. Medical Section.
xLibrary Association Medical Section.

Books & Periodicals in Medical Libraries.
Nichols Pub.
xMedical Section of the Library Association.
ed. Directory of Medical Libraries in the
British Isles. Nichols Pub.
Library Buildings Institute And Alta Workshop - Detroit
- 1965. *see* Library Buildings Institute, Detroit, 1965.
Library Buildings Institute, Detroit, 1965.
xLibrary Buildings Institute And Alta Workshop -
Detroit - 1965.
Libraries: Building for the Future: Proceedings.
ALA.
Library Buildings Institute, San Francisco, 1967.
xLibrary Buildings Institute, San Francisco, June,
1967.
Library Buildings, Innovation for Changing
Needs: Proceedings. ALA.
Library Equipment Institute - New York - July 7-9 1966.
see Library Equipment Institute, 3d, New York, 1966.
Library Equipment Institute - St. Louis - 1964. *see*
Library Equipment Institute, 2d, St. Louis, 1964.
Library Equipment Institute, 2d, St. Louis, 1964.
xLibrary Equipment Institute - St. Louis - 1964.
Library Environment: Aspects of Interior
Planning: Proceedings. ALA.
Library Equipment Institute, 3d, New York, 1966.
xLibrary Equipment Institute - New York - July
7-9 1966.
Procurement of Library Furnishings:
Specifications, Bid Documents, & Evaluation:
Proceedings. ALA.
Library of Congress. *see* United States. Library of
Congress.
Library of Congress, Geography & Map Division
(Washington, D. C.). *see* United States. Library of
Congress. Geography and Map Division.
Library of Congress, Science & Technology Div. *see*
United States. Library of Congress. Science and
Technology Division.
Library of Congress, Washington, D. C. *see* United
States. Library of Congress.
Library of Congress, Washington, D.C. Geography &
Map Division. *see* United States. Library of Congress.
Geography and Map Division.
Libres Entretiens. *see* Libres Entretiens, 2d, Paris?,
1905-1906.
Libres Entretiens, 2d, Paris?, 1905-1906.
xLibres Entretiens.
Sur L'internationalisme. Garland Pub.
Lichfield, N. *see* Lichfield, Nathaniel.
Lichfield, Nathaniel.
xLichfield, N.
Evaluation in the Planning Process. Pergamon.
Lichine, Alexis.
xLichine, Alexis.
Alexis Lichine's Guide to the Wines &
Vineyards of France. Knopf.
Licht, Sidney. *see* Licht, Sidney Herman.
Licht, Sidney Herman.
xLicht, Sidney.
ed. Arthritis & Physical Medicine. Krieger.
Massage, Manipulation & Traction. Krieger.
ed. Stroke & Its Rehabilitation. Williams &
Wilkins.
ed. Therapeutic Electricity & Ultraviolet
Radiation. Krieger.
ed. Therapeutic Heat & Cold. Williams &
Wilkins.
Lichtblau, Myron I., 1925-
xLichtblau, Myron I.
Manuel Galvez. Twayne.
Lichten, Frances.
xLichten, Frances.
Folk Art Motifs of Pennsylvania. Dover.
Folk Art Motifs of Pennsylvania. Peter Smith.
Lichtenberg, D. B. *see* Lichtenberg, Don Bernett.
Lichtenberg, Don Bernett, 1928-
xLichtenberg, D. B.

Unitary Symmetry & Elementary Particles.
Acad Pr.
Lichtenberg, Jacqueline.
xLichtenberg, Jacqueline.
House of Zeor. PB.
Unto Zeor, Forever. Playboy Pbks.
Lichtenberger, E. *see* Lichtenberger, Elisabeth.
Lichtenberger, Elisabeth.
xLichtenberger, E.
The Eastern Alps. Oxford U Pr.
Lichtenberger, Henri.
xLichtenberger, Henri.
Third Reich. Arno.
Lichtenberger, J. P. *see* Lichtenberger, James Pendleton.
Lichtenberger, James Pendleton, 1870-1953
xLichtenberger, J. P.
Divorce: A Social Interpretation. Arno.
Lichtenstein, Grace.
xLichtenstein, Grace.
Desperado. Dial.
A Long Way, Baby: Behind-the-Scenes in
Women's Pro Tennis. Morrow.
Lichtenstein, Sara, 1931-1977
xLichtenstein, Sara.
Delacroix & Raphael. Garland Pub.
Lichtenwalner, Muriel E.
xLichtenwalner, Muriel E.
Teaching & Learning with Early Elementary
Children. Judson.
Lichter, Paul, 1944-
xLichter, Paul.
The Boy Who Dared to Rock: The Definitive
Elvis. Doubleday.
Lichtheim, George.
xLichtheim, George.
Marxism in Modern France. Columbia U Pr.
Lichtman, Allan J.
xLichtman, Allan J.
Historians & the Living Past: The Theory &
Practice of Historical Study. AHM Pub.
Kin & Communities: Families in America.
Smithsonian.
Prejudice & the Old Politics: The Presidential
Election of 1928. U of NC Pr.
Lichtman, Marshall A.
xLichtman, Marshall A.
Hematology for Practitioners. Little.
Lichty, Lawrence W. *see* Lichty, Lawrence Wilson.
Lichty, Lawrence Wilson.
xLichty, Lawrence W.
American Broadcasting: A Source Book on the
History of Radio & Television. Hastings.
Licklider, Heath.
xLicklider, Heath.
Architectural Scale. Braziller.
Licklider, J. C. *see* Licklider, J. C. R.
Licklider, J. C. R.
xLicklider, J. C.
Libraries of the Future. MIT Pr.
Lickona, Thomas.
xLickona, Thomas.
ed. Moral Development & Behavior: Theory,
Research & Social Issues. HR&W.
Lickteig, Mary J.
xLickteig, Mary J.
An Introduction to Children's Literature.
Merrill.
Lid, R. W. *see* Lid, Richard Wald.
Lid, Richard Wald, 1928-
xLid, R. W.
Ford Madox Ford: The Essence of His Art. U
of Cal Pr.
Grooving the Symbol. Free Pr.
Liddell Hart, B. H. *see* Liddell Hart, Basil Henry.
Liddell Hart, Basil H. *see* Liddell Hart, Basil Henry.
Liddell, Henry G. *see* Liddell, Henry George.
Liddell, Henry George.
xLiddell, Henry G.

ed. Greek-English Lexicon. Oxford U Pr.
Liddell, Louise A.
 xLiddell, Louise A.
  Clothes & Your Appearance. Goodheart.
Liddell, Robert, 1908-
 xLiddell, Robert.
  Some Principles of Fiction. Greenwood.
Liddell, Viola G. *see* Liddell, Viola Goode.
Liddell, Viola Goode, 1901-
 xLiddell, Viola G.
  A Place of Springs. U of Ala Pr.
Liddell Hart, Basil Henry, Sir, 1895-1970
 xLiddell Hart, B. H.
  The Real War, 1914-1918. Little.
 xLiddell Hart, Basil H.
  The Defence of Britain. Greenwood.
  Defence of the West. Greenwood.
  Foch, the Man of Orleans. Greenwood.
  The Ghost of Napoleon. Greenwood.
  The Remaking of Modern Armies. Greenwood.
Liddle, Janice.
 xLiddle, Janice.
  Index to Mary Ann Barnes Williams' Origins
   of North Dakota Place Names. N Dak Inst.
Liddy, G. Gordon.
 xLiddy, G. Gordon.
  Out of Control. Berkley Pub.
  Out of Control. St Martin.
Liddy, James, 1934-
 xLiddy, James.
  Corca Bascinn. Humanities.
Lidin, Vladimir. *see* Lidin, Vladimir Germanovich.
Lidin, Vladimir Germanovich, 1894-
 xLidin, Vladimir.
  The Price of Life. Hyperion Conn.
Lidster, Miriam D.
 xLidster, Miriam D.
  Folk Dance Progressions. Greenwood.
Lidstone, Herrick K.
 xLidstone, Herrick K.
  ed. A Tax Guide for Artists & Arts
   Organizations. Lexington Bks.
Lidstone, John.
 xLidstone, John.
  Building with Wire. Van Nos Reinhold.
  Children As Film Makers. Van Nos Reinhold.
  Design Activities for the Classroom. Davis
   Mass.
Lidz, Jane.
 xLidz, Jane.
  Rolling Homes: Handmade Houses on Wheels.
   A & W Pubs.
Lidz, Richard.
 xLidz, Richard.
  Many Kinds of Courage: An Oral History of
   World War II. Putnam.
Lidz, Theodore.
 xLidz, Theodore.
  Origin & Treatment of Schizophrenic
   Disorders. Basic.
Lieb, Julian.
 xLieb, Julian.
  The Crisis Team: A Handbook for the Mental
   Health Professional. Har-Row.
  Integrated Psychiatric Treatment. Har-Row.
Liebaers, Herman.
 xLiebaers, Herman.
  Mostly in the Line of Duty: Thirty Years with
   Books. Kluwer Boston.
Lieban, Richard W. *see* Lieban, Richard Warren.
Lieban, Richard Warren.
 xLieban, Richard W.
  Cebuano Sorcery: Malign Magic in the
   Philippines. U of Cal Pr.
Liebard, Odile. *see* Liebard, Odile M.
Liebard, Odile M.
 xLiebard, Odile.
  Clergy & Laity. McGrath.
Liebeck, Pamela.
 xLiebeck, Pamela.

Vectors & Matrices. Pergamon.
Liebenow, J. Gus, 1925-
 xLiebenow, J. Gus.
  Liberia: The Evolution of Privilege. Cornell U
   Pr.
Lieber, Francis, 1800-1872
 xLieber, Francis.
  On Civil Liberty & Self Government. Da Capo.
Lieber, Harvey.
 xLieber, Harvey.
  Federalism & Clean Waters: The 1972 Water
   Pollution Control Act. Lexington Bks.
Lieber, Mary, 1926-
 xLieber, Mary G.
  A Place Called Empty. Beta Bk.
Lieber, Mary G. *see* Lieber, Mary.
Lieber, Michael D.
 xLieber, Michael D.
  ed. Exiles & Migrants in Oceania. U Pr of
   Hawaii.
Lieber, Robert J.
 xLieber, Robert J.
  British Politics & European Unity: Parties,
   Elites & Pressure Groups. U of Cal Pr.
  Theory & World Politics. Winthrop.
Lieber, Todd M.
 xLieber, Todd M.
  Endless Experiments: Essays on the Heroic
   Experience in American Romanticism. Ohio
   St U Pr.
Lieberg, Owen S.
 xLieberg, Owen S.
  Wonders of Measurement. Dodd.
Lieberman, Archie.
 xLieberman, Archie.
  The Mummies of Guanajuato. Abrams.
Lieberman, Bernhardt, 1929-
 xLieberman, Bernhardt.
  ed. Contemporary Problems in Statistics: A
   Book of Readings for the Behavioral
   Sciences. Oxford U Pr.
  ed. Human Sexual Behavior: A Book of
   Readings. Wiley.
Lieberman, David E., 1954-
 xLieberman, David E.
  ed. Computer Methods: The Fundamentals of
   Digital Nuclear Medicine. Mosby.
Lieberman, David M.
 xLieberman, David M.
  Your Introduction to Real Estate. Van Nos
   Reinhold.
Lieberman, Elias, 1883-1969
 xLieberman, Elias.
  The American Short Story: A Study of the
   Influence of Locality in Its Development.
   Arden Lib.
Lieberman, Ellin.
 xLieberman, Ellin.
  ed. Clinical Pediatric Nephrology. Lippincott.
Lieberman, Florence.
 xLieberman, Florence.
  Social Work with Children. Human Sci Pr.
Lieberman, Fredric.
 xLieberman, Fredric.
  Chinese Music: An Annotated Bibliography.
   Asian Music Pub.
  Chinese Music: An Annotated Bibliography.
   Garland Pub.
Lieberman, Herbert.
 xLieberman, Herbert.
  Brilliant Kids. Macmillan.
  Brilliant Kids. PB.
Lieberman, J. Ben.
 xLieberman, J. Ben.
  Type & Typefaces. Myriade.
Lieberman, Jethro K. *see* Lieberman, Jethro Koller.
Lieberman, Jethro Koller.
 xLieberman, Jethro K.

Free Speech, Free Press, & the Law. Lothrop.
  Privacy & the Law. Lothrop.
Lieberman, Laurence.
 xLieberman, Laurence.
  God's Measurements. Macmillan.
  The Osprey Suicides: Poems. Macmillan.
  Unassigned Frequencies: American Poetry in
   Review, 1964-77. U of Ill Pr.
Lieberman, Leo.
 xLieberman, Leo.
  ed. Dictionary of Correct English Usage. Philos
   Lib.
Lieberman, M. *see* Lieberman, Melvyn.
Lieberman, Maurice.
 xLieberman, Maurice.
  Ear Training & Sight Singing. Norton.
Lieberman, Melvyn.
 xLieberman, M.
  ed. Developmental & Physiological Correlates
   of Cardiac Muscle: Perspectives in
   Cardiovascular Research, Vol. 1. Raven.
Lieberman, Myron.
 xLieberman, Myron.
  Future of Public Education. U of Chicago Pr.
Lieberman, Philip.
 xLieberman, Philip.
  The Speech of Primates. Mouton.
Lieberman, Robert.
 xLieberman, Robert.
  Goobersville Breakdown. Gamma Bks.
Lieberman, Samuel S.
 xLieberman, Samuel S.
  An Economic Approach to Differential
   Demographic Behavior in Turkey. Garland
   Pub.
Lieberman, Saul, 1898-
 xLieberman, Saul.
  Texts & Studies. Ktav.
Lieberman, Sima, 1927-
 xLieberman, Sima.
  ed. Europe & the Industrial Revolution.
   Schenkman.
  The Growth of European Mixed Economies,
   1945-1970: A Concise Study of the
   Economic Evolution of Six Countries.
   Schenkman.
Lieberoff, Allen J.
 xLieberoff, Allen J.
  Good Jobs: High Paying Opportunities
   Working for Yourself or for Others. P-H.
Liebers, Arthur, 1913-
 xLiebers, Arthur.
  How to Get a Civil Service Job. Key Bks.
  How to Get the Job You Want Overseas. Pilot
   Bks.
  How to Raise & Train a Basset Hound. TFH
   Pubns.
  How to Raise & Train a Dalmatian. TFH
   Pubns.
  How to Raise & Train a German Short-Haired
   Pointer. TFH Pubns.
  How to Raise & Train a Pomeranian. TFH
   Pubns.
  How to Raise & Train a Weimaraner. TFH
   Pubns.
  How to Raise & Train a Yorkshire Terrier.
   TFH Pubns.
  How to Start a Profitable Retirement Business.
   Pilot Bks.
  You Can Be a Professional Photographer.
   Lothrop.
Lieberson, Stanley, 1933-
 xLieberson, Stanley.
  Ethnic Patterns in American Cities. Free Pr.
Lieberson, Stanley. *see* Lieberstein, Stanley H.
Lieberstein, Stanley H., 1934-
 xLieberstein, Stanley.

Who Owns What Is in Your Head?: Trade
Secrets & the Mobile Employee. Dutton.

Liebert, Burt.
xLiebert, Burt.
A Schoolwide Secondary Reading Program:
Here's How. Wiley.

Liebert, Robert M.
xLiebert, Robert M.
Developmental Psychology. P-H.
Psychology. Wiley.

Liebert, Roland J.
xLiebert, Roland J.
Disintegration & Political Action: The
Changing Functions of City Governments in
America. Acad Pr.
ed. Power Paradigms & Community Research.
Sage.

Lieberthal, Edwin M.
xLieberthal, Edwin M.
The Complete Book of Fingermath. McGraw.

Lieberthal, Kenneth.
xLieberthal, Kenneth.
Central Documents & Politburo Politics in
China. U of Mich Ctr Chinese.

Liebhafsky, H. A.
xLiebhafsky, Herman A.
Silicones Under the Monogram: A Story of
Industrial Research. Wiley.
Liebhafsky, Herman A. see Liebhafsky, H. A.

Liebig, Justus, Freiherr Von, 1803-1873
xLiebig, Justus Von.
The Natural Laws of Husbandry. Arno.
Liebig, Justus Von. see Liebig, Justus.
Liebler, Joan G. see Liebler, Joan Gratto.

Liebler, Joan Gratto.
xLiebler, Joan G.
Managing Health Records: Administrative
Principles. Aspen Systems.

Lieblich, Gerald S.
xLieblich, Gerald S.
Pre-Algebra Mathematics. Merrill.
Liebling, A. J. see Liebling, Abbott Joseph.
Liebling, Abbott J. see Liebling, Abbott Joseph.

Liebling, Abbott Joseph, 1904-1963
xLiebling, A. J.
Earl of Louisiana. La State U Pr.
The Sweet Science. Greenwood.
xLiebling, Abbott J.
Chicago, the Second City. Greenwood.

Liebling, Herman I.
xLiebling, Herman I.
U. S. Corporate Profitability & Capital
Formation: Are Rates of Return Sufficient?.
Pergamon.

Liebman, Arthur.
xLiebman, Arthur.
Jews & the Left. Wiley.
Latin American University Students: A Six
Nation Study. Harvard U Pr.
Politics of Puerto Rican University Students. U
of Tex Pr.
ed. Science Fiction: Creators & Pioneers.
Rosen Pr.

Liebman, Charles S.
xLiebman, Charles S.
Pressure Without Sanctions: The Influence of
World Jewry on Israeli Policy. Fairleigh
Dickinson.
Liebman, Joshua L. see Liebman, Joshua Loth.

Liebman, Joshua Loth, 1907-1948
xLiebman, Joshua L.
Peace of Mind. NAL.
Peace of Mind. S&S.
Peace of Mind. S&S.

Liebman, Malvina W.
xLiebman, Malvina W.
From Caravan to Casserole: Herbs & Spices in
Legend, History & Recipes. E A Seemann.

Liebman, Seymour B., 1907-
xLiebman, Seymour B.

Exploring the Latin American Mind.
Nelson-Hall.
Liechti, R. see Liechti, Rene.

Liechti, Rene, 1938-
xLiechti, R.
Hip Arthrodesis & Its Problems.
Springer-Verlag.

Liechty, Richard D.
xLiechty, Richard D.
Synopsis of Surgery. Mosby.

Liederbach, Clarence A., 1910-
xLiederbach, Clarence A.
America's Thousand Bishops: From 1513 to
1974, from Abramowicz to Zuroweste. R J
Liederbach.

Liederman, Judith.
xLiederman, Judith.
The Moneyman. HM.
The Moneyman. NAL.

Liefer, Richard.
xLiefer, Richard.
Training Human Service Managers: A
Curriculum Design. Social Matrix.

Liefmann, Robert, 1874-1941
xLiefmann, Robert.
Cartels, Concerns & Trusts. Arno.

Liehm, Antonin J., 1924-
xLiehm, Antonin J.
Closely Watched Films: The Czechoslovak
Experience. M E Sharpe.
Lien, Arnold J. see Lien, Arnold Johnson.

Lien, Arnold Johnson, 1882-
xLien, Arnold J.
Privileges & Immunities of Citizens of the
United States. AMS Pr.

Lien, David A.
xLien, David A.
Complete Guide for Easy Car Care. P-H.
Liener, I. see Liener, Irvin E.

Liener, Irvin E.
xLiener, I.
Toxic Constituents in Plant Foodstuffs. Acad
Pr.

Lienhardt, Godfrey.
xLienhardt, Godfrey.
Divinity & Experience: The Religion of the
Dinka. Oxford U Pr.

Lientz, Bennet P.
xLientz, Bennett P.
Computer Applications in Operations Analysis.
P-H.
Lientz, Bennett P. see Lientz, Bennet P.

Liepmann, Heinrich, 1904-
xLiepmann, Heinrich.
Tariff Levels & the Economic Unity of Europe:
An Examination of Tariff Policy Export
Movements & the Economic Integration of
Europe 1913-1931. Porcupine Pr.
Liere, Edward J. Van. see Van Liere, Edward J.

Liers, Emil E.
xLiers, Emil E.
A Groundhog's Story. Southern Pub.
A Mink's Story. Southern Pub.

Liesener, James W., 1933-
xLiesener, James W.
Systematic Process for Planning Media
Programs. ALA.
Lieth, H. see Lieth, Helmut.

Lieth, Helmut.
xLieth, H.
ed. Primary Productivity of the Biosphere.
Springer-Verlag.

Lieth, R. M. A., 1930-
xLieth, Ronald M.
ed. Preparation & Crystal Growth of Materials
with Layered Structures. Kluwer Boston.
Lieth, Ronald M. see Lieth, R. M. A.

Lietz, Paul S.
xLietz, Paul S.

ed. Calendar of Philippine Documents in the
Ayer Collection of the Newberry Library.
Newberry.
Lievegoed, B. C. see Lievegoed, Bernardus Cornelis
Johannes.

Lievegoed, Bernardus Cornelis Johannes.
xLievegoed, B. C.
The Developing Organization. Celestial Arts.
Lievsay, John L. see Lievsay, John Leon.

Lievsay, John Leon.
xLievsay, John L.
The Seventeenth Century Resolve: A Historical
Anthology of a Literary Form. U Pr of Ky.

Lifchez, Raymond.
xLifchez, Raymond.
Design for Independent Living: The
Environment & Physically Disabled People.
Watson-Guptill.

Life Office Management Association.
xLife Office Management Association.
Canadian, Part 3: A Student Guide. LOMA.
Life Company Operations. LOMA.
Student Guide for Management Principles.
LOMA.
Liff, Alvin. see Liff, Alvin A.

Liff, Alvin A., 1929-
xLiff, Alvin.
Color & Black & White Television Theory &
Servicing. P-H.

Lifshin, Lyn.
xLifshin, Lyn.
Some Madonna Poems. White Pine.
ed. Tangled Vines: A Collection of Mother &
Daughter Poems. Beacon Pr.
Lifton, Betty J. see Lifton, Betty Jean.

Lifton, Betty Jean.
xLifton, Betty J.
The Children of Vietnam. Atheneum.
Lost & Found: The Adoption Experience. Dial.
Twice Born: Memoirs of an Adopted Daughter.
Penguin.
Lifton, Robert J. see Lifton, Robert Jay.

Lifton, Robert Jay, 1926-
xLifton, Robert J.
America & the Asian Revolutions. Transaction
Bks.
Death in Life: Survivors of Hiroshima. S&S.
Revolutionary Immortality: Mao-Tse-Tung &
the Chinese Cultural Revolution. Norton.
Six Lives, Six Deaths: Portraits from Modern
Japan. Yale U Pr.
Liggero, J. see Liggero, John.

Liggero, John.
xLiggero, J.
Successful Approach to High School
Counseling. P-H.

Light, Donald.
xLight, Donald.
ed. Dynamics of University Protest.
Nelson-Hall.
Light, Ivan H. see Light, Ivan Hubert.

Light, Ivan Hubert.
xLight, Ivan H.
Ethnic Enterprise in America: Business &
Welfare Among Chinese, Japanese, & Blacks.
U of Cal Pr.

Light, J. O.
xLight, J. O.
The Financial System. Irwin.

Light, Martin.
xLight, Martin.
The Quixotic Vision of Sinclair Lewis. Purdue.
Lightbody, Donna. see Lightbody, Donna M.

Lightbody, Donna M.
xLightbody, Donna.
Braid Craft. Lothrop.
illus. Hooks & Loops: Beginning Crochet.
Lothrop.

Lighterness, Tony.
xLighterness, Tony.

Living in the Kingdom Here & Now. Logos.
Lightfoot, D. W. see Lightfoot, David.
Lightfoot, David.
xLightfoot, D. W.
Principles of Diachronic Syntax. Cambridge U Pr.
Lightfoot, Georgia F. see Lightfoot, Georgia Frances.
Lightfoot, Georgia Frances.
xLightfoot, Georgia F.
Personality Characteristics of Bright & Dull Children. AMS Pr.
Lightfoot, Gordon.
xLightfoot, Gordon.
The Pony Man. Har-Row.
Lightfoot, Neil R.
xLightfoot, Neil R.
Lessons from the Parables. Baker Bk.
Lightfoot, Sara L. see Lightfoot, Sara Lawrence.
Lightfoot, Sara Lawrence.
xLightfoot, Sara L.
Worlds Apart: Relationships Between Families & Schools. Basic.
Lighthall, Nancy.
xLighthall, Nancy.
Skiing for Women. Chicago Review.
Skiing for Women. ETC Pubns.
Lightman, Alan P., 1948-
xLightman, Alan P.
Problem Book in Relativity & Gravitation. Princeton U Pr.
Lightner, Otto C., 1886-
xLightner, Otto C.
History of Business Depressions: A Vivid Portrayal of Periods of Economic Adversity from the Beginning of Commerce to the Present. B Franklin.
Lightner, Robert P. see Lightner, Robert Paul.
Lightner, Robert Paul.
xLightner, Robert P.
The God of the Bible: An Introduction to the Doctrine of God. Baker Bk.
Neoevangelicalism Today. Reg Baptist.
Prophecy in the Ring. Accent Bks.
Speaking in Tongues & Divine Healing. Reg Baptist.
Truth for the Good Life. Accent Bks.
Lightstone, A. H.
xLightstone, A. H.
Linear Algebra. Irvington.
Lightwood, James T. see Lightwood, James Thomas.
Lightwood, James Thomas, 1856-1944
xLightwood, James T.
Charles Dickens & Music. Haskell.
Charles Dickens & Music. R West.
Lightwood, Martha B.
xLightwood, Martha B.
ed. Public & Business Planning in the United States: A Bibliography. Gale.
Ligon, Ernest M., 1897-
xLigon, Ernest M.
Psychology of Christian Personality. Character Res.
Ligon, Helen H. see Ligon, Helen Hailey.
Ligon, Helen Hailey, 1921-
xLigon, Helen H.
Successful Management Information Systems. Univ Microfilms.
Ligon, Mary G.
xLigon, Mary G.
Teachers Role in Counseling. P-H.
Liguori, F. see Liguori, Fred.
Liguori, Fred.
xLiguori, F.
ed. Automatic Test Equipment: Hardware, Software, & Management. Wiley.
xLiguori, Fred.
ed. Automatic Test Equipment: Hardware, Software & Management. Inst Electrical.
Lihani, John.
xLihani, John.

Bartolome De Torres Naharro. Twayne.
Lucas Fernandez. Twayne.
Lijphart, Arend.
xLijphart, Arend.
Democracy in Plural Societies: A Comparative Exploration. Yale U Pr.
The Politics of Accommodation: Pluralism & Democracy in the Netherlands. U of Cal Pr.
Likert, Rensis, 1903-
xLikert, Rensis.
Human Organization: Its Management & Value. McGraw.
Likoff, William.
xLikoff, William.
ed. Atherosclerosis & Coronary Heart Disease: Twenty Fourth Hahnemann Symposium. Grune.
Liler, M. see Liler, Milica.
Liler, Milica.
xLiler, M.
Reaction Mechanisms in Sulphuric Acid & Other Strong Acid Solutions. Acad Pr.
Liles, B. see Liles, Bruce L.
Liles, Bruce L.
xLiles, B.
Basic Grammar of Modern English. P-H.
xLiles, Bruce L.
An Introduction to Linguistics. P-H.
Linguistics & the English Language: A Transformational Approach. Goodyear.
Liles, Marcia. see Liles, Marcia D.
Liles, Marcia D.
xLiles, Marcia.
The Good Housekeeping Guide to Fixing Things Around the House. PB.
Lilcy, H. I. see Liley, H M I.
Liley, H M I.
xLiley, H. I.
Modern Motherhood: Pregnancy, Childbirth, & the Newborn Baby. Random.
Lilge, Frederic.
xLilge, Frederic.
The Abuse of Learning: The Failure of the German University. Octagon.
Lilienfeld, Abraham M.
xLilienfeld, Abraham M.
Foundations of Epidemiology. Oxford U Pr.
Lilienfeld, Robert.
xLilienfeld, Robert.
Learning to Read Music. T Y Crowell.
Lilienthal, Alfred M.
xLilienthal, Alfred M.
The Zionist Connection: What Price Peace?. Dodd.
Liliuokalani, Queen of the Hawaiian Islands, 1838-1917
xLiliuokalani.
The Kumulipo: A Hawaiian Creation Myth. Pueo Pr.
Liljedahl, J. B. see Liljedahl, John B.
Liljedahl, John B.
xLiljedahl, J. B.
Tractors & Their Power Units. Wiley.
Liljegren, Sten B. see Liljegren, Sten Bodvar.
Liljegren, Sten Bodvar, 1885-
xLiljegren, Sten B.
American & European in the Works of Henry James. Haskell.
Studies in Milton. Folcroft.
Lillard, Richard G. see Lillard, Richard Gordon.
Lillard, Richard Gordon, 1909-
xLillard, Richard G.
Desert Challenge: An Interpretation of Nevada. Greenwood.
The Great Forest. Da Capo.
Lillegraven, Jason A.
xLillegraven, Jason A.
ed. Mesozoic Mammals: The First Two-Thirds of Mammalian History. U of Cal Pr.
Lillesand, Thomas M.
xLillesand, Thomas M.

Remote Sensing & Image Interpretation. Wiley.
Lillibridge, G. D. see Lillibridge, George D.
Lillibridge, George D., 1921-
xLillibridge, G. D.
Images of American Society: A History of the United States. HM.
Lillich, Meredith P., 1932-
xLillich, Meredith P.
The Stained Glass of Saint-Pere de Chartres. Columbia U Pr.
Lillich, Richard B.
xLillich, Richard B.
Humanitarian Intervention & the United Nations. U Pr of Va.
Lillie, Ralph D. see Lillie, Ralph Dougall.
Lillie, Ralph Dougall, 1896-
xLillie, Ralph D.
Histopathologic Technic & Practical Histochemistry. McGraw.
Lillow, Ira.
xLillow, Ira.
Designs for Machine Embroidery. Branford.
Lillyman, William J.
xLillyman, William J.
Reality's Dark Dream: The Narrative Fiction of Ludwig Tieck. De Gruyter.
Lillyquist, Michael J.
xLillyquist, Michael J.
Understanding & Changing Criminal Behavior. P-H.
Lillywhite, Herold S.
xLillywhite, Herold S.
Pediatrician's Handbook of Communication Disorders. Lea & Febiger.
Lim, B. P.
xLim, B. P.
Environmental Factors in the Design of Building Fenestration. Burgess-Intl Ideas.
Lim, David.
xLim, David.
Economic Growth & Development in West Malaysia 1947-1970. Oxford U Pr.
Lim, Pacifico A.
xLim, Pacifico A.
A Guide to Structured COBOL with Efficiency Techniques & Special Algoritms. Van Nos Reinhold.
Lima, Agnes De. see De Lima, Agnes.
Lima, Frank, 1939-
xLima, Frank.
Angel: New Poems. Liveright.
Lima, Robert.
xLima, Robert.
Ramon Del Valle-Inclan. Columbia U Pr.
Liman, Ellen.
xLiman, Ellen.
The Collecting Book. Penguin.
Money Saver's Guide to Decorating. Macmillan.
The Money Saver's Guide to Decorating. Macmillan.
The Spacemaker Book. PB.
Limbacher, James L.
xLimbacher, James L.
Four Aspects of the Film. Arno.
The Song List: A Guide to Contemporary Music from Classical Sources. Pierian.
Limbert, Paul M. see Limbert, Paul Moyer.
Limbert, Paul Moyer, 1897-
xLimbert, Paul M.
Denominational Policies in the Support & Supervision of Higher Education. AMS Pr.
Limburg, James, 1935-
xLimburg, James.
The Prophets & the Powerless. John Knox.
Limburg, Peter. see Limburg, Peter R.
Limburg, Peter R.
xLimburg, Peter.

The Story of Your Heart. Coward.
What's in the Names of Birds. Coward.
What's in the Names of Stars & Constellations.
    Coward.
What's in the Names of Wild Animals.
    Coward.
xLimburg, Peter R.
Chickens, Chickens, Chickens. Elsevier-Nelson.
Engines. Watts.
Oceanographic Institutions: Science Studies the
    Sea. Elsevier-Nelson.
Limerick, Jeffrey.
xLimerick, Jeffrey.
America's Grand Resort Hotels. Pantheon.
Limoge, Aime.
xLimoge, Aime.
An Introduction to Electroanesthesia. Univ
    Park.
Limpert, Rudolf.
xLimpert, Rudolph.
Motor Vehicle Accident Reconstruction &
    Cause Analysis. Michie.
Limpert, Rudolph. *see* Limpert, Rudolf.
Lin, C. C. *see* Lin, Chia-Chiao.
Lin, Chia-Chiao.
xLin, C. C.
Mathematics Applied to Deterministic
    Problems in the Natural Sciences. Macmillan.
Lin, Florence.
xLin, Florence.
Florence Lin's Chinese One-Dish Meals.
    Dutton.
Florence Lin's Chinese Vegetarian Cookbook.
    Dutton.
Florence Lin's Cooking with Fire Pots. Dutton.
Lin, Hazel. *see* Lin, Hazel Ai Chun.
Lin, Hazel Ai Chun, 1913-
xLin, Hazel.
Rachel Weeping for Her Children,
    Uncomforted. Branden.
Lin, N. *see* Lin, Nan.
Lin, Nan.
xLin, N.
Foundations of Social Research. McGraw.
Lin, Shu.
xLin, Shu.
Introduction to Error-Correcting Codes. P-H.
Lin, Steven A. *see* Lin, Steven A. Y.
Lin, Steven A. Y.
xLin, Steven A.
ed. Theory & Measurement of Economic
    Externalities. Acad Pr.
Lin, Y. K. *see* Lin, Yu-Kweng Michael.
Lin, Yu-Kweng Michael, 1923-
xLin, Y. K.
Probabilistic Theory of Structural Dynamics.
    Krieger.
Linart, Charles. *see* Linart, Charles W.
Linart, Charles W.
xLinart, Charles.
How to Increase Your Height. Arco.
Linch, A. L.
xLinch, Adrian L.
Evaluation of Ambient Air Quality by
    Personnel Monitoring. CRC Pr.
Linch, Adrian L. *see* Linch, A. L.
Linck, Orville F.
xLinck, Orville F.
A Passage Through Pakistan. Wayne St U Pr.
Lincoln, Ann.
xLincoln, Ann.
Food for Athletes. Contemp Bks.
Lincoln, Anthony.
xLincoln, Anthony.
Some Political & Social Ideas of English
    Dissent, 1763-1800. Octagon.
Lincoln, C. Eric. *see* Lincoln, Charles Eric.
Lincoln, Charles Eric.
xLincoln, C. Eric.

Martin Luther King, Jr: A Profile. Hill &
    Wang.
My Face Is Black. Beacon Pr.
Sounds of the Struggle: Persons & Perspectives
    in Civil Rights. Peter Smith.
Lincoln, Harry B.
xLincoln, Harry B.
ed. Computer & Music. Cornell U Pr.
Lincoln, Jackson S. *see* Lincoln, Jackson Steward.
Lincoln, Jackson Steward, 1902-1941
xLincoln, Jackson S.
The Dream in Primitive Cultures. Johnson
    Repr.
Lincoln, Jonathan T. *see* Lincoln, Jonathan Thayer.
Lincoln, Jonathan Thayer, 1869-1942
xLincoln, Jonathan T.
The City of the Dinner-Pail. Arno.
Lincoln, Joseph C. *see* Lincoln, Joseph Crosby.
Lincoln, Joseph Colville.
xLincoln, Joseph C.
ed. On Quiet Wings: A Soaring Anthology.
    Northland.
Lincoln, Joseph Crosby, 1870-1944
xLincoln, Joseph C.
Partners of the Tide. AMS Pr.
Lincoln, Rufus.
xLincoln, Rufus.
ed. Papers of Captain Rufus Lincoln of
    Wareham, Mass. Arno.
Lincoln, William C., 1926-
xLincoln, William C.
Personal Bible Study. Bethany Fell.
Lind, Andrew W. *see* Lind, Andrew William.
Lind, Andrew William, 1901-
xLind, Andrew W.
Hawaii's People. U Pr of Hawaii.
Lind, Aulis O.
xLind, Aulis O.
Coastal Landforms of Cat Island, Bahamas: A
    Study of Holocene Accretionary Topography
    & Sea Level Change. U Chicago Dept Geog.
Lind, E. M. *see* Lind, Edna Margaret.
Lind, Earl.
xLind, Earl.
Autobiography of an Androgyne. Arno.
Lind, Edna Margaret.
xLind, E. M.
Some Common Flowering Plants of Uganda.
    Oxford U Pr.
Lind, Ernie.
xLind, Ernie.
The Complete Book of Trick & Fancy
    Shooting. Citadel Pr.
Complete Book of Trick & Fancy Shooting.
    Winchester Pr.
Lind, L. F. *see* Lind, Larry Frederick.
Lind, L. R. *see* Lind, Levi Robert.
Lind, Larry Frederick.
xLind, L. F.
Analysis & Design of Sequential Digital
    Systems. Halsted Pr.
Lind, Levi Robert, 1906-
xLind, L. R.
ed. Twentieth Century Italian Poetry: A
    Bilingual Anthology. Bobbs.
Lind, Owen T., 1934-
xLind, Owen T.
Handbook of Common Methods in Limnology.
    Mosby.
Lindaman, Edward B.
xLindaman, Edward B.
Thinking in the Future Tense. Broadman.
Lindamood, Suzanne.
xLindamood, Suzanne.
Housing, Society & Consumers: An
    Introduction. West Pub.
Lindars, B. *see* Lindars, Barnabas.
Lindars, Barnabas.
xLindars, B.

Christ & Spirit in the New Testament.
    Cambridge U Pr.
Lindau, Joan.
xLindau, Joan.
Mrs. Cooper's Boardinghouse. McGraw.
Lindauer. *see* Lindauer, J. S.
Lindauer, J. S.
xLindauer.
Communicating in Business. Dryden Pr.
xLindauer, Jacqueline S.
Communicating in Business. Saunders.
Lindauer, Jacqueline S. *see* Lindauer, J. S.
Lindauer, Martin.
xLindauer, Martin.
Communication Among Social Bees.
    Atheneum.
Communication Among Social Bees. Harvard
    U Pr.
Lindbeck. *see* Lindbeck, John Robert.
Lindbeck, Assar.
xLindbeck, Assar.
Swedish Economic Policy. U of Cal Pr.
Lindbeck, John R. *see* Lindbeck, John Robert.
Lindbeck, John Robert.
xLindbeck.
Basic Crafts. Bennett Co.
xLindbeck, John R.
Designing Today's Manufactured Products.
    McKnight.
General Industry. Bennett Co.
Lindberg, David C.
xLindberg, David C.
Theories of Vision from Al-Kindi to Kepler. U
    of Chicago Pr.
Lindberg, Donald A. *see* Lindberg, Donald A. B.
Lindberg, Donald A. B.
xLindberg, Donald A.
The Growth of Medical Information Systems in
    the United States. Lexington Bks.
Lindberg, John, 1901-
xLindberg, John.
Foundations of Social Survival. Greenwood.
Lindberg, John S.
xLindberg, John S.
The Background of Swedish Emigration to the
    United States: An Economic & Sociological
    Study in the Dynamics of Migration. Ozer.
Lindberg, Leon N.
xLindberg, Leon N.
The Energy Syndrome: Comparing National
    Responses to the Energy Crisis. Lexington
    Bks.
Lindberg, Lucile.
xLindberg, Lucile.
Early Childhood Education: A Guide for
    Observation & Participation. Allyn.
Lindberg, Roy A.
xLindberg, Roy A.
Materials & Manufacturing Technology. Allyn.
Processes & Materials of Manufacture. Allyn.
What You Should Know About the
    Foundations of Management. Oceana.
Lindberg, Stanley W.
xLindberg, Stanley W.
Van Nostrand's Plain English Handbook. D
    Van Nostrand.
Lindbergh, Anne (Morrow), 1906-
xLindbergh, Anne M.
Bring Me a Unicorn: Diaries & Letters of Anne
    Morrow Lindbergh, 1922-1928. HarBraceJ.
Earth Shine. HarBraceJ.
Gift from the Sea. Pantheon.
Gift from the Sea. Random.
The Unicorn & Other Poems. Random.
Lindbergh, Anne M. *see* Lindbergh, Anne (Morrow).
Lindbergh, Charles A. *see* Lindbergh, Charles Augustus.
Lindbergh, Charles Augustus, 1902-
xLindbergh, Charles A.

Boyhood on the Upper Mississippi: A
Reminiscent Letter. Minn Hist.
Lindblom, C. *see* Lindblom, Charles Edward.
Lindblom, Charles E. *see* Lindblom, Charles Edward.
Lindblom, Charles Edward, 1917-
xLindblom, C.
Policy Making Process. P-H.
xLindblom, Charles E.
Politics & Markets: The World's
Political-Economic Systems. Basic.
Lindblom, J. *see* Lindblom, Johannes.
Lindblom, Johannes, 1882-
xLindblom, J.
Prophecy in Ancient Israel. Fortress.
Lindborg, Kristina.
xLindborg, Kristina.
Five Mexican-American Women in Transition:
A Case Study of Migrants in the Midwest. R
& E Res Assoc.
Lindburg, Donald G., 1932-
xLindburg, Donald G.
The Macaques: Studies in Ecology, Behavior &
Evolution. Van Nos Reinhold.
Linde, Richard W. Te. *see* Te Linde, Richard W.
Lindegren, Erik, 1910-
xLindegren, Erik.
ABC of Lettering & Printing Types. Taplinger.
Lindell, Anne.
xLindell, Anne.
Intensive English for Communication. U of
Mich Pr.
Lindeman, Bruce.
xLindeman, Bruce.
Low Income Housing Subsidies & the Housing
Market: An Economic Analysis. Ga St U
Busn Pub.
Lindeman, Joanne. *see* Lindeman, Joanne Waring.
Lindeman, Joanne Waring.
xLindeman, Joanne.
The Ground Beef Cookbook. Nitty Gritty.
Low Carbohydrate Cookbook. Nitty Gritty.
Lindeman, Richard H. *see* Lindeman, Richard Harold.
Lindeman, Richard Harold, 1926-
xLindeman, Richard H.
Educational Measurement. Scott F.
Lindemann, J. W. *see* Lindemann, John William Richard.
Lindemann, John William Richard, 1900-
xLindemann, J. W.
Old English Preverbal GE, Its Meaning. U Pr
of Va.
Linden, Eugene.
xLinden, Eugene.
Apes, Men & Language. Penguin.
Linden, Glenn M., 1928-
xLinden, Glenn M.
Politics or Principle: Congressional Voting on
the Civil War Amendments & Pro-Negro
Measures, 1838-69. U of Wash Pr.
Linden, Ian.
xLinden, Ian.
Catholics, Peasants & Chewa Resistance in
Nyasaland, 1889-1939. U of Cal Pr.
Linden, Kathryn W.
xLinden, Kathryn W.
Modern Mental Measurement: A Historical
Perspective. HM.
Linden, Millicent.
xLinden, Millicent.
Living in a State of Orgasm. M Linden NY.
Linden, Ronald H. *see* Linden, Ronald Haly.
Linden, Ronald Haly.
xLinden, Ronald H.
Bear & Foxes: The International Relations of
the East European States, 1965-1969. East
Eur Quarterly.
Lindenbaum, S. J.
xLindenbaum, S. J.

Particle-Interaction Physics at High Energies.
Oxford U Pr.
Lindenbaum, Shirley.
xLindenbaum, Shirley.
Kuru Sorcery: Disease & Danger in the New
Guinea Highlands. Mayfield Pub.
Lindenberger, Herbert. *see* Lindenberger, Herbert
Samuel.
Lindenberger, Herbert S. *see* Lindenberger, Herbert
Samuel.
Lindenberger, Herbert Samuel, 1929-
xLindenberger, Herbert.
Georg Buchner. S Ill U Pr.
Historical Drama: The Relation of Literature &
Reality. U of Chicago Pr.
Saul's Fall: A Critical Fiction. Johns Hopkins.
xLindenberger, Herbert S.
On Wordsworth's Prelude. Greenwood.
Lindencrona, G. *see* Lindencrona, Gustaf.
Lindencrona, Gustaf, 1938-
xLindencrona, G.
Trends in Scandinavian Taxation. Kluwer
Boston.
Lindenfeld, Frank.
xLindenfeld, Frank.
Radical Perspectives on Social Problems:
Readings in Critical Sociology. Macmillan.
Lindenmann, J. *see* Lindenmann, Jean.
Lindenmann, Jean.
xLindenmann, J.
Immunological Aspects of Viral Oncolysis.
Springer-Verlag.
Lindenstrauss, Joram.
xLindenstrauss, Joram.
Extension of Compact Operators. Am Math.
Linder. *see* Linder, Carl.
Linder, Bill R. *see* Linder, Billy Royce.
Linder, Billy Royce.
xLinder, Bill R.
How to Trace Your Family History. Popular
Lib.
Linder, Carl.
xLinder.
Filmmaking: A Practical Guide. P-H.
Linder, Erik H. *see* Linder, Erik Hjalmar.
Linder, Erik Hjalmar, 1906-
xLinder, Erik H.
Hjalmar Bergman. Twayne.
Linder, P.
xLinder, P.
Air Filters for Use at Nuclear Facilities.
Unipub.
Linder, Robert D. *see* Linder, Robert Dean.
Linder, Robert Dean.
xLinder, Robert D.
ed. God & Caesar: Case Studies in the
Relationship Between Christianity & the
State. Conf Faith & Hist.
Twilight of the Saints: Biblical Christianity &
Civil Religion in America. Inter-Varsity.
Linder, Roscoe G. *see* Linder, Roscoe George.
Linder, Roscoe George, 1892-
xLinder, Roscoe G.
An Evaluation of the Courses in Education of a
State Teachers College by Teachers in
Service. AMS Pr.
Linderberg, J. *see* Linderberg, Jan.
Linderberg, Jan.
xLinderberg, J.
Propagators in Quantum Chemistry. Acad Pr.
Linderman, Earl. *see* Linderman, Earl W.
Linderman, Earl W.
xLinderman, Earl.
Developing Artistic & Perceptual Awareness:
Art Practice in the Elementary Classroom.
Wm C Brown.
xLinderman, Earl W.

Teaching Secondary School Art: Discovering
Art Objectives, Art Skills, Art History, Art
Ideas. Wm C Brown.
Linderman, Frank B. *see* Linderman, Frank Bird.
Linderman, Frank Bird, 1868-1938
xLinderman, Frank B.
Indian Why Stories: Sparks from War Eagle's
Lodge-Fire. Kraus Repr.
Montana Adventure: The Recollections of
Frank B. Linderman. U of Nebr Pr.
Pretty-shield, Medicine Woman of the Crows.
U of Nebr Pr.
Linderman, Mariene. *see* Linderman, Marlene M.
Linderman, Marlene M.
xLinderman, Mariene.
Art in the Elementary School: Drawing,
Painting & Creating for the Classroom. Wm
C Brown.
Lindert, Peter H.
xLindert, Peter H.
Prices, Jobs & Growth: An Introduction to
Macroeconomics. Little.
Lindesmith, Alfred R. *see* Lindesmith, Alfred Ray.
Lindesmith, Alfred Ray, 1905-
xLindesmith, Alfred R.
Addict & the Law. Ind U Pr.
Lindfors, Bernth.
xLindfors, Bernth.
ed. Black African Literature in English: A
Guide to Information Sources. Gale.
ed. Critical Perspectives on Nigerian
Literatures. Three Continents.
Lindfors, Judith W. *see* Lindfors, Judith Wells.
Lindfors, Judith Wells.
xLindfors, Judith W.
Children's Language & Learning. P-H.
Lindgren, Alvin J.
xLindgren, Alvin J.
Foundations for Purposeful Church
Administration. Abingdon.
Lindgren, Astrid. *see* Lindgren, Astrid Ericsson.
Lindgren, Astrid Ericsson, 1907-
xLindgren, Astrid.
Lotta on Troublemaker Street. Macmillan.
Of Course Polly Can Ride a Bike. Follett.
Pippi in the South Seas. Penguin.
Pippi in the South Seas. Viking Pr.
Pippi on the Run. Viking Pr.
Lindgren, Ernest.
xLindgren, Ernest.
Art of the Film. Macmillan.
Art of the Film. Macmillan.
Lindgren, Henry C. *see* Lindgren, Henry Clay.
Lindgren, Henry Clay, 1914-
xLindgren, Henry C.
Educational Psychology in the Classroom.
Oxford U Pr.
Great Expectations: The Psychology of Money.
W Kaufmann.
An Introduction to Social Psychology. Wiley.
Psychology: An Introduction to a Behavioral
Science. Wiley.
Psychology of Personal Development. Wiley.
Lindgren, K. E.
xLindgren, K. E.
ed. The Corporation & Australian Society. Intl
Pubns Serv.
Lindgren, Raymond E.
xLindgren, Raymond E.
Norway-Sweden: Union, Disunion, &
Scandinavian Integration. Greenwood.
Lindheim, Roslyn.
xLindheim, Roslyn.
Changing Hospital Environments for Children.
Harvard U Pr.
Uncoupling the Radiology System. Hosp Res &
Educ.
Lindholm. *see* Lindholm, Richard Wadsworth.
Lindholm, Richard W. *see* Lindholm, Richard
Wadsworth.

Lindholm, Richard Wadsworth.
   xLindholm.
      Financing & Managing State & Local
         Government. Lexington Bks.
   xLindholm, Richard W.
      Money Management & Institutions. Littlefield.
      Property Taxation & the Finance of Education.
         U of Wis Pr.
      Value-Added Tax & Other Tax Reforms.
         Nelson-Hall.
Lindlahr, Victor H.
   xLindlahr, Victor H.
      The Natural Way to Health. Borgo Pr.
      The Natural Way to Health. Newcastle Pub.
Lindley, D. V. *see* Lindley, Dennis Victor.
Lindley, Dennis V. *see* Lindley, Dennis Victor.
Lindley, Dennis Victor.
   xLindley, D. V.
      Introduction to Probability & Statistics from a
         Bayesian Viewpoint: Pt. 1 Probability.
         Cambridge U Pr.
   xLindley, Dennis V.
      Introduction to Probability & Statistics from a
         Bayesian Viewpoint. Cambridge U Pr.
Lindley, Erica.
   xLindley, Erica.
      Devil in Crystal. NAL.
Lindley, Ernest K. *see* Lindley, Ernest Kidder.
Lindley, Ernest Kidder, 1899-
   xLindley, Ernest K.
      Half Way with Roosevelt. Da Capo.
Lindley, Lester G.
   xLindley, Lester G.
      The Constitution Faces Technology: The
         Relationship of the National Government to
         the Telegraph, 1866-1884. Arno.
Lindley, Mark F. *see* Lindley, Mark Frank.
Lindley, Mark Frank, Sir, 1881-1959
   xLindley, Mark F.
      Acquisition & Government of Backward
         Territory in International Law. Negro U Pr.
Lindman, Harold R.
   xLindman, Harold R.
      Analysis of Variance in Complex Experimental
         Designs. W H Freeman.
Lindmayer, Joseph.
   xLindmayer, Joseph.
      Fundamentals of Semiconductor Devices.
         Krieger.
Lindner, Gert.
   xLindner, Gert.
      Field Guide to Seashells of the World. Van
         Nos Reinhold.
Lindner, Rhoda. *see* Lindner, William A.
Lindner, Robert. *see* Lindner, Robert Mitchell.
Lindner, Robert Mitchell, 1914-
   xLindner, Robert.
      Prescription for Rebellion. Greenwood.
Lindner, William A., 1939-
   xLindner, Rhoda.
      jt. auth. Statistics for Students in the
         Behavioral Sciences. Benjamin-Cummings.
   xLindner, William A.
      Statistics for Students in the Behavioral
         Sciences. Benjamin-Cummings.
Lindo, David K., 1936-
   xLindo, David K.
      Supervision Can Be Easy. Am Mgmt.
Lindop, Edmund.
   xLindop, Edmund.
      An Album of the Fifties. Watts.
      The First Book of Elections. Watts.
Lindow, John.
   xLindow, John.
      Swedish Legends & Folktales. U of Cal Pr.
Lindow, Wesley, 1910-
   xLindow, Wesley.
      Inside the Money Market. Random.
Lindquist, Emory. *see* Lindquist, Emory Kempton.

Lindquist, Emory Kempton, 1908-
   xLindquist, Emory.
      An Immigrant's American Odyssey: A
         Biography of Ernst Skarstedt. Augustana.
      An Immigrant's Two Worlds: A Biography of
         Hjalmar Edgren. Augustana.
Lindquist, Gustavus E. *see* Lindquist, Gustavus Elmer
   Emanuel.
Lindquist, Gustavus Elmer Emanuel, 1886-
   xLindquist, Gustavus E.
      The Indian in American Life. AMS Pr.
Lindquist, Jack.
   xLindquist, Jack.
      ed. Designing Teaching Improvement
         Programs. Coun Advance Small Colleges.
Lindquist, Jennie D. *see* Lindquist, Jennie Dorothea.
Lindquist, Jennie Dorothea.
   xLindquist, Jennie D.
      Golden Name Day. Har-Row.
Lindsay, Alan E.
   xLindsay, Alan E.
      The Cardiac Arrhythmias: An Approach to
         Their Electrocardiographic Recognition. Year
         Bk Med.
Lindsay, Alexander D. *see* Lindsay, Alexander Dunlop.
**Lindsay, Alexander Dunlop, Baron Lindsay of Birker,
1879-1952**
   xLindsay, Alexander D.
      Religion, Science, & Society in the Modern
         World. Arno.
Lindsay, Beverly.
   xLindsay, Beverly.
      ed. Comparative Perspectives of Third World
         Women: The Impact of Race, Sex, & Class.
         Praeger.
Lindsay, David, 1876-1945
   xLindsay, David.
      Devil's Tor. Arno.
Lindsay, Gordon.
   xLindsay, Gordon.
      Amazing Discoveries in the Words of Jesus.
         Christ Nations.
      How to Be Enriched by Giving. Christ
         Nations.
Lindsay, J. *see* Lindsay, John F.
Lindsay, Jack, 1900-
   xLindsay, Jack.
      George Meredith, His Life & Work. Kraus
         Repr.
      Hogarth: His Art & His World. Taplinger.
      The Monster City: Defoe's London,
         1688-1730. St Martin.
      The Normans & Their World. St Martin.
      tr. Ribaldry of Ancient Greece: An Intimate
         Portrait of Greeks in Love. Ungar.
      Song of a Falling World: Culture During the
         Break-up of the Roman Empire (A.D.
         350-600). Hyperion Conn.
      William Morris: His Life & Work. Taplinger.
Lindsay, James A. *see* Lindsay, James Armour.
Lindsay, James Armour, 1897-
   xLindsay, James A.
      Annual & Semiannual Promotion, with Special
         Reference to the Elementary School. AMS
         Pr.
Lindsay, James F.
   xLindsay, James F.
      Dynamics of Physical Circuits & Systems. Intl
         Schol Bk Serv.
Lindsay, Jean. *see* Lindsay, Jean Olivia.
Lindsay, Jean O. *see* Lindsay, Jean Olivia.
Lindsay, Jean Olivia.
   xLindsay, Jean.
      A History of the North Wales Slate Industry.
         David & Charles.
   xLindsay, Jean O.
      Canals of Scotland. Kelley.
Lindsay, Jeanne W. *see* Lindsay, Jeanne Warren.
Lindsay, Jeanne Warren.
   xLindsay, Jeanne W.

      Pregnant Too Soon: Adoption Is an Option.
         EMC.
      Pregnant Too Soon: Adoption Is an Option.
         Morning Glory.
Lindsay, John F.
   xLindsay, J.
      Lunar Stratigraphy & Sedimentology. Elsevier.
Lindsay, John V. *see* Lindsay, John Vliet.
Lindsay, John Vliet.
   xLindsay, John V.
      City. Norton.
      The Edge. Norton.
Lindsay, Joseph.
   xLindsay, Joseph.
      ed. The Aorta. Grune.
Lindsay, Lowell.
   xLindsay, Lowell.
      Anza-Borrego Desert Region. Wilderness.

Lindsay, Michael, Baron Lindsay of Birker, 1909-
   xLindsay, Michael.
      China & the Cold War: A Study in
         International Politics. Hyperion Conn.

Lindsay, Nicholas Vachel.

   xLindsay, Vachel.

      Adventures, Rhymes & Designs. Eakins.
      Letters of Vachel Lindsay. B Franklin.

Lindsay, P. A. *see* Lindsay, Peter A.
Lindsay, Peter A.
   xLindsay, P. A.
      Introduction to Quantum Electronics. Halsted
        Pr.
Lindsay, Peter H.
   xLindsay, Peter H.
      Human Information Processing: An
         Introduction to Psychology. Acad Pr.
Lindsay, Philip.
   xLindsay, Philip.
      The Peasants' Revolt, 1381. Greenwood.
Lindsay, R. Bruce. *see* Lindsay, Robert Bruce.
Lindsay, Rae.
   xLindsay, Rae.
      Alone & Surviving. Walker & Co.
Lindsay, Rae S. *see* Lindsay, Rae Shirley.
Lindsay, Rae Shirley, 1940-
   xLindsay, Rae S.
      Crisis Theory: A Critical Overview. Intl Schol
        Bk Serv.
Lindsay, Robert, 1924-
   xLindsay, Robert.
      ed. Early Concepts of Energy in Atomic
        Physics. DH&R.
Lindsay, Robert B. *see* Lindsay, Robert Bruce.
Lindsay, Robert Bruce, 1900-
   xLindsay, R. Bruce.
      The Control of Energy. Acad Pr.
   xLindsay, Robert B.
      Nature of Physics: A Physicist's Views on the
        History & Philosophy of His Science. Brown
        U Pr.
Lindsay, Thomas. *see* Lindsay, Thomas Somerville
   Reeves.
Lindsay, Thomas Somerville Reeves, 1854-1933
   xLindsay, Thomas.
      Plant Names. Gale.
Lindsay, Vachel. *see* Lindsay, Nicholas Vachel.
Lindsay, Willard L. *see* Lindsay, Willard Lyman.
Lindsay, Willard Lyman, 1926-
   xLindsay, Willard L.
      Chemical Equilibria in Soils. Wiley.
Lindsay, William S. *see* Lindsay, William Schaw.
Lindsay, William Schaw, 1816-1877
   xLindsay, William S.
      History of Merchant Shipping & Ancient
        Commerce. AMS Pr.
Lindsell, Harold, 1913-
   xLindsell, Harold.

God's Incomparable Word. Victor Bks.
God's Incomparable Word. World Wide Pubs.
When You Pray. Baker Bk.
Lindsey, Ben B. *see* Lindsey, Benjamin Barr.
Lindsey, Benjamin Barr.
xLindsey, Ben B.
The Companionate Marriage. Arno.
The Companionate Marriage. Darby Bks.
The Dangerous Life. Arno.
The Revolt of Modern Youth. U of Wash Pr.
Lindsey, C. H.
xLindsey, C. H.
Informal Introduction to Algol 68. Elsevier.
Lindsey, Darryl.
xLindsey, Darryl.
The Design & Drafting of Printed Circuits.
Bishop Graphics.
Lindsey, David.
xLindsey, David.
Americans in Conflict: The Civil War &
Reconstruction. HM.
Lindsey, Dawn.
xLindsey, Dawn.
Duchess of Vidal. Doubleday.
Duchess of Vidal. Playboy Pbks.
Lindsey, Hal.
xLindsey, Hal.
The Late Great Planet Earth. Bantam.
Late Great Planet Earth. Zondervan.
The Liberation of Planet Earth. Bantam.
The Liberation of Planet Earth. Zondervan.
Lindsey, Jim, 1952-
xLindsey, Jim.
In Lieu of Mecca. U of Pittsburgh Pr.
Lindsey, Johanna.
xLindsey, Johanna.
Captive Bride. Avon.
Lindsey, Jonathan A., 1937-
xLindsey, Jonathan A.
Change & Challenge. McGrath.
Lindsey, Ouida. *see* Lindsey, Paul.
Lindsey, Paul.
xLindsey, Ouida.
jt. auth. Breaking the Bonds of Racism. ETC
Pubns.
xLindsey, Paul.
Breaking the Bonds of Racism. ETC Pubns.
Lindsey, Robert.
xLindsey, Robert.
The Falcon & the Snowman: A True Story of
Friendship & Espionage. PB.
Lindskoog, Kathryn.
xLindskoog, Kathryn.
The Gift of Dreams: A Christian View.
Har-Row.
Lindsley, Dan L.
xLindsley, Dan L.
Genetic Variations of Drosophila melanogaster.
Carnegie Inst.
Lindstrom, C. E. *see* Lindstrom, Carl E.
Lindstrom, Carl E.
xLindstrom, C. E.
The Fading American Newspaper. Peter Smith.
Lindstrom, Maurita.
xLindstrom, Maurita.
Conodonts. Elsevier.
Lindstrom, Mauritz. *see* Lindstrom, Maurita.
Lindstrom, Miriam.
xLindstrom, Miriam.
Children's Art: A Study of Normal
Development in Children's Modes of
Visualization. U of Cal Pr.
Lindstrom, Olof, 1939-
xLindstrom, Olof.
Aspects of English Intonation. Humanities.
Lindstrom, Thais S.
xLindstrom, Thais S.
Nikolay Gogol. Twayne.
Lindvall, C. M.
xLindvall, C. Mauritz.

Measuring Pupil Achievement & Aptitude.
HarBraceJ.
Lindvall, C. Mauritz. *see* Lindvall, C. M.
Lindzey, Gardner.
xLindzey, Gardner.
ed. Assessment of Human Motives.
Greenwood.
Projective Techniques & Cross-Cultural
Research. Irvington.
Psychology. Worth.
Line, David.
xLine, David.
Soldier & Me. Har-Row.
Line, Les.
xLine, Les.
The Audubon Society Book of Wild Animals.
Abrams.
The Audubon Society Book of Wild Birds.
Abrams.
The Audubon Society Book of Wildflowers.
Abrams.
Line, W. C.
xLine, Walter C.
News Writing for Non-Professionals.
Nelson-Hall.
Line, Walter C. *see* Line, W. C.
Lineaweaver, Thomas H.
xLineaweaver, Thomas H.
Natural History of Sharks. Lippincott.
Lineback, Neal G.
xLineback, Neal G.
ed. Atlas of Alabama. U of Ala Pr.
Linebarger, Paul M. *see* Linebarger, Paul Myron
Wentworth.
Linebarger, Paul Myron Anthony, 1913-1966
xLinebarger, Paul M.
Government in Republican China. Hyperion
Conn.
Psychological Warfare. Arno.
Linebarger, Paul Myron Wentworth, 1871-1939
xLinebarger, Paul M.
Sun Yat Sen & the Chinese Republic. AMS Pr.
Lineberry, Claude S.
xLineberry, Claude S.
Job Aids. Educ Tech Pubns.
Lineberry, Robert L.
xLineberry, Robert L.
American Public Policy: What Government
Does & What Difference It Makes. Har-Row.
Lineberry, William P.
xLineberry, William P.
ed. American Colleges: The Uncertain Future.
Wilson.
ed. Arms Control. Wilson.
ed. Business of Sports. Wilson.
ed. Colleges at the Crossroads. Wilson.
ed. East Africa. Wilson.
ed. Mass Communications. Wilson.
Priorities for Survival. Wilson.
ed. The Struggle Against Terrorism. Wilson.
Linedecker, Clifford L.
xLinedecker, Clifford L.
The Man Who Killed Boys. St Martin.
Linehan, Don.
xLinehan, Don.
Soft Touch: A Sport That Lets You Touch
Life. Acropolis.
Linehan, Peter.
xLinehan, Peter.
Spanish Church & the Papacy in the Thirteenth
Century. Cambridge U Pr.
Lines, John D. *see* Lines, John Davis.
Lines, John Davis.
xLines, John D.
The Duality of Physical Truth & Cause. Philos
Lib.
Lines, Kenneth.
xLines, Kenneth.

British & Canadian Immigration to the United
States Since 1920. R & E Res Assoc.
Lines, M. E. *see* Lines, Malcolm E.
Lines, M. Vardell.
xLines, Vardell.
Minicomputer Systems. Winthrop.
Lines, Malcolm E.
xLines, M. E.
Principles & Applications of Ferroelectrics &
Related Materials. Oxford U Pr.
Lines, Vardell. *see* Lines, M. Vardell.
Linet, Beverly.
xLinet, Beverly.
Ladd: The Life, the Legend, the Legacy of
Alan Ladd. Arbor Hse.
Linfield, Esther.
xLinfield, Esther.
The Lion of the Kalahari. Greenwillow.
Linfield, Warner M.
xLinfield, Warner M.
ed. Anionic Surfactants. Dekker.
Linfoot, E. H. *see* Linfoot, Edward Hubert.
Linfoot, Edward Hubert, 1905-
xLinfoot, E. H.
Fourier Methods in Optical Image Evaluation.
Focal Pr.
Linfoot, John A.
xLinfoot, John A.
ed. Recent Advances in the Diagnosis &
Treatment of Pituitary Tumors. Raven.
Linford, M. *see* Linford, Madeline.
Linford, Madeline.
xLinford, M.
Mary Wollstonecraft. Gordon Pr.
xLinford, Madeline.
Mary Wollstonecraft. Folcroft.
Linforth, Ivan M. *see* Linforth, Ivan Mortimer.
Linforth, Ivan Mortimer, 1879-
xLinforth, Ivan M.
The Arts of Orpheus. Arno.
Ling, Daniel.
xLing, Daniel.
Aural Habilitation: The Foundations of Verbal
Learning in Hearing-Impaired Children.
Alexander Graham.
Ling, Frederick F. *see* Ling, Frederick Fongsun.
Ling, Frederick Fongsun.
xLing, Frederick F.
Surface Mechanics. Krieger.
Ling, M. *see* Ling, Mona.
Ling, Mona.
xLing, M.
How to Increase Sales & Put Yourself Across
by Telephone. P-H.
Ling, Trevor. *see* Ling, Trevor Oswald.
Ling, Trevor Oswald.
xLing, Trevor.
Buddha, Marx & God: Some Aspects of
Religion in the Modern World. St Martin.
Buddhist Revival in India: Aspects of the
Sociology of Buddhism. St Martin.
Lingard, Joan.
xLingard, Joan.
Across the Barricades. Elsevier-Nelson.
The Clearance. Elsevier-Nelson.
The File on Fraulein Berg. Elsevier-Nelson.
Hostages to Fortune. Elsevier-Nelson.
Odd Girl Out. Elsevier-Nelson.
A Proper Place. Elsevier-Nelson.
The Reunion. Elsevier-Nelson.
The Second Flowering of Emily Mountjoy. St
Martin.
Lingard, John, 1771-1851
xLingard, John.
History & Antiquities of the Anglo-Saxon
Church. Longwood Pr.
Linge, G. J. *see* Linge, G. J. R.
Linge, G. J. R.
xLinge, G. J.

Industrial Awakening: A Geography of
Australian Manufacturing 1788-1890. Bks
Australia.
Lingeman, C. H. *see* Lingeman, Carolyn H.
Lingeman, Carolyn H.
xLingeman, C. H.
ed. Carcinogenic Hormones. Springer-Verlag.
Lingeman, Richard. *see* Lingeman, Richard R.
Lingeman, Richard R.
xLingeman, Richard.
Small Town America: A Narrative History,
1620-the Present. Putnam.
xLingeman, Richard R.
Drugs from A to Z: A Dictionary. McGraw.
Lingenberg, Rolf.
xLingenberg, Rolf.
Metric Planes & Metric Vector Spaces. Wiley.
Lingenfelter, Richard E.
xLingenfelter, Richard E.
ed. Songs of the American West. U of Cal Pr.
Lingren, Wesley E.
xLingren, Wesley E.
Inorganic Nomenclature: A Programmed
Approach. P-H.
Liniger-Goumaz, Max.
xLiniger-Goumaz, Max.
Historical Dictionary of Equatorial Guinea.
Scarecrow.
Linington, Elizabeth.
xLinington, Elizabeth.
Perchance of Death. Doubleday.
Link, A. S. *see* Link, Arthur Stanley.
Link, Arthur S. *see* Link, Arthur Stanley.
Link, Arthur Stanley.
xLink, A. S.
Woodrow Wilson: A Brief Biography. New
Viewpoints.
xLink, Arthur S.
Higher Realism of Woodrow Wilson & Other
Essays. Vanderbilt U Pr.
Woodrow Wilson & the Progressive Era,
1910-1917. Har-Row.
Woodrow Wilson & the Progressive Era:
1910-1917. Har-Row.
Woodrow Wilson: Revolution, War, & Peace.
AHM Pub.
Link, Eugene P. *see* Link, Eugene Perry.
Link, Eugene Perry, 1908-
xLink, Eugene P.
Democratic-Republican Societies, 1790-1800.
Octagon.
Link, F. *see* Link, Frantisek.
Link, Frantisek.
xLink, F.
Eclipse Phenomena in Astronomy.
Springer-Verlag.
Link, Henry C. *see* Link, Henry Charles.
Link, Henry Charles, 1889-1952
xLink, Henry C.
The Return to Religion. Folcroft.
Link, Mark.
xLink, Mark.
In the Stillness Is the Dancing. Argus Comm.
Take off Your Shoes. Argus Comm.
Link, Mark J.
xLink, Mark J.
Christ Teaches Us Today. Loyola.
Link, Robert G. *see* Link, Robert Grant.
Link, Robert Grant, 1918-
xLink, Robert G.
English Theories of Economic Fluctuations,
1815-1848. AMS Pr.
Linke, Lilo.
xLinke, Lilo.
Ecuador: Country of Contrasts. Gordon Pr.
Linker, Robert W. *see* Linker, Robert White.
Linker, Robert White.
xLinker, Robert W.

A Bibliography of Old French Lyrics.
Romance.
Linkh, Richard M.
xLinkh, Richard M.
American Catholicism & European Immigrants
(1900-1924). Ctr Migration.
Linklater, Andro.
xLinklater, Andro.
Amazing Maisie & the Cold Porridge Brigade.
Pantheon.
Linklater, Eric, 1899-1974
xLinklater, Eric.
A Spell for Old Bones. Arno.
Stories of Eric Linklater. Horizon.
Linklater, Kristin.
xLinklater, Kristin.
Freeing the Natural Voice. Drama Bk.
Links, J. G.
xLinks, J. G.
Venice for Pleasure. Dufour.
Venice for Pleasure. FS&G.
Linksz, Arthur.
xLinksz, Arthur.
On Writing, Reading & Dyslexia. Grune.
Linman, J. W. *see* Linman, James W.
Linman, James W., M.d
xLinman, J. W.
Principles of Hematology. Macmillan.
Linn, Charles F.
xLinn, Charles F.
Estimation. T Y Crowell.
Probability. T Y Crowell.
Linn, John G. *see* Linn, John Gaywood.
Linn, John Gaywood.
xLinn, John G.
Theater in the Fiction of Marcel Proust. Ohio
St U Pr.
Linn, Louis, M.d.
xLinn, Louis.
ed. Frontiers in General Hospital Psychiatry.
Intl Univs Pr.
Handbook of Hospital Psychiatry: A Practical
Guide to Therapy. Intl Univs Pr.
Linnaus, Vernon F.
xLinnaus, Vernon F.
Modern College Accounting. HarBraceJ.
Linne, Jean J. *see* Linne, Jean Jorgenson.
Linne, Jean Jorgenson.
xLinne, Jean J.
Basic Techniques for the Medical Laboratory.
McGraw.
Linneman, R. *see* Linneman, Robert E.
Linneman, Robert E., 1928-
xLinneman, R.
Shirt Sleeve Approach to Long Range Planning
for the Smaller Growing Corporation. P-H.
Linneman, William R.
xLinneman, William R.
Richard Hovey. Twayne.
Linney, Romulus, 1930-
xLinney, Romulus.
The Sorrows of Frederick & Holy Ghosts.
HarBraceJ.
Lins, Osman, 1924-
xLins, Osman.
Avalovara. Knopf.
Linsdale, Jean M. *see* Linsdale, Jean Myron.
Linsdale, Jean Myron.
xLinsdale, Jean M.
The Dusky-Footed Wood Rat: A Record of
Observations Made on the Hastings Natural
History Reservation. U of Cal Pr.
Linse, Barbara B. *see* Linse, Barbara Bucher.
Linse, Barbara Bucher, 1924-
xLinse, Barbara B.
Arts & Crafts for All Seasons. Pitman
Learning.
Linse, Linda.
xLinse, Linda.

New Zealand on a Budget. Odyssey Pub Co.
Linsky, Leonard.
xLinsky, Leonard.
Referring. Humanities.
Linsley, Frank.
xLinsley, Frank.
Electrical Drawing for Technicians, 1.
Butterworths.
Linsley, Kenneth W.
xLinsley, Kenneth W.
Advocate for God. Judson.
Linsley, Leslie.
xLinsley, Leslie.
Army Navy Surplus: A Unique Source of
Decorating Ideas. Dell.
Custom Made. Har-Row.
Decoupage for Young Crafters. Dutton.
Photocraft. Delacorte.
Linsley, Ray K.
xLinsley, Ray K.
Hydrology for Engineers. McGraw.
Water Resources Engineering. McGraw.
Linstone, Harold A.
xLinstone, Harold A.
ed. Delphi Method: Techniques &
Applications. A-W.
Linstromberg, Walter W. *see* Linstromberg, Walter
William.
Linstromberg, Walter William, 1912-
xLinstromberg, Walter W.
Organic Chemistry: A Brief Course. Heath.
Organic Experiments. Heath.
Linthicum, M. Channing. *see* Linthicum, Marie
Channing.
Linthicum, Marie Channing.
xLinthicum, M. Channing.
Costume in the Drama of Shakespeare & His
Contemporaries. Hacker.
Linton, Adelin. *see* Linton, Adelin Sumner (Briggs).
Linton, Adelin Sumner (Briggs).
xLinton, Adelin.
Ralph Linton. Columbia U Pr.
Linton, Clarence, 1890-
xLinton, Clarence.
A Study of Some Problems Arising in the
Admission of Students As Candidates for
Professional Degrees in Education. AMS Pr.
Linton, Corinne B.
xLinton, Corrine B.
Hospital-Based Education. Arco.
Linton, Corrine B. *see* Linton, Corinne B.
Linton, Eliza L. *see* Linton, Elizabeth Lynn.
Linton, Elizabeth Lynn, 1822-1898
xLinton, Eliza L.
The Autobiography of Christopher Kirkland,
1885. Garland Pub.
The True History of Joshua Davidson, 1872.
Garland Pub.
Linton, Marigold.
xLinton, Marigold.
The Practical Statistician: Simplified Handbook
of Statistics. Brooks-Cole.
Linton, Ralph.
xLinton, Ralph.
Arts of the South Seas. Arno.
Linton, Robert R. *see* Linton, Robert Ritchie.
Linton, Robert Ritchie, 1900-
xLinton, Robert R.
Atlas of Vascular Surgery. Saunders.
Linton, W. J. *see* Linton, William James.
Linton, William J. *see* Linton, William James.
Linton, William James, 1812-1897
xLinton, W. J.
Life of John Greenleaf Whittier. Folcroft.
xLinton, William J.
Life of John Greenleaf Whittier. Kennikat.
Lints, F. A.
xLints, F. A.

ed. Aging in Drosophila. Mss Info.
  Genetics & Ageing. S Karger.
Lintz, Joseph.
  xLintz, Joseph.
  ed. Remote Sensing of Environment. A-W.
Linz, Peter.
  xLinz, Peter.
  Theoretical Numerical Analysis: An
    Introduction to Advanced Techniques. Wiley.
Linzee, David, 1952-
  xLinzee, David.
  Belgravia. Dell.
  Belgravia. Seaview Bks.
Lion, Edgar, 1920-
  xLion, Edgar.
  Practical Guide to Building Construction. P-H.
Lion, John R.
  xLion, John R.
  The Art of Medicating Psychiatric Patients.
    Williams & Wilkins.
  Evaluation & Management of the Violent
    Patient: Guidelines in the Hospital &
    Institution. C C Thomas.
Lion, Kurt S. *see* Lion, Kurt Siegfried.
Lion, Kurt Siegfried.
  xLion, Kurt S.
  Instrumentation in Scientific Research:
    Electrical Input Transducers. McGraw.
Lionni, Leo, 1910-
  xLionni, Leo.
  illus. A Color of His Own. Pantheon.
  illus. Fish Is Fish. Pantheon.
  illus. Frederick. Pantheon.
  illus. Frederick. Pantheon.
  illus. Geraldine the Music Mouse. Pantheon.
  The Greentail Mouse. Pantheon.
  illus. In the Rabbitgarden. Pantheon.
  Inch by Inch. Astor-Honor.
  On My Beach There Are Many Pebbles.
    Astor-Honor.
  Parallel Botany. Knopf.
  illus. Swimmy. Pantheon.
  illus. Theodore & the Talking Mushroom.
    Pantheon.
Lions, J. L. *see* Lions, Jacques Louis.
Lions, Jacques Louis.
  xLions, J. L.
  Non-Homogeneous Boundary Value Problems
    & Applications. Springer-Verlag.
  Optimal Control of Systems Governed by
    Partial Differential Equations.
    Springer-Verlag.
  Some Aspects of the Optimal Control of
    Distributed Parameter Systems: Proceedings.
    Soc Indus-Appl Math.
Liozner, L. D. *see* Liozner, Lev Davidovich.
Liozner, Lev Davidovich.
  xLiozner, L. D.
  ed. Organ Regeneration: A Study of
    Developmental Biology in Mammals. Plenum
    Pub.
Lipe, Dewey. *see* Wolff, Jurgen.
Lipetz, Ben Ami, 1927-
  xLipetz, Ben-Ami.
  Measurement of Efficiency of Scientific
    Research. Intermedia.
Lipetz, Ben-Ami. *see* Lipetz, Ben Ami.
Lipham, James M.
  xLipham, James M.
  Principal & Individually Guided Education.
    A-W.
Lipke, Jean. *see* Lipke, Jean Coryllel.
Lipke, Jean C. *see* Lipke, Jean Coryllel.
Lipke, Jean Coryllel.
  xLipke, Jean.
  Marriage. Lerner Pubns.
  xLipke, Jean C.

Conception & Contraception. Lerner Pubns.
Dating. Lerner Pubns.
Loving. Lerner Pubns.
Pregnancy. Lerner Pubns.
Puberty & Adolescence. Lerner Pubns.
Lipkin, Gladys B.
  xLipkin, Gladys B.
  Effective Approaches to Patients' Behavior.
    Springer Pub.
Lipkin, Lawrence.
  xLipkin, Lawrence.
  Accountants' Handbook of Formulas & Tables.
    P-H.
Lipkin, Mack.
  xLipkin, Mack.
  Straight Talk About Your Health Care.
    Har-Row.
Lipkin, Martin.
  xLipkin, Martin.
  ed. Gastrointestinal Tract Cancer. Plenum Pub.
Lipkind, William, 1904-
  xLipkind, William.
  Finders Keepers. HarBraceJ.
  Two Reds. HarBraceJ.
Lipking, Lawrence. *see* Lipking, Lawrence I.
Lipking, Lawrence I., 1934-
  xLipking, Lawrence.
  Ordering of the Arts in Eighteenth-Century
    England. Princeton U Pr.
Lipman, Aaron.
  xLipman, Aaron.
  Colombian Entrepreneur in Bogota. U of
    Miami Pr.
Lipman, Bernard S.
  xLipman, Bernard S.
  Clinical Scalar Electrocardiography. Year Bk
    Med.
Lipman, Burton E., 1931-
  xLipman, Burton E.
  Successful Cost Reduction & Control: The
    Probe Systematics Approach. P-H.
Lipman, David.
  xLipman, David.
  The Speed King: Bob Hayes of the Dallas
    Cowboys. Putnam.
Lipman, Jean.
  xLipman, Jean.
  ed. American Folk Painters of Three Centuries.
    Hudson Hills.
Lipman, Jean. *see* Lipman, Jean Herzberg.
Lipman, Jean Herzberg.
  xLipman, Jean.
  Art About Art. Dutton.
  The Flowering of American Folk Art,
    1776-1876. Viking Pr.
Lipman, Matthew.
  xLipman, Matthew.
  ed. Contemporary Aesthetics. Irvington.
  Discovering Philosophy. Irvington.
  Discovering Philosophy. P-H.
  ed. Growing Up with Philosophy. Temple U
    Pr.
  Philosophy in the Classroom. Temple U Pr.
Lipman, Richard. *see* Lipman, Richard P.
Lipman, Richard P.
  xLipman, Richard.
  ed. Pediatrics: PreTest Self-Assessment &
    Review. McGraw-Pretest.
Lipman, Samuel.
  xLipman, Samuel.
  Music After Modernism. Basic.
Lipman, Vivian D. *see* Lipman, Vivian David.
Lipman, Vivian David.
  xLipman, Vivian D.
  Local Government Areas, 1834-1945.
    Greenwood.
Lipowski, Z. *see* Lipowski, Zbigniew Jerzy.
Lipowski, Z. J. *see* Lipowski, Zbigniew Jerzy.
Lipowski, Zbigniew Jerzy.
  xLipowski, Z.

ed. Psychosocial Aspects of Physical Illness. S
    Karger.
  xLipowski, Z. J.
  Delirium: Acute Brain Failure in Man. C C
    Thomas.
  ed. Psychosomatic Medicine: Current Trends &
    Clinical Applications. Oxford U Pr.
Lippard, Lucy R.
  xLippard, Lucy R.
  From the Center: Feminist Essays on Women's
    Art. Dutton.
Lippard, Vernon W., 1905-
  xLippard, Vernon W.
  A Half-Century of American Medical
    Education: 1920-1970. J Macy Foun.
Lippert, Julius, 1839-1909
  xLippert, Julius.
  The Evolution of Culture. Gordon Pr.
Lippett, Peter E.
  xLippett, Peter E.
  Estate Planning: What Anyone Who Owns
    Anything Must Know. Reston.
Lippey, Gerald.
  xLippey, Gerald.
  ed. Computer-Assisted Test Construction. Educ
    Tech Pubns.
Lippiatt, A. *see* Lippiatt, Arthur.
Lippiatt, Arthur, 1936-
  xLippiatt, A.
  Architecture of Small Computer Systems. P-H.
Lippincott, David.
  xLippincott, David.
  Salt Mine. NAL.
  Salt Mine. Viking Pr.
  Savage Ransom. NAL.
  Savage Ransom. Rawson Wade.
Lippincott, Isaac, 1879-
  xLippincott, Isaac.
  A History of Manufactures in the Ohio Valley
    to the Year 1860. Arno.
  A History of Manufactures in the Ohio Valley
    to the Year 1860. Porcupine Pr.
Lippincott, Joseph W. *see* Lippincott, Joseph Wharton.
Lippincott, Joseph Wharton, 1887-
  xLippincott, Joseph W.
  Old Bill, the Whooping Crane. Lippincott.
  Striped Coat, the Skunk. Lippincott.
Lippincott, William T. *see* Lippincott, William Thomas.
Lippincott, William Thomas.
  xLippincott, William T.
  Experimental General Chemistry. HR&W.
Lippitt, Gordon L.
  xLippitt, Gordon L.
  Optimizing Human Resources: Readings in
    Individual & Organization Development.
    A-W.
Lippitt, Peggy.
  xLippitt, Peggy.
  Students Teach Students. Phi Delta Kappa.
Lippitt, Ronald.
  xLippitt, Ronald.
  Dynamics of Planned Change: A Comparative
    Study of Principles & Techniques. HarBraceJ.
Lippitt, Vernon G.
  xLippitt, Vernon G.
  The National Economic Environment.
    McGraw.
  Statistical Sales Forecasting. Finan Exec.
Lippman, Edward A.
  xLippman, Edward A.
  A Humanistic Philosophy of Music. NYU Pr.
  Musical Thought in Ancient Greece. Da Capo.
Lippman, Leopold. *see* Lippman, Leopold D.
Lippman, Leopold D.
  xLippman, Leopold.

Attitudes Toward the Handicapped: A
Comparison Between Europe & the United
States. C C Thomas.
Right to Education: Anatomy of the
Pennsylvania Case & Its Implications for
Exceptional Children. Tchrs Coll.
Lippman, Peter. *see* Lippman, Peter J.
Lippman, Peter J.
xLippman, Peter.
illus. Animals! Animals!. Western Pub.
Lippmann, F. *see* Lippmann, Friedrich.
Lippmann, Friedrich.
xLippmann, F.
Sedimentary Carbonate Minerals.
Springer-Verlag.
Lippmann, Margrit.
xLippmann, Margrit.
Cat Training. TFH Pubns.
Lippmann, Morton.
xLippmann, Morton.
Chemical Contamination in the Human
Environment. Oxford U Pr.
Lippmann, Walter, 1889-
xLippmann, Walter.
Drift & Mastery: An Attempt to Diagnose the
Current Unrest. Greenwood.
An Inquiry into the Principles of the Good
Society. Greenwood.
Men of Destiny. U of Wash Pr.
Public Opinion. Free Pr.
Public Persons. Liveright.
Lipps, Theodor, 1851-1914
xLipps, Theodor.
Psychological Studies. Arno.
Lips, Claude.
xLips, Claude.
Art & Stained Glass. Doubleday.
Lips, Hilary M.
xLips, Hilary M.
The Psychology of Sex Differences. P-H.
Lipschitz, Ceil, 1935-
xLipschitz, Ceil.
An Ecology Craftsbook for the Open
Classroom. Ctr Appl Res.
Lipschultz, Isadore Foreword by. *see* Pollak, Isaac G. G.
Lipschutz, Mark R.
xLipschutz, Mark R.
A Dictionary of African Historical Biography.
Beresford Bk Serv.
Lipscomb, David M.
xLipscomb, David M.
ed. Noise Control: Handbook of Principles &
Practices. Van Nos Reinhold.
Lipscomb, James.
xLipscomb, James.
Cutting Loose. Little.
Lipset, David, 1951-
xLipset, David.
Gregory Bateson: The Legacy of a Scientist.
P-H.
Lipset, Seymour. *see* Lipset, Seymour Martin.
Lipset, Seymour M. *see* Lipset, Seymour Martin.
Lipset, Seymour Martin.
xLipset, Seymour.
The Politics of Unreason: Right Wing
Extremism in America. U of Chicago Pr.
xLipset, Seymour M.
Agrarian Socialism: The Cooperative
Commonwealth Federation in Saskatchewan:
A Study in Political Sociology. U of Cal Pr.
The First New Nation: The United States in
Historical & Comparative Perspective.
Norton.
ed. Politics & the Social Sciences. Oxford U Pr.
Lipsey, Richard G.
xLipsey, Richard G.
Economics. Har-Row.
Lipsitt, Lewis P. *see* Lipsitt, Lewis Paeff.
Lipsitt, Lewis Paeff.
xLipsitt, Lewis P.

Child Development. Scott F.
Lipsitt, Paul D.
xLipsitt, Paul D.
ed. New Directions in Psycholegal Research.
Van Nos Reinhold.
Lipsitz, Joan.
xLipsitz, Joan.
Growing up Forgotten: A Review of Research
& Programs Concerning Early Adolescence.
Lexington Bks.
Lipsky, Louis, 1876-
xLipsky, Louis.
Tales of the Yiddish Rialto: Reminiscences of
Playwrights & Players in New York's Jewish
Theatre in the Early 1900's. Greenwood.
Thirty Years of American Zionism. Arno.
Lipsky, Michael.
xLipsky, Michael.
Commission Politics: The Processing of Racial
Crisis in America. Transaction Bks.
Street-Level Bureaucracy: Dilemmas of the
Individual in Public Services. Basic.
Street-Level Bureaucracy: Dilemmas of the
Individual in Public Services. Russell Sage.
Lipsky, Mortimer, 1915-
xLipsky, Mortimer.
A Tax on Wealth. A S Barnes.
Lipsman, R. L. *see* Lipsman, Ronald L.
Lipsman, Ronald L.
xLipsman, R. L.
Group Representations: A Survey of Some
Current Topics. Springer-Verlag.
Lipson, Dorothy Ann, 1926-
xLipson, Dorothy Ann.
Freemasonry in Federalist Connecticut,
1789-1835. Princeton U Pr.
Lipson, Ephraim, 1888-1960
xLipson, Ephraim.
Europe in the Nineteenth Century, 1815-1914.
Greenwood.
Lipson, H. *see* Lipson, Stephen G.
Lipson, Leslie, 1912-
xLipson, Leslie.
American Governor from Figurehead to
Leader. Greenwood.
Lipson, S. G. *see* Lipson, Stephen G.
Lipson, Stephen G.
xLipson, H.
jt. auth. Optical Physics. Cambridge U Pr.
xLipson, S. G.
Optical Physics. Cambridge U Pr.
Lipson, Stephen H.
xLipson, Stephen H.
Hospital Manpower Budget Preparation
Manual. Health Admin Pr.
Lipsyte, Marjorie, 1932-
xLipsyte, Marjorie.
Hot Type. Doubleday.
Lipsyte, Robert.
xLipsyte, Robert.
The Contender. Har Row.
The Contender. Bantam.
Free to Be Muhammad Ali. Har-Row.
One Fat Summer. Bantam.
One Fat Summer. Har-Row.
Liptak, Bela G.
xLiptak, Bela G.
ed. Instrument Engineers' Handbook. Chilton.
Lipton, Gladys. *see* Lipton, Gladys C.
Lipton, Gladys C.
xLipton, Gladys.
French Bilingual Dictionary: A Beginner's
Guide in Words & Pictures. Barron.
Italian Bilingual Dictionary: A Beginner's
Guide in Words & Pictures. Barron.
Spanish Bilingual Dictionary: A Beginners
Guide in Words & Pictures. Barron.
Lipton, James.
xLipton, James.

An Exaltation of Larks: Or, the Venereal
Game. Penguin.
Exaltation of Larks: The Venereal Game.
Viking Pr.
Lipton, Lenny. *see* Lipton, Leonard.
Lipton, Leonard.
xLipton, Lenny.
Independent Filmmaking. S&S.
Lipton on Filmmaking. S&S.
Lipton, Morris A.
xLipton, Morris A.
ed. Psychopharmacology: A Generation of
Progress. Raven.
Lipton, Sampson.
xLipton, Sampson.
Persistent Pain: Modern Methods of
Treatment. Grune.
Liptzin, Solomon, 1901-
xLiptzin, Solomon.
Historical Survey of German Literature.
Cooper Sq.
Liquori, Marty.
xLiquori, Marty.
On the Run: In Search of the Perfect Race.
Morrow.
Liroff, Richard A.
xLiroff, Richard A.
A National Policy for the Environment: NEPA
& Its Aftermath. Ind U Pr.
Lis, Catharina.
xLis, R.
Poverty & Capitalism in Pre-Industrial Europe:
1350-1850. Humanities.
Lis, R. *see* Lis, Catharina.
Lisann, Maury.
xLisann, Maury.
Broadcasting to the Soviet Union: International
Politics & Radio. Praeger.
Lischer, Richard.
xLischer, Richard.
Marx & Teilhard: Two Ways to the New
Humanity. Orbis Bks.
Lish, Gordon.
xLish, Gordon.
English Grammar. Behavioral Res.
Lisio, Donald J.
xLisio, Donald J.
The President & Protest: Hoover, Conspiracy &
the Bonus Riot. U of Mo Pr.
Lisk, Jill.
xLisk, Jill.
The Struggle for Supremacy in the Baltic,
1600-1725. Hippocrene Bks.
Lisk, R. D.
xLisk, R. D.
Neonatal Hormone Treatment & Adult Sexual
Behavior in Rodents. Mss Info.
Liska, George.
xLiska, George.
Alliances & the Third World. Johns Hopkins.
Career of Empire: America & Imperial
Expansion Over Land & Sea. Johns Hopkins.
Imperial America: The International Politics of
Primacy. Johns Hopkins.
Nations in Alliance: The Limits of
Interdependence. Johns Hopkins.
Quest for Equilibrium: America and the
Balance of Power on Land and Sea. Johns
Hopkins.
Russia & World Order: Strategic Choices & the
Laws of Power in History. Johns Hopkins.
Lisker, Sonia. *see* Lisker, Sonia O.
Lisker, Sonia O.
xLisker, Sonia.
jt. auth. Two Special Cards. HarBraceJ.
xLisker, Sonia O.

I Am. Hastings.
illus. I Can Be. Hastings.
illus. Lost. HarBraceJ.
Two Special Cards. HarBraceJ.
Lisker, Tim. *see* Lisker, Tom.
Lisker, Tom.
xLisker, Tim.
Nellie Bly: First Woman of the News. Silver.
xLisker, Tom.
First to the Top of the World: Admiral Peary
at the North Pole. Silver.
Tall Tales: American Myths. Raintree Pubs.
Lisle, George.
xLisle, George.
Accounting in Theory & Practice. Arno.
Lisle, Laurie.
xLisle, Laurie.
Portrait of an Artist: A Biography of Georgia
O'Keeffe. Seaview Bks.
Lispector, Clarice.
xLispector, Clarice.
Family Ties. U of Tex Pr.
Liss, Howard.
xLiss, Howard.
Baseball's Greatest All-Star Games. McKay.
Fishing Talk for Beginners. Messner.
Football Talk for Beginners. Messner.
The Giant Book of Strange but True Sports
Stories. Random.
Great Drivers, Great Races. Lippincott.
The Great Game of Soccer. Putnam.
Hockey Talk for Beginners. Messner.
More Strange but True Baseball Stories.
Random.
Strange but True Basketball Stories. Random.
Strange but True Hockey Stories. Random.
They Changed the Game: Football's Great
Coaches, Players & Games. Lippincott.
Liss, P. *see* Liss, P. S.
Liss, P. S.
xLiss, P.
Environmental Chemistry. Halsted Pr.
Liss, Robert E.
xLiss, Robert E.
Fading Rainbow. Methuen Inc.
Liss, Sheldon B.
xLiss, Sheldon B.
Century of Disagreement: The Chamizal
Conflict 1864-1964. U Pr of Wash.
Lissak. *see* Lissak, Kalman.
Lissak, K. *see* Lissak, Kalman.
Lissak, Kalman.
xLissak.
Results in Neurochemistry,
Neuroendocrinology, Neurophysiology &
Behavior, Neuropharmacology,
Neuropathology, Cybernetics. Heyden.
xLissak, K.
ed. Results in Neuroanatomy, Motor
Organization, Cerebral Circulation &
Modelling. Intl Pubns Serv.
ed. Results in Neurochemistry,
Neuroendocrinology, Neurophysiology, &
Behavior, Neuropharmacology,
Neurpathology, Cybernetics. Intl Pubns Serv.
List, Friedrich, 1789-1846
xList, Friedrich.
National System of Political Economy. Garland
Pub.
National System of Political Economy. Kelley.
List, Jacob S. *see* List, Jacob Samuel.
List, Jacob Samuel.
xList, Jacob S.
Education for Living. Greenwood.
Lister, Hal.
xLister, Hal.
The Suburban Press: A Separate Journalism.
Lucas.
Lister, I. *see* Lister, Ian.

Lister, Ian.
xLister, I.
Deschooling: A Reader. Cambridge U Pr.
Lister, John W.
xLister, John W.
Arrhythmia Analysis by Intracardiac
Electrocardiography. C C Thomas.
Lister, Margot.
xLister, Margot.
Costumes of Everyday Life: An Illustrated
History of Working Clothes. Plays.
Lister, Martin.
xLister, Martin.
A Journey to Paris in the Year 1698. U of Ill
Pr.
Lister, R. P. *see* Lister, Richard Percival.
Lister, Richard Percival, 1914-
xLister, R. P.
Marco Polo's Travels in Xanadu with Kublai
Khan. Gordon-Cremonesi.
Lister, Robert H. *see* Lister, Robert Hill.
Lister, Robert Hill, 1915-
xLister, Robert H.
The Coombs Site. AMS Pr.
Liston, Maureen. *see* Liston, Maureen R.
Liston, Maureen R.
xListon, Maureen.
Gertrude Stein: An Annotated Critical
Bibliography. Kent St U Pr.
Liston, Robert A.
xListon, Robert A.
By These Faiths: Religions for Today. Messner.
The Charity Racket. Elsevier-Nelson.
Defense Against Tyranny: The Balance of
Power in Government. Messner.
The Edge of Madness: Prisons & Prison
Reform in America. Watts.
Getting in Touch with Your Government.
Messner.
Promise or Peril?: The Role of Technology in
Society. Elsevier-Nelson.
The Right to Know: Censorship in America.
Watts.
The Ugly Palaces: Housing in America. Watts.
Who Stole the Sunset?: Dilemmas in Morality.
Elsevier-Nelson.
Women Who Ruled: Cleopatra to Elizabeth II.
Messner.
Liszt, Franz.
xLiszt, Franz.
Letters of Franz Liszt. Haskell.
Letters of Franz Liszt to Marie Zu
Sayn-Wittgenstein. Greenwood.
Litchfield, Ada B. *see* Litchfield, Ada Bassett.
Litchfield, Ada Bassett.
xLitchfield, Ada B.
A Button in Her Ear. A Whitman.
A Cane in Her Hand. A Whitman.
Litchfield, Edward H. *see* Litchfield, Edward Harold.
Litchfield, Edward Harold, 1914-1968
xLitchfield, Edward H.
Governing Postwar Germany. Kennikat.
Litchfield, Grace D. *see* Litchfield, Grace Denio.
Litchfield, Grace Denio, 1849-1944
xLitchfield, Grace D.
As a Man Sows, & Other Stories. Arno.
Little Venice & Other Stories. Arno.
**Literary Data Processing Conference, Yorktown
Heights, New York.**
xLiterary Data Processing Conference Sept. 9, 10,
11, 1964.
Proceedings. Modern Lang.
Lithgow, Marilyn.
xLithgow, Marilyn.
Quiltmaking & Quiltmakers. T Y Crowell.
Litka, Michael P.
xLitka, Michael P.

Business Law. Grid Pub.
Contemporary Real Estate Incidents. Grid Pub.
Legal Environment of Business: Text Cases &
Readings. Grid Pub.
Litle, William A.
xLitle, William A.
Reliability of Shell Buckling Predictions. MIT
Pr.
Litowinsky, Olga.
xLitowinsky, Olga.
The Dream Book. Coward.
The High Voyage. Viking Pr.
Litschert, Robert J.
xLitschert, Robert J.
The Corporate Role & Ethical Behavior:
Concepts & Cases. Van Nos Reinhold.
Litsey, Sarah.
xLitsey, Sarah.
Toward Mystery. Golden Quill.
Litsky, Frank.
xLitsky, Frank.
Winners on Ice. Watts.
The Winter Olympics. Watts.
Littell, Joseph F.
xLittell, Joseph F.
ed. The Comic Spirit. McDougal-Littell.
ed. The Comic Spirit. Lothrop.
ed. Coping with the Mass Media. Har-Row.
Littell, Philip, 1868-1943
xLittell, Philip.
Books & Things. Arno.
Littell, Robert, 1935-
xLittell, Robert.
The Defection of A. J. Lewinter. Popular Lib.
Read America First. Arno.
Sweet Reason. Popular Lib.
Litterer, Joseph A. *see* Litterer, Joseph August.
Litterer, Joseph August, 1926-
xLitterer, Joseph A.
The Analysis of Organizations. Wiley.
An Introduction to Management. Wiley.
Management: Concepts & Controversies.
Wiley.
Little. *see* Little, Ian Malcolm David.
Little (Arthur D.) Inc.
xA.D. Little, Inc.
Federal Funding of Civilian Research &
Development: A Report to the Experimental
Technology Incentives Program, U. S. Dept.
of Commerce. Westview.
xArthur D. Little Inc.
Civil Aviation Development: A Policy &
Operation Analysis. Irvington.
Corporate Director. CBI Pub.
Little, Bryan. *see* Little, Bryan D. G.
Little, Bryan D. G.
xLittle, Bryan.
Abbeys & Priories of England & Wales.
Holmes & Meier.
English Historic Architecture. Hastings.
Little, Charles E. *see* Little, Charles Eugene.
Little, Charles Eugene, 1838-1918
xLittle, Charles E.
Cyclopedia of Classified Dates, with Exhaustive
Index. Gale.
Little, Clarence C. *see* Little, Clarence Cook.
Little, Clarence Cook, 1888-
xLittle, Clarence C.
Inheritance of Coat Color in Dogs. Howell Bk.
Little, David.
xLittle, David.
American Foreign Policy & Moral Rhetoric:
The Example of Vietnam. Coun Rel & Intl.
Little, Gene.
xLittle, Gene.
Ice Fishing. Contemp Bks.
Little, Graham.
xLittle, Graham.

The Art of Chinese Poetry. U of Chicago Pr.
xLiu, James J.
  Essentials of Chinese Literary Art. Duxbury Pr.
xLiu, James Y.
  Art of Chinese Poetry. U of Chicago Pr.
Liu, James Y. *see* Liu, James J. Y.
Liu, Jung Chao. *see* Liu, Jung-Chao.
Liu, Jung-Chao.
  xLiu, Jung Chao.
  China's Fertilizer Economy. Beresford Bk Serv.
Liu, P. T. *see* Liu, Pan-Tai.
Liu, Pan-Tai.
  xLiu.
  Dynamic Optimization & Mathematical
    Economics. Dekker.
  xLiu, P. T.
    ed. Dynamic Optimization & Mathematical
    Economics. Plenum Pub.
Liu, Wu-Chi, 1907-
  xLiu, Wu-Chi.
  A Short History of Confucian Philosophy.
    Hyperion Conn.
  ed. Sunflower Splendor: Three Thousand Years
    of Chinese Poetry. Doubleday.
  ed. Sunflower Splendor: Three Thousand Years
    of Chinese Poetry. Ind U Pr.
Liulevicius, Arunas. *see* Liulevicius, Arunas Leonardas.
Liulevicius, Arunas Leonardas, 1934-
  xLiulevicius, Arunas.
  Factorization of Cyclic Reduced Powers by
    Secondary Cohomology Operations. Am
    Math.
Live, Anna H. *see* Live, Anna Harris.
Live, Anna Harris.
  xLive, Anna H.
  American Mosaic: Intermediate-Advanced ESL
    Reader. P-H.
Lively, Chauncy, 1919-
  xLively, Chauncy K.
  Chauncy Lively's Flybox: A Portfolio of
    Modern Trout Flies. Stackpole.
Lively, Chauncy K. *see* Lively, Chauncy.
Lively, Jack.
  xLively, Jack.
  Democracy. St Martin.
Lively, Penelope.
  xLively, Penelope.
  Boy Without a Name. Parnassus.
  Fanny's Sister. Dutton.
  The Ghost of Thomas Kempe. Dutton.
  The House in Norham Gardens. Dutton.
  A Stitch in Time. Dutton.
  Treasures of Time. Doubleday.
  The Whispering Knights. Dutton.
Livermore, Elaine.
  xLivermore, Elaine.
  illus. Find the Cat. HM.
  Find the Cat. HM.
  Lost & Found. HM.
  One to Ten, Count Again. HM.
Livermore, George, 1809-1865
  xLivermore, George.
  Historical Research Respecting the Opinions of
    the Founders of the Republic on Negroes As
    Slaves, As Citizens, & As Soldiers. Arno.
Livermore, Robert, 1876-1959
  xLivermore, Robert.
  Bostonians & Bullion: The Journal of Robert
    Livermore, 1892-1915. U of Nebr Pr.
Livermore, Shaw, 1926-
  xLivermore, Shaw.
  Twilight of Federalism: The Disintegration of
    the Federalist Party - 1815-1830. Gordian.
Liversidge, Douglas, 1913-
  xLiversidge, Douglas.
  First Book of the Arctic. Watts.
Livesay, Harold. *see* Livesay, Harold C.
Livesay, Harold C.
  xLivesay, Harold.

Andrew Carnegie & the Rise of Big Business.
    Little.
  xLivesay, Harold C.
  American Made: Men Who Shaped the
    American Economy. Little.
Livesey, Herbert B.
  xLivesey, Herbert B.
  Guide to American Graduate Schools. Penguin.
  Guide to American Graduate Schools. Viking
    Pr.
  Second Chance: Blueprints for Life Change.
    Lippincott.
Livesey, Peter.
  xLivesey, Peter.
  Rock Climbing. Mountaineers.
Livesley, W. J.
  xLivesley, W. J.
  Person Perception in Childhood &
    Adolescence. Wiley.
Liveson, Jay A. *see* Liveson, Jay Allan.
Liveson, Jay Allan.
  xLiveson, Jay A.
  Peripheral Neurology: Case Studies in
    Electrodiagnosis. Davis Co.
Livingood, J. J. *see* Livingood, John Jacob.
Livingood, John J. *see* Livingood, John Jacob.
Livingood, John Jacob, 1903-
  xLivingood, J. J.
  Principles of Cyclic Particle Accelerators.
    Krieger.
  xLivingood, John J.
  Optics of Dipole Magnets. Acad Pr.
Livingston, A. D., 1932-
  xLivingston, A. D.
  Advanced Bass Tackle & Boats. Lippincott.
  Fishing for Bass: Modern Tactics & Tackle.
    Lippincott.
  Fly-Rodding for Bass. Lippincott.
Livingston College.
  xFaculty of Comparative Literature, Livingston
  College.
  A Syllabus of Comparative Literature.
    Scarecrow.
Livingston, Donald. *see* Livingston, Donald W.
Livingston, Donald W.
  xLivingston, Donald.
  ed. Hume: A Re-Evaluation. Fordham.
Livingston, Dorothy M. *see* Livingston, Dorothy
  Michelson.
Livingston, Dorothy Michelson.
  xLivingston, Dorothy M.
  The Master of Light: A Biography of Albert A.
    Michelson. U of Chicago Pr.
Livingston, G. E. *see* Livingston, Gideon Eleazar.
Livingston, G. Herbert. *see* Livingston, George Herbert.
Livingston, George Herbert, 1916-
  xLivingston, G. Herbert.
  The Pentateuch in Its Cultural Environment.
    Baker Bk.
Livingston, Gideon Eleazar.
  xLivingston, G. E.
  ed. Food Service Systems: Analysis, Design &
    Implementation. Acad Pr.
Livingston, Hazel. *see* Livingston, Hazel E.
Livingston, Hazel E.
  xLivingston, Hazel.
  Officer on the Witness Stand. Legal Bk Corp.
Livingston, Jay C.
  xLivingston, Jay C.
  The Fount of Dreams. Metatron Pr.
  The Romantic Muse. Metatron Pr.
Livingston, John C.
  xLivingston, John C.
  Consent of the Governed. Macmillan.
  Fair Game?: Inequality & Affirmative Action.
    W H Freeman.
Livingston, M. Jay.
  xLivingston, M. Jay.
  The Prodigy. Coward.
Livingston, Myra C. *see* Livingston, Myra Cohn.

Livingston, Myra Cohn.
  xLivingston, Myra C.
  ed. Callooh! Callay!: Holiday Poems for Young
    Readers. Atheneum.
  Come Away. Atheneum.
  ed. Listen, Children, Listen: An Anthology of
    Poems for the Very Young. HarBraceJ.
  A Lollygag of Limericks. Atheneum.
  ed. Speak Roughly to Your Little Boy: A
    Collection of Parodies & Burlesques.
    HarBraceJ.
  ed. Tune Beyond Us: A Collection of Poetry.
    HarBraceJ.
Livingston, R. J. *see* Livingston, Robert J.
Livingston, Robert B. *see* Livingston, Robert Burr.
Livingston, Robert Burr, 1918-
  xLivingston, Robert B.
  Sensory Processing, Perception, & Behavior.
    Raven.
Livingston, Robert J.
  xLivingston, R. J.
  ed. Ecological Processes in Coastal & Marine
    Systems. Plenum Pub.
Livingston, Samuel, 1908-
  xLivingston, Samuel.
  Comprehensive Management of Epilepsy in
    Infancy, Childhood & Adolescence. C C
    Thomas.
  Living with Epileptic Seizures. C C Thomas.
Livingston, Virginia W. *see* Livingston, Virginia
  Wuerthele-Caspe.
Livingston, Virginia Wuerthele-Caspe.
  xLivingston, Virginia W.
  Cancer: A New Breakthrough. Reward Bks.
Livingston, William. *see* Livingston, Williams.
Livingston, William S.
  xLivingston, William S.
  ed. Australia, New Zealand, & the Pacific
    Islands Since the First World War. U of Tex
    Pr.
  Federalism & Constitutional Change.
    Greenwood.
  ed. A Prospect of Liberal Democracy. U of Tex
    Pr.
Livingston, Williams.
  xLivingston, William.
  Independent Reflector or, Weekly Essays on
    Sundry Important Subjects More Particularly
    Adapted to the Province of New York.
    Harvard U Pr.
Livingstone, David.
  xLivingstone, David.
  Family Letters: 1841-1856. Greenwood.
  Last Journals of David Livingstone in Central
    Africa, from 1865 to His Death. Greenwood.
  Some Letters from Livingstone, 1840-1872.
    Negro U Pr.
Livingstone, E. A. *see* Livingstone, Elizabeth A.
Livingstone, Elizabeth A.
  xLivingstone, E. A.
  ed. The Concise Oxford Dictionary of the
    Christian Church. Oxford U Pr.
  xLivingstone, Elizabeth A.
  ed. The Concise Oxford Dictionary of the
    Christian Church. Oxford U Pr.
Livingstone, J. L. *see* Livingstone, John Leslie.
Livingstone, J. M., 1925-
  xLivingstone, J. M.
  Britain & the World Economy. Gannon.
  xLivingstone, James V.
  The British Economy in Theory & Practice. St
    Martin.
Livingstone, James V. *see* Livingstone, J. M.
Livingstone, John Leslie.
  xLivingstone, J. L.
  Financial Accounting: An Introductory Study.
    Grid Pub.
Livingstone, Richard W. *see* Livingstone, Richard Winn.
Livingstone, Richard Winn, Sir, 1880-1960
  xLivingstone, Richard W.

Education & the Spirit of the Age. Hyperion
Conn.
Greek Ideals & Modern Life. Biblo.

Livolsi, Virginia A.
xLiVolsi, Virginia A.
Practical Clinical Cytology. C C Thomas.

Livsey, Clara. *see* Livsey, Clara G.

Livsey, Clara G.
xLivsey, Clara.
Marriage Maintenance Manual: How to Get
into It and How to Keep It Going. Dial.

Livshits, M. S. *see* Livshits, Mikhail Samuilovich.

Livshits, Mikhail Samuilovich.
xLivshits, M. S.
Operator Colligations in Hilbert Spaces.
Halsted Pr.

Lizaso, Felix, 1891-
xLizaso, Felix.
Marti, Martyr of Cuban Independence.
Greenwood.

Llano, George A. *see* Llano, George Albert.

Llano, George Albert, 1911-
xLlano, George A.
ed. Antarctic Terrestrial Biology. Am
Geophysical.

Llewellyn, Megan.
xLlewellyn, Megan.
The Eagle of Gwernabwy: Tales from Wales.
Pergamon.

Llewellyn, Richard.
xLlewellyn, Richard.
A Night of Bright Stars. Doubleday.

Llewellyn, Richard. *see* Llewellyn, Richard Richard
David Vivian Llewellyn Lloyd.

**Llewellyn, Richard Richard David Vivian Llewellyn
Lloyd.**
xLlewellyn, Richard.
How Green Was My Valley. Amereon Ltd.
How Green Was My Valley. Dell.
How Green Was My Valley. Macmillan.

Llewellyn, Robert W.
xLlewellyn, Robert W.
Information Systems. P-H.

Llewellyn-Jones, Derek.
xLlewellyn-Jones, Derek.
Everywoman: A Gynaecological Guide for
Life. Merrimack Bk Serv.

Llinas, R.
xLlinas, R.
ed. Frog Neurobiology: A Handbook.
Springer-Verlag.

Lloyd, A. C. *see* Lloyd, Alan C.

Lloyd, A. L. *see* Lloyd, Albert Lancaster.

Lloyd, Alan, 1927-
xLloyd, Alan.
Trade Imperial. Coward.

Lloyd, Alan C.
xLloyd, A. C.
Gregg Typing for Colleges: Intensive Course.
McGraw.
xLloyd, Alan C.
Personal Typing. McGraw.

Lloyd, Albert. *see* Lloyd, Albert L.

Lloyd, Albert L.
xLloyd, Albert.
Deutsch und Deutschland Heute. D Van
Nostrand.
xLloyd, Albert L.
Deutsch Und Deutschland Heute. Van Nos
Reinhold.

Lloyd, Albert Lancaster, 1908-
xLloyd, A. L.
Folk Song in England. Beekman Pubs.
Folk Song in England. Intl Pub Co.

Lloyd, Christopher.
xLloyd, Christopher.
Atlas of Maritime History. Arco.
Nelson & Sea Power. Verry.

Lloyd, Cynthia B.
xLloyd, Cynthia B.

The Economics of Sex Differentials. Columbia
U Pr.

Lloyd, David, 1946-
xLloyd, David.
Finding the Law: A Guide to Legal Research.
Oceana.
Understanding the Uniform Commercial Code.
Oceana.

Lloyd, David. *see* Lloyd, David Wharton.

Lloyd, David K.
xLloyd, David K.
Reliability: Management, Methods &
Mathematics. Lloyd & Lipow.

Lloyd, David Wharton.
xLloyd, David.
Railway Station Architecture. David & Charles.

Lloyd, Ernest M. *see* Lloyd, Ernest Marsh.

Lloyd, Ernest Marsh, 1840-
xLloyd, Ernest M.
A Review of the History of Infantry.
Greenwood.

Lloyd, Errol.
xLloyd, Errol.
illus. Nini at Carnival. T Y Crowell.

Lloyd, Francis E. *see* Lloyd, Francis Ernest.

Lloyd, Francis Ernest, 1868-1947
xLloyd, Francis E.
The Carnivorous Plants. Dover.
The Carnivorous Plants. Peter Smith.

Lloyd, Frederic Ebenezer John, 1859-1933
xLloyd, Frederick E.
ed. Lloyd's Church Musicians Directory. AMS
Pr.

Lloyd, Frederick E. *see* Lloyd, Frederic Ebenezer John.

Lloyd, G. A. *see* Lloyd, Glyn Arthur Simpson.

Lloyd George, David. *see* Lloyd George, David Lloyd
George, 1st Earl.

Lloyd, Glyn Arthur Simpson.
xLloyd, G. A.
Radiology of the Orbit. Saunders.

Lloyd, H. *see* Lloyd, Herbert Mervyn.

Lloyd, Henry D. *see* Lloyd, Henry Demarest.

Lloyd, Henry Demarest, 1847-1903
xLloyd, Henry D.
Lords of Industry. Arno.

Lloyd, Herbert Mervyn.
xLloyd, H.
The Legal Limits of Journalism. Pergamon.

Lloyd, J. A. *see* Lloyd, John Arthur Thomas.

Lloyd, J. M. *see* Lloyd, J. Michael.

Lloyd, J. Michael, 1945-
xLloyd, J. M.
ed. Thermal Imaging Systems. Plenum Pub.

Lloyd, Jean.
xLloyd, Jean.
Sociology & Social Life. D Van Nostrand.

Lloyd, Joan.
xLloyd, Joan.
Guatemala, Land of the Mayas. Greenwood.

Lloyd, John A.
xLloyd, John A.
Snowbound with Mr. Lincoln. Vantage.

Lloyd, John Arthur Thomas, 1870-1956
xLloyd, J. A.
Fyodor Dostoevsky. Arden Lib.
Fyodor Dostoevsky. Cooper Sq.

Lloyd, John W. *see* Lloyd, John William.

Lloyd, John William, 1876-
xLloyd, John W.
Co-Operative & Other Organized Methods of
Marketing California Horticultural Products.
Johnson Repr.

Lloyd, Julius, 1830-1892
xLloyd, Julius.
The Life of Sir Philip Sidney. Folcroft.

Lloyd, L. E. *see* Lloyd, Lewis E.

Lloyd, Lewis E.
xLloyd, L. E.
Fundamentals of Nutrition. W H Freeman.

Lloyd, Llewelyn. *see* Lloyd, Llewelyn Southworth.

Lloyd, Llewelyn Southworth.
xLloyd, Llewelyn.
Intervals, Scales & Temperaments. St Martin.

Lloyd, Lyle L.
xLloyd, Lyle L.
Audiometric Interpretation: A Manual of Basic
Audiometry. Univ Park.
ed. Communication Assessment & Intervention
Strategies. Univ Park.

Lloyd, Margaret.
xLloyd, Margaret.
Borzoi Book of Modern Dance. Dance Horiz.

Lloyd, N. G. *see* Lloyd, Noel Glynne.

Lloyd, Noel Glynne, 1946-
xLloyd, N. G.
Degree Theory. Cambridge U Pr.

Lloyd, P. C. *see* Lloyd, Peter Cutt.

Lloyd, Peter C. *see* Lloyd, Peter Cutt.

Lloyd, Peter Cutt.
xLloyd, P. C.
Power & Independence: Urban Africans'
Perception of Social Inequality. Routledge &
Kegan.
xLloyd, Peter C.
Slums of Hope?: Shanty Towns of the Third
World. St Martin.

Lloyd, Peter E.
xLloyd, Peter E.
Location in Space: A Theoretical Approach to
Economic Geography. Har-Row.

Lloyd, Peter H.
xLloyd, Peter H.
Optical Methods in Ultracentrifugation,
Electrophoresis, & Diffusion. Oxford U Pr.

Lloyd, Robert M.
xLloyd, Robert M.
A Flora of the White Mountains, California &
Nevada. U of Cal Pr.
Systematics of the Onocleoid Ferns. U of Cal
Pr.

Lloyd, Robin.
xLloyd, Robin.
For Money or Love: Boy Prostitution in
America. Ballantine.

Lloyd, Ronald, 1937-
xLloyd, Ronald.
France. Watts.

Lloyd, Ruth.
xLloyd, Ruth.
Creative Keyboard Musicianship: Fundamentals
of Music & Keyboard Harmony Through
Improvisation. Har-Row.

Lloyd, Seton.
xLloyd, Seton.
The Archaeology of Mesopotamia: From the
Old Stone Age to the Persian Conquest.
Thames Hudson.
The Art of the Ancient Near East. Oxford U
Pr.
Foundations in the Dust: A Story of
Mesopotamian Exploration. AMS Pr.
Foundations in the Dust: The Story of
Mesopotamian Exploration. Thames Hudson.

Lloyd George, David Lloyd George, 1st Earl, 1863-1945
xLloyd George, David.
Memoirs of the Peace Conference. Elliots Bks.

Lloyd James, Arthur, 1884-1943
xLloyd James, Arthur.
The Broadcast Word. Greenwood.

Lloyd-Jones, Hugh.
xLloyd-Jones, Hugh.
ed. The Greeks. Arno.
Myths of the Zodiac. St Martin.

Lloyd-Roberts, G. C.
xLloyd-Roberts, G. C.
Hip Disorders in Children. Butterworths.

Llywelyn, Morgan.
xLlywelyn, Morgan.

Lion of Ireland: The Legend of Brian Boru. HM.

Lo Bello, Nino. *see* Lo Bello, Nino D.

Lo, Kenneth. *see* Lo, Kenneth H. C.

Lo, Kenneth H. *see* Lo, Kenneth H. C.

Lo, Kenneth H. C.
  xLo, Kenneth.
    The Encyclopedia of Chinese Cooking. A & W Pubs.
  xLo, Kenneth H.
    Chinese Regional Cooking. Pantheon.
    Quick & Easy Chinese Cooking. HM.

Lo, Winston Wan.
  xLo, Winston Wan.
    The Life & Thought of Yeh Shih. U Presses Fla.

Lo Bello, Nino D.
  xLo Bello, Nino.
    Vatican U.S.A.. Trident.

Loader, J. A., 1945-
  xLoader, Jamer A.
    Polar Structures in the Book of Qohelet. De Gruyter.

Loader, Jamer A. *see* Loader, J. A.

Loades, D. M.
  xLoades, D. M.
    Politics & the Nation 1450-1660: Obedience, Resistance & Public Order. Watts.
    Two Tudor Conspiracies. Cambridge U Pr.

Loan, Charles E. Van. *see* Van Loan, Charles E.

Lobachev, A. N.
  xLobachev, A. N.
    ed. Hydrothermal Synthesis of Crystals. Plenum Pub.

Loban, Walter.
  xLoban, Walter.
    Teaching Language & Literature: Grades Seven to Twelve. HarBraceJ.

Lobb. *see* Lobb, Charlotte.

Lobb, Charlotte.
  xLobb.
    Exploring Careers Through Volunteerism. Rosen Pr.
  xLobb, Charlotte.
    Exploring Apprenticeship Careers. Rosen Pr.
    Exploring Vocational School Careers. Rosen Pr.

Lobban, Richard.
  xLobban, Richard.
    Historical Dictionary of the Republics of Guinea-Bissau & Cape Verde. Scarecrow.

Lobeck, Armin K. *see* Lobeck, Armin Kohl.

Lobeck, Armin Kohl, 1886-
  xLobeck, Armin K.
    Things Maps Don't Tell Us: Adventure into Map Interpretation. Macmillan.

Lobel, Anita.
  xLobel, Anita.
    The Pancake. Greenwillow.
    illus. Potatoes, Potatoes. Har-Row.
    illus. Under a Mushroom. Har-Row.

Lobel, Arnold.
  xLobel, Arnold.

Days with Frog & Toad. Har-Row.
Frog & Toad All Year. Har-Row.
illus. Frog & Toad Are Friends. Har-Row.
illus. Frog & Toad Are Friends. Har-Row.
illus. Frog & Toad Together. Har-Row.
illus. Frog & Toad Together. Har-Row.
illus. Giant John. Har-Row.
illus. Grasshopper on the Road. Har-Row.
illus. Great Blueness & Other Predicaments. Har-Row.
Gregory Griggs & Other Nursery Rhyme People. Greenwillow.
illus. Holiday for Mister Muster. Har-Row.
How the Rooster Saved the Day. Greenwillow.
How the Rooster Saved the Day. Penguin.
illus. On the Day Peter Stuyvesant Sailed into Town. Har-Row.
illus. Owl at Home. Har-Row.
illus. Prince Bertram the Bad. Har-Row.

Lobel, Brana.
  xLobel, Brana.
    The Revenant. Doubleday.
    The Revenant. NAL.

Lobel, Leon.
  xLobel, Leon.
    All About Meat. HarBraceJ.

Lobel, M. D. *see* Lobel, Mary Doreen.

Lobel, Mary Doreen.
  xLobel, M. D.
    ed. Historic Towns: Maps & Plans of Towns & Cities in the British Isles, with Historic Commentaries, from Earliest Times to Circa 1800. Johns Hopkins.

Lobley, Priscilla.
  xLobley, Priscilla.
    Flower Making. Taplinger.
    Flower Making for Beginners. Taplinger.

Lobo, Ben.
  xLobo, Ben.
    Side of the Road: A Hitchhiker's Guide to the United States. SMC.

Locander, William B.
  xLocander, William B.
    Problem Definition in Marketing. Am Mktg.

Lochhead, Jewell, 1888-
  xLochhead, Jewell.
    The Education of Young Children in England. AMS Pr.

Lochhead, Marion.
  xLochhead, Marion.
    Portrait of the Scott Country. Intl Pubns Serv.

Lochman, Jan. *see* Lochman, Jan Milic.

Lochman, Jan Milic.
  xLochman, Jan.
    Living Roots of Reformation. Augsburg.

Lock, F. P.
  xLock, F. P.
    ed. Susanna Centlivre. G K Hall.
    Susanna Centlivre. Twayne.

Lock, Margaret M.
  xLock, Margaret M.
    East Asian Medicine in Urban Japan: Varieties of Medical Experience. U of Cal Pr.

Lockard, Duane.
  xLockard, Duane.
    Basic Cases in Constitutional Law. Macmillan.
    Politics of State & Local Government. Macmillan.

Lockard, William K. *see* Lockard, William Kirby.

Lockard, William Kirby, 1929-
  xLockard, William K.
    Design Drawing. Pepper Pub.
    illus. Design Drawing Experiences. Pepper Pub.
    Drawing As a Means to Architecture. Pepper Pub.

Locke, Alain. *see* Locke, Alain Leroy.

Locke, Alain Leroy, 1886-1954
  xLocke, Alain.

ed. Negro in Art: A Pictorial Record of the Negro Artist & of the Negro Theme in Art. Hacker.
Negro in Art: A Pictorial Record of the Negro Artist & the Negro Theme in Art. Metro Bks.

Locke, David R. *see* Locke, David Ross.

Locke, David Ross, 1833-1888
  xLocke, David R.
    The Demagogue. Irvington.
    The Morals of Abou Ben Adhem. Irvington.
    Nasby in Exile. Arden Lib.
    Nasby in Exile. Irvington.
    A Paper City. Irvington.
    Swingin' Round the Cirkle. Irvington.

Locke, Don.
  xLocke, Don.
    A Fantasy of Reason: The Life & Thought of William Godwin. Routledge & Kegan.

Locke, Edwin A.
  xLocke, Edwin A.
    Guide to Effective Study. Springer Pub.

Locke, Flora M.
  xLocke, Flora M.
    College Mathematics for Business. Wiley.
    Consumer Math: A Guide to Stretching Your Dollar. Wiley.
    Math Shortcuts. Wiley.

Locke, George H. *see* Locke, George Herbert.

Locke, George Herbert, 1870-1937
  xLocke, George H.
    Builders of the Canadian Commonwealth. Arno.

Locke, Harvey J. *see* Locke, Harvey James.

Locke, Harvey James, 1900-
  xLocke, Harvey J.
    Predicting Adjustment in Marriage: A Comparison of a Divorced & a Happily Married Group. Greenwood.

Locke, John.
  xLocke, John.
    The Correspondence of John Locke. Oxford U Pr.
    An Essay Concerning Human Understanding. Collins Pubs.
    Essay Concerning Human Understanding. Dover.
    An Essay Concerning Human Understanding. Dutton.
    An Essay Concerning Human Understanding. Humanities.
    Essay Concerning Human Understanding. NAL.
    An Essay Concerning Human Understanding. Oxford U Pr.
    Essay Concerning Human Understanding. Peter Smith.
    Letter Concerning Toleration. Bobbs.
    Of the Conduct of the Understanding. B Franklin.
    Treatise of Civil Government & a Letter Concerning Toleration. Irvington.
    Two Tracts on Government. Cambridge U Pr.
    Two Treatises of Government. Cambridge U Pr.
    Two Treatises of Government. NAL.

Locke, Lawrence F.
  xLocke, Lawrence F.
    Proposals That Work: A Guide for Planning Research. Tchrs Coll.

Locke, Michael.
  xLocke, Michael.
    Power & Politics in the School System: A Guidebook. Routledge & Kegan.

Locke, Raymond F. *see* Locke, Raymond Friday.

Locke, Raymond Friday.
  xLocke, Raymond F.

Book of the Navajo. Mankind Pub.
    ed. Great Military Battles. Mankind Pub.
Locke, Robert R., 1932-
    xLocke, Robert R.
    French Legitimists & the Politics of Moral
        Order in the Early Third Republic. Princeton
        U Pr.
Locke, W. N. see Locke, William Nash.
Locke, William.
    xLocke, William.
    ed. The Hypothalamus & Pituitary in Health &
        Disease. C C Thomas.
Locke, William Nash, 1901-
    xLocke, W. N.
    Scientific French: A Concise Description of the
        Structural Elements of Scientific & Technical
        French. Krieger.
Lockerbie, Bruce D. see Lockerbie, D. Bruce.
Lockerbie, D. Bruce.
    xLockerbie, Bruce D.
    Who Educates Your Child: A Book for Parents.
        Doubleday.
    xLockerbie, D. Bruce.
    The Apostles' Creed: Do You Really Believe
        It?. Victor Bks.
    The Cosmic Center. Eerdmans.
Lockerbie, Jeanette. see Lockerbie, Jeanette W.
Lockerbie, Jeanette W.
    xLockerbie, Jeanette.
    Living on the Plus Side. Moody.
    More Salt in My Kitchen. Moody.
    When Blood Flows the Heart Grows Softer.
        Tyndale.
Lockerman, Doris.
    xLockerman, Doris.
    Discover Atlanta. S&S.
Lockert, Lacy.
    xLockert, Lacy.
    tr. More Plays by Rivals of Corneille & Racine.
        Vanderbilt U Pr.
    Studies in French-Classical Tragedy. Vanderbilt
        U Pr.
Lockett, F. J.
    xLockett, F. J.
    Nonlinear Viscoelastic Solids. Acad Pr.
Lockett, T. A.
    xLockett, T. A.
    Davenport Pottery & Porcelain: 1794-1887. C
        E Tuttle.
Lockhart, Charles, 1944-
    xLockhart, Charles.
    Bargaining in International Conflicts. Columbia
        U Pr.
Lockhart, J. A. see Lockhart, J. A. R.
Lockhart, J. A. R.
    xLockhart, J. A.
    Introduction to Crop Husbandry. Pergamon.
Lockhart, J. Stewart. see Lockhart, James Haldane
    Stewart.
Lockhart, James. see Lockhart, James Marvin.
Lockhart, James Haldane Stewart, Sir, 1858-1937
    xLockhart, J. Stewart.
    The Lockhart Collection of Chinese Copper
        Coins. Quarterman.
Lockhart, James Marvin.
    xLockhart, James.
    The Men of Cajamarca: A Social &
        Biographical Study of the First Conquerors of
        Peru. U of Tex Pr.
Lockhart, John G. see Lockhart, John Gibson.
Lockhart, John Gibson.
    xLockhart, John G.
    Life of Robert Burns. AMS Pr.
Lockhart, John Gilbert, 1891-
    xLockhart, John G.
    Curses, Lucks & Talismans. Gale.
Lockhart, Noble C. see Lockhart, Noble L.
Lockhart, Noble L.
    xLockhart, Noble C.

AC Circuit Analysis. Van Nos Reinhold.
    xLockhart, Noble L.
    AC Circuit Analysis. Delmar.
Lockhart, Robin B. see Lockhart, Robin Bruce.
Lockhart, Robin Bruce.
    xLockhart, Robin B.
    Ace of Spies. Nordon Pubns.
Locklin, D. Philip. see Locklin, David Philip.
Locklin, David Philip, 1897-
    xLocklin, D. Philip.
    Economics of Transportation. Irwin.
Locklin, Gerald.
    xLocklin, Gerald.
    Two Summer Sequences. Maelstrom.
Lockmiller, David A. see Lockmiller, David Alexander.
Lockmiller, David Alexander, 1906-
    xLockmiller, David A.
    Enoch H. Crowder: Soldier, Lawyer &
        Statesman. U of Mo Pr.
Lockridge, Ernest, 1938-
    xLockridge, Ernest.
    Flying Elbows. Stein & Day.
Lockridge, Frances. see Lockridge, Frances Louise
    (Davis).
Lockridge, Frances Louise (Davis).
    xLockridge, Frances.
    Death of an Angel. Am Repr-Rivercity Pr.
Lockridge, Laurence S., 1942-
    xLockridge, Laurence S.
    Coleridge the Moralist. Cornell U Pr.
Lockridge, Richard, 1898-
    xLockridge, Richard.
    Inspector's Holiday: An Inspector Heimrich
        Mystery. Lippincott.
    One Lady, Two Cats. Lippincott.
    Or Was He Pushed?. Lippincott.
Locks, Mitchell O.
    xLocks, Mitchell O.
    Reliability, Maintainability, and Availability
        Assessment. Hayden.
Locks, Norman.
    xLocks, Norman.
    Familiar Subjects: Polaroid SX-70 Impressions.
        Har-Row.
Lockspeiser, E. see Lockspeiser, Edward.
Lockspeiser, Edward, 1905-
    xLockspeiser, E.
    Debussy: His Life & Mind. Cambridge U Pr.
    xLockspeiser, Edward.
    Debussy. Biblio Dist.
    Debussy, His Life & Mind. Macmillan.
    Music & Painting: A Study in Comparative
        Ideas from Turner to Schoenberg. Har-Row.
Lockwood. see Lockwood, Antony Peter Murray.
Lockwood, A. P. see Lockwood, Antony Peter Murray.
Lockwood, Albert. see Lockwood, Albert Lewis.
Lockwood, Albert Lewis, 1871-1933
    xLockwood, Albert.
    Notes on the Literature of the Piano. Da Capo.
Lockwood, Antony P. see Lockwood, Antony Peter
    Murray.
Lockwood, Antony Peter Murray.
    xLockwood.
    The Membranes of Animal Cells. Univ Park.
    xLockwood, A. P.
    Aspects of the Physiology of Crustacea. W H
        Freeman.
    xLockwood, Antony P.
    Animal Body Fluids & Their Regulation.
        Harvard U Pr.
Lockwood, David G.
    xLockwood, David G.
    Introduction to Stratificational Linguistics.
        HarBraceJ.
Lockwood, Dean P. see Lockwood, Dean Putnam.
Lockwood, Dean Putnam, 1883-
    xLockwood, Dean P.

Survey of Classical Roman Literature. U of
        Chicago Pr.
Lockwood, Deborah. see Lockwood, Deborah L.
Lockwood, Deborah L.
    xLockwood, Deborah.
    Compiled by Library Instruction: A
        Bibliography. Greenwood.
Lockwood, Douglas.
    xLockwood, Douglas.
    We, the Aborigines. Greenwood.
Lockwood, E. H. see Lockwood, Edward Harrington.
Lockwood, Edward Harrington.
    xLockwood, E. H.
    Geometric Symmetry. Cambridge U Pr.
Lockwood, John G. see Lockwood, John George.
Lockwood, John George.
    xLockwood, John G.
    Causes of Climate. Halsted Pr.
Lockwood, Laura E. see Lockwood, Laura Emma.
Lockwood, Laura Emma, 1863-1956
    xLockwood, Laura E.
    Lexicon to the English Poetical Works of John
        Milton. B Franklin.
    Lexicon to the English Poetical Works of John
        Milton. Folcroft.
Lockwood, Luke V. see Lockwood, Luke Vincent.
Lockwood, Luke Vincent.
    xLockwood, Luke V.
    Furniture Collector's Glossary. Da Capo.
Lockwood, M. S. see Lockwood, Mary Smith.
Lockwood, Mary Smith.
    xLockwood, M. S.
    Art Embroidery. Garland Pub.
Lockwood, Stephen C. see Lockwood, Stephen Chapman.
Lockwood, Stephen Chapman.
    xLockwood, Stephen C.
    Augustine Heard & Company: American
        Merchants in China. Harvard U Pr.
Lockwood, W. D. see Lockwood, William Burley.
Lockwood, William Burley.
    xLockwood, W. D.
    A Panorama of Indo-European Languages.
        Humanities.
Lockwood, William W. see Lockwood, William Wirt.
Lockwood, William Wirt, 1906-
    xLockwood, William W.
    Economic Development of Japan: Growth &
        Structural Change, 1868-1938. Princeton U
        Pr.
Lockyer, Herbert.
    xLockyer, Herbert.
    All About Bible Study. Zondervan.
    A Cure for Troubled Hearts. Harvest Hse.
    Dark Threads the Weaver Needs. Revell.
    How to Find Comfort in the Bible. Word Bks.
Lockyer, K. G.
    xLockyer, K. G.
    Introduction to Critical Path Analysis.
        Beekman Pubs.
Lockyer, Roger.
    xLockyer, Roger.
    Habsburg & Bourbon Europe, 1470-1720.
        Longman.
Lodewijk, Tom.
    xLodewijk, Tom.
    The Book of Tulips. Viking Pr..
Lodge, David, 1935-
    xLodge, David.
    Evelyn Waugh. Columbia U Pr.
Lodge, E. C. see Lodge, Eleanor Constance.
Lodge, Edith.
    xLodge, Edith.
    Journey Through Noon. Windy Row.
Lodge, Eleanor. see Lodge, Eleanor Constance.
Lodge, Eleanor C. see Lodge, Eleanor Constance.
Lodge, Eleanor Constance.
    xLodge, E. C.
    English Constitutional Documents, 1307-1485.
        Octagon.
    xLodge, Eleanor.

Loewenstein, Rudolph Maurice.
  xLoewenstein, Rudolph M.
    ed. Psychoanalysis: A General Psychology. Intl
      Univs Pr.
Loewenthal, R. E. *see* Loewenthal, Richard E.
Loewenthal, Richard E.
  xLoewenthal, R. E.
    Carbonate Chemistry of Aquatic Systems:
      Theory & Application. Ann Arbor Science.
Loewer, H. Peter.
  xLoewer, H. Peter.
    illus. Bringing the Outdoors in: How to Do
      Wonders with Vines, Wildflowers, Ferns,
      Moses, Bulbs, Grasses, & Dozens of Other
      Plants Most People Overlook. Walker & Co.
    The Indoor Water Gardener's How to
      Handbook. Walker & Co.
  xLoewer, Peter.
    The Indoor Water Gardener's How-to
      Handbook. Popular Lib.
Loewer, Peter. *see* Loewer, H. Peter.
Loewinsohn, Ron.
  xLoewinsohn, Ron.
    The Leaves. Black Sparrow.
Loewy, A. G. *see* Loewy, Ariel G.
Loewy, Ariel G.
  xLoewy, A. G.
    Cell Structure & Function. HR&W.
Loewy, Herta.
  xLoewy, Herta.
    More About the Backward Child. Philos Lib.
Loewy, Raymond. *see* Loewy, Raymond Fernand.
Loewy, Raymond Fernand, 1893-
  xLoewy, Raymond.
    Industrial Design. Overlook Pr.
Lofaro, Michael A., 1948-
  xLofaro, Michael A.
    The Life & Adventures of Daniel Boone. U Pr
      of Ky.
Lofberg, J. O. *see* Lofberg, John Oscar.
Lofberg, John Oscar, 1882-1932
  xLofberg, J. O.
    Sycophancy in Athens. Ares.
Loffel, E. W. *see* Loffel, Egon W.
Loffel, Egon W.
  xLoffel, E. W.
    Financing Your Business. Wiley.
Loffler, E.
  xLoffler, Ernst.
    Australia. Merrimack Bk Serv.
Loffler, Ernst. *see* Loffler, E.
Lofgren, Ulf.
  xLofgren, Ulf.
    The Boy Who Ate More Than the Giant, &
      Other Swedish Folktales. Philomel.
    tr. Felix Forgetful. Delacorte.
    Swedish Toys, Dolls, & Gifts You Can Make
      Yourself: Traditional Swedish Handicrafts.
      Philomel.
Lofland, John.
  xLofland, John.
    Deviance & Identity. P-H.
    Doomsday Cult: A Study of Conversion,
      Proselytization, & Maintenance of Faith.
      Halsted Pr.
    Doomsday Cult: A Study of Conversion,
      Proselytization, & Maintenance of Faith.
      Irvington.
    Interaction in Everyday Life: Social Strategies.
      Sage.
Lofland, Lyn H.
  xLofland, Lyn H.
    The Craft of Dying: The Modern Face of
      Death. Sage.
    A World of Strangers: Order & Action in
      Urban Public Space. Basic.
Lofthouse, Jessica.
  xLofthouse, Jessica.

Portrait of Lancashire. Intl Pubns Serv.
Lofting, Hugh, 1886-1947
  xLofting, Hugh.
    illus. Doctor Dolittle: A Treasury. Lippincott.
    illus. Doctor Dolittle & the Green Canary.
      Lippincott.
    illus. Doctor Dolittle's Circus. Lippincott.
    illus. Doctor Dolittle's Zoo. Lippincott.
    illus. Story of Mrs. Tubbs. Lippincott.
    Twilight of Magic. Lippincott.
Loftis, John. *see* Loftis, John Clyde.
Loftis, John C. *see* Loftis, John Clyde.
Loftis, John Clyde, 1919-
  xLoftis, John.
    The Spanish Plays of Neoclassical England.
      Yale U Pr.
  xLoftis, John C.
    Steele at Drury Lane. Greenwood.
Loftness, Robert L.
  xLoftness, Robert L.
    Energy Handbook. Van Nos Reinhold.
Lofton, John.
  xLofton, John.
    Insurrection in South Carolina: The Turbulent
      World of Denmark Vesey. Kent St U Pr.
    The Press As Guardian of the First
      Amendment. U of SC Pr.
Lofts, Norah.
  xLofts, Norah.
    The Concubine. Fawcett.
Lofts, Norah. *see* Lofts, Norah Robinson.
Lofts, Norah (Robinson), 1904-
  xLofts, Norah.
    Bride of Moat House. Fawcett.
    Little Wax Doll. Fawcett.
    The Lost Queen. Fawcett.
    Lovers All Untrue. Fawcett.
    The Maude Reed Tale. Dell.
    Out of the Dark. Doubleday.
    Out of the Dark. Fawcett.
Lofts, Norah Ethel (Robinson), 1904-
  xLofts, Norah.
    The House at Old Vine. Fawcett.
    The House at Old Vine. Queens Hse.
    The House at Sunset. Fawcett.
    The House at Sunset. Queens Hse.
Lofts, Norah Robinson, 1904-
  xLofts, Norah.
    Anne Boleyn. Coward.
    Day of the Butterfly. Doubleday.
    The Day of the Butterfly. G K Hall.
    Gad's Hall. Doubleday.
    Haunting of Gad's Hall. Doubleday.
    The Haunting of Gad's Hall. Fawcett.
    The Homecoming. Fawcett.
    The Lonely Furrow. Doubleday.
    The Lonely Furrow. Fawcett.
    Queens of England. Doubleday.
Loftus, Elizabeth. *see* Loftus, Elizabeth F.
Loftus, Elizabeth F., 1944-
  xLoftus, Elizabeth.
    Eyewitness Testimony. Harvard U Pr.
Loftus, John.
  xLoftus, John.
    Toulouse-Lautrec. McGraw.
Logan, Arthur L.
  xLogan, Arthur L.
    Remembering Made Easy. Arc Bks.
Logan, Bob.
  xLogan, Robert.
    The Bulls & Chicago: A Stormy Affair. Follett.
Logan, Frank A.
  xLogan, Frank A.
    Fundamentals of Learning & Motivation. Wm
      C Brown.
    Systematic Analyses of Learning & Motivation.
      Wiley.
Logan, Gene A. *see* Logan, Gene Adams.
Logan, Gene Adams.
  xLogan, Gene A.

Anatomic Kinesiology. Wm C Brown.
Logan, Gerald E.
  xLogan, Gerald E.
    Hallo Deutschland!. Newbury Hse.
Logan, Hugh L. *see* Logan, Hugh Lynn.
Logan, Hugh Lynn.
  xLogan, Hugh L.
    Stress Corrosion of Metals. Wiley.
Logan, Jake.
  xLogan, Jake.
    Across the Rio Grande. Playboy Pbks.
    The Comanche's Woman. Playboy Pbks.
    Outlaw Blood. Playboy Pbks.
    Ride, Slocum, Ride. Playboy Pbks.
    White Hell. Playboy Pbks.
Logan, John A. *see* Logan, John Alexander.
Logan, John Alexander, 1826-1886
  xLogan, John A.
    The Great Conspiracy. Arno.
Logan, John Arthur.
  xLogan, John A.
    No Transfer: An American Security Principle.
      Elliots Bks.
Logan, Joshua.
  xLogan, Joshua.
    Movie Stars, Real People, & Me. Delacorte.
Logan, Margaret, 1936-
  xLogan, Margaret.
    Happy Endings. HM.
    Happy Endings. Popular Lib.
Logan, Mark.
  xLogan, Mark.
    French Kiss. NAL.
Logan, Mary. *see* Logan, Mary Simmerson
  (Cunningham).
Logan, Mary S. *see* Logan, Mary Simmerson
  (Cunningham).
Logan, Mary Simmerson (Cunningham), 1838-1923
  xLogan, Mary.
    Reminiscences of the Civil War &
      Reconstruction. S Ill U Pr.
  xLogan, Mary S.
    The Part Taken by Women in American
      History. Arno.
Logan, Nick.
  xLogan, Nick.
    The Illustrated Encyclopedia of Rock. Crown.
Logan, Rayford W. *see* Logan, Rayford Whittingham.
Logan, Rayford Whittingham.
  xLogan, Rayford W.
    Haiti & the Dominican Republic. Oxford U Pr.
    Intro. by & ed. What the Negro Wants.
      Agathon.
Logan, Robert. *see* Logan, Bob.
Logan, Terence P.
  xLogan, Terence P.
    ed. The Later Jacobean & Caroline Dramatists.
      U of Nebr Pr.
Logan, Wende W. *see* Logan, Wende Westinghouse.
Logan, Wende Westinghouse.
  xLogan, Wende W.
    Breast Carcinoma: The Radiologist's Expanded
      Role. Wiley.
Logan, William. *see* Logan, William Boyd.
Logan, William B. *see* Logan, William Boyd.
Logan, William Boyd.
  xLogan, William.
    Mathematics in Marketing. McGraw.
  xLogan, William B.
    Mathematics in Marketing. McGraw.
Loggins, Vernon, 1893-
  xLoggins, Vernon.
    Andre Chenier: His Life, Death & Glory. Ohio
      U Pr.
    Where the Word Ends: The Life of Louis
      Moreau Gottschalk. La State U Pr.
Logsdon, Gene.
  xLogsdon, Gene.

Successful Berry Growing: How to Plant, Prune, Pick & Preserve Bush & Vine Fruits. Rodale Pr Inc.
Two Acre Eden. Rodale Pr Inc.

Logsdon, John M., 1937-
xLogsdon, John M.
The Decision to Go to the Moon: Project Apollo & the National Interest. U of Chicago Pr.

Logsdon, Joseph.
xLogsdon, Joseph.
Horace White, Nineteenth Century Liberal. Greenwood.

Logsdon, Mayme I.
xLogsdon, Mayme I.
Mathematician Explains. U of Chicago Pr.

Logue, Cal. see Logue, Calvin Mcleod.

Logue, Calvin Mcleod.
xLogue, Cal.
Speaking: Back to Fundamentals. Allyn.

Logue, Christopher.
xLogue, Christopher.
The Magic Circus. Viking Pr.
Ratsmagic. Viking Pr.
Ratsmagic. Pantheon.
Songs. Astor-Honor.

Logue, Jeanne.
xLogue, Jeanne.
The Wonder of It All. Har-Row.

Logue, Patrick E.
xLogue, Patrick E.
Understanding & Living with Brain Damage. C C Thomas.

Logue, William, 1934-
xLogue, William.
Leon Blum: The Formative Years 1872-1914. N Ill U Pr.

Loh, Horace H.
xLoh, Horace H.
ed. Neurochemical Mechanisms of Opiates & Endorphins. Raven.

Loh, Jules.
xLoh, Jules.
Lords of the Earth: The History of the Navajo Indians. Macmillan.

Lohan, Frank.
xLohan, Frank J.
Pen & Ink Techniques. Contemp Bks.

Lohan, Frank J. see Lohan, Frank.

Lohan, Robert.
xLohan, Robert.
ed. Christmas Tales for Reading Aloud. Ungar.
Concise German Grammar for Reference & Review. Ungar.

Lohf, Kenneth A.
xLohf, Kenneth A.
Literary Manuscripts of Hart Crane. Ohio St U Pr.

Lohfink, Gerhard, 1934-
xLohfink, Gerhard.
The Bible, Now I Get It: A Form Criticism Handbook. Doubleday.
The Gospels: God's Word in Human Words. Franciscan Herald.

Lohkamp, Nicholas.
xLohkamp, Nicholas.
The Commandments & the New Morality. St Anthony Mess Pr.

Lohmann, Hartwig.
xLohmann, Hartwig.
I Can Tell You Anything, God. Fortress.

Lohmann, Roger. see Lohmann, Roger A.

Lohmann, Roger A., 1942-
xLohmann, Roger.
Breaking Even: Financial Management in Human Service Organizations. Temple U Pr.

Lohnes, Walter. see Lohnes, Walter F. W.

Lohnes, Walter F. see Lohnes, Walter F. W.

Lohnes, Walter F. W.
xLohnes, Walter.

German: A Structural Approach. Norton.
xLohnes, Walter F.
German: A Structural Approach. Norton.

Lohr, Thomas F.
xLohr, Thomas F.
The Mechanics of the Mind. Venture Bks.

Lohren, Carl.
xLohren, Carl.
One Move to Better Golf. NAL.

Lohse, Bernhard, 1928-
xLohse, Bernhard.
A Short History of Christian Doctrine. Fortress.

Lois, George.
xLois, George.
Art of Advertising: George Lois on Mass Communication. Abrams.

Loisy, Alfred. see Loisy, Alfred Firmin.

Loisy, Alfred F. see Loisy, Alfred Firmin.

Loisy, Alfred Firmin, 1857-1940
xLoisy, Alfred.
The Gospel & the Church. Fortress.
xLoisy, Alfred F.
My Duel with the Vatican: The Autobiography of a Catholic Modernist. Greenwood.

Lojda, Z. see Lojda, Zdenek.

Lojda, Zdenek.
xLojda, Z.
Enzyme Histochemistry: A Laboratory Manual. Springer-Verlag.

Lojko, Grace R.
xLojko, Grace R.
Typewriting Techniques for the Technical Secretary. P-H.

Loke, Y. W.
xLoke, Y. W.
Immunology & Immunopathology of the Human Foetal-Maternal Interaction. Elsevier.

Loken, Chris.
xLoken, Chris.
Come Monday Mornin . M Evans.

Loken, Newton C.
xLoken, Newton C.
The Complete Book of Gymnastics. P-H.
Gymnastics. Sterling.

Lokich, Jacob J.
xLokich, Jacob J.
Primer of Cancer Management. G K Hall.

Lokke, Carl L. see Lokke, Carl Ludwig.

Lokke, Carl Ludwig, 1897-1960
xLokke, Carl L.
France & the Colonial Question: A Study of Contemporary French Opinion, 1763-1801. Octagon.

Lokken, Roy N. see Lokken, Roy Norman.

Lokken, Roy Norman, 1917-
xLokken, Roy N.
David Lloyd, Colonial Lawmaker. U of Wash Pr.

Lolli, Giorgio.
xLolli, Giorgio.
Alcohol in Italian Culture: Food & Wine in Relation to Sobriety Among Italians & Italian Americans. Rutgers Ctr Alcohol.

Loman, Anna.
xLoman, Anna.
Looking at Holland. Lippincott.

Lomas, Charles W. see Lomas, Charles Wyatt.

Lomas, Charles Wyatt.
xLomas, Charles W.
ed. Rhetoric of the British Peace Movement. Phila Bk Co.

Lomask, Milton.
xLomask, Milton.
Andrew Johnson: President on Trial. Octagon.

Lomasney, Eileen.
xLomasney, Eileen.

My Book of Happiness: The Beatitudes for Children. Concordia.
My Book of the Lord's Prayer. Concordia.

Lomax, Alan.
xLomax, Alan.
ed. Folk Song Style & Culture. Transaction Bks.

Lomax, John A. see Lomax, John Avery.

Lomax, John Avery, 1867-1948
xLomax, John A.
Adventures of a Ballad Hunter. Hafner.

Lomax, Louis E., 1922-1970
xLomax, Louis E.
Negro Revolt. Har-Row.
When the Word Is Given...: A Report on Elijah Muhammad, Malcolm X, & the Black Muslim World. Greenwood.

Lombard, Charles M.
xLombard, Charles M.
Joseph de Maistre. Twayne.
Thomas Holley Chivers. Twayne.

Lombard, R. S. see Lombard, Richard S.

Lombard, Richard S.
xLombard, R. S.
American-Venezuelan Private International Law. Oceana.

Lombardi, Guido.
xLombardi, Guido.
Radiology in Neuro-Ophthalmology. Krieger.

Lombardi, John V.
xLombardi, John V.
Decline & Abolition of Negro Slavery in Venezuela, 1820-1854. Greenwood.
People & Places in Colonial Venezuela. Ind U Pr.

Lombardi, Mary, 1940-
xLombardi, Mary.
Brazilian Serial Documents: A Selective & Annotated Guide. Ind U Pr.

Lombardi, Tarky.
xLombardi, Tarky.
Medical Malpractice Insurance: A Legislator's View. Syracuse U Pr.

Lombardy, William.
xLombardy, William.
Chess for Children Step by Step: A New, Easy Way to Learn the Game. Little.
Chess Panorama. Stein & Day.
Guide to Tournament Chess. McKay.

Lombra, Raymond E.
xLombra, Raymond E.
Money & the Financial System: Theory, Institutions & Policy. McGraw.

Lombroso, Cesare.
xLombroso, Cesare.
Crime, Its Causes & Remedies. Patterson Smith.

Lomer, Gerhard R. see Lomer, Gerhard Richard.

Lomer, Gerhard Richard, 1882-
xLomer, Gerhard R.
The Concept of Method. AMS Pr.

Lomnitz, C. see Lomnitz, Cinna.

Lomnitz, Cinna.
xLomnitz, C.
Global Tectonics & Earthquake Risk. Elsevier.

Lomont, John S, 1924-
xLomont, John S.
Applications of Finite Groups. Acad Pr.

London - St. Paul'S Cathedral. see London. St. Paul'S Cathedral.

London, Barbara, 1936-
xLondon, Barbara.

A Short Course in Canon Photography. Curtin
& London.
A Short Course in Minolta Photography.
Curtin & London.
A Short Course in Nikon Photography. Curtin
& London.
A Short Course in Pentax Photography: A
Guide to Great Pictures. Van Nos Reinhold.
A Short Course in Photography. Curtin &
London.
London, Bruce.
xLondon, Bruce.
Metropolis & Nation in Thailand: The Political
Economy of Uneven Development.
Westview.
London, Carolyn.
xLondon, Carolyn.
The Twins Solve the Mystery of the Missing
Money. Moody.
London Chamber of Commerce & Industry. *see* London
Chamber of Commerce and Industry.
London Chamber of Commerce and Industry.
xLondon Chamber of Commerce & Industry.
Trade Contacts in Eastern Europe. Nichols
Pub.
Trade Contacts in West African Countries.
Nichols Pub.
London. City Literary Institute.
xCity Literary Institute Of London.
Tradition & Experiment in Present-Day
Literature. Arno.
xLondon City Literary Institute.
Tradition & Experiment in Present- Day
Literature. Haskell.
London County Council.
xLondon County Council.
Bankside. AMS Pr.
The Parishes of Christ Church & All Saints &
the Liberties of Norton Folgate & the Old
Artillery Ground. AMS Pr.
Survey of London. AMS Pr.
London Dialectical Society.
xLondon Dialectical Society.
Report on Spiritualism: Together with the
Evidence, Oral & Written. Arno.
London, Duke.
xLondon, Duke.
Beautiful Las Vegas. Beautiful Am.
London, H. H. *see* London, Hoyt H.
London, Hannah R. *see* London, Hannah Ruth.
London, Hannah Ruth, 1894-
xLondon, Hannah R.
Portraits of Jews by Gilbert Stuart & Other
Early American Artists. C E Tuttle.
London, Harvey.
xLondon, Harvey.
Dimensions of Personality. Wiley.
ed. Personality: A New Look at Metatheories.
Halsted Pr.
ed. Thought & Feeling: Cognitive Alteration of
Feeling States. Beresford Bk Serv.
London, Herbert I. *see* London, Herbert Ira.
London, Herbert Ira.
xLondon, Herbert I.
The Overheated Decade. NYU Pr.
London, Howard B.
xLondon, Howard B.
The Culture of a Community College. Praeger.
London, Hoyt H., 1900-
xLondon, H. H.
Principles & Techniques of Vocational
Guidance. Merrill.
London, Jack.
xLondon, Jack.

The Assassination Bureau, Ltd.. Penguin.
The Call of the Wild. Biblio Dist.
Call of the Wild. Crown.
The Call of the Wild. Western Pub.
The Call of the Wild. Raintree Pubs.
Call of the Wild. Schol Bk Serv.
The Call of the Wild. Pendulum Pr.
Call of the Wild. Airmont.
Call of the Wild. Macmillan.
Call of the Wild. AMSCO Sch.
Moon-Face, & Other Stories. Arno.
No Mentor but Myself: A Collection of
Articles, Essays, Reviews, & Letters on
Writing & Writers. Kennikat.
South Sea Tales. Macmillan.
Tales of the Fish Patrol. Arno.
Valley of the Moon. Peregrine Smith.
London, Kurt, 1899-
xLondon, Kurt.
Film Music. Arno.
London, Laura.
xLondon, Laura.
The Bad Baron's Daughter. Dell.
London Magazine.
xLondon Magazine.
Coming to London. Arno.
ed. London Magazine Poems, Nineteen
Sixty-One-Sixty-Six. Dufour.
xLondon Magazine Editors.
Leaving School. Dufour.
London Magazine Stories. Dufour.
London Magazine Editors. *see* London Magazine.
London, Mel.
xLondon, Mel.
Getting into Film. Ballantine.
The London Mercury.
xLondon Mercury.
Second Mercury Story Book. Arno.
London Missionary Society.
xLondon Missionary Society.
London Missionary Society's Report of the
Proceedings Against the Late Rev. J. Smith
of Demerara, Who Was Tried Under Martial
Law & Condemned to Death, on a Charge of
Aiding & Assisting in a Rebellion of Negro
Slaves. Negro U Pr.
London. Railway Clearing House.
xLondon Railway Clearing House.
Railway Junction Diagrams 1915. Kelley.
London. St. Paul's Cathedral.
xLondon - St. Paul's Cathedral.
Documents Illustrating the History of St.
Paul's Cathedral. Johnson Repr.
Visitations of Churches Belonging to St. Paul's
Cathedral in 1297 & 1458. Johnson Repr.
xLondon-St. Paul'S Cathedral.
Domesday of Saint Paul of the Year Twelve
Twenty-Two. Johnson Repr.
London, Stationers' Company.
xLondon Stationers' Company.
An Analytical Index to the Ballad-Entries
(1557-1709) in the Registers of the Company
of Stationers of London. Gale.
London Sunday Times. *see* The Times, London.
London Times. *see* The Times, London.
London Times Editors. *see* The Times, London.
London. University.
xUniversity of London.
Catalogue of the Comparative Education
Library, 1st Suppl, Institute of Education. G
K Hall.
Dictionary Catalogue of the London School of
Hygiene & Tropical Medicine. G K Hall.
London. University. Board of Studies in History.
xLondon University, Board of Studies in History.
Tudor Studies Presented to Albert Frederick
Pollard. Arno.
London. University. Contemporary China Institute.
xContemporary China Institute.

ed. A Bibliography of Chinese Newspapers &
Periodicals in European Libraries. Cambridge
U Pr.
London. University. Institute of Advanced Legal Studies.
xInstitute of Advanced Legal Studies, University of
London.
Catalogue of the Library of the Institute of
Advanced Legal Studies. G K Hall.
London. University. Institute of Education.
xUniversity of London, Institute of Education.
Catalogue of the Comparative Education
Library: Second Supplement. G K Hall.
Catalogue of the Comparative Education
Library, University of London, Institute of
Education. G K Hall.
**London. University. Institute of Germanic Languages
and Literatures.**
xLondon. University. Institute of Germanic
Languages & Literatures.
Schiller: Bicentenary Lectures. Ultramarine
Pub.
London. University. Institute of Historical Research.
xUniversity Of London - Institute Of Historical
Research.
Corrections and Additions to the Dictionary of
National Biography Cummulated from the
Bulletin of the Institute of Historical
Research Covering the Years 1923-1963. G
K Hall.
London. University. Library.
xUniversity Of London Library.
Palaeography Collection in the University of
London Library: An Author & Subject
Catalogue. G K Hall.
**London. University. School of Oriental and African
Studies.**
xSchool of Oriental & African Studies, University
of London.
Library Catalogue of the School of Oriental &
African Studies: Third Supplement. G K Hall.
xUniversity of London - School of Oriental &
African Studies.
Library Catalogue of the School of Oriental &
African Studies. G K Hall.
Library Catalogue of the School of Oriental &
African Studies: 2nd Supplement. G K Hall.
London. University. Warburg Institute, Library.
xUniversity Of London - Warburg Institute
Library.
Catalog of the Warburg Institute Library, First
Supplement. G K Hall.
Catalog of the Warburg Institute Library. G K
Hall.
London-St. Paul'S Cathedral. *see* London. St. Paul'S
Cathedral.
Londre, Felicia H. *see* Londre, Felicia Hardison.
Londre, Felicia Hardison, 1941-
xLondre, Felicia H.
Tennessee Williams. Ungar.
Lone, Emma. *see* Lone, Emma Miriam.
Lone, Emma Miriam, 1872-1953
xLone, Emma.
Some Noteworthy Firsts in Europe During the
Fifteenth Century. B Franklin.
Lonergan, Bernard. *see* Lonergan, Bernard J. F.
Lonergan, Bernard J. F.
xLonergan, Bernard.
Subject. Marquette.
Lonetto, Richard.
xLonetto, Richard.
Children's Conceptions of Death. Springer Pub.
Long. *see* Long, Sandra Salser.
Long, Anne, 1926-
xLong, Anne.
The Other Mrs. Wyngate. Beta Bk.
Long Ashton Research Station Symposium, University of
Bristol, Sept. 1971. *see* Long Ashton Symposium, 3d,
University of Bristol, 1971.
Long Ashton Symposium - Fourth, University of Bristol,

September, 1974. *see* Long Ashton Symposium, 4th, University of Bristol, 1973.

Long Ashton Symposium, 3d, University of Bristol, 1971.
xLong Ashton Research Station Symposium, University of Bristol, Sept. 1971.
Fungal Pathogenicity & the Plant's Response: Proceedings. Acad Pr.

Long Ashton Symposium, 4th, University of Bristol, 1973.
xLong Ashton Symposium - Fourth, University of Bristol, September, 1974.
Lactic Acid Bacteria in Beverages & Food: Proceedings. Acad Pr.

Long, B. *see* Long, Beverly Whitaker.

Long, Beverly Whitaker.
xLong, B.
Group Performance of Literature. P-H.

Long, Cathryn. *see* Long, Cathryn J.

Long, Cathryn J.
xLong, Cathryn.
The Future of American Government: What Will It Be?. Allyn.

Long, Charles.
xLong, Charles.
Prevention & Rehabilitation in Ischemic Heart Disease. Williams & Wilkins.

Long, Chuck.
xLong, Chuck.
ed. Pacific Crest Trail Hike Planning Guide. Signpost Bk Pubns.

Long, Claudia.
xLong, Claudia.
Albert's Story. Delacorte.

Long, D. A. *see* Long, Derek Albert.

Long, Dale D.
xLong, Dale D.
Physics Around You. Wadsworth Pub.

Long, David E.
xLong, David E.
ed. The Government & Politics of the Middle East & North Africa. Westview.
The Persian Gulf: An Introduction to Its Peoples, Politics, & Economics. Westview.

Long, David F.
xLong, David F.
How to Organize & Raise Funds for Small Non-Profit Organizations. Groupwork Today.

Long, David F. *see* Long, David Foster.

Long, David Foster.
xLong, David F.
ed. A Documentary History of U. S. Foreign Relations: The Mid-1890's to 1979; Selections from & Additions to Ruhl J. Bartlett's the Record of American Diplomacy. U Pr of Amer.

Long, Derek Albert.
xLong, D. A.
Raman Spectroscopy. McGraw.

Long, Don L.
xLong, Don L.
Introduction to Agribusiness Management. McGraw.

Long, E. B. *see* Long, Everette B.

Long, E. Hudson. *see* Long, Eugene Hudson.

Long, Earlene.
xLong, Earlene.
Johnny's Egg. A-W.

Long, Edward, 1734-1813
xLong, Edward.
History of Jamaica. Biblio Dist.

Long, Edward L. *see* Long, Edward Le Roy.

Long, Edward Le Roy.
xLong, Edward L.
Religious Beliefs of American Scientists. Greenwood.
Survey of Christian Ethics. Oxford U Pr.

Long, Eugene Hudson, 1908-
xLong, E. Hudson.

Compiled by American Drama from Its Beginnings to the Present. AHM Pub.
Mark Twain Handbook. Hendricks House.

Long, Everette B.
xLong, E. B.
Civil War Day by Day: An Almanac 1861-1865. Doubleday.

Long, Frank B. *see* Long, Frank Belknap.

Long, Frank Belknap, 1903-
xLong, Frank B.
Howard Phillips Lovecraft: Dreamer on the Nightside. Arkham.

Long, Frank W.
xLong, Frank W.
Creative Lapidary: Materials, Tools, Techniques, Design. Van Nos Reinhold.

Long, G. Gilbert. *see* Long, George Gilbert.

Long, George.
xLong, George.
Folklore Calendar. Gale.
The Folklore Calendar. Rowman.

Long, George Gilbert.
xLong, G. Gilbert.
Problem Exercises for General Chemistry. Wiley.

Long, Harriet G. *see* Long, Harriet Geneva.

Long, Harriet Geneva, 1897-
xLong, Harriet G.
Rich the Treasure: Public Library Service to Children. ALA.

Long, Hollis M. *see* Long, Hollis Moody.

Long, Hollis Moody, 1900-
xLong, Hollis M.
Public Secondary Education for Negroes in North Carolina. AMS Pr.

Long, Howard De. *see* DeLong, Howard.

Long, Howard R. *see* Long, Howard Rusk.

Long, Howard Rusk, 1906-
xLong, Howard R.
ed. Main Street Militants: An Anthology from "Grassroots Editor". S Ill U Pr.

Long, Huey B.
xLong, Huey B.
Changing Approaches to Studying Adult Education. Jossey-Bass.
Continuing Education of Adults in Colonial America. Syracuse U Cont Ed.

Long, Inez. *see* Long, Inez (Goughnour).

Long, Inez (Goughnour).
xLong, Inez.
Faces Among the Faithful. Brethren.

Long Island Historical Society.
xLong Island Historical Society.
Brooklyn Catalogue of American Genealogies in the Library of the Long Island Historical Society. Genealog Pub.

Long, James D.
xLong, James D.
ed. Classroom Management with Adolescents. Mss Info.

Long, Jean.
xLong, Jean.
How to Paint the Chinese Way. Sterling.

Long, John D. *see* Long, John Davis.

Long, John Davis, 1838-1915
xLong, John D.
After Dinner & Other Speeches. Arno.
The New American Navy. Arno.

Long, Kenneth. *see* Long, Kenneth R.

Long, Kenneth R.
xLong, Kenneth.
Music of the English Church. St Martin.

Long, Laura.
xLong, Laura.
David Farragut: Boy Midshipman. Bobbs.
George Dewey: Vermont Boy. Bobbs.

Long, Leon E., 1933-
xLong, Leon E.

Geology. McGraw.

Long, Maurice W.
xLong, Maurice W.
Radar Reflectivity of Land & Sea. Lexington Bks.

Long, Max F. *see* Long, Max Freedom.

Long, Max Freedom, 1890-
xLong, Max F.
Growing into Light. De Vorss.
Huna Code in Religions. De Vorss.
Psychometric Analysis. De Vorss.

Long, Orie W. *see* Long, Orie William.

Long, Orie William, 1882-
xLong, Orie W.
Literary Pioneers: Early American Explorers of European Culture. Core Collection.

Long, Paul.
xLong, Paul.
All the Answers to All Your Questions About Training Pointing Dogs. Capital Bird.

Long, R. *see* Long, Richard.

Long, R. Gerry.
xLong, R. Gerry.
The Conductor's Workshop: A Workbook for Instrumental Conducting. Wm C Brown.

Long, Ralph B.
xLong, Ralph B.
Structure Worksheets for Contemporary English to Accompany the Sentence & Its Parts. U of Chicago Pr.

Long, Richard.
xLong, R.
Production of Polymer & Plastics Intermediates from Petroleum. Plenum Pub.

Long, Richard A.
xLong, Richard A.
ed. Afro-American Writing: An Anthology of Prose & Poetry. NYU Pr.

Long, Robert P.
xLong, Robert P.
Reference Encyclopedia of Flexographic Equipment & Supplies. North Am Pub Co.
Reference Encyclopedia of Package Printing Techniques & Equipment. North Am Pub Co.

Long, Robert R.
xLong, Robert R.
Mechanics of Solids & Fluids. P-H.

Long, Robert W.
xLong, Robert W.
A Flora of Tropical Florida: A Manual of the Seed Plants & Ferns of Southern Peninsular Florida. Banyan Bks.
Plant Biology: A Laboratory Manual for Elementary Botany. HR&W.

Long, Ruth.
xLong, Ruth.
Student Activities in the Seventies: A Survey Report. Natl Assn Principals.

Long, Ruthanna.
xLong, Ruthanna.
The Great Monster Contest. Western Pub.

Long, Sandra Salser.
xLong.
Transmission: Communication Skills for Technicians. Reston.

Long, Stewart L. *see* Long, Stewart Louis.

Long, Stewart Louis.
xLong, Stewart L.
The Development of the Television Network Oligopoly. Arno.

Long, Valentine.
xLong, Valentine.
Angels in Religion & Art. Franciscan Herald.

Long, William H. *see* Long, William Henry.

Long, William Henry, d. 1896
xLong, William H.
A Dictionary of the Isle of Wight Dialect, & of Provincialisms Used in the Island, with Illustrative Anecdotes & Tales. Folcroft.

Long, William S. *see* Long, William Stuart.

For Whom Are the Stars?. U Pr of Hawaii.
Loomis, Andrew, 1892-
  xLoomis, Andrew.
    Drawing the Head & Hands. Viking Pr.
    Fun with a Pencil. Viking Pr.
Loomis, Charles B. *see* Loomis, Charles Battell.
Loomis, Charles Battell, 1861-1911
  xLoomis, Charles B.
    Cheerful Americans. Arno.
    More Cheerful Americans. Arno.
Loomis, Charles P. *see* Loomis, Charles Price.
Loomis, Charles Price.
  xLoomis, Charles P.
    ed. Social Systems: The Study of Sociology.
    Schenkman.
Loomis, Edward, 1924-
  xLoomis, Edward.
    On Fiction: Critical Essays & Notes. Swallow.
    Vedettes: A Collection of Stories. Swallow.
Loomis, Elias, 1811-1889
  xLoomis, Elias.
    The Recent Progress of Astronomy: Especially
    in the United States. Arno.
Loomis, Gertrude. *see* Loomis, Gertrude (Schoepperle).
Loomis, Gertrude (Schoepperle), 1882-1921
  xLoomis, Gertrude.
    Tristan & Isolt: A Study of the Sources of the
    Romance. B Franklin.
Loomis, Laura A. *see* Loomis, Laura Alandis Hibbard.
Loomis, Laura Alandis Hibbard, 1883-1960
  xLoomis, Laura A.
    Adventures in the Middle Ages: A Memorial
    Collection of Essays & Studies. B Franklin.
    Mediaeval Romance in England: A Study of
    the Sources & Analogues of the Non-Cyclic
    Metrical Romances. Arden Lib.
Loomis, Lynn H.
  xLoomis, Lynn H.
    Advanced Calculus. A-W.
    Calculus. A-W.
    Introduction to Calculus. A-W.
Loomis, Maxine E.
  xLoomis, Maxine E.
    Group Process for Nurses. Mosby.
Loomis, Mildred J.
  xLoomis, Mildred J.
    Go Ahead & Live. Keats.
    Go Ahead & Live. Philos Lib.
Loomis, Noel M.
  xLoomis, Noel M.
    Pedro Vial & the Roads to Santa Fe. U of Okla
    Pr.
Loomis, Roger S. *see* Loomis, Roger Sherman.
Loomis, Roger Sherman, 1887-1966
  xLoomis, Roger S.
    ed. Arthurian Literature in the Middle Ages: A
    Collaborative History. Oxford U Pr.
    Development of Arthurian Romance. Norton.
    Illustrations of Medieval Romance on Tiles
    from Chertsey Abbey. Johnson Repr.
    ed. Studies in Medieval Literature: A Memorial
    Collection of Essays. B Franklin.
Loomis, Ruth.
  xLoomis, Ruth.
    Valley of the Hawk. Dial.
Loomis, Samuel L. *see* Loomis, Samuel Lane.
Loomis, Samuel Lane, 1856-1938
  xLoomis, Samuel L.
    Modern Cities & Their Religious Problems.
    Arno.
Loomis, Ted A.
  xLoomis, Ted A.
    Essentials of Toxicology. Lea & Febiger.
Loomis, William F.
  xLoomis, William F.
    Dictyostelium Discoideum: A Developmental
    System. Acad Pr.
Loon, Dirk Van. *see* Van Loon, Dirk.
Loon, Hendrick W. Van. *see* Van Loon, Hendrick W.
Loon, Hendrick W. Van. *see* Van Loon, Hendrick W.

Loon, Jon C. Van. *see* Van Loon, Jon C.
Looney, J. W.
  xLooney, J. W.
    Estate Planning for Farmers. Doane
    Agricultural.
Looney, Robert E.
  xLooney, Robert E.
    The Economic Development of Panama: The
    Impact of World Inflation on an Open
    Economy. Praeger.
Looper, Travis.
  xLooper, Travis.
    Byron & the Bible: A Compendium of Biblical
    Usage in the Poetry of Lord Byron.
    Scarecrow.
Loor, F.
  xLoor, F.
    ed. B & T Cells in Immune Recognition. Wiley.
Loos. *see* Loos, Anita.
Loos, Amandus W. *see* Loos, Amandus William.
Loos, Amandus William, 1908-
  xLoos, Amandus W.
    ed. Religious Faith & World Culture. Arno.
Loos, Anita, 1894-
  xLoos.
    Cast of Thousands. G&D.
  xLoos, Anita.
    San Francisco: A Screenplay. S Ill U Pr.
Loos, John.
  xLoos, John.
    Chilton's Mobile Home Maintenance Guide.
    Chilton.
Loos, Madge.
  xLoos, Madge.
    Puppet Without Worlds. Golden Quill.
Loos, O. G. *see* Loos, Ottmar.
Loos, Ottmar.
  xLoos, O. G.
    Jordan Pairs. Springer-Verlag.
Loose, K. E. *see* Loose, Kurt Egon.
Loose, Kurt Egon.
  xLoose, K. E.
    ed. Atlas of Angiography. PSG Pub.
Loovis, David.
  xLoovis, David.
    Straight Answers About Homosexuality for
    Straight Readers. B&N.
Lopata, Helena Z. *see* Lopata, Helena Znaniecka.
Lopata, Helena Znaniecka, 1925-
  xLopata, Helena Z.
    Women As Widows: Support Systems. Elsevier.
Lopate, Carol.
  xLopate, Carol.
    Education & Culture in Brooklyn: A History of
    Ten Institutions. Bklyn Educ.
Lopate, Phillip, 1943-
  xLopate, Phillip.
    The Daily Round: New Poems. SUN.
Loper. *see* Loper, Orla E.
Loper, Orla. *see* Loper, Orla E.
Loper, Orla E.
  xLoper.
    Direct Current Fundamentals. Delmar.
  xLoper, Orla.
    Introduction to Electricity & Electronics.
    Delmar.
  xLoper, Orla E.
    Direct Current Fundamentals. Van Nos
    Reinhold.
Lopez, A. *see* Lopez, Adalberto.
Lopez, Adalberto.
  xLopez, A.
    ed. Puerto Rico & the Puerto Ricans: Studies
    in History & Society. Halsted Pr.
  xLopez, Adalberto.
    ed. Puerto Rico & the Puerto Ricans: Studies
    in History & Society. Schenkman.
    Revolt of the Comuneros: A Study in the
    Colonial History of Paraguay. Schenkman.
Lopez, Barry H. *see* Lopez, Barry Holstun.

Lopez, Barry Holstun, 1945-
  xLopez, Barry H.
    Desert Notes: Reflections in the Eye of a
    Raven. Andrews & McMeel.
    Giving Birth to Thunder, Sleeping with His
    Daughter: Coyote Builds North America.
    Andrews & McMeel.
    Of Wolves & Men. Scribner.
    River Notes: The Dance of the Herons.
    Andrews & McMeel.
    River Notes: The Dance of the Herons. Avon.
Lopez, Carlos U.
  xLopez, Carlos U.
    Chilenos in California: A Study of the 1850,
    1852 & 1860 Censuses. R & E Res Assoc.
Lopez, Claude Anne.
  xLopez, Claude-Anne.
    The Private Franklin: The Man & His Family.
    Norton.
Lopez, Claude-Anne. *see* Lopez, Claude Anne.
Lopez, Enrique Hank.
  xLopez, Enrique Hank.
    Eros & Ethos: A Comparative Study of
    Catholic, Jewish & Protestant Sex Behavior.
    P-H.
Lopez, Jorge M.
  xLopez, Jorge M.
    Sidon Sets. Dekker.
Lopez, Nancy.
  xLopez, Nancy.
    The Education of a Woman Golfer.
    Cornerstone.
    The Education of a Woman Golfer. S&S.
Lopez y Rivas, Gilberto.
  xLopez Y Rivas, Gilberto.
    Conquest & Resistance: The Origins of the
    Chicano National Minority. R & E Res
    Assoc.
Lopez-Rey, Jose.
  xLopez-Rey, Jose.
    Goya's Caprichos, Beauty Reason &
    Caricature. Greenwood.
Lopshire, Robert.
  xLopshire, Robert.
    illus. How to Make Snop Snappers & Other
    Fine Things. Greenwillow.
    illus. I Am Better Than You. Har-Row.
    Put Me in the Zoo. Beginner.
    Radio Control Miniature Aircraft. Macmillan.
Lopukhin, Iurii Mikhailovich.
  xLopukhin, Y. M.
    Hemosorption. Mosby.
Lopukhin, Y. M. *see* Lopukhin, Iurii Mikhailovich.
Lora, G. *see* Lora, Guillermo.
Lora, Guillermo.
  xLora, G.
    A History of the Bolivian Labour Movement
    1848-1971. Cambridge U Pr.
Lora, Ronald.
  xLora, Ronald.
    Conservative Minds in America. Greenwood.
Loram, Charles T. *see* Loram, Charles Templeman.
Loram, Charles Templeman, 1879-1940
  xLoram, Charles T.
    Education of the South African Native. Negro
    U Pr.
Lorand, Rhoda L.
  xLorand, Rhoda L.
    Love, Sex & the Teenager. Macmillan.
Lorange, Peter.
  xLorange, Peter.
    Corporate Planning: An Executive Viewpoint.
    P-H.
    Strategic Planning Systems. P-H.
Lorant, Stefan, 1901-
  xLorant, Stefan.
    Pittsburgh: The Story of an American City.
    Authors Edn.
Lorayne, Harry.
  xLorayne, Harry.

Good Memory-Good Student: A Guide to
Remembering What You Learn.
Elsevier-Nelson.
How to Develop a Super-Power Memory.
NAL.
How to Develop a Super-Power Memory. Fell.
The Memory Book. Ballantine.
Memory Book. Stein & Day.
Lorca, Federico Garcia. *see* Garcia Lorca, Federico.
Lorch, Fred W. *see* Lorch, Frederick William.
Lorch, Frederick William, 1893-1967
xLorch, Fred W.
Trouble Begins at Eight: Mark Twain's Lecture
Tours. Iowa St U Pr.
Lorch, Robert S. *see* Lorch, Robert Stuart.
Lorch, Robert Stuart, 1925-
xLorch, Robert S.
Democratic Process & Administrative Law.
Wayne St U Pr.
Public Administration. West Pub.
Lord, B. I. *see* Lord, Brian Iles.
Lord, Brian Iles.
xLord, B. I.
ed. Stem Cells & Tissue Homeostasis.
Cambridge U Pr.
Lord, Clifford L. *see* Lord, Clifford Lee.
Lord, Clifford Lee, 1912-
xLord, Clifford L.
Teaching History with Community Resources.
Tchrs Coll.
Lord, Eda.
xLord, Eda.
Childsplay. S&S.
Matter of Choosing. S&S.
Lord, Edith.
xLord, Edith.
Queen of Sheba's Heirs: Cultural Patterns of
Ethiopia. Acropolis.
Lord, Eleanor L. *see* Lord, Eleanor Louisa.
Lord, Eleanor Louisa, 1866-
xLord, Eleanor L.
Industrial Experiments in the British Colonies
of North America. AMS Pr.
Industrial Experiments in the British Colonies
of North America. B Franklin.
Lord, Francis A. *see* Lord, Francis Alfred.
Lord, Francis Alfred.
xLord, Francis A.
Bands & Drummer Boys of the Civil War. Da
Capo.
Lord, Frederic M.
xLord, Frederic M.
Statistical Theories of Mental Test Scores.
A-W.
Lord, George. *see* Lord, George De Forest.
Lord, George D. *see* Lord, George De Forest.
Lord, George De Forest, 1919-
xLord, George.
ed. Anthology of Poems on Affairs of State:
Augustan Satirical Verse, 1660-1714. Yale U
Pr.
xLord, George D.
Homeric Renaissance: The Odyssey of George
Chapman. Shoe String.
Lord, Guy.
xLord, Guy.
The French Budgetary Process. U of Cal Pr.
Lord, Harold W.
xLord, Harold W.
Noise Control for Engineers. McGraw.
Lord, J. Dennis. *see* Lord, Jerry Dennis.
Lord, James.
xLord, James.
A Giacometti Portrait. FS&G.
Lord, Jeffrey.
xLord, Jeffrey.

The Crystal Seas. Pinnacle Bks.
Ice Dragon. Pinnacle Bks.
Looters of Tharn. Pinnacle Bks.
Lord, Jerry Dennis.
xLord, J. Dennis.
Spatial Perspectives on School Desegregation &
Busing. Assn Am Geographers.
Lord, John V. *see* Lord, John Vernon.
Lord, John Vernon.
xLord, John V.
jt. auth. The Giant Jam Sandwich. HM.
Lord, Kenniston W.
xLord, Kenniston W.
CDP Review Manual: A Data Processing
Handbook. Van Nos Reinhold.
Lord, Lindsay.
xLord, Lindsay.
Nautical Etiquette & Customs. Cornell
Maritime.
Lord, Louis E. *see* Lord, Louis Eleazer.
Lord, Louis Eleazer, 1875-1957
xLord, Louis E.
Aristophanes: His Plays & His Influence.
Cooper Sq.
Lord, May.
xLord, May C.
On a High Hill. Blair.
Lord, May C. *see* Lord, May.
Lord, Moira.
xLord, Moira.
Nightingale Park. NAL.
Lord, Robert H. *see* Lord, Robert Howard.
Lord, Robert Howard, 1885-1954
xLord, Robert H.
Origins of the War of 1870: New Documents
from the German Archives. Russell.
Lord, Russell, 1895-1964
xLord, Russell.
Men of Earth. Arno.
Lord, Shirley.
xLord, Shirley.
The Easy Way to Good Looks. T y Crowell.
Lord, Sterling, 1920-
xLord, Sterling.
Returning the Serve Intelligently. Doubleday.
Lord, Suzanne.
xLord, Suzanne.
American Travelers' Treasury: A Guide to the
Nation's Heirlooms. Morrow.
Lord, Tom F. *see* Lord, Tom Forrester.
Lord, Tom Forrester.
xLord, Tom F.
Decent Housing: A Promise to Keep.
Schenkman.
Lord, Walter, 1917-
xLord, Walter.
The Dawn's Early Light. Norton.
A Night to Remember. HR&W.
Night to Remember. Bantam.
Night to Remember. HR&W.
Lord, Walter E. *see* Lord, Walter Frewen.
Lord, Walter Frewen, 1861-1927
xLord, Walter E.
England & France in the Mediterranean
1660-1830. Kennikat.
Lorde, Audre.
xLorde, Audre.
Coal. Norton.
From a Land Where Other People Live.
Broadside.
Lore, John M.
xLore, John M.
An Atlas of Head & Neck Surgery. Saunders.
Loree, M. Ray.
xLoree, M. Ray.
Psychology of Education. Wiley.
Loree, Sharron.
xLoree, Sharron.

illus. The Sunshine Family & the Pony. HM.
Loren, Charles.
xLoren, Charles.
Classes in the United States: Workers Against
Capitalists. Cardinal Pubs.
Loren, Teri.
xLoren, Teri.
The Dancer's Companion: The Indispensable
Guide to Getting the Most Out of Dance
Classes. Dial.
Lorentz, G. G.
xLorentz, G. G.
ed. Approximation Theory. Acad Pr.
Lorenz, Felix A.
xLorenz, Felix A.
The Only Hope. Southern Pub.
Lorenz, Konrad.
xLorenz, Konrad.
Civilized Man's Eight Deadly Sins. HarBraceJ.
Evolution & Modification of Behavior. U of
Chicago Pr.
On Aggression. HarBraceJ.
Studies in Animal & Human Behaviour.
Harvard U Pr.
The Year of the Greylag Goose. HarBraceJ.
Lorenz, Marian B. *see* Lorenz, Marian Brown.
Lorenz, Marian Brown.
xLorenz, Marian B.
Patterns of American English: A Guide for
Speakers of Other Languages. Oceana.
Lorenzo, Carol L. *see* Lorenzo, Carol Lee.
Lorenzo, Carol Lee.
xLorenzo, Carol L.
The White Sand Road. Har-Row.
Loretto, M. H.
xLoretto, M. H.
Defect Analysis in Electron Microscopy.
Methuen Inc.
Lorge, Irving, 1905-
xLorge, Irving.
Influence of Regularly Interpolated Time
Intervals Upon Subsequent Learning. AMS
Pr.
Lorge Formula for Estimating Difficulty of
Reading Materials. Tchrs Coll.
Lorhan, Paul H., 1908-
xLorhan, Paul H.
Anesthesia for the Aged. C C Thomas.
Lorian, Victor.
xLorian, Victor.
Antibiotics in Laboratory Medicine. Williams &
Wilkins.
Significance of Medical Microbiology in the
Care of Patients. Williams & Wilkins.
Lorillard, Didi.
xLorillard, Didi.
New York City Slicker: A Counterchic Guide
to Manhattan. Viking Pr.
Lorimer, Frank, 1894-
xLorimer, Frank.
Culture & Human Fertility: A Study of the
Relation of Cultural Conditions to Fertility in
Non-Industrial & Transitional Societies.
Greenwood.
The Population of the Soviet Union: History &
Prospects. AMS Pr.
Lorimer, Graeme.
xLorimer, Graeme.
Men Are Like Street Cars. Arno.
Lorimer, Larry. *see* Lorimer, Lawrence T.
Lorimer, Lawrence T.
xLorimer, Larry.
The Tennis Book. Random.
xLorimer, Lawrence T.
The Football Book. Random.
Lorin, Harold.
xLorin, Harold.

Comparative Economic Systems. Har-Row.
Loud, Warren S. *see* Loud, Warren Simms.
Loud, Warren Simms, 1921-
xLoud, Warren S.
Periodic Solutions of Perturbed Second-Order
Autonomous Equations. Am Math.
Louden, J. Keith.
xLouden, J. Keith.
The Effective Director in Action. Am Mgmt.
Louden, Louise.
xLouden, Louise.
Foam & Foam Control. Inst Paper Chem.
Odors & Odor Control. Inst Paper Chem.
Louden, Robert K.
xLouden, Robert K.
Programming the IBM 1130. P-H.
Loudon, David L.
xLoudon, David L.
Consumer Behavior: Concepts & Applications.
McGraw.
Loudon, K. M.
xLoudon, K. M.
Two Mystic Poets & Other Essays. Folcroft.
Loudon, Rodney.
xLoudon, Rodney.
The Quantum Theory of Light. Oxford U Pr.
Lough, John.
xLough, John.
An Introduction to Nineteenth Century France.
Longman.
Writer & Public in France: From the Middle
Ages to the Present Day. Oxford U Pr.
Lough, Marvin D.
xLough, Marvin D.
Newborn Respiratory Care. Year Bk Med.
Pediatric Respiratory Therapy. Year Bk Med.
Loughary, John W. *see* Loughary, John William.
Loughary, John William.
xLoughary, John W.
Helping Others Help Themselves: A Guide to
Counseling Skills. McGraw.
This Isn't Quite What I Had in Mind: A
Career Planning Program for College
Students. Follett.
Lougheed, Victor.
xLougheed, Victor.
Vehicles of the Air: A Popular Exposition of
Modern Aeronautics with Working Drawings.
Arno.
Loughhead, Larue A.
xLoughhead, LaRue A.
Eyewitnesses at the Cross. Judson.
Loughlin, David.
xLoughlin, David.
The Case of Major Fanshawe's Chairs.
Universe.
Loughran, John X.
xLoughran, John X.
Ninety Days to a Better Heart. Arc Bks.
Lougy, Robert E.
xLougy, Robert E.
Charles Robert Maturin. Bucknell U Pr.
Louie, Elaine.
xLouie, Elaine.
Manhattan Clothes Shopping Guide.
Macmillan.
Manhattan Clothes Shopping Guide.
Macmillan.
The Manhattan Home Furnishings Shopping
Guide. Macmillan.
Louie, Kam.
xLouie, Kamm.
Critiques of Confucius in Contemporary China.
St Martin.
Louie, Kamm. *see* Louie, Kam.
Louis, C. J. *see* Louis, Chris John.
Louis, Chris John.
xLouis, C. J.

Tumours: Basic Principles & Clinical Aspects.
Churchill.
Louis Harris & Associates, Inc. *see* Louis Harris and
Associates.
Louis Harris and Associates.
xLouis Harris & Associates, Inc.
Harris Nineteen Seventy-Two American
Women's Opinion Poll. ICPSR.
Louis, Karen S. *see* Louis, Karn Seashore.
Louis, Karn Seashore.
xLouis, Karen S.
ed. Bureaucracy & the Dispersed Organization:
The Educational Extension Agent
Experiment. Ablex Pub.
Louis, Victor. *see* Louis, Victor E.
Louis, Victor E.
xLouis, Victor.
The Coming Decline of the Chinese Empire.
Times Bks.
The Complete Guide to the Soviet Union. St
Martin.
Louis, William R. *see* Louis, Wm. Roger.
Louis, Wm. Roger.
xLouis, William R.
Imperialism at Bay: The United States &
the Decolonization of the British Empire,
1941-1945. Oxford U Pr.
National Security & International Trusteeship
in the Pacific. Naval Inst Pr.
Louisell, David W.
xLouisell, David W.
Federal Evidence. Lawyers Co-Op.
Louisell, William H. *see* Louisell, William Henry.
Louisell, William Henry, 1924-
xLouisell, William H.
Quantum Statistical Properties of Radiation.
Wiley.
Radiation & Noise in Quantum Electronics.
Krieger.
Louisiana District Judges Association.
xLa. Dis. Judges.
Judges of Louisiana. Claitors.
xLockheed Aircraft Corporation.
Of Men & Stars: A History of Lockheed
Aircraft Corporation. Arno.
Louisiana Historical Association.
xLouisiana Historical Association, New Orleans.
Calendar of the Jefferson Davis Post War
Manuscripts in the Louisiana Historical
Association Collection. B Franklin.
Louisiana Historical Association, New Orleans. *see*
Louisiana Historical Association.
Loukes, Harold.
xLoukes, Harold.
Friends & Their Children: A Study in Quaker
Education. Greenwood.
Lounsbury, Floyd G.
xLounsbury, Floyd G.
Oneida Verb Morphology. HRAFP.
Lounsbury, John F.
xLounsbury, John F.
Earth Science. Har-Row.
A Workbook for Weather & Climate. Wm C
Brown.
Lounsbury, John H.
xLounsbury, John H.
A Curriculum for the Middle School Years.
Har-Row.
Lounsbury, Ralph G. *see* Lounsbury, Ralph Greenlee.
Lounsbury, Ralph Greenlee, 1896-
xLounsbury, Ralph G.
British Fishery at Newfoundland, 1634-1763.
Shoe String.
Lounsbury, T. R. *see* Lounsbury, Thomas Raynesford.
Lounsbury, Thomas R. *see* Lounsbury, Thomas
Raynesford.
Lounsbury, Thomas Raynesford, 1838-1915
xLounsbury, T. R.
History of the English Language. Gordon Pr.
xLounsbury, Thomas R.

The Early Literary Career of Robert Browning:
Four Lectures. Norwood Edns.
History of the English Language. R West.
Lounsbury, Warren C.
xLounsbury, Warren C.
Theatre Backstage from A to Z. U of Wash Pr.
Lourie, Dick.
xLourie, Dick.
Anima. Hanging Loose.
Lourie, Richard, 1940-
xLourie, Richard.
Letters to the Future: An Approach to
Sinyavsky-Tertz. Cornell U Pr.
Louthan, William C.
xLouthan, William C.
Politics of Justice: A Study in Law, Social
Science & Public Policy. Kennikat.
Loutit, M. W. *see* Loutit, Margaret W.
Loutit, Margaret W.
xLoutit, M. W.
ed. Microbial Ecology. Springer-Verlag.
Loux, Michael J.
xLoux, Michael J.
Intro. by The Possible & the Actual: Readings
in the Metaphysics of Modality. Cornell U
Pr.
Love, Frank, 1926-
xLove, Frank.
Arizona's Story: A Short History. Pruett.
Love, Glen A., 1932-
xLove, Glen A.
Don Berry. Boise St Univ.
Love, Harold, 1937-
xLove, Harold.
Congreve. Rowman.
Love, Harold D.
xLove, Harold D.
Early Childhood Education: A Methods &
Materials Book. C C Thomas.
Educating Exceptional Children in a Changing
Society. C C Thomas.
Teaching Physically Handicapped Children:
Methods & Materials. C C Thomas.
Love, John. *see* Love, John F.
Love, John F.
xLove, John.
Chess Battle Strategies. Sterling.
Love, Katherine. *see* Love, Katherine Isabel.
Love, Katherine Isabel, 1907-
xLove, Katherine.
ed. Little Laughter. T Y Crowell.
Love, Marie, 1891-
xLove, Marie.
Chronicles of a Texas Pioneer. Stevenson Pr.
Love, Milton. *see* Love, Milton S.
Love, Milton S.
xLove, Milton.
ed. Readings in Ichthyology. Goodyear.
Love, Robert W. *see* Love, Robert William.
Love, Robert William, 1944-
xLove, Robert W.
The Chiefs of Naval Operations. Naval Inst Pr.
Love, Sam.
xLove, Sam.
ed. Ecotage. PB.
Love, Sandra.
xLove, Sandra.
But What About Me. HarBraceJ.
Melissa's Medley. HarBraceJ.
Love, Stephen. *see* Love, Stephen F.
Love, Stephen F.
xLove, Stephen.
Inventory Control. McGraw.
Love, Sydney F.
xLove, Sydney F.
Mastery & Management of Time. P-H.
Planning & Creating Successful Engineered
Designs. Van Nos Reinhold.
Love, T. W.
xLove, T. W.

Stair Builders Handbook. Craftsman.
Love, William. see Love, William D.
Love, William D.
xLove, William.
ed. Options & Perspectives: A Sourcebook of
Innovative Foreign Language Programs in
Action, K-12. Modern Lang.
Lovecraft, H. P. see Lovecraft, Howard Phillips.
Lovecraft, Howard P. see Lovecraft, Howard Phillips.
Lovecraft, Howard Phillips, 1890-1937
xLovecraft, H. P.
Horror in the Museum & Other Revisions.
Arkham.
The Horror in the Museum & Other Revisions.
Ballantine.
xLovecraft, Howard P.
Something About Cats, & Other Pieces. Arno.
Supernatural Horror in Literature. Dover.
Supernatural Horror in Literature. Peter Smith.
Loveday, Alexander, 1888-1962
xLoveday, Alexander.
Reflections on International Administration.
Greenwood.
Loveday, R. see Loveday, Robert.
Loveday, Robert.
xLoveday, Robert.
First Course in Statistics. Cambridge U Pr.
Practical Statistics & Probability. Cambridge U
Pr.
xLoveday, Robert.
Statistics. Cambridge U Pr.
Lovejoy, Arthur O. see Lovejoy, Arthur Oncken.
Lovejoy, Arthur Oncken, 1873-
xLovejoy, Arthur O.
The Reason, The Understanding & Time. Johns
Hopkins.
Reflections on Human Nature. Johns Hopkins.
Lovejoy, David S. see Lovejoy, David Sherman.
Lovejoy, David Sherman, 1919-
xLovejoy, David S.
The Glorious Revolution in America. Har-Row.
Rhode Island Politics & the American
Revolution, 1760-1776. Brown U Pr.
Lovejoy, Elijah P., 1940-
xLovejoy, Elijah P.
Statistics for Math Haters. Har-Row.
Lovejoy, Frederick A.
xLovejoy, Frederick A.
Divestment for Profit. Finan Exec.
Lovejoy, Wallace F. see Lovejoy, Wallace Francis.
Lovejoy, Wallace Francis.
xLovejoy, Wallace F.
Economic Aspects of Oil Conservation
Regulation. Johns Hopkins.
Lovelace, Austin C. see Lovelace, Austin Cole.
Lovelace, Austin Cole.
xLovelace, Austin C.
Music & Worship in the Church. Abingdon.
Lovelace, Linda.
xLovelace, Linda.
Ordeal. Citadel Pr.
Lovelace, Maud H. see Lovelace, Maud Hart.
Lovelace, Maud Hart.
xLovelace, Maud H.
Betsy & Tacy Go Downtown. Har-Row.
Betsy & Tacy Go Downtown. T Y Crowell.
Betsy-Tacy & Tib. Har-Row.
Betsy-Tacy & Tib. T Y Crowell.
Lovelace, Richard F.
xLovelace, Richard F.
Homosexuality & the Church. Revell.
Loveland, D. W. see Loveland, Donald W.
Loveland, Donald W.
xLoveland, D. W.
Automated Theorem Proving: A Logical Basis.
Elsevier.
Loveland, John.
xLoveland, John.

Blessed Assurance: The Life & Hymns of
Fanny J. Crosby. Broadman.
Loveland, Marion, 1917-
xLoveland, Marion F.
America Laughs: A Sampler. Collegium Bk
Pubs.
Loveland, Marion F. see Loveland, Marion.
Loveless, Anthony.
xLoveless, Anthony.
Genetic & Allied Effects of Alkylating Agents.
Pa St U Pr.
Lovell, A. see Lovell, Alan.
Lovell, Alan.
xLovell, A.
Anarchist Cinema. Gordon Pr.
Lovell, Alfred Charles Bernard, Sir, 1913-
xLovell, Bernard.
In the Center of Immensities. Har-Row.
The Origins & International Economics of
Space Exploration. Halsted Pr.
Lovell, Bernard. see Lovell, Alfred Charles Bernard.
Lovell, John C. see Lovell, John Christopher.
Lovell, John Christopher.
xLovell, John C.
Stevedores & Dockers: A Study of Trade
Unionism in the Port of London, 1870-1914.
Kelley.
Lovell, John P., 1932-
xLovell, John P.
Neither Athens nor Sparta: The American
Service Academies in Transition. Ind U Pr.
Lovell, K. see Lovell, Kenneth.
Lovell, Kenneth.
xLovell, K.
The Growth of Basic Mathematical & Scientific
Concepts in Children. Philos Lib.
An Introduction to Human Development. Scott
F.
Lovell, Marc.
xLovell, Marc.
Hand Over Mind. Doubleday.
Lovell, Percy. see Lovell, Percy W.
Lovell, Percy W.
xLovell, Percy.
ed. Parish of St. Pancras. AMS Pr.
Lovell, R. R. see Lovell, Richard Robert Haynes.
Lovell, Richard Robert Haynes.
xLovell, R. R.
Introduction to Clinical Medicine. Intl Schol
Bk Serv.
Lovell, S.
xLovell, S.
An Introduction to Radiation Dosimetry.
Cambridge U Pr.
Lovelock, Christopher. see Lovelock, Christopher H.
Lovelock, Christopher H.
xLovelock, Christopher.
Cases in Public & Nonprofit Marketing.
Scientific Pr.
Lovelock, William.
xLovelock, William.
A Student's Dictionary of Music. Ungar.
Lovelock, Yann.
xLovelock, Yann.
The Vegetable Book: An Unnatural History. St
Martin.
Lovely, Yvonne, 1921-
xLovely, Yvonne.
Practical Secretary's Manual & Guide. P-H.
Loveman, Brian.
xLoveman, Brian.
Chile: The Legacy of Hispanic Capitalism.
Oxford U Pr.
ed. The Politics of Antipolitics: The Military in
Latin America. U of Nebr Pr.
Struggle in the Countryside: A Documentary
Supplement. Intl Development.
Loven, Sven, 1875-
xLoven, Sven.

Origins of the Tainan Culture, West Indies.
AMS Pr.
Loveridge, Raymond.
xLoveridge, Raymond.
Collective Bargaining by National Employees
in the United Kingdom. U of Mich Inst
Labor.
Lovesey, Peter.
xLovesey, Peter.
A Case of Spirits. Penguin.
Swing, Swing Together. Dodd.
Swing, Swing Together. Penguin.
Waxwork. Penguin.
Lovesey, Stephen W.
xLovesey, Stephen W.
Condensed Matter Physics: Dynamic
Correlations. A-W.
Lovett, Clara M. see Lovett, Clara Maria.
Lovett, Clara Maria, 1939-
xLovett, Clara M.
Giuseppe Ferrari & the Italian Revolution. U of
NC Pr.
Lovett, H. Verney. see Lovett, Harrington Verney.
Lovett, Harrington Verney, Sir, 1864-1945
xLovett, H. Verney.
History of the Indian Nationalist Movement.
Kelley.
xLovett, V.
History of the Indian Nationalist Movement.
Biblio Dist.
xLovett, Verney.
A History of the Indian Nationalist Movement.
Intl Pubns Serv.
Lovett, Howard M. see Lovett, Howard Meriwether.
Lovett, Howard Meriwether.
xLovett, Howard M.
Grandmother Stories from the Land of
Used-to-Be. Reprint.
Lovett, Robert M. see Lovett, Robert Morss.
Lovett, Robert Morss, 1870-1956
xLovett, Robert M.
Edith Wharton. Folcroft.
The History of the Novel in England. Folcroft.
History of the Novel in England. Scholarly.
Preface to Fiction: A Discussion of Great
Modern Novels. Arno.
Lovett, Robert W. see Lovett, Robert Woodberry.
Lovett, Robert Woodberry.
xLovett, Robert W.
ed. American Economic & Business History
Information Sources. Gale.
Lovett, V. see Lovett, Harrington Verney.
Lovett, Verney. see Lovett, Harrington Verney.
Lovette, Roger, 1935-
xLovette, Roger.
Journey Toward Joy. Judson.
Lovgren, George. see Lovgren, George K.
Lovgren, George K.
xLovgren, George.
illus. The Art of Inner Seeing. Karl Bern Pubs.
xLovgren, George K.
The Art of Inner Seeing. Karl Bern Pubs.
Lovin, Roger.
xLovin, Roger.
The Complete Motorcycle Nomad: A Guide to
Machines, Equipment, People & Places.
Little.
Lovinger, Sophie L.
xLovinger, Sophie L.
Learning Disabilities & Games. Nelson-Hall.
Lovinggood, Penman.
xLovinggood, Penman.
Famous Modern Negro Musicians. Da Capo.
Lovins, Amory, 1947-
xLovins, Amory B.

Soft Energy Paths: Toward a Durable Peace.
  Ballinger Pub.
Soft Energy Paths: Toward a Durable Peace.
  Har-Row.
World Energy Strategies: Facts, Issues, &
  Options. Har-Row.
Lovins, Amory. see Lovins, Amory B.
Lovins, Amory B.
  xLovins, Amory.
  The Energy Controversy: Soft Path Questions
    & Answers. Friends Earth.
Lovins, Amory B. see Lovins, Amory.
Lovisone, Carter.
  xLovisone, Carter.
  The Disco Hustle. Sterling.
Lovitt, Thomas C.
  xLovitt, Thomas C.
  ed. Classroom Application of Precision
    Teaching. Spec Child.
  In Spite of My Resistance, I've Learned from
    Children. Merrill.
Lovoos, Janice.
  xLovoos, Janice.
  Frederic Whitaker. Northland.
Lovrich, Nicholas P.
  xLovrich, Nicholas P.
  Yugoslavs & Italians in San Pedro: Political
    Culture & Civic Involvement. Ragusan Pr.
Lovy, Charles W.
  xLovy, Charles W.
  Silhouette De la France: A First Reader in
    French Civilization. Wiley.
Low, Abraham A. see Low, Abraham Adolph.
Low, Abraham Adolph, 1891-1954
  xLow, Abraham A.
  Lectures to Relatives of Former Patients. Chris
    Mass.
Low, Alfred D.
  xLow, Alfred D.
  Jews in the Eyes of the Germans: From the
    Enlightenment to Imperial Germany. Inst
    Study Human.
Low, D. A. see Low, Donald Anthony.
Low, David, Sir, 1891-1963
  xLow, David.
  Europe Since Versailles: A History in One
    Hundred Cartoons with a Narrative Text.
    Garland Pub.
Low, Donald.
  xLow, Donald A.
  That Sunny Dome: A Portrait of Regency
    Britain. Rowman.
Low, Donald A. see Low, Donald.
Low, Donald Anthony.
  xLow, D. A.
  Buganda in Modern History. U of Cal Pr.
  ed. Soundings in Modern South Asian History.
    U of Cal Pr.
Low, Elizabeth.
  xLow, Elizabeth.
  Hold Fast the Dream. G&D.
Low, F. see Low, Francis E.
Low, Francis, Sir, 1893-
  xLow, Francis.
  Struggle for Asia. Arno.
Low, Francis E.
  xLow, F.
  Symmetries & Elementary Particles. Gordon.
Low, Janet.
  xLow, Janet.
  Understanding the Stock Market: A Guide for
    Young Investors. Little.
Low, Joseph, 1911-
  xLow, Joseph.

The Christmas Grump. Atheneum.
illus. Five Men Under One Umbrella: And
  Other Ready-to-Read Riddles. Macmillan.
My Dog, Your Dog. Macmillan.
illus. Trust Reba. McGraw.
Low, Richard E.
  xLow, Richard E.
  Modern Economic Organization. Irwin.
Low, Rosemary.
  xLow, Rosemary.
  Parrots: Their Care & Breeding. Sterling.
Low, Sidney J. see Low, Sidney James Mark.
Low, Sidney James Mark.
  xLow, Sidney J.
  History of England During the Reign of
    Victoria, 1837-1901. AMS Pr.
  History of England During the Reign of
    Victoria, 1837-1901. Greenwood.
  History of England During the Reign of
    Victoria, 1837-1907. Haskell.
Low, Theodore L. see Low, Theodore Lewis.
Low, Theodore Lewis, 1915-
  xLow, Theodore L.
  The Educational Philosophy & Practice of Art
    Museums in the United States. AMS Pr.
Low, Vaike.
  xLow, Vaike.
  Drip & Drop: From the Clouds & Back.
    Heineman.
Lowance, Mason I., 1938-
  xLowance, Mason I.
  The Language of Canaan: Metaphor & Symbol
    in New England from the Puritans to the
    Transcendentalists. Harvard U Pr.
  ed. Massachusetts Broadsides of the American
    Revolution. U of Mass Pr.
Lowder, Richard E.
  xLowder, Richard E.
  Cribbage Is the Name of the Game. Har-Row.
Lowe, Alfonso.
  xLowe, Alfonso.
  The Catalan Vengeance. Routledge & Kegan.
Lowe, C. Marshall, 1930-
  xLowe, C. Marshall.
  Value Orientations in Counseling &
    Psychotherapy: The Meanings of Mental
    Health. Carroll Pr.
Lowe, C. R. see Lowe, Christopher R.
Lowe, C. W. see Lowe, Cecil William.
Lowe, Cecil William.
  xLowe, C. W.
  Industrial Statistics. Beekman Pubs.
Lowe, Christopher R.
  xLowe, C. R.
  Affinity Chromatography. Wiley.
  An Introduction to Affinity Chromatography.
    Elsevier.
Lowe, David.
  xLowe, David.
  Costing & Pricing Goods Vehicle Operations.
    Intl Pubns Serv.
  Lost Chicago. HM.
Lowe, E. Nobles. see Lowe, Edwin Nobles.
Lowe, Edwin Nobles.
  xLowe, E. Nobles.
  Legal & Other Aspects of Terrorism. PLI.
Lowe, Gordon K. see Lowe, Gordon R.
Lowe, Gordon R.
  xLowe, Gordon K.
  The Growth of Personality: From Infancy to
    Old Age. Penguin.
  xLowe, Gordon R.
  The Growth of Personality: From Infancy to
    Old Age. Gannon.
Lowe, Jacqueline.
  xLowe, Jacqueline.
  The Language of Show Dancing. Scribner.
Lowe, Jeff.
  xLowe, Jeff.

The Ice Experience. Contemp Bks.
Lowe, Patrica. see Lowe, Patricia Tracy.
Lowe, Patricia Tracy.
  xLowe, Patrica.
  The Tale of the Golden Cockerel. T Y Crowell.
Lowe, Paul. see Lowe, Paul Henry.
Lowe, Paul Henry.
  xLowe, Paul.
  Investment for Production: Managing the Plant
    Investment Process. Halsted Pr.
Lowe, Robert S. see Lowe, Robert William.
Lowe, Robert W. see Lowe, Robert William.
Lowe, Robert William, 1853-1902
  xLowe, Robert S.
  Thomas Betterton. Folcroft.
  xLowe, Robert W.
  Thomas Betterton. AMS Pr.
Lowe, Victor, 1907-
  xLowe, Victor.
  Understanding Whitehead. Johns Hopkins.
Lowe, William, 1929-
  xLowe, William.
  City Life. Hayden.
Lowe, William C.
  xLowe, William C.
  Introduction to Acupuncture Anesthesia. Med
    Exam.
Lowell, A. Lawrence. see Lowell, Abbott Lawrence.
Lowell, Abbot Lawrence, 1856-1943
  xLowell, Abbott L.
  Public Opinion & Popular Government.
    Johnson Repr.
Lowell, Abbott L. see Lowell, Abbott Lawrence.
Lowell, Abbott Lawrence, 1856-1943
  xLowell, A. Lawrence.
  Governments & Parties in Continental Europe.
    Kennikat.
  xLowell, Abbott L.
  At War with Academic Traditions in America.
    Greenwood.
  Public Opinion in War & Peace. Arno.
Lowell, Amy, 1874-1925
  xLowell, Amy.
  Can Grande's Castle. Scholarly.
Lowell, Edward J. see Lowell, Edward Jackson.
Lowell, Edward Jackson, 1845-1894
  xLowell, Edward J.
  Eve of the French Revolution. AMS Pr.
Lowell, Florence.
  xLowell, Florence.
  Be a Guest at Your Own Party. M Evans.
Lowell, Fred R.
  xLowell, Fred R.
  Wheat Market. Keltner.
Lowell, James R. see Lowell, James Russell.
Lowell, James Russell, 1819-1891
  xLowell, James R.
  Among My Books. AMS Pr.
  Among My Books. Arden Lib.
  Among My Books. Folcroft.
  Among My Books. Scholarly.
  Anti-Slavery Papers of James Russell Lowell.
    Negro U Pr.
  Function of the Poet & Other Essays.
    Kennikat.
  Literary Criticism of James Russell Lowell. U
    of Nebr Pr.
  Literary Essays. Arno.
  The Old English Dramatists. R West.
  Uncollected Poems. Greenwood.
Lowell, Josephine (Shaw), 1843-1905
  xLowell, Josephine S.
  Public Relief & Private Charity. Arno.
Lowell, Josephine S. see Lowell, Josephine (Shaw).
Lowell, Mildred H. see Lowell, Mildred Hawksworth.
Lowell, Mildred Hawksworth.
  xLowell, Mildred H.
  Library Management Cases. Scarecrow.
Lowell, Robert, 1917-
  xLowell, Robert.

Day by Day. FS&G.
The Dolphin. FS&G.
History. FS&G.
Imitations. FS&G.
Near the Ocean: Poems. FS&G.
Old Glory. FS&G.
Prometheus Bound. FS&G.
Lowell, S. see Lowell, Seymour.
Lowell, Seymour, 1931-
xLowell, S.
Introduction to Powder Surface Area. Wiley.
Lowen, Alexander.
xLowen, Alexander.
Depression & the Body: The Biological Basis of
Faith & Reality. Penguin.
Lowenberg, Miriam E. see Lowenberg, Miriam Elizabeth.
Lowenberg, Miriam Elizabeth.
xLowenberg, Miriam E.
Food & People. Wiley.
Lowenbraun, Sheila.
xLowenbraun, Sheila.
Teaching Mildly Handicapped Children in
Regular Classes. Merrill.
Lowenfeld, Berthold.
xLowenfeld, Berthold.
The Changing Status of the Blind: From
Separation to Integration. C C Thomas.
Our Blind Children: Growing & Learning with
Them. C C Thomas.
Lowenfeld, Margaret, 1890-
xLowenfeld, Margaret.
The World Technique. Allen Unwin.
Lowenfeld, Viktor.
xLowenfeld, Viktor.
Creative & Mental Growth. Macmillan.
Lowenfels, Albert B.
xLowenfels, Albert B.
Companion Guide to Surgical Diagnosis.
Williams & Wilkins.
Lowenfels, Walter, 1897-
xLowenfels, Walter.
Found Poems & Others. Barlenmir.
Portable Walter: From the Prose & Poetry of
Walter Lowenfels. Intl Pub Co.
The Revolution Is to Be Human. Intl Pub Co.
Lowenherz, Robert J.
xLowenherz, Robert J.
Population. Creative Ed.
Lowenkopf, Martin.
xLowenkopf, Martin.
Politics in Liberia: The Conservative Road to
Development. Hoover Inst Pr.
Lowens, Irving, 1916-
xLowens, Irving.
Music & Musicians in Early America. Norton.
Lowenstein, Bertrand E.
xLowenstein, Bertrand E.
Diabetes: New Look at an Old Problem.
Har-Row.
Lowenstein, Dino. see Lowenstein, Dyno.
Lowenstein, Dyno.
xLowenstein, Dino.
Graphs. Watts.
Lowenthal, Abraham F.
xLowenthal, Abraham F.
Dominican Intervention. Harvard U Pr.
Latin America's Emergence: Toward a U. S.
Response. Foreign Policy.
Lowenthal, David. see Lowenthal, David T.
Lowenthal, David T.
xLowenthal, David.
ed. Therapeutics Through Exercise. Grune.
Lowenthal, Esther, 1883-
xLowenthal, Esther.
Ricardian Socialists. Kelley.
The Ricardian Socialists. Octagon.
Lowenthal, Franklin, 1938-
xLowenthal, Franklin.

Linear Algebra with Linear Differential
Equations. Wiley.
Lowenthal, Leo.
xLowenthal, Leo.
Literature, Popular Culture & Society. Pacific
Bks.
Prophets of Deceit: A Study of the Techniques
of the American Agitator. Pacific Bks.
Lowenthal, Marjorie Fiske.
xLowenthal, Marjorie F.
Aging & Mental Disorder in San Francisco: A
Social Psychiatric Study. Jossey-Bass.
Lowenthal, Marjorie F. see Lowenthal, Majorie Fiske.
Lowenthal, Mark M.
xLowenthal, Mark M.
Crispan Magicker. Avon.
Lowenthal, Max, 1888-
xLowenthal, Max.
Federal Bureau of Investigation. Greenwood.
Lowenthal, Richard, 1908-
xLowenthal, Richard.
World Communism: The Disintegration of a
Secular Faith. Oxford U Pr.
Lower, Arthur R. see Lower, Arthur Reginald Marsden.
Lower, Arthur Reginald Marsden.
xLower, Arthur R.
North American Assault on the Canadian
Forest: A History of the Lumber Trade
Between Canada & the United States.
Greenwood.
Lower, Kenneth F.
xLower, Kenneth F.
The Complete Handbook of Practical Car
Repair. TAB Bks.
Lowery, Barbara.
xLowery, Barbara.
Oil. Watts.
Lowery, Daniel L.
xLowery, Daniel L.
Life & Love: The Commandments for
Teenagers. Paulist Pr.
Lowery, James L.
xLowery, James L.
ed. Case Histories of Tentmakers. Morehouse.
Peers, Tents, & Owls: Some Solutions to
Problems of the Clergy Today. Morehouse.
Lowery, Lawrence. see Lowery, Lawrence F.
Lowery, Lawrence F.
xLowery, Lawrence.
The Everyday Science Sourcebook: Ideas for
Teaching in the Elementary & Middle
School. Allyn.
Lowes, Bryan.
xLowes, Bryan.
Modern Managerial Economics. Intl Pubns
Serv.
Lowes, John L. see Lowes, John Livingston.
Lowes, John Livingston, 1867-1945
xLowes, John L.
Art of Geoffrey Chaucer. Arno.
Art of Geoffrey Chaucer. Folcroft.
Lowi, Theodore J.
xLowi, Theodore J.
Legislative Politics U. S. A. Little.
ed. Nationalizing Government: Public Policies
in America. Sage.
Politics of Disorder. Basic.
The Politics of Disorder. Norton.
xLowi, Theodore S.
The End of Liberalism: The Second Republic
of the United States. Norton.
Lowi, Theodore S. see Lowi, Theodore J.
Lowie, Robert H. see Lowie, Robert Harry.
Lowie, Robert Harry, 1883-1957
xLowie, Robert H.

The Assiniboine. AMS Pr.
The German People: A Social Portrait to 1914.
Octagon.
The Material Culture of the Crow Indians.
AMS Pr.
The Northern Shoshone. AMS Pr.
Notes on Hopi Clans & Hopi Kinship. AMS
Pr.
Primitive Religion. Liveright.
Primitive Society. Liveright.
The Religion of the Crow Indians. AMS Pr.
The Sun Dance of the Crow Indians. AMS Pr.
Toward Understanding Germany. U of Chicago
Pr.
Lowitt, Richard, 1922-
xLowitt, Richard.
America in Depression & War. Forum Pr MO.
George W. Norris: The Making of a
Progressive, 1861 to 1912. Greenwood.
George W. Norris: The Persistence of a
Progressive, 1913-1933. U of Ill Pr.
George W. Norris: The Triumph of a
Progressive, 1933-1944. U of Ill Pr.
Lowitz, Sadyebeth.
xLowitz, Sadyebeth.
Barefoot Abe. Dell.
Lowndes, G. A. see Lowndes, George Alfred Norman.
Lowndes, George Alfred Norman.
xLowndes, G. A.
Silent Social Revolution: An Account of the
Expansion of Public Education in England &
Wales, 1895-1965. Oxford U Pr.
Lowndes, Marie A. see Lowndes, Marie Adelaide Belloc.
Lowndes, Marie Adelaide Belloc, 1868-1947
xLowndes, Marie A.
The End of Her Honeymoon. Arno.
Lowndes, Rosemary.
xLowndes, Rosemary.
A World of Costumes in Cut-Out. HR&W.
Lownds, Camille.
xLownds, Camille.
Foil Around & Stay Fit: Exercise Secrets of a
Fencer. HarBraceJ.
Lowrance, William W., 1943-
xLowrance, William W.
Of Acceptable Risk: Science & the
Determination of Safety. W Kaufmann.
Lowrey, George H.
xLowrey, George H.
Growth & Development of Children. Year Bk
Med.
Lowrey, Janette (Sebring), 1892-
xLowrey, Janette S.
Margaret. Har-Row.
Lowrey, Janette S. see Lowrey, Janette (Sebring).
Lowrie, Samuel H. see Lowrie, Samuel Harman.
Lowrie, Samuel Harman, 1894-
xLowrie, Samuel H.
Culture Conflict in Texas, 1821-1835. AMS Pr.
Lowrie, Walter, 1868-1959
xLowrie, Walter.
Art in the Early Church. Norton.
Art in the Early Church. Peter Smith.
Lowry, Bates.
xLowry, Bates.
ed. The Architecture of Washington, D. C.
Dunlap Soc.
ed. The Architecture of Washington, D.C.
Dunlap Soc.
Renaissance Architecture. Braziller.
Lowry, Beverly.
xLowry, Beverly.
Come Back, Lolly Ray. Doubleday.
Come Back, Lolly Ray. Popular Lib.
Emma Blue. Doubleday.
Emma Blue. Popular Lib.
Lowry, Gertrude S., 1898-
xLowry, Gertrude S.

The Wheel of Truth: An Ancestral Saga.
Exposition.
Lowry, Goodrich.
xLowry, Goodrich.
Streetcar Man: Tom Lowry & the Twin City
Rapid Transit Company. Lerner Pubns.
Lowry, J H.
xLowry, J. H.
World Population & Food Supply.
Crane-Russak Co.
Lowry, James K., 1942-
xLowry, James K.
Soft Bottom Macrobenthic Community of
Arthur Harbor, Antarctica: Paper 1 in
Biology of the Antarctic Seas V. Am
Geophysical.
Lowry, Lois.
xLowry, Lois.
Anastasia Krupnik. HM.
Autumn Street. HM.
Find a Stranger, Say Good-Bye. HM.
Find a Stranger, Say Goodbye. Archway.
Find a Stranger, Say Goodbye. PB.
A Summer to Die. HM.
A Summer to Die. Bantam.
Lowry, M. J. see Lowry, Martin.
Lowry, Malcolm.
xLowry, Malcolm.
Notes on a Screenplay for F. Scott Fitzgerald's
Tender Is the Night. Bruccoli.
October Ferry to Gabriola. NAL.
Under the Volcano. Lippincott.
Under the Volcano. NAL.
Lowry, Martin.
xLowry, M. J.
The World of Aldus Manutius: Business &
Scholarship in Renaissance Venice. Cornell U
Pr.
Lowry, Oliver H.
xLowry, Oliver H.
Flexible System of Enzymatic Analysis. Acad
Pr.
Lowry, Thomas H.
xLowry, Thomas H.
Mechanism & Theory in Organic Chemistry.
Har-Row.
Lowry, Thomas P.
xLowry, Thomas P.
The Clitoris. Green.
Lowry, W. T. see Lowry, William Thomas.
Lowry, William Thomas.
xLowry, W. T.
Forensic Toxicology: Controlled Substances &
Dangerous Drugs. Plenum Pub.
Lowy, Louis.
xLowy, Louis.
Social Work with the Aging: The Challenge &
Promise of the Later Years. Har-Row.
Lowy, Michael.
xLowy, Michael.
The Marxism of Che Guevara: Philosophy,
Economics, & Revolutionary Warfare.
Monthly Rev.
Loy, William G.
xLoy, William G.
Atlas of Oregon. U of Oreg Bks.
Loyd, Lewis C. see Loyd, Lewis Christopher.
Loyd, Lewis Christopher, 1875-1947
xLoyd, Lewis C.
The Origins of Some Anglo-Norman Families.
Genealog Pub.
Loyn, H. R. see Loyn, Henry Royston.
Loyn, Henry Royston.
xLoyn, H. R.
ed. The Reign of Charlemagne: Documents on
Carolingian Government & Administration.
St Martin.
Lozanov, G. see Lozanov, Georgi.
Lozanov, Georgi.
xLozanov, G.

Suggestology & Outlines of Suggestopedy.
Gordon.
Lozowick, Lee.
xLozowick, Lee.
In the Fire. IDHHB.
Lu, David J.
xLu, David J.
Sources of Japanese History. McGraw.
Lu, Pau-Chang, 1930-
xLu, Pau-Chang.
Fluid Mechanics: An Introductory Course.
Iowa St U Pr.
Luard, David Evan Trant, 1926-
xLuard, Evan.
Socialism Without the State. St Martin.
Types of International Society. Free Pr.
Luard, Evan. see Luard, David Evan Trant.
Luard, Nicholas.
xLuard, Nicholas.
The Shadow Spy. Ballantine.
The Shadow Spy. HarBraceJ.
Lubans, John.
xLubans, John.
ed. Progress in Educating the Library User.
Bowker.
ed. Reader in Library Systems Analysis.
IHS-PDS.
Lubavitch Women's Organization.
xLubavitch Womens Organization.
The Spice & Spirit of Kosher-Jewish Cooking.
Lubavitch Women.
Lubavitch Womens Organization. see Lubavitch
Women'S Organization.
Lubbock, Percy, 1879-
xLubbock, Percy.
Earlham. Arden Lib.
Earlham. Greenwood.
Lubchenco, Lula O.
xLubchenco, Lula O.
The High Risk Infant. Saunders.
Lubell, Samuel.
xLubell, Samuel.
The Future While It Happened. Norton.
Lubell, Winifred.
xLubell, Winifred.
Street Markets Around the World. Enslow
Pubs.
Luber, R. F. see Luber, Raymond F.
Luber, Raymond F.
xLuber, R. F.
ed. Partial Hospitalization: A Current
Perspective. Plenum Pub.
Lubich, Chiara, 1920-
xLubich, Chiara.
Servants of All. New City.
That All Men Be One: Origins & Life of the
Focolare Movement. New City.
When Did We See You Lord?. New City.
When Our Love Is Charity. New City.
Lubienska De Lenval, Helena. see Lubienska De Lenval,
Helene.
Lubienska De Lenval, Helene.
xLubienska De Lenval, Helena.
How to Teach Religion. Franciscan Herald.
Lubin, Bernard.
xLubin, Bernard.
Group Psychotherapy: A Bibliography of the
Literature from 1956 Through 1964. Mich St
U Pr.
Lubin, George.
xLubin, George.
Handbook of Fiberglass & Advanced Plastics
Composites. Krieger.
Lubin, Leonard. see Lubin, Leonard B.
Lubin, Leonard B.
xLubin, Leonard.
illus. The White Cat. Little.
Lubke, Wilhelm, 1826-1893
xLubke, Wilhelm.

Ecclesiastical Art in Germany During the
Middle Ages. Longwood Pr.
Luboff, Eileen B. see Luboff, Eileen Baris.
Luboff, Eileen Baris.
xLuboff, Eileen B.
How to Collect Your Child Support &
Alimony. Nolo Pr.
Lubove. see Lubove, Roy.
Lubove, R. see Lubove, Roy.
Lubove, Roy.
xLubove.
Pittsburgh. New Viewpoints.
xLubove, R.
Poverty & Social Welfare in the United States.
Krieger.
xLubove, Roy.
Professional Altruist: The Emergence of Social
Work As a Career, 1880-1930. Atheneum.
Twentieth Century Pittsburgh: Government,
Business & Environmental Change. Wiley.
Lubrano, Linda L.
xLubrano, Linda L.
ed. The Social Context of Soviet Science.
Westview.
Lubs, Herbert. see Lubs, Herbert Augustus.
Lubs, Herbert Augustus.
xLubs, Herbert.
ed. Genetic Counseling. Raven.
Luca, Anthony De. see De Luca, Anthony.
Luca, Louis J. De. see De Luca, Louis J.
Lucarini, Spartaco.
xLucarini, Spartaco.
The Difficult Role of a Father. New City.
Lucas, Alan.
xLucas, Alan.
Illustrated Encyclopedia of Boating. Scribner.
Lucas, Christopher J.
xLucas, Cristopher J.
Our Western Educational Heritage. Macmillan.
Lucas, Clarence, 1866-1947
xLucas, Clarence.
The Story of Musical Form. Longwood Pr.
Lucas, Cristopher J. see Lucas, Christopher J.
Lucas, Dione.
xLucas, Dione.
The Dione Lucas Book of French Cooking.
Little.
Lucas, E. V. see Lucas, Edward Verrall.
Lucas, Edward V. see Lucas, Edward Verrall.
Lucas, Edward Verrall, 1868-1938
xLucas, E. V.
The Colvins & Their Friends. R West.
Reading, Writing & Remembering: A Literary
Record. Arden Lib.
xLucas, Edward V.
Adventures & Misgivings. Arno.
All of a Piece: New Essays. Arno.
Another Book of Verses for Children. Arno.
Compiled by Book of Verses for Children.
Arno.
Cloud & Silver. Arno.
Colvins & Their Friends. Scholarly.
Only the Other Day: A Volume of Essays.
Arno.
Reading, Writing, & Remembering: A Literary
Record. Scholarly.
Lucas, F. L. see Lucas, Frank Laurence.
Lucas, Frank L. see Lucas, Frank Laurence.
Lucas, Frank Laurence, 1894-1967
xLucas, F. L.
Euripides & His Influence. Gordon Pr.
xLucas, Frank L.

Authors Dead & Living. Arno.
Critical Thoughts in Critical Days. Folcroft.
The Criticism of Poetry. Arden Lib.
Criticism of Poetry. Folcroft.
The Drama of Chekhov, Synge, Yeats &
   Pirandello. Gordian.
Euripides & His Influence. Cooper Sq.
Studies French & English. Arno.
Lucas, Henry C.
   xLucas, Henry C.
   Casebook for Management Information
      Systems. McGraw.
   Computer-Based Information Systems in
      Organizations. SRA.
Lucas, Henry S. see Lucas, Henry Stephen.
Lucas, Henry Stephen, 1889-1961
   xLucas, Henry S.
   The Low Countries & the Hundred Years'
      War 1326-1347. Porcupine Pr.
Lucas, I. B. see Lucas, Isaac B.
Lucas, Isaac B.
   xLucas, I. B.
   Dwarf Fruit Trees for Home Gardens. Peter
      Smith.
Lucas, Jack.
   xLucas, Jack.
   Our Polluted Food: A Survey of the Risks.
      Halsted Pr.
Lucas, James. see Lucas, James Sidney.
Lucas, James Sidney.
   xLucas, James.
   Panzer Army Africa. Presidio Pr.
Lucas, Jerry.
   xLucas, Jerry.
   Theomatics: God's Best Kept Secret Revealed.
      Stein & Day.
Lucas, Joseph.
   xLucas, Joseph.
   Life in the Oceans. Dutton.
Lucas, Paul D., 1932-
   xLucas, Paul D.
   Accounting Guide for Construction
      Contractors. Dell.
Lucas, Paul R.
   xLucas, Paul R.
   Valley of Discord: Church & Society Along the
      Connecticut River, 1636-1725. U Pr of New
      Eng.
Lucas, Peter J.
   xLucas, Peter J.
   ed. Exodus. Methuen Inc.
Lucas, R. B. see Lucas, Raleigh Barclay.
Lucas, Raleigh Barclay, M.d.
   xLucas, R. B.
   Pathology of Tumours of the Oral Tissues.
      Churchill.
Lucas, Richard. see Lucas, Richard Melvin.
Lucas, Richard Melvin, 1918-
   xLucas, Richard.
   Common & Uncommon Uses of Herbs for
      Healthful Living. Arc Bks.
   Common & Uncommon Uses of Herbs for
      Healthful Living. P-H.
   Secrets of the Chinese Herbalists. Cornerstone.
   Secrets of the Chinese Herbalists. P-H.
Lucas, Scott, 1937-
   xLucas, Scott.
   The FDA. Celestial Arts.
Lucas, Stephen E.
   xLucas, Stephen E.
   Portents of Rebellion: Rhetoric & Revolution in
      Philadelphia, 1765-1776. Temple U Pr.
Lucas, Ted.
   xLucas, Ted.
   How to Convert to an Electric Car. Crown.
Lucchesi, Bruno.
   xLucchesi, Bruno.
   Modeling the Head in Clay. Watson-Guptill.
Luccock, Halford E. see Luccock, Halford Edward.

Luccock, Halford Edward, 1885-1960
   xLuccock, Halford E.
   American Mirror: Social, Ethical & Religious
      Aspects of American Literature, 1930-1940.
      Cooper Sq.
   Enter the Crocus. Pilgrim NY.
Luccock, Halford Edwards.
   xLuccock, Halford E.
   A Sprig of Holly. Pilgrim NY.
Luce, Arthur A. see Luce, Arthur Aston.
Luce, Arthur Aston, 1882-
   xLuce, Arthur A.
   Life of George Berkeley, Bishop of Cloyne.
      Greenwood.
Luce, Clare (Boothe), 1903-
   xLuce, Clare B.
   Stuffed Shirts. Arno.
Luce, Clare B. see Luce, Clare (Boothe).
Luce, Gladness W. see Luce, Gladness Wharton.
Luce, Gladness Wharton.
   xLuce, Gladness W.
   Hamlet in the Hills: The Story of Parker Hill,
      Vermont. Phoenix Pub.
Luce, Marnie.
   xLuce, Marnie.
   Counting Systems: The Familiar & the
      Unusual. Lerner Pubns.
   One Is Unique. Lerner Pubns.
   Primes Are Builders. Lerner Pubns.
Luce, Robert D. see Luce, Robert Duncan.
Luce, Robert Duncan.
   xLuce, Robert D.
   Individual Choice Behavior: A Theoretical
      Analysis. Greenwood.
Luce, S. B. see Luce, Stephen Bleecker.
Luce, Stanford, 1923-
   xLuce, Stanford.
   A Glossary of Celine's Fiction with English
      Translations. Univ Microfilms.
Luce, Stephen Bleecker, 1827-1917
   xLuce, S. B.
   Naval Songs: A Collection of Original,
      Selected, Traditional Sea Songs. Longwood
      Pr.
Luce, T. J. see Luce, Torrey James.
Luce, Torrey James, 1932-
   xLuce, T. J.
   Livy: The Composition of His History.
      Princeton U Pr.
Luce, Willard.
   xLuce, Willard.
   Utah. Peregrine Smith.
Lucero. see Lucero, Faustina H.
Lucero, Faustina H.
   xLucero.
   Little Indians' ABC. Oddo.
Lucey, Dan.
   xLucey, Dan.
   Living, Loving Generation. Glencoe.
   Living Loving Generation. Our Sunday Visitor.
Lucey, William L. see Lucey, William Leo.
Lucey, William Leo, 1903-
   xLucey, William L.
   Catholic Church in Maine. O'Brien.
Luchs, Alvin S. see Luchs, Alvin Schanfarber.
Luchs, Alvin Schanfarber.
   xLuchs, Alvin S.
   Torchbearers of the Middle Ages. Arno.
Luchs, Esther M. see Luchs, Esther-Martina.
Luchs, Esther-Martina.
   xLuchs, Esther M.
   Yoga for Children. Paulist Pr.
Luchsinger, Judith. see Luchsinger, Judith A. H.
Luchsinger, Judith A. H.
   xLuchsinger, Judith.
   Practical Self-Defense for Women: A Manual
      of Prevention & Escape Techniques. Dillon.
Luchsinger, Vincent P.
   xLuchsinger, Vincent P.

The Systems Approach: A Primer.
   Kendall-Hunt.
Luchterhand, Elmer.
   xLuchterhand, Elmer.
   Choice in Human Affairs: An Application to
      Aging-Accident-Illness Problems. Coll & U
      Pr.
Luciani, V. J.
   xLuciani, V. J.
   Guide to Unusual Contests in America.
      Cologne Pr.
Luciani, Vincent, 1906-
   xLuciani, Vincent.
   A Brief History of Italian Literature. S F
      Vanni.
Luciani, Vincent. see Luciani, Vincnt.
Luciani, Vincnt, 1906-
   xLuciani, Vincent.
   A Concise History of the Italian Theatre. S F
      Vanni.
Luciano, 1934-
   xLuciano.
   Stained Glass Window Art. Music Sales.
Lucid, Daniel P. see Lucid, Daniel Peri.
Lucid, Daniel Peri.
   xLucid, Daniel P.
   ed. Soviet Semiotics: An Anthology. Johns
      Hopkins.
Lucie-Smith, Edward.
   xLucie-Smith, Edward.
   Late Modern: The Visual Arts Since 1945.
      Oxford U Pr.
   Outcasts of the Sea: Pirates & Piracy.
      Paddington.
   ed. Penguin Book of Elizabethan Verse.
      Penguin.
   Symbolist Art. Oxford U Pr.
Lucio, William H.
   xLucio, William H.
   Supervision in Thought & Action. McGraw.
Luciw, Wasyl.
   xLuciw, Wasyl.
   Ukrainians & the Polish Revolt of 1863: A
      Contribution to the History of
      Ukrainian-Polish Relations. Slavia Lib.
Luck, David J. see Luck, David Johnston.
Luck, David Johnston.
   xLuck, David J.
   Marketing Research. P-H.
Luck, G. Coleman.
   xLuck, G. Coleman.
   First Corinthians. Moody.
Luck, G Coleman.
   xLuck, G. Coleman.
   Daniel. Moody.
Luck, J. Murray. see Luck, James Murray.
Luck, James Murray.
   xLuck, J. Murray.
   ed. Modern Switzerland. SPOSS.
Luckau, Alma. see Luckau, Alma Maria.
Luckau, Alma Maria, 1908-
   xLuckau, Alma.
   The German Delegation at the Paris Peace
      Conference. Fertig.
Luckert, Karl W., 1934-
   xLuckert, Karl W.
   Coyoteway: A Navajo Holyway Healing
      Ceremonial. U of Ariz Pr.
   A Navajo Bringing-Home Ceremony: The
      Claus Chee Sonny Version of Deerway
      Ajilee. Mus Northern Ariz.
   The Navajo Hunter Tradition. U of Ariz Pr.
   Navajo Mountain & Rainbow Bridge Religion.
      Mus Northern Ariz.
   Olmec Religion: A Key to Middle America &
      Beyond. U of Okla Pr.
Luckey, Thomas D.
   xLuckey, Thomas D.

Germfree Life & Gnotobiology. Acad Pr.

Luckham, Robin.
　xLuckham, Robin.
　　Nigerian Military: A Sociological Analysis of
　　Authority & Revolt, 1960-67. Cambridge U
　　Pr.
Luckhardt, Mildred C. *see* Luckhardt, Mildred Madeleine
　Corell.
Luckhardt, Mildred Madeleine Corell.
　xLuckhardt, Mildred C.
　　Compiled by Funny Stories to Read or Tell.
　　Abingdon.
Luckin, Joyce.
　xLuckin, Joyce.
　　Easy to Make Puppets. Plays.
Luckmann, Joan.
　xLuckmann, Joan.
　　Medical-Surgical Nursing: A Psychophysiologic
　　Approach. Saunders.
Luckmann, Thomas.
　xLuckmann, Thomas.
　　The Sociology of Language. Bobbs.
Luckyj, George S. *see* Luckyj, George Stephen Nestor.
Luckyj, George Stephen Nestor, 1919-
　xLuckyj, George S.
　　Literary Politics in the Soviet Ukraine
　　1917-1934. Arno.
Ludel, Jacqueline.
　xLudel, Jacqueline.
　　Introduction to Sensory Processes. W H
　　Freeman.
Ludlam, F. H.
　xLudlam, F. H.
　　Clouds & Storms: The Behavior & Effect of
　　Water in the Atmosphere. Pa St U Pr.
Ludlam, James E. *see* Ludlam, James F.
Ludlam, James F.
　xLudlam, James E.
　　Informed Consent. Am Hospital.
Ludlow, Daniel H.
　xLudlow, Daniel H.
　　A Companion to Your Study of the Doctrine &
　　Covenants. Deseret Bk.
Ludlum, Robert, 1927-
　xLudlum, Robert.
　　The Bourne Identity. Marek.
　　The Chancellor Manuscript. Bantam.
　　The Chancellor Manuscript. Dial.
　　The Gemini Contenders. Dell.
　　The Gemini Contenders. Dial.
　　The Holcroft Covenant. Bantam.
　　The Holcroft Covenant. Marek.
　　The Matarese Circle. Bantam.
　　The Matarese Circle. Marek.
　　The Matlock Paper. Dell.
　　The Osterman Weekend. Dell.
　　The Rhinemann Exchange. Dell.
　　The Rhinemann Exchange. Dial.
Ludman, Barbara.
　xLudman, Barbara.
　　Strays. Elsevier-Nelson.
Ludowyk, Evelyn F. *see* Ludowyk, Evelyn Fredrick
　Charles.
Ludowyk, Evelyn Fredrick Charles, 1906-
　xLudowyk, Evelyn F.
　　Understanding Shakespeare. Cambridge U Pr.
Ludwig, Arnold M.
　xLudwig, Arnold M.
　　Principles of Clinical Psychiatry. Free Pr.
Ludwig, Charles, 1918-
　xLudwig, Charles.
　　At the Cross. Pillar Bks.
　　Levi Coffin & the Underground Railroad.
　　Herald Pr.
　　Their Finest Hour. Cook.
Ludwig, D. *see* Ludwig, Donald.
Ludwig, Donald, 1933-
　xLudwig, D.

Stochastic Population Theories.
Springer-Verlag.
Ludwig, Emil, 1881-1948
　xLudwig, Emil.
　　Of Life & Love. Arno.
　　Torch of Freedom. Kennikat.
Ludwig, Ernest E.
　xLudwig, Ernest E.
　　Applied Project Management for the Process
　　Industries. Gulf Pub.
Ludwig, Herbert, 1939-
　xLudwig, Herbert R.
　　Computer Applications & Techniques in
　　Clinical Medicine. Krieger.
Ludwig, Herbert R. *see* Ludwig, Herbert.
Ludwig, Jan.
　xLudwig, Jan K.
　　ed. Philosophy & Parapsychology. Prometheus
　　Bks.
Ludwig, Jan K. *see* Ludwig, Jan.
Ludwig, Jerry. *see* Ludwig, Terry.
Ludwig, Jurgen.
　xLudwig, Jurgen.
　　Current Methods of Autopsy Practice.
　　Saunders.
Ludwig, Terry.
　xLudwig, Jerry.
　　Little Boy Lost. Delacorte.
Ludwigson, Kathryn R.
　xLudwigson, Kathryn R.
　　Edward Dowden. Twayne.
Ludwigson, Raymond.
　xLudwigson, Raymond.
　　A Survey of Bible Prophecy. Zondervan.
Ludz, Peter C. *see* Ludz, Peter Christian.
Ludz, Peter Christian, 1931-
　xLudz, Peter C.
　　Alienation As a Concept in the Social Sciences:
　　A Trend Report & Bibliography Prepared for
　　the International Sociological Association
　　Under the Auspices of the International
　　Committee for Social Science Information &
　　Documentation. Mouton.
　　ed. Changing Party Elite in East Germany.
　　MIT Pr.
　　Dilemmas of the Atlantic Alliance: Two
　　Germanys, Scandinavia, Canada, Nato & the
　　EEC. Praeger.
　　The German Democratic Republic from the
　　Sixties to the Seventies: A Socio-Political
　　Analysis. AMS Pr.
Luebke, Frederick C., 1927-
　xLuebke, Frederick C.
　　ed. Ethnic Voters & the Election of Lincoln. U
　　of Nebr Pr.
　　Immigrants & Politics: The Germans of
　　Nebraska, 1880-1900. U of Nebr Pr.
Luecke, Editha L. *see* Luecke, Editha Louise.
Luecke, Editha Louise, 1894-
　xLuecke, Editha L.
　　Factors Related to Children's Participation in
　　Certain Types of Home Activities. AMS Pr.
Luedemann, Judith. *see* Luedemann, Judith Miner Hine.
Luedemann, Judith Miner Hine.
　xLuedemann, Judith.
　　Ancestry of Harvey Dunn. Globe Pequot.
Lueders, Edward. *see* Lueders, Edward G.
Lueders, Edward G., 1923-
　xLueders, Edward.
　　Carl Van Vechten. Coll & U Pr.
Luenberger, D. G. *see* Luenberger, David G.
Luenberger, David G., 1937-
　xLuenberger, D. G.
　　Optimization by Vector Space Methods. Wiley.
　xLuenberger, David G.

Introduction to Dynamic Systems: Theory,
Models & Applications. Wiley.
Introduction to Linear & Nonlinear
Programming. A-W.
Luening, R. A.
　xLuening, R. A.
　　Farm Management Handbook. Interstate.
Luer, Carlyle A.
　xLuer, Carlyle A.
　　The Native Orchids of Florida. Barron.
　　Native Orchids of Florida. NY Botanical.
Luetscher, G. D. *see* Luetscher, George Daniel.
Luetscher, George Daniel.
　xLuetscher, G. D.
　　Early Political Machinery in the United States.
　　Da Capo.
Luft, Joseph.
　xLuft, Joseph.
　　Group Processes: An Introduction to Group
　　Dynamics. Mayfield Pub.
　　Of Human Interaction. Mayfield Pub.
Lugenbeal, Edward, 1940-
　xLugenbeal, Edward.
　　Who Killed Adam?: A Look at the Major
　　Types of Fossil Man. Southern Pub.
Luger, Harriett. *see* Luger, Harriett Mandelay.
Luger, Harriett Mandelay.
　xLuger, Harriett.
　　Lauren. Viking Pr.
Lugo, James O.
　xLugo, James O.
　　Human Development: A Psychological,
　　Biological, & Sociological Approach to the
　　Life Span. Macmillan.
　　Living Psychology: Research in Action.
　　Macmillan.
Luh, B. S. *see* Luh, Bor Shiun.
Luh, Bor Shiun.
　xLuh, B. S.
　　Commercial Vegetable Processing. AVI.
Luhman, Reid.
　xLuhman, Reid.
　　Race & Ethnic Relations:: The Social &
　　Political Experience of Minority Groups.
　　Wadsworth Pub.
Luijpen, W. A. *see* Luijpen, Wilhelmus Antonius Maria.
Luijpen, Wilhelmus Antonius Maria, 1922-
　xLuijpen, W. A.
　　Existential Phenomenology. Duquesne.
　　First Introduction to Existential
　　Phenomenology. Duquesne.
　xLuijpen, William A.
　　Religion & Atheism. Duquesne.
Luijpen, William A. *see* Luijpen, Wilhelmus Antonius
　Maria.
Luisada , Aldo A. *see* Luisada, Aldo Augusto.
Luisada, Aldo A. *see* Luisada, Aldo Augusto.
Luisada, Aldo Augusto.
　xLuisada , Aldo A.
　　An Atlas of Non-Invasive Techniques: Sound
　　& Pulse Tracings Echograms. C C Thomas.
　xLuisada, Aldo A.
　　A Primer of Cardiac Diagnosis: The Physical &
　　Technical Study of the Cardiac Patient.
　　Green.
　　Pulmonary Edema in Man & Animals. Green.
　　The Sounds of the Diseased Heart. Green.
　　The Sounds of the Normal Heart. Green.
Luisi, Billie.
　xLuisi, Billie.
　　A Practical Guide to Small-Scale Goatkeeping.
　　Rodale Pr Inc.
Luka, Ronald.
　xLuka, Ronald.
　　When a Christian & a Jew Marry. Paulist Pr.
Lukacs, E. *see* Lukacs, Eugene.
Lukacs, Eugene.
　xLukacs, E.
　　Characteristic Functions. Hafner.
　xLukacs, Eugene.

Probability & Mathematical Statistics: An Introduction. Acad Pr.

Lukacs, Georg. *see* Lukacs, Gyorgy.

Lukacs, George. *see* Lukacs, Gyorgy.

Lukacs, Gyorgy, 1885-1971
xLukacs, Georg.
Essays on Thomas Mann. Fertig.
Essays on Thomas Mann. Humanities.
Goethe & His Age. Fertig.
Goethe & His Age. Humanities.
Solzhenitsyn. MIT Pr.
Soul & Form. MIT Pr.
xLukacs, George.
Historical Novel. Humanities.

Lukacs, John. *see* Lukacs, John A.

Lukacs, John A.
xLukacs, John.
The Passing of the Modern Age. Har-Row.
xLukacs, John A.
Decline & Rise of Europe: A Study in Recent History with Particular Emphasis on the Development of a European Consciousness. Greenwood.

Lukaczer, Moses, 1911-
xLukaczer, Moses.
The Federal Buy Indian Program: Promise Versus Performance. Mojave Bks.

Lukas, J. Anthony, 1933-
xLukas, J. Anthony.
Don't Shoot - We Are Your Children. Random.

Lukas, Richard C., 1937-
xLukas, Richard C.
Eagles East: The Army Air Forces & the Soviet Union, 1941-1945. U Presses Fla.

Lukas, Susan. *see* Lukas, Susan Ries.

Lukas, Susan Ries.
xLukas, Susan.
Fat Emily. Stein & Day.

Lukash, William M.
xLukash, William M.
ed. The Systemic Manifestations of Inflammatory Bowel Disease. C C Thomas.

Lukaszewicz, Joseph.
xLukaszewicz, Joseph.
Girys I Biruta: Poemat Z Dawnych Czasow Litewskich. Endurance.

Luke, Barbara.
xLuke, Barbara.
Case Studies in Therapeutic Nutrition. Little.

Luke, Harry C. *see* Luke, Harry Charles Joseph.

Luke, Harry Charles Joseph, Sir, 1884-
xLuke, Harry C.
In the Margin of History. Arno.

Luke, Hugh D.
xLuke, Hugh D.
Automation for Productivity. Krieger.

Luke, Mary.
xLuke, Mary.
The Nonsuch Lure. Berkley Pub.
xLuke, Mary M.
The Nonsuch Lure. Coward.

Luke, Mary M. *see* Luke, Mary.

Luke, Yudell L.
xLuke, Yudell L.
Special Functions & Their Approximations. Acad Pr.

Lukeman, Tim.
xLukeman, Tim.
Rajan. Doubleday.

Lukens, R. J. *see* Lukens, Raymond J.

Lukens, Raymond J.
xLukens, R. J.
Chemistry of Fungicidal Action. Springer-Verlag.

Luker, Benjamin F. *see* Luker, Benjamin Franklin.

Luker, Benjamin Franklin, 1886-
xLuker, Benjamin F.

Use of the Infinitive Instead of a Finite Verb in French. AMS Pr.

Luker, Kristin.
xLuker, Kristin.
Taking Chances: Abortion & the Decision Not to Contracept. U of Cal Pr.

Lukes, Edward A.
xLukes, Edward A.
De Witt Colony of Texas. Jenkins.

Lukes, Steven.
xLukes, Steven.
Power: A Radical View. Humanities.

Lukesova, Milena.
xLukesova, Milena.
The Little Girl & the Rain. HR&W.

Lukinich, Imre, 1880-1950
xLukinich, Imre.
History of Hungary in Biographical Sketches. Arno.

Lukoff, Herman.
xLukoff, Herman.
From Dits to Bits: A Personal History of the Electronic Computer. Intl Schol Bk Serv.

Lukoff, Irving F. *see* Lukoff, Irving Faber.

Lukoff, Irving Faber.
xLukoff, Irving F.
Attitudes Toward Blind Persons. Am Foun Blind.

Lukomskii, A. S. *see* Lukomskii, Aleksandr Sergeevich.

Lukomskii, Aleksandr Sergeevich.
xLukomskii, A. S.
Memoirs of the Russian Revolution. Hyperion Conn.

Lukowski, Susan.
xLukowski, Susan.
Strategy & Tactics for Getting a Government Job. Potomac.

Luks, Alan. *see* Luks, Allan.

Luks, Allan.
xLuks, Alan
ed. Having Been There. Scribner.

Lull, Ramon.
xLull, Ramon.
The Art of Contemplation. Gordon Pr.
The Book of the Lover & the Beloved. Paulist Pr.

Lumb, Fred A.
xLumb, Fred A.
What Every Woman Should Know About Finances. Berkley Pub.
What Every Woman Should Know About Finances. Farnswth Pub.

Lumb, R. D.
xLumb, R. D.
Constitutions of the Australian States. U of Queensland Pr.
The Law of the Sea & Australian off-Shore Areas. U of Queensland Pr.

Lumb, T. W. *see* Lumb, Thomas Wallace.

Lumb, Thomas Wallace.
xLumb, T. W.
Authors of Greece. Kennikat.

Lumbra, Elaine.
xLumbra, Elaine.
ed. The Hoosier Cookbook. Ind U Pr.

Lumbreras, Luis G. *see* Lumbreras, Luis Guillermo.

Lumbreras, Luis Guillermo.
xLumbreras, Luis G.
The Peoples & Cultures of Ancient Peru. Smithsonian.

Lumerman, Harry.
xLumerman, Harry.
Essentials of Oral Pathology. Lippincott.

Lumian, Norman C.
xLumian, Norman C.
Living America. Van Nos Reinhold.

Lumiansky, Robert M. *see* Lumiansky, Robert Mayer.

Lumiansky, Robert Mayer.
xLumiansky, Robert M.

ed. Critical Approaches to Six Major English Works: Beowulf Through Paradise Lost. U of Pa Pr.

Lumley, Brian.
xLumley, Brian.
The Caller of the Black. Arkham.
The Horror at Oakdeene & Others. Arkham.

Lumley, James E. *see* Lumley, James E. A.

Lumley, James E. A.
xLumley, James E.
Real Estate Investment Guide. Realvest Pub Co.

Lumley, John L. *see* Lumley, John Leask.

Lumley, John Leask, 1930-
xLumley, John L.
Stochastic Tools in Turbulence. Acad Pr.

Lumpkin, William L. *see* Lumpkin, William Latane.

Lumpkin, William Latane.
xLumpkin, William L.
Baptist Confessions of Faith. Church History.
Baptist Confessions of Faith. Judson.

Lumpkin, Wilson.
xLumpkin, Wilson.
Removal of the Cherokee Indians from Georgia. Arno.
Removal of the Cherokee Indians from Georgia. Kelley.

Lumsden, George J.
xLumsden, George J.
Impact Management: Personal Power Strategies for Success. Am Mgmt.

Lumsden, Keith G.
xLumsden, Keith G.
ed. Efficiency in Universities: The La Paz Papers. Elsevier.

Luna, Frederick A. De. *see* De Luna, Frederick A.

Luna, Severino N.
xLuna, Severino N.
Born Primitive in the Philippines. S Ill U Pr.

Lunan, Duncan, 1945-
xLunan, Duncan
New Worlds for Old. Morrow.

Lund, Daulatram.
xLund, Daulatram.
Marketing Distribution: A Selected & Annotated Bibliography. Am Mktg.

Lund, Fred B. *see* Lund, Fred Bates.

Lund, Fred Bates, 1865-
xLund, Fred B.
Greek Medicine. AMS Pr.

Lund, James.
xLund, James.
The Ultimate. Riverrun Texas.

Lund, Leonard.
xLund, Leonard.
Corporate Organization for Environmental Policymaking. Conference Bd.
ed. Energy: Update & Outlook - November 1974. Conference Bd.

Lund, Marsha M. *see* Lund, Marsha Mayer.

Lund, Marsha Mayer, 1939-
xLund, Marsha M.
Indian Jewelry: Fact & Fantasy. Paladin Ent.
Indian Jewelry: Fact & Fantasy. Sycamore Island.

Lund, Philip R. *see* Lund, Philip Reginald.

Lund, Philip Reginald.
xLund, Philip R.
Compelling Selling: A Framework for Persuasion. Am Mgmt.

Lund, Preben, 1926-
xLund, Preben.
Generation of Precision Artwork for Printed Circuit Boards. Wiley.

Lund, Raymond D.
xLund, Raymond D.
Development & Plasticity of the Brain: An Introduction. Oxford U Pr.

Lund, Roger D., 1949-
xLund, Roger D.

Restoration & Early Eighteenth-Century
English Literature, 1660-1740: A Selected
Bibliography of Resource Materials. Modern
Lang.
Lund, T. W. *see* Lund, Thomas William May.
Lund, Thomas A. *see* Lund, Thomas Alan.
Lund, Thomas Alan, 1942-
xLund, Thomas A.
American Wildlife Law. U of Cal Pr.
Lund, Thomas William May.
xLund, T. W.
Matthew Arnold: The Message & Meaning of a
Life. Folcroft.
Lunday, Berneice, 1935-
xLunday, Berneice.
Unblessed. Southern Pub.
Lundberg, Donald E.
xLundberg, Donald E.
The Hotel & Restaurant Business. CBI Pub.
The Tourist Business. CBI Pub.
Lundberg, Eric. *see* Lundberg, Erik.
Lundberg, Erik, 1907-
xLundberg, Eric.
Instability & Economic Growth. Yale U Pr.
Lundberg, Ferdinand, 1902-
xLundberg, Ferdinand.
Cracks in the Constitution. Lyle Stuart.
Lundberg, George A. *see* Lundberg, George Andrew.
Lundberg, George Andrew, 1895-
xLundberg, George A.
Can Science Save Us?. Greenwood.
Foundations of Sociology. Greenwood.
Lundblad, Jane.
xLundblad, Jane.
Nathaniel Hawthorne & the Tradition of
Gothic Romance. Haskell.
Lundborg, Louis B.
xLundborg, Louis B.
Future Without Shock. Norton.
Lunde, Alfred E.
xLunde, Alfred E.
Christian Education Thru Music. Evang Tchr.
Lunde, Donald T.
xLunde, Donald T.
The Die Song: A Journey into the Mind of a
Mass Murderer. Norton.
Murder & Madness. Norton.
Murder & Madness. SF Bk Co.
The Next Generation: A Book on Parenting.
HR&W.
Lundegardh, Henrik. *see* Lundegardh, Henrik Gunnar.
Lundegardh, Henrik Gunnar, 1888-
xLundegardh, Henrik.
Environment & Plant Development. Hafner.
Lundell, A. T. *see* Lundell, Albert T.
Lundell, Albert T.
xLundell, A. T.
The Topology of CW Complexes.
Springer-Verlag.
Lundholm, Jean K.
xLundholm, Jean K.
Introduction to Synchronized Swimming.
Burgess.
Lundin, Jack W.
xLundin, Jack W.
A Church for an Open Future: Biblical Roots
& Parish Renewal. Fortress.
Lundin, Robert W.
xLundin, Robert W.
Theories & Systems of Psychology. Heath.
Lundin, Robert W. *see* Lundin, Robert William.
Lundin, Robert William.
xLundin, Robert W.
Personality: A Behavioral Analysis. Macmillan.
Lundkvist, Artur.
xLundkvist, Artur.
Agadir. Ohio U Pr.
Lundman, Richard J., 1944-
xLundman, Richard J.

ed. Police Behavior: A Sociological Perspective.
Oxford U Pr.
Lundquist, James.
xLundquist, James.
Chester Himes. Ungar.
J. D. Salinger. Ungar.
Theodore Dreiser. Ungar.
Lundsten, Lorman L., 1942-
xLundsten, Lorman L.
Market Share Forecasting for Banking Offices.
Univ Microfilms.
Lundstrom, John B.
xLundstrom, John B.
The First South Pacific Campaign: Pacific Fleet
Strategy, December 1941-June 1942. Naval
Inst Pr.
Lundstrom, Lowell.
xLundstrom, Lowell.
How to Enjoy Supernatural Prosperity. Harvest
Hse.
Lungwitz, Anton.
xLungwitz, Anton.
Textbook of Horseshoeing for Horseshoers &
Veterinarians. Oreg St U Pr.
Lunin, Lois F.
xLunin, Lois F.
ed. Health Sciences & Services: A Guide to
Information Sources. Gale.
Lunn, Arnold H. *see* Lunn, Arnold Henry Moore.
Lunn, Arnold Henry Moore, 1888-
xLunn, Arnold H.
The Revolt Against Reason. Greenwood.
Lunn, Eugene.
xLunn, Eugene.
Prophet of Community: The Romantic
Socialism of Gustav Landauer. U of Cal Pr.
Lunn, John E.
xLunn, John E.
Ralph Vaughan Williams: A Pictorial
Biography. Oxford U Pr.
Lunt, William E. *see* Lunt, William Edward.
Lunt, William Edward.
xLunt, William E.
Accounts Rendered by Papal Collectors in
England, 1317-1378. Am Philos.
tr. Papal Revenues in the Middle Ages.
Octagon.
Luoma, Gary A.
xLuoma, Gary A.
Accounting Information in Managerial
Decision-Making for Small & Medium
Manufacturers. Natl Assn Accts.
Luongo, Edward P., 1911-
xLuongo, Edward P.
American Medicine in Crisis. Philos Lib.
Lupo, Alan.
xLupo, Alan.
Liberty's Chosen Home: The Politics of
Violence in Boston. Little.
Lupold, Harry Forrest.
xLupold, Harry Forrest.
The Forgotten People: The Woodland Erie.
Exposition.
Lupton, Edward B. *see* Lupton, Edward Basil.
Lupton, Edward Basil.
xLupton, Edward B.
Dickens, the Immortal. Folcroft.
Lupton, Leonard.
xLupton, Leonard.
Canyon Country. Manor Bks.
Lupton, Thomas, fl. 1583
xLupton, Thomas.
All for Money. AMS Pr.
Lurch, E. Norman.
xLurch, E. Norman.
Fundamentals of Electronics. Wiley.
xLurch, Norman.
Electric Circuit Fundamentals. P-H.
xLurch, Norman E.

Fundamentals of Electronics. Wiley.
Lurch, Norman. *see* Lurch, E. Norman.
Lurch, Norman E. *see* Lurch, E. Norman.
Luria, S. E. *see* Luria, Salvador Edward.
Luria, Salvador Edward.
xLuria, S. E.
General Virology. Wiley.
Life: The Unfinished Experiment. Scribner.
Luria, Zella. *see* Luria, Zella Hurwitz.
Luria, Zella Hurwitz.
xLuria, Zella.
The Psychology of Human Sexuality. Wiley.
Lurie, Adolph G.
xLurie, Adolph G.
Working with the Public Accountant: A Guide
for Managers at All Levels. McGraw.
Lurie, Alison.
xLurie, Alison.
Only Children. Popular Lib.
Only Children. Random.
Only Children. G K Hall.
Real People. Avon.
Lurie, Charles N., 1879-
xLurie, Charles N.
Everyday Sayings: Their Meanings Explained,
Their Origins Given. Gale.
Lurie, Irene.
xLurie, Irene.
ed. Integrating Income Maintenance Programs.
Acad Pr.
Luschei, Martin.
xLuschei, Martin.
The Sovereign Wayfarer: Walker Percy's
Diagnosis of the Malaise. La State U Pr.
Luscombe, T. R.
xLuscombe, T. R.
Builders & Crusaders. Soccer.
Lusk, Harold F.
xLusk, Harold F.
jt. auth. Law of the Real Estate Business.
Irwin.
Luskin, Bernard J.
xLuskin, Bernard J.
Introduction to Economics: A
Performance-Based Learning Guide. HR&W.
Luskin, John.
xLuskin, John.
Lippmann, Liberty & the Press. U of Ala Pr.
Lussier, Ernest, 1911-
xLussier, Ernest.
Adore the Lord: Adoration Viewed Through
the Old Testament. Alba.
Christ's Farewell Discourse. Alba.
The Eucharist: The Bread of Life. Alba.
Getting to Know the Eucharist. Alba.
God Is Love: According to St. John. Alba.
Jesus Christ Is Lord: Adoration Viewed
Through the New Testament. Alba.
Living the Eucharistic Mystery. Alba.
Lust, John B.
xLust, John B.
Drink Your Troubles Away. Lust.
Lustbader, Eric Van. *see* Van Lustbader, Eric.
Lusterman, Seymour.
xLusterman, Seymour.
Industry Roles in Health Care. Conference Bd.
Lustgarten, Karen.
xLustgarten, Karen.
The Complete Guide to Disco Dancing.
Warner Bks.
The Complete Guide to Touch Dancing.
Warner Bks.
Lustgarten, Steven.
xLustgarten, Steven.
Industrial Concentration & Inflation. Am
Enterprise.
Lustick, Ian, 1949-
xLustick, Ian.

Arabs in the Jewish State: Israel's Control of a National Minority. U of Tex Pr.
Lustig, A. see Lustig, Arnost.
Lustig, Arnost.
xLustig, A.
A Prayer for Katerina Horovitzova. Avon.
xLustig, Arnost.
Dita Saxova. Har-Row.
Night and Hope. Avon.
A Prayer for Katerina Horovitzova. Har-Row.
Luszki, Walter A.
xLuszki, Walter A.
How to Test Your Dog's IQ. TAB Bks.
Luterman, David.
xLuterman, David.
Counseling Parents of Hearing-Impaired Children. Little.
Lutgens, F. see Lutgens, Frederick K.
Lutgens, Frederick K.
xLutgens, F.
Atmosphere: An Introduction to Meteorology. P-H.
Luthans, Fred.
xLuthans, Fred.
Contemporary Readings in Organizational Behavior. McGraw.
Introduction to Management: A Contingency Approach. McGraw.
Organizational Behavior. McGraw.
Organizational Behavior Modification. Scott F.
The Practice of Supervision & Management. McGraw.
Social Issues in Business. Macmillan.
Luthe, Wolfgang.
xLuthe, Wolfgang.
Creativity Mobilization Technique. Grune.
Luther, Edward T.
xLuther, Edward T.
Our Restless Earth: The Geologic Regions of Tennessee. U of Tenn Pr.
Luthi, Max, 1909-
xLuthi, Max.
Once Upon a Time: On the Nature of Fairy Tales. Ind U Pr.
Once Upon a Time: On the Nature of Fairy Tales. Ungar.
Luthin, James N.
xLuthin, James N.
Drainage Engineering. Krieger.
Luthin, Reinhard H. see Luthin, Reinhard Henry.
Luthin, Reinhard Henry, 1905-1962
xLuthin, Reinhard H.
The First Lincoln Campaign. Peter Smith.
Luthuli, Albert. see Luthuli, Albert John.
Luthuli, Albert John, 1898-
xLuthuli, Albert.
Let My People Go. NAL.
Lutnick, Solomon.
xLutnick, Solomon.
American Revolution & the British Press, 1775-1783. U of Mo Pr.
Lutoslawski, Wincenty, 1863-
xLutoslawski, Wincenty.
The Origin & Growth of Plato's Logic: With an Account of Plato's Style & the Chronology of His Writings. Irvington.
Lutrin, Carl E.
xLutrin, Carl E.
Pref. by American Public Administration: Concepts & Cases. Mayfield Pub.
Lutterjohann, Martin.
xLutterjohann, Martin.
IQ Tests for School Children: How to Test Your Child's Intelligence. Stein & Day.
Luttrell, Claude.
xLuttrell, Claude.
The Creation of the First Arthurian Romance: A Quest. Northwestern U Pr.
Luttrell, E. S. see Luttrell, Everett Stanley.

Luttrell, Everett Stanley, 1916-
xLuttrell, E. S.
Taxonomy of the Pyrenomycetes. Lubrecht & Cramer.
Luttrell, Guy. see Luttrell, Guy L.
Luttrell, Guy L.
xLuttrell, Guy.
The Instruments of Music. Elsevier-Nelson.
Luttwak, Edward.
xLuttwak, Edward.
Dictionary of Modern War. Har-Row.
The Strategic Balance. Sage.
xLuttwak, Edward N.
The Political Uses of Sea Power. Johns Hopkins.
Sea Power in the Mediterranean: Political Utility & Military Constraints. Sage.
Luttwak, Edward N. see Luttwak, Edward.
Lutyens, David B. see Lutyens, David Bulwer.
Lutyens, David Bulwer.
xLutyens, David B.
Creative Encounter. Humanities.
Lutz, Alma.
xLutz, Alma.
Created Equal: A Biography of Elizabeth Cady Stanton, 1815-1902. Octagon.
Susan B. Anthony: Rebel, Crusader, Humanitarian. Zenger Pub.
Lutz, Bertha.
xLutz, Bertha.
Brazilian Species of Hyla. U of Tex Pr.
Lutz, Charles P.
xLutz, Charles P.
Farming the Lord's Land: Christian Perspectives on American Agriculture. Augsburg.
Lutz, Cora E. see Lutz, Cora Elizabeth.
Lutz, Cora Elizabeth, 1906-
xLutz, Cora E.
Oldest Library Motto & Other Library Essays. Shoe String.
Lutz, Donald S.
xLutz, Donald S.
Popular Consent & Popular Control: Whig Political Theory in the Early State Constitutions. La State U Pr.
Lutz, E. A. see Lutz, Edward Albert.
Lutz, Edward Albert, 1910-
xLutz, E. A.
Some Problems & Alternatives in Developing Federal Block Grants: To States for Public Welfare Purposes. Arno.
Lutz, Frank W.
xLutz, Frank W.
Understanding Educational Organizations: A Field Study Approach. Merrill.
Lutz, Friedrich A. see Lutz, Friedrich August.
Lutz, Friedrich August.
xLutz, Friedrich A.
Theory of Investment of the Firm. Greenwood.
Lutz, Gertrude M. see Lutz, Gertrude May.
Lutz, Gertrude May.
xLutz, Gertrude M.
Song for a New Generation. Golden Quill.
Lutz, Giles. see Lutz, Giles A.
Lutz, Giles A.
xLutz, Giles.
Night of the Cattlemen. PB.
Outcast Gun. Fawcett.
The Shoot Out. PB.
The Stubborn Breed. PB.
xLutz, Giles A.
The Echo. Doubleday.
The Honyocker. Ace Bks.
Killer's Trail. Doubleday.
Lure of the Outlaw Trail. Doubleday.
Night of the Cattlemen. Doubleday.
Relentless Gun. Fawcett.
Lutz, John, 1939-
xLutz, John.

Lazarus Man. Berkley Pub.
Lazarus Man. Morrow.
Lutz, Ralph H. see Lutz, Ralph Haswell.
Lutz, Ralph Haswell, 1886-1968
xLutz, Ralph H.
Fall of the German Empire, 1914-1918. Octagon.
Lutz, Vera. see Lutz, Vera C.
Lutz, Vera C.
xLutz, Vera.
French Planning. Am Enterprise.
Lutzer, Erwin W.
xLutzer, Erwin W.
How in This World Can I Be Holy?. Moody.
You're Richer Than You Think!. Victor Bks.
Lutzow, Count. see Lutzow, Franz Heinrich Hieronymus Valentin.
Lutzow, Francis. see Lutzow, Franz Heinrich Hieronymus Valentin.
Lutzow, Franz. see Lutzow, Franz Heinrich Hieronymus Valentin.
Lutzow, Franz Heinrich Hieronymus Valentin, Graf Von, 1849-1916
xLutzow, Count.
A History of Bohemian Literature. R West.
xLutzow, Francis.
History of Bohemian Literature. Kennikat.
xLutzow, Franz.
Lectures on the Historians of Bohemia. Arno.
Luxemburg, Rosa, 1870-1919
xLuxemburg, Rosa.
The Industrial Development of Poland. Campaigner.
Letters to Karl & Luise Kautsky 1896-1918. Gordon Pr.
Reform or Revolution. Gordon Pr.
Reform or Revolution. Path Pr NY.
Luyben, W. L.
xLuyben, W. L.
Process Modeling, Simulation, & Control for Chemical Engineers. McGraw.
Luza, Radomir.
xLuza, Radomir.
Austro-German Relations in the Anschluss Era. Princeton U Pr.
Luzadder, Warren J. see Luzadder, Warren Jacob.
Luzadder, Warren Jacob.
xLuzadder, Warren J.
Fundamentals of Engineering Drawing for Design, Product Development & Numerical Control. P-H.
Innovative Design with an Introduction to Design Graphics. P-H.
Luzbetak, Louis J.
xLuzbetak, Louis J.
The Church & Cultures: An Applied Anthropology for the Religious Worker. William Carey Lib.
Luzi, Mario.
xLuzi, Mario.
In the Dark Body of Metamorphosis & Other Poems. Norton.
Luzuriaga, Gerardo.
xLuzuriaga, Gerardo.
jt. ed. & ed. The Orgy: Modern One Act Plays from Latin America. UCLA Lat Am Ctr.
Popular Theater for Social Change in Latin America: Essays in Spanish & English. UCLA Lat Am Ctr.
Lwowski, Walter, 1928-
xLwowski, Walter.
Nitrenes. Wiley.
Lyall, Alfred C. see Lyall, Alfred Comyn.
Lyall, Alfred Comyn, Sir, 1835-1911
xLyall, Alfred C.
Studies in Literature & History. Arno.
Lyall, Leslie T.
xLyall, Leslie T.
New Spring in China. Zondervan.
Lybrand, William A. see Lybrand, William Allen.

Lybrand, William Allen, 1925-
  xLybrand, William A.
    A Study on Evaluation of Driver Education.
    Mgmt Info Serv.
Lycan, Gilbert L.
  xLycan, Gilbert L.
    Alexander Hamilton & American Foreign
    Policy: A Design for Greatness. U of Okla
    Pr.
Lycophron.
  xLycophron.
    The Alexandra of Lycophron. Arno.
Lydall, Harold. see Lydall, Harold French.
Lydall, Harold French.
  xLydall, Harold.
    Structure of Earnings. Oxford U Pr.
Lydecker, Beatrice.
  xLydecker, Beatrice.
    Stories the Animals Tell Me. Har-Row.
    What the Animals Tell Me. Har-Row.
    What the Animals Tell Me. NAL.
Lydekker, John W. see Lydekker, John Wolfe.
Lydekker, John Wolfe.
  xLydekker, John W.
    Faithful Mohawks. Friedman.
Lyden, Fremont J.
  xLyden, Fremont J.
    ed. Public Budgeting: Program Planning &
    Evaluation. Rand.
Lydens, Z. Z.
  xLydens, Z. Z.
    A Look at Early Grand Rapids. Kregel.
Lydersen, Aksel.
  xLydersen, Aksel L.
    Fluid Flow & Heat Transfer. Wiley.
Lydersen, Aksel L. see Lydersen, Aksel.
Lydolph, P. see Lydolph, Paul E.
Lydolph, P. E. see Lydolph, Paul E.
Lydolph, Paul E.
  xLydolph, P.
    Geography of the U.S.S.R.. Wiley.
  xLydolph, P. E.
    Climates of the Soviet Union. Elsevier.
Lye, Keith.
  xLye, Keith.
    Minerals & Rocks. Arco.
    Our Planet The Earth. Lerner Pubns.
Lyell, Charles, Sir, Bart, 1797-1875
  xLyell, Charles.
    Principles of Geology: Being an Attempt to
    Explain the Former Changes of the Earth's
    Surface by Reference to Causes Now in
    Operation. Johnson Repr.
Lyell, William A.
  xLyell, William A.
    Lu Hsun's Vision of Reality. U of Cal Pr.
Lyfick, Warren.
  xLyfick, Warren.
    The Punny Pages. Riverhouse Pubns.
Lygre, David. see Lygre, David G.
Lygre, David G.
  xLygre, David.
    Life Manipulation: From Test Tube Babies to
    Aging. Walker & Co.
Lyle, Carl. see Lyle, Carl Blackburn.
Lyle, Carl Blackburn.
  xLyle, Carl.
    Common Clinical Perplexities. Med Exam.
Lyle, Dorothy S. see Lyle, Dorothy Siegert.
Lyle, Dorothy Siegert.
  xLyle, Dorothy S.
    Performance of Textiles. Wiley.
Lyle, E. B.
  xLyle, E. B.
    ed. Ballad Studies. Rowman.
Lyle, Garry.
  xLyle, Garry.
    Let's Visit Greece. John Day.
Lyle, Guy R. see Lyle, Guy Redvers.

Lyle, Guy Redvers, 1907-
  xLyle, Guy R.
    Administration of the College Library. Wilson.
    ed. Praise from Famous Men: An Anthology of
    Introductions. Scarecrow.
Lyle, Katie L. see Lyle, Katie Letcher.
Lyle, Katie Letcher, 1938-
  xLyle, Katie L.
    Fair Day & Another Step Begun. Dell.
    Fair Day & Another Step Begun. Lippincott.
    The Golden Shores of Heaven. Lippincott.
    I Will Go Barefoot All Summer for You.
    Lippincott.
  xLyle, Katie Letcher.
    I Will Go Barefoot All Summer for You. G K
    Hall.
Lyle, Marie C. see Lyle, Marie Caroline.
Lyle, Marie Caroline, 1889-
  xLyle, Marie C.
    The Original Identity of the York & Towneley
    Cycles. Folcroft.
Lyle, Royster.
  xLyle, Royster.
    The Architecture of Historic Lexington. U Pr
    of Va.
Lyle, Sparky.
  xLyle, Sparky.
    The Bronx Zoo. Crown.
    The Bronx Zoo. Dell.
Lyle, Watson.
  xLyle, Watson.
    Camille Saint-Saens, His Life & Art.
    Greenwood.
Lym, Glenn R. see Lym, Glenn Robert.
Lym, Glenn Robert.
  xLym, Glenn R.
    A Psychology of Building: How We Shape &
    Experience Our Structured Spaces. P-H.
Lyman, Dean B. see Lyman, Dean Belden.
Lyman, Dean Belden, 1896-
  xLyman, Dean B.
    Last Lutanist & Other Poems. AMS Pr.
Lyman, Frederick C.
  xLyman, Frederick C.
    Posture of Contemplation. Philos Lib.
Lyman, Helen H., 1910-
  xLyman, Helen H.
    Reading & the Adult New Reader. ALA.
Lyman, Henry, 1915-
  xLyman, Henry.
    Successful Bluefishing. Follett.
    Successful Bluefishing. Intl Marine.
    Tackle Talk. A S Barnes.
Lyman, Howard B. see Lyman, Howard Burbeck.
Lyman, Howard Burbeck, 1920-
  xLyman, Howard B.
    Intelligence, Aptitude & Achievement Testing.
    HM.
Lyman, Nanci A.
  xLyman, Nanci A.
    The Colony of Delaware. Watts.
    The Colony of South Carolina. Watts.
Lyman, Richard W.
  xLyman, Richard W.
    The First Labour Government, 1924. Russell.
Lyman, Stanford M.
  xLyman, Stanford M.
    The Asian in North America. ABC-Clio.
    The Drama of Social Reality. Oxford U Pr.
Lyman, Theodore, 1833-1897
  xLyman, Theodore.
    Meade's Headquarters 1863-1865: Letters of
    Colonel Theodore Lyman from the
    Wilderness to Appomattox. Arno.
Lyman, Tom.
  xLyman, Tom.

    Bouldering & Outcrop Climbing. Greene.
    The Field Book of Mountaineering & Rock
    Climbing. Scribner.
    The Field Book of Mountaineering & Rock
    Climbing. Winchester Pr.
Lynch, Bohun. see Lynch, John Gilbert Bohun.
Lynch, Bohunn. see Lynch, John Gilbert Bohun.
Lynch, David, 1902-
  xLynch, David.
    The Concentration of Economic Power.
    Johnson Repr.
Lynch, Edith M.
  xLynch, Edith M.
    The Woman's Guide to Management.
    Cornerstone.
Lynch, F. D. see Lynch, Francis Dennis.
Lynch, Flann.
  xLynch, Flann.
    Come, Take up Your Cross: The Practical
    Responsibilities of Christians Today. Ave
    Maria.
Lynch, Frances, 1930-
  xLynch, Frances.
    A Dangerous Magic. Fawcett.
    A Dangerous Magic. St Martin.
    The Fine & Handsome Captain. Fawcett.
    Stranger at the Wedding. Fawcett.
    Stranger at the Wedding. St Martin.
Lynch, Francis Dennis.
  xLynch, F. D.
    Clozentropy: A Technique for Studying
    Audience Response to Films. Arno.
Lynch, George.
  xLynch, George.
    Canaries in Color. Sterling.
Lynch, H. see Lynch, Hannah.
Lynch, H. T. see Lynch, Henry T.
Lynch, Hannah, d. 1904
  xLynch, H.
    George Meredith. Haskell.
  xLynch, Hannah.
    George Meredith. Folcroft.
Lynch, Henry T.
  xLynch, H. T.
    ed. Cancer Genetics. C C Thomas.
  xLynch, Henry T.
    ed. Cancer & You. C C Thomas.
Lynch, Hollis R. see Lynch, Hollis Ralph.
Lynch, Hollis Ralph.
  xLynch, Hollis R.
    Edward Wilmot Blyden: Pan-Negro Patriot,
    1832-1912. Oxford U Pr.
Lynch, J. M. see Lynch, James Michael.
Lynch, James J.
  xLynch, James J.
    Box, Pit & Gallery: Stage & Society in
    Johnson's London. Russell.
    The Broken Heart: The Medical Consequences
    of Loneliness. Basic.
Lynch, James Michael.
  xLynch, J. M.
    Microbial Ecology: A Conceptual Approach.
    Halsted Pr.
Lynch, Jane S. see Lynch, Jane Shay.
Lynch, Jane Shay.
  xLynch, Jane S.
    The Women's Guide to Legal Rights. Contemp
    Bks.
Lynch, John, 1904-
  xLynch, John.
    How to Make Mobiles. Viking Pr.
    The Spanish American Revolutions, 1808-1862.
    Norton.
    Spanish Colonial Administration, 1782-1810:
    The Intendant System in the Viceroyalty of
    the Rio De la Plata. Greenwood.
Lynch, John Gilbert Bohun, 1884-
  xLynch, Bohun.

A History of Caricature. Gale.
Max Beerbohm in Perspective. Folcroft.
Max Beerbohm in Perspective. Gale.
Max Beerbohm in Perspective. R West.
xLynch, Bohunn.
Max Beerbohm in Perspective. Haskell.
Lynch, John R. see Lynch, John Roy.
Lynch, John Roy, 1847-1939
xLynch, John R.
Facts of Reconstruction. Arno.
Reminiscences of an Active Life: The
Autobiography of John Roy Lynch. U of
Chicago Pr.
Lynch, Joseph H., 1943-
xLynch, Joseph H.
Simoniacal Entry into Religious Life, 1000 to
1260: A Social, Economic, & Legal Study.
Ohio St U Pr.
Lynch, Kathleen M. see Lynch, Kathleen Martha.
Lynch, Kathleen Martha.
xLynch, Kathleen M.
Congreve Gallery. Octagon.
Lynch, Kevin.
xLynch, Kevin.
Image of the City. MIT Pr.
What Time Is This Place?. MIT Pr.
Lynch, Maureen.
xLynch, Maureen.
Mary Fran & Mo. St Martin.
Lynch, Owen M., 1931-
xLynch, Owen M.
Politics of Untouchability: Social Mobility &
Social Change in a City of India. Columbia U
Pr.
Lynch, Patricia.
xLynch, Patricia.
Brogeen & the Bronze Lizard. Macmillan.
Brogeen Follows the Magic Tune. Macmillan.
Lynch, R. V. see Lynch, Ransom V.
Lynch, Ransom V.
xLynch, R. V.
Calculus with Computer Applications. Wiley.
Lynch, Richard. see Lynch, Richard M.
Lynch, Richard M.
xLynch, Richard.
Accounting for Management: Planning &
Control. McGraw.
Lynch, Thomas. see Lynch, Thomas Dexter.
Lynch, Thomas D. see Lynch, Thomas Dexter.
Lynch, Thomas Dexter, 1942-
xLynch, Thomas.
ed. Contemporary Public Budgeting.
Transaction Bks.
xLynch, Thomas D.
Public Budgeting in America. P-H.
Lynch, Valerie.
xLynch, Valerie.
Exploring the Past. John Day.
Lynch, W. O. see Lynch, William Orlando.
Lynch, William A. see Lynch, William Albert.
Lynch, William Albert, 1917-
xLynch, William A.
Marriage Manual for Catholics. Trident.
Lynch, William F., 1908-
xLynch, William F.
Approach to the Metaphysics of Plato Through
the Parmenides. Greenwood.
Christ & Prometheus: A New Image of the
Secular. U of Notre Dame Pr.
Images of Faith: An Exploration of the Ironic
Imagination. U of Notre Dame Pr.
Lynch, William Orlando.
xLynch, W. O.
Fifty Years of Party Warfare (1789-1837).
Peter Smith.
Lynd, Albert.
xLynd, Albert.
Quackery in the Public Schools. Greenwood.
Lynd, Robert, 1879-1949
xLynd, Robert.

Books & Authors. Arno.
Books & Authors. R West.
Dr. Johnson & Company. Arden Lib.
Dr. Johnson & Company. Folcroft.
Dr. Johnson & Company. Haskell.
Money-Box. Arno.
Old & New Masters. Arno.
Old & New Masters. R West.
Passion of Labour. Arno.
Peal of Bells. Arno.
Peal of Bells. Scholarly.
Solomon in All His Glory. Arno.
Lynd, Staughton.
xLynd, Staughton.
Labor Law for the Rank & Filer. Miles & Weir.
Lynde, John G., 1913-
xLynde, John G.
Thirty-Four Ways to Cast a Fly. A S Barnes.
Lyndoe, Edward.
xLyndoe, Edward.
Astrology for Everyone. Dutton.
Lyndon B. Johnson School of Public Affairs.
xLBJ School of Public Affairs.
Alternate Care for the Elderly: An Annotated
Bibliography. LBJ Sch Public Affairs.
The Arts: Years of Development Time of
Decision. LBJ Sch Public Affairs.
Colonias in the Lower Rio Grande Valley of
South Texas: A Summary Report. LBJ Sch
Public Affairs.
Feasibility of Health Maintenance
Organizations in Texas. LBJ Sch Public
Affairs.
Federal Policies for Equal Educational
Opportunity: Conflict & Confusion. LBJ Sch
Public Affairs.
Financing & Control of Academic Research.
LBJ Sch Public Affairs.
Gold Rush Economics: Developement Planning
in the Persian-Arabian Gulf. LBJ Sch Public
Affairs.
Health of Mexican - Americans in South
Texas. LBJ Sch Public Affairs.
Manpower & Vocational Education Planning
Processes: Four Regional Case Studies. LBJ
Sch Public Affairs.
Meal System for the Elderly: Conventional
Food in Novel Form. LBJ Sch Public Affairs.
The New York City Health & Hospitals
Corporation. LBJ Sch Public Affairs.
Public Policies Affecting Lignite Developement
in Texas. LBJ Sch Public Affairs.
Public Sector Productivity Programs:
Background & Analysis with Special
Reference to State Governments. LBJ Sch
Public Affairs.
Regional Workshops on Texas Women. LBJ
Sch Public Affairs.
Shale Oil Technology: Status of the Industry.
LBJ Sch Public Affairs.
The Sixty-Sixth Texas Legislative Pre-Session
Conference. LBJ Sch Public Affairs.
The Status of Women in Texas: A Preliminary
Assessment. LBJ Sch Public Affairs.
The Supply of Physicians & Physicians'
Incomes Alternative Projections of the
Future. LBJ Sch Public Affairs.
The Third World & International Symbolism.
LBJ Sch Public Affairs.
Toward New Human Rights: The Social
Policies of the Kennedy & Johnson
Administrations. LBJ Sch Public Affairs.
Women in Public Life: Report of a Conference.
LBJ Sch Public Affairs.
Lynds, Beverly T.
xLynds, Beverly T.
ed. Dark Nebulae, Globules, & Protostars. U of
Ariz Pr.
Lyne, Arthur Gordon.
xLyne, Gordon.

Marsupials & Monotremes of Australia.
Taplinger.
Lyne, Gordon. see Lyne, Arthur Gordon.
Lynes, Carlos, 1910-
xLynes, Carlos.
Chateaubriand As a Critic of French Literature.
Johnson Repr.
Lynes, J. A.
xLynes, J. A.
ed. Developments in Lighting. Burgess-Intl
Ideas.
Principles of Natural Lighting. Intl Ideas.
Lynes, Russell, 1910-
xLynes, Russell.
A Surfeit of Honey. Greenwood.
Lyng, Merwin J.
xLyng, Merwin J.
Applied Technical Mathematics. HM.
Dancing Curves: A Dynamic Demonstration of
Geometric Principles. NCTM.
Lyngstad, Sverre.
xLyngstad, Sverre.
Jonas Lie. Twayne.
Lynn, Conrad. see Lynn, Conrad J.
Lynn, Conrad J.
xLynn, Conrad.
There Is a Fountain: The Autobiography of a
Civil Rights Lawyer. Lawrence Hill.
Lynn, David B. see Lynn, David Brandon.
Lynn, David Brandon, 1925-
xLynn, David B.
Daughters & Parents: Past, Present, & Future.
Brooks-Cole.
Lynn, Edward S.
xLynn, Edward S.
Introduction to Fund Accounting. Reston.
Lynn, Elizabeth A.
xLynn, Elizabeth A.
The Dancers of Arun. Berkley Pub.
The Northern Girl. Putnam.
Watchtower. Berkley Pub.
Lynn, Jack, 1927-
xLynn, Jack.
The Turncoat. Delacorte.
Lynn, James T.
xLynn, James T.
The Federal Budget: What Are the Nation's
Priorities?. Am Enterprise.
Lynn, Kenneth S. see Lynn, Kenneth Schuyler.
Lynn, Kenneth Schuyler.
xLynn, Kenneth S.
A Divided People. Greenwood.
The Dream of Success: A Study of the Modern
American Imagination. Greenwood.
Mark Twain & Southwestern Humor.
Greenwood.
Lynn, Laurence E.
xLynn, Laurence E.
The State & Human Services: Organizational
Change in a Political Context. MIT Pr.
Lynn, Loretta.
xLynn, Loretta.
Loretta Lynn: Coal Miner's Daughter. Warner
Bks.
Lynn, R. see Lynn, Richard.
Lynn, Richard.
xLynn, R.
Attention, Arousal & the Orientation Reaction.
Pergamon.
Personality & National Character. Pergamon.
Lynn, Robert. see Lynn, Robert Athan.
Lynn, Robert A. see Lynn, Robert Athan.
Lynn, Robert Athan, 1930-
xLynn, Robert.
Basic Economic Principles. McGraw.
xLynn, Robert A.
Basic Economic Principles. McGraw.
Lynn, Robert J.
xLynn, Robert J.

Introduction to Estate Planning in a Nutshell.
West Pub.
Lynn, Robert W.
xLynn, Robert W.
The Big Little School: Two Hundred Years of
Sunday School. Abingdon.
Lynn, Theodore A.
xLynn, Theodore A.
Introductory Musicianship: A Workbook.
HarBraceJ.
Lynn, Theodore S.
xLynn, Theodore S.
Real Estate Limited Partnerships. Wiley.
Lynton, Harriet R. see Lynton, Harriet Ronken.
Lynton, Harriet Ronken.
xLynton, Harriet R.
The Days of the Beloved. U of Cal Pr.
Lyon, Bryce. see Lyon, Bryce Dale.
Lyon, Bryce D. see Lyon, Bryce Dale.
Lyon, Bryce Dale, 1920-
xLyon, Bryce.
A Constitutional & Legal History of Medieval
England. Norton.
History of the Western World. Rand.
Medieval Finance: A Comparison of Financial
Institutions in Northwestern Europe. Brown
U Pr.
Origins of the Middle Ages: Pirenne's
Challenge to Gibbon. Norton.
xLyon, Bryce D.
From Fief to Indenture: The Transition from
Feudal to Non-Feudal Contract in Western
Europe. Octagon.
Lyon, E. Wilson. see Lyon, Elijah Wilson.
Lyon, Elijah Wilson, 1904-
xLyon, E. Wilson.
Louisiana in French Diplomacy: 1759-1804. U.
of Okla Pr.
Lyon, Eugene, 1929-
xLyon, Eugene.
The Enterprise of Florida: Pedro Menendez de
Aviles & the Spanish Conquest of 1565-1568.
U Presses Fla.
The Search for the Atocha. Har-Row.
Lyon, Harris M. see Lyon, Harris Merton.
Lyon, Harris Merton, 1883-1916
xLyon, Harris M.
Graphics. Arno.
Lyon, Irving W. see Lyon, Irving Whitall.
Lyon, Irving Whitall, 1840-1896
xLyon, Irving W.
Colonial Furniture of New England: A Study
of the Domestic Furniture in Use in the 17th
& 18th Centuries. Dutton.
Lyon, J. C.
xLyon, J. C.
The Fireplace Cookbook. Lightning Tree.
Lyon, John K.
xLyon, John K.
The Database Administrator. Wiley.
Introduction to Data Base Design. Wiley.
Lyon, L. H. see Lyon, Luther H.
Lyon, Leverett S. see Lyon, Leverett Samuel.
Lyon, Leverett Samuel.
xLyon, Leverett S.
Government & Economic Life: Development &
Current Issues of American Public Policy.
Greenwood.
Lyon, Luther H.
xLyon, L. H.
Applied Penmanship. SW Pub.
Lyon, Melvin, 1927-
xLyon, Melvin.
Symbol & Idea in Henry Adams. U of Nebr Pr.
Lyon, Patricia. see Lyon, Patricia J.
Lyon, Patricia J.
xLyon, Patricia.
ed. Native South Americans: Ethnology of the
Least Known Continent. Little.
Lyon, Thoburn C. see Lyon, Thoburn Cassady.

Lyon, Thoburn Cassady, 1896-
xLyon, Thoburn C.
Practical Air Navigation. Jeppesen Sanderson.
Lyon, Thomas, 1912-
xLyon, Thomas.
The Theory of Religious Liberty in England,
1603-1639. Octagon.
Lyon, Thomas J.
xLyon, Thomas J.
Frank Waters. Twayne.
Lyon, Thomas J. see Lyon, Thomas Jefferson.
Lyon, Thomas Jefferson, 1937-
xLyon, Thomas J.
Places, Shadows, Dancing People. Utah St U
Pr.
Lyon, William, 1927-
xLyon, William.
Let Me Live!. Chris Mass.
Lyons. see Lyons, Kathleen M.
Lyons, Arthur.
xLyons, Arthur.
All God's Children. Ballantine.
Castles Burning. HR&W.
Lyons, Barbara.
xLyons, Barbara.
The Brook. Topgallant.
Lyons, Dorothy.
xLyons, Dorothy.
Dark Sunshine. HarBraceJ.
Pedigree Unknown. HarBraceJ.
Lyons, Eugene, 1898-
xLyons, Eugene.
Assignment in Utopia. Greenwood.
Life & Death of Sacco & Vanzetti. Da Capo.
Lyons, Gene M. see Lyons, Gene Martin.
Lyons, Gene Martin.
xLyons, Gene M.
Education & Military Leadership: A Study of
the R.O.T.C.. Greenwood.
Lyons, Grant.
xLyons, Grant.
The Creek Indians. Messner.
Tales the People Tell in Mexico. Messner.
Lyons, H. P. see Lyons, Hugh Peter Carbery.
Lyons, Hugh Peter Carbery.
xLyons, H. P.
Praying Our Prayers. Franciscan Herald.
Lyons, J. B. see Lyons, John Benignus.
Lyons, James W.
xLyons, James W.
Steps into Light: A Prayerbook of Christian
Belief. Ave Maria.
Lyons, Jerry L.
xLyons, Jerry L.
The Designer's Handbook of Pressure Sensing
Devices. Van Nos Reinhold.
Lyons, John.
xLyons, John.
Noam Chomsky. Penguin.
Lyons, John Benignus.
xLyons, J. B.
Oliver St. John Gogarty. Bucknell U Pr.
Lyons, John W., 1930-
xLyons, John W.
Chemistry & Uses of Fire Retardants. Wiley.
Lyons, Joseph.
xLyons, Joseph.
People: An Introduction to Psychology.
Har-Row.
Lyons, Kathleen.
xLyons, Kathleen.
Dear Congressman Howard. Acropolis.
Lyons, Kathleen M.
xLyons.
The Biology of Helminth Parasites. Univ Park.
Lyons, Louis M. see Lyons, Louis Martin.
Lyons, Louis Martin, 1897-
xLyons, Louis M.

Newspaper Story: One Hundred Years of the
Boston Globe. Harvard U Pr.
Lyons, M. see Lyons, Martyn.
Lyons, Martyn.
xLyons, M.
France Under the Directory. Cambridge U Pr.
Lyons, Nan.
xLyons, Nan.
Champagne Blues. Fawcett.
Champagne Blues. S&S.
Someone Is Killing the Great Chefs of Europe.
BJ Pub Group.
Lyons, Nathan.
xLyons, Nathan.
Notations in Passing. MIT Pr.
Lyons, Nick.
xLyons, Nick.
Bright Rivers. Lippincott.
The Sony Vision. Crown.
Lyons, Paul R.
xLyons, Paul R.
Fire in America. Natl Fire Prot.
Operating Fire Department Pumpers. Natl Fire
Prot.
Lyons, Robert. see Lyons, Robert B.
Lyons, Robert B.
xLyons, Robert.
ed. Autobiography: A Reader for Writers.
Oxford U Pr.
Lyons, W. E. see Lyons, William E.
Lyons, W. James. see Lyons, William James.
Lyons, William E.
xLyons, W. E.
The Politics of City-County Merger: The
Lexington-Fayette County Experience. U Pr
of Ky.
Lyons, William James, 1904-
xLyons, W. James.
Impact Phenomena in Textiles. MIT Pr.
Lysaght, A. M. see Lysaght, Averil M.
Lysaght, Averil M.
xLysaght, A. M.
ed. Joseph Banks in Newfoundland &
Labrador, 1766: His Diary, Manuscripts &
Collections. U of Cal Pr.
Lysaght, Sidney R. see Lysaght, Sidney Royse.
Lysaght, Sidney Royse, d. 1941
xLysaght, Sidney R.
Reading of Life. Arno.
Lystad, Mary. see Lystad, Mary H.
Lystad, Mary H.
xLystad, Mary.
The Halloween Parade. Putnam.
Lythgoe, J. N.
xLythgoe, J. N.
The Ecology & Vision. Oxford U Pr.
Lytle, Eldon G.
xLytle, Eldon G.
A Grammar of Subordinate Structures in
English. Mouton.
Lyttle, Richard. see Lyttle, Richard B.
Lyttle, Richard B.
xLyttle, Richard.
How to Beat the High Cost of Sailing.
Contemp Bks.
xLyttle, Richard B.
The Complete Beginner's Guide to
Backpacking. Doubleday.
The Complete Beginner's Guide to Physical
Fitness. Doubleday.
The Complete Beginners Guide to Skiing.
Doubleday.
Getting into Pro Basketball. Watts.
Jogging & Running. Watts.
People of the Dawn. Atheneum.
Lytton, David.
xLytton, David.
Goddam White Man. S&S.
Lytton, Edward B. see Lytton, Edward George Lytton
Bulwer-Lytton, 1st Baron.

Lytton, Edward George Lytton Bulwer-Lytton, 1st
   Baron, 1863-1945
      xLytton, Edward B.
         Last Days of Pompeii. Woodbridge Pr.
M'Bengue, Mamadou S. see M'Bengue, Mamadou Seyni.
M'Bengue, Mamadou Seyni.
      xM'Bengue, Mamadou S.
         Cultural Policy in Senegal. Unipub.
M'Gonigle, R. Michael.
      xM'Gonigle, R. Michael.
         Pollution, Politics, & International Law:
            Tankers at Sea. U of Cal Pr.
Ma, M. T.
      xMa, Mark T.
         Theory & Application of Antenna Arrays.
            Wiley.
Ma, Mark T. see Ma, M. T.
Maarek, Gerard, 1939-
      xMaarek, Gerard.
         Introduction to Karl Marx's 'Das Kapital': A
            Study in Formalisation. Oxford U Pr.
Maas, Henry S.
      xMaas, Henry S.
         ed. Social Service Research: Review of Studies.
            Natl Assn Soc Wrks.
Maas, Peter, 1929-
      xMaas, Peter.
         Made in America. Bantam.
         Made in America. Viking Pr.
Maass, Arthur.
      xMaass, Arthur.
         Design of Water-Resource Systems: New
            Techniques for Relating Economic
            Objectives, Engineering Analysis, &
            Governmental Planning. Harvard U Pr.
         Muddy Waters: The Army Engineers & the
            Nation's Rivers. Da Capo.
Maass, David.
      xMaass, David.
         A Gallery of Waterfowl & Upland Birds.
            Petersen Pub.
Maass, Walter B.
      xMaass, Walter B.
         Country Without a Name: Austria Under Nazi
            Rule, 1938-1945. Ungar.
Mabardi, Georges.
      xMabardi, Georges.
         Vanity Fair's Backgammon to Win. S&S.
Mabbs, A. W.
      xMabbs, A. W.
         Organization of Intermediate Records Storage.
            Unipub.
Mabbutt, J. A.
      xMabbutt, J. A.
         Desert Landforms. MIT Pr.
Mabee, Carleton, 1914-
      xMabee, Carleton.
         American Leonardo: A Life of Samuel F. B.
            Morse. Octagon.
         Black Education in New York State: From
            Colonial to Modern Times. Syracuse U Pr.
Mabey, Richard, 1941-
      xMabey, Richard.
         Plantcraft: A Guide to the Everyday Use of
            Wild Plants. Universe.
Mabie, Hamilton W. see Mabie, Hamilton Wright.
Mabie, Hamilton Wright, 1846-1916
      xMabie, Hamilton W.
         American Ideals, Character & Life. Arno.
         Backgrounds of Literature. Arno.
Mablekos, Van E., 1930-
      xMablekos, Van E.
         Electric Machine Theory for Power Engineers.
            Har-Row.
Mabogunje, Akin L.
      xMabogunje, Akin L.
         Regional Mobility & Resource Development in
            West Africa. McGill-Queens U Pr.
Mabro, Robert.
      xMabro, Robert.

         The Egyptian Economy 1952-1972. Oxford U
            Pr.
Mabry, Edward. see Mabry, Edward A.
Mabry, Edward A.
      xMabry, Edward.
         The Dynamics of Small Group Communication.
            HM.
      xMabry, Edward A.
         The Dynamics of Small Group Communication.
            P-H.
Mabry, T. J. see Mabry, Tom J.
Mabry, Tom J.
      xMabry, T. J.
         Systematic Identification of Flavonoids.
            Springer-Verlag.
Mabus, Eileen Lewis.
      xMabus, Eileen Lewis.
         Music for Tiny Tots: A Teacher's Manual for
            Group Teaching of Four-&-Five-Year-Olds.
            Exposition.
Mac Liammoir, Micheal, 1899-
      xMac Liammoir, Micheal.
         Enter a Goldfish: Memoirs of an Irish Actor,
            Young & Old. Thames Hudson.
MacAdam, David L., 1910-
      xMacAdam, David L.
         ed. Sources of Color Science. MIT Pr.
MacAdams, Cynthia, 1939-
      xMacAdams, Cynthia.
         Emergence. Chelsea Hse.
         Emergence. Dutton.
MacAgy, Douglas. see Macagy, Douglas Guernsey.
Macagy, Douglas Guernsey.
      xMacAgy, Douglas.
         Going for a Walk with a Line: A Step into the
            World of Modern Art. Doubleday.
MacAlister, Ian.
      xMacAlister, Ian.
         Driscoll's Diamonds. Fawcett.
         Valley of the Assassins. Fawcett.
Macalister, R. A. see Macalister, Robert Alexander
   Stewart.
Macalister, Robert A. see Macalister, Robert Alexander
   Stewart.
Macalister, Robert Alexander Stewart, 1870-1950
      xMacalister, R. A.
         The Archaeology of Ireland. Milford Hse.
      xMacalister, Robert A.
         The Archaeology of Ireland. Arno.
Macan, T. T. see Macan, Thomas Townley.
Macan, Thomas Townley.
      xMacan, T. T.
         Ponds & Lakes. Crane-Russak Co.
Macarov, David.
      xMacarov, David.
         Work & Welfare: The Unholy Alliance. Sage.
MacArthur, Catherine.
      xMacArthur, Catherine.
         George's Women. St Martin.
         It Was the Lark. St Martin.
MacArthur, John. see Macarthur, John F.
MacArthur, John F.
      xMacArthur, John.
         Giving God's Way. Tyndale.
MacArthur, Robert H.
      xMacArthur, Roger H.
         Theory of Island Biogeography. Princeton U
            Pr.
MacArthur, Roger H. see Macarthur, Robert H.
MacArthur-Onslow, Annette. see Macarthur-Onslow,
   Annette Rosemary.
Macarthur-Onslow, Annette Rosemary.
      xMacArthur-Onslow, Annette.
         illus. Uhu. Knopf.
Macartney, Carlile A. see Macartney, Carlile Aylmer.
Macartney, Carlile Aylmer, 1895-
      xMacartney, Carlile A.
         National States & National Minorities. Russell.
Macartney, Clarence E. see Macartney, Clarence Edward
   Noble.

Macartney, Clarence Edward Noble, 1879-1957
      xMacartney, Clarence E.
         Grant & His Generals. Arno.
         Lincoln & His Generals. Arno.
Macaulay, David.
      xMacaulay, David.
         illus. Castle. HM.
         Great Moments in Architecture. HM.
         illus. Pyramid. HM.
         illus. Underground. HM.
Macaulay, J. C. see Macaulay, Joseph Cordner.
Macaulay, James, 1817-1902
      xMacaulay, James.
         Doctor Johnson: His Life, Works & Table Talk.
            Folcroft.
Macaulay, Joseph Cordner, 1900-
      xMacaulay, J. C.
         Expository Commentary on Acts. Moody.
         Expository Commentary on Hebrews. Moody.
         Expository Commentary on John. Moody.
Macaulay, Lord. see Macaulay, Thomas Babington
   Macaulay.
Macaulay, Rose, Dame.
      xMacaulay, Rose.
         Personal Pleasures. Arden Lib.
         Personal Pleasures. Arno.
         Personal Pleasures. Darby Bks.
         Some Religious Elements in English Literature.
            Greenwood.
         Some Religious Elements in English Literature.
            Scholarly.
Macaulay, Thomas Babington Macaulay.
      xMacaulay, Lord.
         The History of England. Penguin.
Macauley, Robie.
      xMacauley, Robie.
         A Secret History of Time to Come. Knopf.
Macauley, Ted.
      xMacauley, Ted.
         The Yamaha Legend. St Martin.
MacAvoy, Paul. see Macavoy, Paul W.
MacAvoy, Paul W.
      xMacAvoy, Paul.
         ed. Railroad Revitalization & Regulatory
            Reform. Am Enterprise.
      xMacAvoy, Paul W.
         ed. Deregulation of Cable Television. Am
            Enterprise.
         Economic Effects of Regulation: The
            Trunk-Line Railroad Cartels & the Interstate
            Commerce Commission Before 1900. MIT
            Pr.
         Economic Strategy for Developing Nuclear
            Breeder Reactors. MIT Pr.
         ed. Federal-State Regulation of the Pricing &
            Marketing of Insurance. Am Enterprise.
         Price Controls & the Natural Gas Shortage.
            Am Enterprise.
         Regulated Industries. Norton.
         ed. Regulation of Entry & Pricing in Truck
            Transportation. Am Enterprise.
MacBean, James R. see Macbean, James Roy.
MacBean, James Roy.
      xMacBean, James R.
         Film & Revolution. Ind U Pr.
Macbeth, Ann.
      xMacbeth, Ann.
         Country Woman's Rug Book. Paragraph Pr.
MacBeth, George.
      xMacBeth, George.
         Buying a Heart. Atheneum.
         The Seven Witches. HarBraceJ.
         The Seven Witches. NAL.
         The Survivor. HarBraceJ.
Macbeth, Graham.
      xMacBeth, Graham.
         Observer's Book of Motor Sport. Scribner.
Macbeth, Norman, 1910-
      xMacbeth, Norman.

Darwin Retried: An Appeal to Reason.
Gambit.
MacBride, Roger L. *see* Macbride, Roger Lea.
MacBride, Roger Lea, 1929-
xMacBride, Roger L.
American Electoral College. Caxton.
MacCabe, Colin.
xMacCabe, Colin.
James Joyce & the Revolution of the Word.
B&N.
MacCaffrey, Isabel G. *see* Maccaffrey, Isabel Gamble.
MacCaffrey, Isabel Gamble.
xMacCaffrey, Isabel G.
Paradise Lost As Myth. Harvard U Pr.
Spenser's Allegory: The Anatomy of
Imagination. Princeton U Pr.
MacCallum, Mungo W. *see* Maccallum, Mungo William.
MacCallum, Mungo William, Sir, 1854-1942
xMacCallum, Mungo W.
The Dramatic Monologue in the Victorian
Period. Folcroft.
MacCallum, Reid, 1897-1949
xMacCallum, Reid.
Imitation & Design & Other Essays. U of
Toronto Pr.
Maccallum, Spencer H. *see* Maccallum, Spencer Heath.
MacCallum, Spencer Heath.
xMaccallum, Spencer H.
The Art of Community. Green Hill.
The Art of Community. Humanities.
The Art of the Community. Inst Humane.
MacCann, Donnarae.
xMacCann, Donnarae.
ed. Cultural Conformity in Books for Children:
Further Readings in Racism. Scarecrow.
MacCann, Richard D. *see* Maccann, Richard Dyer.
MacCann, Richard Dyer.
xMacCann, Richard D.
Hollywood in Transition. Greenwood.
The People's Films: A Political History of U.
S. Government Motion Pictures. Hastings.
MacCann, William.
xMacCann, William.
Two Thousand Miles' Ride Through the
Argentine Provinces. AMS Pr.
MacCannell, Dean.
xMacCannell, Dean.
The Tourist: A New Theory of the Leisure
Class. Schocken.
MacCarthy, Desmond, Sir, 1878-1952
xMacCarthy, Desmond.
Criticism. Arden Lib.
Criticism. Arno.
Criticism. Folcroft.
European Tradition in Literature from 1600
Onwards. Folcroft.
The European Tradition in Literature from
1600 Onwards. R West.
Leslie Stephen. Folcroft.
Theatre. Greenwood.
MacCarthy, P. *see* Maccarthy, Peter Arthur Desmond.
MacCarthy, Peter Arthur Desmond.
xMacCarthy, P.
Teaching Pronunciation. Cambridge U Pr.
MacCaskey, Michael.
xMacCaskey, Michael R.
All About Lawns. Ortho.
Award-Winning Small-Space Gardens. Ortho.
MacCaskey, Michael R. *see* Maccaskey, Michael.
Macchiaverna, Paul.
xMacchiaverna, Paul.
Internal Auditing. Conference Bd.
Macciocchi, Maria A. *see* Macciocchi, Maria Antoinetta.
Macciocchi, Maria Antoinetta.
xMacciocchi, Maria A.
Daily Life in Revolutionary China. Monthly
Rev.
Maccioli, Frank J.
xMaccioli, Frank J.

Determination of Toxic Metals & Metalloids in
Ambient Air. Pa St U Pr.
MacClean, Katherine, 1925-
xMacClean, Katherine.
The Trouble with You Earth People. Donning
Co.
MacClintock, Carol. *see* Macclintock, Carol Cook.
MacClintock, Carol Cook, 1910-
xMacClintock, Carol.
ed. Readings in the History of Music in
Performance. Ind U Pr.
MacClintock, Dorcas.
xMacClintock, Dorcas.
Horses As I See Them. Scribner.
A Natural History of Giraffes. Scribner.
A Natural History of Zebras. Scribner.
MacClintock, Lander, 1889-
xMacClintock, Lander.
Age of Pirandello. Kraus Repr.
MacClintock, William D. *see* Macclintock, William
Darnall.
MacClintock, William Darnall, 1858-1936
xMacClintock, William D.
Joseph Warton's Essay on Pope: A History of
the Five Editions. Russell.
MacCloskey, Monro.
xMacCloskey, Monro.
Your Future As a Woman in the Armed
Forces. Rosen Pr.
Your Future in the Military Services. Rosen Pr.
Maccoby, Eleanor E.
xMaccoby, Eleanor E.
ed. The Development of Sex Differences.
Stanford U Pr.
Experiments in Primary Education: Aspects of
Project Follow-Through. HarBraceJ.
The Psychology of Sex Differences. Stanford U
Pr.
Maccoby, Hyam.
xMaccoby, Hyam.
tr. The Day God Laughed: Sayings, Fables &
Entertainments of the Jewish Sages. St
Martin.
MacColl, le Roy Archibald, 1896-
xMacColl, LeRoy A.
Fundamental Theory of Servomechanisms.
Dover.
Fundamental Theory of Servomechanisms.
Peter Smith.
MacColl, LeRoy A. *see* Maccoll, le Roy Archibald.
MacCollam, Joel A., 1946-
xMacCollam, Joel A.
Carnival of Souls: Religious Cults & Young
People. Seabury.
MacCombie, John.
xMacCombie, John.
The Prince & the Genie: A Study of
Rimbaud's Influence on Claudel. U of Mass
Pr.
Macconaill, M. A. *see* Macconaill, Michael Aloysius.
Macconaill, Michael Aloysius.
xMacconaill, M. A.
Muscles & Movements: A Basis for Human
Kinesiology. Krieger.
Maccorkle, Stuart A. *see* Maccorkle, Stuart Alexander.
MacCorkle, Stuart Alexander, 1903-
xMaccorkle, Stuart A.
American Policy of Recognition Towards
Mexico. AMS Pr.
MacCormac, John P. *see* Maccormac, John Patrick.
MacCormac, John Patrick, 1895-
xMacCormac, John P.
This Time for Keeps. Arno.
MacCormack, John R.
xMacCormack, John R.
Revolutionary Politics in the Long Parliament.
Harvard U Pr.
MacCormick, Neil.
xMacCormick, Neil.

Legal Reasoning & Legal Theory. Oxford U Pr.
MacCracken, John H. *see* Maccracken, John Henry.
MacCracken, John Henry, 1875-1948
xMacCracken, John H.
College & Commonwealth, & Other
Educational Papers & Addresses. Arno.
MacCracken, Mary.
xMacCracken, Mary.
A Circle of Children. Lippincott.
Lovey: A Very Special Child. NAL.
MacCulloch, J. Arnott. *see* Macculloch, John Arnott.
MacCulloch, John A. *see* Macculloch, John Arnott.
MacCulloch, John Arnott, 1868-1950
xMacCulloch, J. Arnott.
Medieval Faith & Fable. R West.
xMacCulloch, John A.
The Celtic & Scandinavian Religions.
Greenwood.
The Religion of the Ancient Celts. Folcroft.
MacCunn, John, 1846-1929
xMacCunn, John.
Political Philosophy of Burke. Russell.
MacDermot, Violet.
xMacDermot, Violet.
The Cult of the Seer in the Ancient Middle
East: A Contribution to Current Research on
Hallucinations Drawn from Coptic & Other
Texts. U of Cal Pr.
MacDonagh, Oliver.
xMacDonagh, Oliver.
Early Victorian Government, 1830-1870.
Holmes & Meier.
MacDonagh, Thomas, 1878-1916
xMacDonagh, Thomas.
Thomas Campion & the Art of English Poetry.
Russell.
MacDonald, A. F. *see* Macdonald, Austin Faulks.
Macdonald, A. R.
xMacDonald, A. R.
Prison Secrets. Arno.
Macdonald, Alexander, 1791?-1850
xMacdonald, Alexander.
ed. Letters to the Argyll Family from Elizabeth
Queen of England, Mary Queen of Scots, &
Others. AMS Pr.
Macdonald, Allan H. *see* Macdonald, Allan Houston.
Macdonald, Allan Houston, 1901-1951
xMacdonald, Allan H.
Richard Hovey, Man & Craftsman.
Greenwood.
MacDonald, Austin F. *see* Macdonald, Austin Faulks.
Macdonald, Austin Faulks, 1898-
xMacDonald, A. F.
Federal Aid: A Study of the American Subsidy
System. Arno.
xMacDonald, Austin F.
Government of the Argentine Republic. AMS
Pr.
MacDonald, Betty. *see* Macdonald, Betty (Bard).
MacDonald, Betty (Bard).
xMacDonald, Betty.
Mrs. Piggle-Wiggle. Lippincott.
Mrs. Piggle-Wiggle's Farm. Lippincott.
Mrs. Piggle-Wiggle's Magic. Lippincott.
MacDonald, Charles B.
xMacDonald, Charles B.
Company Commander. Bantam.
Company Commander. Zenger Pub.
MacDonald, Daniel. *see* Macdonald, Daniel J.
MacDonald, Daniel J., 1881-
xMacDonald, Daniel.
Radicalism of Shelley & Its Sources. Phaeton.
xMacDonald, Daniel J.
Radicalism of Shelley & Its Sources. Folcroft.
MacDonald, David D.
xMacDonald, David D.
The Defiant Cadence. FAS Pubs.
Don't Curse the Verse. FAS Pubs.
Macdonald, Donald, 1791-1872
xMacdonald, Donald.

Diaries of Donald Macdonald. Kelley.
Macdonald, Donald F. *see* Macdonald, Donald Farquhar.
Macdonald, Donald Farquhar, 1906-
xMacdonald, Donald F.
Scotland's Shifting Population: 1770-1850.
Porcupine Pr.
MacDonald, Duncan A.
xMacDonald, Duncan A.
Drafting Documents in Plain Language. PLI.
Macdonald, Duncan B. *see* Macdonald, Duncan Black.
Macdonald, Duncan Black, 1863-1943
xMacdonald, Duncan B.
Aspects of Islam. Arno.
Religious Attitude & Life in Islam. AMS Pr.
Macdonald, Elisabeth, 1926-
xMacdonald, Elisabeth.
The House at Gray Eagle. Scribner.
MacDonald, G. *see* Macdonald, George.
Macdonald, George, 1824-1905
xMacDonald, G.
Coin Types: Their Origin & Development.
Longwood Pr.
The Silver Coinage of Crete: A Metrological
Note. Obol Intl.
xMacdonald, George.
At the Back of the North Wind. Biblio Dist.
At the Back of the North Wind. Cook.
At the Back of the North Wind. Garland Pub.
At the Back of the North Wind. Macmillan.
At the Back of the North Wind. Airmont.
At the Back of the North Wind. Schocken.
The Complete Fairy Tales of George
MacDonald. Schocken.
Gold Coast Past & Present: A Short
Description of the Country & Its People.
Negro U Pr.
The Golden Key. FS&G.
Life Essential: The Hope of the Gospel. Shaw
Pubs.
Light Princess. T Y Crowell.
The Light Princess. Dell.
The Light Princess. FS&G.
The Miracles of Our Lord. Shaw Pubs.
Paul Faber, Surgeon. Garland Pub.
The Princess & Curdie. Cook.
The Princess & Curdie. Zondervan.
Princess & Curdie. Macmillan.
Princess & Curdie. Penguin.
The Princess & the Goblin. Cook.
The Princess & the Goblin. Zondervan.
Princess & the Goblin. Penguin.
Princess & the Goblin. Airmont.
Sir Gibbie. Schocken.
Stephen Archer, & Other Tales. Arno.
Macdonald, George. *see* Macdonald, George Everett
Hussey.
Macdonald, George Everett Hussey, 1857-1944
xMacdonald, George.
Fifty Years of Freethought. Gordon Pr.
MacDonald, Gordon.
xMacdonald, Gordon.
The Effective Father. Tyndale.
Macdonald, Greville, 1856-1944
xMacdonald, Greville.
George Macdonald & His Wife. Johnson Repr.
MacDonald, Gwendoline.
xMacdonald, Gwendoline.
Development of Standards & Accreditation in
Collegiate Nursing Education. Lippincott.
Macdonald, Helen G. *see* Macdonald, Helen Grace.
Macdonald, Helen Grace, 1888-
xMacdonald, Helen G.
Canadian Public Opinion on the American
Civil War. Octagon.
MacDonald, Hope.
xMacdonald, Hope.
Discovering How to Pray. Zondervan.
Discovering the Joy of Obedience. Zondervan.
MacDonald, Hugh, 1885-
xMacdonald, Hugh.

ed. Englands Helicon. Harvard U Pr.
Portraits in Prose: A Collection of Characters.
Elliots Bks.
MacDonald, Hugh. *see* Macdonald, Hugh John.
MacDonald, Hugh John.
xMacDonald, Hugh.
Skryabin. Oxford U Pr.
MacDonald, Isobel.
xMacdonald, Isobel.
The Buried Self: A Background to the Poems
of Matthew Arnold. Folcroft.
MacDonald, J. Ramsey. *see* Macdonald, James Ramsay.
MacDonald, James.
xMacDonald, James.
Religion & Myth. Negro U Pr.
MacDonald, James Ramsay, 1866-1937
xMacdonald, J. Ramsey.
National Defence: A Study in Militarism.
Garland Pub.
MacDonald, Janet.
xMacdonald, Janet.
Riding Side Saddle. Transatlantic.
MacDonald, John.
xMacdonald, John.
The Theology of the Samaritans. Allenson.
xMacdonald, John D.
Other Times, Other Worlds. Fawcett.
MacDonald, John. *see* Macdonald, John D.
MacDonald, John B. *see* Macdonald, John Dann.
MacDonald, John D.
xMacdonald, John.
All These Condemned. Fawcett.
xMacdonald, John D.
Area of Suspicion. Fawcett.
Bright Orange for the Shroud. Fawcett.
Bright Orange for the Shroud. Lippincott.
A Bullet for Cinderella. Fawcett.
Cancel All Our Vows. Fawcett.
Clemmie. Fawcett.
The Crossroads. Fawcett.
Cry Hard, Cry Fast. Fawcett.
The Damned. Fawcett.
A Deadly Shade of Gold. Fawcett.
A Deadly Shade of Gold. Lippincott.
Death Trap. Fawcett.
The Deep Blue Good-by. Fawcett.
The Deep Blue Good-by. Lippincott.
The Dreadful Lemon Sky. Fawcett.
The Dreadful Lemon Sky. Lippincott.
The End of Night. Fawcett.
The Girl, the Gold Watch, & Everything.
Fawcett.
One Monday We Killed Them All. Fawcett.
The Only Girl in the Game. Fawcett.
The Price of Murder. Fawcett.
Soft Touch. Fawcett.
Where Is Janice Gantry?. Fawcett.
MacDonald, John D. *see* Macdonald, John Dann.
Macdonald, John Dann, 1916-
xMacdonald, John B.
The Green Ripper. G K Hall.
xMacdonald, John D.

Ballroom of the Skies. Fawcett.
The Brass Cupcake. Fawcett.
Darker Than Amber. Fawcett.
Darker Than Amber: A Travis McGee Story.
Lippincott.
Dead Low Tide. Fawcett.
Deadly Welcome. Fawcett.
Dress Her in Indigo. Fawcett.
Dress Her in Indigo. Lippincott.
The Empty Copper Sea. Fawcett.
The Empty Copper Sea. G K Hall.
The Empty Copper Sea. Lippincott.
Executioners. Fawcett.
A Flash of Green. Fawcett.
Flash of Green. S&S.
Girl in the Plain Brown Wrapper. Fawcett.
Girl in the Plain Brown Wrapper. Lippincott.
The Green Ripper. Fawcett.
The Green Ripper. Lippincott.
The Last One Left. Fawcett.
The Long Lavender Look. Fawcett.
The Long Lavender Look. Lippincott.
Murder for the Bride. Fawcett.
Murder in the Wind. Fawcett.
The Neon Jungle. Fawcett.
Nightmare in Pink. Fawcett.
Nightmare in Pink. G K Hall.
Nightmare in Pink. Lippincott.
On the Run. Fawcett.
One Fearful Yellow Eye. Fawcett.
One Fearful Yellow Eye. Lippincott.
Pale Gray for Guilt. Fawcett.
Pale Gray for Guilt. Lippincott.
A Purple Place for Dying. Fawcett.
The Quick Red Fox. Fawcett.
The Quick Red Fox. Lippincott.
The Scarlet Ruse. G K Hall.
The Scarlet Ruse. Lippincott.
Tan & Sandy Silence. Fawcett.
A Tan & Sandy Silence. Lippincott.
The Turquoise Lament. Fawcett.
Turquoise Lament. Lippincott.
xMacdonald, John S.
A Purple Place for Dying. Lippincott.
Macdonald, John M. *see* Macdonald, John Marshall.
Macdonald, John Marshall, 1920-
xMacdonald, John M.
Armed Robbery: Offenders & Their Victims. C
C Thomas.
Homicidal Threats. C C Thomas.
Indecent Exposure. C C Thomas.
Psychiatry & the Criminal: A Guide to
Psychiatric Examinations for the Criminal
Courts. C C Thomas.
MacDonald, John S. *see* Macdonald, John Dann.
MacDonald, K. L.
xMacDonald, K. L.
Automotive Air Conditioning. Audel.
MacDonald, Keith N. *see* Macdonald, Keith Norman.
MacDonald, Keith Norman, b. 1834
xMacdonald, Keith N.
The Practice of Medicine Among the Burmese.
AMS Pr.
MacDonald, Lorne, 1936-
xMacdonald, Lorne.
Practical Analysis of Amplifier Circuits
Through Experimentation. Tech Ed Pr.
Practical Analysis of Electronic Circuits
Through Experimentation. Tech Ed Pr.
MacDonald, Malcolm, 1932-
xMacdonald, Malcolm.
The Rich Are with You Always. NAL.
Sons of Fortune. Knopf.
Sons of Fortune. NAL.
The Symphonies of Havergal Brian. Taplinger.
The World from Rough Stones. NAL.
xMacdonald, Malcolm R.
The Origin of Johnny. Knopf.
Macdonald, Malcolm R. *see* Macdonald, Malcolm.
Macdonald, Marion E. *see* Macdonald, Marion Ethel.

Macdonald, Marion Ethel, 1893-
  xMacdonald, Marion E.
    The Significance of Various Kinds of
      Preparation for the City-Elementary School
      Principalship in Pennsylvania with
      Implications for a Program for Preparing for
      the Elementary-School Principalship in. AMS
      Pr.
MacDonald, Maurice, 1947-
  xMacDonald, Maurice.
    Food Stamps, & Income Maintenance. Acad
      Pr.
MacDonald, N. see Macdonald, Norman.
Macdonald, Nesta.
  xMacDonald, Nesta.
    Diaghilev Observed by Critics in England &
      the United States, 1911-1929. Dance Horiz.
MacDonald, Norman, 1934-
  xMacDonald, N.
    Time Lags in Biological Models.
      Springer-Verlag.
MacDonald, Peter.
  xMacDonald, Peter.
    Mathematics & Statistics for Scientists &
      Engineers. Van Nos Reinhold.
MacDonald, Philip.
  xMacDonald, Philip.
    The Rasp. Dover.
Macdonald, R. Ross. see Macdonald, Roderick Ross.
Macdonald, R. St. J. see Macdonald, Ronald St. J.
Macdonald, Robert M.
  xMacDonald, Robert M.
    Collective Bargaining in the Automobile
      Industry: A Study of Wage Structure &
      Competitive Relations. Yale U Pr.
Macdonald, Robert W.
  xMacdonald, Robert W.
    League of Arab States: A Study in the
      Dynamics of Regional Organization.
      Princeton U Pr.
Macdonald, Roderick Ross, 1922-
  xMacdonald, R. Ross.
    Indonesian Reference Grammar. Georgetown U
      Pr.
Macdonald, Ronald St. J.
  xMacdonald, R. St. J.
    ed. Canadian Perspectives on International Law
      & Organization. U of Toronto Pr.
Macdonald, Ross, 1915-
  xMacDonald, Ross.
    The Moving Target. Gregg.
    On Crime Writing. Capra Pr.
Macdonald, Shelagh.
  xMacdonald, Shelagh.
    No End to Yesterday. Andre Deutsch.
MacDonald, W. Scott. see Macdonald, Willard Scott.
MacDonald, Willard Scott.
  xMacDonald, W. Scott.
    Focus on Classroom Behavior: Readings &
      Research. C C Thomas.
MacDonald, William, 1863-1938
  xMacDonald, William.
    ed. Documentary Source Book of American
      History 1606-1926. B Franklin.
Macdonald, William K.
  xMacdonald, William K.
    Digging for Gold: Papers on Archaeology for
      Profit. U Mich Mus Anthro.
MacDonald, William L.
  xMacdonald, William L.
    The Pantheon: Design, Meaning & Progeny.
      Harvard U Pr.
Macdonell, A. A. see Macdonell, Arthur Anthony.
Macdonell, Annie.
  xMacdonell, Annie.
    Thomas Hardy. AMS Pr.
    Thomas Hardy. Folcroft.
MacDonell, Arthur A. see Macdonell, Arthur Anthony.
Macdonell, Arthur Anthony, 1854-1930
  xMacdonell, A. A.

Vedic Mythology. Orient Bk Dist.
  xMacDonell, Arthur A.
    History of Sanskrit Literature. Haskell.
    India's Past: A Survey of Her Literatures,
      Religions, Languages & Antiquities. Hyperion
      Conn.
    Vedic Mythology. Gordon Pr.
MacDougall, Bruce.
  xMacDougall, Bruce.
    Rejoice in the Lord. Abingdon.
MacDougall, Curtis. see Macdougall, Curtis Daniel.
MacDougall, Curtis Daniel, 1903-
  xMacDougall, Curtis.
    Hoaxes. Dover.
MacDougall, Hamilton C. see Macdougall, Hamilton
  Crawford.
Macdougall, Hamilton Crawford, 1858-
  xMacDougall, Hamilton C.
    Early New England Psalmody: An Historical
      Appreciation, 1620-1820. Da Capo.
MacDougall, James, 1833-1906
  xMacDougall, James.
    ed. Folk & Hero Tales. AMS Pr.
    Highland Fairy Legends. Rowman.
MacDougall, Ruth D. see Macdougall, Ruth Doan.
MacDougall, Ruth Doan, 1939
  xMacDougall, Ruth D.
    Aunt Pleasantine. Har-Row.
    The Cost of Living. PB.
MacDowall, David W. see Macdowall, David William.
MacDowall, David William.
  xMacDowall, David W.
    The Western Coinages of Nero. Am
      Numismatic.
MacDowell, Douglas M. see Macdowell, Douglas
  Maurice.
MacDowell, Douglas Maurice.
  xMacDowell, Douglas M.
    The Law in Classical Athens. Cornell U Pr.
Mace, Carroll E. see Mace, Carroll Edward.
Mace, Carroll Edward, 1926-
  xMace, Carroll E.
    Two Spanish-Quiche Dance Dramas of
      Rabinal. Tulane Romance Lang.
Mace, David. see Mace, David Robert.
Mace, David R. see Mace, David Robert.
Mace, David Robert.
  xMace, David.
    Marriage Enrichment in the Church.
      Broadman.
  xMace, David R.
    Christian Response to the Sexual Revolution.
      Abingdon.
    Getting Ready for Marriage. Abingdon.
    Success in Marriage. Abingdon.
    Success in Marriage. Abingdon.
Mace, Elisabeth.
  xMace, Elisabeth.
    The Ghost Diviners. Elsevier-Nelson.
    Out There. Greenwillow.
    The Rushton Inheritance. Elsevier-Nelson.
Mace, George, 1934-
  xMace, George.
    Locke, Hobbes, & the Federalist Papers: An
      Essay on the Genesis of the American
      Political Heritage. S Ill U Pr.
Mace, Herbert.
  xMace, Herbert.
    The Complete Handbook of Beekeeping. Van
      Nos Reinhold.
Maceachron, Judith.
  xMacEachron, Judith.
    Tomorrow Is for Weeping. Regmar Pub.
Macedo, Jorge.
  xMacedo, Jorge.
    The Theoretical Basis of the Living System.
      Fireside Bks.
    Theoretical Basis of the Living System. Green.
Macedo, Manuel C.
  xMacedo, Manuel C.

Value Management for Construction. Wiley.
Macey, Robert I.
  xMacey, Robert I.
    Human Physiology. P-H.
Macey, Samuel L.
  xMacey, Samuel L.
    Clocks & the Cosmos: Time in Western Life &
      Thought. Shoe String.
Macfall, Haldane, 1860-1928
  xMacFall, Haldane.
    Ibsen: The Man, His Art & His Significance.
      Folcroft.
MacFarlan, Allan A.
  xMacfarlan, Allan A.
    Boy's Book of Biking. PB.
    Boy's Book of Biking. Archway.
MacFarland, Harold E.
  xMacFarland, Harold E.
    Introduction to Modern Gunsmithing. B&N.
Macfarlane, Aidan, 1939-
  xMacfarlane, Aidan.
    The Psychology of Childbirth. Harvard U Pr.
Macfarlane, Alistair G. see Macfarlane, Alistair George J.
MacFarlane, Alistair George J.
  xMacfarlane, Alistair G.
    Frequency Response Methods in Control
      Systems. Wiley.
Macfarlane, David A.
  xMacfarlane, David A.
    ed. Textbook of Surgery. Churchill.
MacFarlane, W. N. see Macfarlane, William N.
Macfarlane, William N., 1920-
  xMacFarlane, W. N.
    Principles of Small Business Management.
      McGraw.
Macfie, Alec L. see Macfie, Alec Lawrence.
Macfie, Alec Lawrence.
  xMacfie, Alec L.
    Theories of the Trade Cycle. Kelley.
Macfie, Matthew.
  xMacfie, Matthew.
    Vancouver Island & British Columbia: Their
      History, Resources & Prospects. Arno.
MacGaffey, Wyatt.
  xMacGaffey, Wyatt.
    Custom & Government in the Lower Congo. U
      of Cal Pr.
MacGahan, J. A. see Macgahan, Januarius Aloysius.
MacGahan, Januarius Aloysius, 1844-1878
  xMacGahan, J. A.
    Campaigning on the Oxus & the Fall of Khiva.
      Arno.
MacGibbon, David, d. 1902
  xMacGibbon, David.
    The Architecture of Provence & the Riviera.
      Longwood Pr.
MacGillavry, Caroline H. see Macgillavry, Caroline
  Henriette.
MacGillavry, Caroline Henriette, 1904-
  xMacGillavry, Caroline H.
    Fantasy & Symmetry: The Periodic Drawings
      of M. C. Escher. Abrams.
MacGillivray, Ian.
  xMacGillivray, Ian.
    Human Multiple Reproduction. Saunders.
MacGinitie, Harry D. see Macginitie, Harry Dunlap.
Macginitie, Harry Dunlap.
  xMacGinitie, Harry D.
    An Early Middle Eocene Flora from the
      Yellowstone-Absaroka Volcanic Province
      North-Western Wind River Basin, Wyoming.
      U of Cal Pr.
MacGinitie, Walter H.
  xMacGinitie, Walter H.
    ed. Assessment Problems in Reading. Intl
      Reading.
MacGorman, J. W. see Macgorman, Jack W.
MacGorman, Jack W.
  xMacGorman, J. W.

The Gifts of the Spirit. Broadman.
Macgowan, Kenneth, 1888-
xMacgowan, Kenneth.
Early Man in the New World. Peter Smith.
Golden Ages of the Theater: A Classic Now
Revised & Expanded. P-H.
MacGregor, A. J. see Macgregor, Arthur J.
MacGregor, Arthur J., 1939-
xMacGregor, A. J.
Graphics Simplified: How to Plan & Prepare
Effective Charts, Graphs, Illustrations, &
Other Visual Aids. U of Toronto Pr.
MacGregor, Bruce. see Macgregor, Bruce A.
MacGregor, Bruce A.
xMacGregor, Bruce.
Portrait of a Silver Lady: The Train They
Called the California Zephyr. Pruett.
MacGregor, Carol.
xMacGregor, Carol.
Storybook Cookbook. Doubleday.
MacGregor, Ellen.
xMacGregor, Ellen.
Miss Pickerell & the Weather Satellite.
Archway.
Miss Pickerell & the Weather Satellite. PB.
Miss Pickerell Meets Mr. H. U. M.. McGraw.
Miss Pickerell Meets Mr. H. U. M.. PB.
Miss Pickerell Meets Mr. H.U.M.. Archway.
MacGregor, Forbes.
xMacGregor, Forbes.
Scots Proverbs & Rhymes. Folcroft.
MacGregor, Geddes.
xMacGregor, Geddes.
Rhythm of God: A Philosophy of Worship.
Seabury.
Scotland Forever Home: An Introduction to
the Homeland for American & Other Scots.
Dodd.
MacGregor, John Marshall, 1879-1936
xMacGregor, Marshall.
Studies & Diversions in Greek Literature.
Kennikat.
MacGregor, M. H. see Macgregor, Malcolm Herbert.
MacGregor, Malcolm B. see Macgregor, Malcolm Blair.
Macgregor, Malcolm Blair.
xMacGregor, Malcolm B.
The Sources & Literature of Scottish Church
History. Richwood Pub.
MacGregor, Malcolm Herbert, 1926-
xMacGregor, M. H.
The Nature of the Elementary Particle.
Springer-Verlag.
MacGregor, Marshall. see Macgregor, John Marshall.
MacGregor, Ronald N. see Macgregor, Ronald Norman.
MacGregor, Ronald Norman, 1932-
xMacGregor, Ronald N.
Art Plus. McGraw.
MacGregor-Hastie, Roy.
xMacGregor-Hastie, Roy.
Africa: Background for Today. Abelard.
Macgregor-Morris, Pamela.
xMacgregor-Morris, Pamela.
ed. The Book of the Horse. Putnam.
Machado de Assis, Joaquim M. see Machado De Assis,
Joaquim Maria.
Machado, Jeanne. see Machado, Jeanne M.
Machado, Jeanne M.
xMachado, Jeanne.
Early Childhood Experiences in Language Arts.
Delmar.
Machado, Luis A. see Machado, Luis Alberto.
Machado, Luis Alberto.
xMachado, Luis A.
The Right to Be Intelligent. Pergamon.
Machado, Manuel A.
xMachado, Manuel A.

An Industry in Crisis: Mexican-United States
Cooperation in the Control of
Foot-And-Mouth Disease. U of Cal Pr.
Machado De Assis, Joaquim Maria, 1839-1908
xMachado de Assis, Joaquim M.
The Psychiatrist & Other Stories. U of Cal Pr.
MacHaffie, Ingeborg.
xMacHaffie, Ingeborg S.
Of Danish Ways. Dillon.
MacHaffie, Ingeborg S. see Machaffie, Ingeborg.
Machamer, Peter K.
xMachamer, Peter K.
ed. Studies in Perception: Interrelations in the
History of Philosophy & Science. Ohio St U
Pr.
Machan, Tibor R.
xMachan, Tibor R.
ed. The Libertarian Alternative: Essays in
Social & Political Philosophy. Nelson-Hall.
The Pseudo Science of B. F. Skinner. Arlington
Hse.
Machemer, Robert.
xMachemer, Robert.
Vitrectomy. Grune.
Machen, Arthur, 1863-1947
xMachen, Arthur.
Dreads & Drolls. Arno.
Great God Pan. Arno.
House of Souls. Arno.
Machen, J. Gresham. see Machen, John Gresham.
Machen, John Gresham.
xMachen, J. Gresham.
Christianity & Liberalism. Eerdmans.
Origin of Paul's Religion. Eerdmans.
Macherey, Pierre.
xMacherey, Pierre.
A Theory of Literary Production. Routledge &
Kegan.
Machiavelli. see Machiavelli, Niccolo.
Machiavelli, Niccol. see Machiavelli, Niccolo.
Machiavelli, Niccolo.
xMachiavelli
Discourses. Penguin.
The Portable Machiavelli. Viking Pr.
xMachiavelli, Niccol.
Prince. PB.
xMachiavelli, Niccolo.
Art of War. Bobbs.
The Discourses. Routledge & Kegan.
The Living Thoughts of Machiavelli.
Greenwood.
The Prince. Bobbs.
Prince. Dutton.
Prince. NAL.
The Prince. Norton.
Prince. St Martin.
The Prince. U of Dallas Pr.
Prince. Penguin.
The Prince. AHM Pub.
Prince. Airmont.
The Prince & Other Works. Hendricks House.
Machin, G. I. see Machin, G. I. T.
Machin, G. I. T.
xMachin, G. I.
Politics and the Churches in Great Britain,
1832-1868. Oxford U Pr.
Machin, Howard.
xMachin, Howard.
The Prefect in French Public Administration.
St Martin.
Machinability Data Center.
xTheTechnical Staff of the Machinability Data
Center.
ed. Machining Data Handbook. Metcut Res
Assocs.
Machinery & Allied Products Institute Seminar on
Occupational Safety & Health, Washington, D.C.,
1973. see Machinery and Allied Products Institute.
Machinery and Allied Products Institute.
xMachinery & Allied Products Institute Seminar

on Occupational Safety & Health, Washington,
D.C., 1973.
Occupational Safety & Health: A Transcript. M
& A Products.
Machlin, Evangeline.
xMachlin, Evangeline.
Speech for the Stage. Theatre Arts.
Machlin, Milt. see Machlin, Milton.
Machlin, Milton.
xMachlin, Milt.
The Total UFO Story. Dale Books Inc.
Machlis, Joseph, 1906-
xMachlis, Joseph.
Introduction to Contemporary Music. Norton.
Introduction to Contemporary Music. Norton.
Machlis, Leonard.
xMachlis, Leonard.
Plants in Action: A Laboratory Manual of
Plant Physiology. W H Freeman.
Machlup, Fritz, 1902-
xMachlup, Fritz.
The Alignment of Foreign Exchange Rates.
Irvington.
The Alignment of Foreign Exchange Rates.
NYU Pr.
A History of Thought on Economic
Integration. Columbia U Pr.
The Production & Distribution of Knowledge
in the United States. Princeton U Pr.
Machol, Robert E. see Machol, Robert Engel.
Machol, Robert Engel.
xMachol, Robert E.
System Engineering Handbook. McGraw.
Machover, Solomon, 1906-
xMachover, Solomon.
Cultural & Racial Variations in Patterns of
Intellect: Performance of Negro & White
Criminals on the Bellevue Adult Intelligence
Scale. AMS Pr.
Machray, Robert, 1857-1946
xMachray, Robert.
The Little Entente. Fertig.
Macht, Joel, 1938-
xMacht, Joel.
Teaching Our Children. Wiley.
Macht, Lee B.
xMacht, Lee B.
ed. Neighborhood Psychiatry. Lexington Bks.
Maciel, Gary E.
xMaciel, Gary E.
Chemistry. Heath.
MacInnes, Helen.
xMacInnes, Helen.
Above Suspicion. Fawcett.
Above Suspicion. HarBraceJ.
Agent in Place. Fawcett.
Agent in Place. G K Hall.
Agent in Place. HarBraceJ.
Assignment in Brittany. Fawcett.
Assignment in Brittany. HarBraceJ.
Decision at Delphi. Fawcett.
The Double Image. Fawcett.
Double Image. HarBraceJ.
Friends & Lovers. Fawcett.
Horizon. HarBraceJ.
I & My True Love. Fawcett.
I & My True Love. HarBraceJ.
Prelude to Terror. Fawcett.
Prelude to Terror. HarBraceJ.
The Venetian Affair. Fawcett.
Venetian Affair. HarBraceJ.
MacInnes, Hugh.
xMacInnes, Hugh.
Turbochargers. H P Bks.
Macinnis, Joe. see Macinnis, Joseph B.
MacInnis, Joseph B.
xMacinnis, Joe.
Underwater Man. Dodd.
Macintosh, Douglas C. see Macintosh, Douglas Clyde.

Macintosh, Douglas Clyde, 1877-1948
 xMacintosh, Douglas C.
  Theology As an Empirical Science. Arno.
MacIntosh, Duncan.
 xMacintosh, Duncan.
  Chinese Blue & White Porcelain. C E Tuttle.
Macintosh, E. K.
 xMacintosh, E. K.
  Guide to the Rocks, Minerals & Gemstones of
   Southern Africa. Verry.
Macintosh, H. G. see Macintosh, Henry Gordon.
MacIntosh, Harold C., 1940-
 xMacIntosh, Harold C.
  The Chain Saw Craft Book. Pruett.
Macintosh, Henry Gordon.
 xMacintosh, H. G.
  Assessment & the Secondary School Teacher.
   Routledge & Kegan.
Macintosh, J. J. see Macintosh, John James.
MacIntosh, John, 1853-
 xMacintosh, John.
  Life of Robert Burns. AMS Pr.
MacIntosh, John James.
 xMacintosh, J. J.
  ed. Business of Reason. Humanities.
MacIntyre, Alasdair. see Macintyre, Alasdair C.
MacIntyre, Alasdair C.
 xMacIntyre, Alasdair.
  Religious Significance of Atheism. Columbia U
   Pr.
 xMacIntyre, Alasdair C.
  Unconscious: A Conceptual Analysis.
   Humanities.
MacIntyre, C. F. see Macintyre, Carlyle Ferren.
MacIntyre, Carlyle Ferren, 1890-
 xMacIntyre, C. F.
  tr. French Symbolist Poetry. U of Cal Pr.
MacIntyre, Donald G. see Macintyre, Donald G. F. W.
MacIntyre, Donald G. F. W.
 xMacintyre, Donald.
  U-Boat Killer. Naval Inst Pr.
 xMacIntyre, Donald G.
  Fighting Ships & Seamen. Greenwood.
MacIntyre, Elisabeth.
 xMacIntyre, Elisabeth.
  The Purple Mouse. Elsevier-Nelson.
MacIsaac, Fred.
 xMacIsaac, Fred.
  The Hothouse World. Bouregy.
MacIver, Robert M. see Maciver, Robert Morrison.
MacIver, Robert Morrison, 1882-1970
 xMacIver, Robert M.
  Academic Freedom in Our Time. Gordian.
  Leviathan & the People. Kennikat.
  The Nations & the United Nations.
   Greenwood.
MacIvers, Donald.
 xMacivers, Donald.
  Cult of Killers. Nordon Pubns.
Mack, C. see Mack, Cornelius.
Mack, Carol K.
 xMack, Carol K.
  The Chameleon Variant. Dial.
Mack, Cornelius.
 xMack, C.
  Essentials of Statistics for Scientists &
   Technologists. Plenum Pub.
 xMack, Cornelius.
  Essentials of Statistics for Scientists &
   Technologists. Plenum Pub.
Mack, Dorothy.
 xMack, Dorothy.
  The Substitute Bride. Dell.
Mack, Edward C. see Mack, Edward Clarence.
Mack, Edward Clarence, 1904-
 xMack, Edward C.

  Public Schools & British Opinion Since 1860:
   The Relationship Between Contemporary
   Ideas & the Evolution of an English
   Institution. Greenwood.
Mack, Gerstle, 1894-
 xMack, Gerstle.
  Gustave Courbet. Greenwood.
  Paul Cezanne. Octagon.
Mack, Jacque.
 xMack, Jacque.
  Stanley Meets Do Good & Be Bad. Concordia.
Mack, James, 1932-
 xMack, James.
  Psychological Examination & Report Writing.
   Exposition.
Mack, Jerry.
 xMack, Jerry.
  Catfish Farming Handbook. Educator Bks.
Mack, Jim.
 xMack, Jim.
  Haleakala: The Story Behind the Scenery. K C
   Pubns.
Mack, John E., 1929-
 xMack, John E.
  ed. Borderline States in Psychiatry. Grune.
  A Prince of Our Disorder: The Life of T. E.
   Lawrence. Little.
Mack, Karin.
 xMack, Karin.
  Overcoming Writing Blocks. HM.
  Overcoming Writing Blocks. J P Tarcher.
  Overcoming Writing Blocks. St Martin.
Mack, Maynard, 1909-
 xMack, Maynard.
  ed. The Continental Edition of World
   Masterpieces. Norton.
  Garden & the City: Retirement & Politics in
   the Later Poetry of Pope, 1731-1743. U of
   Toronto Pr.
  ed. The Norton Anthology of World
   Masterpieces. Norton.
Mack, Raymond. see Mack, Raymond W.
Mack, Raymond W.
 xMack, Raymond.
  Transforming America: Patterns of Social
   Change. Phila Bk Co.
 xMack, Raymond W.
  ed. Changing South. Transaction Bks.
  ed. Race, Class & Power. Van Nos Reinhold.
  jt. auth. Sociology & Social Life. D Van
   Nostrand.
  Transforming America: Patterns of Social
   Change. Random.
Mack, Sara, 1939-
 xMack, Sara.
  Patterns of Time in Vergil. Shoe String.
Mack, Stan. see Mack, Stanley.
Mack, Stanley.
 xMack, Stan.
  Stan Mack's Real Life Funnies: Guarantee All
   Dialogue Is Reported Verbatim. Putnam.
  illus. Where's My Cheese?. Pantheon.
Mack, Zella.
 xMack, Zella.
  California Paralegal's Handbook. Parker & Son.
Mackail, Denis G. see Mackail, Denis George.
Mackail, Denis George, 1892-
 xMackail, Denis G.
  How Amusing: & a Lot of Other Fables. Arno.
  Tales from Greenery Street. Arno.
Mackail, J. W. see Mackail, John William.
Mackail, John W. see Mackail, John William.
Mackail, John William, 1859-1945
 xMackail, J. W.
  Lectures on Greek Poetry. Biblo.
  Lectures on Greek Poetry. Gordon Pr.
  Life of William Morris. Arno.
  Pope. Gordon Pr.
 xMackail, John W.

  Approach to Shakespeare. AMS Pr.
  Approach to Shakespeare. Arno.
  Classical Studies. Arno.
  Lectures on Poetry. Arno.
  Life of William Morris. Haskell.
  Pope. Folcroft.
  Studies in Humanism. Arno.
  Swinburne: A Lecture Delivered Before the
   University on April 30, 1909. Folcroft.
Mackall, Lucy.
 xMackall, Lucy.
  Lucy's Bag Book. HM.
MacKay, Alfred F.
 xMacKay, Alfred F.
  Arrow's Theorem: the Paradox of Social
   Choice: A Case Study in the Philosophy of
   Economics. Yale U Pr.
MacKay, Angus, 1939-
 xMacKay, Angus.
  Spain in the Middle Ages: From Frontier to
   Empire, 1000-1500. St Martin.
Mackay, Charles, 1814-1889
 xMackay, Charles.
  Extraordinary Popular Delusions & the
   Madness of Crowds. Crown.
  Extraordinary Popular Delusions & the
   Madness of Crowds. FS&G.
  Life & Liberty in America: Or, Sketches of a
   Tour in the United States & Canada in
   1857-58. Johnson Repr.
  ed. Medora Leigh: A History & an
   Autobiography. AMS Pr.
MacKay, David, fl. 1968-
 xMacKay, David.
  ed. Flock of Words: An Anthology of Poetry
   for Children & Others. HarBraceJ.
MacKay, Donald M. see Mackay, Donald Maccrimmon.
MacKay, Donald MacCrimmon, 1922-
 xMacKay, Donald M.
  Human Science & Human Dignity.
   Inter-Varsity.
  Information, Mechanism & Meaning. MIT Pr.
Mackay, I. R. see Mackay, Ian R.
Mackay, Ian R.
 xMackay, I. R.
  ed. Multidisciplinary Gerontology: A Structure
   for Research in Gerontology in a Developed
   Country. S Karger.
MacKay, Ian R. see Mackay, Ian R. A.
MacKay, Ian R. A.
 xMacKay, Ian R.
  Introducing Practical Phonetics. Little.
MacKay, James.
 xMacKay, James.
  Encyclopedia of Small Antiques. Har-Row.
MacKay, James A. see Mackay, James Alexander.
Mackay, James Alexander.
 xMacKay, James A.
  Dictionary of Stamps in Color. Macmillan.
  Encyclopedia of World Stamps, 1945-1975.
   McGraw.
  Value in Coins & Medals. Transatlantic.
Mackay, Kenneth C. see Mackay, Kenneth Campbell.
MacKay, Kenneth Campbell, 1911-
 xMackay, Kenneth C.
  Progressive Movement of 1924. Octagon.
MacKay, Richard V. see Mackay, Richard Vance.
Mackay, Richard Vance.
 xMacKay, Richard V.
  The Law of Guardianships. Oceana.
Mackay, Robert A. see Mackay, Robert Alexander.
Mackay, Robert Alexander, 1894-
 xMackay, Robert A.
  ed. Newfoundland: Economic, Diplomatic &
   Strategic Studies. AMS Pr.
MacKaye, Percy, 1875-1956
 xMacKaye, Percy.
  Tall Tales of the Kentucky Mountains.
   Greenwood.
Mackean, D. J. see Mackean, Donald Gordon.

Mackean, Donald Gordon.
xMackean, D. J.
Introduction to Genetics. Transatlantic.

MacKechnie, John, 1897-
xMackechnie, John.
Compiled by Catalogue of Gaelic Manuscripts in Selected Libraries in Great Britain & Ireland. G K Hall.

MacKeever, Frank C.
xMacKeever, Frank C.
Native & Naturalized Plants of Nantucket. U of Mass Pr.

MacKeever, Maggie.
xMacKeever, Maggie.
A Banbury Tale. Fawcett.
Sweet Vixen. Fawcett.

MacKeith, Ronald. *see* Mackeith, Ronald Charles.

MacKeith, Ronald Charles.
xMacKeith, Ronald.
Infant Feeding & Feeding Difficulties. Churchill.

MacKellar, William.
xMacKellar, William.
The Cat That Never Died. Dodd.
The Ghost of Grannoch Moor. Dodd.
The Silent Bells. Dodd.
The Soccer Orphans. Dodd.

Macken, Walter, 1915-1967
xMacken, Walter.
Flight of the Doves. Macmillan.
Flight of the Doves. Macmillan.
Silent People. Macmillan.

MacKendrick, Louise.
xMacKendrick, Louise.
The Glory Seeker. Belmont-Tower.
Natchez. Belmont Tower.
A Passion for Honor. Nordon Pubns.

MacKendrick, Paul. *see* Mackendrick, Paul Lachlan.

MacKendrick, Paul Lachlan, 1914-
xMacKendrick, Paul.
Athenian Aristocracy, 399 to 31 B. C. Harvard U Pr.
The Greek Stones Speak: The Story of Archaeology in Greek Lands. Norton.
The Mute Stones Speak: The Story of Archaeology in Italy. Norton.

Mackenzie. *see* Mackenzie, Kenneth D.

Mackenzie, Alexander S. *see* Mackenzie, Alexander Slidell.

Mackenzie, Alexander Slidell, 1803-1848
xMackenzie, Alexander S.
The Life of Paul Jones. Arno.

MacKenzie, Andrew.
xMacKenzie, Andrew.
ed. A Gallery of Ghosts: An Anthology of Reported Experience. Taplinger.
Riddle of the Future: A Modern Study of Precognition. Taplinger.

Mackenzie, Charles A.
xMackenzie, Charles A.
Experimental Organic Chemistry. P-H.

Mackenzie, Charles E.
xMackenzie, Charles E.
Coded-Character Sets: History & Development. A-W.

MacKenzie, Charles S.
xMacKenzie, Charles S.
Pascal's Anguish & Joy. Philos Lib.

MacKenzie, Christine B. *see* Mackenzie, Christine Beckwith (Butchart).

MacKenzie, Christine Beckwith (Butchart).
xMacKenzie, Christine B.
Out at Home. Bethany Pr.

MacKenzie, Clara C. *see* Mackenzie, Clara Childs.

MacKenzie, Clara Childs.
xMacKenzie, Clara C.
Sarah Barnwell Elliott. Twayne.

Mackenzie, Compton, Sir, 1883-
xMackenzie, Compton.

Catholicism & Scotland. Kennikat.
Literature in My Time. Arno.
Realms of Silver. Arno.

MacKenzie, David.
xMacKenzie, David.
A History of Russia & the Soviet Union. Dorsey.

MacKenzie, Donald, 1908-
xMacKenzie, Donald.
Raven After Dark. HM.
Raven Settles a Score. Berkley Pub.
Raven Settles a Score. HM.

Mackenzie, Donald. *see* Mackenzie, Donald Alexander.

Mackenzie, Donald Alexander, 1873-1936
xMackenzie, Donald.
Indian Myth & Legend. Longwood Pr.

Mackenzie, Frederick, d. 1824
xMacKenzie, Frederick.
Diary of Frederick MacKenzie. Arno.

Mackenzie, Gregor.
xMackenzie, Gregor.
Memoirs of a Ghillie. David & Charles.

MacKenzie, James, 1680?-1761
xMacKenzie, James.
The History of Health, & the Art of Preserving It. Arno.

Mackenzie, Jeanne.
xMackenzie, Jeanne.
A Victorian Courtship: The Story of Beatrice Potter & Sidney Webb. Oxford U Pr.

Mackenzie, John, 1835-1899
xMackenzie, John.
Day-Dawn in Dark Places: A Story of Wanderings & Work in Bechwanaland. Negro U Pr.

MacKenzie, John S. *see* Mackenzie, John Stuart.

Mackenzie, John Stuart, 1860-1935
xMackenzie, John S.
Lectures on Humanism, with Special Reference to Its Bearings on Sociology. B Franklin.

Mackenzie, Kenneth D.
xMackenzie
A Theory of Group Structures. Gordon.
xMackenzie, Kenneth D.
Organizational Structures. AHM Pub.

MacKenzie, M. M. *see* Mackenzie, Marlin M.

Mackenzie, Manfred, 1934-
xMacKenzie, Manfred.
Communities of Honor & Love in Henry James. Harvard U Pr.

Mackenzie, Marlin M.
xMacKenzie, M. M.
Toward a New Curriculum in Physical Education. McGraw.

MacKenzie, Ossian.
xMacKenzie, Ossian.
ed. Changing World of Correspondence Study: International Readings. Pa St U Pr.

MacKenzie, R. A. *see* Mackenzie, Roderick Andrew Francis.

MacKenzie, Roderick Andrew Francis, 1911-
xMacKenzie, R. A.
Faith & History in the Old Testament. U of Minn Pr.

MacKenzie, W. J. *see* Mackenzie, William James Millar.

MacKenzie, W. Roy. *see* Mackenzie, William Roy.

Mackenzie, W. S.
xMackenzie, W. S.
Atlas of Rock-Forming Minerals in Thin Section. Halsted Pr.

MacKenzie, William C. *see* Mackenzie, William Cook.

Mackenzie, William Cook, 1862-1952
xMackenzie, William C.
The Highlands & Isles of Scotland: A Historical Survey. AMS Pr.

MacKenzie, William J. *see* Mackenzie, William James Millar.

Mackenzie, William James Millar, 1909-
xMackenzie, W. J.

Biological Ideas in Politics: An Essay in Political Adaptivity. St Martin.
xMacKenzie, William J.
Central Administration in Britain. Greenwood.

Mackenzie, William R. *see* Mackenzie, William Roy.

Mackenzie, William Roy, 1883-1957
xMacKenzie, W. Roy.
English Moralities from the Point of View of Allegory. Haskell.
Quest of the Ballad. Haskell.
xMackenzie, William R.
English Moralities from the Point of View of Allegory. Gordian.
The English Moralities from the Point of View of Allegory. Johnson Repr.

Mackenzie-Grieve, Averie. *see* Mackenzie-Grieve, Averil.

Mackenzie-Grieve, Averil.
xMackenzie-Grieve, Averie.
Last Years of the English Slave Trade, Liverpool 1705-1807. Biblio Dist.
xMackenzie-Grieve, Averil.
Clara Novello. Da Capo.

Mackercher, V. M.
xMackercher, V. M.
The Woodworker's Furniture Construction Repair Bible. TAB Bks.

Mackerras, Colin.
xMackerras, Colin.
tr. & ed. The Uighur Empire According to the T'ang Dynastic Histories: A Study in Sino-Uighur Relations, 744-840. U of SC Pr.

Mackesy, Piers.
xMackesy, Piers.
The Coward of Minden: The Affair of Lord George Sackville. St Martin.

Mackey, Douglas A., 1947-
xMackey, Douglas A.
The Rainbow Quest of Thomas Pynchon. Borgo Pr.

Mackey, G. W. *see* Mackey, George Whitelaw.

Mackey, George W. *see* Mackey, George Whitelaw.

Mackey, George Whitelaw, 1916-
xMackey, G. W.
Lectures on the Theory of Functions of a Complex Variable. Krieger.
xMackey, George W.
Induced Representations of Groups & Quantum Mechanics. Benjamin-Cummings.

Mackey, James P. *see* Mackey, James Patrick.

Mackey, James Patrick.
xMackey, James P.
The Problems of Religious Faith. Franciscan Herald.

Mackey, Mary.
xMackey, Mary.
McCarthy's List. Doubleday.

Mackey, Richard T. *see* Mackey, Richard Thomas.

Mackey, Richard Thomas.
xMackey, Richard T.
Bowling. Mayfield Pub.

Mackie, Bob.
xMackie, Bob.
Dressing for Glamour. A & W Pubs.

Mackie, J. L. *see* Mackie, John Leslie.

Mackie, John D. *see* Mackie, John Duncan.

Mackie, John Duncan, 1887-
xMackie, John D.
Earlier Tudors, 1485-1558. Oxford U Pr.

Mackie, John Leslie.
xMackie, J. L.
The Cement of the Universe: A Study of Causation. Oxford U Pr.
Ethics: Inventing Right & Wrong. Penguin.
Problems from Locke. Oxford U Pr.
Truth, Probability, & Paradox: Studies in Philosophical Logic. Oxford U Pr.

Mackie, John M. *see* Mackie, John Milton.

Mackie, John Milton, 1813-1894
xMackie, John M.

From Cape Cod to Dixie & the Tropics. Negro
U Pr.
Mackie, Joyce.
xMackie, Joyce.
Basic Ballet. Penguin.
Mackie, R. K. *see* Mackie, Raymond Keith.
Mackie, Raymond Keith.
xMackie, R. K.
Mathematical Methods for Chemists. Halsted
Pr.
Mackie, Robert L. *see* Mackie, Robert Laird.
Mackie, Robert Laird, 1885-
xMackie, Robert L.
A Short History of Scotland. Arden Lib.
A Short History of Scotland. Folcroft.
Mackie, Romaine P. *see* Mackie, Romaine Prior.
Mackie, Romaine Prior, 1898-
xMackie, Romaine P.
Crippled Children in American Education,
1939-1942. AMS Pr.
Mackillop, James.
xMackillop, James.
Speaking of Words: A Language Reader.
HR&W.
Mackin, Ronald.
xMackin, Ronald.
Exercises in English Patterns & Usage. Oxford
U Pr.
Mackinder, Halford John, Sir, 1861-1947
xMacKinder, Hanford J.
Britain & the British Seas. Greenwood.
Britain & the British Seas. Haskell.
MacKinder, Hanford J. *see* Mackinder, Halford John.
Mackinlay, Malcolm Sterling, 1876-
xMackinlay, Sterling.
Origin & Development of Light Opera. Gordon
Pr.
Mackinlay, Sterling. *see* Mackinlay, Malcolm Sterling.
MacKinnon, D. M. *see* Mackinnon, Donald Mackenzie.
MacKinnon, Donald MacKenzie, 1913-
xMacKinnon, D. M.
The Problem of Metaphysics. Cambridge U Pr.
MacKinnon, Frank.
xMacKinnon, Frank.
The Government of Prince Edward Island. U
of Toronto Pr.
Mackinnon, James, 1860-1945
xMackinnon, James.
The History of Edward the Third: 1327-1377.
Rowman.
MacKinnon, John. *see* Mackinnon, John Ramsay.
Mackinnon, John Ramsay.
xMacKinnon, John.
Borneo. Silver.
Borneo. Time-Life.
In Search of the Red Ape. Ballantine.
In Search of the Red Ape. HR&W.
MacKinnon, L. *see* Mackinnon, Lachlan.
MacKinnon, Lachlan, 1918-
xMacKinnon, L.
Mechanics & Motion. Oxford U Pr.
MacKinnon, Roger A.
xMacKinnon, Roger A.
Psychiatric Interview in Clinical Practice.
Saunders.
Mackintosh, Douglas R.
xMacKintosh, Douglas R.
Systems of Health Care. Westview.
Mackintosh, J. M. *see* Mackintosh, John Malcolm.
Mackintosh, John J. *see* Mackintosh, John Pitcairn.
Mackintosh, John Malcolm.
xMackintosh, J. M.
Strategy & Tactics of Soviet Foreign Policy.
Oxford U Pr.
Mackintosh, John P. *see* Mackintosh, John Pitcairn.
Mackintosh, John Pitcairn, 1929-
xMackintosh, John J.
ed. British Prime Ministers in the Twentieth
Century. St Martin.
xMackintosh, John P.

ed. British Prime Ministers in the Twentieth
Century. St Martin.
Mackintosh, May.
xMackintosh, May.
Balloon Girl. Popular Lib.
Highland Fling. Delacorte.
Mackintosh, N. J. *see* Mackintosh, Nicholas John.
Mackintosh, Nicholas John, 1935-
xMackintosh, N. J.
Psychology of Animal Learning. Acad Pr.
Macklem, P. T. *see* Macklem, Peter T.
Macklem, Peter T.
xMacklem, P. T.
ed. Lung in Transition Between Health &
Disease. Dekker.
Mackler, Ian.
xMackler, Ian.
Pattern for Profit in Southern Africa.
Atheneum.
Macklin, Alys E. *see* Macklin, Alys Eyre.
Macklin, Alys Eyre.
xMacklin, Alys E.
ed. Twenty-Nine Tales from the French. Arno.
Twenty-Nine Tales from the French. Folcroft.
Macklin, Barbara J. *see* Macklin, Barbara June.
Macklin, Barbara June.
xMacklin, Barbara J.
Structural Stability & Culture Change in a
Mexican-American Community. Arno.
Macklin, Michael.
xMacklin, Michael.
When Schools Are Gone: A Projection of the
Thought of Ivan Illich. U of Queensland Pr.
Macksey, Joan.
xMacksey, Joan.
Book of Women's Achievements. Stein & Day.
Macksey, Kenneth.
xMacksey, Kenneth.
History of Land Warfare. Sterling.
MacKsey, Kenneth. *see* Macksey, Kenneth John.
Macksey, Kenneth John.
xMacKsey, Kenneth.
The Partisans of Europe in the Second World
War. Stein & Day.
Mackworth, Cecily.
xMackworth, Cecily.
The Destiny of Isabelle Eberhardt. Ecco Pr.
Mackworth-Praed, C. W. *see* Mackworth-Praed, Cyril
Winthrop.
Mackworth-Praed, Cyril Winthrop.
xMackworth-Praed, C. W.
Birds of Eastern & North Eastern Africa.
Longman.
MacLachlan, Colin M.
xMacLachlan, Colin M.
Criminal Justice in Eighteenth Century
Mexico: A Study of the Tribunal of the
Acordada. U of Cal Pr.
Maclachlan, John M. *see* Maclachlan, John Miller.
Maclachlan, John Miller.
xMaclachlan, John M.
Planning Florida's Health Leadership: Health
& the People in Florida. U Presses Fla.
MacLachlan, Patricia.
xMacLachlan, Patricia.
Arthur, For the Very First Time. Har-Row.
The Sick Day. Pantheon.
Through Grandpa's Eyes. Har-Row.
Maclagan, David, 1932-
xMaclagan, David T.
Adventures into Unknowns: Five Stories for
Young Readers. C E Tuttle.
Maclagan, David T. *see* Maclagan, David.
Maclagan, Robert C. *see* Maclagan, Robert Craig.
Maclagan, Robert Craig, 1839-
xMaclagan, Robert C.
Evil Eye in the Western Highlands. Norwood
Edns.
Maclagan, W. G. *see* Maclagan, William Gauld.

Maclagan, William Gauld.
xMaclagan, W. G.
The Theological Frontier of Ethics: An Essay
Based on the Edward Cadbury Lecture in the
University of Birmingham, 1955-56.
Humanities.
MacLane, S. *see* Maclane, Saunders.
MacLane, Saunders, 1909-
xMacLane, S.
Homology. Springer-Verlag.
MacLaren-Ross, J. *see* Maclaren-Ross, Julian.
Maclaren-Ross, Julian.
xMacLaren-Ross, J.
Doomsday Book. Astor-Honor.
MacLatchie, Sharon.
xMacLatchie, Sharon.
Gardening with Kids. Rodale Pr Inc.
Maclaurin, Colin, 1698-1746
xMacLaurin, Colin.
An Account of Sir Isaac Newton's
Philosophical Discoveries. Adler.
Account of Sir Isaac Newton's Philosophical
Discoveries. Johnson Repr.
Maclay, Edgar S. *see* Maclay, Edgar Stanton.
Maclay, Edgar Stanton, 1863-1919
xMaclay, Edgar S.
A History of American Privateers. Arno.
A History of American Privateers. B Franklin.
Maclay, Elise.
xMaclay, Elise.
Green Winter: Celebrations of Old Age.
Readers Digest Pr.
Maclean, Alan. *see* Maclean, Alan Duart.
Maclean, Alan Duart.
xMaclean, Alan.
ed. Best for Winter. St Martin.
MacLean, Alistair. *see* Maclean, Alistair Stuart.
MacLean, Alistair Stuart, 1922 or 3-
xMaclean, Alistair.
Breakheart Pass. Doubleday.
Breakheart Pass. Fawcett.
Caravan to Vaccares. Fawcett.
Circus. Doubleday.
Circus. Fawcett.
Fear Is the Key. Am Repr-Rivercity Pr.
Fear Is the Key. Fawcett.
The Golden Gate. Fawcett.
The Golden Gate. G K Hall.
The Golden Rendezvous. Fawcett.
Goodbye California. Doubleday.
Goodbye California. Fawcett.
Goodbye California. G K Hall.
Guns of Navarone. Fawcett.
H.M.S. Ulysses. Fawcett.
Ice Station Zebra. Fawcett.
Puppet on a Chain. Fawcett.
South by Java Head. Am Repr-Rivercity Pr.
South by Java Head. Fawcett.
When Eight Bells Toll. Fawcett.
Where Eagles Dare. Doubleday.
Where Eagles Dare. Fawcett.
MacLean, Angus, 1909-
xMacLean, Angus.
Cuentos: Based on the Folk Tales of the
Spanish Californians. Pioneer Pub Co.
Legends of the California Bandidos. Pioneer
Pub Co.
MacLean, Catherine H. *see* Maclean, Catherine
Macdonald.
MacLean, Catherine M. *see* Maclean, Catherine
Macdonald.
Maclean, Catherine Macdonald.
xMaclean, Catherine H.
Dorothy & William Wordsworth. Haskell.
xMaclean, Catherine M.
Dorothy & William Wordsworth. Octagon.
MacLean, Charles.
xMacLean, Charles.

The Wolf Children. Hill & Wang.
The Wolf Children. Penguin.
Maclean, D. see Maclean, Donald.
MacLean, David, 1921-
  xMacLean, David.
    Engine Maintenance & Repair. TAB Bks.
    Hull Care & Repair. TAB Bks.
    Marine Electrical Care & Repair. TAB Bks.
MacLean, David G.
  xMacLean, David G.
    Gene Stratton-Porter: A Bibliography &
      Collector's Guide. Americana Bks.
Maclean, Donald, 1869-
  xMaclean, D.
    Typographia Scoto-Gadelica. Biblio Dist.
Maclean, Ian.
  xMaclean, Ian.
    Statistical Review of Middle East Markets.
      Nichols Pub.
Maclean, Joan.
  xMaclean, Joan.
    English in Basic Medical Science. Oxford U Pr.
MacLean, Malcolm S. see Maclean, Malcolm Shaw.
MacLean, Malcolm Shaw.
  xMacLean, Malcolm S.
    Men & Books. Core Collection.
MacLean, Mavis.
  xMacLean, Mavis.
    Methodological Issues in Social Surveys.
      Humanities.
MacLean, Norman, 1932-
  xMacLean, Norman.
    The Differentiation of Cells. Univ Park.
Maclean, Virginia.
  xMaclean, Virginia.
    Much Entertainment: A Visual & Culinary
      Record of Johnson & Boswell's Tour of
      Scotland in 1773. Liveright.
Maclear, George F. see Maclear, George Frederick.
Maclear, George Frederick, 1833-1902
  xMaclear, George F.
    Apostles of Mediaeval Europe. Arno.
MacLeish. see Macleish, Archibald.
MacLeish, Archibald, 1892-
  xMacLeish.
    Nobodaddy: A Play. R West.
  xMacLeish, Archibald.
    The Human Season: Selected Poems,
      1926-1972. HM.
    Riders on the Earth: Essays & Recollections.
      HM.
    Six Plays. HM.
MacLennan, Beryce W.
  xMaclennan, Beryce W.
    Group Counseling & Psychotherapy with
      Adolescents. Columbia U Pr.
MacLeod, A. J. see Macleod, Alexander Joseph.
Macleod, Alexander Joseph.
  xMacLeod, A. J.
    Instrumental Methods of Food Analysis.
      Halsted Pr.
MacLeod, Anne.
  xMacLeod, Anne S.
    A Moral Tale: Children's Fiction & American
      Culture, 1820-1860. Shoe String.
MacLeod, Anne S. see Macleod, Anne.
MacLeod, Charlotte.
  xMacLeod, Charlotte.
    The Family Vault. Doubleday.
    Rest You Merry. Avon.
    Rest You Merry. G K Hall.
MacLeod, James H., 1925-
  xMacLeod, James H.
    A Method of Proctology. Har-Row.
MacLeod, John. see Macleod, John George.
MacLeod, John George.
  xMacLeod, John.
    Introduction to Clinical Examination.
      Churchill.
MacLeod, Malcolm L. see Macleod, Malcolm Lorimer.

MacLeod, Malcolm Lorimer, 1901-
  xMacLeod, Malcolm L.
    A Concordance to the Poems of Robert
      Herrick. Folcroft.
    Concordance to the Poems of Robert Herrick.
      Haskell.
MacLeod, Murdo J.
  xMacLeod, Murdo J.
    Spanish Central America: A Socioeconomic
      History, 1520-1720. U of Cal Pr.
Macleod, Norman.
  xMacleod, Norman.
    German Lyric Poetry. AMS Pr.
    German Lyric Poetry. R West.
MacLeod, Robert.
  xMacLeod, Robert.
    The Appaloosa. Fawcett.
    The Muleskinner. Fawcett.
MacLiammoir, Michael. see Macliammoir, Micheal.
MacLiammoir, Micheal, 1899-
  xMacLiammoir, Michael.
    The Importance of Being Oscar. Humanities.
MacLure, Millar.
  xMacLure, Millar.
    George Chapman: A Critical Study. U of
      Toronto Pr.
Maclure, William, 1763-1840
  xMaclure, William.
    Opinions on Various Subjects Dedicated to the
      Industrious Producers. B Franklin.
MacLysaght, Edward.
  xMacLysaght, Edward.
    The Surnames of Ireland. Biblio Dist.
MacMahon, A. W. see Macmahon, Arthur Whittier.
MacMahon, Arthur. see Macmahon, Arthur Whittier.
Macmahon, Arthur W. see Macmahon, Arthur Whittier.
Macmahon, Arthur Whittier.
  xMacMahon, A. W.
    The Administration of Federal Work Relief. Da
      Capo.
  xMacmahon, Arthur W.
    Memorandum on the Postwar International
      Information Program of the United States.
      Arno.
Macmahon, Arthur Whittier, 1890-
  xMacMahon, Arthur.
    Administration in Foreign Affairs. U of Ala Pr.
MacMahon, Percy A. see Macmahon, Percy Alexander.
MacMahon, Percy Alexander, 1854-1929
  xMacMahon, Percy A.
    Combinatory Analysis. Chelsea Pub.
MacManus, Seumas, 1869-1960
  xMacmanus, Seumas.
    Dark Patrick. Arno.
    Donegal Fairy Stories. Peter Smith.
    ed. Donegal Fairy Stories. Dover.
MacManus, Susan A.
  xMacManus, Susan A.
    Revenue Patterns in U. S. Cities & Suburbs: A
      Comparative Analysis. Praeger.
MacMillan, Ernest, Sir, 1893-
  xMacmillan, Ernest.
    ed. Music in Canada. Scholarly.
MacMillan, Gail.
  xMacMillan, Gail.
    Inherited Deception. Bouregy.
Macmillan, Harold, 1894-
  xMacmillan, Harold.
    Riding the Storm 1956-1959. Har-Row.
Macmillan, Hugh P. see Macmillan, Hugh Pattison
  Macmillan.
**Macmillan, Hugh Pattison Macmillan, Baron,
1873-1952**
  xMacmillan, Hugh P.
    Law & Other Things. Arno.
MacMillan, Ian. see Macmillan, Ian C.
MacMillan, Ian C., 1940-
  xMacMillan, Ian.

Strategy Formulation: Political Concepts. West
  Pub.
Macmillan Information Division. see Ccm Information
  Corporation.
Macmillan, R. A. see Macmillan, Robert Alexander
  Cameron.
Macmillan, Robert Alexander Cameron.
  xMacmillan, R. A.
    The Crowning Phase of the Critical Philosophy:
      A Study in Kant's Critique of Judgment.
      Garland Pub.
Macmillan, William M. see Macmillan, William Miller.
Macmillan, William Miller, 1885-1974
  xMacmillan, William M.
    Bantu, Boer, & Briton: The Making of the
      South African Native Problem. Greenwood.
MacMillen, Richard E.
  xMacMillen, Richard E.
    Population Ecology, Water Relations & Social
      Behavior of a Southern California Semidesert
      Rodent Fauna. U of Cal Pr.
MacMullen, Ramsay, 1928-
  xMacMullen, Ramsay.
    Constantine. Dial.
MacMunn, George F. see Macmunn, George Fletcher.
MacMunn, George Fletcher, Sir, 1869-1952
  xMacMunn, George F.
    Leadership Through the Ages. Arno.
MacMurchy, Helen, 1862-1940
  xMacMurchy, Helen.
    Almosts: A Study of the Feeble Minded.
      Kennikat.
Macmurray, John, 1891-
  xMacmurray, John.
    ed. Some Makers of the Modern Spirit: A
      Symposium. Arno.
    Structure of Religious Experience. Shoe String.
Macnab, Ian.
  xMacnab, Ian.
    Backache. Williams & Wilkins.
MacNair, Harley F. see Macnair, Harley Farnsworth.
MacNair, Harley Farnsworth.
  xMacNair, Harley F.
    ed. China. Arno.
    Modern Far Eastern International Relations.
      Octagon.
Macnaughton, William R., 1939-
  xMacnaughton, William R.
    Mark Twain's Last Years As a Writer. U of
      Mo Pr.
MacNeal, Kenneth.
  xMacNeal, Kenneth.
    Truth in Accounting. Scholars Bk.
Macneel, Joseph R. see Macneel, Joseph Raymond.
MacNeel, Joseph Raymond, 1890-
  xMacneel, Joseph R.
    Admission of Students As Candidates for
      Master's Degree: A Study of Some Problems
      Encountered in the Admission of Students
      for the Degree of Master of Arts, Teachers
      College, Columbia University. AMS Pr.
MacNeice, Louis, 1907-1963
  xMacNeice, Louis.
    Astrology. Doubleday.
    The Poetry of W. B. Yeats. Greenwood.
    Poetry of W. B. Yeats. Oxford U Pr.
    The Revenant: A Song-Cycle for Hedli
      Anderson. Humanities.
    Varieties of Parable. Cambridge U Pr.
MacNelly, Jeff.
  xMacNelly, Jeff.
    The Very First Shoe Book. Avon.
MacNicholas, John.
  xMacNicholas, John.
    James Joyce's Exiles: A Textual Companion.
      Garland Pub.
MacNicol, Mary.
  xMacNicol, Mary.

Flower Cookery: The Art of Cooking with
Flowers. Fleet.
MacNitt. see Macnitt, Reginald De Koven.
MacNitt, Reginald De Koven.
xMacNitt.
How to Use Astral Power: Key to a Miraculous
New Life. P-H.
MacNutt, Francis.
xMacNutt, Francis.
The Power to Heal. Ave Maria.
Macomber, W. B. see Macomber, William B.
Macomber, William. see Macomber, William B.
Macomber, William B.
xMacomber, W. B.
Anatomy of Disillusion: Martin Heidegger's
Notion of Truth. Northwestern U Pr.
xMacomber, William.
The Angel's Game: A Handbook of Modern
Diplomacy. Stein & Day.
Macomber, William F.
xMacomber, William F.
A Catalogue of Ethiopian Manuscripts. Univ
Microfilm.
Macon, Jorge.
xMacon, Jorge.
Financing Urban & Rural Development
Through Betterment Levies: The Latin
American Experience. Praeger.
Macourek, Milos.
xMacourek, Milos.
Curious Tales. Oxford U Pr.
Macoy Publishing & Masonic Supply Co. see Macoy
Publishing and Masonic Supply Company, New York.
**Macoy Publishing and Masonic Supply Company, New
York.**
xMacoy Publishing & Masonic Supply Co.
Book of the Scarlet Line; Heroines of Jericho
Ritual & Ceremonies. Macoy Pub.
MacPartland, John.
xMacPartland, John.
Conversations with Sheldon. Philos Lib.
MacPeek, Walt, 1942-
xMacPeek, Walt.
Hot Shots of Pro Hockey. Random.
MacPhail, Elizabeth C.
xMacPhail, Elizabeth C.
The Story of New San Diego & of Its Founder
Alonzo E. Horton. San Diego Hist.
MacPhee. see Macphee, Craig Robert.
MacPhee, Craig Robert, 1944-
xMacPhee.
Restrictions on International Trade in Steel.
Lexington Bks.
Macpherson, Alan. see Macpherson, Alan Gibson.
Macpherson, Alan Gibson.
xMacpherson, Alan.
ed. Atlantic Provinces. U of Toronto Pr.
Macpherson, C. B. see Macpherson, Crawford Brough.
Macpherson, Crawford B. see Macpherson, Crawford
Brough.
Macpherson, Crawford Brough.
xMacpherson, C. B.
Real World of Democracy. Oxford U Pr.
xMacpherson, Crawford B.
Political Theory of Possessive Individualism:
Hobbes to Locke. Oxford U Pr.
Macpherson, Ian, 1912-
xMacpherson, Ian.
Art of Illustrating Sermons. Baker Bk.
God's Plan for This Planet. Gospel Pub.
MacPherson, Margaret (Mclean), 1908-
xMacPherson, Margaret M.
Ponies for Hire. HarBraceJ.
MacPherson, Margaret M. see Macpherson, Margaret
(Mclean).
MacPherson, R. C. see Macpherson, Robert C.
MacPherson, Robert C.
xMacPherson, R. C.

Collision Repair Guide. McGraw.
Macquarrie, John.
xMacquarrie, John.
Christian Hope. Seabury.
Dictionary of Christian Ethics. Westminster.
Existentialism. Penguin.
An Existentialist Theology: A Comparison of
Heidegger & Bultmann. Greenwood.
The Humility of God. Westminster.
Martin Heidegger. John Knox.
Principles of Christian Theology. Scribner.
Thinking About God. Har-Row.
MacQueen, Donald R.
xMacQueen, Donald R.
ed. Understanding Sociology Through
Research. A-W.
MacQueen, Jean.
xMacQueen, Jean.
The Living World: Exploring Modern Biology.
P-H.
MacQuitty, William.
xMacQuitty, William.
Ramesses the Great. Crown.
Tutankhamun: The Last Journey. Crown.
MacRae, D. see Macrae, Duncan.
Macrae, Donald G. see Macrae, Donald Gunn.
Macrae, Donald Gunn.
xMacrae, Donald G.
Max Weber. Penguin.
MacRae, Duncan.
xMacRae, D.
Dimensions of Congressional Voting: A
Statistical Study of the House of
Representatives in the Eighty-First Congress.
Octagon.
Parliament Parties & Society in France:
1946-1958. St Martin.
xMacRae, Duncan.
Policy Analysis for Public Decisions. Duxbury
Pr.
MacRae, Norma. see Macrae, Norma M.
MacRae, Norma M., 1924-
xMacRae, Norma.
Mushrooms 'n Bean Sprouts: A First Step for
Would-Be Vegetarians. Pacific Search.
Macrae, Norman, 1923-
xMacrae, Norman.
America's Third Century. HarBraceJ.
Macready, William C. see Macready, William Charles.
Macready, William Charles.
xMacready, William C.
Diaries of William Charles Macready. Arno.
Macridis, Roy. see Macridis, Roy C.
Macridis, Roy C.
xMacridis, Roy.
French Politics in Transition:: The Years After
DeGaulle. Winthrop.
xMacridis, Roy C.
ed. Comparative Politics: Notes & Readings.
Dorsey.
Contemporary Political Ideologies: Movements
& Regimes. Winthrop.
ed. Foreign Policy in World Politics. P-H.
MacRitchie, David, 1851-
xMacritchie, David.
Fians, Fairies & Picts.. Folcroft.
Macrorie, Ken, 1918-
xMacrorie, Ken.
Telling Writing. Hayden.
Telling Writing. Hayden.
Macsai, John.
xMacsai, John.
Housing. Wiley.
MacShane, Frank.
xMacShane, Frank.
ed. Ford Madox Ford: The Critical Heritage.
Routledge & Kegan.
The Life of Raymond Chandler. Penguin.
MacStravic, Robin E.
xMacStravic, Robin E.

Determining Health Needs. Health Admin Pr.
Marketing Health Care. Aspen Systems.
xMacStravic, Robin S.
Marketing by Objectives for Hospitals. Aspen
Systems.
MacStravic, Robin S. see Macstravic, Robin E.
MacStravic, Suellen.
xMacStravic, Suellen.
Print Making. Lerner Pubns.
MacSwiney, Terence. see Macswiney, Terence Joseph.
MacSwiney, Terence Joseph, 1879-1920
xMacSwiney, Terence.
Principles of Freedom. Kennikat.
Mactaggart, Ann.
xMacTaggart, Ann.
Complete Book of Dressmaking. Van Nos
Reinhold.
Macuch, Rudolf.
xMacuch, Rudolf.
Handbook of Classical & Modern Mandaic. De
Gruyter.
Macurdy, Grace H. see Macurdy, Grace Harriet.
Macurdy, Grace Harriet.
xMacurdy, Grace H.
Chronology of the Extant Plays of Euripides.
Haskell.
MacVane, John.
xMacVane, John.
On the Air in World War II. Morrow.
Macvannel, John A. see Macvannel, John Angus.
MacVannel, John Angus, 1871-1915
xMacvannel, John A.
The Educational Theories of Herbart &
Froebel. AMS Pr.
Macvey, John. see Macvey, John W.
Macvey, John W.
xMacvey, John.
Whispers from Space. Macmillan.
xMacvey, John W.
How We Will Reach the Stars. Macmillan.
Space Weapons - Space War. Stein & Day.
MacWilliams, F. J. see Macwilliams, Florence Jessie.
MacWilliams, Florence Jessie.
xMacWilliams, F. J.
The Theory of Error Correcting Codes.
Elsevier.
Macy, Christy.
xMacy, Christy.
Documents. Penguin.
Macy, Jesse, 1842-1919
xMacy, Jesse.
Party Organization & Machinery. Arno.
Political Parties in the United States,
1846-1861. Arno.
Macy, John. see Macy, John Albert.
Macy, John A. see Macy, John Albert.
Macy, John Albert, 1877-1932
xMacy, John.
Edgar Allan Poe. Haskell.
Story of the World's Literature. Liveright.
xMacy, John A.
ed. American Writers on American Literature.
Greenwood.
Edgar Allan Poe. Folcroft.
Macy, John W., 1917-
xMacy, John W.
Public Service: The Human Side of
Government. Har-Row.
Maczak, Antoni.
xMaczak, Antoni.
ed. Natural Resources in European History: A
Conference Report. Johns Hopkins.
Mad.
xMad.
ed. The Pocket. Warner Bks.
xMad Editors.
The Mad Frontier. Warner Bks.
xMad Magazine.
Mad Strikes Back. Ballantine.
xMad Magazine Editors.

ed. The Bedside Mad. Warner Bks.
Boiling Mad. Warner Bks.
Burning Mad. Warner Bks.
The Cuckoo Mad. Warner Bks.
Dirty Old Mad. Warner Bks.
Dr. Jekyll & Mr. Mad. Warner Bks.
Fighting Mad. Warner Bks.
Good 'n' Mad. Warner Bks.
The Greasy Mad. Warner Bks.
Hooked on Mad. Warner Bks.
Hopping Mad. Warner Bks.
Howling Mad. Warner Bks.
The Ides of Mad. Warner Bks.
The Invisible Mad. Warner Bks.
It's a World, World, World, World Mad.
  Warner Bks.
Like Mad. Warner Bks.
The Mad Adventures of Captain Klutz. Warner
  Bks.
Mad Clowns Around. Warner Bks.
Mad Frontier. Warner Bks.
Mad in Orbit. Warner Bks.
Mad Overboard. Warner Bks.
Mad Power. Warner Bks.
Mad Sampler. Warner Bks.
A Mad Scramble. Warner Bks.
A Mad Treasure Chest. Warner Bks.
The Medicine Mad. Warner Bks.
The Non-Violent Mad. Warner Bks.
The Organization Mad. Warner Bks.
The Pocket Mad. Warner Bks.
Polyunsaturated Mad. Warner Bks.
The Portable Mad. Warner Bks.
Questionable Mad. Warner Bks.
Raving Mad. Warner Bks.
Recycled Mad. Warner Bks.
Rip off Mad. Warner Bks.
The Self-Made Mad. Warner Bks.
Son of Mad. Warner Bks.
Steaming Mad. Warner Bks.
The Token Mad. Warner Bks.
The Uncensored Mad. Warner Bks.
The Vintage Mad. Warner Bks.
Voodoo Mad. Warner Bks.
  xMad Magazine Eds.
Three Ring Mad. Warner Bks.
Mad Editors. *see* Mad.
Mad Magazine. *see* Mad.
Mad Magazine Editors. *see* Mad.
Mad Magazine Eds. *see* Mad.
Madachy, Joseph S.
  xMadachy, Joseph S.
  Madachy's Mathematical Recreations. Dover.
Madan, G. R. *see* Madan, Gurmukh Ram.
Madan, Gurmukh Ram.
  xMadan, G. R.
  Western Sociologists on Indian Society: Marx,
    Spencer, Weber, Durkheim, Pareto.
    Routledge & Kegan.
Madan, Raj.
  xMadan, Raj.
  Compiled by Colored Minorities in Great
    Britain: A Comprehensive Bibliography,
    1970-1977. Greenwood.
Madariaga, Salvador De.
  xMadariaga, Salvador de.
  Christopher Columbus: Being the Life of the
    Very Magnificent Lord Don Cristobal Colon.
    Greenwood.
  Disarmament. Kennikat.
  Don Quixote: An Introductory Essay in
    Psychology. Greenwood.
  The Fall of the Spanish American Empire.
    Greenwood.
  Latin America Between the Eagle & the Bear.
    Greenwood.
  xMadariaga, Salvadore De.
  The Fall of the Spanish American Empire.
    Century Bookbindery.
Madariaga, Salvadore De. *see* Madariaga, Salvador De.

Madaus, George F.
  xMadaus, George F.
  School Effectiveness: A Reassessment of the
    Evidence. McGraw.
Madden. *see* Madden, John Patrick Leo.
Madden, Betty. *see* Madden, Betty I.
Madden, Betty I.
  xMadden, Betty.
  Art, Crafts, & Architecture in Early Illinois. U
    of Ill Pr.
Madden, Chris C. *see* Madden, Chris Casson.
Madden, Chris Casson.
  xMadden, Chris C.
  The Summer House Cookbook. HarBraceJ.
Madden, Daniel M.
  xMadden, Daniel M.
  A Religious Guide to Europe. Macmillan.
  A Religious Guide to Europe. Macmillan.
Madden, David, 1933-
  xMadden, David.
  ed. American Dreams, American Nightmares. S
    Ill U Pr.
  A Primer of the Novel: For Readers & Writers.
    Scarecrow.
  ed. Proletarian Writers of the Thirties. S Ill U
    Pr.
  Intro. by & ed. Remembering James Agee. La
    State U Pr.
  ed. Tough Guy Writers of the Thirties. S Ill U
    Pr.
Madden, Dodgsen Hamilton, 1840-1928
  xMadden, Dodgson H.
  Diary of Master William Silence: A Study of
    Shakespeare & Elizabethan Sport. Haskell.
  Diary of Master William Silence: A Study of
    Shakespeare & Elizabethan Sport. R West.
  Diary of Master William Silence: A Study of
    Shakespeare & of Elizabethan Sport.
    Greenwood.
Madden, Dodgson H. *see* Madden, Dodgsen Hamilton.
Madden, Edward H.
  xMadden, Edward H.
  Chauncey Wright & the Foundations of
    Pragmatism. U of Wash Pr.
Madden, James F.
  xMadden, James F.
  The Wonderful World of Maps. Hammond Inc.
Madden, Janice F. *see* Madden, Janice Fanning.
Madden, Janice Fanning.
  xMadden, Janice F.
  The Economics of Sex Discrimination.
    Lexington Bks.
Madden, John L., 1901-
  xMadden, John L.
  Federal & State Lands in Louisiana. Claitors.
Madden, John Patrick Leo.
  xMadden.
  Venous Thromboembolism: Prevention &
    Treatment. ACC.
Madden, Ken.
  xMadden, Ken.
  The Powers of Populations. Chris Mass.
Madden, Lionel.
  xMadden, Lionel.
  The Nineteenth Century Periodical Press in
    Britain: A Bibliography of Modern Studies,
    1901-1971. Garland Pub.
Madden, Loring.
  xMadden, Lorring.
  How to Cope with Your Child's Teacher.
    O'Sullivan Woodside.
Madden, Lorring. *see* Madden, Loring.
Madden, Myron C.
  xMadden, Myron C.
  Raise the Dead!. Word Bks.
Madden, Richard R. *see* Madden, Richard Robert.
Madden, Richard Robert, 1798-1886
  xMadden, Richard R.

Literary Life & Correspondence of the
  Countess of Blessington. AMS Pr.
Madden, Samuel, 1686-1765
  xMadden, Samuel.
  Memoirs of the Twentieth Century: Being
    Original Letters of State Under George the
    Sixth. Garland Pub.
Madders, Jane.
  xMadders, Jane.
  Stress & Relaxation. Arco.
Maddex, James L.
  xMaddex, James L.
  Constitutional Law: Cases & Comments. West
    Pub.
Maddi, Salvatore R.
  xMaddi, Salvatore R.
  ed. Personality Theories: A Comparative
    Analysis. Dorsey.
Maddison, Angus.
  xMaddison, Angus.
  Class Structure & Economic Growth: India &
    Pakistan Since the Moghuls. Norton.
  Economic Growth in Japan & the USSR.
    Norton.
  Economic Growth in the West: Comparative
    Experience in Europe & North America.
    Kraus Repr.
  Economic Growth in the West: Comparative
    Experience in Europe & North America.
    Norton.
Maddock, Brent, 1950-
  xMaddock, Brent.
  The Films of Jacques Tati. Scarecrow.
Maddocks, Melvin.
  xMaddocks, Melvin.
  The Great Liners. Silver.
  The Great Liners. Time-Life.
Maddow, Ben.
  xMaddow, Ben.
  The Asphalt Jungle: A Screenplay. S Ill U Pr
  Faces. A Narrative History of the Portrait in
    Photography. NYGS.
Maddox, Bill.
  xMaddox, Bill.
  Rags & Patches. Follett.
Maddox, Brenda.
  xMaddox, Brenda.
  The Half-Parent: Living with Other People's
    Children. M Evans.
Maddox, Gaynor.
  xMaddox, Gaynor.
  Food & Arthritis. Popular Lib.
  Food & Arthritis. Taplinger.
Maddox, Harry.
  xMaddox, Harry.
  How to Study. Fawcett.
Maddox, I. J. *see* Maddox, Ivor John.
Maddox, Ivor John.
  xMaddox, I. J.
  Elements of Functional Analysis. Cambridge U
    Pr.
  Infinite Matrices of Operators. Springer-Verlag.
Maddox, J. L. *see* Maddox, John Lee.
Maddox, John.
  xMaddox, John.
  Revolution in Biology. Macmillan.
Maddox, John L. *see* Maddox, John Lee.
Maddox, John Lee, 1878-
  xMaddox, J. L.
  The Medicine Man: A Sociological Study of
    the Character & Evolution of Shamanism.
    Gordon Pr.
  xMaddox, John L.
  The Medicine Man: A Sociological Study of
    the Character & Evolution of Shamanism.
    AMS Pr.
Maddox, Marguerite.
  xMaddox, Marguerite.

The Complete Book of Knitting & Crocheting.
PB.
Maddox, Russell W. *see* Maddox, Russell Webber.
Maddox, Russell Webber.
xMaddox, Russell W.
Extraterritorial Powers of Municipalities in the
United States. Oreg St U Pr.
Maddox, William A. *see* Maddox, William Arthur.
Maddox, William Arthur, 1883-1933
xMaddox, William A.
The Free School Idea in Virginia Before the
Civil War: A Phase of Political & Social
Evolution. AMS Pr.
Maddrell, S. H. P.
xMaddrell, Simon H.
Neurosecretion. Halsted Pr.
Maddrell, Simon H. *see* Maddrell, S. H. P.
Maddux, Rachel, 1913-
xMaddux, Rachel.
The Orchard Children. Avon.
Maddux, Thomas R.
xMaddux, Thomas R.
Years of Estrangement: American Relations
with the Soviet Union, 1933 to 1941. U
Presses Fla.
Madeleva, Sister, 1887-1964
xMadeleva.
Pearl: A Study in Spiritual Dryness. Folcroft.
xMadeleva, M.
Pearl: A Study in Spiritual Dryness. Arden Lib.
Pearl: A Study in Spiritual Dryness. Phaeton.
xMadeleva, Mary.
Lost Language & Other Essays on Chaucer.
Russell.
Madeleva, M. *see* Madeleva.
Madeleva, Mary. *see* Madeleva.
Mademoiselle.
xMademoiselle Magazine Editors.
Make It with Mademoiselle. Crown.
Mademoiselle Magazine Editors. *see* Mademoiselle.
Mader, Charles L.
xMader, Charles S.
Numerical Modeling of Detonations. U of Cal
Pr.
Mader, Charles S. *see* Mader, Charles L.
Mader, Chris.
xMader, Chris.
Dow Jones-Irwin Guide to Common Stocks.
Dow Jones-Irwin.
The Dow Jones-Irwin Guide to Real Estate
Investing. Dow Jones-Irwin.
Information Systems: Technology, Economics,
Applications, Management. SRA.
Mader, Friedrich W. *see* Mader, Friedrich Wilhelm.
Mader, Friedrich Wilhelm, 1866-
xMader, Friedrich W.
Distant Worlds: The Story of a Voyage to the
Planets. Hyperion-Conn.
Mader, Sylia S. *see* Mader, Sylvia S.
Mader, Sylvia S.
xMader, Sylia S.
Inquiry into Life. Wm C Brown.
Madge, John H. *see* Madge, John Hylton.
Madge, John Hylton.
xMadge, John H.
Origins of Scientific Sociology. Free Pr.
Madgic, Robert F.
xMadgic, Robert F.
Relevance & the Social Studies: A Conceptual
Analysis. Pitman Learning.
Madgwick, P. J. *see* Madgwick, Peter James.
Madgwick, Peter James.
xMadgwick, P. J.
Introduction to British Politics. Intl Pubns Serv.
Madigan, John C.
xMadigan, John C.

Cerebellum of the Rhesus Monkey: Atlas of
Lobules, Laminae, & Folia, in Sections. Univ
Park.
Madigan, Thomas F., 1891-1936
xMadigan, Thomas F.
Word Shadows of the Great: The Lure of
Autograph Collecting. Gale.
Madison, Arnold.
xMadison, Arnold.
American Global Diplomacy: 1800-1950.
Watts.
Arson!. Watts.
Carry Nation. Elsevier-Nelson.
Drugs & You. Messner.
Great Unsolved Cases. Watts.
Great Unsolved Cases. Dell.
Polish Greats. McKay.
Suicide & Young People. HM.
Madison, Bernice Q.
xMadison, Bernice Q.
Social Welfare in the Soviet Union. Stanford U
Pr.
Madison, James, Pres. U.S., 1751-1836
xMadison, James.
Calendar of the Correspondence of James
Madison. B Franklin.
Complete Madison: His Basic Writings. Kraus
Repr.
Madison, John H., 1918-
xMadison, John H.
Practical Turfgrass Management. Van Nos
Reinhold.
Principles of Turfgrass Culture. Van Nos
Reinhold.
Madison, Winifred.
xMadison, Winifred.
Call Me Danica. Schol Bk Serv.
Getting Out. Follett.
Growing up in a Hurry. Archway.
Growing up in a Hurry. Little.
Growing up in a Hurry. PB.
Maria Luisa. Lippincott.
Marinka, Katinka, & Me (Susie). Bradbury Pr.
Max's Wonderful Delicatessen. Dell.
The Party That Lasted All Summer. Little.
Madler, Trudy.
xMadler, Trudy.
Why Did Grandma Die?. Raintree Child.
Madnick, Stuart. *see* Madnick, Stuart E.
Madnick, Stuart E.
xMadnick, Stuart.
Operating Systems. McGraw.
Madorsky, S. L. *see* Madorsky, Samuel Leo.
Madorsky, Samuel Leo.
xMadorsky, S. L.
Thermal Degradation of Organic Polymers.
Krieger.
Madow, Leo, 1915-
xMadow, Leo.
Anger. Scribner.
Madow, Pauline.
xMadow, Pauline.
ed. Peace Corps. Wilson.
Madox, Thomas, 1666-1727
xMadox, Thomas.
History & Antiquities of the Exchequer of the
Kings of England. Greenwood.
History & Antiquities of the Exchequer of the
Kings of England. Kelley.
Madrigal, Margarita.
xMadrigal, Margarita.
Open Door to Spanish. Regents Pub.
Open Door to Spanish. Regents Pub.
Madsen. *see* Madsen, Sheila K.
Madsen, Axel.
xMadsen, Axel.
Borderlines. Macmillan.
Madsen, Borge G. *see* Madsen, Borge Gedso.
Madsen, Borge Gedso.
xMadsen, Borge G.

Strindberg's Naturalistic Theatre: Its Relation
to French Naturalism. Russell.
Madsen, Brigham D.
xMadsen, Brigham D.
The Lemhi: Sacajawea's People. Caxton.
Madsen, Clifford K.
xMadsen, Clifford K.
Competency-Based Music Education. P-H.
Madsen, Ib.
xMadsen, Ib.
The Classifying Spaces for Surgery &
Cobordism of Manifolds. Princeton U Pr.
Madsen, Richard W.
xMadsen, Richard W.
Statistical Concepts: With Applications to
Business & Economics. P-H.
Madsen, Sheila K.
xMadsen.
The Teacher's Book of Lists. Goodyear.
Madsen, Stephan T. *see* Madsen, Stephan Tschudi.
Madsen, Stephan Tschudi, 1923-
xMadsen, Stephan T.
Art Nouveau. McGraw.
Madsen, Truman. *see* Madsen, Truman G.
Madsen, Truman G.
xMadsen, Truman.
Eternal Man. Deseret Bk.
Madsen, William.
xMadsen, William.
The American Alcoholic: The Nature-Nurture
Controversy in Alcoholic Research &
Therapy. C C Thomas.
Madubuike, Ihechukwu.
xMadubuike, Ihechukwu.
A Handbook of African Names. Three
Continents.
Maeda, F. *see* Maeda, Fumitomo.
Maeda, Fumitomo.
xMaeda, F.
Theory of Symmetric Lattices. Springer-Verlag.
Maeda, Jun.
xMaeda, Jun.
Let's Study Japanese. C E Tuttle.
Maeda, Robert J.
xMaeda, Robert J.
Two Sung Texts on Chinese Painting & the
Landscape Styles of the 11th & 12th
Centuries. Garland Pub.
Maeder, Clara (Fisher).
xMaeder, Clara F.
Autobiography of Clara Fisher Maeder. B
Franklin.
Maeder, Clara F. *see* Maeder, Clara (Fisher).
Maeder, Thomas.
xMaeder, Thomas.
The Unspeakable Crimes of Dr. Petiot. Little.
Maedke, Wilmer O.
xMaedke, Wilmer O.
Consumer Education. Glencoe.
Information & Records Management. Glencoe.
Maegraith, Brian. *see* Maegraith, Brian Gilmore.
Maegraith, Brian Gilmore, 1907-
xMaegraith, Brian.
One World. Humanities.
Maehl, William H. *see* Maehl, William Harvey.
Maehl, William Harvey, 1915-
xMaehl, William H.
Germany in Western Civilization. U of Ala Pr.
Maehr, Martin L.
xMaehr, Martin L.
Culture, Child & School: Sociocultural
Influences on Learning. Brooks-Cole.
Maestro, Betsy.
xMaestro, Betsy.
Busy Day: A Book of Action Words. Crown.
Fat Polka-Dot Cat & Other Haiku. Dutton.
In My Boat. T Y Crowell.
On the Go: A Book of Adjectives. Crown.
Maestro, Giulio.
xMaestro, Giulio.

Leopard Is Sick. Greenwillow.
illus. Tortoise's Tug of War. Bradbury Pr.
xMaestro, Guilio.
Leopard & the Noisy Monkeys. Greenwillow.
Tortoise's Tug of War. Bradbury Pr.
Maestro, Guilio. *see* Maestro, Giulio.
Maestro, Marcello. *see* Maestro, Marcello T.
Maestro, Marcello T., 1907-
xMaestro, Marcello.
Gaetano Filangieri & His Science of
Legislation. Am Philos.
Maeterlinck, Maurice, 1862-1949
xMaeterlinck, Maurice.
Death. Arno.
Light Beyond. Arno.
On Emerson & Other Essays. Core Collection.
Supreme Law. Kennikat.
Maffei, Anthony C.
xMaffei, Anthony C.
Teaching Preschool Math: Foundations &
Activities. Human Sci Pr.
Maffei, Paolo.
xMaffei, Paolo.
Monsters in the Sky. MIT Pr.
Magalaner, Marvin, 1920-
xMagalaner, Marvin.
Fiction of Katherine Mansfield. S Ill U Pr.
Magar, Magar E. *see* Magar, Magar Edward.
Magar, Magar Edward.
xMagar, Magar E.
Data Analysis in Biochemistry & Biophysics.
Acad Pr.
Magarick, Pat. *see* Magarick, Patrick.
Magarick, Patrick.
xMagarick, Pat.
Successful Handling of Casualty Claims.
Boardman.
Magarshack, David.
xMagarshack, David.
Chekhov, a Life. Greenwood.
Dostoevsky. Greenwood.
Magazine, Alan H.
xMagazine, Alan H.
Environmental Management in Local
Government: A Study of Local Response to
Federal Mandate. Praeger.
Magazine Marketing Service.
xMagazine Marketing Service.
M. M. S. County Buying Power Index. Arno.
Magee, Bryan.
xMagee, Bryan.
Democratic Revolution. Dufour.
Men of Ideas. Viking Pr.
Modern British Philosophy. St. Martin.
Magee, John F.
xMagee, John R.
Production Planning & Inventory Control.
McGraw.
Magee, John R. *see* Magee, John F.
Magee, Robert.
xMagee, Robert.
Classic World of Horses. Arco.
Magee, William K. *see* Magee, William Kirkpatrick.
Magee, William Kirkpatrick.
xMagee, William K.
Anglo-Irish Essays. Arno.
Bards & Saints. Folcroft.
Mager, Alison.
xMager, Alison.
ed. Children of the Past in Photographic
Portraits: An Album with 165 Prints. Dover.
Mager, N. H. *see* Mager, Nathan H.
Mager, Nathan H.
xMager, N. H.
ed. The Office Encyclopedia. PB.
xMager, Nathan H.
ed. Complete Letter Writer. PB.
Encyclopedic Dictionary of English Usage.
P-H.
Mager, Robert F. *see* Mager, Robert Frank.

Mager, Robert Frank, 1923-
xMager, Robert F.
Developing Attitude Toward Learning. Pitman
Learning.
Developing Vocational Instruction. Pitman
Learning.
Goal Analysis. Pitman Learning.
Preparing Instructional Objectives. Pitman
Learning.
Maggin, Elliot S.
xMaggin, Elliot S.
Superman: Last Son of Krypton. Warner Bks.
Maggs, Margaret.
xMaggs, Margaret.
The Classroom Survival Book: A Practical
Manual for Teachers. New Viewpoints.
Magi, Giovanna. *see* Magi, Giovonni.
Magi, Giovonni.
xMagi, Giovanna.
Masterpieces of the Louvre & the Jeu De
Paume. Intl Pubns Serv.
Magid, Alvin, 1937-
xMagid, Alvin.
Men in the Middle: Leadership & Role
Conflict in a Nigerian Society. Holmes &
Meier.
Magidoff, Robert.
xMagidoff, Robert.
Guide to Russian Literature: Against the
Background of Russia's General Cultural
Development. NYU Pr.
Magie, Allan. *see* Magie, Allan R.
Magie, Allan R., 1936-
xMagie, Allan.
Pets, People, Plagues. Southern Pub.
Magill, C. P.
xMagill, C. P.
German Literature. Oxford U Pr.
Magill, David.
xMagill, David.
I Can Bake Bread. Dandelion Pr.
I Can Grow Vegetables. Dandelion Pr.
I Can Tell Time. Dandelion Pr.
Magill, Frank N. *see* Magill, Frank Northern.
Magill, Frank Northen, 1907-
xMagill, Frank N.
ed. Cyclopedia of World Authors. Har-Row.
ed. Masterpieces of World Philosophy in
Summary Form. Har-Row.
Magill, Frank Northern.
xMagill, Frank N.
ed. Contemporary Literary Scene II. Salem Pr.
ed. Cyclopedia of Literary Characters.
Har-Row.
Magill, M. J. *see* Magill, M. J. P.
Magill, M. J. P.
xMagill, M. J.
On a General Economic Theory of Motion.
Springer-Verlag.
Magill, Richard A.
xMagill, Richard A.
ed. Children in Sport: A Contemporary
Anthology. Human Kinetics.
Magill, Robert S.
xMagill, Robert S.
Community Decision-Making for Social
Welfare: Federalism, City Government, & the
Poor. Human Sci Pr.
Maginley, C. J.
xMaginley, C. J.
Trains & Boats & Planes & . . .:
Custom-Building Wooden Toys. Dutton.
Trains & Boats & Planes & ...: Custom Building
Wooden Toys. Dutton.
Maginnis, James B.
xMaginnis, James B.
Fundamental ANSI Cobol Programming. P-H.
Magison, E. C. *see* Magison, Ernest C.
Magison, Ernest C.
xMagison, E. C.

Electrical Instruments in Hazardous Locations.
Instru Soc.
Maglio, Vincent J.
xMaglio, Vincent J.
ed. Evolution of African Mammals. Harvard U
Pr.
Magnani, Franco.
xMagnani, Franco.
ed. Living Spaces: 150 Design Ideas from
Around the World. Watson-Guptill.
Magnarella, Paul J.
xMagnarella, Paul J.
The Peasant Venture: Tradition, Migration, &
Change Among Georgian Peasants in Turkey.
G K Hall.
The Peasant Venture: Tradition, Migration &
Change Among Georgian Peasants in Turkey.
Schenkman.
Magner. *see* Magner, Lois N.
Magner, James A. *see* Magner, James Aloysius.
Magner, James Aloysius, 1901-
xMagner, James A.
Men of Mexico. Arno.
Magner, Lois N., 1943-
xMagner.
A History of the Life Sciences. Dekker.
Magner, Monica M. *see* Magner, Monica Mary.
Magner, Monica Mary.
xMagner, Monica M.
Inservice Education Manual for the Nursing
Department. Cath Health.
Magner, Thomas F.
xMagner, Thomas F.
ed. Baltic Linguistics. Pa St U Pr.
Word Accent in Modern Serbo-Croatian. Pa St
U Pr.
Magnes, Judah L. *see* Magnes, Judah Leon.
Magnes, Judah Leon.
xMagnes, Judah L.
Arab-Jewish Unity: Testimony Before the
Anglo-American Inquiry for the Ihud
(Union). Hyperion Conn.
Magnin, Edgar F. *see* Magnin, Edgar Fogel.
Magnin, Edgar Fogel, 1890-
xMagnin, Edgar F.
How to Live a Richer & Fuller Life. Wilshire.
Magnotti, Shirley.
xMagnotti, Shirley.
Masters Theses in Library Science 1960-1969.
Whitston Pub.
Magnus, Bernd.
xMagnus, Bernd.
Nietzsche's Existential Imperative. Ind U Pr.
Magnus, K. *see* Magnus, Kurt.
Magnus, Kurt.
xMagnus, K.
ed. Dynamics of Multibody Systems:
Symposium Munich, Germany, August 29 -
September 3, 1977. Springer-Verlag.
Magnus, Laurie, 1872-1933
xMagnus, Laurie.
A Dictionary of European Literature, Designed
As a Companion to English Studies. Gale.
Dictionary of European Literature, Designed
As a Companion to English Studies. Johnson
Repr.
A History of European Literature. Arden Lib.
History of European Literature. Kennikat.
Magnus, Philip M. *see* Magnus, Philip Montefiore.
Magnus, Philip Montefiore, Sir, Bart, 1906-
xMagnus, Philip M.
Edmund Burke: A Life. Russell.
Magnus, Ralph H.
xMagnus, Ralph H.
ed. Documents on the Middle East. Am
Enterprise.
Magnus, W. *see* Magnus, Wilhelm.
Magnus, Wilhelm.
xMagnus, W.

Formulas & Theorems for the Special
Functions of Mathematical Physics.
Springer-Verlag.
xMagnus, Wilhelm.
Hill's Equation. Dover.

Magnuson, James.
xMagnuson, James.
The Rundown. BJ Pub Group.
The Rundown. Dial.
Magnuson, James. *see* Magnuson, Jim.

Magnuson, Jim.
xMagnuson, James.
Orphan Train. Dial.
Orphan Train. Fawcett.
Orphan Train. G K Hall.

Magnuson, Paul.
xMagnuson, Paul.
Coleridge's Nightmare Poetry. U Pr of Va.
Magnusson, D. *see* Magnusson, David.

Magnusson, David.
xMagnusson, D.
Adjustment: A Longitudinal Study. Halsted Pr.

Magnusson, Magnus.
xMagnusson, Magnus.
Archaeology of the Bible. S&S.

Magocsi, Paul R.
xMagocsi, Paul R.
ed. The Ukrainian Experience in the United
States: A Symposium. Harvard Ukrainian.
Magoffin, Ralph V. *see* Magoffin, Ralph Van Deman.

Magoffin, Ralph Van Deman, 1874-1942
xMagoffin, Ralph V.
A Study of the Topography & Municipal
History of Praeneste. AMS Pr.

Magoon, Robert A.
xMagoon, Robert A.
Education & Psychology: Past, Present, &
Future. Merrill.
Educational Psychology: An Integrated View.
Merrill.

Magor, John, 1915-
xMagor, John.
Our U.F.O. Visitors. Hancock Hse.

Magorian, James.
xMagorian, James.
Phases of the Moon. Black Oak.
Magoun, F. A. *see* Magoun, F. Alexander.

Magoun, F. Alexander.
xMagoun, F. A.
History of Aircraft. Arno.
Magoun, Francis P. *see* Magoun, Francis Peabody.

Magoun, Francis Peabody, 1895-
xMagoun, Francis P.
Chaucer Gazetteer. U of Chicago Pr.
Magrab, E. B. *see* Magrab, Edward B.

Magrab, Edward B.
xMagrab, E. B.
The Measurement of Time-Varying
Phenomena: Fundamentals & Applications.
Krieger.
xMagrab, Edward B.
Environmental Noise Control. Wiley.
Magrab, Phyllis. *see* Magrab, Phyllis R.

Magrab, Phyllis R.
xMagrab, Phyllis.
Psychological Management of Pediatric
Problems. Univ Park.
xMagrab, Phyllis R.
ed. Planning for Services to Handicapped
Persons: Community, Education, Health. P H
Brookes.

Magrane, William G.
xMagrane, William G.
Canine Ophthalmology. Lea & Febiger.

Magriel, Paul.
xMagriel, Paul.
Backgammon. Times Bks.
An Introduction to Backgammon: A
Step-by-Step Guide. Times Bks.
Magriel, Paul. *see* Magriel, Paul David.

Magriel, Paul David, 1906-
xMagriel, Paul.
ed. Nijinsky, Pavlova, Duncan: Three Lives in
Dance. Da Capo.

Magrill, Rose Mary.
xMagrill, Rose Mary.
Compiled by Library Technical Services: A
Selected, Annotated Bibliography.
Greenwood.

Magruder, Gail, 1938-
xMagruder, Gail.
A Gift of Love. Holman.
Magruder, Jeb S. *see* Magruder, Jeb Stuart.

Magruder, Jeb Stuart, 1934-
xMagruder, Jeb S.
From Power to Peace. Word Bks.

Magubane, Bernard.
xMagubane, Bernard.
The Political Economy of Race & Class in
South Africa. Monthly Rev.
Maguire. *see* Maguire, Byron W.
Maguire, B. *see* Maguire, Byron W.
Maguire, Byron. *see* Maguire, Byron W.

Maguire, Byron W., 1931-
xMaguire.
Simple Furniture Making & Refinishing.
Reston.
xMaguire, B.
Carpentry in Commercial Construction. Reston.
xMaguire, Byron.
Carpentry: Framing & Finishing. Reston.
xMaguire, Byron W.
Carpentry in Residential Construction. Reston.
Masonry & Concrete. Reston.

Maguire, Daniel C.
xMaguire, Daniel C.
Death by Choice. Schocken.
The Moral Choice. Doubleday.
The Moral Choice. Winston Pr.

Maguire, Gregory.
xMaguire, Gregory.
The Daughter of the Moon. FS&G.
The Lightning Time. FS&G.
Maguire, J. M. *see* Maguire, John M.

Maguire, Jack R.
xMaguire, Jack R.
Talk of Texas. Shoal Creek Pub.

Maguire, John M.
xMaguire, J. M.
Marx's Theory of Politics. Cambridge U Pr.

Maguire, Robert A., 1930-
xMaguire, Robert A.
ed. Gogol from the Twentieth Century: Eleven
Essays. Princeton U Pr.

Maguire, W. A.
xMaguire, W. A.
The Downshire Estates in Ireland 1801-1845:
The Management of Irish Landed Estates in
the Early Nineteenth Century. Oxford U Pr.
Mahadevan, T. M. *see* Mahadevan, Telliyavaram
Mahadevan Ponnambalam.

**Mahadevan, Telliyavaram Mahadevan Ponnambalam,
1911-**
xMahadevan, T. M.
Ramana Maharshi: The Sage of Arunacala.
Allen Unwin.

Mahaffey, Michael L.
xMahaffey, Michael L.
Teaching Elementary School Mathematics.
Peacock Pubs.
Mahaffy, J. A. *see* Mahaffy, John Pentland.
Mahaffy, J. P. *see* Mahaffy, John Pentland.
Mahaffy, John P. *see* Mahaffy, John Pentland.

Mahaffy, John Pentland, Sir, 1839-1919
xMahaffy, J. A.
A History of Classical Greek Literature.
Gordon Pr.
xMahaffy, J. P.

Greek Life & Thought from the Age of
Alexander to the Roman Conquest. Arno.
A History of Classical Greek Literature. R
West.
Rambles & Studies in Greece. R West.
xMahaffy, John P.
Descartes. Arno.
Old Greek Education. Folcroft.

Mahajan, V. S., 1923-
xMahajan, V. S.
Development Planning: Lessons from the
Japanese Model. South Asia Bks.
Mahajan, Vidya D. *see* Mahajan, Vidya Dhar.

Mahajan, Vidya Dhar.
xMahajan, Vidya D.
Early History of India. Verry.

Mahajan, Vijay.
xMahajan, Vijay.
ed. Systems Analysis in Health Care. Praeger.
Mahalanobis, P. C. *see* Mahalanobis, Prasanta Chandra.

Mahalanobis, Prasanta Chandra, 1893-
xMahalanobis, P. C.
Approach of Operational Research to Planning
in India. Asia.
Rabindranath Tagore's Visit to Canada.
Haskell.
Mahan, Alfred T. *see* Mahan, Alfred Thayer.

Mahan, Alfred Thayer, 1840-1914
xMahan, Alfred T.
Admiral Farragut. Greenwood.
Admiral Farragut. Haskell.
Admiral Farragut. Scholarly.
Influence of Sea Power Upon the French
Revolution & Empire. Scholarly.
Influence of Sea Power Upon the French
Revolution & Empire 1793-1812.
Greenwood.
Life of Nelson: Embodiment of the Sea Power
of Great Britain. Greenwood.
Life of Nelson: The Embodiment of the Sea
Power of Great Britain. Haskell.
Story of the War in South Africa, 1899-1900.
Greenwood.

Mahan, Bill.
xMahan, Bill.
The Moviola Man. Doubleday.

Mahan, Bruce H.
xMahan, Bruce H.
College Chemistry. A-W.

Mahan, Colleen.
xMahan, Colleen.
The Lodge. Doubleday.

Mahan, Philip.
xMahan, Philip.
Alabama Cases on Domestic Relations. U of
Ala Pr.

Mahan, Thomas Jefferson, 1896-
xMahan, Thomas Jefferson.
An Analysis of the Characteristics of
Citizenship. AMS Pr.

Mahanty, J., 1932-
xMahanty, J.
ed. Dispersion Forces. Acad Pr.

Mahapatra, Jayanta.
xMahapatra, Jayanta.
A Rain of Rites. U of Ga Pr.

Mahar, J. Michael.
xMahar, J. Michael.
India: A Critical Bibliography. U of Ariz Pr.

Maharaj, Rabindranath R.
xMaharaj, Rabindranath R.
Death of a Guru. Holman.

Maher, George F.
xMaher, George F.
Hostage: A Police Approach to a
Contemporary Crisis. C C Thomas.

Maher, James T.
xMaher, James T.

The Twilight of Splendor: Chronicles of the
Age of American Palaces. Little.

Maher, John. *see* Maher, John Edward.

Maher, John E. *see* Maher, John Edward.

Maher, John Edward.
xMaher, John.
Ideas About Taxes. Watts.
xMaher, John E.
Ideas About Measuring & Accounting. Watts.
Ideas About Money. Watts.

Maher, Ramona.
xMaher, Ramona.
Alice Yazzie's Year. Coward.

Maheu, Rene.
xMaheu, Rene.
UNESCO in Perspective. Unipub.

Mahfoud, Peter. *see* Mahfoud, Peter J.

Mahfoud, Peter J.
xMahfoud, Peter.
Lebanon & the Turmoil of the Middle East.
Vantage.

Mahgoub, Fatma M., 1917-
xMahgoub, Fatma M.
Linguistic Study of Cairene Proverbs. Res Ctr
Lang Semiotic.

Mahl, George F., 1917-
xMahl, George F.
Psychological Conflict & Defense. HarBraceJ.

Mahl, Mary R.
xMahl, Mary R.
ed. The Female Spectator: English Women
Writers Before 1800. Ind U Pr.

Mahler, Celine. *see* Mahler, Celine Blanchard.

Mahler, Celine Blanchard.
xMahler, Celine.
Once Upon a Quilt: Patchwork Design &
Technique. Van Nos Reinhold.

Mahler, K. *see* Mahler, Kurt.

Mahler, Kurt.
xMahler, K.
Lectures on Transcendental Numbers.
Springer-Verlag.

Mahler, Vincent A.
xMahler, Vincent A.
Dependency Approaches to International
Political Economy: A Cross-National Study.
Columbia U Pr.

Mahler, Walter R. *see* Mahler, Walter Robert.

Mahler, Walter Robert, 1917-
xMahler, Walter R.
Diagnostic Studies. A-W.

Mahmoudi, Jalil.
xMahmoudi, Jalil.
The Story As Told. Kalimat.

Mahon, Derek, 1941-
xMahon, Derek.
Lives. Oxford U Pr.
Night-Crossing. Oxford U Pr.

Mahon, James J. *see* Mahon, James Joseph.

Mahon, James Joseph, 1912-
xMahon, James J.
The Marketing of Professional Accounting
Services. Wiley.

Mahon, John K.
xMahon, John K.
History of the Second Seminole War. U Presses
Fla.

Mahoney. *see* Mahoney, James.

Mahoney, Elizabeth A. *see* Mahoney, Elizabeth Anne.

Mahoney, Elizabeth Anne.
xMahoney, Elizabeth A.
How to Collect and Record a Health History.
Lippincott.

Mahoney, James.
xMahoney.
Journey into Usefulness. Broadman.
xMahoney, James.
Journey into Fullness. Broadman.

Mahoney, Joanne M.
xMahoney, Joanne M.

Guide to Ostomy Nursing Care. Little.

Mahoney, John L.
xMahoney, John L.
The Enlightenment & English Literature: Prose
& Poetry of the Eighteenth Century with
Selected Modern Critical Essays. Heath.

Mahoney, M. J. *see* Mahoney, Michael J.

Mahoney, Michael.
xMahoney, Michael.
The Drawings of Salvator Rosa. Garland Pub.

Mahoney, Michael J.
xMahoney, M. J.
ed. Psychotherapy Process: Current Issues &
Future Directions. Plenum Pub.
xMahoney, Michael J.
Abnormal Psychology: Perspectives on Human
Variance. Har-Row.
Cognition & Behavior Modification. Ballinger
Pub.
Self-Change: Strategies for Solving Personal
Problems. Norton.

Mahood, Kenneth, 1930-
xMahood, Kenneth.
illus. Losing Willy. P-H.

Mahood, M. M. *see* Mahood, Molly Maureen.

Mahood, Molly Maureen.
xMahood, M. M.
The Colonial Encounter: A Reading of Six
Novels. Rowman.

Mahrer, Alvin R.
xMahrer, Alvin R.
ed. Creative Developments in Psychotherapy.
Aronson.
Experiencing: A Humanistic Theory of
Psychology & Psychiatry. Brunner-Mazel.

Mahy, Margaret.
xMahy, Margaret.
The Boy Who Was Followed Home. Watts.
Leaf Magic. Schol Bk Serv.
Lion in the Meadow. Watts.

Mai, Ludwig H
xMai, Ludwig H.
Approach to Economics. Littlefield.
Men & Ideas in Economics: A Dictionary of
World Economists Past & Present. Littlefield.
Men & Ideas in Economics: A Dictionary of
World Economists Past & Present. Rowman.

Maia, Ronaldo.
xMaia, Ronaldo.
Decorating with Flowers. Abrams.

Maidment, William R.
xMaidment, William R.
Librarianship. David & Charles.

Maier, Charles S.
xMaier, Charles S.
ed. The Origins of the Cold War &
Contemporary Europe. New Viewpoints.

Maier, Franz J.
xMaier, Franz J.
Manual of Water Fluoridation Practice.
McGraw.

Maier, Gerhard.
xMaier, Gerhard.
End of the Historical Critical Method.
Concordia.

Maier, Hans, 1931-
xMaier, Hans.
Revolution & Church: The Early History of
Christian Democracy, 1789-1901. U of Notre
Dame Pr.

Maier, Josef, 1911-
xMaier, Josef.
On Hegel's Critique of Kant. AMS Pr.

Maier, Joseph.
xMaier, Joseph.
ed. The Latin American University. U of NM
Pr.

Maier, N. R. *see* Maier, Norman Raymond Frederick.

Maier, Norman. *see* Maier, Norman Raymond Frederick.

Maier, Norman R. *see* Maier, Norman Raymond
Frederick.

Maier, Norman Raymond Frederick.
xMaier, N. R.
Principles of Animal Psychology. Peter Smith.
xMaier, Norman.
Psychological Approach to Literary Criticism.
Folcroft.
xMaier, Norman R.
Problem-Solving Discussions & Conferences:
Leadership Methods & Skills. McGraw.
A Psychological Approach to Literary
Criticism. Arden Lib.
Psychology in Industrial Organizations. HM.

Maier, Paul L.
xMaier, Paul L.
First Easter: The True & Unfamiliar Story in
Words & Pictures. Har-Row.
Pontius Pilate. Tyndale.

Maier, Pauline, 1938-
xMaier, Pauline.
From Resistance to Revolution: Colonial
Radicals & the Development of American
Opposition to Britain, 1765-1776. Knopf.
From Resistance to Revolution: Colonial
Radicals & the Development of American
Opposition to Britain, 1765-1776. Random.

Maier, Richard A.
xMaier, Richard A.
Comparative Animal Behavior. Brooks-Cole.

Maietta, Donald F. *see* Maietta, Donald Francis.

Maietta, Donald Francis.
xMaietta, Donald F.
Baby Learns to Talk. Stanwix.

Mailer, Norman.
xMailer, Norman.
Barbary Shore. Fertig.
The Deer Park. Berkley Pub.
The Deer Park. Fertig.
Deer Park: A Play. Dial.
The Executioner's Song. Little.
The Executioner's Song. Warner Bks.
Existential Errands. NAL.
The Fight. Little.
Of a Fire on the Moon. Little.
Of a Fire on the Moon. NAL.
Prisoner of Sex. NAL.
Some Honorable Men: Political Conventions,
1960-1972. Little.

Maillol, Aristide. *see* Maillol, Aristide Joseph
Boneventure.

Maillol, Aristide Joseph Boneventure, 1861-1944
xMaillol, Aristide.
Maillol Woodcuts: Great Book Illustrations.
Dover.

Main, Edwin M., 1837-
xMain, Edwin M.
Story of the Marches, Battles & Incidents of
the Third United States Colored Cavalry.
Negro U Pr.

Main, Ernest, 1889-
xMain, Ernest.
Palestine at the Crossroads. AMS Pr.

Main, Jackson T. *see* Main, Jackson Turner.

Main, Jackson Turner.
xMain, Jackson T.
Political Parties Before the Constitution.
Norton.
Political Parties Before the Constitution. U of
NC Pr.
The Sovereign States, 1775-1783. New
Viewpoints.

Main, Jody.
xMain, Jody.
Potted Plant Organic Care. Wild Horses Potted
Plant.

Main, Mary. *see* Main, Mary Foster.

Main, Mary Foster.
xMain, Mary.

Evita: The Woman with the Whip. Dodd.
Maine, Henry J. *see* Maine, Henry James Sumner.
Maine, Henry James Sumner.
 xMaine, Henry J.
  International Law. Hyperion Conn.
 xMaine, Henry S.
  Popular Government. Liberty Fund.
Maine De Biran, Pierre, 1766-1824
 xMaine De Biran, Pierre.
  Influence of Habit on the Faculty of Thinking.
  Greenwood.
Maine, Henry S. *see* Maine, Henry James Sumner.
Maine Historical Society.
 xMaine Historical Society.
  The Maine Bicentennial Atlas: An Historical
  Survey. Maine Hist.
  Province & Court Records of Maine. Maine
  Hist.
Maines, Clark, 1945-
 xMaines, Clark.
  The Western Portal of Saint-Loup-De-Naud.
  Garland Pub.
Mainga, Mutumba.
 xMainga, Mutumba.
  Bulozi Under the Luyana Kings: Political
  Evolution & State Formation in Pre-Colonial
  Zambia. Longman.
Maingot. *see* Maingot, Rodney.
Maingot, Rodney, 1893-
 xMaingot.
  Abdominal Operations. ACC.
Mainland, Donald, 1902-
 xMainland, Donald.
  Mainland's Elementary Medical Statistics.
  Univ Microfilms.
  Mainland's Notes on Biometry in Medical
  Research. Univ Microfilms.
Maino, Evelyn.
 xMaino, Evelyn.
  Ornamental Trees: An Illustrated Guide to
  Their Selection & Care. U of Cal Pr.
Mains, Karen B. *see* Mains, Karen Burton.
Mains, Karen Burton.
 xMains, Karen B.
  The Key to a Loving Heart. Cook.
  Open Heart-Open Home. Cook.
  Open Heart-Open Home. NAL.
Mains, Tony.
 xMains, Tony.
  The Retreat from Burma: An Intelligence
  Officer's Personal Story. South Asia Bks.
Mainwaring, W. I. *see* Mainwaring, W. I. P.
Mainwaring, W. I. P.
 xMainwaring, W. I.
  The Mechanism of Action on Androgens.
  Springer-Verlag.
Mainwaring, William L.
 xMainwaring, William L.
  Exploring Oregon's Central & Southern
  Cascades. Westridge.
  Exploring the Oregon Coast. Westridge.
Maiolo, Joseph.
 xMaiolo, Joseph.
  ed. From Three Sides: Reading for Writers.
  P-H.
Maiorana, Victor P.
 xMaiorana, Victor P.
  How to Learn & Study in College. P-H.
Maiorano, Robert.
 xMaiorano, Robert.
  Backstage. Greenwillow.
  Francisco. Macmillan.
Mair, George.
 xMair, George.
  Guide to Successful Real Estate Investing,
  Buying, Financing, & Leasing. P-H.
Mair, Lucy. *see* Mair, Lucy Philip.
Mair, Lucy P. *see* Mair, Lucy Philip.
Mair, Lucy Philip, 1901-
 xMair, Lucy.

  An Introduction to Social Anthropology.
  Oxford U Pr.
  Marriage. Biblio Dist.
  Primitive Government. Peter Smith.
  Primitive Government: A Study of Traditional
  Political Systems in Eastern Africa. Ind U Pr.
 xMair, Lucy P.
  Native Policies in Africa. Negro U Pr.
Mair, W. G. *see* Mair, William George Parker.
Mair, William George Parker.
 xMair, W. G.
  Atlas of the Ultrastructure of Diseased Human
  Muscle. Churchill.
Mairet, Philip. *see* Mairet, Philippe.
Mairet, Philippe, 1886-
 xMairet, Philip.
  Christian Essays in Psychiatry. Philos Lib.
 xMairet, Philippe.
  Pioneer of Sociology: The Life & Letters of
  Patrick Geddes. Hyperion Conn.
Mais, S. P. B. *see* Mais, Stuart Petre Brodie.
Mais, Stuart P. *see* Mais, Stuart Petre Brodie.
Mais, Stuart Petre Brodie, 1885-
 xMais, S. P. B.
  Books & Their Writers. Arden Lib.
 xMais, Stuart P.
  Books & Their Writers. Arno.
  Some Modern Authors. Arno.
  Some Modern Authors. R West.
Maisel. *see* Maisel, Louis.
Maisel, Carolyn.
 xMaisel, Carolyn.
  Witnessing. SBD.
Maisel, E. *see* Maisel, Edward.
Maisel, Edward.
 xMaisel, E.
  Tai-Chi for Health. Wehman.
 xMaisel, Edward.
  Tai Chi for Health. Dell.
  Tai Chi for Health. HR&W.
Maisel, Herbert, 1930-
 xMaisel, Herbert.
  Computers: Programming & Applications. SRA.
  Intro. by Simulation of Discrete Stochastic
  Systems. SRA.
Maisel, L. *see* Maisel, Louis.
Maisel, Louis.
 xMaisel.
  ed. The Future of Political Parties. Sage.
 xMaisel, L.
  ed. Changing Campaign Techniques: Elections
  & Values in Contemporary Democracies.
  Sage.
 xMaisel, Louis.
  ed. The Impact of the Electoral Process. Sage.
Maisel, Sherman J.
 xMaisel, Sherman J.
  Real Estate Investment & Finance. McGraw.
Maislen, Ruth.
 xMaislen, Ruth.
  Eat, Think & Be Thinner: The Weigh of Life
  Way. Sterling.
Maistre, Joseph M. De. *see* Maistre, Joseph Marie.
Maistre, Joseph Marie, Comte De, 1753-1821
 xMaistre, Joseph M. De.
  tr. Letters on the Spanish Inquisition. Schol
  Facsimiles.
Maistrov, L. E. *see* Maistrov, Leonid Efimovich.
Maistrov, Leonid Efimovich.
 xMaistrov, L. E.
  Probability Theory: A Historical Sketch. Acad
  Pr.
Maitland, Antony, 1935-
 xMaitland, Antony.
  illus. Idle Jack. FS&G.
Maitland, Derek, 1943-
 xMaitland, Derek.
  Breaking Out. St Martin.
Maitland, Frederic W. *see* Maitland, Frederic William.

Maitland, Frederic William.
 xMaitland, Frederic W.
  Frederic William Maitland, Historian:
  Selections from His Writings. U of Cal Pr.
 xMaitland, Frederick W.
  Life & Letters of Leslie Stephen. Gale.
Maitland, Frederick W. *see* Maitland, Frederic William.
Maitland, Margaret.
 xMaitland, Margaret.
  The Channings of Everleigh. Belmont-Tower.
  East Side West Side. Belmont-Tower.
Maitland, Peter S.
 xMaitland, Peter S.
  Biology of Fresh Waters. Halsted Pr.
Maitland, S. R. *see* Maitland, Samuel Roffey.
Maitland, Samuel R. *see* Maitland, Samuel Roffey.
Maitland, Samuel Roffey, 1792-1866
 xMaitland, S. R.
  Dark Ages: Essays Illustrating the State of
  Religion & Literature in the Ninth, Tenth,
  Eleventh & Twelfth Centuries. Kennikat.
 xMaitland, Samuel R.
  Chatterton: An Essay. Folcroft.
Maitland-Jones, J. F.
 xMaitland-Jones, J. F.
  Politics in Africa: The Former British
  Territories. Norton.
Maitlis, Peter. *see* Maitlis, Peter M.
Maitlis, Peter M., 1933-
 xMaitlis, Peter.
  Organic Chemistry of Palladium. Acad Pr.
Maitra, Priyatosh.
 xMaitra, Priyatosh.
  Underdevelopment Revisited. South Asia Bks.
Maizell, Robert E. *see* Maizell, Robert Edward.
Maizell, Robert Edward, 1924-
 xMaizell, Robert E.
  How to Find Chemical Information: A Guide
  for Practicing Chemists, Teachers & Students.
  Wiley.
Majault, Joseph.
 xMajault, Joseph.
  Education Documentation Centres in Western
  Europe: A Comparative Study. Unipub.
Majchrowicz, Edward.
 xMajchrowicz, Edward.
  ed. Biochemistry & Pharmacology of Ethanol.
  Plenum Pub.
Majer, M. *see* Majer, Mirko.
Majer, Mirko.
 xMajer, M.
  ed. Strains of Human Viruses. S Karger.
Majerus, Janet, 1936-
 xMajerus, Janet.
  Grandpa & Frank. PB.
  Grandpa & Frank. Lippincott.
Majewski, Henry F.
 xMajewski, Henry P.
  Preromantic Imagination of L. S. Mercier.
  Humanities.
Majewski, Henry P. *see* Majewski, Henry F.
Majid, K. I.
 xMajid, Kamal I.
  Optimum Design of Structures. Halsted Pr.
Majid, Kamal I. *see* Majid, K. I.
Major, Clarence.
 xMajor, Clarence.
  All-Night Visitors. Univ Place.
  ed. Dictionary of Afro-American Slang. Intl
  Pub Co.
  Emergency Exit. Fiction Coll.
  Reflex & Bone Structure. Fiction Coll.
  Swallow the Lake. Columbia U Pr.
  The Syncopated Cakewalk. Barlenmir.
Major, David C.
 xMajor, David C.
  Applied Water Resource Systems Planning.
  P-H.
Major, Diana.
 xMajor, Diana.

The Acquisition of Modal Auxiliaries in the
  Language of Children. Mouton.
Major, Henry D. *see* Major, Henry Dewsbury Alves.
Major, Henry Dewsbury Alves, 1872-
  xMajor, Henry D.
  Civilisation & Religious Values. AMS Pr.
Major, J. Russell. *see* Major, James Russell.
Major, James Russell.
  xMajor, J. Russell.
  Age of the Renaissance & Reformation: A
    Short History. Lippincott.
  The Deputies to the Estates General in
    Renaissance France. Greenwood.
Major, Kevin.
  xMajor, Kevin.
  Hold Fast. Delacorte.
Majors, Judith S. *see* Majors, Judith Soley.
Majors, Judith Soley.
  xMajors, Judith S.
  Sugar Free-That's Me. Apple Pr.
  Sugar Free...That's Me!. Ballantine.
Majstorovic, Stevan.
  xMajstorovic, Stevan.
  Cultural Policy in Yugoslavia. Unipub.
Majumdar, R. C. *see* Majumdar, Ramesh Chandra.
Majumdar, Ramesh Chandra.
  xMajumdar, R. C.
  Historiography in Modern India. Asia.
  Main Currents of Indian History. Humanities.
Majumdar, Tapas.
  xMajumdar, Tapas.
  The Measurement of Utility. Greenwood.
Majumder, Sanat K., 1929-
  xMajumder, Sanat K.
  Drama of Man & Nature. Merrill.
Mak, Lev.
  xMak, Lev.
  From the Night & Other Poems. Ardis Pubs.
Makarova, Natalia.
  xMakarova, Natalia.
  A Dance Autobiography. Knopf.
Makay, J. J. *see* Makay, John J.
Makay, John J.
  xMakay, J. J.
  ed. Speaking with an Audience:
    Communicating Ideas & Attitudes. Har-Row.
  xMakay, John J.
  Speaking with an Audience: Communicating
    Ideas & Attitudes. Kendall-Hunt.
  Speech Communication Now!: An Introduction
    to Rhetorical Influences. Merrill.
Makela, O.
  xMakela, O.
  Cell Interactions & Receptor Antibodies in
    Immune Responses. Acad Pr.
Makens, James C.
  xMakens, James C.
  Canoe Trails Directory. Doubleday.
Maker, C. June.
  xMaker, C. June.
  Providing Programs for the Gifted
    Handicapped. Coun Exc Child.
Makerere University.
  xMakerere University College Library.
  ed. Directory of East African Libraries. Intl
    Pubns Serv.
Makerere University College Library. *see* Makerere
  University.
Makhlis, F. A. *see* Makhlis, Feliks Arkadevich.
Makhlis, Feliks Arkadevich.
  xMakhlis, F. A.
  Radiation Physics & Chemistry of Polymers.
    Halsted Pr.
Maki, Daniel. *see* Maki, Daniel P.
Maki, Daniel P.
  xMaki, Daniel.
  Mathematical Models & Applications: With
    Emphasis on the Social,Life, & Management
    Sciences.. P-H.
  xMaki, Daniel P.

Finite Mathematics. McGraw.
Maki, John M. *see* Maki, John Mcgilvrey.
Maki, John Mcgilvrey, 1909-
  xMaki, John M.
  Conflict & Tension in the Far East: Key
    Documents, 1894-1960. U of Wash Pr.
Makin, Peter.
  xMakin, Peter.
  Provence & Pound. U of Cal Pr.
Makins, Peggy, 1916-
  xMakins, Peggy.
  Evelyn Home's New Handbook of Marriage.
    Merrimack Bk Serv.
Makinson. *see* Makinson, K. Rachel.
Makinson, K. Rachel, 1917-
  xMakinson.
  Shrinkproofing of Wool. Dekker.
Makkai, Adam, 1935-
  xMakkai, Adam.
  Idiom Structure in English. Mouton.
  Readings in Stratificational Linguistics. U of
    Ala Pr.
Makkai, M. *see* Makkai, Michael.
Makkai, Michael.
  xMakkai, M.
  First Order Categorical Logic:
    Model-Theoretical Methods in the Theory of
    Topoi & Related Categories. Springer-Verlag.
Makkreel, Rudolf A., 1939-
  xMakkreel, Rudolf A.
  Dilthey, Philosopher of the Human Studies.
    Princeton U Pr.
Maklan, David M.
  xMaklan, David M.
  The Four-Day Work Week: Blue Collar
    Adjustment to a Nonconventional
    Arrangement of Work & Leisure Time.
    Praeger.
Makos, Christopher, 1948
  xMakos, Christopher.
  White Trash. Stonehill Pub Co.
Makower, Stanley V. *see* Makower, Stanley Victor.
Makower, Stanley Victor.
  xMakower, Stanley V.
  Richard Savage: A Mystery in Biography.
    Kennikat.
  Richard Savage: A Mystery in Biography. R
    West.
Makridakis, Spyros. *see* Makridakis, Spyros G.
Makridakis, Spyros G.
  xMakridakis, Spyros.
  Forecasting: Methods & Applications. Wiley.
Maksimov, M. V. *see* Maksimov, Matvei Vasilevich.
Maksimov, Matvei Vasilevich.
  xMaksimov, M. V.
  Radar Anti-Jamming Techniques. Artech Hse.
Maksymowych, R. *see* Maksymowych, Roman.
Maksymowych, Roman.
  xMaksymowych, R.
  Analysis of Leaf Development. Cambridge U
    Pr.
Malabre, Alfred. *see* Malabre, Alfred L.
Malabre, Alfred L.
  xMalabre, Alfred.
  Understanding the Economy: For People Who
    Can't Stand Economics. NAL.
  xMalabre, Alfred L.
  America's Dilemma: Jobs Vs. Prices. Dodd.
Malalasekera, George P. *see* Malalasekera, Geroge Peiris.
Malalasekera, Geroge Peiris.
  xMalalasekera, George P.
  Buddhism & the Race Question. Greenwood.
Malamud, Bernard.
  xMalamud, Bernard.

Dubin's Lives. Avon.
Dubin's Lives. FS&G.
The Fixer. FS&G.
The Fixer. PB.
Idiots First. FS&G.
Idiots First. PB.
The Magic Barrel. Avon.
The Magic Barrel. FS&G.
The Natural. Avon.
The Natural. FS&G.
Rembrandt's Hat. FS&G.
Rembrandt's Hat. PB.
Malamud, Nathan.
  xMalamud, Nathan.
  Atlas of Neuropathology. U of Cal Pr.
Malan, David H. *see* Malan, David Huntingford.
Malan, David Huntingford.
  xMalan, David H.
  Individual Psychotherapy & the Science of
    Psychodynamics. Butterworths.
Malania, Fae, 1919-
  xMalania, Fae.
  Quantity of a Hazelnut. Knopf.
Malawer, Stuart S.
  xMalawer, Stuart S.
  Studies in International Law. W S Hein.
Malbin, Michael J.
  xMalbin, Michael J.
  ed. Parties. Interest Groups & Campaign
    Finance Laws. Am Enterprise.
Malcolm, Andrew. *see* Malcolm, Andrew I.
Malcolm, Andrew I.
  xMalcolm, Andrew.
  The Tyranny of the Group. Littlefield.
Malcolm, Douglas R.
  xMalcolm, Douglas R.
  How to Build Electronic Projects. McGraw.
Malcolm, George A. *see* Malcolm, George Arthur.
Malcolm, George Arthur, 1881-
  xMalcolm, George A.
  First Malayan Republic: Story of the
    Philippines. AMS Pr.
Malcolm, Ian. *see* Malcolm, Ian Zachary.
Malcolm, Ian Z. *see* Malcolm, Ian Zachary.
Malcolm, Ian Zachary, Sir, 1868-1944
  xMalcolm, Ian.
  The Pursuits of Leisure & Other Essays. R
    West.
  xMalcolm, Ian Z.
  Pursuits of Leisure & Other Essays. Arno.
Malcolm, Norman, 1911-
  xMalcolm, Norman.
  Dreaming. Humanities.
  Memory & Mind. Cornell U Pr.
  Thought & Knowledge: Essays. Cornell U Pr.
Malcolmson, R. W. *see* Malcolmson, Robert W.
Malcolmson, Robert W.
  xMalcolmson, R. W.
  Popular Recreations in English Society,
    1700-1850. Cambridge U Pr.
Maldaver, Alice.
  xMaldaver, Alice.
  Easy Ways to Multiply Your House Plants.
    Elica Bks.
Maldon, Leo D.
  xMaldon, Leo D.
  How to Build with Stone, Brick, Concrete &
    Tile. TAB Bks.
Maldonado-Denis, Manuel, 1933-
  xMaldonado-Denis, Manuel.
  The Emigration Dialectic: Puerto Rico & the
    U. S. A.. Intl Pub Co.
Male, David.
  xMale, David A.
  Approaches to Drama. Allen Unwin.
Male, David A. *see* Male, David.
Male, Emile, 1862-1954
  xMale, Emile.

The Gothic Image: Religious Art in France of
the Thirteenth Century. Har-Row.
Male, George A. *see* Male, George Albert.
Male, George Albert, 1924-
xMale, George A.
The Struggle for Power: Who Controls the
Schools in England & the United States.
Sage.
Male, Roy R.
xMale, Roy R.
Enter, Mysterious Stranger: American Cloistral
Fiction. U of Okla Pr.
ed. Types of Short Fiction. Wadsworth Pub.
Malecot, Gustave.
xMalecot, Gustave.
The Mathematics of Heredity. W H Freeman.
Maleh, Isaac, 1934-
xMaleh, Issac.
Mechanics, Heat, & Sound. Merrill.
Maleh, Issac. *see* Maleh, Isaac.
Malehorn, Hal, 1930-
xMalehorn, Hal.
Encyclopedia of Activities for Teaching Grades
K-3. P-H.
Maler, Karl G. *see* Maler, Karl-Goran.
Maler, Karl-Goran.
xMaler, Karl G.
Economic Measurement of Environmental
Damage: A Technical Handbook. OECD.
Maleske, Herald.
xMaleske, Herald.
Natural Therapy. Mojave Bks.
Malesky, Gaynelle S.
xMalesky, Gaynelle S.
Green Autumn. Golden Quill.
Maleson, Benjamin.
xMaleson, Benjamin.
Leatherwork: A Basic Manual. Little.
Maletta, Gabe J.
xMaletta, Gabe J.
ed. The Aging Nervous System. Praeger.
Maley, A. *see* Maley, Alan.
Maley, Alan.
xMaley, A.
Drama Techniques in Language Learning.
Cambridge U Pr.
Maley, Catherine A.
xMaley, Catherine A.
The Pronouns of Address in Modern Standard
French. Romance.
Maley, Donald, 1918-
xMaley, Donald.
The Industrial Arts Teacher's Handbook:
Techniques, Principles & Methods. Allyn.
Maley, Gerald A.
xMaley, Gerald A.
Logic Design of Transistor Digital Computers.
P-H.
Malherbe, Abraham J.
xMalherbe, Abraham J.
The Cynic Epistles: A Study Edition. Scholars
Pr Ca.
Malherbe, J. A. *see* Malherbe, J. A. G.
Malherbe, J. A. G., 1940-
xMalherbe, J. A.
Microwave Transmission Line Filters. Artech
Hse.
Mali, Paul.
xMali, Paul.
How to Manage by Objectives: A Short Course
for Managers. Wiley.
Improving Total Productivity: MBO Strategies
for Business, Government & Not-for-Profit
Organizations. Wiley.
Malik, Henrick J.
xMalik, Henrick J.

Applied Statistics for Business & Economics.
A-W.
A First Course in Probability & Statistics.
A-W.
Malik, S. C. *see* Malik, Subhash Chandra.
Malik, Subhash Chandra, 1932-
xMalik, S. C.
ed. Dissent, Protest & Reform in Indian
Civilization. South Asia Bks.
Malik, Suneila.
xMalik, Suneila.
Social Integration of Scheduled Castes. South
Asia Bks.
Malin, Irving.
xMalin, Irving.
ed. Critical Views of Isaac Bashevis Singer.
NYU Pr.
Nathanael West's Novels. S Ill U Pr.
Malin, J. C. *see* Malin, James Claude.
Malin, James C. *see* Malin, James Claude.
Malin, James Claude, 1893-
xMalin, J. C.
The Nebraska Question, 1852-1854. Peter
Smith.
xMalin, James C.
Doctors, Devils & the Woman: Fort Scott,
Kansas 1870-1890. Coronado Pr.
Malin, Roni S. *see* Malin, Roni Sue.
Malin, Roni Sue.
xMalin, Roni S.
Only in L. A.: A Guide to Exceptional
Services. Chronicle Bks.
Malinchak, Alan A.
xMalinchak, Alan A.
Crime & Gerontology. P-H.
Maling, Arthur.
xMaling, Arthur.
Decoy. Manor Bks.
The Koberg Link. Har-Row.
Lucky Devil. Har-Row.
Lucky Devil. Har-Row.
The Rheingold Route. Har-Row.
Ripoff. Har-Row.
Schroeder's Game. Har-Row.
Malinin, Theodore. *see* Malinin, Theodore I.
Malinin, Theodore I.
xMalinin, Theodore.
ed. Acute Fluid Replacement in the Therapy of
Shock. Thieme-Stratton.
Surgery & Life: The Extraordinary Career of
Alexis Carrel. HarBraceJ.
Malino, Emily.
xMalino, Emily.
Super Living Rooms. Random.
Malinowski, Bronislaw, 1884-1942
xMalinowski, Bronislaw.
Coral Gardens & Their Magic: A Study of the
Methods of Tilling the Soil & of Agricultural
Rites in the Trobriand Islands. Dover.
Crime & Custom in Savage Society.
Humanities.
Crime & Custom in Savage Society. Littlefield.
The Ethnography of Malinowski: The
Trobriand Islands, 1915-18. Routledge &
Kegan.
Freedom & Civilization. Greenwood.
Malins, D. C.
xMalins, Donald C.
ed. Effects of Petroleum on Arctic & Subarctic
Marine Environments & Organisms:
Biological Effects. Acad Pr.
Malins, Donald C. *see* Malins, D. C.
Malins, Edward.
xMalins, Edward.
A Preface to Yeats. Longman.
A Preface to Yeats. Scribner.
Malins, Peter.
xMalins, Peter.

Peter Malins' Rose Book. Dodd.
Malinvaud, Edmond.
xMalinvaud, Edmond.
The Theory of Unemployment Reconsidered.
Halsted Pr.
Malipiero, Antonio.
xMalipiero, Antonio.
The Book of What & How: An Illustrated
Catalog of the Products & Inventions of the
Modern World. St Martin.
Malis, Jody C. *see* Malis, Jody Cameron.
Malis, Jody Cameron.
xMalis, Jody C.
Office Cookbook. Trident.
Malissa, Hanns.
xMalissa, Hanns.
ed. Analysis of Airborne Particles by Physical
Methods. CRC Pr.
Malkevitch, Joseph.
xMalkevitch, Joseph.
Graphs, Models & Finite Mathematics. P-H.
Malkiel, Burton. *see* Malkiel, Burton Gordon.
Malkiel, Burton G. *see* Malkiel, Burton Gordon.
Malkiel, Burton Gordon.
xMalkiel, Burton.
A Random Walk Down Wall Street. Norton.
xMalkiel, Burton G.
A Random Walk Down Wall Street. Norton.
Strategies & Rational Decisions in the
Securities Options Market. MIT Pr.
Malkiel, Yakov, 1914-
xMalkiel, Yakov.
Etymological Dictionaries: A Tentative
Typology. U of Chicago Pr.
Patterns of Derivational Affixation in the
Cabraniego Dialect of East-Central Asturian.
U of Cal Pr.
Malkin, Michael R., 1943-
xMalkin, Michael R.
Training the Young Actor. A S Barnes.
Malkoff, Karl.
xMalkoff, Karl.
Crowell's Handbook of Contemporary
American Poetry. T Y Crowell.
Muriel Spark. Columbia U Pr.
Mall, E. Jane, 1920-
xMall, E. Jane.
Beyond the Rummage Sale. Abingdon.
How Am I Doing God?. Concordia.
Mallard, William.
xMallard, William.
The Reflection of Theology in Literature: A
Case Study in Theology & Culture. Trinity U
Pr.
Mallarme, Stephane, 1842-1898
xMallarme, Stephane.
Igitur. Press Pegacycle.
Maller, J. *see* Maller, Joshua-O.
Maller, Joshua-O.
xMaller, J.
The Therapeutic Community with Chronic
Mental Patients. S Karger.
Maller, Julius B. *see* Maller, Julius Bernard.
Maller, Julius Bernard, 1901-
xMaller, Julius B.
Cooperation & Competition: An Experimental
Study in Motivation. AMS Pr.
Mallery, Paul.
xMallery, Paul.
The Complete Handbook of Model Railroad
Operations. TAB Bks.
Mallet, David, 1705?-1765
xMallet, David.
Works of David Mallet. AMS Pr.
Mallet, Paul H. *see* Mallet, Paul Henri.
Mallet, Paul Henri, 1730-1807
xMallet, Paul H.
Northern Antiquities. AMS Pr.
Mallett, Jerry J., 1939-
xMallett, Jerry J.

Classroom Reading Games Activities Kit. Ctr
Appl Res.
Mallette, M. Frank. *see* Mallette, Manney Frank.
Mallette, Manney Frank, 1917-
xMallette, M. Frank.
Introductory Biochemistry. Krieger.
Mallin, Jay.
xMallin, Jay.
MERC: American Soldiers of Fortune.
Macmillan.
Merc: American Soldiers of Fortune. NAL.
ed. Strategy for Conquest: Communist
Documents on Guerrilla Warfare. U of
Miami Pr.
Mallin, Samuel B.
xMallin, Samuel B.
Merleau-Ponty's Philosophy. Yale U Pr.
Mallinson, J. H. *see* Mallinson, John H.
Mallinson, Jeremy.
xMallinson, Jeremy.
Earning Your Living with Animals. David &
Charles.
Mallinson, John H.
xMallinson, J. H.
Chemical Plant Design with Reinforced
Plastics. McGraw.
Mallinson, V. *see* Mallinson, Vernon.
Mallinson, Vernon.
xMallinson, V.
The Western European Idea in Education.
Pergamon.
xMallinson, Vernon.
Modern Belgian Literature 1830-1960.
Heinemann Ed.
Mallis, Arnold.
xMallis, Arnold.
American Entomologists. Rutgers U Pr.
Mallison, George.
xMallison, George.
Color at Home & Abroad. AMS Pr.
Mallison, Ruth.
xMallison, Ruth.
Education As Therapy: Suggestions for Work
with Neurologically Impaired Children. Spec
Child.
Mallon, John.
xMallon, John.
Bridge Bidding: Lessons & Quizzes on Goren's
Point Count Method. Macmillan.
Mallon, Richard D.
xMallon, Richard D.
Economic Policymaking in a Conflict Society:
The Argentine Case. Harvard U Pr.
Mallory, Bob F.
xMallory, Bob F.
Physical Geology. McGraw.
Mallory, George.
xMallory, George.
Boswell the Biographer. Gale.
Boswell the Biographer. Gordon Pr.
Boswell the Biographer. R West.
Mallory, Marilyn M. *see* Mallory, Marilyn May.
Mallory, Marilyn May.
xMallory, Marilyn M.
Christian Mysticism: Transcending Techniques.
a Theological Reflection on the Empirical
Testing of the Teaching of St. John of the
Cross.. Humanities.
Mallory, Michael.
xMallory, Michael.
The Sienese Painter Paolo Di Giovanni Fei
(c.1345-1411). Garland Pub.
Mallory, Virgil S. *see* Mallory, Virgil Sampson.
Mallory, Virgil Sampson, 1888-1959
xMallory, Virgil S.
The Relative Difficulty of Certain Topics in
Mathematics for Slow-Moving Ninth Grade
Pupils. AMS Pr.
Mallows, D. F.
xMallows, D. F.

Stress Analysis Problems in SI Units.
Pergamon.
Malloy, James M.
xMalloy, James M.
ed. Authoritarianism & Corporatism in Latin
America. U of Pittsburgh Pr.
The Politics of Social Security in Brazil. U of
Pittsburgh Pr.
Malloy, Merrit.
xMalloy, Merrit.
Things I Meant to Say to You When We Were
Old. Doubleday.
Malloy, Terry.
xMalloy, Terry.
Montessori & Your Child: A Primer for
Parents. Schocken.
Mally, Gerhard.
xMally, Gerhard.
Interdependence: The European-American
Connection in the Global Context. Lexington
Bks.
Malm, William P.
xMalm, William P.
Music Cultures of the Pacific, the Near East &
Asia. P-H.
Malmgren, Ulf, 1937-
xMalmgren, Ulf.
When the Leaves Begin to Fall. Har-Row.
Malmo, R. *see* Malmo, Robert B.
Malmo, Robert B.
xMalmo, R.
On Emotions, Needs, & Our Archaic Brain.
HR&W.
Malmstrom, Jean.
xMalmstrom, Jean.
Grammar Basics: A Reading-Writing Approach.
Hayden.
Malmstrom, Vincent. *see* Malmstrom, Vincent Herschel.
Malmstrom, Vincent Herschel.
xMalmstrom, Vincent.
British Isles. Fideler.
Malnati, Richard J.
xMalnati, Richard J.
ed. Group Procedures for Counselors in
Educational & Community Settings. Mss
Info.
Malnig, Anita.
xMalnig, Anita.
Raggedy Ann & Andy's Dandy Do-It Book.
Western Pub.
Malo, John W.
xMalo, John W.
All-Terrain Adventure Vehicles. Macmillan.
All-Terrain Adventure Vehicles. Macmillan.
The Complete Guide to Houseboating.
Macmillan.
Malo-Juvera, Delores.
xMalo-Juvera, Dolores.
ed. Obstetrical Nursing Continuing Education
Review. Med Exam.
Malo-Juvera, Dolores. *see* Malo-Juvera, Delores.
Malocsay, Zoltan.
xMalocsay, Zoltan.
Galloping Wind. Putnam.
Maloff, Chalda.
xMaloff, Chalda.
Computers in Nutrition. Artech Hse.
Malone. *see* Malone, Michael P.
Malone, David H., 1919-
xMalone, David H.
ed. The Frontiers of Literary Criticism.
Hennessey.
Malone, Dumas, 1892-
xMalone, Dumas.
The Public Life of Thomas Cooper, 1783-1839.
AMS Pr.
Thomas Jefferson As Political Leader.
Greenwood.
Malone, Hugh E.
xMalone, Hugh E.

The Analysis of Rocket Propellants. Acad Pr.
Malone, Joseph J.
xMalone, Joseph J.
Arab Lands of Western Asia. P-H.
Pine Trees & Politics. Arno.
Malone, Kemp, 1889-1971
xMalone, Kemp.
Chapters on Chaucer. Greenwood.
Malone, Laurence Adams.
xMalone, Lawrence A.
How to Mend Your Treasured Porcelain,
China, Glass & Pottery. Reston.
Malone, Lawrence A. *see* Malone, Laurence Adams.
Malone, Maggie, 1942-
xMalone, Maggie.
Classic American Patchwork Quilt Patterns.
Sterling.
Malone, Margaret G. *see* Malone, Margaret Gay.
Malone, Margaret Gay.
xMalone, Margaret G.
Dolly the Dolphin. Messner.
Malone, Mary.
xMalone, Mary.
Actor in Exile: The Life of Ira Aldridge.
Macmillan.
Annie Sullivan. Putnam.
Malone, Michael.
xMalone, Michael.
Dingley Falls. HarBraceJ.
Heroes of Eros: Male Sexuality in the Movies.
Dutton.
Painting the Roses Red. Random.
Malone, Michael P.
xMalone.
Montana's Past: Selected Essays. U of MT
Pubns Hist.
xMalone, Michael P.
Montana: A History of Two Centuries. U of
Wash Pr.
Malone, Midas.
xMalone, Midas.
How to Do Business-Tax Free. Enterprise Del.
Malone, Wex S.
xMalone, Wex S.
Torts in a Nutshell: Injuries to Family, Social
& Trade Relations. West Pub.
Maloney, Clarence.
xMaloney, Clarence.
ed. The Evil Eye. Columbia U Pr.
Maloney, G. T. *see* Maloney, George T.
Maloney, George. *see* Maloney, George A.
Maloney, George A., 1924-
xMaloney, George.
The Breath of the Mystic. Dimension Bks.
Maloney, George T.
xMaloney, G. T.
Chemicals from Pulp & Wood Waste:
Production & Applications. Noyes.
Maloney, Martin. *see* Maloney, Martin Joseph.
Maloney, Martin Joseph.
xMaloney, Martin.
Writing for the Media. P-H.
Maloney, Michael P.
xMaloney, Michael P.
Mental Retardation & Modern Society. Oxford
U Pr.
Psychological Assessment: A Conceptual
Approach. Oxford U Pr.
Maloney, Roy T.
xMaloney, Roy T.
Income Property Illustrated. Delphi Info.
Maloney, Timothy.
xMaloney, Timothy J.
Industrial Solid State Electronics: Devices &
Systems. P-H.
Maloney, Timothy J. *see* Maloney, Timothy.
Malony, H. Newton.
xMalony, H. Newton.

Current Perspectives in the Psychology of
Religion. Eerdmans.
Living the Answers. Abingdon.
Malory, Thomas.
xMalory, Thomas.
Works. Oxford U Pr.
Malott, Richard W.
xMalott, Richard W.
Psychology. Har-Row.
Malouf, David, 1934-
xMalouf, David.
Johnno. Braziller.
The Year of the Foxes & Other Poems.
Braziller.
Maloy, Richard H. *see* Maloy, Richard H. W.
Maloy, Richard H. W.
xMaloy, Richard H.
Your Questions Answered About Florida Law
& Family Relationships in Life & Death.
Windward Pub.
Malpass, Leslie F.
xMalpass, Leslie F.
Human Behavior: A Program for Self
Instruction. McGraw.
Malraux, Andre, 1901-1976
xMalraux, Andre.
Lazarus. Grove.
Lazarus. HR&W.
Man's Hope. Grove.
Malstrom, Stan. *see* Malstrom, Stan D.
Malstrom, Stan D.
xMalstrom, Stan.
Own Your Own Body. Keats.
Maltbie, Milo R. *see* Maltbie, Milo Roy.
Maltbie, Milo Roy, 1871-
xMaltbie, Milo R.
English Local Government of To-Day: A Study
of the Relations of Central & Local
Government. AMS Pr.
Maltby, Arthur.
xMaltby, Arthur.
ed. Classification in the 1970's: A Second
Look. Shoe String.
Ireland in the Nineteenth Century: A Breviate
of Official Publications. Pergamon.
Malthus, Thomas R. *see* Malthus, Thomas Robert.
Malthus, Thomas Robert, 1766-1834
xMalthus, Thomas R.
Definitions in Political Economy. Kelley.
Population: The First Essay. U of Mich Pr.
Maltin, Leonard.
xMaltin, Leonard.
The Art of the Cinematographer: A Survey &
Interviews with Five Masters. Dover.
The Disney Films. Crown.
The Disney Films. Popular Lib.
The Great Movie Shorts. Crown.
Maltz, Albert, 1908-
xMaltz, Albert.
Afternoon in the Jungle: The Selected Short
Stories of Albert Maltz. Liveright.
The Naked City: A Screenplay. S Ill U Pr.
Maltz, Maxwell.
xMaltz, Maxwell.
The Conquest of Frustration. Ballantine.
Creative Living for Today. PB.
Creative Living for Today. S&S.
Psycho-Cybernetics & Self-Fulfillment. Bantam.
Maluccio, Anthony N.
xMaluccio, Anthony N.
Learning from Clients: Interpersonal Helping
As Viewed by Clients & Social Workers. Free
Pr.
Malvern, Gladys.
xMalvern, Gladys.
World of Lady Jane Grey. Vanguard.
Malville, Kim.
xMalville, Kim.

A Feather for Daedalus: Explorations in
Science & Myth. Benjamin-Cummings.
Malvino, A. P. *see* Malvino, Albert Paul.
Malvino, Albert P. *see* Malvino, Albert Paul.
Malvino, Albert Paul.
xMalvino, A. P.
Digital Principles & Applications. McGraw.
xMalvino, Albert P.
Calculus for Electronics. Krieger.
Digital Computer Electronics. McGraw.
Digital Principles & Applications. McGraw.
Electronic Principles. McGraw.
Transistor Circuit Approximations. McGraw.
Transistor Circuit Approximations. McGraw.
Maly, Kurt.
xMaly, Kurt.
Fundamentals of the Computing Sciences. P-H.
Malyshev, A. V. *see* Malyshev, Aleksandr Vasilevich.
Malyshev, Aleksandr Vasilevich.
xMalyshev, A. V.
ed. Studies in Number Theory. Plenum Pub.
Malz, Betty.
xMalz, Betty.
My Glimpse into Eternity. Berkley Pub.
My Glimpse of Eternity. Chosen Bks Pub.
Prayers That Are Answered. Chosen Bks Pub.
Malzberg, Barry N.
xMalzberg, Barry N.
Chorale. Doubleday.
Galaxies. Gregg.
The Gamesman. PB.
ed. Neglected Visions. Doubleday.
Mamak, A. *see* Mamak, Alexander.
Mamak, Alexander.
xMamak, A.
ed. Race, Class & Rebellion in the South
Pacific. Allen Unwin.
Mamalakis, Markos.
xMamalakis, Markos J.
The Growth & Structure of the Chilean
Economy: From Independence to Allende.
Yale U Pr.
Compiled by Historical Statistics of Chile:
National Accounts. Greenwood.
Mamalakis, Markos J. *see* Mamalakis, Markos.
Mamatey, Victor S.
xMamatey, Victor S.
ed. A History of the Czechoslovak Republic,
1918-1948. Princeton U Pr.
Mambert, W. A.
xMambert, W. A.
Presenting Technical Ideas: A Guide to
Audience Communication. Wiley.
A Trip into Your Unconscious. Acropolis.
Mamchak, P. Susan.
xMamchak, P. Susan.
Personalized Behavioral Modification: Practical
Techniques for Elementary Educators. P-H.
Mamdani, Mahmood, 1946-
xMamdani, Mahmood.
Politics & Class Formation in Uganda. Monthly
Rev.
Mamet, David.
xMamet, David.
Reunion & Dark Pony: Two Plays. Grove.
Mamis, Justin.
xMamis, Justin.
When to Sell: Inside Strategies for Stock
Market Profits. FS&G.
Mamot, Patricio R.
xMamot, Patricio R.
Foreign Medical Graduates in America. C C
Thomas.
Mamula, Richard A.
xMamula, Richard A.

Community Placement of the Mentally
Retarded: A Handbook for Community
Agencies and Social Work Practitioners. C C
Thomas.
Manach, Jorge, 1898-1961
xManach, Jorge.
Frontiers in the Americas: A Global
Perspective. Tchrs Coll.
Manahan, Stanley E.
xManahan, Stanley E.
Environmental Chemistry. Prindle.
General Applied Chemistry. Prindle.
Manaka, Yoshio.
xManaka, Yoshio.
The Layman's Guide to Acupuncture.
Weatherhill.
Manard, Barbara B. *see* Manard, Barbara Bolling.
Manard, Barbara Bolling.
xManard, Barbara B.
Old-Age Institutions. Lexington Bks.
Manashil, Gordon B.
xManashil, Gordon B.
Clinical Sialography. C C Thomas.
Manassewitsch, V. *see* Manassewitsch, Vadim.
Manassewitsch, Vadim, 1927-
xManassewitsch, V.
Frequency Synthesizers: Theory & Design.
Wiley.
xManassewitsch, Vadim.
Frequency Synthesizers: Theory & Design.
Wiley.
Manaster, Alfred B., 1938-
xManaster, Alfred B.
Completeness, Compactness & Undecidability:
An Introduction to Mathematical Logic. P-H.
Manaster, Guy J.
xManaster, Guy J.
Adolescent Development & the Life Tasks.
Allyn.
Manceron, Claude.
xManceron, Claude.
The Wind From America. Knopf.
Manchel, Frank.
xManchel, Frank.
An Album of Great Science Fiction Films.
Watts.
The Box-Office Clowns: Bob Hope, Jerry
Lewis, Mel Brooks, Woody Allen. Watts.
Gangsters on the Screen. Watts.
The Talking Clowns: From Laurel & Hardy to
the Marx Brothers. Watts.
Manchester, Eng. Public Libraries. Moss Side Branch.
xManchester, England. Public Libraries, Moss Side
Branch.
Compiled by Thomas De Quincey: A
Bibliography Based Upon the De Quincey
Collection in the Moss Side Library. B
Franklin.
xManhattan Company.
Manna-Hatin: Story of New York. Friedman.
Manchester, England. Public Libraries, Moss Side
Branch. *see* Manchester, Eng. Public Libraries. Moss
Side Branch.
Manchester, Richard N.
xManchester, Richard N.
Pulsars. W H Freeman.
Manchester, William. *see* Manchester, William Raymond.
Manchester, William Raymond.
xManchester, William.
American Caesar: Douglas MacArthur
1880-1964. Little.
Arms of Krupp: 1587-1968. Bantam.
The Arms of Krupp, 1587-1968. Little.
The Glory & the Dream: A Narrative History
of America, 1932-1972. Little.
Mancini, Pat M. *see* Mancini, Pat Mcnees.
Mancini, Pat Mcnees.
xMancini, Pat M.

ed. Contemporary Latin American Short
Stories. Fawcett.
Mancke, Richard. *see* Mancke, Richard B.
Mancke, Richard B., 1943-
xMancke, Richard.
The Failure of U.S. Energy Policy. Columbia U
Pr.
xMancke, Richard B.
Mexican Oil & Natural Gas: Political, Strategic
& Economic Implications. Praeger.
Performance of the Federal Energy Office. Am
Enterprise.
Mancuso, Joseph.
xMancuso, Joseph R.
How to Start, Finance & Manage Your Own
Small Business. P-H.
No Guts - No Glory: How to Fight Dirty
Against Management. Ashley Bks.
Mancuso, Joseph R. *see* Mancuso, Joseph.
Mandal, Anil K.
xMandal, Anil K.
Electron Microscopy of the Kidney in Renal
Disease & Hypertension: A
Clinicopathological Approach. Plenum Pub.
Mandava, N. Bhushan.
xMandava, N. Bhushan.
ed. Plant Growth Substances. Am Chemical.
Mandel, B. J. *see* Mandel, Benjamin J.
Mandel, Barrett J. *see* Mandel, Barrett John.
Mandel, Barrett John.
xMandel, Barrett J.
Literature & the English Department. NCTE.
Mandel, Benjamin J.
xMandel, B. J.
Statistics for Management: A Simplified
Introduction to Statistics. Dangary Pub.
Mandel, Ernest.
xMandel, Ernest.
Decline of the Dollar: A Marxist View of the
Monetary Crisis. Monad Pr.
Introduction to Marxist Economic Theory.
Path Pr NY.
Late Capitalism. Schocken.
Marxist Economic Theory. Monthly Rev.
The Marxist Theory of Alienation. Path Pr
NY.
The Revolutionary Potential of the Working
Class. Path Pr NY.
Mandel, Leon.
xMandel, Leon.
Driven: The American Four-Wheeled Love
Affair. Stein & Day.
Mandel, Morris, 1911-
xMandel, Morris.
Affronts, Insults, & Indignities. Jonathan
David.
A Complete Treasury of Stories for Public
Speakers. Jonathan David.
Mandel, Oscar.
xMandel, Oscar.
Collected Plays. Spectrum Prods.
A Definition of Tragedy. NYU Pr.
The Patriots of Nantucket: A Romantic
Comedy of the American Revolution.
Spectrum Prods.
Mandel, Siegfried.
xMandel, Siegfried.
ed. Contemporary European Novelists. S Ill U
Pr.
Dictionary of Science. Dell.
Mandel, William.
xMandel, William M.
Soviet Women. Doubleday.
Soviet Women. Peter Smith.
Mandel, William M. *see* Mandel, William.
Mandelbaum, Albert J.
xMandelbaum, Albert J.

Fundamentals of Protective Systems: Planning,
Evaluation, Selection. C C Thomas.
Mandelbaum, Allen, 1926-
xMandelbaum, Allen.
Chelmaxioms: The Maxims, Axioms, Maxioms
of Chelm. Godine.
Chelmaxioms: The Maxims Axioms Maxioms
of Chelm. Jewish Pubn.
Journeyman: Poems. Schocken.
Mandelbaum, Bernard, 1922-
xMandelbaum, Bernard.
Add Life to Your Years. G K Hall.
Choose Life. Bloch.
Mandelbaum, David G. *see* Mandelbaum, David
Goodman.
Mandelbaum, David Goodman, 1911-
xMandelbaum, David G.
Human Fertility in India: Social Components &
Policy Perspectives. U of Cal Pr.
The Plains Cree. AMS Pr.
Mandelbaum, Maurice. *see* Mandelbaum, Maurice H.
Mandelbaum, Maurice H., 1908-
xMandelbaum, Maurice.
The Anatomy of Historical Knowledge. Johns
Hopkins.
History, Man, & Reason: A Study in
Nineteenth Century-Thought. Johns Hopkins.
xMandelbaum, Maurice H.
The Problem of Historical Knowledge: An
Answer to Relativism. Arno.
Mandelbaum, Seymour J.
xMandelbaum, Seymour J.
Community & Communications. Norton.
Mandelbrot, Benoit B.
xMandelbrot, Benoit B.
Fractals: Form, Chance, & Dimension. W H
Freeman.
Mandelik, Peter.
xMandelik, Peter.
Compiled by Concordance to the Poetry of
Langston Hughes. Gale.
Mandelker. *see* Mandelker, Daniel R.
Mandelker, Daniel R.
xMandelker.
Housing Subsidies in the United States &
England. Michie.
Mandell, A. J. *see* Mandell, Arnold J.
Mandell, Arnold J.
xMandell, A. J.
ed. Psychochemical Research in Man:
Methods, Strategy & Theory. Acad Pr.
Mandell, Fred.
xMandell, Fred.
The Mourning Road. Micah Pubns.
Mandell, G. L. *see* Mandell, Gerald L.
Mandell, Gerald L.
xMandell, G. L.
Principles & Practice of Infectious Diseases.
Wiley.
Mandell, Lewis.
xMandell, Lewis.
Credit Card Use in the United States. U of
Mich Soc Res.
Mandell, Maurice I.
xMandell, Maurice I.
Advertising. P-H.
Mandell, Richard D.
xMandell, Richard D.
The First Modern Olympics. U of Cal Pr.
xMandell, Richard R.
Nazi Olympics. Macmillan.
Mandell, Richard R. *see* Mandell, Richard D.
Mandell, Robert W.
xMandell, Robert W.
Financing the Capital Requirements of the U.
S. Airline Industry in the 1980's. Lexington
Bks.
Mandell, Sidney, 1904-
xMandell, Sidney.

Laws Governing Banks & Their Customers.
Oceana.
Mandell, Steven L.
xMandell, Steven L.
Computers & Data Processing: Concepts &
Applications. West Pub.
Principles of Data Processing. West Pub.
Mander, Anica V. *see* Mander, Anica Vesel.
Mander, Anica Vesel.
xMander, Anica V.
Feminism As Therapy. Moon Bks.
Feminism As Therapy. Random.
Mander, Jerry.
xMander, Jerry.
Great International Paper Airplane Book. S&S.
The Great International Paper Airplane Book.
S&S.
Mander, John, 1932-
xMander, John.
Berlin: The Eagle & the Bear. Greenwood.
Mander, Linden. *see* Mander, Linden A.
Mander, Linden A, 1897-
xMander, Linden.
Some Dependent Peoples of the South Pacific.
AMS Pr.
Mander, R. *see* Mander, Raymond.
Mander, Raymond.
xMander, R.
Hamlet Through the Ages: A Pictorial Record
from 1709. Gordon Pr.
xMander, Raymond.
Lost Theatres of London. Taplinger.

Musical Comedy: A Story in Pictures.
Taplinger.
Revue: A Story in Pictures. Taplinger.
The Theatres of London. Greenwood.

Theatrical Companion to Shaw: A Pictorial
Record of the First Performance of the Plays
of Bernard Shaw. Folcroft.

Mandera, Franklin R. *see* Mandera, Franklin Richard.

Mandera, Franklin Richard.
xMandera, Franklin R.
An Inquiry into the Effects of Bilingualism on
Native & Non-Native Americans: Viewed in
Sociopsychologic & Cultural Terms. Arno.
Manderscheid, Ronald W.
xManderscheid, Ronald W.
ed. Systems Science & the Future of Health.
Groome Ctr.
Mandeville, John, 1943-
xMandeville, John.
The Complete Old English Sheepdog. Howell
Bk.
Mandich, Donald R., 1925-
xMandich, Donald R.
ed. Foreign Exchange Trading Techniques &
Controls. Am Bankers.
Mandino, Og.
xMandino, Og.
The Christ Commission. T Y Crowell.
Gift of Acabar. Bantam.
The Gift of Acabar. G K Hall.
The Gift of Acabar. Lippincott.
The Greatest Miracle in the World. Bantam.
The Greatest Miracle in the World. Fell.
The Greatest Salesman in the World. Bantam.
Greatest Salesman in the World. Fell.
Mandl. *see* Mandl, Matthew.
Mandl, F. *see* Mandl, Franz.
Mandl, Franz, 1923-
xMandl, F.
Statistical Physics. Wiley.
Mandl, Matthew.
xMandl.
Handbook of Electronic Circuits & Systems.
Reston.
xMandl, Matthew.

Directory of Electronic Circuits: With a
Glossary of Terms. P-H.
Electronic Data Reference Manual. Reston.
Principles of Electronic Communications. P-H.
Solid-State Circuit Design User's Manual.
Reston.
Mandle, Jay. see Mandle, Jay R.
Mandle, Jay R.
xMandle, Jay.
The Plantation Economy: Population &
Economic Change in Guyana, 1838-1960.
Temple U Pr.
xMandle, Jay R.
The Roots of Black Poverty: The Southern
Plantation Economy After the Civil War.
Duke.
Mandle, Joan D.
xMandle, Joan D.
Women & Social Change in America.
Princeton Bk Co.
Mandrou, Robert.
xMandrou, Robert.
Introduction to Modern France, 1500-1640: An
Essay in Historical Psychology. Holmes &
Meier.
Mandry, Kathy.
xMandry, Kathy.
The Cat & the Mouse & the Mouse & the Cat.
Pantheon.
How to Grow a Jelly Glass Farm. Pantheon.
How to Make Elephant Bread. Pantheon.
The World on My Window Sill. Fountain Pub
Co NY.
Manela, Roger.
xManela, Roger.
Health Needs of Children. Sage.
Manella, Douglas.
xManella, Douglas.
Amphoto Guide to Black-&-White Processing
& Printing. Amphoto.
Manenc, J. see Manenc, Jack.
Manenc, Jack.
xManenc, J.
Structural Thermodynamics of Alloys. Kluwer
Boston.
Manera, Anthony S.
xManera, Anthony S.
Solid-State Electronic Circuits for Engineering
Technology. McGraw.
Manes, E. G. see Manes, Ernest G.
Manes, Ernest G., 1943-
xManes, E. G.
Algebraic Theories. Springer-Verlag.
Manes, Stephen.
xManes, Stephen.
The Boy Who Turned into a TV Set. Coward.
Hooples on the Highway. Coward.
Mule in the Mail. Coward.
Manetti, Antonio, 1423-1497
xManetti, Antonio.
Life of Brunelleschi. Pa St U Pr.
Manfred, Frederick.
xManfred, Frederick.
The Conquering Horse. NAL.
Manfred, Frederick. see Manfred, Frederick Feikema.
Manfred, Frederick F. see Manfred, Frederick Feikema.
Manfred, Frederick Feikema, 1912-
xManfred, Frederick.
Lord Grizzly. Gregg.
xManfred, Frederick F.
The Chokecherry Tree. U of NM Pr.
The Golden Bowl. U of NM Pr.
Lord Grizzly. NAL.
Manfred, Freya.
xManfred, Freya.
American Roads: A Book of Poems. Overlook
Pr.
Manfreda, Marguerite L. see Manfreda, Marguerite Lucy.
Manfreda, Marguerite Lucy.
xManfreda, Marguerite L.

Psychiatric Nursing. Davis Co.
Manfredi, John, 1920-
xManfredi, John F.
Periodical Resources in Italian Sociology since
1945. Univ Microfilms.
Manfredi, John F. see Manfredi, John.
Mangalwadi, Vishal.
xMangalwadi, Vishal.
The World of Gurus. Verry.
Mangan, Doreen.
xMangan, Doreen.
How to Be a Super Camp Counselor. Watts.
Mangan, Frances S.
xMangan, Frances S.
Arithmetic for Self-Study. Wadsworth Pub.
Mangan, Frank J.
xMangan, Frank J.
Bordertown Revisited. Mangan Bks.
Mangan, John J. see Mangan, John Joseph.
Mangan, John Joseph, 1857-1935
xMangan, John J.
Life, Character & Influence of Desiderius
Erasmus of Rotterdam. AMS Pr.
Mangano, Antonio.
xMangano, Antonio.
Sons of Italy: A Social & Religious Study of
the Italians in America. Ozer.
Sons of Italy: A Social & Religious Study of
the Italians in America. Russell.
Manganyi, N. C.
xManganyi, Noel C.
Alienation & the Body in Racist Society: A
Study of the Society That Invented Sow.
NOK Pubs.
Manganyi, Noel C. see Manganyi, N. C.
Mangasarian, O. L. see Mangasarian, Olvi L.
Mangasarian, Olvi L., 1934-
xMangasarian, O. L.
ed. Nonlinear Programming 3. Acad Pr.
xMangasarian, Olvi L.
Nonlinear Programming. Krieger.
Mangat Rai, E. N. see Mangat Rai, Edward Nirmal.
Mangat Rai, Edward Nirmal.
xMangat Rai, E. N.
Patterns of Administrative Development in
Independent India. Humanities.
Mange, Alyce E. see Mange, Alyce Edythe.
Mange, Alyce Edythe, 1904-
xMange, Alyce E.
The Near Eastern Policy of the Emperor
Napoleon III. Greenwood.
Mangham, I. L.
xMangham, Iain.
ed. Interactions & Interventions in
Organizations. Wiley.
The Politics of Organizational Change.
Greenwood.
Mangham, Iain. see Mangham, I. L.
Manghnani, Merli H. see Manghnani, Murli H.
Manghnani, Murli H.
xManghnani, Merli H.
High Pressure Research: Applications to
Geophysics. Acad Pr.
Mangione, Jerre. see Mangione, Jerre Gerlando.
Mangione, Jerre Gerlando, 1909-
xMangione, Jerre.
An Ethnic at Large: A Memoir of America in
the Thirties & Forties. Putnam.
Mango, Andrew.
xMango, Andrew.
Turkey. Walker & Co.
Mango, Cyril. see Mango, Cyril A.
Mango, Cyril A.
xMango, Cyril.
Byzantine Architecture. Abrams.
Mangold, Peter.
xMangold, Peter.
Superpower Intervention in the Middle East. St
Martin.
Mangone, G. J. see Mangone, Gerard J.

Mangone, Gerard J.
xMangone, G. J.
ed. Energy Policies of the World. Elsevier.
xMangone, Gerard J.
The Idea & Practice of World Government.
Greenwood.
Mangrum, Charles T.
xMangrum, Charles T.
Developing Competencies in Teaching Reading:
A Modular Program for Preservice &
Inservice Elementary & Middle School
Teachers. Merrill.
Mangrum, Claude T.
xMangrum, Claude T.
The Professional Practitioner in Probation. C C
Thomas.
Mangum, Garth L.
xMangum, Garth L.
A Decade of Manpower Development &
Training. Olympus Pub Co.
Job Market Futurity: Planning & Managing
Local Manpower Programs. Olympus Pub
Co.
Operating Engineers: The Economic History of
a Trade Union. Harvard U Pr.
Mangurian, David.
xMangurian, David.
illus. Children of the Incas. Schol Bk Serv.
Mangus, A. R. see Mangus, Arthur Raymond.
Mangus, Arthur Raymond, 1900-
xMangus, A. R.
Changing Aspects of Rural Relief. Da Capo.
Manhart, Frank. see Manhart, Frank Joseph.
Manhart, Frank Joseph, 1897-
xManhart, Frank.
Random Thoughts in Verse. Hill Hse Pr.
Manhattan, Avro.
xManhattan, Avro.
Catholic Imperialism & World Freedom. Arno.
Catholic Power Today. Lyle Stuart.
The Vatican-Moscow Alliance. Ralston-Pilot.
Manhattan Company. see Manchester, Eng. Public
Libraries. Moss Side Branch.
Manheim, Henry L.
xManheim, Henry L.
Sociological Research: Philosophy & Methods.
Dorsey.
Manheim, Jarol B., 1946-
xManheim, Jarol B.
Deja Vu: American Political Problems in
Historical Perspective. St Martin.
Political Violence in the United States,
1875-1974: A Bibliography. Garland Pub.
The Politics Within: A Primer in Political
Attitudes & Behavior. P-H.
Manheim, Werner.
xManheim, Werner.
Martin Buber. Twayne.
Manheimer, Martha L.
xManheimer, Martha L.
Cataloging & Classification: A Workbook.
Dekker.
OCLC: An Introduction to Searching & Input.
Neal-Schuman.
Style Manual: A Guide for the Preparation of
Reports & Dissertations. Dekker.
Manicas, Peter T.
xManicas, Peter T.
Logic: The Essentials. McGraw.
Manifold, John. see Manifold, John Streeter.
Manifold, John Streeter, 1915-
xManifold, John.
Collected Verse. U of Queensland Pr.
Manifold, Laurie F. see Manifold, Laurie Fraser.
Manifold, Laurie Fraser.
xManifold, Laurie F.
illus. Christmas Window. HM.
Manis, Jerome. see Manis, Jerome G.
Manis, Jerome G.
xManis, Jerome.

Symbolic Interaction: A Reader in Social
Psychology. Allyn.
xManis, Jerome G.
Analyzing Social Problems. HR&W.
Manis, Melvin, 1931-
xManis, Melvin.
Cognitive Processes. Brooks-Cole.
Mankekar, D. R.
xMankekar, D. R.
Accession to Extinction: The Story of Indian
Princes. Intl Bk Dist.
Mankiewicz, Frank.
xMankiewicz, Frank.
Remote Control: Television & the
Manipulation of American Life. Times Bks.
Mankin, Don, 1942-
xMankin, Don.
Toward a Post-Industrial Psychology: Emerging
Perspectives on Technology, Work,
Education & Leisure. Wiley.
Mankin, Linda R.
xMankin, Linda R.
Prelude to Musicianship: Fundamental
Concepts & Skills. HR&W.
Manko, Howard H.
xManko, Howard H.
Effective Technical Speeches & Sessions: A
Guide for Speakers & Program Chairmen.
McGraw.
Mankoff, M. see Mankoff, Milton.
Mankoff, Milton.
xMankoff, M.
Poverty of Progress: The Political Economy of
American Social Problems. HR&W.
Mankowitz, Wolf.
xMankowitz, Wolf.
Dickens of London. Macmillan.
Manley, Albert.
xManley, Albert.
Complete Fencing. Doubleday.
Manley, Deborah.
nManley, Deborah.
All About Me. Raintree Pubs.
Animals All. Raintree Pubs.
Animals One to Ten. Raintree Pubs.
Around the House. Raintree Pubs.
From A to Z. Raintree Pubs.
A New House. Raintree Pubs.
The Other Side. Raintree Pubs.
What Color Is It?. Raintree Pubs.
Where Are We Going?. Raintree Pubs.
Manley, Michael, 1924-
xManley, Michael.
The Politics of Change: A Jamaican Testament.
Howard U Pr.
Manley, Robert. see Manley, Robert H.
Manley, Robert H.
xManley, Robert.
Guyana Emergent: The Post-Independence
Struggle for Nondependent Development. G
K Hall.
xManley, Robert H.
Guyana Emergent: The Post Independence
Struggle for Nondependent Development.
Schenkman.
Manley, Seon.
xManley, Seon.
Adventures in Making: Romance of Crafts
Around the World. Vanguard.
Compiled by Cat Encounters: A Cat-Lover's
Anthology. Lothrop.
Compiled by Fun Phantoms: Tales of Ghostly
Entertainment. Lothrop.
The Ghost in the Far Garden & Other Stories.
Lothrop.
The Haunted Dolls. Doubleday.
ed. Nature's Revenge: Eerie Stories of Revolt
Against the Human Race. Lothrop.
Manley, Timothy M.
xManley, Timothy M.

Outline of Sre Structure. U Pr of Hawaii.
Manlove, C. N. see Manlove, Colin Nicholas.
Manlove, Colin Nicholas, 1942-
xManlove, C. N.
Modern Fantasy: Five Studies. Cambridge U
Pr.
Manly, Richard S. see Manly, Richard Samuel.
Manly, Richard Samuel.
xManly, Richard S.
ed. Adhesion in Biological Systems. Acad Pr.
Manly, William L. see Manly, William Lewis.
Manly, William Lewis, b. 1820
xManly, William L.
Death Valley in '49. Chalfant Pr.
Mann, Abby.
xMann, Abby.
Tuesdays & Thursdays. Doubleday.
Mann, Arthur.
xMann, Arthur.
Immigrants in American Life: Selected
Readings. HM.
The One & the Many: Reflections on the
American Identity. U of Chicago Pr.
Mann, Cameron, Bp, 1851-1932
xMann, Cameron.
Concordance to the English Poems of George
Herbert. Folcroft.
Concordance to the English Poems of George
Herbert. Scholarly.
Mann, Carleton H. see Mann, Carleton Hunter.
Mann, Carleton Hunter, 1886-
xMann, Carleton H.
How Schools Use Their Time: Time Allotment
Practice in 444 Cities. AMS Pr.
Mann, Charles K. see Mann, Charles Kenneth.
Mann, Charles Kenneth.
xMann, Charles K.
Instrumental Analysis. Har-Row.
Mann, Dale.
xMann, Dale.
ed. Making Change Happen?. Tchrs Coll.
Mann, Dean E.
xMann, Dean E.
The Assistant Secretaries: Problems &
Processes of Appointment. Brookings.
Mann, Denese B. see Mann, Denese Berg.
Mann, Denese Berg.
xMann, Denese B.
The Woman in Judaism. Jonathan Pubns.
Mann, Eric.
xMann, Eric.
Comrade George: An Investigation into the
Life, Political Thought, & Assassination of
George Jackson. Har-Row.
Comrade George: An Investigation into the
Life, Political Thought & Assassination of
George Jackson. Peter Smith.
Mann, Floris P. see Mann, Floris Perkins.
Mann, Floris Perkins.
xMann, Floris P.
History of Telfair County from 1812 to 1949.
Reprint.
Mann, George A.
xMann, George A.
Recovery of Reality: Overcoming Chemical
Dependency. Har-Row.
Mann, George B.
xMann, George B.
ABC's of Transistors. Sams.
Mann, Gerald.
xMann, Gerald.
The Seven Deadly Virtues. Word Bks.
Mann, Golo, 1909-
xMann, Golo.
Secretary of Europe: The Life of Friedrich
Gentz, Enemy of Napoleon. Shoe String.
Mann, Heinrich.
xMann, Heinrich.

The Blue Angel. Fertig.
The Blue Angel. Ungar.
Mann, Helen S. see Mann, Helen Scott.
Mann, Helen Scott.
xMann, Helen S.
Charles Ezra Sprague. Arno.
Mann, Henry B. see Mann, Henry Berthold.
Mann, Henry Berthold.
xMann, Henry B.
Addition Theorems: The Addition Theorems of
Group Theory & Number Theory. Krieger.
Mann, Horace, 1796-1859
xMann, Horace.
Lectures on Education. Arno.
Mann, Jack.
xMann, Jack.
Decline & Fall of the New York Yankees.
S&S.
Mann, Jacob, 1888-1940
xMann, Jacob.
Texts & Studies in Jewish History & Literature.
Ktav.
Mann, Jesse A. see Mann, Jesse Aloysius.
Mann, Jesse Aloysius.
xMann, Jesse A.
ed. Approaches to Morality: Readings in Ethics
from Classical Philosophy to Existentialism.
HarBraceJ.
Reflections on Man: Readings in Philosophical
Psychology from Classical Philosophy to
Existentialism. HarBraceJ.
Mann, John. see Mann, John Harvey.
Mann, John Harvey.
xMann, John.
ed. Learning to Be: The Education of Human
Potential. Free Pr.
Mann, Klaus, 1906-1949
xMann, Klaus.
Andre Gide & the Crisis of Modern Thought.
Octagon.
Mephisto. Ballantine.
Mephisto. Random.
Mann, Lawrence.
xMann, Lawrence.
Applied Engineering Statistics for Practicing
Engineers. CBI Pub.
Mann, Lester.
xMann, Lester.
ed. The Human Side of Exceptionality. Grune.
Mann, M. see Mann, Michael.
Mann, Martin.
xMann, Martin.
Peacetime Uses of Atomic Energy. T Y
Crowell.
Mann, Marty, 1904-
xMann, Marty.
Marty Mann Answers Your Questions About
Drinking & Alcoholism. HR&W.
Mann, Mary. see Mann, Mary Tyler (Peabody).
Mann, Mary P. see Mann, Mary Tyler (Peabody).
Mann, Mary Tyler (Peabody), 1806-1887
xMann, Mary.
Life of Horace Mann. Arno.
xMann, Mary P.
Life of Horace Mann. Norwood Edns.
Mann, Michael.
xMann, M.
Workers on the Move: The Sociology of
Relocation. Cambridge U Pr.
xMann, Michael.
Consciousness & Action Among the Western
Working Class. Humanities.
Mann, Peggy.
xMann, Peggy.

Easter Island: Land of Mysteries. HR&W.
Golda: The Life of Israel's Prime Minister.
  WSP.
My Dad Lives in a Downtown Hotel. Avon.
My Dad Lives in a Downtown Hotel.
  Doubleday.
A Present for Yanya. Random.
Street of the Flower Boxes. PB.
Street of the Flower Boxes. Archway.
There Are Two Kinds of Terrible. Doubleday.
There Are Two Kinds of Terrible. Avon.
Twelve Is Too Old. Doubleday.

Mann, Peter, 1948-
  xMann, Peter.
    How to Buy a Used Car Without Getting
      Gypped. B&N.

Mann, Peter H.
  xMann, Peter H.
    Students & Books. Routledge & Kegan.

Mann, Philip A.
  xMann, Philip A.
    Psychological Consultation with a Police
      Department: A Demonstration of
      Cooperative Training in Mental Health. C C
      Thomas.

Mann, Philip H.
  xMann, Philip H.
    Handbook in Diagnostic-Prescriptive Teaching.
      Allyn.

Mann, Roderick, 1922-
  xMann, Roderick.
    Foreign Body. Macmillan.

Mann, Stanley, 1928-
  xMann, Stanley.
    Third Time Lucky. St Martin.
Mann, Stella T. *see* Mann, Stella Terrill.

Mann, Stella Terrill.
  xMann, Stella T.
    Change Your Life Through Faith & Work. De
      Vorss.
    How to Analyze & Overcome Your Fears. De
      Vorss.
    How to Use the Power of Your Word. De
      Vorss.
    How to Use the Power of Your Word. Unity
      Bks.

Mann, Thomas, 1875-1955
  xMann, Thomas.
    The Black Swan. HarBraceJ.
    Black Swan. Knopf.
    Buddenbrooks. Knopf.
    Buddenbrooks. Random.
    Children & Fools. Arno.
    Death in Venice. Modern Lib.
    Nocturnes. Arno.

Mann, Thomas E.
  xMann, Thomas E.
    Unsafe at Any Margin: Interpreting
      Congressional Elections. Am Enterprise.
Mann, W. Edward. *see* Mann, William Edward.

Mann, William.
  xMann, William.
    Lettering & Lettering Display. Van Nos
      Reinhold.
Mann, William. *see* Mann, William S.
Mann, William D. *see* Mann, William D'Alton.

Mann, William D'Alton, 1839-1920
  xMann, William D.
    Fads & Fancies of Representative Americans at
      the Beginning of the Twentieth Century....
      Arno.

Mann, William Edward.
  xMann, W. Edward.
    Orgone, Reich & Eros: Wilhelm Reich's
      Theory of Life Energy. S&S.

Mann, William S.
  xMann, William.
    The Operas of Mozart. Oxford U Pr.
Mann, Zane. *see* Mann, Zane B.

Mann, Zane B., 1924-
  xMann, Zane.
    Fair Winds & Far Places. Dillon.

Manna, Charles.
  xManna, Charlie.
    Loser Is. S&S.
Manna, Charlie. *see* Manna, Charles.
Manna, Z. *see* Manna, Zohar.

Manna, Zohar.
  xManna, Z.
    Studies in Automatic Programming Logic.
      Elsevier.

Manne, Henry G.
  xManne, Henry G.
    ed. Economic Policy & the Regulation of
      Corporate Securities. Am Enterprise.
    The Modern Corporation & Social
      Responsibility. Am Enterprise.
Manne, Henry G. *see* Manne, Henry L.

Manne, Henry L.
  xManne, Henry G.
    ed. Auto Safety Regulation: The Cure or the
      Problem?. T Horton & Dghts.

Mannebach, Wayne C.
  xMannebach, Wayne C.
    Speaking from the Pulpit. Judson.

Manners, Alexandra.
  xManners, Alexandra.
    Candles in the Wood. Berkley Pub.

Manners, David, 1915-
  xManners, David.
    Teach Your Child Self-Defense. Arco.

Manners, David X., 1912-
  xManners, David X.
    Complete Book of Home Workshops. Har-Row.
  xManners, Dick.
    Great Tool Emporium. Dutton.
Manners, Dick. *see* Manners, David X.

Manners, George E.
  xManners, George E.
    Dynamic Incentive Systems. Ga St U Busn
      Pub.

Manners, Gerald.
  xManners, Gerald.
    The Changing World Market for Iron Ore,
      1950-1980: An Economic Geography. Johns
      Hopkins.
    Geography of Energy. Humanities.

Manners, John.
  xManners, John.
    Country Crafts Today. Gale.
    Crafts of the Highlands & Islands. David &
      Charles.

Manners, Robert A.
  xManners, Robert A.
    Southern Paiute & Chemehuevi: An
      Ethnohistorical Report. Clearwater Pub.
Manners, Robert A. *see* Manners, Robert Alan.

Manners, Robert Alan.
  xManners, Robert A.
    ed. Theory in Anthropology: A Sourcebook.
      Aldine Pub.
Manners, Ruth A. *see* Manners, Ruth Ann.

Manners, Ruth Ann.
  xManners, Ruth A.
    The Quick & Easy Vegetarian Cookbook. M
      Evans.

Mannes, David, 1866-1959
  xMannes, David.
    Music Is My Faith: An Autobiography. Da
      Capo.

Mannes, Marya.
  xMannes, Marya.
    Last Rights. NAL.
    Subverse: Rhymes for Our Times. Braziller.

Mannheim, Karl.
  xMannheim, Karl.
    From Karl Mannheim. Oxford U Pr.
    From Karl Mannheim. Oxford U Pr.
Mannin, Ethel. *see* Mannin, Ethel Edith.

Mannin, Ethel Edith, 1900-
  xMannin, Ethel.
    Late Have I Loved Thee. Merrimack Bk Serv.
    The Late Miss Guthrie. Merrimack Bk Serv.
    Pity the Innocent. Merrimack Bk Serv.
    Practitioners of Love. Horizon.
    Sunset Over Dartmoor. Merrimack Bk Serv.
Manning. *see* Manning, Diana Helen.

Manning, Aubrey.
  xManning, Aubrey.
    Introduction to Animal Behavior. A-W.
Manning, Brian. *see* Manning, Brian Stuart.

Manning, Brian Stuart.
  xManning, Brian.
    ed. Politics, Religion & the English Civil War.
      St Martin.
Manning, C. A. *see* Manning, Charles Anthony
  Woodward.

Manning, Caroline.
  xManning, Caroline.
    Immigrant Woman & Her Job. Arno.

Manning, Charles Anthony Woodward.
  xManning, C. A.
    The Nature of International Society. Halsted
      Pr.
Manning, Clarence A. *see* Manning, Clarence Augustus.

Manning, Clarence Augustus, 1893-
  xManning, Clarence A.
    Forgotten Republics. Greenwood.
    History of Modern Bulgarian Literature.
      Greenwood.
    Ukrainian Literature: Studies of the Leading
      Authors. Arno.
Manning, D. J. *see* Manning, David John.

Manning, David John.
  xManning, D. J.
    Liberalism. St Martin.

Manning, Diana Helen.
  xManning.
    Society & Food: The Third World.
      Butterworths.

Manning, Duane.
  xManning, Duane.
    Toward a Humanistic Curriculum. Har-Row.

Manning, Elise W.
  xManning, Elise W.
    Farm Journal's Choice Chocolate Recipes.
      Doubleday.
    ed. Farm Journal's Friendly Food Gifts from
      Your Kitchen. Doubleday.

Manning, Gerry, 1940-
  xManning, Gerry.
    Cobol Basics: A Structured Approach. Random.

Manning, Harvey.
  xManning, Harvey.
    Mountain Flowers. Mountaineers.

Manning, Helen (Taft), 1891-
  xManning, Helen T.
    British Colonial Government After the
      American Revolution, 1782-1820. Shoe
      String.
Manning, Helen T. *see* Manning, Helen (Taft).

Manning, Ian.
  xManning, Ian.
    The Journey to Work. Allen Unwin.

Manning, Jerome A.
  xManning, Jerome A.
    Estate Planning. PLI.
Manning, M. J. *see* Manning, Margaret J.

Manning, Margaret J.
  xManning, M. J.
    Comparative Immunobiology. Halsted Pr.

Manning, Mary.
  xManning, Mary.
    The Last Chronicles of Ballyfungus. Little.

Manning, Olivia.
  xManning, Olivia.

The Battle Lost & Won. Atheneum.
The Danger Tree. Atheneum.
Manning, Owen.
    xManning, Owen.
        The History & Antiquities of the County of
          Surrey. Rowman.
Manning, Peter J., 1942-
    xManning, Peter J.
        Byron & His Fictions. Wayne St U Pr.
Manning, Peter K.
    xManning, Peter K.
        Police Work: The Social Organization of
          Policing. MIT Pr.
        The Sociology of Mental Health & Illness.
          Bobbs.
Manning, Sidney A.
    xInt'l Workshop on Appropriate Tech., Delft Univ.
        of Technology, Sept. 4-7, 1979.
        Fundamental Aspects of Appropriate
          Technology: Proceedings. Sijthoff &
          Noordhoff.
    xManning, Sidney A.
        Classical Psychophysics & Scaling. Krieger.
        Classical Psychophysics & Scaling. McGraw.
Manning, Sidney A. see Manning, Sidney Alpern.
Manning, Sidney Alpern.
    xManning, Sidney A.
        Child & Adolescent Development: A Basic
          Self-Instructional Guide. McGraw.
Manning, W. R. see Manning, William Reginald
    Dermott.
Manning, William. see Manning, William O.
Manning, William O.
    xManning, William.
        ed. Harmfully Involved. Hazelden.
Manning, William R. see Manning, William Ray.
Manning, William Ray, 1871-1942
    xManning, William R.
        ed. Arbitration Treaties Among the American
          Nations, to the Close of the Year 1910.
          Kraus Repr.
        Early Diplomatic Relations between the United
          States & Mexico. AMS Pr.
        Early Diplomatic Relations Between the United
          States & Mexico. Greenwood.
        Early Diplomatic Relations Between the United
          States & Mexico. Scholarly.
        The Nootka Sound Controversy. Arno.
Manning, William Reginald Dermott.
    xManning, W. R.
        High Pressure Engineering. Intl Ideas.
Manning-Sanders, Ruth.
    xManning-Sanders, Ruth.
        A Book of Spooks & Spectres. Dutton.
        Festivals. Dutton.
        Tortoise Tales. Elsevier-Nelson.
Manningham, Mary.
    xManningham, Mary.
        A Mary Mixture. Windy Row.
        Thoughts & Verses. Windy Row.
Mannion, Michael.
    xMannion, Michael.
        Colleen. Belmont-Tower.
Mannucci, P. M. see Mannucci, Pier Mannucio.
Mannucci, Pier Mannucio.
    xMannucci, P. M.
        ed. Platelet Function & Thrombosis: A Review
          of Methods. Plenum Pub.
Mano, M. see Mano, M. Morris.
Mano, M. Morris, 1927-
    xMano, M.
        Digital Logic & Computer Design. P-H.
    xMano, M. Morris.
        Computer Logic Design. P-H.
        Computer System Architecture. P-H.
Manoff, Tom.
    xManoff, Tom.
        The Music Kit. Norton.
Manoharan, S. see Manoharan, Seeniappan.

Manoharan, Seeniappan, 1939-
    xManoharan, S.
        The Oil Crisis: The End of an Era. Intl Pubns
          Serv.
Manolson, Frank.
    xManolson, Frank.
        Living with Your Cat. Penguin.
        Living with Your Cat. Viking Pr.
Manring, Benjamin F. see Manring, Benjamin Franklin.
Manring, Benjamin Franklin, 1866-1946
    xManring, Benjamin F.
        The Conquest of the Coeur D'Alenes,
          Spokanes & Palouses. Ye Galleon.
Mansbach, S. A. see Mansbach, Steven A.
Mansbach, Steven A., 1950-
    xMansbach, S. A.
        Visions of Totality: Laszlo Moholy-Nagy, Theo
          Van Doesburg, & El Lissitzky. Univ
          Microfilms.
Mansbridge, Jane J.
    xMansbridge, Jane J.
        Beyond Adversary Democracy. Basic.
Manschreck, Clyde L. see Manschreck, Clyde Leonard.
Manschreck, Clyde Leonard.
    xManschreck, Clyde L.
        ed. The American Religious Experiment: Piety
          & Practicality. Exploration Pr.
Manschreck, Theo C.
    xManschreck, Theo C.
        ed. Renewal in Psychiatry: A Critical Rational
          Perspective. Halsted Pr.
Mansell, George.
    xMansell, George.
        Anatomy of Architecture. A & W Pubs.
Manser, Ellen.
    xManser, Ellen P.
        ed. Family Advocacy: A Manual for Action.
          Family Serv.
Manser, Ellen P. see Manser, Ellen.
Mansergh, Gerald G.
    xMansergh, Gerald G
        ed. Dynamics of Management by Objectives
          for School Administrators. Interstate.
Mansfield, Alan.
    xMansfield, Alan.
        Handbook of English Costume in the
          Twentieth Century. Plays.
Mansfield, C. M. see Mansfield, Carl M.
Mansfield, Carl M.
    xMansfield, C. M.
        Early Breast Cancer: Its History & Results of
          Treatment. S Karger.
Mansfield, David. see Mansfield, David Hutsby.
Mansfield, David Hutsby.
    xMansfield, David.
        Principles of Physical Chemistry. Heinemann
          Ed.
Mansfield, Edwin.
    xMansfield, Edwin.
        ed. Defense, Science & Public Policy. Norton.
        Economics of Technological Change. Norton.
        Economics: Principles, Problems, Decisions.
          Norton.
        ed. Micro-Economics: Selected Readings.
          Norton.
        ed. Microeconomics: Selected Readings.
          Norton.
        Microeconomics: Theory & Applications.
          Norton.
        Microeconomics: Theory & Applications.
          Norton.
        Principles of Macroeconomics. Norton.
        Principles of Microeconomics. Norton.
        The Production & Application of New
          Industrial Technology. Norton.
Mansfield, Elizabeth.
    xMansfield, Elizabeth.
        A Very Dutiful Daughter. Berkley Pub.
Mansfield, Evelyn A, 1908-
    xMansfield, Evelyn A.

Clothing Construction. HM.
Mansfield, Harvey C., 1932-
    xMansfield, Harvey C.
        Machiavelli's New Modes & Orders: A Study
          of the "Discourses on Livy". Cornell U Pr.
Mansfield, Harvey C. see Mansfield, Harvey Claflin.
Mansfield, Harvey Claflin, 1905-
    xMansfield, Harvey C.
        ed. Congress Against the President. Praeger.
        The Spirit of Liberalism. Harvard U Pr.
Mansfield, Katherine, 1888-1923
    xMansfield, Katherine.
        The Aloe. Fertig.
        The Letters of Katherine Mansfield. Fertig.
        Stories. Random.
        The Urewera Notebook. Oxford U Pr.
Mansfield, Kenneth.
    xMansfield, Kenneth.
        Trout & How to Catch Them. Barrie &
          Jenkins.
Mansfield, Larry E.
    xMansfield, Larry E.
        Linear Algebra with Geometric Applications.
          Dekker.
Mansfield, Maynard J. see Mansfield, Maynard Joseph.
Mansfield, Maynard Joseph, 1930-
    xMansfield, Maynard J.
        Intermediate Real Analysis. Krieger.
Mansfield, Peter, 1928-
    xMansfield, Peter.
        The Arabs. Penguin.
        The Middle East: A Political & Economic
          Survey. Oxford U Pr.
        The Ottoman Empire & Its Successors. St
          Martin.
Mansfield, Ralph.
    xMansfield, Ralph.
        Introduction to Technical Mathematics.
          Har-Row.
Mansfield, T. A. see Mansfield, Terence Arthur.
Mansfield, Terence Arthur.
    xMansfield, T. A.
        ed. Effects of Air Pollutants on Plants.
          Cambridge U Pr.
Mansfield, W. Ed.
    xMansfield, W. Ed.
        An Affirmative Action Program Proposal. Intl
          Personnel Mgmt.
Manske, A. J. see Manske, Arthur John.
Manske, Arthur John, 1907-
    xManske, A. J.
        The Reflection of Teachers' Attitudes in the
          Attitudes of Their Pupils. AMS Pr.
Manson, John A.
    xManson, John A.
        Polymer Blends & Composites. Plenum Pub.
Manson, S. S.
    xManson, S. S.
        Thermal Stress & Low-Cycle Fatigue. McGraw.
Manson-Hing, L. R. see Manson-Hing, Lincoln R.
Manson-Hing, Lincoln R.
    xManson-Hing, L. R.
        Panoramic Dental Radiography. C C Thomas.
    xManson-Hing, Lincoln R.
        Panoramic Dental Radiography. C C Thomas.
Mansour, Joyce.
    xMansour, Joyce.
        Flash Card. Cherry Valley.
Mansuelli, Guido A. see Mansuelli, Guido Achille.
Mansuelli, Guido Achille.
    xMansuelli, Guido A.
        Art of Etruria & Early Rome. Crown.
Mante, Daisy R. see Mante, Daisy Rivers.
Mante, Daisy Rivers.
    xMante, Daisy R.

How to Develop a Model School & Model
    Classrooms for Young Children: A Guide for
    Administrators & Teachers. Project
    Jifunza-Educ.
Mantegazza, P.
    xMantegazza, P.
    ed. Prostaglandins, Peptides & Amines. Acad
        Pr.
Mantel, Gerhard.
    xMantel, Gerhard.
    Cello Technique: Principles & Forms of
        Movement. Ind U Pr.
Mantell, Charles L. *see* Mantell, Charles Letnam.
Mantell, Charles Letnam, 1897-
    xMantell, Charles L.
    Carbon & Graphite Handbook. Krieger.
    Solid Wastes: Origin, Collection, Processing &
        Disposal. Wiley.
Mantell, Martin E., 1936-
    xMantell, Martin E.
    Johnson, Grant, & the Politics of
        Reconstruction. Columbia U Pr.
Manten, A. A.
    xManten, A. A.
    Silurian Reefs of Gotland. Elsevier.
Manter, Harold W. *see* Manter, Harold Winfred.
Manter, Harold Winfred, 1898-
    xManter, Harold W.
    Some North American Fish Trematodes.
        Johnson Repr.
Mantinband, Gerda.
    xMantinband, Gerda.
    Bing, Bong, Bang & Fiddle, Dee, Dee.
        Doubleday.
Mantinband, James. *see* Mantinband, James H.
Mantinband, James H.
    xMantinband, James.
    ed. Dictionary of Latin Literature. Philos Lib.
    xMantinband, James H.
    Dictionary of Greek Literature. Littlefield.
    Dictionary of Latin Literature. Littlefield.
Mantle, Mickey, 1931-
    xMantle, Mickey.
    The Education of a Baseball Player. S&S.
Manton, Jo, 1919-
    xManton, Jo.
    Mary Carpenter & the Children of the Streets.
        Heinemann Ed.
Manton, Joseph E., 1904-
    xManton, Joseph E.
    Stay with Us, Lord!. Our Sunday Visitor.
    Stumbling Toward Heaven. Our Sunday
        Visitor.
Manton, S. M. *see* Manton, Sidnie Milana.
Manton, Sidnie Milana, 1902-
    xManton, S. M.
    The Arthropoda: Habits, Functional
        Morphology & Evolution. Oxford U Pr.
Mantz, R. *see* Mantz, Ruth Elvish.
Mantz, Ruth E. *see* Mantz, Ruth Elvish.
Mantz, Ruth Elvish.
    xMantz, R.
    Life of Katherine Mansfield. Haskell.
    xMantz, Ruth E.
    Critical Bibliography of Katherine Mansfield. B
        Franklin.
    Critical Bibliography of Katherine Mansfield.
        Folcroft.
    The Life of Katherine Mansfield. Scholarly.
Mantzius, Karl, 1860-1921
    xMantzius, Karl.
    History of Theatrical Art in Ancient & Modern
        Times. Peter Smith.
Manuel, Frank E. *see* Manuel, Frank Edward.
Manuel, Frank Edward.
    xManuel, Frank E.

Age of Reason. Cornell U Pr.
    The Politics of Modern Spain. Greenwood.
    A Portrait of Isaac Newton. New Republic.
    The Realities of American-Palestine Relations.
        Greenwood.
    Utopian Thought in the Western World.
        Harvard U Pr.
Manuel, George.
    xManuel, George.
    The Fourth World: An Indian Reality. Free Pr.
Manuel, Yves.
    xManuel, Yves.
    ed. Proteins in Normal & Pathological Urine.
        Univ Park.
Manufacturing Chemists Assn. *see* Manufacturing
    Chemists' Association.
Manufacturing Chemists' Association.
    xManufacturing Chemists Assn.
    Guide to Safety in the Chemical Laboratory.
        Van Nos Reinhold.
Manushkin, Fran.
    xManushkin, Fran.
    Baby. Har-Row.
    Bubblebath!. Har-Row.
    Swinging & Swinging. Har-Row.
Manvell, Roger, 1909-
    xManvell, Roger.
    Chaplin. Little.
    ed. Experiment in the Film. Arno.
    The Hundred Days to Hitler. St Martin.
    Shakespeare & the Film. A S Barnes.
Manville, W. H. *see* Manville, William H.
Manville, William H.
    xManville, W. H.
    Breaking Up. S&S.
    Goodbye. Ballantine.
Manwaring, David R. *see* Manwaring, David Roger.
Manwaring, David Roger, 1933-
    xManwaring, David R.
    Render Unto Caesar: The Flag-Salute
        Controversy. U of Chicago Pr.
Manwaring, George E. *see* Manwaring, George Ernest.
Manwaring, George Ernest.
    xManwaring, George E.
    Floating Republic. Kelley.
Manwell, A. P. *see* Manwell, A. R.
Manwell, A. R.
    xManwell, A. P.
    Hodograph Equations: An Introduction to the
        Mathematical Theory of Plane Transonic
        Flow. Hafner.
Manwill, Marion C.
    xManwill, Marion C.
    How to Shoe a Horse. Arco.
Manypenny, George Washington, 1808-1893
    xManypenny, George Washington.
    Our Indian Wards. Da Capo.
Mao, J. C. *see* Mao, James C. T.
Mao, James C. T., 1926-
    xMao, J. C.
    Quantitative Analysis of Financial Decisions.
        Macmillan.
Mao, Nathan K.
    xMao, Nathan K.
    Li Yu. Twayne.
Mapes, Victor, 1870-1943
    xMapes, Victor.
    Duse & the French. Arno.
    Duse & the French. B Franklin.
Maple, Eric.
    xMaple, Eric.
    The Domain of Devils. R West.
Maple, Terry.
    xMaple, Terry L.
    Orang-Utan Behavior. Van Nos Reinhold.
Maple, Terry L. *see* Maple, Terry.

Maples, Evelyn.
    xMaples, Evelyn.
    The Many Selves of Ann-Elizabeth.
        Independence Pr.
    Norman Learns About the Scriptures. Herald
        Hse.
Mapleton, Robert. *see* Mapleton, Robert A.
Mapleton, Robert A.
    xMapleton, Robert.
    Theory of Charge Exchange. Krieger.
Mapp, Edward.
    xMapp, Edward.
    Directory of Blacks in the Performing Arts.
        Scarecrow.
    ed. Puerto Rican Perspectives. Scarecrow.
Mappen, Marc.
    xMappen, Marc.
    Witches & Historians: Interpretations of Salem
        Witchcraft. Krieger.
Maquet, Jacques. *see* Maquet, Jacques Jerome Pierre.
Maquet, Jacques Jerome Pierre, 1919-
    xMaquet, Jacques.
    Africanity: The Cultural Unity of Black Africa.
        Oxford U Pr.
    Africanity: The Cultural Unity of Black Africa.
        Oxford U Pr.
    Introduction to Aesthetic Anthropology.
        Undena Pubns.
Mara, Tim.
    xMara, Tim.
    The Thames & Hudson Manual of Screen
        Printing. Thames Hudson.
Maradudin, A. A.
    xMaradudin, A. A.
    Lattice Dynamics. Benjamin-Cummings.
Marais, Elizabeth.
    xMarais, Elizabeth.
    Lives Worth Living: The Right of All the
        Handicapped. Intl Schol Bk Serv.
Marais, Eugene N. *see* Marais, Eugene Nielen.
Marais, Eugene Nielen, 1872-1936
    xMarais, Eugene N.
    Soul of the White Ant. Kraus Repr.
Marais, J. S. *see* Marais, Johannes Stephanus.
Marais, Johannes Stephanus.
    xMarais, J. S.
    The Colonisation of New Zealand. Dawson
        Pub.
Maramorosch, K. *see* Maramorosch, Karl.
Maramorosch, Karl.
    xMaramorosch, K.
    ed. Leafhopper Vectors & Plant Disease
        Agents. Acad Pr.
    xMaramorosch, Karl.
    ed. Insect & Plant Viruses: An Atlas. Acad Pr.
Maranda, Pierre.
    xMaranda, Pierre.
    French Kinship Structure & History. Mouton.
    ed. Structural Analysis of Oral Tradition. U of
        Pa Pr.
Marando, Vincent L.
    xMarando, Vincent L.
    The Forgotten Governments: County
        Commissioners As Policy Makers. U Presses
        Fla.
Maranell, Gary M. *see* Maranell, Gary Michael.
Maranell, Gary Michael, 1932-
    xMaranell, Gary M.
    Responses to Religion: Studies in the Social
        Psychology of Religious Belief. Regents Pr
        KS.
Marangell, Virginia J.
    xMarangell, Virginia J.
    Gianna Mia. Dodd.
Maraniss, James E., 1945-
    xMaraniss, James E.
    On Calderon. U of Mo Pr.
Marano, Joseph.
    xMarano, Joseph.

Fundamentals of Mathematics. P-H.
Marasco, Robert.
xMarasco, Robert.
Parlor Games. Delacorte.
Parlor Games. Dell.
Marascuilo, Leonard A.
xMarascuilo, Leonard A.
Nonparametric & Distribution-Free Methods
for the Social Sciences. Brooks-Cole.
Marateck, Samuel L.
xMarateck, Samuel L.
Fortran. Acad Pr.
Maratka, Z.
xMaratka, Z.
ed. Inflammation in Gut: Esophagitis,
Duodenitis, Segmental Colitis. S Karger.
Maravall, Jose.
xMaravall, Jose.
Dictatorship & Political Dissent: Workers &
Students in Franco's Spain. St Martin.
Marbach, Ethel.
xMarbach, Ethel.
Once-Upon-a-Time Saints: Faith-Tales for
Children. St Anthony Mess Pr.
Marber, Scott.
xMarber, Scott.
A Lot of Lumps. SCOAL Pr.
Marble, Annie. *see* Marble, Annie (Russell).
Marble, Annie (Russell), 1864-1936
xMarble, Annie.
Nobel Prize Winners in Literature, 1901-1931.
Arno.
Nobel Prize Winners in Literature, 1901-1931.
R West.
Marburg, Theodore, 1862-1946
xMarburg, Theodore.
Expansion. Garland Pub.
Marc, Olivier, 1930-
xMarc, Olivier.
Psychology of the House. Thames Hudson.
Marcante, Duilio.
xMarcante, Duilio.
This Is Diving: A Complete Underwater
Course. Norton.
Marceau, Felicien, Pseud.
xMarceau, Felicien.
Balzac & His World. Greenwood.
Marceau, Jane.
xMarceau, Jane.
Class & Status in France: Economic Change &
Social Immobility, 1945-1975. Oxford U Pr.
Marceau, Marcel.
xMarceau, Marcel.
illus. The Story of Bip. Har-Row.
**Marcel Grossman Meeting on General Relativity,
1st,trieste, 1975.**
xMarcel Grossman Meeting on General Relativity,
1st, International Center for Theoretical Physics,
University of Trieste, Jul. 1975.
Proceedings. Elsevier.
March, Alden, 1869-1942
xMarch, Alden.
History & Conquest of the Philippines & Our
Other Island Possessions. Arno.
March, Ausias. *see* March, Auzias.
March, Auzias.
xMarch, Ausias.
Ausias March: Selected Poems. Lib Soc Sci.
Ausias March: Selected Poems. U of Tex Pr.
March, Harold, 1896-
xMarch, Harold.
Two Worlds of Marcel Proust. Russell.
March, James G.
xMarch, James G.
Ambiguity & Choice in Organizations.
Universitet.
Organizations. Wiley.
March, Jerry.
xMarch, Jerry.

General Chemistry. Macmillan.
March, L. *see* March, Lionel.
March, Lindsay.
xMarch, Lindsay.
These Cliffs Are Dangerous. S&S.
March, Lionel, 1934-
xMarch, L.
ed. The Architecture of Form. Cambridge U
Pr.
xMarch, Lionel.
The Geometry of Environment: An
Introduction to Spatial Organization in
Design. MIT Pr.
March, N. H. *see* March, Norman Henry.
March, Norman H. *see* March, Norman Henry.
March, Norman Henry.
xMarch, N. H.
Atomic Dynamics in Liquids. Halsted Pr.
ed. Orbital Theories of Molecules & Solids.
Oxford U Pr.
xMarch, Norman H.
Liquid Metals. Pergamon.
March, Peyton C. *see* March, Peyton Conway.
March, Peyton Conway, 1864-1955
xMarch, Peyton C.
Nation at War. Greenwood.
March, Ray A., 1934-
xMarch, Ray A.
Alabama Bound: Forty-Five Years Inside a
Prison System. U of Ala Pr.
Marchalonis, J. J. *see* Marchalonis, John J.
Marchalonis, John J., 1940-
xMarchalonis, J. J.
ed. Comparative Immunology. Halsted Pr.
xMarchalonis, John J.
Immunity in Evolution. Harvard U Pr.
Marchand, Alan P.
xMarchand, Alan P.
ed. Pericyclic Reactions. Acad Pr.
Marchand, C. Roland, 1933-
xMarchand, C. Roland.
The American Peace Movement & Social
Reform, 1898-1918. Princeton U Pr.
Marchand, Erich W.
xMarchand, Erich W.
Gradient Index Optics. Acad Pr.
Marchand, Ernest.
xMarchand, Ernest.
Frank Norris: A Study. Octagon.
Marchand, H. *see* Marchand, Hans.
Marchand, Hans, 1907-
xMarchand, H.
Categories & Types of Present-Day English
Word Formation: A Synchronic-Diacronic
Approach. Adler.
Marchand, James W. *see* Marchand, James Woodrow.
Marchand, James Woodrow, 1926-
xMarchand, James W.
The Sounds & Phonemes of Wulfila's Gothic.
Mouton.
Marchand, Leslie A. *see* Marchand, Leslie Alexis.
Marchand, Leslie Alexis, 1900-
xMarchand, Leslie A.
Byron's Poetry: A Critical Introduction.
Harvard U Pr.
Prefaces to Byron. Norwood Edns.
Marchant, Alexander N. *see* Marchant, Alexander
Nelson De Armond.
Marchant, Alexander Nelson De Armond, 1912-
xMarchant, Alexander N.
From Barter to Slavery: The Economic
Relations of Portuguese & Indians in the
Settlement of Brazil, 1500-1580. Peter Smith.
Marchant, Harold. *see* Marchant, Harold J.
Marchant, Harold J.
xMarchant, Harold.
Adolescent Girls at Risk. Pergamon.
Marchant, Maurice P.
xMarchant, Maurice P.

Participative Management in Academic
Libraries. Greenwood.
Marchant, R. A. *see* Marchant, Ronald Albert.
Marchant, Ralph.
xMarchant, Ralph.
Little Painter. Carolrhoda Bks.
Marchant, Ronald Albert.
xMarchant, R. A.
Where Animals Live. Macmillan.
Marchant, William, 1923-
xMarchant, William.
Firebird. Crown.
The Gentleman Vanishes. St Martin.
Marchbank, Pearce.
xMarchbank, Pearce.
The Illustrated Rock Almanac. Paddington.
Marchbanks, John B., 1914-
xMarchbanks, John B.
Great Doctrines Relating to Salvation.
Loizeaux.
Marchello, J. M.
xMarchello, J. M.
Control of Air Pollution Sources. Dekker.
ed. Gas-Solids Handling in the Process
Industries. Dekker.
xMarchello, Joseph M.
ed. Gas Cleaning for Air Quality Control:
Industrial & Environmental Health & Safety
Requirements. Dekker.
Marchello, Joseph M. *see* Marchello, J. M.
Marchesi, Mathilde. *see* Marchesi, Mathilde Graumann.
Marchesi, Mathilde Graumann, 1822-1913
xMarchesi, Mathilde.
Marchesi & Music: Passages from the Life of a
Famous Singing-Teacher. Da Capo.
Marchesi, Vincent T.
xMarchesi, Vincent T.
ed. Cell Surface Carbohydrates & Biological
Recognition: Proceedings of the ICN-UCLA
Symposium Held at Keystone, Col., Feb.
1977. A R Liss.
Marchetti, Albert.
xMarchetti, Albert.
Common Cures for Common Ailments. Stein &
Day.
Marchiafava, Louis J.
xMarchiafava, Louis J.
The Houston Police, 1878-1948. Rice Univ.
Marchini, Ron.
xMarchini, Ron.
Power Training in Kung-Fu & Karate. Ohara
Pubns.
Marchione, Margherita.
xMarchione, Margherita.
Clemente Rebora. G K Hall.
Clemente Rebora. Twayne.
ed. Twentieth-Century Italian Poetry: A
Bilingual Anthology. Fairleigh Dickinson.
Marchuk, G. I. *see* Marchuk, Gurii Ivanovich.
Marchuk, Gurii Ivanovich.
xMarchuk, G. I.
Monte Carlo Methods in Atmospheric Optics.
Springer-Verlag.
Marcinkowski, M. J.
xMarcinkowski, M. J.
Unified Theory of Mechanical Behavior of
Matter. Wiley.
Marckwardt, Albert. *see* Marckwardt, Albert Henry.
Marckwardt, Albert H. *see* Marckwardt, Albert Henry.
Marckwardt, Albert Henry, 1903-
xMarckwardt, Albert.
Old English Language & Literature. Norton.
xMarckwardt, Albert H.

Characterization in Chaucer's Knight's Tale. Folcroft.
ed. Linguistics in School Programs. U of Chicago Pr.
The Place of Literature in the Teaching of English As a Second or Foreign Language. U Pr of Hawaii.
Marco, Guy. *see* Marco, Guy A.
Marco, Guy A.
xMarco, Guy.
Information on Music: A Handbook of Reference Sources in European Languages. Libs Unl.
xMarco, Guy A.
Information on Music: A Handbook of Reference Sources in European Languages Vol. 1, Basic & Universal Sources. Libs Unl.
Marcoon, Bruce L.
xMarcoon, Bruce L.
Demian Notes. Cliffs.
Marcosson, Isaac F. *see* Marcosson, Isaac Frederick.
Marcosson, Isaac Frederick, 1876-1961
xMarcosson, Isaac F.
Adventures in Interviewing. AMS Pr.
Anaconda. Arno.
Turbulent Years. Arno.
Wherever Men Trade: The Romance of the Cash Register. Arno.
Marcovich, Miroslav.
xMarcovich, Miroslav.
ed. Illinois Classical Studies. U of Ill Pr.
Marcu, Valeriu, 1899-1943?
xMarcu, Valeriu.
Men & Forces of Our Time. Arno.
Marcus, Abraham.
xMarcus, Abraham.
Computers for Technicians. P-H.
Marcus, Adrianne.
xMarcus, Adrianne.
The Chocolate Bible. Putnam.
Faced with Love. SBD.
Marcus, Alfred A. *see* Marcus, Alfred Allen.
Marcus, Alfred Allen, 1950-
xMarcus, Alfred A.
Promise & Performance: Choosing & Implementing an Environmental Policy. Greenwood.
Marcus, Bruce W., 1925-
xMarcus, Bruce W.
Competing for Capital: A Financial Relations Approach. Krieger.
Marcus, Burton.
xMarcus, Burton H.
Marketing Analysis & Decision Making. Little.
Marcus, Burton H. *see* Marcus, Burton.
Marcus, Edward.
xMarcus, Edward.
Economic Progress & the Developing World. Scott F.
Economics. Kendall-Hunt.
Marcus, Eveline.
xMarcus, Eveline.
American Opisthobranch Mollusks. U Miami Marine.
Marcus, Greil.
xMarcus, Greil.
ed. Stranded: Rock & Roll for a Desert Island. Knopf.
Marcus, Henry S.
xMarcus, Henry S.
Federal Port Policy in the United States. MIT Pr.
Marcus, I. M. *see* Marcus, Irwin M.
Marcus, Irwin M.
xMarcus, I. M.
An Interdisciplinary Approach to Accident Patterns in Children. Kraus Repr.
xMarcus, Irwin M.
ed. Currents in Psychoanalysis. Intl Univs Pr.
Marcus, Jacob R. *see* Marcus, Jacob Rader.

Marcus, Jacob Rader, 1896-
xMarcus, Jacob R.
Early American Jewry. Ktav.
Memoirs of American Jews: 1775-1865. Ktav.
Marcus, Kenneth K. *see* Marcus, Kenneth Karl.
Marcus, Kenneth Karl.
xMarcus, Kenneth K.
The National Government & the Natural Gas Industry, 1946-56: A Study in the Making of a National Policy. Arno.
Marcus, Lyn.
xMarcus, Lyn.
Dialectical Economics: An Introduction to Marxist Political Economy. Heath.
Marcus, Marie.
xMarcus, Marie.
Diagnostic Teaching of the Language Arts. Wiley.
Marcus, Marvin, 1927-
xMarcus, Marvin.
ed. Introduction to Modern Algebra. Dekker.
Marcus, Mitchell. *see* Marcus, Mitchell P.
Marcus, Mitchell P.
xMarcus, Mitchell.
Theory of Syntactic Recognition for Natural Language. MIT Pr.
xMarcus, Mitchell P.
Switching Circuits for Engineers. P-H.
Marcus, Phillip L.
xMarcus, Phillip L.
Standish O'Grady. Bucknell U Pr.
Marcus, Ralph, 1900-1956
xMarcus, Ralph.
Law in the Apocrypha. AMS Pr.
Marcus, Rebecca B.
xMarcus, Rebecca B.
Fiesta Time in Mexico. Garrard.
Marcus, Robert D.
xMarcus, Robert D.
ed. America Since 1945. St Martin.
ed. American Scene: Varieties of American History. Irvington.
A Brief History of the United States Since 1945. St Martin.
Grand Old Party: Political Structure in the Gilded Age, 1880-1896. Oxford U Pr.
Marcus, Russell.
xMarcus, Russell.
English-Lao, Lao-English Dictionary. C E Tuttle.
Marcus, Stanley, 1905-
xMarcus, Stanley.
Quest for the Best. Viking Pr.
Marcus, Steven.
xMarcus, Steven.
ed. World of Modern Fiction. S&S.
xMarcus, Stevens.
The Other Victorians: A Study of Sexuality & Pornography in Mid-Nineteenth Century England. NAL.
Marcus, Stevens. *see* Marcus, Steven.
Marcus, Y. *see* Marcus, Yitzhak.
Marcus, Yitzhak.
xMarcus, Y.
Introduction to Liquid State Chemistry. Wiley.
Marcus, D. *see* Marcuse, Dietrich.
Marcuse, Dietrich, 1929-
xMarcuse, D.
Integrated Optics. Wiley.
Principles of Quantum Electronics. Acad Pr.
xMarcuse, Dietrich.
ed. Integrated Optics. Inst Electrical.
Theory of Dielectric Optical Waveguides. Acad Pr.
Marcuse, Herbert, 1898-
xMarcuse, Herbert.

Counterrevolution & Revolt. Beacon Pr.
Negations: Essays in Critical Theory. Beacon Pr.
Soviet Marxism: A Critical Analysis. Columbia U Pr.
Studies in Critical Philosophy. Beacon Pr.
Marcuse, Katherine.
xMarcuse, Katherine.
The Devil's Workshop. Abingdon.
Marcuse, Ludwig, 1894-
xMarcuse, Ludwig.
Soldier of the Church: The Life of Ignatius Loyola. AMS Pr.
Marcuse, Sibyl.
xMarcuse, Sibyl.
Musical Instruments: A Comprehensive Dictionary. Norton.
A Survey of Musical Instruments. Har-Row.
Marcy, Carl. *see* Marcy, Carl Milton.
Marcy, Carl Milton, 1913-
xMarcy, Carl.
Presidential Commissions. Da Capo.
Marcy, Randolph B. *see* Marcy, Randolph Barnes.
Marcy, Randolph Barnes, 1812-1887
xMarcy, Randolph B.
Prairie Traveler. Corner Hse.
Marczali, Henrik.
xMarczali, Henry.
Hungary in the Eighteenth Century. Arno.
Marczali, Henry. *see* Marczali, Henrik.
Marczewski, Jan. *see* Marczewski, Jean.
Marczewski, Jean, 1908-
xMarczewski, Jan.
Inflation & Unemployment in France: A Quantitative Analysis. Praeger.
Marden, Philip S. *see* Marden, Philip Sanford.
Marden, Philip Sanford, 1874-1963
xMarden, Philip S.
Detours (Passable but Unsafe). Arno.
Marder, Arthur. *see* Marder, Arthur Jacob.
Marder, Arthur J. *see* Marder, Arthur Jacob.
Marder, Arthur Jacob.
xMarder, Arthur.
Operation Menace: The Dakar Expedition & the Dudley North Affair. Oxford U Pr.
xMarder, Arthur J.
From the Dardanelles to Oran: Studies of the Royal Navy in War & Peace 1915-1940. Oxford U Pr.
Marder, Daniel.
xMarder, Daniel.
Hugh Henry Brackenridge. Coll & U Pr.
Marder, Herbert.
xMarder, Herbert.
Feminism & Art: A Study of Virginia Woolf. U of Chicago Pr.
Marder, L. *see* Marder, Leslie.
Marder, Leslie.
xMarder, L.
Vector Analysis. Allen Unwin.
Mardin, Yusuf.
xMardin, Yusuf.
Colloquial Turkish. Routledge & Kegan.
Mardock, Robert W. *see* Mardock, Robert Winston.
Mardock, Robert Winston.
xMardock, Robert W.
Reformers & the American Indian. U of Mo Pr.
Mare, Eric De. *see* De Mare, Eric.
Mare, George De. *see* De Mare, George.
Mare, Walter De La. *see* De La Mare, Walter.
Marec, J. P. *see* Marec, Jean Pierre.
Marec, Jean Pierre.
xMarec, J. P.
Optimal Space Trajectories. Elsevier.
Marechera, Dambudzo.
xMarechera, Dambudzo.

The House of Hunger: A Novella & Short
    Stories. Pantheon.
Marei, Sayed.
    xMarei, Sayed A.
    The World Food Crisis. Longman.
Marei, Sayed A. *see* Marei.
Marein, Shirley.
    xMarein, Shirley.
    Stitchery, Needlepoint, Applique & Patchwork:
        A Complete Guide. Penguin.
Marek, George R. *see* Marek, George Richard.
Marek, George Richard.
    xMarek, George R.
    Chopin. Har-Row.
    ed. World Treasury of Grand Opera: Its
        Triumphs, Trials & Great Personalities. Arno.
Marer, Paul.
    xMarer, Paul.
    ed. East European Integration & East-West
        Trade. Ind U Pr.
    Soviet & East European Foreign Trade,
        1946-1969: Statistical Compendium & Guide.
        Ind U Pr.
Mares, Colin.
    xMares, Colin.
    Rapid & Efficient Reading. Emerson.
Maresca, Thomas E.
    xMaresca, Thomas E.
    Pope's Horatian Poems. Ohio St U Pr.
    Three English Epics: Studies of Troilus &
        Criseyde, the Faerie Queene, & Paradise
        Lost. U of Nebr Pr.
Marett, R. R. *see* Marett, Robert Ranulph.
Marett, Robert R. *see* Marett, Robert Ranulph.
Marett, Robert Ranulph, 1866-1943
    xMarett, R. R.
    Psychology & Folklore. Humanities.
    xMarett, Robert R.
    Psychology & Folk-Lore. Gale.
    The Threshold of Religion. AMS Pr.
Marfunin, A. S. *see* Marfunin, Arnol'd Sergeevich.
Marfunin, Arnol'd Sergeevich.
    xMarfunin, A. S.
    Physics of Minerals & Inorganic Materials: An
        Introduction. Springer-Verlag.
    Spectroscopy, Luminescence & Radiation
        Centers in Minerals. Springer-Verlag.
Margenau, H. *see* Margenau, Henry.
Margenau, Henry, 1901-
    xMargenau, H.
    ed. Integrative Principles of Modern Thought.
        Gordon.
    Theory of Intermolecular Forces. Pergamon.
    xMargenau, Henry.
    Ethics & Science. Krieger.
    The Nature of Physical Reality: A Philosophy
        of Modern Physics. Ox Bow.
Marger, Mary A. *see* Marger, Mary Ann.
Marger, Mary Ann.
    xMarger, Mary A.
    Winner at the Dub-Dub Club. Elsevier-Nelson.
Margerison, D.
    xMargerison, D.
    An Introduction to Polymer Chemistry.
        Pergamon.
Margetson, George R. *see* Margetson, George Reginald.
Margetson, George Reginald.
    xMargetson, George R.
    Songs of Life. Arno.
Margiotta, Franklin D.
    xMargiotta, Franklin D.
    ed. The Changing World of the American
        Military. Westview.
Margolese, Richard G, 1935-
    xMargolese, Richard G.
    Doctor's Eat-Hearty Guide for Good Health &
        Long Life. P-H.
Margolies, Edward.
    xMargolies, Edward.

ed. Native Sons Reader. Lippincott.
Margolies, Morris B.
    xMargolies, Morris B.
    Torah - Vision: Sermonic Essays for Our Time.
        Feldheim.
Margolin, Malcolm.
    xMargolin, Malcolm.
    The Earth Manual. HM.
Margolin, Victor, 1941-
    xMargolin, Victor.
    The Golden Age of the American Poster: A
        Concise Edition of the American Poster
        Renaissance. Ballantine.
Margoliouth, H. M. *see* Margoliouth, Herschel Maurice.
Margoliouth, Herschel Maurice, 1887-
    xMargoliouth, H. M.
    Wordsworth & Coleridge 1795-1834. Shoe
        String.
Margolis. *see* Margolis, Simeon.
Margolis, Adele P.
    xMargolis, Adele P.
    The Complete Book of Tailoring. Doubleday.
    Design Your Own Dress Patterns: A Primer in
        Pattern Making for Women Who Like to
        Sew. Doubleday.
Margolis, Art.
    xMargolis, Art.
    The Master Handbook of Electrical Wiring.
        TAB Bks.
    TV Schematics: How to Read Between the
        Lines. TAB Bks.
    TV Trouble Diagnosis Made Easy. TAB Bks.
Margolis, Bruce L.
    xMargolis, Bruce L.
    The Human Side of Accident Prevention:
        Psychological Concepts & Principles Which
        Bear on Industrial Safety. C C Thomas.
Margolis, Diane R. *see* Margolis, Diane Rothbard.
Margolis, Diane Rothbard.
    xMargolis, Diane R.
    The Managers: Corporate Life in America.
        Morrow.
Margolis, John D.
    xMargolis, John D.
    Campus in the Modern World: Twenty-Five
        Essays. Macmillan.
    T. S. Eliot's Intellectual Development,
        1922-1939. U of Chicago Pr.
Margolis, Joseph. *see* Margolis, Joseph Zalman.
Margolis, Joseph Zalman, 1924-
    xMargolis, Joseph.
    Art & Philosophy. Humanities.
Margolis, Max. *see* Margolis, Max Leopold.
Margolis, Max Leopold.
    xMargolis, Max.
    History of the Jewish People. Atheneum.
Margolis, Michael.
    xMargolis, Michael.
    Viable Democracy. Penguin.
    Viable Democracy. St Martin.
Margolis, Neal.
    xMargolis, Neal.
    Accounting Essentials. Wiley.
Margolis, Otto S. *see* Margolis, Otto Schwarz.

Margolis, Otto Schwarz.
    xMargolis, Otto S.
    Grief & the Meaning of the Funeral. Mss Info.

Margolis, R. U. *see* Margolis, Richard U.

Margolis, Richard J.
    xMargolis, Richard J.
    Big Bear, Spare That Tree. Greenwillow.
    Homer the Hunter. Macmillan.

Margolis, Richard U.

    xMargolis, R. U.

ed. Complex Carbohydrates of Nervous Tissue.
    Plenum Pub.
Margolis, Simeon.
    xMargolis.
    The Practice of Medicine: A Self Assessment
        Guide. ACC.
Margolis, Susan, 1941-
    xMargolis, Susan.
    Fame. SF Bk Co.
    Fame. Stein & Day.
Margolius, Sidney, 1911-
    xMargolius, Sidney.
    Innocent Consumer Vs. the Exploiters. Trident.
Margulies, Harold.
    xMargulies, Harold.
    Foreign Medical Graduates in the United
        States. Harvard U Pr.
Margulies, Herbert F.
    xMargulies, Herbert F.
    The Decline of the Progressive Movement in
        Wisconsin 1890-1920. State Hist Soc Wis.
Margulies, N. *see* Margulies, Newton.
Margulies, Newton.
    xMargulies, N.
    Organizational Development: Values Process &
        Technology. McGraw.
    xMargulies, Newton.
    Conceptual Foundations of Organizational
        Development. McGraw.
Margulis, Alexander R.
    xMargulis, Alexander R.
    ed. Alimentary Tract Roentgenology. Mosby.
Marholin, David.
    xMarholin, David.
    ed. Child Behavior Therapy. Halsted Pr.
Mari, Iela.
    xMari, Iela.
    jt. auth. The Apple & the Moth. Pantheon.
    jt. auth. Chicken & the Egg. Pantheon.
Maria, Gary De. *see* De Maria, Gary.
Mariakulandai, A.
    xMariakulandai, A.
    Chemistry of Fertilizers & Manures: A
        Textbook for Students of Agriculture. Asia.
Mariani, Paul L.
    xMariani, Paul L.
    Commentary on the Complete Poems of
        Gerard Manley Hopkins. Cornell U Pr.
Marichal, Juan.
    xMarichal, Juan.
    Pitcher's Story. Doubleday.
Maril, Nadja.
    xMaril, Nadja.
    Me, Molly Midnight, the Artist's Cat. Stemmer
        Hse.
Marill, Alvin H.
    xMarill, Alvin H.
    The Films of Anthony Quinn. Citadel Pr.
    The Films of Sidney Poitier. Citadel Pr.
Marin, John, 1870-1953
    xMarin, John.
    Letters of John Marin. Greenwood.
Marin, Peter.
    xMarin, Peter.
    ed. The Limits of Schooling. P-H.
    Understanding Drug Use: An Adult's Guide to
        Drugs & the Young. Har-Row.
Marinacci, Barbara.
    xMarinacci, Barbara.
    California's Spanish Place-Names: What They
        Mean & How They Got There. Presidio Pr.
Marinaccio, Anthony.
    xMarinaccio, Anthony.
    Human Relations & Cooperative Planning in
        Education & Management. Kendall-Hunt.
    xMarinaccio, M. Maxine.
    jt. auth. Human Relations & Cooperative
        Planning in Education & Management.
        Kendall-Hunt.
Marinaccio, M. Maxine. *see* Marinaccio, Anthony.

Marinaro, Vincent.
xMarinaro, Vincent C.
In the Ring of the Rise. Crown.
Modern Dry-Fly Code. Crown.
Marinaro, Vincent C. see Marinaro, Vincent.
Marine Biological Laboratory & Woods Hole
Oceanographic Institution, Woods Hole,
Massachusetts. see Woods Hole, Mass. Oceanographic
Institution.
Marine Board. see National Academy of Engineering.
Marine Board.
Marine Board, Assembly of Engineering, National
Research Council. see National Research Council.
Marine, Edith L. see Marine, Edith Lucile.
Marine, Edith Lucile, 1893-
xMarine, Edith L.
The Effect of Familiarity with the Examiner
Upon Stanford-Binet Test Performance. AMS
Pr.
Marine Science Instrumentation. see Marine Sciences
Instrumentation Symposium, 5th, Cocoa Beach, Fla.,
1973.
**Marine Sciences Instrumentation Symposium, 5th,
Cocoa Beach, Fla., 1973.**
xMarine Science Instrumentation.
Proceedings. Instru Soc.
Marinelli, Robert P.
xMarinelli, Robert P.
ed. The Psychological & Social Impact of
Physical Disability. Springer Pub.
Mariners Museum Library - Newport News - Virginia.
see Mariner's Museum, Newport News, Va. Library.
Marinetti, Guido. see Marinetti, Guido Vincent.
Marinetti, Guido Vincent, 1918-
xMarinetti, Guido.
ed. Lipid Chromatographic Analysis. Dekker.
Mariner's Museum, Newport News, Va. Library.
xMariners Museum Library - Newport News -
Virginia.
Catalog of Marine Photographs. G K Hall.
Catalog of Marine Prints & Paintings. G K
Hall.
Dictionary Catalog of the Library of the
Mariners Museum. G K Hall.
Maring, Joel M.
xMaring, Joel M.
Historical & Cultural Dictionary of Burma.
Scarecrow.
Marino, Barbara. see Marino, Barbara Pavis.
Marino, Barbara Pavis.
xMarino, Barbara.
Eric Needs Stitches. A-W.
Marino, Dorothy. see Marino, Dorothy (Bronson).
Marino, Dorothy (Bronson), 1912-
xMarino, Dorothy.
Where Are the Mothers?. Lippincott.
Marino, Francis A.
xMarino, Francis A.
Principles of Pharmaceutical Accounting. Lea
& Febiger.
Marino, John, 1948-
xMarino, John.
How to Make Big Money in Real Estate.
Master Key.
Marino, T. J.
xMarino, T. J.
Freelance Photographer's Handbook. Bobbs.
Mario, Thomas.
xMario, Thomas.
Playboy's New Host & Bar Book. Playboy.
Quantity Cooking. AVI.
Marion, Bruce W.
xMarion, Bruce W.
The Food Retailing Industry: Market Structure,
Profits, & Prices. Praeger.
Marion, Frances, 1890-
xMarion, Frances.

Off with Their Heads: A Serio-Comic Tale of
Hollywood. Macmillan.
Valley People. Arno.
Marion, Frieda.
xMarion, Frieda.
China Half-Figures Called Pincushion Dolls. J
Palmer.
The Collector's Encyclopedia of Half Dolls.
Collector Bks.
The Collector's Encyclopedia of Half-Dolls.
Crown.
Marion, Jerry. see Marion, Jerry B.
Marion, Jerry B.
xMarion, Jerry.
Classical Electromagnetic Radiation. Acad Pr.
xMarion, Jerry B.
Classical Electromagnetic Radiation. Acad Pr.
Energy in Perspective. Acad Pr.
General Physics with Bioscience Essays. Wiley.
Mathematical Preparation for General Physics.
HR&W.
Physics & the Physical Universe. Wiley.
Mariscal, R. N. see Mariscal, Richard N.
Mariscal, Richard N., 1935-
xMariscal, R. N.
Experimental Marine Biology. Acad Pr.
Maritain, Jacques, 1882-
xMaritain, Jacques.
Approaches to God. Greenwood.
Art & Scholasticism: With Other Essays. Arno.
A Christian Looks at the Jewish Question.
Arno.
Christianity & Democracy. Arno.
Creative Intuition in Art & Poetry. NAL.
Education at the Crossroads. Yale U Pr.
Existence & the Existent. Greenwood.
On the Church of Christ: The Person of the
Church & Her Personnel. U of Notre Dame
Pr.
On the Philosophy of History. Kelley.
A Preface to Metaphysics: Seven Lectures on
Being. Arno.
Ransoming the Time. Gordian.
Reflections on America. Gordian.
Responsibility of the Artist. Gordian.
True Humanism. Arno.
True Humanism. Greenwood.
Maritain, Raissa.
xMaritain, Raissa.
Raissa's Journal. Magi Bks.
Maritime Transportation Research Board. see National
Research Council. Maritime Transportation Research
Board.
Marius, Richard.
xMarius, Richard.
Bound for the Promised Land. Knopf.
Bound for the Promised Land. NAL.
Coming of Rain. NAL.
Marjoram, D. T. see Marjoram, D. T. E.
Marjoram, D. T. E.
xMarjoram, D. T.
Exercises in Modern Mathematics. Pergamon.
Further Exercises in Modern Mathematics.
Pergamon.
Modern Mathematics in Secondary Schools.
Pergamon.
Mark Age, 1922.
xMark-Age.

Angels & Man. Mark-Age.
Evolution of Man: Two Hundred & Six Million
Years on Earth. Mark-Age.
How to Do All Things: Your Use of Divine
Power. Mark-Age.
Mark Age Period & Program: Entrance to
Golden Age of Aquarius. Mark-Age.
One Thousand Keys to the Truth: Spiritual
Guidelines for Latter Days & Second
Coming. Mark-Age.
Visitors from Other Planets. Mark-Age.
Mark, Alexandra.
xMark, Alexandra.
Astrology for the Aquarian Age. S&S.
Mark, Bernard, 1932-
xMark, Bernard.
Business Management's Guide & Checklist for
the Successful Company Move. Busn Mgmt
Sci.
Mark, Charles.
xMark, Charles.
ed. Sociology of America: A Guide to
Information Sources. Gale.
Mark, Irving.
xMark, Irving.
The Faith of Our Fathers: An Anthology
Expressing the Aspirations of the American
Common Man, 1790-1860. Octagon.
Mark, Jan.
xMark, Jan.
Divide & Rule. T Y Crowell.
Thunder & Lightnings. T Y Crowell.
Under the Autumn Garden. T Y Crowell.
Mark, Melvin.
xMark, Melvin.
Concepts of Thermodynamics. West Pub.
Mark, Michael L.
xMark, Michael L.
Contemporary Music Education. Schirmer Bks.
Mark, Norman.
xMark, Norman.
Norman Mark's Chicago: Walking, Bicycling &
Driving Tours of the City. Chicago Review.
Mark, Richard.
xMark, Richard F.
Memory & Nerve Cell Connections: Criticisms
& Contributions from Developmental
Neurophysiology. Oxford U Pr.
Mark, Richard F. see Mark, Richard.
Mark, Theonie.
xMark, Theonie.
Greek Islands Cooking. David & Charles.
Mark-Age. see Mark Age, 1922.
Markakis, John.
xMarkakis, John.
Ethiopia: Anatomy of a Traditional Polity.
Oxford U Pr.
Markale, J. see Markale, Jean.
Markale, Jean.
xMarkale, J.
Celtic Civilization. Gordon-Cremonesi.
Markel, Geraldine.
xMarkel, Geraldine.
Parents Are to Be Seen & Heard: Assertiveness
in Educational Planning for Handicapped
Children. Impact Pubs Cal.
Markel, J. E. see Markel, John D.
Markel, John D.
xMarkel, J. E.
Linear Prediction of Speech. Springer-Verlag.
Markel, Lester.
xMarkel, Lester.
Global Challenge to the United States: A Study
of the Problems, the Perils, & the Proposed
Solutions Involved in Washington's Search
for a New Role. Fairleigh Dickinson.
Public Opinion & Foreign Policy. Arno.
Markell, Jan, 1944-
xMarkell, Jan.

Gone the Golden Dream. Bethany Fell.
Markert, Christopher.
xMarkert, Christopher.
This Person Is You. Branden.
Marketing Educator'S Conference, Hartford, 1977.
xEducators' Conference of the American
Marketing Association, Hartford, Aug. 7-10,
1977.
Contemporary Marketing Thought - 1977:
Educators' Proceedings. Am Mktg.
Markewich, Reese, 1936-
xMarkewich, Reese.
Definitive Bibliography of Harmonically
Sophisticated Tonal Music. Markewich.
Markey, Frances V. *see* Markey, Frances Virginia.
Markey, Frances Virginia, 1911-
xMarkey, Frances V.
Imaginative Behavior of Preschool Children.
Arno.
Markey, John F. *see* Markey, John Fordyce.
Markey, John Fordyce, 1898-
xMarkey, John F.
The Symbolic Process & It's Integration in
Children: A Study in Social Psychology. U of
Chicago Pr.
Markfield, Wallace.
xMarkfield, Wallace.
Multiple Orgasms. Bruccoli.
Markgraf, Carl.
xMarkgraf, Carl.
Punctuation. Wiley.
Markham, Clements. *see* Markham, Clements Robert.
Markham, Clements R. *see* Markham, Clements Robert.
Markham, Clements Robert, Sir, 1830-1916
xMarkham, Clements.
Incas of Peru. AMS Pr.
xMarkham, Clements R.
tr. & ed. Expeditions into the Valley of the
Amazons, 1539-1540, 1639. B Franklin.
History of Peru. Gordon Pr.
History of Peru. Greenwood.
Markham, Edwin.
xMarkham, Edwin.
Children in Bondage. Arno.
Markham, Gervase, 1568?-1637
xMarkham, Gervase.
The Art of Archerie. Shumway.
Markham, Jesse W. *see* Markham, Jesse William.
Markham, Jesse William, 1916-
xMarkham, Jesse W.
Conglomerate Enterprise & Public Policy.
Harvard Busn.
Fertilizer Industry: Study of an Imperfect
Market. Greenwood.
Horizontal Divestiture & the Petroleum
Industry. Ballinger Pub.
Markham, M. Roland.
xMarkham, M. Roland.
Alcar, the Captive Creole. Arno.
Markin, R. J. *see* Markin, Rom J.
Markin, Rom J.
xMarkin, R. J.
Retailing Management. Macmillan.
xMarkin, Rom J.
Marketing. Wiley.
Markish, Esther, 1912-
xMarkish, Esther.
The Long Return. Ballantine.
Markland, Robert E.
xMarkland, Robert E.
Topics in Management Science. Wiley.
Markle, Allan.
xMarkle, Allan.
ed. Author's Guide to Journals in Psychology,
Psychiatry & Social Work. Haworth Pr.
Markle, Gerald E.
xMarkle, Gerald E.

ed. Politics, Science, & Cancer: The Laetrile
Phenomenon. Westview.
Markle, Joyce B.
xMarkle, Joyce B.
Fighters & Lovers: Theme in the Novels of
John Updike. NYU Pr.
Markley, N. G. *see* Markley, Nelson Groh.
Markley, Nelson Groh.
xMarkley, N. G.
ed. The Structure of Attractors in Dynamical
Systems: Proceedings, North Dakota, June
20-24, 1977. Springer-Verlag.
Markman, Sidney D. *see* Markman, Sidney David.
Markman, Sidney David, 1911-
xMarkman, Sidney D.
Horse in Greek Art. Biblo.
Markoe, Karen.
xMarkoe, Karen.
The Super Duper American History Fun Book.
Watts.
Markoff, Annabelle M. *see* Markoff, Annabelle Most.
Markoff, Annabelle Most.
xMarkoff, Annabelle M.
Teaching Low Achieving Children Reading,
Spelling & Handwriting: Developing
Perceptual Skills with the Graphic Symbols
of the Language. C C Thomas.
Markov, Pavel A. *see* Markov, Pavel Aleksandrovich.
Markov, Pavel Aleksandrovich, 1897-
xMarkov, Pavel A.
The Soviet Theatre. Greenwood.
Markov, Vladimir.
xMarkov, Vladimir.
The Longer Poems of Velimir Khlebnikov.
Greenwood.
Markov, Walter. *see* Markov, Walter M.
Markov, Walter M.
xMarkov, Walter.
Battles of World History. Hippocrene Bks.
Markova, A. K. *see* Markova, Aelita Kapitonovna
Markova, Aelita Kapitonovna.
xMarkova, A. K.
The Teaching & Mastery of Language. M E
Sharpe.
Markow. *see* Markow, Jack.
Markow, Jack, 1905-
xMarkow.
Drawing & Selling Cartoons. G&D.
Drawing Funny Pictures. G&D.
Markowitz, Elysa.
xMarkowitz, Elysa.
Baby Dance: A Comprehensive Guide to
Prenatal & Postpartum Exercise. P-H.
Markowitz, Harry M. *see* Markowitz, Harry Max.
Markowitz, Harry Max, 1927-
xMarkowitz, Harry M.
Portfolio Selection: Efficient Diversification of
Investments. Yale U Pr.
Markowitz, Marvin D.
xMarkowitz, Marvin D.
Cross & Sword: The Political Role of Christian
Missions in the Belgian Congo, 1908-1960.
Hoover Inst Pr.
Markowitz, Milton.
xMarkowitz, Milton.
Rheumatic Fever. Saunders.
Markowski, Michael. *see* Markowski, Michael L.
Markowski, Michael L.
xMarkowski, Michael.
The Encyclopedia of Homebuilt Aircraft. TAB
Bks.
Marks, Alfred H.
xMarks, Alfred H.
Guide to Japanese Prose. G K Hall.
Marks, Barry A. *see* Marks, Barry Alan.
Marks, Barry Alan.
xMarks, Barry A.

E. E. Cummings. Coll & U Pr.
E. E. Cummings. Twayne.
Marks, Burton.
xMarks, Burton.
Give a Magic Show. Schol Bk Serv.
Give a Magic Show!. Lothrop.
Kites for Kids. Lothrop.
Marks, Charles, 1922-
xMarks, Charles.
Carcinoid Tumors: A Clinico-Pathologic Study.
G K Hall.
Portal Venous System. C C Thomas.
Marks, David.
xMarks, David.
The Psychology of the Psychic. Prometheus
Bks.
Marks, Emerson R.
xMarks, Emerson R.
Relativist & Absolutist: The Early Neoclassical
Debate in England. Greenwood.
Marks, F. Helena.
xMarks, F. Helena.
The Sonata, Its Form & Meaning As
Exemplified in the Piano Sonatas by Mozart:
A Descriptive Analysis with Musical
Examples. Hyperion Conn.
Marks, F. Raymond.
xMarks, F. Raymond.
The Lawyer, the Public & Professional
Responsibility. Am Bar Foun.
Marks, Frederick W.
xMarks, Frederick W.
Independence on Trial: Foreign Affairs & the
Making of the Constitution. La State U Pr.
Velvet on Iron: The Diplomacy of Theodore
Roosevelt. U of Nebr Pr.
Marks, Geoffrey.
xMarks, Geoffrey.
The Story of Medicine in America. Scribner.
Marks, Henry S.
xMarks, Henry S.
Who Was Who in Alabama. Strode.
Who Was Who in Florida. Strode.
Marks, J. *see* Marks, John.
Marks, J. M. *see* Marks, James M.
Marks, James. *see* Marks, James M.
Marks, James M., 1921-
xMarks, J. M.
Border Kidnap. Elsevier-Nelson.
Hijacked. Oxford U Pr.
xMarks, James.
Hijacked!. Elsevier-Nelson.
Marks, Jane.
xMarks, Jane.
Help: A Guide to Counseling & Therapy
Without a Hassle. Dell.
Marks, Jeanette. *see* Marks, Jeannette Augustus.
Marks, Jeannette. *see* Marks, Jeannette Augustus.
Marks, Jeannette Augustus, 1875-1964
xMarks, Jeanette.
Genius & Disaster: Studies in Drugs & Genius.
Kennikat.
xMarks, Jeannette.
The Family of the Barrett: A Colonial
Romance. Greenwood.
Marks, John, 1924-
xMarks, J.
A Guide to the Vitamins: Their Role in Health
& Disease. Univ Park.
Marks, John. *see* Marks, John D.
Marks, John D.
xMarks, John.
The Search for the "Manchurian Candidate":
The CIA & Mind Control. McGraw.
The Search for the Manchurian Candidate: The
CIA & Mind Control. Times Bks.
Marks, Joseph E.
xMarks, Joseph E.

ed. The Mathers on Dancing. Dance Horiz.
Marks, Mickey Klar.
  xMarks, Micky K.
    First You Like Me. Schol Bk Serv.
Marks, Micky K. *see* Marks, Mickey Klar.
Marks, Nancy C.
  xMarks, Nancy C.
    Cerebral Palsied & Learning Disabled Children:
    A Handbook Guide to Treatment,
    Rehabilitation & Education. C C Thomas.
Marks, Philip A. *see* Marks, Philip Andre.
Marks, Philip Andre.
  xMarks, Philip A.
    The Actuarial Use of the MMPI with
    Adolescents & Adults. Oxford U Pr.
Marks, Rick.
  xMarks, Rick.
    More Than a Run. J P Tarcher.
    More Than a Run. St Martin.
Marks, Robert W.
  xMarks, Robert W.
    The Dymaxion World of Buckminster Fuller.
    Doubleday.
Marks, Tracy, 1950-
  xMarks, Tracy.
    The Art of Chart Synthesis. Sag Rising.
    ed. Directory of New England Astrologers:
    How to Choose an Astrologer. Sag Rising.
    How to Handle Your T-Square. Sag Rising.
Markson, Elaine.
  xMarkson, Elaine.
    Home Again, Home Again. Morrow.
Markstein, George.
  xMarkstein, George.
    Chance Awakening. Ballantine.
    The Goering Testament. Ballantine.
    Tara Kane. Dell.
    Tara Kane. Stein & Day.
Markun, Maloney P. *see* Markun, Patricia Maloney.
Markun, Patricia Maloney.
  xMarkun, Maloney P.
    The Panama Canal. Watts.
Markus, John, 1911-
  xMarkus, John.
    Modern Electronic Circuits Reference Manual.
    McGraw.
    Sourcebook of Electronic Circuits. McGraw.
Markus, L. *see* Markus, Lawrence.
Markus, Lawrence.
  xMarkus, L.
    Generic Hamiltonian Dynamical Systems Are
    Neither Integrable nor Ergodic. Am Math.
  xMarkus, Lawrence.
    Lectures in Differentiable Dynamics. Am
    Math.
Markus, Rixi.
  xMarkus, Rixi.
    Bridge Around the World. Merrimack Bk Serv.
    Improve Your Bridge. Merrimack Bk Serv.
Markushevich, A. I. *see* Markushevich, Aleksei
  Ivanovich.
Markushevich, Aleksei Ivanovich.
  xMarkushevich, A. I.
    Theory of Functions of a Complex Variable.
    Chelsea Pub.
Markuson, Barbara. *see* Markuson, Barbara Evans.
Markuson, Barbara Evans.
  xMarkuson, Barbara.
    jt. ed. & ed. Networks for Networkers: Critical
    Issues in Cooperative Library Development.
    Neal-Schuman.
Marland, Sidney P. *see* Marland, Sidney Percy.
Marland, Sidney Percy.
  xMarland, Sidney P.
    Career Education: A Proposal for Reform.
    McGraw.
Marlborough, John C. *see* Marlborough, John Churchill,
  1st Duke Of.
Marlborough, John Churchill, 1st Duke Of, 1650-1722
  xMarlborough, John C.

Letters & Dispatches of John Churchill, First
  Duke of Marlborough from 1702-1712.
  Greenwood.
Marlborough, John O. Churchill. *see* Marlborough, John
  C.
Marlborough, Sarah. *see* Marlborough, Sarah (Jennings)
  Churchill.
Marlborough, Sarah (Jennings) Churchill, Duchess Of,
1660-1744
  xMarlborough, Sarah.
    Letters of Sarah, Duchess of Marlborough.
    AMS Pr.
  xMarlborough, Sarah J.
    Letters of Sarah, Duchess of Marlborough.
    Kraus Repr.
Marlborough, Sarah J. *see* Marlborough, Sarah (Jennings)
  Churchill.
Marlow, A. W. *see* Marlow, Andrew W.
Marlow, Andrew W.
  xMarlow, A. W.
    Classic Furniture Projects. Stein & Day.
Marlow, Dorothy R.
  xMarlow, Dorothy R.
    Textbook of Pediatric Nursing. Saunders.
Marlow, H. Carleton.
  xMarlow, H. Carleton.
    The American Search for Woman. ABC-Clio.
Marlow, Joan.
  xMarlow, Joan.
    ed. The Great Women. A & W Pubs.
Marlow, W. H., 1924-
  xMarlow, W. H.
    Mathematics for Operations Research. Wiley.
Marlowe. *see* Marlowe, Christopher.
Marlowe, Ann.
  xMarlowe, Ann.
    Thunder in the Kerk. Dodd.
    The Winnowing Winds. Dodd.
    The Winnowing Winds. NAL.
Marlowe, Christopher.
  xMarlowe.
    Doctor Faustus. Norton.
  xMarlowe, Christopher.
    The Complete Works of Christopher Marlowe.
    Cambridge U Pr.
    Doctor Faustus. AMS Pr.
    Doctor Faustus. Aurora Pubs.
    Doctor Faustus. Methuen Inc.
    Doctor Faustus. NAL.
    Doctor Faustus. PB.
    Doctor Faustus. AHM Pub.
    Works of Christopher Marlowe. AMS Pr.
    The Works of Christopher Marlowe. R West.
Marlowe, Derek.
  xMarlowe, Derek.
    Nightshade. NAL.
    Nightshade. Viking Pr.
    The Rich Boy from Chicago. St Martin.
Marlowe, Don.
  xMarlowe, Don.
    Hollywood That Was. Branch-Smith.
Marlowe, Olwen C.
  xMarlowe, Olwen C.
    Outdoor Design: A Handbook for the Architect
    & Planner. Renouf.
    Outdoor Design: A Handbook for the Architect
    & Planner. Watson-Guptill.
Marlowe, Stephen, 1928-
  xMarlowe, Stephen.
    The Valkyrie Encounter. BJ Pub Group.
Marlowe, Valerious.
  xMarlowe, Valerious.
    How to Write a Book Which the Millions Will
    Want to Read. Am Classical Coll Pr.
Marmarelis, P. Z. *see* Marmarelis, Panos Z.
Marmarelis, Panos Z.
  xMarmarelis, P. Z.
    Analysis of Physiological Systems: The
    White-Noise Approach. Plenum Pub.
  xMarmarelis, V. Z.

    jt. auth. Analysis of Physiological Systems: The
    White-Noise Approach. Plenum Pub.
Marmarelis, V. Z. *see* Marmarelis, Panos Z.
Marmion, Daniel M., 1935-
  xMarmion, Daniel M.
    Handbook of U. S. Colorants for Foods, Drugs
    & Cosmetics. Wiley.
Marmion, Harry A.
  xMarmion, Harry A.
    Case Against a Volunteer Army. Times Bks.
Marmo, V. *see* Marmo, Vladimir.
Marmo, Vladimir.
  xMarmo, V.
    Granite Petrology & the Granite Problem.
    Elsevier.
Marmor, J. *see* Marmor, Judd.
Marmor, Judd.
  xMarmor, J.
    ed. The Interface Between the Psychodynamic
    & Behavioral Therapies. Plenum Pub.
  xMarmor, Judd.
    Homosexual Behavior: A Modern Reappraisal.
    Basic.
Marmor, Leonard.
  xMarmor, Leonard.
    Arthritis Surgery. Lea & Febiger.
Marmor, Theodore R.
  xMarmor, Theodore R.
    The Politics of Medicare. Aldine Pub.
    ed. Poverty Policy: A Compendium of Cash
    Transfer Proposals. Aldine Pub.
Marmorstein, Arthur, 1882-1946
  xMarmorstein, Arthur.
    Studies in Jewish Theology: The Arthur
    Marmorstein Memorial Volume. Arno.
Marmullaku, Ramadan, 1939-
  xMarmullaku, Ramadan.
    Albania & the Albanians. Shoe String.
Marnell, William. *see* Marnell, William H.
Marnell, William H.
  xMarnell, William.
    Vacation Yesterdays of New England.
    Continuum.
  xMarnell, Willim H.
    Light from the West: The Irish Mission & the
    Emergence of Modern Europe. Seabury.
Marnell, Willism H. *see* Marnell, William H.
Marney, Carlyle, 1916-
  xMarney, Carlyle.
    Priests to Each Other. Judson.
Marney, John.
  xMarney, John.
    Liang Chien-Wen Ti. Twayne.
Maron, S. H. *see* Maron, Samuel Herbert.
Maron, Samuel Herbert.
  xMaron, S. H.
    Fundamentals of Physical Chemistry.
    Macmillan.
Marot, Helen, 1865-1940
  xMarot, Helen.
    American Labor Unions. Arno.
    Handbook of Labor Literature. Kelley.
Maroteaux, P.
  xMaroteaux, Pierre.
    Bone Diseases of Children. Lippincott.
Maroteaux, Pierre. *see* Maroteaux, P.
Maroun, F. B.
  xMaroun, F. B.
    Diastematomyelia. Green.
Marovic, D. *see* Marovic, Drazen.
Marovic, Drazen.
  xMarovic, D.
    An Opening Repertoire for Black. David &
    Charles.
  xMarovic, Drazen.
    An Opening Repertoire for Black. Arco.
Marowitz, Charles.
  xMarowitz, Charles.

The Act of Being: Towards a Theory of Acting.
Taplinger.
Marple, Elliot.
xMarple, Elliot.
National Bank of Commerce of Seattle,
1889-1969: Territorial to Worldwide Banking
in Eighty Years, Including the Story of the
Marine Bancorporation. Pacific Bks.
Marple, Raymond P. see Marple, Raymond Parker.
Marple, Raymond Parker, 1899-
xMarple, Raymond P.
Toward a Basic Accounting Philosophy. Natl
Assn Accts.
Marquand, H. A. see Marquand, Hilary Adair.
Marquand, Hilary Adair, 1901-
xMarquand, H. A.
The Dynamics of Industrial Combination.
Arno.
Marquand, John P. see Marquand, John Phillips.
Marquand, John Phillips, 1893-1960
xMarquand, John P.
Last Laugh, Mr. Moto. Popular Lib.
The Late George Apley: A Novel in the Form
of a Memoir. Little.
Thank You, Mr. Moto. Popular Lib.
Marquard, Philip, 1914-
xMarquard, Philip.
Formation of Lay Franciscans. Franciscan
Herald.
Marquart, Frank, 1898-
xMarquart, Frank.
An Auto Worker's Journal: The UAW from
Crusade to One-Party Union. Pa St U Pr.
Marques, Rene.
xMarques, Rene.
The Docile Puerto Rican: Essays. Temple U Pr.
Marquis, Don, 1878-1937
xMarquis, Don.
Archy & Mehitabel. Doubleday.
Archy & Mchitabel. Doubleday.
Cartei, & Other People Arna.
Chapters for the Orthodox. Arno.
Lives & Times of Archy & Mehitabel.
Doubleday.
Sun Dial Time. Arno.
Marquis, Thomas B. see Marquis, Thomas Bailey.
Marquis, Thomas Bailey.
xMarquis, Thomas B.
The Cheyennes of Montana. Ref Pubns.
Custer on the Little Bighorn. Custer.
Marquit, Erwin, 1926-
xMarquit, Erwin.
The Socialist Countries: General Features of
Political, Economic, & Cultural Life. Marxist
Educ.
Marr, G. W. see Marr, Grigor Wilson.
Marr, Grigor Wilson.
xMarr, G. W.
General Engineering Science in SI Units.
Pergamon.
Marr, John S.
xMarr, John S.
A Breath of Air & a Breath of Smoke. M
Evans.
The Food You Eat. M Evans.
The Good Drug & the Bad Drug. M Evans.
Marra, William A.
xMarra, William A.
Happiness & Christian Hope: A
Phenomenological Analysis. Franciscan
Herald.
Marram, Gwen D., 1942-
xMarram, Gwen D.
The Group Approach in Nursing Practice.
Mosby.
Marrin, Albert.
xMarrin, Albert.

The Last Crusade: The Church of England in
the First World War. Duke.
Marriner, Ann, 1943-
xMarriner, Ann.
Current Perspectives in Nursing Management.
Mosby.
A Guide to Nursing Management. Mosby.
The Nursing Process: A Scientific Approach to
Nursing Care. Mosby.
Marriott. see Marriott, Alice Lee.
Marriott, Alice. see Marriott, Alice Lee.
Marriott, Alice L. see Marriott, Alice Lee.
Marriott, Alice Lee, 1910-
xMarriott.
Plains Indian Mythology. NAL.
xMarriott, Alice.
Plains Indian Mythology. T Y Crowell.
xMarriott, Alice L.
Greener Fields: Experiences Among the
American Indians. Greenwood.
Marriott, James W. see Marriott, James William.
Marriott, James William, 1884-1953
xMarriott, James W.
ed. Modern Essays & Sketches. Arno.
Marriott, John. see Marriott, John Arthur Ransome.
Marriott, John A. see Marriott, John Arthur Ransome.
Marriott, John Arthur Ransome, Sir, 1859-1945
xMarriott, John.
English History in English Fiction. Kennikat.
xMarriott, John A.
English Political Institutions: An Introductory
Study. Greenwood.
Marris, Andrew W.
xMarris, Andrew W.
Advanced Dynamics. Krieger.
Marrocco, W. Thomas. see Marrocco, William Thomas.
Marrocco, William Thomas.
xMarrocco, W. Thomas.
Music in America: An Anthology from the
Landing of the Pilgrims to the Close of the
Civil War 1620-1865. Norton.
Marrow, Alfred J. see Marrow, Alfred Jay.
Marrow, Alfred Jay, 1905-
xMarrow, Alfred J.
Practical Theorist: The Life & Work of Kurt
Lewin. Tchrs Coll.
Marrow, Stanley B.
xMarrow, Stanley B.
Christ in Jesus. Paulist Pr.
Marrs, Elijah P., 1840-
xMarrs, Elijah P.
Life & History of the Rev. Elijah P. Marrs.
Arno.
Marrus, Michael R. see Marrus, Michael Robert.
Marrus, Michael Robert.
xMarrus, Michael R.
Politics of Assimilation: A Study of the
French-Jewish Community at the Time of the
Dreyfus Affair. Oxford U Pr.
Marryat. see Marryat, Frederick.
Marryat, Frederick, 1792-1848
xMarryat.
Masterman Ready. Dutton.
xMarryat, Frederick.
Masterman Ready. Garland Pub.
Mars, Charlotte.
xMars, Charlotte.
A Guide to Raising Your Dog Successfully.
Rosen Pr.
Mars, James, b. 1790
xMars, James.
Life of James Mars: A Slave Born & Sold in
Connecticut. Arno.
Marsak, L. M. see Marsak, Leonard Mendes.
Marsak, Leonard Mendes, 1924-
xMarsak, L. M.
ed. The Nature of Historical Inquiry. Krieger.
Marschak, Jacob. see Marschak, Jakob.
Marschak, Jakob.
xMarschak, Jacob.

Economic Theory of Teams. Yale U Pr.
Marschak, Marianne.
xMarschak, Marianne.
Parent-Child Interaction & Youth Rebellion.
Halsted Pr.
Marschak, Thomas. see Marschak, Thomas A.
Marschak, Thomas A.
xMarschak, Thomas.
General Equilibrium with Price-Making Firms.
Springer-Verlag.
Strategy for R & D: Studies in the
Microeconomics of Development.
Springer-Verlag.
Marsden, B. G.
xMarsden, B. G.
The Earth-Moon System. Plenum Pub.
Marsden, Barry M.
xMarsden, Barry M.
The Early Barrow Diggers. Noyes.
Marsden, George M., 1939-
xMarsden, George M.
Evangelical Mind & the New School
Presbyterian Experience: A Case Study of
Thought & Theology in Nineteenth-Century
America. Yale U Pr.
Marsden, H. B. see Marsden, Henry Basil.
Marsden, Henry Basil.
xMarsden, H. B.
ed. Tumours in Children. Springer-Verlag.
Marsden, J. see Marsden, Jerrold E.
Marsden, J. E. see Marsden, Jerrold E.
Marsden, Jerold E. see Marsden, Jerrold E.
Marsden, Jerrold. see Marsden, Jerrold E.
Marsden, Jerrold E.
xMarsden, J.
Calculus. A-W.
xMarsden, J. E.
The Hopf Bifurcation & Its Applications.
Springer-Verlag.
xMarsden, Jerold E.
Vector Calculus. W H Freeman.
xMarsden, Jerrold.
Calculus. Benjamin-Cummings.
xMarsden, Jerry.
Applications of Global Analysis in
Mathematical Physics. Publish or Perish.
Marsden, Jerry. see Marsden, Jerrold E.
Marsden, Neville.
xMarsden, Neville.
Diagnosis Before First Aid: A Manual for
Emergency Care Workers. Churchill.
Marsden, W. E. see Marsden, William Edward.
Marsden, William Edward.
xMarsden, W. E.
North West England. Cambridge U Pr.
Marse, Juan, 1933-
xMarse, Juan.
The Fallen. Little.
Marsella, Elena M. see Marsella, Elena Maria.
Marsella, Elena Maria.
xMarsella, Elena M.
Quest for Eden. Philos Lib.
Marsh. see Marsh, R. Warren.
Marsh, Alan.
xMarsh, Alan.
Protest & Political Consciousness. Sage.
Marsh, Angela.
xMarsh, Angela.
Pirate Treasure. Raintree Child.
Marsh, Dave.
xMarsh, Dave.
Born to Run: The Bruce Springsteen Story.
Doubleday.
Marsh, David C. see Marsh, David Charles.
Marsh, David Charles.
xMarsh, David C.
ed. Introducing Social Policy. Routledge &
Kegan.
Marsh, Edward E. see Marsh, Edward Everett.

Marsh, Edward Everett, 1900-
    xMarsh, Edward E.
        How to Be Healthy with Natural Foods. Arc
        Bks.
Marsh, Frank B. see Marsh, Frank Burr.
Marsh, Frank Burr, 1880-1940
    xMarsh, Frank B.
        The Founding of the Roman Empire.
        Greenwood.
Marsh, Frank L. see Marsh, Frank Lewis.
Marsh, Frank Lewis, 1899-
    xMarsh, Frank L.
        Life, Man & Time. Outdoor Pict.
Marsh, Fredda.
    xMarsh, Fredda.
        Putting It All Together in a Puppet Ministry.
        Gospel Pub.
Marsh, G. P. see Marsh, George Perkins.
Marsh, George E.
    xMarsh, George E.
        The Learning Disabled Adolescent: Program
        Alternatives in the Secondary School. Mosby.
Marsh, George P. see Marsh, George Perkins.
Marsh, George Perkins, 1801-1882
    xMarsh, G. P.
        Intro. by Earth As Modified by Human Action.
        Scholarly.
    xMarsh, George P.
        The Earth As Modified by Human Action.
        Arno.
        Earth As Modified by Human Action.
        Scholarly.
Marsh, Harold.
    xMarsh, Harold.
        Marital Property in Conflict of Laws. U of
        Wash Pr.
Marsh, Jeri.
    xMarsh, Jeri.
        Hurrah for Alexander!. Carolrhoda Bks.
Marsh, John F. see Marsh, John Fitchett.
Marsh, John Fitchett, 1818-1880
    xMarsh, John F.
        Papers Connected with the Affairs of Milton &
        His Family. Folcroft.
Marsh, Ken.
    xMarsh, Ken.
        Independent Video: A Complete Guide to the
        Physics, Operation & Application of the New
        Television for the Student, the Artist & for
        Community TV. S&S.
Marsh, Mary V. see Marsh, Mary Val.
Marsh, Mary Val.
    xMarsh, Mary V.
        Explore & Discover Music: Creative
        Approaches to Music Education in
        Elementary & Middle-Junior High Schools.
        Macmillan.
Marsh, Mathew E.
    xMarsh, Matthew E.
        California Mechanics' Lien Law Handbook.
        Parker & Son.
Marsh, Matthew E. see Marsh, Mathew E.
Marsh, Meredith.
    xMarsh, Meredith.
        Eating Cake. Ballantine.
        Eating Cake. Coward.
        I Had Wild Jack for a Lover. Coward.
        I Had Wild Jack for a Lover. Fawcett.
Marsh, Moreton.
    xMarsh, Moreton.
        Easy Expert in American Antiques: Knowing,
        Finding, Buying & Restoring Early American
        Furniture. Lippincott.
Marsh, Ngaio.
    xMarsh, Ngaio.

        Artists in Crime. Amereon Ltd.
        Artists in Crime. Putnam.
        Clutch of Constables. Amereon Ltd.
        Clutch of Constables. Berkley Pub.
        Colour Scheme. Amereon Ltd.
        Colour Scheme. Berkley Pub.
        Dead Water. Amereon Ltd.
        Death & the Dancing Footman. Amereon Ltd.
        Death & the Dancing Footman. Putnam.
        Death at the Bar. Amereon Ltd.
        Death at the Bar. Berkley Pub.
        Death at the Bar. Berkley Pub.
        Death in a White Tie. Amereon Ltd.
        Death in Ecstasy. Amereon Ltd.
        Death in Ecstasy. BJ Pub Group.
        Death of a Fool. Amereon Ltd.
        Death of a Fool. BJ Pub Group.
        Death of a Peer. Amereon Ltd.
        Death of a Peer. Putnam.
        Died in the Wool. Amereon Ltd.
        Died in the Wool. Berkley Pub.
        Enter a Murderer. Amereon Ltd.
        Enter a Murderer. Berkley Pub.
        Final Curtain. Amereon Ltd.
        Final Curtain. Berkley Pub.
        Final Curtain. BJ Pub Group.
        Grave Mistake. BJ Pub Group.
        Grave Mistake. G K Hall.
        Grave Mistake. Little.
        Hand in Glove. Amereon Ltd.
        Hand in Glove. BJ Pub Group.
        Last Ditch. Berkley Pub.
        Last Ditch. G K Hall.
        Last Ditch. Little.
        Night at the Vulcan. Amereon Ltd.
        Night at the Vulcan. BJ Pub Group.
        Overture to Death. Amereon Ltd.
        Overture to Death. BJ Pub Group.
        Spinsters in Jeopardy. Amereon Ltd.
        Spinsters in Jeopardy. Berkley Pub.
        When in Rome. Amereon Ltd.
        When in Rome. BJ Pub Group.
Marsh, Peter. see Marsh, Peter T.
Marsh, Peter T.
    xMarsh, Peter.
        ed. The Conscience of the Victorian State.
        Syracuse U Pr.
Marsh, Philip M. see Marsh, Philip Merrill.
Marsh, Philip Merrill, 1893-
    xMarsh, Philip M.
        Freneau's Published Prose: A Bibliography.
        Scarecrow.
Marsh, R. W.
    xMarsh, R. W.
        ed. Systemic Fungicides. Halsted Pr.
        ed. Systemic Fungicides. Longman.
Marsh, R. Warren.
    xMarsh.
        Principles of Refrigeration. Delmar.
Marsh, Reginald, 1898-1954
    xMarsh, Reginald.
        Anatomy for Artists. Dover.
        Anatomy for Artists. Gannon.
Marsh, Robert C. see Marsh, Robert Charles.
Marsh, Robert Charles.
    xMarsh, Robert C.
        Toscanini & the Art of Orchestral
        Performance. Greenwood.
Marsh, Roger.
    xMarsh, Roger.
        Imaginative Printmaking. Beekman Pubs.
        Monoprints for the Artist. Transatlantic.
Marsh, William M.
    xMarsh, William M.
        Environmental Analysis: For Land-Use & Site
        Planning. McGraw.
Marsh, Winifred P. see Marsh, Winifred Petchey.
Marsh, Winifred Petchey.
    xMarsh, Winifred P.

        People of the Willow: The Padlimiut Tribe of
        the Caribou Eskimo. Oxford U Pr.
Marshak, Richard. see Marshak, Richard H.
Marshak, Richard H.
    xMarshak, Richard.
        Radiology of the Colon. Saunders.
    xMarshak, Richard H.
        Radiology of the Small Intestine. Saunders.
Marshak, Sondra.
    xMarshak, Sondra.
        Star Trek: The New Voyages. Bantam.
Marshall. see Marshall, Eric.
Marshall, Alexandra.
    xMarshall, Alexandra.
        Gus in Bronze. Knopf.
Marshall, Alfred, 1842-1924
    xMarshall, Alfred.
        Money, Credit & Commerce. Kelley.
        Official Papers. Greenwood.
Marshall, Andrew.
    xMarshall, Andrew.
        Brazil. Walker & Co.
Marshall, Archibald, 1866-1934
    xMarshall, Archibald.
        Clinton Twins, & Other Stories. Arno.
        Clintons, & Others. Arno.
Marshall, Arthur K.
    xMarshall, Arthur K.
        California Probate Procedure. Parker & Son.
Marshall, Bill.
    xMarshall, Bill.
        Bukom. Three Continents.
Marshall, Bill. see Marshall, Bill C.
Marshall, Bill C.
    xMarshall, Bill.
        The Marriage Secret. Hammond Inc.
Marshall, Byron K.
    xMarshall, Byron K.
        Capitalism & Nationalism in Prewar Japan: The
        Ideology of the Business Elite 1868-1941.
        Stanford U Pr.
Marshall, Catherine. see Marshall, Catherine Wood.
Marshall, Catherine Wood, 1914-
    xMarshall, Catherine.
        Beyond Our Selves. Revell.
        Beyond Our Selves. G K Hall.
        Beyond Ourselves. Avon.
        The Helper. Avon.
        The Helper. Chosen Bks Pub.
        The Helper. G K Hall.
        My Personal Prayer Diary. Chosen Bks Pub.
        Something More. Avon.
        Something More. G K Hall.
        Something More. Revell.
Marshall Cavendish Corporation.
    xMarshall Cavendish Editorial Board.
        Carpentry Is Easy - When You Know How.
        Arco.
        Cooking Is Easy - When You Know How.
        Arco.
        Gardening Is Easy - When You Know How.
        Arco.
        History of the Sailing Ship. Arco.
        The Home Bread Baker. Arco.
        Modelling Is Easy - When You Know How.
        Arco.
Marshall Cavendish Editorial Board. see Marshall
    Cavendish Corporation.
Marshall, Chapman F. see Marshall, Chapman Frederick
    Dendy.
Marshall, Chapman Frederick Dendy, 1872-1945
    xMarshall, Chapman F.
        A History of British Railways Down to the
        Year 1830. Oxford U Pr.
Marshall, Charles B. see Marshall, Charles Burton.
Marshall, Charles Burton, 1908-
    xMarshall, Charles B.

American Foreign Policy As a Dimension of
the American Revolution. Am Enterprise.
The Exercise of Sovereignty: Papers on Foreign
Policy. Johns Hopkins.
Marshall, Clifford W., 1928-
xMarshall, Clifford W.
Applied Graph Theory. Wiley.
Marshall, Cyril. *see* Marshall, Cyril Leek.
Marshall, Cyril Leek, 1906-
xMarshall, Cyril.
Foilcraft. Stackpole.
Marshall, Dale R. *see* Marshall, Dale Rogers.
Marshall, Dale Rogers.
xMarshall, Dale R.
The Politics of Participation in Poverty: A Case
Study of the Board of Economic & Youth
Opportunities Agency of Greater Los
Angeles. U of Cal Pr.
ed. Urban Policy Making. Sage.
Marshall, Don B.
xMarshall, Don B.
California Shipwrecks: Footsteps in the Sea.
Superior Pub.
Marshall, Don R., 1939-
xMarshall, Don. R.
Successful Techniques for Solving Employee
Compensation Problems. Wiley.
Marshall, Donald R., 1934-
xMarshall, Donald R.
Frost in the Orchard. Brigham.
Marshall, Dorothy.
xMarshall, Dorothy.
Fanny Kemble. St Martin.
Marshall, Douglas W.
xMarshall, Douglas W.
Campaigns of the American Revolution: An
Atlas of Manuscript Maps. Hammond Inc.
Campaigns of the American Revolution: An
Atlas of Manuscript Maps. U of Mich Pr.
Marshall, Edna M. *see* Marshall, Edna Maytham.
Marshall, Edna Maytham, 1887-
xMarshall, Edna M.
Evaluation of Types of Student-Teaching. AMS
Pr.
Marshall, Edward.
xMarshall, Edward.
Troll Country. Dial.
Marshall, Eric.
xMarshall.
God Is a Good Friend to Have. S&S.
Marshall, F. Ray.
xMarshall, F. Ray.
Cooperatives & Rural Poverty in the South.
Johns Hopkins.
Labor Economics: Wages, Employment &
Trade Unionism. Irwin.
The Negro & Apprenticeship. Johns Hopkins.
xMarshall, Ray.
Human Resource Development in Rural Texas.
U of Tex Busn Res.
The Negro Worker. Phila Bk Co.
Marshall, Florence. *see* Marshall, Florence A. (Thomas).
Marshall, Florence A. (Thomas), 1843-1922
xMarshall, Florence.
Life & Letters of Mary Wollstonecraft Shelley.
Haskell.
Marshall, Frank J. *see* Marshall, Frank James.
Marshall, Frank James.
xMarshall, Frank J.
Chess in an Hour. Arco.
Marshall, Geoffrey.
xMarshall, Geoffrey.
Constitutional Theory. Oxford U Pr.
Restoration Serious Drama. U of Okla Pr.
Marshall, George C. *see* Marshall, George Catlett.
Marshall, George Catlett, 1880-1959
xMarshall, George C.
Memoirs of My Services in the World War:
1917-1918. HM.
Marshall, George W. *see* Marshall, George William.

Marshall, George William.
xMarshall, George W.
Genealogist's Guide. Genealog Pub.
Marshall, Helen Lowrie, 1904-
xMarshall, Helen Lowrie.
Aim for a Star. Doubleday.
Bright Horizons. Doubleday.
Gift of Wonder. Doubleday.
Leave a Touch of Glory. Doubleday.
Quiet Power. Doubleday.
Marshall, Herbert, 1912-
xMarshall, Herbert.
Intro. by The Battleship Potemkin. Avon.
Canadian-American Industry: A Study in
International Investment with an Excursus on
the Canadian Balance of Payments by Frank
A. Knox. Russell.
Marshall, Hermine H.
xMarshall, Hermine H.
Positive Discipline & Classroom Interaction: A
Part of the Teaching-Learning Process. C C
Thomas.
Marshall, I. Howard.
xMarshall, I. Howard.
I Believe in the Historical Jesus. Eerdmans.
Origins of New Testament Christology.
Inter-Varsity.
The Work of Christ. Attic Pr.
Marshall, J. F. *see* Marshall, John Frederick.
Marshall, James.
xMarshall, James.
illus. George & Martha. HM.
illus. George & Martha Encore. HM.
illus. George & Martha One Fine Day. HM.
illus. George & Martha Rise & Shine. HM.
George & Martha Tons of Fun. HM.
Going, Going, Gone?: The Waste of Our
Energy Resources. Coward.
The Guest. HM.
illus. James Marshall's Mother Goose. FS&G.
Law & Psychology in Conflict. Bobbs.
Portly McSwine. HM.
illus. Speedboat. HM.
A Summer in the South. Dell.
illus. A Summer in the South. HM.
illus. What's the Matter with Carruthers?. HM.
Marshall, Joan K.
xMarshall, Joan K.
On Equal Terms: A Thesaurus for Nonsexist
Indexing & Cataloging. Neal-Schuman.
Marshall, John, 1755-1835
xMarshall, John.
Life of George Washington. AMS Pr.
The Life of George Washington. Ridgeway
Bks.
Rail Facts & Feats. Sterling.
Marshall, John C. *see* Marshall, Jon Clark.
Marshall, John Frederick.
xMarshall, J. F.
The British Mosquitoes. Johnson Repr.
Marshall, John P.
xMarshall, John P.
Teacher & His Philosophy. Prof Educ Pubn.
Marshall, Jon Clark.
xMarshall, John C.
Classroom Test Construction. A-W.
Essentials of Testing. A-W.
Marshall, Kathryn.
xMarshall, Kathryn.
Desert Places. Har-Row.
Marshall, L. G.
xMarshall, Larry G.
Evolution of the Borhyaenidae, Extinct South
American Predaceous Marsupials. U of Cal
Pr.
Marshall, Larry G. *see* Marshall, L. G.
Marshall, Lydia.
xMarshall, Lydia.

Nobody Likes to Lose. Childrens.
Marshall, Mac.
xMarshall, Mac.
ed. Beliefs, Behaviors, & Alcoholic Beverages:
A Cross-Cultural Survey. U of Mich Pr.
Weekend Warriors: Alcohol in a Micronesian
Culture. Mayfield Pub.
Marshall, Mary, b. 1780
xMarshall, Mary.
Portraiture of Shakerism. AMS Pr.
Marshall, Mel.
xMarshall, Mel.
Buffalo Hunt. Ballantine.
The Care & Repair of Fishing Tackle.
Winchester Pr.
Cooking Over Coals. Winchester Pr.
How to Fish: A Commonsense Approach.
Winchester Pr.
How to Make Your Own Lures & Flies. T Y
Crowell.
Sierra Summer. U of Nev Pr.
Marshall, N. B. *see* Marshall, Norman Bertram.
Marshall, Norman Bertram.
xMarshall, N. B.
Aspects of Deep Sea Biology. Gordon Pr.
Explorations in the Life of Fishes. Harvard U
Pr.
Life of Fishes. Universe.
Marshall, P. J. *see* Marshall, Peter James.
Marshall, Paul W.
xMarshall, Paul W.
Operations Management: Text & Cases. Irwin.
Marshall, Paule, 1929-
xMarshall, Paule.
Soul Clap Hands & Sing. Chatham Bkseller.
Marshall, Peter.
xMarshall, Peter.
The Light & the Glory. Revell.
Marshall, Peter James.
xMarshall, P. J.
East Indian Fortunes: The British in Bengal in
the Eighteenth Century. Oxford U Pr.
Marshall, Ray. *see* Marshall, F. Ray.
Marshall, Richard H., 1897-
xMarshall, Richard H.
ed. Aspects of Religion in the Soviet Union,
1917-1967. U of Chicago Pr.
Marshall, Robert A. *see* Marshall, Robert Allen.
Marshall, Robert Allen.
xMarshall, Robert A.
The Debit System of Marketing Life & Health
Insurance. Ga St U Busn Pub.
Life Insurance Company Mergers &
Consolidations. Irwin.
Marshall, Robert H. *see* Marshall, Robert Herman.
Marshall, Robert Herman.
xMarshall, Robert H.
The Monetary Process: Essentials of Money &
Banking. HM.
Marshall, Roger.
xMarshall, Roger.
Race to Win. Norton.
Marshall, S. L. *see* Marshall, Samuel Lyman Atwood.
Marshall, Samuel Lyman Atwood, 1900-
xMarshall, S. L.
Fields of Bamboo: Dongtre, Trung Luong &
Hoa Hoi, Three Battles Just Beyond the
South China Sea. Dial.
Marshall, Shelly.
xMarshall, Shelly.
ed. Young, Sober, & Free. Hazelden.
Marshall, Sybil.
xMarshall, Sybil.
Experiment in Education. Cambridge U Pr.
Marshall, T. J. *see* Marshall, Theo John.
Marshall, T. M. *see* Marshall, Thomas Maitland.
Marshall, Theo John.
xMarshall, T. J.

Soil Physics. Cambridge U Pr.

Marshall, Thomas Maitland, 1876-1936
xMarshall, T. M.
History of the Western Boundary of the Louisiana Purchase, 1819-1841. Da Capo.

Marshall, W. see Marshall, William R.

Marshall, William. see Marshall, William Leonard.

Marshall, William H. see Marshall, William Harvey.

Marshall, William Harvey.
xMarshall, William H.
The Structure of Byron's Major Poems. U of Pa Pr.

Marshall, William L. see Marshall, William Leonard.

Marshall, William Leonard, 1944-
xMarshall, William.
Gelignite. Popular Lib.
Skulduggery. HR&W.
xMarshall, William L.
Gelignite. HR&W.

Marshall, William R., 1920-
xMarshall, W.
Administering the Company Personnel Function. P-H.

Marshburn, Joseph H., 1890-
xMarshburn, Joseph H.
Murder & Witchcraft in England, 1550-1640: As Recounted in Pamphlets, Ballads, Broadsides, & Plays. U of Okla Pr.

Marsland, William D. see Marsland, William David.

Marsland, William David.
xMarsland, William D.
Venezuela Through Its History. Greenwood.

Marstin, Ronald.
xMarstin, Ronald.
Beyond Our Tribal Gods: The Maturing of Faith. Orbis Bks.

Marston, Doris. see Marston, Doris E.

Marston, Doris E.
xMarston, Doris.
Exploring Patchwork. Branford.

Marston, Doris Ricker.
xMarston, Doris.
A Guide to Writing History. Writers Digest.

Marston, Hope I. see Marston, Hope Irvin.

Marston, Hope Irvin.
xMarston, Hope I.
Big Rigs. Dodd.
Trucks, Trucking, & You. Dodd.

Marston, John.
xMarston, John.
Antonio's Revenge. Johns Hopkins.
Dutch Courtesan. U of Nebr Pr.

Marston, John E.
xMarston, John E.
Modern Public Relations. McGraw.
Nature of Public Relations. McGraw.

Mart, Donald S.
xMart, Donald S.
The Brand-Name Carbo-Calorie Diet. Doubleday.
The Carbo-Calorie Diet. Doubleday.

Marteau, Robert.
xMarteau, Robert.
Salamander: Selected Poems of Robert Marteau. Princeton U Pr.

Martel, Leon.
xMartel, Leon C.
Lend-Lease, Loans, & the Coming of the Cold War: A Study of the Implementation of Foreign Policy. Westview.

Martel, Leon C. see Martel, Leon.

Martell, Arthur E. see Martell, Arthur Earl.

Martell, Arthur Earl, 1916-
xMartell, Arthur E.
ed. Coordination Chemistry. Am Chemical.

Martell, Paul.
xMartell, Paul.
World Military Leaders. Bowker.

Martellaro, Joseph A.
xMartellaro, Joseph A.

Economic Development in Southern Italy 1950-1960. Intl Schol Bk Serv.

Martenhoff, Jim, 1919-
xMartenhoff, Jim.
The Powerboat Handbook. Follett.

Marteniuk, R. G. see Marteniuk, Ronald G.

Marteniuk, Ronald G.
xMarteniuk, R. G.
Information Processing in Motor Skills. HR&W.

Martens, Frederick H. see Martens, Frederick Herman.

Martens, Frederick Herman, 1874-1932
xMartens, Frederick H.
The Art of the Prima Donna & Concert Singer. Arno.
Leo Ornstein: The Man, His Ideas, His Work. Arno.

Martens, George R.
xMartens, George R.
ed. African Trade Unionism: A Bibliography with a Guide to Trade Union Organizations & Publications. G K Hall.

Martens, Rachel.
xMartens, Rachel.
The How-to Book of Repairing, Rewiring, & Restoring Lamps & Lighting Fixtures. Doubleday.
The How-to Book of Repairing, Rewiring & Restoring Lamps & Lighting Fixtures. Doubleday.

Martens, Rainer, 1942-
xMartens, Rainer.
ed. Joy & Sadness in Children's Sports. Human Kinetics.

Martens, Wilfred, 1935-
xMartens, Wilfred.
River of Glass. Herald Pr.

Martensson, Alf.
xMartensson, Alf.
The Book of Furniture Making. St Martin.
The Woodworker's Bible. Bobbs.

Marti, Donald B.
xMarti, Donald B.
To Improve the Soil & the Mind: Agricultural Societies, Journals & Schools in the Northeastern States, 1791-1865. Univ Microfilms.

Marti, Fritz, 1894-
xMarti, Fritz.
Religion, Reason & Man. Green.

Marti, Jose.
xMarti, Jose.
Inside the Monster: Writings on the United States & American Imperialism. Monthly Rev.
Our America: Writings on Latin America & the Struggle for Cuban Independence. Monthly Rev.

Martialis, Marcus V. see Martialis, Marcus Valerius.

Martialis, Marcus Valerius.
xMartialis, Marcus V.
One Hundred Epigrams of Martial. Perivale Pr.

Martin. see Martin, Nancy.

Martin, A. D. see Martin, Arthur Davis.

Martin, A. G.
xMartin, A. G.
Finishing Processes in Printing. Focal Pr.
Finishing Processes in Printing. Hastings.

Martin, A. S. see Martin, Arthur Shadwell.

Martin, Albert. see Martin, Albert J.

Martin, Albert J., 1929-
xMartin, Albert.
One Man, Hurt. Macmillan.

Martin, Albro.
xMartin, Albro.
Enterprise Denied: Origins of the Decline of American Railroads, 1897-1917. Columbia U Pr.

Martin, Ann.
xMartin, Ann.

The Equestrian Woman. Paddington.

Martin, Ann. see Martin, Ann M.

Martin, Ann Bodenhamer.
xMartin, Ann.
Calico Families. Pelican.

Martin, Ann M., 1925-
xMartin, Ann.
Theory & Practice of Communicating Educational & Vocational Information. HM.

Martin, Anne, 1931-
xMartin, Anne.
Portfolio of Low Expense Art Lessons: Featuring 43 Novel Display Techniques. P-H.

Martin, Aquinata, Sister, 1896-
xMartin, Aquinata.
The Catholic Church on the Nebraska Frontier: 1854-1885. AMS Pr.

Martin, Arthur Davis, 1869-1940
xMartin, A. D.
The Religion of Wordsworth. Haskell.

Martin, Arthur S. see Martin, Arthur Shadwell.

Martin, Arthur Shadwell.
xMartin, A. S.
On Parody. Folcroft.
On Parody. Porter.
xMartin, Arthur S.
On Parody. Arden Lib.

Martin, Asa E. see Martin, Asa Earl.

Martin, Asa Earl, 1885-
xMartin, Asa E.
Anti-Slavery Movement in Kentucky Prior to 1850. Negro U Pr.
xMartin, Asa G.
Our Negro Population: A Sociological Study of the Negroes of Kansas City Missouri. Negro U Pr.

Martin, Asa G. see Martin, Asa Earl.

Martin, B. R. see Martin, Brian Robert Charles.

Martin, Barclay, 1923-
xMartin, Barclay.
Abnormal Psychology. Scott F.
Anxiety & Neurotic Disorders. Wiley.

Martin, Benjamin E. see Martin, Benjamin Ellis.

Martin, Benjamin Ellis, d. 1909
xMartin, Benjamin E.
In the Footprints of Charles Lamb. Folcroft.

Martin, Bernard, 1897-
xMartin, Bernard.
The Ancient Mariner & the Authentic Narrative. Folcroft.
The Existentialist Theology of Paul Tillich. Coll & U Pr.
Strange Vigour: A Biography of Sun Yat-Sen. Kelley.
Strange Vigour: The Biography of Sun Yat-Sen. Kennikat.

Martin, Betty.
xMartin, Betty.
The Principal's Handbook on the School Library Media Center. Gaylord Prof Pubns.

Martin, Bill. see Martin, William Ivan.

Martin, Brian Robert Charles.
xMartin, B. R.
Statistics for Physicists. Acad Pr.

Martin, Bruce.
xMartin, Bruce.
Joints in Buildings. Halsted Pr.

Martin, Burns.
xMartin, Burns.
Allan Ramsay: A Study of His Life & Works. Greenwood.

Martin, C. Leslie.
xMartin, C. Leslie.
Design Graphics. Macmillan.

Martin, Charlotte Bronson W. (Hunnewall), 1871-
xMartin, Charlotte B.
The World & the Aristocrat. Greenwood.

Martin, Charles B. see Martin, Charles Burton.

Martin, Charles Burton.
xMartin, Charles B.

Religious Belief. Cornell U Pr.
Martin, Charles E.
xMartin, Charles E.
ed. Noah's Ark. Random.
Martin, Charles H., 1945-
xMartin, Charles H.
The Angelo Herndon Case & Southern Justice.
La State U Pr.
Martin, Charlotte B. *see* Martin, Chariotte Bronson W.
(Hunnewall).
Martin, Chester. *see* Martin, Chester Bailey.
Martin, Chester Bailey, 1882-
xMartin, Chester.
Foundations of Canadian Nationhood. U of
Toronto Pr.
Martin, Chuck.
xMartin, Chuck.
Law for Tombstone. Belmont-Tower.
Martin, Constance R.
xMartin, Constance R.
Textbook of Endocrine Physiology. Oxford U
Pr.
Martin, Curtis.
xMartin, Curtis.
Colorado Government & Politics. Pruett.
Martin, Cy.
xMartin, Cy.
The Marshal of Packersville. Bouregy.
Martin, D. *see* Martin, Dieter.
Martin, David, 1929-
xMartin, David.
A General Theory of Secularization. Har-Row.
Martin, David. *see* Martin, David A.
Martin, David A.
xMartin, David.
ed. Anarchy & Culture: The Problem of the
Contemporary University. Columbia U Pr.
Breaking the Image: The Sociology of Christian
Theory & Practice. St Martin.
xMartin, David A.
Pacifism: An Historical & Sociological Study.
Schocken.
Martin, David C.
xMartin, David C.
Wilderness of Mirrors. Har-Row.
Martin, David E.
xMartin, David E.
The Marathon Footrace: Performers &
Performances. C C Thomas.
Martin, David G.
xMartin, David G.
Introduction to Psychotherapy. Brooks-Cole.
Personality: Effective & Ineffective.
Brooks-Cole.
Martin, David W., 1943-
xMartin, David W.
Doing Psychology Experiments. Brooks-Cole.
Martin, Dick, 1946-
xMartin, Dick.
The Executive's Guide to Handling a Press
Interview. Pilot Bks.

Martin, Dieter.
xMartin, D.
Dimethyl Sulphoxide. Halsted Pr.

Martin, Dorothy.
xMartin, Dorothy.

Chapter Closed for Peggy. Moody.
Hopes Fulfilled for Peggy. Moody.
tr. Sextette: Translations from the French
Symbolists. AMS Pr.

Martin, Dorothy. *see* Martin, Dorothy McKay.
Martin, Dorothy McKay, 1921-
xMartin, Dorothy.

Mystery of the Jade Earring. Moody.
Mystery of the Missing Bracelets. Moody.
Mystery on the Fourteenth Floor. Moody.
The Other Side of Yesterday. Moody.
Prayer Answered for Peggy. Moody.
Martin, E. W. *see* Martin, Edley Wainright.
Martin, Edgar W. *see* Martin, Edgar Winfield.
Martin, Edgar Winfield, 1910-
xMartin, Edgar W.
The Standard of Living in 1860. Johnson Repr.
Martin, Edley Wainright.
xMartin, E. W.
Computers & Information Systems: An
Introduction. Irwin.
Mathematics for Decision Making: A
Programmed Basic Text. Irwin.
Martin, Edward A. *see* Martin, Edward Alexander.
Martin, Edward Alexander, 1902-
xMartin, Edward A.
Psychology of Funeral Service. E A Martin.
Martin, Edward S. *see* Martin, Edward Sandford.
Martin, Edward Sandford, 1856-1939
xMartin, Edward S.
In a New Century. Arno.
Martin, Edwin. *see* Martin, Edwin W.
Martin, Edwin M.
xMartin, Edwin M.
The Allied Occupation of Japan. Greenwood.
Martin, Edwin W.
xMartin, Edwin.
Southeast Asia & China: The End of
Containment. Westview.
Martin, Eleanor J.
xMartin, Eleanor J.
Rene Marques. Twayne.
Martin, Esmond B. *see* Martin, Esmond Bradley.
Martin, Esmond Bradley.
xMartin, Esmond B.
Zanzibar: Tradition & Revolution. David &
Charles.
Martin, F. David.
xMartin, David
Humanities Through the Arts. McGraw.
xMartin, F. David.
Sculpture & Enlivened Space: Aesthetics &
History. U Pr of Ky.
Martin, Florence.
xMartin, Florence.
Observing National Holidays & Church
Festivals: A Weekday Church School Unit in
Christian Citizenship Series for Grades Three
& Four. Gale.
Martin, Fran. *see* Martin, Frances Gardiner Mcentee.
Martin, Frances Gardiner Mcentee.
xMartin, Fran.
Raven-Who-Sets-Things-Right: Indian Tales of
the Northwest Coast. Har-Row.
Martin, Francis X.
xMartin, Francis X.
ed. Leaders & Men of the Easter Rising:
Dublin 1916. Cornell U Pr.
Martin, Franklin W.
xMartin, Franklin W.
Edible Leaves of the Tropics. Gordon Pr.
Martin, Frederick N.
xMartin, Frederick N.
Introduction to Audiology. P-H.
ed. Pediatric Audiology. P-H.
Martin, Frederick T. *see* Martin, Frederick Townsend.
Martin, Frederick Townsend, 1849-1914
xMartin, Frederick T.
The Passing of the Idle Rich. Arno.
Things I Remember. Arno.
Martin, G. W. *see* Martin, George Willard.
Martin, Ged.
xMartin, Ged.
Episodes of Old Canberra. Bks Australia.
Martin, George.
xMartin, George.

All You Need Is Ears. St Martin.
Martin, George R. *see* Martin, George R. R.
Martin, George R. R.
xMartin, George R.
Songs of Stars & Shadows. PB.
Martin, George W. *see* Martin, George Whitney.
Martin, George Whitney.
xMartin, George W.
The Opera Companion to Twentieth-Century
Opera. Dodd.
Martin, George Willard, 1886-
xMartin, G. W.
Revision of the North Central Tremellales.
Lubrecht & Cramer.
Martin, Gillian.
xMartin, Gillian.
Living Arrows. Scribner.
A Passage of Time. Scribner.
Martin, Gyorgy.
xMartin, Gyorgy.
Hungarian Folk Dances. Intl Pubns Serv.
Martin, Harold C. *see* Martin, Harold Clark.
Martin, Harold Clark.
xMartin, Harold C.
ed. Style in Prose Fiction. Columbia U Pr.
Martin, Harold Clifford, 1913-
xMartin, Harold C.
Introduction to Matrix Methods of Structural
Analysis. McGraw.
Martin, Harold H.
xMartin, Harold H.
Harold Martin Remembers a Place in the
Mountains. Peachtree Pubs.
Martin, Harold P.
xMartin, Harold P.
ed. The Abused Child: A Multidisciplinary
Approach to Developmental Issues &
Treatment. Ballinger Pub.
Martin, Harry.
xMartin, Harry.
Contemporary Homes of the Pacific Northwest.
Madrona Pubs.
Martin, Harry B. *see* Martin, Harry Brownlow.
Martin, Harry Brownlow, 1873-
xMartin, Harry B.
Fifty Years of American Golf. Argosy.
Martin, Howard H. *see* Martin, Howard Hastings.
Martin, Howard Hastings.
xMartin, Howard H.
Communication & Consensus: An Introduction
to Rhetorical Discourse. HarBraceJ.
Martin, Hugh.
xMartin, Hugh.
ed. Christian Social Reformers of the
Nineteenth Century. Arno.
Great Christian Books. Arno.
Great Christian Books. Folcroft.
Martin, I. *see* Martin, Irene.
Martin, Ian K. *see* Martin, Ian Kennedy.
Martin, Ian Kennedy.
xMartin, Ian K.
Rekill. Ballantine.
Martin, Irene.
xMartin, I.
Genesis of the Classical Conditioned Response.
Pergamon.
Martin, J. *see* Martin, James.
Martin, J. R. *see* Martin, John Russell.
Martin, J. T. *see* Martin, John Thomas.
Martin, J. W. *see* Martin, John Wilson.
Martin, James, 1933-
xMartin, J.
Communications Satellite Systems. P-H.
Computer Data Base Organization. P-H.
Design of Real Time Computer Systems. P-H.
xMartin, James.

Design of Man-Computer Dialogues. P-H.
A Pilgrim's Guide to the Holy Land. Westminster.
Principles of Data Base Management. P-H.
Systems Analysis for Data Transmission. P-H.
Martin, James K. *see* Martin, James Kirby.
Martin, James Kirby.
xMartin, James K.
American Revolution: Whose Revolution?. Krieger.
In the Course of Human Events: An Interpretive Exploration of the American Revolution. AHM Pub.
Men in Rebellion: Higher Governmental Leaders & the Coming of the American Revolution. Free Pr.
Men in Rebellion: Higher Governmental Leaders & the Coming of the American Revolution. Rutgers U Pr.
Martin, James M., 1943-
xMartin, James M.
Actualizations: Beyond est. SF Bk Co.
Martin, James T. *see* Martin, James Thomas.
Martin, James Thomas.
xMartin, James T.
Programming Real-Time Computer Systems. P-H.
Martin, Jane R.
xMartin, Jane R.
Choice, Chance & Curriculum. Ohio St U Pr.
Martin, Jay.
xMartin, Jay.
Always Merry & Bright: The Life of Henry Miller. Capra Pr.
Always Merry & Bright: The Life of Henry Miller. Penguin.
Winter Dreams: An American in Moscow. HM.
Martin, Jean L.
xMartin, Jean L.
ed. The Sheldon Memorial Art Gallery Cookbook. Nebraska Art.
Martin, Joan L.
xMartin, Joan L.
Bowling. Wm C Brown.
Martin, Joe. *see* Martin, Joseph William.
Martin, John, 1864-
xMartin, John.
Dictators & Democracies Today. Arno.
Martin, John. *see* Martin, John Joseph.
Martin, John B. *see* Martin, John Biddulph.
Martin, John Bartlow, 1915-
xMartin, John B.
Adlai Stevenson & the World: The Life of Adlai E. Stevenson. Doubleday.
Deep South Says, Never. Negro U Pr.
xMartin, John Bartlow.
Adlai Stevenson of Illinois: The Life of Adlai E. Stevenson. Doubleday.
Martin, John Biddulph.
xMartin, John B.
Grasshopper in Lombard Street. B Franklin.
Martin, John D.
xMartin, John D.
Basic Financial Management. P-H.
Cases in Basic Financial Management. P-H.
Martin, John E. *see* Martin, John Edward.
Martin, John Edward.
xMartin, John E.
Greater London: An Industrial Geography. U of Chicago Pr.
Martin, John F. *see* Martin, John Frederick.
Martin, John Frederick.
xMartin, John F.
Civil Rights & the Crisis of Liberalism: The Democratic Party, 1945-1976. Westview.
Martin, John H. *see* Martin, John Hill.
Martin, John Hill, 1823-1906
xMartin, John H.

Historical Sketch of Bethlehem in Pennsylvania. AMS Pr.
Martin, John Holmes.
xMartin, John H.
Principles of Field Crop Production. Macmillan.
Martin, John Joseph, 1893-
xMartin, John.
Modern Dance. Dance Horiz.
Martin, John Rupert.
xMartin, John.
Baroque. Har-Row.
Martin, John Russell.
xMartin, J. R.
ed. Recommended Guide for the Prediction of the Dispersion of Airborne Effluents. ASME.
Martin, John Thomas.
xMartin, J. T.
Cuticles of Plants. St Martin.
Martin, John Wilson.
xMartin, J. W.
Precipitation Hardening. Pergamon.
Martin, Joseph, 1920-
xMartin, Joseph.
A Guide to Marxism. St Martin.
Martin, Joseph. *see* Martin, Joseph B.
Martin, Joseph B.
xMartin, Joseph.
Clinical Neuroendocrinology. Davis Co.
Martin, Joseph H. *see* Martin, Joseph Howard.
Martin, Joseph Howard, 1932-
xMartin, Joseph H.
Real Estate License Examinations: Salesperson & Broker. Arco.
Martin, Joseph William.
xMartin, Joe.
My First Fifty Years in Politics. Greenwood.
Martin, Julian A.
xMartin, Julian A.
Law Enforcement Vocabulary. C C Thomas.
Martin, Kenneth R. *see* Martin, Kenneth Robert.
Martin, Kenneth Robert, 1921-
xMartin, Kenneth R.
Delaware Goes Whaling, 1833-1845. Eleutherian Mills-Hagley.
Martin, Kingsley, 1897-1969
xMartin, Kingsley.
The Rise of French Liberal Thought: A Study of Political Ideas from Bayle to Condorcet. Greenwood.

Martin, L. F. *see* Martin, Louis F.
Martin, Laurence W.
xMartin, Laurence W.
Strategic Thought in the Nuclear Age. Johns Hopkins.
Martin, Lee J.
xMartin, Lee J.
The Five Hundred Word Theme. P-H.
Martin, Leonard W.
xMartin, Leonard W.
Principles of Economics: Micro. Grid Pub.
Martin, Lester H.
xMartin, Lester H.
This Is the Poodle. TFH Pubns.
Martin, Lillien J. *see* Martin, Lillien Jane.
Martin, Lillien Jane.
xMartin, Lillien J.
Sweeping the Cobwebs. Arno.
Martin, Linette.
xMartin, Linette.
Hans Rookmaaker: A Biography. Inter-Varsity.
Martin, Louis F.
xMartin, L. F.
Storage Batteries & Rechargeable Cell Technology. Noyes.
xMartin, Louis F.
Industrial Water Purification. Noyes.
Martin, Lowell. *see* Martin, Lowell Arthur.

Martin, Lowell Arthur.
xMartin, Lowell.
Library Response to Urban Change: A Study of the Chicago Public Library. ALA.
Martin, Luis.
xMartin, Luis.
Intellectual Conquest of Peru: The Jesuit College of San Pablo, 1568-1767. Fordham.
Martin, Lynne.
xMartin, Lynne.
The Orchid Family. Morrow.
Peacocks. Morrow.
Puffin, Bird of the Open Seas. Morrow.
Martin, M . W. *see* Martin, M. W.
Martin, M. J. *see* Martin, Michael J. C.
Martin, M. Kay.
xMartin, M. Kay.
Female of the Species. Columbia U Pr.
Martin, M. W.
xMartin, M . W.
Let's Talk About the New World of Medicine. Jonathan David.
xMartin, M. W.
A Concise Dictionary of Medicine. Jonathan David.
Martin, Malachi.
xMartin, Malachi.
The Final Conclave. PB.
The Final Conclave. Stein & Day.
Martin, Margaret. *see* Martin, Margaret J.
Martin, Margaret J.
xMartin, Margaret.
Succulents & Their Cultivation. Scribner.
xMartin, Margaret J.
Cacti & Their Cultivation. Merrimack Bk Serv.
Cacti & Their Cultivation. Scribner.
Martin, Margaret R. *see* Martin, Margaret Rhett.
Martin, Margaret Rhett.
xMartin, Margaret R.
Charleston Ghosts. U of SC Pr.
Martin, Marianne W.
xMartin, Maryanne W.
Futurist Art & Theory. Hacker.
Martin, Mary, 1913-
xMartin, Mary.
Mary Martin's Needlepoint. Morrow.
My Heart Belongs. Warner Bks.
Martin, Maryanne W. *see* Martin, Marianne W.
Martin, Melody.
xMartin, Melody.
Mrs. Kamali Would Like to Speak to You About Cloud: Notes from a California Classroom. Dial.
Martin, Michael J. C.
xMartin, M. J.
ed. Case Exercises in Operations Research. Wiley.
Martin, Michael R. *see* Martin, Michael Rheta.
Martin, Michael Rheta.
xMartin, Michael R.
Concise Encyclopedic Guide to Shakespeare. Avon.
Martin, Mildred, 1904-
xMartin, Mildred.
Half-Century of Eliot Criticism: Annotated Bibliography of Books & Articles in English, 1916-1965. Bucknell U Pr.
Martin, Mildred C. *see* Martin, Mildred Crowl.
Martin, Mildred Crowl, 1912-
xMartin, Mildred C.
Chinatown's Angry Angel: The Story of Donaldina Cameron. Pacific Bks.
Martin, Murray S.
xMartin, Murray S.
Budgetary Control in Academic Libraries. Jai Pr.
Martin, Nancy.
xMartin.

Comprehensive Rehabilitation Nursing.
McGraw.
Martin, Norma.
xMartin, Norma.
Divorce, a Christian Dilemma. Herald Pr.
Martin, Patricia M. *see* Martin, Patricia Miles.
Martin, Patricia Miles.
xMartin, Patricia M.
Daniel Boone. Putnam.
The Pumpkin Patch. Putnam.
Rice Bowl Pet. T Y Crowell.
Thomas Alva Edison. Putnam.
Martin, Paul.
xMartin, Paul.
Good Morning, Lord: Devotions for Young
People. Baker Bk.
Good Morning, Lord: More Devotions for
Teens. Baker Bk.
Martin, Percy A. *see* Martin, Percy Alvin.
Martin, Percy Alvin, 1879-1942
xMartin, Percy A.
Latin America & the War. Peter Smith.
Martin, Percy F. *see* Martin, Percy Falcke.
Martin, Percy Falcke, 1861-1941
xMartin, Percy F.
Sudan in Evolution: A Study of the Economic,
Financial & Administrative Conditions of the
Anglo-Egyptian Sudan. Negro U Pr.
Martin, Peter A.
xMartin, Peter A.
A Marital Therapy Manual. Brunner-Mazel.
Martin, Philip. *see* Martin, Philip L.
Martin, Philip L., 1949-
xMartin, Philip.
Contemporary Labor Relations. Wadsworth
Pub.
Martin, Philip R.
xMartin, Philip R.
Auto Mechanics for the Complete Dummy.
Motormatics.
Martin, Priscilla.
xMartin, Priscilla.
Piers Plowman: The Field & the Tower. B&N.
Martin, Purvis L.
xMartin, Purvis L.
Ambulatory Gynecologic Surgery. PSG Pub.
Martin, R. *see* Martin, Roderick.
Martin, R. A. *see* Martin, Raymond A.
Martin, R. C. *see* Martin, Roscoe Coleman.
Martin, R. M. *see* Martin, Richard Milton.
Martin, Rachel.
xMartin, Rachel.
Escape. Accent Bks.
Martin, Ralph, 1942-
xMartin, Ralph.
Hungry for God: Practical Help in Personal
Prayer. Doubleday.
Martin, Raymond. *see* Martin, Raymond A.
Martin, Raymond A.
xMartin, R. A.
Syntactical & Critical Concordance to the
Greek Text of Baruch & the Epistle of
Jeremiah. Biblical Res Assocs.
xMartin, Raymond.
Syntactical Evidence of Semitic Sources in
Greek Documents. Scholars Pr Ca.
Martin, Reed.
xMartin, Reed.
Developing Student Discipline & Motivation: A
Series for Teacher in-Service Training. Res
Press.
Educating Handicapped Children: The Legal
Mandate. Res Press.
Legal Challenges to Behavior Modification:
Trends in Schools, Corrections, & Mental
Health. Res Press.
Martin, Rhona.
xMartin, Rhona.

Gallows Wedding. Berkley Pub.
Gallows Wedding. Coward.
Martin, Richard, M.a.
xMartin, Richard.
The Love That Failed: Ideal & Reality in the
Writings of E. M. Forster. Mouton.
Martin, Richard M. *see* Martin, Richard Milton.
Martin, Richard Milton.
xMartin, R. M.
Logic, Language & Metaphysics. NYU Pr.
Toward a Systematic Pragmatics. Greenwood.
xMartin, Richard M.
Events, Reference & Logical Form. Intl Schol
Bk Serv.
Martin, Robert A.
xMartin, Robert A.
Learning to Change: A Self-Management
Approach to Adjustment. McGraw.
Martin, Robert B. *see* Martin, Robert Bernard.
Martin, Robert Bernard.
xMartin, Robert B.
The Triumph of Wit: A Study of Victorian
Comic Theory. Oxford U Pr.
Martin, Robert H., 1942-
xMartin, Robert H.
Nonlinear Operators & Differential Equations
in Banach Spaces. Wiley.
Martin, Robert H. *see* Martin, Robert Hugh.
Martin, Robert Hugh, 1858-1939
xMartin, Robert H.
Boy of Old Shenandoah. McClain.
Martin, Robert J.
xMartin, Robert J.
All About Witnessing: A Study in the Book of
Acts. Baker Bk.
Martin, Robert K., 1941-
xMartin, Robert K.
The Homosexual Tradition in American Poetry.
U of Tex Pr.
Martin, Robert L.
xMartin, Robert L.
City Moves West: Economic & Industrial
Growth in Central West Texas. U of Tex Pr.
Martin, Robert L. *see* Martin, Robert Lanham.
Martin, Robert Lanham, 1942-
xMartin, Robert L.
Studies in Feedback Shift-Register Synthesis of
Sequential Machines. MIT Pr.
Martin, Roderick.
xMartin, R.
The Sociology of Power. Routledge & Kegan.
Martin, Rolland A.
xMartin, Rollard A.
Occupational Disability: Causes, Prediction,
Prevention. C C Thomas.
Martin, Rollard A. *see* Martin, Rolland A.
Martin, Ronald L.
xMartin, Ronald L.
Official Guide to Marvel Cave. Ozark Mtn
Pubs.
Martin, Roscoe. *see* Martin, Roscoe Coleman.
Martin, Roscoe C. *see* Martin, Roscoe Coleman.
Martin, Roscoe Coleman, 1903-
xMartin, R. C.
The Cities & the Federal System. Arno.
xMartin, Roscoe.
People's Party in Texas: A Study in
Third-Party Politics. U of Tex Pr.
xMartin, Roscoe C.
Decisions in Syracuse. Greenwood.
Government & the Suburban School.
Greenwood.
Grass Roots: Essays. Greenwood.
Martin, Roy, 1943-
xMartin, Roy.
Writing & Defending a Thesis or Dissertation
in Psychology & Education. C C Thomas.
Martin, Russ.
xMartin, Russ.

Rhea. Playboy Pbks.
Martin, Samuel E. *see* Martin, Samuel Elmo.
Martin, Samuel Elmo, 1924-
xMartin, Samuel E.
A Reference Grammar of Japanese. Yale U Pr.
Martin, Sidney W. *see* Martin, Sidney Walter.
Martin, Sidney Walter.
xMartin, Sidney W.
Florida During the Territorial Days. Porcupine
Pr.
Martin, Steve.
xMartin, Steve.
Cruel Shoes. Putnam.
Cruel Shoes. Warner Bks.
Martin, Susan K., 1942-
xMartin, Susan K.
Library Networks 1978-79. Knowledge Indus.
Library Networks: 1980-1981. Knowledge
Indus.
Martin, Terence.
xMartin, Terence.
Instructed Vision: Scottish Common Sense
Philosophy & the Origins of American
Fiction. Kraus Repr.
Nathaniel Hawthorne. Coll & U Pr.
Nathaniel Hawthorne. Twayne.
Martin, Tony, 1942-
xMartin, Tony.
Race First: The Ideological & Organizational
Struggles of Marcus Garvey & the Universal
Negro Improvement Assoc.. Greenwood.
Martin, Valerie.
xMartin, Valerie.
Alexandra. FS&G.
Set in Motion. FS&G.
Martin, Walter. *see* Martin, Walter Ralston.
Martin, Walter Ralston, 1928-
xMartin, Walter.
The Maze of Mormonism. Vision Hse.
Rise of the Cults. Vision Hse.
Martin, Warren B. *see* Martin, Warren Bryan.
Martin, Warren Bryan.
xMartin, Warren B.
Conformity: Standards & Change in Higher
Education. Jossey-Bass.
Martin, Warren S.
xMartin, Warren S.
Personality & Product Symbolism. U of Tex
Busn Res.
Martin, Wayne.
xMartin, Wayne.
Medical Heroes & Heretics. Devin.
Martin, Wendy.
xMartin, Wendy.
ed. American Sisterhood: Writings of the
Feminist Movement from Colonial Times to
the Present. Har-Row.
Love's Journey. Bouregy.
Two Hearts Adrift. Bouregy.
Martin, William A. *see* Martin, William Alexander
Parsons.
Martin, William Alexander Parsons, 1827-1916
xMartin, William A.
The Siege in Peking: China Against the World.
Biblio Dist.
The Siege in Peking: China Against the World.
Scholarly Res Inc.
Martin, William C. *see* Martin, William Curtis.
Martin, William Curtis, 1937-
xMartin, William C.
Christians in Conflict. Ctr Sci Study.
Martin, William Ivan, 1916-
xMartin, Bill.

Palomino Pony. HR&W.
Sounds Around the Clock. HR&W.
Sounds I Remember. HR&W.
Sounds of Home. HR&W.
Sounds of Laughter. HR&W.
Sounds of Numbers. HR&W.
Sounds of the Storyteller. HR&W.
Martin, William J.
xMartin, William J.
ed. Library Services to the Disadvantaged.
Shoe String.
Martin, William O. *see* Martin, William Oliver.
Martin, William Oliver.
xMartin, William O.
Order & Integration of Knowledge.
Greenwood.
Martin, William R.
xMartin, William R.
Music of the Twentieth Century. P-H.
Martin du Gard, Roger, 1881-1958
xMartin Du Gard, Roger.
The Postman. Fertig.
Martin-Doyle, J. L. *see* Martin-Doyle, John Lionel Cyril.
Martin-Doyle, John Lionel Cyril.
xMartin-Doyle, J. L.
Synopsis of Ophthalmology. Year Bk Med.
Martindale, Cyril C. *see* Martindale, Cyril Charlie.
Martindale, Cyril Charlie, 1879-1963
xMartindale, Cyril C.
Faith of the Roman Church. Greenwood.
Martindale, Don. *see* Martindale, Don Albert.
Martindale, Don Albert, 1915-
xMartindale, Don.
Sociological Theory & the Problem of Values.
Merrill.
Martindale, Hilda, 1875-1952
xMartindale, Hilda.
Some Victorian Portraits & Others. Arno.
Some Victorian Portraits & Others. Folcroft.
xMartindale, Hilsa.
Some Victorian Portraits & Others. Century
Bookbindery.
Martindale, Hilsa. *see* Martindale, Hilda.
Martine, James J.
xMartine, James J.
Critical Essays on Arthur Miller. G K Hall.
Martineau, Harriet, 1802-1876
xMartineau, Harriet.
Ireland. Garland Pub.
Martyr Age of the United States. Arno.
Retrospect of Western Travel. Greenwood.
Retrospect of Western Travel. Haskell.
Retrospect of Western Travel. Johnson Repr.
Martineau, James, 1805-1900
xMartineau, James.
A Study of Spinoza. Arno.
Martinelli, Nicholas.
xMartinelli, Nicholas.
Dental Laboratory Technology. Mosby.
Martines, Lauro.
xMartines, Lauro.
Power & Imagination: City-States in
Renaissance Italy. Knopf.
Power & Imagination: City-States in
Renaissance Italy. Random.
Martinez, Julio A.
xMartinez, Julio A.
Compiled by Chicano Scholars & Writers: A
Bio-Bibliographical Directory. Scarecrow.
Martinez, Oscar J. *see* Martinez, Oscar Jaquez.
Martinez, Oscar Jaquez, 1943-
xMartinez, Oscar J.
Border Boom Town: Ciudad Juarez Since 1848.
U of Tex Pr.
Martinez, Rafael V., 1923-
xMartinez, Rafael V.
My House Is Your House. Friend Pr.
Martinez, Ricardo A. *see* Martinez, Ricardo Arguijo.
Martinez, Ricardo Arguijo.
xMartinez, Ricardo A.

ed. Hispanic Culture & Health Care: Fact,
Fiction, Folklore. Mosby.
Martinez, Tomas, 1942-
xMartinez, Tomas.
The Human Marketplace: An Examination of
Private Employment Agencies. Transaction
Bks.
Martinez-Brawley, Emilia E., 1939-
xMartinez-Brawley, Emilia E.
ed. Pioneer Efforts in Rural Social Welfare:
Firsthand Views Since 1908. Pa St U Pr.
Martini, G. A. *see* Martini, Gustav Adolf.
Martini, Gustav Adolf.
xMartini, G. A.
ed. Marburg Virus Disease. Springer-Verlag.
Martini, Luciano.
xMartini, Luciano.
ed. Clinical Neuroendocrinology. Acad Pr.
Martini, Teri.
xMartini, Teri.
All Because of Jill. Westminster.
The Lucky Ghost Shirt. Westminster.
Martini, Therese.
xMartini, Therese.
Dreams to Give. Popular Lib.
Martinis, Gloria. *see* Martinis, Gloria K.
Martinis, Gloria K.
xMartinis, Gloria.
The Two Carolines. Nordon Pubns.
Martino, R. L.
xMartino, R. L.
Project Management. Gordon.
Martino, R L.
xMartino, R. L.
Critical Path Networks. Gordon.
Critical Path Networks. McGraw.
Martino, R. L. *see* Martino, Rocco L.
Martino, Rocco L.
xMartino, R. L.
Integrated Manufacturing Systems. McGraw.
Martinovitch, Nicholas.
xMartinovitch, Nicholas N.
Turkish Theatre. Arno.
Martins, Wilson.
xMartins, Wilson.
The Modernist Idea: A Critical Survey of
Brazilian Writing in the Twentieth Century.
Greenwood.
The Modernist Idea: A Critical Survey of
Brazilian Writing in the Twentieth Century.
NYU Pr.
Martinson, Ida M. *see* Martinson, Ida Marie.
Martinson, Ida Marie.
xMartinson, Ida M.
Mathematics for Health Professionals. Springer
Pub.
Martinussen, Willy, 1938-
xMartinussen, Willy.
The Distant Democracy: Social Inequality,
Political Resources & Political Influence in
Norway. Wiley.
Martof, Bernard S. *see* Martof, Bernard Stephen.
Martof, Bernard Stephen, 1920-
xMartof, Bernard S.
Amphibians & Reptiles of the Carolinas &
Virginia. U of NC Pr.
Marton, Sheila N. *see* Marton, Sheila Nassberg.
Marton, Sheila Nassberg.
xMarton, Sheila N.
Patterned Backgrounds for Needlepoint. Van
Nos Reinhold.
Martorella, P. *see* Martorella, Peter H.
Martorella, Peter H.
xMartorella, P.
Discovering Others. McGraw.
xMartorella, Peter H.
ed. Social Studies Strategies: Theory into
Practice. Har-Row.
Martuza, Victor R.
xMartuza, Victor R.

Applying Norm-Referenced &
Criterion-Referenced Measurement in
Education. Allyn.
Marty, Martin E., 1928-
xMarty, Martin E.
Baptism. Fortress.
The Lord's Supper. Fortress.
A Nation of Behavers. U of Chicago Pr.
The Pro & Con Book of Religious America: A
Bicentennial Argument. Word Bks.
Religion, Awakening & Revolution. McGrath.
The Religious Press in America. Greenwood.
Marty, Sid, 1944-
xMarty, Sid.
Men for the Mountains. Vanguard.
Martyn, Howe.
xMartyn, Howe.
Multinational Business Management. Irvington.
Martyn, J. Louis. *see* Martyn, James Louis.
Martyn, James Louis, 1925-
xMartyn, J. Louis.
History & Theology in the Fourth Gospel.
Abingdon.
Martynov, Ivan I. *see* Martynov, Ivan Ivanovich.
Martynov, Ivan Ivanovich.
xMartynov, Ivan I.
Dmitri Shostakovich, the Man & His Work.
Greenwood.
Martz, Clyde O.
xMartz, Clyde O.
Cases & Materials on the Law of Natural
Resources. Arno.
Martz, John D.
xMartz, John D.
Accion Democratica: Evolution of a Modern
Political Party in Venezuela. Princeton U Pr.
ed. Venezuela: The Democratic Experience.
Praeger.
Martz, Kathren V.
xMartz, Kathren V.
Management of the Patient-Ventilator System:
A Team Approach. Mosby.
Martz, Louis Dohr.
xMartz, Louis L.
Poet of Exile: A Study of Milton's Poetry.
Yale U Pr.
Martz, Louis L. *see* Martz, Louis Lohr.
Martz, Louis Lohr.
xMartz, Louis L.
ed. The Author in His Work: Essays on a
Problem in Criticism. Yale U Pr.
Later Career of Tobias Smollett. Shoe String.
Martz, William J.
xMartz, William J.
Distinctive Voice: Twentieth Century American
Poetry. Scott F.
The Place of the Merchant of Venice in
Shakespeare's Universe of Comedy.
Revisionist Pr.
Maru, Olavi.
xMaru, Olavi.
Digest of Bar Association Ethics Opinions. Am
Bar Foun.
Marulli, Luciana.
xMarulli, Luciana.
Documentation of the United Nations System:
Co-Ordination in Its Bibliographic Control.
Scarecrow.
Maruyama, T. *see* Maruyama, Takeo.
Maruyama, Takeo, 1936-
xMaruyama, T.
Stochastic Problems in Population Genetics.
Springer-Verlag.
Marvan, Jiri.
xMarvan, Jiri.
Prehistoric Slavic Contraction. Pa St U Pr.
Marvell, Charles.
xMarvell, Charles.

In Defense of Nixon: A Study in Political
Psychology & Political Pathology. Am
Classical Coll Pr.

Marvin, Francis S. *see* Marvin, Francis Sydney.

Marvin, Francis Sydney.
xMarvin, Francis S.
ed. Art & Civilization: Essays. Arno.
Comte: The Founder of Sociology. Russell.

Marvin, John T.
xMarvin, John T.
The Complete Cairn Terrier. Howell Bk.
The Complete West Highland White Terrier.
Howell Bk.

Marvin, Philip. *see* Marvin, Philip Roger.

Marvin, Philip Roger, 1916-
xMarvin, Philip.
Product Planning Simplified. Am Mgmt.

Marwell, G. *see* Marwell, Gerald.

Marwell, Gerald.
xMarwell, G.
Cooperation: An Experimental Analysis. Acad
Pr.

Marwick, William H. *see* Marwick, William Hutton.

Marwick, William Hutton.
xMarwick, William H.
Economic Developments in Victorian Scotland.
Kelley.

Marwitt, John P.
xMarwitt, John P.
Median Village & Fremont Culture Regional
Variation. AMS Pr.
Median Village & Fremont Culture Regional
Variation. U of Utah Pr.

Marx, Anne.
xMarx, Anne.
By Way of People. Golden Quill.

Marx, Arthur, 1921-
xMarx, Arthur.
Goldwyn: A Biography of the Man Behind the
Myth. Norton.
Red Skelton. Dutton.

Marx, G. F. *see* Marx, Gertie F.

Marx, Gary T.
xMarx, Gary T.
Protest & Prejudice: A Study of Belief in the
Black Community. Greenwood.

Marx, Gertie F., 1910-
xMarx, G. F.
Clinical Management of Mother & Newborn.
Springer-Verlag.

Marx, Groucho, 1891-
xMarx, Groucho.
Groucho & Me. Manor Bks.

Marx, Herbert L.
xMarx, Herbert L.
ed. Religions in America. Wilson.
ed. The World Food Crisis. Wilson.

Marx, Karl.
xMarx, Karl.

Capital: A Critique of Political Economy.
Random.
Cologne Communist Trial. Beekman Pubs.
The Cologne Communist Trial. Intl Pub Co.
The Communist Manifesto. AHM Pub.
Communist Manifesto. C H Kerr.
Communist Manifesto. Intl Pub Co.
Communist Manifesto. NY Labor News.
Communist Manifesto. Path Pr NY.
Communist Manifesto. Penguin.
Communist Manifesto. WSP.
Contribution to the Critique of Political
Economy. Intl Pub Co.
Critique of Hegel's "Philosophy of Right".
Cambridge U Pr.
Early Writings. McGraw.
Early Writings. Random.
Eastern Question: A Reprint of Letters Written
1853-1856, Dealing with the Events of the
Crimean War. B Franklin.
German Ideology. Intl Pub Co.
The German Ideology. Progress Pubs.
The Grundrisse. Har-Row.
The Grundrisse: Foundations of the Critique of
Political Economy. Random.
Letters to Dr. Kugelmann. Greenwood.
On Society & Social Change. U of Chicago Pr.
Poverty of Philosophy. Intl Pub Co.
Revolution in Spain. Greenwood.
Theories of Surplus Value: Selections. Kelley.

Marx, Melvin H. *see* Marx, Melvin Herman.

Marx, Melvin Herman.
xMarx, Melvin H.
Introduction to Psychology: Problems,
Procedures, & Principles. Macmillan.
Systems & Theories in Psychology. McGraw.

Marx, Milton.
xMarx, Milton.
The Enjoyment of Drama. Irvington.

Marx, Robert F. 1933-
xMarx, Robert F.
Spanish Treasure in Florida Waters: A Billion
Dollar Graveyard. Mariners Boston.

Marx, Samuel, 1902-
xMarx, Samuel.
Queen of the Ritz. Bobbs.

Marxhausen, Joanne.
xMarxhausen, Joanne.
I Am a Tree. Concordia.
I Am People. Concordia.
I Am the Sun. Concordia.
If I Should Die, If I Should Live. Concordia.

Marxhausen, Joanne. *see* Marxhausen, Joannne.

Marxhausen, Joannne.
xMarxhausen, Joanne.
I Am a Cloud. Concordia.

Marxsen, Willi, 1919-
xMarxsen, Willi.
The Beginnings of Christology, Together with
the Lord's Supper As a Christological
Problem. Fortress.
Lord's Supper As a Christological Problem.
Fortress.
Resurrection of Jesus of Nazareth. Fortress.

Mary, 1918-
xMary.
How Does Your Garden Grow?. Potter.

Mary Francis, Sister, P.c.
xMary Francis.
Right to Be Merry. Franciscan Herald.

Marye, George T. *see* Marye, George Thomas.

Marye, George Thomas, 1849-
xMarye, George T.
Nearing the End in Imperial Russia. Arno.

Marygrove College, Detroit.
xMarygrove College, Detroit, Michigan.

Into Her Own: The Status of Woman from
Ancient Times to the End of the Middle
Ages. Arno.

Marygrove College, Detroit, Michigan. *see* Marygrove
College, Detroit.

Maryland Historical Society.
xMaryland Historical Society.
Fund-Publications. AMS Pr.
In Memory of George Peabody. AMS Pr.
Muster Rolls & Other Records of Service of
Maryland Troops in the American Revolution
1775-1783. Genealog Pub.
ed. One Hundred Fiftieth Anniversary of the
Founding of Baltimore: Proceedings. AMS
Pr.

Maryland Hospital Education Institute.
xMaryland Hospital Education Institute.
Controlling Hospital Liability: A Systems
Approach. Am Hospital.
Hospital-Sponsored Ambulatory Care: The
Governing Board's Role. Am Hospital.

Maryland. University. Lower Division Chemistry Staff.
xUniversity of Maryland Staff.
Laboratory Chemistry. Burgess.

Maryk, Michael.
xMaryk, Michael.
Deathbite. Andrews & McMeel.

Marzell, Ernst S.
xMarzell, Ernst S.
Great Inventions. Lerner Pubns.

Marzials, Frank T. *see* Marzials, Frank Thomas.

Marzials, Frank Thomas, Sir, 1840-1912
xMarzials, Frank T.
Browning. Folcroft.
Life of Charles Dickens. Folcroft.

Marzollo, Jean.
xMarzollo, Jean.
Close Your Eyes. Dial.
Learning Through Play. Har-Row.
Learning Through Play. Har-Row
Supertot: Creative Learning Activities for
Children One to Three & Sympathetic
Advice for Their Parents. Har-Row.

Marzuban-Nama.
xMarzuban-Nama.
Tales of Marzuban. Greenwood.

Mas, Frank du. *see* Du Mas, Frank.

Masani, Shakuntala.
xMasani, Shakuntala.
The Story of Indira. Intl Bk Dist.

Masani, Z. *see* Masani, Zareer.

Masani, Zareer.
xMasani, Z.
Indira Gandhi: A Biography. Brown Bk.

Masaryk, Thomas G. *see* Masaryk, Tomas Garrigue.

Masaryk, Tomas G. *see* Masaryk, Tomas Garrigue.

**Masaryk, Tomas Garrigue, Pres. Czechoslovak Republic,
1850-1937**
xMasaryk, Thomas G.
Ideals of Humanity, & How to Work. Arno.
Modern Man & Religion. Arno.
Suicide & the Meaning of Civilization. U of
Chicago Pr.
xMasaryk, Tomas G.
Modern Man & Religion. Greenwood.

Mascetta, Joseph A.
xMascetta, Joseph A.
Modern Chemistry in Review. Barron.

Maschler, Fay.
xMaschler, Fay.
T. G. & Moonie Go Shopping. Doubleday.

Mascord, Ramon.
xMascord, Ramon.
Australian Spiders in Colour. C E Tuttle.

Mascotte, John P.
xMascotte, John P.
Finding Commission Dollars in Your Client's
Financial Statements. Natl Underwriter.

Mase, Darrel J. *see* Mase, Darrel Jay.

Mase, Darrel Jay, 1905-
xMase, Darrel J.
Etiology of Articulatory Speech Defects: A
Comparison of the Incidence of Six Selected
Factors in Children Having Articulatory
Speech Defects, with the Incidence of the
Same Factors in Children Not Having Speech
Defects. AMS Pr.
Masefield, Geoffrey B. *see* Masefield, Geoffrey Bussell.
Masefield, Geoffrey Bussell.
xMasefield, Geoffrey B.
A History of the Colonial Agricultural Service.
Oxford U Pr.
Masefield, John, 1878-1967
xMasefield, John.
Captain Margaret: A Romance. Scholarly.
Chaucer. Folcroft.
ed. My Favourite English Poems. Arno.
Some Memories of W. B. Yeats. Biblio Dist.
Some Memories of W. B. Yeats. Folcroft.
Tarpaulin Muster. Arno.
Masefield, Muriel A. *see* Masefield, Muriel Agnes
Bussell.
Masefield, Muriel Agnes Bussell.
xMasefield, Muriel A.
Peacocks & Primroses: A Survey of Disraeli's
Novels. Kraus Repr.
Maser, Jack D.
xMaser, Jack D.
ed. Efferent Organization & the Integration of
Behavior. Acad Pr.
ed. Psychopathology: Experimental Models. W
H Freeman.
Maser, Werner.
xMaser, Werner.
Hitler's Letters & Notes. Har-Row.
Nuremberg: A Nation on Trial. Scribner.
Maseri, Attilio.
xMaseri, Attilo.
ed. Primary & Secondary Angina Pectoris.
Grune.
Maseri, Attilo. *see* Maseri, Attilio.
Masiello, Joseph.
xMasiello, Joseph.
Family Trouble. PB.
Maskell, David.
xMaskell, David.
The Historical Epic in France 1500-1700.
Oxford U Pr.
Maskelyne, Nevil.
xMaskelyne, Nevil.
Maskelyne on the Performance of Magic.
Dover.
Maskelyne on the Performance of Magic. Peter
Smith.
Maslow, Abraham H. *see* Maslow, Abraham Harold.
Maslow, Abraham Harold.
xMaslow, Abraham H.
The Farther Reaches of Human Nature.
Penguin.
The Journals of A. H. Maslow. Brooks-Cole.
Psychology of Science: A Reconnaissance.
Regnery-Gateway.
Religions, Values, & Peak-Experiences.
Penguin.
Toward a Psychology of Being. Van Nos
Reinhold.
Maslowski, Peter, 1944-
xMaslowski, Peter.
Treason Must Be Made Odious: Military
Occupation & Wartime Reconstruction in
Nashville, Tennessee. 1862-65. Kraus Intl.
Mason, Aaron S.
xMason, Aaron S.
Clinical Handbook of Antipsychotic Drug
Therapy. Brunner Mazel.
Mason, Alpheus T. *see* Mason, Alpheus Thomas.
Mason, Alpheus Thomas, 1899-
xMason, Alpheus T.

Free Government in the Making: Readings in
American Political Thought. Oxford U Pr.
Organized Labor & the Law. Arno.
Security Through Freedom: American Political
Thought & Practice. Cornell U Pr.
Mason, Anita.
xMason, Anita.
An Illustrated Dictionary of Jewellery.
Har-Row.
Mason, Anne.
xMason, Anne.
Swiss Cooking. Transatlantic.
Mason, B. J. *see* Mason, Basil John.
Mason, Basil John.
xMason, B. J.
Clouds, Rain & Rainmaking. Cambridge U Pr.
Mason, Bernard S. *see* Mason, Bernard Sterling.
Mason, Bernard Sterling, 1896-
xMason, Bernard S.
Drums, Tomtoms & Rattles: Primitive
Percussion Instruments for Modern Use.
Peter Smith.
Woodcraft & Camping. Dover.
Mason, Betty.
xMason, Betty.
I Go to School. Broadman.
Mason, Brian.
xMason, Brian.
Principles of Geochemistry. Wiley.
Mason, Bruce B. *see* Mason, Bruce Bonner.
Mason, Bruce Bonner.
xMason, Bruce B.
Constitutional Government in Arizona. Navajo
Coll Pr.
Mason, C. M. *see* Mason, Christopher M.
Mason, C. R. *see* Mason, C. Russell.
Mason, C. Russell.
xMason, C. R.
Art & Science of Protective Relaying. Wiley.
Mason, Carleton D. *see* Mason, Carleton Donald.
Mason, Carleton Donald, 1903-
xMason, Carleton D.
Adaptations of Instruction to Individual
Differences in the Preparation of Teachers in
Normal Schools & Teachers Colleges. AMS
Pr.
Mason, Christopher M.
xMason, C. M.
ed. Effective Management of Resources: The
International Politics of the North Sea.
Nichols Pub.
Mason, Clarence. *see* Mason, Clarence E.
Mason, Clarence E.
xMason, Clarence.
Love Song. Moody.
Mason, Daniel G. *see* Mason, Daniel Gregory.
Mason, Daniel Gregory, 1873-1953
xMason, Daniel G.
Chamber Music of Brahms. AMS Pr.
Chamber Music of Brahms. Arno.
Contemporary Composers. AMS Pr.
Dilemma of American Music, & Other Essays.
Greenwood.
From Grieg to Brahms. AMS Pr.
Orchestral Instruments & What They Do: A
Primer for Concert-Goers. Greenwood.
Tune in America!: A Study of Our Coming
Musical Independence. AMS Pr.
Mason, David, 1939-
xMason, David.
Thalidomide: My Fight. Allen Unwin.
Mason, Dean T.
xMason, Dean T.
Cardiac Emergencies. Williams & Wilkins.
Mason, Donald L.
xMason, Donald L.
The Fine Art of Art Security: Protecting Public
& Private Collections Against Theft, Fire &
Vandalism. Van Nos Reinhold.
Mason, Edward E. *see* Mason, Edward Eaton.

Mason, Edward Eaton, 1920-
xMason, Edward E.
Pref. by Fluid, Electrolyte & Nutrient Therapy
in Surgery. Lea & Febiger.
Mason, Edward S. *see* Mason, Edward Sagendorph.
Mason, Edward Sagendorph, 1899-
xMason, Edward S.
Controlling World Trade: Cartels &
Commodity Agreements. Arno.
ed. Corporation in Modern Society. Atheneum.
ed. Corporation in Modern Society. Harvard U
Pr.
Economic Concentration & the Monopoly
Problem. Atheneum.
Economic Concentration & the Monopoly
Problem. Harvard U Pr.
Economic Development in India & Pakistan.
AMS Pr.
On the Appropriate Size of a Development
Program. AMS Pr.
On the Appropriate Size of a Development
Program. Harvard U Intl Aff.
Mason, Edwin.
xMason, Edwin.
Collaborative Learning. Agathon.
Collaborative Learning. Schocken.
Mason, Emanuel J.
xMason, Emanuel J.
Understanding & Conducting Research:
Applications in Education & the Behavioral
Sciences. McGraw.
Mason, Eugene.
xMason, Eugene.
tr. Aucassin & Nicolette & Other Mediaeval
Romances & Legends. Arden Lib.
Mason, F. Van Wyck. *see* Mason, Van Wyck.
Mason, Frances. *see* Mason, Francis Claiborne.
Mason, Frances (Baker).
xMason, Frances B.
Great Design: Order & Progress in Nature.
Arno.
Mason, Frances B. *see* Mason, Frances (Baker).
Mason, Francis Claiborne.
xMason, Frances.
This Unchanging Mask. AMS Pr.
Mason, Francis Van Wyck, 1901-
xMason, F. Van Wyck.
Maryland Colony. Macmillan.
Mason, Gabriel R. *see* Mason, Gabriel Richard.
Mason, Gabriel Richard.
xMason, Gabriel R.
ed. Great American Liberals. Arno.
Mason, Gene L.
xMason, Gene L.
The Politics of Exploitation. Random.
Mason, George, 1725-1792
xMason, George.
The Papers of George Mason. U of NC Pr.
Mason, George. *see* Mason, George E.
Mason, George E.
xMason, George.
Full Count. Allyn.
On the Level. Allyn.
Mason, George F. *see* Mason, George Frederick.
Mason, George Frederick, 1904-
xMason, George F.
illus. Animal Appetites. Morrow.
illus. Animal Habits. Morrow.
illus. Moose Group. Hastings.
Mason, Germaine.
xMason, Germaine.
Concise Survey of French Literature.
Greenwood.
A Concise Survey of French Literature.
Littlefield.
Mason, Henry L. *see* Mason, Henry Lloyd.
Mason, Henry Lloyd.
xMason, Henry L.

College & University Government: A
    Handbook of Principle & Practice. Tulane
    Stud Pol.
Mason, Herbert, 1932-
    xMason, Herbert.
    The Death of Al-Hallaj: A Dramatic Narrative.
        U of Notre Dame Pr.
    Summer Light. FS&G.
Mason, Herbert M. see Mason, Herbert Molloy.
Mason, Herbert Molloy.
    xMason, Herbert M.
    Secrets of the Supernatural. Schol Bk Serv.
Mason, Hilary, 1895-
    xMason, Hilary.
    Morisco. Atheneum.
    Morisco. Ballantine.
Mason, Isaac, 1822-
    xMason, Isaac.
    Life of Isaac Mason As a Slave. Arno.
Mason, J. Alden. see Mason, John Alden.
Mason, J. E. see Mason, John Edward.
Mason, J. M. see Mason, John Monck.
Mason, James.
    xMason, James.
    Art of Chess. Dover.
Mason, James D.
    xMason, James D.
    Combat Handgun Shooting. C C Thomas.
Mason, Jennie.
    xMason, Jennie.
    Introduction to Word Processing. Bobbs.
Mason, John Alden, 1885-1967
    xMason, J. Alden.
    Ancient Civilizations of Peru. Penguin.
Mason, John B. see Mason, John Brown.
Mason, John Brown.
    xMason, John B.
    Thailand Bibliography. Greenwood.
Mason, John Edward, 1892-
    xMason, J. E.
    Gentlefolk in the Making: Studies in the
        History of English Courtesy Literature &
        Related Topics from 1531 to 1774. Octagon.
Mason, John Monck, 1726-1809
    xMason, J. M.
    Comments on the Last Edition of
        Shakespeare's Plays. AMS Pr.
    Comments on the Several Editions of
        Shakespeare's Plays, Extended to Those of
        Malone & Steevens. AMS Pr.
Mason, Joseph G.
    xMason, Joseph G.
    How to Build Your Management Skills.
        McGraw.
Mason, K. L. see Mason, K. L. J.
Mason, K. L. J.
    xMason, K. L.
    Advanced Spanish Course. Pergamon.
    Spanish Oral Drill Book. Pergamon.
Mason, L. John, 1950-
    xMason, L. John.
    Guide to Stress Reduction. Peace Pr.
Mason, Lauris.
    xMason, Lauris.
    ed. Print Collector's Quarterly: An Anthology
        of Essays on Eminent Printmakers of the
        World. Kraus Intl.
    Compiled by Print Reference Sources: A
        Selected Bibliography, 18th-20th Centuries.
        Kraus Intl.
Mason, Lowell.
    xMason, Lowell.
    Musical Letters from Abroad. Da Capo.
Mason, M. Elizabeth. see Mason, Mary Elizabeth.
Mason, Marion.
    xMason, Marion.
    The Dynamics of Clinical Dietetics. Wiley.
Mason, Mary Elizabeth.
    xMason, M. Elizabeth.

Active Life & Contemplative Life: A Study of
    the Concepts from Plato to the Present.
    Marquette.
Mason, Miriam E. see Mason, Miriam Evangeline.
Mason, Miriam Evangeline, 1899-
    xMason, Miriam E.
    Broomtail, Brother of Lightning. Macmillan.
    Caroline & Her Kettle Named Maud.
        Macmillan.
    Hominy & His Blunt-Nosed Arrow. Macmillan.
Mason, Oliver.
    xMason, Oliver.
    The Gazetteer of England: England's Cities,
        Towns, Villages, & Hamlets: A
        Comprehensive List with Basic Details of
        Each. Rowman.
Mason, Otis T. see Mason, Otis Tufton.
Mason, Otis Tufton, 1838-1908
    xMason, Otis T.
    The Origins of Invention: A Study of Industry
        Among Primitive Peoples. Arno.
    The Origins of Invention: A Study of Industry
        Among Primitive Peoples. MIT Pr.
Mason, Philip.
    xMason, Philip.
    ed. India & Ceylon: Unity & Diversity: A
        Symposium. Oxford U Pr.
    Patterns of Dominance. Oxford U Pr.
    Prospero's Magic: Some Thoughts on Class &
        Race. Greenwood.
    Skinner's Horse. Har-Row.
Mason, Philip P. see Mason, Philip Parker.
Mason, Philip Parker.
    xMason, Philip P.
    Directory of Jewish Archival Institutions.
        Wayne St U Pr.
Mason, R. see Mason, Roger.
Mason, R. H. see Mason, Robert Hal.
Mason, R. H. P.
    xMason, Richard.
    A History of Japan. Free Pr.
Mason, R. Hal. see Mason, Robert Hal.
Mason, Ralph E.
    xMason, R.
    Marketing Practices & Principles. McGraw.
    xMason, Ralph E.
    Cooperative Occupational Education & Work
        Experience in the Curriculum. Interstate.
    Marketing & Distribution. McGraw.
Mason, Richard. see Mason, R. H. P.
Mason, Robert D. see Mason, Robert Deward.
Mason, Robert Deward, 1919-
    xMason, R.
    Essentials of Statistics. P-H.
    xMason, Robert D.
    Statistical Techniques in Business &
        Economics. Irwin.
Mason, Robert E. see Mason, Robert Emmett.
Mason, Robert Emmett.
    xMason, Robert E.
    Contemporary Educational Theory. Longman.
Mason, Robert Hal.
    xMason, R. H.
    The Economics of International Business.
        Krieger.
    xMason, R. Hal.
    The Economics of International Business.
        Wiley.
Mason, Robert L. see Mason, Robert Lee.
Mason, Robert Lee.
    xMason, Robert L.
    How to Choose the Wrong Marriage Partner &
        Live Unhappily Ever After. John Knox.
Mason, Roger, Ph.D.
    xMason, R.
    Petrology of the Metamorphic Rocks. Allen
        Unwin.
Mason, Ronald. see Mason, Ronald Charles.
Mason, Ronald Charles, 1912-
    xMason, Ronald.

The Spirit Above the Dust: A Study of
    Herman Melville. Appel.
Mason, Sheila.
    xMason, Sheila.
    The Toddler. Cambridge U Pr.
Mason, Shirlene.
    xMason, Shirlene.
    Daniel Defoe & the Status of Women. Eden
        Women.
Mason, Stephen F. see Mason, Stephen Finney.
Mason, Stephen Finney, 1923-
    xMason, Stephen F.
    History of the Sciences. Macmillan.
Mason, Stuart, 1872-1927
    xMason, Stuart.
    Oscar Wilde & the Aesthetic Movement.
        Haskell.
Mason, Theodore K.
    xMason, Theodore K.
    On the Ice in Antarctica. Dodd.
    The South Pole Ponies. Dodd.
Mason, Van Wyck, 1897-
    xMason, F. Van Wyck.
    Proud New Flags. Berkley Pub.
Mason, Warren P. see Mason, Warren Perry.
Mason, Warren Perry, 1900-
    xMason, Warren P.
    ed. Crystal Physics of Interaction Processes.
        Acad Pr.
Mason, William, 1829-1908
    xMason, William.
    Memories of a Musical Life. AMS Pr.
    Memories of a Musical Life. Da Capo.
Mason, William H.
    xMason, William H.
    Environmental Problems: Principles, Readings
        & Comments. Wm C Brown.
Masotti, Louis H.
    xMasotti, Louis H.
    ed. Suburbia in Transition. New Viewpoints.
Maspero, Henri, 1883-1945
    xMaspero, Henri.
    China in Antiquity. U of Mass Pr.
Masri, Allan.
    xMasri, Allan.
    The Golden Hills of California: A Descriptive
        Guide to the Mother Lode Counties of the
        Southern Mines. Western Tanager.
Mass, Nathaniel J.
    xMass, Nathaniel J.
    Economic Cycles: An Analysis of Underlying
        Causes. MIT Pr.
    ed. Readings in Urban Dynamics. MIT Pr.
Massabki, Charles.
    xMassabki, Charles.
    Who Is the Holy Spirit?. Alba.
Massachusetts (Colony) Court of Assistants.
    xMassachusetts Colony Court Of Assistants.
    Records of the Court of Assistants of the
        Colony of the Massachusetts Bay, 1630-1692.
        AMS Pr.
**Massachusetts (Colony). Provincial Congress, Feb.-May,
    1775.**
    xProvincial Congress of Massachusetts Colony,
        1775.
    Narrative of the Excursions & Ravages of the
        King's Troops Under Command of General
        Gage. Arno.
Massachusetts Bar Association. see Massachusetts
    Superior Courts.
Massachusetts Colony Court Of Assistants. see
    Massachusetts (Colony) Court of Assistants.
Massachusetts Commission on Cost of Living.
    xMassachusetts Commission on the Cost of Living.
    Report of the Commission on the Cost of
        Living. Arno.
**Massachusetts Commission on Old Age Pensions,
    Annuities and Insurance.**
    xMassachusetts Commission on Old Age Pensions,
        Annuities & Insurance.

Report of the Commission on Old Age
Pensions, Annuities & Insurance. Arno.
Massachusetts Commission on the Cost of Living. *see*
Massachusetts Commission on Cost of Living.
Massachusetts Department of Community Affairs. *see*
Massachusetts. Dept. of Community Affairs.
Massachusetts. Dept. of Community Affairs.
xMassachusetts Department of Community Affairs.
Built to Last: A Handbook on Recycling Old
Buildings. Preservation Pr.
Massachusetts. General Court.
xMassachusetts General Court.
Almshouse Experience: Collected Papers. Arno.
Massachusetts General Hospital. *see* Massachusetts
General Hospital, Boston.
Massachusetts General Hospital, Boston.
xMassachusetts General Hospital.
Manual of Nursing Procedures. Little.
xMassachusetts General Hospital Dietary Dept.
Diet Manual. Little.
Massachusetts General Hospital Dietary Dept. *see*
Massachusetts General Hospital, Boston.
Massachusetts Historical Society. *see* Massachusetts
Historical Society, Boston.
Massachusetts Historical Society, Boston.
xMassachusetts Historical Society.
Historical Index to the Pickering Papers.
Johnson Repr.
xMassachusetts Historical Society, Boston.
Catalog of Manuscripts of the Massachusetts
Historical Society, Boston. G K Hall.
Massachusetts Horticultural Society.
xMassachusetts Horticultural Society, Boston.
Dictionary Catalog of the Library of the
Massachusetts Horticultural Society. G K
Hall.
Massachusetts Sec. of the Commonwealth. *see*
Massachusetts Secretary of the Commonwealth.
Massachusetts Secretary of the Commonwealth.
xMassachusetts Sec. of the Commonwealth.
Statistical Tables Exhibiting the Condition &
Products of Certain Branches of Industry in
Massachusetts. Kelley.
xMassachusetts, Secretary of the Commonwealth.
List of Persons Whose Names Have Been
Changed in Massachusetts, 1780-1892.
Genealog Pub.
**Massachusetts. Special Commission on Investigation of
the Judicial System.**
xSpecial Commission on Investigation of the
Judicial System, Commonwealth of
Massachusetts.
Report: Under Chapter Sixty-Two of the
Resolves of 1935. Arno.
Massachusetts Superior Courts.
xMassachusetts Bar Association.
Superior Court Rules Annotated, 1974. W S
Hein.
Massam, B. H. *see* Massam, Bryan H.
Massam, Bryan. *see* Massam, Bryan H.
Massam, Bryan H.
xMassam, B. H.
The Spatial Structure of Administrative
Systems. Assn Am Geographers.
xMassam, Bryan.
Location & Space in Social Administration.
Halsted Pr.
Massaro, Vincent G.
xMassaro, Vincent G.
A Guide to Forecasting Interest Rates.
Conference Bd.
Massart, D. L.
xMassart, D. L.
Evaluation & Optimization of Laboratory
Methods & Analytical Procedures. Elsevier.
Massee, William E. *see* Massee, William Edman.
Massee, William Edman.
xMassee, William E.

Massee's Guide to Wines of America. Dutton.
Massell, Gregory J., 1925-
xMassell, Gregory L.
Surrogate Proletariat: Moslem Women &
Revolutionary Strategies in Soviet Central
Asia, 1919-1929. Princeton U Pr.
Massell, Gregory L. *see* Massell, Gregory J.
Masselman, George.
xMasselman, George.
Cradle of Colonialism. Elliots Bks.
Massena, Clarence E. Le. *see* Le Massena, Clarence E.
Massengale, John D.
xMassengale, John D.
The Principles & Problems of Coaching. C C
Thomas.
Masserman, J. H. *see* Masserman, Jules Hymen.
Masserman, Jules H. *see* Masserman, Jules Hymen.
Masserman, Jules Hymen, 1905-
xMasserman, J. H.
The Psychiatric Examination. Thieme-Stratton.
xMasserman, Jules H.
Principles & Practice of Biodynamic
Psychotherapy: An Integration Serial
Handbook of Modern Psychiatry.
Thieme-Stratton.
Theory & Therapy of Dynamic Psychiatry.
Aronson.
Massett, Larry.
xMassett, Larry.
Everyman's Guide to Drugs & Medicines.
Luce.
Massey, Charlotte.
xMassey, Charlotte.
The Bride of Invercoe. PB.
Massey, Floyd.
xMassey, Floyd.
Church Administration in the Black
Perspective. Judson.
Massey, Gerald, 1828-1907
xMassey, Gerald.
Gerald Massey's Lectures. Weiser.
Massey, Harrie. *see* Massey, Harrie Stewart Wilson.
Massey, Harrie Stewart Wilson, Sir, 1908-
xMassey, Harrie.
Negative Ions. Cambridge U Pr.
Massey, Howard C.
xMassey, Howard C.
Basic Plumbing Illustrated. Craftsman.
Plumbers Handbook. Craftsman.
Massey, John K.
xMassey, John K.
ed. Comic Spirit in America. Scribner.
Massey, L. D. *see* Massey, Leonard Daniel.
Massey, Leonard Daniel.
xMassey, L. D.
Probability & Statistics. McGraw.
Massey, Raymond.
xMassey, Raymond.
When I Was Young. Little.
Massey, Reginald.
xMassey, Reginald.
The Music of India. Taplinger.
Massey, Robert.
xMassey, Robert.
Formulas for Painters. Watson-Guptill.
Massey, W. S. *see* Massey, William S.
Massey, William S.
xMassey, W. S.
Algebraic Topology: An Introduction.
Springer-Verlag.
Massialas, Byron G., 1929-
xMassialas, Byron G.
Education & the Political System. A-W.
Massie, Diane R. *see* Massie, Diane Redfield.
Massie, Diane Redfield.
xMassie, Diane R.
illus. Briar Rose & the Golden Eggs. Schol Bk
Serv.
illus. Chameleon Was a Spy. T Y Crowell.
xMassie, Dianne.

illus. Monstrous Glisson Glop. Schol Bk Serv.
xMassie, Dianne R.
Monstrous Glisson Glop. Schol Bk Serv.
Massie, Dianne. *see* Massie, Diane Redfield.
Massie, Dianne R. *see* Massie, Diane Redfield.
Massie, Joseph L.
xMassie, Joseph L.
Essentials of Management. P-H.
Massie, Robert. *see* Massie, Robert K.
Massie, Robert K.
xMassie, Robert.
Journey. Knopf.
Journey. Warner Bks.
xMassie, Robert K.
Nicholas & Alexandra. Dell.
Nicholas & Alexandra. Atheneum.
xMassie, Suzanne.
jt. auth. Journey. Knopf.
jt. auth. Journey. Warner Bks.
Massie, Suzanne. *see* Massie, Robert K.
Massignon, Genevieve.
xMassignon, Genevieve.
Folktales of France. U of Chicago Pr.
Massine, Leonide, 1896-
xMassine, Leonide.
Massine on Choreography: Theory & Exercises
in Composition. Merrimack Bk Serv.
Massinger, Philip.
xMassinger, Phillip.
City Madam. U of Nebr Pr.
Massinger, Phillip. *see* Massinger, Philip.
Massingham, Harold J. *see* Massingham, Harold John.
Massingham, Harold John.
xMassingham, Harold J.
ed. Great Victorians. Arno.
Great Victorians. R West.
Massion, J.
xMassion, J.
ed. Cerebro-Cerebellar Interactions. Elsevier.
Masso, Gildo, 1891-
xMasso, Gildo.
Education in Utopias. AMS Pr.
Massoglia, Elinor T. *see* Massoglia, Elinor Tripato.
Massoglia, Elinor Tripato.
xMassoglia, Elinor T.
Early Childhood Education in the Home.
Delmar.
Massola, Aldo.
xMassola, Aldo.
Bunjil's Cave: Myths, Legends & Superstitions
of the Aborigines of South-East Australia.
Humanities.
Masson, David, 1822-1907
xMasson, David.
De Quincey. R West.
DeQuincey. AMS Pr.
Drummond of Hawthornden: The Story of His
Life & Writings. Greenwood.
Drummond of Hawthornden: The Story of His
Life & Writings. Haskell.
Drummond of Hawthornden: The Story of His
Life & Writings. R West.
In the Footsteps of the Poets. Folcroft.
Wordsworth, Shelley, Keats, & Other Essays.
Arno.
Wordsworth, Shelley, Keats, & Other Essays. B
Franklin.
Wordsworth, Shelley, Keats & Other Essays.
Folcroft.
Masson, David. *see* Masson, David Mather.
Masson, David Mather.
xMasson, David.
ed. The Quarrel Between the Earl of
Manchester & Oliver Cromwell: An Episode
of the English Civil War. Johnson Repr.
Masson, Flora.
xMasson, Flora.

Brontes. Folcroft.
Brontes. Kennikat.
Masson, Madeleine.
xMasson, Madeleine.
I Never Kissed Paris Goodbye. David &
Charles.
Masson, Pierre, 1880-1959
xMasson, Pierre.
Human Tumors: Histology, Diagnosis, &
Technique. Wayne St U Pr.
Masson, Thomas L. *see* Masson, Thomas Lansing.
Masson, Thomas Lansing, 1866-1934
xMasson, Thomas L.
Our American Humorists. Arno.
Massry, Shaul G.
xMassry, Shaul G.
Clinical Aspects of Uremia & Dialysis. C C
Thomas.
ed. Renal Handling of Phosphate. Plenum Pub.
Massy, William F.
xMassy, William F.
Stochastic Models of Buying Behavior. MIT Pr.
Mast, Gerald, 1940-
xMast, Gerald.
The Comic Mind: Comedy & the Movies. U of
Chicago Pr.
ed. Film Theory & Criticism: Introductory
Readings. Oxford U Pr.
Filmguide to The Rules of the Game. Ind U
Pr.
Mast, Russel. *see* Mast, Russell L.
Mast, Russell L.
xMast, Russel.
Preach the Word. Faith & Life.
Masten, Arthur H. *see* Masten, Arthur Haynesworth.
Masten, Arthur Haynesworth, 1855-1935
xMasten, Arthur H.
Story of Adirondac. Syracuse U Pr.
Masten, Ric.
xMasten, Ric.
Speaking Poems. Sunflower Ink.
Masterman-Smith, Virginia.
xMasterman-Smith, Virginia.
The Treasure Trap. Schol Bk Serv.
Masters, Anthony, 1940-
xMasters, Anthony.
The Devil's Dominion: The Complete Story of
Hell & Satanism in the Modern World.
Putnam.
Masters, Dexter.
xMasters, Dexter.
jt. ed. & ed. One World or None. Arno.
Masters, Edgar L. *see* Masters, Edgar Lee.
Masters, Edgar Lee, 1869-1950
xMasters, Edgar L.
A Book of Verses. Gordon Pr.
Mark Twain: A Portrait. Biblo.
Whitman. Biblo.
Masters, G. Mallary. *see* Masters, George Mallary.
Masters, George.
xMasters, George.
The Masters Way to Beauty. NAL.
Masters, George Mallary.
xMasters, G. Mallary.
Rabelaisian Dialectic & the Platonic-Hermetic
Tradition. State U NY Pr.
Masters, Gilbert. *see* Masters, Gilbert M.
Masters, Gilbert M.
xMasters, Gilbert.
Introduction to Environmental Science &
Technology. Wiley.
Masters, Hilary.
xMasters, Hilary.
American Marriage. Macmillan.
Masters, James I.
xMasters, James I.
ed. North Fork & Shelter Island Guidebook.
Blue Claw.
Masters, Roger D.
xMasters, Roger D.

The Political Philosophy of Rousseau.
Princeton U Pr.
Masters, Roy.
xMasters, Roy.
How to Conquer Suffering Without Doctors.
Foun Human Under.
How to Control Your Emotions. Foun Human
Under.
How Your Mind Can Keep You Well. Fawcett.
How Your Mind Can Keep You Well. Foun
Human Under.
Masters, William H.
xMasters, William H.
Homosexuality in Perspective. Little.
Human Sexual Inadequacy. Bantam.
Human Sexual Inadequacy. Little.
Masterson, Amanda R.
xMasterson, Amanda R.
ed. Index to the Proceedings of the Lunar &
Planetary Science Conferences, Houston,
Texas, 1970-1978. Pergamon.
Masterson, B. J. *see* Masterson, Byron J.
Masterson, Byron J.
xMasterson, B. J.
Manual of Gynecologic Surgery.
Springer-Verlag.
Masterson, Dan, 1934-
xMasterson, Dan.
On Earth As It Is: Poems. U of Ill Pr.
Masterson, J. B.
xMasterson, J. B.
Rudge. Doubleday.
Masterson, Patrick.
xMasterson, Patrick.
Atheism & Alienation: A Study of the
Philosophical Sources of Contemporary
Atheism. U of Notre Dame Pr.
Masterton, Graham.
xMasterton, Graham.
Rich. PB.
Masterton, William L.
xMasterton, William L.
Chemical Principles. HR&W.
Mathematical Preparation for General
Chemistry. HR&W.
Mastny, Vojtech, 1936-
xMastny, Vojtech.
Czechs Under Nazi Rule: The Failure of
National Resistance, 1939-42. Columbia U
Pr.
Maston, Thomas B. *see* Maston, Thomas Bufford.
Maston, Thomas Bufford, 1897-
xMaston, Thomas B.
God's Will & Your Life. Broadman.
Mastronarde, Donald. *see* Mastronarde, Donald J.
Mastronarde, Donald J.
xMastronarde, Donald.
Contact & Discontinuity: Some Conventions of
Speech & Action on the Greek Tragic Stage.
U of Cal Pr.
Mata, Leonardo J.
xMata, Leonardo J.
The Children of Santa Maria Cauque: A
Prospective Field Study of Health & Growth.
MIT Pr.
Matane, Paulias.
xMatane, Paulias.
My Childhood in New Guinea. Oxford U Pr.
Matarazzo, James M., 1941-
xMatarazzo, James M.
Library Problems in Science & Technology.
Bowker.
Mateer, William H.
xMateer, William H.
Checkless Society: Its Cost Implications for the
Firm. Mich St U Busn.
Matejka, L. *see* Matejka, Ladislav.
Matejka, Ladislav, 1919-
xMatejka, L.

ed. Readings in Soviet Semiotics: Russian
Texts. Mich Slavic Pubns.
Matenko, Percy, 1901-
xMatenko, Percy.
Ludwig Tieck & America. AMS Pr.
Materer, Timothy, 1940-
xMaterer, Timothy.
Vortex: Pound, Eliot, & Lewis. Cornell U Pr.
Materials Advisory Board. *see* National Research
Council. Committee on Ceramic Processing.
Maternity Center Assn. *see* Maternity Center
Association.
Maternity Center Association.
xMaternity Center Assn.
Birth Atlas. Maternity Ctr.
xMaternity Center Association.
Baby Is Born. G&D.
Mates, Julian, 1927-
xMates, Julian.
The American Musical Stage Before 1800.
Rutgers U Pr.
Mathai, A. M.
xMathai, A. M.
Characterizations of the Normal Probability
Law. Halsted Pr.
Generalized Hypergeometric Functions with
Applications in Statistics & Physical Sciences.
Springer-Verlag.
The H-Function with Applications in Statistics
& Other Disciplines. Halsted Pr.
Mathe, G. *see* Mathe, Georges.
Mathe, Georges.
xMathe, G.
ed. Complications of Cancer Chemotherapy.
Springer-Verlag.
Mathematics Research Center, Univ. of Wisconsin,
Advanced Seminar. *see* Advanced Seminar on
Mathematical Programming, Madison, Wis., 1972.
Matheny, Kenneth B.
xMatheny, Kenneth B.
Therapy American Style: Person Power
Through Self-Help. Nelson-Hall.
Mather, Berkely, Pseud.
xMather, Berkely.
The Pagoda Tree. Scribner.
Mather, Cotton.
xMather, Cotton.
The Angel of Bethesda. Am Antiquarian.
Christian Philosopher: A Collection of the Best
Discoveries in Nature, with Religious
Improvements. Schol Facsimiles.
Life of Sir William Phips. AMS Pr.
Life of Sir William Phips. Somerset Pub.
Paterna: The Autobiography of Cotton Mather.
Schol Facsimiles.
Present State of New England. Haskell.
Mather, Eleanore P. *see* Mather, Eleanore Price.
Mather, Eleanore Price, 1910-
xMather, Eleanore P.
Anna Brinton: A Study in Quaker Character.
Pendle Hill.
Mather, Frank J. *see* Mather, Frank Jewett.
Mather, Frank Jewett, 1868-1953
xMather, Frank J.
Estimates in Art. AMS Pr.
Mather, Frederick C. *see* Mather, Frederick Clare.
Mather, Frederick Clare.
xMather, Frederick C.
Public Order in the Age of the Chartists.
Kelley.
Mather, Increase, 1639-1723
xMather, Increase.
Life & Death of That Reverend Man of God,
Mr. Richard Mather. York Mail Print.
Mather, J. Marshall. *see* Mather, Marshall.
Mather, J. Y.
xMather, J. Y.

ed. The Linguistic Atlas of Scotland: Scots
Section. Shoe String.
Mather Jackson, Edward A. *see* Mather Jackson, Edward
Arthur.
Mather, June, 1924-
xMather, June.
Learning Can Be Child's Play: How Parents
Can Help Slower-Than-Average Preschool
Children Learn & Develop Through Play
Experiences. Abingdon.
Mather, Marshall, 1851-1916
xMather, J. Marshall.
Popular Studies of Nineteenth Century Poets.
Folcroft.
Mather, P. M. *see* Mather, Paul M.
Mather, Paul M.
xMather, P. M.
Computational Methods of Multivariate
Analysis in Physical Geography. Wiley.
xMather, Paul M.
Computers in Geography: A Practical
Approach. Biblio Dist.
Mather, Richard, 1596-1669
xMather, Richard.
Church Covenant: Two Tracts. Arno.
Mather, Samuel, 1626-1671
xMather, Samuel.
The Figures or Types of the Old Testament.
Johnson Repr.
Mather Jackson, Edward Arthur, 1899-
xMather Jackson, Edward A.
Nathaniel Hawthorne, a Modest Man.
Greenwood.
Matheron, Georges.
xMatheron, Georges.
Random Sets & Integral Geometry. Wiley.
Mathers, Michael.
xMathers, Michael.
Riding the Rails. Gambit.
Mathes, J. C. *see* Mathes, John C.
Mathes, John C.
xMathes, J. C.
Designing Technical Reports: Writing for
Audiences in Organizations. Bobbs.
Mathes, Stephen J.
xMathes, Stephen J.
Clinical Atlas of Muscle & Musculocutaneous
Flaps. Mosby.
Mathesius, Vilem, 1882-1945
xMathesius, Vilem.
A Functional Analysis of Present Day English
on a General Linguistic Basis. Mouton.
Matheson, Ewing.
xMatheson, Ewing.
The Depreciation of Factories, Mines &
Industrial Undertakings & Their Valuation.
Arno.
Matheson, John R. *see* Matheson, John Ross.
Matheson, John Ross.
xMatheson, John R.
Canada's Flag: A Search for a Country. G K
Hall.
Matheson, Max S.
xMatheson, Max S.
Pulse Radiolysis. Am Chemical.
Matheson, R. *see* Matheson, Ross.
Matheson, Richard, 1926-
xMatheson, Richard.
I Am Legend. Berkley Pub.
The Shores of Space. Berkley Pub.
The Shrinking Man. Berkley Pub.
The Shrinking Man. Gregg.
A Stir of Echoes. Berkley Pub.
Matheson, Ross.
xMatheson, R.
People Development in Developing Countries.
Halsted Pr.
Matheson, Sylvia A.
xMatheson, Sylvia A.

Persia: An Archaeological Guide. Merrimack
Bk Serv.
Mathew, Arnold H. *see* Mathew, Arnold Harris.
Mathew, Arnold Harris, 1852-1919
xMathew, Arnold H.
tr. Old Catholic Missal & Ritual. AMS Pr.
Mathew, Brian.
xMathew, Brian.
Dwarf Bulbs. David & Charles.
The Larger Bulbs. David & Charles.
Mathew, David, Abp, 1902-
xMathew, David.
Acton, the Formative Years. Greenwood.
Celtic Peoples & Renaissance Europe: A Study
of the Celtic & Spanish Influences on
Elizabethan History. Appel.
Lord Acton & His Times. U of Ala Pr.
Mathew, E. T. *see* Mathew, Elangikal Thomas.
Mathew, Elangikal Thomas.
xMathew, E. T.
Agricultural Taxation & Economic
Development in India. Asia.
Mathew, Frank. *see* Mathew, Frank James.
Mathew, Frank James, 1865-1924
xMathew, Frank.
An Image of Shakespeare. Haskell.
An Image of Shakespeare. R West.
Mathews, Chester O. *see* Mathews, Chester Ora.
Mathews, Chester Ora, 1895-
xMathews, Chester O.
The Grade Placement of Curriculum Materials
in the Social Studies. AMS Pr.
Mathews, Cornelius, 1817-1889
xMathews, Cornelius.
The Career of Puffer Hopkins. Mss Info.
The Various Writings of Cornelius Mathews.
AMS Pr.
Mathews, Donald G.
xMathews, Donald G.
Religion in the Old South. U of Chicago Pr.
Slavery & Methodism: A Chapter in American
Morality, 1780-1845. Greenwood.
Mathews, Donald K.
xMathews, Donald K.
Measurement in Physical Education. HR&W.
Mathews, Geda B. *see* Mathews, Geda Bradley.
Mathews, Geda Bradley.
xMathews, Geda B.
What Was That!. Western Pub.
Mathews, Godfrey W.
xMathews, Godfrey W.
Chester Mystery Plays. Folcroft.
Mathews, John J. *see* Mathews, John Joseph.
Mathews, John Joseph, 1895-
xMathews, John J.
Osages: Children of the Middle Waters. U of
Okla Pr.
Sundown. Gregg.
Mathews, John M. *see* Mathews, John Mabry.
Mathews, John Mabry, 1883-
xMathews, John M.
Legislative & Judicial History of the Fifteenth
Amendment. AMS Pr.
Legislative & Judicial History of the Fifteenth
Amendment. Da Capo.
Mathews, Joseph M. *see* Mathews, Joseph Mcdowell.
Mathews, Joseph Mcdowell, 1847-1928
xMathews, Joseph M.
How to Succeed in the Practice of Medicine.
Arno.
Mathews, Louise.
xMathews, Louise.
Bunches & Bunches of Bunnies. Schol Bk Serv.
Bunches & Bunches of Bunnies. Dodd.
Mathews, M. B. *see* Mathews, Martin B.
Mathews, Marcia M.
xMathews, Marcia M.
The Freedom Star. Coward.
Mathews, Martin B., 1912-
xMathews, M. B.

Connective Tissue: Macromolecular Structure
& Evolution. Springer-Verlag.
Mathews, Mitford M. *see* Mathews, Mitford Mcleod.
Mathews, Mitford Mcleod, 1891-
xMathews, Mitford M.
ed. Americanisms: A Dictionary of Selected
Americanisms on Historical Principles. U of
Chicago Pr.
Some Sources of Southernisms. Greenwood.
Mathews, P. M. *see* Mathews, Piravonu Mathews.
Mathews, Piravonu Mathews.
xMathews, P. M.
A Textbook of Quantum Mechanics. McGraw.
Mathews, Richard, 1944-
xMathews, Richard.
Lightning from a Clear Sky: Tolkien, the
Trilogy & the Silmarillion. Borgo Pr.
Worlds Beyond the World: The Fantastic
Vision of William Morris. Borgo Pr.
Mathews, Shailer.
xMathews, Shailer.
Contributions of Science to Religion. Arno.
ed. Dictionary of Religion & Ethics. Gale.
Faith of Modernism. AMS Pr.
Mathews, Sibyl I.
xMathews, Sibyl I.
Charted Designs for Needlemade Rugs. Dover.
Mathews, William S. *see* Mathews, William Smythe
Babcock.
Mathews, William Smythe Babcock.
xMathews, William S.
Pronouncing & Defining Dictionary of Music.
AMS Pr.
Mathews, Willis W., 1917-
xMathews, Willis W.
Atlas of Descriptive Embryology. Macmillan.
Mathews, Winifred, 1894-
xMathews, Winifred.
Dauntless Women: Stories of Pioneer Wives.
Arno.
Mathews, Zena P. *see* Mathews, Zena Pearlstone.
Mathews, Zena Pearlstone.
xMathews, Zena P.
The Relation of Seneca False Face Masks to
Seneca & Ontario Archeology. Garland Pub.
Mathewson, C. H. *see* Mathewson, Champion Herbert.
Mathewson, Champion Herbert, 1881-
xMathewson, C. H.
Critical Shear Stress & Incongruent Shear in
Plastic Deformation. Shoe String.
Mathewson, G. F. *see* Mathewson, G. Frank.
Mathewson, G. Frank.
xMathewson, G. F.
Fiscal Transfer Pricing in Multinational
Corporations. U of Toronto Pr.
Mathewson, Hugh S.
xMathewson, Hugh S.
Respiratory Therapy in Critical Care. Mosby.
Mathewson, Rufus W.
xMathewson, Rufus W.
The Positive Hero in Russian Literature.
Stanford U Pr.
Mathias, Bob.
xMathias, Bob.
Simple Wooden Toymaking. Hamlyn-Amer.
Mathias, William. *see* Mathias, William J.
Mathias, William J.
xMathias, William.
Foundations of Criminal Justice. P-H.
Mathias, Willis D. *see* Mathias, Willis David.
Mathias, Willis David, 1898-
xMathias, Willis D.
Ideas of God & Conduct. AMS Pr.
Mathiassen, Therkel, 1892-
xMathiassen, Therkel.

Archaeological Collections from the Western
   Eskimos. AMS Pr.
Contributions to the Physiography of
   Southampton Island. AMS Pr.
Mathies, Lorraine.
   xMathies, Lorraine.
   Information Sources & Services in Education.
      Phi Delta Kappa.
Mathiesen, Egon, 1907-
   xMathiesen, Egon.
   Oswald the Monkey. Astor-Honor.
Mathiesen, Elva.
   xMathiesen, Elva.
   Sourdough. Mathiesen Edns.
Mathiesen, Thomas.
   xMathiesen, Thomas.
   The Politics of Abolition. Halsted Pr.
Mathieson, Elizabeth L. *see* Mathieson, Elizabeth Laird.
Mathieson, Elizabeth Laird, 1898-
   xMathieson, Elizabeth L.
   The Complete Book of Crochet. T Y Crowell.
Mathieson, Margaret.
   xMathieson, Margaret.
   The Preachers of Culture: A Study of English
      & Its Teachers. Allen Unwin.
   The Preachers of Culture: A Study of English
      & Its Teachers. Rowman.
Mathieson, R. S.
   xMathieson, Raymond S.
   Japan's Role in Soviet Economic Growth:
      Transfer of Technology Since 1965. Praeger.
Mathieson, Raymond S. *see* Mathieson, R. S.
Mathieson, Theodore.
   xMathieson, Theodore.
   Devil & Ben Franklin. S&S.
Mathieson, William L. *see* Mathieson, William Law.
Mathieson, William Law, 1868-
   xMathieson, William L.
   British Slave Emancipation, 1838-1849.
      Octagon.
   British Slavery & Its Abolition, 1834-1838.
      Octagon.
   Great Britain & the Slave Trade, 1839-1865.
      Octagon.
Mathieu, Bertrand.
   xMathieu, Bertrand.
   Orpheus in Brooklyn: Orphism, Rimbaud, &
      Henry Miller. Mouton.
Mathieu, Robert P.
   xMathieu, Robert P.
   Hospital & Nursing Home Management: An
      Instructional & Administrative Manual.
      Saunders.
Mathiot, Madeleine.
   xMathiot, Madeleine.
   ed. Ethnolinguistics: Boas, Sapir, & Whorf
      Revisited. Mouton.
Mathis, B. C. *see* Mathis, B. Claude.
Mathis, B. Claude.
   xMathis, B. C.
   Psychological Foundations of Education:
      Learning & Teaching. Acad Pr.
Mathis, Harry R., 1930-
   xMathis, Harry R.
   Along the Border: A History of Virgilina,
      Virginia & the Surrounding Area in Halifax &
      Mecklenburg Counties in Virginia & Person
      & Granville Counties in North Carolina. Va
      Bk.
Mathis, Jack.
   xMathis, Jack.
   Valley of the Cliffhangers. J Mathis Adv.
Mathis, Robert L.
   xMathis, Robert L.
   Personnel: Contemporary Perspectives &
      Applications. West Pub.
Mathis, Sharon B. *see* Mathis, Sharon Bell.
Mathis, Sharon Bell.
   xMathis, Sharon B.

The Hundred Penny Box. Viking Pr.
Listen for the Fig Tree. Viking Pr.
Ray Charles. T Y Crowell.
Mathisen, Marilyn. *see* Mathisen, Marilyn Purol.
Mathisen, Marilyn Purol.
   xMathisen, Marilyn.
   Apparel & Accessories. McGraw.
Mathur, D. C. *see* Mathur, Dinesh Chandra.
Mathur, Dinesh Chandra.
   xMathur, D. C.
   Naturalistic Philosophies of Experience: Studies
      in James, Dewey & Farber Against the
      Background of Husserl's Phenomenology.
      Green.
Mathur, Gautam.
   xMathur, Gautam.
   Planning for Steady Growth. Kelley.
Mathur, Iqbal.
   xMathur, Iqbal.
   Cases in Financial Management. Macmillan.
   Introduction to Financial Management.
      Macmillan.
Mathur, N. K.
   xMathur, N. K.
   Polymers As Aids in Organic Chemistry. Acad
      Pr.
Mathur, Y. B. *see* Mathur, Yaduvansh Bahadur.
Mathur, Yaduvansh Bahadur, 1929-
   xMathur, Y. B.
   Muslims & Changing India. Verry.
   Women's Education in India. Asia.
Matick, Richard E., 1933-
   xMatick, Richard E.
   Computer Storage Systems & Technology.
      Wiley.
Matin, Philip.
   xMatin, Philip.
   Handbook of Clinical Nuclear Medicine. Med
      Exam.
Matis, J. H. *see* Matis, James H.
Matis, James H.
   xMatis, J. H.
   ed. Compartmental Analysis of Ecosystem
      Models. Intl Co-Op.
Matisoff, Bernard S.
   xMatisoff, Bernard S.
   Handbook of Electronics Manufacturing
      Engineering. Van Nos Reinhold.
Matisoff, James A.
   xMatisoff, James A.
   Blessings, Curses, Hopes, & Fears:
      Psycho-Ostensive Expressions in Yiddish.
      Inst Study Human.
   The Grammar of Lahu. U of Cal Pr.
   The Loloish Tonal Split Revisited. Cellar.
   Variational Semantics in Tibeto-Burman: The
      "Organic" Approach to Linguistic
      Comparison. Inst Study Human.
Matlack, Lucius C.
   xMatlack, Lucius C.
   Antislavery Struggle & Triumph in the
      Methodist Episcopal Church. Negro U Pr.
Matles, James J.
   xMatles, James J.
   Them & Us: Struggles of a Rank-&-File Union.
      P-H.
Matlin, Margaret. *see* Matlin, Margaret W.
Matlin, Margaret W.
   xMatlin, Margaret.
   The Pollyanna Principle: Selectivity in
      Language, Memory, & Thought. Schenkman.
   xMatlin, Margaret W.
   Human Experimental Psychology. Brooks-Cole.
Matlis, Eben, 1923-
   xMatlis, Eben.
   Torsion-Free Modules. U of Chicago Pr.
Matlock, Jack F.
   xMatlock, Jack F.

An Index to the Collected Works of J. V.
   Stalin. Johnson Repr.
Matney, Roy M. *see* Matney, Roy Miller.
Matney, Roy Miller.
   xMatney, Roy M.
   Parallel Computing Structures & Algorithms for
      Logic Design Problems. Mgmt Info Serv.
Matsch, Charles L.
   xMatsch, Charles L.
   North America & the Great Ice Age. McGraw.
Matschat, Cecile H. *see* Matschat, Cecile Hulse.
Matschat, Cecile Hulse.
   xMatschat, Cecile H.
   Suwannee River: Strange Green Land. U of Ga
      Pr.
Matschoss, Conrad, 1871-1942
   xMatschoss, Conrad.
   Great Engineers. Arno.
Matsen, Herbert S. *see* Matsen, Herbert Stanley.
Matsen, Herbert Stanley, 1926-
   xMatsen, Herbert S.
   ed. Alessandro Achillini (1463-1512) & His
      Doctrine of Universals & Transcendentals.
      Bucknell U Pr.
Matson, Clive, 1941-
   xMatson, Clive.
   Space Age. SBD.
Matson, Floyd W.
   xMatson, Floyd W.
   The Idea of Man. Delacorte.
   The Idea of Man. Dell.
Matson, Katinka.
   xMatson, Katinka.
   Short Lives: Portraits of Writers, Painters,
      Poets, Actors, Musicians, & Performers Who
      Died Young. Morrow.
   The Working Actor: A Guide to the
      Profession. Penguin.
   The Working Actor: A Guide to the
      Profession. Viking Pr.
Matson, Peter H.
   xMatson, Peter H.
   A Place in the Country: A Narrative on the
      Imperfect Art of Homesteading & the Value
      of Ignorance. HarBraceJ.
Matson, Robert. *see* Matson, Robert W.
Matson, Robert W.
   xMatson, Robert.
   Compiled by North of San Francisco. Celestial
      Arts.
Matson, Tim, 1943-
   xMatson, Tim.
   Pilobolus. Random.
Matsubara, Hisako.
   xMatsubara, Hisako.
   Samurai. Times Bks.
Matsumoto, Teruo.
   xMatsumoto, Teruo.
   Current Management of Acute Gastrointestinal
      Hemorrhage. C C Thomas.
   Current Management of Trauma in Surgery &
      General Practice. C C Thomas.
Matsumoto, Toru, 1913-
   xMatsumoto, Toru.
   Beyond Prejudice. Arno.
Matsumura, Hideyuki, 1930-
   xMatsumura, Hideyuki.
   Commutative Algebra. Benjamin-Cummings.
Matsunaga, Daigan.
   xMatsunaga, Daigan L.
   Buddhist Concept of Hell. Philos Lib.
Matsunaga, Daigan L. *see* Matsunaga, Daigan.
Matsuoka, y Oko, 1916-
   xMatsuoka, Yoko.
   Daughter of the Pacific. Greenwood.
Matsuoka, Yoko. *see* Matsuoka, y Oko.
Matsushima, J. K. *see* Matsushima, John K.
Matsushima, John K., 1920-
   xMatsushima, J. K.

Feeding Beef Cattle. Springer-Verlag.
Matsushima, Seiz O.
xMatsushima, Seizo.
High-Yielding Rice Cultivation: A Method for
Maximizing Rice Yield Through "Ideal
Plants". Intl Schol Bk Serv.
Matsushima, Seizo. see Matsushima, Seiz O.
Matsushima, Y. see Matsushima, Yozo.
Matsushima, Yozo, 1921-
xMatsushima, Y.
Differentiable Manifolds. Dekker.
Matsushita, Shutaro, 1895-
xMatsushita, Shutaro.
Economic Effects of Public Debts. AMS Pr.
Matsushita, Takaaki.
xMatsushita, Takaaki.
Ink Painting. Weatherhill.
Matt, Stephen R.
xMatt, Stephen R.
Electricity & Basic Electronics. Goodheart.
Mattachine Society. see Mattachine Society of the
Niagara Frontier.
Mattachine Society of the Niagara Frontier.
xMattachine Society.
The Mattachine Review. Arno.
Matteotti, Giacomo, 1885-1924
xMatteotti, Giacomo.
The Fascisti Exposed: A Year of Fascist
Domination. Fertig.
Matter, Joseph A. see Matter, Joseph Allen.
Matter, Joseph Allen, 1901-
xMatter, Joseph A.
Love, Altruism, & World Crisis: The Challenge
of Pitirim Sorokin. Littlefield.
Love, Altruism, & World Crisis: The Challenge
of Pitirim Sorokin. Nelson-Hall.
Mattera, Joanne, 1948-
xMattera, Joanne.
Navajo Techniques for Today's Weaver.
Watson-Guptill.
Matters, Marion. see Matters, Marion E.
Matters, Marion E.
xMatters, Marion.
Compiled by Minnesota State Archives
Preliminary Check List. Minn Hist.
Matteson, D. M. see Matteson, David Maydole.
Matteson, David M. see Matteson, David Maydole.
Matteson, David Maydole, 1871-1949
xMatteson, D. M.
List of Manuscripts Concerning American
History Preserved in European Libraries.
Kraus Repr.
xMatteson, David M.
Organization of the Government Under the
Constitution. Da Capo.
Matteson, David R.
xMatteson, David R.
Adolescence Today: Sex Roles & the Search
for Identity. Dorsey.
Matteson, Esther.
xMatteson, Esther.
Comparative Studies in Amerindian Languages.
Mouton.
Comparative Studies in Amerindian Languages.
Summer Inst Ling.
Matteson, George.
xMatteson, George.
illus. Draggermen: Fishing on Georges Bank.
Schol Bk Serv.
Matthaei, Margaret B., 1921-
xMatthaei, Margaret B.
Reading About Psychology & You. Scott F.
Matthaei, Renate.
xMatthaei, Renate.
Luigi Pirandello. Ungar.
Matthay, Tobias A. see Matthay, Tobias Augustus.
Matthay, Tobias Augustus, 1858-1945
xMatthay, Tobias A.

Musical Interpretation, Its Laws & Principles,
& Their Application in Teaching &
Performing. Arno.
Musical Interpretation, Its Laws & Principles,
& Their Application in Teaching &
Performing. Greenwood.
Matthes, Carole.
xMatthes, Carole.
How Children Are Taught to Read. Prof Educ
Pubn.
Matthew, Brian.
xMatthew, Brian.
Stage Right: How to Run an Amateur Theatre
Group. Transatlantic.
Matthew, Christopher, 1939-
xMatthew, Christopher.
A Different World: Stories of Great Hotels.
Paddington.
Matthew, Donald. see Matthew, Donald James
Alexander.
Matthew, Donald James Alexander, 1930-
xMatthew, Donald.
The Medieval European Community. St
Martin.
The Norman Monasteries & Their English
Possessions. Greenwood.
Matthew, H. C. see Matthew, Henry Colin Gray.
Matthew, Helen G.
xMatthew, Helen G.
ed. Asia in the Modern World. NAL.
Matthew, Henry Colin Gray.
xMatthew, H. C.
The Liberal Imperialists: The Ideas & Politics
of a Post-Gladstonian Elite. Oxford U Pr.
Matthew, James E.
xMatthew, James E.
Literature of Music. Da Capo.
Matthews, A. G. see Matthews, Arnold Gwynne.
Matthews, Alfred W. see Matthews, Alfred Warren.
Matthews, Alfred Warren.
xMatthews, Alfred W.
The Development of St. Augustine from
Neoplatonism to Christianity, 386-391 A.D..
U Pr of Amer.
Matthews, Arnold G. see Matthews, Arnold Gwynne.
Matthews, Arnold Gwynne.
xMatthews, A. G.
Mr. Pepys & Nonconformity. Folcroft.
xMatthews, Arnold G.
Mr. Pepys & Nonconformity. Norwood Edns.
Matthews, Brander, 1852-1929
xMatthews, Brander.
ed. Ballads of Books. Gale.
ed. Ballads of Books. Granger Bk.
Books & Play-Books: Essays on Literature &
the Drama. Arno.
The Development of the Drama. Arno.
Historical Novel, & Other Essays. Arno.
Historical Novel & Other Essays. Gale.
Inquiries & Opinions. Arno.
Outlines in Local Color. Arno.
ed. Papers on Playmaking. Arno.
Stories of the Army. Arno.
Tales of Fantasy & Fact. Arno.
Matthews, Don Q.
xMatthews, Don Q.
The Design of the Management Information
System. Van Nos Reinhold.
Matthews, Douglas.
xMatthews, Douglas.
Sue the B-St-Rds: The Victim's Handbook.
Arbor Hse.
Matthews, Edward.
xMatthews, Edward.
Celebrating Mass with Children: A
Commentary on the Directory of Masses
with Children. Paulist Pr.
Matthews, Ellen.
xMatthews, Ellen.

Getting Rid of Roger. Westminster.
The Trouble with Leslie. Westminster.
Matthews, Esther E., 1918-
xMatthews, Esther E.
Counseling Girls & Women Over the Life
Span. Am Personnel.
Matthews, Fred. see Matthews, Fred H.
Matthews, Fred H.
xMatthews, Fred.
The Quest for an American Sociology: Robert
E. Park & the Chicago School.
McGill-Queens U Pr.
Matthews, G. A.
xMatthews, G. A.
Pesticide Application Methods. Longman.
Matthews, H. see Matthews, Herbert.
Matthews, Herbert.
xMatthews, H.
Surface Wave Filters: Design, Construction, &
Use. Wiley.
Matthews, Herbert L. see Matthews, Herbert Lionel.
Matthews, Herbert Lionel, 1900-
xMatthews, Herbert L.
Cuba. Macmillan.
The Education of a Correspondent.
Greenwood.
Matthews, Honor.
xMatthews, Honor.
The Primal Curse: The Myth of Cain & Abel in
the Theatre. Schocken.
Matthews, J. F. see Matthews, J. H.
Matthews, J. H.
xMatthews, J. F.
Andre Breton. Columbia U Pr.
xMatthews, J. H.
tr. The Custom-House of Desire: A
Half-Century of Surrealist Stories. U of Cal
Pr.
Imagery of Surrealism. Syracuse U Pr.
The Inner Dream: Celine As Novelist. Syracuse
U Pr.
Surrealism & Film. U of Mich Pr.
Surrealism & the Novel. U of Mich Pr.
Surrealist Poetry in France. Syracuse U Pr.
Theatre in Dada & Surrealism. Syracuse U Pr.
Toward the Poetics of Surrealism. Syracuse U
Pr.
Matthews, J. L. see Matthews, John I.
Matthews, Jack.
xMatthews, Jack.
ed. Archetypal Themes in Modern Story. St
Martin.
Charisma Campaigns. HarBraceJ.
Matthews, Jacqueline D.
xMatthews, Jacqueline D.
Association System of the European
Community. Praeger.
Matthews, James. see Matthews, James H.
Matthews, James H., 1942-
xMatthews, James.
Frank O'Connor. Bucknell U Pr.
Matthews, James L. see Matthews, James Lester.
Matthews, James Lester.
xMatthews, James L.
Atlas of Human Histology & Ultrastructure.
Lea & Febiger.
Matthews, John I.
xMatthews, J. L.
Solid State Electronics Concepts. McGraw.
Matthews, Joseph R.
xMatthews, Joseph R.
The County Information Systems Directory.
Lexington Bks.
Matthews, L. Harrison. see Matthews, Leonard Harrison.
Matthews, Lawrence M.
xMatthews, Lawrence M.
Practical Operating Budgeting. McGraw.
Matthews, Leonard Harrison.
xMatthews, L. Harrison.

Penguins, Whalers, & Sealers: A Voyage of
Discovery. Universe.

Matthews, Mervyn.
xMatthews, Mervyn.
ed. Soviet Government: A Selection of Official
Documents on Internal Policies. Taplinger.
Soviet Sociology, 1964-75: A Bibliography.
Praeger.

Matthews, Noel.
xMatthews, Noel.
A Guide to Manuscripts & Documents in the
British Isles Relating to the Far East. Oxford
U Pr.
Materials for West African History in the
Archives of the United Kingdom.
Humanities.

Matthews, P. H. *see* Matthews, Peter H.

Matthews, Patricia.
xMatthews, Patricia.
Love's Avenging Heart. Pinnacle Bks.
Love's Daring Dream. Pinnacle Bks.
Love's Wildest Promise. Pinnacle Bks.

Matthews, Peter H.
xMatthews, P. H.
Generative Grammar & Linguistic Competence.
Allen Unwin.
Inflectional Morphology: A Theoretical Study
Based on Aspects of Latin Verb Conjugation.
Cambridge U Pr.

Matthews, R. E. *see* Matthews, Richard Ellis Ford.

Matthews, Richard Ellis Ford, 1921-
xMatthews, R. E.
Plant Virology. Acad Pr.

Matthews, Robert T.
xMatthews, Robert T.
Engraved Glass & Other Decorated Glass. R T
Matthews.

Matthews, Robley K., 1935-
xMatthews, Robley K.
Dynamic Stratigraphy: An Introduction to
Sedimentation & Stratigraphy. P-H.

Matthews, Sarah H.
xMatthews, Sarah H.
The Social World of Old Women: Management
of Self-Identity. Sage.

Matthews, Vincent.
xMatthews, Vincent.
Laramide Folding Associated with Basement
Block Faulting in Western United States.
Geol Soc.

Matthews, W. Bryan. *see* Matthews, Walter Bryan.
Matthews, W. H. *see* Matthews, William Henry.
Matthews, W. R. *see* Matthews, Walter Robert.

Matthews, Walter Bryan.
xMatthews, W. Bryan.
Multiple Sclerosis: The Facts. Oxford U Pr.

Matthews, Walter Robert, 1881-
xMatthews, W. R.
ed. Christian Faith: Essays in Explanation &
Defence. Arno.

Matthews, William, 1905-
xMatthews, William.

American Diaries: An Annotated Bibliography
of American Diaries Written Prior to the
Year 1861. Canner.
British Autobiographies: An Annotated
Bibliography of British Autobiographies
Published or Written Before 1951. Shoe
String.
British Diaries: An Annotated Bibliography of
British Diaries Written Between 1442-1942.
Peter Smith.
Cockney Past & Present: A Short History of
the Dialect of London. Gale.
The Ill-Framed Knight: A Skeptical Inquiry
into the Identity of Sir Thomas Malory. U of
Cal Pr.
ed. Later Medieval English Prose. Irvington.
ed. Medieval Secular Literature: Four Essays.
U of Cal Pr.
Compiled by Old & Middle English Literature.
AHM Pub.

Matthews, William H. *see* Matthews, William Henry.

Matthews, William Henry, 1919-
xMatthews, W. H.
Mazes & Labyrinths: Their History &
Development. Dover.
Mazes & Labyrinths: Their History &
Development. Peter Smith.
xMatthews, William H.
Earth's Crust. Watts.
Fossils: An Introduction to Prehistoric Life.
Har-Row.
Geology Made Simple. Doubleday.
The Story of Glaciers & the Ice Age. Harvey.
Story of the Earth. Harvey.

Matthews, William K. *see* Matthews, William Kleesmann.

Matthews, William Kleesmann, 1901-
xMatthews, William K.
Structure & Development of Russian.
Greenwood.
xMatthews, William Kleesmann.
ed. Anthology of Modern Estonian Poetry.
Greenwood.

Matthias, John, 1941-
xMatthias, John.
Bucyrus. Swallow.

Matthiessen, F. O. *see* Matthiessen, Francis Otto.

Matthiessen, Francis Otto, 1902-1950
xMatthiessen, F. O.
Achievement of T. S. Eliot: An Essay on the
Nature of Poetry. Oxford U Pr.
American Renaissance: Art & Expression in
the Age of Emerson & Whitman. Oxford U
Pr.
ed. Oxford Book of American Verse. Oxford U
Pr.
Theodore Dreiser. Greenwood.
Theodore Dreiser. R West.

Matthiessen, Peter.
xMatthiessen, Peter.
Far Tortuga. Random.
Oomingmak: The Expedition to the Musk Ox
Island in the Bering Sea. Hastings.

Matti, Jonathan C.
xMatti, Jonathan C.
Silurian & Lower Devonian Basin &
Basin-Slope Limestones, Copenhagen
Canyon, Nevada. Geol Soc.

Mattick, Ilse.
xMattick, Ilse.
Guidelines for Observation & Assessment: An
Approach to Evaluating the Learning
Environment of a Day Care Center. Day
Care & Child Dev.

Mattick, Paul, 1904-
xMattick, Paul.

Anti-Bolshevik Communism. M E Sharpe.
Economics, Politics, & the Age of Inflation. M
E Sharpe.
Marx & Keynes: The Limits of the Mixed
Economy. Porter Sargent.

Mattil, Edward L.
xMattil, Edward L.
Meaning in Crafts. P-H.

Mattingly, Garrett, 1900-
xMattingly, Garrett.
Armada. HM.
Renaissance Diplomacy. HM.
Renaissance Diplomacy. Russell.

Mattingly, George, 1950-
xMattingly, George.
Breathing Space. Blue Wind.

Mattingly, Grayson.
xMattingly, Grayson.
Introducing the Single-Camera VTR System: A
Layman's Guide to Videotape Recording.
Scribner.

Mattingly, Harold, 1884-1964
xMattingly, Harold.
Christianity in the Roman Empire. Norton.
The Imperial Civil Service of Rome. Hyperion
Conn.

Mattingly, M. R. *see* Mattingly, Mary Ramona.

Mattingly, Mary Ramona, Sister.
xMattingly, M. R.
The Catholic Church on the Kentucky
Frontier: 1785-1812. AMS Pr.

Mattingly, Paul H.
xMattingly, Paul H.
The Classless Profession: American Schoolmen
of the Nineteenth Century. NYU Pr.

Mattison, Judith. *see* Mattison, Judith N.

Mattison, Judith N.
xMattison, Judith.
Facing Up. Fortress.
From a Woman's Heart. Augsburg.
Prayers from a Mother's Heart. Augsburg.
Prayers from a Woman's Heart. Augsburg.

Mattlin, Everett. *see* Mattlin, Everett B.

Mattlin, Everett B.
xMattlin, Everett.
Sleep Less, Live More. Lippincott.

Mattman, Lida H.
xMattman, Lida H.
Cell Wall Deficient Forms. CRC Pr.

Mattock, G.
xMattock, G.
ed. New Processes of Waste Water Treatment
& Recovery. Halsted Pr.

Mattoon, Mary Ann.
xMattoon, Mary Ann.
Applied Dream Analysis: A Jungian Approach.
Halsted Pr.

Mattox, Robert.
xMattox, Robert.
The Christian Employee. Logos.

Mattson , James. *see* Mattson, James S.

Mattson, Hans, 1832-1893
xMattson, Hans.
Reminiscences: Story of an Emigrant. Arno.

Mattson, Ivar T.
xMattson, Ivar T.
How to Make Big Money with Little Movies.
PRESCOB.

Mattson, J. *see* Mattson, James S.
Mattson, J. S. *see* Mattson, James S.

Mattson, James S.
xMattson , James.
ed. Computers in Polymer Sciences. Dekker.
xMattson, J.
ed. Spectroscopy & Kinetics. Dekker.
xMattson, J. S.
ed. Computer Fundamentals for Chemists.
Dekker.
xMattson, James S.

ed. Infrared Correlation & Fourier Transform
Spectroscopy. Dekker.
Matunas, Edward.
xMatunas, Edward.
American Ammunition & Ballistics. Winchester
Pr.
Matura, Thaddee.
xMatura, Thaddee.
The Crisis of Religious Life. Franciscan Herald.
Maturin, Charles R. *see* Maturin, Charles Robert.
Maturin, Charles Robert, 1780-1824
xMaturin, Charles R.
The Milesian Chief. Garland Pub.
The Wild Irish Boy. Garland Pub.
xMaturin, Charles Robert.
The Wild Irish Boy. Arno.
Matusow, Allen J.
xMatusow, Allen J.
Farm Policies & Politics in the Truman Years.
Atheneum.
Farm Policies & Politics in the Truman Years.
Harvard U Pr.
Joseph R. McCarthy. P-H.
Matwes, George. *see* Matwes, George J.
Matwes, George J.
xMatwes, George.
A Retailer's Guide to OSHA. Lebhar
Friedman.
Matyi, J. Robert.
xMatyi, Robert.
My God They're Real. Ashley Bks.
Matyi, Robert. *see* Matyi, J. Robert.
Matz, Samuel A.
xMatz, Samuel A.
Bakery Technology & Engineering. AVI.
Cookie & Cracker Technology. AVI.
Matzen, Peter Friedrich.
xMatzen, Peter-Friedrich.
Orthopedic Roentgen Atlas. Grune.
Matzen, Peter-Friedrich. *see* Matzen, Peter Friedrich.
Matzke, Eric.
xMatzke, Eric.
Greenberg's Guide to Marx Trains. Greenberg
Pub Co.
Matzke, Howard A.
xMatzke, Howard A.
Synopsis of Neuroanatomy. Oxford U Pr.
Maud, Ralph.
xMaud, Ralph.
Dylan Thomas in Print: A Bibliographical
History. U of Pittsburgh Pr.
Maude, Angus, 1912-
xMaude, Angus.
South Asia. Dufour.
Maude, Aylmer, 1858-1938
xMaude, Aylmer.
Leo Tolstoy. Haskell.
Leo Tolstoy. R West.
Leo Tolstoy & His Works. Arden Lib.
Leo Tolstoy & His Works. Folcroft.
Leo Tolstoy & His Works. Haskell.
Maude, Francis C. *see* Maude, Francis Cornwallis.
Maude, Francis Cornwallis, 1828-1900
xMaude, Francis C.
Five Years in Madagascar, with Notes on the
Military Situation. Negro U Pr.
Maude, H. E. *see* Maude, Henry Evans.
Maude, Henry Evans, 1906-
xMaude, H. E.
Of Islands & Men: Studies in Pacific History.
Oxford U Pr.
Maude, Jenny M. *see* Maude, Jenny Maria Catherine
Goldschmidt.
Maude, Jenny Maria Catherine Goldschmidt.
xMaude, Jenny M.
The Life of Jenny Lind. Arno.
Maue, Kenneth.
xMaue, Kenneth.

Water in the Lake: Real Events for the
Imagination. Har-Row.
Water in the Lake: Real Events for the
Imagination. Har-Row.
Mauer, George J.
xMauer, George J.
ed. Crises in Campus Management: Case
Studies in the Administration of Colleges &
Universities. Praeger.
Mauger, Emily M.
xMauger, Emily M.
Modern Display Techniques. Fairchild.
Maugham, Robin, 1916-
xMaugham, Robin.
Conversations with Willie: Recollections of W.
Somerset Maugham. S&S.
Somerset & All the Maughams. Greenwood.
Maugham, Somerset W. *see* Maugham, William
Somerset.
Maugham, W. Somerset. *see* Maugham, William
Somerset.
Maugham, William Somerset, 1874-1965
xMaugham, Somerset W.
Vagrant Mood. Kennikat.
xMaugham, W. Somerset.
Ah King. Arno.
The Art of Fiction: An Introduction to Ten
Novels & Their Authors. Arno.
Ashenden, or the British Agent. Arno.
Cakes & Ale. Arno.
Cakes & Ale. Penguin.
Casuarina Tree. Arno.
Catalina: A Romance. Arno.
Christmas Holiday. Arno.
Christmas Holiday. Penguin.
Cosmopolitans. Arno.
Creatures of Circumstance. Arno.
Don Fernando: Or Variations on Some Spanish
Themes. Arno.
For Services Rendered: A Play in Three Acts.
Arno.
France at War. Arno.
The Gentleman in the Parlour: A Record of a
Journey from Rangoon to Haiphong. Arno.
Liza of Lambeth. Arno.
Liza of Lambeth. Penguin.
The Moon & Sixpence. Arno.
The Moon & Sixpence. Penguin.
The Narrow Corner. Arno.
The Narrow Corner. Penguin.
Of Human Bondage. Arno.
Of Human Bondage. Modern Lib.
Of Human Bondage. Penguin.
Of Human Bondage. Random.
Of Human Bondage. Doubleday.
On a Chinese Screen. Arno.
The Painted Veil. Arno.
The Painted Veil. Penguin.
The Razor's Edge. Arno.
The Razor's Edge. Penguin.
Strictly Personal. Arno.
The Summing up. Arno.
The Summing Up. Penguin.
Theatre. Arno.
The Vagrant Mood: Six Essays. Arno.
Mauksch, Ingeborg G.
xMauksch, Ingeborg G.
ed. National Health Insurance. Nursing Res.
Mauldin, Bill. *see* Mauldin, William Henry.
Mauldin, Kenneth, 1918-
xMauldin, Kenneth L.
Table Talk with Jesus. Abingdon.
Mauldin, Kenneth L. *see* Mauldin, Kenneth.
Mauldin, William Henry, 1921-
xMauldin, Bill.
A Sort of a Saga. Norton.
Mauldon, E. *see* Mauldon, Elizabeth.
Mauldon, Elizabeth.
xMauldon, E.

Teaching Gymnastics & Body Control. Plays.
Maull, Linda.
xMaull, Linda.
Getting It All Together: The Down to Earth
Cookbook. Gala Bks.
Maund, Constance.
xMaund, Constance.
Hume's Theory of Knowledge: A Critical
Examination. Russell.
Maunder, P. A.
xMaunder, Peter.
Case Studies in International Economics.
Heinemann Ed.
Case Studies in Macro-Economics. Heinemann
Ed.
Maunder, Peter. *see* Maunder, P. A.
Maunier, Rene, 1887-
xMaunier, Rene.
Manuel Bibliographique Des Sciences Sociales
et Economiques. B Franklin.
Maupin, Armistead.
xMaupin, Armistead.
More Tales of the City. Har-Row.
Tales of the City. Ballantine.
Tales of the City. Har-Row.
Maurello, S Ralph, 1911-
xMaurello, S. Ralph.
Complete Airbrush Book. L Amiel Pub.
Maurer, Armand A. *see* Maurer, Armand Augustine.
Maurer, Armand Augustine.
xMaurer, Armand A.
St. Thomas & Historicity. Marquette.
Maurer, Charles B., 1933-
xMaurer, Charles B.
Call to Revolution: The Mystical Anarchism of
Gustav Landauer. Wayne St U Pr.
Maurer, D. W. *see* Maurer, David W.
Maurer, David W.
xMaurer, D. W.
The Argot of the Racetrack. U of Ala Pr.
Whiz Mob: A Correlation of the Technical
Argot of Pickpockets with Their Behavior
Patterns. U of Ala Pr.
Maurer, H. A. *see* Maurer, Hermann A.
Maurer, H. R. *see* Maurer, H. Rainer.
Maurer, H. Rainer.
xMaurer, H. R.
Disc-Electrophoresis and Related Techniques
of Polyacrylamide Gel Electrophoresis. De
Gruyter.
Maurer, Hermann A., 1941-
xMaurer, H. A.
Data Structures & Programming Techniques.
P-H.
Maurer, Herrymon, 1914-
xMaurer, Herrymon.
ed. Pendle Hill Reader. Arno.
Maurer, James F.
xMaurer, James F.
Hearing & Aging: Tactics for Intervention.
Grune.
Maurer, John G., 1937-
xMaurer, John G.
Work Role Involvement of Industrial
Supervisors. Mich St U Busn.
Maurer, W. D. *see* Maurer, Ward Douglas.
Maurer, Ward Douglas, 1938-
xMaurer, W. D.
The Programmer's Introduction to SNOBOL.
Elsevier.
Mauriac, Francois, 1885-
xMauriac, Francois.
Anguish & Joy of the Christian Life. U of
Notre Dame Pr.
Letters on Art & Literature. Kennikat.
Men I Hold Great. Kennikat.
Maurice, A. B. *see* Maurice, Arthur Bartlett.
Maurice, Arthur B. *see* Maurice, Arthur Bartlett.
Maurice, Arthur Bartlett, 1873-1946
xMaurice, A. B.

History of the Nineteenth Century in
Caricature. Gordon Pr.
The Paris of the Novelists. Gordon Pr.
xMaurice, Arthur B.
Fifth Avenue. Arno.
History of the Nineteenth Century in
Caricature. Cooper Sq.
History of the Nineteenth Century in
Caricature. Gale.
The Paris of the Novelists. Kennikat.
Maurice, Charles E. see Maurice, Charles Edmund.
Maurice, Charles Edmund, 1843-
xMaurice, Charles E.
Revolutionary Movement of 1848-49 in Italy,
Austria, Hungary, & Germany. Scholarly.
Mauriceau, A. M.
xMauriceau, A. M.
The Married Woman's Private Medical
Companion. Arno.
Maurier, Daphne Du. see Du Maurier, Daphne.
Maurin, Peter.
xMaurin, Peter.
Easy Essays. British Am Bks.
Maurino, Ferdinand. see Maurino, Ferdinando Dante.
Maurino, Ferdinando Dante, 1915-
xMaurino, Ferdinand.
Modern Language Dictionary: English-Spanish,
Spanish-English. S&S.
Maurizi, Alex.
xMaurizi, Alex R.
Public Policy & the Dental Care Market. Am
Enterprise.
Maurizi, Alex R. see Maurizi, Alex.
Mauro, Alexander.
xMauro, Alexander.
ed. Muscle Regeneration. Raven.
Maurois, Andre, 1885-1967
xMaurois, Andre.
The Art of Writing. Arno.
Illusions. Columbia U Pr.
Les Illusions. French & Eur.
Lelia: The Life of George Sand. Penguin.
Private Universe. Arno.
Prophets & Poets. Kennikat.
Ricochets: Miniature Tales of Human Life.
Arno.
Mauron, Charles.
xMauron, Charles.
Aesthetics & Psychology. Kennikat.
Maury, Curt.
xMaury, Curt.
Folk Origins of Indian Art. Columbia U Pr.
Maus, Francis L.
xMaus, Francis L.
Economics of Abundance: A Primer of
Economic Law. Caxton.
Mauser, August J.
xMauser, August J.
Assessing the Learning Disabled: Selected
Instruments. Acad Therapy.
Mauser, Ferdinand F.
xMauser, Ferdinand F.
American Business: An Introduction.
HarBraceJ.
Mausner, Bernard, 1920-
xMausner, Bernard.
A Citizen's Guide to the Social Sciences.
Nelson-Hall.
Mausolf, F. see Mausolf, Frederick A.
Mausolf, Frederick A.
xMausolf, F.
The Anatomy of the Ocular Adnexa: Guide to
Orbital Dissection. C C Thomas.
xMausolf, Frederick A.
The Eye & Systemic Disease. Mosby.
Mauss, Evelyn A.
xMauss, Evelyn A.

ed. Conservation of Energy Resources. NY
Acad Sci.
Mauss, Marcel, 1872-1950
xMauss, Marcel.
A General Theory of Magic. Norton.
A General Theory of Magic. Routledge &
Kegan.
Seasonal Variations of the Eskimo: A Study in
Social Morphology. Routledge & Kegan.
Sociology & Psychology: Essays. Routledge &
Kegan.
Mautz, R. K. see Mautz, Robert Kuhn.
Mautz, Robert K. see Mautz, Robert Kuhn.
Mautz, Robert Kuhn.
xMautz, R. K.
Effect of Circumstances on the Application of
Accounting Principles. Finan Exec.
xMautz, Robert K.
Fundamentals of Auditing. Wiley.
Mavrommatis, P. D. see Mavrommatis, Panayotis D.
Mavrommatis, Panayotis D.
xMavrommatis, P. D.
Precalculus Mathematics for Technical
Students. P-H.
Maxa, Rudy.
xMaxa, Rudy.
Dare to Be Great. Morrow.
Maxim, George. see Maxim, George W.
Maxim, George W.
xMaxim, George.
The Very Young: Guiding Children from
Infancy Through the Early Years. Wadsworth
Pub.
Maxim, Hiram P. see Maxim, Hiram Percy.
Maxim, Hiram Percy, 1869-1936
xMaxim, Hiram P.
Genius in the Family. Dover.
Maxon, Hazel C. see Maxon, Hazel Carter.
Maxon, Hazel Carter.
xMaxon, Hazel C.
Opportunities in Free Lance Writing. Natl
Textbk.
Maxon, James C.
xMaxon, James C.
Indians of the Lake Mead Country. Sw Pks
Mnmts.
Maxson, Charles H. see Maxson, Charles Hartshorn.
Maxson, Charles Hartshorn, 1864-
xMaxson, Charles H.
The Great Awakening in the Middle Colonies.
Peter Smith.
Maxted, I. see Maxted, Ian.
Maxted, Ian.
xMaxted, I.
The London Book Trades, 1775-1800: A
Preliminary Checklist of Members. Dawson
Pub.
Maxtone-Graham, John.
xMaxtone-Graham, John.
The Only Way to Cross. Macmillan.
The Only Way to Cross. Macmillan.
Maxtone-Graham, Katrina.
xMaxtone-Graham, Katrina.
Pregnant by Mistake: The Stories of Seventeen
Women. Liveright.
Maxwell, A. E.
xMaxwell, A. E.
The Golden Empire. Fawcett.
Maxwell, A. Graham. see Maxwell, Arthur Graham.
Maxwell, A. S. see Maxwell, Arthur Stanley.
Maxwell, Arthur Graham, 1921-
xMaxwell, A. Graham.
Can God Be Trusted?. Southern Pub.
Maxwell, Arthur Stanley, 1896-
xMaxwell, A. S.
This Is the End. Pacific Pr Pub Assn.
Maxwell, Baldwin, 1893-
xMaxwell, Baldwin.

Studies in Beaumont, Fletcher & Massinger.
Octagon.
Maxwell, Charles H. see Maxwell, Charles Herbert.
Maxwell, Charles Herbert.
xMaxwell, Charles H.
Adventures of the White Girl in Her Search for
God. Folcroft.
Maxwell, D. E. S. see Maxwell, Desmond Ernest
Stewart.
Maxwell, Desmond Ernest Stewart, 1925-
xMaxwell, D. E. S.
Brian Friel. Bucknell U Pr.
Maxwell, E. A. see Maxwell, Edwin Arthur.
Maxwell, Edwin A. see Maxwell, Edwin Arthur.
Maxwell, Edwin Arthur.
xMaxwell, E. A.
Geometry by Transformations. Cambridge U
Pr.
xMaxwell, Edwin A.
Gateway to Abstract Mathematics. Cambridge
U Pr.
Maxwell, Grover.
xMaxwell, Grover.
ed. Induction, Probability, & Confirmation. U
of Minn Pr.
Maxwell, Ian C. see Maxwell, Ian Ramsay.
Maxwell, Ian R. see Maxwell, Ian Ramsay.
Maxwell, Ian Ramsay.
xMaxwell, Ian C.
French Farce & John Heywood. Somerset Pub.
xMaxwell, Ian R.
French Farce & John Heywood. Folcroft.
Maxwell, J. B., 1902-
xMaxwell, J. B.
Data Book on Hydrocarbons: Application to
Process Engineering. Krieger.
Maxwell, James A. see Maxwell, James Ackley.
Maxwell, James Ackley, 1897-
xMaxwell, James A.
Commonwealth-State Financial Relations in
Australia. Intl Schol Bk Serv.
Maxwell, James C. see Maxwell, James Clerk.
Maxwell, James Clerk, 1831-1879
xMaxwell, James C.
Theory of Heat. AMS Pr.
Theory of Heat. Greenwood.
Maxwell, Jessica.
xMaxwell, Jessica.
The Eye-Body Connection. Warner Bks.
Maxwell, Joseph R.
xMaxwell, Joseph R.
Commodity Futures Trading with Moving
Averages. Speer Bks.
Commodity Futures Trading with Point &
Figure Charts. Speer Bks.
Commodity Futures Trading with Stops. Speer
Bks.
Maxwell, Kenneth E., 1908-
xMaxwell, Kenneth E.
Environment of Life. Brooks-Cole.
Maxwell, l E.
xMaxwell, L. E.
Crowded to Christ. Moody.
Maxwell, Morton H.
xMaxwell, Morton H.
ed. Clinical Disorders of Fluid & Electrolyte
Metabolism. McGraw.
Maxwell Museum of Anthropology.
xMaxwell Museum of Anthropology, Univ. of New
Mexico.
Seven Families in Pueblo Pottery. U of NM Pr.
Maxwell Museum of Anthropology, Univ. of New
Mexico. see Maxwell Museum of Anthropology.
Maxwell, Neal A.
xMaxwell, Neal A.

All These Things Shall Give Thee Experience.
Deseret Bk.
Things As They Really Are. Deseret Bk.
Wherefore, Ye Must Press Forward. Deseret
Bk.
Maxwell, Neville. *see* Maxwell, Neville George Anthony.
Maxwell, Neville George Anthony.
xMaxwell, Neville.
China's Road to Development. Pergamon.
Maxwell, Patricia.
xMaxwell, Patricia.
Bride of a Stranger. Fawcett.
How to Become a Christian & Stay One.
Southern Pub.
Night of the Candles. Fawcett.
Sweet Piracy. Fawcett.
Maxwell, W. G. *see* Maxwell, W. G. H.
Maxwell, W. G. H.
xMaxwell, W. G.
Atlas of the Great Barrier Reef. Elsevier.
Maxwell, William, 1908-
xMaxwell, William.
So Long, See You Tomorrow. G K Hall.
So Long, See You Tomorrow. Knopf.
May. *see* May, Frank B.
May, Antionette. *see* May, Antoinette.
May, Antoinette.
xMay, Antionette.
Different Drummers: They Did What They
Wanted. Les Femmes Pub.
May, Arthur J. *see* May, Arthur James.
May, Arthur James, 1899-
xMay, Arthur J.
Passing of the Hapsburg Monarchy, 1914-1918.
U of Pa Pr.
May, Brian.
xMay, Brian.
The Indonesian Tragedy. Routledge & Kegan.
May, C. E. *see* May, Clarence Edward.
May, Clarence Edward, 1903-
xMay, C. E.
Life Under Four Flags in the North River
Basin of Virginia. McClure Printing.
May, Derwent.
xMay, Derwent.
ed. Good Talk: An Anthology from BBC
Radio. Taplinger.
May, Edward. *see* May, Edward C.
May, Edward C.
xMay, Edward.
Family Worship Idea Book. Concordia.
May, Elizabeth, Writer on Music.
xMay, Elizabeth.
ed. Musics of Many Cultures: An Introduction.
U of Cal Pr.
May, Elizabeth E. *see* May, Elizabeth Eckhardt.
May, Elizabeth Eckhardt.
xMay, Elizabeth E.
Independent Living for the Handicapped & the
Elderly. HM.
May, Frank B.
xMay.
Teaching Language As Communication to
Children. Merrill.
May, Gerald. *see* May, Gerald G.
May, Gerald G.
xMay, Gerald.
The Open Way: A Meditation Handbook.
Paulist Pr.
May, Harriett J. *see* May, Harriett Johnson.
May, Harriett Johnson.
xMay, Harriett J.
Enterostomal Therapy. Raven.
May, Henry F. *see* May, Henry Farnham.
May, Henry Fannham, 1915-
xMay, Henry F.
The Enlightenment in America. Oxford U Pr.
The Enlightenment in America. Oxford U Pr.
May, Henry Farnham, 1915-
xMay, Henry F.

End of American Innocence: A Study of the
First Years of Our Own Time, 1912-1917.
New Viewpoints.
The End of American Innocence: A Study of
the First Years of Our Own Time,
1912-1917. Oxford U Pr.
Protestant Churches & Industrial America.
Octagon.
May, Henry J. *see* May, Henry John.
May, Henry John.
xMay, Henry J.
South African Constitution. Greenwood.
May, Herbert G. *see* May, Herbert Gordon.
May, Herbert Gordon.
xMay, Herbert G.
ed. Oxford Bible Atlas. Oxford U Pr.
May, J. Lewis. *see* May, James Lewis.
May, J. P. *see* May, J. Peter.
May, J. Peter.
xMay, J. P.
The Geometry of Iterated Loop Spaces.
Springer-Verlag.
xMay, J. Peter.
Classifying Spaces & Fibrations. Am Math.
May, James D., 1929-
xMay, James D.
Avant-Garde Choral Music: An Annotated
Selected Bibliography. Scarecrow.
May, James Lewis, 1873-
xMay, J. Lewis.
Cardinal Newman. Folcroft.
May, Janice. *see* May, Janice C.
May, Janice C.
xMay, Janice.
Texas Government. McGraw.
May, John R.
xMay, John R.
The Pruning Word: The Parables of Flannery
O'Connor. U of Notre Dame Pr.
Toward a New Earth: Apocalypse in the
American Novel. U of Notre Dame Pr.
May, Julian.
xMay, Julian.
America's Cup Yacht Race. Creative Ed.
Baltimore Colts. Creative Ed.
The Baltimore Colts. Creative Ed.
Boxing's Heavyweight Championship. Creative
Ed.
Cactus Fox. Creative Ed.
Cascade Cougar. Creative Ed.
Dallas Cowboys. Creative Ed.
The Dallas Cowboys. Creative Ed.
Eagles of the Valley. Creative Ed.
The First Living Things. Holiday.
Forest Hills & the American Tennis
Championship. Creative Ed.
Forests That Change Color. Creative Ed.
Giant Condor of California. Creative Ed.
Glacier Grizzly. Creative Ed.
The Grand Prix World Championship. Creative
Ed.
Green Bay Packers. Creative Ed.
The Green Bay Packers. Creative Ed.
How the Animals Came to North America.
Holiday.
How to Build a Body. Creative Ed.
Life Cycle of a Bullfrog. Creative Ed.
Life Cycle of an Opossum. Creative Ed.
Living Blanket on the Land. Creative Ed.
Living Things & Their Young. Follett.
The NBA Playoffs. Creative Ed.
Prairie Has an Endless Sky. Creative Ed.
Prairie Pronghorn. Creative Ed.
The San Diego Chargers. Creative Ed.
The Stanley Cup. Creative Ed.
What Will the Weather Be. Creative Ed.
The World Series. Creative Ed.
May, Julian. *see* May, Julian S.
May, Julian S.
xMay, Julian.

The Student Chemist Explores Computations.
Rosen Pr.
May, Karl. *see* May, Karl Freidrich.
May, Karl Freidrich, 1842-1912
xMay, Karl.
Ardistan & Djinnistan. Bantam.
Ardistan & Djinnistan. Continuum.
May, Lawrence. *see* May, Lawrence A.
May, Lawrence A.
xMay, Lawrence.
Getting the Most Out Your Doctor. Basic.
May, Lola J. *see* May, Lola June.
May, Lola June.
xMay, Lola J.
Teaching Mathematics in the Elementary
School. Free Pr.
May, Philip. *see* May, Philip R.
May, Philip R., 1928-
xMay, Philip.
Which Way to Educate?. Moody.
May, Philip R. *see* May, Philip Ross.
May, Philip Ross.
xMay, Philip R.
Origins of Hydraulic Mining in California.
Holmes.
May, Phillip T.
xMay, Phillip T.
Programming Business Applications in Fortran
IV. HM.
May, Robert. *see* May, Robert G.
May, Robert G.
xMay, Robert.
A Brief Introduction to Managerial & Social
Uses of Accounting. P-H.
xMay, Robert G.
A New Introduction to Financial Accounting.
P-H.
May, Robert M.
xMay, Robert M.
ed. Theoretical Ecology: Principles and
Applications. HR&W.
May, Robin.
xMay, Robin.
A Companion to the Opera. Hippocrene Bks.
May, Rollo.
xMay, Rollo.
The Courage to Create. Norton.
The Courage to Create. Bantam.
ed. Existence: A New Dimension in Psychiatry
& Psychology. S&S.
ed. Existential Psychology. Random.
Love & Will. Dell.
Love & Will. Norton.
The Meaning of Anxiety. Norton.
The Meaning of Anxiety. PB.
Power & Innocence: A Search for the Sources
of Violence. Norton.
Psychology & the Human Dilemma. Norton.
ed. Symbolism in Religion & Literature.
Braziller.
May, Rosalind G.
xMay, Rosalind G.
Exciting Things to Make with Wool String &
Thread. Lippincott.
May, Samuel. *see* May, Samuel Joseph.
May, Samuel J. *see* May, Samuel Joseph.
May, Samuel Joseph, 1797-1871
xMay, Samuel.
Some Recollections of Our Anti-Slavery
Conflict. Mnemosyne.
xMay, Samuel J.
Some Recollections of Our Anti-Slavery
Conflict. Arno.
Some Recollections of Our Antislavery
Conflict. Arno.
May, William. *see* May, William E.
May, William E., 1928-
xMay, William.

On Understanding Human Sexuality.
Franciscan Herald.
xMay, William E.
Christ in Contemporary Thought. Pflaum Pr.
The Nature & Meaning of Chastity. Franciscan
Herald.
The Unity of the Moral & Spiritual Life.
Franciscan Herald.
Mayall, W. H.
xMayall, William H.
Principles in Design. Van Nos Reinhold.
Mayall, William H. see Mayall, W. H.
Maybee, Rolland H. see Maybee, Rolland Harper.
Maybee, Rolland Harper, 1901-
xMaybee, Rolland H.
Railroad Competition & the Oil Trade:
1855-1873. Porcupine Pr.
Maybon, Charles B.
xMaybon, Charles B.
Histoire de la Concession Francaise de
Changhai. AMS Pr.
Mayborn, Mitch.
xMayborn, Mitch.
Stearman Guidebook. Flying Ent.
Maybury, Anne.
xMaybury, Anne.
The Brides of Bellenmore. Ace Bks.
Dark Star. Random.
Falcon's Shadow. Ace Bks.
The House of Fand. Ace Bks.
The Night My Enemy. Ace Bks.
The Pavilion at Monkshood. Ace Bks.
Radiance. Random.
Whisper in the Dark. Ace Bks.
Maybury-Lewis, David.
xMaybury-Lewis, David.
ed. Dialectical Societies: The Ge & Bororo of
Central Brazil. Harvard U Pr.
Mayda, Jaro.
xMayda, Jaro.
Francois Geny & Modern Jurisprudence. La
State U Pr.
Maye, Patricia.
xMaye, Patricia.
Fieldbook of Nature Photography. Sierra.
Mayeda, Noriko.
xMayeda, Noriko.
Tawi Tales: Folktales from Jammu. Am Orient
Soc.
Mayer. see Mayer, Frederick.
Mayer, A. M.
xMayer, A. M.
The Germination of Seeds. Pergamon.
Mayer, Adrian C.
xMayer, Adrian C.
Caste & Kinship in Central India: A Village &
Its Region. U of Cal Pr.
Peasants in the Pacific: A Study of Fiji Indian
Rural Society. U of Cal Pr.
Mayer, Albert I.
xMayer, Albert I.
Story of Old Glory. Childrens.
Mayer, Albert J., 1939-
xMayer, Albert J.
ed. Readings in Management for the Real
Estate Executive. Realtors Natl.
Urban Life & the Struggle to Be Human.
Kendall-Hunt.
Mayer, Allan J.
xMayer, Allan J.
Madam Prime Minister: Margaret Thatcher &
Her Rise to Power. Newsweek.
Mayer, Edmund.
xMayer, Edmund.
Introduction to Dynamic Morphology. Acad
Pr.
Mayer, Egon, 1944-
xMayer, Egon.

From Suburb to Shtetl: The Jews of Boro Park.
Temple U Pr.
Mayer, Frederick, 1921-
xMayer.
Foundations of Education. Merrill.
xMayer, Frederick.
Education for a New Society. Phi Delta Kappa.
xMayer, Frederick A.
A History of Educational Thought. Merrill.
Mayer, Frederick A. see Mayer, Frederick.
Mayer, Greta.
xMayer, Greta.
Learning to Love & Let Go: A Guide to
Helping Children Become Independent.
Jewish Bd Family.
Mayer, Gustav, 1871-1948
xMayer, Gustav.
Friedrich Engels: A Biography. Fertig.
Mayer, H. see Mayer, Henry.
Mayer, Hans E. see Mayer, Hans Eberhard.
Mayer, Hans Eberhard.
xMayer, Hans E.
The Crusades. Oxford U Pr.
Mayer, Harold M. see Mayer, Harold Melvin.
Mayer, Harold Melvin.
xMayer, Harold M.
ed. Readings in Urban Geography. U of
Chicago Pr.
Mayer, Henry.
xMayer, H.
ed. Australian Politics: A Third Reader. Verry.
Mayer, Herbert. see Mayer, Herbert T.
Mayer, Herbert T.
xMayer, Herbert.
Books of the New Testament. Concordia.
xMayer, Herbert T.
Pastoral Care: Its Roots & Renewal. John
Knox.
Mayer, J. P. see Mayer, Jacob Peter.
Mayer, Jacob P. see Mayer, Jacob Peter.
Mayer, Jacob Peter, 1903-
xMayer, J. P.
British Cinemas & Their Audiences. Arno.
Max Weber & German Politics. Arno.
Political Thought in France. Arno.
Intro. by Sociology of Film: Studies &
Documents. Arno.
xMayer, Jacob P.
Alexis de Tocqueville: A Biographical Study in
Political Science. Peter Smith.
xMayer, Jakob P.
Sociology of Film: Studies & Documents. Ozer.
Mayer, Jakob P. see Mayer, Jacob Peter.
Mayer, Jean.
xMayer, Jean.
A Diet for Living. PB.
ed. Food & Nutrition Policy in a Changing
World. Oxford U Pr.
Mayer, K. see Mayer, Robert R.
Mayer, Karl H. see Mayer, Karl Herbert.
Mayer, Karl Herbert.
xMayer, Karl H.
Maya Monuments: Sculptures of Unknown
Provenance in Europe. Acoma Bks.
Mayer, Kurt B. see Mayer, Kurt Bernd.
Mayer, Kurt Bernd, 1916-
xMayer, Kurt B.
Class & Society. Random.
Mayer, Lyle V.
xMayer, Lyle V.
Fundamentals of Voice & Diction. Wm C
Brown.
Mayer, Martin, 1928-
xMayer, Martin.

About Television. Har-Row.
The Bankers. Ballantine.
The Fate of the Dollar. Times Bks.
The Lawyers. Greenwood.
Trigger Points. Har-Row.
Mayer, Mercer, 1943-
xMayer, Mercer.
illus. Ah-Choo. Dial.
Appelard & Liverwurst. Schol Bk Serv.
jt. auth. Boy, a Dog, a Frog & a Friend. Dial.
illus. A Boy, a Dog & a Frog. Dial.
illus. Bubble Bubble. Schol Bk Serv.
illus. East of the Sun & West of the Moon.
Schol Bk Serv.
illus. Frog Goes to Dinner. Dial.
illus. Frog Goes to Dinner. Dial.
illus. Frog on His Own. Dial.
illus. Frog, Where Are You. Dial.
illus. How the Trollusk Got His Hat. Western
Pub.
illus. I Am a Hunter. Dial.
illus. Little Monster at Work. Western Pub.
Little Monster's Bedtime Book. Western Pub.
Little Monster's Counting Book. Western Pub.
illus. Little Monster's Mother Goose. Western
Pub.
Little Monster's Neighborhood. Western Pub.
Little Monster's Word Book. Western Pub.
illus. Liza Lou & the Yeller Belly Swamp.
Schol Bk Serv.
jt. auth. One Frog Too Many. Dial.
Oops. Dial.
illus. Oops. Dial.
illus. Professor Wormbog in Search for the
Zipperump-a-Zoo. Western Pub.
illus. A Silly Story. Schol Bk Serv.
illus. A Special Trick. Dial.
A Special Trick. Dial.
illus. There's a Nightmare in My Closet. Dial.
Mayer, Milton. see Mayer, Milton Sanford.
Mayer, Milton Sanford, 1908-
xMayer, Milton.
The Nature of the Beast. U of Mass Pr.
They Thought They Were Free: The Germans
1933-45. U of Chicago Pr.
Mayer, Morris F. see Mayer, Morris Fritz.
Mayer, Morris Fritz.
xMayer, Morris F.
Group Care of Children: Crossroads &
Transitions. Child Welfare.
Mayer, Paul, 1924-
xMayer, Paul.
Vegetable Cookbook. Nitty Gritty.
Mayer, R. see Mayer, Robert.
Mayer, Ralph, 1895-
xMayer, Ralph.
The Artist's Handbook of Materials &
Techniques. Viking Pr.
Dictionary of Art Terms & Techniques. T Y
Crowell.
The Painter's Craft: An Introduction to
Artists' Methods & Materials. Penguin.
Mayer, Raymond E. see Mayer, Raymond R.
Mayer, Raymond R.
xMayer, Raymond E.
Production & Operations Management.
McGraw.
Mayer, Richard E., 1947-
xMayer, Richard E.
Thinking & Problem Solving: An Introduction
to Human Cognition & Learning. Scott F.
Mayer, Robert, 1934-
xMayer, R.
Los Angeles: A Chronological & Documentary
History, 1542-1976. Oceana.
xMayer, Robert.
The Execution. Viking Pr.
Mayer, Robert. see Mayer, Robert R.
Mayer, Robert R.
xMayer, K.

The Design of Social Policy Research. P-H.
   xMayer, Robert.
      Centrally Planned Change: A Reexamination of
        Theory & Experience. U of Ill Pr.
Mayer, Thomas.
   xMayer, Thomas.
      The Structure of Monetarism. Norton.
Mayeroff, Milton, 1925-
   xMayeroff, Milton.
      On Caring. Har-Row.
      On Caring. Har-Row.
Mayers. *see* Mayers, Marlene Glover.
Mayers, C. P. *see* Mayers, Christopher Paul.
Mayers, Christopher Paul.
   xMayers, C. P.
      Pathology. Arco.
Mayers, Marlene G. *see* Mayers, Marlene Glover.
Mayers, Marlene Glover.
   xMayers.
      Quality Assurance for Patient Care: Nursing
        Perspectives. ACC.
   xMayers, Marlene G.
      A Systematic Approach to the Nursing Care
        Plan. ACC.
Mayers, Marvin K. *see* Mayers, Marvin Keene.
Mayers, Marvin Keene, 1927-
   xMayers, Marvin K.
      Love Goes on Forever. Zondervan.
Mayers, Patrick.
   xMayers, Patrick.
      Lost Bear, Found Bear. A Whitman.
Mayers, W. E. *see* Mayers, William Frederick.
Mayers, William F. *see* Mayers, William Frederick.
Mayers, William Frederick, 1831-1878
   xMayers, W. E.
      The Chinese Reader's Manual: A Handbook of
        Biographical, Historical, Mythological, &
        General Literary Reference. Gordon Pr.
   xMayers, William F.
      The Chinese Reader's Manual: A Handbook of
        Biographical, Historical, Mythological and
        General Literary Reference. Chinese
        Materials.
Mayerson, Evelyn W. *see* Mayerson, Evelyn Wilde.
Mayerson, Evelyn Wilde, 1934-
   xMayerson, Evelyn W.
      Putting the Ill at Ease. Har-Row.
      Sanjo. Lippincott.
      Sanjo. PB.
Mayerson, Philip.
   xMayerson, Philip.
      Classical Mythology in Literature, Art, &
        Music. Wiley.
Mayes, Frances.
   xMayes, Frances.
      After Such Pleasures. Seven Woods Pr.
Mayes, Paul.
   xMayes, Paul.
      ed. Periodicals Administration in Libraries: A
        Collection of Essays. Shoe String.
Mayesky. *see* Mayesky, Mary.
Mayesky, Mary.
   xMayesky.
      Creative Activities for Young Children.
        Delmar.
Mayfield, Jack.
   xMayfield, Jack.
      Loving Strangers. NAL.
Mayfield, John, 1945-
   xMayfield, John.
      Rehearsal for Republicanism: Free Soil & the
        Politics of Antislavery. Kennikat.
Mayfield, Peggy. *see* Mayfield, Peggy M.
Mayfield, Peggy M.
   xMayfield, Peggy.
      Health Assessment: A Modular Approach.
        McGraw.
Mayhall, Jack.
   xMayhall, Jack.

Marriage Takes More Than Love. NavPress.
Mayhall, P. D. *see* Mayhall, Pamela D.
Mayhall, Pamela D.
   xMayhall, P. D.
      Community Relations & the Administration of
        Justice. Wiley.
Mayhar, Ardath.
   xMayhar, Ardath.
      How the Gods Wove in Kyrannon. Doubleday.
Mayhead, Robin.
   xMayhead, Robin.
      Understanding Literature. Cambridge U Pr.
Mayhew, A. L. *see* Mayhew, Anthony Lawson.
Mayhew, Anthony Lawson.
   xMayhew, A. L.
      Concise Dictionary of Middle English from A.
        D. 1150-1580. Folcroft.
Mayhew, David R.
   xMayhew, David R.
      Congress: The Electoral Connection. Yale U
        Pr.
Mayhew, Elizabeth.
   xMayhew, Elizabeth.
      Felicia. PB.
      In the Path of Eagles. PB.
      The Queen of Naples. PB.
Mayhew, Henry, 1812-1887
   xMayhew, Henry.
      London Labour & the London Poor. Biblio
        Dist.
      London Labour & the London Poor. Dover.
Mayhew, Jonathan, 1720-1766
   xMayhew, Jonathan.
      Observations on the Charter & Conduct of the
        Society for the Propagation of the Gospel in
        Foreign Parts; Designed to Show Their
        Non-Conformity to Each Other. Arno.
Mayhew, Lewis B.
   xMayhew, Lewis B.
      Arrogance on Campus. Jossey-Bass.
      Changing the Curriculum. Jossey-Bass.
      Colleges Today & Tomorrow. Jossey-Bass.
      ed. Educational Leadership & Declining
        Enrollments. McCutchan.
      Reform in Graduate & Professional Education.
        Jossey-Bass.
      Surviving the Eighties: Strategies & Procedures
        for Solving Fiscal & Enrollment Problems.
        Jossey-Bass.
Mayhew, Margaret.
   xMayhew, Margaret.
      The Cry of the Owl. Popular Lib.
      The Master of Aysgarth. Popular Lib.
      The Railway King. Doubleday.
Mayhew, Vic.
   xMayhew, Vic.
      Fireball. NAL.
Maykovich, Minako K.
   xMaykovich, Minako K.
      Medical Sociology. Alfred Pub.
Mayle, Peter.
   xMayle, Peter.
      Baby Taming. Crown.
Mayleas, Davidyne.
   xMayleas, Davidyne.
      Rewedded Bliss: Love, Alimony, Incest,
        Ex-Spouses & Other Domestic Blessings.
        Basic.
Maynadier, Gustavus H. *see* Maynadier, Gustavus
Howard.
Maynadier, Gustavus Howard, 1866-1960
   xMaynadier, Gustavus H.
      The Arthur of the English Poets. Johnson
        Repr.
      The Arthur of the English Poets. Octagon.
      Arthur of the English Poets. R West.
Maynard, Charles. *see* Maynard, Charles Clarkson
Martin.
Maynard, Charles Clarkson Martin, Sir, 1870-1945
   xMaynard, Charles.

Murmansk Venture. Arno.
Maynard, Christopher.
   xMaynard, Christopher.
      Prehistoric Life. Watts.
      War Vehicles. Lerner Pubns.
Maynard, Geoffrey.
   xMaynard, Geoffrey.
      Economic Development & the Price Level.
        Kelley.
      A World of Inflation. B&N.
Maynard, Harold B. *see* Maynard, Harold Bright.
Maynard, Harold Bright, 1902-
   xMaynard, Harold B.
      Handbook of Business Administration.
        McGraw.
Maynard, James.
   xMaynard, James.
      Some Microeconomics of Higher Education:
        Economies of Scale. U of Nebr Pr.
Maynard, John, 1941-
   xMaynard, John R.
      Browning's Youth. Harvard U Pr.
Maynard, John R. *see* Maynard, John.
Maynard, John T., 1919-1977
   xMaynard, John T.
      Understanding Chemical Patents: A Guide for
        the Inventor. Am Chemical.
Maynard, L. A. *see* Maynard, Leonard Amby.
Maynard, Leonard A. *see* Maynard, Leonard Amby.
Maynard, Leonard Amby, 1887-
   xMaynard, L. A.
      Animal Nutrition. McGraw.
   xMaynard, Leonard A.
      Animal Nutrition. McGraw.
Maynard, Theodore, 1890-1956
   xMaynard, Theodore.
      The Connection Between the Ballade Chaucer's
        Modification of It, Rime Royal, & the
        Spenserian Stanza. Folcroft.
      De Soto & the Conquistadores. AMS Pr.
      The Humanist As Hero: The Life of Sir
        Thomas More. Hafner.
Mayne, Arthur.
   xMayne, Arthur.
      British Profile Miniaturists. Merrimack Bk
        Serv.
Mayne, E. *see* Mayne, Ethel Colburn.
Mayne, Ethel C. *see* Mayne, Ethel Colburn.
Mayne, Ethel Colburn, d. 1941
   xMayne, E.
      Byron. Gordon Pr.
   xMayne, Ethel C.
      Byron. Arno.
      Byron. R West.
      Byron. Scholarly.
Mayne, Lynn. *see* Mayne, Lynn B.
Mayne, Lynn B.
   xMayne, Lynn.
      Fabric Games. HM.
Mayne, William, 1928-
   xMayne, William.
      Earthfasts. Dutton.
      The Incline. Dutton.
      Max's Dream. Greenwillow.
Mayo, A. D. *see* Mayo, Amory Dwight.
Mayo, Allen.
   xMayo, Allen.
      Contract at Mount Horeb. Tex-Mex.
Mayo, Amory Dwight.
   xMayo, A. D.
      Southern Women in the Recent Educational
        Movement in the South. La State U Pr.
Mayo, Clara. *see* Mayo, Clara Alexandra Weiss.
Mayo, Clara Alexandra Weiss.
   xMayo, Clara.
      Evaluating Research in Social Psychology: A
        Guide for the Consumer. Brooks-Cole.
Mayo Clinic Committee On Dietetics. *see* Mayo Clinic,
Rochester, Minn. Committee on Dietetics.

Mayo Clinic, Rochester, Minn. Committee on Dietetics.
xMayo Clinic Committee On Dietetics.
Mayo Clinic Diet Manual. Saunders.
Mayo, Elton, 1880-1949
xMayo, Elton.
The Human Problems of an Industrial
Civilization. Arno.
The Psychology of Pierre Janet. Greenwood.
Mayo, Henry B. *see* Mayo, Henry Bertram.
Mayo, Henry Bertram, 1911-
xMayo, Henry B.
Introduction to Democratic Theory. Oxford U
Pr.
Mayo, John K.
xMayo, John K.
Educational Reform with Television: The El
Salvador Experience. Stanford U Pr.
Mayo, Katherine, 1868-1940
xMayo, Katherine.
General Washington's Dilemma. Kennikat.
Mayo, Nick.
xMayo, Nick.
The Benefit. Stein & Day.
Mayo, R. Britton.
xMayo, R. Britton.
Corporate Planning & Modeling with Simplan.
A-W.
Mayor, A. Hyatt. *see* Mayor, Alpheus Hyatt.
Mayor, Alpheus Hyatt.
xMayor, A. Hyatt.
Prints & People: A Social History of Printed
Pictures. NYGS.
Mayor, Joseph B. *see* Mayor, Joseph Bickersteth.
Mayor, Joseph Bickersteth, 1828-1916
xMayor, Joseph B.
Chapters on English Metre. AMS Pr.
Chapters on English Metre. Greenwood.
Chapters on English Metre. R West.
Mayor La Guardia's Commission on the Harlem Riot. *see*
New York (City). Mayor La Guardia's Commission on
the Harlem Riot of March 19, 1935.
Mayr, Ernest. *see* Mayr, Ernst.
Mayr, Ernst, 1904-
xMayr, Ernest.
Animal Species & Evolution. Harvard U Pr.
xMayr, Ernest.
Birds of the Southwest Pacific: A Field Guide
to the Birds of the Area Between Samoa,
New Caledonia & Micronesia. C E Tuttle.
Populations, Species, & Evolution: An
Abridgment of Animal Species & Evolution.
Harvard U Pr.
Principles of Systematic Zoology. McGraw.
Mayr, Otto.
xMayr, Otto.
Origins of Feedback Control. MIT Pr.
Mayr-Harting, Henry.
xMayr-Harting, Henry.
The Coming of Christianity to England.
Schocken.
Mays, Benjamin E. *see* Mays, Benjamin Elijah.
Mays, Benjamin Elijah.
xMays, Benjamin E.
Negro's Church. Arno.
Negro's Church. Russell.
Mays, Buddy.
xMays, Buddy.
People of the Sun: Some Out-of-Fashion
Southwesterners. U of NM Pr.
Mays, E. Truman, 1931-
xMays, E. Truman.
Clinical Evaluation of the Critically Injured. C
C Thomas.
Mays, James L. *see* Mays, James Luther.
Mays, James Luther.
xMays, James L.
Ezekiel, Second Isaiah. Fortress.
Mays, Lucinda.
xMays, Lucinda.

The Other Shore. Atheneum.
Mays, Maxine.
xMays, Maxine.
Student Teaching in Special Classes for the
Mentally Retarded. C C Thomas.
Mays, Willie.
xMays, Willie.
Born to Play Ball. Putnam.
Mays, Wolfe.
xMays, Wolfe.
Arthur Koestler. Judson.
Mayston, David J.
xMayston, David J.
The Idea of Social Choice. St Martin.
Mazer, Barry.
xMazer, Barry.
Superstar. Belmont-Tower.
Mazer, Harry.
xMazer, Harry.
Dollar Man. Delacorte.
The Dollar Man. Dell.
Guy Lenny. Delacorte.
Guy Lenny. Dell.
Mazer, Norma.
xMazer, Norma.
A Figure of Speech. Delacorte.
I Trissy. Dell.
I, Trissy. Delacorte.
xMazer, Norma F.
Figure of Speech. Dell.
Mazer, Norma F. *see* Mazer, Norma.
Mazer, Norma Fox, 1931-
xMazer, Norma F.
Mrs. Fish, Ape, & Me the Dump Queen.
Dutton.
Mazgaj, Paul, 1942-
xMazgaj, Paul.
The Action Francaise & Revolutionary
Syndicalism. U of NC Pr.
Maziarz, Edward A.
xMaziarz, Edward A.
Greek Mathematical Philosophy. Ungar.
Mazlish, Bruce, 1923-
xMazlish, Bruce.
In Search of Nixon: A Psychohistorical
Inquiry. Basic.
ed. Railroad & the Space Program: An
Exploration in Historical Analogy. MIT Pr.
The Revolutionary Ascetic: Evolution of a
Political Type. Basic.
Mazmanian, Daniel A.
xMazmanian, Daniel A.
Can Organizations Change?: Environmental
Protection, Citizen Participation, & the Army
Corps of Engineers. Brookings.
Third Parties in Presidential Elections.
Brookings.
Mazo, Joseph H.
xMazo, Joseph H.
Dance Is a Contact Sport. Da Capo.
Prime Movers: The Makers of Modern Dance
in America. Morrow.
Prime Movers: The Makers of Modern Dance
in America. Morrow.
Mazor, L. *see* Mazor, Laszlo.
Mazor, Laszlo.
xMazor, L.
Analytical Chemistry of Organic Halogen
Compounds. Pergamon.
Mazour, Anatole G. *see* Mazour, Anatole Gregory.
Mazour, Anatole Gregory, 1900-
xMazour, Anatole G.
Finland Between East & West. Greenwood.
Mazria, Edward.
xMazria, Edward.
The Passive Solar Energy Book. Rodale Pr Inc.
Mazrui, Ali A.
xMazrui, Ali A.

A World Federation of Cultures: An African
Perspective. Free Pr.
Mazur, Gail.
xMazur, Gail.
Nightfire. Godine.
Mazur, Michael P.
xMazur, Michael P.
Economic Growth & Development in Jordan.
Westview.
Mazur, Ronald M. *see* Mazur, Ronald Michael.
Mazur, Ronald Michael.
xMazur, Ronald M.
Commonsense Sex: A Basis for Discussion &
Reappraisal. Beacon Pr.
Mazurs, Edward G.
xMazurs, Edward G.
Graphic Representations of the Periodic
System During One Hundred Years. U of Ala
Pr.
Mazza, Valentino Del. *see* Del Mazza, Valentino.
Mazzanti, Deborah S. *see* Mazzanti, Deborah Szekely.
Mazzanti, Deborah Szekely.
xMazzanti, Deborah S.
Secrets of the Golden Door. Bantam.
Secrets of the Golden Door. Morrow.
Mazzarino, Santo.
xMazzarino, Santo.
The End of the Ancient World. Greenwood.
Mazzaro, Jerome.
xMazzaro, Jerome.
Postmodern American Poetry. U of Ill Pr.
Profile of William Carlos Williams. Merrill.
Mazze, Edward. *see* Mazze, Edward M.
Mazze, Edward M.
xMazze, Edward.
Personal Selling: Choice Against Chance. West
Pub.
Mazzei, F. *see* Mazzei, Filippo.
Mazzei, Filippo, 1730-1816
xMazzei, F.
Memoirs of the Life & Peregrinations of the
Florentine, Philip Mazzei 1730-1816. Kraus
Repr.
Mazzeo, Joseph A. *see* Mazzeo, Joseph Anthony.
Mazzeo, Joseph Anthony, 1923-
xMazzeo, Joseph A.
Medieval Cultural Tradition in Dante's
Comedy. Greenwood.
Structure & Thought in the Paradiso.
Greenwood.
Varieties of Interpretation. U of Notre Dame
Pr.
Mazzer, S. J.
xMazzer, S. J.
A Monographic Study of the Genus Pouzarella:
A New Genus in the Rhodophyllaceae,
Agaricales, Basidiomycetes. Intl Schol Bk
Serv.
Mazzini, Giuseppe, 1805-1872
xMazzini, Giuseppe.
Mazzini's Letters. Greenwood.
xMazzini, Guiseppe.
Mazzini's Letters. Hyperion Conn.
Mazzini, Guiseppe. *see* Mazzini, Giuseppe.
Mazzocco, Robert.
xMazzocco, Robert.
Trader. Knopf.
Mazzola, Michael L. *see* Mazzola, Michael Lee.
Mazzola, Michael Lee.
xMazzola, Michael L.
Proto-Romance & Sicilian. Humanities.
Mazzolini, R. *see* Mazzolini, Renato.
Mazzolini, Renato, 1950-
xMazzolini, R.
Government Controlled Enterprises:
International Strategic & Policy Decisions.
Wiley.
Mazzotta, Giuseppe, 1942-
xMazzotta, Giuseppe.

Dante, Poet of the Desert: History & Allegory
in the Divine Comedy. Princeton U Pr.
Mbeki, Govan. *see* Mbeki, Govan Archibald Mvunyelwa.
Mbeki, Govan Archibald Mvunyelwa, 1910-
xMbeki, Govan.
South Africa: The Peasant's Revolt. Peter
Smith.
Mberi, Antar. *see* Mberi, Antar Sudan Katara.
Mberi, Antar Sudan Katara.
xMberi, Antar.
ed. Speak Easy - Speak Free. Intl Pub Co.
Mbithi, Philip M.
xMbithi, Philip M.
Self Reliance in Kenya: The Case of Harambee.
Holmes & Meier.
Mbiti, John S.
xMbiti, John S.
African Religions & Philosophy. Doubleday.
McAdams, Alan K.
xMcAdams, Alan K.
Power & Politics in Labor Legislation.
Columbia U Pr.
McAdie, Alexander G. *see* McAdie, Alexander George.
McAdie, Alexander George, 1863-1943
xMcAdie, Alexander G.
Making the Weather. AMS Pr.
McAdoo, Donald.
xMcAdoo, Donald E.
Reflections of the Outer Banks. Island Pub.
McAdoo, Donald E. *see* McAdoo, Donald.
McAfee, Oralie.
xMcAfee, Oralie.
Cooking & Eating with Children: A Way to
Learn. ACEI.
McAleer, Gordon.
xMcAleer, Gordon.
Salaries & Attitudes: A Profile of the Internal
Auditing Profession. Inst Inter Aud.
McAleer, John. *see* McAleer, John J.
McAleer, John J.
xMcAleer, John.
Rex Stout: A Biography. Little.
McAleese, Frank G.
xMcAleese, Frank G.
The Laser Experimenter's Handbook. TAB
Bks.
McAleese, Ray.
xMcAleese, Ray.
ed. Understanding Classroom Life. Humanities.
McAlester, A. Lee. *see* McAlester, Arcie Lee.
McAlester, Arcie Lee, 1933-
xMcAlester, A. Lee.
The History of Life. P-H.
Type Species of Paleozoic Nuculoid Bivalve
Genera. Geol Soc.
McAlexander, Aaron.
xMcAlexander, Aaron.
Hands-on Applied Physics.
Benjamin-Cummings.
McAlister, Joan. *see* McAlister, Joan M.
McAlister, Joan M.
xMcAlister, Joan.
Radionuclide Techniques in Medicine.
Cambridge U Pr.
McAlister, Lyle. *see* McAlister, Lyle N.
McAlister, Lyle N.
xMcAlister, Lyle.
The Fuero Militar in New Spain 1764-1800.
Greenwood.
McAllaster, Elva. *see* McAllaster, Elva Arline.
McAllaster, Elva Arline, 1922-
xMcAllaster, Elva.
Free to Be Single. Christian Herald.
McAllister, Annie L. *see* McAllister, Annie Laurie.
McAllister, Annie Laurie.
xMcAllister, Annie L.
Queen of the Looking-Glass. Berkley Pub.
McAllister, Donald. *see* McAllister, Donald M.
McAllister, Donald M.
xMcAllister, Donald.

Evaluation in Environmental Planning:
Assessing Environmental, Social, Economic &
Political Tradeoffs. MIT Pr.
McAllister, Evelyn D. *see* McAllister, Evelyn Ditton.
McAllister, Evelyn Ditton.
xMcAllister, Evelyn D.
Easy Steps to Safe Swimming. A S Barnes.
McAllister, Samuel W. *see* McAllister, Ward.
McAllister, Ward, 1827-1895
xMcAllister, Samuel W.
Society As I Have Found It. Arno.
xMcAllister, Ward.
Society As I Have Found It. R West.
McAloon, Kenneth.
xMcAloon, Kenneth.
Calculus. HarBraceJ.
Calculus of One Variable. HarBraceJ.
McAlpin, Mary A. *see* McAlpin, Mary Alice Mitchell.
McAlpin, Mary Alice Mitchell, 1908
xMcAlpin, Mary A.
The Relationship of Reading to the Social
Acceptability of Sixth Grade Children. Ams
Pr.
McAlpine, Frank.
xMcAlpine, Frank.
Popular Poetic Pearls & Biographies of Poets.
Arno.
McAlpine, Monica E., 1940-
xMcAlpine, Monica E.
The Genre of Troilus & Criseyde. Cornell U
Pr.
McAnany, Emile G.
xMcAnany, Emile G.
ed. Communications in the Rural Third World:
The Role of Information in Development.
Praeger.
McArthur, A. Verne.
xMcArthur, A. Verne.
Coming Out Cold: Community Reentry from a
State Reformatory. Lexington Bks.
McArthur, Edwin.
xMcArthur, Edwin.
Flagstad: A Personal Memoir. Da Capo.
McArthur, Harvey K.
xMcArthur, Harvey K.
Understanding the Sermon on the Mount.
Greenwood.
McArthur, Lewis A. *see* McArthur, Lewis Ankeny.
McArthur, Lewis Ankeny.
xMcArthur, Lewis A.
Oregon Geographic Names. Oreg Hist Soc.
xMcArthur, Lewis L.
ed. Oregon Geographic Names. Oreg Hist Soc.
McArthur, Lewis L. *see* McArthur, Lewis Ankeny.
McAshan, H. H. *see* McAshan, Hildreth Hoke.
McAshan, Hildreth Hoke.
xMcAshan, H. H.
Competency-Based Education & Behavioral
Objectives. Educ Tech Pubns.
The Goals Approach to Performance
Objectives. HR&W.
McAteer, J. Davitt.
xMcAteer, J. Davitt.
Coal Mine Health & Safety: The Case of West
Virginia. Irvington.
McAulay, Sara.
xMcAulay, Sara.
Catch Rides. Popular Lib.
In Search of the Petroglyph. Coward.
McAuley, Alastair, 1938-
xMcAuley, Alastair.
Economic Welfare in the Soviet Union:
Poverty, Living Standards, & Inequality. U of
Wis Pr.
McAuley, Jack G.
xMcAuley, Jack G.
People to People: Essentials of Personal &
Public Communication. Wadsworth Pub.
McAuley, James J.
xMcAuley, James J.

After the Blizzard: Poems. U of Mo Pr.
McAuley, John.
xMcAuley, John.
Mattress Testing. Cross Country.
McAuley, Mary.
xMcAuley, Mary.
Politics & the Soviet Union. Penguin.
McAuliffe, Kevin.
xMcAuliffe, Kevin.
The Great American Newspaper: The Story of
the Village Voice. Scribner.
McAuliffe, Mary S. *see* McAuliffe, Mary Sperling.
McAuliffe, Mary Sperling, 1943-
xMcAuliffe, Mary S.
Crisis on the Left: Cold War Politics &
American Liberals, 1947-1954. U of Mass Pr.
McAuslan, Patrick.
xMcAuslan, Patrick.
The Ideologies of Planning Law. Pergamon.
McAvoy, Thomas T. *see* McAvoy, Thomas Timothy.
McAvoy, Thomas Timothy, 1903-1969
xMcAvoy, Thomas T.
Father O'Hara of Notre Dame: The
Cardinal-Archbishop of Philadelphia. U of
Notre Dame Pr.
Formation of the American Catholic Minority,
1820-1860. Fortress.
McAvoy, William C.
xMcAvoy, William C.
Dramatic Tragedy. McGraw.
McBain, Ed.
xMcBain, Ed.
Ax. S&S.
The Mugger. Ballantine.
McBain, Howard L. *see* McBain, Howard Lee.
McBain, Howard Lee, 1880-1936
xMcBain, Howard L.
De Witt Clinton & the Origin of the Spoils
System in New York. AMS Pr.
Prohibition Legal & Illegal. Arno.

McBain, Laurie.

xMcBain, Laurie.

Devil's Desire. Avon.

Tears of Gold. Avon.

McBain, Loren D.
xMcBain, Loren D.
Born Again & Living up to It: Guide to Church
Membership. Judson.
McBeath, Marcia.
xMcBeath, Marcia.
Little Changes Mean a Lot: How to Improve
the Behavior of Children & Other Important
People. P-H.
McBee, Alice Eaton.
xMcBee, Alice F.
From Utopia to Florence: The Story of a
Transcendentalist Community in
Northampton, Massachusetts, 1830-1852.
Porcupine Pr.
McBee, Alice F. *see* McBee, Alice Eaton.
McBeth, Leon.
xMcBeth, Leon.
Strange New Religions. Broadman.
Women in Baptist Life. Broadman.
McBey, James.
xMcBey, James.
The Early Life of James McBey: An
Autobiography 1883-1911. Oxford U Pr.
McBirney, Alexander R.
xMcBirney, Alexander R.
Geology & Petrology of the Galapagos Islands.
Geol Soc.
McBoyle, Geoffrey.
xMcBoyle, Geoffrey.
Climate in Review. HM.
McBride. *see* McBride, Helena.

McBride, A. *see* McBride, Alfred.
McBride, Alfred.
  xMcBride.
    Human Dimension of Catechetics. Macmillan.
  xMcBride, A.
    Human Dimension of Catechetics. Glencoe.
  xMcBride, Alfred.
    Catechetics: A Theology of Proclamation.
      Glencoe.
    Human Dimension of Catechetics. Kenedy.
McBride, Angela B. *see* McBride, Angela Barron.
McBride, Angela Barron.
  xMcBride, Angela B.
    The Growth & Development of Mothers.
      Har-Row.
    The Growth & Development of Mothers.
      Har-Row.
    A Married Feminist. Har-Row.
McBride, Carmen.
  xMcBride, Carmen.
    Silent Victory. Nelson-Hall.
McBride, Chris, 1941-
  xMcBride, Chris.
    The White Lions of Timbavati. Bantam.
    The White Lions of Timbavati. Paddington.
McBride, E. B. *see* McBride, Elna Browning.
McBride, Elna Browning.
  xMcBride, E. B.
    Obtaining Generating Functions.
      Springer-Verlag.
McBride, Helena.
  xMcBride.
    Acute Myocardial Infarction. ACC.
McBride, L. R.
  xMcBride, L. R.
    Practical Folk Medicine of Hawaii. Petroglyph.
McBride, Mary M. *see* McBride, Mary Margaret.
McBride, Mary Margaret.
  xMcBride, Mary M.
    Growing up of Mary Elizabeth. Dodd.
McBride, Michele, 1945-
  xMcBride, Michele.
    The Fire That Will Not Die. Chicago Review.
    The Fire That Will Not Die. ETC Pubns.
McBride, Richard.
  xMcBride, Richard.
    Lonely the Autumn Bird: Two Novels.
      Swallow.
McBride, Robert.
  xMcBride, Robert.
    Aspects of Seventeenth-Century French Drama
      & Thought. Rowman.
McBrien, Vincent O. *see* McBrien, Vincent Owen.
McBrien, Vincent Owen, 1916-
  xMcBrien, Vincent O.
    Introduction to Calculus. Irvington.
McBryde, Felix W. *see* McBryde, Felix Webster.
McBryde, Felix Webster, 1908-
  xMcBryde, Felix W.
    Cultural & Historical Geography of Southwest
      Guatemala. Greenwood.
McBryde, Isabel.
  xMcBryde, Isabel.
    Aboriginal Prehistory in New England: An
      Archaeological Survey of Northeastern New
      South Wales. Intl Schol Bk Serv.
McBryde, W. A. *see* McBryde, W. A. E.
McBryde, W. A. E.
  xMcBryde, W. A.
    ed. A Critical Review of Equilibrium Data for
      Proton-and Metal Complexes of
      1,10-Phenanthroline, 2,2'-Bipyridyl & Related
      Compounds: Critical Evaluation of
      Equilibrium Const. in Solution; Part A:
      Stability Const. of Metal Complexes.
      Pergamon.
McBurney, Margaret.
  xMcBurney, Margaret.

Homesteads: Early Buildings & Families from
    Kingston to Toronto. U of Toronto Pr.
McBurney, W. H. *see* McBurney, William Harlin.
McBurney, William Harlin.
  xMcBurney, W. H.
    ed. Four Before Richardson: Selected English
      Novels, 1720-1727. U of Nebr Pr.
McCaba, Joseph.
  xMcCaba, Joseph.
    The Teacher Who Laughs. Reg Baptist.
McCabe, David A. *see* McCabe, David Aloysius.
McCabe, David Aloysius, 1883-
  xMcCabe, David A.
    The Standard Rate in American Trade Unions.
      AMS Pr.
    Standard Rate in American Trade Unions.
      Arno.
McCabe, Dwight.
  xMcCabe, Dwight.
    ed. PCC's Reference Book of Personal &
      Home Computing, 1977. Peoples Computer.
McCabe, Helen M. *see* McCabe, Helen Marie.
McCabe, Helen Marie.
  xMcCabe, Helen M.
    Word Processing: A Systems Approach to the
      Office. HarBraceJ.
McCabe, Herb.
  xMcCabe, Herb.
    Love Letters of Herb & Sandy McCabe.
      Concordia.
McCabe, James D. *see* McCabe, James Dabney.
McCabe, James Dabney, 1842-1883
  xMcCabe, James D.
    Great Fortunes & How They Were Made: Or,
      the Struggles & Triumphs of Our Selfmade
      Men. Arno.
McCabe, Joseph, 1867-1955
  xMcCabe, Joseph.
    George Bernard Shaw: A Critical Study.
      Folcroft.
    George Bernard Shaw: A Critical Study.
      Gordon Pr.
    Rationalist Encyclopaedia: A Book of
      Reference on Religion, Philosophy, Ethics, &
      Science. Gale.
McCabe, Lee, 1939-
  xMcCabe, O. Lee.
    ed. Changing Human Behavior: Current
      Therapies & Future Directions. Grune.
McCabe, O. Lee. *see* McCabe, Lee.
McCafferty, Danelle.
  xMcCafferty, Dannelle.
    How Simple Things Are Made. NAL.
McCafferty, Dannelle. *see* McCafferty, Danelle.
McCafferty, Donald N.
  xMcCafferty, Donald N.
    Successful Field Service Management. Am
      Mgmt.
McCafferty, James A.
  xMcCafferty, James A.
    ed. Capital Punishment. Lieber-Atherton.
McCaffery, Ellen.
  xMcCaffery, Ellen.
    Graphic Astrology: The Astrological Home
      Study Course. Macoy Pub.
McCaffery, Margo, 1938-
  xMcCaffery, Margo.
    Nursing Management of the Patient with Pain.
      Lippincott.
McCaffrey, Anne.
  xMcCaffrey, Anne.

Dragondrums. Atheneum.
Dragondrums. Bantam.
Dragonflight. Ballantine.
Dragonquest. Ballantine.
Dragonsinger. Bantam.
Dragonsinger. Atheneum.
Dragonsong. Atheneum.
Dragonsong. Bantam.
Get off the Unicorn. Ballantine.
Restoree. Ballantine.
The White Dragon. Ballantine.
McCagg, William O.
  xMcCagg, William O.
    ed. Soviet Asian Ethnic Frontiers. Pergamon.
    Stalin Embattled: 1943-1948. Wayne St U Pr.
McCaghy, Charles H.
  xMcCaghy, Charles H.
    Crime in American Society. Macmillan.
McCague, James.
  xMcCague, James.
    The Long Bondage: 1441-1815. Garrard.
    The Office of President. Garrard.
    When Chicago Was Young. Garrard.
    When Cowboys Rode the Chisholm Trail.
      Garrard.
McCahan, David, 1897-
  xMcCahan, David.
    ed. Life Insurance Trends at Mid-Century.
      Irwin.
McCahill, Thomas W.
  xMcCahill, Thomas W.
    The Aftermath of Rape. Lexington Bks.
McCaig, M. *see* McCaig, Malcolm.
McCaig, Malcolm.
  xMcCaig, M.
    Permanent Magnets in Theory & Practice.
      Halsted Pr.
McCain, Garvin.
  xMcCain, Garvin.
    The Game of Science. Brooks-Cole.
McCaleb, James A.
  xMcCaleb, James A.
    Lower Pennsylvanian Ammonoids from the
      Bloyd Formation of Arkansas & Oklahoma.
      Geol Soc.
McCall, Daniel F.
  xMcCall, Daniel F.
    Africa in Time Perspective: A Discussion of
      Historical Reconstruction from Unwritten
      Sources. Oxford U Pr.
McCall, Dorothy.
  xMcCall, Dorothy K.
    Theatre of Jean-Paul Sartre. Columbia U Pr.
McCall, Dorothy K. *see* McCall, Dorothy.
McCall, Dorothy L. *see* McCall, Dorothy Lawson.
McCall, Dorothy Lawson.
  xMcCall, Dorothy L.
    Ranch Under the Rimrock. Binford.
McCall, G. J. *see* McCall, Gerald Joseph Home.
McCall, George A. *see* McCall, George Archibald.
McCall, George Archibald, 1802-1868
  xMcCall, George A.
    Letters from the Frontiers. U Presses Fla.
McCall, George J.
  xMcCall, George J.
    Observing the Law: Field Methods in the
      Study of Crime & the Criminal Justice
      System. Free Pr.
McCall, Gerald Joseph Home.
  xMcCall, G. J.
    ed. The Archean: Search for the Beginning.
      Acad Pr.
McCall, James E. *see* McCall, James Elliott.
McCall, James Elliott.
  xMcCall, James E.
    Fleeting House. Douglas-West.
McCall, John.
  xMcCall, John.

How to Write Themes & Essays. Monarch Pr.
McCall, John P.
   xMcCall, John P.
     Chaucer Among the Gods: The Poetics of
     Classical Myth. Pa St U Pr.
McCall, Morgan W.
   xMcCall, Morgan W.
     Leadership: Where Else Can We Go?. Duke.
McCall, Raymond J. see McCall, Raymond Joseph.
McCall, Raymond Joseph, 1913-
   xMcCall, Raymond J.
     The Varieties of Abnormality: A
     Phenomenological Analysis. C C Thomas.
McCall, Robert B., 1940-
   xMcCall, Robert B.
     Fundamental Statistics for Psychology.
     HarBraceJ.
McCall, Samuel W. see McCall, Samuel Walker.
McCall, Samuel Walker, 1851-1923
   xMcCall, Samuel W.
     Thaddeus Stevens. AMS Pr.
     Thaddeus Stevens. Folcroft.
     Thomas B. Reed. AMS Pr.
McCall, Thomas S.
   xMcCall, Thomas S.
     The Coming Russian Invasion of Israel.
     Moody.
McCall, William A. see McCall, William Anderson.
McCall, William Anderson, 1891-
   xMcCall, William A.
     Correlation of Some Psychological &
     Educational Measurements with Special
     Attention to the Measurement of Mental
     Ability. AMS Pr.
     I Thunk Me a Thaut. Tchrs Coll.
McCall's Editors. see McCall's Magazine.
McCall's Magazine Editors. see McCall's Magazine.
McCall's Needlework. see McCall's Magazine.
McCall's Needlework & Crafts Editors. see McCall's
  Magazine.
McCalla, Thomas R. see McCalla, Thomas Richard.
McCalla, Thomas Richard.
   xMcCalla, Thomas R.
     Introduction to Numerical Methods &
     FORTRAN Programming. Wiley.
McCall's Magazine.
   xMcCall's Editors.
     ed. McCall's Book of Quilts. S&S.
     McCall's Sewing Book. Random.
     The McCalls's Book of Handcraft. Random.
   xMcCall's Magazine Editors.
     McCall's Cooking School Cookbook. Random.
     McCall's Sewing for Your Home. S&S.
   xMcCall's Needlework.
     ed. The McCall's Book of Afghans. S&S.
   xMcCall's Needlework & Crafts Editors.
     The McCall's Book of American's Favorite
     Needlework & Craft. S&S.
     The McCall's Book of Rugmaking. S&S.
     The McCall's Crochet Treasury. S&S.
     McCall's Embroidery Book. S&S.
McCallum, George P.
   xMcCallum, George P.
     More Idiom Drills for Students of English As a
     Second Language. Har-Row.
McCallum, John D. see McCallum, John Dennis.
McCallum, John Dennis, 1924-
   xMcCallum, John D.
     Getting into Pro Football. Watts.
     The World Heavyweight Boxing Championship:
     A History. Chilton.
McCally, Michael.
   xMcCally, Michael.
     ed. Hypodynamics & Hypogravics: The
     Physiology of Inactivity & Weightlessness.
     Acad Pr.
McCameron, Fritz A.
   xMcCameron, Fritz A.

Cobol Logic & Programming. Irwin.
Fortran IV. Irwin.
FORTRAN Logic & Programming. Irwin.
McCammon, R. B. see McCammon, Richard B.
McCammon, Richard B.
   xMcCammon, R. B.
     ed. Concepts in Geostatistics. Springer-Verlag.
McCammon, Robert R.
   xMcCammon, Robert R.
     Baal. Avon.
McCammon, Robert W., 1916-
   xMcCammon, Robert W.
     Human Growth & Development. C C Thomas.
McCampbell, James M.
   xMcCampbell, James M.
     UFOlogy. Celestial Arts.
McCamy, James L. see McCamy, James Lucian.
McCamy, James Lucian, 1906-
   xMcCamy, James L.
     The Quality of the Environment. Free Pr.
McCamy, John C.
   xMcCamy, John C.
     Human Life Styling: Keeping Whole in the
     Twentieth Century. Har-Row.
McCandless, Anthony.
   xMcCandless, Anthony.
     Leap in the Dark. St Martin.
McCandless, Boyd R.
   xMcCandless, Boyd R.
     Adolescents: Behavior & Development.
     HR&W.
McCanles, Michael.
   xMcCanles, Michael.
     Dialectical Criticism & Renaissance Literature.
     U of Cal Pr.
McCann, Franklin T. see McCann, Franklin Thresher.
McCann, Franklin Thresher, 1903-
   xMcCann, Franklin T.
     English Discovery of America to 1585.
     Octagon.
McCann, Garth.
   xMcCann, Garth.
     Edward Abbey. Boise St Univ.
McCann, H. Gilman, 1942-
   xMcCann, H. Gilman.
     Chemistry Transformed: The Paradigmatic Shift
     from Phlogiston to Oxygen. Ablex Pub.
McCann, Philip. see McCann, Phillip.
McCann, Phillip.
   xMcCann, Philip.
     ed. Popular Education & Socialization in the
     Nineteenth Century. Methuen Inc.
McCann, S. M. see McCann, Samuel McDonald.
McCann, Samuel McDonald.
   xMcCann, S. M.
     ed. Endocrine Physiology II. Univ Park.
McCants, Dorothea O. see McCants, Dorothea Olga.
McCants, Dorothea Olga.
   xMcCants, Dorothea O.
     ed. They Came to Louisiana: Letters of a
     Catholic Mission, 1854-1882. La State U Pr.
McCarroll, Tolbert.
   xMcCarroll, Tolbert.
     Exploring the Inner World: A Guidebook for
     Personal Growth & Renewal. NAL.
     Notes from the Song of Life: Spiritual
     Reflections. Celestial Arts.
McCarron, Margaret M., 1928-
   xMcCarron, Margaret M.
     ed. Principles of Clinical Pharmacy Illustrated
     by Clinical Case Studies. Drug Intl Pubns.
McCarry, Charles.
   xMcCarry, Charles.
     The Better Angels. Dutton.
     Double Eagle. Little.
McCarthy , Paul J. see McCarthy, Paul Joseph.
McCarthy, Barry. see McCarthy, Barry W.
McCarthy, Barry W., 1943-
   xMcCarthy, Barry.

What You Still Don't Know About Male
     Sexuality. T Y Crowell.
McCarthy, Cavan, 1943-
   xMcCarthy, Cavan.
     Developing Libraries in Brazil: with a Chapter
     on Paraguay. Scarecrow.
McCarthy, Cormac, 1933-
   xMcCarthy, Cormac.
     Orchard Keeper. Random.
     The Orchard Keeper. SBD.
     Suttree. Random.
McCarthy, Daniel J.
   xMcCarthy, Daniel J.
     Business Policy & Strategy: Concepts &
     Readings. Irwin.
McCarthy, David F.
   xMcCarthy, David F.
     Essentials of Soil Mechanics & Foundations.
     Reston.
McCarthy, David S.
   xMcCarthy, David S.
     Memo to a Weary Sunday School Teacher.
     Judson.
McCarthy, E. Jerome. see McCarthy, Edmund Jerome.
McCarthy, Edmund Jerome.
   xMcCarthy, E. Jerome.
     Essentials of Marketing. Irwin.
     ed. Readings in Basic Marketing. Irwin.
McCarthy, Estelle.
   xMcCarthy, Estelle.
     The Power Picture. Friend Pr.
McCarthy, Eugene. see McCarthy, Eugene J.
McCarthy, Eugene J., 1916-
   xMcCarthy, Eugene.
     Ultimate Tyranny: The Majority Over the
     Majority. HarBraceJ.
   xMcCarthy, Eugene J.
     Other Things & the Aardvark. Doubleday.
McCarthy, Gary.
   xMcCarthy, Gary.
     The Derby Man. Dell.
     The First Sheriff. Doubleday.
     Mustang Fever. Doubleday.
     Showdown at Snakegrass Junction. Dell.
McCarthy, George D.
   xMcCarthy, George D.
     Valuing a Company: Practices & Procedures.
     Wiley.
McCarthy, George W.
   xMcCarthy, George W.
     CBers' Guide to Ham Radio. Van Nos
     Reinhold.
McCarthy, I. E. see McCarthy, Ian Ellery.
McCarthy, Ian Ellery, 1930-
   xMcCarthy, I. E.
     Introduction to Nuclear Theory. Krieger.
McCarthy, J. K. see McCarthy, John Keith.
McCarthy, Jane.
   xMcCarthy, Jane.
     All That Glitters. Bouregy.
     Listen to the Skylark. Bouregy.
McCarthy, John A. see McCarthy, John Aloysius.
McCarthy, John Aloysius, 1942-
   xMcCarthy, John A.
     Christoph Martin Wieland. G K Hall.
     Christoph Martin Wieland. Twayne.
McCarthy, John Keith, 1905-
   xMcCarthy, J. K.
     Patrol into Yesterday: My New Guinea Years
     (1927-1962). Verry.
McCarthy, Justin, 1830-1912
   xMcCarthy, Justin.
     Portraits of the Sixties. Arno.
     Portraits of the Sixties. R West.
McCarthy, M. L.
   xMcCarthy, M. L.

Adapted by The Life of Animals with Hooves. Silver.
Adapted by The Life of Sea Mammals. Silver.
Adapted by The Life of Strange Mammals. Silver.
McCarthy, Mary. *see* McCarthy, Mary Therese.
McCarthy, Mary T. *see* McCarthy, Mary Therese

McCarthy, Mary Therese, 1912-
xMcCarthy, Mary.
Cannibals & Missionaries. Avon.
Cannibals & Missionaries. HarBraceJ.

Cast a Cold Eye. HarBraceJ.
Charmed Life. HarBraceJ.
Company She Keeps. HarBraceJ.

The Group. NAL.
Medina. HarBraceJ.

Memories of a Catholic Girlhood. HarBraceJ.
Memories of a Catholic Girlhood. HarBraceJ.

On the Contrary. Octagon.
Stones of Florence. HarBraceJ.
Stones of Florence. HarBraceJ.
Venice Observed. HarBraceJ.
xMcCarthy, Mary T.
The Company She Keeps. HarBraceJ.
The Group. HarBraceJ.

McCarthy, Melodie A.
xMcCarthy, Melodie A.
Fundamentals of Early Childhood Education. Winthrop.
McCarthy, Patrick J. *see* McCarthy, Patrick Joseph.

McCarthy, Patrick Joseph, 1922-
xMcCarthy, Patrick J.
Matthew Arnold & the Three Classes. Columbia U Pr.

McCarthy, Paul, 1921-
xMcCarthy, Paul.
John Steinbeck. Ungar.

McCarthy, Paul Joseph, 1928-
xMcCarthy , Paul J.
Algebraic Extensions of Fields. Chelsea Pub.
McCarthy, Philip J. *see* McCarthy, Philip John.

McCarthy, Philip John, 1918-
xMcCarthy, Philip J.
Introduction to Statistical Reasoning. Krieger.

McCarthy, Philip L.
xMcCarthy, Philip L.
Diseases of the Oral Mucosa. Lea & Febiger.
McCarthy, Raymond G. *see* McCarthy, Raymond Gerald.

McCarthy, Raymond Gerald, 1901-
xMcCarthy, Raymond G.
ed. Drinking & Intoxication: Selected Readings in Social Attitudes & Controls. Coll & U Pr.
ed. Drinking & Intoxication: Selected Readings in Social Attitudes & Controls. Rutgers Ctr Alcohol.

McCarthy, Thomas, 1954-
xMcCarthy, Thomas.
The First Convention. Humanities.

McCarthy, Timothy, 1940-
xMcCarthy, Timothy.
Marx & the Proletariat: A Study in Social Theory. Greenwood.

McCarthy, Vincent A., 1947-
xMcCarthy, Vincent A.
The Phenomenology of Moods in Kierkegaard. Kluwer Boston.

McCarthy, Willard J.
xMcCarthy, Willard J.
Machine Tool Technology. McKnight.

McCartney, Earl J., 1908-
xMcCartney, Earl J.
Optics of the Atmosphere: Scattering by Molecules & Particles. Wiley.

McCarty, Clifford, 1929-
xMcCarty, Clifford.

Film Composers in America: A Checklist of Their Work. Da Capo.
Published Screenplays: A Checklist. Kent St U Pr.
McCarty, F. M. *see* McCarty, Fred M.

McCarty, Fred M.
xMcCarty, F. M.
The Pelican Guide to Big Bend Country. Pelican.

McCarty, George.
xMcCarty, George.
Calculator Calculus. Burgess.
Calculator Calculus. Educalc Pubns.
Calculator Calculus. Page-Ficklin.
McCarty, Harold H. *see* McCarty, Harold Hull.

McCarty, Harold Hull, 1901-
xMcCarty, Harold H.
Geographic Basis of American Economic Life. Greenwood.
Geographic Basis of American Economic Life. Kennikat.
McCarty, John L. *see* McCarty, John Lawton.

McCarty, John Lawton, 1901-
xMcCarty, John L.
Maverick Town: The Story of Old Tascosa. U of Okla Pr.
McCarty, Marilu H. *see* McCarty, Marilu Hurt.

McCarty, Marilu Hurt.
xMcCarty, Marilu H.
Dollars & Sense: An Introduction to Economics. Scott F.
McCary, James L. *see* McCary, James Leslie.

McCary, James Leslie.
xMcCary, James L.
A Complete Sex Education for Parents, Teenagers, & Young Adults. Van Nos Reinhold.
Freedom & Growth in Marriage. Wiley.
Human Sexuality. D Van Nostrand.
McCasland, S. Vernon. *see* McCasland, Selby Vernon.

McCasland, Selby Vernon.
xMcCasland, S. Vernon.
Religions of the World. Random.

McCaslin, Nellie.
xMcCaslin, Nellie.
Act Now: Plays & Ways to Make Them. S G Phillips.
ed. Children & Drama. Longman.
Creative Drama in the Classroom. Longman.
Creative Dramatics in the Classroom. Longman.
Theatre for Children in the United States: A History. U of Okla Pr.
ed. Theatre for Young Audiences. Longman.

McCaughan, Nano.
xMcCaughan, Nano.
Group Work: Learning & Practice. Allen Unwin.

McCaughey, Elizabeth P., 1948-
xMcCaughey, Elizabeth P.
From Loyalist to Founding Father: The Political Odyssey of William Samuel Johnson. Columbia U Pr.

McCaughey, Robert A.
xMcCaughey, Robert A.
Josiah Quincy, 1772-1864: The Last Federalist. Harvard U Pr.
McCauley, Carole S. *see* McCauley, Carole Spearin.

McCauley, Carole Spearin.
xMcCauley, Carole S.
Surviving Breast Cancer. Dutton.
McCauley, James E. *see* McCauley, James Emmit.

McCauley, James Emmit, 1873-1924
xMcCauley, James E.
A Stove-up Cowboy's Story. SMU Press.

McCauley, Martin.
xMcCauley, Martin.

Marxism-Leninism in the German Democratic Republic: The Socialist Unity Party (SED). B&N.

McCausland, Elizabeth.
xMcCausland, Elizabeth.
Life & Work of Edward Lamson Henry N. A. Da Capo.

McCausland, Ian, 1929-
xMcCausland, Ian.
Introduction to Optimal Control. Krieger.

McCavitt, William E., 1932-
xMcCavitt, William E.
Radio & Television: A Selected, Annotated Bibliography. Scarecrow.

McCaw, Mabel (Niedermeyer).
xMcCaw, Mabel N.
My Friend Next Door. Bethany Pr.
Orange Juice for Terry. Broadman.
McCaw, Mabel N. *see* McCaw, Mabel (Niedermeyer).

McCawley, James D.
xMcCawley, James D.
Adverbs, Vowels, & Other Objects of Wonder. U of Chicago Pr.

McCay, Winsor.
xMcCay, Winsor.
Dreams of the Rarebit Fiend. Dover.
Little Nemo in the Palace of Ice, & Further Adventures. Dover.

McCgwire, Michael.
xMcCGwire, Michael.
ed. Soviet Naval Policy: Objectives & Constraints. Praeger.

McClain, Alva J.
xMcClain, Alva J.
Law & Grace. BMH Bks.
McClain, Charles A. *see* McClain, Charles Allen.

McClain, Charles Allen, 1923-
xMcClain, Charles A.
First Came the Wings. Upper Room.

McClain, Ernest.
xMcClain, Ernest G.
The Myth of Invariance: The Origin of the Gods, Mathematics & Music from the Rg Veda to Plato. N Hays.
McClain, Ernest G. *see* McClain, Ernest.
McClain, J. Dudley. *see* McClain, John Dudley.

McClain, John Dudley.
xMcClain, J. Dudley.
Political Profiles of Black College Students in the South: Socio-Political Attitudes, Preferences, Personality & Characteristics. Resurgens Pubns.
Political Profiles of College Students in the South: Socio-Political Attitudes, Preferences, Personality & Characteristics. Resurgens Pubns.
Political Profiles of White College Students in the South: Socio-Political Attitudes, Preferences, Personality & Characteristics. Resurgens Pubns.
McClane, A. J. *see* McClane, Albert Jules.

McClane, Albert Jules, 1922-
xMcClane, A. J.
McClane's Secrets of Successful Fishing. HR&W.
The Practical Fly Fisherman. Follett.

McClane, Kenneth A., 1951-
xMcClane, Kenneth A.
Moons & Low Times. SBD.
McClary, Ben H. *see* McClary, Ben Harris.

McClary, Ben Harris.
xMcClary, Ben H.
ed. Lovingood Papers, 1965. U of Tenn Pr.
McClary, Jane M. *see* McClary, Jane Mcilvaine.

McClary, Jane Mcilvaine.
xMcClary, Jane M.
A Portion for Foxes. Popular Lib.

McClatchy, J. D., 1945-
xMcClatchy, J. D.

ed. Anne Sexton: The Artist & Her Critics. Ind U Pr.
McClave, Heather.
　xMcClave, Heather.
　　ed. Women Writers of the Short Story: A Collection of Critical Essays. P-H.
McClearn, G. E.
　xMcClearn, G. E.
　　Introduction to Behavioral Genetics. W H Freeman.
McCleary, Elliott.
　xMcCleary, Elliott.
　　The World of Rotary. Rotary Intl.
McCleary, Julia C.
　xMcCleary, Julia C.
　　Cooking Metric Is Fun. HarBraceJ.
McCleary, Richard.
　xMcCleary, Richard.
　　Applied Time Series Analysis for the Social Sciences. Sage.
　　Dangerous Men: The Sociology of Parole. Sage.
McCleary, Robert A.
　xMcCleary, Robert A.
　　Subcortical Mechanisms of Behavior: The Psychological Functions of Primitive Parts of the Brain. Basic.
McClellan, A. L. *see* McClellan, Aubrey Lester.
McClellan, Albert.
　xMcClellan, Albert.
　　Compiled by Meet Southern Baptists. Broadman.
McClellan, Aubrey Lester, 1923-
　xMcClellan, A. L.
　　Tables of Experimental Dipole Moments. W H Freeman.
McClellan, Elisabeth, 1851-1920
　xMcClellan, Elisabeth.
　　Historic Dress in America 1607-1870. Arno.
McClellan, Elizabeth. *see* McClellan, Elizabeth Mary.
McClellan, Elizabeth Mary.
　xMcClellan, Elizabeth.
　　A Part of Me. Grossmont Pr.
McClellan, Foster. *see* McClellan, Foster C.
McClellan, Foster C.
　xMcClellan, Foster.
　　Thoughts for a Friend. Unity Bks.
McClellan, George M. *see* McClellan, George Marion.
McClellan, George Marion, 1860-
　xMcClellan, George M.
　　Old Greenbottom Inn & Other Stories. AMS Pr.
　　Path of Dreams. Arno.
McClellan, Grant. *see* McClellan, Grant S.
McClellan, Grant S.
　xMcClellan, Grant.
　　ed. Canada in Transition. Wilson.
　xMcClellan, Grant S.
　　ed. Civil Rights. Wilson.
　　ed. Consuming Public. Wilson.
　　ed. Protecting Our Environment. Wilson.
　　ed. The Right to Privacy. Wilson.
　　Southern Africa. Wilson.
　　ed. Spain & Portugal: Democratic Beginnings. Wilson.
McClellan, James, 1937-
　xMcClellan, James.
　　Joseph Story & the American Constitution: A Study in Political & Legal Thought. U of Okla Pr.
McClellan, John L. *see* McClellan, John Little.
McClellan, John Little, 1896-
　xMcClellan, John L.
　　Crime Without Punishment. Greenwood.
McClellan, Kenneth.
　xMcClellan, Kenneth.
　　Whatever Happened to Shakespeare?. B&N.
McClellan, W. D. *see* McClellan, Woodford D.
McClellan, Woodford. *see* McClellan, Woodford D.
McClellan, Woodford D.
　xMcClellan, W. D.

Svetozar Markovic & the Origins of Balkan Socialism. Princeton U Pr.
　xMcClellan, Woodford.
　　Revolutionary Exiles: The Russians in the First International & the Paris Commune. Biblio Dist.
McClelland, B. J.
　xMcClelland, B. J.
　　Statistical Thermodynamics. Methuen Inc.
McClelland, Charles E.
　xMcClelland, Charles E.
　　German Historians & England: A Study in Nineteenth Century Views. Cambridge U Pr.
McClelland, D. C. *see* McClelland, David Clarence.
McClelland, David C. *see* McClelland, David Clarence.
McClelland, David Clarence.
　xMcClelland, D. C.
　　The Achievement Motive. Halsted Pr.
　xMcClelland, David C.
　　Achieving Society. Free Pr.
　　The Achieving Society. Halsted Pr.
　　ed. Development of Social Maturity. Irvington.
　　The Drinking Man. Free Pr.
　　ed. Education for Values. Irvington.
　　Power: The Inner Experience. Halsted Pr.
　　Power: The Inner Experience. Irvington.
McClelland, L. *see* McClelland, Lorraine.
McClelland, Lorraine.
　xMcClelland, L.
　　English Sounds & Spelling. P-H.
McClelland, Lucille H. *see* McClelland, Lucille Hudlin.
McClelland, Lucille Hudlin.
　xMcClelland, Lucille H.
　　Textbook for Psychiatric Technicians. Mosby.
McClelland, Nancy. *see* McClelland, Nancy Vincent.
McClelland, Nancy Vincent, 1876-
　xMcClelland, Nancy.
　　Duncan Phyfe & the English Regency. Dover.
McClelland, Peter D.
　xMcClelland, Peter D.
　　Causal Explanation & Model Building in History, Economics, & the New Economic History. Cornell U Pr.
McClements, L. D.
　xMcClements, Leslie.
　　The Economics of Social Security. Heinemann Ed.
McClements, Leslie. *see* McClements, L. D.
McClenaghan, Bruce A.
　xMcClenaghan, Bruce A.
　　Fundamental Movement: A Developmental & Remedial Approach. HR&W.
McClenathan, Louise.
　xMcClenathan, Louise.
　　My Mother Sends Her Wisdom. Morrow.
McClendon, James W. *see* McClendon, James William.
McClendon, James William.
　xMcClendon, James W.
　　Understanding Religious Convictions. U of Notre Dame Pr.
McClennen, Joshua, 1913-
　xMcClennen, Joshua.
　　On the Meaning & Function of Allegory in the English Renaissance. Folcroft.
McCleskey, Clifton.
　xMcCleskey, Clifton.
　　The Government & Politics of Texas. Little.
McClintic, J. Robert, 1928-
　xMcClintic, J. Robert.
　　Basic Anatomy & Physiology of the Human Body. Wiley.
McClintick, David, 1940-
　xMcClintick, David.
　　Stealing from the Rich: The Home Stake Oil Swindle. M Evans.
McClintock, Elizabeth. *see* McClintock, Elizabeth May.
McClintock, Elizabeth May.
　xMcClintock, Elizabeth.

An Annotated Checklist of Woody Ornamental Plants of California, Oregon, & Washington. Ag Sci Pubns.
McClintock, Michael, 1945-
　xMcClintock, Michael.
　　Homeowner's Handbook: What You Need to Know About Buying, Maintaining, Improving, & Running Your Home Successfully. Scribner.
McClinton, Katharine (Morrison).
　xMcClinton, Katherine M.
　　Art Deco: A Guide for Collectors. Potter.
　　Collecting American Victorian Antiques. Wallace-Homestead.
McClinton, Katharine Morrison.
　xMcClinton, Katherine M.
　　An Introduction to Lalique Glass. Wallace-Homestead.
McClinton, Katherine M. *see* McClinton, Katharine (Morrison).
McClinton, Leon.
　xMcClinton, Leon.
　　Cross-Country Runner. Dutton.
McCloskey, Donald N.
　xMcCloskey, Donald N.
　　Economic Maturity & Entrepreneurial Decline: British Iron & Steel, 1870-1913. Harvard U Pr.
McCloskey, Esther.
　xMcCloskey, Esther.
　　This Is the Collie. TFH Pubns.
McCloskey, John Mark.
　xMcCloskey, Mark.
　　Goodbye, but Listen: Poems. Vanderbilt U Pr.
McCloskey, Mark. *see* McCloskey, John Mark.
McCloskey, R. *see* McCloskey, Robert.
McCloskey, Robert, 1914-
　xMcCloskey, R.
　　illus. Lentil. Viking Pr.
　xMcCloskey, Robert.
　　Centerburg Tales. Penguin.
　　illus. Centerburg Tales. Viking Pr.
　　Lentil. Penguin.
　　Lentil. Viking Pr.
　　One Morning in Maine. Penguin.
　　illus. One Morning in Maine. Viking Pr.
McCloskey, Robert G. *see* McCloskey, Robert Green.
McCloskey, Robert Green.
　xMcCloskey, Robert G.
　　American Supreme Court. U of Chicago Pr.
McCloskey, William B., 1928-
　xMcCloskey, William B.
　　The Highliners. McGraw.
McCloy, D.
　xMcCloy, D.
　　The Control of Fluid Power. Halsted Pr.
McCloy, James.
　xMcCloy, James.
　　Dogs at Work. Crown.
McCloy, S. T. *see* McCloy, Shelby Thomas.
McCloy, Shelby T. *see* McCloy, Shelby Thomas.
McCloy, Shelby Thomas, 1898-
　xMcCloy, S. T.
　　The Negro in France. Haskell.
　xMcCloy, Shelby T.
　　Gibbon's Antagonism to Christianity. B Franklin.
　　Government Assistance in Eighteenth Century France. Porcupine Pr.
　　The Negro in the French West Indies. Negro U Pr.
McCluggage, Denise.
　xMcCluggage, Denise.
　　The Centered Skier. Vermont Crossroads.
　　The Centered Skier. Warner Bks.
McClumpha, Charles F. *see* McClumpha, Charles Flint.
McClumpha, Charles Flint, 1863-1933
　xMcClumpha, Charles F.
　　The Alliteration of Chaucer. Folcroft.
McClung, Betty J. *see* McClung, Betty J. Beranek.

McClung, Betty J. Beranek.
  xMcClung, Betty J.
    Something to Say All Through the Day.
    Interstate.
McClung, Jean.
  xMcClung, Jean.
    Effects of High Altitude on Human Birth:
    Observations on Mothers, Placentas, & the
    Newborn in Two Peruvian Populations.
    Harvard U Pr.
McClung, Nellie. *see* McClung, Nellie Letitia (Mooney).
McClung, Nellie Letitia (Mooney), 1873-1951
  xMcClung, Nellie.
    In Times Like These. U of Toronto Pr.
McClung, Robert. *see* McClung, Robert M.
McClung, Robert M.
  xMcClung, Robert.
    Hunted Mammals of the Sea. Morrow.
  xMcClung, Robert M.
    All About Animals & Their Young. Random.
    America's Endangered Birds: Programs &
    People Working to Save Them. Morrow.
    Honker: The Story of a Wild Goose. Morrow.
    Peeper, First Voice of Spring. Morrow.
    illus. Possum. Morrow.
McClung, William A.
  xMcClung, William A.
    The Country House in English Renaissance
    Poetry. U of Cal Pr.
McClure, A. K. *see* McClure, Alexander Kelly.
McClure, Alexander K. *see* McClure, Alexander Kelly.
McClure, Alexander Kelly, 1828-1909
  xMcClure, A. K.
    Our Presidents & How We Make Them. Arno.
  xMcClure, Alexander K.
    Colonel Alexander K. McClure's Recollections
    of Half a Century. AMS Pr.
McClure, Arthur F.
  xMcClure, Arthur F.
    The Truman Administration & the Problems of
    Postwar Labor 1945-1948. Fairleigh
    Dickinson
McClure, Charles R.
  xMcClure, Charles R.
    Information for Academic Library Decision
    Making: The Case for Organizational
    Information Management. Greenwood.
McClure, Charlotte S.
  xMcClure, Charlotte S.
    Gertrude Atherton. Boise St Univ.
    Gertrude Atherton. G K Hall.
    Gertrude Atherton. Twayne.
McClure, Ethel.
  xMcClure, Ethel.
    A Historical Directory of Minnesota Homes for
    the Aged. Minn Hist.
    More Than a Roof: The Development of
    Minnesota Poor Farms & Homes for the
    Aged. Minn Hist.
McClure, Gillian.
  xMcClure, Gillian.
    Fly Home, McDoo. Andre Deutsch.
McClure, James, 1939-
  xMcClure, James.
    Rogue Eagle. Avon.
    Rogue Eagle. Har-Row.
    The Steam Pig. Avon.
    The Steam Pig. Har-Row.
    The Sunday Hangman. Avon.
    The Sunday Hangman. Har-Row.
McClure, Jesse F.
  xMcClure, Jesse F.
    ed. Managing Human Services. Intl Dialogue
    Pr.
McClure, Jon.
  xMcClure, Jon.
    Stretching Your Meat Dollar. BJ Pub Group.
McClure, Jon. *see* McClure, Jon A.
McClure, Jon A.
  xMcClure, Jon.

    Meat Eaters Are Threatened. BJ Pub Group.
McClure, Larry.
  xMcClure, Larry.
    Career Education Survival Manual: A
    Guidebook for Career Educators & Their
    Friends. Olympus Pub Co.
McClure, Louis C.
  xMcClure, Louis C.
    How to Build Low Cost Motor Homes. Trail-R.
McClure, Michael.
  xMcClure, Michael.
    Antechamber & Other Poems. New Directions.
    Hail Thee Who Play. Sand Dollar.
    Josephine the Mouse Singer. New Directions.
McClure, Robert C. *see* McClure, Robert Charles.
McClure, Robert Charles.
  xMcClure, Robert C.
    Cat Anatomy: An Atlas, Text & Dissection
    Guide. Lea & Febiger.
McClure, Ron, 1941-
  xMcClure, Ron.
    Rawlins. Dial.
McCluskey, J. *see* McCluskey, Jim.
McCluskey, Jim.
  xMcCluskey, J.
    Road Form & Townscape. Nichols Pub.
McCluskey, Neil Gerard.
  xMcCluskey, Neil S.
    ed. Catholic University: A Modern Appraisal.
    U of Notre Dame Pr.
McCluskey, Neil S. *see* McCluskey, Neil Gerard.
McClusky, Wanda L.
  xMcClusky, Wanda L.
    Association & Company Publications in Texas,
    1974. U of Tex Busn Res.
McClymer, John F.
  xMcClymer, John F.
    War & Welfare: Social Engineering in America,
    1890-1925. Greenwood.
McCole, C. John, 1905-
  xMcCole, C. John.
    Lucifer at Large. Arno.
    Lucifer at Large. Haskell.
McCollister. *see* McCollister, John.
McCollister, John.
  xMcCollister.
    The Christian Catalogue. Jonathan David.
McCollough, Celeste.
  xMcCollough, Celeste.
    Introduction to Statistical Analysis: A
    Semiprogrammed Approach. McGraw.
McCollough, Charles R., 1934-
  xMcCollough, Charles R.
    Morality of Power: A Notebook on Christian
    Education for Social Change. Pilgrim NY.
McComas, Tom.
  xMcComas, Tom.
    Collecting Toy Trains. Childrens.
McComb, Arthur. *see* McComb, Arthur Kilgore.
McComb, Arthur Kilgore, 1895-
  xMcComb, Arthur.
    Baroque Painters of Italy: An Introductory
    Historical Survey. Russell.
McComb, David G.
  xMcComb, David G.
    Houston, the Bayou City. U of Tex Pr.
McComb, Robert B.
  xMcComb, Robert B.
    Alkaline Phosphatase. Plenum Pub.
McComish, P. B. *see* McComish, Peter Bartholomew.
McComish, Peter Bartholomew.
  xMcComish, P. B.
    Anaesthesia for Neurological Surgery. Year Bk
    Med.
McConathy, Dale.
  xMcConathy, Dale.
    Hollywood Costume. Abrams.
McConkey, Dale. *see* McConkey, Dale D.
McConkey, Dale D.
  xMcConkey, Dale.

    MBO for Nonprofit Organizations. Am Mgmt.
  xMcConkey, Dale D.
    Financial Management by Objectives. P-H.
    How to Manage by Results. Am Mgmt.
    No-Nonsense Delegation. Am Mgmt.
McConkey, James.
  xMcConkey, James.
    Night Stand: A Book of Stories. Cornell U Pr.
    The Tree House Confessions. Dutton.
McConkie, Bruce R.
  xMcConkie, Bruce R.
    The Mortal Messiah: From Bethlehem to
    Calvary. Deseret Bk.
McConkie, Joseph F.
  xMcConkie, Joseph F.
    Seeking the Spirit. Deseret Bk.
McConkie, Oscar W. *see* McConkie, Oscar Walter.
McConkie, Oscar Walter.
  xMcConkie, Oscar W.
    Aaronic Priesthood. Deseret Bk.
    Angels. Deseret Bk.
McConnaughey, Bayard H. *see* McConnaughey, Bayard
Harlow.
McConnaughey, Bayard Harlow, 1916-
  xMcConnaughey, Bayard H.
    Introduction to Marine Biology. Mosby.
McConnel, Frances.
  xMcConnel, Frances.
    ed. One Step Closer: New Poetry by Women
    of the West Coast. Pygmalion Pr.
McConnell, Brian.
  xMcConnell, Brian.
    History of Assassination. Aurora Pubs.
McConnell, Campbell R.
  xMcConnell, Campbell R.
    Economic Issues: A Book of Readings.
    McGraw.
McConnell, Charles.
  xMcConnell, Charles N.
    Home Plumbing Handbook. Audel.
McConnell, Charles N. *see* McConnell, Charles.
McConnell, Frank. *see* McConnell, Frank D.
McConnell, Frank D., 1942-
  xMcConnell, Frank.
    Storytelling & Mythmaking: Images from Film
    & Literature. Oxford U Pr.
  xMcConnell, Frank D.
    Four Postwar American Novelists: Bellow,
    Mailer, Barth, & Pynchon. U of Chicago Pr.
McConnell, Grant.
  xMcConnell, Grant.
    Decline of Agrarian Democracy. Atheneum.
    Private Power & American Democracy.
    Random.
McConnell, John P. *see* McConnell, John Preston.
McConnell, John Preston, 1866-
  xMcConnell, John P.
    Negroes & Their Treatment in Virginia from
    1865-1867. Negro U Pr.
McConnell, Jon P. *see* McConnell, Jon Patrick.
McConnell, Jon Patrick.
  xMcConnell, Jon P.
    Hospitality Management: Avoiding Legal
    Pitfalls. CBI Pub.
McConnell, Robert R., 1945-
  xMcConnell, Robert R.
    Modeling Glass Furnace, Refiner & Forehearth
    Design & Operation for Energy Efficiency &
    Improved Control. Garland Pub.
McConnell, Rosemary.
  xMcConnell, Rosemary.
    The Amazon. Silver.
McConnell, Taylor, 1921-
  xMcConnell, Taylor.
    Group Leadership for Self-Realization. Van
    Nos Reinhold.
McConnell, William J. *see* McConnell, William John.
McConnell, William John.
  xMcConnell, William J.

Frontier Law: A Story of Vigilante Days. AMS
Pr.
McConnico, Charles T.
xMcConnico, Charles T.
Medical Transcriptionist Handbook. C C
Thomas.
McConville, Robert.
xMcConville, Robert.
History of Board Games. Creative Pubns.
McConville, S. see McConville, Sean.
McConville, Sean.
xMcConville, S.
The Use of Imprisonment: Essays in the
Changing State of English Penal Policy.
Routledge & Kegan.
McCook, Henry C. see McCook, Henry Christopher.
McCook, Henry Christopher, 1837-1911
xMcCook, Henry C.
Latimers: A Tale of the Western Insurrection
of 1794. B Franklin.
McCool, Gerald A.
xMcCool, Gerald A.
Catholic Theology in the Nineteenth Century:
The Quest for a Unitary Method. Seabury.
McCord, Howard, 1932-
xMcCord, Howard.
Fire Visions. SBD.
McCord, Jean.
xMcCord, Jean.
Turkeylegs Thompson. Atheneum.
McCord, William. see McCord, William Maxwell.
McCord, William Maxwell, 1930-
xMcCord, William.
Life Styles in the Black Ghetto. Norton.
McCordock, Robert S. see McCordock, Robert Stanley.
McCordock, Robert Stanley, 1897-
xMcCordock, Robert S.
British Far Eastern Policy, 1894-1900.
Octagon.
McCormac, Eugene I. see McCormac, Eugene Irving.
McCormac, Eugene Irving, 1872-1943
xMcCormac, Eugene I.
Colonial Opposition to Imperial Authority
During the French & Indian War. B Franklin.
White Servitude in Maryland, 1634-1820. AMS
Pr.
McCormac, Jack C.
xMcCormac, Jack C.
Structural Analysis. Har-Row.
Structural Steel Design. Har-Row.
McCormack, Andrew Ross, 1943-
xMcCormack, Ross.
Reformers, Rebels, & Revolutionaries: The
Western Canadian Radical Movement
1899-1919. U of Toronto Pr.
McCormack, Erliss.
xMcCormack, Erliss.
How to Raise & Train a Cairn Terrier. TFH
Pubns.
McCormack, Gavan.
xMcCormack, Gavan.
Chang Tso-Lin in Northeast China, 1911-1928:
China, Japan, & the Manchurian Idea.
Stanford U Pr.
McCormack, James E.
xMcCormack, James E.
Early Cognitive Instruction for the Moderately
& Severely Handicapped: Program Guide.
Res Press.
McCormack, John E.
xMcCormack, John E.
Rabbit Tales. Dutton.
McCormack, Lily. see McCormack, Lily Foley.
McCormack, Lily Foley.
xMcCormack, Lily.
I Hear You Calling Me. Greenwood.
McCormack, Mark H.
xMcCormack, Mark H.

The Wonderful World of Professional Golf.
Atheneum.
McCormack, Ross. see McCormack, Andrew Ross.
McCormack, Thomas.
xMcCormack, Thomas.
ed. Afterwords: Novelists on Their Novels.
Har-Row.
McCormack, William. see McCormack, William Charles.
McCormack, William C. see McCormack, William
Charles.
McCormack, William Charles.
xMcCormack, William.
ed. Language & Thought: Anthropological
Issues. Beresford Bk Serv.
xMcCormack, William C.
ed. Language & Thought: Anthropological
Issues. Mouton.
McCormick, Barnes W. see McCormick, Barnes
Warnock.
McCormick, Barnes Warnock, 1926-
xMcCormick, Barnes W.
Aerodynamics, Aeronautics, & Flight
Mechanics. Wiley.
McCormick, Bill.
xMcCormick, Bill.
The Complete Beginner's Guide to Golf.
Doubleday.
McCormick, Brian J. see McCormick, Brian Joseph.
McCormick, Brian Joseph.
xMcCormick, Brian J.
Industrial Relations in the Coal Industry. Shoe
String.
McCormick, Clarence, 1888-
xMcCormick, Clarence.
The Teaching of General Mathematics in the
Secondary Schools of the United States: A
Study of the Development & Present Status
of General Mathematics. AMS Pr.
McCormick, Dell. see McCormick, Dell J.
McCormick, Dell J.
xMcCormick, Dell.
Paul Bunyan Swings His Axe. Schol Bk Serv.
xMcCormick, Dell J.
illus. Paul Bunyan Swings His Axe. Caxton.
McCormick, E. J. see McCormick, Ernest James.
McCormick, E. M. see McCormick, Edward Mack.
McCormick, Edward Mack.
xMcCormick, E. M.
Digital Computer Primer. McGraw.
McCormick, Ernest J. see McCormick, Ernest James.
McCormick, Ernest James.
xMcCormick, E. J.
Human Factors in Engineering & Design.
McGraw.
xMcCormick, Ernest J.
Industrial Psychology. P-H.
Job Analysis: Methods & Applications. Am
Mgmt.
McCormick, J. see McCormick, Jack.
McCormick, Jack.
xMcCormick, J.
Life of the Forest. McGraw.
McCormick, Jim, 1920-
xMcCormick, Jim.
Last Seen Alive. Doubleday.
McCormick, John.
xMcCormick, John.
Catastrophe & Imagination: An Interpretation
of the Recent English & American Novel.
Folcroft.
McCormick, Mary J. see McCormick, Mary Josephine.
McCormick, Mary Josephine, 1903-
xMcCormick, Mary J.
Enduring Values in a Changing Society. Family
Serv.
McCormick, Michael E., 1936-
xMcCormick, Michael E.

ed. Anchoring Systems. Pergamon.
Ocean Engineering Wave Mechanics. Wiley.
McCormick, Richard A.
xMcCormick, Richard A.
ed. Doing Evil to Achieve Good: Moral Choice
in Conflict Situations. Loyola.
McCormick, Richard P.
xMcCormick, Richard P.
Experiment in Independence: New Jersey in
the Critical Period 1781-1789. Rutgers U Pr.
McCormick, Robert. see McCormick, Robert Rutherford.
McCormick, Robert Rutherford, 1880-1955
xMcCormick, Robert.
Freedom of the Press. Arno.
McCormick, Rose M. see McCormick, Rose Matthew.
McCormick, Rose Matthew.
xMcCormick, Rose M.
My Care & Share Book: An
Around-The-World Picture Story. Friend Pr.
McCormick, Thomas C. see McCormick, Thomas
Carson.
McCormick, Thomas Carson, 1892-1954
xMcCormick, Thomas C.
Comparative Study of Rural Relief &
Non-Relief Households. Da Capo.
McCormick, Wilfred.
xMcCormick, Wilfred.
Starmaker. Speller.
McCormick, William F.
xMcCormick, William F.
Atlas of Cerebrovascular Disease. Saunders.
McCorry, Jesse J.
xMcCorry, Jesse J.
Marcus Foster & the Oakland Public Schools:
Leadership in an Urban Bureaucracy. U of
Cal Pr.
McCosh, James, 1811-1894
xMcCosh, James.
Realistic Philosophy Defended in a Philosophic
Series. AMS Pr.
McCourt, James, 1941-
xMcCourt, James.
Mawrdew Czgowchwz. FS&G.
McCourt, Kathleen.
xMcCourt, Kathleen.
Working-Class Women & Grass-Roots Politics.
Ind U Pr.
McCowen, Alec.
xMcCowen, Alec.
Young Gemini. Atheneum.
McCown, Ada C. see McCown, Ada Chenoweth.
McCown, Ada Chenoweth, 1886-
xMcCown, Ada C.
Congressional Conference Committee. AMS Pr.
McCoy, Alfred W.
xMcCoy, Alfred W.
The Politics of Heroin in Southeast Asia.
Har-Row.
McCoy, Barry. see McCoy, Barry M.
McCoy, Barry M.
xMcCoy, Barry.
The Two-Dimensional Ising Model. Harvard U
Pr.
McCoy, Charles A. see McCoy, Charles Allan.
McCoy, Charles Allan, 1920-
xMcCoy, Charles A.
Polk & the Presidency. Haskell.
McCoy, Charles N. see McCoy, Charles Nicholas Reiten.
McCoy, Charles Nicholas Reiten, 1911-
xMcCoy, Charles N.
The Structure of Political Thought: A Study in
the History of Political Ideas. Greenwood.
McCoy, Charles S.
xMcCoy, Charles S.
When gods Change: Hope for Theology.
Abingdon.
McCoy, Donald R.
xMcCoy, Donald R.

Quest & Response: Minority Rights & the
Truman Administration. Regents Pr KS.

McCoy, Doyle, 1917-
xMcCoy, Doyle.
Roadside Wild Fruits of Oklahoma. U of Okla
Pr.

McCoy, Elin.
xMcCoy, Elin.
The Incredible Year-Round Playbook. Random.

McCoy, Esther.
xMcCoy, Esther.
Case Study Houses, 1945-1962. Hennessey.
Richard Neutra. Braziller.

McCoy, Horace, 1897-
xMcCoy, Horace.
I Should Have Stayed Home. Garland Pub.

McCoy, Isaac, 1784-1846
xMcCoy, Isaac.
History of Baptist Indian Missions. Johnson
Repr.

McCoy, J. J. see McCoy, Joseph J.

McCoy, James W.
xMcCoy, James W.
Chemical Analysis of Industrial Water. Chem
Pub.
Chemical Treatment of Cooling Water. Chem
Pub.

McCoy, John H. see McCoy, John Henry.

McCoy, John Henry, 1912-
xMcCoy, John H.
Livestock & Meat Marketing. AVI.

McCoy, Joseph J., 1917-
xMcCoy, J. J.
The Complete Book of Cat Health & Care.
Berkley Pub.
The Complete Book of Dog Training & Care.
Berkley Pub.
In Defense of Animals. HM.
Pet Safety. Watts.

McCoy, Neal. see McCoy, Neal Henry.

McCoy, Neal H. see McCoy, Neal Henry.

McCoy, Neal Henry, 1905-
xMcCoy, Neal.
Introduction to Modern Algebra. Allyn.
xMcCoy, Neal H.
The Theory of Rings. Chelsea Pub.

McCoy, Ralph E. see McCoy, Ralph Edward.

McCoy, Ralph Edward, 1915-
xMcCoy, Ralph E.
Freedom of the Press: An Annotated
Bibliography. S Ill U Pr.

McCoy, Robert A.
xMcCoy, Robert A.
Practical Photography. McKnight.

McCoy, T. L. see McCoy, Terry L.

McCoy, Terry L., 1940-
xMcCoy, T. L.
ed. Dynamics of Population Policy in Latin
America. Ballinger Pub.

McCracken, D. D. see McCracken, Daniel D.

McCracken, Daniel. see McCracken, Daniel D.

McCracken, Daniel D.
xMcCracken, D. D.
A Guide to COBOL Programming. Wiley.
xMcCracken, Daniel.
A Simplified Guide to Structured Cobol
Programming. Wiley.
xMcCracken, Daniel D.
Fortran with Engineering Applications. Wiley.
Guide to Algol Programming. Wiley.
A Guide to Fortran IV Programming. Wiley.
Public Policy & the Expert: Ethical Problems
of the Witness. Coun Rel & Intl.

McCracken, David.
xMcCracken, David.
Junius & Philip Francis. Twayne.

McCracken, George H.
xMcCracken, George H.

Antimicrobial Therapy for Newborns: Practical
Application of Pharmacology to Clinical
Usage. Grune.

McCracken, Harold, 1894-
xMcCracken, Harold.
The American Cowboy. Doubleday.

McCracken, Mary Lou, 1943-
xMcCracken, May Lou.
The Deep South Natural Foods Cookbook. BJ
Pub Group.

McCracken, May Lou. see McCracken, Mary Lou.

McCracken, Paul.
xMcCracken, Paul.
Fiscal Responsibility: Tax Increases or
Spending Cuts?. NYU Pr.

McCracken, Paul W. see McCracken, Paul Winston.

McCracken, Paul Winston.
xMcCracken, Paul W.
The Energy Crisis. Am Enterprise.

McCrady, Edward, 1833-1903
xMcCrady, Edward.
History of South Carolina in the Revolution,
1775-1780. Russell.
History of South Carolina Under the
Proprietary Government, 1670-1719. Russell.
History of South Carolina Under the Royal
Government 1719-1776. Russell.

McCrady, Lady.
xMcCrady, Lady.
illus. Mildred & the Mummy. Holiday.
Miss Kiss & the Nasty Beast. Holiday.

McCraney, William L. see McCraney, William Lloyd.

McCraney, William Lloyd.
xMcCraney, William L.
ed. Readings in Criminal Psychology. Mss Info.

McCrary, Emma.
xMcCrary, Emma J.
Influencing Horses. Printed Horse.

McCrary, Emma J. see McCrary, Emma.

McCrary, Peyton, 1943-
xMcCrary, Peyton.
Abraham Lincoln & Reconstruction: The
Louisiana Experiment. Princeton U Pr.

McCraw, Thomas K.
xMcCraw, Thomas K.
TVA & the Power Fight: 1933-1939.
Lippincott.

McCray, Walter A. see McCray, Walter Arthur.

McCray, Walter Arthur.
xMcCray, Walter A.
Black Folks & Christian Liberty: Black,
Christian, & Free to Be Cultural & Social.
Black Light Fellow.

McCrea, Joan. see McCrea, Joan M.

McCrea, Joan M.
xMcCrea, Joan.
Texas Labor Laws. Gulf Pub.

McCready, Gerald. see McCready, Gerald B.

McCready, Gerald B.
xMcCready, Gerald.
Canadian Marketing Trends. Irwin.
xMcCready, Gerald B.
Profile Canada: Social & Economic Projections.
Irwin.

McCready, Richard R.
xMcCready, Richard R.
Business Mathematics. Wadsworth Pub.

McCready, W. C. see McCready, William C.

McCready, William C.
xMcCready, W. C.
The Ultimate Values of the American
Population. Sage.

McCredie, James R.
xMcCredie, James R.
Fortified Military Camps in Attica. Am Sch
Athens.

McCreery, Charles, 1942-
xMcCreery, Charles.

Psychical Phenomena & the Physical World.
State Mutual Bk.

McCreight, Tim.
xMcCreight, Tim.
Metalworking for Jewelry: Tools, Materials,
Techniques. Van Nos Reinhold.

McCrillis, John O. see McCrillis, John O. C.

McCrillis, John O. C.
xMcCrillis, John O.
Printer's Abecedarium. Godine.

McCrimmon, Barbara.
xMcCrimmon, Barbara.
ed. American Library Philosophy: An
Anthology. Shoe String.

McCrimmon, James M. see McCrimmon, James McNab.

McCrimmon, James McNab.
xMcCrimmon, James M.
Writing with a Purpose. HM.

McCrindle, Jean.
xMcCrindle, Jean.
ed. Dutiful Daughters: Women Talk About
Their Lives. U of Tex Pr.

McCrone, Walter C.
xMcCrone, Walter C.
Polarized Light Microscopy. Ann Arbor
Science.

McCrory, Wallace W.
xMcCrory, Wallace W.
Developmental Nephrology. Harvard U Pr.

McCroskey, James. see McCroskey, James C.

McCroskey, James C.
xMcCroskey, James.
Introduction to Rhetorical Communication.
P-H.
xMcCroskey, James C.
Introduction to Interpersonal Communication.
P-H.

McCrum, Robert.
xMcCrum, Robert.
In the Secret State. S&S.

McCubbin, H. S. see McCubbin, Hamilton I.

McCubbin, Hamilton I.
xMcCubbin, H. S.
Families in the Military System. Sage.

McCue, Marion. see McCue, Marion J.

McCue, Marion J.
xMcCue, Marion.
How to Pick the Right Name for Your Baby.
G&D.

McCuen, Jo Ray.
xMcCuen, Jo Ray.
Readings for Writers. HarBraceJ.
xMcCuen, JoRay.
Readings for Writers. HarBraceJ.

McCuen, JoRay. see McCuen, Jo Ray.

McCullagh, James. see McCullagh, James C.

McCullagh, James C.
xMcCullagh, James.
ed. The Solar Greenhouse Book. Rodale Pr Inc.

McCullen, Maurice.
xMcCullen, Maurice.
A Dictionary of the Characters in George
Meredith's Fiction. Garland Pub.

McCullers, Carson.
xMcCullers, Carson.
The Ballad of the Sad Cafe. Atheneum.

McCullers, Carson. see McCullers, Carson (Smith).

McCullers, Carson (Smith), 1917-
xMcCullers, Carson.
Reflections in a Golden Eye. HM.

McCullers, Levi D. see McCullers, Levis D.

McCullers, Levis D.
xMcCullers, Levi D.
Accounting Theory: Text & Readings. Wiley.
xMcCullers, Levis D.
Introduction to Financial Accounting. Wiley.

McCulley, Johnston, 1883-
xMcCulley, Johnston.
The Mark of Zorro. Am Repr-Rivercity Pr.

McCullin, Don. see McCullin, Donald.

McCullin, Donald, 1935-
  xMcCullin, Don.
    Homecoming. St Martin.
McCullo, Marion. see McCullo, Marion (Biggs).
McCullo, Marion (Biggs).
  xMcCullo, Marion.
    Student Journalist's Proofreader's Manual.
    Rosen Pr.
McCulloch, J. Wallace. see McCulloch, James Wallace.
McCulloch, James A.
  xMcCulloch, James A.
    Medical Greek & Latin Workbook. C C
    Thomas.
McCulloch, James Wallace.
  xMcCulloch, J. Wallace.
    Signs of Stress: The Social Problems of
    Psychiatric Illness. Biblio Dist.
McCulloch, Lou W.
  xMcCulloch, Lous W.
    Paper Americana: A Collector's Guide. A S
    Barnes.
McCulloch, Lous W. see McCulloch, Lou W.
McCulloh, William E.
  xMcCulloh, William E.
    Longus. Irvington.
McCullough. see McCullough, Robert.
McCullough, Ashley M. see McCullough, Ashley Melvin.
McCullough, Ashley Melvin, 1889-
  xMcCullough, Ashley M.
    A Critical Analysis of the Fuel Management
    Program for Schools: Selected New Jersey
    Cities Compared with Nation-Wide Practice.
    AMS Pr.
McCullough, Bonnie R. see McCullough, Bonnie Runyan.
McCullough, Bonnie Runyan.
  xMcCullough, Bonnie R.
    Bonnie's Household Organizer. St Martin.
McCullough, Colleen, 1937-
  xMcCullough, Colleen.
    The Thorn Birds. Avon.
    The Thorn Birds. G K Hall.
    The Thorn Birds. Har-Row.
McCullough, D. R. see McCullough, Dale R.
McCullough, Dale R., 1933-
  xMcCullough, D. R.
    The Tule Elk: Its History, Behavior & Ecology.
    U of Cal Pr.
  xMcCullough, Dale R.
    The George Reserve Deer Herd: Population
    Ecology of a K-Selected Species. U of Mich
    Pr.
McCullough, David. see McCullough, David G.
McCullough, David G.
  xMcCullough, David.
    The Great Bridge. Avon.
    The Great Bridge. S&S.
    Johnstown Flood. S&S.
    The Path Between the Seas: The Creation of
    the Panama Canal 1870-1914. S&S.
    The Path Between the Seas: The Creation the
    Panama Canal 1870-1914. S&S.
McCullough, Edo.
  xMcCullough, Edo.
    World's Fair Midways: An Affectionate
    Account of American Amusement Areas
    from the Crystal Palace to the Crystal Ball.
    Arno.
McCullough, Joseph B.
  xMcCullough, Joseph B.
    Hamlin Garland. Twayne.
McCullough, Marshall E., 1924-
  xMcCullough, Marshall E.
    Optimum Feeding of Dairy Animals for Meat
    & Milk. U of Ga Pr.
McCullough, R. L., 1934-
  xMcCullough, R. L.
    Concepts of Fiber - Resin Composites. Dekker.
McCullough, Robert.
  xMcCullough.

    Pennsylvania Main Line Canal. Am Canal &
    Transport.
McCullough, W. Stewart. see McCullough, William
  Stewart.
McCullough, William J.
  xMcCullough, William J.
    Hold Your Audience: The Way to Success in
    Public Speaking. P-H.
McCullough, William Stewart, 1902-
  xMcCullough, W. Stewart.
    The History & Literature of Palestinian Jews
    from Cyrus to Herod 550 BC - 4 BC. U of
    Toronto Pr.
McCully, Bruce T. see McCully, Bruce Tiebout.
McCully, Bruce Tiebout, 1904-
  xMcCully, Bruce T.
    English Education & the Origins of Indian
    Nationalism. Peter Smith.
McCune, Wesley, 1918-
  xMcCune, Wesley.
    Farm Bloc. Greenwood.
    Nine Young Men. Greenwood.
McCunn, Donald H.
  xMcCunn, Donald H.
    Computer Programing for the Complete Idiot.
    Design Ent SF.
McCunn, Ruthanne L. see McCunn, Ruthanne Lum.
McCunn, Ruthanne Lum.
  xMcCunn, Ruthanne L.
    An Illustrated History of the Chinese in
    America. Design Ent SF.
McCurdy, David W.
  xMcCurdy, David W.
    ed. Issues in Cultural Anthropology: Selected
    Readings. Little.
McCurdy, Dwight R.
  xMcCurdy, Dwight R.
    How to Choose Your Tree: A Guide to
    Parklike Landscaping in Illinois, Indiana, &
    Ohio. S Ill U Pr.
McCurdy, Frances L. see McCurdy, Frances Lea.
McCurdy, Frances Lea, 1906-
  xMcCurdy, Frances L.
    Stump, Bar & Pulpit: Speechmaking on the
    Missouri Frontier. U of Mo Pr.
McCurdy, Harold G. see McCurdy, Harold Grier.
McCurdy, Harold Grier, 1909-
  xMcCurdy, Harold G.
    Chastening of Narcissus. Blair.
    The Personality of Shakespeare: A Venture in
    Psychological Method. Kennikat.
McCurdy, John D. see McCurdy, John Derrickson.
McCurdy, John Derrickson, 1940-1974
  xMcCurdy, John D.
    Visionary Appropriation. Philos Lib.
McCurdy, Richard M.
  xMcCurdy, Richard M.
    Pref. by Qualities & Quantities: Preparation for
    College Chemistry. HarBraceJ.
  xMcCurdy, Richard N.
    Qualities & Quantities in the Laboratory.
    HarBraceJ.
McCurdy, Richard N. see McCurdy, Richard M.
McCurdy, William B.
  xMcCurdy, William B.
    Program Evaluation: A Conceptual Tool Kit for
    Human Service Delivery Managers. Family
    Serv.
McCurry, Dan C.
  xMcCurry, Dan C.
    Intro. by & ed. Cannery Captives: Women
    Workers in the Produce Processing Industry
    (an Original Press Anthology). Arno.
McCurtin, Peter.
  xMcCurtin, Peter.
    Loanshark. Belmont-Tower.
    Minnesota Strip. Belmont Tower.
McCuskey, Dorothy.
  xMcCuskey, Dorothy.

    Bronson Alcott, Teacher. Arno.
McCutchan, Philip, 1920-
  xMcCutchan, Philip.
    Great Yachts. Crown.
    The Guns of Arrest. St Martin.
    Halfhyde Ordered South. St Martin.
  xMcCutchan, Philip D.
    Halfhyde to the Narrows. St Martin.
McCutchan, Philip D. see McCutchan, Philip.
McCutcheon. see McCutcheon, Roger Philip.
McCutcheon, George B. see McCutcheon, George Barr.
McCutcheon, George Barr, 1866-1928
  xMcCutcheon, George B.
    Graustark: The Story of a Love Behind a
    Throne. Scholarly.
McCutcheon, James M.
  xMcCutcheon, James M.
    China & America: A Bibliography of
    Interactions, Foreign & Domestic. U Pr of
    Hawaii.
McCutcheon, James N., 1929-
  xMcCutcheon, James N.
    The Pastoral Ministry. Abingdon.
McCutcheon, Roger P. see McCutcheon, Roger Philip.
McCutcheon, Roger Philip, 1889-
  xMcCutcheon.
    Eighteenth-Century English Literature. R West.
  xMcCutcheon, Roger P.
    Eighteenth-Century English Literature. Arden
    Lib.
McDaniel, Burruss.
  xMcDaniel, Burruss.
    How to Know the Mites & Ticks. Wm C
    Brown.
McDaniel, Gary L.
  xMcDaniel, Gary M.
    Ornamental Horticulture. Reston.
McDaniel, Gary M. see McDaniel, Gary L.
McDaniel, Genevieve Spratt.
  xMcDaniel, Genevieve Spratt.
    Mrs. Spratt's Buffet Cookbook. Exposition.
McDaniel, Herman.
  xMcDaniel, Herman.
    Careers in Computers & Data Processing.
    Petrocelli.
    An Introduction to Decision Logic Tables.
    Petrocelli.
    Personal Records Directory. Petrocelli.
McDaniel, Robert A.
  xMcDaniel, Robert A.
    The Shuster Mission & the Persian
    Constitutional Revolution. Bibliotheca.
McDaniels, Carl.
  xMcDaniels, Carl.
    Developing a Professional Vita or Resume.
    Garrett Pk.
McDarrah, Fred W., 1926-
  xMcDarrah, Fred W.
    ed. Stock Photo & Assignment Source Book:
    Where to Find Photographs Instantly.
    Bowker.
McDavid, James C.
  xMcDavid, James C.
    Police Cooperation & Performance: The
    Greater St. Louis Interlocal Experience. Pa St
    U Pr.
McDavid, John W.
  xMcDavid, John W.
    Understanding Children: Promoting Human
    Growth. Heath.
McDearmon, Kay.
  xMcDearmon, Kay.
    Cougar. Dodd.
    Gorillas. Dodd.
    Rocky Mountain Bighorns. Dodd.
McDermott, Beatrice S.
  xMcDermott, Beatrice S.

ed. Government Regulation of Business
Including Antitrust Information Sources.
Gale.

McDermott, Beverly B. *see* McDermott, Beverly
Brodsky.

McDermott, Beverly Brodsky.
xMcDermott, Beverly B.
illus. The Golem: A Jewish Legend. Lippincott.

McDermott, Gerald.
xMcDermott, Gerald.
illus. & Retold by Anansi the Spider: A Tale
from the Ashanti. HR&W.
illus. Anansi the Spider: A Tale from the
Ashanti. Penguin.
illus. Arrow to the Sun: A Pueblo Indian Tale.
Penguin.
Arrow to the Sun: A Pueblo Indian Tale.
Viking Pr.
illus. Papagayo the Mischief Maker. Windmill
Bks.
The Stonecutter: A Japanese Folk Tale. Viking
Pr.
illus. Sun Flight. Schol Bk Serv.

McDermott, Irene.
xMcDermott, Irene.
Enter the Temple Called Beautiful. De Vorss.

McDermott, John F.
xMcDermott, John F.
ed. Psychiatric Treatment of the Child.
Aronson.
Raising Cain-& Abel, Too: The Parents' Book
of Sibling Rivalry. Wyden.

McDermott, John F. *see* McDermott, John Francis.

McDermott, John Francis.
xMcDermott, John F.
ed. The Frontier Re-Examined. U of Ill Pr.
George Caleb Bingham: River Portraitist. U of
Okla Pr.
ed. The Spanish in the Mississippi Valley:
1762-1804. U of Ill Pr.

McDermott, Robert.
xMcDermott, Robert.
Stop Thief: How to Safeguard & Secure Your
Home & Business. Macmillan.

McDermott, William C. *see* McDermott, William
Coffman.

McDermott, William Coffman.
xMcDermott, William C.
Roman Portraits: The Flavian-Trajanic Period.
U of Mo Pr.

McDiarmid, Norma J.
xMcDiarmid, Norma J.
Loving & Learning: Interacting with Your
Child from Birth to Three. HarBraceJ.
Loving & Learning: Interacting with Your
Child from Birth to Three. HarBraceJ.

McDicken, W. N.
xMcDicken, William N.
Diagnostic Ultrasonics: The Principles & Use of
Instruments. Wiley.

McDicken, William N. *see* McDicken, W. N.

McDill, Edward L. *see* McDill, Edward Lamar.

McDill, Edward Lamar.
xMcDill, Edward L.
Strategies for Success in Compensatory
Education: An Appraisal of Evaluation
Research. Johns Hopkins.
Structure & Process in Secondary Schools: The
Academic Impact of Educational Climates.
Johns Hopkins.

McDill, Wayne.
xMcDill, Wayne.
Evangelism in a Tangled World. Broadman.
Making Friends for Christ. Broadman.
The Power to Become. Revell.

McDonagh, Don.
xMcDonagh, Don.

The Complete Guide to Modern Dance.
Doubleday.
The Complete Guide to Modern Dance.
Popular Lib.
Dance Fever. Random.
How to Enjoy Ballet. Doubleday.
How to Enjoy Ballet. Doubleday.

McDonagh, Edward C.
xMcDonagh, Edward C.
Ethnic Relations in the United States. Negro U
Pr.

McDonagh, Enda.
xMcDonagh, Enda.
Doing the Truth: The Quest for Moral
Theology. U of Notre Dame Pr.
Freedom or Tolerance: The Declaration on
Religious Freedom of Vatican Council Two.
Magi Bks.

McDonald, A. *see* McDonald, Andrew.

McDonald, Alvis E. *see* McDonald, Alvis Edward.

McDonald, Alvis Edward, 1935-
xMcDonald, Alvis E.
A Multiplicity-Independent, Global Iteration
for Meromorphic Functions. Mgmt Info Serv.

McDonald, Andrew, 1942-
xMcDonald, A.
Absence in Strange Countries. U of Queensland
Pr.

McDonald, Angus W., 1941-
xMcDonald, Angus W.
The Urban Origins of Rural Revolution: Elites
& the Masses in Hunan Province, China,
1911-1927. U of Cal Pr.

McDonald, Ann G. *see* McDonald, Ann Gilbert.

McDonald, Ann Gilbert.
xMcDonald, Ann G.
Evolution of the Night Lamp.
Wallace-Homestead.

McDonald, Bernard. *see* McDonald, Bernard R.

McDonald, Bernard R
xMcDonald, Bernard.
Geometric Algebra Over Local Rings. Dekker.
xMcDonald, Bernard R.
Finite Rings with Identity. Dekker.

McDonald, Cleveland.
xMcDonald, Cleveland.
Creating a Successful Christian Marriage. Baker
Bk.
Creating a Successful Christian Marriage. Reg
Baptist.

McDonald, D. L. *see* McDonald, Daniel Lumon.

McDonald, Dan.
xMcDonald, Dan.
The Clyde Puffer. David & Charles.

McDonald, Daniel. *see* McDonald, Daniel Lamont.

McDonald, Daniel Lamont.
xMcDonald, Daniel.
The Language of Argument. Har-Row.

McDonald, Daniel Lumon, 1933-
xMcDonald, D. L.
Comparative Accounting Theory. A-W.

McDonald, Donald, 1857-
xMcDonald, Donald.
Agricultural Writers from Sir Walter of Henley
to Arthur Young 1200-1800. B Franklin.
Catholics in Conversation: Seventeen
Interviews with Leading American Catholics.
Greenwood.

McDonald, Douglas.
xMcDonald, Douglas.
The Price of Punishment: Public Spending for
Corrections in New York. Westview.

McDonald, Elvin.
xMcDonald, Elvin.

Decorative Gardening in Containers.
Doubleday.
Easy Gardens: A Weed Eater Book. Berkley
Pub.
Easy Gardens: A Weed Eater Book. Dorison
Hse.
The Greenhouse Gardener. NAL.
The House Plant Answer Book. Popular Lib.
How to Build Your Own Greenhouse. Popular
Lib.
How to Grow House Plants from Seeds. Van
Nos Reinhold.
How to Grow Vegetables & Herbs from Seeds.
Van Nos Reinhold.
Little Plants for Small Spaces. M Evans.
Little Plants for Small Spaces. Popular Lib.
Plants As Therapy. Popular Lib.
Stop Talking to Your Plants & Listen. T Y
Crowell.
The World Book of House Plants. T Y Crowell.

McDonald, Eugene T.
xMcDonald, Eugene T.
Articulation Testing & Treatment: A
Sensory-Motor Approach. Stanwix.
Cerebral Palsy. P-H.
Understand Those Feelings. Stanwix.

McDonald, Forrest.
xMcDonald, Forrest.
Alexander Hamilton: A Biography. Norton.
Insull. U of Chicago Pr.
The Presidency of George Washington. Norton.
The Presidency of George Washington.
Regents Pr KS.
The Presidency of Thomas Jefferson. Regents
Pr KS.

McDonald, Frank.
xMcDonald, Frank.
Provenance. Avon.
Provenance. Little.

McDonald, G. A. *see* McDonald, George Alexander.

McDonald, George Alexander.
xMcDonald, G. A.
Atlas of Haematology. Churchill.

McDonald, Gerald D. *see* McDonald, Gerald Doan.

McDonald, Gerald Doan.
xMcDonald, Gerald D.
Films of Charlie Chaplin. Citadel Pr.

McDonald, Grace, 1917-
xMcDonald, Grace.
History of the Irish in Wisconsin in the
Nineteenth Century. Arno.

McDonald, Gregory, 1937-
xMcDonald, Gregory.
Confess, Fletch. Avon.
Fletch. Avon.
Fletch's Fortune. Avon.
Flynn. Avon.
Love Among the Mashed Potatoes. Dutton.

McDonald, H. Dermot. *see* McDonald, Hugh Dermot.

McDonald, Hugh Dermot.
xMcDonald, H. Dermot.
Commentary on Colossians & Philemon. Word
Bks.

McDonald, Ian G.
xMcDonald, Ian G.
Introduction to Echocardiography. C C
Thomas.

McDonald, Jack.
xMcDonald, Jack.
How to Make Old-Time Photos. TAB Bks.

McDonald, Jean G.
xMcDonald, Jean G.
Legislators & Patronage in Oklahoma. Univ
OK Gov Res.

McDonald, John. *see* McDonald, John Dennis.

McDonald, John Dennis, 1906-
xMcDonald, John.

The Game of Business. Doubleday.
Strategy in Poker, Business & War. Norton.
McDonald, Kay L.
xMcDonald, Kay L.
The Brightwood Expedition. Liveright.
McDonald, Kendall.
xMcDonald, Kendall.
ed. Great Underwater Adventure Stories.
Pagurian.
McDonald, L. E. *see* McDonald, Leslie Ernest.
McDonald, Leslie Ernest, 1923-
xMcDonald, L. E.
ed. Veterinary Endocrinology & Reproduction.
Lea & Febiger.
McDonald, Linda.
xMcDonald, Linda.
Baby's Recipe Book. A S Barnes.
Everything You Need to Know About Babies.
Oaklawn Pr.
Instant Baby Food. Oaklawn Pr.
McDonald, Lucile. *see* McDonald, Lucile Saunders.
McDonald, Lucile Saunders, 1898-
xMcDonald, Lucile.
The Lake Washington Story. Superior Pub.
McDonald, Lynn.
xMcDonald, Lynn.
The Sociology of Law & Order. Westview.
McDonald, Margaret L. *see* McDonald, Margaret Lamb.
McDonald, Margaret Lamb.
xMcDonald, Margaret L.
The Independent Woman in the Restoration
Comedy of Manners. Humanities.
McDonald, Marjorie, 1926-
xMcDonald, Marjorie.
Not by the Color of Their Skin: The Impact of
Racial Differences on the Child's
Development. Intl Univs Pr.
McDonald, Neil A.
xMcDonald, Neil A.
Politics: A Study of Control Behavior. Rutgers
U Pr.
McDonald, P. *see* McDonald, Peter.
McDonald, Peter.
xMcDonald, P.
Animal Nutrition. Longman.
McDonald, Philip R.
xMcDonald, Philip R.
Factors Influencing Fuel Oil Growth. Arno.
McDonald, Ralph E.
xMcDonald, Ralph E.
Dentistry for the Child & Adolescent. Mosby.
McDonald, Robert A. *see* McDonald, Robert Alexander
Fyfe.
McDonald, Robert Alexander Fyfe, 1878-
xMcDonald, Robert A.
Adjustment of School Organization to Various
Population Groups. AMS Pr.
McDonald, T. Marll. *see* McDonald, Thomas Marll.
McDonald, Thomas Marll.
xMcDonald, T. Marll.
Mathematical Methods for Social &
Management Scientists. HM.
McDonald, Vincent R.
xMcDonald, Vincent R.
The Caribbean Issues of Emergence:
Socio-Economic & Political Perspectives. U
Pr of Amer.
McDonald, W. F. *see* McDonald, William F.
McDonald, William F., 1943-
xMcDonald, W. F.
ed. Criminal Justice & the Victim. Sage.
McDonald, William F. *see* McDonald, William Frank.
McDonald, William Francis, 1898-
xMcDonald, William F.
Federal Relief Administration & the Arts: The
Origins & Administrative History of the Arts
Projects of the Works Progress
Administration. Ohio St U Pr.
McDonald, William Frank.
xMcDonald, William F.

ed. Plea-Bargaining. Lexington Bks.
The Prosecutor. Sage.
McDonald, William J. *see* McDonald, William Joseph.
McDonald, William Joseph.
xMcDonald, William J.
ed. The General Council: Special Studies in
Doctrinal & Historical Background.
Greenwood.
McDonald, Worden.
xMcDonald, Worden.
An Old Guy Who Feels Good. Thorp Springs.
McDonnell. *see* McDonnell, Leo P.
McDonnell, Kilian.
xMcDonnell, Kilian.
Charismatic Renewal & Ecumenism. Paulist Pr.
The Holy Spirit & Power: The Catholic
Charismatic Renewal. Doubleday.
McDonnell, Leo P.
xMcDonnell.
The Use of Hand Woodworking Tools. Delmar.
The Use of Portable Power Tools. Delmar.
xMcDonnell, Leo P.
The Use of Portable Power Tools. Van Nos
Reinhold.
McDonnell, Lois Eddy.
xMcDonnell, Lois Eddy.
Susan Comes Through the Fire. Friend Pr.
McDonnell, Virginia. *see* McDonnell, Virginia B.
McDonnell, Virginia B.
xMcDonnell, Virginia.
Trouble at Mercy Hospital. Doubleday.
McDonough, John.
xMcDonough, John.
Don't Hit Him, He's Dead. Celestial Arts.
McDonough, Martin.
xMcDonough, Martin.
Mastering General Mathematics. Arco.
McDonough, Reginald. *see* McDonough, Reginald M.
McDonough, Reginald M.
xMcDonough, Reginald.
Keys to Effective Motivation. Broadman.
xMcDonough, Reginald M.
Working with Volunteer Leaders in the
Church. Broadman.
McDonough, Susan.
xMcDonough, Susan.
The Complete Book of Questions Cat Owners
Ask Their Vet. Running Pr.
McDougal, Myres S. *see* McDougal, Myres Smith.
McDougal, Myres Smith.
xMcDougal, Myers S.
Human Rights & World Public Order: The
Basic Policies of an International Law of
Human Dignity. Yale U Pr.
McDougall, Donald.
xMcDougall, Donald.
Boswell & Son. St Martin.
Davie. St Martin.
McDougall, Joyce.
xMcDougall, Joyce.
Dialogue with Sammy: A Psycho-Analytical
Contribution to the Understanding of Child
Psychosis. Intl Univs Pr.
McDougall, Mary L. *see* McDougall, Mary Lynn.
McDougall, Mary Lynn.
xMcDougall, Mary L.
The Working Class in Modern Europe. Heath.
McDougall, Ruth B. *see* McDougall, Ruth Bransten.
McDougall, Ruth Bransten.
xMcDougall, Ruth B.
Coffee, Martinis & San Francisco. Presidio Pr.
McDougall, William, 1871-1938
xMcDougall, William.
The Group Mind. Arno.
An Introduction to Social Psychology. Milford
Hse.
Religion & the Sciences of Life: With Other
Essays on Allied Topics. Arno.
McDowall, Arthur S. *see* McDowall, Arthur Sydney.

McDowall, Arthur Sydney, 1877-1933
xMcDowall, Arthur S.
Thomas Hardy: A Critical Study. Folcroft.
McDowell, Bart.
xMcDowell, Bart.
Journey Across Russia: The Soviet Union
Today. Natl Geog.
McDowell, Charles A.
xMcDowell, Charles A.
ed. Mass Spectrometry. Krieger.
ed. Mass Spectrometry. McGraw.
McDowell, Edward A. *see* McDowell, Edward Allison.
McDowell, Edward Allison, 1898-
xMcDowell, Edward A.
Meaning & Message of the Book of Revelation.
Broadman.
McDowell, Ernest R.
xMcDowell, Ernest R.
Checkertail Clan: The 325th Fighter Group in
North Africa & Italy. Aero.
McDowell, John H. *see* McDowell, John Holmes.
McDowell, John Holmes, 1946-
xMcDowell, John H.
Children's Riddling. Ind U Pr.
McDowell, Josh.
xMcDowell, Josh.
More Than a Carpenter. Tyndale.
McDowell, Michael.
xMcDowell, Michael.
The Amulet. Avon.
McDowell, Mildred.
xMcDowell, Mildred.
The Little People. Unicorn Ent.
McDowell, R. B. *see* McDowell, Robert Brendan.
McDowell, Robert B. *see* McDowell, Robert Brendan.
McDowell, Robert Brendan.
xMcDowell, R. B.
Public Opinion & Government Policy in
Ireland, 1801-1846. Greenwood.
xMcDowell, Robert B.
British Conservatism, 1832-1914. Greenwood.
McDowell, Virginia. *see* McDowell, Virginia H.
McDowell, Virginia H.
xMcDowell, Virginia.
Re-Creating: The Experience of Life-Change &
Religion. Beacon Pr.
McEachern, Edna, 1895-
xMcEachern, Edna.
A Survey & Evaluation of the Education of
School Music Teachers in the United States.
AMS Pr.
McEachern, George. *see* McEachern, George Ray.
McEachern, George Ray.
xMcEachern, George.
Growing Fruits, Berries & Nuts in the South.
Pacesetter Pr.
McElderry, Bruce R. *see* McElderry, Bruce Robert.
McElderry, Bruce Robert, 1900-
xMcElderry, Bruce R.
ed. Realistic Movement in American Writing:
1865-1900. Odyssey Pr.
Thomas Wolfe. Coll & U Pr.
Thomas Wolfe. Twayne.
McEleney, Neil J.
xMcEleney, Neil J.
The Growth of the Gospels. Paulist Pr.
McElheran, Brock.
xMcElheran, Brock.
Conducting Technique for Beginners &
Professionals. Oxford U Pr.
McElhinney, M. W.
xMcElhinney, M. W.
Palaeomagnetism & Plate Tectonics. Cambridge
U Pr.
McElrath, William E. *see* McElrath, William N.
McElrath, William N.
xMcElrath, William E.

Judges & Kings: God's Chosen Leaders.
Broadman.

McElreath, T. Jack.
xMcElreath, T. Jack.
IMS Design & Implementation Techniques.
QED Info Sci.

McElroy, Colleen J.
xMcElroy, Colleen J.
Music from Home: Selected Poems. S Ill U Pr.
McElroy, Colleen W. *see* McElroy, Colleen Wilkinson.

McElroy, Colleen Wilkinson.
xMcElroy, Colleen W.
Speech & Language Development of the
Preschool Child: A Survey. C C Thomas.
McElroy, Davis D. *see* McElroy, Davis Dunbar.

McElroy, Davis Dunbar.
xMcElroy, Davis D.
Existentialism & Modern Literature: An Essay
in Existential Criticism. Greenwood.

McElroy, Elam E.
xMcElroy, Elam E.
Applied Business Statistics: An Elementary
Approach. Holden-Day.

McElroy, Jerome L.
xMcElroy, Jerome L.
Consumer Expenditure Patterns: A Survey of
St. Thomas, U. S. V. I., 1975-1976. U Presses
Fla.

McElroy, Joseph.
xMcElroy, Joseph.
Hind's Kidnap: A Pastoral on Familiar Airs.
Ultramarine Pub.
Lookout Cartridge. Knopf.

McElroy, Lee.
xMcElroy, Lee.
Long Way to Texas. Dell.
Long Way to Texas. Doubleday.
McElroy, Robert M. *see* McElroy, Robert McNutt.

McElroy, Robert McNutt, 1872-1959
xMcElroy, Robert M.
Levi Parsons Morton: Banker, Diplomat &
Statesman. Arno.

McElroy, Thomas P., 1914-
xMcElroy, Thomas P.
The Habitat Guide to Birding. Knopf.
McElroy, William D. *see* McElroy, William David.

McElroy, William David, 1917-
xMcElroy, William D.
Cell Physiology & Biochemistry. P-H.

McElvaney, William K., 1928-
xMcElvaney, William K.
Good News Is Bad News Is Good News. Orbis
Bks.

McElveen, Floyd.
xMcElveen, Floyd.
The Mormon Revelations of Convenience.
Bethany Fell.

McElwain, Thomas.
xMcElwain, Thomas.
Mythological Tales & the Allegany Seneca: A
Study of the Socio-Religious Context of
Traditional Oral Phenomena in an Iroquois
Community. Humanities.
McEntee, Howard C. *see* McEntee, Howard Garrett.

McEntee, Howard Garrett, 1905-
xMcEntee, Howard C.
Radio Control Handbook. TAB Bks.
McEntyre. *see* McEntyre, Robert L.

McEntyre, Robert L.
xMcEntyre.
Practical Guide to the Care of the Surgical
Patient. Mosby.

McEvedy, Colin.
xMcEvedy, Colin.
Atlas of African History. Facts on File.
Atlas of African History. Penguin.
Atlas of World Population History. Facts on
File.
Atlas of World Population History. Penguin.
The Penguin Atlas of Ancient History.
Penguin.
Penguin Atlas of Modern History to 1815.
Penguin.

McEvoy, Marjorie.
xMcEvoy, Marjorie.
Echoes from the Past. Doubleday.

McEwan, Ian.
xMcEwan, Ian.
The Cement Garden. S&S.
McEwan, M. J. *see* McEwan, Murray J.

McEwan, Murray J.
xMcEwan, M. J.
The Chemistry of the Atmosphere. Halsted Pr.
McEwan, P. J. *see* McEwan, Peter J. M.

McEwan, Peter J. M.
xMcEwan, P. J.
ed. Nineteenth-Century Africa. Oxford U Pr.
McEwen, F. L. *see* McEwen, Freeman Lester.

McEwen, Freeman Lester.
xMcEwen, F. L.
The Use & Significance of Pesticides in the
Environment. Wiley.

McEwen, Gilbert D.
xMcEwen, Gilbert D.
The Oracle of the Coffee House: John
Dunton's Athenian Mercury. Huntington Lib.

McEwen, Tom.
xMcEwen, Tom.
The Gators: A Story of Florida Football.
Strode.

McEwen, William J.
xMcEwen, William J.
Changing Rural Society: A Study of
Communities in Bolivia. Oxford U Pr.

McFadden, George, 1916-
xMcFadden, George.
Dryden the Public Writer, 1660-1685.
Princeton U Pr.

McFadzean, Ronald.
xMcFadzean, Ronald.
The Life & Work of Alexander Thomson.
Routledge & Kegan.

McFall, Christie.
xMcFall, Christie.
illus. Underwater Continent: The Continental
Shelves. Dodd.
McFall, Robert J. *see* McFall, Robert James.

McFall, Robert James, 1887-
xMcFall, Robert J.
Railway Monopoly & Rate Regulation. AMS
Pr.

McFall, Waddy F., 1917-
xMcFall, Waddy F.
Taxidermy Step by Step. Winchester Pr.
McFarlan, Donald M. *see* McFarlan, Donald Maitland.

McFarlan, Donald Maitland.
xMcFarlan, Donald M.
Who & What & Where in the Bible. John
Knox.
McFarland. *see* McFarland, John Bryan.

McFarland, Andrew S., 1940-
xMcFarland, Andrew S.
Power & Leadership in Pluralist Systems.
Stanford U Pr.
Public Interest Lobbies: Decision Making on
Energy. Am Enterprise.
McFarland, Dalton. *see* McFarland, Dalton E.

McFarland, Dalton E.
xMcFarland, Dalton.
Managerial Achievement: Action Strategies.
P-H.
xMcFarland, Dalton E.
Management: Foundations & Practices.
Macmillan.
ed. Power in Nursing. Nursing Res.
McFarland, Dorothy T. *see* McFarland, Dorothy Tuck.

McFarland, Dorothy Tuck, 1938-
xMcFarland, Dorothy T.
Flannery O'Connor. Ungar.

McFarland, Gerald W., 1938-
xMcFarland, Gerald W.
ed. Mugwumps, Morals, & Politics, 1884-1920.
U of Mass Pr.

McFarland, Grace, 1947-
xMcFarland, Grace.
Official Price Guide to Antiques & Other
Collectibles. Hse of Collectibles.
McFarland, Henry S. *see* McFarland, Henry Stewart
Noel.

McFarland, Henry Stewart Noel.
xMcFarland, Henry S.
Psychology & Teaching. Greenwood.
McFarland, J. *see* McFarland, John Bryan.
McFarland, J. Horace. *see* McFarland, John Horace.

McFarland, John Bryan.
xMcFarland, J.
Postgraduate Surgery Lectures. Butterworths.
xMcFarland, J.
Postgraduate Surgery Lectures-1. Butterworths.

McFarland, John Horace.
xMcFarland, J. Horace.
How to Grow Roses. Macmillan.

McFarland, Kevin.
xMcFarland, Kevin.
Incredible. NAL.

McFarland, M. Carter.
xMcFarland, M. Carter.
The Federal Government & Urban Problems:
HUD: Successes, Failures, & the Fate of Our
Cities. Westview.
McFarland, Philip. *see* McFarland, Philip James.

McFarland, Philip James.
xMcFarland, Philip.
Forms in English Literature. HM.
House Full of Women. S&S.
Perceptions in Literature. HM.
Themes in American Literature. HM.

McFarland, Ronald E.
xMcFarland, Ronald E.
ed. Eight Idaho Poets: An Anthology. U Pr of
Idaho.

McFarland, Walter B.
xMcFarland, Walter B.
Concepts for Management Accounting. Natl
Assn Accts.
McFarland, William N. *see* McFarland, William Norman.

McFarland, William Norman, 1925-
xMcFarland, William N.
Vertebrate Life. Macmillan.

McFarlane, Brian.
xMcFarlane, Brian.
Brian McFarlane's Hockey Quiz. Pagurian.
McFarlane, I. D. *see* McFarlane, Ian Dalrymple.

McFarlane, Ian Dalrymple.
xMcFarlane, I. D.
ed. Renaissance Studies: Six Essays. Rowman.
McFarlane, James W. *see* McFarlane, James Walter.

McFarlane, James Walter.
xMcFarlane, James W.
Ibsen & the Temper of Norwegian Literature.
Octagon.
McFarlane, Judith. *see* McFarlane, Judith M.

McFarlane, Judith M.
xMcFarlane, Judith.
Contemporary Pediatric Nursing: A Conceptual
Approach. Wiley.

McFate, Patricia.
xMcFate, Patricia.
The Writings of James Stephens: Variations on
a Theme of Love. St Martin.

McFather, Nelle.
xMcFather, Nelle.

Dark Refuge. Ace Bks.
McFaul, John M.
xMcFaul, John M.
The Politics of Jacksonian Finance. Cornell U
Pr.
McFeat, Tom.
xMcFeat, Tom.
ed. Indians of the North Pacific Coast. U of
Wash Pr.
McGahern, John, 1934-
xMcGahern, John.
Getting Through. Har-Row.
McGahey, Jeanne.
xMcGahey, Jeanne.
Oregon Winter. Woolmer-Brotherson.
McGann, Anthony F.
xMcGann, Anthony F.
Introduction to Business. Wiley.
McGann, Jerome J.
xMcGann, Jerome J.
Don Juan in Context. U of Chicago Pr.
Swinburne: An Experiment in Criticism. U of
Chicago Pr.
McGarrity, John.
xMcGarrity, John.
Once a Jolly Black Man. David & Charles.
McGarry, Daniel D.
xMcGarry, Daniel D.
Medieval History & Civilization. Macmillan.
Outline of Medieval History. Littlefield.
McGarry, James. *see* McGarry, James P.
McGarry, James P.
xMcGarry, James.
Place Names in the Writings of William Butler
Yeats. Humanities.
McGarry, Michael B.
xMcGarry, Michael B.
Christology After Auschwitz. Paulist Pr.
McGarty, Terrence P., 1943-
xMcGarty, Terrence P.
Stochastic Systems & State Estimation. Wiley.
McGaugh, James L.
xMcGaugh, James L.
ed. Psychobiology: Behavior from a Biological
Perspective. Acad Pr.
McGaughey, C. E., 1905-
xMcGaughey, C. E.
The Hope of the World. Bibl Res Pr.
McGaughey, Janet M. *see* McGaughey, Janet McLoud.
McGaughey, Janet McLoud.
xMcGaughey, Janet M.
Practical Ear Training. Taplinger.
McGaughy, Lane C.
xMcGaughy, Lane C.
Workbook for a Beginning-Intermediate
Grammar of Hellenistic Greek. Scholars Pr
Ca.
McGauhey, P. H. *see* McGauhey, Percy Harold.
McGauhey, Percy Harold.
xMcGauhey, P. H.
Engineering Management of Water Quality.
McGraw.
McGavran, Donald. *see* McGavran, Donald Anderson.
McGavran, Donald A. *see* McGavran, Donald Anderson.
McGavran, Donald Anderson.
xMcGavran, Donald.
Church Growth: Strategies That Work.
Abingdon.
Understanding Church Growth. Eerdmans.
xMcGavran, Donald A.
Ethnic Realities & the Church: Lessons from
India. William Carey Lib.
How to Grow a Church. Regal.
Zaire: Midday in Missions. Judson.
McGaw, Charles. *see* McGaw, Charles J.
McGaw, Charles J., 1910
xMcGaw, Charles.

Acting Is Believing: A Basic Method. HR&W.
Working a Scene: An Actor's Approach.
HR&W.
McGaw, Martha M. *see* McGaw, Martha Mary.
McGaw, Martha Mary, Sister.
xMcGaw, Martha M.
Stevenson in Hawaii. Greenwood.
McGaw, Robert A.
xMcGaw, Robert A.
The Vanderbilt Campus: A Pictorial History.
Vanderbilt U Pr.
McGeachy, D. P. *see* McGeachy, Pat.
McGeachy, Pat, 1929-
xMcGeachy, D. P.
The Gospel According to Andy Capp. John
Knox.
McGee, Cecil.
xMcGee, Cecil.
Drama for Fun. Broadman.
Dramatic Programs for Christmas. Broadman.
McGee, Charles T., 1935-
xMcGee, Charles T.
How to Survive Modern Technology. Keats.
McGee, J. Sears. *see* McGee, James Sears.
McGee, James Sears, 1942-
xMcGee, J. Sears.
The Godly Man in Stuart England: Anglicans,
Puritans & the Two Tables, 1620-1670. Yale
U Pr.
McGee, John S. *see* McGee, John Seneca.
McGee, John Seneca, 1927-
xMcGee, John S.
The Robinson-Patman Act & Effective
Competition. Arno.
McGee, Leo.
xMcGee, Leo.
ed. The Black Rural Landowner--Endangered
Species: Social, Political, & Economic
Implications. Greenwood.
McGee, Mark G.
xMcGee, Mark G.
Introductory Psychology Reader. West Pub.
McGee, Myra.
xMcGee, Myra.
Lester & Mother. Har-Row.
McGee, Thomas D. *see* McGee, Thomas D'Arcy.
McGee, Thomas D'Arcy, 1825-1868
xMcGee, Thomas D.
A History of the Irish Settlers in North
America, from the Earliest Period to the
Census of 1850. Ozer.
McGeehan, Robert, 1933-
xMcGeehan, Robert.
The German Rearmament Question: American
Diplomacy & European Defense After World
War Two. U of Ill Pr.
McGeer, Edith G.
xMcGeer, Edith G.
ed. Kainic Acid As a Tool in Neurobiology.
Raven.
McGerr, Celia, 1956-
xMcGerr, Celia.
Rene Clair. Twayne.
McGervey, John D., 1931-
xMcGervey, John D.
Introduction to Modern Physics. Acad Pr.
McGhee, Edward.
xMcGhee, Edward.
The Chinese Ultimatum. Pinnacle Bks.
McGhee, Robert.
xMcGhee, Robert.
Canadian Arctic Prehistory. Van Nos Reinhold.
McGibony, John R, 1903-
xMcGibony, John R.
Principles of Hospital Administration. Putnam.
McGiffert, A. C. *see* McGiffert, Arthur Cushman.
McGiffert, Arthur C. *see* McGiffert, Arthur Cushman.
McGiffert, Arthur Cushman, 1892-
xMcGiffert, A. C.

Protestant Thought Before Kant. Peter Smith.
xMcGiffert, Arthur C.
Jonathan Edwards. AMS Pr.
McGiffert, Michael.
xMcGiffert, Michael.
ed. Character of Americans: A Book of
Readings. Dorsey.
McGiffert, Robert C., 1922-
xMcGiffert, Robert C.
The Art of Editing the News. Chilton.
McGill, Dan M. *see* McGill, Dan Mays.
McGill, Dan Mays.
xMcGill, Dan M.
ed. All Lines Insurance. Irwin.
Guaranty Fund for Private Pension Obligations.
Irwin.
Life Insurance. Irwin.
Preservation of Pension Benefit Rights. Irwin.
McGill, Michael. *see* McGill, Michael E.
McGill, Michael E.
xMcGill, Michael.
Organization Development for Operating
Managers. Am Mgmt.
xMcGill, Michael E.
Organization Development for Operating
Managers. Am Mgmt.
McGill, Ormond.
xMcGill, Ormond.
Entertaining with Magic. A S Barnes.
How to Produce Miracles. A S Barnes.
How to Produce Miracles. NAL.
Professional Stage Hypnotism. Westwood Pub
Co.
Religious Mysteries of the Orient. A S Barnes.
McGill, T. *see* McGill, Thomas E.
McGill, Thomas E.
xMcGill, T.
Readings in Animal Behavior. HR&W.
McGill University.
xMcGill University, Blacker - Wood Library of
Zoology & Ornithology.
A Dictionary Catalogue of the Blacker - Wood
Library of Zoology & Ornithology. G K Hall.
xMcGill University, Montreal, Institute of Islamic
Studies.
The Library Catalogue of the Institute of
Islamic Studies. G K Hall.
McGill University, Blacker - Wood Library of Zoology &
Ornithology. *see* McGill University.
McGill University, Montreal, Institute of Islamic Studies.
see McGill University.
McGill-Franzen, Anne.
xMcGill-Franzen, Anne.
The Gingerbread Boy. Raintree Child.
The Three Bears. Raintree Child.
The Three Little Pigs. Raintree Child.
McGillem. *see* McGillem, Clare D.
McGillem, Clare D.
xMcGillem.
Continuous & Discrete Signal & System
Analysis. HR&W.
McGilligan, Patrick.
xMcGilligan, Patrick.
Cagney: The Actor As Auteur. A S Barnes.
Cagney: The Actor As Auteur. Da Capo.
McGillis, Glenda, 1926-
xMcGillis, Glenda.
Citrus Cook Book. Golden West Pub.
McGinley, Phyllis.
xMcGinley, Phyllis.
B Book. Macmillan.
McGinn, Maureen.
xMcGinn, Maureen.
I Used to Be an Artichoke. Concordia.
McGinn, Noel F.
xMcGinn, Noel F.

Build a Mill, Build a City, Build a School:
Industrialization, Urbanization, & Education
in Ciudad Guayana. MIT Pr.
Education & Development in Korea. Harvard
U Pr.

McGinnis, Bruce.
xMcGinnis, Bruce.
The Fence. Vanguard.
McGinnis, James B.
xMcGinnis, James B.
Bread & Justice: Toward a New International
Economic Order. Paulist Pr.
McGinnis, Lila. *see* McGinnis, Lila Sprague.
McGinnis, Lila Sprague.
xMcGinnis, Lila.
What Will Simon Say?. Logos.
McGinnis, Michael R.
xMcGinnis, Michael R.
Laboratory Handbook of Medical Mycology.
Acad Pr.
McGinnis, Mildred A.
xMcGinnis, Mildred A.
Aphasic Children: Identification & Education
by the Association Method. Alexander
Graham.
McGinnis, Terri.
xMcGinnis, Terri.
Dr. Terri McGinnis' Dog & Cat Good Food
Book. Taylor & Ng.
McGinnis, William, 1947-
xMcGinnis, William.
Whitewater Rafting. Times Bks.
McGinty, Gerald.
xMcGinty, Gerald P.
Videocassette Recorders: Theory & Servicing.
McGraw.
McGinty, Gerald P. *see* McGinty, Gerald.
McGinty, Park.
xMcGinty, Park.
Interpretation & Dionysos. Method in the
Study of a God. Mouton
McGirt, James E. *see* McGirt, James Ephraim.
McGirt, James Ephraim.
xMcGirt, James E.
The Triumphs of Ephraim. Arno.
McGivney, Raymond.
xMcGivney, Raymond.
Essential Precalculus. Wadsworth Pub.
McGlashan, M. L. *see* McGlashan, Maxwell Len.
McGlashan, Maxwell Len, 1924-
xMcGlashan, M. L.
Chemical Thermodynamics. Am Chemical.
McGloin, Joseph T.
xMcGloin, Joseph T.
Hey, Why Don't We Try Christianity?. Our
Sunday Visitor.
How to Get More Out of the Mass. Liguori
Pubns.
Life of Man in Christ. Glencoe.
McGlynn, Daniel R.
xMcGlynn, Daniel R.
Distributed Processing & Data
Communications. Wiley.
Personal Computing: Home, Professional &
Small Business Applications. Wiley.
McGonagle, Bob.
xMcGonagle, Bob.
Careers in Sports. Lothrop.
xMcGonagle, Robert.
Careers in Aviation in the Sky & on the
Ground. Lothrop.
McGonagle, Robert. *see* McGonagle, Bob.
McGovern, Ann.
xMcGovern, Ann.

If You Lived in Colonial Times. Schol Bk Serv.
If You Lived with the Sioux Indians. Schol Bk
Serv.
If You Lived with the Sioux Indians. Schol Bk
Serv.
Little Whale. Schol Bk Serv.
Mr. Skinner's Skinny House. Schol Bk Serv.
Question & Answer Book About the Human
Body. Random.
Shark Lady: True Adventures of Eugenie
Clark. Schol Bk Serv.
The Underwater World of the Coral Reef.
Schol Bk Serv.
McGovern, George. *see* McGovern, George Stanley.
McGovern, George Stanley, 1922-
xMcGovern, George.
Grassroots: The Autobiography of George
McGovern. Random.
McGovern, John P.
xMcGovern, John P.
Chronobiology in Allergy & Immunology. C C
Thomas.
McGovern, John T. *see* McGovern, John Terence.
McGovern, John Terence, 1876-
xMcGovern, John T.
Diogenes Discovers Us. Arno.
McGovern, William M. *see* McGovern, William
Montgomery.
McGovern, William Montgomery, 1897-1964
xMcGovern, William M.
From Luther to Hitler: The History of
Fascist-Nazi Political Philosophy. AMS Pr.
Strategic Intelligence & the Shape of
Tomorrow. Greenwood.
McGowan, Carl, 1911-
xMcGowan, Carl.
Organization of Judicial Power in the United
States. Northwestern U Pr.
McGowan, Daniel A.
xMcGowan, Daniel A.
Consumer Economics. Rand.
McGowan, Pat. *see* McGowan, Patrick J.
McGowan, Patrick J.
xMcGowan, Pat.
ed. Threats, Weapons, & Foreign Policy. Sage.
xMcGowan, Patrick J.
Demystifying "National Character" in Black
Africa: A Comparative Study of Culture &
Foreign Policy 1979-1980. U of Denver Intl.
McGowan, Richard A.
xMcGowan, Richard A.
Italian Baroque Solo Sonatas for the Recorder
& the Flute. Info Coord.
McGowen, C. H.
xMcGowen, Charles H.
In Six Days. Bible Voice.
McGowen, Charles H. *see* McGowen, C. H.
McGowen, Tom.
xMcGowen, Tom.
Album of Dinosaurs. Rand.
Album of Prehistoric Man. Rand.
Album of Reptiles. Rand.
Album of Sharks. Rand.
Odyssey from River Bend. Little.
McGown, Linda B. *see* McGown, Linda Baine.
McGown, Linda Baine.
xMcGown, Linda B.
How to Obtain Abundant Clean Energy.
Plenum Pub.
McGown, Pearl K. *see* McGown, Pearl Kinnear.
McGown, Pearl Kinnear, 1892-
xMcGown, Pearl K.
Color in Hooked Rugs. OSV Fabric Shop.
Lore & Lure of Hooked Rugs. OSV Fabric
Shop.
Persian Patterns. OSV Fabric Shop.
McGrady, Donald.
xMcGrady, Donald.

Jorge Isaacs. Twayne.
McGrady, Mike.
xMcGrady, Mike.
The Husband's Cookbook. Lippincott.
McGrail, Joie.
xMcGrail, Joie H.
Fighting Back: One Woman's Struggle Against
Cancer. Har-Row.
McGrail, Joie H. *see* McGrail, Joie.
McGrath, Earl J. *see* McGrath, Earl James.
McGrath, Earl James, 1902-
xMcGrath, Earl J.
ed. Prospect for Renewal: The Future of the
Liberal Arts College. Jossey-Bass.
McGrath, Ed, 1950-
xMcGrath, Ed.
Inside the Alaska Pipeline. Celestial Arts.
McGrath, Fergal, 1895-
xMcGrath, Fergal.
Consecration of Learning: Lectures on
Newman's Idea of a University. Fordham.
McGrath, Patricia. *see* McGrath, Patricia L.
McGrath, Patricia L.
xMcGrath, Patricia.
The Unfinished Assignment: Equal Education
for Women. Worldwatch Inst.
McGrath, Robert L., 1935-
xMcGrath, Robert L.
Early Vermont Wall Paintings, 1790-1850. U
Pr of New Eng.
McGrath, Thomas, 1916-
xMcGrath, Thomas.
Letter to an Imaginary Friend. Swallow.
McGrath, William J.
xMcGrath, William J.
Dionysian Art & Populist Politics in Austria.
Yale U Pr.
McGraw, Eloise J. *see* McGraw, Eloise Jarvis
McGraw, Eloise Jarvis.
xMcGraw, Eloise J.
Joel & the Great Merlini. Pantheon.
Master Cornhill. Atheneum.
A Really Weird Summer. Atheneum.
McGraw-Hill. *see* McGraw-Hill Publishing Company,
Inc.
McGraw-Hill Book Company. *see* McGraw-Hill
Publishing Company, Inc.
McGraw-Hill Editors. *see* McGraw-Hill Publishing
Company, Inc.
McGraw-Hill Encyclopedia of Science and Technology.
xMcGraw-Hill Editors.
McGraw-Hill Encyclopedia of Energy.
McGraw.
xMcGraw-Hill Encyclopedia of Science &
Technology Staff.
McGraw-Hill Encyclopedia of Ocean &
Atmospheric Sciences. McGraw.
Modern Men of Science. McGraw.
xStaff of the McGraw-Hill Encyclopedia of Science
& Technology.
McGraw-Hill Encyclopedia of Science &
Technology. McGraw.
McGraw-Hill Publishing Company, Inc.
xDodge Building Cost Services.
Dodge Construction Systems Costs, 1977.
McGraw.
xMcGraw-Hill.
McGraw-Hill Encyclopedia of World
Biography. McGraw.
McGraw-Hill Encyclopedia of World Drama.
McGraw.
xMcGraw-Hill Book Company.
ed. Author's Book. McGraw.
xMcGraw-Hill Editors.

Basic Bibliography of Science & Technology.
　　McGraw.
Dictionary of the Life Sciences. McGraw.
McGraw-Hill Dictionary of Scientific &
　　Technical Terms. McGraw.
McGraw-Hill Encyclopedia of Environmental
　　Science. McGraw.
McGraw-Hill Encyclopedia of Food,
　　Agriculture, & Nutrition. McGraw.
McGraw-Hill Encyclopedia of Science &
　　Technology. McGraw.

McGreevy, Grace.
　　xMcGreevy, Grace.
　　I'm Thirsty Too. A S Barnes.

McGregor, Craig.
　　xMcGregor, Craig.
　　The Great Barrier Reef. Silver.
　　The Great Barrier Reef. Time-Life.

McGregor, Douglas.
　　xMcGregor, Douglas.
　　Human Side of Enterprise. McGraw.
　　Professional Manager. McGraw.

McGregor, John C. see McGregor, John Charles.

McGregor, John Charles, 1905-
　　xMcGregor, John C.
　　The Pool & Irving Villages: A Study of
　　　Hopewell Occupation in the Illinois River
　　　Valley. U of Ill Pr.

McGregor, Lynn.
　　xMcGregor, Lynn.
　　Developments in Drama Teaching. Humanities.

McGregor, R. S. see McGregor, Ronald Stuart.

McGregor, Ronald Stuart.
　　xMcGregor, R. S.
　　Exercises in Spoken Hindi. Cambridge U Pr.

McGruter, Patricia G. see McGruter, Patricia Gaddis.

McGruter, Patricia Gaddis.
　　xMcGruter, Patricia G.
　　The Great American Tofu Cookbook. Autumn
　　　Pr.

McGuane, Thomas.
　　xMcGuane, Thomas.
　　Bushwhacked Piano. S&S.
　　The Bushwhacked Piano. Warner Bks.
　　Ninety-Two in the Shade. FS&G.
　　Ninety-Two in the Shade. Penguin.
　　Panama. FS&G.
　　Panama. Penguin.
　　The Sporting Club. FS&G.
　　The Sporting Club. Penguin.

McGuffey, Verne, 1887
　　xMcGuffey, Verne.
　　Differences in the Activities of Teachers in
　　　Rural One-Teacher Schools & of Grade
　　　Teachers in Cities. AMS Pr.

McGuffey, William H. see McGuffey, William Holmes.

McGuffey, William Holmes.
　　xMcGuffey, William H.
　　Old Favorites from the McGuffey Readers.
　　　Gale.

McGuigan, F. J. see McGuigan, Frank J.

McGuigan, Frank J.
　　xMcGuigan, F. J.
　　Psychophysiological Measurement of Covert
　　　Behavior: A Guide for the Laboratory.
　　　Halsted Pr.
　　xMcGuigan, Frank J.
　　Experimental Psychology: A Methodological
　　　Approach. P-H.

McGuigan, James R.
　　xMcGuigan, James R.
　　Managerial Economics. West Pub.

McGuiness, Kenneth C.
　　xMcGuiness, Kenneth C.
　　How to Take a Case Before the National Labor
　　　Relations Board. BNA.

McGuinness, Arthur E.
　　xMcGuinness, Arthur E.
　　George Fitzmaurice. Bucknell U Pr.

McGuinness, William. see McGuinness, William J.

McGuinness, William J.
　　xMcGuinness, William.
　　Mechanical & Electrical Equipment for
　　　Buildings. Wiley.
　　xMcGuinness, William J.
　　Building Technology: Mechanical & Electrical
　　　Systems. Wiley.

McGuire, C. B.
　　xMcGuire, C. B.
　　Rational Investment Behavior in the Face of
　　　Floods. Mgmt Info Serv.

McGuire, E. Patrick. see McGuire, Edward Patrick.

McGuire, Edward Patrick.
　　xMcGuire, E. Patrick.
　　The Product-Safety Function: Organization &
　　　Operations. Conference Bd.
　　Spin-off Products & Services: The
　　　Commercialization of Internally Supported
　　　Resources. Conference Bd.
　　xMcGuire, Patrick E.
　　Customer Relations in Financial Institutions.
　　　Conference Bd.

McGuire, Frederick L.
　　xMcGuire, Frederick L.
　　An Evaluation of Driver Education: A Study of
　　　History, Philosophy, Research Methodology,
　　　& Effectiveness in the Field of Driver
　　　Education. U of Cal Pr.

McGuire, Jerry, 1934-
　　xMcGuire, Jerry.
　　How to Write, Direct & Produce Effective
　　　Business Films & Documentaries. TAB Bks.
　　Learning How to Fly an Airplane. TAB Bks.

McGuire, Joseph W. see McGuire, Joseph William.

McGuire, Joseph William.
　　xMcGuire, Joseph W.
　　Business & Society. McGraw.

McGuire, Judith W. see McGuire, Judith White
(Brockenbrough).

McGuire, Judith White (Brockenbrough).
　　xMcGuire, Judith W.
　　Diary of a Southern Refugee, During the War.
　　　Arno.

McGuire, Leslie.
　　xMcGuire, Leslie.
　　Susan Perl's Human Body Book. Platt.

McGuire, M. T. see McGuire, Michael T.

McGuire, Martin R. see McGuire, Martin Rawson
Patrick.

McGuire, Martin Rawson Patrick, 1897-
　　xMcGuire, Martin R.
　　Introduction to Classical Scholarship: A
　　　Syllabus & Bibliographical Guide. Intl Schol
　　　Bk Serv.
　　Introduction to Medieval Latin Studies: A
　　　Syllabus & Bibliographical Guide. Intl Schol
　　　Bk Serv.

McGuire, Michael T.
　　xMcGuire, M. T.
　　ed. Ethological Psychiatry: Psychopathology in
　　　the Context of Evolutionary Biology. Grune.

McGuire, Patrick E. see McGuire, Edward Patrick.

McGuire, Paul, 1905-
　　xMcGuire, Paul.
　　A Funeral in Eden. Garland Pub.

McGuire, Richard L.
　　xMcGuire, Richard L.
　　Passionate Attention: An Introduction to
　　　Literary Study. Norton.

McGuire, W. L. see McGuire, William L.

McGuire, William.
　　xMcGuire, William.
　　Matrix Structural Analysis. Wiley.
　　Steel Structures. P-H.

McGuire, William L.
　　xMcGuire, W. L.
　　ed. Estrogen Receptors in Human Breast
　　　Cancer. Raven.
　　xMcGuire, William L.

　　ed. Hormones, Receptors, & Breast Cancer.
　　　Raven.
　　ed. Progesterone Receptors in Normal &
　　　Neoplastic Tissues. Raven.

McGurk, Harry.
　　xMcGurk, Harry.
　　ed. Issues in Childhood Social Development.
　　　Methuen Inc.

McGurn, Robert.
　　xMcGurn, Robert.
　　Golf Power in Motion. Cornerstone.

McGurrin, James.
　　xMcGurrin, James.
　　Bourke Cockran: A Free Lance in American
　　　Politics. Arno.

McHale, J. see McHale, John.

McHale, John.
　　xMcHale, J.
　　World Facts & Trends. Macmillan.
　　xMcHale, John.
　　Changing Information Environment. Westview.
　　The Ecological Context. Braziller.

McHale, Kathryn, 1890-
　　xMcHale, Kathryn.
　　Comparative Psychology & Hygiene of the
　　　Overweight Child. AMS Pr.

McHale, Vincent E.
　　xMcHale, Vincent E.
　　ed. Evaluating Transnational Programs in
　　　Government & Business. Pergamon.

McHale, William R. see McHale, William Ross.

McHale, William Ross.
　　xMcHale, William R.
　　A Silence at Yorktown. Nordon Pubns.

McHarg, Ian L.
　　xMcHarg, Ian L.
　　Design with Nature. Natural Hist.

McHargue, Georgess.
　　xMcHargue, Georgess.
　　A Field Guide to Conservation Archaeology in
　　　North America. Lippincott.
　　Funny Bananas: The Mystery in the Museum.
　　　HR&W.
　　Compiled by Little Victories, Big Defeats: War
　　　As the Ultimate Pollution. Delacorte.
　　Meet the Vampire. Lippincott.
　　Mummies. Lippincott.
　　Private Zoo. Viking Pr.
　　Private Zoo. Penguin.
　　Stoneflight. Avon.
　　The Talking Table Mystery. Doubleday.

McHedlishvili, G. I. see McHedlishvili, Georgii
Iosifovich.

McHedlishvili, Georgii Iosifovich.
　　xMcHedlishvili, G. I.
　　Vascular Mechanisms of the Brain. Plenum
　　　Pub.

McHenry, Dean E. see McHenry, Dean Eugene.

McHenry, Dean Eugene, 1910-
　　xMcHenry, Dean E.
　　Academic Departments: Problems, Variations,
　　　& Alternatives. Jossey-Bass.
　　The Third Force in Canada: The Cooperative
　　　Commonwealth Federation,1932-1948.
　　　Greenwood.

McHenry, Lawrence C., 1929-
　　xMcHenry, Lawrence M.
　　Cerebral Circulation & Stroke. Green.

McHenry, Lawrence M. see McHenry, Lawrence C.

McHenry, Ruth W.
　　xMcHenry, Ruth W.
　　Self-Teaching Tests in Arithmetic for Nurses.
　　　Mosby.

McHoul, Lilian.
　　xMcHoul, Lilian.
　　Wild Flowers of Marin: A Layman's
　　　Handbook. Tamal Land.

McHugh. see McHugh, Mary.

McHugh, Gerald A. see McHugh, Gerald Austin.

McHugh, Gerald Austin.
    xMcHugh, Gerald A.
        Christian Faith & Criminal Justice: Toward a
        Christian Response to Crime & Punishment.
        Paulist Pr.
McHugh, James T.
    xMcHugh, James T.
        Death, Dying & the Law. Our Sunday Visitor.
McHugh, Joseph.
    xMcHugh, Joseph.
        The Apple & the Egg. Celestial Arts.
McHugh, Mary.
    xMcHugh.
        Young People Talk About Death. Watts.
    xMcHugh, Mary.
        Careers in Engineering & Engineering
        Technology. Watts.
        Law & the New Woman. Watts.
McHugh, Paul.
    xMcHugh, Paul.
        Prostitution & Victorian Social Reform: The
        Campaign Against the Contagious Diseases
        Acts. St Martin.
McHugh, Peter, 1929-
    xMcHugh, Peter.
        Defining the Situation: The Organization of
        Meaning in Social Interaction. Bobbs.
McHugh, Roland.
    xMcHugh, Roland.
        Annotations to Finnegans Wake. Johns
        Hopkins.
        The Sigla of Finnegans Wake. U of Tex Pr.
McHugh, Vincent, 1904-
    xMcHugh, Vincent.
        Primer of the Novel. Octagon.
McIlvanney, William, 1936-
    xMcIlvanney, William.
        Laidlaw. Popular Lib.
McIlwain, Charles H. *see* McIlwain, Charles Howard.
McIlwain, Charles Howard, 1871-
    xMcIlwain, Charles H.
        The American Revolution: A Constitutional
        Interpretation. Da Capo.
        American Revolution: A Constitutional
        Interpretation. Cornell U Pr.
McIlwaine, H. R. *see* McIlwaine, Henry Read.
McIlwaine, Henry Read, 1864-1934
    xMcIlwaine, H. R.
        The Struggle of Protestant Dissenters for
        Religious Toleration in Virginia. Johnson
        Repr.
McIlwaine, Shields, 1902-
    xMcIlwaine, Shields.
        Southern Poor White, from Lubberland to
        Tobacco Road. Cooper Sq.
McIlwraith, Archibald K. *see* McIlwraith, Archibald
    Kennedy.
McIlwraith, Archibald Kennedy.
    xMcIlwraith, Archibald K.
        ed. Five Elizabethan Tragedies. Oxford U Pr.
McInerny, Ralph. *see* McInerny, Ralph M.
McInerny, Ralph M.
    xMcInerny, Ralph.
        Bishop As Pawn: A Father Dowling Mystery.
        Vanguard.
        Quick As a Dodo. Vanguard.
McInnes. *see* McInnes, James.
McInnes, Betty, 1931-
    xMcInnes, Betty.
        Controlling the Spread of Infection: A
        Programmed Presentation. Mosby.
McInnes, James.
    xMcInnes.
        Radiographic Anatomy. ACC.
McInnes, John.
    xMcInnes, John.

        The Chocolate Chip Mystery. Garrard.
        Drat the Dragon. Garrard.
        How Pedro Got His Name. Garrard.
        Leo Lion Paints It Red. Garrard.
        On with the Circus. Garrard.
        Who Ever Heard of a Tiger in a Tree. Garrard.
McInnes, John. *see* McInnes, John A.
McInnes, John A.
    xMcInnes, John.
        Goodnight Painted Pony. Garrard.
McInnes, Mary E. *see* McInnes, Mary Elizabeth.
McInnes, Mary Elizabeth, 1931-
    xMcInnes, Mary E.
        ed. Essentials of Communicable Disease.
        Mosby.
McInnes, Neil.
    xMcInnes, Neil.
        The Communist Parties of Western Europe.
        Oxford U Pr.
        French Politics Today: The Future of the Fifth
        Republic. Sage.
McInnis, Raymond G.
    xMcInnis, Raymond G.
        New Perspectives for Reference Service in
        Academic Libraries. Greenwood.
McIntire, C. T.
    xMcIntire, C. T.
        ed. God, History, & Historians: An Anthology
        of Modern Christian Views of History.
        Oxford U Pr.
McIntire, Russell. *see* McIntire, Russell M.
McIntire, Russell M.
    xMcIntire, Russell.
        Live Your Faith!. Pelican.
McIntire, Thomas C., 1942-
    xMcIntire, Thomas C.
        The A to Z Book of Computer Games. TAB
        Bks.
        Software Interpreters for Microcomputers.
        Wiley.
McIntosh, Carey.
    xMcIntosh, Carey.
        The Choice of Life: Samuel Johnson & the
        World of Fiction. Yale U Pr.
McIntosh, D. M. *see* McIntosh, Douglas M.
McIntosh, David S. *see* McIntosh, David Seneff.
McIntosh, David Seneff, 1897-
    xMcIntosh, David S.
        Folk Songs & Singing Games of the Illinois
        Ozarks. S Ill U Pr.
McIntosh, Donald, 1924-
    xMcIntosh, Donald.
        Foundations of Human Society. U of Chicago
        Pr.
McIntosh, Douglas M.
    xMcIntosh, D. M.
        Statistics for the Teacher. Pergamon.
McIntosh, I. G.
    xMcIntosh, I. G.
        The Face of Scotland. Pergamon.
McIntosh, J. A. *see* McIntosh, James Edward Alister.
McIntosh, James Edward Alister.
    xMcIntosh, J. A.
        Mathematical Modelling & Computers in
        Endocrinology. Springer-Verlag.
McIntosh, Maria J. *see* McIntosh, Maria Jane.
McIntosh, Maria Jane, 1803-1878
    xMcIntosh, Maria J.
        Conquest & Self-Conquest. Arno.
McIntosh, P. C. *see* McIntosh, Peter C.
McIntosh, Peter C.
    xMcIntosh, P. C.
        Fair Play: Ethics in Sport & Education.
        Heinemann Ed.
McIntosh, Robert W. *see* McIntosh, Robert Woodrow.

McIntosh, Robert Woodrow.
    xMcIntosh, Robert W.
        Tourism: Principles, Practices, Philosophies.
        Grid Pub.
McIntosh, W. H.
    xMcIntosh, W. H.
        History of Wayne County New York. Yankee
        Ped Bkshop.
McIntyre, C. F. *see* McIntyre, Clara Frances.
McIntyre, Clara Frances.
    xMcIntyre, C. F.
        Ann Radcliffe in Relation to Her Time. Shoe
        String.
McIntyre, Donald M.
    xMcIntyre, Donald M.
        Criminal Justice in the United States. Am Bar
        Foun.
        ed. Law Enforcement in the Metropolis: A
        Working Paper on the Criminal Law System
        in Detroit. Am Bar Foun.
McIntyre, Ida M. *see* McIntyre, Ida Mae.
McIntyre, Ida Mae.
    xMcIntyre, Ida M.
        Unicorn Magic. Garrard.
McIntyre, John T. *see* McIntyre, John Thomas.
McIntyre, John Thomas, 1871-1951
    xMcIntyre, John T.
        Ferment. AMS Pr.
McIntyre, Michael P.
    xMcIntyre, Michael P.
        Physical Geography. Wiley.
McIntyre, Nancy F. *see* McIntyre, Nancy Fair.
McIntyre, Nancy Fair.
    xMcIntyre, Nancy F.
        Earthenware Cookbook. Gala Bks.
        Friends & Lovers Cookbook. Gala Bks.
McIntyre, Thomas J.
    xMcIntyre, Thomas J.
        The Fear Brokers. Pilgrim NY.
McIntyre, Virgie M.
    xMcIntyre, Virgie M.
        Reading Strategies & Enrichment Activities for
        Grades 4-9. Merrill.
McIntyre, Vonda N.
    xMcIntyre, Vonda N.
        The Crystal Ship: Three Original Novellas of
        Science Fiction. Elsevier-Nelson.
        Dreamsnake. HM.
        Fireflood & Other Stories. HM.
McIntyre, W. David. *see* McIntyre, William David.
McIntyre, William David.
    xMcIntyre, W. David.
        The Commonwealth of Nations: Origins and
        Impact, 1869-1971. U of Minn Pr.
McJimsey, Haariet Tilden.
    xMcJimsey, Harriet T.
        Art & Fashion in Clothing Selection. Iowa St U
        Pr.
McJimsey, Harriet T. *see* McJimsey, Haariet Tilden.
McKaig, Thomas H.
    xMcKaig, Thomas H.
        Building Failures: Case Studies of Construction
        & Design. McGraw.
McKain, David W.
    xMcKain, David W.
        ed. Whole Earth: Essays in Appreciation,
        Anger, & Hope. St Martin.
McKain, Robert J.
    xMcKain, Robert J.
        Realize Your Potential. Am Mgmt.
McKale, Donald M., 1943-
    xMcKale, Donald M.
        The Swastika Outside Germany. Kent St U Pr.
McKay, C. E. *see* McKay, Charlotte Elizabeth (Johnson).
McKay, Charles W., 1943-
    xMcKay, Charles W.
        Digital Circuits: A Preparation for
        Microprocessors. P-H.
McKay, Charlotte Elizabeth (Johnson).
    xMcKay, C. E.

Stories of Hospital & Camp. Arno.
McKay, Claude, 1890-1948
xMcKay, Claude.
Banana Bottom. Chatham Bkseller.
Banana Bottom. HarBraceJ.
Home to Harlem. Chatham Bkseller.
A Long Way from Home. Arno.
Long Way from Home. HarBraceJ.
The Negroes in America. Kennikat.
McKay, David. see McKay, David H.
McKay, David H.
xMcKay, David.
Housing & Race in Industrial Society: Civil
Rights & Urban Policy in Britain & the
United States. Rowman.
McKay, Derek.
xMcKay, Derek.
Prince Eugene of Savoy. Thames Hudson.
McKay, Douglas R.
xMcKay, Douglas R.
Carlos Arniches. Twayne.
Enrique Jardiel Poncela. Twayne.
McKay, E. S. see McKay, Edward S.
McKay, Edward S.
xMcKay, E. S.
Marketing Mystique. Am Mgmt.
McKay, Frances P. see McKay, Frances Peabody.
McKay, Frances Peabody.
xMcKay, Frances P.
More Fun Than Heaven. Valkyrie Pr.
McKay, Heather.
xMcKay, Heather.
Heather McKay's Complete Book of Squash.
Ballantine.
McKay, John P.
xMcKay, John P.
A History of Western Society. HM.
McKay, R. B. see McKay, Robert B.
McKay, Robert, 1921-
xMcKay, Robert.
Bordy. Elsevier-Nelson.
Canary Red. Schol Bk Serv.
Dave's Song. Bantam.
The Girl Who Wanted to Run the Boston
Marathon. Elsevier-Nelson.
The Running Back. HarBraceJ.
McKay, Robert B.
xMcKay, R. B.
Reapportionment: The Law & Politics of Equal
Representation. Kraus Repr.
xMcKay, Robert B.
Reapportionment: The Law & Poiitics of Equal
Representation. S&S.
McKay, Ruth C. see McKay, Ruth Capers.
McKay, Ruth Capers, 1902-
xMcKay, Ruth C.
George Gissing & His Critic, Frank
Swinnerton. Arden Lib.
George Gissing & His Critic Frank Swinnerton.
Folcroft.
McKay, Vernon.
xMcKay, Vernon.
Africa in World Politics. Greenwood.
McKean, Dayton D. see McKean, Dayton David.
McKean, Dayton David, 1904-
xMcKean, Dayton D.
Pressures on the Legislature of New Jersey.
Russell.
McKean, H. P. see McKean, Henry P.
McKean, Henry P.
xMcKean, H. P.
Stochastic Integrals. Acad Pr.
McKean, Keith F.
xMcKean, Keith F.
The Moral Measure of Literature. Greenwood.
McKean, Robert C.
xMcKean, Robert C.

Principles & Methods in Secondary Education.
Merrill.
McKearin, Helen.
xMcKearin, Helen.
American Bottles & Flasks & Their Ancestry.
Crown.
McKears, D. W.
xMcKears, D. W.
Surface Anatomy for Radiographers. Year Bk
Med.
McKeating, Henry.
xMcKeating, Henry.
God & the Future. Judson.
Living with Guilt. Judson.
McKechnie, Samuel.
xMcKechnie, Samuel.
Popular Entertainments Through the Ages.
Arno.
Popular Entertainments Through the Ages. R
West.
McKee, Alexander, 1918-
xMcKee, Alexander.
Death Raft: The Human Drama of the Medusa
Shipwreck. Scribner.
McKee, David R. see McKee, David Rice.
McKee, Delber. see McKee, Delber L.
McKee, Edwin D. see McKee, Edwin Dinwiddie.
McKee, Henry S. see McKee, Henry Stewart.
McKee, Thomas H. see McKee, Thomas Hudson.
McKee-Berger-Mansueto. see McKee-Berger-Mansuetto.
McKee-Berger-Mansueto, Inc. see
McKee-Berger-Mansuetto.
McKee-Berger-Mansuetto.
xMcKee-Berger-Mansueto.
Design Cost File Nineteen Seventy-Seven. Van
Nos Reinhold.
xMcKee-Berger-Mansueto, Inc.
Building Cost File, Nineteen Seventy-Eight:
Central Edition. Van Nos Reinhold.
Building Cost File, Nineteen Seventy-Eight:
Eastern Edition. Van Nos Reinhold.
Building Cost File, Nineteen Seventy-Eight:
Southern Edition. Van Nos Reinhold.
Building Cost File, Nineteen Seventy-Eight:
Western Edition. Van Nos Reinhold.
Building Cost File, Nineteen Seventy-Nine:
Unit Prices, Central Edition. Van Nos
Reinhold.
Building Cost File, Nineteen Seventy-Nine:
Unit Prices, Eastern Edition. Van Nos
Reinhold.
Building Cost File, Nineteen Seventy-Nine:
Unit Prices, Southern Edition. Van Nos
Reinhold.
Building Cost File, Nineteen Seventy-Nine:
Unit Prices, Western Edition. Van Nos
Reinhold.
Design Cost File Nineteen Seventy-Nine:
Composite Prices. Van Nos Reinhold.
McKee, David.
xMcKee, David.
Two Admirals. HM.
McKee, David Rice, 1902-
xMcKee, David R.
Simon Tyssot de Patot & the
Seventeenth-Century Background of Critical
Deism. Johnson Repr.
McKee, Delber L., 1923-
xMcKee, Delber.
Chinese Exclusion Versus the Open Door
Policy, 1900-1906: Clashes Over China
Policy in the Roosevelt Era. Wayne St U Pr.
McKee, Edwin Dinwiddie.
xMcKee, Edwin D.
History of the Redwall Limestone of Northern
Arizona. Geol Soc.
McKee, Gerald.
xMcKee, Gerald.

Film Collecting. A S Barnes.
McKee, Henry Stewart.
xMcKee, Henry S.
Journeys in Understanding. Arno.
McKee, James B., 1919-
xMcKee, James B.
Introduction to Sociology. HR&W.
McKee, Jesse O.
xMcKee, Jesse O.
The Choctaws: Cultural Evolution of a Native
American Tribe. U Pr of Miss.
McKee, Thomas Hudson.
xMcKee, Thomas H.
National Conventions & Platforms of All
Political Parties 1789-1905: Convention,
Popular, & Electoral Vote. B Franklin.
McKee, William, Captain, 1895-
xMcKee, William.
ed. Lectures for Bankers & Business
Executives. Arno.
McKee, William D.
xMcKee, William D.
ed. Environmental Problems in Medicine. C C
Thomas.
McKee, William S.
xMcKee, William S.
Federal Taxation of Partnerships & Partners.
Warren.
McKeeman, William M.
xMcKeeman, William M.
Compiler Generator. P-H.
McKeever, J. Ross. see McKeever, James Ross.
McKeever, James M.
xMcKeever, Jim.
Christians Will Go Through the Tribulation: &
How to Prepare for It. Alpha Omega.
McKeever, James Ross, 1910-
xMcKeever, J. Ross.
Apartment Development: Strategy for
Successful Decision Making. Urban Land.
McKeever, Jim. see McKeever, James M.
McKeithan, Daniel M. see McKeithan, Daniel Morley.
McKeithan, Daniel Morley, 1902-
xMcKeithan, Daniel M.
Debt to Shakespeare in Beaumont & Fletcher
Plays. Gordian.
Debt to Shakespeare in the Beaumont &
Fletcher Plays. AMS Pr.
McKellips, Art.
xMcKellips, Art.
Woodcarving for Beginners. Intl Schol Bk Serv.
McKelvey, Blake, 1903-
xMcKelvey, Blake.
American Urbanization: A Comparative
History. Scott F.
McKelvey, James M.
xMcKelvey, James M.
Polymer Processing. Wiley.
McKendrick, Melveena.
xMcKendrick, Melveena.
Ferdinand & Isabella. Am Heritage.
McKendry, Ruth.
xMcKendry, Ruth.
Traditional Quilts & Bed Coverings. Van Nos
Reinhold.
McKenna, G. see McKenna, George.
McKenna, George.
xMcKenna, G.
American Politics: Ideals & Realities. McGraw.
McKenna, Joseph P, 1922-
xMcKenna, Joseph P.
Aggregate Economic Analysis. Dryden Pr.
McKenna, Mary.
xMcKenna, Mary.
A Family. Carillon Bks.
McKenna, Stephen, 1888-
xMcKenna, Stephen.
Tales of Intrigue & Revenge. Arno.
McKenna, Virginia.
xMcKenna, Virginia.

On Playing with Lions. HarBraceJ.

McKenney, James L.
xMcKenney, James L.
Cases in Operations Management. Wiley.

McKenney, Kenneth, 1929-
xMcKenney, Kenneth.
Fire Cloud. Avon.
The Fire Cloud. S&S.
The Firecloud. Avon.
The Moonchild. Avon.
The Moonchild. S&S.

McKenney, Mary, 1946-
xMcKenney, Mary.
Divorce: A Selected Annotated Bibliography.
Scarecrow.

McKenney, Ruth, 1911-
xMcKenney, Ruth.
Industrial Valley. Greenwood.

McKenney, Thomas L. see McKenney, Thomas Loraine.

McKenney, Thomas Loraine, 1785-1859
xMcKenney, Thomas L.
Memoirs, Official & Personal. U of Nebr Pr.

McKenzie, Barbara.
xMcKenzie, Barbara.
ed. Fiction's Journey: 50 Stories. HarBraceJ.
Mary McCarthy. Coll & U Pr.
ed. Process of Fiction: Contemporary Stories &
Criticism. HarBraceJ.

McKenzie, Bruce A.
xMcKenzie, Bruce A.
Understanding & Using Electricity. Interstate.

McKenzie, Dennis J.
xMcKenzie, Dennis J.
Essentials of Real Estate Economics. Wiley.

McKenzie, George W.
xMcKenzie, George W.
The Economics of the Eurocurrency System.
Halsted Pr.

McKenzie, Gordon, 1901-
xMcKenzie, Gordon.
Organic Unity in Coleridge. AMS Pr

McKenzie, Howard L. see McKenzie, Howard Lester.

McKenzie, Howard Lester, 1910-
xMcKenzie, Howard L.
Mealybugs of California: With Taxonomy,
Biology, & Control of North American
Species. U of Cal Pr.

McKenzie, J. see McKenzie, John.

McKenzie, J. Alexander.
xMcKenzie, J. Alexander.
The Omega Document. Bethany Fell.

McKenzie, John.
xMcKenzie, J.
ed. Interactive Computer Graphics in Science
Teaching. Halsted Pr.
xMcKenzie, John.
An Introduction to Developmental Biology.
Halsted Pr.

McKenzie, John L.
xMcKenzie, John L.
Dictionary of the Bible. Macmillan.
The Power & the Wisdom: An Interpretation of
the New Testament. Doubleday.
A Theology of the Old Testament. Doubleday.
Two-Edged Sword: An Interpretation of the
Old Testament. Doubleday.

McKenzie, Sheila C., 1943-
xMcKenzie, Sheila C.
Aging & Old Age. Scott F.

McKeon, Michael, 1943-
xMcKeon, Michael.
Politics & Poetry in Restoration England: The
Case of Dryden's Annus Mirabilis. Harvard
U Pr.

McKeown, Martha F. see McKeown, Martha Ferguson.

McKeown, Martha Ferguson, 1903-
xMcKeown, Martha F.

Come to Our Salmon Feast. Binford.
Them Was the Days: An American Saga of the
'70's. U of Nebr Pr.

McKeown, Thomas.
xMcKeown, Thomas.
An Introduction to Social Medicine.
Lippincott.
The Role of Medicine: Dream, Mirage or
Nemesis?. Princeton U Pr.

McKercher, Berneth N.
xMcKercher, Berneth N.
What You See Is What You Get. Mich St U
Pr.

McKern, Sharon S.

xMcKern, Sharon S.
Living Prehistory: An Introduction to Physical
Anthropology & Archaeology.
Benjamin-Cummings.
The Many Faces of Man. Lothrop.

McKerns, K. W. see McKerns, Kenneth W.

McKerns, Kenneth W.
xMcKerns, K. W.
Hormones & Cancer. Acad Pr.
xMcKerns, Kenneth W.
ed. Synthesis & Release of Adenohypophyseal
Hormones. Plenum Pub.

McKerrow, R. B. see McKerrow, Ronald Brunlees.

McKerrow, Ronald Brunlees, 1872-1940
xMcKerrow, R. B.
Prolegomena for the Oxford Shakespeare: A
Study in Editorial Method. Oxford U Pr.

McKerrow, W. S.
xMcKerrow, W. Stuart.
ed. The Ecology of Fossils: An Illustrated
Guide. MIT Pr.

McKerrow, W. Stuart. see McKerrow, W. S.

McKevitt, Gerald.
xMcKevitt, Gerald.
The University of Santa Clara: A History,
1851-1977. Stanford U Pr.

McKibbin, Jean.
xMcKibbin, Jean.
Cookbook of Foods from Bible Days. Franje.

McKibbin, Lloyd S.
xMcKibbin, Lloyd S.
Horse Owner's Handbook. Saunders.

McKie, Douglas.
xMcKie, Douglas.
The Discovery of Specific & Latent Heats.
Arno.

McKie, Duncan.
xMcKie, Duncan.
Crystalline Solids. Halsted Pr.

McKie, Ronald. see McKie, Ronald Cecil Hamlyn.

McKie, Ronald Cecil Hamlyn, 1909-
xMcKie, Ronald.
The Crushing. Scribner.

McKie, Roy.
xMcKie, Roy.
illus. The Joke Book. Random.
The Riddle Book. Random.

McKiernan, John.
xMcKiernan, John.
Planning & Financing Your New Business: A
Guide to Venture Capital. Tech Mgmt.

McKilligin, Helen R.
xMcKilligin, Helen R.
The First Day of Life: Principles of Neonatal
Nursing. Springer Pub.

McKillip, Patricia. see McKillip, Patricia A.

McKillip, Patricia A.
xMcKillip, Patricia.

The Forgotten Beasts of Eld. Avon.
The Forgotten Beasts of Eld. Atheneum.
Harpist in the Wind. Atheneum.
The House on Parchment Street. Atheneum.
xMcKillip, Patricia A.
The Night Gift. Atheneum.
The Night Gift. Atheneum.
The Riddle-Master of Hed. Ballantine.
The Riddle-Master of Hed. Atheneum.

McKillop, A. B.
xMcKillop, A. B.
A Disciplined Intelligence: Critical Inquiry &
Canadian Thought in the Victorian Era.
McGill-Queens U Pr.

McKillop, Alan D. see McKillop, Alan Dugald.

McKillop, Alan Dugald, 1892-
xMcKillop, Alan D.
The Background of Thomson's Liberty.
Folcroft.
The Background of Thomson's Liberty.
Norwood Edns.
The Early Masters of English Fiction.
Greenwood.

McKillop, Susan R. see McKillop, Susan Regan.

McKillop, Susan Regan.
xMcKillop, Susan R.
Franciabigio. U of Cal Pr.

McKim, Margaret G. see McKim, Margaret Grace.

McKim, Margaret Grace, 1914-
xMcKim, Margaret G.
Guiding Growth in Reading in the Modern
Elementary School. Macmillan.
The Reading of Verbal Material in Ninth
Grade Algebra. AMS Pr

McKim, Robert H.
xMcKim, Robert H.
Experiences in Visual Thinking. Brooks-Cole.

McKinley, Albert E. see McKinley, Albert Edward.

McKinley, Albert Edward, 1870-1936
xMcKinley, Albert E.
Suffrage Franchise in the Thirteen English
Colonies in America. B Franklin.

McKinley, Charles.
xMcKinley, Charles.
Launching Social Security: A Capture &
Record Account, 1935-1937. U of Wis Pr.

McKinley, James.
xMcKinley, James.
Assassination in America. Har-Row.

McKinley, Joe W.
xMcKinley, Joe W.
Fundamentals of Stress Analysis. Intl Schol Bk
Serv.

McKinley, Robin.
xMcKinley, Robin.
Beauty: A Retelling of the Story of Beauty &
the Beast. Har-Row.

McKinnell, Robert C. see McKinnell, Robert Gilmore.

McKinnell, Robert Gilmore.
xMcKinnell, Robert C.
Cloning: A Biologist Reports. U of Minn Pr.

McKinney, David W. see McKinney, David Walter.

McKinney, David Walter.
xMcKinney, David W.
The Authoritarian Personality Studies: An
Inquiry into the Failure of Social Science
Research to Produce Demonstrable
Knowledge. Mouton.

McKinney, Donald, 1909-
xMcKinney, Donald.
Living with Joy. Abingdon.
To Follow a Dream. Broadman.

McKinney, Doug.
xMcKinney, Douglas.
Sam Peckinpah. Twayne.

McKinney, Douglas. see McKinney, Doug.

McKinney, Fred, 1908-
xMcKinney, Fred.

Psychology in Action: Basic Readings.
Macmillan.
McKinney, Gordon B. *see* McKinney, Gordon Bartlett.
McKinney, Gordon Bartlett, 1943-
xMcKinney, Gordon B.
Southern Mountain Republicans, 1865-1900:
Politics & the Appalachian Community. U of
NC Pr.
McKinney, J. Evans. *see* McKinney, Joseph Evans.
McKinney, John C.
xMcKinney, John C.
ed. Aging & Social Policy. Irvington.
McKinney, Joseph Evans, 1913-
xMcKinney, J. Evans.
Decoys of the Susquehanna Flats & Their
Makers. Holly Pr.
McKinney, Richard I. *see* McKinney, Richard Ishmael.
McKinney, Richard Ishmael, 1906-
xMcKinney, Richard I.
Religion in Higher Education Among Negroes.
Arno.
Religion in Higher Education Among Negroes.
Elliots Bks.
McKinney, Wayne C.
xMcKinney, Wayne C.
Archery. Wm C Brown.
McKinnon, Ronald I.
xMcKinnon, Ronald I.
Money & Capital in Economic Development.
Brookings.
Money in International Exchange: The
Convertible Currency System. Oxford U Pr.
McKinsey & Co. *see* McKinsey and Company.
McKinsey and Company.
xMcKinsey & Co.
Arts of Top Management: A McKinsey
Anthology. McGraw.
McKinsey, James O. *see* McKinsey, James Oscar.
McKinsey, James Oscar, 1889-1937
xMcKinsey, James O.
Managerial Accounting. Arno.
McKirahan, Richard D.
xMcKirahan, Richard D.
Plato & Socrates: A Comprehensive
Bibliography, 1958-1973. Garland Pub.
McKitrick, Eric L.
xMcKitrick, Eric L.
Andrew Johnson & Reconstruction. U of
Chicago Pr.
McKitrick, M. *see* McKitrick, Max O.
McKitrick, Max O., 1917-
xMcKitrick, M.
Money Management. McGraw.
McKnight, Bob, 1906-
xMcKnight, Bob.
How to Beat the Claimers. Citadel Pr.
McKnight, Carolyn.
xMcKnight, Carolyn.
Gravetide. St Martin.
The House in the Shadows. St Martin.
McKnight, Edgar V.
xMcKnight, Edgar V.
Meaning in Texts: The Historical Shaping of a
Narrative Hermeneutics. Fortress.
McKnight, George H. *see* McKnight, George Harley.
McKnight, George Harley, 1871-1951
xMcKnight, George H.
English Words & Their Background. Gordian.
McKnight, Hugh.
xMcKnight, Hugh.
Canal & River Craft in Pictures. Kelley.
McKnight, Thomas Lee, 1928-
xMcKnight, Tom.
Feral Livestock in Anglo-America. U of Cal Pr.
xMcKnight, Tom L.
Friendly Vermin: A Survey of Feral Livestock
in Australia. U of Cal Pr.
McKnight, Tom. *see* McKnight, Thomas Lee.
McKnight, Tom L. *see* McKnight, Thomas Lee.

McKown, Robin.
xMcKown, Robin.
Colonial Conquest of Africa. Watts.
The Opium War in China, 1840-1842: The
British Resort to War in Order to Maintain
Their Opium Trade. Watts.
Rakoto & the Drongo Bird. Lothrop.
The World of Mary Cassatt. Dell.
The World of Mary Cassatt. T Y Crowell.
McKuen, Rod.
xMcKuen, Rod.
Alone. PB.
And to Each Season. S&S.
Celebrations of the Heart. S&S.
Come to Me in Silence. S&S.
Coming Close to the Earth. S&S.
In Someone's Shadow. Random.
Love's Been Good to Me. PB.
We Touch the Sky. S&S.
McKusick, Victor. *see* McKusick, Victor A.
McKusick, Victor A.
xMcKusick, Victor.
Human Genetics. P-H.
xMcKusick, Victor A.
ed. Medical Genetic Studies of the Amish:
Selected Papers. Johns Hopkins.
ed. Medical Genetics. HP Pub Co.
Mendelian Inheritance in Man: Catalogs of
Autosomal Dominant, Autosomal Recessive,
& X-Linked Phenotypes. Johns Hopkins.
McLachlan, Dan H.
xMcLachlan, Dan H.
The Fieldbook of Pacific Northwest Sea
Creatures. Naturegraph.
McLachlan, Gordon.
xMcLachlan, Gordon.
ed. Positions, Movements & Directions in
Health Services Research: Proceedings.
Oxford U Pr.
McLachlan, Gordon. *see* Nuffield Provincial Hospitals
Trust.
McLachlan, Herbert, 1876-
xMcLachlan, Herbert.
The Religious Opinions of Milton, Locke &
Newton. Folcroft.
Religious Opinions of Milton, Locke &
Newton. Russell.
McLachlan, J. *see* McLachlan, James.
McLachlan, James, 1932-
xMcLachlan, J.
Princetonians, 1748-1768: A Biographical
Dictionary. Princeton U Pr.
McLafferty, F. W. *see* McLafferty, Fred W.
McLafferty, Fred W.
xMcLafferty, F. W.
ed. Mass Spectrometry of Organic Ions. Acad
Pr.
xMcLafferty, Fred W.
Mass Spectral Correlations. Am Chemical.
McLain, Denny.
xMcLain, Denny.
Nobody's Perfect. Dial.
McLain, Margaret S. *see* McLain, Margaret Starr.
McLain, Margaret Starr.
xMcLain, Margaret S.
Class Piano. Ind U Pr.
McLaine, Ian, 1939-
xMcLaine, Ian.
Ministry of Morale: Home Front Morale &
Ministry of Information in World War II.
Allen Unwin.
McLanathan, Richard. *see* McLanathan, Richard B. K.
McLanathan, Richard B. K.
xMcLanathan, Richard.
Art in America: A Brief History. HarBraceJ.
The Art of Marguerite Stix. Abrams.
McLane, Charles B.
xMcLane, Charles B.

Soviet Policy & the Chinese Communists,
1931-1946. Arno.
Soviet Strategies in Southeast Asia: An
Exploration of Eastern Policy Under Lenin &
Stalin. Princeton U Pr.
McLane, Helen J.
xMcLane, Helen J.
Selecting, Developing & Retaining Women
Executives: A Corporate Strategy for the
Eighties. Van Nos Reinhold.
McLane, John R., 1935-
xMcLane, John R.
Indian Nationalism & the Early Congress.
Princeton U Pr.
McLane, Louis.
xMcLane, Louis.
The Private Journal of Louis McLane, U.S.N.
1844-1848. Dawsons.
McLane, Lucy N. *see* McLane, Lucy Neely.
McLane, Lucy Neely.
xMcLane, Lucy N.
In Tune with Beauty. Pacific Bks.
McLaren, Alan.
xMcLaren, Alan.
Sunny Side up: Diet Cooking the Hospital
Way. Ashley Bks.
McLaren, Ian A.
xMcLaren, Ian A.
Education in a Small Democracy, New
Zealand. Routledge & Kegan.
McLaren, Ian A. *see* McLaren, Ian Alexander.
McLaren, Ian Alexander, 1931-
xMcLaren, Ian A.
Natural Regulation of Animal Populations.
Lieber-Atherton.
McLaren, James C. *see* McLaren, James Clark.
McLaren, James Clark.
xMcLaren, James C.
Theatre of Andre Gide: Evolution of a Moral
Philosopher. Octagon.
McLaughlin, Andrew C. *see* McLaughlin, Andrew
Cunningham.
McLaughlin, Andrew Cunningham, 1861-1947
xMcLaughlin, Andrew C.
Foundations of American Constitutionalism.
Peter Smith.
Lewis Cass. AMS Pr.
Lewis Cass. Chelsea Hse.
McLaughlin, Barry.
xMcLaughlin, Barry.
Learning & Social Behavior. Free Pr.
McLaughlin, Charles.
xMcLaughlin, Charles.
Space Age Dictionary. Van Nos Reinhold.
McLaughlin, Charles A. *see* McLaughlin, Charles Albert.
McLaughlin, Charles Albert.
xMcLaughlin, Charles A.
Laboratory Anatomy of the Rabbit. Wm C
Brown.
McLaughlin, David J., 1936-
xMcLaughlin, David J.
The Executive Money Map. McGraw.
McLaughlin, Doris B.
xMcLaughlin, Doris B.
ed. The Landrum-Griffin Act & Union
Democracy. U of Mich Pr.

McLaughlin, Edward T. *see* McLaughlin, Edward
Tompkins.
McLaughlin, Edward Tompkins, 1860-1893
xMcLaughlin, Edward T.
Studies in Mediaeval Life & Literature. Arno.
McLaughlin, Frank S.
xMcLaughlin, Frank S.
Quantitative Techniques for Management
Decisions. HM.
McLaughlin, Herb.
xMcLaughlin, Herb.

Arizona the Beautiful. Doubleday.
McLaughlin, John C. see McLaughlin, John Cameron.
McLaughlin, John Cameron.
  xMcLaughlin, John C.
    Aspects of the History of English. Irvington.
McLaughlin, John E.
  xMcLaughlin, John E.
    Writing a Job-Winning Resume. P-H.
McLaughlin, Joseph T.
  xMcLaughlin, Joseph T.
    ed. Federal Class Action Digests 1976. PLI.
McLaughlin, Martin M. see McLaughlin, Martin
  Michael.
McLaughlin, Martin Michael.
  xMcLaughlin, Martin M.
    The United States & World Development:
      Agenda 1979. Praeger.
McLaughlin, Mary M. see McLaughlin, Mary Martin.
McLaughlin, Mary Martin, 1919-
  xMcLaughlin, Mary M.
    Intellectual Freedom & Its Limitations in the
      University of Paris in the Thirteenth &
      Fourteenth Centuries. Arno.
McLaughlin, Milbrey W. see McLaughlin, Milbrey
  Wallin.
McLaughlin, Milbrey Wallin.
  xMcLaughlin, Milbrey W.
    Evaluation & Reform: The Elementary &
      Secondary Education Act of 1965, Title I.
      Ballinger Pub.
McLaughlin, Patsy A.
  xMcLaughlin, Patsy A.
    Comparative Morphology of Recent Crustacea.
      W H Freeman.
McLaughlin, Raymond W.
  xMcLaughlin, Raymond W.
    Ethics of Persuasive Preaching. Baker Bk.
McLaughlin, Robert W. see McLaughlin, Robert William.
McLaughlin, Robert William, 1900-
  xMcLaughlin, Robert W.
    Architect: Creating Man's Environment.
      Macmillan.
McLaughlin, Terence.
  xMcLaughlin, Terence.
    If You Like It Don't Eat It: Dietary Fads and
      Fancies. Universe.
McLean. see McLean, Antonia.
McLean, A. see McLean, Alan A.
McLean, Adam. see McLean, Adam C.
McLean, Adam C.
  xMcLean, Adam.
    Geology for Civil Engineers. Allen Unwin.
McLean, Alan A.
  xMcLean, A.
    ed. Occupational Stress. C C Thomas.
McLean, Andrew.
  xMcLean, Andrew.
    illus. The Riverboat Crew. Oxford U Pr.
McLean, Andrew J. see McLean, Andrew James.
McLean, Andrew James.
  xMcLean, Andrew J.
    How to Manage Real Estate Profitably. Delphi
      Info.
    How to Manage Real Estate Profitably. JWP
      Dev.
McLean, Antonia.
  xMcLean.
    Humanism & the Rise of Science in Tudor
      England. N Watson.
McLean, Claire. see McLean, Claire D.
McLean, Claire D.
  xMcLean, Claire.
    The Complete Bouvier Des Flandres.
      Denlingers.
McLean, D. see McLean, Donald.
McLean, Donald, 1915-
  xMcLean, D.
    Mechanical Properties of Metals. Krieger.
McLean, Ephraim R.
  xMcLean, Ephraim R.

Strategic Planning for MIS. Wiley.
McLean, George F.
  xMcLean, George F.
    ed. Religion in Contemporary Thought. Alba.
McLean, Hugh, 1925-
  xMcLean, Hugh.
    Nikolai Leskov: The Man & His Art. Harvard
      U Pr.
McLean, John, 1799-1890
  xMcLean, John.
    Notes of a Twenty-Five Years' Service in the
      Hudson's Bay Territory. Greenwood.
McLean, R. C. see McLean, Robert Colquhoun.
McLean, Robert Colquhoun.
  xMcLean, R. C.
    Textbook of Theoretical Botany. Halsted Pr.
McLean, Ruari.
  xMcLean, Ruari.
    Modern Book Design: From William Morris to
      the Present Day. Oxford U Pr.
McLeave, Hugh.
  xMcLeave, Hugh.
    A Borderline Case. Scribner.
    Double Exposure. Scribner.
McLeay, Alison.
  xMcLeay, Alison.
    The World of the Onedin Line. David &
      Charles.
McLeish, John.
  xMcLeish, John.
    The Psychology of the Learning Group.
      Humanities.
    Soviet Psychology: History, Theory, Content.
      Methuen Inc.
    The Theory of Social Change: Four Views
      Considered. Schocken.
McLeish, Kenneth.
  xMcLeish, Kenneth.
    Food & Drink. Allen Unwin.
McLellan, David.
  xMcLellan, David.
    Friedrich Engels. Penguin.
    Friedrich Engels. Viking Pr.
    Marxism After Marx: An Introduction.
      Har-Row.
McLellan, David S.
  xMcLellan, David S.
    Cold War in Transition. Macmillan.
    Dean Acheson: The State Department Years.
      Dodd.
McLemore. see McLemore, S. Dale.
McLemore, Lelan E.
  xMcLemore, Lelan E.
    Task-Related Norms in a State Legislature: The
      Case of Oklahoma. Univ OK Gov Res.
McLemore, Richard A. see McLemore, Richard Aubrey.
McLemore, Richard Aubrey, 1903-
  xMcLemore, Richard A.
    Franco-American Diplomatic Relations,
      1816-1836. Kennikat.
McLemore, S. Dale.
  xMcLemore.
    Racial & Ethnic Relations in America. Allyn.
McLendon, James.
  xMcLendon, James.
    Eddie Macon's Run. NAL.
    Eddie Macon's Run. Viking Pr.
    Papa Hemingway in Key West. Popular Lib.
McLendon, Jonathon C.
  xMcLendon, Jonathon C.
    A Guide to Reading for Social Studies
      Teachers. Coun Soc Studies.
McLendon, Samuel G. see McLendon, Samuel Guyton.
McLendon, Samuel Guyton.
  xMcLendon, Samuel G.
    History of the Public Domain of Georgia.
      Reprint.
McLenighan, Valjean.
  xMcLenighan, Valjean.

I Know You Cheated. Raintree Pubs.
What You See Is What You Get. Follett.
Women & Science. Raintree Pubs.
McLennan, Barbara. see McLennan, Barbara N.
McLennan, Barbara N., 1940-
  xMcLennan, Barbara.
    Comparative Politics & Public Policy. Duxbury
      Pr.
McLennan, John F. see McLennan, John Ferguson.
McLennan, John Ferguson, 1827-1881
  xMcLennan, John F.
    Primitive Marriage: An Inquiry into the Origin
      of the Form of Capture in Marriage
      Ceremonies. AMS Pr.
McLennan, Roy.
  xMcLennan, Roy.
    Cases in Organisational Behaviour.
      Crane-Russak Co.
McLeod, Alan L. see McLeod, Alan Lindsey.
McLeod, Alan Lindsey, 1928-
  xMcLeod, Alan L.
    ed. Pattern of Australian Culture. Cornell U Pr.
    ed. Pattern of New Zealand Culture. Cornell U
      Pr.
McLeod, Enid.
  xMcLeod, Enid.
    The Order of the Rose: The Life & Ideas of
      Christine de Pizan. Rowman.
McLeod, James R. see McLeod, James Richard.
McLeod, James Richard.
  xMcLeod, James R.
    ed. Theodore Roethke: A Manuscript
      Checklist. Kent St U Pr.
McLeod, Kirsty, 1947-
  xMcLeod, Kirsty.
    Drums & Trumpets: The House of Stuart. HM.
McLeod, Raymond.
  xMcLeod, Raymond.
    Management Information Systems. SRA.
McLeod, Robert W., 1949-
  xMcLeod, Robert W.
    Bank Credit Cards for EFTS: A Cost Benefit
      Analysis. Univ Microfilms.
McLeod, Sterling.
  xMcLeod, Sterling.
    Careers in Consumer Protection. Messner.
    Challenging Careers in Urban Affairs. Messner.
McLeod, Susan H.
  xMcLeod, Susan H.
    Dramatic Imagery in the Plays of John
      Webster. Humanities.
McLin, Jon B.
  xMcLin, Jon B.
    Canada's Changing Defense Policy, 1957-1963:
      The Problems of a Middle Power in Alliance.
      Johns Hopkins.
McLin, Lena.
  xMcLin, Lena.
    Pulse: A History of Music. Kjos.
McLoone, Margo.
  xMcLoone, Margo.
    It's a Girl's Game Too. HR&W.
McLoughlin, Emmett.
  xMcLoughlin, Emmett.
    American Culture & Catholic Schools. Citadel
      Pr.
    American Culture & Catholic Schools. Lyle
      Stuart.
    Famous Ex-Priests. Lyle Stuart.
    Letters to an Ex-Priest. Lyle Stuart.
McLoughlin, William G. see McLoughlin, William
  Gerald.
McLoughlin, William Gerald.
  xMcLoughlin, William G.
    American Evangelicals, 1800-1900: An
      Anthology. Peter Smith.
McLuhan, H. Marshall. see McLuhan, Herbert Marshall.
McLuhan, Herbert Marshall.
  xMcLuhan, H. Marshall.

Gutenberg Galaxy: The Making of Typographic Man. U of Toronto Pr.
xMcLuhan, Marshall.
Gutenberg Galaxy: The Making of Typographic Man. NAL.
Mechanical Bride: Folklore of Industrial Man. Vanguard.
Understanding Media: The Extensions of Man. McGraw.
Understanding Media: The Extensions of Man. NAL.
McLuhan, Marshall. *see* McLuhan, Herbert Marshall.
McLuhan, T. C.
xMcLuhan, T. C.
Touch the Earth: A Self Portrait of Indian Existence. S&S.
McLure, Charles E.
xMcLure, Charles E.
Once Is Enough: The Taxation of Corporate Equity Income. Inst Contemporary.
Value Added Tax, Two Views. Am Enterprise.
McLure, John R. *see* McLure, John Rankin.
McLure, John Rankin, 1888-
xMcLure, John R.
The Ventilation of School Buildings: A Study of Present Practices & Costs in the Light of Experimental Research. AMS Pr.
McLyman, C. *see* McLyman, Colonel William T.
McLyman, Colonel William T., 1932-
xMcLyman, C.
Transformer & Inductor Design Handbook. Dekker.
McMackin. *see* McMackin, Frank Joseph.
McMackin, Frank Joseph, 1888-
xMcMackin.
Mathematics of the Shop. Delmar.
McMahan, Elizabeth.
xMcMahan, Elizabeth.
A Crash Course in Composition. McGraw.
The Writer's Handbook. McGraw.
The Writer's Rhetoric & Handbook. McGraw.
McMahan, John, 1937-
xMcMahan, John W.
Property Development: Effective Decision Making in Uncertain Times. McGraw.
McMahan, John W. *see* McMahan, John.
McMahon, A. Philip. *see* McMahon, Amos Philip.
McMahon, Amos Philip, 1890-1947
xMcMahon, A. Philip.
Preface to an American Philosophy of Art. Kennikat.
McMahon, Clara P. *see* McMahon, Clara Patricia.
McMahon, Clara Patricia, 1910-
xMcMahon, Clara P.
Education in Fifteenth Century England. Greenwood.
McMahon, F. Gilbert. *see* McMahon, Francis Gilbert.
McMahon, Francis Gilbert, 1923-
xMcMahon, F. Gilbert.
ed. Future Trends in Therapeutics. Futura Pub.
McMahon, Frank B.
xMcMahon, Frank B.
Abnormal Behavior: Psychology's View. P-H.
McMahon, Helen.
xMcMahon, Helen.
Criticism of Fiction: A Study of Trends in Atlantic Monthly. AMS Pr.
McMahon, John V. *see* McMahon, John Van Lear.
McMahon, John Van Lear, 1800-1871
xMcMahon, John V.
Historical View of the Government of Maryland: From Its Colonization to the Present Day. Reprint.
McMahon, Joseph H.
xMcMahon, Joseph H.
Humans Being: The World of Jean-Paul Sartre. U of Chicago Pr.
The Imagination of Jean Genet. Greenwood.
McMahon, M. Catharine. *see* McMahon, Mary Catharine.

McMahon, Martin.
xMcMahon, Martin.
Castaneda's the Teachings of Don Juan, a Separate Reality & Journey to Ixtlan Notes. Cliffs.
McMahon, Mary Catharine, Sister.
xMcMahon, M. Catharine.
Aesthetics & Art in the Astree of Honore d'Urfe. AMS Pr.
McMahon, Michael.
xMcMahon, Michael.
ed. Flowering After Frost: The Anthology of Contemporary New England Poetry. Branden.
McMahon, Morgan E.
xMcMahon, Morgan E.
A Flick of the Switch. Vintage Radio.
McMahon, Robert S. *see* McMahon, Robert Sears.
McMahon, Robert Sears.
xMcMahon, Robert S.
Federal Regulation of the Radio & Television Broadcast Industry in the United States: 1927-1959. Arno.
McMahon, Sean.
xMcMahon, Sean.
ed. The Best from "The Bell": Great Irish Writing. Rowman.
McMahon, Thomas.
xMcMahon, Thomas.
McKay's Bees. Har-Row.
The Mass Explained. Carillon Bks.
Principles of American Nuclear Chemistry: A Novel. Little.
McMahon, Thomas. *see* McMahon, Thomas S.
McMahon, Thomas S.
xMcMahon, Thomas.
What, You a Priest!: Father Tom, Pastor. Franciscan Herald.
McMains, Harvey.
xMcMains, Harvey.
ed. Alternatives for Growth: The Engineering & Economics of Natural Resources Development. Ballinger Pub.
McManama, J. *see* McManama, John.
McManama, John.
xMcManama, J.
Effective Program for Teacher-Aide Training. P-H.
xMcManama, John.
Systems Analysis for Effective School Administration. P-H.
McManaway, James G. *see* McManaway, James Gilmer.
McManaway, James Gilmer, 1899-
xMcManaway, James G.
Authorship of Shakespeare. Folger Bks.
McManis, Douglas R.
xMcManis, Douglas R.
European Impressions of the New England Coast, 1497-1620. U Chicago Dept Geog.
McManners, Kelsey.
xMcManners, Kelsey.
Underwater Attack: The First Submarines. Silver.
McManus, Edgar J.
xMcManus, Edgar J.
History of Negro Slavery in New York. Syracuse U Pr.
McManus, Edwin G.
xMcManus, Edwin G.
Palauan-English Dictionary. U Pr of Hawaii.
McManus, George. *see* McManus, George J.
McManus, George J.
xMcManus, George.
In Defense of Prosperity: A Commonsense Case for Capitalism. Chilton.
McManus, Patrick F.
xMcManus, Patrick F.
Kid Camping from Aaaaiii! to Zip. Lothrop.
McMaster, Fitz H. *see* McMaster, Fitz Hugh.

McMaster, Fitz Hugh, 1867-
xMcMaster, Fitz H.
History of Fairfield County, South Carolina, from "Before the White Man Came" to 1942. Reprint.
McMaster, Helen N. *see* McMaster, Helen Neill.
McMaster, Helen Neill.
xMcMaster, Helen N.
Margaret Fuller As a Literary Critic. Folcroft.
Margaret Fuller As a Literary Critic. Gordon Pr.
McMaster, Juliet.
xMcMaster, Juliet.
Thackeray: The Major Novels. U of Toronto Pr.
Trollope's Palliser Novels: Theme & Pattern. Oxford U Pr.
McMasters, William H. *see* McMasters, William Henry.
McMasters, William Henry.
xMcMasters, William H.
Originality, & Other Essays. Arno.
McMath, Robert C., 1944-
xMcMath, Robert C.
Populist Vanguard: A History of the Southern Farmers' Alliance. Norton.
Populist Vanguard: History of Southern Farmer's Alliance. U of NC Pr.
McMenemy, William G. *see* McMenemy, William George.
McMenemy, William George, 1896-
xMcMenemy, William G.
Place of the Circle in Elementary Geometry. Philos Lib.
McMichael, Betty.
xMcMichael, Betty.
The Library & Resource Center in Christian Education. Moody.
McMichael, James, 1939-
xMcMichael, James.
The Lover's Familiar. Godine.
McMichael, Lois.
xMcMichael, Lois.
Compiled by History of Butts County, Georgia 1825-1976. Cherokee.
McMichael, Stanley. *see* McMichael, Stanley L.
McMichael, Stanley L.
xMcMichael, Stanley.
How to Operate a Real Estate Business. P-H.
xMcMichael, Stanley L.
How to Make Money in Real Estate. P-H.
McMillan, Bruce.
xMcMillan, Bruce.
Apples, How They Grow. HM.
Making Sneakers. HM.
The Remarkable Riderless Runaway Tricycle. HM.
xMcMillan, Bruce A.
Punography. Penguin.
McMillan, Bruce A. *see* McMillan, Bruce.
McMillan, Claude.
xMcMillan, Claude.
Mathematical Programming. Wiley.
Systems Analysis: A Computer Approach to Decision Models. Irwin.
McMillan, Constance V. *see* McMillan, Constance Van Brunt.
McMillan, Constance Van Brunt.
xMcMillan, Constance V.
Randy & Janet Jackson: Ready & Right!. EMC.
Steve Cauthen: Million Dollar Baby. EMC.
McMillan, Donald E.
xMcMillan, Donald E.
Central Nervous System Pharmacology: A Self Instruction Text. Little.
McMillan, Earle.
xMcMillan, Earle.
The Gospel According to Mark. Sweet.
McMillan, George.
xMcMillan, George.

Old Breed: A History of the First Marine
Division in World War II. Zenger Pub.
McMillan, James B., 1907-
xMcMillan, James B.
Annotated Bibliography of Southern American
English. U of Miami Pr.
McMillan, Julia A.
xMcMillan, Julia A.
The Whole Pediatrician Catalog. Saunders.
The Whole Pediatrician Catalog: A
Compendium of Clues to Diagnosis &
Management. Saunders.
McMillan, Malcolm C. see McMillan, Malcolm Cook.
McMillan, Malcolm Cook, 1910-
xMcMillan, Malcolm C.
Constitutional Development in Alabama,
1798-1901: A Study in Politics, the Negro, &
Sectionalism. Reprint.
McMillan, Mary L. see McMillan, Mary Lee.
McMillan, Mary Lee.
xMcMillan, Mary L.
Beautiful North Carolina & the World of
Flowers. Moore Pub Co.
McMillan, Patricia H. see McMillan, Patricia Hart.
McMillan, Patricia Hart.
xMcMillan, Patricia H.
Decorating Country-Style: The Look & How to
Have It. Doubleday.
McMillan, Priscilla J. see McMillan, Priscilla Johnson.
McMillan, Priscilla Johnson.
xMcMillan, Priscilla J.
Marina & Lee. Har-Row.
McMillan, William J. see McMillan, William James.
McMillan, William James, 1929-
xMcMillan, William J.
Private School Management. F E Peters.
McMillen, Donald H.
xMcMillen, Donald H.
Chinese Communist Power & Policy in
Xinjiang, 1949-1977. Westview.
McMillen, Neil R., 1939-
xMcMillen, Neil R.
Citizens' Council: Organized Resistance to the
Second Reconstruction, 1954-1964. U of Ill
Pr.
McMillen, S. I. see McMillen, Sim I.
McMillen, Sim I., M.D., 1898-
xMcMillen, S. I.
None of These Diseases. Revell.
McMinn, R. M. see McMinn, Robert Matthew Hay.
McMinn, Robert Matthew Hay.
xMcMinn, R. M.
Color Atlas of Human Anatomy. Year Bk
Med.
McMorries, Edward Y. see McMorries, Edward Young.
McMorries, Edward Young.
xMcMorries, Edward Y.
History of the First Regiment Alabama
Volunteer Infantry, C.S.A.. Arno.
McMullan, J. T. see McMullan, John T.
McMullan, John T.
xMcMullan, J. T.
Energy Resources & Supply. Wiley.
McMullen, David.
xMcMullen, David.
First into the Air: The First Airplanes. Silver.
xMcMullen, Susan.
jt. auth. First into the Air: The First Airplanes.
Silver.
McMullen, John R.
xMcMullen, John R.
Extensions of Positive-Definite Functions. Am
Math.
McMullen, Lorraine.
xMcMullen, Lorraine.
Sinclair Ross. Twayne.
McMullen, Mary, 1920-
xMcMullen, Mary.

Death by Bequest. Penguin.
Man with Fifty Complaints. Doubleday.
The Man with Fifty Complaints. G K Hall.
Prudence Be Damned. Doubleday.
McMullen, Susan. see McMullen, David.
McMullin, Ernan, 1924-
xMcMullin, Ernan.
Newton on Matter & Activity. U of Notre
Dame Pr.
McMurphy, Susannah J. see McMurphy, Susannah Jane.
McMurphy, Susannah Jane, 1881-
xMcMurphy, Susannah J.
Spenser's Use of Ariosto for Allegory. Folcroft.
McMurran, M. W.
xMcMurran, Marshall.
Programming Microprocessors. TAB Bks.
McMurran, Marshall. see McMurran, M. W.
McMurray, George R., 1925-
xMcMurray, George R.
Gabriel Garcia Marquez. Ungar.
Jorge Luis Borges. Ungar.
Jose Donoso. G K Hall.
Jose Donoso. Twayne.
McMurray, William. see McMurray, William J.
McMurray, William J., 1928-
xMcMurray, William.
Literary Realism of William Dean Howells. S
Ill U Pr.
McMurrin, Sterling M.
xMcMurrin, Sterling M.
The Theological Foundations of the Mormon
Religion. U of Utah Pr.
McMurry, Donald L. see McMurry, Donald le Crone.
McMurry, Donald le Crone, 1890-
xMcMurry, Donald L.
The Great Burlington Strike of 1888: A Case
History in Labor Relations. Russell.
McMurry, James.
xMcMurry, James.
Catskill Witch & Other Tales of the Hudson
Valley. Syracuse U Pr.
McMurry, Robert N.
xMcMurry, Robert N.
How to Build a Dynamic Sales Organization.
McGraw.
The Maverick Executive. Am Mgmt.
McMurtrey, Martin.
xMcMurtrey, Martin.
Loose to the Wilds. Har-Row.
McMurtrie, Douglas C. see McMurtrie, Douglas
Crawford.
McMurtrie, Douglas Crawford, 1888-1944
xMcMurtrie, Douglas C.
History of Printing in the United States: The
Story of the Introduction of the Press & of
Its History & Influence. B Franklin.
McMurtry, Jo, 1937-
xMcMurtry, Jo.
Victorian Life & Victorian Fiction: A
Companion for the American Reader. Shoe
String.
McMurtry, Larry.
xMcMurtry, Larry.
Hud. Popular Lib.
The Last Picture Show. Penguin.
Leaving Cheyenne. Penguin.
Somebody's Darling. Popular Lib.
Somebody's Darling. S&S.
McNab, Oliver.
xMcNab, Oliver.
Horror Story. HM.
McNair, James K.
xMcNair, James K.
The Complete Book of Picnics. Ortho.
McNair, Jim, 1934-
xMcNair, Jim.
Experiencing the Holy Spirit. Bethany Fell.
McNair, John F. see McNair, John Frederick Adolphus.
McNair, John Frederick Adolphus.
xMcNair, John F.

Oral Tradition from the Indus. Arno.
McNair, Joseph.
xMcNair, Joseph.
An Odyssey: Poetry & Music. Black River.
McNair, Will. see McNair, Will L.
McNair, Will L.
xMcNair, Will.
Electric Drilling Rig Handbook. Pennwell Pub.
McNair-Wilson, Diana.
xMcNair-Wilson, Diana.
Hungary. David & Charles.
McNairn, Colin H.
xMcNairn, Colin H.
Governmental & Intergovernmental Immunity
in Australia & Canada. U of Toronto Pr.
McNall, Lee. see McNall, Leota Kester.
McNall, Leota K. see McNall, Leota Kester.
McNall, Leota Kester.
xMcNall, Lee.
Current Practice in Obstetric & Gynecologic
Nursing. Mosby.
xMcNall, Leota K.
ed. Current Practice in Obstetric &
Gynecologic Nursing. Mosby.
McNall, Neil A. see McNall, Neil Adams.
McNall, Neil Adams.
xMcNall, Neil A.
An Agricultural History of the Genesee Valley,
1790-1860. Greenwood.
McNall, Preston E. see McNall, Preston Essex.
McNall, Preston Essex.
xMcNall, Preston E.
Our Natural Resources. Interstate.
McNall, Scott G.
xMcNall, Scott G.
The Career of a Radical Rightist: A Study in
Failure. Kennikat.
The Sociological Experience: A Modern
Introduction to Sociology. Little.
ed. The Sociological Perspective: Introductory
Readings. Little.
McNally, Colleen.
xMcNally, Colleen.
Some People Think We Don't Learn Anything
in This School. Ash Lad Pr.
McNally, D., 1934-
xMcNally, D.
Positional Astronomy. Halsted Pr.
McNally, D. W. see McNally, Douglas William.
McNally, Douglas William.
xMcNally, D. W.
Piaget, Education & Teaching. Humanities.
McNally, Fiona.
xMcNally, Fiona.
Women for Hire: A Study of the Female Office
Worker. St Martin.
McNally, Harold J. see McNally, Harold Joseph.
McNally, Harold Joseph, 1913-
xMcNally, Harold J.
The Readability of Certain Type Sizes & Forms
in Sight-Saving Classes. AMS Pr.
McNally, Raymond T., 1931-
xMcNally, Raymond T.
Chaadayev & His Friends: An Intellectual
History of Peter Chaadayev & His Russian
Contemporaries. Diplomatic Fla.
McNally, Robert E.
xMcNally, Robert E.
Council of Trent, the Spiritual Exercises & the
Catholic Reform. Fortress.
McNally, Tom.
xMcNally, Tom.
Fishing. Follett.
Fly Fishing. Har-Row.
Hunting. Follett.

McNamara, Brooks.
xMcNamara, Brooks.

American Playhouse in the Eighteenth
  Century. Harvard U Pr.
Step Right up. Doubleday.
McNamara, J. R. see McNamara, John Regis.

McNamara, Joan.
  xMcNamara, Joan.
    The Adoption Adviser. Dutton.
    The Special Child Handbook. Dutton.

McNamara, John Regis.
  xMcNamara, J. R.
    ed. Behavioral Approaches in Medicine:
      Application & Analysis. Plenum Pub.

McNamara, Patrick H.
  xMcNamara, Patrick H.
    Religion American Style. Har-Row.

McNamara, Peter L.
  xMcNamara, Peter L.
    ed. Critics on Wallace Stevens. U of Miami Pr.

McNamara, William, 1895-
  xMcNamara, William.
    The Catholic Church on the Northern Indiana
      Frontier, 1789-1844. AMS Pr.
    The Human Adventure: Contemplation for
      Everyman. Doubleday.

McNaspy, C. J. see McNaspy, Clement J.
McNaspy, Clement J.
  xMcNaspy, C. J.
    A Guide to Christian Europe. Loyola.

McNaught, Harry.
  xMcNaught, Harry.
    illus. Baby Animals. Random.
    The Truck Book. Random.
    illus. Trucks. Random.

McNaught, Kenneth.
  xMcNaught, Kenneth.
    Prophet in Politics: A Biography of J. S.
      Woodsworth. U of Toronto Pr.
McNaught, Kenneth. see McNaught, Kenneth William
  Kirkpatrick.
McNaught, Kenneth William Kirkpatrick, 1918-
  xMcNaught, Kenneth.
    Pelican History of Canada. Penguin.

McNaughton, Colin.
  xMcNaughton, Colin.
    Anton B. Stanton & the Pirats. Doubleday.
    The Great Zoo Escape. Viking Pr.

McNaughton, Harry H.
  xMcNaughton, Harry H.
    Proofreading & Copyediting: A Practical Guide
      to Style for the 1970's. Hastings.

McNaughton, Patrick R.
  xMcNaughton, Patrick R.
    Secret Sculptures of Komo: Art & Power in
      Bamana (Bambara) Initiation Associations.
      Inst Study Human.

McNaughton, Robert.
  xMcNaughton, Robert.
    Counter-Free Automata. MIT Pr.

McNaughton, Ruth F. see McNaughton, Ruth Flanders.
McNaughton, Ruth Flanders.
  xMcNaughton, Ruth F.
    Imagery of Emily Dickinson. Folcroft.

McNaughton, S. J. see McNaughton, Samuel J.
McNaughton, Samuel J.
  xMcNaughton, S. J.
    General Ecology. HR&W.

McNaughton, Wayne L. see McNaughton, Wayne Leslie.
McNaughton, Wayne Leslie, 1902-
  xMcNaughton, Wayne L.
    Business Basics: An Outline of Business Theory
      & Practice. Littlefield.

McNaughton, William, 1933-
  xMcNaughton, William.

---

    ed. Chinese Literature: An Anthology from the
      Earliest Times to the Present Day. C E
      Tuttle.
    ed. The Confucian Vision. U of Mich Pr.
    ed. The Confucian Vision. U of Mich Pr.
    ed. Taoist Vision. U of Mich Pr.
    ed. The Taoist Vision. U of Mich Pr.

McNeal, James U.
  xMcNeal, James U.
    An Introduction to Consumer Behavior. Wiley.
McNeal, Robert H. see McNeal, Robert Hatch.
McNeal, Robert Hatch, 1930-
  xMcNeal, Robert H.
    Bride of the Revolution: Krupskaya & Lenin. U
      of Mich Pr.

McNee, Robert B., 1922-
  xMcNee, Robert B.
    Primer on Economic Geography. Random.

McNeely, Harol E.
  xMcNeely, Harold E.
    Psychotherapy: The Private & Very Personal
      Viewpoints of Doctor & Patient. Nelson-Hall.
McNeely, Harold E. see McNeely, Harol E.
McNeer, May. see McNeer, May Yonge.
McNeer, May Yonge, 1902-
  xMcNeer, May.
    California Gold Rush. Random.
    Stranger in the Pines. HM.

McNeese, Donald C.
  xMcNeese, Donald G.
    Engineering & Technical Handbook. P-H.
McNeese, Donald G. see McNeese, Donald C.
McNeil, Don.
  xMcNeil, Don.
    The Birdhouse Book: Building Houses, Feeders
      & Baths. Pacific Search.

McNeil, Donald R.
  xMcNeil, Donald R.
    Interactive Data Analysis: A Practical Primer.
      Wiley.

McNeil, Donald S., 1908-
  xMcNeil, Donald S.
    ed. Who's Who in the Jewelry Industry.
      Jewelers Circular.

McNeil, E. see McNeil, Elton Burbank.
McNeil, Elton B. see McNeil, Elton Burbank.
McNeil, Elton Burbank, 1924-1974
  xMcNeil, E.
    Quiet Furies: Man & Disorder. P-H.
  xMcNeil, Elton B.
    The Psychology of Being Human. Har-Row.
    Psychoses. P-H.

McNeil, John D.
  xMcNeil, John D.
    Designing Curriculum: Self Instructional
      Modules. Little.

McNeil, M. see McNeil, Malcolm Roy.
McNeil, Malcolm Roy.
  xMcNeil, M.
    Revised Token Test. Univ Park.

McNeil, Mellicent, 1889-
  xMcNeil, Mellicent.
    A Comparative Study of Entrance to
      Teacher-Training Institutions. AMS Pr.

McNeill, David.
  xMcNeill, David.
    Acquisition of Language: The Study of
      Developmental Psycholinguistics. Har Row.
    The Conceptual Basis of Language. Halsted Pr.

McNeill, George.
  xMcNeill, George.
    The Plantation. Bantam.
McNeill, J. T. see McNeill, John Thomas.
McNeill, Janet.
  xMcNeill, Janet.
    Ever After. Little.
    Monster Too Many. Little.
McNeill, John. see McNeill, John J.
McNeill, John J.
  xMcNeill, John.

    The Church & the Homosexual. Andrews &
      McMeel.

McNeill, John T.
  xMcNeill, John T.
    A History of the Cure of Souls. Har-Row.
McNeill, John T. see McNeill, John Thomas.
McNeill, John Thomas, 1885-
  xMcNeill, J. T.
    The History & Character of Calvinism. Oxford
      U Pr.
  xMcNeill, John T.
    Books of Faith & Power. Arno.
    Celtic Churches: A History, A.D. 200-1200. U
      of Chicago Pr.
    Ecumenical Testimony: The Concern for
      Christian Unity Within the Reformed &
      Presbyterian Churches. Westminster.

McNeill, Joseph. see McNeill, Joseph G.
McNeill, Joseph G.
  xMcNeill, Joseph.
    Principles of Home Inspection: A Guide to
      Residential Construction, Inspection &
      Maintenance. Van Nos Reinhold.
  xMcNeill, Joseph G.
    Homeowner's Guide to Buying, Evaluating &
      Maintaining Your Home. Van Nos Reinhold.

McNeill, Malvina R. see McNeill, Malvina Rosat.
McNeill, Malvina Rosat.
  xMcNeill, Malvina R.
    Guidelines to Problems of Education in Brazil:
      A Review & Selected Bibliography. Tchrs
      Coll.

McNeill, Moyra.
  xMcNeill, Moyra.
    Pulled Thread Embroidery. Taplinger.
    Quilting for Today. Transatlantic.

McNeill, William H. see McNeill, William Hardy.
McNeill, William Hardy, 1917-
  xMcNeill, William H.
    America, Britain & Russia: Their Co-Operation
      & Conflict 1941-1946. Johnson Repr.
    Contemporary World: 1914-Present. Morrow.
    History of Western Civilization: A Handbook.
      U of Chicago Pr.
    ed. Human Migration: Patterns & Policies. Ind
      U Pr.
    Past & Future. U of Chicago Pr.
    Plagues & Peoples. Doubleday.
    A World History. Oxford U Pr.

McNeilly, F S.
  xMcNeilly, F. S.
    Anatomy of Leviathan. St Martin.

McNeir, Waldo F.
  xMcNeir, Waldo F.
    Annotated Bibliography of Edmund Spenser.
      AMS Pr.
    ed. Studies in American Literature. Arno.

McNeish, James.
  xMcNeish, James.
    Belonging: Conversations in Israel. HR&W.

McNelly, Theodore.
  xMcNelly, Theodore.
    Politics & Government in Japan. HM.
    ed. Sources in Modern East Asian History &
      Politics. Irvington.

McNemar, Quinn, 1900-
  xMcNemar, Quinn.
    Psychological Statistics. Wiley.

McNerney, Walter J.
  xMcNerney, Walter J.
    ed. Regionalization & Rural Health Care: An
      Experiment in Three Communitiies. Univ
      Microfilms.

McNesby, Edward J.
  xMcNesby, Edward J.
    Systematic Control of Factory &
      Manufacturing Costs. P-H.

McNett, Dorothy.
  xMcNett, Dorothy.

The Microwave Way. Owlswood Prods.
McNicholas, John.
  xMcNicholas, John.
    The Design of English Elementary & Primary
      Schools: A Select Annotated Bibliography.
      Humanities.
McNichols, Charles L. *see* McNichols, Charles
  Longstreth.
McNichols, Charles Longstreth, 1895-
  xMcNichols, Charles L.
    Crazy Weather. U of Nebr Pr.
    Crazy Weather. Viking Pr.
McNichols, Thomas J.
  xMcNichols, Thomas J.
    Executive Policy & Strategic Planning.
      McGraw.
McNickle, D'Aracy. *see* McNickle, D'Arcy.
McNickle, D'Arcy, 1904-
  xMcNickle, D'Aracy.
    Native American Tribalism: Indian Survivals &
      Renewals. Oxford U Pr.
  xMcNickle, D'Arcy.
    The Surrounded. U of NM Pr.
    They Came Here First: The Epic of the
      American Indian. Octagon.
    They Came Here First: The Epic of the
      American Indian. Har-Row.
McNown, Robert F.
  xMcNown, Robert F.
    Economics in Our Time: Macro Issues. SRA.
McNulty, Faith.
  xMcNulty, Faith.
    The Elephant Who Couldn't Forget. Har-Row.
    The Great Whales. Doubleday.
    How to Dig a Hole to the Other Side of the
      World. Har-Row.
    Prairie Dog Summer. Coward.
    Woodchuck. Har-Row.
McNulty, Henry.
  xMcNulty, Henry.
    Drinking in Vogue. Viking Pr.
McNulty, J. H.
  xMcNulty, J. H.
    Concerning Dickens & Other Literary
      Characters. Folcroft.
McNulty, J. Kneeland.
  xMcNulty, J. Kneeland.
    Effects of Abatement of Domestic Sewage
      Pollution on the Benthos, Volumes of
      Zooplankton, & the Fouling Organisms of
      Biscayne Bay, Florida. U Miami Marine.
McNulty, James E.
  xMcNulty, James E.
    Decision & Influence Processes in Private
      Pension Plans. Irwin.
McNulty, James G.
  xMcNulty, James G.
    Radiology of the Liver. Saunders.
McNulty, John K.
  xMcNulty, John K.
    Federal Income Taxation of Individuals in a
      Nutshell. West Pub.
McOmie, J. F. *see* McOmie, John Frederick William.
McOmie, John Frederick William, 1920-
  xMcOmie, J. F.
    ed. Protective Groups in Organic Chemistry.
      Plenum Pub.
McPartland, John.
  xMcPartland, John.
    No Down Payment. S&S.
McPartland, Joseph F.
  xMcPartland, Joseph F.
    Practical Electricity. McGraw.
McPeek, James A. *see* McPeek, James Andrew
  Scarborough.
McPeek, James Andrew Scarborough.
  xMcPeek, James A.
    Catullus in Strange & Distant Britain. Russell.
McPhail, David. *see* McPhail, David M.

McPhail, David M.
  xMcPhail, David.
    Captain Toad & the Motorbike. Atheneum.
    illus. The Cereal Box. Little.
    illus. Grandfather's Cake. Scribner.
    The Train. Penguin.
    The Train. Little.
    Where Can an Elephant Hide. Doubleday.
McPhee, Allan.
  xMcPhee, Allan.
    Economic Revolution in British West Africa.
      Biblio Dist.
    Economic Revolution in British West Africa.
      Negro U Pr.
McPhee, Arthur, 1945-
  xMcPhee, Arthur G.
    Friendship Evangelism: The Caring Way to
      Share Your Faith. Zondervan.
McPhee, Arthur G. *see* McPhee, Arthur.
McPhee, Carol.
  xMcPhee, Carol.
    Compiled by Feminist Quotations: Voices of
      Rebels, Reformers & Visionaries. T Y
      Crowell.
McPhee, Colin, 1901-1964
  xMcPhee, Colin.
    A House in Bali. AMS Pr.
McPhee Gribble Publishers.
  xMcPhee Gribble Publishers.
    Bottles & Cans. Penguin.
    Constructions: Big Things to Make. Penguin.
    Cover-Ups: Things to Put on Yourself. Penguin.
    Exploring: Getting to Know Your World.
      Penguin.
    Messages: Sending & Receiving Them.
      Penguin.
    Out in the Wilds. Penguin.
    Presents: Making Them to Match People.
      Penguin.
    Smells: Things to Do with Them. Penguin.
McPhee, John. *see* McPhee, John A.
McPhee, John A.
  xMcPhee, John.
    Coming into the Country. FS&G.
    Coming into the Country. Bantam.
    Giving Good Weight. FS&G.
    Levels of the Game. FS&G.
    The Survival of the Bark Canoe. FS&G.
    Survival of the Bark Canoe. Warner Bks.
  xMcPhee, John A.
    Oranges. FS&G.
McPhee, Norma.
  xMcPhee, Norma.
    More Programs & Skits for Young Teens.
      Moody.
McPheeters, D. W.
  xMcPheeters, D. W.
    Camilo Jose Cela. Irvington.
McPherson, David L.
  xMcPherson, David L.
    ed. Instrumentation in the Hearing Sciences.
      Grune.
McPherson, J. H. *see* McPherson, John Hanson Thomas.
McPherson, James A. *see* McPherson, James Alan.
McPherson, James Alan.
  xMcPherson, James A.
    Railroad: Trains & Train People. Random.
McPherson, James M.
  xMcPherson, James M.
    Marching Toward Freedom: The Negro in the
      Civil War 1861-1865. Knopf.
    Struggle for Equality: Abolitionists & the
      Negro in the Civil War & Reconstruction.
      Princeton U Pr.
McPherson, John H. *see* McPherson, John Hanson
  Thomas.
McPherson, John Hanson Thomas, 1865
  xMcPherson, J. H.
    History of Liberia. Johnson Repr.
  xMcPherson, John H.

History of Liberia. AMS Pr.
McPherson, Joseph M. *see* McPherson, Joseph Mckenzie.
McPherson, Joseph Mckenzie, 1875-
  xMcPherson, Joseph M.
    Primitive Beliefs in the North-East of Scotland.
      Arno.
McPherson, Sandra.
  xMcPherson, Sandra.
    Radiation. Ecco Pr.
McPherson, Steven P., 1946-
  xMcPherson, Steven P.
    Respiratory Therapy Equipment. Mosby.
McPherson, William H. *see* McPherson, William Heston.
McPherson, William Heston, 1902-
  xMcPherson, William H.
    Public Employee Relations in West Germany.
      U of Mich Inst Labor.
McPheters, Lee R.
  xMcPheters, Lee R.
    The Economics of Crime & Law Enforcement.
      C C Thomas.
McQuade, Donald.
  xMcQuade, Donald.
    ed. Popular Writing in America: The
      Interaction of Style & Audience. Oxford U
      Pr.
    Thinking in Writing: Structures for
      Composition. Knopf.
McQuaid, Clement.
  xMcQuaid, Clement.
    ed. Gambler's Digest. Follett.
McQuaig, Douglas J.
  xMcQuaig, Douglas J.
    Career Accounting Fundamentals. HM.
    College Accounting Fundamentals. HM.
McQuaker, R. J., 1932-
  xMcQuaker, R. J.
    Computer Choice: A Manual for the
      Practitioner. Elsevier.
McQuarrie, Donald A. *see* McQuarrie, Donald Allan.
McQuarrie, Donald Allan.
  xMcQuarrie, Donald A.
    Statistical Thermodynamics. Har-Row.
McQuay, Earl P.
  xMcQuay, Earl P.
    Go Abraham Go. Accent Bks.
McQueen, Alex S. *see* McQueen, Alexander Stephens.
McQueen, Alexander Stephens, 1889-
  xMcQueen, Alex S.
    History of Charlton County. Reprint.
McQueen, M. *see* McQueen, Matthew.
McQueen, Matthew.
  xMcQueen, M.
    Britain, the EEC & the Developing World.
      Heinemann Ed.
McQueen, William A.
  xMcQueen, William A.
    A Short Guide to English Composition.
      Wadsworth Pub.
McQuillan, Florence. *see* McQuillan, Florence L.
McQuillan, Florence L.
  xMcQuillan, Florence.
    Fundamentals of Nursing Home
      Administration. Saunders.
    Realities of Nursing Management: How to
      Cope. R J Brady.
McQuillin, F. J.
  xMcQuillin, F. J.
    Alicyclic Chemistry. Cambridge U Pr.
    ed. Homogeneous Hydrogenation in Organic
      Chemistry. Kluwer Boston.
McQuinn, Don. *see* McQuinn, Donald E.
McQuinn, Donald E.
  xMcQuinn, Don.
    Targets. Macmillan.
McQuiston, F. W.
  xMcQuiston, Frank W.
    Primary Crushing Plant Design. Soc Mining
      Eng.
McQuiston, Frank W. *see* McQuiston, F. W.

McRae, Robert.
  xMcRae, Robert.
    Leibniz: Perception, Apperception & Thought.
     U of Toronto Pr.
McRae, T. W. *see* McRae, Thomas W.
McRae, Thomas W.
  xMcRae, T. W.
    Statistical Sampling for Audit & Control.
     Wiley.
McRae, William J.
  xMcRae, William J.
    The Dynamics of Spiritual Gifts. Zondervan.
McReynolds, Ginny.
  xMcReynolds, Ginny.
    Alone on a Desert Island. Raintree Pubs.
    Woman Overboard. Raintree Pubs.
    Women in Power. Raintree Pubs.
McReynolds, Jeannie, 1938-
  xMcReynolds, Jeannie.
    Footprints of Providence. Southern Pub.
McReynolds, Leija V.
  xMcReynolds, Leija V.
    Distinctive Feature Analysis of
     Misarticulations. Univ Park.
McReynolds, Paul, 1919-
  xMcReynolds, Paul.
    ed. Advances in Psychological Assessment.
     Jossey-Bass.
    ed. Advances in Psychological Assessment. Sci
     & Behavior.
McReynolds, W. O.
  xMcReynolds, W. O.
    Gas Chromatographic Retention Data. Preston
     Pubns.
McRoberts, Robert L.
  xMcRoberts, Robert L.
    Lip Service. SBD.
McSeveney, Samuel. *see* McSeveney, Samuel T.
McSeveney, Samuel T.
  xMcSeveney, Samuel.
    The Politics of Depression: Political Behavior
     in the Northeast, 1893-1896. Oxford U Pr.
McShane, E. J. *see* McShane, Edward James.
McShane, Edward James, 1904-
  xMcShane, E. J.
    Order-Preserving Maps & Integration
     Processes. Kraus Repr.
    Stochastic Calculus & Stochastic Models. Acad
     Pr.
McShane, Philip.
  xMcShane, Philip.
    Lonergan's Challenge to the University & the
     Economy. U Pr of Amer.
    Music That Is Soundless: An Introduction to
     God for the Graduate. U Pr of Amer.
McShane, Roger B. *see* McShane, Roger Burnham.
McShane, Roger Burnham, 1917-
  xMcShane, Roger B.
    The Foreign Policy of the Attalids of
     Pergamum. U of Ill Pr.
McSherry, James.
  xMcSherry, James.
    History of Maryland. Reprint.
McSorley, Edward, 1902-1966
  xMcSorley, Edward.
    Our Own Kind. Arno.
McSpadden, George E. *see* McSpadden, George Elbert.
McSpadden, George Elbert, 1912-
  xMcSpadden, George E.
    Don Quijote & the Spanish Prologues:
     Glimpses of the Genius of Cervantes at
     Work. Univ Microfilms.
McSpadden, Joseph W. *see* McSpadden, Joseph Walker.
McSpadden, Joseph Walker, 1874-1960
  xMcSpadden, Joseph W.
    ed. Famous Psychic & Ghost Stories. Arno.
McSwain, Romola.
  xMcSwain, Romola.

    The Past & Future People: Tradition & Change
     on a New Guinea Island. Oxford U Pr.
McSweeny, Maxine.
  xMcSweeny, Maxine.
    Christmas Plays for Young Players. A S
     Barnes.
    Creative Children's Theatre for Home, School,
     Church, & Playground. A S Barnes.
McTaggart, David. *see* McTaggart, David Fraser.
McTaggart, David Fraser.
  xMcTaggart, David.
    Greenpeace III: Journey into the Bomb.
     Morrow.
McTaggart, John. *see* McTaggart, John Mctaggart Ellis.
McTaggart, John M. *see* McTaggart, John Mctaggart
  Ellis.
McTaggart, John Mctaggart Ellis.
  xMcTaggart, John.
    Some Dogmas of Religion. Greenwood.
    Some Dogmas of Religion. Kraus Repr.
  xMcTaggart, John M.
    Nature of Existence. Scholarly.
McTaggart, Lynn. *see* McTaggart, Lynne.
McTaggart, Lynne.
  xMcTaggart, Lynn.
    The Baby Brokers: The Marketing of White
     Babies in America. Dial.
McTeer, Ed. *see* McTeer, J. E.
McTeer, J. E., 1903-
  xMcTeer, Ed.
    High Sheriff to the Low Country. Beaufort.
McTyeire, Holland N. *see* McTyeire, Holland Nimmons.
McTyeire, Holland Nimmons.
  xMcTyeire, Holland N.
    Duties of Masters to Servants. Arno.
McVaugh, Rogers, 1909-
  xMcVaugh, Rogers.
    Edward Palmer, Plant Explorer of the
     American West. Theophrastus.
    Ferns of Georgia. U of Ga Pr.
McVeagh, Diana M., 1926-
  xMcVeagh, Diana M.
    Edward Elgar, His Life & Music. Hyperion
     Conn.
McVeigh, J. C.
  xMcVeigh, J. C.
    Sun Power: An Introduction to the
     Applications of Solar Energy. Pergamon.
McVeigh, Malcolm J.
  xMcVeigh, Malcolm J.
    God in Africa: Conceptions of God in African
     Traditional Religion & Christianity. C Stark.
McVey, Frances J. *see* McVey, Frances Jewell.
McVey, Frances Jewell.
  xMcVey, Frances J.
    Uncle Will of Wildwood: Nineteenth-Century
     Life in the Bluegrass. U Pr of Ky.
McVey, Ruth T. *see* McVey, Ruth Thomas.
McVey, Ruth Thomas.
  xMcVey, Ruth T.
    ed. Southeast Asian Transitions: Approaches
     Through Social History. Yale U Pr.
McVoy, L. C. *see* McVoy, Lizzie Carter.
McVoy, Lizzie Carter.
  xMcVoy, L. C.
    Louisiana in the Short Story. Haskell.
McWhirter, J. Jeffries.
  xMcWhirter, J. Jeffries.
    The Learning Disabled Child: A School &
     Family Concern. Res Press.
McWhirter, Louise.
  xMcWhirter, Louise.
    Astrology & Stock Market Forecasting. ASI
     Pubs Inc.
McWhirter, Norris. *see* McWhirter, Norris Dewar.
McWhirter, Norris Dewar.
  xMcWhirter, Norris.

    Guinness Book of Essential Facts. Sterling.
    Guinness Book of Extraordinary Exploits.
     Sterling.
    Guinness Book of Phenomenal Happenings.
     Bantam.
    ed. Guinness Book of Phenomenal Happenings.
     Sterling.
    Guinness Book of Startling Acts & Facts.
     Sterling.
    Guinness Book of World Records. Bantam.
    Guinness Book of World Records 1981.
     Sterling.
    Guinness Book of Young Recordbreakers.
     Sterling.
    Guinness Sports Record Book, 1979-1980.
     Sterling.
McWhorter, Gene.
  xMcWhorter, Gene.
    Understanding Digital Electronics. Tex Instr
     Inc.
McWilliams. *see* McWilliams, Carey.
McWilliams, Carey, 1905-
  xMcWilliams.
    Southern California Country: An Island on the
     Land. R West.
  xMcWilliams, Carey.
    Ambrose Bierce: A Biography. Shoe String.
    Brothers Under the Skin. Little.
    California, the Great Exception. Greenwood.
    Education of Carey McWilliams. S&S.
    Factories in the Field: The Story of the
     Migratory Farm Labor in California. Shoe
     String.
    Ill Fares the Land: Migrants & Migratory
     Labor in the United States. Arno.
    A Mask for Privilege: Anti-Semitism in
     America. Greenwood.
    Prejudice: Japanese-Americans, Symbol of
     Racial Intolerance. Shoe String.
    Southern California Country: An Island on the
     Land. Arno.
McWilliams, Dean.
  xMcWilliams, Dean.
    The Narratives of Michel Butor: The Writer As
     Janus. Ohio U Pr.
McWilliams, Margaret.
  xMcWilliams, Margaret.
    Food Fundamentals. Wiley.
    Fundamentals of Meal Management. Plycon Pr.
    Illustrated Guide to Food Preparation. Plycon
     Pr.
    Modern Food Preservation. Plycon Pr.
McWilliams, Peter.
  xMcWilliams, Peter.
    Catch Me with Your Smile. Blue Mtn Pr CO.
McWilliams, Wilson C.
  xMcWilliams, Wilson C.
    The Idea of Fraternity in America. U of Cal
     Pr.
Meaburn, J. *see* Meaburn, John.
Meaburn, John, 1939-
  xMeaburn, J.
    Detection & Spectrometry of Faint Light.
     Kluwer Boston.
Meacham, Mary, 1946-
  xMeacham, Mary.
    Information Sources in Children's Literature: A
     Practical Reference Guide for Children's
     Librarians, Elementary School Teachers, &
     Students of Children's Literature.
     Greenwood.
Meacham, Standish.
  xMeacham, Standish.
    A Life Apart: The English Working Class,
     1890-1914. Harvard U Pr.
    Lord Bishop: The Life of Samuel Wilberforce,
     1805-1873. Harvard U Pr.
Mead, Arthur Raymond, 1880-
  xMead, Artur R.

The Development of Free Schools in the United States As Illustrated by Connecticut & Michigan. AMS Pr.

Mead, Artur R. *see* Mead, Arthur Raymond.

Mead, C. A. *see* Mead, C. Alden.

Mead, C. Alden.
xMead, C. A.
Symmetry & Chirality. Springer-Verlag.

Mead, Charles W. *see* Mead, Charles Williams.

Mead, Charles Williams, 1845-
xMead, Charles W.
Old Civilizations of Inca Land. Cooper Sq.

Mead, Cyrus D. *see* Mead, Cyrus De Witt.

Mead, Cyrus De Witt, 1875-
xMead, Cyrus D.
The Relations of General Intelligence to Certain Mental & Physical Traits. AMS Pr.

Mead, Edwin D. *see* Mead, Edwin Doak.

Mead, Edwin Doak, 1849-1937
xMead, Edwin D.
The Influence of Emerson. Folcroft.

Mead, Eleanor T. *see* Mead, Eleanor Tyler.

Mead, Eleanor Tyler.
xMead, Eleanor T.
Lay up Your Treasures in Heaven. Logos.

Mead, Frank S. *see* Mead, Frank Spencer.

Mead, Frank Spencer.
xMead, Frank S.
ed. Talking with God: Prayers for Today. Holman.

Mead, Harry.
xMead, Harry.
Inside the North York Moors. David & Charles.

Mead, John T.
xMead, John T.
Marine Refrigeration & Fish Preservation. Busn News.

Mead, Lucia A. *see* Mead, Lucia True (Ames).

Mead, Lucia True (Ames), 1856-1936
xMead, Lucia A.
Law or War?. Garland Pub.

Mead, Margaret.
xMead, Margaret.
And Keep Your Powder Dry: An Anthropologist Looks at America. Arno.
Aspects of the Present. Morrow.
Changing Culture of an Indian Tribe. AMS Pr.
ed. Childhood in Contemporary Cultures. U of Chicago Pr.
Cooperation & Competition Among Primitive Peoples. Peter Smith.
ed. The Golden Age of American Anthropology. Braziller.
Inquiry into the Question of Cultural Stability in Polynesia. AMS Pr.
New Lives for Old: Cultural Transformation-Manus 1928-1953. Greenwood.
Sex & Temperament in Three Primitive Societies. Morrow.
Sex & Temperament in Three Primitive Societies. Peter Smith.
Soviet Attitudes Toward Authority: An Interdisciplinary Approach to Problems of Soviet Character. Greenwood.

Mead, Marian.
xMead, Marian.
Four Studies in Wordsworth. Haskell.
Four Studies in Wordsworth. R West.

Mead, Richard, 1673-1754
xMead, Richard.
A Discourse on the Plague. AMS Pr.

Mead, Rita H.
xMead, Rita H.
Doctoral Dissertations in American Music: A Classified Bibliography. Inst Am Music.

Mead, Robert Douglas.
xMead, Robert Douglas.

The Canoer's Bible. Doubleday.

Mead, Robin.
xMead, Robin.
The Greek Islands. David & Charles.

Mead, Ruth.
xMead, Ruth.
No One Wins Like a Loser. Chr Pubns.

Mead, Sidney E. *see* Mead, Sidney Earl.

Mead, Sidney Earl, 1904-
xMead, Sidney E.
Lively Experiment: The Shaping of Christianity in America. Har-Row.
Love & Learning. New Horizons.

Mead, Stuart B.
xMead, Stuart B.
Mutual Fund & Investment Company Performance in the Fifties. Mich St U Busn.

Mead, Walter J.
xMead, Walter J.
Competition & Oligopsony in the Douglas-Fir Lumber Industry. U of Cal Pr.
ed. U. S. Energy Policy: Errors of the Past, Proposals for the Future. Ballinger Pub.

Mead, William E. *see* Mead, William Edward.

Mead, William Edward, 1860-1949
xMead, William E.
The Grand Tour in the Eighteenth Century. Arno.
Grand Tour in the Eighteenth Century. R West.

Meaddough, R. J.
xMeaddough, R. J.
The Retarded Genius. Troisieme-Canadian.

Meade, Chris.
xMeade, Chris.
Careers with a Railroad. Lerner Pubns.

Meade, J. E. *see* Meade, James Edward.

Meade, James E. *see* Meade, James Edward.

Meade, James Edward, 1907-
xMeade, J. E.
The Intelligent Radical's Guide to Economic Policy: The Mixed Economy. Allen Unwin.
A New-Classical Theory of Economic Growth. Allen Unwin.
xMeade, James E.
Geometry of International Trade. Kelley.

Meade, Marian. *see* Meade, Marion.

Meade, Marion.
xMeade, Marian.
Stealing Heaven: The Love Story of Heloise & Abelard. Morrow.
xMeade, Marion.
Little Book of Big Bad Jokes. Harvey.
Little Book of Big Riddles. Harvey.

Meade, Richard H.
xMeade, Richard H.
History of Thoracic Surgery. C C Thomas.

Meaden, Frank.
xMeaden, Frank.
A Manual of European Bird Keeping. Sterling.

Meader, Clarence L. *see* Meader, Clarence Linton.

Meader, Clarence Linton.
xMeader, Clarence L.
ed. Latin Philology. Johnson Repr.

Meader, Emma B. *see* Meader, Emma Blakely (Grant).

Meader, Emma Blakely (Grant).
xMeader, Emma B.
Teaching Speech in the Elementary School: A Comparative Study of Speech Education in the Elementary Schools of England & of the United States. AMS Pr.

Meader, James L. *see* Meader, James Laurence.

Meader, James Laurence, 1893-
xMeader, James L.
Normal School Education in Connecticut. AMS Pr.

Meader, Robert F. *see* Meader, Robert F. W.

Meader, Robert F. W.
xMeader, Robert F.

Illustrated Guide to Shaker Furniture. Dover.
Illustrated Guide to Shaker Furniture. Peter Smith.

Meader, Stephen W. *see* Meader, Stephen Warren.

Meader, Stephen Warren, 1892-
xMeader, Stephen W.
Buckboard Stranger. HarBraceJ.
Sparkplug of the Hornets. HarBraceJ.

Meadow, Barry.
xMeadow, Barry.
Success at the Harness Races. Citadel Pr.
Success at the Harness Races. Wilshire.

Meadow, Charles. *see* Meadow, Charles T.

Meadow, Charles T.
xMeadow, Charles.
The Analysis of Information Systems. Wiley.
xMeadow, Charles T.
Applied Data Management. Wiley.
Story of Computers. Harvey.

Meadow, Richard H.
xMeadow, Richard H.
ed. Approaches to Faunal Analysis in the Middle East. Peabody Harvard.

Meadows, A. J. *see* Meadows, Arthur Jack.

Meadows, Arthur Jack.
xMeadows, A. J.
Early Solar Physics. Pergamon.
Stellar Evolution. Pergamon.

Meadows, Donella H.

xMeadows, Donella H.

The Limits to Growth: A Report for the Club of Rome's Project on the Predicament of Mankind. Universe.

Meadows, Leon R. *see* Meadows, Leon Renfroe.

Meadows, Leon Renfroe, 1884-
xMeadows, Leon R.
A Study of the Teaching of English Composition in Teachers Colleges of the United States, with a Suggested Course of Procedure. AMS Pr.

Meadows, P. S.
xMeadows, P. S.
An Introduction to Marine Science. Halsted Pr.

Meagher, Jack.
xMeagher, Jack.
Sportsmassage. Doubleday.

Meagher, John. *see* Meagher, John C.

Meagher, John C.
xMeagher, John.
The Gathering of the Ungifted: Toward a Dialogue on Christian Identity. Seabury.

Meagher, Robert. *see* Meagher, Robert E.

Meagher, Robert E.
xMeagher, Robert.
Augustine: An Introduction. Har-Row.
An Introduction to Augustine. NYU Pr.

Meagher, Robert F.
xMeagher, Robert F.
An International Redistribution of Wealth & Power: A Study of the Charter of Economic Rights & Duties of States. Pergamon.

Meagher, Sylvia.
xMeagher, Sylvia.
Accessories After the Fact: The Warren Commission, the Authorities & the Report. Random.

Meaker, Gerald H.
xMeaker, Gerald H.
The Revolutionary Left in Spain: 1914-1923. Stanford U Pr.

Meakin, Annette M. *see* Meakin, Annette M. B.

Meakin, Annette M. B.
xMeakin, Annette M.
Ribbon of Iron. Arno.

Means, Eldred K. *see* Means, Eldred Kurtz.

Means, Eldred Kurtz, 1878-1957
xMeans, Eldred K.
  More E. K. Means. Arno.
Means, Evan.
xMeans, Evan.
  Tennessee Trails. East Woods.
Means, Florence (Crannell), 1891-
xMeans, Florence C.
  Our Cup Is Broken. HM.
  Reach for a Star. HM.
Means, Florence C. see Means, Florence (Crannell).
Means, Gardiner C. see Means, Gardiner Coit.
Means, Gardiner Coit, 1896-
xMeans, Gardiner C.
  Pricing Power & the Public Interest: A Study
    Based on Steel. Arno.
Means, Louis E. see Means, Louis Edgar.
Means, Louis Edgar.
xMeans, Louis E.
  Dynamic Movement Experiences for
    Elementary School Children: Combining the
    Traditional Approach with Movement
    Education to Produce a Physical Education
    That Enhances & Complements Intellectual
    Growth. C C Thomas.
Means, Philip A. see Means, Philip Ainsworth.
Means, Philip Ainsworth, 1892- 1944
xMeans, Philip A.
  Fall of the Inca Empire & the Spanish Rule in
    Peru, 1530-1780. Gordian.
Means, Richard K.
xMeans, Richard K.
  Historical Perspectives on School Health. C B
    Slack.
Means, W. D. see Means, Winthrop Dickinson.
Means, Winthrop Dickinson.
xMeans, W. D.
  Stress & Strain: Basic Concepts of Continuum
    Mechanics for Geologists. Springer-Verlag.
Meany, George.
xMeany, George.
  Government Wage-Price Guideposts in the
    American Economy. NYU Pr.
Meares, Ainslie.
xMeares, Ainslie.
  A System of Medical Hypnosis. Crown.
Meares, P. see Meares, Patrick.
Meares, Patrick.
xMeares, P.
  ed. Membrane Separation Processes. Elsevier.
Mears, Caroline.
xMears, Caroline.
  Music for Today. Oxford U Pr.
Mears, D. C. see Mears, Dana C.
Mears, Dana C.
xMears, D. C.
  Materials in Orthopaedic Surgery. Williams &
    Wilkins.
Mears, Eliot G. see Mears, Eliot Grinnell.
Mears, Eliot Grinnell, 1889-1946
xMears, Eliot G.
  Resident Orientals on the American Pacific
    Coast. Arno.
Mears, Richard C., 1935-
xMears, Richard C.
  Ebb of the River. S&S.
Measell. see Measell, James S.
Measell, James S.
xMeasell.
  An Overview of Speaking Situations. SRA.
Mecacci, Luciano.
xMecacci, Luciano.
  Brain & History: The Relationship Between
    Neurophysiology & Psychology in Soviet
    Research. Brunner-Mazel.
Mecham, J. Lloyd. see Mecham, John Lloyd.
Mecham, John L. see Mecham, John Lloyd.
Mecham, John Lloyd, 1893-
xMecham, J. Lloyd.

  Church & State in Latin America: A History of
    Politico-Ecclesiastical Relations. U of NC Pr.
xMecham, John L.
  Francisco De Ibarra & Nueva Vizcaya.
    Greenwood.
Mecham, Merlin J.
xMecham, Merlin J.
  Language Disorders in Children: A Resource
    Book for Speech-Language Pathologists. C C
    Thomas.
Mechanic, David, 1936-
xMechanic, David.
  Future Issues in Health Care: Social Policy &
    the Rationing of Medical Services. Free Pr.
  The Growth of Bureaucratic Medicine: An
    Inquiry into the Dynamics of Patient
    Behavior & the Organization of Medical
    Care. Wiley.
  Medical Sociology. Free Pr.
  Mental Health & Social Policy. P-H.
  Politics, Medicine & Social Science. Wiley.
  Students Under Stress: A Study in the Social
    Psychology of Adaptation. U of Wis Pr.
Mechanic, Sylvia.
xMechanic, Sylvia.
  Annotated List of Selected United States
    Government Publications Available to
    Depository Libraries. Wilson.
Mechanix Illustrated.
xMechanix Illustrated Editors.
  Car Care. Arco.
  Mechanix Illustrated Fix-It Home Repairs
    Handbook. Arco.
Mechanix Illustrated Editors. see Mechanix Illustrated.
Mechie, Stewart.
xMechie, Stewart.
  The Church & Scottish Social Development,
    1780-1870. Greenwood.
Mechlin, Stuart.
xMechlin, Stuart.
  ed. The Rose. Mayflower Bks.
Meck, Charles R.
xMeck, Charles R.
  Meeting & Fishing the Hatches. Winchester Pr.
Mecklenburger, James.
xMecklenburger, James A.
  Since Feeling Is First. Scott F.
Mecklenburger, James A. see Mecklenburger, James.
Meckler, Alan. see Meckler, Alan M.
Meckler, Alan M.
xMeckler, Alan.
  Oral History Collections. Bowker.
Mecklin, John M. see Mecklin, John Moffatt.
Mecklin, John Moffatt, 1871-1956
xMecklin, John M.
  Democracy & Race Friction: A Study in Social
    Ethics. AMS Pr.
  Story of American Dissent. Kennikat.
Meconis, Charles. see Meconis, Charles A.
Meconis, Charles A., 1945-
xMeconis, Charles.
  With Clumsy Grace: The American Catholic
    Left, 1961-1975. Continuum.
Medalie, Jack H.
xMedalie, Jack H.
  ed. Family Medicine: Principles &
    Applications. Williams & Wilkins.
Medawar, P. B. see Medawar, Peter Brian.
Medawar, Peter Brian, Sir.
xMedawar, P. B.
  Advice to a Young Scientist. Har-Row.
Medbery, James K. see Medbery, James Knowles.
Medbery, James Knowles, 1838-1873
xMedbery, James K.
  Men & Mysteries of Wall Street. Greenwood.
Medborough. see Medborough, James.
Medborough, James.
xMedborough.
  Some Wordsworth Finds?. Folcroft.
Medcalf, G. see Medcalf, Gordon.

Medcalf, Gordon.
xMedcalf, G.
  Marketing & the Brand Manager. Pergamon.
Medcalf, Linda.
xMedcalf, Linda.
  Law & Identity: Lawyers, Native Americans &
    Legal Practice. Sage.
Meddaugh, Susan.
xMeddaugh, Susan.
  illus. Maude & Claude Go Abroad. HM.
Medea, Andra.
xMedea, Andrea.
  Against Rape. FS&G.
Medea, Andrea. see Medea, Andra.
Medeiros, Robert W., 1931-
xMedeiros, Robert W.
  Chemistry: An Interdisciplinary Approach. Van
    Nos Reinhold.
Medema, Ken.
xMedema, Ken.
  Come & See. Word Bks.
Medes, Elizabeth.
xMedes, Elizabeth.
  Exciting River Running in the U.S.. Contemp
    Bks.
Medford, Derek.
xMedford, Derek.
  Environmental Harassment or Technology
    Assessment?. Elsevier.
Medgyessy, Pal.
xMedgyessy, Pal.
  Decomposition of Superpositions of Density
    Functions & Discrete Distributions. Halsted
    Pr.
Medhurst, Kenneth, 1938-
xMedhurst, Kenneth.
  ed. Allende's Chile. St Martin.
xMedhurst, Kenneth M.
  Government in Spain: The Executive at Work.
    Pergamon.
Medhurst, Kenneth M. see Medhurst, Kenneth.
Medical Branch of the University of Texas. see
  University of Texas Medical Branch at Galveston.
Medical Cyclation. Users Conference.
xMedical Cyclotron Users Conference, 4th, Miami,
    1976.
  Medical Cyclotrons in Nuclear Medicine:
    Proceedings. S Karger.
Medical Cyclotron Users Conference, 4th, Miami, 1976.
  see Medical Cyclation. Users Conference.
Medical Economics.
xMedical Economics.
  Antidepressants. Van Nos Reinhold.
  Cartoon Classics. Van Nos Reinhold.
xMedical Economics Company.
  Antidepressants. Med Economics.
  Cartoon Classics. Med Economics.
  Pediatricks. Med Economics.
Medical Economics Company. see Medical Economics.
Medical Group Management Association.
xMedical Group Management Association.
  Organization and Development of a Medical
    Group Practice. Ballinger Pub.
**Medical Institute for Attorneys, 1st, Miami Beach,
  Florida, 1969.**
xUniversity of Miami Law Center & School of
    Medicine.
  Medicine for Attorneys-Orthopedics.
    Trans-Media Pub.
Medical Research Council. Great Britain.
xMedical Research Council of the U. K.
  Aids to the Examination of the Peripheral
    Nervous System. Pendragon Hse.
Medical Research Council of the U. K. see Medical
  Research Council. Great Britain.
Medical Section of the Library Association. see Library
  Association. Medical Section.
Medicinal Chemistry Symposium.
xMedicinal Chemistry Symposium, 20th, New
    York, May 1979.

Drug Action & Design. Mechanism Based on
Enzyme Inhibitors: Proceedings. Elsevier.
Medicinal Chemistry Symposium, 20th, New York, May
1979. see Medicinal Chemistry Symposium.
Medicus, Fritz. see Medicus, Fritz Georg Adolf.
Medicus, Fritz Georg Adolf, 1876-1956
xMedicus, Fritz.
On Being Human: The Life of Truth & Its
Realization. Ungar.
Medina, Arthur.
xMedina, Arthur.
The Businessman's Guide to Puerto Rico.
Puerto Rico Almanacs.
Medina, Jose T. see Medina, Jose Toribio.
Medina, Jose Toribio, 1852-1930
xMedina, Jose T.
Medallas De Proclamaciones y Juras De los
Reyes De Espana En America. Quarterman.
Medina, Pedro De.
xMedina, Pedro De.
A Navigator's Universe: The Libro De
Cosmographia of 1538. U of Chicago Pr.
Medinnus, Gene R. see Medinnus, Gene Roland.
Medinnus, Gene Roland.
xMedinnus, Gene R.
Child & Adolescent Psychology. Wiley.
Child Study & Observation Guide. Wiley.
ed. Readings in the Psychology of Parent-Child
Relations. Wiley.
Meditch, J. S., 1934-
xMeditch, J. S.
Stochastic Optimal Linear Estimation &
Control. McGraw.
Medley, Anthony H. see Medley, H. Anthony.
Medley, H. Anthony.
xMedley, Anthony H.
Sweaty Palms: The Neglected Art of Being
Interviewed. CBI Pub.
xMedley, H. Anthony.
Sweaty Palms: The Neglected Art of Being
Interviewed. Lifetime Learn.
Medley, Morris L.
xMedley, Morris L.
ed. Sociology for the Seventies: A
Contemporary Perspective. Wiley.
Medlicott, W. N. see Medlicott, William Norton.
Medlicott, William Norton, 1900-
xMedlicott, W. N.
Contemporary England: 1914-1964. Longman.
Medlin, Faith.
xMedlin, Faith.
A Gourmet's Book of Beasts. Eriksson.
Medlin, Virgil D.
xMedlin, Virgil D.
ed. The Russian Revolution. Krieger.
Medlycott, James.
xMedlycott, James.
How to Play Squash. Transatlantic.
Mednick, Sarnoff. see Mednick, Sarnoff A.
Mednick, Sarnoff A.
xMednick, Sarnoff.
Psychology: Explorations in Behavior &
Experience. Wiley.
xMednick, Sarnoff A.
Learning. P-H.
Mednikov, Evgenii P. see Mednikov, Evgenii Pavlovich.
Mednikov, Evgenii Pavlovich.
xMednikov, Evgenii P.
Acoustic Coagulation & Precipitation of
Aerosols. Plenum Pub.
Mednis, Edmar, 1937-
xMednis, Edmar.
How to Beat Bobby Fischer. Times Bks.
Practical Endgame Lessons. McKay.
Medoff, Sol.
xMedoff, Sol.
The Student Chemist Explores Atoms &
Molecules. Rosen Pr.
Medved, Eva.
xMedved, Eva.

Food in Theory & Practice. Plycon Pr.
Medved, Harry.
xMedved, Harry.
The Golden Turkey Awards. Putnam.
xMedved, Michael.
jt. auth. The Golden Turkey Awards. Putnam.
Medved, Michael. see Medved, Harry.
Medvedev, P. N. see Medvedev, Pavel Nikolaevich.
Medvedev, Pavel Nikolaevich.
xMedvedev, P. N.
The Formal Method in Literary Scholarship: A
Critical Introduction to Sociological Poetics.
Johns Hopkins.
Medvedev, R. A. see Medvedev, Roi Aleksandrovich.
Medvedev, Roi Aleksandrovich.
xMedvedev, R. A.
Problems in the Literary Biography of Mikhail
Sholokhov. Cambridge U Pr.
xMedvedev, Roy.
The October Revolution. Columbia U Pr.
Medvedev, Roy. see Medvedev, Roi Aleksandrovich.
Medvedev, Roy A. see Medvedev, Zhores
Aleksandrovich.
Medvedev, Sergei V. see Medvedev, Sergei Vasil'Evich.
Medvedev, Sergei Vasil'Evich.
xMedvedev, Sergei V.
Problems of Engineering Seismology. Plenum
Pub.
Medvedev, Zhores A. see Medvedev, Zhores
Aleksandrovich.
Medvedev, Zhores Aleksandrovich.
xMedvedev, Roy A.
jt. auth. A Question of Madness. Norton.
xMedvedev, Zhores A.
Nuclear Disaster in the Urals. Norton.
Nuclear Disaster in the Urals. Random.
A Question of Madness. Norton.
Soviet Science. Norton.
Medvin, Jeannine O'Brien.
xMedvin, O'Brien.
Prenatal Yoga & Natural Birth. Freestone Pub
Co.
Medvin, O'Brien. see Medvin, Jeannine O'Brien.
Medwin, Thomas, 1788-1869
xMedwin, Thomas.
The Life of Percy Bysshe Shelley. Folcroft.
Life of Percy Bysshe Shelley. Scholarly.
Mee, Charles L.
xMee, Charles L.
Meeting at Potsdam. M Evans.
Mee, Graham.
xMee, Graham.
Structure & Performance in Adult Education.
Longman.
Mee, Katherine W. Le. see Le Mee, Katherine W.
Meech, Sanford B. see Meech, Sanford Brown.
Meech, Sanford Brown.
xMeech, Sanford B.
Design in Chaucer's Troilus. Greenwood.
Meehan, E. J.
xMeehan, E. J.
Optical Methods of Analysis. Krieger.
Meehan, Eugene J.
xMeehan, Eugene J.
The Quality of Federal Policymaking:
Programmed Failure in Public Housing. U of
Mo Pr.
Meehan, James R. see Meehan, James Robert.
Meehan, James Robert.
xMeehan, James R.
How to Use the Calculator & Comptometer.
McGraw.
Meehl, Paul E. see Meehl, Paul Everett.
Meehl, Paul Everett, 1920-
xMeehl, Paul E.

Clinical Versus Statistical Prediction: A
Theoretical Analysis & a Review of the
Evidence. U of Minn Pr.
Psychodiagnosis: Selected Papers. Norton.
Psychodiagnosis: Selected Papers. U of Minn
Pr.
Meek, Brian.
xMeek, Brian.
Guide to Good Programming Practice. Halsted
Pr.
ed. Guide to Good Programming Practice.
Wiley.
Meek, Charles Kingsley, 1885-
xMeek, Charles Kingsley.
Northern Tribes of Nigeria: Ethnographical
Account of the Northern Provinces of
Nigeria Together with a Report of the 1921
Decennial Census. Biblio Dist.
Meek, E. S. see Meek, Edward S.
Meek, Edward S.
xMeek, E. S.
Antitumour & Antiviral Substances of Natural
Origin. Springer-Verlag.
Meek, Geoffrey A.
xMeek, Geoffrey A.
Practical Electron Microscopy for Biologists.
Wiley.
Meek, J. L.
xMeek, J. L.
Matrix Structural Analysis. McGraw.
Meek, Margaret.
xMeek, Margaret.
The Cool Web: The Pattern of Children's
Reading. Atheneum.
Meek, Pauline P. see Meek, Pauline Palmer.
Meek, Pauline Palmer.
xMeek, Pauline P.
When Joy Came: The Story of the First
Christmas. Western Pub.
Meeker, Howie.
xMeeker, Howie.
More Hockey Basics from Howie Meeker. P-H.
Meeker, M. E. see Meeker, Michael E.
Meeker, Mary. see Meeker, Mary Nacol.
Meeker, Mary Nacol.
xMeeker, Mary.
Structure of Intellect: Its Interpretation & Uses.
Merrill.
Meeker, Michael E.
xMeeker, M. E.
Literature & Violence in North Arabia.
Cambridge U Pr.
Meekins, Inez P.
xMeekins, Inez P.
Old Dominion Addresses & Ceremonies.
Macoy Pub.
Meeks, Carol B.
xMeeks, Carol B.
Housing. P-H.
Meeks, Cathy.
xMeeks, Cathy.
I Want Somebody to Know My Name. Nelson.
Meeks, Esther. see Meeks, Esther K.
Meeks, Esther K.
xMeeks, Esther.
How New Life Begins. Follett.
Meeks, G. see Meeks, Geoffrey.
Meeks, Geoffrey.
xMeeks, G.
Disappointing Marriage: A Study of the Gains
from Merger. Cambridge U Pr.
Meeks, John E.
xMeeks, John E.
The Fragile Alliance: An Orientation to the
Psychiatric Treatment of the Adolescent.
Krieger.
Meeks, M. Douglas.
xMeeks, M. Douglas.
Origins of the Theology of Hope. Fortress.
Meem, J. L. see Meem, J. Lawrence.

Meem, J. Lawrence, 1915-
xMeem, J. L.
Two Group Reactor Theory. Gordon.
Meen, V. B.
xMeen, V. B.
Crown Jewels of Iran. U of Toronto Pr.
Meenaghan, Thomas M.
xMeenaghan, Thomas M.
Social Policy & Social Welfare: Structure &
Applications. Free Pr.
Meenes, Max.
xMeenes, Max.
Studying & Learning. Phila Bk Co.
Meer, Ron Van Der. see Van Der Meer, Ron.
Meerloo, Abraham M. see Meerloo, Joost Abraham
Maurits.
Meerloo, Joost Abraham Maurits, 1903-
xMeerloo, Abraham M.
Patterns of Panic. Greenwood.
Meerman, Jacob, 1931-
xMeerman, Jacob P.
Public Expenditure in Malaysia: Who Benefits
& Why. Oxford U Pr.
Meerman, Jacob P. see Meerman, Jacob.
Mees, Arthur, 1850-1923
xMees, Arthur.
Choirs & Choral Music. Greenwood.
Choirs & Choral Music. Haskell.
Meeter, Merle.
xMeeter, Merle.
Country of the Risen King: Anthology of
Christian Poetry. Baker Bk.
**Meeting of Consultation of Ministers of Foreign Affairs
of American States, 8th, Punta Del Este, Uruguay.**
xMeeting Of Consultation Of Ministers Of Foreign
Affairs Of The American Republics - 8th - Punta
Del Este - Uruguay - 1962.
Background Memorandum of the Convocation
of the Meeting. OAS.
xMinisters of Foreign Affairs of the American
Republic-8th-Punta Del Este-Uruguay-1962.
Final Act: Meeting of Consultation. OAS.
**Meeting of Experts on the Mechanization of Rice
Production and Processing.**
xMeeting of Experts on the Mechanization of Rice
Production & Processing, Paramaribo, 1971.
Report. Unipub.
Meeting of the Manpower & Social Affairs Committee at
Ministerial Level, 1st, Paris, Mar. 4-5, 1976. see
Organization for Economic Cooperation and
Development. Manpower and Social Affairs
Committee.
Meezan, William.
xMeezan, William.
Adoptions Without Agencies: A Study of
Independent Adoptions. Child Welfare.
Megargee, Edwin I. see Megargee, Edwin Inglee.
Megargee, Edwin Inglee.
xMegargee, Edwin I.
The California Psychological Inventory
Handbook. Jossey-Bass.
Classifying Criminal Offenders: A New System
Based on the MMPI. Sage.
Dynamics of Aggression: Individual, Group &
International Analyses. Har-Row.
Megarry, Jacquetta.
xMegarry, Jacquetta.
ed. Aspects of Simulation & Gaming: An
Anthology of Sagset Journal Volumes.
Nichols Pub.
Megas, Ge Orgios A.
xMegas, Georgios A.
Folktales of Greece. U of Chicago Pr.
Megas, Georgios A. see Megas, Ge Orgios A.
Megateli, Abderrahmane.
xMegateli, Abderrahmane.
Investment Policies of National Oil Companies:
A Comparative Study of Sonatrach, Nioc &
Pemex. Praeger.
Megaw, A. H. see Megaw, Arthur H. S.

Megaw, Arthur H. S.
xMegaw, A. H.
The Church of the Panagia Kanakaria at
Lythrankomi in Cyprus: Its Mosaics &
Frescoes. Dumbarton Oaks.
Megaw, J. V. see Megaw, J. V. S.
Megaw, J. V. S.
xMegaw, J. V.
ed. Hunters, Gatherers & First Farmers Beyond
Europe: An Archaeological Survey.
Humanities.
Megenney, William W.
xMegenney, William W.
A Bahian Heritage: An Ethnolinguistic Study
of African Influences on Bahian Portuguese.
U of NC Pr.
Meggers, Betty J. see Meggers, Betty Jane.
Meggers, Betty Jane.
xMeggers, Betty J.
Prehistoric America: An Ecological
Perspective. Aldine Pub.
Tropical Forest Ecosystems in Africa & South
America: A Comparative Review.
Smithsonian.
Meggett, Joan M., 1909-
xMeggett, Joan M.
Music Periodical Literature: An Annotated
Bibliography of Indexes & Bibliographies.
Scarecrow.
Megginson, Leon C.
xMegginson, Leon C.
Personnel & Human Resources Administration.
Irwin.
Meggitt, M. J.
xMeggitt, M. J.
Desert People: A Study of the Walbiri
Aborigines of Central Australia. U of Chicago
Pr.
Meggs, Brown.
xMeggs, Brown.
Aria. Atheneum.
Meggyesy, Dave, 1941-
xMeggyesy, Dave.
Out of Their League. Warner Bks.
Megill, R. E.
xMegill, R. E.
How to Be a Productive Employee. Pennwell
Pub.
An Introduction to Exploration Economics.
Pennwell Pub.
Megivern, James J.
xMegivern, James J.
ed. Bible Interpretation. McGrath.
Meglin, Nick.
xMeglin, Nick.
On-The-Spot-Drawing. Watson-Guptill.
Megroz, R. see Megroz, Rodolphe Louis.
Megroz, R. L. see Megroz, Rodolphe Louis.
Megroz, Rodolphe Louis, 1891-
xMegroz, R.
Dante Gabriel Rossetti: Painter, Poet of
Heaven in Earth. Haskell.
xMegroz, R. L.
Thirty-One Bedside Essays. Kennikat.
Meguire, K. H. see Meguire, Katherine Hollier.
Meguire, Katherine Hollier.
xMeguire, K. H.
Educating the Mexican Child in the
Elementary School. R & E Res Assoc.
Megyesy, Eugene F.
xMegyesy, Eugene F.
Pressure Vessel Handbook. Pressure.
Mehaffy, Robert E., 1935-
xMehaffy, Robert E.
Writing for the Real World. Scott F.
Mehan, Hugh.
xMehan, Hugh.
The Reality of Ethnomethodology. Wiley.
Mehdi, M. T. see Mehdi, Mohammad Taki.
Mehdi, Mohammad T. see Mehdi, Mohammad Taki.

Mehdi, Mohammad Taki.
xMehdi, M. T.
ed. Palestine & the Bible. New World Press
NY.
xMehdi, Mohammad T.
Peace in the Middle East. New World Press
NY.
Meher Baba, 1894-1969
xMeher Baba.
The Path of Love. Weiser.
Mehl, Duane.
xMehl, Duane.
No More for the Road: One Man's Journey
from Chemical Dependency to Freedom.
Augsburg.
Mehl, Roger.
xMehl, Roger.
Catholic Ethics & Protestant Ethics.
Westminster.
Condition of the Christian Philosopher. Attic
Pr.
Mehler, Alan H. see Mehler, Alan Haskell.
Mehler, Alan Haskell, 1922-
xMehler, Alan H.
Introduction to Enzymology. Acad Pr.
Mehlin, Theodore G. see Mehlin, Theodore Grefe.
Mehlin, Theodore Grefe.
xMehlin, Theodore G.
Astronomy & the Origin of the Earth. Wm C
Brown.
Mehlinger, Howard. see Mehlinger, Howard D.
Mehlinger, Howard D.
xMehlinger, Howard.
Count Witte & the Tsarist Government in the
1905 Revolution. Ind U Pr.
Mehlman, Jeffrey.
xMehlman, Jeffrey.
Revolution & Repetition: Marx-Hugo-Balzac. U
of Cal Pr.
A Structural Study of Autobiography: Proust,
Leiris, Sartre, Levi-Strauss. Cornell U Pr.
Mehlman, Myron A.
xMehlman, Myron A.
ed. Control Processes in Neoplasia. Acad Pr.
ed. Energy Metabolism & the Regulation of
Metabolic Processes in Mitochondria. Acad
Pr.
Mehmet, Ozay.
xMehmet, Ozay.
Economic Planning & Social Justice in
Developing Countries. St Martin.
Mehr. see Mehr, Joseph.
Mehr, Joseph, 1941-
xMehr.
Human Services: Concepts & Intervention
Strategies. Allyn.
Mehr, Robert I. see Mehr, Robert Irwin.
Mehr, Robert Irwin, 1917-
xMehr, Robert I.
Principles of Insurance. Irwin.
Mehra, J. see Mehra, Jagdish.
Mehra, Jagdish.
xMehra, J.
The Solvay Conferences on Physics: Aspects of
the Development of Physics Since 1911.
Kluwer Boston.
Mehra, Raman K.
xMehra, Raman K.
ed. System Identification: Advances & Case
Studies. Acad Pr.
Mehrabian, Albert.
xMehrabian, Albert.

An Approach to Environmental Psychology.
　　MIT Pr.
Basic Dimensions for a General Psychological
　　Theory: Implications for Personality, Social,
　　Environmental & Developmental Studies.
　　Oelgeschlager.
Nonverbal Communication. Aldine Pub.
Silent Messages. Wadsworth Pub.
Tactics of Social Influence. P-H.
Mehren, Arthur T. Von. see Von Mehren, Arthur T.
Mehrens, William A.
　　xMehrens, William A.
　　　　Standardized Tests in Education. HR&W.
Mehrotra, S. R.
　　xMehrotra, S. R.
　　　　Towards India's Freedom & Partition. Advent
　　　　Bk.
　　　　Towards India's Freedom & Partition. Biblio
　　　　Dist.
　　　　Towards India's Freedom & Partition. Intl
　　　　Pubns Serv.
Mehta. see Mehta, Nitin H.
Mehta, Ashoka. see Mehta, Asoka.
Mehta, Asoka.
　　xMehta, Ashoka.
　　　　Reflections on Socialist Era. Verry.
　　xMehta, Asoka.
　　　　India Today. Intl Pubns Serv.
Mehta, Balraj.
　　xMehta, Balraj.
　　　　Crisis of Indian Economy. Intl Pubns Serv.
　　　　Crisis of Indian Economy. Verry.
Mehta, Ghanshyam.
　　xMehta, Ghanshyan.
　　　　The Structure of the Keynesian Revolution. St
　　　　Martin.
Mehta, Ghanshyan. see Mehta, Ghanshyam.
Mehta, Gita.
　　xMehta, Gita
　　　　Karma Cola. S&S.
Mehta, J. K. see Mehta, Jamshed Kaikhusroo.
Mehta, Jamshed K. see Mehta, Jamshed Kaikhusroo.
Mehta, Jamshed Kaikhusroo, 1901-
　　xMehta, J. K.
　　　　Rhyme, Rhythm & Truth in Economics. Asia.
　　xMehta, Jamshed K.
　　　　Economics of Growth. Asia.
Mehta, Nitin H.
　　xMehta.
　　　　Hospital Accounting Systems & Controls. P-H.
Mehta, Rustam J. see Mehta, Rustam Jehangir.
Mehta, Rustam Jehangir, 1912-
　　xMehta, Rustam J.
　　　　Masterpieces of Indian Temples. Intl Pubns
　　　　Serv.
Mehta, Ved. see Mehta, Ved Parkash.
Mehta, Ved Parkash.
　　xMehta, Ved.
　　　　Daddyji. FS&G.
　　　　Daddyji. Oxford U Pr.
　　　　Face to Face. Oxford U Pr.
　　　　Mamaji. Oxford U Pr.
Meidl, J. H. see Meidl, James H.
Meidl, James. see Meidl, James H.
Meidl, James H.
　　xMeidl, J. H.
　　　　Explosive & Toxic Hazardous Materials.
　　　　Glencoe.
　　xMeidl, James.
　　　　Explosive & Toxic Hazardous Materials.
　　　　Glencoe.
Meier, August.
　　xMeier, August.

Black Detroit & the Rise of the UAW. Oxford
　　U Pr.
From Plantation to Ghetto. Hill & Wang.
Negro Thought in America, 1880-1915: Racial
　　Ideologies in the Age of Booker T.
　　Washington. U of Mich Pr.
Negro Thought in America, 1880-1915: Racial
　　Ideologies in the Age of Booker T.
　　Washington. U of Mich Pr.
Meier, G. see Meier, Gerhard.
Meier, Gerald M.
　　xMeier, Gerald M.
　　　　International Economics: The Theory of Policy.
　　　　Oxford U Pr.
　　　　Problems of a World Monetary Order. Oxford
　　　　U Pr.
　　　　Problems of Cooperation for Development.
　　　　Oxford U Pr.
　　　　Problems of Trade Policy. Oxford U Pr.
Meier, Gerhard.
　　xMeier, G.
　　　　Applications of Liquid Crystals.
　　　　Springer-Verlag.
Meier, Hans, 1929-
　　xMeier, Hans.
　　　　Experimental Pharmacogenetics:
　　　　Physiopathology of Heredity &
　　　　Pharmacologic Responses. Acad Pr.
Meier, Heinz K., 1929-
　　xMeier, Heinz K.
　　　　The Swiss-American Historical Society,
　　　　1927-1977. Donning Co.
Meier, Joel F.
　　xMeier, Joel F.
　　　　Backpacking. Wm C Brown.
Meier, John P.
　　xMeier, John P.
　　　　The Vision of Matthew: Christ, Church &
　　　　Morality in the First Gospel. Paulist Pr.
Meier, Matt S.
　　xMeier, Matt S.
　　　　The Chicanos: A History of Mexican
　　　　Americans. Hill & Wang.
　　　　Readings on La Raza: The Twentieth Century.
　　　　Hill & Wang.
　　　　Readings on La Raza: The Twentieth Century.
　　　　Hill & Wang.
Meier, Norman C. see Meier, Norman Charles.
Meier, Norman Charles, 1893-
　　xMeier, Norman C.
　　　　Art in Human Affairs: An Introduction to the
　　　　Psychology of Art. Johnson Repr.
Meier, Paul D.
　　xMeier, Paul D.
　　　　Christian Child Rearing & Personality
　　　　Development. Baker Bk.
Meier, R. C. see Meier, Robert C.
Meier, Robert. see Meier, Robert J.
Meier, Robert C.
　　xMeier, R. C.
　　　　Introduction to Mathematics for Business
　　　　Analysis. McGraw.
Meier, Robert J.
　　xMeier, Robert.
　　　　ed. Evolutionary Models & Studies in Human
　　　　Diversity. Beresford Bk Serv.
Meier-Ruge, W. see Meier-Ruge, William.
Meier-Ruge, William.
　　xMeier-Ruge, W.
　　　　ed. CNS Aging & Its Neuropharmacology:
　　　　Experimental & Clinical Aspects. S Karger.
Meiggs, Russell.
　　xMeiggs, Russell.
　　　　The Athenian Empire. Oxford U Pr.
Meighan, Clement W. see Meighan, Clement Woodward.
Meighan, Clement Woodward.
　　xMeighan, Clement W.

ed. Seven Rock Art Sites in Baja California.
　　Ballena Pr.
Meighan, Thomas.
　　xMeighan, Thomas.
　　　　T. S. Eliot: A Critical Study of His Principles
　　　　& Achievements. Vantage.
Meigs, A. James. see Meigs, Alexander James.
Meigs, Alexander James, 1921-
　　xMeigs, A. James.
　　　　Free Reserves & the Money Supply. U of
　　　　Chicago Pr.
Meigs, W. M. see Meigs, William Montgomery.
Meigs, Walter B.
　　xMeigs, Walter B.
　　　　Financial Accounting. McGraw.
　　　　Modern Advanced Accounting. McGraw.
　　　　Principles of Auditing. Irwin.
Meigs, William M. see Meigs, William Montgomery.
Meigs, William Montgomery, 1852-1929
　　xMeigs, W. M.
　　　　Relation of the Judiciary to the Constitution.
　　　　Da Capo.
　　xMeigs, William M.
　　　　Life of Charles Jared Ingersoll. Da Capo.
　　　　Life of John Caldwell Calhoun. Da Capo.
　　　　Life of Thomas Hart Benton. Da Capo.
Meijer, P. H. see Meijer, Paul Herman Ernst.
Meijer, Paul Herman Ernst, 1921-
　　xMeijer, P. H.
　　　　ed. Quantum Statistical Mechanics. Gordon.
Meijer, Reinder P.
　　xMeijer, Reinder P.
　　　　Literature of the Low Countries: A Short
　　　　History of Dutch Literature in the
　　　　Netherlands & Belgium. Irvington.
Meikle, Jeffrey. see Meikle, Jeffrey L.
Meikle, Jeffrey L., 1949-
　　xMeikle, Jeffrey.
　　　　Twentieth Century Limited: Industrial Design
　　　　in America, 1925-1939. Temple U Pr.
Meikle, Louis S., 1874-
　　xMeikle, Louis S.
　　　　Confederation of the British West Indies
　　　　Versus Annexation to the United States of
　　　　America. Negro U Pr.
Meiklejohn, Alexander, 1872-
　　xMeiklejohn, Alexander.
　　　　Education Between Two Worlds. Arno.
　　　　Experimental College. Arno.
　　　　Liberal College. Arno.
　　　　Political Freedom: The Constitutional Powers
　　　　of the People. Greenwood.
Meiklejohn, Donald.
　　xMeiklejohn, Donald.
　　　　Freedom & the Public: Public & Private
　　　　Morality in America. Syracuse U Pr.
Meiklejohn Civil Liberties Institute.
　　xMeiklejohn Civil Liberties Institute Staff.
　　　　The Pentagon Papers Case Collection:
　　　　Annotated Procedural Guide & Index.
　　　　Meiklejohn Civ Lib.
Meiksin, Z. H.
　　xMeiksin, Z. H.
　　　　Thin & Thick Films for Hybrid
　　　　Microelectronics. Lexington Bks.
Meilach, Dona. see Meilach, Dona Z.
Meilach, Dona Z.
　　xMeilach, Dona.
　　　　Direct Metal Sculpture: Creative Techniques &
　　　　Appreciation. Crown.
　　　　Homemade Liqueurs. Contemp Bks.
　　xMeilach, Dona Z.

Contemporary Art with Wood: Creative
Techniques & Appreciation. Crown.
Contemporary Stone Sculpture: Aesthetics,
Methods, Appreciation. Crown.
Creating Modern Furniture: Trends,
Techniques, Appreciation. Crown.
How to Create Your Own Designs: An
Introduction to Color, Form, Composition for
Artists & Craftsmen. Doubleday.
Macrame Gnomes & Puppets: Creative
Patterns & Ideas. Crown.
xMeilach, Donz Z.
Creating Art with Bread Dough. Crown.
xMeilach, Mel.
jt. auth. Homemade Liqueurs. Contemp Bks.
Meilach, Donz Z. see Meilach, Dona Z.
Meilach, Mel. see Meilach, Dona Z.
Meilach, Michael. see Meilach, Michael D.
Meilach, Michael D.
xMeilach, Michael.
ed. There Shall Be One Christ. Franciscan Inst.
Meilaender, Gilbert, 1946-
xMeilaender, Gilbert.
The Taste for the Other: The Social & Ethical
Thought of C. S. Lewis. Eerdmans.
Meiland, Jack. see Meiland, Jack W.
Meiland, Jack W.
xMeiland, Jack.
First Time in London. Scribner.
xMeiland, Jack W.
Talking About Particulars. Humanities.
Meillet, Antoine, 1866-1936
xMeillet, Antoine.
General Characteristics of the Germanic
Languages. U of Miami Pr.
Introduction a l'Etude Comparative Des
Langues Indo-Europeennes. U of Ala Pr.
Meinardus, Guenter. see Meinardus, Gunter.
Meinardus, Gunter.
xMeinardus, Guenter.
Approximation of Functions: Theory &
Numerical Methods. Springer-Verlag.
Meinardus, Otto F. see Meinardus, Otto Friedrich
August.
Meinardus, Otto Friedrich August.
xMeinardus, Otto F.
St. John of Patmos & the Seven Churches of
the Apocalypse. Caratzas Bros.
St. Paul in Ephesus & the Cities of Galatia &
Cyprus. Caratzas Bros.
St. Paul in Greece. Caratzas Bros.
St. Paul's Last Journey. Caratzas Bros.
Meinel, Aden B.
xMeinel, Aden B.
Applied Solar Energy: An Introduction. A-W.
Meiners, R. K.
xMeiners, R. K.
Everything to Be Endured: An Essay on
Robert Lowell & Modern Poetry. U of Mo
Pr.
Journeying Back to the World: Poems. U of
Mo Pr.
Meinhard, Heinrich.
xMeinhard, Heinrich.
German Wines. Routledge & Kegan.
Meinig, D. W. see Meinig, Donald William.
Meinig, Donald W. see Meinig, Donald William.
Meinig, Donald William, 1924-
xMeinig, D. W.
Imperial Texas: An Interpretive Essay in
Cultural Geography. U of Tex Pr.
xMeinig, Donald W.
Great Columbia Plain: A Historical Geography,
1805-1910. U of Wash Pr.
Meininger, Jut.
xMeininger, Jut.
Success Through Transactional Analysis. NAL.
Meininger, Thomas A.
xMeininger, Thomas A.

Ignatiev & the Establishment of the Bulgarian
Exarchate, 1864-1872: A Study in Personal
Diplomacy. State Hist Soc Wis.
Meinke, Peter.
xMeinke, Peter.
Howard Nemerov. U of Minn Pr.
The Night Train & The Golden Bird. U of
Pittsburgh Pr.
**Meinong, Alexius, Ritter Von Handschuchsheim,
1853-1920**
xMeinong, Alexius.
On Emotional Presentation. Northwestern U
Pr.
Meirovitch, Leonard.
xMeirovitch, Leonard.
Analytical Methods in Vibrations. Macmillan.
Meise, Norman R.
xMeise, Norman R.
Conceptual Design of an Automated National
Library System. Scarecrow.
Meisel, Jerome.
xMeisel, Jerome.
Principles of Electromechanical-Energy
Conversion. McGraw.
Meisel, John.
xMeisel, John.
Working Papers on Canadian Politics.
McGill-Queens U Pr.
Meisel, W. S. see Meisel, William S.
Meisel, William S.
xMeisel, W. S.
Computer-Oriented Approaches to Pattern
Recognition. Acad Pr.
Meiselas, Susan.
xMeiselas, Susan.
Carnival Strippers. FS&G.
Meiselman, David.
xMeiselman, David M.
ed. Varieties of Monetary Experience. U of
Chicago Pr.
Meiselman, David M. see Meiselman, David.
Meiselman, Karin C.
xMeiselman, Karin C.
Incest: A Psychological Study of Causes &
Effects with Treatment Recommendations.
Jossey-Bass.
Meisenzahl, Hilda.
xMeisenzahl, Hilda.
Meisen Breeding Manual. Denlingers.
Meisen Poodle Manual. Denlingers.
Meisner, Maurice. see Meisner, Maurice J.
Meisner, Maurice J., 1931-
xMeisner, Maurice.
Mao's China: A History of the People's
Republic. Free Pr.
Meiss, Millard.
xMeiss, Millard.
The Painter's Choice: Problems in the
Interpretation of Renaissance Art. Har-Row.
Painting in Florence & Siena After the Black
Death: The Arts, Religion & Society in the
Mid-14th Century. Princeton U Pr.
Meissner, William. see Meissner, William W.
Meissner, William W.
xMeissner, William.
The Paranoid Process. Aronson.
xMeissner, William W.
Group Dynamics in the Religious Life. U of
Notre Dame Pr.
Meister, Barbara, 1932-
xMeister, Barbara.
An Introduction to the Art Song. Taplinger.
Nineteenth-Century French Song: Faure,
Chausson, Duparc & Debussy. Ind U Pr.
Meister, Dick.
xMeister, Richard.

A Long Time Coming: The Struggle to
Unionize America's Farm Workers.
Macmillan.
Meister, Jurg.
xMeister, Jurg.
Soviet Warships of the Second World War.
Arco.
Meister, Richard. see Meister, Richard J.
Meister, Richard J., 1938-
xMeister, Richard.
Race & Ethnicity in Modern America. Heath.
Meisterfeld, C. W.
xMeisterfeld, C. W.
Hows & Whys of Psychological Dog Training.
M R K.
Tails' of a Dog Psychoanalyst. M R K.
Meistrell, Lois.
xMeistrell, Lois.
How to Raise & Train a Dachshund. TFH
Pubns.
Meites, Louis.
xMeites, Louis.
Handbook of Analytical Chemistry. McGraw.
Mekhitarian, Arpag.
xMekhitarian, Arpag.
Egyptian Painting. Rizzoli Intl.
Melady, John H. see Melady, John Hayes.
Melady, John Hayes.
xMelady, John H.
Home Owners' Complete Garden Handbook.
G&D.
Melady, Margaret. see Melady, Thomas Patrick.
Melady, Thomas. see Melady, Thomas Patrick.
Melady, Thomas P. see Melady, Thomas Patrick.
Melady, Thomas Patrick.
xMelady, Margaret.
jt. auth. Uganda: The Asian Exiles. Orbis Bks.
xMelady, Thomas.
Uganda: The Asian Exiles. Orbis Bks.
xMelady, Thomas P.
Burundi: The Tragic Years. Orbis Bks.
The Revolution of Color. Greenwood.
Melamed, Myron.
xMelamed, Myron.
The Adult Postoperative Chest. C C Thomas.
Melamed, Myron R.
xMelamed, Myron R.
Flow Cytometry & Sorting. Wiley.
Melanchthon, Philipp.
xMelanchthon, Philipp.
Opera Quae Supersunt Omnia. Johnson Repr.
Meland, Bernard E. see Meland, Bernard Eugene.
Meland, Bernard Eugene, 1899-
xMeland, Bernard E.
Higher Education & the Human Spirit.
Seminary Co-Op.
Reawakening of Christian Faith. Arno.
The Secularization of Modern Cultures.
Seminary Co-Op.
Melander, Lars. see Melander, Lars C. S.
Melander, Lars C. S.
xMelander, Lars.
Reaction Rates of Isotopic Molecules. Wiley.
Melanson, Philip H.
xMelanson, Philip H.
Political Science & Political Knowledge. Pub
Aff Pr.
Melaragno, Ralph J.
xMelaragno, Ralph J.
Tutoring with Students: A Handbook for
Establishing Tutorial Programs in Schools.
Educ Tech Pubns.
Melba, Nellie, Dame, 1861-1931
xMelba, Nellie.
Melodies & Memories. AMS Pr.
Melodies & Memories. Arno.
Melby, Ernest O. see Melby, Ernest Oscar.
Melby, Ernest Oscar, 1891-
xMelby, Ernest O.

The Education of Free Men. Greenwood.

Melcher, Carol R.
  xMelcher, Carol R.
    Horse Care from A to Z. A S Barnes.

Melcher, Daniel.
  xMelcher, Daniel.
    Melcher on Acquisition. ALA.
    Printing & Promotion Handbook: How to Plan,
      Produce, & Use Printing, Advertising &
      Direct Mail. McGraw.

Melcher, Edith, 1901-
  xMelcher, Edith.
    Stage Realism in France Between Diderot &
      Antoine. Russell.

Melcher, James R.
  xMelcher, James R.
    Field Coupled Surface Waves: A Comparative
      Study of Surface-Coupled EHD & MHD
      Systems. MIT Pr.

Melcher, Robert A.
  xMelcher, Robert A.
    Music for Keyboard Harmony. P-H.

Melchinger, Siegfried.
  xMelchinger, Siegfried.
    Anton Chekhov. Ungar.
    Sophocles. Ungar.

Melchiori, Giorgio.
  xMelchiori, Giorgio.
    The Whole Mystery of Art: Pattern into Poetry
      in the Work of W. B. Yeats. Greenwood.

Meldal-Johnsen, Trevor.
  xMeldal-Johnsen, Trevor.
    The Interpol Connection: An Inquiry into the
      International Criminal Police Organization.
      Dial.

Melden, A. I. *see* Melden, Abraham Irving.

Melden, Abraham Irving.
  xMelden, A. I.
    Human Rights. Wadsworth Pub.

Meldman, Monte J.
  xMeldman, Monte J.
    The Problem-Oriented Psychiatric Index &
      Treatment Plans. Mosby.

Meldrum, B. S. *see* Meldrum, Brian S.

Meldrum, Brian S.
  xMeldrum, B. S.
    ed. Primate Models of Neurological Disorders.
      Raven.

Melen, Roger.
  xMelen, Roger.
    ed. Charge-Coupled Devices: Technology &
      Applications. Inst Electrical.
    Understanding CMOS Integrated Circuits.
      Sams.
    Understanding IC Operational Amplifiers.
      Sams.

Melendez, Jesus P. *see* Melendez, Jesus Papoleto.

Melendez, Jesus Papoleto.
  xMelendez, Jesus P.
    Street Poetry and Other Poems. Barlenmir.

Melendy, H. Brett. *see* Melendy, Howard Brett.

Melendy, Howard Brett.
  xMelendy, H. Brett.
    Asians in America: Filipinos, Koreans, & East
      Indians. Twayne.
    The Oriental Americans. Hippocrene Bks.
    The Oriental Americans. Twayne.

Melin, Grace H. *see* Melin, Grace Hathaway.

Melin, Grace Hathaway.
  xMelin, Grace H.
    Dorothea Dix: Girl Reformer. Bobbs.

Melish, John, 1771-1822
  xMelish, John.
    Surveys for Travellers, Emigrants & Others.
      Arno.

Mellaart, James.
  xMellaart, James.

The Archaeology of Ancient Turkey. Rowman.
Earliest Civilizations of the Near East.
  McGraw.
The Neolithic of the Near East. Scribner.

Mellan, I. *see* Mellan, Ibert.

Mellan, Ibert.
  xMellan, I.
    Corrosion Resistant Materials Handbook.
      Noyes.
    Industrial Solvents Handbook. Noyes.

Mellanby, Edward, Sir, 1884-
  xMellanby, Edward.
    Story of Nutritional Research: The Effect of
      Some Dietary Factors on Bones & the
      Nervous System. Vanderbilt U Pr.

Mellard, James C. *see* Mellard, James M.

Mellard, James M.
  xMellard, James C.
    The Authentic Writer: Freshman Rhetoric &
      Composition. Heath.
  xMellard, James M.
    Quaternion: Stories, Poems, Plays, Essays.
      Scott F.

Mellars, Paul.
  xMellars, Paul.
    ed. The Early Postglacial Settlement of
      Northern Europe: An Ecological Perspective.
      U of Pittsburgh Pr.

Mellen, George W. *see* Mellen, George W. F.

Mellen, George W. F.
  xMellen, George W.
    Argument on the Unconstitutionality of
      Slavery, Embracing an Abstract of the
      Proceedings of the National & State
      Conventions on This Subject. AMS Pr.

Mellen, Joan.
  xMellen, Joan.
    Filmguide to The Battle of Algiers. Ind U Pr.
    ed. The World of Luis Bunuel: Essays in
      Criticism. Oxford U Pr.
    ed. The World of Luis Bunuel: Essays in
      Criticism. Oxford U Pr.

Meller, H. E. *see* Meller, Helen Elizabeth.

Meller, Helen Elizabeth.
  xMeller, H. E.
    Leisure & the Changing City, 1870 - 1914.
      Routledge & Kegan.

Meller, Norman.
  xMeller, Norman.
    Congress of Micronesia: Development of the
      Legislative Process in the Trust Territory of
      the Pacific Islands. U Pr of Hawaii.

Meller, Walter C. *see* Meller, Walter Clifford.

Meller, Walter Clifford.
  xMeller, Walter C.
    Ballads of the Forty-Five. Norwood Edns.

Mellerio, Andre, 1862-
  xMellerio, Andre.
    Odilon Redon. Da Capo.

Melling, Joseph.
  xMelling, Joseph.
    ed. Housing, Social Policy & the State. Biblio
      Dist.

Mellinger, Bonnie E. *see* Mellinger, Bonnie Eugenie.

Mellinger, Bonnie Eugenie, 1892-
  xMellinger, Bonnie E.
    Children's Interests in Pictures. AMS Pr.

Mellink, M. J. *see* Mellink, Machteld Johanna.

Mellink, Machteld Johanna.
  xMellink, M. J.
    A Hittite Cemetery at Gordion. Univ Mus of U
      PA.

Mellinkoff, Ruth.
  xMellinkoff, Ruth.
    The Horned Moses in Medieval Art &
      Thought. U of Cal Pr.

Mellon, James.
  xMellon, James.

African Hunter. HarBraceJ.
The Face of Lincoln. Viking Pr.

Mellon, Joseph.
  xMellon, Joseph.
    Hansel & Gretel. Dandelion Pr.
    Sleeping Beauty. Dandelion Pr.
    Snow-White. Dandelion Pr.
    Tom Thumb. Dandelion Pr.

Mellone, Michael.
  xMellone, Michael.
    The Cachet Identifier of U. S. Cacheted First
      Day Covers. FDC Pub.

Mellor, D. H.
  xMellor, David H.
    Matter of Chance. Cambridge U Pr.

Mellor, David H. *see* Mellor, D. H.

Mellor, J. W. *see* Mellor, Joseph William.

Mellor, John W. *see* Mellor, John Williams.

Mellor, John Williams, 1928-
  xMellor, John W.
    Developing Rural India: Plan & Practice.
      Cornell U Pr.

Mellor, Joseph William, 1873-1938
  xMellor, J. W.
    Comprehensive Treatise on Inorganic &
      Theoretical Chemistry. Halsted Pr.

Mellor, M. *see* Mellor, Malcolm.

Mellor, Malcolm.
  xMellor, M.
    ed. Antarctic Snow & Ice Studies. Am
      Geophysical.

Mellor, Roy. *see* Mellor, Roy E. H.

Mellor, Roy E. *see* Mellor, Roy E. H.

Mellor, Roy E. H.
  xMellor, Roy.
    Europe: A Geographical Survey of the
      Continent. Columbia U Pr.
  xMellor, Roy E.
    The Two Germanies: A Modern Geography.
      Har Row.
  xMellor, Roy E. H.
    The Two Germanies: A Modern Geography.
      B&N.

Mellors, Colin.
  xMellors, Colin.
    The British MP: A Socio-Economic Study of
      the House of Commons. Lexington Bks.

Mellott, Douglas W., 1934-
  xMellott, Douglas W.
    Marketing: Principles & Practices. Reston.

Mellows, Joan.
  xMellows, Joan.
    A Different Face. Fawcett.

Mellquist, Jerome.
  xMellquist, Jerome.
    Paul Rosenfeld, Voyager in the Arts. Octagon.

Melmon, Kenneth L., 1934-
  xMelmon, Kenneth L.
    ed. Cardiovascular Drug Therapy. Davis Co.

Melnick, David, 1938-
  xMelnick, David.
    Eclogs. SBD.

Melnick, Jack.
  xMelnick, Jack.
    Step-by-Step Guide to Your Retirement
      Security. Times Bks.

Melnick, Michael.
  xMelnick, Michael.
    ed. External Ear Malformations: Epidemiology,
      Genetics & Natural History. A R Liss.

Melnicove, Betty F.
  xMelnicove, Betty F.
    Crossword Puzzle Dictionary. B&N.

Melnyk, Myron.
  xMelnyk, Myron.
    Principles of Applied Statistics. Pergamon.

Meloan, Clifton. *see* Meloan, Clifton E.

Meloan, Clifton E.
  xMeloan, Clifton.

Food Analysis Laboratory Experiments. AVI.

Melody, Michael E. *see* Melody, Michael Edward.

Melody, Michael Edward.
xMelody, Michael E.
The Apaches: A Critical Bibliography. Ind U
Pr.

Meloe, Torleif.
xMeloe, Torleif.
United States Control of Petroleum Imports: A
Study of the Federal Government's Role in
the Management of Domestic Oil Supplies.
Arno.

Melone, Albert P.
xMelone, Albert P.
North Dakota Lawyers: Mapping the
Socio-Political Dimensions. N Dak Inst.

Melone, Joseph J.
xMelone, Joseph J.
Collectively Bargained Multi-Employer Pension
Plans. Irwin.

Melotti, Umberto, 1940-
xMelotti, Umberto.
Marx & the Third World. Humanities.

Melrose, John.
xMelrose, John.
Bucomco: A Business Communication
Simulation. SRA.

Melsa, James L.
xMelsa, James L.
Computer Programs for Computational
Assistance in the Study of Linear Control
Theory. McGraw.
Decision & Estimation Theory. McGraw.
Linear Control Systems. McGraw.

Melson, G. A. *see* Melson, Gordon A.

Melson, Gordon A., 1937-
xMelson, G. A.
Coordination Chemistry of Macrocyclic
Compounds. Plenum Pub.

Melton, Arthur W. *see* Melton, Arthur Weever.

Melton, Arthur Weever.
xMelton, Arthur W.
ed. Coding Processes in Human Memory.
Halsted Pr.

Melton, David.
xMelton, David.
And God Created.... Independence Pr.
The Survival Kit for Parents of Teenagers. St
Martin.

Melton, J. Gordon.
xMelton, J. Gordon.
Encyclopedia of American Religions. McGrath.
xMelton, James G.
A Directory of Religious Bodies in the United
States. Garland Pub.

Melton, James G. *see* Melton, J. Gordon.

Melton, W. F. *see* Melton, Wightman Fletcher.

Melton, Wightman F. *see* Melton, Wightman Fletcher.

Melton, Wightman Fletcher, 1867-1944
xMelton, W. F.
The Rhetoric of John Donne's Verse. Gordon
Pr.
xMelton, Wightman F.
Rhetoric of John Donne's Verse. Folcroft.

Meltsner, Arnold J.
xMeltsner, Arnold J.
The Politics of City Revenue. U of Cal Pr.

Meltsner, Michael, 1937-
xMeltsner, Michael.
Cruel & Unusual: The Supreme Court &
Capital Punishment. Random.
Public Interest Advocacy: Materials for Clinical
Legal Education. Little.
Short Takes. Random.

Meltzer, David.
xMeltzer, David.
Bark, a Polemic. Capra Pr.

Meltzer, H. *see* Meltzer, Hyman.

Meltzer, Herbert L., 1921-
xMeltzer, Herbert L.

Chemistry of Human Behavior. Nelson-Hall.

Meltzer, Hyman, 1899-
xMeltzer, H.
Humanizing Organizational Behavior. C C
Thomas.
xMeltzer, Hyman.
Children's Social Concepts: A Study of Their
Nature & Development. AMS Pr.

Meltzer, L. E. *see* Meltzer, Lawrence E.

Meltzer, Lawrence E.
xMeltzer, L. E.
Concepts & Practices of Intensive Care for
Nurse Specialists. Charles.
Intensive Coronary Care: A Manual for Nurses.
Charles.

Meltzer, Milton, 1915-
xMeltzer, Milton.
Bread & Roses: The Struggle of American
Labor, 1865 to 1915. Random.
Bread & Roses: The Struggle of American
Labor, 1865-1911. NAL.
Brother, Can You Spare a Dime?: The Great
Depression, 1929-1933. Knopf.
Dorothea Lange: A Photographer's Life.
FS&G.
The Human Rights Book. FS&G.
Hunted Like a Wolf: The Story of the
Seminole War. FS&G.
In Their Own Words: A History of the
American Negro, 1619-1865. T Y Crowell.
The Right to Remain Silent. HarBraceJ.
Taking Root: Jewish Immigrants in America.
Dell.
Taking Root: Jewish Immigrants in America.
FS&G.
World of Our Fathers: The Jews of Eastern
Europe. Dell.
World of Our Fathers: The Jews of Eastern
Europe. FS&G.

Meltzer, Murray A.
xMeltzer, Murray A.
Ophthalmic Plastic Surgery for the General
Ophthalmologist. Williams & Wilkins.

Meltzer, Otto.
xMeltzer, Otto.
Geschichte der Karthager. Arno.

Meltzer, R. *see* Meltzer, Richard.

Meltzer, Richard.
xMeltzer, R.
The Aesthetics of Rock. Ultramarine Pub.

Meltzer, Y. *see* Meltzer, Yale L.

Meltzer, Yale. *see* Meltzer, Yale L.

Meltzer, Yale L.
xMeltzer, Y.
Water-Soluble Polymers: Recent Developments.
Noyes.
xMeltzer, Yale.
Putting Money to Work: An Investment
Primer. P-H.
xMeltzer, Yale L.
Encyclopedia of Enzyme Technology 1973. Fut
Stoch Dynamics.

Melugin, Roy F.
xMelugin, Roy F.
Formation of Isaiah 40-55. De Gruyter.

Melvill, David.
xMelvill, David.
Intro. by The Melvill Book of Roundels. B
Franklin.

Melville, Anne.
xMelville, Anne.
Alexa. Doubleday.
The Lorimer Line. Doubleday.

Melville, Derek.
xMelville, Derek.
Chopin: A Biography, with a Survey of Books,
Editions, & Recordings. Shoe String.

Melville, Dorothy Sutherland.
xMelville, Dorothy Sutherland.

Tyler-Browns of Brattleboro. Exposition.

Melville, Herman, 1819-1891
xMelville, Herman.
The Confidence Man. Hendricks House.
Confidence Man. NAL.
The Confidence-Man. Norwood Edns.
Confidence Man. Norton.
Confidence Man. Airmont.
Omoo. Hendricks House.
Omoo. Northwestern U Pr.
Portable Melville. Penguin.
Shorter Novels of Herman Melville. Liveright.
Typee. NAL.
Typee. Northwestern U Pr.
Typee. Penguin.
Typee. Airmont.

Melville, Jennie.
xMelville, Jennie.
Dragon's Eye. G K Hall.
Dragon's Eye. S&S.
Tarot's Tower. Fawcett.
Tarot's Tower. S&S.

Melville, Joan.
xMelville, Joan.
Step-by-Step Guide to Growing Bonsai Trees.
Hippocrene Bks.

Melville, Keith.
xMelville, Keith.
Communes in the Counter Culture: Origins,
Theories, Styles of Life. Morrow.
Marriage & Family Today. Random.

Melville, Leslie W.
xMelville, Leslie W.
Forms & Agreements on Intellectual Property
& International Licensing. Boardman.

Melvin, J. R. *see* Melvin, James R.

Melvin, James R.
xMelvin, J. R.
The Effects of Energy Price Changes on
Commodity Prices, Interprovincial Trade &
Employment. U of Toronto Pr.

Melvin, Jeanne L.
xMelvin, Jeanne L.
Rheumatic Disease: Occupational Therapy &
Rehabilitation. Davis Co.

Melvin, Kenneth B.
xMelvin, Kenneth B.
ed. Psy Fi One: An Anthology of Psychology
in Science Fiction. Random.

Melvin, Tom, 1935-
xMelvin, Tom.
Practical Psychology in Construction
Management. Van Nos Reinhold.

Melyan, Gary G.
xMelyan, Gary G.
I-Ching: The Hexagrams Revealed. C E Tuttle.

Members of English Dept. of University of Michigan. *see*
Michigan. University. Department of English.

Members of the American Academy of Podiatric Sports
Medicine. *see* American Academy of Podiatric Sports
Medicine.

Members of the American Dietetic Assoc. *see* American
Dietetic Association.

Members of the Staff of the International Monetary
Fund. *see* International Monetary Fund.

Membership Division, Natl. District Attorneys Assn. *see*
National District Attorneys Association.

Memes, John S. *see* Memes, John Smythe.

Memes, John Smythe.
xMemes, John S.
Life of William Cowper. Kennikat.

Memling, Carl.
xMemling, Carl.
Ride, Willy Ride. Follett.

Memmler, Ruth L. *see* Memmler, Ruth Lundeen.

Memmler, Ruth Lundeen.
xMemmler, Ruth L.
Structure & Function of the Human Body.
Lippincott.

Memorial Sloan-Kettering Cancer Center. *see*

Sloan-Kettering Institute for Cancer Research, New York.
Menage, Ronald H. *see* Menage, Ronald Herbert.
Menage, Ronald Herbert.
 xMenage, Ronald H.
  Greenhouse Gardening. Penguin.
Menander, Of Athens.
 xMenander.
  The Dyskolos. NAL.
Menard, Eusebe. *see* Menard, Eusebe M.
Menard, Eusebe M.
 xMenard, Eusebe.
  At All Times, in Every Age. Franciscan Herald.
Menard, H. W. *see* Menard, Henry W.
Menard, Henry W.
 xMenard, H. W.
  Geology, Resources & Society: An Introduction to Earth Science. W H Freeman.
MENC National Committee on Instruction. *see* Music Educator'S National Conference. National Commission on Instruction.
Mencher, Joan P., 1930-
 xMencher, Joan P.
  Agriculture & Social Structure in Tamil Nadu: Past Origins, Present Transformations & Future Prospects. Carolina Acad Pr.
Mencher, Samuel, 1918-1967
 xMencher, Samuel.
  Poor Law to Poverty Program: Economic Security Policy in Britain & the United States. U of Pittsburgh Pr.
Menchin, Robert S.
 xMenchin, Robert S.
  Where There's a Will: A Collection of Wills...Hilarious, Incredible, Bizarre, Witty...Sad. Farnswth Pub.
Mencius.
 xMencius.
  Works of Mencius. Dover.
  Works of Mencius. Peter Smith.
Mencke, John G., 1940-
 xMencke, John G.
  Mulattoes & Race Mixture: American Attitudes & Images, 1865-1918. Univ Microfilms.
Mencken, H. L. *see* Mencken, Henry Louis.
Mencken, Henry L. *see* Mencken, Henry Louis.
Mencken, Henry Louis.
 xMencken, H. L.
  A Gang of Pecksniffs: And Other Comments on Newspaper Publishers, Editors & Reporters. Arlington Hse.
  George Bernard Shaw: His Plays. Glaser.
  George Bernard Shaw: His Plays. Haskell.
  In Defense of Women. Octagon.
  Notes on Democracy. Octagon.
 xMencken, Henry L.
  American Scene: A Reader. Knopf.
  Artist: A Drama Without Words. Folcroft.
  George Bernard Shaw: His Plays. Arden Lib.
  George Bernard Shaw: His Plays. Folcroft.
Mendel Centennial Symposium - Fort Collins - 1965. *see* Mendel Centennial Symposium, Fort Collins, Colorado, 1965.
Mendel Centennial Symposium, Fort Collins, Colorado, 1965.
 xMendel Centennial Symposium - Fort Collins - 1965.
  Heritage from Mendel. U of Wis Pr.
Mendel, Douglas. *see* Mendel, Douglas Heusted.
Mendel, Douglas Heusted, 1921-
 xMendel, Douglas.
  The Politics of Formosan Nationalism. U of Cal Pr.
Mendel, Jerry M., 1938-
 xMendel, Jerry M.
  Discrete Techniques of Parameter Estimation: The Equation Error Formulation. Dekker.
Mendel, Werner M.
 xMendel, Werner M.

  ed. A Celebration of Laughter. Mara.
  ed. The Psychiatric Consultation. Grune.
  Supportive Care: Theory & Technique. Mara.
Mendell, Clarence W. *see* Mendell, Clarence Whittlesey.
Mendell, Clarence Whittlesey.
 xMendell, Clarence W.
  Our Seneca. Shoe String.
Mendelowitz, Daniel M. *see* Mendelowitz, Daniel Marcus.
Mendelowitz, Daniel Marcus.
 xMendelowitz, Daniel M.
  A Guide to Drawing. HR&W.
  A History of American Art. HR&W.
Mendels, Joseph, 1937-
 xMendels, Joseph.
  Concepts of Depression. Wiley.
  Lithium in Medicine. Gordon.
Mendelsohn, Everett.
 xMendelsohn, Everett.
  ed. Human Aspects of Biomedical Innovation. Harvard U Pr.
Mendelsohn, Harold. *see* Mendelsohn, Harold A.
Mendelsohn, Harold A.
 xMendelsohn, Harold.
  The People Choose a President: Influences on Voter Decision Making. Praeger.
Mendelsohn, Jack, 1918-
 xMendelsohn, Jack.
  God, Allah & Ju Ju: Religion in Africa Today. Greenwood.
Mendelsohn, M. *see* Mendelsohn, Martin.
Mendelsohn, M. Stefan. *see* Mendelsohn, Stefan.
Mendelsohn, Martin, 1935-
 xMendelsohn, M.
  Guide to Franchising. Pergamon.
Mendelsohn, Robert O., 1952-
 xMendelsohn, Robert O.
  Towards Efficient Regulation of Air Pollution from Coal-Fired Power Plants. Garland Pub.
Mendelsohn, Robert S.
 xMendelsohn, Robert S.
  Confessions of a Medical Heretic. Contemp Bks.
  Confessions of a Medical Heretic. Warner Bks.
Mendelsohn, Stefan.
 xMendelsohn, M. Stefan.
  Money on the Move: The Modern International Capital Market. McGraw.
Mendelson, Edward.
 xMendelson, Edward.
  ed. Pynchon: A Collection of Critical Essays. P-H.
Mendelson, Elliott.
 xMendelson, Elliott.
  Introduction to Mathematical Logic. Van Nos Reinhold.
Mendelson, Jack H. *see* Mendelson, Jack Harold.
Mendelson, Jack Harold.
 xMendelson, Jack H.
  The Diagnosis & Treatment of Alcoholism. McGraw.
  ed. The Use of Marihuana: A Psychological & Physiological Inquiry. Plenum Pub.
Mendelson, Lee.
 xMendelson, Lee.
  Happy Birthday, Charlie Brown. Random.
Mendelson, Robert E. *see* Mendelson, Robert Eugene.
Mendelson, Robert Eugene.
 xMendelson, Robert E.
  ed. The Politics of Housing in Older Urban Areas. Praeger.
Mendelson, Wallace B.
 xMendelson, Wallace B.
  ed. Human Sleep & Its Disorders. Plenum Pub.
  The Use & Misuse of Sleeping Pills: A Clinical Guide to Treatment. Plenum Pub.
Mendelssohn, Felix Von. *see* Von Mendelssohn, Felix.
Mendelssohn, K. *see* Mendelssohn, Kurt.
Mendelssohn, Kurt.
 xMendelssohn, K.

  The World of Walther Nernst: The Rise & Fall of German Science, 1864-1941. U of Pittsburgh Pr.
 xMendelssohn, Kurt.
  In China Now. Transatlantic.
Mendelssohn-Bartholdy, C. *see* Mendelssohn-Bartholdy, Felix.
Mendelssohn-Bartholdy, F. *see* Mendelssohn-Bartholdy, Karl.
Mendelssohn-Bartholdy, Felix, 1809-1847
 xMendelssohn-Bartholdy, C.
  ed. Letters of Felix Mendelssohn-Bartholdy from 1833-1847. Arno.
 xMendelssohn-Bartholdy, Felix.
  Letters of Felix Mendelssohn-Bartholdy from 1833-1847. Arno.
Mendelssohn-Bartholdy, Karl, 1838-1897
 xMendelssohn-Bartholdy, F.
  Goethe & Mendelssohn. R West.
Mendenhall. *see* Mendenhall, William.
Mendenhall, Charles A.
 xMendenhall, Charles A.
  The Air Racer. Specialty Pr.
Mendenhall, John C. *see* Mendenhall, John Cooper.
Mendenhall, John Cooper, 1886-
 xMendenhall, John C.
  Aureate Terms: A Study in the Literary Diction of the Fifteenth Century. Folcroft.
Mendenhall, Kitty.
 xMendenhall, Kitty.
  Moon of the Lost Frenchman. Bouregy.
Mendenhall, William.
 xMendenhall.
  Statistics for Management & Economics. Duxbury Pr.
  Understanding Statistics. Duxbury Pr.
 xMendenhall, William.
  Introduction to Linear Models & the Design & Analysis of Experiments. Duxbury Pr.
  Introduction to Probability & Statistics. Duxbury Pr.
  Mathematical Statistics with Applications. Duxbury Pr.
  Statistics for Psychology. Duxbury Pr.
  Understanding Statistics. Duxbury Pr.
Mendershausen, Horst.
 xMendershausen, Horst.
  Changes in Income Distribution During the Great Depression. Arno.
  Coping with the Oil Crisis: French & German Experiences. Johns Hopkins.
  Two Postwar Recoveries of the German Economy. Greenwood.
Mendes, Helen.
 xMendes, Helen.
  African Heritage Cookbook. Macmillan.
Mendes-Flohr, Paul R.
 xMendes-Flohr, Paul R.
  The Jew in the Modern World: A Documentary History. Oxford U Pr.
Mendez, Chic.
 xMendez, Chic.
  Beginning Cross-Country Skiing. Prensa Pubns.
Mendez, Eugenio Fernandez. *see* Fernandez Mendez, Eugenio.
Mendilow, Adam A. *see* Mendilow, Adam Abraham.
Mendilow, Adam Abraham.
 xMendilow, Adam A.
  World & Art of Shakespeare. Davey.
Mendis, Garrett C. *see* Mendis, Garrett Champness.
Mendis, Garrett Champness.
 xMendis, Garrett C.
  The Early History of Ceylon & Its Relations with India & Other Foreign Countries. AMS Pr.
Menditto, Joseph.
 xMenditto, Joseph.

Drugs of Addiction & Non-Addiction, Their
Use & Abuse: A Comprehensive
Bibliography. Whitston Pub.
Mendl, R. W. *see* Mendl, Robert William Sigismund.
Mendl, Robert William Sigismund, 1892-
xMendl, R. W.
Revelation in Shakespeare: A Study of the
Supernatural, Religious & Spiritual Elements
in His Art. Humanities.
Mendlewicz, J.
xMendlewicz, J.
ed. Genetic Aspects of Affective Illness:
Current Concepts. Spectrum Pub.
Mendlowitz, Edward, 1942-
xMendlowitz, Edward.
Successful Tax Planning. Boardroom.
Mendlowitz, Milton, 1906-
xMendlowitz, Milton.
Systemic Arterial Hypertension. C C Thomas.
Mendoza, Daniel, 1764-1836
xMendoza, Daniel.
The Memoirs of the Life of Daniel Mendoza.
Arno.
Mendoza, George.
xMendoza, George.
Fearsome Brat. Lothrop.
Fishing the Morning Lonely. Freshet Pr.
Gwot: Horribly Funny Hairticklers. Har-Row.
Hunter I Might Have Been. Astor-Honor.
Practical Man. Lothrop.
Mendras, Henri.
xMendras, Henri.
Vanishing Peasant: Innovation & Change in
French Agriculture. MIT Pr.
Menefee, Selden. *see* Menefee, Selden Cowles.
Menefee, Selden Cowles, 1909-
xMenefee, Selden.
Pais of Manipal. Asia.
Menen, Aubrey.
xMenen, Aubrey.
Art & Money: An Irreverent History. McGraw.
Four Days of Naples. Ballantine.
The Four Days of Naples. Seaview Bks.
Venice. Time-Life.
Venice. Silver.
Menendez, Albert J.
xMenendez, Albert J.
Church-State Relations: An Annotated
Bibliography. Garland Pub.
Religion at the Polls. Westminster.
Menezes, M. N. *see* Menezes, Mary Noel.
Menezes, Mary Noel.
xMenezes, M. N.
British Policy Towards the Amerindians in
British Guiana, 1803-1973. Oxford U Pr.
Meng, S M.
xMeng, S. M.
Tsungli Yamen: Its Organization & Functions.
Harvard U Pr.
Menger, F. M. *see* Menger, Fred M.
Menger, Fred M.
xMenger, F. M.
Problems in Organic Reaction Mechanisms.
Plenum Pub.
xMenger, Frederic M.
Organic Chemistry: A Concise Approach.
Benjamin-Cummings.
Menger, Frederic M. *see* Menger, Fred M.
Menges, Gunter.
xMenges, Gunter.
ed. Information, Inference & Decision. Kluwer
Boston.
Menges, Matthew C. *see* Menges, Matthew Clement.
Menges, Matthew Clement, 1913-
xMenges, Matthew C.
The Concept of Univocity Regarding the
Predication of God & Creature According to
William Ockham. Franciscan Inst.
Menges, Robert J.
xMenges, Robert J.

The Intentional Teacher: Controller, Manager,
Helper. Brooks-Cole.
Mengin, Robert, 1907-
xMengin, Robert.
No Laurels for De Gaulle. Arno.
Menguy, Rene. *see* Menguy, Rene Boris.
Menguy, Rene Boris.
xMenguy, Rene.
Surgery of Peptic Ulcer. Saunders.
Menhennet, David.
xMenhennet, David.
Parliament in Perspective. Dufour.
Menil, Alexander De. *see* De Menil, Alexander N.
Menius, Opal.
xMenius, Opal.
No Escape. Elsevier-Nelson.
Menke, Frank G. *see* Menke, Frank Grant.
Menke, Frank Grant, 1885-1954
xMenke, Frank G.
The Encyclopedia of Sports. A S Barnes.
The Encyclopedia of Sports. Doubleday.
Menke, Werner.
xMenke, Werner.
History of the Trumpet of Bach & Handel.
Brass Pr.
Menken, Adah I. *see* Menken, Adah Isaacs.
Menken, Adah Isaacs, 1835-1868
xMenken, Adah I.
Infelicia. Arno.
Infelicia. Gordon Pr.
Menkes, John H.
xMenkes, John H.
Textbook of Child Neurology. Lea & Febiger.
Mennear. *see* Mennear, John H.
Mennear, John H., 1935-
xMennear.
Cadmium Toxicity. Dekker.
Mennel, Robert M.
xMennel, Robert M.
Thorns & Thistles: Juvenile Delinquents in the
United States, 1825-1940. U Pr of New Eng.
Mennell, John M. *see* Mennell, John Mcm.
Mennell, John Mcm., M.d
xMennell, John M.
Joint Pain: Diagnosis & Treatment Using
Manipulative Techniques. Little.
Mennell, Robert L., 1934-
xMennell, Robert L.
Wills & Trusts in a Nutshell. West Pub.
Menning, Barbara E. *see* Menning, Barbara Eck.
Menning, Barbara Eck.
xMenning, Barbara E.
Infertility: A Guide for the Childless Couple.
P-H.
Menninger Clinic Children's Division. *see* Menninger
Foundation, Topeka, Kansas. Childrens Division.
Menninger, Edwin A. *see* Menninger, Edwin Arnold.
Menninger, Edwin Arnold, 1896-
xMenninger, Edwin A.
Edible Nuts of the World. Horticultural.
Flowering Vines of the World: An
Encyclopedia of Climbing Plants. Hearthside.
Menninger Foundation, Topeka, Kansas.
xMenninger Foundation, Topeka, Kansas.
Catalog of the Menninger Clinic Library. G K
Hall.
**Menninger Foundation, Topeka, Kansas. Childrens
Division.**
xMenninger Clinic Children's Division.
Disturbed Children: Examination & Assessment
Through Team Process. Jossey-Bass.
Menninger, Karl, 1893-
xMenninger, Karl.
Crime of Punishment. Penguin.
Crime of Punishment. Viking Pr.
Whatever Became of Sin?. Bantam.
Whatever Became of Sin?. Dutton.
Menninger, Karl A. *see* Menninger, Karl Augustus.
Menninger, Karl Augustus.
xMenninger, Karl A.

Love Against Hate. HarBraceJ.
Love Against Hate. HarBraceJ.
Mennonite Church.
xMennonite Church.
Mennonite Confession of Faith. Herald Pr.
Menolascino, Frank J.
xMenolascino, Frank J.
Medical Dimensions of Mental Retardation. U
of Nebr Pr.
ed. Psychiatric Aspects of the Diagnosis &
Treatment of Mental Retardation. Spec
Child.
Menon, Bhashkar P.
xMenon, Bhashkar P.
Global Dialogue: The New International
Economic Order. Pergamon.
Menon, Vapal P. *see* Menon, Vapal Pangunni.
Menon, Vapal Pangunni.
xMenon, Vapal P.
The Story of the Integration of the Indian
States. Arno.
Mensch, Pat.
xMensch, Pat.
And Then One Day. Ashley Bks.
Menser, Gary. *see* Menser, Gary P.
Menser, Gary P.
xMenser, Gary.
Hallucinogenic & Poisonous Mushroom Field
Guide. And-or Pr.
Mensh, Ivan N.
xMensh, Ivan N.
Clinical Psychology: Science & Profession.
Macmillan.
Ment, David.
xMent, David.
Building Blocks of Brooklyn: A Study of Urban
Growth. Bklyn Educ.
The Shaping of a City: A Brief History of
Brooklyn. Bklyn Educ.
Mental Health Materials Center. *see* Mental Health
Materials Center, Inc., New York.
Mental Health Materials Center, Inc., New York.
xMental Health Materials Center.
ed. Current Audiovisuals for Mental Health
Education. Marquis.
Mente, Boye De. *see* De Mente, Boye.
Menten, Theodore.
xMenten, Theodore.
ed. Advertising Art in the Art Deco Style.
Dover.
Advertising Art in the Art Deco Style. Peter
Smith.
ed. Chinese Cut Paper Designs. Dover.
Chinese Cut-Paper Designs. Peter Smith.
Mentienne, A. *see* Mentienne, Adrien.
Mentienne, Adrien, b. 1841
xMentienne, A.
La Decouverte de la Photographie en 1839.
Arno.
Menton, Seymour.
xMenton, Seymour.
Prose Fiction of the Cuban Revolution. U of
Tex Pr.
Mentzer, Richard C.
xMentzer, Richard C.
The Core Package. Educ Tech Pubns.
Menuhin, Moshe, 1893-
xMenuhin, Moshe.
Decadence of Judaism in Our Time. New
World Press NY.
The Decadence of Judaism in Our Time.
Noontide.
Menuhin, Yehudi.
xMenuhin, Yehudi.
The Music of Man. Methuen Inc.
Unfinished Journey. Knopf.
Menville, Douglas. *see* Menville, Douglas Alver.
Menville, Douglas Alver.
xMenville, Douglas.

A Historical & Critical Survey of the Science
Fiction Film. Arno.
Menyuk, Paula.
xMenyuk, Paula.
Acquisition & Development of Language. P-H.
The Development of Speech. Bobbs.
Menzel, Donald H. *see* Menzel, Donald Howard.
Menzel, Donald Howard, 1901-
xMenzel, Donald H.
Mathematical Physics. Dover.
Our Sun. Harvard U Pr.
ed. Radio Noise Spectrum. Harvard U Pr.
Menzel, Harold. *see* Menzel, Harold H.
Menzel, Harold H.
xMenzel, Harold.
Write Your Own Will & Avoid Probate. Dale
Books Inc.
Menzies, Robert. *see* Menzies, Robert Gordon.
Menzies, Robert Gordon, Sir, 1894-
xMenzies, Robert.
Central Power in the Australian
Commonwealth: An Examination of the
Growth of Commonwealth Power in the
Australian Federation. U Pr of Va.
Menzies, Robert J. *see* Menzies, Robert James.
Menzies, Robert James.
xMenzies, Robert J.
Abyssal Environment & Ecology of the World
Oceans. Krieger.
Menzies, William W.
xMenzies, William W.
Anointed to Serve: The Story of the
Assemblies of God. Gospel Pub.
Meo, Leila. *see* Meo, Leila M. T.
Meo, Leila M. T.
xMeo, Leila.
Lebanon, Improbable Nation: A Study in
Political Development. Greenwood.
Mera, H. F. *see* Mera, Harry Percival.
Mera, H. P. *see* Mera, Harry Percival.
Mera, H. R. *see* Mera, Harry Percival.
Mera, Harry Percival, 1875-1951
xMera, H. F.
Pueblo Designs: 176 Illustrations of the "Rain
Bird". Dover.
xMera, H. P.
Navajo Textile Arts. Peregrine Smith.
Pueblo Indian Embroidery. Gannon.
xMera, H. R.
Pueblo Designs: 176 Illustrations of the Rain
Bird. Peter Smith.
Mera, Koichi, 1933-
xMera, Koichi.
Income Distribution & Regional Development.
Intl Schol Bk Serv.

Meranto, Philip.
xMeranto, Philip.
Politics of Federal Aid to Education in 1965: A
Study in Political Innovation. Syracuse U Pr.
Meras, Icchokas, 1934-
xMeras, Icchokas.
Stalemate. Lyle Stuart.
Meras, Phyllis.
xMeras, Phyllis.
Christmas Angels. HM.
Vacation Crafts. HM.
Mercadante, James L.
xMercadante, James L.
The Sparterville Surgeon. J L Mercadante.
Mercatante, Anthony. *see* Mercatante, Anthony S.
Mercatante, Anthony S.
xMercatante, Anthony.
Who's Who in Egyptian Mythology. Potter.
xMercatante, Anthony S.
Good & Evil: Mythology & Folklore. Har-Row.
Mercer, A. *see* Mercer, Alan.
Mercer, Alan.
xMercer, A.

Operational Distribution Research: Innovative
Case Studies. Halsted Pr.
Mercer, Cecil D.
xMercer, Cecil D.
Learning Theory Research in Mental
Retardation: Implications for Teaching.
Merrill.
Mercer, Charles.
xMercer, Charles.
The Castle on the River. Popular Lib.
Enough Good Men. Berkley Pub.
Mercer, Charles. *see* Mercer, Charles E.
Mercer, Charles E.
xMercer, Charles.
Adapted by The Battlestar Galactica Story
Book. Putnam.
Gerald Ford. Putnam.
Monsters in the Earth: The Story of
Earthquakes. Putnam.
Murray Hill. Delacorte.
Statue of Liberty. Putnam.
Mercer, Eileen.
xMercer, Eileen.
Let's Make Doll Furniture. Schocken.
Mercer, G. *see* Mercer, Geoffrey.
Mercer, Geoffrey.
xMercer, G.
The Employment of Nurses: Nursing Labour
Turnover in the NHS. Biblio Dist.
Mercer, Henry C. *see* Mercer, Henry Chapman.
Mercer, Henry Chapman, 1856-1930
xMercer, Henry C.
The Hill-Caves of Yucatan: A Search for
Evidence of Man's Antiquity in the Caverns
of Central America. U of Okla Pr.
The Hill-Caves of Yucatan: A Search for
Evidence of Man's Antiquity in the Caverns
of Central America. Zephyrus Pr.
Mercer, James L.
xMercer, James L.
Public Management Systems. Am Mgmt.
Mercer, Jean.
xMercer, Jean.
Small People: How Children Develop & What
You Can Do About It. Nelson-Hall.
Mercer, John.
xMercer, John.
An Introduction to Cinematography. Stipes.
Mercer, Philip. *see* Mercer, Philip C.
Mercer, Philip C.
xMercer, Philip.
Sympathy & Ethics: A Study of the
Relationship Between Sympathy & Morality
with Special Reference to Hume's Treatise.
Oxford U Pr.
Mercer, R. Jack.
xMercer, R. Jack.
The Band Director's Brain Bank. Instrumental
Co.
Mercer, Ramona. *see* Mercer, Ramona Thieme.
Mercer, Ramona Thieme.
xMercer, Ramona.
Perspectives on Adolescent Health Care.
Lippincott.
Mercer, Thomas T.
xMercer, Thomas T.
Aerosol Technology in Hazard Evaluation.
Acad Pr.
Mercer, Walter, 1890-
xMercer, Walter.
Orthopedic Surgery. Williams & Wilkins.
Merchant, Donald J. *see* Merchant, Donald Joseph.
Merchant, Donald Joseph, 1921-
xMerchant, Donald J.
Handbook of Cell & Organ Culture. Burgess.
Merchant, Michael J.
xMerchant, Michael J.
ABC's of Fortran Programming. Wadsworth
Pub.
Mercia, Leonard. *see* Mercia, Leonard S.

Mercia, Leonard S.
xMercia, Leonard.
Raising Poultry the Modern Way. Garden Way
Pub.
Mercier, Jacques, 1946-
xMercier, Jacques.
Ethiopian Magic Scrolls. Braziller.
Mercurio, Joseph A.
xMercurio, Joseph A.
Caning: Educational Rite & Tradition. Syracuse
U Pr.
Meredith, Dale D. *see* Meredith, Dale Dean.
Meredith, Dale Dean.
xMeredith, Dale D.
Design & Planning of Engineering Systems.
P-H.
Meredith, Don.
xMeredith, Don.
Becoming One. Nelson.
Meredith, George, 1828-1909
xMeredith, George.
Diana of the Crossways. Norton.
Diana of the Crossways. Scholarly.
One of Our Conquerors. U of Queensland Pr.
Meredith, P. *see* Meredith, Patrick.
Meredith, Patrick.
xMeredith, P.
Learning, Remembering & Knowing. McKay.
Meredith, Richard C.
xMeredith, Richard C.
The Awakening. St Martin.
Vestiges of Time. Doubleday.
Vestiges of Time. Playboy Pbks.
Mereness, Dorothy A.
xMereness, Dorothy A.
Essentials of Psychiatric Nursing. Mosby.
Mergeler, Karen.
xMergeler, Karen.
Noodle Doodle!: The Art of Creating with
Pasta. Falk Art.
Merha, Lester W. *see* Merha, Lesterwayne.
Merha, Lester Wayne.
xMerha, Lester W.
Return to Elkhorne. Bouregy.
Merhav, Peretz.
xMerhav, Peretz.
The Israeli Left: History, Problems,
Documents. A S Barnes.
Meriam, J. L. *see* Meriam, James L.
Meriam, James L.
xMeriam, J. L.
Dynamics. Wiley.
xMeriam, James L.
Dynamics. Wiley.
Meriam, Junius L. *see* Meriam, Junius Lathrop.
Meriam, Junius Lathrop, 1872-
xMeriam, Junius L.
Normal School Education & Efficiency in
Teaching. AMS Pr.
Merida, Carlos, 1893-
xMerida, Carlos.
Modern Mexican Artists: Critical Notes. Arno.
Merideth, Robert.
xMerideth, Robert.
The Politics of the Universe: Edward Beecher,
Abolition, & Orthodoxy. Vanderbilt U Pr.
Transformations: A Dictionary of
Contemporary Changes. Connect Pr.
Merigan, Thomas C.
xMerigan, Thomas C.
ed. Antivirals with Clinical Potential. U of
Chicago Pr.
Merillat, Herbert C. *see* Merillat, Herbert Christian
Laing.
Merillat, Herbert Christian Laing, 1915-
xMerillat, Herbert C.
ed. Legal Advisers & Foreign Affairs. Oceana.
xMerillat, Herbert L.

Island: A History of the First Marine Division
on Guadalcanal, August 7 - December 9,
Nineteen Forty-Two. Zenger Pub.
Merillat, Herbert L. see Merillat, Herbert Christian
Laing.
Merin, Jennifer.
xMerin, Jennifer.
International Directory of Theatre, Dance, &
Folklore Festivals. Greenwood.
Merin, Joseph H.
xMerin, Joseph H.
ed. Etiology of the Neuroses. Sci & Behavior.
Meritt, Benjamin D. see Meritt, Benjamin Dean.
Meritt, Benjamin Dean, 1899-
xMeritt, Benjamin D.
Athenian Year. U of Cal Pr.
Inscriptions: The Athenian Councillors. Am
Sch Athens.
Meritt, Herbert D. see Meritt, Herbert Dean.
Meritt, Herbert Dean, 1904-
xMeritt, Herbert D.
ed. Old English Prudentius Glosses at
Boulogne-Sur-Mer. AMS Pr.
Some of the Hardest Glosses in Old English.
Stanford U Pr.
Merivale, Herman. see Merivale, Herman Charles.
Merivale, Herman Charles.
xMerivale, Herman.
Life of W. M. Thackeray. Folcroft.
Meriwether, Colyer, d. 1920
xMeriwether, Colyer.
Our Colonial Curriculum. Arden Lib.
Our Colonial Curriculum. Folcroft.
Meriwether, James B.
xMeriwether, James B.
Literary Career of William Faulkner: A
Bibliographical Study. U of SC Pr.
Meriwether, Louise.
xMeriwether, Louise.
The Freedom Ship of Robert Smalls. P-H.
Meriwether, Robert L. see Meriwether, Robert Lee.
Meriwether, Robert Lee, 1890-1958
xMeriwether, Robert L.
The Expansion of South Carolina: 1729-1765.
Porcupine Pr.
Merk, Frederick, 1887-
xMerk, Frederick.
Fruits of Propaganda in the Tyler
Administration. Harvard U Pr.
History of the Westward Movement. Knopf.
The Monroe Doctrine & American
Expansionism 1843-1849. Random.
Oregon Question: Essays in Anglo-American
Diplomacy & Politics. Harvard U Pr.
Merkatz, Irwin R.
xMerkatz, Irwin R.
ed. The Diabetic Pregnancy: A Perinatal
Perspective. Grune.
Merkin, Donald H.
xMerkin, Donald H.
Pregnancy As a Disease: The Pill in Society.
Kennikat.
Merkl, Peter H.
xMerkl, Peter H.
The Making of a Stormtrooper. Princeton U Pr.
Modern Comparative Politics. HR&W.
ed. Western European Party Systems: Trends &
Prospects. Free Pr.
Merklein, Helmut.
xMerklein, Helmut A.
Energy Economics. Gulf Pub.
Merklein, Helmut A. see Merklein, Helmut.
Merkley, Paul.
xMerkley, Paul.
Reinhold Niebuhr: A Political Account.
McGill-Queens U Pr.
Merklin, Lewis.
xMerklin, Lewis.

They Chose Honor: The Problem of
Conscience in Custody. Har-Row.
Merkow, L. P.
xMerkow, L. P.
ed. Oncogenic Adenoviruses. S Karger.
Merle, Robert, 1908-
xMerle, Robert.
Day of the Dolphin. Fawcett.
Merleau-Ponty, Maurice, 1908-1961
xMerleau-Ponty, Maurice.
The Prose of the World. Northwestern U Pr.
Signs. Northwestern U Pr.
Themes from the Lectures at the College de
France, 1952-1960. Northwestern U Pr.
Merlin, Christina.
xMerlin, Christina.
The Spy Concerto. St Martin.
Merlin, Sidney D. see Merlin, Sidney Daniell.
Merlin, Sidney Daniell, 1916-
xMerlin, Sidney D.
Theory of Fluctuations in Contemporary
Economic Thought. AMS Pr.
Merlis, S. see Merlis, Sidney.
Merlis, Sidney.
xMerlis, S.
ed. Non-Scientific Constraints on Medical
Research. Raven.
Mermall, Thomas.
xMermall, Thomas.
The Rhetoric of Humanism: Spanish Culture
After Ortega y Gasset. Bilingual Pr.
Mermelstein, David, 1933-
xMermelstein, David.
The Economic Crisis Reader: Understanding
Depression, Inflation, Unemployment,
Energy, Food, Wage-Price Controls, & Other
Disorders of American & World Capitalism.
Random.
Mermin, N. David.
xMermin, N. David.
Space & Time in Special Relativity. McGraw.
Mermin, Samuel, 1912-
xMermin, Samuel.
Law & the Legal System: An Introduction.
Little.
Meroff, Deborah.
xMeroff, Deborah.
Coronation of Glory: The Story of Lady Jane
Grey. Zondervan.
Merquior, J. G. see Merquior, Jose Guilherme.
Merquior, Jose Guilherme.
xMerquior, J. G.
The Veil & the Mask: Essays on Culture &
Ideology. Routledge & Kegan.
Merrell, David J.
xMerrell, David J.
An Introduction to Genetics. Norton.
Merrell, James L.
xMerrell, James L.
Discover the Word in Print. Bethany Pr.
Merrell, V. Dallas, 1936-
xMerrell, V. Dallas.
Huddling: The Informal Way to Management
Success. Am Mgmt.
Merrens, H. Roy. see Merrens, Harry Roy.
Merrens, Harry Roy.
xMerrens, H. Roy.
ed. The Colonial South Carolina Scene:
Contemporary Views 1697 - 1774. U of SC
Pr.
Merrett, A. J.
xMerrett, A. J.
Capital Budgeting & Company Finance.
Longman.
Merrett, C. E. see Merrett, Christopher Edmond.
Merrett, Christopher Edmond.
xMerrett, C. E.

A Selected Bibliography of Natal Maps. G K
Hall.
Merrett, Stephen.
xMerrett, Stephen.
State Housing in Britain. Routledge & Kegan.
Merriam, Alan P., 1923-
xMerriam, Alan P.
An African World: The Basongye Village of
Lupupa Ngye. Ind U Pr.
Anthropology of Music. Northwestern U Pr.
Congo, Background of Conflict. Northwestern
U Pr.
Merriam, C. Hart. see Merriam, Clinton Hart.
Merriam, C. W. see Merriam, Charles Wolcott.
Merriam, Charles E. see Merriam, Charles Edward.
Merriam, Charles Edward, 1874-
xMerriam, Charles E.
American Political Ideas: Studies in the
Development of American Political Thought
1865-1917. Johnson Repr.
The History of American Political Theories.
Gordon Pr.
History of American Political Theories.
Johnson Repr.
History of American Political Theories. Kelley.
History of American Political Theories. Russell.
History of the Theory of Sovereignty Since
Rousseau. AMS Pr.
Prologue to Politics. Johnson Repr.
Merriam, Charles Wolcott, 1931-
xMerriam, C. W.
Automated Design of Control Systems.
Gordon.
Merriam, Clinton Hart.
xMerriam, C. Hart.
ed. Indian Names for Plants & Animals Among
Californian & Other Western North
American Tribes. Ballena Pr.
Merriam Company. see Merriam (G. and C.) Company,
Publishers, Springfield, Massacheusetts.
Merriam, D. see Merriam, Daniel Francis.
Merriam, D. F. see Merriam, Daniel Francis.
Merriam, Daniel Francis.
xMerriam, D.
Random Processes in Geology. Springer Verlag.
xMerriam, D. F.
ed. Computer Software for the Geosciences:
Proceedings of the Fifth Geochautauqua,
1976. Pergamon.
Merriam, Eve, 1916-
xMerriam, Eve.
The Double Bed. M Evans.
Good Night to Annie. Schol Bk Serv.
A Husband's Notes About Her. Macmillan.
A Husband's Notes About Her. Macmillan.
Inner City Mother Goose. S&S.
The Inner City Mother Goose. S&S.
Rainbow Writing. Atheneum.
There Is No Rhyme for Silver. Atheneum.
Unhurry Harry. Schol Bk Serv.
**Merriam (G. and C.) Company, Publishers, Springfield,
Massacheusetts.**
xMerriam Company.
ed. Liberty's Women. Merriam.
ed. Webster's Big Seven Collegiate Dictionary.
Merriam.
Webster's Biographical Dictionary. Merriam.
ed. Webster's Intermediate Dictionary.
Merriam.
ed. Webster's New Ideal Dictionary. Merriam.
Merriam, George S. see Merriam, George Spring.
Merriam, George Spring, 1843-1914
xMerriam, George S.
Life & Times of Samuel Bowles. Da Capo.
Life & Times of Samuel Bowles. Johnson Repr.
Life & Times of Samuel Bowles. Scholarly.
Negro & the Nation: A History of American
Slavery & Enfranchisement. Negro U Pr.
Merriam, Harold G. see Merriam, Harold Guy.

Merriam, Harold Guy, 1883-
xMerriam, Harold G.
The Golden Valley: Missoula to 1883.
Mountain Pr.
The Long Friendship. Mountain Pr.
Merriam, Kendall.
xMerriam, Kendall A.
Illustrated Dictionary of Lobstering.
Wheelwright.
Merriam, Kendall A. *see* Merriam, Kendall.
Merriam, Sharan B.
xMerriam, Sharan B.
Coping with Male Mid-Life: A Systematic
Analysis Using Literature As a Data Source.
U Pr of Amer.
Merriam, Thornton W. *see* Merriam, Thornton Ward.
Merriam, Thornton Ward, 1894-
xMerriam, Thornton W.
The Relations Between Scholastic Achievement
in a School of Social Work & Six Factors in
Students Background. AMS Pr.
Merrick, Fred.
xMerrick, Fred.
Down on the Farm: A Story of Stanford
Football. Strode.
Merrick, Helen H. *see* Merrick, Helen Hynson.
Merrick, Helen Hynson.
xMerrick, Helen H.
Sweden. Watts.
Merrifield, D. Bruce. *see* Merrifield, Dudley Bruce.
Merrifield, Dudley Bruce, 1921-
xMerrifield, D. Bruce.
Strategic Analysis, Selection, & Management of
R&D Projects. Am Mgmt.
Merrigan, Joseph A.
xMerrigan, Joseph A.
Sunlight to Electricity: Prospects for Solar
Energy Conversion by Photovotaics. MIT Pr.
Merril Library. Special Collections Dept.
xSpecial Collections Department.
Name Index to the Library of Congress
Collection of Mormon Diaries. Utah St U Pr.
Merrill, Arthur A., 1906-
xMerrill, Arthur A.
Chess Openings Simplified. Analysis.
Merrill, Bill.
xMerrill, Bill.
Vacationing with Saddle & Packhorse. Arco.
Merrill, Bill. *see* Merrill, William K.
Merrill, Elizabeth.
xMerrill, Elizabeth.
Dialogue in English Literature. B Franklin.
Dialogue in English Literature. Shoe String.
Merrill, Evelyne S., 1918-
xMerrill, Evelyne S.
The Power of the Word: A Reading &
Language Text. Winthrop.
Merrill, George D.
xMerrill, George D.
A Handbook of Civilization. Kendall-Hunt.
Merrill, George P. *see* Merrill, George Perkins.
Merrill, George Perkins, 1854-1929
xMerrill, George P.
ed. Contributions to a History of American
State Geological & Natural History Surveys.
Arno.
Merrill, Gilbert R. *see* Merrill, Gilbert Roscoe.
Merrill, Gilbert Roscoe.
xMerrill, Gilbert R.
Cotton Drawing & Roving. Textile Bk.
Cotton Opening & Picking. Textile Bk.
Cotton Ring Spinning. Textile Bk.
Merrill, Irving R. *see* Merrill, Irving Rodgers.
Merrill, Irving Rodgers.
xMerrill, Irving R.
Criteria for Planning the College & University
Learning Resources Center. Assn Ed Comm
Tech.
Merrill, James. *see* Merrill, James Ingram.

Merrill, James Ingram.
xMerrill, James.
Scripts for the Pageant. Atheneum.
Merrill, Jean.
xMerrill, Jean.
How Many Kids Are Hiding on My Block. A
Whitman.
The Superlative Horse. A-W.
Merrill, John C. *see* Merrill, John Calhoun.
Merrill, John Calhoun, 1924-
xMerrill, John C.
Existential Journalism. Hastings.
Foreign Press: A Survey of the World's
Journalism. La State U Pr.
The Imperative of Freedom: A Philosophy of
Journalistic Autonomy. Hastings.
Merrill, John R.
xMerrill, John R.
Using Computers in Physics. HM.
Using Computers in Physics. U Pr of Amer.
Merrill, Joseph, 1814-1898
xMerrill, Joseph.
The History of Amesbury & Merrimac,
Massachusetts. Heritage Bk.
Merrill, M. David.
xMerrill, M. David.
Teaching Concepts: An Instructional Design
Guide. Educ Tech Pubns.
TICCIT. Educ Tech Pubns.
Merrill, Maud A. *see* Merrill, Maud Amanda.
Merrill, Maud Amanda, 1888-
xMerrill, Maud A.
Problems of Child Delinquency. Greenwood.
Merrill, Melissa.
xMerrill, Melissa.
Polygamist's Wife. Olympus Pub Co.
Merrill, Paul W. *see* Merrill, Paul Willard.
Merrill, Paul Willard, 1887-1961
xMerrill, Paul W.
Space Chemistry. U of Mich Pr.
Merrill, R. Dale.
xMerrill, R. Dale.
The Church Business Meeting. Judson.
Merrill, Robert.
xMerrill, Robert.
The Divas. Berkley Pub.
The Divas. S&S.
Norman Mailer. G K Hall.
Norman Mailer. Twayne.
Merrill, Selah, 1837-1909
xMerrill, Selah.
Ancient Jerusalem. Arno.
Merrill, Toni.
xMerrill, Toni.
Activities for the Aged & Infirm: A Handbook
for the Untrained Worker. C C Thomas.
Discussion Topics for Oldsters in Nursing
Homes: 365 Things to Talk About. C C
Thomas.
Merrill, W. C. *see* Merrill, William Charles.
Merrill, W. K. *see* Merrill, William K.
Merrill, William Charles, 1934-
xMerrill, W. C.
Panama's Economic Development: The Role of
Agriculture. Iowa St U Pr.
Merrill, William K., 1903-
xMerrill, Bill.
The Hiker's & Backpacker's Handbook. Arc
Bks.
The Survival Handbook. Arc Bks.
xMerrill, W. K.
The Survival Handbook. Winchester Pr.
Merriman, John M.
xMerriman, John M.
The Agony of the Republic: Repression of the
Left in Revolutionary France, 1848-1851.
Yale U Pr.
Merriman, Roger B. *see* Merriman, Roger Bigelow.
Merriman, Roger Bigelow.
xMerriman, Roger B.

Suleiman the Magnificent, 1520-1566. Cooper
Sq.
Merritt, A.
xMerritt, A.
The Fox Woman & Other Stories. Avon.
The Moon Pool. Avon.
xMerritt, Abraham.
The Fox Woman & Other Stories. Arno.
xMerritt, Abraham P.
Moon Pool. Macmillan.
Merritt, Abraham. *see* Merritt, A.
Merritt, Abraham P. *see* Merritt, A.
Merritt, Anna J.
xMerritt, Anna J.
Compiled by Politics, Economics, & Society in
the Two Germanies, 1945-75: A Bibliography
of English-Language Works. U of Ill Pr.
xMerritt, Richard L.
Compiled by Politics, Economics, & Society in
the Two Germanies, 1945-75: A Bibliography
of English-Language Works. U of Ill Pr.
Merritt, F. S. *see* Merritt, Frederick S.
Merritt, Frederick S.
xMerritt, F. S.
Modern Mathematical Methods in Engineering.
McGraw.
xMerritt, Frederick S.
Building Construction Handbook. McGraw.
Building Engineering & Systems Design. Van
Nos Reinhold.
Mathematics Manual: Methods & Principles of
the Various Branches of Mathematics for
Reference Problem Solving & Review.
McGraw.
ed. Standard Handbook for Civil Engineers.
McGraw.
ed. Structural Steel Designer's Handbook.
McGraw.
Merritt, H. Houston. *see* Merritt, Hiram Houston.
Merritt, Herbert E.
xMerritt, Herbert E.
Hydraulic Control Systems. Wiley.
Merritt, Hiram Houston, 1902-
xMerritt, H. Houston.
ed. A Textbook of Neurology. Lea & Febiger.
Merritt, Leroy C. *see* Merritt, Leroy Charles.
Merritt, Leroy Charles, 1912-
xMerritt, Leroy C.
Book Selection & Intellectual Freedom. Wilson.
Reviews in Library Book Selection. Wayne St
U Pr.
Merritt, Richard L.
xMerritt, Richard L.
ed. Communication in International Politics. U
of Ill Pr.
ed. Foreign Policy Analysis. Lexington Bks.
Symbols of American Community, 1735-1775.
Greenwood.
Merritt, Richard L. *see* Merritt, Anna J.
Merry, Suzanne.
xMerry, Suzanne.
Dancer. Scribner.
Merryman, John H. *see* Merryman, John Henry.
Merryman, John Henry.
xMerryman, John H.
The Civil Law Tradition: An Introduction to
the Legal Systems of Western Europe &
Latin America. Stanford U Pr.
ed. Stanford Legal Essays. Stanford U Pr.
Mersand, Joseph. *see* Mersand, Joseph E.
Mersand, Joseph E., 1907-
xMersand, Joseph.
The English Teacher: Basic Traditions &
Successful Innovations. Kennikat.
Spelling Your Way to Success. Barron.
Mersky, Roy. *see* Mersky, Roy M.
Mersky, Roy M.
xMersky, Roy.

ed. Author's Guide to Journals in Law,
    Criminal Justice & Criminology. Haworth Pr.
A Manual on Medical Literature for Law
    Librarians: A Handbook & Annotated
    Bibliography. Glanville.
xMersky, Roy M.
    A Manual on Medical Literature for Law
    Librarians: A Handbook & Annotated
    Bibliography. Oceana.
Mersmann, James F., 1938-
    xMersmann, James F.
    Out of the Vietnam Vortex: A Study of Poets
        & Poetry Against the War. Regents Pr KS.
Merten, George.
    xMerten, George.
    Plays for Puppet Performance. Plays.
Mertens, Joan R.
    xMertens, John R.
    Attic White-Ground: Its Development on
        Shapes Other Than Lekythoi. Garland Pub.
Mertens, John R. *see* Mertens, Joan R.
Mertens, Lawrence E. *see* Mertens, Lawrence Edwin.
Mertens, Lawrence Edwin.
    xMertens, Lawrence E.
    In-Water Photography: Theory & Practice.
        Wiley.
Mertens, Thomas R. *see* Mertens, Thomas Robert.
Mertens, Thomas Robert, 1930-
    xMertens, Thomas R.
    Human Genetics: Readings on the Implications
        of Genetic Engineering. Wiley.
Merton, R. *see* Merton, Robert King.
Merton, Robert K. *see* Merton, Robert King.
Merton, Robert King.
    xMerton, R.
    Science, Technology & Society in Seventeenth
        Century England. Fertig.
    xMerton, Robert K.
    ed. Contemporary Social Problems. HarBraceJ.
    ed. Continuities in Social Research: Studies in
        the Scope & Method of the American
        Soldier. Arno.
    Mass Persuasion: The Social Psychology of a
        War Bond Drive. Greenwood.
    On Theoretical Sociology: Five Essays, Old &
        New. Free Pr.
    ed. Reader in Bureaucracy. Free Pr.
    Science, Technology & Society in Seventeenth
        Century England. Humanities.
    ed. Sociological Traditions from Generation to
        Generation: Glimpses of the American
        Experience. Ablex Pub.
    The Sociology of Science: An Episodic
        Memoir. S Ill U Pr.
    ed. The Sociology of Science in Europe. S Ill U
        Pr.
Merton, T. *see* Merton, Thomas.
Merton, Thomas, 1915-1968
    xMerton, T.
    ed. The Asian Journal of Thomas Merton. New
        Directions.
    xMerton, Thomas.

The Asian Journal of Thomas Merton. New
    Directions.
Catch of Anti-Letters. Andrews & McMeel.
Conjectures of a Guilty Bystander. Doubleday.
Contemplation in a World of Action.
    Doubleday.
Contemplative Prayer. Doubleday.
Disputed Questions. FS&G.
Faith & Violence: Christian Teaching &
    Christian Practice. U of Notre Dame Pr.
Geography of Lograire. New Directions.
Last of the Fathers: Saint Bernard of Clairvaux
    & the Encyclical Letter, Doctor Mellifluus.
    Greenwood.
Life & Holiness. Doubleday.
The Living Bread. FS&G.
Love & Living. Bantam.
Love & Living. FS&G.
The Monastic Journey. Andrews & McMeel.
The Monastic Journey. Doubleday.
My Argument with the Gestapo: A Macaronic
    Journal. New Directions.
No Man Is an Island. HarBraceJ.
The Secular Journal. FS&G.
Seeds of Contemplation. Greenwood.
The Sign of Jonas. Doubleday.
The Sign of Jonas. HarBraceJ.
The Silent Life. FS&G.
Thoughts in Solitude. FS&G.
The Waters of Siloe. HarBraceJ.
Mertz, Herbert.
    xMertz, Herbert.
    Worker's Capitalism. New Visions Pr.
Merwe, H. W. Van Der. *see* Van Der Merwe, H. W.
Merwin, Charles L. *see* Merwin, Charles Lewis.
Merwin, Charles Lewis, 1912-
    xMerwin, Charles L.
    Financing Small Corporations in Five
        Manufacturing Industries: 1926-36. Arno.
Merwin, John.
    xMerwin, John.
    Stillwater Trout. Doubleday.
Merwin, W. S. *see* Merwin, William S.
Merwin, William S., 1927-
    xMerwin, W. S.
    tr. Asian Figures. Atheneum.
    Carrier of Ladders. Atheneum.
    tr. Selected Translations: 1948-1968.
        Atheneum.
    tr. Selected Translations: 1968-1978.
        Atheneum.
    xMerwin, William S.
    Drunk in the Furnace. Macmillan.
Mery, Fernand.
    xMery, Fernand.
    Life History & Magic of the Cat. G&D.
    Life, History & Magic of the Dog. G&D.
Merz, Charles, 1893-
    xMerz, Charles.
    Centerville, U. S. A.. Arno.
    Dry Decade. U of Wash Pr.
Merzbacher, Eugen.
    xMerzbacher, Eugen.
    Quantum Mechanics. Wiley.
Merzer, Meridee.
    xMerzer, Meridee.
    Winning the Diet Wars. HarBraceJ.
Merzkirch, W. *see* Merzkirch, Wolfgang.
Merzkirch, Wolfgang.
    xMerzkirch, W.
    Flow Visualization. Acad Pr.
Mes, G. M.
    xMes, G. M.
    Faith Healing & Religion. Philos Lib.
Meschan, Isadore.
    xMeschan, Isadore.

Analysis of Roentgen Signs in General
    Radiology. Saunders.
An Atlas of Anatomy Basic to Radiology.
    Saunders.
Radiographic Positioning & Related Anatomy.
    Saunders.
Synopsis of Analysis of Roentgen Signs in
    General Radiology. Saunders.
Meschter, Joan W.
    xMeschter, Joan W.
    How to Grow Herbs & Salad Greens Indoors.
        Popular Lib.
Meserve, B. E. *see* Meserve, Bruce Elwyn.
Meserve, Bruce E. *see* Meserve, Bruce Elwyn.
Meserve, Bruce Elwyn.
    xMeserve, B. E.
    Contemporary Mathematics. P-H.
    xMeserve, Bruce E.
    An Introduction to Finite Mathematics. A-W.
Meserve, Walter J.
    xMeserve, Walter J.
    ed. Modern Drama from Communist China.
        NYU Pr.
    ed. Modern Literature from China. NYU Pr.
    Outline History of American Drama.
        Littlefield.
Meshenberg, Michael J.
    xMeshenberg, Michael J.
    ed. Environmental Planning: A Guide to
        Information Sources. Gale.
Meshover, Leonard.
    xMeshover, Leonard.
    The Monkey That Went to School. Follett.
Mesick, Jane L. *see* Mesick, Jane Louise.
Mesick, Jane Louise, 1884-1967
    xMesick, Jane L.
    English Traveller in America, 1785-1835.
        Greenwood.
    English Traveller in America, 1785-1835.
        Scholarly.
Mesics, Emil A.
    xMesics, Emil A.
    Education & Training for Effective Manpower
        Utilization: An Annotated Bibliography. NY
        Sch Indus Rel.
Meskill, Johanna M. *see* Meskill, Johanna Margarete
    Menzel.
Meskill, Johanna Margarete Menzel, 1930-
    xMeskill, Johanna M.
    A Chinese Pioneer Family: The Lins of
        Wu-feng, Taiwan, 1729-1895. Princeton U Pr.
Meskill, John. *see* Meskill, John Thomas.
Meskill, John Thomas, 1925-
    xMeskill, John.
    ed. An Introduction to Chinese Civilization.
        Columbia U Pr.
    An Introduction to Chinese Civilization. Heath.
Mesnard, Jean.
    xMesnard, Jean.
    Pascal. U of Ala Pr.
Mesnet, Marie B. *see* Mesnet, Marie Beatrice.
Mesnet, Marie Beatrice.
    xMesnet, Marie B.
    Graham Greene & the Heart of the Matter: An
        Essay. Greenwood.
Mess, B.
    xMess, B.
    Role of the Pineal Gland in the Regulation of
        Ovulation. Heyden.
    Role of the Pineal Gland in the Regulation of
        Ovulation. Intl Pubns Serv.
Messegue, Maurice.
    xMessegue, Maurice.
    Health Secrets of Plants & Herbs. Morrow.
    Maurice Messegue's Way to Natural Health &
        Beauty. Macmillan.
Messenger, J. C. *see* Messenger, John Cowan.
Messenger, John Cowan, 1920-
    xMessenger, J. C.

Classrooms & Corridors: The Crisis of
Authority in Desegregated Secondary
Schools. U of Cal Pr.

Metz, Rene.
xMetz, Rene.
ed. Informal Groups in the Church: Papers of
the Second Cerdic Colloquium, Strasbourg,
May 13-15, 1971. Pickwick.

Metz, Robert.
xMetz, Robert.
Geology Laboratory Manual: Geology from
New Jersey. RA Corp.

Metzer, Jacob.
xMetzer, Jacob.
Some Economic Aspects of Railroad
Development in Tsarist Russia. Arno.

Metzger, Bruce M. *see* Metzger, Bruce Manning.

Metzger, Bruce Manning.
xMetzger, Bruce M.
Historical & Literary Studies: Pagan, Jewish &
Christian. Eerdmans.
Text of the New Testament: Its Transmission,
Corruption, & Restoration. Oxford U Pr.

Metzger, Charles H. *see* Metzger, Charles Henry.

Metzger, Charles Henry, 1890-
xMetzger, Charles H.
The Prisoner in the American Revolution.
Loyola.

Metzger, Elizabeth.
xMetzger, Elizabeth.
The Breakfast Book: Where to Find the Best
Breakfasts & Brunches in Northern
California. Chronicle Bks.

Metzger, H. *see* Metzger, Hans Ludwig.

Metzger, H. P. *see* Metzger, H. Peter.

Metzger, H. Peter.
xMetzger, H. P.
Atomic Establishment. S&S.

Metzger, Hans Ludwig.
xMetzger, H.
The Human Female Reproductive Tract: A
Scanning Electron Microscopic Atlas.
Springer-Verlag.

Metzger, Jacques. *see* Metzger, Jacques V.

Metzger, Jacques V.
xMetzger, Jacques.
Thiazole & Its Derivatives. Wiley.

Metzger, Norman, 1924-
xMetzger, Norman.
The Health Care Supervisor's Handbook.
Aspen Systems.

Metzger, Therese.
xMetzger, Therese.
Jewish Life in the Middle Ages: Illuminated
Hebrew Manuscripts. Oxford U Pr.

Metzger, Walter P.
xMetzger, Walter P.
Academic Freedom in the Age of the
University. Columbia U Pr.
ed. The Constitutional Status of Academic
Freedom. Arno.
Dimensions of Academic Freedom. U of Ill Pr.
ed. Reader on the Sociology of the Academic
Profession. Arno.

Metzker, Ray. *see* Metzker, Ray K.

Metzker, Ray K.
xMetzker, Ray.
Sand Creatures. Aperture.

Metzler, K. *see* Metzler, Ken.

Metzler, Ken.
xMetzler, K.
Creative Interviewing: The Writer's Guide to
Gathering Information by Asking Questions.
P-H.

Metzler, Lloyd A. *see* Metzler, Lloyd Appleton.

Metzler, Lloyd Appleton.
xMetzler, Lloyd A.
Collected Papers. Harvard U Pr.

Metzler, Paul.
xMetzler, Paul.

Advanced Tennis. Macmillan.
Advanced Tennis. Sterling.
Fine Points of Tennis. Sterling.
Getting Started in Tennis. Macmillan.
Getting Started in Tennis. Sterling.

Metzner, Ralph.
xMetzner, Ralph.
ed. Ecstatic Adventure. Macmillan.

Metzner, Seymour.
xMetzner, Seymour.
One-Minute Game Guide. Pitman Learning.

Meudt, R. *see* Meudt, Rudolf O.

Meudt, R. O. *see* Meudt, Rudolf O.

Meudt, Rudolf O.
xMeudt, R.
Ultrasonoscopic (Real Time) Differential
Diagnosis in Obstetrics & Gynecology.
Springer-Verlag.
xMeudt, R. O.
Ultrasonoscopic Differential Diagnosis in
Obstetrics & Gynecology. Springer-Verlag.

Meuwissen, Hilaire J.
xMeuwissen, Hilaire J.
ed. Combined Immunodeficiency Disease &
Adenosine Deaminase Deficiency: A
Molecular Defect-Proceedings. Acad Pr.

Meves, Eric.
xMeves, Eric.
Guide to Backpacking in the United States.
Macmillan.

Mew, James.
xMew, James.
Drinks of the World. Gale.

Mews, Hazel.
xMews, Hazel.
Reader Instruction in Colleges & Universities:
Teaching the Use of the Library. Shoe String.

Mewshaw, Michael, 1943-
xMewshaw, Michael.
Land Without Shadow. Doubleday.

Mey, Jacob.
xMey, Jacob L.
ed. Pragmalinguistics: Theory & Practice.
Mouton.

Mey, Jacob L. *see* Mey, Jacob.

Meyendorff, Jean, 1926-
xMeyendorff, John.
Byzantine Theology: Historical Trends &
Doctrinal Themes. Fordham.
Christ in Eastern Christian Thought. St
Vladimirs.
Marriage: An Orthodox Perspective. St
Vladimirs.

Meyendorff, John. *see* Meyendorff, Jean.

Meyer, Adolf, 1866-1950
xMeyer, Adolf.
The Commonsense Psychiatry of Dr. Adolf
Meyer: Fifty-Two Selected Papers. Arno.

Meyer, Adolph E. *see* Meyer, Adolphe Erich.

Meyer, Adolphe E. *see* Meyer, Adolphe Erich.

Meyer, Adolphe Erich, 1897-
xMeyer, Adolph E.
Modern European Educators & Their Work.
Arden Lib.
Modern European Educators & Their Work.
Arno.
xMeyer, Adolphe E.
Educational History of the Western World.
McGraw.
Grandmasters of Educational Thought.
McGraw.

Meyer, Alfred. *see* Meyer, Alfred Charles.

Meyer, Alfred Charles, 1914-
xMeyer, Alfred.
Historical Aspects of Cerebral Anatomy.
Oxford U Pr.

Meyer, Alfred G.
xMeyer, Alfred G.
Communism. Random.

Meyer, Balthasar H. *see* Meyer, Balthasar Henry.

Meyer, Balthasar Henry, 1866-1954
xMeyer, Balthasar H.
Railway Legislation in the United States. Arno.
xMeyer, Balthasar Henry.
A History of the Northern Securities Case. Da
Capo.

Meyer, Bernard. *see* Meyer, Bernard Sandler.

Meyer, Bernard Sandler, 1901-
xMeyer, Bernard.
Introduction to Plant Physiology. D Van
Nostrand.

Meyer, C. Kenneth.
xMeyer, C. Kenneth.
An Analysis of Officer Characteristics & Police
Assaults Among Selected South Central
Cities. Univ OK Gov Res.

Meyer, Carl F.
xMeyer, Carl F.
Route Surveying & Design. Har-Row.

Meyer, Carol H., 1924-
xMeyer, Carol H.
Social Work Practice. Free Pr.

Meyer, Carolyn.
xMeyer, Carolyn.
Amish People: Plain Living in a Complex
World. Atheneum.
Bread Book: All About Bread & How to Make
It. HarBraceJ.
C. C. Poindexter. Atheneum.
The Center: From a Troubled Past to a New
Life. Atheneum.
Coconut, the Tree of Life. Morrow.
Lots & Lots of Candy. HarBraceJ.
Mask Magic. HarBraceJ.
The Needlework Book of Bible Stories.
HarBraceJ.
People Who Make Things: How American
Craftsmen Live & Work. Atheneum.

Meyer, Charles R. *see* Meyer, Charles Robert.

Meyer, Charles Robert, 1926-
xMeyer, Charles R.
How to Be a Clown. McKay.
How to Be a Juggler. McKay.
How to Be an Acrobat. McKay.
Touch of God: A Theological Analysis of
Religious Experience. Alba.

Meyer, Clarence.
xMeyer, Clarence.
American Folk Medicine. Formur Intl.
American Folk Medicine. NAL.

Meyer, Daniel P.
xMeyer, Daniel P.
Radar Target Detection: Handbook of Theory
& Practice. Acad Pr.

Meyer, David B., 1923-
xMeyer, David B.
Laboratory Guide for Human Histology.
Wayne St U Pr.

Meyer, David R.
xMeyer, David R.
From Farm to Factory to Urban Pastoralism:
Urban Change in Central Connecticut.
Ballinger Pub.
Spatial Variation of Black Urban Households.
U Chicago Dept Geog.

Meyer, Donald. *see* Meyer, Donald B.

Meyer, Donald B.
xMeyer, Donald.
The Positive Thinkers: Religion As Pop
Psychology from Mary Baker Eddy to Oral
Roberts. Pantheon.
xMeyer, Donald B.
The Protestant Search for Political Realism,
1919-1941. Greenwood.

Meyer, Donald H. *see* Meyer, Donald Harvey.

Meyer, Donald Harvey, 1935-
xMeyer, Donald H.
The Instructed Conscience: The Shaping of the
American National Ethic. U of Pa Pr.

Meyer, Duane. *see* Meyer, Duane Gilbert.

Meyer, Duane Gilbert, 1926-
xMeyer, Duane.
Highland Scots of North Carolina. NC Archives.
Highland Scots of North Carolina, 1732-1776. U of NC Pr.

Meyer, Edith M.
xMeyer, Edith M.
Enjoying Food on a Diabetic Diet. Doubleday.

Meyer, Edith P. *see* Meyer, Edith Patterson.

Meyer, Edith Patterson.
xMeyer, Edith P.
In Search of Peace: The Winners of the Nobel Peace Prize, 1901-1975. Abingdon.

Meyer, Eugene, 1938-
xMeyer, Eugene.
Chemistry of Hazardous Materials. P-H.
Introduction to Modern Chemistry. P-H.
Research in the Psychobiology of Human Behavior. Johns Hopkins.

Meyer, F. B. *see* Meyer, Frederick Brotherton.

Meyer, Frank S.
xMeyer, Frank S.
ed. Breathes There the Man: Heroic Ballads & Poems of the English-Speaking Peoples. Open Court.

Meyer, Fred. *see* Meyer, Fred A.

Meyer, Fred A.
xMeyer, Fred.
ed. Determinants of Law Enforcement Policies. Lexington Bks.

Meyer, Frederick B. *see* Meyer, Frederick Brotherton.

Meyer, Frederick Brotherton, 1847-1929
xMeyer, F. B.
Devotional Commentary on Philippians. Kregel.
Secrets of Christian Living. Good News.
Shepherd Psalm. Chr Lit.
The Shepherd Psalm. Moody.
xMeyer, Frederick B.
The Shepherd Psalm. Kregel.

Meyer, George A.
xMeyer, George A.
The Two Word Verb: A Dictionary of the Verb Preposition Phrases in American English. Mouton.

Meyer, Gunter H.
xMeyer, Gunther H.
Initial Value Methods for Boundary Value Problems: Theory & Applications of Invariant Imbedding. Acad Pr.

Meyer, Gunther H. *see* Meyer, Gunter H.

Meyer, Harvey K. *see* Meyer, Harvey Kessler.

Meyer, Harvey Kessler, 1914-
xMeyer, Harvey K.
Historical Dictionary of Honduras. Scarecrow.
Historical Dictionary of Nicaragua. Scarecrow.

Meyer, Hazel.
xMeyer, Hazel.
Complete Book of Home Freezing. Lippincott.
The Gold in Tin Pan Alley. Greenwood.

Meyer, Henry I.
xMeyer, Henry I.
Corporate Financial Planning Models. Wiley.
The Face of Business. Am Mgmt.

Meyer, Herbert E., 1945-
xMeyer, Herbert E.
The War Against Progress. Storm King.

Meyer, Hermine H. *see* Meyer, Hermine Herta.

Meyer, Hermine Herta.
xMeyer, Hermine H.
The History & Meaning of the Fourteenth Amendment: Judicial Erosion of the Constitution Through the Misuse of the Fourteenth Amendment. Vantage.

Meyer, Jerome. *see* Meyer, Jerome Sydney.

Meyer, Jerome Sydney, 1895-
xMeyer, Jerome.
Puzzle, Quiz & Stunt Fun. Dover.

Meyer, Joachim E. *see* Meyer, Joachim Ernst.

Meyer, Joachim Ernst.
xMeyer, Joachim E.
Death & Neurosis. Intl Univs Pr.

Meyer, John.
xMeyer, John.
Nightchild. PB.

Meyer, John L.
xMeyer, John L.
Get the Right Person for the Job: Managing Interviews & Selecting Employees. P-H.

Meyer, John R. *see* Meyer, John Robert.

Meyer, John Robert.
xMeyer, John R.
ed. Local Public Finance & the Fiscal Squeeze: A Case Study. Ballinger Pub.

Meyer, John S., 1930-
xMeyer, John S.
Review of Pathology. Mosby.

Meyer, John W.
xMeyer, John W.
ed. National Development & the World System: Educational, Economic, & Political Change, 1950-1970. U of Chicago Pr.

Meyer, Jose. *see* Meyer, Jose Maria.

Meyer, Jose Maria.
xMeyer, Jose.
ed. Official Publications of European Governments: An Outline Bibliography of Serials & Important Monographs. B Franklin.

Meyer, Judith W. *see* Meyer, Judith Wangerin.

Meyer, Judith Wangerin, 1943-
xMeyer, Judith W.
Diffusion of an American Montessori Education. U Chicago Dept Geog.

Meyer, Judy A., 1950-
xMeyer, Judy A.
Sewing Dictionary. A S Barnes.

Meyer, Kathleen A. *see* Meyer, Kathleen Allan.

Meyer, Kathleen Allan.
xMeyer, Kathleen A.
Lili. Dillon.

Meyer, Lawrence, 1941-
xMeyer, Lawrence.
A Capitol Crime. Avon.
False Front. Popular Lib.
False Front. Viking Pr.

Meyer, Leo A.
xMeyer, Leo A.
Sheet Metal Layout. McGraw.

Meyer, Leonard B.
xMeyer, Leonard B.
Explaining Music: Essays & Explorations. U of Cal Pr.
Explaining Music: Essays & Explorations. U of Chicago Pr.

Meyer, Lewis, 1913-
xMeyer, Lewis.
Off the Sauce. Macmillan.

Meyer, Lynn.
xMeyer, Lynn.
Paperback Thriller. Avon.

Meyer, M. W. *see* Meyer, Marhsall W.

Meyer, Marhsall W.
xMeyer, M. W.
Change in Public Bureaucracies. Cambridge U Pr.

Meyer, Marshall W.
xMeyer, Marshall W.
Theory of Organizational Structure. Bobbs.

Meyer, Martin. *see* Meyer, Martin J.

Meyer, Martin J.
xMeyer, Martin.
Don't Bank on It. Farnswth Pub.

Meyer, Marvin C. *see* Meyer, Marvin Clinton.

Meyer, Marvin Clinton.
xMeyer, Marvin C.
Essentials of Parasitology. Wm C Brown.

Meyer, Mary K. *see* Meyer, Mary Keysor.

Meyer, Mary Keysor.
xMeyer, Mary K.
ed. Genealogical Research in Maryland: A Guide. Md Hist.

Meyer, Merle. *see* Meyer, Merle E.

Meyer, Merle E.
xMeyer, Merle.
ed. Foundations of Contemporary Psychology. Oxford U Pr.

Meyer, Michael A.
xMeyer, Michael A.
ed. Ideas of Jewish History. Behrman.
The Origins of the Modern Jew: Jewish Identity & European Culture in Germany, 1749-1824. Wayne St U Pr.

Meyer, Michael C.
xMeyer, Michael C.
ed. Supplement to a Bibliography of United States-Latin American Relations Since 1810. U of Nebr Pr.

Meyer, Michael R.
xMeyer, Michael R.
The Astrology of Relationship: A Humanistic Approach to the Practice of Synastry. Doubleday.

Meyer, Milton W. *see* Meyer, Milton Walter.

Meyer, Milton Walter.
xMeyer, Milton W.
China: An Introductory History. Littlefield.
China: An Introductory History. Rowman.
South Asia: A Short History of the Subcontinent. Littlefield.

Meyer, Mitchell.
xMeyer, Mitchell.
Dental Insurance Plans. Conference Bd.
Profile of Employee Benefits. Conference Bd.
Women & Employee Benefits. Conference Bd.

Meyer, Paul Richard.
xMeyer, Paulr.
ed. Papers in Mathematics. NY Acad Sci.

Meyer, Paulr. *see* Meyer, Paul Richard.

Meyer, Philip.
xMeyer, Phillip.
Precision Journalism: A Reporter's Introduction to Social Science Methods. Ind U Pr.

Meyer, Phillip. *see* Meyer, Philip.

Meyer, Priscilla.
xMeyer, Priscilla.
ed. Dostoevsky & Gogol: Texts & Criticism. Ardis Pubs.

Meyer, R. G. *see* Meyer, Robert G.

Meyer, Richard A.
xMeyer, Richard A.
Pediatric Echocardiography. Lea & Febiger.

Meyer, Richard E., 1919-
xMeyer, Richard E.
Introduction to Mathematical Fluid Dynamics. Wiley.

Meyer, Richard H. *see* Meyer, Richard Hemmig.

Meyer, Richard Hemmig.
xMeyer, Richard H.
Bankers' Diplomacy: Monetary Stabilization in the Twenties. Columbia U Pr.

Meyer, Robert A.
xMeyer, Robert A.
Problems in Macroeconomics. HM.
Problems in Price Theory. HM.

Meyer, Robert G., 1942-
xMeyer, R. G.
Integrated-Circuit Operational Amplifiers. Wiley.
xMeyer, Robert G.
ed. Integrated Circuit Operational Amplifiers. Inst Electrical.

Meyer, Robert H. *see* Meyer, Robert Holt.

Meyer, Robert Holt, 1934-
xMeyer, Robert H.
Anatomy of a Theme. Glencoe.

Meyer, Roy W. *see* Meyer, Roy Willard.

Meyer, Roy Willard, 1925-
xMeyer, Roy W.

History of the Santee Sioux: United States
Indian Policy on Trial. U of Nebr Pr.

Meyer, Stuart L., 1937-
xMeyer, Stuart L.
Data Analysis for Scientists & Engineers.
Wiley.

Meyer, Thomas. *see* Meyer, Tom.

Meyer, Tom.
xMeyer, Thomas.
Staves Calends Legends. Jargon Soc.

Meyer, Ursula, 1915-
xMeyer, Ursula.
Conceptual Art. Dutton.

Meyer, William J.
xMeyer, William J.
Public Good & Political Authority: A
Pragmatic Proposal. Kennikat.

Meyer, William R., 1949-
xMeyer, William R.
The Film Buff's Catalog. Arlington Hse.
The Making of the Great Westerns. Arlington
Hse.

Meyer-Arendt, Jurgen. *see* Meyer-Arendt, Jurgen R.

Meyer-Arendt, Jurgen R.
xMeyer-Arendt, Jurgen.
Introduction to Classical & Modern Optics.
P-H.

Meyer-Rey, Ingeborg.
xMeyer-Rey, Ingeborg.
Silly Goose. Carolrhoda Bks.

Meyering, Ralph A.
xMeyering, Ralph A.
Uses of Test Data in Counseling. HM.

Meyerink, George, 1908-
xMeyerink, George.
Appliance Service Handbook. P-H.

Meyerowitz, Eva (Lewin-Richter), 1899-
xMeyerowitz, Eva L.
At the Court of an African King. Humanities.

Meyerowitz, Eva L. *see* Meyerowitz, Eva
(Lewin-Richter).

Meyerowitz, Patricia.
xMeyerowitz, Patricia.
Making Jewelry & Sculpture Through Unit
Construction. Dover.

Meyers, Augustus, 1841-
xMeyers, Augustus.
Ten Years in the Ranks U. S. Army. Arno.

Meyers, C. Edward. *see* Meyers, Charles Edward.

Meyers, Carlton R.
xMeyers, Carlton R.
Measurement in Physical Education. Wiley.

Meyers, Carole T. *see* Meyers, Carole Terwilliger.

Meyers, Carole Terwilliger.
xMeyers, Carole T.
Eating Out with the Kids in San Francisco &
the Bay Area. Carousel Pr.
How to Organize a Babysitting Cooperative &
Get Some Free Time Away from the Kids.
Carousel Pr.

Meyers, Charles Edward, 1912-
xMeyers, C. Edward.
ed. Quality of Life in Severely & Profoundly
Mentally Retarded People: Research
Foundations for Improvement. Am Assn
Mental.

Meyers, Chet.
xMeyers, Chet.
Catching Fish. Dillon.

Meyers, Frederic.
xMeyers, Frederic.
Ownership of Jobs: A Comparative Study. U
Cal LA Indus Rel.

Meyers, Frederick H.
xMeyers, Frederick H.
Review of Medical Pharmacology. Lange.

Meyers, Jeff.
xMeyers, Jeff.

Dallas Cowboys. Macmillan.

Meyers, Jeffrey.
xMeyers, Jeffrey.
George Orwell: An Annotated Bibliography of
Criticism. Garland Pub.
ed. George Orwell: The Critical Heritage.
Routledge & Kegan.
Homosexuality & Literature: 1890-1930.
McGill-Queens U Pr.
Katherine Mansfield: A Biography. New
Directions.
A Reader's Guide to George Orwell.
Littlefield.
T. E. Lawrence: A Bibliography. Garland Pub.

Meyers, L. *see* Meyers, L. Donald.

Meyers, L. Donald.
xMeyers, L.
Expanding the Living Space in Your Home: A
Guide to Remodeling Basements,
Attics,Garages and Porches. Reston.
xMeyers, L. Donald.
Furniture Repair & Refinishing. Reston.
Guide for Outdoor Building & Maintenance.
Reston.

Meyers, Lester, 1902-
xMeyers, Lester.
High-Speed Math. Krieger.

Meyers, Manny, 1930-
xMeyers, Manny.
The Last Mystery of Edgar Allan Poe: The
Troy Dossier. Lippincott.

Meyers, Marvin.
xMeyers, Marvin.
Sources of the American Republic: A
Documentary History of Politics, Society &
Thought. Scott F.

Meyers, Perla.
xMeyers, Perla.
The Peasant Kitchen: A Return to Simple,
Good Food. Har-Row.
Perla Meyer's Market-to-Kitchen Cookbook.
Har-Row.

Meyers, R. A. *see* Meyers, Robert A.

Meyers, Richard.
xMeyers, Richard.
The World of Fantasy Films. A S Barnes.

Meyers, Robert.
xMeyers, Robert.
Like Normal People. McGraw.
Like Normal People. NAL.

Meyers, Robert A., 1936-
xMeyers, R. A.
Coal Desulfurization. Dekker.

Meyers, Rose, 1918-
xMeyers, Rose.
A History of Baton Rouge, 1699-1812. La
State U Pr.

Meyers, Susan.
xMeyers, Susan.
The Truth About Gorillas. Dutton.

Meyers, W. *see* Meyers, William.

Meyers, Walter E. *see* Meyers, Walter Earl.

Meyers, Walter Earl.
xMeyers, Walter E.
Handbook of Contemporary English.
HarBraceJ.

Meyers, William.
xMeyers, W.
ed. Conversion from War to Peace: Social,
Economic, & Political Problems. Gordon.

Meyerson, Edward L. *see* Meyerson, Edward Leon.

Meyerson, Edward Leon.
xMeyerson, Edward L.
Chameleon. Branden.

Meyerson, Martin.
xMeyerson, Martin.

Boston: The Job Ahead. Harvard U Pr.
ed. The Conscience of the City. Braziller.
Gladly Learn & Gladly Teach: Franklin & His
Heirs at the University of Pennsylvania,
1740-1976. U of Pa Pr.
Housing, People, & Cities. McGraw.

Meyerstein, Edward H. *see* Meyerstein, Edward Harry
William.

Meyerstein, Edward Harry William, 1889-1952
xMeyerstein, Edward H.
A Life of Thomas Chatterton. R West.
A Life of Thomas Chatterton. Russell.

Meynell, Alice. *see* Meynell, Alice Christiana Thompson.

Meynell, Alice C. *see* Meynell, Alice Christiana
Thompson.

Meynell, Alice Christiana Thompson, 1847-1922
xMeynell, Alice.
The Rhythm of Life, & Other Essays. Arden
Lib.
xMeynell, Alice C.
Ceres' Runaway & Other Essays. Arno.
The Poems of Alice Meynell. Hyperion Conn.
Prose & Poetry. Arno.

Meynell, Elinor. *see* Meynell, Geoffrey Guy.

Meynell, Esther. *see* Meynell, Esther Hallam
(Moorhouse).

Meynell, Esther Hallam (Moorhouse).
xMeynell, Esther.
Little Chronicle of Magdalena Bach. Ungar.

Meynell, Everard.
xMeynell, Everard.
Life of Francis Thompson. R West.
Life of Francis Thompson. Scholarly.

Meynell, Francis, Sir, 1891-
xMeynell, Francis.
English Printed Books. Folcroft.
English Printed Books. R West.

Meynell, G. G. *see* Meynell, Geoffrey Guy.

Meynell, Geoffrey Guy.
xMeynell, Elinor.
jt. auth. Theory & Practice in Experimental
Bacteriology. Cambridge U Pr.
xMeynell, G. G.
Theory & Practice in Experimental
Bacteriology. Cambridge U Pr.

Meynell, Laurence. *see* Meynell, Laurence Walter.

Meynell, Laurence Walter, 1899-
xMeynell, Laurence.
The Thirteen Trumpeters. Stein & Day.

Meyners, Robert.
xMeyners, Robert.
Sexual Style: Facing & Making Choices About
Sex. HarBraceJ.
Solomon's Sword: Clarifying Values in the
Church. Abingdon.

Meyst, Lucille.
xMeyst, Lucille.
Tyler Lane & the Gold Nugget Mystery.
Moody.

Mez, Adam, 1869-1917
xMez, Adam.
The Renaissance of Islam. AMS Pr.

Mezer, Robert R.
xMezer, Robert R.
Dynamic Psychiatry in Simple Terms. Springer
Pub.

Mezerik, Avrahm G, 1901-
xMezerik, Avrahm G.
ed. Arab Refugees in the Middle East. Intl
Review.
ed. Industrialization of Underdeveloped
Countries. Intl Review.

Mezey, Mathy D. *see* Mezey, Mathy Doval.

Mezey, Mathy Doval.
xMezey, Mathy D.
Health Assessment of the Older Individual.
Springer Pub.

Mi Mi Khaing, Daw.
xMi Mi Khaing, Daw.

Burmese Family. AMS Pr.
Miall, A. B. see Miall, Bernard.
Miall, Antony.
xMiall, Antony.
The Victorian Christmas Book. Pantheon.
xMiall, Peter.
jt. auth. The Victorian Christmas Book.
Pantheon.
Miall, Bernard, 1876-
xMiall, A. B.
Nocturnes & Pastorals. Garland Pub.
Miall, Laurence M. see Miall, Stephen.
Miall, Peter. see Miall, Antony.
Miall, Stephen.
xMiall, Laurence M.
jt. auth. Chemistry, Matter, & Life. Arno.
xMiall, Stephen.
Chemistry, Matter, & Life. Arno.
Miami Symposium on the Prediction of Behavior,
University of Miami, 1968.
xMiami Symposium on the Prediction of Behavior,
1968.
Aversive Stimulation. U of Miami Pr.
Effects of Early Experience. U of Miami Pr.
Miaso, Jozef.
xMiaso, Jozef.
The History of the Education of Polish
Immigrants in the United States. Kosciuszko.
Micarelli, Charles N.
xMicarelli, Charles N.
Manual & Identification Guide to the United
States Regular Issues 1847 Through 1934.
Adriatic Stamp.
Miceli, Vincent P., 1915-
xMiceli, Vincent P.
Gods of Atheism. Arlington Hse.
Micha, Rene.
xMicha, Rene.
Jean Helion. Crown.
Michael, A. M. see Michael, Arayathinal Michael.
Michael, Arayathinal Michael, 1930-
xMichael, A. M.
Irrigation: Theory & Practice. Advent Bk.
Michael, Arnold, 1906-
xMichael, Arnold.
Brothers of the Grape. De Vorss.
Michael, David J., 1944-
xMichael, David J.
Death Tour. Bobbs.
Death Tour. NAL.
Michael, F. see Michael, Franz H.
Michael, Franz. see Michael, Franz H.
Michael, Franz H.
xMichael, F.
The Far East in the Modern World. HR&W.
xMichael, Franz.
The Taiping Rebellion: History & Documents.
U of Wash Pr.
Michael, Henry N.
xMichael, Henry N.
Neolithic Age in Eastern Siberia. Am Philos.
Michael, Ian.
xMichael, Ian.
Gwyn Thomas. Verry.
Michael, Jerome.
xMichael, Jerome.
Crime Law & Social Science. Patterson Smith.
Michael, Paul.
xMichael, Paul.
The Academy Awards: A Pictorial History.
Crown.
Michael, Robert T.
xMichael, Robert T.
The Effect of Education on Efficiency in
Consumption. Natl Bur Econ Res.
Michael, Tom.
xMichael, Tom.
How to Cope in a Computer Age Without
Pulling the Plug. Friend Pr.
Michael, William B. see Michael, William Burton.

Michael, William Burton.
xMichael, William B.
ed. Teaching for Creative Endeavor: Bold New
Venture. AMS Pr.
Michaelis, Bill.
xMichaelis, Bill.
jt. auth. Learning Through Noncompetitive
Activities & Play. Pitman Learning.
xMichaelis, Dolores.
Learning Through Noncompetitive Activities &
Play. Pitman Learning.
Michaelis, Dolores. see Michaelis, Bill.
Michaelis, Johann D. see Michaelis, Johann David.
Michaelis, Johann David, 1717-1791
xMichaelis, Johann D.
Dissertation on the Influence of Opinions on
Language & of Language on Opinions. AMS
Pr.
Michaelis, John. see Michaelis, John Udell.
Michaelis, John Udell, 1912-
xMichaelis, John.
Social Studies for Children: A Guide to Basic
Instruction. P-H.
Michaelis, Meir.
xMichaelis, Meir.
Mussolini & the Jews: German-Italian
Relations & the Jewish Question in Italy
1922-1945. Oxford U Pr.
Michaels, Barbara, 1927-
xMichaels, Barbara.
Wait for What Will Come. Dodd.
Wait for What Will Come. Fawcett.
Wait for What Will Come. G K Hall.
The Walker in Shadows. Dodd.
The Walker in Shadows. G K Hall.
Michaels, Kristin.
xMichaels, Kristin.
A Special Kind of Love. NAL.
Michaels, Leonard, 1933-
xMichaels, Leonard.
Going Places. FS&G.
I Would Have Saved Them If I Could. FS&G.
ed. The State of the Language. U of Cal Pr.
Michaels, Richard M.
xMichaels, Richard M.
Transportation Planning & Policy Decision
Making: Behavioral Science Contributions.
Praeger.
Michaelsen, Katherine J. see Michaelsen, Katherine
Janszky.
Michaelsen, Katherine Janszky, 1944-
xMichaelsen, Katherine J.
Archipenko: A Study of the Early Works,
1908-1920. Garland Pub.
Michaelson, John.
xMichaelson, John.
Tackle Angling. Soccer.
Michaelson, M.
xMichaelson, M.
Metric System & Metric Conversion: A
Checklist of References. Minn Scholarly.
Michaelson, Mike.
xMichaelson, Mike.
Canoeing. Contemp Bks.
The Great Tomato Cookbook. Condor Pub Co.
The Great Tomato Cookbook. Contemp Bks.
The Quick & Delicious Soup Book. Chicago
Review.
Michalak, Donald F.
xMichalak, Donald F.
Making the Training Process Work. Har-Row.
Michalek, Irene R.
xMichalek, Irene R.
When Mercy Seasons Justice: The Spock Trial.
Branden.
Michalopoulos, Andre, 1897-
xMichalopoulos, Andre.
Homer. St Martin.
Homer. Twayne.
Michalos, A. see Michalos, Alex C.

Michalos, Alex C.
xMichalos, A.
Improving Your Reasoning. P-H.
Michalson, G. E.
xMichalson, G. E.
The Historical Dimensions of Rational Faith:
The Role of History in Kant's Religious
Thought. U Pr of Amer.
Michanowsky, George.
xMichanowsky, George.
The Once & Future Star. B&N.
Michaud, Joseph F. see Michaud, Joseph Francois.
Michaud, Joseph Francois, 1767-1839
xMichaud, Joseph F.
History of the Crusades. AMS Pr.
Michaud, Regis, 1880-1939
xMichaud, Regis.
The American Novel To-Day: A Social &
Psychological Study. Greenwood.
Michaud, Roland.
xMichaud, Roland.
illus. Caravans to Tartary. Viking Pr.
xMichaud, Sabrina.
jt. illus. & jt. auth. Caravans to Tartary. Viking
Pr.
Michaud, Sabrina. see Michaud, Roland.
Michaux, Andre, 1746-1802
xMichaux, Andre.
Flora Boreali - Americana. Hafner.
Michaux, Henri, 1899-
xMichaux, Henri.
Ecuador: A Travel Journal. U of Wash Pr.
Micheaux, Oscar, 1884-
xMicheaux, Oscar.
The Case of Mrs. Wingate. AMS Pr.
Conquest: The Story of a Negro Pioneer. Arno.
Conquest: The Story of a Negro Pioneer.
Mnemosyne.
The Masquerade: An Historical Novel. AMS
Pr.
Micheels, William Jordan.
xMicheels, William M.
Measuring Educational Achievement. McGraw.
Micheels, William M. see Micheels, William Jordan.
Michel. see Michel, Anna.
Michel, Aloys A. see Michel, Aloys Arthur.
Michel, Aloys Arthur.
xMichel, Aloys A.
Indus Rivers: A Study of the Effects of
Partition. Yale U Pr.
Michel, Anna.
xMichel.
Little Wild Chimpanzee. Schol Bk Serv.
xMichel, Anna.
Little Wild Chimpanzee. Pantheon.
Little Wild Elephant. Pantheon.
Michel, Anthony N.
xMichel, Anthony N.
Qualitative Analysis of Large Scale Dynamical
Systems. Acad Pr.
Michel, D. see Michel, Dana.
Michel, Dana.
xMichel, D.
Cat in the Box. Wonder.
Michel, Donald E.
xMichel, Donald E.
Music Therapy: An Introduction to Therapy &
Special Education Through Music. C C
Thomas.
Michel, L. A. see Michel, Lois A.
Michel, Laurence. see Michel, Laurence Anthony.
Michel, Laurence Anthony.
xMichel, Laurence.
Thing Contained: Theory of the Tragic. Ind U
Pr.
Michel, Lois A.
xMichel, L. A.
Another Way Out: A Thematic Reader.
HR&W.
Michel, Timothy. see Michel, Timothy M.

Michel, Timothy M.
  xMichel, Timothy.
    Homeowners' Guide to Landscape Design.
    Countryman.
Michelet, Jules.
  xMichelet, Jules.
    History of the French Revolution. U of
    Chicago Pr.
    The People. Gordon Pr.
    The People. U of Ill Pr.
Michelin. see Michelin Tyre Company, Ltd.
Michelin Tyre Company, Ltd.
  xMichelin.
    Michelin Green Guide London. Michelin.
    Michelin Green Guide Rome. Michelin.
    Michelin Green Guide to Hollande. Michelin.
    Michelin Green Guide to Provence Eng..
    Michelin.
Michell, George.
  xMichell, George.
    The Hindu Temple: An Introduction to Its
    Meaning & Forms. Har-Row.
Michell, Humfrey, 1883-
  xMichell, Humphrey.
    Sparta. Cambridge U Pr.
Michell, Humphrey. see Michell, Humfrey.
Michell, John. see Michell, John F.
Michell, John F.
  xMichell, John.
    Natural Likeness: Faces & Figures in Nature.
    Dutton.
    Secrets of the Stones: The Story of
    Astro-Archaeology. Penguin.
Michell, Lewis, Sir, 1842-1928
  xMichell, Lewis.
    The Life & Times of the Right Honourable
    Cecil John Rhodes, 1853-1902. Arno.
    Life & Times of the Right Honourable Cecil
    John Rhodes, 1853-1902. Negro U Pr.
Michelman, Irving S.
  xMichelman, Irving S.
    Consumer Finance: A Case History in
    American Business. Kelley.
Michelozzi, Betty N. see Michelozzi, Betty Neville.
Michelozzi, Betty Neville.
  xMichelozzi, Betty N.
    Coming Alive from Nine to Five: The Career
    Search Handbook. Mayfield Pub.
Michels, Agnes K. see Michels, Agnes Kirsopp.
Michels, Agnes Kirsopp.
  xMichels, Agnes K.
    The Calendar of the Roman Republic.
    Greenwood.
Michels, Joseph W.
  xMichels, Joseph W.
    Dating Methods in Archaeology. Acad Pr.
    The Kaminaljuyu Chiefdom. Pa St U Pr.
Michels, Robert, 1876-1936
  xMichels, Robert.
    Political Parties: A Sociological Study of the
    Oligarchical Tendencies of Modern
    Democracy. Peter Smith.
  xMichels, Roberto.
    First Lectures in Political Sociology. Arno.
Michels, Roberto. see Michels, Robert.
Michels, Rudolf K. see Michels, Rudolf Karl.
Michels, Rudolf Karl, 1901-
  xMichels, Rudolf K.
    Cartels, Combines & Trusts in Post-War
    Germany. AMS Pr.
Michels, Tim.
  xMichels, Timothy I.
    Solar Energy Utilization. Van Nos Reinhold.
Michels, Timothy I. see Michels, Tim.
Michelsohn, David R. see Michelsohn, David Reuben.
Michelsohn, David Reuben.
  xMichelsohn, David R.

Atomic Energy for Human Needs. Messner.
The Cities in Tomorrow's World: Challenges to
  Urban Survival. Messner.
Housing in Tomorrow's World. Messner.
Michelson, Albert A. see Michelson, Albert Abraham.
Michelson, Albert Abraham, 1852-1931
  xMichelson, Albert A.
    Studies in Optics. U of Chicago Pr.
Michelson, Herb.
  xMichelson, Herb.
    Almost a Famous Person. HarBraceJ.
Michelson, Peter.
  xMichelson, Peter.
    The Eater. Swallow.
Michelson, Truman, 1879-1938
  xMichelson, Truman.
    Contributions to Fox Ethnology. Scholarly.
Michelson, William. see Michelson, William M.
Michelson, William M., 1940-
  xMichelson, William.
    Environmental Choice, Human Behavior, &
    Residential Satisfaction. Oxford U Pr.
Michener, James. see Michener, James Albert.
Michener, James A. see Michener, James Albert.
Michener, James Albert, 1907-
  xMichener, James.
    Caravans. Fawcett.
  xMichener, James A.
    The Bridge at Andau. Fawcett.
    Bridge at Andau. Random.
    The Bridges at Toko-Ri. Fawcett.
    Bridges at Toko-Ri. Random.
    Caravans. Random.
    Centennial. Fawcett.
    Centennial. Random.
    Chesapeake. Fawcett.
    Chesapeake. Random.
    Modern Japanese Print: An Appreciation. C E
    Tuttle.
    Presidential Lottery: The Reckless Gamble in
    Our Electoral System. Random.
    Rascals in Paradise. Fawcett.
    Rascals in Paradise. Random.
    Return to Paradise. Fawcett.
    Return to Paradise. Random.
    Tales of the South Pacific. Fawcett.
Michie Co. see Michie Company, Charlottesville, Va.
Michie Company, Charlottesville, Va.
  xMichie Co.
    ed. Burns' Indiana Statutes Title Thirty Five.
    Bobbs.
  xMichie Editorial.
    Delaware Code: Annotated, Revised 1974.
    Michie.
  xMichie Editorial Staff.
    Code of Alabama 1975. Michie.
  xTheMichie Co.
    ed. Indiana Insurance Laws. Bobbs.
Michie Editorial. see Michie Company, Charlottesville,
  Va.
Michie Editorial Staff. see Michie Company,
  Charlottesville, Va.
Michie, Peter S. see Michie, Peter Smith.
Michie, Peter Smith, 1839-1901
  xMichie, Peter S.
    The Life & Letters of Emory Upton. Arno.
Michigan State University. East Lansing.
  xMichigan State University,(East Lansing).
    Dictionary Catalog of the G. Robert Vincent
    Library. G K Hall.
Michigan State University,(East Lansing). see Michigan
  State University. East Lansing.
Michigan. University.
  xUniversity of Michigan.
    ed. Catalogs of the Asia Library, the University
    of Michigan. G K Hall.
    Research Catalog of Maps of America to 1860
    in the William L. Clements Library. G K
    Hall.
  xUniversity of Michigan, Ann Arbor.

Author-Title & Chronological Catalogs of
  Americana, 1493-1860, in the William L.
  Clements Library, University of Michigan,
  Ann Arbor. G K Hall.
**Michigan. University. Center for Programmed Learning
of Business.**
  xCenter For Programmed Learning For Business.
    Retail Salesmanship. A-W.
Michigan. University. Department of English.
  xMembers of English Dept. of University of
    Michigan.
    Essays & Studies in English. Century
    Bookbindery.
  xMichigan University Department of English.
    Studies in Shakespeare, Milton & Donne.
    Haskell.
Michigan. University. English Language Institute.
  xEnglish Language Institute.
    English Conversation Practices. U of Mich Pr.
    English Pattern Practices: Establishing the
    Patterns As Habits. U of Mich Pr.
    Vocabulary in Context. U of Mich Pr.
Michigan. University. Greenland Expeditions 1926-1933.
  xMichigan University Greenland Expeditions
    1926-1933.
    Reports of the Greenland Expeditions of the
    University of Michigan. Greenwood.
Michigan. University. Survey Research Center.
  xStaff of the Survey Research Center.
    Interviewer's Manual. U of Mich Soc Res.
Michman, Ronald. see Michman, Ronald D.
Michman, Ronald D.
  xMichman, Ronald.
    Marketing Channel Strategy: A Selected &
    Annotated Bibliography. Am Mktg.
    Marketing Channels. Grid Pub.
  xMichman, Ronald D.
    ed. Market Segmentation: A Selected &
    Annotated Bibliography. Am Mktg.
    Marketing Channels & Strategies. Grid Pub.
    Strategic Advertising Decisions: Selected
    Readings. Grid Pub.
Michon, J. A. see Michon, John Albertus.
Michon, John Albertus.
  xMichon, J. A.
    ed. Handbook of Psychonomics. Elsevier.
Michor, P. W. see Michor, Peter W.
Michor, Peter W., 1949-
  xMichor, P. W.
    Functors & Categories of Banach Spaces:
    Tensor Products, Operator Ideals & Functors
    on Categories of Banach Spaces.
    Springer-Verlag.
Mick, John.
  xMick, John.
    Bit-Slice Microprocessor Design. McGraw.
Mickel, John.
  xMickel, John.
    The Home Gardener's Book of Ferns. HR&W.
  xMickel, John T.
    How to Know the Ferns & Fern Allies. Wm C
    Brown.
Mickel, John T. see Mickel, John.
Mickelson, Anne Z.
  xMickelson, Anne Z.
    Reaching Out: Sensitivity & Order in Recent
    American Fiction by Women. Scarecrow.
    Thomas Hardy's Women & Men: The Defeat
    of Nature. Scarecrow.
Mickelson, Joel C.
  xMickelson, Joel C.
    Images of the American City in the Arts.
    Kendall-Hunt.
Mickelwait, Donald R.
  xMickelwait, Donald R.
    ed. New Directions in Development: Study of
    U. S. Aid. Westview.
Micklem, Nathaniel, 1888-
  xMicklem, Nathaniel.

Religion. Greenwood.
Micklish, Rita.
  xMicklish, Rita.
    Sugar Bee. Delacorte.
Micks, Marianne H.
  xMicks, Marianne H.
    Future Present: The Phenomenon of Christian
      Worship. Seabury.
Micks, Wilson, 1898-
  xMicks, Wilson.
    Review of Basic French. Oxford U Pr.
Microfilming Corporation of America.
  xMicrofilming Corporation of America.
    Columbia University Oral History Collection:
      An Index to the Memoirs in Part 1 of the
      Microform Edition. Arno.
Micunovic, Veljko, 1916-
  xMicunovic, Veljko.
    Moscow Diary. Doubleday.
Middendorf, J. H. *see* Middendorf, John Harlan.
Middendorf, John Harlan, 1922-
  xMiddendorf, J. H.
    ed. English Writers of the Eighteenth Century.
      Columbia U Pr.
Middendorff, Wolf.
  xMiddendorff, Wolf.
    Effectiveness of Punishment, Especially in
      Relation to Traffic Offenses. Rothman.
Middlebrook, Diane. *see* Middlebrook, Diane Wood.
Middlebrook, Diane Wood.
  xMiddlebrook, Diane.
    Worlds into Words: Understanding Modern
      Poems. Norton.
Middlebrook, Patricia N. *see* Middlebrook, Patricia Niles.
Middlebrook, Patricia Niles.
  xMiddlebrook, Patricia N.
    Social Psychology & Modern Life. Knopf.
Middlebrook, Stanley M. *see* Middlebrook, Stanley
  Musgrave.
Middlebrook, Stanley Musgrave.
  xMiddlebrook, Stanley M.
    How Malaya Is Governed. AMS Pr.
Middlehurst, Barbara M.
  xMiddlehurst, Barbara M.
    ed. Nebulae & Interstellar Matter. U of
      Chicago Pr.
Middlekauff, Robert.
  xMiddlekauff, Robert.
    Ancients & Axioms: Secondary Education in
      Eighteenth-Century New England. Arno.
    Mathers: Three Generations of Puritan
      Intellectuals, 1596-1728. Oxford U Pr.
    The Mathers: Three Generations of Puritan
      Intellectuals, 1596-1728. Oxford U Pr.
Middlekauff, Woodrow W. *see* Middlekauff, Woodrow
  Wilson.
Middlekauff, Woodrow Wilson, 1913-
  xMiddlekauff, Woodrow W.
    The Cephid Stem Borers of California
      (Hymenoptera: Cephidae). U of Cal Pr.
Middleman, Stanley.
  xMiddleman, Stanley.
    Fundamentals of Polymer Processing. McGraw.
Middlemas, Keith. *see* Middlemas, Robert Keith.
Middlemas, Robert Keith, 1935-
  xMiddlemas, Keith.
    The Pursuit of Pleasure. Gordon-Cremonesi.
    The Strategy of Appeasement: The British
      Government & Germany, 1937-1939. Times
      Bks.
Middlemiss, Robert.
  xMiddlemiss, Robert.
    The Lofoten Run. Fawcett.
    The Parrot Man. Fawcett.
Middlemiss, Ross R. *see* Middlemiss, Ross Raymond.
Middlemiss, Ross Raymond.
  xMiddlemiss, Ross R.
    Algebra for College Students. McGraw.
    Analytic Geometry. McGraw.
Middleton. *see* Middleton, Thomas.

Middleton, Bernard C., 1924-
  xMiddleton, Bernard C.
    Restoration of Leather Bindings. ALA.
Middleton, Charles R. *see* Middleton, Charles Ronald.
Middleton, Charles Ronald.
  xMiddleton, Charles R.
    The Administration of British Foreign Policy,
      1782-1846. Duke.
Middleton, Christopher.
  xMiddleton, Christopher.
    Bolshevism in Art & Other Expository
      Writings. Humanities.
    Nonsequences: Self Poems. Norton.
    Pataxanadu & Other Prose. Persea Bks.
Middleton, Drew, 1913-
  xMiddleton, Drew.
    Can America Win the Next War. Scribner.
    The Duel of the Giants: China & Russia in
      Asia. Scribner.
Middleton, Elliott.
  xMiddleton, Elliott.
    Allergy: Principles & Practice. Mosby.
Middleton, John, 1921-
  xMiddleton, John.
    ed. From Child to Adult: Studies in the
      Anthropology of Education. U of Tex Pr.
    ed. Gods & Rituals: Readings in Religious
      Beliefs & Practices. U of Tex Pr.
    Lugbara of Uganda. HR&W.
Middleton, John. *see* Middleton, John Francis
  Marchment.
Middleton, John Francis Marchment, 1921-
  xMiddleton, John.
    Lugbara Religion: Ritual & Authority Among
      an East African People. Oxford U Pr.
Middleton, Katharine.
  xMiddleton, Katharine.
    The Art of Cooking for the Diabetic. Contemp
      Bks.
  xMiddleton, Katharine.
    The Art of Cooking for the Diabetic. NAL.
Middleton, Katherine. *see* Middleton, Katharine.
Middleton, Lamar.
  xMiddleton, Lamar.
    Rape of Africa. Negro U Pr.
    Revolt, U. S. A. Arno.
Middleton, Lucy.
  xMiddleton, Lucy.
    ed. Women in the Labour Movement: The
      British Experience. Rowman.
Middleton, Richard. *see* Middleton, Richard Barham.
Middleton, Richard Barham.
  xMiddleton, Richard.
    Richard Middleton's Letters to Henry Savage.
      Lib Serv Inc.
    Richard Middleton's Letters to Henry Savage.
      R West.
Middleton, Robert.
  xMiddleton, Robert.
    Negotiating on Non-Tariff Distortions of
      Trade: The EFTA Precedents. St Martin.
Middleton, Robert. *see* Middleton, Robert Gordon.
Middleton, Robert G. *see* Middleton, Robert Gordon.
Middleton, Robert Gordon, 1908-
  xMiddleton, Robert.
    Practical Electricity. Audel.
    Radiomans Guide. Audel.
  xMiddleton, Robert G.
    Tape Recorder Servicing Guide. Sams.
    Troubleshooting with the Oscilloscope. Sams.
    TV Troubleshooting & Repair. Hayden.
Middleton, Stanley, 1919-
  xMiddleton, Stanley.
    Ends & Means. Merrimack Bk Serv.
    Still Waters. Merrimack Bk Serv.
Middleton, Thomas.
  xMiddleton.
    A Chaste Maid in Cheapside. Norton.
    A Game at Chess. Norton.
  xMiddleton, Thomas.

A Chaste Maid in Cheapside. Johns Hopkins.
    Game at Chess. Hill & Wang.
    A Game of Chess. Humanities.
    No Wit, No Help Like a Woman's. U of Nebr
      Pr.
    Works of Thomas Middleton. AMS Pr.
Middleton, Thomas H. *see* Middleton, Thomas
  Hazlehurst.
Middleton, Thomas Hazlehurst, 1926-
  xMiddleton, Thomas H.
    Light Refractions. Stein & Day.
    Light Refractions. Verbatim.
Middleton, W. E. *see* Middleton, William Edgar
  Knowles.
Middleton, W. E. Knowles. *see* Middleton, William
  Edgar Knowles.
Middleton, William D., 1928-
  xMiddleton, William D.
    Grand Central ...the World's Greatest Railway
      Terminal. Golden West.
    Railroad Scene. Golden West.
    When the Steam Railroads Electrified.
      Kalmbach.
Middleton, William Edgar Knowles, 1902-
  xMiddleton, W. E.
    History of the Theories of Rain & Other Forms
      of Precipitation. U of Chicago Pr.
  xMiddleton, W. E. Knowles.
    The Experimenters: A Study of the Accademia
      del Cimento. Johns Hopkins.
    A History of the Thermometer & Its Use in
      Meteorology. Johns Hopkins.
Middleton, William S.
  xMiddleton, William S.
    Values in Modern Medicine. U of Wis Pr.
Mid-European Law Project.
  xMid-European Law Project.
    Church & State Behind the Iron Curtain.
      Greenwood.
Midgett, Elwin W.
  xMidgett, Elwin W.
    Accounting Primer. NAL.
Midgley, A. Rees. *see* Midgley, Alvin Rees.
Midgley, Alvin Rees.
  xMidgley, A. Rees.
    ed. Ovarian Follicular Development &
      Function. Raven.
Midgley, David A.
  xMidgley, David A.
    American History: Pre-Colonial to the Present
      Day. Barron.
Midgley, Kenneth.
  xMidgley, Kenneth.
    Garden Design. Merrimack Bk Serv.
Midgley, Mary, 1919-
  xMidgley, Mary.
    Beast & Man: The Roots of Human Nature.
      Cornell U Pr.
    Beast & Man: The Roots of Human Nature.
      NAL.
Midhat, Ali H. *see* Midhat, Ali Haydar.
Midhat, Ali Haydar.
  xMidhat, Ali H.
    The Life of Midhat Pasha. Arno.
Midkiff, Pat.
  xMidkiff, Pat.
    Colonial Furniture for Doll Houses &
      Miniature Rooms. Sterling.
Midlam, Don S.
  xMidlam, Don S.
    Flight of the Lucky Lady. Binford.
Midlarsky, Manus I.
  xMidlarsky, Manus I.
    On War: Political Violence in the International
      System. Free Pr.
Midler, Bette.
  xMidler, Bette.

A View from a Broad. S&S.

Midwest Conference on Ergodic Theory, 1st, Ohio State University, 1970.
xMidwestern Conference on Ergodic Theory, 1st, Ohio State Univ, 1970.
Contributions to Ergodic Theory & Probability: Proceedings. Springer-Verlag.

Midwest Council Association For Latin America - 1967. *see* Association for Latin American Studies. Midwest Council.

Midwest Marxist Scholars Conference.
xMidwest Marxist Scholars Conference.
Marxism & New Left Ideology: Proceedings. Marxist Educ.

Midwest Mechanics Conference.
xMidwestern Mechanics Conference.
Developments in Mechanics: Proceedings. U of Okla Pr.

Midwest Plan Service. *see* Midwest Plan Service, Ames, Iowa.

Midwest Plan Service, Ames, Iowa.
xMidwest Plan Service.
Midwest Plan Service Structures & Environment Handbook. Midwest Plan Serv.
Professional Design Supplement to the MWPS Structures & Environment Handbook. Midwest Plan Serv.

Midwestern Conference on Ergodic Theory, 1st, Ohio State Univ, 1970. *see* Midwest Conference on Ergodic Theory, 1st, Ohio State University, 1970.

Midwestern Mechanics Conference. *see* Midwest Mechanics Conference.

Midwinter, Eric. *see* Midwinter, Eric C.

Midwinter, Eric C.
xMidwinter, Eric.
Make 'em Laugh: Famous Comedians & Their Worlds. Allen Unwin.

Midwinter, John E.
xMidwinter, John E.
Optical Fibers for Transmission. Wiley.

Miedaner, Terrel.
xMiedaner, Terrel.
The Soul of Anna Klane. Ballantine.
The Soul of Anna Klane. Coward.

Miel, Alice, 1906-
xMiel, Alice.
Cooperative Procedures in Learning. Greenwood.

Mields, Hugh.
xMields, Hugh.
Federally Assisted New Communities: New Dimensions in Urban Development. Urban Land.

Miernyk, William H.
xMiernyk, William H.
Air Pollution Abatement & Regional Economic Development: An Input-Output Analysis. Lexington Bks.
Economics. Phila Bk Co.
Economics of Labor & Collective Bargaining. Heath.

Mierow, Charles C. *see* Mierow, Charles Christopher.

Mierow, Charles Christopher, 1883-
xMierow, Charles C.
Hallowed Flame. Trinity U Pr.

Miers, Earl J. *see* Miers, Earl Schenck.

Miers, Earl S. *see* Miers, Earl Schenck.

Miers, Earl Schenck, 1910-
xMiers, Earl J.
Pirate Chase. Williamsburg.
xMiers, Earl S.
The Great Rebellion: The Emergence of the American Conscience. Negro U Pr.

Miers, Suzanne.
xMiers, Suzanne.
Britain & the Ending of the Slave Trade. Holmes & Meier.

Miescher, Peter A.
xMiescher, Peter A.

ed. Textbook of Immunopathology. Grune.

Miessner, B. F. *see* Miessner, Benjamin Franklin.

Miessner, Benjamin Franklin, 1890-
xMiessner, B. F.
On the Early History of Radio Guidance. San Francisco Pr.

Mietus, Norbert J.
xMietus, Norbert J.
Personal Law. SRA.

Miewald, Robert D.
xMiewald, Robert D.
Public Administration: A Critical Perspective. McGraw.

Migdal, A. B. *see* Migdal, Arkadii Beinusovich.

Migdal, Arkadii B. *see* Migdal, Arkadii Beinusovich.

Migdal, Arkadii Beinusovich.
xMigdal, A. B.
Qualitative Methods in Quantum Theory. Benjamin-Cummings.
xMigdal, Arkadii B.
Approximation Methods of Quantum Mechanics. Neo Pr.

Migdal, Joel S.
xMigdal, Joel S.
Palestinian Society & Politics. Princeton U Pr.
Peasants, Politics, & Revolution: Pressures Toward Political & Social Change in the Third World. Princeton U Pr.

Migdalski, Edward C.
xMigdalski, Edward C.
Clay Target Games. Winchester Pr.

Migel, J. Michael.
xMigel, J. Michael.
ed. The Masters on the Dry Fly. Lippincott.
The Stream Conservation Handbook. Crown.
xMigel, Michael.
ed. The Masters on the Dry Fly. Follett.
xMigel, Michael J.
Masters on the Nymph. Doubleday.

Migel, Michael. *see* Migel, J. Michael.

Migel, Michael J. *see* Migel, J. Michael.

Migliore, Daniel L., 1935-
xMigliore, Daniel L.
Called to Freedom: Liberation Theology & the Future of Christian Doctrine. Westminster.

Migliorini, Mario.
xMigliorini, Mario.
Dachshunds. Arco.
German Shorthaired Pointers. Arco.
Secrets of Show Dog Handling. Arco.

Migraine Symposium, 1st, London, 1966.
xMigraine Symposium, 1st, London, 1966.
Background to Migraine: Proceedings. Springer-Verlag.

Mihailovic, Kosta.
xMihailovic, Kosta.
Regional Development: Experiences & Prospects in Eastern Europe. Mouton.

Mihailovich, Vasa D.
xMihailovich, Vasa D.
ed. Contemporary Yugoslav Poetry. U of Iowa Pr.

Mihalas, Dimitri, 1939-
xMihalas, Dimitri.
Stellar Atmospheres. W H Freeman.

Mihalek, R. J.
xMihalek, R. J.
Projective Geometry & Algebraic Structures. Acad Pr.

Mihaly, Mary E.
xMihaly, Mary E.
Getting Your Own Way: A Guide to Growing up Assertively. M Evans.

Mihalyi, Elemer.
xMihalyi, Elemer.
Application of Proteolytic Enzymes to Protein Structure Studies. CRC Pr.

Mihanovich, C. S. *see* Mihanovich, Clement Simon.

Mihanovich, Clement Simon, 1913-
xMihanovich, C. S.

Americanization of the Croats in Saint Louis Missouri During the Past Thirty Years. R & E Res Assoc.

Mikami, Y. *see* Mikami, Yoshio.

Mikami, Yoshio.
xMikami, Y.
The Development of Mathematics in China & Japan. Chelsea Pub.

Mikasinovich, Branko.
xMikasinovich, Branko.
ed. Modern Yugoslav Satire. Cross Cult.

Mikes, George.
xMikes, George.
Charlie: A Novel. Transatlantic.
How to Be Affluent. Heineman.

Mikesell, Raymond F. *see* Mikesell, Raymond Frech.

Mikesell, Raymond Frech.
xMikesell, Raymond F.
Foreign Dollar Balances & the International Role of the Dollar. Natl Bur Econ Res.
New Patterns of World Mineral Development. Natl Planning.
The Rate of Discount for Evaluating Public Projects. Am Enterprise.

Mikhail, E. H.
xMikhail, E. H.
ed. The Art of Brendan Behan. B&N.
Comedy & Tragedy: A Bibliography of Critical Studies. Whitston Pub.
Oscar Wilde: An Annotated Bibliography of Criticism. Rowman.
ed. Oscar Wilde: Interviews & Recollections. B&N.

Mikhailov, V. A. *see* Mikhailov, Valerii Alekseevich.

Mikhailov, Valerii Alekseevich.
xMikhailov, V. A.
Analytical Chemistry of Neptunium. Halsted Pr.

Mikita, Stan.
xMikita, Stan.
Inside Hockey. Contemp Bks.

Miklowitz, Gloria D.
xMiklowitz, Gloria D.
Barefoot Boy. Follett.
Did You Hear What Happened to Andrea?. Delacorte.
Earthquake!. Messner.

Miklowitz, J. *see* Miklowitz, Julius.

Miklowitz, Julius, 1919-
xMiklowitz, J.
The Theory of Elastic Waves & Waveguides. Elsevier.

Miko, Stephen J.
xMiko, Stephen J.
Toward Women in Love: The Emergence of a Lawrentian Aesthetic. Yale U Pr.

Miksche, Ferdinand O. *see* Miksche, Ferdinand Otto.

Miksche, Ferdinand Otto, 1905-
xMiksche, Ferdinand O.
The Failure of Atomic Strategy & a New Proposal for the Defence of the West. Greenwood.

Miksche, J. P. *see* Miksche, Jerome P.

Miksche, Jerome P.
xMiksche, J. P.
ed. Modern Methods in Forest Genetics. Springer-Verlag.

Mikulas, William L.
xMikulas, William L.
Concepts in Learning. HR&W.
ed. Psychology of Learning: Readings. Nelson-Hall.
ed. Readings in Behavior Modification. Mss Info.
ed. Readings in Learning. Mss Info.

Milady Barber Textbook Committee. *see* Milady Publishing Corporation, New York. Textbook Committee of Barbering.

Milady Editors. *see* Milady Publishing Corporation, New York.

Milady Publishing Corporation, New York.
    xMilady Editors.
        Exam Reviews in Hair Structure & Chemistry.
            Milady.
        Practical Beauty Culture Workbook. Milady.
        Tecnicas Modernas Del Peinado. Milady.
        Van Dean Practical Workbook. Milady.
        Van Dean Theory Workbook. Milady.
        Workbook for Beauty Culture Theory. Milady.
    xMilady Staff.
        Cosmetologist's State Board Exam Review in
            Spanish & English. Milady.
        Theory Workbook for Practice & Science of
            Standard Barbering. Milady.
    xMilady Staff Members.
        Van Dean Manual - Professional Techniques
            for Cosmetologists. Milady.
**Milady Publishing Corporation, New York. Textbook
Committee of Barbering.**
    xMilady Barber Textbook Committee.
        Standard Textbook of Professional Barber
            Styling. Milady.
    xTextbook Committee of Barbering.
        Advanced Textbook of Barbering & Men's
            Hairstyling. Milady.
Milady Staff. *see* Milady Publishing Corporation, New
    York.
Milady Staff Members. *see* Milady Publishing
    Corporation, New York.
Milam, Edward E.
    xMilam, Edward E.
        A Practical Guide to Preparing a Corporate
            Income Tax Return. Lawyers & Judges.
        A Practical Guide to Preparing a Tax Return
            for a Closely-Held Corporation. Lawyers &
            Judges.
Milan, Deanne K.
    xMilan, Deanne K.
        Forms of the Essay: The American Experience.
            HarBraceJ.
        Modern College Reading: Techniques with
            Exercises. Scribner.
Milani, Felix.
    xMilani, Felix.
        The Convict. St Martin.
Milani, Lucille.
    xMilani, Lucille.
        Tailoring the Easy Way. P-H.
Milanich, Jerald T.
    xMilanich, Jerald T.
        ed. Tacachale: Essays on the Indians of Florida
            & Southeastern Georgia During the Historic
            Period. U Presses Fla.
Milazzo, Guilio.
    xMilazzo, Guilio.
        Tables of Standard Electrode Potentials. Wiley.
Milazzo, Matteo J.
    xMilazzo, Matteo J.
        The Chetnik Movement & the Yugoslav
            Resistance. Johns Hopkins.
Milbauer, Barbara.
    xMilbauer, Barbara.
        ed. Hunger. PB.
Milberg, Aaron S.
    xMilberg, Aaron S.
        How to Do Your Own Bankruptcy. McGraw.
Milbrath, Lester W.
    xMilbrath, Lester W.
        The Politics of Environmental Policy. Sage.
Milburn, George, 1906-1966
    xMilburn, George.
        No More Trumpets & Other Stories. Arno.
        Oklahoma Town. Arno.
Milburn, J. A. *see* Milburn, John A.
Milburn, John A., 1936-
    xMilburn, J. A.
        Water Flow in Plants. Longman.
Milburn, Robert L. *see* Milburn, Robert Leslie Pollington.
Milburn, Robert Leslie Pollington.
    xMilburn, Robert L.

Early Christian Interpretations of History.
    Greenwood.
Milby, Robert V.
    xMilby, Robert V.
        Plastics Technology. McGraw.
Milch, H. *see* Milch, Henry M. D.
Milch, Henry M. D.
    xMilch, H.
        Osteotomy at the Upper End of Femur.
            Krieger.
Milden, James W. *see* Milden, James Wallace.
Milden, James Wallace.
    xMilden, James W.
        The Family in Past Time: A Guide to the
            Literature. Garland Pub.
Milder, Benjamin.
    xMilder, Benjamin.
        The Fine Art of Prescribing Glasses Without
            Making a Spectacle of Yourself. Triad Pub
            FL.
Mildren, K. W.
    xMildren, K. W.
        ed. Use of Engineering Literature.
            Butterworths.
Milenky, Edward S.
    xMilenky, Edward S.
        Argentina's Foreign Policies. Westview.
Miles. *see* Miles, Bebe.
Miles, A. E. *see* Miles, Albert Edward William.
Miles, Albert Edward William.
    xMiles, A. E.
        Structural & Chemical Organization of Teeth.
            Acad Pr.
Miles, Bebe.
    xMiles.
        Bulbs for the Home Gardener. G&D.
    xMiles, Bebe.
        Designing with Natural Materials. Van Nos
            Reinhold.
Miles, Betty.
    xMiles, Betty.
        All It Takes Is Practice. Dell
        All It Takes Is Practice. Knopf.
        Day of Autumn. Knopf.
        The Real Me. Knopf.
        The Real Me. Avon.
        The Trouble with Thirteen. Avon.
        The Trouble with Thirteen. Knopf.
Miles, Clement A.
    xMiles, Clement A.
        Christmas in Ritual & Tradition, Christian &
            Pagan. Gale.
Miles, Darrell.
    xMiles, Darrell.
        Quantity Cooking: Tested Recipes for Twenty
            or More. Dover.
Miles, Dick.
    xMiles, Dick.
        The Game of Table Tennis. Lippincott.
Miles, Donald. *see* Miles, Donald White.
Miles, Donald White, 1936-
    xMiles, Donald.
        Broadcast News Handbook. Bobbs.
Miles, Dudley H. *see* Miles, Dudley Howe.
Miles, Dudley Howe, 1881-
    xMiles, Dudley H.
        Influence of Moliere on Restoration Comedy.
            Octagon.
Miles, Edward. *see* Miles, Edward L.
Miles, Edward L.
    xMiles, Edward.
        Organizational Arrangements to Facilitate
            Global Management of Fisheries. Johns
            Hopkins.
Miles, Elton, 1917-
    xMiles, Elton.
        Tales of the Big Bend. Tex A&M Univ Pr.
Miles, George C. *see* Miles, George Carpenter.
Miles, George Carpenter, 1904-
    xMiles, George C.

The Coinage of the Arab Amirs of Crete. Am
    Numismatic.
Miles, George H. *see* Miles, George Henry.
Miles, George Henry, 1824-1871
    xMiles, George H.
        A Review of Hamlet. AMS Pr.
        A Review of Hamlet. Folcroft.
Miles, H. *see* Miles, Howard.
Miles, Henry A. *see* Miles, Henry Adolphus.
Miles, Henry Adolphus, 1809-1895
    xMiles, Henry A.
        Lowell, As It Was, & As It Is. Arno.
Miles, Herbert J. *see* Miles, Herbert Jackson.
Miles, Herbert Jackson, 1907-
    xMiles, Herbert J.
        The Dating Game. Zondervan.
        Husband-Wife Equality. Revell.
Miles, Howard.
    xMiles, H.
        Artificial Satellite Observing & Its
            Applications. Elsevier.
Miles, Hugh T. *see* Miles, Hugh Tyler.
Miles, Hugh Tyler, 1943-
    xMiles, Hugh T.
        Horse on Course. A S Barnes.
Miles, J.
    xMiles, J.
        Vegetation Dynamics. Halsted Pr.
        Vegetation Dynamics. Methuen Inc.
Miles, Josephine, 1911-
    xMiles, Josephine.
        Prefabrications. Greenwood.
        Ralph Waldo Emerson. U of Minn Pr.
        Renaissance, Eighteenth-Century & Modern
            Language in English Poetry. R West.
Miles, Judith. *see* Miles, Judith M.
Miles, Judith M., 1937-
    xMiles, Judith.
        Journal from an Obscure Place. Bethany Fell.
Miles, Marc A. 1948-
    xMiles, Marc C.
        Devaluation, the Trade Balance & the Balance
            of Payments. Dekker.
Miles, Marc C. *see* Miles, Marc A.
Miles, Martin J.
    xMiles, Martin J.
        Encyclopedia of Real Estate Formulas &
            Tables. P-H.
Miles, Mary.
    xMiles, Mary.
        Live & Learn: Child Development & the
            Challenge of Parenthood. Schocken.
Miles, Matthew B.
    xMiles, Matthew B.
        ed. Innovation in Education. Tchrs Coll.
Miles, Michael W., 1945-
    xMiles, Michael W.
        The Radical Probe: The Logic of Student
            Rebellion. Atheneum.
Miles, Miska.
    xMiles, Miska.
        Aaron's Door. Little.
        Annie & the Old One. Little.
        Apricot ABC. Little.
        Chicken Forgets. Little.
        Chicken Forgets. Schol Bk Serv.
        Hoagie's Rifle Gun. Little.
        Jenny's Cat. Dutton.
        Nobody's Cat. Little.
        Noisy Gander. Dutton.
        Otter in the Cove. Little.
        Somebody's Dog. Little.
        Swim, Little Duck. Little.
        This Little Pig. Dutton.
Miles, Nelson A. *see* Miles, Nelson Appleton.
Miles, Nelson Appleton, 1839-1925
    xMiles, Nelson A.

Personal Recollections & Observations of
General Nelson A. Miles. Da Capo.

Miles, Patricia.
xMiles, Patricia.
A Disturbing Influence. Lothrop.

Miles, R.
xMiles, Robert.
ed. Racism & Political Action in Britain.
Routledge & Kegan.

Miles, Robert.
xMiles, Robert.
First Principles of the Essay. Har-Row.
Prose Style for the Modern Writer. P-H.
Miles, Robert. *see* Miles, R.

Miles, Rosalind.
xMiles, Rosalind.
The Fiction of Sex: Themes & Functions of Sex
Difference in the Modern Novel. B&N.

Miles, Sally.
xMiles, Sally.
Natural Collage: The Making of Pictures with
Seeds, Leaves & Grasses. Scribner.
Miles, V. C. *see* Miles, Victor Chesney.

Miles, Victor Chesney.
xMiles, V. C.
Thermostatic Control: Principles & Practice.
Transatlantic.

Miles, William, 1942-
xMiles, William.
The Image Makers: A Bibliography of
American Presidential Campaign Biographies.
Scarecrow.

Miles, Wyndham D., 1916-
xMiles, Wyndham D.
ed. American Chemists & Chemical Engineers.
Am Chemical.

Milesko-Pytel, Diana.
xMilesko-Pytel, Diana.
Bicycling the Midwest. Contemp Bks.

Mileur, Jerome M.
xMileur, Jerome M.
Campaigning for the Massachusetts Senate:
Electioneering Outside the Political
Limelight. U of Mass Pr.
Miley, G. H. *see* Miley, George Hunter.
Miley, George H. *see* Miley, George Hunter.

Miley, George Hunter, 1933-
xMiley, G. H.
Intro. by Fusion Energy Conversion. Am
Nuclear Soc.
xMiley, George H.
Fusion Energy Conversion. Am Nuclear Soc.

Miley, Jeanie.
xMiley, Jeannie.
Spread Wide the Curtain. Broadman.
Miley, Jeannie. *see* Miley, Jeanie.

Milford Conference.
xMilford Conference.
Social Case Work: Generic & Specific. Natl
Assn Soc Wkrs.
Milford, T. R. *see* Milford, Theodore Richard.

Milford, Theodore Richard.
xMilford, T. R.
Christian Decision in the Nuclear Age.
Fortress.
Milgram, J. I. *see* Milgram, Joel I.

Milgram, Joel I.
xMilgram, J. I.
Childhood Revisited. Macmillan.

Milgram, Mary.
xMilgram, Mary.
Brothers Are All the Same. Dutton.

Milgram, Morris.
xMilgram, Morris.
Good Neighborhood: The Challenge of Open
Housing. Norton.
Milgram, N. W. *see* Milgram, Norton William.

Milgram, Norton William.
xMilgram, N. W.

Food Aversion Learning. Plenum Pub.

Milgram, Stanley.
xMilgram, Stanley.
Obedience to Authority: An Experimental
View. Har-Row.
ed. Psychology in Today's World. Little.
Milgrim, Shirley. *see* Milgrim, Shirley Gorson.

Milgrim, Shirley Gorson.
xMilgrim, Shirley.
Pathways to Independence: Discovering
Independence National Historical Park.
Chatham Pr.

Milgrom, Harry.
xMilgrom, Harry.
ABC of Ecology. Macmillan.
ABC of Ecology. Macmillan.
ABC Science Experiments. Macmillan.
Adventures with a Cardboard Tube. Dutton.
Adventures with a Straw. Dutton.
Paper Science. Walker & Co.
Understanding Weather. Macmillan.

Milgrom, Peter.
xMilgrom, Peter.
Regulation & the Quality of Dental Care.
Aspen Systems.

Milhaven, John Giles, 1927-
xMilhaven, John Giles.
Toward a New Catholic Morality. Doubleday.

Milhollan, Frank.
xMilhollan, Frank.
From Skinner to Rogers: Contrasting
Approaches to Education. Prof Educ Pubn.
Milhorat, Thomas H. *see* Milhorat, Thomas Herrick.

Milhorat, Thomas Herrick.
xMilhorat, Thomas H.
Pediatric Neurosurgery. Davis Co.

Miliband, Ralph.
xMiliband, Ralph.
Marxism & Politics. Oxford U Pr.
Marxism & Politics. Oxford U Pr.
Parliamentary Socialism: A Study in the
Politics of Labour. Kelley.

Milinaire, Caterine.
xMilinaire, Caterine.
Cheap Chic. Crown.

Milisauskas, Sarunas.
xMilisauskas, Sarunas.
European Prehistory. Acad Pr.

Miljan, Toivo.
xMiljan, Toivo.
The Reluctant Europeans: The Attitudes of the
Nordic Countries Towards European
Integration. McGill-Queens U Pr.
Milkie. *see* Milkie, George M.

Milkie, George M.
xMilkie.
Partnerships & Professional Corporations.
Green.
Mill, Anna J. *see* Mill, Anna Jean.

Mill, Anna Jean.
xMill, Anna J.
Mediaeval Plays in Scotland. Folcroft.
Mill, J. S. *see* Mill, James.

Mill, James.
xMill, J. S.
ed. Analysis of the Phenomena of the Human
Mind. Kelley.
xMill, James.
Analysis of the Phenomena of the Human
Mind. Kelley.
Commerce Defended. Kelley.
Principles of Toleration. B Franklin.
Mill, John S. *see* Mill, John Stuart.

Mill, John Stuart, 1806-1873
xMill, J. S.
On Liberty. Penguin.
xMill, John S.

Auguste Comte & Positivism. U of Mich Pr.
Autobiography. Bobbs.
Collected Works. Gordon Pr.
On Liberty. AHM Pub.
On Liberty. Bobbs.
On Liberty. Hackett Pub.
On Liberty. Norton.
Subjection of Women. MIT Pr.
Utilitarianism. Bobbs.
Utilitarianism. Hackett Pub.
xMill, John Stuart.
Utilitarianism. Collins Pubs.
Mill, P. J. *see* Mill, Peter John.

Mill, Peter John.
xMill, P. J.
Structure & Function of Proprioceptors in the
Invertebrates. Methuen Inc.
Millais, John G. *see* Millais, John Guille.

Millais, John Guille, 1865-1931
xMillais, John G.
Life & Letters of Sir John Everett Millais,
President of the Royal Academy. AMS Pr.

Millar, Andree.
xMillar, Andree.
Orchids of Papua New Guinea: An
Introduction. U of Wash Pr.
Millar, Anthony K. *see* Millar, Anthony Kendal.

Millar, Anthony Kendal.
xMillar, Anthony K.
Plantagenet in South Africa: Lord Charles
Somerset. Oxford U Pr.
Millar, J. H. *see* Millar, John Harold Dundee.

Millar, James R.
xMillar, James R.
ed. The Soviet Rural Community: A
Symposium. U of Ill Pr.

Millar, Jeff, 1942-
xMillar, Jeff.
Private Sector. Dial.
Millar, John F. *see* Millar, John Fitzhugh.

Millar, John Fitzhugh.
xMillar, John F.
American Ships of the Colonial &
Revolutionary Periods. Norton.

Millar, John Harold Dundee.
xMillar, J. H.
Multiple Sclerosis: A Disease Acquired in
Childhood. C C Thomas.

Millar, Margaret.
xMillar, Margaret.
The Murder of Miranda. Random.

Millar, Oliver.
xMillar, Oliver.
The Queen's Pictures. Macmillan.

Millar, Susanna.
xMillar, Susanna.
Psychology of Play. Aronson.
The Psychology of Play. Gannon.
Psychology of Play. Penguin.
Millar, T. B. *see* Millar, Thomas Bruce.

Millar, T. G.
xMillar, T. G.
Long Distance Paths of England & Wales.
David & Charles.

Millar, Thomas Bruce.
xMillar, T. B.
Australia in Peace & War. St Martin.
Australia's Defence. Intl Schol Bk Serv.

Millard, Adele.
xMillard, Adele.
Plants for Kids to Grow Indoors. Sterling.

Millard, Anne.
xMillard, Anne.
Ancient Egypt. Watts.
Millard, B. J. *see* Millard, Brian J.

Millard, Brian J.
xMillard, B. J.
Quantitative Mass Spectrometry. Heyden.

Millard, Reed.
xMillard, Reed.

Careers in Environmental Protection. Messner.
Careers in the Earth Sciences. Messner.
Clean Air-Clean Water for Tomorrow's World.
Messner.

Millas, Jorge.
xMillas, Jorge.
The Intellectual & Moral Challenge of Mass
Society. Univ Microfilms.
Millay, Edna S. *see* Millay, Edna St. Vincent.
Millay, Edna St. Vincent, 1892-1950
xMillay, Edna S.
Renascence & Other Poems. Arno.
xMillay, Edna St. Vincent.
Collected Lyrics. Har-Row.
Collected Lyrics. Har-Row.
Collected Poems. Har-Row.
Letters. Greenwood.
Mille, A. B. De. *see* De Mille, A. B.
Mille, George E. De. *see* De Mille, George E.
Mille, James De. *see* De Mille, James.
Mille, Richard De. *see* De Mille, Richard.
Millen, Bruce H.
xMillen, Bruce H.
The Political Role of Labor in Developing
Countries. Greenwood.
Millen, Nina.
xMillen, Nina.
Children's Festivals from Many Lands. Friend
Pr.
Children's Games from Many Lands. Friend
Pr.
Millenson, J. R. *see* Millenson, John R.
Millenson, John R., 1932-
xMillenson, J. R.
Principles of Behavioral Analysis. Macmillan.
Miller. *see* Miller, Rex.
Miller, A. G. *see* Miller, Albert G.
Miller, Aaron D. *see* Miller, Aaron David.
Miller, Aaron David.
xMiller, Aaron D.
Search for Security: Saudi Arabian Oil &
American Foreign Policy, 1939-1949. U of
NC Pr.
Miller, Abraham H., 1940-
xMiller, Abraham H.
Terrorism & Hostage Negotiations. Westview.
Miller, Albert.
xMiller, Albert.
Elements of Meteorology. Merrill.
Miller, Albert G., 1905-
xMiller, A. G.
ed. Pop-up Book of Boats. Random.
xMiller, Albert G.
Captain Whopper. Astor-Honor.
Mark Twain in Love. HarBraceJ.
Our Friends the ABC's. Bowmar-Noble.
Talking Letters. Bowmar-Noble.
Miller, Albert J. *see* Miller, Albert Jay.
Miller, Albert Jay.
xMiller, Albert J.
Confrontation, Conflict & Dissent: A
Bibliography of a Decade of Controversy,
Nineteen Sixty to Nineteen Seventy.
Scarecrow.
Death: A Bibliographical Guide. Scarecrow.
Miller, Alden D.
xMiller, Alden D.
A Theory of Social Reform: Correctional
Change Processes in Two States. Ballinger
Pub.
Miller, Alexander, 1908-1960
xMiller, Alexander.
Faith & Learning: Christian Faith & Higher
Education in Twentieth Century America.
Greenwood.
Miller, Alfred L. *see* Miller, Alfred Louis.
Miller, Alfred Louis.
xMiller, Alfred L.

Practical Guide on Hearing Impaired Children:
Helpful, Practical Information for Speech &
Hearing Therapists, Audiologists, Physicians,
& Nurses. C C Thomas.
Miller, Alice P.
xMiller, Alice P.
Edmund Burke: A Biography. Allwyn Pr.
Edmund Burke & His World. Devin.
Miller, Amos C.
xMiller, Amos C.
Sir Richard Grenville of the Civil War.
Rowman.
Miller, Ann F.
xMiller, Ann F.
ed. College in Dispersion: Women at Bryn
Mawr, 1896-1975. Westview.
Miller, Arthur, 1915-
xMiller, Arthur.
After the Fall. Bantam.
After the Fall. Penguin.
After the Fall. Viking Pr.
Crucible. Penguin.
Crucible. Viking Pr.
The Crucible. Bantam.
Crucible: Text & Criticism. Penguin.
Portable Arthur Miller. Penguin.
Portable Arthur Miller. Viking Pr.
The Theater Essays of Arthur Miller. Penguin.
The Theater Essays of Arthur Miller. Viking
Pr.
Miller, Arthur R. *see* Miller, Arthur Raphael.
Miller, Arthur Raphael, 1934-
xMiller, Arthur R.
Assault on Privacy: Computers, Data Banks, &
Dossiers. U of Mich Pr.
Miller, Arthur S. *see* Miller, Arthur Selwyn.
Miller, Arthur Selwyn, 1917-
xMiller, Arthur S.
The Modern Corporate State: Private
Governments & the American Constitution.
Greenwood.
The Supreme Court: Myth & Reality.
Greenwood.
Miller, B. D. *see* Miller, Bill David.
Miller, Barbara.
xMiller, Barbara.
Kathy. Revell.
Miller, Barnard S. *see* Miller, Bernard S.
Miller, Barnett. *see* Miller, Barnette.
Miller, Barnette.
xMiller, Barnett.
Leigh Hunt's Relations with Byron, Shelley &
Keats. Folcroft.
The Palace School of Muhammad the
Conqueror. Arno.
xMiller, Barnette.
Leigh Hunt's Relations with Byron, Shelley &
Keats. Octagon.
Miller, Barry, 1946-
xMiller, Barry.
Alphabet World. Macmillan.
Miller, Benjamin F. *see* Miller, Benjamin Frank.
Miller, Benjamin Frank.
xMiller, Benjamin F.
Encyclopedia & Dictionary of Medicine &
Nursing. Saunders.
Freedom from Heart Attacks. S&S.
Miller, Bernard S.
xMiller, Barnard S.
Humanities Approach to the Modern
Secondary School Curriculum. Ctr Appl Res.
Miller, Besse M. *see* Miller, Besse May.
Miller, Besse May.
xMiller.
Legal Secretary's Complete Handbook. P-H.
xMiller, Besse M.
ed. Private Secretary's Encyclopedic
Dictionary. P-H.
Miller, Bill David.
xMiller, B. D.

Local Warning System Definition. Mgmt Info
Serv.
Miller, Brimtom M. *see* Miller, Brinton Marshall.
Miller, Brinton Marshall.
xMiller, Brimtom M.
Industrial Microbiology. McGraw.
Miller, Brown.
xMiller, Brown.
Hiroshima Flows Through Us. Cherry Valley.
Innovation in New Communities. MIT Pr.
Miller, Calvin.
xMiller, Calvin.
The Finale. Inter-Varsity.
The Song. Inter-Varsity.
A View from the Fields. Broadman.
Miller, Carey.
xMiller, Carey.
All About Monsters. EMC.
Miller, Carey D. *see* Miller, Carey Dunlap.
Miller, Carey Dunlap.
xMiller, Carey D.
Fruits of Hawaii: Description, Nutritive Value,
& Recipes. U Pr of Hawaii.
Miller, Carolyn P. *see* Miller, Carolyn Paine.
Miller, Carolyn Paine.
xMiller, Carolyn P.
Captured!. Christian Herald.
Miller, Casey.
xMiller, Casey.
Words & Women. Doubleday.
Miller, Charles A.
xMiller, Charles A.
The Official & Political Manual of the State of
Tennessee. Reprint.
Miller, Charles A. *see* Miller, Charles Allen.
Miller, Charles Allen, 1937-
xMiller, Charles A.
A Catawba Assembly. C A Miller.
Miller, Charles D.
xMiller, Charles D.
Business Mathematics. Scott F.
Miller, Charles D. *see* Miller, Charles David.
Miller, Charles David.
xMiller, Charles D.
Business Mathematics: A Programmed
Approach. Scott F.
Intermediate Algebra: A Text-Workbook. Scott
F.
Introductory Algebra: A Worktext. Scott F.
Mathematics: An Everyday Experience. Scott
F.
Miller, Charles E. *see* Miller, Charles Edward.
Miller, Charles Edward, 1929-
xMiller, Charles E.
Living in Christ: Sacramental & Occasional
Homilies. Alba.
Miller, Charles F., 1941-
xMiller, Charles F.
On Group-Theoretic Decision Problems &
Their Classification. Princeton U Pr.
Miller, Clara B. *see* Miller, Clara Bernice.
Miller, Clara Bernice.
xMiller, Clara B.
Crying Heart. Moody.
Miller, Claude. *see* Miller, Claude Henry.
Miller, Claude Henry.
xMiller, Claude.
Fat & Fed Up: Challenge to Weight Control.
Lyle Stuart.
Miller, D. B.
xMiller, D. B.
Peasants & Politics: Grass Roots Reactions to
Change in Asia. St Martin.
Miller, D. W. *see* Miller, Donald Wesley.
Miller, Daniel.
xMiller, Daniel.

Oncogenesis & Other Pathological Results of
Herpesvirus Infection. Mss Info.
Starting a Small Restaurant: A Guide to
Excellence in the Purveying of Public
Victuals. Harvard Common Pr.
Miller, Daniel. *see* Miller, Daniel Aaron.
Miller, Daniel Aaron, 1943-
xMiller, Daniel.
How to Invest in Real Estate Syndicates. Dow
Jones-Irwin.
Miller, Daniel J.
xMiller, Daniel J.
Guide to the Coastal Marine Fishes of
California. Ag Sci Pubns.
Miller, David, 1935-
xMiller, David.
World Cup: The Argentina Story. Warne.
Miller, David E.
xMiller, David E.
Hole in the Rock: An Epic in the Colonization
of the Great American West. U of Utah Pr.
Miller, David H. *see* Miller, David Harry.
Miller, David Harry.
xMiller, David H.
ed. The Frontier: Comparative Studies. U of
Okla Pr.
Miller, David K.
xMiller, David K.
Fitness: A Lifetime Commitment. Burgess.
Miller, David M.
xMiller, David M.
Hindu Monastic Life: The Monks &
Monasteries of Bhubaneswar. McGill-Queens
U Pr.
John Milton: Poetry. Twayne.
Miller, David M. *see* Miller, David Monroe.
Miller, David Monroe.
xMiller, David M.
Understanding the Metric System: A
Programed Text. Allyn.
Miller, David W., 1940-
xMiller, David W.
Church, State & Nation in Ireland, 1898-1921.
U of Pittsburgh Pr.
Miller, David W. *see* Miller, David Wendell.
Miller, David Wendell.
xMiller, David W.
Executive Decisions & Operations Research.
P-H.
Structure of Human Decisions. P-H.
Miller, Dayton C. *see* Miller, Dayton Clarence.
Miller, Dayton Clarence, 1866-1941
xMiller, Dayton C.
Catalogue of Books & Literary Material
Relating to the Flute & Other Musical
Instruments, with Annotations. Scholarly.
Miller, Delbert C. *see* Miller, Delbert Charles.
Miller, Delbert Charles.
xMiller, Delbert C.
Industrial Sociology: Work in Organizational
Life. Har-Row.
Miller, Della C. *see* Miller, Della Crowder.
Miller, Della Crowder.
xMiller, Della C.
Abraham Lincoln: A Biographic Trilogy in
Sonnet Sequence. Chris Mass.
Miller, Don, 1927-
xMiller, Don.
Hollywood Corral. Popular Lib.
Miller, Don. *see* Miller, Donald C.
Miller, Don C.
xMiller, Donald C.
Ghost Towns of Washington & Oregon. Pruett.
Miller, Donald. *see* Miller, Donald L.
Miller, Donald B. *see* Miller, Donald Britton.
Miller, Donald Britton.
xMiller, Donald B.

Personal Vitality. A-W.
Twice Turned Tales. Vitality Assocs.
Miller, Donald C., 1933-
xMiller, Don.
Ghost Towns of California. Pruett.
Ghost Towns of Wyoming. Pruett.
xMiller, Donald.
Ghost Towns of Nevada. Pruett.
xMiller, Donald C.
Ghosts of the Black Hills. Pictorial Hist.
Miller, Donald C. *see* Miller, Don C.
Miller, Donald G.
xMiller, Donald G.
Fire in Thy Mouth. Baker Bk.
Nature & Mission of the Church. John Knox.
Miller, Donald L., 1944-
xMiller, Donald.
The New American Radicalism: Alfred M.
Bingham & Non-Marxian Insurgency in the
New Deal Era. Kennikat.
Miller, Donald Wesley, 1940-
xMiller, D. W.
The Practice of Coronary Artery Bypass
Surgery. Plenum Pub.
Miller, Donna Mae.
xMiller, Donna Mae.
Coaching the Female Athlete. Lea & Febiger.
Miller, Dorothy. *see* Miller, Dorothy L.
Miller, Dorothy L.
xMiller, Dorothy.
Runaways, Illegal Aliens in Their Own Land:
Implications for Service. Praeger.
Miller, Douglas. *see* Miller, Douglas T.
Miller, Douglas T.
xMiller, Douglas.
Then Was the Future: North in the Age of
Jackson 1815-1850. Knopf.
xMiller, Douglas T.
The Fifties: The Way We Really Were.
Doubleday.
Miller, Dulcy B.
xMiller, Dulcy B.
Nursing Home Organization & Operation. CBI
Pub.
Miller, E. *see* Miller, Elmer S.
Miller, E. Eugene.
xMiller, E. Eugene.
Corrections in the Community: Success Models
in Correctional Reform. Reston.
Miller, Ed L. *see* Miller, Eddie L.
Miller, Eddie L., 1937-
xMiller, Ed L.
God & Reason: A Historical Approach to
Philosophical Theology. Macmillan.
Miller, Edgar.
xMiller, Edgar.
Abnormal Ageing: The Psychology of Senile &
Presenile Dementia. Wiley.
Miller, Edward.
xMiller, Edward.
Medieval England: Rural Society & Economic
Change 1086-1348. Longman.
Prince of Librarians: The Life & Times of
Antonio Panizzi of the British Museum. Ohio
U Pr.
That Noble Cabinet: A History of the British
Museum. Ohio U Pr.
Miller, Edward A. *see* Miller, Edward Alanson.
Miller, Edward Alanson, 1866-
xMiller, Edward A.
History of Educational Legislation in Ohio
from 1803 to 1850. Arno.
Miller, Edward B., 1922-
xMiller, Edward B.
An Administrative Appraisal of the NLRB.
Indus Res Unit-Wharton.
Miller, Edward F. *see* Miller, Edward Frederick.
Miller, Edward Frederick, 1898-
xMiller, Edward F.

Influence of Gesenius on Hebrew
Lexicography. AMS Pr.
Miller, Edwin H. *see* Miller, Edwin Haviland.
Miller, Edwin Haviland.
xMiller, Edwin H.
Melville. Persea Bks.
Miller, Elinor.
xMiller, Elinor.
ed. Plantation, Town, & County: Essays on the
Local History of American Slave Society. U
of Ill Pr.
Miller, Elizabeth W.
xMiller, Elizabeth W.
ed. Negro in America: A Bibliography. Harvard
U Pr.
Miller, Ella M. *see* Miller, Ella May.
Miller, Ella May.
xMiller, Ella M.
I Am a Woman. Moody.
Miller, Ellen C. *see* Miller, Ellen Clare.
Miller, Ellen Clare.
xMiller, Ellen C.
Eastern Sketches: Notes of Scenery, Schools, &
Tent Life in Syria & Palestine. Arno.
Miller, Elmer S.
xMiller, E.
Introduction to Anthropology. P-H.
Introduction to Cultural Anthropology. P-H.
Miller, Elwood. *see* Miller, Elwood L.
Miller, Elwood L.
xMiller, Elwood.
Inflation Accounting. Van Nos Reinhold.
xMiller, Elwood L.
Accounting Problems of Multinational
Enterprises. Lexington Bks.
Miller, Emanuel, 1893-
xMiller, E.
ed. Foundations of Child Psychiatry.
Pergamon.
Miller, Eric J. *see* Miller, Eric John.
Miller, Eric John.
xMiller, Eric J.
ed. Task & Organization. Wiley.
Miller, Ernest L., 1913-
xMiller, Ernest L.
Removable Partial Prosthodontics. Williams &
Wilkins.
Miller, Evelyn.
xMiller, Evelyn.
How to Raise & Train a Boston Terrier. TFH
Pubns.
How to Raise & Train a Bulldog. TFH Pubns.
How to Raise & Train a Cocker Spaniel. TFH
Pubns.
How to Raise & Train a Fox Terrier. TFH
Pubns.
How to Raise & Train a Golden Retriever.
TFH Pubns.
How to Raise & Train a Miniature Pinscher.
TFH Pubns.
How to Raise & Train a Poodle. TFH Pubns.
How to Raise & Train a Pug. TFH Pubns.
How to Raise & Train an Airedale. TFH
Pubns.
Miller, Forrestt A.
xMiller, Forrestt A.
Dmitrii Miliutin & the Reform Era in Russia.
Vanderbilt U Pr.

Miller, Frank B. *see* Miller, Frank Barton.
Miller, Frank Barton.
xMiller, Frank B.
Historical Sources of Personnel Work: An
Annotated Bibliography. NY Sch Indus Rel.
Miller, Franklin.
xMiller, Franklin.
College Physics. HarBraceJ.
Miller Freeman Publications, Inc. *see* Sawmill and
Plywood Clinic Business Management Workshop,
Portland, Oregon, 1976.

Miller, G. Tyler. *see* Miller, George Tyler.
Miller, Gabriel, 1948-
   xMiller, Gabriel.
     Daniel Fuchs. Twayne.
     Screening the Novel: Rediscovered American
      Fiction in Film. Ungar.
Miller, Gale.
   xMiller, Gale.
     Odd Jobs: The World of Deviant Work. P-H.
Miller, Gary. *see* Miller, Gary M.
Miller, Gary A.
   xMiller, Gary A.
     Professional Selling-Inside & Out. Delmar.
Miller, Gary M., 1941-
   xMiller, Gary.
     Linear Circuits for Electronics Technology.
      P-H.
   xMiller, Gary M.
     Modern Electronic Communication. P-H.
Miller, George.
   xMiller, George.
     A Pennsylvania Album: Picture Postcards,
      1900-1930. Pa St U Pr.
Miller, George A. *see* Miller, George Armitage.
Miller, George Armitage, 1920-
   xMiller, George A.
     Communication, Language & Meaning:
      Psychological Perspectives. Basic.
     ed. Psychology & Biology of Language &
      Thought: Essays in Honor of Eric Lenneberg.
      Acad Pr.
     Psychology: The Science of Mental Life.
      Har-Row.
Miller, George E.
   xMiller, George E.
     Educating Medical Teachers. Harvard U Pr.
Miller, George F. *see* Miller, George Frederick.
Miller, George Frederick, 1880-
   xMiller, George F.
     Academy System of the State of New York.
      Arno.
Miller, George H,
   xMiller, George H.
     California Real Estate Appraisal: Residential
      Properties. P-H.
Miller, George H. *see* Miller, George Hall.
Miller, George Hall, 1919-
   xMiller, George H.
     Railroads & the Granger Laws. U of Wis Pr.
Miller, George M. *see* Miller, George Morey.
Miller, George Morey.
   xMiller, George M.
     The Dramatic Element in the Popular Ballad.
      Arden Lib.
     The Dramatic Element in the Popular Ballad.
      Folcroft.
Miller, George N. *see* Miller, George Noyes.
Miller, George Noyes, 1845-1904
   xMiller, George N.
     The Strike of a Sex & Zugassent's Discovery:
      After the Sex Struck. Arno.
Miller, George Tyler, 1931-
   xMiller, G. Tyler.
     Chemistry: A Basic Introduction. Wadsworth
      Pub.
     Chemistry: Principles & Applications.
      Wadsworth Pub.
     Energy & Environment: The Four Energy
      Crises. Wadsworth Pub.
     Living in the Environment. Wadsworth Pub.
     Replenish the Earth: A Primer in Human
      Ecology. Wadsworth Pub.
Miller, George W. *see* Miller, George William.
Miller, George William, 1926-
   xMiller, George W.
     Moral & Ethical Implications of Human Organ
      Transplants. C C Thomas.
Miller, Gerald R.
   xMiller, Gerald R.

     ed. Explorations in Interpersonal
      Communication. Sage.
     An Introduction to Speech Communication.
      Bobbs.
Miller, Glenn H.
   xMiller, Glenn H.
     Basic Chemistry. Har-Row.
Miller, Gordon P. *see* Miller, Gordon Porter.
Miller, Gordon Porter.
   xMiller, Gordon P.
     Life Choices: How to Make the Critical
      Decisions - About Your Education, Career,
      Marriage, Family, Life-Style. T Y Crowell.
Miller, H. A. *see* Miller, Howard A.
Miller, Hannah E. *see* Miller, Hannah Elsas.
Miller, Hannah Elsas, 1926-
   xMiller, Hannah E.
     Films in the Classroom: A Practical Guide.
      Scarecrow.
Miller, Harry H. *see* Miller, Harry Herman.
Miller, Harry Herman, 1900-
   xMiller, Harry H.
     Speaking of Pets. Macmillan.
Miller, Harry M. *see* Miller, Harry Milton.
Miller, Harry Milton, 1895-
   xMiller, Harry M.
     Comparative Studies on Furcocercous
      Cercariae. Johnson Repr.
Miller, Hazen L.
   xMiller, Hazen L.
     Old Au Sable. Eerdmans.
Miller, Heather. *see* Miller, Heather Ross.
Miller, Heather Ross, 1939-
   xMiller, Heather.
     Horse, Horse, Tyger, Tyger. Red Clay.
Miller, Helen Day Hill, 1899-
   xMiller, Helen H.
     Case for Liberty. U of NC Pr.
     George Mason, Gentleman Revolutionary. U of
      NC Pr.
     Historic Places Around the Outer Banks.
      McNally.
Miller, Helen H. *see* Miller, Helen Day Hill.
Miller, Henry, 1891-
   xMiller, Henry.
     Books in My Life. New Directions.
     Collector's Quest: The Correspondence of
      Henry Miller & J. Rives Childs, 1947-1965.
      U Pr of Va.
     Colossus of Maroussi. New Directions.
     Cosmological Eye. New Directions.
     Letters to Anais Nin. Beekman Pubs.
     My Bike & Other Friends. Capra Pr.
     The Nightmare Notebook. New Directions.
     Sunday After the War. New Directions.
     Tropic of Cancer. Grove.
     Tropic of Capricorn. Ballantine.
     Tropic of Capricorn. Grove.
Miller, Henry. *see* Miller, Henry George.
Miller, Henry A. *see* Miller, Henry Arthur.
Miller, Henry Arthur.
   xMiller, Henry A.
     Practical Wiring. Pergamon.
Miller, Henry George.
   xMiller, Henry.
     Medicine & Society. Oxford U Pr.
Miller, Henry S. *see* Miller, Henry Siefke.
Miller, Henry Siefke, 1901-
   xMiller, Henry S.
     Price Control in Fascist Italy. AMS Pr.
Miller, Herb.
   xMiller, Herbert.
     Tools for Active Christians. Bethany Pr.
Miller, Herbert. *see* Miller, Herb.
Miller, Herbert C.
   xMiller, Herbert C.

     ed. Clinical Problems in Pediatrics. Year Bk
      Med.
     Fetal Growth in Humans. Year Bk Med.
Miller, Herbert E.
   xMiller, Herbert E.
     CPA Review Manual. P-H.
Miller, Herman P. *see* Miller, Herman Phillip.
Miller, Herman Phillip, 1921-
   xMiller, Herman P.
     Rich Man, Poor Man. T Y Crowell.
Miller, Howard, 1941-
   xMiller, Howard.
     The Revolutionary College: American
      Presbyterian Higher Education, 1707-1837.
      NYU Pr.
Miller, Howard A.
   xMiller, H. A.
     Particle Board Manufacture. Noyes.
   xMiller, Howard A.
     How to Know the Trees. Wm C Brown.
Miller, Howard S. *see* Miller, Howard Smith.
Miller, Howard Smith, 1936-
   xMiller, Howard S.
     Dollars for Research: Science & Its Patrons in
      Nineteenth-Century America. U of Wash Pr.
Miller, Hugh, 1937-
   xMiller, Hugh.
     Ambulance. Ballantine.
     The Dissector. Ballantine.
     The Dissector. St Martin.
Miller, Hugh M. *see* Miller, Hugh Milton.
Miller, Hugh Milton, 1908-
   xMiller, Hugh M.
     History of Music. B&N.
     Introduction to Music: A Guide to Good
      Listening. B&N.
Miller, Isabel.
   xMiller, Isabel.
     Patience & Sarah. Fawcett.
Miller, J. *see* Miller, John Leslie.
Miller, J. D. *see* Miller, John Donald Bruce.
Miller, J. H. *see* Miller, Jeffrey H.
Miller, J. Hillis. *see* Miller, Joseph Hillis.
Miller, J. Jefferson.
   xMiller, J. Jefferson.
     English Yellow-Glazed Earthenware.
      Smithsonian.

Miller, J. P. *see* Miller, John Parr.
Miller, J. R.
   xMiller, J. R.
     Equal Rights: The Jesuits' Estates Act
      Controversy. McGill-Queens U Pr.
Miller, Jack E., 1930-
   xMiller, Jack E.
     Cooperative Education Workbook for
      Foodservice Hospitality. CBI Pub.
     Menu Pricing & Strategy. CBI Pub.
Miller, James, 1903-
   xMiller, James.
     The Detroit Yiddish Theater, 1920-1937.
      Wayne St U Pr.
     History & Human Existence: From Marx to
      Merleau-Ponty. U of Cal Pr.
Miller, James. *see* Miller, James Clifford.
Miller, James Clifford.
   xMiller, James.
     ed. Benefit Cost Analyses of Social Regulation:
      Case Studies from the Council on Wage &
      Price Stability. Am Enterprise.
Miller, James E. *see* Miller, James Edwin.
Miller, James Edwin, 1920-
   xMiller, James E.

The American Quest for a Supreme Fiction:
Whitman's Legacy in the Personal Epic. U of
Chicago Pr.
Critical Guide to Leaves of Grass. U of
Chicago Pr.
ed. Dimensions of the Short Story: A Critical
Anthology. Har-Row.
A Readers Guide to Herman Melville.
Octagon.
T. S. Eliot's Personal Waste Land: Exorcism of
the Demons. Pa St U Pr.
Miller, James G. *see* Miller, James Grier.
Miller, James Grier.
xMiller, James G.
Living Systems. McGraw.
Miller, James M. *see* Miller, James McDonald.
Miller, James McDonald.
xMiller, James M.
Genesis of Western Culture: The Upper Ohio
Valley, 1800-1825. Da Capo.
Miller, James W. *see* Miller, James Wilkinson.
Miller, James Wilkinson.
xMiller, James W.
Logic Workbook. Oxford U Pr.
Miller, Jane, 1897-
xMiller, Jane.
Lambing Time. Methuen Inc.
Pure Nuisance. Dodd.
Miller, Jarrott T.
xMiller, Jarrott T.
Creative Options Trading. Contemp Bks.

Miller, Jay.

xMiller, Jay.
Nature Crafts. Lerner Pubns.

Miller, Jean. *see* Miller, Jean Baker.

Miller, Jean B. *see* Miller, Jean Baker.

Miller, Jean Baker.
xMiller, Jean.
ed. Psychoanalysis & Women: Contributions to
New Theory & Therapy. Brunner-Mazel.
xMiller, Jean B.
ed. Psychoanalysis & Women. Penguin.
Toward a New Psychology of Women. Beacon
Pr.
Miller, Jean R.
xMiller, Jean R.
Family Focused Care. McGraw.
Miller, Jeffrey. *see* Miller, Jeffrey H.
Miller, Jeffrey H.
xMiller, J. H.
ed. The Operon. Cold Spring Harbor.
xMiller, Jeffrey.
The Operon. Cold Spring Harbor.
xMiller, Jeffrey H.
Experiments in Molecular Genetics. Cold
Spring Harbor.
Miller, Jerome K.
xMiller, Jerome K.
Applying the New Copyright Law: A Guide for
Educators & Librarians. ALA.
Miller, Joaquin, 1841?-1913
xMiller, Joaquin.
Songs of the Sierras. Irvington.
Miller, Joel S.
xMiller, Joel S.
ed. Synthesis & Properties of Low-Dimensional
Materials. NY Acad Sci.
Miller, John.
xMiller, John.
Memoirs of General Miller, in the Service of
the Republic of Peru. AMS Pr.
Miller, John A. *see* Miller, John Anderson.
Miller, John Anderson, 1895-
xMiller, John A.
Master Builders of Sixty Centuries. Arno.
Miller, John C. *see* Miller, John Chester.
Miller, John Chester, 1907-
xMiller, John C.

Crisis in Freedom: The Alien & Sedition Acts.
Little.
The Federalist Era, 1789-1801. Har-Row.
First Frontier: Life in Colonial America. Dell.
Origins of the American Revolution. Stanford
U Pr.
This New Man, the American: The Beginnings
of the American People. McGraw.
Toward a More Perfect Union: The American
Republic 1783-1815. Scott F.
The Wolf by the Ears: Thomas Jefferson &
Slavery. Free Pr.
The Wolf by the Ears: Thomas Jefferson &
Slavery. NAL.
Miller, John Donald Bruce.
xMiller, J. D.
Survey of Commonwealth Affairs: Problems of
Expansion & Attrition 1953-1969. Oxford U
Pr.
Miller, John Leslie.
xMiller, J.
Popery & Politics in England, 1660-1688.
Cambridge U Pr.
Miller, John M. *see* Miller, John Michael.
Miller, John Michael, 1939-
xMiller, John M.
The Contentious Community: Constructive
Conflict in the Church. Westminster.
Miller, John Parr.
xMiller, J. P.
Do You Know Colors?. Random.
Miller, John S. *see* Miller, John Seldon.
Miller, John Seldon, 1918-
xMiller, John S.
Childbirth: A Manual for Pregnancy &
Delivery. Atheneum.
Miller, John W. *see* Miller, John William.
Miller, John William.
xMiller, John W.
The Paradox of Cause & Other Essays. Norton.
Miller, Jonas E.
xMiller, Jonas E.
Prescription for Total Health & Longevity.
Logos.
Miller, Jonathan, 1934-
xMiller, Jonathan.
The Body in Question. Random.
Miller, Joseph, 1899-
xMiller, J.
Aromatic Nucleophilic Substitution. Elsevier.
xMiller, Joseph.
The Arizona Rangers. Hastings.
Fire Department. Miller Bks.
ed. Government & the People. Miller Bks.
Money, Then & Now. Miller Bks.
Miller, Joseph H. *see* Miller, Joseph Hillis.
Miller, Joseph Hillis.
xMiller, J. Hillis.
The Disappearance of God: Five Nineteenth
Century Writers. Harvard U Pr.
xMiller, Joseph H.
Charles Dickens: The World of His Novels.
Harvard U Pr.
Miller, Joseph M.
xMiller, Joseph M.
ed. Readings in Medieval Rhetoric. Ind U Pr.
Miller, Joyce, 1932-
xMiller, Joyce.
In Straw & Story: Christmas Resources for
Home & Church. Brethren.
Miller, Judith G. *see* Miller, Judith Graves.
Miller, Judith Graves.
xMiller, Judith G.
Theater & Revolution in France Since 1968.
French Forum.
Miller, Julian A. *see* Miller, Julian Asher.
Miller, Julian Asher.
xMiller, Julian A.

Breaking Through: Freeing Yourself from Fear,
Helplessness & Depression - Before It's Too
Late. T Y Crowell.
Miller, K. Bruce. *see* Miller, Keith Bruce.
Miller, K. M. *see* Miller, Kenneth M.
Miller, K. S. *see* Miller, Kenneth S.
Miller, Keith.
xMiller, Keith.
The Passionate People: Carriers of the Spirit.
Word Bks.
The Taste of New Wine. Word Bks.
Miller, Keith Bruce.
xMiller, K. Bruce.
Ideology & Moral Philosophy: The Relation of
Moral Ideology to Dynamic Moral
Philosophy. Humanities.
Miller, Kelly, 1863-1939
xMiller, Kelly.
Appeal to Conscience: America's Code of
Caste, a Disgrace to Democracy. Arno.
Out of the House of Bondage. Arno.
Out of the House of Bondage. Schocken.
Race Adjustment: Essays on the Negro in
America. Arno.
Race Adjustment: Essays on the Negro in
America. Mnemosyne.
Miller, Kenneth. *see* Miller, Kenneth Dayton.
Miller, Kenneth Dayton.
xMiller, Kenneth.
Modern Basketball for Women. Merrill.
Miller, Kenneth M.
xMiller, K. M.
Psychological Testing in Personnel Assessment.
Halsted Pr.
Miller, Kenneth S.
xMiller, K. S.
Advanced Trigonometry. Krieger.
xMiller, Kenneth S.
Advanced Real Calculus. Krieger.
An Introduction to Advanced Complex
Calculus. Peter Smith.
An Introduction to Vector Stochastic
Processes. Krieger.
Linear Difference Equations.
Benjamin-Cummings.
Partial Differential Equations in Engineering
Problems. P-H.
Miller, Kent S.
xMiller, Kent S.
ed. Comparative Studies of Blacks & Whites in
the United States. Acad Pr.
The Criminal Justice & Mental Health Systems:
Conflict & Collusion. Oelgeschlager.
Miller, L. B. *see* Miller, Linda B.
Miller, L. F. *see* Miller, Lewis F.
Miller, L. Keith.
xMiller, L. Keith.
Principles of Everyday Behavior Analysis.
Brooks-Cole.
Miller, Larry, 1942-
xMiller, Larry.
Selling in Agribusiness. McGraw.
Miller, Lawrence C.
xMiller, Lawrence C.
Successful Management for Contractors.
McGraw.
Miller, Lee G. *see* Miller, Lee Graham.
Miller, Lee Graham, 1902-1961
xMiller, Lee G.
Story of Ernie Pyle. Greenwood.
Miller, Lee O., 1922-
xMiller, Lee O.
The Great Cowboy Stars of Movies &
Television. Arlington Hse.
Miller, Leonard G.
xMiller, Leonard G.
Double Jeopardy & the Federal System. U of
Chicago Pr.
Miller, Leslie H. *see* Miller, Leslie Haynes.

Miller, Leslie Haynes.
  xMiller, Leslie H.
    College Geometry. Irvington.
Miller, Levi.
  xMiller, Levi.
    ed. Family in Today's Society. Herald Pr.
Miller, Lew, 1917-
  xMiller, Lew A.
    You Can Beat Those Spiritual Blahs. Accent
      Bks.
Miller, Lew A. *see* Miller, Lew.
Miller, Lewis, 1928-
  xMiller, Lewis.
    The Life You Save: A Guide to Getting the
      Best Possible Care from Doctors, Hospitals,
      & Nursing Homes. Morrow.
Miller, Lewis F.
  xMiller, L. F.
    Thick Film Technology & Chip Joining.
      Gordon.
Miller, Lillian B.
  xMiller, Lillian B.
    Patrons & Patriotism: The Encouragement of
      the Fine Arts in the United States,
      1790-1860. U of Chicago Pr.
Miller, Linda B.
  xMiller, L. B.
    World Order & Local Disorder: The United
      Nations & Internal Conflict. Princeton U Pr.
Miller, Louis H.
  xMiller, Louis H.
    ed. Immunity to Blood Parasites of Animals &
      Man. Plenum Pub.
Miller, Lucien.
  xMiller, Lucien.
    Masks of Fiction in Dream of the Red
      Chamber: Myth, Mimesis, & Persona. U of
      Ariz Pr.
Miller, Luree.
  xMiller, Luree.
    Late Bloom: New Lives for Women.
      Paddington.
Miller, Lynn H.
  xMiller, Lynn H.
    ed. Reflections on the Cold War: A Quarter
      Century of American Foreign Policy. Temple
      U Pr.
Miller, Lynne.
  xMiller, Lynne.
    Make Your Own Thing: Games, Puzzles,
      Gimmicks & Gifts. Messner.
Miller, M. *see* Miller, Max H.
Miller, M. W. *see* Miller, Morton W.

Miller, Madeleine S. *see* Miller, Madeleine Sweeny.

Miller, Madeleine Sweeny.

  xMiller, Madeleine S.
    Harper's Encyclopedia of Bible Life. Har-Row.

Miller, Malcolm E. *see* Miller, Malcolm Eugene.

Miller, Malcolm Eugene.
  xMiller, Malcolm E.
    Anatomy of the Dog. Saunders.
Miller, Marcia.
  xMiller, Marcia.
    Deadly Pursuit. Bouregy.
Miller, Martin R.
  xMiller, Martin R.
    Climbing the Corporate Pyramid. Am Mgmt.
Miller, Marv.
  xMiller, Marv.
    Suicide After Sixty: The Final Alternative.
      Springer Pub.
Miller, Marvin G.
  xMiller, Marvin G.
    The Hills & Home. McClain.
Miller, Mary R. *see* Miller, Mary Ruth.
Miller, Mary Ruth.
  xMiller, Mary R.

    Thomas Campbell. Twayne.
Miller, Maureen.
  xMiller, Maureen.
    Help Your Child for Life. Argus Comm.
Miller, Max H.
  xMiller, M.
    ed. The Logic of Language Development in
      Early Childhood. Springer-Verlag.
Miller, May.
  xMiller, May.
    The Clearing & Beyond. Charioteer.
Miller, Merl. *see* Miller, Merl K.
Miller, Merl K.
  xMiller, Merl.
    Home Computers: A Beginner's Glossary &
      Guide. Intl Schol Bk Serv.
  xMiller, Merl K.
    Home Computers: A Beginners Glossary &
      Guide. Dilithium Pr.
Miller, Merle, 1919-
  xMiller, Merle.
    Plain Speaking: An Oral Biography of Harry S.
      Truman. Berkley Pub.
    Plain Speaking: On Oral Biography of Harry S.
      Truman. Berkley Pub.
    What Happened?. St Martin.
Miller, Michael. *see* Miller, Michael M.
Miller, Michael B.
  xMiller, Michael B.
    Current Issues in Clinical Geriatrics. Tiresias
      Pr.
Miller, Michael Charles.
  xMiller, Michael.
    Reef & Beach Life of New Zealand. Intl Pubns
      Serv.
Miller, Michael E.
  xMiller, Michael E.
    Host Defenses in the Human Neonate. Grune.
Miller, Michael M.
  xMiller, Michael.
    Therapeutic Hypnosis. Human Sci Pr.
Miller, Milton L.
  xMiller, Milton L.
    Nostalgia: A Psychoanalytic Study of Marcel
      Proust. Kennikat.
Miller, Morton A., 1914-
  xMiller, Morton A.
    Reading & Writing Short Essays. Random.
Miller, Morton W.
  xMiller, M. W.
    ed. The Dynamics of Meristem Cell
      Populations. Plenum Pub.
Miller, Nancy K., 1941-
  xMiller, Nancy K.
    The Heroine's Text: Readings in the French &
      English Novel, 1722-1782. Columbia U Pr.
Miller, Naomi.
  xMiller, Naomi.
    French Renaissance Fountains. Garland Pub.
Miller, Natalie.
  xMiller, Natalie.
    Story of the Liberty Bell. Childrens.
    Story of the Statue of Liberty. Childrens.
Miller, Nathan, 1900-
  xMiller, Nathan.
    The Child in Primitive Society. Gale.
    The Roosevelt Chronicles. Doubleday.
Miller, Neal E. *see* Miller, Neal Elgar.
Miller, Neal Elgar.
  xMiller, Neal E.
    Social Learning & Imitation. Greenwood.
Miller, Neil.
  xMiller, Neil.
    Conversation in Portuguese: Points of
      Departure. N Miller.
Miller, Nyle H.
  xMiller, Nyle H.

    Great Gunfighters of the Kansas Cowtowns,
      1867-1886. U of Nebr Pr.
Miller, Olga K.
  xMiller, Olga K.
    ed. Genealogical Research for Czech & Slovak
      Americans. Gale.
Miller, Orson K.
  xMiller, Orson K.
    Mushrooms of North America. Dutton.
Miller, Patrick D.
  xMiller, Patrick D.
    The Divine Warrior in Early Israel. Harvard U
      Pr.
Miller, Paul E. *see* Miller, Paul Eduard.
Miller, Paul Eduard, 1903-
  xMiller, Paul E.
    Down Beat's Yearbook of Swing. Greenwood.
Miller, Paul M.
  xMiller, Paul M.
    Peer Counseling in the Church. Herald Pr.
Miller, Paul S.
  xMiller, Paul S.
    Business Math. McGraw.
Miller, Peggy L.
  xMiller, Peggy L.
    Creative Outdoor Play Areas. P-H.
Miller, Perry, 1905-1963
  xMiller, Perry.
    Jonathan Edwards. Greenwood.
    ed. Legal Mind in America: From
      Independence to the Civil War. Cornell U Pr.
    Life of the Mind in America: From the
      Revolution to the Civil War. HarBraceJ.
    The Raven & the Whale: The War of Words &
      Wits in the Era of Poe & Melville.
      Greenwood.
    Religion & Freedom of Thought. Arno.
  xMiller, Perry G.
    Nature's Nation. Harvard U Pr.
Miller, Perry G. *see* Miller, Perry.
Miller, Peter, 1934-
  xMiller, Peter.
    Peter Miller's Ski Almanac. Doubleday.
Miller, Peter. *see* Miller, Peter Michael.
Miller, Peter Michael, 1942-
  xMiller, Peter.
    Personal Habit Control. S&S.
Miller, R. *see* Miller, Roscoe E.
Miller, R. H. *see* Miller, Robert Herschel.
Miller, R. R. *see* Miller, Russell R.
Miller, Randall M.
  xMiller, Randall M.
    ed. Immigrants & Religion in Urban America.
      Temple U Pr.
Miller, Randolph C. *see* Miller, Randolph Crump.
Miller, Randolph Crump, 1910-
  xMiller, Randolph C.
    The American Spirit in Theology. Pilgrim NY.
    ed. Church & Organized Movements. Arno.
    Living with Anxiety. Pilgrim NY.
Miller, Ray.
  xMiller, Ray.
    The Real CORVETTE: An Illustrated History
      of Chevrolet's Sports Car. Evergreen Pr.
Miller, Raymond C. *see* Miller, Raymond Curtis.
Miller, Raymond Curtis.
  xMiller, Raymond C.
    ed. Twentieth-Century Pessimism & the
      American Dream. Greenwood.
Miller, Raymond E. *see* Miller, Raymond Edward.
Miller, Raymond Edward, 1928-
  xMiller, Raymond E.
    Switching Theory. Krieger.
Miller, Rex.
  xMiller.
    Industrial Electricity. Bennett Co.
  xMiller, Rex.

Energy, Electricity & Electronics. Radatron
Corp.
Industrial Electricity. Scribner.
Miller, Richard, 1926-
xMiller, Richard.
English, French, German & Italian Techniques
of Singing: A Study in National Tonal
Preferences & How They Relate to
Functional Efficiency. Scarecrow.
Miller, Richard A., 1911-
xMiller, Richard A.
Bridge Brilliance & Blunders. Dow Jones-Irwin.
Miller, Richard H.
xMiller, Richard H.
ed. The Evolution of the Cold War: From
Confrontation to Containment. Krieger.
Miller, Richard I.
xMiller, Richard I.
Evaluating Faculty Performance. Jossey-Bass.
ed. The Law of War. Lexington Bks.
Legal Aspects of Technology Utilization.
Lexington Bks.
Miller, Richard J.
xMiller, Richard J.
Ancient Japanese Nobility: The Kabane
Ranking System. U of Cal Pr.
Miller, Richard M. *see* Miller, Richard McDermott.
Miller, Richard McDermott, 1922-
xMiller, Richard M.
Figure Sculpture in Wax & Plaster.
Watson-Guptill.
Miller, Richard Ulric.
xMiller, Richard V.
The Impact of Collective Bargaining on
Hospitals. Praeger.
Miller, Richard V. *see* Miller, Richard Ulric.
Miller, Robert F., 1932-
xMiller, Robert F.
One Hundred Thousand Tractors: The MTS &
the Development of Controls in Soviet
Agriculture. Harvard U Pr.
Miller, Robert H., 1942-
xMiller, Robert H.
Textbook of Basic Emergency Medicine.
Mosby.
Miller, Robert Herschel, 1910-
xMiller, R. H.
Power System Operation. McGraw.
Miller, Robert J. *see* Miller, Robert James.
Miller, Robert James, 1923-
xMiller, Robert J.
ed. Religious Ferment in Asia. Regents Pr KS.
Miller, Robert L. *see* Miller, Robert Lee.
Miller, Robert Lee.
xMiller, Robert L.
Linguistic Relativity Principle & Humboldtian
Ethnolinguistics. Mouton.

Miller, Robert Moats.
xMiller, Robert M.

American Protestantism & Social Issues,
1919-1939. Greenwood.

How Shall They Hear Without a Preacher: The
Life of Ernest Fremont Tittle. U of NC Pr.

Miller, Robert P. *see* Miller, Robert Parsons.

Miller, Robert Parsons, 1923-
xMiller, Robert P.
ed. Chaucer: Sources & Backgrounds. Oxford U
Pr.
Miller, Robert W. *see* Miller, Robert William.
Miller, Robert William, 1922-
xMiller, Robert W.
ed. Wallace-Homestead Price Guide to
Antiques & Pattern Glass.
Wallace-Homestead.
Wallace-Homestead Price Guide to Dolls.
Wallace-Homestead.
Miller, Roberta B. *see* Miller, Roberta Baltad.

Miller, Roberta Baltad.
xMiller, Roberta B.
City & Hinterland: A Case Study of Urban
Growth & Regional Developments.
Greenwood.
Miller, Roberta D. *see* Miller, Roberta Delong.
Miller, Roberta Delong.
xMiller, Roberta D.
Psychic Massage. Har-Row.
Miller, Robin.
xMiller, Robin.
Flying Nurse. Taplinger.
Miller, Roger L. *see* Miller, Roger Leroy.
Miller, Roger Leroy.
xMiller, Roger L.
Abortion, Baseball & Weed: Economic Issues
of Our Times. Har-Row.
Economic Issues for Consumers. West Pub.
The Economics of Macro Issues. Har-Row.
Economics of Macro Issues. West Pub.
Economics Today. Har-Row.
Personal Finance Today. West Pub.
Unemployment & Inflation: The New
Economics of the Wage-Price Spiral. West
Pub.
West's Business Law: Text & Cases. West Pub.
Miller, Ron, 1947-
xMiller, Ron.
Compiled by Space Art Poster Book. Stackpole.
Miller, Ronald E.
xMiller, Ronald E.
Modern Mathematical Methods for Economics
& Business. Krieger.
Miller, Roscoe E.
xMiller, R.
ed. Radiographic Contrast Agents. Univ Park.
Miller, Russell E.
xMiller, R. R.
ed. Handbook of Drug Therapy. Elsevier.
xMiller, Russell R.
Drug Effects in Hospitalized Patients:
Experiences of the Boston Collaborative Drug
Surveillance Program, 1966-1975. Wiley.
Miller, Ruth, 1921-
xMiller, Ruth.
The City Rose. McGraw.
High School Hookers. Belmont Tower.
xMiller, Ruth W.
The City Rose. Avon.
Miller, Ruth W.
xMiller, Ruth W.
The Time Minder. Christian Herald.
Miller, Ruth W. *see* Miller, Ruth.
Miller, Sally M., 1937-
xMiller, Sally M.
The Radical Immigrant. Twayne.
Miller, Samuel C.
xMiller, Samuel C.
Neon Techniques & Handling: Handbook of
Neon Sign & Cold Cathode Lighting. Signs of
Times.
Miller, Samuel H. *see* Miller, Samuel Howard.
Miller, Samuel Howard, 1900-
xMiller, Samuel H.
Religion in a Technical Age. Harvard U Pr.
Miller, Sarah W. *see* Miller, Sarah Walton.
Miller, Sarah Walton.
xMiller, Sarah W.
Christmas Drama for Youth. Broadman.
A Variety Book of Puppet Scripts. Broadman.
Miller, Saul.
xMiller, Saul.
After Law School: Finding a Job in a Tight
Market. Little.
Food for Thought: A New Look at Food &
Behavior. P-H.
Miller, Saunders.
xMiller, Saunders.

The Economics of Nuclear & Coal Power.
Praeger.
Miller, Shirley.
xMiller, Shirley.
The Vertical File & Its Satellites: A Handbook
of Acquisition, Processing, & Organization.
Libs Unl.
Miller, Sigmund. *see* Miller, Sigmund Stephen.
Miller, Sigmund Stephen.
xMiller, Sigmund.
Symptoms: The Complete Home Medical
Encyclopedia. T Y Crowell.
Miller, Stanley L.
xMiller, Stanley L.
The Origins of Life on the Earth. P-H.
Miller, Stella. *see* Miller, Stella G.
Miller, Stella G.
xMiller, Stella.
Two Groups of Thessalian Gold. U of Cal Pr.
Miller, Stephen G.
xMiller, Stephen G.
The Prytaneion: Its Function & Architectural
Form. U of Cal Pr.
Miller, Steve, 1950-
xMiller, Steven B.
illus. The Midnight Son. Schol Bk Serv.
Miller, Steven B. *see* Miller, Steve.
Miller, Stewart E.
xMiller, Stewart E.
ed. Optical Fiber Telecommunications. Acad
Pr.
Miller, Theodore K.
xMiller, Theodore K.
The Future of Student Affairs: A Guide to
Student Development for Tomorrow's Higher
Education. Jossey-Bass.
Miller, Theodore R.
xMiller, Theodore R.
Graphic History of the Americas. Krieger.
Miller, Thomas L. *see* Miller, Thomas Lloyd.
Miller, Thomas Lloyd.
xMiller, Thomas L.
Bounty & Donation Land Grants of Texas,
1835-1888. U of Tex Pr.
Public Lands of Texas, 1519-1967. U of Okla
Pr.
Miller, Tom.
xMiller, Tom.
Angler's Guide to Baja California. Baja Trail.
The Assassination Please Almanac. Contemp
Bks.
Miller, Van, 1907-
xMiller, Van.
The Public Administration of American School
Systems. Macmillan.
Miller, Vernon E.
xMiller, Vernon E.
ed. Handy Devices for Farm & Home. Oxmoor
Hse.
Miller, Vernon X.
xMiller, Vernon X.
What Some People Ought to Know About
Personal Injury Law. Vantage.
Miller, Victor B.
xMiller, Victor B.
Therapy in Dynamite. PB.
Miller, Virginia P.
xMiller, Virginia P.
Ukomno'm: The Yuki Indians of Northern
California. Ballena Pr.
Miller, W. H. *see* Miller, Wilma H.
Miller, W. J. *see* Miller, William Jack.
Miller, W. R. *see* Miller, Wilbur R.
Miller, Walter L.
xMiller, Walter L.
The Life & Accomplishments of Herbert
Hoover. Moore Pub Co.
Miller, Walter M., 1923-
xMiller, Walter M.

A Canticle for Leibowitz. Gregg.
Canticle for Leibowitz. Lippincott.
A Canticle for Leibowitz. Bantam.
Miller, Wanda. see Miller, Wanda M.
Miller, Wanda M.
xMiller, Wanda.
Reading Faster & Understanding More.
Winthrop.
Miller, Ward S.
xMiller, Ward S.
Word Wealth. HR&W.
Miller, Warren.
xMiller, Warren.
The Cool World. Fawcett.
Miller, Warren B.
xMiller, Warren B.
ed. The First Child & Family Formation.
Carolina Pop Ctr.
Psyche & Demos: Individual Psychology &
the Issues of Population. Oxford U Pr.
Miller, Warren E. see Miller, Warren Edward.
Miller, Warren Edward.
xMiller, Warren E.
American National Election Studies Data
Sourcebook: 1950-1978. Harvard U Pr.
Miller, Wayne Charles.
xMiller, Wayne Charles.
Compiled by A Comprehensive Bibliography
for the Study of American Minorities. NYU
Pr.
Compiled by A Handbook of American
Minorities. NYU Pr.
Miller, Wick R.
xMiller, W. R.
Acoma Grammar & Texts. U of Cal Pr.
Uto-Aztecan Cognate Sets. U of Cal Pr.
Miller, Wilbur R.
xMiller.
Exploring Careers in Industry. McKnight.
xMiller, W. R.
Instructors & Their Jobs. Am Technical.
xMiller, Wilbur R.
Drafting. McKnight.
Miller, Willard.
xMiller, Willard.
Symmetry Groups & Their Applications. Acad
Pr.
Miller, William.
xMiller, William.
Fishbait: The Memoirs of the Congressional
Doorkeeper. Warner Bks.
The Latins in the Levant: A History of
Frankish Greece. AMS Pr.
ed. Men in Business: Essays on the Historical
Role of the Entrepreneur. Greenwood.
Ottoman Empire & Its Successors, 1801-1927.
Octagon.
Ottoman Empire & Its Successors,1801-1927.
Biblio Dist.
Miller, William A., 1931-
xMiller, William A.
When Going to Pieces Holds You Together.
Augsburg.
Miller, William C., 1925-
xMiller, William C.
Dealing with Stress: A Challenge for
Educators. Phi Delta Kappa.
Teacher Negotiations: A Guide for Bargaining
Teams. P-H.
Miller, William C. see Miller, William Charles.
Miller, William Charles, 1927-
xMiller, William C.
Estimating & Cost Control in Electrical
Construction Design. Van Nos Reinhold.
Estimating & Cost Control in Plumbing Design.
Van Nos Reinhold.
Miller, William D.
xMiller, William D.

Memphis During the Progressive Era,
1900-1917. Brown U Pr.
Miller, William G. see Miller, William Galbraith.
Miller, William Galbraith.
xMiller, William G.
Lectures on the Philosophy of Law, Designed
Mainly As an Introduction to the Study of
International Law. Rothman.
Miller, William H. see Miller, William Hansford.
Miller, William Hansford.
xMiller, William H.
Systematic Parent Training: Procedures, Cases
& Issues. Res Press.
Miller, William Jack, 1927-
xMiller, W. J.
Dairy Cattle Feeding & Nutrition. Acad Pr.
Miller, William R.
xMiller, W. R.
How to Control Your Drinking. P-H.
Miller, William R. see Miller, William Robert.
Miller, William Robert.
xMiller, William R.
Nonviolence: A Christian Interpretation.
Schocken.
Miller, Wilma H.
xMiller, W. H.
The First R: Elementary Reading Today.
HR&W.
xMiller, Wilma H.
Diagnosis & Correction of Reading Difficulties
in Secondary School Students. Ctr Appl Res.
Identifying & Correcting Reading Difficulties in
Children. Ctr Appl Res.
Reading Correction Kit. Ctr Appl Res.
Reading Diagnosis Kit. Ctr Appl Res.
Teaching Reading in the Secondary School. C
C Thomas.
Miller, Wright. see Miller, Wright Watts.
Miller, Wright Watts.
xMiller, Wright.
Who Are the Russians?: A History of the
Russian People. Taplinger.
Miller, Zane L.
xMiller, Zane L.
Boss Cox's Cincinnati: Urban Politics in the
Progressive Era. U of Chicago Pr.
ed. Urban Professionals & the Future of the
Metropolis. Kennikat.
Millerson, Gerald.
xMillerson, Gerald.
Effective TV Production. Focal Pr.
TV Lighting Methods. Focal Pr.
TV Lighting Methods. Hastings.
Millet, Francis D. see Millet, Francis Davis.
Millet, Francis Davis, 1846-1912
xMillet, Francis D.
Capillary Crime, & Other Stories. Arno.
Millett, Allan R. see Millett, Allan Reed.
Millett, Allan Reed.
xMillett, Allan R.
Politics of Intervention: The Military
Occupation of Cuba, 1906-1909. Ohio St U
Pr.
Millett, Fred B. see Millett, Fred Benjamin.
Millett, Fred Benjamin, 1890-
xMillett, Fred B.
Reading Drama. A Method of Analysis with
Selections for Study. Arno.
Millett, J. D. see Millett, John David.
Millett, John D. see Millett, John David.
Millett, John David, 1912-
xMillett, J. D.
The Works Progress Administration in New
York City. Arno.
xMillett, John D.
The Academic Community: An Essay on
Organization. Greenwood.
Politics & Higher Education. U of Ala Pr.
xMillett, John David.

The Process & Organization of Government
Planning. Da Capo.
Millett, Kate.
xMillett, Kate.
The Basement: Meditations on a Human
Sacrifice. S&S.
Flying. Ballantine.
Millett, Ricardo A.
xMillett, Ricardo A.
Examination of "Widespread Citizen
Participation" in the Model Cities Program &
the Demands of Ethnic Minorities for a
Greater Decision-Making Role in American
Cities. R & E Res Assoc.
Millett, Richard.
xMillett, Richard.
ed. The Restless Caribbean: Changing Patterns
of International Relations. Praeger.
Millgate, Michael.
xMillgate, Michael.
The Achievement of William Faulkner. U of
Nebr Pr.
Millham, Spencer.
xMillham, Spencer.
Locking up Children: Secure Provision Within
the Child-Care System. Lexington Bks.
Millhiser, Marlys.
xMillhiser, Marlys.
The Mirror. Fawcett.
The Mirror. Putnam.
Millichap, J Gordon.
xMillichap, J. Gordon.
Febrile Convulsions. Macmillan.
Millichap, Joseph R.
xMillichap, Joseph R.
George Catlin. Boise St Univ.
Hamilton Basso. Twayne.
Milligan, David F. see Milligan, David Fredrick.
Milligan, David Fredrick.
xMilligan, David F.
Fist Puppetry. A S Barnes.
Milligan, Edward A.
xMilligan, Edward A.
Dakota Twilight: The Standing Rock Sioux,
1874-1890. Exposition.
Milligan, John E., 1913-
xMilligan, John E.
Celestial Navigation by H. O. 249. Cornell
Maritime.
Milligan, Nancy G. see Milligan, Nancy Gertrude.
Milligan, Nancy Gertrude, 1889-
xMilligan, Nancy G.
Relationship of the Professed Philosophy to the
Suggested Educational Experiences. AMS Pr.
Milligan, Robert H.
xMilligan, Robert H.
Fetish Folk of West Africa. AMS Pr.
Milligan, Spike. see Milligan, Terence Alan.
Milligan, Terence Alan.
xMilligan, Spike.
Goblins. Merrimack Bk Serv.
Millikan, Max F.
xMillikan, Max F.
A Proposal: Key to an Effective Foreign
Policy. Greenwood.
Millikan, Robert A. see Millikan, Robert Andrews.
Millikan, Robert Andrews, 1868-1953
xMillikan, Robert A.
The Autobiography of Robert A. Millikan.
Arno.
Evolution in Science & Religion. Arden Lib.
Evolution in Science & Religion. Elliots Bks.
Evolution in Science & Religion. Kennikat.
Milliken, Stephen F.
xMilliken, Stephen F.
Chester Himes: A Critical Appraisal. U of Mo
Pr.
Millimaki, Robert H.
xMillimaki, Robert H.

Fingerprint Detective. Lippincott.
Millin, Sarah G. see Millin, Sarah Gertrude Liebson.

Millin, Sarah Gertrude Liebson, 1889-1968
xMillin, Sarah G.
Mary Glenn. Academy Chi Ltd.
The People of South Africa. Greenwood.

Milling, Bryan E.
xMilling, Bryan E.
Handbook of Accounts Receivable Financing:
A Dynamic Approach to Cash Flow &
Profits. Inst Busn Plan.

Millington, Herbert, 1907-
xMillington, Herbert.
American Diplomacy & the War of the Pacific.
Octagon.

Millington, Roger, 1939-
xMillington, Roger.
Crossword Puzzles: Their History & Their Cult.
PB.
Crossword Puzzles: Their History & Their Cult.
Elsevier-Nelson.

Millington, T. Alaric.

xMillington, T. Alaric.
jt. auth. Dictionary of Mathematics. Har-Row.

Millis, H. A. see Millis, Harry Alvin.
Millis, Harry A. see Millis, Harry Alvin.

Millis, Harry Alvin, 1873-1948
xMillis, H. A.
The Japanese Problem in the United States.
Arno.
xMillis, Harry A.
Organized Labor. AMS Pr.

Millis, Walter.
xMillis, Walter.
Abolition of War. Macmillan.
The Martial Spirit. Arno.
This Is Pearl: The United States & Japan, 1941.
Greenwood.

Millman, J. see Millman, Jason.

Millman, Jason.
xMillman, J.
How to Take Tests. McGraw.
xMillman, Jason.
Appraising Educational Research: A Case
Study Approach. P-H.

Millman, Joan.
xMillman, Joan.
Parents As Playmates: A Games Approach to
the Pre-School Years. Human Sci Pr.

Millman, Lawrence.
xMillman, Lawrence.
Our Like Will Not Be There Again: Notes
from the West of Ireland. Little.

Millman, Marcia.
xMillman, Marcia.
Another Voice: Feminist Perspectives on Social
Life & Social Science. Octagon.
Such a Pretty Face: Being Fat in America.
Norton.

Millman, Michael L.
xMillman, Michael L.
Politics & the Expanding Physician Supply.
Allanheld.

Millner, Fredrick L., 1946-
xMillner, Fredrick L.
The Operas of Johann Adolf Hasse. Univ
Microfilms.

Millon, Henry A.
xMillon, Henry A.
ed. Art & Architecture in the Service of
Politics. MIT Pr.
Baroque & Rococo Architecture. Braziller.

Millon, Theodore.
xMillon, Theodore.
ed. Medical Behavioral Science. Saunders.
Millonzi, Joel C. see Millonzi, Joel Carl.

Millonzi, Joel Carl.
xMillonzi, Joel C.
Citizenship in Africa: The Role of Adult
Education in the Political Socialization of
Tanganyika. Maxwell Schl Citizen.

Mills, Alden B. see Mills, Alden Brewster.

Mills, Alden Brewster, 1903-
xMills, Alden B.
Hospital Public Relations Today. Physicians
Rec.

Mills, Barriss.
xMills, Barriss.
Domestic Fables. SBD.

Mills, Belen C. see Mills, Belen Collantes.

Mills, Belen Collantes.
xMills, Belen C.
Understanding the Young Child & His
Curriculum: Selected Readings. Macmillan.

Mills, Burt.
xMills, Burt.
Adventures in Restoring Antique Cars. Dodd.
Auto Restoration from Junker to Jewel.
Motorbooks Intl.
Restoring Convertibles: From Rags to Riches.
Dodd.

Mills, C. Wright. see Mills, Charles Wright.
Mills, Charles W. see Mills, Charles Wright.

Mills, Charles Wright.
xMills, C. Wright.
Marxists. Dell.
Power Elite. Oxford U Pr.
Power Elite. Oxford U Pr.
Puerto Rican Journey: New York's Newest
Migrants. Russell.
Sociological Imagination. Oxford U Pr.
Sociological Imagination. Oxford U Pr.
White Collar: American Middle Classes.
Oxford U Pr.
White Collar: The American Middle Classes.
Oxford U Pr.
xMills, Charles W.
The Causes of World War Three. Greenwood.

Mills, Daniel Q. see Mills, Daniel Quinn.

Mills, Daniel Quinn.
xMills, Daniel Q.
Government, Labor & Inflation: Wage
Stabilization in the United States. U of
Chicago Pr.
Industrial Relations & Manpower in
Construction. MIT Pr.

Mills, Dorothy H. see Mills, Dorothy Hurst.

Mills, Dorothy Hurst.
xMills, Dorothy H.
Spanish Vocabulary & Structure for the Health
Professional. Mills Pub Co.

Mills, Edward D. see Mills, Edward David.

Mills, Edward David.
xMills, Edward D.
National Exhibition Centre: Shop Window for
the World. Beekman Pubs.

Mills, Edwin S.
xMills, Edwin S.
The Economics of Environmental Quality.
Norton.
Urban Economics. Scott F.
Urbanization & Urban Problems. Harvard U Pr.

Mills, Frederick C. see Mills, Frederick Cecil.

Mills, Frederick Cecil, 1892-1964
xMills, Frederick C.
Contemporary Theories of Unemployment & of
Unemployment Relief. AMS Pr.
Economic Tendencies in the United States:
Aspects of Pre-War & Post-War Changes.
Arno.

Mills, Gary B.
xMills, Gary B.
The Forgotten People: Cane River's Creoles of
Color. La State U Pr.

Mills, George. see Mills, George Thompson.

Mills, George Thompson.
xMills, George.
The People of the Saints. Taylor Museum.

Mills, Gordon. see Mills, Gordon H.

Mills, Gordon H., 1914-
xMills, Gordon.
Hamlet's Castle: The Study of Literature As a
Social Experience. U of Tex Pr.
ed. Innocence & Power: Individualism in
Twentieth-Century America. U of Tex Pr.

Mills, H. E. see Mills, Herbert Elmer.
Mills, H. R. see Mills, Henry Robert.
Mills, Harlow B. see Mills, Harlow Burgess.

Mills, Harlow Burgess, 1906-
xMills, Harlow B.
A Century of Biological Research. Arno.

Mills, Helen, 1923-
xMills, Helen.
Commanding Essays. Scott F.
Commanding Paragraphs. Scott F.
Commanding Sentences. Scott F.

Mills, Henry Robert.
xMills, H. R.
Positional Astronomy & Astro-Navigation
Made Easy: A New Approach Using the
Pocket Calculator. Halsted Pr.

Mills, Herbert Elmer, 1861-1946
xMills, H. E.
College Women & the Social Sciences. Arno.

Mills, Howard.
xMills, Howard W.
Peacock, His Circle & His Age. Cambridge U
Pr.

Mills, Howard W. see Mills, Howard.
Mills, J. see Mills, Judson.

Mills, James, 1932-
xMills, James.
On the Edge. Ballantine.
The Truth About Peter Harley. Dutton.

Mills, James D.
xMills, James D.
The Art of Money Making. Arno.

Mills, James P. see Mills, James Philip.

Mills, James Philip, 1890-1960
xMills, James P.
The Lhota Nagas. AMS Pr.
The Rengma Nagas. AMS Pr.

Mills, James R., 1927-
xMills, James R.
The Gospel According to Pontius Pilate.
Revell.
The Gospel According to Pontius Pilate. SF Bk
Co.
Compiled by Poems of Inspiration from the
Masters. Revell.

Mills, Judson, 1931-
xMills, J.
Experimental Social Psychology. Macmillan.

Mills, K. see Mills, Kenneth H.

Mills, Kenneth H.
xMills, K.
Successful Retail Sales. P-H.
xMills, Kenneth H.
Create Distinctive Displays. P-H.

Mills, Lennox A. see Mills, Lennox Algernon.

Mills, Lennox Algernon.
xMills, Lennox A.
British Malaya 1824-1867. AMS Pr.
British Rule in Eastern Asia: A Study of
Contemporary Government & Economic
Development in British Malaya & Hong
Kong. Russell.
Southeast Asia: Illusion & Reality in Politics &
Economics. U of Minn Pr.

Mills, Patrick.
xMills, Patrick.
Rape Intervention Resource Manual. C C
Thomas.

Mills, Paul, 1948-
xMills, Paul.

North Carriageway. Persea Bks.
Third Person. Persea Bks.
Mills, Queenie B. *see* Mills, Queenie Beatrice.
Mills, Queenie Beatrice.
xMills, Queenie B.
Our Town. Allyn.
Mills, Ralph J., 1931-
xMills, Ralph J.
Cry of the Human: Essays on Contemporary
American Poetry. U of Ill Pr.
Richard Eberhart. U of Minn Pr.
Theodore Roethke. U of Minn Pr.
Mills, Richard C. *see* Mills, Richard Charles.
Mills, Richard Charles, 1886-1952
xMills, Richard C.
The Colonization of Australia (1829-42): The
Wakefield Experiment in Empire Building.
Intl Schol Bk Serv.
Mills, Richard L., 1941-
xMills, Richard L.
Statistics for Applied Economics & Business.
McGraw.
Mills, Robert, 1781-1855
xMills, Robert.
Statistics of South Carolina, Including a View
of Its Natural, Civil & Military History,
General & Particular. Reprint.
Mills, Robert E.
xMills, Robert E.
Daughter of Conquest. Nordon Pubns.
Star Fighters. Belmont-Tower.
Star Quest. Belmont-Tower.
Mills, Robin K.
xMills, Robin K.
South Carolina Legal Research Handbook. W S
Hein.
Mills, Roger. *see* Mills, Roger J.
Mills, Roger J.
xMills, Roger.
Tackle Badminton. Soccer.
Mills, Sonya, 1936-
xMills, Sonya.
ed. The Book of Presents: Easy-to-Make Gifts
for Every Occasion. Pantheon.
Mills, Susan W. *see* Mills, Susan Winter.
Mills, Susan Winter.
xMills, Susan W.
Illustrated Index to Traditional American Quilt
Patterns. Arco.
Mills, Theodore M.
xMills, Theodore M.
Sociology of Small Groups. P-H.
Mills, William, 1935-
xMills, William.
I Know a Place: Three Stories. Nightowl.
The Stillness in Moving Things: The World of
Howard Nemerov. Memphis St Univ.
Millspaugh, A. C. *see* Millspaugh, Arthur Chester.
Millspaugh, Arthur Chester, 1883-1955
xMillspaugh, A. C.
The American Task in Persia. Arno.
xMillspaugh, Arthur Chester.
Crime Control by the National Government.
Da Capo.
Millspaugh, Charles F. *see* Millspaugh, Charles Frederick.
Millspaugh, Charles Frederick, 1854-1923
xMillspaugh, Charles F.
American Medicinal Plants: An Illustrated &
Descriptive Guide to Plants Indigenous to &
Naturalized in the United States Which Are
Used in Medicine. Dover.
Millstead, Thomas.
xMillstead, Thomas.
Cave of the Moving Shadows. Dial.
Millward, Roy.
xMillward, Roy.
Landscapes of Britain. David & Charles.
Landscapes of North Wales. David & Charles.
Milman, Donald S.
xMilman, Donald S.

ed. Group Process Today: Evaluation &
Perspective. C C Thomas.
Milman, Henry. *see* Milman, Henry Hart.
Milman, Henry H. *see* Milman, Henry Hart.
Milman, Henry Hart, 1791-1868
xMilman, Henry.
History of Christianity from the Birth of Christ
to the Abolition of Paganism in the Roman
Empire. Church History.
xMilman, Henry H.
History of Christianity from the Birth of Christ
to the Abolition of Paganism in the Roman
Empire. AMS Pr.
Milmine, Georgine.
xMilmine, Georgine.
Life of Mary Baker G. Eddy & the History of
Christian Science. Baker Bk.
Milne, A. A. *see* Milne, Alan Alexander.
Milne, Alan Alexander, 1882-1956
xMilne, A. A.
Christopher Robin Story Book. Dutton.
Gallery of Children. McKay.
Once a Week. Core Collection.
Pooh Story Book. Dutton.
Pooh's Alphabet Book. Dell.
Pooh's Alphabet Book. Dutton.
Pooh's Birthday Book. Dell.
Pooh's Birthday Book. Dutton.
When We Were Very Young. Dutton.
When We Were Very Young. Dutton.
When We Were Very Young. Dell.
Milne, Christopher, 1920-
xMilne, Christopher.
The Enchanted Places. Penguin.
Enchanted Places. Dutton.
Path Through the Trees. Dutton.
Milne, Gordon.
xMilne, Gordon.
American Political Novel. U of Okla Pr.
Milne, J. G. *see* Milne, John Stewart.
Milne, James.
xMilne, James.
London Book Window. Arno.
Milne, John S. *see* Milne, John Stewart.
Milne, John Stewart, 1871-
xMilne, J. G.
Surgical Instruments in Greek & Roman Times.
Ares.
xMilne, John S.
Surgical Instruments in Greek & Roman Times.
Kelley.
Surgical Instruments in Greek & Roman Times.
Milford Hse.
Milne, Joseph G. *see* Milne, Joseph Grafton.
Milne, Joseph Grafton, 1867-1951
xMilne, Joseph G.
Greek & Roman Coins & the Study of History.
Greenwood.
Milne, Katharine.
xMilne, Katharine.
Car Smash. Intl Pubns Serv.
Milne, Lorus. *see* Milne, Lorus Johnson.
Milne, Lorus J. *see* Milne, Lorus Johnson.
Milne, Lorus Johnson.
xMilne, Lorus.
The Animal in Man. McGraw.
The Nature of Plants. Lippincott.
xMilne, Lorus J.
Balance of Nature. Knopf.
Ecology Out of Joint: New Environments &
Why They Happen. Scribner.
Mountains. Silver.
Milne, Robert S. *see* Milne, Robert Scott.
Milne, Robert Scott.
xMilne, Robert S.
Opportunities in Travel Careers. Natl Textbk.
Milne, Roseleen.
xMilne, Roseleen.

Borrowed Plumes. NAL.
Milne, Tom.
xMilne, Tom.
The Cinema of Carl Dreyer. A S Barnes.
Milner, Anita C. *see* Milner, Anita Cheek.
Milner, Anita Cheek.
xMilner, Anita C.
Newspaper Genealogical Column Directory.
Heritage Bk.
Newspaper Indexes: A Location & Subject
Guide for Researchers. Scarecrow.
Milner, Esther.
xMilner, Esther.
The Failure of Success: The Middle Class
Crisis. Green.
Milner, Marion. *see* Milner, Marion (Blackett).
Milner, Marion (Blackett).
xMilner, Marion.
On Not Being Able to Paint. Intl Univs Pr.
Milnes, A. G. *see* Milnes, Arthur George.
Milnes, Arthur George.
xMilnes, A. G.
Deep Impurities in Semiconductors. Wiley.
Semiconductor Devices & Integrated
Electronics. Van Nos Reinhold.
Milnor, J. *see* Milnor, John Willard.
Milnor, John. *see* Milnor, John Willard.
Milnor, John W. *see* Milnor, John Willard.
Milnor, John Willard.
xMilnor, J.
Symmetric Bilinear Forms. Springer-Verlag.
xMilnor, John.
Introduction to Algebraic K-Theory. Princeton
U Pr.
xMilnor, John W.
Characteristic Classes. Princeton U Pr.
Lectures on the H-Cobordism Theorem.
Princeton U Pr.
Milo, Mary.
xMilo, Mary.
A Different Music. Avon.

Milord, Sue.

xMilord, Sue.
Maggie & the Goodbye Gift. Lothrop.

Milsark, Gary L., 1946-

xMilsark, Gary L.
Existential Sentences in English. Garland Pub.
Milson, A. *see* Milson, Anthony.
Milson, Anthony.
xMilson, A.
Principles of Design & Operation of Catering
Equipment. AVI.
Milson, Fred. *see* Milson, Frederick William.
Milson, Frederick William.
xMilson, Fred.
An Introduction to Community Work.
Routledge & Kegan.
An Introduction to Group Work Skill.
Routledge & Kegan.
Milson, Menahem.
xMilson, Menahem.
ed. Society & Political Structure in the Arab
World. Humanities.
Milstein, Ann R. *see* Milstein, Ann Rebecca.
Milstein, Ann Rebecca.
xMilstein, Ann R.
The Paintings of Girolamo Mazzola Bedoli.
Garland Pub.
Milstein, Jeff.
xMilstein, Jeff.
Building Cardboard Dollhouses. Har-Row.
Building Cardboard Toys. Har-Row.
Milstein, Jeffrey S.
xMilstein, Jeffrey S.

The Dynamics of the Vietnam War: A
  Quantitative Analysis & Predictive Computer
  Simulation. Ohio St U Pr.
Milstein, Mike M.
  xMilstein, Mike M.
    Educational Policy-Making & the State
      Legislature: The New York Experience.
      Irvington.
Milthorpe, F. L. see Milthorpe, Frederick Leon.
Milthorpe, Frederick Leon.
  xMilthorpe, F. L.
    Introduction to Crop Physiology. Cambridge U
      Pr.
Milton. see Milton, Arthur.
Milton, Arthur, 1922-
  xMilton.
    Life Insurance Stocks: The Modern Gold Rush.
      Citadel Pr.
Milton, Charles R.
  xMilton, Charles R.
    Ethics & Expediency in Personnel
      Management: A Critical History of Personnel
      Philosophy. U of SC Pr.
Milton, George F. see Milton, George Fort.
Milton, George Fort, 1894-1955
  xMilton, George F.
    Eve of Conflict: Stephen A. Douglas & the
      Needless War. Octagon.
    Use of Presidential Power, 1789-1943.
      Octagon.
Milton, Hilary. see Milton, Hilary H.
Milton, Hilary H.
  xMilton.
    Blind Flight. Watts.
  xMilton, Hilary.
    Mayday! Mayday!. Watts.
Milton, J. see Milton, John.
Milton, J. Susan. see Milton, Janet Susan.
Milton, Janet Susan.
  xMilton, J. Susan.
    Probability Theory with the Essential Analysis.
      A-W.
Milton, John.
  xMilton, J.
    Paradise Lost. Cambridge U Pr.
  xMilton, John.
    Areopagitica. AMS Pr.
    Areopagitica. Saifer.
    Autobiography of John Milton: Milton's Life in
      His Own Words. Folcroft.
    A Brief History of Moscovia & Other Less
      Known Countries Lying Eastward of Russia
      As Far As Cathay: Gather 'd from the
      Writings of Several Eye-Witnesses. Arden
      Lib.
    A Maske: The Earlier Versions. U of Toronto
      Pr.
    Odes, Pastorals, Masques. Cambridge U Pr.
    Paradise Lost. Cambridge U Pr.
    Paradise Lost. Modern Lib.
    Paradise Lost. Norton.
    Paradise Lost. Oxford U Pr.
    Paradise Lost & Selected Poetry & Prose.
      HR&W.
    Paradise Regained: A Poem, in Four Books.
      Arden Lib.
    The Portable Milton. Penguin.
    The Portable Milton. Viking Pr.
Milton, John R.
  xMilton, John R.
    The Literature of South Dakota. Dakota Pr.
    The Novel of the American West. U of Nebr
      Pr.
    Oscar Howe. Dillon.
Milton, Katharine.
  xMilton, Katharine.
    The Foraging Strategy of Howler Monkeys: A
      Study in Economics. Columbia U Pr.
Milton, Katharine. see Milton, Katharine.

Milton, Ohmer.
  xMilton, Ohmer.
    Alternatives to the Traditional: How Professors
      Teach & How Students Learn. Jossey-Bass.
    ed. Learning & the Professors. Ohio U Pr.
Milunsky, Aubrey.
  xMilunsky, Aubrey.
    ed. Genetic Disorders & the Fetus: Diagnosis,
      Prevention, & Treatment. Plenum Pub.
    The Prenatal Diagnosis of Hereditary
      Disorders. C C Thomas.
    Prevention of Genetic Disease & Mental
      Retardation. Saunders.
Milverstedt, Van.
  xMilverstedt, Van.
    On the Boards. Raintree Pubs.
Milward, Alan S.
  xMilward, Alan S.
    The Development of the Economies of
      Continental Europe, 1850-1914. Harvard U
      Pr.
    The Economic Development of Continental
      Europe 1780-1870. Allen Unwin.
Milward, Peter.
  xMilward, Peter.
    Religious Controversies of the Elizabethan Age:
      A Survey of Printed Sources. U of Nebr Pr.
Milwaukee County Welfare Rights Organization.
  xMilwaukee County Welfare Rights Organization.
    Welfare Mothers Speak Out: We Ain't Gonna
      Shuffle Anymore. Norton.
**Milwaukee Curriculum Theory Conference, University of
Wisconsin-Milwaukee, 1976.**
  xCurriculum Theory Conference, University of
    Wisconsin, Milwaukee, November 11-14, 1976.
    Curriculum Theory: Proceedings. Assn
      Supervision.
Mims, Cedric. see Mims, Cedric A.
Mims, Cedric A.
  xMims, Cedric.
    ed. The Pathogenesis of in Infectious Disease.
      Grune.
Mims, Edwin, 1872-1959
  xMims, Edwin.
    Advancing South: Stories of Progress &
      Reaction. Kennikat.
    Christ of the Poets. Greenwood.
    History of Vanderbilt University. Arno.
    Sidney Lanier. Gordon Pr.
    Sidney Lanier. Kennikat.
Mims, Forrest. see Mims, Forrest M.
Mims, Forrest M.
  xMims, Forrest.
    Light-Beam Communications. Sams.
  xMims, Forrest M.
    How to Protect Your CB Rig. Sams.
    LED Circuits & Projects. Sams.
Mims, Stewart L. see Mims, Stewart Lea.
Mims, Stewart Lea, 1880-
  xMims, Stewart L.
    Colbert's West India Policy. Octagon.
Mims, W. B.
  xMims, W. B.
    The Linear Electric Field Effect in
      Paramagnetic Resonance. Oxford U Pr.
Minami, Hiroshi, 1914-
  xMinami, Hiroshi.
    Psychology of the Japanese People. U of
      Toronto Pr.
Minar, William M.
  xMinar, William M.
    Greenhouse Gardening in the South. Pacesetter
      Pr.
Minard, Rosemary.
  xMinard, Rosemary.
    Womenfolk & Fairy Tales. HM.
Minard, Susan.
  xMinard, Susan.

Eat Alone with Your Children & Like It: A
  Cooking Manual for Single Parents.
  Mynabird Pub.
Minarik, Else H. see Minarik, Else Holmelund.
Minarik, Else Holmelund.
  xMinarik, Else H.
    Little Bear. Har-Row.
    Little Bear. Har-Row.
Minarik, John P. see Minarik, John Paul.
Minarik, John Paul.
  xMinarik, John P.
    Patterns in the Dusk. King Pubns.
Minattur, Joseph.
  xMinattur, Joseph.
    Contractual Remedies in Asian Countries.
      Oceana.
Minc, Henryk.
  xMinc, Henryk.
    Permanents. A-W.
Minchin, Harry C. see Minchin, Harry Christopher.
Minchin, Harry Christopher, 1861-1941
  xMinchin, Harry C.
    Talks & Traits. Folcroft.
Minchinton, Walter E.
  xMinchinton, Walter Edward.
    ed. Industrial South Wales, 1750-1914: Essays
      in Welsh Economic History. Biblio Dist.
Minchinton, Walter Edward. see Minchinton, Walter E.
Minckler, Leon S. see Minckler, Leon Sherwood.
Minckler, Leon Sherwood, 1906-
  xMinckler, Leon S.
    Woodland Ecology: Environmental Forestry for
      the Small Owner. Syracuse U Pr.
Mindel, Charles H.
  xMindel, Charles H.
    ed. Ethnic Families in America: Patterns &
      Variations. Elsevier.
Mindell, Earl. see Mindell, Earl L.
Mindell, Earl L.
  xMindell, Earl.
    Earl Mindell's Vitamin Bible. Rawson Wade.
    Earl Mindell's Vitamin Bible. Warner Bks.

Mindess, David.

  xMindess, David.
    Guide to an Effective Kindergarten Program.
      P-H.

Mindess, Harvey.

  xMindess, Harvey.
    Psychology: The Study of People. Goodyear.

Mine, H. see Mine, Hisashi.
Mine, Hisashi.
  xMine, H.
    Markovian Decision Processes. Elsevier.
Minear, Paul S. see Minear, Paul Sevier.
Minear, Paul Sevier, 1906-
  xMinear, Paul S.
    Images of the Church in the New Testament.
      Westminster.
Minehan, Thomas.
  xMinehan, Thomas.
    Boy & Girl Tramps of America. U of Wash Pr.
Miner, Charles S.
  xMiner, Charles S.
    How to Get an Executive Job After 40.
      Macmillan.
Miner, Clarence E. see Miner, Clarence Eugene.
Miner, Clarence Eugene, 1886-
  xMiner, Clarence E.
    Ratification of the Federal Constitution by the
      State of New York. AMS Pr.
Miner, Earl. see Miner, Earl Roy.
Miner, Earl Roy.
  xMiner, Earl.

Intro. by & ed. English Criticism in Japan: Essays by Younger Japanese Scholars on English & Am Literature. Princeton U Pr.

An Introduction to Japanese Court Poetry. Stanford U Pr.

Japanese Linked Poetry: An Account with Translations of Renga & Haikai Sequences. Princeton U Pr.

ed. Literary Uses of Typology: From the Late Middle Ages to the Present. Princeton U Pr.

ed. Stuart & Georgian Moments: Clark Library Seminar Papers on Seventeeth & Eighteenth Century Literature. U of Cal Pr.

Miner, H. Craig.
xMiner, H. Craig.
The Corporation & the Indian: Tribal Sovereignty & Industrial Civilization in Indian Territory. U of Mo Pr.
The End of Indian Kansas: A Study of Cultural Revolution, 1854-1871. Regents Pr KS.

Miner, John B.
xMiner, John B.
Personnel & Industrial Relations: A Managerial Approach. Macmillan.

Miner, Mary G. *see* Miner, Mary Green.

Miner, Mary Green.

xMiner, Mary G.
A Guide to Personnel Management. BNA.

Miner, Maryalice F. *see* Miner, Maryalice Fairbank.

Miner, Maryalice Fairbank.

xMiner, Maryalice F.
Water Fun: Swimming Instruction & Water Games for the Whole Family. P-H.

Miner, Robert.
xMiner, Robert.
Mother's Day. PB.

Miner, Ward. *see* Miner, Ward L.

Miner, Ward L.
xMiner, Ward.
World of William Faulkner. Cooper Sq.

Miner, William H. *see* Miner, William Harvey.

Miner, William Harvey, 1877-1934
xMiner, William H.
ed. Daniel Boone: Contribution Toward a Bibliography of Writings Concerning Daniel Boone. B Franklin.

Miners, N. J.
xMiners, Norman.
The Government & Politics of Hong Kong. Oxford U Pr.

Miners, Norman. *see* Miners, N. J.

Minerva Symposium on Physics, Rehovot, Israel, 1973. *see* Minerva Symposium on Physics, Weizmann Institute of Science, Rehovot, Israel, 1973.

Minerva Symposium on Physics, Weizmann Institute of Science, Rehovot, Israel, 1973.
xMinerva Symposium on Physics, Rehovot, Israel, 1973.
Nuclear Structure Physics: Proceedings. Springer-Verlag.

Minford, P. *see* Minford, Patrick.

Minford, Patrick.
xMinford, P.
Substitution Effects, Speculation & Exchange Rate Stability. Elsevier.

Ming, Dennis. *see* Ming, Dennis L.

Ming, Dennis L.
xMing, Dennis.
Emergency Drug Manual. Reston.

Mingay, G. E.
xMingay, G. E.
The Gentry: The Rise & Fall of a Ruling Class. Longman.

Minge, Ward Alan.
xMinge, Ward Alan.

Acoma: Pueblo in the Sky. U of NM Pr.

Mings, Lonnie C., 1939-
xMings, Lonnie C.
ed. The Pure Land. Moody.

Minieka, Edward.
xMinieka, Edward.
Optimization Algorithms for Networks & Graphs. Dekker.

Minifie, Bernard W.
xMinifie, Bernard W.
Chocolate, Cocoa & Confectionery: Science & Technology. AVI.

Minifie, Fred D.
xMinifie, Fred D.
ed. Communicative & Cognitive Abilities: Early Behavioral Assessment. Univ Park.
Normal Aspects of Speech, Hearing, & Language. P-H.

Minirth, Frank B.
xMinirth, Frank B.
Christian Psychiatry. Revell.

Minish, Gary L.
xMinish, Gary L.
Beef Production & Management. Reston.

Ministers of Foreign Affairs of the American Republic-8th-Punta del Este-Uruguay-1962. *see* Meeting of Consultation of Ministers of Foreign Affairs of American States, 8th, Punta del Este, Uruguay.

Minium, E. W. *see* Minium, Edward W.

Minium, Edward W., 1917-
xMinium, E. W.
Statistical Reasoning in Psychology & Education. Wiley.

Mink, Louis O., 1921-
xMink, Louis O.
A Finnegans Wake Gazetteer. Ind U Pr.

Minkin, Stephen.
xMinkin, Stephen.
A No Doubt Mad Idea. Ross-Back Roads.
xMinkin, Steve.
A No Doubt Mad Idea. Ross Bks.

Minkin, Steve *see* Minkin, Stephen.

Minkin, V. I. *see* Minkin, Vladimir Isaakovich.

Minkin, Vladimir Isaakovich.
xMinkin, V. I.
Dipole Moments in Organic Chemistry. Plenum Pub.

Minkowski, Eugene, 1885-
xMinkowski, Eugene.
Lived Time: Phenomenological & Psychopathological Studies. Northwestern U Pr.

Minna, John D.
xMinna, John D.
Disseminated Intravascular Coagulation in Man. C C Thomas.

Minnaert, M. *see* Minnaert, Marcel Gilles Jozef.
Minnaert, M. J. *see* Minnaert, Marcel Gilles Jozef.

Minnaert, Marcel Gilles Jozef, 1893-
xMinnaert, M.
Nature of Light & Colour in the Open Air. Dover.
xMinnaert, M. J.
Practical Work in Elementary Astronomy. Kluwer Boston.

Minnelli, Vincente.
xMinnelli, Vincente.
I Remember It Well. Berkley Pub.

Minneman, Paul G. *see* Minneman, Paul George.

Minneman, Paul George, 1902-
xMinneman, Paul G.
Large Land Holdings in Ohio & Their Operation. Arno.

Minnery, John.
xMinnery, John.
How to Kill. Paladin Ent.
Improvised Modified Firearms. Paladin Ent.

Minnesota Historical Society.
xMinnesota Historical Society.

Chippewa & Dakota Indians: A Subject Catalog of Books, Pamphlets, Periodical Articles & Manuscripts in the Minnesota Historical Society. Minn Hist.
A Complete Index to the Gopher Historian, 1946-1972. Minn Hist.

Minnesota University - Graduate School. *see* Minnesota. University. Graduate School.

Minnesota. University. Graduate School.
xMinnesota University - Graduate School.
Social Sciences at Mid-Century. Arno.

Minnesota. University. Library. James Ford Bell Collection.
xJames Ford Bell Library, University of Minnesota.
The James Ford Bell Library: An Annotated Catalog of Original Source Materials Relating to the History of European Expansion, 1400-1800. G K Hall.

Minnich, Jerry.
xMinnich, Jerry.
The Earthworm Book: How to Raise & Use Earthworms for Your Farm & Garden. Rodale Pr Inc.
No Time for Houseplants: A Busy Person's Guide to Indoor Gardening. U of Okla Pr.

Minnick, John H. *see* Minnick, John Harper.

Minnick, John Harper.
xMinnick, John H.
An Outline for the Study of Calculus. Har-Row.

Minnick, Wayne C.
xMinnick, Wayne C.
Public Speaking. HM.

Minnigerode, Meade.
xMinnigerode, Meade.
Some Personal Letters of Herman Melville & a Bibliography. Arno.

Minogue, M. *see* Minogue, Martin.

Minogue, Martin.
xMinogue, M.
ed. African Aims & Attitudes: Selected Documents. Cambridge U Pr.

Minor, Andrew C. *see* Minor, Andrew Collier.

Minor, Andrew Collier.
xMinor, Andrew C.
ed. Renaissance Entertainment: Festivities for the Marriage of Cosimo I, Duke of Florence, in 1539. U of Mo Pr.

Minor, Marz.
xMinor, Marz.
The American Indian Craft Book. U of Nebr Pr.

Minor, T. *see* Minor, Theodore E.

Minor, Theodore E.
xMinor, T.
Staphylococci & Their Significance in Foods. Elsevier.

Minot, Charles S. *see* Minot, Charles Sedgwick.

Minot, Charles Sedgwick, 1852-1914
xMinot, Charles S.
The Problem of Age, Growth, & Death. Arno.

Minot, Stephen.
xMinot, Stephen.
Ghost Images. Har-Row.

Minott, Jan.
xMinott, Jan.
Fitting Commercial Patterns: The Minott Method. Burgess.

Minshall, Herbert L., 1912-
xMinshall, Herbert L.
The Broken Stones. Copley Bks.

Minshull, Evelyn. *see* Minshull, Evelyn White.
Minshull, Evelyn W. *see* Minshull, Evelyn White.

Minshull, Evelyn White.
xMinshull, Evelyn.
But I Thought You Really Loved Me. Westminster.
xMinshull, Evelyn W.

The Steps to My Best Friends House. Westminster.

Minsky, Betty J. *see* Minsky, Betty Jane.

Minsky, Betty Jane.
  xMinsky, Betty J.
    Gimmicks Make Money in Retailing. Fairchild.

Minteer, Catherine.
  xMinteer, Catherine.
    Words & What They Do to You: Beginning Lessons in General Semantics for Junior & Senior High School. Inst Gen Semantics.

Minter, Charles R. *see* Minter, Charles Russell.

Minter, Charles Russell, 1947-
  xMinter, Charles R.
    A Processor Design for the Efficient Implementation of APL. Garland Pub.

Minter, Harold A. *see* Minter, Harold Avery.

Minter, Harold Avery, 1892-
  xMinter, Harold A.
    Umpqua Valley, Oregon, & Its Pioneers. Binford.

Minters, Arthur H.
  xMinters, Arthur H.
    Collecting Books for Fun & Profit. Arco.

Minto, William, 1845-1893
  xMinto, William.
    Daniel Defoe. AMS Pr.
    Daniel Defoe. R West.
    The Literature of the Georgian Era. Arden Lib.
    The Literature of the Georgian Era. Folcroft.
    Literature of the Georgian Era. Kennikat.

Minton, Henry L.
  xMinton, Henry L.
    Differential Psychology. Brooks-Cole.

Minton, Penny.
  xMinton, Penny.
    How to Grow Trees Indoors. Doubleday.

Minton, Robert, 1918-
  xMinton, Robert.
    Forest Hills: An Illustrated History. Lippincott.

Minton, S. A. *see* Minton, Sherman A.

Minton, Sherman A.
  xMinton, S. A.
    Venom Diseases. C C Thomas.

Minty, Judith, 1937-
  xMinty, Judith.
    Yellow Dog Journal. Center Pubns.

Mintz, Alan. *see* Mintz, Alan L.

Mintz, Alan L.
  xMintz, Alan.
    George Eliot & the Novel of Vocation. Harvard U Pr.

Mintz, Elizabeth E.
  xMintz, Elizabeth E.
    Marathon Groups: Reality & Symbol. Irvington.

Mintz, Ilse. *see* Mintz, Ilse Schueller.

Mintz, Ilse Schueller, 1904-
  xMintz, Ilse.
    Deterioration in the Quality of Foreign Bonds Issued in the United States, 1920-1930. Arno.

Mintz, Jerome R.
  xMintz, Jerome R.
    Legends of the Hasidim: An Introduction to Hasidic Culture & Oral Tradition in the New World. U of Chicago Pr.

Mintz, Lorelie M. *see* Mintz, Lorelie Miller.

Mintz, Lorelie Miller.
  xMintz, Lorelie M.
    illus. How to Grow Fruits & Berries. Messner.
    illus. Vegetables in Patches & Pots: A Child's Guide to Organic Vegetable Gardening. FS&G.

Mintz, Marilyn D., 1950-
  xMintz, Marilyn D.
    The Martial Arts Film. A S Barnes.

Mintz, Max M., 1919-
  xMintz, Max M.

Gouverneur Morris & the American Revolution. U of Okla Pr.

Mintz, Morton.
  xMintz, Morton.
    Power Inc.: Public & Private Rulers & How to Make Them Accountable. Viking Pr.

Mintz, Ruth F. *see* Mintz, Ruth Finer.

Mintz, Ruth Finer.
  xMintz, Ruth F.
    Modern Hebrew Poetry: A Bilingual Anthology. U of Cal Pr.

Mintz, Sidney W. *see* Mintz, Sidney Wilfred.

Mintz, Sidney Wilfred.
  xMintz, Sidney W.
    An Anthropological Approach to the Afro-American Past: A Caribbean Perspective. Inst Study Human.
    Caribbean Transformations. Aldine Pub.
    Compiled by Papers in Caribbean Anthropology. HRAFP.

Mintzberg, H. *see* Mintzberg, Henry.

Mintzberg, Henry.
  xMintzberg, H.
    Nature of Managerial Work. P-H.
  xMintzberg, Henry.
    The Nature of Managerial Work. Har-Row.

Minuchin, Salvador.
  xMinuchin, Salvador.
    Families & Family Therapy. Harvard U Pr.
    Families of the Slums: An Exploration of Their Structure Treatment. Basic.
    Psychosomatic Families: Anorexia Nervosa in Context. Harvard U Pr.

Minus, Paul M.
  xMinus, Paul M.
    The Catholic Rediscovery of Protestantism: A History of Roman Catholic Ecumenical Pioneering. Paulist Pr.

Mira, Julio A.
  xMira, Julio A.
    Arithmetic Clear & Simple. Har-Row.
    Mathematical Teasers. Har-Row.

Mirabaud, Paul.
  xMirabaud, Paul.
    The Postage Stamps of Switzerland 1843-1862. Quarterman.

Miraglia, Luigi, 1846-1903
  xMiraglia, Luigi.
    Comparative Legal Philosophy Applied to Legal Institutions. Rothman.

Miranda, C. *see* Miranda, Carlo.

Miranda, Carlo.
  xMiranda, C.
    Partial Differential Equations of Elliptic Type. Springer-Verlag.

Mirchuk, Petro.
  xMirchuk, Petro.
    In the German Mills of Death. Vantage.

Mireaux, Emile, 1885-
  xMireaux, Emile.
    Daily Life in the Time of Homer. Macmillan.

Mirengoff, William.
  xMirengoff, William.
    The Comprehensive Employment & Training Act: Impact on People, Places, & Programs: an Interim Report. Natl Acad Pr.

Mirikitani, Leatrice T.
  xMirikitani, Leatrice T.
    Speaking Kapampangan. U Pr of Hawaii.

Mirin, Susan K. *see* Mirin, Susan Kooperstein.

Mirin, Susan Kooperstein.
  xMirin, Susan K.
    ed. Teaching Tomorrow's Nurse: A Nurse Educator Reader. Nursing Res.

Miringoff, Marc L.
  xMiringoff, Marc L.
    Management in Human Service Organizations. Macmillan.

Mirkin, Boris G. *see* Mirkin, Boris Grigorevich.

Mirkin, Boris Grigorevich.
  xMirkin, Boris G.
    Group Choice. Halsted Pr.

Miroff, Bruce.
  xMiroff, Bruce.
    Pragmatic Illusions: The Presidential Politics of John F. Kennedy. Longman.

Miron, Murray S.
  xMiron, Murray S.
    Hostage. Pergamon.

Mironer, Alan.
  xMironer, Alan.
    Engineering Fluid Mechanics. McGraw.

Mirov, Nicholas T. *see* Mirov, Nicholas Tiho.

Mirov, Nicholas Tiho.
  xMirov, Nicholas T.
    The Story of Pines. Ind U Pr.

Mirrielees, Edith R. *see* Mirrielees, Edith Ronald.

Mirrielees, Edith Ronald, 1878-1962
  xMirrielees, Edith R.
    Story Writing. Writer.

Mirsky, Jeannette, 1903-
  xMirsky, Jeannette.
    Balboa: Discoverer of the Pacific. Har-Row.
    Houses of God. U of Chicago Pr.

Mirsky, Reba P. *see* Mirsky, Reba Paeff.

Mirsky, Reba Paeff.
  xMirsky, Reba P.
    Thirty-One Brothers & Sisters. Dell.

Misch, Georg, 1878-1965
  xMisch, Georg.
    A History of Autobiography in Antiquity. Greenwood.

Misch, Robert Jay.
  xMisch, Robert Jay.
    Quick Guide to the Wines of All the Americas. Doubleday.

Mischel, Harriet N.
  xMischel, Harriet N.
    Readings in Personality. HR&W.

Mischel, Theodore.
  xMischel, Theodore.
    ed. Human Action: Conceptual & Empirical Issues. Acad Pr.

Mischel, W. *see* Mischel, Harriet N.

Mischel, Walter.
  xMischel, W.
    Personality & Assessment. Wiley.
  xMischel, Walter.
    Essentials of Psychology. Random.
    Introduction to Personality. HR&W.

Miser, A.
  xMiser, A.
    Factory Store Guide to All New England. Globe Pequot.

Miserez-Schira, Georges.
  xMiserez-Schira, Georges.
    The Art of Painting on Porcelain. Chilton.

Mises, Ludwig Von. *see* Von Mises, Ludwig.

Mises, Richard Von. *see* Von Mises, Richard.

Mish, Charles C. *see* Mish, Charles Carroll.

Mish, Charles Carroll, 1913-
  xMish, Charles C.
    ed. Restoration Prose Fiction, 1666-1700: An Anthology of Representative Pieces. U of Nebr Pr.

Mishara, Brian L.
  xMishara, Brian L.
    Alcohol & Old Age. Grune.

Mishell, D. R.
  xMishell, Daniel R.
    Reproductive Endocrinology, Infertility, & Contraception. Davis Co.

Mishell, Daniel R. *see* Mishell, D. R.

Mishima, Sumie. *see* Mishima, Sumie (Seo).

Mishima, Sumie (Seo).
  xMishima, Sumie.

The Broader Way: A Woman's Life in the
New Japan. Greenwood.
Mishima, Yukio, Pseud.
xMishima, Yukio.
Confessions of a Mask. New Directions.
Mishkin, David J. *see* Mishkin, David Joel.
Mishkin, David Joel.
xMishkin, David J.
The American Colonial Wine Industry: An
Economic Interpretation. Arno.
Mishkin, Julie Russo.
xMishkin, Julie Russo.
The Compleat Belly Dancer. Doubleday.
Mishra, Rammurti S.
xMishra, Rammurti S.
Fundamentals of Yoga: A Handbook of
Theory, Practice & Application. Doubleday.
Mishra, V. M. *see* Mishra, Vishwa Mohan.
Mishra, Vishwa Mohan.
xMishra, V. M.
Law & Disorder: Law Enforcement in
Television Network News. Asia.
Misiak, Henryk.
xMisiak, Henryk.
History of Psychology: An Overview. Grune.
Miskimin, Alice.
xMiskimin, Alice S.
The Renaissance Chaucer. Yale U Pr.
Miskimin, Alice S. *see* Miskimin, Alice.
Miskimin, H. A. *see* Miskimin, Harry A.
Miskimin, Harry A.
xMiskimin, H. A.
Economy of Early Renaissance Europe.
Cambridge U Pr.
xMiskimin, Harry A.
ed. The Medieval City. Yale U Pr.
Money, Prices, & Foreign Exchange in
Fourteenth Century France. Pergamon.
Miskin, Murray.
xMiskin, Murray.
ed. Ultrasound in Pediatrics. Grune.
Mislow, K. *see* Mislow, Kurt.
Mislow, Kurt.
xMislow, K.
Introduction to Stereochemistry.
Benjamin-Cummings.
Misner, Charles W.
xMisner, Charles W.
Gravitation. W H Freeman.
Misra, Atmanand, 1913-
xMisra, Atmanand.
Educational Finance in India. Asia.
Financing of Indian Education. Asia.
Misra, B. B. *see* Misra, Bankey Bihari.
Misra, Bankey Bihari.
xMisra, B. B.
The Administrative History of India,
1834-1947: General Administration. Oxford
U Pr.
The Indian Political Parties: An Historical
Analysis of Political Behavior up to 1947.
Oxford U Pr.
Misra, G. S., 1921-
xMisra, G. S.
Survey of Modern British History. Asia.
Misrow, Jogesh Chander, 1886-
xMisrow, Jogesh Chandler.
East Indian Immigration on the Pacific Coast.
R & E Res Assoc.
Misrow, Jogesh Chandler. *see* Misrow, Jogesh Chander.
Misselwitz, Henry F. *see* Misselwitz, Henry Francis.
Misselwitz, Henry Francis, 1900-
xMisselwitz, Henry F.
The Dragon Stirs: An Intimate Sketchbook of
China's Kuomintang Revolution. Hyperion
Conn.
Missingham, Hal, 1906-
xMissingham, Hal.

Design Focus. Van Nos Reinhold.
Missionary Research Library - New York. *see* New York
(City). Missionary Research Library.
**Mississippi Cooperative Extension Service. Home
Economics Division.**
xMississippi Home Economists.
The Mississippi Cookbook. U Pr of Miss.
Mississippi Department of Archives and History.
xMississippi Department Of Archives And History.
Mississippi Provincial Archives: French
Dominion. AMS Pr.
Mississippi Home Economists. *see* Mississippi
Cooperative Extension Service. Home Economics
Division.
Missouri Association for Criminal Justice.
xMissouri Association For Criminal Justice.
Missouri Crime Survey. Patterson Smith.
M.I.T. Energy Laboratory Policy Study Group.
xM.I.T. Energy Laboratory Policy Study Group.
Energy Self-Sufficiency: An Economic
Evaluation. Am Enterprise.
**M.I.T. Symposium on American Women in Science and
Engineering. 1964.**
xM.I.T. Symposium on American Women in
Science & Engineering, 1964.
Women & the Scientific Professions:
Proceedings. Greenwood.
Mital, K. V.
xMital, K. V.
Optimization Methods in Operations Research
& Systems Analysis. Halsted Pr.
Mitau, G. Theodore.
xMitau, G. Theodore.
Politics in Minnesota. U of Minn Pr.
Mitchel, John, 1815-1875
xMitchel, John.
An Apology for the British Government in
Ireland. AMS Pr.
Mitchel, Monroe.
xMitchel, Monroe.
ed. A Practical Guide to Long Term Care &
Health Services Administration. Panel Pubs.
Mitchel, Ormsby M. *see* Mitchel, Ormsby MacKnight.
Mitchel, Ormsby MacKnight, 1809-1862
xMitchel, Ormsby M.
The Planetary & Stellar Worlds: A Popular
Exposition of the Great Discoveries &
Theories of Modern Astronomy. Arno.
Mitchell. *see* Mitchell, Harry Edward.
Mitchell, A. R. *see* Mitchell, Andrew.
Mitchell, A. Viola.
xMitchell, Viola A.
Camp Counseling. HR&W.
Mitchell, Alice M. *see* Mitchell, Alice Miller.
Mitchell, Alice Miller.
xMitchell, Alice M.
Children & Movies. Ozer.
Mitchell, Andrew.
xMitchell, A. R.
The Finite Element Method in Partial
Differential Equations. Wiley.
Mitchell, Barry.
xMitchell, Barry.
Theory of Categories. Acad Pr.
Mitchell, Basil.
xMitchell, Basil.
Law, Morality & Religion in a Secular Society.
Oxford U Pr.
Mitchell, Bob.
xMitchell, Bob.
Amphoto Guide to Travel Photography.
Amphoto.
Color Printing. Petersen Pub.
Mitchell, Brian. *see* Mitchell, Brian R.
Mitchell, Brian R.
xMitchell, Brian.
European Historical Statistics. Facts on File.
xMitchell, Brian R.

Abstract of British Historical Statistics.
Cambridge U Pr.
Mitchell, Bridger M.
xMitchell, Bridger M.
Peak-Load Pricing: European Lessons for U.S.
Energy Policy. Ballinger Pub.
Mitchell, Broadus, 1892-
xMitchell, Broadus.
Alexander Hamilton. Octagon.
Alexander Hamilton: A Concise Biography.
Oxford U Pr.
Depression Decade: From New Era Through
New Deal 1929-1941. M E Sharpe.
Frederick Law Olmsted, a Critic of the Old
South. AMS Pr.
Industrial Revolution in the South. AMS Pr.
Industrial Revolution in the South. Greenwood.
Postscripts to Economic History. Littlefield.
Mitchell, Bruce, 1944-
xMitchell, Bruce.
Geography & Resource Analysis. Longman.
A Guide to Old English. B&N.
Teachers, Education & Politics: A History of
Organizations of Public School Teachers in
New South Wales. U of Queensland Pr.
Mitchell, Burroughs.
xMitchell, Burroughs.
ed. The Education of an Editor. Doubleday.
Mitchell, Carleton, 1910-
xMitchell, Carleton.
Passage East. Norton.
Mitchell, Christopher.
xMitchell, Christopher.
The Legacy of Populism in Bolivia: From the
MNR to Military Rule. Praeger.
Mitchell, Curtis.
xMitchell, Curtis.
The Perfect Exercise: The Hop, Skip & Jump
Way to Health. PB.
Mitchell, Cynthia.
xMitchell, Cynthia.
Halloweena Hecatee & Other Rhymes to Skip
to. T Y Crowell.
Playtime. Philomel.
Mitchell, Dan. *see* Mitchell, Donald Earl.
Mitchell, Daniel J. *see* Mitchell, Daniel J. B.
Mitchell, Daniel J. B.
xMitchell, Daniel J.
Legal Constraints on Teenage Employment: A
New Look at Child Labor & School-Leaving
Laws. U Cal LA Indus Rel.
Mitchell, David.
xMitchell, David.
Introduction to Logic. Humanities.
Mitchell, David. *see* Mitchell, David J.
Mitchell, David F.
xMitchell, David F.
Oral Diagnosis-Oral Medicine. Lea & Febiger.
Mitchell, David J.
xMitchell, David.
Pirates. Dial.
Mitchell, Don G, 1905-
xMitchell, Don G.
The Challenges Facing Management. NYU Pr.
Mitchell, Donald. *see* Mitchell, Donald William.
Mitchell, Donald Earl.
xMitchell, Dan.
The Souls of Lambs: A Fable. HM.
Mitchell, Donald William, 1911-
xMitchell, Donald.
A History of Russian & Soviet Sea Power.
Macmillan.
Mitchell, Edward J. *see* Mitchell, Edward John.
Mitchell, Edward John.
xMitchell, Edward J.

ed. Oil Pipelines & Public Policy: Analysis of
Proposals for Industry Reform &
Reorganization. Am Enterprise.
Toward Economy in Electric Power. Am
Enterprise.
Mitchell, Edwin V. *see* Mitchell, Edwin Valentine.
Mitchell, Edwin Valentine, 1890-1960
xMitchell, Edwin V.
ed. The Art of Walking. Core Collection.
ed. Encyclopedia of American Politics.
Greenwood.
Horse & Buggy Age in New England. Gale.
It's an Old State of Maine Custom. Thorndike
Pr.
Mitchell, Elaine A. *see* Mitchell, Elaine Allan.
Mitchell, Elaine Allan, 1909-
xMitchell, Elaine A.
Fort Timiskaming & the Fur Trade. U of
Toronto Pr.
Mitchell, Eleanor (Swann).
xMitchell, Eleanor S.
Postscript to Seven Homes. M Jones.
Mitchell, Eleanor S. *see* Mitchell, Eleanor (Swann).
Mitchell, Frances L. *see* Mitchell, Frances Letcher.
Mitchell, Frances Letcher.
xMitchell, Frances L.
Georgia Land & People. Reprint.
Mitchell, G. *see* Mitchell, Gary D.
Mitchell, G. Duncan. *see* Mitchell, Geoffrey Duncan.
Mitchell, Gary D.
xMitchell, G.
Behavioral Sex Differences in Non-Human
Primates. Van Nos Reinhold.
Mitchell, Geoffrey Duncan.
xMitchell, G. Duncan.
ed. A New Dictionary of the Social Sciences.
Aldine Pub.
Mitchell, George, 1944-
xMitchell, George.
I'm Somebody Important: Young Black Voices
from Rural Georgia. U of Ill Pr.
Mitchell, George. *see* Mitchell, George Archibald Grant.
Mitchell, George Archibald Grant.
xMitchell, George.
Essentials of Neuroanatomy. Churchill.
Mitchell, Glenn.
xMitchell, Glenn.
The Collapse of the Dollar & the Approaching
Catastrophe in the World Monetary Order.
Am Classical Coll Pr.
Mitchell, H. L. *see* Mitchell, Harry Leland.
Mitchell, Harry Edward, 1877-
xMitchell.
Exeter & Hampton, New Hampshire, Census &
Business Directory 1908. Heritage Bk.
Mitchell, Harry Leland, 1906-
xMitchell, H. L.
Mean Things Happening in This Land: The
Life & Times of H. L. Mitchell, Cofounder of
the Southern Tenant Farmer's Union.
Universe.
Mitchell, Ingrid, 1935-
xMitchell, Ingrid.
Giving Birth Together: The Modern Parents'
Home Program of Natural Childbirth
Exercises. Continuum.
Mitchell, Irene. *see* Mitchell, Irene Musillo.
Mitchell, Irene Musillo.
xMitchell, Irene.
I Don't Own You So I Can't Give You Away.
Willow River.
Mitchell, J. Clyde. *see* Mitchell, James Clyde.
Mitchell, J. L.
xMitchell, J. L.
Pref. by & ed. Computers in the Humanities. U
of Minn Pr.
Mitchell, J. Pearce. *see* Mitchell, John Pearce.
Mitchell, James, 1926-
xMitchell, James.

Death & Bright Water. G K Hall.
Death & Bright Water. Morrow.
Mitchell, James Clyde.
xMitchell, J. Clyde.
ed. Numerical Techniques in Social
Anthropology. Inst Study Human.
Mitchell, James K. *see* Mitchell, James Kenneth.
Mitchell, James Kenneth, 1930-
xMitchell, James K.
Community Response to Coastal Erosion:
Individual & Collective Adjustments to
Hazard on the Atlantic Shore. U Chicago
Dept Geog.
Fundamentals of Soil Behavior. Wiley.
Mitchell, Jane T. *see* Mitchell, Jane Tucker.
Mitchell, Jane Tucker, 1931-
xMitchell, Jane T.
A Thematic Analysis of Mme. D'Aulnoy's
"Contes De Fees". Romance.
Mitchell, Jean B. *see* Mitchell, Jean Brown.
Mitchell, Jean Brown.
xMitchell, Jean B.
Great Britain: Geographical Essays. Cambridge
U Pr.
Mitchell, Jerome.
xMitchell, Jerome.
Thomas Hoccleve: A Study in Early
Fifteenth-Century English Poetic. U of Ill Pr.
Mitchell, Joan, 1940-
xMitchell, Joan.
Faith: A Persistent Hunger. Winston Pr.
Love, the Language of Caring. Winston Pr.
Price Determination & Prices Policy. Allen
Unwin.
Mitchell, John.
xMitchell, John.
The Curious Naturalist. P-H.
Life of Wallenstein, Duke of Friedland.
Greenwood.
Mitchell, John A. *see* Mitchell, John Ames.
Mitchell, John Ames, 1845-1918
xMitchell, John A.
Drowsy. Arno.
The Last American. Irvington.
The Silent War. Irvington.
That First Affair, - Other Sketches. Arno.
Mitchell, John Pearce, 1880-
xMitchell, J. Pearce.
Stanford University, 1916-1941. Stanford U Pr.
Mitchell, Joseph B. *see* Mitchell, Joseph Brady.
Mitchell, Joseph Brady, 1915-
xMitchell, Joseph B.
Decisive Battles of the American Revolution.
Fawcett.
Mitchell, Joyce. *see* Mitchell, Joyce Slayton.
Mitchell, Joyce S. *see* Mitchell, Joyce Slayton.
Mitchell, Joyce Slayton.
xMitchell, Joyce.
Other Choices for Becoming a Woman. Know
Inc.
xMitchell, Joyce S.

The Classroom Teacher's Workbook for Career
Education. Avon.
Free to Choose: Decision Making for Young
Men. Delacorte.
I Can Be Anything: Careers & Colleges for
Young Women. Bantam.
Other Choices for Becoming a Woman. Dell.
See Me More Clearly: Career & Life Planning
for Teens with Physical Disabilities.
HarBraceJ.
Stopout!: Working Ways to Learn. Avon.
Stopout!: Working Ways to Learn. Garrett Pk.
What's Where: The Official Guide to College
Majors. Avon.
The Work Book: A Guide to Skilled Jobs.
Bantam.
The Work Book: A Guide to Skilled Jobs.
Sterling.
Mitchell, Juliet, 1940-
xMitchell, Juliet.
Psychoanalysis & Feminism. Random.
Mitchell, L. G. *see* Mitchell, Leslie George.
Mitchell, Laisdell.
xMitchell, Laisdell.
Colonel. Arno.
Niram: A Dusky Idyl. Arno.
Mitchell, Larry.
xMitchell, Larry.
The Faggots & Their Friends Between
Revolutions. Calamus Bks.
Mitchell, Leeds.
xMitchell, Leeds.
Introduction to Sailing. Cornerstone.
Mitchell, Leonel. *see* Mitchell, Leonel Lake.
Mitchell, Leonel L. *see* Mitchell, Leonel Lake.
Mitchell, Leonel Lake, 1930-
xMitchell, Leonel.
The Meaning of Ritual. Paulist Pr.
xMitchell, Leonel L.
Baptismal Anointing. U of Notre Dame Pr.
Mitchell, Leslie George.
xMitchell, L. G.
Charles James Fox & the Disintegration of the
Whig Party, 1782-1794. Oxford U Pr.
Mitchell Library, Sydney. *see* Sydney Library of New
South Wales. Mitchell Library.
Mitchell Library, the Library of New South Wales.
(Sydney, Australia). *see* Sydney Library of New South
Wales. Mitchell Library.
Mitchell, Lionel, 1942-
xMitchell, Lionel.
Traveling Light. Seaview Bks.
Mitchell, Loren, 1930-
xMitchell, Loren.
Beautiful San Diego. Beautiful Am.
Mitchell, Malcolm.
xMitchell, Malcolm G.
Propaganda, Polls & Public Opinion: Are the
People Manipulated. P-H.
Mitchell, Malcolm G. *see* Mitchell, Malcolm.
Mitchell, Margaret, 1900-1949
xMitchell, Margaret.
Gone with the Wind. Avon.
Gone with the Wind. Macmillan.
Mitchell, Memory F.
xMitchell, Memory F.
Legal Aspects of Conscription & Exemption in
North Carolina, 1861-1865. U of NC Pr.
Mitchell, Otis C.
xMitchell, Otis C.
Concise History of Western Civilization. Van
Nos Reinhold.
Mitchell, Paige.
xMitchell, Paige.
Covenant. Popular Lib.
Mitchell, Peter, fl. 1968-
xMitchell, Peter.

Great Flower Painters: Four Centuries of Floral
  Art. Overlook Pr.
Mitchell, Ralph.
  xMitchell, Ralph.
    Introduction to Environmental Microbiology.
    P-H.
Mitchell, Richard.
  xMitchell, Richard.
    Less Than Words Can Say. Little.
Mitchell, Richard H.
  xMitchell, Richard H.
    Thought Control in Prewar Japan. Cornell U
    Pr.
Mitchell, Richard L.
  xMitchell, Richard L.
    Radar Signal Simulation. Artech Hse.
Mitchell, Richard S.
  xMitchell, Richard S.
    Variation in the Polygonum Amphibium
    Complex & Its Taxonomic Significance. U of
    Cal Pr.
Mitchell, Richard S. see Mitchell, Richard Scott.
Mitchell, Richard Scott.
  xMitchell, Richard S.
    Mineral Names: What Do They Mean?. Van
    Nos Reinhold.
Mitchell, Robert C. see Mitchell, Robert Cameron.
Mitchell, Robert Cameron.
  xMitchell, Robert C.
    African Primal Religions. Argus Comm.
Mitchell, Robert L., 1944-
  xMitchell, Robert L.
    Tristan Corbiere. G K Hall.
    Tristan Corbiere. Twayne.
Mitchell, Roger.
  xMitchell, Roger.
    Letters from Siberia & Other Poems. SBD.
Mitchell, Roger L., 1932-
  xMitchell, Roger L.
    Crop Growth & Culture. Iowa St U Pr.
Mitchell, Ronald. see Mitchell, Ronald Elwy.
Mitchell, Ronald Elwy, 1905-
  xMitchell, Ronald.
    Opera-Dead or Alive: Production, Performance,
    & Enjoyment of Musical Theatre. U of Wis
    Pr.
Mitchell, Ruth C. see Mitchell, Ruth Comfort.
Mitchell, Ruth Comfort, 1882-1954
  xMitchell, Ruth C.
    Of Human Kindness. AMS Pr.
Mitchell, Ruth K.
  xMitchell, Ruth K.
    Information Science & Computer Basics: An
    Introduction. Shoe String.
Mitchell, S. J. D. see Mitchell, S. John D.
Mitchell, S. John D.
  xMitchell, S. J. D.
    Perse: A History of the Perse School
    1615-1976. Oleander Pr.
Mitchell, S. Weir. see Mitchell, Silas Weir.
Mitchell, Samuel A. see Mitchell, Samuel Alfred.
Mitchell, Samuel Alfred, 1874-
  xMitchell, Samuel A.
    Eclipses of the Sun. Greenwood.
Mitchell, Silas W. see Mitchell, Silas Weir.
Mitchell, Silas Weir, 1829-1914
  xMitchell, S. Weir.
    Doctor & Patient. Arno.
  xMitchell, Silas W.
    Little Stories. Arno.
Mitchell, Stephen.
  xMitchell, Stephen.
    Into the Whirlwind: A Translation of the Book
    of Job. Doubleday.
Mitchell, Stewart, 1892-1957
  xMitchell, Stewart.
    Horatio Seymour of New York. Da Capo.
Mitchell, Susan L.
  xMitchell, Susan L.

George Moore. Kennikat.
Mitchell, Sydney K. see Mitchell, Sydney Knox.
Mitchell, Sydney Knox.
  xMitchell, Sydney K.
    Taxation in Medieval England. Shoe String.
Mitchell, T. F.
  xMitchell, T. F.
    An Introduction to Egyptian Colloquial Arabic.
    Oxford U Pr.
    Principles of Firthian Linguistics. Longman.
Mitchell, Viola A. see Mitchell, A. Viola.
Mitchell, Wesley C. see Mitchell, Wesley Clair.
Mitchell, Wesley Clair, 1874-1948
  xMitchell, Wesley C.
    Business Cycles & Their Causes. U of Cal Pr.
    Business Cycles: The Problem & Its Setting.
    Arno.
    Economic Essays in Honor of Wesley Clair
    Mitchell. Russell.
    Gold, Prices & Wages Under the Greenback
    Standard. Johnson Repr.
    Gold, Prices, & Wages Under the Greenback
    Standard. Kelley.
Mitchell, Will, 1914-
  xMitchell, Will.
    ed. Fuel Cells. Acad Pr.
Mitchell, William E.
  xMitchell, William E.
    Mishpokhe: A Study of New York City Jewish
    Family Clubs. Mouton.
Mitchell, William J. see Mitchell, William John.
Mitchell, William John, 1944-
  xMitchell, William J.
    Computer-Aided Architectural Design. Van
    Nos Reinhold.
Mitchell, Yvonne.
  xMitchell, Yvonne.
    Colette: A Taste of Life. HarBraceJ.
Mitchison, Naomi.
  xMitchison, Naomi.
    The Barbarian. Popular Lib.
Mitchison, Naomi. see Mitchison, Naomi (Haldane).
Mitchison, Naomi (Haldane), 1897-
  xMitchison, Naomi.
    Moral Basis of Politics. Kennikat.
  xMitchison, Naomi M.
    Barbarian Stories. Arno.
    When the Bough Breaks, & Other Stories.
    Arno.
Mitchison, Naomi M. see Mitchison, Naomi (Haldane).
Mitchner, M. see Mitchner, Morton.
Mitchner, Morton.
  xMitchner, M.
    Partially Ionized Gases. Krieger.
Mitchner, Stuart.
  xMitchner, Stuart.
    Indian Action: An American Journey to the
    Great Fair of the East. Little.
Mitchnik, Helen.
  xMitchnik, Helen.
    Egyptian & Sudanese Folk-Tales. Oxford U Pr.
Mitford, Jessica, Hon. 1917-
  xMitford, Jessica.
    Poison Penmanship: The Gentle Art of
    Muckraking. Random.
Mitford, Mary R. see Mitford, Mary Russell.
Mitford, Mary Russell, 1787-1855
  xMitford, Mary R.
    Country Stories. Arno.
    The Letters of Mary Russell Mitford. Folcroft.
    ed. Lights & Shadows of American Life. Mss
    Info.
    ed. Stories of American Life. Mss Info.
Mitford, T. B. see Mitford, Terence Bruce.
Mitford, Terence Bruce.
  xMitford, T. B.
    Inscriptions of Kourion. Am Philos.
Mitgang, Herbert.
  xMitgang, Herbert.

Get These Men Out of the Hot Sun. Arbor
  Hse.
    Return. S&S.
Mithal, H. S. see Mithal, H. S. D.
Mithal, H. S. D.
  xMithal, H. S.
    The Authorship of the Two Italian Gentlemen.
    Folcroft.
Mitnick, Barry M.
  xMitnick, Barry M.
    The Political Economy of Regulation: Creating,
    Designing, & Removing Regulatory Forms.
    Columbia U Pr.
Mitra, Abhijit.
  xMitra, Abhijit.
    Synthesis of Prostaglandins. Wiley.
Mitra, Ashok.
  xMitra, Ashok.
    Calcutta Diary. Biblio Dist.
Mitra, G. see Mitra, Gautam.
Mitra, Gautam.
  xMitra, G.
    Theory & Application of Mathematical
    Programming. Acad Pr.
Mitra, Sanjit K. see Mitra, Sanjit Kumar.
Mitra, Sanjit Kumar.
  xMitra, Sanjit K.
    ed. Active Inductorless Filters. Inst Electrical.
    Active Inductorless Filters. Wiley.
Mitrany, David, 1888-
  xMitrany, David.
    Effect of the War in Southeastern Europe.
    Fertig.
Mitrinovic, D. S. see Mitrinovic, Dragoslav S.
Mitrinovic, Dragoslav S.
  xMitrinovic, D. S.
    Analytic Inequalities. Springer-Verlag.
Mitruka, Brij M.
  xMitruka, Brij M.
    Clinical Biochemical & Hematological
    Reference Values in Normal Experimental
    Animals. Masson Pub.
    Gas Chromatographic Applications in
    Microbiology & Medicine. Wiley.
  xMitruka, M.
    Animals for Medical Research: Models for the
    Study of Human Disease. Krieger.
Mitruka, M. see Mitruka, Brij M.
Mitscher, L. A. see Mitscher, Lester A.
Mitscher, Lester A.
  xMitscher, L. A.
    The Chemistry of Tetracycline Antibiotics.
    Dekker.
Mitscherlich, Alexander.
  xMitscherlich, Alexander.
    The Inability to Mourn: Principles of Collective
    Behavior. Grove.
    The Inability to Mourn: Principles of Collective
    Behavior. Univ Microfilms.
Mitson, Eileen. see Mitson, Eileen Nora.
Mitson, Eileen Nora.
  xMitson, Eileen.
    Reaching for God. Christian Herald.
Mitsui, James M. see Mitsui, James Masao.
Mitsui, James Masao, 1940-
  xMitsui, James M.
    Crossing the Phantom River. Graywolf.
Mitsuko, Iolana.
  xMitsuko, Lolana.
    Honolulu Madam. Holloway.
Mitsuko, Lolana. see Mitsuko, Iolana.
Mittal, K. L.
  xMittal, K. L.
    ed. Surface Contamination: Genesis, Detection,
    & Control. Plenum Pub.
Mittelholzer, Edgar.
  xMittelholzer, Edgar.
    The Old Blood. Fawcett.
Mittelman, James H.
  xMittelman, James H.

Ideology & Politics in Uganda: From Obote to
Amin. Cornell U Pr.
Mittlebeeler, Emmet V.
xMittlebeeler, Emmet V.
African Custom & Western Law: The
Development of the Rhodesian Criminal Law
for Africans. Holmes & Meier.
Mittler, Peter. *see* Mittler, Peter J.
Mittler, Peter J.
xMittler, Peter.
ed. Psychological Assessment of Mental &
Physical Handicaps. Methuen Inc.
Mitton, Bruce. *see* Mitton, Bruce H.
Mitton, Bruce H., 1950-
xMitton, Bruce.
How to Make Your Own Lamps &
Lampshades. TAB Bks.
xMitton, Bruce H.
Photo Display. Doubleday.
Mitton, J. *see* Mitton, Jacqueline.
Mitton, Jacqueline.
xMitton, J.
Concise Book of Astronomy. P-H.

Mitton, Jacqueline. *see* Mitton, Jaqueline.

Mitton, Jaqueline.
xMitton, Jacqueline.
Astronomy: An Introduction for the Amateur
Astronomer. Scribner.

Mitton, Simon, 1946-
xMitton, Simon.
The Crab Nebula. Scribner.
Exploring the Galaxies. Scribner.
ed. Star Atlas. Crown.

Mittra, R. *see* Mittra, Raj.

Mittra, R. A. J. *see* Mittra, Raj.

Mittra, Raj.
xMittra, R.
Analytical Techniques in the Theory of Guided
Waves. Macmillan.
xMittra, R. A. J.
ed. Computer Techniques for Electromagnetics.
Pergamon.

Mittra, Sid, 1930-
xMittra, Sid.
Personal Finance: Lifetime Management by
Objectives. Har-Row.

Mittwer, Henry.
xMittwer, Henry.
Art of Chabana: Flowers for the Tea
Ceremony. C E Tuttle.

Mittwoch, Ursula.
xMittwoch, Ursula.
Genetics of Sex Differentiation. Acad Pr.

Mitz, Rick.
xMitz, Rick.
Aim for a Job in the Record Business. Rosen
Pr.

Mitzman, Max E.
xMitzman, Max E.
George Baxter & the Baxter Prints. David &
Charles.

Miura, Akira, 1927-
xMiura, Akira.
English Loanwords in Japanese: A Selection. C
E Tuttle.

Mixco, Mauricio J.
xMixco, Mauricio J.
Cochimi & Proto-Yuman: Lexical & Syntactic
Evidence for a New Language Family in
Lower Calif. U of Utah Pr.

Mixon, S. R. *see* Mixon, Shirley R.

Mixon, Shirley R.
xMixon, S. R.
Handbook of Data Processing Administration,
Operations, & Procedures. Am Mgmt.

Mixter, Keith E. *see* Mixter, Keith Eugene.

Mixter, Keith Eugene, 1922-
xMixter, Keith E.
General Bibliography for Music Research. Info
Coord.

Miyamori, Asataro, 1869-1952
xMiyamori, Asataro.
ed. Masterpieces of Japanese Poetry, Ancient
& Modern. Greenwood.

Miyamori, Asataro. *see* Miyamori, Asator O.

Miyamori, Asatoro, 1869-1952
xMiyamori, Asataro.
ed. Anthology of Haiku, Ancient & Modern.
Greenwood.

Miyashita, Tadao, 1909-
xMiyashita, Tadao.
The Currency & Financial System of Mainland
China. Da Capo.

Miyazaki, Ichisada, 1901-
xMiyazaki, Ichisada.
China's Examination Hell: The Civil Service
Examinations of Imperial China. Weatherhill.

Miyazawa, K. *see* Miyazawa, Kenichi.

Miyazawa, Kenichi, 1925-
xMiyazawa, K.
Input-Output Analysis & the Structure of
Income Distribution. Springer-Verlag.

Miyoshi, Masao.
xMiyoshi, Masao.
Accomplices of Silence: The Modern Japanese
Novel. U of Cal Pr.

Miyoshi, Masao. *see* Miyoshi, Masoa.

Miyoshi, Masoa.
xMiyoshi, Masao.
As We Saw Them: The First Japanese Embassy
to the United States (1860). U of Cal Pr.

Mize, Jan L. *see* Mize, Jan Lee.

Mize, Jan Lee.
xMize, Jan L.
Essentials of Structured Cobol Programming.
Wadsworth Pub.

Mize, Joe H.
xMize, Joe H.
Essentials of Simulation. P-H.
Operations Planning & Control. P-H.

Mizener, Arthur.
xMizener, Arthur.
A Catalogue of the First Editions of Archibald
MacLeish. Folcroft.
ed. F. Scott Fitzgerald: A Collection of Critical
Essays. P-H.
Far Side of Paradise: A Biography of F. Scott
Fitzgerald. HM.

Mizerak, Steve.
xMizerak, Steve.
Inside Pocket Billiards. Contemp Bks.

Mizrahi, Abe.
xMizrahi, Abe.
Calculus with Applications to Business & the
Life Sciences. Wiley.
Finite Mathematics with Applications for
Business & Social Sciences. Wiley.

Mizruchi, Ephraim H. *see* Mizruchi, Ephraim Harold.

Mizruchi, Ephraim Harold.
xMizruchi, Ephraim H.
ed. Substance of Sociology: Codes, Conduct &
Consequences. Irvington.

Mizuki, John, 1922-
xMizuki, John.
The Growth of Japanese Churches in Brazil.
William Carey Lib.

Mizumura, Kazue.
xMizumura, Kazue.
illus. Flower Moon Snow: A Book of Haiku. T
Y Crowell.
If I Built a Village.... T Y Crowell.
illus. If I Were a Cricket.... T Y Crowell.
illus. If I Were a Mother.... T Y Crowell.

Mizushima, Masataka, 1923-
xMizushima, Masataka.

Quantum Mechanics of Atomic Spectra &
Atomic Structure. Benjamin-Cummings.
The Theory of Rotating Diatomic Molecules.
Krieger.

Mizushima, San-Ichiro. *see* Mizushima, San'Ichiro.

Mizushima, San'Ichiro, 1899-
xMizushima, San-Ichiro.
Structure of Molecules & Internal Rotation.
Acad Pr.

Mlynar, Zdenek.
xMlynar, Zdenek.
Night Frost in Prague: The End of Humane
Socialism. Karz Pub.

Moakley, Gertrude.
xMoakley, Gertrude.
Tarot Cards Painted by Bonifacio Bembo for
the Visconti-Sforza Family. NY Pub Lib.

Moan, Terrence.
xMoan, Terry.
Deadly Frost. Rawson Wade.

Moan, Terry. *see* Moan, Terrence.

Moat, Albert G.
xMoat, Albert G.
Microbial Physiology. Wiley.

Moates, Danny R.
xMoates, Danny R.
Introduction to Cognitive Psychology.
Wadsworth Pub.

Moburg, Lawrence. *see* Moburg, Lawrence G.

Moburg, Lawrence G.
xMoburg, Lawrence.
Inservice Teacher Training in Reading. Intl
Reading.

Moche. *see* Moche, Dinah L.

Moche, Dinah. *see* Moche, Dinah L.

Moche, Dinah L., 1936-
xMoche.
The Star Wars Question & Answer Book
About Space. Schol Bk Serv.
xMoche, Dinah.
Mars. Watts.
xMoche, Dinah L.
The Astronauts. Random.
Life in Space. A & W Pubs.
The Star Wars Question & Answer Book
About Space. Random.

Mock, Elizabeth B. *see* Mock, Elizabeth Bauer.

Mock, Elizabeth Bauer.
xMock, Elizabeth B.
The Architecture of Bridges. Arno.

Mock, James R. *see* Mock, James Robert.

Mock, James Robert.
xMock, James R.
Words That Won the War: The Story of the
Committee on Public Information,
1917-1919. Russell.

Mock, Theodore J.
xMock, Theodore J.
Measurement, Accounting, & Organizational
Information. Wiley.

Mockerie, Parmenas G. *see* Mockerie, Parmenas
Githendu.

Mockerie, Parmenas Githendu.
xMockerie, Parmenas G.
An African Speaks for His People. AMS Pr.

Mockett, Douglas A. *see* Mockett, Douglas A. J.

Mockett, Douglas A. J.
xMockett, Douglas A.
How to Travel for Free. Phoenix Pr CA.

Mockler, Robert J.
xMockler, Robert J.
Business & Society. Har-Row.
Guidelines for More Effective Planning &
Management of Franchise Systems. Ga St U
Busn Pub.

Mode, Peter G. *see* Mode, Peter George.

Mode, Peter George.
xMode, Peter G.

The Complete Pun Book. Citadel Pr.
Moger, Byron.
  xMoger, Byron J.
    How to Buy a House. Lyle Stuart.
Moger, Byron J. *see* Moger, Byron.
Moghdam, Dineh, 1946-
  xMoghdam, Dineh.
    Computers in Newspaper Publishing: User
      Oriented Systems. Dekker.
Moghissi, Kamran. *see* Moghissi, Kamran S.
Moghissi, Kamran S.
  xMoghissi, Kamran.
    Controversies in Contraception. Williams &
      Wilkins.
Moglen, Helene, 1936-
  xMoglen, Helene.
    Charlotte Bronte: The Self Conceived. Norton.
Mogulof, Melvin B.
  xMogulof, Melvin B.
    Citizen Participation: A Review & Commentary
      on Federal Policies & Practices. Urban Inst.
Mohan, John.
  xMohan, John.
    Freestyle Skiing. Winchester Pr.
Mohanty, Gopal.
  xMohanty, Gopal.
    Lattice Path Counting & Applications. Acad
      Pr.
Mohanty, J. N, 1928-
  xMohanty, J. N.
    Edmund Husserl's Theory of Meaning. Kluwer
      Boston.
Mohl, Raymond A.
  xMohl, Raymond A.
    Poverty in New York, 1783-1825. Oxford U
      Pr.
Mohlenbrock, Robert H.
  xMohlenbrock, Robert H.
    Distribution of Illinois Vascular Plants. S Ill U
      Pr.
    Ferns. S Ill U Pr.
    Flora of Southern Illinois. S Ill U Pr.
    Flowering Plants: Hollies to Loasas. S Ill U Pr.
    Guide to the Vascular Flora of Illinois. S Ill U
      Pr.
Mohler, James A.
  xMohler, James A.
    The Sacrament of Suffering. Fides Claretian.
Mohler, R. R. *see* Mohler, Ronald R.
Mohler, Ronald R.
  xMohler, R. R.
    Optimal Control of Nuclear Reactors. Acad Pr.
    ed. Recent Developments in Variable Structure
      Systems, Economics & Biology.
      Springer-Verlag.
Mohn, N. Carroll.
  xMohn, N. Carroll.
    Compensation of Professionals: A Selected &
      Annotated Bibliography. U of Tex Busn Res.
Mohn, Peter. *see* Mohn, Peter B.
Mohn, Peter B.
  xMohn, Peter.
    Golden Knights. Childrens.
    Thunderbirds. Childrens.
  xMohn, Peter B.
    Cross-Country Skiing. Crestwood Hse.
Mohney, Russ.
  xMohney, Russ.
    The Dogfish Cookbook. Pacific Search.
Moholy-Nagy, Laszlo, 1895-1946
  xMoholy-Nagy, Laszlo.
    Painting, Photography, & Film. MIT Pr.
Mohonk Conference on the Negro Question.
  xMohonk Conference on the Negro Question.
    First & Second. Negro U Pr.
Mohr, Anton, 1890-1968
  xMohr, Anton.
    The Oil War. Hyperion Conn.
Mohr, Charles E.
  xMohr, Charles E.

    ed. Celebrated American Caves. Rutgers U Pr.
    Life of the Cave. McGraw.
    The World of the Bat. Lippincott.
Mohr, H. *see* Mohr, Hans.
Mohr, Hans, 1930-
  xMohr, H.
    Lectures on Structure & Significance of
      Science. Springer-Verlag.
Mohr, J. Gilbert. *see* Mohr, John Gilbert.
Mohr, James C.
  xMohr, James C.
    The Radical Republicans & Reform in New
      York During Reconstruction. Cornell U Pr.
    ed. Radical Republicans in the North: State
      Politics during Reconstruction. Johns
      Hopkins.
Mohr, John Gilbert.
  xMohr, J. Gilbert.
    Fiberglass. Van Nos Reinhold.
Mohr, Nicholasa.
  xMohr, Nicholasa.
    Felita. Dial.
    In Nueva York. Dial.
    illus. Nilda. Har-Row.
Mohrig, J. *see* Mohrig, Jerry R.
Mohrig, Jerry R.
  xMohrig, J.
    Laboratory Experiments in Organic Chemistry.
      D Van Nostrand.
Mohrman, Dick.
  xMohrman, Dick.
    Let It Show: Natural Expressions of the
      Spirit-Controlled Life. Christian Herald.
Mohs, Frederic E. *see* Mohs, Frederic Edward.
Mohs, Frederic Edward, 1910-
  xMohs, Frederic E.
    Chemosurgery: Microscopically Controlled
      Surgery for Skin Cancer. C C Thomas.
Moien, Mary.
  xMoien, Mary.
    Inpatient Utilization of Short-Stay Hospitals by
      Diagnosis, United States, 1973. Natl Ctr
      Health Stats.
Moir, Alfred.
  xMoir, Alfred.
    Caravaggio & His Copyists. NYU Pr.
Moir, Esther.
  xMoir, Esther.
    Discovery of Britain: The English Tourists,
      1540-1840. Humanities.
Moise, E. E. *see* Moise, Edwin E.
Moise, Edwin E.
  xMoise, E. E.
    Geometric Topology in Dimensions 2 & 3.
      Springer-Verlag.
  xMoise, Edwin E.
    Calculus. A-W.
Moise, Lotte E.
  xMoise, Lotte E.
    As up We Grew with Barbara. Dillon.
Moiseiwitsch, Benjamin L. *see* Moiseiwitsch, Benjamin
  Lawrence.
Moiseiwitsch, Benjamin Lawrence.
  xMoiseiwitsch, Benjamin L.
    Integral Equations. Longman.
Mojtabai, A. G., 1937-
  xMojtabai, A. G.
    Mundome. S&S.
    A Stopping Place. S&S.
Mojumdar, Kanchanmoy, 1935-
  xMojumdar, Kanchanmoy.
    Anglo-Nepalese Relations in the Nineteenth
      Century. South Asia Bks.
Mojzer, Miklos.
  xMojzer, Miklos.
    Intro. by Dutch Genre Paintings. Branden.
Mokgatle, Naboth, 1911-
  xMokgatle, Naboth.

    The Autobiography of an Unknown South
      African. U of Cal Pr.
Mokyr, Joel.
  xMokyr, Joel.
    Industrialization in the Low Countries,
      1795-1850. Yale U Pr.
Molan, Dorothy L. *see* Molan, Dorothy Lennon.
Molan, Dorothy Lennon.
  xMolan, Dorothy L.
    Teaching Middlers. Judson.
Molarsky, Osmond.
  xMolarsky, Osmond.
    A Different Ball Game. Coward.
    The Fearless Leroy. Walck.
    Right Thumb, Left Thumb. A-W.
Molau, Gunther E.
  xMolau, Gunther E.
    ed. Colloidal & Morphological Behavior of
      Block & Graft Copolymers. Plenum Pub.
Moldafsky, Annie.
  xMoldafsky, Annie.
    Welcome to the Real World: A Guide to
      Making Your First Personal Financial, &
      Career Decisions. Doubleday.
Moldea, Dan E., 1950-
  xMoldea, Dan E.
    The Hoffa Wars: Teamsters, Rebels, Politicians
      & the Mob. Paddington.
Molden, Fritz.
  xMolden, Fritz.
    Exploding Star: A Young Austrian Against
      Hitler. Morrow.
Moldenke, H. N. *see* Moldenke, Harold Norman.
Moldenke, Harold Norman.
  xMoldenke, H. N.
    Plants of the Bible. Wiley.
Moldestad, J. *see* Moldestad, Johan.
Moldestad, Johan, 1946-
  xMoldestad, J.
    Computations in Higher Types.
      Springer-Verlag.
Moldvay, Albert.
  xMoldvay, Albert.
    Photographing Amsterdam. Amphoto.
    Photographing London. Amphoto.
    Photographing Mexico City & Acapulco.
      Amphoto.
    Photographing New York. Amphoto.
    Photographing Paris. Amphoto.
Mole, Michaela M.
  xMole, Michaela M.
    ed. Away We Go!: A Guidebook of Family
      Trips to Places of Interest in New Jersey,
      Nearby Pennsylvania & New York. Rutgers
      U Pr.
Mole, Robert L., 1923-
  xMole, Robert L.
    Montagnards of South Vietnam: A Study of
      Nine Tribes. C E Tuttle.
    Thai Values & Behavior Patterns. C E Tuttle.
Molen, Robert Vander. *see* Vander Molen, Robert.
Molen, Ronald L.
  xMolen, Ronald L.
    House, Plus Environment. Olympus Pub Co.
Moles, Ian, 1935-
  xMoles, Ian.
    A Majority of One: Tom Aikens &
      Independent Politics in Townsville. U of
      Queensland Pr.
Molesworth. *see* Molesworth, Mary Louisa Stewart.
Molesworth, Charles.
  xMolesworth, Charles.
    The Fierce Embrace: A Study of Contemporary
      American Poetry. U of Mo Pr.
Molesworth, Mary L. *see* Molesworth, Mary Louisa
  Stewart.

Molesworth, Mary Louisa Stewart.
  xMolesworth.
    The Cuckoo Clock. Biblio Dist.
  xMolesworth, Mary L.
    The Cuckoo Clock. Mayflower Bks.
Molesworth, William N. see Molesworth, William
  Nassau.
Molesworth, William Nassau, 1816-1890
  xMolesworth, William N.
    History of the Reform Bill of 1832. Kelley.
Moley, Raymond, 1886-
  xMoley, Raymond.
    After Seven Years. Da Capo.
    Our Criminal Courts. Arno.
    Politics & Criminal Prosecution. Arno.
Molho, Anthony.
  xMolho, Anthony.
    Florentine Public Finances in the Early
      Renaissance, 1400-1433. Harvard U Pr.
Moliere. see Moliere, Jean Baptiste Poquelin.
Moliere, Jean B. see Moliere, Jean Baptiste Poquelin.
Moliere, Jean Baptiste. see Moliere, Jean Baptiste
  Poquelin.
Moliere, Jean Baptiste Poquelin.
  xMoliere.
    One-Act Comedies of Moliere. Ungar.
    Le Tartuffe. French & Eur.
  xMoliere, Jean B.
    Tartuffe. Bobbs.
    Tartuffe. Larousse.
    Tartuffe. AHM Pub.
    Tartuffe. Barron.
  xMoliere, Jean Baptiste.
    Tartuffe. HarBraceJ.
Molina, Claude.
  xMolina, Claude.
    Broncho-Pulmonary Immunopathology.
      Churchill.
Molinie, M. D. see Molinie, Marie Dominique.
Molinie, Marie Dominique.
  xMolinie, M. D.
    The Struggle of Jacob. Paulist Pr.
Molinsky, Steven J.
  xMolinsky, Steven J.
    Side by Side: English Grammar Through
      Guided Conversations. P-H.
Molitor, Joseph W.
  xMolitor, Joseph W.
    Architectural Photography. Wiley.
Moll, Elick.
  xMoll, Elick.
    Image of Tallie. S&S.
Moll, Helmut, 1927-
  xMoll, Helmut.
    Atlas of Pediatric Diseases. Saunders.
Moll, Lane de. see De Moll, Lane.
Moll, Richard.
  xMoll, Richard.
    Playing the Private College Admissions Game.
      Penguin.
    Playing the Private College Admissions Game.
      Times Bks.
Molland, Einar, 1908-
  xMolland, Einar.
    Church Life in Norway: 1800-1950.
      Greenwood.
Molle, W. see Molle, Willem.
Molle, Willem.
  xMolle, W.
    Regional Disparity & Economic Development
      in the European Community. Allanheld.
Mollenhoff, Clark R.
  xMollenhoff, Clark R.
    The President Who Failed: Carter Out of
      Control. Macmillan.
Moller, C. see Moller, Christian.
Moller, Christian, 1904-
  xMoller, C.

Theory of Relativity. Oxford U Pr.
Moller, Clifford B.
  xMoller, Clifford B.
    Architectural Environment & Our Mental
      Health. Horizon.
Moller, James H.
  xMoller, James H.
    Essentials of Pediatric Cardiology. Davis Co.
Moller, K. D. see Moller, Karl Dieter.
Moller, Karl Dieter.
  xMoller, K. D.
    Far-Infrared Spectroscopy. Wiley.
Moller, Mary E. see Moller, Mary Elkins.
Moller, Mary Elkins, 1929-
  xMoller, Mary E.
    Thoreau in the Human Community. U of Mass
      Pr.
Mollo, Andrew.
  xMollo, Andrew.
    Army Uniforms of World War 1. Arco.
    Naval, Marine & Air Force Uniforms of World
      War 2. Macmillan.
Mollo, Boris.
  xMollo, Boris.
    Uniforms of the Imperial Russian Army.
      Sterling.
Molloy, Al.
  xMolloy, Al.
    Contemporary Squash. Contemp Bks.
Molloy, Anne S. see Molloy, Anne Stearns (Baker).
Molloy, Anne Stearns (Baker).
  xMolloy, Anne S.
    Girl from Two Miles High. Hastings.
Molloy, John. see Molloy, John T.
Molloy, John T.
  xMolloy, John.
    Dress for Success. Warner Bks.
  xMolloy, John T.
    Dress for Success. Warner Bks.
Molnar, Agnes.
  xMolnar, Agnes.
    illus. Jack & the Beanstalk. Knopf.
Molnar, John E. see Molnar, John Edgar.
Molnar, John Edgar.
  xMolnar, John E.
    Author-Title Index to Joseph Sabin's
      Dictionary of Books Relating to America.
      Scarecrow.
Molnar, Thomas. see Molnar, Thomas Steven.
Molnar, Thomas Steven.
  xMolnar, Thomas.
    Authority & Its Enemies. Arlington Hse.
    Future of Education. Fleet.
Molner, J. see Molner, Joseph G.
Molner, Joseph G., M.D., 1907-
  xMolner, J.
    Stay Well Every Year of Your Life: Dr.
      Molners Guide to Total Health. P-H.
Moloney, James. see Moloney, James H.
Moloney, James C. see Moloney, James Clark.
Moloney, James Clark, 1900-
  xMoloney, James C.
    Understanding the Japanese Mind. Greenwood.
Moloney, James H.
  xMoloney, James.
    Encyclopedia of American Cars, 1930-1942.
      Crestline.
Molony, Chartres J. see Molony, John Chartres.
Molony, John Chartres, 1877-
  xMolony, Chartres J.
    Riddle of the Irish. Kennikat.
Molony, John N. see Molony, John Neylon.
Molony, John Neylon.
  xMolony, John N.
    The Emergence of Political Catholicism in
      Italy: Partito Populare 1919-1926. Rowman.
Molseed, Elwood, 1938-1967
  xMolseed, Elwood.

The Genus Tigridia (Iridaceae) of Mexico &
  Central America. U of Cal Pr.
Molter, Rita.
  xMolter, Rita.
    ed. Parents' Magazine Cookbook. Nelson.
Moltmann, Jurgen.
  xMoltmann, Jurgen.
    The Passion for Life: A Messianic Lifestyle.
      Fortress.
    Religion & Political Society. E Mellen.
Moltmann-Wendel, Elisabeth.
  xMoltmann-Wendel, Elisabeth.
    Liberty, Equality, Sisterhood: On the
      Emancipation of Women in Church &
      Society. Fortress.
Molz, Kathleen R. see Molz, Redmond Kathleen.
Molz, Redmond Kathleen, 1928-
  xMolz, Kathleen R.
    Federal Policy & Library Support. MIT Pr.
Momaday, N. Scott. see Momaday, Natachee Scott.
Momaday, Natachee S. see Momaday, Natachee Scott.
Momaday, Natachee Scott.
  xMomaday, N. Scott.
    House Made of Dawn. Har-Row.
    House Made of Dawn. Har-Row.
  xMomaday, Natachee S.
    Owl in the Cedar Tree. Northland.
Momboisse, Raymond M.
  xMomboisse, Raymond M.
    Community Relations & Riot Prevention. C C
      Thomas.
    Industrial Security for Strikes, Riots &
      Disasters. C C Thomas.
Momyer, William W.
  xMomyer, William W.
    Airpower in Three Wars. Arno.
Monaco, James.
  xMonaco, James.
    American Film Now: The People, the Power,
      the Money, the Movies. Oxford U Pr.
    Books About Film: A Bibliographical Checklist.
      NY Zoetrope.
    How to Read a Film: The Art, Technology,
      Language, History & Theory of Film &
      Television. Oxford U Pr.
Monaco, P. see Monaco, Paul.
Monaco, Paul.
  xMonaco, P.
    Cinema & Society: France & Germany During
      the Twenties. Elsevier.
Monaco, Richard.
  xMonaco, Richard.
    The Grail War. PB.
    The Logic of Poetry. McGraw.
    Parsival: Or a Knight's Tale. Macmillan.
Monaghan, Frank.
  xMonaghan, Frank J.
    Analytic Relaxation Therapy: A Psychoanalytic
      Technique. Kendall-Hunt.
Monaghan, Frank J. see Monaghan, Frank.
Monaghan, James, 1891-
  xMonaghan, James.
    Overland Trail. Arno.
  xMonaghan, Jay.
    Australians & the Gold Rush: California &
      Down Under, 1849-1854. U of Cal Pr.
Monaghan, Jay. see Monaghan, James.
Monahan, Brent J. see Monahan, Brent Jeffrey.
Monahan, Brent Jeffrey.
  xMonahan, Brent J.
    The Art of Singing: A Compendium of
      Thoughts on Singing Published Between 1777
      & 1927. Scarecrow.
Monahan, Evelyn.
  xMonahan, Evelyn.
    Put Your Psychic Powers to Work: A Practical
      Guide to Parapsychology. Nelson-Hall.
    Secrets of Meta-Cosmic Projection. P-H.
Monahan, John, 1946-
  xMonahan, John.

ed. Community Mental Health & the Criminal
    Justice System. Pergamon.
Monahan, Michael, 1865-1933
    xMonahan, Michael.
    Attic Dreamer. Arno.
    Nemesis. Arno.
Monahan, Peter J.
    xMonahan, Peter J.
    ed. Comic Vision. McGraw.
Monat, Alan.
    xMonat, Alan.
    ed. Stress and Coping: An Anthology.
        Columbia U Pr.
Monbeck, Michael E.
    xMonbeck, Michael E.
    The Meaning of Blindness: Attitudes Toward
        Blindness & Blind People. Ind U Pr.
Monboddo, James B. *see* Monboddo, James Burnett.
Monboddo, James Burnett, Lord, 1714-1799
    xMonboddo, James B.
    Of the Origin & Progress of Language. AMS
        Pr.
Moncrieff, A. R. *see* Moncrieff, Ascott Robert Hope.
Moncrieff, Ascott Robert Hope, 1846-1927
    xMoncrieff, A. R.
    Romance & Legend of Chivalry. Folcroft.
Moncrif, Francois A. De. *see* Moncrif, Francois Augustin
    Paradis De.
Moncrif, Francois Augustin Paradis de, 1687-1770
    xMoncrif, Francois A. De.
    Adventures of Zeloide & Amanzarifdine. Arno.
Moncur, John P.
    xMoncur, John P.
    Developing Your Speaking Voice. Har-Row.
Moncure, Jane B. *see* Moncure, Jane Belk.
Moncure, Jane Belk.
    xMoncure, Jane B.
    Animal, Animal, Where Do You Live?. Childs
        World.
    The Bunny Who Knew All About Plants.
        Childs World.
    But I'm Thankful, I Really Am!. Childs World.
    Fall Is Here!. Childs World.
    The Gift of Christmas. Childs World.
    I Never Say I'm Thankful, but I Am. Childs
        World.
    If a Dinosaur Came to Dinner. Childs World.
    Magic Monsters Learn About Health.
        Childrens.
    Magic Monsters Learn About Health. Childs
        World.
    Magic Monsters Learn About Manners.
        Childrens.
    Magic Monsters Learn About Manners. Childs
        World.
    Magic Monsters Look for Colors. Childs
        World.
    Magic Monsters Look for Shapes. Childs
        World.
    My "b" Sound Box. Childs World.
    My Baby Brother Needs a Friend. Childs
        World.
    My Baby Brother Needs Me. Childs World.
    My "c" Sound Box. Childs World.
    My "d" Sound Box. Childs World.
    My "g" Sound Box. Childs World.
    My "j" Sound Box. Childs World.
    My "k" Sound Box. Childs World.
    My "l" Sound Box. Childs World.
    My "m" Sound Box. Childs World.
    My "n" Sound Box. Childs World.
    My "w" Sound Box. Childs World.
    One Little World. Childs World.
    Our Birthday Book. Childs World.
    Our Christmas Book. Childs World.
    Our Halloween Book. Childs World.
    Our Mother's Day Book. Childs World.
    Our Thanksgiving Book. Childs World.
    Our Valentine Book. Childs World.
    People Who Help People. Childs World.

Plants Give Us Many Kinds of Food. Childs
        World.
    Play with A & T. Childs World.
    Play with E & D. Childs World.
    Play with I & G. Childs World.
    Play with O & G. Childs World.
    Play with U & G. Childs World.
    Rhyme Me a Rhyme. Childs World.
    Riddle Me a Riddle. Childs World.
    Short A & Long A Play a Game. Childs
        World.
    Short E & Long E Play a Game. Childs World.
    Short I & Long I Play a Game. Childs World.
    Short O & Long O Play a Game. Childs
        World.
    Short U & Long U Play a Game. Childs World.
    Summer Is Here!. Childs World.
    Thank You, Animal Friends. Childs World.
    Thank You, God, for Fall. Childs World.
    Thank You, God, for Spring. Childs World.
    Thank You, God, for Summer. Childs World.
    Thank You, God, for Winter. Childs World.
    Thank You, Lord, for Me. Childs World.
    Try on a Shoe. Childs World.
    When I'm Afraid. Childs World.
    Where Things Belong. Childs World.
    Wishes, Whispers & Secrets. Childs World.
Mondelli, Rudolph J.
    xMondelli, Rudolph J.
    French Conversational Review Grammar. Van
        Nos Reinhold.
Mondy, Robert W. *see* Mondy, Robert William.
Mondy, Robert William, 1907-
    xMondy, Robert W.
    Pioneers & Preachers: Stories of the Old
        Frontier. Nelson-Hall.
Monette, Paul.
    xMonette, Paul.
    The Gold Diggers. Avon.
    Taking Care of Mrs. Carroll. Avon.
Money, John, Ph.D.
    xMoney, John.
    Experience & Identity: Birmingham & the West
        Midlands 1760-1800. McGill-Queens U Pr.
Money-Kyrle, R. E. *see* Money-Kyrle, Roger Ernle.
Money-Kyrle, Roger Ernle, 1898-
    xMoney-Kyrle, R. E.
    Psychoanalysis & Politics: A Contribution to
        the Psychology of Politics & Morals.
        Greenwood.
Moneyhon, Carl H., 1944-
    xMoneyhon, Carl H.
    Republicanism in Reconstruction Texas. U of
        Tex Pr.
Mongait, A. L. *see* Mongait, Aleksandr Lvovich.
Mongait, Aleksandr Lvovich.
    xMongait, A. L.
    Archaeology in the U. S. S. R.. Peter Smith.
Mongan, Agnes.
    xMongan, Agnes.
    ed. One Hundred Master Drawings.
        Greenwood.
Monger, George W.
    xMonger, George W.
    The End of Isolation: British Foreign Policy,
        1900-1907. Greenwood.
Mongolia Society.
    xMongolia Society.
    Bulletin. Mongolia.
Mongoven, Anne Marie.
    xMongoven, Anne Marie.
    Signs of Catechesis: An Overview of the
        National Catechetical Directory. Paulist Pr.
Monif, Gilles R. *see* Monif, Gilles R. G.
Monif, Gilles R. G.
    xMonif, Gilles R.
    ed. Infectious Diseases in Obstetrics &
        Gynecology. Har-Row.
Monin, A. S. *see* Monin, Andrei Sergeevich.

Monin, Andrei Sergeevich.
    xMonin, A. S.
    Variability of the Oceans. Wiley.
Monin, J. P.
    xMonin, J. P.
    Initiation to the Mathematics of the Processes
        of Diffusion, Contagion & Propagation.
        Mouton.
Monjo, F. N.
    xMonjo, F. N.
    Drinking Gourd. Har-Row.
    Indian Summer. Har-Row.
    One Bad Thing About Father. Har-Row.
    Poor Richard in France. Dell.
    The Porcelain Pagoda. Viking Pr.
    xMonjo, Ferdinand N.
    Pirates in Panama. S&S.
Monjo, Ferdinand N. *see* Monjo, F. N.
Monk, Abraham.
    xMonk, Abraham.
    ed. The Age of Aging: A Reader in Social
        Gerontology. Prometheus Bks.
Monk, C. J. E. *see* Monk, Cyril John Elmes.
Monk, Cyril John Elmes.
    xMonk, C. J. E.
    Orthopaedics for Undergraduates. Oxford U Pr.
Monk, Edwin.
    xMonk, Edwin.
    Modern Boat Building. Scribner.
Monk, J. D. *see* Monk, James Donald.
Monk, J. Donald. *see* Monk, James Donald.
Monk, James Donald, 1930-
    xMonk, J. D.
    Mathematical Logic. Springer-Verlag.
    xMonk, J. Donald.
    Introduction to Set Theory. Krieger.
Monk, K. *see* Monk, Kathleen.
Monk, Kathleen.
    xMonk, K.
    Fun with Fabric Printing. Textile Bk.
    xMonk, Kathleen.
    Fun with Fabric Printing. Taplinger.
Monk, Robert. *see* Monk, Robert C.
Monk, Robert C.
    xMonk, Robert.
    Exploring Religious Meaning. P-H.
Monkerud, Donald.
    xMonkerud, Donald.
    Self-Defense for Women. Wm C Brown.
Monkhouse, A. *see* Monkhouse, Allan Noble.
Monkhouse, Allan. *see* Monkhouse, Allan Noble.
Monkhouse, Allan Noble, 1858-1936
    xMonkhouse, A.
    Books & Plays. R West.
    xMonkhouse, Allan.
    Books & Plays. Arno.
    Books & Plays. R West.
Monkhouse, F. J. *see* Monkhouse, Francis John.
Monkhouse, Francis John.
    xMonkhouse, F. J.
    A Dictionary of the Natural Environment.
        Halsted Pr.
Monkkonen, Eric H., 1942-
    xMonkkonen, Eric H.
    The Dangerous Class: Crime & Poverty in
        Columbus, Ohio, 1860-1885. Harvard U Pr.
Monks Of Solesmes. *see* Catholic Church. Pope.
Monmonier, Mark S.
    xMonmonier, Mark S.
    Maps, Distortion, & Meaning. Assn Am
        Geographers.
Monnerot, Jules.
    xMonnerot, Jules.
    Sociology of Communism. Greenwood.
Monnet, Jean, 1888-
    xMonnet, Jean.
    Memoirs. Doubleday.
Monod, Jacques.
    xMonod, Jacques.

ed. Of Microbes & Life. Columbia U Pr.
Monod, Sylvere, 1921-
xMonod, Sylvere.
Dickens the Novelist. U of Okla Pr.
Monro, David H. *see* Monro, David Hector.
Monro, David Hector.
xMonro, David H.
Godwin's Moral Philosophy: An Interpretation
of William Godwin. Greenwood.
Monro, Donald M.
xMonro, Donald M.
Computing with Fortran: A Practical Course.
Intl Schol Bk Serv.
Monro, Harold, 1879-1932
xMonro, Harold.
Some Contemporary Poets. Folcroft.
Monro, Hector.
xMonro, Hector.
The Ambivalence of Bernard Mandeville.
Oxford U Pr.
Monro, Margaret T. *see* Monro, Margaret Theodora.
Monro, Margaret Theodora, 1896-
xMonro, Margaret T.
Book of Unlikely Saints. Arno.
Monroe, Alan D.
xMonroe, Alan D.
Public Opinion in America. Har-Row.
Monroe, Alan H. *see* Monroe, Alan Houston.
Monroe, Alan Houston.
xMonroe, Alan H.
jt. auth. Principles of Speech Communication.
Scott F.
Monroe, Charles R.
xMonroe, Charles R.
Profile of the Community College: A
Handbook. Jossey-Bass.
Monroe City County Fine Arts Council. *see* Monroe City
Fine Arts Council.
Monroe City Fine Arts Council.
xMonroe City County Fine Arts Council.
Brighten the Corner. Monroe County Lib.
Monroe, Day, 1888-
xMonroe, Day.
Chicago Families: A Study of Unpublished
Census Data. Arno.
Monroe, James T.
xMonroe, James T.
Hispano-Arabic Poetry: A Student Anthology.
U of Cal Pr.
Shu'Ubiyya in Al'Andalus: The Risala of Ibn
Garcia & Five Refutations. U of Cal Pr.
Monroe, Lewis B. *see* Monroe, Lewis Baxter.
Monroe, Lewis Baxter, 1825?-1879
xMonroe, Lewis B.
ed. Dialogues & Dramas. Arno.
ed. Humorous Readings. Arno.
Monroe, Lynn L. *see* Monroe, Lynn Lee.
Monroe, Lynn Lee.
xMonroe, Lynn L.
The Old-Time Bicycle Book. Carolrhoda Bks.
Monroe, Marion, 1898-
xMonroe, Marion.
Growing into Reading: How Readiness for
Reading Develops at Home & at School.
Greenwood.
Monroe, Paul, 1869-1947
xMonroe, Paul.
ed. Cyclopedia of Education. Gale.
Founding of the American Public School
System: A History of Education in the
United States; from the Early Settlements to
the Close of the Civil War Period. Hafner.
A Text-Book in the History of Education.
Norwood Edns.
Textbook in the History of Education. AMS
Pr.
Monroe, R. E. *see* Monroe, Russell R.
Monroe, Robert A.
xMonroe, Robert A.

Journeys Out of the Body. Doubleday.
Monroe, Russell R.
xMonroe, R. E.
ed. Psychiatric Epidemiology & Mental Health
Planning. Am Psychiatric.
xMonroe, Russell R.
Brain Dysfunction in Aggressive Criminals.
Lexington Bks.
Monroe, Tom, 1940-
xMonroe, Tom.
Clutch & Flywheel Handbook. H P Bks.
How to Rebuild Your Small-Block Ford. H P
Bks.
Monroe, Walter S. *see* Monroe, Walter Scott.
Monroe, Walter Scott, 1882-1961
xMonroe, Walter S.
Teaching-Learning Theory & Teacher
Education, 1890-1950. Greenwood.
Monroe, Will S. *see* Monroe, Will Seymour.
Monroe, Will Seymour, 1863-1939
xMonroe, Will S.
Comenius & the Beginnings of Educational
Reform. Arno.
History of the Pestalozzian Movement in the
United States. Arno.
Monroney, A. S. *see* Monroney, A. S. Mike.
Monroney, A. S. Mike, 1902-
xMonroney, A. S.
Strengthening of American Political
Institutions. Kennikat.
Monrotus, Steven C.
xMonrotus, Steven C.
Practical Pharmacology for the Dental
Hygienist. Saunders.
Monroy, A. *see* Monroy, Alberto.
Monroy, Alberto.
xMonroy, A.
Introductory Concepts in Developmental
Biology. U of Chicago Pr.
Monsanto Research Corp.
xMonsanto Research Corporation.
Potential Pollutants from Petrochemical
Processes. Technomic.
Monsanto Research Corporation. *see* Monsanto Research
Corp.
Monsarrat, Ann.
xMonsarrat, Ann.
And the Bride Wore...: The Story of the White
Wedding. Dodd.
Monsarrat, Nicholas, 1910-
xMonsarrat, Nicholas.
The Cruel Sea. Bantam.
Cruel Sea. Knopf.
The Master Mariner: Running Proud. Morrow.
The Master Mariner: Running Proud. Popular
Lib.
Monsarrat at Sea. Popular Lib.
Monsen, Joseph. *see* Monsen, R. Joseph.
Monsen, R. Joseph.
xMonsen, Joseph.
Business & the Changing Environment.
McGraw.
Monserud, Wilma.
xMonserud, Wilma.
Common Wild Flowers of Minnesota. U of
Minn Pr.
Monsma, Timothy, 1933-
xMonsma, Timothy.
An Urban Strategy for Africa. William Carey
Lib.
Monson, Karen.
xMonson, Karen.
Alban Berg. HM.
Monson, Richard S.
xMonson, Richard S.
Fundamentals of Organic Chemistry. McGraw.
Monson, Samuel C. *see* Monson, Samuel Christian.
Monson, Samuel Christian, 1919-
xMonson, Samuel C.

Word Building. Macmillan.
Monson, Thomas S., 1927-
xMonson, Thomas S.
Be Your Best Self. Deseret Bk.
Monsour, Sally.
xMonsour, Sally.
Music in Open Education. Ctr Appl Res.
Montag, Mildred L. *see* Montag, Mildred Louise.
Montag, Mildred Louise.
xMontag, Mildred L.
Handbook of Fundamental Nursing
Techniques. Wiley.
Montagna, Paul D.
xMontagna, Paul D.
Certified Public Accounting: A Sociological
View of a Profession in Change. Scholars Bk.
Montagna, William.
xMontagna, William.
Nonhuman Primates in Biomedical Research. U
of Minn Pr.
Montagu. *see* Montagu, Ashley.
Montagu, A. *see* Montagu, Ashley.
Montagu, Ashley, 1905-
xMontagu.
On Being Human. Dutton.
xMontagu, A.
The Practice of Love. P-H.
xMontagu, Ashley.
Culture & the Evolution of Man. Oxford U Pr.
The Elephant Man: A Study in Human
Dignity. Dutton.
The Human Connection. McGraw.
ed. Learning Non-Aggression: The Experience
of Non-Literate Societies. Oxford U Pr.
ed. Learning Non-Aggression: The Experience
of Non-Literate Societies. Oxford U Pr.
ed. Meaning of Love. Greenwood.
The Nature of Human Aggression. Oxford U
Pr.
Race & IQ. Oxford U Pr.
Race & IQ. Oxford U Pr.
ed. Sociobiology Examined. Oxford U Pr.
Montagu, Ashley. *see* Montagu, Ashley Montague
Francis Ashley Montagu.
**Montagu, Ashley Montague Francis Ashley Montagu,
1905-**
xMontagu, Ashley.
Natural Superiority of Women. Macmillan.
The Natural Superiority of Women. Macmillan.
Montagu, Jeremy.
xMontagu, Jeremy.
The World of Baroque & Classical Musical
Instruments. Overlook Pr.
Montagu, Mary (Pierrepont) Wortley.
xMontagu, Mary W.
Letters & Works of Lady Mary Wortley
Montagu. AMS Pr.
Nonsense of Common Sense, 1737-1738. AMS
Pr.
Montagu, Mary W. *see* Montagu, Mary (Pierrepont)
Wortley.
Montagu-Nathan. *see* Montagu-Nathan, Montagu.
Montagu-Nathan, M. *see* Montagu-Nathan, Montagu.
Montagu-Nathan, Montagu.
xMontagu-Nathan.
Glinka. AMS Pr.
xMontagu-Nathan, M.
History of Russian Music. Biblo.
A History of Russian Music. Longwood Pr.
xMontagu-Nathan, Montagu.
Contemporary Russian Composers. Greenwood.
Contemporary Russian Composers. Scholarly.
Montague, Charles E. *see* Montague, Charles Edward.
Montague, Charles Edward, 1867-1928
xMontague, Charles E.

Action & Other Stories. Arno.
Disenchantment. Greenwood.
Dramatic Values. Greenwood.
Dramatic Values. Scholarly.
Fiery Particles. Scholarly.

Montague, Gene.
xMontague, Gene.
Experience of Literature. P-H.

Montague, George T.
xMontague, George T.
Building Christ's Body: The Dynamics of
Christian Living According to St. Paul.
Franciscan Herald.
The Holy Spirit: Growth of Biblical Tradition.
Paulist Pr.

Montague, Joel B., Jr
xMontague, Joel B.
Class & Nationality: English & American
Studies. Coll & U Pr.

Montague, John.
xMontague, John.
Chosen Light. Swallow.

Montalban, Ricardo.
xMontalban, Ricardo.
Reflections: A Life in Two Worlds. Doubleday.

Montale, Eugenio.
xMontale, Eugenio.
The Storm & Other Poems. Field Oberlin.

Montana Historical Socety. see Montana. Historical
Society.

Montana. Historical Society.
xMontana Historical Socety.
ed. Not in Precious Metals Alone: A
Manuscript History of Montana. MT Hist
Soc.

Montapert, Alfred A. see Montapert, Alfred Armand.

Montapert, Alfred Armand.
xMontapert, Alfred A.
Distilled Wisdom. Bks of Value.
Compiled by Distilled Wisdom. Borden.
Supreme Philosophy of Man: The Laws of Life.
Borden.

Monteath, C. D. see Monteath, G. D.

Monteath, G. D.
xMonteath, C. D.
Applications of the Electromagnetic
Reciprocity Principle. Pergamon.

Montefiore, Alan.
xMontefiore, Alan.
A Modern Introduction to Moral Philosophy.
Routledge & Kegan.

Montefiore, C. G. see Montefiore, Claude Joseph
Goldsmid.

Montefiore, Claude G. see Montefiore, Claude Joseph
Goldsmid.

Montefiore, Claude J. see Montefiore, Claude Joseph
Goldsmith.

Montefiore, Claude Joseph Goldsmid.
xMontefiore, C. G.
ed. A Rabbinic Anthology. Schocken.
xMontefiore, Claude G.
Some Elements of the Religious Teaching of
Jesus According to the Synoptic Ospels.
Arno.
The Synoptic Gospels. Ktav.

Montefiore, Claude Joseph Goldsmith, 1858-1938
xMontefiore, Claude J.
Lectures on the Origin & Growth of Religion
As Illustrated by the Religion of the Ancient
Hebrews. AMS Pr.

Monteilhet, Hubert.
xMonteilhet, Hubert.
Cupid's Executioners. S&S.

Monteiro, Lois A.
xMonteiro, Lois A.
Monitoring Health Status & Medical Care.
Ballinger Pub.

Monteiro, Mariana.
xMonteiro, Mariana.

Legends & Popular Tales of the Basque People.
Arno.
Legends & Popular Tales of the Basque People.
Gordon Pr.

Monteleone, Thomas. see Monteleone, Thomas F.

Monteleone, Thomas F.
xMonteleone, Thomas.
The Secret Sea. Popular Lib.

Montelius, Oscar, 1843-1921
xMontelius, Oscar.
Civilisation of Sweden in Heathen Times.
Johnson Repr.

Montenegro, Marilyn.
xMontenegro, Marilyn.
Chicanos & Mexican-Americans: Ethnic
Self-Identification & Attitudinal Differences.
R & E Res Assoc.

Monter, E. W. see Monter, E. William.

Monter, E. William.
xMonter, E. W.
Calvin's Geneva. Krieger.
xMonter, E. William.
ed. European Witchcraft. Wiley.

Montero, Darell. see Montero, Darrel.

Montero, Darrel.
xMontero, Darell.
Vietnamese Americans: Patterns of
Resettlement & Socioeconomic Adaption in
the United States. Westview.

Montesano, Philip M.
xMontesano, Phillip.
Some Aspects of the Free Negro Question in
San Francisco. R & E Res Assoc.

Montesano, Phillip. see Montesano, Philip M.

Montesquieu, C. de. see Montesquieu, Charles Louis De
Secondat, Baron De la Brede et De.

**Montesquieu, Charles Louis de Secondat, baron de La
Brede et de, 1689-1755**
xMontesquieu, C. de.
Spirit of the Laws. Hafner.
xMontesquieu, Charles-Louis.
Oeuvres Completes. French & Eur.

Montesquieu, Charles-Louis. see Montesquieu, Charles
Louis De Secondat, Baron De la Brede et De.

Montessori, Maria, 1870-1952
xMontessori, Maria.
Child in the Family. Avon.
Childhood Education. NAL.
The Discovery of the Child. Ballantine.
Dr. Montessori's Own Handbook. Schocken.
From Childhood to Adolescence: Including
Erdkinder & the Function of the University.
Schocken.
The Montessori Elementary Material.
Schocken.
The Montessori Method. Norwood Edns.
The Montessori Method. Schocken.

Montessori, Mario M.
xMontessori, Mario M.
Education for Human Development:
Understanding Montessori. Schocken.

Montet, Pierre, 1885-1966
xMontet, Pierre.
Everyday Life in Egypt in the Days of
Ramesses the Great. Greenwood.

Montez, Lola, 1818-1861
xMontez, Lola.
The Arts of Beauty: Or, Secrets of a Lady's
Toilet, with Hints to Gentlemen on the Art
of Fascinating. Ecco Pr.

Montgomery, A. T. see Montgomery, A. Thompson.

Montgomery, A. Thompson.
xMontgomery, A. T.
Financial Accounting Information: An
Introduction to Its Preparation & Use. A-W.
xMontgomery, A. Thompson.

Managerial Accounting Information: An
Introduction to Its Content & Usefulness.
A-W.

Montgomery, Bernard. see Montgomery, Bernard Law
Montgomery, Ist Viscount.

**Montgomery, Bernard Law Montgomery, Ist Viscount,
1887-**
xMontgomery, Bernard.
Approach to Sanity: A Study of East-West
Relations. Arno.

Montgomery, Brian.
xMontgomery, Brian.
A Field-Marshal in the Family: A Personal
Biography of Montgomery of Alamein.
Taplinger.

Montgomery, Charles F.
xMontgomery, Charles F.
A History of American Pewter. Dutton.

Montgomery, D. see Montgomery, Deane.

Montgomery, David C. see Montgomery, David
Campbell.

Montgomery, David Campbell, 1936-
xMontgomery, David C.
Theory of the Unmagnetized Plasma. Gordon.

Montgomery, Deane.
xMontgomery, D.
Topological Transformation Groups. Krieger.

Montgomery, Douglas C.
xMontgomery, Douglas C.
Design & Analysis of Experiments. Wiley.
Forecasting & Time Series Analysis. McGraw.

Montgomery, E. S. see Montgomery, Edward Samuel.

Montgomery, Edward.
xMontgomery, Edward.
Useful Knots for Everyone. Scribner.

Montgomery, Edward Samuel, 1912-
xMontgomery, E. S.
The Thoroughbred. Arco.

Montgomery, Elizabeth. see Montgomery, Elizabeth
Rider.

Montgomery, Elizabeth R. see Montgomery, Elizabeth
Rider.

Montgomery, Elizabeth Rider.
xMontgomery, Elizabeth.
The Builder Also Grows. Ashley Bks.
xMontgomery, Elizabeth R.
Duke Ellington: King of Jazz. Garrard.
Trouble Is His Name. Garrard.

Montgomery, Guy.
xMontgomery, Guy.
ed. Concordance to the Poetical Works of John
Dryden. Russell.

Montgomery, H. see Montgomery, Herbert.

Montgomery, H. L. see Montgomery, Hugh L.

Montgomery, Herb. see Montgomery, Herbert.

Montgomery, Herbert.
xMontgomery, H.
Mongoose Magoo. Oddo.
xMontgomery, Herb.
Love & Let Grow: Reflections on Family
Living. Winston Pr.

Montgomery, Hugh L.
xMontgomery, H. L.
Topics in Multiplicative Number Theory.
Springer-Verlag.

Montgomery, James A. see Montgomery, James Alan.

Montgomery, James Alan, 1866-1949
xMontgomery, James A.
Arabia & the Bible. Ktav.

Montgomery, John.
xMontgomery, John.
Foxy & the Badgers. Schocken.

Montgomery, John D. see Montgomery, John Dickey.

Montgomery, John Dickey.
xMontgomery, John D.
ed. Patterns of Policy: Comparative &
Longitudinal Studies of Population Events.
Transaction Bks.

Montgomery, John W. see Montgomery, John Warwick.

Montgomery, John Warwick.
  xMontgomery, John W.
    Damned Through the Church. Bethany Fell.
    History & Christianity. Inter-Varsity.
Montgomery, K. Leon.
  xMontgomery, K. Leon.
    Document Retrieval Systems: Factors Affecting
      Search Time. Dekker.
Montgomery, L. M.
  xMontgomery, L. M.
    Anne of Avonlea. Bantam.
    Anne of Green Gables. Bantam.
    Anne of Green Gables. Buccaneer Bks.
Montgomery, Louise, 1864-
  xMontgomery, Louise.
    Mrs. Mahoney of the Tenement. Arno.
Montgomery, Marion.
  xMontgomery, Marion.
    Eliot's Reflective Journey to the Garden.
      Whitston Pub.
    The Reflective Journey Toward Order: Essays
      on Dante, Wordsworth, Eliot, & Others. U of
      Ga Pr.
Montgomery, Mary.
  xMontgomery, Mary.
    History of Legislation & Policy Formation of
      the Central Valley Project. Arno.
Montgomery Museum of Fine Art. see Montgomery
  Museum of Fine Arts.
Montgomery Museum of Fine Arts.
  xMontgomery Museum of Fine Art.
    Walter Gaudnek Retrospective. Montgomery
      Mus.
  xMontgomery Museum of Fine Arts.
    American Art, Nineteen Thirty-Four to
      Nineteen Fifty-Six: Selections from the
      Whitney Museum of American Art.
      Montgomery Mus.
    American Fashion Designs by Wilson Folmar.
      Montgomery Mus.
    Art Inc: American Paintings from Corporate
      Collections. Montgomery Mus.
    Spaces & Places: Views of Montgomery's Built
      Environment. Montgomery Mus.
Montgomery, R. H. see Montgomery, Richard H.
Montgomery, Richard H.
  xMontgomery, R. H.
    The Solar Decision Book: Your Guide to
      Making a Sound Investment. Wiley.
Montgomery, Robert, 1904-
  xMontgomery, Robert.
    Open Letter from a Television Viewer.
      Heineman.
Montgomery, Robert. see Montgomery, Robert John.
Montgomery, Robert B. see Montgomery, Robert Bruce.
Montgomery, Robert Bruce.
  xMontgomery, Robert B.
    Long Divorce. Greenwood.
Montgomery, Robert H. see Montgomery, Robert
  Hiester.
Montgomery, Robert Hiester, 1872-1953
  xMontgomery, Robert H.
    Auditing Theory & Practice. Arno.
    Fifty Years of Accountancy. Arno.
Montgomery, Robert John.
  xMontgomery, Robert.
    A New Examination of Examinations.
      Routledge & Kegan.
Montgomery, Robert L. see Montgomery, Robert Leo.
Montgomery, Robert Langford.
  xMontgomery, Robert L.
    The Reader's Eye: Studies in Didactic Literary
      Theory from Dante to Tasso. U of Cal Pr.
    Symmetry & Sense: The Poetry of Sir Philip
      Sidney. Greenwood.
Montgomery, Robert Leo, 1927-
  xMontgomery, Robert L.

    A Master Guide to Public Speaking. Har-Row.
    Memory Made Easy: The Complete Book of
      Memory Training. Am Mgmt.
Montgomery, Robin.
  xMontgomery, Robin.
    The History of Montgomery County. Jenkins.
Montgomery, Royal E. see Montgomery, Royal Ewert.
Montgomery, Royal Ewert, 1896-
  xMontgomery, Royal E.
    Industrial Relations in the Chicago Building
      Trades. Arno.
Montgomery, Royce L.
  xMontgomery, Royce L.
    Human Anatomy Review. Arco.
Montgomery, Ruth. see Montgomery, Ruth Shick.
Montgomery, Ruth Shick, 1912-
  xMontgomery, Ruth.
    Strangers Among Us: Enlightened Beings from
      a World to Come. Coward.
    The World Before. Coward.
    The World Before. Fawcett.
    A World Beyond: A Startling Message from
      the Eminent Psychic Arthur Ford from
      Beyond the Grave. Coward.
Montgomery, Rutherford G. see Montgomery,
  Rutherford George.
Montgomery, Rutherford George, 1896-
  xMontgomery, Rutherford G.
    The Capture of the Golden Stallion. Little.
    Carcajou. Caxton.
    Pekan the Shadow. Caxton.
  xMontgomery, Ruthford G.
    Living Wilderness. Caxton.
Montgomery, Ruthford G. see Montgomery, Rutherford
  George.
Montgomery, Vivian.
  xMontgomery, Vivian.
    Mr. Jellybean. Shoal Creek Pub.
Montgomery, Walter.
  xMontgomery, Walter.
    ed. American Art & American Art Collections.
      Garland Pub.
Montgomery Ward. see Ward (Montgomery) and
  Company.
Montgomery Ward & Co. see Ward (Montgomery) and
  Company.
Montgomery, William W., 1923-
  xMontgomery, William W.
    Surgery of the Upper Respiratory System. Lea
      & Febiger.
Monthan, Doris. see Monthan, Doris Born.
Monthan, Doris Born.
  xMonthan, Doris.
    R. C. Gorman: The Lithographs. Northland.
Montias, John M. see Montias, John Michael.
Montias, John Michael, 1928-
  xMontias, John M.
    Central Planning in Poland. Greenwood.
Montilla, M. Robert.
  xMontilla, M. Robert.
    ed. Correctional Facilities Planning. Lexington
      Bks.
Montoye, Henry J. see Montoye, Henry Joseph.
Montoye, Henry Joseph.
  xMontoye, Henry J.
    An Introduction to Measurement in Physical
      Education. Allyn.
Montresor, Beni.
  xMontresor, Beni.
    illus. Bedtime. Har-Row.
Montreville, Doris De. see De Montreville, Doris.
Montroll, John.
  xMontroll, John.
    Origami for the Enthusiast: Step-by-Step
      Instructions in Over 700 Diagrams. Dover.
Montross, Lois (Seyster), 1897-
  xMontross, Lois S.
    Among Those Present. Arno.
Montross, Lois S. see Montross, Lois (Seyster).

Monty Python.
  xMonty Python's Flying Circus.
    Monty Python & the Holy Grail. Methuen Inc.
Monty Python's Flying Circus. see Monty Python.
Monypenny, William F. see Monypenny, William
  Flavelle.
Monypenny, William Flavelle.
  xMonypenny, William F.
    Life of Benjamin Disraeli, Earl of Beaconsfield.
      Russell.
Moodie, Graeme C.
  xMoodie, Graeme C.
    Power & Authority in British Universities.
      McGill-Queens U Pr.
Moodie, Michael, 1948-
  xMoodie, Michael.
    Sovereignty, Security & Arms. Sage.
Moodie, William.
  xMoodie, William.
    Hypnosis in Treatment. Emerson.
Moody, Anne, 1940-
  xMoody, Anne.
    Coming of Age in Mississippi. Dell.
Moody, Bert.
  xMoody, Bert.
    Ocean Ships. Intl Pubns Serv.
Moody Bible Institute of Chicago.
  xMoody Press Editors.
    Bible Concordance. Moody.
    ed. Esto Creemos: What Christians Believe.
      Moody.
    Second Coming of Christ. Moody.
Moody, Elizabeth.
  xMoody, Elizabeth.
    Patty Cake. Times Bks.
Moody, Eric N.
  xMoody, Eric N.
    Compiled by An Index to the Publications of
      the Nevada Historical Society, 1907-1971.
      Nevada Hist Soc.
Moody, Ernest. see Moody, Ernest Addison.
Moody, Ernest A. see Moody, Ernest Addison.
Moody, Ernest Addison, 1903-
  xMoody, Ernest.
    Studies in Medieval Philosophy, Science &
      Logic: Collected Papers, 1933-1969. U of Cal
      Pr.
  xMoody, Ernest A.
    Logic of William of Ockham. Russell.
    Truth & Consequence in Mediaeval Logic.
      Greenwood.
Moody, J. Carroll.
  xMoody, J. Carroll.
    Credit Union Movement: Origins &
      Development, 1850-1970. U of Nebr Pr.
Moody, James, 1744-1809
  xMoody, James.
    Lieutenant James Moody's Narrative of His
      Exertions & Sufferings in the Cause of
      Government, Since the Year 1776. Arno.
Moody, John, 1868-1958
  xMoody, John.
    The Long Road Home: An Autobiography.
      Arno.
Moody, Joseph N. see Moody, Joseph Nestor.
Moody, Joseph Nestor, 1904-
  xMoody, Joseph N.
    French Education Since Napoleon. Syracuse U
      Pr.
Moody, Marvin D.
  xMoody, Marvin D.
    The Interior Article in De-Compounds in
      French: Agent De Police Versus Agent De la
      Police. U Pr of Amer.
Moody, Paul A. see Moody, Paul Amos.
Moody, Paul Amos, 1903-
  xMoody, Paul A.

Story of Silent Night. Concordia.

Moore, John Trotwood, 1858-1929
xMoore, John T.
Songs & Stories from Tennessee. Arno.

Moore, John W.
xMoore, Elizabeth A.
jt. auth. Environmental Chemistry. Acad Pr.
xMoore, John W.
Chemistry. McGraw.
Environmental Chemistry. Acad Pr.

Moore, John W. *see* Moore, John Weeks.

Moore, John Weeks, 1807-1889
xMoore, John W.
Complete Encyclopaedia of Music: Elementary,
Technical, Historical, Biographical, Vocal, &
Instrumental. Scholarly.
Moore's Historical, Biographical, &
Miscellaneous Gatherings. Gale.

Moore, John Wilson.
xMoore, John W.
ed. Membranes, Ions, & Impulses. Plenum Pub.

Moore, Josiah Staunton, 1843-
xMoore, J. Staunton.
The Annals & History of Henrico Parish,
Diocese of Virginia, & St. John's P. E.
Church. Genealog Pub.

Moore, Keith L.
xMoore, Keith L.
Clinically Oriented Anatomy. Williams &
Wilkins.

Moore, Kendall. *see* Moore, Kendall H.

Moore, Kendall H.
xMoore, Kendall.
The Surgical Beauty Racket. Ashley Bks.

Moore, Kenneth, 1930-
xMoore, Kenneth.
Those of the Street: The Catholic-Jews of
Mallorca. U of Notre Dame Pr.

Moore, Kenneth C., 1934-
xMoore, Kenneth C.
Airport, Aircraft & Airline Security.
Butterworths.

Moore, L. Hugh.
xMoore, L. Hugh.
A Concise Handbook of English Composition.
P-H.

Moore, Lilian.
xMoore, Lilian.
The Duport Mystery. Johnson Repr.
I Feel the Same Way. Atheneum.
Little Raccoon & Poems from the Woods.
McGraw.
Little Raccoon & the Thing in the Pool.
McGraw.
Riddle Walk. Garrard.

Moore, Lillian.
xMoore, Lillian.
Images of the Dance: Historical Treasures of
the Dance Collection, 1581-1861. NY Pub
Lib.

Moore, Lolita D. *see* Moore, Lolita Daneo.

Moore, Lolita Daneo, 1928-
xMoore, Lolita D.
Italian Herb Cooking. Richboro Pr.

Moore, Lorna G., 1946-
xMoore, Lorna G.
Biocultural Basis of Health: Expanding Views
of Medical Anthropology. Mosby.

Moore, Lucia. *see* Moore, Lucia Wilkins.

Moore, Lucia Wilkins, 1887-
xMoore, Lucia.
The Wheel & the Hearth. Ballantine.

Moore, M. J.
xMoore, M. J.
Two-Phase Steam Flow in Turbines &
Separators: Theory, Instrumentation,
Engineering. McGraw.

Moore, Marcia.
xMoore, Marcia.

Diet, Sex & Yoga. Arcane Pubns.
Reincarnation, Key to Immortality. Arcane
Pubns.

Moore, Margaret. *see* Moore, Margaret (Whiteside).

Moore, Margaret (Whiteside), Mrs, 1906-
xMoore, Margaret.
A Study of Young High School Graduates.
AMS Pr.

Moore, Margaret R.
xMoore, Margaret.
Pepito's Speech at the United Nations.
Carolrhoda Bks.

Moore, Marianne, 1887-
xMoore, Marianne.
Collected Poems. Macmillan.

Moore, Marie A. *see* Moore, Marie Antoinette.

Moore, Marie Antoinette.
xMoore, Marie A.
The Mastiff. Denlingers.

Moore, Marvin, 1937-
xMoore, Marvin.
How to Handle Your Imagination. Southern
Pub.
Sacrifice. Southern Pub.
Television & the Christian Home. Pacific Pr
Pub Assn.
xMoore, Marvin H.
How to Handle Competition. Southern Pub.
xMoore, Marvin L.
Witnesses Through Trial. Southern Pub.

Moore, Marvin H. *see* Moore, Marvin.

Moore, Marvin L. *see* Moore, Marvin.

Moore, Mary Lou.
xMoore, Mary Lou.
Realities in Childbearing. Saunders.

Moore, Matthew T., 1901-
xMoore, Matthew T.
Archives of the International Congresses &
Society of Neuropathology: 1952-1977. Lea
& Febiger.

Moore, Maxine, 1927-
xMoore, Maxine.
That Lonely Game: Melville, "Mardi", & the
Almanac. U of Mo Pr.

Moore, N. Hudson. *see* Moore, Hannah Hudson.

Moore, Norman D.
xMoore, Norman D.
Dictionary of Business, Finance, & Investment.
Investor's Syst.

Moore, P. D. *see* Moore, Peter D.

Moore, Patrick.
xMoore, Patrick.
Amateur Astronomy. Norton.
Can You Speak Venusian?: A Guide to
Independent Thinkers. Norton.
Craters of the Moon: An Observational
Approach. Norton.
Guide to Mars. Norton.
Mars. Crown.
New Challenge to the Stars. Rand.
The Next Fifty Years in Space. Taplinger.
Observer's Book of Astronomy. Scribner.
Pocket Guide to Astronomy. S&S.
Sun. Norton.
Suns, Myths & Men. Norton.
Survey of the Moon. Norton.

Moore, Patrick Foreword by. *see* Blunck, Jurgen.

Moore, Patsie S. *see* Moore, Harvey Daniel.

Moore, Paul, 1919-
xMoore, Paul.
Take a Bishop Like Me. Har-Row.

Moore, Peter D.
xMoore, P. D.
An Illustrated Guide to Pollen Analysis.
Halsted Pr.

Moore, Philip S. *see* Moore, Philip Samuel.

Moore, Philip Samuel, 1900-
xMoore, Philip S.

Century of Law at Notre Dame. U of Notre
Dame Pr.

Moore, Preston L.
xMoore, Preston L.
Drilling Practices Manual. Pennwell Pub.

Moore, R. I. *see* Moore, Robert Ian.

Moore, R. J. *see* Moore, Robin James.

Moore, R. Laurence. *see* Moore, Robert Laurence.

Moore, Ralph L.
xMoore, Ralph L.
Neutralization of Waste Water by pH Control.
Instru Soc.

Moore, Rayburn S., 1920-
xMoore, Rayburn S.
Paul Hamilton Hayne. Twayne.

Moore, Raylyn.
xMoore, Raylyn.
What Happened to Emily Goode After the
Great Exhibition. Donning Co.

Moore, Richter H.
xMoore, Richter H.
Readings in Criminal Justice. Bobbs.

Moore, Robert E. *see* Moore, Robert Etheridge.

Moore, Robert Etheridge, 1920-
xMoore, Robert E.
Hogarth's Literary Relationships. Octagon.

Moore, Robert H. *see* Moore, Robert Hamilton.

Moore, Robert Hamilton, 1913-
xMoore, Robert H.
Effective Writing. HR&W.
Handbook of Effective Writing. HR&W.

Moore, Robert Ian, 1941-
xMoore, R. I.
The Origins of European Dissent. St Martin.

Moore, Robert L., 1949-
xMoore, Robert L.
Economic Principles in Action. P-H.
ed. Sources of Vitality in American Church
Life. Exploration Pr.

Moore, Robert L. *see* Moore, Robert Lee.

Moore, Robert Laurence.
xMoore, R. Laurence.
In Search of White Crows: Spiritualism,
Parapsychology, & American Culture. Oxford
U Pr.

Moore, Robert Lee, 1882-
xMoore, Robert L.
Foundations of Point Set Theory. Am Math.

Moore, Robin James.
xMoore, R. J.
The Crisis of Indian Unity, 1917-1940. Oxford
U Pr.

Moore, Ronald.
xMoore, Ronald.
Legal Norms & Legal Science: A Critical Study
of Kelsen's Pure Theory of Law. U Pr of
Hawaii.

Moore, Rosalie, 1910-
xMoore, Rosalie.
Of Singles & Doubles. Woolmer-Brotherson.

Moore, Russell F. *see* Moore, Russell Franklin.

Moore, Russell Franklin, 1920-
xMoore, Russell F.
ed. Law for Executives. Am Mgmt.

Moore, Ruth N. *see* Moore, Ruth Nulton.

Moore, Ruth Nulton.
xMoore, Ruth N.
The Ghost Bird Mystery. Herald Pr.
Peace Treaty. Herald Pr.
Tomas & the Talking Birds. Herald Pr.
Wilderness Journey. Herald Pr.

Moore, Sally F. *see* Moore, Sally Falk.

Moore, Sally Falk, 1924-
xMoore, Sally F.
Power & Property in Inca Peru. Greenwood.
ed. Secular Ritual. Humanities.
ed. Symbol & Politics in Communal Ideology:
Cases & Questions. Cornell U Pr.

Moore, Samuel, 1877-
xMoore, Samuel.

Historical Outlines of English Sounds &
Inflections. Wahr.
Moore, Shirley T.
xMoore, Shirley T.
A Vegetarian Diet: What It Is, How to Make It
Healthful & Enjoyable. Woodbridge Pr.
Moore, Sonia.
xMoore, Sonia.
Training an Actor: The Stanislavski System in
Class. Penguin.
Moore, Stanley B.
xMoore, Stanley B.
illus. Ornamental Horticulture As a Vocation.
Mor-Mac.
Moore, T. C. *see* Moore, Thomas C.
Moore, T. Sturge. *see* Moore, Thomas Sturge.
Moore, T. W.
xMoore, T. W.
Educational Theory: An Introduction.
Routledge & Kegan.
Moore, Thomas, 1779-1852
xMoore, Thomas.
Memoirs, Journal & Correspondence of
Thomas Moore. Scholarly.
Memoirs of the Life of the Rt. Hon. Richard
Brinsley Sheridan. Arno.
The Poetical Works of Thomas Moore. AMS
Pr.
Moore, Thomas C.
xMoore, T. C.
Biochemistry & Physiology of Plant Hormones.
Springer-Verlag.
Moore, Thomas G. *see* Moore, Thomas Gale.
Moore, Thomas Gale.
xMoore, Thomas G.
Economics of the American Theater. Duke.
Uranium Enrichment & Public Policy. Am
Enterprise.
Moore, Thomas S. *see* Moore, Thomas Sturge.
Moore, Thomas Sturge, 1870-1944
xMoore, T. Sturge.
Poems of T. Sturge Moore. Scholarly.
xMoore, Thomas S.
Some Soldier Poets. Arno.
Moore, Vardine, 1906-
xMoore, Vardine.
Pre-School Story Hour. Scarecrow.
Moore, W. E. *see* Moore, Wilbert Ellis.
Moore, W. G. *see* Moore, Wilfred George.
Moore, Waddy W. *see* Moore, Waddy William.
Moore, Waddy William.
xMoore, Waddy W.
Arkansas in the Gilded Age, 1874-1900. Rose
Pub.
Moore, Walter L.
xMoore, Walter L.
ed. Effects of Watershed Changes on
Streamflow. U of Tex Pr.
Moore, Walter L. *see* Moore, Walter Lane.
Moore, Walter Lane, 1905-
xMoore, Walter L.
Outlines for Preaching. Broadman.
Moore, Ward, 1903-
xMoore, Ward.
Bring the Jubilee. Avon.
Moore, Wilbert E. *see* Moore, Wilbert Ellis.
Moore, Wilbert Ellis.
xMoore, W. E.
World Modernization: The Limits of
Convergence. Elsevier.
xMoore, Wilbert E.
Industrial Relations & the Social Order. Arno.
Moore, Wilfred George, 1907-
xMoore, W. G.
A Dictionary of Geography: Definitions &
Explanations of Terms Used in Physical
Geography. B&N.
Moore, Will Grayburn.
xMoore, W. G.

The Tutorial System & Its Future. Pergamon.
Moore, William, fl. 1970-
xMoore, William.
The Thin Yellow Line. St Martin.
Moore, William Edgar.
xMoore, Wilbert E.
Creative & Critical Thinking. HM.
Moore, William T.
xMoore, William T.
Dateline Chicago: A Veteran Newsman Recalls
Its Heyday. Taplinger.
Moore-Betty, Maurice.
xMoore-Betty, Maurice.
Cooking for Occasions. D White.
The Maurice Moore-Betty Cookbook. Bobbs.
Moore-Landecker, Elizabeth.
xMoore-Landecker, Elizabeth.
Fundamentals of the Fungi. P-H.
Moorehead, Alan, 1910-
xMoorehead, Alan.
Cooper's Creek. St Martin.
No Room in the Ark. Har-Row.
White Nile. Har-Row.
Moorehead, Cleatus.
xMoorehead, Cleatus.
Math Made Fun for the Young Child.
Broadman.
Moores, Larry.
xMoores, Lawrence.
Thieves in the Schoolhouse. Ashley Bks.
Moores, Lawrence. *see* Moores, Larry.
Moorey, Peter R. *see* Moorey, Peter Roger Stuart.
Moorey, Peter Roger Stuart.
xMoorey, Peter R.
ed. The Origins of Civilization. Oxford U Pr.
Moorhead, James H.
xMoorhead, James H.
American Apocalypse: Yankee Protestants &
the Civil War, 1860-1869. Yale U Pr.
Moorhead, Lucy.
xMoorhead, Lucy.
Entertaining in Washington. Putnam.
Moorhead, Max L.
xMoorhead, Max L.
The Apache Frontier: Jacobo Ugarte &
Spanish-Indian Relations in Northern New
Spain, 1769-1791. U of Okla Pr.
The Presidio: Bastion of the Spanish
Borderlands. U of Okla Pr.
Moorhead, Ted B.
xMoorhead, Ted B.
How to Be a Family & Survive. Word Bks.
Moorhouse, Earl.
xMoorhouse, Earl.
Wake up! It's a Crash. Paddington.
Moorhouse, Geoffrey, 1931-
xMoorhouse, Geoffrey.
The Boat & the Town. Little.
The Fearful Void. Lippincott.
Moorhouse, Walter W. *see* Moorhouse, Walter Wilson.
Moorhouse, Walter Wilson, 1913-
xMoorhouse, Walter W.
Study of Rocks in Thin Section. Har-Row.
Moorman, Charles.
xMoorman, Charles.
An Arthurian Dictionary. U Pr of Miss.
Editing the Middle English Manuscript. U Pr
of Miss.
The Works of the "Gawain" Poet. U Pr of
Miss.
Moorman, John R. *see* Moorman, John Richard
Humpidge.
Moorman, John Richard Humpidge, Bp. of Ripon.
xMoorman, John R.
A History of the Church in England.
Morehouse.
Moorman, Thomas.
xMoorman, Thomas.

How to Make Your Science Project Scientific.
Atheneum.
How to Make Your Science Project Scientific.
Atheneum.
How to Work Toward Agreement. Atheneum.
Moors, H. G.
xMoors, H. G.
ed. Population & Family in the Low Countries.
Kluwer Boston.
Moorsteen, Richard. *see* Moorsteen, Richard Harris.
Moorsteen, Richard Harris, 1926-
xMoorsteen, Richard.
Prices & Production of Machinery in the Soviet
Union 1928-1958. Harvard U Pr.
Remaking China Policy: U. S. -China Relations
& Governmental Decisionmaking. Harvard U
Pr.
Moos, Malcolm C. *see* Moos, Malcolm Charles.
Moos, Malcolm Charles, 1916-
xMoos, Malcolm C.
Politics, Presidents, & Coat Tails. Greenwood.
Moos, R. H. *see* Moos, Rudolf H.
Moos, Rudolf. *see* Moos, Rudolf H.
Moos, Rudolf H.
xMoos, R. H.
Environment & Utopia: A Synthesis. Plenum
Pub.
xMoos, Rudolf.
Environment & Utopia: A Synthesis. Plenum
Pub.
xMoos, Rudolf H.
Evaluating Correctional & Community Settings.
Wiley.
Evaluating Treatment Environments: A Social
Ecological Approach. Wiley.
The Human Context: Environmental
Determinants of Behavior. Wiley.
Moose, J. W. *see* Moose, John W.
Moose, John W.
xMoose, J. W.
The Application of Comparative Morphology
in the Identification of Intestinal Parasites. C
C Thomas.
Mooser, Stephen.
xMooser, Stephen.
The Ghost with the Halloween Hiccups. Avon.
The Ghost with the Halloween Hiccups. Watts.
Monster Fun. Messner.
Moossa, A. R.
xMoossa, A. R.
Tumors of the Pancreas. Williams & Wilkins.
Moote, A. Lloyd. *see* Moote, Alanson Lloyd.
Moote, Alanson Lloyd.
xMoote, A. Lloyd.
Revolt of the Judges: The Parlement of Paris &
the Fronde, 1643-1652. Princeton U Pr.
Moots, Philip R.
xMoots, Philip R.
Church & Campus: Legal Issues in Religiously
Affiliated Higher Education. U of Notre
Dame Pr.
Mopsik, Stanley I.
xMopsik, Stanley I.
An Education Handbook for Parents of
Handicapped Children. Abt Assoc.
Moraes, Francis Robert Frank Moraes.
xMoraes, Frank.
India Today. Macmillan.
Moraes, Frank. *see* Moraes, Francis Robert Frank
Moraes.
Moragas, Augusto.
xMoragas, Augusto.
Atlas of Neonatal Histopathology. Saunders.
Morain, Lloyd.
xMorain, Lloyd L.
The Human Cougar. Prometheus Bks.
Morain, Lloyd L. *see* Morain, Lloyd.
Morales, Francisco, 1937-
xMorales, Francisco.

Ethnic & Social Background of the Franciscan
Friars in Seventeenth Century Mexico.
AAFH.

Morales, Pablo.
xMorales, Pablo.
Victim for Hire. Nordon Pubns.
Moran. *see* Moran, M. Marcus.
Moran, Emilio F.
xMoran, Emilio F.
Human Adaptability: An Introduction to
Ecological Anthropology. Duxbury Pr.
Moran, Gabriel.
xMoran, Gabriel.
Catechesis of Revelation. Seabury.
Education Toward Adulthood. Paulist Pr.
Theology of Revelation. Seabury.
Moran, George, 1942-
xMoran, George.
Eggs. Workman Pub.
Moran, Joan M. *see* Moran, Joan May.
Moran, Joan May.
xMoran, Joan M.
Leisure Activities for the Mature Adult.
Burgess.
Moran, John. *see* Moran, John H.
Moran, John H.
xMoran, John.
Toward the World & Wisdom of Wittgenstein's
"Tractatus". Mouton.
Moran, Joseph M.
xMoran, Joseph M.
Introduction to Environmental Science. W H
Freeman.
An Introduction to Environmental Sciences.
Little.
Moran, Lois.
xMoran, Lois.
ed. The Craftsman's Cookbook. Am Craft.
Moran, M. Marcus.
xMoran.
Applied Business Mathematics. Holbrook.
Moran, Martha (Manker).
xMoran, Martha Manker.
Sugar & Mr. Duck. Exposition.
Moran, Martha Manker. *see* Moran, Martha (Manker).
Moran, Michael. *see* Moran, Michael C.
Moran, Michael C.
xMoran, Michael.
Standards Relating to Appeals & Collateral
Review. Ballinger Pub.
Moran, Miriam G.
xMoran, Miriam G.
ed. Death: Jesus Made It All Different. Keats.
ed. What You Should Know About Women's
Lib. Keats.
Moran, P. A. *see* Moran, Partick Alfred Pierce.
Moran, Partick Alfred Pierce, 1917-
xMoran, P. A.
The Theory of Storage. Methuen Inc.
Morand, Paul, 1888-
xMorand, Paul.
Green Shoots. Arno.
Morante, Elsa, 1916-
xMorante, Elsa.
History: A Novel. Knopf.
Morariu, Mircea A.
xMorariu, Mircea A.
Major Neurological Syndromes. C C Thomas.
Morath, Inge.
xMorath, Inge.
Chinese Encounters. FS&G.
Moravcsik, J. M. *see* Moravcsik, J. M. E.
Moravcsik, J. M. E.
xMoravcsik, J. M.
ed. Logic & Philosophy for Linguists: A Book
of Readings. Humanities.
Logic & Philosophy for Linguists: A Book of
Readings. Mouton.
Moravetz, Bruno, 1921-
xMoravetz, Bruno.

The Big Book of Mountaineering. Barron.
Moravia, Alberto, 1907-
xMoravia, Alberto.
Bought & Sold. Manor Bks.
Command, & I Will Obey You. Manor Bks.
The Conformist. Greenwood.
Conjugal Love. Manor Bks.
The Fetish & Other Stories. Greenwood.
Racconti di Alberto Moravia. Irvington.
Two: A Phallic Novel. FS&G.
Two: A Phallic Novel. Manor Bks.
Two Women. Manor Bks.
Morawetz, David.
xMorawetz, David.
The Andean Group: A Case Study in
Economic Integration Among Developing
Countries. MIT Pr.
Twenty-Five Years of Economic Development:
1950 to 1975. Johns Hopkins.
Morawetz, Thomas, 1942-
xMorawetz, Thomas.
Wittgenstein & Knowledge: The Importance of
on Certainty. Humanities.
Wittgenstein & Knowledge: The Importance of
"On Certainty". U of Mass Pr.
xMorawetz, Thomas A.
The Philosophy of Law: An Introduction.
Macmillan.
Morawetz, Thomas A. *see* Morawetz, Thomas.
Morawski, Stefan.
xMorawski, Stefan.
Inquiries into the Fundamentals of Aesthetics.
MIT Pr.
Moray, Neville.
xMoray, Neville.
Listening & Attention. Gannon.
Morazan, Ronald R.
xMorazan, Ronald R.
Biographical Sketches of the Veterans of the
Battalion of Orleans, 1814 - 1815. Legacy
Pub Co.
Moraze, Charles, 1913-
xMoraze, Charles.
French & the Republic. Kennikat.
The Logic of History. Mouton.
Mordden, Ethan, 1947-
xMordden, Ethan.
A Guide to Orchestral Music: The Handbook
for Non-Musicians. Oxford U Pr.
Mordecai, John, Sir, 1903-
xMordecai, John.
Federation of the West Indies. Northwestern U
Pr.
Mordell, Albert, 1885-
xMordell, Albert.
Literature of Ecstasy.. Arden Lib.
The Literature of Ecstasy. Folcroft.
Literature of Ecstasy. Kennikat.
Mordell, L. J. *see* Mordell, Louis Joel.
Mordell, Louis Joel, 1888-
xMordell, L. J.
Diophantine Equations. Acad Pr.
Mordue, W.
xMordue, W.
Insect Physiology. Halsted Pr.
More, Charles A. *see* More, Charles Albert.
More, Charles Albert.
xMore, Charles A.
French Volunteer of the War of Independence.
Kennikat.
More, Daphne.
xMore, Daphne.
Ideas for Interesting Gardens. David &
Charles.
More, Hannah, 1745-1833
xMore, Hannah.
Strictures on the Modern System of Female
Education. Garland Pub.
More, Harry W.
xMore, Harry W.

ed. Contemporary Criminal Justice. Justice Sys.
Critical Issues in Law Enforcement. Anderson
Pub Co.
Effective Police Administration: A Behavioral
Approach. West Pub.
More, Paul E. *see* More, Paul Elmer.
More, Paul Elmer, 1864-1937
xMore, Paul E.
Catholic Faith. Kennikat.
Christ of the New Testament. Greenwood.
Christ the Word. Greenwood.
On Being Human. Arno.
On Being Human. Folcroft.
Pages from an Oxford Diary. Kennikat.
Platonism. AMS Pr.
Platonism. Greenwood.
Platonism. R West.
More, Shankar S. *see* More, Shankar Shantaram.
More, Shankar Shantaram, 1899-1965
xMore, Shankar S.
Remodelling of Democracy for Afro-Asian
Nations. Greenwood.
More, Thomas, Sir, Saint, 1478-1535
xMore, Thomas.
The Correspondence of Sir Thomas More.
Arno.
Thomas More's Prayer Book: A Facsimile
Reproduction of the Annotated Pages. Yale
U Pr.
Utopia. Norton.
Utopia. PB.
Utopia. Penguin.
Utopia. Yale U Pr.
Utopia. AHM Pub.
Morea, Peter. *see* Morea, Peter C.
Morea, Peter C.
xMorea, Peter.
Guidance, Selection, & Training: Ideas &
Applications. Routledge & Kegan.
Moreau, Claude.
xMoreau, Claude.
Moulds, Toxins & Food. Wiley.
Moreau, David.
xMoreau, David.
Look Behind You!: An Alphabetical Guide to
Executive Survival. Morrow.
Moreau, Genevieve.
xMoreau, Genevieve.
The Restless Journey of James Agee. Morrow.
Moreby, D. H.
xMoreby, D. H.
Personnel Management in Merchant Ships.
Pergamon.
Morehart, Grover C. *see* Morehart, Grover Cleveland.
Morehart, Grover Cleveland, 1885-
xMorehart, Grover C.
The Legal Status of City School Boards. AMS
Pr.
Morehead, A. H. *see* Morehead, Albert Hodges.
Morehead, Albert H. *see* Morehead, Albert Hodges.
Morehead, Albert Hodges, 1909-
xMorehead, A. H.
Complete Guide to Winning Poker. S&S.
xMorehead, Albert H.
Complete Guide to Winning Poker. S&S.
Morehead, Anne E. *see* Morehead, Donald M.
Morehead, Donald M.
xMorehead, Anne E.
jt. ed. Normal & Deficient Child Language.
Univ Park.
xMorehead, Donald M.
ed. Normal & Deficient Child Language. Univ
Park.
Morehead, Joe, 1931-
xMorehead, Joe.
Theory & Practice in Library Education: The
Teaching-Learning Process. Libs Unl.
Morehead, Judith.
xMorehead, Judith.

Texas Wild Game Cookbook. Encino Pr.

Morehouse, Chauncey A.
  xMorehouse, Chauncey A.
    Statistical Principles & Procedures with
      Applications for Physical Education. Lea &
      Febiger.

Morehouse, Kathleen M. see Morehouse, Kathleen
  Moore.

Morehouse, Kathleen Moore.
  xMorehouse, Kathleen M.
    Rain on the Just: A Novel. S Ill U Pr.

Morehouse, Laurence. see Morehouse, Laurence
  Englemohr.

Morehouse, Laurence Englemohr.
  xMorehouse, Laurence.
    Maximum Performance. PB.
  xMorehouse, Lawrence E.
    Maximum Performance. S&S.

Morehouse, Lawrence E. see Morehouse, Laurence
  Englemohr.

Morehouse, Ward, 1898-1966
  xMorehouse, Ward.
    George M. Cohan, Prince of the American
      Theater. Greenwood.

Morel, Alice.
  xMorel, Alice.
    Urologic Endoscopic Procedures. Mosby.

Morel, E. D. see Morel, Edmund Dene.
Morel, Edmund D. see Morel, Edmund Dene.

Morel, Edmund Dene, 1873-1924
  xMorel, E. D.
    Great Britain & the Congo: The Pillage of the
      Congo Basin. Fertig.
  xMorel, Edmund D.
    British Case in French Congo: The Story of a
      Great Injustice, Its Causes & Its Lessons.
      Negro U Pr.
    Truth & the War. Garland Pub.

Morel, Juliette.
  xMorel, Juliette.
    Lingerie Parisienne. St Martin.

Moreland, A. see Moreland, Arthur.

Moreland, Arthur.
  xMoreland, A.
    Dickens Landmarks in London. Gordon Pr.
  xMoreland, Arthur.
    Dickens Landmarks in London. Haskell.

Morell, Jonathan A. see Morell, Jonathan Alan.

Morell, Jonathan Alan, 1946-
  xMorell, Jonathan A.
    Program Evaluation in Social Research.
      Pergamon.

Morell, Parker, 1906-1943
  xMorell, Parker.
    Diamond Jim: The Life & Times of James
      Buchanan Brady. AMS Pr.

Morelli, Remo.
  xMorelli, Remo.
    ed. Clinical Studies of Complement. Mss Info.

Moreno, Eduardo, 1936-
  xMoreno, Eduardo.
    The Films of Susan Hayward. Citadel Pr.

Moreno, Elizabeth.
  xMoreno, Elizabeth.
    Firm Your Fanny. Putnam.

Moreno, Francisco Jose.
  xMoreno, Francisco Jose.
    Legitimacy & Stability in Latin America: A
      Study of Chilean Political Culture. NYU Pr.

Moreno, J. L. see Moreno, Jacob L.

Moreno, Jacob L., 1892-
  xMoreno, J. L.
    Sociometry & the Science of Man. Beacon Hse.
    Who Shall Survive: Foundations of Sociometry,
      Group Psychotherapy & Sociodrama. Beacon
      Hse.

Moreno, Jose A. see Moreno, Jose Antonio.

Moreno, Jose Antonio, 1928-
  xMoreno, Jose A.

Barrios in Arms: Revolution in Santo Domingo.
    U of Pittsburgh Pr.

Moreno, Leonides.
  xMoreno, Leonides.
    Of Stone & Tears. Greenfld Rev Pr.

Morenz, Siegfried.
  xMorenz, Siegfried.
    Egyptian Religion. Cornell U Pr.

Moret, A. see Moret, Alexandre.

Moret, Alexandre, 1868-1938
  xMoret, A.
    From Tribe to Empire: Social Organization
      Among the Primitives & in the Ancient East.
      Cooper Sq.
  xMoret, Alexandre.
    The Nile & Egyptian Civilization. Routledge &
      Kegan.

Moreton, Bernard.
  xMoreton, Bernard.
    The Eighth-Century Gelasian Sacramentary: A
      Study in Tradition. Oxford U Pr.

Moreton, N. Edwina.
  xMoreton, N. Edwina.
    East Germany & the Warsaw Alliance: The
      Politics of Detente. Westview.

Morewedge, Parviz.
  xMorewedge, Parviz.
    ed. Islamic Philosophical Theology. State U
      NY Pr.

Morey, Charles R. see Morey, Charles Rufus.

Morey, Charles Rufus, 1877-1955
  xMorey, Charles R.
    Christian Art. Norton.
    Christian Art. Peter Smith.

Morey, Joan.
  xMorey, Joan.
    Let's Look at Houses & Homes. A Whitman.
    Let's Look at Houses & Homes. Soccer.

Morey, Robert A., 1946-
  xMorey, Robert A.
    How to Answer a Jehovah's Witness. Bethany
      Fell.

Morey, Walt.
  xMorey, Walt.
    Gentle Ben. Avon.
    Gentle Ben. Dutton.

Morey, Walt. see Morey, Walter.

Morey, Walter.
  xMorey, Walt.
    Canyon Winter. Dutton.
    Deep Trouble. Dutton.
    Operation Blue Bear: A True Story. Dutton.

Morford, Henry, 1823-1881
  xMorford, Henry.
    The Days of Shoddy: A Novel of the Great
      Rebellion in 1861. Arno.

Morgan. see Morgan, Lewis B.
Morgan, A. E. see Morgan, Arthur Eustace.
Morgan, Alfred. see Morgan, Alfred Powell.
Morgan, Alfred P. see Morgan, Alfred Powell.

Morgan, Alfred Powell, 1889-
  xMorgan, Alfred.
    First Chemistry Book for Boys & Girls.
      Scribner.
  xMorgan, Alfred P.
    How to Use Tools. Arco.

Morgan, Alison, 1930-
  xMorgan, Alison.
    All Kinds of Prickles. Elsevier-Nelson.
    A Boy Called Fish. Har-Row.

Morgan, Alun, 1928-
  xMorgan, Alun.
    Modern Jazz: A Survey of Developments Since
      1939. Greenwood.

Morgan, Arthur E. see Morgan, Arthur Eustace.

Morgan, Arthur Ernest, 1878-
  xMorgan, Arthur E.

Dams & Other Disasters: A Century of the
    Army Corps of Engineers in Civil Works.
    Porter Sargent.
    Edward Bellamy. Porcupine Pr.
    The Philosophy of Edward Bellamy.
      Greenwood.
    The Philosophy of Edward Bellamy. Hyperion
      Conn.

Morgan, Arthur Eustace, 1886-
  xMorgan, A. E.
    Some Problems of Shakespeare's Henry the
      Fourth. Folcroft.
  xMorgan, Arthur E.
    English Domestic Drama. Folcroft.

Morgan, Augustus De. see De Morgan, Augustus.
Morgan, Barbara K. see Morgan, Barbara Kysor.

Morgan, Barbara Kysor.
  xMorgan, Barbara K.
    Obstacle Course. Chronicle Bks.

Morgan, Bayard Q. see Morgan, Bayard Quincy.

Morgan, Bayard Quincy, 1883-
  xMorgan, Bayard Q.
    A Critical Bibliography of German Literature
      in English Translation, 1481-1927. Scarecrow.

Morgan, Brian.
  xMorgan, Brian.
    Osteomalacia, Renal Osteodystrophy &
      Osteoporosis. C C Thomas.

Morgan, Brian Stanford.
  xMorgan, Bryan.
    Men & Discoveries in Mathematics.
      Transatlantic.

Morgan, Bryan. see Morgan, Brian Stanford.
Morgan, C. Lloyd. see Morgan, Conwy Lloyd.

Morgan, Campbell G.
  xMorgan, G. Campbell.
    Preaching. Baker Bk.

Morgan, Carl H. see Morgan, Carl Hamilton.

Morgan, Carl Hamilton, 1901-
  xMorgan, Carl H.
    Layman's Introduction to the New Testament.
      Judson.

Morgan, Charles, 1930-
  xMorgan, Charles.
    One Man, One Voice. HR&W.
    A Time to Speak. HR&W.

Morgan, Christopher. see Morgan, Christopher P.

Morgan, Christopher P.
  xMorgan, Christopher.
    ed. The Byte Book of Computer Music.
      McGraw.

Morgan, Clifford T. see Morgan, Clifford Thomas.

Morgan, Clifford Thomas.
  xMorgan, Clifford T.
    Brief Introduction to Psychology. McGraw.
    How to Study. McGraw.
    Introduction to Psychology. McGraw.

Morgan, Conwy Lloyd, 1852-1936
  xMorgan, C. Lloyd.
    Habit & Instinct. Arno.

Morgan, D. H. see Morgan, D. H. J.

Morgan, D. H. J.
  xMorgan, D. H.
    Social Theory & the Family. Routledge &
      Kegan.

Morgan, Dale L. see Morgan, Dale Lowell.

Morgan, Dale Lowell, 1914-
  xMorgan, Dale L.
    Humboldt, Highroad of the West. Arno.

Morgan, Dan, 1937-
  xMorgan, Dan.
    Merchants of Grain. Viking Pr.
  xMorgan, Daniel.
    Merchants of Grain. Penguin.

Morgan, Daniel. see Morgan, Dan.

Morgan, David, 1937-
  xMorgan, David.

The Capitol Press Corps: Newsmen & the
Governing of New York State. Greenwood.
Suffragists & Liberals: The Politics of Woman
Suffrage in England. Rowman.
Morgan, David J., 1947-
xMorgan, David J.
Patterns of Population Distribution: A
Residential Preference Model & Its Dynamic.
U Chicago Dept Geog.
Morgan, David P. see Morgan, David Page.
Morgan, David Page, 1927-
xMorgan, David P.
ed. Canadian Steam. Kalmbach.
ed. Steam's Finest Hour. Kalmbach.
Morgan, David R.
xMorgan, David R.
Handbook of State Policy Indicators. Univ OK
Gov Res.
Oklahoma State Finance: A Longitudinal &
Comparative Overview. Univ OK Gov Res.
Morgan, David T.
xMorgan, David T.
North Carolinians in the Continental Congress.
Blair.
Morgan, David W., 1938-
xMorgan, David W.
The Socialist Left & the German Revolution: A
History of the German Independent Social
Democratic Party, 1917-1922. Cornell U Pr.
Morgan, Dyfnallt.
xMorgan, Dyfnallt.
D. Gwenallt Jones (1899-1968). Verry.
Morgan, E. J. see Morgan, Edward James Ranembe.
Morgan, E. Victor. see Morgan, Edward Victor.
Morgan, Edmund M. see Morgan, Edmund Morris.
Morgan, Edmund Morris, 1878-
xMorgan, Edmund M.
ed. Some Problems of Proof Under the
Anglo-American System of Litigation.
Greenwood.
Morgan, Edmund S. see Morgan, Edmund Sears.
Morgan, Edmund Sears.
xMorgan, Edmund S.
American Slavery - American Freedom: The
Ordeal of Colonial Virginia. Norton.
The Challenge of the American Revolution.
Norton.
The Meaning of Independence: John Adams,
George Washington, & Thomas Jefferson.
Norton.
The Meaning of Independence: John Adams,
George Washington, Thomas Jefferson. U Pr
of Va.
The Puritan Dilemma: The Story of John
Winthrop. Little.
The Puritan Family: Religion & Domestic
Relations in Seventeenth-Century New
England. Greenwood.
ed. Puritan Political Ideas 1558-1794. Bobbs.
Morgan, Edward James Ranembe.
xMorgan, E. J.
Early Adelaide Architecture 1836-1886.
Oxford U Pr.
Morgan, Edward P., 1945-
xMorgan, Edward P.
Inequality in Classroom Learning: Schooling &
Democratic Citizenship. Praeger.
Morgan, Edward Victor.
xMorgan, E. Victor.
Theory & Practice of Central Banking
1797-1913. Kelley.
xMorgan, Edward Victor.
Theory & Practice of Central Banking,
1797-1913. Biblio Dist.
Morgan, Elaine.
xMorgan, Elaine.

The Descent of Woman. Bantam.
The Descent of Woman. Stein & Day.
Falling Apart: The Rise & Fall of Urban
Civilization. Bantam.
Falling Apart: The Rise & Fall of Urban
Civilization. Stein & Day.
Morgan, Everett J.
xMorgan, Everett J.
ed. Christian Witness in the Secular City.
Loyola.
Morgan, Florence H.
xMorgan, Florence H.
Experiences. HarBraceJ.
Morgan, Fred. see Morgan, Fred T.
Morgan, Fred T.
xMorgan, Fred.
Uwharrie Magic. Moore Pub Co.
xMorgan, Fred T.
Ghost Tales of the Uwharries. Blair.
Morgan, Frederick, 1922-
xMorgan, Frederick.
Death Mother & Other Poems. U of Ill Pr.
The Tarot of Cornelius Agrippa. Sagarin Pr.
Morgan, G. see Morgan, Gwyneth.
Morgan, G. Campbell.
xMorgan, G. Campbell.
God's Last Word to Man: Studies in Hebrews.
Baker Bk.
Morgan, G. Campbell. see Morgan, George Campbell.
Morgan, George, 1854-1936
xMorgan, George.
Life of James Monroe. AMS Pr.
Morgan, George Campbell, 1863-1945
xMorgan, G. Campbell.
Analyzed Bible. Revell.
Answers of Jesus to Job. Baker Bk.
Triumphs of Faith. Baker Bk.
Morgan, Glenn G.
xMorgan, Glenn G.
Soviet Administrative Legality: The Role of the
Attorney General's Office. Stanford U Pr.
Morgan, Gwyneth.
xMorgan, G.
Life in a Medieval Village. Cambridge U Pr.
Morgan, H. G. see Morgan, Howard Gethin.
Morgan, H. Wayne. see Morgan, Howard Wayne.
Morgan, Hank. see Morgan, Julie.
Morgan, Harry, 1926-
xMorgan, Harry.
The Learning Community: A Humanistic
Cookbook for Teachers. Merrill.
xMorgan, Harry W.
Perspective Drawing for the Theatre. Drama
Bk.
Morgan, Harry T. see Morgan, Harry Titterton.
Morgan, Harry Titterton, 1872-
xMorgan, Harry T.
Chinese Symbols & Superstitions. Gale.
Morgan, Harry W. see Morgan, Harry.
Morgan, Helen L.
xMorgan, Helen L.
Maria Mitchell, First Lady of American
Astronomy. Westminster.
Morgan, Henry.
xMorgan, Henry.
Dogs. HM.
Toro. Belmont-Tower.
Morgan, Howard Gethin.
xMorgan, H. G.
Death Wishes?: The Understanding &
Management of Deliberate Self-Harm. Wiley.
Morgan, Howard W. see Morgan, Howard Wayne.
Morgan, Howard Wayne.
xMorgan, H. Wayne.
Eugene V. Debs: Socialist for President.
Greenwood.
xMorgan, Howard W.

ed. American Socialism 1900-1960. Peter
Smith.
America's Road to Empire: The War with
Spain & Overseas Expansion. Wiley.
Morgan, J. see Morgan, John W.
Morgan, James A.
xMorgan, James A.
The Art & Science of Medical Radiography.
Cath Health.
Morgan, James A. see Morgan, James Appleton.
Morgan, James Appleton, 1845-1928
xMorgan, James A.
ed. Mrs. Shakespeare's Second Marriage. AMS
Pr.
Morgan, James E., 1926-
xMorgan, James E.
Principles of Administrative & Supervisory
Management. P-H.
Morgan, James N.
xMorgan, James N.
Productive Americans: A Study of How
Individuals Contribute to Economic Progress.
U of Mich Soc Res.
Morgan, James P. see Morgan, James Plummer.
Morgan, James Plummer.
xMorgan, James P.
Mudlumps at the Mouth of South Pass,
Mississippi River: Sedimentology,
Paleontology, Structure, Origin, & Relation to
Deltaic Processes. La State U Pr.
Morgan, Jane.
xMorgan, Jane.
Nicknames: Their Origins & Social
Consequences. Routledge & Kegan.
Morgan, Janet B. see Morgan, Janet Barton.
Morgan, Janet Barton.
xMorgan, Janet B.
Take with You Words. Golden Quill.
Morgan, Janet P.
xMorgan, Janet P.
The House of Lords & the Labour
Government, 1964-1970. Oxford U Pr.
Morgan, Joe P.
xMorgan, Joe P.
Radiology in Veterinary Orthopedics. Lea &
Febiger.
Morgan, John, 1735-1789
xMorgan, John.
A Discourse Upon the Institution of Medical
Schools in America. Arno.
Morgan, John C. see Morgan, John Crossley.
Morgan, John Crossley, 1941-
xMorgan, John C.
Becoming Old: An Introduction to Social
Gerontology. Springer Pub.
Morgan, John H. see Morgan, John Henry.
Morgan, John Henry, 1945-
xMorgan, John H.
In Search of Meaning: From Freud to Teilhard
De Chardin (an Analysis of the Classic
Statements). U Pr of Amer.
Morgan, John W., 1946-
xMorgan, J.
A Product Formula for Surgery Obstructions.
Am Math.
Morgan, Jonnie. see Morgan, Jonnie R.
Morgan, Jonnie R.
xMorgan, Jonnie.
History of Wichita Falls. Nortex Pr.
Morgan, Joseph, 1909-
xMorgan, Joseph.
Introduction to Geometrical & Physical Optics.
Krieger.
The Physical Basis of Musical Sound. Krieger.
xMorgan, Joseph R.
Oahu Environments. Intl Schol Bk Serv.
Morgan, Joseph R. see Morgan, Joseph.
Morgan, Julie.
xMorgan, Hank.

photos by Speedboat Racing. Lippincott.
xMorgan, Julie C.
Speedboat Racing. Lippincott.
Morgan, Julie C. *see* Morgan, Julie.
Morgan, Kay S. *see* Morgan, Kay Summersby.
Morgan, Kay Summersby.
xMorgan, Kay S.
Past Forgetting: My Love Affair with Dwight
D. Eisenhower. S&S.
Morgan, L. H. *see* Morgan, Lewis Henry.
Morgan, Lael.
xMorgan, Lael.
Tatting: A New Look at the Old Art of
Making Lace. Doubleday.
Morgan, Len.
xMorgan, Len.
Airliners of the World. Arco.
Morgan, Lewis. *see* Morgan, Lewis Henry.
Morgan, Lewis B.
xMorgan.
A Casebook for School Counselors. Am
Personnel.
Morgan, Lewis H. *see* Morgan, Lewis Henry.
Morgan, Lewis Henry, 1818-1881
xMorgan, L. H.
Ancient Society: Or Researches in the Lines of
Human Progress from Savagery Through
Barbarism to Civilization. Peter Smith.
xMorgan, Lewis.
Ancient Society. Gordon Pr.
xMorgan, Lewis H.
American Beaver & His Works. B Franklin.
Ancient Society. NY Labor News.
Morgan, Marabel.
xMorgan, Marabel.
Total Joy. Berkley Pub.
Total Joy. Revell.
The Total Woman. Revell.
Morgan, Marilyn A.
xMorgan, Marilyn A.
ed. Managing Career Development. Van Nos
Reinhold.
Morgan, Meredith. *see* Morgan, Meredith W.
Morgan, Meredith W.
xMorgan, Meredith.
Optics of Ophthalmic Lenses. Prof Press.
Morgan, Michael. *see* Morgan, Michael Cooke.
Morgan, Michael Cooke.
xMorgan, Michael.
Lenin. Free Pr.
Lenin. Lib Soc Sci.
Lenin. Ohio U Pr.
Morgan, Murray. *see* Morgan, Murray Cromwell.
Morgan, Murray Cromwell, 1916-
xMorgan, Murray.
The Last Wilderness. U of Wash Pr.
One Man's Gold Rush: A Klondike Album. U
of Wash Pr.
Puget's Sound: A Narrative of Early Tacoma &
the Southern Sound. U of Wash Pr.
Morgan, Ora S. *see* Morgan, Ora Sherman.
Morgan, Ora Sherman, 1877-
xMorgan, Ora S.
ed. Agricultural Systems of Middle Europe: A
Symposium. AMS Pr.
Morgan, Patricia.
xMorgan, Patricia.
Child Care: Sense & Fable. Intl Pubns Serv.
Delinquent Fantasies. Transatlantic.
Morgan, Patrick M., 1940-
xMorgan, Patrick M.
Deterrence: A Conceptual Analysis. Sage.
Morgan, Paul.
xMorgan, Paul.
The D.C. Dialect: How to Master the New
Language of Washington in Ten Easy
Lessons. NYU Pr.
Morgan, Paula.
xMorgan, Paula.

Sol's Daughter. G&D.
Morgan, R. P. C. *see* Morgan, Royston Philip Charles.
Morgan, Raleigh, 1916-
xMorgan, Raleigh.
The Regional French of County Beauce,
Quebec. Mouton.
Morgan, Raymond C.
xMorgan, Raymond C.
The Angels Do Not Forget. Law & Justice.
Morgan, Richard E., 1937-
xMorgan, Richard E.
The Politics of Religious Conflict: Church &
State in America. U Pr of Amer.
The Supreme Court & Religion. Free Pr.
Morgan, Rita, 1905-
xMorgan, Rita.
Arbitration in the Men's Clothing Industry in
New York City: A Case Study of Industrial
Arbitration & Conference Method with
Particular Reference to Its Educational
Implications. AMS Pr.
Morgan, Robert, 1944-
xMorgan, Robert.
Groundwork. Gnomon Pr.
Trunk & Thicket. SBD.
Morgan, Robert J.
xMorgan, Robert J.
Governing Soil Conservation: Thirty Years of
the New Decentralization. Johns Hopkins.
A Whig Embattled: The Presidency Under
John Tyler. Shoe String.
Morgan, Robert P.
xMorgan, Robert P.
Science & Technology for Development: The
Role of U. S. Universities. Pergamon.
Morgan, Roberta, 1953-
xMorgan, Roberta.
Main Event: The World of Professional
Wrestling. Dial.
Morgan, Robin.
xMorgan, Robin.
Going Too Far: The Personal Chronicle of a
Feminist. Random.
ed. Going Too Far: The Personal Chronicle of
a Feminist. Random.
Morgan, Royston Philip Charles.
xMorgan, R. P. C.
Soil Erosion. Longman.
Morgan, Sarah.
xMorgan, Sarah.
The Church Supper: New Trends in Cooking
for Crowds. Bethany Pr.
Morgan, Speer, 1949-
xMorgan, Speer.
Belle Starr: A Novel. Little.
Frog Gig & Other Stories. U of Mo Pr.
Morgan, Susan, 1943-
xMorgan, Susan.
In the Meantime: Character & Perception in
Jane Austen's Fiction. U of Chicago Pr.
Morgan, T. L. *see* Morgan, Terry.
Morgan, Ted, 1932-
xMorgan, Ted.
Maugham. S&S.
On Becoming American. HM.
Morgan, Terry.
xMorgan, T. L.
Fighter Aircraft of the United States. Arco.
Morgan, Thomas B. *see* Morgan, Thomas Brynmor.
Morgan, Thomas Brynmor, 1886-
xMorgan, Thomas B.
Speaking of Cardinals. Arno.
Morgan, Thomas H. *see* Morgan, Thomas Hunt.
Morgan, Thomas Hunt, 1866-1945
xMorgan, Thomas H.
The Mechanism of Mendelian Heredity.
Johnson Repr.
Theory of the Gene. Hafner.
Morgan, Tom, 1950-
xMorgan, Tom.

The Building Book. P-H.
Morgan, W. B. *see* Morgan, William Basil.
Morgan, W. Scott.
xMorgan, W. Scott.
History of the Wheel & Alliance & the
Impending Revolution. B Franklin.
Morgan, William, 1944-
xMorgan, William.
Louisville: Architecture & the Urban
Environment. Bauhan.
Morgan, William Basil.
xMorgan, W. B.
Agricultural Geography. St Martin.
Agriculture in the Third World: A Spatial
Analysis. Westview.
Morgan, William J., 1924-
xMorgan, William J.
Hospitality Personnel Management. CBI Pub.
Morgan, William L.
xMorgan, William L.
Clinical Approach to the Patient. Saunders.
Morgan, William S.
xMorgan, William S.
Principles & Practices in Freshman
Composition. Macmillan.
Morgan, Winona L. *see* Morgan, Winona Louise.
Morgan, Winona Louise, 1907-
xMorgan, Winona L.
The Family Meets the Depression: A Study of
a Group of Highly Selected Families.
Greenwood.
Morgan, Wynn L.
xMorgan, Wynn L.
The Ice Man. Dell.
Morgan-Grenville, Gerard.
xMorgan-Grenville, Gerard.
Cruising the Sahara. David & Charles.
Morganstern, Stanley, 1941-
xMorganstern, Stanley.
Legal Protection in Garnishment &
Attachment. Oceana.
Legal Regulation of Consumer Credit. Oceana.
xMorganstern, Stanley M.
Legal Protection for the Consumer. Oceana.
Morganstern, Stanley M. *see* Morganstern, Stanley.
Morgenroth, Barbara.
xMorgenroth, Barbara.
Last Junior Year. Atheneum.
Ride a Proud Horse. Atheneum.
Tramps Like Us. Atheneum.
Morgenstein, Gary.
xMorgenstein, Gary.
Take Me Out to the Ballgame. St Martin.
Morgenstern, Christian.
xMorgenstern, Christian.
The Gallows Songs. U of Cal Pr.
Morgenstern, Murry.
xMorgenstern, Murry.
Psychology in the Vocational Rehabilitation of
the Mentally Retarded. C C Thomas.
Morgenstern, Oskar.
xMorgenstern, Oskar.
Mathematical Theory of Expanding &
Contracting Economies. Lexington Bks.
On the Accuracy of Economic Observations.
Princeton U Pr.
Morgenstern, Sam.
xMorgenstern, Sam.
ed. Composers on Music: An Anthology of
Composers Writings from Palestrino to
Copland. Greenwood.
Morgenthau, Hans J. *see* Morgenthau, Hans Joachim.
Morgenthau, Hans Joachim.
xMorgenthau, Hans J.

ed. Germany & the Future of Europe. U of
Chicago Pr.
ed. Peace, Security & the United Nations.
Arno.
Politics Among Nations: The Struggle for
Power & Peace. Knopf.
xMorgenthau, Hans W.
Politics in the Twentieth Century. U of
Chicago Pr.
Morgenthau, Hans W. *see* Morgenthau, Hans Joachim.
Morgenthau, Ruth S. *see* Morgenthau, Ruth Schachter.
Morgenthau, Ruth Schachter.
xMorgenthau, Ruth S.
Political Parties in French-Speaking West
Africa. Oxford U Pr.
Morholt, Evelyn.
xMorholt, Evelyn.
Sourcebook for the Biological Sciences.
HarBraceJ.
Moriarty, Alice E. *see* Moriarty, Alice Ewell.
Moriarty, Alice Ewell.
xMoriarty, Alice E.
ed. Adolescent Coping. Grune.
Moriarty, Barry M.
xMoriarty, Barry M.
Industrial Location & Community
Development. U of NC Pr.
Moriarty, F.
xMoriarty, F.
ed. Organochlorine Insecticides: Persistent
Organic Pollutants. Acad Pr.
Moriarty, G. P. *see* Moriarty, Gerald Patrick.
Moriarty, Gerald P. *see* Moriarty, Gerald Patrick.
Moriarty, Gerald Patrick, 1863-
xMoriarty, G. P.
Dean Swift & His Writings. Haskell.
xMoriarty, Gerald P.
Dean Swift & His Writings. Folcroft.
Moriarty, James R. *see* Moriarty, James Robert.
Moriarty, James Robert.
xMoriarty, James R.
Chinigchinix, an Indigenous California Indian
Religion. Southwest Mus.
Morice, Anne.
xMorice, Anne.
Death of a Wedding Guest. St Martin.
Murder by Proxy. St Martin.
Morick, Harold.
xMorick, Harold.
Challenges to Empiricism. Hackett Pub.
Challenges to Empiricism. Wadsworth Pub.
Morikawa, Jitsuo.
xMorikawa, Jitsuo.
Biblical Dimensions of Church Growth. Judson.
Morin, Claude.
xMorin, Claude.
Braided Cord Animals You Can Make.
Sterling.
Quebec versus Ottawa: The Struggle for
Self-Government, 1960-1972. U of Toronto
Pr.
Morin, Relman, 1907-1973
xMorin, Relman.
East Wind Rising: A Long View of the Pacific
Crisis. Greenwood.
Morin, Thomas D., 1938-
xMorin, Thomas D.
Mariano Picon Salas. Twayne.
Morinaga, H. *see* Morinaga, Haruhiko.
Morinaga, Haruhiko.
xMorinaga, H.
In-Beam Gamma-Ray Spectroscopy. Elsevier.
Morino, Claudio.
xMorino, Claudio.
Church & State in the Teaching of St.
Ambrose. Intl Schol Bk Serv.
Morioka, Kiyomi, 1923-
xMorioka, Kiyomi.

Religion in Changing Japanese Society. Intl
Schol Bk Serv.
Morishima, M. *see* Morishima, Michio.
Morishima, Michio, 1923-
xMorishima, M.
The Economic Theory of Modern Society.
Cambridge U Pr.
Marx's Economics: A Dual Theory of Value &
Growth. Cambridge U Pr.
The Working of Econometric Models.
Cambridge U Pr.
Morison, Elting E. *see* Morison, Elting Elmore.
Morison, Elting Elmore.
xMorison, Elting E.
Admiral Sims & the Modern American Navy.
Russell.
Men, Machines, & Modern Times. MIT Pr.
Morison, J. C. *see* Morison, James Augustus Cotter.
Morison, James Augustus Cotter, 1832-1888
xMorison, J. C.
Gibbon. AMS Pr.
Gibbon. R West.
xMorison, James C.
Gibbon. Arden Lib.
Gibbon. R West.
Morison, James C. *see* Morison, James Augustus Cotter.
Morison, Richard.
xMorison, Richard.
Humanist Scholarship & Public Order: Two
Tracts Against the Pilgrimage of Grace, & a
Collection of Related Contemporary
Documents. Folger Bks.
Morison, S. *see* Morison, Stanley.
Morison, Samuel E. *see* Morison, Samuel Eliot.
Morison, Samuel Eliot, 1887-
xMorison, Samuel E.
Builders of the Bay Colony. AMS Pr.
Builders of the Bay Colony. HM.
Christopher Columbus, Mariner. Little.
Christopher Columbus, Mariner. NAL.
A Concise History of the American Republic.
Oxford U Pr.
Dissent in Three American Wars. Harvard U
Pr.
The Growth of the American Republic. Oxford
U Pr.
Growth of the American Republic. Oxford U
Pr.
The Intellectual Life of Colonial New England.
Greenwood.
Intellectual Life of Colonial New England.
Cornell U Pr.
Oxford History of the American People. NAL.
Oxford History of the American People.
Oxford U Pr.
The Oxford History of the American People.
Oxford U Pr.
ed. Sources & Documents Illustrating the
American Revolution, 1764-1788, & the
Formation of the Federal Constitution.
Oxford U Pr.
The Two-Ocean War: A Short History of
United States Navy in the Second World
War. Little.
Morison, Stanley, 1889-1967
xMorison, S.
Fra Luca De Pacioli of Borgo S. Sepolcro.
Kraus Repr.
xMorison, Stanley.
John Fell, the University Press & the Fell
Types. Garland Pub.
Likeness of Thomas More: An Iconographical
Survey of Three Centuries. Fordham.
Tally of Types. Cambridge U Pr.
Moritz, Alan R. *see* Moritz, Alan Richards.
Moritz, Alan Richards.
xMoritz, Alan R.
jt. auth. Handbook of Legal Medicine. Mosby.
Moritz, Karl P. *see* Moritz, Karl Philipp.

Moritz, Karl Philipp, 1757-1793
xMoritz, Karl P.
Anton Reiser: A Psychological Novel.
Hyperion Conn.
Moritz, L. A.
xMoritz, L. A.
Grain-Mills & Flour in Classical Antiquity.
Arno.
Moriyama, Iwao. *see* Moriyama, Iwao Milton.
Moriyama, Iwao Milton.
xMoriyama, Iwao.
Cardiovascular Diseases in the United States.
Harvard U Pr.
Morize, Andre, 1883-
xMorize, Andre.
Problems & Methods of Literary History.
Biblo.
Morizot, Carol A. *see* Morizot, Carol Ann.
Morizot, Carol Ann.
xMorizot, Carol A.
Child of Scorn: A Mind Play in Three Parts &
Numerous Voices. Harold Hse.
Survivors & Other Poems. Harold Hse.
Morken, Linda O. *see* Morken, Lucinda Oakland.
Morken, Lucinda Oakland.
xMorken, Linda O.
Lines Across My Sky. Windy Row.
Morlan, Don B.
xMorlan, Don M.
Specific Situations in Effective Oral
Communication. Bobbs.
Morlan, Don M. *see* Morlan, Don B.
Morlan, J. E. *see* Morlan, John E.
Morlan, John E.
xMorlan, J. E.
Preparation of Inexpensive Teaching Materials.
Har-Row.
Morlan, Robert L. *see* Morlan, Robert Loren.
Morlan, Robert Loren, 1920-
xMorlan, Robert L.
American Government: Policy & Process. HM.
Political Prairie Fire: The Nonpartisan
League, 1915-1922. Greenwood.
Morland, J. Kenneth. *see* Morland, John Kenneth.
Morland, John Kenneth.
xMorland, J. Kenneth.
ed. Not So Solid South: Anthropological
Studies in a Regional Subculture. U of Ga Pr.
Morley, Christopher. *see* Morley, Christopher Darlington.
Morley, Christopher Darlington, 1890-1957
xMorley, Christopher.
Parnassus on Wheels. Lippincott.
Prefaces Without Books: Prefaces &
Introductions to Thirty Books. U of Tex Hum
Res.
Morley, David.
xMorley, David C.
See How They Grow: Monitoring Child
Growth for Appropriate Health Care in
Developing Countries. Oxford U Pr.
Morley, David C.
xMorley, David C.
Halfway up the Mountain. Revell.
Morley, David C. *see* Morley, David.
Morley, Edith J. *see* Morley, Edith Julia.
Morley, Edith Julia, 1875-
xMorley, Edith J.
Works of Sir Philip Sidney. Folcroft.
Morley, Felix.
xMorley, Felix.
ed. Aspects of the Depression. Arno.
The Power in the People. Green Hill.
Power in the People. Inst Humane.
The Power in the People. Nash Pub.
Morley, Henry, 1822-1894
xMorley, Henry.
Journal of a London Playgoer. Humanities.
Morley, Hugh. *see* Morley, Hugh M.
Morley, Hugh M.
xMorley, Hugh.

Pope & the Press. U of Notre Dame Pr.
Morley, Iris, 1910-
xMorley, Iris.
Proud Paladin. Arno.
Morley, James W. *see* Morley, James William.
Morley, James William.
xMorley, James W.
ed. Deterrent Diplomacy: Japan, Germany, &
the USSR, 1935-1940. Columbia U Pr.
Morley, John. *see* Morley, John Morley.
Morley, John M. *see* Morley, John Morley.
Morley, John Morley, Viscount, 1838-1923
xMorley, John.
Burke. AMS Pr.
Burke. Arden Lib.
Life of William Ewart Gladstone. R West.
The Life of William Ewart Gladstone.
Scholarly.
Nineteenth Century Essays. U of Chicago Pr.
Studies in Literature. R West.
xMorley, John M.
Burke. R West.
Critical Miscellanies. Arno.
Critical Miscellanies. Folcroft.
Life of William Ewart Gladstone. Greenwood.
Oracles on Man & Government. Arno.
Morley, Margaret.
xMorley, Margaret.
The Films of Laurence Olivier. Citadel Pr.
Morley, Michael.
xMorley, Michael.
Brecht: A Study. Rowman.
Morley, Muriel E.
xMorley, Muriel E.
Cleft Palate & Speech. Churchill.
Morley, Robert.
xMorley, Robert.
Robert Morley's Book of Bricks. Putnam.
Morley, Sheridan, 1941-
xMorley, Sheridan.
Marlene Dietrich. McGraw.
Oscar Wilde. HR&W.
Review Copies: Plays and Players in London
1970-74. Rowman.
Morley, T. P. *see* Morley, Thomas P.
Morley, Thomas.
xMorley, Thomas.
A Plain & Easy Introduction to Practical
Music. Norton.
Morley, Thomas P.
xMorley, T. P.
ed. Current Controversies in Neurosurgery.
Saunders.
Morman, Jean M. *see* Morman, Jean Mary.
Morman, Jean Mary.
xMorman, Jean M.
Art: Tempo of Today. Art Educ.
Mornay, Philippe De.
xMornay, Philippe de.
A Woorke Concerning the Trewnesse of the
Christian Religion. Schol Facsimiles.
Mornay, Philippe De. *see* Mornay, Philippe de.
Mornell, Pierre.
xMornell, Pierre.
Passive Men, Wild Women. Ballantine.
Passive Men, Wild Women. S&S.
Morner, Magnus.
xMorner, Magnus.
Race Mixture in the History of Latin America.
Little.
Morneweck, Evelyn (Foster).
xMorneweck, Evelyn F.
Chronicles of Stephen Foster's Family.
Kennikat.
Morneweck, Evelyn F. *see* Morneweck, Evelyn (Foster).
Morningstar, Connie, 1927-
xMorningstar, Connie.
Early Utah Furniture. Utah St U Pr.
Moroney, R. M. *see* Moroney, Robert.

Moroney, Robert, 1936-
xMoroney, R. M.
The Family & the State: Considerations for
Social Policy. Longman.
Morowitz, Harold J.
xMorowitz, Harold J.
Ego Niches: An Ecological View of
Organizational Behavior. Ox Bow.
Foundations of Bioenergetics. Acad Pr.
Life on the Planet Earth. Norton.
xMorowitz, Lucille S.
jt. auth. Life on the Planet Earth. Norton.
Morowitz, Lucille S. *see* Morowitz, Harold J.
Morphet. *see* Morphet, Clive.
Morphet, Clive.
xMorphet.
Galileo & Copernican Astronomy: A Scientific
World View Defined. Butterworths.
Morphet, Edgar L. *see* Morphet, Edgar Leroy.
Morphet, Edgar Leroy, 1895-
xMorphet, Edgar L.
The Measurement & Interpretation of School
Building Utilization. AMS Pr.
Morrah, Dermot, 1896-
xMorrah, Dermot.
The Mummy Case. Garland Pub.
Morrall, John B.
xMorrall, John B.
Aristotle. Allen Unwin.
Morray, Joseph P., 1916-
xMorray, Joseph P.
From Yalta to Disarmament: Cold War Debate.
Greenwood.
Morrell, David.
xMorrell, David.
The Last Reveille. Fawcett.
Last Reveille. M Evans.
Morrell, Ottoline. *see* Morrell, Ottoline Violet Anne
Cavendish-Bentinck.
**Morrell, Ottoline Violet Anne Cavendish-Bentinck,
Lady, 1873-1938**
xMorrell, Ottoline.
Ottoline at Garsington: Memoirs of Lady
Ottoline Morrell, 1915-1918. Knopf.
Morrell, R.
xMorrell, R.
Common Malayan Butterflies. Intl Pubns Serv.
Morrell, Roy.
xMorrell, Roy.
Thomas Hardy: The Will & the Way. Folcroft.
Morrell, Sydney.
xMorrell, Sydney.
Spheres of Influence. Arno.
Morrell, W. P. *see* Morrell, William Parker.
Morrell, William H.
xMorrell, William H.
The Energy Miser's Manual. Grist Mill.
Morrell, William P. *see* Morrell, William Parker.
Morrell, William Parker, 1899-
xMorrell, W. P.
Gold Rushes. Dufour.
xMorrell, William P.
The Anglican Church in New Zealand: A
History. Intl Pubns Serv.
Morressy, John.
xMorressy, John.
The Drought on Ziax II. Walker & Co.
Under a Calculating Star. Popular Lib.
Morrill, Bernard.
xMorrill, Bernard.
An Introduction to Equilibrium
Thermodynamics. Pergamon.
Morrill, J. S.
xMorrill, J. S.
The Revolt of the Provinces: Conservatives &
Radicals in the English Civil War, 1630-1650.
Allen Unwin.
Morrill, J. S. *see* Morrill, John Stephen.
Morrill, John Stephen.
xMorrill, J. S.

The Cheshire Grand Jury, 1625-1959: A Social
& Administrative Study. Humanities.
Morrill, Richard L.
xMorrill, Richard L.
The Geography of Poverty in the United
States. McGraw.
Morrill, Sibley S.
xMorrill, Sibley S.
Ambrose Bierce, F. A. Mitchell-Hedges & the
Crystal Skull. Cadleon Pr.
Morrin, Helen C. *see* Morrin, Helen Clanton.
Morrin, Helen Clanton.
xMorrin, Helen C.
Communication for Nurses. Littlefield.
Morris. *see* Morris, Robert Ada.
Morris, A. E. *see* Morris, Anthony Edwin James.
Morris, A. J. Anthony.
xMorris, Anthony J.
Radicalism Against War 1906-1914: The
Advocacy of Peace & Retrenchment.
Rowman.
Morris, Aldyth, 1901-
xMorris, Aldyth.
Damien. U Pr of Hawaii.
Morris, Allen. *see* Morris, Allen Covington.
Morris, Allen Covington, 1909-
xMorris, Allen.
Florida Place Names. U of Miami Pr.
Morris, Alton C. *see* Morris, Alton Chester.
Morris, Alton Chester.
xMorris, Alton C.
College English: The First Year. HarBraceJ.
Morris, Alvin L.
xMorris, Alvin L.
ed. Dental Specialties in General Practice.
Saunders.
Morris, Ann A. *see* Morris, Ann Axtell.
Morris, Ann Axtell, 1900-
xMorris, Ann A.
Digging in the Southwest. Peregrine Smith.
Morris, Anthony Edwin James.
xMorris, A. E.
Precast Concrete in Architecture.
Watson-Guptill.
Morris, Anthony J. *see* Morris, A. J. Anthony.
Morris, Arthur S. *see* Morris, Arthur Stephen.
Morris, Arthur Stephen.
xMorris, Arthur S.
South America. B&N.
Morris, Arval A.
xMorris, Arval A.
The Constitution & American Education. West
Pub.
Morris, Audrey S. *see* Morris, Audrey Stone.
Morris, Audrey Stone.
xMorris, Audrey S.
One Thousand Inspirational Things. Dutton.
Morris, Bernard S.
xMorris, Bernard S.
Imperialism & Revolution: An Essay for
Radicals. Ind U Pr.
Morris, Bertram, 1908-
xMorris, Bertram.
Institutions of Intelligence. Ohio St U Pr.
Morris, Bruce R. *see* Morris, Bruce Robert.
Morris, Bruce Robert, 1909-
xMorris, Bruce R.
The Economics of the Special Taxation of
Chain Stores. Arno.
Morris, C. *see* Morris, Charles G.
Morris, C. Robert. *see* Morris, Clarence.
Morris, Charles. *see* Morris, Charles William.
Morris, Charles G.
xMorris, C.
Psychology: An Introduction. P-H.
Morris, Charles R.
xMorris, Charles R.

The Cost of Good Intentions: New York City
& the Liberal Experiment. Norton.
Morris, Charles R. *see* Morris, Charles Richard.
Morris, Charles Richard.
xMorris, Charles R.
Locke, Berkeley, Hume. Greenwood.
Morris, Charles W. *see* Morris, Charles William.
Morris, Charles William, 1901-
xMorris, Charles.
Festival. Braziller.
The Pragmatic Movement in American
Philosophy. Braziller.
Signification & Significance: A Study of the
Relations of Signs & Values. MIT Pr.
Signs, Language & Behavior. Braziller.
xMorris, Charles W.
Logical Positivism, Pragmatism & Scientific
Empiricism. AMS Pr.
Paths of Life: Preface to a World Religion. U
of Chicago Pr.
Varieties of Human Value. U of Chicago Pr.
Morris, Cheryl H. *see* Morris, Cheryl Haun.
Morris, Cheryl Haun, 1947-
xMorris, Cheryl H.
The Cutting Edge: The Life of John Rogers. U
of Okla Pr.
Morris, Christopher.
xMorris, C.
The Tudors. Watts.
Morris, Clarence, 1903-
xMorris, C. Robert.
jt. auth. Morris on Torts. Foundation Pr.
xMorris, Clarence.
ed. Great Legal Philosophers: Selected
Readings in Jurisprudence. U of Pa Pr.
Morris on Torts. Foundation Pr.
Morris, Colin. *see* Morris, Colin M.
Morris, Colin M.
xMorris, Colin.
Bugles in the Afternoon. Westminster.
Morris, D. Hampton. *see* Morris, Drewry Hampton.
Morris, Dan.
xMorris, Dan.
Complete Fish Cookbook. Bobbs.
The Complete Fish Cookbook. Follett.
The Complete Outdoor Cookbook. Dutton.
Fisherman's Almanac. Macmillan.
Morris, David. *see* Morris, David J.
Morris, David J.
xMorris, David.
Neighborhood Power: The New Localism.
Beacon Pr.
Morris, David J. *see* Morris, David Joseph.
Morris, David Joseph.
xMorris, David J.
Introduction to Communication Command &
Control Systems. Pergamon.
Morris, Dean.
xMorris, Dean.
Animals That Burrow. Raintree Child.
Animals That Live in Shells. Raintree Child.
Cats. Raintree Child.
Dinosaurs & Other First Animals. Raintree
Child.
Dogs. Raintree Child.
Endangered Animals. Raintree Child.
Frogs & Toads. Raintree Child.
Insects That Live in Families. Raintree Child.
Monkeys & Apes. Raintree Child.
Spiders. Raintree Child.
Morris, Desmond.
xMorris, Desmond.
Animal Days. Morrow.
The Human Zoo. Dell.
Human Zoo. Dell.
Morris, Drewry Hampton, 1945-
xMorris, D. Hampton.

Stephane Mallarme, Twentieth-Century
Criticism, 1901-1971. Romance.
Morris, E. C., 1855-
xMorris, Elias C.
Sermons, Addresses & Reminiscences &
Important Correspondence, with a Picture
Gallery of Eminent Ministers & Scholars.
Arno.
Morris, Earl W.
xMorris, Earl W.
Housing, Family, & Society. Wiley.
Morris, Edita, 1902-
xMorris, Edita.
Life, Wonderful Life. Braziller.
Morris, Edmund.
xMorris, Edmund.
The Rise of Theodore Roosevelt. Ballantine.
The Rise of Theodore Roosevelt. Coward.
Morris, Edward A., 1925-
xMorris, Edward A.
The Demagogue's Disease. World Wide Prods.
Morris, Elias C. *see* Morris, E. C.
Morris, Elisabeth (Woodbridge), 1870-
xMorris, Elizabeth.
Days Out & Other Papers. Arno.
Jonathan Papers. Arno.
More Jonathan Papers. Arno.
Morris, Elizabeth. *see* Morris, Elisabeth (Woodbridge).
Morris, Elizabeth A. *see* Morris, Elizabeth Ann.
Morris, Elizabeth Ann, 1932-
xMorris, Elizabeth A.
Basketmaker Caves in the Prayer Rock
District, Northeastern Arizona. U of Ariz Pr.
Morris, Elizabeth H. *see* Morris, Elizabeth Hunt.
Morris, Elizabeth Hunt, 1892-
xMorris, Elizabeth H.
Personal Traits & Success in Teaching. AMS
Pr.
Morris, Ernest.
xMorris, Ernest.
Legends O' the Bells: Being a Collection of
Legends, Traditions, Folktales, Myths Etc
Centred Around the Bells of All Lands.
Folcroft.
Morris, Faye.
xMorris, Faye.
They Claimed a Desert. Ye Galleon.
Morris, Freda.
xMorris, Freda.
Hypnosis with Friends & Lovers. Har-Row.
Morris, G. S. *see* Morris, G. S. Don.
Morris, G. S. Don.
xMorris, G. S.
How to Change the Games Children Play.
Burgess.
Morris, George H.
xMorris, George H.
Hunter Seat Equitation. Doubleday.
Morris, Gouverneur, 1752-1816
xMorris, Gouverneur.
Diary & Letters of Gouverneur Morris. Da
Capo.
A Diary of the French Revolution. Arno.
Diary of the French Revolution. Greenwood.
Incandescent Lily, & Other Stories. Arno.
Morris, Harriet. *see* Morris, Harriett.
Morris, Harriett.
xMorris, Harriet.
Art of Korean Cooking. C E Tuttle.
Morris, Henry. *see* Morris, Henry M.
Morris, Henry M.
xMorris, Henry.
Explore the Word. CLP Pubs.
xMorris, Henry M.
Baptism: How Important Is It?. Accent Bks.
Morris, Henry M. *see* Morris, Henry Madison.

Morris, Henry Madison, 1918-
xMorris, Henry M.
Applied Hydraulics in Engineering. Wiley.
Evolution & the Modern Christian. Presby &
Reformed.
The Remarkable Birth of Planet Earth. Bethany
Fell.
The Remarkable Birth of Planet Earth. CLP
Pubs.
Sampling the Psalms. CLP Pubs.
Symposium on Creation. Baker Bk.
Twilight of Evolution. Baker Bk.
Morris, Herbert, 1928-
xMorris, Herbert.
ed. Freedom & Responsibility: Readings in
Philosophy & Law. Stanford U Pr.
The Masked Citadel: The Significance of the
Title of Stendhal's La Chartreuse de Parme.
U of Cal Pr.
On Guilt & Innocence: Essays in Legal
Philosophy & Moral Psychology. U of Cal Pr.
Morris, Homer L. *see* Morris, Homer Lawrence.
Morris, Homer Lawrence, 1886-1951
xMorris, Homer L.
Parliamentary Franchise Reform in England
from 1885 to 1918. AMS Pr.
Morris, Hugh.
xMorris, Hugh.
The Art of Kissing. Doubleday.
Morris, Ivan. *see* Morris, Ivan I.
Morris, Ivan I.
xMorris, Ivan.
Tale of Genji Scroll. Kodansha.
The World of the Shining Prince: Court Life in
Ancient Japan. Penguin.
Morris, J. N. *see* Morris, Jeremy Noah.
Morris, James, 1926-
xMorris, James.
Farewell the Trumpets: An Imperial Retreat.
HarBraceJ.
Great Port: A Passage Through New York.
HarBraceJ.
Heaven's Command: An Imperial Progress.
HarBraceJ.
Pax Britannica: The Climax of an Empire.
HarBraceJ.
Places. HarBraceJ.
Morris, James. *see* Morris, James Humphry.
Morris, James A., 1933-
xMorris, James A.
Art of Conversation: The Magic Key to
Personal & Social Popularity. P-H.
Morris, James Humphry, 1926-
xMorris, James.
The World of Venice. HarBraceJ.
The World of Venice. HarBraceJ.
Morris, James M. *see* Morris, James Matthew.
Morris, James Matthew, 1935-
xMorris, James M.
Our Maritime Heritage: Maritime
Developments & Their Impact on American
Life. U Pr of Amer.
Morris, Jan, 1926-
xMorris, Jan.
Conundrum. HarBraceJ.
Conundrum. NAL.
Destinations: Essays from ROLLING STONE.
Oxford U Pr.
ed. The Oxford Book of Oxford. Oxford U Pr.
Morris, Jeannie.
xMorris, Jeannie.
Brian Piccolo: A Short Season. Dell.
Morris, Jeffrey B. *see* Morris, Richard Brandon.
Morris, Jeremy Noah.
xMorris, J. N.
Uses of Epidemiology. Churchill.
Morris, Jim, 1940-
xMorris, Jim.

The Sheriff of Purgatory. Doubleday.
War Story. Sycamore Island.
Morris, Joe A. *see* Morris, Joe Alex.
Morris, Joe Alex, 1904-
  xMorris, Joe A.
    Deadline Every Minute: The Story of the
    United Press. Greenwood.
Morris, John.
  xMorris, John.
    The Checkerboard Caper. Citadel Pr.
    How Mad Tulloch Was Taken Away.
    Merrimack Bk Serv.
    Managing the Library Fire Risk. U Cal Risk
    Management.
Morris, John N.
  xMorris, John N.
    The Life Beside This One. Atheneum.
Morris, John W. *see* Morris, John Wesley.
Morris, John Wesley, 1907-
  xMorris, John W.
    Ghost Towns of Oklahoma. U of Okla Pr.
Morris, Johnny.
  xMorris, Johnny.
    ed. The Faber Book of Animal Stories.
    Merrimack Bk Serv.
Morris, Joseph, 1942-
  xMorris, Joseph.
    Psychology & Teaching: A Humanistic View.
    Random.
Morris, Kathleen.
  xMorris, Kathleen.
    Mara. Dell.
Morris, Kelso B.
  xMorris, Kelso B.
    Fundamental Chemical Equilibria:
    Nonionic-Ionic. Gordon.
Morris, Kenneth, 1879-
  xMorris, Kenneth.
    Book of the Three Dragons. Arno.
    The Fates of the Princes of Dyfed. Borgo Pr.
    The Fates of the Princes of Dyfed. Newcastle
    Pub.
    Golden Threads in the Tapestry of History.
    Point Loma Pub.
Morris, Kenneth T.
  xMorris, Kenneth T.
    Controversial Issues in Human Relations
    Training Groups. C C Thomas.
Morris, Langdon E. *see* Morris, Langdon Emmons.
Morris, Langdon Emmons.
  xMorris, Langdon E.
    Denver Landmarks. C W Cleworth.
Morris, Larry W. *see* Morris, Larry Wayne.
Morris, Larry Wayne.
  xMorris, Larry W.
    Extraversion & Introversion: An Interactional
    Perspective. Halsted Pr.
Morris, Leon, 1914-
  xMorris, Leon.
    Apocalyptic. Eerdmans.
    Apostolic Preaching of the Cross. Eerdmans.
    Cross in the New Testament. Eerdmans.
    I Believe in Revelation. Eerdmans.
Morris, Lloyd. *see* Morris, Lloyd R.
Morris, Lloyd R.
  xMorris, Lloyd.
    Incredible New York: High Life & Low Life of
    the Last Hundred Years. Arno.
  xMorris, Lloyd R.
    Celtic Dawn: A Survey of the Renascence in
    Ireland, 1889-1916. Cooper Sq.
Morris, Madeleine C., 1915-
  xMorris, Madeleine C.
    The Amazing Power of Solar-Kinetics. P-H.
Morris, Mair.
  xMorris, Mair.
    Creative Thread Design. Branford.
Morris, Milton D.
  xMorris, Milton D.

The Politics of Black America. Har-Row.
Morris, Monica B., 1928-
  xMorris, Monica B.
    An Excursion into Creative Sociology.
    Columbia U Pr.
Morris, Norval.
  xMorris, Norval.
    The Future of Imprisonment. U of Chicago Pr.
    The Habitual Criminal. Greenwood.
    Honest Politicians Guide to Crime Control. U
    of Chicago Pr.
    Letter to the President on Crime Control. U of
    Chicago Pr.
Morris, P. M. *see* Morris, Vince.
Morris, Paul D.
  xMorris, Paul D.
    Love Therapy. Tyndale.
Morris, Peter, 1937-
  xMorris, Peter.
    Embattled Shadows: A History of Canadian
    Cinema, 1895-1939. McGill-Queens U Pr.
Morris, R. C.
  xMorris, Ralph C.
    Air Conditioning Cutter's Ready Reference.
    Busn News.
Morris, R. Winston.
  xMorris, R. Winston.
    ed. Tuba Music Guide. Instrumental Co.
Morris, Ralph C. *see* Morris, R. C.
Morris, Reginald O. *see* Morris, Reginald Owen.
Morris, Reginald Owen, 1886-1948
  xMorris, Reginald O.
    Foundations of Practical Harmony &
    Counterpoint. Greenwood.
    Structure of Music: An Outline for Students.
    Oxford U Pr.
Morris, Richard B. *see* Morris, Richard Brandon.
Morris, Richard Brandon, 1904-
  xMorris, Jeffrey B.
    jt. ed. Encyclopedia of American History.
    Har-Row.
  xMorris, Richard B.
    The American Revolution Reconsidered.
    Greenwood.
    Basic Documents in American History.
    Krieger.
    ed. Basic Documents in American History. Van
    Nos Reinhold.
    ed. Encyclopedia of American History.
    Har-Row.
    First Book of the American Revolution. Watts.
    First Book of the Constitution. Watts.
    First Book of the Founding of the Republic.
    Watts.
    Government & Labor in Early America.
    Octagon.
    ed. Great Presidential Decisions: State Papers
    That Changed the Course of History.
    Har-Row.
    ed. Hope & Anguish in Foreign Relations,
    1962-1975. McGraw.
Morris, Richard S., 1947-
  xMorris, Richard S.
    Bum Rap on America's Cities: The Real
    Causes of Urban Decay. P-H.
Morris, Robert.
  xMorris, Robert.
    Feasible Planning for Social Change. Columbia
    U Pr.
    Freemasonry in the Holy Land: Handmarks of
    Hiram's Builders. Arno.
    Self-Destruct: Dismantling America's Internal
    Security. Arlington Hse.
    Social Policy of the American Welfare State:
    An Introduction to Policy Analysis.
    Har-Row.
    The Truth About the American Flag.
    Wynnehaven.
Morris, Robert A. *see* Morris, Robert Ada.

Morris, Robert Ada.
  xMorris.
    Dolphin. Schol Bk Serv.
  xMorris, Robert A.
    Dolphin. Har-Row.
Morris, Robert J.
  xMorris, Robert J.
    The Contemporary Peruvian Theatre. Tex Tech
    Pr.
Morris, Robert K.
  xMorris, Robert K.
    ed. The Achievement of William Styron. U of
    Ga Pr.
    Continuance & Change: Contemporary British
    Novel Sequence. S Ill U Pr.
    Paradoxes of Order: Some Perspectives on the
    Fiction of V. S. Naipaul. U of Mo Pr.
Morris, Ronald W. *see* Morris, Ronald W. B.
Morris, Ronald W. B.
  xMorris, Ronald W.
    The Prehistoric Rock Art of Galloway & the
    Isle of Man. Sterling.
Morris, Rosamound.
  xMorris, Rosamund.
    ed. Great Detective Stories. Lion.
Morris, Rosamund. *see* Morris, Rosamound.
Morris, Scot.
  xMorris, Scot.
    The Book of Strange Facts & Useless
    Information. Doubleday.
Morris, Thomas D., 1938-
  xMorris, Thomas D.
    Free Men All: The Personal Liberty Laws of
    the North, 1780-1861. Johns Hopkins.
Morris, Thomas V.
  xMorris, Thomas V.
    Francis Schaeffer's Apologetics: A Critique.
    Moody.
Morris, Van Cleve.
  xMorris, Van Cleve.
    Existentialism in Education: What It Means.
    Har-Row.
Morris, Victor P. *see* Morris, Victor Pierpont.
Morris, Victor Pierpont, 1891-
  xMorris, Victor P.
    Oregon's Experience with Minimum Wage
    Legislation. AMS Pr.
Morris, Vince.
  xMorris, P. M.
    The Illustrated Guide to Karate. Van Nos
    Reinhold.
Morris, Warren B. *see* Morris, Warren Bayard.
Morris, Warren Bayard, 1948-
  xMorris, Warren B.
    The Revisionist Historians & German War
    Guilt. Revisionist Pr.
Morris, Wesley.
  xMorris, Wesley.
    Friday's Footprint: Structuralism & the
    Articulated Text. Ohio St U Pr.
    Toward a New Historicism. Princeton U Pr.
Morris, William.
  xMorris, William.
    Collected Works. Gordon Pr.
    Early Romances in Prose & Verse. Rowman.
    The Letters of William Morris to His Family &
    Friends. AMS Pr.
    The Wood Beyond the World. Dover.
    The Wood Beyond the World. Peter Smith.
Morris, William. *see* Morris, William Thomas.
Morris, William C. *see* Morris, William Clinton.
Morris, William Clinton.
  xMorris, William C.
    Organization Behavior in Action: Skill Building
    Experiences. West Pub.
Morris, William D. *see* Morris, William Dale.
Morris, William Dale.
  xMorris, William D.

The Christian Origins of Social Revolt.
Hyperion Conn.
Morris, William O.
xMorris, William O.
Dental Litigation. Michie.
Morris, William T. see Morris, William Thomas.
Morris, William Thomas, 1928-
xMorris, William.
Engineering Economic Analysis. Reston.
xMorris, William T.
Decentralization in Management Systems: An
Introduction to Design. Ohio St U Pr.
Decision Analysis. Grid Pub.
Implementation Strategies for Industrial
Engineers. Grid Pub.
Morris, Willie.
xMorris, Willie.
Good Old Boy. Yoknapatawpha.
North Toward Home. Larlin Corp.
Morris, Wright, 1910-
xMorris, Wright.
Cause for Wonder. U of Nebr Pr.
Ceremony in Lone Tree. U of Nebr Pr.
The Deep Sleep. U of Nebr Pr.
Earthly Delights, Unearthly Adornments:
American Writers As Image Makers.
Har-Row.
The Field of Vision. U of Nebr Pr.
Fire Sermon. U of Nebr Pr.
The Home Place. U of Nebr Pr.
In Orbit. U of Nebr Pr.
Pref. by The Inhabitants. Da Capo.
A Life. U of Nebr Pr.
What a Way to Go. U of Nebr Pr.
The Works of Love. U of Nebr Pr.
Morris-Jones, Wyndraeth H. see Morris-Jones,
Wyndraeth Humphreys.
Morris-Jones, Wyndraeth Humphreys.
xMorris-Jones, Wyndraeth H.
Parliament in India. Greenwood.
Morrisett, Lloyd M. see Morrisett, Lloyd N.
Morrisett, Lloyd N., 1893-
xMorrisett, Lloyd M.
Letters of Recommendation: A Study of
Letters of Recommendation As an
Instrument in the Selection of Secondary
School Teachers. AMS Pr.
Morrisey, George L.
xMorrisey, George L.
Appraisal & Development Through Objectives
& Results. A-W.
Morrisey, T. J. see Morrisey, Thomas J.
Morrisey, Thomas, 1952-
xMorrisey, Thomas.
Twenty American Peaks & Crags. Contemp
Bks.
Morrisey, Thomas J.
xMorrisey, T. J.
ed. Pollution Control Problems & Related
Federal Legislation. Mss Info.
Morrish, Alan H. see Morrish, Allan H.
Morrish, Allan H.
xMorrish, Alan H.
The Physical Principles of Magnetism. Krieger.
Morrish, Ivor.
xMorrish, Ivor.
Aspects of Educational Change. Allen Unwin.
Morrison, Arthur, 1863-1945
xMorrison, Arthur.
Chronicles of Martin Hewitt. Arno.
Martin Hewitt, Investigator. Arno.
Martin Hewitt, Investigator. Hyperion Conn.
Tales of Mean Streets. Arno.
Morrison, Chaplain W.
xMorrison, Chaplain W.
Democratic Politics & Sectionalism: The
Wilmot Proviso Controversy. U of NC Pr.
Morrison, Charles C. see Morrison, Charles Clayton.
Morrison, Charles Clayton, 1874-
xMorrison, Charles C.

Unfinished Reformation. Arno.
Morrison, Charles E. see Morrison, Charles Edward.
Morrison, Charles Edward.
xMorrison, Charles E.
Strategies of Survival: The Foreign Policy
Dilemmas of Smaller Asian States. St Martin.
Morrison, Clinton, 1924-
xMorrison, Clinton.
An Analytical Concordance to the Revised
Standard Version of the New Testament.
Westminster.
Morrison, Coleman.
xMorrison, Coleman.
The Torch Lighters Revisited. Intl Reading.
Morrison, D. F. see Morrison, Donald F.
Morrison, Delmont.
xMorrison, Delmont.
Sensory-Motor Dysfunction & Therapy in
Infancy & Early Childhood. C C Thomas.
Morrison, Denton E.
xMorrison, Denton E.
Collective Behavior: A Bibliography. Garland
Pub.
Energy II: A Bibliography of 1975-1976 Social
Science & Related Literature. Garland Pub.
ed. Significance Test Controversy: A Reader.
Aldine Pub.
Morrison, Diana.
xMorrison, Diana.
A Glossary of Sanskrit from the Spiritual
Tradition of India. Nilgiri Pr.
Morrison, Donald F.
xMorrison, D. F.
Multivariate Statistical Methods. McGraw.
Morrison, Eleanor S. see Morrison, Eleanor Shelton.
Morrison, Eleanor Shelton.
xMorrison, Eleanor S.
ed. Human Sexuality: Contemporary
Perspectives. Mayfield Pub.
Morrison, Florence.
xMorrison, Florence.
The Cockeyed Boom Shack Cat & Other
Stories. Mojave Bks.
Morrison, Frank.
xMorrison, Frank.
Adventure Stories for Boys. Denison.
Morrison, Fred L.
xMorrison, Fred L.
Courts & the Political Process in England.
Sage.
Morrison, George R.
xMorrison, George R.
Liquidity Preferences of Commercial Banks. U
of Chicago Pr.
Morrison, George S.
xMorrison, George S.
Early Childhood Education Today. Merrill.
Parent Involvement in the Home, School &
Community. Merrill.
Morrison, Hugh.
xMorrison, Hugh.
Directing in the Theatre. Theatre Arts.
Morrison, Hugh. see Morrison, Hugh Sinclair.
Morrison, Hugh Sinclair, 1905-
xMorrison, Hugh.
Louis Sullivan: Prophet of Modern
Architecture. Greenwood.
Louis Sullivan: Prophet of Modern
Architecture. Peter Smith.
Morrison, Jacob H.
xMorrison, Jacob H.
Historic Preservation Law. Preservation Pr.
Morrison, James H. see Morrison, James Harris.
Morrison, James Harris.
xMorrison, James H.
Practical Transactional Analysis in
Management. A-W.
Morrison, James Horne, 1872-
xMorrison, James H.

Streams in the Desert: A Picture of Life in
Livingstonia. Negro U Pr.
Morrison, James K.
xMorrison, James K.
A Consumer Approach to Community
Psychology. Nelson-Hall.
Morrison, James W. see Morrison, James Warner.
Morrison, James Warner, 1940-
xMorrison, James W.
Air Traffic Controller. Arco.
Certificate in Data Processing Examination.
Arco.
Civil Engineering Technician. Arco.
Engineering Fundamentals. Arco.
The Florida Literacy Test: Statewide
Assessment Program of Basic Skills &
Functional Literacy. Arco.
Fundamentals of Engineering: Home Study
Preparation for the Engineer-in-Training
Examination. Arco.
Instrument Pilot Examination. Arco.
Mechanical Engineering Technician. Arco.
Principles of Data Processing. Arco.
Professional Engineering Registration: Problems
& Solutions. Arco.
Morrison, Jim, 1943-1971
xMorrison, Jim.
The Bank of America of Louisiana.
Zeppelin-IBM.
Morrison, John. see Morrison, John W.
Morrison, John H. see Morrison, John Harrison.
Morrison, John Harrison, 1841-1917
xMorrison, John H.
History of American Steam Navigation.
Gordon Pr.
History of New York Ship Yards. Friedman.
Morrison, John W.
xMorrison, John.
Modern Japanese Fiction. Greenwood.
Morrison, Joseph L.
xMorrison, Joseph L.
Governor O. Max Gardner: A Power in North
Carolina & New Deal Washington. U of NC
Pr.
Morrison, Kristin.
xMorrison, Kristin.
In Black & White. Free Pr.
Morrison, L. Jed. see Morrison, Leland Jed.
Morrison, L. M. see Morrison, Lester M.
Morrison, Leland Jed.
xMorrison, L. Jed.
The Onset of Parenthood: A Comprehensive,
Illustrated Guide to Pregnancy, Birth &
Infant Care. Horizon Utah.
Morrison, Lester M.
xMorrison, L. M.
Coronary Heart Disease & the
Mucopolysaccharides (Glycosaminoglycans).
C C Thomas.
Morrison, Lillian.
xMorrison, Lillian.
ed. Diller, a Dollar: Rhymes & Sayings for the
Ten O'Clock Scholar. T Y Crowell.
The Sidewalk Racer & Other Poems of Sports
& Motion. Lothrop.
Morrison, M. A. see Morrison, Michael A.
Morrison, Marsh, 1902-
xMorrison, Marsh.
Doctor Morrison's Miracle Body Tune-up for
Rejuvenated Health. P-H.
Doctor Morrison's Miracle Body Tune-up for
Rejuvenated Health. P-H.
Morrison, Martin E.
xMorrison, Martin E.
ed. Official Rules of Chess. McKay.
Morrison, Mary. see Morrison, Mary Chase.
Morrison, Mary Chase.
xMorrison, Mary.

Approaching the Gospels. Pendle Hill.
Re-Conciliation: The Hidden Hyphen. Pendle
    Hill.
Morrison, Michael A.
    xMorrison, M. A.
    Quantum States of Atoms, Molecules, & Solids.
        P-H.
Morrison, N. *see* Morrison, Norman.
Morrison, Norman.
    xMorrison, N.
    Introduction to Sequential Smoothing &
        Prediction. McGraw.
Morrison, Patton N.
    xMorrison, Patton N.
    Perceptions of the Police Organization: A
        Sociometric Analysis. Univ OK Gov Res.
Morrison, Perry D., 1919-
    xMorrison, Perry D.
    Career of the Academic Librarian: A Study of
        the Social Origins, Educational Attainments,
        Vocational Experience & Personality
        Characteristics of a Group of American
        Academic Librarians. ALA.
Morrison, Phylis, 1927-
    xMorrison, Phylis.
    Spiders' Games: A Book for Beginning
        Weavers. U of Wash Pr.
Morrison, Phyllis. *see* Morrison, Phyllis C.
Morrison, Phyllis C., 1923-
    xMorrison, Phyllis.
    The Business Office. McGraw.
Morrison, Ralph.
    xMorrison, Ralph.
    DC Amplifiers in Instrumentation. Krieger.
    Grounding & Shielding Techniques in
        Instrumentation. Wiley.
Morrison, Robert. *see* Morrison, Robert J.
Morrison, Robert J.
    xMorrison, Robert.
    The Contact Lens Book. Cornerstone.
    xMorrison, Robert J.
    The Contact Lens Book. Chatham Sq.
Morrison, S. Roy. *see* Morrison, Stanley Roy.
Morrison, Sean.
    xMorrison, Sean.
    illus. Armor. T Y Crowell.
Morrison, Stanley Roy.
    xMorrison, S. Roy.
    The Chemical Physics of Surfaces. Plenum Pub.
Morrison, T. F. *see* Morrison, Thomas Fairchild.
Morrison, Theodore.
    xMorrison, Theodore.
    Chautauqua: A Center for Education, Religion,
        & the Arts in America. U of Chicago Pr.
Morrison, Thomas Fairchild, 1901-
    xMorrison, T. F.
    Human Physiology. HR&W.
Morrison, Thomas K.
    xMorrison, Thomas K.
    Manufactured Exports from Developing
        Countries. Praeger.
Morrison, Toni.
    xMorrison, Toni.
    Song of Solomon. NAL.
    Sula. Knopf.
Morrison, Velma F. *see* Morrison, Velma Ford.
Morrison, Velma Ford.
    xMorrison, Velma F.
    There's Only One You: The Story of Heredity.
        Messner.
Morrison, Veronique.
    xMorrison, Veronique.
    ed. Tout a Fait Francais. Norton.
Morrison, W. I. *see* Morrison, William Ian.
Morrison, Wilbur H., 1915-
    xMorrison, Wilbur H.
    Point of No Return: The Story of the
        Twentieth Air Force. Times Bks.
Morrison, William Ian.
    xMorrison, W. I.

Input Output Methods in Urban & Regional
    Planning: A Practical Guide. Pergamon.
Morriss, L. L.
    xMorriss, L. L.
    The Sound of Boldness. Broadman.
Morriss, Margaret S. *see* Morriss, Margaret Shove.
Morriss, Margaret Shove, 1884-
    xMorriss, Margaret S.
    Colonial Trade of Maryland, 1689-1715. AMS
        Pr.
    Colonial Trade of Maryland 1689-1715.
        Porcupine Pr.
Morrissey, L. J.
    xMorrissey, L. J.
    Gulliver's Progress. Shoe String.
Morrow, Annette S. *see* Morrow, Annette Schaefer.
Morrow, Annette Schaefer.
    xMorrow, Annette S.
    Haiku of Hawaii. C E Tuttle.
Morrow, Felix.
    xMorrow, Felix.
    Revolution & Counter-Revolution in Spain.
        Path Pr NY.
Morrow, Glen R. *see* Morrow, Glenn Raymond.
Morrow, Glenn R. *see* Morrow, Glenn Raymond.
Morrow, Glenn Raymond, 1895-
    xMorrow, Glen R.
    Ethical & Economic Theories of Adam Smith.
        Kelley.
    xMorrow, Glenn R.
    Plato's Law of Slavery in Its Relation to Greek
        Law. Arno.
Morrow, James.
    xMorrow, James.
    Media & Kids: Real-World Learning in the
        Schools. Hayden.
Morrow, Mable.
    xMorrow, Mable.
    Indian Rawhide: An American Folk Art. U of
        Okla Pr.
Morrow, Ralph E. *see* Morrow, Ralph Ernest.
Morrow, Ralph Ernest.
    xMorrow, Ralph E.
    Northern Methodism & Reconstruction. Mich
        St U Pr.
Morrow, Robert M., 1931-
    xMorrow, Robert M.
    Handbook of Immediate Overdentures. Mosby.
Morrow, William L. *see* Morrow, William Lockhart.
Morrow, William Lockhart, 1935-
    xMorrow, William L.
    Public Administration: Politics, Policy & the
        Political System. Random.
Morsberger, Robert E. *see* Morsberger, Robert Eustis.
Morsberger, Robert Eustis, 1929-
    xMorsberger, Robert E.
    Commonsense Grammar & Style. T Y Crowell.
Morscheck, Charles R.
    xMorscheck, Charles R.
    Relief Sculpture for the Facade of the Certosa
        di Pavia, 1473-1499. Garland Pub.
Morse, Ann.
    xMorse, Ann.
    Forward Roll. EMC.
    Olivia Newton-John. Creative Ed.
Morse, Ann. *see* Morse, Charles.
Morse, C. G. *see* Morse, Christopher George John.
Morse, Charles.
    xMorse, Ann.
    jt. auth. Lee Trevino. Creative Ed.
    xMorse, Charles.
    Arthur Ashe. Creative Ed.
    Carly Simon. Creative Ed.
    Johnny Unitas. Creative Ed.
    Lee Trevino. Creative Ed.
    Let This Be a Day for Grandparents. St Marys.
    Pancho Gonzales. Creative Ed.
    Peggy Fleming. Creative Ed.
Morse, Christopher, 1935-
    xMorse, Christopher.

The Logic of Promise in Moltmann's Theology.
    Fortress.
Morse, Christopher George John, 1947-
    xMorse, C. G.
    Torts in Private International Law. Elsevier.
Morse, David.
    xMorse, David.
    Grandfather Rock: The New Poetry & the Old.
        Delacorte.
Morse, Dean.
    xMorse, Dean.
    Peripheral Worker. Columbia U Pr.
Morse, Donald R.
    xMorse, Donald R.
    Clinical Endodontology: A Comprehensive
        Guide to Diagnosis, Treatment & Prevention.
        C C Thomas.
    Stress & Relaxation: Application to Dentistry.
        C C Thomas.
Morse, Edward L.
    xMorse, Edward L.
    Foreign Policy & Interdependence in Gaullist
        France. Princeton U Pr.
Morse, Flo.
    xMorse, Flo.
    How Does It Feel to Be a Tree?. Schol Bk
        Serv.
Morse, Grant W.
    xMorse, Grant W.
    A Complete Guide to Organizing &
        Documenting Research Papers. Fleet.
    Concise Guide to Library Research. Fleet.
Morse, Herbert, 1854-
    xMorse, Herbert.
    Back to Shakespeare. Kennikat.
Morse, J. Mitchell. *see* Morse, Josiah Mitchell.
Morse, Jarvis M. *see* Morse, Jarvis Means.
Morse, Jarvis Means, 1899-
    xMorse, Jarvis M.
    A Neglected Period in Connecticut's History,
        1818-1850. Octagon.
Morse, Jerome G.
    xMorse, Jerome G.
    Energy Resources in Colorado: Coal, Oil Shale
        & Uranium. Westview.
Morse, John T. *see* Morse, John Torrey.
Morse, John Torrey, 1840-1937
    xMorse, John T.
    Abraham Lincoln. AMS Pr.
    Abraham Lincoln. R West.
    ed. Thomas Jefferson. AMS Pr.
    Thomas Jefferson. Chelsea Hse.
Morse, Josiah Mitchell, 1912-
    xMorse, J. Mitchell.
    Prejudice & Literature. Temple U Pr.
Morse, Marston.
    xMorse, Martson.
    Critical Point Theory in Global Analysis &
        Differential Topology. Acad Pr.
Morse, Martson. *see* Morse, Marston.
Morse, Milton. *see* Morse, Milton A.
Morse, Milton A.
    xMorse, Milton.
    Modern Real Estate Practice in Texas. Real
        Estate Ed Co.
Morse, Peter.
    xMorse, Peter.
    Popular Art: The Example of Jean Charlot.
        Capra Pr.
Morse, Peter H., 1935-
    xMorse, Peter H.
    Vitreoretinal Disease: A Manual for Diagnosis
        & Treatment. Year Bk Med.
Morse, Philip M. *see* Morse, Philip Mccord.
Morse, Philip Mccord, 1903-
    xMorse, Philip M.

In at the Beginnings: A Physicist's Life. MIT
Pr.
Thermal Physics. Benjamin-Cummings.

Morse, R. C.
xMorse, R. C.
An A,B,C of Publishing Literary Magazines.
Upsala Coll.

Morse, Randy.
xMorse, Randy.
The Mountains of Canada. Mountaineers.

Morse, Roger A.
xMorse, Roger A.
The Complete Guide to Beekeeping. Dutton.
ed. Honey Bee Pests, Predators, & Diseases.
Cornell U Pr.

Morse, Samuel F. see Morse, Samuel Finley Breese.

Morse, Samuel Finley Breese, 1791-1872
xMorse, Samuel F.
Imminent Dangers to the Free Institutions of
the United States Through Foreign
Immigration & the Present State of the
Naturalization Laws. Arno.
xMorse, Samuel Finley Breese.
Foreign Conspiracy Against the Liberties of the
United States: The Numbers of Brutus. Arno.

Morse, Samuel French, 1916-
xMorse, Samuel F.
Changes. Swallow.

Morse, Stephen J.
xMorse, Stephen J.
Psychotherapies: A Comparative Casebook.
HR&W.

Morse, Wayne L. see Morse, Wayne Lyman.

Morse, Wayne Lyman.
xMorse, Wayne L.
Survey of the Administration of Criminal
Justice in Oregon: Final Report on 1771
Felony Cases in Multnomah County Report
Number One. Arno.

Morse, William C. see Morse, William Charles.

Morse, William Charles
xMorse, William C.
ed. Humanistic Teaching for Exceptional
Children: An Introduction to Special
Education. Syracuse U Pr.

Morse, William R. see Morse, William Reginald.

Morse, William Reginald, 1974-
xMorse, William R.
Chinese Medicine. AMS Pr.

Morselli, P. L.
xMorselli, Paolo L.
ed. Drug Disposition During Development.
Halsted Pr.

Morselli, Paolo L. see Morselli, P. L.

Morson, B. C.
xMorson, Bosil C.
The Pathogenesis of Colorectal Cancer.
Saunders.

Morson, Bosil C. see Morson, B. C.

Morson, Lillian I.
xMorson, Lillian I.
An English Guide for Court Reporters.
Vantage.

Morss, Elliott R.
xMorss, Elliott R.
Government Information Management: A
Counter-Report to the Commission on
Federal Paperwork. Westview.

Mort, Paul R., 1894-
xMort, Paul R.
The Measurement of Educational Need: A
Basis for Distributing State Aid. AMS Pr.

Mort, Terry A.
xMort, Terry A.
Systematic Selling: How to Influence the
Buying Decision Process. Am Mgmt.

Mortell, Arthur.
xMortell, Arthur.

Anatomy of a Successful Salesman. Farnswth
Pub.

Mortensen, C. David.
xMortensen, C. David.
Basic Readings in Communication Theory.
Har-Row.
Communication: The Study of Human
Interaction. McGraw.

Mortensen, Enok, 1902-
xMortensen, Enok.
Danish-American Life & Letters: A
Bibliography. Arno.

Mortensen, William.
xMortensen, William.
Monsters & Madonnas. Arno.

Mortenson, William P. see Mortenson, William Peter.

Mortenson, William Peter, 1895-
xMortenson, William P.
Modern Marketing of Farm Products.
Interstate.

Mortimer, Charles E.
xMortimer, Charles E.
Chemistry: A Conceptual Approach. D Van
Nostrand.

Mortimer, John. see Mortimer, John Clifford.

Mortimer, John Clifford, 1923-
xMortimer, John.
Rumpole of the Bailey. Penguin.

Mortimer, Penelope, 1918-
xMortimer, Penelope.
About Time: An Aspect of an Autobiography.
Doubleday.
The Pumpkin Eater. Daughters.

Mortimer, Rex. see Mortimer, Rex Alfred.

Mortimer, Rex Alfred.
xMortimer, Rex.
Indonesian Communism Under Sukarno:
Ideology & Politics, 1959-1965. Cornell U Pr.

Mortimer, Robert A.
xMortimer, Robert A.
The Third World Coalition in International
Politics. Praeger.

Mortimer, W. Golden.
xMortimer, W. Golden.
The History of Coca: The Divine Plant of the
Incas. And-or Pr.

Morton. see Morton, Leslie Thomas.
Morton, A. L. see Morton, Arthur Leslie.
Morton, A. Q. see Morton, Andrew Queen.

Morton, Adam.
xMorton, Adam.
A Guide Through the Theory of Knowledge.
Dickenson.

Morton, Andrew O. see Morton, Andrew Queen.

Morton, Andrew Queen.
xMorton, A. Q.
A Critical Concordance to the Acts of the
Apostles. Biblical Res Assocs.
xMorton, Andrew O.
Literary Detection: How to Prove Authorship
& Fraud in Literature & Documents.
Scribner.

Morton, Arthur Leslie, 1903-
xMorton, A. L.
The Everlasting Gospel: A Study in the
Sources of William Blake. Folcroft.
ed. Freedom in Arms: A Selection of Leveller
Writings. Intl Pub Co.

Morton, Barbara. see Morton, Barbara M.

Morton, Barbara M.
xMorton, Barbara.
VD: A Guide for Nurses & Counselors. Little.

Morton, Brenda.
xMorton, Brenda.

Cuddly Dolls & How to Dress Them.
Taplinger.
Do-It-Yourself Dinosaurs: Imaginative Toycraft
for Beginners. Taplinger.
Floppy Toys. Taplinger.
Mascot Toys: Simple Toys to Make from
Sponges. Taplinger.
Sleeve Puppets. Taplinger.
Soft Toys Made Easy. Taplinger.

Morton, Carl P. see Morton, Carl Patrick.

Morton, Carl Patrick.
xMorton, Carl P.
Desiring Stone. Windy Row.

Morton, Frederic.
xMorton, Frederic.
A Nervous Splendor: Vienna 1888-1889. Little.
A Nervous Splendor: Vienna 1888-1889.
Penguin.

Morton, Grace M. see Morton, Grace Margaret.

Morton, Grace Margaret.
xMorton, Grace M.
Arts of Costume & Personal Appearance.
Wiley.

Morton, H. V. see Morton, Henry Canova Vollam.
Morton, Harry. see Morton, Henry Albert.

Morton, Henry Albert.
xMorton, Harry.
And Now New Zealand. Intl Pubns Serv.

Morton, Henry Canova Vollam.
xMorton, H. V.
In Search of the Holy Land. Dodd.
The Magic of Ireland. Dodd.

Morton, Henry W.
xMorton, Henry W.
Soviet Politics & Society in the 1970's. Free
Pr.

Morton, Jacqueline.
xMorton, Jacqueline.
English Grammar for Students of French.
Olivia & Hill.

Morton, Jane, 1931-
xMorton, Jane.
Running Scared. Elsevier-Nelson.

Morton, Jeffrey B.
xMorton, Jeffrey B.
Introduction to Basic. Intl Schol Bk Serv.

Morton, John B. see Morton, John Bingham.

Morton, John Bingham, 1893-
xMorton, John B.
Hilaire Belloc: A Memoir. Folcroft.

Morton, Joyce.
xMorton, Joyce.
Edge of Fear. Bouregy.
Legal Secretarial Procedures. P-H.

Morton, Judy C. see Morton, Judy Corey.

Morton, Judy Corey.
xMorton, Judy C.
Dental Teamwork Strategies: Interpersonal &
Organizational Approaches. Mosby.

Morton, Julia F. see Morton, Julia Frances.

Morton, Julia Frances, 1912-
xMorton, Julia F.
Folk Remedies of the Low Country. E A
Seemann.

Morton, Kathryn.
xMorton, Kathryn.
Aid & Dependence: British Aid to Malawi.
Holmes & Meier.

Morton, Leslie Thomas.
xMorton.
Use of Medical Literature. Butterworths.

Morton, Malvin.
xMorton, Malvin.
ed. Can Public Welfare Keep Pace. Columbia U
Pr.

Morton, Miriam.
xMorton, Miriam.

Growing Old. PB.
Moss, Gordon E. *see* Moss, Gordon Ervin.
Moss, Gordon Ervin, 1937-
xMoss, Gordon E.
Illness, Immunity & Social Interaction: The
Dynamics of Biosocial Resonation. Wiley.
Moss, Howard, 1922-
xMoss, Howard.
Instant Lives. Avon.
A Swimmer in the Air: Poems. Greenwood.
Moss, Leonard.
xMoss, Leonard.
Arthur Miller. Coll & U Pr.
Arthur Miller. Twayne.
Moss, Martha, 1948-
xMoss, Martha.
Photography Books Index: A Subject Guide to
Photo Anthologies. Scarecrow.
Moss, Michael S.
xMoss, Michael S.
Workshop of the British Empire: Engineering &
Shipbuilding in the West of Scotland.
Fairleigh Dickinson.
Moss, Morris H.
xMoss, Morris H.
Schaum's Outline of Tax Accounting.
McGraw.
Moss, Orlando, 1931-
xMoss, Orlando.
Complete Handbook for Teaching Small Vocal
Ensembles. P-H.
Moss, Robert, 1946-
xMoss, Robert.
Chile's Marxist Experiment. Halsted Pr.
Moss, Stanley.
xMoss, Stanley.
Skull of Adam. Horizon.
Moss, Stirling, 1929-
xMoss, Stirling.
How to Watch Motor Racing. Dodd.
Moss, Thelma.
xMoss, Thelma.
The Body Electric: A Personal Journey into the
Mysteries of Parapsychological Research,
Bioenergy & Kirlian Photography. J P
Tarcher.
Moss, Warner, 1902-
xMoss, Warner.
Political Parties in the Irish Free State. AMS
Pr.
Moss, William T.
xMoss, William T.
Radiation Oncology: Rationale, Technique,
Results. Mosby.
Moss, William W., 1935-
xMoss, William W.
Oral History Program Manual. Praeger.
Moss-Salentijn, Letty.
xMoss-Salentijn, Letty.
Dental & Oral Tissues: An Introduction for
Paraprofessionals in Dentistry. Lea &
Febiger.
Orofacial Histology & Embryology: A Visual
Integration. Davis Co.
Mosse, Claude, Docteur Es Lettres.
xMosse, Claude.
Athens in Decline 404-86 B. C.. Routledge &
Kegan.
Mosse, George L. *see* Mosse, George Lachmann.
Mosse, George Lachmann.
xMosse, George L.

Germans & Jews: The Right, the Left, & the
Search for a 'third Force' in Pre-Nazi
Germany. Fertig.
The Nationalization of the Masses: Political
Symbolism & Mass Movements in Germany,
from the Napoleonic Wars Through the Third
Reich. Fertig.
The Nationalization of the Masses: Political
Symbolism & Mass Movements in Germany
from the Napoleonic Wars Through the Third
Reich. NAL.
Nazism: A Historical & Comparative Analysis
of National Socialism. Transaction Bks.
The Reformation. HR&W.
Reformation. Peter Smith.
Toward the Final Solution: A History of
European Racism. Fertig.
Toward the Final Solution: A History of
European Racism. Har-Row.
Mosse, W. E. *see* Mosse, Walter Eugen.
Mosse, Walter Eugen.
xMosse, W. E.
Liberal Europe: The Age of Bourgeois Realism
1848-1875. HarBraceJ.
Liberal Europe: The Age of Bourgeois Realism
1848-1875. Transatlantic.
Mossek, M.
xMossek, M.
Palestine Immigration Policy Under Sir Herbert
Samuel: British, Zionist & Arab Attitudes.
Biblio Dist.
Mossell, N. F., Mrs, 1855-
xMossell, N. F.
The Work of the Afro-American Woman.
Arno.
Mosshammer, Alden A.
xMosshammer, Alden A.
The Chronicle of Eusebius & Greek
Chronographic Tradition. Bucknell U Pr.
Mossi, John P.
xMossi, John P.
Modern Liturgy Handbook: A Study and
Planning Guide for Worship. Paulist Pr.
Mossin, Jan.
xMossin, Jan.
The Economic Efficiency of Financial Markets.
Lexington Bks.
Theory of Financial Markets. P-H.
Mossman, Frank H. *see* Mossman, Frank Homer.
Mossman, Frank Homer.
xMossman, Frank H.
Financial Dimensions of Marketing
Management. Wiley.
Mossman, Harland W. *see* Mossman, Harland Winfield.
Mossman, Harland Winfield.
xMossman, Harland W.
Comparative Morphology of the Mammalian
Ovary. U of Wis Pr.
Mossman, Keith.
xMossman, Keith.
Indoor Light Gardening. Branford.
Mossman, Philip L.
xMossman, Philip L.
A Problem-Oriented Approach to Stroke
Rehabilitation. C E Tuttle.
Mossman, Tam.
xMossman, Tam.
Gardens That Care for Themselves: How to
Grow Neater, Healthier Plants, Cut Your
Outdoor Chores in Half. Doubleday.
Mossner, Ernest C. *see* Mossner, Ernest Campbell.
Mossner, Ernest Campbell, 1907-
xMossner, Ernest C.
The Life of David Hume. Oxford U Pr.
Mosston, Muska.
xMosston, Muska.
Developmental Movement. Merrill.
Most, Bernard.
xMost, Bernard.

illus. If the Dinosaurs Came Back. HarBraceJ.
illus. My Very Own Octopus. HarBraceJ.
illus. There's an Ant in Anthony. Morrow.
Most, Kenneth S.
xMost, Kenneth S.
Accounting Theory. Grid Pub.
Most, William G. *see* Most, William George.
Most, William George, 1914-
xMost, William G.
Latin by the Natural Method. Lawrence.
Mosteller, F. R. *see* Mosteller, Frederick.
Mosteller, Frederick.
xMosteller, F. R.
Probability & Statistics. A-W.
xMosteller, Frederick.
Data Analysis & Regression: A Second Course
in Statistics. A-W.
Moster, Mary Beth.
xMoster, Mary Beth.
Living with Cancer. Moody.
Mostert, Noel.
xMostert, Noel.
Supership. Knopf.
Supership. Warner Bks.
Mostofsky, David I.
xMostofsky, David I.
ed. Stimulus Generalization. Stanford U Pr.
Mostow, G. D. *see* Mostow, George D.
Mostow, George D.
xMostow, G. D.
ed. Mathematical Models for Cell
Rearrangement. Yale U Pr.
Strong Rigidity of Locally Symmetric Spaces.
Princeton U Pr.
Mostow, Mark A. *see* Mostow, Mark Alan.
Mostow, Mark Alan, 1948-
xMostow, Mark A.
Continuous Cohomology of Spaces with Two
Topologies. Am Math.
Mostowski, A. *see* Mostowski, Andrzej.
Mostowski, Andrej. *see* Mostowski, Andrzej.
Mostowski, Andrzej.
xMostowski, A.
Foundational Studies: Selected Works. Elsevier.
xMostowski, Andrej.
Thirty Years of Foundational Studies: Lectures
on the Development of Mathematical Logic
& the Study of the Foundations of
Mathematics in 1930-1964. Biblio Dist.
Motamen, Homa.
xMotamen, Homa.
Expenditure of Oil Revenue: An Optimal
Control Approach with Application to the
Iranian Economy. St Martin.
Motani, Nizar.
xMotani, Nizar.
On His Majesty's Service in Uganda: The
Origins of Uganda's African Civil Service,
1912-1914. Maxwell Schl Citizen.
Mote, Frederick W., 1922-
xMote, Frederick W.
Intellectual Foundations of China. Knopf.
The Mother Earth News.
xMother Earth News Staff.
Handbook of Homemade Power. Bantam.
Mother Earth News Staff. *see* The Mother Earth News.
Mothershead, Harmon R. *see* Mothershead, Harmon
Ross.
Mothershead, Harmon Ross.
xMothershead, Harmon R.
Swan Land & Cattle Company, Ltd. U of Okla
Pr.
Mothersill, Mary.
xMothersill, Mary.
ed. Ethics. Macmillan.
Mothner, Ira.
xMothner, Ira.
Woodrow Wilson, Champion of Peace. Watts.
Motion, Andrew, 1952-
xMotion, Andrew.

The Pleasure Steamers. Persea Bks.
Motley, Pseud.
xMotley.
Theatre Props. Drama Bk.
Motley. *see* Motley, Michael T.
Motley, Annette.
xMotley, Annette.
The Sins of the Lion. Stein & Day.
Motley, Brian.
xMotley, Brian.
Money, Income, & Wealth: The
Macroeconomics of a Monetary Economy.
Heath.
Motley, James M. *see* Motley, James Marvin.
Motley, James Marvin, 1877-
xMotley, James M.
Apprenticeship in American Trade Unions.
AMS Pr.
Motley, John J.
xMotley, John J.
Now Hear This!: Histories of U. S. Ships in
World War II. Zenger Pub.
Motley, Michael T.
xMotley.
Orientations to Language & Communication.
SRA.
Motley, R. W. *see* Motley, Robert W.
Motley, Robert W.
xMotley, R. W.
Q Machines. Acad Pr.
Motley, Wilma E.
xMotley, Wilma E.
Ethics, Jurisprudence & History for the Dental
Hygienist. Lea & Febiger.
Motolinia, Toribio, d. 1568
xMotolinia, Toribio.
History of the Indians of New Spain.
Greenwood.
Moton, Robert R. *see* Moton, Robert Russa.
Moton, Robert Russa, 1867-1940
xMoton, Robert R.
Finding a Way Out: An Autobiography. Negro
U Pr.
The Motor Cycle.
xThe Motor Cycle Staff.
Motor Cycles & How to Manage Them. British
Bk Ctr.
The Motor Cycle Staff. *see* The Motor Cycle.
Motor Vehicle Manufacturers Association of the U.S.A.
xMotor Vehicle Manufacturers Association of the
United States.
Automobiles of America: Milestones, Pioneers,
Roll Call, Highlights. Wayne St U Pr.
Motorola, Inc.
xMotorola, Inc.
Integrated Circuits: Design Principles &
Fabrication. McGraw.
Motorola Inc. *see* Motorola Semiconductor Products Inc.
Motorola Semiconductor Products Inc.
xMotorola Inc.
Microprocessor Applications Manual. McGraw.
Motoyama, Hiroshi.
xMotoyama, Hiroshi.
Science & the Evolution of Consciousness:
Chakras, Ki, & Psi. Autumn Pr.
Mott, Abigail (Field).
xMott, Alexander.
Compiled by Narratives of Colored Americans.
Arno.
Mott, Alexander. *see* Mott, Abigail (Field).
Mott, John R. *see* Mott, John Raleigh.
Mott, John Raleigh, 1865-1955
xMott, John R.
The Evangelization of the World in This
Generation. Arno.
Mott, L. C. *see* Mott, Leslie Charles.
Mott, Lawrence, 1881-1931
xMott, Lawrence.

White Darkness: & Other Stories of the Great
Northwest. Arno.
Mott, Leslie Charles.
xMott, L. C.
Engineering Drawing & Construction. Oxford
U Pr.
Mott, Lewis F. *see* Mott, Lewis Freeman.
Mott, Lewis Freeman, 1863-1941
xMott, Lewis F.
The Provencal Lyric. Folcroft.
Mott, Michael.
xMott, Michael.
Absence of Unicorns, Presence of Lions:
Poems. Little.
Mott, N. F. *see* Mott, Nevill Francis.
Mott, Nevill Francis.
xMott, N. F.
Theory of Atomic Collisions. Oxford U Pr.
Mott, Pearle G., 1885-
xMott, Pearle G.
History of Davis & Canaan Valley. McClain.
Mott, Robert L.
xMott, Robert L.
Applied Fluid Mechanics. Merrill.
Applied Strength of Materials. P-H.
Mott, Russell. *see* Mott, Russell C.
Mott, Russell C.
xMott, Russell.
Total Book of House Plants. Delacorte.
Mott, Thomas B. *see* Mott, Thomas Bentley.
Mott, Thomas Bentley, 1865-
xMott, Thomas B.
Twenty Years As Military Attache. Arno.
Mottahedeh, Roy P., 1940-
xMottahedeh, Roy P.
Loyalty & Leadership in an Early Islamic
Society. Princeton U Pr.
Motte, Ellen N. La. *see* La Motte, Ellen N.
Motte, Jacob R. *see* Motte, Jacob Rhett.
Motte, Jacob Rhett, 1811-1868
xMotte, Jacob R.
Journey into Wilderness: An Army Surgeon's
Account of Life in Camp & Field During the
Creek & Seminole Wars, 1836-1838. U
Presses Fla.
Motter, Alton M.
xMotter, Alton M.
ed. Preaching About Death: Eighteen Sermons
Dealing with the Experience of Death from
the Christian Perspective. Fortress.
Mottley, Charles C.
xMottley, Charles C.
The Mustard Seed. Popular Lib.
xMottley, Charles M.
jt. auth. The Mustard Seed. Popular Lib.
Mottley, Charles M. *see* Mottley, Charles C.
Motto, Jerome A.
xMotto, Jerome A.
Standards for Suicide Prevention & Crisis
Centers. Human Sci Pr.
Mottram, Anthony.
xMottram, Tony.
Play Better Tennis. Arc Bks.
Play Better Tennis. Arco.
Skills & Tactics of Tennis. Arco.
Mottram, Ralph H. *see* Mottram, Ralph Hale.
Mottram, Ralph Hale, 1883-
xMottram, Ralph H.
Armistice & Other Memories: Forming a
Pendant to the 'Spanish Farm Trilogy'. Arno.
Mottram, Tony. *see* Mottram, Anthony.
Motulsky, A. G. *see* Motulsky, Arno G.
Motulsky, Arno G.
xMotulsky, A. G.
ed. Human Genetic Variation in Response to
Medical & Environmental Agents:
Pharmacogenetics & Ecogenetics.
Springer-Verlag.
xMotulsky, Arno G.

Genetic Counseling. Mss Info.
Motz, Lloyd.
xMotz, Lloyd.
Essentials of Astronomy. Columbia U Pr.
ed. Rediscovery of the Earth. Van Nos
Reinhold.
This Is Astronomy. Columbia U Pr.
Mouat, Lucia.
xMouat, Lucia.
Back to Business: A Woman's Guide to
Reentering the Job Market. NAL.
Back to Business: A Woman's Guide to
Reentering the Job Market. Sovereign Bks.
Moudgal, N. R.
xMoudgal, N. R.
Gonadotropins & Gonadal Function. Acad Pr.
Mouffe, Chantal.
xMouffe, Chantal.
Gramsci & Marxist Theory. Routledge &
Kegan.
Moul, Keith. *see* Moul, Keith R.
Moul, Keith R.
xMoul, Keith.
Theodore Roethke's Career: An Annotated
Bibliography. G K Hall.
Mould, J. Albert.
xMould, J. Albert.
Review Text in General Science. AMSCO Sch.
Moule, A. C. *see* Moule, Arthur Christopher.
Moule, Arthur Christopher, 1873-1957
xMoule, A. C.
Christians in China Before the Year 1550.
Gordon Pr.
Christians in China Before the Year 1550.
Octagon.
Moule, C. F. *see* Moule, Charles Francis Digby.
Moule, Charles F. *see* Moule, Charles Francis Digby.
Moule, Charles Francis Digby.
xMoule, C. F.
The Holy Spirit. Eerdmans.
The Origin of Christology. Cambridge U Pr.
xMoule, Charles F.
Meaning of Hope: A Biblical Exposition with
Concordance. Fortress.
Moule, H. C. G. *see* Moule, Handley Carr Glyn.
Moule, Handley Carr Glyn, Bp. of Durham, 1841-1920
xMoule, H. C. G.
Person & Work of the Holy Spirit. Kregel.
Studies in Hebrews. Kregel.
Moulton, Elizabeth.
xMoulton, Elizabeth.
Fatal Demonstrations. Har-Row.
Moulton, Eugene R.
xMoulton, Eugene R.
Communication: A Creative Process. Burgess.
Moulton, Forest R. *see* Moulton, Forest Ray.
Moulton, Forest Ray, 1872-1952
xMoulton, Forest R.
Periodic Orbits. Johnson Repr.
Moulton, Harland B.
xMoulton, Harland B.
From Superiority to Parity: The United States
and the Strategic Arms Race, 1961-1971.
Greenwood.
Moulton, Harold G. *see* Moulton, Harold Glenn.
Moulton, Harold Glenn, 1883-
xMoulton, Harold G.
Can Inflation Be Controlled. Anderson Kramer.
Capital Expansion, Employment & Economic
Stability. Arno.
Financial Organization & the Economic
System. Arno.
The Financial Organization of Society. Arno.
The Formation of Capital. Arno.
The French Debt Problem. Johnson Repr.
Germany's Capacity to Pay: A Study of the
Reparation Problem. Johnson Repr.
World War Debt Settlements. Johnson Repr.
Moulton, Harold K. *see* Moulton, Harold Keeling.

Moulton, Harold Keeling.
  xMoulton, Harold K.
    ed. The Analytical Greek Lexicon Revised.
    Zondervan.
Moulton, J. L. see Moulton, James Louis.
Moulton, Jack. see Moulton, Jack E.
Moulton, Jack E, 1922-
  xMoulton, Jack.
    ed. Tumors in Domestic Animals. U of Cal Pr.
Moulton, James Louis.
  xMoulton, J. L.
    Battle for Antwerp: The Liberation of the City
    & the Opening of the Scheldt 1944. Intl
    Pubns Serv.
Moulton, Phillips P., 1909-
  xMoulton, Phillips P.
    The Living Witness of John Woolman. Pendle
    Hill.
Moulton, Ron. see Moulton, Ron Godfrey.
Moulton, Ron Godfrey.
  xMoulton, Ron.
    Kites. Transatlantic.
Moulton, William G. see Moulton, William Gamwell.
Moulton, William Gamwell, 1914-
  xMoulton, William G.
    Linguistic Guide to Language Learning.
    Modern Lang.
    Sounds of English & German. U of Chicago Pr.
Mouly, George J.
  xMouly, George J.
    Educational Research: The Art & Science of
    Investigation. Allyn.
Mounier, Emmanuel, 1905-1950
  xMounier, Emmanuel.
    Personalism. U of Notre Dame Pr.
Mount, E. see Mount, Ellis.
Mount, Ellis.
  xMount, E.
    Guide to Basic Information Sources in
    Engineering. J Norton Pubs.
  xMount, Ellis.
    ed. Guide to Basic Information Sources in
    Engineering. Halsted Pr.
Mount, Ferdinand, 1939-
  xMount, Ferdinand.
    The Theatre of Politics. Schocken.
Mount Holyoke College.
  xMount Holyoke College.
    Those Having Torches. Arno.
Mount, Tom.
  xMount, Tom.
    The New Practical Diving: A Complete
    Manual for Compressed Air Divers. U of
    Miami Pr.
    Practical Diving: A Complete Manual for
    Compressed Air Divers. U of Miami Pr.
Mountain. see Mountain, Robert.
Mountain, Robert.
  xMountain.
    Journey Under the Sea. Vermont Crossroads.
Mountain States Telephone & Telegraph Company. see
    Mountain States Telephone and Telegraph Company.
Mountain States Telephone and Telegraph Company.
  xMountain States Telephone & Telegraph
    Company.
    Pricing in Regulated Industries Theory &
    Application Two. Mountain St Tel.
Mountbatten, Earl. see Mountbatten, Louis Mountbatten.
Mountbatten, Louis Mountbatten, Earl, 1900-
  xMountbatten, Earl.
    Intro. by An Introduction to Polo. J A Allen.
Mountcastle, Vernon B.
  xMountcastle, Vernon B.
    Medical Physiology. Mosby.
Mountcastle, William W., 1925-
  xMountcastle, William W.

    Religion in Planetary Perspective: A
    Philosophy of Comparative Religion.
    Abingdon.
Mountfield, David, 1938-
  xMountfield, David.
    A History of Polar Exploration. Dial.
Mountford, Alan.
  xMountford, Alan.
    English in Agriculture. Oxford U Pr.
    English in Workshop Practice. Oxford U Pr.
Mountjoy, Alan B.
  xMountjoy, Alan B.
    ed. The Third World: Problems & Perspectives.
    St Martin.
Mountney, George J.
  xMountney, George J.
    Poultry Products Technology. AVI.
Mourad, Samiha.
  xMourad, Samiha.
    Understanding & Programming Computers.
    Exposition.
Mourant, A. E. see Mourant, Arthur Ernest.
Mourant, Arthur Ernest.
  xMourant, A. E.
    The Genetics of the Jews. Oxford U Pr.
Mourant, John A. see Mourant, John Arthur.
Mourant, John Arthur, 1903-
  xMourant, John A.
    Readings in the Philosophy of Religion. Peter
    Smith.
Mourelatos, Alexander P. D., 1936-
  xMourelatos, Alexander P. D.
    ed. The Pre-Socratics: A Collection of Critical
    Essays. Doubleday.
Mourey, Gabriel, 1865-1943
  xMourey, Gabriel.
    Art Nouveau Jewellery & Fans. Peter Smith.
Moursund, Janet.
  xMoursund, Janet P.
    Learning & the Learner.. Brooks-Cole.
Moursund, Janet P. see Moursund, Janet.
Moustakas, Clark. see Moustakas, Clark E.
Moustakas, Clark E.
  xMoustakas, Clark.
    Individuality & Encounter: A Brief Journey
    into Loneliness & Sensitivity Groups.
    Howard Doyle.
  xMoustakas, Clark E.
    Alive & Growing Teacher. Philos Lib.
    Children in Play Therapy. Aronson.
    Creative Life. Van Nos Reinhold.
    Finding Yourself, Finding Others. P-H.
    Learning to Be Free. P-H.
    Loneliness. P-H.
    Loneliness & Love. P-H.
    Psychotherapy with Children: The Living
    Relationship. Har-Row.
Mouw, Richard. see Mouw, Richard J.
Mouw, Richard J.
  xMouw, Richard.
    Politics & the Biblical Drama. Eerdmans.
Mouzelis, Nicos P.
  xMouzelis, Nicos P.
    Modern Greece: Facets of Underdevelopment.
    Holmes & Meier.
    Organisation & Bureaucracy: An Analysis of
    Modern Theories. Aldine Pub.
Movius, Hallam L. see Movius, Hallam Leonard.
Movius, Hallam Leonard, 1907-
  xMovius, Hallam L.
    ed. Excavation of the Abri Pataud, Les Eyzies
    (Dordogne). Peabody Harvard.
Mow, Anna B.
  xMow, Anna B.
    Springs of Love. Brethren.
Mowat, A. P. see Mowat, Alex P.
Mowat, Alex P.
  xMowat, A. P.

    Liver Disorders in Childhood. Butterworths.
Mowat, Barbara A.
  xMowat, Barbara A.
    The Dramaturgy of Shakespeare's Romances.
    U of Ga Pr.
Mowat, C. L. see Mowat, Charles Loch.
Mowat, Charles Loch, 1911-1970
  xMowat, C. L.
    Great Britain Since 1914. Cornell U Pr.
Mowat, Farley, 1921-
  xMowat, Farley.
    And No Birds Sang. Little.
    The Curse of the Viking Grave. Little.
    The Desperate People. Little.
    The Dog Who Wouldn't Be. Bantam.
    The Dog Who Wouldn't Be. Little.
    Dog Who Wouldn't Be. BJ Pub Group.
    Lost in the Barrens. Little.
Mowat, Robert B. see Mowat, Robert Balmain.
Mowat, Robert Balmain, 1883-1941
  xMowat, Robert B.
    Age of Reason: The Continent of Europe in the
    Eighteenth Century. Russell.
    Diplomacy of Napoleon. Russell.
    England in the Eighteenth Century. Folcroft.
    History of European Diplomacy, 1451-1789.
    Shoe String.
Mowbray, R. M.
  xMowbray, R. M.
    Psychology in Relation to Medicine. Churchill.
Mower, A. Glenn. see Mower, Alfred Glenn.
Mower, Alfred Glenn.
  xMower, A. Glenn.
    The United States, the United Nations, &
    Human Rights: The Eleanor Roosevelt &
    Jimmy Carter Eras. Greenwood.
Mowinckel, Sigmund. see Mowinckel, Sigmund Olaf
    Plytt.
Mowinckel, Sigmund Olaf Plytt, 1884-
  xMowinckel, Sigmund.
    Psalms in Israel's Worship. Abingdon.
Mowitz, Robert J.
  xMowitz, Robert J.
    Profile of a Metropolis: A Case Book. Wayne
    St U Pr.
Mowle, Frederic J.
  xMowle, Frederic J.
    Systematic Approach to Digital Logic Design.
    A-W.
Mowoe, Isaac J. see Mowoe, Isaac James.
Mowoe, Isaac James.
  xMowoe, Isaac J.
    ed. The Performance of Soldiers As Governors:
    African Politics & the African Military. U Pr
    of Amer.
Mowrer, Edgar A. see Mowrer, Edgar Ansel.
Mowrer, Edgar Ansel.
  xMowrer, Edgar A.
    Umano & the Price of Lasting Peace. Philos
    Lib.
Mowrer, Ernest R. see Mowrer, Ernest Russell.
Mowrer, Ernest Russell, 1895-
  xMowrer, Ernest R.
    Family Disorganization: An Introduction to a
    Sociological Analysis. Arno.
Mowrer, O. Hobart. see Mowrer, Orval Hobart.
Mowrer, Orval Hobart, 1907-
  xMowrer, O. Hobart.
    Learning Theory & Behavior. Krieger.
    Learning Theory & Personality Dynamics:
    Selected Papers. Krieger.
Mowrer, Paul S. see Mowrer, Paul Scott.
Mowrer, Paul Scott, 1887-
  xMowrer, Paul S.
    This Teeming Earth. Golden Quill.
Mowry, George E. see Mowry, George Edwin.

Mowry, George Edwin, 1909-
xMowry, George E.
Another Look at the Twentieth - Century South. La State U Pr.
California Progressives. Times Bks.
ed. Twenties: Fords, Flappers, & Fanatics. P-H.
ed. Twenties: Fords, Flappers & Fanatics. Peter Smith.
Mowry, Sylvester, 1830-1871
xMowry, Sylvester.
Arizona & Sonora: The Geography, History, & Resources of the Silver Region of North America. Arno.
Mowschenson, P. M. *see* Mowschenson, Peter M.
Mowschenson, Peter M.
xMowschenson, P. M.
Aids to Undergraduate Surgery. Churchill.
Mowshowitz, Abbe.
xMowshowitz, Abbe.
Conquest of Will: Information Processing in Human Affairs. A-W.
Mowvley, Harry.
xMowvley, Harry.
Reading the Old Testament Prophets Today. John Knox.
Moxcey, Mary E. *see* Moxcey, Mary Eliza.
Moxcey, Mary Eliza, 1875-
xMoxcey, Mary E.
Some Qualities Associated with Success in the Christian Ministry. AMS Pr.
Moxon, Joseph.
xMoxon, Joseph.
Mechanick Exercises on the Whole Art of Printing. Dover.
Moy-Thomas, J. A. *see* Moy-Thomas, James Alan.
Moy-Thomas, James Alan.
xMoy-Thomas, J. A.
Palaeozoic Fishes. HR&W.
Moya, Frank, 1929-
xMoya, Frank.
Fundamentals of Management for the Physician. C C Thomas.
Moyd, Olin P.
xMoyd, Olin P.
Redemption in Black Theology. Judson.
Moyer, Cecil C.
xMoyer, Cecil C.
Historic Ranchos of San Diego. Copley Bks.
Moyer, Elgin S. *see* Moyer, Elgin Sylvester.
Moyer, Elgin Sylvester, 1890-
xMoyer, Elgin S.
Who Was Who in Church History. Keats.
Moyer, K. E. *see* Moyer, Kenneth Evan.
Moyer, Kenneth E. *see* Moyer, Kenneth Evan.
Moyer, Kenneth Evan, 1919-
xMoyer, K. E.
Neuroanatomy. Har-Row.
xMoyer, Kenneth E.
The Psychobiology of Aggression. Har-Row.
Moyer, Reed.
xMoyer, Reed.
Competition in the Midwestern Coal Industry. Harvard U Pr.
Moyes, Patricia.
xMoyes, Patricia.
The Coconut Killings. HR&W.
The Coconut Killings. Penguin.
The Curious Affair of the Third Dog. Penguin.
How to Talk to Your Cat. HR&W.
Who Is Simon Warwick?. HR&W.
Moyle, Peter B.
xMoyle, Peter B.
Inland Fishes of California. U of Cal Pr.
Moyles, R. G.
xMoyles, R. G.
ed. English-Canadian Literature to 1900: A Guide to Information Sources. Gale.
Moynahan, Julian, 1925-
xMoynahan, Julian.

Deed of Life: The Novels & Tales of D. H. Lawrence. Princeton U Pr.
Pairing off. Nordon Pubns.
Moynihan, Daniel P. *see* Moynihan, Daniel Patrick.
Moynihan, Daniel Patrick.
xMoynihan, Daniel P.
ed. On Understanding Poverty: Perspectives from the Social Sciences. Basic.
Politics of a Guaranteed Income: The Nixon Administration & the Family Assistance Plan. Random.
Moynihan, Donald T.
xMoynihan, Donald T.
Skin Deep: The Making of a Plastic Surgeon. Little.
Moynihan, Elizabeth B.
xMoynihan, Elizabeth B.
Paradise As a Garden: In Persia & Mughal India. Braziller.
Moynihan, James H.
xMoynihan, James H.
The Life of Archbishop John Ireland. Arno.
Moynihan, William T.
xMoynihan, William T.
Craft & Art of Dylan Thomas. Cornell U Pr.
Mozart, Johann Chrysostom Wolfgang Amadeus.
xMozart, Wolfgang A.
Letters of Wolfgang Amadeus Mozart. Dover.
Mozart, Wolfgang A. *see* Mozart, Johann Chrysostom Wolfgang Amadeus.
Mozzochi, C. J. *see* Mozzochi, Charles J.
Mozzochi, Charles J.
xMozzochi, C. J.
On the Pointwise Convergence of Fourier Series. Springer-Verlag.
Symmetric Generalized Topological Structures. Exposition.
Mrabet, Mohammed.
xMrabet, Mohammed.
The Beach Cafe & The Voice. Black Sparrow.
Look & Move on. Black Sparrow.
MRC Symposium-1971. *see* Symposium on Nonlinear Functional Analysis, Madison, Wis., 1971.
Mroczkowski, George.
xMroczkowski, George.
Professional Treasure Hunter. Ram Pub.
Mrowec, S. *see* Mrowec, Stanisaw.
Mrowec, Stanisaw.
xMrowec, S.
Defects & Diffusion in Solids: An Introduction. Elsevier.
Mtewa, Mekki.
xMtewa, Mekki.
Public Policy & Development Politics: The Politics of Technical Expertise in Africa. U Pr of Amer.
Muccigrosso, Robert.
xMuccigrosso, Robert.
American Gothic: The Mind & Art of Ralph Adams Cram. U Pr of Amer.
Muchnic, Helen.
xMuchnic, Helen.
From Gorky to Pasternak: Six Writers in Soviet Russia. Octagon.
Muchow, David J.
xMuchow, David J.
The Vanishing Congress: Where Has All the Power Gone?. North Am Intl.
Muck, Otto. *see* Muck, Otto Heinrich.
Muck, Otto Heinrich.
xMuck, Otto.
The Secret of Atlantis. PB.
The Secret of Atlantis. Times Bks.
Muckelroy, K. *see* Muckelroy, Keith.
Muckelroy, Keith, 1951-
xMuckelroy, K.
Maritime Archaeology. Cambridge U Pr.
Muckle, D. S. *see* Muckle, David Sutherland.
Muckle, David Sutherland.
xMuckle, D. S.

Femoral Neck Fractures & Hip Joint Injuries. Wiley.
Mudd, Charles S.
xMudd, Charles S.
Speech: Content & Communication. Har-Row.
Muddiman, Bernard.
xMuddiman, Bernard.
Men of the Nineties. Folcroft.
Mudford, Peter.
xMudford, Peter.
The Art of Celebration. Merrimack Bk Serv.
Mudge, Arthur E.
xMudge, Arthur E.
Value Engineering: A Systematic Approach. McGraw.
Mudge, Isadore G. *see* Mudge, Isadore Gilbert.
Mudge, Isadore Gilbert.
xMudge, Isadore G.
A Thackeray Dictionary: The Characters & Scenes of the Novels & Short Stories Alphabetically Arranged. Folcroft.
Mudie, Colin.
xMudie, Colin.
Power Boats. Transatlantic.
Mudrick, Marvin.
xMudrick, Marvin.
Books Are Not Life but Then What Is?. Oxford U Pr.
On Culture & Literature. Horizon.
Mudroch, Vaclav.
xMudroch, Vaclav.
The Wyclyf Tradition. Ohio U Pr.
Muehl, William.
xMuehl, William.
All the Damned Angels. Pilgrim NY.
Muehrcke, P. *see* Muehrcke, Phillip.
Muehrcke, Phillip.
xMuehrcke, P.
Thematic Cartography. Assn Am Geographers.
xMuehrcke, Phillip C.
Map Use: Reading, Analysis & Interpretation. JP Pubns WI.
Muehrcke, Phillip C. *see* Muehrcke, Phillip.
Muehsam, G. *see* Muehsam, Gerd.
Muehsam, Gerd, 1913-
xMuehsam, G.
Guide to Basic Information Sources in the Visual Arts. J Norton Pubs.
xMuehsam, Gerd.
ed. French Painters & Paintings from the Fourteenth Century to Post-Impressionism. Ungar.
Mueller, Charles S.
xMueller, Charles S.
Thank God I'm a Teenager. Augsburg.
Mueller, Claus, 1941-
xMueller, Claus.
The Politics of Communication: A Study in the Political Sociology of Language, Socialization, & Legitimation. Oxford U Pr.
Mueller, D. C. *see* Mueller, Dennis C.
Mueller, Dale M. J.
xMueller, Dale M. J.
The Peristome of Fissidens limbatus Sullivant. U of Cal Pr.
Mueller, Dennis C.
xMueller, D. C.
Public Choice. Cambridge U Pr.
Mueller, Francis J.
xMueller, Francis J.
General Mathematics for College Students. P-H.
Intermediate Algebra. P-H.
Mueller, G. *see* Mueller, Gerhard G.
Mueller, Georgiana.
xMueller, Georgiana.
How to Raise & Train a Greyhound. TFH Pubns.
Mueller, Gerhard G.
xMueller, G.

Accounting: A Book of Readings. HR&W.
Mueller, Gerhard O. see Mueller, Gerhard O. W.
Mueller, Gerhard O. W.
  xMueller, Gerhard O.
    Sexual Conduct & the Law. Oceana.
  xMueller, Gerhard O. W.
    Comparative Criminal Procedure. NYU Pr.
Mueller, Gustav. see Mueller, Gustav Emil.
Mueller, Gustav Emil, 1898-
  xMueller, Gustav.
    Instead of a Biography. Philos Lib.
Mueller, Henry R. see Mueller, Henry Richard.
Mueller, Henry Richard, 1887-1937
  xMueller, Henry R.
    Whig Party in Pennsylvania. AMS Pr.
Mueller, Herbert C.
  xMueller, Herbert C.
    Learning to Teach Through Playing: A Brass
      Method. A-W.
Mueller, Ivan I. see Mueller, Ivan Istvan.
Mueller, Ivan Istvan.
  xMueller, Ivan I.
    Introduction to Surveying. Ungar.
Mueller, John. see Mueller, John E.
Mueller, John E.
  xMueller, John.
    Dance Film Directory: An Annotated &
      Evaluative Guide to Films on Ballet &
      Modern Dance. Princeton Bk Co.
Mueller, John H. see Mueller, John Henry.
Mueller, John Henry, 1895-
  xMueller, John H.
    The American Symphony Orchestra: A Social
      History of Musical Taste. Greenwood.
    Statistical Reasoning in Sociology. HM.
Mueller, John T. see Mueller, John Theodore.
Mueller, John Theodore, 1885-
  xMueller, John T.
    Great Missionaries to China. Arno.
    Great Missionaries to the Orient. Arno.
Mueller, Kate (Hevner), 1898-
  xMueller, Kate H.
    Twenty-Seven Major American Symphony
      Orchestras: A History & Analysis of Their
      Repertoires, Seasons 1842-43 Through
      1969-1970. Ind U Pr.
Mueller, Kate H. see Mueller, Kate (Hevner).
Mueller, Lisel.
  xMueller, Lisel.
    Life of a Queen. Juniper Pr WI.
Mueller, Max G. see Mueller, Max Gerhard.
Mueller, Max Gerhard, 1927-
  xMueller, Max G.
    ed. Readings in Macroeconomics. HR&W.
Mueller, Pat.
  xMueller, Pat.
    Intramural-Recreational Sports: Programming &
      Administration. Wiley.
Mueller, Robert K. see Mueller, Robert Kirk.
Mueller, Robert Kirk.
  xMueller, Robert K.
    Board Compass: What It Means to Be a
      Director in a Changing World. Lexington
      Bks.
Mueller, W. see Mueller, William Joseph.
Mueller, Walter, 1932-
  xMueller, Walter.
    Grammatical Aids for Students of New
      Testament Greek. Eerdmans.
Mueller, Willard F. see Mueller, Willard Fritz.
Mueller, Willard Fritz.
  xMueller, Willard F.
    Primer on Monopoly & Competition. Random.
Mueller, William Joseph, 1927-
  xMueller, W.
    Avenues to Understanding: Dynamics of
      Therapeutic Interactions. P-H.
Mueller, William R.
  xMueller, William R.

Anatomy of Robert Burton's England. Folcroft.
Muench, Bonnie. see Muench, David.
Muench, David.
  xMuench, Bonnie.
    illus. Sierra Nevada. Graphic Arts Ctr.
  xMuench, David.
    Arizona. Rand.
    photos by Colorado. Graphic Arts Ctr.
    Colorado. Rand.
    Lewis & Clark Country. Beautiful Am.
    The National Parks. Rand.
    photos by Sierra Nevada. Graphic Arts Ctr.
    photos by Utah. Graphic Arts Ctr.
Muench, Josef.
  xMuench, Josef.
    photos by Arizona II. Graphic Arts Ctr.
Muench, K. H. see Muench, Karl H.
Muench, Karl H.
  xMuench, K. H.
    ed. The Genetic Basis for Human Disease.
      Elsevier.
Mueser, Anne M. see Mueser, Anne Marie.
Mueser, Anne Marie.
  xMueser, Anne M.
    The Picture Story of Jockey Steve Cauthen.
      Messner.
Muessig, Raymond. see Muessig, Raymond Henry.
Muessig, Raymond Henry.
  xMuessig, Raymond.
    Aphorisms on Education. Phi Delta Kappa.
Muetterties, Earl L.
  xMuetterties, Earl L.
    ed. Boron Hydride Chemistry. Acad Pr.
Muffoletto, Anna.
  xMuffoletto, Anna.
    Art of Sicilian Cooking. Doubleday.
Mufti, I. H.
  xMufti, I. H.
    Computational Methods in Optimal Control
      Problems. Springer-Verlag.
Muga, Bruce J. see Muga, Bruce Jennings.
Muga, Bruce Jennings.
  xMuga, Bruce J.
    Dynamic Analysis of Ocean Structures. Plenum
      Pub.
Mugge, M. see Mugge, Maximilian August.
Mugge, Maximilian A. see Mugge, Maximilian August.
Mugge, Maximilian August, 1878-
  xMugge, M.
    Friedrich Nietzsche. Gordon Pr.
  xMugge, Maximilian A.
    Friedrich Nietzsche. Kennikat.
Muggenthaler, August K. see Muggenthaler, August Karl.
Muggenthaler, August Karl, 1927-
  xMuggenthaler, August K.
    German Raiders of World War II. P-H.
Muggeridge, Malcolm, 1903-
  xMuggeridge, Malcolm.
    Christ & the Media. Eerdmans.
    Earnest Atheist: A Study of Samuel Butler.
      Haskell.
    Earnest Atheist: A Study of Samuel Butler. R
      West.
    Something Beautiful for God: Mother Teresa of
      Calcutta. Doubleday.
    Things Past. Morrow.
    A Third Testament. Little.
    A Twentieth Century Testimony. Nelson.
Muggia, Franco. see Muggia, Franco M.
Muggia, Franco M.
  xMuggia, Franco.
    ed. Lung Cancer: Progress in Therapeutic
      Research. Raven.
Mugglestone, Patricia.
  xMugglestone, Patricia.
    Planning & Using the Blackboard. Allen
      Unwin.
Mughisuddin, Mohammed.
  xMughisuddin, Mohammed.

    ed. Conflict & Cooperation in the Persian Gulf.
      Praeger.
Mugnier, George F. see Mugnier, George Francois.
Mugnier, George Francois.
  xMugnier, George F.
    Louisiana Images, 1880-1920: A Photographic
      Essay. La State U Pr.
Muhlen, Herbert. see Muhlen, Heribert.
Muhlen, Heribert.
  xMuhlen, Herbert.
    A Charismatic Theology: Initiation in the
      Spirit. Paulist Pr.
Muhler, Joseph C. see Muhler, Joseph Charles.
Muhler, Joseph Charles.
  xMuhler, Joseph C.
    ed. Fluorine & Dental Health: The
      Pharmacology & Toxicology of Fluorine.
      Kennikat.
Muhly, James D. see Muhly, James David.
Muhly, James David.
  xMuhly, James D.
    Copper & Tin: The Distribution of Mineral
      Resources & the Nature of the Metals Trade
      in the Bronze Age, Including Supplement.
      Shoe String.
Muir, Edward.
  xMuir, Edward.
    The Social Studies Student Investigates
      American Law. Rosen Pr.
Muir, Edwin, 1887-1959
  xMuir, Edwin.
    Collected Poems. Oxford U Pr.
    Estate of Poetry. Harvard U Pr.
    Politics of King Lear. Folcroft.
    The Politics of King Lear. Gordon Pr.
    Politics of King Lear. Haskell.
Muir, Frank.
  xMuir, Frank.
    Christmas Customs & Traditions. Taplinger.
    What-A-Mess, the Good. Doubleday.
Muir, I. F. see Muir, Ian Fraser Kerr.
Muir, Ian Fraser Kerr.
  xMuir, I. F.
    Burns & Their Treatment. Year Bk Med.
Muir, John, 1838-1914
  xMuir, John.
    The Cruise of the Corwin: Journal of the Arctic
      Expedition of 1881 in Search of De Long &
      the Jeannette. Larlin Corp.
    Gentle Wilderness: The Sierra Nevada. Sierra.
    My First Summer in the Sierra. HM.
    My First Summer in the Sierra. Larlin Corp.
    Our National Parks. AMS Pr.
    Our National Parks. Scholarly.
    Our National Parks. Scholars Ref Lib.
    Steep Trails. Larlin Corp.
    Stickeen. Larlin Corp.
    Stickeen. R West.
    Stickeen: The Story of a Dog. Doubleday.
    Travels in Alaska. AMS Pr.
    Travels in Alaska. HM.
    Travels in Alaska. Scholarly.
    Wilderness Essays. Peregrine Smith.
Muir, Kenneth.
  xMuir, Kenneth.
    An Introduction to Elizabethan Literature.
      Phila Bk Co.
    Shakespeare's Comic Sequence. B&N.
    Shakespeare's Sonnets. Allen Unwin.
    Shakespeare's Tragic Sequence. B&N.
    The Sources of Shakespeare's Plays. Yale U Pr.
Muir, M. M. see Muir, Matthew Moncrieff Pattison.
Muir, Matthew Moncrieff Pattison, 1848-1931
  xMuir, M. M.
    A History of Chemical Theories & Laws. Arno.
Muir, Ramsay, 1872-1941
  xMuir, Ramsay.

America the Golden. Arno.
Expansion of Europe: The Culmination of
Modern History. Kennikat.
Interdependent World & Its Problems.
Kennikat.
Muir, William.
xMuir, William.
The Life of Mohammad from Original Sources.
AMS Pr.
Muir, William K.
xMuir, William K.
Prayer in the Public Schools: Law & Attitude
Change. U of Chicago Pr.
Muirden, James.
xMuirden, James.
Astronomy with Binoculars. T Y Crowell.
Muirhead, Desmond.
xMuirhead, Desmond.
Palms. King.
Muirhead, H. see Muirhead, Hugh.
Muirhead, Hugh.
xMuirhead, H.
Notes on Elementary Particle Physics.
Pergamon.
Muirhead, James F. see Muirhead, James Fullarton.
Muirhead, James Fullarton, 1853-1934
xMuirhead, James F.
America the Land of Contrasts: A Briton's
View of His American Kin. Da Capo.
Muirhead, John H. see Muirhead, John Henry.
Muirhead, John Henry, 1855-1940
xMuirhead, John H.
The Use of Philosophy: Californian Addresses.
Greenwood.
Mujeeb, Mohammed, 1902-
xMujeeb, Mohammed.
World History: Our Heritage. Asia.
Mujica, Francisco.
xMujica, Francisco.
History of the Skyscraper. Da Capo.
Mujumdar, A S.
xMujumdar, Arun S.
ed. Advances in Drying. Hemisphere Pub.
Mujumdar, Arun S. see Mujumdar, A. S.
Mukarovsky, Jan.
xMukarovsky, Jan.
The Word & Verbal Art: Selected Essays by
Jan Mukarovsky. Yale U Pr.
Mukasa, Ham.
xMukasa, Ham.
Uganda's Katikiro in England. Arno.
Mukerjee, Radhakamal, 1889-
xMukerjee, Radhakamal.
Destiny of Civilization. Asia.
Mukerji, Dhan G. see Mukerji, Dhan Gopal.
Mukerji, Dhan Gopal.
xMukerji, Dhan G.
Gay-Neck: The Story of a Pigeon. Dutton.
Mukherjea, A.
xMukherjea, A.
ed. Real & Functional Analysis. Plenum Pub.
Mukherjea, A. see Mukherjea, Arunava.
Mukherjea, Arunava.
xMukherjea, A.
Measures on Topological Semi-Groups:
Convolution Products & Random Walks.
Springer-Verlag.
Mukherjee, K. K. see Mukherjee, Krishna Kumar.
Mukherjee, Kanai L.
xMukherjee, Kanai L.
Introductory Mathematics for the Clinical
Laboratory. Am Soc Clinical.
xMukherjee, Kanai Lai.
Review of Clinical Laboratory Methods: A Key
Word Index System. Mosby.
Mukherjee, Kanai Lai. see Mukherjee, Kanai L.
Mukherjee, Krishna Kumar, 1928-
xMukherjee, K. K.

Economics for Engineers. Asia.
Mukherjee, Sudhansu B. see Mukherjee, Sudhansu
Bhusan.
Mukherjee, Sudhansu Bhusan, 1923-
xMukherjee, Sudhansu B.
The Age Distribution of the Indian Population:
A Reconstruction for the States & Territories,
1881-1961. U Pr of Hawaii.
Mukherji, A. K. see Mukherji, Anil K.
Mukherji, Anil K.
xMukherji, A. K.
Analytical Chemistry of Zirconium & Hafnium.
Pergamon.
Mukhia, Harbans.
xMukhia, Harbans.
Historians & Historiography During the Reign
of Akbar. Verry.
Mulac, Margaret E. see Mulac, Margaret Elizabeth.
Mulac, Margaret Elizabeth, 1912-
xMulac, Margaret E.
Educational Games for Fun. Har-Row.
Perceptual Games & Activities. Har-Row.
Mulcahy, Kevin V.
xMulcahy, Kevin V.
America Votes: What You Should Know About
Elections Today. P-H.
Mulcahy, Risteard.
xMulcahy, Risteard.
Beat Heart Disease!. Arco.
Mulder. see Mulder, Carol Woodbridge.
Mulder, Carol Woodbridge.
xMulder.
Imported Foundation Stock of North American
Arabian Horses. Borden.
Mulder, J. W. see Mulder, Johannes Wilhelmus
Franciscus.
Mulder, Johannes Wilhelmus Franciscus.
xMulder, J. W.
Theory of the Linguistic Sign. Mouton.
Mulder, John M.
xMulder, John M.
Religion in American History: Interpretive
Essays. P-H.
Woodrow Wilson: The Years of Preparation.
Princeton U Pr.
Mulder, Mauk.
xMulder, Mauk.
The Daily Power Game. Kluwer Boston.
Mulder, Ronald A.
xMulder, Ronald A.
The Insurgent Progressives in the United States
Senate & the New Deal, 1933-1939. Garland
Pub.
Mulder, William.
xMulder, William.
ed. Among the Mormons: Historic Accounts by
Contemporary Observers. U of Nebr Pr.
Muldoon, James, 1935-
xMuldoon, James.
ed. The Expansion of Europe: The First Phase.
U of Pa Pr.
Muldoon, Paul.
xMuldoon, Paul.
Mules. Wake Forest.
Mulford, Clarence. see Mulford, Clarence Edward.
Mulford, Clarence Edward, 1883-
xMulford, Clarence.
Hopalong Cassidy. Amereon Ltd.
Hopalong Cassidy & the Eagles Brood.
Amereon Ltd.
Hopalong Cassidy Returns. Amereon Ltd.
Hopalong Cassidy Serves a Writ. Amereon Ltd.
Hopalong Cassidy Takes Cards. Amereon Ltd.
Hopalong Cassidy's Protege. Amereon Ltd.
On the Trail of the Tumbling T. Amereon Ltd.
Orphan. Amereon Ltd.
Mulford, David C.
xMulford, David C.

Northern Rhodesia General Election, 1962.
Oxford U Pr.
Mulford, Elisha, 1833-1885
xMulford, Elisha.
Nation: The Foundations of Civil Order &
Political Life in the United States. Kelley.
Mulgan, Alan. see Mulgan, Alan Edward.
Mulgan, Alan Edward, 1881-1962
xMulgan, Alan.
Literature & Authorship in New Zealand.
Folcroft.
Mulgan, John, 1911-1945
xMulgan, John.
An Introduction to English Literature. Arden
Lib.
Mulhall, M. G. see Mulhall, Michael George.
Mulhall, Michael G. see Mulhall, Michael George.
Mulhall, Michael George, 1836-1900
xMulhall, M. G.
Dictionary of Statistics. Gordon Pr.
xMulhall, Michael G.
Dictionary of Statistics. Gale.
The English in South America. Arno.
Industries & Wealth of Nations. Johnson Repr.
Mulhauser, Roland. see Mulhauser, Roland A.
Mulhauser, Roland A.
xMulhauser, Roland.
More Vitamins & Minerals with Fewer
Calories. C E Tuttle.
xMulhauser, Roland A.
This Will Kill You Cookbook. C E Tuttle.
Mulhauser, Ruth E., 1913-
xMulhauser, Ruth E.
Maurice Sceve. Twayne.
Mulhearn, John.
xMulhearn, John.
The Psychiatric Hospital Today: A Quality
Profile. Ballinger Pub.
Mulhern, James, 1890-
xMulhern, James.
History of Secondary Education in
Pennsylvania. Arno.
Mulholland, Jim.
xMulholland, Jim.
Abbott & Costello Book. Popular Lib.
Mulholland, John, 1898-
xMulholland, John.
Beware Familiar Spirits. Arno.
Mulkay, Michael. see Mulkay, Michael Joseph.
Mulkay, Michael Joseph.
xMulkay, Michael.
Science & the Sociology of Knowledge. Allen
Unwin.
Mullan, Sean.
xMullan, Sean.
Essentials of Neurosurgery for Students &
Practitioners. Springer Pub.
Mullaney, Sean.
xMullaney, Sean.
Taking up Sculpture. Taplinger.
Mullany, Peter F.
xMullany, Peter F.
Religion & the Artifice of Jacobean & Caroline
Drama. Humanities.
Mullard, Chris, 1944-
xMullard, Chris.
On Being Black in Britain. Inscape Corp.
Mullen, Chris.
xMullen, Chris.
Cigarette Pack Art. St Martin.
Mullen, Edward J., 1942-
xMullen, Edward J.
Carlos Pellicer. Twayne.
Evaluation of Social Intervention. Jossey-Bass.
Mullen, Frank. see Mullen, William F.
Mullen, John. see Mullen, John Joseph.
Mullen, John Joseph.
xMullen, John.

In a Year of Our Lord: A Memoir of American
Innocence. Arbor Hse.

Mullen, Thomas James, 1934-
xMullen, Tom.
Parables for Parents & Other Original Sinners.
Word Bks.
Mullen, Tom. see Mullen, Thomas James.

Mullen, William F.
xMullen, Frank.
ed. The Government & Politics of Washington
State. Wash St U Pr.
xMullen, William F.
Presidential Power & Politics. St Martin.

Mullenbach, Philip.
xMullenbach, Philip.
Civilian Nuclear Power: Economic Issues &
Policy Formation. Kraus Repr.

Mullenix, Dennis.
xMullenix, Dennis.
Antiques: A Browser's Handbook. Har-Row.

Muller, Alois, 1924-
xMuller, Alois.
Catechetics for the Future. Seabury.
Democratization of the Church. Seabury.
Ongoing Reform of the Church. Seabury.

Muller, Antal.
xMuller, Antal.
Quantum Mechanics: A Physical World
Picture. Pergamon.

Muller, Charles R.
xMuller, Charles R.
The Shaker Way. Ohio Antique Rev.

Muller, Charlotte (Feldman), 1921-
xMuller, Charlotte F.
Light Metals Monopoly. AMS Pr.
Muller, Charlotte F. see Muller, Charlotte (Feldman).
Muller, E. see Muller, Edward John.

Muller, Edward J.
xMuller, Edward J.
Architectural Drawing & Light Construction.
P-H.
Muller, Edward J. see Muller, Edward John.

Muller, Edward John, 1916-
xMuller, E.
Reading Architectural Working Drawings. P-H.
xMuller, Edward J.
Reading Architectural Working Drawings. P-H.
Muller, F. M. see Muller, Frits Mari.

Muller, Frits Mari, 1907-
xMuller, F. M.
Seedlings of the North-Western European
Lowland: A Flora of Seedlings. Unipub.

Muller, Gilbert H.
xMuller, Gilbert H.
The Short Prose Reader. McGraw.

Muller, H. G. see Muller, Hans Gerd.

Muller, H. J. see Muller, Hermann Joseph.

Muller, Hans Gerd, 1928-
xMuller, H. G.
An Introduction to Food Rheology.
Crane-Russak Co.
Muller, Herbert J. see Muller, Herbert Joseph.

Muller, Herbert Joseph, 1905-
xMuller, Herbert J.
Children of Frankenstein: A Primer on Modern
Technology & Human Values. Ind U Pr.
Religion & Freedom in the Modern World. U
of Chicago Pr.
Uses of the Past: Profiles of Former Societies.
Oxford U Pr.

Muller, Hermann, 1829-1883
xMuller, Hermann.
The Fertilisation of Flowers. Arno.
Muller, Hermann J. see Muller, Hermann Joseph.

Muller, Hermann Joseph.
xMuller, H. J.
Studies in Genetics: The Selected Papers of H.
J. Muller. Ind U Pr.
xMuller, Hermann J.

The Modern Concept of Nature. State U NY
Pr.
Muller, James A. see Muller, James Arthur.

Muller, James Arthur, 1884-1945
xMuller, James A.
Stephen Gardiner & the Tudor Reaction.
Octagon.

Muller, Jorg.
xMuller, Jorg.
The Changing City. Atheneum.
The Changing Countryside. Atheneum.

Muller, Joseph Emile.
xMuller, Joseph-Emile.
A Century of Modern Painting. L Amiel Pub.
Velazquez. Transatlantic.
Muller, Joseph-Emile. see Muller, Joseph Emile.
Muller, Karl O. see Muller, Karl Otfried.

Muller, Karl Otfried.
xMuller, Karl O.
History of the Literature of Ancient Greece.
Kennikat.
Introduction to a Scientific System of
Mythology. Arno.

Muller, Peter O.
xMuller, Peter O.
The Outer City: Geographical Consequences of
the Urbanization of the Suburbs. Assn Am
Geographers.

Muller, Philippe.
xMuller, Philippe.
Tasks of Childhood. McGraw.

Muller, Richard S.
xMuller, Richard S.
Device Electronics for Integrated Circuits.
Wiley.
Muller, Rudolf O. see Muller, Rudolf Olimpio.

Muller, Rudolf Olimpio.
xMuller, Rudolf O.
Spectrochemical Analysis by X-Ray
Fluorescence. Plenum Pub.
Muller, Theresa G. see Muller, Theresa Grace.

Muller, Theresa Grace.
xMuller, Theresa G.
Fundamentals of Psychiatric Nursing.
Littlefield.

Muller, Thomas.
xMuller, Thomas.
Fiscal Impacts of Land Development: A
Critique of Methods & Review of Issues.
Urban Inst.

Muller, Walter H.
xMuller, Walter H.
Botany: A Functional Approach. Macmillan.

Muller-Reuter, Theodor, 1858-1919
xMuller-Reuter, Theodor.
Lexikon der Deutschen Konzertliteratur. Da
Capo.
Mullett, Charles F. see Mullett, Charles Frederic.

Mullett, Charles Frederic, 1902-
xMullett, Charles F.
Fundamental Law & the American Revolution,
1760-1776. Octagon.

Mullick, K. S.
xMullick, K. S.
Tangled Tapes: The Inside Story of Indian
Broadcasting. South Asia Bks.

Mulligan, Bill, 1942-
xMulligan, Bill.
The Vegetable Gardener's Answer Book. Van
Nos Reinhold.

Mulligan, James J.
xMulligan, James J.
The Christian Experience. Alba.
Mulligan, Joseph F. see Mulligan, Joseph Francis.

Mulligan, Joseph Francis, 1920-
xMulligan, Joseph F.
Practical Physics: The Production &
Conservation of Energy. McGraw.

Mulligan, Mary.
xMulligan, Mary.

Denver Guidebook. Johnson Colo.
Mulligan, Mary A. see Mulligan, Mary Ann.

Mulligan, Mary Ann.
xMulligan, Mary A.
Integrating Music with Other Studies. Ctr Appl
Res.

Mullin, Donald C.
xMullin, Donald C.
The Development of the Playhouse: A Survey
of Theatre Architecture from the Renaissance
to the Present. U of Cal Pr.

Mullin, Michael.
xMullin, Michael.
Compiled by Theatre at Stratford-Upon-Avon:
A Catalogue-Index to Productions of the
Shakespeare Memorial-Royal Shakespeare
Theatre, 1879 to 1978. Greenwood.

Mullin, Ray C.
xMullin, Ray C.
Electrical Wiring Residential: Code, Theory,
Plans Specifications, Installation Methods.
Van Nos Reinhold.

Mullin, Virginia L.
xMullin, Virginia L.
Chemistry Experiments for Children. Dover.

Mullin, William F., 1921-
xMullin, William F.
ABC's of Capacitors. Sams.

Mullings, Llewellyn M.
xMullings, Llewellyn M.
Economic Development. Mss Info.

Mullins, Carolyn J.
xMullins, Carolyn J.
A Guide to Writing & Publishing in the Social
& Behavioral Sciences. Wiley.
Mullins, Edgar Y. see Mullins, Edgar Young.

Mullins, Edgar Young, 1860-1928
xMullins, Edgar Y.
Baptist Beliefs. Judson.

Mullins, Hugh A, 1886-
xMullins, Hugh A.
Marine Insurance Digest. Cornell Maritime.

Mullins, June.
xMullins, June B.
A Teacher's Guide to Management of
Physically Handicapped Students. C C
Thomas.
Mullins, June B. see Mullins, June.

Mullish, Henry.
xMullish, Henry.
A Business-Like Approach to Cobol. Har-Row.
The Complete Pocket Calculator Handbook.
Macmillan.
How to Get the Most Out of Your Pocket
Calculator. Macmillan.
Introduction to Computer Programming.
Gordon.

Mulloy, Elizabeth D.
xMulloy, Elizabeth D.
The History of the National Trust for Historic
Preservation, 1963-1973. Preservation Pr.

Multhauf, Robert P.
xMulthauf, Robert P.
Neptune's Gift: A History of Common Salt.
Johns Hopkins.
The Origins of Chemistry. N Watson.
Mulvaney, J. E. see Mulvaney, John Edward.

Mulvaney, John Edward.
xMulvaney, J. E.
Practical Business Models. Halsted Pr.

Mulvey, Charles.
xMulvey, Charles.
The Economic Analysis of Trade Unions. St
Martin.
Mulvey, Mary D. see Mulvey, Mary Doris.

Mulvey, Mary Doris, Sister.
xMulvey, Mary D.
French Catholic Missionaries in the Present
United States (1604-1791). AMS Pr.
Mulvey, Ruth W. see Mulvey, Ruth Watt.

The Beggar Maid: Stories of Flo & Rose. Knopf.

Munro, Alistair.
xMunro, A.
Psychiatry for Social Workers. Pergamon.
Munro, Dana G. *see* Munro, Dana Gardner.
Munro, Dana Gardner, 1892-
xMunro, Dana G.
Five Republics of Central America: Their Political & Economic Development & Their Relations with the United States. Russell.
Munro, Donald J.
xMunro, Donald J.
The Concept of Man in Contemporary China. U of Mich Pr.
The Concept of Man in Early China. Stanford U Pr.
Munro, Douglas.
xMunro, Douglas.
Alexandre Dumas Pere: A Bibliography of Works Translated into English to 1910. Garland Pub.
Munro, J. Forbes.
xMunro, J. Forbes.
Africa & the International Economy, 1800-1960: An Introduction to the Modern Economic History of Africa South of the Sahara. Rowman.
Colonial Rule & the Kamba: Social Change in the Kenya Highlands 1889-1939. Oxford U Pr.
Munro, Jim L.
xMunro, Jim L.
Administrative Behavior & Police Organization. Anderson Pub Co.
Classes, Conflict & Control: Studies in Criminal Justice Management. Anderson Pub Co.
Munro, John.
xMunro, John.
A Trip to Venus: A Novel. Hyperion Conn.
Munro, John M.
xMunro, John M.
A Mutual Concern: The Story of the American University of Beirut. Caravan Bks.
Munro, Margaret.
xMunro, Margaret.
The Psychology & Education of the Young: A Guide to the Principles of Development, Learning & Assessment. Heinemann Ed.
Munro, Neil G. *see* Munro, Neil Gordon.
Munro, Neil Gordon.
xMunro, Neil G.
Prehistoric Japan. Johnson Repr.
Munro, William B. *see* Munro, William Bennett.
Munro, William Bennett, 1875-1957
xMunro, William B.
ed. Documents Relating to the Seigniorial Tenure in Canada, 1598-1854. Greenwood.
Munroe, C. J.
xMunroe, C. J.
The Smallholder's Guide. David & Charles.
Munroe, John A., 1914-
xMunroe, John A.
Colonial Delaware: A History. Kraus Intl.
History of Delaware. U Delaware Pr.
Munroe, Robert L.
xMunroe, Robert L.
Cross-Cultural Human Development. Brooks-Cole.
xMunroe, Ruth H.
jt. auth. Cross-Cultural Human Development. Brooks-Cole.
Munroe, Ruth H. *see* Munroe, Robert L.
Munrow, David.
xMunrow, David.
Instruments of the Middle Ages & Renaissance. Oxford U Pr.
Munsell, Joel, 1808-1880
xMunsell, Joel.

Chronology of the Origin & Progress of Paper & Paper-Making. Garland Pub.

Munsey, Cecil.
xMunsey, Cecil.
The Illustrated Guide to Collecting Bottles. Dutton.
Munshower. *see* Munshower, Suzanne L.
Munshower, Suzanne L.
xMunshower.
Diane Keaton Scrapbook. G&D.
Munsinger, Harry.
xMunsinger, Harry.
Fundamentals of Child Development. HR&W.
Readings in Child Development. HR&W.
Munson, Amelia H.
xMunson, Amelia H.
Ample Field: Books & Young People. ALA.
Munson, Carlton E.
xMunson, Carlton E.
ed. Social Work Supervision: Classic Statements & Critical Issues. Free Pr.
Munson, Charles J.
xMunson, Charles J.
Westward to Paradise. U Pr of Idaho.
Munson, Dee.
xMunson, Dee.
ed. The Canning & Freezing Book. Delair.
Munson, Gorham B. *see* Munson, Gorham Bert.
Munson, Gorham Bert, 1896-1969
xMunson, Gorham B.
Destinations: A Canvass of American Literature Since 1900. AMS Pr.
Destinations: A Canvass of American Literature Since 1900. Scholarly.
The Dilemma of the Liberated: An Interpretation of Twentieth Century Humanism. Kennikat.
Style & Form in American Prose. Kennikat.
Munson, Kenneth. *see* Munson, Kenneth G.
Munson, Kenneth G.
xMunson, Kenneth.
Fighters in Service: Attack & Training Aircraft Since 1960. Macmillan.
xMunson, Kenneth G.
Famous Aircraft of All Time. Arco.
Munson, Ron. *see* Munson, Ronald.
Munson, Ronald, 1939-
xMunson, Ron.
Intervention & Reflection: Basic Issues in Medical Ethics. Wadsworth Pub.
Munson, Thomas N.
xMunson, Thomas N.
Reflective Theology: Philosophical Orientations in Religion. Greenwood.
Munson, Tunie.
xMunson, Tunie.
A Fistful of Sun. Lothrop.
Munster, Andrew. *see* Munster, Andrew M.
Munster, Andrew M., 1935-
xMunster, Andrew.
Burn Care for the House Officer. Williams & Wilkins.
xMunster, Andrew M.
Surgical Anatomy for Clinical Examination. C C Thomas.
ed. Surgical Immunology. Grune.
Munsterberg, Hugo, 1863-1916
xMunsterberg, Hugo.

American Patriotism, and Other Social Studies. Arno.
American Problems, from the Point of View of a Psychologist. Arno.
The Art of Modern Japan: From the Meiji Restoration to the Meiji Centennial, 1868-1968. Hacker.
Arts of Japan: An Illustrated History. C E Tuttle.
Folk Arts of Japan. C E Tuttle.
The History of Women Artists. Potter.
Psychology & Industrial Efficiency. Arno.
Psychology & Industrial Efficiency. Hive Pub.
Munsterberg, Margarete. *see* Munsterberg, Margarete Anna Adelheid.
Munsterberg, Margarete Anna Adelheid, 1889-
xMunsterberg, Margarete.
ed. A Harvest of German Verse. Granger Bk.
Munsterhjelm, Erik, 1905-
xMunsterhjelm, Erik.
A Dog Named Wolf. Dell.
Munthe, Wilhelm, 1883-
xMunthe, Wilhelm.
American Librarianship from a European Angle: An Attempt at the Evaluation of Policies & Activities. Shoe String.
Munts, Raymond, 1923-
xMunts, Raymond.
Bargaining for Health: Labor Unions, Health Insurance, & Medical Care. U of Wis Pr.
Muntzing, L. Manning.
xMuntzing, L. Manning.
International Instruments of Nuclear Technology Transfer. Am Nuclear Soc.
Munves, James.
xMunves, James.
The FBI & the CIA: Secret Agents & American Democracy. HarBraceJ.
Thomas Jefferson & the Declaration of Independence. Scribner.
The Treasure of Diogenes Sampuez. Schol Bk Serv.
Munz, Peter, 1921-
xMunz, Peter.
Place of Hooker in the History of Thought. Greenwood.
When the Golden Bough Breaks: Structuralism or Typology?. Routledge & Kegan.
Munz, Philip A. *see* Munz, Philip Alexander.
Munz, Philip Alexander, 1892-
xMunz, Philip A.
California Desert Wildflowers. U of Cal Pr.
California Spring Wildflowers: From the Base of the Sierra Nevada & Southern Mountains to the Sea. U of Cal Pr.
A Flora of Southern California. U of Cal Pr.
Munzert, Alfred. *see* Munzert, Alfred W.
Munzert, Alfred W.
xMunzert, Alfred.
National Directory of External Degree Programs. Dutton.
xMunzert, Alfred W.
National Directory of External Degree Programs. Hemisphere NY.
Muppet Show.
xMuppet Show People.
The Muppet Show Book. Bantam.
Muppet Show People. *see* Muppet Show.
Murach, Mike.
xMurach, Mike.
Business Data Processing. SRA.
Standard COBOL. SRA.
Murakami, S. *see* Murakami, Shingo.
Murakami, Shingo.
xMurakami, S.
On Automorphisms of Siegel Domains. Springer-Verlag.
Murakami, Y. *see* Murakami, Yasusuke.
Murakami, Yasusuke, 1931-
xMurakami, Y.

Logic & Social Choice. Routledge & Kegan.
Muraoka, Kageo.
  xMuraoka, Kageo.
    Folk Arts & Crafts of Japan. Weatherhill.
Murari, Timeri.
  xMurari, Timeri.
    Lovers Are Not People. Morrow.
    The Oblivion Tapes. Berkley Pub.
Murase, Miyeko.
  xMurase, Miyeko.
    The Arts of Japan. McGraw.
Murat, Felix.
  xMurat, Felix.
    The Last Days of the U. S. A.,. F Murat.
Murat, J. see Murat, Jacques.
Murat, Jacques.
  xMurat, J.
    A Lover's Cock & Other Gay Poems.
      Bookpeople.
Murayama, T. see Murayama, Takayuki.
Murayama, Takayuki.
  xMurayama, T.
    Dynamic Mechanical Analysis of Polymeric
      Material. Elsevier.
Murbarger, Nell, 1909-
  xMurbarger, Nell.
    Sovereigns of the Sage: True Stories of People
      & Places in the Great Sagebrush Kingdom of
      the Western United States. Treasure Chest.
Murch, Alma E. see Murch, Alma Elizabeth.
Murch, Alma Elizabeth.
  xMurch, Alma E.
    Development of the Detective Novel.
      Greenwood.
Murch, Gerald M., 1940-
  xMurch, Gerald M.
    ed. Studies in Perception. Bobbs.
Murchie, Guy, 1907-
  xMurchie, Guy.
    Music of the Spheres: The Material Universe
      from Atom to Quasar, Simply Explained.
      Peter Smith.
    Music of the Spheres: The Material Universe
      from Atom to Quasar, Simply Explained.
      Dover.
Murchison, Carl. see Murchison, Carl Allanmore.
Murchison, Carl A. see Murchison, Carl Allanmore.
Murchison, Carl Allanmore, 1887-
  xMurchison, Carl.
    The Case for and Against Psychical Belief.
      Arno.
    ed. Foundations of Experimental Psychology.
      Johnson Repr.
  xMurchison, Carl A.
    ed. Handbook of General Experimental
      Psychology. Russell.
Murchison, Irene.
  xMurchison, Irene.
    Legal Accountability in the Nursing Process.
      Mosby.
Murchison, Irene A.
  xMurchison, Irene A.
    Legal Foundations of Nursing Practice.
      Macmillan.
Murck, Christian F.
  xMurck, Christian F.
    ed. Artists & Traditions: Uses of the Past in
      Chinese Culture. Princeton U Pr.
Murdick, Robert. see Murdick, Robert G.
Murdick, Robert C. see Murdick, Robert G.
Murdick, Robert G.
  xMurdick, Robert.
    Accounting Information Systems. P-H.
  xMurdick, Robert C.
    Introduction to Management Information
      Systems. P-H.
  xMurdick, Robert G.

Business Policy: A Framework for Analysis.
  Grid Pub.
Information Systems for Modern Management.
  P-H.
Murdoch, David C. see Murdoch, David Carruthers.
Murdoch, David Carruthers.
  xMurdoch, David C.
    Linear Algebra. Wiley.
Murdoch, Iris.
  xMurdoch, Iris.
    Bruno's Dream. Penguin.
    The Nice & the Good. Penguin.
    The Sea, the Sea. Penguin.
    The Sea, the Sea. Viking Pr.
    A Word Child. Penguin.
    A Word Child. Viking Pr.
Murdoch, Joseph S. see Murdoch, Joseph S. F.
Murdoch, Joseph S. F.
  xMurdoch, Joseph S.
    ed. Golf: A Guide to Information Sources.
      Gale.
Murdock, Carol. see Murdock, Carol Vevjoda.
Murdock, Carol Vevjoda.
  xMurdock, Carol.
    Single Parents Are People, Too!. Butterick Pub.
Murdock, Clark A.
  xMurdock, Clark A.
    Defense Policy Formation: A Comparative
      Analysis of the McNamara Era. State U NY
      Pr.
Murdock, James. see Murdock, James W.
Murdock, James W.
  xMurdock, James.
    Fluid Mechanics & Its Applications. HM.
Murdock, Kenneth B. see Murdock, Kenneth Ballard.
Murdock, Kenneth Ballard, 1895-
  xMurdock, Kenneth B.
    Increase Mather: The Foremost American
      Puritan. Russell.
Murdock, Steven H.
  xMurdock, Steven H.
    Energy Development in the Western United
      States: Impact on Rural Areas. Praeger.
Murdock, Tony.
  xMurdock, Tony.
    Gymnastics for Girls. Plays.
Mure, G. R. see Mure, Geoffrey Reginald Gilchrist.
Mure, Geoffrey Reginald Gilchrist.
  xMure, G. R.
    Aristotle. Greenwood.
    Idealist Epilogue. Oxford U Pr.
Muret, Charlotte (Touzalin).
  xMuret, Charlotte T.
    French Royalist Doctrines Since the
      Revolution. Octagon.
Muret, Charlotte T. see Muret, Charlotte (Touzalin).
Muret, M. see Muret, Maurice.
Muret, Maurice, 1870-
  xMuret, M.
    The Twilight of the White Races. Gordon Pr.
  xMuret, Maurice.
    Twilight of the White Races. Negro U Pr.
Murfin, Marjorie E.
  xMurfin, Marjorie E.
    Reference Service: An Annotated Bibliographic
      Guide. Libs Unl.
Murfin, Ross C.
  xMurfin, Ross C.
    Swinburne, Hardy, Lawrence, & the Burden of
      Belief. U of Chicago Pr.
Murfree, Mary N. see Murfree, Mary Noailles.
Murfree, Mary Noailles, 1850-1922
  xMurfree, Mary N.

Bushwhackers, & Other Stories. Arno.
In the Tennessee Mountains. Irvington.
In the Tennessee Mountains. U of Tenn Pr.
Prophet of the Great Smoky Mountains. AMS
  Pr.
The Story of Old Fort Loudon. Irvington.
Murg, Gary E.
  xMurg, Gary E.
    Labor Relations Law: Canada, Mexico, &
      Western Europe. PLI.
Murger, Henri.
  xMurger, Henri.
    Latin Quarter: Scenes De la Vie De Boheme.
      Hyperion Conn.
Murgo, John D.
  xMurgo, John D.
    ed. Readings in the Economics of Education.
      Mss Info.
Murguia, Edward.
  xMurguia, Edward.
    Assimilation, Colonialism & the Mexican
      American People. U of Tex Pr.
Murie, Olaus J. see Murie, Olaus Johan.
Murie, Olaus Johan, 1889-1963
  xMurie, Olaus J.
    A Field Guide to Animal Tracks. HM.
Muriuki, Godfrey.
  xMuriuki, Godfrey.
    A History of the Kikuyu 1500-1900. Oxford U
      Pr.
Murnane, Richard J.
  xMurnane, Richard J.
    The Impact of School Resources on the
      Learning of Inner City Children. Ballinger
      Pub.
Muro, Diane P.
  xMuro, Diane P.
    Police Careers for Women. Messner.
Muro, James J.
  xMuro, James J.
    Counseling in the Elementary & Middle
      Schools: A Pragmatic Approach. Wm C
      Brown.
Muroga, Saburo.
  xMuroga, Saburo.
    Logic Design & Switching Theory. Wiley.
Murphey, Cecil. see Murphey, Cecil B.
Murphey, Cecil B.
  xMurphey, Cecil.
    But God Has Promised. Creation Hse.
  xMurphey, Cecil B.
    Somebody Knows I'm Alive. John Knox.
    When in Doubt, Hug 'em: How to Develop a
      Caring Church. John Knox.
Murphey, Rhoads, 1919-
  xMurphey, Rhoads.
    The Outsiders: The Western Experience in
      India & China. U of Mich Pr.
    Patterns on the Earth: Introduction to
      Geography. Rand.
Murphey, Sara.
  xMurphey, Sara.
    Animal Hat Shop. Follett.
Murphey, Wayne K.
  xMurphey, Wayne K.
    Wood As an Industrial Arts Material.
      Pergamon.
Murphy. see Murphy, Joseph.
Murphy, Agnes. see Murphy, Agnes G.
Murphy, Agnes G.
  xMurphy, Agnes.
    Melba: A Biography. Da Capo.
  xMurphy, Agnes G.
    Melba: A Biography. AMS Pr.
Murphy, Arthur E. see Murphy, Arthur Edward.
Murphy, Arthur Edward, 1901-1962
  xMurphy, Arthur E.
    The Uses of Reason. Greenwood.
Murphy, Arthur L.
  xMurphy, Arthur L.

The First Falls on Monday. U of Toronto Pr.
Murphy, Barbara.
  xMurphy, Barbara.
    Thor Heyerdahl & the Reed Boat RA.
      Lippincott.
  xMurphy, Barbara B.
    Home Free. Delacorte.
Murphy, Barbara B. *see* Murphy, Barbara Beasley.
Murphy, Barbara Beasley.
  xMurphy, Barbara B.
    No Place to Run. Archway.
    No Place to Run. Bradbury Pr.
    No Place to Run. PB.
Murphy, Bill. *see* Murphy, William E.
Murphy, Bob.
  xMurphy, Bob.
    Christianity Rubs Holes in My Religion.
      Hunter Bks.
Murphy, Carol R.
  xMurphy, Carol R.
    The Sound of Silence: Moving with T'ai Chi.
      Pendle Hill.
Murphy, Charles F.
  xMurphy, Charles F.
    Working Plans for Working Decoys.
      Winchester Pr.
Murphy, Chester W.
  xMurphy, Chet.
    Advanced Tennis. Wm C Brown.
Murphy, Chet. *see* Murphy, Chester W.
Murphy, Chuck, 1922-
  xMurphy, Chuck.
    Fundamentals of the Faith. Abingdon.
    There's No Business Like God's Business.
      Abingdon.
Murphy, D. J.
  xMurphy, D. J.
    T. J. Ryan: A Political Biography. U of
      Queensland Pr.
Murphy, Daniel B. *see* Murphy, Daniel Barker.
Murphy, Daniel Barker.
  xMurphy, Daniel B.
    Foundations of College Chemistry. Wiley.
Murphy, Dennis D.
  xMurphy, Dennis D.
    Directory of Conservative & Libertarian
      Serials, Publishers, & Freelance Markets. D
      D Murphy.
Murphy, E. A. *see* Murphy, Edmond A.
Murphy, E. Jefferson.
  xMurphy, E. Jefferson.
    Creative Philanthropy: Carnegie Corporation in
      Africa, 1953-74. Tchrs Coll.
    History of African Civilization. Dell.
    History of African Civilization. T Y Crowell.
    Teaching Africa Today: A Handbook for
      Teachers & Curriculum Planners. Schol Bk
      Serv.
    Understanding Africa. T Y Crowell.
Murphy, Earl F. *see* Murphy, Earl Finbar.
Murphy, Earl Finbar, 1928-
  xMurphy, Earl F.
    Energy & Environmental Balance. Pergamon.
Murphy, Edmond A.
  xMurphy, E. A.
    Principles of Genetic Counseling. Year Bk
      Med.
  xMurphy, Edmond A.
    The Logic of Medicine. Johns Hopkins.
    Probability in Medicine. Johns Hopkins.
Murphy, Edward F., 1921-
  xMurphy, Edward F.
    The Crown Treasury of Relevant Quotations.
      Crown.
Murphy, Edward J.
  xMurphy, Edward J.
    Life to the Full. Our Sunday Visitor.
Murphy, Elspeth. *see* Murphy, Elspeth Campbell.
Murphy, Elspeth Campbell.
  xMurphy, Elspeth.

The World Is Me. Cook.
Murphy, Frank D., 1918-
  xMurphy, Frank D.
    Administrative Manual Guidelines for
      Hospitals. G K Hall.
Murphy, Gardner.
  xMurphy, Gardner.
    ed. Asian Psychology. Irvington.
    Challenge of Psychical Research: A Primer of
      Parapsychology. Greenwood.
    Freeing Intelligence Through Teaching: A
      Dialectic of the Rational & the Personal.
      Greenwood.
    Historical Introduction to Modern Psychology.
      HarBraceJ.
    Introduction to Psychology. Greenwood.
    Psychological Thought from Pythagoras to
      Freud: An Informal Introduction. HarBraceJ.
    Public Opinion & the Individual: A
      Psychological Study of Student Attitudes on
      Public Questions, with a Retest Five Years
      Later. Russell.
Murphy, George G. *see* Murphy, George Gregory S.
Murphy, George Gregory S., 1924-
  xMurphy, George G.
    Soviet Mongolia: A Study of the Oldest
      Political Satellite. U of Cal Pr.
Murphy, Gerald. *see* Murphy, Gerald Patrick.
Murphy, Gerald Patrick.
  xMurphy, Gerald.
    ed. Prostatic Cancer. PSG Pub.
Murphy, Gwendolen.
  xMurphy, Gwendolen.
    A Cabinet of Characters. Norwood Edns.
    ed. A Cabinet of Characters. Scholarly.
Murphy, Henry C. *see* Murphy, Henry Cruse.
Murphy, Henry Cruse.
  xMurphy, Henry C.
    Anthology of New Netherland. Friedman.
Murphy, Herta A.
  xMurphy, Herta A.
    Effective Business Communications. McGraw.
Murphy, Howard A. *see* Murphy, Howard Ansley.
Murphy, Howard Ansley.
  xMurphy, Howard A.
    Creative Harmony & Musicianship: An
      Introduction to the Structure of Music. P-H.
Murphy, Jack, 1923-
  xMurphy, Jack.
    Abe & Me. Joyce Pr.
Murphy, James A. *see* Murphy, James Anthony.
Murphy, James Anthony.
  xMurphy, James A.
    ed. Plant Engineering Management. SME.
Murphy, James F., 1932-
  xMurphy, James F.
    Quonsett. Avon.
Murphy, James F. *see* Murphy, James Frederick.
Murphy, James Frederick.
  xMurphy, James F.
    Delivery of Community Leisure Services: An
      Holistic Approach. Lea & Febiger.
    Leisure Service Delivery System: A Modern
      Perspective. Lea & Febiger.
Murphy, James J. *see* Murphy, James Jerome.
Murphy, James Jerome.
  xMurphy, James J.
    Debater's Guide. Bobbs.
    Medieval Rhetoric: A Select Bibliography. U of
      Toronto Pr.
Murphy, James K.
  xMurphy, James K.
    Will N. Harben. Twayne.
Murphy, James L.
  xMurphy, James L.
    An Archeological History of the Hocking
      Valley. Ohio U Pr.
Murphy, James M. *see* Murphy, James Martin.
Murphy, James Martin, 1917-
  xMurphy, James M.

Laws, Courts, & Lawyers: Through the Years
    in Arizona. U of Ariz Pr.
Murphy, Jeffrie G.
  xMurphy, Jeffrie G.
    Punishment & Rehabilitation. Wadsworth Pub.
Murphy, Jim.
  xMurphy, Jim.
    Harold Thinks Big. Crown.
    Rat's Christmas Party. P-H.
    Weird & Wacky Inventions. Crown.
Murphy, John A. *see* Murphy, John Albert.
Murphy, John Albert, 1936-
  xMurphy, John A.
    The Homeowner's Energy Guide: How to Beat
      the Heating Game. T Y Crowell.
Murphy, John D., 1921-
  xMurphy, John D.
    Luganda-English Dictionary. Intl Schol Bk
      Serv.
Murphy, John J. *see* Murphy, John Joseph.
Murphy, John Joseph, 1914-
  xMurphy, John J.
    The Book of Pidgin English. AMS Pr.
Murphy, Joseph, 1898-
  xMurphy.
    Infinite Power for Richer Living. Parker Pub
      So.
    Secrets of the I Ching. P-H.
  xMurphy, Joseph.
    Amazing Laws of Cosmic Mind Power. P-H.
    Amazing Laws of Cosmic Mind Power. P-H.
    Cosmic Power Within You. P-H.
    Great Bible Truths for Human Problems. De
      Vorss.
    How to Attract Money. De Vorss.
    How to Use Your Healing Power. De Vorss.
    Infinite Power for Richer Living. P-H.
    Infinite Power for Richer Living. P-H.
    Peace Within Yourself. De Vorss.
    Power of Your Subconscious Mind. P-H.
    Pray Your Way Through It. De Vorss.
    Psychic Perception: The Magic of Extrasensory
      Power. P-H.
    Psychic Perception: The Magic of Extrasensory
      Power. P-H.
    Secrets of the I Ching. P-H.
Murphy, Joseph Francis.
  xMurphy, Joseph L.
    Spellbound & Other Poems. Devin.
Murphy, Joseph L. *see* Murphy, Joseph Francis.
Murphy, Keith.
  xMurphy, Keith.
    Battle of the Alamo. Raintree Child.
Murphy, Lawrence R., 1942-
  xMurphy, Lawrence R.
    Frontier Crusader-William F. M. Arny.. U of
      Ariz Pr.
Murphy, Leonard J. *see* Murphy, Leonard J. T.
Murphy, Leonard J. T.
  xMurphy, Leonard J.
    History of Urology. C C Thomas.
Murphy, M. A. *see* Murphy, Michael A.
Murphy, M. J. *see* Murphy, Martin J.
Murphy, Mabel (Ansley).
  xMurphy, Mabel A.
    When America Was Young. Arno.
Murphy, Mabel A. *see* Murphy, Mabel (Ansley).
Murphy, Marcy.
  xMurphy, Marcy.
    Handbook of Library Regulations. Dekker.
Murphy, Margaret. *see* Murphy, Margaret Deeds.
Murphy, Margaret D. *see* Murphy, Margaret Deeds.
Murphy, Margaret Deeds.
  xMurphy, Margaret.
    Meat Makes the Meal. Berkley Pub.
  xMurphy, Margaret D.
    Meat Makes the Meal. Dorison Hse.
Murphy, Martin J.
  xMurphy, M. J.

ed. In Vitro Aspects of Erythropoiesis.
Springer-Verlag.
Murphy, Michael.
xMurphy, Michael.
Golf in the Kingdom. Dell.
Psychic Side of Sports. A-W.
Murphy, Michael A.
xMurphy, M. A.
Aptian & Albian Tetragonitidae (Ammonoidea)
from Northern California. U of Cal Pr.
The Aptian Cenomanian Members of the
Ammonite Genus Tetragonites. U of Cal Pr.
Murphy, Michael J.
xMurphy, Michael J.
Cambridge Newspapers & Opinion, 1780-1850.
Oleander Pr.
Murphy, Nonie C.
xMurphy, Nonie C.
Mutual Arrangements. Berkley Pub.
Mutual Arrangements. S&S.
Murphy, Pat. *see* Murphy, Shirley Rousseau.
Murphy, Patricia, 1931-
xMurphy, Patricia.
A Special Way for the Special Child in the
Regular Classroom. Acad Therapy.
Murphy, Patrick T.
xMurphy, Patrick T.
Our Kindly Parent - the State: The Juvenile
Justice System & How It Works. Penguin.
Murphy, Paul L., 1923-
xMurphy, Paul L.
Constitution in Crisis Times, 1918-1969.
Har-Row.
Murphy, R. *see* Murphy, Rosalie.
Murphy, Richard. *see* Murphy, Richard W.
Murphy, Richard C.
xMurphy, Richard C.
Care & Feeding of Trees. Crown.
Murphy, Richard T. *see* Murphy, Richard Thomas
Aquinas.
Murphy, Richard Thomas Aquinas, 1908-
xMurphy, Richard T.
Days of Glory: The Passion, Death, &
Resurrection of Jesus Christ. Servant.
Murphy, Richard W.
xMurphy, Richard.
Status & Conformity. Silver.
xMurphy, Richard W.
Status & Conformity. Time-Life.
World of Cezanne. Time-Life.
World of Cezanne. Silver.
Murphy, Robert. *see* Murphy, Robert William.
Murphy, Robert D.
xMurphy, Robert D.
Mass Communication & Human Interaction.
HM.
Murphy, Robert D. *see* Murphy, Robert Daniel.
Murphy, Robert Daniel, 1894-
xMurphy, Robert D.
Diplomat Among Warriors. Greenwood.
Murphy, Robert Francis, 1924-
xMurphy, Robert.
An Overture to Social Anthropology. P-H.
Murphy, Robert William.
xMurphy, Robert.
The Stream. FS&G.
Murphy, Roland. *see* Murphy, Roland Edmund.
Murphy, Roland E. *see* Murphy, Roland Edmund.
Murphy, Roland Edmund, 1917-
xMurphy, Roland.
ed. Theology, Exegesis, & Proclamation.
Seabury.
xMurphy, Roland E.
The Psalms, Job. Fortress.
Murphy, Rosalie.
xMurphy, R.
ed. Contemporary Poets of the English
Language. St Martin.
Murphy, Roy E.
xMurphy, Roy E.

Adaptive Processes in Economic Systems.
Acad Pr.
Murphy, Shirley. *see* Murphy, Shirley Rousseau.
Murphy, Shirley R. *see* Murphy, Shirley Rousseau.
Murphy, Shirley Rousseau.
xMurphy, Pat.
Mrs. Tortino's Return to the Sun. Lothrop.
xMurphy, Shirley.
jt. auth. Mrs. Tortino's Return to the Sun.
Lothrop.
xMurphy, Shirley R.
The Castle of Hape. Atheneum.
The Flight of the Fox. Atheneum.
The Grass Tower. Atheneum.
Poor Jenny, Bright As a Penny. Viking Pr.
The Ring of Fire. Avon.
The Ring of Fire. Atheneum.
Silver Woven in My Hair. Atheneum.
Soonie & the Dragon. Atheneum.
The Wolf Bell. Atheneum.
The Wolf Bell. Avon.
Murphy, Terry.
xMurphy, Terry.
Some of My Best Friends Are Animals.
Paddington.
Murphy, Thomas. *see* Murphy, Thomas P.
Murphy, Thomas P., 1931-
xMurphy, Thomas.
Inside the Bureaucracy: The View from the
Assistant Secretary's Desk. Westview.
xMurphy, Thomas P.
Government Management Internships &
Executive Development. Lexington Bks.
Pressures Upon Congress: Legislation by
Lobby. Barron.
ed. Urban Indicators: A Guide to Information
Sources. Gale.
Murphy, Thomas W.
xMurphy, Thomas W.
The Wedding Cake House: The World of
George W. Bourne. Durrell.
Murphy, Tom, 1935-
xMurphy, Tom.
Aspen Incident. NAL.
Aspen Incident. St Martin.
Murphy, Walter. *see* Murphy, Walter F.
Murphy, Walter F.
xMurphy, Walter.
American Democracy. HR&W.
xMurphy, Walter F.
ed. Courts, Judges & Politics: An Introduction
to the Judicial Process. Random.
The Vicar of Christ. Ballantine.
The Vicar of Christ. Macmillan.
Murphy, Wendy B.
xMurphy, Wendy B.
Gardening Under Lights. Silver.
Murphy, William E.
xMurphy, Bill.
Lifetime Treasury of Tested Tennis Tips:
Secrets of Winning Play. P-H.
Murphy, William F. *see* Murphy, William Francis.
Murphy, William Francis, 1906-
xMurphy, William F.
The Tactics of Psychotherapy: An Application
of Psychoanalytic Theory to Psychotherapy.
Intl Univs Pr.
Murphy, William M. *see* Murphy, William Michael.
Murphy, William Michael, 1916-
xMurphy, William M.
Prodigal Father: The Life of John Butler Yeats,
1839-1922. Cornell U Pr.
Murr, L. *see* Murr, Lawrence Eugene.
Murr, Lawrence E. *see* Murr, Lawrence Eugene.
Murr, Lawrence Eugene.
xMurr, L.
Solid State Electronics. Dekker.
xMurr, Lawrence E.

ed. Metallurgical Applications of Bacterial
Leaching & Related Microbiological
Phenomena. Acad Pr.
Murray. *see* Murray, John Edward.
Murray, A. A.
xMurray, A. A.
Anybody's Spring. Vanguard.
Murray, A. R. *see* Murray, Alexander Rainy Maclean.
Murray, Albert.
xMurray, Albert.
Stomping the Blues. McGraw.
Murray, Alexander Rainy Maclean.
xMurray, A. R.
An Introduction to Political Philosophy.
Routledge & Kegan.
Murray, Alice E. *see* Murray, Alice Effie.
Murray, Alice Effie, 1877-
xMurray, Alice E.
A History of the Commercial & Financial
Relations Between England & Ireland from
the Period of the Restoration. Arno.
History of the Commercial & Financial
Relations Between England & Ireland from
the Period of the Restoration. B Franklin.
Murray, Amelia M. *see* Murray, Amelia Matilda.
Murray, Amelia Matilda, 1795-1884
xMurray, Amelia M.
Letters from the United States, Cuba &
Canada. Negro U. Pr.
Murray, Andrew, 1828-1917
xMurray, Andrew.
Confession & Forgiveness. Zondervan.
The Geographical Distribution of Mammals.
Arno.
How to Raise Your Children for Christ.
Bethany Fell.
Key to the Missionary Problem. Chr Lit.
Like Christ. Bethany Fell.
The Master's Indwelling. Bethany Fell.
The Spirit of Christ. Bethany Fell.
Spirit of Christ. Chr Lit.
Murray, Bertram G.
xMurray, Bertram G.
Population Dynamics: Alternative Models.
Acad Pr.
Murray, Bruce C.
xMurray, Bruce C.
Flight to Mercury. Columbia U Pr.
Murray, Charles A.
xMurray, Charles A.
Beyond Probation: Juvenile Corrections & the
Chronic Delinquent. Sage.
Murray, Chris.
xMurray, Chris.
Youth in Contemporary Society: Theoretical &
Research Perspectives. Humanities.
Murray, D. M. *see* Murray, Donald Mcleish.
Murray, David C. *see* Murray, David Christie.
Murray, David Christie, 1847-1907
xMurray, David C.
My Contemporaries in Fiction. Folcroft.
Murray, David L. *see* Murray, David Leslie.
Murray, David Leslie, 1883-
xMurray, David L.
Pragmatism. AMS Pr.
Murray, Donald Mcleish.
xMurray, D. M.
Noodle Words: An Introduction to Chinese &
Japanese Characters. C E Tuttle.
Murray, E. C. *see* Murray, Eustace Clare Grenville.
Murray, Edward.
xMurray, Edward.
The Cinematic Imagination: Writers & the
Motion Pictures. Ungar.
Fellini the Artist. Ungar.
Nine American Film Critics: Study of Theory
& Practice. Ungar.
Murray, Eustace Clare Grenville, 1824-1881
xMurray, E. C.

Side-Lights on English Society: Sketches from
Life, Social & Satirical. Gale.
Side-Lights on English Society: Sketches from
Life, Social & Satirical. R West.
Sidelights on English Society: Sketches from
Life, Social & Satirical. R West.
Murray, F. J. *see* Murray, Francis Joseph.
Murray, Frances.
xMurray, Frances.
Castaway. Scribner.
The Dear Colleague. PB.
Murray, Francis J. *see* Murray, Francis Joseph.
Murray, Francis Joseph, 1911-
xMurray, F. J.
Applied Mathematics: An Intellectual
Orientation. Plenum Pub.
Existence Theorems for Ordinary Differential
Equations. Krieger.
xMurray, Francis J.
Introduction to Linear Transformations in
Hilbert Space. Kraus Repr.
Murray, Frank B.
xMurray, Frank B.
ed. Critical Features of Piaget's Theory of the
Development of Thought. Mss Info.
Murray, G. E., 1945-
xMurray, G. E.
Repairs: Poems. U of Mo Pr.
Murray, George, 1900-1970
xMurray, George M.
The Press & the Public: The Story of the
British Press Council. S Ill U Pr.
Murray, George M. *see* Murray, George.
Murray, George W. *see* Murray, George William.
Murray, George William, 1885-
xMurray, George W.
Sons of Ishmael: A Study of the Egyptian
Bedouin. AMS Pr.
Murray, Gilbert, 1866-
xMurray, Gilbert.
Aristophanes: A Study. Russell.
Classical Tradition in Poetry. Russell.
Euripides & His Age. Greenwood.
Five Stages of Greek Religion. Greenwood.
History of Ancient Greek Literature. Folcroft.
Humanist Essays. Allen Unwin.
Stoic, Christian & Humanist. Arno.
Murray, Grace A.
xMurray, Grace A.
Personalities of the Eighteenth Century.
Folcroft.
Murray, H. J. R.
xMurray, J. H.
A History of Board Games Other Than Chess.
Hacker.
Murray, Henry A. *see* Murray, Henry Arthur.
Murray, Henry Arthur, 1892-
xMurray, Henry A.
Golf Secret. Emerson.
Murray, J. *see* Murray, John Iv.
Murray, J. D. *see* Murray, James Dickson.
Murray, J. H. *see* Murray, H. J. R.
Murray, James Dickson.
xMurray, J. D.
Asymptotic Analysis. Oxford U Pr.
Lectures on Nonlinear-Differential-Equation
Models in Biology. Oxford U Pr.
Murray, Jan.
xMurray, Jan.
Dance Now. Penguin.
Murray, Jerry.
xMurray, Jerry.
Getting into Radio-Controlled Sports. Putnam.
Your Used Car: Selecting It & Making It Like
New. Putnam.
Murray, Jim.
xMurray, Jim.

Contemporary Weight Training. Contemp Bks.
Inside Bodybuilding. Contemp Bks.
Inside Weight Lifting & Weight Training.
Contemp Bks.
Murray, John, 1898-
xMurray, John.
Christian Baptism. Presby & Reformed.
Divorce. Presby & Reformed.
Imputation of Adam's Sin. Presby & Reformed.
The Media Law Dictionary. U Pr of Amer.
Murray, John Edward.
xMurray.
Cases & Materials on Contracts. Michie.
Murray on Contracts. Michie.
Murray, John F. *see* Murray, John Frederic.
Murray, John Frederic, 1927-
xMurray, John F.
The Normal Lung: The Basis for Diagnosis &
Treatment of Pulmonary Disease. Saunders.
Murray, John IV.
xMurray, J.
Lord Byron & His Detractors. Haskell.
Murray, John J. *see* Murray, John Joseph.
Murray, John Joseph, 1915-
xMurray, John J.
Antwerp in the Age of Plantin & Brueghel. U
of Okla Pr.
Murray, John W. *see* Murray, John William.
Murray, John William.
xMurray, John W.
An Atlas of British Recent Foraminiferids.
Heinemann Ed.
Murray, Ken, 1903-
xMurray, Ken.
Golden Days of San Simeon. Doubleday.
Murray, Les. *see* Murray, les A.
Murray, les A., 1938-
xMurray, Les.
The Peasant Mandarin: Prose Pieces. U of
Queensland Pr.
Murray, Linda.
xMurray, Linda.
The High Renaissance & Mannerism: Italy, the
North, & Spain, 1500-1600. Oxford U Pr.
Michelangelo. Oxford U Pr.
Murray, M. *see* Murray, Malinda.
Murray, Malinda.
xMurray, M.
Fundamentals of Nursing. P-H.
xMurray, Malinda.
Fundamentals of Nursing. P-H.
Murray, Margaret. *see* Murray, Margaret Alice.
Murray, Margaret A. *see* Murray, Margaret Alice.
Murray, Margaret Alice.
xMurray, Margaret.
God of the Witches. Oxford U Pr.
xMurray, Margaret A.
Egyptian Sculpture. Greenwood.
Egyptian Temples. AMS Pr.
Murray, Marian.
xMurray, Marian.
Circus: From Rome to Ringling. Greenwood.
Hunting for Fossils: A Guide to Finding &
Collecting Fossils in All Fifty States.
Macmillan.
Plant Wizard: The Life of Lue Gim Gong.
Macmillan.
Murray, Melba W.
xMurray, Melba W.
Engineered Report Writing. Pennwell Pub.
Murray, Michele.
xMurray, Michele.
Nellie Cameron. HM.
Murray, Mimi.
xMurray, Mimi.
Women's Gymnastics: Coach, Participant,
Spectator. Allyn.
Murray, Nicholas, 1802-1861
xMurray, Nicholas.

Letters to the Right Rev. John Hughes, Roman
Catholic Bishop of New York. Arno.
Murray, Pauli, 1910-
xMurray, Pauli.
Proud Shoes: The Story of an American
Family. Har-Row.
Proud Shoes: The Story of an American
Family. Har-Row.
Proud Shoes: The Story of an American
Family. Reprint.
Murray, Peter.
xMurray, Peter.
The Architecture of the Italian Renaissance.
Schocken.
The Art of the Renaissance. Oxford U Pr.
A Dictionary of Art & Artists. Gannon.
A Dictionary of Art & Artists. Penguin.
Murray, R. C. *see* Murray, Raymond C.
Murray, Ralph L.
xMurray, Ralph L.
Signs of the Savior. Broadman.
Murray, Raymond C.
xMurray, R. C.
Forensic Geology: Earth Sciences & Criminal
Investigation. Rutgers U Pr.
Murray, Rebecca.
xMurray, Rebecca.
ed. History of the Public School Kindergarten
in North Carolina. Mss Info.
Murray, Robbie.
xMurray, Robbie.
The Gentle Art of Horsebreaking. A S Barnes.
Murray, Robert. *see* Murray, Robert William.
Murray, Robert F.
xMurray, Robert F.
ed. The Genetic, Metabolic & Developmental
Aspects of Mental Retardation. C C Thomas.
Murray, Robert H. *see* Murray, Robert Henry.
Murray, Robert Henry, 1874-1947
xMurray, Robert H.
Group Movements Throughout the Ages. Arno.
Murray, Robert William, 1914-
xMurray, Robert.
How to Buy the Right House at the Right
Price. Macmillan.
Murray, Roger F.
xMurray, Roger F.
Economic Aspects of Pensions: A Summary
Report. Natl Bur Econ Res.
Murray, Roger N.
xMurray, Roger N.
Wordsworth's Style: Figures & Themes in the
Lyrical Ballads of 1800. U of Nebr Pr.
Murray, Ronald O.
xMurray, Ronald O.
The Radiology of Skeletal Disorders: Exercises
in Diagnosis. Churchill.
Murray, Rosemary.
xMurray, Rosemary.
Current Perspectives in Rehabilitation Nursing.
Mosby.
Practical Modern Weaving. Van Nos Reinhold.
Murray, Ruth.
xMurray, Ruth B.
Nursing Assessment & Health Promotion
Through the Life Span. P-H.
Nursing Concepts for Health Promotion. P-H.
The Nursing Process in Later Maturity. P-H.
Murray, Ruth B. *see* Murray, Ruth.
Murray, Ruth L. *see* Murray, Ruth Lovell.
Murray, Ruth Lovell.
xMurray, Ruth L.
Dance in Elementary Education: A Program
for Boys & Girls. Har-Row.
Murray, Simon.
xMurray, Simon.
Legionnaire: My Five Years in the French
Foreign Legion. Times Bks.
Murray, Spence. *see* Murray, Spencer.

Murray, Spencer.
xMurray, Spence.
ed. Chevrolet Tune-up & Repair. Petersen Pub.
ed. Chevy-GMC Pickup Repair. Petersen Pub.
ed. Dodge Pickup Repair. Petersen Pub.
ed. How to Tune Your Car. Petersen Pub.
Murray, William, 1926-
xMurray, William.
Horse Fever. Dodd.
Malibu. Coward.
Murray, William D.
xMurray, William D.
Paper Folding for Beginners. Gannon.
Paperfolding for Beginners. Dover.
Murray, William G. *see* Murray, William Gordon.
Murray, William Gordon, 1903-
xMurray, William G.
Farm Appraisal & Valuation. Iowa St U Pr.
Murray-Aynsley. *see* Murray-Aynsley, Harriet Georgiana
Maria (Manners-Sutton).
Murray-Aynsley, Harriet G. *see* Murray-Aynsley, Harriet
Georgiana Maria (Manners-Sutton).
Murray-Aynsley, Harriet Georgiana Maria
(Manners-Sutton), 1827?-1898
xMurray-Aynsley.
Symbolism of the East & West. Kennikat.
xMurray-Aynsley, Harriet G.
Symbolism of the East & West. Gale.
Murray-Brown, Jeremy, 1932-
xMurray-Brown, Jeremy.
Faith & the Flag: The Opening of Africa. Allen
Unwin.
Kenyatta. Allen Unwin.
Kenyatta. Dutton.
Portraits of Power. Times Bks.
Murray-Smith, S. *see* Murray-Smith, Stephen.
Murray-Smith, Stephen.
xMurray-Smith, S.
Melbourne Studies in Education 1974. Intl
Schol Bk Serv.
ed. Melbourne Studies in Education 1976. Intl
Schol Bk Serv.
xMurray-Smith, Stephen.
ed. Melbourne Studies in Education 1973. Intl
Schol Bk Serv.
ed. Melbourne Studies in Education 1975. Intl
Schol Bk Serv.
ed. Melbourne Studies in Education 1977. Intl
Schol Bk Serv.
Murrell, John N. *see* Murrell, John Norman.
Murrell, John Norman.
xMurrell, John N.
The Chemical Bond. Wiley.
Valence Theory. Wiley.
Murrill, Paul W.
xMurrill, Paul W.
An Introduction to Cobol Programming.
Har-Row.
Introduction to Computer Science. Har-Row.
Murrill, Rupert I. *see* Murrill, Rupert Ivan.
Murrill, Rupert Ivan.
xMurrill, Rupert I.
Cranial & Postcranial Skeletal Remains from
Easter Island. U of Minn Pr.
Murrin, Michael.
xMurrin, Michael.
The Allegorical Epic: Essays in Its Rise &
Decline. U of Chicago Pr.
Murry, J. Middleton. *see* Murry, John Middleton.
Murry, John M. *see* Murry, John Middleton.
Murry, John Middleton, 1889-1957
xMurry, J. Middleton.
The Challenge of Schweitzer. Folcroft.
xMurry, John M.

Aspects of Literature. Arno.
Pencillings. Arno.
Problem of Style. Oxford U Pr.
Reminiscences of D. H. Lawrence. Arno.
Studies in Keats. Haskell.
Studies in Keats, New & Old. Folcroft.
Murschetz, Luis.
xMurschetz, Luis.
tr. A Hamster's Journey. P-H.
Mursell, James. *see* Mursell, James Lockhart.
Mursell, James L. *see* Mursell, James Lockhart.
Mursell, James Lockhart, 1893-
xMursell, James.
Psychology of Music. Scholarly.
xMursell, James L.
The Psychology of Music. Greenwood.
The Psychology of Music. Johnson Repr.
Murstein, Bernard I.
xMurstein, Bernard I.
Exploring Intimate Life Styles. Springer Pub.
Love, Sex, & Marriage Through the Ages.
Springer Pub.
Murtagh, William J.
xMurtagh, William J.
Moravian Architecture & Town Planning:
Bethlehem, Pennsylvania, and Other 18th
Century American Settlements. U of NC Pr.
Murtaugh, Daniel M. *see* Murtaugh, Daniel Maher.
Murtaugh, Daniel Maher.
xMurtaugh, Daniel M.
Piers Plowman & the Image of God. U Presses
Fla.
Murton, R. K.
xMurton, R. K.
Avian Breeding Cycles. Oxford U Pr.
Murty, Katta G., 1936-
xMurty, Katta G.
Linear & Combinatorial Programming. Wiley.
Murtz, Harold A.
xMurtz, Harold A.
ed. Gun Digest Book of Exploded Firearms
Drawings. Follett.
Muscatine, Charles.
xMuscatine, Charles.
The Borzoi College Reader. Knopf.
ed. Borzoi College Reader. Knopf.
Chaucer & the French Tradition: A Study in
Style & Meaning. U of Cal Pr.
Muschamp, Herbert.
xMuschamp, Herbert M.
File Under Architecture. MIT Pr.
Muschamp, Herbert M. *see* Muschamp, Herbert.
Muscio, Bernard.
xMuscio, Bernard.
Lectures on Industrial Psychology. Hive Pub.
Muse, Benjamin.
xMuse, Benjamin.
American Negro Revolution: From
Nonviolence to Black Power, 1963-1967. Ind
U Pr.
Muse, Vance, 1949-
xMuse, Vance.
Don't Buy a Car Made on Monday. PB.
Museler, Wilhelm, 1887-1952
xMuseler, Wilhelm.
Riding Logic. Arco.
Muser, Curt.
xMuser, Curt.
Compiled by Facts & Artifacts of Ancient
Middle America: A Glossary of Terms &
Words Used in the Archaeology & Art
History of Pre-Columbian Mexico & Central
America. Dutton.
Museum Council of Philadelphia.
xMuseum Council of Philadelphia.

ed. Guide to Museums in the Delaware Valley.
Art Alliance.
ed. A Guide to Museums of the Delaware
Valley. A S Barnes.
Museum of Concord Antiquarian Society. *see* Concord,
Mass. Antiquarian Museum.
Museum Of Modern Art. *see* Museum of Modern Art.
New York.
Museum of Modern Art. New York.
xMuseum Of Modern Art.
Bulletin of the Museum of Modern Art,
1933-1963. Arno.
xMuseum of Modern Art, New York.
Catalog of the Library of the Museum of
Modern Art, New York. G K Hall.
Museum of New Mexico Press. *see* Museum of New
Mexico. Santa Fe.
Museum of New Mexico. Santa Fe.
xMuseum of New Mexico Press.
ed. Navajo Weaving Handbook. Museum NM
Pr.
Musgrave, Anthony, 1849-1912
xMusgrave, Anthony.
Studies in Political Economy. Kelley.
Musgrave, Clifford.
xMusgrave, Clifford.
Life in Brighton, from the Earliest Times to the
Present. Shoe String.
Musgrave, Florence.
xMusgrave, Florence.
Two Dates for Mike. Hastings.
Two Dates for Mike. G K Hall.
Musgrave, G. Ray. *see* Musgrave, George Ray.
Musgrave, George Ray, 1922-
xMusgrave, G. Ray.
Individualized Instruction: Teaching Strategies
Focusing on the Learner. Allyn.
Musgrave, Richard. *see* Musgrave, Richard Abel.
Musgrave, Richard A. *see* Musgrave, Richard Abel.
Musgrave, Richard Abel.
xMusgrave, Richard.
Public Finance in Theory & Practice. McGraw.
xMusgrave, Richard A.
Public Finance in Theory & Practice. McGraw.
Musgrave, Ted R.
xMusgrave, Ted R.
Understanding Problems for Chemical
Principles. HR&W.
Musgraves, Don.
xMusgraves, Don.
One More Time. Bethany Fell.
Musgrove, Bill.
xMusgrove, Bill.
Fur Trapping. Winchester Pr.
Musgrove, Gordon.
xMusgrove, Gordon.
The Pathfinder Force: The History of 8 Group.
Hippocrene Bks.
Musgrove, Margaret.
xMusgrove, Margaret.
Ashanti to Zulu: African Traditions. Dial.
xMusgrove, Margaret W.
Ashanti to Zulu: African Traditions. Dial.
Musgrove, Margaret W. *see* Musgrove, Margaret.
Musgrove, Philip.
xMusgrove, Philip.
Consumer Behavior in Latin America: Income
& Spending of Families in Ten Andean
Cities. Brookings.
Musgrove, Richard W. *see* Musgrove, Richard Watson.
Musgrove, Richard Watson, 1840-1914
xMusgrove, Richard W.

History of the Town of Bristol, New
　　Hampshire. NH Pub Co.
Musgrove, S. *see* Musgrove, Sydney.
Musgrove, Sydney.
　　xMusgrove, S.
　　　T. S. Eliot & Walt Whitman. Folcroft.
　　　T. S. Eliot & Walt Whitman. Gordon Pr.
　　xMusgrove, Sydney.
　　　T. S. Eliot & Walt Whitman. Haskell.
Musheno, Elizabeth J.
　　xMusheno, Elizabeth J.
　　　The Home Decorating Sewing Book.
　　　　Macmillan.
Mushkin, Selma J.
　　xMushkin, Selma J.
　　　Biomedical Research: Costs & Benefits.
　　　　Ballinger Pub.
　　　ed. Health: What Is It Worth?: Measures of
　　　　Health Benefits. Pergamon.
　　　Personnel Management & Productivity in City
　　　　Government. Lexington Bks.
　　　ed. Public Prices for Public Products. Urban
　　　　Inst.
Music Education National Conference. *see* Music
　　Educators'National Conference.
Music Educators National Conference. *see* Music
　　Educators'National Conference.
Music Educators'National Conference.
　　xMusic Education National Conference.
　　　Study of Music in the Elementary School: A
　　　　Conceptual Approach. Music Ed.
　　xMusic Educators National Conference.
　　　Perspectives in Music Education. Music Ed.
　　　Power of Music. Music Ed.
　　　ed. The School Music Program: Description &
　　　　Standards. Music Ed.
　　　Selective Music Lists: Instrumental Solos &
　　　　Ensembles. Music Ed.
　　　Selective Music Lists: Vocal Solos &
　　　　Ensembles. Music Ed.
　　　Teacher Education in Music. Music Ed.
　　　Toward an Aesthetic Education. Music Ed.
**Music Educators' National Conference. National
Commission on Instruction.**
　　xMENC National Committee on Instruction.
　　　ed. Selected Instructional Programs in Music.
　　　　Music Ed.
Musick, Archie L. *see* Musick, Ruth Ann.
Musick, Phil.
　　xMusick, Phil.
　　　Who Was Roberto: A Biography of Roberto
　　　　Clemente. Doubleday.
Musick, Ruth A. *see* Musick, Ruth Ann.
Musick, Ruth Ann.
　　xMusick, Archie L.
　　　illus. Coffin Hollow & Other Ghost Tales. U Pr
　　　　of Ky.
　　xMusick, Ruth A.
　　　Coffin Hollow & Other Ghost Tales. U Pr of
　　　　Ky.
Musiker, Reuben.
　　xMusiker, Reuben.
　　　Guide to Cape of Good Hope Official
　　　　Publications, 1854-1910. G K Hall.
　　　South African Bibliography: A Survey of
　　　　Bibliographies & Bibliographical Work.
　　　　Rowman.
Musil, Alois, 1868-1944
　　xMusil, Alois.
　　　The Northern Hegaz: A Topographical
　　　　Itinerary. AMS Pr.
　　　Northern Negd: A Topographical Itinerary.
　　　　AMS Pr.
　　　Palmyrena: A Topographical Itinerary. AMS
　　　　Pr.
Musleah, Ezekiel N.
　　xMusleah, Ezekiel N.
　　　On the Banks of the Ganga: The Sojourn of
　　　　Jews in Calcutta. Chris Mass.
Musmanno, Michael A. *see* Musmanno, Michael Angelo.

Musmanno, Michael Angelo.
　　xMusmanno, Michael A.
　　　That's My Opinion. Michie.
Musolf, Lloyd D.
　　xMusolf, Lloyd D.
　　　Federal Examiners & the Conflict of Law &
　　　　Administration. AMS Pr.
　　　Federal Examiners & the Conflict of Law &
　　　　Administration. Greenwood.
　　　Malaysia's Parliamentary System:
　　　　Representative Politics & Policymaking in a
　　　　Divided Society. Westview.
Musselman, Donald. *see* Musselman, Donald Lee.
Musselman, Donald Lee.
　　xMusselman, Donald.
　　　Lesson Plans in Accounting. Interstate.
Mussen, Paul. *see* Mussen, Paul Henry.
Mussen, Paul H. *see* Mussen, Paul Henry.
Mussen, Paul Henry.
　　xMussen, Paul.
　　　Psychological Development of the Child. P-H.
　　　Psychology: An Introduction. Heath.
　　xMussen, Paul H.
　　　Child Development & Personality. Har-Row.
　　　Essentials of Child Development & Personality.
　　　　Har-Row.
　　　Psychological Development of the Child. P-H.
Musset, Alfred de, 1810-1857
　　xMusset, Alfred de.
　　　The Confession of a Child of the Century.
　　　　Hyperion Conn.
Musset, Lucien.
　　xMusset, Lucien.
　　　The Germanic Invasions: The Making of
　　　　Europe AD 400-600. Pa St U Pr.
Mussey, Henry R. *see* Mussey, Henry Raymond.
Mussey, Henry Raymond, 1875-1940
　　xMussey, Henry R.
　　　Combination in the Mining Industry: A Study
　　　　in Concentration in Lake Superior Iron Ore
　　　　Production. AMS Pr.
Mussner, Franz.
　　xMussner, Franz.
　　　Christ & the End of the World: A Biblical
　　　　Study in Eschatology. U of Notre Dame Pr.
Mussolini, Benito.
　　xMussolini, Benito.
　　　My Autobiography. Greenwood.
Musson, A. E. *see* Musson, Albert Edward.
Musson, Albert Edward, 1920-
　　xMusson, A. E.
　　　The Growth of British Industry. Holmes &
　　　　Meier.
Mussulman, Joseph A.
　　xMussulman, Joseph A.
　　　The Uses of Music: An Introduction to Music
　　　　in Contemporary American Life. P-H.
Mustafa, Husain. *see* Mustafa, Husain M.
Mustafa, Husain M.
　　xMustafa, Husain.
　　　Postal Technology & Management. Lomond.
Mustard, W. P. *see* Mustard, Wilfred Pirt.
Mustard, Wilfred P. *see* Mustard, Wilfred Pirt.
Mustard, Wilfred Pirt, 1864-1932
　　xMustard, W. P.
　　　Classical Echoes in Tennyson. Haskell.
　　xMustard, Wilfred P.
　　　Classical Echoes in Tennyson. Folcroft.
Muste, A. J. *see* Muste, Abraham John.
Muste, Abraham John, 1885-1967
　　xMuste, A. J.
　　　Non-Violence in an Aggressive World. Ozer.
Mustill, Norman O. *see* Mustill, Norman Ogue.
Mustill, Norman Ogue.
　　xMustill, Norman O.
　　　Twinpak. Ultramarine Pub.
Musurillo, Herbert A. *see* Musurillo, Herbert Anthony.
Musurillo, Herbert Anthony.
　　xMusurillo, Herbert A.

Symbol & Myth in Ancient Poetry.
　　Greenwood.
Mutambirwa, James A. *see* Mutambirwa, James A.
　　Chamunorwa.
Mutambirwa, James A. Chamunorwa, 1938-
　　xMutambirwa, James A.
　　　The Rise of Settler Power in Southern
　　　　Rhodesia (Zimbabwe) 1898-1923. Fairleigh
　　　　Dickinson.
Mutch, Ronnie.
　　xMutch, Ronnie.
　　　Mutch About Horses. Arco.
Mutch, Thomas A., 1931-
　　xMutch, Thomas A.
　　　The Geology of Mars. Princeton U Pr.
　　　Geology of the Moon: A Stratigraphic View.
　　　　Princeton U Pr.
Muth, Richard F., 1927-
　　xMuth, Richard F.
　　　Cities & Housing: The Spatial Pattern of Urban
　　　　Residential Land Use. U of Chicago Pr.
　　　Public Housing: an Economic Evaluation. Am
　　　　Enterprise.
Muth, Robert G.
　　xMuth, Robert G.
　　　Renal Medicine. C C Thomas.
Muth, Thomas A.
　　xMuth, Thomas A.
　　　State Interest in Cable Communications. Arno.
Muther, Richard.
　　xMuther, Richard.
　　　Systematic Handling Analysis. CBI Pub.
Mutherich, Florentine.
　　xMutherich, Florentine.
　　　Intro. by Carolingian Painting. Braziller.
Muthesius, Hermann.
　　xMuthesius, Hermann.
　　　The English House. Rizzoli Intl.
Muthesius, Stefan.
　　xMuthesius, Stefan.
　　　The High Victorian Movement in Architecture
　　　　1850-1870. Routledge & Kegan.
Mutschmann, H. *see* Mutschmann, Heinrich.
Mutschmann, Heinrich, 1885-1955
　　xMutschmann, H.
　　　Origin & Meaning of Young's Night Thoughts.
　　　　Folcroft.
　　xMutschmann, Heinrich.
　　　The Origin & Meaning of Young's Night
　　　　Thoughts. R West.
Mutwa, Vusamazulu C. *see* Mutwa, Vusamazulu Credo.
Mutwa, Vusamazulu Credo, 1921 (ca.)-
　　xMutwa, Vusamazulu C.
　　　Indaba My Children. Humanities.
Muuss, Rolf E. *see* Muuss, Rolf Eduard Helmut.
Muuss, Rolf Eduard Helmut, 1924-
　　xMuuss, Rolf E.
　　　Adolescent Behavior & Society: A Book of
　　　　Readings. Random.
　　xMuuss, Rolfe.
　　　Theories of Adolescence. Peter Smith.
Muuss, Rolfe. *see* Muuss, Rolf Eduard Helmut.
Muybridge, Eadweard, 1830-1904
　　xMuybridge, Eadweard.
　　　Animals in Motion. Dover.
　　　Human Figure in Motion. Dover.
Muysken, P. *see* Muysken, Pieter.
Muysken, Pieter.
　　xMuysken, P.
　　　Syntactic Developments in the Verb Phrase of
　　　　Ecuadorian Quechua. Humanities.
Muyskens, James L., 1942-
　　xMuyskens, James L.
　　　The Sufficiency of Hope: Conceptual
　　　　Foundations of Religion. Temple U Pr.
Mwase, George Simeon.
　　xMwase, George Simeon.

Strike a Blow & Die: A Narrative of Race
Relations in Colonial Africa. Harvard U Pr.

Myatt, L. J.
xMyatt, L. J.
Symmetrical Components. Pergamon.

Mycue, Edward, 1937-
xMycue, Edward.
Damage Within the Community. Panjandrum.

Mydans, Carl.
xMydans, Carl.
More Than Meets the Eye. Greenwood.

Myer, Donna.
xMyer, Donna.
Answers to Your Mushroom Questions Plus
Recipes. Mushroom Cave.

Myer, Isaac, 1836-1902
xMyer, Isaac.
Qabbalah: The Philosophical Writings of
Solomon Ben Yehudah Ibn Gabirol. Gordon
Pr.

Myer, John C. see Myer, John Colby.

Myer, John Colby.
xMyer, John C.
The Psychology of Western Culture. Philos Lib.

Myer, John N. see Myer, John Nicholas.

Myer, John Nicholas, 1897-
xMyer, John N.
Accounting for Non-Accountants. Dutton.

Myerhoff, Barbara.
xMyerhoff, Barbara.
Life's Career--Aging: Cultural Variations on
Growing Old. Sage.
xMyerhoff, Barbara G.
ed. Life's Career-Aging: Cultural Variations on
Growing Old. Sage.

Myerhoff, Barbara. see Myerhoff, Barbara G.

Myerhoff, Barbara G.
xMyerhoff, Barbara.
Number Our Days. Dutton.
Number Our Days. S&S.

Myerhoff, Barbara G. see Myerhoff, Barbara.

Myers, A. see Myers, Alan L.

Myers, A. R. see Myers, Alec Reginald.

Myers, Alan L.
xMyers, A.
Introduction to Chemical Engineering
Computer Calculations. P-H.

Myers, Albert C. see Myers, Albert Cook.

Myers, Albert Cook, 1874-
xMyers, Albert C.
ed. Narratives of Early Pennsylvania, West
New Jersey & Delaware, 1630-1707. B&N.

Myers, Alec Reginald.
xMyers, A. R.
England in the Late Middle Ages. Gannon.
England in the Late Middle Ages. Penguin.
London in the Age of Chaucer. U of Okla Pr.
Parliaments & Estates in Europe: To 1789.
HarBraceJ.
Parliaments & Estates in Europe to 1789. N
Watson.

Myers, Alonyo F. see Myers, Alonzo Franklin.

Myers, Alonzo Franklin, 1893-
xMyers, Alonyo F.
A Teacher-Training Program for Ohio. AMS
Pr.

Myers, Amy.
xMyers, Amy.
I Know a Monster. A W.

Myers, Andrew B.
xMyers, Andrew B.
ed. Century of Commentary on the Works of
Washington Irving, 1860-1974. Sleepy
Hollow.

Myers, Arthur.
xMyers, Arthur.
Analysis: The Short Story. Foothills Pr.
Kids Do Amazing Things. Random.

Myers, B. S. see Myers, Bernard Samuel.

Myers, Barbara.
xMyers, Barbara.
Christmas Cookies & Candies. Rawson Wade.

Myers, Bernard Samuel, 1908-
xMyers, B. S.
Art & Civilization. McGraw.

Myers, Bernice.
xMyers, Bernice.
illus. The Apple War. Schol Bk Serv.
illus. Little John Bear in the Big City. Schol Bk
Serv.

Myers, C. V.
xMyers, C. V.
The Coming Deflation: Its Dangers -- &
Opportunities. Arlington Hse.

Myers, Carole R. see Myers, Carole Robbins.

Myers, Carole Robbins.
xMyers, Carole R.
A Primer of Left-Handed Embroidery.
Scribner.

Myers, Charles A. see Myers, Charles Andrew.

Myers, Charles Andrew, 1913-
xMyers, Charles A.
Computers in Knowledge Based Fields. MIT
Pr.
The Dynamics of a Labor Market: A Study the
Impact of Employment Changes on Labor
Mobility, Job Satisfactions, & Company &
Union Policies. Greenwood.
ed. Impact of Computers on Management. MIT
Pr.

Myers, Charles S. see Myers, Charles Samuel.

Myers, Charles Samuel, 1873-1946
xMyers, Charles S.
Industrial Psychology. Arno.

Myers, Constance A. see Myers, Constance Ashton.

Myers, Constance Ashton.
xMyers, Constance A.
The Prophet's Army: Trotskyists in America
1928-1941. Greenwood.

Myers, David C. see Myers, David G.

Myers, David G.
xMyers, David C.
The Human Puzzle: Psychological Research &
Christian Belief. Har-Row.

Myers, Donald G.
xMyers, Donald G.
Individual Educational Programming for All
Teachers of the Special Needs Learner. C C
Thomas.
The Right-to-Education Child: A Curriculum
for the Severely & Profoundly Mentally
Retarded. C C Thomas.

Myers, Ernest R., 1935-
xMyers, Ernest R.
The Community Psychology Concept:
Integrating Theory, Education & Practice in
Psychology, Social Work & Public
Administration. U Pr of Amer.

Myers, Eugene A.
xMyers, Eugene A.
Arabic Thought & the Western World in the
Golden Age of Islam. Ungar.

Myers, F. W. see Myers, Frederic William Henry.

Myers, Frank.
xMyers, Frank.
Soldiering in Dakota Among the Indians in
1865. Ye Galleon.

Myers, Frederic W. see Myers, Frederic William Henry.

Myers, Frederic William Henry, 1843-1901
xMyers, F. W.
Wordsworth. AMS Pr.
Wordsworth. Arden Lib.
Wordsworth. Folcroft.
xMyers, Frederic W.
The Subliminal Consciousness. Arno.

Myers, Gary.
xMyers, Gary.

The House of the Worm. Arkham.

Myers, Gerald E.
xMyers, Gerald E.
Insurance Manual for Libraries. ALA.

Myers, Glenford J., 1946-
xMyers, Glenford J.
The Art of Software Testing. Wiley.
Software Reliability: Principles & Practices.
Wiley.

Myers, Gustavus, 1872-1942
xMyers, Gustavus.
Ending of Hereditary American Fortunes.
Kelley.
The History of American Idealism. AMS Pr.
History of Canadian Wealth. Argosy.
History of Tammany Hall. B Franklin.
History of Tammany Hall. Dover.
History of Tammany Hall. Peter Smith.

Myers, H. M. see Myers, Howard M.

Myers, Harold.
xMyers, Harold.
Table Tennis. Merrimack Bk Serv.

Myers, Hector F.
xMyers, Hector F.
Compiled by Black Child Development in
America, 1927-1977: An Annotated
Bibliography. Greenwood.

Myers, Henry A. see Myers, Henry Alonzo.

Myers, Henry Alonzo, 1906-
xMyers, Henry A.
Are Men Equal: An Inquiry into the Meaning
of American Democracy. Cornell U Pr.
Spinoza-Hegel Paradox: A Study of the Choice
Between Traditional Idealism & Systematic
Pluralism. B Franklin.

Myers, Henry S.
xMyers, Henry S.
Fundamentally Speaking. Strawberry Hill.

Myers, Howard M.
xMyers, H. M.
Fluorides & Dental Fluorosis. S Karger.

Myers, J. Arthur. see Myers, Jay Arthur.

Myers, J. M. see Myers, Jacob Martin.

Myers, Jacob Martin, 1904-
xMyers, J. M.
Grace & Torah. Fortress.

Myers, James E.
xMyers, James E.
The Bridge of Time: A View of the Israeli
People. A S Barnes.

Myers, James H.
xMyers, James H.
Market Structure Analysis. Am Mktg.

Myers, James T.
xMyers, James T.
The American Way: An Introduction to the U.
S. Government & Politics. Heath.

Myers, Jay A. see Myers, Jay Arthur.

Myers, Jay Arthur, 1888-
xMyers, J. Arthur.
Masters of Medicine: An Historical Sketch of
the College of Medical Sciences of the
University of Minnesota, 1888-1966. Green.
xMyers, Jay A.
Tuberculosis: A Half-Century of Study &
Conquest. Green.

Myers, Jerome L.
xMyers, Jerome L.
Fundamentals of Experimental Design. Allyn.

Myers, John B. see Myers, John Brown.

Myers, John Brown, 1844 or 45-1915
xMyers, John B.
Thomas J. Comber, Missionary Pioneer to the
Congo. Negro U Pr.

Myers, John H. see Myers, John Holmes.

Myers, John Holmes, 1915-
xMyers, John H.
Auditing Cases. Northwestern U Pr.

Myers, John M. see Myers, John Myers.

Myers, John Myers.
xMyers, John M.
  The Alamo. U of Nebr Pr.
  Doc Holliday. U of Nebr Pr.
  The Last Chance: Tombstone's Early Years. U
    of Nebr Pr.
Myers, Kenneth. *see* Myers, Kenneth A.
Myers, Kenneth A.
xMyers, Kenneth.
  North Atlantic Security: The Forgotten Flank?.
    Sage.
Myers, Kenneth H. *see* Myers, Kenneth Holston.
Myers, Kenneth Holston, 1919-
xMyers, Kenneth H.
  Marketing Policy Determination by a Major
    Firm in a Capital Goods Industry. Arno.
Myers, L. M. *see* Myers, Louis McCorry.
Myers, Leopold H. *see* Myers, Leopold Hamilton.
Myers, Leopold Hamilton, 1881-1944
xMyers, Leopold H.
  Clio. Scholarly.
Myers, Lonny.
xMyers, Lonny.
  Adultery & Other Private Matters: Your Right
    to Personal Freedom in Marriage.
    Nelson-Hall.
Myers, Lou.
xMyers, Lou.
  Absent & Accounted for. Workman Pub.
Myers, Louis McCorry.
xMyers, L. M.
  Guide to American English. P-H.
  The Roots of Modern English. Little.
Myers, Margaret. *see* Myers, Margaret Good.
Myers, Margaret G. *see* Myers, Margaret Good.
Myers, Margaret Good, 1899-
xMyers, Margaret.
  Monetary Proposals for Social Reform. AMS
    Pr.
xMyers, Margaret G.
  Financial History of the United States.
    Columbia U Pr.
Myers, Mary R. *see* Myers, Mary Ruth.
Myers, Mary Ruth.
xMyers, Mary R.
  A Journey to Cuzco. Coward.
Myers, Max. *see* Myers, Maxmilian Hardy.
Myers, Maxmilian Hardy, 1922-
xMyers, Max.
  Max Myers' New Guide to a Successful Small
    Tax Client Practice. P-H.
Myers, Nancy.
xMyers, Nancy.
  The Math Book. Hafner.
Myers, Norma.
xMyers, Norma.
  Gifts from the Kitchen. Bobbs.
Myers, Norman.
xMyers, Norman.
  The Long African Day. Macmillan.
Myers, Phyllis.
xMyers, Phyllis.
  Neighborhood Conservation: Lessons from
    Three Cities. Conservation Foun.
Myers, R. B.
xMyers, R. B.
  The Gamma Particle: A Study of
    Cell-Organelle Interactions in the
    Development of the Water Mold
    Blastocladiella Emersonii. S Karger.
Myers, Ramon H. *see* Myers, Ramon Hawley.
Myers, Ramon Hawley, 1929-
xMyers, Ramon H.
  ed. Selected Essays in Chinese Economic
    Development. Garland Pub.
Myers, Robert J. *see* Myers, Robert Julius.
Myers, Robert Julius, 1912-
xMyers, Robert J.

  Coverage of Out-of-Hospital Prescription Drugs
    Under Medicare. Am Enterprise.
  Indexation of Pension & Other Benefits. Irwin.
  Medicare. Irwin.
Myers, Robert M. *see* Myers, Robert Manson.
Myers, Robert Manson.
xMyers, Robert M.
  ed. The Children of Pride: A True Story of
    Georgia & the Civil War. Yale U Pr.
  ed. A Georgian at Princeton. HarBraceJ.
Myers, Rollo H.
xMyers, Rollo H.
  Debussy. Hyperion Conn.
Myers, Stanley E., 1926-
xMyers, Stanley E.
  RPG II with Business Applications. Reston.
Myers, Steven.
xMyers, Steven.
  The Enchanted Sticks. Coward.
Myers, W. D. *see* Myers, William D.
Myers, Walter. *see* Myers, Walter Dean.
Myers, Walter D. *see* Myers, Walter Dean.
Myers, Walter Dean.
xMyers, Walter.
  Social Welfare. Watts.
xMyers, Walter D.
  Brainstorm. Dell.
  Brainstorm. Watts.
  The Dancers. Schol Bk Serv.
  The Dragon Takes a Wife. Bobbs.
  Fast Sam, Cool Clyde, & Stuff. Viking Pr.
  It Ain't All for Nothin'. Avon.
  It Ain't All for Nothin'. Viking Pr.
  Mojo & the Russians. Viking Pr.
  Mojo & the Russians. Avon.
  The Young Landlords. Viking Pr.
Myers, Walter L. *see* Myers, Walter Lawrence.
Myers, Walter Lawrence.
xMyers, Walter L.
  The Later Realism: A Study of
    Characterization in the British Novel. Arno.
Myers, William D.
xMyers, W. D.
  Droplet Model of Atomic Nuclei. IFI Plenum.
Myers, William S. *see* Myers, William Starr.
Myers, William Starr.
xMyers, William S.
  Hoover Administration: A Documented
    Narrative. Scholarly.
  The Maryland Constitution of 1864. AMS Pr.
Myerson, Abraham, 1881-1948
xMyerson, Abraham.
  The Inheritance of Mental Diseases. Arno.
  The Nervous Housewife. Arno.
Myerson, Joel.
xMyerson, Joel.
  ed. The American Renaissance in New
    England. Gale.
  ed. Antebellum Writers in New York & the
    South. Gale.
  ed. Critical Essays on Margaret Fuller. G K
    Hall.
  Margaret Fuller: A Descriptive Bibliography. U
    of Pittsburgh Pr.
  New England Transcendentalists & the DIAL:
    A History of the Magazine & Its
    Contributors. Fairleigh Dickinson.
Myerson, Kathleen. *see* Myerson, Kathleen R.
Myerson, Kathleen R.
xMyerson, Kathleen.
  Introduction to Data Processing. Petrocelli.
Myerson, Michael, 1940-
xMyerson, Michael.
  Nothing Could Be Finer. Intl Pub Co.
Myhill, Henry.
xMyhill, Henry.

  The Loire Valley: Plantagenet & Valois.
    Merrimack Bk Serv.
  North of the Pyrenees. Transatlantic.
  Portugal. Transatlantic.
Myhr, Ivar L. *see* Myhr, Ivar Lou.
Myhr, Ivar Lou, 1902-
xMyhr, Ivar L.
  The Evolution & Practice of Milton's Epic
    Theory. Arden Lib.
  Evolution & Practice of Milton's Epic Theory.
    Folcroft.
Myint, H.
xMyint, H.
  Intro. by The Economics of the Developing
    Countries. Humanities.
Mykian, M. *see* Mykian, W.
Mykian, W.
xMykian, M.
  Numerology Made Easy. Wilshire.
Myklestad, J. Meyer. *see* Myklestad, Johannes Meyer.
Myklestad, Johannes Meyer.
xMyklestad, J. Meyer.
  English-Norwegian, Norwegian-English
    Dictionary. Saphrograph.
Mykura, H. *see* Mykura, Helmut.
Mykura, Helmut.
xMykura, H.
  Solid Surfaces & Interfaces. Routledge &
    Kegan.
Mylander, Charles.
xMylander, Charles.
  Secrets for Growing Churches. Har-Row.
Myles, Margaret. *see* Myles, Margaret F.
Myles, Margaret F.
xMyles, Margaret.
  A Textbook for Midwives. Churchill.
Myller, Rolf.
xMyller, Rolf.
  From Idea into House. Atheneum.
  illus. How Big Is a Foot. Atheneum.
  illus. Symbols & Their Meaning. Atheneum.
Mylonas, Anastassios D. *see* Mylonas, Anastassios
  Demosthenes.
Mylonas, Anastassios Demosthenes, 1925-
xMylonas, Anastassios D.
  Prisoners' Attitudes Toward Law & Legal
    Institutions. R & E Res Assoc.
Mynatt, Constance V. *see* Mynatt, Constance Virginia.
Mynatt, Constance Virginia.
xMynatt, Constance V.
  Folk Dancing for Students & Teachers. Wm C
    Brown.
Myra, Harold. *see* Myra, Harold Lawrence.
Myra, Harold Lawrence.
xMyra, Harold.
  Easter Bunny, Are You for Real?. Nelson.
  Love Notes to Jeanette. Victor Bks.
Myrdal, Alva. *see* Myrdal, Alva Reimer.
Myrdal, Alva Reimer, 1902-
xMyrdal, Alva.
  The Game of Disarmament: How the United
    States & Russia Run the Arms Race.
    Pantheon.
Myrdal, Gunnar, 1898-
xMyrdal, Gunnar.
  Against the Stream: Critical Essays on
    Economics. Random.
  American Dilemma. Har-Row.
  An American Dilemma. Pantheon.
  Objectivity in Social Research. Pantheon.
Myrdal, Jan.
xMyrdal, Jan.
  The Silk Road: A Journey from the High
    Pamirs & Ili Through Sinkiang & Kansu.
    Pantheon.
Myrer, Anton.
xMyrer, Anton.
  Once an Eagle. Berkley Pub.
Myres, John Linton, Sir, 1869-1954
xMyres, John Linton.

Geographical History in Greek Lands. Greenwood.

Myres, Sandra L.
xMyres, Sandra L.
ed. Ho for California: Women's Overland Diaries from the Huntington Library. Huntington Lib.
The Ranch in Spanish Texas 1691-1800. Tex Western.
Myrick. *see* Myrick, Jean Lockwood.
Myrick, David. *see* Myrick, David F.
Myrick, David F.
xMyrick, David.
Railroads of Arizona. Howell-North.
Myrick, Jean Lockwood.
xMyrick.
Ninety-Nine Pockets. Lantern.
Myrick, Mildred.
xMyrick, Mildred.
Ants Are Fun. Har-Row.
Myrick, William J.
xMyrick, William J.
Coordination: Concept or Reality?: A Study of Libraries in a University System. Scarecrow.
Myron. *see* Myron, Robert.
Myron, Nancy.
xMyron, Nancy.
ed. Lesbianism & the Women's Movement. Diana Pr.
Myron, Robert.
xMyron.
Prehistoric Art. G&D.
xMyron, Robert.
Modern Art in America. Macmillan.
Myrsiades, Kostas.
xMyrsiades, Kostas.
Takis Papatsonis. Twayne.
Myrus, Don. *see* Myrus, Donald.
Myrus, Donald, 1927-
xMyrus, Don.
Dog Catalog. Macmillan.
Dog Catalog. Macmillan.
xMyrus, Donald.
Ballads, Blues, & the Big Beat. Macmillan.
I Like Jazz. Macmillan.
Mysak. *see* Mysak, Edward Damien.
Mysak, Edward Damien, 1930-
xMysak.
Pathologies of Speech Systems. Williams & Wilkins.
Mysels, Karol J.
xMysels, Karol J.
Introduction to Colloid Chemistry. Krieger.
Mystery Writers of America.
xMystery Writers of America.
Mystery Writers Handbook. Writers Digest.
Mystic Seaport Museum, Inc. *see* Mystic Seaport, Mystic, Connecticut.
Mystic Seaport, Mystic, Connecticut.
xMystic Seaport Museum, Inc.
International Congress of Maritime Museums, 3rd Conference: Proceedings, 1978. Univ Microfilms.
Naamani, Israel T.
xNaamani, Israel T.
The State of Israel. Behrman.
Nab Broadcast Engineering Conference, 24th, Washington, D.C., 1970.
xNational Association of Broadcasters Engineering Conference, 1970.
Technical Papers. TAB Bks.
Nab Broadcast Engineering Conference, 27th, Washington, 1973.
xNational Association of Broadcasters Engineering Conference, 1973.
Technical Papers. TAB Bks.
Nabbes, Thomas.
xNabbes, Thomas.

Works of Thomas Nabbes. Arno.
Nabholtz, John R.
xNabholtz, John R.
The Prose of the British Romantic Movement. Macmillan.
Nabokov, Nicolas, 1903-
xNabokov, Nicolas.
Old Friends & New Music. Greenwood.
Nabokov, Peter.
xNabokov, Peter.
ed. Native American Testimony: An Anthology of Indian & White Relations. First Encounter to Dispossession. T Y Crowell.

Nabokov, Vladimir. *see* Nabokov, Vladimir Vladimirovich.

Nabokov, Vladimir Vladimirovich.
xNabokov, Vladimir.
Annotated Lolita. McGraw.
Laughter in the Dark. New Directions.
Look at the Harlequins. McGraw.
Nikolai Gogol. New Directions.
Pale Fire. Berkley Pub.
Pale Fire. Putnam.
Pale Fire. Putnam.
Portable Nabokov. Penguin.
Real Life of Sebastian Knight. New Directions.
Strong Opinions. McGraw.
Nabuco, Carolina.
xNabuco, Carolina.
Life of Joaquim Nabuco. Greenwood.
Nabuco, Joaquim, 1849-1910
xNabuco, Joaquim.
Abolitionism: The Brazilian Antislavery Struggle. U of Ill Pr.
Nacci, Chris N.
xNacci, Chris N.
Ignacio Manuel Altamirano. Twayne.
Nachalo, Sophia.
xNachalo, Sophia.
Letters of Insurgents. Black & Red.
Nachant, Frances G. *see* Nachant, Frances Grant.
Nachant, Frances Grant.
xNachant, Frances G.
Song of Peace. Golden Quill.
Nachbin, L. *see* Nachbin, Leopoldo.
Nachbin, Leopoldo.
xNachbin, L.
Holomorphic Functions, Domains of Holomorphy & Local Properties. Elsevier.
Topology & Order. Krieger.
xNachbin, Leopoldo.
The Haar Integral. Krieger.
Nachmias, David.
xNachmias, David.
Bureaucratic Culture: Citizens & Administrators in Israel. St Martin.
Nachod, Joy N. *see* Nachod, Joy Nevill.
Nachod, Joy Nevill.
xNachod, Joy N.
Of Prisoners...Poets...& People. Vantage.
Nachtmann, Francis W. *see* Nachtmann, Francis Weldon.
Nachtmann, Francis Weldon, 1913-
xNachtmann, Francis W.
Exercises in French Phonics. Scott F.
French Review for Reading Improvement. Macmillan.
Naclerio, Emil A.
xNaclerio, Emil A.
Chest Injuries: Physiologic Principles & Emergency Management. Grune.
NACUBO. *see* National Association of College and University Business Officers.
Naczi, Frances D.
xNaczi, Frances D.
Without Bombast & Blunder: An Executive's Guide to Effective Writing. Farnswth Pub.
Nadas, Alexander S. *see* Nadas, Alexander Sander.

Nadas, Alexander Sander, 1913-
xNadas, Alexander S.
Pediatric Cardiology. Saunders.
Nadeau, Maurice.
xNadeau, Maurice.
The Greatness of Flaubert. Open Court.
Nadeau, Ray E.
xNadeau, Ray E.
Speech Communication: A Career Education Approach. A-W.
Speech-Communication: A Modern Approach. A-W.
xNadeau, Raymond E.
Speech Communication: A Career Education Approach. A-W.
Nadeau, Raymond E. *see* Nadeau, Ray E.
Nadeau, Remi. *see* Nadeau, Remi A.
Nadeau, Remi A.
xNadeau, Remi.
California: The New Society. Greenwood.
Nadel, Ethan R.
xNadel, Ethan R.
ed. Problems with Temperature Regulation During Exercise. Acad Pr.
Nadel, Ira B. *see* Nadel, Ira Bruce.
Nadel, Ira Bruce.
xNadel, Ira B.
ed. Victorian Artists & the City: A Collection of Critical Essays. Pergamon.
Nadel, Mark V.
xNadel, Mark V.
Corporations & Political Accountability. Heath.
Nadel, Myron H. *see* Nadel, Myron Howard.
Nadel, Myron Howard.
xNadel, Myron H.
ed. The Dance Experience: Readings in Dance Appreciation. Universe.
Nadel, Siegfried F. *see* Nadel, Siegfried Frederick.
Nadel, Siegfried Frederick, 1903-1956
xNadel, Siegfried F.
The Nuba: An Anthropological Study of the Hill Tribes in Kordofan. AMS Pr.
Naden, Corinne. *see* Naden, Corinne J.
Naden, Corinne J.
xNaden, Corinne.
Driving Your Bike Safely. Messner.
xNaden, Corinne J.
The Colony of New Jersey. Watts.
Let's Find Out About Frogs. Watts.
Woodlands Around the World. Watts.
Nader, George.
xNader, George.
Chrome. BJ Pub Group.
Nader, Helen, 1936-
xNader, Helen.
The Mendoza Family in the Spanish Renaissance, 1350-1550. Rutgers U Pr.
Nader, Laura.
xNader, Laura.
ed. The Disputing Process in Ten Societies. Columbia U Pr.
Nader, Ralph.
xNader, Ralph.
The Menace of Atomic Energy. Norton.
Taming the Giant Corporation. Norton.
Nadiri, M. Ishaq.
xNadiri, M. Ishaq.
Disequilibrium Model of Demand for Factors of Production. Natl Bur Econ Res.
Nadler, Bob.
xNadler, Bob.
Advanced B & W Darkroom Book. Amphoto.
The Color Printing Manual. Amphoto.
xNadler, Robert.
The Color Printing Manual. Amphoto.
Nadler, David.
xNadler, David A.

Feedback & Organization Development: Using
Data-Based Methods. A-W.
Managing Organizational Behavior. Little.
Nadler, David A. see Nadler, David.

Nadler, Leonard.
xNadler, Leonard.
The Conference Book. Gulf Pub.
Developing Human Resources. Learning
Concepts.

Nadler, Myra, 1945-
xNadler, Myra.
ed. How to Start an Audiovisual Collection.
Scarecrow.
Nadler, Paul. see Nadler, Paul S.
Nadler, Paul S.
xNadler, Paul.
Commercial Banking in the Economy.
Random.
xNadler, Paul S.
Commercial Banking in the Economy.
Random.

Nadler, Susan, 1947-
xNadler, Susan.
The Butterfly Convention. Dial.
Nadler, Zeace. see Nadler, Leonard.
Naegele, John A.
xNaegele, John A.
Air Pollution Damage to Vegetation. Am
Chemical.
Naert, P. A.
xNaert, P. A.
Building Implementable Marketing Models.
Kluwer Boston.
Naeseth, Henriette C. see Naeseth, Henriette C K.
Naeseth, Henriette C K.
xNaeseth, Henriette C.
The Swedish Theatre of Chicago: 1868-1950.
Augustana Coll.
Naeve, Virginia.
xNaeve, Virginia.
ed. Changeover: Drive for Peace. Swallow.
Naftalin, Rose.
xNaftalin, Rose.
Grandma Rose's Book of Sinfully Delicious
Snacks, Nibbles, Noshes & Other Delights.
Random.
Naftolin, F.
xNaftolin, Frederick.
ed. Dilation of the Uterine Cervix: Connective
Tissue Biology & Clinical Management.
Raven.
Naftolin, Frederick. see Naftolin, F.
Nafziger, E. Wayne.
xNafziger, E. Wayne.
Class, Caste, & Entrepreneurship: A Study of
Indian Industrialists. U Pr of Hawaii.
Nafziger, Ralph O.
xNafziger, Ralph O.
ed. Introduction to Journalism Research.
Greenwood.
Nag, B. R.
xNag, B. R.
Theory of Electrical Transport in
Semi-Conductors. Pergamon.
Nagahiro, Toshio.
xNagahiro, Toshio.
Great Sculpture of the Far East. Morrow.
Nagai, Kafu, 1879-1959
xNagai, Kafu.
Geisha in Rivalry. C E Tuttle.
Nagaishi, C. see Nagaishi, Ch Uz O.
Nagaishi, Ch Uz O.
xNagaishi, C.
Functional Anatomy & Histology of the Lung.
Univ Park.
Nagarajan, K. see Nagarajan, Krishnaswami.

Nagarajan, Krishnaswami, 1893-
xNagarajan, K.
Chronicles of Kedaram. Asia.
Nagata, M. see Nagata, Masayoshi.
Nagata, Masayoshi, 1927-
xNagata, M.
Local Rings. Krieger.
Polynomial Rings & Affine Spaces. Am Math.
xNagata, Masayoshi.
Field Theory. Dekker.
Nagatani, K. see Nagatani, Keizo.
Nagatani, Keizo.
xNagatani, K.
Monetary Theory. Elsevier.
Nagatsuka, Ruyji. see Nagatsuka, Ryuji.
Nagatsuka, Ryuji.
xNagatsuka, Ruyji.
I Was a Kamikaze. Macmillan.
Nagel, Ernest.
xNagel, Ernest.
Godel's Proof. NYU Pr.
Observation & Theory in Science. Johns
Hopkins.
Principles of the Theory of Probability. U of
Chicago Pr.
Structure of Science: Problems in the Logic of
Scientific Explanation. HarBraceJ.
Teleology Revisited & Other Essays in the
Philosophy & History of Science. Columbia U
Pr.
Nagel, Shirley.
xNagel, Shirley.
Escape from the Tower. Creative Ed.
Nagel, Stuart S.
xNagel, Stuart S.
Decision Theory & the Legal Process.
Lexington Bks.
ed. Environmental Politics. Praeger.
Nagel, T. see Nagel, Thomas.
Nagel, Thomas.
xNagel, T.
Mortal Questions. Cambridge U Pr.
Nagenda, John.
xNagenda, John.
Frwd. by Mukasa. Macmillan.
Nagera, Humberto.
xNagera, Humberto.
Female Sexuality & the Oedipus Complex.
Aronson.
Nagi, Saad. see Nagi, Saad Zaghloul.
Nagi, Saad Zaghloul.
xNagi, Saad.
ed. The Social Contexts of Research. Krieger.
Nagin, Paul. see Nagin, Paul A.
Nagin, Paul A.
xNagin, Paul.
BASIC with Style: Programming Proverbs.
Hayden.
Nagle, D. Brendan, 1936-
xNagle, D. Brendan.
The Ancient World: A Social & Cultural
History. P-H.
Nagle, James J.
xNagle, James J.
Heredity & Human Affairs. Mosby.
Nagle, John D. see Nagle, John David.
Nagle, John David.
xNagle, John D.
The National Democratic Party:
Right-Radicalism in the Federal Republic of
Germany. U of Cal Pr.
System and Succession: The Social Bases of
Political Elite Recruitment. U of Tex Pr.
Nagle, Judy, 1929-
xNagle, Judy.
The Responsive Arts. Alfred Pub.
Nagler, A. M. see Nagler, Alois Maria.
Nagler, Alois Maria, 1907-
xNagler, A. M.

The Medieval Religious Stage: Shapes &
Phantoms. Yale U Pr.
Theatre Festivals of the Medici, 1539-1637. Da
Capo.
Nagrath, I. J.
xNagrath, I. J.
Control Systems Engineering. Halsted Pr.
Nagy, B. see Nagy, Bartholomew J.
Nagy, Bartholomew J., 1927-
xNagy, B.
Carbonaceous Meteorites. Elsevier.
Nagy, Gregory.
xNagy, Gregory.
Comparative Studies in Greek & Indic Meter.
Harvard U Pr.
Greek Dialects & the Transformation of an
Indo-European Process. Harvard U Pr.
Nagy, Steven.
xNagy, Steven.
Citrus Science & Technology. AVI.
Nagy-Talavera, Nicholas M., 1929-
xNagy-Talavera, Nicholas M.
Green Shirts & the Others: A History of
Fascism in Hungary & Rumania. Hoover Inst
Pr.
Nahas, Gabriel G., 1920-
xNahas, Gabriel G.
Keep off the Grass: A Scientific Enquiry into
the Biological Effects of Marijuana.
Pergamon.
Nahas, Rebecca.
xNahas, Rebecca.
The New Couple: Women & Gay Men.
Seaview Bks.
Nahi, Nasser E., 1933-
xNahi, Nasser E.
Estimation Theory & Applications. Krieger.
Nahikian, Howard M.
xNahikian, Howard M.
Modern Algebra for Biologists. U of Chicago
Pr.
Nahm, Milton C. see Nahm, Milton Charles.
Nahm, Milton Charles, 1903-
xNahm, Milton C.
Aesthetic Experience & Its Presuppositions.
Russell.
The Artist As Creator: An Essay of Human
Freedom. Univ Microfilms.
Nahmad, H. M.
xNahmad, H. M.
Compiled by A Portion in Paradise: And Other
Jewish Folktales. Schocken.
Naib, Zuher M.
xNaib, Zuher M.
ed. Cytology Examination Review Book. Med
Exam.
Exfoliative Cytopathology. Little.
Naidech, Howard J.
xNaidech, Howard J.
Radiologic Technology Examination Review.
Arco.
Naidu, D. S. see Naidu, Devara Satyanarayana.
Naidu, Devara Satyanarayana, 1898-
xNaidu, D. S.
Engineering Materials & Their Testing. Asia.
Naierman, Naomi.
xNaierman, Naomi.
Community Mental Health Centers: A Decade
Later. Abt Assoc.
Naifeh. see Naifeh, Steven W.
Naifeh, Steven W.
xNaifeh.
Moving up: The Successful Man's Guide to
Impeccable Taste. St Martin.
Naik, J. A.
xNaik, J. A.
An Alternative Polity for India. Verry.
Naik, M. K.
xNaik, M. K.

Mulk Raj Anand. InterCulture.

Naile, Florence.
xNaile, Florence.
America's Master of Bee Culture: The Life of
L. L. Langstroth. Cornell U Pr.

Naim, C. M.
xNaim, C. M.
Pref. by Iqbal, Jinnah, & Pakistan: The Vision
& the Reality. Maxwell Schl Citizen.
Readings in Urdu: Prose & Poetry. U Pr of
Hawaii.

Naima. *see* Naima, Mustafa.

Naima, Mustafa, 1652-1715
xNaima.
Annals of the Turkish Empire from 1591 to
1659 of the Christian Era. Arno.

Naiman, Arnold.
xNaiman, Arnold.
Understanding Statistics. McGraw.

Naimark, Norman M.
xNaimark, Norman M.
A History of the "Proletariat": The Emergence
of Marxism in the Kingdom of Poland,
1870-1887. East Eur Quarterly.

Naimpally, S. A.
xNaimpally, S. A.
Proximity Spaces. Cambridge U Pr.

Naipaul, Shiva, 1945-
xNaipaul, Shiva.
North of South: An African Journey. Penguin.

Naipaul, V. S. *see* Naipaul, Vidiadhar Surajprasad.

Naipaul, Vidiadhar Surajprasad.
xNaipaul, V. S.
A Bend in the River. Knopf.
A Bend in the River. Random.
A House for Mr. Biswas. Penguin.
India: A Wounded Civilization. Knopf.
India: A Wounded Civilization. Random.
The Return of Eva Peron with the Killings in
Trinidad. Knopf.
The Suffrage of Elvira. Penguin.

Nair, K. K., 1918-
xNair, K. K.
A Profile of Indian Culture. InterCulture.

Nair, Kannan K.
xNair, Kannan K.
Politics & Society in South Eastern Nigeria,
1841-1906: A Study of Power, Diplomacy, &
Commerce in Old Cabar. Northwestern U Pr.

Nair, Kusum.
xNair, Kusum.
In Defense of the Irrational Peasant: Indian
Agriculture After the Green Revolution. U of
Chicago Pr.

Nair, Sreekantan S.
xNair, Sreekantan S.
On Certain Priority Queues. Mgmt Info Serv.

Nairn, John A. *see* Nairn, John Arbuthnot.

Nairn, John Arbuthnot, 1874-
xNairn, John A.
Authors of Rome. Folcroft.
Authors of Rome. Kennikat.

Nairn, R. C.
xNairn, R. C.
Fluorescent Protein Tracing. Churchill.

Nairn, Ronald C.
xNairn, Ronald C.
Wealth of Nations in Crisis. Bayland Pub.

Nairne, Carolina O. *see* Nairne, Carolina Oliphant
Nairne.

Nairne, Carolina Oliphant Nairne.
xNairne, Carolina O.
The Life & Songs of the Baroness Nairne, with
a Memoir & Poems of Caroline Oliphant the
Younger. AMS Pr.

Nais Committee for International & World Education.
see National Association of Independent Schools.
Committee for International and World Education.

NAIS Task Force on Secondary Mathematics.
xNAIS Task Force on Secondary Mathematics.

Graphing, Factoring Quadratic Trinomials.
NAIS.
Quadratic Functions & Equivalence. NAIS.
Signed Numbers, Linear Functions, Surface
Area Blocks. NAIS.

NAIS Teacher Services Committee. *see* National
Association of Independent Schools. Teacher Service
Committee.

Naisawald, L. Van Loan.
xNaisawald, L. VanLoan.
Intro. by In Some Foreign Field: The Story of
Four British Graves on the Outer Banks.
Blair.

Naisawald, L. VanLoan. *see* Naisawald, L. Van Loan.

Naish, Camille, 1945-
xNaish, Camille.
A Genetic Approach to Structures in the Work
of Jean Genet. Harvard U Pr.

Naito, Hiroshi.
xNaito, Hiroshi.
Retold by Legends of Japan. C E Tuttle.

Najarian, Haig H. *see* Najarian, Haig Hagop.

Najarian, Haig Hagop, 1925-
xNajarian, Haig H.
ed. Textbook of Medical Parasitology. Krieger.

Najarian, Peter, 1940-
xNajarian, Peter.
Voyages. Ararat Pr.

Najder, Z. *see* Najder, Zdzisaw.

Najder, Zdzisaw.
xNajder, Z.
Values & Evaluations. Oxford U Pr.

Najita, Tetsuo.
xNajita, Tetsuo.
Japan: The Intellectual Foundations of Modern
Japanese Politics. U of Chicago Pr.

Nakagami, Y. *see* Nakagami, Yoshiomi.

Nakagami, Yoshiomi.
xNakagami, Y.
Duality for Crossed Products of Von Neumann
Algebras. Springer-Verlag.

Nakagawa, Sensaka. *see* Nakagawa, Sensaku.

Nakagawa, Sensaku, 1910-
xNakagawa, Sensaka.
Kutani Ware. Kodansha.

Nakamoto, Kazno. *see* Nakamoto, Kazuo.

Nakamoto, Kazuo, 1922-
xNakamoto, Kazno.
Spectroscopy & Structure of Metal Chelate
Compounds. Krieger.
xNakamoto, Kazuo.
Infrared & Raman Spectra of Inorganic &
Coordination Compounds. Wiley.

Nakamura, Hajime, 1912-
xNakamura, Hajime.
Gotama Buddha. Buddhist Bks.
Parallel Developments: A Comparative History
of Ideas. Kodansha.

Nakamura, Robert M.
xNakamura, Robert M.
Immunopathology: Clinical Laboratory
Concepts & Methods. Little.

Nakamura, Shoichiro, 1935-
xNakamura, Shoichiro.
Computational Methods in Engineering &
Science: With Applications to Fluid
Dynamics & Nuclear Systems. Wiley.

Nakano, Hidegoro, 1909-
xNakano, Hidegoro.
Linear Lattices. Wayne St U Pr.

Nakano, Tomio, 1891-1948
xNakano, Tomio.
Ordinance Power of the Japanese Emperor.
AMS Pr.

Nakao, M. *see* Nakao, Makoto.

Nakao, Makoto.
xNakao, M.

ed. Active Transport. Univ Park.
Organization of Energy Transducing
Membranes. Univ Park.

Nakata, y Ujiro O, 1905-
xNakata, Yujiro.
The Art of Japanese Calligraphy. Weatherhill.

Nakata, Yujiro. *see* Nakata, y Ujiro O.

Nakata, Yuri.
xNakata, Yuri.
From Press to People: Collecting & Using U. S.
Government Publications. ALA.
Organizing a Local Government Documents
Collection. ALA.

Nakatani, Chiyoko.
xNakatani, Chiyoko.
illus. My Day on the Farm. T Y Crowell.

Nakayama, Ichiro, 1898_-
xNakayama, Ichiro.
Industrialization of Japan. U Pr of Hawaii.

Nakayama, Shigeru, 1928-
xNakayama, Shigeru.
History of Japanese Astronomy: Chinese
Background & Western Impact. Harvard U
Pr.

Nakhleh, Emile A., 1938-
xNakhleh, Emile A.
Arab-American Relations in the Persian Gulf.
Am Enterprise.
Bahrain: Political Development in a
Modernizing Society. Lexington Bks.

Nakhleh, K. *see* Nakhleh, Khalil.

Nakhleh, Khalil.
xNakhleh, K.
The Sociology of the Palestinians. St Martin.

Nakosteen, Mehdi. *see* Nakosteen, Mehdi Khan.

Nakosteen, Mehdi Khan, 1904-
xNakosteen, Mehdi.
The History & Philosophy of Education. Wiley.

Nalbandian, Louise.
xNalbandian, Louise Z.
The Armenian Revolutionary Movement: The
Development of Armenian Political Parties
Through the Nineteenth Century. U of Cal
Pr.

Nalbandian, Louise Z. *see* Nalbandian, Louise.

Nalbantian, Suzanne, 1950-
xNalbantian, Suzanne.
The Symbol of the Soul from Holderlin to
Yeats: A Study in Metonymy. Columbia U
Pr.

Nalivkin, D. V. *see* Nalivkin, Dmitrii Vasilevich.

Nalivkin, Dmitrii Vasilevich, 1889-
xNalivkin, D. V.
Geology of the U.S.S.R.. U of Toronto Pr.

Nallin, W. E. *see* Nallin, Walter Edward.

Nallin, Walter Edward, 1918-
xNallin, W. E.
Musical Idea: A Consideration of Music & Its
Ways. Macmillan.

Nalty, Bernard C.
xNalty, Bernard C.
ed. Wrecks, Rescues & Investigations: Selected
Documents of the U. S. Coast Guard & Its
Predecessors. Scholarly Res Inc.

Nam, Koon Woo.
xNam, Koon Woo.
The North Korean Communist Leadership,
1945-1965: A Study of Factionalism &
Political Consolidation. U of Ala Pr.

Namath, Joe. *see* Namath, Joe Willie.

Namath, Joe Willie.
xNamath, Joe.
A Matter of Style. Little.

Namba, M. *see* Namba, Makoto.

Namba, Makoto, 1943-
xNamba, M.
Families of Meromorphic Functions on
Compact Riemann Surfaces. Springer-Verlag.

Name, Willard G. Van. *see* Van Name, Willard G.
Namee, J. William Van. *see* Van Namee, J. William.

Names, Larry. *see* Names, Larry D.
Names, Larry D.
xNames, Larry.
The Legend of Eagle Claw. Independence Pr.
Twice Dead. Nordon Pubns.
xNames, Larry D.
The Shaman's Secret. Doubleday.
Namias, June.
xNamias, June.
First Generation: In the Words of Twentieth -
Century American Immigrants. Beacon Pr.
Namier, L. B. *see* Namier, Lewis Bernstein.
Namier, Lewis. *see* Namier, Lewis Bernstein.
Namier, Lewis B. *see* Namier, Lewis Bernstein.
Namier, Lewis Bernstein, Sir, 1888-1960
xNamier, L. B.
Diplomatic Prelude, 1938-1939. Fertig.
xNamier, Lewis.
England in the Age of the American
Revolution. St Martin.
Personalities & Powers. Greenwood.
xNamier, Lewis B.
In the Margin of History. Arno.
Namikawa, Banri, 1931-
xNamikawa, Banri.
Spain. Kodansha.
Namioka, Lensey.
xNamioka, Lensey.
Samurai & the Long-Nosed Devils. Dell.
White Serpent Castle. Dell.
Nanassy, L. *see* Nanassy, Louis C.
Nanassy, Louis C.
xNanassy, L.
General Business & Economic Understandings.
P-H.
xNanassy, Louis C.
Principles & Trends in Business Education.
Bobbs.
ed. Readings in Teaching Business Subjects.
Pitman Learning.
Reference Manual for Office Workers.
Glencoe.
Reference Manual for Office Workers.
Macmillan.
Nanavati, Manilal B. *see* Nanavati, Manilal Balabhai.
Nanavati, Manilal Balabhai.
xNanavati, Manilal B.
Group Prejudices in India: A Symposium.
Greenwood.
Nance, John, 1935-
xNance, John.
The Gentle Tasaday: A Stone Age People in
the Philippine Rain Forest. HarBraceJ.
The Mud Pie Dilemma: A Master Potter's
Struggle to Make Art & Ends Meet. Intl
Schol Bk Serv.
Nance, Joseph M. *see* Nance, Joseph Milton.
Nance, Joseph Milton.
xNance, Joseph M.
After San Jacinto: The Texas-Mexican
Frontier, 1836-1841. U of Tex Pr.
Attack & Counterattack: The Texas-Mexican
Frontier, 1842. U of Tex Pr.
Nance, Virginia L. *see* Nance, Virginia Lindblad.
Nance, Virginia Lindblad.
xNance, Virginia L.
Golf. Wm C Brown.
Nance, William L.
xNance, William L.
Worlds of Truman Capote. Stein & Day.
Nanda, B. R.
xNanda, B. R.
ed. Studies in Modern Indian History.
Kennikat.
Nanda, B. R. *see* Nanda, Bal Ram.
Nanda, Bal Ram.
xNanda, B. R.

Gokhale, Gandhi & the Nehrus: Studies in
Indian Nationalism. St Martin.
Gokhale: The Indian Moderates & the British
Raj. Princeton U Pr.
The Nehrus: Motilal & Jawaharlal. U of
Chicago Pr.
Nanda, Navin C.
xNanda, Navin C.
Clinical Echocardiography. Mosby.
Nandakumar, Prema.
xNandakumar, Prema.
The Glory & the Good: Essays on Literature.
Dynamic Learn Corp.
Nandan, Yash.
xNandan, Yash.
Compiled by The Durkheimian School: A
Systematic & Comprehensive Bibliography.
Greenwood.
Nandy, K. *see* Nandy, Kalidas.
Nandy, Kalidas.
xNandy, K.
ed. Geriatric Psychopharmacology. Elsevier.
ed. Senile Dementia: a Biomedical Approach:
Proceedings of the Conference at St. Louis,
Missouri, March 1978. Elsevier.
Nanfria, Linda.
xNanfria, Linda.
Beat the Super Markets!. Impact Pub.
Beat the Supermarkets. Delphi Info.
Nankivell, John H. *see* Nankivell, John Henry.
Nankivell, John Henry, 1884-
xNankivell, John H.
History of the Twenty Fifth Regiment: United
States Infantry 1869-1926. Old Army.
Nannes, Caspar H. *see* Nannes, Caspar Harold.
Nannes, Caspar Harold.
xNannes, Caspar H.
Politics in the American Drama. Intl Schol Bk
Serv.
Nanney, J. Louis.
xNanney, J. Louis.
Trigonometry: A Skills Approach. Allyn.
xNanney, Louis.
Developing Skills in Algebra: A Lecture
Worktext. Allyn.
Nanney, Louis. *see* Nanney, J. Louis.
Nansen, Fridtjof, 1861-1930
xNansen, Fridtjof.
Adventure, & Other Papers. Arno.
Armenia & the Near East. Da Capo.
In Northern Mists: Arctic Exploration in Early
Times. AMS Pr.
In Northern Mists: Arctic Exploration in Early
Times. Greenwood.
ed. Norwegian North Polar Expedition
1893-96: Scientific Results. Greenwood.
Nanyenya-Takirambudde, Peter.
xNanyenya-Takirambudde, Peter.
Technology Transfer & International Law.
Praeger.
Napear, Peggy.
xNapear, Peggy.
Brain Child: A Mother's Diary. Har-Row.
Napier, Augustus.
xNapier, Augustus Y.
The Family Crucible. Bantam.
The Family Crucible. Har-Row.
Napier, Augustus Y. *see* Napier, Augustus.
Napier, B. D. *see* Napier, Bunyan Davie.
Napier, B. Davie. *see* Napier, Bunyan Davie.
Napier, Bunyan Davie.
xNapier, B. D.
On New Creation. La State U Pr.
xNapier, B. Davie.
Come Sweet Death: A Quintet from Genesis.
Pilgrim NY.
Napier, J. R. *see* Napier, John Russell.
Napier, John. *see* Napier, John Russell.
Napier, John Russell.
xNapier, J. R.

Primates & Their Adaptations. Carolina
Biological.
xNapier, John.
The Human Hand. Carolina Biological.
Napier, Prue. *see* Napier, Prue H.
Napier, Prue H.
xNapier, Prue.
Chimpanzees. McGraw.
Napier, William. *see* Napier, William Francis Patrick.
Napier, William Francis Patrick.
xNapier, William.
History of the War in the Peninsula. U of
Chicago Pr.
Napoleoni, Claudio.
xNapoleoni, Claudio.
Economic Thought of the Twentieth Century.
Biblio Dist.
Economic Thought of the Twentieth Century.
Intl Pubns Serv.
Napoli, Donna J. *see* Napoli, Donna Jo.
Napoli, Donna Jo.
xNapoli, Donna J.
ed. Elements of Tone, Stress, & Intonation.
Georgetown U Pr.
Syntactic Argumentation. Georgetown U Pr.
Napolitane, Catherine.
xNapolitane, Catherine.
Living & Loving After Divorce. NAL.
Nara, Harry R.
xNara, Harry R.
Vector Mechanics for Engineers. Krieger.
Narain, A. K.
xNarain, A. K.
Coin Types of the Indo-Greek Kings. Ares.
Naranjo, Claudio.
xNaranjo, Claudio.
On the Psychology of Meditation. Penguin.
Narasimhamurty, T. S.
xNarasimhamurty, T. S.
Photoelastic & Electro-Optic Properties of
Crystals. Plenum Pub.
Narasimhan, C. V. *see* Narasimhan, Chakravarthi V.
Narasimhan, Chakravarthi V., 1915-
xNarasimhan, C. V.
Regionalism in the United Nations. Asia.
Naravane, Vishwanath S.
xNaravane, Vishwanath S.
Ananda K. Coomaraswamy. G K Hall.
Ananda K. Coomaraswamy. Twayne.
Narayan, B. K.
xNarayan, B. K.
Anwar el Sadat: Man with a Mission. Intl
Pubns Serv.
Narayan, Ongkar, 1926-
xNarayan, Ongkar.
Bye Bye Mista. Philos Lib.
Narayan, R. K., 1906-
xNarayan, R. K.
Grateful to Life & Death. Mich St U Pr.
The Guide: A Novel. Penguin.
A Painter of Signs. Viking Pr.
Printer of Malgudi. Mich St U Pr.
Narayana, T. V. *see* Narayana, Tadepalli Venkata.
Narayana, Tadepalli Venkata, 1930-
xNarayana, T. V.
Lattice Path Combinatorics with Statistical
Applications. U of Toronto Pr.
Nardin, Jane, 1944-
xNardin, Jane.
Those Elegant Decorums: The Concept of
Propriety in Jane Austen's Novels. State U
NY Pr.
Nardone, Thomas R.
xNardone, Thomas R.
ed. Classical Vocal Music in Print. Musicdata.
ed. Organ Music in Print. Musicdata.
Naremore, James.
xNaremore, James.

The World Without a Self: Virginia Woolf &
the Novel. Yale U Pr.

Narici, Lawrence.
xNarici, Lawrence.
Functional Analysis & Valuation Theory.
Dekker.

Narkiewicz, Olga A.
xNarkiewicz, Olga A.
The Green Flag: Polish Populist Politics,
1867-1970. Rowman.

Narkiss, Bezalel.
xNarkiss, Bezalel.
The Armenian Art Treasures of Jerusalem.
Caratzas Bros.

Narlikar, Jayant V. *see* Narlikar, Jayant Vishnu.

Narlikar, Jayant Vishnu, 1938-
xNarlikar, Jayant V.
The Structure of the Universe. Oxford U Pr.

Narodny, Ivan.
xNarodny, Ivan.
American Artists. Arno.

Naroll, Raoul.
xNaroll, Raoul.
Worldwide Theory Testing. HRAFP.

Narramore, Bruce.
xNarramore, Bruce.
Adolescence Is Not an Illness. Revell.
Parenting with Love & Limits. Zondervan.
You're Someone Special. Zondervan.

Narramore, Clyde M. *see* Narramore, Clyde Maurice.

Narramore, Clyde Maurice, 1916-

xNarramore, Clyde M.

Encyclopedia of Psychological Problems.
Zondervan.
How to Handle Pressure. Tyndale.
How to Tell Your Children About Sex.
Zondervan.

Narus, Donald J.
xNarus, Donald J.
Great American Woodies & Wagons. Crestline.

Narver, John C.
xNarver, John C.
Conglomerate Mergers & Market Competition.
U of Cal Pr.

Nasar, S. A.
xNasar, S. A.
Linear Motion Electric Machines. Wiley.

Nasatir, Abraham P. *see* Nasatir, Abraham Phineas.

Nasatir, Abraham Phineas, 1904-
xNasatir, Abraham P.
Borderland in Retreat: From Spanish Louisiana
to the Far Southwest. U of NM Pr.
ed. Manuel Lisa. Argosy.

Nasaw, David.
xNasaw, David.
Schooled to Order: A Social History of Public
Schooling in the United States. Oxford U Pr.

Nascher, Ignatz L. *see* Nascher, Ignatz Leo.

Nascher, Ignatz Leo, 1863-
xNascher, Ignatz L.
Geriatrics: The Diseases of Old Age & Their
Treatment. Arno.

Nascimento, Edson Arantes Do, 1940-
xNascimento, Edson Arantes do.
Learning Soccer with Pele. Lippincott.

Nash, A. E. *see* Nash, A. E. Keir.

Nash, A. E. Keir.
xNash, A. E.
Oil Pollution & the Public Interest: A Study of
the Santa Barbara Oil Spill. Inst Gov Stud
Berk.

Nash, Arnold S. *see* Nash, Arnold Samuel.

Nash, Arnold Samuel.
xNash, Arnold S.

ed. Protestant Thought in the Twentieth
Century: Whence & Whither?. Greenwood.

Nash, Barbara.
xNash, Barbara.
Tap Dance. Wm C Brown.

Nash, Bruce. *see* Nash, Bruce M.

Nash, Bruce M.
xNash, Bruce.
Whatever Happened to Blue Suede Shoes: A
Nostalgia Quiz Book of the Fifties. G&D.

Nash, David T.
xNash, David T.
Coronary!: Prediction & Prevention. NAL.
Coronary: Prediction & Prevention. Scribner.
Dr. Nash's Natural Diet Book. G&D.

Nash, Donald J.
xNash, Donald J.
Individual Identification & the Law
Enforcement Officer. C C Thomas.

Nash, E. *see* Nash, E. J. H.

Nash, E. J. H.
xNash, E.
How to Succeed in the Christian Life.
Inter-Varsity.

Nash, F. C. *see* Nash, Frederick C.

Nash, Frederick C., 1922-
xNash, F. C.
Automotive Technology. McGraw.

Nash, Gary B.
xNash, Gary B.
Class & Society in Early America. P-H.
ed. Great Fear: Race in the Mind of America.
HR&W.
ed. The Private Side of American History:
Readings in Everyday Life. HarBraceJ.
The Urban Crucible: Social Change, Political
Consciousness, & the Origins of the
American Revolution. Harvard U Pr.

Nash, Gerald D.
xNash, Gerald D.
The American West in the Twentieth Century:
A Short History of an Urban Oasis. U of NM
Pr.
Issues in American Economic History: Selected
Readings. Heath.
State Government & Economic Development.
Arno.

Nash, Henry T.
xNash, Henry T.
American Foreign Policy: Changing
Perspectives on National Security. Dorsey.

Nash, Howard P. *see* Nash, Howard Pervear.

Nash, Howard Pervear, 1900-
xNash, Howard P.
A Naval History of the Civil War. A S Barnes.
Stormy Petrel: The Life & Times of General
Benjamin F. Butler, 1818-1893. Fairleigh
Dickinson.
Third Parties in American Politics. Pub Aff Pr.

Nash, J. C. *see* Nash, John C.

Nash, J. M. *see* Nash, Jonathon M.

Nash, Jay R. *see* Nash, Jay Robert.

Nash, Jay Robert.
xNash, Jay R.
Among the Missing: An Anecdotal History of
Missing Persons from 1800 to Present. S&S.
Citizen Hoover: A Critical Study of the Life &
Times of J. Edgar Hoover & His FBI.
Nelson-Hall.
Darkest Hours: A Narrative Encyclopedia of
World Wide Disasters from Ancient Times to
the Present. Nelson-Hall.
On All Fronts. December Pr.

Nash, John, 1920-
xNash, John.
Developmental Psychology: A Psychobiological
Approach. P-H.

Nash, John C., 1947-
xNash, J. C.

Compact Numerical Methods for Computers:
Linear Algebra & Functional Minimization.
Halsted Pr.

Nash, Jonathon M.
xNash, J. M.
ed. Modeling, Simulation, Testing, &
Measurements for Solar Energy Systems.
ASME.

Nash, June. *see* Nash, June C.

Nash, June C.
xNash, June.
ed. Ideology & Social Change in Latin
America. Gordon.
ed. Popular Participation in Social Change:
Cooperatives, Collectives, & Nationalized
Industry. Beresford Bk Serv.
We Eat the Mines & the Mines Eat Us:
Dependency & Exploitation in Bolivian Tin
Mines. Columbia U Pr.

Nash, Mary, 1925-
xNash, Mary.
While Mrs. Coverlet Was Away. Little.

Nash, N. Richard.
xNash, N. Richard.
The Last Magic. Atheneum.

Nash, Ogden.
xNash, Ogden.
The Cruise of the Aardvark. M Evans.
The Old Dog Barks Backwards. Little.
Parents Keep Out: Elderly Poems for
Youngerly Readers. Little.
There's Always Another Windmill. Little.

Nash, Paul.
xNash, Paul.
The Educated Man: Studies in the History of
Educational Thought. Krieger.
ed. History & Education: The Educational Uses
of the Past. Phila Bk Co.

Nash, Peter G.
xNash, Peter G.
ed. Appropriate Units for Collective
Bargaining. PLI.

Nash, Robert.
xNash, Robert.
Bringing Christ Back. Our Sunday Visitor.

Nash, Roderick.
xNash, Roderick.
American Environment: Readings in the
History of Conservation. A-W.
ed. Environment & Americans: The Problem of
Priorities. Krieger.
From These Beginnings: A Biographical
Approach to American History. Har-Row.

Nash, Ronald H.
xNash, Ronald H.
The Light of the Mind: St. Augustine's Theory
of Knowledge. U Pr of Ky.

Nash, Rose.
xNash, Rose.
Turkish Intonation: An Instrumental Study.
Mouton.

Nash, Roy.
xNash, Roy.
Classrooms Observed: The Teacher's
Perception & the Pupil's Performance.
Routledge & Kegan.
Conquest of Brazil. Biblo.
Teacher Expectations & Pupil Learning.
Routledge & Kegan.

Nash, Valery.
xNash, Valery.
The Narrows. Cleveland St Univ Poetry Ctr.

Nash, Willard L. *see* Nash, Willard Lee.

Nash, Willard Lee, 1898-
xNash, Willard L.

A Study of the Stated Aims & Purposes of the
Departments of Military Science & Tactics &
Physical Education in the Land-Grant
Colleges of the United States. AMS Pr.

Nashelsky, Louis.
xNashelsky, Louis.
Introduction to Digital Computer Technology.
Wiley.

Nasir, Sari J.
xNasir, Sari J.
The Arabs & the English. Longman.

Naslund, B. see Naslund, Bertil.

Naslund, Bertil, 1933-
xNaslund, B.
An Analysis of Economic Size Distributions.
Springer-Verlag.

Nason, T. see Nason, Thelma Campbell.

Nason, Thelma. see Nason, Thelma Campbell.

Nason, Thelma Campbell.
xNason, T.
No Golden Cities. Macmillan.
xNason, Thelma.
Our Statue of Liberty. Follett.

Nasr, Raja. see Nasr, Raja Tewfik.

Nasr, Raja Tewfik, 1929-
xNasr, Raja.
Learn to Read Arabic. Intl Bk Ctr.

Nasr, Sayyed H. see Nasr, Seyyed Hossein.

Nasr, Seyyed H. see Nasr, Seyyed Hossein.

Nasr, Seyyed Hossein.
xNasr, Sayyed H.
Sufi Essays. State U NY Pr.
xNasr, Seyyed H.
Ideals & Realities of Islam. Beacon Pr.
Sufi Essays. Schocken.

Nasri, William Z.
xNasri, William Z.
Crisis in Copyright. Dekker.

Nass, Gilbert D.
xNass, Gilbert D.
Marriage & the Family. A-W.

Nass, Leonard. see Nass, Leonard I.

Nass, Leonard I.
xNass, Leonard.
ed. Encyclopedia of PVC. Dekker.

Nass, Stanley.
xNass, Stanley.
Crisis Intervention. Kendall-Hunt.
Turn Your Life Around: Self-Knowledge for
Self Improvement. P-H.

Nassar, Eugene P. see Nassar, Eugene Paul.

Nassar, Eugene Paul.
xNassar, Eugene P.
Rape of Cinderella: Essays in Literary
Continuity. Ind U Pr.

Nassau, Robert H. see Nassau, Robert Hamill.

Nassau, Robert Hamill, 1835-1921
xNassau, Robert H.
In an Elephant Corral: And Other Tales of
West African Experiences. Negro U Pr.
Where Animals Talk: West African Folk Lore
Tales. Negro U Pr.

Nasser, Essam, 1931-
xNasser, Essam.
Fundamentals of Gaseous Ionization & Plasma
Electronics. Wiley.

Nasser, Munir K., 1936-
xNasser, Munir K.
Press, Politics, & Power: Egypt's Heikal &
Al-Ahram. Iowa St U Pr.

Nassi, Robert J.
xNassi, Robert J.
Review Text in Spanish Three Years. AMSCO
Sch.

Nassiet, Claude.
xNassiet, Claude.
What to Make with Nuts & Grains. Sterling.

NASSP. see National Association of Secondary School
Principals.

Nast, Thomas, 1840-1902
xNast, Thomas.
Thomas Nast's Christmas Drawings. Dover.
Thomas Nast's Christmas Drawings. Peter
Smith.

Nastasescu, C. see Nastasescu, Constantin.

Nastasescu, Constantin.
xNastasescu, C.
Graded & Filtered Rings & Modules.
Springer-Verlag.

**NASW Professional Symposium on Social Work, 4th,
Hollywood, Florida, 1975.**
xFourth Symposium, Oct. 22-25, 1975.
Social Work in Practice: Proceedings. Natl
Assn Soc Wkrs.

**NASW Professional Symposium of Social Work Practice
and Social Justice, 3d, New Orleans, 1972.**
xThird Symposium, New Orleans, Nov. 26-29,
1972.
Social Work Practice and Social Justice:
Proceedings. Natl Assn Soc Wkrs.

Natale, Gloria.
xNatale, Gloria.
The Pregnant Woman's Beauty Book. Morrow.

Natale, Samuel.
xNatale, Samuel M.
Pastoral Counselling: Reflections & Concerns.
Paulist Pr.

Natale, Samuel M. see Natale, Samuel.

Natan, Alex, 1906-
xNatan, Alex.
ed. German Men of Letters: Twelve Literary
Essays. Dufour.

Natanson, I. see Natanson, Isidor Pavlovich.

Natanson, Isidor Pavlovich.
xNatanson, I.
Summation of Infinitesimal Quantities. College
Mktg Grp.
Summation of Infinitesimal Quantities. Gordon.

Natanson, Maurice. see Natanson, Maurice Alexander.

Natanson, Maurice Alexander, 1924-
xNatanson, Maurice.
A Critique of Jean-Paul Sartre's Ontology.
Haskell.
The Journeying Self: A Study in Philosophy &
Social Role. A-W.

Natella, A. A. see Natella, Arthur A.

Natella, Arthur A.
xNatella, A. A.
The Spanish in America, 1513-1974: A
Chronology & Fact Book. Oceana.

Nath, B. see Nath, Bhaskardev.

Nath, Bhaskardev.
xNath, B.
Intro. by Fundamentals of Finite Elements for
Engineers. Humanities.

Nath, R.
xNath, R.
History of Decorative Art in Mughal
Architecture. Orient Bk Dist.
History of Decorative Art in Mughal
Architecture. South Asia Bks.

Nath, S. K.
xNath, S. K.
Reappraisal of Welfare Economics. Kelley.

Nathan, Andrew. see Nathan, Andrew James.

Nathan, Andrew J. see Nathan, Andrew James.

Nathan, Andrew James.
xNathan, Andrew.
Peking Politics, 1918-1923: Factionalism & the
Failure of Constitutionalism. U of Cal Pr.
xNathan, Andrew J.

History of the China International Famine
Relief Commission. Harvard U Pr.
Modern China, 1840-1972: An Introduction to
Sources & Research Aids. U of Mich Ctr
Chinese.

Nathan, Carl F.
xNathan, Carl F.
Plague Prevention & Politics in Manchuria,
1910-1931. Harvard U Pr.

Nathan, George J. see Nathan, George Jean.

Nathan, George Jean.
xNathan, George J.
The American Credo: A Contribution Toward
the Interpretation of the National Mind.
Octagon.
Art of the Night. Fairleigh Dickinson.
Autobiography of an Attitude. Scholarly.
Critic & the Drama. Fairleigh Dickinson.
Materia Critica. Fairleigh Dickinson.
Materia Critica. R West.
Passing Judgments. Arno.
Passing Judgments. Fairleigh Dickinson.
Passing Judgments. Greenwood.
Passing Judgments. Johnson Repr.
The World in Falseface. Fairleigh Dickinson.
The World in Falseface. R West.

Nathan, Hans, 1910-
xNathan, Hans.
Dan Emmett & the Rise of Early Negro
Minstrelsy. U of Okla Pr.

Nathan, James A.
xNathan, James A.
The Future of United States Naval Power. Ind
U Pr.

Nathan, Joan.
xNathan, Joan.
The Flavor of Jerusalem. Little.

Nathan, Maud. see Nathan, Maud Nathan.

Nathan, Maud Nathan, 1862-
xNathan, Maud.
Once Upon a Time & Today. Arno.

Nathan, Norman.
xNathan, Norman.
Prince William B.: The Philosophical
Conceptions of William Blake. Mouton.

Nathan, Otto.
xNathan, Otto.
Nazi Economic System: Germany's
Mobilization for War. Russell.

Nathan, Peter E.
xNathan, Peter E.
Psychopathology & Society. McGraw.

Nathan, Richard P.
xNathan, Richard P.
Compiled by America's Governments: A Fact
Book of Census Data on the Organization,
Finances & Employment of Federal, State &
Local Governments. Wiley.
Monitoring Revenue Sharing. Brookings.
Revenue Sharing: The Second Round.
Brookings.

Nathan, Robert.
xNathan, Robert.
Portrait of Jennie. Dell.
Portrait of Jennie. Knopf.
Sir Henry. Borgo Pr.

Nathan, Robert L. see Nathan, Robert Louis.

Nathan, Robert Louis.
xNathan, Robert L.
The Dreamtime. Overlook Pr.

Nathan, Robert S. see Nathan, Robert Stuart.

Nathan, Robert Stuart.
xNathan, Robert S.

Amusement Park. Dial.
Amusement Park. Fawcett.
Nathans, Elizabeth S. *see* Nathans, Elizabeth Studley.
Nathans, Elizabeth Studley.
  xNathans, Elizabeth S.
    Losing the Peace: Georgia Republicans &
    Reconstruction, 1865-1871. La State U Pr.
Nathanson, Bernard N.
  xNathanson, Bernard N.
    Aborting America. Doubleday.
Nathanson, E. M., 1928-
  xNathanson, E. M.
    The Latecomers. PB.
Nathanson, Fred E.
  xNathanson, Fred E.
    Radar Design Principles: Signal Processing &
    the Environment. McGraw.
Nathanson, Jerome.
  xNathanson, Jerome.
    ed. Individual Excellence & Social
    Responsibility. Prometheus Bks.
Nathenson, Michael B.
  xNathenson, Michael B.
    Using Student Feedback to Improve Learning
    Materials. Biblio Dist.
Nation, James E.
  xNation, James E.
    Diagnosis of Speech & Language Disorders.
    Mosby.
Nation, John.
  xNation, John.
    Customs of Respect: The Traditional Basis of
    Fijian Communal Politics. Bks Australia.
The Nation (New York).
  xNation Magazine.
    View of the Nation: 1955-1959. Arno.
Nation Magazine. *see* The Nation (New York).
Nation, Rhoda.
  xNation, Rhoda.
    Mary Bought a Little Lamb, & This Is How
    She Cooked It. Intl Pubns Serv
    Mary Bought a Little Lamb & This Is How She
    Cooked It. Reed.
National Academy of Arbitrators.
  xNational Academy Of Arbitrators - Meetings 1-7.
    Profession of Labor Arbitration: Proceedings.
    BNA.
  xNational Academy Of Arbitrators - 18th Meeting.
    Proceedings. BNA.
  xNational Academy of Arbitrators, Annual
    Meeting.
    Arbitration of Subcontracting & Wage
    Incentive Disputes: Proceedings. BNA.
  xNational Academy of Arbitrators-11th Annual
    Meeting.
    Arbitrator & the Parties: Proceedings. BNA.
  xNational Academy of Arbitrators-12th Annual
    Meeting.
    Arbitration & the Law: Proceedings. BNA.
  xNational Academy of Arbitrators-13th Annual
    Meeting.
    Challenges to Arbitration: Proceedings. BNA.
  xNational Academy of Arbitrators-14th Annual
    Meeting.
    Arbitration & Public Policy: Proceedings. BNA.
  xNational Academy of Arbitrators-15th Annual
    Meeting.
    Collective Bargaining & the Arbitrator's Role:
    Proceedings. BNA.
  xNational Academy of Arbitrators-16th Annual
    Meeting.
    Labor Arbitration & Industrial Change:
    Proceedings. BNA.
  xNational Academy of Arbitrators-17th Annual
    Meeting.
    Labor Arbitration: Perspectives & Problems:
    Proceedings. BNA.
  xNational Academy of Arbitrators-20th Annual
    Meeting.

Arbitrator, the NLRB, & the Courts:
  Proceedings. BNA.
xNational Academy of Arbitrators-21st Annnual
  Meeting.
  Developments in American & Foreign
  Arbitration: Proceedings. BNA.
xNational Academy of Arbitrators-22nd Annual
  Meeting.
  Arbitration & Social Change: Proceedings.
  BNA.
xNational Academy of Arbitrators-23nd Annual
  Meeting.
  Arbitration & the Expanding Role of Neutrals:
  Proceedings. BNA.
xNational Academy of Arbitrators-24th Annual
  Meeting.
  Arbitration & the Public Interest: Proceedings.
  BNA.
xNational Academy of Arbitrators-25th Annual
  Meeting.
  Labor Arbitration at the Quarter-Century
  Mark: Proceedings. BNA.
xNational Academy of Arbitrators-26th Meeting.
  Arbitration of Interest Disputes: Proceedings.
  BNA.
xNational Academy of Arbitrators-27th Annual
  Meeting.
  Arbitration, 1974: Proceedings. BNA.
xNational Academy of Arbitrators-28th Annual
  Meeting.
  Arbitration, 1975: Proceedings. BNA.
xNational Academy of Arbitrators-29th Annual
  Meeting.
  Arbitration, 1976: Proceedings. BNA.
xThirtieth Annual Meeting of the National
  Academy of Arbitrators.
  Arbitration-1977: Proceedings. BNA.
National Academy Of Arbitrators - Meetings 1-7. *see*
  National Academy of Arbitrators.
National Academy Of Arbitrators - 18th Meeting. *see*
  National Academy of Arbitrators.
National Academy of Arbitrators, Annual Meeting. *see*
  National Academy of Arbitrators.
National Academy of Arbitrators-11th Annual Meeting.
  see National Academy of Arbitrators.
National Academy of Arbitrators-12th Annual Meeting.
  see National Academy of Arbitrators.
National Academy of Arbitrators-13th Annual Meeting.
  see National Academy of Arbitrators.
National Academy of Arbitrators-14th Annual Meeting.
  see National Academy of Arbitrators.
National Academy of Arbitrators-15th Annual Meeting.
  see National Academy of Arbitrators.
National Academy of Arbitrators-16th Annual Meeting.
  see National Academy of Arbitrators.
National Academy of Arbitrators-17th Annual Meeting.
  see National Academy of Arbitrators.
National Academy of Arbitrators-20th Annual Meeting.
  see National Academy of Arbitrators.
National Academy of Arbitrators-21st Annnual Meeting.
  see National Academy of Arbitrators.
National Academy of Arbitrators-22nd Annual Meeting.
  see National Academy of Arbitrators.
National Academy of Arbitrators-23nd Annual Meeting.
  see National Academy of Arbitrators.
National Academy of Arbitrators-24th Annual Meeting.
  see National Academy of Arbitrators.
National Academy of Arbitrators-25th Annual Meeting.
  see National Academy of Arbitrators.
National Academy of Arbitrators-26th Meeting. *see*
  National Academy of Arbitrators.
National Academy of Arbitrators-27th Annual Meeting.
  see National Academy of Arbitrators.
National Academy of Arbitrators-28th Annual Meeting.
  see National Academy of Arbitrators.
National Academy of Arbitrators-29th Annual Meeting.
  see National Academy of Arbitrators.
National Academy of Engineering.
  xNational Academy Of Engineering.

Application of Technology to Improve
  Productivity in the Service Sector of the
  National Economy. Natl Acad Pr.
Costs of Health Care Facilities. Natl Acad Pr.
The Engineer and the City. Natl Acad Pr.
Engineering & Medicine. Natl Acad Pr.
National Academy of Engineering Memorial
  Tributes. Natl Acad Pr.
State of the Nation's Air Transportation
  System. Natl Acad Pr.
Transportation & the Prospects for Improved
  Efficiency. Natl Acad Pr.
U. S. Energy Prospects: An Engineering
  Viewpoint. Natl Acad Pr.
xNational Academy of Sciences, National
  Academy of Engineering.
  Man, Materials, & Environment. MIT Pr.
National Academy of Engineering. Advisory Committee
on Issues in Educational Technology.
  xAdvisory Committee on Issues in Educational
  Technology.
    Issues & Public Policies in Educational
    Technology: To Realize the Promise.
    Lexington Bks.
National Academy of Engineering. Committee on Power
Plant Siting.
  xCommittee on Power Plant Siting.
    Engineering for Resolution of the
    Energy-Environment Dilemma. Natl Acad
    Pr.
National Academy of Engineering. Committee on the
Interplay of Engineering with Biology and Medicine.
  xCommittee on Interplay of Engineering with
  Biology & Medicine.
    Study of Engineering in Medicine & Health
    Care. Natl Acad Pr.
National Academy of Engineering. Marine Board.
  xMarine Board.
    Toward Fulfillment of a National Ocean
    Commitment. Natl Acad Pr.
National Academy of Engineering. Task Group on
Industrial Activity.
  xCommittee On Interplay Of Engineering With
  Biology And Medicine.
    Assessment of Industrial Activity in the Field
    of Biomedical Engineering. Natl Acad Pr.
National Academy of Science, National Research
  Council. *see* National Research Council.
National Academy of Sciences. *see* National Academy of
  Sciences, Washington, D.C.
National Academy Of Sciences - Division Of
  Mathematics Committee On Support Of Research In
  Mathematical Sciences. *see* National Research
  Council. Panel on Undergraduate Education in
  Mathematics.
National Academy of Sciences Agricultural Board. *see*
  National Research Council. Committee on Genetic
  Vulnerability of Major Crops.
National Academy Of Sciences Division Of Physical
  Sciences. *see* Conference on Semiconductor
  Nuclear-Particle Detectors and Circuits, Gatlinburg,
  Tenn., 1967.
National Academy of Sciences, National Academy of
  Engineering. *see* National Academy of Engineering.
National Academy Of Sciences Office Of Scientific
  Personnel. *see* National Research Council. Office of
  Scientific Personnel. Research Division.
National Academy of Sciences, Washington, D.C.
  xBiology And Agriculture Division.
    Biochronometry. Natl Acad Pr.
  xDietary Allowances Committee.
    Recommended Dietary Allowances. Natl Acad
    Pr.
  xDiv. of Earth Sciences.
    Geographical Perspectives & Urban Problems.
    Natl Acad Pr.
  xDivision Of Behavioral Sciences.
    Behavioral Science Research in New Guinea.
    Natl Acad Pr.
  xDivision of Biology & Agriculture.

Alternative Sources of Protein for Animal
Production. Natl Acad Sci.
Degradation of Synthetic Organic Molecules in
the Biosphere. Natl Acad Pr.
xDivision Of Biology And Agriculture.
Eutrophication: Causes, Consequences,
Correctives. Natl Acad Pr.
Principles of Plant & Animal Pest Control.
Natl Acad Pr.
U. S. - Canadian Tables of Feed Composition.
Natl Acad Pr.
xDivision of Chemistry & Chemical Technology.
Critical Evaluation of Chemical & Physical
Structural Information. Natl Acad Pr.
Principles for Evaluating Chemicals in the
Environment. Natl Acad Pr.
Specifications & Criteria for Biochemical
Compounds. Natl Acad Pr.
xDivision of Chemistry and Chemical Technology.
Characterization of Macromolecular Structure.
Natl Acad Pr.
Chemical Structure Information Handling: A
Review of the Literature, 1962-1968. Natl
Acad Pr.
Survey of Chemical Notation Systems. Natl
Acad Pr.
xDivision Of Earth Sciences.
Japanese Colonization in Eastern Paraguay.
Natl Acad Pr.
Rock-Mechanics Research in the U. S. Natl
Acad Pr.
xDivision Of Engineering.
Rapid Excavation: Significance, Needs
Opportunities. Natl Acad Pr.
xDivision of Mathematics - Committee on Support
of Research in Mathematical Sciences.
Mathematical Sciences: A Report. Natl Acad
Pr.
xDivision of Medical Sciences.
Contraception: Science, Technology &
Application. Natl Acad Pr.
Phototherapy in the Newborn: An Overview.
Natl Acad Pr.
xDivision of Medical Sciences, Assembly of Life
Sciences, National Research Council.
Chlorine & Hydrogen Chloride. Natl Acad Pr.
xDivision of Medical Sciences, National Research
Council.
Copper. Natl Acad Pr.
Genetic Screening: Programs, Principles &
Research. Natl Acad Pr.
xDivision of Medical Sciences, NRC.
Preservation of Red Blood Cells. Natl Acad Pr.
xDivision Of Physical Sciences.
Physics in Perspective, Vol. 1. Natl Acad Pr.
Research in Optical Spectroscopy: Present
Status & Prospects. Natl Acad Pr.
Research in Solid State Sciences: Opportunities
& Relevance to National Needs. Natl Acad
Pr.
xNational Academy of Sciences.

Aircraft: Civil & Military. Technomic.
Biographical Memoirs. Natl Acad Pr.
Biographical Memoirs, Vol. 49. Natl Acad Pr.
Current Status of Modular Coordination. Natl
Acad Pr.
Documentation of Building Science Literature.
Natl Acad Pr.
Effect of Genetic Variance on Nutritional
Requirements of Animals. Natl Acad Pr.
Energy Systems of Extended Endurance in the
1-100 Kilowatt Range for Undersea
Applications. Natl Acad Pr.
Feasibility of a Global Observation & Analysis
Experiment. Natl Acad Pr.
ed. Fire Dynamics & Scenarios. Technomic.
Index to the Literature of Semiconductor
Detectors. Natl Acad Pr.
Insulated Masonry Cavity Walls. Natl Acad Pr.
Marine Chemistry. Natl Acad Pr.
Materials: State of the Art. Technomic.
Mechanical Fasteners for Industrial Curtain
Walls. Natl Acad Pr.
Nutrient Requirements of Sheep. Natl Acad Pr.
Plastics in Building Illumination. Natl Acad Pr.
Prefinishing of Exterior Building Components.
Natl Acad Pr.
Principles of Plant & Animal Pest Control.
Natl Acad Pr.
Prospects of the World Food Supply. Natl
Acad Pr.
Public Entrance Doors. Natl Acad Pr.
Reform of Medical Education. Natl Acad Pr.
The Rehabilitation Potential of Western Coal
Lands. Ballinger Pub.
Science & Technology: A Five-Year Outlook.
W H Freeman.
xNational Materials Advisory Board.
National Materials Policy. Natl Acad Pr.
**National Academy of Sciences. Washington, D.C.,
Committe on Research in the Life Sciences.**
xCommittee On Research In The Life Sciences.
Life Sciences. Natl Acad Pr.
**National Academy of Sciences, Washington, D.C.,
Committee on the Survey of Materials Science and
Engineering.**
xScience & Public Policy Comm., Comm. on the
Survey of Materials Science & Engineering.
Materials & Man's Needs. Natl Acad Pr.
**National Accreditation Council for Agencies Serving the
Blind and Visually Handicapped.**
xNational Accreditation Council for Agencies
Serving the Blind & Visually Handicapped.
Section C-4, Physical Facilities. NACASBVH.
Section D-6, Vocational Services.
NACASBVH.
Standards for Production of Reading Materials
for the Blind & Visually Handicapped.
NACASBVH.
National Air & Space Museum Library Staff. see
National Air and Space Museum.
National Air and Space Museum.
xNational Air & Space Museum Library Staff.
ed. The International Handbook of Aerospace
Awards & Trophies. Smithsonian.
National Army Museum.
xNational Army Museum, London.
War and Weapons. Watts.
National Army Museum, London. see National Army
Museum.
National Art Education Assn. see National Art
Education Association.
National Art Education Association.
xNational Art Education Assn.
Job Description in the Business World of Art
& Design. Natl Gallery Art.
Youth Art Month. Natl Gallery Art.
xNational Art Education Association.

American Artist Art School Directory:
1976-77. Natl Art Ed.
Art Education for the Disadvantaged Child.
Natl Art Ed.
Art in American Higher Institutions. Natl Art
Ed.
Black Art: A Bibliography. Natl Art Ed.
Careers in Art. Natl Art Ed.
College & University Acceptance of High
School Art Credits for Admission. Natl Art
Ed.
Report on the Nineteenth World Congress of
INSEA. Natl Art Ed.
Teaching Art As a Career. Natl Art Ed.
National Assn. of College & University Business Officers.
see National Association of College and University
Business Officers.
**National Association for the Advancement of Colored
People.**
xNational Association For The Advancement Of
Colored People.
Crisis, A Record of the Darker Races. Negro U
Pr.
Thirty Years of Lynching in the United States,
1889-1918. Arno.
Thirty Years of Lynching in the United States,
1889-1918. Negro U Pr.
**National Association for the Promotion of Social
Science. Committee on Trades' Societies.**
xNational Association for the Promotion of Social
Science Trades' Societies Committee.
Trades' Societies & Strikes. Kelley.
National Association of Accountants.
xNational Association of Accountants.
ed. Management Accounting for Multinational
Corporations. Natl Assn Accts.
ed. Managing Price Level Accounting. Natl
Assn Accts.
ed. Managing the Cash Flow. Natl Assn Accts.
xNational Association of Accounting Editorial
Staff.
ed. Management Reporting Under Inflation.
Natl Assn Accts.
National Association of Accounting Editorial Staff. see
National Association of Accountants.
National Association of Broadcasters.
xNational Association of Broadcasters.
Broadcasting & the Bill of Rights: Statements
on the White Bill. B Franklin.
National Association of Broadcasters Engineering
Conference, 1970. see Nab Broadcast Engineering
Conference, 24th, Washington, D.C., 1970.
National Association of Catholic Chaplains.
xNational Association of Catholic Chaplins.
Fear Not, I Am with You. Alba.
National Association of College & University Business
Officers. see National Association of College and
University Business Officers.
**National Association of College and University Business
Officers.**
xNACUBO.
Financial Responsibilities of Governing Boards
of Trustees. Natl Assn Coll.
xNational Assn. of College & University Business
Officers.
College & University Business Administration.
Natl Assn Coll.
xNational Association of College & University
Business Officers.
Energy Management for Colleges &
Universities. Natl Assn Coll.
A Planning Manual for Colleges. Natl Assn
Coll.
National Association of Credit Management.
xNational Association of Credit Management.

Digest of Commercial Laws of the World.
Oceana.
Patent-Trademark Law & Practice. Oceana.

National Association of Home Builders of the United States.
xNational Association of Home Builders.
PUD: A Flexible Concept for Land Use,
Shelter & Community. Urban Land.
Residential Site Planning. Natl Assn Home.
Residential Storm Water Management:
Objectives, Principles, & Design
Considerations. Urban Land.
jt. auth. Residential Streets: Objective
Principles & Design Considerations. Urban
Land.
Residential Streets: Objectives, Principles, &
Design Considerations.. Natl Assn Home.

National Association of Independent Schools.
xNational Association of Independent Schools.
Accounting for Independent Schools. NAIS.
A Teacher's Notebook: English 5-9. NAIS.
A Teacher's Notebook: French. NAIS.
A Teacher's Notebook: German. NAIS.
A Teacher's Notebook: Language Arts, K-4.
NAIS.
A Teacher's Notebook: Mathematics, K-9.
NAIS.

**National Association of Independent Schools.
Committee for International and World Education.**
xNais Committee for International & World
Education.
ed. Internationalize Your School. NAIS.

National Association of Independent Schools. Library Committee.
xNational Association of Independent Schools,
Library Committee.
Compiled by Books for Secondary School
Libraries. Bowker.

National Association of Independent Schools. Teacher Service Committee.
xNAIS Teacher Services Committee.
Interdependence: A Handbook for
Environmental Education. NAIS.

National Association of Legal Assistants.
xNational Association of Legal Assistants Inc.
Manual for Legal Assistants. West Pub.

National Association of Secondary School Principals.
xNASSP.
Student Activities in Secondary Schools: A
Bibliography. Natl Assn Principals.
Twenty-Five Action-Learning Schools. Natl
Assn Principals.
xNational Association of Secondary School
principals.
The Assistant Principalship. Natl Assn
Principals.
Junior High-School Principalship. Natl Assn
Principals.
National Honor Society Handbook. Natl Assn
Principals.
National Junior Honor Society Handbook. Natl
Assn Principals.
Student Council Adviser. Natl Assn Principals.
Student Council Handbook. Natl Assn
Principals.
Student Learning Styles: Diagnosing &
Prescribing Programs. Natl Assn Principals.
xNational Associaton of Secondary School
Principals.
NASSP Commencement Manual. Natl Assn
Principals.

National Association of Social Workers.
xNational Association of Social Workers.

The Handbook on the Private Practice of
Social Work. Natl Assn Soc Wkrs.
Manual for Adjudication of Grievances. Natl
Assn Soc Wkrs.
Preventive Intervention in Social Work. Natl
Assn Soc Wkrs.

National Associaton of Secondary School Principals. *see*
National Association of Secondary School Principals.

National Audubon Society.
xAudubon Society.
One Hundred Two Favorite Audubon Birds of
America. Crown.

National Biomedical Sciences Instrumentation Symposium.
xRocky Mountain Bioengineering Symposium,
12th.
Biomedical Sciences Instrumentation:
Proceedings. Instru Soc.
xRocky Mt. Bioengineering Symposium, 13th, &
International ISA Biomedical Sciences
Instrumentation Symposium, 13th May 1976,
Laramie, WY.
Biomedical Sciences Instrumentation:
Proceedings. Instru Soc.

National Board on Graduate Education.
xNational Board on Graduate Education.
Graduate School Adjustments to the New
Depression in Higher Education. Natl Acad
Pr.
Minority Group Participation in Graduate
Education. Natl Acad Pr.
Science Development: An Evaluation Study.
Natl Acad Pr.

National Book League. *see* National Book League,
London.
National Book League Exhibitions London. *see* National
Book League, London.

National Book League, London.
xNational Book League.
Children's Books of Yesterday. Gale.
xNational Book League Exhibitions London.
English Poetry. Greenwood.

National Building Agency.
xNational Building Agency.
External Works Detail Sheets. Nichols Pub.

National Bureau Committee For Economic Research. *see*
Universities-National Bureau Committee for Economic
Research.

National Bureau of Economic Research.
xNational Bureau Of Economic Research.
Measurement & Interpretation of Job
Vacancies. Natl Bur Econ Res.
Transportation Economics. Natl Bur Econ Res.

National Bureau of Standards. *see* United States.
National Bureau of Standards.

National Canners Association.
xNational Canners Association Staff.
ed. Laboratory Manual for Food Canners &
Processors. AVI.

National Canners Association Staff. *see* National Canners
Association.

National Cash Register Company, Dayton, Ohio.
xTheNational Cash Register Company.
NCR Data Communications Concepts. E & L
Instru.

National Center for Health Statistics. *see* United States.
National Center for Health Statistics.

National Center for Resource Recovery.
xNational Center for Resource Recovery, Inc.
Incineration: A State of the Art Study.
Lexington Bks.
Sanitary Landfill. Lexington Bks.

National Center for State Courts.
xNational Center for State Courts.

Administrative Unification of the Maine State
Courts: Full Report. Natl Ctr St Courts.
Audio-Video Technology & the Courts: Guide
for Court Managers. Natl Ctr St Courts.
Business Equipment & the Courts. Natl Ctr St
Courts.
Business Equipment & the Courts: Reference
Guide. Natl Ctr St Courts.
Clemency: Legal Authority, Procedure &
Structure. Natl Ctr St Courts.
Data Processing & the Courts: Guide for Court
Managers. Natl Ctr St Courts.
Facets of the Jury System: A Survey. Natl Ctr
St Courts.
Justice Delayed: The Pace of Litigation in
Urban Trial Courts. Natl Ctr St Courts.
Maine Traffic Court Study: Executive
Summary. Natl Ctr St Courts.
Maine Traffic Court Study: Full Report. Natl
Ctr St Courts.
Managing to Reduce Delay. Natl Ctr St
Courts.
Microfilm & the Courts: Reference Manual.
Natl Ctr St Courts.
Parajudges: Their Role in Today's Court
Systems. Natl Ctr St Courts.
Planning in State Courts: A Survey of the State
of the Art. Natl Ctr St Courts.
Pretrial Delay: A Review & Bibliography. Natl
Ctr St Courts.
Rural Courts: The Effect Ofspace & Distance
on the Administration of Justice. Natl Ctr St
Courts.
State Courts: Options for the Future. Natl Ctr
St Courts.
A Unified Court System for Vermont: Full
Report. Natl Ctr St Courts.
Wisconsin Appellate Practice & Procedure
Study: Final Report. Natl Ctr St Courts.
Workload Measures in the Court. Natl Ctr St
Courts.
xNational Center for State Courts, Denver.
Policymakers' Views Regarding Issues in the
Operation & Evaluation of Pretrial Release &
Diversion Programs: Findings from a
Questionnaire Survey. Natl Ctr St Courts.

National Center for State Courts, Denver. *see* National
Center for State Courts.

National Child Labor Committee, New York.
xNational Child Labor Committee, 1905.
Proceedings. Arno.

National Child Labor Committee, 1905. *see* National
Child Labor Committee, New York.

National Clearing House for Bilingual Education.
xNational Clearinghouse for Bilingual Education.
Bibliography of English As a Second Language
Materials: Grades K-3. Natl Clearinghse
Bilingual Ed.
A Bibliography of English As a Second
Language Materials: Grades 4-12. Natl
Clearinghse Bilingual Ed.
English As a Second Language Bibliography:
Adults. Natl Clearinghse Bilingual Ed.
Resources in Bilingual Education: A
Preliminary Guide to Government Agency
Programs of Interest to Minority Language
Groups. Natl Clearinghse Bilingual Ed.
Sources of Materials for Minority Languages:
A Preliminary List. Natl Clearinghse
Bilingual Ed.

National Clearinghouse for Bilingual Education. *see*
National Clearing House for Bilingual Education.

National Commission for the Study of Nursing and Nursing Education.
xNational Commission for the Study of Nursing &
Nursing Education.

National District Attorneys Association.
  xMembership Division, Natl. District Attorneys
    Assn.
      National Directory. Natl Dist Atty.
      ed. National Prosecutor Survey. Natl Dist
        Atty.
  xNational District Attorneys Assoc.
      National Prosecution Standards. Natl Dist
        Atty.
National Education Association. *see* National Education
  Association of the United States.
National Education Association of the United States.
  xNational Education Association.
      Ability Grouping. NEA.
      Anxiety As Related to Thinking & Forgetting.
        NEA.
      Class Size. NEA.
      Code of Student Rights & Responsibilities.
        NEA.
      Community Decision-Making for Education
        Associations. NEA.
      Coping with Disruptive Behavior. NEA.
      Corporal Punishment Task Force Report.
        NEA.
      Curriculum for the Seventies: An Agenda for
        Invention. NEA.
      Developing Citizen Committees for Education
        Associations. NEA.
      Discipline & Learning: An Inquiry into
        Student-Teacher Relationships. NEA.
      Discipline in the Classroom. NEA.
      Educational Games & Simulations. NEA.
      Educational Media. NEA.
      Environment & Population: A Sourcebook for
        Teachers. NEA.
      Evaluation & Reporting of Student
        Achievement. NEA.
      Feedback Process for Education Associations.
        NEA.
      Financial Program for Today's Schools. NEA.
      Financing Education: Who Benefits? Who
        Pays?. NEA.
      Fiscal Planning for Schools in Transition.
        NEA.
      Group Processes in Elementary & Secondary
        Schools. NEA.
      A Guide to Planning & Conducting
        Environmental Study Area Workshops. NEA.
      High Spots in State School Legislation: January
        1 - August 31,1972. NEA.
      How Adults Can Learn More, Faster. Natl
        Assn Con Adult Ed.
      Humanizing Education in the Seventies:
        Imperatives & Strategies-Report of the 12th
        Annual Conference on Civil & Human Rights
        in Education. NEA.
      Instructional Materials: Their Selection &
        Purchase. NEA.
      Interdependence in School Finance: The City,
        the State, the Nation. NEA.
      Internal PR for Education Associations. NEA.
      Learning Process. NEA.
      Lessons from the Teacher Corps. NEA.
      Local-State-Federal Partnership in School
        Finance. NEA.
      Manual on Standards Affecting School
        Personnel in the United States. NEA.
      Media & the Culturally Different Learner.
        NEA
      Motivation in Teaching & Learning. NEA.
      National Professional Accrediting Agencies.
        NEA.
      NEA Handbook for Local, State, & National
        Associations 1977-78. NEA.
      On Staying Awake: Talks with Teachers. NEA.
      Planning the Evaluation of Educators: A
        Simulation. NEA.
      Portable Videotape Recorder, A Guide for
        Teachers. NEA.
      PR in PN for Education Associations. NEA.

      Primer in Publicity for Education Associations.
        NEA.
      Real World of the Beginning Teacher. NEA.
      Reform of Urban Schools. NEA.
      Rescheduled School Year. NEA.
      Salary Schedule Provisions for Full-Time
        Guidance Counselors,1971-72. NEA.
      School Finance Campaign Handbook for
        Education Associations. NEA.
      Schools & Cable Television. NEA.
      Schools Are People: An Anthology of Stories
        Highlighting the Human Drama of Teaching
        & Learning. NEA.
      Selected Guide to Curriculum Literature: An
        Annotated Bibliography. NEA.
      Sensory Factors in the School Learning
        Environment. NEA.
      Source Materials for Teachers of Foreign
        Languages: An Annotated Bibliography.
        NEA.
      Sources of Information on Student Aid. NEA.
      Student Displacement Exclusion. NEA.
      Style Manual for Writers & Editors. NEA.
      Teacher Strikes,Work Stoppages and
        Interruptions of Service,1970-71. NEA.
      Teachers in Television & Other Media. NEA.
      Teaching Toward Inquiry. NEA.
      Time for Priorities: Financing the Schools for
        the 70's. NEA.
      Tips for the PR Chairman. NEA.
      Trends in Financing Public Education. NEA.
      Unfinished Stories for Use in the Classroom.
        NEA.
National Education Association of the United States.
  Department of School Nurses.
  xDepartment of School Nurses.
      Department-Wide Study of School Nurse
        Practices. Natl Assn Sch Nurses.
National Extension Homemakers Council.
  xNational Extension Homemakers Council.
      Treasure Trails in the USA. North Plains.
National Farm Institute.
  xNational Farm Institute.
      Seventies: Challenge & Opportunity. Iowa St U
        Pr.
National Federation of Abstracting and Indexing
  Services.
  xNational Federation of Abstracting & Indexing
    Services.
      Key Papers: On the Use of Computer-Based
        Bibliographic Services. NFAIS.
      On-Line Commands Chart: A Quick Users
        Guide for Bibliographic Search Systems.
        NFAIS.
National Fire Protection Assn. *see* National Fire
  Protection Association.
National Fire Protection Association.
  xNational Fire Protection Assn.
      Features of Fire Department Pumpers. Natl
        Fire Prot.
  xNational Fire Protection Association.
      Danger!: Fire Fighters at Work Safety One.
        Natl Fire Prot.
      The Fire Department Safety Program: Safety
        Two. Natl Fire Prot.
      Hydraulics for the Fire Service: Hydraulic
        Field Equations. Natl Fire Prot.
      Successful Public Relations - the What, Why,
        Who, How, Where & When. Natl Fire Prot.
  xNFPA.

      The Fire Fighter & Plastics in a Changing
        Environment. Natl Fire Prot.
      Handling Hazardous Materials Transportation
        Emergencies. Natl Fire Prot.
      Instructor's Manual to Accompany
        Management in the Fire Service. Natl Fire
        Prot.
      National Electrical Code, 1978. Natl Fire Prot.
      Thak Vehicle Fire Fighting. Natl Fire Prot.
National Fire Protection Association. Forest Committee.
  xNFPA Forest Committee.
      Chemicals for Forest Fire Fighting. Natl Fire
        Prot.
National Fire Protection Association. Sectional
  Committee on Protective Equipment for Fire
  Fighters.
  xCommittee On Urban Technology - Division Of
    Engineering.
      Long-Range Planning for Urban Research &
        Development: Technological Considerations.
        Natl Acad Pr.
  xSectional Committee on Protective Equipment.
      Fire Officer's Guide, Breathing Apparatus for
        the Fire Service. Natl Fire Prot.
National Football League.
  xNational Football League.
      Official Encyclopedic History of Professional
        Football. Macmillan.
National Football League Properties. Inc.
  xNational Football League Properties Inc.
      The NFL's Official Encyclopedic History of
        Professional Football. Macmillan.
National Forum Foundation.
  xNational Forum Foundation Staff.
      Seeing Ourselves. Am Guidance.
National Forum Foundation Staff. *see* National Forum
  Foundation.
National Foundation for Educational Research in
  England and Wales.
  xNational Foundation for Educational Research in
    England & Wales.
      Register of Educational Research in the United
        Kingdom, 1973-76. Humanities.
      Register of Educational Research in the UK:
        1976-1977. Humanities.
      The Register of Research in the United
        Kingdom: 1977-78. Humanities.
National Foundation for Educational Research in
  England and Wales. School to University Research
  Unit.
  xNational Foundation for Educational Research.
      Prediction of Academic Success. Humanities.
National Gallery of Canada.
  xNational Gallery of Canada. (Ottawa).
      Catalogue of the Library of the National
        Gallery of Canada. G K Hall.
National Gallery of Canada. (Ottawa). *see* National
  Gallery of Canada.
National Geographic Society.
  xNational Geographic Society.

ed. The Age of Chivalry. Natl Geog.
ed. The Alps. Natl Geog.
ed. American Mountain People. Natl Geog.
ed. As We Live & Breathe: The Challenge of Our Environment. Natl Geog.
ed. The Craftsman in America. Natl Geog.
ed. Everyday Life in Bible Times. Natl Geog.
ed. The Incredible Incas & Their Timeless Land. Natl Geog.
ed. Life in Rural America. Natl Geog.
ed. Man's Best Friend. Natl Geog.
ed. Nomads of the World. Natl Geog.
ed. Primitive Worlds: People Lost in Time. Natl Geog.
Those Inventive Americans. Natl Geog..
ed. Undersea Treasures. Natl Geog.
ed. Wilderness U.S.A.. Natl Geog.
ed. The World of the American Indian. Natl Geog.
National Incinerator Conference - 1970. *see* National Incinerator Conference, Cincinnati, 1970.
National Incinerator Conference, Cincinnati, 1970.
xNational Incinerator Conference - 1970.
Proceedings. ASME.
National Incinerator Conference, New York, 1972.
xNational Incinerator Conference, New York City, June, 1972.
Proceedings. ASME.
National Information Center for Educational Media.
xNational Information Center for Educational Media.
Index to Educational Audio Tapes. Univ SC Natl Info.
Index to Educational Overhead Transparencies. Univ SC Natl Info.
Index to Educational Records. Univ SC Natl Info.
Index to Educational Slides. Univ SC Natl Info.
Index to Educational Video Tapes. Univ SC Natl Info.
Index to Eight-mm Motion Cartridges. Univ SC Natl Info.
Index to Environmental Studies - Multimedia. Univ SC Natl Info.
Index to Environmental Studies: Multimedia. Univ SC Natl Info.
Index to Health & Safety Education - Multimedia. Univ SC Natl Info.
Index to Health & Safety Education: Multimedia. Univ SC Natl Info.
Index to Producers & Distributors. Univ SC Natl Info.
Index to Psychology - Multimedia. Univ SC Natl Info.
Index to Psychology: Multimedia. Univ SC Natl Info.
Index to Sixteen-mm Educational Films. Univ SC Natl Info.
Index to Thirty-Five-mm Filmstrips. Univ SC Natl Info.
Index to Vocational & Technical Education - Multimedia. Univ SC Natl Info.
Index to Vocational & Technical Education: Multimedia. Univ SC Natl Info.
Index to 16mm Educational Films. Univ SC Natl Info.
Index to 35mm Filmstrips. Univ SC Natl Info.
Index to 8mm Motion Cartridges. Univ SC Natl Info.
NICEM Index to Non-Print Special Education Materials: Multimedia (Learner Volume). Univ SC Natl Info.
NICEM Index to Non-Print Special Education Materials: Multimedia (Professional Volume). Univ SC Natl Info.
NICEM Update of Nonbook Media. Univ SC Natl Info.
NICSEM Special Education Thesaurus. Univ SC Natl Info.

National Information Center for Educational Media. *see* National Information Center for Special Education Materials.
National Information Center for Special Education Materials.
xNational Information Center for Educational Media.
Special Education Index to Learner Materials. Univ SC Natl Info.
xNational Information Center for Special Education Materials.
Index to Media & Materials for the Deaf, Hard of Hearing, Speech Impaired. Univ SC Natl Info.
Index to Media & Materials for the Visually Handicapped, Orthopedically Impaired, Other Health Impaired. Univ SC Natl Info.
Index to Visually Handicapped, Orthopedically Impaired, Other Health Impaired. Univ SC Natl Info.
Master Catalog of NIMIS-NICSEM Special Education Information. Univ SC Natl Info.
Special Education Index to Assessment Devices. Univ. SC Natl Info.
Special Education Index to Inservice Training Materials. Univ. SC Natl Info.
National Institute for Foodservice Industry. *see* National Institute for the Foodservice Industry.
National Institute for the Foodservice Industry.
xNational Institute for Foodservice Industry.
Applied Foodservice Sanitation. Heath.
National Institute of Mental Health. *see* United States. National Institute of Mental Health. Program Analysis and Evaluation Branch.
National Interracial Conference. *see* National Interracial Conference, 1st, Cincinnati, 1925.
National Interracial Conference, 1st, Cincinnati, 1925.
xNational Interracial Conference.
Toward Interracial Cooperation. Negro U Pr.
National Invitational Conference on the Independent Student, Dallas, 1974.
xNational Invitational Conference on the Independent Student.
Who Pays? Who Benefits?. College Bd.
National Judicial College.
xNational Judicial College.
Judicial Function Outline. Natl Judicial Coll.
Significant State Appellate Decisions. Natl Judicial Coll.
National Lampoon.
xNational Lampoon.
A Dirty Book. NAL.
xNational Lampoon Editors.
ed. The Job of Sex. Warner Bks.
National Lampoon Editors. *see* National Lampoon.
National Lawyers Guild.
xNational Lawyers Guild.
Representation of Witnesses Before Federal Grand Juries. Boardman.
National Lawyers Guild. 1977 Middle East Delegation.
xNational Lawyers Guild 1977 Middle East Delegation.
Treatment of Palestinians in Israeli-Occupied West Bank & Gaza. Natl Lawyers Guild.
National League of American Pen Women.
xNational League Of American Pen Women.
ed. Historic Homes of Alabama & Their Traditions. Southern U Pr.
National Material Advisory Board. *see* National Research Council. Committee on Structural Adhesives for Aerospace Use.
National Materials Advisory Board. *see* National Research Council. Ad Hoc Committee on the Fundamentals of Amorphous Semiconductors.
National Materials Advisory Board, National Research Council. *see* National Research Council. Committee on Electroslag Remelting and Plasma Arc Melting.
National Medicolegal Symposium, Las Vegas, 1973.
xNational Medicolegal Symposium 1973.

Proceedings. AMA.
National Medicolegal Symposium 1973. *see* National Medicolegal Symposium, Las Vegas, 1973.
National Micrographics Assn. *see* National Micrographics Association.
National Micrographics Association.
xNational Micrographics Assn.
Document Mark (Blip) Used in Image Mark Retrieval Systems: ANSI-NMA MS8-1979. Natl Micrograph.
Format & Coding for Computer Output Microfilm: ANSI-NMA MS2-1978. Natl Micrograph.
Guide to Micrographic Equipment: RS15-1979. Natl Micrograph.
Identification of Microforms: ANSI-NMA MS19-1978. Natl Micrograph.
Microfilm Readers: ANSI-NMA MS20-1979. Natl Micrograph.
Microfilming Newspapers: ANSI-NMA MS111-1977. Natl Micrograph.
Practice for Uniform Product Disclosure for Unitized Microform Readers (Microfiche, Jackets & Image Cards): NMA MS22-1979. Natl Micrograph.
Specifications for Sixteen & Thirty-Five Millimeter Microfilms in Roll Form: ASNI-NMA MS14-1978. Natl Micrograph.
National Municipal League. Committee on Metropolitan Government.
xNational Municipal League, Committee on Metropolitan Government.
The Government of Metropolitan Areas in the United States. Arno.
National Museum of Natural History.
xSmithsonian Institution, Washington, D.C. National Museum of Natural History.
Catalog to Manuscripts at the National Anthropological Archives. G K Hall.
National Negro Conference - 1909. *see* National Negro COnference, New York, 1909.
National Negro Conference, New York, 1909.
xNational Negro Conference - 1909.
Proceedings. Arno.
National Notary Association.
xEditors of The National Notary Magazine of the National Notary Assn.
ed. The California Notary Law Primer. Natl Notary.
National Observer. *see* National Observer (The).
National Observer (The).
xNational Observer.
Twenty Modern Men. R West.
National Paint & Coatings Association. *see* National Paint and Coatings Association.
National Paint and Coatings Association.
xNational Paint & Coatings Association.
The Household Paint Selector. B&N.
National Planning Association.
xNational Planning Association.
The Creole Petrolum Corporation in Venezuela. Arno.
The Economic State of New England: Report of the Committee of New England of the National Planning Association. Kennikat.
The Firestone Operations in Liberia. Arno.
The General Electric Company in Brazil. Arno.
Stanvac in Indonesia. Arno.
The United Fruit Company in Latin America. Arno.
National Police Convention. *see* National Police Convention, St. Louis, 1871.
National Police Convention, St. Louis, 1871.
xNational Police Convention.
Official Proceedings of the National Police Convention. Arno.
National Press Club Of Washington. *see* National Press Club of Washington, Washington, D.C.
National Press Club of Washington, Washington, D.C.
xNational Press Club Of Washington.

Dateline: Washington, the Story of National
Affairs Journalism in the Life & Times of the
National Press Club. Greenwood.
National Radio Institute Staff. *see* National Radio
Institute, Washington, D.C.
National Radio Institute, Washington, D.C.
xNational Radio Institute Staff.
Mathematics for Electronic-Electricity..
Hayden.
National Register Publishing Co.
xNational Register Publishing Co.
The Official Museum Directory. Natl Register.
Standard Directory of Advertisers: Classified
Edition. Natl Register.
Standard Directory of Advertisers:
Geographical Edition. Natl Register.
Standard Directory of Advertising Agencies.
Natl Register.
National Research Center of the Arts.
xNational Research Center of the Arts.
Americans & the Arts:: A Survey of Public
Opinion. Am Council Arts.
A Second Look: The Non-Profit Arts &
Cultural Industry of New York State
1975-76. Pub Ctr Cult Res.
National Research Council.
xMarine Board, Assembly of Engineering, National
Research Council.
Mining in the Outer Continental Shelf & in the
Deep Ocean. Natl Acad Pr.
xNational Academy of Science, National Research
Council.
Toward an Understanding of Metropolitan
America. Har-Row.
xNational Academy Of Sciences.
Resources & Man: A Study &
Recommendations by the Committee on
Resources & Man. W H Freeman.
xNational Research Council.
Earth & Human Affairs. Har-Row
Introductory Meteorology. Elliots Bks.
Invisible University: Postdoctoral Education in
the United States. Natl Acad Pr.
Mineral Resources & the Environment. Natl
Acad Pr.
National Research Council. *see* National Research
Council. Committee on Animal Nutrition.
National Research Council - Committee For The Survey
Of Chemistry. *see* National Research Council.
Committee for the Survey of Chemistry.
**National Research Council. Ad Hoc Committee on
Materials and Processes for Electron Devices.**
xNational Materials Advisory Board.
Materials & Processes for Electron Devices.
Natl Acad Pr.
**National Research Council. Ad Hoc Committee on the
Fundamentals of Amorphous Semiconductors.**
xNational Materials Advisory Board.
Fundamentals of Amorphous Semiconductors.
Natl Acad Pr.
**National Research Council. Ad Hoc Panel on Yield of
Electronic Materials and Devices.**
xNational Materials Advisory Board.
Yield of Electronic Materials & Devices. Natl
Acad Pr.
**National Research Council. Advisory Committee for
Assessment of University-Based Institutes for
Research on Poverty.**
xAdvisory Committee For Assessment Of
University Based Institutes For Research On
Poverty.
Policy & Program Research in a University
Setting: A Case Study. Natl Acad Pr.
**National Research Council. Board on Agriculture and
Renewable Resources.**
xAgriculture & Renewable Resources Board,
National Research Council.

Urea & Other Nonprotein Nitrogen
Compounds in Animal Nutrition. Natl Acad
Pr.
xBoard on Agriculture & Renewable Resources.
African Agricultural Research Capabilities. Natl
Acad Pr.
Agricultural Production Efficiency. Natl Acad
Pr.
Climate & Food: Climatic Fluctuation & U. S.
Agricultural Production. Natl Acad Pr.
Enhancement of Food Production for the
United States: World Food & Nutrition
Study. Natl Acad Pr.
Genetic Improvement of Seed Proteins. Natl
Acad Pr.
Nutrient Requirements of Non Human
Primates. Natl Acad Pr.
xBoard on Agriculture and Renewable Resources,
National Research Council.
Renewable Resources for Industrial Materials.
Natl Acad Pr.
**National Research Council. Board on Mineral and
Energy Sources.**
xBoard on Mineral & Energy Resources.
Radioactive Wastes at the Hanford
Reservation. Natl Acad Pr.
Redistribution of Accessory Elements in
Mining & Mineral Processing: Coal & Oil
Shale. Natl Acad Pr.
Surface Mining of Non-Coal Minerals. Natl
Acad Pr.
Technological Innovation & Forces for Change
in the Mineral Industry. Natl Acad Pr.
**National Research Council. Board on Toxicology and
Environmental Health Hazards.**
xBoard on Toxicology & Environmental Health
Hazards.
Odors from Stationary & Mobile Sources. Natl
Acad Pr.
**National Research Council. Commission on Natural
Resources.**
xCommission on Natural Resources, National
Research Council.
The Shallow Land Burial of Low-Level
Radioactively Contaminated Solid Waste.
Natl Acad Pr.
xEnvironmental Studies Board Commission on
Natural Resources, National Research Council.
Decision Making for Regulating Chemicals in
the Environment. Natl Acad Pr.
**National Research Council. Commision on
Sociotechnical Systems.**
xNational Research Council, Commission on
Sociotechnical Systems.
Materials Technology in the Near-Term
Energy Program. Natl Acad Pr.
National Research Council, Commission on
Sociotechnical Systems. *see* National Research
Council. Commision on Sociotechnical Systems.
**National Research Council. Committee for the Survey of
Chemistry.**
xNational Research Council - Committee For The
Survey Of Chemistry.
Nuclear Chemistry: A Current Review. Natl
Acad Pr.
**National Research Council. Committee on Agriculture
Land Use and Wildlife Resources.**
xCommittee On Agricultural Land Use And
Wildlife Resources.
Land Use & Wildlife Resources. Natl Acad Pr.
**National Research Council. Committee on Animal
Health.**
xCommittee on Animal Health.
A Nationwide System for Animal Health
Surveillance. Natl Acad Sci.
**National Research Council. Committee on Animal
Nutrition.**
xNational Research Council.

World Food & Nutrition Study: Potential
Contributions of Research, Commission on
International Relations. Natl Acad Pr.
xNational Research Council, Committee on Animal
Nutrition.
Nutrients & Toxic Substances in Water for
Livestock & Poultry. Natl Acad Pr.
**National Research Council. Committee on Animal
Nutrition. Subcommittee on Feed Composition.**
xCommittee on Animal Nutrition, Agricultural
Board.
Atlas of Nutritional Data on United States &
Canadian Feeds. Natl Acad Pr.
**National Research Council. Committee on Animal
Nutrition. Subcommittee on Fluorosis.**
xCommittee on Animal Nutrition.
Effects of Fluorides in Animals. Natl Acad Pr.
**National Research Council. Committee on Atmospheric
Sciences.**
xCommittee On Atmospheric Sciences.
Atmospheric Sciences & Man's Needs:
Priorities for the Future. Natl Acad Pr.
Weather & Climate Modification. Natl Acad
Pr.
**National Research Council. Committee on Biologic
Effects of Atmospheric Pollutants.**
xCommittee on Biologic Effects of Atmosphere
Pollutants.
Particulate Polycyclic Organic Matter. Natl
Acad Pr.
xCommittee On Biological Effects Of Atmospheric
Pollutants.
Fluorides. Natl Acad Pr.
Lead: Airborne Lead in Perspective. Natl Acad
Pr.
**National Research Council. Committee on Ceramic
Processing.**
xMaterials Advisory Board.
Ceramic Processing. Natl Acad Pr.
**National Research Council. Committee on Electroslag
Remelting and Plasma Arc Melting.**
xNational Materials Advisory Board, National
Research Council.
Electroslag Remelting & Plasma Arc Melting.
Natl Acad Pr.
**National Research Council. Committee on Energy and
the Environment. Implications of Environmental
Regulations for Energy Production and Consumption.**
xBoard on Energy Studies.
Implications of Environmental Regulations for
Energy Production & Consumption. Natl
Acad Pr.
**National Research Council. Committee on Federal
Agency Evaluation Research.**
xCommittee on Federal Agency Evaluation
Research, National Research Council.
Protecting Individual Privacy in Evaluation
Research. Natl Acad Pr.
**National Research Council. Committee on Foreign
Relations.**
xCommittee On Foreign Relations.
Decade of American Foreign Policy, Basic
Documents 1941-1949. Scholarly.
**National Research Council. Committee on Genetic
Vulnerability of Major Crops.**
xNational Academy of Sciences Agricultural
Board.
Genetic Vulnerability of Major Crops. Natl
Acad Sci.
**National Research Council. Committee on Hazardous
Materials, Advisory to the United States Coast
Guard.**
xCommittee on Hazardous Materials.
Pressure Relieving Systems for Marine Bulk
Liquid Cargo Containers. Natl Acad Pr.
**National Research Council. Committee on Maternal
Nutrition.**
xFood and Nutrition Board - Division of Biology
and Agriculture.

Maternal Nutrition & the Course of Pregnancy. Natl Acad Pr.

National Research Council. Committee on Medical and Biologic Effects of Environmental Pollutants.
xCommittee on Medical and Biologic Effects of Environmental Pollutants, National Research Council.
Selenium. Natl Acad Pr.
xNational Research Council, Division of Medical Sciences, Medical & Biologic Effects of Environmental Pollutants.
ed. Ozone & Other Photochemical Oxidants. Natl Acad Pr.

National Research Council. Committee on Mineral Resources and the Environment.
xCommittee on Mineral Resources & Environment, National Research Council.
Reserves & Resources of Uranium in the United States: Mineral Resources & the Environment Supplementary Report. Natl Acad Pr.
xCommittee on Mineral Resources & the Environment, National Research Council.
Coal Workers' Pneumoconiosis-Medical Considerations, Some Social Implications: Mineral Resources & the Environment Supplementary Report. Natl Acad Pr.
Resource Recovery from Municipal Solid Wastes: Mineral Resources & the Environment Supplementary Report. Natl Acad Pr.

National Research Council. Committee on Nuclear Sciences.
xCommittee On Nuclear Science.
Source Material for Radiochemistry. Natl Acad Pr.
xCommittee On Nuclear Sciences.
Geochronology of North America. Natl Acad Pr.

National Research Council. Committee on Oceanography.
xCommittee On Oceanography.
Oceanic Quest: The International Decade of Ocean Exploration. Natl Acad Pr.
Oceanography Nineteen Sixty-Six: Achievements & Opportunites. Natl Acad Pr.
Radioactivity in the Marine Environment. Natl Acad Pr.
Recommended Procedures for Measuring Productivity of Plankton Standing Stock & Related Ocean Properties. Natl Acad Pr.
Scientific Exploration of the South Pacific. Natl Acad Pr.
Wastes Management Concepts for the Coastal Zone. Natl Acad Pr.

National Research Council. Committee on Orthodontic Conditions.
xAssembly of Life Sciences, National Research Council.
Seriously Handicapping Orthodontic Conditions. Natl Acad Pr.

National Research Council. Committee on Pollution.
xCommittee On Pollution.
Waste Management & Control. Natl Acad Sci.

National Research Council. Committee on Problems of Drug Dependence.
xThirty-Seventh Annual Scientific Meeting of the Committee on Problems of Drug Dependence Division of Medical Sciences, National Research Council.
Problems of Drug Dependence 1975: Proceedings. Natl Acad Pr.

National Research Council. Committee on Salmonella.
xCommittee On Salmonella - Division Of Biology And Agriculture.

Evaluation of the Salmonella Problem. Natl Acad Pr.

National Research Council. Committee on Social and Behavioral Urban Research.
xCommittee On Social And Behavioral Urban Research - Division Of Behavioral Sciences.
Strategic Approach to Urban Research & Development: Social & Behavioral Science Considerations. Natl Acad Pr.

National Research Council. Committee on Specifications of the Food Chemicals Codex.
xFood Protection Committee.
Food Chemicals Codex. Natl Acad Pr.

National Research Council. Committee on Structural Adhesives for Aerospace Use.
xNational Material Advisory Board.
ed. Structural Adhesives with Emphasis on Aerospace Application. Dekker.

National Research Council. Committee on the Alaska Earthquake.
xCommittee on the Alaska Earthquake.
The Great Alaska Earthquake of 1964: Biology. Natl Acad Pr.
The Great Alaska Earthquake of 1964: Geology. Natl Acad Pr.
Great Alaska Earthquake of 1964: Human Ecology. Natl Acad Pr.
Great Alaska Earthquake of 1964: Hydrology. Natl Acad Pr.
The Great Alaska Earthquake of 1964: Oceanography & Coastal Engineering. Natl Acad Pr.

National Research Council. Committee on Transportaion.
xCommittee on Transportation, Assembly of Engineering, Natl. Research Council.
A Review of Short Haul Passenger Transportation. Natl Acad Pr.
xCommittee On Underwater Telecommunications Division Of Physical Sciences.
Present & Future Civil Uses of Underwater Sound. Natl Acad Pr.

National Research Council. Committee on Vocational Education Research and Development.
xCommittee on Vocational Education Research & Development, National Research Council.
Assessing Vocational Education Research & Development. Natl Acad Pr.

National Research Council. Disposal Study Steering Comittee.
xOcean Affairs Board, Natl. Research Council.
Disposal in the Marine Environment: An Oceanographic Assessment. Natl Acad Pr.

National Research Council, Division of Medical Sciences, Medical & Biologic Effects of Environmental Pollutants. *see* National Research Council. Committee on Medical and Biologic Effects of Environmental Pollutants.

National Research Council, Food & Nutrition Board. *see* National Research Council. Food and Nutrition Board.

National Research Council. Food and Nutrition Board.
xFood & Nutrition Board.
Folic Acid: Biochemistry & Physiology in Relation to the Human Nutrition Requirement. Natl Acad Pr.
Human Vitamin B-Six Requirements. Natl Acad Pr.
Laboratory Indices of Nutritional Status in Pregnancy. Natl Acad Pr.
Nutrition and Fertility Interrelationships. Natl Acad Pr.
xNational Research Council, Food & Nutrition Board.
Proposed Fortification Policy for Cereal-Grain Products. Natl Acad Pr.

National Research Council. Food Protection Committee.
xCommittee On Food Protection.

Evaluation of Public Health Hazards from Microbiological Contamination of Foods. Natl Acad Pr.
xCommittee on Food Protection, NRC.
The Use of Chemicals in Food Production, Processing, Storage & Distribution. Natl Acad Pr.
xFood Protection Committee.
Food Colors. Natl Acad Pr.

National Research Council. Geophysics Research Board.
xGeophysics Research Board.
Climate, Climatic Change & Water Supply. Natl Acad Pr.
Continental Scientific Drilling. Natl Acad Pr.
Impact of Technology on Geophysics. Natl Acad Pr.
Solid-Earth Geophysics: Survey & Outlook. Natl Acad Pr.
xGeophysics Research Board, National Research Council.
Geophysical Predictions. Natl Acad Pr.

National Research Council. Institute of Laboratory Animal Resources.
xInstitute Of Laboratory Animal Research.
Laboratory Animals in Gerontological Research. Natl Acad Sci.
xInstitute Of Laboratory Animal Resources.
Amphibians: Guidelines for the Breeding, Care & Management of Laboratory Animals. Natl Acad Pr.
Animal Models for Biochemical Research. Natl Acad Pr.
Animal Models for Biomedical Research. Natl Acad Pr.
Coturnix (Coturnix Coturnix Japonica): Standards & Guidelines for the Breeding, Care, & Management of Laboratory Animals. Natl Acad Pr.
Defining the Laboratory Animal. Natl Acad Pr.
Dogs: Standards & Guidelines for the Breeding, Care, & Management of Laboratory Animals. Natl Acad Pr.
Fishes: Guidelines for the Breeding, Care, & Management of Laboratory Animals. Natl Acad Sci.
Guide to Infectious Diseases of Mice & Rats. Natl Acad Pr.
Laboratory Animal Housing. Natl Acad Pr.
Laboratory Animal Medical Subject Headings. Natl Acad Pr.
Research in Zoos & Aquariums. Natl Acad Pr.
Ruminants: Cattle, Sheep & Goats, Guidelines for Breeding, Care & Management of Laboratory Animals. Natl Acad Pr.

National Research Council. International Marine Sciences Affairs Panel.
xOcean Affairs Board.
International Marine Science Affairs. Natl Acad Pr.

National Research Council. Maritime Transportation Research Board.
xMaritime Transportation Research Board.
Legal Impediments to International Intermodal Transportation. Natl Acad Pr.
Maritime Metrication: A Recommended Metric Conversion Plan for the U.S. Maritime Industry. Natl Acad Pr.
Port Development in the United States. Natl Acad Pr.

National Research Council, Maritime Transportation Research Board. *see* National Research Council. Panel on Strategy for Developing Nuclear-Powered Merchant Ships.

National Research Council. Ocean Science Committee.
xOcean Affairs Board, National Research Council.
U. S. Directory of Marine Scientists 1975. Natl Acad Pr.

National Research Council. Office of Scientific Personnel.
xOffice Of Scientific Personnel.

Doctorate Production in United States
Universities, 1920-1962, with Baccalaureate
Origins of Doctorates in Sciences, Arts &
Professions. Natl Acad Pr.
Profiles of PhD's in the Sciences. Natl Acad
Pr.
xScientific Personnel Office.
The Science Committee. Natl Acad Pr.
**National Research Council. Office of Scientific
Personnel. Research Division.**
xNational Academy Of Sciences Office Of
Scientific Personnel.
Careers of PhD's. Natl Acad Sci.
xOffice Of Scientific Personnel.
Doctorate Recipients from United States
Universities, 1958-1966. Natl Acad Pr.
Mobility of PhD's: Before & After the
Doctorate. Natl Acad Pr.
**National Research Council. Panel on Basic Chemical
Research in Government Laboratories.**
xCommittee For The Survey Of Chemistry.
Basic Chemical Research in Government
Laboratories. Natl Acad Pr.
**National Research Council. Panel on Chemical
Dynamics.**
xCommittee for the Survey of Chemistry.
Chemical Dynamics. Natl Acad Pr.
**National Research Council. Panel on Orientations for
Geochemistry.**
xU.S. National Committee for Geochemistry, Div.
of Earth Sciences.
Orientations in Geochemistry. Natl Acad Pr.
**National Research Council. Panel on Planetary
Astronomy.**
xSpace Science Board.
Planetary Astronomy: An Appraisal of
Ground-Based Opportunities. Natl Acad Pr.
**National Research Council. Panel on Seismograph
Networks.**
xCommittee on Seismology.
ed. Global Earthquake Monitoring: Its Uses,
Potentials, & Support Requirements. Natl
Acad Pr.
**National Research Council. Panel on Short-Range
Prediction.**
xCommittee on Atmospheric Sciences.
ed. Severe Storms: Predicion, Detection &
Warning. Natl Acad Pr.
**National Research Council. Panel on Strategy for
Developing Nuclear-Powered Merchant Ships.**
xNational Research Council, Maritime
Transportation Research Board.
Nuclear Merchant Ships. Natl Acad Pr.
**National Research Council. Panel on Undergraduate
Education in Mathematics.**
xNational Academy Of Sciences - Division Of
Mathematics Committee On Support Of
Research In Mathematical Sciences.
Mathematical Sciences: Undergraduate
Education. Natl Acad Pr.
**National Research Council. Space Radiation Study
Panel.**
xSpace Science Board.
Radiobiological Factors in Manned Space
Flight. Natl Acad Pr.
National Research Council. Space Science Board.
xSpace Science Board.
Human Factors in Long-Duration Space Flight.
Natl Acad Pr.
**National Research Council. Study Panel on Assessing
Potential Ocean Pollutants.**
xOcean Affairs Board.
Assessing Potential Ocean Pollutants. Natl
Acad Pr.
**National Research Council. Subcommittee on Beef
Cattle Nutrition.**
xCommittee on Animal Nutrition Board on
Agriculture & Renewable Resources, Natl
Research Council.

Nutrient Requirements of Beef Cattle. Natl
Acad Pr.
**National Research Council. Subcommittee on Prenatal
and Postnatal Mortality in Bovines.**
xCommittee On Animal Health.
Prenatal & Postnatal Mortality in Cattle. Natl
Acad Sci.
National Resources Defense Council.
xThe Natural Resources Defense Council.
Land Use Controls in New York State: A
Handbook on the Legal Rights of Citizens.
Dial.
National Retail Merch. Assn. *see* National Retail
Merchants Association.
National Retail Merchant Assn. *see* National Retail
Merchants Association.
National Retail Merchants Assn. *see* National Retail
Merchants Association.
National Retail Merchants Association.
xNational Retail Merch. Assn.
How to Profit from Radio Advertising. Natl
Ret Merch.
Retailing Job Analysis & Job Evaluation. Natl
Ret Merch.
xNational Retail Merchant Assn.
Cost Control Through Improved Personnel
Practices. Natl Ret Merch.
xNational Retail Merchants Assn.
Briefs: A Supplement to Rising Electrical
Rates: a Blueprint for Action. Natl Ret
Merch.
Executive Compensation Survey of the Retail
Industry. Natl Ret Merch.
Financial & Operating Results of Department
& Specialty Stores of 1976. Natl Ret Merch.
Manual for Reducing Transportation Costs.
Natl Ret Merch.
Measuring Executive & Employee. Natl Ret
Merch.
Merchandising & Operating Results of
Department & Specialty Stores of 1975. Natl
Ret Merch.
OCR-A Cost Benefit Study. Natl Ret Merch.
OCR-A Implementation Handbook. Natl Ret
Merch.
Organization Survival & Growth Including
Management by Objectives. Natl Ret Merch.
POS Update. Natl Ret Merch.
Practical Communications. Natl Ret Merch.
Retail Accounting Manual. Natl Ret Merch.
Shopping Center Useful Lives: An Economic
Analysis. Natl Ret Merch.
Visual Merchandising. Natl Ret Merch.
xNational Retail Merchants Association.
OCR: A Users Guide. Natl Ret Merch.
xNatl Retail Merchants Assn.
Executive Compensation Survey of the Retail
Industry. Natl Ret Merch.
xNRMA.
Measuring Executive & Employee
Performance: Updating Appraisal Methods.
Natl Ret Merch.
Personnel Practices of the Retail Industry. Natl
Ret Merch.
ed. Profitable Retail Television Advertising.
Natl Ret Merch.
ed. Retailer's Guide to Shopping Center
Leasing. Natl Ret Merch.
National Safety Council.
xNational Safety Council.

Aviation Ground Operations Handbook. Natl
Safety Coun.
Forging Safety Manual. Natl Safety Coun.
Guards Illustrated. Natl Safety Coun.
Handbook of Accident Prevention. Natl Safety
Coun.
Industrial Safety Data Sheet. Natl Safety Coun.
Making Safety Work. McGraw.
Meat Industry Safety Guidelines. Natl Safety
Coun.
Motor Fleet Safety Manual. Natl Safety Coun.
School Transporation: A Guide for Supervisors.
Natl Safety Coun.
Small Fleet Guide. Natl Safety Coun.
Supervisors Safety Manual. Natl Safety Coun.
xNational Safety Council Staff.
Handbook of Occupational Safety & Health.
Natl Safety Coun.
Industrial Noise & Hearing Conservation. Natl
Safety Coun.
National Safety Council Staff. *see* National Safety
Council.
National School Public Relations Association.
xNational School Public Relations Association.
Conference Planner: A Guide to Good
Education Meetings. Natl Sch PR.
Conference Time for Teachers & Parents. Natl
Sch PR.
IGE: Individually Guided Education & the
Multiunit School. Natl Sch Pr.
Working with Parents: A Guide for Classroom
Teachers & Other Educators. Natl Sch Pr.
National Science Teachers Association.
xNational Science Teachers Association.
Metric Is Coming. Natl Sci Tchrs.
National Society for the Study of Education.
xNational Society for the Study of Education.
Graduate Study in Education: 50th Yearbook.
U of Chicago Pr.
National Society of Colonial Dames of America. *see*
National Society of the Colonial Dames of America.
National Society of Public Accountants.
xNational Society of Public Accountants.
Portfolio of Accounting Systems for Small &
Medium-Sized Businesses. P-H.
National Society of Sales Training Executives.
xNational Society of Sales Training Executives.
Management of Sales Training. A-W.
Sales Manager As a Trainer. A-W.
National Society of the Colonial Dames of America.
xNational Society of Colonial Dames of America.
Church Music & Musical Life in Pennsylvania
in the Eighteenth Century. AMS Pr.
xNational Society Of The Colonial Dames Of
America.
American War Songs. Gale.
Catalogue of the Genealogical & Historical
Library of the Colonial Dames of the State of
New York. Gale.
**National Symposium on Thermal Pollution, Vanderbilt
University, 1968.**
xNational Symposium on Thermal Pollution.
Proceedings: Biological Aspects of Thermal
Pollution. Vanderbilt U Pr.
Proceedings: Engineering Aspects of Thermal
Pollution. Vanderbilt U Pr.
National Task Force on Citizenship Education.
xNational Task Force on Citizenship Education.
Education for Responsible Citizenship: A
National Task Force Report. McGraw.
**National Trust for Historic Preservation in the United
States.**
xNational Trust for Historic Preservation.

Nauman, St. Elmo.
  xNauman, Elmo.
    Exorcism Through the Ages. Citadel Pr.
  xNauman, St. Elmo.
    Dictionary of American Philosophy. Littlefield.
    Dictionary of American Philosophy. Philos Lib.
    Dictionary of Asian Philosophies. Philos Lib.
    Exorcism Through the Ages. Philos Lib.
Naumann, Friedrich, 1860-1919
  xNaumann, Friedrich.
    Central Europe. Greenwood.
Naumann, Marina Turkevich, 1938-
  xNaumann, Marina Turkevich.
    Blue Evenings in Berlin: Nabokov's Short
      Stories of the 1920s. NYU Pr.
Naumenko, E. V. see Naumenko, Evgenii Vladimirovich.
Naumenko, Evgenii Vladimirovich.
  xNaumenko, E. V.
    Central Regulation of the Pituitary-Adrenal
      Complex. Plenum Pub.
Naumes, William.
  xNaumes, William.
    Cases for Organizational Strategy & Policy.
      HR&W.
    Entrepreneurial Manager in the Small Business:
      Text Readings & Cases. A-W.
Naunton, Ralph F.
  xNaunton, Ralph F.
    ed. Evoked Electrical Activity in the Auditory
      Nervous System. Acad Pr.
Naur, Peter.
  xNaur, Peter.
    Concise Survey of Computer Methods. Van
      Nos Reinhold.
Nauss, Robert M., 1947-
  xNauss, Robert M.
    Parametric Integer Programming. U of Mo Pr.
Nauta, Doede, 1934-
  xNauta, Doede.
    The Meaning of Information. Mouton.
Navajo School of Indian Basketry. see Navajo School of
  Indian Basketry, Los Angeles.
Navajo School of Indian Basketry, Los Angeles.
  xNavajo School Of Indian Basketry.
    Indian Basket Weaving. Dover.
  xTheNavajo School of Indian Basketry.
    Indian Basket Weaving. Peter Smith.
Navarra, John G. see Navarra, John Gabriel.
Navarra, John Gabriel.
  xNavarra, John G.
    The Development of Scientific Concepts in a
      Young Child: A Case Study. Greenwood.
    Earth, Space, & Time: An Introduction to
      Earth Science. Wiley.
  xNavarra, John Gabriel.
    Superboats. Doubleday.
    Supercars. Doubleday.
    Superplanes. Doubleday.
    Supertrains. Doubleday.
Navarre, Yves, 1940-
  xNavarre, Yves.
    Sweet Tooth. Riverrun Texas.
Navarro, Vicente.
  xNavarro, Vincent.
    Medicine Under Capitalism. N Watson.
Navarro, Vincent. see Navarro, Vicente.
Nave, Carl R.
  xNave, Carl R.
    Physics for the Health Sciences. Saunders.
Navia, Luis E.
  xNavia, Luis E.
    A Bridge to the Stars: Our Ancient Cosmic
      Legacy. Avery Pub.
Naviaux, James L.
  xNaviaux, James L.
    Horses in Health & Disease. Arco.
Navin, Thomas R.
  xNavin, Thomas R.

    Copper Mining & Management. U of Ariz Pr.
    Whitin Machine Works Since 1831: A Textile
      Machinery Company in an Industrial Village.
      Russell.
Navone, John. see Navone, John J.
Navone, John J.
  xNavone, John.
    The Jesus Story: Our Life As Story in Christ.
      Liturgical Pr.
Nawaz, Tawfique.
  xNawaz, Tawfique.
    Compiled by The New International Economic
      Order: A Bibliography. Greenwood.
Nawrocki, Dennis A. see Nawrocki, Dennis Alan.
Nawrocki, Dennis Alan.
  xNawrocki, Dennis A.
    Art in Detroit Public Places. Wayne St U Pr.
Nay, W. Robert.
  xNay, W. Robert.
    Multimethod Clinical Assessment. Halsted Pr.
Nayacakalou, R. R., 1927-
  xNayacakalou, R. R.
    Leadership in Fiji. Oxford U Pr.
Nayar, Kuldip.
  xNayar, Kuldip.
    Distant Neighbours: Tale of the Subcontinent.
      Intl Bk Dist.
Nayfeh, Ali H. see Nayfeh, Ali Hasan.
Nayfeh, Ali Hasan.
  xNayfeh, Ali H.
    Nonlinear Oscillations. Wiley.

Nayler, J. L. see Nayler, Joseph Lawrence.

Nayler, Joseph Lawrence.

  xNayler, J. L.
    Dictionary of Mechanical Engineering.
      Butterworths.

Naylon, J see Naylon, John.

Naylon, John.
  xNaylon, J.
    Andalusia. Oxford U Pr.
Naylor, Bernard.
  xNaylor, Bernard.
    ed. Directory of Libraries & Special Collections
      on Latin America & the West Indies.
      Humanities.
Naylor, David T., 1941-
  xNaylor, David T.
    Law, Order, & Justice. Hayden.
Naylor, Edward W. see Naylor, Edward Woodall.
Naylor, Edward Woodall, 1867-1934
  xNaylor, Edward W.
    The Poets & Music. Da Capo.
    The Poets & Music. Hyperion Conn.
Naylor, John.
  xNaylor, John.
    Practical Marketing Audits: A Guide to
      Increased Profitability. Halsted Pr.
Naylor, John F., 1937-
  xNaylor, John F.
    ed. British Aristocracy & the Peerage Bill of
      1719. Oxford U Pr.
Naylor, L. H. see Naylor, Louis Hastings.
Naylor, Louis Hastings, 1896-
  xNaylor, L. H.
    Chateaubriand & Virgil. Johnson Repr.
Naylor, Phyllis R. see Naylor, Phyllis Reynolds.
Naylor, Phyllis Reynolds.
  xNaylor, Phyllis R.
    Eddie, Incorporated. Atheneum.
    Getting Along in Your Family. Abingdon.
    Getting Along with Your Friends. Abingdon.
    How I Came to Be a Writer. Atheneum.
    How Lazy Can You Get?. Atheneum.
    In Small Doses. Atheneum.
Naylor, Robert E.
  xNaylor, Robert E.

    Baptist Deacon. Broadman.
Naylor, Rod.
  xNaylor, Rod.
    Woodcarving Techniques. David & Charles.
Naylor, Thomas H.
  xNaylor, Thomas H.
    Computer Simulation Techniques. Wiley.
    Corporate Planning Models. A-W.
    Simplan: A Computer Based Planning System
      for Government. Duke.
    Simulation Models in Corporate Planning.
      Praeger.
    Strategies for Change in the South. U of NC
      Pr.
Nayman, Jacqueline.
  xNayman, Jacqueline.
    Atlas of Wildlife. T Y Crowell.
Nayyar, D. see Nayyar, Deepak.
Nayyar, Deepak.
  xNayyar, D.
    India's Exports & Export Policies in the
      1960's. Cambridge U Pr.
Nazel, Joseph.
  xNazel, Joseph.
    Paul Robeson: Biography of a Proud Man.
      Holloway.
NCTE Committee to Review Standardized Tests. see
  National Council of Teachers of English. Committee
  to Review Standardized Tests.
Ndeti, Kivuto.
  xNdeti, Kivuto.
    Cultural Policy in Kenya. Unipub.
Ne'Eman, Yuval.
  xNe'eman, Yuval.
    Algebraic Theory of Particle Physics: Hadron
      Dynamics in Terms of Unitary Spin Currents.
      Benjamin-Cummings.
Nead, Daniel W. see Nead, Daniel Wunderlich.
Nead, Daniel Wunderlich, 1858-
  xNead, Daniel W.
    The Pennsylvania-German in the Settlement of
      Maryland. Genealog Pub.
Neagley, Ross L. see Neagley, Ross Linn.
Neagley, Ross Linn.
  xNeagley, Ross L.
    Handbook for Effective Supervision of
      Instruction. P-H.
Neal, Arminta.
  xNeal, Arminta.
    Exhibits for the Small Museum: A Handbook.
      AASLH.
Neal, Avon.
  xNeal, Avon.
    Scarecrows. Potter.
Neal, B. G. see Neal, Bernard George.
Neal, Bernard George.
  xNeal, B. G.
    Structural Theorems & Their Applications.
      Pergamon.
Neal, Berniece R. see Neal, Berniece Roer.
Neal, Berniece Roer.
  xNeal, Berniece R.
    Chicken. Dandelion Pr.
Neal, Charles D.
  xNeal, Charles D.
    Build Your Own Greenhouse: How to
      Construct, Equip, & Maintain It. Chilton.
    Build Your Own Tennis Court: Constructing,
      Subcontracting, Equipping, & Maintaining
      Indoor & Outdoor Courts. Chilton.
    Do-It-Yourself Housebuilding Step-by-Step.
      Stein & Day.
Neal, Emily G. see Neal, Emily Gardiner.
Neal, Emily Gardiner.
  xNeal, Emily G.
    In the Midst of Life. Dutton.
Neal, Ernest. see Neal, Ernest G.
Neal, Ernest G.
  xNeal, Ernest.

Badgers. Sterling.
xNeal, Ernest G.
Woodland Ecology. Harvard U Pr.
Neal, Fred W. see Neal, Fred Warner.
Neal, Fred Warner.
xNeal, Fred W.
ed. Detente or Debacle: Common Sense U.
S.-Soviet Relations. Norton.
Neal, Harry E. see Neal, Harry Edward.
Neal, Harry Edward, 1906-
xNeal, Harry E.
The Secret Service in Action. Elsevier-Nelson.
The Story of Offshore Oil. Messner.
Neal, Helen.
xNeal, Helen.
The Politics of Pain. McGraw.
Neal, James M.
xNeal, James M.
Newswriting & Reporting. Iowa St U Pr.
Neal, John R. see Neal, John Randolph.
Neal, John Randolph, 1874-
xNeal, John R.
Disunion & Restoration in Tennessee. Arno.
Neal, Julia.
xNeal, Julia.
By Their Fruits: The Story of Shakerism in
South Union, Kentucky. Porcupine Pr.
Neal, Larry, 1937-
xNeal, Larry.
Hoodoo Hollerin Bebop Ghosts. Howard U Pr.
Neal, Lois S.
xNeal, Lois S.
Abstracts of Vital Records from Raleigh, North
Carolina, Newspapers 1799-1819. Reprint.
Neal, Patsy.
xNeal, Patsy.
Coaching Methods for Women. A-W.
Neal, R. E. see Neal, Raymond Elwood.
Neal, Raymond Elwood.
xNeal, R. E.
Chemistry: With Selected Principles of Physics.
McGraw.
Neal, Steve, 1949-
xNeal, Steve.
The Eisenhowers: Reluctant Dynasty.
Doubleday.
Neal, W. Keith.
xNeal, W. Keith.
Great British Gunmakers 1740-1790: The
History of John Twigg & the Packington
Guns. Biblio Dist.
Neale, C. M. see Neale, Charles Montague.
Neale, Charles Montague, 1856-
xNeale, C. M.
An Index to Pickwick. Arden Lib.
An Index to Pickwick. Folcroft.
Neale, J. E. see Neale, John Ernest.
Neale, John E. see Neale, John Ernest.
Neale, John Ernest.
xNeale, J. E.
The Age of Catherine de Medici. Merrimack
Bk Serv.
xNeale, John E.
Age of Catherine De Medici. Har-Row.
Neale, John M.
xNeale, John M.
Contemporary Readings in Psychopathology.
Wiley.
Science & Behavior: An Introduction to the
Methods of Research. P-H.
Neale, John M. see Neale, John Mason.
Neale, John Mason, 1818-1866
xNeale, John M.
A History of the Holy Eastern Church. AMS
Pr.
Hymns of the Eastern Church. AMS Pr.
Neale, R. G. see Neale, Robert George.
Neale, R. S.
xNeale, R. S.

Class & Ideology in the Nineteenth Century.
Routledge & Kegan.
Neale, Robert E.
xNeale, Robert E.
The Art of Dying. Har-Row.
Neale, Robert George.
xNeale, R. G.
Great Britain & United States Expansion:
1898-1900. Mich St U Pr.
Neale, Walter, 1873-1933
xNeale, Walter.
Life of Ambrose Bierce. AMS Pr.
Life of Ambrose Bierce. R West.
Sovereignty of the States, an Oration: Address
to the Survivors of the Eighth Virginia
Regiment. B Franklin.
Neale, Walter C.
xNeale, Walter C.
The British Economy: Toward a Decent
Society. Grid Pub.
Economic Change in Rural India: Land Tenure
& Reform in Uttar Pradish, 1800-1955.
Kennikat.
Monies in Societies. Chandler & Sharp.
Neale-Silva, Eduardo.
xNeale-Silva, Eduardo.
Horizonte Humano: Vida De Jose Eustasio
Rivera. U of Wis Pr.
Lengua Hispanica Moderna. HR&W.
Neame, K. D.
xNeame, K. D.
Liquid Scintillation Counting. Halsted Pr.
Nearing, Helen.
xNearing, Helen.
Building & Using Our Sun-Heated Greenhouse:
Grow Vegetables All Year-Round. Garden
Way Pub.
Living the Good Life: How to Live Sanely &
Simply in a Troubled World. Schocken.
Nearing, Homer, 1915-
xNearing, Homer.
English Historical Poetry. Arden Lib.
Nearing, Scott, 1883-
xNearing, Scott.
Anthracite: An Instance of Natural Resource
Monopoly. Arno.
Civilization & Beyond: Learning from History.
Soc Sci Inst.
The Conscience of a Radical. Soc Sci Inst.
Dollar Diplomacy: A Study in American
Imperialism. Arno.
Whither China?: An Economic Interpretation
of Recent Events in the Far East. Hyperion
Conn.
Neary, Peter.
xNeary, Peter.
ed. By Great Waters: A Newfoundland &
Labrador Anthology. U of Toronto Pr.
Neatby, L. H. see Neatby, Leslie H.
Neatby, Leslie H.
xNeatby, L. H.
Discovery in Russian & Siberian Waters. Ohio
U Pr.
Neave, Airey, 1916-
xNeave, Airey.
On Trial at Nuremberg. Little.
Neave, Guy. see Neave, Guy R.
Neave, Guy R.
xNeave, Guy.
How They Fared: The Impact of the
Comprehensive School Upon the University.
Routledge & Kegan.
Nebenzahl, Kenneth.
xNebenzahl, Kenneth.
Commentary by Atlas of the American
Revolution. Rand.
Nebergall, William H. see Nebergall, William Harrison.
Nebergall, William Harrison.
xNebergall, William H.

General Chemistry. Heath.
Nebraska Curriculum Development Center.
xNebraska Curriculum Development Center.
Nebraska Curriculum for English: Grade 12,
Unit 114, Rhetoric. U of Nebr Pr.
Nebraska Curriculum for English, Grade 1:
Units 1-12. U of Nebr Pr.
Nebraska Curriculum for English, Grade 10:
Units 99-100, Man & Moral Law. U of Nebr
Pr.
Nebraska Curriculum for English, Grade 10:
Units 97-98, Man & Nature. U of Nebr Pr.
Nebraska Curriculum for English, Grade 2:
Units 13-22. U of Nebr Pr.
Nebraska Curriculum for English, Grade 3:
Units 23-33. U of Nebr Pr.
Nebraska Curriculum for English, Grade 4:
Units 34-44. U of Nebr Pr.
Nebraska Curriculum for English, Grade 5:
Units 45-57. U of Nebr Pr.
Nebraska Curriculum for English, Grade 6:
Units 58-70. U of Nebr Pr.
Nebraska Curriculum for English, Grade 7:
Units 77-79, Language & Its Written Uses,
Form Classes, the Dictionary Phonology &
Spelling. U of Nebr Pr.
Nebraska Curriculum for English, Grade 8:
Units 80-81, Literature: the Making of
Heroes. U of Nebr Pr.
Nebraska Curriculum for English, Grade 9:
Units 89-90, the Rhetoric of Literature. U of
Nebr Pr.
Nebraska Curriculum for English, Grade 9:
Units 94-96, Language & Its Written Uses. U
of Nebr Pr.
Nebraska Curriculum for English: Language
Explorations for the Elementary Grades. U of
Nebr Pr.
Nebraska Curriculum for English: Poetry for
the Elementary Grades. U of Nebr Pr.
Nebraska Symposium on Motivation.
xNebraska Symposium on Motivation.
Proceedings. U of Nebr Pr.
Nebraska Symposium on Motivation, 1963.
xNebraska Symposium on Motivation, 1963.
Proceedings. U of Nebr Pr.
Nebraska Symposium on Motivation, 1964.
xNebraska Symposium on Motivation, 1964.
Proceedings. U of Nebr Pr.
Nebylitsyn, V. D. see Nebylitsyn, Vladimir Dmitrievich.
Nebylitsyn, Vladimir Dmitrievich.
xNebylitsyn, V. D.
Fundamental Properties of the Human Nervous
System. Plenum Pub.
Nechamkin, Howard, 1918-
xNechamkin, Howard.
Chemistry of the Elements. McGraw.
Nechas, James W. see Nechas, James William.
Nechas, James William.
xNechas, James W.
Synonomy, Repetition, & Restatement in the
Vocabulary of Herman Melville's
Moby-Dick. Norwood Edns.
Necheles, Ruth F., 1936-
xNecheles, Ruth F.
Abbe Gregoire, 1787-1831: The Odyssey of an
Egalitarian. Greenwood.
Necheles, Thomas F., 1933-
xNecheles, Thomas F.
ed. The Acute Leukemias. Thieme-Stratton.
Necker, Claire.
xNecker, Claire.
The Cat's Got Our Tongue. Scarecrow.
Four Centuries of Cat Books: A Bibliography,
1570-1970. Scarecrow.
The Natural History of Cats. Dell.
Necker, Willy.
xNecker, Willy.
How to Train the Family Dog. G&D.
Neckers, D. C. see Neckers, Douglas C.

Neckers, Douglas C.
xNeckers, D. C.
Mechanistic Organic Photochemistry. Krieger.
Neckers, James W. see Neckers, James Winfred.
Neckers, James Winfred, 1902-
xNeckers, James W.
The Building of a Department: Chemistry at
Southern Illinois University, 1927-1967. S Ill
U Pr.
Nederhood, Joel. see Nederhood, Joel H.
Nederhood, Joel H.
xNederhood, Joel.
Promises, Promises, Promises. Bd of Pubns
CRC.
Nedjati, Z. M. see Nedjati, Zaim M.
Nedjati, Zaim M.
xNedjati, Z. M.
Human Rights Under the European
Convention. Elsevier.
Nedler, Shari. see Nedler, Shari E.
Nedler, Shari E.
xNedler, Shari.
Working with Parents: Guidelines for Early
Childhood & Elementary Teachers.
Wadsworth Pub.
Nee, Kay B. see Nee, Kay Bonner.
Nee, Kay Bonner.
xNee, Kay B.
Powhatan. Dillon.
Nee, Victor.
xNee, Victor G.
Longtime Californ: A Documentary Study of
an American Chinatown. HM.
Nee, Victor G. see Nee, Victor.
Needham, Barrie.
xNeedham, D. Barrie.
How Cities Work: An Introduction. Pergamon.
Needham, Christopher D. see Needham, Christopher
Donald.
Needham, Christopher Donald.
xNeedham, Christopher D.
ed. Study of Subject Bibliography with Special
Reference to the Social Sciences. U of Md
Lib Serv.
Needham, D. Barrie. see Needham, Barrie.
Needham, David C., 1929-
xNeedham, David C.
Birthright!: Christian, Do You Know Who You
Are?. Multnomah.
Needham, Douglas.
xNeedham, Douglas.
The Economics of Industrial Structure,
Conduct & Performance. St Martin.
Needham, Henry Beach, 1871-1915
xNeedham, Henry Beach.
Double Squeeze. Arno.

Needham, James G. see Needham, James George.
Needham, James George.
xNeedham, James G.
Guide to the Study of Freshwater Biology.
Holden-Day.
Needham, Joseph.
xNeedham, Joseph.
ed. Background to Modern Science. Arno.
Clerks & Craftsmen in China & the West:
Lectures & Addresses on the History of
Science & Technology. Cambridge U Pr.
The Grand Titration: Science & Society in East
& West. U of Toronto Pr.
A History of Embryology. Arno.
Order & Life. MIT Pr.
Needham, Rodney.
xNeedham, Rodney.

Primordial Characters. U Pr of Va.
ed. Right & Left: Essays on Dual Symbolic
Classification. U of Chicago Pr.
Structure & Sentiment: A Test Case in Social
Anthropology. U of Chicago Pr.
Symbolic Classification. Goodyear.

Needham, Ted.

xNeedham, Ted.
Alcatraz. Celestial Arts.

Needleman, Jacob.
xNeedleman, Jacob.
Religion for a New Generation. Macmillan.
ed. Speaking of My Life: The Art of Living in
the Cultural Revolution. Har-Row.
ed. Understanding the New Religions. Seabury.

Needleman, Martin L.

xNeedleman, Martin L.
Guerrillas in the Bureaucracy: The Community
Planning Experiment in the United States.
Wiley.

Needleman, S. B. see Needleman, Saul Ben.

Needleman, Saul Ben, 1927-
xNeedleman, S. B.
ed. Advanced Methods in Protein Sequence
Determination. Springer-Verlag.
ed. Protein Sequence Determination: A
Sourcebook of Methods & Techniques.
Springer-Verlag.
Needler, Martin C.
xNeedler, Martin C.
An Introduction to Latin American Politics:
The Structure of Conflict. P-H.
Political Systems of Latin America. Van Nos
Reinhold.
Politics & Society in Mexico. U of NM Pr.
Needy, Charles. see Needy, Charles W.
Needy, Charles W.
xNeedy, Charles.
Regulation-Induced Distortions. Lexington Bks.
Neel, Ann F. see Neel, Ann Maria (Filinger).
Neel, Ann Maria (Filinger), 1927-
xNeel, Ann F.
Theories of Psychology: A Handbook.
Schenkman.
Neel, Richard E.
xNeel, Richard E.
Readings in Price Theory. SW Pub.
Neelankavil, James P.
xNeelankavil, James P.
Advertising Self-Regulation: A Global
Perspective. Hastings.
Neeld, Judith.
xNeeld, Judith.
Scripts for a Life in Three Parts. Stone
Country.
Neely, Charles.
xNeely, Charles.
Tales & Songs of Southern Illinois. R West.
Neely, Henry M. see Neely, Henry Milton.
Neely, Henry Milton, 1877-
xNeely, Henry M.
Primer for Star-Gazers. Har-Row.
Neely, John, 1920-
xNeely, John.
Practical Metallurgy & Materials of Industry.
Wiley.
Neely, Richard.
xNeely, Richard.
Lies. BJ Pub Group.
Neeper, Cary.
xNeeper, Cary.

A Place Beyond Man. Dell.
Neeraj, 1938-
xNeeraj.
Nehru & Democracy in India. Intl Pubns Serv.
Neese, Harvey C.
xNeese, Harvey C.
The Almanac of Rural Living. Morrow.
The Almanac of Rural Living. N & N
Resources.
Nef, John U. see Nef, John Ulric.

Nef, John Ulric, 1899-
xNef, John U.
Conquest of the Material World. U of Chicago
Pr.
Cultural Foundations of Industrial Civilization.
Shoe String.

Neff, Charles.
xNeff, Charles.
Aids to Curriculum Planning English Language
Arts K-12. NCTE.

Neff, Emery. see Neff, Emery Edward.
Neff, Emery E. see Neff, Emery Edward.
Neff, Emery Edward, 1892-
xNeff, Emery.
Carlyle. Russell.
A Revolution in European Poetry, 1660-1900.
Octagon.
xNeff, Emery E.
The Poetry of History: The Contribution of
Literature & Literary Scholarship to the
Writing of History Since Voltaire. Columbia
U Pr.
Neff, Fred.
xNeff, Fred.
Karate Is for Me. Lerner Pubns.
Running Is for Me. Lerner Pubns.
Neff, Herbert. see Neff, Herbert B.
Neff, Herbert B.
xNeff, Herbert.
Teaching Handicapped Children Easily: A
Manual for the Average Classroom Teacher
Without Specialized Training. C C Thomas.
Neff, Ivan C.
xNeff, Ivan C.
Dictionary of Oriental Rugs: With a
Monograph on Identification by Weave. Van
Nos Reinhold.
Neff, Mariam. see Neff, Miriam.
Neff, Miriam.
xNeff, Mariam.
Discover Your Worth. Victor Bks.

Neff, Walter S. see Neff, Walter Scott.
Neff, Walter Scott, 1910-
xNeff, Walter S.
Work & Human Behavior. Aldine Pub.
Negandhi, Anant R.
xNegandhi, Anant R.
Comparative Management. Irvington.
The Frightening Angels: A Study of U. S.
Multinationals in Developing Nations. Kent
St U Pr.
Private Foreign Investment Climate in India.
Mich St U Busn.
Work Organization Research: American &
European Perspectives. Kent St U Pr.
Negin, Elliott, 1954-
xNegin, Elliott.
Celebrities Sweepsteaks. Methuen Inc.
Negishi, Ei-Ichi, 1935-
xNegishi, Ei-Ichi.
Organometallics in Organic Synthesis: General
Discussions & Organometallics of Main
Group Metals in Organic Synthesis. Wiley.
Negley, Glenn. see Negley, Glenn Robert.
Negley, Glenn Robert, 1907-
xNegley, Glenn.

Utopian Literature: A Bibliography with a
Supplementary Listing of Works Influential in
Utopian Thought. Regents Pr KS.
Negoita, C. V. see Negoita, Constantin Virgil.
Negoita, Constantin Virgil.
xNegoita, C. V.
Applications of Fuzzy Sets to Systems
Analysis. Halsted Pr.
Negrin, S. see Negrin, Su.
Negrin, Su.
xNegrin, S.
ed. The Great Harmony: Teachings &
Observations of the Way of the Universe.
Times Change.
Negro Young People's Christian & Educational Congress
Atlanta 1902. see Negro Young People'S Christian
and Educational Congress, Atlanta, 1902.
**Negro Young People'S Christian and Educational
Congress, Atlanta, 1902.**
xNegro Young People's Christian & Educational
Congress Atlanta 1902.
United Negro: His Problems & His Progress.
Negro U Pr.
Negroponte, Nicholas.
xNegroponte, Nicholas.
Soft Architecture Machines. MIT Pr.
Negus, R. W., 1916-
xNegus, R. W.
Fundamentals of Finite Mathematics. Wiley.
Nehari, Zeev, 1915-
xNehari, Zeev.
Conformal Mapping. Dover.
Nehemkis, Peter. see Nehemkis, Peter Raymond.
Nehemkis, Peter Raymond.
xNehemkis, Peter.
Latin America: Myth & Reality. Greenwood.
Neher, Clark D.
xNeher, Clark D.
ed. Modern Thai Politics: From Village to
Nation. Schenkman.
Politics in Southeast Asia. Schenkman.

Nehrling, Arno.

xNehrling, Arno.

Easy Gardening with Drought - Resistant
Plants. Dover.

Easy Gardening with Drought-Resistant Plants.
Peter Smith.

Neiburger, Morris.
xNeiburger, Morris.
Understanding Our Atmospheric Environment.
W H Freeman.
Neidecker, Elizabeth. see Neidecker, Elizabeth A.
Neidecker, Elizabeth A.
xNeidecker, Elizabeth.
School Programs in Speech-Language:
Organization & Management. P-H.
Neider, Charles, 1915-
xNeider, Charles.
ed. Stature of Thomas Mann. Arno.
Neidhardt, W. S. see Neidhardt, Wilfried.
Neidhardt, Wilfried.
xNeidhardt, W. S.
Fenianism in North America. Pa St U Pr.
Neidig, Kenneth L.
xNeidig, Kenneth L.
Music Director's Complete Handbook of
Forms. P-H.
Neidle, Cecyle S.
xNeidle, Cecyle S.
America's Immigrant Women. Hippocrene Bks.
America's Immigrant Women. Twayne.
Great Immigrants. Twayne.
Neier, Areyeh, 1937-
xNeier, Aryeh.

Crime & Punishment: A Radical Solution. Stein
& Day.
Neier, Aryeh. see Neier, Areyeh.
Neifeld, Morris R.
xNeifeld, Morris R.
Cooperative Consumer Credit. Arno.
Neiger, A.
xNeiger, A.
Atlas of Practical Proctology. Krieger.
Neighbour, Ralph W. see Neighbour, Ralph Webster.
Neighbour, Ralph Webster, 1929-
xNeighbour, Ralph W.
This Gift Is Mine. Broadman.
The Touch of the Spirit. Broadman.
Neigoff, Anne.
xNeigoff, Anne.
Dinner's Ready. A Whitman.
The Energy Workers. A Whitman.
Neigoff, Mike.
xNeigoff, Mike.
Goal to Go. A Whitman.
It Will Never Be the Same Again. HR&W.
Neihardt, John G. see Neihardt, John Gneisenau.
Neihardt, John Gneisenau, 1881-1973
xNeihardt, John G.
Collected Poems of John G. Neihardt.
Greenwood.
Patterns & Coincidences: A Sequel to "All Is
But a Beginning". U of Mo Pr.
Neil. see Neil, Thomas C.
Neil Brice Memorial Symposium, Frascati, 1974.
xNeil Brice Memorial Symposium, Frascati, Italy,
May 28-June 1 1974.
The Magnetospheres of the Earth & Jupiter:
Proceedings. Kluwer Boston.
Neil, J. Meredith, 1937-
xNeil, J. Meredith.
Toward a National Taste: America's Quest for
Aesthetic Independence. U Pr of Hawaii.
Neil, Randy.
xNeil, Randy.
The Official Cheerleader's Handbook. S&S.
Neil, Thomas C., 1939-
xNeil.
Interpersonal Communications for Criminal
Justice Personnel. Allyn.
Neil, William, 1909-
xNeil, William.
ed. Concise Dictionary of Religious Quotations.
Eerdmans.
The Difficult Sayings of Jesus. Eerdmans.
Neilan, Edward.
xNeilan, Edward.
Future of the China Market: Prospects for
Sino-American Trade. Am Enterprise.
Neilan, Sarah.
xNeilan, Sarah.
An Air of Glory. Morrow.
Neill, A. S. see Neill, Alexander Sutherland.
Neill, Alexander Sutherland, 1883-
xNeill, A. S.
Summerhill: A Radical Approach to Child
Rearing. PB.
Summerhill for & Against. PB.
Neill, John R.
xNeill, John R.
Practical Manual of Psychiatric Consultation.
Williams & Wilkins.
Neill, Kenneth.
xNeill, Kenneth.
The Irish People: An Illustrated History.
Mayflower Bks.
Neill, Robert.
xNeill, Robert.
The Devil's Door. St Martin.
Neill, Stephen C. see Neill, Stephen Charles.
Neill, Stephen Charles, Bp.
xNeill, Stephen C.

The Christian Society. Greenwood.
Neill, Wilfred T.
xNeill, Wilfred T.
Archeology & a Science of Man. Columbia U
Pr.
Geography of Life. Columbia U Pr.
Twentieth-Century Indonesia. Columbia U Pr.
Neill, William A.
xNeill, William A.
Butterflies Afield in the Pacific Northwest.
Pacific Search.
Neilson, Charles.
xNeilson, Charles.
Original, Compiled & Corrected Account of
Burgoyne's Campaign. Kennikat.

Neilson, Katharine B. see Neilson, Katharine Bishop.
Neilson, Katharine Bishop.
xNeilson, Katharine B.
Filippino Lippi, a Critical Study. Greenwood.
Neilson, Marguerite.
xNeilson, Marguerite.
The Bride of Alderburn. Berkley Pub.
Neilson, William A. see Neilson, William A. W.
Neilson, William A. W.
xNeilson, William A.
Proposals for Legislative Reform Aiding the
Consumer of Funeral Industry Products &
Services. Continent Assn Funeral.

Neilson, Winthrop.

xNeilson, Winthrop.
The Ring & the River. Putnam.

Neiman, Fraser.
xNeiman, Fraser.
Matthew Arnold. Twayne.
Neiman, Leroy, 1927-
xNeiman, LeRoy.
Horses. Abrams.
Neimark, Anne E.
xNeimark, Anne E.
Sigmund Freud: The World Within. HarBraceJ.
Touch of Light: The Story of Louis Braille.
HarBraceJ.
Neimark, Maria. see Neimark, Mariia Solomonovna.
Neimark, Mariia Solomonovna.
xNeimark, Maria.
Personality Orientation. Educ Tech Pubn.
Neinstein, Raymond L.
xNeinstein, Raymond L.
The Ghost Country: A Study of the Novels of
Larry McMurtry. Creative Arts Bk.
Neisser, U. see Neisser, Ulric.
Neisser, Ulric.
xNeisser, U.
Cognitive Psychology. P-H.
xNeisser, Ulric.
Cognition & Reality: Principles & Implications
of Cognitive Psychology. W H Freeman.
Neisworth, John. see Neisworth, John T.
Neisworth, John T.
xNeisworth, John.
Retardation: Issues, Assessment & Intervention.
McGraw.
Nekipelov, Victor. see Nekipelov, Viktor.
Nekipelov, Viktor.
xNekipelov, Victor.
Institute of Fools: Notes from Serbsky. FS&G.
Nekrasov, Nikolai A. see Nekrasov, Nikolai Alekseevich.
Nekrasov, Nikolai Alekseevich.
xNekrasov, Nikolai A.
Who Can Be Happy & Free in Russia. AMS
Pr.
Who Can Be Happy & Free in Russia ?.
Hyperion Conn.
Nelkin, Dorothy.
xNelkin, Dorothy.

On the Season: Aspects of the Migrant Labor
System. NY Sch Indus Rel.
The Politics of Housing Innovation: The Fate
of the Civilian Industrial Technology
Program. Braziller.
Nell, Onora.
xNell, Onora.
Acting on Principle: An Essay in Kantian
Ethics. Columbia U Pr.
Nell, W. C. see Nell, William Cooper.
Nell, William C. see Nell, William Cooper.
Nell, William Cooper, 1816-1874
xNell, W. C.
The Colored Patriots of the American
Revolution. Gordon Pr.
xNell, William C.
Colored Patriots of the American Revolution.
Arno.
Nelli, Humbert S., 1930-
xNelli, Humbert S.
The Business of Crime: Italians & Syndicate
Crime in the United States. Oxford U Pr.
Nelligan, John E. see Nelligan, John Emmett.
Nelligan, John Emmett.
xNelligan, John E.
White Pine Empire: The Life of a Lumberman.
North Star.
Nellis, John R.
xNellis, John R.
A Theory of Ideology: The Tanzanian
Example. Oxford U Pr.
Nellis, Muriel.
xNellis, Muriel.
The Female Fix. HM.
Nelms, Clarice.
xNelms, Clarice.
Developing Leadership in Recreation. Pacific
Coast.
Nelson. see Nelson, Walter Henry.
Nelson, Alan H.
xNelson, Alan H.
The Medieval English Stage: Corpus Christi
Pageants & Plays. U of Chicago Pr.
Nelson, Alice R. see Nelson, Alice Ruth Moore Dunbar.
Nelson, Alice Ruth Moore Dunbar, 1875-1935
xNelson, Alice R.
The Goodness of St. Rocque & Other Stories.
AMS Pr.
Nelson, Alvin F. see Nelson, Alvin Fredolph.
Nelson, Alvin Fredolph.
xNelson, Alvin F.
Inquiry & Reality: A Discourse in Pragmatic
Synthesis. Tex Christian.
Nelson, Anna K. see Nelson, Anna Kasten.
Nelson, Anna Kasten.
xNelson, Anna K.
ed. The Records of Federal Officials: A
Selection of Materials from the National
Study Commission on Records & Documents
of Federal Officials. Garland Pub.
Nelson Associates. see Nelson Associates, Inc.
Nelson Associates, Inc.
xNelson Associates.
Public Library Systems in the United States: A
Survey of Multijurisdictional Systems. ALA.
Nelson, Bert.
xNelson, Bert.
ed. The Little Red Book: Metric Conversion
Tables & Other Useful Information for the
Track Fan, Athlete, Coach & Official.
Tafnews.
Nelson, Beth, 1926-
xNelson, Beth.
George Crabbe & the Progress of
Eighteenth-Century Narrative Verse.
Bucknell U Pr.
Nelson, Betty Lou.
xNelson, Betty Lou.
A Diabetic Party Cookbook. Booklore Pubs.
Nelson, Bobby J. see Nelson, Bobby Jack.

Nelson, Bobby Jack.
xNelson, Bobby J.
Brothers. Macmillan.
Nelson, Bruce W. see Nelson, Bruce Warren.
Nelson, Bruce Warren.
xNelson, Bruce W.
ed. Environmental Framework of Coastal Plain
Estuaries. Geol Soc.
Nelson, Bryan, 1932-
xNelson, Bryan.
Azraq: Desert Oasis. Ohio U Pr.
The Gannet. Buteo.
Nelson, C. Ellis. see Nelson, Carl Ellis.
Nelson, C. V. see Nelson, Clifford V.
Nelson, Carl A.
xNelson, Carl A.
Mechanical Trades Pocket Manual. Audel.
Nelson, Carl Ellis, 1916-
xNelson, C. Ellis.
Don't Let Your Conscience Be Your Guide.
Paulist Pr.
Where Faith Begins. John Knox.
Nelson, Cary.
xNelson, Cary.
The Incarnate Word: Literature As Verbal
Space. U of Ill Pr.
Nelson, Clifford V.
xNelson, C. V.
The Theoretical Basis of Electrocardiology.
Oxford U Pr.
Nelson, Conny. see Nelson, Conny E.
Nelson, Conny E.
xNelson, Conny.
Homer's Odyssey: A Critical Handbook.
Wadsworth Pub.
Nelson, Daniel.
xNelson, Daniel.
A Checklist of Writings on the Economic
History of the Greater
Philadelphia-Wilmington Region. Eleutherian
Mills-Hagley
Frederick W. Taylor & the Rise of Scientific
Management. U of Wis Pr.
Nelson, Darrel.
xNelson, Darrell.
Little Millard Mustardseed. Cook.
Nelson, Darrell. see Nelson, Darrel.
Nelson, Dee J. see Nelson, Dee Jay.

Nelson, Dee Jay.

xNelson, Dee J.
Life Force in the Great Pyramids. De Vorss.

Nelson, Dick.

xNelson, Dick.
Desert Survival. Tecolote Pr.
Hiker's Guide to the Superstition Mountains.
Tecolote Pr.

Nelson, Donald F., 1929-
xNelson, Donald F.
Portrait of the Artist As Hermes: A Study of
Myth & Psychology in Thomas Mann's
Felix-Krull. U of NC Pr.
Nelson, Donald F. see Nelson, Donald Frederick.
Nelson, Donald Frederick, 1930-
xNelson, Donald F.
Electric, Optic, & Acoustic Interactions in
Dielectrics. Wiley.
Nelson, Donald M. see Nelson, Donald Marr.
Nelson, Donald Marr, 1888-1959
xNelson, Donald M.
Arsenal of Democracy: The Story of American
War Production. Da Capo.
Nelson, E. Clifford, 1911-
xNelson, E. Clifford.
ed. Lutherans in North America. Fortress.
Nelson, Edward W. see Nelson, Edward William.

Nelson, Edward William, 1855-1934
xNelson, Edward W.
Lower California & Its Natural Resources.
Manessier.
Nelson, Eugene. see Nelson, Eugene Walter.
Nelson, Eugene Walter, 1914-
xNelson, Eugene.
Practical Aspects of Texas Real Estate Law.
Austin Pr.
Nelson, Gary J.
xNelson, Gary J.
ed. Blood Lipids & Lipoproteins: Quantitation,
Composition & Metabolism. Krieger.
Nelson, Gayle L.
xNelson, Gayle L.
ESL Operations: Techniques for Learning
While Doing. Newbury Hse.
Nelson, George, 1908-
xNelson, George.
How to See: Visual Adventures in a World
God Never Made. Little.
Problems of Design. Watson-Guptill.
Problems of Design. Watson-Guptill.
Nelson, George R.
xNelson, George R.
ed. Freedom & Welfare: Social Patterns in the
Northern Countries of Europe. Greenwood.
Nelson, Gideon E.
xNelson, Gideon E.
Biological Principles with Human Perspectives.
Wiley.
Fundamental Concepts of Biology. Wiley.
Nelson, Glenn C.
xNelson, Glenn C.
Ceramics: A Potter's Handbook. HR&W.
Nelson, Hallie F., 1905-
xNelson, Hallie M.
South of the Cottonwood Tree. Purcells.
Nelson, Hallie M. see Nelson, Hallie F.
Nelson, Harry.
xNelson, Harry.
Introduction to Physical Anthropology. West
Pub.
Nelson, Harry W. see Nelson, Harry William.
Nelson, Harry William.
xNelson, Harry W.
Not of This Star Dust & Other Poems. Blue
Leaf.
Nelson, Helge, 1882-
xNelson, Helge.
The Swedes & the Swedish Settlements in
North America. Arno.
Nelson, Howard J.
xNelson, Howard J.
The Los Angeles Metropolitan Experience:
Uniqueness, Generality & the Goal of the
Good Life. Ballinger Pub.
Nelson, Indiana.
xNelson, Indiana.
Truckstop. St Martin.
Nelson, J. Craig. see Nelson, James Craig.
Nelson, J. S. see Nelson, Joseph S.
Nelson, Jack.
xNelson, Jack.
The Censors & the Schools. Greenwood.
Nelson, Jack A.
xNelson, Jack A.
Hunger for Justice: The Politics of Food &
Faith. Orbis Bks.
Nelson, Jack K.
xNelson, Jack K.
The Measurement of Physical Performance:
Resource Guide with Laboratory
Experiments. Burgess.
Nelson, Jack L.
xNelson, Jack L.
Values & Society. Hayden.
Nelson, James Craig, 1932-
xNelson, J. Craig.

Abraham Cowley: The Muse's Hannibal.
Russell.
Last Four Lives of Annie Besant. U of Chicago
Pr.
Netherton, Cliff, 1910-
xNetherton, Cliff.
Angling & Casting: A Manual for Self & Class
Instruction. A S Barnes.
Netherton, Morris.
xNetherton, Morris.
Past Lives Therapy. Ace Bks.
Past Lives Therapy. Morrow.
Netherton, Nan.
xNetherton, Nan.
Fairfax County, Virginia: A History. Fairfax
County.
Nethery, Susan.
xNethery, Susan.
One Year & Counting: Breast Cancer, My
World, & Me. Baker Bk.
Netschert, Bruce C. see Netschert, Bruce Carlton.
Netschert, Bruce Carlton.
xNetschert, Bruce C.
The Future Supply of Oil & Gas: A Study of
the Availability of Crude Oil, Natural Gas, &
Natural Gas Liquids in the United States in
the Period Through 1975. Greenwood.
Netsky, Martin G.
xNetsky, Martin G.
The Choroid Plexus in Health & Disease. U Pr
of Va.
Nettel, Reginald, 1899-
xNettel, Reginald.
The Orchestra in England: A Social History.
Scholarly.
Nettels, Curtis P. see Nettels, Curtis Putnam.
Nettels, Curtis Putnam.
xNettels, Curtis P.
George Washington & American Independence.
Greenwood.
Money Supply of the American Colonies
Before 1720. Kelley.
Netter, Frank. see Netter, Frank Henry.
Netter, Frank Henry, 1906-
xNetter, Frank.
Fad Diets Can Be Deadly: The Safe Sure, Way
to Weight Loss & Good Nutrition.
Exposition.
Nettesheim, P.
xNettesheim, P.
Organ & Tissue Regeneration in Mammals.
Mss Info.
Nettl, Bruno, 1930-
xNettl, Bruno.
ed. Eight Urban Musical Cultures: Tradition &
Change. U of Ill Pr.
Folk & Traditional Music of the Western
Continents. P-H.
Folk Music in the United States: An
Introduction. Wayne St U Pr.
Music in Primitive Culture. Harvard U Pr.
Theory & Method in Ethnomusicology. Free
Pr.
Nettl, J P.
xNettl, J. P.
Soviet Achievement. HarBraceJ.
Nettl, Paul, 1889-
xNettl, Paul.
Forgotten Musicians. Greenwood.
National Anthems. Ungar.
Nettlau, Max, 1865-1944
xNettlau, Max.
Anarchy Through the Times. Gordon Pr.
Nettleford, Rex. see Nettleford, Rex M.
Nettleford, Rex M., 1933-
xNettleford, Rex.
Identity, Race, & Protest in Jamaica. Morrow.
Nettler, Gwynn.
xNettler, Gwynn.

Explaining Crime. McGraw.
Nettleship, Richard L. see Nettleship, Richard Lewis.
Nettleship, Richard Lewis, 1846-1892
xNettleship, Richard L.
Lectures on the Republic of Plato. Folcroft.
Lectures on the Republic of Plato. R West.
Theory of Education in the Republic of Plato.
Tchrs Coll.
Nettleton, David, 1918-
xNettleton, David.
Our Infallible Bible. Reg Baptist.
Nettleton, George H. see Nettleton, George Henry.
Nettleton, George Henry.
xNettleton, George H.
ed. British Dramatists from Dryden to
Sheridan. Folcroft.
ed. British Dramatists from Dryden to
Sheridan. S Ill U Pr.
ed. Specimens of the Short Story. Arno.
Nettleton, L. L. see Nettleton, Lewis Lomat.
Nettleton, Lewis Lomat, 1896-
xNettleton, L. L.
Gravity & Magnetics in Oil Prospecting.
McGraw.
Netzer, Dick.
xNetzer, Dick.
Economics of the Property Tax. Brookings.
Netzer, Lanore A.
xNetzer, Lanore A.
Strategies for Instructional Management. Allyn.
Neu, Charles E.
xNeu, Charles E.
The Troubled Encounter: The United States &
Japan. Krieger.
Neubardt, Selig.
xNeubardt, Selig.
Concept of Contraception. Trident.
Neubauer, Peter. see Neubauer, Peter B.
Neubauer, Peter B.
xNeubauer, Peter.
The Process of Child Development. NAL.
Neubeck, Deborah K.
xNeubeck, Deborah K.
Guide to the Microfilm Edition of The Frank
B. Kellogg Papers. Minn Hist.
Neubeck, Kenneth J.
xNeubeck, Kenneth J.
Corporate Response to Urban Crisis. Lexington
Bks.
Neubeck, Kenneth J. see Neubeck, Kenneth John.
Neubeck, Kenneth John, 1943-
xNeubeck, Kenneth J.
Social Problems: A Critical Approach. Scott F.
Neubecker, Ottfried, 1908-
xNeubecker, Ottfried.
A Guide to Heraldry. McGraw.
Neuber, Keith A.
xNeuber, Keith A.
Needs Assessment: A Model for Community
Planning. Sage.
Neuberger, Egon.
xNeuberger, Egon.
Comparative Economic Systems: A
Decision-Making Approach. Allyn.
Neuberger, Richard L. see Neuberger, Richard Lewis.
Neuberger, Richard Lewis, 1912-1960
xNeuberger, Richard L.
Lewis & Clark Expedition. Random.
Neubert, Hermann K. see Neubert, Hermann K P.
Neubert, Hermann K P.
xNeubert, Hermann K.
Instrument Transducers: An Introduction to
Their Performance & Design. Oxford U Pr.
Neuburger, Hugh. see Neuburger, Hugh M.
Neuburger, Hugh M., 1943-
xNeuburger, Hugh.
German Banks & German Economic Growth
from Unification to World War I. Arno.
Neuer, Kathleen.
xNeuer, Kathleen.

The Inn Book: A Field Guide to Old Inns &
Good Food in New York, New Jersey,
Eastern Pennsylvania, Delaware &
Connecticut. Random.
Neufeld, John.
xNeufeld, John.
Edgar Allan. NAL.
Edgar Allan. S G Phillips.
Freddy's Book. Avon.
Freddy's Book. Random.
Sunday Father. NAL.
Touching. S G Phillips.
Neufeld, Maurice F.
xNeufeld, Maurice F.
Poor Countries & Authoritarian Rule. NY Sch
Indus Rel.
Neufert, Ernst.
xNeufert, Ernst.
Architects' Data. Beekman Pubs.
Neufville, Richard De. see De Neufville, Richard.
Neugebauer, O. see Neugebauer, Otto.
Neugebauer, Otto, 1899-
xNeugebauer, O.
A History of Ancient Mathematical
Astronomy. Springer-Verlag.
Neugebauer, Wilbert.
xNeugebauer, Wilbert.
Marine Aquarium Fish Identifier. Sterling.
Neugeboren, Jay.
xNeugeboren, Jay.
Corky's Brother. FS&G.
Neuhaus, Eugen.
xNeuhaus, Eugen.
Drawn from Memory: A Self-Portrait. Pacific
Bks.
Neuhaus, O. W. see Neuhaus, Otto Wilhelm.
Neuhaus, Otto Wilhelm.
xNeuhaus, O. W.
ed. Fish in Research. Acad Pr.
Neuhaus, Richard J. see Neuhaus, Richard John.
Neuhaus, Richard John.
xNeuhaus, Richard J.
Freedom for Ministry. Har-Row.
Neuhaus, Robert. see Neuhaus, Robert H.
Neuhaus, Robert H.
xNeuhaus, Robert.
Family Crises. Merrill.
Neujahr, James. see Neujahr, James L.
Neujahr, James L., 1939-
xNeujahr, James.
The Individualized Instruction Game. Tchrs
Coll.
Neukrantz, Klaus, 1897-ca. 1943
xNeukrantz, Klaus.
Barricades in Berlin. Banner Pr IL.
Neulinger, John.
xNeulinger, John.
The Psychology of Leisure: Research
Approaches to the Study of Leisure. C C
Thomas.
Neuman, Daniel M., 1944-
xNeuman, Daniel M.
The Life of Music in North India: The
Organization of an Artistic Tradition. Wayne
St U Pr.
Neuman, Donald.
xNeuman, Donald B.
Experiences in Science for Young Children.
Delmar.
Neuman, Donald B. see Neuman, Donald.
Neuman, Robert W.
xNeuman, Robert W.
The Sonota Complex & Associated Sites on the
Northern Great Plains. Nebraska Hist.
Neuman, Stephanie G.
xNeuman, Stephanie G.

America Through British Eyes. Peter Smith.
American States During & After the
   Revolution, 1775-1798. Kelley.
Evening Post: A Century of Journalism.
   Russell.
Hamilton Fish: The Inner History of the Grant
   Administration. Ungar.
History of the Bank of New York & Trust
   Company, 1784-1934. Arno.
Nevins, Deborah.
   xNevins, Deborah.
   The Architect's Eye: American Architectural
      Drawings 1799-1978. Pantheon.
Nevins, Francis M.
   xNevins, Francis M.
   Corrupt & Ensnare. Putnam.
Nevins, William, 1797-1835
   xNevins, William.
   Thoughts on Popery. Arno.
Nevinson, Henry W. see Nevinson, Henry Woodd.
Nevinson, Henry Woodd, 1856-1941
   xNevinson, Henry W.
   Books & Personalities. Arno.
   Books & Personalities. R West.
   Farewell to America. Gordon Pr.
   In the Dark Backward. Arno.
   Thomas Hardy. Folcroft.
   Thomas Hardy. Haskell.
Nevison, John M.
   xNevison, John M.
   Little Book of Basic Style: How to Write a
      Program You Can Read. A-W.
Nevius, Blake.
   xNevius, Blake.
   Compiled by American Novel: Sinclair Lewis
      to the Present. AHM Pub.
   Cooper's Landscapes: An Essay on the
      Picturesque Vision. U of Cal Pr.
   Edith Wharton: A Study of Her Fiction. U of
      Cal Pr.
New, Christopher.
   xNew, Christopher.
   Goodbye Chairman Mao. Coward.
   Goodbye Chairman Mao. Popular Lib.
New Dimensions Foundation.
   xNew Dimensions Foundation.
   ed. The New Healers. And-Or Pr.
New England Coastal Zone Management Conference,
   4th, Durham, N.H., 1974.
   xNew England Coastal Zone Management
      Conference, Fourth.
   Perspectives on Oil Refineries & Offshore
      Unloading Facilities: Proceedings. URI MAS.
New Games Foundation.
   xNew Games Foundation.
   The New Games Book. Doubleday.
New Jersey. Adjutant General's Office.
   xNew Jersey Adjutant-General's Office.
   Records of Officers & Men of New Jersey in
      Wars, 1791-1815. Genealog Pub.
New Jersey Adjutant-General's Office. see New Jersey.
   Adjutant General'S Office.
New Jersey Conference Of Social Work. see New Jersy
   Conference of Social Work. Interracial Committee.
New Jersey Conference of Social Work. Interracial
   Committee.
   xNew Jersey Conference   f Social Work.
   Negro in New Jersey. Negro U Pr.
New Jersey. Governor's Select Commission on Civil
   Disorder.
   xState of New Jersey Governor's Select
      Commission on Civil Disorder.
   Report on Action: An Investigation into the
      Causes & Events of the 1967 Newark Race
      Riots. Humanities.
New, John F. see New, John F. H.
New, John F. H.
   xNew, John F.

Anglican & Puritan: The Basis of Their
   Opposition, 1558-1640. Stanford U Pr.
ed. Oliver Cromwell: Pretender, Puritan,
   Statesman, Paradox?. Krieger.
New, Melvyn.
   xNew, Melvyn.
   Laurence Sterne As Satirist: A Reading of
      Tristram Shandy. U Presses Fla.
New Mexico (Ter.). Bureau of Immigration.
   xTheTerritorial Bureau of Immigration.
   The Resources of New Mexico. Gannon.
New Orleans Academy Of Ophthalmology. see New
   Orleans Academy of Opthalmology.
New Orleans Academy of Opthalmology.
   xNew Orleans Academy Of Ophthalmology.
   Symposium on Cataracts. Mosby.
   Symposium on Contact Lenses. Mosby.
   Symposium on the Cornea. Mosby.
   xNew Orleans Academy of Opthalmology.
   Symposium on Glaucoma: Transactions of the
      New Orleans Academy of Opthalmology.
      Mosby.
   Symposium on Medical & Surgical Diseases of
      the Cornea. Mosby.

New Orleans Museum of Art.
   xNew Orleans Museum of Art.
   Diverse Images. Amphoto.

New, Peter.
   xNew, Peter J.
   George Crabbe's Poetry. St Martin.
New, Peter J. see New, Peter.

New Statesman.
   xNew Statesman.
   New Statesmanship. Arno.

New York Academy of Medicine.

   xNew York Academy Of Medicine.
   Author Catalog of the Library of the New
      York Academy of Medicine, Second
      Supplement. G K Hall.
   Freud & Contemporary Culture. Arno.
   Frontiers in Medicine. Arno.
   Future in Medicine: The March of Medicine,
      1949, Laity Lectures, No. 14. Arno.
   Landmarks in Medicine. Arno.
   March of Medicine Laity Lectures, No. 4.
      Arno.
   March of Medicine, Laity Lectures No. 5.
      Arno.
   March of Medicine, Laity Lectures No. 6.
      Arno.
   March of Medicine, Laity Lectures No. 7.
      Arno.
   March of Medicine: Lectures to the Laity,
      1943. Arno.
   Medicine & Anthropology. Arno.
   Medicine & Science. Arno.
   Medicine in a Changing Society. Arno.
   Medicine in the Postwar World: The March of
      Medicine, 1947, Laity Lectures, No. 12.
      Arno.
   Medicine Today: The March of Medicine, 1946
      (Laity Lectures, No. 11). Arno.
   Milestones in Medicine. Arno.
   Ministry & Medicine in Human Relations.
      Arno.
   Modern Attitudes in Psychiatry. Arno.
   Perspectives in Medicine. Arno.
   Portrait Catalog. G K Hall.
   Portrait Catalog: Third Supplement, 1971-1975.
      G K Hall.
   Society & Medicine. Arno.
   Subject Catalog of the Library of the New
      York Academy of Medicine. G K Hall.
New York Adjutant-General's Office. see New York
   (State). Adjutant-General's Office.

New York. Botanical Garden.
   xNew York Botanical Garden.
   Index to Economic Botany: Volumes 1-20,
      1947-1966. NY Botanical.
   Mycologia Index: Volumes 1-58, 1909-1966.
      NY Botanical.
   Wild Flowers of the Northeastern States.
      McGraw.
New York (City). Board of Aldermen.
   xBoard Of Aldermen.
   Police in New York City: An Investigation.
      Arno.
New York (City). Board of Aldermen (1902-1937).
   Committee on General Welfare.
   xNew York City. Board of Aldermen. Committee
      on General Welfare.
   Preliminary Report of the Committee on
      General Welfare in the Matter of a Request
      of the Conference of Organized Labor
      Relative to Educational Facilities. Meeting of
      June 26, 1917. Arno.
New York (City). Board of Education.
   xBoard Of Education Of The City Of New York.
   Nonstandard Dialect. NCTE.
New York (City). Botanical Garden. Library.
   xTheNew York Botanical Garden Library.
   Catalog of the Manuscript & Archival
      Collections and Index to the Correspondence
      of John Torrey. G K Hall.
New York (City). City University of New York. Center
   for Puerto Rican Studies. History Task Force.
   xHistory Task Force, Centro de Estudios
      Puertorriquenos.
   Labor Migration Under Capitalism: The Puerto
      Rican Experience. Monthly Rev.
New York City. Board of Aldermen. Committee on
   General Welfare. see New York (City). Board of
   Aldermen (1902-1937). Committee on General
   Welfare.
New York City Commission. see New York (State).
   Staten Island Improvement Commission.
New York City Graph Theory Conference, 1st, St.
   John's University, 1970.
   xNew York City Graph Theory Conference, 1st,
      1970.
   Recent Trends in Graph Theory: Proceedings.
      Springer-Verlag.
New York (City). Mayor La Guardia's Commission on
   the Harlem Riot of March 19, 1935.
   xMayor La Guardia's Commission on the Harlem
      Riot.
   Complete Report of Mayor La Guardia's
      Commission on the Harlem Riot of March
      19, 1935. Arno.
New York (City). Metropolitan Museum of Art.
   xCuratorial Staff, Metropolitan Museum of Art.
   Metropolitan Museum of Art: Notable
      Acquisitions, 1965-1975. Metro Mus Art.
   xMetropolitan Museum of Art (New York).
   Library Catalog of the Metropolitan Museum
      of Art. G K Hall.
   xMetropolitan Museum of Art Curatorial Staff.
   Great Paintings from the Metropolitan
      Museum of Art. Abrams.
   xMetropolitan Museum of Art, New York.
   Library Catalog of the Metropolitan Museum
      of Art, New York. G K Hall.
   xTheMetropolitan Museum of Art.
   Treasures from the Bronze Age of China: An
      Exhibition from the People's Republic of
      China. Ballantine.
   jt. auth. The Vikings. Morrow.
New York (City). Missionary Research Library.
   xMissionary Research Library - New York.
   Dictionary Catalog of the Missionary Research
      Library. G K Hall.
New York (City). Public Library.
   xNew York Public Library.

Ancient Egypt: Sources of Information in the
New York Public Library. Kraus Repr.
Dictionary Catalog of the Schomburg
Collection of Negro Literature & History,
Supplement 1974. G K Hall.
The Eno Collection of New York City Views.
Gale.
Modern Egypt: A List of References to
Material in the New York Public Library.
Kraus Repr.
New York Public Library in Fiction, Poetry &
Children's Literature. NY Pub Lib.
Sixty-Four Treasures. NY Pub Lib.
**New York (City). Public Library. Local History and
Genealogy Division.**
xNew York Public Library, Research Libraries,
Local History & Genealogy Division.
United States Local History Catalog. G K Hall.
New York (City). Public Library. Research Libraries.
xNew York Public Library, Research Libraries.
Bibliographic Guide to Black Studies. G K
Hall.
Bibliographic Guide to Black Studies: 1977. G
K Hall.
Bibliographic Guide to Business & Economics.
G K Hall.
Bibliographic Guide to Business & Economics:
1977. G K Hall.
Bibliographic Guide to Conference
Publications. G K Hall.
Bibliographic Guide to Conference
Publications: 1977. G K Hall.
Bibliographic Guide to Government
Publications. G K Hall.
Bibliographic Guide to Government
Publications U.S.: 1977. G K Hall.
Bibliographic Guide to Law: 1977. G K Hall.
Bibliographic Guide to Music. G K Hall.
Bibliographic Guide to Music: 1977. G K Hall.
Bibliographic Guide to Technology. G K Hall.
Catalog of Government Publications,
Economics Division. G K Hall.
Catalog of the Theatre & Drama Collections:
First Supplement to Pt. 2, Theatre Collection.
G K Hall.
Catalog of the Theatre & Drama Collections. G
K Hall.
Dictionary Catalog & Shelf List of the Spencer
Collection of Illustrated Books & Manuscripts
& Fine Bindings. G K Hall.
Dictionary Catalog of Jewish Collection. G K
Hall.
Dictionary Catalog of the Albert A. & Henry
W. Berg Collection of English & American
Literature, First Supplement. G K Hall.
Dictionary Catalog of the Art & Architecture
Division, The Research Libraries of The New
York Public Library. G K Hall.
Dictionary Catalog of the Dance Collection,
Performing Arts Research Center. G K Hall.
Dictionary Catalog of the Henry W. & Albert
A. Berg Collection of English & American
Literature. G K Hall.
Dictionary Catalog of the History of the
Americas Collection. G K Hall.
Dictionary Catalog of the History of the
Americas Collection, First Supplement. G K
Hall.
Dictionary Catalog of the Jewish Collection,
First Supplement. G K Hall.
Dictionary Catalog of the Local History &
Genealogy Division. G K Hall.
Dictionary Catalog of the Manuscript Division.
G K Hall.
Dictionary Catalog of the Map Division. G K
Hall.
Dictionary Catalog of the Music Collection. G
K Hall.
Dictionary Catalog of the Music Collection,
Supplement II. G K Hall.

Dictionary Catalog of the Oriental Collection:
First Supplement. G K Hall.
Dictionary Catalog of the Oriental Collection.
G K Hall.
The Dictionary Catalog of the Prints Division.
G K Hall.
Dictionary Catalog of the Rare Book Division:
First Supplement. G K Hall.
Dictionary Catalog of the Rare Book Division.
G K Hall.
Dictionary Catalog of the Schomburg
Collection of Negro Literature & History. G
K Hall.
Music Subject Headings. G K Hall.
Subject Catalog of the World War One
Collection. G K Hall.
Subject Headings. G K Hall.
Theatre Subject Headings. G K Hall.
xNew York Public Library, the Research Libraries.
Dictionary Catalog of the Slavonic Collection.
G K Hall.
xResearch Libraries of the New York Public
Library.
ed. Bibliographic Guide to Dance: 1978. G K
Hall.
Catalog of Government Publications,
Supplement 1974. G K Hall.
Catalog of the Theatre & Drama Collections,
Supplement 1974. G K Hall.
Dictionary Catalog of Materials on New York
City. G K Hall.
Dictionary Catalog of the Art & Architecture
Division, Supplement 1974. G K Hall.
xTheResearch Libraries of New York Public
Library.
Bibliographic Guide to North American
History, 1977. G K Hall.
xTheResearch Libraries of the New York Public
Library.
Bibliographic Guide to Art & Architecture,
1977. G K Hall.
Bibliographic Guide to Dance: Nineteen
Seventy-Nine. G K Hall.
Bibliographic Guide to Dance, 1977. G K Hall.
Bibliographic Guide to Government
Publications Foreign, 1977. G K Hall.
Bibliographic Guide to Psychology, 1977. G K
Hall.
Bibliographic Guide to Theatre Arts, 1977. G
K Hall.
Dictionary Catalog of the Music Collection,
Supplement 1974. G K Hall.
The Imprint Catalog in the Rare Book
Division: The Research Libraries of the New
York Public Library. G K Hall.
New York Community Trust.
xNew York Community Trust.
Heritage of New York: A Walking Guide.
Fordham.
Heritage of New York: Historic-Landmark
Plaques of the New York Community Trust.
Fordham.
New York Constitutional Convention, 1821. see New
York (State). Constitutional Convention, 1821.
New York Heart Association.
xNew York Heart Association.
Nomenclature & Criteria for Diagnosis of the
Heart & Great Vessels. Little.
New York Historical Society.
xNew York Historical Society.
Catalogue of American Portraits in the New
York Historical Society. Yale U Pr.
Collections of the New York Historical
Society, First Series. AMS Pr.
Colonel Stephen Kemble's Journals & British
Army Orders, 1775-1778. Irvington.
New York Institute of Technology.
xNew York Institute Of Technology.

Algebra & Trigonometry. McGraw.
A Programmed Course in Basic Electricity.
McGraw.
Programmed Course in Basic Electronics.
McGraw.
A Programmed Course in Basic Pulse Circuits.
McGraw.
New York, Kings Country, Grand Jury. see Kings Co.,
N.Y. Grand Jury.
New York. Museum of Modern Art.
xNew York Museum Of Modern Art.
Modern Architecture in England. Greenwood.
Vincent Van Gogh. Greenwood.
New York (State). Adjutant-General's Office.
xNew York Adjutant-General's Office.
Index of Awards on Claims of the Soldiers of
the War of 1812. Genealog Pub.
**New York (State). Commission for Detecting and
Defeating Conspiracies, 1777-1778.**
xAlbany County Sessions.
Minutes of the Commissioners for Detecting &
Defeating Conspiracies in the State of New
York. Da Capo.
New York (State). Commission on Cultural Resources.
xNew York State Commission on Cultural
Resources.
Cultural Resource Development: A Planning
Survey & Analysis. Praeger.
**New York (State). Commission on Relief for Widowed
Mothers.**
xNew York State Commission on Relief for
Widowed Mothers.
Report of the New York State Commission on
Relief for Widowed Mothers. Arno.
New York (State). Constitutional Convention, 1821.
xNew York Constitutional Convention, 1821.
Reports of the Proceedings & Debates. Da
Capo.
New York (State). Crime Commission.
xNew York State, Crime Commission.
Crime & the Community. Arno.
**New York (State). Legislature. Assembly. Committee on
State Prisons.**
xNew York State, Committee on State Prisons.
Investigation of the New York State Prisons.
Arno.
**New York (State). Legislature. Joint Committee
Investigatng Seditious Activities.**
xNew York State Joint Legislative Committee
Investigating Seditious Activities.
Revolutionary Radicalism. Da Capo.
**New York (State). Staten Island Improvement
Commission.**
xNew York City Commission.
Report of a Preliminary Scheme of
Improvements: Staten Island. Arno.
New York (State). Supreme Court. Appellate Division.
xNew York State, Supreme Court, Appellate
Division.
The Investigation of the Magistrated Courts in
the First Judicial Department & the
Magistrates Thereof, & of Attorneys-at-Law
Practicing in Said Courts: Final Report of
Samuel Seabury, Referee. Arno.
New York Public Library. see New York (City). Public
Library.
New York Public Library, Research Libraries. see New
York (City). Public Library. Research Libraries.
New York Public Library, the Research Libraries. see
New York (City). Public Library. Research Libraries.
New York State Commission on Cultural Resources. see
New York (State). Commission on Cultural Resources.
New York State Commission on Relief for Widowed
Mothers. see New York (State). Commission on Relief
for Widowed Mothers.
New York State, Committee on State Prisons. see New
York (State). Legislature. Assembly. Committee on
State Prisons.
New York State, Crime Commission. see New York
(State). Crime Commission.

New York State Joint Legislative Committee
  Investigating Seditious Activities. *see* New York
  (State). Legislature. Joint Committee Investigatng
  Seditious Activities.
New York State, Supreme Court, Appellate Division. *see*
  New York (State). Supreme Court. Appellate Division.
The New York Times.
  xNew York Times.
    The Complete Book of Tennis: A New York
      Times Scrapbook History. Bobbs.
    Directory of the Film. Arno.
    Give Us This Day...: A Report on the World
      Food Crisis. Arno.
    jt. auth. The New York Times Atlas of the
      World. Times Bks.
  xTheNew York Times.
    The Complete Book of Baseball. Bobbs.
    The Complete Book of Football: A New York
      Times Scrapbook History. Bobbs.
    The Complete Book of Golf. Bobbs.
New York Times Company.
  xTheNew York Times Co.
    The New York Times Index: 1973.
      Microfilming Corp.
New York Times Information Bank. *see* New York
  Times Information Bank (Firm).
New York Times Information Bank (Firm).
  xNew York Times Information Bank.
    Key Issues: Issues & Events of 1978 from the
      New York Times Information Bank. Bowker.
New York University.
  xNew York University.
    Anglo-American Legal History Series. Oceana.
    Library Catalog of the Conservation Center of
      the Institute of Fine Arts. G K Hall.
New York University. Division of General Education.
  xNew York University, Division of General
    Education.
    Conference on Practice & Procedure Under the
      Immigration & Nationality Act
      (McCarran-Walter Act) Held on June 13,
      1953: Proceedings. Greenwood
New York University. Libraries.
  xNew York University Libraries.
    Fales Library Checklist. AMS Pr.
    Fales Library Checklist: First Supplement.
      AMS Pr.
    Fales Library Checklist: Second Supplement.
      AMS Pr.
New York Writer's Program. *see* Writers' Program. New
  York.
The New Yorker.
  xNew Yorker.
    New Yorker Book of War Pieces. Arno.
    The New Yorker Twenty-Fifth Anniversary
      Album 1925-1950. Har-Row.
  xNew Yorker Editors.
    ed. The New Yorker Book of Poems. Morrow.
  xNew Yorker Magazine.
    How to Get Things Done in New York: Urban
      Strategist. Dutton.
  xTheNew Yorker.
    The New Yorker Album of Drawings. Penguin.
  xTheNew Yorker Magazine.
    Fifty-Five Short Stories from the New Yorker,
      1940-1949. S&S.
New Yorker Editors. *see* The New Yorker.
New Yorker Magazine. *see* The New Yorker.
Newall, Venetia.
  xNewall, Venetia.
    Egg at Easter: A Folklore Study. Ind U Pr.
Newberg, Norman A.
  xNewberg, Norman A.
    Affective Education in Philadelphia. Phi Delta
      Kappa.
Newberry Library. *see* Newberry Library, Chicago.
Newberry Library - Chicago. *see* Newberry Library,
  Chicago.
Newberry Library, Chicago.
  xNewberry Library.

Bibliographical Inventory to the Early Music in
  the Newberry Library, Chicago, Illinois. G K
  Hall.
Narratives of Captivity Among the Indians of
  North America, with Supplement I. Gale.
xNewberry Library - Chicago.
  Catalogue of the Greenlee Collection. G K
    Hall.
  Dictionary Catalog of the Edward E. Ayer
    Collection of Americana & American Indians,
    First Supplement. G K Hall.
  Dictionary Catalogue of the History of Printing
    from the John M. Wing Foundation. G K
    Hall.
  Genealogical Index of the Newberry
    Library,Chicago. G K Hall.
Newbigin, James E. *see* Newbigin, James Edward Lesslie.
Newbigin, James Edward Lesslie, Bp.
  xNewbigin, James E.
    The Reunion of the Church: A Defence of the
      South India Scheme. Greenwood.
Newbold, E. B.
  xNewbold, E. B.
    Coventry Old & New. Intl Pubns Serv.
Newbold, H. L. *see* Newbold, Herbert Leon.
Newbold, Herbert Leon, 1921-
  xNewbold, H. L.
    Dr. Newbold's Revolutionary New Discoveries
      About Weight Loss: How to Master the
      Hidden Food & Environmental Allergies
      That Make You Fat. NAL.
    Mega-Nutrients for Your Nerves. Berkley Pub.
    Vitamin C Against Cancer. Ballantine.
    Vitamin C Against Cancer. Stein & Day.
Newbolt, Henry J. *see* Newbolt, Henry John.
Newbolt, Henry John, Sir, 1862-1938
  xNewbolt, Henry J.
    Studies, Green & Gray. Arno.
Newborn, Monroe.
  xNewborn, Monroe.
    Computer Chess. Acad Pr.
Newborn, Sasha.
  xNewborn, Sasha.
    The Basement. Mudborn.
Newbrough, E. T.
  xNewbrough, E. T.
    Effective Maintenance Management:
      Organization, Motivation, & Control in
      Industrial Maintenance. McGraw.
Newbrun. *see* Newbrun, Ernest.
Newbrun, Ernest.
  xNewbrun.
    Cariology. Williams & Wilkins.
Newbury, Colin. *see* Newbury, Colin W.
Newbury, Colin W.
  xNewbury, Colin.
    Tahiti Nui: Change & Survival in French
      Polynesia, 1767-1945. U Pr of Hawaii.
Newbury, Josephine.
  xNewbury, Josephine.
    More Kindergarten Resources. John Knox.
Newby, Eric.
  xNewby, Eric.
    The Big Red Train Ride. Penguin.
    The Big Red Train Ride. St Martin.
Newby, F. *see* Newby, Frank.
Newby, Frank.
  xNewby, F.
    How to Find Out About Patents. Pergamon.
Newby, Hayes A.
  xNewby, Hayes A.
    Audiology. P-H.
Newby, Howard.
  xNewby, Howard.
    Social Change in Rural England. U of Wis Pr.
Newby, I. A. *see* Newby, Idus A.
Newby, Idus A.
  xNewby, I. A.

Challenge to the Court: Social Scientists & the
  Defense of Segregation, 1954-1966. La State
  U Pr.
ed. Civil War & Reconstruction, 1850-1877.
  Irvington.
Jim Crow's Defense: Anti-Negro Thought in
  America, 1900-1930. La State U Pr.
The South: A History. HR&W.
Newby, James E. *see* Newby, James Edward.
Newby, James Edward.
  xNewby, James E.
    Black Authors & Education: An Annotated
      Bibliography of Books. U Pr of Amer.
Newby, P. H. *see* Newby, Percy Howard.
Newby, Percy Howard, 1918-
  xNewby, P. H.
    Maria Edgeworth. Folcroft.
Newcity, Michael A.
  xNewcity, Michael A.
    Copyright Law in the Soviet Union. Praeger.
Newcomb, Duane. *see* Newcomb, Duane G.
Newcomb, Duane G.
  xNewcomb, Duane.
    The Complete Vegetable Gardener's
      Sourcebook. Avon.
    The Poor Man's Road to Riches. P-H.
    Word Power Makes the Difference: Making
      What You Write Pay off. P-H.
  xNewcomb, Duane G.
    Spare-Time Fortune Guide. P-H.
    Spare-Time Fortune Guide. P-H.
Newcomb, Franc (Johnson).
  xNewcomb, Franc J.
    Hosteen Klah: Navaho Medicine Man & Sand
      Painter. U of Okla Pr.
    Navaho Neighbors. U of Okla Pr.
Newcomb, Franc J. *see* Newcomb, Franc (Johnson).
Newcomb, Horace.
  xNewcomb, Horace.
    TV the Most Popular Art. Doubleday.
Newcomb, Robert M.
  xNewcomb, Robert M.
    Planning the Past: Historical Landscape
      Resources & Recreation. Shoe String.
Newcomb, Simon, 1835-1909
  xNewcomb, Simon.
    A Critical Examination of Our Financial Policy
      During the Southern Rebellion. Garland Pub.
    Critical Examination of Our Financial Policy
      During the Southern Rebellion. Greenwood.
    Plain Man's Talk on the Labor Question.
      Arno.
    Principles of Political Economy. Kelley.
Newcomb, T. P.
  xNewcomb, T. P.
    Braking of Road Vehicles. Bentley.
Newcomb, Theodore M. *see* Newcomb, Theodore Mead.
Newcomb, Theodore Mead, 1903-
  xNewcomb, Theodore M.
    The Acquaintance Process. Irvington.
    ed. College Peer Groups: Problems & Prospects
      for Research. NORC.
Newcomb, W. W. *see* Newcomb, William Wilmon.
Newcomb, Wilburn W. *see* Newcomb, Wilburn Wendell.
Newcomb, Wilburn Wendell, 1935-
  xNewcomb, Wilburn W.
    Wood Stove Handbook. Audel.
Newcomb, William Wilmon, 1921-
  xNewcomb, W. W.
    North American Indians: An Anthropological
      Perspective. Goodyear.
Newcombe, D. *see* Newcombe, David S.
Newcombe, David S.
  xNewcombe, D.
    Inherited Biochemical Disorders & Uric Acid
      Metabolism. Univ Park.
Newcombe, Jack.
  xNewcombe, Jack.

Game of Football. Garrard.
Newcombe, Josephine M. *see* Newcombe, Josephine
Marjorie.
Newcombe, Josephine Marjorie.
xNewcombe, Josephine M.
Leonid Andreyev. Ungar.
Newcomer, C. Armour. *see* Newcomer, Christopher
Armour.
Newcomer, Christopher Armour.
xNewcomer, C. Armour.
Cole's Cavalry: Or, Three Years in the Saddle
in the Shenandoah Valley. Arno.
Newcomer, James.
xNewcomer, James.
Maria Edgeworth. Bucknell U Pr.
Newcomer, Mabel, 1891-
xNewcomer, Mabel.
A Century of Higher Education for American
Women. Zenger Pub.
Newcomer, Phyllis L.
xNewcomer, Phyllis L.
Psycholinguistics in the Schools. Merrill.
Newell. *see* Newell, Peter.
Newell, A. Donald.
xNewell, A. Donald.
Gunstock Finishing & Care. Stackpole.
Newell, Adnah C. *see* Newell, Adnah Clifton.
Newell, Adnah Clifton.
xNewell, Adnah C.
Coloring, Finishing & Painting Wood. Bennett
Co.
Newell, Allen.
xNewell, Allen.
Human Problem Solving. P-H.
Newell, Barbara W. *see* Newell, Barbara Warne.
Newell, Barbara Warne.
xNewell, Barbara W.
Chicago & the Labor Movement: Metropolitan
Unionism in the 1930's. U of Ill Pr.
Newell, Clarence A. *see* Newell, Clarence Albert.
Newell, Clarence Albert, 1914-
xNewell, Clarence A.
Class Size & Adaptability, Including
Observations on Invention: A Study of
Selected Elementary School Classes in New
Jersey. AMS Pr.
Newell, David. *see* Newell, David McCheyne.
Newell, David M. *see* Newell, David McCheyne.
Newell, David McCheyne, 1898-
xNewell, David.
The Trouble of It Is. Knopf.
xNewell, David M.
If Nothin' Don't Happen. Knopf.
Newell, Dianne.
xNewell, Dianne.
The Failure to Preserve the Queen City Hotel,
Cumberland, Maryland. Preservation Pr.
Newell, E. T. *see* Newell, Edward Theodore.
Newell, Edward Theodore, 1886-1941
xNewell, E. T.
Some Cypriote "Alexanders". Obol Intl.
Newell, Frank W.
xNewell, Frank W.
Ophthalmology: Principles & Concepts. Mosby.
Newell, G. F. *see* Newell, Gordon Frank.
Newell, Gordon. *see* Newell, Gordon R.
Newell, Gordon Frank, 1925-
xNewell, G. F.
Approximate Stochastic Behavior of n-Server
Service Systems with Large n.
Springer-Verlag.
Newell, Gordon R.
xNewell, Gordon.
Pacific Tugboats. Superior Pub.
Newell, Hope. *see* Newell, Hope Hockenberry.
Newell, Hope Hockenberry.
xNewell, Hope.
The Little Old Woman Who Used Her Head &
Other Stories. Elsevier-Nelson.
Newell, J. David. *see* Newell, James David.

Newell, James David, 1939-
xNewell, J. David.
ed. Philosophy & Common Sense. U Pr of
Amer.
Newell, Peter, 1862-1924
xNewell.
Topsys & Turvys. Dover.
Newell, R. R.
xNewell, R. R.
Automatic Artifact Registration & Systems for
Archaeological Analysis with the Philips
P1100 Computer: A Mesolithic Test-Case.
Humanities.
Newell, Richard S., 1933-
xNewell, Richard S.
Politics of Afghanistan. Cornell U Pr.
Newell, Robert H. *see* Newell, Robert Henry.
Newell, Robert Henry, 1836-1901
xNewell, Robert H.
Orpheus C. Kerr Papers. AMS Pr.
Newell, Virginia K.
xNewell, Virginia K.
ed. Black Mathematicians & Their Works.
Dorrance.
Newell, William H. *see* Newell, William Hare.
Newell, William Hare.
xNewell, William H.
ed. Ancestors. Beresford Bk Serv.
Newfarmer, Richard. *see* Newfarmer, Richard S.
Newfarmer, Richard S.
xNewfarmer, Richard.
Transnational Conglomerates & the Economics
of Dependent Development. Jai Pr.
Newfield, Jack.
xNewfield, Jack.
Bread & Roses Too. Dutton.
Newhall, Beaumont, 1908-
xNewhall, Beaumont.
The Daguerreotype in America. Dover.
The Daguerreotype in America. Peter Smith.
Newhall, Richard A. *see* Newhall, Richard Ager.
Newhall, Richard Ager.
xNewhall, Richard A.
English Conquest of Normandy, 1416-1424: A
Study in Fifteenth Century Warfare. Russell.
Newhall, Sue M. *see* Newhall, Sue Mayes.
Newhall, Sue Mayes.
xNewhall, Sue M.
Devil in God's Old Man. Norton.
Newhouse, Bertha S.
xNewhouse, Bertha S.
How to Prepare for the Graduate Management
Admission Test. McGraw.
Newhouse, Flower A. *see* Newhouse, Flower Arlene
(Sechler).
Newhouse, Flower Arlene (Sechler), 1909-
xNewhouse, Flower A.
Songs of Deliverance. Christward.
Newhouse, John.
xNewhouse, John.
Cold Dawn: The Story of SALT. HR&W.
Collision in Brussels: The Common Market
Crisis of 30 June 1965. Norton.
Newhouse, Joseph P.
xNewhouse, Joseph P.
Economics of Medical Care: A Policy
Perspective. A-W.
Newhouse, Neville H.
xNewhouse, Neville H.
Joseph Conrad. Arco.
Newitt, Jane.
xNewitt, Jane.
Future Trends in Education Policy. Lexington
Bks.
Newland, Chester A.
xNewland, Chester A.
ed. MBO & Productivity Bargaining in the
Public Sector. Intl Personnel Mgmt.
Newland, D. E. *see* Newland, David Edward.

Newland, David Edward.
xNewland, D. E.
An Introduction to Random Vibrations &
Spectral Analysis. Longman.
Newland, Kathleen.
xNewland, Kathleen.
International Migration: The Search for Work.
Worldwatch Inst.
Newland, T. Ernest.
xNewland, T. Ernest.
Gifted in Socio-Educational Perspective. P-H.
Newlin, Claude M. *see* Newlin, Claude Milton.
Newlin, Claude Milton.
xNewlin, Claude M.
Life & Writings of Hugh Henry Brackenridge.
Appel.
Newlin, Paul.
xNewlin, Paul.
It Had to Be a Woman. Stein & Day.
Newlon, Clarke.
xNewlon, Clarke.
Fighting Douglas MacArthur. Dodd.
The Men Who Made Mexico. Dodd.
Southern Africa, The Critical Land. Dodd.
Newlove, Donald.
xNewlove, Donald.
Leo & Theodore. Dutton.
Newlun, Chester O. *see* Newlun, Chester Otto.
Newlun, Chester Otto, 1888-
xNewlun, Chester O.
Teaching Children to Summarize in Fifth
Grade History. AMS Pr.
Newlyn, Walter T. *see* Newlyn, Walter Tessier.
Newlyn, Walter Tessier.
xNewlyn, Walter T.
Theory of Money. Oxford U Pr.
Newman. *see* Newman, Gerald.
Newman, Anabel P.
xNewman, Anabel P.
Adult Basic Education: Reading. Allyn.
Newman, Andrea, 1938-
xNewman, Andrea.
An Evil Streak. PB.
Newman, Anne.
xNewman, Anne.
ed. Bear Crossings: An Anthology of North
American Poets. New South Co.
Newman, Arnold, 1918-
xNewman, Arnold.
The Great British. NYGS.
photos by The Great British. U of Chicago Pr.
Newman, Barbara M.
xNewman, Barbara M.
ed. Development Through Life: A Case Study
Approach. Dorsey.
Development Through Life: A Psychosocial
Approach. Dorsey.
xNewman, Barbara W.
An Introduction to the Psychology of
Adolescence. Dorsey.
Newman, Barbara W. *see* Newman, Barbara M.
Newman, Bernard H.
xNewman, Bernard H.
Business Communications: A Managerial
Approach. Monongahela Pub.
Newman, Bertram, 1886-
xNewman, Bertram.
Edmund Burke. Arno.
Edmund Burke. R West.
Jonathan Swift. Folcroft.
Newman, Charles. *see* Newman, Charles Hamilton.
Newman, Charles Hamilton.
xNewman, Charles.
ed. Prose for Borges. Northwestern U Pr.
Newman, Charles L.
xNewman, Charles L.

Personnel Practices in Adult Parole Systems. C
C Thomas.
Sourcebook on Probation, Parole & Pardons. C
C Thomas.
Newman, Daisy.
xNewman, Daisy.
I Take Thee, Serenity. HM.
Newman, Danny.
xNewman, Danny.
Subscribe Now!: Building Arts Audiences
Through Dynamic Subscription Promotion.
Pub Ctr Cult Res.
Newman, David. *see* Newman, David Bruce.
Newman, David Bruce.
xNewman, David.
Space Vehicle Electronics. Van Nos Reinhold.
Newman, Donald J.
xNewman, Donald J.
Introduction to Criminal Justice. Har-Row.
Newman, E. *see* Newman, Ernest.
Newman, Edwin S.

xNewman, Edwin.
A Civil Tongue. Bobbs.
A Civil Tongue. Warner Bks.
Strictly Speaking: Will America Be the Death
of English?. Bobbs.
Sunday Punch. Berkley Pub.
Sunday Punch. HM.

xNewman, Edwin S.
Civil Liberty & Civil Rights. Oceana.
Freedom Reader. Oceana.

Newman, Ernest, 1868-1959
xNewman, E.
The Life of Richard Wagner. Cambridge U Pr.
xNewman, Ernest.
Gluck & the Opera: A Study in Musical
History. AMS Pr.
Gluck & the Opera: A Study in Musical
History. Greenwood.
A Musical Motley. Da Capo.
Richard Strauss. Arno.
Richard Strauss. Greenwood.
Newman, Eugene. *see* Newman, Eugene J.
Newman, Eugene J.
xNewman, Eugene.
Restoration Radical: Robert Blum & the
Challenge of German Democracy, 1807-1848.
Branden.
Newman, F. X.
xNewman, Francis X.
ed. Meaning of Courtly Love. State U NY Pr.
Newman, Francis W. *see* Newman, Francis William.
Newman, Francis William, 1805-1897
xNewman, Francis W.
Anglo-Saxon Abolition of Negro Slavery.
Negro U Pr.
Newman, Francis X. *see* Newman, F. X.
Newman, Gerald.
xNewman.
The Concise Encyclopedia of Sports. Watts.
xNewman, Gerald.
The Changing Eskimos. Watts.
ed. The Concise Encyclopedia of Sports. Watts.
Lebanon. Watts.
xNewman, Gerry.
Compiled by Encyclopedia of Health & the
Human Body. Watts.
Newman, Gerry. *see* Newman, Gerald.
Newman, Graeme. *see* Newman, Graeme R.
Newman, Graeme R.
xNewman, Graeme.
The Punishment Response. Har-Row.
xNewman, Graeme R.

Comparative Deviance: Perception & Law in
Six Cultures. Elsevier.
ed. Crime & Deviance: A Comparative
Perspective. Sage.
Understanding Violence. Har-Row.
Newman, Grant.
xNewman, Grant.
Teaching Children Music: Fundamentals of
Music & Method. Wm C Brown.
Newman, Harold.
xNewman, Harold.
An Illustrated Dictionary of Glass. Thames
Hudson.
Reading Disabilities: Selections on
Identification & Treatment. Odyssey Pr.
Newman, Henry S. *see* Newman, Henry Stanley.
Newman, Henry Stanley.
xNewman, Henry S.
Banani: The Transition from Slavery to
Freedom in Zanzibar & Pemba. Negro U Pr.
Newman, Horatio H. *see* Newman, Horatio Hackett.
Newman, Horatio Hackett, 1875-
xNewman, Horatio H.
ed. Evolution, Genetics & Eugenics.
Greenwood.
Twins: A Study of Heredity & Environment. U
of Chicago Pr.
Newman, Hubert N.
xNewman, Hubert N.
Dental Plaque: The Ecology of the Flora on
Human Teeth. C C Thomas.
Newman, James W.
xNewman, James W.
Release Your Brakes!. Warner Bks.
Newman, Joel.
xNewman, Joel.
A Thematic Index to the Works of Salamon
Rossi. Eur-Am Music.
Newman, John. *see* Newman, John Henry.
Newman, John H. *see* Newman, John Henry.
Newman, John Henry.
xNewman, John.
Apologia Pro Vita Sua. Collins Pubs.
Apologia Pro Vita Sua. HM.
xNewman, John H.
Apologia Pro Vita Sua. Norton.
Apologia Pro Vita Sua: Being a History of His
Religious Opinions. Oxford U Pr.
Arians of the Fourth Century. Chr Classics.
Essay in Aid Grammar of Assent. Chr Classics.
An Essay in Aid of a Grammar of Assent. U of
Notre Dame Pr.
Meditations & Devotions. Chr Classics.
xNewman, John Henry Cardinal.
Apologia Pro Vita Sua. Doubleday.
Newman, John Henry Cardinal. *see* Newman, John
Henry.
Newman, John N. *see* Newman, John Nicholas.
Newman, John Nicholas, 1935-
xNewman, John N.
Marine Hydrodynamics. MIT Pr.
Newman, Joseph W.
xNewman, Joseph W.
Consumers' Information-Seeking Processes for
Fashion Goods: A Literature Review. U
Mich Busn Div Res.
Newman, Karl J. *see* Newman, Karl John.
Newman, Karl John.
xNewman, Karl J.
European Democracy Between the Wars. U of
Notre Dame Pr.
Newman, L. B. *see* Newman, Louis B.
Newman, Lea B. *see* Newman, Lea Bertani Vozar.
Newman, Lea Bertani Vozar.
xNewman, Lea B.
A Reader's Guide to the Short Stories of
Nathaniel Hawthorne. G K Hall.
Newman, Louis B.
xNewman, L. B.

Friction Materials: Recent Advances. Noyes.
Newman, M. *see* Newman, Morton.
Newman, M. Haskell. *see* Newman, Meshach Haskell.
Newman, Margaret A.
xNewman, Margaret A.
Theory Development in Nursing. Davis Co.
Newman, Melvin S. *see* Newman, Melvin Spencer.
Newman, Melvin Spencer.
xNewman, Melvin S.
An Advanced Organic Laboratory Course.
Macmillan.
Newman, Meshach Haskell.
xNewman, M. Haskell.
ed. Handbook of Ear, Nose & Throat
Emergencies. Med Exam.
Newman, Mildred.
xNewman, Mildred.
ed. How to Be Awake & Alive. Ballantine.
How to Take Charge of Your Life. Bantam.
How to Take Charge of Your Life. HarBraceJ.
Newman, Morris.
xNewman, Morris.
Integral Matrices. Acad Pr.
Newman, Morton.
xNewman, M.
Standard Cantilever Retaining Walls. McGraw.
xNewman, Morton.
Standard Structural Details for Building
Construction. McGraw.
Newman, Oscar.
xNewman, Oscar.
Community of Interest. Doubleday.
Newman, Parley W., 1923-
xNewman, Parley W.
Opportunities in Speech Pathology. Natl
Textbk.
Newman, Patty.
xNewman, Patty.
Do It up Brown. Reward Bks.
Pass the Poverty Please. Constructive Action.
Newman, Paul, 1945-
xNewman, Paul.
The Hill of the Dragon: An Enquiry into the
Nature of Dragon Legends. Rowman.
No Place to Play. Wonder.
Newman, Richard.
xNewman, Richard.
Index to Birthplaces of American Authors. G
K Hall.
Newman, Robert, 1909-
xNewman, Robert.
The Case of the Vanishing Corpse. Atheneum.
Night Spell. Atheneum.
The Twelve Labors of Hercules. T Y Crowell.
Newman, Robert C.
xNewman, Robert C.
Baptists & the American Tradition. Reg
Baptist.
Newman, Robert C. *see* Newman, Robert Chapman.
Newman, Robert Chapman.
xNewman, Robert C.
Genesis One & the Origin of the Earth. Baker
Bk.
Newman, Ruby A.
xNewman, Ruby A.
Tour for Seven. MN Pubs.
Newman, Ruth G.
xNewman, Ruth G.
Groups in Schools. S&S.
Newman, Shirlee. *see* Newman, Shirlee Petkin.
Newman, Shirlee P. *see* Newman, Shirlee Petkin.
Newman, Shirlee Petkin.
xNewman, Shirlee.
Tell Me Grandma Tell Me,Grandpa. HM.
xNewman, Shirlee P.
Marian Anderson: Lady from Philadelphia.
Westminster.
Newman, Shirley.
xNewman, Shirley.

A Child's Introduction to the Early Prophets.
Behrman.
Newman, Thelma R.
xNewman, Thelma R.
The Complete Book of Making Miniatures: For
Room Settings & Dollhouses. Crown.
Crafting with Plastics. Chilton.
Innovative Printmaking: The Making of Two
and Three Dimensional Prints & Multiples.
Crown.
Leather As Art & Craft. Crown.
Plastics As an Art Form. Chilton.
Newman, Virginia H. *see* Newman, Virginia Hunt.
Newman, Virginia Hunt.
xNewman, Virginia H.
Teaching an Infant to Swim. HarBraceJ.
Teaching an Infant to Swim. HarBraceJ.
Newman, Walter S.
xNewman, Walter S.
ed. Amerinds & Their Paleoenvironments in
Northeastern North America. NY Acad Sci.
Newman, William. *see* Newman, William M.
Newman, William H. *see* Newman, William Herman.
Newman, William Herman, 1909-
xNewman, William H.
Administrative Action: The Techniques of
Organization & Management. P-H.
Process of Management: The Concepts,
Behavior & Practice. P-H.
Strategy, Policy & Central Management. SW
Pub.
Newman, William J.
xNewman, William J.
Liberalism & the Retreat from Politics.
Braziller.
Newman, William M.
xNewman, William.
Principles of Interactive Computer Graphics.
McGraw.
xNewman, William M.
American Pluralism. A Study of Minority
Groups & Social Theory. Har-Row.
Principles of Interactive Computer Graphics.
McGraw.
Newman, William S.
xNewman, William S.
Sonata in the Baroque Era. Norton.
Newmann, Dana.
xNewmann, Dana.
Teacher's Almanack: Practical Ideas for Every
Day of the School Year. Ctr Appl Res.
Newmans, Evans.
xNewmans, Evans.
The True Story of the Notorious Jesse James.
Exposition.
Newmarch, Rosa. *see* Newmarch, Rosa Harriet
(Jeaffreson).
Newmarch, Rosa H. *see* Newmarch, Rosa Harriet
(Jeaffreson).
Newmarch, Rosa Harriet (Jeaffreson), 1857-1940
xNewmarch, Rosa.
The Concert-Goer's Library of Descriptive
Notes. Arno.
The Music of Czechoslovakia. Da Capo.
xNewmarch, Rosa H.
The Concert-Goer's Library of Descriptive
Notes. Scholarly.
Newmark, J. *see* Newmark, Joseph.
Newmark, Joseph.
xNewmark, J.
Statistics & Probability in Modern Life.
HR&W.
Newmark, M. E. *see* Newmark, Michael E.
Newmark, Maxim.
xNewmark, Maxim.
Dictionary of Spanish Literature. Greenwood.
Dictionary of Spanish Literature. Littlefield.
Newmark, Michael E.
xNewmark, M. E.

ed. Genetics of Epilepsy: A Review. Raven.
Newmark, N. M. *see* Newmark, Nathan Mortimore.
Newmark, Nathan Mortimore.
xNewmark, N. M.
Fundamentals of Earthquake Engineering. P-H.
Newmeyer, Frederick J.
xNewmeyer, Frederick J.
English Aspectual Verbs. Mouton.
Newmeyer, William L.
xNewmeyer, William L.
Primary Care of Hand Injuries. Lea & Febiger.
Newnan, Donald G.
xNewnan, Donald G.
Civil Engineering License Review. Eng Pr.
Engineering Economic Analysis. Eng Pr.
Engineering Fundamentals: Examination
Review. Wiley.
Newport Harbor Art Museum.
xNewport Harbor Art Museum.
Just Before the War: Urban America from 1935
to 1941. October.
Newport, M. Gene. *see* Newport, Marvin Gene.
Newport, Marvin Gene.
xNewport, M. Gene.
Supervisory Management: Tools & Techniques.
West Pub.
Newquist, Roy.
xNewquist, Roy.
Conversations with Joan Crawford. Citadel Pr.
ed. Counterpoint. S&S.
Newsom, C. *see* Newsom, Carroll Vincent.
Newsom, Carroll Vincent, 1904-
xNewsom, C.
Roots of Christianity. P-H.
Newsom, Doug.
xNewsom, Doug.
This Is PR: The Realities of Public Relations.
Wadsworth Pub.
Newsom, Robert, 1944-
xNewsom, Robert.
Dickens on the Romantic Side of Familiar
Things: Bleak House & the Novel Tradition.
Columbia U Pr.
Newsome, Audrey.
xNewsome, Audrey.
Student Counselling in Practice. Verry.
Newsome, David, 1929-
xNewsome, David.
Two Classes of Men: Platonism & English
Romantic Thought. St Martin.
Newsome, James D., 1931-
xNewsome, James D.
By the Waters of Babylon: An Introduction to
the History & Theology of the Exile. John
Knox.
Newson, E. F. *see* Newson, E. F. Peter.
Newson, E. F. Peter.
xNewson, E. F.
Management Science & the Manager: A
Casebook. P-H.
Newstrom, John. *see* Newstrom, John W.
Newstrom, John W.
xNewstrom, John.
Contingency Approach to Management
Readings. McGraw.
Newton, A. Edward. *see* Newton, Alfred Edward.
Newton, Alfred Edward, 1864-1940
xNewton, A. Edward.
End Papers: Literary Recreations. Kennikat.
Newton, Alice S. *see* Newton, Alice Spohn.
Newton, Alice Spohn.
xNewton, Alice S.
Paths of Wondering. Golden Quill.
Newton, Annabel.
xNewton, Annabel.
Wordsworth in Early American Criticism.
Folcroft.
Newton, Arthur P. *see* Newton, Arthur Percival.
Newton, Arthur Percival, 1873-1942
xNewton, Arthur P.

ed. Great Age of Discovery. Arno.
ed. Great Age of Discovery. B Franklin.
Newton, B. *see* Newton, Brian.
Newton, Brian.
xNewton, B.
The Generative Interpretation of Dialect: A
Study of Modern Greek Phonology.
Cambridge U Pr.
Newton, Carolyn.
xNewton, Carolyn.
Outdoor Mississippi. U Pr of Miss.
xNewton, Carolyn S.
Meet Mississippi. Strode.
Newton, Carolyn S. *see* Newton, Carolyn.
Newton, D. B.
xNewton, D. B.
Bounty on Bannister. Berkley Pub.
Broken Spur. Berkley Pub.
Newton, Derek A.
xNewton, Derek A.
Think Like a Man, Act Like a Lady, Work
Like a Dog. Doubleday.
Newton, Donald G.
xNewton, Donald G.
Fluid Power for Technicians. P-H.
Newton, Esther.
xNewton, Esther.
Mother Camp: Female Impersonators in
America. U of Chicago Pr.
Newton, G. W. *see* Newton, Grant W.
Newton, Grant W.
xNewton, G. W.
Bankruptcy & Insolvency Accounting: Practice
& Procedure. Ronald Pr.
xNewton, Grant W.
Certificate in Management Accounting Review.
Har-Row.
Newton, Helmut, 1920-
xNewton, Helmut.
Sleepless Nights. Congreve Pub.
Sleepless Nights. S&S.
White Women. Congreve Pub.
White Women. Stonehill Pub Co.
Newton, Huey P.
xNewton, Huey P.
Insights & Poems. City Lights.
Revolutionary Suicide. HarBraceJ.
Newton, Ian.
xNewton, Ian.
Population Ecology of Raptors. Buteo.
Newton, Isaac, 1642-1727
xNewton, Isaac.
Mathematical Papers of Isaac Newton.
Cambridge U Pr.
Mathematical Papers of Isaac Newton:
1691-1695. Cambridge U Pr.
Mathematical Principles of Natural Philosophy.
Dawson Pub.
Mathematical Principles of Natural Philosophy.
Philos Lib.
xNewton, Issac.
The Mathematical Principles of Natural
Philosophy. Dawson Pub.
Newton, Issac. *see* Newton, Isaac.
Newton, J. *see* Newton, Joseph.
Newton, James R.
xNewton, James R.
Forest Log. T Y Crowell.
The March of the Lemmings. T Y Crowell.
Newton, John R. *see* Newton, John Roy.
Newton, John Roy.
xNewton, John R.
Reading in Your School. McGraw.
Newton, Joseph, 1909-
xNewton, J.
Extractive Metallurgy. Wiley.
Newton, Joseph F. *see* Newton, Joseph Fort.
Newton, Joseph Fort, 1876-1950
xNewton, Joseph F.

The Builders: A Story and Study of
Freemasonry. Macoy Pub.
ed. The Religion of Masonry: An
Interpretation. Macoy Pub.
Some Living Masters of the Pulpit: Studies in
Religious Personality. Arno.
Newton, Margaret.
xNewton, Margaret.
Dyslexia: A Guide for Teachers & Parents.
Verry.
Newton, Mariana.
xNewton, Mariana.
Cerebral Palsy: Speech, Hearing, & Language
Problems. Cliffs.
Newton, Michael, 1951-
xNewton, Michael.
A Case of Conspiracy. Holloway.
Monsters, Mysteries & Man. A-W.
Newton, Norman T., 1898-
xNewton, Norman T.
Design on the Land: The Development of
Landscape Architecture. Harvard U Pr.
Newton, Robert R.
xNewton, Robert R.
Ancient Astronomical Observations & the
Accelerations of the Earth & Moon. Johns
Hopkins.
Ancient Planetary Observations & the Validity
of Ephemeris Time. Johns Hopkins.
The Crime of Claudius Ptolemy. Johns
Hopkins.
Medieval Chronicles & the Rotation of the
Earth. Johns Hopkins.
Newton, Roger G.
xNewton, Roger G.
The Complex J-Plane: Complex Angular
Momentum in Nonrelativistic Quantum
Scattering Theory. Benjamin-Cummings.
Newton, Ronald C., 1933-
xNewton, Ronald C.
German Buenos Aires, 1900-1933: Social
Change & Cultural Crisis. U of Tex Pr.
Newton, S. A. *see* Newton, Stuart A.
Newton, Stuart A.
xNewton, S. A.
Whitlathe Walrus. SBD.
Newton, Suzanne.
xNewton, Suzanne.
Reubella & the Old Focus Home. Westminster.
Newton, Thomas H.
xNewton, Thomas H.
ed. Radiology of the Skull & Brain. Mosby.
Newton, V. M. *see* Newton, Virgil Miller.
Newton, Virgil Miller.
xNewton, V. M.
Crusade for Democracy. Iowa St U Pr.
Newton, William T.
xNewton, William T.
Radioassay in Clinical Medicine. C C Thomas.
Newton-Smith, W.
xNewton-Smith, W. H.
The Structure of Time. Routledge & Kegan.
Newton-Smith, W. H. *see* Newton-Smith, W.
Ney, John, 1923-
xNey, John.
Ox Goes North: More Trouble for the Kid at
the Top. Har-Row.
Ox Under Pressure. Lippincott.
Nezlin, R. S. *see* Nezlin, Roald Solomonovich.
Nezlin, Roald Solomonovich.
xNezlin, R. S.
ed. Structure & Biosynthesis of Antibodies.
Plenum Pub.
NFPA. *see* National Fire Protection Association.
NFPA Forest Committee. *see* National Fire Protection
Association. Forest Committee.
Ngata, Apirana N. *see* Ngata, Apirana Turupa.
Ngata, Apirana Turupa, Sir, 1874-1950
xNgata, Apirana N.

Complete Manual of Maori Grammar &
Conversation, with Vocabulary. AMS Pr.
Niatum, Duane, 1938-
xNiatum, Duane.
Ascending Red Cedar Moon. Har-Row.
Niazi, Sarfaraz, 1949-
xNiazi, Sarfaraz.
Textbook of Biopharmaceutics & Clinical
Pharmacokinetics. ACC.

Nibbelink, Don. *see* Nibbelink, Don D.

Nibbelink, Don D.

xNibbelink, Don.
Picturing the Times of Your Life. Amphoto.

Niblett, William R. *see* Niblett, William Roy.

Niblett, William Roy.
xNiblett, William R.
Education, the Lost Dimension. Greenwood.
Nibley. *see* Nibley, Hugh.
Nibley, Hugh, 1910-
xNibley.
An Approach to the Book of Mormon. Deseret
Bk.
Nicander.
xNicander.
The Poems & Poetical Fragments. Arno.
Nicanor, Precioso M.
xNicanor, Precioso M.
Martyrs Never Die. Pre-Mer.
Nicephorus.
xNicephorus.
Nicephori Archiepiscopi Constantinopolitani
Opuscula Historica. Arno.
Nichol, John, 1833-1894
xNichol, John.
American Literature, an Historical Sketch.
Gordon Pr.
Byron. AMS Pr.
Byron. R West.
Nicholas. *see* Nicholas, James Karl.
Nicholas, Anna K. *see* Nicholas, Anna Katherine.
Nicholas, Anna Katherine.
xNicholas, Anna K.
The Nicholas Guide to Dog Judging. Howell
Bk.
Nicholas, Barry.
xNicholas, Barry.
Introduction to Roman Law. Oxford U Pr.
Nicholas, David R.
xNicholas, David R.
What's a Woman to Do in Church?. BMH Bks.
Nicholas, Edward, 1906-
xNicholas, Edward.
Hours & the Ages: Sequence of Americans.
Kennikat.
Nicholas, H. G. *see* Nicholas, Herbert George.
Nicholas, Herbert. *see* Nicholas, Herbert George.
Nicholas, Herbert George.
xNicholas, H. G.
The Nature of American Politics. Oxford U Pr.
xNicholas, Herbert.
Britain & the U. S. A.. Johns Hopkins.
Nicholas, J. E. *see* Nicholas, John Edward.
Nicholas, J. F. *see* Nicholas, John F.
Nicholas, J. Karl. *see* Nicholas, James Karl.
Nicholas, James Karl.
xNicholas.
Rhetorical Models for Effective Writing.
Winthrop.
xNicholas, J. Karl.
Rhetorical Models for Effective Writing.
Winthrop.
Nicholas, John Edward.
xNicholas, J. E.

Chemical Kinetics: A Modern Survey of Gas
Reactions. Halsted Pr.
Nicholas, John F.
xNicholas, J. F.
An Atlas of Models of Crystal Surfaces.
Gordon.
Nicholas, Susan C. *see* Nicholas, Susan Cary.
Nicholas, Susan Cary.
xNicholas, Susan C.
Rights & Wrongs: Women's Struggle for Legal
Equality. Feminist Pr.
Nicholas, Ted, 1934-
xNicholas, Ted.
How to Form Your Own Professional
Corporation. Enterprise Del.
How to Get Out If You're in Over Your Head.
Enterprise Del.
How to Self Publish Your Own Book & Make
It a Best Seller. Enterprise Del.
Where the Money Is & How to Get It.
Enterprise Del.
Nicholas, Tim.
xNicholas, Tim.
More Than Just Talk. Home Mission.
Nicholas, Tracy.
xNicholas, Tracy.
Rastafari: A Way of Life. Doubleday.
Nicholas Ii.
xNicholas II.
The Letters of the Tsar to the Tsaritsa,
(1914-1917). Hoover Inst Pr.
Nicholds, Elizabeth.
xNicholds, Elizabeth.
In-Service Casework Training. Columbia U Pr.
Primer of Social Casework. Columbia U Pr.
Nicholl, Worth L.
xNicholl, Worth L.
The Rhetoric of Cultural Pluralism Vs. the
Drive Toward Total Assimilation: The
Mexican American Cultural Component of
Federally Funded Bilingual Projects. R & E
Res Assoc.
Nicholls, A. J. *see* Nicholls, Anthony James.
Nicholls, Anthony James, 1934-
xNicholls, A. J.
Weimar & the Rise of Hitler. St Martin.
Nicholls, C. S. *see* Nicholls, Christine Stephanie.
Nicholls, Christine Stephanie.
xNicholls, C. S.
Swahili Coast: Politics, Diplomacy & Trade on
the East African Littoral, 1798-1856. Holmes
& Meier.
Nicholls, D. *see* Nicholls, David.
Nicholls, David, 1936-
xNicholls, D.
Inorganic Chemistry in Liquid Ammonia.
Elsevier.
xNicholls, David.
From Dessalines to Duvalier: Race, Colour &
National Independence in Haiti. Cambridge
U Pr.
Nicholls, George, Sir, 1781-1865
xNicholls, George.
History of the Irish Poor Law. Kelley.
History of the Scotch Poor Law. Kelley.
Nicholls, John E.
xNicholls, John E.
Structure & Design of Programming Languages.
A-W.
Nicholls, Peter, 1939-
xNicholls, Peter.
ed. The Science Fiction Encyclopedia.
Doubleday.
ed. The Science Fiction Encyclopedia.
Doubleday.
Nicholls, Richard, 1949-
xNicholls, Richard E.
The Plant Buyer's Handbook: A Consumer's
Guide to Buying House Plants. Running Pr.
Nicholls, Richard E. *see* Nicholls, Richard.

Nicholls, Roger A. *see* Nicholls, Roger Archibald.
Nicholls, Roger Archibald, 1922-
    xNicholls, Roger A.
        Nietzsche in the Early Work of Thomas Mann.
          Russell.
Nicholls, William H. *see* Nicholls, William Hord.
Nicholls, William Hord, 1914-
    xNicholls, William H.
        Southern Tradition & Regional Progress.
          Greenwood.
Nichols, Arlene O. *see* Nichols, Arlene Odom.
Nichols, Arlene Odom.
    xNichols, Arlene O.
        Pearls for Nursing Practice. Lippincott.
Nichols, Claude A. *see* Nichols, Claude Andrew.
Nichols, Claude Andrew, 1877-
    xNichols, Claude A.
        Moral Education Among the North American
          Indians. AMS Pr.
Nichols, David.
    xNichols, David.
        Echinoderms. Humanities.
Nichols, David A., 1939-
    xNichols, David A.
        Lincoln & the Indians: Civil War Policy &
          Politics. U of Mo Pr.
Nichols, David H. *see* Nichols, David Harry.
Nichols, David Harry.
    xNichols, David H.
        Vaginal Surgery. Williams & Wilkins.
Nichols, E. D. *see* Nichols, Eugene Douglas.
Nichols, Eugene Douglas, 1923-
    xNichols, E. D.
        Pre-Algebra Mathematics. HR&W.
Nichols, Frances Sellman Gaither.
    xNichols, Francis S.
        Compiled by Index to Schoolcraft's "Indian
          Tribes of the United States". Scholarly.
Nichols, Francis S. *see* Nichols, Frances Sellman Gaither.
Nichols, Frank.
    nNichols, Frank.
        Theory & Practice of Body Massage. Milady.
Nichols, Fred J., 1939-
    xNichols, Fred J.
        Anthology of Neo-Latin Poetry. Yale U Pr.
Nichols, Frederick D. *see* Nichols, Frederick Doveton.
Nichols, Frederick Doveton.
    xNichols, Frederick D.
        Thomas Jefferson Landscape Architect. U Pr of
          Va.
Nichols, Gerald E.
    xNichols, Gerald E.
        Programmed Cost Accounting: A Participative
          Approach. Irwin.
Nichols, Harold.
    xNichols, Harold.
        Local Studies Librarianship. K G Saur.
Nichols, Herbert L. *see* Nichols, Herbert Lownds.
Nichols, Herbert Lownds, 1908-
    xNichols, Herbert L.
        Intro. by Cooking with Understanding. North
          Castle.
        Excavator Operation. North Castle.
Nichols, J. Randall.
    xNichols, J. Randall.
        Building the Word: The Dynamics of
          Communication & Preaching. Har-Row.
Nichols, James H. *see* Nichols, James Hastings.
Nichols, James Hastings, 1915-
    xNichols, James H.
        Democracy & the Churches. Greenwood.
        History of Christianity, 1650-1950:
          Secularization of the West. Wiley.
Nichols, James L. *see* Nichols, James Lynn.
Nichols, James Lynn.
    xNichols, James L.
        Confederate Quartermaster in the
          Trans-Mississippi. U of Tex Pr.
Nichols, James R., 1938-
    xNichols, James R.

        Children of the Sea. Blair.
Nichols, James R. *see* Nichols, James Robinson.
Nichols, James Robinson, 1819-1888
    xNichols, James R.
        Chemistry of the Farm & the Sea. Arno.
Nichols, John, 1745-1826
    xNichols, John.
        Progresses, Processions & Magnificent
          Festivities of King James First, His Royal
          Consort, Family & Court. AMS Pr.
        Progresses, Processions & Magnificent
          Festivities of King James the First, His Royal
          Consort, Family & Court. B Franklin.
        Progresses, Processions & Magnificent
          Festivities of King James First, His Royal
          Consort, Family & Court. Kraus Repr.
        The Sterile Cuckoo. PB.
Nichols, John. *see* Nichols, John Treadwell.
Nichols, John T. *see* Nichols, John Treadwell.
Nichols, John Treadwell.
    xNichols, John.
        If Mountains Die: A New Mexico Memoir.
          Knopf.
    xNichols, John T.
        A Ghost in the Music. HR&W.
Nichols, K. M. *see* Nichols, Kathryn Marion.
Nichols, Kathryn Marion.
    xNichols, K. M.
        Stratigraphy & Depositional History of the Star
          Peak Group (Triassic) Northwestern Nevada.
          Geol Soc.
Nichols, Leigh.
    xNichols, Leigh.
        The Key to Midnight. PB.
Nichols, M. P. *see* Nichols, Michael P.
Nichols, Marie H. *see* Nichols, Marie Hochmuth.
Nichols, Marie Hochmuth.
    xNichols, Marie H.
        Rhetoric & Criticism. La State U Pr.
Nichols, Marion.
    xNichols, Marion.
        Encyclopedia of Embroidery Stitches, Including
          Crewel. Dover.
        Encyclopedia of Embroidery Stitches, Including
          Crewel. Peter Smith.
Nichols, Mary G. *see* Nichols, Mary Sargeant Gove.
Nichols, Mary Sargeant Gove, 1810-1884
    xNichols, Mary G.
        Reminiscences of Edgar Allan Poe. Folcroft.
        Reminiscences of Edgar Allan Poe. Haskell.
Nichols, Michael P.
    xNichols, M. P.
        Catharsis in Psychotherapy. Halsted Pr.
Nichols, Nell B. *see* Nichols, Nell Beaubien.
Nichols, Nell Beaubien.
    xNichols, Nell B.
        Farm Journal's Cook It Your Way. Doubleday.
        Farm Journal's Freezing & Canning Cookbook.
          Doubleday.
        Homemade Candy. Doubleday.
Nichols, R. *see* Nichols, Ralph G.
Nichols, R. W.
    xNichols, R. W.
        ed. Pressure Vessel Engineering Technology.
          Intl Ideas.
Nichols, Ralph G.
    xNichols, R.
        Are You Listening?. McGraw.
Nichols, Ray. *see* Nichols, Ray L.
Nichols, Ray L.
    xNichols, Ray.
        Treason, Tradition, & the Intellectual: Julien
          Benda & Political Discourse. Regents Pr KS.
Nichols, Robert, 1919-
    xNichols, Robert.
        Arrival. New Directions.
        Exile. New Directions.
        The Harditts in Sawna. New Directions.
Nichols, Roger.
    xNichols, Roger.

        Debussy. Oxford U Pr.
        Ravel. Biblio Dist.
Nichols, Roger L.
    xNichols, Roger L.
        General Henry Atkinson: A Western Military
          Career. U of Okla Pr.
Nichols, Roy C., 1918-
    xNichols, Roy C.
        Footsteps in the Sea. Abingdon.
Nichols, Roy F. *see* Nichols, Roy Franklin.
Nichols, Roy Franklin, 1896-
    xNichols, Roy F.
        Advance Agents of American Destiny.
          Greenwood.
        Democratic Machine, 1850-1854. AMS Pr.
Nichols, Ruth.
    xNichols, Ruth.
        The Marrow of the World. Atheneum.
        Song of the Pearl. Bantam.
        Song of the Pearl. Atheneum.
Nichols, Sarah.
    xNichols, Sarah.
        Charity. Popular Lib.
        Grave's Company. Popular Lib.
        The Sunless Day. Popular Lib.
Nichols, Theo.
    xNichols, Theo.
        Living with Capitalism: Class Relations & the
          Modern Factory. Routledge & Kegan.
Nichols, Thomas L. *see* Nichols, Thomas Low.
Nichols, Thomas Low, 1815-1901
    xNichols, Thomas L.
        Forty Years of American Life. Johnson Repr.
        Forty Years of American Life. Negro U Pr.
        Journal in Jail. Arno.
Nichols, Warren W.
    xNichols, Warren W.
        ed. Senescence: Dominant or Recessive in
          Somatic Cell Crosses. Plenum Pub.
Nicholson, Anne M. *see* Nicholson, Anne Mary.
Nicholson, Anne Mary, 1965-
    xNicholson, Anne M.
        The Concept Standard: An Historical Survey of
          What Men Have Conceived As Constituting
          or Determining Life Values. AMS Pr.
Nicholson, B. E. *see* Nicholson, Barbara Evelyn.
Nicholson, Barbara E. *see* Nicholson, Barbara Evelyn.
Nicholson, Barbara Evelyn.
    xNicholson, B. E.
        Oxford Book of Food Plants. Oxford U Pr.
        The Oxford Book of Trees. Oxford U Pr.
        Oxford Book of Wild Flowers. Oxford U Pr.
    xNicholson, Barbara E.
        The Oxford Book of Garden Flowers. Oxford
          U Pr.
Nicholson, Christina.
    xNicholson, Christina.
        The Power & the Passion. Fawcett.
        The Savage Sands. Coward.
        The Savage Sands. Fawcett.
Nicholson, E. W. *see* Nicholson, Ernest Wilson.
Nicholson, Edward A.
    xNicholson, Edward A.
        Business Responsibility & Social Issues. Merrill.

Nicholson, Edward Williams Byron.
    xNicholson, Edward W.
        Golspie: Contributions to Its Folklore. R West.
Nicholson, Edwin, 1891-
    xNicholson, Edwin.
        Education & the Boy Scout Movement in
          America. AMS Pr.
Nicholson, Ernest Wilson.
    xNicholson, E. W.
        Preaching to the Exiles: A Study of the Prose
          Tradition in the Book of Jeremiah. Schocken.
Nicholson, George A. *see* Nicholson, George Albert.
Nicholson, George Albert.
    xNicholson, George A.

English Words with Native Roots & with
Greek, Latin, or Romance Suffixes. AMS Pr.
Nicholson, H. B. see Nicholson, Henry B.
Nicholson, Heather J. see Nicholson, Heather Johnston.
Nicholson, Heather Johnston.
xNicholson, Heather J.
Distant Hunger: Agriculture, Food & Human
Values. Purdue Res Foun.
Nicholson, Henry B.
xNicholson, H. B.
ed. Origins of Religious Art & Iconography in
Preclassic Mesoamerica. UCLA Lat Am Ctr.
Two Aztec Wood Idols: Iconographic &
Chronologic Analysis. Dumbarton Oaks.
Nicholson, J. B. see Nicholson, J. B. R.
Nicholson, J. B. R.
xNicholson, J. B.
The British Army of the Crimea. Hippocrene
Bks.
The Gurkha Rifles. Hippocrene Bks.
Nicholson, J. Shield. see Nicholson, Joseph Shield.
Nicholson, James W. see Nicholson, James William.

Nicholson, James William, 1844-1917
xNicholson, James W.
Plane Trigonometry. Claitors.
Stories of Dixie. Claitors.

Nicholson, John, of Hull, Eng.

xNicholson, John.
The Folk Speech of East Yorkshire.. Folcroft.

Nicholson, Joseph S. see Nicholson, Joseph Shield.
Nicholson, Joseph Shield, 1850-1927
xNicholson, J. Shield.
The Effects of Machinery on Wages. Arno.
xNicholson, Joseph S.
Strikes & Social Problems. Arno.
Nicholson, Lewis E.
xNicholson, Lewis E.
ed. Anthology of Beowulf Criticism. U of
Notre Dame Pr.
Nicholson, Luree.
xNicholson, Luree.
How to Fight Fair with Your Kids...& Win.
HarBraceJ.
Nicholson, Margaret.
xNicholson, Margaret.
Practical Style Guide for Authors & Editors.
HR&W.
Nicholson, Norman, 1914-
xNicholson, Norman.
H. G. Wells. Folcroft.
Portrait of the Lakes. Intl Pubns Serv.
Nicholson, Reynold A. see Nicholson, Reynold Alleyne.
Nicholson, Reynold Alleyne, 1868-1945
xNicholson, Reynold A.
Literary History of the Arabs. Cambridge U Pr.
A Literary History of the Arabs. R West.
Nicholson, Shirley J.
xNicholson, Shirley S.
Nature's Merry - Go - Round. Theos Pub Hse.
Nicholson, Shirley S. see Nicholson, Shirley J.
Nicholson, T. R. see Nicholson, Timothy Robin.
Nicholson, Timothy Robin.
xNicholson, T. R.
Passenger Cars, 1863-1904. Macmillan.
Passenger Cars, 1905-1912. Macmillan.
Passenger Cars, 1913-1923. Macmillan.
Nicholson, Watson, 1866-1951
xNicholson, Watson.
Struggle for a Free Stage in London. Arno.
Nicholson, William.
xNicholson, William.
illus. Clever Bill. FS&G.
Nicholson, William J. see Nicholson, William Jamieson.
Nicholson, William Jamieson.
xNicholson, William J.

ed. Health Effects of Halogenated Aromatic
Hydrocarbons. NY Acad Sci.
Nickel, Mildred L.
xNickel, Mildred L.
Let's Find Out About a Book. Watts.
Steps to Service: A Handbook of Procedures
for the School Library Media Center. ALA.
Nickel, P. E. see Nickel, Paul E.
Nickel, Paul E.
xNickel, P. E.
Economic Impacts & Linkages of the Canadian
Mining Industry. Renouf.

Nickell, Lesley J.
xNickell, Lesley J.
The White Queen. St Martin.
Nickels, Martin K.
xNickels, Martin K.
The Study of Physical Anthropology &
Archaeology. Har-Row.
Nickels, William G.
xNickels, William G.
Marketing Communications & Promotion. Grid
Pub.
xNickels, Williams G.
Marketing Principles: A Broadened Concept of
Marketing. P-H.
Nickels, Williams G. see Nickels, William G.
Nickerson, Charles A.
xNickerson, Charles A.
Statistical Analysis for Decision Making.
Petrocelli.
Taxes & You. Petrocelli.
Nickerson, Clarence B., 1906-
xNickerson, Clarence B.
Accounting Handbook for Non-Accountants.
CBI Pub.
Nickerson, Jane S. see Nickerson, Jane Soames.
Nickerson, Jane Soames.
xNickerson, Jane S.
Homage to Malthus. Kennikat.
Nickerson, R. see Nickerson, Robert C.
Nickerson, Robert C., 1946-
xNickerson, R.
Fundamentals of Fortran Programming.
Winthrop.
xNickerson, Robert C.
Fundamentals of Fortran Programming.
Winthrop.
Nickey, J. M.
xNickey, J. M.
The Stoneworker's Bible. TAB Bks.
Nicklaus, Carol.
xNicklaus, Carol.
illus. Harry the Hider. Avon.
illus. Harry the Hider. Watts.
Nicklaus, Jack.
xNicklaus, Jack.
Golf My Way. S&S.
Golf My Way. S&S.
Greatest Game of All: My Life in Golf. S&S.
On & Off the Fairway: A Pictorial
Autobiography. S&S.
Take a Tip from Me. S&S.
Nickles, Olga, 1932-
xNickles, Olga.
The Dairy Cookbook. Celestial Arts.
Nickless, Graham.
xNickless, Graham.
ed. Inorganic Sulphur Chemistry. Elsevier.
Nickol, Brent B.
xNickol, Brent B.
ed. Host-Parasite Interfaces. Acad Pr.
Nickson, Jack W.
xNickson, Jack W.
Economics & Social Choice. McGraw.
Nickson, Richard, 1917-
xNickson, Richard.

Staves: A Book of Songs. Moretus Pr.
Nicod, Jean, 1893-1924
xNicod, Jean.
Geometry & Induction: Containing Geometry
in the Sensible World & the Logical Problem
of Induction. U of Cal Pr.
Nicol, D. M. see Nicol, Donald Macgillivray.
Nicol, Donald. see Nicol, Donald Macgillivray.
Nicol, Donald M. see Nicol, Donald Macgillivray.
Nicol, Donald Macgillivray.
xNicol, D. M.
Church & Society in the Last Centuries of
Byzantium. Cambridge U Pr.
xNicol, Donald.
The Last Centuries of Byzantium. Humanities.
xNicol, Donald M.
The Last Centuries of Byzantium. Beekman
Pubs.
Nicol, Gladys.
xNicol, Gladys.
Athens. David & Charles.
Nicola, Toufick, 1894-
xNicola, Toufick.
Atlas of Orthopaedic Exposures. Krieger.
Nicolaides, Kimon, 1891-1938
xNicolaides, Kimon.
Natural Way to Draw: A Working Plan for Art
Study. HM.
Nicolau, C. see Nicolau, Claude.
Nicolau, Claude.
xNicolau, C.
ed. Structural & Kinetic Approach to Plasma
Membrane Functions: Proceedings,Grignon,
September 6-9, 1976. Springer-Verlag.
Nicolay, Helen, 1866-1954
xNicolay, Helen.
Lincoln's Secretary: A Biography of John G.
Nicolay. Greenwood.
Nicolay, John G. see Nicolay, John George.
Nicolay, John George.
xNicolay, John G.
Abraham Lincoln: A History. U of Chicago Pr.
Nicole, Christopher.
xNicole, Christopher.
Black Dawn. NAL.
Black Dawn. St Martin.
Caribee. NAL.
The Devil's Own. NAL.
Sunset. NAL.
Sunset. St Martin.
Nicolin, Curt.
xNicolin, Curt.
Private Industry in a Public World. A-W.
Nicolini, Gerard.
xNicolini, Gerard.
The Ancient Spaniards. Saxon.
Nicolis, G.
xNicolis, G.
ed. Membranes, Dissipative Structures &
Evolution. Wiley.
Nicoll, Allardyce, 1894-
xNicoll, Allardyce.
British Drama. B&N.
British Drama. R West.
Dryden & His Poetry. Folcroft.
Dryden As an Adapter of Shakespeare. AMS
Pr.
Dryden As an Adapter of Shakespeare.
Folcroft.
The English Stage. Folcroft.
English Theatre: A Short History. Greenwood.
Film & Theatre. Arno.
The Theatre & Dramatic Theory. Greenwood.
Nicoll, Bruce H. see Nicoll, Bruce Hilton.
Nicoll, Bruce Hilton.
xNicoll, Bruce H.
Compiled by Nebraska: A Pictorial History. U
of Nebr Pr.
Nicoll, Helen.
xNicoll, Helen.

Meg's Eggs. Penguin.
Nicoll, Henry J. *see* Nicoll, Henry James.
Nicoll, Henry James.
　xNicoll, Henry J.
　　Thomas Carlyle. Arden Lib.
　　Thomas Carlyle. Folcroft.
Nicoll, M. *see* Nicoll, Maurice.
Nicoll, Maurice, 1884-
　xNicoll, M.
　　The Mark. Weiser.
Nicolson, Harold. *see* Nicolson, Harold George.
Nicolson, Harold George, Sir, 1886-
　xNicolson, Harold.
　　Some People. Popular Lib.
　　Swinburne & Baudelaire. Folcroft.
Nicolson, Iain.
　xNicolson, Iain.
　　Road to the Stars. Morrow.
　　The Road to the Stars. NAL.
　　Simple Astronomy. Scribner.
Nicolson, John, 1876-
　xNicolson, John.
　　Some Folk Tales & Legends of Shetland.
　　Folcroft.
Nicolson, Marjorie H. *see* Nicolson, Marjorie Hope.
Nicolson, Marjorie Hope, 1894-
　xNicolson, Marjorie H.
　　Pepys' Diary & the New Science. U Pr of Va.
Nicolson, Nigel.
　xNicolson, Nigel.
　　The Himalayas. Silver.
　　The Himalayas. Time-Life.
　　People & Parliament. Greenwood.
　　Portrait of a Marriage. Atheneum.
Nida, Eugene A. *see* Nida, Eugene Albert.
Nida, Eugene Albert, 1914-
　xNida, Eugene A.
　　Toward a Science of Translating: With Special
　　Reference to Principles & Procedures
　　Involved in Bible Translating. Humanities.
Nidditch, P. H.
　xNidditch, P. H.
　　The Development of Mathematical Logic.
　　Routledge & Kegan.
Nideffer, Robert. *see* Nideffer, Robert M.
Nideffer, Robert M.
　xNideffer, Robert.
　　The Inner Athlete: Mind Plus Muscle for
　　Winning. T Y Crowell.
　xNideffer, Robert M.
　　A.C.T.-Attention Control Training: How to Get
　　Control of Your Mind Through Total
　　Concentration. Wyden.
　xNideffer, Robert N.
　　How to Put Anxiety Behind You. Stein & Day.
Nideffer, Robert N. *see* Nideffer, Robert M.
Nidetch, Jean.
　xNidetch, Jean.
　　The Story of Weight Watchers. NAL.
　　Weight Watchers New Program Cookbook.
　　NAL.
Nie, Norman H.
　xNie, Norman H.
　　The Changing American Voter. Harvard U Pr.
Niebel, B. W. *see* Niebel, Benjamin W.
Niebel, Benjamin W.
　xNiebel, B. W.
　　Product Design & Process Engineering.
　　McGraw.
Niebling, Richard. *see* Niebling, Richard F.
Niebling, Richard F.
　xNiebling, Richard.
　　ed. Journey of Poems. Dell.
Nieboer, Joe.
　xNieboer, Joe.
　　How to Be a Happy Christian. Loizeaux.
　　One Another: Or, How to Get Along with
　　Other Christians. Loizeaux.
Niebuhr, H. Richard. *see* Niebuhr, Helmut Richard.

Niebuhr, Helmut Richard, 1894-
　xNiebuhr, H. Richard.
　　Christ & Culture. Har-Row.
　　Christ & Culture. Peter Smith.
　　Meaning of Revelation. Macmillan.
Niebuhr, Reinhold, 1892-
　xNiebuhr, Reinhold.
　　Christian Realism & Political Problems. Kelley.
　　Christianity & Power Politics. Shoe String.
　　The Contribution of Religion to Social Work.
　　AMS Pr.
　　Leaves from the Notebook of a Tamed Cynic.
　　Har-Row.
　　Love & Justice: Selections from the Shorter
　　Writings of Reinhold Niebuhr. Peter Smith.
　　Moral Man & Immoral Society: A Study in
　　Ethics & Politics. Scribner.
　　Structure of Nations & Empires: A Study of
　　the Recurring Patterns & Problems of the
　　Political Order in Relation to the Unique
　　Problems of the Nuclear Age. Kelley.
Nieburg, Harold L.
　xNieburg, Harold L.
　　In the Name of Science. Times Bks.
Nieburgs, H E.
　xNieburgs, H. E.
　　Cytologic Technics for Office & Clinic. Grune.
Niederer, Frances J.
　xNiederer, Frances J.
　　Hollins College: An Illustrated History. U Pr of
　　Va.
Niederhoffer, Arthur.
　xNiederhoffer, Arthur.
　　The Ambivalent Force. HR&W.
Niedermayer, Franz.
　xNiedermayer, Franz.
　　Jose Ortega y Gasset. Ungar.
Niedermeyer, Ernst, 1920-
　xNiedermeyer, Ernst.
　　Compendium of the Epilepsies. C C Thomas.
Niehans, Jurg.
　xNiehans, Jurg.
　　The Theory of Money. Johns Hopkins.
Niehans, Paul, 1882-
　xNiehans, Paul.
　　Introduction to Cellular Therapy. Cooper Sq.
Niehaus, Richard J.
　xNiehaus, Richard J.
　　Computer-Assisted Human Resources Planning.
　　Wiley.
Niel, Robert Van. *see* Van Niel, Robert.
Nield, Dorothea.
　xNield, Dorothea.
　　Adventures in Patchwork. Transatlantic.
Nield, J. *see* Nield, Jonathan.
Nield, Jonathan, 1863-
　xNield, J.
　　A Guide to the Best Historical Novels & Tales.
　　Gordon Pr.
　xNield, Jonathan.
　　Guide to the Best Historical Novels & Tales. B
　　Franklin.
　　A Guide to the Best Historical Novels & Tales.
　　Longwood Pr.
Nielsen, Andreas, 1899-1957
　xNielsen, Andreas.
　　German Air Force General Staff. Arno.
Nielsen, D. R. *see* Nielsen, Donald R.
Nielsen, Donald R.
　xNielsen, D. R.
　　Nitrogen in the Environment. Acad Pr.
Nielsen, Duane M.
　xNielsen, Duane M.
　　Reading & Career Education. Intl Reading.
Nielsen, Jens.
　xNielsen, Jens.
　　How to Save or Make Thousands When You
　　Buy or Sell Your House. Doubleday.
Nielsen, Kai.
　xNielsen, Kai.

Contemporary Critiques of Religion. Seabury.
　　Ethics Without God. Prometheus Bks.
Nielsen, Kaj L. *see* Nielsen, Kaj Leo.
Nielsen, Kaj Leo, 1914-
　xNielsen, Kaj L.
　　College Mathematics. Cliffs.
　　College Mathematics. Har-Row.
　　Differential Equations. Har-Row.
Nielsen, L. E. *see* Nielsen, Lawrence E.
Nielsen, Lawrence E.
　xNielsen, L. E.
　　Mechanical Properties of Polymers &
　　Composites. Dekker.
　xNielsen, Lawrence E.
　　Mechanical Properties of Polymers &
　　Composites. Dekker.
Nielsen, Niels C. *see* Nielsen, Niels Christian.
Nielsen, Niels Christian, 1921-
　xNielsen, Niels C.
　　The Crisis of Human Rights. Nelson.
Nielsen, Swen C.
　xNielsen, Swen C.
　　General Organizational & Administrative
　　Concepts for University Police. C C Thomas.
Nielsen, Waldemar A.
　xNielsen, Waldemar A.
　　Africa. Atheneum.
Nieman, Donald G.
　xNieman, Donald G.
　　To Set the Law in Motion: The Freedmen's
　　Bureau & the Legal Rights of Blacks,
　　1865-1868. Kraus Intl.
Niemann, Bernard J.
　xNiemann, Bernard J.
　　An Annotated Bibliography of Land Planning
　　& Land Information Systems. Vance Biblios.
Niemann, John O.
　xNiemann, John O.
　　The Bank Income Tax Return Manual with
　　Specimen Filled in Returns. Warren.
Nieman Reports.
　xNieman Reports.
　　ed. Reading, Writing & Newspapers: A Special
　　Issue Devoted Wholly to a Discussion of the
　　Conditions That Affect Newspaper Writing.
　　Johnson Repr.
Niemann, Walter.
　xNiemann, Walter.
　　Brahms. Cooper Sq.
Niemeyer, E. V. *see* Niemeyer, Eberhardt Victor.
Niemeyer, Eberhardt Victor.
　xNiemeyer, E. V.
　　Revolution at Queretaro: The Mexican
　　Constitutional Convention of 1916-1917. U
　　of Tex Pr.
Niemeyer, Glenn A.
　xNiemeyer, Glenn A.
　　Automotive Career of Ransom E. Olds. Mich
　　St U Busn.
Niemeyer, N. *see* Niemeyer, Nannie.
Niemeyer, Nannie.
　xNiemeyer, N.
　　Children & Childhood. Folcroft.
Niemi, Albert W.
　xNiemi, Albert W.
　　Gross State Product & Productivity in the
　　Southeast. U of NC Pr.
Niemi, John A.
　xNiemi, John A.
　　ed. Mass Media & Adult Education. Educ
　　Tech Pubns.
Niemi, Richard. *see* Niemi, Richard G.
Niemi, Richard G.
　xNiemi, Richard.
　　Probability Models of Collective Decision
　　Making. Merrill.
　xNiemi, Richard G.

ed. Controversies in American Voting
Behavior. W H Freeman.
How Family Members Perceive Each Other:
Political & Social Attitudes in Two
Generations. Yale U Pr.
Nienhauser, William H.
xNienhauser, William H.
Liu Tsung-Yuan. Twayne.
P'I Jih-Hsiu. Twayne.
Nierenberg, Gerard I.
xNierenberg, Gerard I.
Fundamentals of Negotiating. Dutton.
How to Give & Receive Advice. PB.
How to Give & Receive Advice. S&S.
How to Read a Person Like a Book.
Cornerstone.
Nierman, Judith.
xNierman, Judith.
ed. Edna St. Vincent Millay: A Reference
Guide. G K Hall.
Nies, Richard, 1928-
xNies, Richard C.
The Security of Salvation. Southern Pub.
Nies, Richard C. *see* Nies, Richard.
Nietzel, Michael. *see* Nietzel, Michael T.
Nietzel, Michael T.
xNietzel, Michael.
Crime & Its Modification: A Social Learning
Perspective. Pergamon.
Nietzsche, F. *see* Nietzsche, Friedrich Wilhelm.
Nietzsche, Friedrich. *see* Nietzsche, Friedrich Wilhelm.
Nietzsche, Friedrich Wilhelm, 1844-1900
xNietzsche, F.
The Portable Nietzsche. Viking Pr.
xNietzsche, Friedrich.
The Antichrist. Arno.
A Nietzsche Reader. Penguin.
Portable Nietzsche. Penguin.
Nieuwenhuys, R.
xNieuwenhuys, R.
The Human Central Nervous System: A
Pictorial Survey. Springer-Verlag.
Nieuwenhuys, Rob. *see* Nieuwenhuys, Robert.
Nieuwenhuys, Robert, 1908-
xNieuwenhuys, Rob.
Memory & Agony: Dutch Stories from
Indonesia. Twayne.
Nieuwenhuysen, J. P.
xNieuwenhuysen, J. P.
ed. Australian Economic Policy. Intl Schol Bk
Serv.
The Australian Prices Justification Tribunal.
Intl Schol Bk Serv.
Competition in Australian Bookselling: Resale
Price Maintenance & After. Intl Schol Bk
Serv.
xNieuwenhuysen, John P.
ed. Australian Trade Practices: Readings. Biblio
Dist.
Nieuwenhuysen, John P. *see* Nieuwenhuysen, J. P.
Nieuwhoff, Constance.
xNieuwhoff, Constance.
Contemporary Lace Making. Van Nos
Reinhold.
Nievergelt, Jurg.
xNievergelt, Jurg.
Computer Approaches to Mathematical
Problems. P-H.
Nievo, Ippolito, 1831-1861
xNievo, Ippolito.
Castle of Fratta. Greenwood.
Niewyk, Donald L., 1940-
xNiewyk, Donald L.
Socialist, Anti-Semite, & Jew: German Social
Democracy Confronts the Problem of
Anti-Semitism, 1918-1933. La State U Pr.
Nigeria. Cocoa Marketing Board.
xNigerian Cocoa Marketing Board.

Nigerian Cocoa Farmers. Greenwood.
Nigerian Cocoa Marketing Board. *see* Nigeria. Cocoa
Marketing Board.
Nigh, Edward.
xNigh, Edward.
The Formula Book 3. Andrews & McMeel.
Nightingale, Earl.
xNightingale, Earl.
This Is Earl Nightingale. Doubleday.
Nightingale, Florence, 1820-1910
xNightingale, Florence.
Notes on Nursing. Biblio Dist.
Notes on Nursing: What It Is, & What It Is
Not. Dover.
Notes on Nursing: What It Is & What It Is
Not. Lippincott.
Notes on Nursing: What It Is & What It Is
Not. Peter Smith.
Nightingale, R. H. *see* Nightingale, Reuben H.
Nightingale, Reuben H.
xNightingale, R. H.
Crossing Jordan at Flood Tide. Pacific Pr Pub
Assn.
Nigro, Felix A.
xNigro, Felix A.
Modern Public Administration. Har-Row.
Nigrosh, Leon I.
xNigrosh, Leon I.
Claywork: Form & Idea in Ceramic Design.
Davis Mass.
Low Fire: Other Ways to Work in Clay. Davis
Mass.
Nihon Boeki Shinkokai.
xJapan External Trade Organization & Press
International, Ltd. (Tokyo).
China: A Business Guide. Intl Pubns Serv.
Nihon No Sanko Tosho Henshu Iinkai.
xNihon No Sankotosho.
Guide to Japanese Reference Books. ALA.
Nihon No Sankotosho. *see* Nihon No Sanko Tosho
Henshu Iinkai.
Nihon Sugakkai.
xIyanaga, Shokichi.
Encyclopedic Dictionary of Mathematics. MIT
Pr.
Niiniluoto, I. *see* Niiniluoto, Ilkka.
Niiniluoto, Ilkka.
xNiiniluoto, I.
Theoretical Concepts & Hypothetico-Inductive
Inference. Kluwer Boston.
Nijinsky, Romola. *see* Nijinsky, Romola (De Pulszky).
Nijinsky, Romola (De Pulszky).
xNijinsky, Romola.
Last Years of Nijinsky. AMS Pr.
Nijinsky. AMS Pr.
Nijkamp, P. *see* Nijkamp, Peter.
Nijkamp, Peter.
xNijkamp, P.
Theory & Application of Environmental
Economics. Elsevier.
xNijkamp, Peter.
Multidimensional Spatial Data & Decision
Analysis. Wiley.
Nikaido, Hukukane, 1923-
xNikaido, Hukukane.
Convex Structures & Economic Theory. Acad
Pr.
Monopolistic Competition & Effective
Demand. Princeton U Pr.
Nikelly, Arthur G.
xNikelly, Arthur G.
Achieving Competence & Fulfillment.
Brooks-Cole.
Nikitin, Nikolai. *see* Nikitin, Nikolai Nikolaevich.
Nikitin, Nikolai Nikolaevich.
xNikitin, Nikolai.
Night & Other Stories. Strathcona.
Nikolaieff, George A.
xNikolaieff, George A.

Computers & Society. Wilson.
ed. President & the Constitution. Wilson.
Niland, Deborah.
xNiland, Deborah.
illus. ABC of Monsters. McGraw.
Niles, Blair.
xNiles, Blair.
Strange Brother. Arno.
Niles, Kathryn B. *see* Niles, Kathryn Bele.
Niles, Kathryn Bele.
xNiles, Kathryn B.
Food Preparation Recipes. Wiley.
Niles, Nathan O.
xNiles, Nathan O.
Calculus with Analytic Geometry. P-H.
Plane Trigonometry. Wiley.
Nilsen, Don L. *see* Nilsen, Don Lee Fred.
Nilsen, Don Lee Fred.
xNilsen, Don L.
The Instrumental Case in English: Syntactic &
Semantic Considerations. Mouton.
Toward a Semantic Specification of Deep Case.
Mouton.
Nilsen, Thomas R.
xNilsen, Thomas R.
Ethics of Speech Communication. Bobbs.
Nilsson, Anne.
xNilsson, Anne.
The Art of Home Cheesemaking. Woodbridge
Pr.
Nilsson, B. H. *see* Nilsson, Bengt-Herman.
Nilsson, Bengt-Herman.
xNilsson, B. H.
Competing in Cross-Country Skiing. Sterling.
Nilsson, Martin P. *see* Nilsson, Martin Persson.
Nilsson, Martin Persson, 1874-1967
xNilsson, Martin P.
The Dionysiac Mysteries of the Hellenistic &
Roman Age. Arno.
Homer & Mycenae. Cooper Sq.
Homer & Mycenae. U of Pa Pr.
Nilsson, Nils A. *see* Nilsson, Nils Ake.
Nilsson, Nils Ake.
xNilsson, Nils A.
Osip Mandelstam: Five Poems. Humanities.
Nilsson, Nils J., 1933-
xNilsson, Nils J.
Learning Machines: Foundations of Trainable
Pattern-Classifying Systems. McGraw.
Principles of Artificial Intelligence. Tioga Pub
Co.
Problem-Solving Methods in Artificial
Intelligence. McGraw.
Nilus. *see* Nilus, Sergei Aleksandrovich.
Nilus, Sergei Aleksandrovich.
xNilus.
Protocols of the Learned Elders of Zion.
Gordon Pr.
Nim, P. S.
xNim, P. S.
Double Mobius Sphere. PB.
Nimeth, Albert J.
xNimeth, Albert J.
Of Course I Love You. Franciscan Herald.
Sudden Thoughts. Franciscan Herald.
Nimetz, Michael.
xNimetz, Michael.
Humor in Galdos: A Study of the "Novelas
Contemporaneas". Yale U Pr.
Nimmer, Melville B.
xNimmer, Melville B.
Cases & Materials on Copyright & Other
Aspects of Law Pertaining to Literary,
Musical & Artistic Works. West Pub.
Nimmer, Raymond T.
xNimmer, Raymond T.

The Omnibus Hearing: An Experiment in
Relieving Inefficiency, Unfairness & Judicial
Delay. Am Bar Foun.
Prosecutor Disclosure & Judicial Reform: The
Omnibus Hearing in Two Courts. Am Bar
Foun.
Two Million Unnecessary Arrests: Removing a
Social Service Concern from the Criminal
Justice System. Am Bar Foun.
Nimmo, Dan. *see* Nimmo, Dan D.
Nimmo, Dan D.
xNimmo, Dan.
Candidates & Their Images: Concepts, Methods
& Findings. Goodyear.
Political Patterns in America: Conflict
Representation & Resolution. W H Freeman.
Political Persuaders: The Techniques of
Modern Election Campaigns. P-H.
Nimnicht, Nona, 1930-
xNimnicht, Nona.
In the Museum Naked. Second Coming.
Nimocks, Patricia E.
xNimocks, Patricia E.
The Craft of Decoupage. Scribner.
Decoupage. Scribner.
Nimoy, Leonard.
xNimoy, Leonard.
I Am Not Spock. Ballantine.
I Am Not Spock. Celestial Arts.
Nimuendaju, Curt.
xNimuendaju, Curt.
The Serente. AMS Pr.
The Serente. Southwest Mus.
Nin, Anais, 1903-
xNin, Anais.
Delta of Venus: Erotica. HarBraceJ.
Diary of Anais Nin. HarBraceJ.
The Diary of Anais Nin, 1947-1955.
HarBraceJ.
The Diary of Anais Nin, 1947-1955.
HarBraceJ.
The Diary of Anais Nin: 1955-1966.
HarBraceJ.
The Diary of Anais Nin: 1955-1966.
HarBraceJ.
Four-Chambered Heart. Swallow.
In Favor of the Sensitive Man & Other Essays.
HarBraceJ.
Linotte: The Early Diary of Anais Nin
1914-1920. HarBraceJ.
Nind, T. *see* Nind, T E W.
Nind, T. E. *see* Nind, T E W.
Nind, T E W.
xNind, T.
Principles of Oil Well Production. McGraw.
xNind, T. E.
Principles of Oil Well Production. McGraw.
Ninde, Edward S. *see* Ninde, Edward Summerfield.
Ninde, Edward Summerfield, 1866-1935
xNinde, Edward S.
The Story of the American Hymn. AMS Pr.
Nininger, H. H. *see* Nininger, Harvey Harlow.
Nininger, Harvey Harlow, 1887-
xNininger, H. H.
Ask a Question About Meteorites. Am
Meteorite.
Find a Falling Star. Eriksson.
Ninth International Summer School of Brain Research.
see International Summer School of Brain Research,
9th, Amsterdam, 1975.
Nir, I. *see* Nir, Isaac.
Nir, Isaac.
xNir, I.
ed. The Pineal Gland: Proceedings of the
International Symposium, Jerusalem, Nov.
14-17, 1977. Springer-Verlag.
Nirdlinger, Charles F. *see* Nirdlinger, Charles Frederic.
Nirdlinger, Charles Frederic.
xNirdlinger, Charles F.

Four Short Plays. Core Collection.
Nirenberg, Jesse S.
xNirenberg, Jesse S.
Breaking Through to Each Other: Creative
Persuasion on the Job & in the Home.
Har-Row.
Getting Through to People. P-H.
Nirenberg, L.
xNirenberg, Louis.
Lectures on Linear Partial Differential
Equations. Am Math.
Nirenberg, Louis. *see* Nirenberg, L.
Nisbet, Ada.
xNisbet, Ada.
Dickens & Ellen Ternan. U of Cal Pr.
Nisbet, Richard.
xNisbet, Richard.
Capacity of Negroes for Religious & Moral
Improvement Considered. Negro U Pr.
Nisbet, Robert.
xNisbet, Robert.
History of the Idea of Progress. Basic.
Sociology As an Art Form. Oxford U Pr.
Sociology As an Art Form. Oxford U Pr.
Nisbet, Robert. *see* Nisbet, Robert A.
Nisbet, Robert A.
xNisbet, Robert.
Sociology of Emile Durkheim. Oxford U Pr.
Twilight of Authority. Oxford U Pr.
Twilight of Authority. Oxford U Pr.
Nisbet, Ulric.
xNisbet, Ulric.
Onlie Begetter. Haskell.
Nisbett, Alec.
xNisbett, Alec.
The Use of Microphones. Focal Pr.
Nish, Dale L., 1932-
xNish, Dale L.
Creative Woodturning. Brigham.
Nish, Ian H. *see* Nish, Ian Hill.
Nish, Ian Hill.
xNish, Ian H.
Alliance in Decline: A Study in
Anglo-Japanese Relations 1908-23.
Humanities.
The Anglo-Japanese Alliance: The Diplomacy
of Two Island Empires. Greenwood.
Nishida, A. *see* Nishida, Atsuhiro.
Nishida, Atsuhiro, 1936-
xNishida, A.
Geomagnetic Diagnosis of the Magnetosphere.
Springer-Verlag.
Nishida, Kitaro, 1870-1945
xNishida, Kitaro.
Art & Morality. U Pr of Hawaii.
Nishihara, Masashi.
xNishihara, Masashi.
Golkar & the Indonesian Elections of 1971.
Cornell Mod Indo.
Nishijima, K. *see* Nishijima, Kazuhiko.
Nishijima, Kazuhiko, 1912-
xNishijima, K.
Fields & Particles: Field Theory & Dispersion
Relations. Benjamin-Cummings.
Nishimura, Shizuya, 1929-
xNishimura, Shizuya.
Decline of Inland Bills of Exchange in the
London Money Market, 1855-1913.
Cambridge U Pr.
Nishioka, Hayward, 1942-
xNishioka, Hayward.
Foot Throws Karate, Judo & Self-Defense.
Ohara Pubns.
Nishiyama, Zenji, 1901-
xNishiyama, Zenji.
Martensitic Transformation. Acad Pr.
Niskanen, William A., 1933-
xNiskanen, William A.

Structural Reform of the Federal Budget
Process. Am Enterprise.
Tax & Expenditure Limitation by
Constitutional Amendment: Four Perspectives
on the California Initiative. Inst Gov Stud
Berk.
Nissenbaum, Stephen.
xNissenbaum, Stephen.
Sex, Diet & Debility in Jacksonian America:
Sylvester Graham & Health Reform.
Greenwood.
Nissenson, S. G. *see* Nissenson, Samuel George.
Nissenson, Samuel George, 1884-
xNissenson, S. G.
The Patroon's Domain. Octagon.
Nissman, Albert.
xNissman, Albert.
Organizing & Developing a Summer
Professional Workshop. Shoe String.
Nist, John. *see* Nist, John A.
Nist, John A.
xNist, John.
Speaking into Writing: A Guidebook for
English Composition. St Martin.
Structural History of English. St Martin.
Niswander, G. Donald.
xNiswander, G. Donald.
A Panorama of Suicide: A Casebook of
Psychological Autopsies. C C Thomas.
Niswander, Kenneth R.
xNiswander, Kenneth R.
Obstetrics: Essentials of Clinical Practice.
Little.
Niswonger, C. Rollin. *see* Niswonger, Clifford Rollin.
Niswonger, Clifford Rollin.
xNiswonger, C. Rollin.
Accounting Principles. SW Pub.
Nitchie, Edward. *see* Nitchie, Edward Bartlett.
Nitchie, Edward Bartlett, 1876-1917
xNitchie, Edward.
How to Read Lips for Fun & Profit. Dutton
Nitchie, Elizabeth, 1889-
xNitchie, Elizabeth.
Mary Shelley, Author of Frankenstein.
Greenwood.
Reverend Colonel Finch. AMS Pr.
Nitchie, George W. *see* Nitchie, George Wilson.
Nitchie, George Wilson, 1921-
xNitchie, George W.
Human Values in the Poetry of Robert Frost:
A Study of a Poet's Convictions. Gordian.
Marianne Moore: An Introduction to the
Poetry. Columbia U Pr.
Nitecki, Zbigniew.
xNitecki, Zbigniew.
Differentiable Dynamics: An Introduction to
the Orbit Structure of Diffeomorphisms. MIT
Pr.
Nitobe, Inaz O, 1862-1933
xNitobe, Inazo O.
The Intercourse Between the United States &
Japan: An Historical Sketch. AMS Pr.
Nitobe, Inazo O. *see* Nitobe, Inaz O.
Nitti, Francesco S. *see* Nitti, Francesco Saverio.
Nitti, Francesco Saverio, 1868-1953
xNitti, Francesco S.
Population & the Social System. Arno.
Nitzan, M.
xNitzan, Menachem.
ed. The Influence of Maternal Hormones on
the Fetus & Newborn. S Karger.
Nitzan, Menachem. *see* Nitzan, M.
Nitze, Paul H.
xNitze, Paul H.
The Fateful Ends & Shades of SALT:
Past...Present... & Yet to Come.
Crane-Russak Co.
Nitze, William A. *see* Nitze, William Albert.
Nitze, William Albert, 1876-1957
xNitze, William A.

Aaron Burr & the American Literary
Imagination. Greenwood.
Nolan, D. see Nolan, Dennis.
Nolan, David.
xNolan, David.
ed. Dante Commentaries: Eight Studies of the
Divine Comedy. Rowman.
Nolan, Dennis.
xNolan, D.
Alphabrutes. P-H.
xNolan, Dennis.
Alphabrutes. P-H.
Monster Bubbles: A Counting Book. P-H.
illus. Witch Bazooza. P-H.
Nolan, Frederick.
xNolan, Frederick.
Brass Target. BJ Pub Group.
Nolan, James, 1949-
xNolan, James.
What Moves Is Not the Wind. Columbia U Pr.
Nolan, James L. see Nolan, James Lee.
Nolan, James Lee.
xNolan, James L.
Discovery of the Lost Art Treasures of
California's First Mission. Copley Bks.
Nolan, Janette. see Nolan, Janette Gay.
Nolan, Janette Gay, 1942-
xNolan, Janette.
Bundaberg, History, & People. U of
Queensland Pr.
Nolan, Jeannette (Covert), 1896-
xNolan, Jeannette C.
Little Giant: Stephen A. Douglas. Messner.
Nolan, Jeannette C. see Nolan, Jeannette (Covert).
Nolan, Madeena S. see Nolan, Madeena Spray.
Nolan, Madeena Spray.
xNolan, Madeena S.
My Daddy Don't Go to Work. Carolrhoda
Bks.
Nolan, Michael, d. 1827
xNolan, Michael.
A Treatise of the Laws for the Relief &
Settlement of the Poor. Garland Pub.
Nolan, Paul T.
xNolan, Paul T.
Marc Connelly. Twayne.
Nolan, R. L. see Nolan, Richard L.
Nolan, Richard L.
xNolan, R. L.
Introduction to Computing Through the BASIC
Language. HR&W.
Nolan, William F., 1928-
xNolan, William F.
Dashiell Hammett: A Casebook. McNally.
ed. Ray Bradbury Companion: A Life & Career
History, Photolog, & Comprehensive
Checklist of Writings, with Facsimiles from
Ray Bradbury's Unpublished & Uncollected
Works in All Media. Gale.
Noland, Aaron.
xNoland, Aaron.
The Founding of the French Socialist Party,
1893-1905. Fertig.
Noland, George B.
xNoland, George B.
General Biology. Mosby.
Noland, Robert L., 1928-
xNoland, Robert L.
ed. Counseling Parents of the Ill & the
Handicapped. C C Thomas.
Counseling Parents of the Mentally Retarded:
A Sourcebook. C C Thomas.
Nolde, O. Frederick. see Nolde, Otto Frederick.
Nolde, Otto Frederick, 1899-
xNolde, O. Frederick.
ed. Toward World-Wide Christianity. Kennikat.
Nolen, Barbara, 1902-
xNolen, Barbara.

Ethiopia. Watts.
Nolen, William A., 1928-
xNolen, William A.
Spare Parts for the Human Body. Random.
A Surgeon's World. Random.
Noli, Jean, 1928-
xNoli, Jean.
The Admiral's Wolfpack. Zebra.
Nolin, Bertil.
xNolin, Bertil.
Georg Brandes. Twayne.
Noll, Edward M.
xNoll, Edward M.
CB Test Equipment & Measurements. Sams.
First-Class Radiotelephone License Handbook.
Sams.
Ham & CB Antenna Dimension Charts.
Editors.
Marine Radiotelegraph Operator License
Handbook. Sams.
Oscilloscope Applications & Experiments.
Sams.
Radio Transmitter Principles & Projects.
Editors.
Noll, James W. see Noll, James William.
Noll, James William.
xNoll, James W.
ed. Foundations of Education in America: An
Anthology of Major Thoughts & Significant
Actions. Har-Row.
Noll, Kenneth E.
xNoll, Kenneth E.
Air Monitoring Survey Design. Ann Arbor
Science.
ed. Power Generation: Air Pollution
Monitoring & Control. Ann Arbor Science.
Noll, Roger G.
xNoll, Roger G.
Economic Aspects of Television Regulation.
Brookings.
Reforming Regulation: An Evaluation of the
Ash Council Proposals. Brookings.
Noll, Victor H. see Noll, Victor Herbert.
Noll, Victor Herbert, 1900-
xNoll, Victor H.
Introduction to Educational Measurement.
HM.
ed. Readings in Educational Psychology.
Macmillan.
Noll, W. see Noll, Walter.
Noll, Walter, 1907-
xNoll, W.
The Foundations of Mechanics &
Thermodynamics: Selected Papers.
Springer-Verlag.
Nollen, Stanley D.
xNollen, Stanley D.
Permanent Part-Time Employment: The
Manager's Perspective. Praeger.
Nolte, Claude B.
xNolte, Claude B.
Optimum Pipe Size Selection. Gulf Pub.
Optimum Pipe Size Selection. Trans Tech.
Nolte, Fred O. see Nolte, Fred Otto.
Nolte, Fred Otto, 1894-
xNolte, Fred O.
The Early Middle Class Drama. Folcroft.
Nolte, Lawrence W.
xNolte, Lawrence W.
ed. Fundamentals of Public Relations:
Professional Guidelines, Concepts &
Integrations. Pergamon.
Nolte, M. see Nolte, Mervin Chester.
Nolte, M. Chester. see Nolte, Mervin Chester.
Nolte, Mervin Chester.
xNolte, M.

Guide to School Law. P-H.
xNolte, M. Chester.
Duties & Liabilities of School Administrators.
P-H.
Nolte, Robert C.
xNolte, Robert C.
Residential Construction Wiring. SRA.
Nolte, William A. see Nolte, William Anthony.
Nolte, William Anthony, 1913-
xNolte, William A.
Oral Microbiology. Mosby.
Nolte, William H.
xNolte, William H.
H. L. Mencken, Literary Critic. Columbia U
Pr.
H. L. Mencken, Literary Critic. U of Wash Pr.
Noma, Seiroku.
xNoma, Seiroku.
Arts of Japan. Kodansha.
Nomizu, Katsumi, 1924-
xNomizu, Katsumi.
Fundamentals of Linear Algebra. Chelsea Pub.
Nomokonov, V. P. see Nomokonov, Vladimir P.
Nomokonov, Vladimir P.
xNomokonov, V. P.
Theory of Seismic Prospecting Instruments.
Gordon.
Nonet, Philippe.
xNonet, Philippe.
Administrative Justice: Advocacy & Change in
a Government Agency. Russell Sage.
Law & Society in Transition: Toward
Responsive Law. Octagon.
Nonhebel, D. C.
xNonhebel, D. C.
Radicals. Cambridge U Pr.
Nonte, George. see Nonte, George C.
Nonte, George C.
xNonte, George.
Firearms Encyclopedia. Har-Row.
Modern Handloading. Winchester Pr.
xNonte, George C.
Combat Handguns. Stackpole.
Handloading for Handgunners. Follett.
Pistolsmithing. Stackpole.
Noojin, Ray O.
xNoojin, Ray O.
Dermatology for Students. C C Thomas.
Noonan, D. P. see Noonan, Daniel P.
Noonan, Daniel P.
xNoonan, D. P.
The Passion of Fulton Sheen. Dodd.
Noonan, Hugh.
xNoonan, Hugh.
Companion to the Clams. Franciscan Herald.
Noonan, John P. see Noonan, John Patrick.
Noonan, John Patrick, 1892-
xNoonan, John P.
General Metaphysics. Loyola.
Noonan, John T. see Noonan, John Thomas.
Noonan, John Thomas, 1926-
xNoonan, John T.
The Antelope: The Ordeal of the Recaptured
Africans in the Administrations of James
Monroe & John Quincy Adams. U of Cal Pr.
Power to Dissolve: Lawyers & Marriages in the
Courts of the Roman Curia. Harvard U Pr.
Noordergraaf, Abraham.
xNoordergraaf, Abraham.
Circulatory System Dynamics. Acad Pr.
Noordman, L. G. see Noordman, Leonhard G. M.
Noordman, Leonhard G. M., 1940-
xNoordman, L. G.
Inferring from Language. Springer-Verlag.
Noordman-Vonk, W. see Noordman-Vonk, Wietske.
Noordman-Vonk, Wietske, 1939-
xNoordman-Vonk, W.

Retrieval from Semantic Memory.
Springer-Verlag.

Noory, Samuel, 1910-
xNoory, Samuel J.
Dictionary of Pronunciation. A S Barnes.

Noory, Samuel J. *see* Noory, Samuel.

Noose, Theodore, 1930-
xNoose, Theodore.
Hollywood Film Acting. A S Barnes.

Nora, James J.
xNora, James J.
Genetics & Counseling in Cardiovascular
Diseases. C C Thomas.

Nora, Paul F.
xNora, Paul F.
ed. Operative Surgery: Principles &
Techniques. Lea & Febiger.

Norback, C. T. *see* Norback, Craig T.

Norback, Craig. *see* Norback, Craig T.

Norback, Craig T.
xNorback, C. T.
Everything You Can Get from the Government
for Free or Almost for Free. Van Nos
Reinhold.
xNorback, Craig.
New American Guide to Athletics, Sports, &
Recreation. NAL.
xNorback, Craig T.
ed. Corporate Publications in Print. McGraw.
jt. auth. Newsweek Travel Guide of the United
States. Newsweek.

Norback, Peter G.
xNorback, P. G.
jt. auth. Everything You Can Get from the
Government for Free or Almost for Free.
Van Nos Reinhold.
xNorback, Peter.
jt. auth. New American Guide to Athletics,
Sports, & Recreation. NAL.
xNorback, Peter G.
Newsweek Travel Guide of the United States.
Newsweek.

Norbeck, Edward, 1915-
xNorbeck, Edward.
Changing Japan. HR&W.
Country to City: The Urbanization of a
Japanese Hamlet. U of Utah Pr.
ed. Study of Japan in the Behavioral Sciences.
Rice Univ.

Norbeck, Jack.
xNorbeck, Jack.
Encyclopedia of American Steam Traction on
Engines. Crestline.

Norberg, Kenneth D. *see* Norberg, Kenneth Delbert.

Norberg, Kenneth Delbert, 1909-
xNorberg, Kenneth D.
American Democracy & Secondary Education:
A Study of Some Tendencies & Conceptions
of Youth Education in the United States.
AMS Pr.

Norberg-Schulz, Christian.
xNorberg-Schulz, Christian.
Baroque Architecture. Abrams.
Intentions in Architecture. MIT Pr.
Late Baroque & Rococo Architecture. Abrams.
Meaning in Western Architecture. Rizzoli Intl.

Norbury, Paul.
xNorbury, Paul.

Business in Japan: A Guide to Japanese
Business Practice & Procedure. Halsted Pr.
ed. Business in Japan: A Guide to Japanese
Business Practice & Procedure. Westview.

Norbye, Jan. *see* Norbye, Jan P.

Norbye, Jan P.
xNorbye, Jan.
The Complete Handbook of Front Wheel Drive
Cars. TAB Bks.
Modern Diesel Cars. TAB Bks.
Streamlining & Car Aerodynamics. TAB Bks.
xNorbye, Jan P.
Buick: The Postwar Years. Motorbooks Intl.
The Car & Its Wheels: A Guide to Modern
Suspension Systems. TAB Bks.
The Complete Handbook of Automotive Power
Trains. TAB Bks.

Norcliffe, G. B.
xNorcliffe, G. B.
Inferential Statistics for Geographers: An
Introduction. Halsted Pr.

Nord, David P. *see* Nord, David Paul.

Nord, David Paul.
xNord, David P.
A Guide to Old Wade House Historical Site.
State Hist Soc Wis.

Nord, Walter R.
xNord, Walter R.
ed. Concepts & Controversy in Organizational
Behavior. Goodyear.

Nordby, Conrad H. *see* Nordby, Conrad Hjalmar.

Nordby, Conrad Hjalmar, 1867-1900
xNordby, Conrad H.
Influence of Old Norse Literature Upon
English Literature. AMS Pr.

Nordby, Vernon J.
xNordby, Vernon J.
A Guide to Psychologists & Their Concepts. W
H Freeman.

Norden, Carroll R. *see* Norden, Carroll Raymond.

Norden, Carroll Raymond, 1920
xNorden, Carroll R.
Deserts. Raintree Child.

Norden, Eduard, 1868-1941
xNorden, Eduard.
Aus Altromischen Priesterbuchern. Arno.

Nordenskiold, Erland, Friherre, 1877-1932
xNordenskiold, Erland.
The Changes in the Material Culture of Two
Indian Tribes Under the Influence of New
Surroundings. AMS Pr.
The Copper & Bronze Ages in South America.
AMS Pr.
The Ethnography of South America Seen from
Mojos in Bolivia. AMS Pr.
An Historical & Ethnological Survey of the
Cuna Indians. AMS Pr.
ed. Origin of the Indian Civilizations in South
America. AMS Pr.

Nordenskiold, Gustaf E. *see* Nordenskiold, Gustaf Erik
Adolf.

Nordenskiold, Gustaf Erik Adolf, 1968-1895
xNordenskiold, Gustaf E.
The Cliff Dwellers of the Mesa Verde,
Southwestern Colorado: Their Pottery &
Implements. AMS Pr.
xNordenskiold, Gustaf N.
The Cliff Dwellers of the Mesa Verde,
Southwestern Colorado: Their Pottery &
Implements. Rio Grande.

Nordenskiold, Gustaf N. *see* Nordenskiold, Gustaf Erik
Adolf.

Nordenskjold, Otto.
xNordenskjold, Otto.
Antarctica: Or Two Years Amongst the Ice of
the South Pole. Shoe String.

Nordgaard, M. A. *see* Nordgaard, Martin Andrew.

Nordgaard, Martin Andrew, 1882-
xNordgaard, M. A.

An Historical Survey of Algebraic Methods of
Approximating the Roots of Numerical
Higher Equations up to the Year 1819. AMS
Pr.

Nordhaus. *see* Nordhaus, William D.

Nordhaus, George W.
xNordhaus, George W.
Insurance Agency Advertising & Public
Relations. Merritt Co.

Nordhaus, William D.
xNordhaus.
The Efficient Use of Energy Resources. Yale U
Pr.

Nordhoff, Charles, 1830-1901
xNordhoff, Charles.
Cape Cod, & All Along Shore: Stories. Arno.
Communistic Societies of the United States:
From Personal Visit & Observation. Dover.
Northern California, Oregon & the Sandwich
Islands. Ten Speed Pr.

Nordhoff, Charles. *see* Nordhoff, Charles Bernard.

Nordhoff, Charles Bernard.
xNordhoff, Charles.
Pitcairn's Island. Little.
Pitcairn's Island. PB.

Nordholm, Harriet.
xNordholm, Harriet.
Learning Music: Musicianship for the
Elementary Classroom Teacher. P-H.

Nordin, B. E. *see* Nordin, B. E. C.

Nordin, B. E. C.
xNordin, B. E.
Calcium, Phosphate & Magnesium Metabolism:
Clinical Physiology & Diagnostic Procedures.
Churchill.

Nordin, D. *see* Nordin, Dayton W.

Nordin, D. Sven. *see* Nordin, Dennis Sven.

Nordin, Dayton W.
xNordin, D.
How to Organize & Direct the Church Choir.
P-H.

Nordin, Dennis Sven, 1942-
xNordin, D. Sven.
Rich Harvest: A History of the Grange,
1867-1900. U Pr of Miss.

Nordling, Jo Anne.
xNordling, Jo Anne.
Dear Faculty: A Discovery Method Guidebook
to the High-School Library. Faxon.

Nordlinger, Eric A.
xNordlinger, Eric A.
Conflict Regulation in Divided Societies.
Harvard U Intl Aff.

Nordly, Carl L. *see* Nordly, Carl Leonard.

Nordly, Carl Leonard, 1901-
xNordly, Carl L.
The Administration of Intramural Athletics for
Men in Colleges & Universities. AMS Pr.

Nordoff, Paul.
xNordoff, Paul.
Creative Music Therapy: Individualized
Treatment for the Handicapped Child. T Y
Crowell.
Music Therapy in Special Education. T Y
Crowell.

Nordstrom, Carl.
xNordstrom, Carl.
Frontier Elements in a Hudson River Village.
Kennikat.

Nordtvedt, Matilda.
xNordtvedt, Matilda.
Defeating Despair & Depression. Moody.
Fat Alfie & the Feather Caper. Moody.
Living Beyond Depression. Bethany Fell.

Nordyke, Eleanor C.
xNordyke, Eleanor C.
The Peopling of Hawaii. U Pr of Hawaii.

Nordyke, Lewis.
xNordyke, Lewis.

Cattle Empire: The Fabulous Story of the 3,000,000 Acre XIT. Arno.

Norell, Irene P.
xNorell, Irene P.
Literature of the Filipino-American in the United States: A Selective & Annotated Bibliography. R & E Res Assoc.

Noren, Catherine.
xNoren, Catherine H.
The Camera of My Family. Knopf.

Noren, Catherine H. *see* Noren, Catherine.

Norenberg, W. *see* Norenberg, Wolfgang.

Norenberg, Wolfgang.
xNorenberg, W.
Introduction to the Theory of Heavy-Ion Collisions. Springer-Verlag.

Norfleet, Barbara.
xNorfleet, Barbara.
The Champion Pig: Great Moments in Everyday Life. Godine.
The Champion Pig: Great Moments in Everyday Life. Penguin.
Wedding. S&S.

Norfolk, Donald, 1931-
xNorfolk, Donald.
The Habits of Health. Avon.

Norgate, Gerald le Grys, 1866-
xNorgate, LeGrys G.
The Life of Sir Walter Scott. Haskell.

Norgate, Kate.
xNorgate, Kate.
England Under the Angevin Kings. B Franklin.
England Under the Angevin Kings. Haskell.
Richard the Lion Heart. Russell.

Norgate, LeGrys G. *see* Norgate, Gerald le Grys.

Norgren, Paul H. *see* Norgren, Paul Herbert.

Norgren, Paul Herbert.
xNorgren, Paul H.
Toward Fair Employment. Columbia U Pr.

Norgrove, Ross.
xNorgrove, Ross.
The Charter Game: How to Make Money Sailing Your Own Boat. Intl Marine.

Norick, Sylvester.
xNorick, Sylvester.
Outdoor Life in the Menominee Forest. Franciscan Herald.

Norkin, S. B. *see* Norkin, Sim Borisovich.

Norkin, Sim Borisovich.
xNorkin, S. B.
Differential Equations of the Second Order with Retarded Argument: Some Problems of the Theory of Vibrations of Systems with Retardation. Am Math.

Norlen, Urban.
xNorlen, Urban.
Simulation Model Building: A Statistical Approach to Modelling in the Social Sciences with the Simulation. Halsted Pr.

Norlie, Olaf M. *see* Norlie, Olaf Morgan.

Norlie, Olaf Morgan, 1876-1962
xNorlie, Olaf M.
History of the Norwegian People in America. Haskell.

Norlin, George, 1871-1942
xNorlin, George.
Integrity in Education, & Other Papers. Arno.

Norling, Bernard, 1924-
xNorling, Bernard.
Towards a Better Understanding of History. U of Notre Dame Pr.

Norman. *see* Norman, Barry.

Norman, A. *see* Norman, A. Vesey B.

Norman, A. V. *see* Norman, A. Vesey B.

Norman, A. Vesey B.
xNorman, A.
English Weapons & Warfare. P-H.
xNorman, A. V.

A History of War & Weapons: 449 to 1660 (English Warfare from the Anglo-Saxons to Cromwell). T Y Crowell.

Norman, Albert, 1914-
xNorman, Albert.
Operation Overlord, Design & Reality: The Allied Invasion of Western Europe. Greenwood.

Norman, Arthur Geoffrey, 1905-
xNorman, Geoffrey A.
ed. Soybean Physiology, Agronomy, & Utilization. Acad Pr.

Norman, Barry.
xNorman.
The Hollywood Greats. Watts.

Norman, C. H.
xNorman, C. H.
Revolutionary Spirit in Modern Literature & Drama & the Class War in Europe: 1918-36. Folcroft.

Norman, Charles, 1904-
xNorman, Charles.
The Case of Ezra Pound. Ultramarine Pub.

Norman, Colin, 1946-
xNorman, Colin.
Knowledge & Power: The Global Research & Development Budget. Worldwatch Inst.
Soft Technologies, Hard Choices. Worldwatch Inst.

Norman, David F.
xNorman, David F.
Practical CB Radio Troubleshooting & Repair. TAB Bks.

Norman, Donald A.
xNorman, Donald A.
Explorations in Cognition. W H Freeman.
Memory & Attention: An Introduction to Human Information Processing. Wiley.

Norman, E. Herbert, 1909-1957
xNorman, E. Herbert.
Soldier & Peasant in Japan: The Origins of Conscription. AMS Pr.

Norman, E. R. *see* Norman, Edward R.

Norman, Edward. *see* Norman, Edward R.

Norman, Edward R.
xNorman, E. R.
Christianity & the World Order. Oxford U Pr.
xNorman, Edward.
History of Modern Ireland. U of Miami Pr.

Norman, Elizabeth.
xNorman, Elizabeth.
Castle Cloud. Avon.
If the Reaper Ride. Avon.

Norman, Ernest L.
xNorman, Ernest L.
The Anthenium. Unarius.
Cosmic Continuum. Unarius.
Infinite Contact. Unarius.
Infinite Perspectus. Unarius.
Tempus Interludium. Unarius.
The Truth About Mars. Unarius.

Norman, Frank.
xNorman, Frank.
The Dead Butler Caper. St Martin.

Norman, Geoffrey A. *see* Norman, Arthur Geoffrey.

Norman, George, 1946-
xNorman, George.
Economies of Scale, Transport Costs, & Location. Kluwer Boston.

Norman, Geraldine.
xNorman, Geraldine.
Nineteenth Century Painters & Painting: A Dictionary. U of Cal Pr.

Norman, Gertrude.
xNorman, Gertrude.
ed. Letters of Composers: An Anthology 1603-1945. Greenwood.

Norman, Hilda. *see* Norman, Hilda Laura.

Norman, Hilda Laura, 1892-
xNorman, Hilda.
Swindlers & Rogues in French Drama. Kennikat.

Norman, J. R. *see* Norman, John Roxborough.

Norman, James, 1912-
xNorman, James.
Ancestral Voices: Decoding Ancient Languages. Schol Bk Serv.

Norman, James W. *see* Norman, James William.

Norman, James William, 1884-
xNorman, James W.
A Comparison of Tendencies in Secondary Education in England & the United States. AMS Pr.

Norman, John.
xNorman, John.
Explorers of Gor. DAW Bks.
Hunters of Gor. DAW Bks.
Imaginative Sex. DAW Bks.
Marauders of Gor. DAW Bks.

Norman, John Roxborough.
xNorman, J. R.
A History of Fishes. Halsted Pr.

Norman, M. Frank.
xNorman, M. Frank.
Markov Processes & Learning Models. Acad Pr.

Norman, Marc, 1941-
xNorman, Marc.
Oklahoma Crude. Popular Lib.

Norman, Maxwell H.
xNorman, Maxwell H.
How to Read & Study for Success in College. HR&W.
Successful Reading: Key to Our Dynamic Society. HR&W.

Norman, Philip, 1842-1931
xNorman, Philip.
London Signs & Inscriptions. Gale.

Norman, R. O. *see* Norman, Richard Oswald Chandler.

Norman, Richard Oswald Chandler.
xNorman, R. O.
Principles of Organic Synthesis. Methuen Inc.

Norman, Richard W. Van. *see* Van Norman, Richard W.

Norman, Sylva, 1901-
xNorman, Sylva.
Contemporary Essays. R West.

Norman, Victor D.
xNorman, Victor D.
Education, Learning & Productivity. Universitet.

Normano, Joao F. *see* Normano, Joao Frederico.

Normano, Joao Frederico.
xNormano, Joao F.
The Japanese in South America: An Introductory Survey with Special Reference to Peru. AMS Pr.
The Struggle for South America, Economy & Ideology. Greenwood.

Norona, Delf, 1895-
xNorona, Delf.
ed. Cyclopedia of United States Postmarks & Postal History. Quarterman.

Norrie, D. H.
xNorrie, D. H.
An Introduction to Finite Element Analysis. Acad Pr.
xNorrie, Douglas H.
ed. The Finite Element Method: Fundamentals & Applications. Acad Pr.

Norrie, Douglas H. *see* Norrie, D. H.

Norris, A. H. *see* Norris, Arthur H.

Norris, Arthur H.
xNorris, A. H.

The Central Nervous System & Aging. Mss
Info.
Norris, Charles G. see Norris, Charles Gilman.
Norris, Charles Gilman, 1881-1945
xNorris, Charles G.
Frank Norris. Folcroft.
Norris, Clarence.
xNorris, Clarence.
The Last of the Scottsboro Boys: An
Autobiography. Putnam.
Norris, Faith.
xNorris, Faith G.
ed. Men in Exile. Oreg St U Pr.
Norris, Faith G. see Norris, Faith.

Norris, Frank. see Norris, Frank Benjamin Franklin
Norris.
Norris, Frank Benjamin Franklin Norris, 1870-1902
xNorris, Frank.

Frank Norris of "the Wave": Stories & Sketches
from the San Francisco Weekly 1893 to
1897. Folcroft.
The Octopus: A Story of California. Bentley.
The Pit: A Story of Chicago. Bentley.
The Pit: A Story of Chicago. Peter Smith.
The Pit: A Story of Chicago. R West.
The Pit. Brown Bk.
The Pit. Lighthouse Pr NY.
Pit. AMSCO Sch.
Vandover & the Brute. U of Nebr Pr.

Norris, Geoffrey.
xNorris, Geoffrey.
Rakhmaninov. Biblio Dist.
Rakhmaninov. Littlefield.
Norris, H. T.
xNorris, H. T.
The Tuaregs: Their Islamic Legacy & Its
Diffusion in the Sahel. Intl Schol Bk Serv.
Norris, James A. see Norris, James Alfred.
Norris, James Alfred, 1929-
xNorris, James A.
First Afghan War: 1838-42. Cambridge U Pr.
Norris, James S., 1915-
xNorris, James S.
Advertising. Reston.
Norris, Kathleen. see Norris, Kathleen Thompson.
Norris, Kathleen Thompson, 1880-1966
xNorris, Kathleen.
The Angel in the House. Am Repr-Rivercity
Pr.
Baker's Dozen. Arno.
Norris, Kenneth S. see Norris, Kenneth Stafford.
Norris, Kenneth Stafford.
xNorris, Kenneth S.
The Porpoise Watcher. Norton.
Norris, Kerstin.
xNorris, Kerstin.
Say It in Swedish. Dover.
Norris, Louanne.
xNorris, Louanne.
An Oak Tree Dies & a Journey Begins. Crown.
Norris, Lynne, 1931-
xNorris, Lynne.
Can a Woman Over Forty?. Olive Pr Pubns.
Norris, Marilyn W. see Norris, Marilyn White.
Norris, Marilyn White.
xNorris, Marilyn W.
Caring for Kids. McGraw.
Norris, Martin J.
xNorris, Martin J.
The Law of Maritime Personal Injuries.
Lawyers Co-Op.
The Law of Seamen. Lawyers Co-Op.
Norris, R. M. see Norris, Robert Matheson.
Norris, Robert Matheson.
xNorris, R. M.
Geology of California. Wiley.
Norris, Willa.
xNorris, Willa.

The Career Information Service. Rand.
Norse, Harold.
xNorse, Harold.
Carnivorous Saint: Gay Poems 1941-1976.
Bookpeople.
Norstog, Knut.
xNorstog, Knut.
Plant Biology. HR&W.
North. see North, Robert Carver.
**North American Symposium on Carbenoxolone,
Montreal, Quebec, 1975.**
xNorth American Symposium on Carbenoxolone,
Montreal, 1975.
Proceedings. Elsevier.
North, Anthony.
xNorth, Anthony.
Strike Deep. Dial.
North Atlantic Treaty Organization.
xNATO.
Software Engineering Concepts & Techniques.
Van Nos Reinhold.
**North Atlantic Treaty Organization. Advisory Group for
Aerospace Research and Development. Avionics
Panel.**
xAGARD-NATO.
Radar Techniques for Detection Tracking &
Navigation. Gordon.
**North Atlantic Treaty Organization. Advisory Group for
Aerospace Research and Development. Combustion
and Propulsion Panel.**
xAGARD-NATO.
Physics & Technology of Ion Motors. Gordon.
North British Locomotive Co. see North British
Locomotive Company.
North British Locomotive Company.
xNorth British Locomotive Co.
Catalogue of Narrow Gauge Locomotives.
Kelley.
North, C.
xNorth, C.
Plant Breeding & Genetics in Horticulture.
Halsted Pr.
North Carolina. Adjutant General's Department.
xNorth Carolina Adjutant-Genearal's Office.
Muster Rolls of the Soldiers of the War of
1812 Detached from the Militia of North
Carolina in 1812 & 1814. Genealog Pub.
North Carolina Adjutant-Genearal's Office. see North
Carolina. Adjutant General's Department.
North Carolina Federation of Music Clubs.
xNorth Carolina Federation of Music Clubs.
North Carolina Musicians. Scholarly.
North Carolina General Assembly.
xNorth Carolina General Assembly.
Colonial Records of North Carolina,
1662-1776. AMS Pr.
Index to Colonial & State Records of North
Carolina, 1662-1790. AMS Pr.
State Records of North Carolina, 1777-1790.
AMS Pr.
North Carolina Museum Of Art. see North Carolina.
Museum of Art, Raleigh.
North Carolina. Museum of Art, Raleigh.
xNorth Carolina Museum Of Art.

ed. Acquisitions from N. C. Annuals, 1946-66.
NCMA.
ed. American Paintings Since Nineteen
Hundred from the Permanent Collection.
NCMA.
ed. Catalogue of Paintings: American Paintings
to 1900. NCMA.
ed. Catalogue of Paintings: British Paintings to
1900. NCMA.
ed. The Door. NCMA.
ed. E. L. Kirchner, German Expressionist: A
Loan Exhibition. NCMA.
ed. Exhibition No. 1 from the Permanent
Collection. NCMA.
ed. French Painting of the Last Half of the
Nineteenth Century. NCMA.
ed. Henry Pearson: A Retrospective Exhibition.
NCMA.
ed. John Derrickson McCurdy (1940-1974): A
Memorial Exhibition. NCMA.
ed. Josef Albers: Loan Exhibition. NCMA.
ed. Masterpieces of Art: In Memory of W. R.
Valentiner, 1880-1958. NCMA.
ed. North Carolina Collects: A Loan Exhibition
of North Carolina Owned Art Objects.
NCMA.
ed. North Carolina Craftsmen Exhibition, 1971.
NCMA.
ed. Paul Hudgins, 1940-1968: A Memorial
Exhibition. NCMA.
ed. Pottery of Marguerite Wildenhain: A
Selection of Her Recent Work. NCMA.
ed. Robert F. Phifer Collection. NCMA.
A Selection from The Birds of America by
John J. Audubon. NCMA.
ed. Selections from the Collection of Mr. &
Mrs. Harry L. Dalton. NCMA.
ed. Two Hundred Years of the Visual Arts in
North Carolina. NCMA.
ed. William C. A. Frerichs 1829-1905: A
Retrospective Exhibition. NCMA.
North Carolina Poetry Society.
xNorth Carolina Poetry Society.
Time for Poetry. Blair.
North Carolina. University.
xNorth Carolina University.
University of North Carolina Studies in the
Germanic Language & Literatures. AMS Pr.
North Carolina. University. Division of the Humanities.
xUniversity of North Carolina Division of the
Humanities.
State University Surveys the Humanities. Arno.
**North Carolina. University. Woman's College,
Greensboro.**
xUniversity of North Carolina Woman's College
Faculty.
Walter Clinton Jackson Essays in the Social
Sciences. Arno.
North, Diane M. see North, Diane M. T.
North, Diane M. T.
xNorth, Diane M.
Samuel Peter Heintzelman & the Sonora
Exploring & Mining Company. U of Ariz Pr.
North East London Polytechnic.
xNorth East London Polytechnic London,
England.
The Psychology Readings Catalogue of the
North East London Polytechnic, London,
England. G K Hall.
North East London Polytechnic London, England. see
North East London Polytechnic.
**North Eastern Regional Antipollution Conference, 6th,
University of Rhode Island, 1975.**
xNorth Eastern Regional Antipollution Conference,
6th, 1975.
Energy from Solid Waste
Utilization-(Proceedings of Anerac '75
Conference. Technomic.
North, Elizabeth, 1932-
xNorth, Elizabeth.

Pelican Rising. Academy Chi Ltd.
North, Emily.
xNorth, Emily.
Old Friends, New Friends. Childrens.
North, Gary.
xNorth, Gary.
Introduction to Christian Economics. Presby &
Reformed.
xNorth, Gary K.
None Dare Call It Witchcraft. Arlington Hse.
North, Gary K. *see* North, Gary.
North, Helen.
xNorth, Helen.
From the Myth to Icon: Reflections of Greek
Ethical Doctrine in Literature & Art. Cornell
U Pr.
North, Howard.
xNorth, Howard.
Expressway. S&S.
North, Jessica.
xNorth, Jessica.
The High Valley. NAL.
Legend of the Thirteenth Pilgrim. Coward.
The Legend of the Thirteenth Pilgrim. NAL.
North, Joseph.
xNorth, Joseph.
No Men Are Strangers. Intl Pub Co.
North, Joseph H.
xNorth, Joseph H.
The Early Development of the Motion Picture,
1887-1909. Arno.
North, Liisa.
xNorth, Liisa.
Civil-Military Relations in Argentina, Chile, &
Peru. U of Cal Intl St.
North, Mack O.
xNorth, Mack O.
Commercial Chicken Production Manual. AVI.
North, Marion.
xNorth, Marion.
ed. Personality Assessment Through
Movement. Plays.
North, P. M. *see* North, Peter Machin.
North, Peter Machin.
xNorth, P. M.
ed. The Private International Law of
Matrimonial Causes in the British Isles & the
Republic of Ireland. Elsevier.
North, Robert C. *see* North, Robert Carver.
North, Robert Carver.
xNorth.
The Foreign Relations of China. Duxbury Pr.
xNorth, Robert C.
Chinese Communism. McGraw.
Content Analysis: A Handbook with
Applications for the Study of International
Crisis. Northwestern U Pr.
The World That Could Be. Norton.
The World That Could Be. Norton.
North, Sterling.
xNorth, Sterling.
Rascal: A Memoir of a Better Era. Dutton.
North, Susanna.
xNorth, Susanna.
Traveling Alone: A Practical Guide for
Business Women. Cornerstone.
North, Wheeler. *see* North, Wheeler J.
North, Wheeler J.
xNorth, Wheeler.
Underwater California. U of Cal Pr.
Northam, J. *see* Northam, John Richard.
Northam, John Richard, 1922-
xNortham, J.
Ibsen: A Critical Study. Cambridge U Pr.
Northcott, Cecil. *see* Northcott, William Cecil.
Northcott, Clarence H. *see* Northcott, Clarence Hunter.
Northcott, Clarence Hunter, 1880-
xNorthcott, Clarence H.
Australian Social Development. AMS Pr.
Northcott, D. G. *see* Northcott, Douglas Geoffrey.

Northcott, Douglas G. *see* Northcott, Douglas Geoffrey.
Northcott, Douglas Geoffrey.
xNorthcott, D. G.
Affine Sets & Affine Groups. Cambridge U Pr.
Finite Free Resolutions. Cambridge U Pr.
A First Course of Homological Algebra.
Cambridge U Pr.
xNorthcott, Douglas G.
Ideal Theory. Cambridge U Pr.
Introduction to Homological Algebra.
Cambridge U Pr.
Lessons on Rings, Modules & Multiplicities.
Cambridge U Pr.
Northcott, William Cecil.
xNorthcott, Cecil.
People of the Bible. Westminster.
Northcott, Winifred H.
xNorthcott, Winifred H.
ed. Curriculum Guide: Hearing-Impaired
Children, Birth to Three Years, & Their
Parents. Alexander Graham.
Northeastern University - Dodge Library, Boston. *see*
Northeastern University, Boston. Dodge Library.
Northeastern University, Boston. Dodge Library.
xNortheastern University - Dodge Library, Boston.
Selective Bibliography in Science &
Engineering. G K Hall.
**Northeastern Women's Geoscientists Conference, 1st,
St. Lawrence University, 1976.**
xNortheastern Women's Geoscientists Conference,
First.
Women in Geology: Proceedings. Ash Lad Pr.
Northedge, F. S.
xNorthedge, F. S.
ed. The Foreign Policies of the Powers. Free
Pr.
The Foreign Policies of the Powers. Merrimack
Bk Serv.
ed. The Use of Force in International
Relations. Free Pr.
Northen, Helen.
xNorthen, Helen.
Social Work with Groups. Columbia U Pr.
Northen, Henry. *see* Northen, Henry T.
Northen, Henry T.
xNorthen, Henry.
Ingenious Kingdom: The Remarkable World of
Plants. P-H.
xNorthen, Henry T.
Greenhouse Gardening. Wiley.
Northen, Rebecca T. *see* Northen, Rebecca Tyson.
Northen, Rebecca Tyson, 1910-
xNorthen, Rebecca T.
Home Orchid Growing. Van Nos Reinhold.
Miniature Orchids. Van Nos Reinhold.
Orchids As House Plants. Dover.
Orchids As House Plants. Peter Smith.
Northern. *see* Northern, Jerry L.
Northern, Jerry L.
xNorthern.
Hearing in Children. Williams & Wilkins.
Northouse, Cameron.
xNorthouse, Cameron.
ed. Articles on English Literature: A
Comprehensive Bibliography 1900-1975. New
London Pr.
Sylvia Plath & Anne Sexton: A Reference
Guide. G K Hall.
Northrip, John W.
xNorthrip, John W.
Introduction to Biomechanic Analysis of Sport.
Wm C Brown.
Northrop, E. P. *see* Northrop, Eugene Purdy.
Northrop, Eugene Purdy, 1908-1969
xNorthrop, E. P.
Riddles in Mathematics: A Book of Paradoxes.
Krieger.
Northrop, Filmer S. *see* Northrop, Filmer Stuart Cuckow.
Northrop, Filmer Stuart Cuckow, 1893-
xNorthrop, Filmer S.

ed. Ideological Differences & World Order:
Studies in the Philosophy & Science of the
World's Cultures. Greenwood.
The Logic of the Sciences & the Humanities.
Greenwood.
Northrop Institute Of Technology. *see* Northrop Institute
of Technology, Inglewood, Calif.
Northrop Institute of Technology, Inglewood, Calif.
xNorthrop Institute Of Technology.
Basic Science for Aerospace Vehicles.
McGraw.
Electricity & Electronics for Aerospace
Vehicles. McGraw.
Maintenance & Repair of Aerospace Vehicles.
McGraw.
Northrop, Kenneth.
xNorthrop, Kenneth.
A Violent World Ahead. Inst Econ Pol.
Northrop, Mildred B. *see* Northrop, Mildred Benedict.
Northrop, Mildred Benedict, 1903-1963
xNorthrop, Mildred B.
Control Policies of the Reichsbank, 1924-1933.
AMS Pr.
Northrup, David.
xNorthrup, David.
Trade Without Rulers: Pre-Colonial Economic
Development in South-Eastern Nigeria.
Oxford U Pr.
Northrup, Herbert R. *see* Northrup, Herbert Roof.
Northrup, Herbert Roof.
xNorthrup, Herbert R.
Impact of the AT&T-EEO Consent Decree.
Indus Res Unit-Wharton.
Manpower in the Retail Pharmacy Industry.
Indus Res Unit-Wharton.
The Objective Selection of Supervisors: A
Study of Informal Industry Practice & Two
Models for Improved Supervisor Selection.
Indus Res Unit-Wharton.
Northup, Geoge Tyler, 1874-
xNorthup, George T.
Introduction to Spanish Literature. U of
Chicago Pr.
Northup, George T. *see* Northup, Geoge Tyler.
Northup, Solomon, b. 1808
xNorthup, Solomon.
Twelve Years a Slave. La State U Pr.
Northwest Regional Educational Laboratory.
xNorthwest Regional Educational Laboratory.
Advertising Techniques & Consumer Fraud.
McGraw.
Buying & Caring for Your Car & Insurance for
Your Life, Health & Possessions. McGraw.
Comparison Shopping & Caring for Your
Personal Possessions. McGraw.
Counting Money & Making Change & Making
a Budget. McGraw.
Housing: Buying a House, Buying a Mobile
Home. McGraw.
Housing: Moving on Getting Utilities & Using
Them Wisely. McGraw.
Housing: What Are Your Needs, Renting a
Place to Live. McGraw.
Introduction to Data Processing. Pitman
Learning.
Ordering from Catalogs & Dining Out.
McGraw.
Using Credit & Banking Services &
Understanding Income Tax. McGraw.
Northwestern University. *see* Northwestern University,
Evanston, Ill.
Northwestern University, Evanston, Ill.
xNorthwestern University.

ed. English Romantic Poetry & Prose. Oxford U Pr.

Wordsworth & the Art of Landscape. Haskell.

Noyes, Sybil.
xNoyes, Sybil.
Genealogical Dictionary of Maine & New Hampshire. Genealog Pub.

Noyle, Ken.
xNoyle, Ken.
The Geisha Diary. Berkley Pub.
The Geisha Diary. Berkley Pub.

Noz, Marilyn E.
xNoz, Marilyn E.
Radiation Protection in the Radiologic & Health Sciences. Lea & Febiger.

Nozick, Robert.
xNozick, Robert.
Anarchy, State & Utopia. Basic.

Nriagu, J. O. *see* Nriagu, Jerome O.

Nriagu, Jerome O.
xNriagu, J. O.
ed. The Biogeochemistry of Lead in the Environment. Elsevier.

NRMA. *see* National Retail Merchants Association.

Nsarkoh, J. K.
xNsarkoh, J. K.
Local Government in Ghana. Oxford U Pr.

Nuclear Energy Policy Study Group.
xNuclear Energy Policy Study Group.
Nuclear Power Issues and Choices. Ballinger Pub.

Nueces County Historical Society.
xNueces County Historical Society.
The History of Neuces County. Jenkins.
Nueces County, Texas. Jenkins.

Nuechterlein, Donald E. *see* Nuechterlein, Donald Edwin.

Nuechterlein, Donald Edwin, 1925-
xNuechterlein, Donald E.
National Interests & Presidential Leadership: The Setting of Priorities. Westview.
Thailand & the Struggle for Southeast Asia. Cornell U Pr.

Nuffield Provincial Hospitals Trust.
xMcLachlan, Gordon.
ed. Patterns for Uncertainty?: Planning for the Greater Medical Profession. Oxford U Pr.

Nugent, Donald, 1930-
xNugent, Donald.
Ecumenism in the Age of the Reformation: The Colloquy of Poissy. Harvard U Pr.

Nugent, Nancy.
xNugent, Nancy.
How to Get Along with Your Stomach: A Complete Guide to the Prevention & Treatment of Stomach Distress. Doubleday.
How to Get Along with Your Stomach: A Complete Guide to the Prevention & Treatment of Stomach Distress. Little.

Nugent, Nell M. *see* Nugent, Nell Marion.

Nugent, Nell Marion.
xNugent, Nell M.
Cavaliers & Pioneers: Abstracts of Virginia Land Patents & Grants 1623-1666. Genealog Pub.
Cavaliers & Pioneers: Abstracts of Virginia Land Patents & Grants, 1666-1695. VA State Lib.

Nugent, Robert.
xNugent, Robert.
Paul Eluard. Twayne.

Nugent, Walter T. *see* Nugent, Walter T. K.

Nugent, Walter T. K.
xNugent, Walter T.
Money Question During Reconstruction. Norton.
xNugent, Walter T. K.

From Centennial to World War: American Society, 1876-1917. Bobbs.

Null, Gary.
xNull, Gary.
The Complete Handbook of Nutrition. Dell.
The Complete Handbook of Nutrition. Speller.
The Complete Question & Answer Book of Natural Therapy. Speller.
Food Combining Handbook. BJ Pub Group.
Grow Your Own Food Organically. Speller.
How to Turn Ideas into Dollars. Pilot Bks.
The Natural Organic Beauty Book. Speller.
Profitable Part-Time, Home Based, Businesses. Pilot Bks.
Protein for Vegetarians. BJ Pub Group.

Null, Harold R., 1929-
xNull, Harold R.
Phase Equilibrium in Process Design. Krieger.

Nulsen, David.
xNulsen, David.
How to Live Like a Millionaire on an Average Income. Trail-R.

Nulsen, David R.
xNulsen, David R.
How to Build Patios, Porches, Carports & Storage Sheds for Mobile Homes. Trail-R.

Nultsch, Wilhelm.
xNultsch, Wilhelm.
General Botany. Acad Pr.

Nulty, Leslie.
xNulty, Leslie.
The Green Revolution in West Pakistan: Implications of Technological Change. Irvington.

Numbers, Ronald L.
xNumbers, Ronald L.
Almost Persuaded: American Physicians & Compulsory Health Insurance, 1912-1920. Johns Hopkins.
Creation by Natural Law: Laplace's Nebular Hypothesis in American Thought. U of Wash Pr.
ed. The Education of American Physicians: Historical Essays. U of Cal Pr.

Nunberg, Herman, 1884-
xNunberg, Herman.
Curiosity. Intl Univs Pr.

Nunez, Benjamin.
xNunez, Benjamin.
Dictionary of Afro-Latin American Civilization. Greenwood.

Nunez, Nemours H. *see* Nunez, Nemours Henry.

Nunez, Nemours Henry.
xNunez, Nemours H.
Chien Negre: A Tale of the Vaudoux. Arno.

Nunn, G. Raymond. *see* Nunn, Godfrey Raymond.

Nunn, Godfrey Raymond, 1918-
xNunn, G. Raymond.
Asian Libraries & Librarianship: An Annotated Bibliography of Selected Books & Periodicals & a Draft Syllabus. Scarecrow.
Publishing in Mainland China. MIT Pr.
Compiled by Southeast Asian Periodicals: An International Union List. Merrimack Bk Serv.

Nunn, J. F. *see* Nunn, John Francis.

Nunn, John Francis.
xNunn, J. F.
Applied Respiratory Physiology. Butterworths.

Nunn, Louie B.
xNunn, Louie B.
The Public Papers of Governor Louie B. Nunn, 1967-1971. U Pr of Ky.

Nunn, Richard. *see* Nunn, Richard V.

Nunn, Richard V.
xNunn, Richard.
Home Paint Book. Oxmoor Hse.
xNunn, Richard V.
Easy Auto Repairs. Oxmoor Hse.
Easy Home Plumbing. Oxmoor Hse.
Easy Kitchen Remodeling. Oxmoor Hse.
Floors & Floorcoverings. Oxmoor Hse.
Furniture Repair & Refinishing. Oxmoor Hse.
Home Storage. Oxmoor Hse.

Nunn, W. C. *see* Nunn, William Curtis.

Nunn, William Curtis, 1908-
xNunn, W. C.
Peace Unto You. G&D.
Somervell: Story of a Texas County. Tex Christian.

Nunnally, Jim C. *see* Nunnally, Jum C.

Nunnally, Jum. *see* Nunnally, Jum C.

Nunnally, Jum C.
xNunnally, Jim C.
Educational Measurement & Evaluation. McGraw.
Introduction to Psychological Measurement. McGraw.
Introduction to Statistics for Psychology & Education. McGraw.
xNunnally, Jum.
Psychometric Theory. McGraw.

Nunnally, S. W., 1927-
xNunnally, S. W.
Construction Methods & Management. P-H.

Nunnery, Michael Y.
xNunnery, Michael Y.
Politics, Power, Polls, & School Elections. McCutchan.

Nurnberg, M. *see* Nurnberg, Maxwell.

Nurnberg, Maxwell.
xNurnberg, M.
Fun with Words. P-H.

Nurnberg, Maxwell. *see* Nurnberg, Maxwell W.

Nurnberg, Maxwell W.
xNurnberg, Maxwell.
All About Words: An Adult Approach to Vocabulary Building. NAL.

Nursing Development Conference Group.
xNursing Development Conference Group.
Concept Formalization in Nursing: Process & Product. Little.

Nursing Theories Conference Group.
xNursing Theories Conference Group.
Nursing Theories: The Base for Professional Nursing Practice. P-H.

Nussbaum, Frederick L. *see* Nussbaum, Frederick Louis.

Nussbaum, Frederick Louis, 1885-
xNussbaum, Frederick L.
Commercial Policy in the French Revolution: A Study of the Career of G. J. A. Ducher. AMS Pr.

Nussbaum, Hedda.
xNussbaum, Hedda.
Animals Build Amazing Homes. Random.
Plants Do Amazing Things. Random.

Nussbaum, Martin.
xNussbaum, Martin.
Opportunities in Electronic Data Processing. Natl Textbk.

Nussenzveig, H. M. *see* Nussenzveig, Herch Moyses.

Nussenzveig, Herch Moyses.
xNussenzveig, H. M.
Causality & Dispersion Relations. Acad Pr.
Introduction to Quantum Optics. Gordon.

Nute, Donald, 1947-
xNute, Donald.
Topics in Conditional Logic. Kluwer Boston.

Nute, Grace L. *see* Nute, Grace Lee.

Nute, Grace Lee, 1895-
xNute, Grace L.

Caesars of the Wilderness: Medard Chouart,
Sieur des Groseilliers & Pierre Esprit
Radisson, 1618-1710. Minn Hist.
Rainy River Country: A Brief History of the
Region Bordering Minnesota & Ontario.
Minn Hist.
xNute, Grace Lee.
Caesars of the Wilderness: Medard Chouart,
Sieurdes Groseilliers & Pierre Espirt
Radisson, 1618-1710. Arno.
Nutman, P. S.
xNutman, P. S.
ed. Symbiotic Nitrogen Fixation in Plants.
Cambridge U Pr.
Nutrition Department, Johns Hopkins Hospital. *see* Johns
Hopkins Hospital, Baltimore. Nutrition Dept.
Nutt, Alfred. *see* Nutt, Alfred Trubner.
Nutt, Alfred T. *see* Nutt, Alfred Trubner.
Nutt, Alfred Trubner, 1856-1910
xNutt, Alfred.
Fairy Mythology of Shakespeare. Folcroft.
xNutt, Alfred T.
Critical Study of Gaelic Literature
Indispensable for the History of the Gaelic
Race. B Franklin.
Cuchulainn, the Irish Achilles. AMS Pr.
Fairy Mythology of Shakespeare. AMS Pr.
Fairy Mythology of Shakespeare. Haskell.
Legends of the Holy Grail. AMS Pr.
Ossian & Ossianic Literature. AMS Pr.
Nutt, Grady.
xNutt, Grady.
The Gospel According to Norton. Broadman.
So Good, So Far. Impact Tenn.
Nutt, Merle C.
xNutt, Merle C.
Functional Plant Planning, Layout & Materials
Handling. Exposition.
Meeting the Challenge of Supervision.
Exposition.
Nuttall, Jeff
xNuttall, Jeff.
Common Factors-Vulgar Factions. Routledge &
Kegan.
King Twist: A Portrait of Frank Randle.
Routledge & Kegan.
Objects. SBD.
Nuttall, Leonard J. *see* Nuttall, Leonard John.
Nuttall, Leonard John, 1887-
xNuttall, Leonard J.
Progress in Adjusting Differences of Amount of
Educational Opportunity Offered Under the
County Unit Systems of Maryland & Utah.
AMS Pr.
Nuttall, Thomas, 1786-1859
xNuttall, Thomas.
Genera of North American Plants. Hafner.
A Journal of Travels into the Arkansas
Territory During the Year 1819. U of Okla
Pr.
Nutter, G. Warren.
xNutter, G. Warren.
Central Economic Planning: The Visible Hand.
Am Enterprise.
Enterprise Monopoly in the United States,
1899-1958. Columbia U Pr.
Freedom in a Revolutionary Economy. Am
Enterprise.
Growth of Government in the West. Am
Enterprise.
The Strange World of Ivan Ivanov. Green Hill.
The Strange World of Ivan Ivanov. Humanities.
The Strange World of Ivan Ivanov. Inst
Humane.
Nuttin, Jozef, 1909-
xNuttin, Jozef.
Psychoanalysis & Personality: A Dynamic
Theory of Normal Personality. Greenwood.
Nwabueze, B. O. *see* Nwabueze, Benjamin Obi.

Nwabueze, Benjamin Obi.
xNwabueze, B. O.
Constitutionalism in the Emergent States.
Fairleigh Dickinson.
Presidentialism in Commonwealth Africa. St
Martin.
Nwulia, Moses. *see* Nwulia, Moses D. E.
Nwulia, Moses D. E., 1932-
xNwulia, Moses.
Britain & Slavery in East Africa. Three
Continents.
Nyad, Diana.
xNyad, Diana.
Other Shores. Random.
Nyangoni, Christopher.
xNyangoni, Christopher.
ed. Zimbabwe Independence Movements:
Select Documents. B&N.
Nyasaland Economic Symposium - Blantyre Nyasaland.
see Nyasaland Economic Symposium, Blantyre,
Nyasaland.
Nyasaland Economic Symposium, Blantyre, Nyasaland.
xNyasaland Economic Symposium - Blantyre
Nyasaland.
Economic Development in Africa. Kelley.
Nybakken, Oscar E. *see* Nybakken, Oscar Edward.
Nybakken, Oscar Edward, 1904-
xNybakken, Oscar E.
Greek & Latin in Scientific Terminology. Iowa
St U Pr.
Nyce, Vera.
xNyce, Vera.
A Jolly Christmas at the Patterprints. Schol Bk
Serv.
Nye, Beverly K., 1934-
xNye, Beverly K.
A Family Raised on Rainbows. Writers Digest.
A Family Raised on Sunshine. Writers Digest.
Nye, Edgar W. *see* Nye, Edgar Wilson.
Nye, Edgar Wilson.
xNye, Edgar W.
A Guest at the Ludlow. Irvington.
Thinks. Irvington.
Nye, F. Ivan. *see* Nye, Francis Ivan.
Nye, Francis Ivan, 1918-
xNye, F. Ivan.
Family Relationships & Delinquent Behavior.
Greenwood.
Nye, Joseph S.
xNye, Joseph S.
Pan-Africanism & East African Integration.
Harvard U Pr.
Nye, Nelson.
xNye, Nelson.
Bancroft's Banco. Ace Bks.
Bandido. Ace Bks.
Death Valley Slim. Ace Bks.
The One-Shot Kid. Ace Bks.
Quick Fire Hombre. Belmont-Tower.
Sudden Country. Ace Bks.
Nye, O. B. *see* Nye, Osborne Barr.
Nye, Osborne Barr.
xNye, O. B.
Generic Revision & Skeletal Morphology of
Some Cerioporid Cyclostomes. Paleo Res.
Nyc, P. H. *see* Nye, Peter Hague.
Nye, Peter Hague.
xNye, P. H.
Solute Movement in the Soil-Root System. U
of Cal Pr.
Nye, Robert.
xNye, Robert.
Divisions on a Ground. Persea Bks.
The Mathematical Princess & Other Stories.
Hill & Wang.
Merlin. Bantam.
Merlin. Putnam.
Tales I Told My Mother. Hill & Wang.
Taliesin. Hill & Wang.
Nye, Robert. *see* Nye, Robert Evans.

Nye, Robert A.
xNye, Robert A.
The Origins of Crowd Psychology: Gustave le
Bon & the Crisis of Mass Democracy in the
Third Republic. Sage.
Nye, Robert D.
xNye, Robert D.
What Is B. F. Skinner Really Saying?. P-H.
Nye, Robert E. *see* Nye, Robert Evans.
Nye, Robert Evans.
xNye, Robert.
Music in the Elementary School. P-H.
xNye, Robert E.
Essentials of Teaching Elementary School
Music. P-H.
Nye, Russel. *see* Nye, Russel Blaine.
Nye, Russel B. *see* Nye, Russel Blaine.
Nye, Russel Blaine, 1913-
xNye, Russel.
The Unembarrassed Muse: The Popular Arts in
America. Dial.
xNye, Russel B.
Cultural Life of the New Nation: 1776-1830.
Har-Row.
Society & Culture in America: 1830-1860.
Har-Row.
xNye, Russell B.
Society & Culture in America: 1830-1860.
Har-Row.
Nye, Russell B. *see* Nye, Russel Blaine.
Nye, Vernice T. *see* Nye, Vernice Trousdale.
Nye, Vernice Trousdale.
xNye, Vernice T.
Music for Young Children. Wm C Brown.
Nye, W. P. *see* Nye, William Preston.
Nye, Wilbur S. *see* Nye, Wilbur Sturtevant.
Nye, Wilbur Sturtevant, 1898-
xNye, Wilbur S.
Bad Medicine & Good: Tales of the Kiowas. U
of Okla Pr.
Carbine & Lance: The Story of Old Fort Sill. U
of Okla Pr.
Plains Indian Raiders: The Final Phases of
Warfare from the Arkansas to the Red River.
U of Okla Pr.
Nye, William Preston, 1917-
xNye, W. P.
Nectar & Pollen Plants of Utah. Utah St U Pr.
Nyerere, Julius K. *see* Nyerere, Julius Kambarage.
Nyerere, Julius Kambarage, Pres. Tanzania, 1922-
xNyerere, Julius K.
Crusade for Liberation. Oxford U Pr.
Nyerges, Christopher.
xNyerges, Christopher.
The Urban Wilderness. Peace Pr.
Nygaard, Joseph M. *see* Nygaard, Joseph Magnus.
Nygaard, Joseph Magnus, 1922-
xNygaard, Joseph M.
The Counselor & Student's Legal Rights. HM.
Nygren, William V.
xNygren, William V.
Business Forms Management. Am Mgmt.
Nyhus, Lloyd M.
xNyhus, Lloyd M.
Hernia. Lippincott.
Surgery of the Stomach & Duodenum. Little.
Nykodym, Nick.
xNykodym, Nick.
Business & Organizational Communication: An
Experiential Skill Building Approach. Grid
Pub.
Nylander, Jane C., 1938-
xNylander, Jane C.
Fabrics for Historic Buildings. Preservation Pr.
Nylen. *see* Nylen, David W.
Nylen, Anna-Maja, 1912-
xNylen, Anna-Maja.
Swedish Handcraft. Van Nos Reinhold.
Nylen, David W.
xNylen.

Advertising: Planning, Implementation &
Control. SW Pub.
Nyman, C. J. *see* Nyman, Carl John.
Nyman, Carl John.
xNyman, C. J.
Problems for General Chemistry & Qualitative
Analysis. Wiley.
Nyman, Michael.
xNyman, Michael.
Experimental Music: Cage & Beyond. Schirmer
Bks.
Nymeyer, Robert, 1910-
xNymeyer, Robert.
Carlsbad, Caves, & a Camera. Zephyrus Pr.
Nyomarkay, Joseph.
xNyomarkay, Joseph.
Charisma & Factionalism in the Nazi Party. U
of Minn Pr.
Nyquist, Thomas E.
xNyquist, Thomas E.
Toward a Theory of the African Upper Stratum
in South Africa. Ohio U Ctr Intl.
Nystrom, Carolyn.
xNystrom, Carolyn.
Angels & Me. Creation Hse.
Forgive Me If I'm Frayed Around the Edges.
Moody.
I Learn About the Bible. Creation Hse.
Nystrom, Harry, 1936-
xNystrom, Harry.
Creativity & Innovation. Wiley.
Nystrom, J. Warren. *see* Nystrom, John Warren.
Nystrom, John Warren.
xNystrom, J. Warren.
The Common Market. Van Nos Reinhold.
Nystrom, P. *see* Nystrom, Paul C.
Nystrom, Paul C.
xNystrom, P.
ed. Prescriptive Models of Organizations.
Elsevier.
Nystrom, Paul H. *see* Nystrom, Paul Henry.
Nystrom, Paul Henry, 1878-
xNystrom, Paul H.
Economics of Retailing. Arno.
The Economics of Retailing. R West.
Nyswander, Marie.
xNyswander, Marie.
Drug Addict As a Patient. Grune.
Nyvlt, J. *see* Nyvlt, Jaroslav.
Nyvlt, Jaroslav.
xNyvlt, J.
Solid-Liquid Phase Equilibria. Elsevier.
Nzimiro, Francis Ikenna, 1927-
xNzimiro, Ikenna.
Studies in Ibo Political Systems: Chieftaincy &
Politics in Four Niger States. Biblio Dist.
Nzimiro, Ikenna. *see* Nzimiro, Francis Ikenna.
O Hehir, Diana, 1929-
xO Hehir, Diana.
Summoned: Poems. U of Mo Pr.
O'Ballance, Edgar.
xO'Ballance, Edgar.
Arab Guerilla Power. Shoe String.
Language of Violence: The Blood Politics of
Terrorism. Presidio Pr.
O'Banion, Terry, 1936-
xO'Banion, Terry.
Organizing Staff Development Programs That
Work. Am Assn Comm Jr Coll.
Teachers for Tomorrow: Staff Development in
the Community-Junior College. U of Ariz Pr.
O'Bannon, George W.
xO'Bannon, George W.
Turkoman Carpet. Biblio Dist.
O'Barr, William M.
xO'Barr, William M.
ed. Survey Research in Africa: Its Applications
& Limits. Northwestern U Pr.
O'Brian, Patrick.
xO'Brian, Patrick.

Desolation Island. Stein & Day.
The Mauritius Command. Stein & Day.
O'Brien. *see* O'Brien, Kevin P.
O'Brien, Barbara.
xO'Brien, Barbara.
Operators & Things: The Inner Life of a
Schizophrenic. A S Barnes.
O'Brien, Bonnie Ball.
xO'Brien, Bonnie Ball.
Promises Kept. Broadman.
O'Brien, Claire.
xO'Brien, Claire.
Everything a Girl Needs to Know to Be
Beautifully Healthy. Har-Row.
O'Brien, D. P. *see* O'Brien, Denis Patrick.
O'Brien, David J., 1941-
xO'Brien, David J.
Neighborhood Organization & Interest-Group
Processes. Princeton U Pr.
The Renewal of American Catholicism. Oxford
U Pr.
The Renewal of American Catholicism. Paulist
Pr.
ed. Renewing the Earth: Catholic Documents
on Peace, Justice & Liberation. Doubleday.
O'Brien, David M.
xO'Brien, David M.
Privacy, Law & Public Policy. Praeger.
O'Brien, David W.
xO'Brien, David W.
California Disability Benefits Handbook.
Winter Brook.
California Employer-Employee Benefits
Handbook. Winter Brook.
O'Brien, Denis P. *see* O'Brien, Denis Patrick.
O'Brien, Denis Patrick.
xO'Brien, D. P.
The Classical Economists. Oxford U Pr.
Competition Policy, Profitability & Growth.
Holmes & Meier.
xO'Brien, Denis P.
Information Agreements, Competition &
Efficiency. Kelley.
O'Brien, Edna.
xO'Brien, Edna.
I Hardly Knew You. Avon.
A Rose in the Heart. Avon.
A Rose in the Heart. Doubleday.
O'Brien, Edward J. *see* O'Brien, Edward Joseph
Harrington.
O'Brien, Edward Joseph Harrington, 1890-1941
xO'Brien, Edward J.
The Advance of the American Short Story.
Folcroft.
The Advance of the American Short Story.
Scholarly.
O'Brien, Eris M. *see* O'Brien, Eris Michael.
O'Brien, Eris Michael, 1895-
xO'Brien, Eris M.
Foundation of Australia, 1786-1800: A Study
in English Criminal Practice & Penal
Colonization in the Eighteenth Century.
Greenwood.
O'Brien, F. T. *see* O'Brien, Frederick Thomas.
O'Brien, Fitz James, 1828-1862
xO'Brien, Fitz-James.
Diamond Lens & Other Stories. AMS Pr.
Diamond Lens & Other Stories. Scholarly.
O'Brien, Fitz-James. *see* O'Brien, Fitz James.
O'Brien, Frederick Thomas.
xO'Brien, F. T.
Early Solent Steamers: A History of Local
Steam Navigation. David & Charles.
O'Brien, Grace.
xO'Brien, Grace.

The Golden Age of German Music & Its
Origins. Hyperion Conn.
The Golden Age of Italian Music. Hyperion
Conn.
O'Brien, Isidore, 1895-1953
xO'Brien, Isidore.
Francis of Assisi: Mirror Christ. Franciscan
Herald.
Life of Christ. Dghtrs St Paul.
O'Brien, J. Stephen.
xO'Brien, Stephen.
The Supreme Court & the Religion-Education
Controversy: A Tightrope to Entanglement.
Moore Pub Co.
O'Brien, James. *see* O'Brien, James Howard.
O'Brien, James F. *see* O'Brien, James Francis.
O'Brien, James Francis, 1917-
xO'Brien, James F.
Design by Accident. Peter Smith.
O'Brien, James Howard, 1919-
xO'Brien, James.
Liam O'Flaherty. Bucknell U Pr.
O'Brien, James J. *see* O'Brien, James Jerome.
O'Brien, James Jerome.
xO'Brien, James J.
Contractor's Management Handbook.
McGraw.
Value Analysis in Design & Construction.
McGraw.
O'Brien, John M.
xO'Brien, John M.
Medieval Church. Littlefield.
O'Brien, John P. *see* O'Brien, John Patrick.
O'Brien, John Patrick, 1925-
xO'Brien, John P.
ed. Gas Turbines for Automotive Use. Noyes.
O'Brien, John T.
xO'Brien, John T.
ed. Crime & Justice in America. Pergamon.
O'Brien, Katherine L. *see* O'Brien, Kathryn L.
O'Brien, Kathryn L, 1898-
xO'Brien, Katherine L.
Advanced French. Wiley.
O'Brien, Kevin P.
xO'Brien.
Criminalistics: Theory & Practice. Allyn.
O'Brien, Linda.
xO'Brien, Linda.
Computers. Watts.
O'Brien, Marian M. *see* O'Brien, Marian Maeve.
O'Brien, Marian Maeve.
xO'Brien, Marian M.
The Collector's Guide to Dollhouses &
Dollhouse Miniatures. Dutton.
O'Brien, Martin.
xO'Brien, Martin.
ed. Travel in Vogue. Mayflower Bks.
O'Brien, Mary T.
xO'Brien, Mary T.
Total Care of the Stroke Patient. Little.
O'Brien, Maureen J.
xO'Brien.
The Care of the Elderly Person: A Guide for
the Licensed Practical Nurse. Mosby.
O'Brien, Michael, 1908-
xO'Brien, Michael.
The Idea of the American South: 1920-1941.
Johns Hopkins.
To a Dark Moon. Valkyrie Pr.
O'Brien, Michael J. *see* O'Brien, Michael Joseph.
O'Brien, Michael Joseph.
xO'Brien, Michael J.
Irish Settlers in America: A Consolidation of
Articles from the Journal of the American
Irish Historical Society. Genealog Pub.
O'Brien, Patrick, 1941-
xO'Brien, Patrick.
Disordered Mind: What We Now Know About
Schizophrenia. P-H.
O'Brien, Patrick. *see* O'Brien, Patrick Karl.

O'Brien, Patrick Karl.
  xO'Brien, Patrick.
    Economic Growth in Britain & France
      1780-1914: Two Paths to the Twentieth
      Century. Allen Unwin.
O'Brien, Richard, 1934-
  xO'Brien, Richard.
    Collecting Toys: A Collector's Identification &
      Value Guide. Crown.
    The Golden Age of Comic Books, 1937-1945.
      Ballantine.
    Publicity: How to Get It. B&N.
    Publicity: How to Get It. Har-Row.
O'Brien, Richard B. see O'Brien, Richard Barry.
O'Brien, Richard Barry, 1847-1918
  xO'Brien, Richard B.
    Life of Charles Stewart Parnell, 1846-1891.
      Haskell.
    Life of Charles Stewart Parnell, 1846-1891. R
      West.
O'Brien, Richard C.
  xO'Brien, Richard C.
    Dental Radiography: An Introduction for
      Dental Hygienists & Assistants. Saunders.
O'Brien, Richard J. see O'Brien, Richard James.
O'Brien, Richard James, 1922-
  xO'Brien, Richard J.
    A Descriptive Grammar of Ecclesiastical Latin
      Based on Modern Structural Analysis.
      Loyola.
O'Brien, Rita C. see O'Brien, Rita Cruise.
O'Brien, Rita Cruise.
  xO'Brien, Rita C.
    ed. The Political Economy of
      Underdevelopment: Dependence in Senegal.
      Sage.
O'Brien, Robert C.
  xO'Brien, Robert C.
    Silver Crown. Atheneum.
O'Brien, Robert W. see O'Brien, Robert William.
O'Brien, Robert William, 1907-
  xO'Brien, Robert W.
    The College Nisei. Arno.
O'Brien, Robert Y. see O'Brien, Robert Yorke.
O'Brien, Robert Yorke.
  xO'Brien, Robert Y.
    Clarity in Religious Education. Religious Educ.
O'Brien, Saliee.
  xO'Brien, Saliee.
    The Bride of Gaylord Hall. PB.
    Night of the Scorpion. Berkley Pub.
O'Brien, Seumas, 1880-
  xO'Brien, Seumas.
    Duty & Other Irish Comedies. Core Collection.
O'Brien, Stephen. see O'Brien, J. Stephen.
O'Brien, Tim.
  xO'Brien, Tim.
    Northern Lights. Delacorte.
O'Brien, Timothy R.
  xO'Brien, Timothy R.
    Radiographic Diagnosis of Abdominal
      Disorders in the Dog & Cat: Radiographic
      Interpretation, Clinical Signs,
      Pathophysiology. Saunders.
O'Brien, W. M. see O'Brien, William M.
O'Brien, William, 1852-1928
  xO'Brien, William.
    When We Were Boys. AMS Pr.
    When We Were Boys. Garland Pub.
O'Brien, William. see O'Brien, William Joseph.
O'Brien, William J. see O'Brien, William James.
O'Brien, William James.
  xO'Brien, William J.
    Stories to the Dark: Explorations in Religious
      Imagination. Paulist Pr.
O'Brien, William Joseph.
  xO'Brien, William.

An Outline of Dental Materials & Their
  Selection. Saunders.
O'Brien, William M.
  xO'Brien, W. M.
    ed. Piroxicam. Grune.
O'Brien, William V. see O'Brien, William Vincent.
O'Brien, William Vincent.
  xO'Brien, William V.
    U.S. Military Intervention: Law & Morality.
      Sage.
O'Brine, Manning, 1915-
  xO'Brine, Manning.
    Pale Moon Rising. St Martin.
O'Broin, Leon, 1902-
  xO'Broin, Leon.
    Dublin Castle & the 1916 Rising. NYU Pr.
O'Byrne, John C.
  xO'Byrne, John C.
    Deskbook for Illinois Estate Planners. Michie.
    Farm Income Tax Manual. A Smith Co.
O'Callaghan, Edmund B. see O'Callaghan, Edmund
  Bailey.
O'Callaghan, Edmund Bailey, 1797-1880
  xO'Callaghan, Edmund B.
    List of Editions of the Holy Scriptures & Parts
      Thereof Printed in American Previous to
      1860. Gale.
    Lists of Inhabitants of Colonial New York.
      Genealog Pub.
O'Callaghan, Jerry A.
  xO'Callaghan, Jerry A.
    The Disposition of the Public Domain in
      Oregon. Arno.
O'Callaghan, Joseph F.
  xO'Callaghan, Joseph F.
    A History of Medieval Spain. Cornell U Pr.
O'Casey, Sean, 1880-1964
  xO'Casey, Sean.
    The Harvest Festival: A Play in Three Acts.
      NY Pub Lib.
O'Collins, Gerald.
  nO'Collins, Gerald.
    The Calvary Christ. Westminster.
    The Case Against Dogma. Paulist Pr.
    The Cross Today: An Evaluation of the
      Current Theological Reflections of the Cross
      of Christ. Paulist Pr.
    Foundations of Theology. Loyola.
    The Resurrection of Jesus Christ. Judson.
O'Connell, April.
  xO'Connell, April.
    Choice & Change: Psychology of Adjustment,
      Growth & Creativity. P-H.
O'Connell, Brian J.
  xO'Connell, Brian J.
    Blacks in White-Collar Jobs. Allanheld.
O'Connell, C. B.
  xO'Connell, C. B.
    Home Furnishing Self Help. Scarecrow.
O'Connell, Charles, 1900-
  xO'Connell, Charles.
    The Other Side of the Record. Greenwood.
O'Connell, D. P. see O'Connell, Daniel Patrick.
O'Connell, Daniel Patrick.
  xO'Connell, D. P.
    The Influence of Law on Sea Power. Naval
      Inst Pr.
O'Connell, David.
  xO'Connell, David.
    Louis-Ferdinand Celine. Twayne.
O'Connell, Desmond. see O'Connell, Desmond H.
O'Connell, Desmond H.
  xO'Connell, Desmond.
    Aim for a Job in the Bakery Industry. Rosen
      Pr.
  xO'Connell, Desmond H.
    Aim for a Job in the Bakery Industry. Arco.
O'Connell, James.
  xO'Connell, James.

Education & Power in Nigeria. Holmes &
  Meier.
O'Connell, James F.
  xO'Connell, James F.
    The Prehistory of Surprise Valley. Ballena Pr.
O'Connell, Jean S.
  xO'Connell, Jean S.
    The Dollhouse Caper. T Y Crowell.
    The Dollhouse Caper. Schol Bk Serv.
O'Connell, Jeffrey.
  xO'Connell, Jeffrey.
    Ending Insult to Injury: No-Fault Insurance for
      Products & Services. U of Ill Pr.
    The Lawsuit Lottery: Only the Lawyers Win.
      Free Pr.
O'Connell, Jeremiah J. see O'Connell, Jeremiah Joseph.
O'Connell, Jeremiah Joseph, 1821-1894
  xO'Connell, Jeremiah J.
    Catholicity in the Carolinas & Georgia: Leaves
      of Its History. Reprint.
O'Connell, M. R. see O'Connell, Marvin Richard.
O'Connell, Marvin Richard.
  xO'Connell, M. R.
    Thomas Stapleton & the Counter Reformation.
      Elliots Bks.
O'Connell, Peggy.
  xO'Connell, Peggy.
    Aim for a Job As a Waiter or Waitress. Arco.
O'Connell, R. F. see O'Connell, Robert F.
O'Connell, Richard.
  xO'Connell, Richard.
    ed. Apollo's Day: Seventeenth Century Songs.
      Atlantis Edns.
    Deaths & Distances. Atlantis Edns.
O'Connell, Robert F.
  xO'Connell, R. F.
    ed. The Freshwater Aquarium. Arco.
    The Marine Aquarium for the Home Aquarist.
      Great Outdoors.
O'Connell, Robert J.
  xO'Connell, Robert J.
    Art & the Christian Intelligence in St.
      Augustine. Harvard U Pr.
O'Connell, Sandra E., 1940-
  xO'Connell, Sandra E.
    The Manager As Communicator. Har-Row.
O'Connell, Thomas E.
  xO'Connell, Thomas E.
    Community Colleges: A President's View. U of
      Ill Pr.
O'Connell, Timothy E.
  xO'Connell, Timothy E.
    Principles for a Catholic Morality. Seabury.
    Principles for a Catholic Morality. Seabury.
O'Connell, V. see O'Connell, Vincent.
O'Connell, Vincent.
  xO'Connell, V.
    Choice & Change: An Introduction to the
      Psychology of Growth. P-H.
O'Connell, Walter E.
  xO'Connell, Walter E.
    Action Therapy & Adlerian Theory: Selected
      Papers. A Adler Inst.
    ed. Psychotherapy: Theoretical & Technical
      Readings. Mss Info.
O'Connor, A. M. see O'Connor, Anthony Michael.
O'Connor, Anthony M. see O'Connor, Anthony
  Michael.
O'Connor, Anthony Michael.
  xO'Connor, A. M.
    An Economic Geography of East Africa.
      Westview.
  xO'Connor, Anthony M.

The Geography of Tropical African
  Development: A Study of Spatial Patterns of
  Economic Change Since Independence.
  Pergamon.
The Geography of Tropical African
  Development. Pergamon.
O'Connor, Colin.
  xO'Connor, Colin.
  Design of Bridge Superstructures. Wiley.
O'Connor, Connie, 1932-
  xO'Connor, Connie.
  The Leisure Wasters. A S Barnes.
O'Connor, Daniel.
  xO'Connor, Daniel.
  The Images of Jesus: Exploring the Metaphors
    in Matthew's Gospel. Winston Pr.
O'Connor, Daniel J. see O'Connor, Daniel John.
O'Connor, Daniel John, 1914-
  xO'Connor, Daniel J.
  ed. Critical History of Western Philosophy.
    Free Pr.
O'Connor, Edward D. see O'Connor, Edward Dennis.
O'Connor, Edward Dennis.
  xO'Connor, Edward D.
  Pentecostal Movement in the Catholic Church.
    Ave Maria.
O'Connor, Edwin.
  xO'Connor, Edwin.
  Last Hurrah. Bantam.
  The Last Hurrah. Little.
O'Connor, Elizabeth.
  xO'Connor, Elizabeth.
  Journey Inward, Journey Outward. Har-Row.
  Our Many Selves. Har-Row.
O'Connor, Flannery.
  xO'Connor, Flannery.
  The Complete Stories. FS&G.
  The Habit of Being: Letters. FS&G.
O'Connor, Francis V.
  xO'Connor, Francis V.
  ed. Art for the Millions: Essays from the
    1930's by Artists & Administrators of the
    WPA Federal Art Project. NYGS.
O'Connor, Garry.
  xO'Connor, Garry.
  The Pursuit of Perfection: A Life of Maggie
    Teyte. Atheneum.
O'Connor, Harvey, 1897-
  xO'Connor, Harvey.
  The Guggenheims: The Making of an
    American Dynasty. Arno.
O'Connor, J. F. see O'Connor, James Francis Thaddeus.
O'Connor, J. J. see O'Connor, James J.
O'Connor, Jack, 1902-
  xO'Connor, Jack.
  The Art of Hunting Big Game in North
    America. Knopf.
  Hunting Rifle. Winchester Pr.
  The Rifle Book. Knopf.
O'Connor, James. see O'Connor, James R.
O'Connor, James Francis Thaddeus, 1884-1949
  xO'Connor, J. F.
  The Banking Crisis & Recovery Under the
    Roosevelt Administration. Da Capo.
O'Connor, James J.
  xO'Connor, J. J.
  Standard Handbook of Lubrication
    Engineering. McGraw.
O'Connor, James R.
  xO'Connor, James.
  The Fiscal Crisis of the State. St Martin.
  Origins of Socialism in Cuba. Cornell U Pr.
O'Connor, John.
  xO'Connor, John.
  Free, Adult, Uncensored: The Living History of
    the Federal Theatre Project. New Republic.
O'Connor, John E.
  xO'Connor, John E.

ed. American History, American Film:
  Interpreting the Hollywood Image. Ungar.
  Teaching History with Film. Am Hist Assn.
O'Connor, John J. see O'Connor, John Joseph.
O'Connor, John Joseph, 1918 (june 15)-
  xO'Connor, John J.
  Amadis De Gaule & Its Influence on
    Elizabethan Literature. Rutgers U Pr.
O'Connor, John T.
  xO'Connor, John T.
  Negotiator Out of Season: The Career of
    Wilhelm Egon von Furstenberg (i629-1704).
    U of Ga Pr.
O'Connor, June.
  xO'Connor, June.
  The Quest for Political & Spiritual Liberation:
    A Study in the Thought of Sri Aurobindo
    Ghose. Fairleigh Dickinson.
O'Connor, Karen.
  xO'Connor, Karen.
  Working with Horses: A Roundup of Careers.
    Dodd.
O'Connor, Katherine H.
  xO'Connor, Katherine H.
  Read & Do: Learning to Follow Written
    Directions. Johnny Reads.
O'Connor, Maeve.
  xO'Connor, Maeve.
  The Scientist As Editor: Guidelines for Editors
    of Books & Journals. Wiley.
O'Connor, Mark, 1945-
  xO'Connor, Mark.
  Reef Poems. U of Queensland Pr.
O'Connor, Mary I. see O'Connor, Mary Irene.
O'Connor, Mary Irene, Sister.
  xO'Connor, Mary I.
  Study of the Sources of Han D'Islande & Their
    Significance in the Literary Development of
    Victor Hugo. AMS Pr.
O'Connor, Michael J. see O'Connor, Michael Joseph
  Lalor.
O'Connor, Michael Joseph Lalor, 1907-
  xO'Connor, Michael J.
  Origins of Academic Economics in the United
    States. Garland Pub.
O'Connor, N. see O'Connor, Neil.
O'Connor, Neil.
  xO'Connor, N.
  ed. Present Day Russian Psychology.
    Pergamon.
O'Connor, R. F. see O'Connor, Raymond F.
O'Connor, R. M. see O'Connor, Raymond M.
O'Connor, R. T. see O'Connor, Robert T.
O'Connor, Raymond F.
  xO'Connor, R. F.
  Chemical Principles & Their Biological
    Implications. Wiley.
O'Connor, Raymond G. see O'Connor, Raymond Gish.
O'Connor, Raymond Gish.
  xO'Connor, Raymond G.
  Diplomacy for Victory: FDR & Unconditional
    Surrender. Norton.
  Force & Diplomacy: Essays Military &
    Diplomatic. U of Miami Pr.
  Perilous Equilibrium: The United States & the
    London Naval Conference of 1930.
    Greenwood.
O'Connor, Raymond M.
  xO'Connor, R. M.
  Commodity Classification & Naming. Intl
    Pubns Serv.
O'Connor, Richard, 1915-
  xO'Connor, Richard.
  Gould's Millions. Greenwood.
O'Connor, Richard L.
  xO'Connor, Richard L.
  Arthroscopy. Lippincott.
O'Connor, Robert T.
  xO'Connor, R. T.

ed. Instrumental Analysis of Cotton Cellulose
  & Modified Cotton Cellulose. Dekker.
O'Connor, Rochelle.
  xO'Connor, Rochelle.
  Managing Corporate Development. Conference
    Bd.
  Planning Under Uncertainty: Multiple
    Scenarios & Contingency Planning.
    Conference Bd.
O'Connor, Rod, 1934-
  xO'Connor, Rod.
  Fundamentals of Chemistry. Har-Row.
O'Connor, Thomas H.
  xO'Connor, Thomas H.
  The Disunited States: The Era of Civil War &
    Reconstruction. Har-Row.
O'Connor, Vincent F.
  xO'Connor, Vincent F.
  Mathematics on the Playground. Raintree
    Child.
O'Connor, William V. see O'Connor, William Van.
O'Connor, William Van, 1915-1966
  xO'Connor, William V.
  Ezra Pound. U of Minn Pr.
  xO'Connor, William Van.
  Tangled Fire of William Faulkner. Gordian.
O'Crouley, Pedro A. see O'Crouley, Pedro Alonso.
O'Crouley, Pedro Alonso.
  xO'Crouley, Pedro A.
  A Description of the Kingdom of New Spain. J
    Howell.
O'Daffer, Phares. see O'Daffer, Phares G.
O'Daffer, Phares G.
  xO'Daffer, Phares.
  Geometry: An Investigative Approach. A-W.
O'Daly, Bill.
  xO'Daly, Bill.
  The Whale in the Web. Copper Canyon.
O'Day, Alan.
  xO'Day, Alan.
  ed. The Edwardian Age: Conflict & Stability,
    1900-1914. Shoe String.
O'Day, Rosemary.
  xO'Day, Rosemary.
  ed. Continuity & Change: Personnel &
    Administration of the Church in England,
    1500-1642. Humanities.
  The English Clergy: The Emergence &
    Consolidation of a Profession, 1558-1642.
    Humanities.
O'Dea, D. J. see O'Dea, Desmond James.
O'Dea, Desmond James, 1942-
  xO'Dea, D. J.
  Cyclical Indicators for the Post War British
    Economy. Cambridge U Pr.
O'Dea, T. see O'Dea, Thomas F.
O'Dea, Thomas F.
  xO'Dea, T.
  Sociology of Religion. P-H.
  xO'Dea, Thomas F.
  Readings on the Sociology of Religion. P-H.
O'Dell, De Forest, 1898-
  xO'Dell, De Forest.
  The History of Journalism Education in the
    United States. AMS Pr.
O'Dell, Paul.
  xO'Dell, Paul.
  Griffith & the Rise of Hollywood. A S Barnes.
O'Dell, Scott, 1903-
  xO'Dell, Scott.

The Captive. HM.
illus. Carlota. HM.
Carlota. Dell.
Child of Fire. Dell.
Child of Fire. G K Hall.
Child of Fire. HM.
Dark Canoe. HM.
Journey to Jericho. HM.
Sarah Bishop. HM.
O'Dell, Sterg.
xO'Dell, Sterg.
A Chronological List of Prose Fiction in
English Printed in England & Other
Countries 1475-1640. Folcroft.
Chronological List of Prose Fiction in English
Printed in England & Other Countries,
1475-1640. Kraus Repr.
O'Doherty, E. F. *see* O'Doherty, Eamonn Feichin.
O'Doherty, Eamon F. *see* O'Doherty, Eamonn Feichin.
O'Doherty, Eamonn Feichin.
xO'Doherty, E. F.
The Religious Formation of the Adolescent.
Alba.
The Religious Formation of the Elementary
School Child. Alba.
xO'Doherty, Eamon F.
Religion & Psychology. Alba.
O'Doherty, Neil.
xO'Doherty, Neil.
Atlas of the Newborn. Lippincott.
O'Donnell, E. P. *see* O'Donnell, Edwin P.
O'Donnell, Edwin P., 1895-1943
xO'Donnell, E. P.
The Great Big Doorstep: A Delta Comedy. S
Ill U Pr.
O'Donnell, Elliot, 1872-1965
xO'Donnell, Elliot.
The Sorcery Club. Arno.
O'Donnell, F. Hugh. *see* O'Donnell, Frank Hugh
Macdonald.
O'Donnell, Frank Hugh Macdonald, 1848-1916
xO'Donnell, F. Hugh.
History of the Irish Parliamentary Party.
Kennikat.
O'Donnell, J. H. *see* O'Donnell, James H.
O'Donnell, James H.
xO'Donnell, J. H.
Principles of Radiation Chemistry. Elsevier.
xO'Donnell, James H.
Southern Indians in the American Revolution.
U of Tenn Pr.
O'Donnell, James J. *see* O'Donnell, James Joseph.
O'Donnell, James Joseph, 1950-
xO'Donnell, James J.
Cassiodorus. U of Cal Pr.
O'Donnell, John H. *see* O'Donnell, John Hugh.
O'Donnell, John Hugh, 1895-1947
xO'Donnell, John H.
The Catholic Hierarchy of the United States,
1790-1922. AMS Pr.
O'Donnell, John L.
xO'Donnell, John L.
Analysis of Foreign Trade Statistics of the
Michigan Customs District, 1951-53,
1958-59. Mich St U Busn.
O'Donnell, Kenneth P.
xO'Donnell, Kenneth P.
Johnny, We Hardly Knew Ye: Memories of
John Fitzgerald Kennedy. Little.
O'Donnell, Lillian.
xO'Donnell, Lillian.
Aftershock. Putnam.
Falling Star. Putnam.
No Business Being a Cop. Fawcett.
No Business Being a Cop. Putnam.
O'Donnell, M. J. *see* O'Donnell, Michael J.
O'Donnell, Michael J., 1952-
xO'Donnell, M. J.

Computing in Systems Described by Equations.
Springer-Verlag.
O'Donnell, Paul T.
xO'Donnell, Paul T.
The Practice of Real Estate. HR&W.
Principles of Real Estate. HR&W.
O'Donnell, Pierce.
xO'Donnell, Pierce.
Toward a Just & Effective Sentencing System:
Agenda for Legislative Reform. Praeger.
O'Donnell, Roy. *see* O'Donnell, Roy C.
O'Donnell, Roy C.
xO'Donnell, Roy.
Syntax of Kindergarten & Elementary School
Children: A Transformational Analysis.
NCTE.
O'Donnell, Terence.
xO'Donnell, Terence.
Portland: A Historical Sketch & Guide. Oreg
Hist Soc.
O'Donnell, Thomas J., 1938-
xO'Donnell, Thomas J.
The Confessions of T. E. Lawrence: The
Romantic Hero's Presentation of Self. Ohio
U Pr.
O'Donnell, Thomas J. *see* O'Donnell, Thomas Joseph.
O'Donnell, Thomas Joseph, 1918-
xO'Donnell, Thomas J.
Medicine & Christian Morality. Alba.
O'Donoghue, D. J. *see* O'Donoghue, David James.
O'Donoghue, David J. *see* O'Donoghue, David James.
O'Donoghue, David James, 1866-1917
xO'Donoghue, D. J.
ed. The Humour of Ireland. R West.
xO'Donoghue, David J.
The Life & Writings of James Clarence
Mangan. Johnson Repr.
O'Donoghue, Martin.
xO'Donoghue, Martin.
Economic Dimensions in Education. Beresford
Bk Serv.
O'Donovan, Thomas R.
xO'Donovan, Thomas R.
ed. Ambulatory Surgical Centers: Development
& Management. Aspen Systems.
O'Driscoll, Gerald P.
xO'Driscoll, Gerald P.
ed. Adam Smith & Modern Political Economy:
Bicentennial Essays on the Wealth of
Nations. Iowa St U Pr.
Economics As a Coordination Problem: The
Contributions of Friedrich A. Hayek. Inst
Humane.
O'Driscoll, Herbert.
xO'Driscoll, Herbert.
A Certain Life: Contemporary Meditations on
the Way of Christ. Seabury.
O'Driscoll, Kenneth. *see* O'Driscoll, Kenneth F.
O'Driscoll, Kenneth F.
xO'Driscoll, Kenneth.
Nature & Chemistry of High Polymers. Van
Nos Reinhold.
O'Dwyer, M. F. *see* O'Dwyer, Michael Francis.
O'Dwyer, Michael Francis.
xO'Dwyer, M. F.
Valency. Springer-Verlag.
O'Faolain, Sean, 1900-
xO'Faolain, Sean.
A Summer in Italy. Devin.
O'Farrell, P. *see* O'Farrell, Patrick James.
O'Farrell, P. J. *see* O'Farrell, Patrick James.
O'Farrell, Patrick James.
xO'Farrell, P.
The Catholic Church in Australia: A Short
History, 1788-1967. Verry.
xO'Farrell, P. J.
England & Ireland Since 1800. Oxford U Pr.
O'Flaherty, Fred.
xO'Flaherty, Fred.

The Chemistry & Technology of Leather.
Krieger.
O'Flaherty, James C.
xO'Flaherty, James C.
ed. Studies in Nietzsche & the Classical
Tradition. U of NC Pr.
O'Flaherty, Joseph S., 1915-
xO'Flaherty, Joseph S.
Those Powerful Years: The South Coast & Los
Angeles 1887-1917. Exposition.
O'Flaherty, Liam, 1897-
xO'Flaherty, Liam.
The Informer. HarBraceJ.
Informer. NAL.
O'Flaherty, Patrick.
xO'Flaherty, Patrick.
The Rock Observed: Studies in the Literature
of Newfoundland. U of Toronto Pr.
O'Flaherty, Wendy D. *see* O'Flaherty, Wendy Doniger.
O'Flaherty, Wendy Doniger.
xO'Flaherty, Wendy D.
Asceticism & Eroticism in the Mythology of
Siva. Oxford U Pr.
ed. The Critical Study of Sacred Texts.
Lancaster-Miller.
The Origins of Evil in Hindu Mythology. U of
Cal Pr.
Women, Androgynes, & Other Mythical
Beasts. U of Chicago Pr.
O'Gallagher, Liam.
xO'Gallagher, Liam.
Planet Noise. Ultramarine Pub.
O'Gorman, James F.
xO'Gorman, James F.
The Architecture of the Monastic Library in
Italy 1300-1600: Catalogue with Introductory
Essay. NYU Pr.
O'Gorman, Patricia.
xO'Gorman, Patricia W.
Patios & Gardens of Mexico. Architectural.
Patios & Gardens of Mexico. Hastings.
O'Gorman, Patricia W. *see* O'Gorman, Patricia.
O'Grady, Desmond.
xO'Grady, Desmond.
Deschooling Kevin Carew. David & Charles.
The Gododdin. Humanities.
O'Grady, Joseph P.
xO'Grady, Joseph P.
How the Irish Became Americans. Twayne.
ed. The Immigrants' Influence on Wilson's
Peace Policies. U Pr of Ky.
O'Grady, Leslie.
xO'Grady, Leslie.
The Artist's Daughter. St Martin.
O'Grady, Philippe.
xO'Grady, Philippe.
Escape from the Island of Ice. Raintree Pubs.
O'Hanlon, Jacklyn.
xO'Hanlon, Jacklyn.
The Door. Dial.
Fair Game. Dial.
The Other Michael. Dial.
O'Hara, Charles E.
xO'Hara, Charles E.
Fundamentals of Criminal Investigation. C C
Thomas.
An Introduction to Criminalistics: The
Application of the Physical Sciences to the
Detection of Crime. Ind U Pr.
O'Hara, Frank.
xO'Hara, Frank.
Art Chronicles: 1954-1966. Braziller.
Meditations in an Emergency. Grove.
O'Hara, Frederic J., 1917-
xO'Hara, Frederic J.
ed. Reader in Government Documents.
IHS-PDS.
O'Hara, John.
xO'Hara, John.

Assembly. Popular Lib.
Assembly. Random.
The Ewings. Popular Lib.
The Ewings. Random.
Good Samaritan & Other Stories. Random.
Hope of Heaven. Popular Lib.
The Horse Knows the Way. Popular Lib.
Horse Knows the Way. Random.
The O'Hara Generation. Popular Lib.
O'Hara Generation. Random.
Pal Joey. Popular Lib.
A Rage to Live. Popular Lib.
Sweet & Sour. Popular Lib.
Two by O'Hara. HarBraceJ.

O'Hara, Mary.
  xO'Hara, Mary.
  Green Grass of Wyoming. Dell.
  Green Grass of Wyoming. Lippincott.
  Musical in the Making. Taplinger.
  My Friend Flicka. Dell.
  My Friend Flicka. Lippincott.
  Sometimes Sad, Sometimes Glad. Friend Pr.
O'Hara, William T.
  xO'Hara, William T.
  The Student - the College - the Law. Tchrs
    Coll.
O'Hare, John. see O'Hare, John M.
O'Hare, John M., 1927-
  xO'Hare, John.
  Ornashious. Red Dust.
O'Hare, Kate R. see O'Hare, Kate Richards.
O'Hare, Kate Richards, 1877-1948
  xO'Hare, Kate R.
  In Prison. U of Wash Pr.
O'Hare, Padraic.
  xO'Hare, Padraic.
  ed. Tradition & Transformation in Religious
    Education. Religious Educ.
O'Hehir, Brendan.
  xO'Hehir, Brendan.
  A Classical Lexicon for Finnegans Wake: A
    Glossary of the Greek & Latin in Major
    Works of Joyce. U of Cal Pr.
O'Higgins, Harvey J. see O'Higgins, Harvey Jerrold.
O'Higgins, Harvey Jerrold, 1876-1929
  xO'Higgins, Harvey J.
  Alias Walt Whitman.. Folcroft.
  Some Distinguished Americans: Imaginary
    Portraits. Arno.
O'Higgins, Paul.
  xO'Higgins, Paul.
  Workers' Rights. Merrimack Bk Serv.
O'Kane, Dick.
  xO'Kane, Dick.
  Simple Auto Repair. Doubleday.
O'Kane, Richard H., 1911-
  xO'Kane, Richard H.
  Clear the Bridge!: The War Patrols of the
    U.S.S. Tang. Rand.
O'Keefe, Dan.
  xO'Keefe, Daniel.
  The Cheese Buyer's Handbook. McGraw.
O'Keefe, Daniel. see O'Keefe, Dan.
O'Keefe, John. see O'Keefe, John M.
O'Keefe, John M.
  xO'Keefe, John.
  The Hippocampus As a Cognitive Map. Oxford
    U Pr.
O'Keeffe, Georgia, 1887-
  xO'Keeffe, Georgia.
  Georgia O'Keeffe. Penguin.
  Georgia O'Keeffe. Viking Pr.
  Some Memories of Drawings. Atlantis.
O'Kelly, Charlotte. see O'Kelly, Charlotte G.
O'Kelly, Charlotte G.
  xO'Kelly, Charlotte.
  Women & Men in Society. Van Nos Reinhold.
O'Laoghaire, D. T.
  xO'Laoghaire, D. T.

Optimal Expansion of a Water Resources
  System. Acad Pr.
O'Leary, Cornelius.
  xO'Leary, Cornelius.
  Irish Elections, 1918 - 1977: Parties, Voters &
    Proportional Representation. St Martin.
O'Leary, De Lacy E. see O'Leary, De Lacy Evans.
O'Leary, De Lacy Evans, 1872-
  xO'Leary, De Lacy E.
  Arabia Before Muhammad. AMS Pr.
O'Leary, Greg.
  xO'Leary, Greg.
  The Shaping of Chinese Foreign Policy. St
    Martin.
O'Leary, K. Daniel.
  xO'Leary, K. Daniel.
  ed. Classroom Management: The Successful
    Use of Behavior Modification. Pergamon.
O'Leary, Lawrence R.
  xO'Leary, Lawrence R.
  The Selection & Promotion of the Successful
    Police Officer. C C Thomas.
O'Loughlin, C. see O'Loughlin, Carleen.
O'Loughlin, Carleen.
  xO'Loughlin, C.
  National Economic Accounting. Pergamon.
O'Loughlin, Michael, 1936-
  xO'Loughlin, Michael.
  The Garlands of Repose: The Literary
    Celebration of Civic & Retired Leisure, the
    Tradition of Homer & Vergil, Horace &
    Montaigne. U of Chicago Pr.
O'Malia, Thomas J.
  xO'Malia, Thomas J.
  Banker's Guide to Financial Statements.
    Bankers.
O'Malley, Bert W.
  xO'Malley, Bert W.
  ed. Hormone Action. Acad Pr.
O'Malley, C. D. see O'Malley, Charles Donald.
O'Malley, Charles Donald.
  xO'Malley, C. D.
  ed. Leonardo's Legacy: An International
    Symposium. U of Cal Pr.
O'Malley, John. see O'Malley, William J.
O'Malley, John R.
  xO'Malley, John R.
  Circuit Analysis. P-H.
O'Malley, John W.
  xO'Malley, John W.
  Praise & Blame in Renaissance Rome:
    Rhetoric, Doctrine, & Reform in the Sacred
    Orators of the Papal Court, C. Fourteen Fifty
    to Fifteen Twenty-One. Duke.
O'Malley, L. S. see O'Malley, Lewis Sydney Steward.
O'Malley, Lewis Sydney Steward.
  xO'Malley, L. S.
  ed. Modern India & the West: A Study of the
    Interaction of Their Civilizations. Oxford U
    Pr.
O'Malley, Martin J.
  xO'Malley, Martin J.
  The Lun Yu of Kung Fu. M J O'Malley.
O'Malley, Robert E.
  xO'Malley, Robert E.
  Introduction to Singular Perturbations. Acad
    Pr.
O'Malley, William J.
  xO'Malley, John.
  Fifth Week. Loyola.
  xO'Malley, William J.
  Meeting the Living God. Paulist Pr.
O'Mara, Ruth H. see O'Mara, Ruth Hatcher.
O'Mara, Ruth Hatcher.
  xO'Mara, Ruth H.
  Easy Knitting: Children's Sizes 4 to 14. PB.
O'Mary, C. C.
  xO'Mary, Clayton C.

ed. Commercial Beef Cattle Production. Lea &
  Febiger.
O'Mary, Clayton C. see O'Mary, C. C.
O'Meara, Carra F. see O'Meara, Carra Ferguson.
O'Meara, Carra Ferguson.
  xO'Meara, Carra F.
  The Iconography of the Facade of
    Saint-Gilles-Du-Gard. Garland Pub.
O'Meara, J. Roger. see O'Meara, John Roger.
O'Meara, John Roger.
  xO'Meara, J. Roger.
  Retirement: Reward or Rejection?. Conference
    Bd.
O'Meara, O. T. see O'Meara, Onorato Timothy.
O'Meara, Onorato Timothy, 1928-
  xO'Meara, O. T.
  Introduction to Quadratic Forms.
    Springer-Verlag.
  Lectures on Linear Groups. Am Math.
  xO'Meara, Timothy.
  Symplectic Groups. Am Math.
O'Meara, Timothy. see O'Meara, Onorato Timothy.
O'Meara, Walter.
  xO'Meara, Walter.
  Guns at the Forks. U of Pittsburgh.
O'Meara, Walter. see O'Meara, Walter Andrew.
O'Meara, Walter Andrew.
  xO'Meara, Walter.
  Castle Danger. Manor Bks.
O'Morrow, Gerald S.
  xO'Morrow, Gerald S.
  Therapeutic Recreation: A Helping Profession.
    Reston.
O'Muircheartaigh, Colm A.
  xO'Muircheartaigh, Colm A.
  The Analysis of Survey Data. Wiley.
O'Nan, Michael.
  xO'Nan, Michael.
  Linear Algebra. HarBraceJ.
O'Neal, Bill, 1942-
  xO'Neal, Bill.
  Encyclopedia of Western Gunfighters. U of
    Okla Pr.
O'Neal, William B. see O'Neal, William Bainter.
O'Neal, William Bainter.
  xO'Neal, William B.
  ed. Architecture in Virginia: An Official Guide
    to Four Centuries of Building in the Old
    Dominion. Walker & Co.
O'Neil, Daniel J. see O'Neil, Daniel John.
O'Neil, Daniel John, 1936-
  xO'Neil, Daniel J.
  Church Lobbying in a Western State: A Case
    Study on Abortion Legislation. U of Ariz Pr.
O'Neil, Harold F., 1943-
  xO'Neil, Harold F.
  ed. Learning Strategies. Acad Pr.
O'Neil, P. see O'Neil, Peter V.
O'Neil, Peter V.
  xO'Neil, P.
  Fundamental Concepts of Topology. Gordon.
O'Neil, Robert M.
  xO'Neil, Robert M.
  The Courts, Government, & Higher Education.
    Comm Econ Dev.
  Discriminating Against Discrimination:
    Preferential Admissions & the DeFunis Case.
    Ind U Pr.
O'Neil, Russell.
  xO'Neil, Russell.
  Country Club. PB.
  Devil's Profession. S&S.
O'Neil, Will.
  xO'Neil, Will.
  The Libyan Kill. Norton.
O'Neill, Bard.
  xO'Neill, Bard.

Armed Struggle in Palestine: A Political -
Military Analysis. Westview.
Revolutionary Warfare in the Middle East: The
Israelis vs. the Fedayeen. Paladin Ent.

O'Neill, Carol L.
xO'Neill, Carol L.
Complete Guide to Editorial Freelancing.
Dodd.

O'Neill, Catherine, 1950-
xO'Neill, Catherine.
The Daffodil Farmer. Wash Writers Pub.

O'Neill, Colman E.
xO'Neill, Colman E.
Meeting Christ in the Sacraments. Alba.

O'Neill, Dan.
xO'Neill, Dan.
The Collective Unconscience of Odd Bodkins.
New Glide.

O'Neill, Dave M., 1933-
xO'Neill, Dave M.
The Federal Government & Manpower: A
Critical Look at the MDTA-Institutional &
Job Corps Program. Am Enterprise.

O'Neill, Eugene. see O'Neill, Eugene Gladstone.

O'Neill, Eugene Gladstone, 1888-1953
xO'Neill, Eugene.
More Stately Mansions. Yale U Pr.

O'Neill, Frank.
xO'Neill, Frank.
Sports Conditioning: Getting in Shape, Playing
Your Best, & Preventing Injuries. Doubleday.

O'Neill, James M. see O'Neill, James Milton.

O'Neill, James Milton, 1881-
xO'Neill, James M.
Catholicism & American Freedom. Greenwood.
xO'Neill, James Milton.
Religion & Education Under the Constitution.
Da Capo.

O'Neill, John, 1933-
xO'Neill, John.
ed. On Critical Theory. Continuum.
Perception, Expression, & History: The Social
Phenomenology of Maurice Merleau-Ponty.
Northwestern U Pr.

O'Neill, Judith, fl. 1967-
xO'Neill, Judith.
ed. Critics on Charlotte & Emily Bronte. U of
Miami Pr.
ed. Critics on Jane Austen. U of Miami Pr.
ed. Critics on Marlowe. U of Miami Pr.
Martin Luther. Lerner Pubns.
Martin Luther. Cambridge U Pr.

O'Neill, Lois Decker.
xO'Neill, Lois Decker.
ed. Women's Book of World Records &
Achievements. Doubleday.

O'Neill, Michael E.
xO'Neill, Michael E.
Criminal Justice Group Training: A
Facilitator's Handbook. Univ Assocs.
Criminal Justice Planning: A Practical
Approach. Justice Sys.

O'Neill, Nena.
xO'Neill, Nena.
The Marriage Premise. M Evans.
Open Marriage: A New Life Style for Couples.
M Evans.
Open Marriage: A New Lifestyle for Couples.
Avon.

O'Neill, Olivia.
xO'Neill, Olivia.
Indigo Nights. Berkley Pub.

O'Neill, Onora.
xO'Neill, Onora.
ed. Having Children: Philosophical & Legal
Reflections on Parenthood. Oxford U Pr.

O'Neill, Patrick, 1945-
xO'Neill, Patrick.

Gunter Grass: A Bibliography 1955-75. U of
Toronto Pr.

O'Neill, R. see O'Neill, Robert.
O'Neill, Reginald. see O'Neill, Reginald F.

O'Neill, Reginald F.
xO'Neill, Reginald.
ed. Readings in Epistemology. Irvington.

O'Neill, Robert.
xO'Neill, R.
English in Situations. Oxford U Pr.

O'Neill, Robert J. see O'Neill, Robert John.

O'Neill, Robert John.
xO'Neill, Robert J.
German Army & the Nazi Party, 1933-39.
Heineman.

O'Neill, Timothy P.
xO'Neill, Timothy P.
Life & Tradition in Rural Ireland. Biblio Dist.

O'Neill, Timothy R.
xO'Neill, Timothy R.
The Individuated Hobbit: Jung, Tolkien & the
Archetypes of Middle-Earth. HM.

O'Neill, W. L. see O'Neill, William L.
O'Neill, William. see O'Neill, William L.

O'Neill, William D.
xO'Neill, William D.
Systems Analysis: Theory & Applications.
Waveland Pr.

O'Neill, William L.
xO'Neill, W. L.
ed. The American Sexual Dilemma. Krieger.
xO'Neill, William.
The Progressive Years: America Comes of Age.
Dodd.
xO'Neill, William L.
Coming Apart: An Informal History of
America in the 1960's. Times Bks.
Divorce in the Progressive Era. New
Viewpoints.
Divorce in the Progressive Era. Yale U Pr.
The Progressive Years: America Comes of Age.
Har-Row.

O'Neill, Ynez V. see O'Neill, Ynez Viole.

O'Neill, Ynez Viole.
xO'Neill, Ynez V.
Speech & Speech Disorders in Western
Thought Before 1600. Greenwood.

O'Nell, Carl W., 1925-
xO'Nell, Carl W.
Dreams, Culture & the Individual. Chandler &
Sharp.

O'Quinn, Garland.
xO'Quinn, Garland.
Developmental Gymnastics: Building Physical
Skills for Children. U of Tex Pr.

O'Quinn, Hazel H. see O'Quinn, Hazel Hedick.

O'Quinn, Hazel Hedick.
xO'Quinn, Hazel H.
Rhyming at the Kitchen Sink. Jenkins.

O'Rahilly, Thomas F. see O'Rahilly, Thomas Francis.

O'Rahilly, Thomas Francis.
xO'Rahilly, Thomas F.
Danfhocail: Irish Epigrams in Verse. AMS Pr.

O'Regan, Susan K. see O'Regan, Suzanne K.

O'Regan, Suzanne K.
xO'Regan, Susan K.
Neil Diamond. Creative Ed.

O'Reilly, Barbi. see O'Reilly, Barbi Leifert.

O'Reilly, Barbi Leifert.
xO'Reilly, Barbi.
Manhattan Dance School Directory. Dekker.

O'Reilly, E. see O'Reilly, Edward.

O'Reilly, Edward.
xO'Reilly, E.
A Chronological Account of Nearly Four
Hundred Irish Writers. Biblio Dist.
xO'Reilly, Edward.
Brown Pelican at the Pond. Manzanita Pr.

O'Reilly, P H. see O'Reilly, Patrick Henry.

O'Reilly, Patrick Henry.
xO'Reilly, P H.
Nuclear Medicine in Urology & Nephrology.
Butterworths.

O'Reilly, Robert C., 1928-
xO'Reilly, Robert C.
Understanding Collective Bargaining in
Education: Negotiations, Contracts &
Disputes Between Teachers & Boards.
Scarecrow.

O'Reilly, Sean, 1922-
xO'Reilly, Sean.
Meet the Centers. Creative Ed.
Meet the Coaches. Creative Ed.
Meet the Forwards. Creative Ed.
Meet the Guards. Creative Ed.

O'Rourke, A. Desmond. see O'Rourke, Andrew
Desmond.

O'Rourke, Andrew Desmond, 1938-
xO'Rourke, A. Desmond.
Changing Dimensions of U. S. Agricultural
Policy. P-H.

O'Rourke, Edward. see O'Rourke, Edward W.

O'Rourke, Edward W.
xO'Rourke, Edward.
Gift of Gifts. Paulist Pr.
xO'Rourke, Edward W.
Self Help Works. Paulist Pr.

O'Rourke, Frank, 1916-
xO'Rourke, Frank.
The Abduction of Virginia Lee. Manor Bks.

O'Rourke, J. J. see O'Rourke, James J.

O'Rourke, James J.
xO'Rourke, J. J.
The Problem of Freedom in Marxist Thought:
An Analysis of the Treatment of Human
Freedom by Marx, Engels, Lenin &
Contemporary Soviet Philosophy. Kluwer
Boston.

O'Rourke, Joseph, 1928-
xO'Rourke, Joseph P.
Toward a Science of Vocabulary Development.
Mouton.

O'Rourke, Joseph P. see O'Rourke, Joseph.
O'Rourke, Karen. see O'Rourke, Karen A.

O'Rourke, Karen A.
xO'Rourke, Karen.
Nurse Power: Unions & the Law. R J Brady.

O'Rourke, Maire, 1926-
xO'Rourke, Maire.
Charles Du Bos: "Exaltation" & Creative
Criticism with Special Reference to the
Period 1919-1927". Univ Microfilms.

O'Rourke, Thomas P. see O'Rourke, Thomas Patrick.

O'Rourke, Thomas Patrick, 1889-
xO'Rourke, Thomas P.
The Franciscan Missions in Texas (1690-1793).
AMS Pr.

O'Rourke, Timothy. see O'Rourke, Timothy G.

O'Rourke, Timothy G.
xO'Rourke, Timothy.
The Impact of Reapportionment. Transaction
Bks.

O'Rourke, William.
xO'Rourke, William.
On the Job: Fiction About Work by
Contemporary American Writers. Random.

O'Shaughnessy, Arthur. see O'Shaughnessy, Arthur
William Edgar.
O'Shaughnessy, Arthur E. see O'Shaughnessy, Arthur
William Edgar.

O'Shaughnessy, Arthur William Edgar, 1844-1881
xO'Shaughnessy, Arthur.
Music & Moonlight. Garland Pub.
Songs of a Worker. Garland Pub.
xO'Shaughnessy, Arthur E.
Poems of Arthur O'Shaughnessy. Greenwood.

O'Shaughnessy, Edith, 1870-1939
xO'Shaughnessy, Edith.

Oates, Whitney Jennings, 1904-
　xOates, Whitney J.
　　Aristotle & the Problem of Value. Princeton U
　　Pr.
Oatley, Keith.
　xOatley, Keith.
　　Perceptions & Representations: The Theoretical
　　Bases of Brain Research & Psychology. Free
　　Pr.
Oatman, Eric F.
　xOatman, Eric F.
　　ed. Crime & Society. Wilson.
　　ed. Medical Care in the United States. Wilson.
Obelkevich, James.
　xObelkevich, James.
　　Religion & Rural Society: South Lindsey,
　　1825-1875. Oxford U Pr.
Ober, Kenneth H.
　xOber, Kenneth H.
　　Meir Goldschmidt. Twayne.
Ober, William B.
　xOber, William B.
　　Boswell's Clap & Other Essays: Medical
　　Analyses of Literary Men's Afflictions. S Ill
　　U Pr.
Oberer, Walter E.
　xOberer, Walter E.
　　Cases & Materials on Labor Law: Collective
　　Bargaining in a Free Society. West Pub.
Oberg, Arthur, 1938-
　xOberg, Arthur.
　　Anna's Song. U of Wash Pr.
　　Modern American Lyric: Lowell, Berryman,
　　Creeley, & Plath. Rutgers U Pr.
Oberg, Kalervo, 1901-1973
　xOberg, Kalervo.
　　Indian Tribes of Northern Mato Grosso, Brazil.
　　AMS Pr.
　　The Terena & the Caduveo of Southern Mato
　　Grosso, Brazil. AMS Pr.
Oberhettinger, F. see Oberhettinger, Fritz.
Oberhettinger, Fritz.
　xOberhettinger, F.
　　Tables of Bessel Transforms. Springer-Verlag.
　　Tables of Mellin Transforms. Springer-Verlag.
　xOberhettinger, Fritz.
　　Fourier Expansions: A Collection of Formulas.
　　Acad Pr.
Oberholzer, Emil, 1926-
　xOberholzer, Emil.
　　Delinquent Saints: Disciplinary Action in the
　　Early Congregational Churches of
　　Massachusetts. AMS Pr.
Oberley, Edith T.
　xOberley, Edith T.
　　Understanding Your New Life with Dialysis:
　　Patient Guide for Physical & Psychological
　　Adjustment to Maintenance Dialysis. C C
　　Thomas.
Obermaier, Hugo, 1877-1946
　xObermaier, Hugo.
　　Fossil Man in Spain. AMS Pr.
　　Fossil Man in Spain. Greenwood.
Oberman, Joseph.
　xOberman, Joseph.
　　Planning & Managing the Economy of the
　　City: Policy Guidelines for the Metropolitan
　　Mayor. Irvington.
Oberman, R. M. see Oberman, Roelof Maarten Marie.
Oberman, Roelof Maarten Marie.
　xOberman, R. M.
　　Digital Circuits for Binary Arithmetic. Halsted
　　Pr.
　　Digital Circuits for Binary Arithmetic. Wiley.
Obermeyer, Henry.
　xObermeyer, Henry.
　　Successful Advertising Management. McGraw.
Obermeyer, Thomas.
　xObermeyer, Thomas.

Architectural Technology. McGraw.
Oberrecht, Ken. see Oberrecht, Kenn.
Oberrecht, Kenn.
　xOberrecht, Ken.
　　The Outdoor Photographer's Handbook.
　　Winchester Pr.
　xOberrecht, Kenn.
　　The Great Outdoors Catalog. Winchester Pr.
　　The Practical Angler's Guide to Successful
　　Fishing. Winchester Pr.
Oberst, Byron B.
　xOberst, Byron B.
　　Practical Guidance for Office Pediatric &
　　Adolescent Practice. C C Thomas.
Obert, Jessie C. see Obert, Jessie Craig.
Obert, Jessie Craig, 1911-
　xObert, Jessie C.
　　Community Nutrition. Wiley.
Oberteuffer, Del. see Oberteuffer, Delbert.
Oberteuffer, Delbert, 1901-
　xOberteuffer, Del.
　　Concepts & Convictions. AAHPER.
Obiechina, Emanuel N. see Obiechina, Emmanuel N.
Obiechina, Emmanual. see Obiechina, Emmanuel N.
Obiechina, Emmanuel N., 1933-
　xObiechina, Emanuel N.
　　Onitsha Market Literature. Holmes & Meier.
　xObiechina, Emmanual.
　　Onitsha Market Literature. Heinemann Ed.
Oblad, Alex. see Oblad, Alex Golden.
Oblad, Alex Golden.
　xOblad, Alex.
　　ed. Thermal Hydrocarbon Chemistry. Am
　　Chemical.
Obolensky, Chloe.
　xObolensky, Chloe.
　　The Russian Empire: A Portrait in
　　Photographs. Random.
Oboler, Eli M.
　xOboler, Eli M.
　　Ideas & the University Library: Essays of an
　　Unorthodox Academic Librarian. Greenwood.
Obrist, Paul A.
　xObrist, Paul A.
　　ed. Cardiovascular Psychophysiology: Current
　　Issues in Response Mechanisms, Biofeedback
　　& Methodology. Aldine Pub.
Observer. see The Observer, London.
The Observer, London.
　xObserver.
　　Observer Profiles. Arno.
Obst, Frances M. see Obst, Frances Melanie.
Obst, Frances Melanie.
　xObst, Frances M.
　　Art & Design for Home Living. Macmillan.
Obudho, Constance E.
　xObudho, Constance E.
　　Compiled by Human Nonverbal Behavior: An
　　Annotated Bibliography. Greenwood.
Obudho, R. A. see Obudho, Robert A.
Obudho, Robert A.
　xObudho, R. A.
　　ed. Development of Urban Systems in Africa.
　　Praeger.
　　Periodic Markets, Urbanization, & Regional
　　Planning: A Case Study from Western Kenya.
　　Greenwood.
Ocean Affairs Board. see National Research Council.
　International Marine Sciences Affairs Panel.
Ocean Affairs Board, National Research Council. see
　National Research Council. Ocean Science
　Committee.
Ocean Affairs Board, Natl. Research Council. see
　National Research Council. Disposal Study Steering
　Comittee.
Ochester, Ed.
　xOchester, Ed.

Dancing on the Edges of Knives: Poems. U of
Mo Pr.
Ochiai, Hidy.
　xOchiai, Hidy.
　　The Essence of Self-Defense. Contemp Bks.
Ochs, Donovan J.
　xOchs, Donovan J.
　　A Brief Introduction to Speech. HarBraceJ.
Ochs, Elinor.
　xOchs, Elinor.
　　ed. Developmental Pragmatics. Acad Pr.
Ochse, Orpha. see Ochse, Orpha Caroline.
Ochse, Orpha Caroline, 1925-
　xOchse, Orpha.
　　The History of the Organ in the United States.
　　Ind U Pr.
Ochsner, John L.
　xOchsner, John L.
　　Coronary Artery Surgery. Lea & Febiger.
Ockerman, Herbert W.
　xOckerman, Herbert W.
　　Source Book for Food Scientists. AVI.
O.C.L.C. see Ohio College Library Center.
Ocran, Emanuel B. see Ocran, Emanuel Benjamin.
Ocran, Emanuel Benjamin.
　xOcran, Emanuel B.
　　Ocran's Acronyms: A Dictionary of
　　Abbreviations & Acronyms Used in Scientific
　　& Technical Writing. Routledge & Kegan.
Ocvirk, Otto G.
　xOcvirk, Otto G.
　　Art Fundamentals: Theory & Practice. Wm C
　　Brown.
Odahl, Charles M. see Odahl, Charles Matson.
Odahl, Charles Matson, 1944-
　xOdahl, Charles M.
　　Catilinarian Conspiracy. Coll & U Pr.
Odaka, Kunio, 1908-
　xOdaka, Kunio.
　　Toward Industrial Democracy: Management &
　　the Workers in Modern Japan. Harvard U Pr.
Oddo, Gilbert L. see Oddo, Gilbert Lawrence.
Oddo, Gilbert Lawrence.
　xOddo, Gilbert L.
　　Freedom & Equality: Civil Liberties & the
　　Supreme Court. Goodyear.
Oddo, Vincent.
　xOddo, Vincent.
　　Playing & Teaching the Strings. Wadsworth
　　Pub.
Ode, James. see Ode, James A.
Ode, James A.
　xOde, James.
　　Brass Instruments in Church Services.
　　Augsburg.
Odegaard, Charles E. see Odegaard, Charles Edwin.
Odegaard, Charles Edwin, 1911-
　xOdegaard, Charles E.
　　Vassi & Fideles in the Carolingian Empire.
　　Octagon.
Odegard, Gordon.
　xOdegard, Gordon.
　　Modeling the Clinchfield Railroad in N Scale.
　　Kalmbach.
Odegard, Peter H., 1901-1966
　xOdegard, Peter H.
　　Pressure Politics: The Story of the Anti-Saloon
　　League. Octagon.
Odell, Audrey.
　xOdell, Audrey.
　　Anna's Woods. Brown Penny.
Odell, George C. see Odell, George Clinton Densmore.
Odell, George Clinton Densmore, 1866-1949
　xOdell, George C.
　　Annals of the New York Stage. AMS Pr.
　　Simile & Metaphor in the English & Scottish
　　Ballads. Arden Lib.
Odell, Louise M. see Odell, Louise Minter.

Odell, Louise Minter.
  xOdell, Louise M.
    You & the Senior Boom: New Challenges &
      Opportunities for All. Exposition.
Odell, Peter R.
  xOdell, Peter R.
    An Economic Geography of Oil. Greenwood.
    Economies & Societies in Latin America: A
      Geographical Interpretation. Wiley.
    Oil & World Power: Background to the Oil
      Crisis. Penguin.
    Oil & World Power: Background to the Oil
      Crisis. Taplinger.
Odell, William D.
  xOdell, William D.
    Principles of Competitive Protein Binding
      Assays. Lippincott.
Oden, Clifford.
  xOden, Clifford.
    Thank God I Have Cancer!. Arlington Hse.
Oden, J. T. see Oden, John Tinsley.
Oden, John Tinsley, 1936-
  xOden, J. T.
    Finite Elements of Nonlinear Continua.
      McGraw.
    Variational Methods in Theoretical Mechanics.
      Springer-Verlag.
Oden, Marilyn B. see Oden, Marilyn Brown.
Oden, Marilyn Brown.
  xOden, Marilyn B.
    The Courage to Care. Abingdon.
Oden, Thomas C.
  xOden, Thomas C.
    Agenda for Theology. Har-Row.
    The Intensive Group Experience: The New
      Pietism. Westminster.
Odenweller, Arthur L. see Odenweller, Arthur Leonard.
Odenweller, Arthur Leonard, 1879-
  xOdenweller, Arthur L.
    Predicting the Quality of Teaching: The
      Predictive Value of Certain Traits for
      Effectiveness in Teaching. AMS Pr.
Odescalchi, Esther K. see Odescalchi, Esther Kando.
Odescalchi, Esther Kando.
  xOdescalchi, Esther K.
    The Little Shoe That Ran Away. Cyclopedia.
Odhiambo, E. S. see Odhiambo, E. S. Atieno.
Odhiambo, E. S. Atieno.
  xOdhiambo, E. S.
    A History of East Africa. Longman.
Odiorne, George S.
  xOdiorne, George S.
    How Managers Make Things Happen. P-H.
    MBO II: A System of Managerial Leadership
      for the 80's. Pitman Learning.
    Personal Effectiveness: A Strategy for Success.
      MBO Inc.
Odishaw, Hugh.
  xOdishaw, Hugh.
    ed. Challenges of Space. U of Chicago Pr.
Odlaug, Theron O. see Odlaug, Theron Oswald.
Odlaug, Theron Oswald, 1911-
  xOdlaug, Theron O.
    Laboratory Anatomy of the Fetal Pig. Wm C
      Brown.
Odle, Joe T.
  xOdle, Joe T.
    Coming of the King. Broadman.
Odlozilik, Otakar, 1899-
  xOdlozilik, Otakar.
    The Hussite King: Bohemia in European
      Affairs, 1440-1471. Rutgers U Pr.
Odor, Ruth.
  xOdor, Ruth.

    Lori's Day. Childs World.
    Please. Childrens.
    Thanks. Childrens.
  xOdor, Ruth S.
    Cissy, the Pup. Childs World.
    A Friend Is One Who Helps. Childs World.
    Glad. Childs World.
    Growing up. Childs World.
    Happiest Day. Childs World.
    Please. Childs World.
    The Pup Who Did As She Pleased. Childs
      World.
    Thanks. Childs World.
Odor, Ruth S. see Odor, Ruth.
Odum, Eugene P. see Odum, Eugene Pleasants.
Odum, Eugene Pleasants, 1913-
  xOdum, Eugene P.
    Fundamentals of Ecology. HR&W.
Odum, Howard. see Odum, Howard Washington.
Odum, Howard T.
  xOdum, Howard T.
    Energy Basis for Man & Nature. McGraw.
Odum, Howard W. see Odum, Howard Washington.
Odum, Howard Washington, 1884-
  xOdum, Howard.
    Southern Regions of the United States.
      Agathon.
  xOdum, Howard W.
    American Sociology: The Story of Sociology in
      the United States Through 1950. Greenwood.
    Negro Workaday Songs. Negro U Pr.
    Race & Rumors of Race: Challenge to
      American Crisis. Negro U Pr.
    ed. Southern Pioneers in Social Interpretation.
      Arno.
Odwarka, Karl.
  xOdwarka, Karl.
    A Word Frequency Study of Basic German
      Textbooks. Univ Microfilms.
Ody, Kenneth.
  xOdy, Kenneth.
    Paper Folding & Paper Sculpture. Emerson.
OECD. see Organization for Economic Cooperation and
  Development.
OECD Conference February 4-6, 1975. see Conference
  on Computer-Telecommunications Policy, Paris, 1975.
OECD Staff. see Organization for Economic Cooperation
  and Development.
Oechsli, Kelly.
  xOechsli, Kelly.
    ed. Humpty Dumpty's Bedtime Stories. Schol
      Bk Serv.
Oechsner, Carl, 1936-
  xOechsner, Carl.
    Ossining New York: An Informal Bicentennial
      History. North River.
Oehlbeck, J. Tracy.
  xOehlbeck, J. Tracy.
    The Consumer's Guide to Life Insurance. BJ
      Pub Group.
Oehme. see Oehme, Frederick W.
Oehme, Frederick W.
  xOehme.
    Toxicity of Heavy Metals in the Environment.
      Dekker.
Oehmichen, M. see Oehmichen, Manfred.
Oehmichen, Manfred.
  xOehmichen, M.
    Mononuclear Phagocytes in the Central
      Nervous System: Origin, Mode of
      Distribution, & Function of Progressive
      Microglia, Perivascular Cells of Intracerebral
      Vessels, Free Subarachnoidal Cells, &
      Epiplexus Cells. Springer-Verlag.
Oehser, Paul H. see Oehser, Paul Henry.

Oehser, Paul Henry, 1904-
  xOehser, Paul H.
    Sons of Science: The Story of the Smithsonian
      Institution & Its Leaders. Greenwood.
Oenslager, Donald, 1902-
  xOenslager, Donald.
    Stage Design: Four Centuries of Scenic
      Invention. Viking Pr.
Oesterreicher, John M., 1904-
  xOesterreicher, John M.
    Five in Search of Wisdom. U of Notre Dame
      Pr.
Oestreich, Alan E.
  xOestreich, Alan E.
    Pediatric Radiology. Med Exam.
Oetteking, Bruno, 1871-
  xOetteking, Bruno.
    Craniology of the North Pacific Coast. AMS
      Pr.
Oetting. see Oetting, Rae.
Oetting, R. see Oetting, Rae.
Oetting, Rae.
  xOetting.
    The Gray Ghosts of Gotham. Oddo.
  xOetting, R.
    Prairie Dog Town. Oddo.
    When Jesus Was a Lad. Oddo.
Oetting, Robert B.
  xOetting, R.
    Quetico Wolf. Oddo.
Oettinger, K. see Oettinger, Katherine Brownell.
Oettinger, Katherine Brownell.
  xOettinger, K.
    Not My Daughter: Facing up to Adolescent
      Pregnancy. P-H.
Offe, Claus.
  xOffe, Claus.
    Industry & Inequality: The Achievement
      Principle in Work & Social Status. St Martin.
Offen, Carol.
  xOffen, Carol.
    Country Music: The Poetry. Ballantine.
Office of Information, Gov't of Papua New Guinea. see
  Papua New Guinea. Office of Information.
Office Of Scientific Personnel. see National Research
  Council. Office of Scientific Personnel. Research
  Division.
Office Strategic Services. see United States. Office of
  Strategic Services.
Officer, Lawrence H.
  xOfficer, Lawrence H.
    Econometric Model of Canada Under the
      Fluctuating Exchange Rate. Harvard U Pr.
Officials of the National Oceanic & Atmospheric
  Administration. see United States. National Oceanic
  and Atmospheric Administration.
Offit, Sidney.
  xOffit, Sidney.
    The Adventures of Homer Fink. Schol Bk Serv.
    Only a Girl Like You. Coward.
Offner, Arnold. see Offner, Arnold A.
Offner, Arnold A.
  xOffner, Arnold.
    American Appeasement: United States Foreign
      Policy & Germany, 1933-1938. Norton.
  xOffner, Arnold A.
    American Appeasement: United States Foreign
      Policy & Germany 1933-1938. Harvard U Pr.
    The Origins of the Second World War:
      American Foreign Policy & World Politics,
      1917-1941. HR&W.
Offner, Herman L. see Offner, Herman Leroy.
Offner, Herman Leroy, 1903-
  xOffner, Herman L.
    Administrative Procedures for Changing
      Curriculum Patterns for Selected State
      Teachers Colleges. AMS Pr.
Offord, Carl R. see Offord, Carl Ruthven.
Offord, Carl Ruthven.
  xOfford, Carl R.

The White Face. AMS Pr.

Ofice of Strategic Services. *see* United States. Office of Strategic Services.

Ofosu-Appiah, L. H.
xOfosu-Appiah, L. H.
People in Bondage: African Slavery in the Modern Era. Lerner Pubns.

Ofshe, Lynne.
xOfshe, Lynne.
Utility & Choice in Social Interaction. Irvington.

Ofshe, Richard.
xOfshe, Richard J.
Sociology of the Possible. P-H.

Ofshe, Richard J. *see* Ofshe, Richard.

Ogan, Margaret. *see* Ogan, Margaret Nettles.

Ogan, Margaret Nettles.
xOgan, Margaret.
Grand National Racer. Westminster.
Raceway Charger. Westminster.

Ogasapian, John.
xOgasapian, John.
Organ Building in New York City,1700 to 1900. Organ Lit.

Ogata, Katshuiko. *see* Ogata, Katsuhiko.
Ogata, Katsuhiko.
xOgata, Katshuiko.
System Dynamics. P-H.
xOgata, Katsuhiko.
Modern Control Engineering. P-H.
Ogawa, Dennis. *see* Ogawa, Dennis M.
Ogawa, Dennis M.
xOgawa, Dennis.
ed. From Japs to Japanese: The Evolution of Japanese-American Stereotypes. McCutchan.
Ogawa, Hirohide.
xOgawa, Hirohide
Enlightenment Through the Art of Basketball. Oleander Pr.
Ogburn, Carlton. *see* Ogburn, Charlton.
Ogburn, Charlton, 1911-
xOgburn, Carlton.
Winter Beach. PB.
xOgburn, Charlton.
The Adventure of Birds. Morrow.
Adventure of Birds. Morrow.
The Continent in Our Hands. Morrow.
Railroads: The Great American Adventure. Natl Geog.
The Southern Appalachians: A Wilderness Quest. Morrow.
The Winter Beach. Morrow.
The Winter Beach. Morrow.
Winter Beach. S&S.
Ogburn, William F. *see* Ogburn, William Fielding.
Ogburn, William Fielding, 1886-1959
xOgburn, William F.
ed. American Society in Wartime. Da Capo.
Ogden, Adele, 1902-
xOgden, Adele.
The California Sea Otter Trade: 1784-1848. U of Cal Pr.
Ogden, Edith B. *see* Ogden, Edith Bolan.
Ogden, Edith Bolan.
xOgden, Edith B.
The Ferns of Maine. Thorndike Pr.
Ogden, Gina.
xOgden, Gina.
When a Family Needs Therapy: A Practical Assessment Guide for Parents, Lay Therapists, & Professionals. Beacon Pr.
Ogden, R. James.
xOgden, R. James.
ed. Going Public with One's Faith. Judson.
Ogden, Richard W.
xOgden, Richard W.

How to Succeed in Business & Marriage. Am Mgmt.
Manage Your Plant for Profit & Your Promotion. Am Mgmt.
Ogden, Samuel. *see* Ogden, Samuel R.
Ogden, Samuel R.
xOgden, Samuel.
Step by Step to Organic Vegetable Growing. Rodale Pr Inc.
xOgden, Samuel R.
Pan & Griddle Cakes. Greene.
Ogden, Schubert M. *see* Ogden, Schubert Miles.
Ogden, Schubert Miles, 1928-
xOgden, Schubert M.
Faith & Freedom: Toward a Theology of Liberation. Abingdon.
Ogdin, Carol A. *see* Ogdin, Carol Anne.
Ogdin, Carol Anne, 1941-
xOgdin, Carol A.
Microcomputer Management & Programming. P-H.
Software Design for Microcomputers. P-H.
Ogdon, Donald P. *see* Ogdon, Donald Potter.
Ogdon, Donald Potter, 1923-
xOgdon, Donald P.
Psychodiagnostics & Personality Assessment: A Handbook. Western Psych.
Ogg, David, 1887-1965
xOgg, David.
England in the Reign of Charles II. Greenwood.
Ogg, Frederic A. *see* Ogg, Frederic Austin.
Ogg, Frederic Austin.
xOgg, Frederic A.
Economic Development of Modern Europe. Scholarly.
Opening of the Mississippi: A Struggle for Supremacy in the American Interior. Cooper Sq.
Opening of the Mississippi: A Struggle for Supremacy in the American Interior. Greenwood.
Opening of the Mississippi: A Struggle for Supremacy in the American Interior. Haskell.

Ogilvie, Elisabeth, 1917-
xOgilvie, Elisabeth.
A Dancer in Yellow. McGraw.
The Devil in Tartan. McGraw.
The Dreaming Swimmer. Avon.
The Dreaming Swimmer. McGraw.
Where the Lost Aprils Are. Avon.
xOgilvie, Elizabeth.
An Answer in the Tide. McGraw.
Ebbing Tide. Amereon Ltd.
High Tide at Noon. Amereon Ltd.
Storm Tide. Amereon Ltd.

Ogilvie, Elizabeth. *see* Ogilvie, Elisabeth.

Ogilvie, Lloyd. *see* Ogilvie, Lloyd John.

Ogilvie, Lloyd J. *see* Ogilvie, Lloyd John.

Ogilvie, Lloyd John.
xOgilvie, Lloyd.
Let God Love You. Word Bks.
xOgilvie, Lloyd J.
A Life Full of Surprises. Abingdon.

Ogilvie, M. A. *see* Ogilvie, Malcolm Alexander.

Ogilvie, Malcolm Alexander.
xOgilvie, M. A.
Wild Geese. Buteo.
Ogilvie, R. M. *see* Ogilvie, Robert Maxwell.
Ogilvie, Robert Maxwell.
xOgilvie, R. M.

Early Rome & the Etruscans. Humanities.
Latin & Greek: A History of the Influence of the Classics on English Life from 1600 to 1918. Shoe String.
The Library of Lactantius. Oxford U Pr.
Ogilvy, David, 1911-
xOgilvy, David.
Confessions of an Advertising Man. Atheneum.
Ogilvy, J. D. *see* Ogilvy, Jack David Angus.
Ogilvy, Jack David Angus.
xOgilvy, J. D.
Books Known to the English, 497-1066. Medieval Acad.
Ogilvy, James A.
xOgilvy, James A.
Many Dimensional Man: Decentralizing Self, Society & the Sacred. Oxford U Pr.
Ogle, Arthur, 1871-
xOgle, Arthur.
Canon Law in Mediaeval England: An Examination of William Lyndwood's Provinciale. B Franklin.
Oglesby, Clarkson H. *see* Oglesby, Clarkson Hill.
Oglesby, Clarkson Hill.
xOglesby, Clarkson H.
Highway Engineering. Wiley.
Oglesby, Francis C.
xOglesby, Francis C.
Examination of a Decision Procedure. Am Math.
Oglesby, William B.
xOglesby, William B.
Referral in Pastoral Counseling. Abingdon.
Oglesby, William B. *see* Oglesby, William P.
Oglesby, William P.
xOglesby, William B.
Biblical Themes for Pastoral Care. Abingdon.
Ogletree, Earl J.
xOgletree, Earl J.
Education of the Spanish Speaking Urban Child: A Book of Readings. C C Thomas.
The Unit Plan: A Plan for Curriculum Organizing & Teaching. U Pr of Amer.
Ogul, Morris S., 1931-
xOgul, Morris S.
Congress Oversees the Bureaucracy: Studies in Legislative Supervision. U of Pittsburgh Pr.
Oh, Tai K.
xOh, Tai K.
The Asian Brain Drain: A Factual & Casual Analysis. R & E Res Assoc.
Ohanian, Hans C.
xOhanian, Hans C.
Gravitation & Space Time. Norton.
Ohio College Library Center.
xO.C.L.C.
Design of Formats & Packs of Catalog Cards. Ohio St U Lib.
On-Line Cataloging. Ohio St U Lib.
Ohio Family Historians.
xOhio Family Historians.
Eighteen Thirty Federal Population Census Index of Ohio. Ohio Lib Foun.
Eighteen Twenty Federal Population Census Index of Ohio. Ohio Lib Foun.
Ohio State University. *see* Ohio State University, Bowling Green.
Ohio State University, Bowling Green.
xOhio State University.
Democracy in Transition. Norwood Edns.
Nursing Skills. Reston.
Ohio. State University, Columbus. Research Foundation.
xOhio State University Research Foundation.
Toilet Training: Help for the Delayed Learner. McGraw.
Ohio State University Research Foundation. *see* Ohio. State University, Columbus. Research Foundation.
Ohles, John F.
xOhles, John F.

Introduction to Teaching. Phila Bk Co.
Principles & Practice of Teaching: Selected
Readings. Phila Bk Co.
Ohlin, Bertil. see Ohlin, Bertil Gotthard.

Ohlin, Bertil Gotthard, 1899-
xOhlin, Bertil.
The Problem of Employment Stabilization.
Greenwood.
Ohlsen, M. M. see Ohlsen, Merle M.

Ohlsen, Merle M.
xOhlsen, M. M.
Group Counseling. HR&W.
xOhlsen, Merle M.
Guidance Services in the Modern School.
HarBraceJ.
Marriage Counseling in Groups. Res Press.

Ohlsen, Woodrow.
xOhlsen, Woodrow.
ed. From Paragraph to Essay: Readings for
Progress in Writing. Scribner.
Ohlson, Margaret. see Ohlson, Margaret Alexander.

Ohlson, Margaret Alexander.
xOhlson, Margaret.
Experimental & Therapeutic Dietetics. Burgess.
Ohmann, Richard. see Ohmann, Richard Malin.

Ohmann, Richard Malin.
xOhmann, Richard.
English in America: A Radical View of the
Profession. Oxford U Pr.
English in America: A Radical View of the
Profession. Oxford U Pr.
Ohmer, M. M. see Ohmer, Merlin Maurice.

Ohmer, Merlin Maurice.
xOhmer, M. M.
Mathematics for a Liberal Education. A-W.
Ohno, S. see Ohno, Susumu.

Ohno, Susumu.
xOhno, S.
Evolution by Gene Duplication.
Springer-Verlag.
Major Sex-Determining Genes. Springer-Verlag.

Ohnysty, James.
xOhnysty, James.
Aids to Ethics & Professional Conduct for
Student Radiologic Technologists. C C
Thomas.
Ohringer, Fred. see Ohringer, Frederic.

Ohringer, Frederic.
xOhringer, Fred.
photos by Portrait of the Theatre. Crown.

Ohrling, Staffan.
xOhrling, Staffan.
Rural Change & Spatial Re-Organization in Sri
Lanka: Barriers Against Development of
Traditional Sinhalese Local Communities.
Humanities.
Ohrn, Karin B. see Ohrn, Karin Becker.

Ohrn, Karin Becker, 1946-
xOhrn, Karin B.
Dorothea Lange & the Documentary Tradition.
La State U Pr.

Ohrt, Wallace L.
xOhrt, Wallace L.
The Rogue I Remember. Mountaineers.
Ohto, M. see Ohto, Masao.

Ohto, Masao, 1929-
xOhto, M.
Cholangiography & Pancreatography. Univ
Park.

Oinas, Felix J.
xOinas, Felix J.
The Study of Russian Folklore. Mouton.
Ojakangas, Beatrice. see Ojakangas, Beatrice A.

Ojakangas, Beatrice A.
xOjakangas, Beatrice.
Gourmet Cooking for Two. Crown.
xOjakangas, Beatrice A.
Finnish Cook Book. Crown.

Ojala, Aatos.
xOjala, Aatos.

Aestheticism & Oscar Wilde. R West.

Ojala, Jeanne A.
xOjala, Jeanne A.
Auguste De Colbert: Aristocratic Survival in an
Era of Upheaval, 1793-1809. U of Utah Pr.

Ojetti, Ugo, 1871-1946
xOjetti, Ugo.
As They Seemed to Me. Arno.

**Oji Seminar on Physics of Highly Excited States in
Solid S, Tomakomai, Japan, 1975.**
xOji Seminar, Tomakomai, Japan, Sept. 9-13, 1975.
Physics of Highly Excited States in Solids:
Proceedings. Springer-Verlag.
Oji Seminar, Tomakomai, Japan, Sept. 9-13, 1975. see
Oji Seminar on Physics of Highly Excited States in
Solid S, Tomakomai, Japan, 1975.

Okara, Gabriel, 1921-
xOkara, Gabriel.
The Fisherman's Invocation. Heinemann Ed.

Okasha, Elisabeth.
xOkasha, Elizabeth.
Hand-List of Anglo-Saxon Non-Runic
Inscriptions. Cambridge U Pr.
Okasha, Elizabeth. see Okasha, Elisabeth.

Okazaki, Joji, 1925-
xOkazaki, Joji.
Pure Land Buddhist Painting. Kodansha.
Okazaki, Joji. see Okazaki, J Oji.

Oke, T. R.
xOke, T. R.
Boundary Layer Climates. Methuen Inc.
Okigbo, P. N. see Okigbo, Pius Nwabufo C.
Okigbo, Pius N. see Okigbo, Pius Nwabufo C.

Okigbo, Pius Nwabufo C, 1924-
xOkigbo, P. N.
Nigerian Public Finance. Northwestern U Pr.
xOkigbo, Pius N.
Africa & the Common Market. Northwestern
U Pr.
Okimoto, Jean D. see Okimoto, Jean Davies.

Okimoto, Jean Davies.
xOkimoto, Jean D.
My Mother Is Not Married to My Father.
Putnam.
Okin, Susan M. see Okin, Susan Moller.

Okin, Susan Moller.
xOkin, Susan M.
Women in Western Political Thought.
Princeton U Pr.

Oklahoma. University. Executive Planning Committee.
xUniversity Of Oklahoma Executive Planning
Committee.
Future of the University: A Report to the
People. U of Okla Pr.
Okoli, Ekwueme F. see Okoli, Ekwueme Felix.

Okoli, Ekwueme Felix, 1929-
xOkoli, Ekwueme F.
Institutional Structure & Conflict in Nigeria. U
Pr of Amer.

Okonek, Christian.
xOkonek, Christian.
Vector Bundles on Complex Projective Spaces.
Birkhauser.

Okpaku, Joseph.
xOkpaku, Joseph.
ed. Nigeria, Dilemma of Nationhood: An
African Analysis of the Biafran Conflict.
Greenwood.
ed. Nigeria-Dilemma of Nationhood: An
African Analysis of the Biafran Conflict.
Okpaku Communications.

Okrent, Daniel.
xOkrent, Daniel.
The Ultimate Baseball Book. HM.

Oksenberg, Michel.
xOksenberg, Michel.
ed. Dragon & Eagle: United States-China
Relations: Past & Future. Basic.
Oktavec, Frank L. see Oktavec, Frank Leopold.

Oktavec, Frank Leopold, 1897-
xOktavec, Frank L.
The Professional Education of Special Men
Teachers of Physical Education in Prussia.
AMS Pr.

Okubo, Akira.
xOkubo, Akira.
Oceanic Mixing. Mgmt Info Serv.
Okuma, Thomas M. see Okuma, Thomas Masaji.

Okuma, Thomas Masaji.
xOkuma, Thomas M.
Angola in Ferment: The Background &
Prospects of Angolan Nationalism.
Greenwood.

Okun, Arthur M.
xOkun, Arthur M.
ed. Brookings Papers on Economic Activity.
Brookings.
ed. Curing Chronic Inflation. Brookings.
Okun, Daniel A. see Okun, Daniel Alexander.

Okun, Daniel Alexander.
xOkun, Daniel A.
Regionalization of Water Management: A
Revolution in England & Wales. Burgess-Intl
Ideas.
Okun, M. see Okun, Mitchell.

Okun, Mitchell.
xOkun, M.
The Challenge of America. HR&W.
Okun, S. B. see Okun, Semen Bentsionovich.

Okun, Semen Bentsionovich.
xOkun, S. B.
The Russian-American Company. Octagon.
Okutani, T. see Okutani, Takashi.

Okutani, Takashi.
xOkutani, T.
Systematics, Distribution & Abundance of the
Epiplanktonic Squid. U of Cal Pr.

Okwuosa, V. E. Akubueze.
xOkwuosa, Vincent A.
In the Name of Christianity: The Missionaries
in Africa. Dorrance.
Okwuosa, Vincent A. see Okwuosa, V. E. Akubueze.

Olafson, Frederick A.
xOlafson, Frederick A.
The Dialectic of Action: A Philosophical
Interpretation of History & the Humanities.
U of Chicago Pr.

Olaloku, F. Akin.
xOlaloku, F. Akin.
The Structure of the Nigerian Economy. St
Martin.

Olander, Joseph D.
xOlander, Joseph D.
ed. Arthur C. Clarke. Taplinger.
ed. Criminal Justice Through Science Fiction.
New Viewpoints.

Olbrich, Emil, d. 1906
xOlbrich, Emil.
Development of Sentiment on Negro Suffrage
to 1860. Arno.

Olbricht, Thomas H.
xOlbricht, Thomas H.
Informative Speaking. Scott F.
Olcott, Henry S. see Olcott, Henry Steel.

Olcott, Henry Steel, 1832-1907
xOlcott, Henry S.
Inside the Occult: The True Story of Madame
H. P. Blavatsky. Running Pr.
People from the Other World. C E Tuttle.

Olcott, Jack.
xOlcott, Jack.

Coaching the Quarterback. P-H.
Complete Book of Triple Option Football. P-H.
Complete Guide to the Fifty Defenses in
   Football. P-H.
Football Coach's Guide to Successful Pass
   Defense. P-H.
Football's Seven Best Offenses. P-H.
Old Slave Mart Museum & Library. see Old Slave Mart
   Museum and Library.
Old Slave Mart Museum and Library.
   xOld Slave Mart Museum & Library.
   Catalog of the Old Slave Mart Museum &
      Library. G K Hall.
Oldale, Adrienne.
   xOldale, Adrienne.
   Plant Propagation in Pictures. David & Charles.
Oldenberg, Otto.
   xOldenberg, Otto.
   Introduction to Atomic & Nuclear Physics.
      Krieger.
Oldenburg, Claes, 1929-
   xOldenburg, Claes.
   Injun & Other Histories. Ultramarine Pub.
Oldenburg, E. William.
   xOldenburg, E. William.
   Potawatomi Indian Summer. Eerdmans.
Oldenquist, Andrew.
   xOldenquist, Andrew.
   Moral Philosophy: Text & Readings. HM.
Older, Julia.
   xOlder, Julia.
   The New Hampshire Dining Guide: A
      Compendium of Dining Places of Note &
      Flavorful Recipes Therefrom. Phoenix Pub.
Oldfield, George S.
   xOldfield, George S.
   Implications of Regulation on Bank Expansion:
      A Simulation Analysis. Jai Pr.
Oldfield, Pamela.
   xOldfield, Pamela.
   The Halloween Pumpkin. Childrens.
   Simon's Extra Gran. Childrens.
Oldham, Dale.
   xOldham, Dale.
   Badlands Drifter. Nordon Pubns.
Oldham, Doug.
   xOldham, Doug.
   I Don't Live There Anymore. Impact Tenn.
Oldham, Joseph H. see Oldham, Joseph Houldsworth.
Oldham, Joseph Houldsworth, 1874-1969
   xOldham, Joseph H.
   Christianity & the Race Problem. Negro U Pr.
Oldham, Keith B.
   xOldham, Keith B.
   The Fractional Calculus: Theory &
      Applications, Differentiation & Integration to
      Arbitrary Order. Acad Pr.
Olding, R. K. see Olding, Raymond Knox.
Olding, Raymond Knox, 1929-ed
   xOlding, R. K.
   ed. Readings in Library Cataloguing. Shoe
      String.
Oldman, Oliver. see Oldman, Oliver Sanford.
Oldman, Oliver Sanford.
   xOldman, Oliver.
   Financing Urban Development in Mexico City:
      A Case Study of Property Tax, Land Use,
      Housing, & Urban Planning. Harvard U Pr.
Oldroyd, Harold.
   xOldroyd, Harold.
   Insects & Their World. U of Chicago Pr.
Olds, Carl D. see Olds, Carl Douglas.
Olds, Carl Douglas, 1912-
   xOlds, Carl D.

Continued Fractions. Math Assn.
Olds, Helen (Diehl), 1895-
   xOlds, Helen D.
   Detour for Meg. Archway.
   Detour for Meg. PB.
Olds, Helen D. see Olds, Helen (Diehl).
Olds, James.
   xOlds, James.
   Drives & Reinforcements: Behavioral Studies of
      Hypothalamic Functions. Raven.
Olds, Marshall.
   xOlds, Marshall.
   Analysis of the Interchurch World Movement
      Report on the Steel Strike. Arno.
   Analysis of the Interchurch World Movement
      Report on the Steel Strike. Da Capo.
Olds, R. J.
   xOlds, R. J.
   Color Atlas of Microbiology. Year Bk Med.
Olds, Robert.
   xOlds, Robert.
   Helldiver Squadron: The Story of Carrier
      Bombing Squadron 17 with Task Force 58.
      Zenger Pub.
Olds, Sarah E., 1875-1963
   xOlds, Sarah E.
   Twenty Miles from a Match: Homesteading in
      Western Nevada. U of Nev Pr.
Olds, Sharon.
   xOlds, Sharon.
   Satan Says. U of Pittsburgh Pr.
Olds, W. J. see Olds, Wilbert J.
Olds, Wilbert J.
   xOlds, W. J.
   Lubricants,Cutting Fluids & Coolants. CBI Pub.
Oldsey, Bernard. see Oldsey, Bernard Stanley.
Oldsey, Bernard Stanley, 1923-
   xOldsey, Bernard.
   Hemingway's Hidden Craft: The Writing of "A
      Farewell to Arms". Pa St U Pr.
Oldson, William O., 1940-
   xOldson, William O.
   The Historical & Nationalistic Thought of
      Nicolae Iorga. East Eur Quarterly.
Oleksy, Jerome E.
   xOleksy, Jerome E.
   Practical Solid-State Circuit Design. Sams.
Oleksy, Walter. see Oleksy, Walter G.
Oleksy, Walter G., 1930-
   xOleksy, Walter.
   If I'm Lost, How Come I Found You?.
      McGraw.
   It's Women's Work, Too!. Messner.
   Laugh, Clown, Cry: The Story of Charlie
      Chaplin. Raintree Pubs.
Olendorff, Richard. see Olendorff, Richard R.
Olendorff, Richard R.
   xOlendorff, Richard.
   Golden Eagle Country. Knopf.
Oles, Carole.
   xOles, Carole.
   The Loneliness Factor. Tex Tech Pr.
Olesen, Henning L. see Olesen, Henning Lind.
Olesen, Henning Lind.
   xOlesen, Henning L.
   Radiation Effects on Electronic Systems.
      Plenum Pub.
Olesen, Virginia L.
   xOlesen, Virginia L.
   The Silent Dialogue: A Study in the Social
      Psychology of Professional Socialization.
      Jossey-Bass.
Olesha, Iurii Karlovich, 1899-1960
   xOlesha, Yury.
   No Day Without a Line. Ardis Pubs.
Olesha, Yury. see Olesha, Iurii Karlovich.
Olesker, J. Bradford, 1949-
   xOlesker, J. Bradford.

No Place Like Home. PB.
Oleson, Alexandra.
   xOleson, Alexandra.
   ed. Organization of Knowledge in Modern
      America, 1860-1920. Johns Hopkins.
   ed. The Pursuit of Knowledge in the Early
      American Republic: American Scientific &
      Learned Societies from Colonial Times to the
      Civil War. Johns Hopkins.
Oleson, Karen E.
   xOleson, Karen E.
   Floral Patterns for Needlecraft & the
      Decorative Arts. Van Nos Reinhold.
Olgin, Joseph.
   xOlgin, Joseph.
   Illustrated Football Dictionary for Young
      People. P-H.
   Illustrated Football Dictionary for Young
      People. Harvey.
Olgin, Moissaye J. see Olgin, Moissaye Joseph.
Olgin, Moissaye Joseph, 1874-1939
   xOlgin, Moissaye J.
   Guide to Russian Literature, 1820-1917.
      Russell.
Olien, Michael D.
   xOlien, Michael D.
   The Human Myth: An Introduction to
      Anthropology. Har-Row.
Olin, George.
   xOlin, George.
   House in the Sun. SW Pks Mnmts.
Olin, John C.
   xOlin, John C.
   Six Essays on Erasmus & a Translation of
      Erasmus' Letter to Carondelet 1523.
      Fordham.
Olin, Spencer C.
   xOlin, Spencer C.
   California's Prodigal Sons: Hiram Johnson &
      the Progressives. U of Cal Pr.
Olin, William F., 1979-
   xOlin, William F.
   Escape from Utopia: My Ten Years in
      Synanon. Unity Pr.
Oliner, A. A. see Oliner, Arthur A.
Oliner, Arthur A.
   xOliner, A. A.
   Acoustic Surface Waves. Springer-Verlag.
Oliner, Pearl. see Oliner, Pearl M.
Oliner, Pearl M.
   xOliner, Pearl.
   Teaching Elementary Social Studies: A
      Rational & Humanistic Approach. HarBraceJ.
Olinick, Michael.
   xOlinick, Michael.
   Introduction to Mathematical Models in the
      Social & Life Sciences. A-W.
Olins, Wally.
   xOlins, Wally.
   The Corporate Personality: An Inquiry into the
      Nature of Corporate Identity. Mayflower Bks.
Oliphant, Margaret. see Oliphant, Margaret Oliphant
   Wilson.
Oliphant, Margaret O. see Oliphant, Margaret Oliphant
   Wilson.
Oliphant, Margaret Oliphant Wilson, 1828-1897
   xOliphant, Margaret.
   Memoir of the Life of Laurence Oliphant & of
      Alice Oliphant, His Wife. Arno.
   xOliphant, Margaret O.
   Literary History of England in the End of the
      Eighteenth & Beginning of the Nineteenth
      Century. AMS Pr.
   The Perpetual Curate. Garland Pub.
   Stories of the Seen & the Unseen. Arno.
   xOliphant, Margaret W.
   Cervantes. Folcroft.
Oliphant, Margaret W. see Oliphant, Margaret Oliphant
   Wilson.
Oliva , Peter F. see Oliva, Peter F.

Oliva, Peter F.
xOliva , Peter F.
Supervision for Today's Schools. Har-Row.

Olive, Gloria.
xOlive, Gloria.
Mathematics for Liberal Arts Students. Macmillan.

Oliveira, Antonio Ramos. *see* Ramos Oliveira, Antonio.

Oliver, A. P. *see* Oliver, Arthur Peter Hoblyn.

Oliver, Albert I.
xOliver, Albert I.
Curriculum Improvement: A Guide to Problems, Principles, & Process. Har-Row.

Oliver, Andrew, 1906-
xOliver, Andrew.
Portraits of John & Abigail Adams. Harvard U Pr.
The Portraits of John Marshall. U Pr of Va.
Portraits of John Quincy Adams & His Wife. Harvard U Pr.

Oliver, Arthur Peter Hoblyn.
xOliver, A. P.
Guide to Shells. Times Bks.

Oliver, Dexter.
xOliver, Dexter.
I Want to Be. Third World.

Oliver, Donald W.
xOliver, Donald W.
Education & Community: A Radical Critique of Innovative Schooling. McCutchan.
Teaching Public Issues in the High School. Utah St U Pr.

Oliver, Douglas. *see* Oliver, Douglas L.

Oliver, Douglas L.
xOliver, Douglas.
The Pacific Islands. U Pr of Hawaii.

Oliver, E. J. *see* Oliver, Edward James.

Oliver, Edward James, 1911-
xOliver, E. J.
Honore De Balzac. Macmillan.

Oliver, Ethel R. *see* Oliver, Ethel Ross.

Oliver, Ethel Ross.
xOliver, Ethel R.
Aleutian Boy. Binford.

Oliver, Fay C. *see* Oliver, Fay Conlee.

Oliver, Fay Conlee.
xOliver, Fay C.
Christian Growth Through Meditation. Judson.

Oliver, Frances.
xOliver, Frances.
All Souls: A Family Album. St Martin.
The Tourist Season. Merrimack Bk Serv.

Oliver, Frank J.
xOliver, Frank J.
Practical Relay Circuits. Hayden.

Oliver, Frederick S. *see* Oliver, Frederick Scott.

Oliver, Frederick Scott, 1864-1934
xOliver, Frederick S.
Endless Adventure. AMS Pr.

Oliver, H. J. *see* Oliver, Harold James.

Oliver, H. M. *see* Oliver, Henry Madison.

Oliver, Harold J. *see* Oliver, Harold James.

Oliver, Harold James.
xOliver, H. J.
Problem of John Ford. R West.
xOliver, Harold J.
The Art of E. M. Forster. Folcroft.

Oliver, Henry M. *see* Oliver, Henry Madison.

Oliver, Henry Madison, 1912-
xOliver, H. M.
Critique of Socioeconomic Goals. Kraus Repr.
xOliver, Henry M.
Economic Opinion & Policy in Ceylon. Duke.

Oliver, J. W. *see* Oliver, John Walter.

Oliver, James H. *see* Oliver, James Henry.

Oliver, James Henry.
xOliver, James H.
Civilizing Power: A Study of the Panathenaic Discourse of Aelius Aristides Against the Background of Literature & Cultural Conflict. Am Philos.

Oliver, John E.
xOliver, John E.
Climate & Man's Environment: An Introduction to Applied Climatology. Wiley.

Oliver, John Walter.
xOliver, J. W.
The Life of William Beckford. Folcroft.

Oliver, Lincoln I.
xOliver, Lincoln I.
Association of Health Attitudes & Perceptions for Youths 12-17 Years of Age & Their Parents, United States, 1966-70. Natl Ctr Health Stats.

Oliver, Martha H.
xOliver, Martha H.
Add a Few Sprouts-to Eat Better for Less Money. Keats.

Oliver, Mary. *see* Oliver, Mary Jane.

Oliver, Mary Jane, 1935-
xOliver, Mary.
Twelve Moons. Little.

Oliver, Michael F. *see* Oliver, Michael Francis.

Oliver, Michael Francis.
xOliver, Michael F.
Coronary Heart Disease in Young Women. Churchill.

Oliver, Ray. *see* Oliver, Raymond.

Oliver, Raymond, 1921-
xOliver, Ray.
Principles of the Use of Radioisotope Tracers in Clinical & Research Investigations. Pergamon.

Oliver, Robert S., 1919-
xOliver, Robert S.
The Sketch. Van Nos Reinhold.

Oliver, Robert T. *see* Oliver, Robert Tarbell.

Oliver, Robert Tarbell, 1909-
xOliver, Robert T.
History of Public Speaking in America. Greenwood.

Oliver, Samuel P. *see* Oliver, Samuel Pasfield.

Oliver, Samuel Pasfield, 1838-1907
xOliver, Samuel P.
True Story of the French Dispute in Madagascar. Negro U Pr.

Oliver, Stanley.
xOliver, Stanley.
ed. Accountants Guide to Management Techniques. Herman Pub.

Oliver, W. H. *see* Oliver, William Hosking.

Oliver, William Hosking.
xOliver, W. H.
Prophets & Millennialists: The Uses of Biblical Prophecy in England from the 1790s to the 1840s. Oxford U Pr.

Oliver Brachfeld, F.
xOliver Brachfeld, F.
Inferiority Feelings in the Individual & the Group. Greenwood.

Oliverio, A. *see* Oliverio, Alberto.

Oliverio, Alberto.
xOliverio, A.
ed. Genetics, Environment & Intelligence. Elsevier.

Olivero, Federico, 1878-
xOlivero, Federico.
Edgar Allan Poe. AMS Pr.

Olivero, James L.
xOlivero, James L.
ed. Educational Manpower: From Aides to Differentiated Staff Patterns. Ind U Pr.

Oliveroff, Andre.
xOliveroff, Andre.
Flight of the Swan: A Memory of Anna Pavlova. Da Capo.

Olivier, Sydney H. *see* Olivier, Sydney Haldane Olivier.

Olivier, Sydney Haldane Olivier, Baron, 1859-1943
xOlivier, Sydney H.
White Capital & Coloured Labour. Negro U Pr.
White Capital & Coloured Labour. Russell.

Olivieri, Joseph B.
xOlivieri, Joseph B.
How to Design Heating-Cooling Comfort Systems. Busn News.

Olivo. *see* Olivo, C. Thomas.

Olivo, C. Thomas.
xOlivo.
Basic Blueprint Reading & Sketching. Delmar.
xOlivo, C. Thomas.
Basic Blueprint Reading & Sketching. Van Nos Reinhold.
Fundamentals of Applied Physics. Delmar.
xOlivo, Thomas P.
jt. auth. Basic Blueprint Reading & Sketching. Van Nos Reinhold.
jt. auth. Fundamentals of Applied Physics. Delmar.

Olivo, Thomas P. *see* Olivo, C. Thomas.

Olken, Ilene T.
xOlken, Ilene T.
ed. Racconti Del Novecento: Forti E. Deboli. P-H.

Olkhovsky, Andrey. *see* Olkhovsky, Andrey Vasilyevich.

Olkhovsky, Andrey Vasilyevich, 1900-
xOlkhovsky, Andrey.
Music Under the Soviets: The Agony of an Art. Greenwood.

Olkin, Ingram.
xOlkin, Ingram.
ed. Contributions to Probability & Statistics: Essays in Honor of Harold Hotelling. Stanford U Pr.
Probability Models & Applications. Macmillan.

Ollard, Richard. *see* Ollard, Richard Lawrence.

Ollard, Richard Lawrence.
xOllard, Richard.
The Image of the King: A Biography of Charles I & Charles II. Atheneum.

Olle, James G. *see* Olle, James Gordon Herbert.

Olle, James Gordon Herbert.
xOlle, James G.
Library History. K G Saur.

Ollen, Gunnar, 1913-
xOllen, Gunnar.
August Strindberg. Ungar.

Oller, John. *see* Oller, John W.

Oller, John W.
xOller, John.
Research in Language Testing. Newbury Hse.

Ollier, Claude.
xOllier, Claude.
Law & Order. Red Dust.

Olliver, Jane.
xOlliver, Jane.
ed. The Living World. Watts.

Olmos, Ralph A.
xOlmos, Ralph A.
An Introduction to Police-Community Relations: A Guide for the Pre-Service Student & Practicing Police Officer. C C Thomas.

Olmstead, A. T. *see* Olmstead, Albert Ten Eyck.

Olmstead, Alan H.
xOlmstead, Alan H.
In Praise of Seasons. Har-Row.

Olmstead, Albert Ten Eyck, 1880- 1945
xOlmstead, A. T.
History of Assyria. U of Chicago Pr.
xOlmstead, Arthur T.
History of the Persian Empire. U of Chicago Pr.

Olmstead, Arthur T. *see* Olmstead, Albert Ten Eyck.

Olmsted, D. L. *see* Olmsted, David Lockwood.

Olmsted, David Lockwood, 1926-
  xOlmsted, D. L.
    A History of Palaihnihan Phonology. U of Cal
      Pr.
Olmsted, Denison, 1791-1859
  xOlmsted, Denison.
    Memoir of Eli Whitney, Esq.. Arno.
Olmsted, Elizabeth H.
  xOlmsted, Elizabeth H.
    ed. Music Library Association Catalog of Cards
      for Printed Music, 1953-1972: A Supplement
      to the Library of Congress Catalogs.
      Rowman.
Olmsted, Frederick L. *see* Olmsted, Frederick Law.
Olmsted, Frederick Law, 1822-1903
  xOlmsted, Frederick L.
    Journey in the Back Country. B Franklin.
    Journey in the Seaboard Slave States, with
      Remarks on Their Economy. Negro U Pr.
    Public Parks & the Enlargement of Towns.
      Arno.
Olmsted, John.
  xOlmsted, John C.
    Victorian Novel Illustration: A Selected
      Checklist 1900-1976. Garland Pub.
Olmsted, John C. *see* Olmsted, John.
Olmsted, John M. *see* Olmsted, John Meigs Hubbell.
Olmsted, John Meigs Hubbell, 1911-
  xOlmsted, John M.
    Advanced Calculus. P-H.
    Calculus with Analytic Geometry. Irvington.
    Intermediate Analysis: An Introduction to
      Theory of Functions of One Real Variable.
      Irvington.
    Prelude to Calculus & Linear Algebra.
      Irvington.
Olmsted, Lorena A. *see* Olmsted, Lorena Ann.
Olmsted, Lorena Ann.
  xOlmsted, Lorena A.
    Journey to Adventure. Bouregy.
  xOlmsted, Lorena Ann.
    Dangerous Memory. Bouregy.
Olmsted, Robert P.
  xOlmsted, Robert P.
    Prairie Rails. McMillan.
Olness, Karen.
  xOlness, Karen.
    Raising Happy, Healthy Children.
      Meadowbrook Pr.
Olney, James.
  xOlney, James.
    The Rhizome & the Flower: The Perennial
      Philosophy--Yeats & Jung. U of Cal Pr.
Olney, Judith.
  xOlney, Judith.
    Comforting Food. Atheneum.
    Summer Food. Atheneum.
Olney, Julian.
  xOlney, Julian.
    Beyond Broadway. Dorrance.
Olney, Richard.
  xOlney, Richard.
    illus. Simple French Food. Atheneum.
Olney, Ross.
  xOlney, Ross.
    Football. Western Pub.
    Hockey. Western Pub.
Olorunsola, Victor A., 1939-
  xOlorunsola, Victor A.
    Soldiers & Power: The Development
      Performance of the Nigerian Military
      Regime. Hoover Inst Pr.
Olschki, Leonardo.
  xOlschki, Leonardo.
    Marco Polo's Asia: An Introduction to His
      "Description of the World" Called "Il
      Milione". U of Cal Pr.
    Marco Polo's Precursors. Octagon.
Olsen, Alfa-Betty.
  xOlsen, Alfa-Betty.

    Omnivores: They Said They Would Eat
      Anything--& They Did. Viking Pr.
Olsen, Austin.
  xOlsen, Austin.
    Corcho Bliss. S&S.
Olsen, Don.
  xOlsen, Don.
    Nature's Candles. A S Barnes.
Olsen, Donald J.
  xOlsen, Donald J.
    The Growth of Victorian London. Holmes &
      Meier.
Olsen, E. A. *see* Olsen, Einar A.
Olsen, Edward G. *see* Olsen, Edward Gustave.
Olsen, Edward Gustave.
  xOlsen, Edward G.
    Life-Centering Education. Pendell Pub.
Olsen, Einar A.
  xOlsen, E. A.
    Adrift on a Raft. Oddo.
    Lobster King. Oddo.
Olsen, Evelyn G. *see* Olsen, Evelyn Guard.
Olsen, Evelyn Guard.
  xOlsen, Evelyn G.
    Indian Blood. McClain.
Olsen, Fred, 1891-
  xOlsen, Fred.
    On the Trail of the Arawaks. U of Okla Pr.
Olsen, George H. *see* Olsen, George Henry.
Olsen, George Henry.
  xOlsen, George H.
    The Beginner's Handbook of Electronics. P-H.
Olsen, Hans C. *see* Olsen, Hans Christian.
Olsen, Hans Christian, 1892-
  xOlsen, Hans C.
    The Work of Boards of Education. AMS Pr.
Olsen, Ib S. *see* Olsen, Ib Spang.
Olsen, Ib Spang.
  xOlsen, Ib S.
    tr. The Boy in the Moon. Schol Bk Serv.
Olsen, Jack.
  xOlsen, Jack.
    The Girls in the Office. PB.
    Night of the Grizzlies. NAL.
Olsen, James T.
  xOlsen, James T.
    Aretha Franklin. Creative Ed.
Olsen, Larry D. *see* Olsen, Larry Dean.
Olsen, Larry Dean, 1939-
  xOlsen, Larry D.
    Outdoor Survival Skills. Brigham.
    Outdoor Survival Skills. PB.
Olsen, M. *see* Olsen, Marvin Elliott.
Olsen, M. E. *see* Olsen, Marvin Elliott.
Olsen, Mahlon E. *see* Olsen, Mahlon Ellsworth.
Olsen, Mahlon Ellsworth, 1873-1952
  xOlsen, Mahlon E.
    History of the Origin & Progress of
      Seventh-Day Adventists. AMS Pr.
Olsen, Marvin Elliott.
  xOlsen, M.
    The Process of Social Organization: Power in
      Social Systems. HR&W.
  xOlsen, M. E.
    Power in Societies. Macmillan.
Olsen, Otto H.
  xOlsen, Otto H.
    Carpetbagger's Crusade: The Life of Albion
      Winegar Tourgee. Johns Hopkins.
Olsen, Richard G.
  xOlsen, Richard G.
    Immunology & Immunopathology of Domestic
      Animals. C C Thomas.
Olsen, Stanley J. *see* Olsen, Stanley John.
Olsen, Stanley John, 1919-
  xOlsen, Stanley J.
    Osteology for the Archaeologist. Peabody
      Harvard.
Olsen, Stein H. *see* Olsen, Stein Haugom.

Olsen, Stein Haugom, 1946-
  xOlsen, Stein H.
    The Structure of Literary Understanding.
      Cambridge U Pr.
Olsen, T. V.
  xOlsen, T. V.
    Canyon of the Gun. Fawcett.
Olsen, Tillie.
  xOlsen, Tillie.
    Silences. Delacorte.
Olsen, Udia G.
  xOlsen, Udia G.
    Preparing the Manuscript. Writer.
Olshaker, Bennett, 1921-
  xOlshaker, Bennett.
    What Shall We Tell the Kids?. Arbor Hse.
Olshavsky, Richard W., 1941-
  xOlshavsky, Richard W.
    No More Butts: A Psychologist's Approach to
      Quitting Cigarettes. Ind U Pr.
Olshen, Barry N.
  xOlshen, Barry N.
    John Fowles. Ungar.
Olson. *see* Olson, Bruce.
Olson, Adolf, 1886-
  xOlson, Adolf.
    A Centenary History As Related to the Baptist
      General Conference of America. Arno.
Olson, Alden C.
  xOlson, Alden C.
    Impact of Valuation Requirements on the
      Preferred Stock Investment Policies of Life
      Insurance Companies. Mich St U Busn.
Olson, Alfred. *see* Olson, Alfred C.
Olson, Alfred C.
  xOlson, Alfred.
    ed. Immobilized Enzymes in Food & Microbial
      Processes. Plenum Pub.
Olson, Alton T.
  xOlson, Alton T.
    Mathematics Through Paper Folding. NCTM.
Olson, Bruce.
  xOlson.
    Bruchko. Creation Hse.
Olson, C. L.
  xOlson, C. L.
    Collective Ion Acceleration. Springer-Verlag.
Olson, Charles, 1910-1970
  xOlson, Charles.
    Call Me Ishmael. City Lights.
    Maximus Poems. Corinth Bks.
    Special View of History. SBD.
  xOlson, Charles F.
    Additional Prose: A Bibliography on America,
      Proprioception & Other Notes & Essays.
      Four Seasons Foun.
Olson, Charles E.
  xOlson, Charles E.
    Cost Considerations for Efficient Electricity
      Supply. Mich St U Busn.
Olson, Charles F. *see* Olson, Charles.
Olson, Clarinda E.
  xOlson, Clarinda E.
    Basic Science for Dental Auxiliaries. P-H.
Olson, David C. *see* Olson, David C. B.
Olson, David C. B., 1904-
  xOlson, David C.
    Life on the Upper Michigan Frontier. Branden.
Olson, David H. *see* Olson, David H.L.
Olson, David H.L.
  xOlson, David H.
    ed. Inventory of Marriage & Family Literature.
      Sage.
Olson, David J.
  xOlson, David J.
    Governing the United States: To Keep the
      Republic in Its Third Century. McGraw.
Olson, David R.
  xOlson, David R.

Cognitive Development: The Childs
Acquisition of Diagonality. Acad Pr.
ed. Media & Symbols: The Forms of
Expression, Communication, & Education. U
of Chicago Pr.
Olson, Dean F. *see* Olson, Dean Francis.
Olson, Dean Francis.
xOlson, Dean F.
Alaska Reindeer Herdsmen: A Study of Native
Management in Transition. U of Wash Pr.
Olson, Donald.
xOlson, Donald.
Sleep Before Evening. St Martin.
Olson, Elder, 1909-
xOlson, Elder.
ed. Aristotle's Poetics & English Literature: A
Collection of Critical Essays. U of Chicago
Pr.
Collected Poems. U of Chicago Pr.
Olson, Ernst W. *see* Olson, Ernst Wilhelm.
Olson, Ernst Wilhelm.
xOlson, Ernst W.
History of the Swedes of Illinois. Arno.
Olson, Everett C. *see* Olson, Everett Claire.
Olson, Everett Claire.
xOlson, Everett C.
Concepts of Evolution. Merrill.
Olson, Gene, 1922-
xOlson, Gene.
Bailey & the Bearcat. Westminster.
Drop into Hell. Westminster.
Pistons & Powderpuffs. Westminster.

Olson, Gloria. *see* Olson, Gloria Preston.

Olson, Gloria P. *see* Olson, Gloria Preston.

Olson, Gloria Preston, 1933-
xOlson, Gloria.
Culinary Classics. Sherbourne.
xOlson, Gloria P.
Culinary Classics. Sherbourne.

Olson, Harry A., 1944-
xOlson, Harry A.
Early Recollections: Their Use in Diagnosis &
Psychotherapy. C C Thomas.

Olson, Harry E., 1934-
xOlson, Harry E.
Monday Morning Christianity. Augsburg.
Physician Recruitment & the Hospital. Am
Hospital.

Olson, James S. *see* Olson, James Stuart.

Olson, James Stuart, 1946-
xOlson, James S.
The Ethnic Dimension in American History. St
Martin.

Olson, Joan.
xOlson, Joan.
California Times & Trails. Windyridge.
Olson, Joanne P.
xOlson, Joanne P.
Learning to Teach Reading in the Elementary
School: Utilizing the Competency Based
Instructional System. Macmillan.
Olson, Ken.
xOlson, Ken.
Can You Wait till Friday?: The Psychology of
Hope. Fawcett.
Olson, Lois E. *see* Olson, Lois Ellen.
Olson, Lois Ellen, 1941-
xOlson, Lois E.
Meeting Him in the Wilderness: A True Story
of Adventure & Faith. Doubleday.
Olson, Lynn.
xOlson, Lynn.
Classroom-Tested Techniques for Elementary
Teachers. Ctr Appl Res.
Olson, Mancur, Jr.
xOlson, Mancur.

Logic of Collective Action: Public Goods & the
Theory of Groups. Harvard U Pr.
Olson, Mckinley C.
xOlson, McKinley C.
Unacceptable Risk: The Nuclear Power
Controversy. Bantam.
Olson, Michael L.
xOlson, Michael L.
Barai Sentence Structure & Embedding.
Summer Inst Ling.
Olson, Nancy B.
xOlson, Nancy B.
ed. Combined Indexes to the Library of
Congress Classification Schedules. US Hist
Doc.
ed. Library of Congress Classification Number
Index to the MARC Data Base, 1968-1978.
Carrollton Pr.
Olson, Nat. *see* Olson, Nathanael.
Olson, Nathanael.
xOlson, Nat.
How to Win Your Family to Christ. Good
News.
Olson, O. Charles, 1913-
xOlson, O. Charles.
Prevention of Football Injuries: Protecting the
Health of the Student Athlete. Lea &
Febiger.
Olson, Paul R. *see* Olson, Paul Richard.
Olson, Paul Richard.
xOlson, Paul R.
Circle of Paradox: Time & Essence in the
Poetry of Juan Ramon Jimenez. Johns
Hopkins.
Olson, Raymond E.
xOlson, Raymond E.
ed. Contemporary Philosophy in Scandinavia.
Johns Hopkins.
Olson, Reuben M.
xOlson, Reuben M.
Essentials of Engineering Fluid Mechanics.
Har-Row.
Olson, Robert E.
xOlson, Robert E.
ed. Protein-Calorie Malnutrition. Acad Pr.
Olson, Robert G. *see* Olson, Robert Goodwin.
Olson, Robert Goodwin, 1924-
xOlson, Robert G.
Ethics: A Short Introduction. Random.
Introduction to Existentialism. Dover.
An Introduction to Existentialism. Peter Smith.
Meaning & Argument: Elements of Logic.
HarBraceJ.
Olson, Selma.
xOlson, Selma.
Ana Mistral. Double M Pr.
Olson, Sheldon R., 1944-
xOlson, Sheldon R.
Ideas & Data: The Process & Practice of Social
Research. Dorsey.
Olson, Sherry. *see* Olson, Sherry H.
Olson, Sherry H.
xOlson, Sherry.
Baltimore. Ballinger Pub.
xOlson, Sherry H.
Depletion Myth: A History of Railroad Use of
Timber. Harvard U Pr.
Olson, Sigurd F.
xOlson, Sigurd F.
The Hidden Forest. Penguin.
Open Horizons. Knopf.
Sigurd F. Olson's Wilderness Days. Knopf.
Olson, Ted, 1899-
xOlson, Ted.
Stranger & Afraid. AMS Pr.
Olson, Toby.
xOlson, Toby.
Home. Membrane Pr.
Olson, Virgil J.
xOlson, Virgil J.

Capitol Reef: The Story Behind the Scenery. K
C Pubns.
Olson, W. G. *see* Olson, William George.
Olson, W. P. *see* Olson, Willard Paul.
Olson, Willard C. *see* Olson, Willard Clifford.
Olson, Willard Clifford, 1899-
xOlson, Willard C.
The Measurement of Nervous Habits in
Normal Children. Greenwood.
Olson, Willard Paul, 1939-
xOlson, W. P.
ed. Quantitative Modeling of Magnetospheric
Processes. Am Geophysical.
Olson, William George.
xOlson, W. G.
Charismatic Church. Bethany Fell.
Olsson, Axel A. *see* Olsson, Axel Adolf.
Olsson, Axel Adolf.
xOlsson, Axel A.
Neogene Mollusks from Northwestern
Ecuador. Paleo Res.
Some Tertiary Mollusks from South Florida &
the Caribbean. Paleo Res.
Olsson, Karl A.
xOlsson, Karl A.
By One Spirit. Covenant.
Find Your Self in the Bible: A Guide to
Relational Bible Study for Small Groups.
Augsburg.
Meet Me on the Patio: New Relational Bible
Studies for Individuals & Groups. Augsburg.
Olsson, Margareta, 1927-
xOlsson, Margareta.
Intelligibility: An Evaluation of Some Features
of English Produced by Swedish 14 Years
Olds. Humanities.
Olsson, Sten Erik.
xOlsson, Sten-Erik.
Radiological Diagnosis in Canine & Feline
Emergencies: An Atlas of Thoracic &
Abdominal Changes. Lea & Febiger.
Olsson, Sten-Erik. *see* Olsson, Sten Erik.
Olstad, Charles.
xOlstad, Charles.
Creative Spanish. Har-Row.
Olszowy, Damon R.
xOlszowy, Damon R.
Horticulture for the Disabled & Disadvantaged.
C C Thomas.
Olton, Charles S., 1938-
xOlton, Charles S.
Artisans for Independence: Philadelphia
Mechanics & the American Revolution.
Syracuse U Pr.
Olton, D. *see* Olton, David S.
Olton, David S.
xOlton, D.
Biofeedback: Clinical Applications in
Behavioral Medicine. P-H.
Oltorf, Frank C. *see* Oltorf, Frank Calvert.
Oltorf, Frank Calvert.
xOltorf, Frank C.
Marlin Compound: Letters of a Singular
Family. U of Tex Pr.
Oltrogge, David.
xOltrogge, David.
Two Studies in Middle American Comparative
Linguistics. Summer Inst Ling.
Olver, F. W. *see* Olver, Frank W. J.
Olver, Frank W. J., 1924-
xOlver, F. W.
Introduction to Asymptotics & Special
Functions. Acad Pr.
Olwell, C. *see* Olwell, Carol.
Olwell, Carol.
xOlwell, C.
A Gift to the Street. Antelope Island.
Olweus, Dan, 1931-
xOlweus, Dan.

Aggression in the Schools: Bullies & Whipping Boys. Halsted Pr.

Olyanova, Nadya.
xOlyanova, Nadya.
Psychology of Handwriting. Wilshire.

Olympic Mountain Rescue. *see* Olympic Mountain Rescue (Society).

Olympic Mountain Rescue (Society).
xOlympic Mountain Rescue.
Climber's Guide to the Olympic Mountains. Mountaineers.

Olynyk, Roman.
xOlynyk, Stephen D.
In Defense of the Ukrainian Cause. Chris Mass.

Olynyk, Stephen D. *see* Olynyk, Roman.

Olyslager Organisation.
xOlyslager Organisation.
Commercial Vehicles. Intl Pubns Serv.
Military Wheeled Vehicles. Intl Pubns Serv.
xOlyslager Organization.
American Cars of the 1930's. Warne.
American Cars of the 1940's. Warne.
American Cars of the 1950's. Warne.
American Cars of the 1960's. Warne.
American Trucks of the Early Thirties. Warne.
American Trucks of the Late Thirties. Warne.
Armour on Wheels to Nineteen Forty-Two. Warne.
British Cars of the Early Fifties. Warne.
British Cars of the Late Forties. Warne.
British Cars of the Late Thirties. Warne.
Buses & Coaches from 1940. Warne.
Cross Country Cars from 1945. Warne.
Earth Movers. Warne.
Fairground & Circus Transport. Warne.
Fire & Crash Tenders from 1950. Warne.
Fire Fighting Vehicles. Warne.
Half-Tracks. Warne.
Jeep. A Pictorial History. Warne.
Motorcycles & Scooters from 1945. Warne.
Motorcycles Pre-1945. Warne.
The Observer's Book of Automobiles. Scribner.
Passenger Vehicles: 1893-1940. Warne.
Scammell Vehicles. Warne.
Tanks & Transport Vehicles of World War Two. Warne.
Wrecker & Recovery Vehicles. Warne.

Olyslager Organization. *see* Olyslager Organisation.

Olzendam, Roderic Marble.
xOlzendam, Roderick M.
It Came to Pass in the San Juan Islands. Binford.

Olzendam, Roderick M. *see* Olzendam, Roderic Marble.

Omaggio, Alice C.
xOmaggio, Alice C.
Games & Simulations in the Foreign Language Classroom. Ctr Appl Ling.

Oman, Charles. *see* Oman, Charles William Chadwick.

Oman, Charles Chichele, 1901
xOman, Charles.
English Engraved Silver. Merrimack Bk Serv.

Oman, Charles W. *see* Oman, Charles William Chadwick.

Oman, Charles William Chadwick, Sir, 1860-1946
xOman, Charles.
History of England. Arno.
xOman, Charles W.
A History of the Art of War in the Sixteenth Century. AMS Pr.
Unfortunate Colonel Despard & Other Studies. B Franklin.

Oman, John W. *see* Oman, John Wood.

Oman, John Wood, 1860-1939
xOman, John W.
The Natural & the Supernatural. Arno.

Oman, Robert M.
xOman, Robert M.

An Introduction to Radiologic Science. McGraw.

Omarr, Sydney.
xOmarr, Sydney.
Sydney Omarr's Astrological Guide for You in 1981. NAL.

Omeltchenko, Stephen. *see* Omeltchenko, Stephen William.

Omeltchenko, Stephen William.
xOmeltchenko, Stephen.
A Quantitative & Comparative Study of the Vocalism of the Latin Inscriptions of North American, Britain, Dalmatia, & the Balkans. U of NC Pr.

Omer, George E.
xOmer, George E.
Management of Peripheral Nerve Problems. Saunders.

Omer, Jane. *see* Omer, Jane L.

Omer, Jane L.
xOmer, Jane.
Evaluating the Audiogram. Interstate.

Omholt, A. *see* Omholt, Anders.

Omholt, Anders.
xOmholt, A.
Optical Aurora. Springer-Verlag.

Ominde, S. H. *see* Ominde, Simeon H.

Ominde, Simeon H.
xOminde, S. H.
ed. Studies in East African Geography & Development. U of Cal Pr.

Ominsky, Elaine.
xOminsky, Elaine.
Jon O: A Special Boy. P-H.

Ommanney, F. D. *see* Ommanney, Francis Downes.

Ommanney, Francis Downes.
xOmmanney, F. D.
Frogs, Toads & Newts. McGraw.

Omori, Annie S. *see* Omori, Annie Shepley.

Omori, Annie Shepley.
xOmori, Annie S.
tr. Diaries of Court Ladies of Old Japan. AMS Pr.

Omran , Abdel R. *see* Omran, Abdel R.

Omran, Abdel R.
xOmran , Abdel R.
ed. Liberalization of Abortion Laws: Implications. Carolina Pop Ctr.
xOmran, Abdel R.
ed. Community Medicine in Developing Countries. Springer Pub.

Omrcanin, Ivo.
xOmrcanin, Ivo.
Diplomatic & Political History of Croatia. Dorrance.
Economic Wealth of Croatia. Dorrance.

On, D. *see* On, Danny.

On, Danny.
xOn, D.
Plants of Waterton-Glacier National Parks. Mountain Pr.

Onak, Thomas.
xOnak, Thomas.
Organoborane Chemistry. Acad Pr.

Onate, Andres D., 1940-
xOnate, Andres D.
Chairman Mao & the Chinese Communist Party. Nelson-Hall.

Ondaatje, Michael, 1943-
xOndaatje, Michael.
The Collected Works of Billy the Kid. Norton.
The Collected Works of Billy the Kid. Wingbow Pr.
Coming Through Slaughter. Avon.
Coming Through Slaughter. Norton.

Onderdonk, Henry, 1804-1886
xOnderdonk, Henry.

Documents & Letters Intended to Illustrate the Revolutionary Incidents of Queens County. Friedman.

Oneal, James, 1875-
xOneal, James.
Workers in American History. Arno.

Oneal, Zibby.
xOneal, Zibby.
The Language of Goldfish. Viking Pr.
Turtle & Snail. Lippincott.

Oneida Community. *see* Oneida, Ltd.

Oneida, Ltd.
xOneida Community.
Annual Report: 1848-1851. AMS Pr.
Bible Communism. Porcupine Pr.
Bible Communism: A Compilation from the Annual Reports & Other Publications of the Oneida Association & Its Branches. AMS Pr.

Onesti, Gaddo.
xOnesti, Gaddo.
Hypertension: Mechanisms, Diagnosis & Treatment. Davis Co.

Onetti, Juan C. *see* Onetti, Juan Carlos.

Onetti, Juan Carlos, 1909-
xOnetti, Juan C.
A Brief Life. Viking Pr.

Ong, Walter J.
xOng, Walter J.
The Presence of the Word: Some Prolegomena for Cultural & Religious History. Yale U Pr.

Oniciu, L. *see* Oniciu, Liviu.

Oniciu, Liviu.
xOniciu, L.
Fuel Cells. Intl Schol Bk Serv.

Onions, Charles T. *see* Onions, Charles Talbut.

Onions, Charles Talbut.
xOnions, Charles T.
ed. Oxford Dictionary of English Etymology. Oxford U Pr.

Onions, Oliver, Pseud.
xOnions, Oliver.
In Accordance with Evidence. Garland Pub.

Onoda, George Y.
xOnoda, George Y.
ed. Ceramic Processing Before Firing. Wiley.

Onoda, Hiroo.
xOnoda, Hiroo.
No Surrender: My Thirty-Year War. Kodansha.

Onopa, Robert.
xOnopa, Robert.
The Pleasure Tube. Berkley Pub.

Onorato, Richard J.
xOnorato, Richard J.
Character of the Poet: Wordsworth in the Prelude. Princeton U Pr.

Onosko, Tim.
xOnosko, Tim.
Wasn't the Future Wonderful?: A View of Trends & Technology from the 1930's. Dutton.

Onstad, Esther.
xOnstad, Esther.
Courage for Today - Hope for Tomorrow: A Study of the Revelation. Augsburg.

Onstott, Kyle, 1886-
xOnstott, Kyle.
Drum. Fawcett.
Master of Falconhurst. Fawcett.

Ooms, Herman.
xOoms, Herman.
Charismatic Bureaucrat: A Political Biography of Matsudaira Sadanobu, 1758-1829. U of Chicago Pr.

Oort, F.
xOort, F.
Commutative Group Schemes. Springer-Verlag.

Oost, Stewart I. *see* Oost, Stewart Irvin.

Oost, Stewart Irvin, 1922-
xOost, Stewart I.

Galla Placidia Augusta: A Biographical Essay.
U of Chicago Pr.

Oosterhuis, Huub.
xOosterhuis, Huub.
Open Your Hearts. Seabury.

Oosting, Henry J. see Oosting, Henry John.

Oosting, Henry John, 1903-
xOosting, Henry J.
The Study of Plant Communities: An
Introduction to Plant Ecology. W H
Freeman.

Oparin, A. I. see Oparin, Aleksandr Ivanovich.

Oparin, Aleksandr Ivanovich, 1894-
xOparin, A. I.
Genesis & Evolutionary Development of Life.
Acad Pr.
The Origin of Life. Gannon.
xOparin, Alexander I.
Origin of Life. Dover.

Oparin, Alexander I. see Oparin, Aleksandr Ivanovich.

OPEC (Organization of Petroleum Exporting
Companies). see Organization of Petroleum Exporting
Countries.

Openshaw, Howard.
xOpenshaw, Howard.
Race & Residence: An Analysis of Property
Values in Transitional Areas, Atlanta,
Georgia, 1960-1971. Ga St U Busn Pub.

Operations Research Group. see Operations Research,
Inc.

Operations Research, Inc.
xOperations Research Group.
India in Perspective: Development Issues.
Verry.

Ophthalmic Microsurgery Study Group.
xSymposium of the Ophthalmic Microsurgery
Study Group, 2nd, Buergenstock, 1968.
Microsurgery in Glaucoma: Proceedings. S
Karger.
Microsurgery of Cataract, Vitreous &
Astigmatism. S Karger.

Ophuls, William, 1934-
xOphuls, William.
Ecology & the Politics of Scarcity: Prologue to
a Political Theory of Steady State. W H
Freeman.

Opie, Amelia A. see Opie, Amelia Alderson.

Opie, Amelia Alderson, 1769-1853
xOpie, Amelia A.
Memorials of the Life of Amelia Opie. AMS
Pr.

Opie, Iona. see Opie, Iona Archibald.

Opie, Iona Archibald.
xOpie, Iona.
Lore & Language of School Children. Oxford
U Pr.
ed. Oxford Dictionary of Nursery Rhymes.
Oxford U Pr.
ed. Oxford Nursery Rhyme Book. Oxford U
Pr.

Opie, Robert. see Opie, Robert T.

Opie, Robert T.
xOpie, Robert.
Rev'rund, Get Your Gun. Creation Hse.

Opler, M. E. see Opler, Morris Edward.

Opler, Morris E. see Opler, Morris Edward.

Opler, Morris Edward, 1907-
xOpler, M. E.
Childhood & Youth in Jicarilla Apache Society.
Southwest Mus.
xOpler, Morris E.
Childhood & Youth in Jicarilla Apache Society.
AMS Pr.

Oppe, T. E. see Oppe, Thomas Ernest.

Oppe, Thomas Ernest.
xOppe, T. E.
ed. Early Management of Handicapping
Disorders. Elsevier.

Oppen, George.
xOppen, George.

Of Being Numerous. New Directions.

Oppenheim, A. see Oppenheim, Alan V.

Oppenheim, A. K.
xOppenheim, A. K.
Impact of Aerospace Technology on Studies of
the Earth's Atmosphere. Pergamon.

Oppenheim, A. Leo, 1904-
xOppenheim, A. Leo.
Ancient Mesopotamia: Portrait of a Dead
Civilization. U of Chicago Pr.
Letters from Mesopotamia: Official, Business,
& Private Letters on Clay Tablets from Two
Millennia. U of Chicago Pr.

Oppenheim, Abraham N. see Oppenheim, Abraham
Naftali.

Oppenheim, Abraham Naftali, 1924-
xOppenheim, Abraham N.
Questionnaire Design & Attitude Measurement.
Basic.

Oppenheim, Alan V., 1937-
xOppenheim, A.
Applications of Digital Signal Processing. P-H.
xOppenheim, Alan V.
Digital Signal Processing. P-H.

Oppenheim, E. Phillips. see Oppenheim, Edward Phillips.

Oppenheim, Edward P. see Oppenheim, Edward Phillips.

Oppenheim, Edward Phillips, 1866-1946
xOppenheim, E. Phillips.
The Great Impersonation. Dover.
xOppenheim, Edward P.
Ask Miss Mott. Arno.

Oppenheim, Felix. see Oppenheim, Felix E.

Oppenheim, Felix E., 1913-
xOppenheim, Felix.
Moral Principles in Political Philosophy. Phila
Bk Co.

Oppenheim, Frank M., 1925-
xOppenheim, Frank M.
Royces Voyage Down Under: A Journey of the
Mind. U Pr of Ky.

Oppenheim, Irene.
xOppenheim, Irene.
Consumer Skills. Bennett Co.

Oppenheim, James, 1882-1932
xOppenheim, James.
Pay Envelopes: Tales of the Mill, the Mine &
the City Street. Arno.

Oppenheim, Joanne.
xOppenheim, Joanne.
Black Hawk, Frontier Warrior. Troll Assocs.
Mrs. Peloki's Snake. Dodd.

Oppenheim, Micha F. see Oppenheim, Micha Falk.

Oppenheim, Micha Falk.
xOppenheim, Micha F.
The Study & Practice of Judaism: A Selected,
Annotated List. Torah Res.

Oppenheim, Norbert.
xOppenheim, Norbert.
Applied Models in Urban & Regional Analysis.
P-H.

Oppenheim, S. Chesterfield. see Oppenheim, Saul
Chesterfield.

Oppenheim, Saul Chesterfield.
xOppenheim, S. Chesterfield.
ed. The Lawyer's Robinson-Patman Act
Sourcebook: Opinions of the FTC & the
Courts, & Related Materials. Little.

Oppenheimer. see Oppenheimer, Steven B.

Oppenheimer, Carl H.
xOppenheimer, Carl H.
ed. Environmental Data Management. Plenum
Pub.

Oppenheimer, Doug.
xOppenheimer, Doug.
Sun Valley: A Biography. R O Beatty Assocs.

Oppenheimer, Ernest J., 1924-
xOppenheimer, Ernest J.

A Realistic Approach to U. S. Energy
Independence. Pen & Podium.

Oppenheimer, Franz, 1864-1943
xOppenheimer, Franz.
The State. Free Life.

Oppenheimer, Heinrich, Ph.D.
xOppenheimer, Heinrich.
Rationale of Punishment. Patterson Smith.

Oppenheimer, J. R. see Oppenheimer, J. Robert.

Oppenheimer, J. Robert.
xOppenheimer, J. R.
Lectures on Electrodynamics. Gordon.

Oppenheimer, Joan. see Oppenheimer, Joan L.

Oppenheimer, Joan L.
xOppenheimer, Joan.
Working on It. HarBraceJ.

Oppenheimer, Samuel P.
xOppenheimer, Samuel P.
Directing Construction for Profit: Business
Aspects of Contracting. McGraw.

Oppenheimer, Steven B., 1944-
xOppenheimer.
Introduction to Embryonic Development.
Allyn.

Oppler, Alfred C. see Oppler, Alfred Christian.

Oppler, Alfred Christian, 1893-
xOppler, Alfred C.
Legal Reform in Occupied Japan: A Participant
Looks Back. Princeton U Pr.

Oppler, Ellen C.
xOppler, Ellen C.
Fauvism Reexamined. Garland Pub.

Opsahl, Paul D.
xOpsahl, Paul D.
The Holy Spirit in the Life of the Church:
From Biblical Times to the Present.
Augsburg.

Optner, Stanford L.
xOptner, Stanford L.
Systems Analysis for Business Management.
P-H.

Orage, Alfred R. see Orage, Alfred Richard.

Orage, Alfred Richard, 1873-1934
xOrage, Alfred R.
Readers & Writers. Arno.

Oraison, Marc.
xOraison, Marc.
The Homosexual Question. Har-Row.
Morality for Our Time. Doubleday.

Oraker, James R.
xOraker, James R.
Almost Grown: A Christian Guide for Parents
of Teenagers. Har-Row.

Oram, James, 1936-
xOram, James.
The People's Pope: The Story of Karol Wojtyla
of Poland. Chronicle Bks.

Oram, R. B. see Oram, Robert Bruce.

Oram, Robert Bruce.
xOram, R. B.
Cargo Handling in a Modern Port. Pergamon.

Orange, Anne.
xOrange, Anne.
The Flower Book. Lerner Pubns.
The Leaf Book. Lerner Pubns.

Orange County Genealogical Society.
xOrange County Genealogical Society.
Index to the Eighteen Eighty-One Ruttenber &
Clark History of Orange County, New York.
Orange County Genealog.

Oras, Ants, 1900-
xOras, Ants.
Critical Ideas of T. S. Eliot. Folcroft.
On Some Aspects of Shelley's Poetic Imagery.
Folcroft.
Pause Patterns in Elizabethan & Jacobean
Drama: An Experiment in Prosody. U
Presses Fla.

Oravetz, Jules. see Oravetz, Jules A.

The Theater of the Marvelous: Surrealism &
the Contemporary Stage. NYU Pr.

Orenstein, Henry.
xOrenstein, Henry.
Gaon: Conflict & Cohesion in an Indian
Village. Princeton U Pr.

Orf, Gerhard, 1935-
xOrf, G.
Critical Resection Length & Gap Distance in
Peripheral Nerves: Experimental &
Morphological Studies. Springer-Verlag.

Orfield, Gary.
xOrfield, Gary.
Congressional Power: Congress & Social
Change. HarBraceJ.

Orfield, Lester Bernhardt.
xOrfield, Lester B.
Cases & Materials on International Law.
Michie.
Criminal Procedure from Arrest to Appeal.
Greenwood.

Orford, Jim.
xOrford, Jim.
Alcoholism: A Comparison of Treatment &
Advice, with a Study of the Influence of
Marriage. Oxford U Pr.

Orga, Ates.
xOrga, Ates.
Chopin: His Life & Times. Two Continents.
The Proms. David & Charles.

Organ, Troy Wilson.
xOrgan, Troy W.
The Hindu Quest for the Perfection of Man.
Ohio U Pr.

Organick, Elliott Irving, 1925-
xOrganick, Elliot I.
The Multics System: An Examination of Its
Structure. MIT Pr.

Organization of the Petroleum Exporting Countries. *see*
Organization of Petroleum Exporting Countries.

Orgel, Doris.
xOrgel, Doris.
A Certain Magic. Dell.
A Certain Magic. Dial.
Cindy's Snowdrops. Knopf.
The Devil in Vienna. Dial.
Retold by Little John. FS&G.
The Mulberry Music. Har-Row.

Orgel, Irene.
xOrgel, Irene.
Odd Tales of Irene Orgel. Eakins.

Orgill, Douglas, 1922-
xOrgill, Douglas.
The Astrid Factor. State Mutual Bk.
The Sixth Winter. S&S.

Orgler, Yair. *see* Orgler, Yair E.

Orgler, Yair E.
xOrgler, Yair.
Bank Capital. Van Nos Reinhold.

Orians, Gordon H.
xOrians, Gordon H.
Some Adaptations of Marsh-Nesting
Blackbirds. Princeton U Pr.

Oriental Economist. *see* Oriental Economists.

Oriental Economists.
xOriental Economist.
ed. New Japanese-English Dictionary of
Economic Terms. Intl Pubns Serv.

Oriental Institute. *see* Chicago. University. Oriental
Institute.

Orieux, Jean, 1907-
xOrieux, Jean.
Voltaire. Doubleday.

Origo, Iris. *see* Origo, Iris (Cutting).

Origo, Iris (Cutting), Marchesa, 1902-
xOrigo, Iris.
Images & Shadows: Part of a Life. HarBraceJ.

Orilia, Lawrence.
xOrilia, Lawrence.

Introduction to Business Data Processing.
McGraw.

Oringel, Robert S.
xOringel, Robert S.
Audio Control Handbook: For Radio &
Television Broadcasting. Hastings.

Orita, Zenji.
xOrita, Zenji.
I-Boat Captain. Major Bks.

Oriti, Ronald. *see* Oriti, Ronald A.

Oriti, Ronald A.
xOriti, Ronald.
Introduction to Astronomy. Glencoe.

Orkin, Mark. *see* Orkin, Mark M.

Orkin, Mark M.
xOrkin, Mark.
Murrican Huh?. Vanguard.

Orkin, Ruth.
xOrkin, Ruth.
ed. A World Through My Window. Har-Row.
A World Through My Window. Har-Row.

Orland, Leonard.
xOrland, Leonard.
Prisons: Houses of Darkness. Free Pr.

Orlandi, F.
xOrlandi, F.
ed. Liver & Drugs. Acad Pr.

Orlando, Francesco, 1934-
xOrlando, Francesco.
Toward a Freudian Theory of Literature: With
an Analysis of Racine's Phedre. Johns
Hopkins.

Orlans, Harold, 1921-
xOrlans, Harold.
Stevenage: A Sociological Study of a New
Town. Greenwood.

Orleans, Jacob S. *see* Orleans, Jacob Samuel.

Orleans, Jacob Samuel, 1899-
xOrleans, Jacob S.
A Study of the Nature of Difficulty. AMS Pr.

Orleans, Peter.
xOrleans, Peter.
ed. Race Change & Urban Society. Sage.

Orlich, Donald C.
xOrlich, Donald C.
Teaching Strategies: A Guide to Better
Instruction. Heath.

Orlicky, Joseph.
xOrlicky, Joseph A.
Material Requirements Planning: The New
Way of Life in Production & Inventory
Management. McGraw.

Orlicky, Joseph A. *see* Orlicky, Joseph.

Orlik, Peter B.
xOrlik, Peter B.
Broadcast Copywriting. Allyn.

Orlinsky, David E.
xOrlinsky, David O.
Varieties of Psychotherapeutic Experience.
Tchrs Coll.

Orlinsky, David O. *see* Orlinsky, David E.

Orlinsky, Harry M. *see* Orlinsky, Harry Meyer.

Orlinsky, Harry Meyer, 1908-
xOrlinsky, Harry M.
Ancient Israel. Cornell U Pr.

Orlob, Helen.
xOrlob, Helen.
The Northeast Passage: Black Water, White
Ice. Elsevier-Nelson.

Orloff, Neil.
xOrloff, Neil.
The Environmental Impact Statement Process:
A Guide to Citizen Action. Info Resources.

Orlosky, Donald E.
xOrlosky, Donald E.
Curriculum Development: Issues & Insights.
Rand.

Orlovsky, Peter, 1933-
xOrlovsky, Peter.

Clean Asshole Poems & Smiling Vegetable
Songs. City Lights.

Orlow, Dietrich.
xOrlow, Dietrich.
The History of the Nazi Party, 1919-1933. U
of Pittsburgh Pr.
The History of the Nazi Party, 1933-1945. U
of Pittsburgh Pr.

Orman, John M.
xOrman, John M.
Presidential Secrecy & Deception: Beyond the
Power to Persuade. Greenwood.

Orman, Tony.
xOrman, Tony.
Trout with Nymph. Intl Pubns Serv.

Ormandy, P. G.
xOrmandy, P. G.
An Introduction to Metallurgical Laboratory
Techniques. Pergamon.

Ormerod, Henry A. *see* Ormerod, Henry Arderne.

Ormerod, Henry Arderne, 1886-1964
xOrmerod, Henry A.
Piracy in the Ancient World: An Essay in
Mediterranean History. Rowman.

Ormerod, M. B. *see* Ormerod, Milton Blackburn.

Ormerod, Milton Blackburn.
xOrmerod, M. B.
Pupils Attitudes to Science: A Review of
Research. Humanities.

Ormes, Robert M.
xOrmes, Robert M.
Guide to the Colorado Mountains. Swallow.

Ormond, Brande.
xOrmond, Brande.
Museum Masterpieces in Needlepoint. HM.
Needlepoints to Go: Small Projects for Spare
Moments. HM.

Ormond, Clyde, 1906-
xOrmond, Clyde.
Complete Book of Outdoor Lore. Har-Row.
How to Track & Find Game. T Y Crowell.
Outdoorsman's Handbook. Berkley Pub.

Ormond, Leonee.
xOrmond, Leonee.
Lord Leighton. Yale U Pr.
xOrmond, Richard.
jt. auth. Lord Leighton. Yale U Pr.

Ormond, Richard. *see* Ormond, Leonee.

Ormond, Suzanne.
xOrmond, Suzanne.
Favorite New Orleans Recipes. Pelican.

Ormondroyd, Edward.
xOrmondroyd, Edward.
Broderick. Parnassus.
Imagination Greene. Parnassus.
Theodore. Parnassus.
Theodore's Rival. Parnassus.

Ormont, Louis. *see* Ormont, Louis R.

Ormont, Louis R.
xOrmont, Louis.
The Practice of Conjoint Therapy: Combining
Individual & Group Treatment. Human Sci
Pr.

Ormsby, Frank, 1947-
xOrmsby, Frank.
A Store of Candles. Oxford U Pr.

Ornati, Oscar A.
xOrnati, Oscar A.
Poverty Amid Affluence: A Report on a
Research Project Carried Out at the New
School for Social Research. Kraus Repr.

Ornduff, Robert.
xOrnduff, Robert.
Introduction to California Plant Life. U of Cal
Pr.

Ornstein, Allan C.
xOrnstein, Allan C.

Education & Social Inquiry. Peacock Pubs.
Looking into Teaching: An Introduction to
American Education. Rand.
Reforming Metropolitan Schools. Goodyear.
Ornstein, J. Alan.
xOrnstein, J. Alan.
The Lion's Share: A Combat Manual for the
Divorcing Male. Times Bks.
Ornstein, Norman J.
xOrnstein, Norman J.
ed. Changing Congress: The Committee
System. Am Acad Pol Soc Sci.
Interest Groups, Lobbying & Policymaking.
Congr Quarterly.
Ornstein, Robert.
xOrnstein, Robert.
The Moral Vision of Jacobean Tragedy.
Greenwood.
Ornstein, Robert E. *see* Ornstein, Robert Evans.
Ornstein, Robert Evans.
xOrnstein, Robert E.
ed. The Nature of Human Consciousness: A
Book of Readings. W H Freeman.
The Psychology of Consciousness. HarBraceJ.
The Psychology of Consciousness. Penguin.
The Psychology of Consciousness. Viking Pr.
Ornstein, Stanley. *see* Ornstein, Stanley I.
Ornstein, Stanley I.
xOrnstein, Stanley.
Industrial Concentration & Advertising
Intensity. Am Enterprise.
Ornstien, Edwin J.
xOrnstien, Edwin J.
Marketing of Money. Beekman Pubs.
Orpe, Frank.
xOrpe, Frank.
Dare to Be Brave. Alpha Pubns.
Orr, Alexandra. *see* Orr, Alexandra (Leighton).
Orr, Alexandra (Leighton).
xOrr, Alexandra.
Life & Letters of Robert Browning. R West.
xOrr, Alexandra L.
Life & Letters of Robert Browning.
Greenwood.
Orr, Alexandra L. *see* Orr, Alexandra (Leighton).
Orr, Clyde.
xOrr, Clyde.
Filtration: Principles & Practices. Dekker.
Orr, Daniel.
xOrr, Daniel.
Property, Markets, & Government
Intervention: A Textbook in Microeconomic
Theory & Its Current Applications.
Goodyear.
Orr, David W.
xOrr, David W.
ed. The Global Predicament: Ecological
Perspectives on World Order. U of NC Pr.
Orr, Frank.
xOrr, Frank.
Great Goalies of Pro Hockey. Random.
Great Moments in Auto Racing. Random.
Story of Hockey. Random.
World's Great Race Drivers. Random.
Orr, J. Edwin. *see* Orr, James Edwin.
Orr, J. M. *see* Orr, James Mcconnell.
Orr, James Edwin, 1912-
xOrr, J. Edwin.

Evangelical Awakenings in Africa. Bethany
Fell.
Evangelical Awakenings in Eastern Asia.
Bethany Fell.
Intro. by Evangelical Awakenings in Latin
America. Bethany Fell.
Evangelical Awakenings in Southern Asia.
Bethany Fell.
Evangelical Awakenings in the South Seas.
Bethany Fell.
The Faith That Persuades. Har-Row.
Orr, James F.
xOrr, James F.
The American National Park System: A
Selected Review. Vance Biblios.
Technology Transfer & the Diffusion of
Innovations: A Working Bibliography with
Annotations. Vance Biblios.
Orr, James Mcconnell.
xOrr, J. M.
Libraries As Communication Systems.
Greenwood.
Orr, Larry L.
xOrr, Larry L.
Income, Employment & Urban Residential
Location. Acad Pr.
Orr, Leon.
xOrr, Leon.
Unleashed. Southern Pub.
Orr, Leonard, 1953-
xOrr, Leonard.
A Catalogue Checklist of English Prose
Fiction: 1750-1800. Whitston Pub.
Orr, Robert T. *see* Orr, Robert Thomas.
Orr, Robert Thomas, 1908-
xOrr, Robert T.
The Little-Known Pika. Macmillan.
Marine Mammals of California. U of Cal Pr.
Orr, W. D. *see* Orr, William D.
Orr, William D.
xOrr, W. D.
Conversational Computers. Krieger.
Orr, William I. *see* Orr, William Ittner.
Orr, William Ittner, 1919-
xOrr, William I.
Radio Handbook. Editors.
Orrey, Leslie.
xOrrey, Leslie.
ed. The Encyclopedia of Opera. Scribner.
Orrick, James B. *see* Orrick, James Bentley.
Orrick, James Bentley.
xOrrick, James B.
Matthew Arnold & Goethe. Folcroft.
Matthew Arnold & Goethe. Haskell.
Orser, Mary.
xOrser, Mary.
What's My Sign?. Har-Row.
Orser, W. Edward.
xOrser, W. Edward.
Searching for a Viable Alternative: The
Macedonia Cooperative Community, 1937 to
1958. B Franklin.
Orsini, Gian N. *see* Orsini, Gian Napoleone Giordano.
Orsini, Gian Napoleone Giordano, 1903-
xOrsini, Gian N.
Organic Unity in Ancient & Later Poetics: The
Philosophical Foundations of Literary
Criticism. S Ill U Pr.
T. S. Eliot & the Doctrine of Dramatic
Conventions. Folcroft.
Orsini, Joseph. *see* Orsini, Joseph E.
Orsini, Joseph E.
xOrsini, Joseph.
Papa Bear's Favorite Italian Dishes. Logos.
Orso, Kathryn W. *see* Orso, Kathryn Wickey.
Orso, Kathryn Wickey.
xOrso, Kathryn W.

Parenthood: A Commitment in Faith.
Morehouse.
Ortali, Raymond.
xOrtali, Raymond.
Aujourd'hui. HarBraceJ.
Ortega y Gasset, Jose, 1883-1955
xOrtega Y Gasset, Jose.
Idea of Principle in Leibnitz & the Evolution of
Deductive Theory. Norton.
Meditations on Quixote. Norton.
Origin of Philosophy. Norton.
Orten, James M.
xOrten, James M.
Human Biochemistry. Mosby.
Orth, Samuel P. *see* Orth, Samuel Peter.
Orth, Samuel Peter, 1873-1922
xOrth, Samuel P.
Centralization of Administration in Ohio. AMS
Pr.
ed. Readings on the Relation of Government to
Property & Industry. Arno.
Orthodox Eastern Church.
xOrthodox Eastern Church.
The General Menaion, or the Book of Services
Common to the Festivals of Our Lord Jesus
Christ, of the Holy Virgin, & of the Different
Orders of Saints. Eastern Orthodox.
Liturgies of Saints Mark, James, Clement,
Chrysostom, & the Church of Malabar. AMS
Pr.
Liturgies of Saints Mark, James, Clement,
Chrysostom, Basil. AMS Pr.
Offices of the Oriental Church. AMS Pr.
Prayers for the Dead. Eastern Orthodox.
Service to a Fool for Christ Sake. Eastern
Orthodox.
Synod of Sixteen Seventy Two: Acts &
Decrees of the Jerusalem Synod Held Under
Dositheus, Containing the Confession
Published Name of Cyril Lukaris. AMS Pr.
Orthodox Eastern Church. Russian.
xOrthodox Eastern Church--Russian.
Service to St. Tikhon of Zadonsk (Text in Old
Church Slavonic). Eastern Orthodox.
Orthodox Eastern Church. Synod of Jerusalem, 1672.
xOrthodox Eastern Church-Synod of Jerusalem.
Acts & Decrees of the Synod of Jerusalem,
1672. Eastern Orthodox.
Orthodox Eastern Church--Russian. *see* Orthodox
Eastern Church. Russian.
Orthodox Eastern Church-Synod of Jerusalem. *see*
Orthodox Eastern Church. Synod of Jerusalem, 1672.
Ortiz, Elisabeth L. *see* Ortiz, Elisabeth Lambert.
Ortiz, Elisabeth Lambert.
xOrtiz, Elisabeth L.
A Book of Latin American Cooking. Knopf.
The Book of Latin-American Cooking.
Random.
The Complete Book of Caribbean Cooking. M
Evans.
The Complete Book of Mexican Cooking. M
Evans.
Ortiz, Juan C. *see* Ortiz, Juan Carlos.
Ortiz, Juan Carlos, 1934-
xOrtiz, Juan C.
The Disciple. Creation Hse.
Ortleb, Charles.
xOrtleb, Charles.
Another Cat Book. St Martin.
Ortlund, Anne.
xOrtlund, Anne.
The Disciplines of the Beautiful Woman. Word
Bks.
Ortlund, Raymond C.
xOrtlund, Raymond C.
Lord, Make My Life a Miracle. Regal.
Ortmayer, Roger.
xOrtmayer, Roger.

Sing & Pray & Shout Hurrah. Friend Pr.
Orton, Colin G.
xOrton, Colin G.
Radiological Physics Examination Review
Book. Med Exam.
Orton, Gavin, 1943-
xOrton, Gavin.
Eyvind Johnson. Twayne.
Orton, Harold.
xOrton, Harold.
ed. The Linguistic Atlas of England.
Humanities.
A Word Geography of England. Acad Pr.
Orton, Mildred E. *see* Orton, Mildred Ellen.
Orton, Mildred Ellen, 1911-
xOrton, Mildred E.
Cooking with Wholegrains. FS&G.
Orton, Vrest.
xOrton, Vrest.
Dreiserana: A Book About His Books. Folcroft.
Dreiserana: A Book About His Books. Haskell.
Ortony, Andrew, 1942-
xOrtony, Andrew.
ed. Metaphor & Thought. Cambridge U Pr.
Ortzen, Len.
xOrtzen, Len.
Famous Stories of the Resistance. St Martin.
Strange Stories of UFOs. Taplinger.
Orum, Anthony M.
xOrum, Anthony M.
Introduction to Political Sociology: The Social
Anatomy of Body Politics. P-H.
Orvis, Marianne D. *see* Orvis, Marianne Dwight.
Orvis, Marianne Dwight, 1816-1901
xOrvis, Marianne D.
Letters from Brook Farm: 1841-1847.
Porcupine Pr.
Orwell, George, 1903-1950
xOrwell, George.
Animal Farm. NAL.
Animal Farm. HarBraceJ.
Clergyman's Daughter. HarBraceJ.
Collection of Essays. HarBraceJ.
Dickens, Dali, & Others. HarBraceJ.
Dickens, Dali & Others. HarBraceJ.
Down & Out in Paris & London. HarBraceJ.
The English People. Haskell.
Homage to Catalonia. HarBraceJ.
The Lion & the Unicorn: Socialism & the
English Genius. AMS Pr.
Orwin, Christabel S. *see* Orwin, Christabel Susan
(Lowry).
Orwin, Christabel Susan (Lowry).
xOrwin, Christabel S.
History of British Agriculture, 1864-1914.
Humanities.
Orzech, Morris.
xOrzech, Morris.
The Brauer Group of Commutative Rings.
Dekker.
Orzel, Nick.
xOrzel, Nick.
ed. Eight Plays from Off-Off Broadway. Bobbs.
Osaragi, Jir O, Pseud.
xOsaragi, Jiro.
Homecoming. C E Tuttle.
Homecoming. Greenwood.
Osaragi, Jiro. *see* Osaragi, Jir O.
Osato, Sono, 1919-
xOsato, Sono.
Distant Dances. Knopf.
Osborn. *see* Osborn, Michael.
Osborn, Albert S. *see* Osborn, Albert Sherman.
Osborn, Albert Sherman, 1858-1946
xOsborn, Albert S.
Questioned Documents. Nelson-Hall.
Questioned Documents. Patterson Smith.
Osborn, Arthur W. *see* Osborn, Arthur Walter.
Osborn, Arthur Walter, 1891-
xOsborn, Arthur W.

Cosmic Womb: An Interpretation of Man's
Relationship to the Infinite. Theos Pub Hse.
Future Is Now: The Significance of
Precognition. Theos Pub Hse.
Osborn, D. Keith.
xOsborn, D. Keith.
Discipline & Classroom Management. Ed
Assocs.
Early Childhood Education in Historical
Perspective. Ed Assocs.
xOsborn, Janie D.
jt. auth. Discipline & Classroom Management.
Ed Assocs.
Osborn, David, 1923-
xOsborn, David.
The French Decision. Doubleday.
Osborn, E. *see* Osborn, Eric Francis.
Osborn, Edward B. *see* Osborn, Edward Bolland.
Osborn, Edward Bolland, 1867-1967
xOsborn, Edward B.
Literature & Life: Things Seen, Heard & Read.
Arno.
Osborn, Eric Francis.
xOsborn, E.
Ethical Patterns in Early Christian Thought.
Cambridge U Pr.
Osborn, Fairfield, 1887-1969
xOsborn, Fairfield.
Limits of the Earth. Greenwood.
Osborn, Frederic J. *see* Osborn, Frederic James.
Osborn, Frederic James, 1885-
xOsborn, Frederic J.
Green-Belt Cities. Schocken.
Osborn, Henry F. *see* Osborn, Henry Fairfield.
Osborn, Henry Fairfield, 1857-1935
xOsborn, Henry F.
Cope. Master Naturalist: Life & Letters of
Edward Drinker Cope, with a Bibliography of
His Writings. Arno.
Osborn, Jack L.
xOsborn, Jack L.
Personal Information: Privacy at the
Workplace. Am Mgmt.
Osborn, James.
xOsborn, James.
Area, Development Policy, & the Middle City
in Malaysia. U Chicago Dept Geog.
Osborn, Janie D. *see* Osborn, D. Keith.
Osborn, Jean S., 1943-
xOsborn, Jean S.
Green Glass Wings. Libra.
Osborn, John F.
xOsborn, John F.
Statistical Exercises in Medical Research.
Halsted Pr.
Osborn, Louise B. *see* Osborn, Louise Brown.
Osborn, Louise Brown.
xOsborn, Louise B.
The Life, Letters & Writings of John Hoskyns,
1566-1638. Shoe String.
Osborn, Mary E. *see* Osborn, Mary Elizabeth.
Osborn, Mary Elizabeth.
xOsborn, Mary E.
Who Tempers the Wind. Swallow.
Osborn, Michael, 1937-
xOsborn.
Orientations to Rhetorical Style. SRA.
Osborn, Richard K.
xOsborn, Richard K.
Foundations of Neutron Transport Theory.
Gordon.
Osborn, Robert. *see* Osborn, Robert Chesley.
Osborn, Robert Chesley.
xOsborn, Robert.
Dying to Smoke. HM.
Osborn Festival of Phobias. Liveright.
Osborn, Roger.
xOsborn, Roger.
Mathematics of Investment. Jenkins.
Osborn, Ruth H. *see* Osborn, Ruth Helm.

Osborn, Ruth Helm.
xOsborn, Ruth H.
Developing New Horizons for Women.
McGraw.
Osborn, Scott C. *see* Osborn, Scott Compton.
Osborn, Scott Compton.
xOsborn, Scott C.
Richard Harding Davis. G K Hall.
Richard Harding Davis. Twayne.
Osborn, Susan M.
xOsborn, Susan M.
Assertive Training for Women. C C Thomas.
Osborne, Agnes E. *see* Osborne, Agnes Elizabeth.
Osborne, Agnes Elizabeth, 1901-
xOsborne, Agnes E.
The Relationship Between Certain
Psychological Tests & Shorthand
Achievement. AMS Pr.
Osborne, Alan. *see* Osborne, Alan R.
Osborne, Alan R.
xOsborne, Alan.
ed. An In-Service Handbook for Mathematics
Education. NCTM.
Osborne, Algernon A. *see* Osborne, Algernon Ashburner.
Osborne, Algernon Ashburner, 1882-
xOsborne, Algernon A.
Speculation on the New York Stock Exchange,
September, 1904-March, 1907. AMS Pr.
Osborne, Anne.
xOsborne, Anne.
The Analyst. Dell.
The Analyst. Morrow.
Osborne, Arthur, 1906-
xOsborne, Arthur.
Ramana Maharshi & the Path of
Self-Knowledge. Weiser.
Osborne, Carl A.
xOsborne, Carl A.
Canine & Feline Urology. Saunders.
Osborne, Cecil. *see* Osborne, Cecil G.
Osborne, Cecil G.
xOsborne, Cecil.
The Art of Learning to Love Yourself.
Zondervan.
Art of Understanding Your Mate. Zondervan.
Art of Understanding Yourself. Zondervan.
xOsborne, Cecil G.
The Art of Becoming a Whole Person. Word
Bks.
The Art of Getting Along with People.
Zondervan.
Prayer & You. Word Bks.
Release from Fear & Anxiety. Word Bks.
Osborne, Charles, 1927-
xOsborne, Charles.
Complete Operas of Verdi. Knopf.
ed. The Dictionary of Composers. Taplinger.
W. H. Auden: The Life of a Poet. HarBraceJ.
Osborne, Denis.
xOsborne, Denis.
The Andromedans & Other Parables of Science
& Faith. Inter-Varsity.
Osborne, Grant R.
xOsborne, Grant R.
Handbook for Bible Study. Baker Bk.
Osborne, Harold, 1905-
xOsborne, Harold.
Abstraction & Artifice in Twentieth Century
Art. Oxford U Pr.
ed. Aesthetics. Oxford U Pr.
Aesthetics & Criticism. Greenwood.
ed. Oxford Companion to Art. Oxford U Pr.
ed. The Oxford Companion to the Decorative
Arts. Oxford U Pr.
Osborne, Helena.
xOsborne, Helena.
The Joker. Coward.
White Poppy. PB.
Osborne, James I. *see* Osborne, James Insley.

Osborne, James Insley, 1887-
    xOsborne, James I.
        Arthur Hugh Clough. Folcroft.
Osborne, Jerry.
    xOsborne, Jerry.
        A Guide to Record Collecting. O'Sullivan
        Woodside.
Osborne, John.
    xOsborne, John.
        The Third Year of the Nixon Watch. Liveright.
Osborne, Juanita T. see Osborne, Juanita Tyree.
Osborne, Juanita Tyree.
    xOsborne, Juanita T.
        The Ashes of Windrow. Bouregy.
        Dark Season at Aerie. Bouregy.
    xOsborne, Juanita Tyree.
        The House on Hibiscus Hill. Bouregy.
Osborne, Lilly D. see Osborne, Lilly De Jongh.
Osborne, Lilly De Jongh.
    xOsborne, Lilly D.
        Indian Crafts of Guatemala & El Salvador. U
        of Okla Pr.
Osborne, M. see Osborne, Milton E.
Osborne, M. R. see Osborne, Michael Robert.
Osborne, Maggie.
    xOsborne, Maggie.
        Alexa. NAL.
Osborne, Margaret.
    xOsborne, Margaret.
        Collies. Arco.
        Collies. Palmetto Pub.
Osborne, Martha L. see Osborne, Martha Lee.
Osborne, Martha Lee, 1928-
    xOsborne, Martha L.
        Woman in Western Thought. Random.
Osborne, Michael Robert.
    xOsborne, M. R.
        ed. Simulation & Modelling. U of Queensland
        Pr.
Osborne, Milton. see Osborne, Milton E.
Osborne, Milton E.
    xOsborne, M.
        Region of Revolt: Focus on Southeast Asia.
        Pergamon.
    xOsborne, Milton.
        Before Kampuchea: Preludes to Tragedy. Allen
        Unwin.
    xOsborne, Milton E.
        French Presence in Cochinchina & Cambodia:
        Rule & Response 1859-1905. Cornell U Pr.
        Strategic Hamlets in South Viet-Nam: A
        Survey & a Comparison. Cornell SE Asia.
Osborne, R. T. see Osborne, Robert Travis.
Osborne, Robert Travis.
    xOsborne, R. T.
        ed. Human Variation: The Biopsychology of
        Age, Race, & Sex. Acad Pr.
Osborne, William S.
    xOsborne, William S.
        Caroline M. Kirkland. Twayne.
Osbourne, Lloyd, 1868-1947
    xOsbourne, Lloyd.
        Love, the Fiddler. Arno.
Osburn, Burl N. see Osburn, Burl Neff.
Osburn, Burl Neff.
    xOsburn, Burl N.
        Measured Drawings of Early American
        Furniture. Dover.
        Measured Drawings of Early American
        Furniture. Peter Smith.
        Pewter-Working: Instructions & Projects.
        Dover.
Osburn, Charles B.
    xOsburn, Charles B.
        Academic Research & Library Resources:
        Changing Patterns in America. Greenwood.
Osdol, Bob M. Van. see Van Osdol, Bob M.
Osdol, William R. Van. see Van Osdol, William R.
Osee, Johan.
    xOsee, Johan.

Call of the Virgin at San Damiano. Chris Mass.
Osei, G. K. see Osei, Gabriel Kingsley.
Osei, Gabriel Kingsley.
    xOsei, G. K.
        Caribbean Women: Their History & Habits.
        Intl Pubns Serv.
Oser, Jacob, 1915-
    xOser, Jacob.
        Evolution of Economic Thought. HarBraceJ.
Osgood, C. G. see Osgood, Charles Grosvenor.
Osgood, Charles.
    xOsgood, Charles.
        Nothing Could Be Finer Than a Crisis That Is
        Minor in the Morning. HR&W.
Osgood, Charles E. see Osgood, Charles Egerton.
Osgood, Charles Egerton.
    xOsgood, Charles E.
        An Alternative to War or Surrender. U of Ill
        Pr.
        Cross-Cultural Universals of Affective
        Meaning. U of Ill Pr.
Osgood, Charles G. see Osgood, Charles Grosvenor.
Osgood, Charles Grosvenor, 1871-1964
    xOsgood, C. G.
        The Classical Mythology of Milton's English
        Poems. Irvington.
    xOsgood, Charles G.
        Classical Mythology of Milton's English
        Poems. Gordian.
        Classical Mythology of Milton's English
        Poems. Haskell.
        Concordance to the Poems of Edmund
        Spenser. Peter Smith.
        Creed of a Humanist. U of Wash Pr.
        Spenser & the Enchanted Glass. Folcroft.
Osgood, Cornelius, 1905-
    xOsgood, Cornelius.
        The Chinese: A Study of a Hong Kong
        Community. U of Ariz Pr.
        Contributions to the Ethnography of the
        Kutchin. HRAFP.
        Ingalik Material Culture. HRAFP.
Osgood, Dewitt S.
    xOsgood, DeWitt S.
        Preparing for the Latter Rain. Southern Pub.
Osgood, Don.
    xOsgood, Don.
        Pressure Points: The Christian's Response to
        Stress. Christian Herald.
Osgood, Ernest S. see Osgood, Ernest Staples.
Osgood, Ernest Staples.
    xOsgood, Ernest S.
        Day of the Cattleman. U of Chicago Pr.
Osgood, Herbert L. see Osgood, Herbert Levi.
Osgood, Herbert Levi, 1855-1918
    xOsgood, Herbert L.
        American Colonies in the Eighteenth Century.
        Peter Smith.
Osgood, Judy.
    xOsgood, Judy.
        How to Beat the Grade Game. Condor Pub
        Co.
Osgood, Robert E. see Osgood, Robert Endicott.
Osgood, Robert Endicott.
    xOsgood, Robert E.
        Alliances & American Foreign Policy. Johns
        Hopkins.
        America & the World: From the Truman
        Doctrine to Vietnam. Johns Hopkins.
        Force, Order, & Justice. Johns Hopkins.
        Limited War Revisited. Westview.
Osgood, Samuel. see Osgood, Samuel M.
Osgood, Samuel M.
    xOsgood, Samuel.
        French Royalism Under the Third & Fourth
        Republics. Hyperion Conn.
Osgood, William R.
    xOsgood, William R.

Basics of Successful Business Planning. Am
        Mgmt.
Osherson, Samuel, 1945-
    xOsherson, Samuel D.
        Holding on or Letting Go: Men & Career
        Change at Midlife. Free Pr.
Osherson, Samuel D. see Osherson, Samuel.
Osiek, Betty T. see Osiek, Betty Tyree.
Osiek, Betty Tyree.
    xOsiek, Betty T.
        Jose Asuncion Silva. Twayne.
Osinski, F. W. see Osinski, Franklin W. W.
Osinski, Franklin W. W.
    xOsinski, F. W.
        ed. Toward Gog & Magog or?: A Critical
        Review of the Literature of Adult Group
        Discussion. Syracuse U Cont Ed.
Osipow, Lloyd I.
    xOsipow, Lloyd I.
        Surface Chemistry: Theory & Industrial
        Applications. Krieger.
Osipow, Samuel H.
    xOsipow, Samuel H.
        ed. Strategies in Counseling for Behavior
        Change. P-H.
        A Survey of Counseling Methods. Dorsey.
        Theories of Career Development. P-H.
Osis, K Arlis.
    xOsis, Karlis.
        At the Hour of Death. Avon.
Osis, Karlis, 1917-
    xOsis, Karlis.
        Deathbed Observations by Physicians &
        Nurses. Parapsych Foun.
Osis, Karlis. see Osis, K Arlis.
Oskamp, S. see Oskamp, Stuart.
Oskamp, Stuart.
    xOskamp, S.
        Attitudes & Opinions. P-H.
Osler, William, Sir, Bart, 1849-1919
    xOsler, William.
        The Evolution of Modern Medicine: A Series
        of Lectures Delivered at Yale University on
        the Silliman Foundation in April, 1913. Arno.
        Student Life, & Other Essays. Arno.
Osman, Betty. see Osman, Betty B.
Osman, Betty B.
    xOsman, Betty.
        Learning Disabilities: A Family Affair.
        Random.
    xOsman, Betty B.
        Learning Disabilities: A Family Affair. Warner
        Bks.
Osmond, Edward, 1900-
    xOsmond, Edward.
        illus. Animals of Central Asia. Abelard.
Osmond, John.
    xOsmond, John.
        Creative Conflict: The Politics of Welsh
        Devolution. Routledge & Kegan.
Osmond, Liz.
    xOsmond, Liz.
        People in Europe. Allen Unwin.
Osmond, Marie.
    xOsmond, Marie.
        Marie Osmond's Guide to Beauty, Health &
        Style. S&S.
Osofsky, Barbara L.
    xOsofsky, Barbara L.
        Homological Dimensions of Modules. Am
        Math.
Osofsky, Howard J., 1935-
    xOsofsky, Howard J.
        The Pregnant Teen-Ager: A Medical,
        Educational, & Social Analysis. C C Thomas.
Osofsky, Joy D.
    xOsofsky, Joy D.

ed. The Handbook of Infant Development.
Wiley.
Osofsky, Stephen.
xOsofsky, Stephen.
Peter Kropotkin. G K Hall.
Peter Kropotkin. Twayne.
Ossar, Michael, 1938-
xOssar, Michael.
Anarchism in the Dramas of Ernst Toller. State
U N Y Pr.
Osserman, Robert.
xOsserman, Robert.
Two-Dimensional Calculus. Krieger.
Ossoli, Margaret F. see Ossoli, Sarah Margaret (Fuller).
Ossoli, Sarah M. see Ossoli, Sarah Margaret (Fuller).
Ossoli, Sarah Margaret (Fuller).
xOssoli, Margaret F.
Love Letters of Margaret Fuller 1845-1846.
AMS Pr.
Memoirs of Margaret Fuller Ossoli. B Franklin.
Memoirs of Margaret Fuller Ossoli. R West.
Papers on Literature & Art. AMS Pr.
Summer on the Lakes. Haskell.
xOssoli, Sarah M.
Love-Letters of Margaret Fuller, 1845-1846.
Greenwood.
Ost, Hans.
xOst, Hans.
Leonardo-Studien. De Gruyter.
Osten, Gar.
xOsten, Gar.
The Astrological Chart of the United States
from 1776 to 2141. Stein & Day.
Osten, Hans Henning Von Der, 1899-1960
xOsten, Hans Von Der.
Explorations in Hittite Asia Minor,
Greenwood.
Osten, Hans Von Der. see Osten, Hans Henning Von
Der.
Oster, George F.
xOster, George F.
Caste & Ecology in the Social Insects.
Princeton U Pr.
Oster, Harry.
xOster, Harry.
Living Country Blues. Gale.
Living Country Blues. T Y Crowell.
Oster, Kenneth.
xOster, Kenneth.
Islam Reconsidered: A Brief Historical
Background to the Religion & Thought of the
Moslem World. Exposition.
Oster, Ludwig.
xOster, Ludwig.
Modern Astronomy. Holden-Day.
Osterbrock, Donald E.
xOsterbrock, Donald E.
Astrophysics of Gaseous Nebulae. W H
Freeman.
Osterburg, James W.
xOsterburg, James W.
Crime Laboratory: Case Studies of Scientific
Criminal Investigation. Ind U Pr.
Osterholm, Jewell L.
xOsterholm, Jewell L.
The Pathophysiology of Spinal Cord Trauma. C
C Thomas.
Osterhout, Marilyn M.
xOsterhout, Marilyn M.
ed. Decontamination & Decommissioning of
Nuclear Facilities. Plenum Pub.
Osterlund, Steven, 1943-
xOsterlund, Steven.
Twenty Love Poems. Windflower Pr.
Osterwald, Doris B.
xOsterwald, Doris B.

Cinders & Smoke: A Mile by Mile Guide for
the Durango to Silverton Narrow Gauge
Trip. Western Guideways.
Osteryoung, Jerome S.
xOsteryoung, Jerome S.
Analytical Techniques for Financial
Management. Grid Pub.
Capital Budgeting: Long-Term Asset Selection.
Grid Pub.
Financial Management: Self-Correcting
Problems. Grid Pub.
Osteyee, D. B. see Osteyee, David Bridston.
Osteyee, David Bridston.
xOsteyee, D. B.
Information Weight of Evidence, the
Singularity Between Probability Measures &
Signal Detection. Springer-Verlag.
Osthaus, Carl R.
xOsthaus, Carl R.
Freedmen, Philanthropy & Fraud: A History of
the Freedman's Savings Bank. U of Ill Pr.
Ostheimer, John M.
xOstheimer, John M.
Nigerian Politics. Har-Row.
Ostler, George.
xOstler, George.
ed. Little Oxford Dictionary of Current
English. Oxford U Pr.
Ostlere, Gordon.
xOstlere, Gordon.
Anaesthetics for Medical Students. Churchill.
Ostman, Ronald E. see Ostman, Ronald Elroy.
Ostman, Ronald Elroy.
xOstman, Ronald E.
Communication Research & Drug Education.
Sage.
Ostow, Miriam.
xOstow, Miriam.
Work & Welfare in New York City. Johns
Hopkins.
Ostow, Mortimer.
xOstow, Mortimer.
ed. The Psychodynamic Approach to Drug
Therapy. Van Nos Reinhold.
Ostrander, Gilman M. see Ostrander, Gilman Marston.
Ostrander, Gilman Marston, 1923-
xOstrander, Gilman M.
A Profile History of the United States.
McGraw.
Ostrander, Kate.
xOstrander, Kate.
Dance with a Ghost. Berkley Pub.
Ostrander, Nancy. see Ostrander, Sheila.
Ostrander, Raymond H.
xOstrander, Raymond H.
A Values Approach to Educational
Administration. Krieger.
Ostrander, Sheila.
xOstrander, Nancy.
jt. auth. Superlearning. Delacorte.
xOstrander, Sheila.
Psychic Discoveries Behind the Iron Curtain.
Bantam.
Superlearning. Delacorte.
Superlearning. Dell.
Ostransky, Leroy.
xOstransky, Leroy.
The Anatomy of Jazz. Greenwood.
Understanding Jazz. P-H.
Ostrofsky, Benjamin, 1925-
xOstrofsky, Benjamin.
Design, Planning & Development
Methodology. P-H.
Ostrom, Elinor.
xOstrom, Elinor.
Patterns of Metropolitan Policing. Ballinger
Pub.
Ostrom, John. see Ostrom, John Ward.
Ostrom, John H.
xOstrom, John.

The Strange World of Dinosaurs. Putnam.
Ostrom, John Ward, 1903-
xOstrom, John.
Better Paragraphs. Har-Row.
Ostrom, T. G. see Ostrom, Theodore Gleason.
Ostrom, Theodore Gleason, 1916-
xOstrom, T. G.
Finite Translation Planes. Springer-Verlag.
Ostrom, Vincent.
xOstrom, Vincent.
ed. Comparing Urban Service Delivery
Systems: Structure & Performance. Sage.
The Intellectual Crisis in American Public
Administration. U of Ala Pr.
Ostrovskii, Nikolai A. see Ostrovskii, Nikolai
Alekseevich.
Ostrovskii, Nikolai Alekseevich.
xOstrovskii, Nikolai A.
Born of the Storm. Hyperion Conn.
Ostrovsky, Erika.
xOstrovsky, Erika.
Celine & His Vision. NYU Pr.
Eye of Dawn: The Rise & Fall of Mata Hari. G
K Hall.
Eye of Dawn: The Rise & Fall of Mata Hari.
Macmillan.
Ostrower, Gary B., 1939-
xOstrower, Gary B.
Collective Insecurity: The United States and
the League of Nations During the Early
Thirties. Bucknell U Pr.
Ostwald, Martin, 1922-
xOstwald, Martin.
Nomos & the Beginnings of the Athenian
Democracy. Greenwood.
Ostwald, Peter F.
xOstwald, Peter F.
ed. Communication & Social Interaction:
Clinical & Therapeutic Aspects of Human
Behavior. Grune.
Ostwald, Phillip F., 1931-
xOstwald, Phillip F.
Cost Estimating for Engineering &
Management. P-H.
ed. Manufacturing Cost Estimating. SME.
Ostyn, Paul.
xOstyn, Paul.
Fluent Spoken French. Har-Row.
Osuna, Juan J. see Osuna, Juan Jose.
Osuna, Juan Jose, 1884-1950
xOsuna, Juan J.
Education in Porto Rico. AMS Pr.
A History of Education in Puerto Rico. Arno.
A History of Education in Puerto Rico. U of
PR Pr.
A History of Education in Puerto Rico. Univ
Place.
Osuntokun, Akinjide.
xOsuntokun, Akinjide.
Nigeria in the First World War. Humanities.
Oswald, F. see Oswald, Frederick William.
Oswald, Frederick William.
xOswald, F.
Ranger's Guide to Useful Plants of Eastern
Wilds. Chris Mass.
Oswalt, Wendell. see Oswalt, Wendell H.
Oswalt, Wendell H.
xOswalt, Wendell.
Understanding Our Culture: An
Anthropological View. HR&W.
xOswalt, Wendell H.
An Anthropological Analysis of Food-Getting
Technology. Wiley.
Eskimos & Explorers. Chandler & Sharp.
This Land Was Theirs: A Study of North
American Indians. Wiley.
Otaala, Barnabas.
xOtaala, Barnabas.

The Development of Operational Thinking in Primary School Children: An Examination of Some Aspects of Piaget's Theory Among the Iteso Children of Uganda. Tchrs Coll.

Otero, Lisandro, 1932-
xOtero, Lisandro.
Cultural Policy in Cuba. Unipub.

Otis, Amos.
xOtis, Amos.
Genealogical Notes of Barnstable Families. Genealog Pub.

Otis, Brooks.
xOtis, Brooks.
Ovid As an Epic Poet. Cambridge U Pr.

Otis, George.
xOtis, George.
The Solution to Crisis America. Bible Voice.

Otite, Onigu.
xOtite, Onigu.
Autonomy & Dependence: The Urhobo Kingdom of Okpe in Modern Nigeria. Northwestern U Pr.

Otnes, Robert K.
xOtnes, Robert K.
Digital Time Series Analysis. Wiley.

Ott. *see* Ott, Lyman.

Ott, David J.
xOtt, David J.
Federal Budget Policy. Brookings.

Ott, Frederick W.
xOtt, Frederick W.
The Films of Carole Lombard. Citadel Pr.
The Films of Fritz Lang. Citadel Pr.

Ott, Heinrich.
xOtt, Heinrich.
God. John Knox.

Ott, Henry W., 1936-
xOtt, Henry W.
Noise Reduction Techniques in Electronic Systems. Wiley.

Ott, John.
xOtt, John.
Work As You Like It: A Look at Unusual Jobs. Messner.

Ott, John. *see* Ott, John Nash.

Ott, John Nash, 1909-
xOtt, John.
How to Write & Deliver a Speech. Cornerstone.
How to Write & Deliver a Speech. Trident.

Ott, Jonathan.
xOtt, Jonathan.
Hallucinogenic Plants of North America. Wingbow Pr.

Ott, Lyman.
xOtt.
Introduction to Statistical Methods & Data Analysis. Duxbury Pr.
xOtt, Lyman.
Statistics: A Tool for the Social Sciences. Duxbury Pr.

Ott, Thomas O., 1938-
xOtt, Thomas O.
The Haitian Revolution, 1789-1804. U of Tenn Pr.

Ott, Wayne.
xOtt, Wayne R.
Environmental Indices: Theory & Practice. Ann Arbor Science.

Ott, Wayne R. *see* Ott, Wayne.

Ottaway, David.
xOttaway, David.
Algeria: The Politics of a Socialist Revolution. U of Cal Pr.

Ottaway, Hugh.
xOttaway, Hugh.
Vaughan Williams Symphonies. U of Wash Pr.

Ottaway, Richard N.
xOttaway, Richard N.

Change Agents at Work. Greenwood.

Otte, Elmer.
xOtte, Elmer.
Rehearse Before You Retire. Retirement Res.

Otten, Charlotte M., 1915-
xOtten, Charlotte M.
ed. Aggression & Evolution. Wiley.
ed. Anthropology & Art: Readings in Cross-Cultural Aesthetics. U of Tex Pr.

Otten, Terry.
xOtten, Terry.
The Deserted Stage: The Search for Dramatic Form in Nineteenth-Century England. Ohio U Pr.

Ottenberg, Miriam.
xOttenberg, Miriam.
The Pursuit of Hope. Rawson Wade.

Ottensmann, John R.
xOttensmann, John R.
The Changing Spatial Structure of American Cities. Lexington Bks.

Ottley, Reginald.
xOttley, Reginald.
Boy Alone. HarBraceJ.

Ottman, Robert. *see* Ottman, Robert W.

Ottman, Robert W.
xOttman, Robert.
Programmed Rudiments of Music. P-H.
xOttman, Robert W.
Advanced Harmony: Theory & Practice. P-H.
Music for Sight Singing. P-H.

Otto, Henry J. *see* Otto, Henry John.

Otto, Henry John.
xOtto, Henry J.
Principles of Elementary Education. Greenwood.

Otto, Herbert. *see* Otto, Herbert Arthur.

Otto, Herbert A. *see* Otto, Herbert Arthur.

Otto, Herbert Arthur.
xOtto, Herbert.
Total Sex. NAL.
xOtto, Herbert A.
ed. Dimensions in Wholistic Healing: New Frontiers in the Treatment of the Whole Person. Nelson-Hall.
Guide to Developing Your Potential. Wilshire.
ed. Marriage & Family Enrichment: New Perspectives & Programs. Abingdon.

Otto, P. *see* Otto, Peter.

Otto, Peter.
xOtto, P.
Atlas of Rectoscopy & Colonoscopy. Springer-Verlag.

Otto, Rudolf, 1869-1937
xOtto, Rudolf.
Idea of the Holy: An Inquiry into the Non-Rational Factor in the Idea of the Divine & Its Relation to the Rational. Oxford U Pr.

Otto, Svend.
xOtto, Svend.
illus. Taxi Dog. Schol Bk Serv.

Otto, Walter F. *see* Otto, Walter Friedrich.

Otto, Walter Friedrich, 1874-1958
xOtto, Walter F.
The Homeric Gods: The Spiritual Significance of Greek Religion. Arno.
The Homeric Gods: The Spiritual Significance of Greek Religion. Thames Hudson.

Otto, Wayne.
xOtto, Wayne.
Corrective & Remedial Teaching. HM.
Focused Reading Instruction. A-W.
How to Teach Reading. A-W.
Inservice Education to Improve Reading Instruction. Intl Reading.
Objective Based Reading. A-W.
Reading Problems: A Multidisciplinary Perspective. A-W.

Ottoson, H. W. *see* Ottoson, Howard W.

Ottoson, Howard W.
xOttoson, H. W.
Land & People in the Northern Plains Transition Area. Arno.

Otway, Thomas.
xOtway, Thomas.
The Orphan. U of Nebr Pr.
Venice Preserved. U of Nebr Pr.

Otway-Ruthven, A. J. *see* Otway-Ruthven, Annette Jocelyn.

Otway-Ruthven, Annette Jocelyn, 1909-
xOtway-Ruthven, A. J.
A History of Medieval Ireland. St Martin.

Otwell, John H.
xOtwell, John H.
And Sarah Laughed: The Status of Woman in the Old Testament. Westminster.

Oubre, Claude F., 1936-
xOubre, Claude F.
Forty Acres & a Mule: The Freedmen's Bureau & Black Land Ownership. La State U Pr.

Ouden, Bernard D. *see* Ouden, Bernard D. Den.

Ouden, Bernard D. Den.
xOuden, Bernard D.
The Fusion of Naturalism & Humanism. U Pr of Amer.

Ouei, Mimi. *see* Ouei, Mimie.

Ouei, Mimie.
xOuei, Mimi.
The Art of Chinese Cooking. Random.

Ouellette, R. P.
xOuellette, R. P.
Computer Techniques in Environmental Science. Van Nos Reinhold.

Ouellette, Raymond.
xOuellette, Raymond.
Holistic Healing & the Edgar Cayce Readings. Aero Pr.

Ouellette, Robert J., 1938-
xOuellette, Robert J.
Understanding Chemistry. Har-Row.

Ourada, Patricia K. *see* Ourada, Patrick K.

Ourada, Patrick K., 1926-
xOurada, Patricia K.
The Menominee Indians: A History. U of Okla Pr.

Oursler, Fulton, 1893-1952
xOursler, Fulton.
Fulton Oursler's Greatest: The Greatest Book Ever Written, The Greatest Story Ever Told, The Greatest Faith Ever Known. Doubleday.

Ousby, Ian, 1947-
xOusby, Ian.
A Reader's Guide to Fifty American Novels. B&N.

Ousby, William J.
xOusby, William J.
Theory & Practice of Hypnotism. Arc Bks.
The Theory & Practice of Hypnotism. Arco.

Ouseley, William G. *see* Ouseley, William Gore.

Ouseley, William Gore, Sir, 1797-1866
xOuseley, William G.
Remarks on the Statistics & Political Institutions of the United States. Arno.

Ouseph, P. J., 1933-
xOuseph, P. J.
Introduction to Nuclear Radiation Detectors. Plenum Pub.

Ouspensky, Leonid. *see* Ouspensky, Leonide.

Ouspensky, Leonide.
xOuspensky, Leonid.
Theology of the Icon. St Vladimirs.

Ouston, Philip.
xOuston, Philip A.
The Imagination of Maurice Barres. U of Toronto Pr.

Ouston, Philip A. *see* Ouston, Philip.

Outdoor Life.
xOutdoor Life Editors.

Outdoor Life's Deer Hunting Book. Har-Row.
Outdoor Life Editors. see Outdoor Life.
Outerbridge, David.
  xOuterbridge, David.
    The Last Shepherds. Viking Pr.
Outhwaite, William.
  xOuthwaite, William.
    Understanding Social Life: The Method Called
      Verstehen. Allen Unwin.
    Understanding Social Life: The Method Called
      Verstehen. Holmes & Meier.
Outka, Gene. see Outka, Gene H.
Outka, Gene H.
  xOutka, Gene.
    Agape: An Ethical Analysis. Yale U Pr.
Outler, Albert C. see Outler, Albert Cook.
Outler, Albert Cook.
  xOutler, Albert C.
    The Relationships Among the Gospels: An
      Interdisciplinary Dialogue. Trinity U Pr.
Outwater, Christopher.
  xOutwater, Christopher.
    Guide to Practical Holography. Pentangle Pr.
Ouzer, Louis.
  xOuzer, Louis.
    Contemporary Musicians in Photographs.
      Dover.
Ovard, Glen.
  xOvard, Glen F.
    Administration of the Changing Secondary
      School. Macmillan.
Ovard, Glen F.
  xOvard, Glen F.
    Change & Secondary School Administration: A
      Book of Readings. Macmillan.
Ovard, Glen F. see Ovard, Glen.
Ovchinnikov, Iurii Anatol'Evich.
  xOvchinnikov Y A
    ed. Frontiers in Bioorganic Chemistry &
      Molecular Biology. Elsevier.
Ovchinnikov, Iurii Anatolevich.
  xOvchinnikov, Y. A.
    Membrane Active Complexones. Elsevier.
Ovchinnikov, Y. A. see Ovchinnikov, Iurii Anatolevich.
Ovenden, Graham.
  xOvenden, Graham.
    The Illustrators of Alice in Wonderland. St
      Martin.
Over, Raymond Van. see Van Over, Raymond.
Overacker, Louise, 1891-
  xOveracker, Louise.
    Money in Elections. Arno.
    Presidential Campaign Funds. AMS Pr.
    The Presidential Primary. Arno.
Overall, John E. see Overall, John Ernest.
Overall, John Ernest.
  xOverall, John E.
    Applied Multivariate Analysis. McGraw.
Overbeck, Cynthia.
  xOverbeck, Cynthia.
    The Butterfly Book. Lerner Pubns.
    Curly the Piglet. Carolrhoda Bks.
    The Fruit Book. Lerner Pubns.
    The Vegetable Book. Lerner Pubns
Overbeck, Wayne.
  xOverbeck, Wayne.
    Mass Media Law in California. Kendall-Hunt.
Overbeek, Johannes.
  xOverbeek, Johannes.
    ed. The Evolution of Population Theory: A
      Documentary Sourcebook. Greenwood.
    The Population Challenge: A Handbook for
      Non-Specialists. Greenwood.
Overbeek, Ross A.
  xOverbeek, Ross A.
    Assembler Language with ASSIST. SRA.
Overbey, David.
  xOverbey, David.

    ed. Springtime in Italy: A Reader on
      Neo-Realism. Shoe String.
Overcash, J. P. Foreword by. see Edmond, J. B.
Overcash, Michael R.
  xOvercash, Michael R.
    ed. Environmental Impact of Nonpoint Source
      Pollution. Ann Arbor Science.
Overholser, Stephen.
  xOverholser, Stephen.
    Field of Death. Doubleday.
Overholt, W. H. see Overholt, William H.
Overholt, William. see Overholt, William H.
Overholt, William A.
  xOverholt, William A.
    Religion in American Colleges & Universities.
      Am Personnel.
Overholt, William H.
  xOverholt, W. H.
    Asia's Nuclear Future. Westview.
  xOverholt, William.
    The Future of Brazil. Westview.
Overholts, Lee O. see Overholts, Lee Oras.
Overholts, Lee Oras, 1890-1946
  xOverholts, Lee O.
    Polyporaceae of the United States, Alaska, &
      Canada. U of Mich Pr.
Overholtzer, Arthur E., 1910-
  xOverholtzer, Arthur E.
    Classic Guitar Making. Brock Pub.
Overlach, Theodore W. see Overlach, Theodore William.
Overlach, Theodore William, 1887-
  xOverlach, Theodore W.
    Foreign Financial Control in China. Arno.
Overlie, George.
  xOverlie, George.
    illus. Tallest Tree. Lerner Pubns.
Overman, Michael.
  xOverman, Michael
    Understanding Sound, Video, & Film
      Recording. TAB Bks.
    Understanding Telecommunications. Intl Pubns
      Serv.
Overmyer, Daniel L., 1935-
  xOvermyer, Daniel L.
    Folk Buddhist Religion: Dissenting Sects in
      Late Traditional China. Harvard U Pr.
Overmyer, Grace.
  xOvermyer, Grace.
    America's First Hamlet. Greenwood.
Overs, Robert P.
  xOvers, Robert P.
    Avocational Activities for the Handicapped: A
      Handbook for Avocational Counseling. C C
      Thomas.
Overseas Assignment Directory Service.
  xEditors of the Overseas Assignment Directory.
    Business with China. Knowledge Indus.
Overseas Development Institute. see Overseas
  Development Institute, London.
Overseas Development Institute, London.
  xOverseas Development Institute.
    Development Guide. Allen Unwin.
Overstake, Charles P.
  xOverstake, Charles P.
    Stuttering: A New Look at an Old Problem
      Based on Neurophysiological Aspects. C C
      Thomas.
Overstreet, Bonaro W. see Overstreet, Bonaro Wilkinson.
Overstreet, Bonaro Wilkinson, 1902-
  xOverstreet, Bonaro W.
    How to Think About Ourselves. Norton.
    Signature: New & Selected Poems. Norton.
Overstreet, H. A. see Overstreet, Harry Allen.
Overstreet, Harry A. see Overstreet, Harry Allen.
Overstreet, Harry Allen, 1875-
  xOverstreet, H. A.
    Mature Mind. Watts.
    Strange Tactics of Extremism. Norton.
  xOverstreet, Harry A.

    Guide to Civilized Leisure. Arno.
Overton, D. E. see Overton, Donald E.
Overton, Donald E.
  xOverton, D. E.
    Stormwater Modeling. Acad Pr.
Overton, Grant. see Overton, Grant Martin.
Overton, Grant M. see Overton, Grant Martin.
Overton, Grant Martin, 1887-1930
  xOverton, Grant.
    Cargoes for Crusoes. R West.
  xOverton, Grant M.
    Authors of the Day: Studies in Contemporary
      Literature. Arno.
    Authors of the Day: Studies in Contemporary
      Literature. R West.
    Cargoes for Crusoes. Arno.
    When Winter Comes to Main Street. Arno.
    When Winter Comes to Main Street. R West.
    Women Who Make Our Novels. Arno.
    Women Who Make Our Novels. R West.
Overton, Jenny.
  xOverton, Jenny.
    Creed Country. Macmillan.
Overton, Richard C. see Overton, Richard Cleghorn.
Overton, Richard Cleghorn, 1907-
  xOverton, Richard C.
    Gulf to Rockies: The Heritage of the Fort
      Worth & Denver-Colorado & Southern
      Railways, 1861-1898. U of Tex Pr.
Overton, Ron.
  xOverton, Ron.
    Dead Reckoning. Street Pr.
Ovesen, Ellis.
  xOvesen, Ellis.
    Lives Touch. St Marys.
Ovington, Mary W. see Ovington, Mary White.
Ovington, Mary White, 1865-1951
  xOvington, Mary W
    Half a Man: The Status of the Negro in New
      York. Negro U Pr.
    Half a Man: The Status of the Negro in New
      York. Schocken.
Ovington, Ray.
  xOvington, Ray.
    America's Best Fresh Water Fishing. Jonathan
      David.
    Freshwater Fishing. Dutton.
    How to Take Trout on Wet Flies & Nymphs.
      Freshet Pr.
    Pelican. Great Outdoors.
    Tactics on Trout. Knopf.
    The Trout & the Fly. Dutton.
Owen. see Owen, John D.
Owen, A. L.
  xOwen, A. L.
    The Famous Druids: A Survey of Three
      Centuries of English Literature in the Druids.
      Greenwood.
Owen, A. R. see Owen, a R G.
Owen, A. R. G.
  xOwen, A. R.
    Can We Explain the Poltergeist. Garrett-Helix.
Owen, Albert K. see Owen, Albert Kimsey.
Owen, Albert Kimsey.
  xOwen, Albert K.
    Integral Cooperation: It's Practical Application.
      Porcupine Pr.
Owen, Bruce M.
  xOwen, Bruce M.
    Economics & Freedom of Expression: Media
      Structure & the First Amendment. Ballinger
      Pub.
Owen, Charles A. see Owen, Charles Abraham.
Owen, Charles Abraham, 1914-
  xOwen, Charles A.
    ed. Discussions of the Canterbury Tales.
      Greenwood.
Owen, Charles Archibald, 1915-
  xOwen, Charles A.

The Diagnosis of Bleeding Disorders. Little.
Owen, D. F.
  xOwen, D. F.
    Animal Ecology in Tropical Africa. Longman.
Owen, D. F. *see* Owen, Denis Frank.
Owen, David, 1938-
  xOwen, David.
    Human Rights. Norton.
    The Politics of Defence. Taplinger.
Owen, Denis Frank.
  xOwen, D. F.
    Tropical Butterflies: The Ecology & Behaviour
      of Butterflies in the Tropics with Special
      Reference to African Species. Oxford U Pr.
Owen, Dilys.
  xOwen, Dilys.
    Leo Possessed. HarBraceJ.
Owen, Dolores. *see* Owen, Dolores B.
Owen, Dolores B.
  xOwen, Dolores.
    Abstracts & Indexes in Science & Technology:
      A Descriptive Guide. Scarecrow.
Owen, G. Frederick. *see* Owen, George Frederick.
Owen, Geoffrey, 1934-
  xOwen, Geoffrey.
    Industry in the U. S. A. Gannon.
Owen, George E. *see* Owen, George Ernest.
Owen, George Ernest, 1922-
  xOwen, George E.
    Fundamentals of Scientific Mathematics. Johns
      Hopkins.
Owen, George Frederick, 1897-
  xOwen, G. Frederick.
    The Holy Land. Beacon Hill.
Owen, Guy.
  xOwen, Guy.
    ed. Contemporary Poetry of North Carolina.
      Blair.
Owen, Harold, 1872-1930
  xOwen, Harold.
    Common Sense About Shaw. Arden Lib.
    Common Sense About Shaw. Folcroft.
Owen, Harrison, 1936-
  xOwen, Harrison.
    illus. When the Devil Dances. Mara.
Owen, John B. *see* Owen, John Beresford.
Owen, John Beresford.
  xOwen, John B.
    The Eighteenth Century, 1714-1815. Norton.
    The Eighteenth Century: 1714-1815. Rowman.
Owen, John D.
  xOwen.
    Working Hours: An Economic Analysis.
      Lexington Bks.
Owen, Norman G.
  xOwen, Norman G.
    ed. Compadre Colonialism: Studies on the
      Philippines Under American Rule. Ctr S&SE
      Asian.
Owen, Pat.
  xOwen, Pat.
    Story of Royal Copenhagen Christmas Plates.
      Viking Import.
Owen, R. C. *see* Owen, Roger C.
Owen, Raymond E.
  xOwen, Raymond E.
    A Survey Manual for State Legislators. U Ctr
      Intl St.
Owen, Richard, Sir, 1804-1892
  xOwen, Richard.
    The Eye of the Gods. NAL.
    A History of British Fossil Mammals & Birds.
      AMS Pr.
    Nightmare. St Martin.
    On the Anatomy of Vertebrates. AMS Pr.
Owen, Richard S. *see* Owen, Richard Startin.
Owen, Richard Startin.
  xOwen, Richard S.
    The Life of Richard Owen. AMS Pr.
Owen, Robert D. *see* Owen, Robert Dale.

Owen, Robert Dale, 1801-1877
  xOwen, Robert D.
    Hints on Public Architecture. Da Capo.
Owen, Roger C.
  xOwen, R. C.
    North American Indians: A Sourcebook.
      Macmillan.
Owen, Steven V.
  xOwen, Steven V.
    Educational Psychology: An Introduction.
      Little.
Owen, Sylvia C., 1899-
  xOwen, Sylvia C.
    The Complete Puli. Howell Bk.
Owen, T. C. *see* Owen, Terence C.
Owen, T. R. *see* Owen, Thomas Richard.
Owen, Terence C., 1930-
  xOwen, T. C.
    Characterization of Organic Compounds by
      Chemical Methods: An Introductory
      Laboratory Textbook. Dekker.
Owen, Thomas M. *see* Owen, Thomas Mcadory.
Owen, Thomas Mcadory, 1866-1920
  xOwen, Thomas M.
    History of Alabama & Dictionary of Alabama
      Biography. Reprint.
Owen, Thomas Richard.
  xOwen, T. R.
    The Geological Evolution of the British Isles.
      Pergamon.
Owen, W. J. *see* Owen, Warwick Jack Burgoyne.
Owen, Warwick Jack Burgoyne.
  xOwen, W. J.
    Wordsworth As Critic. U of Toronto Pr.
Owen, Wilfred.
  xOwen, Wilfred.
    The Accessible City. Brookings.
    Cities in the Motor Age. Cooper Sq.
    Distance & Development: Transport &
      Communications in India. Brookings.
    Strategy for Mobility. Greenwood.
Owen, William B. *see* Owen, William Bishop.
Owen, William Bishop.
  xOwen, William B.
    Homeric Vocabularies: Greek & English
      Word-Lists for the Study of Homer. U of
      Okla Pr.
Owens, Bill.
  xOwens, Bill.
    Suburbia. Working Pr CA.
    Working: I Do It for the Money. S&S.
Owens, Edgar.
  xOwens, Edgar.
    Development Reconsidered: Bridging the Gap
      Between Government & People. Lexington
      Bks.
Owens, Elisabeth A.
  xOwens, Elisabeth A.
    The Foreign Tax Credit: A Study of the Credit
      for Foreign Taxes Under United States
      Income Tax Law. Harvard Law Intl Tax.
    Indirect Credit: A Study of Various Foreign
      Tax Credits Granted to Domestic
      Shareholders Under U.S. Income Tax Law.
      Harvard Law Intl Tax.
Owens, Frank J.
  xOwens, Frank J.
    ed. Magnetic Resonance of Phase Transitions.
      Acad Pr.
Owens, Jimmy.
  xOwens, Jimmy.
    If My People...: A Handbook for National
      Intercession. Word Bks.
Owens, Joan L. *see* Owens, Joan Llewelyn.
Owens, Joan Llewelyn.
  xOwens, Joan L.
    The Graduate's Guide to the Business World.
      Leviathan Hse.
Owens, Joseph.
  xOwens, Joseph.

History of Ancient Western Philosophy. P-H.
St. Thomas Aquinas on the Existence of God:
    Collected Papers of Joseph Owens. State U
    NY Pr.
Owens, Leslie H. *see* Owens, Leslie Howard.
Owens, Leslie Howard.
  xOwens, Leslie H.
    This Species of Property: Slave Life & Culture
      in the Old South. Oxford U Pr.
Owens, Richard. *see* Owens, Richard E.
Owens, Richard E.
  xOwens, Richard.
    Carnival Glass Tumblers. Wallace-Homestead.
Owens, Robert G.
  xOwens, Robert G.
    Administering Change in Schools. P-H.
    Organizational Behavior in Schools. P-H.
Owens, Virginia S. *see* Owens, Virginia Stem.
Owens, Virginia Stem.
  xOwens, Virginia S.
    A Taste of Creation. Judson.
Owens, W. *see* Owens, William A.
Owens, William A., 1905-
  xOwens, W.
    Look to the River. McGraw.
  xOwens, William A.
    This Stubborn Soil. Scribner.
Owensby, Clenton E., 1940-
  xOwensby, Clenton E.
    Kansas Prairie Wildflowers. Iowa St U Pr.
Ower, Ernest.
  xOwer, Ernest.
    Measurement of Air Flow. Pergamon.
Ower, John.
  xOwer, John.
    Legendary Acts. U of Ga Pr.
Owicki, Susan S. *see* Owicki, Susan Speer.
Owicki, Susan Speer.
  xOwicki, Susan S.
    Axiomatic Proof Techniques for Parallel
      Programs. Garland Pub.
Owings, Marvin A. *see* Owings, Marvin Alpheus.
Owings, Marvin Alpheus.
  xOwings, Marvin A.
    Arts in the Middle English Romances. AMS
      Pr.
Owlett, F. *see* Owlett, F. C.
Owlett, F. C.
  xOwlett, F.
    Francis Thompson. Arden Lib.
  xOwlett, F. C.
    Francis Thompson. Folcroft.
Owre, H. B. *see* Owre, Harding Boehme.
Owre, Harding Boehme.
  xOwre, H. B.
    Copepods of the Florida Current. U Miami
      Marine.
Owsley, Frank L. *see* Owsley, Frank Lawrence.
Owsley, Frank Lawrence, 1890-
  xOwsley, Frank L.
    Plain Folk of the Old South. Times Bks.
Owst, Gerald R. *see* Owst, Gerald Robert.
Owst, Gerald Robert, 1894-
  xOwst, Gerald R.
    Preaching in Medieval England: An
      Introduction to Sermon Manuscripts of the
      Period c. 1350-1450. Russell.
Owusu, Maxwell.
  xOwusu, Maxwell.
    Uses & Abuses of Political Power: A Case
      Study of Continuity & Change in the Politics
      of Ghana. U of Chicago Pr.
Oxenbury, Helen.
  xOxenbury, Helen.
    The Queen & Rosie Randall. Morrow.
Oxendine, J. *see* Oxendine, Joseph B.
Oxendine, Joseph B.
  xOxendine, J.
    Psychology of Motor Learning. P-H.
Oxenfeldt, Alfred R. *see* Oxenfeldt, Alfred Richard.

Oxenfeldt, Alfred Richard, 1917-
xOxenfeldt, Alfred R.
Cost-Benefit Analysis for Executive Decision Making: The Danger of Plain Common Sense. Am Mgmt.
Pricing Strategies. Am Mgmt.

Oxenhandler, Neal.
xOxenhandler, Neal.
Change of Gods. HarBraceJ.

Oxford Liberal Group.
xOxford Liberal Group.
Radical Alternative: Studies in Liberalism. Greenwood.

Oxford. University.
xOxford University.
Register of the Visitors of the University of Oxford, from A.D. 1647 to A.D. 1658. Johnson Repr.
xUniversity Of Oxford.
Report of the Committee on Relations with Junior Members. Oxford U Pr.
University of Oxford: Report of Commission for Inquiry. Oxford U Pr.

Oxford University - Bodleian Library. *see* Oxford. University. Bodleian Library.

Oxford. University. Bodleian Library.
xOxford University - Bodleian Library.
ed. Catalogue of a Collection of Early Newspapers & Essayists. Kelley.

Oxford University British Commonwealth Group.
xOxford University, British Commonwealth Group.
Germany's Colonial Demands. Greenwood.

Oxford University Press.
xThe Cartographic Department of Oxford University Press.
ed. The New Oxford Atlas. Oxford U Pr.

Oxford University. Taylor Institution. *see* Oxford. University. Taylor Instituluion.

Oxford. University. Taylor Instilutulon.
xOxford University. Taylor Institution.
Studies in European Literature, Being the Taylorian Lectures 1920-1930. Arno.

Oxley, Mary B. *see* Oxley, Mary Boone.

Oxley, Mary Boone, 1928-
xOxley, Mary B.
Illustrated Guide to Individualized Kindergarten Instruction. P-H.

Oxnam, Garfield B. *see* Oxnam, Garfield Bromley.

Oxnam, Garfield Bromley, Bp, 1891-1963
xOxnam, Garfield B.
I Protest. Greenwood.
Preaching in a Revolutionary Age. Arno.

Oxtoby, J. C. *see* Oxtoby, John C.

Oxtoby, John C.
xOxtoby, J. C.
Measure & Category: A Survey of the Analogies Between Topological & Measure Spaces. Springer-Verlag.

Oxtoby, Willard G. *see* Oxtoby, Willard Gurdon.

Oxtoby, Willard Gurdon.
xOxtoby, Willard G.
Some Inscriptions of the Safaitic Bedouin. Am Orient Soc.

Oyama, Mas. *see* Oyama, Masutatsu.

Oyama, Masutatsu.
xOyama, Mas.
This Is Karate. Wehman.
xOyama, Masutatsu.
This Is Karate. Japan Pubns.

Oyama, T. *see* Oyama, Tsutomu.

Oyama, Tsutomu, 1923-
xOyama, T.
Anesthetic Management of Endocrine Disease. Springer-Verlag.

Oyebola, Areoye.
xOyebola, Areoye.
Black Man's Dilemma. Vantage.

Oyediran, Oyeleye.
xOyediran, Oyeleye.

ed. Nigerian Government & Politics Under Military Rule 1966-1979. St Martin.

Oyer, E. Jane. *see* Oyer, Herbert J.
Oyer, H. J. *see* Oyer, Herbert J.

Oyer, Herbert J.
xOyer, E. Jane.
jt. ed. Aging & Communication. Univ Park.
xOyer, H. J.
The Aural Rehabilitation Process: A Conceptual Framework Analysis. HR&W.
xOyer, Herbert J.
ed. Aging & Communication. Univ Park.
ed. Communication for the Hearing Handicapped: An International Perspective. Univ Park.

Oyle, Irving, 1925-
xOyle, Irving.
The New American Medicine Show: Discovering the Healing Connection. Unity Pr.

Oz, Amos.
xOz, Amos.
Touch the Water, Touch the Wind. Bantam.
Touch the Water, Touch the Wind. HarBraceJ.

Ozanam, Antoine Frederic.
xOzanam, Frederick.
Franciscan Poets of the Thirteenth Century. Kennikat.

Ozanam, Frederick. *see* Ozanam, Antoine Frederic.

Ozawa, Terutomo.
xOzawa, Terutomo.
Multinationalism, Japanese Style: The Political Economy of Outward Dependency. Princeton U Pr.

Ozenfant. *see* Ozenfant, Amedee.
Ozenfant, A. *see* Ozenfant, Amedee.

Ozenfant, Amedee, 1886-
xOzenfant.
Foundations of Modern Art. Arden Lib.
xOzenfant, A.
Foundations of Modern Art. Peter Smith.
xOzenfant, Amedee.
Foundations of Modern Art. Dover.

Ozer, Mark N.
xOzer, Mark N.
ed. A Cybernetic Approach to the Assessment of Children: Toward a More Humane Use of Human Beings. Westview.

Ozias, Blake.
xOzias, Blake.
All About Wine. T Y Crowell.

Ozisik, M. Necati.
xOzisik, M. Necati.
Heat Conduction. Wiley.
Radiative Transfer & Interactions with Conduction & Convection. Wiley.

Ozment, Steven E.
xOzment, Steven E.
ed. Reformation in Medieval Perspective. New Viewpoints.
The Reformation in the Cities: The Appeal of Protestantism to Sixteenth-Century Germany & Switzerland. Yale U Pr.

Ozmon, Howard.
xOzmon, Howard.
Dialogue in the Philosophy of Education. Merrill.

Ozonoff, M. B.
xOzonoff, M. B.
Pediatric Orthopedic Radiology. Saunders.

P-H Editorial Staff. *see* Prentice-Hall, Inc.
P-H Staff. *see* Prentice-Hall, Inc.

P'Bitek, Okot, 1931-
xP'Bitek, Okot.
The Hare & the Hornbill. Heinemann Ed.

Paalman, Anthony.
xPaalman, Anthony.
Training Showjumpers. J A Allen.

Paarlberg, Don. *see* Paarlberg, Donald.

Paarlberg, Donald.
xPaarlberg, Don.
Great Myths of Economics. Green Hill.
Great Myths of Economics. Humanities.
Great Myths of Economics. Inst Humane.
Subsidized Food Consumption. Am Enterprise.

Paaswell, Robert E.
xPaaswell, Robert E.
Problems of the Carless. Praeger.

Paavo Nurmi Symposium, 1st, Finland, 1969. *see* Paavo Nurmi Symposium, 1st, Porvoo, Finland,1969.

Paavo Nurmi Symposium, 1st, Porvoo, Finland,1969.
xPaavo Nurmi Symposium, 1st, Finland, 1969.
Thrombosis & Coronary Heart Disease: Proceedings. S Karger.

Paavo Nurmi Symposium, 2d, Porvoo, Finland, 1971.
xPaavo Nurmi Sympposium, 2nd, Porvoo, September 1971.
Early Diagnosis of Coronary Heart Disease: Proceedings. S Karger.

Paavo Nurmi Symposium 3d, Helsinki, 1975.
xPaavo Nurmi Symposium, 3rd, Helsinki, 1975.
Physical Activity & Coronary Heart Disease: Proceedings. S Karger.

Paavo Nurmi Symposium, 3rd, Helsinki, 1975. *see* Paavo Nurmi Symposium 3d, Helsinki, 1975.

Paavo Nurmi Sympposium, 2nd, Porvoo, September 1971. *see* Paavo Nurmi Symposium, 2d, Porvoo, Finland, 1971.

Pace, C. Robert. *see* Pace, Charles Robert.

Pace, Charles Robert, 1912-
xPace, C. Robert.
Measuring Outcomes of College: Fifty Years of Findings & Recommendations for the Future. Jossey-Bass.

Pace, Dale K.
xPace, Dale K
A Christian's Guide to Effective Jail & Prison Ministries. Revell.

Pace, David. *see* Pace, David E.

Pace, David E.
xPace, David.
Direct Participation in Action: The New Bureaucracy. Lexington Bks.

Pace, Dean F. *see* Pace, Dean Francis.

Pace, Dean Francis.
xPace, Dean F.
Negotiation & Management of Defense Contracts. Wiley.

Pace, Eric, 1936-
xPace, Eric.
Nightingale. Random.

Pace, J. Blair, 1916-
xPace, J. Blair.
Pain: A Personal Experience. Nelson-Hall.

Pace, R. Wayne.
xPace, R. Wayne.
The Human Transaction: Facets, Functions, & Forms of Interpersonal Communication. Scott F.
Techniques of Effective Communication. A-W.

Pace, Richard, 1482 (ca.)-1536
xPace, Richard.
De Fructu Qui Ex Doctrina Percipitur: The Benefit of a Liberal Education. Ungar.

Pacey, Arnold.
xPacey, Arnold.
The Maze of Ingenuity: Ideas & Idealism in the Development of Technology. Holmes & Meier.
The Maze of Ingenuity: Ideas & Idealism in the Development of Technology. MIT Pr.

Pacey, Desmond, 1917-
xPacey, Desmond.
Creative Writing in Canada: A Short History of English-Canadian Literature. Greenwood.

Pacey, Lorene M.
xPacey, Lorene M.

ed. Readings in the Development of Settlement
Work. Arno.
Pach, Walter, 1883-1958
xPach, Walter.
Masters of Modern Art. Arno.
Queer Thing, Painting: Forty Years in the
World of Art. Arno.
Pachauri, R. K.
xPachauri, R. K.
The Dynamics of Electrical Energy Supply &
Demand: An Economic Analysis. Praeger.
Energy & Economic Development in India.
Praeger.
Pacheco, Ferdie.
xPacheco, Ferdie.
Fight Doctor. S&S.
Pachmuss, Temira, 1927-
xPachmuss, Temira.
ed. Women Writers in Russian Modernism: An
Anthology. U of Ill Pr.
Pacholczyk, A. G., 1935-
xPacholczyk, A. G.
Radio Astrophysics: Nonthermal Processes in
Galactic & Extragalactic Sources. W H
Freeman.
Radio Galaxies: Radiation Transfer, Dynamics,
Stability & Evolution of a Synchroton
Plasmon. Pergamon.
Pachter, Henry M. *see* Pachter, Henry Maximilan.
Pachter, Henry Maximilan, 1907-
xPachter, Henry M.
Modern Germany: A Social, Cultural, &
Political History. Westview.
Pachucki, Chester, 1917-
xPachucki, Chester.
Mathematics for Industrial Technicians. P-H.
Paci, Enzo, 1911-
xPaci, Enzo.
The Function of the Sciences & the Meaning
of Man. Northwestern U Pr.
Pacific Northwest Laboratory. *see* Battelle Memorial
Institute, Columbus, Ohio. Pacific Northwest
Laboratory, Richland, Wash.
Pacifici, Sergio.
xPacifici, Sergio.
A Guide to Contemporary Italian Literature:
From Futurism to Neorealism. S Ill U Pr.
Pack, Alice C.
xPack, Alice C.
Learning to Type in English As a Second
Language. U Pr of Amer.
Pack, Frank.
xPack, Frank.
Preaching to Modern Man. Bibl Res Pr.
Pack, G. T. *see* Pack, George Thomas.
Pack, George Thomas.
xPack, G. T.
ed. Tumors of the Liver. Springer-Verlag.
Pack, Howard.
xPack, Howard.
Structural Change & Economic Policy in Israel.
Yale U Pr.
Pack, Robert.
xPack, Robert.
How to Catch a Crocodile. Knopf.
Waking to My Name: New & Selected Poems.
Johns Hopkins.
xPack, Robert M.
Nothing but Light. Rutgers U Pr.
Pack, Robert M. *see* Pack, Robert.
Pack, S. W. *see* Pack, S. W. C.
Pack, S. W. C.
xPack, S. W.
Operation HUSKY: The Allied Invasion of
Sicily. Hippocrene Bks.
Packard. *see* Packard, Sidney.
Packard, Bob.
xPackard, Bob.

The Pro. Nordon Pubns.
Packard, David W.
xPackard, David W.
Concordance to Livy. Harvard U Pr.
Packard, Earl L. *see* Packard, Earl Leroy.
Packard, Earl Leroy, 1885-
xPackard, Earl L.
Fossil Edentates of Oregon. Oreg St U Pr.
Packard, Edward.
xPackard, Edward.
The Third Planet from Altair. Lippincott.
The Third Planet from Altair. Bantam.
Packard, Elizabeth P. *see* Packard, Elizabeth Parsons
Ware.
Packard, Elizabeth Parsons Ware, 1816-1895
xPackard, Elizabeth P.
Great Disclosure of Spiritual Wickedness in
High Places: With Appeal to the Government
to Protect the Inalienable Rights of Married
Women. Arno.
Packard, Frederic A. *see* Packard, Frederick Adolphus.
Packard, Frederick Adolphus, 1794-1867
xPackard, Frederic A.
Daily Public School in the United States. Arno.
Packard, George V., 1932-
xPackard, George V.
That Grail Song, Sam, One More Time.
Gambit.
Packard, L. B. *see* Packard, Laurence Bradford.
Packard, Laurence Bradford, 1887-
xPackard, L. B.
The Age of Louis XIV. HR&W.
Packard, Philip C.
xPackard, Philip C.
Critical Path Analysis for Development
Administration. Mouton.
Packard, Robert G.
xPackard, Robert G.
Psychology of Learning & Instruction: A
Performance Based Course. Merrill.
Packard, Sidney.
xPackard.
Fashion Buying & Merchandising. Fairchild.
xPackard, Sidney.
The Buying Game: Fashion Buying &
Merchandising. Fairchild.
Consumer Behavior & Fashion Marketing. Wm
C Brown.
Packard, Vance. *see* Packard, Vance Oakley.
Packard, Vance Oakley, 1914-
xPackard, Vance.
Nation of Strangers. PB.
The People Shapers. Bantam.
The People Shapers. Little.
Packard, Vernal S.
xPackard, Vernal S.
Processed Foods & the Consumer: Additives,
Labeling, Standards & Nutrition. U of Minn
Pr.
Packard, William.
xPackard, William.
The American Experience. Barlenmir.
First Selected Poems. Pylon.
Four Plays. Living Poets.
Packenham, Robert A.
xPackenham, Robert A.
Liberal America & the Third World: Political
Development Ideas in Foreign Aid & Social
Science. Princeton U Pr.
Packer, Bernard.
xPacker, Bernard.
The Second Death of Samuel Auer. HarBraceJ.
Packer, Boyd K.
xPacker, Boyd K.
Eternal Love. Deseret Bk.
Teach Ye Diligently. Deseret Bk.
Packer, Clinton L.
xPacker, Clinton L.

Preparing Hospital Management for Labor
Contract Negotiations. Am Hospital.
Packer, Herbert L.
xPacker, Herbert L.
Ex-Communist Witnesses: Four Studies in Fact
Finding. Stanford U Pr.
The Limits of the Criminal Sanction. Stanford
U Pr.
Packer, J. I.
xPacker, James I.
Evangelism & the Sovereignty of God.
Inter-Varsity.
Packer, James I. *see* Packer, J. I.
Packer, Lester.
xPacker, Lester.
Experiments in Cell Physiology. Acad Pr.
Packer, Paul C. *see* Packer, Paul Clifford.
Packer, Paul Clifford, 1886-
xPacker, Paul C.
Housing of High School Programs. AMS Pr.
Packer, Peter.
xPacker, Peter.
Death of the Other Self. Belmont-Tower.
Packman, Jean.
xPackman, Jean.
The Child's Generation: Child Care Policy
from Curtis to Houghton. Biblio Dist.
Packwood, William T.
xPackwood, William T.
College Student Personnel Services. C C
Thomas.
Padden, R. C.
xPadden, R. C.
Hummingbird & the Hawk: Conquest &
Sovereignty in the Valley of Mexico,
1503-1541. Har-Row.
Hummingbird & the Hawk: Conquest &
Sovereignty in the Valley of Mexico,
1503-1541. Ohio St U Pr.
Paddock, John.
xPaddock, John.
ed. Ancient Oaxaca: Discoveries in Mexican
Archeology & History. Stanford U Pr.
Paddock, Nancy.
xPaddock, Nancy.
A Dark Light. Vanilla.
Paddock, Paul.
xPaddock, Paul.
China Diary: Crisis Diplomacy in Dairen. Iowa
St U Pr.
Padelford, Frederick M. *see* Padelford, Frederick
Morgan.
Padelford, Frederick Morgan, 1875-1942
xPadelford, Frederick M.
Early Sixteenth Century Lyrics. AMS Pr.
Old English Musical Terms. Longwood Pr.
Paden, Donald W.
xPaden, Donald W.
An Introduction to Economic Analysis. West
Pub.
Paden, John N.
xPaden, John N.
ed. African Experience. Northwestern U Pr.
Religion & Political Culture in Kano. U of Cal
Pr.
Padfield, Harland.
xPadfield, Harland.
Farmers, Workers, & Machines: Technological
& Social Change in Farm Industries of
Arizona. U of Ariz Pr.
Padgett, Leonard. *see* Padgett, Leonard E.
Padgett, Leonard E.
xPadgett, Leonard.
Pairpoint Glass. Wallace-Homestead.
Padgett, Ron.
xPadgett, Ron.
Tulsa Kid. Z Pr.
Padgett, W. J.
xPadgett, W. J.

Laws of Large Numbers for Normed Linear
      Spaces & Certain Frechet Spaces.
      Springer-Verlag.
Padilla, George M.
   xPadilla, George M.
      Cell Cycle Controls. Acad Pr.
      Cell Cycle: Gene-Enzyme Interactions. Acad
      Pr.
Padmore, George, 1903-1959
   xPadmore, George.
      How Britain Rules Africa. Negro U Pr.
      Life & Struggles of Negro Toilers. Sun Dance
      Bks.
Padover, Saul K. *see* Padover, Saul Kussiel.
Padover, Saul Kussiel, 1905-
   xPadover, Saul K.
      French Institutions: Values & Politics.
      Greenwood.
Padulo, Louis.
   xPadulo, Louis.
      System Theory: A Unified State-Space
      Approach to Continuous & Discrete Systems.
      Hemisphere Pub.
Paelian, G. *see* Paelian, Garabed Hagop.
Paelian, Garabed Hagop, 1880-
   xPaelian, G.
      Nicholas Roerich. Aqua Educ.
Paelinck, J. H. *see* Paelinck, Jean H. P.
Paelinck, Jean H. P.
   xPaelinck, J. H.
      Spatial Econometrics. Lexington Bks.
Paetow, L. J. *see* Paetow, Louis John.
Paetow, Louis John, 1880-1928
   xPaetow, L. J.
      The Arts Course at Medieval Universities with
      Special Reference to Grammar & Rhetoric.
      Irvington.
Paetro, Maxine.
   xPaetro, Maxine.
      How to Put Your Book Together & Get a Job
      in Advertising. Dutton.
      How to Put Your Book Together & Get a Job
      in Advertising. Executive Comm.
Paff, George H. *see* Paff, George Hugo.
Paff, George Hugo, 1905-
   xPaff, George H.
      Anatomy of the Head & Neck. Saunders.
Paffard, Michael.
   xPaffard, Michael.
      The Unattended Moment: Excerpts from
      Autobiographies with Hints & Guesses.
      Allenson.
Pagano, Jo, 1906-
   xPagano, Jo.
      Golden Wedding. Arno.
Page. *see* Page, Thomas.
Page, Benjamin. *see* Page, Benjamin I.
Page, Benjamin I.
   xPage, Benjamin.
      Choices & Echoes in Presidential Elections:
      Rational Man & Electoral Democracy. U of
      Chicago Pr.
Page, Charles H. *see* Page, Charles Hunt.
Page, Charles Hunt.
   xPage, Charles H.
      ed. Sociology & Contemporary Education.
      Phila Bk Co.
Page, Chester H. *see* Page, Chester Hall.
Page, Chester Hall.
   xPage, Chester H.
      The Algebra of Electronics. Krieger.
Page, David P. *see* Page, David Perkins.
Page, David Perkins, 1810-1848
   xPage, David P.
      Theory & Practice of Teaching. Arno.
Page, David S.
   xPage, David S.
      Principles of Biological Chemistry. Prindle.
Page, Denys. *see* Page, Denys Lionel.
Page, Denys L. *see* Page, Denys Lionel.

Page, Denys Lionel.
   xPage, Denys.
      Folktales in Homer's Odyssey. Harvard U Pr.
   xPage, Denys L.
      History & the Homeric Iliad. U of Cal Pr.
Page, E. S.
   xPage, E. S.
      Information, Representation & Manipulation in
      a Computer. Cambridge U Pr.
Page, I. H. *see* Page, Irvine Heinly.
Page, Irvine Heinly.
   xPage, I. H.
      ed. Angiotensin. Springer-Verlag.
Page, J. S. *see* Page, John S.
Page, Jack. *see* Page, Jake.
Page, Jake.
   xPage, Jack.
      Shoot the Moon. Bobbs.
Page, James O.
   xPage.
      Effective Company Command for Company
      Officers in the Professional Fire Service.
      Borden.
Page, John S.
   xPage, J. S.
      Estimator's Piping Manhour Manual. Gulf Pub.
   xPage, John S.
      Estimator's Electrical Man-Hour Manual. Gulf
      Pub.
      Estimator's Equipment Installation Man-Hour
      Manual. Gulf Pub.
      Estimator's General Construction Man-Hour
      Manual. Gulf Pub.
      Estimator's Man-Hour Manual on Heating, Air
      Conditioning, Ventilating & Plumbing. Gulf
      Pub.
Page, Kirby, 1890-1957
   xPage, Kirby.
      Dollars & World Peace. Garland Pub.
Page, Marian, 1918-
   xPage, Marian.
      Furniture Designed by Architects.
      Watson-Guptill.
      Historic Houses Restored & Preserved.
      Watson-Guptill.
      Historic Houses Restored & Preserved.
      Watson-Guptill.
Page, Norman.
   xPage, Norman.
      Thomas Hardy. Routledge & Kegan.
Page, Robert C. *see* Page, Robert Collier.
Page, Robert Collier, 1908-
   xPage, Robert C.
      Occupational Health & Mantalent
      Development. Fireside Bks.
      Occupational Health & Mantalent
      Development. Green.
Page, Robert M. *see* Page, Robert Morris.
Page, Robert Morris, 1903-
   xPage, Robert M.
      The Origin of Radar. Greenwood.
Page, Ruth.
   xPage, Ruth.
      Page by Page. Dance Horiz.
Page, S. W. *see* Page, Stanley W.
Page, Stanley W.
   xPage, S. W.
      Lenin & World Revolution. Peter Smith.
   xPage, Stanley W.
      The Formation of the Baltic States: A Study of
      the Effects of Great Power Politics Upon the
      Emergence of Lithuania,Latvia, & Estonia.
      Fertig.
Page, T. *see* Page, Talbot.
Page, Talbot.
   xPage, T.

Economics of Involuntary Transfers: A Unified
      Approach to Pollution & Congestion
      Externalities. Springer-Verlag.
Page, Thomas, 1942-
   xPage.
      New York. Bonanza.
   xPage, Thomas.
      The Spirit. Ballantine.
Page, Thomas N. *see* Page, Thomas Nelson.
Page, Thomas Nelson, 1853-1922
   xPage, Thomas N.
      Bred in the Bone. Arno.
      The Burial of the Guns. Mss Info.
      The Negro: The Southerner's Problem.
      Johnson Repr.
      On Newfound River. AMS Pr.
      Pastime Stories. Arno.
      Stories of the South. Arno.
Page, Warren.
   xPage, Warren.
      The Accurate Rifle. Follett.
      The Accurate Rifle. Winchester Pr.
      Topological Uniform Structures. Wiley.
Page, William D.
   xPage, William D.
      Teaching Reading Comprehension: Theory &
      Practice. NCTE.
Paget, George Edward.
   xPaget, O. G.
      Quality Control in Toxicology. Univ Park.
Paget, John, 1811-1898
   xPaget, John.
      Paradoxes & Puzzles, Historical, Judicial &
      Literary. AMS Pr.
Paget, Julian, Sir.
   xPaget, Julian
      The Story of the Guards. Presidio Pr.
Paget, O. G. *see* Paget, George Edward.
Paget, Richard A. *see* Paget, Richard Arthur Surtees.
Paget, Richard Arthur Surtees.
   xPaget, Richard A.
      Human Speech: Some Observations,
      Experiments, & Conclusions As to the
      Origin, Purpose, & Possible Improvement of
      Human Speech. AMS Pr.
Paget, Stephen, 1855-1926
   xPaget, Stephen.
      I Have Reason to Believe. Arno.
      I Wonder: Essays for the Young People. Arno.
Paget, Violet, 1856-1935
   xPaget, Violet.
      For Maurice: Five Unlikely Stories. Arno.
Pagliaro, Penny.
   xPagliaro, Penny.
      ed. I Like Poems & Poems Like Me. Pr
      Pacifica.
Pagoulatos, Angelos.
   xPagoulatos, Angelos.
      Major Determinants Affecting the Demand &
      Supply of Energy Resources: An Analysis of
      the Petroleum Market. Arno.
Paher, Stanley W.
   xPaher, Stanley W.
      Death Valley Ghost Towns. Nevada Pubns.
Pahissa, Jaime, 1880-
   xPahissa, Jaime.
      Manuel De Falla, His Life & Works. Hyperion
      Conn.
Pahl, R. E. *see* Pahl, Raymond Edward.
Pahl, Raymond Edward.
   xPahl, R. E.
      Patterns of Urban Life. Humanities.
      ed. Readings in Urban Sociology. Pergamon.
Pahz, James A. *see* Pahz, Jim.
Pahz, Jim.
   xPahz, James A.

Total Communication: The Meaning Behind
the Movement to Expand Educational
Opportunities for Deaf Children. C C
Thomas.
Pai, Anna C., 1935-
xPai, Anna C.
Foundations of Genetics: A Science for
Society. McGraw.
Pai, Young, 1929-
xPai, Young.
Teaching, Learning, & the Mind. HM.
Paige, David.
xPaige, David.
Carol Burnett. Creative Ed.
Johnny Carson. Creative Ed.
Liza Minnelli. Creative Ed.
Lucille Ball. Creative Ed.
Mary Tyler Moore. Creative Ed.
Paul Newman. Creative Ed.
Pro Baseball: An Almanac of Facts & Records.
Creative Ed.
Pro Basketball: An Almanac of Facts &
Records. Creative Ed.
Pro Football: An Almanac of Facts & Records.
Creative Ed.
Sidney Poitier. Creative Ed.
Paige, Harry W., 1922-
xPaige, Harry W.
Songs of the Teton Sioux. Westernlore.
Paige, Jeffery M.
xPaige, Jeffery M.
Agrarian Revolution: Social Movements &
Export Agriculture in the Underdeveloped
World. Free Pr.
Paige, Joseph.
xPaige, Joseph.
The Law Nobody Knows: Enlargement of the
Constitution - Treaties & Executive
Agreements. Vantage.
Paige, Richard E., 1904-
xPaige, Richard E.
Complete Guide to Making Money with Your
Ideas & Inventions. B&N.
Paige, Roger.
xPaige, Roger.
Dealing with Divorce. Herald Hse.
Paige, Woodrow.
xPaige, Woodrow.
Orange Madness: The Incredible Odyssey of
the Denver Broncos. T Y Crowell.
Paik, Woon Ki.
xPaik, Woon Ki.
Protein Methylation. Wiley.
Paillot, Jean Le. see Le Paillot, Jean.
Pain, Barry, 1864-1928
xPain, Barry.
The Short Story. Folcroft.
The Short Story. R West.
xPain, Barry E.
Humorous Stories. Arno.
Pain, Barry E. see Pain, Barry.
Paine. see Paine, Frank T.
Paine, Frank T.
xPaine.
Organizational Strategy & Policy. Dryden Pr.
xPaine, Frank T.
Organizational Strategy & Policy. HR&W.
Paine, Geoffrey. see Paine, Gregory Lansing.
Paine, Gregory Lansing.
xPaine, Geoffrey.
Southern Prose Writers: Representative
Selections, with Introduction, Bibliography &
Notes. Arden Lib.
Paine, John K. see Paine, John Knowles.
Paine, John Knowles, 1839-1906
xPaine, John K.
History of Music to the Death of Schubert. Da
Capo.
Paine, Lauran.
xPaine, Lauran.

Assassins' World. Taplinger.
Paine, R. see Paine, Robert Treat.
Paine, Robert T. see Paine, Robert Treat.
Paine, Robert Treat.
xPaine, R.
Art & Architecture of Japan. Viking Pr.
xPaine, Robert T.
The Art & Architecture of Japan. Penguin.
Paine, Roberta M.
xPaine, Roberta M.
Looking at Architecture. Lothrop.
Paine, Ruth B. see Paine, Ruth Benson.
Paine, Ruth Benson, 1927-
xPaine, Ruth B.
Thematic Analysis of Francois Mauriac's
"Genitrix, le Desert De L'amour, & le Noeud
De Viperes". Romance.
Paine, Thomas.
xPaine, Thomas.
Common Sense. Penguin.
Common Sense & Other Political Writings.
Bobbs.
Painter, Ann F.
xPainter, Ann F.
ed. Reader in Classification & Descriptive
Cataloging. IHS-PDS.
Painter, Dean E., 1916-
xPainter, Dean E.
Air Pollution Technology. Reston.
Painter, F. V. see Painter, Franklin Verzelius Newton.
Painter, Franklin V. see Painter, Franklin Verzelius
Newton.
Painter, Franklin Verzelius Newton, 1852-1931
xPainter, F. V.
A History of Education. Norwood Edns.
xPainter, Franklin V.
History of Education. AMS Pr.
History of Education. Scholarly.
Painter, George D. see Painter, George Duncan.
Painter, George Duncan, 1914-
xPainter, George D.
Marcel Proust: A Biography. Random.
Painter, John.
xPainter, John.
Reading John's Gospel Today. John Knox.
Painter, Nell I. see Painter, Nell Irvin.
Painter, Nell Irvin.
xPainter, Nell I.
Exodusters: Black Migration to Kansas After
Reconstruction. Knopf.
Exodusters: Black Migration to Kansas After
Reconstruction. Norton.
Painter, Sidney, 1902-
xPainter, Sidney.
Mediaeval Society. Cornell U Pr.
Studies in the History of the English Feudal
Barony. AMS Pr.
Studies in the History of the English Feudal
Barony. Octagon.
Painter, William, 1540?-1594
xPainter, William.
Palace of Pleasure: Elizabethan Versions of
Italian & French Novels. Peter Smith.
Painter, William H., 1927-
xPainter, William H.
Corporate & Tax Aspects of Closely Held
Corporations. Little.
Federal Regulation of Insider Trading. Michie.
Pais, Ettore, 1856-1939
xPais, Ettore.
Ancient Legends of Roman History. Arno.
Paish, Wilf. see Paish, Wilfred Henry Charles.
Paish, Wilfred Henry Charles.
xPaish, Wilf.
Diet in Sport. Sterling.
Introduction to Athletics. Transatlantic.
Paisley Abbey.
xPaisley Abbey.
Registrum Monasterii De Passelet. AMS Pr.
Pajgrt, O. see Pajgrt, Oldrich.

Pajgrt, Oldrich.
xPajgrt, O.
ed. Processing of Polyester Fibres. Elsevier.
Pakenham, Thomas, Hon, 1933-
xPakenham, Thomas.
The Boer War. Random.
Pakula, Marion B. see Pakula, Marion Broome.
Pakula, Marion Broome.
xPakula, Marion B.
Needlepoint Patterns for Signs & Sayings.
Crown.
Needlepoint Plaids. Crown.
Pal, Pratapaditya.
xPal, Pratapaditya.
Bronzes of Kashmir. Hacker.
The Divine Presence: Asian Sculptures from
the Collection of Mr. & Mrs. Harry Lenart.
LA Co Art Mus.
The Ideal Image: The Gupta Sculptural
Tradition & Its Influence. Asia Soc.
Nepal: Where the Gods Are Young.
Weatherhill.
Pal, R.
xPal, R.
ed. The Use of Genetics in Insect Control.
Elsevier.
Pala, Dolores.
xPala, Dolores.
Trumpet for a Walled City. Fawcett.
Palache, J. G. see Palache, John Garber.
Palache, John G. see Palache, John Garber.
Palache, John Garber.
xPalache, J. G.
Gautier & the Romantics. Gordon Pr.
xPalache, John G.
Gautier & the Romantics. Arden Lib.
Gautier & the Romantics. Folcroft.
Gautier & the Romantics. R West.
Palacios, Argentina.
xPalacios, Argentina.
The Knight & the Squire: A Retelling of the
Adventures of Don Quixote & Sancho Panza,
Based on Cervantes' Don Quixote De la
Mancha. Doubleday.
Palais, James B., 1934-
xPalais, James B.
Politics & Policy in Traditional Korea,
1864-1876. Harvard U Pr.
Palais, Richard S.
xPalais, Richard S.
Foundations of Global Nonlinear Analysis.
Benjamin-Cummings.
Palamas, K Ost Es.
xPalamas, Kostes.
The Twelve Words of the Gypsy. Memphis St
Univ.
Twelve Words of the Gypsy. U of Nebr Pr.
Palamas, Kostes. see Palamas, K Ost Es.
Palamountain, Joseph C. see Palamountain, Joseph
Cornwall.
Palamountain, Joseph Cornwall, 1920-
xPalamountain, Joseph C.
Politics of Distribution. Greenwood.
Palau, Luis, 1934-
xPalau, Luis.
Heart After God: Running with David.
Multnomah.
Palay, Steven.
xPalay, Steven.
I Love My Grandma. Raintree Pubs.
Palazzo, Tony, 1905-
xPalazzo, Tony.
illus. Animal Family Album. Lion.
Palen, J. John.
xPalen, J. John.
City Scenes: Problems & Prospects. Little.
xPalen, John.
Social Problems. McGraw.
Palen, Jennie. see Palen, Jennie M.

Palen, Jennie M.
 xPalen, Jennie.
  Stranger Let Me Speak. Golden Quill.
Palen, John. *see* Palen, J. John.
Palermo, David S. *see* Palermo, David Stuart.
Palermo, David Stuart.
 xPalermo, David S.
  Psychology of Language. Scott F.
Palermo, Patrick F.
 xPalermo, Patrick F.
  Lincoln Steffens. G K Hall.
  Lincoln Steffens. Twayne.
Paletta, Jeanne L. *see* Paletta, Jeanne Lynch.
Paletta, Jeanne Lynch.
 xPaletta, Jeanne L.
  Gynecologic Nursing. Med Exam.
Paletz, David L.
 xPaletz, David L.
  Politics in Public Service Advertising on
   Television. Praeger.
Paley, Alan L.
 xPaley, Alan L.
  Confucius, Ancient Chinese Philosopher.
   SamHar Pr.
  Edgar Allan Poe, American Poet & Mystery
   Writer. SamHar Pr.
  Munich & the Sudeten Crisis. SamHar Pr.
  Sigmund Freud, Father of Psychoanalysis.
   SamHar Pr.
Paley, Vivian G. *see* Paley, Vivian Gussin.
Paley, Vivian Gussin, 1929-
 xPaley, Vivian G.
  White Teacher. Harvard U Pr.
Paley, William, 1743-1905
 xPaley, William.
  The Principles of Moral & Political Philosophy.
   Garland Pub.
  The Principles of Moral & Political Philosophy.
   St Thomas.
Paley, William S. *see* Paley, William Samuel.
Paley, William Samuel, 1901-
 xPaley, William S.
  As It Happened: A Memoir. Doubleday.
Palgrave, Francis T. *see* Palgrave, Francis Turner.
Palgrave, Francis Turner.
 xPalgrave, Francis T.
  Francis Turner Palgrave: His Journals &
   Memories of His Life. AMS Pr.
  ed. Golden Treasury of the Best Songs &
   Lyrical Poems in the English Language.
   Oxford U Pr.
 xPalgrave, Gwenllian F.
  ed. Francis Turner Palgrave: His Journals &
   Memories of His Life. AMS Pr.
Palgrave, Gwenllian F. *see* Palgrave, Francis Turner.
Palgrave, Robert H. *see* Palgrave, Robert Harry Inglis.
Palgrave, Robert Harry Inglis, Sir, 1827-1919
 xPalgrave, Robert H.
  Bank Rate & the Money Market in England,
   France, Germany, Holland, & Belgium
   1844-1900. Greenwood.
Palin, Michael.
 xPalin, Michael.
  Ripping Yarns. Pantheon.
Paliouras, John D.
 xPaliouras, John D.
  Complex Variables for Scientists & Engineers.
   Macmillan.
Palisca, Claude. *see* Palisca, Claude V.
Palisca, Claude V.
 xPalisca, Claude.
  Baroque Music. P-H.
 xPalisca, Claude V.
  Baroque Music. P-H.
Palladian, Arthur.
 xPalladian, Arthur.

  Careers in Soccer. Lerner Pubns.
  Careers in the Air Force. Lerner Pubns.
  Careers in the Army. Lerner Pubns.
  Careers in the Navy. Lerner Pubns.
Palladin, A. V. *see* Palladin, Aleksandr Vladimirovich.
Palladin, Aleksandr Vladimirovich.
 xPalladin, A. V.
  ed. Protein Metabolism of the Brain. Plenum
   Pub.
Pallasch, Thomas J.
 xPallasch, Thomas J.
  Clinical Drug Therapy in Dental Practice. Lea
   & Febiger.
  Synopsis of Pharmacology for Students in
   Dentistry. Lea & Febiger.
Palley, Marian L. *see* Palley, Marian Lief.
Palley, Marian Lief.
 xPalley, Marian L.
  ed. Race, Sex, & Policy Problems. Lexington
   Bks.
Pallis, Marco, 1895-
 xPallis, Marco.
  Peaks & Lamas. Biblio Dist.
  Peaks & Lamas. Gordon Pr.
Palliser. *see* Palliser, Palliser and Co., Firm, Architects.
Palliser & Palliser. *see* Palliser, Palliser and Co., Firm,
 Architects.
Palliser, Bury. *see* Palliser, Fanny (Marryat).
Palliser, Fanny (Marryat), 1805-1878
 xPalliser, Bury.
  History of Lace. Charles River Bks.
 xPalliser, Fanny M.
  Historic Devices, Badges, & War-Cries. Gale.
  History of Lace. Gale.
Palliser, Fanny M. *see* Palliser, Fanny (Marryat).
Palliser, John, 1807-1887
 xPalliser, John.
  Solitary Rambles & Adventures of a Hunter in
   the Prairies. C E Tuttle.
Palliser, Palliser & Co. *see* Palliser, Palliser and Co.,
 Firm, Architects.
Palliser, Palliser and Co., Firm, Architects.
 xPalliser & Palliser.
  Palliser's Model Homes. Am Life Foun.
 xPalliser, Palliser & Co.
  Palliser's Model Homes, Eighteen
   Seventy-Eight. Glenwood.
Palliser, Palliser and Co., Firm, Architects.
 xPalliser.
  Palliser's New Cottage Homes & Details. Da
   Capo.
Pallister, John.
 xPallister, John C.
  In the Steps of the Great American
   Entomologist, Frank Eugene Lutz. Natural
   Sci Youth.
Pallister, John C. *see* Pallister, John.
Pallottino, Massimo.
 xPallottino, Massimo.
  The Etruscans. Ind U Pr.
  The Etruscans. Penguin.
Palm, Franklin C. *see* Palm, Franklin Charles.
Palm, Franklin Charles, 1890-
 xPalm, Franklin C.
  The Economic Policies of Richelieu. Johnson
   Repr.
  Politics & Religion in Sixteenth-Century
   France: A Study of the Career of Henry of
   Montmorency-Damville, Uncrowned King of
   the South. Peter Smith.
Palm, Goran.
 xPalm, Goran.
  The Flight from Work. Cambridge U Pr.
Palma, A. F. De. *see* De Palma, A. F.
Palma, Anthony D.
 xPalma, Anthony D.
  The Spirit: God in Action. Gospel Pub.
Palma, Guiseppe Di. *see* Di Palma, Giuseppe.
Palma, Marigloria.
 xPalma, Marigloria.

  Cuentos De la Abeja Encinta. U of PR Pr.
Palma, Mary M. *see* Palma, Mary Martin.
Palma, Mary Martin.
 xPalma, Mary M.
  Reflections. Golden Quill.
Palmen, Eric H. *see* Palmen, Erik Herbert.
Palmen, Erik Herbert.
 xPalmen, Eric H.
  Atmospheric Circulation Systems: Their
   Structure & Physical Interpretation. Acad Pr.
Palmer, Earl F.
 xPalmer, Earl F.
  The Intimate Gospel: Studies in John. Word
   Bks.
Palmer, A. *see* Palmer, Alvin E.
Palmer, Abram. *see* Palmer, Abram Smythe.
Palmer, Abram S. *see* Palmer, Abram Smythe.
Palmer, Abram Smythe.
 xPalmer, Abram.
  Folk-Etymology: A Dictionary of Verbal
   Corruptions or Words Perverted in Form.
   Haskell.
 xPalmer, Abram S.
  Folk-Etymology: A Dictionary of Verbal
   Corruptions or Words Perverted in Form or
   Meaning, by False Derivation or Mistaken
   Analogy. Johnson Repr.
  Some Curios from a Word-Collector's Cabinet.
   Gale.
Palmer, Adrienne.
 xPalmer, Adrienne.
  Dealer's Choice. Belmont-Tower.
Palmer, Alan. *see* Palmer, Alan Warwick.
Palmer, Alan Warwick.
 xPalmer, Alan.
  Gardeners of Salonika. S&S.
Palmer, Alvin E.
 xPalmer, A.
  Planning the Office Landscape. McGraw.
Palmer, Andrew C.
 xPalmer, Andrew C.
  Structural Mechanics. Oxford U Pr.
Palmer, B. I. *see* Palmer, Bernard Ira.
Palmer, Bernard. *see* Palmer, Bernard Alvin.
Palmer, Bernard Alvin, 1914-
 xPalmer, Bernard.
  Nothing Is Impossible. Moody.
Palmer, Bernard Ira, 1910-
 xPalmer, B. I.
  From Little Acorns: The Library Profession in
   Britain. Asia.
Palmer, Bruce.
 xPalmer, Bruce.
  Many Are the Hearts. S&S.
Palmer, C. Everard.
 xPalmer, C. Everard.
  Dog Called Houdini. Andre Deutsch.
Palmer, C. Harvey. *see* Palmer, Charles Harvey.
Palmer, Charles Harvey, 1919-
 xPalmer, C. Harvey.
  Optics: Experiments and Demonstrations.
   Johns Hopkins.
Palmer, Christopher.
 xPalmer, Christopher.
  Delius: Portrait of a Cosmopolitan. Holmes &
   Meier.
Palmer, D. G.
 xPalmer, D. G.
  Introduction to Air Pollution. Intl Pubns Serv.
Palmer, Dave R. *see* Palmer, Dave Richard.
Palmer, Dave Richard, 1934-
 xPalmer, Dave R.
  Summons of the Trumpet: U.S.-Vietnam in
   Perspective. Presidio Pr.
Palmer, David S. *see* Palmer, David Scott.
Palmer, David Scott, 1937-
 xPalmer, David S.
  Peru: The Authoritarian Tradition. Praeger.
Palmer, Doris M.
 xPalmer, Doris M.

ed. Sources of Information on the European
Communities. Merrimack Bk Serv.
Palmer, Doug.
xPalmer, Doug.
In Quire. SBD.
Moon Services. SBD.
Palmer, E. A. *see* Palmer, Robert E. A.
Palmer, E. Lawrence. *see* Palmer, Ephraim Laurence.
Palmer, Earl F. *see* Palmer.
Palmer, Eddy D.
xPalmer, Eddy D.
Practical Points in Gastroenterology. Med
Exam.

Palmer, Edgar Z. *see* Palmer, Edgar Zavitz.
Palmer, Edgar Zavitz.
xPalmer, Edgar Z.
I Will Lift up Mine Eyes. Word Serv.

Palmer, Edwin. *see* Palmer, Edwin Obadiah.

Palmer, Edwin H.
xPalmer, Edwin H.
Person & Ministry of the Holy Spirit: The
Traditional Calvinistic Perspective. Baker Bk.
Palmer, Edwin Obadiah, 1872-
xPalmer, Edwin.
History of Hollywood. Garland Pub.
Palmer, Ephraim Laurence.
xPalmer, E. Lawrence.
Fieldbook of Natural History. McGraw.
Palmer, Eustace.
xPalmer, Eustace.
The Growth of the African Novel. Heinemann
Ed.
Palmer, Frederick, 1873-1958
xPalmer, Frederick.
America in France. Greenwood.
Palmer, George E.
xPalmer, George E.
The Law of Restitution. Little.
Palmer, George H. *see* Palmer, George Herbert.
Palmer, George Herbert, 1842-1933
xPalmer, George H.
Altruism: Its Nature & Varieties. Greenwood.
Autobiography of a Philosopher. Greenwood.
Autobiography of a Philosopher. Johnson Repr.
Problem of Freedom. AMS Pr.
Palmer, H. E. *see* Palmer, Harold E.
Palmer, Harold E.
xPalmer, H. E.
A Grammar of Spoken English. Cambridge U
Pr.
xPalmer, Harold E.
Principles of Language Study. Oxford U Pr.
This Language-Learning Business. Norwood
Edns.
Palmer, Henrietta R. *see* Palmer, Henrietta Raymer.
Palmer, Henrietta Raymer, 1867-
xPalmer, Henrietta R.
List of English Editions & Translations of
Greek & Latin Classics Printed Before 1641.
Folcroft.
Palmer, Herbert E. *see* Palmer, Herbert Edward.
Palmer, Herbert Edward, 1880-
xPalmer, Herbert E.
Post Victorian Poetry. Folcroft.
Palmer, Herbert R. *see* Palmer, Herbert Richmond.
Palmer, Herbert Richmond, Sir, 1877-
xPalmer, Herbert R.
Bornu Sahara & Sudan. Negro U Pr.
Palmer, Ian R.
xPalmer, Ian R.
Data Base Systems: A Practical Reference.
QED Info Sci.
Palmer, James O.
xPalmer, James O.
Psychological Assessment of Children. Wiley.
Palmer, Jeffrey.
xPalmer, Jeffrey.

The Business Tenderfoot's Guide to Tax
Avoidance. Shrewd Info.
Palmer, Jerry.
xPalmer, Jerry.
Thrillers: Genesis & Structure of a Popular
Genre. St Martin.
Palmer, Jim.
xPalmer, Jim.
Pitching. Atheneum.
Palmer, Joe H. *see* Palmer, Joseph Hill.
Palmer, John D.
xPalmer, John D.
An Introduction to Biological Rhythms. Acad
Pr.
Palmer, John L. *see* Palmer, John Logan.
Palmer, John Leslie, 1885-1944
xPalmer, John L.
Comedy. Folcroft.
The Future of the Theatre. Folcroft.
Palmer, John Logan.
xPalmer, John L.
ed. Creating Jobs: Public Employment
Programs & Wage Subsidies. Brookings.
Inflation, Unemployment, & Poverty.
Lexington Bks.
Palmer, John M. *see* Palmer, John Mcauley.
Palmer, John Mcauley, 1870-1955
xPalmer, John M.
America in Arms. Arno.
General Von Steuben. Kennikat.
Palmer, John Milton, 1922-
xPalmer, John M.
Anatomy for Speech & Hearing. Har-Row.
Palmer, Joseph Hill, 1904-1952
xPalmer, Joe H.
This Was Racing. Henry Clay.
Palmer, Julia R. *see* Palmer, Julia Reed.
Palmer, Julia Reed.
xPalmer, Julia R.
Read for Your Life: Two Successful Efforts to
Help People Read & an Annotated List of
Books That Made Them Want to. Scarecrow.
Palmer, Julian A. *see* Palmer, Julian Arthur Beaufort.
Palmer, Julian Arthur Beaufort.
xPalmer, Julian A.
Mutiny Outbreak at Meerut in 1857.
Cambridge U Pr.
Palmer, K. N.
xPalmer, K. N.
Dust Explosions & Fires. Methuen Inc.
Palmer, Kenneth T.
xPalmer, Kenneth T.
ed. Studies in American Politics. Mss Info.
Palmer, Kingsley.
xPalmer, Kingsley.
The Folklore of Somerset. Rowman.
Oral Folk Tales of Wessex. David & Charles.
Palmer, L. R. *see* Palmer, Leonard Robert.
Palmer, Leonard R. *see* Palmer, Leonard Robert.
Palmer, Leonard Robert, 1906-
xPalmer, L. R.
The Greek Language. Humanities.
The Latin Language. Humanities.
xPalmer, Leonard R.
Mycenaeans & Minoans: Aegean Prehistory in
the Light of the Linear B Tablets.
Greenwood.
Palmer, M. Lynn.
xPalmer, M. Lynn.
Manual for Functional Training. Davis Co.
Palmer, Mabel (Atkinson), 1876-
xPalmer, Mabel A.
The History of the Indians in Natal.
Greenwood.
Palmer, Mabel A. *see* Palmer, Mabel (Atkinson).
Palmer, Marjorie.
xPalmer, Marjorie.
Bride's Book of Ideas. Tyndale.
Palmer, Mary.
xPalmer, Mary.

Sound Exploration & Discovery. Ctr Appl Res.
Palmer, Michael, 1943-
xPalmer, Michael.
The Circular Gates. Black Sparrow.
Palmer, Michele.
xPalmer, Michele.
Zoup Soup. Rocking Horse.
Palmer, Nicholas.
xPalmer, Nicholas.
The Comprehensive Guide to Board
Wargaming. McGraw.

Palmer, Pat.
xPalmer, Patricia.
Liking Myself. Impact Pubs Cal.
Palmer, Patricia. *see* Palmer, Pat.
Palmer, Peggy, 1941-
xPalmer, Peggy.
Classroom Craft Activities: Featuring 50
Seasonal Ideas. P-H.
Palmer, R. R. *see* Palmer, Robert Roswell.
Palmer, Ransford W.
xPalmer, Ransford W.
Caribbean Dependence on the United States
Economy. Praeger.
Palmer, Richard, 1904-
xPalmer, Richard.
Starting School: A Study in Policies. Verry.
Palmer, Richard P.
xPalmer, Richard P.
Case Studies in Library Computer Systems.
Bowker.
Palmer, Robert.
xPalmer, Robert.
A Tale of Two Cities: Memphis Rock, New
Orleans Roll. Inst Am Music.
Palmer, Robert E. A.
xPalmer, E. A.
Archaic Community of the Romans. Cambridge
U Pr.
Palmer, Robert R. *see* Palmer, Robert Roswell.
Palmer, Robert Roswell.
xPalmer, R. R.
World of the French Revolution. Har-Row.
xPalmer, Robert R.
A History of the Modern World. Knopf.
Twelve Who Ruled: The Year of the Terror in
the French Revolution. Princeton U Pr.
Palmer, Robin.
xPalmer, Robin.
Dictionary of Mythical Places. Walck.
Palmer, Roger F.
xPalmer, Roger F.
ed. Horizons in Clinical Pharmacology. Dekker.
Palmer, Rose A. *see* Palmer, Rose Amelia.
Palmer, Rose Amelia.
xPalmer, Rose A.
The North American Indians: An Account of
the American Indians North of Mexico.
Cooper Sq.
Palmer, Roy, fl. 1971-
xPalmer, Roy.
The Folklore of Warwickshire. Rowman.
Palmer, Samuel, 1805-1881
xPalmer, Samuel.
The Letters of Samuel Palmer. Oxford U Pr.
Palmer, Spencer J.
xPalmer, Spencer W.
The Expanding Church. Deseret Bk.
Palmer, Spencer W. *see* Palmer, Spencer J.
Palmer, Stanley H.
xPalmer, Stanley H.
Economic Arithmetic: A Guide to the
Statistical Sources of English Commerce,
Industry & Finance, 1700-1850. Garland Pub.
Palmer, Stuart. *see* Palmer, Stuart Hunter.
Palmer, Stuart Hunter, 1924-
xPalmer, Stuart.

Understanding Other People. Fawcett.
Palmer, Sushma.
xPalmer, Sushma.
Pediatric Nutrition in Developmental
Disorders. C C Thomas.
Palmer, Ted.
xPalmer, Ted.
Correctional Intervention & Research: Current
Issues & Future Prospects. Lexington Bks.
Palmer, Thomas W. see Palmer, Thomas Waverly.
Palmer, Thomas Waverly, 1891-
xPalmer, Thomas W.
Gringo Lawyer. U Presses Fla.
Guide to the Law & Legal Literature of Spain.
Hyperion Conn.
Palmer, Tim.
xPalmer, Tim.
Rivers of Pennsylvania. Pa St U Pr.
Palmer, Tobias.
xPalmer, Tobias.
Angel in My House. Ave Maria.
Palmer, Tony, 1941-
xPalmer, Tony.
All You Need Is Love: The Story of Popular
Music. Penguin.
Palmer, Vernon V.
xPalmer, Vernon V.
Legal System of Lesotho. Michie.
Palmer, Walter L.
xPalmer, Walter L.
ed. Gastric Irradiation in Peptic Ulcer. U of
Chicago Pr.
Palmer, William J.
xPalmer, William J.
The Fiction of John Fowles: Tradition, Art, &
the Loneliness of Selfhood. U of Mo Pr.
Palmer, Winthrop. see Palmer, Winthrop Bushnell.
Palmer, Winthrop Bushnell.
xPalmer, Winthrop.
Theatrical Dancing in America. A S Barnes.
Palmeri, Joseph.
xPalmeri, Joseph.
Conversational & Cultural French. P-H.
Palmier, Leslie H.
xPalmier, Leslie H.
Indonesia. Walker & Co.
Palmore, Erdman. see Palmore, Erdman Ballagh.
Palmore, Erdman Ballagh, 1930-
xPalmore, Erdman.
The Honorable Elders: A Cross-Cultural
Analysis of Aging in Japan. Duke.
ed. International Handbook on Aging:
Contemporary Developments & Research.
Greenwood.
ed. Normal Aging 1: Reports from the Duke
Longitudinal Study, 1955-1969. Duke.
ed. Normal Aging 2: Reports from the Duke
Longitudinal Study, 1970-1973. Duke.
Palmour, Vernon E.
xPalmour, Vernon E.
Compiled by A Study of the Characteristics,
Costs, & Magnitude of Interlibrary Loans in
Academic Libraries. Greenwood.
Palmquist, Roland. see Palmquist, Roland E.
Palmquist, Roland E.
xPalmquist, Roland.
Answers on Blueprint Reading. Audel.
Palms, Roger C.
xPalms, Roger C.
The Christian & the Occult. Judson.
God Holds Your Tomorrows. Augsburg.
God's Promises for You. Revell.
Palombara, Joseph G. La. see La Palombara, Joseph G.
Palombo, Stanley R.
xPalombo, Stanley R.
Dreaming & Memory: A New
Information-Processing Model. Basic.
Paloyan, Edward.
xPaloyan, Edward.

Endocrine Surgery. Year Bk Med.
Hyperparathyroidism. Grune.
Palter, Robert M.
xPalter, Robert M.
Whitehead's Philosophy of Science. U of
Chicago Pr.
Paltock, Robert, 1697-1767
xPaltock, Robert.
Life & Adventures of Peter Wilkins. Hyperion
Conn.
The Life & Adventures of Peter Wilkins.
Oxford U Pr.
Paltridge, G. see Paltridge, G. W.
Paltridge, G. W.
xPaltridge, G.
Radiative Processes in Meteorology &
Climatology. Elsevier.
Palubinskas, F. see Palubinskas, Feliksas.
Palubinskas, Feliksas.
xPalubinskas, F.
Guidebook to Worldwide Marketing.
Technomic.
Paludan, Jacob, 1896-
xPaludan, Jacob.
Jorgen Stein. U of Wis Pr.
Paludan, Lis.
xPaludan, Lis.
Easy Embroidery. Taplinger.
Paludan, Philip S. see Paludan, Phillip S.
Paludan, Phillip S., 1938-
xPaludan, Philip S.
A Covenant with Death: The Constitution,
Law, & Equality in the Civil War Era. U of
Ill Pr.
Palumbo, D. J. see Palumbo, Dennis James.
Palumbo, Dennis. see Palumbo, Dennis James.
Palumbo, Dennis J. see Palumbo, Dennis James.
Palumbo, Dennis James, 1925-
xPalumbo, D. J.
American Politics. A-W.
xPalumbo, Dennis.
ed. Urban Policy: A Guide to Information
Sources. Gale.
xPalumbo, Dennis J.
Statistics in Political & Behavioral Science.
Columbia U Pr.
Palumbo, E. see Palumbo, Edward M.
Palumbo, Edward M.
xPalumbo, E.
The Literary Use of Formulas in Guthlac II &
Their Relation to Felix's Vita Sancti
Guthlaci. Mouton.
Paluszny, Maria J.
xPaluszny, Maria J.
Autism: A Practical Guide for Parents &
Professionals. Syracuse U Pr.
Pambrun, Andrew. see Pambrun, Andrew Dominique.
Pambrun, Andrew Dominique, 1822-1895
xPambrun, Andrew.
Sixty Years on the Frontier in the Pacific
Northwest. Ye Galleon.
Pampana, Emilio.
xPampana, Emilio.
Textbook of Malaria Eradication. Oxford U Pr.
Pampe, William R.
xPampe, William R.
ed. Maps & Geological Publications of the
United States: A Layman's Guide. Am Geol.
Pamplin, Brian R.
xPamplin, Brian R.
Crystal Growth. Pergamon.
Pampuch, R. see Pampuch, Roman.
Pampuch, Roman.
xPampuch, R.
Ceramic Materials: An Introduction to Their
Properties. Elsevier.
Pan Am. see Pan American World Airways, Inc.
Pan Am World Airways. see Pan American World
Airways, Inc.

Pan Am World Airways, Inc. see Pan American World
Airways, Inc.
Pan American Union.
xPan American Union.
ed. Mexico. Gordon Pr.
Pan American World Airways, Inc.
xPan Am.
Pan Am World Guide. McGraw.
xPan Am World Airways.
ed. Pan Am's U. S. A. Guide. McGraw.
xPan Am World Airways, Inc.
Pan Am's World Guide. McGraw.
Pan, Lynn.
xPan, Lynn.
Alcohol in Colonial Africa. Rutgers Ctr
Alcohol.
Panagopoulos, Beata K. see Panagopoulos, Beata Maria.
Panagopoulos, Beata Maria, 1925-
xPanagopoulos, Beata K.
Cistercian & Mendicant Monasteries in
Medieval Greece. U of Chicago Pr.
Panagopoulos, Epaminodes P. see Panagopoulos,
Epaminondes P.
Panagopoulos, Epaminondes P.
xPanagopoulos, Epaminodes P.
New Smyrna: An Eighteenth Century Greek
Odyssey. Holy Cross Orthodox.
Pananides, Nicholas A.
xPananides, Nicholas A.
Introductory Astronomy. A-W.
Panares, R. Rodrigo.
xPanares, R. Rodrigo.
Energy, Organization & Life. Ed Methods.
Panassie, Hughes. see Panassie, Hugues.
Panassie, Hugues.
xPanassie, Hughes.
Hot Jazz: The Guide to Swing Music. Negro U
Pr.
xPanassie, Hugues.
Guide to Jazz. Greenwood.
Louis Armstrong. Da Capo.
The Real Jazz. Greenwood.
Panati, Charles, 1943-
xPanati, Charles.
Links. Berkley Pub.
Links. HM.
Panchev, S. see Panchev, Stoicho.
Panchev, Stoicho.
xPanchev, S.
Random Functions & Turbulence. Pergamon.
Panda, N.
xPanda, N.
Principles of Host-Plant Resistance to Insect
Pests. Allanheld.
Pandey, B. N. see Pandey, Bishwa Nath.
Pandey, Bishwa Nath, 1929-
xPandey, B. N.
Nehru. Stein & Day.
Pandit, D. P. see Pandit, Dhairyabala Prabodh.
Pandit, Dhairyabala Prabodh.
xPandit, D. P.
Earning One's Livelihood in Mahuva. Asia.
Pandit, M. P. see Pandit, Madhav Pundalik.
Pandit, Madhav Pundalik, 1918-
xPandit, M. P.
Occult Lines Behind Life. Auromere.
Pandolfini, Bruce.
xPandolfini, Bruce.
Let's Play Chess!: A Step by Step Guide for
Beginners. Wanderer Bks.
Let's Play Chess: A Step-by-Step Guide for
Beginners. Messner.
Pandosy, Marie C. see Pandosy, Marie Charles.
Pandosy, Marie Charles.
xPandosy, Marie C.
Grammar & Dictionary of the Yakama
Language. AMS Pr.
Panek, Leroy.
xPanek, Leroy.

Watteau's Shepherds: The Detective Novel in
Britain 1914-1940. Bowling Green Univ.
Panel on Geography in the Two-Year Colleges.
xPanel on Geography in the Two-Year Colleges.
Geography in the Two-Year Colleges: No. 10.
Assn Am Geographers.
**Panel on Radon in Uranium Mining, Washington, D.C.,
1973.**
xPanel, Washington D.C., Sept. 4-7, 1973.
Radon in Uranium Mining: Proceedings.
Unipub.
**Panel on the Use of Nuclear Techniques for Studying
Animal Protein Production from Non-Protein
Nitrogen, Vienna, 1971.**
xResearch Co-Ordination Meeting & Panel.
Tracer Studies on Non-Protein Nitrogen for
Ruminants II: Proceedings. Unipub.
Panel, Washington D.C., Sept. 4-7, 1973. *see* Panel on
Radon in Uranium Mining, Washington, D.C., 1973.
Panella, Vincent.
xPanella, Vincent.
The Other Side: Growing up Italian in
America. Doubleday.
Paneth, Donald.
xPaneth, Donald.
Current Affairs Atlas. Facts on File.
Pang, Eul-Soo.
xPang, Eul-Soo.
Bahia in the First Brazilian Republic:
Coronelismo & Oligarchies, 1889-1934. U
Presses Fla.
Pang, Shin H.
xPang, Shin Hak.
Acupuncture Treatment. Dong Nam P & C.
Pang, Shin Hak. *see* Pang, Shin H.
Pangborn, Edgar.
xPangborn, Edgar.
Davy. Ballantine.
Davy. Garland Pub.
Good Neighbors & Other Strangers.
Macmillan.
Pangburn, Jessie M. *see* Pangburn, Jessie May.
Pangburn, Jessie May, 1889-
xPangburn, Jessie M.
The Evolution of the American Teachers
College. AMS Pr.
Panger, Daniel.
xPanger, Daniel.
The Dance of the Wild Mouse. Entwhistle Bks.
Ol' Prophet Nat. Blair.
Pangonis, William J.
xPangonis, William J.
Angular Scattering Functions for Spherical
Particles. Wayne St U Pr.
Panikkar, K. M. *see* Panikkar, Kavalam Madhava.
Panikkar, K. Madhu. *see* Panikkar, Kavalam
Madhusudan.
Panikkar, Kavalam M. *see* Panikkar, Kavalam
Madhusudan.
Panikkar, Kavalam Madhava, 1896-1963
xPanikkar, K. M.
An Autobiography. Oxford U Pr.
xPanikkar, Kavalam M.
In Defense of Liberalism. Asia.
Panikkar, Kavalam Madhusudan, 1923-
xPanikkar, K. Madhu.
Revolution in Africa. Greenwood.
xPanikkar, Kavalam M.
Angola in Flames. Asia.
Panikkar, Raimundo. *see* Panikkar, Raymond.
Panikkar, Raymond, 1918-
xPanikkar, Raimundo.
Intrareligious Dialogue. Paulist Pr.
Panitch, Leo.
xPanitch, Leo.
ed. The Canadian State: Political Economy &
Political Power. U of Toronto Pr.
Pankey, William R. *see* Pankey, William Russell.
Pankey, William Russell.
xPankey, William R.

Edge of Paradise: Fifty Years in the Pulpit.
McClain.
Pankhurst, Estelle S. *see* Pankhurst, Estelle Sylvia.
Pankhurst, Estelle Sylvia, 1882-
xPankhurst, Estelle S.
Ex-Italian Somaliland. Greenwood.
Panko, Stephen M.
xPanko, Stephen M.
Martin Buber. Word Bks.
Pankove, Jacques I., 1922-
xPankove, Jacques I.
Optical Processes in Semiconductors. Dover.
Pannain, Guido, 1891-
xPannain, Guido.
Modern Composers. Arno.
Pannell, Henry C. *see* Pannell, Henry Clifton.
Pannell, Henry Clifton, 1896-1946
xPannell, Henry C.
The Preparation & Work of Alabama High
School Teachers. AMS Pr.
Pannenberg. *see* Pannenberg, Wolfhart.
Pannenberg, Wolfhart, 1928-
xPannenberg.
Spirit, Faith & Church. Westminster.
xPannenberg, Wolfhart.
Human Nature, Election & History.
Westminster.
The Idea of God & Human Freedom.
Westminster.
Theology & the Kingdom of God. Westminster.
Theology & the Philosophy of Science.
Westminster.
Pano, Nicholas C.
xPano, Nicholas C.
The People's Republic of Albania. Johns
Hopkins.
Panofsky, Erwin, 1892-1968
xPanofsky, Erwin.
Gothic Architecture & Scholasticism. NAL.
Idea: A Concept in Art Theory. Har-Row.
Idea: A Concept in Art Theory. U of SC Pr.
Renaissance & Renascences in Western Art.
Har-Row.
Studies in Iconology: Humanistic Themes in
the Art of the Renaissance. Har-Row.
Studies in Iconology: Humanistic Themes in
the Art of the Renaissance. Peter Smith.
Panov, V. *see* Panov, Vasilii Nikolaevich.
Panov, Valery.
xPanov, Valery.
To Dance. Avon.
Panov, Vasilii Nikolaevich.
xPanov, V.
A Course in the Openings. Pergamon.
Panova, V. *see* Panova, Vera Fedorovna.
Panova, Vera F. *see* Panova, Vera Fedorovna.
Panova, Vera Fedorovna, 1905-1973
xPanova, V.
On Faraway Street. Braziller.
xPanova, Vera F.
The Factory. Hyperion-Conn.
Span of the Year. Hyperion-Conn.
Panshin, Alexis J. *see* Panshin, Alexis John.
Panshin, Alexis John.
xPanshin, Alexis J.
Textbook of Wood Technology. McGraw.
Pansini, Anthony J.
xPansini, Anthony J.
Maximizing Management Effectiveness.
Greenvale.
Undergrounding Electric Lines. Hayden.
Undergrounding Telephone Lines. Hayden.
Pansky, Ben.
xPansky, Ben.
Dynamic Anatomy & Physiology. Macmillan.
Pantaleoni, C. A.
xPantaleoni, C. A.

California Criminal Law: A Guide for
Policemen. P-H.
Pantano, Steve.
xPantano, Steve.
The Sun Never Shines. Coral Reef.
Pantelidis, Veronica.
xPantelidis, Veronica S.
The Arab World: Libraries & Librarianship
1960-1976; a Bibliography. Merrimack Bk
Serv.
Pantelidis, Veronica S. *see* Pantelidis, Veronica.
Pantell, Dora. *see* Pantell, Dora F.
Pantell, Dora F.
xPantell, Dora.
If Not Now, When: The Many Meanings of
Black Power. Delacorte.
Pantell, Robert. *see* Pantell, Robert H.
Pantell, Robert H.
xPantell, Robert.
Taking Care of Your Child: A Parents' Guide
to Medical Care. A-W.
Pantelouris, E. M.
xPantelouris, E. M.
Introduction to Animal Physiology &
Physiological Genetics. Pergamon.
Panter-Brick, Simone.
xPanter-Brick, Simone.
Gandhi Against Machiavellism: Non-Violence
in Politics. Asia.
Panter-Downes, Mollie, 1906-
xPanter-Downes, Mollie.
At the Pines: Swinburne & Watts-Dunton in
Putney. Gambit.
London War Notes, 1939-1945. FS&G.
Ooty Preserved: A Victorian Hill Station in
India. FS&G.
Pantin, Gerard.
xPantin, Gerard.
A Mole Cricket Called Servol: An Account of
Experiences in Education & Community
Development in Trinidad & Tobago, West
Indies. Pergamon.
Pantridge, J. F.
xPantridge, J. F.
The Acute Coronary Attack. Grune.
Panum, Hortense.
xPanum, Hortense.
Stringed Instruments of the Middle Ages, Their
Evolution & Development. Greenwood.
Panunzio, Constantine. *see* Panunzio, Constantine Maria.
Panunzio, Constantine M. *see* Panunzio, Constantine
Maria.
Panunzio, Constantine Maria, 1884-1964
xPanunzio, Constantine.
Immigration Crossroads. Ozer.
xPanunzio, Constantine M.
Soul of an Immigrant. Arno.
Panzar, John C., 1947-
xPanzar, John C.
Regulation, Service Quality, & Market
Performance: A Model of Airline Rivalry.
Garland Pub.
Panzarella, Andrew.
xPanzarella, Andrew.
Religion & Human Experience. St Marys.
Panzetta, Anthony F., 1934-
xPanzetta, Anthony F.
Community Mental Health: Myth & Reality.
Lea & Febiger.
Pao, Y. H. *see* Pao, Yoh-Han.
Pao, Yoh-Han.
xPao, Y. H.
ed. Optoacoustic Spectroscopy & Detection.
Acad Pr.
Paola, Tomie de. *see* De Paola, Tomie.
Paoletti, John T.
xPaoletti, John T.

The Siena Baptistry Font: A Study of an Early
Renaissance Collaborative Program,
1416-1434. Garland Pub.

Paoli, Arturo.
xPaoli, Arturo.
Freedom to Be Free. Orbis Bks.
Meditations on Saint Luke. Orbis Bks.

Paolino, Ernest N.
xPaolino, Ernest N.
The Foundations of the American Empire:
William Henry Seward & U.S. Foreign
Policy. Cornell U Pr.

Paolino, Thomas J.
xPaolino, Thomas J.
The Alcoholic Marriage: Alternative
Perspectives. Grune.
ed. Marriage & Marital Therapy:
Psychoanalytic, Behavioral & Systems Theory
Perspectives. Brunner-Mazel.

Paolo, Tomie De. see De Paola, Tomie.

Paolozzi. see Paolozzi, Gabriel J.

Paolozzi, Gabriel J.
xPaolozzi.
Conversation in Italian: Points of Departure. D
Van Nostrand.
xPaolozzi, Gabriel J.
Conversation in Italian: Points of Departure. D
Van Nostrand.

Paolucci, Anne.
xPaolucci, Anne.
From Tension to Tonic: The Plays of Edward
Albee. S Ill U Pr.
Pirandello's Theater: The Recovery of the
Modern Stage for Dramatic Art. S Ill U Pr.

Paolucci, Beatrice.
xPaolucci, Beatrice.
Family Decision Making: An Ecosystem
Approach. Wiley.
Personal Perspectives: A Guide to Decision
Making. McGraw.

Paor, Maire De. see De Paor, Maire.

Pap, Leo.
xPap, Leo.
The Portuguese in the United States: A
Bibliography. Ctr Migration.

Papachristou, Judith.
xPapachristou, Judith.
Women Together: A History in Documents of
the Women's Movement in the United
States. Knopf.

Papadaki, Stamo.
xPapadaki, Stamo.
Oscar Niemeyer. Braziller.

Papademetriou, George C.
xPapademetriou, George C.
An Introduction to Saint Gregory Palamas.
Philos Lib.

Papadopoullos, Theodore H.
xPapadopoullos, Theodore H.
Studies & Documents Relating to the History
of the Greek Church & People Under
Turkish Domination. AMS Pr.

Papadopoulo, Alexandre.
xPapadopoulo, Alexandre.
Islam & Muslim Art. Abrams.

Papadopoulos, C. see Papadopoulos, Christos.

Papadopoulos, Christos.
xPapadopoulos, C.
True Visual Magnitude Photographic Star
Atlas. Pergamon.

Papageorgiou, George J.
xPapageorgiou, George J.
Mathematical Land Use Theory. Lexington
Bks.

Papagiannis, Michael D., 1932-
xPapagiannis, Michael D.
Space Physics & Space Astronomy. Gordon.

Papahadjopoulos, D.
xPapahadjopoulos, Demetrios.

ed. Liposomes & Their Uses in Biology &
Medicine. NY Acad Sci.

Papahadjopoulos, Demetrios. see Papahadjopoulos, D.

Papajewski, Helmut, 1903-
xPapajewski, Helmut.
Thornton Wilder. Ungar.

Papalia, Diane E.
xPapalia, Diane E.
A Child's World: Infancy Through
Adolescence. McGraw.
Human Development. McGraw.

Papandreou, Andreas G. see Papandreou, Andreas
George.

Papandreou, Andreas George.
xPapandreou, Andreas G.
Paternalistic Capitalism. U of Minn Pr.

Papanek, Ernst.
xPapanek, Ernst.
Out of the Fire. Morrow.

Papanek, Gustav F. see Papanek, Gustav Fritz.

Papanek, Gustav Fritz.
xPapanek, Gustav F.
A Plan for Planning: The Need for a Better
Method of Assisting Underdeveloped
Countries on Their Economic Policies. AMS
Pr.

Papanek, Victor. see Papanek, Victor J.

Papanek, Victor J.
xPapanek, Victor.
How Things Don't Work. Pantheon.

Papanikolas, Helen Z. see Papanikolas, Helen Zeese.

Papanikolas, Helen Zeese.
xPapanikolas, Helen Z.
ed. The Peoples of Utah. Utah St Hist Soc.

Papanoutsos, E. P.
xPapanoutsos, Evangelos P.
Foundations of Knowledge. State U NY Pr.

Papanoutsos, Evangelos P. see Papanoutsos, E. P.

Papapetrou, A. see Papapetrou, Achilleus.

Papapetrou, Achilleus.
xPapapetrou, A.
Lectures on General Relativity. Kluwer Boston.

Paparella, Michael M.
xPaparella, Michael M.
Otolaryngology. Saunders.

Papashvily, George.
xPapashvily, George.
Anything Can Happen. Har-Row.

Pape, D. see Pape, Donna Lugg.

Pape, D. L. see Pape, Donna Lugg.

Pape, Donna. see Pape, Donna Lugg.

Pape, Donna L. see Pape, Donna Lugg.

Pape, Donna Lugg.
xPape, D.
Gerbil for a Friend. P-H.
xPape, D. L.
Liz Dearly's Silly Glasses. Oddo.
Professor Fred & the Fid Fuddlephone. Oddo.
xPape, Donna.
Mrs. Twitter the Animal Sitter. Garrard.
xPape, Donna L.
Doghouse for Sale. Garrard.
Leo Lion Looks for Books. Garrard.
Play Ball, Joey Kangaroo!. Garrard.
The Snoino Mystery. Garrard.
Taffy Finds a Halloween Witch. Garrard.
Where Is My Little Joey?. Garrard.

Pape, Dorothy.
xPape, Dorothy R.
In Search of Gods Ideal Woman: A Personal
Examination of the New Testament.
Inter-Varsity.

Pape, Dorothy R. see Pape, Dorothy.

Pape, Gordon.
xPape, Gordon.
Chain Reaction. Bantam.
Chain Reaction. Viking Pr.

Pape, Greg, 1947-
xPape, Greg.

Border Crossings. U of Pittsburgh Pr.

Pape, Mary.
xPape, Mary.
Growing up with Music: Musical Experiences
in the Infant School. Oxford U Pr.

Papenfuse, Edward C.
xPapenfuse, Edward C.
ed. A Biographical Dictionary of the Maryland
Legislature, 1635-1789. Johns Hopkins.
In Pursuit of Profit: The Annapolis Merchants
in the Era of the American Revolution,
1763-1805. Johns Hopkins.
Maryland: A New Guide to the Old Line
State. Johns Hopkins.

Paper, Jordan D.
xPaper, Jordan D.
Guide to Chinese Prose. G K Hall.

Paperny, Myra.
xPaperny, Myra.
The Wooden People. Little.

Papers from the Thomas Gray Bicentenary Conference at
Carleton University. see Thomas Grey Bicentenary
Conference, Carleton University, 1971.

Papers Presented at the Conference,Convened by the
American Jewish Historical Society & the Theodor
Herzl Foundation in New York City,December
26-27,1955. see American Jewish Historical Society.

Papers Presented Before the College of Sports Medicine.
see American College of Sports Medicine.

Papillon, Alfred L.
xPapillon, Alfred L.
Foundations of Educational Research. U Pr of
Amer.

Papineau, David, 1947-
xPapineau, David.
For Science in the Social Sciences. St Martin.

Papini, Giovanni, 1881-1956
xPapini, Giovanni.
Dante Vivo. Kennikat.
Dante Vivo. R West.

Papinot, E. see Papinot, Edmond.

Papinot, Edmond, b. 1860
xPapinot, E.
Historical & Geographical Dictionary of Japan.
C E Tuttle.

Papoulis, Athanasios, 1921-
xPapoulis, Athanasios.
Fourier Integral & Its Applications. McGraw.
Probability, Random Variables & Stochastic
Processes. McGraw.
Signal Analysis. McGraw.
Systems & Transforms with Applications in
Optics. McGraw.

Pappas, George, 1929-
xPappas, George.
Concepts in Art & Education: An Anthology of
Current Issues. Macmillan.

Pappas, George. see Pappas, George Sotiros.

Pappas, George Sotiros, 1942-
xPappas, George.
ed. Justification & Knowledge: New Studies in
Epistemology. Kluwer Boston.

Pappas, Lou S. see Pappas, Lou Seibert.

Pappas, Lou Seibert.
xPappas, Lou S.
Bread Baking. Nitty Gritty.
Crockery Pot Cookbook. Nitty Gritty.
Entertaining the Slim Way. A-W.
Greek Cooking. Har-Row.
International Fish Cookery. One Hund One
Prods.

Pappas, S. Peter. see Pappas, Socrates Peter.

Pappas, Socrates Peter, 1936-
xPappas, S. Peter.
ed. UV Curing: Science & Technology. Tech
Marketing.

Papper, E. M.
xPapper, E. M.

Anesthesiology - Progress Since 1940. U of
　　Miami Pr.
Papper, Solomon, 1922-
　　xPapper, Solomon.
　　　Clinical Nephrology. Little.
Papsidero, Joseph. *see* Papsidero, Joseph A.
Papsidero, Joseph A.
　　xPapsidero, Joseph.
　　　Chance for Change: Implications of a Chronic
　　　　Disease Module Study. Mich St U Pr.
Papua New Guinea. Office of Information.
　　xOffice of Information, Gov't of Papua New
　　　Guinea.
　　　Papua New Guinea. U Pr of Hawaii.
Papy. *see* Papy, Frederique.
Papy, Frederique.
　　xPapy.
　　　Graph Games. T Y Crowell.
Paquette, L. A. *see* Paquette, Leo A.
Paquette, Leo A.
　　xPaquette, L. A.
　　　Principles of Modern Heterocyclic Chemistry.
　　　　Benjamin-Cummings.
Paquin, J. R.
　　xPaquin, Joseph R.
　　　Fractions to Millimeters. Indus Pr.
Paquin, Joseph R. *see* Paquin, J. R.
Parachek, Ralph E.
　　xParachek, Ralph E.
　　　Desert Architecture. Parr AZ.
Parad, Howard J.
　　xParad, Howard J.
　　　ed. Crisis Intervention: Selected Readings.
　　　　Family Serv.
Paradis, James G., 1942-
　　xParadis, James G.
　　　T. H. Huxley: Man's Place in Nature. U of
　　　　Nebr Pr.
Paramount Pictures Corporation. *see* Paramount Pictures,
　　Inc.
Paramount Pictures, Inc.
　　xParamount Pictures Corporation.
　　　The Mork & Mindy Super Activity Book.
　　　　G&D.
Paranjpe, A. C.
　　xParanjpe, A. C.
　　　In Search of Identity. Halsted Pr.
Paranka, Stephen.
　　xParanka, Stephen.
　　　Business Applications of Decision Sciences.
　　　　Van Nos Reinhold.
Parapsychological Association.
　　xParapsychological Association.
　　　Research in Parapsychology 1972: Abstracts &
　　　　Papers from the 15th Annual Convention of
　　　　the Parapsychological Association, 1972.
　　　　Scarecrow.
　　　Research in Parapsychology 1973: Abstracts &
　　　　Papers from the 16th Annual Convention of
　　　　the Parapsychological Association, 1973.
　　　　Scarecrow.
　　　Research in Parapsychology 1974: Abstracts &
　　　　Papers from the 17th Annual Convention of
　　　　the Parapsychological Association, 1974.
　　　　Scarecrow.
　　　Research in Parapsychology 1975: Abstracts &
　　　　Papers from the 18th Annual Convention of
　　　　the Parapsychological Association, 1975.
　　　　Scarecrow.
　　　Research in Parapsychology 1976: Abstracts &
　　　　Papers from the 19th Annual Convention of
　　　　the Parapsychological Association, 1976.
　　　　Scarecrow.
Paraquin, Charles H.
　　xParaquin, Charles H.
　　　Eye Teasers: Optical Illusion Puzzles. Sterling.
Parasnis, D S.
　　xParasnis, D. S.

Principles of Applied Geophysics. Methuen
　　Inc.
Parcel, Guy S.
　　xParcel, Guy S.
　　　First Aid in Emergency Care. Mosby.
　　　Teaching Myself About Asthma. Mosby.
Pardey, Larry. *see* Pardey, Lin.
Pardey, Lin.
　　xPardey, Larry.
　　　jt. auth. The Care & Feeding of the Offshore
　　　　Crew. Norton.
　　　jt. auth. Seraffyn's European Adventures.
　　　　Norton.
　　xPardey, Lin.
　　　The Care & Feeding of the Offshore Crew.
　　　　Norton.
　　　Seraffyn's European Adventures. Norton.
Pardi, Marco M.
　　xPardi, Marco M.
　　　Death: An Anthropological Perspective. U Pr
　　　　of Amer.
Pardo Bazan, Emilia, Condesa De, 1852-1921
　　xPardo Bazan, Emilia.
　　　The Son of the Bondwoman. Fertig.
Pardoe, E. F. *see* Pardoe, Frank Ernest.
Pardoe, Frank Ernest.
　　xPardoe, E. F.
　　　Communication in Writing. Pergamon.
Pardoe, T. Earl, 1885-
　　xPardoe, T. Earl.
　　　Pantomimes for Stage & Study. Arno.
Pardon, William, 1947-
　　xPardon, William.
　　　Local Surgery & the Exact Sequence of a
　　　　Localization for Wall Groups. Am Math.
Pare, Ambroise, 1510?-1590
　　xPare, Ambroise.
　　　Apologie & Treatise of Ambroise Pare:
　　　　Containing the Voyages Made into Divers
　　　　Places with Many of His Writings Upon
　　　　Surgery. Dover.
Pare, E G.
　　xPare, E. G.
　　　Descriptive Geometry. Macmillan.
Pare, Madeline F. *see* Pare, Madeline Ferrin.
Pare, Madeline Ferrin.
　　xPare, Madeline F.
　　　Arizona Pageant: A Short History of the 48th
　　　　State. AZ Hist Foun.
Paredes, Americo.
　　xParedes, Americo.
　　　ed. Folktales of Mexico. U of Chicago Pr.
　　　ed. Toward New Perspectives in Folklore. U of
　　　　Tex Pr.

Parelius, Ann P. *see* Parelius, Ann Parker.

Parelius, Ann Parker.

　　xParelius, Ann P.
　　　The Sociology of Education. P-H.

Parens, Henri.
　　xParens, Henri.
　　　Dependence in Man: A Psychoanalytic Study.
　　　　Intl Univs Pr.
Parent, Gail.
　　xParent, Gail.
　　　David Meyer Is a Mother. Har-Row.
Parenteau, Shirley.
　　xParenteau, Shirley.
　　　Secrets of Scarlet. Childrens.
　　　A Space Age Cookbook for Kids. P-H.
　　　The Talking Coffins of Cryo City.
　　　　Elsevier-Nelson.
Parenti, Michael, 1933-
　　xParenti, Michael.
　　　Democracy for the Few. St Martin.
　　　Power & the Powerless. St Martin.
Parenti, Umberto.
　　xParenti, Umberto.

The World of Butterflies & Moths. Putnam.
Parents Nursery School.
　　xParents Nursery School.
　　　Kids Are Natural Cooks. HM.
　　xTheParents Nursery School.
　　　Kids Are Natural Cooks. HM.
Pares, Bernard, Sir, 1867-1949
　　xPares, Bernard.
　　　A History of Russia. AMS Pr.
　　　A History of Russia. Random.
Pares, Richard, 1902-1958
　　xPares, Richard.
　　　Colonial Blockade & Neutral Rights
　　　　1739-1763. Porcupine Pr.
Paret, Peter.
　　xParet, Peter.
　　　Clausewitz & the State. Oxford U Pr.
　　　ed. Frederick the Great: A Profile. Hill &
　　　　Wang.
Pareto, Vilfredo.
　　xPareto, Vilfredo.
　　　Compendium of General Sociology. U of Minn
　　　　Pr.
　　　Sociological Writings. Rowman.
Paretti, Sandra.
　　xParetti, Sandra.
　　　The Drums of Winter. M Evans.
　　　The Drums of Winter. NAL.
　　　The Magic Ship. St Martin.
Parfit, Michael.
　　xParfit, Michael.
　　　Last Stand at Rosebud Creek: The Story of
　　　　Eighteen People & a Power Plant. Dutton.
Parfitt, Rebecca R. *see* Parfitt, Rebecca Rowe.
Parfitt, Rebecca Rowe.
　　xParfitt, Rebecca R.
　　　Birth Primer: A Source Book of Traditional &
　　　　Alternative Methods in Labor & Delivery.
　　　　Facts on File.
　　　The Birth Primer: A Source Book of
　　　　Traditional & Alternative Methods in Labor
　　　　& Delivery. NAL.
　　　The Birth Primer: A Source Book of
　　　　Traditional & Alternative Methods in Labor
　　　　& Delivery. Running Pr.
Pargeter, Edith.
　　xPargeter, Edith.
　　　The Marriage of Meggotta. Popular Lib.
　　　The Marriage of Meggotta. Viking Pr.
Parham, Barbara.
　　xParham, Barbara.
　　　What's Wrong with Eating Meat?. Ananda
　　　　Marga.
Parham, William E., 1922-
　　xParham, Wm. E.
　　　Syntheses & Reactions in Organic Chemistry.
　　　　Krieger.
Parham, Wm. E. *see* Parham, William E.
Parigi, Sam F. *see* Parigi, Sam Frank.
Parigi, Sam Frank.
　　xParigi, Sam F.
　　　A Case Study of Latin American Unionization
　　　　in Austin, Texas. Arno.
Parikh. *see* Parikh, Jitendra C.
Parikh, Jitendra C.
　　xParikh.
　　　Group Symmetries in Nuclear Structure.
　　　　Plenum Pub.
Parikh, V. M.
　　xParikh, V. M.
　　　Absorption Spectroscopy of Organic Molecules.
　　　　A-W.
Parins, James W.
　　xParins, James W.
　　　Concordance to Conrad's Victory. Garland
　　　　Pub.
Paris. Assemblee Electorale.
　　xParis Assemblee Electorale.

Assemblee Electorale De Paris, 18 Novembre
1790-15, Juin 1791. AMS Pr.
Assemblee Electorale De Paris, 2 Septembre
1972. AMS Pr.
Assemblee Electorale De Paris, 26 Aout
1791-12 Aout 1792. AMS Pr.

Paris, Bernard J.
xParis, Bernard J.
Character & Conflict in Jane Austen's Novels:
A Psychological Approach. Wayne St U Pr.
Experiments in Life: George Eliot's Quest for
Values. Wayne St U Pr.
A Psychological Approach to Fiction: Studies
in Thackeray, Stendhal, George Eliot,
Dostoevsky, & Conrad. Ind U Pr.

Paris. Bibliotheque Nationale.
xBibliotheque Nationale.
Catalogue General Des Livres Imprimes:
Auteurs, Collectivites, Auteurs Anonymes
(1960-1969). French & Eur.
Catalogue Generale Des Livres Imprimes:
Auteurs, Collectivities-Auteurs, Anonymes,
1960-1969. French & Eur.
xBibliotheque Nationale. Departement des
Imprimes, Paris.
Catalogue de l'histoire de l'Afrique. B
Franklin.
Catalogue des ouvrages de Chateaubriand. B
Franklin.
xBibliotheque Nationale, Paris.
Catalogue de l'histoire de l'Amerique. B
Franklin.
Inventaire de la Collection Anisson sur
l'histoire de l'imprimerie et la librarie. B
Franklin.
xParis. Bibliotheque Nationale.
Cinquantenaire du symbolisme: Exposition de
manuscrits autographes, estamps, peintures,
sculptures, editions rares, portraits, objets
d'art. AMS Pr.

Paris. Commune, 1789-1794.
xCommune de Paris, 1789-1794.
Actes de la Commune de Paris pendant la
Revolution. AMS Pr.
Paris, Gaston. *see* Paris, Gaston Bruno Paulin.
Paris, Gaston B. *see* Paris, Gaston Bruno Paulin.
Paris, James D. *see* Paris, James Daniel.
Paris, William F. *see* Paris, William Francklyn.

**Paris- Dauphine Conference on Money and
International Monetary Problems, 3d, 1974.**
xThird Paris-Dauphine Conference on Money &
International Monetary Problems, March 28-30,
1974.
Recent Issues in International Monetary
Economics: Proceedings. Elsevier.

Paris. Ecole Pratique Des Hautes Etudes.
xCentre De Mathematique Sociale Ecole Des
Hautes Etudes En Sciences Sociales.
Combinatorics Graphs & Algebra. Mouton.

Paris, Gaston Bruno Paulin, 1839-1903
xParis, Gaston.
Mediaeval French Literature. Arno.
xParis, Gaston B.
Francois Villon. AMS Pr.

Paris, James Daniel, 1908-
xParis, James D.
Monetary Policies of the United States,
1932-1938. AMS Pr.

Paris, Lena.
xParis, Lena.
Mom Is Single. Childrens.

Paris, Scott G., 1946-
xParis, Scott G.
Propositional Logical Thinking &
Comprehension of Language Connectives: A
Developmental Analysis. Mouton.

Paris. Universite. Bibliotheque.
xParis Universite Bibliotheque.

Catalogue De la Reserve Seizieme Siecle, De la
Bibliotheque De l'Universite De Paris
1501-1540. B Franklin.
Catalogue Des Incunables De la Bibliotheque
De l'Universite De Paris. B Franklin.

Paris, William Francklyn, 1871-1954
xParis, William F.
Personalities in American Art. Arno.

Pariser, E. R. *see* Pariser, Ernst R.

Pariser, Ernst R.
xPariser, E. R.
Fish Protein Concentrate: Panacea for Protein
Malnutrition?. MIT Pr.

Parish. *see* Parish, Peggy.

Parish, Helen R. *see* Parish, Helen Rand.

Parish, Helen Rand.
xParish, Helen R.
Estebanico. Viking Pr.

Parish, J. H. *see* Parish, John Howard.

Parish, James R. *see* Parish, James Robert.

Parish, James Robert.
xParish, James R.
Film Directors: A Guide to Their American
Films Scarecrow.
The Funsters. Arlington Hse.
Great Gangster Pictures. Scarecrow.
Great Movie Heroes. B&N.
ed. The Great Movie Series. A S Barnes.
The Great Science Fiction Pictures. Scarecrow.
The Great Spy Pictures. Scarecrow.
The Great Western Pictures. Scarecrow.
The Hollywood Beauties. Arlington Hse.
Hollywood Character Actors. Arlington Hse.
Hollywood on Hollywood. Scarecrow.
Hollywood's Great Love Teams. Arlington
Hse.
Hollywood's Great Love Teams. Rainbow Bks.
The Leading Ladies. Arlington Hse.
The Leading Ladies. Rainbow Bks.
The Swashbucklers. Arlington Hse.
The Swashbucklers. Rainbow Bks.
The Tough Guys. Arlington Hse.
The Tough Guys. Rainbow Bks.

Parish, John Howard.
xParish, J. H.
ed. Developmental Biology of Prokaryotes. U
of Cal Pr.

Parish, Peggy.
xParish.
Teach Us, Amelia Bedelia. Schol Bk Serv.
xParish, Peggy.

Amelia Bedelia. Har-Row.
Amelia Bedelia. Schol Bk Serv.
Amelia Bedelia Helps Out. Greenwillow.
Be Ready at Eight. Macmillan.
Beginning Mobiles. Macmillan.
Clues in the Woods. Dell.
Clues in the Woods. Macmillan.
Clues in the Woods. Macmillan.
Come Back, Amelia Bedelia. Har-Row.
Come Back, Amelia Bedelia. Har-Row.
Costumes to Make. Macmillan.
Dinosaur Time. Har-Row.
Good Work, Amelia Bedelia. Avon.
Good Work, Amelia Bedelia. Greenwillow.
Granny & the Desperadoes. Macmillan.
Granny & the Indians. Macmillan.
Granny & the Indians. Macmillan.
Granny, the Baby, & the Big Gray Thing.
Macmillan.
Granny, the Baby, & the Big Gray Thing.
Macmillan.
Let's Be Early Settler's with Daniel Boone.
Har-Row.
Let's Be Indians. Har-Row.
Let's Celebrate: Holiday Decorations You Can
Make. Greenwillow.
Little Indian. S&S.
My Golden Book of Manners. Western Pub.
Ootah's Lucky Day. Har-Row.
Pirate Island Adventure. Macmillan.
Play Ball, Amelia Bedelia. Har-Row.
Play Ball, Amelia Bedelia. Har-Row.
Teach Us, Amelia Bedelia. Greenwillow.
Thank You, Amelia Bedelia. Har-Row.
Zed & the Monsters. Doubleday.

Parish, Peter.
xParish, Peter.
The Doctors & Patients Handbook of
Medicines & Drugs. Knopf.
Parish, W. A. *see* Parish, W. Alton.

Parish, W. Alton.
xParish, W. A.
Essentials of Business Mathematics. HR&W.
Parish, William J. *see* Parish, William Jackson.

Parish, William Jackson.
xParish, William J.
Charles Ilfeld Company: A Study in the Rise &
Decline of Mercantile Capitalism in New
Mexico. Harvard U Pr.

Parisi, Alfred F.
xParisi, Alfred F.
Noninvasive Approaches to Cardiovascular
Diagnosis. ACC.
Parisi, D. *see* Parisi, Domenico.

Parisi, Domenico.
xParisi, D.
Essentials of Grammar. Acad Pr.
Parizeau, Alice. *see* Parizeau, Alice Poznanska.

Parizeau, Alice Poznanska.
xParizeau, Alice.
The Canadian Criminal Justice System.
Lexington Bks.
Park, Charles F. *see* Park, Charles Frederick.

Park, Charles Frederick.
xPark, Charles F.
Earthbound: Minerals, Energy & Man's Future.
Freeman C.
Ore Deposits. W H Freeman.
Park, Clara C. *see* Park, Clara Claiborne.

Park, Clara Claiborne.
xPark, Clara C.
The Siege. Humanities.
Park, D. A. *see* Park, David.

Park, David, 1919-
xPark, D. A.
Classical Dynamics & Its Quantum Analogues.
Springer-Verlag.
Park, David. *see* Park, David Allen.

Park, David Allen, 1919-
xPark, David.

From Evolution to Creation: A Personal
Testimony. CLP Pubs.
Parker, Gary E. *see* Parker, Gary.
Parker, Geoffrey, 1933-
xParker, Geoffrey.
The Countries of Community Europe: A
Geographical Survey of Contemporary Issues.
St Martin.
Parker, Harry, 1887-
xParker, Harry.
Simplified Design of Reinforced Concrete.
Wiley.
Simplified Design of Structural Steel. Wiley.
Simplified Design of Structural Wood. Wiley.
Simplified Engineering for Architects &
Builders. Wiley.
Simplified Mechanics & Strength of Materials.
Wiley.
Simplified Site Engineering for Architects &
Builders. Wiley.
Parker, Harry L. *see* Parker, Harry Lee.
Parker, Harry Lee.
xParker, Harry L.
Clinical Studies in Neurology. C C Thomas.
Parker, Homer W., 1921-
xParker, Homer W.
Air Pollution. P-H.
Parker, J. D. *see* Parker, Jerald D.
Parker, James.
xParker, James.
jt. auth. Glossary of Terms Used in Heraldry.
Gale.
Glossary of Terms Used in Heraldry. C E
Tuttle.
Parker, James E., 1938-
xParker, James E.
Programmed Guide to Tax Research
Wadsworth Pub.
Parker, James T.
xParker.
Official Guide to Pocket Knives. Hse of
Collectibles.
Parker, James L. *see* Parker, James Laurie.
Parker, James Laurie.
xParker, James L.
FORTRAN Programming & WATFIV. SRA.
Parker, James T. *see* Parker, James Thompson.
Parker, James Thompson.
xParker, James T.
Delphi Survey: CBAE Through the Eyes of
Leading Educators. Pitman Learning.
Parker, Jerald D.
xParker, J. D.
Introduction to Fluid Mechanics & Heat
Transfer. A-W.
Parker, Jeri, 1939-
xParker, Jeri.
Uneasy Survivors: Five Women Writers.
Peregrine Smith.
Parker, John R.
xParker, John R.
A Musical Biography. Info Coord.
Parker, Joseph F.
xParker, Joseph F.
Prayers at Sea. Naval Inst Pr.
Parker, K. Langloh. *see* Parker, Catherine Somerville
(Field).
Parker, Kenneth.
xParker, Kenneth.
ed. The South African Novel in English:
Essays in Criticism & Society. Holmes &
Meier.
Parker, Kittie F.
xParker, Kittie F.
An Illustrated Guide to Arizona Weeds. U of
Ariz Pr.
Parker, Lois M.
xParker, Lois M.

Thee, Patience. Review & Herald.
Parker, Margaret, 1941-
xParker, Margaret.
The Didactic Structure & Content of el Libro
De Calila E Digna. Ediciones.
Parker, Mark.
xParker, Mark.
Horses, Airplanes, & Frogs. Childs World.
Parker, Nancy W. *see* Parker, Nancy Winslow.
Parker, Nancy Winslow.
xParker, Nancy W.
The Crocodile Under Louis Finneberg's Bed.
Dodd.
illus. Love from Uncle Clyde. Dodd.
Mrs. Wilson Wanders Off. Dodd.
The Ordeal of Byron B. Blackbear. Dodd.
illus. The Party at the Old Farm: A Halloween
Story. Atheneum.
Poofy Loves Company. Dodd.
Parker, Norton S.
xParker, Norton S.
Audiovisual Script Writing. Rutgers U Pr.
Parker, Oren W. *see* Parker, Wilford Oren.
Parker, Patricia A., 1946-
xParker, Patricia A.
Inescapable Romance: Studies in the Poetics of
a Mode. Princeton U Pr.
Parker, Paul E.
xParker, Paul E.
What's a Nice Person Like You Doing Sick?.
Creation Hse.
Parker, Phyllis R., 1947-
xParker, Phyllis R.
Brazil & the Quiet Intervention. U of Tex Pr.
Parker Pub. Editorial Staff. *see* Parker Publishing
Company.
Parker Publishing Company.
xParker Pub. Editorial Staff.
Business Etiquette Handbook. 1-11.
One Hundred Fifty Five Office Shortcuts &
Time Savers for the Secretary. P-H.
Parker Prosperity Program. P-H.
Secretary's Desk Book. P-H.
Successful Secretary. P-H.
Parker, R. A. *see* Parker, Richard Alexander.
Parker, R. H. *see* Parker, Robert Henry.
Parker, R. S. *see* Parker, Robert Stewart.
Parker, Reeve.
xParker, Reeve.
Coleridge's Meditative Art. Cornell U Pr.
Coleridge's Meditative Art. Irvington.
Parker, Richard, 1915-
xParker, Richard.
Quarter Boy. Elsevier-Nelson.
Parker, Richard A. *see* Parker, Richard Anthony.
Parker, Richard Alexander, 1898-
xParker, R. A.
Claude De l' Estoille, Poet & Dramatist,
1597-1652. Johnson Repr.
Parker, Richard Anthony, 1905-
xParker, Richard A.
Demotic Mathematical Papyri. Brown U Pr.
The Edifice of Taharqa by the Sacred Lake of
Karnak. Brown U Pr.
Parker, Robert Andrew.
xParker, Robert A.
Sweet Betsy from Pike: A Song from the Gold
Rush Days. Viking Pr.
Parker, Robert B., 1932-
xParker, Robert B.
God Save the Child. Berkley Pub.
The Godwulf Manuscript. Berkley Pub.
The Judas Goat. Berkley Pub.
Promised Land. Berkley Pub.
Parker, Robert Henry.
xParker, R. H.
ed. Readings in the Concept & Measurement of
Income. Cambridge U Pr.
Parker, Robert P. *see* Parker, Robert Prescott.

Parker, Robert Prescott.
xParker, Robert P.
Teaching English in the Secondary School.
Free Pr.
Parker, Robert Stewart.
xParker, R. S.
Government of New South Wales. U of
Queensland Pr.
Parker, Roger Hill.
xParker, R. H.
An Introduction to Chemical Metallurgy.
Pergamon.
Parker, Rolland S.
xParker, Rolland S.
Effective Decisions & Emotional Fulfillment.
Nelson-Hall.
Living Single Successfully: How to Be Your
Own Person with or Without a Partner.
Watts.
Psychology & Counseling Careers. Watts.
Parker, Rollin J.
xParker, Rollin J.
Permanent Magnets & Their Applications.
Wiley.
Parker, Ronald K.
xParker, Ronald K.
Day Care & Preschool Services: Trends &
Issues. Avatar Pr.
Parker, S. R. *see* Parker, Stanley Robert.
Parker, Samuel C. *see* Parker, Samuel Chester.
Parker, Samuel Chester, 1880-1924
xParker, Samuel C.
History of Modern Elementary Education.
Littlefield.
Parker, Stanley. *see* Parker, Stanley Robert.
Parker, Stanley Robert.
xParker, S. R.
The Sociology of Industry. Allen Unwin.
xParker, Stanley.
The Sociology of Leisure. Allen Unwin.
Sociology of Leisure. Intl Pubns Serv.
Parker, Theodore, 1810-1860
xParker, Theodore.
A Discourse of Matters Pertaining to Religion.
Arno.
Parker, W. H. *see* Parker, William Hosken.
Parker, Watson.
xParker, Watson.
Gold in the Black Hills. U of Okla Pr.
Parker, Wendy.
xParker, Wendy.
The Christmas Doll. HR&W.
Parker, Wilford Oren.
xParker, Oren W.
Scene Design & Stage Lighting. HR&W.
Parker, William.
xParker, William.
Homosexuality Bibliography: Supplement,
1970-1975. Scarecrow.
Paris Bourse & French Finance with Reference
to Organized Speculation in New York. AMS
Pr.
Parker, William B. *see* Parker, William Belmont.
Parker, William Belmont, 1871-1934
xParker, William B.
Chileans of To-Day. Kraus Repr.
Life & Public Services of Justin Smith Morrill.
Da Capo.
Paraguayans of To-Day. Kraus Repr.
Parker, William Hosken, 1910-
xParker, W. H.
Health & Disease in Farm Animals: An
Introduction to Farm Animal Medicine.
Pergamon.
Parker, Willis Dye, 1908-
xParker.
Modern Chinchilla Fur Farming. Borden.
Parker, Xenia L. *see* Parker, Xenia Ley.
Parker, Xenia Ley.
xParker, Xenia L.

Creative Handweaving. Dial.
  ed. Wooden Toys. Dutton.
Parker-Rhodes, A. F. see Parker-Rhodes, Arthur
  Frederick Parker.
Parker-Rhodes, Arthur Frederick Parker, 1914-
  xParker-Rhodes, A. F.
    Inferential Semantics. Humanities.
Parkes, Alan. see Parkes, Alan S.
Parkes, Alan S.
  xParkes, Alan.
    Patterns of Sexuality & Reproduction. Oxford
    U Pr.
Parkes, E. W. see Parkes, Edward Walter.
Parkes, Edward Walter, 1926-
  xParkes, E. W.
    Braced Frameworks: An Introduction to the
    Theory of Structures. Pergamon.
Parkes, Henry B. see Parkes, Henry Bamford.
Parkes, Henry Bamford, 1904-
  xParkes, Henry B.
    History of Mexico. HM.
    History of Mexico. HM.
    Jonathan Edwards, the Fiery Puritan. AMS Pr.
Parkes, James. see Parkes, James William.
Parkes, James William, 1896-
  xParkes, James.
    Antisemitism. Times Bks.
Parkey, Robert W.
  xParkey, Robert W.
    ed. Clinical Nuclear Cardiology. ACC.
Parkhouse, Bonnie L.
  xParkhouse, Bonnie L.
    Women Who Win: Exercising Your Rights in
    Sports. P-H.
Parkhurst, Charles H. see Parkhurst, Charles Henry.
Parkhurst, Charles Henry, 1842-1933
  xParkhurst, Charles H.
    Our Fight with Tammany. Arno.
Parkin, Andrew.
  xParkin, Andrew.
    The Dramatic Imagination of W. B. Yeats.
    B&N.
Parkin, Charles W.
  xParkin, Charles W.
    Moral Basis of Burke's Political Thought: An
    Essay. Russell.
Parkin, David J.
  xParkin, David J.
    Neighbours & Nationals in an African City
    Ward. U of Cal Pr.
Parkin, Michael.
  xParkin, Michael.
    ed. Inflation in the World Economy. U of
    Toronto Pr.
Parkin, Molly, 1932-
  xParkin, Molly.
    Full up!. St Martin.
Parkin, P. H. see Parkin, Peter Hubert.
Parkin, Peter Hubert.
  xParkin, P. H.
    Acoustics, Noise & Buildings. Merrimack Bk
    Serv.
Parkins, Almon E. see Parkins, Almon Ernest.
Parkins, Almon Ernest, 1879-1940
  xParkins, Almon E.
    Historical Geography of Detroit. Kennikat.
    South, Its Economic-Geographic Development.
    Greenwood.

Parkinson, C. Northcote. see Parkinson, Cyril Northcote.
Parkinson, Cyril Northcote, 1909-
  xParkinson, C. Northcote.
    The Fur-Lined Mousetrap. Hippocrene Bks.
    Gunpowder, Treason & Plot. St Martin.
    Industrial Disruption. Hippocrene Bks.
    Parkinson's Law & Other Studies in
      Administration. Ballantine.
    Touch & Go. G K Hall.
    Touch & Go. Playboy Pbks.
Parkinson, Ethelyn. see Parkinson, Ethelyn M.

Parkinson, Ethelyn M.
  xParkinson, Ethelyn.
    Rupert Piper & the Boy Who Could Knit.
    Abingdon.
Parkinson, George H. see Parkinson, George Henry
  Radcliffe.
Parkinson, George Henry Radcliffe.
  xParkinson, George H.
    Georg Lukacs. Routledge & Kegan.
Parkinson, James, 1755-1824
  xParkinson, James.
    Organic Remains of a Former World. Arno.
Parkinson, James W.
  xParkinson, James W.
    Focus on Your Language. Bobbs.
Parkinson, John A.
  xParkinson, John A.
    An Index to the Vocal Works of Thomas
    Augustine Arne & Michael Arne. Info Coord.
Parkinson, Norman, 1913-
  xParkinson, Norman.
    Sisters Under the Skin. St Martin.

Parkinson, Roger.
  xParkinson, Roger.
    The Encyclopedia of Modern War. Stein &
    Day.
Parkinson, Thomas. see Parkinson, Thomas Francis.

Parkinson, Thomas Francis, 1920-

  xParkinson, Thomas.
    Protect the Earth. City Lights.
    What the Blindman Saw: Or Twenty-Five
    Years of the Endless War. Thorp Springs.
Parkinson, Tom.
  xParkinson, Tom.
    The Circus Moves by Rail. Pruett.

Parkman, Frances. see Parkman, Francis.
Parkman, Francis, 1823-1893
  xParkman, Frances.
    Oregon Trail. U of Wis Pr.
  xParkman, Francis.
    Oregon Trail. NAL.
    Oregon Trail. Airmont.
    Oregon Trail. Watts.
Parkman, R. see Parkman, Ralph.
Parkman, Ralph.
  xParkman, R.
    The Cybernetic Society. Pergamon.
Parks, Alex L. see Parks, Alex Leon.
Parks, Alex Leon, 1925-
  xParks, Alex L.
    Law of Tug, Tow & Pilotage. Cornell Maritime.
Parks, Dennis.
  xParks, Dennis.
    A Potter's Guide to Raw Glazing & Oil Firing.
    Scribner.
Parks, Douglas R.
  xParks, Douglas R.
    A Grammar of Pawnee. Garland Pub.
Parks, E. T. see Parks, E. Taylor.
Parks, E. Taylor.
  xParks, E. T.
    Colombia & the United States. Gordon Pr.
  xParks, E. Taylor.
    Colombia & the United States. Arno.
Parks, Edd W. see Parks, Edd Winfield.
Parks, Edd Winfield, 1906-
  xParks, Edd W.
    Ante-Bellum Southern Literary Critics.
    Greenwood.
Parks, George B. see Parks, George Bruner.
Parks, George Bruner, 1890-
  xParks, George B.
    Richard Hakluyt & the English Voyages.
    Ungar.
Parks, Gordon, 1912-
  xParks, Gordon.

Born Black. Lippincott.
Choice of Weapons. Har-Row.
A Choice of Weapons. Har-Row.
Flavio. Norton.
The Learning Tree. Fawcett.
Parks, Joseph H. see Parks, Joseph Howard.
Parks, Joseph Howard.
  xParks, Joseph H.
    Joseph E. Brown of Georgia. La State U Pr.
Parks, Marshall M.
  xParks, Marshall M.
    Ocular Motility & Strabismus. Har-Row.
Parks, Mercer H.
  xParks, Mercer H.
    The Task Worthy of Travail. Pacesetter Pr.
Parks, Paul B.
  xParks, Paul B.
    Model of an Ablating Solid Hydrogen Pellet in
    a Plasma. Garland Pub.
Parks, R. D., 1935-
  xParks, R. D.
    ed. Superconductivity. Dekker.
Parks, Robert J.
  xParks, Robert J.
    European Origins of the Economic Ideas of
    Alexander Hamilton. Arno.
Parkus, H. see Parkus, Heinz.
Parkus, Heinz, 1909-
  xParkus, H.
    Thermoelasticity. Springer-Verlag.
Parkyn, George W.
  xParkyn, George W.
    Towards a Conceptual Model of Life-Long
    Education. Unipub.
Parlato, Salvatore J., 1931-
  xParlato, Salvatore J.
    Superfilms: An International Guide to Award
    Winning Educational Films. Scarecrow.
Parler, Mary C. see Parler, Mary Celestia.
Parler, Mary Celestia.
  xParler, Mary C.
    An Arkansas Ballet Book. Folcroft.
Parlett, Beresford N.
  xParlett, Beresford N.
    The Symmetric Eigenvalue Problem. P-H.
Parliamentary Debates, Great Britain. see Great Britain.
    Parliament.
Parlin, Bradley W.
  xParlin, Bradley W.
    Immigrant Professionals in the United States:
    Discrimination in the Scientific Labor
    Market. Praeger.
Parman, Donald L.
  xParman, Donald L.
    The Navajos & the New Deal. Yale U Pr.
Parmelee, C. W. see Parmelee, Cullen Warner.
Parmelee, Cullen Warner, 1874-1947
  xParmelee, C. W.
    Ceramic Glazes. CBI Pub.
Parmenter, Ross.
  xParmenter, Ross.
    Explorer, Linguist & Ethnologist: A Descriptive
    Bibliography of the Published Works of
    Alphonse Louis Pinart, with Notes on His
    Life. Southwest Mus.
Parmet, Herbert S.
  xParmet, Herbert S.
    The Democrats: The Years After FDR.
    Macmillan.
    Democrats: The Years After FDR. Oxford U
    Pr.
    Jack: The Struggles of John F. Kennedy. Dial.
Parnall, Peter.
  xParnall, Peter.
    A Dog's Book of Birds. Scribner.
Parnes, Robert, 1931-
  xParnes, Robert.
    Canoeing the Jersey Pine Barrens. East Woods.
Parnwell, E. C.
  xParnwell, E. C.

Oxford Picture Dictionary of American
English. Oxford U Pr.
Parole Commission, Commonwealth of Pennsylvania. *see*
Pennsylvania. Parole Commission.
Parpart, Arthur K. *see* Parpart, Arthur Kemble.
Parpart, Arthur Kemble.
xParpart, Arthur K.
ed. Chemistry & Physiology of Growth.
Kennikat.
Parr, A. H.
xParr, Adolph H.
Rendezvous with the Unknown. Dghtrs St
Paul.
Parr, Adolph H. *see* Parr, A. H.
Parr, Johnstone, 1911-
xParr, Johnstone.
Tamburlaine's Malady: & Other Essays on
Astrology in Elizabethan Drama. Greenwood.
Parr, Letitia.
xParr, Letitia.
When Sea & Sky Are Blue. Scroll Pr.
Parr, Lucy.
xParr, Lucy.
True Stories of Mormon Pioneer Courage.
Horizon Utah.
xParr, Lucy C.
Not of the World: A Living Account of the
United Order. Horizon Utah.
Parr, Lucy C. *see* Parr, Lucy.
Parr, Robert E.
xParr, Robert E.
Principles of Mechanical Design. McGraw.
Parr, William M., 1916-
xParr, William M.
Executive's Guide to Effective Letters &
Reports. P-H.
Parrack, James D.
xParrack, James D.
The Naturalist in Majorca. David & Charles
Parramore, Thomas C.
xParramore, Thomas C.
Carolina Quest. P-H.
Parrell, Mary Agnes.
xParrell, Mary Agnes.
Profiles of Dobbs Ferry. Oceana.
Parrinder, Edward G. *see* Parrinder, Edward Geoffrey.
Parrinder, Edward Geoffrey.
xParrinder, Edward G.
Book of World Religions. Dufour.
xParrinder, Geoffrey.
Religion in an African City. Negro U Pr.
Parrinder, Geoffrey.
xParrinder, Geoffrey.
Introduction to Asian Religions. Oxford U Pr.
Parrinder, Geoffrey. *see* Parrinder, Edward Geoffrey.
Parrinder, Patrick.
xParrinder, Patrick.
Authors & Authority: A Study of English
Literary Criticism & Its Relation to Culture,
1750-1900. Routledge & Kegan.
ed. H. G. Wells: The Critical Heritage.
Routledge & Kegan.
Parrington, Vernon L. *see* Parrington, Vernon Louis.
Parrington, Vernon Louis, 1871-1929
xParrington, Vernon L.
ed. The Connecticut Wits. Peter Smith.
Parrino, John J., 1941-
xParrino, John J.
From Panic to Power: The Positive Use of
Stress. Wiley.
Parris, C. *see* Parris, Crawley A.
Parris, Crawley A.
xParris, Crawley A.
Mastering Executive Arts & Skills. P-H.
Parris, Judith H.
xParris, Judith H.
The Convention Problem: Issues in Reform of
Presidential Nominating Procedures.
Brookings.
Parrish, John A. *see* Parrish, John Albert.

Parrish, John Albert, 1939-
xParrish, John A.
Dermatology & Skin Care. McGraw.
Parrish, Louis.
xParrish, Louis.
Cooking As Therapy. Arbor Hse.
Parrish, Mary V. *see* Parrish, Mary Virginia.
Parrish, Mary Virginia, 1911-
xParrish, Mary V.
Then Comes the Joy. Abingdon.
Parrish, Michael E.
xParrish, Michael E.
Securities Regulation & the New Deal. Yale U
Pr.
Parrish, Noel F. *see* Parrish, Noel Francis.
Parrish, Noel Francis.
xParrish, Noel F.
Behind the Sheltering Bomb. Arno.
Parrish, Robert.
xParrish, Robert.
Growing up in Hollywood. HarBraceJ.
Parrish, Stephen M. *see* Parrish, Stephen Maxfield.
Parrish, Stephen Maxfield.
xParrish, Stephen M.
The Art of the Lyrical Ballads. Harvard U Pr.
ed. Concordance to the Poems of W. B. Yeats.
Cornell U Pr.
Parrish, Thomas. *see* Parrish, Thomas D.
Parrish, Thomas D.
xParrish, Thomas.
ed. The Simon & Schuster Encyclopedia of
World War II. S&S.
Parrot, Friedrich. *see* Parrot, Friedrich von.
Parrot, Friedrich von, 1791-1841
xParrot, Friedrich.
Journey to Ararat. Arno.
Parrott, Thomas M. *see* Parrott, Thomas Marc.
Parrott, Thomas Marc.
xParrott, Thomas M.
Companion to Victorian Literature. Kelley.
Parry. *see* Parry, Gareth.
Parry, Adam.
xParry, Adam.
Studies in Fifth-Century Thought & Literature.
Cambridge U Pr.
Parry, Albert W. *see* Parry, Albert William.
Parry, Albert William, 1874-1950
xParry, Albert W.
Education in England in the Middle Ages.
AMS Pr.
Parry, Benita.
xParry, Benita.
Delusions & Discoveries: Studies on India in
the British Imagination 1880-1930. U of Cal
Pr.
Parry, Charles. *see* Parry, Charles Hubert Hastings.
Parry, Charles H. *see* Parry, Charles Hubert Hastings.
Parry, Charles Hubert Hastings.
xParry, Charles.
Style in Musical Art. Scholarly.
xParry, Charles H.
Evolution of the Art of Music. Greenwood.
Style in Musical Art. Hyperion Conn.
Parry, Clive.
xParry, Clive.
ed. Commonwealth International Law Cases.
Oceana.
Parry, Edward A. *see* Parry, Edward Abbott.
Parry, Edward Abbott, Sir, 1863-1943
xParry, Edward A.
The Overbury Mystery: A Chronicle of Fact &
Drama of the Law. Arno.
Vagabonds All. Arno.
What the Judge Thought. Arno.
Parry, Ellwood.
xParry, Ellwood.
The Image of the Indian & the Black Man in
American Art, 1590-1900. Braziller.
Parry, Gareth.
xParry.

Birds of Prey. S&S.
Parry, Geraint.
xParry, Geraint.
John Locke. Allen Unwin.
Parry, H. B. *see* Parry, Herbert Butler.
Parry, Herbert Butler.
xParry, H. B.
ed. Population & Its Problems: A Plain Man's
Guide. Oxford U Pr.
Parry, J. H.
xParry, John H.
ed. Establishment of the European Hegemony:
1415-1715: Trade & Exploration in the Age
of the Renaissance. Har-Row.
Parry, J. H. *see* Parry, John Horace.
Parry, J. P. *see* Parry, Jonathan P.
Parry, John H. *see* Parry, John Horace.
Parry, John Horace.
xParry, J. H.
The Discovery of South America. Taplinger.
xParry, John H.
The Discovery of the Sea. Dial.
Spanish Seaborne Empire. Knopf.
Spanish Theory of Empire in the Sixteenth
Century. Folcroft.
The Spanish Theory of Empire in the Sixteenth
Century. Octagon.
Parry, Jonathan P.
xParry, J. P.
Caste & Kinship in Kangra. Routledge &
Kegan.
Parry, Leonard A. *see* Parry, Leonard Arthur.
Parry, Leonard Arthur.
xParry, Leonard A.
History of Torture in England. Patterson
Smith.
Some Famous Medical Trials. Kelley.
Parry, M. L. *see* Parry, Martin L.
Parry, Marian.
xParry, Marian.
I Am a Big Help. Greenwillow.
Parry, Martin L.
xParry, M. L.
Climatic Change, Agriculture, & Settlement.
Shoe String.
Parry, Megan.
xParry, Megan.
Stenciling. Van Nos Reinhold.
Parry, Michael. *see* Parry, Michel.
Parry, Michel.
xParry, Michael.
Chariots of Fire. Popular Lib.
xParry, Michel.
ed. The Devil's Children. Berkley Pub.
ed. Great Black Magic Stories. Taplinger.
Hounds of Hell: Stories of Canine Horror &
Fantasy. Taplinger.
ed. Savage Heroes: Tales of Magical Fantasy.
Taplinger.
ed. The Supernatural Solution: Chilling Stories
of Spooks & Sleuths. Taplinger.
Parry, Pamela J. *see* Parry, Pamela Jeffcott.
Parry, Pamela Jeffcott.
xParry, Pamela J.
Compiled by Photography Index: A Guide to
Reproductions. Greenwood.
Parry, Richard. *see* Parry, Richard Albert.
Parry, Richard Albert.
xParry, Richard.
Guide to Counselling & Basic Psychotherapy.
Churchill.
Parry, William.
xParry, William.
Entropy & Generators in Ergodic Theory.
Benjamin-Cummings.
Parry, William E. *see* Parry, William Edward.
Parry, William Edward, Sir, 1790-1855
xParry, William E.

Journal of a Second Voyage for the Discovery
of a Northwest Passage from the Atlantic to
the Pacific. Greenwood.
Journal of a Voyage for the Discovery of a
Northwest Passage from the Atlantic to the
Pacific, Performed in the Years 1819-20.
Greenwood.
Parsley, Mary.
xParsley, Mary.
ed. I Can Choose My Bedtime Story. G&D.
Parson, Thomas E.
xParson, Thomas E.
How to Dance. Har-Row.
Parsonage, N. G. *see* Parsonage, Neville George.
Parsonage, Neville George.
xParsonage, N. G.
ed. Disorder in Crystals. Oxford U Pr.
Parsons, Burke A. *see* Parsons, Burke Adrian.
Parsons, Burke Adrian.
xParsons, Burke A.
British Trade Cycles & American Bank Credit:
Some Aspects of Economic Fluctuations in
the United States, 1815-1840. Arno.
Parsons, C. G. *see* Parsons, Charles Grandison.
Parsons, Charles Grandison, 1807-1864
xParsons, C. G.
Inside View of Slavery: Or a Tour Among the
Planters. Argosy.
Parsons, Charles S. *see* Parsons, Charles Sumner.
Parsons, Charles Sumner.
xParsons, Charles S.
The Dunlaps & Their Furniture. U of Mass Pr.
Parsons, Cheryl.
xParsons, Cheryl.
Schools in an Urban Community: A Study of
Carbrook, 1870-1965. Routledge & Kegan.
Parsons, Derrick.
xParsons, Derrick.
Do Your Own Horse. J A Allen.
Parsons, E. M.
xParsons, E. M.
Fargo. Fawcett.
Parsons, Edwin C.
xParsons, Edwin C.
I Flew with the Lafayette Escadrille. Arno.
Parsons, Ellen.
xParsons, Ellen.
Rainy Day Together. Har-Row.
Parsons, Elsie W. *see* Parsons, Elsie Worthington
(Clews).
Parsons, Elsie W. C. *see* Parsons, Elsie Worthington
(Clews).
Parsons, Elsie Worthington (Clews), 1875-1941
xParsons, Elsie W.
Educational Legislation & Administration of
the Colonial Governments. Arno.
xParsons, Elsie W. C.
Taos Pueblo. Johnson Repr.
Parsons, F. *see* Parsons, Frederick Gymer.
Parsons, F. G. *see* Parsons, Frederick Gymer.
Parsons, Florence M. *see* Parsons, Florence Mary
(Wilson).
Parsons, Florence Mary (Wilson), 1864-1934
xParsons, Florence M.
Incomparable Siddons. Arno.
Parsons, Frances T. *see* Parsons, Frances Theodora
(Smith) Dana.
Parsons, Frances Theodora (Smith) Dana, 1861-1952
xParsons, Frances T.
How to Know the Ferns: A Guide to the
Names, Haunts, & Habits of Our Common
Ferns. Dover.
Parsons, Frank, 1854-1908
xParsons, Frank.
Choosing a Vocation. Agathon.
Parsons, Frank A. *see* Parsons, Frank Alvah.
Parsons, Frank Alvah, 1868-
xParsons, Frank A.

The Psychology of Dress. Gale.
Parsons, Frederick Gymer, 1863-1943
xParsons, F.
The Earlier Inhabitants of London. Gordon Pr.
xParsons, F. G.
Earlier Inhabitants of London. Kennikat.
Parsons, H. Rosamond.
xParsons, Rosamond H.
Anglo-Norman Books of Courtesy & Nurture.
Haskell.
Parsons, Howard L.
xParsons, Howard L.
ed. Marx & Engels on Ecology. Greenwood.
Parsons, Ian. *see* Parsons, Ian Macnaghten.
Parsons, Ian Macnaghten.
xParsons, Ian.
Poetry for Pleasure: A Choice of Poetry &
Verse on a Variety of Themes. Norton.
Parsons, J. J. *see* Parsons, James Jerome.
Parsons, Jack.
xParsons, Jack.
Population Fallacies. Merrimack Bk Serv.
Parsons, James B. *see* Parsons, James Bunyan.
Parsons, James Bunyan.
xParsons, James B.
The Peasant Rebellions of the Late Ming
Dynasty. U of Ariz Pr.
Parsons, James J. *see* Parsons, James Jerome.
Parsons, James Jerome, 1915-
xParsons, J. J.
Antioquia's Corridor to the Sea: An Historical
Geography of the Settlement of Uraba. U of
Cal Pr.
xParsons, James J.
Antioqueno Colonization in Western Colombia.
U of Cal Pr.
Parsons, Jeffrey R.
xParsons, Jeffrey R.
Prehistoric Settlement Patterns in the Texcoco
Region, Mexico. U Mich Mus Anthro.
Parsons, John A. *see* Parsons, John Anthony.
Parsons, John Anthony.
xParsons, John A.
ed. Peptide Hormones. Univ Park.
Parsons, Kermit C. *see* Parsons, Kermit Carlyle.
Parsons, Kermit Carlyle, 1927-
xParsons, Kermit C.
Cornell Campus: A History of Its Planning &
Development. Cornell U Pr.
Parsons, Kitty.
xParsons, Kitty.
Ancestral Timber. Golden Quill.
Down to Earth. Golden Quill.
Parsons, Langdon.
xParsons, Langdon.
Atlas of Pelvic Operations. Saunders.
Gynecology. Saunders.
Parsons, M. L. *see* Parsons, Michael Loewen.
Parsons, Malcolm.
xParsons, Malcolm.
Tuberculous Meningitis: A Handbook for
Clinicians. Oxford U Pr.
Parsons, Michael Loewen.
xParsons, M. L.
Atlas of Spectral Interferences in ICP
Spectroscopy. Plenum Pub.
Handbook of Flame Spectroscopy. Plenum Pub.
Parsons, Philip A. *see* Parsons, Philip Archibald.
Parsons, Philip Archibald, 1879-1943
xParsons, Philip A.
Responsibility for Crime: An Investigation of
the Nature & Causes of Crime & a Means of
Its Prevention. AMS Pr.
Parsons, Rosamond H. *see* Parsons, H. Rosamond.
Parsons, S. A. *see* Parsons, Stanley Alfred James.
Parsons, Samuel B. *see* Parsons, Samuel Bowne.
Parsons, Samuel Bowne, 1819-1906
xParsons, Samuel B.

Parsons on the Rose. E M Coleman Ent.
Parsons School of Design, New York.
xParsons School of Design Students.
Parsons Bread Book. Har-Row.
Parsons School of Design Students. *see* Parsons School of
Design, New York.
Parsons, Stanley Alfred James.
xParsons, S. A.
How to Find Out About Engineering.
Pergamon.
Parsons, Stanley B.
xParsons, Stanley B.
The Populist Context: Rural Versus Urban
Power on a Great Plains Frontier.
Greenwood.
Parsons, Talcott, 1902-
xParsons, Talcott.
Action Theory & the Human Condition. Free
Pr.
The Evolution of Societies. P-H.
Politics and Social Structure. Free Pr.
Social System. Free Pr.
Social Systems & the Evolution of Action
Theory. Free Pr.
Sociological Theory & Modern Society. Free
Pr.
Structure & Process in Modern Societies. Free
Pr.
ed. Toward a General Theory of Action.
Harvard U Pr.
Parsons, Theophilus.
xParsons, Theophilus.
Memoir of Theophilus Parsons. Da Capo.
Parsons, Thomas W., 1826-1915
xParsons, Thomas W.
Incidents & Experiences in the Life of Thomas
W. Parsons from 1826 to 1900. U Pr of Ky.
Parsons, Virginia.
xParsons, Virginia.
Rainbow Rhymes. Western Pub.
Parsons, Wilfrid, 1887-
xParsons, Wilfrid.
Which Way, Democracy?. Arno.
Parsons, William B. *see* Parsons, William Barclay.
Parsons, William Barclay, 1859-1932
xParsons, William B.
An American Engineer in China. Chinese
Materials.
An American Engineer in China. Garland Pub.
Engineers & Engineering of the Renaissance.
MIT Pr.
Parsons, William E. *see* Parsons, William Edward.
Parsons, William Edward, 1936-
xParsons, William E.
Silly Putty & Other Children's Sermons.
Abingdon.
Parsonson, S. L.
xParsonson, S. L.
Pure Mathematics. Cambridge U Pr.
Parsson, Jens O.
xParsson, Jens O.
Dying of Money: Lessons of the Great German
& American Inflations. Wellspring Pr.
Parston, Gregory.
xParston, Gregory.
Planners, Politics & Health Services. Biblio
Dist.
Partee, Barbara H. *see* Partee, Barbara Hall.
Partee, Barbara Hall.
xPartee, Barbara H.
Subject & Object in Modern English. Garland
Pub.
Partee, Charles.
xPartee, Charles.
ed. Calvin & Classical Philosophy (1977).
Heinman.
Parthasarathy, K. R.
xParthasarathy, K. R.

Multipliers on Locally Compact Groups.
Springer-Verlag.
Positive Definite Kernels, Continuous Tensor
Products, & Central Limit Theorems of
Probability Theory. Springer-Verlag.
Probability Measures on Metric Spaces. Acad
Pr.
Parthasarathy, T.
xParthasarathy, T.
Some Topics in Two-Person Games. Elsevier.
Parthe, Erwin.
xParthe, Erwin.
Crystal Chemistry of Tetrahedral Structures.
Gordon.
Partin, Earl.
xPartin, Earl.
And This Is How It Is. Harlo Pr.
Partington, Geoffrey.
xPartington, Geoffrey.
Women Teachers in the Twentieth Century in
England & Wales. Humanities.
Partington, I. see Partington, Ian.
Partington, Ian.
xPartington, I.
Applied Economics in Banking & Finance.
Oxford U Pr.
Partington, Martin.
xPartington, Martin.
ed. Welfare Law & Policy: Studies in Teaching,
Practice & Research. Nichols Pub.
Partington, Paul G.
xPartington, Paul G.
Who's Who on the Postage Stamps of Eastern
Europe. Scarecrow.
Partlow, Miriam, 1893-
xPartlow, Miriam.
Liberty, Liberty County & the Atascosito
District. Jenkins.
Partner, Peter.
xPartner, Peter.
Renaissance Rome: A Portrait of a Society,
1500-1559. U of Cal Pr.
Partnow, Elaine.
xPartnow, Elaine.
ed. The Quotable Woman. Corwin.
Parton, James, 1822-1891
xParton, James.
Captains of Industry: Or, Men of Business Who
Did Something Besides Making Money; a
Book for Young Americans. Arno.
Partridge. see Partridge, Eric.
Partridge, A. C. see Partridge, Astley Cooper.
Partridge, Ashley C. see Partridge, Astley Cooper.
Partridge, Astley Cooper.
xPartridge, A. C.
Orthography in Shakespeare & Elizabethan
Drama: A Study of Colloquial Contractions,
Elision, Prosody, & Punctuation. U of Ncbr
Pr.
xPartridge, Ashley C.
A Substantive Grammar of Shakespeare's
Non-Dramatic Texts. U Pr of Va.
Partridge, Edward B. see Partridge, Edward Bellamy.
Partridge, Edward Bellamy, 1916-
xPartridge, Edward B.
The Broken Compass: A Study of the Major
Comedies of Ben Jonson. Greenwood.
Partridge, Eric, 1894-
xPartridge.
Concise Usage & Abusage. British Bk Ctr.
xPartridge, Eric.

Adventuring Among Words. Arno.
A Charm of Words: Essays & Papers on
Language. Arno.
ed. A Dictionary of Forces' Slang: 1939-1945.
Arno.
Literary Sessions. Arno.
Literary Sessions. Folcroft.
Words at War, Words at Peace: Essays on
Language in General & Particular Words.
Arno.
Words at War, Words at Peace: Essays on
Language in General & Particular Words.
Folcroft.
Words, Words, Words!. Arno.
Words, Words, Words. Folcroft.
Partridge, Ernest D. see Partridge, Ernest Dealton.
Partridge, Ernest Dealton, 1906-
xPartridge, Ernest D.
Leadership Among Adolescent Boys. AMS Pr.
Partridge, Frances.
xPartridge, Frances.
A Pacifist's War. Universe.
Partridge, Loren. see Partridge, Loren W.
Partridge, Loren W.
xPartridge, Loren.
A Renaissance Likeness: Art & Culture in
Raphael's Julius II. U of Cal Pr.
Partridge, P. H. see Partridge, Percy Herbert.
Partridge, Percy Herbert, 1910-
xPartridge, P. H.
Society, Schools & Progress in Australia.
Pergamon.
Parturier, Francoise.
xParturier, Francoise.
Open Letter to Men. Houghton.
Parulski, George.
xParulski, George.
A Path to Oriental Wisdom: Introductory
Studies in Eastern Philosophy. Ohara Pubns.
Parvan, Vasile, 1882-1927
xParvan, Vasile.
Dacia: An Outline of the Early Civilizations of
the Carpatho-Danubian Countries.
Greenwood.
Parvati, Jeannine.
xParvati, Jeannine.
Hygieia: A Woman's Herbal. Freestone Pub
Co.
Parzen, Emanuel, 1929-
xParzen, Emanuel.
Stochastic Processes. Holden-Day.
Pasachoff, Jay M.
xPasachoff, Jay M.
Astronomy Now. HR&W.
Contemporary Astronomy. HR&W.
Pasadena Art Alliance. see Pasadena. Art Museum. Art
Alliance.
Pasadena. Art Museum. Art Alliance.
xPasadena Art Alliance.
All Things Wise & Wonderful. Pasadena Art.
Wish You Were Here. Pasadena Art.
Pascal, A. Michael.
xPascal, A. Michael.
Hospital Security & Safety. Aspen Systems.
Pascal, Blaise.
xPascal, Blaise.
Pensees. Dutton.
Pensees. French & Eur.
Pensees. Larousse.
Pensees. Penguin.
The Thoughts of Blaise Pascal. Greenwood.
Pascal, Francine.
xPascal, Francine.

The Hand-Me-Down Kid. Viking Pr.
Hangin' Out with Cici. Viking Pr.
Hangin' Out with Cici. Archway.
Hangin' Out with Cici. PB.
My First Love & Other Disasters. Dell.
My First Love & Other Disasters. Viking Pr.
Pascal, Harold.
xPascal, Harold J.
The Marijuana Maze. Alba Bks.
Pascal, Harold J. see Pascal, Harold.
Pascal, Pierre, 1890-
xPascal, Pierre.
The Religion of the Russian People. St
Vladimirs.
Pascal, Roy, 1904-
xPascal, Roy.
The Dual Voice: Free Indirect Speech & Its
Functioning in the Nineteenth Century
European Novel. Rowman.
German Literature in the Sixteenth &
Seventeenth Centuries:
Renaissance-Reformation-Baroque.
Greenwood.
Growth of Modern Germany. Russell.
Paschal, George H.
xPaschal, George H.
One Hundred Years of Challenge & Change: A
History of the Synod of Texas of the United
Presbyterian Church in the U.S.A. Trinity U
Pr.
Paschal, George W. see Paschal, George Washington.
Paschal, George Washington, 1812-1878
xPaschal, George W.
Ninety-Four Years - Agnes Paschal. Reprint.
Paschall. see Paschall, Henry Franklin.
Paschall, Henry Franklin.
xPaschall.
ed. Teacher's Bible Commentary. Broadman.
Pascoe, Delmer J.
xPascoe, Delmer J.
ed. Quick Reference to Pediatric Emergencies.
Lippincott.
Pascoe, K. J.
xPascoe, K. J.
Properties of Materials for Electrical Engineers.
Wiley.
Pascoe, Rob, 1953-
xPascoe, Rob.
The Manufacture of Australian History. Oxford
U Pr.
Pascoe, Robert D., 1943-
xPascoe, Robert D.
Fundamentals of Solid-State Electronics. Wiley.
Pasdermadjian, Hrant, 1904-1954
xPasdermadjian, Hrant.
The Department Store: Its Origins Evolution &
Economics. Arno.
Pasek, Jan C. see Pasek, Jan Chryzostom.
Pasek, Jan Chryzostom.
xPasek, Jan C.
Memoirs of the Polish Baroque: The Writings
of Jan Chryzostom Pasek, a Squire of the
Commonwealth of Poland & Lithuania. U of
Cal Pr.
Pashko, Stanley, 1913-
xPashko, Stanley.
Ferguson Jenkins: The Quiet Winner. Putnam.
Pasika, W. M. see Pasika, Wallace M.
Pasika, Wallace M.
xPasika, W. M.
ed. Advances in Macromolecular Chemistry.
Acad Pr.
Pasinetti, Luigi. see Pasinetti, Luigi L.
Pasinetti, Luigi L.
xPasinetti, Luigi.
Essays on the Theory of Joint Production.
Columbia U Pr.
Paskewitz, Daniel F.
xPaskewitz, Daniel F.

Student Effectiveness: A Group Approach to
Self-Managed Learning. U Pr of Amer.
Paskins, B. A. see Paskins, Barrie.
Paskins, Barrie.
xPaskins, B. A.
The Ethics of War. U of Minn Pr.
Pasley, Virginia. see Pasley, Virginia Schmitz.
Pasley, Virginia Schmitz, 1905-
xPasley, Virginia.
In Celebration of Food. S&S.
Pasmore, William A.
xPasmore, William A.
ed. Sociotechnical Systems: A Sourcebook.
Univ Assocs.
Paso, Alfonso.
xPaso, Alfonso.
Usted Puede Ser un Asesino. Irvington.
Pasolini, Pier P. see Pasolini, Pier Paolo.
Pasolini, Pier Paolo, 1922-1975
xPasolini, Pier P.
A Violent Life. Garland Pub.
Pasquali, Nicolo, d 1757
xPasquali, Nicolo.
Thorough-Bass Made Easy. Oxford U Pr.
Pass, G. see Pass, Geoffrey.
Pass, Geoffrey.
xPass, G.
Practical Inorganic Chemistry: Preparations,
Reactions & Instrumental Methods. Methuen
Inc.
Passadore, Wanda.
xPassadore, Wanda.
Needlework Book. S&S.
Passage, Charles E.
xPassage, Charles E.
Friedrich Schiller. Ungar.
Passavant, Johann D. see Passavant, Johann David.
Passavant, Johann David, 1787-1861
xPassavant, Johann D.
Raphael of Urbino & His Father Giovanni
Santi. Garland Pub.
Passell, Peter.
xPassell, Peter.
The Best Encore. Ballantine.
How to. Ballantine.
How to. FS&G.
Passett, Barry A.
xPassett, Barry A.
Leadership Development for Public Service.
Gulf Pub.
Passi, I. B. see Passi, Inder Bir S.
Passi, Inder Bir S., 1939-
xPassi, I. B.
Group Rings & Their Augmentation Ideals.
Springer-Verlag.
Passin, Herbert.
xPassin, Herbert.
ed. Encounter at Shimoda: Search for a New
Pacific Partnership. Westview.
Society & Education in Japan. Tchrs Coll.
Passman, D. S. see Passman, Donald S.
Passman, Donald S., 1940-
xPassman, D. S.
Permutation Groups. Benjamin-Cummings.
xPassman, Donald S.
The Algebraic Structure of Group Rings.
Wiley.
xPassman, R. D.
Infinite Group Rings. Dekker.
Passman, Jerome.
xPassman, Jerome.
Publish What You Write. Graystone Pub Co.
Passman, R. D. see Passman, Donald S.
Passmore, John. see Passmore, John Arthur.
Passmore, John Arthur.
xPassmore, John.
A Hundred Years of Philosophy. Penguin.
Passons, W. see Passons, William R.
Passons, William R.
xPassons, W.

Gestalt Approaches in Counseling. HR&W.
Passos, John Dos. see Dos Passos, John.
Passow, A. H. see Passow, A. Harry.
Passow, A. Harry.
xPassow, A. H.
The National Case Study: An Empirical
Comparative Study of Twenty-One
Educational Systems. Krieger.
xPassow, A. Harry.
ed. Developing Programs for the Educationally
Disadvantaged. Tchrs Coll.
Passwater, Richard. see Passwater, Richard A.
Passwater, Richard A.
xPasswater, Richard.
The Easy No-Flab Diet. Marek.
Pastan, Linda, 1932-
xPastan, Linda.
Aspects of Eve: Poems. Liveright.
The Five Stages of Grief: Poems. Norton.
Perfect Circle of the Sun. Swallow.
Pasternak, Bill.
xPasternak, Bill.
The Practical Handbook of Amateur Radio FM
& Repeaters. TAB Bks.
Pasternak, Burton.
xPasternak, Burton.
Introduction to Kinship & Social Organization.
P-H.
Pasternak, C. A. see Pasternak, Charles Alexander.
Pasternak, Charles Alexander.
xPasternak, C. A.
An Introduction to Human Biochemistry.
Oxford U Pr.
Pasternak, Michael G.
xPasternak, Michael G.
Helping Kids Learn Multi-Cultural Concepts: A
Handbook of Strategies. Res Press.
Pasto, Daniel. see Pasto, Daniel J.
Pasto, Daniel J.
xPasto, Daniel.
Organic Structure Determination. P-H.
xPasto, Daniel J.
Laboratory Text for Organic Chemistry: A
Source Book of Chemical & Physical
Techniques. P-H.
Pastor, Peter.
xPastor, Peter.
Hungary Between Wilson & Lenin: The
Hungarian Revolution of 1918-1919 & the
Big Three. East Eur Quarterly.
Pasvolsky, Leo, 1893-1953
xPasvolsky, Leo.
Economic Nationalism of the Danubian States.
Johnson Repr.
Paszkiewicz, H. see Paszkiewicz, Henryk.
Paszkiewicz, Henryk, 1897-
xPaszkiewicz, H.
Origin of Russia. Gordon Pr.
Origin of Russia. Kraus Repr.
xPaszkiewicz, Henryk.
Origin of Russia. Philos Lib.
Pasztory, Esther.
xPasztory, Esther.
The Iconography of the Teotihuacan Tlaloc.
Dumbarton Oaks.
Patai, Raphael, 1910-
xPatai, Raphael.
The Arab Mind. Scribner.
Jordan, Lebanon, & Syria: An Annotated
Bibliography. Greenwood.
The Messiah Texts. Avon.
Patai, S. see Patai, Saul.
Patai, Saul.
xPatai, S.
ed. Chemistry of Acyl Halides. Wiley.
Chemistry of the Azido Group. Wiley.
The Chemistry of the Diazonium & Diazo
Groups. Wiley.
xPatai, Saul.

The Chemistry of Amidines & Imidates. Wiley.
Chemistry of Carboxylic Acids & Esters.
Wiley.
Pataki-Schweizer, K. J.
xPataki-Schweizer, K. J.
A New Guinea Landscape: Community, Space
& Time in the Eastern Highlands. U of Wash
Pr.
Patch, Blanche. see Patch, Blanche Eliza.
Patch, Blanche Eliza, 1878-
xPatch, Blanche.
Thirty Years with G. B. S.. R West.
Patch, Howard R. see Patch, Howard Rollin.
Patch, Howard Rollin, 1889-1963
xPatch, Howard R.
On Rereading Chaucer. Harvard U Pr.
Other World, According to Descriptions in
Medieval Literature. Octagon.
Patch, Robert C.
xPatch, Robert C.
Illustrated Stories About the New Testament.
Promised Land.
Patchell, Mary. see Patchell, Mary Frances Corinne.
Patchell, Mary Frances Corinne.
xPatchell, Mary.
Palmerin Romances in Elizabethan Prose
Fiction. AMS Pr.
Patchen, Kenneth, 1911-
xPatchen, Kenneth.
But Even So. New Directions.
Hallelujah Anyway. New Directions.
In Quest of Candlelighters. New Directions.
Journal of Albion Moonlight. New Directions.
Love Poems. City Lights.
Patchen's Lost Plays. Capra Pr.
Wonderings. New Directions.
Patchen, Martin.
xPatchen, Martin.
Some Questionnaire Measures of Employee
Motivation & Morale. U of Mich Soc Res.
Pate, Bille. see Pate, Billie.
Pate, Billie.
xPate, Bille.
Touch Life. Broadman.
Pate, Don, 1951-
xPate, Don.
Episodes at the Olive Press. Southern Pub.
Pate, John B. see Pate, John Ben.
Pate, John Ben, 1874-
xPate, John B.
History of Turner County. Reprint.
Patel, Dinker I.
xPatel, Dinker I.
Exurbs: Urban Residential Developments in the
Countryside. U Pr of Amer.
Patel, M. L.
xPatel, M. L.
Changing Land Problems of Tribal India. Intl
Pubns Serv.
Patel, Satyavrata R. see Patel, Satyavrata Ramdas.
Patel, Satyavrata Ramdas.
xPatel, Satyavrata R.
The Soul of India. Intl Pubns Serv.
Pateman, Carole.
xPateman, Carole.
Participation & Democratic Theory. Cambridge
U Pr.
Patent, Dorothy H. see Patent, Dorothy Hinshaw.
Patent, Dorothy Hinshaw.
xPatent, Dorothy H.

Animal & Plant Mimicry. Holiday.

Bears of the World. Holiday.

Fish & How They Reproduce. Holiday.

Frogs, Toads, Salamanders & How They Reproduce. Holiday.

How Insects Communicate. Holiday.

Plants & Insects Together. Holiday.

Raccoons, Coatimundis, & Their Family. Holiday.

The World of Worms. Holiday.

Pater, Walter. *see* Pater, Walter Horatio.

Pater, Walter H. *see* Pater, Walter Horatio.

Pater, Walter Horatio, 1839-1894

xPater, Walter.

Appreciations: With an Essay on Style. Folcroft.

Greek Studies: A Series of Essays. Arden Lib.

Letters of Walter Pater. Oxford U Pr.

Marius the Epicurean. Garland Pub.

The Renaissance. Academy Chi Ltd.

Renaissance. R West.

Uncollected Essays. Folcroft.

xPater, Walter H.

The Renaissance. Folcroft.

Uncollected Essays. AMS Pr.

Uncollected Essays. Arden Lib.

Paterson, Antoinette M. *see* Paterson, Antoinette Mann.

Paterson, Antoinette Mann.

xPaterson, Antoinette M.

Francis Bacon & Socialized Science. C C Thomas.

Infinite Worlds of Giordano Bruno. C C Thomas.

Paterson, Arthur Henry.

xPaterson, J.

The Homes of Tennyson. Haskell.

The Homes of Tennyson. R West.

Paterson, D. G.

xPaterson, Donald G.

British Direct Investment in Canada, 1890-1914. U of Toronto Pr.

Paterson, Diane, 1946-

xPaterson, Diane.

The Bathtub Ocean. Dial.

Eat!. Dial.

illus. Eat!. Dial.

illus. If I Were A Toad. Dial.

Paterson, Donald G. *see* Paterson, D. G.

Paterson, George W.

xPaterson, George W.

The Cardiac Patient. Augsburg.

Paterson, Isabel. *see* Paterson, Isabel (Bowler).

Paterson, Isabel (Bowler).

xPaterson, Isabel.

God of the Machine. Arno.

xPaterson, Isabel B.

God of the Machine. Arno.

Paterson, Isabel B. *see* Paterson, Isabel (Bowler).

Paterson, J. *see* Paterson, Arthur Henry.

Paterson, James, 1005-1876

xPaterson, James.

The Contemporaries of Burns, & the More Recent Poets of Ayrshire, with Selections from Their Writings. AMS Pr.

Paterson, Josephine G.

xPaterson, Josephine G.

Humanistic Nursing. Wiley.

Paterson, Katherine.

xPaterson, Katherine.

Angels & Other Strangers: Family Christmas Stories. T Y Crowell.

Bridge to Terabithia. T Y Crowell.

Bridge to Terabithia. Avon.

The Great Gilly Hopkins. Avon.

The Great Gilly Hopkins. T Y Crowell.

The Master Puppeteer. T Y Crowell.

Of Nightingales That Weep. Avon.

Of Nightingales That Weep. T Y Crowell.

The Sign of the Chrysanthemum. T Y Crowell.

The Sign of the Chrysanthemum. Avon.

Paterson, Linda M.

xPaterson, Linda M.

Troubadours & Eloquence. Oxford U Pr.

Paterson, M. S. *see* Paterson, Mervyn Silas.

Paterson, Mervyn Silas, 1953-

xPaterson, M. S.

Experimental Rock Deformation: The Brittle Field. Springer-Verlag.

Paterson, R. W. *see* Paterson, Ronald William Keith.

Paterson, Ronald William Keith.

xPaterson, R. W.

Values, Education & the Adult. Routledge & Kegan.

Paterson, Thomas. *see* Paterson, Thomas G.

Paterson, Thomas G.

xPaterson, Thomas.

The Origins of the Cold War. Heath.

xPaterson, Thomas G.

American Foreign Policy: A History. Heath.

ed. American Imperialism & Anti-Imperialism. AHM Pub.

ed. Cold War Critics: Alternatives to American Foreign Policy in the Truman Years. New Viewpoints.

On Every Front: The Making of the Cold War. Norton.

Paterson, William D. *see* Paterson, William Brown.

Paterson, William Brown, 1912-

xPaterson, William B.

Marine Engine Room Blue Book. Cornell Maritime.

Pathria, R. K.

xPathria, R. K.

The Theory of Relativity. Pergamon.

Patil, D. R., 1915-

xPatil, D. R.

ed. Cultural History from the Vayu Purana. Verry.

xPatil, D. Rajaram.

Cultural History from the Vayu Purana. Orient Bk Dist.

Patil, D. Rajaram. *see* Patil, D. R.

Patinkin, Don.

xPatinkin, Don.

Money, Interest, & Prices: An Integration of Monetary & Value Theory. Har-Row.

Patitucci, Frank M.

xPatitucci, Frank M.

Improving Cash Management in Local Government: A Comprehensive Approach. Municipal.

Patka, Frederick.

xPatka, Frederick.

Dialogues on the Future of Man. Philos Lib.

ed. Existentialist Thinkers & Thought. Citadel Pr.

Paton, A. *see* Paton, Alan.

Paton, Alan.

xPaton, A.

Instrument of Thy Peace: The Prayer of St. Francis. Seabury.

xPaton, Alan.

Creative Suffering: The Ripple of Hope. Pilgrim NY.

Cry, the Beloved Country. Scribner.

Tales from a Troubled Land. Scribner.

Paton, David.

xPaton, David.

The Relation of Angioid Streaks to Systemic Disease. C C Thomas.

Paton, David M.

xPaton, David M.

ed. The Mechanism of Neuronal & Extraneuronal Transport of Catecholamines. Raven.

ed. The Release of Catecholamines from Adrenergic Neurons. Pergamon.

Paton, G. W. *see* Paton, George Whitecross.

Paton, George Whitecross.

xPaton, G. W.

ed. A Textbook of Jurisprudence. Oxford U Pr.

xPaton, George Whitecross.

A Textbook of Jurisprudence. Oxford U Pr.

Paton, H. J. *see* Paton, Herbert James.

Paton, Herbert James, 1887-

xPaton, H. J.

The Categorical Imperative: A Study in Kant's Moral Philosophy. U of Pa Pr.

Paton, W. D. *see* Paton, William Drummond Macdonald.

Paton, William A. *see* Paton, William Andrew.

Paton, William Agnew, 1848-1918

xPaton, William A.

Down the Islands: A Voyage to the Caribbees. Negro U Pr.

Paton, William Andrew.

xPaton, William A.

Principles of Accounting. Arno.

Paton, William Drummond Macdonald.

xPaton, W. D.

ed. Cannabis & Its Derivatives: Pharmacology & Experimental Psychology. Oxford U Pr.

Paton Walsh, Jill, 1937-

xPaton Walsh, Jill.

Children of the Fox. FS&G.

The Huffler. FS&G.

Patourel, John Le. *see* Le Patourel, John.

Patrascu, Anghel.

xPatrascu, Anghel.

Construction Cost Engineering. Craftsman.

Patraw, Pauline M. *see* Patraw, Pauline Mead.

Patraw, Pauline Mead, 1904-

xPatraw, Pauline M.

Flowers of the Southwest Mesas. Sw Pks Mnmts.

Patrick, Alison.

xPatrick, Alison.

The Men of the First French Republic: Political Alignments in the National Convention of 1792. Johns Hopkins.

Patrick, Clarence H. *see* Patrick, Clarence Hodges.

Patrick, Clarence Hodges, 1907-

xPatrick, Clarence H.

Alcohol, Culture & Society. AMS Pr.

Patrick, Dale.

xPatrick, Dale.

Arguing with God: The Angry Prayers of Job. Bethany Pr.

Patrick, Dale R.

xPatrick, Dale R.

Industrial Electrical Systems. Sams.

Industrial Electronic Systems. Sams.

Patrick, George Z. *see* Patrick, George Zinovei.

Patrick, George Zinovei, 1886-1946

xPatrick, George Z.

Popular Poetry in Soviet Russia. Arno.

Patrick, Gloria.

xPatrick, Gloria.

This Is. Carolrhoda Bks.

Patrick, Hugh. *see* Patrick, Hugh T.

Patrick, Hugh T.

xPatrick, Hugh.

ed. Asia's New Giant: How the Japanese Economy Works. Brookings.

Patrick, John M. *see* Patrick, John Marton.

Patrick, John Marton, 1922-

xPatrick, John M.

Artillery & Warfare During the Thirteenth &
Fourteenth Centuries. Utah St U Pr.

Patrick, Johnstone G.
xPatrick, Johnstone G.
Under the Mistletoe. Windy Row.

Patrick, Maxine.
xPatrick, Maxine.
The Abducted Heart. NAL.
Bayou Bride. NAL.
Snowbound Heart. NAL.

Patrick, R. *see* Patrick, Ruth J.

Patrick, Ruth J.
xPatrick, R.
Study of Library Co-Operatives Networks &
Demonstration Projects. K G Saur.

Patrick, Ted.
xPatrick, Ted.
Let Our Children Go. Ballantine.

Patrick, Vincent.
xPatrick, Vincent.
The Pope of Greenwich Village. PB.
The Pope of Greenwich Village. Seaview Bks.

Patrick, W. B.
xPatrick, W. B.
Letter to the Ghosts. SBD.

Patrides, C. A.
xPatrides, C. A.
Milton & the Christian Tradition. Shoe String.

Patrikas, Elaine O.

xPatrikas, Elaine O.

Medical Records Administration Continuing
Education Review. Med Exam.

Patt, Donald I.
xPatt, Donald I.
An Introduction to Modern Genetics. A-W.

Patte, Daniel.
xPatte, Daniel.
Early Jewish Hermeneutic in Palestine.
Scholars Pr Ca.

Pattee, Fred L. *see* Pattee, Fred Lewis.

Pattee, Fred Lewis, 1863-1950
xPattee, Fred L.
First Century of American Literature,
1770-1870. Cooper Sq.
First Century of American Literature,
1770-1870. R West.
History of American Literature Since 1870.
Cooper Sq.

Pattemore, Arnel W.
xPattemore, Arnel W.
Art & Environment: An Art Resource for
Teachers. Van Nos Reinhold.

Patten, Bernard C., 1931-
xPatten, Bernard C.
ed. Systems Analysis & Simulation in Ecology.
Acad Pr.

Patten, Bradley M. *see* Patten, Bradley Merrill.

Patten, Bradley Merrill, 1889-
xPatten, Bradley M.
Early Embryology of the Chick. McGraw.
Foundations of Embryology. McGraw.

Patten, J. *see* Patten, John.

Patten, John.
xPatten, J.
ed. Pre-Industrial England: Geographical
Essays. Dawson Pub.

Patten, Lewis B.
xPatten, Lewis B.

Cheyenne Captives. NAL.
Death Rides a Black Horse. Doubleday.
Death Rides a Black Horse. NAL.
Giant on Horse Back. Ace Bks.
The Law in Cottonwood. Doubleday.
The Law in Cottonwood. NAL.
Man Outgunned. G K Hall.
The Trail of the Apache Kid. Doubleday.
The Trail of the Apache Kid. NAL.
xPatten, Lewis G.
Death Rides a Black Horse. G K Hall.

Patten, Lewis G. *see* Patten, Lewis B.

Patten, Marguerite.

xPatten, Marguerite.
The Epicure's Book of Steak & Beef Dishes.
Knapp Pr.
The Epicure's Book of Steak & Beef Dishes.
Sovereign Bks.

Patten, Priscilla.
xPatten, Priscilla.
jt. auth. Before the Times. Strawberry Hill.

Patten, Robert L.
xPatten, Robert L.
Charles Dickens & His Publishers. Oxford U
Pr.

Patten, Simon. *see* Patten, Simon Nelson.

Patten, Simon N. *see* Patten, Simon Nelson.

Patten, Simon Nelson, 1852-1922
xPatten, Simon.
The Economic Basis of Protection. Garland
Pub.
The Theory of Prosperity. Garland Pub.
xPatten, Simon N.
The Economic Basis of Protection. Arno.
The Theory of Dynamic Economics. Hyperion
Conn.

Patten, Thomas H. *see* Patten, Thomas Henry.

Patten, Thomas Henry, 1929-
xPatten, Thomas H.
Pay: Employee Compensation & Incentive
Plans. Free Pr.

Patterson. *see* Patterson, Cecil Holden.

Patterson, A. M. *see* Patterson, Austin McDowell.

Patterson, Annabel M.
xPatterson, Annabel M.
Marvell & the Civic Crown. Princeton U Pr.

Patterson, Austin McDowell, 1876-
xPatterson, A. M.
German-English Dictionary for Chemists.
Wiley.

Patterson, Bob E.
xPatterson, Bob E.
Reinhold Niebuhr. Word Bks.

Patterson, C. H. *see* Patterson, Cecil Holden.

Patterson, C. Stuart. *see* Patterson, Charles Stuart.

Patterson, Caleb P. *see* Patterson, Caleb Perry.

Patterson, Caleb Perry, 1880-
xPatterson, Caleb P.
The Constitutional Principles of Thomas
Jefferson. Arno.
The Constitutional Principles of Thomas
Jefferson. Peter Smith.
Negro in Tennessee, 1790-1865. Negro U Pr.

Patterson, Cecil Holden, 1912-
xPatterson.
Readings in Rehabilitation Counseling. Stipes.
xPatterson, C. H.
Foundations for a Theory of Instruction &
Educational Psychology. Har-Row.
Relationship Counseling & Psychotherapy.
Har-Row.
Theories of Counseling & Psychotherapy.
Har-Row.

Patterson, Charles I. *see* Patterson, Charles Ivey.

Patterson, Charles Ivey, 1913-
xPatterson, Charles I.

The Daemonic in the Poetry of John Keats.
Lib Soc Sci.

Patterson, Charles Stuart.
xPatterson, C. Stuart.
Principles of Chemistry. Irvington.

Patterson, Colin.
xPatterson, Colin.
Evolution. Cornell U Pr.

Patterson, Craig.
xPatterson, Craig.
Mountain Wilderness Survival. And-or Pr.

Patterson, David S., 1937-
xPatterson, David S.
Toward a Warless World: The Travail of the
American Peace Movement, 1887-1914. Ind
U Pr.

Patterson, David W.
xPatterson, David W.
ed. Crime & Criminal Justice. Mss Info.

Patterson, Edwin W. *see* Patterson, Edwin Wilhite.

Patterson, Edwin Wilhite, 1889-
xPatterson, Edwin W.
Legal Protection of Private Pension
Expectations. Irwin.

Patterson, Ernest M. *see* Patterson, Ernest Minor.

Patterson, Ernest Minor, 1879-
xPatterson, Ernest M.
Economic Bases of Peace. Kennikat.

Patterson, Floyd.
xPatterson, Floyd.
Inside Boxing. Contemp Bks.

Patterson, Frederick D. *see* Patterson, Frederick
Douglass.

Patterson, Frederick Douglass, 1901-
xPatterson, Frederick D.
The College Endowment Funding Plan. ACE.

Patterson, G. A.
xPatterson, G. A.
Energy Analysis with a Pocket Calculator.
Basic Sci Pr.
Engine Thermodynamics with a Pocket
Calculator. Basic Sci Pr.

Patterson, Gardner.
xPatterson, Gardner.
Discrimination in International Trade: The
Policy Issues, 1945-1965. Princeton U Pr.

Patterson, Geoffrey.
xPatterson, Geoffrey.
The Oak. Andre Deutsch.

Patterson, George J.
xPatterson, George J.
ed. Plastics Book List. Technomic.

Patterson, Gerald R. *see* Patterson, Gerald Roy.

Patterson, Gerald Roy.
xPatterson, Gerald R.
Living with Children: New Methods for
Parents & Teachers. Res Press.

Patterson, Harriet-Louise H. *see* Patterson,
Harriet-Louise Holland.

Patterson, Harriet-Louise Holland, 1903-
xPatterson, Harriet-Louise H.
Come with Me to the Holy Land. Judson.

Patterson, Harry. *see* Patterson, Henry.

Patterson, Henry.
xPatterson, Harry.
The Valhalla Exchange. Fawcett.
The Valhalla Exchange. G K Hall.
The Valhalla Exchange. Stein & Day.

Patterson, James, 1947-
xPatterson, James.
The Thomas Berryman Number. Ballantine.
The Thomas Berryman Number. Little.
Virgin. McGraw.

Patterson, James T.
xPatterson, James T.
Congressional Conservatism & the New Deal:
The Growth of the Conservative Coalition in
Congress, 1933-1939. U Pr of Ky.

Patterson, Janet. *see* Patterson, Janet M.

Patterson, Janet M.
xPatterson, Janet.
How to Live with a Pregnant Wife. Nelson.

Patterson, K. David.
xPatterson, K. David.
The Northern Gabon Coast to 1875. Oxford U Pr.

Patterson, Katheryn.
xPatterson, Katheryn.
No Time for Tears. Johnson Chi.

Patterson, Leroy, 1918-
xPatterson, Pat.
After You've Said "I Believe". Tyndale.

Patterson, Lillie.
xPatterson, Lillie.
Christmas Feasts & Festivals. Garrard.
Christmas in America. Garrard.
Christmas Trick or Treat. Garrard.
Coretta Scott King. Garrard.
The Grouchy Santa. Garrard.
Halloween. Garrard.
Haunted Houses on Halloween. Garrard.
The Jack-O'-Lantern Trick. Garrard.
Jenny, the Halloween Spy. Garrard.
Martin Luther King, Jr: Man of Peace. Garrard.
Meet Miss Liberty. Macmillan.

Patterson, Lyman R. see Patterson, Lyman Ray.

Patterson, Lyman Ray.
xPatterson, Lyman R.
Copyright in Historical Perspective. Vanderbilt U Pr.

Patterson, Margaret C.
xPatterson, Margaret C.
ed. Literary Research Guide. Gale.

Patterson, Pat. see Patterson, Leroy.

Patterson, Raymond. see Patterson, Raymond Albert.

Patterson, Raymond Albert, 1856-1909
xPatterson, Raymond.
The Negro & His Needs. Arno.

Patterson, Rebecca.
xPatterson, Rebecca.
Emily Dickinson's Imagery. U of Mass Pr.
The Riddle of Emily Dickinson. Cooper Sq.

Patterson, Richard N. see Patterson, Richard North.

Patterson, Richard North.
xPatterson, Richard N.
The Lasko Tangent. Ballantine.
The Lasko Tangent. Norton.

Patterson, Richard O.
xPatterson, Richard O.
The Mandarin from Salem. Philos Lib.

Patterson, Roy, 1926-
xPatterson, Roy.
ed. Modern Concepts in Clinical Allergy. Krieger.

Patterson, Samuel C. see Patterson, Samuel Charles.

Patterson, Samuel Charles.
xPatterson, Samuel C.
A More Perfect Union: Introduction to American Government. Dorsey.

Patterson, Sarah.
xPatterson, Sarah.
The Distant Summer. S&S.
A Distant Summer. Archway.
The Distant Summer. PB.

Patterson, Stephen E., 1937-
xPatterson, Stephen E.
Political Parties in Revolutionary Massachusetts. U of Wis Pr.

Patterson, T. William. see Patterson, Theodore William.

Patterson, Theodore William.
xPatterson, T. William.

Land Use Planning: Techniques of Implementation. Van Nos Reinhold.

Patterson, Thomas C.
xPatterson, Thomas C.
America's Past: A New World Archaeology. Scott F.
Pattern & Process in the Early Intermediate Period Pottery of the Central Coast of Peru. U of Cal Pr.

Patterson, Zella J. see Patterson, Zella J. Black.

Patterson, Zella J. Black.
xPatterson, Zella J.
Langston University: A History. U of Okla Pr.

Patti, Charles.
xPatti, Charles.
Food Book: What You Eat from A-Z. Fleet.

Patti, Charles H.
xPatti, Charles H.
Advertising Management: Cases & Concepts. Grid Pub.

Pattinson, J. S.
xPattinson, J. S.
The Symbolism of the Rubaiyat of Omar Khayyam. Folcroft.

Pattison, Bruce.
xPattison, Bruce.
Music & Poetry of the English Renaissance. Arden Lib.
Music & Poetry of the English Renaissance. Da Capo.
Music & Poetry of the English Renaissance. Folcroft.

Pattison, E. Mansell, 1933-
xPattison, E. Mansell.
Pastor & Parish: A Systems Approach. Fortress.

Pattison, E. Mansell. see Pattison, S. Mansell.

Pattison, Mark, 1813-1884
xPattison, Mark.
Suggestions on Academical Organisation with Especial Reference to Oxford. Arno.

Pattison, O. R. see Pattison, Olive Ruth Brown.

Pattison, Olive Ruth Brown.
xPattison, O. R.
Left Behind. Revell.

Pattison, Robert.
xPattison, Robert.
The Child Figure in English Literature. U of Ga Pr.
Tennyson & Tradition. Harvard U Pr.

Pattison, S. Mansell, 1933-
xPattison, E. Mansell.
The Experience of Dying. P-H.

Patton, A. R. see Patton, Arthur R.

Patton, Arthur R.
xPatton, A. R.
Solar Energy for Heating & Cooling of Buildings. Noyes.

Patton, Bobby R.
xPatton, Bobby R.
Decision-Making Group Interaction. Har-Row.

Patton, Carl V.
xPatton, Carl V.
Academia in Transition: Mid-Career Change or Early Retirement. Abt Assoc.

Patton, F. Lester. see Patton, Francis Lester.

Patton, Frances G. see Patton, Frances Gray.

Patton, Frances Gray.
xPatton, Frances G.
Good Morning Miss Dove. PB.
Good Morning, Miss Dove. Dodd.

Patton, Francis Lester, 1891-
xPatton, F. Lester.
Diminishing Returns in Agriculture. AMS Pr.

Patton, Harald Smith, 1889-1945
xPatton, Harold S.
Grain Growers' Cooperation in Western Canada. AMS Pr.

Patton, Harold S. see Patton, Harald Smith.

Patton, Harry D. see Patton, Harry Dickson.

Patton, Harry Dickson.
xPatton, Harry D.
Introduction to Basic Neurology. Saunders.

Patton, Julia, 1873-
xPatton, Julia.
The English Village: A Literary Study. Folcroft.
The English Village: A Literary Study, 1750-1850. Arden Lib.

Patton, Michael Q. see Patton, Michael Quinn.

Patton, Michael Quinn.
xPatton, Michael Q.
Utilization-Focused Evaluation. Sage.

Patton, Sadie. see Patton, Sadie Smathers.

Patton, Sadie Smathers.
xPatton, Sadie.
The Story of Henderson County. Reprint.

Patton, Temple C.
xPatton, Temple C.
Paint Flow & Pigment Dispersion: A Rheological Approach to Coating & Ink Technology. Wiley.

Patton, W. see Patton, W. J.

Patton, W. J.
xPatton, W.
Materials in Industry. P-H.
Mechanical Power Transmission. P-H.
xPatton, William J.
Kinematics. Reston.

Patton, William J. see Patton, W. J.

Patty, F. A. see Patty, Frank Arthur.

Patty, Frank Arthur, 1897-
xPatty, F. A.
Industrial Hygiene & Toxicology. Wiley.

Patty, William L.
xPatty, William L.
Need to Read. Van Nos Reinhold.

Paturi, Felix. see Paturi, Felix R.

Paturi, Felix R.
xPaturi, Felix.
Prehistoric Heritage. Scribner.

Patz. see Patz, Nancy.

Patz, Nancy.
xPatz.
Nobody Knows I Have Delicate Toes. Watts.

Pau, Hans.
xPau, Hans.
Differential Diagnosis of Eye Diseases. Saunders.

Pauk, Walter.
xPauk, Walter.
How to Read Creative Literature. SRA.
How to Read Factual Literature. SRA.
How to Study in College. HM.
Reading for Facts. Longman.

Paul, Aileen.
xPaul, Aileen.
The Kid's Diet Cookbook. Doubleday.

Paul, Andrew, 1907-
xPaul, Andrew.
History of the Beja Tribes of the Sudan. Biblio Dist.

Paul, Barbara.
xPaul, Barbara.
Pillars of Salt. NAL.

Paul, Burton, 1931-
xPaul, Burton.
Kinematics & Dynamics of Planar Machinery. P-H.

Paul, C. Kegan. see Paul, Charles Kegan.

Paul Carus Memorial Symposium, Peru, Illinois, 1957.
xPaul Carus Memorial Symposium, Peru, Illinois, 1957.
Modern Trends in World Religions. Arno.

Paul, Charles Kegan, 1828-1902
xPaul, C. Kegan.
Memories. R West.

Paul, Charlotte.
xPaul, Charlotte.

A Child Is Missing. Berkley Pub.
Gold Mountain. Ace Bks.
Paul, D. R. see Paul, Donald R.
Paul, Diane B.
xPaul, Diane B.
The Politics of the Property Tax. Lexington
Bks.
Paul, Donald R.
xPaul, D. R.
ed. Polymer Blends. Acad Pr.
Paul, Ellen F. see Paul, Ellen Frankel.
Paul, Ellen Frankel.
xPaul, Ellen F.
Moral Revolution & Economic Science: The
Demise of Laissez-Faire in Nineteenth
Century British Political Economy.
Greenwood.
Paul, Elliot H. see Paul, Elliot Harold.
Paul, Elliot Harold, 1891-
xPaul, Elliot H.
Life & Death of a Spanish Town. Greenwood.
That Crazy American Music. Kennikat.
Paul, Florrie.
xPaul, Florrie.
How to Create Incredible Edibles: An
Illustrated Guide to Imaginative Food
Presentation. Norman Pub.
Paul, Grace.
xPaul, Grace.
Your Future in Medical Technology. Rosen Pr.
Paul, Harry W.
xPaul, Harry W.
The Edge of Contingency: French Catholic
Reaction to Scientific Change from Darwin
to Duhem. U Presses Fla.
The Sorcerer's Apprentice: The French
Scientist's Image of German Science,
1840-1919. U Presses Fla.
Paul, Herbert. see Paul, Herbert Woodfield.
Paul, Herbert W. see Paul, Herbert Woodfield.
Paul, Herbert Woodfield, 1853-1935
xPaul, Herbert.
Stray Leaves. Folcroft.
xPaul, Herbert W.
Men & Letters. Arno.
Men & Letters. R West.
Paul, I. H. see Paul, Irving H.
Paul, Irving H.
xPaul, I. H.
The Form & Technique of Psychotherapy. U of
Chicago Pr.
Paul, J. K.
xPaul, J. K.
Fruit & Vegetable Juice Processing. Noyes.
ed. Methanol Technology & Application in
Motor Fuels. Noyes.
ed. Passive Solar Energy Design & Materials.
Noyes.
Solar Heating & Cooling: Recent Advances.
Noyes.
Paul, James C. see Paul, James C. N.
Paul, James C. N.
xPaul, James C.
Federal Censorship: Obscenity in the Mail.
Greenwood.
Paul, James L.
xPaul, James L.
ed. Child Advocacy Within the System.
Syracuse U Pr.
Mainstreaming: A Practical Guide. Schocken.
Mainstreaming: A Practical Guide. Syracuse U
Pr.
Paul, John, 1922-
xPaul, John.
Cell & Tissue Culture. Churchill.
Paul, John R. see Paul, John Rodman.
Paul, John Rodman, 1893-
xPaul, John R.

Clinical Epidemiology. U of Chicago Pr.
Paul, Justus F.

xPaul, Justus F.
The Badger State: A Documentary History of
Wisconsin. Eerdmans.

Paul, Kathleen.

xPaul, Kathleen.
Aries. Creative Ed.
Taurus. Creative Ed.
Paul, Leslie A. see Paul, Leslie Allen.
Paul, Leslie Allen, 1905-
xPaul, Leslie A.
Meaning of Human Existence. Greenwood.
Paul, Lester W.
xPaul, Lester W.
The Essentials of Roentgen Interpretation.
Har-Row.
Paul, Oglesby, 1916-
xPaul, Oglesby.
ed. Angina Pectoris. Krieger.
Paul, Paula G.
xPaul, Paula G.
Inn of the Clowns. Bouregy.
Paul, Pauline C.
xPaul, Pauline C.
ed. Food Theory & Applications. Wiley.
Paul, Raymond.
xPaul, Raymond.
ed. Perception & Persuasion: A New Approach
to Effective Writing. Har-Row.
Paul, Richard S.
xPaul, Richard S.
Algebra & Trigonometry: For College Students.
Reston.
Contemporary Technical Mathematics with
Calculus. P-H.
Essentials of Technical Mathematics with
Calculus. P-H.
Paul, Rodman W. see Paul, Rodman Wilson.
Paul, Rodman Wilson.
xPaul, Rodman W.
California Gold: The Beginning of Mining in
the Far West. U of Nebr Pr.
The Frontier & the American West. AHM Pub.
Paul, Sherman.
xPaul, Sherman.
Edmund Wilson: A Study of Literary Vocation
in Our Time. U of Ill Pr.
The Music of Survival: A Biography of a Poem
by William Carlos Williams. U of Ill Pr.
Olson's Push: Origin, Black Mountain, &
Recent American Poetry. La State U Pr.
Paul, Virginia.
xPaul, Virginia.
The Homestead Cookbook: Pioneer Receipts,
Remedies & Reminders. Superior Pub.
Paulding, James K. see Paulding, James Kirke.
Paulding, James Kirke, 1778-1860
xPaulding, James K.
Life of Washington. Kennikat.
Pauley, Steven. see Pauley, Steven E.
Pauley, Steven E.
xPauley, Steven.
Technical Report Writing Today. HM.
Pauli, Eugen.
xPauli, Eugen.
Classical Cooking the Modern Way. CBI Pub.
Pauli, Reinhold, 1823-1882
xPauli, Reinhold.
Life of Alfred the Great. AMS Pr.
Pauling, Linus. see Pauling, Linus Carl.
Pauling, Linus Carl, 1901-
xPauling, Linus.

Nature of the Chemical Bond & the Structure
of Molecules & Crystals: An Introduction to
Modern Structural Chemistry. Cornell U Pr.
No More War!. Greenwood.

Paull, H. M. see Paull, Harry Major.

Paull, Harry Major, 1854-1934

xPaull, H. M.
Literary Ethics: A Study in the Growth of the
Literary Conscience. Kennikat.
Literary Ethics: A Study in the Growth of the
Literary Conscience. R West.

Paull, Rachel K. see Paull, Rachel Krebs.

Paull, Rachel Krebs.

xPaull, Rachel K.

Geology of Wisconsin & Upper Michigan:

Including Parts of Adjacent States.

Kendall-Hunt.

Paullin, C. O. see Paullin, Charles Oscar.

Paullin, Charles Oscar.

xPaullin, C. O.
Guide to the Materials in London Archives for
the History of the United States Since 1783.
Kraus Repr.

Pauls, Ferdinand.

xPauls, Ferdinand.
Building Juniors. Cook.

Paulsell, William O.

xPaulsell, William O.
Taste & See: A Personal Guide to the Spiritual
Life. St Mary's.

Paulsen, F. Robert. see Paulsen, Frank Robert.

Paulsen, Frank Robert.

xPaulsen, F. Robert.
American Education: Challenges & Images. U
of Ariz Pr.
ed. Changing Dimensions in International
Education. U of Ariz Pr.

Paulsen, Friedrich, 1846-1908

xPaulsen, Friedrich.
German Education Past & Present. AMS Pr.

Paulsen, Gary.

xPaulsen, Gary.

The Building a New, Buying an Old, Remodeling a Used, Comprehensive Home & Shelter How to Do It Book. P-H.

Canoeing, Kayaking & Rafting. Messner.

Careers in an Airport. Raintree Pubs.

The CB Radio Caper. Raintree Pubs.

The Curse of the Cobra. Raintree Pubs.

Downhill, Hotdogging, & Cross-Country--If the Snow Isn't Sticky. Raintree Pubs.

Facing off, Checking, & Goaltending--Perhaps. Raintree Pubs.

Farm Machines. Raintree Pubs.

The Foxman. Elsevier-Nelson.

Going Very Fast in a Circle--If You Don't Run Out of Gas. Raintree Pubs.

The Golden Stick. Raintree Pubs.

The Green Recruit. Independence Pr.

Hiking & Backpacking. Messner.

Launching, Floating High & Landing--If Your Pilot Light Doesn't Go Out. Raintree Pubs.

The Night the White Deer Died. Elsevier-Nelson.

Riding, Roping, & Bulldogging - Almost. Raintree Pubs.

The Spitball Gang. Elsevier-Nelson.

Successful Home Repair: When Not to Call the Contractor. Structures Pub.

Track, Enduro, & Motocross--Unless You Fall Over. Raintree Pubs.

TV & Movie Animals. Messner.

Paulsen, Monrad C.
xPaulsen, Monrad C.
ed. Legal Institutions Today & Tomorrow: The Centennial Conference Volume of the Columbia Law School. Greenwood.

Paulsen, Vic. see Paulsen, Victor Perry.

Paulsen, Victor Perry.
xPaulsen, Vic.
Improved Orthography: An Aid to Reading Thinkript Pubs.

Paulson, Ivar, 1922-1966
xPaulson, Ivar.
Old Estonian Folk Religion. Res Ctr Lang Semiotic.

Paulson, Michael G.
xPaulson, Michael G.
The Fallen Crown: Three French Mary Stuart Plays of the Seventeenth Century. U Pr of Amer.

Paulson, Moses, 1897-
xPaulson, Moses.
ed. Gastroenterologic Medicine. Lea & Febiger.

Paulson, R. Lee, 1933-
xPaulson, R. Lee.
The Computer Challenge in Retailing. Lebhar Friedman.

Paulson, Ronald.
xPaulson, Ronald.
Hogarth, His Life, Art, & Times. Yale U Pr.
Popular & Polite Art in the Age of Hogarth & Fielding. U of Notre Dame Pr.
Theme & Structure in Swift's Tale of a Tub. Shoe String.

Paulson, Ross E.
xPaulson, Ross E.
Radicalism & Reform: The Vrooman Family & American Social Thought, 1837-1937. U Pr of Ky.
Women's Suffrage & Prohibition: A Comparative Study of Equality & Social Control. Scott F.

Paulston, C. see Paulston, Christina Bratt.

Paulston, Christina Bratt.
xPaulston, C.
Teaching English As a Second Language: Techniques & Procedures. Winthrop.

Paulston, Roland G. see Paulston, Rolland G.

Paulston, Rolland G.
xPaulston, Roland G.
Society, Schools & Progress in Peru. Pergamon.
xPaulston, Rolland G.
Conflicting Theories of Social & Educational Change: A Typological Review. U Ctr Intl St.
ed. Non-Formal Education: An Annotated International Bibliography. Irvington.

Paulu, Burton, 1910-
xPaulu, Burton.
British Broadcasting in Transition. U of Minn Pr.

Paulus, Paul B.
xPaulus, Paul B.
ed. Psychology of Group Influence. L Erlbaum Assocs.

Paulus, Trina.
xPaulus, Trina.
Hope for the Flowers. Paulist Pr.

Paulus, Virginia.
xPaulus, Virginia.
ed. Housing: A Bibliography, 1960-72. AMS Pr.

Pauly, Reinhard G.
xPauly, Reinhard G.
Music & the Theater: An Introduction to Opera. P-H.
Music in the Classic Period. P-H.

Paupst, James. see Paupst, James C.

Paupst, James C.
xPaupst, James.
The Sleep Book. Macmillan.

Pausanias.
xPausanias.
Guide to Greece. Penguin.

Paust, Gil.
xPaust, Gil.
The Complete Beginner's Guide to Horseback Riding. Doubleday.

Paust, Jordan L.
xPaust, Jordan L.
Business Law Text. West Pub.

Pauw, John W. De. see De Pauw, John W.

Pauw, Linda G. De. see De Pauw, Linda G.

Pauwels, Louis, Aug. 2, 1920-
xPauwels, Louis.
Gurdjieff. Weiser.
Impossible Possibilities. Avon.

Pavalko, Ronald M.
xPavalko, Ronald M.
ed. Sociological Perspectives on Occupations. Peacock Pubs.
ed. Sociology of Education: A Book of Readings. Peacock Pubs.

Pavese, Cesare.
xPavese, Cesare.
The Devil in the Hills. Greenwood.

Pavey, Peter.
xPavey, Peter.
illus. One Dragon's Dream. Bradbury Pr.

Pavia, Donald L.
xPavia, Donald L.
Introduction to Organic Laboratory Techniques: A Contemporary Approach. HR&W.
Introduction to Spectroscopy: A Guide for Students of Organic Chemistry. HR&W.

Pavlak, Thomas J.
xPavlak, Thomas J.
Ethnic Identification & Political Behavior. R & E Res Assoc.

Pavlakis, Christopher.
xPavlakis, Christopher.
The American Music Handbook. Free Pr.

Pavletich, Aida.
xPavletich, Aida.
Rock-A-Bye Baby. Doubleday.

Pavlich, Vita.
xPavlich, Vita.

Survival Kit for Substitutes: Activities That Work in Elementary Classrooms. Schol Bk Serv.

Pavlidis, T. see Pavlidis, Theodosios.

Pavlidis, Theodosios.
xPavlidis, T.
Structural Pattern Recognition. Springer-Verlag.

Pavlov, Boris. see Pavlov, Boris Alekseevich.

Pavlov, Boris Alekseevich.
xPavlov, Boris.
Organic Chemistry. Beekman Pubs.
Organic Chemistry. Gordon.

Pavlov, Ivan P. see Pavlov, Ivan Petrovich.

Pavlov, Ivan Petrovich.
xPavlov, Ivan P.
Conditioned Reflexes: An Investigation of the Physiological Activity of the Cerebral Cortex. Dover.

Pavy, Robert N.
xPavy, Robert N.
The Teacher's & Doctor's Guide to a Practical Approach to Learning Problems. C C Thomas.

Pawelek, S. see Pawelek, Stanley John.

Pawelek, Stanley John.
xPawelek, S.
Introduction to Industrial Drafting. Glencoe.

Pawlak, Elizabeth A.
xPawlak, Elizabeth A.
Essentials of Periodontics. Mosby.

Pawley, Bernard C.
xPawley, Bernard C.
An Anglican View of the Vatican Council. Greenwood.

Pawley, Martin.
xPawley, Martin.
Garbage Housing. Krieger.

Pawlikowski, John.
xPawlikowski, John T.
What Are They Saying About Christian-Jewish Relations?. Paulist Pr.

Pawlikowski, John T. see Pawlikowski, John.

Pawlina, Albert M.
xPawlina, Albert M.
The Family Prescription & Medication Guide. P-H.

Pax, Wolfgang E.
xPax, Wolfgang E.
In the Footsteps of Jesus. L Amiel Pub.

Paxman, Shirley B. see Paxman, Shirley Brockbank.

Paxman, Shirley Brockbank.
xPaxman, Shirley B.
Homespun: Domestic Arts & Crafts of Mormon Pioneers. Deseret Bk.

Paxson, Frederic L. see Paxson, Frederic Logan.

Paxson, Frederic Logan, 1877-1948
xPaxson, Frederic L.
History of the American Frontier: 1763-1893. Larlin Corp.
Independence of the South-American Republics: A Study in Recognition & Foreign Policy. Cooper Sq.
Last American Frontier. Cooper Sq.

Paxton, Albert. see Paxton, Albert S.

Paxton, Albert S.
xPaxton, Albert.
National Repair & Remodeling Estimator: 1981. Craftsman.

Paxton, John.
xPaxton, John.
ed. A Dictionary of the European Economic Community. Facts on File.
World Legislatures. St Martin.

Paxton, R. R. see Paxton, Ralph Robert.

Paxton, Ralph Robert, 1920-
xPaxton, R. R.
Manufactured Carbon: A Self-Lubricating Material for Mechanical Devices. CRC Pr.

Paxton, Robert O.
xPaxton, Robert O.

Europe in the Twentieth Century. HarBraceJ.
Paye, Burall. see Paye, Burrall.
Paye, Burrall, 1938-
xPaye, Burall.
Secrets of the Passing-Dribbling Game Offense.
P-H.
xPaye, Burrall.
Coaching the Full Court Man-to-Man Press.
P-H.
Payer, Cheryl, 1940-
xPayer, Cheryl.
ed. Commodity Trade of the Third World.
Halsted Pr.
The Debt Trap: The IMF & the Third World.
Monthly Rev.
Paylin, Jolie, 1913-
xPaylin, Jolie.
Cutover Country: Jolie's Story. Iowa St U Pr.
Nels Oskar. Iowa St U Pr.
Paylore, Patricia.
xPaylore, Patricia.
ed. Arid-Lands Research Institutions: A World
Directory, 1977. U of Ariz Pr.
Payn, James, 1830-1898
xPayn, James.
Lost Sir Massingberd: A Romance of Real Life.
Arno.
Some Literary Recollections. R West.
Payne. see Payne, Stanley G.
Payne, Alma. see Payne, Alma Smith.
Payne, Alma Smith.
xPayne, Alma.
The Baby Food Book. Little.
Payne, Ben I. see Payne, Ben Iden.
Payne, Ben Iden, 1881-1976
xPayne, Ben I.
Life in a Wooden O: Memoirs of the Theatre.
Yale U Pr.
Payne, Beverly C.
xPayne, Beverly C.
The Quality of Medical Care: Evaluation &
Improvement. Hosp Res & Educ.
Payne, Blanche.
xPayne, Blanche.
History of Costume: From the Ancient
Egyptians to the Twentieth Century.
Har-Row.
Payne, C. J. see Payne, Christopher J.
Payne, Charles.
xPayne, Charles.
The American Ballet Theatre. Knopf.
Payne, Charles A.
xPayne, Charles A.
Physical Science: Principles & Applications.
Wm C Brown.
Payne, Charlotte.
xPayne, Charlotte.
The Glitterati. Morrow.
Payne, Christopher J.
xPayne, C. J.
ed. Caring for Deprived Children: International
Case Studies of Residential Setting. St
Martin.

Payne, Daniel A. see Payne, Daniel Alexander.
Payne, Daniel Alexander, Bp, 1811-1893
xPayne, Daniel A.
History of the African Methodist Episcopal
Church. Arno.
Payne, Darwin.
xPayne, Darwin.
Initiative in Energy: Dresser Industries, Inc.
1880-1978. S&S.
Payne, Darwin R. see Payne, Darwin Reid.
Payne, Darwin Reid.
xPayne, Darwin R.

Design for the Stage: First Steps. S Ill U Pr.
Materials & Craft of the Scenic Model. S Ill U
Pr.
Payne, David A.
xPayne, David A.
The Assessment of Learning: Cognitive &
Affective. Heath.
ed. Specification & Measurement of Learning
Outcomes. Wiley.
Payne, Doris (Palmer).
xPayne, Doris P.
Captain Jack, Modoc Renegade. Binford.
Payne, Doris B. see Payne, Dorris B.
Payne, Doris P. see Payne, Doris (Palmer).
Payne, Dorris B.
xPayne, Doris B.
ed. Psychiatric-Mental Health Nursing. Med
Exam.
Payne, Elizabeth. see Payne, Elizabeth Ann.
Payne, Elizabeth Ann.
xPayne, Elizabeth.
Meet the North American Indians. Random.
Meet the Pilgrim Fathers. Random.
Payne, H. F. see Payne, Henry Fleming.
Payne, Henry Fleming.
xPayne, H. F.
Organic Coating Technology. Wiley.
Payne, Howard C.
xPayne, Howard C.
As the Storm Clouds Gathered: European
Perceptions of American Foreign Policy in
the 1930's. Moore Pub Co.
Payne, J. Barton. see Payne, John Barton.
Payne, James L.
xPayne, James L.
Incentive Theory & Political Process:
Motivation & Leadership in the Dominican
Republic. Lytton Pub.
Principles of Social Science Measurement.
Lytton Pub.
Payne, James S.
xPayne, James S.
Education & Rehabilitation Techniques. Human
Sci Pr.
Living in the Classroom: The Currency-Based
Token Economy. Human Sci Pr.
Payne, Joan B. see Payne, Joan Balfour.
Payne, Joan Balfour.
xPayne, Joan B.
illus. Leprechaun of Bayou Luce. Hastings.
illus. Raven & Other Fairy Tales. Hastings.
Payne, John Barton, 1922-
xPayne, J. Barton.
Theology of the Older Testament. Zondervan.
Payne, Les. see Payne, Leslie.
Payne, Leslie.
xPayne, Les.
The Life & Death of the SLA. Ballantine.
Payne, Lucile Vaughan.
xPayne, Lucille V.
Lively Art of Writing. NAL.
Payne, Lucille V. see Payne, Lucile Vaughan.
Payne, M. A. see Payne, Muriel Amy.
Payne, May D. see Payne, May De Forest.
Payne, May De Forest.
xPayne, May D.
Compiled by Melodic Index to the Works of
Johann Sebastian Bach. AMS Pr.
Payne, Michael. see Payne, Michael Noel.
Payne, Michael Noel.
xPayne, Michael.
Pre-Calculus Mathematics. HR&W.
Payne, Muriel A. see Payne, Muriel Amy.
Payne, Muriel Amy.
xPayne, M. A.
Oliver Untwisted. Johnson Repr.
xPayne, Muriel A.
Oliver Untwisted. Gordon Pr.
Payne, Peter L. see Payne, Peter Lester.

Payne, Peter Lester.
xPayne, Peter L.
Colvilles & the Scottish Steel Industry. Oxford
U Pr.
Payne, Pierre Stephen Robert, 1911-
xPayne, Robert.
By Me, William Shakespeare. Everest Hse.
The Life & Death of Adolf Hitler. Popular Lib.
The Life & Death of Trotsky. McGraw.
Massacre. Macmillan.
A Rage for China. HR&W.
Payne, Richard. see Payne, Richard A.
Payne, Richard A.
xPayne, Richard.
How to Get a Better Job Quicker. NAL.
xPayne, Richard A.
How to Get a Better Job Quicker. NAL.
How to Get a Better Job Quicker. Taplinger.

Payne, Richard J.
xPayne, Richard J.
Discovery in Advertising. Paulist Pr.

Payne, Robert. see Payne, Pierre Stephen Robert.

Payne, Rolce R. see Payne, Rolce Redard.

Payne, Rolce Redard.

xPayne, Rolce R.
An Illustrated & Annotated Guide to New
England Gardens Open to the Public.
Godine.

Payne, Selma.
xPayne, Selma.
Cooking with Exotic Fruit. David & Charles.
Payne, Stanley. see Payne, Stanley le Baron.
Payne, Stanley G.
xPayne.
Politics & Society in Twentieth-Century Spain.
New Viewpoints.
xPayne, Stanley G.
Falange: A History of Spanish Fascism.
Stanford U Pr.
A History of Spain & Portugal. U of Wis Pr.
Politics & the Military in Modern Spain.
Stanford U Pr.
Spanish Revolution. Norton.
Payne, Stanley le Baron, 1911-
xPayne, Stanley.
Art of Asking Questions. Princeton U Pr.
Payne, Stepen.
xPayne, Stephen.
Raiders of the Rimrock. Assoc Bk.
Payne, Stephen. see Payne, Stepen.
Payne, William M. see Payne, William Morton.
Payne, William Morton, 1858-1919
xPayne, William M.
Greater English Poets of the Nineteenth
Century. Arno.
Paynter, John H. see Paynter, John Henry.
Paynter, John Henry.
xPaynter, John H.
Fugitives of the Pearl. AMS Pr.
Paysan, Klaus.
xPaysan, Klaus.
illus. Creatures of Pond & Pool. Lerner Pubns.
Domestic Pets. Lerner Pubns.
Payson, D. see Payson, Dale.
Payson, Dale.
xPayson, D.
Almost Twins. P-H.
Payson, Harold H.
xPayson, Harold H.
Instant Boats. Intl Marine.
Payson, Herb.
xPayson, Herb.
Blown Away. Sail Bks.
Payson, Huldah S. see Payson, Huldah Smith.
Payson, Huldah Smith.
xPayson, Huldah S.

Museum Collections of the Essex Institute.
  Essex Inst.
Payton, Everett J.
  xPayton, Everett J.
    I Won't Be Crippled When I See Jesus.
      Augsburg.
Payton, George T.
  xPayton, George T.
    Patrol Procedure. Legal Bk Corp.
Payton, Mary.
  xPayton, Mary.
    The Observer's Book of Glass. Scribner.
Paz, Azaria.
  xPaz, Azaria.
    Introduction to Probabilistic Automata. Acad
      Pr.
Paz, Mario.
  xPaz, Mario.
    Structural Dynamics: Theory & Computation.
      Van Nos Reinhold.
Pazhayatil, Harshajan.
  xPazhayatil, Harshajan.
    Counseling & Health Care. Franciscan Herald.
Peabody, Francis G. see Peabody, Francis Greenwood.
Peabody, Francis Greenwood, 1847-1936
  xPeabody, Francis G.
    Reminiscences of Present-Day Saints. Arno.
Peabody Museum of Archaeology & Ethnology. see
  Harvard University. Peabody Museum of Archaeology
  and Ethnology.
Peabody, Richard, 1951-
  xPeabody, Richard.
    I'm in Love with the Morton Salt Girl.
      Paycock Pr.
Peace, Adrian J.
  xPeace, Adrian J.
    Choice, Class & Conflict: A Study of Southern
      Nigerian Factory Workers. Humanities.
Peace, R. see Peace, Richard.
Peace, Richard.
  xPeace, R.
    Learning to Love God. Inter-Varsity.
    Learning to Love Ourselves. Inter-Varsity.
    Learning to Love People. Inter-Varsity.
Peaceman, D. W. see Peaceman, Donald W.
Peaceman, Donald W.
  xPeaceman, D. W.
    Fundamentals of Numerical Reservoir
      Simulation. Elsevier.
Peach, William. see Peach, William Nelson.
Peach, William Nelson, 1912-
  xPeach, William.
    The Security Affiliates of National Banks.
      AMS Pr.
Peacher, Georgiana.
  xPeacher, Georgiana.
    How to Improve Your Speaking Voice. Fell.
Peachey, L. D. see Peachey, Lee D.
Peachey, Lee D.
  xPeachey, L. D.
    Muscle & Motility. McGraw.
Peacock, J. see Peacock, James L.
Peacock, James L.
  xPeacock, J.
    Human Direction: An Evolutionary Approach
      to Social & Cultural Anthropology. P-H.
  xPeacock, James L.
    Muslim Puritans: Reformist Psychology in
      Southeast Asian Islam. U of Cal Pr.
    Purifying the Faith: The Muhammadijah
      Movement in Indonesian Islam.
      Benjamin-Cummings.
Peacock, Ronald, 1907-
  xPeacock, Ronald.
    The Art of Drama. Greenwood.
Peacock, Thomas L. see Peacock, Thomas Love.
Peacock, Thomas Love, 1785-1866
  xPeacock, Thomas L.

Nightmare Abbey. Norton.
    The Pleasures of Peacock: Comprising in
      Whole or in Part the Seven Novels of
      Thomas Love Peacock. Greenwood.
Peak, Hugh S.
  xPeak, Hugh S.
    Supermarket Merchandising & Management.
      P-H.
Peake, Cyrus H. see Peake, Cyrus Henderson.
Peake, Cyrus Henderson, 1900-
  xPeake, Cyrus H.
    Nationalism & Education in Modern China.
      Fertig.
Peake, Harold. see Peake, Harold John Edward.
Peake, Harold J. see Peake, Harold John Edward.
Peake, Harold John Edward, 1867-1946
  xPeake, Harold.
    The Origins of Agriculture. Arden Lib.
  xPeake, Harold J.
    The Origins of Agriculture. AMS Pr.
Peake, Jacqueline.
  xPeake, Jacqueline.
    The Housewife Handyperson. TAB Bks.
Peake, Katy.
  xPeake, Katy.
    The Indian Heart of Carrie Hodges. Viking Pr.
Peake, Mervyn. see Peake, Mervyn Laurence.
Peake, Mervyn Laurence, 1911-1968
  xPeake, Mervyn.
    Gormenghast. Ballantine.
Peale, Norman V. see Peale, Norman Vincent.
Peale, Norman Vincent, 1898-
  xPeale, Norman V.
    Amazing Results of Positive Thinking. Fawcett.
    The Amazing Results of Positive Thinking.
      Revell.
    The Art of Real Happiness. Fawcett.
    Bible Stories. Watts.
    A Guide to Confident Living. Fawcett.
    Guide to Confident Living. P-H.
    Inspiring Messages for Daily Living. P-H.
    Power of Positive Thinking. Fawcett.
    Power of Positive Thinking. Gibson.
    Power of Positive Thinking. P-H.
    Power of Positive Thinking. Revell.
    Sin, Sex & Self-Control. Fawcett.
    Stay Alive All Your Life. Fawcett.
    The Tough-Minded Optimist. Fawcett.
  xPeale, Norman Vincent.
    Norman Vincent Peale's Treasury of Courage
      & Confidence. Doubleday.
Pearce, A. Philippa. see Pearce, Ann Philippa.
Pearce, Ann Philippa.
  xPearce, A. Philippa.
    The Minnow Leads to Treasure. Gregg.
  xPearce, Philippa.
    Tom's Midnight Garden. Dell.
  xPearce, Phillipa.
    Tom's Midnight Garden. Lippincott.
Pearce, Charles E.
  xPearce, Charles E.
    Polly Peachum: The Story of Lavinia Fenton -
      "the Beggar's Opera". Arno.
    Polly Peachum: The Story of Lavinia Fenton &
      the Beggar's Opera. R West.
Pearce, Colin.
  xPearce, Colin.
    Prediction Techniques for Marketing Planners:
      The Practical Application of Forecasting
      Methods to Business Problems. Intl Pubns
      Serv.
Pearce, David W. see Pearce, David William.
Pearce, David William.
  xPearce, David W.
    Environmental Economics. Longman.
    ed. The Valuation of Social Cost. Allen Unwin.
Pearce, Evelyn. see Pearce, Evelyn Clare.
Pearce, Evelyn Clare.
  xPearce, Evelyn.

A General Textbook of Nursing: A
      Compendium of Nursing Knowledge.
      Merrimack Bk Serv.
    Medical & Nursing Dictionary &
      Encyclopaedia. Merrimack Bk Serv.
Pearce, G. H. see Pearce, Gerald H.
Pearce, Gerald H.
  xPearce, G. H.
    The Medical Report & Testimony. Allen
      Unwin.
Pearce, Helen R. see Pearce, Helen Ruth.
Pearce, Helen Ruth, 1928-
  xPearce, Helen R.
    The Hop Industry in Australia. Intl Schol Bk
      Serv.
Pearce, J. Kenneth. see Pearce, John Kenneth.
Pearce, J. Winston.
  xPearce, J. Winston.
    Planning Your Preaching. Broadman.
  xPearce, Winton J.
    I Believe. Broadman.
Pearce, John Kenneth.
  xPearce, J. Kenneth.
    Logging & Pulpwood Production. Wiley.
Pearce, M. J.
  xPearce, M. J.
    Workbook of Analytical & Descriptive
      Bibliography. Shoe String.
Pearce, Mary. see Pearce, Mary Emily.
Pearce, Mary Emily.
  xPearce, Mary.
    Apple Tree, Lean Down. Ballantine.
    Apple Tree Lean Down. St Martin.
Pearce, Peter.
  xPearce, Peter.
    Experiments in Form: A Foundation Course in
      Three-Dimensional Design. Van Nos
      Reinhold
    Polyhedra Primer. Van Nos Reinhold.
    Structure in Nature Is a Strategy for Design.
      MIT Pr.
Pearce, Philippa. see Pearce, Ann Philippa.
Pearce, Phillipa. see Pearce, Ann Philippa.
Pearce, Richard, 1932-
  xPearce, Richard.
    Stages of the Clown: Perspectives on Modern
      Fiction from Dostoyevsky to Beckett. S Ill U
      Pr.
Pearce, Roy H. see Pearce, Roy Harvey.
Pearce, Roy Harvey.
  xPearce, Roy H.
    ed. Colonial American Writing. Peter Smith.
    Continuity of American Poetry. Princeton U
      Pr.
    Historicism Once More: Problems & Occasions
      for the American Scholar. Princeton U Pr.
Pearce, T. M. see Pearce, Thomas Matthews.
Pearce, T. S.
  xPearce, T. S.
    George Eliot. Rowman.
    T. S. Eliot. Arco.
Pearce, Thomas Matthews, 1902-
  xPearce, T. M.
    Mary Hunter Austin. Coll & U Pr.
    Mary Hunter Austin. Irvington.
Pearce, William W.
  xPearce, William W.
    Caught in the Act: The True Adventures of a
      Divorce Detective. Stein & Day.
Pearce, Winton J. see Pearce, J. Winston.
Pearcy, C.
  xPearcy, C.
    ed. Topics in Operator Theory. Am Math.
  xPearcy, Carl M.
    Some Recent Developments in Operator
      Theory. Am Math.
Pearcy, Carl M. see Pearcy, C.
Pearcy, G. Etzel. see Pearcy, George Etzel.
Pearcy, George Etzel, 1905-
  xPearcy, G. Etzel.

Supercounties, U. S. A.. Plycon Pr.
Thirty-Eight State U.S.A. Plycon Pr.
World Sovereignty. Plycon Pr.
Peare, Catherine O. see Peare, Catherine Owens.
Peare, Catherine Owens.
   xPeare, Catherine O.
   FDR Story. T Y Crowell.
   Mary McLeod Bethune. Vanguard.
Pearl, David.
   xPearl, David.
   A Textbook of Muslim Law. Biblio Dist.
Pearl, Jack.
   xPearl, Jack.
   Lepke. PB.

Pearl, Leon.
   xPearl, Leon.
   Descartes. Twayne.

Pearl, Raymond.
   xPearl, Raymond.
   The Ancestry of the Long-Lived. Arno.

Pearl, Richard M.
   xPearl, Richard M.
   Fallen from Heaven: Meteorites & Man. Earth
     Science.
Pearl, Richard M. see Pearl, Richard Maxwell.
Pearl, Richard Maxwell, 1913-
   xPearl, Richard M.
   Atlas of Crystal Stereograms. Earth Science.
   Geology. Cliffs.
   Geology. Har-Row.
   How to Know the Minerals & Rocks. NAL.
   Wonders of Gems. Dodd.
   Wonders of Rocks & Minerals. Dodd.

Pearlman, Barbara.
   xPearlman, Barbara.
   Barbara Pearlman's Dance Exercises.
     Doubleday.
Pearlman, Daniel. see Pearlman, Daniel D.

Pearlman, Daniel D.
   xPearlman, Daniel.
   Guide to Rapid Revision. Odyssey Pr.

Pearlman, Moshe, 1911-
   xPearlman, Moshe.
   In the Footsteps of the Prophets. T Y Crowell.
Pearlman, Myer.
   xPearlman, Myer.
   Let's Meet the Holy Spirit. Gospel Pub.

Pearlman, Ruth.
   xPearlman, Ruth.
   Feeding Your Baby the Safe & Healthy Way.
     Random.
Pearlstein, S. see Pearlstein, Stanley.
Pearlstein, Stanley.
   xPearlstein, S.
   Psychiatry, the Law & Mental Health. Oceana.
Pearman, William I. see Pearman, William Irvin.
Pearman, William Irvin, 1903-
   xPearman, William I.
   Support of State Educational Programs by
     Dedication of Specific Revenues & by
     General Revenue Appropriations: A Study of
     Certain Factors Which Relate to the
     Adoption & Use of These General Policies by
     State Governments. AMS Pr.
Pears, David. see Pears, David Francis.
Pears, David Francis.
   xPears, David.
   Ludwig Wittgenstein. Penguin.
   Ludwig Wittgenstein. Viking Pr.
Pears, Edwin, Sir, 1835-1919
   xPears, Edwin.

Destruction of the Greek Empire & the Story
   of the Capture of Constantinople by the
   Turks. Greenwood.
Destruction of the Greek Empire & the Story
   of the Capture of Constantinople by the
   Turks. Haskell.
Life of Abdul Hamid. Arno.
Pearsall, Ronald, 1927-
   xPearsall, Ronald.
   Collecting & Restoring Scientific Instruments.
     Arco.
   Collecting Mechanical Antiques. Arco.
   Edwardian Popular Music. Fairleigh Dickinson.
Pearsall, Thomas E.
   xPearsall, Thomas E.
   Audience Analysis for Technical Writing.
     Glencoe.
   How to Write for the World of Work. HR&W.
Pearse, Andrew. see Pearse, Andrew Chernocke.
Pearse, Andrew Chernocke.
   xPearse, Andrew.
   Latin American Peasant. Biblio Dist.
Pearse, John B. see Pearse, John Barnard.
Pearse, John Barnard, 1842-1914
   xPearse, John B.
   A Concise History of the Iron Manufacture of
     the American Colonies up to the Revolution
     & of Pennsylvania Until the Present Time. B
     Franklin.
Pearse, Padraic, 1879-1916
   xPearse, Padraic.
   The Murder Machine & Other Essays. Irish Bk
     Ctr.
Pearson. see Pearson, Craig.
Pearson, Arnold.
   xPearson, Arnold.
   Early Churches of Washington State. U of
     Wash Pr.
Pearson, Bruce L., 1932-
   xPearson, Bruce L.
   Introduction to Linguistic Concepts. Knopf.
Pearson, C. C. see Pearson, Charles Chilton.
Pearson, Carol.
   xPearson, Carol.
   Who Am I This Time?: Female Portraits in
     British & American Literature. McGraw.
Pearson, Catherine.
   xPearson, Catherine.
   Discovery in Literature. Paulist Pr.
Pearson, Charles Chilton.
   xPearson, C. C.
   Readjuster Movement in Virginia. Peter Smith.

Pearson, Charles H. see Pearson, Charles Henry.
Pearson, Charles Henry, 1830-1894
   xPearson, Charles H.
   Early & Middle Ages of England. Kennikat.
Pearson, Charles T.
   xPearson, Charles T.
   The Indomitable Tin Goose: The True Story of
     Preston Tucker & His Car. Motorbooks Intl.
Pearson, Craig.
   xPearson.
   On Your Own. McGraw.
Pearson, Drew.
   xPearson, Drew.
   The Nine Old Men. Da Capo.
Pearson, E. Norman.
   xPearson, E. Norman.
   Space Time & Self. Theos Pub Hse.
Pearson, Edmund. see Pearson, Edmund Lester.
Pearson, Edmund L. see Pearson, Edmund Lester.
Pearson, Edmund Lester, 1880-1937
   xPearson, Edmund.
   Queer Books. Kennikat.
   xPearson, Edmund L.
   Books in Black or Red. Arno.
Pearson, Elizabeth W. see Pearson, Elizabeth Ware.
Pearson, Elizabeth Ware.
   xPearson, Elizabeth W.

   ed. Letters from Port Royal, 1862-1868. Arno.
Pearson, Emil, 1897-
   xPearson, Emil.
   People of the Aurora. Beta Bk.
Pearson, Frank A. see Pearson, Frank Ashmore.
Pearson, Frank Ashmore.
   xPearson, Frank A.
   World's Hunger. Kennikat.
Pearson, Geoffrey.
   xPearson, Geoffrey.
   The Deviant Imagination: Psychiatry, Social
     Work & Social Change. Holmes & Meier.
Pearson, Hesketh, 1887-1964
   xPearson, Hesketh.
   Common Misquotations. Folcroft.
   Dizzy: The Life & Nature of Benjamin
     Disraeli, Earl of Beaconsfield. Greenwood.
   Doctor Darwin. Folcroft.
   George Bernard Shaw: His Life & Personality.
     Atheneum.
   The Life of Oscar Wilde. Greenwood.
   The Man Whistler. Taplinger.

Pearson, Ian.
   xPearson, Ian.
   English in Biological Science. Oxford U Pr.

Pearson, Jeanne.

   xPearson, Jeanne.
   illus. Pony in the Yard. Denison.

Pearson, Jerry D. see Pearson, Jerry Dean.

Pearson, Jerry Dean.
   xPearson, Jerry D.
   Thermodynamic Properties of Combustion
     Gases. Iowa St U Pr.
Pearson, John, 1930-
   xPearson, John.
   The Sitwells: A Family's Biography.
     HarBraceJ.
   The Sun's Birthday. Doubleday.
Pearson, John G.
   xPearson, John G.
   Math Skills for the Sciences. Wiley.
Pearson, John S. see Pearson, John Samuel.
Pearson, John Samuel.
   xPearson, John S.
   Ocean Floor Mining. Noyes.
Pearson, Jonathan, 1813-1887
   xPearson, Jonathan.
   Contributions for the Genealogies of the
     Descendants of the First Settlers of the
     Patent & City of Schenectady N.Y. from
     1662 to 1800. Genealog Pub.
Pearson, Judy C.
   xPearson, Judy C.
   Understanding & Sharing: An Introduction to
     Speech Communication. Wm C Brown.
Pearson, Karl, 1857-1936
   xPearson, Karl.
   The Grammar of Science. Peter Smith.
Pearson, Karl G.
   xPearson, Karl G.
   Real Estate: Principles & Practices. Grid Pub.
Pearson, Leonard.
   xPearson, Leonard.
   Psychologist's Eat-Anything Diet. Popular Lib.
Pearson, Lester B.
   xPearson, Lester B.
   Democracy in World Politics. Princeton U Pr.
   Diplomacy in the Nuclear Age. Greenwood.
Pearson, Linda Buck.
   xPearson, Linda J.
   Geriatric Clinical Protocols. Lippincott.
Pearson, Linda J. see Pearson, Linda Buck.
Pearson, Lionel. see Pearson, Lionel Ignacius Cusack.
Pearson, Lionel Ignacius Cusack.
   xPearson, Lionel.

The Local Historians of Attica. Greenwood.
Popular Ethics in Ancient Greece. Stanford U
Pr.
Pearson, Lorentz C.
xPearson, Lorentz C.
Principles of Agronomy. Van Nos Reinhold.

Pearson, Norman H. see Pearson, Norman Holmes.
Pearson, Norman Holmes, 1909-
xPearson, Norman H.
ed. Decade: A Collection of Poems from the
First Ten Years of The Wesleyan Poetry
Program. Columbia U Pr.
Pearson, P. D. see Pearson, P. David.
Pearson, P. David.
xPearson, P. D.
Teaching Reading Comprehension. HR&W.
Pearson, Paul B.
xPearson, Paul P.
ed. Nutrition, Food & Man: An
Interdisciplinary Perspective. U of Ariz Pr.
Pearson, Paul D. see Pearson, Paul David.
Pearson, Paul David, 1936-
xPearson, Paul D.
Alvar Aalto & the International Style.
Watson-Guptill.
Pearson, Paul P. see Pearson, Paul B.
Pearson, Ralph G.
xPearson, Ralph G.
Symmetry Rules for Chemical Reactions:
Orbital Topology & Elementary Processes.
Wiley.
Pearson, Raymond.
xPearson, Raymond.
The Russian Moderates & the Crisis of Tsarism
1914-1917. B&N.
Pearson, Richard J.
xPearson, Richard J.
Archaeology of the Ryukyu Islands: A
Regional Chronology from 3000 B. C. to the
Historic Period. U Pr of Hawaii.
Pearson, Ronald. see Pearson, Ronald George.
Pearson, Ronald George.
xPearson, Ronald.
Avian Brain. Acad Pr.
Pearson, Scott R.
xPearson, Scott R.
Commodity Exports & African Economic
Development. Lexington Bks.
Pearson, Sidney A.
xPearson, Sidney A.
Arthur Koestler. Twayne.
Pearson, Susan.
xPearson, Susan.
Everybody Knows That!. Dial.
Monday I Was an Alligator. Lippincott.
Monnie Hates Lydia. Dial.
That's Enough for One Day, J.P.!. Dial.
Pearson, William, 1922-
xPearson, William.
Hunt the Man Down. S&S.
Pearson, William B. see Pearson, William Burton.
Pearson, William Burton.
xPearson, William B.
Crystal Chemistry & Physics of Metals &
Alloys. Wiley.
Peart, Alan T. see Peart, Alan Thomas.
Peart, Alan Thomas.
xPeart, Alan T.
Design of Project Management Systems &
Records. CBI Pub.
Peary, Gerald.
xPeary, Gerald.
ed. The Classic American Novel & the Movies.
Ungar.
ed. The Modern American Novel & the
Movies. Ungar.
Peary, Josephine D. see Peary, Josephine Diebitsch.
Peary, Josephine Diebitsch.
xPeary, Josephine D.

My Arctic Journal: A Year Among Ice-Fields
& Eskimos. AMS Pr.

Peary, Robert Edwin, 1856-1920
xPeary, Robert E.

xPeary, Robert E.
Commentary by My Arctic Journal: A Year
Among Ice-Fields & Eskimos. AMS Pr.
The North Pole: Its Discovery in 1909 Under
the Auspices of the Peary Arctic Club. Arden
Lib.
Pease, Edward M. see Pease, Edward Monroe Joseph.
Pease, Edward Monroe Joseph.
xPease, Edward M.
Calculus with Analytic Geometry. Wiley.
Pease, Esther E. see Pease, Esther Elizabeth.
Pease, Esther Elizabeth, 1911-
xPease, Esther E.
Modern Dance. Wm C Brown.
Pease, Jack G.
xPease, Jack G.
Arithmetic Fundamentals. Merrill.
Pease, Jane. see Pease, Jane H.
Pease, Jane H.
xPease, Jane.
They Who Would Be Free: The Blacks' Search
for Freedom. Atheneum.
xPease, Jane H.
ed. The Antislavery Argument. Irvington.
Pease, Otis. see Pease, Otis A.
Pease, Otis A.
xPease, Otis.
ed. Progressive Years: The Spirit &
Achievement of American Reform. Braziller.
The Responsibilities of American Advertising:
Private Control & Public Influence,
1920-1940. Arno.
xPease, Otis A.
Parkman's History: The Historian As Literary
Artist. Shoe String.
Pease, William H. see Pease, William Henry.
Pease, William Henry.
xPease, William H.
Bound with Them in Chains: A Biographical
History of the Antislavery Movement.
Greenwood.
jt. auth. They Who Would Be Free: The
Blacks' Search for Freedom. Atheneum.
Peat, Marwick, Mitchell & Co. see Peat, Marwick,
Mitchell and Company.
Peat, Marwick, Mitchell and Company.
xPeat, Marwick, Mitchell & Co.
ed. Taxation of Intercompany Transactions in
Selected Countries in Europe & the USA.
Kluwer Boston.
Peatling, John H.
xPeatling, John H.
Career Development: Designing Self. Accel
Devel.
Peatman, J. B. see Peatman, John B.
Peatman, John B.
xPeatman, J. B.
Design of Digital Systems. McGraw.
Peattie, Roderick, 1891-1955
xPeattie, Roderick.
Geography in Human Destiny. Kennikat.
Pebworth, Ted-Larry.
xPebworth, Ted-Larry.
Owen Felltham. Twayne.
Peccei, A. see Peccei, Aurelio.
Peccei, Aurelio.
xPeccei, A.
Chasm Ahead. Macmillan.
xPeccei, Aurelio.
The Human Quality. Pergamon.
Pechman, Joseph A., 1918-
xPechman, Joseph A.
Federal Tax Policy. Norton.
xPechman, Joseph A. A.

Federal Tax Policy. Brookings.
xPechman, Joseph A. B.
Who Bears the Tax Burden?. Brookings.
xPechman, Joseph A. K.
Work Incentives & Income Guarantees: The
New Jersey Negative Income Tax
Experiment. Brookings.
Pechman, Joseph A. A. see Pechman, Joseph A.
Pechman, Joseph A. B. see Pechman, Joseph A.
Pechman, Joseph A. K. see Pechman, Joseph A.
Pecht, I. see Pecht, Israel.
Pecht, Israel.
xPecht, I.
ed. Chemical Relaxation in Molecular Biology.
Springer-Verlag.
Pechter, E. see Pechter, Edward.
Pechter, Edward.
xPechter, E.
Dryden's Classical Theory of Literature.
Cambridge U Pr.
Pechuro, N. S.
xPechuro, N. S.
ed. Organic Reactions in Electrical Discharges.
Plenum Pub.
Peck, Abraham J.
xPeck, Abraham J.
Radicals & Reactionaries: The Crisis of
Conservatism in Wilhelmine Germany. U Pr
of Amer.
Peck, Daniel H. see Peck, H. Daniel.
Peck, David R.
xPeck, David R.
American Marxist Literary Criticism:
1926-1941-a Bibliography. Am Inst Marxist.
Peck, David W.
xPeck, David W.
Decision at Law. Greenwood.
Peck, Dennis L.
xPeck, Dennis L.
Fatalistic Suicide. R & E Res Assoc.
Peck, Ellis L.
xPeck, Ellis L.
Space Rocks & Buffalo Grass. Peach
Enterprises.
Peck, George. see Peck, George Terhune.
Peck, George Terhune, 1916-
xPeck, George.
Simplicity: A Rich Quaker's View. Pendle Hill.
Peck, George W. see Peck, George Wilbur.
Peck, George Wilbur, 1840-1916
xPeck, George W.
The Grocery Man & Peck's Bad Boy.
Irvington.
Peck, H. Daniel.
xPeck, Daniel H.
A World by Itself: The Pastoral Moment in
Cooper's Fiction. Yale U Pr.
Peck, Harry T. see Peck, Harry Thurston.
Peck, Harry Thurston, 1856-1914
xPeck, Harry T.
The Personal Equation. Arno.
Peck, Johanne.
xPeck, Johanne.
Pref. by Young Children's Behavior:
Implementing Your Goals. Humanics Ltd.
Peck, John, 1941-
xPeck, John.
The Broken Blockhouse-Wall. Godine.
Peck, Judith.
xPeck, Judith.
Leap to the Sun: Learning Through Dynamic
Play. P-H.
Peck, Leilani B. see Peck, Leilani Brinkley.
Peck, Leilani Brinkley, 1945-
xPeck, Leilani B.
Focus on Food. McGraw.
Peck, Louis F, 1904-
xPeck, Louis F.
Life of Matthew G. Lewis. Harvard U Pr.
Peck, M. Scott. see Peck, Morgan Scott.

Peck, Matilda J.
  xPeck, R.
      Teaching Ideas That Make Learning Fun. P-H.
Peck, Morgan Scott, 1936-
  xPeck, M. Scott.
      The Road Less Traveled: A New Psychology of
      Love, Traditional Values & Spiritual Growth.
      S&S.
Peck, Paul L. see Peck, Paul Lachlan.
Peck, Paul Lachlan.
  xPeck, Paul L.
      Intermediate Spiritual Metaphysics. Mojave
      Bks.
Peck, Paula.
  xPeck, Paula.
      Art of Fine Baking. S&S.
      Art of Fine Baking. S&S.
      Art of Good Cooking. S&S.
Peck, R. see Peck, Matilda J.
Peck, Ralph B. see Peck, Ralph Brazelton.
Peck, Ralph Brazelton.
  xPeck, Ralph B.
      Foundation Engineering. Wiley.
Peck, Ralph H.
  xPeck, Ralph H.
      Hotel & Motel Careers. Watts.
Peck, Richard.
  xPeck, Richard.
      Are You in the House Alone?. Dell.
      Are You in the House Alone?. Viking Pr.
      Don't Look & It Won't Hurt. Avon.
      Don't Look & It Won't Hurt. HR&W.
      Dreamland Lake. Avon.
      Dreamland Lake. HR&W.
      The Ghost Belonged to Me. Avon.
      The Ghost Belonged to Me. Viking Pr.
      Ghosts I Have Been. Dell.
      Ghosts I Have Been. Viking Pr.
      Amanda Miranda. Viking Pr.
      Monster Night at Grandma's House. Penguin.
      Monster Night at Grandma's House. Viking Pr.
      Secrets of a Shopping Mall. Dell.
      Secrets of the Shopping Mall. Delacorte.
      ed. Sounds & Silences. Dell.
Peck, Robert.
  xPeck, Robert N.
      Path of Hunters: Animal Struggle in a
      Meadow. Knopf.
Peck, Robert N. see Peck, Robert Newton.
Peck, Robert Newton.
  xPeck, Robert N.
      Clunie. Knopf.
      A Day No Pigs Would Die. Knopf.
      Eagle Fur. Avon.
      Eagle Fur. Knopf.
      Hamilton. Little.
      Hub. Knopf.
      Mr. Little. Doubleday.
      Patooie. Knopf.
      Rabbits & Redcoats. Regional Ctr Educ.
      Rabbits & Redcoats. Walker & Co.
      Secrets of Successful Fiction. Writers Digest.
      Soup. Dell.
      Soup. Knopf.
      Soup & Me. Dell.
      Soup & Me. Knopf.
      Soup for President. Knopf.
      Soup's Drum. Knopf.
  xPeck, Robert Newton.
      Basket Case. Doubleday.
      Last Sunday. Doubleday.
Peck, Ruth. see Peck, Ruth L.
Peck, Ruth L.
  xPeck, Ruth.
      Art & Language Lessons in the Elementary
      Classroom. P-H.
  xPeck, Ruth L.

      Art Lessons on a Shoestring: New Ideas for
      Practical Art Lessons in the Elementary
      School. P-H.
      Art Lessons That Teach Children About Their
      Natural Environment. P-H.
Peck, Theodore P.
  xPeck, Theodore P.
      ed. Employee Counseling in Industry &
      Government: A Guide to Information
      Sources. Gale.
      ed. Occupational Safety & Health: A Guide to
      Information Sources. Gale.
Peck, William. see Peck, William A.
Peck, William A.
  xPeck, William.
      Anatomy of Local Radio-TV Copy. TAB Bks.
Peckham, Elsie Maye.
  xPeckham, Elsie Maye.
      Sugarless Cookery for the Gourmet: Delectable
      Dietetic Dishes for Sugar-Restricted Diets.
      Exposition.
Peckham, Gladys C.
  xPeckham, Gladys C.
      Foundations of Food Preparation. Macmillan.
Peckham, Harry H. see Peckham, Harry Houston.
Peckham, Harry Houston.
  xPeckham, Harry H.
      Gotham Yankee: A Biography of William
      Cullen Bryant. Russell.
Peckham, Herbert D.
  xPeckham, Herbert D.
      Computers, BASIC & Physics. A-W.
      Hands-on Basic with a Pet. McGraw.
Peckham, Howard H. see Peckham, Howard Henry.
Peckham, Howard Henry, 1910-
  xPeckham, Howard H.
      Pontiac & the Indian Uprising. Russell.
Peckham, J. see Peckham, John M.
Peckham, J. Brian. see Peckham, John Brian.
Peckham, John Brian.
  xPeckham, J. Brian.
      Development of the Late Phoenician Scripts.
      Harvard U Pr.
Peckham, John M.
  xPeckham, J.
      Master Guide to Income Property Brokerage.
      P-H.
Peckham, Morse.
  xPeckham, Morse.
      Explanation & Power: The Control of Human
      Behavior. Continuum.
      Triumph of Romanticism: Collected Essays. U
      of SC Pr.
Peckner, Donald.
  xPeckner, Donald.
      ed. Strengthening of Metals. Krieger.
Pecktal, L. see Pecktal, Lynn.
Pecktal, Lynn.
  xPecktal, L.
      Designing & Painting for the Theatre. HR&W.
Pecsok, Robert L.
  xPecsok, Robert L.
      Modern Methods of Chemical Analysis. Wiley.
Pedder, I. J.
  xPedder, I. J.
      Genetics: A Basic Guide. Norton.
Peddersen, Ray. see Peddersen, Raymond B.
Peddersen, Raymond B.
  xPeddersen, Ray.
      Specs: The Comprehensive Foodservice
      Purchasing and Specification Manual. CBI
      Pub.
Peddie, Robert A. see Peddie, Robert Alexander.
Peddie, Robert Alexander, 1869-1951
  xPeddie, Robert A.
      Place-Names in Imprints: An Index to the
      Latin & Other Forms Used on Title-Pages.
      Gale.
Peddle, Frank.
  xPeddle, Frank.

      Thought & Being: Hegel's Criticism of Kant's
      System of Cosmological Ideas. U Pr of Amer.
Peden, Margaret S. see Peden, Margaret Sayers.
Peden, Margaret Sayers.
  xPeden, Margaret S.
      Emilio Carballido. Twayne.
Peden, William. see Peden, William Harwood.
Peden, William Harwood, 1913-
  xPeden, William.
      Night in Funland & Other Stories. La State U
      Pr.
Pedersen, Frank A.
  xPedersen, Frank A.
      ed. The Father-Infant Relationship:
      Observational Studies in Family Settings.
      Praeger.
Pederson, Carl S. see Pederson, Carl Severin.
Pederson, Carl Severin, 1897-
  xPederson, Carl S.
      Microbiology of Food Fermentations. AVI.
Pederson, Duane.
  xPederson, Duane.
      How to Establish a Jail & Prison Ministry.
      Nelson.
Pederson, E. O. see Pederson, Eldor Olin.
Pederson, Eldor Olin.
  xPederson, E. O.
      Transportation in Cities. Pergamon.
Pedicord, Harry W. see Pedicord, Harry William.

Pedicord, Harry William.
  xPedicord, Harry W.
      Theatrical Public in the Time of Garrick. S Ill
      U Pr.

Pedigo, Virginia G.

  xPedigo, Virginia G.

      History of Patrick & Henry Counties, Virginia.
      Regional.

Pedler, Kit.
  xPedler, Kit.
      Brainrack. PB.
Pedley, John G. see Pedley, John Griffiths.
Pedley, John Griffiths.
  xPedley, John G.
      Ancient Literary Sources on Sardis. Harvard U
      Pr.
Pedlosky, J. see Pedlosky, Joseph.
Pedlosky, Joseph.
  xPedlosky, J.
      Geophysical Fluid Dynamics. Springer-Verlag.
Pedoe, Arthur.
  xPedoe, Arthur.
      Life Insurance, Annuities, & Pensions: A
      Canadian Text. U of Toronto Pr.
Pedoe, Dan. see Pedoe, Daniel.
Pedoe, Daniel.
  xPedoe, Dan.
      Circles, a Mathematical View. Dover.
      The Gentle Art of Mathematics. Dover.
      Geometry & the Liberal Arts. St Martin.
  xPedoe, Daniel.
      A Geometric Introduction to Linear Algebra.
      Chelsea Pub.
Pedretti, Carlo.
  xPedretti, Carlo.
      Leonardo Da Vinci: The Royal Palace at
      Romorantin. Harvard U Pr.
Pedrick, Bob.
  xPedrick, Bob.
      The Confident Parent. Cook.
Pedrini, Duilio T. see Pedrini, Duilio Thomas.
Pedrini, Duilio Thomas.
  xPedrini, Duilio T.

Pedrini Supplementary Aid to the Administration of the Stanford-Binet Intelligence Scale (Form L-M): A Handbook. Western Psych.

Peebles, P. J. *see* Peebles, Phillip James Edwin.

Peebles, Peyton Z.

xPeebles, Peyton Z.
Communication System Principles. A-W.

Peebles, Phillip James Edwin.

xPeebles, P. J.

The Large-Scale Structure of the Universe.

Princeton U Pr.

Peebles, Robert W. *see* Peebles, Robert Whitney.
Peebles, Robert Whitney.
xPeebles, Robert W.
Leonard Covello: A Study of an Immigrants Contribution to New York City. Arno.
Peed, Dorothy Myers.
xPeed, Dorothy Myers.
The Art of Communication: A Self-Help Course in Basics. Exposition.
Peel, Colin. *see* Peel, Colin D.
Peel, Colin D.
xPeel, Colin.
Flameout. St Martin.
Hell Seed. St Martin.
Nightdive. St Martin.
xPeel, Colin D.
Night Dive. Playboy Pbks.
Peel, E. A. *see* Peel, Edwin Arthur.
Peel, Edwin Arthur.
xPeel, E. A.
Pupils Thinking. Philos Lib.
Peel, J. *see* Peel, John.
Peel, J. H. *see* Peel, John Hugh Brignal.
Peel, John.
xPeel, J.
Textbook of Contraceptive Practice. Cambridge U Pr.
Peel, John D. *see* Peel, John Donald.
Peel, John Donald.
xPeel, John D.
Fundamentals of Training for Security Officers: A Comprehensive Guide to What You Should Be, Know & Do to Have a Successful Career As a Private Patrolman or Security Officer. C C Thomas.
Story of Private Security. C C Thomas.
Peel, John Hugh Brignal, 1913-
xPeel, J. H.
Along the Pennine Way. David & Charles.
Peel's England. David & Charles.
Peel, Robert, 1909-
xPeel, Robert.
The Creed of a Victorian Pagan. Octagon.
Mary Baker Eddy: The Years of Authority. HR&W.
Mary Baker Eddy: The Years of Discovery. Chr Science.
Peel, Roy V. *see* Peel, Roy Victor.
Peel, Roy Victor, 1896-
xPeel, Roy V.
ed. Ombudsman or Citizen's Defender: A Modern Institution. Am Acad Pol Soc Sci.
Peele, Stanton.
xPeele, Stanton.
Love & Addiction. NAL.
Love & Addiction. Taplinger.
Peelman, Nancy.
xPeelman, Nancy.
The Plants of the Bible. Morehouse.
Peeples, Edwin A. *see* Peeples, Edwin Augustus.
Peeples, Edwin Augustus.
xPeeples, Edwin A.

Hole in the Hill. Peeples.
Professional Storywriter's Handbook. Peeples.
Peer Review Committee of the American Psychiatric Assn. *see* American Psychiatric Association. Peer Review Committee.
Peerman, Dean G.
xPeerman, Dean G.
ed. A Handbook of Christian Theologians. Abingdon.
Handbook of Christian Theologians. Abingdon.
ed. Handbook of Christian Theologians. NAL.
Peers, E. A. *see* Peers, Edgar Allison.
Peers, E. Allison. *see* Peers, Edgar Allison.
Peers, Edgar A. *see* Peers, Edgar Allison.
Peers, Edgar Allison.
xPeers, E. A.
Spirit of Flame: A Study of St. John of the Cross. Morehouse.
xPeers, E. Allison.
ed. A Critical Anthology of Spanish Verse. Gordon Pr.
xPeers, Edgar A.
Catalonia Infelix. Folcroft.
ed. Critical Anthology of Spanish Verse. Greenwood.
Ramon Lull: A Biography. B Franklin.
Spanish Golden Age Poetry & Drama. AMS Pr.
Spirit of Flame: A Study of St. John of the Cross. Folcroft.
xPeers, Edgar Allison.
ed. Spanish Golden Age in Poetry & Drama. Phaeton.
Peers, Frank W.
xPeers, Frank W.
Politics of Canadian Broadcasting, 1920-1951. U of Toronto Pr.
The Public Eye: Television & the Politics of Canadian Broadcasting, 1952-68. U of Toronto Pr.
Peers, W. R. *see* Peers, William R.
Peers, William R.
xPeers, W. R.
The My Lai Inquiry. Norton.
Peery, David J.
xPeery, David J.
Aircraft Structures. McGraw.
Peery, Nelson.
xPeery, Nelson.
The Negro National Colonial Question. Workers Pr.
Peet, Bill.
xPeet, Bill.
illus. The Ant & the Elephant. HM.
Buford, the Little Bighorn. HM.
illus. Caboose Who Got Loose. HM.
Capyboppy. HM.
illus. Countdown to Christmas. Childrens.
Cowardly Clyde. HM.
Cyrus the Unsinkable Sea Serpent. HM.
Farewell to Shady Glade. HM.
illus. Fly Homer Fly. HM.
illus. The Gnats of Knotty Pine. HM.
illus. How Droofus the Dragon Lost His Head. HM.
Randy's Dandy Lions. HM.
Randy's Dandy Lions. HM.
illus. Whingdingdilly. HM.
Peet, Creighton, 1899-
xPeet, Creighton.
Eye on the Sky: How Aircraft Controllers Work. Macrae.
First Book of Skyscrapers. Watts.
Peet, Louise J. *see* Peet, Louise Jenison.
Peet, Louise Jenison.
xPeet, Louise J.
Household Equipment. Wiley.
Peeters, Peter.
xPeeters, Peter.

Can We Avoid a Third World War Around 2010?. Holmes & Meier.
Peets, Elbert, 1886-1968
xPeets, Elbert.
On the Art of Designing Cities: Selected Essays of Elbert Peets. MIT Pr.
Peffer, E Louise.
xPeffer, E. Louise.
The Closing of the Public Domain: Disposal & Reservation Policies, 1900-50. Arno.
Peffer, Nathaniel, 1890-
xPeffer, Nathaniel.
Far East: A Modern History. U of Mich Pr.
The White Man's Dilemma: Climax of the Age of Imperialism. Arno.
Peffer, Randall S.
xPeffer, Randall S.
The Watermen. Johns Hopkins.
Peffer, William A. *see* Peffer, William Alfred.
Peffer, William Alfred, 1831-1912
xPeffer, William A.
The Farmer's Side, His Troubles & Their Remedy. Hyperion Conn.
Pefley, Richard. *see* Pefley, Richard K.
Pefley, Richard K.
xPefley, Richard.
Mechanical Engineering License Review. Eng Pr.
Pegels, C. C. *see* Pegels, C. Carl.
Pegels, C. Carl.
xPegels, C. C.
Systems Analysis for Production Operations. Gordon.
xPegels, C. Carl.
BASIC: A Computer Programming Language with Business & Management Applications. Holden-Day.
Pegnetter, Richard.
xPegnetter, Richard.
Public Employment Bibliography. NY Sch Indus Rel.
Pegram, Louis.
xPegram, Louis.
The Complete Whippet. Howell Bk.
Pegram, Wayne F., 1938-
xPegram, Wayne F.
Practical Guidelines for Developing the High School Band. P-H.
Pegues, A. W., 1859-
xPegues, Albert W.
Our Baptist Ministers & Schools. Johnson Repr.
Pegues, Albert W. *see* Pegues, A. W.
Pei, Mario. *see* Pei, Mario Andrew.
Pei, Mario A. *see* Pei, Mario Andrew.
Pei, Mario Andrew, 1901-
xPei, Mario.
Story of Language. NAL.
Story of Language. Lippincott.
The Story of Latin & the Romance Languages. Har-Row.
Story of the English Language. S&S.
xPei, Mario A.
Families of Words. AMS Pr.
French Precursors of the Chanson De Roland. AMS Pr.
Glossary of Linguistic Terminology. Columbia U Pr.
Peierls, Rudolf. *see* Peierls, Rudolf Ernst.
Peierls, Rudolf E. *see* Peierls, Rudolf Ernst.
Peierls, Rudolf Ernst, 1907-
xPeierls, Rudolf.
Surprises in Theoretical Physics. Princeton U Pr.
xPeierls, Rudolf E.
Quantum Theory of Solids. Oxford U Pr.
Peikari, Behrouz.
xPeikari, Behrouz.

Fundamentals of Network Analysis & Synthesis. P-H.

Peinovich, M. P. *see* Peinovich, Michael P.

Peinovich, Michael P., 1944-
xPeinovich, M. P.
Old English Noun Morphology: A Diachronic Study. Elsevier.

Peirce, Ebenezer W. *see* Peirce, Ebenezer Weaver.

Peirce, Ebenezer Weaver, 1822-1903
xPeirce, Ebenezer W.
Peirce's Colonial Lists: Civil, Military & Professional Lists of Plymouth & Rhode Island Colonies. Genealog Pub.

Peirce, Neal R.
xPeirce, Neal R.
People's President: The Electoral College in American History & the Direct Vote Alternative. S&S.

Peissel, Michel, 1937-
xPeissel, Michel.
Zanskar: The Hidden Kingdom. Dutton.

Peithmann, Irvin M.
xPeithmann, Irvin M.
Broken Peace Pipes: A Four-Hundred Year History of the American Indian. C C Thomas.

Peixotto, Jessica B. *see* Peixotto, Jessica Blanche.

Peixotto, Jessica Blanche, 1864-1941
xPeixotto, Jessica B.
Getting & Spending at the Professional Standard of Living: A Study of the Costs off Living an Academic Life. Arno.

Pejovich, Svetozar.
xPejovich, Svetozar.
Life in the Soviet Union: A Report Card on Socialism. Fisher Inst.
Market Planned Economy of Yugoslavia. U of Minn Pr.

Pekelis, Alexander H. *see* Pekelis, Alexander Haim.

Pekelis, Alexander Haim.
xPekelis, Alexander H.
Law & Social Action: Selected Essays of Alexander H. Pekelis. Da Capo.

Pekic, Borislav, 1930-
xPekic, Borislav.
The Houses of Belgrade. HarBraceJ.

Pekkanen, John, 1939-
xPekkanen, John.
Best Doctors in the U. S.: A Guide to the Finest Specialists, Hospitals, & Health Centers. Seaview Bks.
The Best Doctors in the U. S.: A Guide to the Finest Specialists, Hospitals & Health Centers in America. Wideview Bks.

Pelavin, Cheryl.
xPelavin, Cheryl.
illus. There Once Was a Cat. Dial.

Pelcovits, Nathan A. *see* Pelcovits, Nathan Albert.

Pelcovits, Nathan Albert, 1912-
xPelcovits, Nathan A.
Old China Hands & the Foreign Office. Octagon.

Pelegrino, Donald A.
xPelegrino, Donald A.
Research Methods for Recreation & Leisure: A Theoretical & Practical Guide. Wm C Brown.

Pelfrey, William V.
xPelfrey, William V.
The Evolution of Criminology. Anderson Pub Co.

Pelgrave, E. J.
xPelgrave, E. J.
Adapted by The Nightingale. Abelard.

Pelgrin, Mark, 1908 or 9-1956
xPelgrin, Mark.
And a Time to Die. Theos Pub Hse.

Pelham, David.
xPelham, David.

The Penguin Book of Kites. Penguin.

Pelham, Thomas G.
xPelham, Thomas G.
State Land-Use Planning & Regulation: Florida, the Model Code, & Beyond. Lexington Bks.

Pelikan, Jiri, 1923-
xPelikan, Jiri.
Socialist Opposition in Eastern Europe: The Czechoslovak Example. St Martin.

Pell, Arthur R.
xPell, Arthur R.
The College Graduate Guide to Job Finding. Monarch Pr.

Pell, P. S. *see* Pell, Peter S.

Pell, Peter S.
xPell, P. S.
ed. Developments in Highway Pavement Engineering. Burgess-Intl Ideas.

Pellegrini, Angelo M.
xPellegrini, Angelo M.
Food-Lover's Garden. Knopf.
Food-Lover's Garden. Madrona Pubs.

Pellegrino, Edmund D.
xPellegrino, Edmund D.
Humanism & the Physician. U of Tenn Pr.

Peller, Sigismund, 1890-
xPeller, Sigismund.
Not in My Time: The Story of a Doctor. Philos Lib.

Pellerite, James.
xPellerite, James J.
Performance Methods for Flutists. Zalo.

Pellerite, James J. *see* Pellerite, James.

Pellet, E. J. *see* Pellet, Eleanor Jane.

Pellet, Eleanor Jane, 1877-
xPellet, E. J.
A Forgotten French Dramatist, Gabriel Gilbert. Johnson Repr.

Pelletier, S. W., 1924-
xPelletier, S. W.
Chemistry of the Alkaloids. Van Nos Reinhold.

Pellettieri, L. *see* Pellettieri, Luigi.

Pellettieri, Luigi.
xPellettieri, L.
Surgical Versus Conservative Treatment of Intracranial Arteriovenous Malformations. Springer-Verlag.

Pellew, John C., 1903-
xPellew, John C.
John Pellew Paints Watercolors. Watson-Guptill.
Painting Maritime Landscapes. Watson-Guptill.

Pelling, Henry.
xPelling, Henry.
American Labor. U of Chicago Pr.
The British Communist Party: A Historical Profile. Humanities.
A History of British Trade Unionism. St Martin.
The Origins of the Labour Party, 1880-1900. Oxford U Pr.

Pellissier, Georges. *see* Pellissier, Georges Jacques Maurice.

Pellissier, Georges Jacques Maurice, 1852-1918
xPellissier, Georges.
Literary Movement in France During the Nineteenth Century. Arno.

Pellowski, Anne.
xPellowski, Anne.
The World of Storytelling. Bowker.

Pells, Edward G. *see* Pells, Edward George.

Pells, Edward George.
xPells, Edward G.
European, Coloured & Native Education in South Africa, 1652-1928. AMS Pr.

Peloubet, Francis N. *see* Peloubet, Francis Nathan.

Peloubet, Francis Nathan.
xPeloubet, Francis N.

Peloubet's Bible Dictionary. Zondervan.

Pelt, Adrian.
xPelt, Adrian.
Libyan Independence & the United Nations: A Case of Planned Decolonization. Yale U Pr.

Pelt, Ethel Van. *see* Van Pelt, Ethel.

Pelt, Sydney J. Van. *see* Van Pelt, Sydney J.

Pelta, Kathy.
xPelta, Kathy.
There's a Job for You in Food Service: A Career Guide. Dodd.

Peltason, J. W. *see* Peltason, Jack Walter.

Peltason, Jack Walter.
xPeltason, J. W.
Fifty-Eight Lonely Men: Southern Federal Judges & School Desegregation. U of Ill Pr.
ed. Students & Their Institutions: A Changing Relationship. ACE.

Pelto, Pertti J.

xPelto, Pertti J.

Anthropological Research: The Structure of Inquiry. Cambridge U Pr.

Pelton, Barry. *see* Pelton, Barry C.

Pelton, Barry C.
xPelton, Barry.
Tennis. Goodyear.
xPelton, Barry C.
Badminton. P-H.
Tennis. Goodyear.

Pelton, Joseph N.
xPelton, Joseph N.
ed. Economic & Policy Problems in Satellite Communications. Praeger.
Global Communications Satellite Policy: INTELSAT, Politics & Functionalism. Lomond.

Pelton, Leroy H.
xPelton, Leroy H.
The Psychology of Nonviolence. Pergamon.

Pelton, Robert. *see* Pelton, Robert W.

Pelton, Robert W., 1934-
xPelton, Robert.
Confrontations with the Devil. PB.
xPelton, Robert W.
Ancient Secrets of Fortunetelling. A S Barnes.
Confrontations with the Devil. A S Barnes.
In My Name Shall They Cast Out Devils. A S Barnes.

Peltzman, Sam.
xPeltzman, Sam.
Regulation of Automobile Safety. Am Enterprise.

Pelz, Stephen E.
xPelz, Stephen E.
Race to Pearl Harbor: The Failure of the Second London Naval Conference & the Onset of World War Two. Harvard U Pr.

Pelzel, Thomas.
xPelzel, Thomas.
Anton Raphael Mengs & Neoclassicism. Garland Pub.

Pelzer, Louis.
xPelzer, Louis.
Cattlemen's Frontier: A Record of the Trans-Mississippi Cattle Industry 1850-1890. Russell.
Marches of the Dragoons in the Mississippi Valley: 1833-1850. Arno.

Pember, Don. *see* Pember, Don R.

Pember, Don R., 1939-
xPember, Don.
Mass Media in America. SRA.
xPember, Don R.

Mass Media Law. Wm C Brown.
Privacy & the Press: The Law, the Mass Media, & the First Amendment. U of Wash Pr.

Pemberton, Caroline H.
xPemberton, Caroline H.
Stephen the Black. Arno.

Pemberton, J. E. *see* Pemberton, John E.

Pemberton, John E.
xPemberton, J. E.
British Official Publications. Pergamon.

Pemberton, Margaret.
xPemberton, Margaret.
The Guilty Secret. St Martin.

Pemberton, T. Edgar. *see* Pemberton, Thomas Edgar.
Pemberton, Thomas E. *see* Pemberton, Thomas Edgar.

Pemberton, Thomas Edgar, 1849-1905
xPemberton, T. Edgar.
Dicken's London: Or London in the Works of Charles Dickens. Haskell.
xPemberton, Thomas E.
The Life of Bret Harte. Arno.

Pemberton, William E. *see* Pemberton, William Erwin.

Pemberton, William Erwin, 1940-
xPemberton, William E.
Bureaucratic Politics: Executive Reorganization During the Truman Administration. U of Mo Pr.

Pemble, John.
xPemble, John.
The Raj, the Indian Mutiny, & the Kingdom of Oudh, 1801-1859. Fairleigh Dickinson.

Pembrook, Linda.
xPembrook, Linda.
How to Beat Fatigue. Avon.

Pempel, T. J., 1942-
xPempel, T. J.
Patterns of Japanese Policy Making. Experiences from Higher Education. Westview.

Pena, William.
xPena, William.
Problem Seeking: An Architectural Programming Primer. CBI Pub.

Penalosa, Fernando.
xPenalosa, Fernando.
Class Consciousness & Social Mobility in a Mexican-American Community. R & E Res Assoc.

Pence, R. W. *see* Pence, Raymond Woodbury.

Pence, Raymond Woodbury.
xPence, R. W.
Grammar of Present-Day English. Macmillan.

Penchoen, Thomas G.
xPenchoen, Thomas G.
Tamazight of the Ayt Ndhir. Undena Pubns.

Pender. *see* Pender, Roy G.

Pender, Roy G.
xPender.
Mauser Pocket Pistols: 1910-1946. Borden.

Pendergast, James F.
xPendergast, James F.
Cartier's Hochelaga & the Dawson Site. McGill-Queens U Pr.

Pendergast, Kathleen.
xPendergast, Kathleen F.
Building Good Speech. Stanwix.

Pendergast, Kathleen F. *see* Pendergast, Kathleen.
Pendergrass, Bonnie B. *see* Pendergrass, Bonnie Baack.

Pendergrass, Bonnie Baack.
xPendergrass, Bonnie B.
Public Power, Politics & Technology in the Eisenhower & Kennedy Years: The Hanford Dual-Purpose Reactor Controversy, 1956-1962. Arno.

Pendergrass, Virginia E.
xPendergrass, Virginia E.

ed. Women Winning: A Handbook for Action Against Sex Discrimination. Nelson-Hall.

Penders, C. L. M.
xPenders, C. L. M.
The Life & Times of Sukarno. Fairleigh Dickinson.

Pendery, Rosemary.
xPendery, Rosemary.
A Home for Hopper. Morrow.

Pendle, G. *see* Pendle, George.

Pendle, George.
xPendle, G.
Argentina. Gordon Pr.
Paraguay: A Riverside Nation. Gordon Pr.
xPendle, George.
History of Latin America. Penguin.

Pendle, Karin, 1939-
xPendle, Karin.
Eugene Scribe & French Opera of the Nineteenth Century. Univ Microfilms.

Pendleton, Don.
xPendleton, Don.
Acapulco Rampage. Pinnacle Bks.
Canadian Crisis. Pinnacle Bks.
Colorado Kill Zone. Pinnacle Bks.

Pendleton, James M. *see* Pendleton, James Madison.

Pendleton, James Madison, 1811-1891
xPendleton, James M.
Baptist Church Manual. Broadman.

Pendleton, Louis. *see* Pendleton, Louis Beauregard.

Pendleton, Louis Beauregard, 1861-1939
xPendleton, Louis.
In the Okefenokee: A Story of War Time and the Great Georgia Swamp. Arno.

Pendleton, Mary.
xPendleton, Mary.
Navajo & Hopi Weaving Techniques. Macmillan.
Navajo & Hopi Weaving Techniques. Macmillan.

Pendleton, Winston K.
xPendleton, Winston K.
How to Make Money Speaking. Pelican.

Pendorf, James G.
xPendorf, James G.
Church Organization: A Manual for Effective Local Church Administration. Morehouse.

Penfield, Marc.
xPenfield, Marc.
An Astrological Who's Who. Arcane Pubns.

Penfield, Wilder.
xPenfield, Wilder.
Speech & Brain-Mechanisms. Atheneum.
Speech & Brain-Mechanisms. Princeton U Pr.

Penfold, Gerda.
xPenfold, Gerda.
Done with Mirrors. Vagabond Pr.

Peng, Syd S., 1939-
xPeng, Syd S.
Coal Mine Ground Control. Wiley.

Pengelly, L. D.
xPengelly, L. D.
ed. Loaded Breathing: Proceedings, International Symposium on the Effects of Mechanical Loads on Breathing, April 12-14, 1973 Under the Auspices of McMaster University, Hamilton, Canada. Churchill.

Penick, James L.
xPenick, James L.
Progressive Politics & Conservation: The Ballinger-Pinchot Affair. U of Chicago Pr.

Penland. *see* Penland, Patrick R.

Penland, Patrick R.
xPenland.
Group Dynamics & Individual Development. Dekker.

Penman, Bruce.
xPenman, Bruce.

ed. Five Italian Renaissance Comedies. Penguin.

Penman, Kenneth A.
xPenman, Kenneth A.
Planning Physical Education & Athletic Facilities in Schools. Wiley.
Using Statistics in Teaching Physical Education: A Linear Programmed Presentation. Wiley.

Penn, Elizabeth H. *see* Penn, Elizabeth Hall.

Penn, Elizabeth Hall.
xPenn, Elizabeth H.
Individualized Arts & Crafts Lessons for the Elementary School. P-H.

Penn, I. Garland. *see* Penn, Irvine Garland.

Penn, Irvine Garland, 1867-1930
xPenn, I. Garland.
Afro-American Press & Its Editors. Arno.

Penn, Irving.
xPenn, Irving.
Worlds in a Small Room. Viking Pr.

Penn, William, 1644-1718
xPenn, William.
Some Fruits of Solitude in Reflections & Maxims. Folcroft.

Penna. *see* Penna, Carlos Victor.

Penna, Carlos Victor.
xPenna.
National Library & Information Services: A Handbook for Planners. Butterworths.

Pennak, Robert W. *see* Pennak, Robert William.

Pennak, Robert William.
xPennak, Robert W.
Collegiate Dictionary of Zoology. Wiley.
Fresh-Water Invertebrates of the United States. Wiley.

Pennell, E. R. *see* Pennell, Elizabeth Robins.
Pennell, Elizabeth. *see* Pennell, Elizabeth Robins.
Pennell, Elizabeth R. *see* Pennell, Elizabeth Robins.

Pennell, Elizabeth Robins, 1855-1936
xPennell, E. R.
Mary Wollstonecraft Godwin. Gordon Pr.
xPennell, Elizabeth.
Charles Godfrey Leland: A Biography. R West.
xPennell, Elizabeth R.
Charles Godfrey Leland: A Biography. Arno.
Life of James McNeill Whistler. AMS Pr.
The Life of James McNeill Whistler. R West.
Mary Wollstonecraft Godwin. Folcroft.

Penner, Jonathan, 1940-
xPenner, Jonathan.
Going Blind. G K Hall.
Going Blind. S&S.
xPenner, Jonathon.
Going Blind. BJ Pub Group.

Penner, Jonathon. *see* Penner, Jonathan.
Penner, Lucille R. *see* Penner, Lucille Recht.

Penner, Lucille Recht.
xPenner, Lucille R.
The Honey Book. Hastings.

Penney, James F.
xPenney, James F.
Perspective & Challenge in College Personnel Work. C C Thomas.

Penney, Richard L.
xPenney, Richard L.
Penguins Are Coming. Har-Row.

Penney, Sharon H. *see* Penney, Sherry.

Penney, Sherry.
xPenney, Sharon H.
Patrician in Politics: Daniel Dewey Barnard of New York. Kennikat.

Penniman, Clara.
xPenniman, Clara.
State Income Taxation. Johns Hopkins.

Penniman, Howard R. *see* Penniman, Howard Rae.

Penniman, Howard Rae, 1916-
xPenniman, Howard R.

ed. Canada at the Polls: The General Election
of 1974. Am Enterprise.
ed. French National Assembly Elections of
1978. Am Enterprise.
ed. Israel at the Polls: The Knesset Elections of
1977. Am Enterprise.
Penning-Rowsell, E. *see* Penning-Rowsell, Edmund.
Penning-Rowsell, Edmund.
xPenning-Rowsell, E.
The Benefits of Flood Alleviation: A Manual of
Assessment Techniques. Lexington Bks.
Penninger, Frieda E. *see* Penninger, Frieda Elaine.
Penninger, Frieda Elaine.
xPenninger, Frieda E.
William Caxton. Twayne.
Pennington, Eunice. *see* Pennington, Eunice (Randolph).
Pennington, Eunice (Randolph), 1923-
xPennington, Eunice.
History of the Ozarks. Pennington.
Pennington, James, 1777-1862
xPennington, James.
Currency of the British Colonies. Kelley.
Pennington, Jerry.
xPennington, Jerry.
How to Sell Your House for More Than It's
Worth. Playboy Pbks.
Pennington, Lee.
xPennington, Lee.
I Knew a Woman. Love Street.
Pennington, Levi T. *see* Pennington, Levi Talbott.
Pennington, Levi Talbott, 1875-
xPennington, Levi T.
Rambling Recollections of Ninety Happy
Years. Binford.
Pennington, M. Basil.
xPennington, M. Basil.
The Centering Prayer: Renewing an Ancient
Christian Prayer Form. Doubleday.
Daily We Touch Him: Practical Religious
Experiences. Doubleday.
Pennington, Robert R.
xPennington, Robert R.
Stannary Law: A History of the Mining Law of
Cornwall & Devon. David & Charles.
Pennock, J. R. *see* Pennock, James Roland.
Pennock, J. Roland. *see* Pennock, James Roland.
Pennock, James R. *see* Pennock, James Roland.
Pennock, James Roland.
xPennock, J. R.
Democratic Political Theory. Princeton U Pr.
xPennock, J. Roland.
ed. Coercion. Lieber-Atherton.
ed. Participation in Politics. Lieber-Atherton.
ed. Privacy. Lieber-Atherton.
ed. Property. NYU Pr.
xPennock, James R.
Liberal Democracy: Its Merits & Prospects.
Greenwood.
Pennsylvania (Colony).
xPennsylvania Colony.
Colonial Records of Pennsylvania. AMS Pr.
Pennsylvania Colony. *see* Pennsylvania (Colony).
Pennsylvania Hall Association. *see* Pennsylvania Hall
Association, Philadelphia.
Pennsylvania Hall Association, Philadelphia.
xPennsylvania Hall Association.
History of Pennsylvania Hall. Negro U Pr.
Pennsylvania. Laws, Statutes, Etc.
xGuardians Of The Poor.
Compilation of the Poor Laws of the State of
Pennsylvania from the Year 1700 to 1788,
Inclusive. Arno.
Pennsylvania. Parole Commission.
xParole Commission, Commonwealth of
Pennsylvania.
The Report of the Pennsylvania State Parole
Commission to the Legislature, 1927 Part I,
& Part Ii. Arno.
Pennsylvania. University.
xUniversity of Pennsylvania.

Animal Locomotion: The Muybridge Work at
the University of Pennsylvania. Arno.
Catalog of the Edgar Fahs Smith Memorial
Collection in the History of Chemistry. G K
Hall.
Catalog of the Programmschriften Collection.
G K Hall.
Pennsylvania University - Department of History. *see*
Pennsylvania. University. Department of History.
Pennsylvania. University. Bicentennial Conference.
xPennsylvania University Bicentennial Conference.
Conservation of Renewable Natural Resources.
Kennikat.
Fluid Mechanics & Statistical Methods in
Engineering. Kennikat.
Religion & the Modern World. Kennikat.
Studies in Civilization. Kennikat.
Studies in Economics & Industrial Relations.
Kennikat.
Studies in Political Science & Sociology.
Kennikat.
Studies in the Arts & Architecture. Kennikat.
Studies in the History of Science. Kennikat.
Pennsylvania. University. Department of History.
xPennsylvania University - Department Of History.
Translations & Reprints from the Original
Sources of European History. AMS Pr.
**Pennsylvania. University. Institute of Contemporary
Art.**
xUniversity of Pennsylvania, Institute of
Contemporary Art.
Robert Morris: Projects. U of Pa Contemp Art.
Pennsylvania. University. Library.
xPennsylvania University Library.
Changing Patterns of Scholarship & the Future
of Research Libraries. Arno.
Penoyre, John.
xPenoyre, John.
Houses in the Landscape: A Regional Study of
Vernacular Building Styles in England &
Wales. Merrimack Bk Serv.
Penrod, James.
xPenrod, James.
The Dancer Prepares: Modern Dance for
Beginners. Mayfield Pub.
Penrose, Edith T. *see* Penrose, Edith Tilton.
Penrose, Edith Tilton.
xPenrose, Edith T.
The Economics of the International Patent
System. AMS Pr.
The Economics of the International Patent
System. Greenwood.
The Theory of the Growth of the Firm. M E
Sharpe.
Penrose, Ernest F. *see* Penrose, Ernest Francis.
Penrose, Ernest Francis.
xPenrose, Ernest F.
Population Theories & Their Application: With
Special Reference to Japan. Greenwood.
xPenrose, Ernest Francis.
European Imperialism & the Partition of
Africa. Biblio Dist.
Penrose, Harald.
xPenrose, Harald.
No Echo in the Sky. Arno.
Penrose, O. *see* Penrose, Oliver.
Penrose, Oliver.
xPenrose, O.
Foundations of Statistical Mechanics: A
Deductive Treatment. Pergamon.
Penry, J. K. *see* Penry, J. Kiffin.
Penry, J. Kiffin.
xPenry, J. K.
ed. Complex Partial Seizures & Their
Treatment. Raven.
Pensare, C.
xPensare, C.

Rape of Nations: A Study in Societal
Economics. Goss.
Penson, John B.
xPenson, John B.
Agricultural Finance: An Introduction to Micro
& Macro Concepts. P-H.
Pentagram. *see* Pentagran Productions.
Pentagran Productions.
xPentagram.
Pentagram: The Work of Five Designers.
Watson-Guptill.
Pentecost, J. Dwight.
xPentecost, J. Dwight.
Glory of God. Multnomah.
The Sermon on the Mount: Contemporary
Insights for a Christian Life Style.
Multnomah.
Things Which Become Sound Doctrine.
Zondervan.
Penton, Anne.
xPenton, Anne.
Customs & Cookery in the Perigord & Quercy.
David & Charles.
Pentony, De Vere. *see* Pentony, DeVere Edwin.
Pentony, DeVere Edwin.
xPentony, De Vere.
Unfinished Rebellions. Jossey-Bass.
Penzel, Frederick, 1948-
xPenzel, Frederick.
Theatre Lighting Before Electricity. Columbia
U Pr.
Penzer, Mark.
xPenzer, Mark.
The Powerboater's Bible. Doubleday.
Penzer, N. M. *see* Penzer, Norman Mosley.
Penzer, Norman M. *see* Penzer, Norman Mosley.
Penzer, Norman Mosley, 1892-
xPenzer, N. M.
An Annotated Bibliography of Sir Richard
Francis Burton. Dawson Pub.
xPenzer, Norman M.
Annotated Bibliography of Sir Richard Francis
Burton. B Franklin.
Penzler, Otto.
xPenzler, Otto.
Danger! White Water. Troll Assocs.
The Great Detectives. Little.
ed. The Great Detectives. Penguin.
Hunting the Killer Shark. Troll Assocs.
Penzoldt, Peter.
xPenzoldt, Peter.
Supernatural in Fiction. Humanities.
People's Bicentennial Commission.
xPeople's Bicentennial Committee.
America's Birthday. S&S.
People's Bicentennial Committee. *see* People's
Bicentennial Commission.
Peoples, Edward E.
xPeoples, Edward E.
Readings in Correctional Casework &
Counseling. Goodyear.
Readings in Criminal Justice: An Introduction
to the System. Goodyear.
People's Lobby.
xPeople's Lobby.
National Initiative & Vote of Confidence.
People's Lobby.

People's Press.
xPeoples Press.
The Earth Belongs to the People: Ecology &
Power. Peoples Pr.

Peoples Press. *see* People's Press.

Pepe. *see* Pepe, Phil.

Pepe, Phil.

xPepe.

No-Hitter. Schol Bk Serv.
Pepe, Thomas J.
    xPepe, Thomas J.
        A Guide for Understanding School Law.
        Interstate.
Peper. see Peper, Eric.
Peper, Eric.
    xPeper.
        ed. Mind-Body Integration: Essential Readings
        in Biofeedback. Plenum Pub.
Pepinsky, Harold B.
    xPepinsky, Harold B.
        People & Information. Pergamon.
Pepinsky, Harold E.
    xPepinsky, Harold E.
        Crime Control Strategies: An Introduction to
        the Study of Crime. Oxford U Pr.
Peppe, Rodney.
    xPeppe, Rodney.
        Humphrey the Number Horse: Fun with
        Counting & Multiplication. Viking Pr.
        Odd One Out. Penguin.
        Odd One Out. Viking Pr.
        Three Little Pigs. Lothrop.
Pepper, Adeline.
    xPepper, Adeline.
        Tours of Historic New Jersey. Rutgers U Pr.
Pepper, Art.
    xPepper, Art.
        Straight Life: The Story of Art Pepper.
        Schirmer Bks.
Pepper, Curtis G.
    xPepper, Curtis G.
        Pope's Back Yard. FS&G.
Pepper, Elizabeth.
    xPepper, Elizabeth.
        A Guide to Magical & Mystical Sites: Europe
        & the British Isles. Har-Row.
Pepper, Robert M.
    xPepper, Robert M.
        The Formation of the Public Broadcasting
        Service. Arno.
Pepper, Roger S., 1916-
    xPepper, Roger S.
        Pressure Groups Among "Small Businessmen".
        Arno.
Pepper, Stephen C. see Pepper, Stephen Coburn.
Pepper, Stephen Coburn, 1891-
    xPepper, Stephen C.
        Aesthetic Quality: A Contextualistic Theory of
        Beauty. Greenwood.
        Principles of Art Appreciation. Greenwood.
        The Sources of Value. U of Cal Pr.
Pepper, Suzanne.
    xPepper, Suzanne.
        Civil War in China: The Political Struggle,
        1945-1949. U of Cal Pr.
Pepper, William, 1847-1947
    xPepper, William.
        The Medical Side of Benjamin Franklin.
        Argosy.
Peppin, Brigid.
    xPeppin, Brigid.
        Fantasy: The Golden Age of Fantastic
        Illustration. NAL.
Peppler, Alice S. see Peppler, Alice Stolper.
Peppler, Alice Stolper.
    xPeppler, Alice S.
        Divorced & Christian. Concordia.
Peppler, Henry J.
    xPeppler, Henry J.
        ed. Microbial Technology. Krieger.
Peppler, Mary Jo, 1944-
    xPeppler, Mary Jo.
        Inside Volleyball for Women. Contemp Bks.
Pepys, Samuel.
    xPepys, Samuel.

Diary of Samuel Pepys. AMS Pr.
Diary of Samuel Pepys. Peter Smith.
The Illustrated Pepys: Extracts from the Diary.
    U of Cal Pr.
Pepys' Memoires of the Royal Navy. Haskell.
Pepys on the Restoration Stage. Arno.
A Pepysian Garland: Black-Letter Broadside
    Ballads of the Years 1595-1639, Chiefly from
    the Collection of Samuel Pepys. Harvard U
    Pr.
Pequegnat, Willis E.
    xPequegnat, Willis E.
        ed. Contributions on the Biology of the Gulf of
        Mexico. Gulf Pub.
Perard, Victor. see Perard, Victor Semon.
Perard, Victor Semon, 1870-1957
    xPerard, Victor.
        How to Sketch. G&D.
Peray, K. see Peray, Kurt E.
Peray, Kurt E.
    xPeray, K.
        Cement Manufacturer's Handbook. Chem Pub.
Perchik, Simon.
    xPerchik, Simon.
        Both Hands Screaming. SBD.
Percival, Elizabeth.
    xPercival, Elizabeth.
        Chemistry & Enzymology of Marine Algal
        Polysaccharides. Acad Pr.
Percival, Harold W. see Percival, Harold Waldwin.
Percival, Harold Waldwin, 1868-
    xPercival, Harold W.
        Democracy Is Self-Government. Word Foun.
        Masonry & Its Symbols, in Light of "Thinking
        & Destiny". Word Foun.
Percival, J. see Percival, Jan.
Percival, Jan.
    xPercival, J.
        Complete Guide to Total Fitness. P-H.
    xPercival, Jan
        The Complete Guide to Total Fitness. Methuen
        Inc.
Percival, John.
    xPercival, John.
        The World of Diaghilev. Crown.
Percival, M. see Percival, Mary S.
Percival, Mary S.
    xPercival, M.
        Floral Biology. Pergamon.
Percival, Milton O. see Percival, Milton Oswin.
Percival, Milton Oswin, 1883-
    xPercival, Milton O.
        Reading of Moby Dick. Octagon.
Percival, Robert.
    xPercival, Robert.
        Holland & Brew's Manual of Obstetrics.
        Churchill.
Percus, J. K. see Percus, Jerome Kenneth.
Percus, Jerome Kenneth.
    xPercus, J. K.
        Combinatorial Methods. Springer-Verlag.
Percy, Bernard.
    xPercy, Bernard.
        Help Your Child in School. P-H.
Percy, Christopher V. see Percy, Christopher Vane.
Percy, Christopher Vane.
    xPercy, Christopher V.
        The Glass of Lalique: A Collector's Guide.
        Scribner.
Percy, George.
    xPercy, George.
        Observations Gathered Out of a Discourse of
        the Plantation of the Southern Colony of
        Virginia by the English, 1606. U Pr of Va.
Percy, Larry.
    xPercy, Larry.
        Advertising Strategy: A Communication
        Theory Approach. Praeger.
Percy, Walker, 1916-
    xPercy, Walker.

The Last Gentleman. FS&G.
The Moviegoer. Avon.
The Moviegoer. FS&G.
Moviegoer. Knopf.
The Second Coming. FS&G.
Perdue, Virginia.
    xPerdue, Virginia.
        Alarum & Excursion. Garland Pub.
Pereira, Antonio O. see Pereira, Antonio Olavo.
Pereira, Antonio Olavo.
    xPereira, Antonio O.
        Marcore. U of Tex Pr.
Perella, Nicolas J. see Perella, Nicolas James.
Perella, Nicolas James, 1927-
    xPerella, Nicolas J.
        Night & the Sublime in Giacomo Leopardi. U
        of Cal Pr.
Perelman, Chaim.
    xPerelman, Charles.
        Historical Introduction to Philosophical
        Thinking. Random.
Perelman, Charles. see Perelman, Chaim.
Perelman, Michael.
    xPerelman, Michael.
        Farming for Profit in a Hungry World: Capital
        & the Crisis in Agriculture. Allanheld.
Perelman, S. J. see Perelman, Sidney Joseph.
Perelman, Sidney J. see Perelman, Sidney Joseph.
Perelman, Sidney Joseph, 1904-
    xPerelman, S. J.
        Crazy Like a Fox. Random.
        Eastward Ha!. S&S.
    xPerelman, Sidney J.
        Baby, It's Cold Inside. S&S.
        Eastward Ha!. S&S.
        Ill-Tempered Clavichord. S&S.
        Swiss Family Perelman. S&S.
Perera, Frederica P.
    xPerera, Frederica P.
        Respirable Particles: Impact of Airborne Fine
        Particulates on Health & Environment.
        Ballinger Pub.

Perera, Padma. see Perera, Padma, Hejmadi.
Perera, Padma, Hejmadi.
    xPerera, Padma.
        Dr. Salaam, & Other Stories of India. Capra Pr.

Perera, Thomas. see Perera, Thomas Biddle.

Perera, Thomas Biddle.

    xPerera, Thomas.
        Louder & Louder: The Dangers of Noise
        Pollution. Watts.

Perera, Victor, 1934-
    xPerera, Victor.
        The Conversion. SBD.
Peres, Richard, 1947-
    xPeres, Richard.
        Dealing with Employment Discrimination.
        McGraw.
        Preventing Discrimination Complaints: A
        Guide for Supervisors. McGraw.
Peretz, Don, 1922-
    xPeretz, Don.
        The Government & Politics of Israel.
        Westview.
Peretz, Isaac L. see Peretz, Isaac Loeb.
Peretz, Isaac Loeb, 1851-1915
    xPeretz, Isaac L.
        Peretz. Arno.
        Stories & Pictures. Gordon Pr.
Perez, Bernard, 1836-1903
    xPerez, Bernard.
        The First Three Years of Childhood. Arno.
Perez, Eugene.
    xPerez, Eugene.

Avocado Pit Grower's Indoor How-To-Book. Walker & Co.
Citrus Seed Grower's Indoor How-to Book. Dodd.

Perper, Joshua A.
xPerper, Joshua A.
Microscopic Diagnosis in Forensic Pathology. C C Thomas.

Perper, R. J.
xPerper, R. J.
ed. Mechanisms of Tissue Injury with Reference to Rheumatoid Arthritis. NY Acad Sci.

Perpillou, Aime V. *see* Perpillou, Aime Vincent.

Perpillou, Aime Vincent, 1902-
xPerpillou, Aime V.
Human Geography. Longman.

Perrault, Charles, 1628-1703
xPerrault, Charles.
Cinderella. Bradbury Pr.
Cinderella. Scribner.
Cinderella. T Y Crowell.
Cinderella. Troll Assocs.
Cinderella. French & Eur.
Perrault's Fairy Tales. Gannon.
Perrault's Fairy Tales. Dover.
Popular Tales. Arno.
Puss in Boots. Scribner.
Puss-in-Boots. T Y Crowell.
Puss in Boots. Troll Assocs.

Perrault, Pierre, 1611-1680 (ca.)
xPerrault, Pierre.
On the Origin of Springs. Hafner.

Perreault, John, 1937-
xPerreault, John.
Luck. Kulchur Foun.

Perrella, Robert.
xPerrella, Robert.
They Call Me the Show Biz Priest. PB.

Perren, Richard.
xPerren, Richard.
The Meat Trade in Britain, 1840-1914. Routledge & Kegan.

Perret, Jacques, 1901-
xPerret, Jacques.
Horace. NYU Pr.

Perrett, Geoffrey.
xPerrett, Geoffrey.
Days of Sadness, Years of Triumph: The American People, 1939-1945. Penguin.

Perrin, Charles. *see* Perrin, Charles L.

Perrin, Charles L., 1938-
xPerrin, Charles.
Mathematics for Chemists. Wiley.

Perrin, Elula.
xPerrin, Elula.
So Long As There Are Women. Morrow.
Women Prefer Women. Bantam.
Women Prefer Women. Morrow.

Perrin, Joseph Marie, 1905-
xPerrin, Joseph-Marie.
Mary Mother of Christ & of Christians. Alba.

Perrin, Joseph-Marie. *see* Perrin, Joseph Marie.

Perrin, Noel.
xPerrin, Noel.
Dr. Bowdler's Legacy: A History of Expurgated Books in England & America. U Pr of New Eng.
First Person Rural: Essays of a Sometime Farmer. Godine.
First Person Rural: Essays of a Sometime Farmer. Penguin.
Giving up the Gun: Japan's Reversion to the Sword, 1543-1879. Godine.
Giving up the Gun: Japan's Reversion to the Sword, 1543-1879. G K Hall.

Perrin, Norman.
xPerrin, Norman.

The Promise of Bultmann. Fortress.
The Resurrection According to Matthew Mark & Luke. Fortress.

Perrin, Porter G. *see* Perrin, Porter Gale.

Perrin, Porter Gale.
xPerrin, Porter G.
Reference Handbook of Grammar & Usage. Morrow.

Perrin, Robert, 1939-
xPerrin, Robert.
Jewels. Stein & Day.

Perrin, Ursula, 1935-
xPerrin, Ursula.
Heart Failures. Avon.
Heart Failures. Doubleday.

Perrine, Garrith D.
xPerrine, Garrith D.
Administration of Justice: Principles & Procedures. West Pub.

Perrine, Laurence.
xPerrine, Laurence.
Dimensions of Drama. HarBraceJ.
Sound & Sense: An Introduction to Poetry. HarBraceJ.
ed. Story & Structure. HarBraceJ.

Perrone, Vito.
xPerrone, Vito.
The Abuses of Standardized Testing. Phi Delta Kappa.

Perrot, Charles. *see* Perrot, Georges.

Perrot, Georges, 1832-1914
xPerrot, Charles.
History of Art in Phrygia, Lydia, Caria, & Lycia. Longwood Pr.

Perrot, Jean, fl. 1965-
xPerrot, Jean.
The Organ from Its Invention in the Hellenistic Period to the End of the Thirteenth Century. Oxford U Pr.

Perrow, Charles.
xPerrow, Charles.
Complex Organizations: A Critical Essay. Scott F.
Organizational Analysis: A Sociological View. Brooks-Cole.

Perrucci, Robert.
xPerrucci, Robert.
Circle of Madness: On Being Insane & Institutionalized in America. P-H.
Profession Without Community: Engineers in American Society. Phila Bk Co.

Perry, A. H.
xPerry, A. H.
The Ocean-Atmosphere System. Longman.

Perry, Andrew.
xPerry, Andrew.
The Practical Carpenter. T Y Crowell.

Perry, Anne.
xPerry, Anne.
The Cater Street Hangman. Fawcett.
The Cater Street Hangman. St Martin.

Perry, Ben E. *see* Perry, Ben Edwin.

Perry, Ben Edwin, 1892-1968
xPerry, Ben E.
The Ancient Romances: A Literary-Historical Account of Their Origins. U of Cal Pr.

Perry, Bill.
xPerry, William.
Our Threatened Wildlife: An Ecological Study. Coward.

Perry, Bliss, 1860-1954
xPerry, Bliss.

Amateur Spirit. Arno.
American Mind. Kennikat.
Park-Street Papers. Arno.
Powers at Play. Arno.
A Study of Poetry. Folcroft.
Study of Poetry. Kennikat.
Study of Poetry. R West.
A Study of Prose Fiction. Folcroft.

Perry, C. C. *see* Perry, Charles C.

Perry, Charles C.
xPerry, C. C.
Strain Gage Primer. McGraw.

Perry, David.
xPerry, David.
Grox & Eugene. Knopf.

Perry, Edith (Weir), 1875-
xPerry, Edith W.
Altar Guild Manual. Morehouse.

Perry, Edith W. *see* Perry, Edith (Weir).

Perry, F. M. *see* Perry, Frances Melville.

Perry, Frances M. *see* Perry, Frances Melville.

Perry, Frances Melville.
xPerry, F. M.
The Art of Story-Writing. Folcroft.
xPerry, Frances M.
The Art of Story-Writing. Norwood Edns.

Perry, Frederick, 1857-
xPerry, Frederick.
Fair Winds & Foul: A Narrative of Daily Life Aboard an American Clipper Ship. E M Coleman Ent.

Perry, George G. *see* Perry, George Gresley.

Perry, George Gresley.
xPerry, George G.
ed. Religious Pieces in Prose & Verse. Kraus Repr.

Perry, George R., 1939-
xPerry, George R.
Slow Pitch Softball. A S Barnes.

Perry, George S. *see* Perry, George Sessions.

Perry, George Sessions, 1910-1956
xPerry, George S.
Cities of America. Arno.
Hold Autumn in Your Hand. U of NM Pr.

Perry, Henry T. *see* Perry, Henry Ten Eyck.

Perry, Henry Ten Eyck.
xPerry, Henry T.
Masters of Dramatic Comedy & Their Social Themes. Kennikat.

Perry, J. W. *see* Perry, John Weir.

Perry, Jacquelin.
xPerry, Jacquelin.
Principles of Lower-Extremity Bracing. Am Phys Therapy Assn.

Perry, John, 1943-
xPerry, John.
ed. Personal Identity. U of Cal Pr.

Perry, John. *see* Perry, John Sherwood.

Perry, John A. *see* Perry, John Ambrose.

Perry, John Ambrose.
xPerry, John A.
Contemporary Society: An Introduction to Social Science. Har-Row.
The Social Web: An Introduction to Sociology. Har-Row.

Perry, John Howard, 1895-
xPerry, Robert H.
Chemical Engineers' Handbook. McGraw.

Perry, John Sherwood.
xPerry, John.
The Ovarian Cycle of Mammals. Hafner.

Perry, John W. *see* Perry, John Weir.

Perry, John Weir.
xPerry, J. W.
Lord of the Four Quarters: Myths of the Royal Father. Macmillan.
xPerry, John W.

The Far Side of Madness. P-H.
Lord of the Four Quarters: Myths of the Royal
Father. Braziller.
Perry, Joseph B.
xPerry, Joseph B.
Collective Behavior: Response to Social Stress.
West Pub.
Perry, Josephine.
xPerry, Josephine.
Cookies from Many Lands. Dover.
Perry, K. R. *see* Perry, Keith Robert.
Perry, Keith Robert.
xPerry, K. R.
The Bourgeois Century: A History of Europe
1780-1870. Humanities.
Perry, Kenneth F. *see* Perry, Kenneth Frederick.
Perry, Kenneth Frederick, 1902-
xPerry, Kenneth F.
An Experiment with a Diversified Art
Program. AMS Pr.
Perry, Lewis.
xPerry, Lewis C.
Childhood Marriage & Reform: Henry Clarke
Wright, 1797-1870. U of Chicago Pr.
Perry, Lewis C. *see* Perry, Lewis.
Perry, Lily M. *see* Perry, Lily May.
Perry, Lily May.
xPerry, Lily M.
Medicinal Plants of East & Southeast Asia:
Attributed Properties & Uses. MIT Pr.
Perry, Lloyd. *see* Perry, Lloyd Merle.
Perry, Lloyd M. *see* Perry, Lloyd Merle.
Perry, Lloyd Merle.
xPerry, Lloyd.
Evangelistic Preaching. Moody.
Getting the Church on Target. Moody.
xPerry, Lloyd M.
How to Get More from Your Bible. Baker Bk.
Perry, Mary E. *see* Perry, Mary Elizabeth.
Perry, Mary Elizabeth, 1937-
xPerry, Mary E.
Crime & Society in Early Modern Seville. U Pr
of New Eng.
Perry, Octavia J. *see* Perry, Octavia Jordan.
Perry, Octavia Jordan.
xPerry, Octavia J.
My Head's High from Proudness. Blair.
Perry, Patricia.
xPerry, Patricia.
Fabulous Fit. Butterick Pub.
Mommy & Daddy Are Divorced. Dial.
Perry, Phyllis J. *see* Perry, Phyllis Jean.
Perry, Phyllis Jean.
xPerry, Phyllis J.
Let's Look at Frogs. Denison.
Let's Look at Moths & Butterflies. Denison.
Let's Look at Seashells. Denison.
Let's Look at Snails. Denison.
A Look at Colorado. Pruett.
Spiders. Denison.
Perry, Ralph B. *see* Perry, Ralph Barton.
Perry, Ralph Barton, 1876-1957
xPerry, Ralph B.
Annotated Bibliography of the Writings of
William James. Folcroft.
Annotated Bibliography of the Writings of
William James. Norwood Edns.
Annotated Bibliography of the Writings of
William James. Verbeke.
In the Spirit of William James. Greenwood.
Puritanism & Democracy. Vanguard.
Realms of Value: A Critique of Human
Civilization. Greenwood.
Perry, Richard, 1944-
xPerry, Richard.

Changes. Bobbs.
Life at the Sea's Frontiers. Taplinger.
Life in Desert & Plain. Taplinger.
Life in Forest & Jungle. Taplinger.
The World of the Giant Panda. Taplinger.
The World of the Jaguar. Taplinger.
World of the Walrus. Taplinger.
Perry, Richard L.
xPerry, Richard L.
ed. Sources of Our Liberties: Documentary
Origins of Individual Liberties in the United
States Constitution & Bill of Rights. NYU Pr.
Perry, Ritchie, 1942-
xPerry, Ritchie.
Bishop's Pawn. Pantheon.
Perry, Robert H. *see* Perry, John Howard.
Perry, Robin.
xPerry, Robin.
Creative Professional Photography. Ziff-Davis
Pub.
Perry, Roger.
xPerry, Roger.
ed. Handbook of Air Pollution Analysis.
Methuen Inc.
Wonders of Llamas. Dodd.
Perry, Roland, 1946-
xPerry, Roland.
Program for a Puppet. Crown.
Perry, Ronald, 1932-
xPerry, Ronald.
Denizens. Random.
Perry, Ronald W.
xPerry, Ronald W.
Racial Discrimination & Military Justice.
Praeger.
Perry, Rosalie S. *see* Perry, Rosalie Sandra.
Perry, Rosalie Sandra.
xPerry, Rosalie S.
Charles Ives & the American Mind. Kent St U
Pr.
Perry, S. G. *see* Perry, Sidney George.
Perry, Sidney George.
xPerry, S. G.
Practical Liquid Chromatography. Plenum Pub.
Practical Liquid Chromatography. Plenum Pub.
Perry, T. Anthony. *see* Perry, Theodore Anthony.
Perry, T. W. *see* Perry, Tilden Wayne.
Perry, Theodore Anthony.
xPerry, T. Anthony.
Art & Meaning in Berceo's Vida De Santa
Oria. Yale U Pr.
Perry, Thomas D.
xPerry, Thomas D.
Moral Reasoning & Truth: An Essay in
Philosophy & Jurisprudence. Oxford U Pr.
Perry, Thomas W. *see* Perry, Thomas Whipple.
Perry, Thomas Whipple, 1925-
xPerry, Thomas W.
Public Opinion, Propaganda, & Politics in
Eighteenth-Century England: A Study of the
Jew Bill of 1753. Harvard U Pr.
Perry, Tilden Wayne.
xPerry, T. W.
Feed Formulations. Interstate.
Perry, W. J. *see* Perry, William James.
Perry, William. *see* Perry, Bill.
Perry, William E.
xPerry, William E.
How to Manage Management. Vanguard.
Perry, William J. *see* Perry, William James.
Perry, William James.
xPerry, W. J.
Origin of Magic & Religion. Kennikat.
xPerry, William J.
Children of the Sun: A Study in the Early
History of Civilization. Scholarly.
Perry, William S. *see* Perry, William Stevens.
Perry, William Stevens, Bp, 1832-1893
xPerry, William S.

Historical Collections Relating to the American
Colonial Church. AMS Pr.
Perry, Wilma I.
xPerry, Wilma I.
Awake the Sleeping Giant Within You. Revell.
Perry-Cowen, Frances.
xPerry-Cowen, Frances.
Chautauqua to Opera: An Autobiography of a
Voice Teacher & Daughter of a Chautauqua
Pioneer. Exposition.
Pers, Jessica S.
xPers, Jessica S.
Government As Parent: Administering Foster
Care in California. Inst Gov Stud Berk.
Persaud, T. V. *see* Persaud, T. V. N.
Persaud, T. V. N.
xPersaud, T. V.
Prenatal Pathology: Fetal Medicine. C C
Thomas.
Persell, Caroline H. *see* Persell, Caroline Hodges.
Persell, Caroline Hodges.
xPersell, Caroline H.
Quality, Careers & Training in Educational &
Social Research. Gen Hall.
Persico, Joseph. *see* Persico, Joseph E.
Persico, Joseph E.
xPersico, Joseph.
The Spiderweb. Crown.
Persing, Louisa.
xPersing, Louisa.
ed. Life Is a Moody Rainbow: A Collection of
Modern Poetry. Palomar.
Persinger, Michael A.
xPersinger, Michael A.
Space-Time Transients & Unusual Events.
Nelson-Hall.
Persky, Serge M., 1870-1938
xPersky, Serge M.
Contemporary Russian Novelists. Arno.
Person, Henry A. *see* Person, Henry Axel.
Person, Henry Axel, 1903-
xPerson, Henry A.
ed. Cambridge Middle English Lyrics.
Greenwood.
Person, Peter P.
xPerson, Peter P.
Introduction to Christian Education. Baker Bk.
Person, R. V. *see* Person, Russell V.
Person, Russell V.
xPerson, R. V.
Calculus with Analytic Geometry. HR&W.
xPerson, Russell V.
Essentials of Mathematics. Wiley.
Persons, Benjamin S.
xPersons, Benjamin S.
Laterite: Genesis, Location, Use. Plenum Pub.
Persons, Stow, 1913-
xPersons, Stow.
American Minds: A History of Ideas. Krieger.
The Decline of American Gentility. Columbia
U Pr.
Perusse, Roland I.
xPerusse, Roland I.
ed. Directory of Caribbean Scholars. Gordon
Pr.
Historical Dictionary of Haiti. Scarecrow.
Pervin, Lawrence A.
xPervin, Lawrence A.
ed. College Dropout & the Utilization of
Talent. Princeton U Pr.
Pesando, James E.
xPesando, James E.
ed. Public & Private Pensions in Canada: An
Economic Analysis. U of Toronto Pr.
Pescatello, Ann.
xPescatello, Ann.
ed. Female & Male in Latin America: Essays.
U of Pittsburgh Pr.
xPescatello, Ann M.

Power & Pawn: The Female in Iberian
Families, Societies & Cultures. Greenwood.
Pescatello, Ann M. see Pescatello, Ann.
Pesce, Amadeo. see Pesce, Amadeo J.
Pesce, Amadeo J.
xPesce, Amadeo.
ed. Fluorescence Spectroscopy: An
Introduction for Biology & Medicine.
Dekker.
Pesce, Giovanni, 1918-
xPesce, Giovanni.
And No Quarter: An Italian Partisan in World
War II-Memoirs of Giovanni Pesce. Ohio U
Pr.
Peschel, Enid R. see Peschel, Enid Rhodes.
Peschel, Enid Rhodes.
xPeschel, Enid R.
ed. Medicine & Literature. N Watson.
Pesek, Boris P.
xPesek, Boris P.
Gross National Product of Czechoslovakia in
Monetary & Real Terms, 1946-58. U of
Chicago Pr.
Pesek, Ludek.
xPesek, Ludek.
Trap for Perseus. Bradbury Pr.
Pesez, M. see Pesez, Maurice.
Pesez, Maurice.
xPesez, M.
Colorimetric & Fluorimetric Analysis of
Organic Compounds & Drugs. Dekker.
Peshkin, Alan.
xPeshkin, Alan.
Growing up American: Schooling & the
Survival of Community. U of Chicago Pr.
Pesin, Ivan N. see Pesin, Ivan Nikolaevich.
Pesin, Ivan Nikolaevich.
xPesin, Ivan N.
Classical & Modern Integration Theories. Acad
Pr.
Peskett, Hugh.
xPeskett, Hugh.
Discover Your Ancestors: A Quest for Your
Roots. Arco.
Peskin, Dean B.
xPeskin, Dean B.
The Corporate Casino: How Managers Win &
Lose at the Biggest Game in Town. Am
Mgmt.
Sacked!: What to Do When You Lose Your
Job. Am Mgmt.
Pessagno, Emile A.
xPessagno, Emile A.
Radiolarian Zonation & Stratigraphy of the
Upper Cretaceous Portion of the Great
Valley Sequence, California Coast Ranges.
Am Mus Natl Hist.
Pessemier, Edgar A., 1922-
xPessemier, Edgar A.
Product Management: Strategy & Organization.
Wiley.
Pessen, D.
xPessen, D.
The Design & Application of Programmable
Sequence Controllers for Automation
Systems. Longman.
Pessen, Edward, 1920-
xPessen, Edward.
The Many-Faceted Jacksonian Era: New
Interpretations. Greenwood.
Riches, Class, & Power Before the Civil War.
Heath.
Pesso, Albert.
xPesso, Albert.
Experience in Action: A Psychomotor
Psychology. NYU Pr.
Pestana, Carlos.
xPestana, Carlos.

Fluids & Electrolytes in the Surgical Patient.
Williams & Wilkins.
Pester, Ann E.
xPester, Ann E.
Dictionary of Needlepoint Stitches. Western
Pub.
Pestolesi, Robert A.
xPestolesi, Robert A.
Creative Administration in Physical Education
& Athletics. P-H.
Pesznecker, Betty L.
xPesznecker, Betty L.
Psychiatric Content in the Nursing Curriculum:
A Study of Integration Process. U of Wash
Pr.
Peter, John D. see Peter, John Desmond.
Peter, John Desmond.
xPeter, John D.
Critique of Paradise Lost. Shoe String.
Peter, Laurence J.
xPeter, Laurence J.
Peter's People. Morrow.
Prescriptive Teaching. McGraw.
Peter, Madeleine.
xPeter, Madeleine.
Favorite Recipes of the Great Women Chefs of
France. HR&W.
Peter, Mary.
xPeter, Mary.
Collecting Victorian Jewellery. Emerson.
Collecting Victorian Jewellery.
Wallace-Homestead.
Peterkin, Julia.
xPeterkin, Julia.
A Plantation Christmas. Arno.
A Plantation Christmas. Larlin Corp.
Peterkin, Julia. see Peterkin, Julia (Mood).
Peterkin, Julia (Mood), 1880-1961
xPeterkin, Julia.
Bright Skin. Larlin Corp.
Peterman, Ruth.
xPeterman, Ruth.
My World Is Growing Larger. Tyndale.
Peters. see Peters, Ellen A.
Peters, Alan.
xPeters, Alan.
The Fine Structure of the Nervous System: The
Neurons & Supporting Cells. Saunders.
Peters, Charles.
xPeters, Charles.
The Culture of Bureaucracy. HR&W.
How Washington Really Works. A-W.
Inside the System. HR&W.
Peters, Charles C. see Peters, Charles Clinton.
Peters, Charles Clinton.
xPeters, Charles C.
Statistical Procedures & Their Mathematical
Bases. Greenwood.
Peters, Cortez.
xPeters, Cortez W.
Cortez Peters Championship Typing Drills.
McGraw.
Peters, Cortez W. see Peters, Cortez.
Peters, D. A. see Peters, David A.
Peters, Daniel.
xPeters, Daniel.
Border Crossings. Har-Row.
Peters, David A.
xPeters, D. A.
The Principles & Practice of Supervision.
Pergamon.
Peters, David W. see Peters, David Wilbur.
Peters, David Wilbur, 1889-
xPeters, David W.
The Status of the Married Woman Teacher.
AMS Pr.
Peters, Dennis G.
xPeters, Dennis G.

Chemical Separations & Measurements: Theory
& Practice of Analytical Chemistry. HR&W.
Peters, Don, 1943-
xPeters, Don.
Mondeb: An Advanced M6800 Monitor
Debugger. McGraw.
Peters, Donald. see Peters, Donald L.
Peters, Donald L.
xPeters, Donald.
For the Time of Your Life. Rosen Pr.
xPeters, Donald L.
Early Childhood. Brooks-Cole.
Peters, Edward. see Peters, Edward M.
Peters, Edward I.
xPeters, Edward I.
Introduction to Chemical Principles. HR&W.
Problem Solving for Chemistry. HR&W.
Peters, Edward M.
xPeters, Edward.
ed. First Crusade: The Chronicle of Fulcher of
Chartres & Other Source Materials. U of Pa
Pr.
Peters, Elizabeth.
xPeters, Elizabeth.
Crocodile on the Sandbank. Dodd.
Crocodile on the Sandbank. Fawcett.
Crocodile on the Sandbank. G K Hall.
Devil-May-Care. Dodd.
Devil-May-Care. Fawcett.
Legend in Green Velvet. Dodd.
Street of the Five Moons. Dodd.
Street of the Five Moons. Fawcett.
Summer of the Dragon. Dodd.
Summer of the Dragon. Fawcett.
Peters, Elizabeth. see Peters, Elizabeth C.
Peters, Elizabeth C.
xPeters, Elizabeth.
Pour Lire et Parler. Loyola.
Peters, Ellen A., 1930-
xPeters.
Negotiable Instruments Primer. Michie.
Peters, F. E. see Peters, Francis E.
Peters, Francis E.
xPeters, F. E.
Aristotle & the Arabs: The Aristotelian
Tradition in Islam. NYU Pr.
Greek Philosophical Terms: A Historical
Lexicon. NYU Pr.
Peters, G. see Peters, Georges.
Peters, Geoff.
xPeters, Geoff.
Woodturning. Arc Bks.
Peters, Georges.
xPeters, G.
ed. Control Mechanisms of Drinking.
Springer-Verlag.
Peters, H. F. see Peters, Heinz Frederick.
Peters, Harry B.
xPeters, Harry B.
Literature of the Woodwind Quintet.
Scarecrow.
Peters, Harry T. see Peters, Harry Twyford.
Peters, Harry Twyford, 1881-1948
xPeters, Harry T.
America on Stone: The Other Printmakers to
the American People. Arno.
California on Stone. Arno.
Peters, Harvey W., 1909-
xPeters, Harvey W.
America's Coming Bankruptcy: How the
Government Is Wrecking Your Dollar.
Arlington Hse.
Peters, Heinz Frederick.
xPeters, H. F.
Rainer Maria Rilke: Masks & the Man.
Gordian.
Peters, J.
xPeters, J.

The Communist Party: A Manual on
Organization. Proletarian Pubs.
Peters, J. see Peters, Jean.
Peters, Jean.
xPeters, J.
Collectible Books: Some New Paths. Pacific Bk
Ctr.
xPeters, Jean.
ed. The Bookman's Glossary. Bowker.
ed. Collectible Books: Some New Paths.
Bowker.
Peters, Joan.
xPeters, Joan.
Creative Masks for Stage & School. Plays.
Peters, John M. see Peters, John Marshall.
Peters, John Marshall, 1941-
xPeters, John M.
Building an Effective Adult Education
Enterprise. Jossey-Bass.
Peters, Joseph P.
xPeters, Joseph P.
A Guide to Strategic Planning for Hospitals.
Am Hospital.
Compiled by Indian Battles & Skirmishes on
the American Frontier 1790-1898. Arno.
Peters, Lloyd, 1902-
xPeters, Lloyd.
Lionhead Lodge. Ye Galleon.
Peters, M. S. see Peters, Max Stone.
Peters, Madison C. see Peters, Madison Clinton.
Peters, Madison Clinton, 1859-1918
xPeters, Madison C.
Wit & Wisdom of the Talmud. Folcroft.
Peters, Margaret.
xPeters, Margaret W.
The Ebony Book of Black Achievement.
Johnson Chi.
Peters, Margaret W. see Peters, Margaret.
Peters, Margot.
xPeters, Margot.
Bernard Shaw & the Actresses. Doubleday.
Peters, Max.
xPeters, Max.
Barron's How to Prepare for High School
Entrance Examinations. Barron.
Peters, Max S. see Peters, Max Stone.
Peters, Max Stone.
xPeters, M. S.
Plant Design & Economics for Chemical
Engineers. McGraw.
xPeters, Max S.
Plant Design & Economics for Chemical
Engineers. McGraw.
Peters, Mike.
xPeters, Mike.
The Nixon Chronicles. Lorenz Pr.
Peters, R. H. see Peters, Raymond Harry.
Peters, R. S. see Peters, Richard Stanley.
Peters, Raymond Harry, 1918-
xPeters, R. H.
Textile Chemistry. Textile Bk.
Peters, Richard S. see Peters, Richard Stanley.
Peters, Richard Stanley.
xPeters, R. S.
Authority, Responsibility & Education. Allen
Unwin.
Concept of Motivation. Humanities.
Education & the Education of Teachers.
Routledge & Kegan.
xPeters, Richard S.
Hobbes. Greenwood.
Peters, Robert. see Peters, Robert Louis.
Peters, Robert L. see Peters, Robert Louis.
Peters, Robert Louis, 1924-
xPeters, Robert.
The Great American Poetry Bake-off.
Scarecrow.
The Sow's Head & Other Poems. SBD.
Sow's Head & Other Poems. Wayne St U Pr.
xPeters, Robert L.

Songs for a Son. Norton.
Peters, Roger.
xPeters, Roger.
Mammalian Communication: A Behavioral
Analysis of Meaning. Brooks-Cole.
Peters, Ronald M.
xPeters, Ronald M.
The Massachusetts Constitution of 1780: A
Social Compact. U of Mass Pr.
Peters, S. see Peters, Stan.
Peters, Stan.
xPeters, S.
How to Select & Develop Athletes for Winning
High School Football. P-H.
Peters, Stanley, 1941-
xPeters, Stanley.
ed. Goals of Linguistic Theory. P-H.
Peters, Ted, 1941-
xPeters, Ted.
Fear, Faith, & the Future: Affirming Christian
Hope in the Face of Doomsday Prophecies.
Augsburg.
Futures--Human & Divine. John Knox.
UFOs-God's Chariots?: Flying Saucers in
Politics, Science & Religion. John Knox.
Peters, Victor.
xPeters, Victor.
All Things Common: The Hutterian Way of
Life. U of Minn Pr.
Peters, Virginia B. see Peters, Virginia Bergman.
Peters, Virginia Bergman, 1918-
xPeters, Virginia B.
The Florida Wars. Shoe String.
Peters, W. see Peters, Wallace.
Peters, Wallace.
xPeters, W.
Chemotherapy & Drug Resistance in Malaria.
Acad Pr.
Peters, William C.
xPeters, William C.
Exploration & Mining Geology. Wiley.
Peters, William E. see Peters, William Edwards.
Peters, William Edwards, 1857-1952
xPeters, William E.
Ohio Lands & Their History. Arno.
Petersen, Arnold.
xPetersen, Arnold.
Constitution of the United States: Founding of
the Bourgeois Republic. NY Labor News.
Daniel De Leon: Social Architect. NY Labor
News.
The Supreme Court. NY Labor News.
Petersen, Barbara A. see Petersen, Barbara Ellingson.
Petersen, Barbara Ellingson, 1945-
xPetersen, Barbara A.
Ton und Wort: The Lieder of Richard Strauss.
Univ Microfilms.
Petersen, David M.
xPetersen, David M.
Corrections: Problems & Prospects. P-H.
ed. Police Work: Strategies & Outcomes in
Law Enforcement. Sage.
Petersen, Eggert.
xPetersen, Eggert.
A Reassessment of the Concept of Criminality:
An Analysis of Criminal Behavior in Terms
of Individual & Current Environment: the
Application of a Stochastic Model. Halsted
Pr.
Petersen, Gwen.
xPetersen, Gwen.
Ranch Woman's Manual. North Plains.
Petersen, Gwenn B. see Petersen, Gwenn Boardman.
Petersen, Gwenn Boardman.
xPetersen, Gwenn B.

Across the Bridge to China. Elsevier-Nelson.
The Moon in the Water: Understanding
Tanizaki, Kawabata, & Mishima. U Pr of
Hawaii.
Petersen, J. Allan.
xPetersen, J. Allan.
Conquering Family Stress. Victor Bks.
Petersen, Johanna.
xPetersen, Johanna.
Careers with a Fire Department. Lerner Pubns.
Careers with the Postal Service. Lerner Pubns.
Petersen, John E.
xPetersen, John E.
ed. Essays in Public Finance & Financial
Management: State & Local Perspectives.
Chatham Hse Pubs.
Petersen, K. E. see Petersen, Karl Endel.
Petersen, Karen D. see Petersen, Karen Daniels.
Petersen, Karen Daniels.
xPetersen, Karen D.
Plains Indian Art from Fort Marion. U of Okla
Pr.
Petersen, Karl Endel, 1943-
xPetersen, K. E.
Brownian Motion, Hardy Spaces & Bounded
Mean Oscillation. Cambridge U Pr.
Petersen, Kate O. see Petersen, Kate Oelzner.
Petersen, Kate Oelzner.
xPetersen, Kate O.
Sources of the Parson's Tale. AMS Pr.
Petersen, Kristelle L.
xPetersen, Kristelle L.
The Single Person's Home-Buying Handbook.
Dutton.
xPetersen, Kristellie L.
Single Person's Home-Buying Handbook.
Dutton.
Petersen, Kristellic L. see Petersen, Kristelle L.
Petersen, Morris S.
xPetersen, Morris S.
Historical Geology of North America. Wm C
Brown.
Petersen, N. B. see Petersen, Nicholas B.
Petersen, Nicholas B.
xPetersen, N. B.
Edible Starches & Starch-Derived Syrups.
Noyes.
Petersen, Norman R., 1933-
xPetersen, Norman R.
Literary Criticism for New Testament Critics.
Fortress.
Petersen, Paul.
xPetersen, Paul.
The Crystal Fortress. PB.
Fools of the Trade. PB.
Petersen, Rodney.
xPetersen, Rodney A.
The Philosophy of a Peasant. InterAction.
Petersen, Rodney A. see Petersen, Rodney.
Petersen, W. P.
xPetersen, W. P.
Meditation Made Easy. Watts.
Petersen, William.
xPetersen, William.
Malthus. Harvard U Pr.
Petersen, William J.
xPetersen, William J.
Meet Me on the Mountain. Victor Bks.
Those Curious New Cults. Keats.
Petersham, Maud. see Petersham, Maud (Fuller).
Petersham, Maud (Fuller).
xPetersham, Maud.
jt. auth. Box with Red Wheels. Macmillan.
jt. auth. The Box with Red Wheels. Macmillan.
Let's Learn About Silk. Harvey.
Let's Learn About Sugar. Harvey.
Petersohn, Henry H.
xPetersohn, Henry H.

Freedom & Franchise: The Political Career of
B. Gratz Brown. U of Mo Pr.

Peterson, Paul.
xPeterson, Paul.
Working in Animal Science. McGraw.
Peterson, Paul W. see Peterson, Paul Willard.
Peterson, Paul Willard, 1912-
xPeterson, Paul W.
Natural Singing & Expressive Conducting.
Blair.
Peterson, Penelope L.
xPeterson, Penelope L.
ed. Research on Teaching: Concepts, Findings
& Implications. McCutchan.
Peterson, Peter Victor.
xPeterson, Victor P.
jt. auth. Native Trees of the Sierra Nevada. U
of Cal Pr.
Peterson, Philip L.
xPeterson, Philip L.
Concepts & Language: An Essay in Generative
Semantics & the Philosophy of Language.
Mouton.
Peterson, R. see Peterson, Richard A.
Peterson, R. F. see Peterson, Russell Francis.
Peterson, R. J. see Peterson, Robert J.
Peterson, Randolph L.
xPeterson, Randolph L.
North American Moose. U of Toronto Pr.
Peterson, Raymond M.
xPeterson, Raymond M.
Medical Problems in the Classroom: An
Educator's Guide. C C Thomas.
Peterson, Rein.
xPeterson, Rein.
Decision Systems for Inventory Management &
Production Planning. Wiley.
Peterson, Richard. see Peterson, Richard F.
Peterson, Richard A.
xPeterson, R.
Industrial Order & Social Policy. P-H.
xPeterson, Richard A.
ed. The Production of Culture. Sage.
Peterson, Richard F.
xPeterson, Richard.
Mary Lavin. Twayne.
Peterson, Robert C., 1921-
xPeterson, Robert C.
Understand Accounting-Fast. McGraw.
Peterson, Robert J.
xPeterson, R. J.
Hydrogenation Catalysts. Noyes.
Peterson, Robert L.
xPeterson, Robert L.
Career Motivations of Administrators & Their
Impact in the European Community. U of
Denver Intl.
Peterson, Robert M. see Peterson, Robert Martin.
Peterson, Robert Martin.
xPeterson, Robert M.
A Case Study of a Northern California Indian
Tribe: Cultural Change to 1860. R & E Res
Assoc.
Peterson, Robin.
xPeterson, Robin.
ed. Ecology & the Market Place. Mss Info.
Marketing: A Contemporary Introduction.
Wiley.
Marketing in Action: An Experiential
Approach. West Pub.
xPeterson, Robin T.
Personal Selling: An Introduction. Wiley.
Peterson, Robin T. see Peterson, Robin.
Peterson, Roger T. see Peterson, Roger Tory.
Peterson, Roger Tory.
xPeterson, Roger T.

The Birds. Silver.
Birds. Silver.
A Field Guide to the Birds of Texas &
Adjacent States. HM.
A Field Guide to Wildflowers of Northeastern
& North-Central North America. HM.
Penguins. HM.
Peterson, Russell Francis.
xPeterson, R. F.
Silently, by Night. McGraw.
Peterson, Ruth S. see Peterson, Ruth Streeter.
Peterson, Ruth Streeter.
xPeterson, Ruth S.
Stretch Out My Golden Wing. Windy Row.
Peterson, Shailer. see Peterson, Shailer Alvarey.
Peterson, Shailer A. see Peterson, Shailer Alvarey.
Peterson, Shailer Alvarey, 1908-
xPeterson, Shailer.
ed. Comprehensive Review for Dental
Hygienists. Mosby.
xPeterson, Shailer A.
Preparing to Enter Dental School. P-H.
Preparing to Enter Medical School. P-H.
Preparing to Enter Pharmacy School. P-H.
Peterson, Susan.
xPeterson, Susan.
The Living Tradition of Maria Martinez.
Kodansha.
Peterson, Thomas V. see Peterson, Thomas Virgil.
Peterson, Thomas Virgil, 1943-
xPeterson, Thomas V.
Ham & Japheth: The Mythic World of Whites
in the Antebellum South. Scarecrow.
Peterson, Thurman S. see Peterson, Thurman Stewart.
Peterson, Thurman Stewart.
xPeterson, Thurman S.
Intermediate Algebra for College Students.
Har-Row.
Peterson, Trudy H. see Peterson, Trudy Huskamp.
Peterson, Trudy Huskamp, 1945-
xPeterson, Trudy H.
Agricultural Exports, Farm Income, & the
Eisenhower Administration. U of Nebr Pr.
Peterson, Victor P. see Peterson, Peter Victor.
Peterson, Violet E.
xPeterson, Violet E.
Library Instruction Guide: Suggested Courses
for Use by Librarians & Teachers in Junior &
Senior High Schools. Shoe String.
Peterson, W. see Peterson, Willis L.
Peterson, W. Wesley. see Peterson, William Wesley.
Peterson, Walfred H. see Peterson, Walfred Hugo.
Peterson, Walfred Hugo.
xPeterson, Walfred H.
Thy Liberty in Law. Broadman.
Peterson, William Wesley, 1924-
xPeterson, W. Wesley.
Introduction to Programming Languages. P-H.
Peterson, Willis.
xPeterson, Willis.
A Guide to Better Nature Photography.
Beautiful Am.
Peterson, Willis L.
xPeterson, W.
Introduction to Economics. P-H.
Petersson, Robert T. see Petersson, Robert Torsten.
Petersson, Robert Torsten.
xPetersson, Robert T.
Art of Ecstasy: Teresa, Bernini & Crashaw.
Atheneum.
Petesch, Natalie L. see Petesch, Natalie L. M.
Petesch, Natalie L. M., 1924-
xPetesch, Natalie L.
After the First Death, There Is No Other. U of
Iowa Pr.
Petherbridge, Elizabeth.
xPetherbridge, Elizabeth.
Paper Sculpture Step by Step. Transatlantic.
Pethick, Derek, 1920-
xPethick, Derek.

First Approaches to the Northwest Coast. U of
Wash Pr.
Pethig, Ronald.
xPethig, Ronald.
Dielectric & Electronic Properties of Biological
Materials. Wiley.
Pethybridge. see Pethybridge, Roger William.
Pethybridge, Roger William, 1934-
xPethybridge.
History of Postwar Russia. NAL.
Petit, Gaston.
xPetit, Gaston.
Evolving Techniques in Japanese Woodblock
Prints. Kodansha.
Petit, Paul.
xPetit, Paul.
Pax Romana. U of Cal Pr.
Petit, Thomas A.
xPetit, Thomas A.
Fundamentals of Management Coordination:
Supervisors, Middle Managers, & Executives.
Wiley.
Petite, Irving, 1920-
xPetite, Irving.
Meander to Alaska. Seattle Bk.
Petitjean, Pierre, 1947-
xPetitjean, Pierre.
tr. Backstage. Viking Pr.
Backstage: With the Ballet. Penguin.
Petlock, Alice.
xPetlock, Alice.
Young, Bold & Beautiful. Grossmont Pr.
Petrakis, Harry M. see Petrakis, Harry Mark.
Petrakis, Harry Mark.
xPetrakis, Harry M.
Nick the Greek. Doubleday.
Petrarca, Francesco, 1304-1374
xPetrarca, Francesco.
The Life of Solitude. Hyperion Conn.
Love Rimes of Petrarch. Greenwood.
Sonnets & Songs. AMS Pr.
Petras, James. see Petras, James F.
Petras, James F., 1937-
xPetras, James.
Critical Perspectives on Imperialism & Social
Class in the Third World. Monthly Rev.
Politics & Social Forces in Chilean
Development. U of Cal Pr.
Politics & Social Structure in Latin America.
Monthly Rev.
xPetras, James F.
The Nationalization of Venezuelan Oil.
Praeger.
Petrement, Simone.
xPetrement, Simone.
Simone Weil: A Life. Pantheon.
Petres, J.
xPetres, J.
Dermatosurgery. Springer-Verlag.
Petreshene, Susan S.
xPetreshene, Susan S.
A Complete Guide to Learning Centers.
Pendragon Hse.
Petri, Darlene.
xPetri, Darlene.
The Hurt & Healing of Divorce. Cook.
Petrich, M. see Petrich, Mario.
Petrich, Mario.
xPetrich, M.
Categories of Algebraic Systems: Vector &
Projective Spaces, Semigroups, Rings &
Lattices. Springer-Verlag.
xPetrich, Mario.
Introduction to Semigroups. Merrill.
Lectures in Semigroups. Wiley.
Petrides, Platon, 1912-
xPetrides, Platon.

Diabetes Mellitus: Theory & Management.
Urban & S.

Petrie, Alexander.
xPetrie, Alexander.
An Introduction to Roman History, Literature
& Antiquities. Greenwood.

Petrie, Asenath.
xPetrie, Asenath.
Individuality in Pain & Suffering. U of Chicago
Pr.

Petrie, Charles A. see Petrie, Charles Alexander.

Petrie, Charles Alexander, Sir, Bart, 1895-
xPetrie, Charles A.
The Victorians. Greenwood.

Petrie, Ferdinand, 1925-
xPetrie, Ferdinand.
Drawing Landscapes in Pencil. Watson-Guptill.

Petrie, George, 1866-1947
xPetrie, George.
Church & State in Early Maryland. AMS Pr.
Church & State in Early Maryland. Johnson
Repr.

Petrie, Graham.
xPetrie, Graham.
The Cinema of Francois Truffaut. A S Barnes.

Petrie, Paul.
xPetrie, Paul.
The Academy of Goodbye. U Pr of New Eng.

Petrie, Paul. see Petrie, Paul James.

Petrie, Paul James, 1928-
xPetrie, Paul.
From Under the Hill of Night: Poems.
Vanderbilt U Pr.

Petrie, Sidney.
xPetrie, Sidney.
Hypno-Cybernetics: Helping Yourself to a Rich
New Life. NAL.
Hypno-Cybernetics: Helping Yourself to a Rich
New Life. P-H.
Martinis & Whipped Cream: The New
Carbo-Cal Way to Lose Weight & Stay Slim.
P-H.
Martinis & Whipped Cream: The New
Carbo-Cal Way to Lose Weight & Stay Slim.
P-H.
The Wonder Protein Diet: Miracle Way to
Better Health & Longer Life. P-H.

Petrie, W. M. see Petrie, William Matthew Flinders.

Petrie, William Matthew Flinders, Sir, 1853-1942
xPetrie, W. M.
Arts & Crafts of Ancient Egypt. Attic Bks.
Religious Life in Ancient Egypt. Cooper Sq.

Petrillo, H. V.
xPetrillo, H. V.
Processing Securities Transactions:
Administrative Procedures of Brokerage
Firms. Ronald Pr.

Petrillo, Madeline.
xPetrillo, Madeline.
Emotional Care of Hospitalized Children: An
Environmental Approach. Lippincott.

Petrocelli, Orlando. see Petrocelli, Orlando R.

Petrocelli, Orlando R.
xPetrocelli, Orlando.
The Pact. PB.
xPetrocelli, Orlando R.
Olympia's Inheritance. Pinnacle Bks.

Petrone, Fred R.
xPetrone, Fred R.
The Developmental Kindergarten:
Individualized Instruction Through
Diagnostic Grouping. C C Thomas.

Petroni, Frank A.
xPetroni, Frank A.
Two, Four, Six, Eight, When You Gonna
Integrate?. Liveright.

Petronius Arbiter.
xPetronius Arbiter.

The Works of Petronius Arbiter, in Prose &
Verse. AMS Pr.

Petropulos, John A. see Petropulos, John Anthony.

Petropulos, John Anthony.
xPetropulos, John A.
Politics & Statecraft in the Kingdom of Greece,
1833-1843. Princeton U Pr.

Petrov, I. P. see Petrov, Iurii Petrovich.

Petrov, Iurii Petrovich.
xPetrov, I. P.
Variational Methods in Optimum Control
Theory. Acad Pr.

Petrov, M. P. see Petrov, Mikhail Platonovich.

Petrov, Mikhail Platonovich, 1906-
xPetrov, M. P.
Deserts of the World. Halsted Pr.

Petrov, V. V. see Petrov, Valentin Vladimirovich.

Petrov, Valentin Vladimirovich.
xPetrov, V. V.
Sums of Independent Random Variables.
Springer-Verlag.

Petrov, Vladimir, 1915-
xPetrov, Vladimir.
Money & Conquest: Allied Occupation
Currencies in World War II. Johns Hopkins.

Petrova, Nina.
xPetrova, Nina.
The Best of Russian Cooking. Crown.

Petrovich, Michael B. see Petrovich, Michael Boro.

Petrovich, Michael Boro.
xPetrovich, Michael B.
A History of Modern Serbia, 1804-1918.
HarBraceJ.

Petrucci, Kenneth. see Petrucci, Kenneth R.

Petrucci, Kenneth R.
xPetrucci, Kenneth.
Soul's Eye. Branden.

Petrucci, Ralph H.
xPetrucci, Ralph H.
General Chemistry: Principles & Modern
Applications. Macmillan.

Pett, Stephen.
xPett, Stephen.
Pulpit of Bones. Morrow.

Pettee, George S. see Pettee, George Sawyer.

Pettee, George Sawyer, 1904-
xPettee, George S.
Process of Revolution. Fertig.

Pettengill, Samuel B. see Pettengill, Samuel Barrett.

Pettengill, Samuel Barrett, 1886-
xPettengill, Samuel B.
Hot Oil: The Problem of Petroleum. Hyperion
Conn.

Pettepiece, Thomas G.
xPettepiece, Thomas G.
Visions of a World Hungry: Study, Prayer, &
Action. Upper Room.

Petter, Helen M. see Petter, Helen Mary.

Petter, Helen Mary.
xPetter, Helen M.
The Oxford Almanacks. Oxford U Pr.

Petter, Henri.
xPetter, Henri.
Early American Novel. Ohio St U Pr.

Petterssen, Sverre, 1898-
xPetterssen, Sverre.
Introduction to Meteorology. McGraw.

Pettersson, Hans, 1888-
xPettersson, Hans.
Ocean Floor. Hafner.

Petteruto, Ray.
xPetteruto, Ray.
How to Open & Operate a Restaurant: A
Step-by-Step Guide to Financial Success. Van
Nos Reinhold.

Pettey, Richard J.
xPettey, Richard J.

In His Footsteps: The Priest in the Catholic
Charismatic Renewal. Paulist Pr.

Petti, Anthony G.
xPetti, Anthony G.
English Literary Hands from Chaucer to
Dryden. Harvard U Pr.

Pettibone, Marian H.
xPettibone, Marian H.
Some Scale-Bearing Polychaetes of Puget
Sound & Adjacent Waters. U of Wash Pr.

Pettifer, Ernest W. see Pettifer, Ernest William.

Pettifer, Ernest William, 1882-1962
xPettifer, Ernest W.
Punishments of Former Days. Beekman Pubs.
Punishments of Former Days. Charles River
Bks.

Pettigrew, Shirley.
xPettigrew, Shirley.
There Was an Old Lady. Coward.

Pettigrew, T. F. see Pettigrew, Thomas F.

Pettigrew, Thomas F.
xPettigrew, T. F.
Racially Separate or Together. McGraw.
xPettigrew, Thomas F.
ed. Racial Discrimination in the United States.
Har-Row.
The Sociology of Race Relations: Reflection &
Reform. Free Pr.

Pettijohn, F. J. see Pettijohn, Francis John.

Pettijohn, Francis John, 1904-
xPettijohn, F. J.
Sedimentary Rocks. Har-Row.

Pettingill, Amos, 1900-
xPettingill, Amos.
The White-Flower-Farm Garden Book. Little.

Pettingill, Olin S. see Pettingill, Olin Sewall.

Pettingill, Olin Sewall, 1907-
xPettingill, Olin S.
A Guide to Bird Finding East of the
Mississippi. HM.
A Guide to Bird Finding East of the
Mississippi. Oxford U Pr.
Ornithology in Laboratory & Field. Burgess.

Pettingill, William L. see Pettingill, William Leroy.

Pettingill, William Leroy.
xPettingill, William L.
Bible Questions Answered. Zondervan.

Pettit, Arthur G.
xPettit, Arthur G.
Mark Twain & the South. U Pr of Ky.

Pettit, Clyde Edwin.
xPettit, Clyde Edwin.
The Experts. Lyle Stuart.

Pettit, Florence. see Pettit, Florence Harvey.

Pettit, Florence H. see Pettit, Florence Harvey.

Pettit, Florence Harvey.
xPettit, Florence.
Christmas All Around the House: Traditional
Decorations You Can Make. T Y Crowell.
xPettit, Florence H.
America's Indigo Blues: Resist - Printed &
Dyed Textiles of the Eighteenth Century.
Hastings.
America's Printed & Painted Fabrics,
1600-1900. Hastings.
How to Make Whirligigs & Whimmy Diddles
& Other American Folkcraft Objects. T Y
Crowell.
illus. The Stamp-Pad Printing Book. T Y
Crowell.

Pettit, G. R. see Pettit, George R.

Pettit, George R.
xPettit, G. R.
Synthetic Peptides. Elsevier.
xPettit, George R.
Synthetic Nucleotides. Van Nos Reinhold.
Synthetic Peptides. Acad Pr.
Synthetic Peptides. Van Nos Reinhold.

Pettit, Henry, 1906-
xPettit, Henry.

A Bibliography of Young's Night Thoughts.
  Folcroft.
Pettit, Hermon.
  xPettit, Hermon.
    Intro. by Jubilee!!: The Autobiography of
      Hermon Pettit. Bookmates Intl.
Pettit, Paul.
  xPettit, Paul.
    Prehistoric Dartmoor. David & Charles.
Pettit, Philip, 1945-
  xPettit, Philip.
    The Concept of Structuralism: A Critical
      Analysis. U of Cal Pr.
Pettitt, Stephen, 1945-
  xPettitt, Stephen.
    Dennis Brain: A Biography. Taplinger.
Pettman, Ralph.
  xPettman, Ralph.
    ed. Moral Claims in World Affairs. St Martin.
    State & Class: A Sociology of International
      Affairs. St Martin.
Pettofrezzo, Anthony J.
  xPettofrezzo, Anthony J.
    Elementary Algebra: A Programmed Approach.
      Scott F.
    Matrices & Transformations. Dover.
Petty. *see* Petty, Walter Thomas.
Petty, Barbara.
  xPetty, Barbara.
    Bad Blood. Dell.
Petty, David L.
  xPetty, David L.
    An Analysis of Attitudes & Behaviors of
      Young Adults Toward the Aged. R & E Res
      Assoc.
Petty, George R.
  xPetty, George R.
    Project Occult: The Ordered Computer
      Collation of Unprepared Literary Text. NYU
      Pr.
Petty, Jo.
  xPetty, Jo.
    Compiled by Apples of Gold. Gibson.
    Gifts for the Graduate. Revell.
    Golden Prayers. Doubleday.
    Life Is for Living. Revell.
    Words of Silver & Gold. G K Hall.
    Compiled by Words of Silver & Gold. Revell.
Petty, Julian J. *see* Petty, Julian Jay.
Petty, Julian Jay.
  xPetty, Julian J.
    The Growth & Distribution of Population in
      South Carolina. Reprint.
Petty, Roy.
  xPetty, Roy.
    Contemporary Tennis. Contemp Bks.
    Home Birth. Quality Bks IL.
Petty, Ryan.
  xPetty, Ryan L.
    The Great Garage Sale Success Book: How to
      Make a Lot More Money (& Have a Better
      Time) with Your Garage Sale. Provision.
Petty, Ryan L. *see* Petty, Ryan.
Petty, Thomas E. *see* Petty, Thomas L.
Petty, Thomas L.
  xPetty, Thomas E.
    ed. Chronic Obstructive Pulmonary Disease.
      Dekker.
  xPetty, Thomas L.
    For Those Who Live & Breathe: A Manual for
      Patients with Emphysema & Chronic
      Bronchitis. C C Thomas.
Petty, Walter. *see* Petty, Walter Thomas.
Petty, Walter T. *see* Petty, Walter Thomas.
Petty, Walter Thomas, 1918-
  xPetty.
    Developing Children's Language. Allyn.
  xPetty, Walter.

Experiences in Language: Tools & Techniques
  for Language Arts Methods. Allyn.
  xPetty, Walter T.
    ed. Curriculum for the Modern Elementary
      School. Rand.
    Experiences in Language: Tools & Techniques
      for Language Arts Methods. Allyn.
Petuchowski, Jakob J. *see* Petuchowski, Jakob Josef.
Petuchowski, Jakob Josef.
  xPetuchowski, Jakob J.
    ed. Understanding Jewish Prayer. Ktav.
  xPetuchowski, Jakob L.
    The Lord's Prayer & Jewish Liturgy. Seabury.
Petuchowski, Jakob L. *see* Petuchowski, Jakob Josef.
Petulla, Joseph M.
  xPetulla, Joseph M.
    American Environmentalism: Values, Tactics,
      Priorities. Tex A&M Univ Pr.
Petzal, David E.
  xPetzal, David E.
    ed. The Expert's Book of Big Game Hunting in
      North America. S&S.
    ed. The Expert's Book of Upland Bird &
      Water-Fowl Hunting. S&S.
Petzold, Paul.
  xPetzold, Paul.
    The All in One Cine Book. Focal Pr.
    Effects & Experiments in Photography. Focal
      Pr.
Peucker, T. J. *see* Peucker, Thomas K.
Peucker, Thomas K.
  xPeucker, T. J.
    Computer Cartography. Assn Am Geographers.
Peurifoy, Robert L. *see* Peurifoy, Robert Leroy.
Peurifoy, Robert Leroy, 1902-
  xPeurifoy, Robert L.
    Construction Planning, Equipment, & Methods.
      McGraw.
    Estimating Construction Costs. McGraw.
    Formwork for Concrete Structures. McGraw.
Peusner, Leonardo, 1943-
  xPeusner, Leonardo.
    Concepts in Bioenergetics. P-H.
Pevear, Richard, 1943-
  xPevear, Richard.
    Night Talk & Other Poems. Princeton U Pr.
Pevsner, Nicholas. *see* Pevsner, Nikolaus.
Pevsner, Nikolaus, Sir, 1902-
  xPevsner, Nicholas.
    Some Architectural Writers of the Nineteenth
      Century. Oxford U Pr.
  xPevsner, Nikolaus.
    Academies of Art, Past & Present. Da Capo.
    A History of Building Types. Princeton U Pr.
    The Sources of Modern Architecture & Design.
      Oxford U Pr.
    Studies in Art, Architecture, & Design. Walker
      & Co.
Pevsner, Stella.
  xPevsner, Stella.
    And You Give Me a Pain, Elaine. HM.
    Call Me Heller, That's My Name. HM.
    Cute Is a Four Letter Word. HM.
Pevzner, L. V. *see* Pevzner, Leonid Zalmanovich.
Pevzner, Leonid Zalmanovich.
  xPevzner, L. V.
    Functional Biochemistry of the Neuroglia.
      Plenum Pub.
Pexieder, T. *see* Pexieder, Tomas.
Pexieder, Tomas, 1941-
  xPexieder, T.
    Cell Death in the Morphogenesis &
      Teratogenesis of the Heart. Springer-Verlag.
Peyre, Henri, 1901-
  xPeyre, Henri.

The Failures of Criticism. Cornell U Pr.
French Literary Imagination & Dostoevsky &
  Other Essays. U of Ala Pr.
French Novelists of Today. Oxford U Pr.
Literature & Sincerity. Greenwood.
Louis Menard. AMS Pr.
Marcel Proust. Columbia U Pr.
Observations on Life, Literature & Learning in
  America. S Ill U Pr.
Victor Hugo: Philosophy & Poetry. U of Ala
  Pr.
What Is Symbolism?. U of Ala Pr.
Peyser, Joan.
  xPeyser, Joan.
    Boulez. Schirmer Bks.
Peyton, K. M.
  xPeyton, K. M.
    The Maplin Bird. Gregg.
    Marion's Angels. Oxford U Pr.
    A Midsummer Night's Death. Philomel.
    A Pattern of Roses. T Y Crowell.
    illus. Pennington's Last Term. T Y Crowell.
    Prove Yourself a Hero. Philomel.
    Prove Yourself a Hero. Dell.
Peyton, Leslie.
  xPeyton, Leslie.
    A Layman's Bible Digest. Revell.
Pezdek, Robert V.
  xPezdek, Robert V.
    Public Employment Bibliography. NY Sch
      Indus Rel.
Pezeu-Massabuau, Jacques.
  xPezeu-Massabuau, Jacques.
    The Japanese Islands: A Physical & Social
      Geography. C E Tuttle.
Pezzano, Chuck.
  xPezzano, Chuck.
    Professional Bowlers Association Guide to
      Better Bowling. S&S.
    Professional Bowler's Association Guide to
      Better Bowling. S&S.
Pezzini, Wilma.
  xPezzini, Wilma.
    The Tuscan Cookbook. Atheneum.
Pezzullo, Thomas R.
  xPezzullo, Thomas R.
    Salary Equity: Detecting Sex Bias in Salaries
      Among College & University Professors.
      Lexington Bks.
Pfadt, Robert E.
  xPfadt, Robert E.
    Fundamentals of Applied Entomology.
      Macmillan.
Pfaff, Martin.
  xPfaff, Martin.
    Grants & Exchange. Elsevier.
Pfaffenberger, Roger C.
  xPfaffenberger, Roger C.
    Mathematical Programming for Economics &
      Business. Iowa St U Pr.
Pfafflin, James. *see* Pfafflin, James R.
Pfafflin, James R.
  xPfafflin, James.
    The Encyclopedia of Environmental Science &
      Engineering. Gordon.
Pfahl, Peter B. *see* Pfahl, Peter Blair.
Pfahl, Peter Blair, 1919-
  xPfahl, Peter B.
    Retail Florist Business. Interstate.
Pfaltz, Marilyn.
  xPfaltz, Marilyn.
    How to Move Your Family Successfully. H P
      Bks.
Pfaltzgraff, Robert. *see* Pfaltzgraff, Robert L.
Pfaltzgraff, Robert L.
  xPfaltzgraff, Robert.
    ed. Study of International Relations: A Guide
      to Information Sources. Gale.
  xPfaltzgraff, Robert L.

Britain Faces Europe: 1957 to 1967. U of Pa
Pr.

Pfanzagl, Johann.
xPfanzagl, Johann.
Theory of Measurement. Intl Pubns Serv.

Pfarr, Paul.
xPfarr, Paul.
Build Your Own Log Cabin. Winchester Pr.

Pfatteicher, Philip H.
xPfatteicher, Philip H.
Manual on the Liturgy: Lutheran Book of
Worship. Augsburg.

Pfeffer, Alan J. see Pfeffer, Jay Alan.

Pfeffer, Irving.
xPfeffer, Irving.
Insurance & Economic Theory. Irwin.

Pfeffer, Jay Alan, 1907-
xPfeffer, Alan J.
German Review Grammar. Heath.

Pfeffer, Jeffrey.
xPfeffer, Jeffrey.
The External Control of Organizations: A
Resource Dependence Perspective. Har-Row.
Organizational Design. AHM Pub.
xTrade & Technical Press Editors.
Principles of Pneumatics. Renouf.

Pfeffer, Leo, 1910-
xPfeffer, Leo.
Creeds in Competition: A Creative Force in
American Culture. Greenwood.

Pfeffer, Rose, 1908-
xPfeffer, Rose.
Nietzsche: Disciple of Dionysus. Bucknell U
Pr.

Pfeffer, Susan B. see Pfeffer, Susan Beth.

Pfeffer, Susan Beth.
xPfeffer, Susan B.
Just Between Us. Delacorte.
Marly the Kid. Dell.
xPfeffer, Susan Beth.
Marly the Kid. Doubleday.

Pfeffer, Washek F.
xPfeffer, Washek F.
Integrals & Measures. Dekker.

Pfeifer, Carl J.
xPfeifer, Carl J.
The Living Faith in a World of Change. Ave
Maria.
Living Water: Prayers of Our Heritage. Paulist
Pr.

Pfeiffer, C. Boyd.
xPfeiffer, C. Boyd.
Field Guide to Outdoor Photography.
Stackpole.
Tackle Craft. Crown.

Pfeiffer, Charles F.
xPfeiffer, Charles F.
Baker's Pocket Atlas of the Bible. Baker Bk.
ed. Dead Sea Scrolls & the Bible. Baker Bk.
Outline of Old Testament History. Moody.
Ras Shamra & the Bible. Baker Bk.

Pfeiffer, Guy O.
xPfeiffer, Guy O.
The Household Environment & Chronic Illness:
Guidelines for Constructing & Maintaining a
Less Polluted Residence. C C Thomas.

Pfeiffer, J. William.
xPfeiffer, J. William.
Reference Guide to Handbooks & Annuals.
Univ Assocs.

Pfeiffer, John B.
xPfeiffer, John B.
ed. Sulfur Removal & Recovery from Industrial
Processes. Am Chemical.

Pfeiffer, John R.
xPfeiffer, John R.
Fantasy & Science Fiction: A Critical Guide.
Filter.

Pfeiffer, Paul E.
xPfeiffer, Paul E.

Concepts of Probability Theory. Dover.
ed. Introduction to Applied Probability. Acad
Pr.

Pfeiffer, Philip A.
xPfeiffer, Philip A.
Pensacola's Currency Issuing Banks & Their
Bank Notes, 1833-1935. Pfeiffer.

Pfeiffer, Rudolf. see Pfeiffer, Rudolph.

Pfeiffer, Rudolph, 1889-
xPfeiffer, Rudolf.
History of Classical Scholarship from 1300 to
1850. Oxford U Pr.

Pfennigstorf, Werner.
xPfennigstorf, Werner.
Legal Expense Insurance: The European
Experience in Financing Legal Services. Am
Bar Foun.
ed. Legal Service Plans: Approaches to
Regulation. Am Bar Foun.

Pfiffner, James P.
xPfiffner, James P.
The President, the Budget, & Congress:
Impoundment & the 1974 Budget Act.
Westview.

Pflanze, Otto.
xPflanze, Otto.
The Unification of Germany, 1848-1871.
Krieger.

Pflaum-Connor, Susanna.
xPflaum-Connor, Susanna.
ed. Aspects of Reading Education. McCutchan.

Pfleiderer, Otto, 1839-1908
xPfleiderer, Otto.
Philosophy & Development of Religion. AMS
Pr.

Pfloog, Jan.
xPfloog, Jan.
illus. Animal Friends & Neighbors. Western
Pub.
illus. The Cat Book. Western Pub.
illus. The Farm Book. Western Pub.
The Fox Book. Western Pub.
illus. Puppies Are Like That. Random.

Pflug, Betsy.
xPflug, Betsy.
Boxed-in Doll Houses. Lippincott.
illus. Funny Bags. Lippincott.

Pfnister, Allan O.
xPfnister, Allan O.
Planning for Higher Education: Background &
Application. Westview.

Phadke, Sindhu V. see Phadke, Sindhu Vaman.

Phadke, Sindhu Vaman.
xPhadke, Sindhu V.
Licensing of Child Care in California,
1911-1961. R & E Res Assoc.

Phadnis, Urmila.
xPhadnis, Urmila.
Religion & Politics in Sri Lanka. South Asia
Bks.

Phaff, H. J. see Phaff, Herman Jan.

Phaff, Herman Jan.
xPhaff, H. J.
The Life of Yeasts. Harvard U Pr.

Phantom, D. S.
xPhantom, D. S.
Texas Rising. S & S Pr TX.

Phares, Donald.
xPhares, Donald.
ed. A Decent Home & Environment: Housing
Urban America. Ballinger Pub.

Phares, E. Jerry.
xPhares, E. Jerry.
Clinical Psychology: Concepts, Methods, &
Profession. Dorsey.

Phares, Ross.
xPhares, Ross.

Cavalier in the Wilderness: The Story of the
Explorer & Trader Louis Juchereau De St.
Denis. Peter Smith.
Governors of Texas. Pelican.

Pharmaceutical Society of Great Britain, London.
xPharmaceutical Society of Great Britain.
British National Formulary: 1976-1978.
Rittenhouse.
ed. British Pharmacopoeia. Rittenhouse.
European Pharmacopoeia. Rittenhouse.
ed. The Pharmaceutical Codex. Rittenhouse.
ed. Pharmaceutical Handbook. Rittenhouse.
Supplement to British Pharmaceutical Codex.
Rittenhouse.

Pharmacology of Thermoregulation Symposium, 2nd,
Paris, 1974. see Symposium on the Pharmacology of
Thermoregulation.

Pharmacology of Thermoregulation, 3rd Symposium,
Banff, Alberta, Sept. 1976. see Symposium on the
Pharmacology of Thermoregulation.

Pharr, Clyde, 1883-
xPharr, Clyde.
Homeric Greek: A Book for Beginners. U of
Okla Pr.

Phayer, J. Michael.
xPhayer, J. Michael.
Sexual Liberation & Religion in Nineteenth
Century Europe. Rowman.

Phelan, Gladys K.
xPhelan, Gladys K.
Family Relationships. Burgess.

Phelan, John L. see Phelan, John Leddy.

Phelan, John Leddy, 1924-
xPhelan, John L.
Hispanization of the Philippines: Spanish Aims
& Filipino Responses, 1565-1700. U of Wis
Pr.
The People & the King: The Comunero
Revolution in Colombia, 1781. U of Wis Pr.

Phelan, John M.
xPhelan, John M.
Disenchantment: Meaning & Morality in the
Media. Hastings.
Mediaworld: Programming the Public.
Continuum.

Phelan, Mary K. see Phelan, Mary Kay.

Phelan, Mary Kay.
xPhelan, Mary K.
The Burning of Washington: August 1814. T Y
Crowell.
Four Days in Philadelphia- 1776. T Y Crowell.
Fourth of July. T Y Crowell.
Martha Berry. T Y Crowell.
The Story of the Boston Massacre. T Y
Crowell.
The Story of the Boston Tea Party. T Y
Crowell.
Story of the Great Chicago Fire, 1871. T Y
Crowell.
The Story of the Louisiana Purchase. T Y
Crowell.

Phelan, Richard M.
xPhelan, Richard M.
Automatic Control Systems. Cornell U Pr.
Fundamentals of Mechanical Design. McGraw.

Phelan, Terry W. see Phelan, Terry Wolfe.

Phelan, Terry Wolfe.
xPhelan, Terry W.
The S. S. Valentine. Schol Bk Serv.
The Week Mom Unplugged the TVs. Schol Bk
Serv.

Phelan, Thomas P. see Phelan, Thomas Patrick.

Phelan, Thomas Patrick, 1870-
xPhelan, Thomas P.
Catholics in Colonial Days. Gale.

Phelps, Albert.
xPhelps, Albert.
Louisiana: A Record of Expansion. AMS Pr.

Phelps, Amos A. see Phelps, Amos Augustus.

Phelps, Amos Augustus, 1805-1847
xPhelps, Amos A.
Lectures on Slavery & Its Remedy. Scholarly.
Phelps, Arthur L. see Phelps, Arthur Leonard.
Phelps, Arthur Leonard, 1887-
xPhelps, Arthur L.
Canadian Writers. Arno.
Phelps, Clyde William, 1897-
xPhelps, William C.
The Foreign Expansion of American Banks:
American Branch Banking Abroad. Arno.
Phelps, Dean, 1929-
xPhelps, Dean.
And Now We'll Play a Man's Game: Montana
Stories. Holmgangers.
Phelps, Edmund S.
xPhelps, Edmund S.
ed. Problems of the Modern Economy. Norton.
Phelps, Orme W. see Phelps, Orme Wheclock.
Phelps, Orme Wheclock.
xPhelps, Orme W.
Introduction to Labor Economics. Krieger.
Phelps, Robert.
xPhelps, Robert.
ed. Literary Life: A Scrapbook Almanac of the
Anglo-American Literary Scene from 1900 to
1950. FS&G.
Phelps, Robert H.
xPhelps, Robert H.
Libel: Rights, Risks, Responsibilities. Dover.
Phelps, Stanlee.
xPhelps, Stanlee.
The Assertive Woman. Impact Pubs Cal.
Phelps, Thomas R.
xPhelps, Thomas R.
Introduction to Criminal Justice. Goodyear.
Phelps, William C. see Phelps, Clyde William.
Phelps, William L. see Phelps, William Lyon.
Phelps, William Lyon, 1865-1943
xPhelps, William L.
Adventures & Confessions. Arno.
Some Makers of American Literature. Arno.
Some Makers of American Literature. Folcroft.
Twentieth Century Theatre: Observations on
the Contemporary English & American Stage.
Arno.
Phenix, Philip H. see Phenix, Philip Henry.
Phenix, Philip Henry, 1915
xPhenix, Philip H.
Education & the Common Good: A Moral
Philosophy of the Curriculum. Greenwood.
Realms of Meaning: A Philosophy of the
Curriculum for General Education. McGraw.
Phi Delta Kappa Symposium on Educational Research,
9th, Syracuse University, 1968.
xPhi Delta Kappa Symposium on Educational
Research - 9th.
Bayesian Statistics. Peacock Pubs.
Phibbs, Brendan.
xPhibbs, Brendan.
The Human Heart: A Guide to Heart Disease.
Mosby.
Phifer, Keith R.
xPhifer, Keith R.
Whole in One. Key Ray Pub.
Phifer, Kenneth G.
xPhifer, Kenneth G.
Tales of Human Frailty & the Gentleness of
God. John Knox.
Philadelphia Bureau of Municipal Research. see Bureau
of Municipal Research, Philadelphia.
Philadelphia Co., Grand Jury.
xSpecial Grand Jury, Commonwealth of
Pennsylvania.
Investigation of Vice, Crime & Law
Enforcement. Arno.
Philadelphia Library Co. see Philadelphia. Library
Company.
Philadelphia. Library Company.
xPhiladelphia Library Co.

American Song Sheets, Slip Ballads & Poetical
Broadsides, 1850-1870. Kraus Repr.
Philadelphia. Maritime Museum.
xPhiladelphia Maritime Museum.
George Robert Bonfield: Philadelphia Marine
Painter, 1805 to 1898. Phila Maritime Mus.
Philadelphia. Mayor.
xPhiladelphia Office of Mayor.
Record of Indentures (1771-1773): Excerpted
from the Pennsylvania-German Society
Proceedings and Addresses 16. Genealog
Pub.
Philadelphia Museum of Art. see Philadelphia Museum of
Arts.
Philadelphia Museum of Arts.
xPhiladelphia Museum of Art.
The Second Empire, Eighteen Fifty-Two to
Eighteen Seventy: Art in France Under
Napoleon III. Wayne St U Pr.
Philadelphia Office of Mayor. see Philadelphia. Mayor.
Philadelphia Suburban School Study Council. Group A.
xPhiladelphia Suburban School Study Council
Group A.
Improving Programs for the Gifted. Interstate.
Improving Today's Curriculum for Tomorrow's
Challenges. Interstate.
Philadelphia Suburban School Study Council. Group B.
xPhiladelphia Suburban School Study Council
Group B.
Educated Child. Interstate.
Junior High School Years. Interstate.
Southeast Asia & the Soviet Union. Interstate.
Study of World Cultures in Secondary Schools.
Interstate.
Philbrick, Helen. see Philbrick, Helen Louise Porter.
Philbrick, Helen Louise Porter.
xPhilbrick, Helen.
The Bug Book: Harmless Insect Controls.
Garden Way Pub.
Philbrick, John. see Philbrick, John H.
Philbrick, John H.
xPhilbrick, John.
Gardening for Health & Nutrition. Har-Row.
Philbrook, Clem.
xPhilbrook, Clem.
Captured by the Abnakis. Hastings.
Ollie, the Backward Forward. Hastings.
Ollie's Team & the Alley Cats. Hastings.
Ollie's Team & the Baseball Computer.
Hastings.
Ollie's Team & the Football Computer.
Hastings.
Ollie's Team & the Million Dollar Mistake.
Hastings.
Ollie's Team Plays Biddy Baseball. Hastings.
Philby, H. St. J. see Philby, Harry St. John Bridger.
Philby, Harry S. see Philby, Harry St. John Bridger.
Philby, Harry St. John Bridger, 1885-
xPhilby, H. St. J.
Arabia of the Wahhabis. Biblio Dist.
xPhilby, Harry S.
Arabia of the Wahhabis. Arno.
xPhilby, J. B.
Arabian Highlands. Da Capo.
Arabian Oil Ventures. Mid East Inst.
Philby, J. B. see Philby, Harry St. John Bridger.
Philco Tech. Rep. Institute. see Philco Technical
Institute, Philadelphia.
Philco Technical Institute, Philadelphia.
xPhilco Tech. Rep. Institute.
Electronic Troubleshooting: A Self-Instructional
Programmed Manual. P-H.
Philcox, Norman W.
xPhilcox, Norman W.
An Introduction to Organized Crime. C C
Thomas.
Philip, A. E. see Philip, Alistair E.
Philip, Alex J. see Philip, Alexander John.
Philip, Alexander John.
xPhilip, Alex J.

Dickens Dictionary. B Franklin.
Dickens Dictionary. R West.
Philip, Alistair E.
xPhilip, A. E.
Social Work Research & the Analysis of Social
Data. Pergamon.
Philip, G. D. see Philip, George D. E.
Philip, George D. E.
xPhilip, G. D.
The Rise & Fall of the Peruvian Military
Radicals 1968-1976. Humanities.
Philipp, Elliot. see Philipp, Elliot Elias.
Philipp, Elliot Elias, 1915-
xPhilipp, Elliot.
Overcoming Childlessness: Its Causes & What
to Do About Them. Taplinger.
Philipp, Emanuel L. see Philipp, Emanuel Lorenz.
Philipp, Emanuel Lorenz.
xPhilipp, Emanuel L.
Political Reform in Wisconsin: A Historical
Review of the Subjects of Primary Election,
Taxation & Railway Regulation. State Hist
Soc Wis.
Philippakis, Andreas. see Philippakis, Andreas S.
Philippakis, Andreas S.
xPhilippakis, Andreas.
Structured COBOL. McGraw.
xPhilippakis, Andreas S.
Cobol for Business Applications. McGraw.
Information Systems Through COBOL.
McGraw.
Philippatos, George C.
xPhilippatos, George C.
Case Studies in Basic Finance. HR&W.
Philippi, Herbert.
xPhilippi, Herbert.
Stagecraft & Scene Design. HM.
Philippovich von Philippsberg, Eugen, 1858-1917
xPhilippovich Von Philippsberg, Eugen.
History of the Bank of England & Its Financial
Services to the State. Hyperion Conn.
Philips, C. M. see Philips, Cyril Henry.
Philips, Cyril Henry.
xPhilips, C. M.
ed. Partition of India: Policies & Perspectives
1935-1947. MIT Pr.
Philips, David.
xPhilips, David.
Crime & Authority in Victorian England: The
Black Country 1835-1860. Rowman.
Philips, Judson. see Philips, Judson Pentecost.
Philips, Judson Pentecost, 1903-
xPhilips, Judson.
Backlash. Dodd.
Death Is a Dirty Trick. Dodd.
Five Roads to Death. Dodd.
Philipson, David, 1862-1949
xPhilipson, David.
Old European Jewries. AMS Pr.
Reform Movement in Judaism. Ktav.
Philipson, Morris. see Philipson, Morris H.
Philipson, Morris H., 1926-
xPhilipson, Morris.
Everything Changes. Pantheon.
Philipson, Susan S. see Philipson, Susan Sacher.
Philipson, Susan Sacher.
xPhilipson, Susan S.
Lion for Niccolby. Pantheon.
Phillimore, W. P. see Phillimore, William Phillimore
Watts.
Phillimore, William P. see Phillimore, William Phillimore
Watts.
Phillimore, William Phillimore Watts, 1853-1913
xPhillimore, W. P.
How to Write the History of a Family: A
Guide for the Genealogist. Gale.
xPhillimore, William P.
Indexes to Irish Wills. Genealog Pub.
Phillip, P. Joseph.
xPhillip, P. Joseph.

Seasonal Patterns of Hospital Activity.
Lexington Bks.

Phillippo, Gene.
xPhillippo, Gene.
The Professional Guide to Real Estate
Development. Dow Jones-Irwin.

Phillipps, Evelyn M. *see* Phillipps, Evelyn March.
Phillips. *see* Phillips, Michael.
Phillips, A. A. *see* Phillips, Arthur Angell.
Phillips, Bernard. *see* Phillips, Bernard S.
Phillips, Betty L. *see* Phillips, Betty Lou.

Phillips Brooks House.
xHarvard University, Phillips Brooks House
Association.
Religion & Modern Life. Arno.

Phillips, C. A. *see* Phillips, Chester Arthur.
Phillips, C. G. *see* Phillips, Charles Garrett.
Phillips, Charles F. *see* Phillips, Charles Fox.
Phillips, Charles S. *see* Phillips, Charles Stanley.
Phillips, Clifton J. *see* Phillips, Clifton Jackson.

Phillips Collection, Washington, D.C.
xThePhillips Collection.
A Collection in the Making: Works from the
Phillips Collection. U of Chicago Pr.

Phillips, Evelyn March, d. 1915
xPhillipps, Evelyn M.
The Venetian School of Painting. Arno.

Phillips, Almarin.
xPhillips, Almarin.
ed. Promoting Competition in Regulated
Markets. Brookings.

Phillips, Ann Patricia.
xPhillips, Patricia.
Prehistory of Europe. Ind U Pr.

Phillips, Ann-Victoria.
xPhillips, Ann-Victoria.
The Complete Book of Roller Skating.
Workman Pub.

Phillips, Anthony.
xPhillips, Anthony.
God B. C.. Oxford U Pr.

Phillips, Arthur.
xPhillips, Arthur.
Marriage Laws in Africa. Oxford U Pr.
ed. Survey of African Marriage & Family Life.
AMS Pr.

Phillips, Arthur Angell.
xPhillips, A. A.
In Fealty to Apollo. Intl Schol Bk Serv.

Phillips, Bernard, 1915-1974
xPhillips, Bernard.
Religion & the Life of Man. CSA Pr.

Phillips, Bernard S.
xPhillips, Bernard.
Worlds of the Future: Exercises in the
Sociological Imagination. Merrill.

Phillips, Betty J.
xPhillips, Betty J.
Manual of Echocardiographic Techniques.
Saunders.

Phillips, Betty Lou.
xPhillips, Betty L.
The Picture Story of Nancy Lopez. Messner.
xPhillips, Betty Lou.
Earl Campbell, Houston Oiler Superstar.
McKay.

Phillips, Bob, 1940-
xPhillips, Bob.
The All American Joke Book. Harvest Hse.

Phillips, Celeste R., 1933-
xPhillips, Celeste R.
Family-Centered Maternity Newborn Care: A
Basic Text. Mosby.

Phillips, Charles Fox.
xPhillips, Charles F.
illus. The Hoity-Toity Mouse & Other Bayou
Tales. Doubleday.

Phillips, Charles Garrett.
xPhillips, C. G.

ed. Corticospinal Neurones: Their Role in
Movement. Acad Pr.

Phillips, Charles Stanley, 1883-
xPhillips, Charles S.
Church in France, 1789-1848. Russell.
Church in France, 1848-1907. Russell.

Phillips, Chester Arthur.
xPhillips, C. A.
Banking & the Business Cycle: A Study of the
Great Depression in the United States. Arno.

Phillips, Claude S.
xPhillips, Claude S.
Development of Nigerian Foreign Policy.
Northwestern U Pr.

Phillips, Clifton Jackson.
xPhillips, Clifton J.
Indiana in Transition: The Emergence of an
Industrial Commonwealth, 1880-1920. Ind U
Pr.

Phillips, D. C. *see* Phillips, Denis Charles.
Phillips, D. E. *see* Phillips, Eustace Dockray.
Phillips, D. Z. *see* Phillips, Dewi Zephaniah.
Phillips, Daniel E. *see* Phillips, Daniel Edward.

Phillips, Daniel Edward, 1865-
xPhillips, Daniel E.
Human Element in Literature. Kennikat.

Phillips, Dave.
xPhillips, Dave.
Graphic & Op-Art Mazes. Dover.

Phillips, David A. *see* Phillips, David Atlee.

Phillips, David Atlee.
xPhillips, David A.
The Great Texas Murder Trials: A Compelling
Account of the Sensational T. Cullen Davis
Case. Macmillan.

Phillips, David G. *see* Phillips, David Graham.

Phillips, David Gordon.
xPhillips, David G.
Federal-State Relations & the Control of
Atomic Energy. Arno.

Phillips, David Graham, 1867-1911
xPhillips, David G.
The Deluge. Irvington.
The Deluge. Johnson Repr.
The Deluge. Mss Info.
Light-Fingered Gentry. Johnson Repr.
Susan Lenox: Her Fall & Rise. Arden Lib.
Susan Lenox: Her Fall & Rise. Popular Lib.

Phillips, David M.
xPhillips, David M.
Spermiogenesis. Acad Pr.

Phillips, Debora.
xPhillips, Debora.
How to Fall Out of Love. HM.
How to Fall Out of Love. Popular Lib.

Phillips, Denis Charles.
xPhillips, D. C.
Holistic Thought in Social Science. Stanford U
Pr.

Phillips, Dewi Zephaniah.
xPhillips, D. Z.
Religion Without Explanation. Biblio Dist.

Phillips, E. Bryant. *see* Phillips, Elmo Bryant.
Phillips, E. L. *see* Phillips, Ewing Lakin.
Phillips, E. Lakin. *see* Phillips, Ewing Lakin.

Phillips, E. Lee.
xPhillips, E. Lee.
Prayers for Worship. Word Bks.

Phillips, Elmo Bryant.
xPhillips, E. Bryant.
ed. How to Manage Your Personal Finances: A
Short Course for Professionals. Wiley.

Phillips, Eustace Dockray.
xPhillips, D. E.
Aspects of Greek Medicine. St Martin.

Phillips, Ewing Lakin, 1915-
xPhillips, E. L.
Day to Day Anxiety Management. Krieger.
xPhillips, E. Lakin.

Counseling & Psychotherapy: A Behavioral
Approach. Wiley.
ed. The Social Skills Basis of Psychopathology:
Alternatives to Abnormal Psychology. Grune.

Phillips, F. C. *see* Phillips, Frank Coles.

Phillips, Frank Coles, 1902-
xPhillips, F. C.
An Introduction to Crystallography. Halsted
Pr.

Phillips, Fred, Sir, 1918-
xPhillips, Fred.
Freedom in the Caribbean: A Study in
Constitutional Change. Oceana.

Phillips, Fred M.
xPhillips, Fred M.
Desert People & Mountain Men: Exploration
of the Great Basin 1824-1865. Chalfant Pr.

Phillips, Gene D.
xPhillips, Gene D.
Evelyn Waugh's Officers, Gentlemen &
Rogues: The Fact Behind His Fiction. Nelson
Hall.
The Films of Tennessee Williams. Art Alliance.
Ken Russell. Twayne.
Stanley Kubrick: A Film Odyssey. Popular Lib.

Phillips, Gerald M.
xPhillips, Gerald M.
Communication & the Small Group. Bobbs.
Structuring Speech: A How-to-Do-It-Book
About Public Speaking. Bobbs.

Phillips, H. M. *see* Phillips, Herbert Moore.

Phillips, Helen Upson.
xPhillips, Helen V.
Essentials of Social Group Work Skill. Folcroft.

Phillips, Helen V. *see* Phillips, Helen Upson.

Phillips, Henry, 1838-1895
xPhillips, Henry.
Historical Sketches of the Paper Currency of
the American Colonies Prior to the Adoption
of the Federal Constitution. B Franklin.

Phillips, Henry A. *see* Phillips, Henry Albert.

Phillips, Henry Albert, 1880-1951
xPhillips, Henry A.
Art in Short Story Narration. R West.

Phillips, Herbert Moore, 1908-
xPhillips, H. M.
Educational Cooperation Between Developed &
Developing Countries. Praeger.
Planning Educational Assistance for the Second
Development Decade. Unipub.

Phillips, Herbert P.
xPhillips, Herbert P.
Thai Peasant Personality: The Patterning of
Interpersonal Behavior in the Village of Bang
Chan. U of Cal Pr.

Phillips, Hubert, 1891-
xPhillips, Hubert.
Profitable Poker. Arc Bks.
xPhillips, Hubert C.
My Best Puzzles in Logic & Reasoning. Dover.
My Best Puzzles in Mathematics. Dover.

Phillips, Hubert C. *see* Phillips, Hubert.

Phillips, James C.
xPhillips, James C.
Covalent Bonding in Crystals, Molecules &
Polymers. U of Chicago Pr.

Phillips, James E. *see* Phillips, James Emerson.

Phillips, James Emerson, 1912-
xPhillips, James E.
Images of a Queen: Mary Stuart in
Sixteenth-Century Literature. U of Cal Pr.

Phillips, James W. *see* Phillips, James Wendell.

Phillips, James Wendell, 1922-
xPhillips, James W.
Alaska-Yukon Place Names. U of Wash Pr.

Phillips, Jayne A. *see* Phillips, Jayne Anne.

Phillips, Jayne Anne, 1952-
xPhillips, Jayne A.

Chronicles of St. Tid. Arno.
A Deal with the Devil. Arno.
Human Boy. Arno.
Human Boy & the War. Arno.
Peacock House, & Other Mysteries. Arno.
The Torch, & Other Tales. Arno.
Philp, Howard L. see Philp, Howard Littleton.
Philp, Howard Littleton.
xPhilp, Howard L.
Freud & Religious Belief. Greenwood.
Philpott, A. R. see Philpott, Alexis Robert.
Philpott, Alexis R. see Philpott, Alexis Robert.
Philpott, Alexis Robert.
xPhilpott, A. R.
Dictionary of Puppetry. Plays.
ed. Eight Plays for Hand Puppets. Plays.
Let's Look at Puppets. A Whitman.
xPhilpott, Alexis R.
ed. Puppets & Therapy. Plays.
Philpott, Kent.
xPhilpott, Kent.
The Gay Theology. Logos.
If the Devil Wrote a Bible. Logos.
Phinney, Robert A.
xPhinney, Robert A.
ed. History of the Earth's Crust: A
Symposium. Princeton U Pr.
Phippen, George.
xPhippen, George.
The Life of a Cowboy. U of Ariz Pr.
Phipps, Antony A.
xPhipps, Antony A.
The Homebuying Guide. Abt Assoc.
Phipps, Charles T. see Phipps, Charles Thomas.
Phipps, Charles Thomas.
xPhipps, Charles T.
Browning's Clerical Characters. Humanities.
Phipps, Frances, 1924-
xPhipps, Frances.
Collector's Complete Dictionary of American
Antiques. Doubleday.
Phipps, Lloyd J. see Phipps, Lloyd James.
Phipps, Lloyd James.
xPhipps, Lloyd J.
Handbook on Agricultural Education in Public
Schools. Interstate.
Mechanics in Agriculture. Interstate.
Phipps, Ramsay W. see Phipps, Ramsay Weston.
Phipps, Ramsay Weston, 1838-1923
xPhipps, Ramsay W.
The Armies of the First French Republic & the
Rise of the Marshals of Napoleon I.
Greenwood.
Phipps, William E., 1930-
xPhipps, William E.
Influential Theologians on Wo-Man. U Pr of
Amer.
Phipps, Wilma J.
xPhipps, Wilma J.
Medical-Surgical Nursing: Concepts & Clinical
Practice. Mosby.
Phipson, Joan.
xPhipson, Joan.
The Cats. Atheneum.
Family Conspiracy. HarBraceJ.
The Family Conspiracy. HarBraceJ.
Fly Free. Atheneum.
Fly into Danger. Atheneum.
Horse with Eight Hands. Atheneum.
When the City Stopped. Atheneum.
Phister, Montgomery, 1926-
xPhister, Montgomery.
Data Processing Technology & Economics.
Digital Pr.
Data Processing Technology & Economics.
Santa Monica Pub.
Photiadis, John D.
xPhotiadis, John D.

ed. Change in Rural Appalachia: Implications
for Action Programs. U of Pa Pr.
Photographers' Gallery.
xThePhotographer's Gallery.
Reading Photographs: Understanding the
Aesthetics of Photography. Pantheon.
Photoplay Research Society.
xPhotoplay Research Society.
Opportunities in the Motion Picture Industry &
How to Qualify for Positions in Its Many
Branches. Arno.
Pi Sigma Alpha. Committee on Publications.
xPi Sigma Alpha Committee on Publications.
Major Problems in State Constitutional
Revision. Greenwood.
Pia, H. W. see Pia, Hans Werner.
Pia, Hans Werner.
xPia, H. W.
ed. Cerebral Angiomas: Advances in Diagnosis
& Therapy. Springer-Verlag.
ed. Spinal Angiomas: Advances in Diagnosis &
Therapy. Springer-Verlag.
Pia, Jack.
xPia, Jack.
Nazi Regalia. Ballantine.
Piaget, Jean, 1896-
xPiaget, Jean.
Child's Conception of Movement & Speed.
Basic.
The Child's Conception of Space. Humanities.
Child's Conception of Space. Norton.
Child's Conception of Time. Basic.
Genetic Epistemology. Columbia U Pr.
Genetic Epistemology. Norton.
The Grasp of Consciousness: Action &
Concept in the Young Child. Harvard U Pr.
Insights & Illusions of Philosophy. NAL.
Mechanisms of Perception. Basic.
Memory & Intelligence. Basic.
Origin of the Idea of Chance in Children.
Norton.
Psychology & Epistemology. Penguin.
Psychology of the Child. Basic.
Structuralism. Har-Row.
Success & Understanding. Harvard U Pr.
Understanding Causality. Norton.
Pialorsi, Frank.
xPialorsi, Frank P.
ed. Teaching the Bilingual: New Methods &
Old Traditions. U of Ariz Pr.
Pialorsi, Frank P. see Pialorsi, Frank.
Pian, Rulan C. see Pian, Rulan Chao.
Pian, Rulan Chao.
xPian, Rulan C.
Sonq Dynasty Musical Sources & Their
Interpretation. Harvard U Pr.
Syllabus for Mandarin Primer. Harvard U Pr.
Piana, Angelina La. see La Piana, Angelina.
Pianka, Eric R.
xPianka, Eric R.
Evolutionary Ecology. Har-Row.
Piano Teachers Congress Members. see Piano Teachers
Congress of New York.
Piano Teachers Congress of New York.
xPiano Teachers Congress Members.
Technical Control for the Modern Pianist:
Finger Exercises Used by Members of the
Piano Teachers Congress of N.Y., Inc..
Kenyon.
Piasecki, Jan Aleksander.
xPiasecki, Jan Aleksander.
The Origin of the Universe. Philos Lib.
Piazza, Paul, 1941-
xPiazza, Paul.
Christopher Isherwood: Myth & Anti-Myth.
Columbia U Pr.
Picano, Felice, 1944-
xPicano, Felice.

The Deformity Lover & Other Poems. Sea
Horse.
Eyes. Arbor Hse.
Eyes. Dell.
The Lure. Delacorte.
The Lure. Dell.
Picard, Barbara L. see Picard, Barbara Leonie.
Picard, Barbara Leonie.
xPicard, Barbara L.
The Odyssey of Homer. Oxford U Pr.
Picard, Jacques L., 1950-
xPicard, Jacques L.
Marketing Decisions for European Operations
in the U.S.. Univ Microfilms.
Picard, M. D. see Picard, M. Dane.
Picard, M. Dane, 1927-
xPicard, M. D.
Grit & Clay. Elsevier.
xPicard, M. Dane.
Sedimentary Structures of Ephemeral Streams.
Elsevier.
Picasso, Pablo, 1881-1973
xPicasso, Pablo.
Hunk of Skin. City Lights.
Piccard, Betty. see Piccard, Betty J.
Piccard, Betty J.
xPiccard, Betty.
An Introduction to Social Work: A Primer.
Dorsey.
Piccard, J. see Piccard, Jacques.
Piccard, Jacques.
xPiccard, J.
Sun Beneath the Sea. Intl Pubns Serv.
Piccigallo, Philip R., 1949-
xPiccigallo, Philip R.
The Japanese on Trial: Allied War Crimes
Operations in the East, 1945-1951. U of Tex
Pr.
Piccinni, Niccolo.
xPiccinni, Niccolo.
Catone in Utica. Garland Pub.
Piccione, Sandi, 1938-
xPiccione, Sandi.
Polar Sun. Slow Loris.
Pichon, Charles, 1893-1963
xPichon, Charles.
Vatican & Its Role in World Affairs.
Greenwood.
Pick, Albert.
xPick, Albert.
Standard Catalog of World Paper Money.
Krause Pubns.
Pick, Arnold, 1851-1924
xPick, Arnold.
Aphasia.. C C Thomas.
Pick, Christopher C.
xPick, Christopher C.
Oil Machines. Raintree Pubs.
Pick, Franz.
xPick, Franz.
Silver-How & Where to Buy & Hold It. Pick
Pub.
Pick, Joseph, 1908-1968
xPick, Joseph.
Autonomic Nervous System: Morphological,
Comparative, Clinical & Surgical Aspects.
Lippincott.
Pick, M. see Pick, Milos.
Pick, Milos.
xPick, M.
Theory of the Earth's Gravity Field. Elsevier.
Pick, Robert, 1898-
xPick, Robert.
The Last Days of Imperial Vienna. Dial.
Pickard, P. M.
xPickard, P. M.
The Activity of Children. Humanities.
Pickard, P. M. see Pickard, Phyllis M.
Pickard, Phyllis M.
xPickard, P. M.

If You Think Your Child Is Gifted. Allen
Unwin.
xPickard, Phyllis M.
If You Think Your Child Is Gifted. Shoe
String.
Pickard, S. see Pickard, Samuel Thomas.
Pickard, Samuel T. see Pickard, Samuel Thomas.
Pickard, Samuel Thomas, 1828-1915
xPickard, S.
Whittier-Land: A Handbook of North Essex.
Haskell.
xPickard, Samuel T.
Life & Letters of John Greenleaf Whittier.
Haskell.
Life & Letters of John Greenleaf Whittier. R
West.
Picken, Laurence.
xPicken, Lawrence.
Folk Musical Instruments of Turkey. Oxford U
Pr.
Picken, Lawrence. see Picken, Laurence.
Picken, Mary (Brooks).
xPicken, Mary B.
Needlepoint for Everyone. Har-Row.
Picken, Mary B. see Picken, Mary (Brooks).
Pickens, Richard.
xPickens, Richard.
How to Punt, Pass & Kick. Random.
Pickens, William, 1881-
xPickens, William.
American Aesop: Negro & Other Humor. AMS
Pr.
The Vengeance of the Gods & Three Other
Stories of Real American Color Line Life.
AMS Pr.
The Vengeance of the Gods; & Three Other
Stories of Real American Color Line Life.
Arno.
Picker, Fred.
xPicker, Fred.
The Fine Print. Amphoto.
Pickering, Ernest. see Pickering, Ernest D.
Pickering, Ernest D.
xPickering, Ernest.
Biblical Separation: The Struggle for a Pure
Church. Reg Baptist.
Pickering, F. P. see Pickering, Frederick Pickering.
Pickering, Frederick Pickering, 1909-
xPickering, F. P.
Literature & Art in the Middle Ages. U of
Miami Pr.
Pickering, H. S. see Pickering, Henry Sinclair.
Pickering, Henry Sinclair.
xPickering, H. S.
The Covalent Bond. Crane-Russak Co.
Pickering, James H.
xPickering, James H.
ed. The City in American Literature. Har-Row.
ed. The World Turned Upside Down: The
Prose and Poetry of the American
Revolution. Kennikat.
Pickering, James S. see Pickering, James Sayre.
Pickering, James Sayre.
xPickering, James S.
Asterisks: A Book of Astronomical Footnotes.
Dodd.
Captives of the Sun. Dodd.
Pickering, Jerry V., 1931-
xPickering, Jerry V.
Theatre: A History of the Art. West Pub.
Pickering, W. F. see Pickering, William F.
Pickering, W. S. see Pickering, W. S. F.
Pickering, W. S. F.
xPickering, W. S.
ed. Durkheim: Essays on Morals & Education.
Routledge & Kegan.
Pickering, Wilbur. see Pickering, Wilbur N.
Pickering, Wilbur N.
xPickering, Wilbur.

The Identity of the New Testament, Text.
Nelson.
xPickering, Wilbur N.
The Identity of the New Testament Text.
Nelson.
Pickering, William F.
xPickering, W. F.
Pollution Evaluation: The Quantitative Aspects.
Dekker.
Pickert, G. see Pickert, Gunter.
Pickert, Gunter, 1917-
xPickert, G.
Projektive Ebenen. Springer-Verlag.
Pickett, D. J. see Pickett, David J.
Pickett, David J.
xPickett, D. J.
Electrochemical Reactor Design. Elsevier.
Pickett, George E. see Pickett, George Edward.
Pickett, George Edward.
xPickett, George E.
Soldier of the South: General Pickett's War
Letters to His Wife. Arno.
Pickett, Hale C. see Pickett, Hale Clifford.
Pickett, Hale Clifford, 1892-
xPickett, Hale C.
An Analysis of Proofs & Solutions of Exercises
Used in Plane Geometry Tests. AMS Pr.
Pickett, John D.
xPickett, John D.
Expansion of Thought. Exposition.
Pickett, L. M. see Pickett, Leonard M.
Pickett, Leonard M.
xPickett, L. M.
Centre Game & Danish Gambit. Hippocrene
Bks.
Pickett, Robert S.
xPickett, Robert S.
House of Refuge: Origins of Juvenile Reform in
New York State, 1815-1857. Syracuse U Pr.
Pickett, William P. see Pickett, William Passmore.
Pickett, William Passmore, 1855-
xPickett, William P.
Negro Problem: Abraham Lincoln's Solution.
Negro U Pr.
Pickford, J. see Pickford, John Aston.
Pickford, John Aston.
xPickford, J.
Analysis of Water Surge. Gordon.
Pickle, Hal. see Pickle, Hal B.
Pickle, Hal B.
xPickle, Hal.
Introduction to Business. Goodyear.
Pickles, Dorothy M. see Pickles, Dorothy Maud.
Pickles, Dorothy Maud.
xPickles, Dorothy M.
The Fifth French Republic. Greenwood.
France Between the Republics. Russell.
Pickowicz, Paul.
xPickowicz, Paul.
Marxist Literary Thought & China: A
Conceptual Framework. IEAS Ctr Chinese
Stud.
Pico della Mirandola, Giovanni. see Pico Della
Mirandola, Giovanni Francesco.
Pico della Mirandola, Giovanni Francesco, 1470-1533
xPico della Mirandola, Giovanni.
On the Imagination. Greenwood.
Picon-Salas, Mariano, 1901-
xPicon-Salas, Mariano.
A Cultural History of Spanish America: From
Conquest to Independence. U of Cal Pr.
Picou, J. Steven.
xPicou, J. Steven.
Career Behavior of Special Groups. Merrill.
Piddington, J. H. see Piddington, Jack Hobart.
Piddington, Jack Hobart.
xPiddington, J. H.
Cosmic Electrodynamics. Krieger.
Pidgin, Charles F. see Pidgin, Charles Felton.

Pidgin, Charles Felton.
xPidgin, Charles F.
The Chronicles of Quincy Adams Sawyer,
Detective. Arno.
Piekalkiewicz, Jaroslaw.
xPiekalkiewicz, Jaroslaw.
Communist Local Government: A Study of
Poland. Ohio U Pr.
Public Opinion Polling in Czechoslovakia,
1968-1969: Results & Analysis of Surveys
Conducted During the Dubcek Era.
Irvington.
Pielou, E. C., 1924-
xPielou, E. C.
Biogeography. Wiley.
Mathematical Ecology. Wiley.
Population & Community Ecology: Principles
& Methods. Gordon.
xPielou, Evelyn C.
Ecological Diversity. Wiley.
Pielou, Evelyn C. see Pielou, E. C.
Pienaar, William J. see Pienaar, William J. B.
Pienaar, William J. B.
xPienaar, William J.
English Influences in Dutch Literature & Justus
Van Effen As Intermediary. Kennikat.
Piepenburg, Robert.
xPiepenburg, Robert.
Raku Pottery. Macmillan.
Pieper, Elizabeth.
xPieper, Elizabeth.
A School for Tommy. Childs World.
Pieper, Josef, 1904-
xPieper, Josef.
Leisure: The Basis of Culture. NAL.
Pieper, Thomas. see Pieper, Thomas I.
Pieper, Thomas I.
xPieper, Thomas.
Fort Laurens, 1778-1779: The Revolutionary
War in Ohio. Kent St U Pr.
Pierce, A. J. see Pierce, Anthony J.
Pierce, Anne E. see Pierce, Anne Elise.
Pierce, Anne Elise.
xPierce, Anne E.
Musicianship for the Elementary Teacher:
Theory & Skills Through Songs. McGraw.
Pierce, Anthony J.
xPierce, A. J.
Victorian & Edwardian Children from Old
Photographs. David & Charles.

Pierce, Barbara B.
xPierce, Barbara B.
The Design of Poetry. Pendulum Pr.

Pierce, Barbara H. see Pierce, Barbara Hanson.

Pierce, Barbara Hanson.
xPierce, Barbara H.
Junior Year in Britain: Where to Go-How to
Apply-What to Expect. Petersons Guides.
Pierce, Bessie L. see Pierce, Bessie Louise.
Pierce, Bessie Louise, 1890-
xPierce, Bessie L.
Civic Attitudes in American School Textbooks.
Arno.
Public Opinion & the Teaching of History in
the United States. Da Capo.
Pierce, Dale. see Pierce, Dale D.
Pierce, Dale D.
xPierce, Dale.
The Wind Blows Death. Grossmont Pr.
Pierce, David. see Pierce, David Alan.
Pierce, David Alan, 1936-
xPierce, David.
Learning Exercises in Astronomy. HR&W.
Pierce, Donald S.
xPierce, Donald S.
ed. The Total Care of Spinal Cord Injuries.
Little.
Pierce, Edward L. see Pierce, Edward Lillie.

Pierce, Edward Lillie, 1829-1897
xPierce, Edward L.
Memoir & Letters of Charles Sumner. Arno.
Pierce, Frederick E. *see* Pierce, Frederick Erastus.
Pierce, Frederick Erastus, 1878-1935
xPierce, Frederick E.
The Collaboration of Webster & Dekker. Folcroft.
The Collaboration of Webster & Dekker. Norwood Edns.
The Collaboration of Webster & Dekker. Shoe String.
Currents & Eddies in the English Romantic Generation. Arno.
Pierce, G. A.
xPierce, G. A.
Dickens Dictionary: A Key to the Plots-Characters in the Tales of Charles Dickens. Kraus Repr.
Pierce, G. Barry. *see* Pierce, Gordon Barry.
Pierce, Gordon Barry.
xPierce, G. Barry.
Cancer: A Problem of Developmental Biology. P-H.
Pierce, J. *see* Pierce, James Smith.
Pierce, Jack.
xPierce, Jack.
illus. The Freight Train Book. Carolrhoda Bks.
illus. The State Fair Book. Carolrhoda Bks.
Pierce, James S. *see* Pierce, James Smith.
Pierce, James Smith.
xPierce, J.
From Abacus to Zeus: A Handbook of Art History. P-H.
xPierce, James S.
Paul Klee & Primitive Art. Garland Pub.
Pierce, Joe E.
xPierce, Joe E.
A Theory of Language, Culture & Human Behavior. Hapi Pr.
Understanding the Middle East. C E Tuttle.
Pierce, John C.
xPierce, John C.
ed. The Electorate Reconsidered. Sage.
Pierce, John E. *see* Pierce, John Eugene.
Pierce, John Eugene.
xPierce, John E.
Development of Comprehensive Insurance for the Household. Irwin.
Pierce, John R. *see* Pierce, John Robinson.
Pierce, John Robinson, 1910-
xPierce, John R.
Almost All About Waves. MIT Pr.
Pierce, Jotham D.
xPierce, Jotham D.
Construction Contracts. PLI.
Pierce, Noel, 1907-
xPierce, Noel.
Praetorius Point. Coward.
Pierce, Paul.
xPierce, Paul P.
Take an Alternate Route. Sherbourne.
Pierce, Paul P. *see* Pierce, Paul.
Pierce, Phil E., 1912-
xPierce, Philip E.
ed. Pungent Prayers. Abingdon.
Pierce, Philip E. *see* Pierce, Phil E.
Pierce, R. C.
xPierce, R. C.
Operational Mathematics for Business. Wadsworth Pub.
Pierce, R. S. *see* Pierce, Richard S.
Pierce, Rice A. *see* Pierce, Rice Alexander.
Pierce, Rice Alexander, 1916-
xPierce, Rice A.
Leading Dynamic Bible Study. Religious Activ.
Pierce, Richard.
xPierce, Richard.

The Other Side of Hate. Manor Bks.
Pierce, Richard S.
xPierce, R. S.
Compact Zero-Dimensional Metric Spaces of Finite Type. Am Math.
Pierce, Robert, 1915-
xPierce, Robert.
Look & Laugh. Western Pub.

Pierce, Robert N.
xPierce, Robert N.
Keeping the Flame: Media & Government in Latin America. Hastings.
Pierce, Roy.
xPierce, Roy.
Contemporary French Political Thought. Oxford U Pr.
French Politics & Political Institutions. Har-Row.
Pierce, W. C. *see* Pierce, Willis Conway.
Pierce, W. H.
xPierce, W. H.
Thirteen Years of Travel & Exploration in Alaska: 1877-1889. Alaska Northwest.
Pierce, Walter D.
xPierce, Walter D.
Objectives & Methods for Secondary Teaching. P-H.
Pierce, William.
xPierce, William.
Historical Introduction to the Marprelate Tracts: A Chapter in the Evolution of Religious & Civil Liberty in England. B Franklin.
Pierce, Willis Conway, 1895-
xPierce, W. C.
Quantitative Analysis. Wiley.
Piercy, Josephine K. *see* Piercy, Josephine Ketcham.
Piercy, Josephine Ketcham.
xPiercy, Josephine K.
Anne Bradstreet. Coll & U Pr.
Studies in Literary Types in Seventeenth Century America, 1607-1710. Shoe String.
Piercy, Marge.
xPiercy, Marge.
Going Down Fast. Trident.
The Last White Class: A Play About Neighborhood Terror. Crossing Pr.
The Twelve-Spoked Wheel Flashing. Knopf.
Pierik, Robert.
xPierik, Robert.
Archy's Dream World. Morrow.
Rookfleas in the Cellar. Westminster.
Pieris, Ralph.
xPieris, Ralph.
Asian Development Styles. South Asia Bks.
Piermattei, D L.
xPiermattei, D. L.
An Atlas of Surgical Approaches to the Bones of the Dog & Cat. Saunders.
Pierog, Sophie H.
xPierog, Sophie H.
Medical Care of the Sick Newborn. Mosby.
Pieron, Henri, 1881-1964
xPieron, Henri.
Thought & the Brain. Arno.
Pieroni, David. *see* Pieroni, David T.
Pieroni, David T.
xPieroni, David.
Physician Compensation. Aspen Systems.
Pierpont, John, 1785-1866
xPierpont, John.
Anti-Slavery Poems. Irvington.
Pierpont Morgan Library. *see* Pierpont Morgan Library, New York.
Pierpont Morgan Library, New York.
xPierpont Morgan Library.

British Watercolors, Seventeen Fifty to Eighteen Fifty. Pierpont Morgan.
Treasures from the Pierpont Morgan Library. Pierpont Morgan.
Pierquin, Bernard.
xPierquin, Bernard.
Brachytherapy. Green.
Pierre, Andrew J.
xPierre, Andrew J.
ed. Arms Transfers & American Foreign Policy. NYU Pr.
Pierre, Joseph H.
xPierre, Joseph H.
When Timber Stood Tall. Superior Pub.
Piers, Maria W.
xPiers, Maria W.
Infanticide. Norton.
ed. Play & Development: A Symposium. Norton.
Pierson, Don, 1944-
xPierson, Don.
Renaldo Nehemiah: The Bionic Hurdler. Childrens.
Pierson, Irene. *see* Pierson, Irene Dorothy.
Pierson, Irene Dorothy.
xPierson, Irene.
Campus Cues. Interstate.
Pierson, Jan.
xPierson, Jan.
Mystery of Five Finger Island. Tyndale.
Pierson, Richard N.
xPierson, Richard N.
ed. Quantitative Nuclear Cardiography. Wiley.
Pierson, Robert H.
xPierson, Robert H.
How to Become a Successful Christian Leader. Pacific Pr Pub Assn.
Pierson, Stanley, 1925-
xPierson, Stanley.
British Socialists: The Journey from Fantasy to Politics. Harvard U Pr.
Marxism & the Origins of British Socialism: The Struggle for a New Consciousness. Cornell U Pr.
Pierson, Welcome D.
xPierson, Welcome D.
Defense Attorney & Basic Defense Tactics. Michie.
Pietermaritzburg - University Of Natal - Department Of Economics. *see* Pietermaritzburg. University of Natal. Department of Economics.
Pietermaritzburg. University of Natal. Department of Economics.
xPietermaritzburg - University Of Natal - Department Of Economics.
Durban Housing Survey: A Study of Housing in a Multi-Racial Community. Negro U Pr.
Pietermaritzburg. University of Natal. Department of Sociology and Social Work.
xPietermaritzburg-University of Natal-Department of Sociology & Social Work.
Small Towns of Natal, a Socioeconomic Sample Survey. Negro U Pr.
Pietermaritzburg-University of Natal-Department of Sociology & Social Work. *see* Pietermaritzburg. University of Natal. Department of Sociology and Social Work.
Pieters, A. *see* Pieters, Albertus.
Pieters, Albertus, 1869-
xPieters, A.
Can We Trust Bible History. Rose Pub MI.
Pieterse, Cosmo.
xPieterse, Cosmo.
ed. Protest & Conflict in African Literature. Holmes & Meier.
Pietrasinski, Z. *see* Pietrasinski, Zbigniew.
Pietrasinski, Zbigniew.
xPietrasinski, Z.

The Art of Learning. Pergamon.
The Psychology of Efficient Thinking.
Pergamon.

Pietri, Pedro, 1944-
xPietri, Pedro.
Puerto Rican Obituary. Monthly Rev.

Pietrkiewicz, Jerzy.
xPietrkiewicz, Jerzy.
Compiled by Five Centuries of Polish Poetry,
1450-1970. Greenwood.

Pietro, Anthony San. *see* San Pietro, Anthony.

Pietrofesa, John J.
xPietrofesa, John J.
Authentic Counselor. Rand.
Career Development: Theory & Research.
Grune.
Counseling: Theory, Research & Practice.
Rand.

Pietrzyk, Donald J.
xPietrzyk, Donald J.
Analytical Chemistry. Acad Pr.

Pietsch, A. *see* Pietsch, Albrecht.

Pietsch, Albrecht.
xPietsch, A.
Operator Ideals. Elsevier.

Pietsch, William V.
xPietsch, William V.
Human Be-Ing: How to Have a Creative
Relationship Instead of a Power Struggle.
Lawrence Hill.
Human Be-Ing: How to Have a Creative
Relationship Instead of a Power Struggle.
NAL.

Pietschmann, H. *see* Pietschmann, Herbert.

Pietschmann, Herbert, 1936-
xPietschmann, H.
Formulae & Results in Weak Interactions.
Springer-Verlag.

Piggott, Derek.
xPiggott, Derek.
Understanding Gliding: The Principles of
Soaring Flight. B&N.

Piggott, F. T. *see* Piggott, Francis Taylor.

Piggott, Francis Taylor.
xPiggott, F. T.
The Music & Musical Instruments of Japan. Da
Capo.

Piggott, Stuart.
xPiggott, Stuart.
Antiquity Depicted: Aspects of Archaeological
Illustration. Thames Hudson.
ed. Approach to Archaeology. McGraw.

Pigman, W. *see* Pigman, William Ward.

Pigman, William Ward.
xPigman, W.
Carbohydrates: Chemistry & Biochemistry.
Acad Pr.

Pignani, Tullio J.
xPignani, Tullio J.
Modern Analytic Geometry. Heath.

Pignatti, Terisio, 1920-
xPignatti, Terisio.
Canaletto. Barron.
The Golden Century of Venetian Painting.
Braziller.

Pigors, Paul. *see* Pigors, Paul John William.

Pigors, Paul John William.
xPigors, Paul.
The Pigors Incident Process of Case Study.
Educ Tech Pubns.

Pigou, Arthur C. *see* Pigou, Arthur Cecil.

Pigou, Arthur Cecil, 1877-1959
xPigou, Arthur C.

Economics in Practice: Six Lectures on Current
Issues. Hyperion Conn.
Employment & Equilibrium: A Theoretical
Discussion. Greenwood.
Employment & Equilibrium: A Theoretical
Discussion. Kelley.
Essays in Economics. Hyperion Conn.
Income: An Introduction to Economics.
Greenwood.
Industrial Fluctuations. Kelley.
Protective & Preferential Import Duties.
Kelley.
Riddle of the Tariff. Kelley.
Theory of Unemployment. Kelley.
The Veil of Money. Greenwood.
xPigou, Arthur Cecil.
Industrial Fluctuations. Biblio Dist.
Protective & Preferential Import Duties. Biblio
Dist.
Theory of Unemployment. Biblio Dist.

Pigozzi, Jean C.
xPigozzi, Jean C.
Pigozzi's Journal of the Seventies. Doubleday.

Pike, D. *see* Pike, Douglas.

Pike, Dag.
xPike, Dag.
Power Boats in Rough Seas. Scribner.

Pike, Diane K. *see* Pike, Diane Kennedy.

Pike, Diane Kennedy.
xPike, Diane K.
Channeling Love Energy. L P Pubns.
Cosmic Unfoldment: The Individualizing
Process As Mirrored in the Life of Jesus. L P
Pubns.

Pike, Douglas.
xPike, D.
Australia: The Quiet Continent. Cambridge U
Pr.
xPike, Douglas.
Paradise of Dissent: South Australia
1829-1857. Intl Schol Bk Serv.

Pike, Douglas. *see* Pike, Douglas Eugene.

Pike, Douglas Eugene, 1924-
xPike, Douglas.
History of Vietnamese Communism 1925-1976.
Hoover Inst Pr.

Pike, E. Royston. *see* Pike, Edgar Royston.

Pike, Earl A.
xPike, Earl A.
Protection Against Bombs & Incendiaries: For
Business, Industrial & Educational
Institutions. C C Thomas.

Pike, Edgar Royston, 1896-
xPike, E. Royston.
Human Documents of the Lloyd George Era.
St Martin.
Political Parties & Policies: A Popular
Explanation of the Principles of the Chief
Political Parties & a Guide to Understanding
of Current Politics. Greenwood.
xPike, Royston E.
ed. Human Documents of Adam Smith's Time.
Allen Unwin.
Human Documents of the Lloyd George Era.
Allen Unwin.

Pike, Fredrick B.
xPike, Fredrick B.
ed. Freedom & Reform in Latin America. U of
Notre Dame Pr.
Hispanismo, 1898-1936: Spanish Conservatives
& Liberals & Their Relations with Spanish
America. U of Notre Dame Pr.

Pike, Joseph B. *see* Pike, Joseph Brown.

Pike, Joseph Brown, 1866-
xPike, Joseph B.
Classical Studies & Sketches. Arno.

Pike, K. L. *see* Pike, Kenneth Lee.

Pike, Kenneth L. *see* Pike, Kenneth Lee.

Pike, Kenneth Lee.
xPike, K. L.

Grammatical Analysis. Summer Inst Ling.
xPike, Kenneth L.
The Intonation of American English.
Greenwood.
Tagmemic & Matrix Linguistics Applied to
Selected African Languages. Summer Inst
Ling.

Pike, Louise.
xPike, Louise.
Southern Echoes. Arno.

Pike, Nelson.
xPike, Nelson.
God & Timelessness. Schocken.

Pike, Nicholas. *see* Pike, Nicolas.

Pike, Nicolas, U.S. Consul, Port Louis, Mauritius.
xPike, Nicholas.
Sub-Tropical Rambles in the Land of the
Aphanapteryx: Personal Experiences,
Adventures, & Wanderings in & Around the
Island of Mauritus. Arno.

Pike, Robert E. *see* Pike, Robert Everding.

Pike, Robert Everding.
xPike, Robert E.
Tall Trees, Tough Men. Norton.

Pike, Royston E. *see* Pike, Edgar Royston.

Pike, Ruth, 1931-
xPike, Ruth.
Aristocrats & Traders: Sevillian Society in the
Sixteenth Century. Cornell U Pr.

Pilat, Oliver. *see* Pilat, Oliver Ramsay.

Pilat, Oliver Ramsay, 1903-
xPilat, Oliver.
Pegler, Angry Man of the Press. Greenwood.

Pilbeam, David. *see* Pilbeam, David R.

Pilbeam, David R.
xPilbeam, David.
The Ascent of Man: An Introduction to
Human Evolution. Macmillan.

Pilbrow, Richard.
xPilbrow, Richard.
Stage Lighting. Drama Bk.

Pilcher, R. *see* Pilcher, Roy.

Pilcher, Rosamunde.
xPilcher, Rosamunde.
Another View. St Martin.
Day of the Storm. Ballantine.
The Day of the Storm. St Martin.
Under Gemini. Ballantine.
Under Gemini. St Martin.

Pilcher, Roy.
xPilcher, R.
Appraisal & Control of Project Costs. McGraw.

Pile, John.
xPile, John.
ed. Drawings of Architectural Interiors.
Watson-Guptill.

Pile, John. *see* Pile, John F.

Pile, John F.
xPile, John.
Open Office Planning: A Handbook for Interior
Designers & Architects. Watson-Guptill.
xPile, John F.
Design: Purpose, Form, & Meaning. Norton.
Design: Purpose, Form & Meaning. U of Mass
Pr.
Modern Furniture. Wiley.

Pile, Stephen.
xPile, Stephen.
The Incomplete Book of Failures: The Official
Handbook of the Not-Terribly-Good Club of
Great Britain. Dutton.

Pile, William, Sir, 1919-
xPile, William.
The Department of Education & Science. Allen
Unwin.

Pilisuk, Marc.
xPilisuk, Marc.
ed. How We Lost the War on Poverty.
Transaction Bks.

Pilkey, W. D. *see* Pilkey, Walter D.

Pilkey, Walter D.
xPilkey, W. D.
ed. System Identification of Vibrating Structures: Mathematical Models from Test Data. ASME.

xPilkey, Walter D.
Modern Formulas for Statics & Dynamics: A Stress & Strain Approach. McGraw.

Pilkington, William T.
xPilkington, William T.
ed. Western Movies. U of NM Pr.

Pillai, C. A. Joachim.
xPillai, C. Joachim.
Early Missionary Preaching: A Study of Luke's Report in Acts 13. Exposition.
xPillai, Joachim.
The Apostolic Interpretation of History: A Commentary on Acts 13: 16-41. Exposition.

Pillai, C. Joachim. *see* Pillai, C. A. Joachim.
Pillai, Joachim. *see* Pillai, C. A. Joachim.

Pillai, K. C.
xPillai, K. C.
Light Through an Eastern Window. Speller.

Pillin, William.
xPillin, William.
Pavanne for a Fading Memory. Swallow.

Pilling, Arnold R.
xPilling, Arnold R.
Aborigine Culture History: A Survey of Publications 1954-1957. Wayne St U Pr.

Pilling, Doria.
xPilling, Doria.
Controversial Issues in Child Development. Schocken.

Pilling, M. J.
xPilling, M. J.
Reaction Kinetics. Oxford U Pr.

Pillsbury. *see* Pillsbury Company.

Pillsbury Company.
xPillsbury.
Breads Cook Book. S&S.
Pillsbury Bake-Offs: Cake & Frosting Cook Books. S&S.
Pillsbury Bake-Offs: Cookie Book. S&S.
Pillsbury Bake-Offs: Dessert Cookbook. S&S.
Pillsbury Bake-Offs: Main Dish Cookbook. S&S.
Pillsbury Entertainment Guide. S&S.
Pillsbury Slim & Sensible Cook Book. S&S.

Pillsbury, Donald M. *see* Pillsbury, Donald Marion.

Pillsbury, Donald Marion.
xPillsbury, Donald M.
A Manual of Dermatology. Saunders.

Pillsbury, Parker, 1809-1898
xPillsbury, Parker.
Acts of the Anti-Slavery Apostles. Arno.
Acts of the Anti-Slavery Apostles. Negro U Pr.

Pillsbury, W. *see* Pillsbury, Walter Bowers.
Pillsbury, Walter B. *see* Pillsbury, Walter Bowers.

Pillsbury, Walter Bowers, 1872-1960
xPillsbury, W.
The Psychology of Language. R West.
xPillsbury, Walter B.
Attention. Arno.

Pilon, A. Barbara.
xPilon, A. Barbara.
Teaching Language Arts Creatively in the Elementary Grades. Wiley.

Pilon, Juliana G. *see* Pilon, Juliana Geran.

Pilon, Juliana Geran, 1947-
xPilon, Juliana G.
Notes from the Other Side of Night. Regnery-Gateway.

Pilpel, Robert H.
xPilpel, Robert H.

To the Honor of the Fleet. Atheneum.

Pilz, G. *see* Pilz, Gunter.

Pilz, Gunter.
xPilz, G.
Near Rings: The Theory & Its Application. Elsevier.

Pilzer, Jay, 1946-
xPilzer, Jay.
Anti-Semitism & Jewish Nationalism. Donning Co.

Pim, Alan. *see* Pim, Alan William.

Pim, Alan William, Sir, 1871-1958
xPim, Alan.
Financial & Economic History of the African Tropical Territories. Argosy.

Pimbley, George H.
xPimbley, George H.
Eigenfunction Branches of Nonlinear Operators & Their Bifurcations. Springer-Verlag.

Pimentel, David.
xPimentel, David.
Food, Energy & Society. Halsted Pr.
ed. World Food, Pest Losses & the Environment. Westview.

Pimentel, George C.
xPimentel, George C.
Chemical Bonding Clarified Through Quantum Mechanics. Holden-Day.
Understanding Chemical Thermodynamics. Holden-Day.
Understanding Chemistry. Holden-Day.

Pimsleur, Paul.
xPimsleur, Paul.
C'est la Vie. HarBraceJ.
C'est la Vie: Lectures d'aujourd'hui. HarBraceJ.

Pinar, William.
xPinar, William.
ed. Curriculum Theorizing: The Reconceptualists. McCutchan.

Pinchas, S. *see* Pinchas, Shraga.

Pinchas, Shraga.
xPinchas, S.
Infrared Spectra of Labelled Compounds. Acad Pr.

Pinchbeck, Ivy, 1898-
xPinchbeck, Ivy.
Women Workers & the Industrial Revolution, 1750-1850. Biblio Dist.
Women Workers & the Industrial Revolution, 1750-1850. Kelley.

Pinchot, Amos R. *see* Pinchot, Amos Richard Eno.

Pinchot, Amos Richard Eno.
xPinchot, Amos R.
History of the Progressive Party, 1912-1916. Greenwood.

Pinchot, Ann.
xPinchot, Ann.
Certain Rich Girls. Arbor Hse.
Certain Rich Girls. Bantam.

Pinchot, Gifford, 1865-1946
xPinchot, Gifford.
The Fight for Conservation. U of Wash Pr.

Pinckney, Cathey.
xPinckney, Cathey.
The Encyclopedia of Medical Tests. PB.

Pinckney, Elise. *see* Pinckney, Eliza (Lucas).

Pinckney, Eliza (Lucas).
xPinckney, Elise.
ed. Letterbook of Eliza Lucas Pinckney, 1739-1762. U of NC Pr.

Pincoffs, Edmund. *see* Pincoffs, Edmund L.

Pincoffs, Edmund L.
xPincoffs, Edmund.
Rationale of Legal Punishment. Humanities.

Pincus, Cynthia S. *see* Pincus, Cynthia Sterling.

Pincus, Cynthia Sterling.
xPincus, Cynthia S.
Double Duties: An Action Plan for the Working Wife. Chatham Sq.

Pincus, Edward.
xPincus, Edward.
Guide to Film Making. NAL.

Pincus, Gregory, 1903-
xPincus, Gregory.
ed. Control of Fertility. Acad Pr.

Pincus, J. J. *see* Pincus, Jonathan J.

Pincus, Jonathan J., 1939-
xPincus, J. J.
Pressure Groups & Politics in Antebellum Tariffs. Columbia U Pr.

Pincus, Lee.
xPincus, Lee.
The Songwriters' Success Manual. Music Pr.

Pincus, Leo I.
xPincus, Leo I.
Practical Boiler Water Treatment: Including Air Conditioning Systems. McGraw.

Pincus, Lily.
xPincus, Lily.
Secrets in the Family. Har-Row.
Secrets in the Family. Pantheon.

Pincus, Stanley.
xPincus, Stanley.
Respiratory Therapist Manual. Bobbs.

Pinder, G. F. *see* Pinder, George Francis.

Pinder, George Francis.
xPinder, G. F.
Finite Element Simulation in Surface & Subsurface Hydrology. Acad Pr.

Pinder-Wilson, R. *see* Pinder-Wilson, Ralph H.

Pinder-Wilson, Ralph H.
xPinder-Wilson, R.
ed. Paintings from Islamic Lands. U of SC Pr.

Pindyck, Robert S.
xPindyck, Robert S.
Econometric Models & Economic Forecasts. McGraw.
The Structure of World Energy Demand. MIT Pr.

Pine, L. G. *see* Pine, Leslie Gilbert.

Pine, Leslie Gilbert.
xPine, L. G.
Princes of Wales. C E Tuttle.
Story of Titles. C E Tuttle.

Pine, Mary A.
xPine, Mary A.
Informal Education, Self-Concept, & Reading Achievement: A Research Study. R & E Res Assoc.

Pine, Stanley H.
xPine, Stanley H.
Organic Chemistry. McGraw.

Pine, Tillie S.
xPine, Tillie S.
Africans Knew. McGraw.
The Arabs Knew. McGraw.
Energy All Around. McGraw.
Incas Knew. McGraw.

Pine, V. R. *see* Pine, Vanderlyn R.

Pine, Vanderlyn R.
xPine, V. R.
Caretaker of the Dead: The American Funeral Director. Halsted Pr.
xPine, Vanderlyn R.
ed. Acute Grief & the Funeral. C C Thomas.
Introduction to Social Statistics. P-H.

Pinegar, Ed J.
xPinegar, Ed J.
ed. Fatherhood. Deseret Bk.

Pines, Maya.
xPines, Maya.

The Brain Changers: Scientists & the New
Mind Control. HarBraceJ.
Inside the Cell: The New Frontier of Medical
Science. Enslow Pubs.
Revolution in Learning: The Years from Birth
to Six. Har-Row.

Pines, Philip A.
xPines, Philip A.
The Complete Book of Harness Racing. Arco.

Pinet, F. see Pinet, Francois.

Pinet, Francois, 1927-
xPinet, F.
Selective Bronchography & Bronchial Brushing.
Springer-Verlag.

Pinger, W. R. see Pinger, Wilhelm Robert Richard.

Pinger, Wilhelm Robert Richard, 1873-1917
xPinger, W. R.
Laurence Sterne & Goethe. Folcroft.

Pingry, Jack R.
xPingry, Jack R.
ed. Industrial Marketing: A Selected &
Annotated Bibliography. Am Mktg.

Pinion, F. B.
xPinion, F. B.
A Bronte Companion: Literary Assessment,
Background & Reference. B&N.
A D. H. Lawrence Companion: Life, Thought
& Works. B&N.

Pink, Marilyn.
xPink, Marilyn.
How to Catalogue Works of Art: A Guide for
the Private Collector. Mus Sys.

Pinkard, Bruce, 1932-
xPinkard, Bruce.
Creative Techniques in Studio Photography.
Lippincott.

Pinker, Robert.
xPinker, Robert.
The Idea of Welfare. Heinemann Ed.

Pinkerton, Allan, 1819-1884
xPinkerton, Allan.
Criminal Reminiscences & Detective Sketches.
Arno.
Criminal Reminiscences & Detective Sketches.
Mss Info.
Criminal Reminiscences & Detective Sketches.
Somerset Pub.
The Expressman & the Detective. Arno.
Professional Thieves & the Detective. AMS Pr.
Strikers, Communists, Tramps & Detectives.
Arno.

Pinkerton, Kathrene. see Pinkerton, Kathrene Sutherland
Gedney.

Pinkerton, Kathrene Sutherland Gedney, 1887-1967
xPinkerton, Kathrene.
A Home in the Wilds. Taplinger.

Pinkerton, Todd, 1917-
xPinkerton, Todd.
Breaking Communication Barriers with
Roleplay. John Knox.

Pinkley, Virgil.
xPinkley, Virgil.
Eisenhower Declassified. Revell.

Pinkney, D. H. see Pinkney, David H.

Pinkney, David H.
xPinkney, D. H.
The French Revolution of 1830. Princeton U
Pr.

Pinkney, William, Bp, 1810-1883
xPinkney, William.
Life of William Pinkney. Da Capo.

Pinkstaff, Marlene A. see Pinkstaff, Marlene Arthur.

Pinkstaff, Marlene Arthur.
xPinkstaff, Marlene A.

jt. auth. Personal Skill Building for the
Emerging Manager. CBI Pub.
Women at Work: Overcoming the Obstacles.
A-W.

Pinkster, H.
xPinkster, H.
On Latin Adverbs. Elsevier.

Pinkwater, D. Manus.
xPinkwater, D. Manus.
Lizard Music. Dell.
Lizard Music. Dodd.

Pinkwater, D. Manus. see Pinkwater, Daniel Manus.

Pinkwater, Daniel M. see Pinkwater, Daniel Manus.

Pinkwater, Daniel Manus, 1941-
xPinkwater, D. Manus.
illus. Fat Men from Space. Dell.
The Hoboken Chicken Emergency. P-H.
The Hoboken Chicken Emergency. Schol Bk
Serv.
xPinkwater, Daniel M.
Alan Mendelsohn, the Boy from Mars. Dutton.
Fat Men from Space. Dodd.
The Last Guru. Bantam.
The Last Guru. Dodd.
illus. Pickle Creature. Schol Bk Serv.
Return of the Moose. Dodd.
The Wuggie Norple Story. Schol Bk Serv.

Pinkwater, Manus.
xPinkwater, Manus.
Around Fred's Bed. P-H.

Pinney, Edward L.
xPinney, Edward L.
ed. Comparative Politics and Political Theory:
Essays Written in Honor of Charles
Baskervill Robson. U of NC Pr.

Pinney, Edward L. see Pinney, Edward Lowell.

Pinney, Edward Lowell, 1925-
xPinney, Edward L.
First Group Psychotherapy Book. C C Thomas.

Pinnock, Clark H., 1937-
xPinnock, Clark H.
Defense of Biblical Infallibility. Presby &
Reformed.
Grace Unlimited. Bethany Fell.

Pinsker, Harold. see Pinsker, Harold M.

Pinsker, Harold M.
xPinsker, Harold.
ed. Information Processing in the Nervous
System. Raven.

Pinsker, Sanford.
xPinsker, Sanford.
The Comedy That "Hoits": An Essay on the
Fiction of Philip Roth. U of Mo Pr.
Still Life & Other Poems. Greenfld Rev Pr.

Pinsky, Robert.
xPinsky, Robert.
An Explanation of America. Princeton U Pr.

Pinson. see Pinson, William M.

Pinson, William M.
xPinson.
The Local Church in Ministry. Broadman.
xPinson, William M.
Applying the Gospel: Suggestions for Christian
Social Action in the Local Church.
Broadman.
Compiled by An Approach to Christian Ethics:
The Life Contribution, & Thought of T. B.
Maston. Broadman.
Families with Purpose. Broadman.

Pinson, William W. see Pinson, William Washington.

Pinson, William Washington, 1854-1930
xPinson, William W.
In White & Black: A Story. Arno.

Pinta, Maurice.
xPinta, Maurice.

ed. Atomic Absorption Spectrometry. Halsted
Pr.
Modern Methods for Trace Element Analysis.
Ann Arbor Science.

Pintauro, Joseph.
xPintauro, Joseph.
Cold Hands. NAL.
Cold Hands. S&S.

Pintauro, N. D. see Pintauro, Nicholas.

Pintauro, Nicholas.
xPintauro, N. D.
Food Flavoring Processes. Noyes.
Food Packaging. Noyes.
Sweeteners & Enhancers. Noyes.

Pintel, Gerald.
xPintel, Gerald.
Retailing. P-H.

Pinter, Harold, 1930-
xPinter, Harold.
Betrayal. Grove.
Betrayal. Grove.
No Man's Land. Grove.
No Man's Land. Grove.

Pinto, Alexandre A. Serpa. see Serpa Pinto, Alexandre A.

Pinto, Roger.
xPinto, Roger.
Aspects De L'evolution Gouvernementale De
L'indochine Francaise. AMS Pr.

Pinto, V. de Sola. see Pinto, Vivian de Sola.

Pinto, Vivian de Sola, 1895-
xPinto, V. de Sola.
Enthusiast in Wit: Portrait of John Wilmot Earl
of Rochester, 1647-1680. U of Nebr Pr.

Pintoro, John.
xPintoro, John.
The Summoning. Avon.

Pinza, Ezio.
xPinza, Ezio.
Ezio Pinza: An Autobiography. Arno.

Pioneer Club, Birmingham, Ala.
xPioneers Club of Birmingham.
Early Days in Birmingham. Southern U Pr.

Pioneers Club of Birmingham. see Pioneer Club,
Birmingham, Ala.

Piotrkowski, Chaya S.
xPiotrkowski, Chaya S.
Work & the Family System: A Naturalistic
Study of Working-Class &
Lower-Middle-Class Families. Free Pr.

Piotrowska, Irena (Gebocka), 1904-
xPiotrowska, Irena G.
Art of Poland. Arno.

Piotrowska, Irena G. see Piotrowska, Irena (Gebocka).

Piotrowski, Roman, 1898-
xPiotrowski, Roman.
Cartels & Trusts: Their Origin & Historical
Development, from the Economic & Legal
Aspects. Porcupine Pr.

Piotrowski, Zygmunt A. see Piotrowski, Zygmunt a L.

Piotrowski, Zygmunt a L.
xPiotrowski, Zygmunt A.
Perceptanalytic Executive Scale: A Tool for the
Selection of Top Managers. Grune.

Pious, Richard M., 1944-
xPious, Richard M.
The American Presidency. Basic.
Civil Rights & Liberties in the 1970's.
Random.

Piozzi, Hester. see Piozzi, Hester Lynch Salusbury
Thrale.

Piozzi, Hester Lynch Salusbury Thrale, 1741-1821
xPiozzi, Hester.
Autobiography, Letters, & Literary Remains of
Mrs. Piozzi (Thrale). AMS Pr.
xPiozzi, Hesther L.
Anecdotes of Samuel Johnson. Arno.

Piozzi, Hesther L. see Piozzi, Hester Lynch Salusbury
Thrale.

Pipa, Arshi, 1920-
xPipa, Arshi.

Montale & Dante. U of Minn Pr.
Pipard, Maurice.
  xPipard, Maurice.
    Games for a Rainy Day. Watts.
Pipe, Ann K. *see* Pipe, Ann Kimball.
Pipe, Ann Kimball.
  xPipe, Ann K.
    Reproducing Furniture in Miniature. Contemp
    Bks.
Pipe, Peter.
  xPipe, Peter.
    Objectives-Tool for Change. Pitman Learning.
    Practical Programming. Krieger.
Piper, C. B.
  xPiper, C. B.
    Introduction to Arithmetic. Philos Lib.
Piper, David.
  xPiper, David.
    The Companion Guide to London. Scribner.
    The Genius of British Painting. Morrow.
Piper, David W. *see* Piper, David Warren.
Piper, David Warren.
  xPiper, David W.
    The Changing University: A Report on the
    Staff Development in Universities Programme
    72-74. Humanities.
Piper, H. Beam.
  xPiper, H. Beam.
    Lord Kalvan of Otherwhen. Garland Pub.
    Space Viking. Ace Bks.
    Space Viking. Garland Pub.
Piper, H. W. *see* Piper, Herbert Walter.
Piper, Henry D. *see* Piper, Henry Dan.
Piper, Henry Dan.
  xPiper, Henry D.
    ed. Fitzgerald's the Great Gatsby: The Novel,
    the Critics, the Background. Scribner.
Piper, Herbert Walter, 1915-
  xPiper, H. W.
    Nature & the Supernatural in the Ancient
    Mariner. Folcroft.
Piper, James. *see* Piper, Jim.
Piper, Jim.
  xPiper, James.
    Personal Filmmaking. Reston.
Piper, Patricia L. *see* Piper, Patricia Luster.
Piper, Patricia Luster.
  xPiper, Patricia L.
    Manual on K F: The Library of Congress
    Classification Schedule for Law of the United
    States. Rothman.
Piper, Robert J.
  xPiper, Robert J.
    Opportunities in Architecture Today. Natl
    Textbk.
Piper, Roger.
  xPiper, Roger.
    Story of Computers. HarBraceJ.
Piper, Steven, d. 1970
  xPiper, Steven.
    The North Ships: The Life of a Trawlerman.
    David & Charles.
Piper, Terrence. *see* Piper, Terrence J.
Piper, Terrence J.
  xPiper, Terrence.
    Teacher Supervision Through Behavioral
    Objectives: An Operationally Described
    System. P H Brookes.
Piper, Watty.
  xPiper, Watty.
    ed. The Little Engine That Could. Platt.
    The Little Engine That Could. Platt.
    The Little Engine That Could. Schol Bk Serv.
Piper, William. *see* Piper, William Bowman.
Piper, William Bowman, 1927-
  xPiper, William.
    An Anthology of Heroic-Couplet Poetry. Univ
    Microfilms.
Pipes, L. A. *see* Pipes, Louis Albert.

Pipes, Louis Albert, 1910-
  xPipes, L. A.
    Applied Mathematics for Engineers &
    Physicists. McGraw.
Pipes, Richard.
  xPipes, Richard.
    ed. Soviet Strategy in Europe. Crane-Russak
    Co.
Pipes, Thomas V.
  xPipes, Thomas V.
    The Pipes Fitness Test & Prescription. J P
    Tarcher.
Pipkin, Charles W. *see* Pipkin, Charles Wooten.
Pipkin, Charles Wooten, 1899-1941
  xPipkin, Charles W.
    Duty of the Educated Mind. Kennikat.
Pipkin, J. J. *see* Pipkin, James Jefferson.
Pipkin, James Jefferson, 1861-
  xPipkin, J. J.
    The Story of a Rising Race. Arno.
Pipkin, John M. *see* Pipkin, John Moses.
Pipkin, John Moses.
  xPipkin, John M.
    Half-a-Love. Windy Row.
    Half After Love. Moore Pub Co.
Pippard, A. B.
  xPippard, A. B.
    The Dynamics of Conduction Electrons.
    Gordon.
  xPippard, Brian.
    The Physics of Vibration. Cambridge U Pr.
Pippard, Brian. *see* Pippard, A. B.
Pippin, Wilbur.
  xPippin, Wilbur.
    Catwise. Knopf.
Pipping, Ella.
  xPipping, Ella.
    Soldier of Fortune: The Story of a Nineteenth
    Century Adventurer. Gambit.
Pirages, Dennis.
  xPirages, Dennis.
    The New Context for International Relations:
    Global Ecopolitics. Duxbury Pr.
  xPirages, Dennis C.
    ed. The Sustainable Society: Implications for
    Limited Growth. Praeger.
Pirages, Dennis C. *see* Pirages, Dennis.
Piranesi, Giovanni B. *see* Piranesi, Giovanni Battista.
Piranesi, Giovanni Battista.
  xPiranesi, Giovanni B.
    Giovanni Battista Piranesi: Drawings in the
    Pierpont Morgan Library. Dover.
    The Prisons (Le Carceri): The Complete First
    & Second States. Dover.
Pirenne, Henri, 1862-1935
  xPirenne, Henri.
    Early Democracies in the Low Countries:
    Urban Society & Political Conflict in the
    Middle Ages & the Renaissance. Norton.
Pirenne, M. H. *see* Pirenne, Maurice Henri Leonard.
Pirenne, Maurice Henri Leonard.
  xPirenne, M. H.
    Optics, Painting & Photography. Cambridge U
    Pr.
Pires-Ferreira, Jane W.
  xPires-Ferreira, Jane W.
    Formative Mesoamerican Exchange Networks
    with Special Reference to the Valley of
    Oaxaca. U Mich Mus Anthro.
Pirie, N. W. *see* Pirie, Norman W.
Pirie, Norman W.
  xPirie, N. W.
    ed. Food Protein Sources. Cambridge U Pr.
    Leaf Protein & Other Aspects of Fodder
    Fractionation. Cambridge U Pr.
Pirone, Pascal P. *see* Pirone, Pascal Pompey.
Pirone, Pascal Pompey, 1907-
  xPirone, Pascal P.

Diseases & Pests of Ornamental Plants. Wiley.
Pirozzolo, Francis J.
  xPirozzolo, Francis J.
    The Neuropsychology of Developmental
    Reading Disorders. Praeger.
Pirson, S. J. *see* Pirson, Sylvain Joseph.
Pirson, Sylvain Joseph, 1905-
  xPirson, S. J.
    Geologic Well Log Analysis. Gulf Pub.
Pirt, S. J.
  xPirt, S. John.
    Principles of Microbe & Cell Cultivation.
    Halsted Pr.
Pirt, S. John. *see* Pirt, S. J.
Pisar, Samuel.
  xPisar, Samuel.
    Of Blood & Hope. Little.
Piscataqua Garden Club.
  xThePiscatagua Gardening Club.
    Compiled by Gardening from the Merrimack to
    the Kennebec: A Personal Approach to
    Growing Flowers, Herbs, Fruits & Vegetables.
    Heritage Bk.
Pisello, Daniel M.
  xPisello, Daniel M.
    Gravitation, Electromagnetism & Quantized
    Charge: The Einstein Insight. Ann Arbor
    Science.
Pisemskii, Aleksei F. *see* Pisemskii, Aleksei
    Feofilaktovich.
Pisemskii, Aleksei Feofilaktovich, 1820-1881
  xPisemskii, Aleksei F.
    One Thousand Souls. Greenwood.
    One Thousand Souls. Hyperion Conn.
    The Simpleton. Hyperion Conn.
Piserchia, Doris.
  xPiserchia, Doris.
    Earthchild. DAW Bks.
    Spaceling. DAW Bks.
Pisk, Litz.
  xPisk, Litz.
    The Actor & His Body. Theatre Arts.
Pistole, Jesse R.
  xPistole, Jesse R.
    Criminal Law for Peace Officers. Reston.
Piston, Walter, 1894-
  xPiston, Walter.
    Orchestration. Norton.
Pitavy, Francois.
  xPitavy, Francois.
    Faulkner's Light in August. Ind U Pr.
Pitcairne, Archibald.
  xPitcairne, Archibald.
    The Assembly. Purdue.
Pitcher, Evelyn G. *see* Pitcher, Evelyn Goodenough.
Pitcher, Evelyn Goodenough.
  xPitcher, Evelyn G.
    Helping Young Children Learn. Merrill.
Pitcher, George.
  xPitcher, George.
    Theory of Perception. Princeton U Pr.
Pitcher, H. J. *see* Pitcher, Harvey J.
Pitcher, Harvey J.
  xPitcher, H. J.
    Understanding the Russians. Intl Pubns Serv.
Pitcher, Seymour M. *see* Pitcher, Seymour Maitland.
Pitcher, Seymour Maitland.
  xPitcher, Seymour M.
    ed. Two Creative Traditions in English Poetry.
    Arno.
Pitchford, J. D.
  xPitchford, J. D.
    Applications of Control Theory to Economic
    Analysis. Elsevier.
Pitkin, Hanna F. *see* Pitkin, Hanna Fenichel.
Pitkin, Hanna Fenichel.
  xPitkin, Hanna F.
    The Concept of Representation. U of Cal Pr.
Pitkin, Thomas M.
  xPitkin, Thomas M.

The Captain Departs: Ulysses S. Grant's Last
Campaign. S Ill U Pr.
Grant the Soldier. Acropolis.
Pitman, E. J. *see* Pitman, Edwin J. G.
Pitman Editors. *see* Pitman, Firm, Publishers, New York.
Pitman, Edwin J. G.
xPitman, E. J.
Some Basic Theory for Statistical Inference.
Methuen Inc.
Pitman, Firm, Publishers, New York.
xPitman Editors.
Pitman Accelerated Speed Drill Book. Pitman
Learning.
Pitman, Frank W. *see* Pitman, Frank Wesley.
Pitman, Frank Wesley.
xPitman, Frank W.
Development of the British West Indies,
1700-1763. Shoe String.
Pitman, Walter G.
xPitman, Walter G.
The Baptists & Public Affairs in the Province
of Canada: 1840-1867. Arno.
Pitot, Henry C., 1930-
xPitot, Henry C.
Fundamentals of Oncology. Dekker.
Pitt, D. C. *see* Pitt, David C.
Pitt, David C.
xPitt, D. C.
Using Historical Sources in Anthropology &
Sociology. HR&W.
xPitt, David C.
ed. Development from Below: Anthropologists
& Development Situations. Beresford Bk
Serv.
Pitt, Leonard.
xPitt, Leonard.
California Controversies: Major Issues in the
History of the State. Scott F.
The Decline of the Californio: A Social
History of the Spanish-Speaking Californians,
1846-1890. U of Cal Pr.
Pitt, Valerie.
xPitt, Valerie.
A Closer Look at Ants. Watts.
Let's Find Out About Communications. Watts.
Let's Find Out About Manners. Watts.
Let's Find Out About Names. Watts.
Let's Find Out About Neighbors. Watts.
Let's Find Out About Streets. Watts.
Let's Find Out About the City. Watts.
Let's Find Out About the Community. Watts.
xPitt, Valerie H.
ed. The Penguin Dictionary of Physics.
Penguin.
Pitt, Valerie H. *see* Pitt, Valerie.
Pitt-Rivers, A. H. *see* Pitt-Rivers, Augustus Henry
Lane-Fox.
Pitt-Rivers, Augustus. *see* Pitt-Rivers, Augustus Henry
Lane-Fox.
Pitt-Rivers, Augustus H. *see* Pitt-Rivers, Augustus Henry
Lane-Fox.
Pitt-Rivers, Augustus Henry Lane-Fox, 1827-1900
xPitt-Rivers, A. H.
Antique Works of Art from Benin. Hacker.
xPitt-Rivers, Augustus.
Antique Works of Art from Benin. Dover.
xPitt-Rivers, Augustus H.
The Evolution of Culture, & Other Essays.
AMS Pr.
Pitt-Rivers, Julian. *see* Pitt-Rivers, Julian Alfred.
Pitt-Rivers, Julian Alfred.
xPitt-Rivers, Julian.
People of the Sierra. U of Chicago Pr.
Pitt-Watson, Ian, 1881-1955
xPitt-Watson, Ian.
Preaching: A Kind of Folly. Westminster.
Pittard, Kay.
xPittard, Kay.

Comparative Morphology of the Life Stages of
Cryptocellus Pelaezi (Arachnida, Ricinulei).
Tex Tech Pr.
Pittenger, Donald B.
xPittenger, Donald B.
Projecting State & Local Populations. Ballinger
Pub.
Pittenger, Norman. *see* Pittenger, William Norman.
Pittenger, Owen E. *see* Pittenger, Owen Ernest.
Pittenger, Owen Ernest.
xPittenger, Owen E.
Learning Theories in Educational Practice: An
Integration of Psychological Theory &
Educational Philosophy. Wiley.
Pittenger, Peggy J. *see* Pittenger, Peggy Jett.
Pittenger, Peggy Jett.
xPittenger, Peggy J.
The Back-Yard Foal. Arco.
The Back-Yard Horse. Arco.
Pittenger, W. Norman. *see* Pittenger, William Norman.
Pittenger, William N. *see* Pittenger, William Norman.
Pittenger, William Norman, 1905-
xPittenger, Norman.
After Death-Life in God. Seabury.
The Holy Spirit. Pilgrim NY.
Loving Says It All. Pilgrim NY.
xPittenger, W. Norman.
Trying to Be a Christian. Pilgrim NY.
xPittenger, William N.
The Historic Faith & a Changing World.
Greenwood.
Pittman, Blair.
xPittman, Blair.
photos by The Natural World of the Texas Big
Thicket. Tex A&M Univ Pr.
Pittman, David J. *see* Pittman, David Joshua.
Pittman, David Joshua, 1927-
xPittman, David J.
ed. Alcoholism. Har-Row.
Pittman, Philip.
xPittman, Philip.
The Present State of the European Settlements
on the Mississippi. Memphis St Univ.
The Present State of the European Settlements
on the Mississippi. U Presses Fla.
Pittock, Joan.
xPittock, Joan.
The Ascendancy of Taste: The Achievement of
Joseph & Thomas Warton. Routledge &
Kegan.
Pittock, Malcolm.
xPittock, Malcolm.
Ernst Toller. Twayne.
Pitts, Forrest R. *see* Pitts, Forrest Ralph.
Pitts, Forrest Ralph, 1924-
xPitts, Forrest R.
Japan. Fideler.
Pitts, Michael R.
xPitts, Michael R.
Famous Movie Detectives. Scarecrow.
Hollywood on Record: The Film Stars'
Discography. Scarecrow.
Radio Soundtracks: A Reference Guide.
Scarecrow.
Pitts, V. Peter.
xPitts, V. Peter.
Concept Development & the Development of
the God Concept in the Child: A
Bibliography. Character Res.
Pittsburgh. University. Bureau of Business Research.
xUniversity of Pittsburgh, Bureau of Business
Research.
Small Business Bibliography. Arno.
Pitz, Henry C. *see* Pitz, Henry Clarence.
Pitz, Henry Clarence, 1895-
xPitz, Henry C.

Charcoal Drawing. Watson-Guptill.
Drawing Outdoors. Watson-Guptill.
How to Draw Trees. Watson-Guptill.
Ink Drawing Techniques. Watson-Guptill.
Pivar, William. *see* Pivar, William H.
Pivar, William H.
xPivar, William.
Real Estate Ethics. Follett.
Real Estate Ethics. Real Estate Ed Co.
xPivar, William H.
California Real Estate License Preparation
Text. P-H.
Survival Manual for Nursing Students. HR&W.
Work Experience Handbook. Har-Row.
Piven, Frances. *see* Piven, Frances Fox.
Piven, Frances F. *see* Piven, Frances Fox.
Piven, Frances Fox.
xPiven, Frances.
Poor People's Movements: Why They Succeed,
How They Fail. Pantheon.
xPiven, Frances F.
Poor People's Movements: Why They Succeed,
How They Fail. Random.
Pivovarov, A. A. *see* Pivovarov, Anatolii Aleksandrovich.
Pivovarov, Anatolii Aleksandrovich.
xPivovarov, A. A.
Thermal Conditions in Freezing Lakes &
Rivers. Halsted Pr.
Thermal Conditions in Freezing Lakes &
Rivers. Krieger.
Pizarro, P. *see* Pizarro, Pedro.
Pizarro, Pedro.
xPizarro, P.
Relation of the Discovery & Conquest of the
Kingdoms of Peru. Kraus Repr.
xPizarro, Pedro.
Relation of the Discovery & Conquest of the
Kingdoms of Peru. Longwood Pr.
Pizer, Donald.
xPizer, Donald.
Hamlin Garland's Early Work & Career.
Russell.
The Literary Criticism of Frank Norris.
Russell.
Realism & Naturalism in Nineteenth-Century
American Literature. Russell.
Pizer, Hank.
xPizer, Hank.
The Post Partum Book: How to Cope with &
Enjoy the First Year of Parenting. Grove.
Pizer, Vernon, 1918-
xPizer, Vernon.
Glorious Triumphs: Athletes Who Conquered
Adversity. Dodd.
Ink, Ark., & All That: How American Places
Got Their Names. Putnam.
Shortchanged by History: America's Neglected
Innovators. Putnam.
PLA Audiovisual Committee. *see* Public Library
Association. Audio Visual Committee.
Plaat, Otto, 1924-
xPlaat, Otto.
Ordinary Differential Equations. Holden-Day.
Place, Irene. *see* Place, Irene Magdaline Glazik.
Place, Irene M. *see* Place, Irene Magdaline Glazik.
Place, Irene Magdaline Glazik.
xPlace, Irene.
Executive Secretarial Procedures. McGraw.
Fundamental Filing Practice. P-H.
xPlace, Irene M.
Filing & Records Management. P-H.
Place, J. A. *see* Place, Janey Ann.
Place, Janey Ann, 1946-
xPlace, J. A.
The Non-Western Films of John Ford. Citadel
Pr.
Place, Lucille.
xPlace, Lucille.

Fell's Beginner's Guide to Bridge for All Ages. Fell.

Place, Marian T. *see* Place, Marian Templeton.

Place, Marian Templeton.
xPlace, Marian T.
The Boy Who Saw Bigfoot. Dodd.
Comanches & Other Indians of Texas. HarBraceJ.
Gold Down Under: Story of the Australian Gold Rush. Macmillan.
Nobody Meets Bigfoot. Dodd.
On the Track of Bigfoot. Dodd.
xPlace, Marion T.
On the Track of Big Foot. Archway.
On the Track of Bigfoot. PB.

Place, Marion T. *see* Place, Marian Templeton.

Place, Robin.
xPlace, Robin.
Introduction to Archaeology. Philos Lib.

Plackett, R. L.
xPlackett, Robert L.
Analysis of Categorical Data. Hafner.

Plackett, Robert L. *see* Plackett, R. L.

Plageman. *see* Plageman, Karen.

Plageman, Karen.
xPlageman.
Bundt Cakes. Owlswood Prods.
xPlageman, Karen.
Good, Hearty Soups. Owlswood Prods.
Natural Fiber Cooking. Owlswood Prods.

Plagemann, Bentz, 1913-
xPlagemann, Bentz.
How to Write a Story. Lothrop.

Plakidas, A. G. *see* Plakidas, Antonios George.

Plakidas, Antonios George, 1895-
xPlakidas, A. G.
Strawberry Diseases. La State U Pr.

Plaks, Andrew H., 1945-
xPlaks, Andrew H.
Archetype & Allegory in the Dream of the Red Chamber. Princeton U Pr.
ed. Chinese Narrative: Critical & Theoretical Essays. Princeton U Pr.

Plamenatz, J. P. *see* Plamenatz, John Petrov.

Plamenatz, John.
xPlamenatz, John.
Democracy & Illusion: An Examination of Certain Aspects of Modern Democratic Theory. Longman.

Plamenatz, John P. *see* Plamenatz, John Petrov.

Plamenatz, John Petrov.
xPlamenatz, J. P.
Consent, Freedom & Political Obligation. Oxford U Pr.
xPlamenatz, John P.
German Marxism & Russian Communism. Greenwood.

Plamondon, Ann L.
xPlamondon, Ann L.
Whitehead's Organic Philosophy of Science. State U NY Pr.

Planck, Charles R.
xPlanck, Charles R.
The Changing Status of German Reunification in Western Diplomacy, 1955-1966. Johns Hopkins.

Planck, Max K. *see* Planck, Max Karl Ernst Ludwig.

Planck, Max Karl Ernst Ludwig, 1858-1947
xPlanck, Max K.
Where Is Science Going?. AMS Pr.

Plane, Donald R.
xPlane, Donald R.
Operations Research for Managerial Decisions. Irwin.
Statistics for Management Decisions. Business Pubns.

Plank, J. Van Der. *see* Van Der Plank, J. E.

Plank, John N. *see* Plank, John Nathan.

Plank, John Nathan.
xPlank, John N.

ed. Cuba & the United States: Long Range Perspectives. Brookings.

Planned Parenthood of New York City.
xPlanned Parenthood of NYC.
Abortion: A Woman's Guide. PB.

Planned Parenthood of NYC. *see* Planned Parenthood of New York City.

Planning Research Corporation.
xPlanning Research Corporation.
Application & System Design Study for Cost-Effective Solar Photovoltaic Systems at Federal Installations. Solar Energy Info.

Plano, Jack. *see* Plano, Jack C.

Plano, Jack C.
xPlano, Jack.
The American Political Dictionary. HR&W.
International Relations Dictionary. New Issues MI.
xPlano, Jack C.
The American Political Dictionary. HR&W.

Plansee Seminar De Re Metallica - 5th - Reutte - 1964. *see* Plansee Seminar De Re Metallica, 5th, Reuttle, Austria, 1964.

Plansee Seminar De Re Metallica, 5th, Reuttle, Austria, 1964.
xPlansee Seminar De Re Metallica - 5th - Reutte - 1964.
Metals for Space Travel: Lectures held at the Fifth Plansee Seminar. Springer Verlag.
Metals for the Space Age: Papers presented at the Fifth Plansee Seminar. Springer-Verlag.

Plant, James S. *see* Plant, James Stuart.

Plant, James Stuart, 1890-1947
xPlant, James S.
Personality & the Cultural Pattern. Octagon.

Plant, Raymond.
xPlant, Raymond.
Community & Ideology: An Essay in Applied Social Philosophy. Routledge & Kegan.

Plante, Jacques, 1929-
xPlante, Jacques.
Goaltending. Macmillan.

Plantinga, Alvin.
xPlantinga, Alvin.
God & Other Minds: A Study of the Rational Justification of Belief in God. Cornell U Pr.
God, Freedom, & Evil. Eerdmans.

Plantinga, Theodore, 1947-
xPlantinga, Theodore.
Historical Understanding in the Thought of Wilhelm Dilthey. U of Toronto Pr.

Plants, H. *see* Plants, Helen Lester.

Plants, Helen. *see* Plants, Helen Lester.

Plants, Helen Lester.
xPlants, H.
Programmed Topics in Statics & Strength of Materials. McGraw.
xPlants, Helen.
Introduction to Statics. West Pub.

Planz, Allen, 1937-
xPlanz, Allen.
Night for Rioting. Swallow.

Plaskow, Judith.
xPlaskow, Judith.
Sex, Sin & Grace: Women's Experience & the Theologies of Reinhold Niebuhr & Paul Tillich. U Pr of Amer.

Plasterer, Nicholas N.
xPlasterer, Nicholas N.
Assignment Jonesville: A News Reporting Workbook. La State U Pr.

Plastics Conference.
xPlastics Conference, 2nd Annual.
From Recession to Recovery: Proceedings. BCC.

Plastics Conference, 2nd Annual. *see* Plastics Conference.

Plater, William M., 1945-
xPlater, William M.

The Grim Phoenix: Reconstructing Thomas Pynchon. Ind U Pr.

Plath, David W.
xPlath, David W.
ed. Aware of Utopia. U of Ill Pr.

Plath, Iona.
xPlath, Iona.
illus. Decorative Arts of Sweden. Dover.
Decorative Arts of Sweden. Peter Smith.

Plath, Karl. *see* Plath, Karl R.

Plath, Karl R.
xPlath, Karl.
The Annual School Plan. Natl Assn Principals.

Plath, Sylvia.
xPlath, Sylvia.
Colossus & Other Poems. Knopf.
Colossus & Other Poems. Random.

Platnauer, Maurice.
xPlatnauer, Maurice.
Latin Elegiac Verse: A Study of the Metrical Usages of Tibullus, Propertius, & Ovid. Shoe String.
Life & Reign of the Emperor Lucius Septimius Severus. Greenwood.

Plato.
xPlato.
The Euthydemus of Plato. Arno.
Gorgias. Bobbs.
Gorgias. Oxford U Pr.
Gorgias. Penguin.
The Gorgias of Plato. Arno.
The Laws. Basic.
Laws. Harvard U Pr.
Laws. Penguin.
The Laws of Plato. Arno.
Meno. Bobbs.
Meno. Cambridge U Pr.
Meno. Hackett Pub.
The Platonic Epistles. Arno.
Plato's Euthyphro, Apology of Socrates & Crito. AMS Pr.
Plato's Republic. Airmont.
Protagoras. Bobbs.
Protagoras. Cambridge U Pr.
The Republic. AHM Pub.
Republic. Cambridge U Pr.
Republic. Dutton.
The Republic. Hackett Pub.
Republic. Harvard U Pr.
Republic. Modern Lib.
Republic. Random.
Republic. Penguin.
The Sophistes & Politicus of Plato. Arno.
Symposium of Plato. Branden.
The Symposium of Plato. U of Mass Pr.
The Theaetetus of Plato. Arno.
The Theaetetus of Plato. Hackett Pub.
Works of Plato. AMS Pr.
Works of Plato. Modern Lib.

Plato, Chris C.
xPlato, Chris C.
ed. Dermatoglyphics-Fifty Years Later. A R Liss.

Platon.
xPlaton.
Orthodox Doctrine of the Apostolic Eastern Church: A Compendium of Christian Theology. AMS Pr.

Platonov, Andrei. *see* Platonov, Andrei Platonovich.

Platonov, Andrei Platonovich, 1899-1951
xPlatonov, Andrei.
Chevengur. Ardis Pubs.

Platt, Alan.
xPlatt, Alan.
ed. Congress & Arms Control. Westview.

Platt, Anthony M.
xPlatt, Anthony M.

The Child Savers: The Invention of
Delinquency. U of Chicago Pr.

Platt, Arthur, 1860-1925
xPlatt, Arthur.
Nine Essays. Arno.

Platt, Charles.
xPlatt, Charles.
Outdoor Survival. Watts.
Popular Superstitions. Gale.
Sweet Evil. Berkley Pub.

Platt, Colin.
xPlatt, Colin.
The Atlas of Medieval Man. St Martin.
Medieval Southampton: The Port & Trading
Community A. D. 1000-1600. Routledge &
Kegan.
The Monastic Grange in Medieval England: A
Reassessment. Fordham.

Platt, D. C. see Platt, Desmond Christopher St. Martin.

Platt, Desmond Christopher St. Martin.
xPlatt, D. C.
Latin America & British Trade: 1806-1914.
Humanities.

Platt, Frederic W.
xPlatt, Frederic W.
Case Studies in Emergency Medicine. Little.

Platt, Frederick, 1946-
xPlatt, Frederick.
America's Gilded Age. A S Barnes.

Platt, Jennifer.
xPlatt, Jennifer.
Realities of Social Research. Halsted Pr.

Platt, Jerome J.
xPlatt, Jerome J.
ed. The Psychological Consultant. Grune.

Platt, John A.
xPlatt, John A.
Whispers from Old Genesee & Echoes of the
Salmon River. Ye Galleon.

Platt, John R. see Platt, John Rader.

Platt, John Rader, 1918-
xPlatt, John R.
The Excitement of Science. Greenwood.
Perception & Change: Projections for Survival.
U of Mich Pr.
The Step to Man. Krieger.

Platt, Kenneth B.
xPlatt, Kenneth B.
Salmon River Saga. Ye Galleon.

Platt, Kin.
xPlatt, Kin.
The Ape Inside Me. Lippincott.
Boy Who Could Make Himself Disappear.
Dell.
Chloris & the Creeps. Dell.
Chloris & the Weirdos. Bantam.
Chloris & the Weirdos. Bradbury Pr.
The Doomsday Gang. Greenwillow.
Dracula, Go Home. Dell.
Dracula, Go Home. Watts.

Platt, Lee F. see Platt, Lee Frew.

Platt, Lee Frew.
xPlatt, Lee F.
The Real Estate Examination Study Guide.
Inscape Corp.

Platt, Rutherford H.
xPlatt, Rutherford H.
Frwd. by Open Land in Urban Illinois: Roles of
the Citizen Advocate. N Ill U Pr.

Platt, Thomas C. see Platt, Thomas Collier.

Platt, Thomas Collier.
xPlatt, Thomas C.
The Autobiography of Thomas Collier Platt.
Arno.

Platt, Washington.
xPlatt, Washington.
National Character in Action: Intelligence
Factors in Foreign Relations. Rutgers U Pr.

Platt, William R., 1915-
xPlatt, William R.

Color Atlas & Textbook of Hematology.
Lippincott.

Platte, Hans.
xPlatte, Hans.
Color Prints International. Universe.

Plattel, Martin G., 1921-
xPlattel, Martin G.
Utopian & Critical Thinking. Duquesne.

Platten, David, 1947-
xPlatten, David.
The Outdoor Survival Handbook. David &
Charles.

Plattner, Marc F., 1945-
xPlattner, Marc F.
Rousseau's State of Nature: An Interpretation
of the Discourse on Inequality. N Ill U Pr.

Platts, Beryl.
xPlatts, Beryl.
A History of Greenwich. David & Charles.

Platts, John T. see Platts, John Thompson.

Platts, John Thompson, 1830-1904
xPlatts, John T.
A Dictionary of Urdu Classical Hindi &
English. Intl Pubns Serv.
Dictionary of Urdu, Classical Hindi, & English.
Oxford U Pr.

Platts, Mark. see Platts, Mark De Bretton.

Platts, Mark De Bretton, 1947-
xPlatts, Mark.
ed. Reference, Truth & Reality: Essays on the
Philosophy of Language. Routledge & Kegan.
Ways of Meaning: An Introduction to a
Philosophy of Language. Routledge & Kegan.

Platzer, Norbert A. see Platzer, Norbert A. J.

Platzer, Norbert A. J.
xPlatzer, Norbert A.
ed. Polymerization Kinetics & Technology. Am
Chemical.
ed. Polymerization Reactions & New Polymers.
Am Chemical.

Plaut, James S. see Plaut, James Sachs.

Plaut, James Sachs, 1912-
xPlaut, James S.
Steuben Glass. Peter Smith.

Plautus. see Plautus, Titus Maccius.

Plautus, Titus Maccius.
xPlautus.
Amphitryon & Two Other Plays. Norton.
Casina. Cambridge U Pr.
Menaechmus Twins & Two Other Plays.
Norton.

Plavchan, Ronald J. see Plavchan, Ronald Jan.

Plavchan, Ronald Jan.
xPlavchan, Ronald J.
A History of Anheuser-Busch, 1852-1933.
Arno.

Playbody Editors. see Playboy.

Playboy.
xPlaybody Editors.
Playboy's Party Jokes. Playboy Pbks.
xPlayboy Editors.
Best from Playboy No. Three. Trident.
Best from Playboy No. Two. Trident.
Playboy's Party Jokes. Playboy Pbks.
Playboy's Party Jokes No. 3. Playboy Pbks.
xPlayboy Magazine Editors.
Playboy Advisor. PB.
ed. Playboy's Party Joke Books. PB.
Playboy's Party Jokes. Playboy Pbks.
Playboy's Party Jokes, No. 5. Playboy Pbks.
Playboy's Ribald Classics. PB.

Playboy Editors. see Playboy.

Playboy Magazine Editors. see Playboy.

Player, Mack A.
xPlayer, Mack A.
Cases & Materials on Employment
Discrimination Law. West Pub.

Playfair, Nigel R. see Playfair, Nigel Ross.

Playfair, Nigel Ross.
xPlayfair, Nigel R.

Story of the Lyric Theatre, Hammersmith.
Arno.

Pleasants, Henry.
xPleasants, Henry.
Agony of Modern Music. S&S.
The Great American Popular Singers. S&S.

Pleasants, Mary M. see Pleasants, Mary Minta.

Pleasants, Mary Minta, 1853-
xPleasants, Mary M.
Which One? & Other Ante Bellum Days..
Arno.

Pleasants, Samuel A. see Pleasants, Samuel Augustus.

Pleasants, Samuel Augustus, 1918-
xPleasants, Samuel A.
Fernando Wood of New York. AMS Pr.

Pleck, Elizabeth H.
xPleck, Elizabeth H.
The American Man. P-H.

Pleck, Joseph H.
xPleck, Joseph H.
ed. Men & Masculinity. P-H.

Pledger, D. M. see Pledger, David M.

Pledger, David M.
xPledger, D. M.
Complete Guide to Demolition. Longman.

Pleeter, Saul, 1944-
xPleeter, Saul.
Economic Impact Analysis: Methodology &
Applications. Kluwer Boston.

Plekhanov, G. see Plekhanov, Georgii Valentinovich.

Plekhanov, G. V. see Plekhanov, Georgii Valentinovich.

Plekhanov, George V. see Plekhanov, Georgii
Valentinovich.

Plekhanov, Georgii Valentinovich, 1856-1918
xPlekhanov, G.
Fundamental Problems of Marxism. Arden Lib.
xPlekhanov, G. V.
Fundamental Problems of Marxism. Beekman
Pubs.
History of Russian Social Thought. Fertig.
xPlekhanov, George V.
Fundamental Problems of Marxism. Intl Pub
Co.

Plenary Sessions of the First World Congress on
Chemical Engineering, Amsterdam, June 28-July 1,
1976. see World Congress on Chemical Engineering,
1st, Amsterdam, 1976.

Pleninger, Andrew.
xPleninger, Andrew.
How to Survive & Market Yourself in
Management. Am Mgmt.

Plescia, Joseph, 1928-
xPlescia, Joseph.
The Oath & Perjury in Ancient Greece. U
Presses Fla.

Plessen, Elisabeth.
xPlessen, Elisabeth.
Such Sad Tidings. Viking Pr.

Plessen, Elizabeth. see Plessen, Elisabeth.

Plesset, Isabel R. see Plesset, Isabel Rosanoff.

Plesset, Isabel Rosanoff, 1912-
xPlesset, Isabel R.
Noguchi & His Patrons. Fairleigh Dickinson.

Plessis, N. Du. see Du Plessis, N.

Plessner, Helmuth, 1892-
xPlessner, Helmuth.
Laughing & Crying: A Study of the Limits of
Human Behavior. Northwestern U Pr.

Pletcher, David M.
xPletcher, David M.
The Diplomacy of Annexation: Texas, Oregon,
& the Mexican War. U of Mo Pr.

Plewig, G. see Plewig, Gerd.

Plewig, Gerd.
xPlewig, G.
Acne: Morphogenesis & Treatment.
Springer-Verlag.

Plews, R. W.
xPlews, R. W.

ed. Analytical Methods Used in Sugar
Refining. Burgess-Intl Ideas.

Plimmer, Charlotte.

xPlimmer, Charlotte.
London: A Visitor's Companion. Norton.

Plimpton, George.

xPlimpton, George.
One for the Record: The Inside Story of Hank
Aaron's Chase for the Home-Run Record.
Har-Row.
Paper Lion. NAL.

Pliner. *see* Pliner, Patricia.
Pliner, Patricia.
xPliner.
ed. Perception of Emotion in Self & Others.
Plenum Pub.
Plischke, Elmer, 1914-
xPlischke, Elmer.
American Foreign Relations: A Bibliography of
Official Sources. Johnson Repr.
Conduct of American Diplomacy. Greenwood.
Ploeger, Jo-Ann. *see* Ploeger, Joann.
Ploeger, Joann.
xPloeger, Jo-Ann.
Slim Living Day by Day. Tyndale.
Plog, Fred.
xPlog, Fred.
Anthropology: Decisions, Adaptation &
Evolution. Knopf.
Cultural Anthropology. Knopf.
xPlog, Fred T.
A Study of Prehistoric Change. Acad Pr.
Plog, Fred T. *see* Plog, Fred.
Plomer, H. R. *see* Plomer, Henry Robert.
Plomer, Henry Robert, 1856-1928
xPlomer, H. R.
English Printers' Ornaments. B Franklin.
Plomer, William. *see* Plomer, William Charles Franklyn.
Plomer, William C. *see* Plomer, William Charles
Franklyn.
Plomer, William Charles Franklyn, 1903-1973
xPlomer, William.
The Autobiography of William Plomer.
Taplinger.
xPlomer, William C.
Remarks When Opening the George Gissing
Exhibition at the National Book
League,London. Folcroft.
Plonsky, Carolyn G.
xPlonsky, Carolyn G.
Consumer Health: Protecting Your Health &
Money. Har-Row.
Plonus, Martin. *see* Plonus, Martin A.
Plonus, Martin A.
xPlonus, Martin.
Applied Electromagnetics. McGraw.
Ploss, Sidney I.
xPloss, Sidney L.
Conflict & Decision-Making in Soviet Russia:
A Case Study of Agricultural Policy,
1953-1963. Princeton U Pr.
Ploss, Sidney L. *see* Ploss, Sidney I.
Plotkin, Frederick.
xPlotkin, Frederick.
Faith & Reason: Essays in the Religious &
Scientific Imagination. Philos Lib.
Plotnicov, Leonard.
xPlotnicov, Leonard.
Strangers to the City: Urban Man in Jos,
Nigeria. U of Pittsburgh Pr.
Plotnik, Arthur.
xPlotnik, Arthur.
Library Life - American Style: A Journalist's
Field Report. Scarecrow.
Plotz, Helen.
xPlotz, Helen.

As I Walked Out One Evening: A Book of
Ballads. Greenwillow.
ed. The Gift Outright: America to Her Poets.
Greenwillow.
ed. Imagination's Other Place: Poems of
Science & Mathematics. T Y Crowell.
ed. Life Hungers to Abound: Poems of the
Family. Greenwillow.
This Powerful Rhyme: A Book of Sonnets.
Greenwillow.
Plowden, Alison.
xPlowden, Alison.
The House of Tudor. Stein & Day.
Plowman, Thomas.
xPlowman, Thomas.
Craft Pottery. ARS Ceramica.
Pluckhan, Margaret. *see* Pluckhan, Margaret L.
Pluckhan, Margaret L.
xPluckhan, Margaret.
Human Communication: The Matrix of
Nursing. McGraw.
Plucknett, Donald L.
xPlucknett, Donald L.
Small-Scale Processing & Storage of Tropical
Root Crops. Westview.
Plum, Fred.
xPlum, Fred.
ed. The Diagnosis of Stupor & Coma. Davis
Co.
Plumb, Barbara.
xPlumb, Barbara.
Houses Architects Live in. Penguin.
Houses Architects Live in. Viking Pr.
Plumb, J. *see* Plumb, John Harold.
Plumb, J. H. *see* Plumb, John Harold.
Plumb, John H. *see* Plumb, John Harold.
Plumb, John Harold, 1911-
xPlumb, J.
The First Four Georges. Watts.
xPlumb, J. H.
England in the Eighteenth Century. Gannon.
Intro. by The English Heritage. Forum Pr MO.
The First Four Georges. Little.
xPlumb, John H.
England in the Eighteenth Century. Penguin.
Men & Centuries. Greenwood.
Plumb, S. C. *see* Plumb, Stephen C.
Plumb, Stephen C.
xPlumb, S. C.
Introduction to Fortran: A Program for
Self-Instruction. McGraw.
Plumer, William.
xPlumer, William.
Life of William Plumer. Da Capo.
Plumer, William S. *see* Plumer, William Swan.
Plumer, William Swan, 1802-1880
xPlumer, William S.
Commentary on Romans. Kregel.
Plumly, Stanley.
xPlumly, Stanley.
In the Outer Dark: Poems. La State U Pr.
Out-of-the-Body Travel. Ecco Pr.
Plummer, Charles C.
xPlummer, Charles C.
Physical Geology. Wm C Brown.
Plummer, Gail.
xPlummer, Gail.
The Business of Show Business. Greenwood.
Plummer, William J., 1927-
xPlummer, William J.
A Quail in the Family. Fawcett.
Plumridge, John H. *see* Plumridge, John Henry.
Plumridge, John Henry, 1894-
xPlumridge, John H.
Hospital Ships & Ambulance Trains.
Hippocrene Bks.
Plunket, Jean R. *see* Plunket, Jean Reasoner.
Plunket, Jean Reasoner.
xPlunket, Jean R.

Faces That Won't Sit Still: Celebrated Subjects
by a Prominent Portrait Artist & How They
Were Captured. Acropolis.
Plunkett, E. R. *see* Plunkett, Edmond Robert.
Plunkett, Edmond Robert, 1922-
xPlunkett, E. R.
Folk Name & Trade Diseases. Barrett Bk.
Occupational Diseases: A Syllabus of Signs &
Symptoms. Barrett Bk.
Plunkett, James, 1920-
xPlunkett, James.
Farewell Companions. Coward.
Plunkett, W. Richard. *see* Plunkett, Warren Richard.
Plunkett, Warren Richard.
xPlunkett, W. Richard.
Introduction to Business: A Functional
Approach. Wm C Brown.
Supervision: The Direction of People at Work.
Wm C Brown.
Plutchik, Robert.
xPlutchik, Robert.
Foundations of Experimental Research.
Har-Row.
Plutschow, Herbert. *see* Plutschow, Herbert E.
Plutschow, Herbert E.
xPlutschow, Herbert.
Introducing Kyoto. Kodansha.
Plymell, Charles.
xPlymell, Charles.
Are You a Kid?. Cherry Valley.
Poague, Leland A., 1948-
xPoague, Leland A.
The Cinema of Ernst Lubitsch. A S Barnes.
The Cinema of Frank Capra: An Approach to
Film Comedy. A S Barnes.
Pobee, J. S.
xPobee, John S.
Toward an African Theology. Abingdon.
Pobee, John S. *see* Pobee, J. S.
Poche, Emanuel.
xPoche, Emanuel.
Porcelain Marks of the World. Arco.
Pochedly, C. *see* Pochedly, Carl.
Pochedly, Carl.
xPochedly, C.
ed. Acute Childhood Leukemia. S Karger.
xPochedly, Carl.
Cancer in Children: Reasons for Hope. Ashley
Bks.
The Child with Leukemia. C C Thomas.
Leukemia & Lymphoma in the Nervous
System. C C Thomas.
Pochmann, Henry A. *see* Pochmann, Henry August.
Pochmann, Henry August, 1901-
xPochmann, Henry A.
German Culture in America: Philosophical &
Literary Influences 1600-1900. Greenwood.
Pocknee, Cyril E. *see* Pocknee, Cyril Edward.
Pocknee, Cyril Edward.
xPocknee, Cyril E.
Christian Altar in History & Today. Allenson.
Pocock. *see* Pocock, Robine.
Pocock, Douglas. *see* Pocock, Douglas Charles David.
Pocock, Douglas Charles David.
xPocock, Douglas.
Images of the Urban Environment. Columbia U
Pr.
Pocock, J. G. *see* Pocock, John Greville Agard.
Pocock, John Greville Agard.
xPocock, J. G.
Ancient Constitution & the Feudal Law: A
Study of English Historical Thought in the
17th Century. Norton.
Pocock, Robine.
xPocock.
The Burmese Cat. David & Charles.
xPocock, Robine.

Norman Mailer. Viking Pr.

Performing Self: Compositions & Decompositions in the Languages of Contemporary Life. Oxford U Pr.

World Elsewhere: The Place of Style in American Literature. Oxford U Pr.

A World Elsewhere: The Place of Style in American Literature. Oxford U Pr.

Poirot, James L.
xPoirot, James L.
Computer Science for the Teacher. Sterling Swift.

Pois, Robert A.
xPois, Robert A.
Bourgeois Democrats of Weimar Germany. Am Philos.
Friedrich Meinecke & German Politics in the Twentieth Century. U of Cal Pr.

Poister, Theodore H.
xPoister, Theodore H.
Applied Program Evaluation in Local Government. Lexington Bks.

Poitier, Sidney.
xPoitier, Sidney.
This Life. Knopf.

Pokorny, George.
xPokorny, George.
International Directory of Mountaineering Clubs & Organizations. Mountain Pr.

Pokorny, Joel.
xPokorny, Joel.
ed. Congenital & Acquired Color Vision Defects. Grune.

Pokotilov, Dmitrii. see Pokotilov, Dmitrii Dmitrievich.

Pokotilov, Dmitrii Dmitrievich.
xPokotilov, Dmitrii.
History of the Eastern Mongols During the Ming Dynasty from 1368-1631. Porcupine Pr.

Pokras, Fran.
xPokras, Fran.
Leaving. BJ Pub Group.

Pokress, E.
xPokress, E.
Advertising & Public Relations. Aurea.

Polack, Frank M., 1929-
xPolack, Frank M.
Corneal Transplantation. Grune.

Polak, A. Laurence. see Polak, Alfred Laurence.

Polak, Alfred Laurence.
xPolak, A. Laurence.
More Legal Fictions: Series of Cases from Shakespeare. Arden Lib.
xPolak, Alfred S.
More Legal Fictions: A Series of Cases from Shakespeare. AMS Pr.

Polak, Alfred S. see Polak, Alfred Laurence.

Polak, Johan.
xPolak, Johan.
illus. True-To-Life ABC Book Including Numbers. G&D.

Polakoff, Claire.
xPolakoff, Claire.
Into Indigo: African Textiles & Dyeing Techniques. Doubleday.

Polakoff, Keith I. see Polakoff, Keith Ian.

Polakoff, Keith Ian.
xPolakoff, Keith I.
Generations of Americans: A History of the United States. St Martin.
The Politics of Inertia: The Election of 1876 & the End of Reconstruction. La State U Pr.

Polakoff, Murray A. see Polakoff, Murray Emanuel.

Polakoff, Murray E. see Polakoff, Murray Emanuel.

Polakoff, Murray Emanuel.
xPolakoff, Murray A.
Financial Institutions & Markets. HM.
xPolakoff, Murray E.
Financial Institutions & Markets. HM.

Poland, D. see Poland, Douglas.

Poland, Douglas.
xPoland, D.
Cooperative Equilibria in Physical Biochemistry. Oxford U Pr.

Polansky, Norman A. see Polansky, Norman Alburt.

Polansky, Norman Alburt, 1918-
xPolansky, Norman A.
ed. Social Work Research: Methods for the Helping Professions. U of Chicago Pr.

Polanyi, Karl, 1886-1964
xPolanyi, Karl.
Primitive, Archaic & Modern Economies: Essays of Karl Polanyi. Beacon Pr.

Polanyi, Michael, 1891-
xPolanyi, Michael.
The Contempt of Freedom: The Russian Experiment & After. Arno.
The Logic of Liberty: Reflections & Rejoinders. U of Chicago Pr.
Meaning. U of Chicago Pr.
Study of Man. U of Chicago Pr.
Tacit Dimension. Doubleday.

Polatin, Phillip.
xPolatin, Phillip.
How Psychiatry Helps. Macmillan.

Pole, J. R. see Pole, Jack Richon.

Pole, Jack Richon.
xPole, J. R.
Paths to the American Past. Oxford U Pr.
Political Representation in England & the Origins of the American Republic. St Martin.
Political Representation in England & the Origins of the American Republic. U of Cal Pr.
The Pursuit of Equality in American History. U of Cal Pr.
ed. The Revolution in America, 1754-1788: Documents & Commentaries. Stanford U Pr.

Pole, Thomas, 1753-1829
xPole, Thomas.
History of the Origin & Progress of Adult Schools. Kelley.

Polednak, Anthony P.
xPolednak, Anthony P.
The Longevity of Athletes. C C Thomas.

Poledor, Andrew P., 1927-
xPoledor, Andrew P.
Determining the Feasibility of a Total Convenience Food System. CBI Pub.

Poleman, Horace I. see Poleman, Horace Irvin.

Poleman, Horace Irvin, 1905-
xPoleman, Horace I.
Census of Indic Manuscripts in the United States & Canada. Kraus Repr.

Poleman, Thomas T.
xPoleman, Thomas T.
The Papaloapan Project: Agricultural Development in the Mexican Tropics. Stanford U Pr.

Polemis, Aphrodite.
xPolemis, Aphrodite.
Aphrodite's Kitchen: Homestyle Greek Cooking. Western Pub.

Polenberg, Richard.
xPolenberg, Richard.
One Nation Divisible: Class, Race, & Ethnicity in the United States Since 1938. Viking Pr.
Reorganizing Roosevelt's Government: The Controversy Over Executive Reorganization, 1936-1939. Harvard U Pr.

Polentz, Lloyd M.
xPolentz, Lloyd M.
Engineering Fundamentals for Professional Engineers' Examinations. McGraw.

Polese, Carolyn.
xPolese, Carolyn.
Something About a Mermaid. Dutton.

Polette, Nancy.
xPolette, Nancy.

Celebrating with Books. Scarecrow.

Developing Methods of Inquiry: A Source Book for Elementary Media Personnel. Scarecrow.

E Is for Everybody: A Manual for Bringing Fine Picture Books into the Hands & Hearts of Children. Scarecrow.

Reading Guidance in a Media Age. Scarecrow.

Polevoi, Boris N. see Polevoi, Boris Nikolaevich.

Polevoi, Boris Nikolaevich.
xPolevoi, Boris N.
Story About a Real Man. Greenwood.

Polezhaev, L. V. see Polezhaev, Lev Vladimirovich.

Polezhaev, Lev Vladimirovich.
xPolezhaev, L. V.
Loss & Restoration of Regenerative Capacity in Tissues & Organs of Animals. Harvard U Pr.
Organ Regeneration in Animals: Recovery of Organ Regeneration Ability in Animals. C C Thomas.

Polgar, Steven.
xPolgar, Steven.
ed. Population, Ecology, & Social Evolution. Beresford Bk Serv.

Polgreen, John.
xPolgreen, John.
Earth in Space. Random.
Sunlight & Shadows. Doubleday.

Polhamus, Jean B. see Polhamus, Jean Burt.

Polhamus, Jean Burt.
xPolhamus, Jean B.
Dinosaur Do's & Don'ts. P-H.

Polhemus, Robert M.
xPolhemus, Robert M.
The Changing World of Anthony Trollope. U of Cal Pr.

Poli, Bernard J.
xPoli, Bernard J.
Ford Madox Ford & the Transatlantic Review. Syracuse U Pr.

Poliakov, Leon, 1910-
xPoliakov, Leon.
The Aryan Myth: A History of Racist & Nationalist Ideas in Europe. NAL.
Harvest of Hate: The Nazi Program for the Destruction of the Jews in Europe. Greenwood.
Harvest of Hate: The Nazi Program for the Destruction of the Jews of Europe. Schocken.

Poliakova, Liudmila V. see Poliakova, Liudmila Viktorovna.

Poliakova, Liudmila Viktorovna.
xPoliakova, Liudmila V.
Soviet Music. Hyperion Conn.

Police Department, Los Angeles. see Los Angeles. Police Department.

Polikoff, Alexander.
xPolikoff, Alexander.
Housing the Poor: The Case for Heroism. Ballinger Pub.

Polin, Claire C. see Polin, Claire C. J.

Polin, Claire C. J.
xPolin, Claire C.
Music of the Ancient Near East. Greenwood.

Poling, David, 1928-
xPoling, David.
To Be Born Again: The Conversion Phenomenon. Doubleday.

Poling, Lena. see Poling, Lena E.

Poling, Lena E.
xPoling, Lena.
A History of the City of Shinnston. McClain.

Polisensky, J. V. see Polisensky, Josef V.

Polisensky, Josef V.
xPolisensky, J. V.
The Thirty Years War. U of Cal Pr.

Polish Institute of Arts & Sciences in America, N.Y., 1966. see Polish Institute of Arts and Sciences in America.

Polish Institute of Arts and Sciences in America.
xPolish Institute of Arts & Sciences in America, N.Y., 1966.
Studies in Polish Civilization: Selected Papers. Polish Inst Arts.
Polishook, Irwin H.
xPolishook, Irwin H.
Rhode Island & the Union, 1774-1795. Northwestern U Pr.
Polites, George W.
xPolites, George W.
Precalculus Mathematics: A Study of Functions. Har-Row.
Polites, Nicholas.
xPolites, Nicholas.
The Architecture of Leandro V. Locsin. Weatherhill.
Politi, Leo, 1908-
xPoliti, Leo.
illus. Butterflies Come. Scribner.
illus. Little Leo. Scribner.
Political & Economic Planning. *see* Political and Economic Planning.
Political and Economic Planning.
xPolitical & Economic Planning.
World Population & Resources: A Report. Hyperion Conn.
Politz, Murray J.
xPolitz, Murray J.
Clinical Podiatric Laboratory Diagnosis. Futura Pub.
Politzer, R. L. *see* Politzer, Robert Louis.
Politzer, Robert L. *see* Politzer, Robert Louis.
Politzer, Robert Louis.
xPolitzer, R. L.
Peldanos. Wiley.
xPolitzer, Robert L.
Active Review of French: Selected Patterns, Vocabulary & Pronunciation Problems for Speakers of English. Wiley.
Speaking German. P-H.
Teaching English As a Second Language. Krieger.
Teaching French: An Introduction to Applied Linguistics. Wiley.
Polivka, Raymond P. *see* Polivka, Raymond Peter.
Polivka, Raymond Peter.
xPolivka, Raymond P.
APL: The Language & Its Usage. P-H.
Poliziano, Angelo, 1454-1494
xPoliziano, Angelo.
The Stanze of Angelo Poliziano. U of Mass Pr.
Poljakoff-Mayber, A. *see* Poljakoff-Mayber, Alexandra.
Poljakoff-Mayber, Alexandra.
xPoljakoff-Mayber, A.
ed. Plants in Saline Environments. Springer-Verlag.
Polk, Dora.
xPolk, Dora.
The Gilt Feather. Doubleday.
Polk, Frank, 1908-
xPolk, Frank.
F-F-F-Frank Polk: An Uncommonly Frank Autobiography. Northland.
Polk, Lee.
xPolk, Lee.
The Incredible Television Machine. Macmillan.
Polk, Noel.
xPolk, Noel.
ed. Requiem for a Nun: A Concordance to the Novel. Univ Microfilms.
xPolk, Noel E.
ed. Anthology of Mississippi Writers. U Pr of Miss.
Polk, Noel E. *see* Polk, Noel.
Polk, William R. *see* Polk, William Roe.
Polk, William Roe, 1929-
xPolk, William R.

The Elusive Peace: The Middle East in the Twentieth Century. St Martin.
Polking, Kirk.
xPolking, Kirk.
ed. Law & the Writer. Writers Digest.
The Private Pilot's Dictionary & Handbook. Arco.
Polkinghorn, R. Stephen. *see* Polkinghorn, Robert Stephen.
Polkinghorn, Robert Stephen.
xPolkinghorn, R. Stephen.
Micro-Theory & Economic Choices. Irwin.
Poll, Richard. *see* Poll, Richard Douglas.
Poll, Richard D. *see* Poll, Richard Douglas.
Poll, Richard Douglas.
xPoll, Richard.
Intro. by Utah's History. Brigham.
xPoll, Richard D.
ed. Utah's History. Brigham.
Poll, Solomon.
xPoll, Solomon.
Ancient Thoughts in Modern Perspective: A Contemporary View of the Bible. Philos Lib.
Poll, Toni L., 1948-
xPoll, Toni L.
Complete Handbook of Secondary School Dance Activities. P-H.
Pollack. *see* Pollack, Herman W.
Pollack, Bary W.
xPollack, Bary W.
Compiler Techniques. Van Nos Reinhold.
Pollack, Doreen.
xPollack, Doreen.
Educational Audiology for the Limited Hearing Infant. C C Thomas.
Pollack, Ervin H. *see* Pollack, Ervin Harold.
Pollack, Ervin Harold, 1913-
xPollack, Ervin H.
Jurisprudence: Principles & Applications. Ohio St U Pr.
Pollack, Erwin. *see* Pollack, Erwin W.
Pollack, Erwin W.
xPollack, Erwin.
Spanish-Speaking Students & Guidance. HM.
Pollack, Harriet.
xPollack, Harriet.
Civil Liberties & Civil Rights in the United States. West Pub.
Pollack, Herman. *see* Pollack, Herman W.
Pollack, Herman W.
xPollack.
Materials Science & Metallurgy. Reston.
xPollack, Herman.
Manufacturing & Machine Tool Operations. P-H.
Pollack, Jack H. *see* Pollack, Jack Horrison.
Pollack, Jack Horrison.
xPollack, Jack H.
Dr. Sam: An American Tragedy. Avon.
Pollack, Michael C.
xPollack, Michael C.
Amplification for the Hearing Impaired. Grune.
Pollack, Neuman. *see* Pollack, Neuman F.
Pollack, Neuman F., 1947-
xPollack, Neuman.
Fundamentals of American Government: A Programmed Approach. Allyn.
Pollack, Norman.
xPollack, Norman.
ed. Populist Mind. Bobbs.
ed. The Populist Mind. Irvington.
Pollack, R. S. *see* Pollack, Robert S.
Pollack, Robert, 1926-
xPollack, Robert.
ed. Readings in Mammalian Cell Culture. Cold Spring Harbor.
Pollack, Robert S.
xPollack, R. S.

Tumor Surgery of the Head & Neck. S Karger.
Pollack, Rosalind S.
xPollack, R. S.
The Individual's Rights & International Organization. Smith Coll.
Pollack, Sandy.
xPollack, Sandy.
Alternative Careers for Teachers. Harvard Common Pr.
Pollack, Simon R.
xPollack, Simon R.
Jewish Wit for All Occasions. A & W Pubs.
Pollak, Felix.
xPollak, Felix.
Subject to Change. Juniper Pr WI.
Pollak, G.
xPollak, G.
ed. Algebraic Theory of Semigroups. Elsevier.
Pollak, Isaac.
xPollak, Isaac G. G.
The World of the Diamond. Exposition.
Pollak, Isaac G. G. *see* Pollak, Isaac.
Pollak, James. *see* Pollak, James S.
Pollak, James S., 1909-
xPollak, James.
The Golden Egg. Garland Pub.
Pollak, Otto, 1908-
xPollak, Otto.
The Criminality of Women. A S Barnes.
The Criminality of Women. Greenwood.
Invitation to a Dialogue: Union & Separation in Family Life. Spectrum Pub.
Polland, Barbara K. *see* Polland, Barbara Kay.
Polland, Barbara Kay.
xPolland, Barbara K.
Feelings: Inside You & Outloud Too. Celestial Arts.
Pollard, A. H. *see* Pollard, Alfred Hurlstone.
Pollard, Alfred Hurlstone.
xPollard, A. H.
Demographic Techniques. Pergamon.
Pollard, Alfred W. *see* Pollard, Alfred William.
Pollard, Alfred William, 1859-1944
xPollard, Alfred W.
Chaucer. AMS Pr.
Chaucer. Arno.
Chaucer. Greenwood.
Fifteenth Century Prose & Verse. Cooper Sq.
Fine Books. Cooper Sq.
Pollard, Arthur.
xPollard, Arthur.
Anthony Trollope. Routledge & Kegan.
Crabbe: The Critical Heritage. Routledge & Kegan.
Pollard, Edward A. *see* Pollard, Edward Alfred.
Pollard, Edward Alfred, 1831-1872
xPollard, Edward A.
Lost Cause Regained. AMS Pr.
Lost Cause Regained. Arno.
Pollard, Harold R.
xPollard, Harold R.
Developments in Management Thought. Crane-Russak Co.
Pollard, Harry, 1919-
xPollard, Harry.
The Theory of Algebraic Numbers. Math Assn.

Pollard, Hugh B. *see* Pollard, Hugh Bertie Campbell.
Pollard, Hugh Bertie Campbell, 1888-
xPollard, Hugh B.
The History of Firearms. B Franklin.
Pollard, J. H.
xPollard, J. H.
Mathematical Models for the Growth of Human Populations. Cambridge U Pr.
Pollard, Jack.
xPollard, Jack.

ed. Australian & New Zealand Fishing. Intl
   Pubns Serv.
Compiled by Surfrider. Taplinger.
Swimming Australian Style. Soccer.
Pollard, James E. *see* Pollard, James Edward.

Pollard, James Edward, 1894-
xPollard, James E.
   The Presidents & the Press. Octagon.
   Presidents & the Press: Truman to Johnson.
      Pub Aff Pr.

Pollard, Marie B.
xPollard, Marie B.
   Growing Child in Contemporary Society.
      Glencoe.

Pollard, Michael.
xPollard, Michael.
   How Things Work. Larousse.

Pollard, Morris.
xPollard, Morris.
   ed. Antiviral Mechanisms. Acad Pr.

Pollard, Percival, 1869-1911
xPollard, Percival.
   Their Day in Court. Johnson Repr.

Pollard, Richard. *see* Pollard, Richard N.

Pollard, Richard N.
xPollard, Richard.
   From Human Sentience to Drama: Principles
      of Critical Analysis, Tragic & Comedic. Ohio
      U Pr.

Pollard, Sidney.
xPollard, Sidney.
   Development of the British Economy:
      1914-1967. St Martin.

Pollard, William L.
xPollard, William L.
   A Study of Black Self Help. R & E Res Assoc.
Pollarolo, Carlo F. *see* Pollarolo, Carlo Francesco.

Pollarolo, Carlo Francesco.
xPollarolo, Carlo F.
   Gl'inganni felici. Garland Pub.

Pollay, Richard W.
xPollay, Richard W.
   ed. Information Sources in Advertising History.
      Greenwood.

Poller, R. C., 1928-
xPoller, R. C.
   Chemistry of Organotin Compounds. Acad Pr.
Polley, Howard F. *see* Polley, Howard Freeman.

Polley, Howard Freeman.
xPolley, Howard F.
   Rheumatologic Interviewing & Physical
      Examination of the Joints. Saunders.
Polley, Joseph. *see* Polley, Joseph H.

Polley, Joseph H., 1919-
xPolley, Joseph.
   Applied Real Estate Math. Reston.
xPolley, Joseph H.
   Applied Real Estate Math. Reston.

Polley, Judith.
xPolley, Judith.
   Passion's Prisoner. Dell.
   Val Verde. Delacorte.

Polley, Maxine.
xPolley, Maxine.
   Disco Basics. P-H.
Polliack, A. *see* Polliack, Aaron.

Polliack, Aaron, 1939-
xPolliack, A.
   Normal, Transformed & Leukemic Leukocytes:
      A Scanning Electron Microscopy Atlas.
      Springer-Verlag.

Pollin, Alice M.
xPollin, Alice M.
   ed. Concordancias de la obra poetica de
      Eugenio Florit. NYU Pr.
Pollin, Burton R. *see* Pollin, Burton Ralph.

Pollin, Burton Ralph.
xPollin, Burton R.
   Dictionary of Names & Titles in Poe's
      Collected Works. Da Capo.
   Discoveries in Poe. U of Notre Dame Pr.

Pollins, Harold.
xPollins, Harold.
   Britain's Railways: An Industrial History.
      Rowman.
Pollio, H. R. *see* Pollio, Howard R.

Pollio, Howard R.
xPollio, H. R.
   Psychology & the Poetics of Growth:
      Figurative Language in Psychology,
      Psychotherapy, & Education. Halsted Pr.
xPollio, Howard R.
   The Psychology of Symbolic Activity. A-W.

Pollis, Adamantia.
xPollis, Adamantia.
   ed. Human Rights: Cultural & Ideological
      Perspectives. Praeger.

Pollitt, J. J. *see* Pollitt, Jerry Jordan.

Pollitt, Jerry Jordan.
xPollitt, J. J.
   Art & Experience in Classical Greece.
      Cambridge U Pr.

Pollitt, Ronald.
xPollitt, Ronald.
   ed. Portraits in British History. Dorsey.

Pollock, Bruce.
xPollock, Bruce.
   It's Only Rock & Roll. HM.
   Me, Minsky, & Max. HM.

Pollock, Dean, 1897-
xPollock, Dean.
   Joseph, Chief of the Nez Perce. Binford.

Pollock, Frederick, Sir, Bart, 1845-1937
xPollock, Frederick.
   Expansion of the Common Law. Rothman.

Pollock, James K. *see* Pollock, James Kerr.

Pollock, James Kerr, 1898-
xPollock, James K.
   Money & Politics Abroad. Arno.

Pollock, Michael L.
xPollock, Michael L.
   Heart Disease & Rehabilitation. HM Prof Med
      Div.
Pollock, Norman C. *see* Pollock, Norman Charles.

Pollock, Norman Charles.
xPollock, Norman C.
   Studies in Emerging Africa. Rowman.

Pollock, Penny.
xPollock, Penny.
   Ants Don't Get Sunday off. Putnam.
   The Slug Who Thought He Was a Snail.
      Putnam.
Pollock, Ted. *see* Pollock, Theodore Marvin.

Pollock, Theodore Marvin, 1929-
xPollock, Ted.
   The Rainbow Man. McGraw.
Pollock, Thomas C. *see* Pollock, Thomas Clark.

Pollock, Thomas Clark, 1902-
xPollock, Thomas C.
   Nature of Literature: Its Relation to Science,
      Language & Human Experiences. Gordian.

Pollock, Vera.
xPollock, Vera.
   Newsprint. Inst Paper Chem.

Pollowitz, Melinda.
xPollowitz, Melinda.
   Cinnamon Cane. Har-Row.

Polo, Marco.
xPolo, Marco.
   The Description of the World. AMS Pr.

Poloma, Margaret M.
xPoloma, Margaret M.
   Contemporary Sociological Theory. Macmillan.
Polovko, A. M. *see* Polovko, Anatolii Mikhailovich.

Polovko, Anatolii Mikhailovich.
xPolovko, A. M.
   Fundamentals of Reliability Theory. Acad Pr.

Polow, Nancy.
xPolow, Nancy.
   An Articulation Curriculum for the S Sound. C
      C Thomas.
xPolow, Nancy G.
   A Stuttering Manual for the Speech Therapist.
      C C Thomas.
Polow, Nancy G. *see* Polow, Nancy.

Pols, Edward.
xPols, Edward.
   Meditation on a Prisoner: Towards
      Understanding Action & Mind. S Ill U Pr.
   Whitehead's Metaphysics: A Critical
      Examination of Process & Reality. S Ill U Pr.
Polsby, Nelson. *see* Polsby, Nelson W.

Polsby, Nelson W.
xPolsby, Nelson.
   Presidential Elections: Strategies of American
      Electoral Politics. Scribner.
xPolsby, Nelson W.
   Community Power & Political Theory: A
      Further Look at Problems of Evidence &
      Inference. Yale U Pr.
   ed. Reapportionment in the 1970s. U of Cal Pr.

Polseno, Jo.
xPolseno, Jo.
   illus. Secrets of a Cypress Swamp: The Natural
      History of Okefenokee. Western Pub.
   This Hawk Belongs to Me. McKay.

Polsky, Howard W.
xPolsky, Howard W.
   Cottage Six: Social System of Delinquent Boys
      in Residential Treatment. Krieger.
   Dynamics of Residential Treatment: A Social
      System Analysis. U of NC Pr.
   ed. Social System Perspectives in Residential
      Institutions. Mich St U Pr.

Polsky, Milton E.
xPolsky, Milton E.
   Let's Improvise: Becoming Creative, Expressive
      & Spontaneous Through Drama. P-H.
   Today's Young Stars of Stage & Screen. Watts.

Polsky, Ned.
xPolsky, Ned.
   Hustlers, Beats & Others. Doubleday.

Polsky, Samuel.
xPolsky, Samuel.
   ed. Medico-Legal Reader. Oceana.

Polson, C. J. *see* Polson, Cyril John.

Polson, Cyril John.
xPolson, C. J.
   Essentials of Forensic Medicine. Pergamon.

Polster, Erving.
xPolster, Irving.
   Gestalt Therapy Integrated: Contours of
      Theory & Practice. Random.

Polster, Irving. *see* Polster, Erving.

Polt, John H. *see* Polt, John Herman Richard.

Polt, John Herman Richard, 1929-
xPolt, John H.
   Gaspar Melchor de Jovellanos. Irvington.

Polten, Eric P.
xPolten, Eric P.

Critique of the Psycho-Physical Identity Theory: A Refutation of Scientific Materialism & an Establishment of Mind-Matter Dualism by Means of Philosophy & Scientific Method. Mouton.

Polunin, Miriam.
xPolunin, Miriam.
The Right Way to Eat: To Feel Good-or Even Better. Biblio Dist.

Polunin, Oleg.
xPolunin, Oleg.
The Concise Flowers of Europe. Oxford U Pr.

Polunin, Vladimir.
xPolunin, Vladimir.
The Continental Method of Scene Painting. Da Capo.

Polushkin, Maria.
xPolushkin, Maria.
Who Said Meow?. Crown.

Polvay, Marina.
xPolvay, Marina.
All Along the Danube: Classic Cookery from the Great Cuisines of Eastern Europe. P-H.

Polya, George.
xPolya, George.
Complex Variables. Wiley.
xPolya, Gyorgy.
Mathematical Discovery on Understanding, Learning & Teaching Problem Solving. Wiley.
Polya, Gyorgy. see Polya, George.

Polybius.
xPolybius.
Histories. Harvard U Pr.
The Histories of Polybius. Greenwood.

Polzin, Robert.
xPolzin, Robert.
Late Biblical Hebrew: Toward an Historical Typology of Biblical Hebrew Prose. Scholars Pr Ca.

Pomada, Elizabeth.
xPomada, Elizabeth.
Places to Go with Children in Northern California. Chronicle Bks.

Pomare, Maui.
xPomare, Maui.
Legends of the Maori. AMS Pr.
Pomerance, Herbert. see Pomerance, Herbert H.

Pomerance, Herbert H., 1918-
xPomerance, Herbert.
Growth Standards in Children. Har-Row.

Pomerance, Michla.
xPomerance, Michla.
The Advisory Function of the International Court in the League & U N Eras. Johns Hopkins.

Pomerantz, Charlotte.
xPomerantz, Charlotte.
The Ballad of the Long-Tailed Rat. Macmillan.
The Downtown Fairy Godmother. A-W.
The Princess & the Admiral. A-W.
The Tamarindo Puppy & Other Poems. Greenwillow.

Pomeranz, Felix.
xPomeranz, Felix.
Pensions: An Accounting & Management Guide. Ronald Pr.
Pomeranz, Y. see Pomeranz, Yeshajahu.

Pomeranz, Yeshajahu.
xPomeranz, Y.
Bread Science & Technology. AVI.

Pomerleau, Ovide F.
xPomerleau, Ovide F.
Break the Smoking Habit: A Behavioral Program for Giving up Cigarettes. Res Press.

Pomeroy, Claire, 1928-
xPomeroy, Claire.
Fight It Out, Work It Out, Love It Out. NAL.
Pomeroy, Earl S. see Pomeroy, Earl Spencer.

Pomeroy, Earl Spencer, 1915-
xPomeroy, Earl S.

Pacific Outpost: American Strategy in Guam & Micronesia. Russell.
The Pacific Slope: A History of California, Oregon, Washington, Idaho, Utah, & Nevada. U of Wash Pr.

Pomeroy, Lawrence R., 1925-
xPomeroy, Lawrence R.
ed. Cycles of Essential Elements. Acad Pr.

Pomeroy, Marnie.
xPomeroy, Marnie.
Calendar for Dinah. Masterwork Pr.

Pomeroy, Sarah B.
xPomeroy, Sarah B.
Goddesses, Whores, Wives, & Slaves: Women in Classical Antiquity. Schocken.
Pomeroy, Wardell B. see Pomeroy, Wardell Baxter.

Pomeroy, Wardell Baxter.
xPomeroy, Wardell B.
Boys & Sex. Delacorte.
Girls & Sex. Delacorte.

Pomeroy, William J., 1916-
xPomeroy, William J.
American Made Tragedy: Neo colonialism & Dictatorship in the Philippines. Intl Pub Co.
American Neo-Colonialism: Its Emergence in the Philippines & Asia. Intl Pub Co.
ed. Guerrilla Warfare & Marxism: A Collection of Writings from Karl Marx to the Present. Intl Pub Co.
Pomfret, John E. see Pomfret, John Edwin.

Pomfret, John Edwin, 1898-
xPomfret, John E.
Struggle for Land in Ireland 1800-1923. Russell.

Pommery, Jean.
xPommery, Jean.
How Human the Animals. Stein & Day.
What to Do till the Veterinarian Comes. Chilton

Pomper, Gerald M.
xPomper, Gerald M.
Party Renewal in America: Theory & Practice. Praeger.

Pomper, Philip.
xPomper, Philip.
Sergei Nechaev. Rutgers U Pr.

Pompilio, Loretta.
xPompilio, Loretta.
Soft People: The Art of Dollcrafting. Crossing Pr.

Pomroy, Martha.
xPomroy, Martha.
What Every Woman Needs to Know About the Law. Doubleday.

Ponasse, Daniel.
xPonasse, Daniel.
Mathematical Logic. Gordon.

Ponchaud, Francois, 1939-
xPonchaud, Francois.
Cambodia: Year Zero. HR&W.
Pond, Alonzo W. see Pond, Alonzo William.

Pond, Alonzo William, 1894-
xPond, Alonzo W.
The Desert World. Greenwood.

Pond, Desmond.
xPond, Desmond.
Counselling in Religion & Psychiatry. Oxford U Pr.

Pond, Grace.
xPond, Grace.
The Intelligent Cat. Dial.
The Intelligent Cat. Putnam.
Longhaired Cat. Arco.

Pond, Jean, 1929-
xPond, Jean.
Surviving. Ace Bks.
Pond, John. see Pond, John H.

Pond, John H., 1923-
xPond, John.

Your Future in Personnel Work. Rosen Pr.
Pond, Seymour G. see Pond, Seymour Gates.

Pond, Seymour Gates, 1896-
xPond, Seymour G.
History & Romance of Exploration, Told with Pictures. Cooper Sq.

Pond, Wilson G.
xPond, Wilson G.
The Biology of the Pig. Cornell U Pr.
Swine Production in Temperate & Tropical Environments. W H Freeman.

Ponder, Catherine.
xPonder, Catherine.
Dynamic Laws of Healing. De Vorss.
Open Your Mind to Prosperity. Unity Bks.
Pray & Grow Rich. P-H.
Prospering Power of Love. Unity Bks.

Ponder, James A.
xPonder, James A.
Evangelism Men: Proclaiming Doctrines of Salvation. Broadman.

Pong, David.
xPong, David.
A Critical Guide to the Kwangtung Provincial Archives Deposited at the Public Record Office, London. Harvard U Pr.

Ponge, Francis.
xPonge, Francis.
Sun Placed in the Abyss & Other Texts. SUN.
Things. SBD.

Poniachek, Harvey A.
xPoniachek, Harvey A.
Monetary Independence Under Flexible Exchange Rates. Lexington Bks.

Ponicsan, Darryl.
xPonicsan, Darryl.
The Accomplice. D Ponicsan.
Last Detail. NAL.
Tom Mix Died for Your Sins. D Ponicsan.
Tom Mix Died for Your Sins. Delacorte.

Ponnamperuma, Cyril, 1923-
xPonnamperuma, Cyril.
ed. Chemical Evolution of the Giant Planets. Acad Pr.

Ponse, Barbara.
xPonse, Barbara.
Identities in the Lesbian World: The Social Construction of Self. Greenwood.
Ponsioen, J. A. see Ponsioen, Johannes Antonius.

Ponsioen, Johannes Antonius, 1911-
xPonsioen, J. A.
Analysis of Social Change Reconsidered: A Sociological Study. Mouton.
Ponsonby, Arthur. see Ponsonby, Arthur Ponsonby.

Ponsonby, Arthur Ponsonby, Baron, 1871-1946
xPonsonby, Arthur.
British Diarists. Arden Lib.
British Diarists. Folcroft.

Ponsor, Y. R.
xPonsor, Y. R.
Gawain & the Green Knight: Adventure at Camelot. Macmillan.

Ponte, Lowell, 1946-
xPonte, Lowell.
The Cooling. P-H.
Ponti. see Ponti, Irene Y.

Ponti, Irene Y.
xPonti.
A Guide for Financing School Food & Nutrition Services. Assn Sch Busn.
Pontifical Academy of Sciences, 1975. see Pontificia Accademia Delle Scienze, Rome.

Pontifical Institute of Mediaeval Studies.
xPontifical Institute of Mediaeval Studies, Toronto.

Dictionary Catalog of the Library of the
Pontifical Institute of Mediaeval Studies:
First Supplement. G K Hall.
Dictionary Catalogue of the Library of the
Pontifical Institute of Mediaeval Studies:
First Supplement. G K Hall.
xPontifical Institute of Medieval Studies, Ontario.
Dictionary Catalogue of the Library of the
Pontifical Institute of Medieval Studies. G K
Hall.
Pontifical Institute of Medieval Studies, Ontario. *see*
Pontifical Institute of Mediaeval Studies.
Pontificia Academia Scientiarum - Study Week - 1964.
see Pontificia Accademia Delle Scienze, Rome.
Pontificia Accademia Delle Scienze, Rome.
xPontifical Academy of Sciences, 1975.
Biological & Artificial Membranes &
Desalination of Water: Proceedings. Elsevier.
xPontificia Academia Scientiarum - Study Week -
1964.
Brain & Conscious Experience. Springer-Verlag.
Pontiflet, Ted.
xPontiflet, Ted.
Poochie. Dial.
Pooch, U. *see* Pooch, U. W.
Pooch, U. W.
xPooch, U.
Designing Microcomputer Systems. Hayden.
xPooch, Udo W.
Minicomputers: Hardware, Software, &
Selection. West Pub.
Pooch, Udo W. *see* Pooch, U. W.
Pool, Bernard.
xPool, Bernard.
Navy Board Contracts, 1660-1832: Contract
Administration Under the Navy Board. Shoe
String.
Pool, D. Ian. *see* Pool, David Ian.
Pool, David Ian.
xPool, D. Ian.
The Maori Population of New Zealand
1769-1971. Oxford U Pr.
Pool, Eugene.
xPool, Eugene.
The Captain of Battery Park. A-W.
Pool, Gerald M. Van. *see* Van Pool, Gerald M.
Pool, J. Lawrence. *see* Pool, James Lawrence.
Pool, James Lawrence, 1906-
xPool, J. Lawrence.
Your Brain & Nerves. Scribner.
Pool, Jonathan.
xPool, Jonathan.
Computer Assisted Instruction in Political
Science. Am Political.
Pool, Phoebe.
xPool, Phoebe.
Impressionism. Oxford U Pr.
Poole, Adrian.
xPoole, Adrian.
Gissing in Context. Rowman.
Poole, Charles P.
xPoole, Charles P.
Relaxation in Magnetic Resonance: Dielectric
& Mossbauer Applications. Acad Pr.
Poole, Ernest, 1880-1950
xPoole, Ernest.
The Bridge: My Own Story. Johnson Repr.
His Family. Larlin Corp.
His Family. Lighthouse Pr NY.
Poole, Frederick K. *see* Poole, Frederick King.
Poole, Frederick King.
xPoole, Frederick K.
Jordan. Watts.
Jordan. Watts.
Southeast Asia. Watts.
Thailand. Watts.
Poole, Gray.
xPoole, Gray J.
Architects & Man's Skyline. Dodd.
Poole, Gray J. *see* Poole, Gray.

Poole, James.
xPoole, James.
Badminton. Goodyear.
Poole, Josephine.
xPoole, Josephine.
Moon Eyes. Little.
Poole, Keith B.
xPoole, Keith B.
Ghosts of Wessex. David & Charles.
Poole, Kenyon E. *see* Poole, Kenyon Edwards.
Poole, Kenyon Edwards, 1909-
xPoole, Kenyon E.
German Financial Policies, 1932-1939. Gordon
Pr.
German Financial Policies, 1932-1939. Russell.
Poole, Michael.
xPoole, Michael.
Workers Participation in Industry. Routledge &
Kegan.
Poole, Peter A.
xPoole, Peter A.
Eight Presidents & Indochina. Krieger.
Poole, Robert. *see* Poole, Robert W.
Poole, Robert W., 1944-
xPoole, Robert.
Cutting Back City Hall. Universe.
xPoole, Robert W.
An Introduction to Quantitative Ecology.
McGraw.
Poole, Shona C. *see* Poole, Shona Crawford.
Poole, Shona Crawford.
xPoole, Shona C.
The Christmas Cookbook. Atheneum.
Poole, Susan. *see* Poole, Susan D.
Poole, Susan D.
xPoole, Susan.
Nathan Hale. Dandelion Pr.
Poole, Victoria.
xPoole, Victoria.
Thursday's Child. Little.
Poole, William, 1937-
xPoole, William.
Money & the Economy: A Monetarist View.
A-W.
Pooley, Robert C. *see* Pooley, Robert Cecil.
Pooley, Robert Cecil, 1898-
xPooley, Robert C.
Teaching English Grammar. Irvington.
The Teaching of English Usage. NCTE.
Poonen, Zac.
xPoonen, Zac.
Where Do I Go from Here, God?. Tyndale.
Poore, Benjamin P. *see* Poore, Benjamin Perley.
Poore, Benjamin Perley, 1820-1887
xPoore, Benjamin P.
ed. Descriptive Catalogue of the Government
Publications of the United States, September
5, 1774 - March 4, 1881. Johnson Repr.
The Federal & State Constitutions, Colonial
Charters, & Other Organic Laws of the U. S.
Compiled Under an Order of the United
States Senate. B Franklin.
Perley's Reminiscences of Sixty Years in the
National Metropolis. AMS Pr.
Poore, Henry R. *see* Poore, Henry Rankin.
Poore, Henry Rankin, 1859-1940
xPoore, Henry R.
Composition in Art. Dover.
Composition in Art. Peter Smith.
Poort, Jon M. *see* Poort, Jon Michael.
Poort, Jon Michael, 1936-
xPoort, Jon M.
Historical Geology: Interpretations &
Applications. Burgess.
Poovey, W. A. *see* Poovey, William Arthur.
Poovey, William Arthur, 1913-
xPoovey, W. A.

The Days Before Christmas: How Your Family
Can Prepare for the Coming of Jesus.
Augsburg.
The Days Before Easter. Augsburg.
The Days of Pentecost: Devotions, Customs, &
Summertime Activities to Celebrate the
Season of the Spirit. Augsburg.
Faith Is the Password: Meditations on Romans.
Augsburg.
Let Us Adore Him: Dramas & Meditations for
Advent, Christmas, Epiphany. Augsburg.
ed. Planning a Christian Funeral: A Minister's
Guide. Augsburg.
The Prayer He Taught: Seven Dramas &
Meditations on the Lord's Prayer. Augsburg.
Popa, Vasko.
xPopa, Vasko.
The Little Box. Charioteer.
Pope, Alan.
xPope, Alan.
High-Speed Wind Tunnel Testing. Krieger.
Low-Speed Wind Tunnel Testing. Wiley.
Pope, Alexander.
xPope, Alexander.
Memoirs of the Extraordinary Life, Works &
Discoveries of Martinus Scriblerus. Russell.
Rape of the Lock. Aurora Pubs.
The Rape of the Lock. Dover.
The Rape of the Lock. Methuen Inc.
Rape of the Lock. Oxford U Pr.
Works of Alexander Pope. Gordian.
Pope, Arthur U. *see* Pope, Arthur Upham.
Pope, Arthur Upham, 1881-1969
xPope, Arthur U.
An Introduction to Persian Art Since the
Seventh Century A. D. Greenwood.
Masterpieces of Persian Art. Greenwood.
Pope, Clayne L.
xPope, Clayne L.
The Impact of the Ante-Bellum Tariff on
Income Distribution. Arno.
Pope, Dudley.
xPope, Dudley.
Great Gamble. S&S.
Triton Brig. PB.
Pope, Elizabeth M. *see* Pope, Elizabeth Marie.
Pope, Elizabeth Marie, 1917-
xPope, Elizabeth M.
Paradise Regained: The Tradition & the Poem.
Russell.
The Perilous Gard. HM.
Pope, Hugh.
xPope, Hugh.
English Versions of the Bible. Greenwood.
Pope, J. K. *see* Pope, J. Keith.
Pope, J. Keith, 1919-
xPope, J. K.
Decade of Adventure. Singer Island.
Pope, Jesse E. *see* Pope, Jesse Eliphalet.
Pope, Jesse Eliphalet, 1869-
xPope, Jesse E.
ed. Clothing Industry in New York. B
Franklin.
Pope, John.
xPope, John.
Tour Through the Southern & Western
Territories of the United States of North
America, the Spanish Dominions on the
River Mississippi & the Floridas, the
Countries of the Creek Nations, & Many
Uninhabited Parts. Arno.
A Tour Through the Southern & Western
Territories of the United States of
North-America: The Spanish Dominions on
the River Mississippi, & the Floridas. the
Countries of the Creek Nations; & Many
Uninhabited Parts. U Presses Fla.
Pope, Joyce.
xPope, Joyce.

A Closer Look at Jungles. Watts.
Pope, K. S. see Pope, Kenneth S.
Pope, Kenneth S.
xPope, K. S.
ed. The Stream of Consciousness: Scientific
Investigations into the Flow of Human
Experience. Plenum Pub.
Pope, Lillie.
xPope, Lillie.
Guidelines to Teaching Remedial Reading.
Book-Lab.
Tutor!: A Handbook for Tutorial Programs.
Book-Lab.
Pope, Margaret M. see Pope, Margaret Mcconkie.
Pope, Margaret Mcconkie.
xPope, Margaret M.
War on Weight. Brigham.
Pope, Maurice.
xPope, Maurice.
The Ancient Greeks: How They Lived &
Worked. Dufour.
Pope, Myrtle P. see Pope, Myrtle Pihlman.
Pope, Myrtle Pihlman.
xPope, Myrtle P.
Critical Bibliography of Works by & About
Francis Thompson. NY Pub Lib.
Pope, Norris, 1945-
xPope, Norris.
Dickens & Charity. Columbia U Pr.
Pope, Robert G.
xPope, Robert G.
Half-Way Covenant: Church Membership in
Puritan New England. Princeton U Pr.
Pope, Ruth V. see Pope, Ruth Vesta.
Pope, Ruth Vesta, 1891-
xPope, Ruth V.
Factors Affecting the Elimination of Women
Students from Selected Coeducational
Colleges of Liberal Arts. AMS Pr.
Pope, Saxton T.
xPope, Saxton T.
Bows & Arrows. U of Cal Pr.
Pope, Whitney.
xPope, Whitney.
Durkheim's Suicide: A Classic Analyzed. U of
Chicago Pr.
Pope-Hennessy, John. see Pope-Hennessy, John
Wyndham.
Pope-Hennessy, John Wyndham, Sir, 1913-
xPope-Hennessy, John.
Luca della Robbia. Cornell U Pr.
Portrait in the Renaissance. Princeton U Pr.
Popejoy, Bill.
xPopejoy, Bill.
The Case for Divine Healing. Gospel Pub.
Popenoe, David, 1932-
xPopenoe, David.
Sociology. P-H.
The Suburban Environment: Sweden & the
United States. U of Chicago Pr.
Popescu, Julian.
xPopescu, Julian.
Let's Visit Russia. John Day.
Popham, E. see Popham, Estelle L.
Popham, Estelle L.
xPopham, E.
A Teaching-Learning System for Business
Education. McGraw.
Popham, G. T.
xPopham, G. T.
Government in Britain. Pergamon.
Popham, James. see Popham, W. James.
Popham, W. see Popham, W. James.
Popham, W. James.
xPopham, James.
Establishing Instructional Goals. P-H.
Planning an Instructional Sequence. P-H.
xPopham, W.
Systematic Instruction. P-H.
xPopham, W. James.

Advising Schools: A Handbook for Concerned
Citizens. Instruct Object.
Criterion-Referenced Measurement. P-H.
Uses of Instructional Objectives: A Personal
Perspective. Pitman Learning.
Popiel, W. J., 1932-
xPopiel, W. J.
Introduction to Colloid Science. Exposition.
Popkin, Gary. see Popkin, Gary S.
Popkin, Gary S.
xPopkin, Gary.
Introduction to Data Processing. HM.
Popkin, Michael.
xPopkin, Michael.
ed. Modern Black Writers. Ungar.
Popkin, Richard H. see Popkin, Richard Henry.
Popkin, Richard Henry, 1923-
xPopkin, Richard H.
The History of Scepticism from Erasmus to
Spinoza. U of Cal Pr.
Popkin, Samuel. see Popkin, Samuel L.
Popkin, Samuel L.
xPopkin, Samuel.
The Rational Peasant: The Political Economy
of Rural Society in Vietnam. U of Cal Pr.
Popko, Kathleen M.
xPopko, Kathleen M.
Regulatory Controls: Implications for the
Community Hospital. Lexington Bks.
Poplasen, Ilija.
xPoplasen, Ilija.
Computerized Two & Three Dimensional
Finite Existents Analysis. MIR PA.
Pople, J. A. see Pople, John A.
Pople, John A.
xPople, J. A.
Approximate Molecular Orbital Theory.
McGraw.
Poplin, Dennis E.
xPoplin, Dennis E.
Communities: A Survey of Theories &
Methods of Research. Macmillan.
Popoff, Irmis B.
xPopoff, Irmis B.
Gurdjieff: His Work on Myself ... with Others
... for the Work. Weiser.
Popov, A. A. see Popov, Andrei Aleksandrovich.
Popov, Andrei Aleksandrovich.
xPopov, A. A.
Nganasan: The Material Culture of the Tavgi
Samoyeds. Res Ctr Lang Semiotic.
Popov, Egor P. see Popov, Egor Paul.
Popov, Egor Paul.
xPopov, Egor P.
Introduction to Mechanics of Solids. P-H.
Popovic, Vojin.
xPopovic, Vojin.
Hypothermia in Biology & in Medicine. Grune.
Popovics, Sandor, 1921-
xPopovics, Sandor.
Concrete Making Materials. McGraw.
Popp, A. John.
xPopp, A. John.
ed. Neural Trauma. Raven.
Popp, Dennis.
xPopp, Dennis.
Ice Racing. Lerner Pubns.
Popp, Edward E.
xPopp, Edward E.
The Great Cookie Jar: Taking the Mysteries
Out of the Money System. Wis Ed Fund.
Money, Bona Fide or Non-Bona Fide. Wis Ed
Fund.
Popp, H. see Popp, Herbert.
Popp, Herbert.
xPopp, H.

ed. Classification of Algebraic Varieties &
Compact Complex Manifolds.
Springer-Verlag.
Popp, Lothar.
xPopp, Lothar.
Ultrasound in Obstetrics & Gynecology.
McGraw.
Popper, Frank.
xPopper, Frank.
President's Commissions. Kraus Repr.
Popper, Karl R. see Popper, Karl Raimund.
Popper, Karl Raimund, 1902-
xPopper, Karl R.
Conjectures & Refutations: The Growth of
Scientific Knowledge. Har-Row.
The Logic of Scientific Discovery. Basic.
Logic of Scientific Discovery. Har-Row.
Objective Knowledge: An Evolutionary
Approach. Oxford U Pr.
The Poverty of Historicism. Har-Row.
Popper, William, 1874-1963
xPopper, William.
Censorship of Hebrew Books. B Franklin.
Censorship of Hebrew Books. Ktav.
Poppke, William R. see Poppke, William Randolph.
Poppke, William Randolph.
xPoppke, William R.
How to Catch a Crab. Stein & Day.
Popplewell, George.
xPopplewell, George.
Modern Weightlifting & Powerlifting.
Merrimack Bk Serv.
Poppy, Willard J.
xPoppy, Willard J.
Exploring the Physical Sciences. P-H.

Popular Science Authors. see Popular Science Publishing
Company, New York.
Popular Science Publishing Company, New York.
xPopular Science Authors.
Woodworking Projects for the Home.
Har-Row.
Popular Council, New York.
xPopulation Council.
Catalogue of the Population Council Library. G
K Hall.
The Population Council: A Chronicle of the
First Twenty-Five Years, 1952-1977.
Population Coun.
Population Council. see Popular Council, New York.
Population Institute.
xPopulation Institute.
The Population Activist's Handbook.
Macmillan.
Population Activist's Handbook. Macmillan.
Population Reference Bureau. see Population Reference
Bureau, Washington, D.C.
Population Reference Bureau Editors. see Population
Reference Bureau, Washington, D.C.
Population Reference Bureau, Washington, D.C.
xPopulation Reference Bureau.
People!. Columbia Bks.
xPopulation Reference Bureau Editors.
World Population Growth & Response
1965-1975: A Decade of Global Action.
Population Ref.
Porambo, Ron.
xPorambo, Ron.
No Cause for Indictment: An Autopsy of
Newark. HR&W.
Porat, Dan I.
xPorat, Dan I.
Introduction to Digital Techniques. Wiley.
Porat, Frieda.
xPorat, Frieda.
Changing Your Life Style. Lyle Stuart.
Porch, Douglas.
xPorch, Douglas.

Army & Revolution: France 1815-1848.
Routledge & Kegan.
The Portuguese Armed Forces & the
Revolution. Hoover Inst Pr.
Porche, Francois, 1877-1944
xPorche, Francois.
Charles Baudelaire. Folcroft.
Porges, G.
xPorges, G.
Applied Acoustics. Halsted Pr.
Porges, Irwin.
xPorges, Irwin.
Edgar Rice Burroughs: The Man Who Created
Tarzan. Ballantine.
Edgar Rice Burroughs: The Man Who Created
Tarzan. Brigham.
Porges, S. W. see Porges, Stephen W.
Porges, Stephen W.
xPorges, S. W.
ed. Psychophysiology. Acad Pr.
Pories, Walter J.
xPories, Walter J.
ed. Clinical Applications of Zinc Metabolism. C
C Thomas.
Porn, Ingmar.
xPorn, Ingmar.
The Logic of Power. Biblio Dist.
Porrier, Herbert Le. see Le Porrier, Herbert.
Port, Michael. see Port, Michael Harry.
Port, Michael Harry.
xPort, Michael.
ed. The Houses of Parliament. Yale U Pr.
Port, Sidney C.
xPort, Sidney C.
Brownian Motion & Classical Potential Theory.
Acad Pr.
Portal, Gerald H. see Portal, Gerald Herbert.
Portal, Gerald Herbert.
xPortal, Gerald H.
British Mission to Uganda in 1893. Negro U
Pr.
Portalie, Eugene, 1852-1909
xPortalie, Eugene.
A Guide to the Thought of Saint Augustine.
Greenwood.
Porte, Joel.
xPorte, Joel.
Representative Man: Ralph Waldo Emerson in
His Time. Oxford U Pr.
Portenier, Lillian G. see Portenier, Lillian Gertrude.
Portenier, Lillian Gertrude, 1890-
xPortenier, Lillian G.
Pupils of Low Mentality in High School. AMS
Pr.
Porteous, Alvin C., 1922-
xPorteous, Alvin C.
Preaching to Suburban Captives. Judson.
Porteous, J. Douglas. see Porteous, John Douglas.
Porteous, John Douglas.
xPorteous, J. Douglas.
Environment & Behavior: Planning & Everyday
Urban Life. A-W.
Porter, A. Kingsley. see Porter, Arthur Kingsley.
Porter, A. N. see Porter, Andrew N.
Porter, Albert W.
xPorter, Albert W.
The Art of Sketching. Davis Mass.
Porter, Andrew N.
xPorter, A. N.
The Origins of the South African War: Joseph
Chamberlain & the Diplomacy of Imperialism
1895-1899. St Martin.
Porter, Archie, 1924-
xPorter, Archie.
Complete Book of the Man for Man Defense.
P-H.
Porter, Arthur K. see Porter, Arthur Kingsley.
Porter, Arthur Kingsley.
xPorter, A. Kingsley.

Lombard Architecture. Hacker.
Spanish Romanesque Sculpture. Hacker.
xPorter, Arthur K.
Crosses & Culture of Ireland. Arno.
The Crosses & Culture of Ireland. Elliots Bks.
Porter, Barton.
xPorter, Barton.
Listen to the Millrace. M J Stone.
Porter, Bern. see Porter, Bernard H.
Porter, Bernard.
xPorter, Bernard.
The Lion's Share: A Short History of British
Imperialism, 1850-1970. Longman.
Porter, Bernard H.
xPorter, Bern.
I've Left. Ultramarine Pub.
xPorter, Bernard H.
I've Left. Porter.
I've Left. Univ Microfilms.
Porter, Bertha.
xPorter, Bertha.
Topographical Bibliography of Ancient
Egyptian Hieroglyphic Texts, Reliefs &
Paintings III: Memphis Part 2. Intl Schol Bk
Serv.
Porter, Burton F. see Porter, Burton Frederick.
Porter, Burton Frederick.
xPorter, Burton F.
The Good Life: Alternatives in Ethics.
Macmillan.
Porter, Cedric L. see Porter, Cedric Lambert.
Porter, Cedric Lambert, 1905-
xPorter, Cedric L.
Taxonomy of Flowering Plants. W H Freeman.
Porter, Charles W. see Porter, Charles Wesley.
Porter, Charles Wesley, 1904-
xPorter, Charles W.
The Career of Theophile Delcasse. Greenwood.
Porter, Curt C., 1914-
xPorter, Curt C.
Chemical Mechanisms of Drug Action. C C
Thomas.
Porter, Dale H.
xPorter, Dale H.
Abolition of the Slave Trade in England,
1784-1807. Shoe String.
Porter, Darwin.
xPorter, Darwin.
Marika. Arbor Hse.
Marika. Berkley Pub.
Porter, David L., 1941-
xPorter, David L.
Congress & the Waning of the New Deal.
Kennikat.
Porter, Dorothy B. see Porter, Dorothy Burnett.
Porter, Dorothy Burnett, 1905-
xPorter, Dorothy B.
ed. Afro-Braziliana: A Working Bibliography.
G K Hall.
Porter, Eliot.
xPorter, Eliot.
Appalachian Wilderness: The Great Smoky
Mountains. Dutton.
Porter, Elizabeth.
xPorter, Elizabeth.
Water Management in England & Wales.
Cambridge U Pr.
Porter, Enid.
xPorter, Enid.
The Folklore of East Anglia. Rowman.
Porter, Gareth, 1942-
xPorter, Gareth.
A Peace Denied: The United States, Vietnam,
& the Paris Agreement. Ind U Pr.
Porter, Gene S. see Porter, Gene Stratton.
Porter, Gene Stratton, 1863-1924
xPorter, Gene S.

At the Foot of the Rainbow. Am
Repr-Rivercity Pr.
Freckles. Harmony & Co.
Freckles. Scholarly.
Porter, George, 1910-
xPorter, George.
World of the Frog & the Toad. Lippincott.
Porter, George H. see Porter, George Henry.
Porter, George Henry, 1878-
xPorter, George H.
Ohio Politics During the Civil War Period.
AMS Pr.
Porter, George R. see Porter, George Richardson.
Porter, George Richardson.
xPorter, George R.
Progress of the Nation. Kelley.
Porter, H. C. see Porter, Harry Culverwell.
Porter, Harry Culverwell.
xPorter, H. C.
Inconstant Savage: England & the North
American Indian, 1500-1660. Biblio Dist.
ed. Puritanism in Tudor England. U of SC Pr.
Reformation & Reaction in Tudor Cambridge.
Shoe String.
Porter, Henry, fl. 1599
xPorter, Henry.
Two Angry Women of Abingdon. AMS Pr.
Porter, J. A. see Porter, Joseph Ashby.
Porter, J. R. see Porter, Joshua Roy.
Porter, Jack W.
xPorter, Jack W.
The Catholic Church in Greencastle, Putnam
County, Indiana 1848-1978. St Paul the
Apostle.
Porter, James A. see Porter, James Amos.
Porter, James Amos, 1905-
xPorter, James A.
Modern Negro Art. Arno.
Porter, Joe A. see Porter, Joe Ashby.
Porter, Joe Ashby, 1942-
xPorter, Joe A.
Eelgrass. New Directions.
Porter, John A. see Porter, John Addison.
Porter, John Addison, 1856-1900
xPorter, John A.
The City of Washington, Its Origin &
Administration. AMS Pr.
The City of Washington, Its Origin &
Administration. Johnson Repr.
Porter, John R., 1932-
xPorter, John R.
Dating Habits of Young Black Americans: And
Almost Everybody Else's Too. Kendall-Hunt.
Porter, Jonathan.
xPorter, Jonathan.
Tseng Kuo-Fan's Private Bureaucracy. IEAS
Ctr Chinese Stud.
Porter, Joseph Ashby, 1942-
xPorter, J. A.
The Drama of Speech Acts: Shakespeare's
Lancastrian Tetralogy. U of Cal Pr.
Porter, Joshua Roy.
xPorter, J. R.
ed. Animals in Folklore. Rowman.
Porter, Katherine A. see Porter, Katherine Anne.
Porter, Katherine Anne, 1894-
xPorter, Katherine A.
The Collected Stories of Katherine Anne
Porter. HarBraceJ.
Collected Stories of Katherine Anne Porter.
NAL.
Days Before. Arno.
Porter, Keith R.
xPorter, Keith R.
Fine Structure of Cells & Tissues. Lea &
Febiger.
Porter, Kenneth W. see Porter, Kenneth Wiggins.
Porter, Kenneth Wiggins, 1905-
xPorter, Kenneth W.

The Negro on the American Frontier. Arno.
Porter, Kent.
   xPorter, Kent.
      Building Model Ships from Scratch. TAB Bks.
Porter, Kirk H. *see* Porter, Kirk Harold.
Porter, Kirk Harold, 1891-
   xPorter, Kirk H.
      History of Suffrage in the United States. AMS
        Pr.
      History of Suffrage in the United States.
        Greenwood.
Porter, Larry. *see* Porter, Larry C.
Porter, Larry C.
   xPorter, Larry.
      Illustrated Stories from Church History.
        Promised Land.
Porter, Laurence M., 1936-
   xPorter, Laurence M.
      The Literary Dream in French Romanticism: A
        Psychoanalytic Interpretation. Wayne St U
        Pr.
Porter, Luz. *see* Porter, Luz Sobong.
Porter, Luz Sobong.
   xPorter, Luz.
      Child Health Nursing Review. Arco.
Porter, M. Gilbert.
   xPorter, M. Gilbert.
      Whence the Power?: The Artistry & Humanity
        of Saul Bellow. U of Mo Pr.
Porter, Michael E., 1947-
   xPorter, Michael E.
      Interbrand Choice Strategy, & Bilateral Market
        Power. Harvard U Pr.
Porter, Noah, 1811-1892
   xPorter, Noah.
      American Colleges & the American Public.
        Arno.
Porter, Pat. *see* Porter, Patricia A.
Porter, Patricia A.
   xPorter, Pat.
      Active English: Understand, Practice,
        Communicate. P-H.
Porter, Peter.
   xPorter, Peter.
      Last of England. Oxford U Pr.
      Preaching to the Converted. Oxford U Pr.
Porter, Philip W. *see* Porter, Philip Wiley.
Porter, Philip Wiley.
   xPorter, Philip W.
      Cleveland: Confused City on a Seesaw. Ohio St
        U Pr.
Porter, R. *see* Porter, Raymond J.
Porter, Raymond J.
   xPorter, R.
      Brendan Behan. Columbia U Pr.
   xPorter, Raymond J.
      P. H. Pearse. Twayne.
Porter, Richard D. *see* Porter, Richard Dawson.
Porter, Richard Dawson.
   xPorter, Richard D.
      Introduction to Fibre Bundles. Dekker.
Porter, Robert G.
   xPorter, Robert G.
      Preparation of Computerized Index to
        Nonfiction of Thomas Mann. Rice Univ.
Porter, Robert P. *see* Porter, Robert Percival.
Porter, Robert Percival, 1852-1917
   xPorter, Robert P.
      Industrial Cuba. Gordon Pr.
Porter, Russell W. *see* Porter, Russell Williams.
Porter, Russell Williams, 1871-1949
   xPorter, Russell W.
      The Arctic Diary of Russell Williams Porter. U
        Pr of Va.
Porter, Sheena.
   xPorter, Sheena.
      Nordy Bank. Oxford U Pr.
Porter, Sylvia. *see* Porter, Sylvia Field.
Porter, Sylvia Field, 1913-
   xPorter, Sylvia.

Sylvia Porter's New Money Book for the 80's.
      Avon.
Porter, Tom.
   xPorter, Tom.
      Color for Architecture. Van Nos Reinhold.
      How Architects Visualize. Van Nos Reinhold.
Porter, Willard H., 1920-
   xPorter, Willard H.
      How to Enjoy the Quarter Horse. A S Barnes.
Porter, William E. *see* Porter, William Earl.
Porter, William Earl.
   xPorter, William E.
      Assault on the Media: The Nixon Years. U of
        Mich Pr.
Porterfield, Bill.
   xPorterfield, Bill.
      A Loose Herd of Texans. Tex A&M Univ Pr.
Porterfield, Nolan.
   xPorterfield, Nolan.
      Jimmie Rodgers: The Life & Times of
        America's Blue Yodeler. U of Ill Pr.
Porterfield, William M. *see* Porterfield, William W.
Porterfield, William W.
   xPorterfield, William M.
      Concepts of Chemistry. Norton.
Porteus, Stanley D. *see* Porteus, Stanley David.
Porteus, Stanley David, 1883-
   xPorteus, Stanley D.
      Century of Social Thinking in Hawaii. Pacific
        Bks.
      A Psychologist of Sorts: The Autobiography &
        Publications of the Inventor of the Porteus
        Maze Tests. Pacific Bks.
      The Psychology of a Primitive People: Study of
        the Australian Aborigine. Arno.
Portis, Charles.
   xPortis, Charles.
      The Dog of the South. Knopf.
      Norwood. S&S.
Portland Cement Association. *see* Portland Cement
   Association, Chicago.
Portland Cement Association, Chicago.
   xPortland Cement Association.
      Administrative Practices in Concrete
        Construction. Wiley.
      Basic Concrete Construction Practices. Wiley.
      Concrete Construction & Estimates. Craftsman.
      Concrete Inspection Procedures. Wiley.
      Design & Construction of Large-Panel
        Concrete Structures (EBO96D):
        Methodology. Portland Cement.
      Design & Construction of Large-Panel
        Concrete Structures (EBO95D): Special
        Topics. Portland Cement.
      Design & Construction of Large-Panel
        Concrete Structures, Report 4: A Design
        Approach to General Structural Integrity.
        Portland Cement.
      Principles of Quality Concrete. Wiley.
      Special Concretes, Mortars, & Products. Wiley.
Portman, David N.
   xPortman, David N.
      ed. Early Reform in American Higher
        Education. Nelson-Hall.
Portman, John. *see* Portman, John Calvin.
Portman, John Calvin.
   xPortman, John.
      The Architect As Developer. McGraw.
Portmann, Adolf, 1897-
   xPortmann, Adolf.
      Animal Forms & Patterns: A Study of the
        Appearance of Animals. Schocken.
Portmann, Michel.
   xPortmann, Michel.
      The Ear & Temporal Bone. Masson Pub.
Portney, Gerald L.
   xPortney, Gerald L.
      Glaucoma Guidebook. Lea & Febiger.
Portnoy, Julius, 1910-
   xPortnoy, Julius.

Music in the Life of Man. Greenwood.
Portugal, Pamela R. *see* Portugal, Pamela Rainbear.
Portugal, Pamela Rainbear.
   xPortugal, Pamela R.
      A Place for Human Beings. Wild Horses Potted
        Plant.
Portuges, Paul, 1945-
   xPortuges, Paul.
      The Visionary Poetics of Allen Ginsberg.
        Ross-Erikson.
Posavac, Emil J.
   xPosavac, Emile J.
      Program Evaluation: Methods & Case Studies.
        P-H.
Posavac, Emile J. *see* Posavac, Emil J.
Poschinger, Margarete. *see* Poschinger, Margarete
   (Landau).
Poschinger, Margarete (Landau), Edle Von, 1862-
   xPoschinger, Margarete.
      Life of the Emperor Frederick.. Scholarly.
Posell, Elsa. *see* Posell, Elsa Z.
Posell, Elsa Z.
   xPosell, Elsa.
      This Is an Orchestra. HM.
Poser, S. *see* Poser, Sigrid.
Poser, Sigrid, 1941-
   xPoser, S.
      Multiple Sclerosis: An Analysis of 812 Cases
        by Means of Electronic Data Processing.
        Springer-Verlag.
Posey, Jeanne K.
   xPosey, Jeanne K.
      The Horse Buyer's Guide. A S Barnes.
      The Rider's Handbook. Arco.
Posey, Rollin B. *see* Posey, Rollin Bennett.
Posey, Rollin Bennett, 1907-
   xPosey, Rollin B.
      American Government. Littlefield.
Posey, Walter B. *see* Posey, Walter Brownlow.
Posey, Walter Brownlow, 1900-
   xPosey, Walter B.
      The Development of Methodism in the Old
        Southwest: 1783-1824. Porcupine Pr.
Positron Annihilation Conference - Wayne State
   University - 1965. *see* Positron Annihilation
   Conference, Wayne State University, 1965.
**Positron Annihilation Conference, Wayne State
   University, 1965.**
   xPositron Annihilation Conference - Wayne State
      University - 1965.
      Positron Annihilation: Proceedings. Acad Pr.
Posner, Arlene.
   xPosner, Arlene.
      China: A Resource & Curriculum Guide. U of
        Chicago Pr.
Posner, Charles.
   xPosner, Charles.
      Reflections on the Revolution in France: 1968.
        Peter Smith.
Posner, Ernst.
   xPosner, Ernst.
      American State Archives. U of Chicago Pr.
Posner, George J.
   xPosner, George J.
      Course Design: A Guide to Curriculum
        Development for Teachers. Longman.
Posner, Richard.
   xPosner, Richard.
      The Lovers. Fawcett.
Posner, Richard A.
   xPosner, Richard A.
      Economic Analysis of Law. Little.
      Regulation of Advertising by the FTC. Am
        Enterprise.
Posner, Zalman I.
   xPosner, Zalman I.

Think Jewish: A Contemporary View of
Judaism, a Jewish View of Today's World.
Kesher.

Pospisil, Leopold J.
xPospisil, Leopold J.
The Ethnology of Law. Benjamin-Cummings.
The Kapauku Papuans of West New Guinea.
HR&W.

Possien, Wilma M.
xPossien, Wilma M.
They All Need to Talk: Oral Communication
in the Language Arts Program. P-H.

Post, Albert, 1915-
xPost, Albert.
Popular Freethought in America, 1825-1850.
Octagon.

Post, C. Gordon. see Post, Charles Gordon.
Post, Chandler R. see Post, Chandler Rathfon.

Post, Chandler Rathfon, 1881-1959
xPost, Chandler R.
Mediaeval Spanish Allegory. Greenwood.

Post, Charles G. see Post, Charles Gordon.

Post, Charles Gordon, 1903-
xPost, C. Gordon.
Supreme Court & Political Questions. Da Capo.
xPost, Charles G.
The Supreme Court & Political Questions.
AMS Pr.

Post, Henry.
xPost, Henry.
The Ultimate Man. Berkley Pub.

Post, J. B., 1937-
xPost, J. B.
An Atlas of Fantasy. Ballantine.

Post, John D. see Post, John Dexter.

Post, John Dexter, 1925-
xPost, John D.
The Last Great Subsistence Crisis in the
Western World. Johns Hopkins.

Post, K. W. see Post, Kenneth William John.
Post, Kenneth. see Post, Kenneth William John.

Post, Kenneth William John.
xPost, K. W.
The Price of Liberty: Personality & Politics in
Colonial Nigeria. Cambridge U Pr.
xPost, Kenneth.
Structure & Conflict in Nigeria. U of Wis Pr.

Post, Laurens Van Der. see Van Der Post, Laurens.
Post, Melville. see Post, Melville Davisson.
Post, Melville D. see Post, Melville Davisson.

Post, Melville Davisson, 1871-1930
xPost, Melville.
The Strange Schemes of Randolph Mason.
Arno.
xPost, Melville D.
The Complete Uncle Abner. Pubs Inc.
The Strange Schemes of Randolph Mason.
Hyperion Conn.
The Strange Schemes of Randolph Mason.
Lighthouse Pr NY.

Post, Richard S.
xPost, Richard S.
ed. Combating Crime Against Small Business.
C C Thomas.
Security Administration: An Introduction. C C
Thomas.

Post, Seymour C.
xPost, Seymour C.
ed. Moral Values & the Superego Concept in
Psychoanalysis. Intl Univs Pr.

Postal , Bernard. see Postal, Bernard.

Postal, Bernard.
xPostal , Bernard.
Jewish Landmarks of New York: A Travel
Guide & History. Fleet.
xPostal, Bernard.
American Jewish Landmarks: A Travel Guide
and History. Fleet.

Postal, Paul M. see Postal, Paul Martin.

Postal, Paul Martin, 1936-
xPostal, Paul M.
Some Syntactic Rules in Mohawk. Garland
Pub.

Postan, M. M. see Postan, Michael Moissey.

Postan, Michael Moissey, 1898-
xPostan, M. M.
Fact & Relevance: Essays on Historical
Method. Cambridge U Pr.
Medieval Trade & Finance. Cambridge U Pr.

Poste. see Poste, George.
Poste, G. see Poste, George.

Poste, George.
xPoste.
ed. Dynamic Aspects of Cell Surface
Organization. Elsevier.
The Synthesis, Assembly & Turnover of Cell
Surface Components. Elsevier.
xPoste, G.
ed. Membrane Fusion. Elsevier.

Postell, Catherine.
xPostell, Catherine.
On Toplecote Bayou. Arno.

Posten, Margaret L.
xPosten, Margaret L.
Lucky You. Denison.
This Is the Place - Iowa. Iowa St U Pr.

Poster, Mark.
xPoster, Mark.
Critical Theory of the Family. Continuum.
Critical Theory of the Family. Seabury.
The Utopian Thought of Restif de la Bretonne.
NYU Pr.

Posternak, Theodore.
xPosternak, Theodore.
Cyclitols. Holden-Day.
The Cyclitols. Intl Pubns Serv.

Postgate, J. R. see Postgate, John Raymond.

Postgate, John Raymond.
xPostgate, J. R.
ed. Chemistry & Biochemistry of Nitrogen
Fixation. Plenum Pub.
The Sulphate Reducing Bacteria. Cambridge U
Pr.

Postgate, Raymond. see Postgate, Raymond William.

Postgate, Raymond William.
xPostgate, Raymond.
Plain Man's Guide to Wine. Intl Pubns Serv.
Story of a Year: 1848. Greenwood.

Postlethwait, P. W. see Postlethwait, Raymond W.

Postlethwait, Raymond W.
xPostlethwait, P. W.
Surgery of the Esophagus. ACC.

Postlethwait, S. N. see Postlethwait, Samuel N.

Postlethwait, Samuel N.
xPostlethwait, S. N.
The Audio-Tutorial Approach to Learning:
Through Independent Study & Integrated
Experiences. Burgess.

Postma, H. L. see Postma, Lidia.

Postma, Lidia.
xPostma, H. L.
The Witch's Garden. McGraw.
xPostma, Lidia.
illus. The Stolen Mirror. McGraw.

Postman, Leo. see Postman, Leo Joseph.

Postman, Leo Joseph.
xPostman, Leo.
ed. Norms of Word Association. Acad Pr.

Postman, Neil.
xPostman, Neil.
How to Recognize a Good School. Phi Delta
Kappa.
Teaching As a Conserving Activity. Delacorte.
Teaching As a Conserving Activity. Dell.
Teaching As a Subversive Activity. Delacorte.
Teaching As a Subversive Activity. Dell.

Posyniak, Henry.
xPosyniak, Henry.

Guide to Accounting Principles, Practices &
Systems for Nursing Homes. Cath Health.

Posz, Gary S.
xPosz, Gary S.
Administrative Alternatives in Development
Assistance. Ballinger Pub.

Poteat, Hubert M. see Poteat, Hubert McNeill.

Poteat, Hubert McNeill, 1886-1958
xPoteat, Hubert M.
Practical Hymnology. AMS Pr.

Poteet, David.
xPoteet, David.
How to Trace Your Family Tree. Bethany Fell.
How to Trace Your Family Tree. Jeremy Bks.

Poteet, G. Howard.
xPoteet, G. Howard.
Complete Guide to the Use & Maintenance of
Hand & Power Tools. P-H.
Complete Illustrated Guide to Basic Carpentry.
P-H.
How to Live in Your Van & Love It!. Trail-R.
Published Radio, Television & Film Scripts: A
Bibliography. Whitston Pub.
Workbench Guide to Tape Recorder Servicing.
P-H.
xPoteet, George H.
Film Criticism in Popular American
Periodicals, 1933-1967. Revisionist Pr.

Poteet, George H. see Poteet, G. Howard.
Potholm, C. see Potholm, Christian P.
Potholm, Christian. see Potholm, Christian P.

Potholm, Christian P.
xPotholm, C.
The Theory & Practice of African Politics.
P-H.
xPotholm, Christian.
ed. Southern Africa in Perspective: Essays in
Regional Politics. Free Pr.

Potok, Chaim.
xPotok, Chaim.
In the Beginning. Fawcett.
In the Beginning. Knopf.
Promise. Fawcett.
Promise. Knopf.

Potomac Corral of the Westerners. see Westerners, the
Potomac Corral.

Potonniee, Georges.
xPotonniee, Georges.
The History of the Discovery of Photography.
Arno.

Pottebaum, Gerard. see Pottebaum, Gerard A.

Pottebaum, Gerard A.
xPottebaum, Gerard.
Festival of Art. Augsburg.
xPottebaum, Gerard A.
Wonderings. St Marys.

Pottenger, Francis M. see Pottenger, Francis Marion.

Pottenger, Francis Marion.
xPottenger, Francis M.
Fundamentals of Chemistry. Scott F.

Potter. see Potter, Beatrix.
Potter, Allen. see Potter, Allen Meyers.

Potter, Allen Meyers, 1924-
xPotter, Allen.
Organized Groups in British National Politics.
Greenwood.

Potter, B. see Potter, Beatrix.

Potter, Beatrix, 1866-1943
xPotter.
Tale of Peter Rabbit. Schol Bk Serv.
xPotter, B.
The Tailor of Gloucester. Watts.
The Tale of Benjamin Bunny. Watts.
The Tale of Squirrel Nutkin. Watts.
xPotter, Beatrix.

Appley Dapply's Nursery Rhymes. Warne.
The Art of Beatrix Potter. Warne.
Cecily Parsley's Nursery Rhymes. Warne.
Fairy Caravan. Warne.
Letters to Children. Walker & Co.
Tailor of Gloucester. Phila Free Lib.
The Tailor of Gloucester. Dover.
illus. Tailor of Gloucester. Warne.
Tale of Benjamin Bunny. Warne.
The Tale of Benjamin Bunny. Dover.
Tale of Jemima Puddle Duck. Warne.
Tale of Johnny Townmouse. Warne.
Tale of Little Pig Robinson. Warne.
The Tale of Mr. Jeremy Fisher. Dover.
The Tale of Mrs. Tiggy-Winkle. Dover.
Tale of Mrs. Tiggy-Winkle. Warne.
Tale of Mrs. Tittlemouse. Warne.
Tale of Peter Rabbit. Schol Bk Serv.
Tale of Peter Rabbit. Warne.
Tale of Peter Rabbit. Western Pub.
The Tale of Peter Rabbit. Dover.
Tale of Peter Rabbit. Troll Assocs.
Tale of Pigling Bland. Warne.
Tale of Squirrel Nutkin. Warne.
The Tale of Squirrel Nutkin. Dover.
Tale of the Flopsy Bunnies. Warne.
Tale of Timmy Tiptoes. Warne.
Tale of Tom Kitten. Warne.
Tale of Two Bad Mice. Warne.
The Tale of Two Bad Mice. Dover.
Potter, Beverly A.
xPotter, Beverly A.
Turning Around: The Behavioral Approach to
Managing People. Am Mgmt.
Potter, C. F. *see* Potter, Charles Francis.
Potter, Charles Francis, 1885-
xPotter, C. F.
The Lost Years of Jesus Revealed. Fawcett.
Potter, D. E. *see* Potter, David E.
Potter, David,
xPotter, David.
Frwd. by & ed. Colonial Idiom. S Ill U Pr.
Debating in the Colonial Chartered Colleges:
An Historical Survey, 1642 to 1900. AMS
Pr.
Potter, David E.
xPotter, D. E.
Computational Physics. Wiley.
Potter, David M. *see* Potter, David Morris.
Potter, David Morris.
xPotter, David M.
Division & the Stresses of Reunion: 1845-1876.
Scott F.
Freedom & Its Limitations in American Life.
Stanford U Pr.
The Impending Crisis: 1848-1861. Har-Row.
Lincoln & His Party in the Secession Crisis.
AMS Pr.
People of Plenty: Economic Abundance & the
American Character. U of Chicago Pr.
The South & the Concurrent Majority. La State
U Pr.
Potter, Edgar. *see* Potter, Edgar R.
Potter, Edgar R.
xPotter, Edgar.
Cowboy Slang. Superior Pub.
Potter, Edith L. *see* Potter, Edith Louise.
Potter, Edith Louise, 1901-
xPotter, Edith L.
Normal & Abnormal Development of the
Kidney. Year Bk Med.
Potter, Elaine.
xPotter, Elaine.
The Press As Opposition: The Political Role of
South African Newspapers. Rowman.
Potter, Elisha R. *see* Potter, Elisha Reynolds.
Potter, Elisha Reynolds, 1811-1882
xPotter, Elisha R.

Memoir Concerning the French Settlements &
French Settlers in the Colony of Rhode
Island. Genealog Pub.
Potter, Elmer B. *see* Potter, Elmer Belmont.
Potter, Elmer Belmont, 1908-
xPotter, Elmer B.
Nimitz. Naval Inst Pr.
Potter, F. F. *see* Potter, Frederick Felix.
Potter, Frederick Felix.
xPotter, F. F.
Teaching of Arithmetic. Philos Lib.
Potter, Guy D., 1928-
xPotter, Guy D.
Sectional Anatomy & Tomography of the
Head. Grune.
Potter, J. M. *see* Potter, Jack M.
Potter, J. Reid.
xPotter, J. Reid.
North Carolina Appellate Handbook. Michie.
Potter, Jack M.
xPotter, J. M.
Capitalism & the Chinese Peasant: Social &
Economic Change in a Hong Kong Village. U
of Cal Pr.
xPotter, Jack M.
Thai Peasant Social Structure. U of Chicago Pr.
Potter, James L.
xPotter, James L.
Theory of Networks & Lines. P-H.
Potter, Jeffrey.
xPotter, Jeffrey.
Men, Money & Magic: The Story of Dorothy
Schiff. Coward.
Men, Money & Magic: The Story of Dorothy
Schiff. NAL.
Potter, Jerry. *see* Potter, Jerry Allen.
Potter, Jerry A. *see* Potter, Jerry Allen.
Potter, Jerry Allen.
xPotter, Jerry.
Silence in Eden. T Y Crowell.
xPotter, Jerry A.
Silence in Eden. Popular Lib.
Potter, John M.
xPotter, John M.
The Practical Management of Head Injuries.
Year Bk Med.
Potter, John M. *see* Potter, John Mason.
Potter, John Mason.
xPotter, John M.
Thirteen Desperate Days. Astor-Honor.
Potter, Joy H. *see* Potter, Joy Hambuechen.
Potter, Joy Hambuechen.
xPotter, Joy H.
Elio Vittorini. Twayne.
Potter, Karl. *see* Potter, Karl H.
Potter, Karl H.
xPotter, Karl.
ed. Indian Metaphysics & Epistemology: The
Tradition of Nyaya-Vaisesika up to Gangesa.
Encyclopedia of Indian Philosophies.
Princeton U Pr.
xPotter, Karl H.
Presuppositions of India's Philosophies.
Greenwood.
Potter, Leo G. *see* Potter, Leo Goodwin.
Potter, Leo Goodwin, 1901-
xPotter, Leo G.
My Bible Is Jesus. Bethany Pr.
Potter, Lois.
xPotter, Lois.
A Preface to Milton. Longman.
Potter, Marian.
xPotter, Marian.
The Shared Room. Morrow.
Potter, Merle C.
xPotter, Merle C.
Mathematical Methods in the Physical
Sciences. P-H.
Potter, Murray A. *see* Potter, Murray Anthony.

Potter, Murray Anthony, 1871-1915
xPotter, Murray A.
Four Essays. Kraus Repr.
Potter, Norman N.
xPotter, Norman N.
Food Science. AVI.
Potter, Norris W. *see* Potter, Norris Whitfield.
Potter, Norris Whitfield, 1904-
xPotter, Norris W.
Punahou Story. Pacific Bks.
Potter, Philip J., 1895-
xPotter, Philip J.
Power Plant Theory & Design. Wiley.
Potter, Reuben. *see* Potter, Reuben Marmaduke.
Potter, Reuben Marmaduke, 1802-1890
xPotter, Reuben.
The Fall of the Alamo. Otterden.
Potter, S. *see* Potter, Simeon.
Potter, Simeon.
xPotter, S.
Modern Linguistics. Westview.
xPotter, Simeon.
Our Language. R West.
Potter, Stephen.
xPotter, Stephen.
ed. The Muse in Chains: A Study in Education.
Folcroft.
Pedigree: The Origins of Words from Nature.
Taplinger.
Potter, Sulamith H. *see* Potter, Sulamith Heins.
Potter, Sulamith Heins.
xPotter, Sulamith H.
Family Life in a Northern Thai Village: A
Study of the Structural Significance of
Women. U of Cal Pr.
Potter, T. *see* Potter, Thomas C.
Potter, T. W. *see* Potter, Timothy W.
Potter, Thelma M. *see* Potter, Thelma Maude.
Potter, Thelma Maude, 1910-
xPotter, Thelma M.
An Analysis of the Work of General Clerical
Employees. AMS Pr.
Potter, Thomas C.
xPotter, T.
Informal Reading Diagnosis: A Practical Guide
for the Classroom Teacher. P-H.
xPotter, Thomas C.
Informal Reading Diagnosis: A Practical Guide
for the Classroom Teacher. P-H.
Potter, Timothy W.
xPotter, T. W.
The Changing Landscape of South Etruria. St
Martin.
Potter, Vincent G.
xPotter, Vincent G.
Charles S. Peirce on Norms & Ideals. U of
Mass Pr.
Potterbaum, Charlene.
xPotterbaum, Charlene.
Thanks Lord, I Needed That. Logos.
Potterton, Homan.
xPotterton, Homan.
The National Gallery London. Thames
Hudson.
Potthoff, Harvey H.
xPotthoff, Harvey H.
Loneliness: Understanding & Dealing with It.
Abingdon.
Understanding Loneliness. B&N.
Pottinger, David. *see* Pottinger, David Thomas.
Pottinger, David Thomas, 1884-1958
xPottinger, David.
Printers & Printing. Arno.
Pottinger, George.
xPottinger, George.
The Court of the Medici. Rowman.
Pottle, Ralph R.
xPottle, Ralph R.

Tuning the School Band & Orchestra. Pottle.
Potts, Charles, 1943-
  xPotts, Charles.
    The Golden Calf. Litmus.
    The Opium Must Go Thru. Litmus.
    Valga Krusa. Litmus.
Potts, James L.
  xPotts, James L.
    jt. auth. Prisoner's Self Help Litigation Manual.
    Lexington Bks.
Potts, L. J. *see* Potts, Leonard James.
Potts, Leonard James, 1897-
  xPotts, L. J.
    Comedy. R West.
Potts, Malcolm.
  xPotts, Malcolm.
    Abortion. Cambridge U Pr.
Potts, Marie, 1895-
  xPotts, Marie.
    The Northern Maidu. Naturegraph.
Potts, Marion.
  xPotts, Marion.
    Structure & Development in Child Language:
    The Preschool Years. Cornell U Pr.
Potts, Nancy. *see* Potts, Nancy D.
Potts, Nancy D.
  xPotts, Nancy.
    Loneliness: Living Between the Times. Victor
    Bks.
  xPotts, Nancy D.
    Counseling with Single Adults. Broadman.
Potts, Renfrey B. *see* Potts, Renfrey Burnard.
Potts, Renfrey Burnard.
  xPotts, Renfrey B.
    Flows in Transportation Networks. Acad Pr.
Potts, Willard, 1929-
  xPotts, Willard.
    ed. Portraits of the Artist in Exile:
    Recollections of James Joyce by Europeans.
    U of Wash Pr.
Potts, William, 1868-1947
  xPotts, William.
    Banbury Cross & the Rhyme. Folcroft.
Potvin, Denis.
  xPotvin, Denis.
    Power on Ice. Har-Row.
Potzl, Otto.
  xPotzl, Otto.
    Preconscious Stimulation in Dreams,
    Associations & Images: Classical Studies. Intl
    Univs Pr.
Pough, Frederick H.
  xPough, Frederick H.
    A Field Guide to Rocks & Minerals. HM.
Pough, Richard H. *see* Pough, Richard Hooper.
Pough, Richard Hooper, 1904-
  xPough, Richard H.
    Audubon Land Bird Guide: Small Land Birds
    of Eastern & Central North America from
    Southern Texas to Central Greenland.
    Doubleday.
Pouillon, Fernand.
  xPouillon, Fernand.
    Stones of the Abbey. HarBraceJ.
Poulantzas, Nicos. *see* Poulantzas, Nicos Ar.
Poulantzas, Nicos Ar.
  xPoulantzas, Nicos.
    State, Power, Socialism. Schocken.
Poulet, Georges.
  xPoulet, Georges.
    Proustian Space. Johns Hopkins.
    Studies in Human Time. Greenwood.
Poulet, Virginia.
  xPoulet, Virginia.
    Blue Bug Goes to the Library. Childrens.
Poulin, Clarence.
  xPoulin, Clarence.

Tailoring Suits the Professional Way. Bennett
    Co.
Poullada, Leon B., 1913-
  xPoullada, Leon B.
    Reform & Rebellion in Afghanistan, 1919-1929:
    King Amanullah's Failure to Modernize a
    Tribal Society. Cornell U Pr.
Poulose, T. T.
  xPoulose, T. T.
    ed. Indian Ocean Power Rivalry. Intl Pubns
    Serv.
Poulson, Barry W. *see* Poulson, Barry Warren.
Poulson, Barry Warren, 1937-
  xPoulson, Barry W.
    Value Added in Manufacturing, Mining, &
    Agriculture in the American Economy from
    1809 to 1839. Arno.
Poulsson, Emilie.
  xPoulsson, Emilie.
    Finger Plays for Nursery & Kindergarten.
    Gannon.
    Finger Plays for Nursery & Kindergarten.
    Dover.
Poulter, Nick.
  xPoulter, Nick.
    Growing Vines. British Bk Ctr.
Poulton, E. C.
  xPoulton, E. C.
    Environment & Human Efficiency. C C
    Thomas.
    The Environment at Work. C C Thomas.
Pound, Arthur, 1884-1966
  xPound, Arthur.
    The Golden Earth: The Story of Manhattan's
    Landed Wealth. Arno.
Pound, Ezra. *see* Pound, Ezra Loomis.
Pound, Ezra L. *see* Pound, Ezra Loomis.
Pound, Ezra Loomis.
  xPound, Ezra.
    Ezra Pound & Music: The Complete Criticism.
    New Directions.
    Guide to Kulchur. New Directions.
    How to Read. Gordon Pr.
    How to Read. Haskell.
    Letters of Ezra Pound. Haskell.
    Letters to Ibbotson. Natl-Poet Univ ME.
    Literary Essays. New Directions.
    Pavannes & Divagations. New Directions.
  xPound, Ezra L.
    Literary Essays. Greenwood.
Pound, Louise, 1872-1958
  xPound, Louise.
    Nebraska Folklore. Greenwood.
Pound, Roscoe, 1870-1964
  xPound, Roscoe.
    Criminal Justice in America. Da Capo.
    The Development of Constitutional Guarantees
    of Liberty. Greenwood.
    Law & Morals. Kelley.
    Law & Morals. Rothman.
    Organization of Courts. Greenwood.
Pounders, Margaret.
  xPounders, Margaret.
    Laws of Love. Unity Bks.
Pounds. *see* Pounds, Norman John Greville.
Pounds, Norman J. *see* Pounds, Norman John Greville.
Pounds, Norman John Greville.
  xPounds.
    World Geography. SW Pub.
    World Geography. SW Pub.
  xPounds, Norman J.
    ed. Geographical Essays on Eastern Europe.
    Greenwood.
Pountney, Kate.
  xPountney, Kate.
    illus. Creative Crafts for Children. Merrimack
    Bk Serv.
Pourade, Richard F.
  xPourade, Richard F.

    The Call to California. Copley Bks.
    City of the Dream. Copley Bks.
    The Silver Dons. Copley Bks.
Pourbaix, Marcel. *see* Pourbaix, Marcel Jean Nestor.
Pourbaix, Marcel Jean Nestor.
  xPourbaix, Marcel.
    Lectures on Electrochemical Corrosion. Plenum
    Pub.
Povoledo, D.
  xPovoledo, D.
    ed. Humic Substances: Their Structure &
    Function in the Biosphere. Unipub.
Powdermaker, Hortense, 1903-
  xPowdermaker, Hortense.
    Copper Town: Changing Africa, the Human
    Situation on the Rhodesian Copperbelt.
    Greenwood.
    Life in Lesu: The Study of a Melanesian
    Society in New Ireland. AMS Pr.
    Stranger & Friend: The Way of an
    Anthropologist. Norton.
    Stranger & Friend: The Way of an
    Anthropologist. Norton.
Powell, A. E. *see* Powell, Arthur Edward.
Powell, Aaron M. *see* Powell, Aaron Macy.
Powell, Aaron Macy, 1832-1899
  xPowell, Aaron M.
    Personal Reminiscences of the Anti-Slavery &
    Other Reforms & Reformers. Negro U Pr.
Powell, Al.
  xPowell, Al.
    Astonishing & True-Stories of the Speedway.
    Messner.
Powell, Alan. *see* Powell, Alan Walter.
Powell, Alan Walter, 1936-
  xPowell, Alan.
    Patrician Democrat: The Political Life of
    Charles Cowper 1843-1870. Intl Schol Bk
    Serv.
Powell, Ann.
  xPowell, Ann.
    The Origins of Western Art. HarBraceJ.
    The Origins of Western Art. HarBraceJ.
Powell, Anthony. *see* Powell, Anthony Dymoke.
Powell, Anthony Dymoke, 1905-
  xPowell, Anthony.
    What's Become of Waring?. Popular Lib.
Powell, Anton.
  xPowell, Anton.
    Ancient Greeks. Watts.
Powell, Arthur Edward, 1882-
  xPowell, A. E.
    Solar System. Theos Pub Hse.
Powell, Arthur G., 1937-
  xPowell, Arthur G.
    The Uncertain Profession: Harvard & the
    Search for Educational Authority. Harvard U
    Pr.
Powell, Barbara, 1929-
  xPowell, Barbara.
    How to Raise a Successful Daughter.
    Nelson-Hall.
Powell, C. Randall.
  xPowell, C. Randall.
    Career Planning & Placement Today.
    Kendall-Hunt.
Powell, Chilton L. *see* Powell, Chilton Latham.
Powell, Chilton Latham, 1885-
  xPowell, Chilton L.
    English Domestic Relations, 1487-1653: A
    Study of Matrimony & Family Life in Theory
    & Practice As Revealed by the Literature,
    Law & History of the Period. Russell.
Powell, Claire.
  xPowell, Claire.
    The Meaning of Flowers: A Garland of Plant
    Lore & Symbolism from Popular Custom &
    Literature. Shambhala Pubns.
Powell, David E.
  xPowell, David E.

Antireligious Propaganda in the Soviet Union:
A Study of Mass Persuasion. MIT Pr.

Powell, Dilys.
xPowell, Dilys.
Descent from Parnassus. Arno.

Powell, Edgar.
xPowell, Edgar.
ed. The Peasants' Rising & the Lollards. AMS Pr.

Powell, Elwin H. see Powell, Elwin Humphreys.

Powell, Elwin Humphreys, 1925-
xPowell, Elwin H.
Design of Discord: Studies of Anomie. Oxford U Pr.

Powell, Evan.
xPowell, Evan.
Complete Guide to Home Appliance Repair. Har-Row.

Powell, Fern.
xPowell, Fern.
Porcupine & the Tiger. Lothrop.

Powell, Fred.
xPowell, Fred.
Bartender's Standard Manual. B&N.
Bartender's Standard Manual. Educator Bks.

Powell, Fred W. see Powell, Fred Wilbur.

Powell, Fred Wilbur, 1881-1943
xPowell, Fred W.
The Bureau of Animal Industry: Its History, Activities & Organization. AMS Pr.
The Bureau of Mines: Its History, Activities & Organization. AMS Pr.
The Bureau of Plant Industry: Its History, Activities & Organization. AMS Pr.

Powell, Frederick Y. see Powell, Frederick York.

Powell, Frederick York, 1850-1904
xPowell, Frederick Y.
Some Words on Allegory in England. Folcroft.

Powell, Gordon. see Powell, Gordon George.

Powell, Gordon George, 1911-
xPowell, Gordon.
Power Through Acceptance: The Secret of Serenity. Christian Herald.

Powell, Harold.
xPowell, Harold.
Pottery for Beginners. Sterling.

Powell, Hickman.
xPowell, Hickman.
Ninety Times Guilty. Arno.

Powell, J. C.
xPowell, J. C.
American Siberia: Or, Fourteen Years Experience in a Southern Convict Camp. Arno.
The American Siberia, or: Fourteen Years' Experience in a Southern Convict Camp. U Presses Fla.

Powell, J. Lewis.
xPowell, J. Lewis.
Executive Speaking: An Acquired Skill. BNA.

Powell, J. M. see Powell, Joseph Michael.

Powell, J. W.
xPowell, John W.
Canyons of the Colorado. Argosy.

Powell, James.
xPowell, James.
Deathwind. Doubleday.

Powell, James D.
xPowell, James D.
Building Plastic Ship Models. A S Barnes.

Powell, James M.
xPowell, James M.
ed. Medieval Studies: An Introduction. Syracuse U Pr.

Powell, Jay.
xPowell, Jay.
Quileute: An Introduction to the Indians of La Push. U of Wash Pr.

Powell, Jesse J. see Powell, Jesse Jerome.

Powell, Jesse Jerome, 1891-
xPowell, Jesse J.
A Study of Problem Material in High School Algebra. AMS Pr.

Powell, John. see Powell, John Joseph.

Powell, John H. see Powell, John Harvey.

Powell, John Harvey, 1914-
xPowell, John H.
Bring Out Your Dead: The Great Plague of Yellow Fever in Philadelphia in 1793. Arno.

Powell, John J.
xPowell, John J.
Golden State & Its Resources. Arno.

Powell, John Joseph, 1925-
xPowell, John.
A Reason to Live, a Reason to Die. Argus Comm.
Unconditional Love. Argus Comm.

Powell, John W. see Powell, J. W.

Powell, Joseph Michael.
xPowell, J. M.
ed. Australian Space, Australian Time: Geographical Perspectives. Oxford U Pr.
Environmental Management in Australia, 1788-1914: Guardians, Improvers & Profit: an Introductory Survey. Oxford U Pr.
The Public Lands of Australia Felix: Settlement & Land Appraisal in Victoria 1834-91 with Special Reference to the Western Plains. Oxford U Pr.

Powell, K. G.
xPowell, Ken.
English Historical Facts, 1485-1603. Rowman.

Powell, Ken. see Powell, K. G.

Powell, L. see Powell, Lawrie W.

Powell, Lawrence C. see Powell, Lawrence Clark.

Powell, Lawrence Clark, 1906-
xPowell, Lawrence C.
Books in My Baggage: Adventures in Reading & Collecting. Greenwood.
From the Heartland: Profiles of People & Places of the Southwest & Beyond. Northland.
The Little Package: Pages on Literature & Landscape from a Traveling Bookman's Life. Arno.
A Passion for Books. Greenwood.

Powell, Lawrence N.
xPowell, Lawrence N.
New Masters: Northern Planters During the Civil War & Reconstruction. Yale U Pr.

Powell, Lawrie W.
xPowell, L.
Metals in the Liver. Dekker.

Powell, M. J. V. see Powell, Michael John Vivian.

Powell, Mary.
xPowell, Mary.
Orthopaedic Nursing. Churchill.

Powell, Michael.
xPowell, Michael.
The Red Shoes. Avon.

Powell, Michael John Vivian.
xPowell, M. J. V.
ed. House Builders Reference Book. Butterworths.

Powell, Neil.
xPowell, Neil.
At the Edge. Persea Bks.
Carpenters of Light: Some Contemporary English Poets. B&N.

Powell, Orrin E. see Powell, Orrin Edwin.

Powell, Orrin Edwin, 1889-
xPowell, Orrin E.
Educational Returns at Varying Expenditure Levels: A Basis for Relating Expenditures to Outcomes in Education. AMS Pr.

Powell, P. see Powell, Paul.

Powell, Paul.
xPowell, P.

Chemistry of the Non-Metals. Methuen Inc.

Powell, Paul W.
xPowell, Paul W.
How to Make Your Church Hum. Broadman.

Powell, Ray M.
xPowell, Ray M.
Accounting Procedures for Institutions. U of Notre Dame Pr.
Budgetary Control Procedures for Institutions. U of Notre Dame Pr.
Management Procedures for Institutions. U of Notre Dame Pr.

Powell, Reed M. see Powell, Reed Madsen.

Powell, Reed Madsen.
xPowell, Reed M.
Race, Religion, & the Promotion of the American Executive. Ohio St U Admin Sci.

Powell, Robert B. see Powell, Robert Blake.

Powell, Robert Blake.
xPowell, Robert B.
Antique Shaving Mugs of the United States. R B Powell.
Occupational & Fraternal Shaving Mugs of the United States. R B Powell.

Powell, Roger.
xPowell, Roger.
Equilibrium Thermodynamics in Petrology: An Introduction. Har-Row.

Powell, Russell H., 1943-
xPowell, Russell H.
ed. Handbooks & Tables in Science & Technology. Oryx Pr.

Powell, Sumner C. see Powell, Sumner Chilton.

Powell, Sumner Chilton, 1924-
xPowell, Sumner C.
Puritan Village: The Formation of a New England Town. Columbia U Pr.

Powell, T. G. see Powell, Thomas George Eyre.

Powell, Terry.
xPowell, Terry.
Nobody's Perfect. Victor Bks.

Powell, Thomas F.
xPowell, Thomas F.
Josiah Royce. Twayne.

Powell, Thomas George Eyre, 1916-
xPowell, T. G.
Prehistoric Art. Oxford U Pr.

Powell, Thomas R. see Powell, Thomas Reed.

Powell, Thomas Reed, 1880-1955
xPowell, Thomas R.
Vagaries & Varieties in Constitutional Interpretation. AMS Pr.

Powell, Virgil S.
xPowell, Virgil S.
From the Slave Cabin of Yani. Exposition.

Powell, William, 1949-
xPowell, William.
The Anarchist Cookbook. Lyle Stuart.
The First Casualty. Lyle Stuart.

Powell, William S. see Powell, William Stevens.

Powell, William Stevens, 1919-
xPowell, William S.
North Carolina. Tchrs Coll.
North Carolina Colony. Macmillan.
North Carolina Gazetteer. U of NC Pr.

Powelson, John P., 1920-
xPowelson, John P.
Institutions of Economic Growth: A Theory of Conflict Management in Developing Countries. Princeton U Pr.

Power.
xPower Editors.
Plant Energy System: Energy Systems Engineering. McGraw.

Power, Barbara.
xPower, Barbara.
I Wish Laura's Mommy Was My Mommy. Lippincott.

Power, D'Arcy, Sir, 1855-1941
xPower, D'Arcy.

ed. British Masters of Medicine. Arno.

Power Editors. *see* Power.

Power, Effie. *see* Power, Effie Louise.

Power, Effie Louise.
xPower, Effie.
Bag O' Tales: 63 Famous Stories for
Storytellers. Peter Smith.

Power, Eileen. *see* Power, Eileen Edna.

Power, Eileen Edna, 1889-1940
xPower, Eileen.
Medieval People. B&N.
Medieval People. Har-Row.
Medieval Women. Cambridge U Pr.

Power, Elaine.
xPower, Elaine.
Horse in New Zealand. Intl Pubns Serv.

Power, Henry M.
xPower, Henry M.
Introduction to Dynamics & Control. McGraw.

Power Instrumentation Symposium, May 22-25, 1977,
New Orleans. *see* International Isa Power
Instrumentation Symposium.

Power, Jonathan.
xPower, Jonathan.
World of Hunger: A Strategy for Survival.
Transatlantic.
xPower, Jonothan.
Migrant Workers in Western Europe & the
United States. Pergamon.

Power, Jonothan. *see* Power, Jonathan.

Power, Jules.
xPower, Jules.
How Life Begins. S&S.

Power, Lawrence.
xPower, Lawrence.
Diabetes Outpatient Care Through Physician
Assistants: A Model for Health Maintenance
Organizations. C C Thomas.

Power, Mary J. *see* Power, Mary James.

Power, Mary James, Sister, 1894-1967
xPower, Mary J.
In the Name of the Bee: The Significance of
Emily Dickinson. Biblo.

Power, P. *see* Power, Paul W.

Power, Paul W.
xPower, P.
The Role of the Family in the Rehabilitation of
the Physically Disabled. Univ Park.

Power, Rex.
xPower, Rex.
How to Beat Police Radar...& Do It Legally.
Arco.

Power, Thomas C.
xPower, Thomas C.
Practical Shop Mathematics. McGraw.

Powers, Bill.
xPowers, Bill.
Break Him Down!. Watts.
illus. Flying High. Watts.
A Test of Love. Watts.
A Test of Love. Dell.

Powers, Bob, 1924-
xPowers, Bob.
South Fork Country. Westernlore.

Powers, Bruce P.
xPowers, Bruce P.
Christian Leadership. Broadman.

Powers, C. F.
xPowers, C. F.
Practical Guide to Bills of Lading. Oceana.

Powers, David G. *see* Powers, David Guy.

Powers, David Guy.
xPowers, David G.
First Book of How to Make a Speech. Watts.
First Book of How to Run a Meeting. Watts.

Powers, David L.
xPowers, David L.
Boundary Value Problems. Acad Pr.

Powers, Edward A.
xPowers, Edward A.

Process in Relationship: Marriage & Family.
West Pub.
Signs of Shalom. Pilgrim NY.

Powers, Elizabeth, 1944-
xPowers, Elizabeth.
The Journal of Madame Royale. Walker & Co.
Switzerland. Kodansha.

Powers, Gene R.
xPowers, Gene R.
Cleft Palate. Bobbs.

Powers, Hugh.
xPowers, Hugh.
Food Power: Nutrition & Your Child's
Behavior. St Martin.

Powers, James.
xPowers, James.
Estate of Grace. Har-Row.

Powers, Jo Marie, 1935-
xPowers, Jo Marie.
Basics of Quantity Food Production. Wiley.

Powers, John, 1948-
xPowers, John.
The Short Season: A Boston Celtics Diary,
1977-1978. Har-Row.

Powers, John R.
xPowers, John R.
Do Black Patent Leather Shoes Really Reflect
up?. Contemp Bks.
Do Black Patent Leather Shoes Really Reflect
Up?. Popular Lib.

Powers, Marion D.
xPowers, Marion D.
The Legal Citation Directory. Franas Pr.

Powers, Mark. *see* Powers, Mark J.

Powers, Mark J.
xPowers, Mark.
Getting Started in Commodity Futures Trading.
Investor Pubns.

Powers, Melvin, 1922-
xPowers, Melvin.
Practical Guide to Self-Hypnosis. Wilshire.

Powers, P. W. *see* Powers, Philip W.

Powers, Pauline S.
xPowers, Pauline S.
Obesity: The Regulation of Weight. Williams &
Wilkins.

Powers, Philip W.
xPowers, P. W.
How to Dispose of Toxic Substances &
Industrial Wastes. Noyes.

Powers, Richard. *see* Powers, Richard B.

Powers, Richard B.
xPowers, Richard.
Fundamentals of Behavior. West Pub.

Powers, Richard H. *see* Powers, Richard Howard.

Powers, Richard Howard.
xPowers, Richard H.
Edgar Quinet: A Study in French Patriotism.
SMU Press.

Powers, Robert M.
xPowers, Robert M.
Planetary Encounters. Stackpole.

Powers, Ron.
xPowers, Ron.
Face Value. Dell.

Powers, Samuel R. *see* Powers, Samuel Ralph.

Powers, Samuel Ralph, 1887-1970
xPowers, Samuel R.
A Diagnostic Study of the Subject Matter of
High School Chemistry. AMS Pr.

Powers, Thetis.
xPowers, Thetis.
Little Book of Daffinitions. Harvey.

Powers, Thomas, 1940 (dec. 12)-
xPowers, Thomas.
The Man Who Kept the Secrets: Richard
Helms & the CIA. Knopf.

Powers, Thomas E.
xPowers, Thomas E.

Invitation to a Great Experiment: Exploring
the Possibility That God Can Be Known.
Doubleday.

Powers, Thomas F.
xPowers, Thomas F.
ed. Educating for Careers: Policy Issues in a
Time of Change. Pa St U Pr.
Introduction to Management in the Hospitality
Industry. Wiley.

Powers, William K.
xPowers, William K.
Oglala Religion. U of Nebr Pr.

Powicke, Frederick J. *see* Powicke, Frederick James.

Powicke, Frederick James, 1854-1935
xPowicke, Frederick J.
Cambridge Platonists. Shoe String.

Powicke, Frederick M. *see* Powicke, Frederick Maurice.

Powicke, Frederick Maurice, Sir, 1879-1963
xPowicke, Frederick M.
The Christian Life in the Middle Ages & Other
Essays. Greenwood.
Modern Historians & the Study of History:
Essays & Papers. Greenwood.
Reformation in England. Oxford U Pr.
Thirteenth Century, 1216-1307. Oxford U Pr.
xPowicke, Maurice.
Medieval England, 1066-1485. Oxford U Pr.

Powicke, Maurice. *see* Powicke, Frederick Maurice.

Powledge, Fred.
xPowledge, Fred.
Born on the Circus. HarBraceJ.

Powles, J. G.
xPowles, J. G.
Particles & Their Interactions. A-W.

Pownall, Glen.
xPownall, Glen.
Lighting Crafts. Intl Pubns Serv.

Pownall, Thomas, 1722-1805
xPownall, Thomas.
A Topographical Description of the Dominions
of the United States of America. Arno.

Powsner, Edward R.
xPowsner, Edward R.
Diagnostic Nuclear Medicine. Grune.

Powys, John C. *see* Powys, John Cowper.

Powys, John Cowper.
xPowys, John C.
The Meaning of Culture. Greenwood.
Visions & Revisions: A Book of Literary
Devotions. Core Collection.

Powys, Llewelyn, 1884-1939
xPowys, Llewelyn.
Baker's Dozen. Arno.
Earth Memories. Arno.
Ebony & Ivory. Arden Lib.
Ebony & Ivory. Arno.
The Pathetic Fallacy: A Study of Christianity.
R West.
Rats in the Sacristy. Arno.
Thirteen Worthies. Arno.

Powys, T. F. *see* Powys, Theodore Francis.

Powys, Theodore F. *see* Powys, Theodore Francis.

Powys, Theodore Francis, 1875-1953
xPowys, T. F.
Mark Only. Scholarly.
xPowys, Theodore F.
Fables. Scholarly.
Left Leg. Arno.
Two Thieves. Arno.
Unclay. Scholarly.
White Paternoster, & Other Stories. Arno.

Poyer, Joe.
xPoyer, Joe.
The Contract. Atheneum.
Tunnel War. Atheneum.

Poynter, Dan.
xPoynter, Dan.

The Parachute Manual: A Technical Treatise
on the Parachute. Parachuting Pubns.
Parachuting: The Skydivers' Handbook.
Parachuting Pubns.
The Self-Publishing Manual: How to Write,
Print & Sell Your Own Book. Parachuting
Pubns.

Poynter, Margaret.
xPoynter, Margaret.
Crazy Minnie. Creative Ed.
Frisbee Fun. PB.
The Racquetball Book. Messner.
Search & Rescue: The Team & the Missions.
Atheneum.
The Zoo Lady: Belle Benchley & the San
Diego Zoo. Dillon.
xPoynter, Margaret R.
Frisbee Fun. Messner.
Poynter, Margaret R. see Poynter, Margaret.

Pozen, Robert.
xPozen, Robert C.
Legal Choices for State Enterprises in the
Third World. NYU Pr.
Pozen, Robert C. see Pozen, Robert.

Poznanski, Andrew K.
xPoznanski, Andrew K.
Practical Approaches to Pediatric Radiology.
Year Bk Med.
Pracy, R. see Pracy, Robert.

Pracy, Robert.
xPracy, R.
Ear, Nose, Throat: Surgery & Nursing. Wiley.
Prada, Beatriz-Maria. see Prada, Beatry-Maria.

Prada, Beatry-Maria.
xPrada, Beatriz-Maria.
Great Quick & Easy Cooking. Ballantine.

Prade, Ernstfried.
xPrade, Ernstfried.
Windsurfing. Sterling.

Prado, Caio.
xPrado, Caio.
The Colonial Background of Modern Brazil. U
of Cal Pr.

Prado, Holly.
xPrado, Holly.
Nothing Breaks off at the Edge. SBD.
Praeger, R. L. see Praeger, Robert Lloyd.

Praeger, Robert Lloyd, 1865-1953
xPraeger, R. L.
An Account of the Sempervivum Group.
Lubrecht & Cramer.

Prager, Annabelle.
xPrager, Annabelle.
The Surprise Party. Dell.

Prager, Arthur.
xPrager, Arthur.
World War II Resistance Stories. Watts.
xPrager, Emily.
jt. auth. World War II Resistance Stories.
Watts.
Prager, Emily. see Prager, Arthur.

Prager, Frank D.
xPrager, Frank D.
Mariano Taccola & His Book De Ingeneis.
MIT Pr.
Prago, A. see Prago, Albert.

Prago, Albert.
xPrago, A.
Intro. by The Revolutions in Spanish America:
The Independence Movements of 1808-1825.
Macmillan.
xPrago, Albert.
The Revolutions in Spanish America: The
Independence Movements of 1808-1825.
Macmillan.
Prahl-Andersen, B. see Prahl-Andersen, Birte.

Prahl-Andersen, Birte.
xPrahl-Andersen, B.

ed. A Mixed-Longitudinal, Interdisciplinary
Study of Growth & Developement. Acad Pr.

Prakash, Shamsher.
xPrakash, Shamsher.
Problems in Soil Mechanics. Asia.
Prall, S. E. see Prall, Stuart E.

Prall, Stuart E.
xPrall, S. E.
Puritan Revolution: A Documentary History.
Peter Smith.

Prance, Ghillean T.
xPrance, Ghillean T.
The Amazon Forest & River. Barron.

Prange, Erwin E.
xPrange, Erwin E.
How to Pray for Your Children. Bethany Fell.

Pranger, Robert J.
xPranger, Robert J.
Action, Symbolism & Order: The Existential
Dimensions of Politics in Modern
Citizenship. Vanderbilt U Pr.
Defense Implications of International
Indeterminacy. Am Enterprise.
ed. Detente & Defense: A Reader. Am
Enterprise.
Implications of the 1976 Arab-Israeli Military
Status. Am Enterprise.
Toward a Realistic Military Assistance
Program. Am Enterprise.
Prasad, Bimal. see Prasad, Bimla.

Prasad, Bimla, 1925-
xPrasad, Bimal.
Indo-Soviet Relations, 1947 to 1972: A
Documentary Study. Intl Pubns Serv.

Prasad, Kedar N.
xPrasad, Kedar N.
Human Radiation Biology. Har-Row.
xPrasad, Keder N.
Regulation of Differentiation in Mammalian
Nerve Cells. Plenum Pub.
Prasad, Keder N. see Prasad, Kedar N.
Prasad, Prakash C. see Prasad, Prakash Charan.

Prasad, Prakash Charan, 1938-
xPrasad, Prakash C.
Foreign Trade & Commerce in Ancient India.
South Asia Bks.
Prasad, Rai A. see Prasad, Rai Akhilendra.

Prasad, Rai Akhilendra, 1932-
xPrasad, Rai A.
Socialist Thought in Modern India. Intl Pubns
Serv.
Socialist Thought in Modern India. South Asia
Bks.

Prasad, Rajendra, Pres. India.
xPrasad, Rajendra.
At the Feet of Mahatma Gandhi. Greenwood.

Prasad, S. Benjamin.
xPrasad, S. Benjamin.
An Introduction to Multinational Management.
P-H.
Prasad, S. N. see Prasad, Sri Nandan.

Prasad, Sri Nandan.
xPrasad, S. N.
Survey of Work Done in the Military History
of India. South Asia Bks.
Prashad, G. see Prashad, Ganesh.

Prashad, Ganesh, 1913-
xPrashad, G.
Nehru: A Study in Colonial Liberalism. Verry.
Prassel, Frank R. see Prassel, Frank Richard.

Prassel, Frank Richard, 1937-
xPrassel, Frank R.
Criminal Law, Justice & Society. Goodyear.
Introduction to American Criminal Justice.
Har-Row.

Pratchett, Terry.
xPratchett, Terry.
The Dark Side of the Sun. St Martin.

Prater, Arnold.
xPrater, Arnold.

How to Beat the Blahs. Harvest Hse.
How to Tangibilitate. Nelson.

Prather, Hugh.
xPrather, Hugh.
I Touch the Earth, the Earth Touches Me.
Doubleday.
Notes on Love & Courage. Doubleday.

Prather, Ray.
xPrather, Ray.
illus. Anthony & Sabrina. Macmillan.
illus. Double-Dog-Dare. Macmillan.
illus. The Ostrich Girl. Scribner.

Prather, Ronald E.
xPrather, Ronald E.
Discrete Mathematical Structures for Computer
Science. HM.

Pratley, Gerald.
xPratley, Gerald.
The Cinema of David Lean. A S Barnes.
The Cinema of John Huston. A S Barnes.
Pratson, Fred. see Pratson, Frederick John.
Pratson, Frederick J. see Pratson, Frederick John.

Pratson, Frederick John.
xPratson, Fred.
photos by The Special World of the Artisan.
HM.
xPratson, Frederick J.
A Guide to Atlantic Canada. Chatham Pr.
Pratt. see Pratt, Cranford.

Pratt, Annis.
xPratt, Annis.
Dylan Thomas' Early Prose: A Study in
Creative Mythology. U of Pittsburgh Pr.

Pratt, Cranford.
xPratt.
Peace, Justice & Reconciliation in the
Arab-Israeli Conflict: A Christian Perspective.
Friend Pr.

Pratt, David, 1939-
xPratt, David.
How to Find & Measure Bias in Textbooks.
Educ Tech Pubns.
Pratt, Edward E. see Pratt, Edward Ewing.

Pratt, Edward Ewing, 1886-
xPratt, Edward E.
Industrial Causes of Congestion of Population
in New York City. AMS Pr.

Pratt, Fletcher, 1897-1956
xPratt, Fletcher.
Civil War. Doubleday.
Stanton, Lincoln's Secretary of War.
Greenwood.

Pratt, George C.
xPratt, George C.
Spellbound in Darkness: A History of the
Silent Film. NYGS.

Pratt, Gerald Hillary, 1903-
xPratt.
Vascular Surgery: Guide & Handbook. Green.

Pratt, Henry J., 1934-
xPratt, Henry J.
The Gray Lobby. U of Chicago Pr.
Liberalization of American Protestantism: A
Case Study in Complex Organizations.
Wayne St U Pr.
Pratt, J. G. see Pratt, Joseph Gaither.
Pratt, J. M. see Pratt, John Macdonald.
Pratt, James. see Pratt, Joanne Henderson.
Pratt, James B. see Pratt, James Bissett.

Pratt, James Bissett, 1875-1944
xPratt, James B.
Matter & Spirit: A Study of Mind & Body in
Their Relation to the Spiritual Life.
Greenwood.
Naturalism. Kennikat.
The Pilgrimage of Buddhism & a Buddhist
Pilgrimage. AMS Pr.
Pratt, Joanne H. see Pratt, Joanne Henderson.

Pratt, Joanne Henderson.
xPratt, James.

jt. auth. Environmental Encounter: Experiences
in Decision-Making for the Built & the
Natural Environment. Reverchon Pr.
xPratt, Joanne H.
Environmental Encounter: Experiences in
Decision-Making for the Built & the Natural
Environment. Reverchon Pr.

Pratt, John Macdonald.
xPratt, J. M.
Inorganic Chemistry of Vitamin B1120. Acad
Pr.
Pratt, John W. *see* Pratt, John Webb.
Pratt, John Webb.
xPratt, John W.
Religion, Politics, & Diversity: The
Church-State Theme in New York History.
Cornell U Pr.
Pratt, Joseph Gaither, 1910-
xPratt, J. G.
On the Evaluation of Verbal Material in
Parapsychology. Parapsych Foun.
Pratt, Julius W. *see* Pratt, Julius William.
Pratt, Julius William, 1888-
xPratt, Julius W.
A History of United States Foreign Policy.
P-H.
Pratt, Laurence, 1890-
xPratt, Laurence.
I Remember Portland. Binford.
Pratt, Lois. *see* Pratt, Lois Verveer.
Pratt, Lois Verveer, 1924-
xPratt, Lois.
Family Structure & Effective Health Behavior:
The Energized Family. HM.
Pratt, Mary L. *see* Pratt, Mary Louise.
Pratt, Mary Louise, 1948-
xPratt, Mary L.
Toward a Speech Act Theory of Literary
Discourse. Ind U Pr.
Pratt, Mike.
xPratt, Mike.
Own a Steel Boat. Intl Marine.
Pratt, N. S.
xPratt, Stephen.
French Revolution. John Day.
Pratt, Norma F. *see* Pratt, Norma Fain.
Pratt, Norma Fain.
xPratt, Norma F.
Morris Hillquit: A Political History of an
American Jewish Socialist. Greenwood.
Pratt, Stephen. *see* Pratt, N. S.
Pratt, Theodore, 1901-
xPratt, Theodore.
Story of Boca Raton. Great Outdoors.
Pratt, Vaughan R.
xPratt, Vaughan R.
Shellsort & Sorting Networks. Garland Pub.
Pratt, Vernon.
xPratt, Vernon.
The Philosophy of the Social Sciences.
Methuen Inc.
Pratt, Waldo S. *see* Pratt, Waldo Selden.
Pratt, Waldo Selden.
xPratt, Waldo S.
Music of the Pilgrims: A Description of the
Psalm-Book Brought to Plymouth in 1620.
Russell.
Pratt, Walter F., 1946-
xPratt, Walter F.
Privacy in Britain. Bucknell U Pr.
Pratt, William. *see* Pratt, William Crouch.
Pratt, William B.
xPratt, William B.
The Anticancer Drugs. Oxford U Pr.
Chemotherapy of Infection. Oxford U Pr.
Pratt, William Crouch, 1927-
xPratt, William.

ed. Fugitive Poets: Modern Southern Poetry in
Perspective. Dutton.
Pratt, William K.
xPratt, William K.
Digital Image Processing. Wiley.
Pratt-Butler, Grace K.
xPratt-Butler, Grace K.
Let Them Write Creatively. Merrill.
Pratte, Richard.
xPratte, Richard.
Pluralism in Education: Conflict, Clarity, &
Commitment. C C Thomas.
Prausnitz, J. *see* Prausnitz, J. M.
Prausnitz, J. M.
xPrausnitz, J.
Computer Calculations for Multicomponent
Vapor-Liquid & Liquid-Liquid Equilibrium.
P-H.
Prawer, Joshua.
xPrawer, Joshua.
The World of the Crusaders. Times Bks.
Prawer, S. S. *see* Prawer, Siegbert Saloman.
Prawer, Siegbert Saloman, 1925-
xPrawer, S. S.
Caligari's Children: The Film As Tale of
Terror. Oxford U Pr.
Pray, Isaac C. *see* Pray, Isaac Clarke.
Pray, Isaac Clarke, 1813-1869
xPray, Isaac C.
Memoirs of James Gordon Bennett & His
Times. Arno.
Praz, Mario, 1896-
xPraz, Mario.
Conversation Pieces: A Survey of the Informal
Group Portrait in Europe & America. Pa St
U Pr.
Prcela, John.
xPrcela, John.
Operation Slaughterhouse: Eyewitness
Accounts of Post War Massacres in
Yugoslavia. Dorrance.
Prebble, John, 1915-
xPrebble, John.
The Lion in the North: A Personal View of
Scotland's History. Intl Pubns Serv.
Prebish, Charles S.
xPrebish, Charles S.
American Buddhism. Duxbury Pr.
Preble, Duane.
xPreble, Duane.
Artforms. Har-Row.
Predmore, Helen R., 1893-
xPredmore, Helen R.
Chester, N.Y. Presbyterian Church: A History.
Lib Res.
Predmore, Richard L. *see* Predmore, Richard Lionel.
Predmore, Richard Lionel.
xPredmore, Richard L.
Cervantes. Dodd.
Lorca's New York Poetry: Social Injustice,
Dark Love, Lost Faith. Duke.
World of Don Quixote. Harvard U Pr.
Pree, Mildred De. *see* DePree, Mildred.
Prehn, Monika.
xPrehn, Monika.
A Christmas Crib. Taplinger.
Prehoda, Robert W.
xPrehoda, Robert W.
Your Next Fifty Years. Ace Bks.
Preibisch, P. *see* Preibisch, Paul.
Preibisch, Paul, 1851-
xPreibisch, P.
Two Studies on the Roman Pontifices. Arno.
Preinreich, Gabriel A. *see* Preinreich, Gabriel A. D.
Preinreich, Gabriel A. D., 1893-
xPreinreich, Gabriel A.
The Nature of Dividends. Arno.
Preis, S. *see* Preis, Sandra.
Preis, Sandra.
xPreis, S.

Arithmetic. P-H.
xPreis, Sandra.
Arithmetic. P-H.
Preiss, Byron.
xPreiss, Byron.
The Beach Boys. Ballantine.
The One Year Affair. Workman Pub.
Preiss, Jack. *see* Preiss, Jack Joseph.
Preiss, Jack J. *see* Preiss, Jack Joseph.
Preiss, Jack Joseph, 1919-
xPreiss, Jack.
Camp William James. Argo Bks.
xPreiss, Jack J.
Examination of Role Theory: The Case of the
State Police. U of Nebr Pr.
Preiswerk, Roy.
xPreiswerk, Roy.
ed. Documents on International Relations in
the Caribbean. Intl Pubns Serv.
Prejean, Blanche. *see* Prejean, Blanche G.
Prejean, Blanche G.
xPrejean, Blanche.
Programmed News Style. P-H.
Preliminary Commission of Inquiry. *see* Commission of
Inquiry into the Charges Made Against Leon Trotsky
in the Moscow Trials. Preliminary Commission,
Coyoacan, Mexico, 1937.
Preller, Victor.
xPreller, Victor.
Divine Science & the Science of God: A
Reformulation of Thomas Aquinas. Princeton
U Pr.
Prelutsky, Jack.
xPrelutsky, Jack.
Circus. Macmillan.
Circus. Macmillan.
The Mean Old Mean Hyena. Greenwillow.
Nightmares: Poems to Trouble Your Sleep.
Greenwillow.
Pack Rat's Day & Other Poems. Macmillan.
The Queen of Eene. Greenwillow.
Rainy Rainy Saturday. Greenwillow.
Rolling Harvey Down the Hill. Greenwillow.
Toucans Two & Other Poems. Macmillan.
Preminger, Alex. *see* Preminger, Alexander S.
Preminger, Alexander S.
xPreminger, Alex.
ed. The Princeton Encyclopedia of Poetry &
Poetics. Princeton U Pr.
Premm, Mathias, 1890-
xPremm, Mattias.
Dogmatic Theology for the Laity. TAN Bks
Pubs.
Premm, Mattias. *see* Premm, Mathias.
Prendergast, Christopher.
xPrendergast, Christopher.
Balzac: Fiction & Melodrama. Holmes &
Meier.
Prendergast, Roy M., 1943-
xPrendergast, Roy M.
A Neglected Art: A Critical Study of Music in
Films. NYU Pr.
Prendergast, William B.
xPrendergast, William M.
Mutual & Balanced Force Reduction: Issues &
Prospects. Am Enterprise.
Prendergast, William M. *see* Prendergast, William B.
Prenshaw, Peggy. *see* Prenshaw, Peggy Whitman.
Prenshaw, Peggy Whitman.
xPrenshaw, Peggy.
ed. Eudora Welty: Critical Essays. U Pr of
Miss.
Prentice, Ann E.
xPrentice, Ann E.
Public Library Finance. ALA.
Prentice, Archibald, 1792-1857
xPrentice, Archibald.

Prentice-Hall, Inc.
    xPrentice-Hall Editorial Staff.
        Accountant's Factomatic. P-H.
        Common Secretarial Mistakes & How to Avoid
            Them. P-H.
        Corporate Treasurer's & Controller's
            Encyclopedia. P-H.
        Corporate Treasurer's & Controller's
            Encyclopedia. P-H.
        Director's & Officer's Complete Letter Book.
            P-H.
        Encyclopedia of Accounting Systems. P-H.
        Federal Tax Course, 1979. P-H.
        Handbook of Forms & Reports for Forty-Eight
            Representative Accounting Systems. P-H.
        Handbook of Successful Operating Systems &
            Procedures, with Forms. P-H.
        Handbook of Successful School Administration.
            P-H.
        Legal Secretary's Encyclopedic Dictionary.
            P-H.

Prentice, William Kelly, 1871-1964
    xPrentice, William K.
        Ancient Greeks: Studies Toward a Better
            Understanding of the Ancient World. Russell.
        Those Ancient Dramas Called Tragedies.
            Russell.
Prentiss, Stan. see Prentiss, Stanton Rust.
Prentiss, Stanton Rust.
    xPrentiss, Stan.
        Admiral Color TV Service Manual. TAB Bks.
Prenzel, Howard V., 1911-
    xPrenzel, Howard V.
        Dynamic Trendline Charting. P-H.
Pres, Terrence Des. see Des Pres, Terrence.
Presbrey, Frank S. see Presbrey, Frank Spencer.
Presbrey, Frank Spencer, 1855-1936
    xPresbrey, Frank S.
        History & Development of Advertising.
            Greenwood.
Presbyterian Church in the United States of America.
    xPresbyterian Church In The United States Of
        America.
        Records of the Presbyterian Church in the
            United States of America, 1706-1788. Arno.
Prescod, Stephen V.
    xPrescod, Stephen V.
        Audiological Handbook of Hearing Disorders.
            Van Nos Reinhold.
Prescot, Dray.
    xPrescot, Dray.
        A Life for Kregen. DAW Bks.
Prescott, Anne L. see Prescott, Anne Lake.
Prescott, Anne Lake, 1936-
    xPrescott, Anne L.
        French Poets & the English Renaissance:
            Yale U Pr.
Prescott, Arthur T. see Prescott, Arthur Taylor.
Prescott, Arthur Taylor.
    xPrescott, Arthur T.
        ed. Drafting the Federal Constitution:
            Greenwood.
Prescott, D. see Prescott, David M.
Prescott, D. M. see Prescott, David M.
Prescott, David M., 1926-
    xPrescott, D.
        Reproduction of Eukaryotic Cells. Carolina
            Biological.
    xPrescott, D. M.
        Reproduction of Eukaryotic Cells. Acad Pr.
Prescott, Ernest.
    xPrescott, Ernest.
        Flying Creatures. Watts.
Prescott, Frank W. see Prescott, Frank Williams.
Prescott, Frank Williams.
    xPrescott, Frank W.

        The Politics of the Veto of Legislation in New
            York State. U Pr of Amer.
Prescott, G. W. see Prescott, Gerald Webber.
Prescott, Gerald Webber, 1899-
    xPrescott, G. W.
        Algae of the Western Great Lakes Area. Wm
            C Brown.
        How to Know the Aquatic Plants. Wm C
            Brown.
Prescott, H. F. see Prescott, Hilda Frances Margaret.
Prescott, Henry W. see Prescott, Henry Washington.
Prescott, Henry Washington, 1874-
    xPrescott, Henry W.
        Development of Virgil's Art. Russell.
Prescott, Hilda F. see Prescott, Hilda Frances Margaret.
Prescott, Hilda Frances Margaret, 1896-
    xPrescott, H. F.
        Spanish Tudor. AMS Pr.
    xPrescott, Hilda F.
        Friar Felix at Large. Greenwood.
Prescott, J. R. see Prescott, John Robert Victor.
Prescott, James R.
    xPrescott, James R.
        Economic Aspects of Public Housing. Sage.
Prescott, John Robert Victor.
    xPrescott, J. R.
        Boundaries & Frontiers. Rowman.
        Frontiers of Asia & Southeast Asia. Intl Schol
            Bk Serv.
Prescott, W. H. see Prescott, William Hickling.
Prescott, William H. see Prescott, William Hickling.
Prescott, William Hickling, 1796-1859
    xPrescott, W. H.
        Correspondence of William Hickling Prescott,
            1833-1847. Da Capo.
    xPrescott, William H.
        Conquest of Peru. NAL.
        History of the Conquest of Mexico. Dutton.
        History of the Conquest of Mexico. U of
            Chicago Pr.
President's Commission On Immigration. see United
    States. President'S Commission on Immigration and
    Naturalization.
President'S Commission On Law Enforcement And
    Administration Of Justice. see United States.
    President'S Commission on Law Enforcement and
    Administration of Justice.
President's Commission on the Health Needs of the
    Nation. see United States. President'S Commission on
    the Health Needs of the Nation.
**President's Conference on Home Building and Home
    Ownership.**
    xPresident's Conference On Home Building And
        Home Ownership.
        Negro Housing. Negro U Pr.
President's Research Committee on Social Trends.
    xPresident's Research Committee on Social
        Trends.
        Recent Social Trends in the United States.
            Arno.
    xPresidents Research Committee On Social Trends.
        Recent Social Trends in the United States.
            Greenwood.
Presley, Dee.
    xPresley, Dee.
        Elvis We Love You Tender. Delacorte.
        Elvis, We Love You Tender. Dell.
Presley, Horton.
    xPresley, Horton.
        Restoring & Collecting Antique Reed Organs.
            TAB Bks.
Presley, Vester.
    xPresley, Vester.
        A Presley Speaks. Wimmer Bks.

Presno, V. see Presno, Vincent.
Presno, Vincent.

    xPresno, V.

        The Value Realms: Activities for Helping
            Students Develop Values. Tchrs Coll.
Press. see Press, Hans Jurgen.
Press, Charles.
    xPress, Charles.
        State & Community Governments in the
            Federal System. Wiley.
Press, Frank.
    xPress, Frank.
        Earth. W H Freeman.
Press, Hans J. see Press, Hans Jurgen.
Press, Hans Jurgen.
    xPress.
        The Adventures of the Black Hand Gang.
            Schol Bk Serv.
    xPress, Hans J.
        The Adventures of the Black Hand Gang. P-H.
Press, Irwin.
    xPress, Irwin.
        Urban Place & Process: Readings in the
            Anthropology of Cities. Macmillan.
Press, John.
    xPress, John.
        Chequer'd Shade: Reflections on Obscurity in
            Poetry. Oxford U Pr.
        Map of Modern English Verse. Oxford U Pr.
Pressau, Jack R. see Pressau, Jack Renard.
Pressau, Jack Renard, 1933-
    xPressau, Jack R.
        I'm Saved, You're Saved--Maybe. John Knox.
Presseisen, B. see Presseisen, Barbara Z.
Presseisen, Barbara Z.
    xPresseisen, B.
        ed. Language & Operational Thought. Plenum
            Pub.
Presser, Harriet B.
    xPresser, Harriet B.
        Sterilization & Fertility Decline In Puerto Rico.
            Greenwood.
Pressland, David.
    xPressland, David.
        The Art of the Tin Toy. Crown.
Pressly, Thomas J.
    xPressly, Thomas J.
        Americans Interpret Their Civil War. Free Pr.
Pressman, Abraham I.
    xPressman, Abraham I.
        Switching & Linear Power Supply, Power
            Converter Design. Hayden.
Pressman, David, 1937-
    xPressman, David R.
        Patent It Yourself!: How to Protect, Patent &
            Market Your Inventions. McGraw.
Pressman, David R. see Pressman, David.
Pressman, Jeffrey L.
    xPressman, Jeffrey L.
        Federal Programs & City Politics: The
            Dynamics of the Aid Process in Oakland. U
            of Cal Pr.
        Implementation; How Great Expectations in
            Washington Are Dashed in Oakland: Or Why
            It's Amazing That Federal Programs Work at
            All, This Being the Saga of the Economic
            Development Administration As Told to by
            Two Sympathetic Observers Who Seek to
            Build Morals on Ruined Hopes. U of Cal Pr.
Pressman, Maurice J.
    xPressman, Maurice J.
        Workmen's Compensation in Maryland.
            Michie.
Presson, Hazel.
    xPresson, Hazel.
        Student Journalist & Interviewing. Rosen Pr.
Prest, A. R. see Prest, Alan Richmond.
Prest, Alan Richmond.
    xPrest, A. R.
        ed. The UK Economy: Manual of Applied
            Economics. Beekman Pubs.
Prest, John. see Prest, John M.

Prest, John M.
xPrest, John.
Lord John Russell. U of SC Pr.
Prestage, Edgar, 1869-1951
xPrestage, Edgar.
ed. Chapters in Anglo-Portuguese Relations. Greenwood.
Presthus, R. see Presthus, Robert Vance.
Presthus, Robert. see Presthus, Robert Vance.
Presthus, Robert Vance.
xPresthus, R.
Public Administration. Wiley.
xPresthus, Robert.
Men at the Top: A Study in Community Power. Oxford U Pr.
Preston, Adrian. see Preston, Adrian W.
Preston, Adrian W.
xPreston, Adrian.
ed. Swords & Covenants. Rowman.
Preston, C. see Preston, Christopher J.
Preston, Charles, 1921-
xPreston, Charles.
ed. The Wall Street Journal Cartoon Portfolio. Dow Jones-Irwin.
Preston, Christopher J.
xPreston, C.
Random Fields. Springer-Verlag.
Preston, Edna M. see Preston, Edna Mitchell.
Preston, Edna Mitchell.
xPreston, Edna M.
Pop Corn & Ma Goodness. Penguin.
Where Did My Mother Go?. Schol Bk Serv.
Preston, Everett C. see Preston, Everett Conant.
Preston, Everett Conant, 1898-
xPreston, Everett C.
Principles & Statutory Provisions Relating to Recreational, Medical & Social Welfare Services of the Public Schools. AMS Pr.
Preston, Gerald C.
xPreston, Gerald C.
Modern Analytic Geometry. Har-Row.
Preston, Howard L.
xPreston, Howard L.
Automobile Age Atlanta: The Making of a Southern Metropolis, 1900-1935. U of Ga Pr.
Preston, Hugh.
xPreston, Hugh.
Feast in the Morning. St Martin.
Preston, Ivan L., 1931-
xPreston, Ivan L.
The Great American Blow-up: Puffery in Advertising & Selling. U of Wis Pr.
Preston, Ivy.
xPreston, Ivy.
Romance in Glenmore Street. Ace Bks.
Preston, K. see Preston, Kendall.
Preston, Kendall.
xPreston, K.
ed. Digital Processing of Biomedical Images. Plenum Pub.
Preston, Lee E.
xPreston, Lee E.
Private Management & Public Policy: The Principle of Public Responsibility. P-H.
Preston, M. A. see Preston, Melvin Alexander.
Preston, Margaret (Junkin), 1820-1897
xPreston, Margaret J.
Aunt Dorothy: An Old Virginia Plantation Story. Arno.
Preston, Margaret J. see Preston, Margaret (Junkin).
Preston, Melvin Alexander.
xPreston, M. A.
Structure of the Nucleus. A-W.
Preston, P. see Preston, Paul.
Preston, Paul, 1944-
xPreston, P.
Communication for Managers. P-H.
Preston, Philip.
xPreston, Philip.

White Mountains-West. Waumbek.
Preston, R. see Preston, Ralph Clausius.
Preston, Ralph Clausius, 1908-
xPreston, R.
Teaching Social Studies in the Elementary School. HR&W.
Preston, Raymond.
xPreston, Raymond.
Chaucer. Greenwood.
Chaucer. Norwood Edns.
Preston, Richard A. see Preston, Richard Arthur.
Preston, Richard Arthur.
xPreston, Richard A.
Canada & "Imperial Defense": A Study of the Origins of the British Commonwealth's Defense Organization, 1867-1919. Duke.
Men in Arms: A History of Warfare & Its Interrelationships with Western Society. HR&W.
Men in Arms: A History of Warfare & Its Interrelationships with Western Society. Praeger.
Preston, T. R. see Preston, Thomas Reginald.
Preston, Thomas. see Preston, Thomas R.
Preston, Thomas R.
xPreston, Thomas.
Not in Timon's Manner: Feeling Misanthropy, & Satire in Eighteenth-Century England. U of Ala Pr.
Preston, Thomas Reginald.
xPreston, T. R.
Intensive Beef Production. Pergamon.
Preston, Wheeler.
xPreston, Wheeler.
American Biographies. Gale.
Preston, William H. see Preston, William Hall.
Preston, William Hall.
xPreston, William H.
ed. Fathers Are Special. Broadman.
Prestressed Concrete Institute.
xPrestressed Concrete Institute.
Architectural Precast Concrete Drafting Handbook. P-H.
Prestwich, Michael.
xPrestwich, Michael.
The Three Edwards: War & State in England, 1272-1377. St Martin.
Preterm, Inc.
xPreterm Institute.
Exploring Human Sexuality. Schenkman.
Sex Counseling by Telephone. Schenkman.
Preterm Institute. see Preterm, Inc.
Pretest Series. see Pretest Service, Inc.
Pretest Series Editors. see Pretest Service, Inc.
Pretest Service, Inc.
xPretest Series.
ed. PreTest for Physicians Preparing for the VISA Qualifying Examination. McGraw-Pretest.
ed. PreTest for Students Preparing for the National Board Examination. McGraw-Pretest.
ed. PreTest for Students Preparing for the State Board Examinations for Practical Nurse Licensure. McGraw-Pretest.
xPretest Series Editors.
Pretest for Physicians Preparing for the Federation Licensing Examination Flex. McGraw-Pretest.
xPreTest Service, Inc.
Internal Medicine: PreTest Self-Assessment & Review. McGraw.
Pretner, Lee.
xPretner, Lee.
Pro Sports Trivia. Watts.
Preto-Rodas, Richard A.
xPreto-Rodas, Richard A.

Negritude As a Theme in the Poetry of the Portuguese-Speaking World. U Presses Fla.
Prettyman, Barrett, 1925-
xPrettyman, Barrett.
Death & the Supreme Court. HarBraceJ.
Preu, James. see Preu, James A.
Preu, James A.
xPreu, James.
The Dean & the Anarchist. Haskell.
xPreu, James A.
Dean & the Anarchist. U Presses Fla.
Preus, David W.
xPreus, David W.
Go with the Gospel. Augsburg.
Preus, Robert D., 1924-
xPreus, Robert D.
Theology of Post-Reformation Lutheranism. Concordia.
Preuss, Arthur, 1871-1934
xPreuss, Arthur.
ed. Dictionary of Secret & Other Societies. Gale.
Preuss, Karen.
xPreuss, Karen.
ed. Life Time: A New Image of Aging. Unity Pr.
Preussler, Otfried.
xPreussler, Otfried.
Adventures of Strong Vanya. Abelard.
Previn, Andre.
xPrevin, Andre.
Orchestra. Doubleday.
Previte-Orton, C. W. see Previte-Orton, Charles William.
Previte-Orton, Charles W. see Previte-Orton, Charles William.
Previte-Orton, Charles William, 1877-1947
xPrevite-Orton, C. W.
Political Satire in English Poetry. Haskell.
xPrevite-Orton, Charles W.
Political Satire in English Poetry. Russell.
Previts, Gary J. see Previts, Gary John.
Previts, Gary John.
xPrevits, Gary J.
A History of Accounting in America: An Historical Interpretation of the Cultural Significance of Accounting. Wiley.
Prewitt, Kenneth.
xPrewitt, Kenneth.
An Introduction to American Government. Har-Row.
Preziosi, Donald, 1941-
xPreziosi, Donald.
The Semiotics of the Built Environment: An Introduction to Architectonic Analysis. Ind U Pr.
Priamo, Carol, 1947-
xPriamo, Carol.
The General Store. McGraw.
Pribram, Alfred F. see Pribram, Alfred Francis.
Pribram, Alfred Francis, 1859-1941
xPribram, Alfred F.
Austrian Foreign Policy, 1908-1918. Shoe String.
Pribram, Karl H.
xPribram, Karl H.
Freud's "Project" Reassessed: Preface to Contemporary Cognitive Theory & Neuropsychology. Basic.
Price, A. Rae.
xPrice, A. Rae.
Developing Your Vocabulary. Wm C Brown.
Price, Alan. see Price, Alan Frederick.
Price, Alan Frederick.
xPrice, Alan.
Synge & Anglo-Irish Drama. Russell.
Price, Alfred.
xPrice, Alfred.

Focke-Wulf 190 at War. Scribner.
Instruments of Darkness: The History of
Electronic Warfare. Scribner.
Price, Anthony.
xPrice, Anthony.
Tomorrow's Ghost. Doubleday.
Price, Archibald G. *see* Price, Archibald Grenfell.
Price, Archibald Grenfell, Sir, 1892-
xPrice, Archibald G.
White Settlers & Native Peoples: An Historical
Study of Racial Contacts Between
English-Speaking Whites & Aboriginal
Peoples in the United States, Canada,
Australia, & New Zealand. Greenwood.
White Settlers in the Tropics. AMS Pr.
Price, Arthur J.
xPrice, Arthur J.
Appreciation of Joseph Conrad. Folcroft.
Price, Barbara A. *see* Price, Barbara Anne.
Price, Barbara Anne.
xPrice, Barbara A.
Federico Fellini: An Annotated International
Bibliography. Scarecrow.
Price, Barrie.
xPrice, Barry.
The Lea-Francis Story. David & Charles.
Price, Barry. *see* Price, Barrie.
Price, Billy L.
xPrice, Billy L.
Homeowner's Guide to Saving Energy. TAB
Bks.
Price, Brick.
xPrice, Brick.
BSA Service-Repair Handbook: All 500 &
650cc Unit Construction Twins. Clymer
Pubns.
Price, C. C. *see* Price, Charles Coale.
Price, Cecil. *see* Price, Cecil John Layton.
Price, Cecil John Layton.
xPrice, Cecil.
Theatre in the Age of Garrick. Rowman.
Price, Charles Coale, 1913-
xPrice, C. C.
Geometry of Molecules. McGraw.
Price, Colin.
xPrice, Colin.
Landscape Economics. Holmes & Meier.
Price, David L. *see* Price, David Lynn.
Price, David Lynn.
xPrice, David L.
Oil & Middle East Security. Sage.
The Western Sahara. Sage.
Price, Derek de Solla. *see* Price, Derek John De Solla.
Price, Derek J. *see* Price, Derek John De Solla.
Price, Derek John De Solla.
xPrice, Derek de Solla.
Gears from the Greeks: The Antikythera
Mechanism, a Calendar Computer from ca 80
B. C.. Am Philos.
xPrice, Derek J.
Little Science, Big Science. Columbia U Pr.
Price, E. A., 1925-
xPrice, E. A.
Introduction to Algebra. Arc Bks.
Price, E. W.
xPrice, E. W.
Acts in Prayer. Broadman.
Price, Edna C. *see* Price, Edna Calkins.
Price, Edna Calkins.
xPrice, Edna C.
Burro Bill & Me. Strawberry Valley.
Price, Edward O.
xPrice, Edward O.
Animal Behavior in Laboratory & Field. W H
Freeman.
Price, Emerson.
xPrice, Emerson.

Inn of That Journey. Popular Lib.
Inn of That Journey. S Ill U Pr.
Price, Eugenia.
xPrice, Eugenia.
Don Juan McQueen. Bantam.
Don Juan McQueen. Lippincott.
God Speaks to Women Today. Zondervan.
Leave Your Self Alone. Zondervan.
Lighthouse. Bantam.
Lighthouse. Lippincott.
Maria. Bantam.
Maria. Lippincott.
No Pat Answers. Bantam.
No Pat Answers. Zondervan.
Price, F. W. *see* Price, Frederick William.
Price, Flo.
xPrice, Flo.
Casseroles I Have Known. Word Bks.
Super Salads. Word Bks.
Price, Frank J. *see* Price, Frank James.
Price, Frank James, 1917-
xPrice, Frank J.
Troy H. Middleton: A Biography. La State U
Pr.
Price, Frederick G. *see* Price, Frederick George Hilton.
Price, Frederick George Hilton, 1842-1909
xPrice, Frederick G.
Handbook of London Bankers: With Some
Account of Their Predecessors, the Early
Goldsmiths. B Franklin.
Price, Frederick William.
xPrice, F. W.
Price's Textbook of the Practice of Medicine.
Oxford U Pr.
Price, G. Ward. *see* Price, George Ward.
Price, George, 1901-
xPrice, George.
Browse at Your Own Risk S&S.
Price, George M. *see* Price, George Moses.
Price, George Moses, 1864-1942
xPrice, George M.
Modern Factory: Safety, Sanitation & Welfare.
Arno.
Price, George R.
xPrice, George R.
Reading Shakespeare's Plays: A Guide for
College Students. Barron.
Thomas Dekker. Irvington.
Price, George Ward, 1886-
xPrice, G. Ward.
I Know These Dictators. Kennikat.
Price, H. H. *see* Price, Henry Habberley.
Price, H. T. *see* Price, Hereward Thimbleby.
Price, Harry, 1881-1948
xPrice, Harry.
Fifty Years of Psychical Research: A Critical
Survey. Arno.
Price, Henry Habberley, 1899-
xPrice, H. H.
Thinking & Representation. Haskell.
Price, Hereward T. *see* Price, Hereward Thimbleby.
Price, Hereward Thimbleby, 1880-1964
xPrice, H. T.
Construction in Shakespeare. Folcroft.
xPrice, Hereward T.
Construction in Shakespeare. Norwood Edns.
Price, Hugh D. *see* Price, Hugh Douglas.
Price, Hugh Douglas.
xPrice, Hugh D.
The Negro & Southern Politics: A Chapter of
Florida History. Greenwood.
Price, Irving.
xPrice, Irving.
How to Get Top Dollar for Your Home. Times
Bks.
Price, Jacob M.
xPrice, Jacob M.

France & the Chesapeake: A History of the
French Tobacco Monopoly, 1674-1791, & of
Its Relationship to the British & American
Tobacco Trades. U of Mich Pr.
Price, James E.
xPrice, James E.
Analysis of a Middle Mississippian House in
Butler County, Missouri. Mus Anthro Mo.
Dalton, Occupation of the Ozark Border. Mus
Anthro Mo.
Price, James L.
xPrice, James L.
The Study of Turnover. Iowa St U Pr.
Price, Jane, 1944-
xPrice, Jane.
How to Have a Child & Keep Your Job. St
Martin.
Price, Jeanne.
xPrice, Jeanne.
Grading Techniques for Modern Design.
Fairchild.
Price, John. *see* Price, John Richard.
Price, John A., 1933-
xPrice, John A.
Native Studies: American & Canadian Indians.
McGraw.
Price, John F. *see* Price, John Frederick.
Price, John Frederick, 1943-
xPrice, John F.
Lie Groups & Compact Groups. Cambridge U
Pr.
Price, John Richard, 1941-
xPrice, John.
America at the Crossroads. Tyndale.
Price, Jonathan, 1941-
xPrice, Jonathan.
Classic Scenes. NAL.
ed. Critics on Robert Lowell. U of Miami Pr.
Price, Julia S.
xPrice, Julia S.
The Off-Broadway Theater. Greenwood.
Price, L. W. *see* Price, Larry W.
Price, Larkin B.
xPrice, Larkin B.
ed. Marcel Proust: A Critical Panorama. U of
Ill Pr.
Price, Larry W.
xPrice, L. W.
Periglacial Environment, Permafrost & Man.
Assn Am Geographers.
Price, Louise, 1892-
xPrice, Louise.
Creative Group Work on the Campus: A
Developmental Study of Certain Aspects of
Student Life. AMS Pr.
Price, Martin, 1920-
xPrice, Martin.
ed. Dickens: A Collection of Critical Essays.
P-H.
Swift's Rhetorical Art: A Study in Structure &
Meaning. S Ill U Pr.
Price, Mary R. *see* Price, Mary Roper.
Price, Mary Roper.
xPrice, Mary R.
Portrait of Britain in the Middle Ages,
1066-1485. Oxford U Pr.
Price, Michael H.
xPrice, Michael H.
Forgotten Horrors: Early Talkie Chillers from
Poverty Row. A S Barnes.
Price, Michelle.
xPrice, Michelle.
Mean Melissa. Bradbury Pr.
Price, Miles O. *see* Price, Miles Oscar.
Price, Miles Oscar.
xPrice, Miles O.
Effective Legal Research. Kelley.
Effective Legal Research. Little.
Effective Legal Research. Rothman.
Price, Monroe E. *see* Price, Monroe Edwin.

Price, Monroe Edwin, 1938-
  xPrice, Monroe E.
    Law & the American Indian: Readings, Notes
    & Cases. Michie.
Price, Nancy, 1925-
  xPrice, Nancy.
    An Accomplished Woman. Coward.
    An Accomplished Woman. NAL.
Price, Nelson L.
  xPrice, Nelson L.
    How to Find Out Who You Are. Broadman.
    Supreme Happiness. Broadman.
Price, Nicholas. see Price, Nicholas C.
Price, Nicholas C.
  xPrice, Nicholas.
    Principles & Problems in Physical Chemistry
    for Biochemists. Oxford U Pr.
Price, Oliver R. see Price, Oliver Ray.
Price, Oliver Ray.
  xPrice, Oliver R.
    High Leverage Real Estate Investments: Inside
    Secrets of Using OPM. P-H.
Price, Peter W.
  xPrice, Peter W.
    Evolutionary Biology of Parasites. Princeton U
    Pr.
    Insect Ecology. Wiley.
Price, R. D. see Price, Roger.
Price, R. F.
  xPrice, R. F.
    Reference Book of English Words & Phrases
    for Foreign Science Students. Pergamon.
  xPrice, Ronald F.
    Marx & Education in Russia & China.
    Rowman.
Price, Ray G.
  xPrice, Ray G.
    Business & You As a Consumer, Worker &
    Citizen. McGraw.
Price, Reynolds, 1933-
  xPrice, Reynolds.
    A Generous Man. Atheneum.
    Generous Man. Avon.
    A Long & Happy Life. Atheneum.
    A Long & Happy Life. Avon.
    Love & Work. Atheneum.
    Permanent Errors. Atheneum.
Price, Richard, 1941-
  xPrice, Richard.
    The Guiana Maroons: A Historical &
    Bibliographical Introduction. Johns Hopkins.
    ed. Maroon Societies: Rebel Slave
    Communities in the Americas. Johns
    Hopkins.
    ed. Maroon Societies: Rebel Slave
    Communities in the Americas. Peter Smith.
    Review of the Principal Questions in Morals. B
    Franklin.
    A Review of the Principal Questions in Morals.
    Oxford U Pr.
Price, Robert, 1900-
  xPrice, Robert.
    Johnny Appleseed: Man & Myth. Peter Smith.
Price, Robert M.
  xPrice, Robert M.
    Society & Bureaucracy in Contemporary
    Ghana. U of Cal Pr.
    U.S. Foreign Policy in Sub-Saharan Africa:
    National Interest & Global Strategy. U of Cal
    Intl St.
Price, Roger.
  xPrice, R. D.
    French Second Republic: A Social History.
    Cornell U Pr.
  xPrice, Roger.
    Droodles. Price Stern.
    The French Second Republic: A Social History.
    David & Charles.
    Oodles of Droodles. Price Stern.
Price, Ronald F. see Price, R. F.

Price, Seymour G.
  xPrice, Seymour G.
    A Guide to Monitoring & Controlling Utility
    Costs. BNA.
Price, Steve, 1947-
  xPrice, Steve.
    Wild Places of the South. East Woods.
Price, Steven D.
  xPrice, Steven D.
    A Panorama of American Horses. Barre.
    Teaching Riding at Summer Camps. Greene.
Price, Susan.
  xPrice, Susan.
    The Devil's Piper. Greenwillow.
    Home from Home. Merrimack Bk Serv.
Price, Sylvia. see Price, Sylvia Anderson.
Price, Sylvia Anderson.
  xPrice, Sylvia.
    Pathophysiology: Clinical Concepts of Disease
    Processes. McGraw.

Price, Thomas Randolph, 1839-1903
  xPrice, Thomas R.
    Construction & Types of Shakespeare's Verse
    As Seen in the Othello. AMS Pr.
    Construction & Types of Shakespeare's Verse
    As Seen in the Othello. R West.
Price, Vincent Foreword by. see King, Robert B.
Price, W. C. see Price, William Charles.
Price, W. J. see Price, William John.
Price, Walter. see Price, Walter K.
Price, Walter K.
  xPrice, Walter.
    In the Final Days. Moody.
  xPrice, Walter K.
    The Coming Antichrist. Moody.
    The Prophet Joel & the Day of the Lord.
    Moody.
Price, Warren C.
  xPrice, Warren C.
    Annotated Journalism Bibliography, 1958-1968.
    U of Minn Pr.
    Eugene Register-Guard. Binford.
Price Waterhouse & Co. see Price Waterhouse and
Company.
Price Waterhouse and Company.
  xPrice Waterhouse & Co.
    Compiled by Abingdon Clergy Income Tax
    Guide, 1979. Abingdon.
    ed. Abingdon Clergy Income Tax Guide, 1981
    Edition for 1980 Returns. Abingdon.
    Rev. by Abingdon Clergy Income Tax Guide,
    1980. Abingdon.
Price, Willard, 1887-
  xPrice, Willard.
    African Adventure. John Day.
Price, Willet J.
  xPrice, Willet J.
    Boots & Forceps. Iowa St U Pr.
Price, William Charles.
  xPrice, W. C.
    The Uncertainty Principle & Foundations of
    Quantum Mechanics: A Fifty Years' Survey.
    Wiley.
Price, William H. see Price, William Hyde.
Price, William Hyde.
  xPrice, William H.
    The English Patents of Monopoly. AMS Pr.
Price, William John, 1924-
  xPrice, W. J.
    Spectrochemical Analysis by Atomic
    Absorption. Heyden.
Price-Williams, Douglass R. see Price-Williams, Douglass
Richard.
Price-Williams, Douglass Richard.
  xPrice-Williams, Douglass R.
    Explorations in Cross-Cultural Psychology.
    Chandler & Sharp.
Prichard, Anita.
  xPrichard, Anita.

    Anita Prichard's Complete Candy Cookbook.
    Crown.
Prichard, Elizabeth. see Prichard, Elizabeth R.
Prichard, Elizabeth R.
  xPrichard, Elizabeth.
    ed. Social Work with the Dying Patient & the
    Family. Columbia U Pr.
Prichard, Hesketh. see Prichard, Hesketh Vernon
Hesketh.
Prichard, Hesketh Vernon Hesketh, 1876-1922
  xPrichard, Hesketh.
    Where Black Rules White: A Journey Across &
    About Hayti. Biblio Dist.
    Where Black Rules White: A Journey Across &
    About Hayti. Humanities.
Prichard, John F.
  xPrichard, John F.
    Advanced Periodontal Disease: Surgical &
    Prosthetic Management. Saunders.
    The Diagnosis & Treatment of Periodontal
    Disease. Saunders.
Prichard, Keith W.
  xPrichard, Keith W.
    Concepts & Theories in Sociology of
    Education. Prof Educ Pubn.
Prickett, Stephen.
  xPrickett, Stephen.
    Victorian Fantasy. Ind U Pr.
Priddy, Frances.
  xPriddy, Frances.
    Challenge for Angel. Westminster.
    Ghosts of Lee House. Doubleday.
Pride, Kitty.
  xPride, Kitty.
    Chatino Syntax. Summer Inst Ling.
Pride, William M.
  xPride, William M.
    Marketing: Basic Concepts & Decisions. HM.
Prideaux, J. D. C. A.
  xPrideaux, John.
    English Narrow Gauge Railway. David &
    Charles.
Prideaux, John. see Prideaux, J. D. C. A.
Prideaux, Tom.
  xPrideaux, Tom.
    Cro-Magnon Man. Time-Life.
    Cro-Magnon Man. Silver.
    World of Delacroix. Time-Life.
    World of Delacroix. Silver.
    World of Whistler. Time-Life.
    World of Whistler. Silver.
Prideaux, William F. see Prideaux, William Francis.
Prideaux, William Francis, 1840-1914
  xPrideaux, William F.
    Notes for a Bibliography of Edward
    FitzGerald. B Franklin.
    Notes for a Bibliography of Edward Fitzgerald.
    R West.
Pridham, G. J.
  xPridham, G. J.
    Solid State Circuits. Pergamon.
Pridham, Geoffrey, 1942-
  xPridham, Geoffrey.
    Christian Democracy in Western Germany. St
    Martin.
Pridmore, F. see Pridmore, Mayor F.
Pridmore, Mayor F.
  xPridmore, F.
    Modern Coins & Notes of Cyprus. Intl Pubns
    Serv.
Prieditis, Arthur, 1909-
  xPrieditis, Arthur.
    The Fate of the Nations. Llewellyn Pubns.
Prier, J. see Prier, James E.
Prier, James E.
  xPrier, J.
    Australia Antigen. Univ Park.
Priesing, Elwood R.
  xPriesing, Elwood R.

Music & the Dance. Exposition.

Priest, Christopher.
xPriest, Christopher.
Anticipations. Scribner.
Darkening Island. Ultramarine Pub.
Indoctrinaire. Ultramarine Pub.
An Infinite Summer. Scribner.
The Perfect Lover. Scribner.

Priest, Jean H., 1928-
xPriest, Jean H.
Medical Cytogenetics & Cell Culture. Lea &
Febiger.

Priest, Joseph.
xPriest, Joseph.
Problems of Our Physical Environment: Energy
- Transportation - Pollution. A-W.

Priest, Loring B. see Priest, Loring Benson.

Priest, Loring Benson.
xPriest, Loring B.
Uncle Sam's Stepchildren: The Reformation of
United States Indian Policy, 1865-1887.
Octagon.
Uncle Sam's Stepchildren: The Reformation of
United States Indian Policy, 1865-1887. U of
Nebr Pr.

Priest, Robert G.
xPriest, Robert G.
Insanity: A Study of Major Psychiatric
Disorders. Biblio Dist.

Priester, Gertrude A. see Priester, Gertrude Ann.

Priester, Gertrude Ann.
xPriester, Gertrude A.
Let's Talk About God: Devotions for Families
with Young Children. Westminster.

Priestley, Harold E. see Priestley, Harold Edford.

Priestley, Harold Edford.
xPriestley, Harold E.
Truly Bizarre. Sterling.

Priestley, Herbert I. see Priestley, Herbert Ingram.

Priestley, Herbert Ingram, 1875-1944
xPriestley, Herbert I.
Coming of the White Man: 1492-1848. New
Viewpoints.
Jose De Galvez, Visitor General of New Spain
1765-1771. Porcupine Pr.

Priestley, J. B. see Priestley, John Boynton.

Priestley, John B. see Priestley, John Boynton.

Priestley, John Boynton, 1894-
xPriestley, J. B.
Charles Dickens & His World. Scribner.
English Humour. Folcroft.
English Humour. R West.
English Humour. Stein & Day.
English Novel. Scholarly.
Instead of the Trees: A Final Chapter of
Autobiography. Stein & Day.
Particular Pleasures. Stein & Day.
Thoughts in the Wilderness. Kennikat.
xPriestley, John B.
Balconinny. Arno.
Delight. Arno.
Eden End: A Play in Three Acts. Greenwood.
English Comic Characters. Phaeton.
The English Comic Characters. Somerset Pub.
The English Novel. Arden Lib.
English Novel. Folcroft.
Figures in Modern Literature. Arno.
George Meredith. Scholarly.
I for One. Arno.
The Other Place: & Other Stories of the Same
Sort. Arno.

Priestley, Joseph, 1733-1804
xPriestley, Joseph.

A Continuation of the Letters to the
Philosophers & Politicians of France on the
Subject of Religion, & of the Letters to a
Philosophical Unbeliever in Answer to Mr.
Paine's Age of Reason. Kraus Repr.
Disquisitions Relating to Matter & Spirit.
Arno.
Historical Account of the Navigable Rivers,
Canals, & Railways Throughout Great
Britain. Kelley.
Memoirs of Dr. Joseph Priestley, to the Year
1795, Written by Himself, with a
Continuation,.... Kraus Repr.

Priestley, Lee.
xPriestley, Lee.
America's Space Shuttle. Messner.

Priestly, E. B.
xPriestly, E. B.
Introduction to Liquid Crystals. Plenum Pub.

Prieto. see Prieto, Mariana Beeching De.

Prieto, Mariana B. see Prieto, Mariana Beeching De.

Prieto, Mariana Beeching De.
xPrieto.
Pablo's Petunias. Oddo.
xPrieto, Mariana B.
ed. Play It in Spanish: Spanish Games & Folk
Songs for Children. John Day.

Prifti, Peter R.
xPrifti, Peter R.
Socialist Albania Since 1944: Domestic &
Foreign Developments. MIT Pr.

Prigmore, Charles S.
xPrigmore, Charles S.
Social Welfare Policy: Analysis & Formulation.
Heath.
Social Work in Iran Since the White
Revolution. U of Ala Pr.

Priluck, H. M. see Priluck, Herbert M.

Priluck, Herbert M.
xPriluck, H. M.
Practical CPM for Construction. Means.

Prima, Diane Di. see Di Prima, Diane.

Primack, M. L. see Primack, Martin L.

Primack, Martin, 1929-
xPrimack, Martin L.
Farm Formed Capital in American Agriculture,
1850-1910. Arno.

Primack, Martin L.
xPrimack, M. L.
An Economic History of the United States.
A-W.
xPrimack, Martin L.
An Economic History of the United States.
Benjamin-Cummings.

Primack, Martin L. see Primack, Martin.

Primak, W. see Primak, William.

Primak, William, 1917-
xPrimak, W.
The Compacted States of Vitreous Silica.
Gordon.

Primeau, Ronald.
xPrimeau, Ronald.
ed. Influx: Essays on Literary Influence.
Kennikat.
The Rhetoric of Television. Longman.

Primer, Ben, 1949-
xPrimer, Ben.
Protestants & American Business Methods.
Univ Microfilms.

Primm, James N. see Primm, James Neal.

Primm, James Neal, 1918-
xPrimm, James N.
The American Experience. Forum Pr MO.
The American Experience. Ind Sch Pr.

Primrose, S. B.
xPrimrose, S. B.
Introduction to Modern Virology. Halsted Pr.

Prince, Alison.
xPrince, Alison.

The Doubting Kind. Morrow.
The Turkey's Nest. Morrow.

Prince, F. T. see Prince, Frank Templeton.

Prince, Frank Templeton.
xPrince, F. T.
Afterword on Rupert Brooke. SBD.
Collected Poems. Sheep Meadow.

Prince, Gary M.
xPrince, Gary M.
Vanya & the Clay Queen. Carolrhoda Bks.

Prince, George M., 1918-
xPrince, George M.
Practice of Creativity: A Manual for Dynamic
Group Problem Solving. Har-Row.
The Practice of Creativity: A Manual for
Dynamic Group Problem Solving. Macmillan.

Prince, Gerald.
xPrince, Gerald.
A Grammar of Stories: An Introduction.
Mouton.

Prince, J. Dyneley. see Prince, John Dyneley.

Prince, J. H. see Prince, Jack Harvey.

Prince, Jack Harvey.
xPrince, J. H.
How Animals Hunt. Elsevier-Nelson.
Plants That Eat Animals. Elsevier-Nelson.

Prince, John D. see Prince, John Dyneley.

Prince, John Dyneley, 1868-1945
xPrince, J. Dyneley.
Assyrian Primer: An Inductive Method of
Learning the Cuneiform Characters. AMS Pr.
xPrince, John D.
Fragments from Babel. AMS Pr.
Passamaquoddy Texts. AMS Pr.

Prince, L. Bradford. see Prince, le Baron Bradford.

Prince, le Baron Bradford, 1840-1922
xPrince, L. Bradford,
Spanish Mission Churches of New Mexico. Rio
Grande.

Prince, Morton.
xPrince, Morton.
Clinical & Experimental Studies in Personality.
Greenwood.
Dissociation of a Personality: A Biographical
Study in Abnormal Psychology. Greenwood.
The Dissociation of a Personality: A
Biographical Study in Abnormal Psychology.
Johnson Repr.
The Dissociation of a Personality: The Hunt
for the Real Miss Beauchamp. Oxford U Pr.
The Unconscious: The Fundamentals of Human
Personality Normal & Abnormal. Arno.

Prince, Patricia.
xPrince, Patricia.
The Contreras Clinic Laetrile Cookbook.
Devin.

Prince, Walter F. see Prince, Walter Franklin.

Prince, Walter Franklin, 1863-1934
xPrince, Walter F.
Noted Witnesses for Psychic Occurrences.
Univ Bks.

Prince, William M. see Prince, William Meade.

Prince, William Meade, 1893-1951
xPrince, William M.
Southern Part of Heaven. U of NC Pr.

Prince, William R. see Prince, William Robert.

Prince, William Robert, 1795-1869
xPrince, William R.
Prince's Manual of Roses. E M Coleman Ent.

**Princeton Bicentennial Conference on the Future of
Nuclear Science, Princeton University, 1946.**
xPrinceton Bicentennial Conference On The Future
Of Nuclear Science.
Physical Science & Human Values, a
Symposium. Greenwood.

Princeton Center for Infancy. see Princeton Center for
Infancy and Early Childhood.

Princeton Center for Infancy & Early Childhood. see
Princeton Center for Infancy and Early Childhood.

Princeton Center for Infancy and Early Childhood.
  xPrinceton Center for Infancy.
    Growing-up Years: Your Child's Record Keeping Book. Doubleday.
    The Parenting Advisor. Doubleday.
  xPrinceton Center for Infancy & Early Childhood.
    First Twelve Months of Life. G&D.
  xThePrinceton Center for Infancy.
    Parents' Yellow Pages. Doubleday.
Princeton University.
  xPrinceton University.
    Dictionary Catalog of the Princeton University Plasma Physics Laboratory Library. G K Hall.
Princeton University - Office of Population Research. see Princeton University. Office of Population Research.
Princeton University, Library.
  xPrinceton University Library.
    Robert Louis Stevenson: Catalogue. Princeton Lib.
Princeton University. Office of Population Research.
  xPrinceton University - Office of Population Research.
    Population Index Bibliography Cumulated 1935-1968 by Authors & Geographical Areas. G K Hall.
Prindiville, Kathleen.
  xPrindiville, Kathleen.
    First Ladies. Macmillan.
Prindl, Andreas R.
  xPrindl, Andreas R.
    Foreign Exchange Risk. Wiley.
Prindle, Paul W. see Prindle, Paul Wesley.
Prindle, Paul Wesley, 1903-
  xPrindle, Paul W.
    Descendants of John & Mary Jane (Cunningham) Gillespie. NY Pub Lib.
Pringle, David.
  xPringle, David.
    Earth Is the Alien Planet: J. G. Ballard's Four-Dimensional Nightmare. Borgo Pr.
Pringle, Henry F. see Pringle, Henry Fowles.
Pringle, Henry Fowles, 1897-1958
  xPringle, Henry F.
    Alfred E. Smith: A Critical Study. AMS Pr.
    Alfred E. Smith: A Critical Study. Scholarly.
Pringle, Laurence.
  xPringle, Laurence.
    Dinosaurs & Their World. HarBraceJ.
    Dinosaurs & Their World. HarBraceJ.
Pringle, Laurence. see Pringle, Laurence P.
Pringle, Laurence P.
  xPringle, Laurence.
    Chains, Webs, & Pyramids: The Flow of Energy in Nature. T Y Crowell.
    Follow a Fisher. T Y Crowell.
    From Pond to Prairie: The Changing World of a Pond & Its Life. Macmillan.
    The Gentle Desert: Exploring an Ecosystem. Macmillan.
    Listen to the Crows. T Y Crowell.
    Nuclear Power: From Physics to Politics. Macmillan.
    Only Earth We Have. Macmillan.
    Only Earth We Have. Macmillan.
    Our Hungry Earth: The World Food Crisis. Macmillan.
    Twist, Wiggle, & Squirm: A Book About Earthworms. T Y Crowell.
Pringle, M. A.
  xPringle, M. A.
    Journey in East Africa: Towards the Mountains of the Moon. Arno.
Pringle, M. L. see Pringle, Mia Lilly (Kellmer).
Pringle, Mia Lilly (Kellmer).
  xPringle, M. L.
    ed. Caring for Children: A Symposium on Co-Operation in Child Care. Humanities.
Pringle, R. M.
  xPringle, R. M.

Generalized Inverse Matrices with Applications to Statistics. Hafner.
Pringle, Robert, 1936-
  xPringle, Robert M.
    Rajahs & Rebels: The Ibans of Sarawak Under Brooke Rule, 1841-1941. Cornell U Pr.
Pringle, Robert M. see Pringle, Robert.
Prins, H. A. see Prins, Herschel A.
Prins, Herschel A.
  xPrins, H. A.
    Social Work & Medical Practice. Pergamon.
Print Project.
  xPrint Project.
    The Unusual-by-Mail Catalog. St Martin.
Printz, Peggy.
  xPrintz, Peggy.
    Commune: Life in Rural China. Dodd.
Prinz, Joachim, 1902-
  xPrinz, Joachim.
    Popes from the Ghetto: A View of Medieval Christendom. Schocken.
Prinz, Martin.
  xPrinz, Martin.
    ed. Simon & Schuster's Guide to Rocks & Minerals. S&S.
Priolo, Anthony. see Priolo, Joan B.
Priolo, Joan. see Priolo, Joan B.
Priolo, Joan B.
  xPriolo, Anthony.
    jt. auth. Ceramics by Coil & Slab. Sterling.
  xPriolo, Joan.
    Ceramics by Coil & Slab. Sterling.
Prior, Arthur N.
  xPrior, Arthur N.
    The Doctrine of Propositions & Terms. U of Mass Pr.
    Logic & the Basis of Ethics. Oxford U Pr.
    Objects of Thought. Oxford U Pr.
    Papers in Logic & Ethics. U of Mass Pr.
    Papers on Time & Tense. Oxford U Pr.
    Time & Modality. Greenwood.
    Worlds, Times & Selves. U of Mass Pr.
Prior, Edward S. see Prior, Edward Schroder.
Prior, Edward Schroder, 1852-1932
  xPrior, Edward S.
    The Cathedral Builders in England. Longwood Pr.
    History of Gothic Art in England. Beekman Pubs.
    History of Gothic Art in England. Charles River Bks.
Prior, Matthew.
  xPrior, Matthew.
    The Literary Works of Matthew Prior. Oxford U Pr.
Prior, Moody E. see Prior, Moody Erasmus.
Prior, Moody Erasmus, 1901-
  xPrior, Moody E.
    The Drama of Power: Studies in Shakespeare's History Plays. Northwestern U Pr.
Prior, Peter J.
  xPrior, Peter J.
    Leadership Is Not a Bowler Hat. David & Charles.
Prishvin, Mikhail. see Prishvin, Mikhail Mikhailovich.
Prishvin, Mikhail Mikhailovich, 1873-1954
  xPrishvin, Mikhail.
    The Root of Life. Macmillan.
Prison Discipline Society. see Prison Discipline Society, Boston.
Prison Discipline Society, Boston.
  xPrison Discipline Society.
    Reports of the Prison Discipline Society, Boston: Reports 1-29, 1826-1854. Patterson Smith.
Pritchard, Alan.
  xPritchard, Alan.

A Guide to Computer Literature: An Introductory Survey of the Sources of Information. Shoe String.
Pritchard, Anthony.
  xPritchard, Anthony.
    Racing Sports Car. Norton.
Pritchard, Arnold, 1949-
  xPritchard, Arnold.
    Catholic Loyalism in Elizabethan England. U of NC Pr.
Pritchard, Colin.
  xPritchard, Colin.
    Social Work: Reform or Revolution?. Routledge & Kegan.
Pritchard, D. Brine.
  xPritchard, D. Brine.
    The Right Way to Play Chess. B&N.
    The Right Way to Play Chess. Emerson.
Pritchard, D. C. see Pritchard, David Christopher.
Pritchard, David Christopher, 1928-
  xPritchard, D. C.
    Lighting. Longman.
Pritchard, Earl H. see Pritchard, Earl Hampton.
Pritchard, Earl Hampton, 1907-
  xPritchard, Earl H.
    Anglo-Chinese Relations During the Seventeenth & Eighteenth Centuries. Octagon.
Pritchard, H. Baden. see Pritchard, Henry Baden.
Pritchard, Henry Baden, 1841-1884
  xPritchard, H. Baden.
    About Photography & Photographers. Arno.
Pritchard, J. A. see Pritchard, John A. T.
Pritchard, John A. T.
  xPritchard, J. A.
    Quantitative Methods in On-Line Systems. Hayden.
Pritchard, John P. see Pritchard, John Paul.
Pritchard, John Paul, 1902-
  xPritchard, John P.
    Criticism in America: An Account of the Development of Critical Techniques from the Early Period of the Republic to the Middle Years of the Twentieth Century. U of Okla Pr.
    A Literary Approach to the New Testament. U of Okla Pr.
    Literary Wise Men of Gotham: Criticism in New York, 1815-1860. Greenwood.
Pritchard, Miriam C. see Pritchard, Miriam Carol.
Pritchard, Miriam Carol, 1906-1950
  xPritchard, Miriam C.
    The Mechanical Ability of Subnormal Boys. AMS Pr.
Pritchard, N. H. see Pritchard, Norman H.
Pritchard, Norman H., 1939-
  xPritchard, N. H.
    Eecchhooeess. NYU Pr.
Pritchard, Peter.
  xPritchard, Peter.
    Manual of Primary Health Care: Its Nature & Organization. Oxford U Pr.
Pritchard, R.
  xPritchard, R.
    Handbook of Industrial Gas Utilization: Engineering Principles & Practices. Van Nos Reinhold.
Pritchard, Robert. see Pritchard, Robert E.
Pritchard, Robert E., 1941-
  xPritchard, Robert.
    Operational Financial Management. P-H.
Pritchard, Violet.
  xPritchard, Violet.
    English Medieval Graffiti. Cambridge U Pr.
Pritchard, William H.
  xPritchard, William H.
    Lives of the Modern Poets. Oxford U Pr.
Pritchett, C. H. see Pritchett, Charles Herman.
Pritchett, C. Herman. see Pritchett, Charles Herman.
Pritchett, C. W. see Pritchett, Craig.

Pritchett, Charles H. see Pritchett, Charles Herman.
Pritchett, Charles Herman, 1907-
  xPritchett, C. H.
    The American Constitutional System. McGraw.
  xPritchett, C. Herman.
    Civil Liberties & the Vinson Court. U of
      Chicago Pr.
  xPritchett, Charles H.
    The American Constitutional System. McGraw.
  xPritchett, G. Herman.
    The Federal System in Constitutional Law.
      P-H.
Pritchett, Craig.
  xPritchett, C. W.
    Sicilian Scheveningen. David & Charles.
Pritchett, Elaine. see Pritchett, Elaine H.
Pritchett, Elaine H.
  xPritchett, Elaine.
    Student Journalist & the Newsmagazine
      Format. Rosen Pr.
Pritchett, G. Herman. see Pritchett, Charles Herman.
Pritchett, Oliver.
  xPritchett, Oliver.
    A Prize Paradise. St Martin.
Pritchett, Reuel B.
  xPritchett, Reuel B.
    On the Ground Floor of Heaven. Brethren.
Pritchett, S. Travis.
  xPritchett, S. Travis.
    Individual Annuities As a Source of Retirement
      Income. LOMA.
Pritchett, V. S. see Pritchett, Victor Sawdon.
Pritchett, Victor S. see Pritchett, Victor Sawdon.
Pritchett, Victor Sawdon, 1900-
  xPritchett, V. S.
    Balzac. Knopf.
    Camberwell Beauty & Other Stories. Random.
    The Gentle Barbarian: The Life & Work of
      Turgenev. Random.
    On the Edge of the Cliff: Short Stories.
      Random.
    Selected Stories. Random.
    The Spanish Temper. Greenwood.
  xPritchett, Victor S.
    Books in General. Greenwood.
    In My Good Books. Kennikat.
    London Perceived. HarBraceJ.
Pritchett, W. Kendrick. see Pritchett, William Kendrick.
Pritchett, William Kendrick.
  xPritchett, W. Kendrick.
    The Choiseul Marble. U of Cal Pr.
    The Greek State at War. U of Cal Pr.
Pritchett, William L.
  xPritchett, William L.
    Properties & Management of Forest Soils.
      Wiley.
Pritikin, Nathan.
  xPritikin, Nathan.
    The Pritikin Program for Diet & Exercise.
      Bantam.
Pritikin, Roland I.
  xPritikin, Roland I.
    Essentials of Ophthalmology. Moore Pub Co.
Pritsker, A. Alan. see Pritsker, A. Alan B.
Pritsker, A. Alan B., 1933-
  xPritsker, A. Alan.
    The Gasp IV Simulation Language. Wiley.
    Introduction to Simulation & Slam. Halsted Pr.
    Modeling & Analysis Using Q-Gert Networks.
      Halsted Pr.
Pritzker, Wendy, 1941-
  xPritzker, Wendy.
    Natural Foods & Vitamins Handbook. Arc Bks.
Probabilistic Conference, the University of Victoria,
  August 1974. see Conference on Probabilistic Methods
  in Differential Equations, University of Victoria, 1974.
Probert, S. D.
  xProbert, S. D.

    ed. Thermal Insulation. Burgess-Intl Ideas.
Probert, Walter.
  xProbert, Walter.
    Law, Language & Communication. C C
      Thomas.
Proby, Kathryn H. see Proby, Kathryn Hall.
Proby, Kathryn Hall, 1921-
  xProby, Kathryn H.
    Audubon in Florida: With Selections from the
      Writings of John James Audubon. U of
      Miami Pr.
Probyn, Clive T.
  xProbyn, Clive T.
    ed. The Art of Jonathan Swift. B&N.
Probyn, Walter, 1931-
  xProbyn, Walter.
    Angel Face: The Making of a Criminal. Allen
      Unwin.
Proceedings of the Colloquium on Numerical Analysis,
  Lausanne, Oct. 11-13, 1976. see Colloquium on
  Numerical Analysis, Lausanne, Switzerland, 1976.
Proceedings of the Kew Chromosome Conference -
  Jodrell Laboratory, England. see Kew Chromosome
  Conference, Kew, England, 1976.
Prochaska, James O.
  xProchaska, James O.
    Systems of Psychotherapy: A Transtheoretical
      Analysis. Dorsey.
Prochnow, H. see Prochnow, Herbert Victor.
Prochnow, Herbert V. see Prochnow, Herbert Victor.
Prochnow, Herbert Victor, 1897-
  xProchnow, H.
    The Successful Speakers Handbook. P-H.
  xProchnow, Herbert V.
    American Financial Institutions. Arno.
    jt. auth. Dictionary of Wit, Wisdom, & Humor.
      Baker Bk.
    ed. Dilemmas Facing the Nation. Har-Row.
    Federal Reserve System. Har-Row
    Speaker's Book of Illustrations. Baker Bk.
    The Successful Speaker's Handbook. P-H.
    jt. auth. The Toastmaster's Treasure Chest.
      Har-Row.
Procter, Ben H.
  xProcter, Ben H.
    Not Without Honor: The Life of John H.
      Reagan. U of Tex Pr.
Procter, Bryan W. see Procter, Bryan Waller.
Procter, Bryan Waller, 1787-1874
  xProcter, Bryan W.
    Life of Edmund Kean. Arno.
Proctor, Charles W.
  xProctor, Charles W.
    Authorities & Rights of Interstate Truckers.
      Michie.
Proctor, Ellen A.
  xProctor, Ellen A.
    A Brief Memoir of Christina G. Rossetti.
      Folcroft.
Proctor, John.
  xProctor, John.
    Color in Plants & Flowers. Everest Hse.
Proctor, Marion.
  xProctor, Marion B.
    Figure Skating. Wm C Brown.
Proctor, Marion B. see Proctor, Marion.
Proctor, Michael. see Proctor, Michael C. F.
Proctor, Michael C. F.
  xProctor, Michael.
    The Pollination of Flowers. Taplinger.
Proctor, Nick H.
  xProctor, Nick H.
    Chemical Hazards of the Workplace.
      Lippincott.
Proctor, Richard M.
  xProctor, Richard M.
    Principles of Pattern for Craftsmen and
      Designers. Van Nos Reinhold.
Proctor, Samuel.
  xProctor, Samuel.

    ed. Eighteenth Century Florida & Its
      Borderlands. U Presses Fla.
    ed. Eighteenth Century Florida & the
      Revolutionary South. U Presses Fla.
Proctor, Sigmund K. see Proctor, Sigmund Kluss.
Proctor, Sigmund Kluss.
  xProctor, Sigmund K.
    Thomas De Quincey's Theory of Literature.
      Octagon.
Proctor, Thomas, fl. 1578
  xProctor, Thomas.
    Gorgeous Gallery of Gallant Inventions, 1578.
      Russell.
Proctor, William.
  xProctor, William.
    The Born-Again Christian Catalog: A Complete
      Sourcebook for Evangelicals. M Evans.
Proddow, Penelope.
  xProddow, Penelope.
    Art Tells a Story: Greek & Roman Myths.
      Doubleday.
Proefriedt, W. see Proefriedt, William A.
Proefriedt, William A.
  xProefriedt, W.
    The Teacher You Choose to Be. HR&W.
Proehl, Stephen.
  xProehl, Steven.
    Over Cape Cod & the Islands. HM.
Proehl, Steven. see Proehl, Stephen.
Proetz, Victor, 1897-1966
  xProetz, Victor.
    Astonishment of Words: An Experiment in the
      Comparison of Languages. U of Tex Pr.
Professional Golfer's Asso. see Professional Golfers'
  Association of America.
Professional Golfers' Association of America.
  xProfessional Golfer's Asso.
    Golf. British Bk Ctr.
Professional Staff of Hewlett-Woodmere Public Library.
  see Hewlett-Woodmere Public Library.
Proffer, Carl R.
  xProffer, Carl R.
    ed. Ardis Anthology of Recent Russian
      Literature. Random.
    ed. A Book of Things About Vladimir
      Nabokov. Ardis Pubs.
    ed. From Karamzin to Bunin: An Anthology of
      Russian Short Stories. Ind U Pr.
  xProffer, Ellendea.
    jt. ed. Ardis Anthology of Recent Russian
      Literature. Random.
Proffer, Ellendea. see Proffer, Carl R.
Profio, A. Edward, 1931-
  xProfio, A. Edward.
    Experimental Reactor Physics. Wiley.
    Radiation Shielding & Dosimetry. Wiley.
Proger, Samuel.
  xProger, Samuel.
    A Career in Primary Care. Ballinger Pub.
Progoff, Ira.
  xProgoff, Ira.
    At a Journal Workshop: The Basic Text &
      Guide for Using the Intensive Journal.
      Dialogue Hse.
    Image of an Oracle: A Report on Research into
      the Mediumship of Eileen J. Garrett.
      Garrett-Helix.
**Program on Hospital Finance, Accounting, and
Administration, 26th, Indiana University,1968.**
  xProgram On Hospital-Finance-Accounting And
    Administration - 26th.
    Financial Implications for Hospitals in
      Comprehensive Health Care Planning:
      Proceedings. Ind U Busn Res.
Program On Hospital-Finance-Accounting And
  Administration - 26th. see Program on Hospital
  Finance, Accounting, and Administration, 26th,
  Indiana University,1968.
Programa De Proyecto Frontera.
  xPrograma de Proyecto Frontera.

Ya Lo Leo. Barron.
**Programa Regional Del Empleo Para America Latina y
el Caribe.**
xRegional Employment Programme for Latin
America & the Caribbean.
Employment in Latin America. Praeger.
Programming Symposium, Paris, 1974.
xColloque Sur la Programmation, Paris, 9-11 April,
1974.
Programming Symposium: Proceedings.
Springer-Verlag.

The Progressive Grocer.

xProgressive Grocer Magazine Staff.

Grocery Retailing in the Eighties. Prog Grocer.

Progressive Grocer Magazine Staff. see The Progressive

Grocer.

Progressive Grocer's Marketing Guidebook.

xProgressive Grocer's Marketing Guidebook Staff.

Display & Merchandising Idea Book. Prog

Grocer.

New Idea Book. Prog Grocer.

Project Squid Workshop on Transonic Flows in

Turbomechanics, Naval Post Graduate School, 1976.

xProject SQUID Workshop on Transonic Flow

Problems in Turbomachinery, Feb. 1976.

Transonic Flow Problems in Turbomachinery:

Proceedings. Hemisphere Pub.

Project Squid Workshop on Turbulence in Internal

Flows: Turbomachinery and Other Applications,

Airlie House, 1976.

xProject Squid Workshop on Turbulence in
Internal Flows: Turbomachinery & Other

Applications, Airlie House, Warrenton, Va., June
14-15, 1976.

Turbulence in Internal Flows: Turbomachinery

& Other Engineering Applications,

Proceedings. Hemisphere Pub.

Prokes, J. see Prokes, Josef.
Prokes, Josef.
xProkes, J.
Hydraulic Mechanisms in Automation.
Elsevier.
Prokop, Dave.
xProkop, Dave.
ed. The Dart Book. Anderson World.
Prokop, Jan, 1934-
xProkop, Jan.
ed. Computers in the Navy. Naval Inst Pr.
Prokop, Phyllis S. see Prokop, Phyllis Stillwell.
Prokop, Phyllis Stillwell.
xProkop, Phyllis S.
How to Wake up Singing. Broadman.
Prokosch, Frederi.
xProkosch, Frederic.
A Ballad of Love. Greenwood.
Prokosch, Frederic, 1908-
xProkosch, Frederic.

America, My Wilderness. FS&G.
The Idols of the Cave. Greenwood.
Night of the Poor. Greenwood.
Prokosch, Frederic. see Prokosch, Frederi.
Prolla, J. B. see Prolla, Joao B.
Prolla, Joao B.
xProlla, J. B.
Approximation of Vector Valued Functions.
Elsevier.
Prolman, Marilyn.
xProlman, Marilyn.
Story of the Capitol. Childrens.
Story of the Constitution. Childrens.
Promersberger, W. J. see Promersberger, William J.
Promersberger, William J.
xPromersberger, W. J.
Modern Farm Power. Reston.
xPromersberger, William J.
Modern Farm Power. P-H.
Pronikov, A. S. see Pronikov, Aleksandr Sergeevich.
Pronikov, Aleksandr Sergeevich.
xPronikov, A. S.
Dependability & Durability Engineering
Products. Butterworths.
Pronko, Leonard C. see Pronko, Leonard Cabell.
Pronko, Leonard Cabell.
xPronko, Leonard C.
Avant Garde: The Experimental Theater in
France. Greenwood.
Eugene Ionesco. Columbia U Pr.
Georges Feydeau. Ungar.
Guide to Japanese Drama. G K Hall.
Theater East & West: Perspectives Toward a
Total Theater. U of Cal Pr.
Pronzini, Bill.
xPronzini, Bill.
ed. Bug-Eyed Monsters. HarBraceJ.
Games. Fawcett.
Labyrinth. St Martin.
Panic. PB.
Undercurrent. PB.
The Vanished. PB.
Werewolf!. Arbor Hse.
Proper, Churchill. see Proper, Churchill H.
Proper, Churchill H.
xProper, Churchill.
Indian Crafts. SamHar Pr.
Propes, Stephen. see Propes, Steve.
Propes, Steve.
xPropes, Stephen.
Those Oldies but Goodies: A Guide to 50's
Record Collecting. Macmillan.
xPropes, Steve.
Golden Goodies: A Guide to 50's & 60's
Popular Rock & Roll Record Collecting.
Chilton.
Prophet, Elizabeth C. see Prophet, Elizabeth Clare.
Prophet, Elizabeth Clare.
xProphet, Elizabeth C.
The Great White Brotherhood in the Culture,
History and Religion of America. Summit
Univ.
Proprietary Association.
xProprietary Association.
Responsible Self-Medication. Proprietary Assn.
Propst, Louise, 1907-
xPropst, Louise.
An Analytical Study of Shelley's Versification.
Arden Lib.
Analytical Study of Shelley's Versification.
Folcroft.
Prose, Francine, 1947-
xProse, Francine.
Animal Magnetism. Berkley Pub.
Animal Magnetism. Putnam.
Marie Laveau. Berkley Pub.
Proske, B. G. see Proske, Beatrice Irene (Gilman).
Proske, Beatrice G. see Proske, Beatrice Irene (Gilman).
Proske, Beatrice Irene (Gilman), 1899-
xProske, B. G.

Pompeo Leoni: Work in Marble & Alabaster in
Relation to Spanish Sculpture. Hispanic Soc.
xProske, Beatrice G.
Archer Milton Huntington. Hispanic Soc.
Proskine, Alec.
xProskine, Alec.
No Two Rivers Alike: Fifty Canoeable Rivers
of New York & Pennsylvania. Crossing Pr.
Prosper, Peter A.
xProsper, Peter A.
Concentration & the Rate of Change of Wages
in the United States, 1950-1962. Arno.
xWorld Bank.
ed. Yugoslavia: Self-Management Socialism &
the Challenges of Development. Johns
Hopkins.
Prossdorf. see Prossdorf, Siegfried.
Prossdorf, Siegfried.
xProssdorf.
Some Classes of Singular Equations. Elsevier.
Prosser, C. Ladd. see Prosser, Clifford Ladd.
Prosser, Clifford Ladd, 1907-
xProsser, C. Ladd.
Comparative Animal Physiology. HR&W.
Prosser, Eleanor.
xProsser, Eleanor.
Drama & Religion in the English Mystery
Plays: A Re-Evaluation. Stanford U Pr.
Hamlet & Revenge. Stanford U Pr.
Prosser, Hilary.
xProsser, Hilary.
Perspectives on Foster Care. Humanities.
Prosser, Michael H., 1936-
xProsser, Michael H.
The Cultural Dialogue: An Introduction to
Intercultural Communication. HM.
Prosser, Robert.
xProsser, Robert.
Geology Explained in the Lake District. David
& Charles.
Prostano, Emanuel T.
xProstano, Emanuel T.
Audiovisual Media & Libraries: Selected
Readings. Libs Unl.
Law Enforcement: A Selective Bibliography.
Libs Unl.
Protein Advisory Group of the United Nations Systems.
xProtein Advisory Group of the United Nations
System.
Nutritional Improvement of Food Legumes by
Breeding. Wiley.
Protein-Calorie Advisory Group. see Protein-Calorie
Advisory Group of the United Nations Systems.
**Protein-Calorie Advisory Group of the United Nations
Systems.**
xProtein-Calorie Advisory Group.
The P A G Compendium. Halsted Pr.
Protell, Martin R.
xProtell, Martin R.
Psychodynamics in Dental Practice. C C
Thomas.
Prothero, R. Mansell.
xProthero, R. Mansell.
ed. Geography of Africa: Regional Essays on
Fundamental Characteristics, Issues &
Problems. Routledge & Kegan.
ed. People & Land in Africa South of the
Sahara: Readings in Social Geography.
Oxford U Pr.
Protheroe, W. see Protheroe, W. M.
Protheroe, W. M.
xProtheroe, W.
Exploring the Universe. Merrill.
Prothro, Edwin T. see Prothro, Edwin Terry.
Prothro, Edwin Terry.
xProthro, Edwin T.

Changing Family Patterns in the Arab East.
Syracuse U Pr.
Child Rearing in the Lebanon. Harvard U Pr.
Psychology: A Biosocial Study of Behavior.
Greenwood.
Prothro, James W. see Prothro, James Warren.
Prothro, James Warren, 1922-
xProthro, James W.
Dollar Decade: Business Ideas in the 1920's.
Greenwood.
Prothro, Vivian C.
xProthro, Vivian C.
Information Management Systems: A Data
Base Primer. Van Nos Reinhold.
Protter, M. H. see Protter, Murray H.
Protter, Murray H.
xProtter, M. H.
A First Course in Real Analysis.
Springer-Verlag.
xProtter, Murray H.
Analytic Geometry. A-W.
Calculus for College Students. A-W.
Calculus with Analytic Geometry: A First
Course. A-W.
College Calculus with Analytic Geometry.
A-W.
Proud, Franklin.
xProud, Franklin.
Where the Wind Is Wild. PB.
Proud, Franklin. see Proud, Franklin M.
Proud, Franklin M., 1920-
xProud, Franklin.
The Walking Wind. St Martin.
xProud, Franklin M.
The Golden Triangle. St Martin.
Proudfoot, L.
xProudfoot, L.
Dryden's Aeneid & Its Seventeenth Century
Predecessors. Folcroft.
Proudfoot, Malcolm J. see Proudfoot, Malcolm Jarvis.
Proudfoot, Malcolm Jarvis.
xProudfoot, Malcolm J.
Population Movements in the Caribbean.
Negro U Pr.
Proudfoot, Mary M. see Proudfoot, Mary Macdonald.
Proudfoot, Mary Macdonald.
xProudfoot, Mary M.
Britain & the United States in the Caribbean: A
Comparative Study in Methods of
Development. Greenwood.
Proudfoot, Merrill.
xProudfoot, Merrill.
Diary of a Sit-In. Coll & U Pr.
Proudfoot, Wayne, 1939-
xProudfoot, Wayne.
God & the Self: Three Types of Philosophy of
Religion. Bucknell U Pr.
Proudhon, P. J. see Proudhon, Pierre Joseph.
Proudhon, P-J. see Proudhon, Pierre Joseph.
Proudhon, Pierre Joseph, 1809-1865
xProudhon, P. J.
General Idea of the Revolution in the
Nineteenth Century. Gordon Pr.
xProudhon, P-J.
The Principle of Federation. U of Toronto Pr.
Proulx, Donald A., 1939-
xProulx, Donald A.
Local Differences & Time Differences in Nasca
Pottery. U of Cal Pr.
Prouse, Howard L.
xProuse, Howard L.
Principles of Mathematics. Scott F.
Proust, Marcel, 1871-1922
xProust, Marcel.

Captive. Random.
Cities of the Plain. Random.
Past Recaptured. Random.
Past Recaptured. Random.
Remembrance of Things Past. Random.
Sweet Cheat Gone. Random.
Prout, Ebenezer, 1835-1909
xProut, Ebenezer.
Applied Forms: A Sequel to Musical Form.
AMS Pr.
Applied Forms: A Sequel to Musical Form.
Scholarly.
Double Counterpoint & Canon. Greenwood.
Double Counterpoint & Canon. Haskell.
Fugue. Greenwood.
Fugue. Haskell.
Fugue. Scholarly.
Instrumentation. Haskell.
Instrumentation. Scholarly.
Musical Form. AMS Pr.
Musical Form. Scholarly.
The Orchestra. Scholarly.
Prout, Henry G. see Prout, Henry Goslee.
Prout, Henry Goslee.
xProut, Henry G.
A Life of George Westinghouse. Arno.
Prouty, Olive H. see Prouty, Olive Higgins.
Prouty, Olive Higgins.
xProuty, Olive H.
Conflict. Popular Lib.
Provence, Sally. see Provence, Sally A.
Provence, Sally A.
xProvence, Sally.
The Challenge of Daycare. Yale U Pr.
Guide for the Care of Infants in Groups. Child
Welfare.
Provensen, Alice.
xProvensen, Alice.
Our Animal Friends at Maple Hill Farm.
Random.
Provensen Book of Fairy Tales. Random.
Provenzo, E. see Provenzo, Eugene F.
Provenzo, Eugene F.
xProvenzo, E.
Historian's Toybox: Children's Toys from the
Past You Can Make Yourself. P-H.
Provincial Archives of British Columbia, Victoria. see
British Columbia. Provincial Archives.
Provincial Congress of Massachusetts Colony, 1775. see
Massachusetts (Colony). Provincial Congress,
Feb.-May, 1775.
Provine, William. see Provine, William B.
Provine, William B.
xProvine, William.
Origins of Theoretical Population Genetics. U
of Chicago Pr.
Provizer, Norman W.
xProvizer, Norman W.
ed. Analyzing the Third World: Essays from
"Comparative Politics". Schenkman.
Provus, Malcolm. see Provus, Malcolm M.
Provus, Malcolm D. see Provus, Malcolm M.
Provus, Malcolm M., 1928-1975
xProvus, Malcolm.
Teaching for Relevance. Whitchall Co.
xProvus, Malcolm D.
The Grand Experiment: The Life and Death of
the TTT Program As Seen Through the Eyes
of Its Evaluators. McCutchan.
Proxmire, William.
xProxmire, William.
Can Small Business Survive?. Arno.
The Fleecing of America. HM.
Prpic, G. J. see Prpic, George J.
Prpic, George J.
xPrpic, G. J.
A Century of World Communism: Selective
Chronological Outline. Barron.
xPrpic, George J.

Croatian Immigrants in America. Philos Lib.
The Croatian Immigrants in America. R & E
Res Assoc.
The Croatian Immigrants in America. Ragusan
Pr.
South Slavic Immigration in America. Twayne.
Prucha, F. P. see Prucha, Francis Paul.
Prucha, Francis P. see Prucha, Francis Paul.
Prucha, Francis Paul.
xPrucha, F. P.
Broadax & Bayonet: The Role of the United
States Army in the Development of the
Northwest, 1815-1860. Peter Smith.
Indian in American History. HR&W.
xPrucha, Francis P.
American Indian Policy in Crisis: Christian
Reformers & the Indian,1865-1900. U of
Okla Pr.
ed. Americanizing the American Indians:
Writings by the Friends of the Indian,
1880-1900. Harvard U Pr.
ed. Americanizing the American Indians:
Writings by the "Friends of the Indian,"
1880-1900. U of Nebr Pr.
Broadax & Bayonet: The Role of the United
States Army in the Development of the
Northwest, Seventeen Ninety to Eighteen
Thirty-Four. U of Nebr Pr.
ed. Documents of United States Indian Policy.
U of Nebr Pr.
Indian Peace Medals in American History. U
of Nebr Pr.
xPrucha, Francis Paul.
A Guide to the Military Posts of the United
States 1789-1895. State Hist Soc Wis.
Prudden. see Prudden, Suzy.
Prudden, Bonnie, 1911-
xPrudden, Bonnie.
How to Keep Your Child Fit from Birth to Six.
Har-Row.
Prudden, Suzy.
xPrudden.
Suzy Prudden's Family Fitness Book. S&S.
xPrudden, Suzy.
See How They Run: Suzy Prudden's Running
Book for Kids. G&D.
Suzy Prudden's Family Fitness Book. G&D.
Suzy Prudden's Spot Reducing Program.
Workman Pub.
Prudden, T. M. see Prudden, Theodore Mitchell.
Prudden, Theodore Mitchell.
xPrudden, T. M.
About Lobsters. Wheelwright.
Pruden, Donald, 1934-
xPruden, Donald.
Around Town Cycling. Anderson World.
**Prudential Insurance Company of America, Newark,
New Jersey.**
xPrudential Insurance Company of America.
Health Insurance Fundamentals. Wiley.
Life Insurance Fundamentals. Wiley.
New York State Insurance Law. Wiley.
Prudhommeaux, Jules see Prudhommeaux, Jules Jean.
Prudhommeaux, Jules Jean, 1869-
xPrudhommeaux, Jules.
Icarie et Son Fondateur, Etienne Cabet:
Contribution a L'etude Du Socialisme
Experimental. Porcupine Pr.
Pruett, James W.
xPruett, James W.
Compiled by Studies in Musicology: Essays in
History, Style and Bibliography of Music in
Memory of Glenn Haydon. Greenwood.
Prufer, Olaf H.
xPrufer, Olaf H.
ed. Studies in Ohio Archaeology. Kent St U Pr.
Prugovecki, Eduard.
xPrugovecki, Eduard.

Quantum Mechanics in Hilbert Space. Acad Pr.

Pruitt, Dean G.
xPruitt, Dean G.
Problem Solving in the Department of State. U of Denver Intl.

Pruitt, Ida.
xPruitt, Ida.
A China Childhood. Chinese Materials.
Old Madam Yin: A Memoir of Peking Life. Stanford U Pr.

Pruitt, Joann.
xPruitt, JoAnn.
Looking for Tomorrow. Broadman.

Prusek, J. see Prusek, Jaroslav.

Prusek, Jaroslav.
xPrusek, J.
Chinese Statelets & the Northern Barbarians in the Period 1400-300 B. C.. Kluwer Boston.
xPrusek, Jaroslav.
ed. Dictionary of Oriental Literatures. Basic.

Prussia. Armee.
xPrussia Kriegsministerium.
Regulations for the Prussian Infantry: To Which Is Added the Prussian Tactick. Greenwood.

Prussia. Armee. Kavallerie.
xPrussia Kriegsministerium.
Regulations for the Prussian Cavalry. Greenwood.

Prussia Kriegsministerium. see Prussia. Armee. Kavallerie.

Prussin, Labelle.
xPrussin, Labelle.
Architecture in Northern Ghana: A Study of Forms & Functions. U of Cal Pr.

Pruter, A. T.
xPruter, A. T.
The Columbia River Estuary & Adjacent Ocean Waters: Bioenvironmental Studies. U of Wash Pr.

Prutton, M.
xPrutton, M.
Surface Physics. Oxford U Pr.

Prybyla, Jan S.
xPrybyla, Jan S.
The Chinese Economy: Problems & Policies. U of SC Pr.
ed. Comparative Economic Systems. Irvington.

Pryce, Dick.
xPryce, Dick.
Hunting for Beginners: An Introduction to Hunting Guns & Gun Safety. Follett.

Pryce, Roy.
xPryce, Roy.
Politics of the European Community. Rowman.

Pryce-Jones, David, 1936-
xPryce-Jones, David.
ed. Evelyn Waugh & His World. Little.
Vienna. Time-Life.

Pryke, Richard.
xPryke, Richard.
The British Rail Problem: A Case Study in Economic Disaster. Westview.
Public Enterprise in Practice. St Martin.

Pryluck, Calvin.
xPryluck, Calvin.
Sources of Meaning in Motion Pictures & Television. Arno.

Prynne, William, 1600-1669
xPrynne, William.
Histrio-Mastix: The Player's Scourge, or Actors Tragedy. Johnson Repr.

Pryor, Dennis.
xPryor, Dennis.
Focus on Milton Moon. U of Queensland Pr.

Pryor, Frederic. see Pryor, Frederic L.

Pryor, Frederic L.
xPryor, Frederic.
Public Expenditures in Communist & Capitalist Nations. Yale U Pr.

Pryor, Helen (Brenton), 1897-
xPryor, Helen B.
Lou Henry Hoover, Gallant First Lady. Dodd.

Pryor, Helen B. see Pryor, Helen (Brenton).

Pryor, Hugh C. see Pryor, Hugh Clark.

Pryor, Hugh Clark, 1881-
xPryor, Hugh C.
Graded Units in Student-Teaching. AMS Pr.

Pryor, Robin. see Pryor, Robin J.

Pryor, Robin J.
xPryor, Robin.
ed. Migration & Development in South-East Asia: A Demographic Perspective. Oxford U Pr.

Pryor, Roger A. see Pryor, Sara Agnes (Rice).

Pryor, Sara Agnes (Rice), 1830-1912
xPryor, Roger A.
Reminiscences of Peace & War. Arno.

Pryor, William A.
xPryor, William A.
ed. Free Radicals in Biology. Acad Pr.

Pryse, Marjorie, 1948-
xPryse, Marjorie.
The Mark & the Knowledge: Social Stigma in Classic American Fiction. Ohio St U Pr.

Pryse-Phillips, William.
xPryse-Phillips, William.
Essential Neurology. Med Exam.

Przemieniecki, J S.
xPrzemieniecki, J. S.
Theory of Matrix Structural Analysis. McGraw.

Przetak, Louis.
xPrzetak, Louis.
Standard Details for Fire-Resistive Building Construction. McGraw.

Przhevalskii, Nikolai M. see Przhevalskii, Nikolai Mikhailovich.

Przhevalskii, Nikolai Mikhailovich, 1839-1888
xPrzhevalskii, Nikolai M.
From Kulja, Across the Tian Shan to Lob-Nor. Greenwood.

Psacharopoulos, George.
xPsacharopoulos, George.
Returns to Education: An International Comparison. Elsevier.

Psathas, George.
xPsathas, George.
ed. Everyday Language: Studies in Ethno-Methodology. Halsted Pr.

Pshenichnyi, B. N. see Pshenichnyi, Boris Nikolaevich.

Pshenichnyi, Boris Nikolaevich.
xPshenichnyi, B. N.
Necessary Conditions for an Extremum. Dekker.

Pszczola, Lorraine.
xPszczola, Lorraine.
Archery. HR&W.

Public Archives of Canada. see Canada. Public Archives.

Public Archives of Canada (Ottawa). see Canada. Public Archives.

Public Library Association. Audio Visual Committee.
xPLA Audiovisual Committee.
Guidelines for Audiovisual Materials & Services for Large Public Libraries. ALA.
Recommendations for Audiovisual Materials & Services for Small & Medium- Sized Public Libraries. ALA.

Public Record Office Of Great Britain. see Great Britain. Public Record Office.

Public Service Materials Center.
xPublic Service Materials Center.
ed. Foundations That Send Their Annual Report. Public Serv Materials.
ed. The Survey of Grant Making Foundations: 1980-81 Edition. Public Serv Materials.

Publisher's Editorial Staff. see Indiana. Laws, Statues, Etc.

Pucci, Cora.
xPucci, Cora.
Pottery: A Basic Manual. Little.

Pucci, Pietro.
xPucci, Pietro.
The Violence of Pity in Euripides' Medea. Cornell U Pr.

Puckett, John R., 1931-
xPuckett, John R.
Guide to an Effective Physical Education Program. P-H.

Puckett, N. Niles. see Puckett, Newbell Niles.

Puckett, Newbell N. see Puckett, Newbell Niles.

Puckett, Newbell Niles.
xPuckett, N. Niles.
Folk Beliefs of the Southern Negro. Greenwood.
xPuckett, Newbell N.
Folk Beliefs of the Southern Negro. Patterson Smith.

Puckett, Richard H.
xPuckett, Richard H.
Introduction to Mathematical Economics: Matrix Algebra & Linear Economic Models. Heath.

Puckette, Clara C. see Puckette, Clara Childs.

Puckette, Clara Childs.
xPuckette, Clara C.
Edisto, A Sea Island Principality. Seaforth Pubns.

Puddephatt, R. J.
xPuddephatt, R. J.
The Chemistry of Gold. Elsevier.
The Periodic Table of the Elements. Oxford U Pr.

Pudney, John, 1909-
xPudney, John.
Brunel & His World. Transatlantic.
ed. Flight & Flying. D White.
John Wesley & His World. Scribner.
Lewis Carroll & His World. Scribner.

Puerto Rican Forum.
xPuerto Rican Forum.
The Puerto Rican Community Development Project. Arno.

Puerto Rico. University. Department of Spanish.
xDepartamento De Espanol, Facultad De Estudios Generales, UPR.
Manual De Nociones y Ejercicios Gramaticales: Unidad De Composicion y Otras Destrezas Linguisticas. U of PR Pr.

Pugel, Thomas A.
xPugel, Thomas A.
International Market Linkages & U.S. Manufacturing: Prices, Profits, & Patterns. Ballinger Pub.

Puget, Rene.
xPuget, Rene.
Long Haul. S&S.

Puget Sound Mycological Society.
xPuget Sound Mycological Society.
Wild Mushroom Recipes. Pacific Search.

Pugh, Anthony.
xPugh, Anthony.
Polyhedra: A Visual Approach. U of Cal Pr.

Pugh, Anthony R.
xPugh, Anthony R.
Balzac's Recurring Characters. U of Toronto Pr.

Pugh, Derek S. see Pugh, Derek Salman.

Pugh, Derek Salman.
xPugh, Derek S.
Organizational Structure Extensions & Replications: The Aston Program II. Lexington Bks.

Pugh, Edwin. see Pugh, Edwin William.

Pugh, Edwin W. see Pugh, Edwin William.

Pugh, Edwin William, 1874-1930
xPugh, Edwin.

Charles Dickens: Apostle of the People.
Haskell.
xPugh, Edwin W.
The Charles Dickens Originals. AMS Pr.
Charles Dickens: The Apostle of the People.
AMS Pr.
Pugh, Ellen.
xPugh, Ellen.
The Adventures of Yoo-Lah-Teen: A Legend
of the Salish Coastal Indians. Dial.
More Tales from the Welsh Hills. Dodd.
Tales from the Welsh Hills. Dodd.
Pugh, Eric.
xPugh, Eric.
Third Dictionary of Acronyms &
Abbreviations: More Abbreviations in
Management, Technology, & Information
Science. Shoe String.
Pugh, H. L. see Pugh, H. Ll. D.
Pugh, H. Ll. D.
xPugh, H. L.
ed. Mechanical Behaviour of Materials Under
Pressure. Intl Ideas.
Pugh, J. C. see Pugh, John Charles.
Pugh, John Charles.
xPugh, J. C.
Surveying for Field Scientists. U of Pittsburgh
Pr.
Pugh, Ralph B. see Pugh, Ralph Bernard.
Pugh, Ralph Bernard, 1910-
xPugh, Ralph B.
Imprisonment in Medieval England. Cambridge
U Pr.
Pugmire, Donald R. see Pugmire, Donald Ross.
Pugmire, Donald Ross, 1902-
xPugmire, Donald R.
The Administration of Personnel in
Correctional Institutions in New York State.
AMS Pr.
Pugmire, M. C. see Pugmire, Mary Carolyn Weller.
Pugmire, Mary Carolyn Weller,
xPugmire, M. C.
Experiences in Music for Young Children.
Delmar.
Puharich, Andrija.
xPuharich, Andrija.
Time No Longer. Stein & Day.
Puhn, Fred.
xPuhn, Fred.
How to Make Your Car Handle. H P Bks.
Puiboube, Daniel.
xPuiboube, Daniel.
The Art of Making Miniature Models. Arco.
Puig, Manuel.
xPuig, Manuel.
Kiss of the Spider Woman. Knopf.
Kiss of the Spider Woman. Random.
Pula, James S., 1946-
xPula, James S.
The French in America, 1488-1974: A
Chronology & Fact Book. Oceana.
The History of a German-Polish Civil War
Brigade. R & E Res Assoc.
Pulaski, Mary A. see Pulaski, Mary Ann Spencer.
Pulaski, Mary Ann Spencer.
xPulaski, Mary A.
Step by Step Guide to Correct English. Arco.
Understanding Piaget: An Introduction to
Children's Cognitive Development. Har-Row.
Puleo, Nicole.
xPuleo, Nicole.
Drag Racing. Lerner Pubns.
Pulgar, Fernando Del.
xPulgar, Fernando Del.
Claros Varones De Castilla. Oxford U Pr.
Puligandla, R., 1930-
xPuligandla, R.
Fundamentals of Indian Philosophy. Abingdon.
Pulkingham, Betty.
xPulkingham, Betty.

Little Things in the Hands of a Big God. Word
Bks.
Pullen, Keats A., 1916-
xPullen, Keats A.
Design of Transistor Circuits, with
Experiments. Sams.
Pulliam, H. Ronald.
xPulliam, H. Ronald.
Programmed to Learn: An Essay on the
Evolution of Culture. Columbia U Pr.
Pulliam, John D.
xPulliam, John D.
History of Education in America. Merrill.
Pullias, Earl V. see Pullias, Earl Vivon.
Pullias, Earl Vivon.
xPullias, Earl V.
Teacher Is Many Things. Ind U Pr.
Pullman, Bernard, 1919-
xPullman, Bernard.
ed. Quantum Mechanics of Molecular
Conformations. Wiley.
Pullum, Geoffrey K.
xPullum, Geoffrey K.
Rule Interaction & the Organization of a
Grammar. Garland Pub.
Pullum, Thomas W.
xPullum, Thomas W.
Measuring Occupational Inheritance. Elsevier.
Pulman, Jack.
xPulman, Jack.
Collision. Atheneum.
Puls, Herta.
xPuls, Herta.
Art of Cutwork & Applique: Historic, Modern
& Kuna Indian. Branford.
Pulszky, Agost, 1846-1901
xPulszky, Agost.
The Theory of Law & Civil Society. Hyperion
Conn.
Pulszky, Ferencz A. see Pulszky, Ferencz Aurelius.
Pulszky, Ferencz Aurelius.
xPulszky, Ferencz A.
White, Red, Black. Johnson Repr.
Pultick and Simpson, Firm, Auctioneers, London.
xPuttick and Simpson.
Bibliotheca Mejicana. B Franklin.
Pulvertaft, R. G. see Pulvertaft, R. Guy.
Pulvertaft, R. Guy.
xPulvertaft, R. G.
Hand. Butterworths.
Pulvino, Charles J.
xPulvino, Charles J.
Financial Counseling: Interviewing Skills.
Kendall-Hunt.
Pumerantz, P. see Pumerantz, Philip.
Pumerantz, Philip.
xPumerantz, P.
Establishing Interdisciplinary Programs in the
Middle School. P-H.
Pumper, Robert W. see Pumper, Robert William.
Pumper, Robert William.
xPumper, Robert W.
Essentials of Medical Virology. Saunders.
Pumpian-Mindlin, Eugene.
xPumpian-Mindlin, Eugene.
ed. Psychoanalysis As Science: The Hixon
Lectures on the Scientific Status of
Psychoanalysis. Greenwood.
Pumroy, Donald K. see Pumroy, Donald Keith.
Pumroy, Donald Keith.
xPumroy, Donald K.
Modern Childrearing: A Behavioral Approach.
Nelson-Hall.
Pun, Lucas.
xPun, Lucas.
Introduction to Optimization Practice. Wiley.
Punch (London).
xPunch Magazine.
Century of Punch Cartoons. S&S.
Punch Magazine. see Punch (London).

Punch, Maurice.
xPunch, Maurice.
Policing the Inner City: A Study of
Amsterdam's Warmoesstraat. Shoe String.
Pundt, Alfred G. see Pundt, Alfred George.
Pundt, Alfred George, 1904-
xPundt, Alfred G.
Arndt & the Nationalist Awakening in
Germany. AMS Pr.
Puner, Morton.
xPuner, Morton.
Vital Maturity: Living Longer & Better.
Universe.
Pungor, E. see Pungor, Erno.
Pungor, Erno.
xPungor, E.
Flame Photometry Theory. Van Nos Reinhold.
Punke, Harold H. see Punke, Harold Herman.
Punke, Harold Herman, 1900-
xPunke, Harold H.
Education, Lawlessness & Political Corruption
in America. Chris Mass.
The Teacher & the Courts. Interstate.
Punnett, R. M. see Punnett, Robert Malcolm.
Punnett, Robert Malcolm.
xPunnett, R. M.
British Government & Politics. Norton.
Puopolo, Vito.
xPuopolo, Vito.
Music Fundamentals. Schirmer Bks.
Puotinen, Arthur E. see Puotinen, Arthur Edwin.
Puotinen, Arthur Edwin.
xPuotinen, Arthur E.
Finnish Radicals & Religion in Midwestern
Mining Towns: 1865-1914. Arno.
Pupin, Michael. see Pupin, Michael Idvorsky.
Pupin, Michael Idvorsky, 1858-1935
xPupin, Michael.
From Immigrant to Inventor. Arno.
Puppi, G.
xPuppi, G.
ed. Old & New Problems in Elementary
Particles. Acad Pr.
Puppi, Lionello.
xPuppi, Lionello.
Andrea Palladio. NYGS.
Purcell, Edmund S. see Purcell, Edmund Sheridan.
Purcell, Edmund Sheridan, 1824?-1899
xPurcell, Edmund S.
Life of Cardinal Manning, Archbishop of
Westminster. R West.
Purcell, Edward A.
xPurcell, Edward A.
The Crisis of Democratic Theory: Scientific
Naturalism & the Problem of Value. U Pr of
Ky.
Purcell, Edwin J. see Purcell, Edwin Joseph.
Purcell, Edwin Joseph, 1901-
xPurcell, Edwin J.
Analytic Geometry. Irvington.
Calculus with Analytic Geometry. P-H.
Purcell, Elizabeth.
xPurcell, Elizabeth.
ed. World Trends in Medical Education:
Faculty, Students, & Curriculum. Johns
Hopkins.
Purcell, Hugh.
xPurcell, Hugh.
Mao Tse-Tung. St Martin.
Purcell, John.
xPurcell, John.
ed. The Control of Work. Holmes & Meier.
Purcell, William P.
xPurcell, William P.
Strategy of Drug Design: A Guide to Biological
Activity. Wiley.
Purdom, P. Walton, 1917-
xPurdom, P. Walton.

ed. Environmental Health. Acad Pr.
Purdy, James.
 xPurdy, James.
  Children Is All. New Directions.
  In a Shallow Grave. Arbor Hse.
Purdy, Robert L., 1921-
 xPurdy, Robert L.
  Successful High School Athletic Program. P-H.
Purdy, Strother B., 1932-
 xPurdy, Strother B.
  The Hole in the Fabric: Science, Contemporary
  Literature, & Henry James. U of Pittsburgh
  Pr.
Purdy, Susan.
 xPurdy, Susan.
  illus. Christmas Decorations for You to Make.
  Lippincott.
Purdy, Susan. *see* Purdy, Susan Gold.
Purdy, Susan G. *see* Purdy, Susan Gold.
Purdy, Susan Gold, 1939-
 xPurdy, Susan.
  Holiday Cards for You to Make. Lippincott.
 xPurdy, Susan G.
  Jewish Holiday Cookbook. Watts.
Purefoy, George W., 1809-1880
 xPurefoy, George W.
  History of the Sandy Creek Baptist
  Association, from Its Organization in A. D.
  1758 to 1858. Arno.
Puri, Baij N. *see* Puri, Baij Nath.
Puri, Baij Nath.
 xPuri, Baij N.
  India Under the Kushanas. Paragon.
Puri, M. L. *see* Puri, Madan Lal.
Puri, Madan Lal.
 xPuri, M. L.
  Nonparametric Methods in Multivariate
  Analysis. Wiley.
Puri, Subhash C.
 xPuri, Subhash C.
  Statistical Quality Control for Food &
  Agricultural Scientists. G K Hall.
Purington, Robert C. *see* Purington, Robert G.
Purington, Robert G.
 xPurington, Robert C.
  Fire Fighting Hydraulics. McGraw.
Purkis, John. *see* Purkis, John Arthur.
Purkis, John A. *see* Purkis, John Arthur.
Purkis, John Arthur, 1933-
 xPurkis, John.
  A Preface to Wordsworth. Longman.
 xPurkis, John A.
  The Icelandic Jaunt: A Study of the
  Expeditions Made by Morris to Iceland in
  1871 & 1873. Folcroft.
Purkiser, W. T.
 xPurkiser, W. T.
  When You Get to the End of Yourself. Baker
  Bk.
Purpel, David. *see* Purpel, David E.
Purpel, David E.
 xPurpel, David.
  ed. Moral Education...It Comes with the
  Territory. Phi Delta Kappa.
Pursell, Margaret S. *see* Pursell, Margaret Sanford.
Pursell, Margaret Sanford.
 xPursell, Margaret S.
  Boots the Kitten. Carolrhoda Bks.
  Marigold the Goldfish. Carolrhoda Bks.
  Polly the Guinea Pig. Carolrhoda Bks.
Pursell, Thomas. *see* Pursell, Thomas F.
Pursell, Thomas F.
 xPursell, Thomas.
  Bicycles on Parade. Lerner Pubns.
 xPursell, Thomas F.
  The Burning Barn Mystery. Carolrhoda Bks.
  The Prize Tomatoes Mystery. Carolrhoda Bks.
Pursey, Helen L.
 xPursey, Helen L.

Wild Flowers. Transatlantic.
Pursh, Frederick.
 xPursh, Frederick.
  Journal of a Botanical Excursion in the
  Northeastern Parts of the States of
  Pennsylvania & New York During the Year
  1807. Friedman.
Pursley, Robert. *see* Pursley, Robert D.
Pursley, Robert D.
 xPursley, Robert.
  Introduction to Criminal Justice. Glencoe.
Purtill, Richard. *see* Purtill, Richard L.
Purtill, Richard L., 1931-
 xPurtill, Richard.
  Thinking About Ethics. P-H.
  Thinking About Religion: A Philosophical
  Introduction to Religion. P-H.
 xPurtill, Richard L.
  Logical Thinking. Har-Row.
Purtilo, David T.
 xPurtilo, David T.
  A Survey of Human Diseases. A-W.
Purves, Alan C.
 xPurves, Alan C.
  ed. Educational Policy & International
  Assessment: Implications of the IEA Surveys
  of Achievement. McCutchan.
Purves, Lloyd, 1912-
 xPurves, Lloyd.
  Lloyd Purves on Closing Sales. P-H.
Puryear, Elmer L.
 xPuryear, Elmer L.
  Democratic Party Dissension in North
  Carolina, 1928-1936. U of NC Pr.
Pusateri, C. Joseph.
 xPusateri, C. Joseph.
  Enterprise in Radio: WWL & the Business of
  Broadcasting in America. U Pr of Amer.
Pusey, Merlo J. *see* Pusey, Merlo John.
Pusey, Merlo John, 1902-
 xPusey, Merlo J.
  Eugene Meyer. Knopf.
  The Supreme Court Crisis. Da Capo.
Pusey, Nathan M. *see* Pusey, Nathan Marsh.
Pusey, Nathan Marsh, 1907-
 xPusey, Nathan M.
  Age of the Scholar: Observations on Education
  in a Troubled Decade. Harvard U Pr.
Pusey, William A. *see* Pusey, William Allen.
Pusey, William Allen, 1865-1940
 xPusey, William A.
  The History of Dermatology. AMS Pr.
Pushaw, David R., 1926-
 xPushaw, David R.
  Teach Your Child to Talk: A Parent Guide.
  Dantree Pr.
  Teach Your Child to Talk: A Parent Guide.
  Intl Schol Bk Serv.
Pushkarev, Boris.
 xPushkarev, Boris S.
  Public Transportation & Land Use Policy. Ind
  U Pr.
Pushkarev, Boris S. *see* Pushkarev, Boris.
Pushkarnath, 1910-
 xPushkarnath.
  Potato in Sub-Tropics. South Asia Bks.
Pushkin, Aleksandr Sergeevich.
 xPushkin, Alexander.
  Eugene Onegin. Dutton.
  Eugene Onegin. Penguin.
  Eugene Onegin. Viking Pr.
  A Journey to Arzrum. Ardis Pubs.
  Little Tragedies. Kent St U Pr.
Pushkin, Alexander. *see* Pushkin, Aleksandr Sergeevich.
Pusic, Eugen.
 xPusic, Eugen.
  Social Welfare & Social Development. Mouton.
Pustay, John S.
 xPustay, John S.

Counterinsurgency Warfare. Free Pr.
Puter, S. A. *see* Puter, Stephen A. Douglas.
Puter, Stephen A. Douglas.
 xPuter, S. A.
  Looters of the Public Domain: Embracing a
  Complete Exposure of the Fraudulent System
  of Acquiring Titles to the Public Lands of the
  United States. Arno.
Puth, Robert C. *see* Puth, Robert Christian.
Puth, Robert Christian, 1936-
 xPuth, Robert C.
  Supreme Life: The History of a Negro Life
  Insurance Company. Arno.
Puthucheary, Mavis.
 xPuthucheary, Mavis.
  The Politics of Administration: The Malaysian
  Experience. Oxford U Pr.
Putnam, Alice.
 xPutnam, Alice.
  The Spy Doll. Elsevier-Nelson.
Putnam, Bertha H. *see* Putnam, Bertha Haven.
Putnam, Bertha Haven, 1872-1960
 xPutnam, Bertha H.
  ed. Enforcement of the Statutes of Labourers
  During the First Decade After the Black
  Death, 1349-59. AMS Pr.
Putnam, Bluford H.
 xPutnam, Bluford H.
  ed. The Monetary Approach to International
  Adjustment. Praeger.
Putnam, Calvin R. *see* Putnam, Calvin Richard.
Putnam, Calvin Richard, 1924-
 xPutnam, Calvin R.
  Commutation Properties of Hilbert Space
  Operators & Related Topics. Springer-Verlag.
Putnam, Emily J. *see* Putnam, Emily James (Smith).
Putnam, Emily James (Smith).
 xPutnam, Emily J.
  Candaules' Wife, & Other Old Stories. Arno.
Putnam, Frank W.
 xPutnam, Frank W.
  ed. The Plasma Proteins: Structure, Function,
  & Genetic Control. Acad Pr.
Putnam, George H. *see* Putnam, George Haven.
Putnam, George Haven, 1844-1930
 xPutnam, George H.
  Censorship of the Church of Rome & Its
  Influence Upon the Production &
  Distribution of Literature. Arno.
Putnam, Hilary.
 xPutnam, Hilary.
  Meaning & the Moral Sciences. Routledge &
  Kegan.
Putnam, Jackson K., 1929-
 xPutnam, Jackson K.
  Old-Age Politics in California: From
  Richardson to Reagan. Stanford U Pr.
Putnam, James J. *see* Putnam, James Jackson.
Putnam, James Jackson, 1846-1918
 xPutnam, James J.
  Human Motives. Arno.
Putnam, Peter.
 xPutnam, Peter.
  Triumph of the Seeing Eye. Har-Row.
 xPutnam, Peter B.
  Love in the Lead: The Fifty-Year Miracle of
  the Seeing Eye Dog. Dutton.
Putnam, Peter B. *see* Putnam, Peter.
Putnam, R. E.
 xPutnam, Robert.
  Architectural & Building Trades Dictionary.
  Am Technical.
Putnam, Robert. *see* Putnam, R. E.
Putnam, Robert D.
 xPutnam, Robert D.
  Comparative Study of Political Elites. P-H.
Putnam, Roy C., 1928-
 xPutnam, Roy C.
  Those He Came to Save. Abingdon.
Putnam, William C. *see* Putnam, William Clement.

Putnam, William Clement.
　xPutnam, William C.
　　Geology. Oxford U Pr.
Putnik, Edwin. see Putnik, Edwin V.
Putnik, Edwin V.
　xPutnik, Edwin.
　　Art of Flute Playing. Summy.
Putt, Arlene M.
　xPutt, Arlene M.
　　General Systems Theory Applied to Nursing.
　　Little.
Puttcamp, Rita.
　xPuttcamp, Rita.
　　Operation Bro-Kee. Concordia.
Putte, S. C. Van Der. see Van Der Putte, S. C.
Puttick and Simpson. see Pultick and Simpson, Firm,
　Auctioneers, London.
Puttkammer, Ernst W. see Puttkammer, Ernst Wilfred.
Puttkammer, Ernst Wilfred, 1891-
　xPuttkammer, Ernst W.
　　Administration of Criminal Law. U of Chicago
　　Pr.
Puttock, A. G.
　xPuttock, A. G.
　　Dictionary of Heraldry & Related Subjects.
　　Genealog Pub.
Putz, Helmut.
　xPutz, Helmut.
　　Adventures of Good Comrade Schweik. Ungar.
Puu, T. see Puu, Tonu.
Puu, Tonu.
　xPuu, T.
　　The Allocation of Road Capital in
　　Two-Dimensional Space: A Continuous
　　Approach. Elsevier.
Puzo, Mario.
　xPuzo, Mario.
　　The Dark Arena. Fawcett.
　　Fools Die: A Novel. Putnam.
　　The Godfather. Putnam
　　The Godfather. NAL.
　　The Godfather Papers & Other Confessions.
　　Putnam.
Puzzo, Dante A. see Puzzo, Dante Anthony.
Puzzo, Dante Anthony, 1918-
　xPuzzo, Dante A.
　　Spanish Civil War. Van Nos Reinhold.
Pye, David. see Pye, David W.
Pye, David W., 1914-
　xPye, David.
　　The Nature & Aesthetics of Design. Van Nos
　　Reinhold.
　　Nature & Art of Workmanship. Cambridge U
　　Pr.
Pye, Lloyd.
　xPye, Lloyd.
　　That Prosser Kid. Arbor Hse.
　　That Prosser Kid. Fawcett.
Pye, Lucian W., 1921-
　xPye, Lucian W.
　　Mao Tse-Tung: The Man in the Leader. Basic.
　　Politics, Personality, & Nation Building:
　　Burma's Search for Identity. Greenwood.
　　Southeast Asia's Political Systems. P-H.
Pye, Michael, 1946-
　xPye, Michael.
　　Moguls: Inside the Business of Show Business.
　　HR&W.
　　The Movie Brats: How the Film Generation
　　Took Over Hollywood. HR&W.
　　Skilful Means: A Concept in Mahayana
　　Buddhism. Biblio Dist.
Pyenson, Louis, 1909-
　xPyenson, Louis L.
　　Fundamentals of Entomology & Plant
　　Pathology. AVI.
Pyenson, Louis L. see Pyenson, Louis.
Pyk, Ann.
　xPyk, Ann.

　　The Hammer of Thunder. Putnam.
Pykare, Nina.
　xPykare, Nina.
　　Love's Promise. Dell.
Pyke, Gertrude V.
　xPyke, Gertrude V.
　　Student Nurse. Southern Pub.
　xPyke, Helen G.
　　jt. auth. Student Nurse. Southern Pub.
Pyke, Helen G. see Pyke, Gertrude V.
Pyke, Magnus.
　xPyke, Magnus.
　　Butter Side up!: The Delights of Science.
　　Sterling.
Pyle, Ernest Taylor, 1900-1945
　xPyle, Ernie.
　　Here Is Your War. Arno.
Pyle, Ernie. see Pyle, Ernest Taylor.
Pyle, Gerald F.
　xPyle, Gerald F.
　　Applied Medical Geography. Halsted Pr.
　　The Spatial Dynamics of Crime. U Chicago
　　Dept Geog.
Pyle, Howard.
　xPyle, Howard.
　　illus. Men of Iron. Har-Row.
　　Men of Iron. Airmont.
　　The Story of the Champions of the Round
　　Table. Peter Smith.
　　illus. The Story of the Champions of the Round
　　Table. Dover.
Pyle, Sara.
　xPyle, Sara.
　　Canoeing & Rafting: The Complete
　　Where-to-Go Guide to America's Best Tame
　　& Wild Waters. Morrow.
Pyle, Steve.
　xPyle, Steve.
　　Mopeds: The Complete Guide. Stein & Day.
Pyle, Theresa P. see Pyle, Theresa Permelia.
Pyle, Theresa Permelia, 1904-
　xPyle, Theresa P.
　　The Teacher's Dependency Load. AMS Pr.
Pyle, William. see Pyle, William W.
Pyle, William W.
　xPyle, William.
　　Fundamental Accounting Principles. Irwin.
　xPyle, William W.
　　Fundamental Accounting Principles. Irwin.
Pylee, M. V. see Pylee, Moolamattom Varkey.
Pylee, Moolamattom Varkey, 1922-
　xPylee, M. V.
　　Constitutional Government in India. Asia.
Pyles, Rudd.
　xPyles, Rudd.
　　How to Become an Expert Recreational Skier.
　　Norton.
Pyles, Thomas, 1905-
　xPyles, Thomas.
　　Origins & Development of the English
　　Language. HarBraceJ.
Pym, Barbara.
　xPym, Barbara.
　　Excellent Women. Dutton.
　　Excellent Women. Har-Row.
　　Glass of Blessings. Dutton.
　　Quartet in Autumn. Dutton.
　　Quartet in Autumn. G K Hall.
　　Quartet in Autumn. Har-Row.
　　The Sweet Dove Died. Dutton.
　　The Sweet Dove Died. Har-Row.
Pym, Bridget.
　xPym, Bridget.
　　Pressure Groups & the Permissive Society.
　　David & Charles.
Pym, David.
　xPym, David.

　　The Religious Thought of Samuel Taylor
　　Coleridge. B&N.
　　The Religious Thought of Samuel Taylor
　　Coleridge. Humanities.
Pynchon, Thomas.
　xPynchon, Thomas.
　　Gravity's Rainbow. Bantam.
　　Gravity's Rainbow. Penguin.
　　Gravity's Rainbow. Viking Pr.
Pyne, Zoe K. see Pyne, Zoe Kendrick.
Pyne, Zoe Kendrick.
　xPyne, Zoe K.
　　Giovanni Pierluigi Da Palestrina, His Life &
　　Times. Arno.
　　Giovanni Pierluigi Da Palestrina, His Life &
　　Times. Greenwood.
Pynoos, Jon.
　xPynoos, Jon.
　　ed. Housing Urban America. Aldine Pub.
Pyrah, G B.
　xPyrah, G. B.
　　Imperial Policy & South Africa, 1902-1910.
　　Greenwood.
Pyrah, L. N. see Pyrah, Leslie Norman.
Pyrah, Leslie Norman.
　xPyrah, L. N.
　　Renal Calculus. Springer-Verlag.
Pyron, Cherry.
　xPyron, Cherry.
　　ed. The Forgotten Art of Making
　　Old-Fashioned Pickles, Relishes, Chutneys,
　　Sauces & Catsups, Mincemeat, Beverages &
　　Syrups. Yankee Bks.
Pyster, Arthur.
　xPyster, Arthur B.
　　Compiler Design & Construction. Van Nos
　　Reinhold.
Pyster, Arthur B. see Pyster, Arthur.
Pyziur, Eugene, 1917-
　xPyziur, Eugene.
　　Doctrine of Anarchism of Michael A. Bakunin.
　　Regnery-Gateway.
Qayum, Abdul.
　xQayum, Abdul.
　　Social Cost-Benefit Analysis. Hapi Pr.
Qazi, M. A.
　xQazi, M. A.
　　What's in a Muslim Name. Kazi Pubns.
Quaal, Ward L.
　xQuaal, Ward L.
　　Broadcast Management: Radio & Television.
　　Hastings.
Quackenbush, Robert. see Quackenbush, Robert M.
Quackenbush, Robert M.
　xQuackenbush, Robert.
　　illus. Animal Cracks. Lothrop.
　　illus. Calling Doctor Quack. Lothrop.
　　Detective Mole & the Circus Mystery.
　　Lothrop.
　　Detective Mole & the Seashore Mystery.
　　Lothrop.
　　illus. Moose's Store. Lothrop.
　　ed. Movie Monsters & Their Masters: The
　　Birth of the Horror Film. A Whitman.
　　illus. Piet Potter's First Case. McGraw.
　　illus. There'll Be a Hot Time in the Old Town
　　Tonight. Lippincott.
Quade, E. see Quade, Edward S.
Quade, Edward S.
　xQuade, E.
　　Analysis for Public Decisions. Elsevier.
Quagliata, Narcissus.
　xQuagliata, Narcissus.
　　Stained Glass from Mind to Light: An Inquiry
　　into the Nature of the Medium. Mattole Pr.
Quaife, G. R. see Quaife, Geoffrey Robert.
Quaife, Geoffrey Robert.
　xQuaife, G. R.

Wanton Wenches & Wayward Wives: Peasants & Illicit Sex in Early Seventeenth Century England. Rutgers U Pr.

Quale, G. Robina. *see* Quale, Gladys Robina.

Quale, Gladys Robina, 1931-
xQuale, G. Robina.
Eastern Civilizations. P-H.

Qualey, Carlton C. *see* Qualey, Carlton Chester.

Qualey, Carlton Chester, 1904-
xQualey, Carlton C.
Norwegian Settlement in the United States. Arno.

Qualls, C. B. *see* Qualls, C. Brandon.

Qualls, C. Brandon.
xQualls, C. B.
ed. The Prevention of Sexual Disorders: Issues & Approaches. Plenum Pub.

Quance, Frank M. *see* Quance, Frank Melville.

Quance, Frank Melville, 1883-
xQuance, Frank M.
Part-Time Types of Elementary Schools in New York City: A Comparative Study of Pupil Achievement. AMS Pr.

Quandt, Jean B.
xQuandt, Jean B.
From the Small Town to the Great Community: The Social Thought of Progressive Intellectuals. Rutgers U Pr.

Quandt, William B.
xQuandt, William B.
Decade of Decisions: American Policy Toward the Arab-Israeli Conflict, 1967-1976. U of Cal Pr.
The Politics of Palestinian Nationalism. U of Cal Pr.
Revolution & Political Leadership Algeria 1954-1968. MIT Pr.

Quante, Wolfgang.
xQuante, Wolfgang.
The Exodus of Corporate Headquarters from New York City. Praeger.

Quantz, Johann J. *see* Quantz, Johann Joachim.

Quantz, Johann Joachim.
xQuantz, Johann J.
On Playing the Flute. Schirmer Bks.

Quarantelli, E. L. *see* Quarantelli, Enrico Louis.

Quarantelli, Enrico Louis, 1924-
xQuarantelli, E. L.
Disasters: Theory & Research. Sage.

Quaritch, Bernard.
xQuaritch, Bernard.
Contributions Towards a Dictionary of English Book-Collectors. B Franklin.

Quarles, Benjamin.
xQuarles, Benjamin.
Allies for Freedom: Blacks & John Brown. Oxford U Pr.
Frederick Douglass. Atheneum.
The Negro in the American Revolution. Norton.
Negro in the American Revolution. U of NC Pr.
Negro in the Making of America. Macmillan.

Quarles, Francis.
xQuarles, Francis.
Complete Works in Prose & Verse. Adler.
Complete Works in Prose & Verse. AMS Pr.

Quarles, John.
xQuarles, John.
Cleaning up America: An Insider's View of the Environmental Protection Agency. HM.

Quast, Emilie.
xQuast, Emilie.
An Index & Bibliography to Douglas C. McMurtrie's, "A History of Printing in the United States". B Franklin.

Quat, Helen.
xQuat, Helen.

Wonderful World of Freezer Cooking. Hearthside.
Wonderful World of Freezer Cooking. NAL.

Quay, Herbert C. *see* Quay, Herbert Callister.

Quay, Herbert Callister.
xQuay, Herbert C.
Psychopathological Disorders of Childhood. Wiley.

Quay, Richard H.
xQuay, Richard H.
Compiled by Index to Anthologies on Postsecondary Education, 1960-1978. Greenwood.

Quayle, Eric.
xQuayle, Eric.
Old Cook Books: An Illustrated History. Dutton.

Quayle, Margaret S. *see* Quayle, Margaret Sidney.

Quayle, Margaret Sidney, 1889-
xQuayle, Margaret S.
A Study of Some Aspects of Satisfaction in the Vocation of Stenography. AMS Pr.

Qubain, Fahim I. *see* Qubain, Fahim Issa.

Qubain, Fahim Issa, 1924-
xQubain, Fahim I.
Crisis in Lebanon. Mid East Inst.

Quebbeman, Frances E.
xQuebbeman, Frances E.
Medicine in Territorial Arizona. AZ Hist Foun.

Quebedeaux, Richard.
xQuebedeaux, Richard.
ed. Evangelical-Unification Dialogue. Unif Theol Seminary.

Queen, Ellery. *see* Queen, Ellery Pseud. of Frederic Dannay and Manfred Lee.

Queen, Ellery Pseud. of Frederic Dannay and Manfred Lee.
xQueen, Ellery.
The Spanish Cape Mystery. NAL.

Queenan, John T.
xQueenan, John T.
Modern Management of the Rh Problem. Har-Row.

Queensberry, Francis A. *see* Queensberry, Francis Archibald Kelhead Douglas.

Queensberry, Francis Archibald Kelhead Douglas, 1896-
xQueensberry, Francis A.
Oscar Wilde & the Black Douglas. Folcroft.

Queensland. University, Brisbane. Library.
xUniversity of Queensland, Department of Physics.
Useful Formulae in Elementary Physics & International Standard Units. U of Queensland Pr.

Queneau, Raymond, 1903-
xQueneau, Raymond.
The Flight of Icarus. New Directions.

Quennell, Peter, 1905-
xQuennell, Peter.
Affairs of the Mind: The Salon in Europe & America from the 18th to the 20th Century. New Republic.
Aspects of Seventeenth Century Verse. Arden Lib.
Aspects of Seventeenth Century Verse. Folcroft.
Byron. Haskell.
ed. Byron. Merrimack Bk Serv.
Byron: The Years of Fame. Shoe String.
The Colosseum. Newsweek.

Quenouille, M. H.
xQuenouille, M. H.
Rapid Statistical Calculations: A Collection of Distribution-Free & Easy Methods of Estimation & Testing. Hafner.

Quere, Ralph W.
xQuere, Ralph W.
Evangelical Witness: The Message Medium, Mission, & Method of Evangleism. Augsburg.

Quereshi, M. Y. *see* Quereshi, Mohammed Younus.

Quereshi, Mohammed Younus, 1929-
xQuereshi, M. Y.
Statistics & Behavior: An Introduction. U Pr of Amer.

Queriere, Yves de La. *see* La Queriere, Yves de.

Quesada, Fernando.
xQuesada, Fernando.
Argentine Anarchism & La Protesta. Gordon Pr.

Quesnell, John G.
xQuesnell, John G.
Marriage: A Discovery Together. Fides Claretian.
xQuesnell, John Q.
The Family Planning Dilemma Revisited. Franciscan Herald.

Quesnell, John Q. *see* Quesnell, John G.

Quesnell, Quentin.
xQuesnell, Quentin.
His Word Endures. Alba Bks.

Quest, Erica.
xQuest, Erica.
The October Cabaret. Doubleday.
The Silver Castle. Doubleday.

Quester, G. H. *see* Quester, George H.

Quester, George H.
xQuester, G. H.
Offense & Defense in the International System. Wiley.
xQuester, George H.
The Politics of Nuclear Proliferation. Johns Hopkins.

Queux, William Le. *see* Le Queux, William.

Quevedo y Villegas, Francisco G. de. *see* Quevedo y Villegas, Francisco Gomez De.

Quevedo y Villegas, Francisco Gomez De, 1580-1645
xQuevedo y Villegas, Francisco G. de.
Choice Humorous Satirical Works. Hyperion Conn.

Quezon, Manuel L. *see* Quezon, Manuel Luis.

Quezon, Manuel Luis, Pres. Philippines, 1878-1944
xQuezon, Manuel L.
Good Fight. AMS Pr.

Quible, Z. *see* Quible, Zane K.

Quible, Zane K., 1942-
xQuible, Z.
Introduction to Administrative Office Management. Winthrop.
xQuible, Zane K.
Introduction to Administrative Office Management. Winthrop.
Introduction to Word Processing. Winthrop.

Quick, Ellen K. *see* Quick, Ellen Kaufman.

Quick, Ellen Kaufman.
xQuick, Ellen K.
Teaching Responsibility to Psychiatric Inpatients: A Behavioral-Humanistic Approach. Gateway Book.

Quick, Horace F. *see* Quick, Horace Floyd.

Quick, Horace Floyd, 1915-
xQuick, Horace F.
Population Ecology. Pegasus.

Quick, James.
xQuick, James.
Fishing the Nymph. Ronald Pr.

Quick, John, 1931-
xQuick, John.
Artist's & Illustrator's Encyclopedia. McGraw.
Dictionary of Weapons & Military Terms. McGraw.

Quick, Thomas. *see* Quick, Thomas L.

Quick, Thomas L.
xQuick, Thomas.
Understanding People at Work: A Manager's Guide to the Behavioral Sciences. Exec Ent.
xQuick, Thomas L.
The Quick Motivation Method. St Martin.

Quicke, Kenneth.
xQuicke, Kenneth.

Immortal Henry: The Story of a Lipizzaner
Stallion. Merrimack Bk Serv.
Quiggin, Alison Hingston, 1874-
xQuiggin, Aliston H.
A Survey of Primitive Money: The Beginnings
of Currency. AMS Pr.
Quiggin, Aliston H. *see* Quiggin, Alison Hingston.
Quigley, Dorothy A.
xQuigley, Dorothy A.
The Quigley Book of the Pekingese. Howell
Bk.
Quigley, Harold S. *see* Quigley, Harold Scott.
Quigley, Harold Scott, 1889-
xQuigley, Harold S.
China's Politics in Perspective. Greenwood.
Far East: An International Survey. Johnson
Repr.
Quigley, Joan.
xQuigley, Joan.
Astrology for Adults. HR&W.
Astrology for Adults. Warner Bks.
Quigley, John.
xQuigley, John.
Queen's Royal. Fawcett.
Quigley, John. *see* Quigley, John B.
Quigley, John B.
xQuigley, John.
The Soviet Foreign Trade Monopoly:
Institutions and Laws. Ohio St U Pr.
Quigley, Stacy.
xQuigley, Stacy.
Do I Have to?. Raintree Child.
Quill, J. Michael.
xQuill, J. Michael.
Prelude to the Radicals: The North &
Reconstruction During 1865. U Pr of Amer.
Quillen, D. G. *see* Quillen, Daniel G.
Quillen, Daniel G.
xQuillen, D. G.
Homotopical Algebra. Springer-Verlag.
Quillen, Ruthellen, 1951-
xQuillen, Ruthellen.
Magdalen. Sibyl-Child.
Quiller, Andrew.
xQuiller, Andrew.
The Gladiator: The Hill of the Dead. Pinnacle
Bks.
Quiller-Couch, Arthur. *see* Quiller-Couch, Arthur
Thomas.
Quiller-Couch, Arthur T. *see* Quiller-Couch, Arthur
Thomas.
Quiller-Couch, Arthur Thomas, Sir, 1863-1944
xQuiller-Couch, Arthur.
ed. English Sonnets. Granger Bk.
On the Art of Writing. Folcroft.
ed. The Oxford Book of English Verse.
Granger Bk.
The Oxford Book of Victorian Verse. Granger
Bk.
xQuiller-Couch, Arthur T.
Astonishing History of Troy Town. Dutton.
ed. English Sonnets. Arno.
I Saw Three Ships, & Other Winter's Tales.
Arno.
Old Fires & Profitable Ghosts: A Book of
Stories. Arno.
Quilligan, E. J. *see* Quilligan, Edward J.
Quilligan, Edward J.
xQuilligan, E. J.
ed. Fetal & Maternal Medicine. Wiley.
Quimby, Charles W.
xQuimby, Charles W.
Law for the Medical Practitioner. Health
Admin Pr.
Quimby, George I. *see* Quimby, George Irving.
Quimby, George Irving, 1913-
xQuimby, George I.

Indian Culture & European Trade Goods: The
Archaeology of the Historic Period in the
Western Great Lakes Region. Greenwood.
Quimby, Ian M. *see* Quimby, Ian M. G.
Quimby, Ian M. G.
xQuimby, Ian M.
ed. American Furniture & Its Makers. U of
Chicago Pr.
Quimby, Myrtle.
xQuimby, Myrtle.
Cougar. Abelard.
Quimby, Robert S.
xQuimby, Robert S.
Background of Napoleonic Warfare: The
Theory of Military Tactics in
Eighteenth-Century France. AMS Pr.
Quimme, Peter.
xQuimme, Peter.
The Signet Book of American Wine. NAL.
The Signet Book of Cheese. NAL.
The Signet Book of Coffee & Tea. NAL.
Quin-Harkin, Janet.
xQuin-Harkin, Janet.
Benjamin's Balloon. Parents.
Septimus Bean & His Amazing Machine.
Parents.
Quinault, R.
xQuinault, R.
ed. Popular Protest & Public Order: Six Studies
in British History, 1790-1920. St Martin.
Quincey, Thomas De. *see* De Quincey, Thomas.
Quincy, Joseph. *see* Quincy, Josiah.
Quincy, Josiah, 1772-1864
xQuincy, Joseph.
The History of Harvard University. Arno.
xQuincy, Josiah.
Memoir of the Life of Josiah Quincy. Da Capo.
Quine, Willard. *see* Quine, Willard Van Orman.
Quine, Willard V. *see* Quine, Willard Van Orman.
Quine, Willard Van Orman.
xQuine, Willard.
From a Logical Point of View:
Logico-Philosophical Essays. Har-Row.
xQuine, Willard V.
Mathematical Logic. Harvard U Pr.
Word & Object. MIT Pr.
Quinlan, Charles.
xQuinlan, Charles.
Orthographic Projection Simplified. McKnight.
Quinlan, Edith.
xQuinlan, Edith.
In gods We Trust. Accent Bks.
Quinlan, Sterling.
xQuinlan, Sterling.
The Hundred Million Dollar Lunch. O'Hara.
Inside ABC: American Broadcasting
Company's Rise to Power. Hastings.
Quinley, Harold E.
xQuinley, Harold E.
Anti-Semitism in America. Free Pr.
Quinn, A. D. *see* Quinn, Alonzo Def.
Quinn, Alonzo Def.
xQuinn, A. D.
Design & Construction of Ports & Marine
Structures. McGraw.
Quinn, Arthur H. *see* Quinn, Arthur Hobson.
Quinn, Arthur Hobson, 1875-
xQuinn, Arthur H.
Edgar Allan Poe: A Critical Biography. Cooper
Sq.
Edith Wharton. Folcroft.
Quinn, Bernard.
xQuinn, Bernard.
Apostolic Regions of the United States: 1971.
Glenmary Res Ctr.
Distribution of Catholic Priests in the United
States: 1971. Glenmary Res Ctr.
The Small Rural Parish. Glenmary Res Ctr.
Quinn, Bernetta. *see* Quinn, Mary Bernetta.

Quinn, Carin.
xQuinn, Carin.
Your Career As a Physician. Arco.
Quinn, David B. *see* Quinn, David Beers.
Quinn, David Beers.
xQuinn, David B.
ed. North American Discovery, Circa
1000-1612. U of SC Pr.
Quinn, Derry.
xQuinn, Derry.
The Fear of God. St Martin.
The Limbo Connection. Penguin.
The Solstice Man. St Martin.
Quinn, Edward. *see* Quinn, Edward G.
Quinn, Edward G.
xQuinn, Edward.
The Major Shakespearean Tragedies: A Critical
Bibliography. Free Pr.
xQuinn, Edward G.
Relevants. Free Pr.
Quinn, Esther C. *see* Quinn, Esther Casier.
Quinn, Esther Casier.
xQuinn, Esther C.
Quest of Seth for the Oil of Life. U of Chicago
Pr.
Quinn, Gardner.
xQuinn, Gardner.
Valentine Crafts & Cookbook. Harvey.
Quinn, James A. *see* Quinn, James Alfred.
Quinn, James Alfred, 1895-
xQuinn, James A.
Human Ecology. Shoe String.
Quinn, Jim.
xQuinn, Jim.
Word of Mouth: A Completely New Kind of
Guide to New York City Restaurants.
Lippincott.
Quinn, John R.
xQuinn, John R.
Nature's World Records. Schol Bk Serv.
Nature's World Records. Walker & Co.
The Summer Woodlands. Chatham Pr.
Quinn, Kenneth.
xQuinn, Kenneth.
Texts & Contexts: The Roman Writers & Their
Audience. Routledge & Kegan.
Quinn, Loyd Y. *see* Quinn, Loyd Yost.
Quinn, Loyd Yost, 1917-
xQuinn, Loyd Y.
Immunological Concepts. Iowa St U Pr.
Quinn, Mary Bernetta.
xQuinn, Bernetta.
Ezra Pound: An Introduction to the Poetry.
Columbia U Pr.
Quinn, Patrick F. *see* Quinn, Patrick Francis.
Quinn, Patrick Francis, 1918-
xQuinn, Patrick F.
French Face of Edgar Poe. S Ill U Pr.
Quinn, Philip L.
xQuinn, Philip L.
Divine Commands & Moral Requirements.
Oxford U Pr.
Quinn, Robert P.
xQuinn, Robert P.
The Chosen Few: A Study of Discrimination in
Executive Selection. U of Mich Soc Res.
Quinn, T. F. *see* Quinn, Terence Frederick James.
Quinn, Terence Frederick James.
xQuinn, T. F.
Application of Modern Physical Techniques of
Tribology. Van Nos Reinhold.
Quinn, Terry, 1945-
xQuinn, Terry.
The Great Bridge Conspiracy. St Martin.
Quinn, Thomas, 1947-
xQuinn, Thomas.
Dairy Farm Management. Delmar.
Dairy Farm Management. Van Nos Reinhold.
Quinn, Thomas M.
xQuinn, Thomas M.

The Uniform Commercial Code Commentary &
Law Digest. Warren.
Quinn, Vincent. *see* Quinn, Vincent Gerard.
Quinn, Vincent Gerard, 1926-
xQuinn, Vincent.
Hilda Doolittle (H. D.). Irvington.
Quinn, Wayne, 1941-
xQuinn, Wayne.
The Art of Wayne Quinn. New Glide.
Quinney, Richard.
xQuinney, Richard.
Capitalist Society: Readings for a Critical
Sociology. Dorsey.
ed. Criminal Justice in America: A Critical
Understanding. Little.
Criminology. Little.
Critique of Legal Order: Crime control in
Capitalist Society. Little.
Quinones, Ricardo. *see* Quinones, Ricardo J.
Quinones, Ricardo J.
xQuinones, Ricardo.
Dante Alighieri. Twayne.
xQuinones, Ricardo J.
The Renaissance Discovery of Time. Harvard
U Pr.
Quinones De Perez, Josefina.
xQuinones De Perez, Josefina.
Maquinas De Oficina. U of PR Pr.
Quint, Howard H.
xQuint, Howard H.
ed. Men, Women & Issues in American
History. Dorsey.
Profile in Black & White: A Frank Portrait of
South Carolina. Greenwood.
Quintana, Ricardo.
xQuintana, Ricardo.
ed. English Poetry of the Mid & Late
Eighteenth Century: An Historical
Anthology. Greenwood.
Swift: An Introduction. Greenwood.
Two Augustans: John Locke, Jonathan Swift. U
of Wis Pr.
ed. Two Hundred Poems. Arno.
Quintilianus, Marcus F. *see* Quintilianus, Marcus Fabius.
Quintilianus, Marcus Fabius.
xQuintilianus, Marcus F.
Quintilian As Educator: Selections from the
Institutio Oratoria of Marcus Fabius
Quintilianus. Irvington.
Quinton, Anthony.
xQuinton, Anthony.
The Nature of Things. Routledge & Kegan.
Utilitarian Ethics. St Martin.
Quirin, William L.
xQuirin, William L.
Probability & Statistics. Har-Row.
Winning at the Races: Computer Discoveries in
Thoroughbred Handicapping. Morrow.
Quirk, James.
xQuirk, James.
Introduction to General Equilibrium Theory &
Welfare Economics. McGraw.
Quirk, John. *see* Quirk, John E.
Quirk, John E.
xQuirk, John.
No Red Ribbons. Devin.
Quirk, Lawrence J.
xQuirk, Lawrence J.
Films of Fredric March. Citadel Pr.
Films of Ingrid Bergman. Citadel Pr.
Films of Joan Crawford. Citadel Pr.
Films of Paul Newman. Citadel Pr.
The Films of Robert Taylor. Citadel Pr.
The Films of Ronald Colman. Citadel Pr.
The Films of Warren Beatty. Citadel Pr.
The Films of William Holden. Citadel Pr.
The Great Romantic Films. Citadel Pr.
Quirk, Randolph.
xQuirk, Randolph.

The Concessive Relation in Old English
Poetry. Shoe String.
An Old English Grammar. Methuen Inc.
Quirk, Robert E.
xQuirk, Robert E.
Affair of Honor: Woodrow Wilson & the
Occupation of Vera Cruz. Norton.
Quirk, Thomas J., 1939-
xQuirk, Thomas J.
Psychological Research: How to Do It. Wiley.
Quirke, Lillian M. *see* Quirke, Lillian Mary.
Quirke, Lillian Mary.
xQuirke, Lillian M.
The Rug Book: How to Make All Kinds of
Rugs. P-H.
Quoist, Michael. *see* Quoist, Michel.
Quoist, Michel.
xQuoist, Michael.
Prayers. Avon.
xQuoist, Michel.
Christ Is Alive. Doubleday.
Meaning of Success. Fides Claretian.
Prayers. Andrews & McMeel.

Ra, Jong Oh.
xRa, Jong Oh.
Labor at the Polls: Union Voting in Presidential
Elections, 1952-1976. U of Mass Pr.
Raab, Carl. *see* Raab, Carl M.
Raab, Carl M.
xRaab, Carl.
Budding Wonders: The Flowering Plants.
Rosen Pr.
The Student Biologist Explores Genetics.
Rosen Pr.
Raab, Lawrence, 1946-
xRaab, Lawrence.
The Collector of Cold Weather. Ecco Pr.
Raab, Robert.
xRaab, Robert A.
Coping with Divorce. Rosen Pr.
Raab, Robert A. *see* Raab, Robert.
Raab, W. *see* Raab, Wolfgang.
Raab, Wolfgang.
xRaab, W.
The Treatment of Mycosis with Imidazole
Derivatives. Springer-Verlag.
Raack, R. C.
xRaack, Richard C.
Fall of Stein. Harvard U Pr.
Raack, Richard C. *see* Raack, R. C.
Rabalais, J. Wayne, 1944-
xRabalais, J. Wayne.
Principles of Ultraviolet Photoelectron
Spectroscopy. Wiley.
Rabald, Erich, 1899-
xRabald, Erich.
Corrosion Guide. Elsevier.
Raban, Jonathan.
xRaban, Jonathan.
Arabia: A Journey Through the Labyrinth.
S&S.
Arabia: A Journey Through the Labyrinth.
S&S.
Rabassa, Clementine C. *see* Rabassa, Clementine
Christos.
Rabassa, Clementine Christos.
xRabassa, Clementine C.
Demetrio Aguilera-Malta & Social Justice: The
Tertiary Phase of Epic Tradition in Latin
American Literature. Fairleigh Dickinson.
Rabb, Kate (Milner).
xRabb, Kate M.
National Epics. Arno.
Rabb, Kate M. *see* Rabb, Kate (Milner).
Rabb, Theodore K.
xRabb, Theodore K.

Family in History: Interdisciplinary Essays.
Har-Row.
The Family in History: Interdisciplinary
Essays. Octagon.
The Struggle for Stability in Early Modern
Europe. Oxford U Pr.
Rabbath, Antoine, 1867-1913
xRabbath, Antoine.
Documents Inedits Pour Servir a l'Histoire Du
Christianisme En Orient. AMS Pr.
Rabbitt, Thomas, 1943-
xRabbitt, Thomas.
Exile. U of Pittsburgh Pr.
Rabe, Bernice. *see* Rabe, Berniece.
Rabe, Berniece.
xRabe, Bernice.
Who's Afraid?. Dutton.
xRabe, Berniece.
The Girl Who Had No Name. Dutton.
The Orphans. Dutton.
Rabe, David.
xRabe, David.
In the Boom Boom Room. Knopf.
Streamers. Knopf.
Rabelais, Francois.
xRabelais, Francois.
Gargantua & Pantagruel. AMS Pr.
Gargantua & Pantagruel. Penguin.
The Portable Rabelais. Penguin.
Raben, Joseph.
xRaben, Joseph.
Computer Assisted Research in the
Humanities: A Directory of Scholars Active,
1966-1972. Pergamon.
Raben, Marguerite.
xRaben, Marguerite.
Textile Mill. Watts.
Rabenort, William L. *see* Rabenort, William Louis.
Rabenort, William Louis, 1870-
xRabenort, William L.
Spinoza As Educator. AMS Pr.
Raber, Dorothy A., 1930-
xRaber, Dorothy A.
Protestantism in Changing Taiwan: A Call to
Creative Response. William Carey Lib.
Rabin, Albert I.
xRabin, Albert I.
ed. Clinical Psychology: Issues of the Seventies.
Mich St U Pr.
Rabin, Carol. *see* Rabin, Carol Price.
Rabin, Carol Price.
xRabin, Carol.
A Guide to Music Festivals in America.
Berkshire Traveller.
Rabin, Chaim.
xRabin, Chaim.
Qumran Studies. Greenwood.
Qumran Studies. Schocken.
Rabin, Coleman. *see* Rabin, Coleman Berley.
Rabin, Coleman Berley.
xRabin, Coleman.
Radiology of the Chest. Williams & Wilkins.
Rabin, Gil.
xRabin, Gil.
Changes. Har-Row.
Rabin, Lucy F. *see* Rabin, Lucy Feiden.
Rabin, Lucy Feiden.
xRabin, Lucy F.
Ford Madox Brown & the Pre-Raphaelite
History-Picture. Garland Pub.
Rabin, M. *see* Rabin, Michael Oser.
Rabin, Michael Oser, 1931-
xRabin, M.
Automata on Infinite Objects & Church's
Problem. Am Math.
Rabin, Robert. *see* Rabin, Robert L.
Rabin, Robert L.
xRabin, Robert.

Perspectives on the Administrative Process.
Little.

Rabin, Yitzhak, 1922-
  xRabin, Yitzhak.
    The Rabin Memoirs. Little.
Rabiner, Lawrence R.
  xRabiner, Lawrence R.
    Digital Processing of Speech Signals. P-H.
    ed. Digital Signal Processing. Inst Electrical.
    Digital Signal Processing. Wiley.
    Theory & Application of Digital Signal
      Processing. P-H.
Rabinovich, I. *see* Rabinovich, Itamar.
Rabinovich, I. B. *see* Rabinovich, Izrail Beniaminovich.
Rabinovich, Itamar.
  xRabinovich, I.
    ed. From June to October: The Middle East
      Between 1967 & 1973. Transaction Bks.
Rabinovich, Izrail Beniaminovich.
  xRabinovich, I. B.
    Influence of Isotopy on the Physicochemical
      Properties of Liquids. Plenum Pub.
Rabinovitz, Francine F.
  xRabinovitz, Francine F.
    City Politics & Planning. Aldine Pub.
Rabinow, Paul.
  xRabinow, Paul.
    ed. Interpretive Social Science: A Reader. U of
      Cal Pr.
    Reflections on Fieldwork in Morocco. U of Cal
      Pr.
Rabinowich, Ellen.
  xRabinowich, Ellen.
    Horses & Foals. Watts.
    The Loch Ness Monster. Watts.
    Rock Fever. Watts.
Rabinowicz, Ernest.
  xRabinowicz, Ernest.
    Friction & Wear of Materials. Wiley.
    Introduction to Experimentation. A-W.
Rabinowicz, Harry M., 1919-
  xRabinowicz, Harry M.
    World of Hasidism. Hartmore.
Rabinowitsch, Wolf Z. *see* Rabinowitsch, Wolf Zeev.
Rabinowitsch, Wolf Zeev, 1900-
  xRabinowitsch, Wolf Z.
    Lithuanian Hasidism. Schocken.
Rabinowitz, Dorothy.
  xRabinowitz, Dorothy.
    About the Holocaust: What We Know & How
      We Know It. Am Jewish Comm.
Rabinowitz, Howard N., 1942-
  xRabinowitz, Howard N.
    Race Relations in the Urban South 1865-1890.
      Oxford U Pr.
    Race Relations in the Urban South, 1865-1890.
      U of Ill Pr.
Rabinowitz, Jack G.
  xRabinowitz, Jack G.
    Pediatric Radiology. Lippincott.
Rabinowitz, Louis I. *see* Rabinowitz, Louis Isaac.
Rabinowitz, Louis Isaac, 1906-
  xRabinowitz, Louis I.
    Torah & Flora. Hebrew Pub.
Rabinowitz, Sandy.
  xRabinowitz, Sandy.
    A Colt Named Mischief. Doubleday.
    What's Happening to Daisy?. Har-Row.
Rabkin, Eric S.
  xRabkin, Eric S.
    Arthur C. Clarke. Borgo Pr.
    The Fantastic in Literature. Princeton U Pr.
Rabkin, Richard, 1932-
  xRabkin, Richard.
    Strategic Psychotherapy: Brief & Symptomatic
      Treatment. Basic.
Raboff, Ernest. *see* Raboff, Ernest Lloyd.
Raboff, Ernest Lloyd.
  xRaboff, Ernest.

Marc Chagall. Doubleday.
    Pablo Picasso. Doubleday.
    Paul Klee. Doubleday.
Rabushka, Alvin.
  xRabushka, Alvin.
    Caseworkers or Police?: How Tenants See
      Public Housing. Hoover Inst Pr.
    Old Folks at Home. Free Pr.
    Race & Politics in Urban Malaya. Hoover Inst
      Pr.
    A Theory of Racial Harmony. U of SC Pr.
    Value for Money: The Hong Kong Budgetary
      Process. Hoover Inst Pr.
Raccagni, Michelle, 1939-
  xRaccagni, Michelle.
    The Modern Arab Woman: A Bibliography.
      Scarecrow.
Race, George J.
  xRace, George J.
    Basic Urinalysis. Har-Row.
Rachels, James, 1941-
  xRachels, James.
    Understanding Moral Philosophy. Dickenson.
Rachie, Kenneth O.
  xRachie, Kenneth O.
    Pearl Millet. Pa St U Pr.
Rachlin, Harvey.
  xRachlin, Harvey.
    The Songwriter's Handbook. T Y Crowell.
Rachlin, Howard, 1935-
  xRachlin, Howard.
    Introduction to Modern Behaviorism. W H
      Freeman.
Rachlin, Nahid.
  xRachlin, Nahid.
    Foreigner. Norton.
Rachlin, Robert.
  xRachlin, Robert.
    Return on Investment: Strategies for Profit.
      Marr Pubns.
    Return on Investment: Strategies for Profit.
      P-H.
Rachman, Arnold W.
  xRachman, Arnold W.
    Identity Group Psychotherapy with
      Adolescents. C C Thomas.
Rachman, David. *see* Rachman, David J.
Rachman, David J.
  xRachman, David.
    Marketing Strategy & Structure. P-H.
  xRachman, David J.
    Business Today. Random.
    Modern Marketing. Dryden Pr.
Rachman, S. *see* Rachman, Stanley.
Rachman, Stanley.
  xRachman, S.
    ed. Contributions to Medical Psychology.
      Pergamon.
    Critical Essays on Psychoanalysis. Pergamon.
    Obsessions & Compulsions. P-H.
  xRachman, Stanley J.
    Fear & Courage. W H Freeman.
Rachman, Stanley J. *see* Rachman, Stanley.
Rachmaninoff, Sergei, 1873-1943
  xRachmaninoff, Sergei.
    Rachmaninoff's Recollections Told to Oskar
      Von Riesemann. Arno.
Racine, Jean. *see* Racine, Jean Baptiste.
Racine, Jean B. *see* Racine, Jean Baptiste.
Racine, Jean Baptiste.
  xRacine, Jean.
    Andromaque. French & Eur.
  xRacine, Jean B.
    Andromache. Barron.
    Andromaque. Larousse.
    Britannicus. Cambridge U Pr.
    Britannicus. French & Eur.
Racine, Michel L., 1945-
  xRacine, Michel L.

The Arithmetics of Quadratic Jordan Algebras.
      Am Math.
Racker, Efraim, 1913-
  xRacker, Efraim.
    ed. Membranes of Mitochondria &
      Chloroplasts. Am Chemical.
  xRacker, Efriam.
    Science & the Cure of Diseases: Letters to
      Members of Congress. Princeton U Pr.
Racker, Efriam. *see* Racker, Efraim.
Rackham, Arthur, 1867-1939
  xRackham, Arthur.
    illus. Fairy Tales from Many Lands. Penguin.
    Rackham's Color Illustrations for Wagner's
      Ring. Dover.
Rackley, Charles E.
  xRackley, Charles E.
    Coronary Artery Disease: Recognition &
      Management. Futura Pub.
Rackman, Emanuel.
  xRackman, Emanuel.
    One Man's Judaism. Philos Lib.
Racle, Fred. *see* Racle, Fred A.
Racle, Fred A.
  xRacle, Fred.
    Introduction to Evolution. P-H.
Racster, Olga.
  xRacster, Olga.
    The Master of the Russian Ballet: The
      Memoirs of Cav. Enrico Cecchetti. Da Capo.
Racz, Sandor D., 1934-
  xRacz, Sandor D.
    Carburetor Basics, Trouble-Shooting &
      Rebuilding. Racz Pub.
Raczkowski, George.
  xRaczkowski, George.
    Principles of Machine Dynamics. Gulf Pub.
Rada, Richard T.
  xRada, Richard T.
    ed. Clinical Aspects of the Rapist. Grune.
Radano, Gene.
  xRadano, Gene.
    Stories Cops Only Tell Each Other. Stein &
      Day.
Radcliff, Ruth K.
  xRadcliff, Ruth K.
    Calculation of Drug Dosages: A Workbook.
      Mosby.
Radcliffe, Ann. *see* Radcliffe, Ann (Ward).
Radcliffe, Ann (Ward), 1764-1823
  xRadcliffe, Ann.
    Castles of Athlin & Dunbayne: A Highland
      Story. Arno.
    Sicilian Romance. Arno.
  xRadcliffe, Ann W.
    Castles of Athlin & Dunbayne: A Highland
      Story. Johnson Repr.
    Sicilian Romance. Johnson Repr.
Radcliffe, Ann W. *see* Radcliffe, Ann (Ward).
Radcliffe, C. W. *see* Radcliffe, Charles W.
Radcliffe, Charles W.
  xRadcliffe, C. W.
    The Patellar-Tendon-Bearing Below-Knee
      Prosthesis. U of Cal Pr.
Radcliff, Cyril John Radcliffe, 1st Viscount.
  xRadcliffe, Cyril J.
    Law & Its Compass. Northwestern U Pr.
Radcliffe, Cyril J. *see* Radcliff, Cyril John Radcliffe, 1st
  Viscount.
Radcliffe, George L. *see* Radcliffe, George Lovic Pierce.
Radcliffe, George Lovic Pierce, 1877-
  xRadcliffe, George L.
    Governor Thomas H. Hicks of Maryland & the
      Civil War. AMS Pr.
Radcliffe, James E.
  xRadcliffe, James E.
    The Case or Controversy Provision. Pa St U
      Pr.
Radcliffe, Janette.
  xRadcliffe, Janette.

Gift of Violets. Dell.
Radcliffe, P. *see* Radcliffe, Philip.
Radcliffe, Peter.
　xRadcliffe, Peter.
　　Land of Mountains: Hiking & Climbing in New
　　Zealand. Mountaineers.
Radcliffe, Philip.
　xRadcliffe, P.
　　Beethoven's String Quartets. Cambridge U Pr.
　xRadcliffe, Philip.
　　Mendelssohn. Biblio Dist.
　　Mendelssohn. Littlefield.
Radcliffe, W. *see* Radcliffe, William.
Radcliffe, William, 1856-1938
　xRadcliffe, W.
　　Fishing from the Earliest Times. Ares.
　xRadcliffe, William.
　　Fishing from the Earliest Times. B Franklin.
　　Origin of the New System of Manufacture
　　Commonly Called Power Loom Weaving.
　　Kelley.
Radcliffe-Brown, Alfred R. *see* Radcliffe-Brown, Alfred
　Reginald.
Radcliffe-Brown, Alfred Reginald, 1881-
　xRadcliffe-Brown, Alfred R.
　　Andaman Islanders. Free Pr.
Raddatz, Fritz J. *see* Raddatz, Fritz Joachim.
Raddatz, Fritz Joachim.
　xRaddatz, Fritz J.
　　Karl Marx: A Political Biography. Little.
Radding, Charles.
　xRadding, Charles.
　　The Modern Presidency. Watts.
Rade, Lennart.
　xRade, Lennart.
　　Take a Chance with Your Calculator:
　　Probability Problems for Programmable
　　Calculators. Dilithium Pr.
Radek, Karl, 1885-1939
　xRadek, Karl.
　　Portraits & Pamphlets. Arno.
Rademacher, Hans.
　xRademacher, Hans.
　　Dedekind Sums. Math Assn.
　　Lectures on Elementary Number Theory.
　　Krieger.
Rademacher, William J., 1928-
　xRademacher, William J.
　　Working with Parish Councils. Alba Bks.
Rader, Brian F.
　xRader, Brian F.
　　The Political Outsiders: Blacks & Indians in a
　　Rural Oklahoma County. R & E Res Assoc.
Rader, M. *see* Rader, Melvin Miller.
Rader, Melvin. *see* Rader, Melvin Miller.
Rader, Melvin M. *see* Rader, Melvin Miller.
Rader, Melvin Miller.
　xRader, M.
　　Art & Human Values. P-H.
　xRader, Melvin.
　　False Witness. U of Wash Pr.
　　Marx's Interpretation of History. Oxford U Pr.
　xRader, Melvin M.
　　Ethics & Society: An Appraisal of Social
　　Ideals. Greenwood.
　　Presiding Ideas in Wordsworth's Poetry.
　　Gordian.
Rader, Trout, 1938-
　xRader, Trout.
　　The Economics of Feudalism. Gordon.
　　Theory of General Economic Equilibrium.
　　Acad Pr.
　　Theory of Microeconomics. Acad Pr.
Radetzki, Marian.
　xRadetzki, Marian.
　　Aid & Development: A Handbook for Small
　　Donors. Irvington.
Radford, Albert E.
　xRadford, Albert E.

Manual of the Vascular Flora of the Carolinas.
U of NC Pr.
Radford, G. H. *see* Radford, George Heynes.
Radford, George Heynes, Sir, 1851-1937
　xRadford, G. H.
　　Shylock & Others: Eight Studies. Arno.
Radford, Jean.
　xRadford, Jean.
　　Norman Mailer: A Critical Study. B&N.
Radford, K. J.
　xRadford, K. J.
　　Complex Decision Problems: An Integrated
　　Strategy for Resolution. Reston.
　　Information Systems for Strategic Decisions.
　　Reston.
　　Information Systems in Management. Reston.
　　Strategic Planning: An Analytical Approach.
　　Reston.
Radhakrishnan. *see* Radhakrishnan, Sarvepalli.
Radhakrishnan, S. *see* Radhakrishnan, Sarvepalli.
Radhakrishnan, Sarvepalli, Pres. India, 1888-
　xRadhakrishnan.
　　Indian Philosophy. Orient Bk Dist.
　xRadhakrishnan, S.
　　Eastern Religions & Western Thought. Oxford
　　U Pr.
　　The Hindu View of Life. Allen Unwin.
　　An Idealist View of Life. Allen Unwin.
　xRadhakrishnan, Sarvepalli.
　　An Idealist View of Life. AMS Pr.
　xRadhakrishnan, Sarvepelli.
　　Indian Philosophy. Humanities.
Radhakrishnan, Sarvepelli. *see* Radhakrishnan, Sarvepalli.
Radin, Beryl.
　xRadin, Beryl.
　　Implementation, Change, in the Federal
　　Bureaucracy: School Desegregation Policy in
　　HEW, 1964-1968. Tchrs Coll.
Radin, Max, 1880-1850
　xRadin, Max.
　　Law As Logic & Experience. Shoe String.
　　ed. Law Dictionary. Oceana.
　　The Lawful Pursuit of Gain. Arno.
Radin, Paul, 1883-1959
　xRadin, Paul.
　　African Folktales. Princeton U Pr.
　　ed. African Folktales & Sculpture. Princeton U
　　Pr.
　　Indians of South America. Greenwood.
　　Literary Aspects of North American
　　Mythology. Arden Lib.
　　Literary Aspects of North American
　　Mythology. Folcroft.
　　Literary Aspects of North American
　　Mythology. Norwood Edns.
　　Primitive Man As a Philosopher. Peter Smith.
　　Primitive Man As Philosopher. Dover.
　　Primitive Religion: Its Nature & Origin. Dover.
　　World of Primitive Man. Dutton.
Radine, Lawrence B.
　xRadine, Lawrence B.
　　The Taming of the Troops: Social Control in
　　the United States Army. Greenwood.
Radio Electronics Staff. *see* Radio-Electronics.
Radio-Electronics.
　xRadio Electronics Staff.
　　Transistor Techniques. TAB Bks.
　xRadio-Electronics Staff.
　　Radio-Electronics Hobby Projects. TAB Bks.
Radio-Electronics Staff. *see* Radio-Electronics.
Raditsa, Leo.
　xRaditsa, Leo.
　　Some Sense About Wilhelm Reich. Philos Lib.
Radius, Marianne. *see* Radius, Mariannwe.
Radius, Mariannwe.
　xRadius, Marianne.
　　Ninety Story Sermons for Children's Church.
　　Baker Bk.
Radke, Don, 1940-
　xRadke, Don.

Cheese Making at Home: The Complete
Illustrated Guide. Doubleday.
Radl, Shirley. *see* Radl, Shirley L.
Radl, Shirley L.
　xRadl, Shirley.
　　And the Pursuit of Happiness. A & W Pubs.
　　How to Be a Mother & a Person, Too. Rawson
　　Wade.
　xRadl, Shirley L.
　　ed. And the Pursuit of Happiness.
　　Metamorphosis Pr.
Radlauer, E. *see* Radlauer, Edward.
Radlauer, Ed. *see* Radlauer, Edward.
Radlauer, Edward.
　xRadlauer, E.
　　jt. auth. Buggy-Go-Round. Watts.
　　jt. auth. Chopper Cycle. Watts.
　　Foolish Filly. Watts.
　　jt. auth. Horsing Around. Watts.
　　jt. auth. On the Drag Strip. Watts.
　　jt. auth. On the Sand. Watts.
　　On the Water. Watts.
　　Racing on the Wind. Watts.
　xRadlauer, Ed.
　　Gymnastics School. Watts.
　　photos by & jt. auth. Miniatures. Childrens.
　　Monster Mania. Childrens.
　　Pursuit School. Watts.
　　Race Car Drivers School. Watts.
　　Racing Numbers. Childrens.
　　illus. Roller Skate Mania. Childrens.
　　Some Basics About Bicycles. Childrens.
　　Some Basics About Motorcycles. Childrens.
　　Some Basics About Skateboards. Childrens.
　　Some Basics About Vans. Childrens.
　　illus. Some Basics About Water Skiing.
　　Childrens.
　　photos by Trucks. Childrens.
　xRadlauer, Edward.
　　Bicycle Motocross. Childrens.
　　CB Radio. Childrens.
　　Dinosaur Mania. Childrens.
　　Drag Racing: Quarter Mile Thunder. Abelard.
　　photos by Fast, Faster, Fastest. Childrens.
　　Flying Mania. Childrens.
　　Horse Show Challenge. Childrens.
　　Model Trains. Childrens.
　　Monkey Mania. Childrens.
　　Ready, Get Set, Whoa!. Childrens.
　　Some Basics About Hang Gliding. Childrens.
　　Some Basics About Running. Childrens.

Radlauer, Ruth. *see* Radlauer, Ruth Shaw.

Radlauer, Ruth S. *see* Radlauer, Ruth Shaw.

Radlauer, Ruth Shaw.

　xRadlauer, Ruth.

　　illus. Acadia National Park. Childrens.
　　illus. Bryce Canyon National Park. Childrens.
　　Great Smoky Mountains National Park.
　　Childrens.
　　Haleakala National Park. Childrens.
　　illus. Hawaii Volcanoes National Park.
　　Childrens.
　　Olympic National Park. Childrens.
　xRadlauer, Ruth S.
　　Everglades National Park. Childrens.
　　Glacier National Park. Childrens.
　　Grand Canyon National Park. Childrens.
Radler, Don. *see* Radler, Don H.
Radler, Don H.
　xRadler, Don.
　　How Congress Works. NAL.
Radley, Gail.
　xRadley, Gail.
　　The Night Stella Hid the Stars. Crown.
Radlow, James, 1925-
　xRadlow, James.

Finite Mathematics for Business, Economics, & Social Science. Duxbury Pr.

Radnoti, Miklos.
xRadnoti, Miklos.
Forced March: Selected Poems. Persea Bks.

Rado, T. *see* Rado, Tibor.

Rado, Tibor, 1895-
xRado, T.
On the Problem of Plateau - Subharmonic Functions. Springer-Verlag.

Radocy, Rudolf E.
xRadocy, Rudolf E.
Psychological Foundations of Musical Behavior. C C Thomas.

Radosevich, G. E. *see* Radosevich, George.

Radosevich, George.
xRadosevich, G. E.
Evolution & Administration of Colorado Water Law: 1876-1976. WRP.

Radosh, R. *see* Radosh, Ronald.

Radosh, Ronald.
xRadosh, R.
ed. Debs. Brown Bk.
xRadosh, Ronald.
ed. Debs. P-H.
Prophets on the Right: Profiles of Conservative Critics of American Globalism. Free Life.
Prophets on the Right: Profiles of Conservative Critics of American Globalism. S&S.

Radovic, Igor. *see* Radovic, Igor D.

Radovic, Igor D.
xRadovic, Igor.
How to Manage the Boss: The Radovic Rule. Brown Bk.

Radvanyi, Janos.
xRadvanyi, Janos.
Delusion & Reality: Gambits, Hoaxes, & Diplomatic One-Upmanship in Vietnam. Regnery-Gateway.
Hungary & the Superpowers: The 1956 Revolution & Realpolitik. Hoover Inst Pr.

Radwanski, George.
xRadwanski, George.
Trudeau. Taplinger.

Radwin, George E.
xRadwin, George E.
Murex Shells of the World: An Illustrated Guide to the Muricidae. Stanford U Pr.

Radzinowicz, Leon.
xRadzinowicz, Leon.
ed. Crime & Justice. Basic.
The Growth of Crime: The International Experience. Basic.
Ideology & Crime. Columbia U Pr.

Radzinowicz, Mary Ann.
xRadzinowicz, Mary Ann.
Toward Samson Agonistes: The Growth of Milton's Mind. Princeton U Pr.

Rae, Douglas W.
xRae, Douglas W.
ed. Public Policy & Public Choice. Sage.

Rae, Gwynedd.
xRae, Gwynedd.
Mary Plain Omnibus. Routledge & Kegan.

Rae, John, 1931-
xRae, John.
Conscience & Politics: British Government & the Conscientious Objector to Military Service, 1916-1919. Oxford U Pr.
Contemporary Socialism. Norwood Edns.

Rae, John B. *see* Rae, John Bell.

Rae, John Bell, 1911-
xRae, John B.
American Automobile: A Brief History. U of Chicago Pr.
Climb to Greatness: The American Aircraft Industry, 1920-1960. MIT Pr.

Rae, Rusty.
xRae, Rusty.

The World's Biggest Motorcycle Race: The Daytona 200. Lerner Pubns.

Rae, Wesley D.
xRae, Wesley D.
Thomas Lodge. Irvington.

Raedler, A.
xRaedler, A.
The Development of the Visual System of the Albino Rat. Springer-Verlag.
Influences of Experimental Brain Edema on the Development of Visual Systems. Springer-Verlag.

Raeff, Marc.
xRaeff, Marc.
Origins of the Russian Intelligentsia: The Eighteenth-Century Nobility. HarBraceJ.

Rael, Juan B. *see* Rael, Juan Bautista.

Rael, Juan Bautista.
xRael, Juan B.
Cuentos Espanoles De Colorado y Nuevo Mejico: Spanish Tales from Colorado & New Mexico. Arno.

Raelson, Jeffrey E.
xRaelson, Jeffrey E.
Getting to Know German Wines. Banyan Bks.

Rafelson, Max E.
xRafelson, Max E.
Basic Biochemistry. Macmillan.

Raffaele, Joseph A.
xRaffaele, Joseph A.
The Economic Development of Nations. Phila Bk Co.

Raffauf, Robert F. *see* Raffauf, Robert Francis.

Raffauf, Robert Francis.
xRaffauf, Robert F.
Handbook of Alkaloids & Alkaloid-Containing Plants. Wiley.
Introduction to Drug Analysis. Davis Co.

Raffel, Burton.
xRaffel, Burton.
ed. Anthology of Modern Indonesian Poetry. State U NY Pr.
Development of Modern Indonesian Poetry. State U NY Pr.
From the Vietnamese: Ten Centuries of Poetry. October.

Raffel, Jeffrey A.
xRaffel, Jeffrey A.
The Politics of School Desegregation: The Metropolitan Remedy in Delaware. Temple U Pr.
Systematic Analysis of University Libraries: Application of Cost-Benefit Analysis to the M. I. T. Libraries. MIT Pr.

Raffel, Stanley.
xRaffel, Stanley.
Matters of Fact: A Sociological Inquiry. Routledge & Kegan.

Raffensperger, John G.
xRaffensperger, John G.
Acute Abdomen in Infancy & Childhood. Lippincott.

Rafferty, Kathleen.
xRafferty, Kathleen.
ed. Dell Crossword Dictionary. Delacorte.
The Dell Crossword Dictionary. Dell.
ed. Dell Crossword Dictionary. Dell.

Rafferty, S. S.
xRafferty, S. S.
Fatal Flourishes. Avon.

Raffles, Stamford. *see* Raffles, Thomas Stamford.

Raffles, Thomas Stamford, Sir, 1781-1826
xRaffles, Stamford.
Statement of the Services of Sir Stamford Raffles. Oxford U Pr.

Rafroidi, Patrick.
xRafroidi, Patrick.

Irish Literature in English: The Romantic Period (1789-1850). Humanities.
The Irish Short Story. Humanities.

Ragan, Donal M.
xRagan, Donal M.
Structural Geology: An Introduction to Geometrical Techniques. Wiley.

Ragan, Pauline K.
xRagan, Pauline K.
ed. Aging Parents. USC Andrus Geron.

Ragan, W. B. *see* Ragan, William Burk.

Ragan, William Burk.
xRagan, W. B.
Modern Elementary Curriculum. HR&W.

Raghunathan, M. S.
xRaghunathan, M. S.
Discrete Subgroups of Lie Groups. Springer-Verlag.

Ragosta, Millie J.
xRagosta, Millie J.
The House on Curtin Street. Doubleday.

Ragsdale, John G.
xRagsdale, John G.
Dutch Oven Cooking. Pacesetter Pr.

Ragsdale, Kenneth B. *see* Ragsdale, Kenneth Baxter.

Ragsdale, Kenneth Baxter, 1917-
xRagsdale, Kenneth B.
Quicksilver: Terlingua & the Chisos Mining Company. Tex A&M Univ Pr.

Raguin, Y. *see* Raguin, Yves.

Raguin, Yves, 1912-
xRaguin, Y.
How to Pray Today. Abbey.

Ragusa, Olga.
xRagusa, Olga.
Luigi Pirandello. Columbia U Pr.

Ragussis, Michael.
xRagussis, Michael.
The Subterfuge of Art: Language & the Romantic Tradition. Johns Hopkins.

Raheja, P. C.
xRaheja, P. C.
Soil Productivity & Crop Growth. Asia.

Rahill, Frank.
xRahill, Frank.
World of Melodrama. Pa St U Pr.

Rahimtoola, Shahbudin H.
xRahimtoola, Shahbudin H.
Coronary Bypass Surgery. Davis Co.
ed. Infective Endocarditis. Grune.

Rahman, Fazlur, 1919-
xRahman, Fazlur.
Islam. U of Chicago Pr.

Rahman, N. A. *see* Rahman, Najeeb Abdur.

Rahman, Najeeb Abdur.
xRahman, N. A.
Exercises in Probability & Statistics for Mathematics Undergraduates. Hafner.

Rahmlow, Harold F.
xRahmlow, Harold F.
Objectives-Based Testing: A Guide to Effective Test Development. Educ Tech Pubns.
PLATO. Educ Tech Pubns.
The Teaching-Learning Unit. Educ Tech Pubns.

Rahn, Joan E. *see* Rahn, Joan Elma.

Rahn, Joan Elma, 1929-
xRahn, Joan E.
Biology: The Science of Life. Macmillan.
Grocery Store Botany. Atheneum.
Grocery Store Zoology: Bones & Muscles. Atheneum.
How Plants Are Pollinated. Atheneum.
More About What Plants Do. Atheneum.
Nature in the City: Plants. Raintree Pubs.

Rahn, John.
xRahn, John.
Basic Atonal Theory. Longman.

Rahner, Hugo, 1900-1968
xRahner, Hugo.

Greek Myths & Christian Mystery. Biblo.
Rahner, Karl, 1904-
xRahner, Karl.
ed. Encyclopedia of Theology: The Concise
Sacramentum Mundi. Seabury.
Meditations on Freedom & the Spirit. Seabury.
Meditations on Hope & Love. Seabury.
Meditations on the Sacraments. Seabury.
On Prayer. Paulist Pr.
Opportunities for Faith: Elements of a Modern
Spirituality. Seabury.
The Priesthood. Seabury.
The Religious Life Today. Seabury.
The Spirit in the Church. Seabury.
Spirit in the World. Seabury.
Theological Investigations. Seabury.
Rahul, Ram.
xRahul, Ram.
Modern Central Asia. Advent Bk.
Rahv, Betty T.
xRahv, Betty T.
From Sartre to the New Novel. Kennikat.
Rahv, Philip, 1908-
xRahv, Philip.
Image & Idea: Fourteen Essays on Literary
Themes. Greenwood.
Literature in America: An Anthology of
Literary Criticism.. Peter Smith.
Rai, Kul B.
xRai, Kul B.
Political Science Statistics. Shoe String.
Rai, Lala Lajpat. see Lajpat Rai, Lala.
Raichur, S. see Raichur, Satish.
Raichur, Satish.
xRaichur, S.
ed. The Politics of Aid, Trade & Investment.
Halsted Pr.
Raiffa, Howard.
xRaiffa, Howard.
Applied Statistical Decision Theory. MIT Pr.
Decision Analysis: Introductory Lectures on
Choices Under Uncertainty. A-W.
Railey, William E. see Railey, William Edward.
Railey, William Edward, 1852-
xRailey, William E.
History of Woodford County, Kentucky.
Regional.
Railton, Stephen, 1948-
xRailton, Stephen.
Fenimore Cooper: A Study of His Life &
Imagination. Princeton U Pr.
Raimes, Ann, 1938-
xRaimes, Ann.
Focus on Composition. Oxford U Pr.
Raimo, John.
xRaimo, John W.
ed. A Guide to Manuscripts Relating to
America in Great Britain & Ireland: Crick &
Alman. Meckler Bks.
Raimo, John W. see Raimo, John.
Raimondi, Anthony J.
xRaimondi, Anthony J.
Pediatric Neuroradiology. Saunders.
Rain, Thomas.
xRain, Thomas.
Browning for Beginners. Haskell.
Browning for Beginners. R West.
Rainbolt, Richard.
xRainbolt, Richard.
Boxing's Heavyweight Champions. Lerner
Pubns.
Football's Clever Quarterbacks. Lerner Pubns.
Football's Rugged Running Backs. Lerner
Pubns.
Hockey's Top Scorers. Lerner Pubns.
Raine, Craig.
xRaine, Craig.

A Martian Sends a Postcard Home. Oxford U
Pr.
The Onion, Memory. Oxford U Pr.
Raine, K. see Raine, Kathleen Jessie.
Raine, Kathleen.
xRaine, Kathleen.
Death in Life & Life in Death: Cuchulain
Comforted & News for the Delphic Oracle.
Humanities.
Raine, Kathleen. see Raine, Kathleen Jessie.
Raine, Kathleen Jessie, 1908-
xRaine, K.
Blake & Antiquity. Princeton U Pr.
xRaine, Kathleen.
Blake & the New Age. Allen Unwin.
From Blake to a Vision. Humanities.
The Lion's Mouth. Braziller.
The Lost Country. Humanities.
The Oval Portrait & Other Poems. SBD.
Raine, William M. see Raine, William MacLeod.
Raine, William MacLeod.
xRaine, William M.
Arizona Guns. Popular Lib.
Colorado. Amereon Ltd.
Range Beyond the Law. Popular Lib.
Raines, John C.
xRaines, John C.
Attack on Privacy. Judson.
Illusions of Success. Judson.
ed. Marxism & Radical Religion: Essays
Toward a Revolutionary Humanism. Temple
U Pr.
Raines, Margaret.
xRaines, Margaret.
Consumers' Management. Bennett Co.
Raines, Max R.
xRaines, Max R.
Developing Constituency Programs in
Community Colleges. Am Assn Comm Jr
Coll.
Raines, Robert A. see Raines, Robert Arnold.
Raines, Robert Arnold.
xRaines, Robert A.
Creative Brooding. Macmillan.
Going Home. Har-Row.
Living the Questions. Word Bks.
Lord, Could You Make It a Little Better?.
Word Bks.
New Life in the Church. Har-Row.
Rainey, Homer P. see Rainey, Homer Price.
Rainey, Homer Price, 1896-
xRainey, Homer P.
How Fare American Youth?. Arno.
Rainey, Patricia A. see Rainey, Patricia Ann.
Rainey, Patricia Ann.
xRainey, Patricia A.
Illusions: A Journey into Perception. Shoe
String.
Rainolds, John.
xRainolds, John.
The Overthrow of Stage-Plays. Johnson Repr.
Rainsford, George N.
xRainsford, George N.
Congress & Higher Education in the
Nineteenth Century. U of Tenn Pr.
Raintree. see Raintree, Diane.
Raintree, Diane.
xRaintree.
The Household Book of Hints & Tips.
Jonathan David.
xRaintree, Diane.
ed. The Household Book of Hints & Tips.
Ballantine.
Rainville, Earl D. see Rainville, Earl David.
Rainville, Earl David, 1907-
xRainville, Earl D.
Special Functions. Chelsea Pub.
Rainwater, Dorothy. see Rainwater, Dorothy T.
Rainwater, Dorothy T.
xRainwater, Dorothy.

Encyclopedia of American Silver
Manufacturers. Wallace-Homestead.
Raison, Timothy, 1929-
xRaison, Timothy.
Power & Parliament. Biblio Dist.
Raisz, Erwin J. see Raisz, Erwin Josephus.
Raisz, Erwin Josephus, 1893-
xRaisz, Erwin J.
Principles of Cartography. McGraw.
Rait, Robert S. see Rait, Robert Sangster.
Rait, Robert Sangster, Sir, 1874-1936
xRait, Robert S.
Life in the Medieval University. Gordon Pr.
Life in the Medieval University. Kraus Repr.
Raizer, Iurii Petrovich.
xRaizer, Y. P.
ed. Laser Induced Discharge Phenomena.
Plenum Pub.
Raizer, Y. P. see Raizer, Iurii Petrovich.
Raizis, M. Byron.
xRaizis, M. Byron.
Dionysios Solomos. Twayne.
Raj, Des.
xRaj, Des.
Design of Sample Surveys. McGraw.
Raj, Jagdish, 1929-
xRaj, Jagdish.
Mutiny & British Land Policy in North India,
1856-1868. Asia.
Raj, Prakash A.
xRaj, Praskah A.
Kathmandu & the Kingdom of Nepal. Two
Continents.
Raj, Praskah A. see Raj, Prakash A.
Rajan, B. see Rajan, Balachandra.
Rajan, Balachandra.
xRajan, B.
T. S. Eliot: A Study of His Writings by Several
Hands. Haskell.
xRajan, Balachandra.
The Overwhelming Question: A Study of the
Poetry of T. S. Eliot. U of Toronto Pr.
Paradise Lost & the Seventeenth Century
Reader. U of Mich Pr.
ed. The Prison & the Pinnacle. U of Toronto
Pr.
Rajan, M. S. see Rajan, Mannaraswamighala Sreeranga.
Rajan, Mannaraswamighala Sreeranga.
xRajan, M. S.
Sovereignty Over Natural Resources.
Humanities.
Rajaratnam, N.
xRajaratnam, N.
Turbulent Jets. Elsevier.

Rajcsanyi, P. M. see Rajcsanyi, Peter M.

Rajcsanyi, Peter M.

xRajcsanyi, P. M.
High-Speed Liquid Chromatography. Dekker.

Rajec, E. M. see Rajec, Elizabeth M.
Rajec, Elizabeth M.
xRajec, E. M.
The Study of Names in Literature: A
Bibliography. K G Saur.
Rajhans, Gyan S.
xRajhans, Gyan S.
Engineering Aspects of Asbestos Dust Control.
Ann Arbor Science.
Rajka, Georg.
xRajka, George.
Atopic Dermatitis. Saunders.
Rajka, George. see Rajka, Georg.
Raju, P. T. see Raju, Poolla Tirupati.
Raju, Poolla T. see Raju, Poolla Tirupati.
Raju, Poolla Tirupati, 1902-
xRaju, P. T.

Introduction to Comparative Philosophy. S Ill
U Pr.
xRaju, Poolla T.
Pref. by Idealistic Thought of India. Johnson
Repr.
Rakel, Robert E.
xRakel, Robert E.
Principles of Family Medicine. Saunders.
Rakes, Charles. *see* Rakes, Charles D.
Rakes, Charles D.
xRakes, Charles.
Integrated Circuit Projects. Sams.
Rakestraw, Lawrence.
xRakestraw, Lawrence.
A History of Forest Conservation in the Pacific
Northwest, 1891-1913. Arno.
Rakich, Jonathon S.
xRakich, Jonathon S.
Hospital Organization & Management: Text &
Readings. Halsted Pr.
Rakoff, V. M.
xRakoff, Vivian M.
ed. Psychiatric Diagnosis. Brunner-Mazel.
Rakoff, Vivian M. *see* Rakoff, V. M.
Rakosi, Carl, 1903-
xRakosi, Carl.
Amulet. Black Sparrow.
Ex Cranium, Night. Black Sparrow.
Rakove, Milton L.
xRakove, Milton L.
ed. Arms & Foreign Policy in the Nuclear Age.
Oxford U Pr.
Don't Make No Waves - Don't Back No
Losers: An Insider's Analysis of the Daley
Machine. Ind U Pr.
Rakow, Robert.
xRakow, Robert.
Podiatric Management of the Diabetic Foot.
Futura Pub.
Rakowitz, Elly.
xRakowitz, Elly.
Living With Your New Baby: A Postpartum
Guide for Mothers & Fathers. Watts.
Rakowski, John, 1922-
xRakowski, John.
Cooking on the Road. Anderson World.
Raktoe. *see* Raktoe, B. L.
Raktoe, B. L.
xRaktoe.
Basic Applied Statistics. Dekker.
Raleigh, John H. *see* Raleigh, John Henry.
Raleigh, John Henry, 1920-
xRaleigh, John H.
The Chronicle of Leopold & Molly Bloom:
"Ulysses" As Narrative. U of Cal Pr.
Matthew Arnold & American Culture. Peter
Smith.
Matthew Arnold & American Culture. U of Cal
Pr.
Raleigh, Walter.
xRaleigh, Walter.
Sir Walter Raleigh Selections from His
"Historie of the World," His Letters, Etc.
Folcroft.
Raleigh, Walter. *see* Raleigh, Walter Alexander.
Raleigh, Walter A. *see* Raleigh, Walter Alexander.
Raleigh, Walter Alexander, Sir, 1861-1922
xRaleigh, Walter.
English Novel: Being a Short Sketch of Its
History from the Earliest Times to the
Appearance of Waverly. Folcroft.
English Novel: Being a Short Sketch of Its
History from the Earliest Times to the
Appearance of Waverly. Scholarly.
On Writing & Writers. R West.
Style. Folcroft.
xRaleigh, Walter A.
Wordsworth. Scholarly.
Raley, Tom.
xRaley, Tom.

Rodeo Fever: A Collection of Poems Capturing
the Spirit of Rodeo. Latigo Pr.
Ralfe, James, fl. 1820-1829
xRalfe, James.
The Naval Biography of Great Britain:
Consisting of Historical Memoirs of Those
Officers of the British Navy Who
Distinguished Themselves During the Reign
of His Majesty George III. Irvington.
Ralfs, J. *see* Ralfs, John.
Ralfs, John.
xRalfs, J.
British Desmidieae. Lubrecht & Cramer.
Rall, Eilene M.
xRall, Eilene M.
Structures in Composition. Scott F.
Ralli, Augustus, 1875-
xRalli, Augustus.
Christians at Mecca. Kennikat.
Guide to Carlyle. Haskell.
Guide to Carlyle. R West.
Later Critiques. Dynamic Learn Corp.
xRalli, Augustus J.
Later Critiques. Arno.
Later Critiques. R West.
Ralli, Augustus J. *see* Ralli, Augustus.
Ralls, Kenneth. *see* Ralls, Kenneth M.
Ralls, Kenneth M.
xRalls, Kenneth.
Introduction to Materials Science &
Engineering. Wiley.
Ralph, Julian, 1853-1903
xRalph, Julian.
Prince of Georgia, & Other Tales. Arno.
Ralph, L. Philip. *see* Ralph, Philip Lee.
Ralph Nader Congress Project.
xRalph Nader Congress Project.
Ruling Congress: How the House & Senate
Rules Govern the Legislative Process.
Penguin.
Ralph, Philip Lee, 1905-
xRalph, L. Philip.
The Renaissance in Perspective. St Martin.
Ralston, A. *see* Ralston, Anthony.
Ralston, Alma P. *see* Ralston, Alma Payne.
Ralston, Alma Payne.
xRalston, Alma P.
Pressure Cooking. Nitty Gritty.
Ralston, Anthony.
xRalston, A.
A First Course in Numerical Analysis.
McGraw.
xRalston, Anthony.
Introduction to Programming & Computer
Science. Krieger.
ed. Mathematical Methods for Digital
Computers. Wiley.
Ralston, Jackson H. *see* Ralston, Jackson Harvey.
Ralston, Jackson Harvey.
xRalston, Jackson H.
Law & Procedure of International Tribunals.
Garland Pub.
Ralston, John.
xRalston, John.
Coaching Today's Athlete: A Football
Textbook. Mayfield Pub.
Ralston, Susan E.
xRalston, Susan E.
Review & Application of Clinical
Pharmacology. Lippincott.
Ralston, W. R. *see* Ralston, William Ralston Shedden.
Ralston, William Ralston Shedden, 1828-1889
xRalston, W. R.
Songs of the Russian People: As Illustrative of
Slavonic Mythology & Russian Social Life.
Haskell.
Ram, N. V. *see* Ram, N. V. Raghu.
Ram, N. V. Raghu, 1931-
xRam, N. V.

Games Bureaucrats Play. Advent Bk.
Rama.
xRama, Swami.
Pref. by Living with the Himalayan Masters:
Spiritual Experiences of Swami Rama.
Himalayan Intl Inst.
Rama, Swami. *see* Rama.
Ramacciotti, Mary D. *see* Ramacciotti, Mary Dominic.
Ramacciotti, Mary Dominic, Sister.
xRamacciotti, Mary D.
Syntax of Il Fiore & of Dante's Inferno As
Evidence in the Question of the Authorship
of Il Fiore. AMS Pr.
Ramachandran, G.
xRamachandran, G.
ed. Gandhi: His Relevance for Our Times.
World Without War.
Ramaer, R.
xRamaer, R.
Steam Locomotives of the East African
Railways. David & Charles.
Ramage, C. S.
xRamage, C. S.
Monsoon Meteorology. Acad Pr.
Ramalingam, P., 1941-
xRamalingam, P.
Systems Analysis for Managerial Decisions: A
Computer Approach. Wiley.
Ramalingam, Vimala.
xRamalingam, Vimala.
ed. Medicinal Plants. Mss Info.
Ramamurti. *see* Ramamurti, Chinni Pennathur.
Ramamurti, Chinni Pennathur.
xRamamurti.
Orthopaedics in Primary Care. Williams &
Wilkins.
Ramamurty, Bhaskara K. *see* Ramamurty, K. Bhaskara.
Ramamurty, K. Bhaskara, 1924-
xRamamurty, Bhaskara K.
Aldous Huxley: A Study of His Novels. Asia.
Raman, T. A., 1907-1961
xRaman, T. A.
India. Fideler.
Ramanujan, A. K., 1929-
xRamanujan, A. K.
tr. Speaking of Siva. Penguin.
Ramaswamy, M.
xRamaswamy, M.
Creative Role of the Supreme Court of the
United States. Russell.
Ramazani, Rouhollah K., 1928-
xRamazani, Rouhollah K.
Foreign Policy of Iran, 1500-1941: A
Developing Nation in World Affairs. U Pr of
Va.
Ramazanoglu, Gulseren.
xRamazanoglu, Gulseren.
Turkish Embroidery. Van Nos Reinhold.
Rambach, Pierre, 1925-
xRambach, Pierre.
The Secret Message of Tantric Buddhism.
Rizzoli Intl.
Rambaud, Alfred N. *see* Rambaud, Alfred Nicolas.
Rambaud, Alfred Nicolas, 1842-1905
xRambaud, Alfred N.
De Byzantino Hippodromo et Circensibus
Factionibus. B Franklin.
Ramberg, Bennett.
xRamberg, Bennett.
The Seabed Arms Control Negotiations: A
Study of Multilateral Arms Control
Diplomacy. U of Denver Intl.
Ramdohr, P. *see* Ramdohr, Paul.
Ramdohr, Paul, 1890-
xRamdohr, P.
The Ore Minerals & Their Intergrowths.
Pergamon.
xRamdohr, Paul.

The Ore Minerals & Their Intergrowths.
Pergamon.

Ramer, Ernest L.
xRamer, Ernest L.
The Catholic Church of the Future. Exposition.

Rames, H. B., 1914-
xRames, H. B.
Dynamics of Motivating Prospects to Buy.
P-H.

Ramfjord, Sigurd. see Ramfjord, Sigurd Peder.

Ramfjord, Sigurd P. see Ramfjord, Sigurd Peder.

Ramfjord, Sigurd Peder.
xRamfjord, Sigurd.
Occlusion. Saunders.
xRamfjord, Sigurd P.
Periodontology & Periodontics. Saunders.

Raming, Ida.
xRaming, Ida.
The Exclusion of Women from the Priesthood:
Divine Law or Sex Discrimination?.
Scarecrow.

Ramirez, Bruno.
xRamirez, Bruno.
When Workers Fight: The Politics of Industrial
Relations in the Progressive Era, 1898-1916.
Greenwood.

Ramirez, Carolyn.
xRamirez, Carolyn.
Foot & Feet. Harvey.

Ramirez, Efren C. see Ramirez, Efren Convento.

Ramirez, Efren Convento, 1941-
xRamirez, Efren C.
In Pursuit of Images. SF Arts & Letters.

Ramm, Hartmut, 1942-
xRamm, Hartmut.
The Marxism of Regis Debray: Between Lenin
& Guevara. Regents Pr KS.

Ramo, Simon.
xRamo, Simon.
Extraordinary Tennis for the Ordinary Player.
Crown.
ed. Peacetime Uses of Outer Space.
Greenwood.

Ramon y Cajal, Santiago, 1852-1934
xRamon Y Cajal, Santiago.
Structure of Ammon's Horn. C C Thomas.
Structure of the Retina. C C Thomas.

Ramond, Charles.
xRamond, Charles.
The Art of Using Science in Marketing.
Har-Row.

Ramos, Gloria.
xRamos, Gloria.
Careers in Construction. Lerner Pubns.

Ramos, Graciliano, 1892-1953
xRamos, Graciliano.
Anguish. Greenwood.

Ramos, Samuel.
xRamos, Samuel.
Profile of Man & Culture in Mexico. U of Tex
Pr.

Ramos, Suzanne.
xRamos, Suzanne.
The Complete Book of Child Custody. Putnam.

Ramos, Teresita V.
xRamos, Teresita V.
Tagalog Dictionary. U Pr of Hawaii.
Tagalog for Beginners. U Pr of Hawaii.
Tagalog Structures. U Pr of Hawaii.

Ramos Oliveira, Antonio, 1907-
xRamos Oliveira, Antonio.
Politics, Economics & Men of Modern Spain,
1808-1946. Arno.

Ramous, Arthur. see Ramous, Arthur J.

Ramous, Arthur J.
xRamous, Arthur.
Applied Kinematics. P-H.

Rampersad, Arnold.
xRampersad, Arnold.

The Art & Imagination of W. E. B. Dubois.
Harvard U Pr.

Rampp, Donald L.
xRampp, Donald L.
Auditory Processing & Learning Disabilities.
Cliffs.
Classroom Activities for Auditory Perceptual
Disorders. Interstate.

Rams, E. see Rams, Edwin M.

Rams, Edwin. see Rams, Edwin M.

Rams, Edwin M.
xRams, E.
Rams' Real Estate Appraising Handbook. P-H.
xRams, Edwin.
Analysis & Valuation of Retail Locations.
Reston.

Ramsahoye, Fenton H. see Ramsahoye, Fenton H W.

Ramsahoye, Fenton H W.
xRamsahoye, Fenton H.
The Development of Land Law in British
Guiana. Oceana.

Ramsay, A. T. see Ramsay, Anthony Thomas Stanley.

Ramsay, Anthony Thomas Stanley.
xRamsay, A. T.
Oceanic Micropalaeontology. Acad Pr.

Ramsay, David, 1749-1815
xRamsay, David.
History of the American Revolution. Russell.

Ramsay, E. Mary. see Ramsay, Emily Mary.

Ramsay, Emily Mary, 1863-
xRamsay, E. Mary.
Christian Science & Its Discoverer. Chr
Science.

Ramsay, Jack.
xRamsay, Jack.
The Coach's Art. Intl Schol Bk Serv.

Ramsay, James A. see Ramsay, James Arthur.

Ramsay, James Arthur.
xRamsay, James A.
Experimental Basis of Modern Biology.
Cambridge U Pr.

Ramsay, James H. see Ramsay, James Henry.

Ramsay, James Henry, Sir, Bart, 1832-1925
xRamsay, James H.
History of the Revenues of the Kings of
England 1066-1399. Kelley.

Ramsay, Marion L. see Ramsay, Marion Livingston.

Ramsay, Marion Livingston, 1897-
xRamsay, Marion L.
Pyramids of Power: The Story of Roosevelt,
Insull & the Utility Wars. Da Capo.

Ramsay, W. M. see Ramsay, William Mitchell.

Ramsay, William M. see Ramsay, William Mitchell.

Ramsay, William Mitchell, Sir, 1851-1939
xRamsay, W. M.
The Church in the Roman Empire Before A.
D. 170. Longwood Pr.
The Historical Geography of Asia Minor.
Cooper Sq.
xRamsay, William M.
The Cities & Bishoprics of Phrygia. Arno.

Ramsdale, Jeanne. see Ramsdale, Jeanne Alice.

Ramsdale, Jeanne Alice.
xRamsdale, Jeanne.
Persian Cats. TFH Pubns.
Persian Cats & Other Longhairs. TFH Pubns.

Ramsden, Caroline.
xRamsden, Caroline.
Racing Without Tears. J A Allen.

Ramsden, John, 1947-
xRamsden, John.
The Age of Balfour & Baldwin: 1902-1940.
Longman.

Ramseur, Nancy. see Ramseur, Nancy Fairley.

Ramseur, Nancy Fairley.
xRamseur, Nancy.
Where to Find Tomorrow: A Zero-Cost Road
to Better Public Schools. Regnery-Gateway.

Ramsey, A. Michael. see Ramsey, Arthur Michael.

Ramsey, Arthur M. see Ramsey, Arthur Michael.

Ramsey, Arthur Michael, Abp. of Canterbury, 1904-
xRamsey, A. Michael.
The Charismatic Christ. Morehouse.
xRamsey, Arthur M.
Come Holy Spirit. Morehouse.
Future of the Christian Church. Morehouse.
xRamsey, Michael.
Canterbury Pilgrim. Seabury.

Ramsey, C. G. see Ramsey, Charles George.

Ramsey, Charles George.
xRamsey, C. G.
Architectural Graphic Standards. Wiley.

Ramsey, F. P. see Ramsey, Frank Plumpton.

Ramsey, Frank Plumpton, 1903-1930
xRamsey, F. P.
Intro. by Foundations: Essays in Philosophy,
Logic, Mathematics & Economics.
Humanities.

Ramsey, Frederic, 1915-
xRamsey, Frederick.
A Guide to Longplay Jazz Records. Da Capo.

Ramsey, Frederick. see Ramsey, Frederic.

Ramsey, Ian T.
xRamsey, Ian T.
On Being Sure in Religion. Humanities.
ed. Prospect for Metaphysics: Essays of
Metaphysical Exploration. Greenwood.

Ramsey, J. G. see Ramsey, James Gettys McGready.

Ramsey, Jackson E. see Ramsey, Jackson Eugene.

Ramsey, Jackson Eugene, 1938-
xRamsey, Jackson E.
Research & Development: Project Selection
Criteria. Univ Microfilms.

Ramsey, James Gettys McGready, 1797-1884
xRamsey, J. G.
Annals of Tennessee to the End of the
Eighteenth Century. Arno.

Ramsey, Jarold, 1937-
xRamsey, Jarold.
Coyote Was Going There: Indian Literature of
the Oregon Country. U of Wash Pr.
Love in an Earthquake. U of Wash Pr.

Ramsey, Julian.
xRamsey, Julian W.
My Brother's Keeper. Windy Row.

Ramsey, Julian W. see Ramsey, Julian.

Ramsey, Michael. see Ramsey, Arthur Michael.

Ramsey, Paul.
xRamsey, Paul.
Ethics at the Edges of Life: Medical & Legal
Intersections. Yale U Pr.
The Ethics of Fetal Research. Yale U Pr.
Fabricated Man: The Ethics of Genetic
Control. Yale U Pr.
The Fickle Glass: A Study of Shakespeare's
Sonnets. AMS Pr.
Limits of Nuclear War: Thinking About the
Do-Able & the Un-Do-Able. Coun Rel &
Intl.
ed. Study of Religion in Colleges &
Universities. Princeton U Pr.

Ramsey, Robert H. see Ramsey, Robert Henderson.

Ramsey, Robert Henderson, 1909-
xRamsey, Robert H.
Men & Mines of Newmont: A Fifty Year
History. Octagon.

Ramsey, Robert W. see Ramsey, Robert Wayne.

Ramsey, Robert Wayne.
xRamsey, Robert W.
Carolina Cradle: Settlement of the Northwest
Carolina Frontier, 1747-1762. U of NC Pr.

Ramseyer, Lloyd L.
xRamseyer, Lloyd L.
More Excellent Way. Faith & Life.

Ramstad, Josie W. see Ramstad, Josie Winship.

Ramstad, Josie Winship.
xRamstad, Josie W.
Ferocious Sarah. Talespinner.

Ramus, J., 1940-
xRamus, J.

Developmental Sequence of the Marine Red
Alga Pseudogloiophloea in Culture. U of Cal
Pr.
Ramusack, Barbara. *see* Ramusack, Barbara N.
Ramusack, Barbara N.
xRamusack, Barbara.
The Princes of India in the Twilight of Empire:
Dissolution of a Patron-Client System
1914-1939. Ohio St U Pr.
Ranadive, K. R.
xRanadive, K. R.
Income Distribution: The Unsolved Puzzle.
Oxford U Pr.
Rancier, Esther.
xRancier, Esther.
Matchcovers: A Guide to Collecting. Century
Hse.
Rand, Ann.
xRand, Ann.
Listen, Listen. HarBraceJ.
Rand, Ayn.
xRand, Ayn.
Anthem. Caxton.
Anthem. NAL.
Atlas Shrugged. NAL.
Atlas Shrugged. Random.
An Introduction to Objectivist Epistemology.
NAL.
Rand, Benjamin, 1856-1934
xRand, Benjamin.
ed. The Classical Moralists: Selections
Illustrating Ethics from Socrates to
Martineau. Peter Smith.
ed. The Classical Psychologists: Selections
Illustrating Psychology from Anaxagoras to
Wundt. Peter Smith.
Rand, Christopher.
xRand, Christopher.
Changing Landscape: Salisbury, Connecticut.
Oxford U Pr.
Puerto Ricans. Oxford U Pr.
Rand, E. M. *see* Rand, Edward Kennard.
Rand, Edward K. *see* Rand, Edward Kennard.
Rand, Edward Kennard, 1871-1945
xRand, E. M.
Founders of the Middle Ages. Peter Smith.
xRand, Edward K.
The Building of Eternal Rome. Cooper Sq.
Founders of the Middle Ages. Dover.
Rand, Howard B, 1889-
xRand, Howard B.
Hour Cometh. Destiny.
Marvels of Prophecy. Destiny.
Rand, James. *see* Rand, James S.
Rand, James S.
xRand, James.
The Great Sky & the Silence. McGraw.
Rand, John. *see* Rand, John A.
Rand, John A.
xRand, John.
People's Lewiston - Auburn, Maine 1875-1975.
Wheelwright.
Rand McNally. *see* Rand McNally and Company.
Rand McNally and Company.
xRand McNally.
Dist-O-Map. Rand.
Guide to Florida. Rand.
xRand McNally Editors.
Rand McNally Handy Railroad Atlas of the
United States. Rand.
Zip Code Atlas. Rand.
Rand McNally Editors. *see* Rand McNally and Company.
Rand, Silas T. *see* Rand, Silas Tertius.
Rand, Silas Tertius, 1810-1889
xRand, Silas T.
Legends of the Micmacs. Johnson Repr.
Randall, Alice E. *see* Randall, Alice Elizabeth (Sawtelle).
Randall, Alice Elizabeth (Sawtelle), 1865-1909
xRandall, Alice E.

Sources of Spenser's Classical Mythology.
AMS Pr.
The Sources of Spenser's Classical Mythology.
Gordon Pr.
Sources of Spenser's Classical Mythology. R
West.
Randall, Bob.
xRandall, Bob.
The Fan. Random.
The Fan. Warner Bks.
Randall, Bruce.
xRandall, Bruce.
Barbell Way to Physical Fitness. Doubleday.
Randall, Charles A. *see* Randall, Charles Addison.
Randall, Charles Addison.
xRandall, Charles A.
ed. Extra-Terrestrial Matter. N Ill U Pr.
Randall, Clarence B. *see* Randall, Clarence Bernard.
Randall, Clarence Bernard.
xRandall, Clarence B.
Systems & Procedures for Business Data
Processing. SW Pub.
Randall, Dale B. *see* Randall, Dale B. J.
Randall, Dale B. J.
xRandall, Dale B.
Golden Tapestry: A Critical Survey of
Non-Chivalric Spanish Fiction in English
Translation, 1543-1657. Duke.
Jonson's Gypsies Unmasked: Background &
Theme of the Gypsies Metamorphos'd. Duke.
Joseph Conrad & Warrington Dawson: The
Record of a Friendship. Duke.
Randall, Daniel R. *see* Randall, Daniel Richard.
Randall, Daniel Richard, 1864-1936
xRandall, Daniel R.
Cooperation in Maryland & the South. AMS
Pr.
A Puritan Colony in Maryland. AMS Pr.
A Puritan Colony in Maryland. Johnson Repr.
Randall, Dudley, 1914-
xRandall, Dudley.
After the Killing. Broadside.
Cities Burning. Broadside.
ed. For Malcolm: Poems on the Life & Death
of Malcolm X. Broadside.
Randall, Florence.
xRandall, Florence.
Getting a Job. Pitman Learning.
Randall, Florence E. *see* Randall, Florence Engel.
Randall, Florence Engel, 1917-
xRandall, Florence E.
The Almost Year. Schol Bk Serv.
Randall, Frank A. *see* Randall, Frank Alfred.
Randall, Frank Alfred, 1883-
xRandall, Frank A.
History of the Development of Building
Construction in Chicago. Arno.
Randall, Gerald.
xRandall, Gerald.
Church Furnishing & Decoration in England &
Wales. Holmes & Meier.
Randall, Henry S. *see* Randall, Henry Stephens.
Randall, Henry Stephens, 1811-1876
xRandall, Henry S.
Life of Thomas Jefferson. Arno.
xRandall, Henry Stephens.
The Life of Thomas Jefferson. Da Capo.
Randall, James, 1938-
xRandall, James.
Cities & Other Disasters. Broadside.
Randall, James G. *see* Randall, James Garfield.
Randall, James Garfield.
xRandall, James G.
Civil War & Reconstruction. Heath.
The Civil War & Reconstruction. Little.
Constitutional Problems Under Lincoln. Peter
Smith.
Randall, John E., 1924-
xRandall, John E.

Caribbean Reef Fishes. TFH Pubns.
Randall, John H. *see* Randall, John Herman.
Randall, John Herman, 1899-
xRandall, John H.
Aristotle. Columbia U Pr.
How Philosophy Uses Its Past. Columbia U Pr.
Nature & Historical Experience: Essays in
Naturalism & the Theory of History.
Columbia U Pr.
Plato: Dramatist of the Life of Reason.
Columbia U Pr.
Problem of Group Responsibility to Society.
Arno.
Readings in Philosophy. Har-Row.
Randall, John L.
xRandall, John L.
Parapsychology & the Nature of Life.
Har-Row.
Randall, Jon C., 1942-
xRandall, Jon C.
Indigoes. Broadside.
Randall, Lyman. *see* Randall, Lyman K.
Randall, Lyman K.
xRandall, Lyman.
Your Future As an Airline Steward-Stewardess.
Rosen Pr.
Randall, Margaret. *see* Randall, Margaret (Randall).
Randall, Margaret (Randall), 1936-
xRandall, Margaret.
Part of the Solution: Portrait of a
Revolutionary. New Directions.
Randall, Marta.
xRandall, Marta.
A City in the North. Warner Bks.
Journey. PB.
Randall, Monica.
xRandall, Monica.
The Mansions of Long Island's Gold Coast.
Hastings.
Randall, Richard S.
xRandall, Richard S.
Censorship of the Movies: The Social &
Political Control of a Mass Medium. U of
Wis Pr.
Randall, Robert W., 1925-
xRandall, Robert W.
Real Del Monte: A British Mining Venture in
Mexico. U of Tex Pr.
Randall, Rona, Pseud.
xRandall, Rona.
The Eagle at the Gate. Avon.
Eagle at the Gate. Coward.
The Eagle at the Gate. G K Hall.
The Mating Dance. Coward.
Randall-Maciver, David, 1873-1945
xRandall-MacIver, David.
Greek Cities in Italy & Sicily. Greenwood.
Randel, Don M. *see* Randel, Don Michael.
Randel, Don Michael.
xRandel, Don M.
Responsorial Psalm Tones for the Mozarabic
Office. Princeton U Pr.
Randel, William. *see* Randel, William Peirce.
Randel, William P. *see* Randel, William Peirce.
Randel, William Peirce, 1909-
xRandel, William.
Edward Eggleston. Coll & U Pr.
xRandel, William P.
Edward Eggleston. Peter Smith.
Randell, B. *see* Randell, Brian.
Randell, Brian, 1936-
xRandell, B.
ed. The Origins of Digital Computers: Selected
Papers. Springer-Verlag.
Randell, J. E. *see* Randell, John Edward.
Randell, John Edward, 1934-
xRandell, J. E.

ed. Ambient Energy & Building Design.
Longman.
Randhawa, Bikkar S.
xRandhawa, Bikkar S.
ed. Visual Learning, Thinking, &
Communication. Acad Pr.
Randle, Paul A.
xRandle, Paul A.
Financial Planning for the Professional. Utah St
U Pr.
Managing Your Money: An Investment Guide
for Professionals & Entrepreneurs. CBI Pub.
Managing Your Money: An Investment Guide
for Professionals & Entrepreneurs. Lifetime
Learn.
Randle, Robert F.
xRandle, Robert F.
Origins of Peace: A Study of Peacemaking &
the Structure of Peace Settlements. Free Pr.
Randles, Ronald H.
xRandles, Ronald H.
Introduction to the Theory of Nonparametric
Statistics. Wiley.
Randolph, D. A. *see* Randolph, Donald Allen.
Randolph, David J. *see* Randolph, David James.
Randolph, David James, 1934-
xRandolph, David J.
God's Party: A Guide to New Forms of
Worship. Abingdon.
Randolph, Donald Allen.
xRandolph, D. A.
Eugenio de Ochoa y el Romanticismo Espanol.
U of Cal Pr.
Randolph, Edmund, 1753-1813
xRandolph, Edmund.
History of Virginia. U Pr of Va.
Randolph, Francis L. *see* Randolph, Francis Lewis.
Randolph, Francis Lewis, 1951-1974
xRandolph, Francis L.
Studies for a Byron Bibliography. Sutter House.

Randolph, Judson. *see* Randolph, Judson G.
Randolph, Judson G.
xRandolph, Judson.
The Injured Child: Surgical Management. Year
Bk Med.
Randolph, Lillian.
xRandolph, Lillian L.
Third-Party Settlement of Disputes in Theory
and Practice. Oceana.
Randolph, Lillian L. *see* Randolph, Lillian.
Randolph, Paul H. *see* Randolph, Paul Herbert.
Randolph, Paul Herbert.
xRandolph, Paul H.
Applied Linear Optimization. Grid Pub.
Randolph, Polley A. *see* Randolph, Polley Ann.

Randolph, Polley Ann.

xRandolph, Polley A.
ed. Readings in Ecology. Mss Info.

Randolph, Robert M., 1934-
xRandolph, Robert M.
Planagement: Moving Concept into Reality.
Learning Concepts.
Randolph, Sarah N. *see* Randolph, Sarah Nicholas.
Randolph, Sarah Nicholas, 1839-1892
xRandolph, Sarah N.
The Domestic Life of Thomas Jefferson. U Pr
of Va.
Domestic Life of Thomas Jefferson. Ungar.
Randolph, Theron G.
xRandolph, Theron G.
Human Ecology & Susceptibility to the
Chemical Environment. C C Thomas.
Randolph, Vance, 1892-
xRandolph, Vance.

Ozark Folklore: A Bibliography. Res Ctr Lang
Semiotic.
ed. Who Blowed up the Church House? &
Other Ozark Folk Tales. Greenwood.
Rane, Bill, 1927-
xRane, Bill.
Talfulano. The Smith.
Rang, Mercer.
xRang, Mercer.
Anthology of Orthopaedics. Churchill.
Children's Fractures. Lippincott.
Ranganathan, D. *see* Ranganathan, Darshan.
Ranganathan, Darshan.
xRanganathan, D.
Challenging Problems in Organic Reaction
Mechanisms. Acad Pr.
xRanganathan, Darshan.
Further Challenging Problems in Organic
Reaction Mechanisms. Acad Pr.
Rangappa, K. S.
xRangappa, K. S.
Indian Dairy Products. Asia.
Rangarajan, L. N.
xRangarajan, L. N.
Commodity Conflict: The Political Economy of
International Commodity Negotiations.
Cornell U Pr.
Range, Dale G.
xRange, Dale G.
ed. Aspects of Early Childhood Education:
Theory to Research to Practice. Acad Pr.
Ranger, T. O. *see* Ranger, Terence O.
Ranger, Terence O.
xRanger, T. O.
African Voice in Southern Rhodesia.
Northwestern U Pr.
The African Voice in Southern Rhodesia: 1898
to 1930. Intl Pubns Serv.
ed. Aspects of Central African History.
Northwestern U Pr.
Dance & Society in Eastern Africa 1890-1970:
The Beni Ngoma. U of Cal Pr.
ed. The Historical Study of African Religion. U
of Cal Pr.
ed. Themes in the Christian History of Central
Africa. U of Cal Pr.
Ranis, Gustav.
xRanis, Gustav.
ed. Government & Economic Development.
Yale U Pr.
Ranis, P. *see* Ranis, Peter.
Ranis, Peter, 1935-
xRanis, P.
Five Latin American Nations: A Comparative
Political Study. Macmillan.
Rank, Hugh.
xRank, Hugh.
Edwin O'Connor. Twayne.
Rank, Otto, 1884-1939
xRank, Otto.
The Don Juan Legend. Princeton U Pr.
Truth & Reality. Norton.
Rank, Richard.
xRank, Richard.
Criminal Justice Systems of the
Latin-American Nations: A Bibliography of
the Primary & Secondary Literature.
Rothman.
Ranke, Kurt.
xRanke, Kurt.
Folktales of Germany. U of Chicago Pr.
Ranke, Leopold. *see* Ranke, Leopold Von.
Ranke, Leopold Von, 1795-1886
xRanke, Leopold.
History of the Latin & Teutonic Nations. R
West.
Rankin, Guy R.
xRankin, Guy R.

The Professional Handbook for Patrol &
Security Guards. Exposition.
Rankin, H. D.
xRankin, H. D.
Archilochus of Paros. Noyes.
Rankin, Hugh. *see* Rankin, Hugh F.
Rankin, Hugh F.
xRankin, Hugh.
The Golden Age of Piracy. Williamsburg.
xRankin, Hugh F.
North Carolina Continentals. U of NC Pr.
Pirates of Colonial North Carolina. NC
Archives.
Rankin, John, 1793-1886
xRankin, John.
Letters on American Slavery. Negro U Pr.
Rankin, Judy.
xRankin, Judy.
A Natural Way to Golf Power. Cornerstone.
A Natural Way to Golf Power. Har-Row.
Rankin, Karl L. *see* Rankin, Karl Lott.
Rankin, Karl Lott, 1898
xRankin, Karl L.
China Assignment. U of Wash Pr.
Rankin, Marie, 1896-
xRankin, Marie.
Children's Interests in Library Books of
Fiction. AMS Pr.
Rankin, Marni.
xRankin, Marni.
The Getaway Guide: Short Vacations in the
Pacific Northwest. Pacific Search.
Rankin, Mary B. *see* Rankin, Mary Backus.
Rankin, Mary Backus.
xRankin, Mary B.
Early Chinese Revolutionaries: Radical
Intellectuals in Shanghai & Chekiang,
1902-1911. Harvard U Pr.
Rankin, Molly K.
xRankin, Molly K.
I Heard Singing. Pacific Pr Pub Assn.
Rankin, T. E. *see* Rankin, Thomas Ernest.
Rankin, Thomas E. *see* Rankin, Thomas Ernest.
Rankin, Thomas Ernest, 1872-1953
xRankin, T. E.
American Writers of the Present Day. R West.
xRankin, Thomas E.
American Writers of the Present Day:
1890-1920. Folcroft.
Rankine, John.
xRankine, John.
Lunar Attack. Amereon Ltd.
Lunar Attack. PB.
Rankow, Robin M.
xRankow, Robin M.
Diseases of the Salivary Glands. Saunders.
Ranlett, John G.
xRanlett, John G.
Money & Banking: An Introduction to
Analysis & Policy. Wiley.
Ranly, Don M., 1938-
xRanly, Don M.
illus. Synopsis of Craniofacial Growth. ACC.
Ranney, Austin.
xRanney, Austin.
Curing the Mischiefs of Faction: Party Reform
in America. U of Cal Pr.
Democracy & the American Party System.
Greenwood.
Participation in American Presidential
Nominations - 1976. Am Enterprise.
Pathways to Parliament: Candidate Selection in
Britain. U of Wis Pr.
Ranney, David. *see* Ranney, David C.
Ranney, David C.
xRanney, David.
Planning & Politics in the Metropolis. Merrill.
Ranney, Edward.
xRanney, Edward.

Stonework of the Maya. U of NM Pr.
Ranney, M. *see* Ranney, Maurice William.
Ranney, M. W. *see* Ranney, Maurice William.
Ranney, M. William. *see* Ranney, Maurice William.
Ranney, Maurice William, 1934-
xRanney, M.
Crude Oil Drilling Fluids. Noyes.
xRanney, M. W.
Fertilizer Additives & Soil Conditioners.
Noyes.
Heat Exchange Fluids & Techniques. Noyes.
Offshore Oil Technology: Recent
Developments. Noyes.
xRanney, M. William.
ed. Functional Fluids for Industry,
Transportation & Aerospace. Noyes.
Rannie, David W. *see* Rannie, David Watson.
Rannie, David Watson, 1857-1923
xRannie, David W.
Daniel Defoe. Folcroft.
Wordsworth & His Circle. Haskell.
Wordsworth & His Circle. R West.
Ransel, David L.
xRansel, David L.
The Politics of Catherinian Russia: The Panin
Party. Yale U Pr.
Ransford, H. Edward.
xRansford, H. Edward.
Race & Class in American Society: Black,
Chicano, Anglo. Schenkman.
Ransom, C. J.
xRansom, C. J.
The Age of Velikovsky. Kronos Pr.
Ransom, David F.
xRansom, David F.
George Keller, Architect. Stowe-Day.
Ransom, Grayce A.
xRansom, Grayce A.
Preparing to Teach Reading. Little.
Ransom, Harry H. *see* Ransom, Harry Howe.
Ransom, Harry Howe, 1922-
xRansom, Harry H.
Intelligence Establishment. Harvard U Pr.
Ransom, Jay E. *see* Ransom, Jay Ellis.
Ransom, Jay Ellis, 1914-
xRansom, Jay E.
Gems & Minerals of America: A Guide to
Rock Collecting. Har-Row.
The Gold Hunter's Field Book: How & Where
to Prospect for Colors, Nuggets, & Mineral
Ores of Gold by Amateur Serious Followers
of Jason & the Golden Fleece. Har-Row.
Ransom, John C. *see* Ransom, John Crowe.
Ransom, John Crowe, 1888-1974
xRansom, John C.
The New Criticism. Greenwood.
World's Body. La State U Pr.
Ransom, Timothy W.
xRansom, Timothy W.
The Beach Troop of the Gombe. Bucknell U
Pr.
Ransom, Will, 1878-1955
xRansom, Will.
Private Presses & Their Books. AMS Pr.
Ransom, William R. *see* Ransom, William Richard.
Ransom, William Richard, 1876-
xRansom, William R.
Pastimes with String & Paper. Chris Mass.
Ransome, Arthur, 1884-1967
xRansome, Arthur.
Edgar Allan Poe: A Critical Study. Folcroft.
Edgar Allan Poe: A Critical Study. Haskell.
Oscar Wilde: A Critical Study. Folcroft.
Portraits & Speculations. Folcroft.
Ranson, Joseph.
xRanson, Joseph.
Songs of the Wexford Coast. Norwood Edns.
Ransone, Coleman B. *see* Ransone, Coleman Bernard.
Ransone, Coleman Bernard, 1920-
xRansone, Coleman B.

Office of Governor in the United States. Arno.
Rantz, Marilyn. *see* Rantz, Marilyn J.
Rantz, Marilyn J.
xRantz, Marilyn.
Lifting, Moving & Transferring Patients: A
Manual. Mosby.
xRantz, Marilyn J.
Lifting, Moving & Transferring Patients: A
Manual. Mosby.
Rantzen, M. J. *see* Rantzen, Mannas Joel.
Rantzen, Mannas Joel, 1900-
xRantzen, M. J.
Little Ship Astro-Navigation. Barrie & Jenkins.
Ranucci, Ernest R.
xRanucci, Ernest R.
Curiosities of the Cube. T Y Crowell.
Ranum, Orest. *see* Ranum, Orest A.
Ranum, Orest A.
xRanum, Orest.
Artisans of Glory: Writers & Historical
Thought in Seventeenth-Century France. U
of NC Pr.
ed. National Consciousness, History, &
Political Culture in Early-Modern Europe.
Johns Hopkins.
Ranwell, D. S.
xRanwell, D. S.
Ecology of Salt Marshes & Sand Dunes.
Methuen Inc.
Rao, Anthony.
xRao, Anthony.
illus. The Highlights Book of Nursery Rhymes.
Highlights.
Rao, C. N. *see* Rao, Chintamani Nagesa Ramachandra.
Rao, C. N. R. *see* Rao, Chintamani Nagesa
Ramachandra.
Rao, C. R. *see* Rao, Calyampudi Radhakrishna.
Rao, Calyampudi Radhakrishna.
xRao, C. R.
Advanced Statistical Methods in Biometric
Research. Hafner.
Generalized Inverse of Matrices & Its
Applications. Wiley.
Rao, Chintamani N. *see* Rao, Chintamani Nagesa
Ramachandra.
Rao, Chintamani Nagesa Ramachandra.
xRao, C. N.
Spectroscopy in Inorganic Chemistry. Acad Pr.
Ultra-Violet & Visible Spectroscopy: Chemical
Applications. Butterworths.
xRao, C. N. R.
ed. Solid State Chemistry. Dekker.
xRao, Chintamani N.
Chemical Applications of Infrared
Spectroscopy. Acad Pr.
Rao, Guthikonda V.
xRao, Guthikonda V.
Complex Digital Control Systems. Van Nos
Reinhold.
Rao, K. L. *see* Rao, K. L. Seshagiri.
Rao, K. L. Seshagiri, 1929-
xRao, K. L.
Mahatma Gandhi & Comparative Religion.
South Asia Bks.
xRao, K. L. Seshagiri.
Mahatma Gandhi & Comparative Religion.
Orient Bk Dist.
Rao, Potluri.
xRao, Potluri M.
Applied Econometrics. Wadsworth Pub.
Rao, Potluri M. *see* Rao, Potluri.
Rao, S. S.
xRao, S. S.
Optimization: Theory & Applications. Halsted
Pr.
Rao, Shikaripur R. *see* Rao, Shikaripur Ranganatha.
Rao, Shikaripur Ranganatha, 1922-
xRao, Shikaripur R.
Lothal & the Indus Civilization. Asia.
Rao, Y. Lakshmana. *see* Rao, Y. V. Lakshmana.

Rao, Y. V. Lakshmana.
xRao, Y. Lakshmana.
Communication & Development: A Study of
Two Indian Villages. U of Minn Pr.
Rapaport, David.
xRapaport, David.
Diagnostic Psychological Testing. Intl Univs Pr.
The History of the Concept of Association of
Ideas. Intl Univs Pr.
Structure of Psychoanalytic Theory: A
Systematizing Attempt. Intl Univs Pr.
Rapaport, Elliot.
xRapaport, Elliot.
Current Controversies in Cardiovascular
Disease. Saunders.
Rapaport, Felix T.
xRapaport, Felix T.
ed. Human Transplantation. Grune.
Rapaport, Howard G.
xRapaport, Howard G.
Complete Allergy Guide. S&S.
Rapee, Erno.
xRapee, Erno.
Encyclopedia of Music for Pictures. Arno.
Raper, Arthur F. *see* Raper, Arthur Franklin.
Raper, Arthur Franklin, 1899-
xRaper, Arthur F.
Preface to Peasantry: A Tale of Two Black Belt
Counties. Arno.
Preface to Peasantry: A Tale of Two Black Belt
Counties. Atheneum.
Raph, Theodore.
xRaph, Theodore.
The Songs We Sang: A Treasury of American
Popular Music. A S Barnes.
Raphael, Alice. *see* Raphael, Alice Pearl.
Raphael, Alice Pearl, 1887-
xRaphael, Alice.
Goethe & the Philosophers' Stone: Symbolical
Patterns in the Parable & the Second Part of
Faust. Garrett-Helix.
Raphael, Bertram.
xRaphael, Bertram.
The Thinking Computer: Mind Inside Matter.
W H Freeman.
Raphael, Chaim.
xRaphael, Chaim.
Encounters with the Jewish People. Behrman.
Raphael, David D. *see* Raphael, David Daiches.
Raphael, David Daiches.
xRaphael, David D.
Paradox of Tragedy. Arno.
Raphael, Elaine.
xRaphael, Elaine.
jt. auth. Donkey & Carlo. Har-Row.
Raphael, Frederic, 1931-
xRaphael, Frederic.
The Glittering Prizes. Penguin.
Glittering Prizes. St Martin.
Raphael, Jesse S. *see* Raphael, Jesse Scharff.
Raphael, Jesse Scharff, 1894-
xRaphael, Jesse S.
Governmental Regulation of Business. Free Pr.
Raphael, Lois A. *see* Raphael, Lois Alward (Childs).
Raphael, Lois Alward (Childs), 1900-
xRaphael, Lois A.
Cape-To-Cairo Dream: A Study in British
Imperialism. Octagon.
Raphael, Marc L. *see* Raphael, Marc Lee.
Raphael, Marc Lee.
xRaphael, Marc L.
Understanding American Jewish Philanthropy.
Ktav.
Raphael, Rick.
xRaphael, Rick.
Code Three. S&S.
Raphael, Robert, 1927-
xRaphael, Robert.
Richard Wagner. Twayne.
Rapisardi, Carmelino J. *see* Rapisardi, Carmelino John.

Rapisardi, Carmelino John, 1925-
xRapisardi, Carmelino J.
Then, Now, & Forever. Brasch & Brasch.
Rapoport, A. see Rapoport, Amnon.
Rapoport, Amnon.
xRapoport, A.
Coalition Formation by Sophisticated Players.
Springer-Verlag.
Rapoport, Amos.
xRapoport, Amos.
House Form & Culture. P-H.
Human Aspects of Urban Form: Towards a
Man-Environment Approach to Urban Form
& Design. Pergamon.
Rapoport, Anatol, 1911-
xRapoport, Anatol.
Fights, Games, & Debates. U of Mich Pr.
Two-Person Game Theory: The Essential Ideas.
U of Mich Pr.
Two-Person Game Theory: The Essential Ideas.
U of Mich Pr.
Rapoport, I. M. see Rapoport, Ilia Markovich.
Rapoport, Ilia Markovich.
xRapoport, I. M.
Dynamics of Elastic Containers Partially Filled
with Liquid. Springer-Verlag.
Rapoport, Paul.
xRapoport, Paul.
Opus Est: Six Composers from Northern
Europe. Taplinger.

Rapoport, Rhona.

xRapoport, Rhona.
Leisure & the Family Life Cycle. Routledge &
Kegan.
jt. ed. Working Couples. Har-Row.

Rapp, Doris J.

xRapp, Doris J.
Allergies & Your Child. HR&W.
Allergies & Your Family. Sterling.

Rapp, Kenneth W.

xRapp, Kenneth W.
West Point: Whistler in Cadet Gray, & Other
Stories About the United States Military
Academy. North River.

Rapp, Richard T.
xRapp, Richard T.
Industry & Economic Decline in Seventeenth
Century Venice. Harvard U Pr.
Rapp, William G.
xRapp, William G.
Construction of Structural Steel Building
Frames. Wiley.
Rappaport, Alfred.
xRappaport, Alfred.
Framework for Financial Reporting by
Diversified Companies. Natl Assn Accts.
Information for Decision-Making: Quantitative
& Behavioral Dimensions. P-H.
Rappaport, Armin.
xRappaport, Armin.
The British Press & Wilsonian Neutrality. Peter
Smith.
ed. The Monroe Doctrine. Krieger.
Rappaport, Ernest A.
xRappaport, Ernest A.
Anti-Judaism: A Psychohistory. Perspective
Chicago.
Rappaport, Julian.
xRappaport, Julian.

Innovations in Helping Chronic Patients:
College Students in a Mental Institution.
Acad Pr.
Rappaport, Roy A.
xRappaport, Roy A.
Ecology, Meaning, & Religion. North Atlantic.
Rappaport, Sheldon R.
xRappaport, Sheldon R.
Public Education for Children with Brain
Dysfunction. Syracuse U Pr.
Rappeport, Rhoda.
xRappeport, Rhoda.
Fred Shero: A Kaleidoscopic View of the
Philadelphia Flyers' Coach. St Martin.
Rappoport, Angelo S. see Rappoport, Angelo Solomon.
Rappoport, Angelo Solomon, 1871-1950
xRappoport, Angelo S.
Mediaeval Legends of Christ. Folcroft.
Rappoport, Ken.
xRappoport, Ken.
The Syracuse Football Story. Strode.
The Trojans: A Story of Southern California
Football. Strode.
Rappoport, Leon.
xRappoport, Leon.
Personality Development: The Chronology of
Experience. Scott F.
Rapport, Samuel. see Rapport, Samuel Berder.

Rapport, Samuel Berder.

xRapport, Samuel.
ed. Anthropology. NYU Pr.
ed. Archaeology. NYU Pr.
ed. Astronomy. NYU Pr.
ed. Engineering. NYU Pr.
ed. Mathematics. NYU Pr.

Rapson, Richard L.
xRapson, Richard L.
ed. Cult of Youth in Middle-Class America.
Heath.
The Pursuit of Meaning: America - 1600-2000.
U Pr of Amer.

Raring, Richard H.
xRaring, Richard H.
Crib Death: Scourge of Infants Shame of
Society. Exposition.
Rasbach, Roger.
xRasbach, Roger.
The Provident Planner: A Blueprint for Homes,
Communities & Lifestyles. Walker & Co.
Rasch, Heinz.
xRasch, Heinz.
Some Roots of Modern Architecture.
Transatlantic.
Rasch, Philip J.
xRasch, Philip J.
Weight Training. Wm C Brown.
Raschke, Carl A.
xRaschke, Carl A.
The Alchemy of the Word: Language & the
End of Theology. Scholars Pr Ca.
The Interruption of Eternity: Modern
Gnosticism & the Origins of the New
Religious Consciousness. Nelson-Hall.
Religion & the Human Image. P-H.
Rascoe, Burton.
xRascoe, Burton.
H. L. Mencken. Folcroft.
Theodore Dreiser. Folcroft.
Theodore Dreiser. Haskell.
Rash, J. E. see Rash, John E.
Rash, J. Keogh.
xRash, J. Keogh.

Health Education Curriculum: A Guide for
Curriculum Development in Health
Education. Wiley.
Rash, John E.
xRash, J. E.
Freeze-Fracture: Methods, Artifacts, &
Interpretations. Raven.
Rashdall, Hastings.
xRashdall, Hastings.
Ideas & Ideals. Arno.
Rasiowa, Helen. see Rasiowa, Helena.
Rasiowa, Helena.
xRasiowa, Helen.
Introduction to Modern Mathematics. Elsevier.
Raskin, Allen.
xRaskin, Allen.
ed. Psychiatric Symptoms & Cognitive Loss in
the Elderly: Evaluation & Assessment
Technique. Halsted Pr.
Raskin, Barbara.
xRaskin, Barbara.
Out of Order. S&S.
Raskin, Ellen.
xRaskin, Ellen.
illus. And It Rained. Atheneum.
illus. Figgs & Phantoms. Dutton.
illus. Franklin Stein. Atheneum.
illus. Franklin Stein. Atheneum.
Ghost in a Four-Room Apartment. Atheneum.
illus. Moose, Goose & Little Nobody. Schol Bk
Serv.
Nothing Ever Happens on My Block.
Atheneum.
illus. Nothing Ever Happens on My Block.
Atheneum.
Nothing Ever Happens on My Block. Schol Bk
Serv.
illus. Spectacles. Atheneum.
illus. Spectacles. Atheneum.
Tattooed Potato & Other Clues. Dutton.
Twenty-Two, Twenty-Three. Atheneum.
Who, Said Sue, Said Whoo?. Atheneum.
Who, Said Sue, Said Whoo?. Atheneum.
Raskin, Eugene.
xRaskin, Eugene.
Architecturally Speaking. Bloch.
Architecture & People. P-H.
Raskin, Joseph.
xRaskin, Joseph.
Of Whales & Wolves & Other Adventures in
Early America. Lothrop.
Spies & Traitors: Tales of the Revolutionary &
Civil Wars. Lothrop.
Tales Our Settlers Told. Lothrop.
Raskin, Michael M., 1942-
xRaskin, Michael M.
Comparative Abdominal & Pelvic Anatomy by
Computed Tomography & Ultrasound. CRC
Pr.
Raskin, Neil H.
xRaskin, Neil H.
Headache. Saunders.
Rasmussen, Henry, 1939-
xRasmussen, Henry.
Classic Cars. Times Bks.
European Sports Cars of the Fifties. Picturama.
Rasmussen, Jorgen S. see Rasmussen, Jorgen Scott.
Rasmussen, Jorgen Scott.
xRasmussen, Jorgen S.
Retrenchment & Revival: A Study of the
Contemporary British Liberal Party. U of
Ariz Pr.
Rasmussen, Knud J. see Rasmussen, Knud Johan Victor.
Rasmussen, Knud Johan Victor, 1879-1933
xRasmussen, Knud J.

Intellectual Culture of the Copper Eskimos.
AMS Pr.
Intellectual Culture of the Iglulik Eskimos.
AMS Pr.
The People of the Polar North: A Record....
AMS Pr.
Rasmussen, Louis J.
xRasmussen, Louis J.
San Francisco Ship Passenger Lists. Genealog
Pub.
Rasmussen, R. Kent.
xRasmussen, R. Kent.
Historical Dictionary of Rhodesia-Zimbabwe.
Scarecrow.
Rasmussen, Steen E. see Rasmussen, Steen Eiler.
Rasmussen, Steen Eiler, 1898-
xRasmussen, Steen E.
Experiencing Architecture. MIT Pr.
Rasmussen, Theodore.
xRasmussen, Theodore.
ed. Functional Neurosurgery. Raven.
Rasool, S. I.
xRasool, S. I.
Chemistry of the Lower Atmosphere. Plenum
Pub.
Rasor, Eugene L., 1936-
xRasor, Eugene L.
Reform in the Royal Navy: A Social History of
the Lower Deck, 1850-80. Shoe String.
Raspail, Jean.
xRaspail, Jean.
The Camp of the Saints. Ace Bks.
The Camp of the Saints. Scribner.
Rasputin, Valentin. see Rasputin, Valentin Grigorevich.
Rasputin, Valentin Grigorevich.
xRasputin, Valentin.
Farewell to Matyora, A Novel. Macmillan.
Live & Remember. Macmillan.
Rassi, J. see Rassi, Judith A.
Rassi, Judith A., 1939-
xRassi, J.
Supervision in Audiology. Univ Park.
Rassias, John.
xRassias, John A.
Le Francais: Depart-Arrivee. Har-Row.
Rassias, John A. see Rassias, John.
Rassieur, Charles L., 1938-
xRassieur, Charles L.
The Problem Clergymen Don't Talk About.
Westminster.
Rassinier, Paul.
xRassinier, Paul.
The Drama of the European Jews.
Steppingstones.
Rassner, Gernot.
xRassner, Gernot.
Atlas of Dermatology. Urban & S.
Rast, Walter E., 1930-
xRast, Walter E.
Joshua, Judges, Samuel, Kings. Fortress.
Raswan, Carl R. see Raswan, Carl Reinhard.
Raswan, Carl Reinhard.
xRaswan, Carl R.
Drinkers of the Wind. Darby Bks.
Ratch, Jerry.
xRatch, Jerry.
Puppet X. Shameless Hussy.
Ratchford, B. U. see Ratchford, Benjamin Ulysses.
Ratchford, Benjamin U. see Ratchford, Benjamin Ulysses.
Ratchford, Benjamin Ulysses, 1902-
xRatchford, B. U.
American State Debts. AMS Pr.
xRatchford, Benjamin U.
Public Expenditures in Australia. Duke.
Ratcliff, Carter.
xRatcliff, Carter.
Fever Coast. Kulchur Foun.
Ratcliff, John D. see Ratcliff, John Drury.
Ratcliff, John Drury, 1903-
xRatcliff, John D.

Modern Miracle Men. Arno.
Ratcliff, Richard. see Ratcliff, Richard Updegraff.
Ratcliff, Richard Updegraff, 1906-
xRatcliff, Richard.
Real Estate Analysis. McGraw.
Ratcliffe, Robert H., 1918-
xRatcliffe, Robert H.
ed. Great Cases of the Supreme Court. HM.
Ratermanis, J. B.
xRatermanis, J. B.
Comic Style of Beaumarchais. Greenwood.
Rath, Eric, 1911-
xRath, Eric.
Container Systems. Wiley.
Rath, Frederick L.
xRath, Frederick L.
A Guide to Historic Preservation, Historical
Agencies, & Museum Practices: A Selective
Bibliography. Fenimore Bk.
Rath, Jo Anne, 1947-
xRath, Jo Anne.
Antique & Unusual Thimbles. A S Barnes.
Rath, R. John. see Rath, Reuben John.
Rath, Reuben J. see Rath, Reuben John.
Rath, Reuben John, 1910-
xRath, R. John.
Provisional Austrian Regime in
Lombardy-Venetia, 1814-1815. U of Tex Pr.
xRath, Reuben J.
Fall of the Napoleonic Kingdom of Italy 1814.
Octagon.
Rathbone, Belinda.
xRathbone, Belinda.
ed. One of a Kind: Recent Polaroid Color
Photography. Godine.
Rathbone, Josephine L. see Rathbone, Josephine
Langworthy.
Rathbone, Josephine Langworthy, 1899-
xRathbone, Josephine L.
Relaxation. Lea & Febiger.
Rathbone, Julian.
xRathbone, Julian.
Carnival. St Martin.
The Euro-Killers. Pantheon.
Rathborne, Isabel E. see Rathborne, Isabel Elisabeth.
Rathborne, Isabel Elisabeth, 1901-
xRathborne, Isabel E.
Meaning of Spenser's Fairyland. Russell.
Rather, Dan.
xRather, Dan.
The Camera Never Blinks: Adventures of a TV
Journalist. Ballantine.
The Camera Never Blinks: Adventures of a TV
Journalist. Morrow.
The Palace Guard. Warner Bks.
Rather, L. J.
xRather, L. J.
The Dream of Self-Destruction: Wagner's Ring
& the Modern World. La State U Pr.
The Genesis of Cancer: A Study in the History
of Ideas. Johns Hopkins.
Rather, Lois, 1905-
xRather, Lois.
Bufano & the U. S. A.. Rather Pr.
J. Ross Browne, Adventurer. Rather Pr.
Rathi, Manohar.
xRathi, Manohar.
ed. Perinatal Medicine: Clinical & Biochemical
Aspects. Hemisphere Pub.
Rathmell, J. see Rathmell, John M.
Rathmell, John M.
xRathmell, J.
Marketing in the Service Sector. Winthrop.
Raths, James. see Raths, James D.
Raths, James D.
xRaths, James.
Studying Teaching. P-H.
Raths, Louis. see Raths, Louis Edward.
Raths, Louis E. see Raths, Louis Edward.

Raths, Louis Edward.
xRaths, Louis.
Teaching for Learning. Merrill.
xRaths, Louis E.
Meeting the Needs of Children: Creating Trust
& Security. Merrill.
Rathus, Spencer A.
xRathus, Spencer A.
Adjustment & Growth: The Challenges of Life.
HR&W.
Ratigan, William.
xRatigan, William.
Great Lakes Shipwrecks & Survivals.
Eerdmans.
Rational Dress Association.
xRational Dress Association.
Exhibition Catalogue, 1883 & Gazette,
1888-1889. Garland Pub.
Ratkevich, Ron. see Ratkevich, Ronald Paul.
Ratkevich, Ronald P. see Ratkevich, Ronald Paul.
Ratkevich, Ronald Paul.
xRatkevich, Ron.
Field Guide to New Mexico Fossils. Dinograph
SW.
xRatkevich, Ronald P.
Dinosaurs of the Southwest. U of NM Pr.
Ratliff, Richard C.
xRatliff, Richard C.
American Government. Cliffs.
Constitutional Rights of College Students: A
Study in Case Law. Scarecrow.
Ratner, A. M. see Ratner, Anatolii Markovich.
Ratner, Anatolii Markovich.
xRatner, A. M.
Spectral, Spatial, & Temporal Properties of
Lasers. Plenum Pub
Ratner, Leonard G.
xRatner, Leonard G.
Music: The Listener's Art. McGraw.
Ratner, Moses, 1895-
xRatner, Moses.
Theory & Criticism of the Novel in France
from L'Astree to 1750. Russell.
Ratner, Rochelle.
xRatner, Rochelle.
Combing the Waves. Hanging Loose.
Ratner, Ronnie S. see Ratner, Ronnie Steinberg.
Ratner, Ronnie Steinberg.
xRatner, Ronnie S.
ed. Equal Employment Policy for Women:
Strategies for Implementation in the United
States, Canada & Western Europe. Temple U
Pr.
Ratner, Sidney.
xRatner, Sidney.
The Evolution of the American Economy:
Growth, Welfare & Decision Making. Basic.
Taxation & Democracy in America. Octagon.
Ratterree, Dee.
xRatterree, Dee.
Compiled by The Great International Quiz
Book: Neatness Counts. Lippincott.
Ratti, J. S.
xRatti, J. S.
College Algebra. Macmillan.
Ratti, O. see Ratti, Oscar.
Ratti, Oscar.
xRatti, O.
Secrets of the Samurai: A Survey of the
Martial Arts of Feudal Japan. C E Tuttle.
Rattner, Abraham.
xRattner, Abraham.
Abraham Rattner. Abrams.
Rattray, Jeannette (Edwards), 1893-
xRattray, Jeannette E.
The Perils of the Port of New York: Maritime
Disasters from Sandy Hook to Execution
Rocks. Dodd.
Rattray, Jeannette E. see Rattray, Jeannette (Edwards).
Rattray, R. S. see Rattray, Robert Sutherland.

Rattray, Robert S. see Rattray, Robert Sutherland.
Rattray, Robert Sutherland, 1881-1938
  xRattray, R. S.
    Ashanti. Oxford U Pr.
  xRattray, Robert S.
    Ashanti. Negro U Pr.
    Religion & Art in Ashanti. AMS Pr.
    Religion & Art in Ashanti. Oxford U Pr.
Ratzinger, Joseph.
  xRatzinger, Joseph.
    Faith & the Future. Franciscan Herald.
    Introduction to Christianity. Seabury.
    Living with the Church. Franciscan Herald.
Ratzlaff, John T.
  xRatzlaff, John T.
    Dr. Nikola Tesla Bibliography. Ragusan Pr.
Rau, John. see Rau, John G.
Rau, John G.
  xRau, John.
    Optimization & Probability in Systems
      Engineering (70). Van Nos Reinhold.
  xRau, John G.
    Environmental Impact Analysis Handbook.
      McGraw.
Rau, Joseph L.
  xRau, Joseph L.
    Respiratory Therapy Pharmacology. Year Bk
      Med.
Rau, Margaret.
  xRau, Margaret.
    The Giant Panda at Home. Knopf.
    The Gray Kangaroo at Home. Knopf.
    Our World: The People's Republic of China.
      Messner.
    The People of New China. Messner.
    The Snow Monkey at Home. Knopf.
Rau, Sandy.
  xRau, Sandy.
    How Not to Raise Cain. Victor Bks.
Raubinger, Frederick M.
  xRaubinger, Frederick M.
    Development of Secondary Education.
      Macmillan.
    Leadership in the Secondary School. Merrill.
Rauch, Basil, 1908-
  xRauch, Basil.
    American Interest in Cuba, 1848-1855.
      Octagon.
    The History of the New Deal, 1933-1938.
      Octagon.
Rauch, David. see Rauch, David B.
Rauch, David B.
  xRauch, David.
    Priorities in Adult Education. Adult Ed.
    Priorities in Adult Education. Macmillan.
Rauch, H. W.
  xRauch, H. W.
    Ceramic Fibers & Fibrous Composite Materials.
      Acad Pr.
Rauch, Hans-Georg, 1939-
  xRauch, Hans-Georg.
    The Lines Are Coming: A Book About
      Drawing. Scribner.
Rauch, Irmengard.
  xRauch, Irmengard.
    ed. Approaches in Linguistic Methodology. U
      of Wis Pr.
Raucher, Herman.
  xRaucher, Herman.
    There Should Have Been Castles. Delacorte.
Raudkivi, A. J.
  xRaudkivi, A. J.
    Advanced Fluid Mechanics: An Introduction.
      Halsted Pr.
    Analysis of Groundwater Flow. Halsted Pr.
    Loose Boundary Hydraulics. Pergamon.
Raudsepp, Eugene.
  xRaudsepp, Eugene.
    Creative Growth Games. HarBraceJ.
Rausch, D. O. see Rausch, Donald O.

Rausch, Donald O.
  xRausch, D. O.
    ed. Lead-Zinc Update. Soc Mining Eng.
Rausch, Edward N.
  xRausch, Edward N.
    Financial Management for Small Business. Am
      Mgmt.
Rausch, Erwin, 1923-
  xRausch, Erwin.
    Balancing Needs of People & Organizations:
      The Linking Elements Concept. BNA.
Rauschenbach, Hans S.
  xRauschenbach, Hans S.
    Solar Cell Array Design Handbook: The
      Principles & Technology of Photovoltaic
      Energy Conversion. Van Nos Reinhold.
Rauschenberg, Roy A. see Rauschenberg, Roy Anthony.
Rauschenberg, Roy Anthony, 1929-
  xRauschenberg, Roy A.
    Daniel Carl Solander, Naturalist on the
      "Endeavour". Am Philos.
Rauschenbusch, Walter, 1861-1918
  xRauschenbusch, Walter.
    Theology for the Social Gospel. Abingdon.
Rauschning, Hermann, 1887-
  xRauschning, Hermann.
    Men of Chaos. Arno.
    The Revolution of Nihilism: Warning to the
      West. AMS Pr.
    The Revolution of Nihilism: Warning to the
      West. Arno.
Raush, Charlotte L. see Raush, Harold L.
Raush, Harold L.
  xRaush, Charlotte L.
    jt. auth. Halfway House Movement: A Search
      for Sanity. Irvington.
  xRaush, Harold L.
    Halfway House Movement: A Search for
      Sanity. Irvington.
Raushenbush, Esther.
  xRaushenbush, Esther.
    The Student & His Studies. Columbia U Pr.
Raushenbush, Winifred.
  xRaushenbush, Winifred.
    Robert E. Park: Biography of a Sociologist.
      Duke.
Rausser, Gordon. see Rausser, Gordon C.
Rausser, Gordon C.
  xRausser, Gordon.
    Dynamic Agricultural Systems: Economic,
      Prediction & Control. Elsevier.
Raven, Anton A. see Raven, Anton Adolph.
Raven, Anton Adolph.
  xRaven, Anton A.
    Hamlet Bibliography & Reference Guide,
      1877-1935. Russell.
Raven, Charles Earle, 1885-1964
  xRaven, Charles Earle.
    Apollinarianism: An Essay on the Christology
      of the Early Church. AMS Pr.
Raven, Francis. see Raven, Francis Harvey.
Raven, Francis H. see Raven, Francis Harvey.
Raven, Francis Harvey, 1928-
  xRaven, Francis.
    Automatic Control Engineering. McGraw.
  xRaven, Francis H.
    Mathematics of Engineering Systems. McGraw.
Raven, Jon.
  xRaven, Jon.
    The Folklore of Staffordshire. Rowman.
Raven, Peter H.
  xRaven, Peter H.
    Native Shrubs of Southern California. U of Cal
      Pr.
    Origin & Relationships of the California Flora.
      U of Cal Pr.
Raven, Ronald W. see Raven, Ronald William.
Raven, Ronald William.
  xRaven, Ronald W.

    ed. Outlook on Cancer. Plenum Pub.
    ed. Principles of Surgical Oncology. Plenum
      Pub.
Raven, Simon.
  xRaven, Simon.
    Brother Cain. S&S.
    Decline of the Gentleman. S&S.
    Doctors Wear Scarlet. S&S.
    Feathers of Death. S&S.
    The Survivors. Intl Pubns Serv.
Ravenal, Earl C.
  xRavenal, Earl C.
    ed. Peace with China?: U. S. Decisions for
      Asia. Liveright.
Ravenel, Daniel, 1789-1873
  xRavenel, Daniel.
    Liste Des Francois et Suisses: From an Old
      Manuscript List of French & Swiss
      Protestants Settled in Charleston. Genealog
      Pub.
Ravenel, Henry E. see Ravenel, Henry Edmund.
Ravenel, Henry Edmund, 1856-1939
  xRavenel, Henry E.
    Ravenel Records. Larlin Corp.
Ravenette, A. T.
  xRavenette, A. T.
    Dimensions of Reading Difficulties. Pergamon.
Ravenhill, Leonard.
  xRavenhill, Leonard.
    America Is Too Young to Die. Bethany Fell.
Ravenscroft, Donald R.
  xRavenscroft, Donald R.
    Taxation & Foreign Currency: The Income Tax
      Consequences of Foreign Exchange
      Transactions & Exchange Rate Fluctuations.
      Harvard Law Intl Tax.
Raverat, Gwen. see Raverat, Gwendolen Mary Darwin.
Raverat, Gwendolen Mary Darwin, 1885-1957
  xRaverat, Gwen.
    Period Piece. Merrimack Bk Serv.
    Period Piece. Norton.
Ravich, M. G. see Ravich, Mikhail Grigorevich.
Ravich, Mikhail Grigorevich.
  xRavich, M. G.
    Crystalline Basement of the Antarctic Platform.
      Halsted Pr.
Ravin, A. see Ravin, Abe.
Ravin, Abe, 1908-
  xRavin, A.
    Auscultation of the Heart. Year Bk Med.
Ravin, Arnold W. see Ravin, Arnold Warren.
Ravin, Arnold Warren.
  xRavin, Arnold W.
    Evolution of Genetics. Acad Pr.
Ravindranath, B.
  xRavindranath, B.
    Power System Protection & Switchgear.
      Halsted Pr.
Ravitch, Mark M., 1910-
  xRavitch, Mark M.
    Congenital Deformities of the Chest Wall &
      Their Operative Correction. Saunders.
    Pediatric Surgery. Year Bk Med.
    Repair of Hernias. Year Bk Med.
Ravitch, Norman.
  xRavitch, Norman.
    Sword & Mitre: Government & Episcopate in
      France & England in the Age of Aristocracy.
      Mouton.
Ravitz, Abe C.
  xRavitz, Abe C.
    Alfred Henry Lewis. Boise St Univ.
    David Graham Phillips. Coll & U Pr.
    David Graham Phillips. Irvington.
Raw, Barbara C. see Raw, Barbara Catherine.
Raw, Barbara Catherine.
  xRaw, Barbara C.

The Art & Background of Old English Poetry.
St Martin.
Rawding, F. W.
xRawding, F. W.
The Buddha. Cambridge U Pr.
Rawick, George P., 1929-
xRawick, George P.
ed. The American Slave: A Composite
Autobiography, Supplement Series 1.
Greenwood.
Rawidowicz, Simon, 1897-1957
xRawidowicz, Simon.
Studies in Jewish Thought. Jewish Pubn.
Rawles, William A., 1863-1936
xRawles, William A.
Centralizing Tendencies in the Administration
of Indiana. AMS Pr.
Rawley, James A.
xRawley, James A.
Edwin D. Morgan, 1811-1833: Merchant in
Politics. AMS Pr.
ed. Lincoln & Civil War Politics. Krieger.
Lincoln & Civil War Politics. Peter Smith.
Race & Politics: Bleeding Kansas & the
Coming of the Civil War. Lippincott.
Race & Politics: Bleeding Kansas & the
Coming of the Civil War. U of Nebr Pr.
Turning Points of the Civil War. U of Nebr Pr.
Rawlings, Edna I.
xRawlings, Edna I.
Psychotherapy for Women: Treatment Toward
Equality. C C Thomas.
Rawlings, Ronald.
xRawlings, Ronald.
Antique-Hunter's Handbook. David & Charles.
Rawlins, Jack P.
xRawlins, Jack P.
Thackeray's Novels: A Fiction That Is True. U
of Cal Pr.
Rawlins, N. Omri. *see* Rawlins, Nolan Omri.
Rawlins, Nolan Omri, 1938-
xRawlins, N. Omri.
Introduction to Agribusiness. P-H.
Rawlins, Ray, 1917-
xRawlins, Ray.
The Stein & Day Book of World Autographs.
Stein & Day.
Rawlins, Winifred.
xRawlins, Winifred.
Fire Within. Golden Quill.
Rawlinson, Alfred E. *see* Rawlinson, Alfred Edward
John.
Rawlinson, Alfred Edward John, Bp. of Derby, 1884-
xRawlinson, Alfred E.
Christ in the Gospels. Greenwood.
Rawlinson, D. H. *see* Rawlinson, David H.
Rawlinson, David H.
xRawlinson, D. H.
Practice of Criticism. Cambridge U Pr.
Rawlinson, John L.
xRawlinson, John L.
China's Struggle for Naval Development,
1839-1895. Harvard U Pr.
Rawls, John, 1921-
xRawls, John.
Theory of Justice. Harvard U Pr.
Rawls, Wendall. *see* Rawls, Wendell.
Rawls, Wendell.
xRawls, Wendall.
Cold Storage. S&S.
Rawls, Wilson.
xRawls, Wilson.
Summer of the Monkeys. Doubleday.
Rawnsley, H. *see* Rawnsley, Hardwicke Drummond.
Rawnsley, Hardwicke Drummond, 1851-1920
xRawnsley, H.
Memories of the Tennysons. Haskell.
Rawski, Evelyn S. *see* Rawski, Evelyn Sakakida.
Rawski, Evelyn Sakakida.
xRawski, Evelyn S.

Education & Popular Literacy in Ch'ing China.
U of Mich Pr.
Rawski, Thomas G., 1943-
xRawski, Thomas G.
China's Transition to Industrialism: Producer
Goods & Economic Development in the
Twentieth Century. U of Mich Pr.
Economic Growth & Employment in China.
Oxford U Pr.
Rawson, Beryl.
xRawson, Beryl.
Politics of Friendship: Pompey & Cicero. Intl
Schol Bk Serv.
Rawson, C. J. *see* Rawson, Claude Julien.
Rawson, Claude Julien.
xRawson, C. J.
Gulliver & the Gentle Reader: Studies in Swift
& Our Time. Routledge & Kegan.
Rawson, Clayton, 1906-
xRawson, Clayton.
Death from a Top Hat. Gregg.
Rawson, Donald. *see* Rawson, Donald William.
Rawson, Donald William.
xRawson, Donald.
Unions & Unionists in Australia. Allen Unwin.
Rawson, Geoffrey.
xRawson, Geoffrey.
Pandora's Last Voyage. HarBraceJ.
Rawson, Marion (Nicholl), 1878-1956
xRawson, Marion N.
Little Old Mills. Johnson Repr.
Rawson, Marion N. *see* Rawson, Marion (Nicholl).
Rawson, Robert R. *see* Rawson, Robert Rees.
Rawson, Robert Rees.
xRawson, Robert R.
Monsoon Lands of Asia. Beresford Bk Serv.
Rawson, Ruth, 1913-
xRawson, Ruth.
Acting. Rosen Pr.
Ray. *see* Ray, Mary Frey.
Ray, Ajit K. *see* Ray, Ajit Kumar.
Ray, Ajit Kumar.
xRay, Ajit K.
The Religious Ideas of Rammohun Roy: A
Survey of His Writings on Religion
Particularly in Persian, Sanskrit, & Bengali.
South Asia Bks.
Ray, Ann, 1937-
xRay, Ann.
Journey into Light. Univ of Trees.
Ray, Benjamin C., 1940-
xRay, Benjamin C.
African Religions: Symbol, Ritual &
Community. P-H.
Ray, Charles D. *see* Ray, Charles Dean.
Ray, Charles Dean.
xRay, Charles D.
ed. Medical Engineering. Year Bk Med.
Ray, Colin. *see* Ray, Colin H.
Ray, Colin H.
xRay, Colin.
ed. Library Service to Children: An
International Survey. K G Saur.
Ray, Cyril, 1908-
xRay, Cyril.
Cognac. Stein & Day.
The Complete Book of Spirits & Liqueurs.
Macmillan.
Cyril Ray's Book of Wine. Morrow.
Ray on Wine. Biblio Dist.
Ray, Delmas D.
xRay, Delmas D.
Accounting & Business Fluctuations. U Presses
Fla.
Ray, Dorothy J. *see* Ray, Dorothy Jean.
Ray, Dorothy Jean.
xRay, Dorothy J.

Aleut & Eskimo Art: Tradition & Innovation in
South Alaska. U of Wash Pr.
Artists of the Tundra & the Sea. U of Wash Pr.
Ray, George. *see* Ray, George E.
Ray, George E.
xRay, George.
Incorporating the Professional Practice. P-H.
xRay, George E.
Financial Incentives for Executives:
Wealth-Building Programs Techniques. P-H.
Ray, Gordon N. *see* Ray, Gordon Norton.
Ray, Gordon Norton, 1915-
xRay, Gordon N.
Buried Life: A Study of the Relation Between
Thackeray's Fiction & His Personal History.
Folcroft.
H. G. Wells & Rebecca West. Yale U Pr.
The Illustrator & the Book in England,
1790-1914. Oxford U Pr.
Thackeray. Octagon.
Ray, Isaac, 1807-1881
xRay, Isaac.
Contributions to Mental Pathology (1873)..
Schol Facsimiles.
Ray, J. D.
xRay, J. D.
The Archive of Hor. Intl Schol Bk Serv.
Ray, J. Edgar. *see* Ray, Jesse Edgar.
Ray, James L. *see* Ray, James Lee.
Ray, James Lee.
xRay, James L.
Global Politics. HM.
Ray, Jesse Edgar, 1888-
xRay, J. Edgar.
Art of Bricklaying. Bennett Co.
Ray, Jo A. *see* Ray, Jo Anne.
Ray, Jo Anne.
xRay, Jo A.
Careers in Computers. Lerner Pubns.
Careers in Football. Lerner Pubns.
Careers in Hockey. Lerner Pubns.
Careers with a Police Department. Lerner
Pubns.
Careers with a Television Station. Lerner
Pubns.
Ray, John, 1627-1705
xRay, John.
The Correspondence of John Ray. Arno.
Ray, Joseph M. *see* Ray, Joseph Malchus.
Ray, Joseph Malchus.
xRay, Joseph M.
The President: Rex, Princeps, Imperator?. Tex
Western.
Ray, Juliana.
xRay, Juliana.
Crochet Designs from Hungary. Dover.
Crochet Designs from Hungary. Peter Smith.
Ray, Marvin E.
xRay.
Finance. Winthrop.
Ray, Mary, 1932-
xRay, Mary.
The Ides of April. FS&G.
Song of Thunder. Merrimack Bk Serv.
Standing Lions. Merrimack Bk Serv.
Ray, Mary Frey.
xRay.
Exploring Professional Cooking. Bennett Co.
Ray, Michael L.
xRay, Michael L.
Communicating with Consumers: The
Information Processing Approach. Sage.
Ray, N. *see* Ray, Nigel.
Ray, Nigel.
xRay, N.
Normal Structures & Bordism Theory, with
Applications to MSp. Am Math.
Ray, Nihar-Ranjan, 1903-
xRay, Niharranjan.

Nationalism in India: An Historical Analysis of
Its Stresses & Strains. Intl Pubns Serv.

Ray, Niharranjan. *see* Ray, Nihar-Ranjan.

Ray, Oakley S. *see* Ray, Oakley Stern.

Ray, Oakley Stern.
xRay, Oakley S.
Drugs, Society & Human Behavior. Mosby.

Ray, P. M. *see* Ray, Peter Martin.

Ray, Paul C.
xRay, Paul C.
Surrealist Movement in England. Cornell U Pr.

Ray, Peter Martin.
xRay, P. M.
Living Plant. HR&W.

Ray, Rajat K.
xRay, Rajat K.
Industrialization in India: Growth & Conflict in
the Private Corporate Sector, 1914-47.
Oxford U Pr.

Ray, Sandy F.
xRay, Sandy F.
Journeying Through a Jungle. Broadman.

Ray, Satyajit, 1922-
xRay, Satyajit.
Our Films, Their Films. South Asia Bks.

Ray, Sheila. *see* Ray, Shelia G. Bannister.

Ray, Shelia G. Bannister.
xRay, Sheila.
Children's Librarianship. K G Saur.

Ray, Shreela.
xRay, Shreela.
Night Conversations with None Other.
Dustbooks.

Ray, Sibnarayan, 1921-
xRay, Sibnarayan.
ed. Gandhi, India & the World: An
International Symposium. Temple U Pr.

Ray, Sidney. *see* Ray, Sidney F.

Ray, Sidney F.
xRay, Sidney.
The Lens in Action. Focal Pr.
xRay, Sidney F.
The Focalguide to Close-Ups. Focal Pr.
Lens in Action. Hastings.

Ray, Sidney H. *see* Ray, Sidney Herbert.

Ray, Sidney Herbert, 1858-1939.
xRay, Sidney H.
A Comparative Study of the Melanesian Island
Languages. AMS Pr.

Ray, Talton F.
xRay, Talton F.
The Politics of the Barrios of Venezuela. U of
Cal Pr.

Ray, Verne F. *see* Ray, Verne Frederick.

Ray, Verne Frederick, 1905-
xRay, Verne F.
The Sanpoil & Nespelem: Salishan Peoples of
Northeastern Washington. AMS Pr.

Ray, W. Harmon. *see* Ray, Willis Harmon.

Ray, W. J. *see* Ray, William J.

Ray, William J., 1932-
xRay, W. J.
Evaluation of Clinical Biofeedback. Plenum
Pub.

Ray, William S. *see* Ray, William Samuel.

Ray, William Samuel, 1917-
xRay, William S.
Statistics in Psychological Research.
Macmillan.

Ray, Willis H. *see* Ray, Willis Harmon.

Ray, Willis Harmon, 1940-
xRay, W. Harmon.
Advanced Process Control. McGraw.
ed. Distributed Parameter Systems:
Identification, Estimation & Control. Dekker.
xRay, Willis H.
Process Optimization with Applications in
Metallurgy & Chemical Engineering. Wiley.

Ray, Worth S. *see* Ray, Worth Stickley.

Ray, Worth Stickley, 1877-
xRay, Worth S.
The Mecklenburg Signers & Their Neighbors.
Genealog Pub.

Rayan, Samuel.
xRayan, Samuel.
The Holy Spirit: Heart of the Gospel &
Christian Hope. Orbis Bks.

Rayback, J. G. *see* Rayback, Joseph G.

Rayback, Joseph G.
xRayback, J. G.
History of American Labor. Macmillan.
xRayback, Joseph G.
History of American Labor. Free Pr.

Rayburn, Robert G. *see* Rayburn, Robert Gibson.

Rayburn, Robert Gibson, 1915-
xRayburn, Robert G.
O Come, Let Us Worship: Corporate Worship
in the Evangelical Church. Baker Bk.

Raycraft, Don. *see* Raycraft, Donald R.

Raycraft, Donald R.

xRaycraft, Don.
Wallace-Homestead Price Guide to American
Country Antiques. Wallace-Homestead.

xRaycraft, Donald R.
Early American Folk & Country Antiques. C E
Tuttle.

Rayfield, Donald, 1942-
xRayfield, Donald.
The Dream of Lhasa: The Life of Nikolay
Przhevalsky (1839-88), Explorer of Central
Asia. Ohio U Pr.

Raygor, Alton L. *see* Raygor, Alton Lamon.

Raygor, Alton Lamon.
xRaygor, Alton L.
Systems for Study. McGraw

Raymond, Antonin, 1888-
xRaymond, Antonin.
Antonin Raymond: An Autobiography. C E
Tuttle.

Raymond, Boris, 1925-
xRaymond, Boris.
Krupskaia & Soviet Russian Librarianship:
1917-1939. Scarecrow.

Raymond, D. *see* Raymond, Dorothy Maclean.

Raymond, Dora (Neill), 1889-
xRaymond, Dora N.
British Policy & Opinion During the
Franco-Prussian War. AMS Pr.

Raymond, Dora N. *see* Raymond, Dora (Neill).

Raymond, Dorothy.
xRaymond, Dorothy.
Stalking the Stone Crab. Great Outdoors.

Raymond, Dorothy Maclean.
xRaymond, D.
Individualizing Reading in the Elementary
School. P-H.

Raymond, Ellsworth. *see* Raymond, Ellsworth Lester.

Raymond, Ellsworth Lester, 1912-
xRaymond, Ellsworth.
The Soviet State. NYU Pr.

Raymond, Ernest, 1888-
xRaymond, Ernest.
In the Steps of St. Francis. Franciscan Herald.

Raymond, George.
xRaymond, George.
Memoirs of Robert William Elliston. Arno.

Raymond, George L. *see* Raymond, George Lansing.

Raymond, George Lansing, 1839-1929.
xRaymond, George L.
The Orator's Manual: A Practical &
Philosophical Treatise on Vocal Culture,
Emphasis & Gesture. Arno.

Raymond, Howard W.
xRaymond, Howard W.

Fundamentals of Abdominal Sonography: A
Teaching Approach. Grune.

Raymond, Irving W. *see* Raymond, Irving Woodworth.

Raymond, Irving Woodworth, 1898-
xRaymond, Irving W.
Teaching of the Early Church on the Use of
Wine & Strong Drink. AMS Pr.

Raymond, James C., 1940-
xRaymond, James C.
Writing (Is an Unnatural Act). Har-Row.

Raymond, Janice G.
xRaymond, Janice G.
The Transsexual Empire: The Making of the
She-Male. Beacon Pr.

Raymond, Louise.
xRaymond, Louise.
Adoption & After. Har-Row.

Raymond, Robert L. *see* Raymond, Robert Lovejoy.

Raymond, Robert Lovejoy, 1874-
xRaymond, Robert L.
At a Dollar a Year: Ripples on the Edge of the
Maelstrom. Arno.

Raymond, Thomas L. *see* Raymond, Thomas Lynch.

Raymond, Thomas Lynch, 1875-1928
xRaymond, Thomas L.
Stephen Crane. Folcroft.

Raymond, Wayne.
xRaymond, Wayne.
ed. Southeast Asia, an Emerging Center of
World Influence?: Economic & Resource
Considerations. Ohio U Ctr Intl.

Raymont, J. E. *see* Raymont, John E. G.

Raymont, John E. G.
xRaymont, J. E.
Plankton & Productivity in the Oceans.
Pergamon.

Raynal, Guillaume T. *see* Raynal, Guillaume Thomas
Francois.

Raynal, Guillaume Thomas Francois, 1713-1796
xRaynal, Guillaume T.
The Revolution of America. Irvington.

Raynal, Maurice.
xRaynal, Maurice.
Modern French Painters. Arno.

Rayner, Claire.
xRayner, Claire.
The Body Book. Barron.
Charing Cross. Putnam.
Covent Garden. NAL.
Covent Garden. Putnam.
Gower Street. S&S.
Paddington Green. Fawcett.

Rayner, D. H. *see* Rayner, Dorothy Helen.

Rayner, Dorothy H. *see* Rayner, Dorothy Helen.

Rayner, Dorothy Helen.
xRayner, D. H.
Stratigraphy of the British Isles. Cambridge U
Pr.
xRayner, Dorothy H.
Stratigraphy of the British Isles. Cambridge U
Pr.

Rayner, Mary.
xRayner, Mary.
Garth Pig & the Ice Cream Lady. Atheneum.

Raynes, Jean.
xRaynes, Jean.
The Blood Carnelian. Doubleday.
Legacy of the Wolf. Doubleday.
Legacy of the Wolf. Playboy Pbks.

Raynolds, Robert, 1902-1965
xRaynolds, Robert.
Thomas Wolfe: Memoir of a Friendship. U of
Tex Pr.

Raynor, Dorka.
xRaynor, Dorka.

ed. Grandparents Around the World. A
Whitman.
ed. My Friends Live in Many Places. A
Whitman.
illus. This Is My Father & Me. A Whitman.
Raynor, Henry.
xRaynor, Henry.
The Orchestra: A History. Scribner.
Raynor, John, 1942-
xRaynor, John.
Anatomy & Physiology. Har-Row.
Rayson, Steven.
xRayson, Steven.
The Crows of War. Atheneum.
Raz, Joseph.
xRaz, Joseph.
ed. Practical Reasoning. Oxford U Pr.
Razzi, James.
xRazzi, James.
illus. Don't Open This Box. Schol Bk Serv.
illus. Star-Spangled Fun!: Things to Make, Do
& See from American History. Schol Bk
Serv.
Rca Corporation.
xRCA Staff.
RCA Color-TV Service Handbook. RCA Dist
Spec Prods.
RCA Electro-Optics Handbook. RCA Solid
State.
RCA Power Transistors. RCA Solid State.
RCA RF Power Transistor Manual: RFM-430.
RCA Solid State.
RCA Solid State Servicing. RCA Dist Spec
Prods.
RCA Staff. see Rca Corporation.
Re, Edward D.
xRe, Edward D.
Brief Writing & Oral Argument. Oceana.
Brief Writing & Oral Argument. Trans-Media
Pub.
Re, Frank M.
xRe, Frank M.
Re Views. F M Re.
Rea, John.
xRea, John.
Building a Hospital: A Primer for
Administrators. Am Hospital.
A Look at Scotland & the Macdonalds. Eilean
Ban Pub.
Read. see Read, Anne.
Read, Allen W. see Read, Allen Walker.
Read, Allen Walker.
xRead, Allen W.
Classic American Graffiti: Lexical Evidence
from Folk Epigraphy in Western North
America; a Glossarial Study of the Low
Element in the English Vocabulary.
Maledicta.
Read, Ann. see Read, Anne.
Read, Anne.
xRead.
Edgar Cayce Diet & Health. Warner Bks.
xRead, Ann.
Edgar Cayce on Diet & Health. Warner Bks.
Read, B. E. see Read, Bryan Eric.
Read, Benjamin M. see Read, Benjamin Maurice.
Read, Benjamin Maurice, 1853-1927
xRead, Benjamin M.
Illustrated History of New Mexico. Arno.
Read, Beryl J.
xRead, Beryl J.
Pip's Mountain. Zondervan.
The Runaway Girl. Zondervan.
Read, Bryan Eric.
xRead, B. E.
Determination of Dynamic Properties of
Polymers & Composites. Halsted Pr.
Read, Charles, 1940-
xRead, Charles.

Children's Categorization of Speech Sounds in
English. NCTE.
Read, Clark P., 1921-
xRead, Clark P.
Parasitism & Symbiology: An Introductory
Text.. Wiley.
Read, David H. see Read, David Haxton Carswell.
Read, David Haxton Carswell.
xRead, David H.
Unfinished Easter: Sermons on the Ministry.
Har-Row.
Read, Don.
xRead, Don.
Complete Football Passing Game. P-H.
Read, Donald. see Read, Donald A.
Read, Donald A.
xRead, Donald.
The Concept of Health. Holbrook.
xRead, Donald A.
The Concept of Health. Allyn.
Creative Teaching in Health. Macmillan.
Drugs & People. Allyn.
Looking in: Exploring One's Personal Health
Values. P-H.
xRead, Donald C.
Humanistic Education Sourcebook. P-H.
Read, Donald C. see Read, Donald A.
Read, Elfreida, 1920-
xRead, Elfreida.
Brothers by Choice. FS&G.
Read, Frank T.
xRead, Frank T.
Let Them Be Judged: The Judicial Integration
of the Deep South. Scarecrow.
Read, Gardner, 1913-
xRead, Gardner.
Contemporary Instrumental Techniques.
Schirmer Bks.
Style & Orchestration. Schirmer Bks.
Thesaurus of Orchestral Devices. Greenwood.
Read, H. E. see Read, Herbert Edward.
Read, Herbert. see Read, Herbert Edward.
Read, Herbert E. see Read, Herbert Edward.
Read, Herbert Edward, Sir, 1893-1968
xRead, H. E.
English Stained Glass. Kraus Repr.
xRead, Herbert.
Annals of Innocence & Experience. Haskell.
Art & Industry: The Principles of Industrial
Design. Peter Smith.
Art of Sculpture. Princeton U Pr.
Green Child. New Directions.
The Meaning of Art. Arden Lib.
xRead, Herbert E.
Collected Essays in Literary Criticism.
Hyperion Conn.
In Defence of Shelley & Other Essays. Arno.
ed. Surrealism. Somerset Pub.
The True Voice of Feeling: Studies in English
Romantic Poetry. AMS Pr.
Read, Hollis, 1802-1887
xRead, Hollis.
Negro Problem Solved: Or, Africa As She Was,
As She Is, & As She Shall Be, Her Curse &
Her Cure. Arno.
Negro Problem Solved: Or, Africa As She Was,
As She Is, & As She Shall Be. Negro U Pr.
Read, Miss.
xRead.
No Holly for Miss Quinn. HM.
Read, James M. see Read, James Morgan.
Read, James Morgan, 1908-
xRead, James M.
Atrocity Propaganda, 1914-1919. Arno.
Read, Jean B.
xRead, Jean B.
ed. McCall's Book of Entertaining. Random.
Read, Kenneth E.
xRead, Kenneth E.

The High Valley. Columbia U Pr.
High Valley. Scribner.
Read, Leonard E. see Read, Leonard Edward.
Read, Leonard Edward, 1898-
xRead, Leonard E.
Accent on the Right. Foun Econ Ed.
Awake for Freedom's Sake. Foun Econ Ed.
Castles in the Air. Foun Econ Ed.
Comes the Dawn. Foun Econ Ed.
Coming Aristocracy. Foun Econ Ed.
Deeper Than You Think. Foun Econ Ed.
Free Market & Its Enemy. Foun Econ Ed.
Freedom Freeway. Foun Econ Ed.
Let Freedom Reign. Foun Econ Ed.
The Love of Liberty. Foun Econ Ed.
Talking to Myself. Foun Econ Ed.
Then Truth Will Out. Foun Econ Ed.
Read, Margaret.
xRead, Margaret.
Ngoni of Nyasaland. Biblio Dist.
Read, Mary L. see Read, Mary Lyle.
Read, Mary Lyle.
xRead, Mary L.
The Ghost of Emma Louise. Abingdon.
Read, Maureen H. see Read, Maureen Hay.
Read, Maureen Hay, 1937-
xRead, Maureen H.
Like a Watered Garden. Herald Pr.
Read, Opie. see Read, Opie Percival.
Read, Opie Percival.
xRead, Opie.
The Carpetbagger: A Novel. Arno.
Mark Twain & I. Folcroft.
Read, Piers P. see Read, Piers Paul.
Read, Piers Paul, 1941-
xRead, Piers P.
Alive: The Story of the Andes Survivors. Avon.
A Married Man. Lippincott.
Polonaise. Avon.
Polonaise. Lippincott.
The Professor's Daughter. Avon.
xRead, Piers Paul.
Alive: The Story of the Andes Survivors.
Lippincott.
The Upstart. Avon.
Read, Ronald C.
xRead, Ronald C.
ed. Graph Theory & Computing. Acad Pr.
Read, William H.
xRead, William.
America's Mass Media Merchants. Johns
Hopkins.
Reade, Aleyn L. see Reade, Aleyn Lyell.
Reade, Aleyn Lyell.
xReade, Aleyn L.
Johnsonian Gleanings. Octagon.
Reade, Charles, 1814-1884
xReade, Charles.
Works of Charles Reade. AMS Pr.
Reade, W. H. see Reade, William Henry Vincent.
Reade, William Henry Vincent, 1872-1943
xReade, W. H.
Moral System of Dante's Inferno. Kennikat.
Reade, Winwood, 1838-1875
xReade, Winwood.
The Outcast. Darby Bks.
Reader, John.
xReader, John.
Pyramids of Life: Illuminations of Nature's
Fearful Symmetry. Lippincott.
The Reader'S Digest.
xBoard of Publication of the Reorganized Church
of Jesus Christ of Latter Day Saints.
ed. Doctrine & Covenants. Herald Hse.
xReader's Digest.
Joy of Nature. Norton.
Reader's Digest Crafts & Hobbies. Norton.
Reader's Digest Stories Behind Everyday
Things. Norton.
xReader's Digest Editors.

ed. The Art of Living. Berkley Pub.
Book of Christmas. Norton.
ed. Secrets of the Past. Berkley Pub.
ed. Tests & Teasers. Berkley Pub.
xReaders Digest.
Animals Can Be Almost Human. Norton.
Complete Guide to Needlework. Norton.
Success with House Plants. Norton.
Treasury for Young Readers. Norton.
xReaders Digest Editorial Staff.
Animals You Will Never Forget. Norton.
xReaders Digest Editors.
Family Word Finder. Norton.
The Story of America. Norton.
xReaders' Digest Editors.
ed. How to Live on Your Income. Norton.
xTheReader's Digest.
ed. The World's Best Fairy Tales. Norton.
Reader's Digest Association, London. *see* Reader's
Digest Association, Ltd.
Reader's Digest Association, Ltd.
xReader's Digest Association, London.
Encyclopaedia of Garden Plants & Flowers.
Norton.
Reader's Digest Editors. *see* The Reader's Digest.
Readers Digest. *see* The Reader's Digest.
Readers Digest Editorial Staff. *see* The Reader's Digest.
Readers Digest Editors. *see* The Reader's Digest.
Readers' Digest Editors. *see* The Reader's Digest.
Readey, Helen.
xReadey, Helen.
Introduction to Nursing Essentials: A
Handbook. Mosby.
Mathematical Concepts for Nursing: A
Workbook. A-W.
Reading, Gerald R. *see* Reading, Gerald Rufus Isaacs, 2d
Marquis Of.
Reading, Gerald Rufus Isaacs, 2d Marquis Of, 1889-
xReading, Gerald R.
The South Sea Bubble. Greenwood.
Reading, H. G.
xReading, H. G.
ed. Sedimentary Environments & Facies.
Elsevier.
Reading, Hugo F.
xReading, Hugo F.
A Dictionary of the Social Sciences. Routledge
& Kegan.
Reading Laboratory, Inc.
xTheReading Laboratory.
Double Your Reading Speed. Fawcett.
Ready, John. *see* Ready, John F.
Ready, John F.
xReady, John.
ed. Lasers in Modern Industry. SME.
Reagan, Charles. *see* Reagan, Charles E.
Reagan, Charles E.
xReagan, Charles.
ed. Studies in the Philosophy of Paul Ricoeur.
Ohio U Pr.
xReagan, Charles E.
Ethics for Scientific Researchers. C C Thomas.
Reagan, Cora L. *see* Reagan, Cora Lee.
Reagan, Cora Lee.
xReagan, Cora L.
Handbook of Auditory Perceptual Training. C
C Thomas.
Reagan, J. W. *see* Reagan, James William.
Reagan, James William.
xReagan, J. W.
The Cells of Uterine Adenocarcinoma. S
Karger.
Reagan, Nancy.
xReagan, Nancy.
Nancy. Morrow.
Reagan, Wes.
xReagan, Wesley.
Return to Identity. Standard Pub.
Reagan, Wesley. *see* Reagan, Wes.

Real Estate Research Corporation.
xReal Estate Research Corporation.
Air Rights & Highways. Urban Land.
Selling the Solar House. Solar Energy Info.
Reale, Giovanni.
xReale, Giovanni.
The Concept of First Philosophy & the Unity
of the Metaphysics of Aristotle. State U NY
Pr.
Reams, Bernard D.
xReams, Bernard D.
Law for the Businessman. Oceana.
Reamy, Tom.
xReamy, Tom.
Blind Voices. Berkley Pub.
Blind Voices. Putnam.
San Diego Lightfoot Sue & Other Stories.
Earthlight.
Reaney, Gilbert.
xReaney, Gilbert.
Guillaume De Machaut. Oxford U Pr.
Reaney, P. H. *see* Reaney, Percy Hide.
Reaney, Percy Hide.
xReaney, P. H.
A Dictionary of British Surnames. Routledge &
Kegan.
The Origin of English Place-Names. Routledge
& Kegan.
The Origin of English Surnames. Routledge &
Kegan.
Rearden, Jim.
xRearden, Jim.
Wonders of Caribou. Dodd.
Reardon, Bernard M. *see* Reardon, Bernard M. G.
Reardon, Bernard M. G.
xReardon, Bernard M.
ed. Liberal Protestantism. Stanford U Pr.
Reardon, Joan.
xReardon, Joan.
Poetry by American Women, 1900-1975: A
Bibliography. Scarecrow.
Reardon, Maureen.
xReardon, Maureen.
Match Point. Raintree Pubs.
Reardon, Ray.
xReardon, Ray.
Classic Snooker. David & Charles.
Reardon, Robert C.
xReardon, Robert C.
Facilitating Career Development: Strategies for
Counselors. C C Thomas.
Rearick, Elizabeth C. *see* Rearick, Elizabeth Charlotte.
Rearick, Elizabeth Charlotte, 1899-
xRearick, Elizabeth C.
Dances of the Hungarians. AMS Pr.
Reaske, Christopher R. *see* Reaske, Christopher Russell.
Reaske, Christopher Russell.
xReaske, Christopher R.
College Writer's Guide to the Study of
Literature. Phila Bk Co.
Reasoner, Charles. *see* Reasoner, Charles F.
Reasoner, Charles F., 1925-
xReasoner, Charles.
Portfolio of Working Materials for
Individualized Instruction. P-H.
Reaver, J. Russell. *see* Reaver, Joseph Russell.
Reaver, Joseph Russell, 1915-
xReaver, J. Russell.
O'Neill Concordance. Gale.
Reaves, Rhod, 1932-
xReaves, Rhod.
Football's "Combo" Defensive System. P-H.
The Multiple Power I Offense. P-H.
Reavin, Sam.
xReavin, Sam.
Hurray for Captain Jane. Schol Bk Serv.
Reavis, Charles A.
xReavis, Charles A.

Teacher Improvement Through Clinical
Supervision. Phi Delta Kappa.
Reay, D. A. *see* Reay, David Anthony.
Reay, David A. *see* Reay, David Anthony.
Reay, David Anthony.
xReay, D. A.
Industrial Energy Conservation: A Handbook
for Engineers & Managers. Pergamon.
xReay, David A.
Industrial Energy Conservation: A Handbook
for Engineers & Managers. Pergamon.
Reay, John R. *see* Reay, John Robert.
Reay, John Robert, 1934-
xReay, John R.
Generalizations of a Theorem of Caratheodory.
Am Math.
Reay, Tony.
xReay, Tony.
The Illustrated Guide to Judo. Van Nos
Reinhold.
Reb, Paul.
xReb, Paul.
Confessions of a Future Scotsman. Braziller.
Reband, P.
xReband, P.
Related Mathematics for Carpenters. Am
Technical.
Rebane, K. K. *see* Rebane, Karl-Samuel.
Rebane, Karl-Samuel.
xRebane, K. K.
Impurity Spectra of Solids: Elementary Theory
of Vibrational Structure. Plenum Pub.
Rebay, Luciano.
xRebay, Luciano.
Alberto Moravia. Columbia U Pr.
Rebell, Gerbert.
xRebell, Gerbert.
ed. Dermatophytes: Their Recognition &
Identification. U of Miami Pr.
Reber, Vera B. *see* Reber, Vera Blinn.
Reber, Vera Blinn, 1941-
xReber, Vera B.
British Mercantile Houses in Buenos Aires,
1810-1880. Harvard U Pr.
Rebhorn, Eldon.
xRebhorn, Eldon.
Woodturning. McKnight.
Rebhorn, Wayne A., 1943-
xRebhorn, Wayne A.
Courtly Performances: Masking & Festivity in
Castiglione's "Book of the Courtier". Wayne
St U Pr.
Reboul, Antoine, 1914-
xReboul, Antoine.
Thou Shalt Not Kill. S G Phillips.
Rebuffat, Gaston.
xRebuffat, Gaston.
Men & the Matterhorn. Oxford U Pr.
On Ice & Snow & Rock. Oxford U Pr.
Recami, E. *see* Recami, Erasmo.
Recami, Erasmo.
xRecami, E.
ed. Tachyons, Monopoles & Related Topics:
Proceedings of the First Session of the
Interdisciplinary Seminars on "Tachyons &
Related Topics," Erice, September 1976.
Elsevier.
Recamier, Jeanne F. *see* Recamier, Jeanne Francoise
Julie Adelaide Bernard.
**Recamier, Jeanne Francoise Julie Adelaide Bernard,
1777-1849**
xRecamier, Jeanne F.
Memoirs & Correspondence of Madame
Recamier. AMS Pr.
Rech, R. *see* Rech, Richard H.
Rech, Richard H.
xRech, R.

ed. Introduction to Psychopharmacology.
Raven.

Rechy, John.
xRechy, John.
City of Night. Ballantine.
City of Night. Grove.
The Vampires. Grove.

Reck, Andrew J., 1927-
xReck, Andrew J.
Speculative Philosophy: A Study of Its Nature,
Types, & Uses. U of NM Pr.

Reck, David.
xReck, David.
Music of the Whole Earth. Scribner.

Reck, Gregory C. *see* Reck, Gregory G.

Reck, Gregory G., 1944-
xReck, Gregory C.
In the Shadow of Tlaloc: Life in a Mexican
Village. Penguin.

Reck, Rima D. *see* Reck, Rima Drell.

Reck, Rima Drell.
xReck, Rima D.
Literature & Responsibility: The French
Novelist in the Twentieth Century. La State
U Pr.

Reck, Vera T.
xReck, Vera T.
Boris Pil'niak: A Soviet Writer in Conflict with
the State. McGill-Queens U Pr.

Reckless, Walter C. *see* Reckless, Walter Cade.

Reckless, Walter Cade.
xReckless, Walter C.
The Prevention of Juvenile Delinquency: An
Experiment. Ohio St U Pr.

Recktenwald, Horst C. *see* Recktenwald, Horst Claus.

Recktenwald, Horst Claus.
xRecktenwald, Horst C.
Tax Incidence & Income Redistribution: An
Introduction. Wayne St U Pr.

Record Controls, Inc.,. *see* Record Controls, Inc.,
Chicago.

Record Controls, Inc., Chicago.
xRecord Controls, Inc.,
A Guide to the Retention & Preservation of
Records (with Destruction Schedules).
Hospital Finan.

Record, Nancy A.
xRecord, Nancy A.
illus. Coffers & Cabinets. Lerner Pubns.
illus. Come to the Table. Lerner Pubns.

Record, Wilson, 1916-
xRecord, Wilson.
Negro & the Communist Party. Atheneum.
The Negro & the Communist Party.
Greenwood.

Records, Raymond E., 1930-
xRecords, Raymond E.
Physiology of the Human Eye & Visual
System. Har-Row.

Rector, Frank.
xRector, Frank.
The Nazi Extermination of Homosexuals. Stein
& Day.

Rector, Margaret H. *see* Rector, Margaret Hayden.

Rector, Margaret Hayden.
xRector, Margaret H.
Norton & Gus. Grossmont Pr.

Rector, Robert E.
xRector, Robert E.
Finite Mathematics & Its Applications. HM.

**Red Cross. United States. American National Red
Cross.**
xAmerican National Red Cross.

Adapted Aquatics: Swimming for Persons with
Physical or Mental Impairments. Doubleday.
Advanced First Aid & Emergency Care.
Doubleday.
Basic First Aid. Doubleday.
Canoeing. Doubleday.
Family Health & Home Nursing. Doubleday.
Standard First Aid & Personal Safety.
Doubleday.
xAmerican Red Cross.
ed. Home Nursing Textbook. Doubleday.
ed. Lifesaving, Rescue & Water Safety.
Doubleday.

Reda, Mario.
xReda, Mario.
ed. Systems & Processes: Collected Works in
Sociology. Coll & U Pr.

Redbook Editors. *see* Redbook Magazine.

Redbook Magazine.
xRedbook Editors.
We Are Proud to Announce. Walker & Co.
xRedbook Magazine.
Expectant Mother: A Reassuring Guide to the
Special Demands of Pregnancy & Childbirth.
Trident.

Redcliffe-Maud, J. *see* Redcliffe-Maud, John Primat
Redcliffe-Maud.

Redcliffe-Maud, John Primat Redcliffe-Maud.
xRedcliffe-Maud, J.
English Local Government Reformed. Oxford
U Pr.
xRedcliffe-Maud, Lord.
English Local Government Reformed. Oxford
U Pr.

Redcliffe-Maud, Lord. *see* Redcliffe-Maud, John Primat
Redcliffe-Maud.

Redd, William. *see* Redd, William H.

Redd, William H.
xRedd, William.
Take Charge: A Personal Guide to Behavior
Modification. Random.
xRedd, William H.
Take Charge: A Personal Guide to Behavior
Modification. Random.

Reddan, Minnie.
xReddan, Minnie.
The Church of St. Helen, Bishopsgate. AMS
Pr.

Reddaway, W. W. *see* Reddaway, William Fiddian.

Reddaway, William F. *see* Reddaway, William Fiddian.

Reddaway, William Fiddian, 1872-1949
xReddaway, W. W.
ed. Cambridge History of Poland. Octagon.
xReddaway, William F.
Frederick the Great & the Rise of Prussia.
Greenwood.
Frederick the Great & the Rise of Prussia.
Haskell.
Frederick the Great & the Rise of Prussia.
Scholarly.
Problems of the Baltic. AMS Pr.

Redden, Kenneth. *see* Redden, Kenneth Robert.

Redden, Kenneth Robert.
xRedden, Kenneth.
Legal System of Ethiopia. Michie.

Redden, Martha R. *see* Redden, Martha Ross.

Redden, Martha Ross.
xRedden, Martha R.
Barrier-Free Meetings: A Guide for
Professional Associations. AAAS.

Redder, Ronald. *see* Redder, Ronald M.

Redder, Ronald M.
xRedder, Ronald.
Perforated Mood-Swing Book. Concordia.

Reddick, Bryan.
xReddick, Bryan.
Student Journalist & Effective Writing Style.
Rosen Pr.

Reddick, De Witt C. *see* Reddick, De Witt Carter.

Reddick, De Witt Carter, 1904-
xReddick, De Witt C.
The Mass Media & the School Newspaper.
Wadsworth Pub.

Reddick, John.
xReddick, John.
The Danzig Trilogy of Gunter Grass: A Study
of the Tin Drum, Cat & Mouse, & Dog
Years. HarBraceJ.

Reddick, Kate.
xReddick, Kate.
Horses. Bantam.

Reddick, William J., 1890-1965
xReddick, William J.
Standard Musical Repertoire with Accurate
Timings. Greenwood.

Reddin, W. J. *see* Reddin, William J.

Reddin, William J.
xReddin, W. J.
Effective Management by Objectives: The 3-D
Method of MBO. McGraw.

Redding, David A.
xRedding, David A.
Lives He Touched: The Relationships of Jesus.
Har-Row.
The Parables He Told. Har-Row.
The Prayers I Love. Strawberry Hill.

Redding, Harold T.
xRedding, Harold T.
The Dun & Bradstreet Handbook of Credits &
Collections. T Y Crowell.

Redding, Jay S. *see* Redding, Jay Saunders.

Redding, Jay Saunders, 1906-
xRedding, Jay S.
To Make a Poet Black. Core Collection.

Redding, Robert, 1930-
xRedding, Robert W.
Starring Robert Benchley: "Those Magnificent
Movie Shorts". U of NM Pr.

Redding, Robert H.
xRedding, Robert H.
Alaska Pipeline. Childrens.

Redding, Robert W. *see* Redding, Robert.

Reddy, Anne W. *see* Reddy, Anne Waller.

Reddy, Anne Waller.
xReddy, Anne W.
Richmond City, Virginia, Marriage Bonds
1797-1853. Genealog Pub.

Redei, L. *see* Redei, Laszlo.

Redei, Laszlo.
xRedei, L.
Foundation of Euclidean & Non-Euclidean
Geometries According to F. Klein. Pergamon.

Redekop, Calvin. *see* Redekop, Calvin Wall.

Redekop, Calvin Wall, 1925-
xRedekop, Calvin.
Free Church & Seductive Culture. Herald Pr.

Redfern, Barrie.
xRedfern, Barrie.
Local Radio. Focal Pr.

Redfern, H. B. *see* Redfern, Hildred Betty.

Redfern, Hildred Betty.
xRedfern, H. B.
Concepts in Modern Educational Dance. Plays.

Redfern, W. D.
xRedfern, Walter D.
Private World of Jean Giono. Duke.

Redfern, Walter D. *see* Redfern, W. D.

Redfield, Isaac F. *see* Redfield, Isaac Fletcher.

Redfield, Isaac Fletcher, 1804-1876
xRedfield, Isaac F.
A Practical Treatise Upon the Law of
Railways. Arno.
A Practical Treatise Upon the Law of
Railways. Johnson Repr.

Redfield, James M., 1935-
xRedfield, James M.

Nature & Culture in the Iliad: The Tragedy of Hector. U of Chicago Pr.

Redfield, Malissa.
xRedfield, Malissa.
Scenes from Country Life. P-H.

Redfield, Robert, 1897-
xRedfield, Robert.
The Folk Culture of Yucatan. Gordon Pr.
Folk Culture of Yucatan. U of Chicago Pr.
Primitive World & Its Transformations. Cornell U Pr.

Redford, E. S. *see* Redford, Emmette Shelburn.

Redford, Emmette S. *see* Redford, Emmette Shelburn.

Redford, Emmette Shelburn, 1904-
xRedford, E. S.
Ideal & Practice in Public Administration. U of Ala Pr.
xRedford, Emmette S.
Administration of National Economic Control. Johnson Repr.
Democracy in the Administrative State. Oxford U Pr.
ed. Public Administration & Policy Formation: Studies in Oil, Gas, Banking, River Development, & Corporate Investigations. Greenwood.
Regulatory Process: With Illustrations from Commercial Aviation. U of Tex Pr.

Redford, Ken.
xRedford, Ken.
Success in Golf. Transatlantic.

Redford, M. H. *see* Redford, Myron H.

Redford, Myron H.
xRedford, M. H.
ed. The Condom: Increasing Utilization in the U. S.. San Francisco Pr.

Redford, Robert.
xRedford, Robert.
The Outlaw Trail. G&D.

Redgrove, Peter.
xRedgrove, Peter.
Dr. Faust's Sea-Spiral Spirit, & Other Poems. Routledge & Kegan.
Weddings at Nether Powers & Other New Poems. Routledge & Kegan.

Redinbaugh, L. D. *see* Redinbaugh, Larry D.

Redinbaugh, Larry D.
xRedinbaugh, L. D.
Retailing Management: A Planning Approach. McGraw.
xRedinbaugh, Larry D.
Small Business Management: A Planning Approach. West Pub.

Redinger, Ruby V. *see* Redinger, Ruby Virginia.

Redinger, Ruby Virginia, 1915-
xRedinger, Ruby V.
George Eliot: The Emergent Self. Knopf.

Redington, Robert J.
xRedington, Robert J.
Survey of the Appalachians. Taconic Pubs.

Redish, Martin H.
xRedish, Martin H.
The Constitutionality of Medical Malpractice Reform Legislation: A Supplemental Report. Am Hospital.
Legislative Response to the Medical Malpractice Crisis: Constitutional Implications. Am Hospital.

Redivo, Hugo.
xRedivo, Hugo.
The Okanagan. Oxford U Pr.

Redl, Fritz.
xRedl, Fritz.
Children Who Hate: The Disorganization & Breakdown of Behavior Controls. Free Pr.
Controls from Within: Techniques for the Treatment of the Aggressive Child. Free Pr.
When We Deal with Children: Selected Writings. Free Pr.

Redlich, Frederick C. *see* Redlich, Fredrick Carl.

Redlich, Fredrick Carl.
xRedlich, Frederick C.
Theory & Practice of Psychiatry. Basic.

Redlich, Norman.
xRedlich, Norman.
Professional Responsibility: A Problem Approach. Little.

Redlich, Otto, 1896-
xRedlich, Otto.
Thermodynamics: Fundamentals, Applications. Elsevier.

Redman, Barbara J.
xRedman, Barbara J.
Consumer Behavior: Theory & Applications. AVI.

Redman, Barbara K. *see* Redman, Barbara Klug.

Redman, Barbara Klug.
xRedman, Barbara K.
The Process of Patient Teaching in Nursing. Mosby.

Redman, Ben R. *see* Redman, Ben Ray.

Redman, Ben Ray, 1896-1961
xRedman, Ben R.
Edwin Arlington Robinson. Arden Lib.
Edwin Arlington Robinson. Folcroft.
Edwin Arlington Robinson. Gordon Pr.
Edwin Arlington Robinson. Haskell.

Redman, Eric.
xRedman, Eric.
The Dance of Legislation. S&S.
The Dance of Legislation. S&S.

Redman, Helen C.
xRedman, Helen C.
Computed Tomography of the Body. Saunders.

Redman, Jane.
xRedman, Jane.
Frame-Loom Weaving. Van Nos Reinhold.

Redman, Martin.
xRedman, Martin.
Superbike: Modern High Performance Motorcycles. Har-Row.

Redmond, Eugene.
xRedmond, Eugene.
In a Time of Rain & Desire: New Love Poems. Black River.

Redmond, Gerald, 1934-
xRedmond, Gerald.
Caledonian Games in Nineteenth-Century America. Fairleigh Dickinson.

Redmore, Fred H.
xRedmore, Fred H.
Fundamentals of Chemistry. P-H.

Redo, S. Frank.
xRedo, S. Frank.
Atlas of Surgery in the First Six Months of Life. Har-Row.
Principles of Surgery in the First Six Months of Life. Har-Row.

Redon, Odilon.
xRedon, Odilon.
Graphic Works of Odilon Redon. Dover.

Redondo, Diego.
xRedondo, Diego.
Growing up Healthy. Condor Pub Co.

Redpath, James, 1833-1891
xRedpath, James.
Echoes of Harper's Ferry. Arno.
Echoes of Harper's Ferry. Negro U Pr.

Redpath, Peter A.
xRedpath, Peter A.
A Simplified Introduction to the Wisdom of St. Thomas. U Pr of Amer.

Redstone, Louis G.
xRedstone, Louis G.
Art in Architecture. McGraw.

Ree, J. *see* Ree, Jonathan.

Ree, Jonathan, 1948-
xRee, J.
Philosophy & Its Past. Humanities.
xRee, Jonathan.

Descartes. Universe.

Ree, Stephen, 1852-
xRee, Stephen.
Gordon Ballads. Norwood Edns.

Reebenacker, Noel.
xReebenacker, Noel.
How to Develop a Successful High School Passing Attack. P-H.

Reece, Colleen L.
xReece, Colleen L.
In Search of Twilight. Bouregy.

Reece, Eileen.
xReece, Eileen.
The Dieting Gourmet. Allen Unwin.
Soups for All Seasons & a Collation of Sandwiches. Allen Unwin.

Reece, Jack E.
xReece, Jack E.
The Bretons Against France: Ethnic Minority Nationalism in Twentieth-Century France. U of NC Pr.

Reed, A. W. *see* Reed, Alfred Hamish.

Reed, Alexander W. *see* Reed, Alexander Ward.

Reed, Alexander Ward.
xReed, Alexander W.
Ocean Waste Disposal Practices. Noyes.

Reed, Alexander Wyclif.
xReed, A. W.
Aboriginal Legends: Animal Tales. Reed.

Reed, Alfred Hamish, 1875-
xReed, A. W.
The Story of New Zealand. Reed.

Reed, Alfred Z. *see* Reed, Alfred Zantzinger.

Reed, Alfred Zantzinger, 1875-1949
xReed, Alfred Z.
Present-Day Law Schools in the United States & Canada. Arno.

Reed, Barry. *see* Reed, Barry C.

Reed, Barry C.
xReed, Barry.
The Verdict. S&S.

Reed, Betty J. *see* Reed, Betty Jane.

Reed, Betty Jane.
xReed, Betty J.
Are You a Kangaroo?. Denison.
Flyin' with a Lion. Denison.
Golfin' with a Dolphin. Denison.
A Horse of Course. Denison.
Laugh with a Giraffe. Denison.
More Mom for Tom. Denison.
Such a Fuss with a Hippopotamus. Denison.
They Left the Moon Too Soon. Denison.

Reed, Carl.
xReed, Carl.
Art from Scrap. Davis Mass.

Reed, Carroll. *see* Reed, Carroll E.

Reed, Carroll E.
xReed, Carroll.
Dialects of American English. U of Mass Pr.

Reed, Charles A.
xReed, Charles A.
ed. Origins of Agriculture. Beresford Bk Serv.

Reed, Constance.
xReed, Constance.
How to Be Beautiful After the Baby Comes. Watts.

Reed, E. *see* Reed, Edward Wilson.

Reed, Edward.
xReed, Edward.
ed. Readings for Democrats. Oceana.

Reed, Edward W. *see* Reed, Edward Wilson.

Reed, Edward Wilson.
xReed, E.
Commercial Banking. P-H.
xReed, Edward W.
Casebook in Commercial Banking. P-H.

Reed, Eugene E. *see* Reed, Eugene Elliott.

Reed, Eugene Elliott.
xReed, Eugene E.

The Civilized Vs. Civilization: Primitivism in
the Literature of German Pre-Romanticism.
U Pr of Idaho.

Reed, Evelyn.
xReed, Evelyn.
Problems of Women's Liberation: A Marxist
Approach. Path Pr NY.

Reed, Frank A., 1895-
xReed, Frank A.
Lumberjack Sky Pilot. North Country.

Reed, Germaine M., 1929-
xReed, Germaine M.
David French Boyd: Founder of Louisiana
State University. La State U Pr.

Reed, Graham.
xReed, Graham.
Magical Miracles You Can Do.
Elsevier-Nelson.

Reed, Graham. see Reed, Graham F.

Reed, Graham F.
xReed, Graham.
The Psychology of Anomalous Experience: A
Cognitive Approach. Humanities.

Reed, Gretchen M. see Reed, Gretchen Mayo.

Reed, Gretchen Mayo.
xReed, Gretchen M.
Regulation of Fluid & Electrolyte Balance: A
Programmed Instruction in Clinical
Physiology. Saunders.

Reed, Gwendolyn. see Reed, Gwendolyn E.

Reed, Gwendolyn E.
xReed, Gwendolyn.
Adam & Eve. Lothrop.
Talkative Beasts: Myths, Fables, & Poems of
India. Lothrop.

Reed, H. Clay. see Reed, Henry Clay.

Reed, Henry, 1808-1854
xReed, Henry.
Lectures on English History & Tragic Poetry
As Illustrated by Shakespeare. R West.

Reed, Henry Clay, 1899-
xReed, H. Clay.
Delaware Colony. Macmillan.

Reed, Irving B.
xReed, Irving B.
The Latin American Scene of the Seventies: A
Basic Fact Book. AISI.

Reed, Ishmael, 1938-
xReed, Ishmael.
Flight to Canada. Random.
The Free Lance Pallbearers. Avon.
The Free-Lance Pallbearers. Chatham Bkseller.
The Last Days of Louisiana Red. Avon.
The Last Days of Louisiana Red. Random.

Reed, James.
xReed, James.
The Border Ballads. Humanities.
From Private Vice to Public Virtue: The Birth
Control Movement & American Society
Since 1830. Basic.

Reed, John, 1887-1920
xReed, John.
Adventures of a Young Man: Short Stories
from Life. City Lights.
Daughter of the Revolution, & Other Stories.
Arno.
Insurgent Mexico. Greenwood.
Insurgent Mexico. Intl Pub Co.
Ten Days That Shook the World. Penguin.
Ten Days That Shook the World. Random.
Ten Days That Shook the World. Intl Pub Co.

Reed, John F. see Reed, John Ford.

Reed, John Ford, 1911-
xReed, John F.
Valley Forge, Crucible of Victory. Freneau.

Reed, John H., 1937-
xReed, John H.

The Application of Operations Research to
Court Delay. Irvington.

Reed, John R.
xReed, John R.
Perception & Design in Tennyson's "Idylls of
the King". Ohio U Pr.

Reed, Joseph W.
xReed, Joseph W.
Faulkner's Narrative. Yale U Pr.

Reed, Kathlyn L.
xReed, Kathlyn L.
Concepts of Occupational Therapy. Williams &
Wilkins.

Reed, Kenneth, 1944-
xReed, Kenneth.
Mennonite Soldier. Herald Pr.

Reed, Kit.
xReed, Kit.
Magic Time. Putnam.

Reed, Langford, 1889-
xReed, Langford.
The Complete Limerick Book: The Origin,
History & Achievements of the Limerick.
Gale.
The Life of Lewis Carroll. Folcroft.

Reed, M. see Reed, Mortimer P.

Reed, M. C. see Reed, Michael.

Reed, Mark L.
xReed, Mark L.
Wordsworth: The Chronology of the Early
Years, 1770-1799. Harvard U Pr.
Wordsworth: The Chronology of the Middle
Years, 1800-1815. Harvard U Pr.

Reed, Michael.
xReed, M. C.
Abstract Non Linear Wave Equations.
Springer-Verlag.

Reed, Mortimer P,
xReed, M.
Handbook of Vacation House Planning &
Building. P-H.

Reed, Nelson.
xReed, Nelson.
The Caste War of Yucatan. Stanford U Pr.

Reed, P. B. see Reed, Prentiss B.

Reed, Philip, 1908-
xReed, Philip.
Mother Goose & Nursery Rhymes.
Regnery-Gateway.

Reed, Prentiss B.
xReed, P. B.
Adjustment of Property Losses. McGraw.
xReed, Prentiss B.
Adjustment of Property Losses. McGraw.

Reed, Rex.
xReed, Rex.
People Are Crazy Here. Delacorte.
Travolta to Keaton. Berkley Pub.
Travolta to Keaton. Morrow.

Reed, Richard E.
xReed, Richard Ernie.
Return to the City: How to Restore Old
Buildings & Ourselves in America's Historic
Urban Neighborhoods. Doubleday.

Reed, Richard Ernie. see Reed, Richard E.

Reed, Richard J. see Reed, Richard Jay.

Reed, Richard Jay, 1928-
xReed, Richard J.
Cutaneous Vasculitides: Immunologic &
Histologic Correlations. Am Soc Clinical.

Reed, Robert. see Reed, Robert Carroll.

Reed, Robert C. see Reed, Robert Carroll.

Reed, Robert Carroll, 1937-
xReed, Robert.
The Streamline Era. Golden West.
xReed, Robert C.
The New York Elevated. A S Barnes.

Reed, Robert R. see Reed, Robert Rentoul.

Reed, Robert Rentoul, 1911-
xReed, Robert R.

Occult on the Tudor & Stuart Stage. Chris
Mass.

Reed, Rowena.
xReed, Rowena A.
Combined Operations in the Civil War. Naval
Inst Pr.

Reed, Rowena A. see Reed, Rowena.

Reed, Rowland I.
xReed, Rowland I.
Applications of Mass Spectrometry to Organic
Chemistry. Acad Pr.

Reed, Ruth, 1898-
xReed, Ruth.
The Illegitimate Family in New York City: Its
Treatment by Social & Health Agencies.
Arno.
Negro Illegitimacy in New York City. AMS
Pr.

Reed, Stephen K.
xReed, Stephen K.
Psychological Processes in Pattern Recognition.
Acad Pr.

Reed, Thomas B.
xReed, Thomas B.
Free Energy of Formation of Binary
Compounds: An Atlas of Charts for High
Temperature Chemical Calculations. MIT Pr.

Reed, Tim.
xReed, Tim.
The Loom Book. Scribner.

Reed, Wallace E.
xReed, Wallace E.
Areal Interaction in India: Commodity Flows
of the Bengal-Bihar Industrial Area. U
Chicago Dept Geog.

Reed, Walter L.
xReed, Walter L.
Meditations on the Hero: A Study of the
Romantic Hero in Nineteenth-Century
Fiction. Yale U Pr.

Reed, William, 1929-
xReed, William.
Olaf Wieghorst. Northland.

Reeder, Carolyn.
xReeder, Carolyn.
Shenandoah Heritage: The Story of the People
Before the Park. Potomac Appalach.

Reeder, M. M. see Reeder, Maurice M.

Reeder, Maurice M.
xReeder, M. M.
ed. Gamuts in Radiology: Comprehensive Lists
of Roentgen Differentials Diagnosis.
Pergamon.

Reeder, Rudolph R. see Reeder, Rudolph Rex.

Reeder, Rudolph Rex, 1859-
xReeder, Rudolph R.
How Two Hundred Children Live & Learn.
Arno.

Reeder, Sharon. see Reeder, Sharon J.

Reeder, Sharon J.
xReeder, Sharon.
Maternity Nursing. Lippincott.

Reeder, W. Donald.
xReeder, W. Donald.
Letters of John & Jude. Moody.

Reedstrom, Ernest L. see Reedstrom, Ernest Lisle.

Reedstrom, Ernest Lisle.
xReedstrom, Ernest L.
Bugles, Banners & War Bonnets. Caxton.

Reedy, George. see Reedy, George E.

Reedy, George E., 1917-
xReedy, George.
The Presidency in Flux. Columbia U Pr.
Twilight of the Presidency. NAL.
xReedy, George E.
The Presidency. Arno.

Reefman, William E.
xReefman, William E.

How to Sell Your Own Invention. Halls of Ivy.

Reeh, Merrill J.
  xReeh, Merrill J.
    Practical Ophthalmic Plastic & Reconstructive
    Surgery. Lea & Febiger.

Reekie, Duncan W. see Reekie, W. Duncan.

Reekie, R. Fraser. see Reekie, Ronald Fraser.

Reekie, Ronald Fraser.
  xReekie, R. Fraser.
    Design in the Built Environment. Crane-Russak
    Co.

Reekie, W. Duncan.
  xReekie, Duncan W.
    Profits, Politics & Drugs. Holmes & Meier.
  xReekie, W. Duncan.
    Give Us This Day: An Economic Critique of
    Political Intervention Between Men &
    Women & Their Daily Bread. Transatlantic.
    Industry, Prices & Markets. Halsted Pr.

Reeman, Douglas.
  xReeman, Douglas.
    The Deep Silence. Berkley Pub.
    The Deep Silence. Putnam.
    The Greatest Enemy. Putnam.
    His Majesty's U-Boat. Berkley Pub.
    His Majesty's U-Boat. Berkley Pub.
    The Last Raider. Berkley Pub.
    A Prayer for the Ship. Putnam.
    Rendezvous-South Atlantic. Putnam.
    A Ship Must Die. Morrow.
    Strike from the Sea. Berkley Pub.
    Strike from the Sea. Morrow.
    Surface with Daring. Berkley Pub.
    Surface with Daring. Putnam.

Rees, A. R. see Rees, Alun Rocyn.

Rees, Albert, 1921-
  xRees, Albert.
    The Economics of Trade Unions. U of Chicago
    Pr.
    The Economics of Work & Pay. Har-Row.
    Workers & Wages in an Urban Labor Market.
    U of Chicago Pr.

Rees, Alun Rocyn, 1932-
  xRees, A. R.
    Growth of Bulbs: Applied Aspects of the
    Physiology of Ornamental Bulbous Corp
    Plants. Acad Pr.

Rees, Barbara.
  xRees, Barbara.
    Harriet Dark: Branwell Bronte's Lost Novel.
    Gordon-Cremonesi.

Rees, Clair. see Rees, Clair F.

Rees, Clair F.
  xRees, Clair.
    Off Road Vehicle Digest. Follett.
  xRees, Clair F.
    Beginner's Guide to Guns & Shooting. Follett.

Rees, D. Morgan. see Rees, David Morgan.

Rees, David, 1936-
  xRees, David.
    The Exeter Blitz. Elsevier-Nelson.
    Quintin's Man. Elsevier-Nelson.

Rees, David Morgan.
  xRees, D. Morgan.
    Industrial Archaeology of Wales. David &
    Charles.

Rees, Ennis.
  xRees, Ennis.
    Brer Rabbit & His Tricks. A-W.
    Fables from Aesop. Oxford U Pr.
    Pun Fun. Abelard.

Rees, Goronwy, 1909-
  xRees, Goronwy.
    Chapter of Accidents. Open Court.

Rees, H. H.
  xRees, H. H.

Insect Biochemistry. Methuen Inc.

Rees, Hubert.
  xRees, Hubert.
    Chromosome Genetics. Univ Park.

Rees, James, 1802-1885
  xRees, James.
    The Life of Edwin Forrest. Longwood Pr.

Rees, Joan.
  xRees, Joan.
    Fulke Greville, Lord Brooke, 1554-1628: A
    Critical Biography. U of Cal Pr.
    Shakespeare & the Story: Aspects of the
    Creation. Humanities.

Rees, Leighton.
  xRees, Leighton.
    Darts. Atheneum.

Rees, Margaret A.
  xRees, Margaret A.
    Alfred de Musset. Irvington.

Rees, Paul. see Rees, Paul Klein.

Rees, Paul K. see Rees, Paul Klein.

Rees, Paul Klein.

  xRees, Paul.
    Intermediate Algebra. McGraw.
    Principles of Mathematics. P-H.

  xRees, Paul K.
    Algebra & Trigonometry. McGraw.
    Algebra, Trigonometry & Analytic Geometry.
    McGraw.

    Analytic Geometry. P-H.
    Calculus with Analytic Geometry. McGraw.
    College Algebra. McGraw.

Rees, Philip H., 1944-

  xRees, Philip H.
    Residential Patterns in American Cities: 1960.
    U Chicago Dept Geog.

Rees, Richard, Sir, Bart.
  xRees, Richard.
    Simone Weil: A Sketch for a Portrait. S Ill U
    Pr.

Rees, Robert A.
  xRees, Robert A.
    ed. Fifteen American Authors Before 1900:
    Bibliographic Essays on Research &
    Criticism. U of Wis Pr.

Rees, Samuel, 1936-
  xRees, Samuel.
    David Jones. Twayne.

Rees, William, 1887-
  xRees, William.
    A History of the Order of St. John of
    Jerusalem in Wales & on the Welsh Border:
    Including an Account of the Templars. AMS
    Pr.

Reese, Alexander, 1881-1969
  xReese, Alexander.
    Approaching Advent of Christ. Kregel.

Reese, Algernon B.
  xReese, Algernon B.
    Tumors of the Eye. Har-Row.

Reese, David M. see Reese, David Meredith.

Reese, David Meredith, 1800-1861
  xReese, David M.
    Humbugs of New York. Arno.

Reese, Ellen P.
  xReese, Ellen P.
    Human Behavior: Analysis & Application. Wm
    C Brown.

Reese, Ernst S.
  xReese, Ernst S.
    Contrasts in Behavior: Adaptations in the
    Aquatic & Terrestrial Environments. Wiley.

Reese, Gustave, 1899-
  xReese, Gustave.

Fourscore Classics of Music Literature. Da
  Capo.
  Music in the Renaissance. Norton.

Reese, Hayne W. see Reese, Hayne Waring.

Reese, Hayne Waring, 1931-
  xReese, Hayne W.
    Perception of Stimulus Relations:
    Discrimination Learning & Transposition.
    Acad Pr.

Reese, Herbert H. see Reese, Herbert Harshman.

Reese, Herbert Harshman.
  xReese, Herbert H.
    Arabian Horse Breeding. Borden.

Reese, John. see Reese, John Henry.

Reese, John Henry.
  xReese, John.
    Angel Range. Nordon Pubns.
    Halter-Broke. BJ Pub Group.
    Legacy of a Land Hog. Doubleday.
    A Pair of Deuces. Doubleday.

Reese, Michael, 1942-
  xReese, Michael.
    Collector's Guide to Luger Values. Pelican.

Reese, Richard M. see Reese, Richard Martin.

Reese, Richard Martin.
  xReese, Richard M.
    Marketing of a Forest Product: A
    Chance-Constrained Transportation Model. U
    of Tex Busn Res.

Reese, Terence.
  xReese, Terence.
    Backgammon the Modern Game. Cornerstone.
    Begin Bridge with Reese. NAL.
    Begin Bridge with Reese. Sterling.
    Bridge at the Top. Merrimack Bk Serv.
    Bridge Conventions, Finesses & Coups. Dover.
    Bridge for Bright Beginners. Dover.
    The Most Puzzling Situations in Bridge Play.
    NAL.
    The Most Puzzling Situations in Bridge Play.
    Sterling.
    Those Extra Chances in Bridge. Fell.
    When to Duck--When to Win in Bridge. Fell.
    Winning at Casino Gambling: An International
    Guide. Sterling.
  xReese, Terrence.
    Play Bridge with Reese. Dover.

Reese, Terrence. see Reese, Terence.

Reese, Thomas. see Reese, Thomas Ford.

Reese, Thomas Ford.
  xReese, Thomas.
    The Architecture of Ventura Rodriguez.
    Garland Pub.

Reese, Trevor R. see Reese, Trevor Richard.

Reese, Trevor Richard.
  xReese, Trevor R.
    Colonial Georgia: A Study in British Imperial
    Policy in the Eighteenth Century. U of Ga
    Pr.

Reesink, Maryke.
  xReesink, Maryke.
    Two Windmills. HarBraceJ.

Reeve, Arthur B. see Reeve, Arthur Benjamin.

Reeve, Arthur Benjamin, 1880-1936
  xReeve, Arthur B.
    The Silent Bullet: The Adventures of Craig
    Kennedy, Scientific Detective. Arno.

Reeve, Carl.
  xReeve, Carl.
    James Connolly & the United States: The Road
    to the 1916 Irish Rebellion. Humanities.
    Life & Times of Daniel De Leon. Am Inst
    Marxist.
    The Life & Times of Daniel De Leon.
    Humanities.

Reeve, E. G.
  xReeve, E. G.

Validation of Selection Boards; & Procedures
As Exemplified in a Study of the War Office
Selection Boards. Acad Pr.

Reeve, F. A.
xReeve, Frank Albert.
The Cambridge Nobody Knows. Oleander Pr.

Reeve, F. D. see Reeve, Franklin D.

Reeve, Frank Albert. see Reeve, F. A.

Reeve, Franklin D., 1928-
xReeve, F. D.
The Brother. FS&G.
tr. & ed. Nineteenth-Century Russian Plays.
Norton.
tr. & ed. Twentieth-Century Russian Plays: An
Anthology. Norton.
White Colors. FS&G.
xReeve, Franklin D.
ed. Contemporary Russian Drama. Irvington.

Reeve, W. D.
xReeve, W. D.
Public Administration in Siam. AMS Pr.
The Republic of Korea: A Political &
Economic Study. Greenwood.

Reeve, William C., 1943-
xReeve, William C.
Georg Buchner. Ungar.

Reeves. see Reeves, David S.

Reeves, C. M.
xReeves, C. M.
An Introduction to Logical Design of Digital
Circuits. Cambridge U Pr.

Reeves, Charles E. see Reeves, Charles Everand.

Reeves, Charles Everand, 1889-
xReeves, Charles E.
An Analysis of Janitor Service in Elementary
Schools. AMS Pr.

Reeves, David S.
xReeves.
ed. Laboratory Methods in Antimicrobial
Chemotherapy. Churchill.

Reeves, Dona B.
xReeves, Dona B.
ed. Retrospect & Retrieval: The German
Element in Review, Essays on Cultural
Preservation. Univ Microfilms.

Reeves, Elton. see Reeves, Elton T.

Reeves, Elton T.
xReeves, Elton.
How to Get Along with (Almost) Everybody.
Citadel Pr.

Reeves, Floyd. see Reeves, Floyd Wesley.

Reeves, Floyd W. see Reeves, Floyd Wesley.

Reeves, Floyd Wesley.
xReeves, Floyd.
Instructional Problems in the University.
Greenwood.
xReeves, Floyd W.
ed. Instructional Problems in the University.
AMS Pr.

Reeves, Henry, 1939-
xReeves, Henry.
In a Meadow's Calm. Windy Row.

Reeves, James.
xReeves, James.
Arcadian Ballads. Heinemann Ed.
ed. Cassell Book of English Poetry. Har-Row.
The Clever Mouse. Merrimack Bk Serv.
Commitment to Poetry. Heinemann Ed.
Dialogue & Drama. Heinemann Ed.
Inside Poetry. Heinemann Ed.
Understanding Poetry. Heinemann Ed.

Reeves, John, 1752?-1829
xReeves, John.
History of the English Law, from the Time of
the Saxons, to the End of the Reign of Philip
& Mary. Rothman.
History of the Government of the Island of
Newfoundland. Johnson Repr.
Murder by Microphone. Doubleday.

Reeves, John R. see Reeves, John Richard T.

Reeves, John Richard T.
xReeves, John R.
Questions & Answers About Acne. P-H.

Reeves, Michael.
xReeves, Michael.
Travolta: A Photo Bio. BJ Pub Group.

Reeves, Miriam. see Reeves, Miriam G.

Reeves, Miriam G.
xReeves, Miriam.
Felicianas of Louisiana. Claitors.
xReeves, Miriam G.
Governors of Louisiana. Pelican.

Reeves, P.
xReeves, P.
The Bacteriocins. Springer-Verlag.

Reeves, Richard.
xReeves, Richard.
Convention. HarBraceJ.
A Ford, Not a Lincoln. HarBraceJ.

Reeves, Robert B.
xReeves, Robert B.
Pastoral Care of the Dying & Bereaved:
Selected Readings. H S Pub Corp.

Reeves, Robert N. see Reeves, Robert Nicholas.

Reeves, Robert Nicholas.
xReeves, Robert N.
The Ridiculous to the Delightful: Comic
Characters in Sidney's New Arcadia.
Harvard U Pr.

Reeves, Rosser.
xReeves, Rosser.
Reality in Advertising. Knopf.

Reeves, Thomas C., 1936-
xReeves, Thomas C.
ed. Foundations Under Fire. Cornell U Pr.

Reeves, William J. see Reeves, William Joseph.

Reeves, William Joseph.
xReeves, William J.
Librarians As Professionals: The Occupation's
Impact on Library Work Arrangements.
Lexington Bks.

Reeves, Wilson A.
xReeves, Wilson A.
Fire Resistant Textiles Handbook. Technomic.

Reff, Theodore.
xReff, Theodore.
Degas: The Artist's Mind. Har-Row.

Regan, D. E. see Regan, David E.

Regan, David E.
xRegan, D. E.
Local Government & Education. Allen Unwin.

Regan, J. Peter. see Regan, James Peter.

Regan, James Peter.
xRegan, J. Peter.
Massachusetts Real Estate Principles &
Practices. Winthrop.

Regan, Richard J.
xRegan, Richard J.
Private Conscience & Public Law: The
American Experience. Fordham.

Regazzi, John J.
xRegazzi, John J.
A Guide to Indexed Periodicals in Religion.
Scarecrow.

Regelski, Thomas A., 1941-
xRegelski, Thomas A.
Principles & Problems of Music Education.
P-H.

Regener, Eric.
xRegener, Eric.
Pitch Notation & Equal Temperament: A
Formal Study. U of Cal Pr.

Regensburg, Jeannette, 1898-
xRegensburg, Jeannette.
Toward Education for Health Professions.
Har-Row.

Regensburg, Jeannette. see Regensburg, Jeanette.

Regenstein, Lewis.
xRegenstein, Lewis.
The Politics of Extinction: The Shocking Story
of the World's Endangered Wildlife.
Macmillan.

Regensteiner, Else, 1906-
xRegensteiner, Else.
The Art of Weaving. Textile Bk.
Art of Weaving. Van Nos Reinhold.

Reger, Roger.
xReger, Roger.
Preschool Programming of Children with
Disabilities. C C Thomas.
Special Education: Children with Learning
Problems. Oxford U Pr.

Regier, Marilyn C.
xRegier, Marilyn C.
Social Policy in Action: Perspectives on the
Implementation of Alcoholism Reforms.
Lexington Bks.

Reginald, R.
xReginald, R.
Contemporary Science Fiction Authors. Arno.
ed. They: Three Parodies of H. Rider
Haggard's She. Arno.
xReginald, Robert.
ed. Science Fiction & Fantasy Literature: A
Checklist from 1700 to 1974...with
Contemporary Science Fiction Authors II.
Gale.

Reginald, Robert. see Reginald, R.

**Regional Conference on Relativity, University of
Pittsburgh, 1970.**
xRegional Conference on Relativity, Univ. of
Pittsburgh, July 13-17, 1970.
Methods of Local & Global Differential
Geometry in General Relativity: Proceedings.
Springer-Verlag

Regional Employment Programme for Latin America &
the Caribbean. see Programa Regional Del Empleo
Para America Latina y el Caribe.

Regional Environmental Management, San Diego, Ca.,
1973. see National Conference on Regional
Environmental Management, San Diego, Calif., 1973.

Regional Plan Association. see Regional Plan
Association, New York.

Regional Plan Association, New York.
xRegional Plan Association.
From Plan to Reality. Arno.
Office Industry: Patterns of Growth &
Location. MIT Pr.

Regional Science Association.
xRegional Science Association, Far East
Conference, 1st.
Paper & Proceedings. Intl Schol Bk Serv.

Regional Science Association, Far East Conference, 1st.
see Regional Science Association.

Regional Symposium, Panama, 1973. see Symposium on
Equality of Opportunity in Employment in
Theamerican Region, Panama, 1973.

Register, Susanne. see Register, Susanne Haines.

Register, Susanne Haines, 1947-
xRegister, Susanne.
Take It All off. Beta Bk.

Register, W. Raymond, 1937-
xRegister, W. Raymond.
Discovery by Lamplight. Golden Quill.

Regnery, Dorothy F.
xRegnery, Dorothy F.
An Enduring Heritage: Historic Buildings of
the San Francisco Peninsula. Stanford U Pr.

Regnery, Henry, 1912-
xRegnery, Henry.
Memoirs of a Dissident Publisher. HarBraceJ.

Regnier, Edme, 1920-
xRegnier, Edme.
There Is a Cure for the Common Cold. P-H.

Regniers, Beatrice S. De. see De Regniers, Beatrice S.

Regosin, Richard. see Regosin, Richard L.

Regosin, Richard L., 1937-
xRegosin, Richard.

The Matter of My Book: Montaigne's "Essais"
As the Book of the Self. U of Cal Pr.

Regush, Nicholas. see Regush, Nicholas M.

Regush, Nicholas M.

xRegush, Nicholas.
The New Consciousness Catalog. Putnam.

xRegush, Nicholas M.
Human Aura. Berkley Pub.

Reh, A. M. see Reh, Albert M.
Reh, Albert M., 1922-
xReh, A. M.
Continuing German: A Bridge to Literature.
McGraw.
Reh, E. see Reh, Emma.
Reh, Emma.
xReh, E.
Manual on Household Food Consumption
Surveys. Unipub.
Rehberg, Richard A.
xRehberg, Richard A.
Class & Merit in the American High School:
An Assessment of the Revisionist &
Meritocratic Arguments. Longman.
Rehder, Helmut.
xRehder, Helmut.
ed. Literary Symbolism: A Symposium. U of
Tex Pr.
Rehder, Jessie. see Rehder, Jessie C.
Rehder, Jessie C.
xRehder, Jessie.
ed. Act of Writing. Odyssey Pr.
Rehfisch, Farnham.
xRehfisch, Farnham.
ed. Gypsies, Tinkers, & Other Travellers. Acad
Pr.
Rehg, Kenneth L.
xRehg, Kenneth L.
Ponapean-English Dictionary. U Pr of Hawaii.
Rehkopf, Donald C.
xRehkopf, Donald C.
ed. Portraits in Words: An Introduction to the
Study of Biography. Odyssey Pr.
Rehmus, Charles M.
xRehmus, Charles M.
ed. Public Employment Labor Relations: An
Overview of Eleven Nations. U of Mich Inst
Labor.
Rehor, John A., 1929-
xRehor, John A.
Nickel Plate Story. Kalmbach.
Rehrauer, George.
xRehrauer, George.
The Film User's Handbook: A Basic Manual
for Managing Library Film Services. Bowker.
Reich, Charles A.
xReich, Charles A.
Greening of America: How the Youth
Revolution Is Trying to Make America
Liveable. Random.
The Sorcerer of Bolinas Reef. Random.
Reich, Emil, 1854-1910
xReich, Emil.
Hungarian Literature: Historical & Critical
Survey. Arno.
Reich, Hanns.
xReich, Hanns.
ed. Children & Their Fathers. Hill & Wang.
ed. Children & Their Mothers. Hill & Wang.
ed. Laughing Camera for Children. Hill &
Wang.
Reich, Helen.
xReich, Helen.
College Housemother. Interstate.
Reich, L. see Reich, Leo.
Reich, Larry.
xReich, Laurence.

From Fat to Skinny. Playboy Pbks.
Reich, Laurence. see Reich, Larry.
Reich, Leo.
xReich, L.
Autoxidation of Hydrocarbons & Polyolefins:
Kinetics & Mechanisms. Dekker.
Reich, Paul R. see Reich, Paul Richard.
Reich, Paul Richard.
xReich, Paul R.
Hematology: Physiopathologic Basis for
Clinical Practice. Little.
Reich, Warren T.
xReich, Warren T.
ed. Encyclopedia of Bioethics. Free Pr.
Reich, Wilhelm, 1897-1957
xReich, Wilhelm.
Cancer Biopathy. FS&G.
Character Analysis. FS&G.
Character Analysis. S&S.
Early Writings. FS&G.
Listen, Little Man!. FS&G.
Listen, Little Man. Octagon.
The Mass Psychology of Fascism. FS&G.
The Mass Psychology of Fascism. PB.
The Mass Psychology of Fascism. S&S.
Reichard, Gary W., 1943-
xReichard, Gary W.
The Reaffirmation of Republicanism:
Eisenhower & the Eighty-Third Congress. U
of Tenn Pr.
Reichard, Gladys A. see Reichard, Gladys Amanda.
Reichard, Gladys Amanda, 1893-1955
xReichard, Gladys A.
Melanesian Design: A Study of Style in Wood
& Tortoiseshell Carving. AMS Pr.
Navaho Grammar. AMS Pr.
Navaho Religion: A Study of Symbolism.
Princeton U Pr.
Navajo Shepherd & Weaver. Rio Grande.
Spider Woman: A Story of Navajo Weavers &
Chanters. Rio Grande.
Reichard, Richard W., 1923-
xReichard, Richard W.
Crippled from Birth: German Social
Democracy 1844-1870. Iowa St U Pr.
Reichard, Robert. see Reichard, Robert S.
Reichard, Robert S.
xReichard, Robert.
Figure Finaglers. McGraw.
Reichel, Levin T. see Reichel, Levin Theodore.
Reichel, Levin Theodore, 1812-1878
xReichel, Levin T.
Moravians in North Carolina: An Authentic
History. Genealog Pub.
Reichenbach, Bruce R.
xReichenbach, Bruce R.
Cosmological Argument: A Reassessment. C C
Thomas.
Reichenbach, Hans.
xReichenbach, Hans.
Axiomatization of the Theory of Relativity. U
of Cal Pr.
From Copernicus to Einstein. Dover.
Laws, Modalities, & Counterfactuals. U of Cal
Pr.
Reichert, Katharine E.
xReichert, Katharine E.
Primary Care of Young Adults: A
Practitioner's Manual. Med Exam.
Reichert, Richard.
xReichert, Richard.
Simulation Games for Religious Education.
John Knox.
Simulation Games for Religious Education. St
Marys.
Teaching Sacraments to Youth. Paulist Pr.
xReichert, Richard J.
A Learning Process for Religious Education.
Pflaum Pr.
Reichert, Richard J. see Reichert, Richard.

Reichert, Sara.
xReichert, Sara.
In Wisdom & the Spirit: A Religious Education
Program for Those Over Sixty-Five. Paulist
Pr.
Reichert, William O.
xReichert, William O.
Partisans of Freedom: A Study in American
Anarchism. Bowling Green Univ.
Reichl, L. E.
xReichl, R. E.
A Modern Course in Statistical Physics. U of
Tex Pr.
Reichl, R. E. see Reichl, L. E.
Reichler, Joe.
xReichler, Joseph L.
The World Series: A 75th Anniversary. S&S.
Reichler, Joseph L. see Reichler, Joe.
Reichlin, Seymour.
xReichlin, Seymour.
ed. The Hypothalamus. Raven.
Reichman, Charles.
xReichman, Charles.
Guide to the Manufacture of Sweaters, Knit
Shirts & Swimwear. Textile Bk.
Reichwein, Adolf, 1898-1944
xReichwein, Adolf.
China and Europe: Intellectual and Artistic
Contacts in the Eighteenth Century. Chinese
Materials.
Reid, Alan, fl. 1973-
xReid, Alan.
Concise Encyclopedia of the Second World
War. Beekman Pubs.
Reid, Alastair.
xReid, Alastair.
Ounce, Dice, Trice. Gregg.
Ounce, Dice, Trice. Little.
Reid, Alexander J. see Reid, Alexander James.
Reid, Alexander James.
xReid, Alexander J.
Roots of Lomomba: Mongo Land. Exposition.
Reid, Alfred S.
xReid, Alfred S.
Furman University: Toward a New Identity,
1925-1975. Duke.
Reid, Allan L.
xReid, Allan L.
Modern Applied Salesmanship. Goodyear.
Reid, B. L. see Reid, Benjamin Lawrence.
Reid, Benjamin Lawrence.
xReid, B. L.
The Lives of Roger Casement. Yale U Pr.
Reid, Charles, 1937-
xReid, Charles.
Figure Painting in Watercolor. Watson-Guptill.
Flower Painting in Oil. Watson-Guptill.
Flower Painting in Watercolor. Watson-Guptill.
Portrait Painting in Watercolor.
Watson-Guptill.
Reid, Charles F. see Reid, Charles Frederick.
Reid, Charles Frederick.
xReid, Charles F.
Education in the Territories & Outlying
Possessions of the United States. AMS Pr.
Reid, Charles R., 1926-
xReid, Charles R.
Environment & Learning: The Prior Issues.
Fairleigh Dickinson.
Reid, Christopher.
xReid, Christopher.
Arcadia. Oxford U Pr.
Reid, Constance.
xReid, Constance.
Hilbert. Springer-Verlag.
Reid, Dorothy E.
xReid, Dorothy E.
Coach into Pumpkin. AMS Pr.
Reid, Duncan E.
xReid, Duncan E.

Principles & Management of Human
Reproduction. Saunders.

Reid, E. *see* Reid, Eric.

Reid, E. Emmet. *see* Reid, Ebenezer Emmet.

Reid, Ebenezer Emmet, 1872-
xReid, E. Emmet.
Chemistry through the Language Barrier: How
to Scan Chemical Articles in Foreign
Languages with Emphasis on Russian &
Japanese. Johns Hopkins.

Reid, Ed.
xReid, Ed.
Green Felt Jungle. PB.

Reid, Eric, 1922-
xReid, E.
Cell Populations. Halsted Pr.
ed. Plant Organelles. Halsted Pr.
xReid, Eric.
ed. Assay of Drugs & Other Trace Compounds
in Biological Fluids. Elsevier.
ed. Membranous Elements & Movement of
Molecules. Halsted Pr.

Reid, Escott.
xReid, Escott.
Strengthening the World Bank. U of Chicago
Pr.

Reid, Forrest, 1876-1947
xReid, Forrest.
Pender Among the Residents. Scholarly.
Pirates of the Spring. Folcroft.
Pirates of the Spring. Scholarly.
Uncle Stephen. Scholarly.

Reid, Francis.
xReid, Francis.
Stage Lighting Handbook. Theatre Arts.

Reid, G. A.
xReid, G. A.
Pitman Shorthand. Pitman Learning.

Reid, George K. *see* Reid, George Kell.

Reid, George H., 1924-
xReid, George H.
Boatmen's Guide to Light Salvage. Cornell
Maritime.

Reid, George Kell.
xReid, George K.
Ecology of Inland Waters & Estuaries. Van
Nos Reinhold.

Reid, Giorgina.
xReid, Giorgina.
How to Hold up a Bank. A S Barnes.

Reid, Gordon.
xReid, Gordon.
Politics of Financial Control: The Role of the
House of Commons. Humanities.

Reid, Ian.
xReid, Ian.
The Short Story. Methuen Inc.

Reid, Ira D. *see* Reid, Ira De Augustine.

Reid, Ira De Augustine.
xReid, Ira D.
In a Minor Key: Negro Youth in Story & Fact.
Greenwood.
Negro Immigrant: His Background,
Characteristics & Social Adjustment,
1899-1937. AMS Pr.
Negro Immigrant: His Background,
Characteristics and Social Adjustment,
1899-1937. Arno.

Reid, J. B.
xReid, J. B.
Complete Word & Phrase Concordance to the
Poems & Songs of Robert Burns. B Franklin.
A Complete Word & Phrase Concordance to
the Poems & Songs of Robert Burns. R West.
ed. Complete Word & Phrase Concordance to
the Poems & Songs of Robert Burns. Russell.

Reid, J. H. *see* Reid, J H Stewart.

Reid, J H Stewart, 1909-
xReid, J. H.

Origins of the British Labour Party. U of Minn
Pr.

Reid, James. *see* Reid, James W.

Reid, James M.
xReid, James M.
Effective Letters: A Program for
Self-Instruction. McGraw.

Reid, James W.
xReid, James.
The Offering. BJ Pub Group.

Reid, Jan.
xReid, Jan.
The Improbable Rise of Redneck Rock. Da
Capo.
The Improbable Rise of Redneck Rock.
Heidelberg Pubs.

Reid, Jimmy, 1932-
xReid, Jimmy.
Reflections of a Clyde-Built Man. Intl Schol Bk
Serv.

Reid, Jo.
xReid, Jo.
Stove Book. St Martin.

Reid, John C. *see* Reid, John Calvin.

Reid, John Calvin, 1901-
xReid, John C.
Marriage Covenant. John Knox.

Reid, John P. *see* Reid, John Phillip.

Reid, John Phillip.
xReid, John P.
Chief Justice: The Judicial World of Charles
Doe. Harvard U Pr.
In a Defiant Stance: The Conditions of Law in
Massachusetts Bay, the Irish Comparison, &
the Coming of the American Revolution. Pa
St U Pr.
In a Rebellious Spirit: The Argument of Facts,
the Liberty Riot, & the Coming of the
American Revolution. Pa St U Pr.
xReid, John Phillip.
An American Judge: Marmaduke Dent of West
Virginia. NYU Pr.

Reid, John T. *see* Reid, John Turner.

Reid, John Turner, 1908-
xReid, John T.
Spanish American Images of the United
States, 1790-1960. U Presses Fla.

Reid, Joseph L.
xReid, Joseph L.
Northwest Pacific Ocean Waters in Winter.
Johns Hopkins.

Reid, l Leon.
xReid, L. Leon.
Annotated Bibliography of Selected References
in Cerebral Palsy. Stanwix.

Reid, Larry.
xReid, Larry.
Accessories for Your Sports Car. TAB Bks.
TSD Rallying with a Programmable Calculator.
TAB Bks.

Reid, Loren. *see* Reid, Loren Dudley.

Reid, Loren Dudley, 1905-
xReid, Loren.
Speaking Well. McGraw.
Teaching Speech. McGraw.

Reid, Margaret G. *see* Reid, Margaret Gilpin.

Reid, Margaret Gilpin, 1896-
xReid, Margaret G.
Consumers & the Market. Arno.
Food for People. Arno.

Reid, Margaret I. *see* Reid, Margaret Isabelle.

Reid, Margaret Isabelle.
xReid, Margaret I.
Guidance in the Secondary School: An
Annotated Bibliography of Literature,
Materials & Tests. Humanities.
A Matter of Choice: A Study of Guidance &
Subject Options. Humanities.

Reid, Mildred I.
xReid, Mildred I.

The Devil's Handmaidens. Burkehaven Pr.
Over Fool's Hill. Burkehaven Pr.

Reid, Patrick R., 1910-
xReid, Patrick R.
The Colditz Story. Greenwood.

Reid, Randall.
xReid, Randall.
Fiction of Nathanael West: No Redeemer, No
Promised Land. U of Chicago Pr.
Lost & Found. S&S.

Reid, Robert. *see* Reid, Robert William.

Reid, Robert William.
xReid, Robert.
Marie Curie. NAL.
My Children, My Children. HarBraceJ.

Reid, Rolland R.
xReid, Rolland R.
Precambrian Geology of North Snowy Block,
Beartooth Mountains, Montana. Geol Soc.

Reid, Russell M.
xReid, Russell M.
Human Population Genetics. Burgess.

Reid, Sue T. *see* Reid, Sue Titus.

Reid, Sue Titus.
xReid, Sue T.
Crime & Criminology. HR&W.
Population Crisis: An Interdisciplinary
Perspective. Scott F.

Reid, Thomas, 1710-1796
xReid, Thomas.
Inquiry into the Human Mind. U of Chicago
Pr.
Thomas Reid's Inquiry & Essays. Bobbs.

Reid, Thomas F.
xReid, Thomas F.
The Exploding Church. Logos.

Reid, Victor S. *see* Reid, Victor Stafford.

Reid, Victor Stafford, 1913-
xReid, Victor S.
The Leopard. Chatham Bkseller.
The Leopard. Macmillan.

Reid, Virginia. *see* Reid, Virginia M.

Reid, Virginia M.
xReid, Virginia.
Reading Ladders for Human Relations. ACE.

Reid, W. S. *see* Reid, William Stanford.

Reid, W. T. *see* Reid, William Thomas.

Reid, Walter.
xReid, Walter.
The Meaning of Company Accounts. Beekman
Pubs.
Meaning of Company Accounts. Herman Pub.

Reid, Whitelaw.
xReid, Whitelaw.
After the War: A Tour of the Southern States,
1865-1866. Peter Smith.
American & English Studies. Arno.

Reid, William A. *see* Reid, William Arbuckle.

Reid, William Arbuckle.
xReid, William A.
Thinking About the Curriculum: The Nature &
Treatment of Curriculum Problems.
Routledge & Kegan.

Reid, William H., 1945-
xReid, William H.
Basic Intensive Psychotherapy. Brunner-Mazel.
Psychiatry for the House Officer. Brunner
Mazel.
ed. The Psychopath: A Comprehensive Study
of Antisocial Disorders & Behaviors.
Brunner-Mazel.

Reid, William J. *see* Reid, William James.

Reid, William James.
xReid, William J.
Brief & Extended Casework. Columbia U Pr.
Task-Centered Casework. Columbia U Pr.
Task-Centered Practice. Columbia U Pr.
Task-Centered System. Columbia U Pr.

Reid, William Stanford, 1913-
xReid, W. S.

ed. The Reformation: Revival or Revolution?.
Krieger.
Reid, William T. *see* Reid, William Thomas.
Reid, William Thomas, oct. 4, 1907-
xReid, W. T.
Riccati Differential Equations. Acad Pr.
xReid, William T.
Ordinary Differential Equations. Krieger.
Reidenberg, Marcus. *see* Reidenberg, Marcus M.
Reidenberg, Marcus M., 1934-
xReidenberg, Marcus.
Renal Function & Drug Action. Saunders.
Reidy, Brian.
xReidy, Brian.
Guide to World Commodity Markets. Nichols
Pub.
Reif, Arnold E.
xReif, Arnold E.
Immunity & Cancer in Man: An Introduction.
Dekker.
Reif, Frederick, 1927-
xReif, Frederick.
Fundamentals of Statistical & Thermal Physics.
McGraw.
Reif, Rita.
xReif, Rita.
Home - It Takes More Than Money. Times
Bks.
Reifert, Gail.
xReifert, Gail.
Women Who Fought: An American History.
Dermody.
Reiff, Florence M.
xReiff, Florence M.
Steps in Home Living. Bennett Co.
Reiff, R. *see* Reiff, Robert F.
Reiff, Robert.
xReiff, Robert.
Memory & Hypnotic Age Regression:
Developmental Aspects of Cognitive
Function Explored Through Hypnosis. Intl
Univs Pr.
Reiff, Robert F., 1918-
xReiff, R.
Renoir. McGraw.
xReiff, Robert F.
A Stylistic Analysis of Arshile Gorky's Art
from 1943-1948. Garland Pub.
Reiff, Stephanie.
xReiff, Stephanie A.
Secrets of Tut's Tomb & the Pyramids.
Raintree Pubs.
Reiff, Stephanie A. *see* Reiff, Stephanie.
Reiffel, James.
xReiffel, James.
ed. Psychosocial Aspects of Cardiovascular
Disease: The Life-Threatened Patient, the
Family & the Staff. Columbia U Pr.
Reiffel, Leonard.
xReiffel, Leonard.
The Contaminant. Dell.
The Contaminant. Har-Row.
Reifsnyder, William. *see* Reifsnyder, William E.
Reifsnyder, William E.
xReifsnyder, William.
Hut Hopping in the Austrian Alps. Sierra.
xReifsnyder, William E.
Radiant Energy in Relation to Forests. AMS
Pr.
Reiger, John F.
xReiger, John F.
American Sportsmen & the Origins of
Conservation. Winchester Pr.
Reigh, Mildred.
xReigh, Mildred.

Algebra Review Manual: Program for Self
Instruction. McGraw.
Brief Algebra Review Manual: A Program for
Self-Instruction. McGraw.
Reik, Theodor, 1888-
xReik, Theodor.
From Thirty Years with Freud. Greenwood.
Psychology of Sex Relations. Greenwood.
Reiley, H. Edward.
xReiley, H. Edward.
Introductory Horticulture. Delmar.
Introductory Horticulture. Van Nos Reinhold.
Reill, Peter H. *see* Reill, Peter Hanns.
Reill, Peter Hanns.
xReill, Peter H.
The German Enlightenment & the Rise of
Historicism. U of Cal Pr.
Reilley, C. N. *see* Reilley, Charles N.
Reilley, Charles N.
xReilley, C. N.
Experiments for Instrumental Methods.
Krieger.
Reilly, Alayne P.
xReilly, Alayne P.
America in Contemporary Soviet Literature.
NYU Pr.
Reilly, Catherine W.
xReilly, Catherine W.
English Poetry of the First World War: A
Bibliography. St Martin.
Reilly, Dorothy E.
xReilly, Dorothy E.
ed. Teaching & Evaluating the Affective
Domain in Nursing Programs. C B Slack.
Reilly, Edgar M.
xReilly, Edgar M.
The Audubon Illustrated Handbook of
American Birds. Interbk Inc.
Reilly, Elizabeth C. *see* Reilly, Elizabeth Carroll.
Reilly, Elizabeth Carroll.
xReilly, Elizabeth C.
Dictionary of Colonial American Printer's
Ornaments & Illustrations. Am Antiquarian.
Reilly, Francis E. *see* Reilly, Francis Eagan.
Reilly, Francis Eagan, 1922-
xReilly, Francis E.
Charles Peirce's Theory of Scientific Method.
Fordham.
Reilly, Harold J.
xReilly, Harold J.
Edgar Cayce Handbook for Health Through
Drugless Therapy. BJ Pub Group.
The Edgar Cayce Handbook for Health
Through Drugless Therapy. Macmillan.
Reilly, John M.
xReilly, John M.
ed. Richard Wright: The Critical Reception. B
Franklin.
Reilly, Joseph J. *see* Reilly, Joseph John.
Reilly, Joseph John, 1881-1951
xReilly, Joseph J.
Of Books & Men. Arno.
Reilly, Mary.
xReilly, Mary.
Play As Exploratory Learning: Studies of
Curiosity Behavior. Sage.
Reilly, Philip, 1947-
xReilly, Philip.
Genetics, Law, & Social Policy. Harvard U Pr.
Reilly, Richard W.
xReilly, Richard W.
ed. Fiber Deficiency & Colonic Disorders.
Plenum Pub.
Reilly, Robert T.
xReilly, Robert T.
Rebels in the Shadows. U of Pittsburgh Pr.
Reilly, Robin.
xReilly, Robin.

William Pitt the Younger. Putnam.
Reilly, Theresa M., 1919-
xReilly, Theresa M.
Legal Secretary's Word Finder & Desk Book.
P-H.
Reilly, William J. *see* Reilly, William John.
Reilly, William John, 1899-
xReilly, William J.
Marketing Investigations. Arno.
Reiman, Donald H.
xReiman, Donald H.
ed. The Evidence of the Imagination: Studies
of Interactions Between Life & Art in English
Romantic Literature. NYU Pr.
Percy Bysshe Shelley. St Martin.
Percy Bysshe Shelley. Twayne.
Reiman, Jeffrey H.
xReiman, Jeffrey H.
The Rich Get Richer & the Poor Get Prison:
Ideology, Class & Criminal Justice. Wiley.
Reimers, D. M. *see* Reimers, David M.
Reimers, David M.
xReimers, D. M.
ed. Racism in the United States: An American
Dilemma?. Krieger.
xReimers, David M.
White Protestantism & the Negro. Oxford U
Pr.
Reimers, Henry L.
xReimers, Henry L.
The Abrams Story. Ye Galleon.
Reimold, Orlando S., 1910-1977
xReimold, Orlando S.
One Mind's Eye-View of the Mind. Philos Lib.
Reimold, Robert J.
xReimold, Robert J.
Ecology of Halophytes. Acad Pr.
Rein, Irving J.
xRein, Irving J.
The Great American Communication
Catalogue. P-H.
The Public Speaking Book. Scott F.
Reinach, Jacquelyn.
xReinach, Jacquelyn.
Carefree Cooking. Hearthside.
Goose Goofs off. HR&W.
ed. Happy Birthday Unicorn. HR&W.
Me Too, Iguana. HR&W.
Octopus Protests. HR&W.
Quail Can't Decide. HR&W.
Rest Rabbit Rest. HR&W.
Who Stole Alligator's Shoe?. HR&W.
Reinaud, Joseph T. *see* Reinaud, Joseph Toussaint.
Reinaud, Joseph Toussaint, 1795-1867
xReinaud, Joseph T.
Relations Politiques et Commerciales De
l'Empire Romain Avec l'Asie Orientale. B
Franklin.
Reinders, Robert C. *see* Reinders, Robert Clemens.
Reinders, Robert Clemens, 1926-
xReinders, Robert C.
End of an Era: New Orleans 1850-1860.
Pelican.
Reineck, H. E. *see* Reineck, Hans-Erich.
Reineck, Hans-Erich.
xReineck, H. E.
Depositional Sedimentary Environments: With
Reference to Terrigenous Clastics.
Springer-Verlag.
Reinecke. *see* Reinecke, John A.
Reinecke, John A.
xReinecke.
Introduction to Business: A Contemporary
View. Allyn.
Reinecke, R. *see* Reinecke, Robert D.
Reinecke, Robert D.
xReinecke, R.
Refraction: A Programmed Text. ACC.
Reiner, Beatrice S. *see* Reiner, Beatrice Simcox.

By the Sweat of Their Brow: Mexican
Immigrant Labor in the United States,
1900-1940. Greenwood.
Reisman, A. see Reisman, Arnold.
Reisman, Arnold, 1934 (aug. 2)-
xReisman, A.
Industrial Inventory Control. Gordon.
xReisman, Arnold.
Systems Analysis in Health-Care Delivery.
Lexington Bks.
Reisman, Fredricka K.
xReisman, Fredricka K.
A Guide to the Diagnostic Teaching of
Arithmetic. Merrill.
Reisman, J. H. see Reisman, John M.
Reisman, J. M. see Reisman, John M.
Reisman, John M.
xReisman, J. H.
A History of Clinical Psychology. Halsted Pr.
xReisman, J. M.
Principles of Psychotherapy with Children.
Wiley.
xReisman, John M.
Anatomy of Friendship. Irvington.
Reisman, Michael. see Reisman, William Michael.
Reisman, W. Michael. see Reisman, William Michael.
Reisman, William Michael, 1939-
xReisman, Michael.
Art of the Possible: Diplomatic Alternatives in
the Middle East. Princeton U Pr.
xReisman, W. Michael.
Folded Lies: Bribery, Crusades, & Reforms.
Free Pr.
Reisner, G. A. see Reisner, George Andrew.
Reisner, George Andrew, 1867-1942
xReisner, G. A.
Excavations at Kerma. Kraus Repr.
Reiss, Albert J.
xReiss, Albert J.
Occupations & Social Status. Arno.
Reiss, Edmund.
xReiss, Edmund.
William Dunbar. Twayne.
Reiss, Ira L.
xReiss, Ira L.
Family Systems in America. HR&W.
Reiss, James.
xReiss, James.
The Breathers. Ecco Pr.
Reiss, Johanna.
xReiss, Johanna.
The Journey Back. T Y Crowell.
Reissner, Will.
xReissner, Will.
ed. Dynamics of World Revolution Today.
Path Pr NY.
Reister, Floyd N. see Reister, Floyd Nester.
Reister, Floyd Nester.
xReister, Floyd N.
ed. Private Aviation: A Guide to Information
Sources. Gale.
Reit, Seymour.
xReit, Seymour.
All Kinds of Planes. Western Pub.
All Kinds of Ships. Western Pub.
All Kinds of Trains. Western Pub.
Bugs Bunny Goes to the Dentist. Western Pub.
Child of the Navajos. Dodd.
The Easy How-to Book. Western Pub.
Sails, Rails & Wings. Western Pub.
Tweety & Sylvester: Birds of a Feather.
Western Pub.
Reiter, R. J. see Reiter, Russel J.
Reiter, Rayna R.
xReiter, Rayna R.
ed. Toward an Anthropology of Women.
Monthly Rev.
Reiter, Russel J.
xReiter, R. J.

ed. The Pineal & Reproduction. S Karger.
Reiter, Seymour.
xReiter, Seymour.
A Study of Shelley's Poetry. Lib Soc Sci.
Reith, Edward J.
xReith, Edward J.
Atlas of Descriptive Histology. Har-Row.
Reithmaier, L. W. see Reithmaier, Larry W.
Reithmaier, Larry. see Reithmaier, Larry W.
Reithmaier, Larry W.
xReithmaier, L. W.
Instrument Pilot's Guide. Aero.
Private Pilot's Guide. Aero.
xReithmaier, Larry.
Aircraft Mechanic's Shop Manual. Palomar
Bks.
Flight Planning Guide for Pilots. Aero.
Radar Guide for Pilots. Aero.
Reitinger, Frank F.
xReitinger, Frank F.
Common Snakes of South East Asia & Hong
Kong. Heinemann Ed.
Reitman, Sandford W.
xReitman, Sandford W.
Foundations of Education for Prospective
Teachers. Allyn.
Reitz, John R.
xReitz, John R.
Foundations of Electromagnetic Theory. A-W.
Reitz, Rosetta.
xReitz, Rosetta.
Menopause: A Positive Approach. Chilton.
Menopause: A Positive Approach. Penguin.
Reitze, Arnold W.
xReitze, Arnold W.
Environmental Planning: Law of Land &
Resources. North Am Intl.
Reizenstein, Milton.
xReizenstein, Milton.
The Economic History of the Baltimore &
Ohio Railroad. 1827-1853. AMS Pr.
Economic History of the Baltimore & Ohio
Railroad: 1827-1853. Johnson Repr.
Reizes, Haim.
xReizes, Haim.
The Mechanics of Vehicle Collisions. C C
Thomas.
Rejai, Mostafa.
xRejai, Mostafa.
The Comparative Study of Revolutionary
Strategy. Longman.
Decline of Ideology?. Lieber-Atherton.
Leaders of Revolution. Sage.
Rejda, L. J.
xRejda, L. J.
Industrial Motor Users' Handbook of
Insulation for Rewinds. Elsevier.
Rekoff. see Rekoff, Michael G.
Rekoff, Michael G.
xRekoff.
Analog Computer Programming. Merrill.
Rekosh, Lois.
xRekosh, Lois.
Basic Social Studies Skills. McGraw.
Rektorys, Karel.
xRektorys, Karel.
Variational Methods in Mathematics, Science
& Engineering. Kluwer Boston.
Reliability Analysis Center.
xReliability Analysis Center.
Hybrid Microcircuit Reliability Compiled by
IIT Research Institute, Chicago. Pergamon.
Reller, L. Barth.
xReller, L. Barth.
Clinical Internal Medicine. Little.
Relyea, Suzanne. see Relyea, Suzanne L.
Relyea, Suzanne L.
xRelyea, Suzanne.

Signs, Systems, & Meanings: A Contemporary
Semiotic Reading of Four Moliere Plays.
Columbia U Pr.
Remak, J. see Remak, Joachim.
Remak, Joachim, 1920-
xRemak, J.
The Origins of the Second World War. P-H.
xRemak, Joachim.
Gentle Critic: Theodor Fontane & German
Politics, 1848-1898. Syracuse U Pr.
ed. Nazi Years: A Documentary History. P-H.
The Origins of World War I. HR&W.
Reman, Edward.
xReman, Edward.
The Norse Discoveries & Explorations in
America. Greenwood.
Remarque, Erich M. see Remarque, Erich Maria.
Remarque, Erich Maria, 1898-1970
xRemarque, Erich M.
All Quiet on the Western Front. Fawcett.
All Quiet on the Western Front. Little.
Rembar, Charles.
xRembar, Charles.
The Law of the Land. S&S.
Perspective. Arbor Hse.
Rementeria, Jose L. see Rementeria, Jose Luis.
Rementeria, Jose Luis, 1931-
xRementeria, Jose L.
ed. Drug Abuse in Pregnancy & Neonatal
Effects. Mosby.
Remer, C. F. see Remer, Charles Frederick.
Remer, Charles F. see Remer, Charles Frederick.
Remer, Charles Frederick, 1889-
xRemer, C. F.
Readings in Economics for China. Garland
Pub.
xRemer, Charles F.
Foreign Investments in China. Fertig.
Remers, William A. see Remers, William Alan.
Remers, William Alan, 1932-
xRemers, William A.
The Chemistry of Antitumor Antibiotics.
Wiley.
Remick, Cecile P.
xRemick, Cecile P.
An Annotated Bibliography of Works on
Juvenile Delinquency in America & Britain in
the Nineteenth Century. R West.
Remington, Frederic, 1861-1909
xRemington, Frederic.
Crooked Trails. Arno.
Crooked Trails. Irvington.
Illustrations of Frederic Remington. Crown.
Remington's Frontier Sketches. B Franklin.
Stories of Peace & War. Arno.
Remington, Jack S.
xRemington, Jack S.
ed. Infectious Diseases of the Fetus &
Newborn Infant. Saunders.
Remington, R. see Remington, Richard Delleraine.
Remington, Richard Delleraine.
xRemington, R.
Statistics with Applications to the Biological &
Health Sciences. P-H.
Remini, Robert V. see Remini, Robert Vincent.
Remini, Robert Vincent, 1921-
xRemini, Robert V.

ed. The Age of Jackson. U of SC Pr.
ed. Andrew Jackson. Chelsea Hse.
Andrew Jackson. Har-Row.
Andrew Jackson. Twayne.
Andrew Jackson & the Course of American
  Empire, 1767-1821. Har-Row.
The Election of Andrew Jackson. Greenwood.
Election of Andrew Jackson. Har-Row.
Compiled by The Era of Good Feelings & the
  Age of Jackson, 1816-1841. AHM Pub.
Martin Van Buren & the Making of the
  Democratic Party. Norton.
The Revolutionary Age of Andrew Jackson.
  Avon.
The Revolutionary Age of Andrew Jackson.
  Har-Row.
Remizov, Aleksei. *see* Remizov, Aleksei Mikhailovich.
Remizov, Aleksei M. *see* Remizov, Aleksei Mikhailovich.
Remizov, Aleksei Mikhailovich, 1877-1957
  xRemizov, Aleksei.
    On a Field Azure. Greenwood.
  xRemizov, Aleksei M.
    The Clock. Hyperion Conn.
    On a Field Azure. Hyperion Conn.
Remling, John, 1928-
  xRemling, John.
    Brakes. Wiley.
    Steering & Suspension. Wiley.
Remmers, Hermann H. *see* Remmers, Hermann Henry.
Remmers, Hermann Henry, 1892-
  xRemmers, Hermann H.
    Anti-Democratic Attitudes in American
      Schools. Northwestern U Pr.
    Introduction to Opinion & Attitude
      Measurement. Greenwood.
Remmling, Gunter W.
  xRemmling, Gunter W.
    South American Sociologists: A Directory. U
      of Tex Pr.
Remnant, G. L.
  xRemnant, G. L.
    Catalogue of Misericords in Great Britain.
      Oxford U Pr.
Remnant, Mary.
  xRemnant, Mary.
    Musical Instruments of the West. St Martin.
Remson, Susan T.
  xRemson, Susan T.
    Calculations for the Medical Laboratory. Little.
Remy, Bob.
  xRemy, Bob.
    Louisiana Sports Encyclopedia. Pelican.
Remy, Pierre Jean.
  xRemy, Pierre-Jean.
    Maria Callas. St Martin.
Remy, Pierre-Jean. *see* Remy, Pierre Jean.
Renal Stone Research Symposium, Madrid, Sept. 1972.
  see International Symposium on Renal Stone
  Research, Madrid, 1972.
Renaldi, Thomas W. *see* Renaldi, Thomas Wayne.
Renaldi, Thomas Wayne.
  xRenaldi, Thomas W.
    The Two Versions of Mariano Azuela's "Los
      De Abajo": A Comparative Study. Gordon
      Pr.
Renan, Ernest, 1823-1892
  xRenan, Ernest.
    Lectures on the Influence of the Institutions,
      Thought & Culture of Rome, on Christianity
      & the Development of the Catholic Church.
      AMS Pr.
Renard, Georges. *see* Renard, Georges Francois.
Renard, Georges Francois, 1847-1930
  xRenard, Georges.
    Guilds in the Middle Ages. Kelley.
Renaud, Georges.
  xRenaud, Georges.
    Art of the Checkmate. Dover.
Renault, Mary.
  xRenault, Mary.

The Bull from the Sea. Random.
Fire from Heaven. Pantheon.
Fire from Heaven. Random.
The Last of the Wine. Random.
The Mask of Apollo. Bantam.
The Nature of Alexander. Pantheon.
North Face. Popular Lib.
North Face. Queens Hse.
The Persian Boy. Bantam.
The Persian Boy. Pantheon.
The Praise Singer. Bantam.
The Praise Singer. Pantheon.
Promise of Love. BJ Pub Group.
Promise of Love. Queens Hse.
Return to Night. BJ Pub Group.
Return to Night. Queens Hse.
Renay, Liz.
  xRenay, Liz.
    My Face for the World to See. Lyle Stuart.
Rendall, Jane, 1945-
  xRendall, Jane.
    The Origins of the Scottish Enlightenment:
      1707-1776. St Martin.
Rendell, Joan.
  xRendell, Joan.
    Collecting Out of Doors. Routledge & Kegan.
Rendell, Ruth, 1930-
  xRendell, Ruth.
    A Demon in My View. Doubleday.
    A Guilty Thing Surprised. Ballantine.
    A Judgement in Stone. Doubleday.
    A Judgement in Stone. G K Hall.
    Make Death Love Me. Bantam.
    Make Death Love Me. Doubleday.
    Make Death Love Me. G K Hall.
    Means of Evil: Five Mystery Stories by an
      Edgar-Award Winning Writer. Doubleday.
Render, Barry
  xRender, Barry.
    Management Science: A Self-Correcting
      Approach. Allyn.
Rendina, George, 1923-
  xRendina, George.
    Experimental Methods in Modern
      Biochemistry. HR&W.
Rendleman, Ron.
  xRendleman, Ron.
    Tears for a King. Jeremy Bks.
Rendon, Gabino.
  xRendon, Gabino.
    Prediction of Adjustment Outcomes of Rural
      Migrants to the City. R & E Res Assoc.
Reneau, John P.
  xReneau, John P.
    ed. Evoked Response Audiometry: A Topical &
      Historical Review. Univ Park.
Renehan, Robert, 1935-
  xRenehan, Robert.
    Greek Textual Criticism: A Reader. Harvard U
      Pr.
Renfield, Richard.
  xRenfield, Richard.
    If Teachers Were Free. Dell.
Renford, Beverly.
  xRenford, Beverly.
    Bibliographic Instruction: A Handbook.
      Neal-Schuman.
Renfrew, C. E.
  xRenfrew, C. E.
    Speech Disorders in Children. Pergamon.
Renfrew, Colin, 1937-
  xRenfrew, Colin.
    ed. British Prehistory: A New Outline. Noyes.
    ed. Transformations: Mathematical Approaches
      to Culture Change. Acad Pr.
Renfroe, Earl W.
  xRenfroe, Earl W.
    Edgewise. Lea & Febiger.
Renfroe, O. S.
  xRenfroe, O. S.

ed. Building Materials from Solid Wastes.
  Noyes.
Rengers, Rosemary.
  xRengers, Rosemary.
    Design & Social Planning in Housing for the
      Elderly, 1975-1977: An Annotated
      Bibliography. Vance Biblios.
Rengger, J. R. *see* Rengger, Johann Rudolph.
Rengger, Johann R. *see* Rengger, Johann Rudolph.
Rengger, Johann Rudolph.
  xRengger, J. R.
    jt. auth. The Reign of Doctor Joseph Gaspard
      Roderick De Francia in Paraguay: Being an
      Account of a Six Years' Residence in That
      Republic from July 1819 to May 1825.
      Documentary Pubns.
  xRengger, Johann R.
    Reign of Doctor Joseph Gaspard Roderick De
      Francia, in Paraguay. Kennikat.
Renick, Marion.
  xRenick, Marion.
    The Famous Forward Pass Pair. Scribner.
    Take a Long Jump. Scribner.
Renier, Elizabeth.
  xRenier, Elizabeth.
    Landscape of the Heart. Fawcett.
Renken, Aleda.
  xRenken, Aleda.
    Trouble at Briden High. Concordia.
    The Two Christmases. Concordia.
Renn, Derek F. *see* Renn, Derek Frank.
Renn, Derek Frank.
  xRenn, Derek F.
    Norman Castles of Britain. Humanities.
Rennell, Francis J. *see* Rennell, Francis James Rennell
  Rodd.
Rennell, Francis James Rennell Rodd, Baron, 1895-
  xRennell, Francis J.
    British Military Administration of Occupied
      Territories in Africa During the Years of
      1941-1947. Greenwood.
Renner, Al G.
  xRenner, Al G.
    How to Build a Better Mousetrap Car -- &
      Other Experimental Science Fun. Dodd.
    How to Make & Use Electric Motors. Putnam.
Renner, B.
  xRenner, B.
    Current Algebras & Their Applications.
      Pergamon.
Renner, John. *see* Renner, John M.
Renner, John M.
  xRenner, John.
    Source Book on South American Geography.
      Intl Pubns Serv.
Renner, John W. *see* Renner, John Wilson.
Renner, John Wilson.
  xRenner, John W.
    Teaching Science in the Elementary School.
      Har-Row.
Renner, K. Edward, 1936-
  xRenner, K. Edward.
    What's Wrong with the Mental Health
      Movement. Nelson-Hall.
Renner, Louis L.
  xRenner, Louis L.
    Pioneer Missionary to the Bering Strait
      Eskimos: Bellarmine Lafortune, S. J.. Binford.
Rennert, Amy.
  xRennert, Amy.
    Making It in Photography. Putnam.
Rennert, Hugo A. *see* Rennert, Hugo Albert.
Rennert, Hugo Albert, 1858-1927
  xRennert, Hugo A.
    Life of Lope De Vega. Arno.
    Spanish Pastoral Romances. Biblo.
Rennie, M. K.
  xRennie, M. K.
    Logic Theory & Practice. U of Queensland Pr.
Rennie, Ysabel F. *see* Rennie, Ysabel Fisk.

Rennie, Ysabel Fisk, 1918-
  xRennie, Ysabel F.
    The Argentine Republic. Greenwood.
Reno, Marie. see Reno, Marie R.
Reno, Marie R.
  xReno, Marie.
    Final Proof. Popular Lib.
Reno, Ottie W.
  xReno, Ottie W.
    Pitching Championship Horseshoes. A S
    Barnes.
Reno, Richard R.
  xReno, Richard R.
    Profitable Real Estate Exchanging &
    Counseling. P-H.
Renoir, Jean, 1894-
  xRenoir, Jean.
    My Life & My Films. Atheneum.
Renou, Louis, 1896-1966
  xRenou, Louis.
    ed. Hinduism. Braziller.
Renouard, Yves.
  xRenouard, Yves.
    Avignon Papacy, 1305-1403. Shoe String.
Renouf, Peter L. see Renouf, Peter le Page.
Renouf, Peter le Page, Sir, 1822-1897
  xRenouf, Peter L.
    Lectures on the Origin & Growth of Religion
    As Illustrated by the Religion of Ancient
    Egypt. AMS Pr.
Rensberger, Boyce.
  xRensberger, Boyce.
    The Cult of the Wild. Doubleday.
    The Cult of the Wild. Doubleday.
Rensberger, John M.
  xRensberger, John M.
    Entoptychine Pocket Gophers (Mammalia,
    Geomyoidea) of the Early Miocene John Day
    Formation, Oregon. U of Cal Pr.
Rensch, Bernard. see Rensch, Bernhard.
Rensch, Bernhard, 1900-
  xRensch, Bernard.
    Evolution Above the Species Level. Columbia
    U Pr.
Renshaw, Domeena C.
  xRenshaw, Domeena C.
    The Hyperactive Child. Little.
    The Hyperactive Child. Nelson-Hall.
Renshon, Stanley A. see Renshon, Stanley Allen.
Renshon, Stanley Allen.
  xRenshon, Stanley A.
    Psychological Needs & Political Behavior: A
    Theory of Personality & Political Efficacy.
    Free Pr.
Rensselaer, John K. Van. see Van Rensselaer, John K.
Rensselaer, Phillip Van. see Van Rensselaer, Phillip.
Renstrom, Richard C.
  xRenstrom, Richard C.
    Great Motorcycle Legends. Aztex.
Rentzel, Lance, 1943-
  xRentzel, Lance.
    When All the Laughter Died in Sorrow.
    Bantam.
Renwick, A. M.
  xRenwick, A. M.
    Story of the Church. Eerdmans.
Renwick, Ethel. see Renwick, Ethel Hulbert.
Renwick, Ethel Hulbert.
  xRenwick, Ethel.
    The Real Food Cookbook. Zondervan.
Renwick, F. B. see Renwick, Fred Blackwell.
Renwick, Fred Blackwell, 1930-
  xRenwick, F. B.
    Introduction to Investments & Finance: Theory
    and Analysis. Macmillan.
Renwick Gallery.
  xRenwick Gallery of the National Collection of
    Fine Arts.

Shaker: Furniture & Objects from the Faith &
  Andrew Deming Andrews Collection.
  Smithsonian.
Renwick Gallery of the National Collection of Fine Arts.
  see Renwick Gallery.
Renyi, Alfred.
  xRenyi, Alfred.
    Dialogues on Mathematics. Holden-Day.
    Foundations of Probability. Holden-Day.
    tr. Letters on Probability. Wayne St U Pr.
Renzo, D. De. see De Renzo, D.
Renzo, D. J. De. see De Renzo, D. J.
Renzoni, Tommy.
  xRenzoni, Tommy.
    Baccarat: Everything You Want to Know
    About Playing & Winning. Citadel Pr.
Replogle, Justin. see Replogle, Justin Maynard.
Replogle, Justin Maynard, 1929-
  xReplogle, Justin.
    Auden's Poetry. U of Wash Pr.
Report of Round Table, European Conference of
  Ministers of Transport on Transport Economics, 34th,
  Paris, May 6-7, 1976. see Round Table on Transport
  Economics, 34th, Paris, 1976.
Report of the Twentieth Century Fund Task Force on
  Broadcasting & the Legislature. see Twentieth Century
  Fund. Task Force on Broadcasting and the Legislature.
Reports on Astronomy. see International Astronomical
  Union.
Repplier, Agnes, 1855-1950
  xRepplier, Agnes.
    Americans & Others. Arno.
    Books & Men. Folcroft.
    Compromises. AMS Pr.
    Compromises. Greenwood.
    Compromises. Scholarly.
    Counter-Currents. Arno.
    Counter-Currents. R West.
    In Our Convent Days. AMS Pr.
    In Our Convent Days. Scholarly.
    Under Dispute. Arno.
Reps, John W. see Reps, John William.
Reps, John William.
  xReps, John W.
    Cities of the American West: A History of
    Frontier Urban Planning. Princeton U Pr.
    Monumental Washington: The Planning &
    Development of the Capital Center.
    Princeton U Pr.
Repton, Humphry, 1752-1818
  xRepton, Humphry.
    The Art of Landscape Gardening.
    Theophrastus.
Reque, John.
  xReque, John.
    The Student Journalist & Staff Management.
    Rosen Pr.
Reschke, Elaine M., 1931-
  xReschke, Elaine M.
    The Medical Office: Organization &
    Management. Har-Row.
Reschke, Robert C.
  xReschke, Robert C.
    Successful How to Build Your Own Home.
    Structures Pub.
    Successful Roofing & Siding. Structures Pub.
Rescorla, Robert A.
  xRescorla, Robert A.
    Pavlovian Second-Order Conditioning: Studies
    in Associative Learning. Halsted Pr.
Research & Education Association Staff. see Research
  and Education Association.
Research and Education Association.
  xResearch & Education Association Staff.

The Calculus Problem Solver: A Supplement to
  Any Class Text. Res & Educ.
The Electric Circuits Problem Solver: A
  Supplement to Any Class Text. Res & Educ.
The Geometry Problem Solver: A Supplement
  to Any Class Text. Res & Educ.
The Linear Algebra Problem Solver: A
  Supplement to Any Class Text. Res & Educ.
The Mechanics Problem Solver: A Supplement
  to Any Class Text. Res & Educ.
Modern Energy Technology: Nuclear, Coal,
  Petroleum, Gas, Solar, Geothermal, Fuel
  Cells, Oil Shale, Tar Sands, Organic Wastes.
  Res & Educ.
  ed. Modern Pollution Control Technology: Air
  Pollution Control, Water Pollution Control,
  Solid Wastes Disposal. Res & Educ.
The Organic Chemistry Problem Solver: A
  Supplement to Any Class Text. Res & Educ.
Research Co-Ordination Meeting & Panel. see Panel on
  the Use of Nuclear Techniques for Studying Animal
  Protein Production from Non-Protein Nitrogen,
  Vienna, 1971.
Research Conference in Industrial Relations, 13th,
  University of California, Los Angeles, 1970.
    xAnnual Research Conference, 13th, UCLA, 1970.
    The Generation Gap: Implications for
    Labour-Management Relations: Proceedings.
    U Cal LA Indus Rel.
Research Conference in Industrial Relations, 14th,
  University of California, Los Angeles, 1971.
    xAnnual Research Conference, 14th, UCLA, 1972.
    National Incomes Policy & Manpower
    Problems: Proceedings. U Cal LA Indus Rel.
Research for Better Schools, Inc.
  xResearch for Better Schools, Inc.
    Educational Reform for a Changing Society.
    Allyn.
    The Future of Education: Perspectives on
    Tomorrow's Schooling. Allyn.
Research Libraries of the New York Public Library. see
  New York (City). Public Library. Research Libraries.
Reseck, John, 1935-
  xReseck, John.
    Marine Biology. Reston.
Resek, Carl.
  xResek, Carl.
    ed. The Progressives. Bobbs.
Reshetar, John S. see Reshetar, John Stephen.
Reshetar, John Stephen.
  xReshetar, John S.
    Soviet Polity: Government & Politics & in the
    U.S.S.R. Dodd.
    The Soviet Polity: Government & Politics in
    the U.S.S.R.. Har-Row.
Reshevsky. see Reshevsky, Samuel.
Reshevsky, Samuel, 1911-
  xReshevsky.
    Art of Positional Play. McKay.
  xReshevsky, Samuel.
    Great Chess Upsets. Arco.
Resick, Matthew C.
  xResick, Matthew C.
    Intercollegiate & Interscholastic Athletics for
    Men & Women. A-W.
    Modern Administrative Practices in Physical
    Education & Athletics. A-W.
Resnick, Daniel P. see Resnick, Daniel Philip.
Resnick, Daniel Philip.
  xResnick, Daniel P.
    White Terror & the Political Reaction After
    Waterloo. Harvard U Pr.
Resnick, Lauren B.
  xResnick, Lauren B.
    ed. Theory & Practice of Early Reading. L
    Erlbaum Assocs.
Resnick, Marvin D.
  xResnick, Marvin D.

Practical Composition for the Contemporary
Student. Har-Row.
Resnick, Michael.
xResnick, Michael.
Gymnastics & You: The Whole Story of the
Sport. Rand.
Resnick, Seymour.
xResnick, Seymour.
ed. Anthology of Spanish Literature in English
Translation. Ungar.
Essential Spanish Grammar. Dover.
Essential Spanish Grammar. Gannon.
Resnik, H. L. *see* Resnik, H. L. P.
Resnik, H. L. P.
xResnik, H. L.
Teaching Outlines in Suicide Studies & Crisis
Intervention. Charles.
Teaching Outlines in Suicide Studies & Crisis
Intervention. R J Brady.
Resnikoff, George J.
xResnikoff, George J.
Tables of the Non-Central T-Distribution:
Density Function, Cumulative Distribution
Function, & Percentage Points. Stanford U
Pr.
Resnikoff, H. L.
xResnikoff, H. L.
Mathematics in Civilization. Irvington.
Resource Publications, Inc.
xResource Publications, Inc. Staff.
MusiCatalog. Resource Pubns.
Resource Publications, Inc. Staff. *see* Resource
Publications, Inc.
Resources for the Future.
xResources for the Future, Inc.
jt. auth. Land Economics Research: Papers
Presented at a Symposium Held at Lincoln,
Nebraska, June 16-23, 1961. AMS Pr.
The Nation Looks at Its Resources: Report of
the Mid-Century Conference of Resources for
the Future. Washington, D.C., Dec. 2-4,
1953. AMS Pr.
Publications of Resources for the Future, Inc..
AMS Pr.
xResources for the Future Staff.
Agricultural Development in the Mekong
Basin: Goals, Priorities, & Strategies. Johns
Hopkins.
Design for a Worldwide Study of Regional
Development: A Report to the United
Nations on a Proposed Research-Training
Program. Johns Hopkins.
Forest Credit in the United States: A Survey of
Needs & Facilities. Johns Hopkins.
U. S. Energy Policies: An Agenda for
Research. Johns Hopkins.
Resources for the Future, Inc. *see* Resources for the
Future.
Resources for the Future Staff. *see* Resources for the
Future.
Ressner, Philip.
xRessner, Phillip.
Dudley Pippin's Summer. Har-Row.
Ressner, Phillip. *see* Ressner, Philip.
Rest, Friedrich, 1913-
xRest, Friedrich.
Our Christian Symbols. Pilgrim NY.
Rest, James R.
xRest, James R.
Development in Judging Moral Issues. U of
Minn Pr.
Restak, Richard M., 1942-
xRestak, Richard M.
The Brain: The Last Frontier. Warner Bks.
Premeditated Man: Bioethics & the Control of
Future Human Life. Penguin.
Restany, Pierre.
xRestany, Pierre.

Cesar. Abrams.
Resume Service.
xResume Service Staff.
Resumes That Get Jobs. Arco.
Resume Service Staff. *see* Resume Service.
Reswick, James. *see* Reswick, James B.
Reswick, James B.
xReswick, James.
Introduction to Dynamic Systems. P-H.
Retallack, Dorothy. *see* Retallack, Dorothy L.
Retallack, Dorothy L.
xRetallack, Dorothy.
The Sound of Music & Plants. De Vorss.
Retherford, Robert D.
xRetherford, Robert D.
The Changing Sex Differential in Mortality.
Greenwood.
Rethmel, R. C.
xRethmel, Robert C.
Backpacking. Follett.
Rethmel, Robert C. *see* Rethmel, R. C.
Reti, Richard, 1889-1929
xReti, Richard.
Masters of the Chessboard. Dover.
Reti, Rudolph R. *see* Reti, Rudolph Richard.

Reti, Rudolph Richard, 1885-
xReti, Rudolph R.
The Thematic Process in Music. Greenwood.

Rettich, Margaret. *see* Rettich, Margret.

Rettich, Margret.
xRettich, Margaret.
The Silver Touch & Other Family Christmas
Stories. Morrow.

xRettich, Margret.
The Tightwad's Curse & Other Pleasantly
Chilling Stories. Morrow.

Rettig, Richard. *see* Rettig, Richard A.
Rettig, Richard A.
xRettig, Richard.
Cancer Crusade: The Story of the National
Cancer Act of 1971. Princeton U Pr.
Rettig, Robert B.
xRettig, Robert B.
Guide to Cambridge Architecture: Ten Walking
Tours. MIT Pr.
Reu, Johann M. *see* Reu, Johann Michael.
Reu, Johann Michael, 1869-1943
xReu, Johann M.
Thirty-Five Years of Luther Research. AMS
Pr.
Reuben, David. *see* Reuben, David, R.
Reuben, David, R.
xReuben, David.
Everything You Always Wanted to Know
About Nutrition. Avon.
Everything You Always Wanted to Know
About Nutrition. G K Hall.
Everything You Always Wanted to Know
About Nutrition. S&S.
Reubens, Beatrice G.
xReubens, Beatrice G.
Preparation for Work: A Cross-Country
Analysis. Allanheld.
Reuber, G. L. *see* Reuber, Grant L.
Reuber, Grant L.
xReuber, G. L.
Britain's Export Trade with Canada. U of
Toronto Pr.
Reul, Myrtle R.
xReul, Myrtle R.
Practical Approach to Marriage. Mich St U Pr.
Reumann, John. *see* Reumann, John Henry Paul.
Reumann, John Henry Paul.
xReumann, John.

ed. Studies in Lutheran Hermeneutics. Fortress.
Reunert, Theodore.
xReunert, Theodore.
Diamonds & Gold in South Africa. Arno.
Reusch, William. *see* Reusch, William H.
Reusch, William H., 1931-
xReusch, William.
An Introduction to Organic Chemistry. Holden
Day.
Reuschlein, Harold G. *see* Reuschlein, Harold Gill.
Reuschlein, Harold Gill.
xReuschlein, Harold G.
Handbook on the Law of Agency &
Partnership. West Pub.
Reuss, Frederick G.
xReuss, Frederick G.
Fiscal Policy for Growth Without Inflation:
The German Experiment. Johns Hopkins.
Reuter, Edward B. *see* Reuter, Edward Byron.
Reuter, Edward Byron, 1880-1946
xReuter, Edward B.
The Mulatto in the United States: Including a
Study of the Role of Mixed Blood Races
Throughout the World. Johnson Repr.
Race Mixture: Studies in Intermarriage &
Miscegenation. Johnson Repr.
Reuter, Frank. *see* Reuter, Frank Theodore.
Reuter, Frank Theodore.
xReuter, Frank.
Catholic Influence on American Colonial
Policies, 1898-1904. U of Tex Pr.
Reuter, Margaret.
xReuter, Margaret.
Careers in a Police Department. Raintree Pubs.
Earthquakes: Our Restless Planet. Raintree
Pubs.
My Mother Is Blind. Childrens.
You Can Depend on Me. Childrens.
Reuter, Stewart R.
xReuter, Stewart R.
Gastrointestinal Angiography. Saunders.
Reuther, Victor. *see* Reuther, Victor G.
Reuther, Victor G., 1912-
xReuther, Victor.
The Brothers Reuther & the Story of the
UAW: A Memoir. HM.
Reutter, K. *see* Reutter, Klaus.
Reutter, Klaus, 1937-
xReutter, K.
Taste Organ in the Bullhead (Teleostei).
Springer-Verlag.
Revankar, Ratna G.
xRevankar, Ratna G.
The Indian Constitution: A Case Study of
Backward Classes. Fairleigh Dickinson.
Revault, Jacques.
xRevault, Jacques.
Designs & Patterns from North African
Carpets & Textiles. Dover.
Designs & Patterns from North African
Carpets & Textiles. Peter Smith.
Revel, Jean Francois.
xRevel, Jean-Francois.
On Proust. Open Court.
The Totalitarian Temptation. Penguin.
Revel, Jean-Francois. *see* Revel, Jean Francois.
Revell, Don, 1954-
xRevell, Don.
The Broken Juke. Iris Pr.
Revell, Dorothy T. *see* Revell, Dorothy Tompkins.
Revell, Dorothy Tompkins.
xRevell, Dorothy T.
Gourmet Recipes for Diabetics: The
International Diabetic Diet Book. C C
Thomas.
Revell, Peter.
xRevell, Peter.
Paul Laurence Dunbar. Twayne.
Revelle, Charles.
xReVelle, Charles S.

Sourcebook on the Environment: The Scientific
Perspective. HM.

ReVelle, Charles S. *see* Revelle, Charles.

Reverby, Susan.

xReverby, Susan.
ed. Health Care in America: Essays in Social
History. Temple U Pr.

Revesz, Geza, 1878-1955
xRevesz, Geza.
The Origins & Prehistory of Language.
Greenwood.
Psychology of a Musical Prodigy. Arno.
Psychology of a Musical Prodigy. Greenwood.
The Psychology of a Musical Prodigy. Johnson
Repr.

Revesz, Pal.
xRevesz, Pal.
Laws of Large Numbers. Acad Pr.

Revill, Janie.
xRevill, Janie.
A Compilation of the Original Lists of
Protestant Immigrants to South Carolina,
1763-1773. Genealog Pub.

Revlin, Russell.
xRevlin, Russell.
ed. Human Reasoning. Halsted Pr.

Revsine, Lawrence.
xRevsine, Lawrence.
Replacement Cost Accounting. P-H.

Rewadikar, Nalini, 1939-
xRewadikar, Nalini.
Conference Diplomacy Austrian Model: A
Study of the Dynamics of Negotiations &
Disengagement of Big Powers. Intl Pubns
Serv.

Rewald, John, 1912-
xRewald, John.
History of Impressionism. NYGS.

Rex, Barbara.
xRex, Barbara.
I Want to Be in Love Again. Norton.

Rex, John.
xRex, John.
ed. Approaches to Sociology: An Introduction
to the Major Trends in British Sociology.
Routledge & Kegan.
Colonial Immigrants in a British City: A Class
Analysis. Routledge & Kegan.
Race, Colonialism & the City. Routledge &
Kegan.
Sociology & the Demystification of the Modern
World. Routledge & Kegan.

Rex, Walter E.
xRex, Walter E.
Pascal's Provincial Letters: An Introduction.
Holmes & Meier.

Rexford, Eveoleen N.
xRexford, Eveoleen N.
ed. Infant Psychiatry: A New Synthesis. Yale
U Pr.

Rexilius, Barbara G. *see* Rexilius, Barbara Goff.
Rexilius, Barbara Goff.
xRexilius, Barbara G.
Chest Drainage & Suction. Davis Co.

Rexine, John E.
xRexine, John E.
Religion in Plato & Cicero. Greenwood.

Rexroat, Stephen.
xRexroat, Stephen V.
The Sunday School Spirit. Gospel Pub.

Rexroat, Stephen V. *see* Rexroat, Stephen.
Rexroth, Kenneth, 1905-
xRexroth, Kenneth.

An Autobiographical Novel. Ross-Erikson.
Collected Longer Poems. New Directions.
The Morning Star. New Directions.
tr. One Hundred More Poems from the
Japanese. New Directions.
tr. One Hundred Poems from the Chinese.
New Directions.
tr. One Hundred Poems from the Japanese.
New Directions.

Rey, Charles F. *see* Rey, Charles Fernand.
Rey, Charles Fernand, 1877-
xRey, Charles F.
In the Country of the Blue Nile. Negro U Pr.
Real Abyssinia. Negro U Pr.

Rey, H. A. *see* Rey, Hans Augusto.

Rey, Hans Augusto, 1898-
xRey, H. A.

illus. Curious George. HM.
illus. Curious George Gets a Medal. HM.
Curious George Goes to the Hospital. HM.
illus. Curious George Learns the Alphabet.
HM.
Curious George Rides a Bike. HM.
illus. Curious George Takes a Job. HM.
illus. Find the Constellations. HM.

Rey, J. J. *see* Rey, William J. J.
Rey, Judy-Lynn Del. *see* Del Rey, Judy-Lynn.
Rey, Lester Del. *see* Del Rey, Lester.
Rey, Margaret. *see* Rey, Margret Elisabeth (Waldstein).
Rey, Margret Elisabeth (Waldstein).

xRey, Margaret.
jt. auth. Curious George Goes to the Hospital.
HM.

Rey, William J. J., 1940-
xRey, J. J.
Robust Statistical Methods. Springer-Verlag.
Reyburn, H. A. *see* Reyburn, Hugh Adam.
Reyburn, Hugh Adam.
xReyburn, H. A.
Nietzsche: The Story of a Human Philosopher.
Greenwood.

Reyburn, Wallace.
xReyburn, Wallace.
Flushed with Pride: The Story of Thomas
Crapper. P-H.
Twickenham: The Story of a Rugby Ground.
Allen Unwin.

Reychler, Luc.
xReychler, Luc.
Patterns of Diplomatic Thinking: A Cross
National Study of Structural &
Social-Psychological Determinants. Praeger.

Reyes, Alfonso, 1889-1959
xReyes, Alfonso.
Position of America & Other Essays. Arno.

Reyes, Ignacio, 1917-
xReyes, Ignacio.
A Survey of the Problems Involved in the
Americanization of the Mexican-American. R
& E Res Assoc.

Reyes, Jose S., 1899-
xReyes, Jose S.
Legislative History of America's Economic
Policy Toward the Philippines. AMS Pr.

Reyna, Jose L. *see* Reyna, Jose Luis.
Reyna, Jose Luis.
xReyna, Jose L.
ed. Authoritarianism in Mexico. Inst Study
Human.
xReyna, Jose' L.
ed. Authoritarianism in Mexico. Inst Study
Human.

Reyna, Jose' L. *see* Reyna, Jose Luis.
Reyna, Rudy De. *see* De Reyna, Rudy.
Reyner, J. H. *see* Reyner, John Hereward.
Reyner, John Hereward.
xReyner, J. H.

No Easy Immortality. Allen Unwin.
Reynierse, James H.
xReynierse, James H.
ed. Current Issues in Animal Learning: A
Colloquium. U of Nebr Pr.

Reynolds, A. J.
xReynolds, A. J.
Turbulent Flows in Engineering. Wiley.

Reynolds, Barbara.
xReynolds, Barbara.
Concise Cambridge Italian Dictionary.
Cambridge U Pr.

Reynolds, Bede, 1892-
xReynolds, Bede.
Let's Mend the Mess. Alba Bks.

Reynolds, Bonnie J. *see* Reynolds, Bonnie Jones.
Reynolds, Bonnie Jones.
xReynolds, Bonnie J.
The Confetti Man. Ballantine.
Confetti Man. Stein & Day.

Reynolds, Clark G.
xReynolds, Clark G.
Command of the Sea: The History & Strategy
of Maritime Empires. Morrow.
Famous American Admirals. Van Nos
Reinhold.
The Fast Carriers: The Forging of an Air Navy.
Krieger.

Reynolds, David K.
xReynolds, David K.
Endangered Hope: Experiences in Psychiatric
Aftercare Facilities. U of Cal Pr.

Reynolds, Donald E., 1931-
xReynolds, Donald E.
Editors Make War: Southern Newspapers in
the Secession Crisis. Vanderbilt U Pr.

Reynolds, Donald M.
xReynolds, Donald M.
Hiram Powers & His Ideal Sculpture. Garland
Pub.

Reynolds, E. E. *see* Reynolds, Ernest Edwin.
Reynolds, E. G. *see* Reynolds, Edmund George Barton.
Reynolds, Earle L.
xReynolds, Earle L.
The Forbidden Voyage. Greenwood.

Reynolds, Edmund George Barton.
xReynolds, E. G.
Target Rifle Shooting. Barrie & Jenkins.

Reynolds, Elhanan W. *see* Reynolds, Elhanan
Winchester.
Reynolds, Elhanan Winchester, 1827-1867
xReynolds, Elhanan W.
True Story of the Barons of the South: Or, the
Rationale of the American Conflict. Negro U
Pr.

Reynolds, Emily B. *see* Reynolds, Emily Bellinger.
Reynolds, Emily Bellinger.
xReynolds, Emily B.
The County Offices & Officers of Barnwell
County, S. C., 1775-1975: A Record. Reprint.

Reynolds, Ernest E. *see* Reynolds, Ernest Edwin.
Reynolds, Ernest Edwin, 1894-
xReynolds, E. E.
The Life & Death of St. Thomas More: The
Field Is Won. B&N.
xReynolds, Ernest E.
Thomas More & Erasmus. Fordham.

Reynolds, G. F. *see* Reynolds, George Fullmer.
Reynolds, George F. *see* Reynolds, George Fullmer.
Reynolds, George Fullmer, 1877-
xReynolds, G. F.
Some Principles of Elizabethan Staging. AMS
Pr.
xReynolds, George F.
Some Principles of Elizabethan Staging.
Folcroft.

Reynolds, George G. *see* Reynolds, George Greenwood.
Reynolds, George Greenwood, 1885-
xReynolds, George G.

Distribution of Power to Regulate Interstate Carriers Between the Nation & the States. AMS Pr.

Reynolds, George S. *see* Reynolds, George Stanley.

Reynolds, George Stanley, 1936-
xReynolds, George S.
A Primer of Operant Conditioning. Scott F.

Reynolds, George W. *see* Reynolds, George William MacArthur.

Reynolds, George William MacArthur, 1814-1879
xReynolds, George W.
The Necromancer: A Romance. Arno.

Reynolds, Graham.
xReynolds, Graham.
Turner. Oxford U Pr.

Reynolds, Helen W. *see* Reynolds, Helen Wilkinson.

Reynolds, Helen Wilkinson.
xReynolds, Helen W.
Dutch Houses in the Hudson Valley Before 1776. Dover.
Dutch Houses in the Hudson Valley Before 1776. Peter Smith.

Reynolds, James A.
xReynolds, James A.
Catholic Emancipation Crisis in Ireland, 1823-1829. Greenwood.

Reynolds, Jane L.
xReynolds, Jane L.
Music Lessons That Are Easy to Teach. P-H.
Music Lessons You Can Teach. P-H.

Reynolds, Jean K. *see* Reynolds, Jean Kirk.

Reynolds, Jean Kirk.
xReynolds, Jean K.
Compiled by How to Choose & Use Child Care. Broadman.

Reynolds, John E. *see* Reynolds, John Everett.

Reynolds, John Everett.
xReynolds, John E.
ed. Readings in Natural Resource Economics. Mss Info.

Reynolds, John H. *see* Reynolds, John Hamilton.

Reynolds, John Hamilton.
xReynolds, John H.
The Letters of John Hamilton Reynolds. U of Nebr Pr.

Reynolds, Joyce.
xReynolds, Joyce.
Puppet Shows That Reach & Teach Children. Gospel Pub.

Reynolds, Lloyd G. *see* Reynolds, Lloyd George.

Reynolds, Lloyd George.
xReynolds, Lloyd G.
ed. Agriculture in Development Theory. Yale U Pr.
Current Issues of Economic Policy. Irwin.
Economics: A General Introduction. Irwin.
Image & Reality in Economic Development. Yale U Pr.
Macroeconomics: Analysis & Policy. Irwin.
Microeconomics: Analysis & Policy. Irwin.
Readings in Labor Economics & Labor Relations. P-H.

Reynolds, M. *see* Reynolds, Morgan.

Reynolds, Mack.
xReynolds, Mack.
The Cosmic Eye. Nordon Pubns.
Earth Unaware. Nordon Pubns.
The Fracas Factor. Nordon Pubns.
Puerto Rican Patriot: The Life of Luis Munoz Rivera. Macmillan.

Reynolds, Marjorie.
xReynolds, Marjorie.
Dark Horse Barnaby. Macmillan.
Horse Called Mystery. Har-Row.
Horse Called Mystery. Har-Row.
Ride the Wild Storm. Macmillan.

Reynolds, Martha May, 1893-
xReynolds, Marthay M.

Negativism of Pre-School Children: An Observational & Experimental Study. AMS Pr.

Reynolds, Marthay M. *see* Reynolds, Martha May.

Reynolds, Mary (Trackett), 1914-
xReynolds, Mary T.
Interdepartmental Committees in the National Administration, 1932-1936. AMS Pr.

Reynolds, Mary T. *see* Reynolds, Mary (Trackett).

Reynolds, Maynard C. *see* Reynolds, Maynard Clinton.

Reynolds, Maynard Clinton.
xReynolds, Maynard C.
ed. Teaching Exceptional Children in All America's Schools: A First Course for Teachers & Principals. Coun Exc Child.

Reynolds, Michael.
xReynolds, Michael.
Engine-Driving Life: Stirring Adventures & Incidents in the Lives of Locomotive Engine-Drivers. Hastings.

Reynolds, Michael M.
xReynolds, Michael M.
ed. Guide to Theses & Dissertations: An Annotated, International Bibliography of Bibliographies. Gale.
ed. Reader in Library & Information Services. IHS-PDS.
ed. Reader in Library Cooperation. IHS-PDS.
ed. Reader in the Academic Library. IHS-PDS.

Reynolds, Michele.
xReynolds, Michele.
Critters' Kitchen. Atheneum.

Reynolds, Moira D. *see* Reynolds, Moira Davison.

Reynolds, Moira Davison.
xReynolds, Moira D.
Aim for a Job in the Medical Laboratory. Rosen Pr.

Reynolds, Morgan.
xReynolds, M.
ed. Public Expenditures, Taxes & the Distribution of Income: The U.S. 1950, 1961, 1970. Acad Pr.

Reynolds, Nancy, 1938-
xReynolds, Nancy.
ed. The Dance Catalog. Crown.

Reynolds, P. A. *see* Reynolds, Philip Alan.

Reynolds, Paul D. *see* Reynolds, Paul Davidson.

Reynolds, Paul Davidson.
xReynolds, Paul D.
Primer in Theory Construction. Bobbs.

Reynolds, Paul R. *see* Reynolds, Paul Revere.

Reynolds, Paul Revere, 1904-
xReynolds, Paul R.
Professional Guide to Marketing Manuscripts. Writer.
The Writing & Selling of Fiction. Morrow.

Reynolds, Philip A. *see* Reynolds, Philip Alan.

Reynolds, Philip Alan.
xReynolds, P. A.
The Historian As Diplomat: Charles Kingsley Webster & the United Nations 1939-1946. Biblio Dist.
xReynolds, Philip A.
British Foreign Policy in the Inter-War Years. Greenwood.

Reynolds, Reginald, 1905-
xReynolds, Reginald.
White Sahibs in India. Greenwood.

Reynolds, Robert L. *see* Reynolds, Robert Leonard.

Reynolds, Robert Leonard.
xReynolds, Robert L.
Europe Emerges: Transition Toward an Industrial World-Wide Society, 600-1750. U of Wis Pr.

Reynolds, Roger E., 1936-
xReynolds, Roger E.

The Ordinals of Christ from Their Origins to the Twelfth Century. De Gruyter.

Reynolds, Stephen, 1937-
xReynolds, Stephen.
Christian Religious Tradition. Dickenson.

Reynolds, Tim.
xReynolds, Tim.
Que. Halty Ferguson.

Reynolds, William C. *see* Reynolds, William Craig.

Reynolds, William Craig.
xReynolds, William C.
Engineering Thermodynamics. McGraw.
Thermodynamics. McGraw.

Reynolds, William L., 1945-
xReynolds, William L.
Judicial Process in a Nutshell. West Pub.

Rezak, Richard.
xRezak, Richard.
ed. Contributions on the Geological & Geophysical Oceanography of the Gulf of Mexico. Gulf Pub.

Rezazadeh, Reza.
xRezazadeh, Reza.
Political Parties in Colombia: Continuity in Political Style. Univ Microfilms.

Rezler, Julius. *see* Rezler, Julius Stephen.

Rezler, Julius Stephen.
xRezler, Julius.
Automation & Industrial Labor. Phila Bk Co.

Rezneck, Samuel.
xRezneck, Samuel.
The Saga of an American Jewish Family Since the Revolution: A History of the Family of Jonas Phillips. U Pr of Amer.

Reznik, John W.
xReznik, John W.
Racquetball. Sterling.

Reznikoff, Charles, 1894-
xReznikoff, Charles.
Holocaust. Black Sparrow.

Reznikoff, S. C., 1930-
xReznikoff, S. C.
Specifications for Commercial Interiors: Professional Liabilities, Regulations, & Performance Criteria. Watson-Guptill.

Rha, Chokyun.
xRha, Chokyun.
ed. Theory, Determination & Control of Physical Properties of Food Materials. Kluwer Boston.

Rhea, Carolyn.
xRhea, Carolyn.
Glimpses of God's Presence. Broadman.
My Heart Kneels, Too. G&D.
Such Is My Confidence. G&D.

Rhea, Nicholas.
xRhea, Nicholas.
Constable on the Hill. St Martin.

Rhead, Louis, 1857-1926
xRhead, Louis.
illus. Bait Angling for Common Fishes. C E Tuttle.

Rhee, Jhoon. *see* Rhee, Jhoon Goo.

Rhee, Jhoon Goo.
xRhee, Jhoon.
Hwa-Rang & Chung-Mu of Tae Kwon Do Hyung. Ohara Pubns.
Won-Hyo & Yul-Kok of Tae Kwon Do Hyung. Ohara Pubns.

Rhees, William J. *see* Rhees, William Jones.

Rhees, William Jones, 1830-1907
xRhees, William J.
An Account of the Smithsonian Institution: Its Founder, Building, Operations, Etc.. Arno.

Rheims, Maurice.
xRheims, Maurice.
The Glorious Obsession. St Martin.

Rhein, Francis B. *see* Rhein, Francis Bayard.

Rhein, Francis Bayard.
xRhein, Francis B.

Understanding the New Testament. Barron.
Rhein, Phillip H.
xRhein, Phillip H.
Albert Camus. Twayne.
Rheinfelder, William A.
xRheinfelder, William A.
CATV Circuit Engineering. TAB Bks.
Rheingold, Paul D.
xRheingold, Paul D.
ed. Product Liability: Law, Practice, Science.
PLI.
Rheinheimer, G. *see* Rheinheimer, Gerhard.
Rheinheimer, Gerhard, 1927-
xRheinheimer, G.
Aquatic Microbiology. Wiley.
xRheinheimer, Gerhard.
Aquatic Microbiology. Wiley.
Rheinstein, Max, 1899-
xRheinstein, Max.
Marriage Stability, Divorce, & the Law. U of
Chicago Pr.
Rheinstrom, Carroll.
xRheinstrom, Carroll.
Psyching the Ads: The Case Book of
Advertising; the Methods & Results of 180
Advertisements. Arno.
Rhett, Blanche S. *see* Rhett, Blanche Salley.
Rhett, Blanche Salley.
xRhett, Blanche S.
Two Hundred Years of Charleston Cooking. U
of SC Pr.
Rhie, Marylin M.
xRhie, Marylin M.
Fo-Kuang Ssu: Literary Evidences & Buddhist
Images. Garland Pub.
Rhine. *see* Rhine, Joseph Banks.
Rhine, J. B. *see* Rhine, Joseph Banks.
Rhine, Joseph Banks, 1895-
xRhine.
Parapsychology Today. Citadel Pr.
xRhine, J. B.
The Reach of the Mind. Morrow.
Rhinehart, Luke.
xRhinehart, Luke.
The Dice Man. PB.
Rhiner, Gladys.
xRhiner, Gladys.
Jimmy Goes Camping. Broadman.
Rho, M. *see* Rho, Mannque.
Rho, Mannque.
xRho, M.
ed. Mesons in Nuclei. Elsevier.
Rhoades, Robert B., 1942-
xRhoades, Robert B.
Medical Aspects of the Imported Fire Ant. U
Presses Fla.
Rhoads, Sharon A. *see* Rhoads, Sharon Ann.
Rhoads, Sharon Ann.
xRhoads, Sharon A.
Cooking with Sea Vegetables. Autumn Pr.
Rhoads, Steven E.
xRhoads, Steven E.
Valuing Life: Public Policy Dilemmas.
Westview.
Rhoads, William B.
xRhoads, William B.
The Colonial Revival. Garland Pub.
Rhodabarger. *see* Rhodabarger, T. Dale.
Rhodabarger, T. D. *see* Rhodabarger, T. Dale.
Rhodabarger, T. Dale.
xRhodabarger.
Personal Money Management for Physicians.
Van Nos Reinhold.
xRhodabarger, T. D.
Personal Money Management for Physicians.
Med Economics.
Rhode, Eric, 1934-
xRhode, Eric.

A History of the Cinema: From Its Origins to
1970. Hill & Wang.
Rhode, Irma.
xRhode, Irma.
Practical Entertaining. Atheneum.
Rhode Island Historical Society.
xRhode Island Historical Society.
Rhode Island Land Evidences, Vol. 1:
1648-1696. Genealog Pub.
Rhode, Robert B. *see* Rhode, Robert Bartlett.
Rhode, Robert Bartlett.
xRhode, Robert B.
Introduction to Photography. Macmillan.
Rhoden, Chris C.
xRhoden, Chris C.
Economics: Facts, Theory & Policy. Wiley.
Rhoderick, E. H.
xRhoderick, E. H.
Metal-Semiconductor Contacts. Oxford U Pr.
Rhodes, A. *see* Rhodes, Alan.
Rhodes, Alan.
xRhodes, A.
Principles of Industrial Microbiology.
Pergamon.
Rhodes, Bennie, 1927-
xRhodes, Bennie.
Calculator Word Games. Mott Media.
Rhodes, Buck A., 1935-
xRhodes, Buck A.
ed. Quality Control in Nuclear Medicine:
Radiopharmaceuticals, Instrumentation &
in-Vitro Assays. Mosby.
Rhodes, C. K. *see* Rhodes, Charles K.
Rhodes, C. O.
xRhodes, C. O.
Let's Look at Musical Instruments & the
Orchestra. A Whitman.
Rhodes, Charles K.
xRhodes, C. K.
ed. Excimer Lasers. Springer-Verlag.
Rhodes, Daniel, 1911-
xRhodes, Daniel.
Clay & Glazes for the Potter. Chilton.
Stoneware & Porcelain: The Art of High-Fired
Pottery. Chilton.
Rhodes, Eugene M. *see* Rhodes, Eugene Manlove.
Rhodes, Eugene Manlove, 1869-1934
xRhodes, Eugene M.
Paso Por Aqui. U of Okla Pr.
The Proud Sheriff. U of Okla Pr.
Trusty Knaves. U of Okla Pr.
Rhodes, Evan H.
xRhodes, Evan H.
The Carrion Eaters. Stein & Day.
Rhodes, Frank H. *see* Rhodes, Frank Harold Trevor.
Rhodes, Frank Harold Trevor.
xRhodes, Frank H.
ed. Conodont Paleozoology. Geol Soc.
Geology. Western Pub.
Rhodes, Irma. *see* Rhodes, Irma G.
Rhodes, Irma G.
xRhodes, Irma.
Flashbacks: Poems for Children. Dragons
Teeth.
Rhodes, J. D. *see* Rhodes, John David.
Rhodes, James F. *see* Rhodes, James Ford.
Rhodes, James Ford, 1848-1927
xRhodes, James F.
Historical Essays. Kennikat.
History of the United States from the
Compromise of 1850. U of Chicago Pr.
Rhodes, John David.
xRhodes, J. D.
Theory of Electrical Filters. Wiley.
Rhodes, Lelia G.
xRhodes, Lelia G.
Jackson State University: The First Hundred
Years, 1877-1977. U Pr of Miss.
Rhodes, P. J. *see* Rhodes, Peter John.

Rhodes, Peter John.
xRhodes, P. J.
Athenian Boule. Oxford U Pr.
Rhodes, Philip.
xRhodes, Philip.
The Value of Medicine. Allen Unwin.
Rhodes, R. C.
xRhodes, R. L.
ed. Homeowner's Security Handbook. ASTM.
Rhodes, R. L. *see* Rhodes, R. C.
Rhodes, Richard.
xRhodes, Richard.
Holy Secrets. Bantam.
Holy Secrets. Doubleday.
Looking for America: A Writer's Odyssey.
Doubleday.
Looking for America: A Writer's Odyssey.
Penguin.
The Ozarks. Time-Life.
The Ozarks. Silver.
Rhodes, Robert P.
xRhodes, Robert P.
The Insoluble Problems of Crime. Wiley.
Rhodes, Russell. *see* Rhodes, Russell L.
Rhodes, Russell L.
xRhodes, Russell.
The Styx Complex. Dodd.
Rhodes, Thomas J.
xRhodes, Thomas J.
Industrial Instruments for Measurement &
Control. McGraw.
Rhodin, Eric, 1916-
xRhodin, Eric.
The Good Greenwood. Westminster.
Rhodin, Johannes A. *see* Rhodin, Johannes A. G.
Rhodin, Johannes A. G.
xRhodin, Johannes A
An Atlas of Histology. Oxford U Pr.
xRhodin, Johannes G.
Histology: A Text & Atlas. Oxford U Pr.
Rhodin, Johannes G. *see* Rhodin, Johannes A. G.
Rhondda, Margaret H. *see* Rhondda, Margaret Haig
(Thomas) Mackworth.
**Rhondda, Margaret Haig (Thomas) Mackworth,
Viscountess, 1883-**
xRhondda, Margaret H.
Notes on the Way. Arno.
xRhondda, Viscountess.
Notes on the Way. R West.
Rhondda, Viscountess. *see* Rhondda, Margaret Haig
(Thomas) Mackworth.
Rhone, L. C.
xRhone, L. C.
Total Auto Body Repair. Bobbs.
Rhymer, Joseph.
xRhymer, Joseph.
Companion to the Good News, Old Testament.
World Bible.
Rhyne, Jennings J. *see* Rhyne, Jennings Jefferson.
Rhyne, Jennings Jefferson, 1897-
xRhyne, Jennings J.
Some Southern Cotton Mill Workers & Their
Villages. Arno.
Rhys, Ernest, 1859-1946
xRhys, Ernest.
Browning & His Poetry. AMS Pr.
Browning & His Poetry. Folcroft.
The Golden Treasury of Longer Poems.
Century Bookbindery.
ed. The Golden Treasury of Longer Poems.
Granger Bk.
Rhys, Horton.
xRhys, Horton.
Theatrical Trip for a Wager. Arno.
Rhys, Jean.
xRhys, Jean.

After Leaving Mr. Mackenzie. Har-Row.
After Leaving Mr. Mackenzie. Random.
Good Morning, Midnight. Random.
Left Bank, & Other Stories. Arno.
Quartet. Har-Row.
Quartet. Random.
Smile Please: An Unfinished Autobiography.
Har-Row.
Rhys, John, Sir, 1840-1915
xRhys, John.
Celtic Folklore, Welsh & Manx. Johnson Repr.
Lectures on the Origin & Growth of Religion
As Illustrated by Celtic Heathendom. AMS
Pr.
Rhys, Keidrych.
xRhys, Keidrych.
ed. Modern Welsh Poetry. Granger Bk.
Rial, Arlyne F.
xRial, Arlyne F.
Speed Reading Made Easy. Doubleday.
Riasanovsky, Nicholas V. see Riasanovsky, Nicholas
Valentine.
Riasanovsky, Nicholas Valentine, 1923-
xRiasanovsky, Nicholas V.
A History of Russia. Oxford U Pr.
A Parting of the Ways: Government & the
Educated Public in Russia, 1801-1855.
Oxford U Pr.
The Teaching of Charles Fourier. U of Cal Pr.
Riaud, Alexis.
xRiaud, Alexis.
The Holy Spirit Acting in Our Souls. Alba.
Ribenboim, P. see Ribenboim, Paulo.
Ribenboim, Paulo.
xRibenboim, P.
Algebraic Numbers. Wiley.
Ribera y Tarrago, Julian, 1858-1934
xRibera y Tarrago, Julian.
Historia De la Musica Arabe Medieval y Su
Influencia En la Espanola. AMS Pr.
Ribicoff, Abraham. see Ribicoff, Abraham A.
Ribicoff, Abraham A.
xRibicoff, Abraham.
Politics: The American Way. Allyn.
Riblet, Carl.
xRiblet, Carl.
The Solid Gold Copy Editor. Beresford Bk
Serv.
Ribner, Irving.
xRibner, Irving.
The English History Play in the Age of
Shakespeare. Octagon.
Patterns in Shakespearian Tragedy. Rowman.
Tudor & Stuart Drama. AHM Pub.
Ribton-Turner, C. J. see Ribton-Turner, Charles James.
Ribton-Turner, Charles James.
xRibton-Turner, C. J.
A History of Vagrants and Vagrancy, and
Beggars and Begging. Patterson Smith.
Ricardo, Don.
xRicardo, Don.
Early California & Mexico Cook Book. Borden.
Riccardi, Vincent M.
xRiccardi, Vincent M.
The Genetic Approach to Human Disease.
Oxford U Pr.
Riccardo, Edward P.
xRiccardo, Edward P.
Introduction to Humanistic Philosophy.
Kendall-Hunt.
Ricchiuti, Paul. see Ricchiuti, Paul B.
Ricchiuti, Paul B.
xRicchiuti, Paul.
I Found a Feather. Pacific Pr Pub Assn.
Let's Play Make Believe. Pacific Pr Pub Assn.
Ricci, a James.
xRicci, A. James.
Understanding & Training Horses. Lippincott.
Ricci, Benjamin.
xRicci, Benjamin.

Experiments in the Physiology of Human
Performance. Lea & Febiger.
Ricci, Corrado, 1858-1934
xRicci, Corrado.
North Italian Painting of the Cinquecento:
Piedmont, Liguria, Lombardy, Emilia.
Hacker.
Ricci, David M.
xRicci, David M.
Community Power & Democratic Theory: The
Logic of Political Analysis. Random.
Ricci, Mark.
xRicci, Mark.
The Films of John Wayne. Citadel Pr.
Ricciardi, L. M. see Ricciardi, Luigi M.
Ricciardi, Luigi M., 1942-
xRicciardi, L. M.
Diffusion Processes & Related Topics in
Biology. Springer-Verlag.
Riccio, Anthony C.
xRiccio, Anthony C.
Establishing Guidance Programs in Secondary
Schools. HM.
Ricciuti, Edward R.
xRicciuti, Edward R.
Catch a Whale by the Tail. Har-Row.
The Devil's Garden: Facts & Folklore of
Perilous Plants. Walker & Co.
Donald & the Fish That Walked. Har-Row.
Plants in Danger. Har-Row.
Sounds of Animals at Night. Har-Row.
Wildlife of the Mountains. Abrams.
Rice, Alice Caldwell Hegan, 1870-1942
xRice, Alice H.
Mrs. Wiggs of the Cabbage Patch. U Pr of Ky.
Rice, Alice H. see Rice, Alice Caldwell Hegan.
Rice, Allen T. see Rice, Allen Thorndike.
Rice, Allen Thorndike, 1851-1889
xRice, Allen T.
ed. Reminiscences of Abraham Lincoln.
Haskell.
Rice, Anne, 1941-
xRice, Anne.
The Feast of All Saints. S&S.
Rice, Benjamin, 1902-
xRice, Benjamin.
Old Farmer's Almanac's Book of Country
Essays. Yankee Bks.
Rice, Bernard J.
xRice, Bernard J.
Algebra & Trigonometry. Prindle.
College Algebra. Prindle.
Plane Trigonometry. Prindle.
Rice, Bradley R. see Rice, Bradley Robert.
Rice, Bradley Robert, 1948-
xRice, Bradley R.
Progressive Cities: The Commission
Government Movement in America,
1901-1920. U of Tex Pr.
Rice, Brian.
xRice, Brian.
The English Sunrise. Music Sales.
Rice, Charles E.
xRice, Charles E.
Freedom of Association. NYU Pr.
Rice, Craig S.
xRice, Craig S.
Power Secrets of Managing People. P-H.
Rice, David. see Rice, David Talbot.
Rice, David G. see Rice, David Gordon.
Rice, David Gordon, 1938-
xRice, David G.
Dual-Career Marriage: Conflict & Treatment.
Free Pr.
Rice, David T. see Rice, David Talbot.
Rice, David Talbot, 1903-
xRice, David T.
Icons & Their History. Overlook Pr.
xRice, David T.

Art of the Byzantine Era. Oxford U Pr.
Rice, Eddy, 1911-
xRice, Eddy.
How to Eat Better & Spend Less: A Complete
Guide to Vegetable Gardening. Reston.
How to Grow, Preserve & Store All the Food
You Need. Reston.
Rice, Edward.
xRice, Edward.
illus. Babylon, Next to Nineveh: Where the
World Began. Schol Bk Serv.
illus. The Five Great Religions. Schol Bk Serv.
Rice, Edward. see Rice, Edward E.
Rice, Edward E., 1918-
xRice, Edward.
Marx, Engels & the Workers of the World.
Schol Bk Serv.
Rice, Edward E. see Rice, Edward Earl.
Rice, Edward Earl.
xRice, Edward E.
Mao's Way. U of Cal Pr.
Rice, Edwin W. see Rice, Edwin Wilbur.
Rice, Edwin Wilbur, 1831-1929
xRice, Edwin W.
Sunday-School Movement, 1780-1917, & the
American Sunday-School Union, 1817-1917.
Arno.
Rice, Emmett A. see Rice, Emmett Ainsworth.
Rice, Emmett Ainsworth.
xRice, Emmett A.
A Brief History of Physical Education. Wiley.
Rice, Eugene F.
xRice, Eugene F.
The Renaissance Idea of Wisdom. Greenwood.
Rice, Eve.
xRice, Eve.
Ebbie. Penguin.
Ebbie. Greenwillow.
Goodnight, Goodnight. Greenwillow.
Oh, Lewis!. Penguin.
illus. Oh, Lewis!. Macmillan.
Once in a Wood: Ten Tales from Aesop.
Greenwillow.
Papa's Lemonade & Other Stories.
Greenwillow.
Rice, F. Philip.
xRice, F. Philip.
Marriage & Parenthood. Allyn.
Morality & Youth: A Guide for Christian
Parents. Westminster.
Outdoor Life Gun Data Book. Har-Row.
The Working Mother's Guide to Child
Development. P-H.
Rice, Frank M.
xRice, Frank M.
English & Its Teaching. Prof Educ Pubn.
Rice, George H. see Rice, George Hall.
Rice, George Hall, 1923-
xRice, George H.
ed. Industrial Organizations: Selected Readings.
Austin Pr.
Rice, Hazel V.
xRice, Hazel V.
Gastrointestinal Nursing. Med Exam.
Rice, Helen S. see Rice, Helen Steiner.
Rice, Helen Steiner.
xRice, Helen S.
Life Is Forever. Revell.
Lovingly: Poems for All Seasons. Revell.
Somebody Loves You. Revell.
Rice, Homer.
xRice, Homer.
Homer Rice on Triple Option Football. P-H.
Rice, Howard C. see Rice, Howard Crosby.
Rice, Howard Crosby, 1904-
xRice, Howard C.
ed. Thomas Jefferson's Paris. Princeton U Pr.
Rice, J. M. see Rice, Joseph Mayer.
Rice, J. R. see Rice, John K.

Chemically Induced Dynamic Nuclear &
Electron Polarizations-Cidnp & Cidep.
Springer-Verlag.

Richard, Frederick S.
xRichard, Frederick S.
Hispanoamerica moderna. HarBraceJ.
Richard, J. see Richard, Jean.
Richard, J. F. see Richard, Jean Francois.
Richard, Jean, 1921 (feb. 7)-
xRichard, J.
The Latin Kingdom of Jerusalem. Elsevier.
Richard, Jean Francois.
xRichard, J. F.
Posterior & Predictive Densities for
Simultaneous Equation Models.
Springer-Verlag.
Richards. see Richards, William Graham.
Richards, Alan J.
xRichards, Alan J.
British Birds: A Field Guide. David & Charles.
Richards, Alun.
xRichards, Alun.
Barque Whisper. St Martin.

Richards, Arlene. see Richards, Arlene Kramer.
Richards, Arlene K. see Richards, Arlene Kramer
Richards, Arlene Kramer.
xRichards, Arlene.
How to Get It Together When Your Parents
Are Coming Apart. Bantam.
How to Get It Together When Your Parents
Are Coming Apart. McKay.
xRichards, Arlene K.
Boy Friends, Girl Friends, Just Friends.
Atheneum.

Richards, Aubrey I. see Richards, Audrey Isabel.
Richards, Audrey Isabel, 1899-
xRichards, Aubrey I.
Hunger & Work in a Savage Tribe: A
Functional Study of Nutrition Among the
Southern Bantu. Peter Smith.
Richards, B. see Richards, Bryan E.
Richards, Barry.
xRichards, Barry.
The Barry Richards Story. Merrimack Bk Serv.
Richards, Bernard F. see Richards, Bertrand F.
Richards, Bertrand F.
xRichards, Bernard F.
Gene Stratton Porter. Twayne.
Richards, Bryan E.
xRichards, B.
ed. Measurement of Unsteady Fluid Dynamic
Phenomena. Hemisphere Pub.
Richards, C. J. see Richards, Clement John.
Richards, Cara. see Richards, Cara Elizabeth.
Richards, Cara E. see Richards, Cara Elizabeth.
Richards, Cara Elizabeth, 1927-
xRichards, Cara.
People in Perspective: An Introduction to
Cultural Anthropology. Random.
xRichards, Cara E.
People in Perspective: An Introduction to
Cultural Anthropology. Random.
Richards, Caroline.
xRichards, Caroline.
Sweet Country. HarBraceJ.
Richards, Clement John.
xRichards, C. J.
Mechanical Engineering in Radar &
Communications. Van Nos Reinhold.
Richards, David A. see Richards, David A. J.
Richards, David A. J.
xRichards, David A.
The Moral Criticism of Law. Dickenson.
A Theory of Reasons for Action. Oxford U Pr.
Richards, David G. see Richards, David Gleyre.
Richards, David Gleyre, 1935-
xRichards, David G.

Georg Buchner. State U NY Pr.
Richards, Denis.
xRichards, Denis.
Portal of Hungerford: The Life of Marshal of
the Royal Air Force Viscount Portal of
Hungerford KG, GCB, OM, DSO, MC.
Holmes & Meier.
Richards, Dorothy F. see Richards, Dorothy Fay.
Richards, Dorothy Fay.
xRichards, Dorothy F.
Abe Lincoln, Make It Right!. Childs World.
Thomas James the Second & Friends. Childs
World.
Richards, Edward A. see Richards, Edward Ames.
Richards, Edward Ames, 1898-1964
xRichards, Edward A.
Hudibras in the Burlesque Tradition. Octagon.
Richards, Elizabeth A.
xRichards, Elizabeth A.
ed. Market Information & Research in Fashion
Management. Am Mktg.
Richards, Eugene.
xRichards, Eugene.
Few Comforts or Surprises: The Arkansas
Delta. MIT Pr.
Richards, Fred.
xRichards, Fred.
Homonovus: The New Man. Publishers
Consult.
Richards, Gerald F.
xRichards, Gerald F.
Tax-Planning Opportunities. Wiley.
Richards, Guy, 1905-
xRichards, Guy.
Imperial Agent: The Goleniewski-Romanov
Case. Devin.
Richards, Harold. see Richards, Harold Marshall
Sylvester.
Richards, Harold Marshall Sylvester.
xRichards, Harold.
Earthquake. Southern Pub.
Richards, Henry M. see Richards, Henry Melchior
Muhlenberg.
Richards, Henry Melchior Muhlenberg, 1848-1935
xRichards, Henry M.
The Pennsylvania-German in the Revolutionary
War, 1775-1783. Genealog Pub.
Richards, Hubert. see Richards, Hubert J.
Richards, Hubert J, 1921-
xRichards, Hubert.
Reading Paul Today: A New Introduction to
the Man & His Letters. John Knox.
xRichards, Hubert J.
ABC of the Bible. Glencoe.
Richards, J. F.
xRichards, J. F.
Mughal Administration in Golconda. Oxford U
Pr.
Richards, J. W.
xRichards, J. W.
Introduction to Industrial Sterilization. Acad
Pr.
Richards, Jean H. see Richards, Jean Hosking.
Richards, Jean Hosking.
xRichards, Jean H.
A Boy Named Jesus. Broadman.
Richards, Jeffrey.
xRichards, Jeffrey.
The Popes & the Papacy in the Early Middle
Ages, 476-752. Routledge & Kegan.
Richards, Jill.
xRichards, Jill.
Classroom Language: What Sort?. Allen Unwin.
Richards, Joyce.
xRichards, Joyce.
More Easy Answers. Platt.
Richards, Judith.
xRichards, Judith.

The Sounds of Silence. Putnam.
Summer Lightning. Avon.
Summer Lightning. St Martin.
Richards, Kenneth. see Richards, Kenneth G.
Richards, Kenneth G.
xRichards, Kenneth.
Story of the Gettysburg Address. Childrens.
Richards, Kent D., 1938-
xRichards, Kent D.
Isaac I. Stevens: Young Man in a Hurry.
Brigham.
Richards, Larry E.
xRichards, Larry E.
Business Statistics: Why & When. McGraw.
Richards, Laura E. see Richards, Laura Elizabeth
(Howe).
Richards, Laura Elizabeth (Howe), 1850-1943
xRichards, Laura E.
Abigail Adams & Her Times. Gale.
Richards, Lawrence O.
xRichards, Lawrence O.
Creative Bible Teaching. Moody.
How Far I Can Go. Zondervan.
How I Can Experience God. Zondervan.
How I Can Make Decisions. Zondervan.
A Theology of Christian Education. Zondervan.
Richards, le Grand, Bp, 1886-
xRichards, LeGrand.
Marvelous Work & a Wonder. Deseret Bk.
Richards, LeGrand. see Richards, le Grand.
Richards, Leonard L.
xRichards, Leonard L.
Gentlemen of Property & Standing:
Anti-Abolition Mobs in Jacksonian America.
Oxford U Pr.
Gentlemen of Property and Standing:
Anti-Abolition Mobs in Jacksonian America.
Oxford U Pr.
Richards, Leyton. see Richards, Leyton Price.
Richards, Leyton Price, 1879-1948
xRichards, Leyton.
Realistic Pacifism: The Ethics of War & the
Politics of Peace. Garland Pub.
Richards, Lockie.
xRichards, Lockie.
Dressage: Begin the Right Way. David &
Charles.
Richards, M. see Richards, Michael W.
Richards, Martin G. see Richards, Martin Gomm.
Richards, Martin Gomm.
xRichards, Martin G.
A Disaggregate Travel Demand Model.
Lexington Bks.
Richards, Mary C. see Richards, Mary Caroline.
Richards, Mary Caroline.
xRichards, Mary C.
Centering in Pottery, Poetry, & the Person.
Columbia U Pr.
The Crossing Point: Selected Talks & Writings.
Columbia U Pr.
Richards, Max D. see Richards, Max De Voe.
Richards, Max De Voe, 1923-
xRichards, Max D.
Intermediate & Long-Term Credit for Small
Corporations. Arno.
Readings in Management. SW Pub.
Richards, Michael W.
xRichards, M.
Focalguide to Bird Photography. Focal Pr.
Richards, Nat, 1942-
xRichards, Nat.
Otis Dunn-Manhunter. Ashley Bks.
Richards, Norman.
xRichards, Norman.

The Complete Beginner's Guide to Soaring & Hang Gliding. Doubleday.
Story of Monticello. Childrens.
Story of Old Ironsides. Childrens.
Story of the Declaration of Independence. Childrens.
Story of the Mayflower Compact. Childrens.
Trucks & Supertrucks. Doubleday.
Richards, O. W. see Richards, Owain Westmacott.
Richards, Owain Westmacott, 1901-
  xRichards, O. W.
  The Species of Pseudomasaris Ashmead (Hymenoptera: Masaridae). U of Cal Pr.
Richards, P. W. see Richards, Paul Westmacott.
Richards, Pamela.
  xRichards, Pamela.
  Crime As Play: Delinquency in a Middle Class Suburb. Ballinger Pub.
Richards, Paul Westmacott.
  xRichards, P. W.
  Life of the Jungle. McGraw.
Richards, Peter G.
  xRichards, Peter G.
  The Backbenchers. Humanities.
  Reformed Local Government System. Allen Unwin.
Richards, R. J.
  xRichards, R. J.
  An Introduction to Dynamics & Control. Longman.
Richards, R. K. see Richards, Richard Kohler.
Richards, Richard D. see Richards, Richard David.
Richards, Richard David.
  xRichards, Richard D.
  Early History of Banking in England. Kelley.
Richards, Richard Davison, 1927-
  xRichards, Richard D.
  ed. Ophthalmologic Disorders: A Practitioner's Guide. Med Exam.
Richards, Richard Kohler, 1921-
  xRichards, R. K.
  Digital Design. Krieger.
Richards, Robert F. see Richards, Robert Fulton.
Richards, Robert Fulton.
  xRichards, Robert F.
  ed. Concise Dictionary of American Literature. Greenwood.
Richards, Robert K.
  xRichards, Robert K.
  Continuing Medical Education: Perspectives, Problems, Prognosis. Yale U Pr.
Richards, Ruth.
  xRichards, Ruth.
  Let's Do Yoga. HR&W.
Richards, Stanleu. see Richards, Stanley.
Richards, Stanley, 1918-
  xRichards, Stanleu.
  Great Rock Musicals. Stein & Day.
  xRichards, Stanley.
  ed. America on Stage: Ten Great Plays of American History. Doubleday.
  ed. Twenty One-Act Plays: An Anthology for Amateur Performing Groups. Doubleday.
Richards, Vyvyan.
  xRichards, Vyvyan.
  Portrait of T. E. Lawrence. Haskell.
Richards, W. G. see Richards, William Graham.
Richards, William Graham.
  xRichards.
  Quantum Pharmacology. Butterworths.
  xRichards, W. G.
  Structure & Spectra of Atoms. Wiley.
Richardson. see Richardson, James H.
Richardson, A. E. see Richardson, Albert Edward.
Richardson, Alan, 1905-
  xRichardson, Alan.

  ed. Dictionary of Christian Theology. Westminster.
  Theological Word Book of the Bible. Macmillan.
Richardson, Albert E. see Richardson, Albert Edward.
Richardson, Albert Edward.
  xRichardson, A. E.
  The Old Inns of England. Arno.
  xRichardson, Albert E.
  The Art of Architecture. Greenwood.
Richardson, Alphyn P. see Richardson, Alphyon Perry.
Richardson, Alphyon Perry, 1875-1949
  xRichardson, Alphyn P.
  Barnegat Ways. Arno.
Richardson, Arleta.
  xRichardson, Arleta.
  More Stories from Grandma's Attic. Cook.
Richardson, B. A. see Richardson, Barry A.
Richardson, Barry A.
  xRichardson, B. A.
  Wood Construction. Longman.
  xRichardson, Barry A.
  Wood Preservation. Longman.
Richardson, Bessie E. see Richardson, Bessie Ellen.
Richardson, Bessie Ellen, 1901-
  xRichardson, Bessie E.
  Old Age Among the Ancient Greeks: The Greek Portrayal of Old Age in Literature, Art & Inscriptions. Greenwood.
Richardson, Bill.
  xRichardson, Bill.
  The Appaloosa. Arco.
Richardson, C. James.
  xRichardson, C. James.
  Contemporary Social Mobility. Nichols Pub.
Richardson, Cyril A. see Richardson, Cyril Albert.
Richardson, Cyril Albert.
  xRichardson, Cyril A.
  Education of Teachers in England, France & the U.S.A. Greenwood.
Richardson, Cyril C. see Richardson, Cyril Charles.
Richardson, Cyril Charles, 1909-
  xRichardson, Cyril C.
  Christianity of Ignatius of Antioch. AMS Pr.
  The Church Through the Centuries. AMS Pr.
  ed. Early Christian Fathers. Macmillan.
Richardson, Don.
  xRichardson, Don.
  Peace Child. Regal.
Richardson, Donald V.
  xRichardson, Donald V.
  ed. Handbook of Rotating Electric Machinery. Reston.
Richardson, Dorothy Lee.
  xRichardson, Dorthy L.
  Half-Seen Face. Bauhan.
Richardson, Dorthy L. see Richardson, Dorothy Lee.
Richardson, Elmo. see Richardson, Elmo R.
Richardson, Elmo R.
  xRichardson, Elmo.
  The Presidency of Dwight D. Eisenhower. Regents Pr KS.
Richardson, Gary L.
  xRichardson, Gary L.
  A Primer of Structured Program Design. Petrocelli.
Richardson, George B. see Richardson, George Barclay.
Richardson, George Barclay.
  xRichardson, George B.
  Economic Theory. Humanities.
Richardson, Grace.
  xRichardson, Grace.
  Apples Every Day. Har-Row.
Richardson, H. D. see Richardson, Harold Davis.
Richardson, H. Edward. see Richardson, Harold Edward.
Richardson, H. L.
  xRichardson, H. L.
  What Makes You Think We Read the Bills?. Caroline Hse.
Richardson, H. W. see Richardson, Harry Ward.

Richardson, Harold Davis.
  xRichardson, H. D.
  Developmental Counseling in Education. HM.
Richardson, Harold Edward.
  xRichardson, H. Edward.
  How to Think & Write. Scott F.
Richardson, Harry W. see Richardson, Harry Ward.
Richardson, Harry Ward.
  xRichardson, H. W.
  Regional Growth Theory. Halsted Pr.
  xRichardson, Harry W.
  Economic Aspects of the Energy Crisis. Lexington Bks.
  Regional Economics. U of Ill Pr.
Richardson, Hazel A.
  xRichardson, Hazel A.
  Games for the Elementary School Grades. Burgess.
Richardson, Henry B. see Richardson, Henry Brush.
Richardson, Henry Brush, 1889-
  xRichardson, Henry B.
  Etymological Vocabulary to the Libro De Buen Amor of Juan Ruiz, Arcipreste De Hita. AMS Pr.
Richardson, Herbert, Mrs.
  xRichardson, Herbert.
  The Old English Newspaper. Folcroft.
Richardson, Ivan L.
  xRichardson.
  Public Administration: Government in Action. Merrill.
Richardson, J. D.
  xRichardson, J. D.
  Essentials of Aviation Management. Kendall-Hunt.
Richardson, J. David.
  xRichardson, J. David.
  Understanding International Economics: Theory & Practice. Little.
Richardson, J. H. see Richardson, James H.
Richardson, Jack, 1935-
  xRichardson, Jack.
  Memoir of a Gambler. S&S.
Richardson, Jacques.
  xRichardson, Jacques.
  ed. Integrated Technology Transfer. Lomond.
Richardson, James, 1950-
  xRichardson, James.
  Thomas Hardy: The Poetry of Necessity. U of Chicago Pr.
Richardson, James H.
  xRichardson.
  Systematic Materials Analysis. Acad Pr.
  xRichardson, J. H.
  ed. Systematic Materials Analysis. Acad Pr.
Richardson, James L.
  xRichardson, James L.
  Germany & the Atlantic Alliance: The Interaction of Strategy & Politics. Harvard U Pr.
Richardson, James T.
  xRichardson, James T.
  Organized Miracles: A Study of a Contemporary, Youth, Communal, Fundamentalist Organization. Transaction Bks.
Richardson, James W. see Richardson, James Walls.
Richardson, James Walls, 1893-
  xRichardson, James W.
  Problems of Articulation Between the Units of Secondary Education. AMS Pr.
Richardson, Joanna.
  xRichardson, Joanna.
  The Disastrous Marriage: A Study of George IV & Caroline of Brunswick. Greenwood.
  Enid Starkie. Macmillan.
  The Pre-Eminent Victorian: A Study of Tennyson. Greenwood.
  Zola. St Martin.
Richardson, Joe M. see Richardson, Joe Martin.

Richardson, Joe Martin.
  xRichardson, Joe M.
    The Negro in the Reconstruction of Florida,
      1865-1877. Trend House.
Richardson, John, Sir, 1787-1865
  xRichardson, John.
    Arctic Searching Expedition: A Journal of a
      Boat Voyage Through Rupert's Land & the
      Arctic Sea, in Search of the Discovery Ships
      Under Command of Sir John Franklin.
      Greenwood.
    The Canadian Brothers: Or the Prophecy
      Fulfilled: a Tale of the Late American War.
      U of Toronto Pr.
    Fauna Boreali-Americana. Arno.
    ed. The Human Dimension of Foreign Policy:
      An American Perspective. Am Acad Pol Soc
      Sci.
Richardson, John A. see Richardson, John Adkins.
Richardson, John Adkins.
  xRichardson, John A.
    Art: The Way It Is. P-H.
    The Complete Book of Cartooning. P-H.
    Modern Art & Scientific Thought. U of Ill Pr.
Richardson, John H. see Richardson, John Henry.
Richardson, John Henry, 1890-
  xRichardson, John H.
    Economic Disarmament: A Study of
      International Cooperation. AMS Pr.
    Economic Disarmament: A Study on
      International Cooperation. Greenwood.
Richardson, John M. see Richardson, John Martin.
Richardson, John Martin, 1938-
  xRichardson, John M.
    Partners in Development: An Analysis of
      AID-University Relations, 1950-1966. Mich
      St U Pr.
Richardson, John T. see Richardson, John T. E.
Richardson, John T. E.
  xRichardson, John T.
    The Grammar of Justification: An
      Interpretation of Wittgenstein's Philosophy of
      Language. St Martin.
    Mental Imagery & Human Memory. St Martin.
Richardson, Jonathan.
  xRichardson, Jonathan.
    jt. auth. Explanatory Notes & Remarks on
      Milton's Paradise Lost. AMS Pr.
Richardson, Joseph G. see Richardson, Joseph Gibbons.
Richardson, Joseph Gibbons, 1836-1886
  xRichardson, Joseph G.
    Long Life & How to Reach It.. Arno.
Richardson, Kay.
  xRichardson, Kay.
    Briarwood Summer. Bouregy.
    Come to Greenleaves. Bouregy.
Richardson, Lewis F. see Richardson, Lewis Fry.
Richardson, Lewis Fry.
  xRichardson, Lewis F.
    Arms & Insecurity: A Mathematical Study of
      the Causes & Origins of War. Univ
      Microfilms.
Richardson, Lloyd I.
  xRichardson, Lloyd I.
    A Mathematics Activity Curriculum for Early
      Childhood & Special Education. Macmillan.
Richardson, Lyon N. see Richardson, Lyon Norman.
Richardson, Lyon Norman, 1898-
  xRichardson, Lyon N.
    History of Early American Magazines,
      1741-1789. Octagon.
Richardson, M. see Richardson, Moses.
Richardson, Miles, 1932-
  xRichardson, Miles.
    ed. The Human Mirror: Material & Spatial
      Images of Man. La State U Pr.
Richardson, Moses, 1911-
  xRichardson, M.

    Fundamentals of Mathematics. Macmillan.
Richardson, Mozelle.
  xRichardson, Mozelle.
    Daughter of the Sacred Mountain. Morrow.
    The Song of India. G K Hall.
Richardson, Nancy.
  xRichardson, Nancy.
    How to Stencil & Decorate Furniture &
      Tinware. Ronald Pr.
Richardson, Norman. see Richardson, W. Norman.
Richardson, Norman W. see Richardson, W. Norman.
Richardson, Peter, 1935-
  xRichardson, Peter.
    Paul's Ethic of Freedom. Westminster.
Richardson, R. C.
  xRichardson, R. C.
    The Debate on the English Revolution. St
      Martin.
Richardson, Reed C., 1917-
  xRichardson, Reed C.
    Collective Bargaining by Objectives: A Positive
      Approach. P-H.
Richardson, Richard E. see Richardson, Richard
  Edgeworth.
Richardson, Richard Edgeworth.
  xRichardson, Richard E.
    The Dental Assistant. McGraw.
Richardson, Ruth, 1894-
  xRichardson, Ruth.
    Florencio Sanchez & the Argentine Theatre.
      Gordon Pr.
Richardson, S. D. see Richardson, Stanley Dennis.
Richardson, Samuel, 1689-1761
  xRichardson, Samuel.
    The History of Sir Charles Grandison. Oxford
      U Pr.
Richardson, Selma K.
  xRichardson, Selma K.
    Periodicals for School Media Programs. ALA.
Richardson, Stanley Dennis, 1925-
  xRichardson, S. D.
    Forestry in Communist China. Johns Hopkins.
Richardson, Terry. see Richardson, Terry A.
Richardson, Terry A.
  xRichardson, Terry.
    A Guide to Metrics. Prakken.
    Modern Industrial Plastics. Bobbs.
Richardson, Tony.
  xRichardson, Tony.
    ed. Concepts of Modern Art. Har-Row.
Richardson, Vokes, 1924-
  xRichardson, Vokes.
    Not All Our Pride. Braziller.
Richardson, W. J. see Richardson, Wallace J.
Richardson, W. Norman.
  xRichardson, Norman.
    Plants, Agriculture, & Human Society.
      Benjamin-Cummings.
  xRichardson, Norman W.
    Evolution, Human Ecology, & Society.
      Macmillan.
Richardson, Wallace G.
  xRichardson, Wallace G.
    The Spiritual Value of Gem Stones. De Vorss.
Richardson, Wallace J.
  xRichardson, W. J.
    Cost Improvement, Work Sampling & Short
      Interval Scheduling. Reston.
Richardson, Walter C. see Richardson, Walter Cecil.
Richardson, Walter Cecil, 1902-
  xRichardson, Walter C.
    Mary Tudor, the White Queen. U of Wash Pr.
Richardson, William, 1743-1814
  xRichardson, William.
    Anecdotes of the Russian Empire. Da Capo.
Richardson, Willis, 1889-
  xRichardson, Willis.

    ed. Plays & Pageants from the Life of the
      Negro. Core Collection.
Richardson, Wyman, 1896-1953
  xRichardson, Wyman.
    House on Nauset Marsh. Chatham Pr.
Richason, Benjamin F.
  xRichason, Benjamin F.
    Introduction to Remote Sensing of the
      Environment. Kendall-Hunt.
Riche, Pierre.
  xRiche, Pierre.
    Daily Life in the World of Charlemagne. U of
      Pa Pr.
Richens, Alan.
  xRichens, Alan.
    Drug Treatment of Epilepsy. Year Bk Med.
Richer, Paul. see Richer, Paul Marie Louis Pierre.
Richer, Paul Marie Louis Pierre, 1849-1933
  xRicher, Paul.
    Artistic Anatomy. Watson-Guptill.
Riches, Naomi, 1895-
  xRiches, Naomi.
    Agricultural Revolution in Norfolk. Biblio Dist.
    Agricultural Revolution in Norfolk. Kelley.
Riches, Robert J.
  xRiches, Robert J.
    Breeding Snakes in Captivity. Arco.
    Breeding Snakes in Captivity. Palmetto Pub.
Richet, Charles. see Richet, Charles Robert.
Richet, Charles Robert, 1850-1935
  xRichet, Charles.
    The Natural History of a Savant. Arno.
Richetto. see Richetto, Gary M.
Richetto, Gary M.
  xRichetto.
    Fundamentals of Interviewing. SRA.
Richey, Dave. see Richey, David.
Richey, David, 1939-
  xRichey, Dave.
    Steelheading for Everybody. Stackpole.
  xRichey, David.
    The Brown Trout Fisherman's Guide. Dutton.
    A Child's Introduction to the Outdoors.
      Pigurian.
    Dardevle's Guide to Fishing. Dorrance.
    Fly Hatches. Dutton.
Richey, E. T. see Richey, Eldred Thurston.
Richey, Eldred Thurston.
  xRichey, E. T.
    EEG Instrumentation and Technology. C C
      Thomas.
Richey, Elinor.
  xRichey, Elinor.
    Remain to Be Seen: Historic California Houses
      Open to the Public. Howell-North.
    The Ultimate Victorians of the Continental
      Side of San Francisco Bay. Howell-North.
Richey, Robert. see Richey, Robert William.
Richey, Robert William.
  xRichey, Robert.
    Planning for Teaching: An Introduction to
      Education. McGraw.
Richey, Russell E.
  xRichey, Russell E.
    ed. American Civil Religion. Har-Row.
    ed. Denominationalism. Abingdon.
Richie, David S., 1908-
  xRichie, David S.
    Memories & Meditations of a Workcamper.
      Pendle Hill.
Richie, Donald, 1924-
  xRichie, Donald.
    The Films of Akira Kurosawa. U of Cal Pr.
    George Stevens: An American Romantic.
      Museum Mod Art.
Richland, W. Bernard.
  xRichland, W. Bernard.
    You Can Beat City Hall. Rawson Wade.
Richler, Mordecai.
  xRichler, Mordecai.

ed. Causes of Postoperative Death in Children: Analysis & Therapeutic Implications. Urban & S.

ed. Long-Term Surgical Results in Children. Urban & S.

Neonatal Surgery. Butterworths.

Ricklefs, M. C.
xRicklefs, M. C.
Indonesian Manuscripts in Great Britain: A Catalogue of Manuscripts in Indonesian Languages in British Public Collections. Oxford U Pr.

Ricklefs, Robert E.
xRicklefs, Robert E.
Ecology. Chiron Pr.

Ricks, Charlotte. *see* Ricks, Charlotte Hall.

Ricks, Charlotte Hall.
xRicks, Charlotte.
Look at Me. HM.

Rico, Ul De. *see* De Rico, Ul.

Ricoeur, Paul.
xRicoeur, Paul.
The Conflict of Interpretations: Essays on Hermeneutics. Northwestern U Pr.
Freud & Philosophy: An Essay on Interpretation. Yale U Pr.

Riddel, Joseph N.
xRiddel, Joseph N.
Clairvoyant Eye: The Poetry & Poetics of Wallace Stevens. La State U Pr.

Riddell, George. *see* Riddell, George Allardice Riddell.

Riddell, George A. *see* Riddell, George Allardice Riddell.

Riddell, George Allardice Riddell, Baron, 1865-1934
xRiddell, George.
More Things That Matter. Arno.
xRiddell, George A.
Some Things That Matter. Arno.

Riddell, Jim.
xRiddell, Jim.
Career Decision Making. Broadman.

Riddle, Donald W. *see* Riddle, Donald Wayne.

Riddle, Donald Wayne, 1894-
xRiddle, Donald W.
Congressman Abraham Lincoln. Greenwood.

Riddle, Douglas F.
xRiddle, Douglas F.
Analytic Geometry with Vectors. Wadsworth Pub.
Calculus & Analytic Geometry. Wadsworth Pub.

Riddle, Jeff. *see* Riddle, Jeff C. Davis.

Riddle, Jeff C. *see* Riddle, Jeff C. Davis.

Riddle, Jeff C. Davis, 1863-
xRiddle, Jeff.
Indian History of the Modoc War. Pine Cone Pubs.
xRiddle, Jeff C.
The Indian History of the Modoc War. Urion Pr Oreg.

Riddle, Lawrence M. *see* Riddle, Lawrence Melville.

Riddle, Lawrence Melville, 1884-
xRiddle, Lawrence M.
The Genesis & Sources of Pierre Corneille's Tragedies from Medee to Pertharite. Johnson Repr.

Riddle, Maxwell.
xRiddle, Maxwell.
The Complete Alaskan Malamute. Howell Bk.
This Is the Chihuahua. TFH Pubns.

Riddle, Pamela.
xRiddle, Pamela.
The Complete Sausage Cookbook. SF Bk Co.

Rideal, Eric K. *see* Rideal, Eric Keightley.

Rideal, Eric Keightley, Sir, 1890-
xRideal, Eric K.
Concepts in Catalysis. Acad Pr.

Rideing, William H. *see* Rideing, William Henry.

Rideing, William Henry, 1853-1918
xRideing, William H.

The Boyhood of Living Authors. R West.

Ridenour, Fritz.
xRidenour, Fritz.
How to Be a Christian in an Unchristian World. Regal.
I'm a Good Man, But. Regal.
So What's the Difference?. Regal.

Rideout, R. W.
xRideout, R. W.
The Right to Membership of a Trade Union. Greenwood.

Rider, Alice D. *see* Rider, Alice Damon.

Rider, Alice Damon, 1895-
xRider, Alice D.
A Story of Books & Libraries. Scarecrow.

Rider, Barry. *see* Rider, Barry Alexander K.

Rider, Barry Alexander K.
xRider, Barry.
The Regulation of Insider Trading. Oceana.

Rider, Bertha C. *see* Rider, Bertha Carr.

Rider, Bertha Carr.
xRider, Bertha C.
The Greek House: Its History & Development from the Neolithic Period to the Hellenistic Age. Longwood Pr.

Rider, Dan, 1869-
xRider, Dan.
Adventures with Bernard Shaw. Folcroft.
Adventures with Bernard Shaw. Haskell.

Rider, Frederick.
xRider, Frederick.
The Dialectic of Selfhood in Montaigne. Stanford U Pr.

Rider, Rowland W.
xRider, Rowland W.
Sixshooters & Sagebrush: Cowboy Stories of the Southwest. Brigham.

Ridge, J. D. *see* Ridge, John Drew.

Ridge, John Drew, 1909-
xRidge, J. D.
Annotated Bibliographies of Mineral Deposits in Africa Asia (Exclusive of the USSR) & Australasia. Pergamon.

Ridge, John R. *see* Ridge, John Rollin.

Ridge, John Rollin, 1827-1867
xRidge, John R.
Life & Adventures of Joaquin Murieta, the Celebrated California Bandit. U of Okla Pr.

Ridge, M. *see* Ridge, Martin.

Ridge, Martin.
xRidge, M.
ed. America's Frontier Story: A Documentary History of Westward Expansion. Krieger.
xRidge, Martin.
ed. America's Frontier Story: A Documentary History of Westward Expansion. Krieger.

Ridgely, J. V. *see* Ridgely, Joseph Vincent.

Ridgely, Joseph Vincent.
xRidgely, J. V.
Nineteenth Century Southern Literature. U Pr of Ky.

Ridgeway, James, 1936-
xRidgeway, James.
Politics of Ecology. Dutton.
Who Owns the Earth?. Macmillan.

Ridgeway, Rick.
xRidgeway, Rick.
The Boldest Dream: The Story of Twelve Who Climbed Mount Everest. HarBraceJ.

Ridgeway, William, Sir, 1853-1926
xRidgeway, William.
The Origin & Influence of the Thoroughbred Horse. Arno.
The Origin of Metallic Currency & Weight Standards. Attic Bks.

Ridgway, Alan.
xRidgway, Alan.
An Illustrated Guide to Antique Collecting. St Martin.

Ridgway, Arlene M. *see* Ridgway, Arlene Martin.

Ridgway, Arlene Martin, 1936-
xRidgway, Arlene M.
ed. Chicken Foot Soup & Other Recipes from the Pine Barrens. Rutgers U Pr.

Ridgway, Brunilde S. *see* Ridgway, Brunilde Sismondo.

Ridgway, Brunilde Sismondo, 1929-
xRidgway, Brunilde S.
The Archaic Style in Greek Sculpture. Princeton U Pr.

Ridgway, John. *see* Ridgway, John M.

Ridgway, John M.
xRidgway, John.
Amazon Journey. Doubleday.

Ridgway, Lorna.
xRidgway, Lorna.
Family Grouping in the Primary School. Agathon.

Ridl, Charles. *see* Ridl, Charles G.

Ridl, Charles G.
xRidl, Charles.
How to Develop a Deliberate Basketball Offense. P-H.

Ridle, Julia B. *see* Ridle, Julia Brown.

Ridle, Julia Brown.
xRidle, Julia B.
ed. Hog Wild. Har-Row.

Ridley, B. K.
xRidley, Brian K.
The Physical Environment. Halsted Pr.

Ridley, Brian K. *see* Ridley, B. K.

Ridley, F. *see* Ridley, Frederick F.

Ridley, F. F. *see* Ridley, Frederick F.

Ridley, Frederick F.
xRidley, F.
Public Administration in France. Routledge & Kegan.
xRidley, F. F.
ed. Government & Administration in Western Europe. St Martin.

Ridley, James, 1736-1765
xRidley, James.
The History of James Lovegrove, Esq., 1761. Garland Pub.

Ridley, Jasper G. *see* Ridley, Jasper Godwin.

Ridley, Jasper Godwin.
xRidley, Jasper G.
Nicholas Ridley: A Biography. R West.

Ridley, M. R. *see* Ridley, Maurice Roy.

Ridley, Maurice Roy, 1890-
xRidley, M. R.
On Reading Shakespeare. Folcroft.

Ridley, Michael.
xRidley, Michael.
Buddhism. Sterling.

Ridley, Nancy.
xRidley, Nancy.
Portrait of Northumberland. Intl Pubns Serv.

Ridolfi, Roberto, 1895-
xRidolfi, Roberto.
The Life of Girolamo Savonarola. Greenwood.

Ridout, Samuel, 1855-1930
xRidout, Samuel.
Lectures on the Tabernacle. Loizeaux.

Ridpath, Ian.
xRidpath, Ian.
Worlds Beyond: A Report on the Search for Life in Space. Har-Row.

Ridpath, Paule.
xRidpath, Paule.
Possum Moods. Taplinger.

Riebel, John P.
xRiebel, John P.
How to Write Reports, Papers, Theses Articles. Arco.

Rieber, Robert W.
xRieber, Robert W.

ed. Applied Psycholinguistics & Mental Health.
Plenum Pub.
ed. The Problem of Stuttering: Theory &
Therapy. Elsevier.
Pref. by & ed. The Psychological Foundations
of Criminal Justice: Historical Perspectives on
Forensic Psychology. John Jay Pr.

Riechel, Klaus-Walter.
xRiechel, Klaus-Walter.
Economic Effects of Exchange-Rate Changes.
Lexington Bks.

Riede, David G.
xRiede, David G.
Swinburne: A Study of Romantic Mythmaking.
U Pr of Va.

Riedel, Donald C.
xRiedel, Donald C.
ed. Patient Care Evaluation in Mental Health
Programs. Ballinger Pub.

Riedel, Eunice.
xRiedel, Eunice.
The Book of the Bible. Morrow.

Riedel, F. Carl. *see* Riedel, Frederick Carl.

Riedel, Frederick Carl, 1902-
xRiedel, F. Carl.
Crime & Punishment in the Old French
Romances. AMS Pr.

Rieder, Robert J.
xRieder, Robert J.
Law Enforcement Information Systems. C C
Thomas.

Riedesel, C. Alan.
xRiedesel, C. Alan.
Teaching Elementary School Mathematics.
P-H.

Riedl, F. *see* Riedl, Frigyes.
Riedl, Frederick. *see* Riedl, Frigyes.

Riedl, Frigyes, 1856-1921
xRiedl, F.
A History of Hungarian Literature. Gordon Pr.
xRiedl, Frederick.
History of Hungarian Literature. Gale.

Riedl, R. *see* Riedl, Rupert.

Riedl, Rupert.
xRiedl, R.
Order in Living Organisms: A Systems
Analysis of Evolution. Wiley.

Riedman, Sarah R. *see* Riedman, Sarah Regal.

Riedman, Sarah Regal, 1902-
xRiedman, Sarah R.
Food for People. Abelard.
Gardening Without Soil. Watts.
How Man Discovered His Body. Abelard.
How Wildlife Survives Natural Disasters.
McKay.
Spiders. Watts.

Riedmann. *see* Riedmann, Agnes Czerwinski.

Riedmann, Agnes Czerwinski.
xRiedmann.
The Story of Adamsville. Wadsworth Pub.

Riedt, Heinz, 1919-
xRiedt, Heinz.
Carlo Goldoni. Ungar.

Riefenstahl, Leni.
xRiefenstahl, Leni.
The Last of the Nuba. Har-Row.
The People of Kau. Har-Row.

Rieff, Philip, 1922-
xRieff, Philip.
Triumph of the Therapeutic: Uses of Faith
After Freud. Har-Row.

Riegel, J. A. *see* Riegel, Jay Arthur.

Riegel, Jay Arthur.
xRiegel, J. A.
Comparative Physiology of Renal Excretion.
Hafner.

Riegel, Klaus F.
xRiegel, Klaus F.

Psychology, Mon Amour: A Countertext. HM.
Psychology of Development & History. Plenum
Pub.

Riegel, R. *see* Riegel, Robert.

Riegel, Robert.
xRiegel, R.
Insurance Principles & Practices: Property &
Liability. P-H.

Riegel, Robert E. *see* Riegel, Robert Edgar.

Riegel, Robert Edgar, 1897-
xRiegel, Robert E.
American Women: A Story of Social Change.
Fairleigh Dickinson.
The Story of the Western Railroads: From
1852 Through the Reign of the Giants. U of
Nebr Pr.

Rieger, James, 1936-
xRieger, James.
Mutiny Within. Braziller.

Rieger, Shay.
xRieger, Shay.
Our Family. Lothrop.

Riegert, Ray, 1947-
xRiegert, Ray.
Hidden Hawaii: An Adventurer's Guide.
And-Or Pr.

Riegler, Gordon A. *see* Riegler, Gordon Arthur.

Riegler, Gordon Arthur, 1901-
xRiegler, Gordon A.
The Socialization of the New England Clergy
1800-1860. Porcupine Pr.

Riegler, Hubert F.
xRiegler, Hubert F.
Surface Anatomy for Coaches & Athletic
Trainers. C C Thomas.

Riehl. *see* Riehl, Joan P.
Riehl, C. Luise. *see* Riehl, Carmella Luise.

Riehl, Carmella Luise.
xRiehl, C. Luise.
Family Nursing. Bennett Co.

Riehl, Joan P.
xRiehl.
Conceptual Models for Nursing Practice. ACC.

Rieke, H. H. *see* Rieke, Herman H.

Rieke, Herman H.
xRieke, H. H.
Compaction of Argillaceous Sediments.
Elsevier.

Rieke, Jane. *see* Rieke, Jane A.

Rieke, Jane A.
xRieke, Jane.
Teaching Strategies for Language Development.
Grune.

Rieke, Richard D.
xRieke, Richard D.
Argumentation & the Decision Making
Process. Wiley.

Riekhoff, Harold Von. *see* Von Riekhoff, Harald.

Riekkinen, Paavo.
xRiekkinen, Paavo.
The Nature of Multiple Sclerosis. Mss Info.

Riemann, H. *see* Riemann, Hans.

Riemann, Hans, 1920-
xRiemann, H.
Food-Borne Infections & Intoxications. Acad
Pr.

Riemann, Hugo, 1849-1919
xRiemann, Hugo.
Dictionary of Music. Da Capo.
Dictionary of Music. Scholarly.

Riemcke, Cal, 1926-
xRiemcke, Cal.
Guard Freedom Offense for Winning
Basketball. P-H.

Riemer, Barry M.
xRiemer, Barry M.
The Great American Con Machine. Ashley
Bks.

Riemsdijk, H. C. *see* Riemsdijk, H. C. Van.

Riemsdijk, H. C. Van.
xRiemsdijk, H. C.
A Case Study in Syntactic Markedness: The
Binding Nature of Prepositional Phrases.
Humanities.

Riendeau, Albert J.
xRiendeau, Albert J.
Advisory Committees for Occupational
Education: A Guide to Organization &
Operation. McGraw.

Riese, Hertha. *see* Riese, Hertha Pataky.

Riese, Hertha Pataky.
xRiese, Hertha.
ed. Historical Explorations in Medicine &
Psychiatry. Springer Pub.

Rieselbach, Leroy N.
xRieselbach, Leroy N.
Congressional Politics. McGraw.
The Congressional System: Notes & Readings.
Duxbury Pr.
ed. People vs. Government: The
Responsiveness of American Institutions. Ind
U Pr.

Riesen, Austin H. *see* Riesen, Austin Herbert.

Riesen, Austin Herbert.
xRiesen, Austin H.
Developmental Neuropsychology of Sensory
Deprivation. Acad Pr.

Riesenberg, Felix, 1879-1939
xRiesenberg, Felix.
Pacific Ocean. Arno.

Riesenfeld, Stefan A. *see* Riesenfeld, Stefan Albrecht.

Riesenfeld, Stefan Albrecht, 1908-
xRiesenfeld, Stefan A.
Cases & Materials on Creditors' Remedies &
Debtors' Protection. West Pub.
Protection of Coastal Fisheries Under
International Law. Johnson Repr.

Rieser, Max.
xRieser, Max.
An Analysis of Poetic Thinking. Wayne St U
Pr.

Rieser, P. *see* Rieser, Peter.

Rieser, Peter.
xRieser, P.
Insulin, Membranes & Metabolism. Krieger.

Riesman, David.
xRiesman, David.
Academic Values & Mass Education. McGraw.
Constraint & Variety in American Education.
U of Nebr Pr.
Medicine in Modern Society. Core Collection.

Riesman, Paul.
xRiesman, Paul.
Freedom in Fulani Social Life: An
Introspective Ethnography. U of Chicago Pr.

Riess, Walter.
xRiess, Walter.
Christ's Love Will Make You Live. Concordia.

Riesser, J. *see* Riesser, Jacob.

Riesser, Jacob, 1853-1932
xRiesser, J.
The German Great Banks & Their
Concentration in Connection with the
Economic Development of Germany. Arno.

Riessman, Frank, 1924-
xRiessman, Frank.
The Inner City Child. Har-Row.

Riesz, Elizabeth. *see* Riesz, Elizabeth Dunkman.

Riesz, Elizabeth Dunkman.
xRiesz, Elizabeth.
First Years of a Down's Syndrome Child. Spec
Child.

Rietstap, Johannes B. *see* Rietstap, Johannes Baptist.

Rietstap, Johannes Baptist, 1828-1891
xRietstap, Johannes B.
Armorial General. Genealog Pub.

Rietti, Mario.
xRietti, Mario.

Money & Banking in Latin America. Praeger.
Rife, J. Merle. *see* Rife, John Merle.
Rife, John Merle, 1895-
xRife, J. Merle.
The Nature & Origin of the New Testament.
Philos Lib.

Riffel, Herman. *see* Riffel, Herman H.
Riffel, Herman H.
xRiffel, Herman.
Voice of God. Tyndale.
Riffel, M. *see* Riffel, M. J.
Riffel, M. J.
xRiffel, M.
How to Combine Wild Imagination with
Creative Thinking to Make Big Money in
Real Estate. P-H.
Rifi, M. R.
xRifi, M. R.
Introduction to Organic Electrochemistry.
Dekker.
Rifkin, Bernard.
xRifkin, Bernard.
American Labor Sourcebook. McGraw.
Rifkin, Jeremy.
xRifkin, Jeremy.
The Emerging Order: God in the Age of
Scarcity. Putnam.
The North Will Rise Again: Pensions, Politics
& Power in the 1980s. Beacon Pr.
Rifkin, Shepard, 1918-
xRifkin, Shepard.
McQuaid in August. Doubleday.
Rifkind, Basil M.
xRifkind, Basil M.
ed. Hyperlipidemia: Diagnosis & Therapy.
Grune.
Rifkind, Carole
xRifkind, Carole.
Field Guide to American Architecture. NAL.
Field Guide to American Architecture. NAL.
Main Street: The Face of Urban America.
Har-Row.
Main Street: The Face of Urban America.
Har-Row.
Rifkind, R. A. *see* Rifkind, Richard A.
Rifkind, Richard A.
xRifkind, R. A.
Fundamentals of Hematology. Year Bk Med.
Riga, Frank P.
xRiga, Frank P.
Index to the London Magazine. Garland Pub.
Rigaud, Milo, 1904-
xRigaud, Milo.
Secrets of Voodoo. PB.
Rigaud, Stephen P. *see* Rigaud, Stephen Peter.
Rigaud, Stephen Peter.
xRigaud, Stephen P.
Historical Essay on the First Publication of Sir
Isaac Newton's Principia. Johnson Repr.
Rigby, Andrew.
xRigby, Andrew.
Communes in Britain. Routledge & Kegan.
Rigby, Peter.
xRigby, Peter J.
Cattle & Kinship Among the Gogo: A
Semi-Pastoral Society of Central Tanzania.
Cornell U Pr.
Rigby, Peter J. *see* Rigby, Peter.
Rigdon, Charles.
xRigdon, Charles.
Diosa. PB.
The Last Ball. Trident.
Rigg, Donald C.
xRigg, Donald C.
Prentice-Hall Workbook for Writers. P-H.
Riggs, Carol.
xRiggs, Carol.

Herbs: Leaves of Magic: The Care, Culture &
Cooking of Herbs. Sycamore Island.
Riggs, Charles H., Jr
xRiggs, Charles H.
Criminal Asylum in Anglo-Saxon Law. U
Presses Fla.
Riggs, Douglas S. *see* Riggs, Douglas Shepard.
Riggs, Douglas Shepard, M.D.
xRiggs, Douglas S.
Mathematical Approach to Physiological
Problems: A Critical Primer. MIT Pr.
Riggs, Fred W. *see* Riggs, Fred Warren.
Riggs, Fred Warren.
xRiggs, Fred W.
Formosa Under Chinese Nationalist Rule.
Octagon.
Pressures on Congress: A Study of the Repeal
of Chinese Exclusion. Greenwood.
Thailand: The Modernization of a Bureaucratic
Polity. U Pr of Hawaii.
Riggs, J. *see* Riggs, James L.
Riggs, James L.
xRiggs, J.
Industrial Organization & Management.
McGraw.
xRiggs, James L.
Economic Decision Models for Engineers &
Managers. McGraw.
Engineering Economics. McGraw.
Industrial Organization & Management.
McGraw.
Introduction to Operations Research &
Management Science: A General Systems
Approach. McGraw.
Riggs, Noel V. *see* Riggs, Noel Victor.
Riggs, Noel Victor.
xRiggs, Noel V
Quantum Chemistry: Elementary Principles &
Methods. Macmillan.
Riggs, Ralph M, 1895-
xRiggs, Ralph M.
The Story of the Future. Gospel Pub.
Riggs, Robert E. *see* Riggs, Robert Edwon.
Riggs, Robert Edwon.
xRiggs, Robert E.
Beyond Functionalism: Attitudes Toward
International Organization in Norway & the
United States. U of Minn Pr.
Riggs, Stephen R. *see* Riggs, Stephen Return.
Riggs, Stephen Return, 1812-1883
xRiggs, Stephen R.
Dakota Grammar, Texts & Ethnography. AMS
Pr.
Mary & I: Forty Years with the Sioux. Corner
Hse.
Riggs, Webster.
xRiggs, Webster.
Pediatric Chest Roentgenology: Recognizing
the Abnormal. Green.
Riggs, William G.
xRiggs, William G.
The Christian Poet in Paradise Lost. U of Cal
Pr.
Righter, Rosemary.
xRighter, Rosemary.
Whose News?: Politics, the Press & the Third
World. Times Bks.
Rigsbee, David.
xRigsbee, David.
ed. The Ardis Anthology of New American
Poetry. Ardis Pubs.
Rigsby, Lewis W. *see* Rigsby, Lewis Wiley.
Rigsby, Lewis Wiley.
xRigsby, Lewis W.
Historic Georgia Families. Genealog Pub.
Riis, Jacob A. *see* Riis, Jacob August.
Riis, Jacob August, 1849-1914
xRiis, Jacob A.

Children of the Poor. Arno.
The Children of the Poor. Johnson Repr.
The Children of the Poor. Mss Info.
Children of the Tenements. Arno.
Children of the Tenements. Century
Bookbindery.
Children of the Tenements. Irvington.
How the Other Half Lives: Studies Among the
Tenements of New York. Harvard U Pr.
How the Other Half Lives: Studies Among the
Tenements of New York. Peter Smith.
Nibsy's Christmas. Arno.
Out of Mulberry Street. Irvington.
Theodore Roosevelt, the Citizen. AMS Pr.
Theodore Roosevelt, the Citizen. Scholarly.

Riker, Audrey. *see* Riker, Audrey Palm.

Riker, Audrey Palm.

xRiker, Audrey.
Married Life. Bennett Co.
Me: Understanding Myself & Others. Bennett
Co.
Riker, Tom.

xRiker, Tom.
City & Suburban Gardens: Frontyards,
Backyards, Terraces, Rooftops & Window
Boxes. P-H.
The Gardener's Catalogue. Morrow.
The Guide to Buying Plants. Morrow.
Rikhoff, Jean.
xRikhoff, Jean.
Buttes Landing. Dial.
One of the Raymonds. Dial.
One of the Raymonds. Fawcett.
The Sweetwater. Dial.
Rikhye, Indar J. *see* Rikhye, Indar Jit.
Rikhye, Indar Jit.
xRikhye, Indar J.
The Thin Blue Line: International
Peacekeeping & Its Future. Yale U Pr.
Rikitake, T. *see* Rikitake, Tsuneji.
Rikitake, Tsuneji, 1921-
xRikitake, T.
Earthquake Prediction. Elsevier.
Rikon, Irving.
xRikon, Irving.
Peace As It Can Be. Philos Lib.
Riley, Carroll L.
xRiley, Carroll L.
Origins of Civilization. S Ill U Pr.
Riley, Charles M.
xRiley, Charles M.
Our Mineral Resources: An Elementary
Textbook in Economic Geology. Krieger.
Riley, D. *see* Riley, Denis.
Riley, Denis.
xRiley, D.
World Weather & Climate. Cambridge U Pr.
xRiley, Denis R.
World Vegetation. Cambridge U Pr.
Riley, Denis R. *see* Riley, Denis.
Riley, Dick.
xRiley, Dick.
ed. The Bedside, Bathtub & Armchair
Companion to Agatha Christie. Ungar.
ed. Critical Encounters: Writers & Themes in
Science Fiction. Ungar.
Riley, Elizabeth.
xRiley, Elizabeth.
Compiled by Love Poems. Arno.
Riley, Franklin L. *see* Riley, Franklin Lafayette.
Riley, Franklin Lafayette, 1868-1929
xRiley, Franklin L.

Colonial Origins of New England Senates.
   AMS Pr.
Colonial Origins of New England Senates.
   Johnson Repr.
Riley, Gary L.
   xRiley, Gary L.
      ed. Governing Academic Organizations: New
      Problems, New Perspectives. McCutchan.
Riley, Herbert P. *see* Riley, Herbert Parkes.
Riley, Herbert Parkes, 1904-
   xRiley, Herbert P.
      Introduction to Genetics & Cytogenetics.
      Hafner.
Riley, Isaac H. *see* Riley, Isaac Woodbridge.
Riley, Isaac Woodbridge, 1869-1933
   xRiley, Isaac H.
      The Meaning of Mysticism. Folcroft.
   xRiley, Woodbridge.
      Men & Morals: The Story of Ethics. Ungar.
Riley, James W. *see* Riley, James Whitcomb.
Riley, James Whitcomb, 1849-1916
   xRiley, James W.
      The Boss Girl: A Christmas Story, & Other
      Sketches. Arno.
      A Child-World. Arno.
      The Complete Works of James Whitcomb
      Riley. AMS Pr.
      Letters of James Whitcomb Riley. AMS Pr.
Riley, John.
   xRiley, John.
      Ancient & Modern. SBD.
      A Legend of St. Anthony. SBD.
Riley, John J.
   xRiley, John J.
      A History of the American Soft Drink
      Industry: Bottled Carbonated Beverages,
      1807-1957. Arno.
Riley, Mary Ann K.
   xRiley, Mary Ann K.
      Case Studies in Nursing Fundamentals.
      Macmillan.
Riley, Matilda W. *see* Riley, Matilda White.
Riley, Matilda White, 1911-
   xRiley, Matilda W.
      ed. Aging from Birth to Death:
      Interdisciplinary Perspectives. Westview.
      ed. Sociological Research. HarBraceJ.
Riley, Michael J.
   xRiley, Michael J.
      Basic Orienteering. Contemp Bks.
Riley, Miles O. *see* Riley, Miles O'Brien.
Riley, Miles O'Brien, 1937-
   xRiley, Miles O.
      Set Your House in Order: A Practical Way to
      Prepare for Death. Doubleday.
Riley, Sue, 1946-
   xRiley, Sue.
      Success. Childs World.
Riley, Sue. *see* Riley, Susan.
Riley, Sue S. *see* Riley, Susan.
Riley, Susan, 1946-
   xRiley, Sue.
      Afraid. Childs World.
   xRiley, Sue S.
      How to Generate Values in Young Children:
      Integrity, Honesty, Individuality,
      Self-Confidence, & Wisdom. New South Co.
Riley, Woodbridge. *see* Riley, Isaac Woodbridge.
Riley-Smith, Jonathan. *see* Riley-Smith, Jonathan Simon
   Christopher.
Riley-Smith, Jonathan Simon Christopher, 1938-
   xRiley-Smith, Jonathan.
      What Were the Crusades?. Rowman.
Rilke, Rainer M. *see* Rilke, Rainer Maria.
Rilke, Rainer Maria.
   xRilke, Rainer M.

Duino Elegies. U of Cal Pr.
Duino Elegies & the Sonnets to Orpheus. HM.
Lay of the Love & Death of Cornet
   Christopher Rilke. Norton.
Letters to a Young Poet. Norton.
The Life of the Virgin Mary. Greenwood.
Nine Plays. Ungar.
Rodin. Haskell.
Rodin. Peregrine Smith.
Selected Poems of Rainer Maria Rilke: A
   Translation from the German &
   Commentary. Har-Row.
Sonnets to Orpheus. Norton.
Sonnets to Orpheus. U of Cal Pr.
Where Silence Reigns: Selected Prose. New
   Directions.
Rilla, Wolf. *see* Rilla, Wolf Peter.
Rilla, Wolf Peter.
   xRilla, Wolf.
      The Illusionists. BJ Pub Group.
      The Illusionists. St Martin.
Rima, I. H. *see* Rima, Ingrid H.
Rima, Ingrid H., 1925-
   xRima, I. H.
      Development of Economic Analysis. Irwin.
Rimberg, David.
   xRimberg, David.
      Utilization of Waste Heat from Power Plants.
      Noyes.
Rimer, J. Thomas.
   xRimer, J. Thomas.
      Guide to Japanese Poetry. G K Hall.
Rimmer, C. Brandon. *see* Rimmer, Charles Brandon.
Rimmer, Charles Brandon, 1917-
   xRimmer, C. Brandon.
      Religion in Shreds. Aragorn Bks.
Rimmer, Robert. *see* Rimmer, Robert H.
Rimmer, Robert H.
   xRimmer, Robert.
      The Premar Experiments. NAL.
   xRimmer, Robert H.
      Proposition Thirty-One. NAL.
      That Girl from Boston. Irvington.
      That Girl from Boston. NAL.
Rinaldi, Augusto.
   xRinaldi, Augusto.
      The Complete Book of Mushrooms: Over 1,000
      Species & Varieties of American, European,
      & Asiatic Mushrooms. Crown.
Rinaldi, S. *see* Rinaldi, Sergio.
Rinaldi, Sergio.
   xRinaldi, S.
      ed. Topics in Combinatorial Optimization.
      Springer-Verlag.
   xRinaldi, Sergio.
      Modeling & Control of River Quality.
      McGraw.
Rinaldo, C. L.
   xRinaldo, C. L.
      Dark Dreams. Har-Row.
Rinder, Walter.
   xRinder, Walter.
      Aura of Love. Celestial Arts.
      Follow Your Heart. Celestial Arts.
      Friends & Lovers. Celestial Arts.
      The Humanness of You. Celestial Arts.
      Love Is an Attitude. Celestial Arts.
      A Promise of Change. Celestial Arts.
      Spectrum of Love. Celestial Arts.
      This Time Called Life. Celestial Arts.
Rindfleisch, Norval.
   xRindfleisch, Norval.
      In Loveless Clarity & Other Stories. SBD.
Rindfuss, R. R. *see* Rindfuss, Ronald R.
Rindfuss, Ronald R.
   xRindfuss, R. R.
      ed. Postwar Fertility Trends & Differentials in
      the United States. Acad Pr.
Rinehart, John S. *see* Rinehart, John Sargent.

Rinehart, John Sargent, 1915-
   xRinehart, John S.
      Stress Transients in Solids. HyperDynamics.
Rinehart, Mary R. *see* Rinehart, Mary Roberts.
Rinehart, Mary Roberts.
   xRinehart, Mary R.
      Circular Staircase. Lighthouse Pr NY.
      The Circular Staircase. Pubs Inc.
Ring, Alfred. *see* Ring, Alfred A.
Ring, Alfred A.
   xRing, Alfred.
      Real Estate Principles & Practices. P-H.
   xRing, Alfred A.
      Real Estate Principles & Practices. P-H.
      Valuation of Real Estate. P-H.
Ring, B. Albert. *see* Ring, Benjamin Albert.
Ring, Benjamin Albert, 1920-
   xRing, B. Albert.
      The Neglected Cause of Stroke: Occlusion of
      the Smaller Intracranial Arteries & Their
      Diagnosis by Cerebral Angiography. Green.
Ringe, Donald A.
   xRinge, Donald A.
      Charles Brockden Brown. Coll & U Pr.
Ringel, G. *see* Ringel, Gerhard.
Ringel, Gerhard.
   xRingel, G.
      Map Color Theorem. Springer-Verlag.
Ringel, William E.
   xRingel, William E.
      Identification & Police Line-Ups. Gould.
      Obscenity Law Today. Gould.
Ringenberg, Lawrence A.
   xRingenberg, Lawrence A.
      College Geometry. Krieger.
Ringer, Fritz K., 1934-
   xRinger, Fritz K.
      Education & Society in Modern Europe. Ind U
      Pr.
Ringgold, Gene.
   xRinggold, Gene.
      Chevalier: The Films & Career of Maurice
      Chevalier. Citadel Pr.
      Films of Bette Davis. Citadel Pr.
      Films of Cecil B. DeMille. Citadel Pr.
      Films of Frank Sinatra. Citadel Pr.
Ringgren, Helmer, 1917-
   xRinggren, Helmer.
      Religions of the Ancient Near East.
      Westminster.
Ringi, Kjell.
   xRingi, Kjell.
      illus. Stranger. Random.
      The Sun & the Cloud. Har-Row.
Ringness, Thomas A.
   xRingness, Thomas A.
      The Affective Domain in Education. Little.
Ringstad, M. *see* Ringstad, Muriel E.
Ringstad, Muriel E.
   xRingstad, M.
      Adventures on Library Shelves. Oddo.
Ringwood, A. E., 1930-
   xRingwood, A. E.
      Origin of the Earth & Moon. Springer-Verlag.
   xRingwood, Alfred E.
      Composition & Petrology of the Earth's
      Mantle. McGraw.
Ringwood, Alfred E. *see* Ringwood, A. E.
Rink, Hinrich J. *see* Rink, Hinrich Johannes.
Rink, Hinrich Johannes, 1819-1893
   xRink, Hinrich J.
      Tales & Traditions of the Eskimo, with a
      Sketch of Their Habits, Religion, Language &
      Other Peculiarities. AMS Pr.
Rinker, Richard N.
   xRinker, Richard N.
      The East Burlap Parables. U of Nebr Pr.
Rinker, Rosalind.
   xRinker, Rosalind.

Ask Me Lord, I Want to Say Yes. Logos.
Communicating Love Through Prayer.
Zondervan.
How to Have Family Prayers. Zondervan.
Open Heart. Zondervan.
Prayer: Conversing with God. Zondervan.
Praying Together. Zondervan.

Rinkoff, Barbara.
xRinkoff, Barbara.
Guess What Grasses Do. Lothrop.
Guess What Rocks Do. Lothrop.
Map Is a Picture. T Y Crowell.
No Pushing, No Ducking: Safety in the Water.
Lothrop.
Troublesome Tuba. Lothrop.

Rinsland, Henry D. see Rinsland, Henry Daniel.

Rinsland, Henry Daniel, 1889-
xRinsland, Henry D.
Analysis of Completion Sentences &
Arithmetical Problems As Items for
Intelligence Tests. AMS Pr.

Rinsler, Norma.
xRinsler, Norma.
Gerard de Nerval. Humanities.

Rintala, Marvin.
xRintala, Marvin.
The Constitution of Silence: Essays on
Generational Themes. Greenwood.
Four Finns: Political Profiles. U of Cal Pr.

Rintels, David W.
xRintels, David W.
Clarence Darrow: A One-Man Play.
Doubleday.

Rinzler, Alan.
xRinzler, Alan.
Bob Dylan: The Illustrated Record. Crown.

Rinzler, Carol A. see Rinzler, Carol Ann.

Rinzler, Carol Ann.
xRinzler, Carol A.
The Dictionary of Medical Folklore. T Y
Crowell.

Riordan, Francis E. see Riordan, Francis Ellen.

Riordan, Francis Ellen, Sister, 1915-
xRiordan, Francis E.
Concept of Love in the French Catholic
Literary Revival. AMS Pr.

Riordan, Robert C.
xRiordan, Robert C.
Alternative Schools in Action. Phi Delta
Kappa.

Rios, Jorge C.
xRios, Jorge G.
Clinical Electrocardiographic Correlations.
Davis Co.

Rios, Jorge G. see Rios, Jorge C.

Ripa, Cesare, fl. 1600
xRipa, Cesare.
Iconologia. Garland Pub.

Ripa, Louis C. see Ripa, Louis Carl.

Ripa, Louis Carl.
xRipa, Louis C.
Surveying Manual. McGraw.

Riper, Charles G. Van. see Van Riper, Charles G.
Riper, Charles Van. see Van Riper, Charles.
Riper, Guernsey Van. see Van Riper, Guernsey.

Ripin, Edwin M.
xRipin, Edwin M.
The Instrument Catalogs of Leopoldo
Franciolini. Eur-Am Music.

Ripka, Hubert, 1895-1958
xRipka, Hubert.
Czechoslovakia Enslaved: The Story of the
Communist Coup D'Etat. Hyperion Conn.

Ripka, L. V.
xRipka, L. V.
Plumbing Installation & Design. Am Technical.

Ripley, Randall B.
xRipley, Randall B.

American National Government & Public
Policy. Free Pr.
Congress: Process & Policy. Norton.
Congress, the Bureaucracy & Public Policy.
Dorsey.
Congress, the Bureaucracy, & the Public
Policy. Dorsey.
ed. National Government & Policy in the
United States. Peacock Pubs.
The Politics of Economic & Human Resource
Development. Bobbs.

Ripley, Robert. see Ripley, Robert le Roy.

Ripley, Robert le Roy, 1893-1949
xRipley, Robert.
Ripley's Believe It or Not. Western Pub.

Ripley, S. Dillon. see Ripley, Sidney Dillon.

Ripley, Sidney Dillon, 1913-
xRipley, S. Dillon.
Cabinets Lost & Found. Shoe String.

Ripley, William Z. see Ripley, William Zebina.

Ripley, William Zebina, 1867-1941
xRipley, William Z.
Financial History of Virginia 1609-1776. AMS
Pr.
Financial History of Virginia 1609-1776. B
Franklin.
The Races of Europe: A Sociological Study.
Johnson Repr.

Ripnen, Kenneth H.
xRipnen, Kenneth H.
Office Space Administration. McGraw.

Ripoll, Carlos.
xRipoll, Carlos.
Conciencia Intelectual De America: Antologia
Del Ensayo Hispanoamericano. E Torres &
Sons.

Ripon Society.
xRipon Society.
Jaws of Victory: The Game Plan Politics of
1972, the Crisis of the Republican Party, &
the Future of the Constitution. Little.

Rippa, Alexander S. see Rippa, S. Alexander.

Rippa, S. Alexander.
xRippa, Alexander S.
Education in a Free Society: An American
History. Longman.

Rippley, La Vern. see Rippley, Lavern.

Rippley, Lavern.
xRippley, La Vern.
The German-Americans. Twayne.

Rippon, Marion.
xRippon, Marion.
Lucien's Tombs. Doubleday.

Rippon, Michelle.
xRippon, Michelle.
Combining Sentences. HarBraceJ.

Rippy, James F. see Rippy, James Fred.

Rippy, James Fred, 1892-
xRippy, James F.
Globe & Hemisphere: Latin America's Place in
the Post-War Foreign Relations of the United
States. Greenwood.
Latin America & the Industrial Age.
Greenwood.

Ririe, Robert L.
xRirie, Robert L.
Let's Cook Dutch!: A Complete Guide for the
Dutch Oven Chef. Horizon Utah.

Ris, Thomas F.
xRis, Thomas F.
The Neat Stuff Something-to-Do Book.
Messner.
The Neat Stuff Something-to-Do Book. S&S.

Rischin, Moses, 1925-
xRischin, Moses.
Immigration & the American Tradition. Bobbs.
The Promised City: New York's Jews,
1870-1914. Harvard U Pr.

Risebero, Bill, 1938-
xRisebero, Bill.

The Story of Western Architecture. Scribner.

Riseborough, Donald. see Riseborough, Donald J.

Riseborough, Donald J.
xRiseborough, Donald.
ed. Canada & the French. Facts on File.

Risenhoover, Morris.
xRisenhoover, Morris.
Artists As Professors: Conversations with
Musicians, Painters, Sculptors. U of Ill Pr.

Riser, Wayne. see Riser, Wayne H.

Riser, Wayne H.
xRiser, Wayne.
Your Future in Veterinary Medicine. Arco.
xRiser, Wayne H.
Your Future in Veterinary Medicine. Rosen Pr.

Rishabhchand.
xRishabhchand.
Integral Yoga of Sri Aurobindo. Assoc Bk.
The Integral Yoga of Sri Aurobindo. Matagiri.

Rising, Gerald R.
xRising, Gerald R.
The Third "R": Mathematics Teaching for
Grades K-8. Wadsworth Pub.

Rising, James S.
xRising, James S.
Engineering Graphics: Communication,
Analysis, & Creative Design. Kendall-Hunt.

Risjord, Norman K.
xRisjord, Norman K.
Forging the American Republic, 1760-1815.
A-W.

Risku, Cillay.
xRisku, Cillay.
White Midnight. Playboy Pubs.

Risley, George, 1910-
xRisley, George.
Modern Industrial Marketing. McGraw.

Riso, Don R. see Riso, Don Richard.

Riso, Don Richard.
xRiso, Don R.
ed. The Incredible Illustrated Electricity Book.
Pathmark Bks.

Risom, Ole.
xRisom, Ole.
I Am a Kitten. Western Pub.
I Am a Puppy. Western Pub.

Risse, Guenter B.
xRisse, Guenter B.
ed. Medicine Without Doctors: Home Health
Care in American History. N Watson.

Risser, Hubert E.
xRisser, Hubert E.
The Economics of the Coal Industry.
Greenwood.

Rissi, Mathias.
xRissi, Mathias.
The Future of the World: An Exegetical Study
of Revelation 19.11-22.15. Allenson.

Rissover, F. see Rissover, Fredric.

Rissover, Fredric.
xRissover, F.
Mass Media & the Popular Arts. McGraw.

Rist, J. M. see Rist, John M.

Rist, John M.
xRist, J. M.
On the Independence of Matthew & Mark.
Cambridge U Pr.
Stoic Philosophy. Cambridge U Pr.
xRist, John M.
ed. The Stoics. U of Cal Pr.

Rist, Ray C.
xRist, Ray C.

ed. Desegregated Schools: Appraisals of an
 American Experiment. Acad Pr.
Education, Social Science, & the Judicial
 Process. Tchrs Coll.
Guestworkers in Germany: Prospects for
 Pluralism. Praeger.
ed. Pornography Controversy: Changing Moral
 Standards in American Life. Transaction Bks.
ed. Restructuring American Education:
 Innovations & Alternatives. Transaction Bks.

Ritch, Ocee.
 xRitch, Ocee.
  The Lincoln Continental. Motorbooks Intl.

Ritcheson, Charles R.
 xRitcheson, Charles R.
  Aftermath of Revolution: British Policy Toward
   the United States, 1783-1795. Norton.
  Aftermath of Revolution: British Policy Toward
   the United States, 1783-1795. SMU Press.

Ritchie, Carson I. *see* Ritchie, Carson I. A.
Ritchie, Carson I. A.
 xRitchie, Carson I.
  Art of the Eskimo. A S Barnes.
  The Decorated Gun. A S Barnes.
  Frontier Parish: An Account of the Society for
   the Propagation of the Gospel & the
   Anglican Church in America, Drawn from
   the Records of the Bishop of London.
   Fairleigh Dickinson.
 xRitchie, Carson I. A.
  Art in Paper. A S Barnes.

Ritchie, Dave. *see* Ritchie, David.
Ritchie, David.
 xRitchie, Dave.
  Ski the Canadian Way. P-H.

Ritchie, Donald. *see* Ritchie, Donald D.
Ritchie, Donald D.
 xRitchie, Donald.
  Biology. A-W.
  Biology. Monarch Pr.

Ritchie, Eveline.
 xRitchie, Eveline.
  Taking Out My Bucketful. Accent Bks.

Ritchie, George. *see* Ritchie, George L.
Ritchie, George G.
 xRitchie, George G.
  Return from Tomorrow. Chosen Bks Pub.

Ritchie, George L.
 xRitchie, George.
  Electronics Construction & Assembly. P-H.

Ritchie, Hugh, 1864-1948
 xRitchie, Hugh.
  The Navicert System During the World War.
   Johnson Repr.

Ritchie, J. B.
 xRitchie, J. B.
  Organization & People: Readings, Cases &
   Exercises in Organizational Behavior. West
   Pub.

Ritchie, James L.
 xRitchie, James L.
  Thallium--201 Myocardial Imaging. Raven.

Ritchie, Jane. *see* Ritchie, Jane Beaglehole.
Ritchie, Jane Beaglehole.
 xRitchie, Jane.
  Growing up in New Zealand. Allen Unwin.
  Growing up in Polynesia. Allen Unwin.

Ritchie, Jo-An.
 xRitchie, Jo-An.
  Jonie Goes to Academy. Southern Pub.
  Jonie Graduates. Southern Pub.
  Jonie's Direct Line. Southern Pub.

Ritchie, John. *see* Ritchie, John Douglas.
Ritchie, John Douglas.
 xRitchie, John.
  Australia As Once We Were. Holmes & Meier.

Ritchie, Judith.
 xRitchie, Judith.
  Holy Days: Holidays. Mott Media.

Ritchie, Lewis A. *see* Ritchie, Lewis Anselm Da Costa.

Ritchie, Lewis Anselm Da Costa, 1886-
 xRitchie, Lewis A.
  Naval Occasions, & Some Traits of the
   Sailorman. Arno.

Ritchie, Paul.
 xRitchie, Paul.
  Australia. Macmillan.

Ritchie, Robert C., 1938-
 xRitchie, Robert C.
  The Duke's Province: A Study of New York
   Politics & Society, 1664-1691. U of NC Pr.

Ritchie, Robert F., 1930-
 xRitchie, Robert F.
  ed. Automated Immunoanalysis. Dekker.

Ritger, Dick.
 xRitger, Dick.
  The Complete Guide to Bowling Spares. Ritger
   Sports.

Ritner, Peter V. *see* Ritner, Peter Vaughan.
Ritner, Peter Vaughan.
 xRitner, Peter V.
  Death of Africa. Macmillan.

Ritota, Michael C., 1914-
 xRitota, Michael C.
  Diagnostic Electrocardiography. Lippincott.

Ritschel, W. A.
 xRitschel, W. A.
  Handbook of Basic Pharmacokinetics. Drug
   Intl Pubns.

Ritsko, Alan J.
 xRitsko, Alan J.
  Lighting for Location Motion Pictures. Van
   Nos Reinhold.

Ritson, Joseph, 1752-1803
 xRitson, Joseph.
  Northern Garlands. Folcroft.
  Remarks, Critical & Illustrative, on the Text &
   Notes of the Last Edition of Shakspeare.
   AMS Pr.

Rittenhouse, Jessie B. *see* Rittenhouse, Jessie Belle.
Rittenhouse, Jessie Belle, 1869-1948
 xRittenhouse, Jessie B.
  Little Book of American Poets, 1787-1900. R
   West.
  The Little Book of Modern Verse: A Selection
   from the Work of Contemporaneous
   American Poets. Arden Lib.

Rittenhouse, Mignon.
 xRittenhouse, Mignon.
  Amazing Nellie Bly. Arno.

Ritter, Dale F.
 xRitter, Dale F.
  Process Geomorphology. Wm C Brown.

Ritter, Frederic L. *see* Ritter, Frederic Louis.
Ritter, Frederic Louis, 1834-1891
 xRitter, Frederic L.
  Music in America. Johnson Repr.

Ritter, Gerhard.
 xRitter, Gerhard.
  Frederick the Great: A Historical Profile. U of
   Cal Pr.

Ritter, Jess, 1930-
 xRitter, Jess.
  Fixins. Cal Living Bks.

Ritter, Karl, 1779-1859
 xRitter, Karl.
  Comparative Geography. AMS Pr.
  Comparative Geography of Palestine & the
   Sinaitic Peninsula. Greenwood.
  Comparative Geography of Palestine & the
   Sinaitic Peninsula. Haskell.

Ritter, Lawrence S.
 xRitter, Lawrence S.
  The Image of Their Greatness: An Illustrated
   History of Baseball from 1900 to the Present.
   Crown.
  Principles of Money, Banking, & Financial
   Markets. Basic.

Ritter, Margaret.
 xRitter, Margaret.

The Burning Woman. Berkley Pub.
 The Burning Woman. Putnam.

Ritter, Paul, 1925-
 xRitter, Paul.
  Planning for Man & Motor. Pergamon.

Ritterbush, Philip. *see* Ritterbush, Philip C.
Ritterbush, Philip C.
 xRitterbush, Philip.
  Overtures to Biology: Speculations of
   Eighteenth Century Naturalists. Elliots Bks.
 xRitterbush, Philip C.
  Art of Organic Forms. Smithsonian.
  ed. Let the Entire Community Become Our
   University. Acropolis.

Rittershausen, B. *see* Rittershausen, Brian.
Rittershausen, Brian.
 xRittershausen, B.
  Popular Orchids. Verry.
 xRittershausen, W.
  jt. auth. Popular Orchids. Verry.
Rittershausen, W. *see* Rittershausen, Brian.

Ritz, David.
 xRitz, David.
  Search for Happiness. S&S.

Ritzer. *see* Ritzer, George.
Ritzer, George.
 xRitzer.
  Sociology: A Multiple Paradigm Science. Allyn.
 xRitzer, George.
  Issues, Debates & Controversies: An
   Introduction to Sociology. Allyn.

Rius.
 xRIUS.
  Cuba for Beginners. Path Pr NY.

Rivadeneyra, Antonio De Solis Y. *see* Solis Y
 Rivadeneyra, Antonio De.
River Oaks Garden Club.
 xRiver Oaks Garden Club.
  ed. Garden Book for Houston & the Gulf
   Coast. Pacesetter Pr.

Rivera, Julius, 1917-
 xRivera, Julius.
  Latin America: A Sociocultural Interpretation.
   Halsted Pr.
  Latin America: A Sociocultural Interpretation.
   Irvington.

Rivera, Robert V. De. *see* De Rivera, Robert V.
Rivers, Caryl.
 xRivers, Caryl.
  Beyond Sugar & Spice: How Women Grow,
   Learn, & Thrive. Putnam.

Rivers, Gayle.
 xRivers, Gayle.
  The Five Fingers. Bantam.
  The Five Fingers. Doubleday.

Rivers, James W. *see* Rivers, Jim W.
Rivers, Jim W.
 xRivers, James W.
  From the Chicago Notebook: Memories of the
   South Side. Spoon Riv Poetry.

Rivers, Patrick.
 xRivers, Patrick.
  The Survivalists. Universe.

Rivers, R. W. *see* Rivers, Robert W.
Rivers, Robert W.
 xRivers, R. W.
  Traffic Accident Investigators' Handbook. C C
   Thomas.

Rivers, Thomas, 1798-1877
 xRivers, Thomas.
  The Rose Amateur's Guide. E M Coleman
   Ent.

Rivers, W. *see* Rivers, William Halse Rivers.
Rivers, W. L. *see* Rivers, William L.
Rivers, Wilga. *see* Rivers, Wilga M.
Rivers, Wilga M.
 xRivers, Wilga.

A Practical Guide to the Teaching of French. Oxford U Pr.
A Practical Guide to the Teaching of German. Oxford U Pr.
xRivers, Wilga M.
A Practical Guide to the Teaching of Spanish. Oxford U Pr.
Psychologist & the Foreign-Language Teacher. U of Chicago Pr.
Teaching Foreign Language Skills. U of Chicago Pr.
Rivers, William H. see Rivers, William Halse Rivers

Rivers, William Halse Rivers, 1864-1922
xRivers, W.
Social Organization. Dawson Pub.
xRivers, William H.
Medicine, Magic & Religion. AMS Pr.
Social Organization. AMS Pr.

Rivers, William L.
xRivers, W.
Finding Facts: Interviewing, Observing, Using Reference Sources. P-H.
xRivers, W. L.
Mass Media & Modern Society. HR&W.
xRivers, William L.
Responsibility in Mass Communication. Har-Row.
Rivers-Coffey, Rachel.
xRivers-Coffey, Rachel.
A Horse Like Mr. Ragman. Schol Bk Serv.
A Horse Like Mr. Ragman. Scribner.
Rives, William C. see Rives, William Cabell.
Rives, William Cabell, 1793-1868
xRives, William C.
History of the Life & Times of James Madison Arno.
Rivet, A. L. see Rivet, Albert Lionel Frederick.
Rivet, Albert Lionel Frederick.
xRivet, A. L.
The Place-Names of Roman Britain. Princeton U Pr.
Rivett, Kenneth.
xRivett, Kenneth.
ed. Australia & the Non-White Migrant. Intl Schol Bk Serv.
Rivett-Carnac, Charles.
xRivett-Carnac, Charles.
Pursuit in the Wilderness. Intl Pubns Serv.
Riviere, Claude, fl. 1969-
xRiviere, Claude.
Guinea: The Mobilization of a People. Cornell U Pr.
Riviere, J. see Riviere, Jacques.
Riviere, Jacques.
xRiviere, J.
Industrial Applications of Microbiology. Halsted Pr.
Rivkin, Arnold.
xRivkin, Arnold.
Nation-Building in Africa: Problems & Prospects. Rutgers U Pr.
Rivkin, Solomon. see Rivkin, Solomon Lazarevich.
Rivkin, Solomon Lazarevich.
xRivkin, Solomon.
Thermodynamic Derivatives for Water & Steam. Halsted Pr.
Rivkin, Steven R.
xRivkin, Steven R.
Cable Television: A Guide to Federal Regulations. Crane-Russak Co.
Rivlin, Alice M.
xRivlin, Alice M.

ed. Ethical & Legal Issues of Social Experimentation. Brookings.
ed. Planned Variation in Education: Should We Give up or Try Harder?. Brookings.
Systematic Thinking for Social Action. Brookings.
Rivlin, Harry N. see Rivlin, Harry Nathaniel.
Rivlin, Harry Nathaniel, 1904-
xRivlin, Harry N.
Functional Grammar. AMS Pr.
Rivlin, Richard. see Rivlin, Richard S.
Rivlin, Richard S.
xRivlin, Richard.
ed. Riboflavin. Plenum Pub.
Rivlin, Theodore J., 1926-
xRivlin, Theodore J.
The Chebyshev Polynomials. Wiley.
Riwkin-Brick, Anna.
xRiwkin-Brick, Anna.
photos by Gennet Lives in Ethiopia. Macmillan.
Rix, Herbert D. see Rix, Herbert David.
Rix, Herbert David, 1908-
xRix, Herbert D.
Rhetoric in Spenser's Poetry. Arden Lib.
Rhetoric in Spenser's Poetry. Folcroft.
Rixom, M. R.
xRixom, M. R.
Chemical Admixtures for Concrete. Methuen Inc.
Rixon, A. E.
xRixon, A. E.
Fossil Animal Remains: Their Preparation and Conservation. Humanities.
Rizal y Alonso, Jose, 1861-1896
xRizal Y Alonso, Jose.
Lost Eden: Noli Me Tangere. Greenwood.
Rizza, Paul F.
xRizza, Paul F.
Pennsylvania Atlas: A Thematic Atlas of the Keystone State. Ptolemy Pr.
Rizzi, Marcia S. see Rizzi, Marcia Salo.
Rizzi, Marcia Salo.
xRizzi, Marcia S.
Some Pictures from My Life: A Diary. Times Change.
Rizzo, Mario J.
xRizzo, Mario J.
ed. Time, Uncertainty & Disequilibrium: Exploration of Austrian Themes. Lexington Bks.
Rizzo, Raymond.
xRizzo, Raymond.
The Total Actor. Odyssey Pr.
Rizzuto, Ana-Maria.
xRizzuto, Ana-Maria.
The Birth of the Living God: A Psychoanalytic Study. U of Chicago Pr.
Rizzuto, Anthony.
xRizzuto, Anthony.
Style & Theme in Reverdy's les Ardoises Du Toit. U of Ala Pr.
Rizzuto, Jim, 1939-
xRizzuto, Jim.
Modern Hawaiian Gamefishing. U Pr of Hawaii.
Rjndt, Philippe Van. see Van Rjndt, Philippe.
Rjndt, Phillipe Van. see Van Rjndt, Phillipe.
Roach, Abby M. see Roach, Abby Meguire.
Roach, Abby Meguire.
xRoach, Abby M.
Some Successful Marriages. Arno.
Roach, Don.
xRoach, Don.
Basic College Chemistry. McGraw.
Roach, Eugene. see Roach, Eugene G.
Roach, Eugene G.
xRoach, Eugene.
Purdue Perceptual-Motor Survey. Merrill.
Roach, F. E. see Roach, Franklin Evans.

Roach, Franklin Evans.
xRoach, F. E.
The Light of the Night Sky. Kluwer Boston.
Roach, Fred.
xRoach, Fred.
Let's Talk: Ideas to Trigger Family Conversation. Revell.
Roach, Helen P. see Roach, Helen Pauline.
Roach, Helen Pauline, 1903-
xRoach, Helen P.
History of Speech Education at Columbia College, 1754-1940. AMS Pr.
Roach, John. see Roach, John Peter Charles.
Roach, John Peter Charles.
xRoach, John.
Public Examinations in England, 1850-1900. Cambridge U Pr.
Roach, Marilynne. see Roach, Marilynne K.
Roach, Marilynne K.
xRoach, Marilynne.
Two Roman Mice. T Y Crowell.
xRoach, Marilynne K.
Presto: Or the Adventures of a Turnspit Dog. HM.
Roach, Mary Ellen.
xRoach, Mary Ellen.
ed. Dress, Adornment, & the Social Order. Wiley.
Roache, Patrick J.
xRoache, Patrick J.
Computational Fluid Dynamics. Hermosa.
Roadarmel, Gordon C., 1932-
xRoadarmel, Gordon C.
tr. Modern Hindi Short Stories. U of Cal Pr.
Roadarmel, Paul.
xRoadarmel, Paul.
The Kaligarh Fault. Har-Row.
Roads and Transportation Association of Canada. Project Committee on Urban Transportation Planning.
xRoads and Transportation Association of Canada, Committee on Urban Transportation.
Urban Transportation Planning Guide. U of Toronto Pr.
Roaf, Robert.
xRoaf, Robert.
Posture. Acad Pr.
Roark, Dallas M., 1931-
xRoark, Dallas M.
Dietrich Bonhoeffer. Word Bks.
Roark, Raymond J. see Roark, Raymond Jefferson.
Roark, Raymond Jefferson, 1890-
xRoark, Raymond J.
Formulas for Stress & Strain. McGraw.
Roat, Evelyn C.
xRoat, Evelyn C.
The Museum of Northern Arizona. Mus Northern Ariz.
Roazen, Paul, 1936-
xRoazen, Paul.
Freud & His Followers. Knopf.
Freud & His Followers. NAL.
Sigmund Freud. P-H.
Roback, A. A. see Roback, Abraham Aaron.
Roback, Abraham A. see Roback, Abraham Aaron.
Roback, Abraham Aaron, 1890-1965
xRoback, A. A.
ed. The Albert Schweitzer Jubilee Book. Greenwood.
History of Psychology & Psychiatry. Philos Lib.
The Story of Yiddish Literature. Gordon Pr.
xRoback, Abraham A.

History of Psychology & Psychiatry.
Greenwood.
ed. Present-Day Psychology: An Original
Survey of Departments, Branches, Methods
& Phases, Including Clinical & Dynamic
Psychology. Greenwood.

Roback, Howard B.
xRoback, Howard B.
ed. Group Psychotherapy Research:
Commentaries & Selected Readings. Krieger.
Robacker, Ada F. *see* Robacker, Earl Francis.
Robacker, Earl Francis.
xRobacker, Ada F.
Spatterware & Sponge: Hardy Perennials of
Ceramics. A S Barnes.
Robarts, Edward.
xRobarts, Edward.
The Marquesan Journal of Edward Robarts:
1797-1824. U Pr of Hawaii.
Robb. *see* Robb, Stephen.
Robb, Dale, 1921-
xRobb, Dale.
Love & Living Together. Fortress.
Robb, David M. *see* Robb, David Metheny.
Robb, David Metheny, 1903-
xRobb, David M.
The Art of the Illuminated Manuscript. A S
Barnes.
The Art of the Illuminated Manuscript. Art
Alliance.
Robb, George P. *see* Robb, George Paul.
Robb, George Paul.
xRobb, George P.
Assessment of Individual Mental Ability.
Har-Row.
Robb, James W. *see* Robb, James Willis.
Robb, James Willis.
xRobb, James W.
Patterns of Image & Structure in the Essays of
Alfonso Reyes. AMS Pr.
Robb, Janet H. *see* Robb, Janet Henderson.
Robb, Janet Henderson, 1896-
xRobb, Janet H.
Primrose League 1883-1906. AMS Pr.
Robb, Margaret D.
xRobb, Margaret D.
Dynamics of Motor-Skill Acquisition. P-H.
Robb, Mary M. *see* Robb, Mary Margaret.
Robb, Mary Margaret, 1900-
xRobb, Mary M.
Oral Interpretation of Literature in American
Colleges & Universities. Johnson Repr.
Robb, Mel. *see* Robb, Melvin. H.
Robb, Melvin. H.
xRobb, Mel.
Teacher Assistants. Merrill.
Robb, Nesca A. *see* Robb, Nesca Adeline.
Robb, Nesca Adeline.
xRobb, Nesca A.
Four in Exile. Folcroft.
Neoplatonism of the Italian Renaissance.
Octagon.
Robb, Stephen, 1939-
xRobb.
Fundamentals of Evidence & Argument. SRA.
Robb, Stewart.
xRobb, Stewart.
Prophecies on World Events by Nostradamus.
Liveright.
Robbe-Grillet, Alain, 1922-
xRobbe-Grillet, Alain.
Topology of a Phantom City. Grove.
Topology of a Phantom City. Grove.
Robben, John.
xRobben, John.
Coming to My Senses. Ballantine.
Robbins, Ann Brokaw Roe, 1905-
xRobbins, Ann R.

How to Grow Annuals. Dover.
How to Grow Annuals. Peter Smith.
Robbins, Ann R. *see* Robbins, Ann Brokaw Roe.
Robbins, Arthur.
xRobbins, Arthur.
Creative Art Therapy. Brunner-Mazel.
Robbins, Charles L. *see* Robbins, Charles Leonidas.
Robbins, Charles Leonidas, 1876-1938
xRobbins, Charles L.
Teachers in Germany in the Sixteenth Century:
Conditions in Protestant Elementary &
Secondary Schools. AMS Pr.
Robbins, Christopher, 1946-
xRobbins, Christopher.
Air America. Putnam.
Robbins, Clarence R.
xRobbins, Clarence R.
The Chemical & Physical Behavior of Human
Hair. Van Nos Reinhold.
Robbins, Daniel.
xRobbins, Daniel.
Painting Between the Wars: 1918-1940.
McGraw.
Robbins, Harold.
xRobbins, Harold.
A Stone for Danny Fisher. PB.
Robbins, Herbert.
xRobbins, Herbert.
Introduction to Statistics. SRA.
Robbins, Ireene.
xRobbins, Irene.
Arts & Crafts Media Ideas for the Elementary
Teacher. P-H.
Robbins, Irene. *see* Robbins, Ireene.
Robbins, James G.
xRobbins, James G.
Effective Communication for Today's Manager.
Lebhar Friedman.
Robbins, Jhan.
xRobbins, Jhan.
Anatomy of a Prostitute. NAL.
Robbins, Keith.
xRobbins, Keith.
The Abolition of War: The 'peace Movement'
in Britain, 1914-1919. Verry.
John Bright. Routledge & Kegan.
Robbins, Lionel. *see* Robbins, Lionel Charles Robbins.
Robbins, Lionel C. *see* Robbins, Lionel Charles Robbins.
Robbins, Lionel Charles Robbins, Baron, 1898-
xRobbins, Lionel.
Great Depression. Arno.
xRobbins, Lionel C.
The Theory of Economic Policy in English
Classical Political Economy. Porcupine Pr.
Robbins, Martin. *see* Robbins, Martin H.
Robbins, Martin D.
xRobbins, Martin D.
Who Runs the Computer?: Strategies for the
Management of Computers in Higher
Education. Westview.
Robbins, Martin H.
xRobbins, Martin.
Reply to the Headlines: Poems 1965-1970.
Swallow.
Robbins, Patricia.
xRobbins, Patricia.
Antics. S&S.
Robbins, Peter.
xRobbins, Peter.
ed. Guide to Precious Metals & Their Markets.
Nichols Pub.
Guide to Precious Metals & Their Markets.
Van Nos Reinhold.
Robbins, Ray F., 1915-
xRobbins, Ray F.
The Revelation of Jesus Christ. Broadman.
Robbins, Rossell H. *see* Robbins, Rossell Hope.
Robbins, Rossell Hope, 1912-
xRobbins, Rossell H.

Encyclopedia of Witchcraft & Demonology.
Crown.
Robbins, Roy M. *see* Robbins, Roy Marvin.
Robbins, Roy Marvin.
xRobbins, Roy M.
Our Landed Heritage: The Public Domain,
1776-1970. U of Nebr Pr.
Robbins, Ruth.
xRobbins, Ruth.
illus. Taliesin & King Arthur. Parnassus.
Robbins, Stanley L.
xRobbins, Stanley L.
Pathologic Basis of Disease. Saunders.
Robbins, Thomas. *see* Robbins, Tom.
Robbins, Tom.
xRobbins, Thomas.
Even Cowgirls Get the Blues. Bantam.
xRobbins, Tom.
Even Cowgirls Get the Blues. HM.
Robbins, Vesta D. *see* Robbins, Vesta O.
Robbins, Vesta O.
xRobbins, Vesta D.
No Coward Soul. Iowa St U Pr.
Robboy, Howard.
xRobboy, Howard.
ed. Social Interaction: Introductory Readings in
Sociology. St Martin.
Robe, Stanley. *see* Robe, Stanley Linn.
Robe, Stanley L. *see* Robe, Stanley Linn.
Robe, Stanley Linn, 1915-
xRobe, Stanley.
Hispanic Folktales from New Mexico:
Narratives from the R.D. Jameson Collection.
U of Cal Pr.
xRobe, Stanley L.
Amapa Storytellers. U of Cal Pr.
Azuela & the Mexican Underdogs. U of Cal Pr.
Robeck, Nesta De. *see* De Robeck, Nesta.
Robens, Howard.
xRobens, Howard.
Hambro's Itch. Doubleday.
Roberg, Roy R.
xRoberg, Roy R.
ed. The Changing Police Role: New
Dimensions & New Issues. Justice Sys.
Police Management & Organizational Behavior:
A Contingency Approach. West Pub.
Roberge, James K., 1938-
xRoberge, James K.
Operational Amplifiers: Theory & Practice.
Wiley.
Roberson, Cliff, 1937-
xRoberson, Cliff.
Legal Guide for Pilots & Owners. TAB Bks.
Roberson, Ed.
xRoberson, Ed.
Etai-Eken. U of Pittsburgh Pr.
Roberson, John A.
xRoberson, John A.
Engineering Fluid Mechanics. HM.
Robert. *see* Robert, Paul.
Robert Bentley, Inc.
xRobert Bentley, Inc.
Audi Fox Service Manual, 1973, 1974, 1975,
1976, 1977, 1978, 1979. Bentley.
Capri Complete Service Manual 1970-1975.
Bentley.
Toyota Corolla 1600 Service Manual, 1975,
1976, 1977, 1978, 1979. Bentley.
Volkswagen Rabbit Diesel Service Manual,
1977-1981. Bentley.
Volkswagen Rabbit-Scirocco Service Manual,
Gasoline Models, 1975, 1976, 1977, 1978,
1979. Bentley.
Volkswagen Rabbit-Scirocco Service Manual,
1980-1981: Gasoline Models. Bentley.
Robert, Carl, 1850-1922
xRobert, Carl.

Archaeologische Hermeneutik: Anleitung Zur Deutung Klassischer Bildwerke. Arno.

Robert, Charles E. see Robert, Charles Edwin.

Robert, Charles Edwin.
xRobert, Charles E.
Negro Civilization in the South. Arno.

Robert, Guy.
xRobert, Guy.
Lemieux. Vanguard.

Robert, Henry M. see Robert, Henry Martyn.

Robert, Henry Martyn, 1837-1923
xRobert, Henry M.
Parliamentary Practice: An Introduction to Parliamentary Law. Halsted Pr.

Robert J. Brady Company.
xEducation & Training Systems Division of the Robert J. Brady Co.
Brady's Programmed Introduction to Microbiology. Lippincott.
Brady's Programmed Orientation to Medical Terminology. Lippincott.

Robert, Marthe.
xRobert, Marthe.
The Old & the New: From Don Quixote to Kafka. U of Cal Pr.

Robert, Paul.
xRobert.
Dictionnaire Alphabetique et Analogique De la Langue Francaise. French & Eur.

Robertiello, Richard. see Robertiello, Richard C.

Robertiello, Richard C.
xRobertiello, Richard.
Hold Them Very Close, Then Let Them Go: How to Be an Authentic Parent. Dial.
xRobertiello, Richard C.
A Man in the Making: Grandfathers, Fathers, & Sons. Marek.

Roberts. see Roberts, Nigel Keith.

Roberts, Albert F., 1911
xRoberts, Albert F.
Geotechnology: An Introductory Text for Students & Engineers. Pergamon.

Roberts, Albert R.
xRoberts, Albert R.
ed. Childhood Deprivation. C C Thomas.
Readings in Prison Education. C C Thomas.

Roberts, Alice C. see Roberts, Alice Calvert.

Roberts, Alice Calvert.
xRoberts, Alice C.
Aphasic Child: A Neurological Basis for His Education & Rehabilitation. C C Thomas.

Roberts, Allen E.
xRoberts, Allen E.
G. Washington; Master Mason. Macoy Pub.

Roberts, Alvin.
xRoberts, Alvin.
Psychosocial Rehabilitation of the Blind. C C Thomas.

Roberts, Andrew.
xRoberts, Andrew.
A History of Zambia. Holmes & Meier.
xRoberts, Andrew O.
A History of the Bemba: Political Growth & Change in North-Eastern Zambia Before 1900. U of Wis Pr.

Roberts, Andrew O. see Roberts, Andrew.

Roberts, Arthur. see Roberts, Arthur D.

Roberts, Arthur D.
xRoberts, Arthur.
Programming for Numerical Control Machines. McGraw.

Roberts, Arthur J.
xRoberts, Arthur J.
The American Diesel Locomotive. A S Barnes.

Roberts, B. T. see Roberts, Benjamine Titus.

Roberts, Benjamine Titus, 1823-1893
xRoberts, B. T.
Holiness Teachings. Schmul Pub Co.

Roberts, Blaine.
xRoberts, Blaine.
Modern Mathematics & Economic Analysis. Norton.

Roberts, Brian.
xRoberts, Brian.
Churchills in Africa. Taplinger.
Diamond Magnates. Scribner.

Roberts, Bruce.
xRoberts, Bruce.
Where Time Stood Still: A Portrait of Appalachia. Macmillan.

Roberts, Bryan. see Roberts, Bryan R.

Roberts, Bryan R., 1939-
xRoberts, Bryan.
Cities of Peasants: The Political Economy of Urbanization in the Third World. Sage.

Roberts, Catherine.
xRoberts, Catherine.
Science, Animals & Evolution: Reflections on Some Unrealized Potentials of Biology & Medicine. Greenwood.

Roberts, Cecil E., 1919-
xRoberts, Cecil E.
A Soldier from Texas. Branch-Smith.

Roberts, Cecilia M.
xRoberts, Cecilia M.
Doctor & Patient in the Teaching Hospital: A Tale of Two Life-Worlds. Lexington Bks.

Roberts, Charles C. see Roberts, Charles Clifton.

Roberts, Charles Clifton.
xRoberts, Charles C.
Tangled Justice: Some Reasons for a Change of Policy in Africa. Negro U Pr.

Roberts, Charles E., 1942-
xRoberts, Charles E.
Ordinary Differential Equations: A Computational Approach. P-H.

Roberts, Charles G. see Roberts, Charles George Douglas.

Roberts, Charles George Douglas, Sir, 1860-1943
xRoberts, Charles G.
By the Marshes of Minas. Arno.

Roberts, Clarence.
xRoberts.
Sharing of Scripture. Paulist Pr.

Roberts, D. F. see Roberts, Derek Frank.

Roberts, Daniel A.
xRoberts, Daniel A.
Fundamentals of Plant Pathology. W H Freeman.

Roberts, David.
xRoberts, David.
Adventure at Murray's: A Strange Shopping Trip. Creative Ed.
Lost City of the Incas. Rand.
Paternalism in Early Victorian England. Rutgers U Pr.

Roberts, David D., 1943-
xRoberts, David D.
The Syndicalist Tradition & Italian Fascism. U of NC Pr.

Roberts, David R.
xRoberts, David R.
Executive Compensation. Free Pr.

Roberts, Derek Frank.
xRoberts, D. F.
Climate & Human Variability. Benjamin-Cummings.

Roberts, Derrell C.
xRoberts, Derrell C.
Joseph E. Brown & the Politics of Reconstruction. U of Ala Pr.

Roberts, Dick, 1939-
xRoberts, Dick.
Pref. by Capitalism in Crisis. Path Pr NY.

Roberts, Don D.
xRoberts, Don D.
Existential Graphs of Charles S. Peirce. Mouton.

Roberts, Douglas L.
xRoberts, Douglas L.
The Dynamics of Dental Practice Administration: A Guide for Efficient Dental Health Care Delivery. Med Exam.

Roberts, Duane F.
xRoberts, Duane F.
Marketing & Leasing of Office Space. Inst Real Estate.

Roberts, Duke.
xRoberts, Willis J.
Introduction to Modern Police Firearms. Glencoe.

Roberts, E. see Roberts, Eugene.

Roberts, Edgar. see Roberts, Edgar V.

Roberts, Edgar V.
xRoberts, Edgar.
A Practical College Rhetoric: Writing Themes & Tests. Winthrop.

Roberts, Elizabeth M. see Roberts, Elizabeth Madox.

Roberts, Elizabeth Madox.
xRoberts, Elizabeth M.
The Great Meadow. AMS Pr.
The Great Meadow. Mockingbird Bks.

Roberts, Eric B.
xRoberts, Eric B.
From Football to Finance: The Story of Brady Keys Jr. HarBraceJ.

Roberts, Ernie.
xRoberts, Ernie.
Worker's Control. Allen Unwin.

Roberts, Eugene.
xRoberts, E.
ed. GABA in Nervous System Function. Raven.

Roberts, Evelyn.
xRoberts, Evelyn.
Heaven Has a Floor. Damascus Hse.
His Darling Wife, Evelyn: The Autobiography of Mrs. Oral Roberts. G K Hall.

Roberts, Florence B. see Roberts, Florence Bright.

Roberts, Florence Bright, 1941-
xRoberts, Florence B.
Perinatal Nursing: Care of Newborns & Their Families. McGraw.
Review of Pediatric Nursing. Mosby.

Roberts, Francis Warren.
xRoberts, Warren.
Jane Austen & the French Revolution. St Martin.

Roberts, Fred M.
xRoberts, Fred M.
Nikonos Photography: The Camera & the System. F M Roberts.

Roberts, Fred S.
xRoberts, Fred S.
Discrete Mathematical Models with Applications to Social Biological & Environmental Problems. P-H.

Roberts, G. K. see Roberts, Geoffrey K.

Roberts, Geoffrey K.
xRoberts, G. K.
Dictionary of Political Analysis. St Martin.
xRoberts, Geoffrey K.
Political Parties & Pressure Groups in Britain. St Martin.

Roberts, Geoffrey R.
xRoberts, Geoffrey R.
English in Primary Schools. Routledge & Kegan.

Roberts, George O.
xRoberts, George O.
Afro-Arab Fraternity: The Roots of Terramedia. Sage.

Roberts, George W.
xRoberts, George W.

The Population of Jamaica. Kraus Repr.
Roberts, Glyn C.
   xRoberts, Glyn C.
      Social Science of Play, Games & Sport:
         Learning Experiences. Human Kinetics.
Roberts, H. H. *see* Roberts, Helen Heffron.
Roberts, H. J. *see* Roberts, Hyman Jacob.
Roberts, Helen H. *see* Roberts, Helen Heffron.
Roberts, Helen Heffron, 1888-
   xRoberts, H. H.
      Ancient Hawaiian Music. Kraus Repr.
   xRoberts, Helen H.
      Ancient Hawaiian Music. Peter Smith.
Roberts, Hugh. *see* Roberts, M. Hugh P.
Roberts, Hyman Jacob, 1924-
   xRoberts, H. J.
      Causes, Ecology & Prevention of Traffic
         Accidents: With Emphasis Upon Traffic
         Medicine, Epidemiology Sociology &
         Logistics. C C Thomas.
Roberts, J.
   xRoberts, J.
      Practical Plant Physiology. Longman.
Roberts, J. *see* Roberts, Jane.
Roberts, J. Fraser. *see* Roberts, John Alexander Fraser.
Roberts, J. M. *see* Roberts, John Morris.
Roberts, J. W., 1918-
   xRoberts, J. W.
      Letters of John. Sweet.
Roberts, Jane, 1929-
   xRoberts, J.
      Adventures in Consciousness: An Introduction
         to Aspect Psychology. P-H.
   xRoberts, Jane.
      The Coming of Seth. PB.
      Emir's Education in the Proper Use of Magical
         Powers. Delacorte.
      How to Develop Your ESP Power. Fell.
      The Nature of Personal Reality: A Seth Book.
         P-H.
      Psychic Politics: An Aspect Psychology Book.
         P-H.
      The World View of Paul Cezanne: A Psychic
         Interpretation. P-H.
Roberts, Janet L. *see* Roberts, Janet Louise.
Roberts, Janet Louise.
   xRoberts, Janet L.
      The Dornstein Icon. PB.
Roberts, Jeanne A. *see* Roberts, Jeanne Addison.
Roberts, Jeanne Addison.
   xRoberts, Jeanne A.
      Shakespeare's English Comedy: The Merry
         Wives of Windsor in Context. U of Nebr Pr.
Roberts, John. *see* Roberts, John G.
Roberts, John Alexander Fraser, 1899-
   xRoberts, J. Fraser.
      Introduction to Medical Genetics. Oxford U
         Pr.
Roberts, John G.
   xRoberts, John.
      Industrialization of Japan. Watts.
   xRoberts, John G.
      The Colonial Conquest of Asia. Watts.
Roberts, John Morris, 1928-
   xRoberts, J. M.
      The French Revolution. Oxford U Pr.
      History of the World. Knopf.
Roberts, John R. *see* Roberts, John Richard.
Roberts, John Richard.
   xRoberts, John R.
      George Herbert: An Annotated Bibliography of
         Modern Criticism, 1905-1974. U of Mo Pr.
Roberts, John S.
   xRoberts, John S.
      The Latin Tinge: The Impact of Latin
         American Music on the United States.
         Oxford U Pr.
Roberts, Joseph M., 1927-
   xRoberts, Joseph M.

O.S.H.A. Compliance Manual. Reston.
Roberts, June C. *see* Roberts, June Carver.
Roberts, June Carver.
   xRoberts, June C.
      Born in the Spring: A Collection of Spring
         Wildflowers. Ohio U Pr.
Roberts, Karlene H.
   xRoberts, Karlene H.
      Developing an Interdisciplinary Science of
         Organizations. Jossey-Bass.
Roberts, Keith, 1935-
   xRoberts, Keith.
      The Chalk Giants. Berkley Pub.
      Pavane. Berkley Pub.
Roberts, Kenneth.
   xRoberts, Kenneth.
      Arundel. Fawcett.
      Arundel. Doubleday.
      The Character Training Industry: Adventure
         Training Schemes in Britain. David &
         Charles.
      Northwest Passage. Fawcett.
      Northwest Passage. Doubleday.
Roberts, Kenneth. *see* Roberts, Kenneth Lewis.
Roberts, Kenneth H.
   xRoberts, Kenneth H.
      Primer for Film-Making: A Complete Guide to
         16mm & 35mm Film Production. Pegasus.
Roberts, Kenneth J., 1930-
   xRoberts, Kenneth J.
      The Rest of the Week. Our Sunday Visitor.
Roberts, Kenneth Lewis, 1885-1957
   xRoberts, Kenneth.
      The Lively Lady. Doubleday.
      Lively Lady. Fawcett.
      Oliver Wiswell. Doubleday.
      Oliver Wiswell. Fawcett.
      Rabble in Arms. Fawcett.
      Rabble in Arms. Doubleday.
Roberts, Launey F.
   xRoberts, Launey F.
      ed. Individualizing Instruction in Educational
         Administration: A Performance-Based
         Worktext. Mss Info.
Roberts, Laurance O. *see* Roberts, Laurance P.
Roberts, Laurance P.
   xRoberts, Laurance O.
      Roberts' Guide to Japanese Museums.
         Kodansha.
   xRoberts, Laurence P.
      A Dictionary of Japanese Artists: Painting,
         Sculpture, Ceramics, Prints, Lacquer.
         Weatherhill.
Roberts, Laurence P. *see* Roberts, Laurance P.
Roberts, Louise A.
   xRoberts, Louise A.
      How to Write for Business. Har-Row.
Roberts, Lydia J. *see* Roberts, Lydia Jane.
Roberts, Lydia Jane.
   xRoberts, Lydia J.
      Patterns of Living in Puerto Rican Families.
         Arno.
Roberts, M. Hugh P.
   xRoberts, Hugh.
      An Urban Profile of the Middle East. St
         Martin.
Roberts, M. W. *see* Roberts, Meirion Wynn.
Roberts, Martha G. *see* Roberts, Martha Gaby.
Roberts, Martha Gaby.
   xRoberts, Martha G.
      Honeymaid: The Story of Silver Dollar Tabor.
         Golden Bell.
Roberts, Mary Carter.
   xRoberts, Mary-Carter.
      Little Brother Fate. FS&G.
Roberts, Mary-Carter. *see* Roberts, Mary Carter.
Roberts, Meirion Wynn.
   xRoberts, M. W.

Chemistry of the Metal-Gas Interface. Oxford
   U Pr.
Roberts, Melville.
   xRoberts, Melville.
      Atlas of the Human Brain in Section. Lea &
         Febiger.
Roberts, Mervin F.
   xRoberts, Mervin F.
      Guinea Pigs for Beginners. TFH Pubns.
      The Tide Marsh Guide. Dutton.
Roberts, Michael, 1908-
   xRoberts, Michael.
      British Diplomacy & Swedish Politics,
         1758-1773. U of Minn Pr.
      Critique of Poetry. Folcroft.
      Modern Mind. Arno.
      T. E. Hulme. Haskell.
Roberts, Moss, 1937-
   xRoberts, Moss.
      tr. & ed. Chinese Fairy Tales & Fantasies.
         Pantheon.
Roberts, Nadine H.
   xRoberts, Nadine H.
      The Complete Handbook of Taxidermy. TAB
         Bks.
Roberts, Nancy, 1924-

   xRoberts, Nancy.
      Appalachian Ghosts. Doubleday.
      Ghosts of the Carolinas. McNally.
Roberts, Neal. *see* Roberts, Neal Alison.
Roberts, Neal A. *see* Roberts, Neal Alison.
Roberts, Neal Alison.
   xRoberts, Neal.
      ed. Property Tax Preferences for Agricultural
         Land. Allanheld.
   xRoberts, Neal A.
      Property Tax Preferences for Agricultural
         Land. Universe.
Roberts, Neil.
   xRoberts, Neil.
      George Eliot: Her Beliefs & Her Art. U of
         Pittsburgh Pr.
Roberts, Nigel K. *see* Roberts, Nigel Keith.
Roberts, Nigel Keith.
   xRoberts.
      The Cardiac Conducting System & the HIS
         Bundle Electrogram. ACC.
   xRoberts, Nigel K.
      Cardiac Arrhythmias in the Neonate, Infant &
         Child. ACC.
Roberts, Oral.
   xRoberts, Oral.
      Daily Blessing: A Guide to Seed-Faith Living.
         Revell.
Roberts, Patrick.
   xRoberts, Patrick.
      Psychology of Tragic Drama. Routledge &
         Kegan.
Roberts, Paul.
   xRoberts, Paul.
      Modern Grammar. HarBraceJ.
   xRoberts, Paul M.
      Understanding Grammar. Har-Row.
Roberts, Paul C. *see* Roberts, Paul Craig.
Roberts, Paul Craig.
   xRoberts, Paul C.
      Marx's Theory of Exchange, Alienation &
         Crisis. Hoover Inst Pr.
Roberts, Paul H. *see* Roberts, Paul Harry.
Roberts, Paul Harry.
   xRoberts, Paul H.
      An Introduction to Magnetohydrodynamics.
         Elsevier.
Roberts, Paul M. *see* Roberts, Paul.
Roberts, Peter, 1859-1932
   xRoberts, Peter.

Anthracite Coal Communities. Greenwood.
Anthracite Coal Communities: A Study of the
Demography, the Social, Educational &
Moral Life of the Anthracite Regions. Arno.

Roberts, Peter C.
xRoberts, Peter C.
Modelling Large Systems: Limits to Growth
Revisited. Halsted Pr.

Roberts, Ron E.
xRoberts, Ron E.
Social Movements: Between the Balcony & the
Barricade. Mosby.

Roberts, Royston M.
xRoberts, Royston M.
Modern Experimental Organic Chemistry.
HR&W.

Roberts, S. *see* Roberts, Sidney.

Roberts, Samuel J.
xRoberts, Samuel J.
Survival or Hegemony?: The Foundations of
Israeli Foreign Policy. Johns Hopkins.

Roberts, Sanford M.
xRoberts, Sanford M.
Dynamic Programming in Chemical
Engineering & Process Control. Acad Pr.

Roberts, Sidney.
xRoberts, S.
ed. Mechanisms, Regulation & Special
Functions of Protein Synthesis in the Brain.
Elsevier.

Roberts, Simon.
xRoberts, Simon.
Order & Dispute: An Introduction to Legal
Anthropology. St Martin.

Roberts, Stephen. *see* Roberts, Stephen Henry.
Roberts, Stephen H. *see* Roberts, Stephen Henry.

Roberts, Stephen Henry, Sir, 1901-
xRoberts, Stephen.
The House That Hitler Built. Gordon Pr.
xRoberts, Stephen H.
History of Australian Land Settlement
1788-1920. Johnson Repr.
Population Problems of the Pacific. AMS Pr.

Roberts, Suzanne.
xRoberts, Suzanne.
Danger in Paradise. Bouregy.

Roberts, Suzanne. *see* Roberts, Suzanne Fleisher.

Roberts, Suzanne Fleisher, 1922-
xRoberts, Suzanne.
Gracie. Doubleday.

Roberts, Sydney C. *see* Roberts, Sydney Castle.

Roberts, Sydney Castle, Sir, 1887-1966
xRoberts, Sydney C.
Thomas Gray of Pembroke. Folcroft.

Roberts, T. R. *see* Roberts, Terence Robert.

Roberts, Terence Robert, 1943-
xRoberts, T. R.
Radiochromatography: The Chromatography &
Electrophoresis of Radiolabelled Compounds.
Elsevier.

Roberts, Thom.
xRoberts, Thom.
Summerdog. Avon.

Roberts, Thomas J. *see* Roberts, Thomas John.

Roberts, Thomas John.
xRoberts, Thomas J.
When Is Something Fiction?. S Ill U Pr.

Roberts, Vera M. *see* Roberts, Vera Mowry.

Roberts, Vera Mowry.
xRoberts, Vera M.
Nature of Theatre. Har-Row.

Roberts, W. G. *see* Roberts, William Geoffrey.
Roberts, W. Rhys. *see* Roberts, William Rhys.
Roberts, Walter A. *see* Roberts, Walter Adolphe.

Roberts, Walter Adolphe, 1886-
xRoberts, Walter A.
Caribbean: The Story of Our Sea of Destiny.
Negro U Pr.
The Moralist. AMS Pr.

Roberts, Walter O. *see* Roberts, Walter Orr.

Roberts, Walter Orr.
xRoberts, Walter O.
The Climate Mandate. W H Freeman.

Roberts, Warren. *see* Roberts, Francis Warren.

Roberts, Will Davis.
xRoberts, Willo D.
The Radkin Revenge. Popular Lib.

Roberts, Willard L. *see* Roberts, Willard Lincoln.

Roberts, Willard Lincoln.
xRoberts, Willard L.
Encyclopedia of Minerals. Van Nos Reinhold.

Roberts, William, fl. 1763
xRoberts, William.
Account of the First Discovery & Natural
History of Florida. U Presses Fla.
Earlier History of English Bookselling. Gale.
The Earlier History of English Bookselling.
Gordon Pr.
xRoberts, William P.
At the Door Knocking. Pflaum Pr.

Roberts, William C. *see* Roberts, William Clifford.

Roberts, William Clifford, 1932-
xRoberts, William C.
Congenital Heart Disease in Adults. Davis Co.

Roberts, William Geoffrey.
xRoberts, W. G.
The Quest for Oil. S G Phillips.

Roberts, William P. *see* Roberts, William.
Roberts, William R. *see* Roberts, William Rhys.

Roberts, William Rhys., 1858-1929
xRoberts, W. Rhys.
Greek Rhetoric & Literary Criticism. Folcroft.
xRoberts, William R.
Greek Rhetoric & Literary Criticism. Cooper
Sq.

Roberts, Willis J. *see* Roberts, Duke.

Roberts, Willo D. *see* Roberts, Willo Davis.

Roberts, Willo Davis.
xRoberts, Willo D.
Cade Curse. Popular Lib.
Dark Dowry. Popular Lib.
Don't Hurt Laurie!. Atheneum.
More Minden Curses. Atheneum.

Roberts-Jones, Philippe.
xRoberts-Jones, Philippe.
Beyond Time & Place: Non-Realist Painting in
the Nineteenth Century. Oxford U Pr.

Robertshaw, D.
xRobertshaw, D.
Environmental Physiology II. Univ Park.

Robertson. *see* Robertson, Stuart.

Robertson, A. T.
xRobertson, A. T.
Paul, the Interpreter of Christ. Broadman.
Some Minor Characters in the New Testament.
Baker Bk.
Some Minor Characters in the New Testament.
Broadman.

Robertson, Alden.
xRobertson, Alden.
The No Baloney Sandwich Book. Doubleday.

Robertson, Alec.
xRobertson, Alec.
ed. Pelican History of Music. Penguin.

Robertson, Alec. *see* Robertson, Alec. Collingwood
Cuthbert.

Robertson, Alec. Collingwood Cuthbert.
xRobertson, Alec.
Dvorak. Biblio Dist.
Dvorak. Littlefield.

Robertson, Andrew. *see* Robertson, Andrew Beaumont.

Robertson, Andrew Beaumont, 1921-
xRobertson, Andrew.
Strategic Marketing: A Business Response to
Consumerism. Halsted Pr.

Robertson, Angus.
xRobertson, Angus.

ed. From Television to Home Computer: The
Future of Consumer Electronics. Sterling.

Robertson, Archibald, 1886-
xRobertson, Archibald.
Morals in World History. Haskell.

Robertson, C. M. *see* Robertson, Martin.
Robertson, C. N. *see* Robertson, Constance Noyes.
Robertson, Charles G. *see* Robertson, Charles Grant.

Robertson, Charles Grant, Sir, 1869-1948
xRobertson, Charles G.
Chatham & the British Empire. Verry.

Robertson, Christina. *see* Robertson, Christina A.

Robertson, Christina A., 1944-
xRobertson, Christina.
Divorce & Decision-Making: A Woman's
Guide. Follett.

Robertson, Constance N. *see* Robertson, Constance
Noyes .

Robertson, Constance Noyes.
xRobertson, C. N.
Oneida Community Profiles. Syracuse U Pr.

xRobertson, Constance N.
Oneida Community: The Breakup, 1876 - 1881.
Syracuse U Pr.

Robertson, D. B.
xRobertson, D. B.
Reinhold Niebuhr's Works: A Bibliography. G
K Hall.

Robertson, D. W. *see* Robertson, Durant Waite.

Robertson, Dan H.
xRobertson, Dan H.
Sales Management: Decision Making for
Improved Profitability. Macmillan.

Robertson, David. *see* Robertson, David Bruce.

Robertson, David Bruce.
xRobertson, David.
A Theory of Party Competition. Wiley.

Robertson, David H. *see* Robertson, David Herlie.

Robertson, David Herlie.
xRobertson, David H.
Manual of Clinical Pharmacology. Williams &
Wilkins.

Robertson, David M.
xRobertson, David M.
The Nervous System. Williams & Wilkins.

Robertson, Dennis H. *see* Robertson, Dennis Holme.

Robertson, Dennis Holme, 1890-1963
xRobertson, Dennis H.
Economic Commentaries. Greenwood.
Economic Commentaries. Hyperion Conn.
Essays in Monetary Theory. Hyperion Conn.

Robertson, Don, 1929-
xRobertson, Don.
The Greatest Thing That Almost Happened.
Warner Bks.
Praise the Human Season. Ballantine.
Victoria at Nine. Ballantine.

Robertson, Donald, 1919-
xRobertson, Donald.
Pre-Columbian Architecture. Braziller.

Robertson, Donald S. *see* Robertson, Donald Struan.

Robertson, Donald Struan, 1885-1961
xRobertson, Donald S.
Greek & Roman Architecture. Cambridge U
Pr.

Robertson, Dorothy L. *see* Robertson, Dorothy Lewis.

Robertson, Dorothy Lewis.
xRobertson, Dorothy L.
Fairy Tales from the Philippines. Dodd.
Fairy Tales from Viet Nam. Dodd.

Robertson, Durant W. *see* Robertson, Durant Waite.

Robertson, Durant Waite.
xRobertson, D. W.
Literature of Medieval England. McGraw.
Preface to Chaucer: Studies in Medieval
Perspectives. Princeton U Pr.
xRobertson, Durant W.
Chaucer's London. Wiley.

Robertson, E. Graeme. *see* Robertson, Edward Graeme.

Robertson, Edward Graeme.
  xRobertson, E. Graeme.
    Cast Iron Decoration: A World Survey.
      Watson-Guptill.
Robertson, Edwin H. see Robertson, Edwin Hanton.
Robertson, Edwin Hanton.
  xRobertson, Edwin H.
    Dietrich Bonhoeffer. John Knox.
Robertson, Eric S. see Robertson, Eric Sutherland.
Robertson, Eric Sutherland.
  xRobertson, Eric S.
    Life of Henry Wadsworth Longfellow. Arden
      Lib.
    Life of Henry Wadsworth Longfellow. Folcroft.
    Life of Henry Wadsworth Longfellow.
      Kennikat.
Robertson, Esmonde M. see Robertson, Esmonde
  Manning.
Robertson, Esmonde Manning, 1923-
  xRobertson, Esmonde M.
    Mussolini As Empire-Builder: Europe & Africa,
      1932-36. St Martin.
Robertson, F. W. see Robertson, Frederick William.
Robertson, Frederick William, 1816-1853
  xRobertson, F. W.
    Lectures on the Influence of Poetry &
      Wordsworth. Kennikat.
    Lectures on the Influence of Poetry &
      Wordsworth. R West.
Robertson, George, 1918-
  xRobertson, George.
    Port. Merrimack Bk Serv.
Robertson, George. see Robertson, George Scott.
Robertson, George C. see Robertson, George Croom.
Robertson, George Croom, 1842-1892
  xRobertson, George C.
    Hobbes. AMS Pr.
    Hobbes. R West.
    Hobbes. Scholarly.
Robertson, George Scott, Sir, 1852-1916
  xRobertson, George.
    Chitral: The Story of a Minor Siege. Oxford U
      Pr.
Robertson, Hector M. see Robertson, Hector Menteith.
Robertson, Hector Menteith.
  xRobertson, Hector M.
    South Africa: Economic & Political Aspects.
      Duke.
Robertson, Ian.
  xRobertson, Ian.
    ed. Race & Politics in South Africa.
      Transaction Bks.
    Social Problems. Random.
    Sociology. Worth.
Robertson, Irvine.
  xRobertson, Irvine G.
    What the Cults Believe. Moody.
Robertson, Irvine G. see Robertson, Irvine.
Robertson, J. see Robertson, John Mackinnon.
Robertson, J. A. see Robertson, James Alexander.
Robertson, J. G. see Robertson, John George.
Robertson, J. M. see Robertson, John Mackinnon.
Robertson, Jack. see Robertson, Jack C.
Robertson, Jack C.
  xRobertson, Jack.
    Selling to the Federal Government: A Guide
      for Business. McGraw.
  xRobertson, Jack C.
    Auditing. Business Pubns.
Robertson, Jack R.
  xRobertson, Jack R.
    Genitourinary Problems in Women. C C
      Thomas.
Robertson, James Alexander, 1873-
  xRobertson, J. A.
    List of Documents in Spanish Archives
      Relating to the History of the United States.
      Kraus Repr.
Robertson, James C.
  xRobertson, James C.

    Introduction to Fire Prevention. Glencoe.
Robertson, James I.
  xRobertson, James I.
    Compiled by An Index-Guide to the Southern
      Historical Society Papers, 1876-1959. Kraus
      Intl.
    Stonewall Brigade. La State U Pr.
Robertson, James L. see Robertson, James Logie.
Robertson, James Logie, 1846-1922
  xRobertson, James L.
    In Scottish Fields. AMS Pr.
Robertson, Jason.
  xRobertson, Jason.
    How to Win in a Job Interview. P-H.
Robertson, John G. see Robertson, John George.
Robertson, John George, 1867-1933
  xRobertson, J. G.
    Goethe. Haskell.
    Goethe. R West.
    Goethe & the Twentieth Century. Haskell.
    The Life & Work of Goethe. Haskell.
  xRobertson, John G.
    Goethe & Byron. Folcroft.
    The Life & Work of Goethe, 1749-1832. Arno.
    The Life & Work of Goethe 1749-1832.
      Folcroft.
Robertson, John M. see Robertson, John Mackinnon.
Robertson, John Mackinnon, 1856-1933
  xRobertson, J.
    Modern Humanists Reconsidered. Gordon Pr.
  xRobertson, J. M.
    Baconian Heresy: A Confutation. Scholarly.
    Modern Humanists Reconsidered. Haskell.
    The Problem of "Hamlet". Folcroft.
    The Problems of the Shakespeare Sonnets.
      Haskell.
  xRobertson, John M.
    Baconian Heresy: A Confutation. Folcroft.
    Criticisms. Folcroft.
    Croce As Shakespearean Critic. Folcroft.
    Meaning of Liberalism. Kennikat.
    The Problem of the Merry Wives of Windsor.
      Folcroft.
Robertson, Joseph F.
  xRobertson, Joseph F.
    Motion Picture Distribution Handbook. TAB
      Bks.
Robertson, Josephine.
  xRobertson, Josephine.
    Garden Meditations. Abingdon.
    Meditations for the Later Years. Abingdon.
Robertson, Keith.
  xRobertson, Keith.
    In Search of a Sandhill Crane. Penguin.
    In Search of a Sandhill Crane. Viking Pr.
    Tales of Myrtle the Turtle. Viking Pr.
Robertson, Kirk.
  xRobertson, Kirk.
    Under the Weight of the Sky. Cherry Valley.
Robertson, Laurel.
  xRobertson, Laurel.
    Laurel's Kitchen: A Handbook for Vegetarian
      Cookery & Nutrition. Bantam.
    Laurel's Kitchen: A Handbook for Vegetarian
      Cookery & Nutrition. Nilgiri Pr.
Robertson, Leon. see Robertson, Leon S.
Robertson, Leon S.
  xRobertson, Leon.
    Medical Sociology: A General Systems
      Approach. Nelson-Hall.
Robertson, Martin.
  xRobertson, C. M.
    History of Greek Art. Cambridge U Pr.
  xRobertson, Martin.
    Greek Painting. Rizzoli Intl.
Robertson, Mary.
  xRobertson.

    Practical Correspondence for Colleges. SW
      Pub.
Robertson, Neville L.
  xRobertson, Neville L.
    Education in South Africa. Phi Delta Kappa.
Robertson, Noel.
  xRobertson, Noel.
    ed. The Archaeology of Cyprus: Recent
      Developments. Noyes.
Robertson, Pauline D. see Robertson, Pauline Durrett.
Robertson, Pauline Durrett.
  xRobertson, Pauline D.
    Panhandle Pilgrimage: Illustrated Tales Tracing
      History in the Texas Panhandle. Staked
      Plains.
Robertson, Priscilla. see Robertson, Priscilla (Smith).
Robertson, Priscilla (Smith).
  xRobertson, Priscilla.
    Revolutions of 1848: A Social History.
      Princeton U Pr.
Robertson, Roland.
  xRobertson, Roland.
    Meaning & Change: Explorations in the
      Cultural Sociology of Modern Societies. NYU
      Pr.
    The Sociological Interpretation of Religion.
      Schocken.
Robertson, Ross M.
  xRobertson, Ross M.
    History of the American Economy. HarBraceJ.
Robertson, Stuart.
  xRobertson.
    Development of Modern English. P-H.
Robertson, Thomas A., 1897-
  xRobertson, Tomas.
    Baja California & Its Missions. La Siesta.
Robertson, Thomas S.
  xRobertson, Thomas S.
    Televised Medicine Advertising & Children.
      Praeger.
Robertson, Tomas. see Robertson, Thomas A.
Robertson, William S. see Robertson, William Spence.
Robertson, William Spence, 1872-
  xRobertson, William S.
    France & Latin-American Independence.
      Octagon.
    Life of Miranda. Cooper Sq.
Robertson, Wilmot.
  xRobertson, Wilmot.
    Dispossessed Majority. Devin.
    The Dispossessed Majority. Howard Allen.
Robeson, Kenneth.
  xRobeson, Kenneth.
    Purple Dragon. Bantam.
Robey, Cora L.
  xRobey, Cora L.
    Handbook of Basic Writing Skills. HarBraceJ.
Robichaud, Beryl.
  xRobichaud, Beryl.
    Introduction to Data Processing. McGraw.
    Vegetation of New Jersey: A Study of
      Landscape Diversity. Rutgers U Pr.
Robichaux, Albert. see Robichaux, Albert J.
Robichaux, Albert J.
  xRobichaux, Albert.
    Louisiana Census & Militia Lists: 1770-1789.
      Polyanthos.
Robicheaux, Robert A.
  xRobicheaux, Robert A.
    Marketing: Contemporary Dimensions. HM.
Robicsek, Francis.
  xRobicsek, Francis.
    photos by The Smoking Gods: Tobacco in
      Maya Art, History, & Religion. U of Okla Pr.
Robie, Joan H. see Robie, Joan Hake.

Robie, Joan Hake.
  xRobie, Joan H.
    What Your Handwriting Tells About You.
      Broadman.
Robin, 1944-1975
  xRobin.
    Don't Bury Me 'til I'm Dead. Accent Bks.
Robin. *see* Robin, Melvin B.
Robin, Donald. *see* Robin, Donald P.
Robin, Donald P.
  xRobin, Donald.
    Marketing: Basic Concepts for
      Decision-Making. Har-Row.
Robin, Gerald D., 1936-
  xRobin, Gerald D.
    Introduction to the Criminal Justice System:
      Principles, Procedures, Practice. Har-Row.
Robin, Melvin B.
  xRobin.
    Higher Excited States of Polyatomic Molecules.
      Acad Pr.
Robin, P. Ansell. *see* Robin, Percy Ansell.
Robin, Percy Ansell.
  xRobin, P. Ansell.
    Animal Lore in English Literature. Folcroft.
Robin, Richard S.
  xRobin, Richard S.
    ed. Annotated Catalogue of the Papers of
      Charles S. Peirce. U of Mass Pr.
Robin, Suni, 1951-
  xRobin, Suni.
    illus. The Fiddler, the Fire, & the Feast.
      Dawne-Leigh.
Robinet, Harriette.
  xRobinet, Harriette G.
    Ride the Red Cycle. HM.
Robinet, Harriette G. *see* Robinet, Harriette.
Robinett, Betty W. *see* Robinett, Betty Wallace.
Robinett, Betty Wallace.
  xRobinett, Betty W.
    Teaching English to Speakers of Other
      Languages: Substance & Technique. U of
      Minn Pr.
Robinette, Gary O.
  xRobinette, Gary O.
    Parking Lot Landscape Development. Environ
      Des VA.
Robinette, Margaret A., 1932-
  xRobinette, Margaret A.
    Outdoor Sculpture: Object & Environment.
      Watson-Guptill.
Robins, Denise.
  xRobins, Denise.
    Dance in the Dust. Avon.
    Desert Rapture. Avon.
    Give Me Back My Heart. Avon.
    I, Too, Have Loved. Avon.
    Love Me No More. Avon.
    Meet Me in Monte Carlo. Avon.
    The Uncertain Heart. Avon.
Robins, E. *see* Robins, Elizabeth.
Robins, Elizabeth, 1862-1952
  xRobins, E.
    Ibsen & the Actress. Haskell.
  xRobins, Elizabeth.
    Ancilla's Share: An Indictment of Sex
      Antagonism. Hyperion-Conn.
Robins, Eric.
  xRobins, Eric.
    Ebony Ark: Black Africa's Battle to Save Its
      Wild Life. Taplinger.
Robins, Lee N.
  xRobins, Lee N.
    ed. The Social Consequences of Psychiatric
      Illness. Brunner-Mazel.
Robins, Madeleine.
  xRobins, Madeleine.
    Althea. Fawcett.
Robins, R. H. *see* Robins, Robert Henry.
Robins, R. S. *see* Robins, Robert S.

Robins, Robert Henry.
  xRobins, R. H.
    General Linguistics: An Introductory Survey.
      Longman.
    A Short History of Linguistics. Longman.
Robins, Robert S.
  xRobins, R. S.
    Psychopathology & Political Leadership. Tulane
      Stud Pol.
Robinson, A. *see* Robinson, Abraham.
Robinson, A. R.
  xRobinson, A. R.
    Theodor Fontane: An Introduction to the Man
      & His Work. Verry.
Robinson, Abraham, 1918-1974
  xRobinson, A.
    Complete Theories. Elsevier.
Robinson, Adjai.
  xRobinson, Adjai.
    Three African Tales. Putnam.
Robinson, Albert G. *see* Robinson, Albert Gardner.
Robinson, Albert Gardner, 1855-1932
  xRobinson, Albert G.
    Cuba, Old & New. Negro U Pr.
Robinson, Alice. *see* Robinson, Alice M.
Robinson, Alice M.
  xRobinson, Alice.
    Your Future in Nursing Careers. Arco.
    Your Future in Nursing Careers. Rosen Pr.
Robinson, Anthony.
  xRobinson, Anthony.
    Easy Way. S&S.
Robinson, Arthur.
  xRobinson, Arthur.
    ed. Sex Chromosome Aneuploidy: Prospective
      Studies on Children. A R Liss.
Robinson, Arthur E. *see* Robinson, Arthur Elsworth.
Robinson, Arthur Elsworth, 1881-
  xRobinson, Arthur E.
    The Professional Education of Elementary
      Teachers in the Field of Arithmetic. AMS Pr.
Robinson, Arthur H. *see* Robinson, Arthur Howard.
Robinson, Arthur Howard, 1915-
  xRobinson, Arthur H.
    Look of Maps: An Examination of
      Cartographic Design. U of Wis Pr.
    The Nature of Maps: Essays Toward
      Understanding Maps & Mapping. U of
      Chicago Pr.
Robinson, B. W. *see* Robinson, Basil William.
Robinson, Barbara.
  xRobinson, Barbara.
    The Best Christmas Pageant Ever. Avon.
    The Best Christmas Pageant Ever. Avon.
    The Best Christmas Pageant Ever. Har-Row.
Robinson, Barry.
  xRobinson, Barry.
    On the Beat: Policemen at Work. HarBraceJ.
Robinson, Basil William.
  xRobinson, B. W.
    The Arts of the Japanese Sword. Merrimack
      Bk Serv.
Robinson, Charles A. *see* Robinson, Charles Alexander.
Robinson, Charles Alexander, 1900-
  xRobinson, Charles A.
    Athens in the Age of Pericles. U of Okla Pr.
    First Book of Ancient Rome. Watts.
    History of Alexander the Great. Kraus Repr.
Robinson, Charles E. *see* Robinson, Charles Edson.
Robinson, Charles Edson, 1836-1925
  xRobinson, Charles E.
    A Concise History of the United Society of
      Believers Called Shakers. Hyperion Conn.
Robinson, Charles H. *see* Robinson, Charles Henry.
Robinson, Charles Henry, 1861-1925
  xRobinson, Charles H.
    Nigeria, Our Latest Protectorate. Negro U Pr.
Robinson, Charles M. *see* Robinson, Charles Mulford.
Robinson, Charles Mulford, 1869-1917
  xRobinson, Charles M.

    Modern Civic Art: Or, the City Made
      Beautiful. Arno.
Robinson, Christopher.
  xRobinson, Christopher.
    Lucian & His Influence in Europe. U of NC
      Pr.
Robinson, Corinne H. *see* Robinson, Corinne Hogden.
Robinson, Corinne Hogden.
  xRobinson, Corinne H.
    Fundamentals of Normal Nutrition. Macmillan.
  xRobinson, Corrine H.
    Basic Nutrition & Diet Therapy. Macmillan.
Robinson, Corrine H. *see* Robinson, Corinne Hogden.
Robinson, Cyril E. *see* Robinson, Cyril Edward.
Robinson, Cyril Edward, 1884-
  xRobinson, Cyril E.
    Everyday Life in Ancient Greece. AMS Pr.
    Everyday Life in Ancient Greece. Greenwood.
Robinson, D. J. *see* Robinson, Derek John Scott.
Robinson, Daniel N., 1937-
  xRobinson, Daniel N.
    Enlightened Machine: An Analytical
      Introduction to Neuropsychology. Columbia
      U Pr.
Robinson, Daniel S. *see* Robinson, Daniel Sommer.
Robinson, Daniel Sommer, 1888-
  xRobinson, Daniel S.
    ed. The Story of Scottish Philosophy: A
      Compendium of Selections from the Writings
      of Nine Pre-Eminent Scottish Philosophers,
      with Biobibliographical Essays. Greenwood.
Robinson, David, 1941-
  xRobinson, David.
    From Drinking to Alcoholism: A Sociological
      Commentary. Wiley.
    Gerbils. Arco.
    The History of World Cinema. Stein & Day.
    Reflections. HR&W
Robinson, David. *see* Robinson, David Wallace.
Robinson, David A. *see* Robinson, David Alexander.
Robinson, David Alexander, 1909-
  xRobinson, David A.
    Accounts Receivable & Inventory Lending:
      How to Establish & Operate a Department.
      Bankers.
Robinson, David M. *see* Robinson, David Moore.
Robinson, David Moore.
  xRobinson, David M.
    A Study of the Greek Love Names. AMS Pr.
    A Study of the Greek Love-Names. Arno.
Robinson, David Wallace.
  xRobinson, David.
    Sources of the African Past. Holmes & Meier.
Robinson, Derek, 1932 (apr. 12)-
  xRobinson, Derek.
    The Eldorado Network. Norton.
Robinson, Derek John Scott.
  xRobinson, D. J.
    Finiteness Conditions & Generalized Soluble
      Groups. Springer-Verlag.
Robinson, Donald. *see* Robinson, Donald L.
Robinson, Donald L., 1936-
  xRobinson, Donald.
    Slavery in the Structure of American Politics,
      1765-1820. Norton.
Robinson, Dorothy. *see* Robinson, Dorothy W.
Robinson, Dorothy R. *see* Robinson, Dorothy Redus.
Robinson, Dorothy Redus.
  xRobinson, Dorothy R.
    The Bell Rings at Four: A Black Teacher's
      Chronicle of Change. Madrona Pr.
Robinson, Dorothy W.
  xRobinson, Dorothy.
    The Legend of Africania. Johnson Chi.
Robinson, Douglas H. *see* Robinson, Douglas Hill.
Robinson, Douglas Hill, 1918-
  xRobinson, Douglas H.
    Giants in the Sky: A History of the Rigid
      Airship. U of Wash Pr.
Robinson, E. A. *see* Robinson, Edward Austin George.

Robinson, E. John, 1932-
  xRobinson, E. John.
    Master Class in Seascape Painting.
    Watson-Guptill.
Robinson, Edgar E. see Robinson, Edgar Eugene.
Robinson, Edgar Eugene, 1887-
  xRobinson, Edgar E.
    Presidential Vote, 1896-1932. Octagon.
    They Voted for Roosevelt: The Presidential
    Vote, 1932-1944. Octagon.
Robinson, Edward, 1897-
  xRobinson, Edward.
    Lawrence - the Story of His Life. R West.
    Lawrence the Rebel. Folcroft.
    Lawrence, the Story of His Life. Norwood
    Edns.
Robinson, Edward Austin George.
  xRobinson, E. A.
    ed. The Economic Development of Bangladesh
    Within a Socialist Framework: Proceedings of
    a Conference Held by the International
    Economic Association at Daca. Halsted Pr.
Robinson, Edward J.
  xRobinson, Edward J.
    Public Relations & Survey Research: Achieving
    Organizational Goals in a Communication
    Context. Irvington.
Robinson, Edwin A. see Robinson, Edwin Arlington.
Robinson, Edwin Arlington, 1869-1935
  xRobinson, Edwin A.
    The Children of the Night. Gordon Pr.
    Edwin Arlington Robinson's Letters to Edith
    Brower. Harvard U Pr.
    Selected Letters of Edwin Arlington Robinson.
    Greenwood.
    Van Zorn: A Comedy in Three Acts. AMS Pr.
Robinson, Enders A.
  xRobinson, Enders A.
    Geophysical Signal Analysis. P-H.
    Introduction to Infinitely Many Variates.
    Hafner.
    Multichannel Time Series Analysis with Digital
    Computer Programs. Holden-Day.
    Random Wavelets & Cybernetic Systems.
    Hafner.
Robinson, Francis, 1910-
  xRobinson, Francis.
    Celebration: The Metropolitan Opera.
    Doubleday.
Robinson, Francis P. see Robinson, Francis Pleasant.
Robinson, Francis Pleasant, 1906-
  xRobinson, Francis P.
    Effective Study. Har-Row.
Robinson, Frank M.
  xRobinson, Frank M.
    The Power. Berkley Pub.
Robinson, Franklin W. see Robinson, Franklin Westcott.
Robinson, Franklin Westcott.
  xRobinson, Franklin W.
    ed. The Meaning of Mannerism. U Pr of New
    England.
Robinson, Fred C.
  xRobinson, Fred C.
    Old English Literature: A Select Bibliography.
    U of Toronto Pr.
Robinson, Frederick W. see Robinson, Frederick William.
Robinson, Frederick William, 1830-1901
  xRobinson, Frederick W.
    Church & Chapel, 1863. Garland Pub.
    No Church. Garland Pub.
Robinson, G. W. see Robinson, G. W. S.
Robinson, G. W. S.
  xRobinson, G. W.
    Guernsey. David & Charles.
Robinson, George L. see Robinson, George Livingstone.
Robinson, George Livingstone, 1864-
  xRobinson, George L.
    Twelve Minor Prophets. Baker Bk.
Robinson, Gertrude.
  xRobinson, Gertrude.

    David Urquhart: Some Chapters in the Life of
    a Victorian Knight Errant of Justice &
    Liberty. Kelley.
Robinson, Gilmer G. see Robinson, Gilmer George.
Robinson, Gilmer George.
  xRobinson, Gilmer G.
    The Basic Guide to Fly Fishing. A S Barnes.
Robinson, Glen O.
  xRobinson, Glen O.
    The Administrative Process. West Pub.
Robinson, H. Alan.
  xRobinson, H. Alan.
    ed. Fusing Reading Skills & Content. Intl
    Reading.
    ed. Reading & Writing Instruction in the
    United States: Historical Trends. Intl
    Reading.
    Teaching Reading & Study Strategies: The
    Content Areas. Allyn.
Robinson, H. Russell.
  xRobinson, H. Russell.
    The Armour of Imperial Rome. Scribner.
Robinson, H. Wheeler. see Robinson, Henry Wheeler.
Robinson, Harry M. see Robinson, Harry Maximillan.
Robinson, Harry Maximillan.
  xRobinson, Harry M.
    A Dictionary of Dermatologic Therapy. Yorke
    Med.
Robinson, Henry C. see Robinson, Henry Crabb.
Robinson, Henry Crabb.
  xRobinson, Henry C.
    Diary, Reminiscences, & Correspondence of
    Henry Crabb Robinson. AMS Pr.
Robinson, Henry M. see Robinson, Henry Morton.
Robinson, Henry Morton.
  xRobinson, Henry M.
    The Cardinal. PB.
Robinson, Henry P. see Robinson, Henry Peach.
Robinson, Henry Peach.
  xRobinson, Henry P.
    The Art & Practice of Silver Printing. Arno.
    Letters on Landscape Photography. Arno.
Robinson, Henry W. see Robinson, Henry Wheeler.
Robinson, Henry Wheeler, 1872-1945
  xRobinson, H. Wheeler.
    Corporate Personality in Ancient Israel.
    Fortress.
  xRobinson, Henry W.
    Inspiration & Revelation in the Old Testament.
    Greenwood.
Robinson, Herbert S. see Robinson, Herbert Spencer.
Robinson, Herbert Spencer.
  xRobinson, Herbert S.
    The Dictionary of Biography. Littlefield.
    Dictionary of Biography. Peter Smith.
    The Dictionary of Biography. Rowman.
Robinson, Hilary.
  xRobinson, Hilary.
    Somerville & Ross: A Critical Appreciation. St
    Martin.
Robinson, Ian.
  xRobinson, Ian.
    Chaucer & the English Tradition. Cambridge U
    Pr.
  xRobinson, Ian S.
    Authority & Resistance in the Investiture
    Contest. Holmes & Meier.
Robinson, Ian S. see Robinson, Ian.
Robinson, J. see Robinson, John.
Robinson, J. A.
  xRobinson, J. A.
    Looking at Language. Routledge & Kegan.
Robinson, J. Armitage. see Robinson, Joseph Armitage.
Robinson, J. E. see Robinson, James.
Robinson, J. Hedley.
  xRobinson, J. Hedley.

    Astronomy Data Book. David & Charles.
    Astronomy Data Book. Halsted Pr.
    Using the Telescope: A Handbook for
    Astronomers. Halsted Pr.
Robinson, J. Lewis. see Robinson, John Lewis.
Robinson, J. Lister.
  xRobinson, J. Lister.
    Mechanics of Materials. Krieger.
Robinson, J. S., 1936-
  xRobinson, J. S.
    Corrosion Inhibitors: Recent Developments.
    Noyes.
    ed. Fiber-Forming Polymers: Recent Advances.
    Noyes.
Robinson, Jacob, 1889-
  xRobinson, Jacob.
    Palestine & the United Nations: Prelude to
    Solution. Greenwood.
Robinson, Jacob S.
  xRobinson, Jacob S.
    A Journal of the Santa Fe Expedition Under
    Colonel Doniphan. Da Capo.
Robinson, James, 1938-
  xRobinson, J. E.
    Fundamentals for Mathematics: A Foundation
    for Decisions. A-W.
Robinson, James H. see Robinson, James Harvey.
Robinson, James Harvey, 1863-1936
  xRobinson, James H.
    Humanizing of Knowledge. Arno.
Robinson, James M. see Robinson, James Mcconkey.
Robinson, James Mcconkey.
  xRobinson, James M.
    ed. The Later Heidegger & Theology.
    Greenwood.
    Problem of History in Mark. Allenson.
Robinson, James W., 1923-
  xRobinson, James W.
    Atomic Absorption Spectroscopy. Dekker.
Robinson, James W. see Robinson, James William.
Robinson, James William.
  xRobinson, James W.
    ed. Introduction to Labor. P-H.
Robinson, Jan. see Robinson, Jan M.
Robinson, Jan M.
  xRobinson, Jan.
    The Story of WARPLE. Aurora Pubs.
Robinson, Jay.
  xRobinson, Jay.
    The Comeback. Chosen Bks Pub.
Robinson, Jean. see Robinson, Jean O.
Robinson, Jean O.
  xRobinson, Jean.
    Strange but Wonderful Cosmic Awareness of
    Duffy Moon. HM.
    The Strange but Wonderful Cosmic Awareness
    of Duffy Moon. Dell.
Robinson, Jerry.
  xRobinson, Jerry.
    Skippy & Percy Crosby. HR&W.
Robinson, Jill, 1936-
  xRobinson, Jill.
    Perdido. Knopf.
    Perdido. PB.
Robinson, Joan, 1903-
  xRobinson, J.
    Intro. by Accumulation of Capital. Monthly
    Rev.
  xRobinson, Joan.

Accumulation of Capital. St Martin.
An American Legal Almanac: Law in All
   States Summary & Update. Oceana.
Aspects of Development & Underdevelopment.
   Cambridge U Pr.
Economic Heresies: Some Old-Fashioned
   Questions in Economic Theory. Basic.
The Generalisation of the General Theory &
   Other Essays. St Martin.
An Introduction to Modern Economics.
   McGraw.
Robinson, Joan. see Robinson, Joan G.
Robinson, Joan G.
   xRobinson, Joan.
   The Dark House of the Sea Witch. Coward.
Robinson, John, 1909-
   xRobinson, J.
   Highways & Our Environment. McGraw.
   Integrated Theory of Finite Element Methods.
      Wiley.
Robinson, John. see Robinson, John W.
Robinson, John A. see Robinson, John Arthur Thomas.
Robinson, John Arthur Thomas, Bp, 1919-
   xRobinson, John A.
   Can We Trust the New Testament?. Eerdmans.
   Exploration into God. Stanford U Pr.
   Honest to God. Westminster.
   The Human Face of God. Westminster.
   Jesus & His Coming. Westminster.
   Truth Is Two-Eyed. Westminster.
   Wrestling with Romans. Westminster.
Robinson, John B. see Robinson, John Beverly.
Robinson, John Beverly, Sir Bart, 1791-1863
   xRobinson, John B.
   Canada, & the Canada Bill. Johnson Repr.
Robinson, John L. see Robinson, John Lewis.
Robinson, John Lewis.
   xRobinson, J. Lewis.
   ed. British Columbia. U of Toronto Pr.
   xRobinson, John L.
   Geography of Canada. Greenwood.
Robinson, John P.
   xRobinson, John.
   How Americans Use Time: A
      Social-Psychological Analysis of Everyday
      Behavior. Praeger.
   xRobinson, John P.
   How Americans Used Time in 1965. Univ
      Microfilms.
Robinson, John R. see Robinson, John Robert.
Robinson, John Robert, 1850-1910
   xRobinson, John R.
   The Last Earls of Barrymore, 1769-1824. Arno.
Robinson, John T.
   xRobinson, John T.
   Early Hominid Posture & Locomotion. U of
      Chicago Pr.
Robinson, John W.
   xRobinson, John.
   Camping & Climbing in Baja. La Siesta.
   Los Angeles in Civil War Days. Dawsons.
Robinson, Joseph Armitage, 1858-1933
   xRobinson, J. Armitage.
   Commentary on Ephesians. Kregel.
Robinson, Julian.
   xRobinson, Julian.
   Instant Dress Making: The Three-in-One
      Guide. Transatlantic.
Robinson, Keith.
   xRobinson, Keith.
   ed. Extending Economics Within the
      Curriculum. Routledge & Kegan.
Robinson, Leonard. see Robinson, Leonard A.
Robinson, Leonard A.
   xRobinson, Leonard.
   Light at the Tunnel End. McClain.
Robinson, Lisa.
   xRobinson, Lisa.

Psychiatric Nursing As a Human Experience.
   Saunders.
Psychological Aspects of the Care of
   Hospitalized Patients. Davis Co.
Robinson, Lois.
   xRobinson, Lois.
   Guided Writing & Free Writing: A Text in
      Composition for English As a Second
      Language. Har-Row.
Robinson, Louie.
   xRobinson, Louis.
   Arthur Ashe, Tennis Champion. Doubleday.
Robinson, Louis. see Robinson, Louie.
Robinson, Louis N. see Robinson, Louis Newton.
Robinson, Louis Newton, 1880-
   xRobinson, Louis N.
   History & Organization of Criminal Statistics
      in the United States. Patterson Smith.
Robinson, Luther E. see Robinson, Luther Emerson.
Robinson, Luther Emerson, 1867-
   xRobinson, Luther E.
   Abraham Lincoln As a Man of Letters.
      Folcroft.
Robinson, M. see Robinson, Marguerite S.
Robinson, M. J. see Robinson, Maxwell James.
Robinson, Margaret. see Robinson, Margaret E.
Robinson, Margaret E.
   xRobinson, Margaret.
   Schools & Social Work. Routledge & Kegan.
Robinson, Marguerite S.
   xRobinson, M.
   Political Structure in a Changing Sinhalese
      Village. Cambridge U Pr.
Robinson, Marie (Nyswander).
   xRobinson, Marie N.
   Power of Sexual Surrender. NAL.
Robinson, Marie N. see Robinson, Marie (Nyswander).
Robinson, Maxwell James.
   xRobinson, M. J.
   Paediatric Problems in Tropical Countries.
      Churchill.
Robinson, Michael C.
   xRobinson, Michael C.
   Water for the West: The Bureau of
      Reclamation, 1902-1977. Am Public Works.
Robinson, Nancy K.
   xRobinson, Nancy K.
   Wendy & the Bullies. Hastings.
Robinson, Nancy M.
   xRobinson, Nancy M.
   A World of Children: Daycare & Preschool
      Institutions. Brooks-Cole.
Robinson, Neil.
   xRobinson, Neil.
   Lion of Scotland. Intl Pubns Serv.
Robinson, Nicholas A.
   xRobinson, Nicholas A.
   Historic Preservation Law. PLI.
Robinson, O. Preston.
   xRobinson, O. Preston.
   Christ's Eternal Gospel: Do the Dead Sea
      Scrolls, the Pseudepigrapha, & Other Ancient
      Records Challenge or Support the Bible?.
      Deseret Bk.
Robinson, P. G. see Robinson, Peter G.
Robinson, Paul W., 1942-
   xRobinson, Paul W.
   Fundamentals of Experimental Psychology: A
      Comparative Approach. P-H.
Robinson, Pauline C.
   xRobinson, Pauline C.
   ESP (English for Specific Purposes): The
      Present Position. Pergamon.
Robinson, Peggy.
   xRobinson, Peggy.
   The Portland Walkbook. P Robinson.
   The Portland Walkbook. Victoria Hse.
Robinson, Percy, 1863-
   xRobinson, Percy.

Handel & His Orbit. Da Capo.
Robinson, Peter. see Robinson, William Peter.
Robinson, Peter G., 1935-
   xRobinson, P. G.
   Marine Engineer's Guide to Fluid Flow.
      Cornell Maritime.
Robinson, Peter M.
   xRobinson, Peter M.
   Practical Fungal Physiology. Wiley.
Robinson, Peter S.
   xRobinson, Peter S.
   ed. Foundation Guide for Religious Grant
      Seekers. Scholars Pr Ca.
Robinson, R. A. see Robinson, Raoul A.
Robinson, Raoul A., 1928-
   xRobinson, R. A.
   Plant Pathosystems. Springer-Verlag.
Robinson, Ray, Dec. 4, 1930-
   xRobinson, Ray.
   Greatest World Series Thrillers. Random.
Robinson, Ray. see Robinson, Ray V. F.
Robinson, Ray V. F.
   xRobinson, Ray.
   Housing Economics & Public Policy. Holmes &
      Meier.
Robinson, Richard.
   xRobinson, Richard.
   An Atheist's Values. Biblio Dist.
   Definition. Oxford U Pr.
Robinson, Richard A. see Robinson, Richard Alan
   Hodgson.
Robinson, Richard Alan Hodgson.
   xRobinson, Richard A.
   The Origins of Franco's Spain: The Right, the
      Republic & Revolution, 1931-1936. U of
      Pittsburgh Pr.
Robinson, Richard H., 1926-
   xRobinson, Richard H.
   ed. Chinese Buddhist Verse. Greenwood.
Robinson, Robert L.
   xRobinson, Robert L.
   Complete Course in Professional Locksmithing.
      Nelson-Hall.
   How to Burglar-Proof Your Home.
      Nelson-Hall.
Robinson, Roland. see Robinson, Roland I.
Robinson, Roland I.
   xRobinson, Roland.
   Financial Markets: The Accumulation &
      Allocation of Wealth. McGraw.
   xRobinson, Roland I.
   Financial Markets: The Accumulation &
      Allocation of Wealth. McGraw.
Robinson, Romney, 1913-
   xRobinson, Romney.
   Edward H. Chamberlin. Columbia U Pr.
Robinson, Rowland E. see Robinson, Rowland Evans.
Robinson, Rowland Evans, 1833-1900
   xRobinson, Rowland E.
   Uncle Lisha's Shop. Irvington.
Robinson, Roy.
   xRobinson, Roy.
   Genetics for Cat Breeders. Pergamon.
Robinson, Russell D.
   xRobinson, Russell D.
   Group Dynamics for Student Activities. Natl
      Assn Principals.
Robinson, Samuel A.
   xRobinson, Samuel A.
   ed. Beyond Identity: Education & the Future
      Role of Black Americans, a Book of
      Readings. Univ Microfilms.
Robinson, Sharon, 1938-
   xRobinson, Sharon.
   Contemporary Basketry. Davis Mass.
Robinson, Sol.
   xRobinson, Sol.
   Guidelines for News Reporters. TAB Bks.
Robinson, Spider.
   xRobinson, Spider.

Roche, George Charles.
  xRoche, G.
    The Balancing Act: Quota Hiring in Higher
      Education. Open Court.
  xRoche, George C.
    Education in America. Foun Econ Ed.
Roche, Jerome.
  xRoche, Jerome.
    Palestrina. Oxford U Pr.
Roche, John F. see Roche, John Francis.
Roche, John Francis, 1925-
  xRoche, John F.
    Joseph Reed: A Moderate in the American
      Revolution. AMS Pr.
Roche, Mazo. see De La Roche, Mazo.
Roche, Mazo De La. see De La Roche, Mazo.
Roche, P. K. see Roche, Patricia K.
Roche, Patricia K.
  xRoche, P. K.
    Dollhouse Magic: How to Make & Find Simple
      Dollhouse Furniture. Dial.
    Dollhouse Magic: How to Make & Find Simple
      Dollhouse Furniture. Dial.
    illus. Good-Bye, Arnold. Dial.
Roche, Regina M. see Roche, Regina Maria Dalton.
Roche, Regina Maria Dalton, 1764?-1845
  xRoche, Regina M.
    Nocturnal Visit: A Tale. Arno.
Roche De Coppens, Peter.
  xRoche De Coppens, Peter.
    The Spiritual Perspective: Key Issues &
      Themes Interpreted from the Standpoint of
      Spiritual Consciousness. U Pr of Amer.
Rocher, Gregory De.
  xRocher, Gregory De.
    ed. Rabelais's Laughers & Joubert's Traite du
      Ris. U of Ala Pr.
Rochester, C. H. see Rochester, Colin H.
Rochester, Colin H.
  xRochester, C. H.
    Acidity Functions. Acad Pr.
Rochester Conference on Superconductivity in D- and
  F-Band Metals, 1976.
  xAIP Conference, Univ. of Rochester, 1971.
    Superconductivity in D- & F- Band Metals:
      Proceedings. Am Inst Physics.
Rochester, Devereaux.
  xRochester, Devereaux.
    Full Moon to France. Har-Row.
Rochester Folk Art Guild.
  xRochester Folk Art Guild.
    More Simple Dishes. Rochester Folk Art.
Rochester, S. R. see Rochester, Sherry.
Rochester, Sherry.
  xRochester, S. R.
    Crazy Talk: A Study of Discourse of
      Schizophrenic Speakers. Plenum Pub.
Rochlin, Gene I.
  xRochlin, Gene I.
    Plutonium, Power, & Politics: International
      Arrangements for the Disposition of Spent
      Nuclear Fuel. U of Cal Pr.
Rock, David.
  xRock, David.
    ed. Argentina in the Twentieth Century. U of
      Pittsburgh Pr.
Rock, Gail.
  xRock, Gail.
    Addie & the King of Hearts. Bantam.
    Addie & the King of Hearts. Knopf.
    A Dream for Addie. Bantam.
    A Dream for Addie. Knopf.
    The House Without a Christmas Tree. Knopf.
    The House Without a Christmas Tree. Bantam.
    The Thanksgiving Treasure. Knopf.
    The Thanksgiving Treasure. Bantam.
Rock, Howard B., 1944-
  xRock, Howard B.
    Artisans of the New Republic: Tradesmen of
      New York City in the Age of Jefferson. NYU
      Pr.
Rock, Irvin.
  xRock, Irvin.
    An Introduction to Perception. Macmillan.
    Orientation & Form. Acad Pr.
Rock, James M.
  xRock, James M.
    ed. Money, Banking & Macroeconomics: A
      Guide to Information Sources. Gale.
Rock Mechanics Symposium. see Rock Mechanics
  Symposium, Detroit, 1973.
Rock Mechanics Symposium, Detroit, 1973.
  xRock Mechanics Symposium.
    Proceedings: AMD. ASME.
Rock, Paul. see Rock, Paul Elliott.
Rock, Paul Elliott.
  xRock, Paul.
    The Making of Symbolic Interactionism.
      Rowman.
Rock, Philip. see Rock, Phillip.
Rock, Phillip, 1927-
  xRock, Phillip.
    The Passing Bells. Dell.
  xRock, Phillip.
    The Passing Bells. Seaview Bks.
Rock, Robert T. see Rock, Robert Thomas.
Rock, Robert Thomas, 1903-
  xRock, Robert T.
    The Influence Upon Learning of the
      Quantitative Variation of After-Effects. AMS
      Pr.
Rock, Ronald. see Rock, Ronald S.
Rock, Ronald S.
  xRock, Ronald.
    Hospitalization & Discharge of the Mentally
      Ill. U of Chicago Pr.
Rock, Sidney.
  xRock, Sidney.
    Career Mathematics: Practical Applications for
      Nonmechanical & Business Occupations.
      Hayden.
Rock, William R.
  xRock, William R.
    British Appeasement in the 1930's. Norton.
Rockefeller Brothers Foundation. see Rockefeller
  Foundation.
Rockefeller, Edwin S.
  xRockefeller, Edwin S.
    Antitrust Questions & Answers. BNA.
    Desk Book of FTC Practice & Procedure. PLI.
Rockefeller Foundation.
  xRockefeller Brothers Foundation.
    The Use of Land. T Y Crowell.
Rockefeller, John D. see Rockefeller, John Davison.
Rockefeller, John Davison, 1839-1937
  xRockefeller, John D.
    Random Reminiscences of Men & Events.
      Arno.
Rockefeller, Nelson A. see Rockefeller, Nelson Aldrich.
Rockefeller, Nelson Aldrich, 1908-
  xRockefeller, Nelson A.
    Future of Federalism. Atheneum.
    Future of Federalism. Harvard U Pr.
Rockefeller University, New York.
  xThe Rockefeller University & State University of
    New York, Nov. 26-27, 1965.
    The Future of Biology. State U NY Pr.
Rocker, Rudolf, 1873-1958
  xRocker, Rudolf.
    Nationalism & Culture. M E Coughlin.
    Nationalism & Culture. Revisionist Pr.
Rockland, C. see Rockland, Charles.
Rockland, Charles, 1947-
  xRockland, C.
    Hypoellipticity & Eigenvalue Asymptotics.
      Springer-Verlag.
Rockland, Mae S. see Rockland, Mae Shafter.

Rockland, Mae Shafter.
  xRockland, Mae S.
    The Work of Our Hands: Jewish Needlecraft
      for Today. Schocken.
Rockley, Alicia A. see Rockley, Alicia Margaret
  (Tyssen-Amherst) Cecil.
Rockley, Alicia Margaret (Tyssen-Amherst) Cecil,
  Baroness, d. 1941
  xRockley, Alicia A.
    History of Gardening in England. Gale.
Rockman, Bert A.
  xRockman, Bert A.
    Studying Elite Political Culture: Problems in
      Design & Interpretation. U Ctr Intl St.
Rockmore, Renee.
  xRockmore, Renee.
    The Carpet Garden. T Y Crowell.
  xRockmore, Steve.
    jt. auth. The Carpet Garden. T Y Crowell.
Rockmore, Steve. see Rockmore, Renee.
Rockness, Miriam H. see Rockness, Miriam Huffman.
Rockness, Miriam Huffman, 1944-
  xRockness, Miriam H.
    Keep These Things, Ponder Them in Your
      Heart: Reflections of a Mother. Abingdon.
    Keep These Things, Ponder Them in Your
      Heart: Reflections of a Mother. Doubleday.
Rockoff, Hugh.
  xRockoff, Hugh.
    The Free Banking Era: A Re-Examination.
      Arno.
Rocks, Lawrence.
  xRocks, Lawrence E.
    The Energy Crisis. Crown.
Rocks, Lawrence E. see Rocks, Lawrence.
Rockstein, Morris.
  xRockstein, Morris.
    ed. Biochemistry of Insects. Acad Pr.
Rockstro, William S. see Rockstro, William Smyth.
Rockstro, William Smyth, 1823-1895
  xRockstro, William S.
    A General History of Music from the Infancy
      of the Greek Drama to the Present Period.
      Longwood Pr.
Rockwell. see Rockwell, Anne F.
Rockwell, Anne. see Rockwell, Anne F.
Rockwell, Anne F.
  xRockwell.
    A Bump in the Night. Schol Bk Serv.
  xRockwell, Anne.
    illus. The Awful Mess. Schol Bk Serv.
    Blackout. Macmillan.
    illus. The Bump in the Night. Greenwillow.
    Buster & the Bogeyman. Schol Bk Serv.
    illus. Games (& How to Play Them). T Y
      Crowell.
    illus. Gift for a Gift. Schol Bk Serv.
    The Girl with a Donkey Tail. Dutton.
    Gogo's Car Breaks Down. Doubleday.
    Gogo's Car Breaks Down. Schol Bk Serv.
    Gogo's Pay Day. Doubleday.
    Gollywhopper Egg. Macmillan.
    The Gollywhopper Egg. Macmillan.
    illus. Henry the Cat & the Big Sneeze.
      Greenwillow.
    illus. Honk Honk!. Dutton.
    I Like the Library. Dutton.
    No More Work. Greenwillow.
    illus. Paul & Arthur & the Little Explorer.
      Schol Bk Serv.
    illus. The Story Snail. Macmillan.
    The Supermarket. Macmillan.
    illus. Tuhurahura & the Whale. Schol Bk Serv.
Rockwell, Charles, Reverend, 1806-1882
  xRockwell, Charles.
    Catskill Mountains & the Region Around.
      Hope Farm.
Rockwell, F. see Rockwell, F. A.
Rockwell, F. A.
  xRockwell, F.

How to Write Nonfiction That Sells. Contemp
Bks.
xRockwell, F. A.
How to Write Plots That Sell. Contemp Bks.
Modern Fiction Techniques. Writer.
Rockwell, F. F. see Rockwell, Frederick Frye.
Rockwell, Frederick Frye.
xRockwell, F. F.
The Complete Book of Bulbs. Lippincott.
Rockwell, George L. see Rockwell, George Lounsbury.
Rockwell, George Lounsbury, 1869-
xRockwell, George L.
History of Ridgefield, Connecticut. Harbor Hill
Bks.
Rockwell, Harlow.
xRockwell, Harlow.
The Compost Heap. Doubleday.
illus. I Did It. Macmillan.
Look at This. Macmillan.
My Dentist. Greenwillow.
illus. My Doctor. Macmillan.
My Kitchen. Greenwillow.
Printmaking. Doubleday.
Rockwell, Jane.
xRockwell, Jane.
Cats & Kittens. Archway.
Cats & Kittens. Watts.
Dogs & Puppies. Archway.
Dogs & Puppies. PB.
Dogs & Puppies. Watts.
Rockwell, Mabel. see Rockwell, Mabel M.
Rockwell, Mabel M.
xRockwell, Mabel.
California's Sea Frontier. McNally.
Rockwell, Molly. see Rockwell, Norman.
Rockwell, Norman.
xRockwell, Norman.
Norman Rockwell: A Sixty-Year Retrospective.
Abrams.
Norman Rockwell's Americana ABC. Dell.
Rockwell, Thomas.
xRockwell, Thomas.
How to Eat Fried Worms. Dell.
How to Eat Fried Worms. Watts.
The Neon Motorcycle. Watts.
The Portmanteau Book. Bantam.
The Portmanteau Book. Little.
The Thief. Dell.
The Thief. Delacorte.
Rockwood, Charles A.
xRockwood, Charles A.
ed. Fractures. Lippincott.
Rockwood, Charles E. see Rockwood, Charles Edward.
Rockwood, Charles Edward, 1932-
xRockwood, Charles E.
National Incomes Policy for Inflation Control.
U Presses Fla.
Rockwood, Joyce.
xRockwood, Joyce.
Enoch's Place. HR&W.
Groundhog's Horse. HR&W.
Long Man's Song. Dell.
Long Man's Song. HR&W.
To Spoil the Sun. Dell.
To Spoil the Sun. HR&W.
Rockwood, Raymond O. see Rockwood, Raymond
Oxley.
Rockwood, Raymond Oxley.
xRockwood, Raymond O.
ed. Carl Becker's Heavenly City Revisited.
Shoe String.
Rocky Mountain Bioengineering Symposium, 12th. see
National Biomedical Sciences Instrumentation
Symposium.
Rocky Mt. Bioengineering Symposium, 13th, &
International ISA Biomedical Sciences Instrumentation

Symposium, 13th May 1976, Laramie, WY. see
National Biomedical Sciences Instrumentation
Symposium.
Rocq, Margaret M. see Rocq, Margaret Miller.
Rocq, Margaret Miller.
xRocq, Margaret M.
ed. California Local History: A Bibliography &
Union List of Library Holdings. Stanford U
Pr.
Rodale, J. I. see Rodale, Jerome Irving.
Rodale, Jerome I. see Rodale, Jerome Irving.
Rodale, Jerome Irving, 1898-
xRodale, J. I.
Complete Book of Minerals for Health. Rodale
Pr Inc.
Synonym Finder. Rodale Pr Inc.
Word Finder. Rodale Pr Inc.
xRodale, Jerome I.
Natural Way to Better Eyesight. BJ Pub
Group.
Rodd, L. C. see Rodd, Lewis Charles.
Rodd, Lewis Charles.
xRodd, L. C.
Compiled by The Australian Essay. Verry.
Rodda, J. C.
xRodda, J. C.
Systematic Hydrology. Butterworths.
xRodda, John C.
Facets of Hydrology. Wiley.
Rodda, John C. see Rodda, J. C.
Roddewig, Richard.
xRoddewig, Richard J.
Green Bans: The Birth of Australian
Environmental Politics. Allanheld.
Roddewig, Richard J. see Roddewig, Richard.
Roddick, Ellen.
xRoddick, Ellen.
Together. PB.
Together. St Martin.
Roddon, G. see Roddon, Guy.
Roddon, Guy.
xRoddon, G.
Pastel Painting Techniques. David & Charles.
xRoddon, Guy.
Pastel Painting Techniques. Larousse.
Roddy, D.
xRoddy, D.
Introduction to Microelectronics. Pergamon.
Roddy, Lee.
xRoddy, Lee.
In Search of Historic Jesus. Bantam.
Rodechko, James P. see Rodechko, James Paul.
Rodechko, James Paul.
xRodechko, James P.
Patrick Ford & His Search for America: A
Case Study of Irish-American Journalism,
1870-1913. Arno.
Rodee, C. see Rodee, Carlton Clymer.
Rodee, Carlton Clymer.
xRodee, C.
Introduction to Political Science. McGraw.
Rodee, Marian E.
xRodee, Marian E.
Southwestern Weaving. U of NM Pr.
Rodefeld, Richard D., 1943-
xRodefeld, Richard D.
Change in Rural America: Causes,
Consequences & Alternatives. Mosby.
Roden, Claudia.
xRoden, Claudia.
Coffee. Merrimack Bk Serv.
Roden, Martin. see Roden, Martin S.
Roden, Martin S.
xRoden, Martin.
Analog & Digital Communication Systems.
P-H.
Roden, Shelly.
xRoden, Shelly.

When Puppets Talk, Everybody Listens. Victor
Bks.
Rodenmayer, Robert L. see Rodenmayer, Robert N. N.
Rodenmayer, Robert N. N.
xRodenmayer, Robert L.
Thanks Be to God. Attic Pr.
Roderus, Frank.
xRoderus, Frank.
Hell Creek Cabin. Doubleday.
Sheepherding Man. Doubleday.
Rodes, John E.
xRodes, John E.
Germany: A History. Krieger.
Rodewald, Cosmo.
xRodewald, Cosmo.
Money in the Age of Tiberius. Rowman.
Rodger, Alan.
xRodger, Alan.
Owners & Neighbours in Roman Law. Oxford
U Pr.
Rodger, L. W. see Rodger, Leslie W.
Rodger, Leslie W.
xRodger, L. W.
Marketing Concepts & Strategies in the Next
Decade. Halsted Pr.
Marketing in a Competitive Economy. Halsted
Pr.
xRodger, Leslie W.
Marketing in a Competitive Economy. Intl
Pubns Serv.
Rodgers, Allan. see Rodgers, Allan L.
Rodgers, Allan L.
xRodgers, Allan.
Economic Development in Retrospect: The
Italian Model & Its Significance for Regional
Planning in Market Oriented Economies.
Halsted Pr.
Rodgers, Andrew D. see Rodgers, Andrew Denny.
Rodgers, Andrew Denny, 1900-
xRodgers, Andrew D.
Liberty Hyde Bailey: A Story of American
Plant Sciences. Hafner.
Rodgers, Audrey T.
xRodgers, Audrey T.
The Universal Drum: Dance Imagery in the
Poetry of Eliot, Crane, Roethke & Williams.
Pa St U Pr.
Rodgers, Bill.
xRodgers, Bill.
Marathoning. S&S.
Rodgers, Bruce.
xRodgers, Bruce.
The Queen's Vernacular: A Gay Lexicon. S&S.
Rodgers, Carolyn. see Rodgers, Carolyn M.
Rodgers, Carolyn M.
xRodgers, Carolyn.
Songs of a Black Bird. Third World.
xRodgers, Carolyn M.
How I Got Ovah: New & Selected Poems.
Doubleday.
Rodgers, Daniel T.
xRodgers, Daniel T.
The Work Ethic in Industrial America:
1850-1920. U of Chicago Pr.
Rodgers, David L. see Rodgers, David Leigh.
Rodgers, David Leigh.
xRodgers, David L.
World Alone. Libra.
Rodgers, Dorothy. see Rodgers, Dorothy F.
Rodgers, Dorothy F., 1909-
xRodgers, Dorothy.
House in My Head. Atheneum.
Rodgers, Edith (Cooperrider), 1893-
xRodgers, Edith C.
Discussion of Holidays in the Later Middle
Ages. AMS Pr.
Rodgers, Edith C. see Rodgers, Edith (Cooperrider).
Rodgers, Frederick A.
xRodgers, Frederick A.

Let's Do Some Cooking. Burgess.
Rodgers, H. J.
xRodgers, H. J.
Twenty-Three Years Under a Skylight; or, Life & Experiences of a Photographer. Arno.
Rodgers, Harrell R.
xRodgers, Harrell R.
Poverty Amid Plenty: A Political & Economic Analysis. A-W.
Rodgers, Joseph L. see Rodgers, Joseph Lee.
Rodgers, Joseph Lee.
xRodgers, Joseph L.
Citizen Committees: A Guide to Their Use in Local Government. Ballinger Pub.
Rodgers, Mary.
xRodgers, Mary.
Freaky Friday. Har-Row.
Freaky Friday. Har-Row.
Freaky Friday. Har-Row.
Rodgers, Pepper.
xRodgers, Pepper.
Installing Football's Wishbone T Attack. P-H.
Rodgers, Peter R. see Rodgers, Peter Rowland.
Rodgers, Peter Rowland.
xRodgers, Peter R.
Rock & Mineral Collecting in Britain. Merrimack Bk Serv.
Rodgers, Richard, 1902-
xRodgers, Richard.
Musical Stages: An Autobiography. Random.
Rodgers, William D.
xRodgers, William D.
Be Thou Pleased to Dwell with Me. Accent Bks.
Cult Sunday. Accent Bks.
Rodgers, William H, 1920-
xRodgers, William H.
Cases & Materials on Energy & Natural Resources Law. West Pub.
Rodgers, William P.
xRodgers, William P.
Introduction to System Safety Engineering. Krieger.
Rodgers-Rose, la Frances.
xRodgers-Rose, La Frances.
ed. The Black Woman. Sage.
Rodin, Alvin E.
xRodin, Alvin E.
The Influence of Matthew Baillie's Morbid Anatomy: Biography, Evaluation & Reprint. C C Thomas.
Rodin, Burt. see Rodin, Burton.
Rodin, Burton.
xRodin, Burt.
Calculus with Analytic Geometry. P-H.
xRodin, R.
Principal Functions. Springer-Verlag.
Rodin, R. see Rodin, Burton.
Rodionov, Dmitrii A. see Rodionov, Dmitrii Alekseevich.
Rodionov, Dmitrii Alekseevich.
xRodionov, Dmitrii A.
Distribution Functions of the Element & Mineral Contents of Igneous Rocks. Plenum Pub.
Roditi, Edouard.
xRoditi, Edouard.
The Delights of Turkey: Twenty Tales. New Directions.
Rodman, F. Robert. see Rodman, Francis Robert.
Rodman, Francis Robert, 1934-
xRodman, F. Robert.
Not Dying. Random.
Rodman, Hyman.
xRodman, Hyman.

Lower-Class Families: The Culture of Poverty in Negro Trinidad. Oxford U Pr.
ed. Marriage, Family & Society: A Reader. Phila Bk Co.
Teaching About Families: Text Book Evaluations & Recommendations for Secondary Schools. Howard Doyle.
Rodman, Julius.
xRodman, Julius Scammon.
The Kahuna Sorcerers of Hawaii, Past & Present: With a Glossary of Ancient Religious Terms & the Books of the Hawaiian Royal Dead. Exposition.
Rodman, Julius Scammon. see Rodman, Julius.
Rodman, Margaret.
xRodman, Margaret.
The Pacification of Melanesia. Univ Microfilms.
Rodman, Morton J.
xRodman, Morton J.
Clinical Pharmacology in Nursing. Lippincott.
Pharmacology & Drug Therapy in Nursing. Lippincott.
Rodman, Selden, 1909-
xRodman, Selden.
Insiders: Rejection & Rediscovery of Man in the Arts of Our Time. La State U Pr.
South America of the Poets. S Ill U Pr.
Rodney, Janet.
xRodney, Janet.
Crystals. North Atlantic.
Rodney, L. S. see Rodney, Lynn Smith.
Rodney, Lynn Smith, 1915-
xRodney, L. S.
Administration of Public Recreation. Wiley.
Rodney, Walter.
xRodney, Walter.
How Europe Underdeveloped Africa. Howard U Pr.
Rodney, William.
xRodney, William.
Soldiers of the International: A History of the Communist Party of Canada, 1919-1929. U of Toronto Pr.
Rodnick, David, 1908-
xRodnick, David.
The Fort Belknap Assiniboine of Montana: A Study in Culture Change. AMS Pr.
Strangled Democracy: Czechoslovakia 1948-1969. Caprock Pr.
Rodowsky, Colby. see Rodowsky, Colby F.
Rodowsky, Colby F.
xRodowsky, Colby.
Evy-Ivy-Over. Watts.
Rodrigues, Jose H. see Rodrigues, Jose Honorio.
Rodrigues, Jose Honorio, 1913-
xRodrigues, Jose H.
Brazil & Africa. U of Cal Pr.
Rodrigues, Raymond J.
xRodrigues, Raymond J.
A Guidebook for Teaching Literature. Allyn.
Rodriguez, Alejandro, 1918-
xRodriguez, Alejandro.
Handbook of Child Abuse & Neglect. Med Exam.
Rodriguez, F. see Rodriguez, Ferdinand.
Rodriguez, Ferdinand, 1928-
xRodriguez, F.
Principles of Polymer Systems. McGraw.
Rodriguez, Louis J.
xRodriguez, Louis J.
The Economics of Education. Prof Educ Pubn.
Rodriguez, Mario, 1922-
xRodriguez, Mario.
The Cadiz Experiment in Central America, 1808-1826. U of Cal Pr.
Rodriguez, Rita M.
xRodriguez, Rita M.

International Financial Management. P-H.
Rodriguez, Roy C.
xRodriguez, Roy D.
Mexican-American Civic Organizations: Political Participation & Political Attitudes. R & E Res Assoc.
Rodriguez, Roy D. see Rodriguez, Roy C.
Rodway, A. E. see Rodway, Allan Edwin.
Rodway, Allan E. see Rodway, Allan Edwin.
Rodway, Allan Edwin.
xRodway, A. E.
ed. Godwin & the Age of Transition. Haskell.
xRodway, Allan E.
Godwin & the Age of Transition. Folcroft.
Rodwell, Peter.
xRodwell, Peter.
Gymnastics: Progressive Practices and Modern Coaching. Emerson.
Rodwin, Lloyd.
xRodwin, Lloyd.
Planning Urban Growth & Regional Development: The Experience of the Guayana Program of Venezuela. MIT Pr.
Rodzinski, Halina.
xRodzinski, Halina.
Our Two Lives. Scribner.
Rodzinski, Witold.
xRodzinski, Witold.
History of China. Pergamon.
Roe, A. K. see Roe, Anne K.
Roe, Anne, 1904-
xRoe, Anne.
The Psychology of Occupations. Arno.
Roe, Anne K.
xRoe, A. K.
Learning Experience Guides for Nursing Students. Wiley.
Roe, Daphne A.
xRoe, Daphne A.
Alcohol & the Diet. AVI.
Clinical Nutrition for the Health Scientist. CRC Pr.
Drug Induced Nutritional Deficiencies. AVI.
Roe, Derek. see Roe, Derek Arthur.
Roe, Derek Arthur.
xRoe, Derek.
Prehistory: An Introduction. U of Cal Pr.
Roe, E. P. see Roe, Edward Payson.
Roe, Edward P. see Roe, Edward Payson.
Roe, Edward Payson, 1838-1888
xRoe, E. P.
Barriers Burned Away. Scholarly.
xRoe, Edward P.
Barriers Burned Away. AMS Pr.
Barriers Burned Away. Irvington.
Roe, Frances M. see Roe, Frances Marie Antoinette Mack.
Roe, Frances Marie Antoinette Mack, Mrs.
xRoe, Frances M.
Army Letters from an Officer's Wife, 1871-1888. Arno.
Roe, Frank G. see Roe, Frank Gilbert.
Roe, Frank Gilbert.
xRoe, Frank G.
The Indian & the Horse. U of Okla Pr.
Roe, Frederic W. see Roe, Frederick William.
Roe, Frederick W. see Roe, Frederick William.
Roe, Frederick William, 1874-
xRoe, Frederic W.
Thomas Carlyle As a Critic of Literature. Octagon.
xRoe, Frederick W.
Thomas Carlyle As a Critic of Literature. Folcroft.
Roe, Herbert C. see Roe, Herbert Charles.
Roe, Herbert Charles, 1873-1923
xRoe, Herbert C.

The Rare Quarto Edition of Lord Byron's
"Fugitive Pieces". Arden Lib.
The Rare Quarto Edition of Lord Byron's
"Fugitive Pieces". Folcroft.
Roe, L. B., 1928-
xRoe, L. B.
Practices & Procedures of Industrial Electrical
Design. McGraw.
Roe, Paul F.
xRoe, Paul F.
Choral Music Education. P-H.
Roe, Peter. *see* Roe, Peter G.
Roe, Peter G.
xRoe, Peter.
A Further Exploration of the Rowe Chavin
Seriation & its Implications for North Central
Coast Chronology. Dumbarton Oaks.
Roe, W. H. *see* Roe, William Henry.
Roe, William H. *see* Roe, William Henry.
Roe, William Henry.
xRoe, W. H.
Principalship. Macmillan.
xRoe, William H.
The Principalship. Macmillan.
Roeber, Richard J. *see* Roeber, Richard J. C.
Roeber, Richard J. C.
xRoeber, Richard J.
The Organization in a Changing Environment.
A-W.
Roebling, Karl.
xRoebling, Karl.
Pentecostals Around the World. Exposition.
Roebuck, Alan D.
xRoebuck, Alan D.
How to Put up Your Own Post-Frame House
& Cabin. TAB Bks.
Roebuck, Carl. *see* Roebuck, Carl Angus.
Roebuck, Carl Angus, 1914-
xRoebuck, Carl.
ed. Muses at Work: Arts, Crafts, & Professions
in Ancient Greece & Rome. MIT Pr.
World of Ancient Times. Scribner.
Roebuck, J. A. *see* Roebuck, John Arthur.
Roebuck, John Arthur.
xRoebuck, J. A.
Engineering Anthropometry Methods. Wiley.
Roebuck, Julian B.
xRoebuck, Julian B.
The Rendezvous: A Case Study of an
After-Hours Club. Free Pr.
Roeck, Alan L.
xRoeck, Alan L.
Twenty-Four Hours a Day for Everyone.
Hazelden.
Roedell, Wendy C. *see* Roedell, Wendy Conklin.
Roedell, Wendy Conklin.
xRoedell, Wendy C.
Gifted Young Children. Tchrs Coll.
Roeder, Kenneth D. *see* Roeder, Kenneth David.
Roeder, Kenneth David, 1908-
xRoeder, Kenneth D.
Nerve Cells and Insect Behavior. Harvard U
Pr.
Roederer, J. G. *see* Roederer, Juan G.
Roederer, Juan G., 1929-
xRoederer, J. G.
Dynamics of Geomagnetically Trapped
Radiation. Springer-Verlag.
Roehm, Marjorie (Catlin).
xRoehm, Marjorie C.
ed. The Letters of George Catlin & His Family:
A Chronicle of the American West. U of Cal
Pr.
Roehm, Marjorie C. *see* Roehm, Marjorie (Catlin).
Roelandt, J. *see* Roelandt, Jos.
Roelandt, Jos.
xRoelandt, J.
Practical Echocardiology. Res Stud Pr.
Roelker, Nancy L. *see* Roelker, Nancy Lyman.

Roelker, Nancy Lyman.
xRoelker, Nancy L.
Queen of Navarre, Jeanne D'Albret,
1528-1572. Harvard U Pr.
Roelofs, Robert. *see* Roelofs, Robert T.
Roelofs, Robert T.
xRoelofs, Robert.
Environment & Society: A Book of Readings
on Environmental Policy, Attitudes & Values.
P-H.
Roels, Oswald A.
xRoels, Oswald A.
ed. Hudson River Colloquium. NY Acad Sci.
Roemer, Kenneth. *see* Roemer, Kenneth M.
Roemer, Kenneth M., 1945-
xRoemer, Kenneth.
The Obsolete Necessity: America in Utopian
Writings, 1888-1900. Kent St U Pr.
xRoemer, Kenneth M.
ed. America As Utopia: Collected Essays. B
Franklin.
Roemer, Michael.
xRoemer, Michael.
The Appraisal of Development Projects: A
Practical Guide to Project Analysis with Case
Studies & Solutions. Praeger.
Fishing for Growth: Export-led Development
in Peru, 1950-1967. Harvard U Pr.
Roemer, Milton I. *see* Roemer, Milton Irwin.
Roemer, Milton Irwin, 1916-
xRoemer, Milton I.
Systems of Health Care. Springer Pub.
Roemer, Theodore, Father, 1889-
xRoemer, Theodore.
The Ludwig-Missionsverein & the Church in
the United States (1838-1918). AMS Pr.
Roen, Samuel.
xRoen, Samuel.
Murder of a Little Girl. Chateau Pub.
Roenigk, Henry H.
xRoenigk, Henry H.
Leg Ulcers: Medical & Surgical Management.
Har-Row.
Roepke, Howard G.
xRoepke, Howard G.
Readings in Economic Geography. Wiley.
Roes, Carol.
xRoes, Carol.
Children's Hulas from Hawaii. M Loke.
Roesch, Roberta.
xRoesch, Roberta.
There's Always a Right Job for Every Woman.
Berkley Pub.
Roesel, Catherine E.
xRoesel, Catherine E.
Immunology: A Self-Instructional Approach.
McGraw.
Roeseler, W. G.
xRoeseler, W. G.
Alternative Goals of Urbanization for America.
EMR Pubns.
General Policies & Principles for Prototype
Zoning Ordinances & Related Measures.
EMR Pubns.
Roessler, R. *see* Roessler, Richard.
Roessler, Richard.
xRoessler, R.
Psychosocial Adjustment to Disability. Univ
Park.
Roethke, Theodore, 1908-1963
xRoethke, Theodore.
Collected Poems. Doubleday.
Far Field. Doubleday.
Roetter, Charles.
xRoetter, Charles.
The Art of Psychological Warfare. Stein &
Day.
Roff, Merrill. *see* Roff, Merrill Flagg.
Roff, Merrill Flagg.
xRoff, Merrill.

ed. Life History Research in Psychopathology.
U of Minn Pr.
Rogal, Samuel J.
xRogal, Samuel J.
A Chronological Outline of British Literature.
Greenwood.
Teaching Composition in Senior High School.
Littlefield.
Rogalin, Wilma. *see* Rogalin, Wilma C.
Rogalin, Wilma C.
xRogalin, Wilma.
Women's Guide to Management Positions.
S&S.
Rogers, A. *see* Rogers, Alan.
Rogers, A. Robert, 1927-
xRogers, A. Robert.
The Humanities: A Selective Guide to
Information Sources. Libs Unl.
Rogers, Agnes L. *see* Rogers, Agnes Low.
Rogers, Agnes Low, 1884-1943
xRogers, Agnes L.
Experimental Tests of Mathematical Ability &
Their Prognostic Value. AMS Pr.
Rogers, Alan.
xRogers, A.
ed. Group Projects in Local History. Dawson
Pub.
xRogers, Alan.
ed. From Revolution to Republic: A
Documentary Reader. Schenkman.
Rogers, Andrei.
xRogers, Andrei.
Introduction to Multiregional Mathematical
Demography. Krieger.
Matrix Analysis of Interregional Population
Growth & Distribution. U of Cal Pr.
Matrix Methods in Urban & Regional Analysis.
Holden-Day.
Rogers, Ann.
xRogers, Ann.
The New Cookbook for Poor Poets & Others.
Scribner.
Rogers, Archibald, 1917-
xRogers, Archibald C.
Monticello Fault. Moore Pub Co.
Rogers, Archibald C. *see* Rogers, Archibald.
Rogers, Arthur K. *see* Rogers, Arthur Kenyon.
Rogers, Arthur Kenyon, 1868-1936
xRogers, Arthur K.
Morals in Review. AMS Pr.
Socratic Problem. Russell.
Rogers, Augustus J. *see* Rogers, Augustus James.
Rogers, Augustus James, 1929-
xRogers, Augustus J.
Choice: An Introduction to Economics. P-H.
Rogers, Barbara, 1935-
xRogers, Barbara.
The Doomsday Scroll. Dell.
The Doomsday Scroll. Dodd.
Project Web. Dodd.
White Wealth & Black Poverty: American
Investments in Southern Africa. Greenwood.
Rogers, Bernard, 1893-
xRogers, Bernard.
Art of Orchestration: Principles of Tone Color
in Modern Scoring. Greenwood.
Rogers, Carl. *see* Rogers, Carl Ransom.
Rogers, Carl R. *see* Rogers, Carl Ransom.
Rogers, Carl Ransom, 1902-
xRogers, Carl.
Carl Rogers on Personal Power. Delacorte.
Carl Rogers on Personal Power. Dell.
Freedom to Learn: A View of What Education
Might Become. Merrill.
xRogers, Carl R.

Measuring Personality Adjustment in Children Nine to Thirteen Years of Age. AMS Pr.
Therapist's View of Personal Goals. Pendle Hill.

Rogers, Cyril A.
xRogers, Cyril A.
Racial Themes in Southern Rhodesia: The Attitudes & Behavior of the White Population. Kennikat.

Rogers, Cyril H.
xRogers, Cyril H.
Budgerigars. Palmetto Pub.
Canaries. Arco.
Canaries. Palmetto Pub.
Foreign Birds. Arco.
Foreign Birds. Palmetto Pub.
Parrots. Arco.

Rogers, Dale E. *see* Rogers, Dale Evans.
Rogers, Dale Evans.
xRogers, Dale E.
Angel Unaware. Pillar Bks.
Angel Unaware. Revell.
Let Freedom Ring. G K Hall.
Where He Leads. Pillar Bks.
Where He Leads. Revell.
Woman. Revell.

Rogers, David, 1930-
xRogers, David.
Can Business Management Save the Cities?: The Case of New York. Free Pr.
Somewhere There's Music. St Martin.

Rogers, David C. *see* Rogers, David C. D.
Rogers, David C. D.
xRogers, David C.
Essentials of Business Policy. Har-Row.

Rogers, David F.
xRogers, David F.
Mathematical Elements for Computer Graphics. McGraw.

Rogers, Diane P.
xRogers, Diane P.
Inside World Politics 1974. Allyn.

Rogers, Dilwyn J.
xRogers, Dilwyn J.
ed. A Bibliography of African Ecology: A Geographically & Topically Classified List of Books & Articles. Greenwood.

Rogers, Donald, 1923-
xRogers, Donald.
The Donald Rogers Illustrated Handbook of Arts & Crafts Lesson Plans for the Elementary Teacher: An Innovative Classroom-Tested Approach. P-H.

Rogers, Donald B., 1931-
xRogers, Donald B.
In Praise of Learning. Abingdon.

Rogers, Donald I.
xRogers, Donald I.
Since You Went Away. Arlington Hse.

Rogers, Dorothy, 1914-
xRogers, Dorothy.
The Adult Years: An Introduction to Aging. P-H.
Child Psychology. Brooks-Cole.
Issues in Adult Development. Brooks-Cole.
Issues in Life-Span Human Development. Brooks-Cole.
Psychology of Adolescence. P-H.

Rogers, Dorothy S.
xRogers, Dorothy S.
Retailing: Cases for Analysis. Grid Pub.

Rogers, E. M. *see* Rogers, Eric Malcolm.
Rogers, E. N.
xRogers, E. N.
Fasting: The Phenomenon of Self-Denial. Elsevier-Nelson.

Rogers, Edith R. *see* Rogers, Edith Randam.
Rogers, Edith Randam, 1924-
xRogers, Edith R.

The Perilous Hunt: Symbols in Hispanic & European Balladry. U Pr of Ky.

Rogers, Eric Malcolm, 1902-
xRogers, E. M.
Teaching Physics for the Inquiring Mind. Princeton U Pr.

Rogers, Everett M.
xRogers, Everett M.
Communication in Organizations. Free Pr.
Communication Strategies for Family Planning. Free Pr.

Rogers, F. E. *see* Rogers, Francis Emil.
Rogers, Florence K.
xRogers, Florence K.
Another Little Mouth to Feed!. S&S.
Parenting the Difficult Child. Chilton.

Rogers, Francis, 1870-1951
xRogers, Francis.
Some Famous Singers of the 19th Century. Arno.

Rogers, Francis Emil.
xRogers, F. E.
Illustrations in Applied Network Theory. Crane-Russak Co.

Rogers, Francis M. *see* Rogers, Francis Millet.
Rogers, Francis Millet.
xRogers, Francis M.
Atlantic Islanders of the Azores & Madeiras. Chris Mass.
Quest for Eastern Christians: Travels & Rumor in the Age of Discovery. U of Minn Pr.

Rogers, G. L. *see* Rogers, Gordon Leonard.
Rogers, George C.
xRogers, George C.
Evolution of a Federalist: William Loughton Smith of Charleston, 1758-1812. U of SC Pr.
History of Georgetown County, South Carolina. U of SC Pr

Rogers, Gordon Leonard, 1916-
xRogers, G. L.
Noncoherent Optical Processing. Wiley.

Rogers, H. C. *see* Rogers, Hugh Cuthbert Basset.
Rogers, Harold, 1907-
xRogers, Harold.
A Handful of Quietness. G K Hall.

Rogers, Hartley, 1926-
xRogers, Hartley.
Theory of Recursive Functions & Effective Computability. McGraw.

Rogers, Horatio.
xRogers, Horatio.
World War I through My Sights. Presidio Pr.

Rogers, Hugh Cuthbert Basset.
xRogers, H. C.
The British Army of the Eighteenth Century. Hippocrene Bks.

Rogers, J. A. *see* Rogers, Joel Augustus.
Rogers, J. W. *see* Rogers, John W.
Rogers, Jack. *see* Rogers, Jack Bartlett.
Rogers, Jack Bartlett.
xRogers, Jack.
The Authority & Interpretation of the Bible: An Historical Approach. Har-Row.

Rogers, James T.
xRogers, James T.
The Calculating Book: Fun & Games with Your Pocket Calculator. Random.

Rogers, Jan F. *see* Rogers, Jan Faulk.
Rogers, Jan Faulk.
xRogers, Jan F.
First Lady: Rosalynn Carter. Childrens.
Georgia: Home of President Jimmy Carter. Childrens.

Rogers, Joel A. *see* Rogers, Joel Augustus.
Rogers, Joel Augustus, 1880-
xRogers, J. A.
From "Superman to Man". H M Rogers.
World's Great Men of Color. Macmillan.
xRogers, Joel A.

From Superman to Man. Arno.
Rogers, John W.
xRogers, J. W.
Coil Slitting. Pergamon.

Rogers, Katharine M.
xRogers, Katharine M.
ed. Before Their Time: Six Women Writers of the Eighteenth Century. Ungar.

Rogers, Kenneth.
xRogers, Kenneth.
Advanced Calculus. Merrill.

Rogers, L. R. *see* Rogers, Leonard Robert.
Rogers, Leonard Robert, 1924-
xRogers, L. R.
Relief Sculpture. Oxford U Pr.

Rogers, Lindsay, 1891-
xRogers, Lindsay.
The American Senate. Johnson Repr.

Rogers, Malcolm J. *see* Rogers, Malcolm Jennings.
Rogers, Malcolm Jennings.
xRogers, Malcolm J.
Ancient Hunters of the Far West. Copley Bks.

Rogers, Marc.
xRogers, Marc.
Garden Way's Growing & Saving Vegetable Seeds. Garden Way Pub.

Rogers, Mary, 1929-
xRogers, Mary.
Mary Rogers on Pottery & Porcelain. Watson-Guptill.
Women & Money. Avon.
Women & Money. McGraw.
Women & Money. SF Bk Co.

Rogers, Michael.
xRogers, Michael.
Biohazard. Avon.
Biohazard. Knopf.

Rogers, Natalie
xRogers, Natalie.
Farewell Fatigue. Arco.

Rogers, Pamela.
xRogers, Pamela.
The Rare One. Elsevier-Nelson.

Rogers, Pat.
xRogers, Pat.
The Augustan Vision. Methuen Inc.
Robinson Crusoe. Allen Unwin.

Rogers, Paul.
xRogers, Paul.
Reinforced Concrete Design for Buildings. Van Nos Reinhold.
Steel Columns Eccentrically Loaded. Ungar.

Rogers, Peter.
xRogers, Peter D.
Everyday Problems in Public Health. Davis Co.

Rogers, Peter D. *see* Rogers, Peter.
Rogers, Peter V.
xRogers, Peter V.
Tragedy Is My Parish: Working for God in the Streets of New Orleans. Macmillan.

Rogers, Raymond A.
xRogers, Raymond A.
How to Report Research & Development Findings to Management. Pilot Bks.

Rogers, Robert, 1928-
xRogers, Robert.
Metaphor: A Psychoanalytic View. U of Cal Pr.
Psychoanalytic Study of the Double in Literature. Wayne St U Pr.

Rogers, Robert M. *see* Rogers, Robert Mark.
Rogers, Robert Mark, 1933-
xRogers, Robert M.
Respiratory Intensive Care. C C Thomas.

Rogers, Robert W. *see* Rogers, Robert William.
Rogers, Robert William, 1864-1930
xRogers, Robert W.
A History of Babylonia & Assyria. Arno.

Rogers, Rolf E.
xRogers, Rolf E.

Max Weber's Ideal Type Theory. Philos Lib.

Rogers, Rosemary.
 xRogers, Rosemary.
  The Crowd Pleasers. Avon.
  Dark Fires. Avon.
Rogers, Ruth H.
 xRogers, Ruth H.
  Fluid Mechanics. Routledge & Kegan.
Rogers, Samuel, 1894-
 xRogers, Samuel.
  Balzac & the Novel. Octagon.
Rogers, Sinclair.
 xRogers, Sinclair.
  ed. Children & Language: Readings in Early
   Language & Socialization. Oxford U Pr.
Rogers, Theresa F.
 xRogers, Theresa F.
  Printers Face Automation: The Impact of
   Technology on Work & Retirement Among
   Skilled Craftsmen. Lexington Bks.
Rogers, Thomas, 1927-
 xRogers, Thomas.
  The Confession of a Child of the Century. S&S.
  Leicester's Ghost. Newberry.
  Leicester's Ghost. U of Chicago Pr.
Rogers, Thomas F.
 xRogers, Thomas F.
  Superfluous Men & the Post-Stalin Thaw: The
   Alienated Hero in Soviet Prose During the
   Decade 1953-1963. Mouton.
Rogers, Vincent R. *see* Rogers, Vincent Robert.
Rogers, Vincent Robert.
 xRogers, Vincent R.
  Open Education: Critique & Assessment. Assn
   Supervision.
Rogers, Walter E. *see* Rogers, Walter Edmund.
Rogers, Walter Edmund, 1946-
 xRogers, Walter E.
  Program Facilities: Planning for Needs. GS.
Rogers, Will, 1879-1935
 xRogers, Will.
  The Illiterate Digest. Gale.
Rogers, William G. *see* Rogers, William Garland.
Rogers, William Garland, 1896-
 xRogers, William G.
  When This You See Remember Me: Gertrude
   Stein in Person. Greenwood.
Rogers, William R.
 xRogers, William R.
  ed. Nourishing the Humanistic in Medicine:
   Interactions with the Social Sciences. U of
   Pittsburgh Pr.
Rogers, William W. *see* Rogers, William Warren.
Rogers, William Warren.
 xRogers, William W.
  One-Gallused Rebellion: Agrarianism in
   Alabama, 1865-1896. La State U Pr.
Rogers, Wynn.
 xRogers, Wynn.
  Advanced Badminton. Wm C Brown.
Rogerson, J. W. *see* Rogerson, John William.
Rogerson, John William.
 xRogerson, J. W.
  Anthropology & the Old Testament. John
   Knox.
Rogerson, Sidney, 1894-
 xRogerson, Sidney.
  Propaganda in the Next War. Arno.
  Propaganda in the Next War. Garland Pub.
Rogg, Eleanor M. *see* Rogg, Eleanor Meyer.
Rogg, Eleanor Meyer.
 xRogg, Eleanor M.
  The Assimilation of Cuban Exiles: The Role of
   Community & Class. Fed Legal Pubns.
Rogge, Benjamin A.
 xRogge, Benjamin A.
  Can Capitalism Survive?. Liberty Fund.
Roggenkamp, K. W. *see* Roggenkamp, Klaus W.
Roggenkamp, Klaus W.
 xRoggenkamp, K. W.

Lattices Over Orders 1. Springer-Verlag.
Lattices Over Orders 2. Springer-Verlag.
Rogger, Hans.
 xRogger, Hans J.
  National Consciousness in Eighteenth-Century
   Russia. Harvard U Pr.
Rogger, Hans J. *see* Rogger, Hans.
Rogin, Gilbert, 1929-
 xRogin, Gilbert.
  Preparations for the Ascent. Random.
Rogin, Leo, 1893-1947
 xRogin, Leo.
  The Introduction of Farm Machinery in Its
   Relation to the Productivity of Labor in the
   Agriculturei of the U. S. During the
   Nineteenth Century. Johnson Repr.
Rogliatti, Gianni.
 xRogliatti, Gianni.
  Great Collectors' Cars. G&D.
Rogness, Alvin N., 1906-
 xRogness, Alvin N.
  Book of Comfort. Augsburg.
  Touch of His Love: Devotions for Every
   Season. Augsburg.
Rogo, D. Scott.
 xRogo, D. Scott.
  An Experience of Phantoms. Taplinger.
  Parapsychology: A Century of Inquiry.
   Taplinger.
  Phone Calls from the Dead. P-H.
  The Poltergeist Experience. Penguin.
 xRogo, Scott.
  An Experience of Phantoms. Dell.
Rogo, Scott. *see* Rogo, D. Scott.
Rogoff, Abraham M. *see* Rogoff, Abraham Meyer.
Rogoff, Abraham Meyer, 1894-
 xRogoff, Abraham M.
  Formative Years of the Jewish Labor
   Movement in the United States: (1890-1900).
   Greenwood.
Rogoff, Mortimer.
 xRogoff, Mortimer.
  Calculator Navigation. Norton.
Rogovin, Anne.
 xRogovin, Anne.
  Let Me Do It!. T Y Crowell.
Rogovin, Z. A.
 xRogovin, Z. A.
  ed. Advances in Polymer Science. Halsted Pr.
Rogow, Arnold A.
 xRogow, Arnold A.
  Power, Corruption, & Rectitude. Greenwood.
Rogowski, Ronald.
 xRogowski, Ronald.
  Rational Legitimacy: A Theory of Political
   Support. Princeton U Pr.
Roguet, A. M., 1906-
 xRoguet, A. M.
  Homilies for the Celebration of Marriage.
   Franciscan Herald.
Rohan, Donald.
 xRohan, Donald.
  The Browning Touch. Dial.
Rohatgi, V. K., 1939-
 xRohatgi, Vijay K.
  An Introduction to Probability Theory &
   Mathematical Statistics. Wiley.
Rohatgi, Vijay K. *see* Rohatgi, V. K.
Rohatgi-Mukherjee, K. K.
 xRohatgi-Mukherjee, K. K.
  Fundamentals of Photochemistry. Halsted Pr.
Rohatyn, Dennis A.
 xRohatyn, Dennis A.
  Two Dogmas of Philosophy & Other Essays in
   the Philosophy of Philosophy. Fairleigh
   Dickinson.
Rohde, David W.
 xRohde, David W.

Supreme Court Decision Making. W H
 Freeman.
Rohde, Eleanor S. *see* Rohde, Eleanour Sinclair.
Rohde, Eleanour S. *see* Rohde, Eleanour Sinclair.
Rohde, Eleanour Sinclair.
 xRohde, Eleanor S.
  Culinary & Salad Herbs: Their Cultivation &
   Food Values with Recipes. Peter Smith.
  The Old English Herbals. Peter Smith.
 xRohde, Eleanor S.
  Garden of Herbs. Dover.
  A Garden of Herbs. Peter Smith.
Roheim, Geza, 1891-1953
 xRoheim, Geza.
  Animism, Magic & the Divine King. Intl Univs
   Pr.
  Australian Totemism: A Psycho-Analytic Study
   in Anthropology. Humanities.
  Gates of the Dream. Intl Univs Pr.
Roherty, James M. *see* Roherty, James Michael.
Roherty, James Michael, 1926-
 xRoherty, James M.
  Decisions of Robert S. McNamara: A Study of
   the Role of the Secretary of Defense. U of
   Miami Pr.
  Intro. by & ed. Defense Policy Formation:
   Towards Comparative Analysis. Carolina
   Acad Pr.
Rohkamm, R. *see* Rohkamm, Reinhard.
Rohkamm, Reinhard, 1946-
 xRohkamm, R.
  Degeneration & Regeneration in Neurons of
   the Cerebellum. Springer-Verlag.
Rohlen, Thomas P.
 xRohlen, Thomas P.
  For Harmony & Strength: Japanese
   White-Collar Organization in Anthropological
   Perspective. U of Cal Pr.
Rohmer, Eric, 1920-
 xRohmer, Eric.
  Six Moral Tales. Viking Pr.
Rohmer, Sax.
 xRohmer, Sax.
  The Mask of Fu Manchu. Am Repr-Rivercity
   Pr.
Rohn, Arthur H., 1929-
 xRohn, Arthur H.
  Cultural Change & Continuity on Chapin
   Mesa. Regents Pr KS.
Rohner, Ronald P.
 xRohner, Ronald P.
  They Love Me, They Love Me Not: A
   Worldwide Study of the Effects of Parental
   Acceptance & Rejection. HRAFP.
Rohr, Donald G.
 xRohr, Donald G.
  Origins of Social Liberalism in Germany. U of
   Chicago Pr.
Rohrberger, Mary.
 xRohrberger, Mary.
  Story to Anti-Story. HM.
 xRohrberger, Mary H.
  The Art of Katherine Mansfield. Univ
   Microfilms.
Rohrberger, Mary H. *see* Rohrberger, Mary.
Rohrer, Daniel M.
 xRohrer, Daniel M.
  Freedom of Speech & Human Rights: An
   International Perspective. Kendall-Hunt.
  Mass Media, Freedom of Speech, &
   Advertising: A Study in Communication Law.
   Kendall-Hunt.
Rohrer, Gertrude M. *see* Rohrer, Gertrude Martin.
Rohrer, Gertrude Martin.
 xRohrer, Gertrude M.
  Music & Musicians of Pennsylvania. Friedman.
Rohrer, Virginia.
 xRohrer, Virginia.

How to Eat Right & Feel Great. Tyndale.
Rohrlich, Chester.
　xRohrlich, Chester.
　　Organizing Corporate & Other Business
　　Enterprises. Bender.
Rohrlich, F.
　xRohrlich, F.
　　Classical Charged Particles. A-W.
Rohrs, Richard C.
　xRohrs, Richard C.
　　The Germans in Oklahoma. U of Okla Pr.
Rohwer. *see* Rohwer, Jurgen.
Rohwer, Jurgen.
　xRohwer.
　　Superpower Confrontation on the Seas: Naval
　　Development & Strategy Since 1945. Sage.
Roider, Karl A.
　xRoider, Karl A.
　　Reluctant Ally: Austria's Policy in the
　　Austro-Turkish War, 1737-1739. La State U
　　Pr.
Roinestad, Soren C.
　xRoinestad, Soren C.
　　A Hundred Years with the Norwegians in the
　　East Bay. R & E Res Assoc.
Roiphe, Anne. *see* Roiphe, Anne Richardson.
Roiphe, Anne Richardson, 1935-
　xRoiphe, Anne.
　　Long Division. S&S.
　　Torch Song. FS&G.
　　Torch Song. NAL.
Rojankovsky, Feodor, 1891-
　xRojankovsky, Feodor.
　　illus. Animals in the Zoo. Knopf.
　　illus. Animals on the Farm. Knopf.
Rokeach, Milton.
　xRokeach, Milton.
　　The Nature of Human Values. Free Pr.
　　Understanding Human Values: Individual &
　　Societal. Free Pr.
Rokes, Willis P. *see* Rokes, Willis Park.
Rokes, Willis Park.
　xRokes, Willis P.
　　Human Relations in Handling Insurance
　　Claims. Irwin.
　　Frwd. by No-Fault Insurance. Merritt Co.
Rokosz, Francis M.
　xRokosz, Francis M.
　　Structured Intramurals. HR&W.
Roland, Alan.
　xRoland, Alan.
　　Career & Motherhood: Struggles for a New
　　Identity. Human Sci Pr.
Roland, Albert.
　xRoland, Albert.
　　Great Indian Chiefs. Macmillan.
　　Profiles from the New Asia. Macmillan.
Roland, Alex, 1944-
　xRoland, Alex.
　　Underwater Warfare in the Age of Sail. Ind U
　　Pr.
Roland, Charles P.
　xRoland, Charles P.
　　Confederacy. U of Chicago Pr.
Roland de la Platiere, Marie. *see* Roland De la Platiere,
　Marie Jeanne Phlipon.
Roland, Jean Claude.
　xRoland, Jean-Claude.
　　Atlas of Cell Biology. Little.
Roland, Jean-Claude. *see* Roland, Jean Claude.
Roland, Maxwell.
　xRoland, Maxwell.
　　Response to Contraception. Saunders.
Roland, Nicholas.
　xRoland, Nicholas.
　　Natural Causes. Aurora Pubs.
Roland De la Platiere, Marie Jeanne Phlipon.
　xRoland de la Platiere, Marie.

The Private Memoirs of Madame Roland.
AMS Pr.
Roleder, George.
　xRoleder, George.
　　Marriage Means Encounter. Wm C Brown.
Rolerson, Darrell A.
　xRolerson, Darrell A.
　　Boy & a Deer. Dodd.
　　A Boy Called Plum. Dodd.
Rolett, Karin.
　xRolett, Karin.
　　Organizing Community Resources in Sexuality
　　Counseling & Family Planning for the
　　Retarded: a Community Workers' Manual.
　　Carolina Pop Ctr.
Roley, V. Vance, 1951-
　xRoley, V. Vance.
　　A Structural Model of the U. S. Government
　　Securities Market. Garland Pub.
Rolf, Robert.
　xRolf, Robert.
　　Masamune Hakucho. Twayne.
Rolfe, Frederick C. *see* Rolfe, Frederick William.
Rolfe, Frederick W. *see* Rolfe, Frederick William.
Rolfe, Frederick William, 1860-1913
　xRolfe, Frederick C.
　　Nicholas Crabbe: Or, The One & the Many, a
　　Romance. Greenwood.
　xRolfe, Frederick W.
　　A History of the Borgias. Greenwood.
　　In His Own Image. Arno.
Rolfe, John, 1585-1622
　xRolfe, John.
　　True Relation of the State of Virginia Lefte by
　　Sir Thomas Dale, Knight, in May Last 1616.
　　U Pr of Va.
Rolfe, John C. *see* Rolfe, John Carew.
Rolfe, John Carew, 1859-1943
　xRolfe, John C.
　　Cicero & His Influence. Cooper Sq.
Rolfe, Sidney E.
　xRolfe, Sidney E.
　　The Great Wheel: The World Monetary
　　System - a Reinterpretation. Times Bks.
　　The Great Wheel: The World, Monetary
　　System; a Reinterpretation. McGraw.
Rolfe, Stan. *see* Rolfe, Stanley Theodore.
Rolfe, Stanley Theodore.
　xRolfe, Stan.
　　Fracture & Fatigue Control in Structures:
　　Applications of Fracture Mechanics. P-H.
Rolfe, William J. *see* Rolfe, William James.
Rolfe, William James, 1827-1910
　xRolfe, William J.
　　Life of William Shakespeare. AMS Pr.
　　Life of William Shakespeare. R West.
Roll, Eric. *see* Roll, Erich.
Roll, Erich, 1907-
　xRoll, Eric.
　　The Combined Food Board: A Study in
　　Wartime International Planning. Stanford U
　　Pr.
　　A History of Economic Thought. Irwin.
　　A History of Economic Thought. Merrimack
　　Bk Serv.
Roll, William. *see* Roll, William George.
Roll, William G. *see* Roll, William George.
Roll, William George, 1926-
　xRoll, William.
　　Poltergeist. NAL.
　xRoll, William G.
　　The Poltergeist. Scarecrow.
Roll, Winifred, Lady.
　xRoll, Winifred.
　　Mary I: The History of an Unhappy Tudor
　　Queen. P-H.
Rollain. *see* Rollain, Philip J.
Rollain, Philip J.
　xRollain.

Exploring Electricity-Electronics with the
Electrical Team. Delmar.
Rolland, Romain.
　xRolland, Romain.
　　Musical Tour Through the Land of the Past.
　　Arno.
　　Musicians of To-Day. Arno.
　　Some Musicians of Former Days. Arno.
Rollband, James.
　xRollband, Jim.
　　The Long & the Short of Chinese Cooking.
　　Crossing Pr.
Rollband, Jim. *see* Rollband, James.
Rolle, Andrew. *see* Rolle, Andrew F.
Rolle, Andrew F.
　xRolle, Andrew.
　　The Italian Americans: Troubled Roots. Free
　　Pr.
　xRolle, Andrew F.
　　California: A History. AHM Pub.
　　Immigrant Upraised: Italian Adventurers &
　　Colonists in an Expanding America. U of
　　Okla Pr.
Rolle, Richard.
　xRolle, Richard.
　　Selected Works of Richard Rolle, Hermit.
　　Hyperion Conn.
Roller, David C.
　xRoller, David C.
　　ed. The Encyclopedia of Southern History. La
　　State U Pr.
Rolleston, Maud.
　xRolleston, Maud.
　　Talks with Lady Shelley. Folcroft.
Rolleston, Sara E. *see* Rolleston, Sara Emerson.
Rolleston, Sara Emerson.
　xRolleston, Sara E.
　　photos by Heritage Houses: The American
　　Tradition in Connecticut, 1660-1900. Viking
　　Pr.
　　Historic Houses & Interiors in Southern
　　Connecticut. Hastings.
Rolleston, T. W. *see* Rolleston, Thomas William Hazen.
Rolleston, Thomas W. *see* Rolleston, Thomas William
　Hazen.
Rolleston, Thomas William Hazen, 1857-1920
　xRolleston, T. W.
　　Life of Gotthold Ephraim Lessing. R West.
　xRolleston, Thomas W.
　　Life of Gotthold Ephraim Lessing. Kennikat.
Rollin, Bernard E.
　xRollin, Bernard E.
　　Natural & Conventional Meaning: An
　　Examination of the Distinction. Mouton.
Rollin, Betty.
　xRollin, Betty.
　　First, You Cry. Lippincott.
　　First You Cry. NAL.
Rollin, F. A. *see* Rollin, Frank A.
Rollin, Frank A.
　xRollin, F. A.
　　Life and Public Services of Martin R. Delany.
　　Kraus Repr.
Rolling Stone.
　xRolling Stone.
　　The Rolling Stone Book of Days: 1980.
　　Macmillan.
　　The Rolling Stone History of the Sixties.
　　Random.
　xRolling Stone Editors.
　　Dancing Madness. Doubleday.
　　Rolling Stone Interviews, No. 1. Warner Bks.
　xRolling Stone Magazine Editors.
　　The Rolling Stone Record Review, No. 2. PB.
　xRolling Stone Magazines Editors.
　　ed. Knocking on Dylan's Door. PB.
　xRolling Stone Press.

Rolling Stone Illustrated History of Rock & Roll. Random.

The Rolling Stone Illustrated History of Rock & Roll, 1950-1980. Random.

The Rolling Stone Visits Saturday Night Live. Doubleday.

Rolling Stone Editors. see Rolling Stone.

Rolling Stone Magazine Editors. see Rolling Stone.

Rolling Stone Magazines Editors. see Rolling Stone.

Rolling Stone Press. see Rolling Stone.

Rollins, Bryant.
xRollins, Bryant.
Danger Song. Macmillan.

Rollins, Charlemae. see Rollins, Charlemae Hill.

Rollins, Charlemae H. see Rollins, Charlemae Hill.

Rollins, Charlemae Hill.
xRollins, Charlemae.
Famous American Negro Poets. Dodd.
xRollins, Charlemae H.
They Showed the Way: Forty American Negro Leaders. T Y Crowell.

Rollins, George W. see Rollins, George Watson.

Rollins, George Watson.
xRollins, George W.
The Struggle of the Cattleman, Sheepman & Settler for Control of Lands in Wyoming, 1867-1910. Arno.

Rollins, Hyder E. see Rollins, Hyder Edward.

Rollins, Hyder Edward, 1889-1958
xRollins, Hyder E.
Contribution to the History of English Commonwealth Drama. Haskell.
Troilus-Cressida Story from Chaucer to Shakespeare. Haskell.

Rollins, Marion J. see Rollins, Marion Josephine (Benedict).

Rollins, Marion Josephine (Benedict), 1898-
xRollins, Marion J.
The God of the Old Testament in Relation to War. AMS Pr.

Rollins, Nancy.
xRollins, Nancy.
Child Psychiatry in the Soviet Union: Preliminary Observations. Harvard U Pr.

Rollins, Philip. see Rollins, Philip Ashton.

Rollins, Philip A. see Rollins, Philip Ashton.

Rollins, Philip Ashton.
xRollins, Philip.
The Cowboy: An Unconventional History of Civilization on the Old-Time Cattle Range. U of NM Pr.
xRollins, Philip A.
The Cowboy: An Unconventional History of Civilization on the Old Time Cattle Range. Kelley.

Rollins, Reed C. see Rollins, Reed Clark.

Rollins, Reed Clark.
xRollins, Reed C.
Genus Lesquerella (Cruciferae) in North America. Harvard U Pr.

Rollo, Vera A. Foster.
xRollo, Vera F.
Maryland's Constitution & Government. Maryland Hist Pr.

Rollo, Vera F. see Rollo, Vera A. Foster.

Rolls, E. T.
xRolls, E. T.
The Brain & Reward. Pergamon.

Rolo, Charles J. see Rolo, Charles James.

Rolo, Charles James, 1916-
xRolo, Charles J.
ed. Psychiatry in American Life. Arno.

Roloff, Leland H.
xRoloff, Leland H.
The Perception & Evocation of Literature. Scott F.

Roloff, Marie B. see Roloff, Marie Brady.

Roloff, Marie Brady.
xRoloff, Marie B.

Lester Roloff: Living by Faith. Nelson.

Roloff, Michael. see Roloff, Michael E.

Roloff, Michael E.
xRoloff, Michael.
ed. Persuasion: New Directions in Theory & Research. Sage.

Rolph, Earl R. see Rolph, Earl Robert.

Rolph, Earl Robert, 1910-
xRolph, Earl R.
Theory of Fiscal Economics. Greenwood.
The Theory of Fiscal Economics. U of Cal Pr.

Rolph, Elizabeth.
xRolph, Elizabeth S.
Nuclear Power & the Public Safety: A Study in Regulation. Lexington Bks.

Rolph, Elizabeth S. see Rolph, Elizabeth.

Rolston, Holmes, 1900-
xRolston, Holmes.
The Apostle Peter Speaks to Us Today. John Knox.

Rolvaag, O. E. see Rolvaag, Ole Edvart.

Rolvaag, Ole Edvart, 1876-1931
xRolvaag, O. E.
Giants in the Earth. Darby Bks.
Giants in the Earth. Har-Row.

Romaine, Lawrence B., 1900-
xRomaine, Lawrence B.
A Guide to American Trade Catalogs, 1744-1900. Arno.

Romaine, Mertie E., 1893-
xRomaine, Mertie E.
General Tom Thumb & His Lady. W S Sullwold.

Romains, Jules, 1885-1972
xRomains, Jules.
Eyeless Sight. Citadel Pr.
Open Letter Against a Vast Conspiracy. Heineman.

Roman, Charles V. see Roman, Charles Victor.

Roman, Charles Victor, 1864-
xRoman, Charles V.
American Civilization & the Negro. Arno.

Roman, Daniel D.
xRoman, Daniel D.
Science, Technology, & Innovation: A Systems Approach. Grid Pub.

Roman, Kenneth.
xRoman, Kenneth.
How to Advertise. St Martin.

Roman, Klara G. see Roman, Klara Goldzieher.

Roman, Klara Goldzieher.
xRoman, Klara G.
Encyclopedia of the Written Word: A Lexicon for Graphology & Other Aspects of Writing. Ungar.

Roman, Lulu.
xRoman, Lulu.
Lulu. Revell.

Roman, Mel. see Roman, Melvin.

Roman, Melvin.
xRoman, Mel.
The Disposable Parent: The Case for Joint Custody. HR&W.

Roman, Murray, 1920-
xRoman, Murray.
Telephone Marketing Techniques. Am Mgmt.

Roman, Paul. see Roman, Paul M.

Roman, Paul M.
xRoman, Paul.
ed. The Sociology of Psychotherapy. Aronson.
xRoman, Paul M.
Explorations in Psychiatric Sociology. Davis Co.
Sociological Perspectives on Community Mental Health. Davis Co.

Roman, Stephen B.
xRoman, Stephen B.
The Responsible Society. Two Continents.

Romanek, Enid W. see Romanek, Enid Warner.

Romanek, Enid Warner.
xRomanek, Enid W.
Teddy. Scribner.

Romanek, Richard J., 1933-
xRomanek, Richard J.
Introduction to Electronic Technology. P-H.

Romano, Albert.
xRomano, Albert.
Applied Statistics for Science & Industry. Allyn.

Romano, John.
xRomano, John.
ed. Adaptation. Kennikat.
Dickens & Reality. Columbia U Pr.

Romanos, Michael C.
xRomanos, Michael C.
ed. Western European Cities in Crisis. Lexington Bks.

Romanov, Panteleimon S. see Romanov, Panteleimon Sergeevich.

Romanov, Panteleimon Sergeevich, 1884-1938
xRomanov, Panteleimon S.
On the Volga & Other Stories. Hyperion Conn.

Romanowitz, H. A. see Romanowitz, Harry Alex.

Romanowitz, Harry Alex.
xRomanowitz, H. A.
Introduction to Electronics. Wiley.

Romans, J. Thomas.
xRomans, J. Thomas.
Capital Exports & Growth Among U.S. Regions. Columbia U Pr.

Romans, John R.
xRomans, John R.
The Meat We Eat. Interstate.

Romashko, Sandra.
xRomashko, Sandra D.
Living Coral & Other Inhabitants of the Reef. Windward Pub.
Wild Ducks & Geese of North America. Windward Pub.

Romashko, Sandra D. see Romashko, Sandra.

Romberg, Bertil.
xRomberg, Bertil.
Carl Jonas Love Almqvist. Twayne.

Romberg, Jenean.
xRomberg, Jenean.
Let's Discover Crayon. Ctr Appl Res.
Let's Discover Mobiles. Ctr Appl Res.
Let's Discover Paper. Ctr Appl Res.
Let's Discover Papier-Mache. Ctr Appl Res.
Let's Discover Printing. Ctr Appl Res.
Let's Discover Puppets. Ctr Appl Res.
Let's Discover Tempera. Ctr Appl Res.
Let's Discover Tissue. Ctr Appl Res.
Let's Discover Watercolor. Ctr Appl Res.
Let's Discover Weaving. Ctr Appl Res.

Romberg, Thomas A.
xRomberg, Thomas A.
Individually Guided Mathematics. A-W.

Rome, Claire.
xRome, Claire.
An Owl Came to Stay. Crown.

Romer, Alfred, 1906-
xRomer, Alfred.
ed. Radiochemistry & the Discovery of Isotopes. Dover.

Romer, Alfred. see Romer, Alfred Sherwood.

Romer, Alfred S. see Romer, Alfred Sherwood.

Romer, Alfred Sherwood, 1894-
xRomer, Alfred.
Osteology of the Reptiles. U of Chicago Pr.
xRomer, Alfred S.
Osteology of the Reptiles. U of Chicago Pr.

Romer, Robert H.
xRomer, Robert H.
Energy: An Introduction to Physics. W H Freeman.

Romer, Terry L., 1946-
xRomer, Terry L.

Complete Kindergarten Handbook. P-H.
Romera-Navarro, M. *see* Romera-Navarro, Miguel.
Romera-Navarro, Miguel, 1888-
xRomera-Navarro, M.
Estudios Sobre Gracian. U of Tex Pr.
Romero, Francisco, 1891-1962
xRomero, Francisco.
Theory of Man. U of Cal Pr.
Romero, George.
xRomero, George.
Dawn of the Dead. St Martin.
Romero, Jose L. *see* Romero, Jose Luis.
Romero, Jose Luis, 1909-
xRomero, Jose L.
A History of Argentine Political Thought.
Stanford U Pr.
Romey, Bill.
xRomey, Bill.
Confluent Education in Science. Ash Lad Pr.
Romine, Carrie, 1915-
xRomine, Carrie.
Ready-to-Teach Crafts Activities for the
Elementary School. P-H.
Romine, Jack S.
xRomine, Jack S.
Writing Sentences: A Self-Teaching Guide to
Grammar, Structure, & Sentence Combining.
HR&W.
Rommel, Erwin, 1891-1944
xRommel, Erwin.
Attacks. Athena Pr.
Rommen, Heinrich A. *see* Rommen, Heinrich Albert.
Rommen, Heinrich Albert, 1897-1967
xRommen, Heinrich A.
The Natural Law. Arno.
Romney, George, 1734-1802
xRomney, George.
Drawings of Romney. Borden.
Romney, Marion G., 1897-
xRomney, Marion G.
Learning for the Eternities. Deseret Bk.
Romney, S. *see* Romney, Seymour L.
Romney, Seymour. *see* Romney, Seymour L.
Romney, Seymour L.
xRomney, S.
Gynecology & Obstetrics: The Health Care of
Women. McGraw.
xRomney, Seymour.
ed. Gynecology & Obstetrics: The Health Care
of Women. McGraw.
Romo, Ida.
xRomo, Ida.
Homestyle Mexican Cooking. Rand.
Romualdez, Daniel.
xRomualdez, Daniel.
China: A Personal Encounter with the People's
Republic. P-H.
Romulo, Carlos P. *see* Romulo, Carlos Pena.
Romulo, Carlos Pena, 1899-
xRomulo, Carlos P.
Crusade in Asia: Philippine Victory.
Greenwood.
I See the Philippines Rise. AMS Pr.
Ronai, Lili.
xRonai, Lili.
Corals. T Y Crowell.
Ronald, D. W.
xRonald, D. W.
The Longmoor Military Railway. David &
Charles.
Ronander, Albert C.
xRonander, Albert C.
Guide to the Pilgrim Hymnal. Pilgrim NY.
Ronay, Gabriel.
xRonay, Gabriel.
The Truth About Dracula. Stein & Day.
Rondell, Florence.
xRondell, Florence.

Adopted Family. Crown.
Rondileau, Adrian, 1912-
xRondileau, Adrian.
Education for Installment Buying. AMS Pr.
Rondinelli, Dennis A.
xRondinelli, Dennis A.
Planning Development Projects. DH&R.
Ronen. *see* Ronen, Dov.
Ronen, Dov.
xRonen.
The Quest for Self-Determination. Yale U Pr.
xRonen, Dov.
Dahomey: Between Tradition & Modernity.
Cornell U Pr.
Ronfeldt, David.
xRonfeldt, David F.
Atencingo: The Politics of Agrarian Struggle in
a Mexican Ejido. Stanford U Pr.
Ronfeldt, David F. *see* Ronfeldt, David.
Rongen, Bjorn, 1906-
xRongen, Bjorn.
Anna of the Bears. FS&G.
Rongstad, James.
xRongstad, James.
How to Respond to the Lodge. Concordia.
Ronk, A. T. *see* Ronk, Albert T.
Ronk, Albert T.
xRonk, A. T.
History of Brethren Missionary Movements.
Brethren Ohio.
Ronken, Harriet O.
xRonken, Harriet O.
Administering Changes: A Case Study of
Human Relations in a Factory. Greenwood.
Ronsard, Pierre de.
xRonsard, Pierre De.
Poems of Pierre de Ronsard. U of Cal Pr.

Rood, Arnold.
xRood, Arnold.
ed. Edward Gordon Craig, Artist of the
Theatre, 1872-1966: A Memorial Exhibition
in the Amsterdam Gallery. Arno.
Rood, Ronald. *see* Rood, Ronald N.
Rood, Ronald N.
xRood, Ronald.
Animals Nobody Loves. Greene.
How Do You Spank a Porcupine. Trident.
The Loon in My Bathtub. Greene.
Possum in the Parking Lot. S&S.
Roody, Peter.
xRoody, Peter.
Medical Abbreviations & Acronyms. McGraw.
Roof, Katharine M. *see* Roof, Katharine Metcalf.
Roof, Katharine Metcalf.
xRoof, Katharine M.
The Life & Art of William Merritt Chase.
Hacker.
Roof, Wade C. *see* Roof, Wade Clark.
Roof, Wade Clark.
xRoof, Wade C.
ed. Race & Residence in American Cities. Am
Acad Pol Soc Sci.
Rook, Douglas L.
xRook, Douglas N.
The Sound of Thought. Windy Row.
Rook, Douglas N. *see* Rook, Douglas L.
Rook, E. C. *see* Rook, Emma Cecilia.
Rook, Emma Cecilia.
xRook, E. C.
ed. Drills & Marches. Arno.
Rooke, Leon.
xRooke, Leon.
The Broad Back of the Angel. Fiction Coll.
Last One Home Sleeps in the Yellow Bed:
Stories. La State U Pr.
Rooke, M. Leigh. *see* Rooke, Mabel Leigh.
Rooke, Mabel Leigh.
xRooke, M. Leigh.

Benefaction or Bondage?: Social Policy & the
Aged. U Pr of Amer.
Rookmaaker, H. R. *see* Rookmaaker, Hendrik Roelof.
Rookmaaker, Hendrik Roelof, 1922-1977
xRookmaaker, H. R.
Art Needs No Justification. Inter-Varsity.
Modern Art & the Death of a Culture.
Inter-Varsity.
Room, Adrian.
xRoom, Adrian.
The Penguin Dictionary of Confusibles.
Penguin.
Room's Dictionary of Confusibles. Routledge
& Kegan.
Room, Graham.
xRoom, Graham.
The Sociology of Welfare: Social Policy,
Stratification & Political Order. St Martin.
Roome, Katherine A. *see* Roome, Katherine A. Davis.
Roome, Katherine A. Davis.
xRoome, Katherine A.
The Letter of the Law. Random.
Rooney, James R.
xRooney, James R.
Autopsy of the Horse: Technique &
Interpretation. Krieger.
The Sick Horse: Causes, Symptoms, &
Treatment. A S Barnes.
Rooney, John F.
xRooney, John F.
The Recruiting Game: Toward a New System
of Intercollegiate Sports. U of Nebr Pr.
Roonwal, M. L.
xRoonwal, M. L.
Primates of South Asia: Ecology, Sociobiology,
& Behavior. Harvard U Pr.
Roop, Eugene F., 1942-
xRoop, Eugene F.
Living the Biblical Story. Abingdon.
Roos, Bernard W.
xRoos, Bernard W.
Analytic Functions & Distributions in Physics
& Engineering. Krieger.
Roos, Robert W. De. *see* De Roos, Robert W.
Roosbroeck, G. L. Van. *see* Van Roosbroeck, G. L.
Roose, Kenneth D.
xRoose, Kenneth D.
Economics of Recession & Revival: An
Interpretation of 1937-38. Shoe String.
Roose, Robert W. *see* Roose, Robert Welburne.
Roose, Robert Welburne.
xRoose, Robert W.
ed. Handbook of Energy Conservation for
Mechanical Systems in Buildings. Van Nos
Reinhold.
Roosen, William J. *see* Roosen, William James.
Roosen, William James.
xRoosen, William J.
Age of Louis XIV: The Rise of Modern
Diplomacy. Schenkman.
Roosens, Eugeen, 1934-
xRoosens, Eugeen.
Mental Patients in Town Life: Geel - Europe's
First Therapeutic Community. Sage.
Rooses, Max, 1839-1914
xRooses, Max.
Art in Flanders. AMS Pr.
Roosevelt, Eleanor. *see* Roosevelt, Eleanor Roosevelt.
Roosevelt, Eleanor Roosevelt, 1884-1962
xRoosevelt, Eleanor.
This I Remember. Greenwood.
Roosevelt, Elliott, 1910-
xRoosevelt, Elliott.
As He Saw It. Greenwood.
Roosevelt, F. D. *see* Roosevelt, Franklin Delano.
Roosevelt, Franklin Delano, Pres. U.s, 1882-1945
xRoosevelt, F. D.
On Our Way. Da Capo.
Roosevelt, James.
xRoosevelt, James.

A Family Matter. S&W.
   ed. Liberal Papers. Arno.
Roosevelt, Nicholas, 1893-
   xRoosevelt, Nicholas.
   Good Cooking. Macmillan.
Roosevelt, Ruth.
   xRoosevelt, Ruth.
   Living in Step. McGraw.
   Living in Step. Stein & Day.
Roosevelt, Theodore, Pres. U.s, 1858-1919
   xRoosevelt, Theodore.
   Gouverneur Morris. AMS Pr.
   Gouverneur Morris. Chelsea Hse.
   Gouverneur Morris. Haskell.
   Gouverneur Morris. Scholarly.
   History As Literature & Other Essays.
     Kennikat.
   Hunting Trips of a Ranchman. Irvington.
   Maxims. Irvington.
   Outdoor Pastimes of an American Hunter.
     Arno.
   Ranch Life & the Hunting Trail. Arno.
   Realizable Ideals. Arno.
   Strenuous Life: Essays & Addresses. Scholarly.
   Thomas H. Benton. AMS Pr.
   Thomas Hart Benton. Haskell.
   Thomas Hart Benton. Scholarly.
Root, E. Merrill. *see* Root, Edward Merrill.
Root, Edward Merrill, 1895-
   xRoot, E. Merrill.
   America's Steadfast Dream. Western Islands.
   Children of the Morning. Golden Quill.
   Like White Birds Flying. Golden Quill.
Root, Elihu.
   xRoot, Elihu.
   Addresses on Government & Citizenship.
     Arno.
   Addresses on International Subjects. Arno.
   Men & Policies: Addresses. Arno.
Root, George F. *see* Root, George Frederick.
Root, George Frederick, 1820-1895
   xRoot, George F.
   The Story of a Musical Life: An
     Autobiography. Da Capo.
Root, Kathleen (Berger).
   xRoot, Kathleen B.
   Medical Typing Practice. McGraw.
Root, Kathleen B. *see* Root, Kathleen (Berger).
Root, Leon.
   xRoot, Leon.
   The Bad Back Exercise Book. Warner Bks.
   Oh, My Aching Back: A Doctor's Guide to
     Your Back Pain & How to Control It.
     McKay.
Root, Oren, 1911-
   xRoot, Oren.
   Persons & Persuasions. Norton.
Root, Pat.
   xRoot, Pat.
   Devil of the Stairs. S&S.
   Evil Became Them. S&S.
Root, Robert K. *see* Root, Robert Kilburn.
Root, Robert Kilburn, 1877-1950
   xRoot, Robert K.
   Classical Mythology in Shakespeare. Gordian.
Root, Waverley. *see* Root, Waverley Lewis.
Root, Waverley Lewis, 1903-
   xRoot, Waverley.
   Food of France. Knopf.
   The Food of France. Random.
Root, Wells.
   xRoot, Wells.
   Writing the Script: A Practical Guide for Films
     & Television. HR&W.
Root, William P. *see* Root, William Pitt.
Root, William Pitt, 1941-
   xRoot, William P.
   Storm & Other Poems. Atheneum.
Root, William S.
   xRoot, William S.

Standard Bidding. Crown.
Root, Winfred T. *see* Root, Winfred Trexler.
Root, Winfred Trexler, 1879-1947
   xRoot, Winfred T.
   Relations of Pennsylvania with the British
     Government, 1696-1765. AMS Pr.
   Relations of Pennsylvania with the British
     Government, 1696-1765. B Franklin.
Rooth, Anne R. *see* Rooth, Anne Reed.
Rooth, Anne Reed.
   xRooth, Anne R.
   The Ninth Car. Putnam.
Rooth, Gosta.
   xRooth, Gosta.
   Acid Base & Electrolyte Balance. Year Bk
     Med.
Rootham, Helen.
   xRootham, Helen.
     ed. Kossovo, Heroic Songs of the Serbs. Core
     Collection.
Roots, Clive, 1935-
   xRoots, Clive.
   Animal Invaders. Universe.
Roots, Ivan A. *see* Roots, Ivan Alan.
Roots, Ivan Alan.
   xRoots, Ivan A.
   Commonwealth & Protectorate: The English
     Civil War & Its Aftermath. Greenwood.
Rope, Frederick T. *see* Rope, Frederick Thornton.
Rope, Frederick Thornton, 1909-
   xRope, Frederick T.
   Opinion Conflict & School Support. AMS Pr.
Roper, Alan.
   xRoper, Alan.
   Arnold's Poetic Landscapes. Johns Hopkins.
Roper, C. A. *see* Roper, Carl A.
Roper, Carl A.
   xRoper, C. A.
   Complete Handbook of Locks & Locksmithing.
     TAB Bks.
Roper, Daniel C. *see* Roper, Daniel Calhoun.
Roper, Daniel Calhoun.
   xRoper, Daniel C.
   Fifty Years of Public Life. Greenwood.
Roper, Derek.
   xRoper, Derek.
   Reviewing Before the Edinburgh, 1788-1802. U
     Delaware Pr.
Roper, Donna C., 1944-
   xRoper, Donna C.
   Archaeological Survey & Settlement Pattern
     Models in Central Illinois. Kent St U Pr.
Roper, Freeman C. *see* Roper, Freeman Clarke Samuel.
Roper, Freeman Clarke Samuel, 1819-1896
   xRoper, Freeman C.
   Catalogue of Works on the Microscope & of
     Those Referring to Microscopical Subjects in
     the Library of Freeman C. S. Roper. N T
     Smith.
Roper, L. V.
   xRoper, L. V.
   Death As in Matador. Popular Lib.
Roper, Les V., Jr.
   xRoper, Les V.
   The Overlord. BJ Pub Group.
Roper, Steve.
   xRoper, Steve.
   Climber's Guide to the High Sierra. Sierra.
   Climbers Guide to Yosemite Valley. Sierra.
   Fifty Classic Climbs of North America. Sierra.
Ropes, Marian W. *see* Ropes, Marian Wilkins.
Ropes, Marian Wilkins, 1903-
   xRopes, Marian W.
   Systemic Lupus Erythematosus. Harvard U Pr.
Ropke, Wilhelm, 1899-1966
   xRopke, Wilhelm.
   International Economic Disintegration.
     Porcupine Pr.
   The Social Crisis of Our Time. Hyperion Conn.
Ropp, Robert S. De. *see* De Ropp, Robert S.

Roppen, Georg.
   xRoppen, Georg.
   Evolution & Poetic Belief: A Study in Some
     Victorian & Modern Writers. Somerset Pub.
Rorabacher, Louise E. *see* Rorabacher, Louise Elizabeth.
Rorabacher, Louise Elizabeth, 1906-
   xRorabacher, Louise E.
   Assignments in Exposition. Har-Row.
   A Concise Guide to Composition. Har-Row.
   Frank Dalby Davison. G K Hall.
   Frank Dalby Davison. Twayne.
Rordorf, Willy.
   xRordorf, Willy.
   The Eucharist of the Early Christians. Pueblo
     Pub Co.
Rorem, Ned, 1923-
   xRorem, Ned.
   An Absolute Gift: A New Diary. S&S.
   Critical Affairs: A Composer's Journal.
     Braziller.
   Music from Inside Out. Braziller.
Rorig, Fritz, 1882-1952
   xRorig, Fritz.
   The Medieval Town. U of Cal Pr.
Rorres, Chris.
   xRorres, Chris.
   Applications of Linear Algebra. Wiley.
Rorty, Amelie.
   xRorty, Amelie O.
     ed. Explaining Emotions. U of Cal Pr.
     ed. The Identities of Persons. U of Cal Pr.
Rorty, Amelie O. *see* Rorty, Amelie.
Rorty, James, 1890-1973
   xRorty, James.
   Our Master's Voice: Advertising. Arno.
Rorty, Richard.
   xRorty, Richard.
     ed. Linguistic Turn: Recent Essays in
     Philosophical Method. U of Chicago Pr.
   Philosophy & the Mirror of Nature. Princeton
     U Pr.
Rorvik, David. *see* Rorvik, David M.
Rorvik, David M.
   xRorvik, David.
   In His Image: The Cloning of a Man. PB.
   xRorvik, David M.
   Decompression Babies. Dodd.
   In His Image: The Cloning of a Man.
     Lippincott.
Rosa, Alfred. *see* Rosa, Alfred F.
Rosa, Alfred F.
   xRosa, Alfred.
   Salem, Transcendentalism, & Hawthorne.
     Fairleigh Dickinson.
   xRosa, Alfred F.
     ed. Contemporary Fiction in America &
     England, 1950-1970: A Guide to Information
     Sources. Gale.
Rosa, Peter De. *see* De Rosa, Peter.
Rosander, A. C. *see* Rosander, Arlyn Custer.
Rosander, Arlyn Custer, 1903-
   xRosander, A. C.
   Case Studies in Sample Design. Dekker.
Rosario, Jose C. *see* Rosario, Jose Colomban.
Rosario, Jose Colomban.
   xRosario, Jose C.
   The Development of the Puerto Rican Jibaro &
     His Present Attitude Towards Society. Arno.

Rosato, Dominick. *see* Rosato, Dominick V.

Rosato, Dominick V.

   xRosato, Dominick.

   Markets for Plastics. Van Nos Reinhold.

Rosberg, Carl Gustav.
   xRosberg, Carl G.

ed. Socialism in Sub-Saharan Africa: A New
Assessment. U of Cal Intl St.

Rosberger, Paul.
xRosberger, Paul.
The Theory of Total Consonance. Fairleigh
Dickinson.

Rosborough, E H.
xRosborough, E. H.
Tying & Fishing the Fuzzy Nymphs. Stackpole.

Rosbottom, Ronald C., 1942-
xRosbottom, Ronald C.
Choderlos De Laclos. Twayne.

Rosch, Eleanor.
xRosch, Eleanor.
ed. Cognition & Categorization. Halsted Pr.

Roscher, Wilhelm Georg Friedrich, 1817-1894
xRoscher, William.
Principles of Political Economy. Arno.
Roscher, William. *see* Roscher, Wilhelm Georg Friedrich.
Roscoe, E. S. *see* Roscoe, Edward Stanley.
Roscoe, Edward S. *see* Roscoe, Edward Stanley.

Roscoe, Edward Stanley, 1849-1932
xRoscoe, E. S.
Aspects of Doctor Johnson. Folcroft.
xRoscoe, Edward S.
The English Scene in the Eighteenth Century.
Folcroft.
Roscoe, J. T. *see* Roscoe, John T.

Roscoe, John.
xRoscoe, John.
Soul of Central Africa: A General Account of
the Mackie Ethnological Expedition. Negro
U Pr.
Twenty-Five Years in East Africa. Negro U Pr.

Roscoe, John T.
xRoscoe, J. T.
Fundamental Research Statistics for the
Behavioral Sciences. HR&W.

Roscoe, William.
xRoscoe, William.
The Life & Pontificate of Leo the Tenth.
Ridgeway Bks.
Rosden. *see* Rosden, George Eric.

Rosden, George Eric.
xRosden.
jt. auth. The Law of Advertising. Bender.
Rose. *see* Rose, Caroline (Baer).

Rose, Al.
xRose, Al.
Eubie Blake. Schirmer Bks.
Rose, Alan H. *see* Rose, Alan Henry.

Rose, Alan Henry, 1938-
xRose, Alan H.
Demonic Vision: Racial Fantasy & Southern
Fiction. Shoe String.

Rose, Albert, 1910-
xRose, Albert.
Concepts in Photoconductivity & Allied
Problems. Krieger.

Rose, Alexander.
xRose, Alexander.
Hamilton Club. S&S.
Rose, Anne. *see* Rose, Anne K.

Rose, Anne K.
xRose, Anne.
As Right As Right Can Be. Dial.
As Right As Right Can Be. Dial.
How Does a Czar Eat Potatoes?. Lothrop.
Spider in the Sky. Har-Row.
The Talking Turnip. Parents.
The Triumphs of Fuzzy Fogtop. Dial.

Rose, Anthony H.
xRose, Anthony H.
ed. Thermobiology. Acad Pr.
Rose, Arnold. *see* Rose, Arnold Marshall.
Rose, Arnold M. *see* Rose, Arnold Marshall.

Rose, Arnold Marshall, 1918-
xRose, Arnold.

Negro in America: The Condensed Version of
Gunnar Myrdal's an American Dilemma.
Peter Smith.
xRose, Arnold M.
ed. Institutions of Advanced Societies. U of
Minn Pr.
Libel & Academic Freedom: A Lawsuit Against
Political Extremists. U of Minn Pr.
Sociology: The Study of Human Relations.
Phila Bk Co.
Theory & Method in Social Sciences.
Greenwood.
Rose, Burton D. *see* Rose, Burton David.

Rose, Burton David.
xRose, Burton D.
Clinical Physiology of Acid Base & Electrolyte
Disorders. McGraw.
Pathophysiology of Renal Disease. McGraw.

Rose, Carol M.
xRose, Carol M.
Some Emerging Issues in Legal Liability of
Children's Agencies. Child Welfare.

Rose, Caroline (Baer), 1913-
xRose.
The Study of Sociology. Merrill.
Rose, Clifford F. *see* Rose, Frank Clifford.

Rose, Darrell E.
xRose, Darrell E.
Audiological Assessment. P-H.

Rose, David P.
xRose, David P.
Endocrinology of Cancer. CRC Pr.
Rose, Edgar. *see* Rose, Edgar A.

Rose, Edgar A.
xRose, Edgar.
Housing for the Aged. Lexington Bks.

Rose, Elliot.
xRose, Elliot.
A Razor for a Goat: A Discussion of Certain
Problems in the History of Witchcraft &
Diabolism. U of Toronto Pr.

Rose, Ernest Andreas Gottlieb, 1899-
xRose, Ernst.
A History of German Literature. NYU Pr.

Rose, Ernst, 1899-
xRose, Ernst.
Faith from the Abyss: Hermann Hesse's Way
from Romanticism to Modernity. NYU Pr.
Rose, Ernst. *see* Rose, Ernest Andreas Gottlieb.

Rose, Ethne.
xRose, Ethne.
Dolls. Scribner.

Rose, Evelyn.
xRose, Evelyn.
The Complete International Jewish Cookbook.
B&N.
The Complete International Jewish Cookbook.
St Martin.

Rose, Francis.
xRose, Francis.
The Observer's Book of Wild Flowers.
Scribner.

Rose, Frank.
xRose, Frank.
Real Men. Doubleday.

Rose, Frank Clifford.
xRose, Clifford F.
Migraine: The Facts. Oxford U Pr.

Rose, George G.
xRose, George G.
ed. Atlas of Vertebrate Cells in Tissue Culture.
Acad Pr.
ed. Cinemicrography in Cell Biology. Acad Pr.

Rose, Gerald.
xRose, Gerald.

The Tiger-Skin Rug. P-H.

Rose, Gordon.
xRose, Gordon.
Counselling & School Social Work: An
Experimental Study. Wiley.

Rose, Harold M.
xRose, Harold M.
Lethal Aspects of Urban Violence. Lexington
Bks.

Rose, Helen.
xRose, Helen.
Begin to Live. St Martin.
Rose, Herbert J. *see* Rose, Herbert Jennings.

Rose, Herbert Jennings, 1883-
xRose, Herbert J.
ed. Gods & Heroes of the Greeks: An
Introduction to Greek Mythology. Peter
Smith.
Primitive Culture in Italy. Arno.
Religion in Greece & Rome. Har-Row.

Rose, Howard N.
xRose, Howard N.
A Thesaurus of Slang. Gale.
Rose, J. Holland. *see* Rose, John Holland.

Rose, Jeanne, 1940-
xRose, Jeanne.
Jeanne Rose's Herbal Guide to Inner Health.
G&D.

Rose, Jerry D., 1933-
xRose, Jerry D.
Introduction to Sociology. Rand.
Peoples: The Ethnic Dimension in Human
Relations. Rand.
Rose, John H. *see* Rose, John Holland.

Rose, John Holland, 1855-1942
xRose, J. Holland.
The Mediterranean in the Ancient World.
Ares.
xRose, John H.
Mediterranean in the Ancient World.
Greenwood.

Rose, Joseph A.
xRose, Joseph A.
How to Be Successful. McClain.

Rose, Joseph L.
xRose, Joseph L.
Basic Physics in Diagnostic Ultrasound. Wiley.

Rose, Karen.
xRose, Karen.
In the Land of the Mind. Atheneum.

Rose, L. M., Ph.d
xRose, L. M.
The Application of Mathematical Modelling to
Process Development & Design. Halsted Pr.
Rose, Leesha. *see* Rose, Leesha, 1922.

Rose, Leesha, 1922.
xRose, Leesha.
The Tulips Are Red. A S Barnes.

Rose, Leo E.
xRose, Leo E.
Nepal: Profile of a Himalayan Kingdom.
Westview.
The Politics of Bhutan. Cornell U Pr.
Politics of Nepal: Persistence & Change in an
Asian Monarchy. Cornell U Pr.

Rose, Linda C.
xRose, Linda C.
Disease Beliefs in Mexican-American
Communities. R & E Res Assoc.
Rose, Lisle A. *see* Rose, Lisle Abbott.

Rose, Lisle Abbott, 1936-
xRose, Lisle A.
The Long Shadow: Reflections on the Second
World War Era. Greenwood.

Rose, Margaret A.
xRose, Margaret A.

Parody-Meta-Fiction: An Analysis of Parody
  As a Critical Mirror to the Writing &
  Reception of Fiction. Biblio Dist.
Reading the Young Marx & Engels: Poetry,
  Parody & the Censor. Rowman.
Rose, Mark.
  xRose, Mark.
    Spenser's Art: A Companion to Book One of
      the Faerie Queene. Harvard U Pr.
Rose, Martial.
  xRose, Martial.
    E. M. Forster. Arco.
Rose, Michael, 1937-
  xRose, Michael.
    Servants of Post-Industrial Power: Sociologie
      Du Travail in Modern France. M E Sharpe.
Rose, Michael T.
  xRose, Michael T.
    A Prayer for Relief: The Constitutional
      Infirmities of the Military Academies'
      Conduct, Honor, & Ehtics Systems.
      Rothman.
Rose, N. A.
  xRose, N. A.
    Gentile Zionists: Study in Anglo-Zionist
      Diplomacy 1929-1939. Biblio Dist.
Rose, Pete.
  xRose, Pete.
    Charlie Hustle. P-H.
    Charlie Hustle. P-H.
    Pete Rose: My Life in Baseball. Doubleday.
Rose, Peter I. see Rose, Peter Isaac.
Rose, Peter Isaac, 1933-
  xRose, Peter I.
    ed. Nation of Nations: The Ethnic Experience
      & the Racial Crisis. Random.
    ed. Socialization & the Life Cycle. St Martin.
    Sociology: Inquiring into Society. Har-Row.
    Strangers in Their Midst: Small-Town Jews &
      Their Neighbors. Richwood Pub.
    ed. The Study of Society: An Integrated
      Anthology. Random.
    The Subject Is Race: Traditional Ideologies &
      the Teaching of Race Relations. Oxford U Pr.
Rose, Peter L. De. see De Rose, Peter L.
Rose, R. B.
  xRose, R. B.
    Gracchus Babeuf: The First Revolutionary
      Communist. Stanford U Pr.
Rose, Richard.
  xRose, Richard.
    Can Government Go Bankrupt?. Basic.
    Governing Without Consensus: An Irish
      Perspective. Beacon Pr.
    The Problem of Party Government. Free Pr.
Rose, Ronald, 1920-
  xRose, Ronald.
    illus. Ngari the Hunter. HarBraceJ.
Rose, Saul.
  xRose, Saul.
    Socialism in Southern Asia. Octagon.
Rose, Sheldon D.
  xRose, Sheldon D.
    Group Therapy: A Behavioral Approach. P-H.
Rose, Tom, 1928-
  xRose, Tom.
    Economics: Principles & Policy from a
      Christian Perspective. American Ent Texas.
    Economics: Principles & Policy, from a
      Christian Perspective. Inst Free Enterprise.
    Economics: Principles & Policy from a
      Christian Perspective. Mott Media.
    How to Succeed in Business: A Resource Unit
      on Understanding Business & Getting Ahead
      in the Business World. American Ent Texas.
    How to Succeed in Business: A Resource Unit
      on Understanding Business & Getting Ahead
      in the Business World. Inst Free Enterprise.
Rose, Warren.
  xRose, Warren.

Logistics Management: Systems &
  Components. Wm C Brown.
Rose, Wendy.
  xRose, Wendy.
    Hopi Roadrunner, Dancing. Greenfld Rev Pr.
Rose, Will. see Rose, Will P.
Rose, Will P.
  xRose, Will.
    The Vanishing Village. Twines Catskill.
Rose, William.
  xRose, William.
    ed. Contemporary Movements in European
      Literature. Arno.
    Contemporary Movements in European
      Literature. R West.
Rose, William K., 1935-
  xRose, William K.
    Astrophysics. Irvington.
Rose, Willie L. see Rose, Willie Lee Nichols.
Rose, Willie Lee Nichols, 1927-
  xRose, Willie L.
    Rehearsal for Reconstruction: The Port Royal
      Experiment. Oxford U Pr.
    Rehearsal for Reconstruction: The Port Royal
      Experiment. Oxford U Pr.
Rose-Ackerman, Susan.
  xRose-Ackerman, Susan.
    Corruption: A Study in Political Economy.
      Acad Pr.
Rose-Troup, Frances. see Rose-Troup, Frances (James).
Rose-Troup, Frances (James), 1859-
  xRose-Troup, Frances.
    Massachusetts Bay Company & Its
      Predecessors. Kelley.
Rosebault, Charles J.
  xRosebault, Charles J.
    When Dana Was the Sun: A Story of Personal
      Journalism. Greenwood.
Rosebery, A. P. see Rosebery, Archibald Philip Primrose,
  5th Earl Of.
Rosebery, Archibald P. see Rosebery, Archibald Philip
  Primrose, 5th Earl Of.
**Rosebery, Archibald Philip Primrose, 5th Earl Of,
  1847-1929**
  xRosebery, A. P.
    Lord Rosebery's North American Journal
      1873. Shoe String.
  xRosebery, Archibald P.
    Pitt. AMS Pr.
    Pitt. Greenwood.
Rosebrock, Ellen F. see Rosebrock, Ellen Fletcher.
Rosebrock, Ellen Fletcher.
  xRosebrock, Ellen F.
    Counting-House Days in South Street: New
      York's Early Brick Seaport Buildings. South
      St Sea Mus.
    South Street: A Photographic Guide to New
      York City's Historic Seaport. Dover.
    South Street: A Photographic Guide to New
      York City's Historic Seaport. Peter Smith.
Rosebush, Waldo E. see Rosebush, Waldo Emerson.
Rosebush, Waldo Emerson, 1889-1961
  xRosebush, Waldo E.
    American Firearms & the Changing Frontier.
      Eastern Wash.
Rosecrance, R. N.
  xRosecrance, R. N.
    Australian Diplomacy & Japan, 1945-51. Intl
      Schol Bk Serv.
Rosecrance, Richard N.
  xRosecrance, Richard N.
    Action & Reaction in World Politics:
      International Systems in Perspective.
      Greenwood.
    Defense of the Realm: British Strategy in the
      Nuclear Epoch. Columbia U Pr.
    ed. Dispersion of Nuclear Weapons: Strategy &
      Politics. Columbia U Pr.
Rosecrans, Glen.
  xRosecrans, Glen.

A Music Notation Primer. Music Sales.
  xRosecrans, Glen R.
    A Music Notation Primer. Music Sales.
Rosecrans, Glen R. see Rosecrans, Glen.
Rosefielde, Steven.
  xRosefielde, Steven.
    ed. World Communism at the Crossroads:
      Military Ascendancy, Political Economy &
      Human Welfare. Kluwer Boston.
Rosefsky, Robert. see Rosefsky, Robert S.
Rosefsky, Robert S.
  xRosefsky, Robert.
    The Ins & Outs of Moving. Follett.
Rosegger, Gerhard.
  xRosegger, Gerhard.
    The Economics of Production & Innovation:
      An Industrial Perspective. Pergamon.
Roseliep, Raymond, 1917-
  xRoseliep, Raymond.
    Love Makes the Air Light. Norton.
Roseman, Curtis C.
  xRoseman, Curtis C.
    Changing Migration Patterns Within the United
      States. Assn Am Geographers.
Roseman, Edward.
  xRoseman, Edward.
    Confronting Nonpromotability: How to
      Manage a Stalled Career. Am Mgmt.
Rosemergy, John C., 1921-
  xRosemergy, John C.
    Celestial Horizons: A Concise View of the
      Universe. Allyn.
Rosen, A. see Rosen, Arnold.
Rosen, Arnold.
  xRosen, A.
    Word Processing. P-H.
Rosen, Bernard.
  xRosen, Bernard.
    Strategies of Ethics. HM.
Rosen, C. see Rosen, George.
Rosen, Charles, 1927-
  xRosen, Charles.
    Arnold Schoenberg. Viking Pr.
    The Classical Style: Haydn, Mozart,
      Beethoven. Norton.
    The Classical Style: Haydn, Mozart,
      Beethoven. Viking Pr.
Rosen, David H., 1945-
  xRosen, David H.
    Lesbianism: A Study of Female Homosexuality.
      C C Thomas.
Rosen, Elliot A., 1928-
  xRosen, Elliot A.
    Hoover, Roosevelt, and the Brains Trust: From
      Depression to New Deal. Columbia U Pr.
Rosen, Ephraim.
  xRosen, Ephraim.
    Abnormal Psychology. HR&W.
Rosen, Esther K. see Rosen, Esther Katz.
Rosen, Esther Katz, 1896-
  xRosen, Esther K.
    A Comparison of the Intellectual &
      Educational Status of Neurotic & Normal
      Children in Public Schools. AMS Pr.
Rosen, George, 1920-
  xRosen, C.
    Some Aspects of Industrial Finance in India.
      Free Pr.
  xRosen, George.
    Democracy & Economic Change in India. U of
      Cal Pr.
    History of Public Health. MD Pubns.
    Peasant Society in Changing Economy:
      Comparative Development in Southeast Asia
      & India. U of Ill Pr.
Rosen, Gerald. see Rosen, Gerald M.
Rosen, Gerald M., 1945-
  xRosen, Gerald.

The Relaxation Book: An Illustrated Self-Help
Program. P-H.

Rosen, Harold J.
xRosen, Harold J.
Construction Materials Evaluation & Selection:
A Systematic Approach. Wiley.

Rosen, Hugh.
xRosen, Hugh.
Pathway to Piaget: A Guide for Clinicians,
Educators, & Developmentalists. Postgrad
Intl.

Rosen, John N., 1902-
xRosen, John N.
Direct Psychoanalytic Psychiatry. Grune.

Rosen, Lawrence, 1941-
xRosen, Lawrence.
American Indians & the Law. Transaction Bks.
The Delinquent & Non-Delinquent in a High
Delinquent Area. R & E Res Assoc.

Rosen, Lawrence R.
xRosen, Lawrence R.
Calculator Mathematics for the Real Estate
Professional. Dow Jones-Irwin.
When & How to Profit from Buying & Selling
Gold. Dow Jones-Irwin.

Rosen, Marvin.
xRosen, Marvin.
ed. The History of Mental Retardation:
Collected Papers. Univ Park.
Notes & Blots from a Psychologist's Desk.
Nelson-Hall.

Rosen, Marvin J.
xRosen, Marvin J.
Introduction to Photography: A Self Directing
Approach. HM.

Rosen, Milton J.
xRosen, Milton J.
Surfactants & Interfacial Phenomena. Wiley.

Rosen, Ned A.
xRosen, Ned A.
Leadership Change & Work-Group Dynamics:
An Experiment. Cornell U Pr.

Rosen, Paul L.
xRosen, Paul L.
The Supreme Court & Social Science. U of Ill
Pr.

Rosen, Pauline.
xRosen, Pauline.
Bottle Beauty, Guide to Arranging with
Bottles. P Rosen.

Rosen, Philip, 1928-
xRosen, Philip.
The Neglected Dimension: Ethnicity in
American Life. U of Notre Dame Pr.
Rosen, R. D. see Rosen, Richard Dean.

Rosen, Richard Dean, 1949-
xRosen, R. D.
Psychobabble. Atheneum.
Psychobabble. Avon.

Rosen, Stanley, 1929-
xRosen, Stanley.
G. W. F. Hegel: An Introduction to the
Science of Wisdom. Yale U Pr.

Rosen, Stephen, 1934-
xRosen, Stephen.
Weathering: How the Atmosphere Conditions
Your Body, Your Mind, Your Moods & Your
Health. M Evans.
Rosen, Stephen. see Rosen, Steven.

Rosen, Steven.
xRosen, Stephen.
The Logic of International Relations. Winthrop.
xRosen, Steven J.
The Logic of International Relations. Winthrop.
Rosen, Steven J. see Rosen, Steven.

Rosen, Winifred.
xRosen, Winifred.
Cruisin for a Bruisin. Knopf.
Marvin's Manhole. Dial.
Rosenau, J. N. see Rosenau, James N.

Rosenau, James N.
xRosenau, J. N.
National Leadership & Foreign Policy: A Case
Study in the Mobilization of Public Support.
Princeton U Pr.
xRosenau, James N.
The Dramas of Political Life. Duxbury Pr.
In Search of Global Patterns. Free Pr.
Race in International Politics: A Dialogue in
Five Parts. U of Denver Intl.
Scientific Study of Foreign Policy. Nichols
Pub.
Study of Global Interdependence: Essays on
the Transnationalization of World Affairs.
Nichols Pub.
Study of Political Adaptation. Nichols Pub.
Rosenbach, Joseph B. see Rosenbach, Joseph Bernhardt.

Rosenbach, Joseph Bernhardt, 1897-1951
xRosenbach, Joseph B.
College Algebra. Wiley.
College Algebra with Trigonometry. Wiley.
Rosenbauer, Donna. see Rosenbauer, Donna L.

Rosenbauer, Donna L.
xRosenbauer, Donna.
Introduction to Fire Protection Law. Natl Fire
Prot.

Rosenbaum, C. Peter.
xRosenbaum, C. Peter.
ed. Psychiatric Treatment: Crisis, Clinic &
Consultation. McGraw.

Rosenbaum, Helen.
xRosenbaum, Helen.
Don't Swallow the Avocado Pit-- & What to
Do with the Rest of It. Popular Lib.
Don't Swallow the Avocado Pit & What to Do
with the Rest of It. Eriksson.

Rosenbaum, Jean.
xRosenbaum, Jean.
How to Avoid Divorce. Har-Row.
Living with Teenagers. Stein & Day.
Stepparenting. Chandler & Sharp.
Stepparenting. Dutton.

Rosenbaum, Kurt.
xRosenbaum, Kurt.
Community of Fate: German-Soviet Diplomatic
Relations, 1922-1928. Syracuse U Pr.

Rosenbaum, Max.
xRosenbaum, Max.
ed. Group Psychotherapy & Group Function.
Basic.
The Intensive Group Experience. Free Pr.
Rosenbaum, Max. see Rosenbaum, Max Comp.

Rosenbaum, Max Comp.
xRosenbaum, Max.
ed. Group Psychotherapy from the Southwest.
Gordon.

Rosenbaum, Myron G.
xRosenbaum, Myron G.
Understanding Arthritis. Green.
Rosenbaum, Peter. see Rosenbaum, Peter S.

Rosenbaum, Peter S.
xRosenbaum, Peter.
Peer-Mediated Instruction. Tchrs Coll.
xRosenbaum, Peter S.
Grammar of English Predicate Complement
Constructions. MIT Pr.
Rosenbaum, Stanford P. see Rosenbaum, Stanford
Patrick.

Rosenbaum, Stanford Patrick.
xRosenbaum, Stanford P.
ed. Concordance to the Poems of Emily
Dickinson. Cornell U Pr.

Rosenbaum, Walter A.
xRosenbaum, Walter A.
The Politics of Environmental Concern.
HR&W.
The Politics of Environmental Concern.
Praeger.

Rosenberg, Alan L.
xRosenberg, Alan L.

ed. Living with Your Arthritis: A Home
Program for Arthritis Management. Arco.
Rosenberg, Arnold. see Rosenberg, Arnold S.

Rosenberg, Arnold S.
xRosenberg, Arnold.
The Social Studies Student Investigates
Modern Wars. Rosen Pr.

Rosenberg, Bernard.
xRosenberg, Bernard.
The Real Tinsel. Macmillan.
Rosenberg, Carroll S. see Rosenberg, Carroll Smith.

Rosenberg, Carroll Smith.
xRosenberg, Carroll S.
Religion & the Rise of the American City: The
New York City Mission Movement,
1812-1870. Cornell U Pr.

Rosenberg, Charles E.
xRosenberg, Charles E.
Cholera Years: The United States in 1832,
1849, & 1866. U of Chicago Pr.
ed. The Family in History. U of Pa Pr.
No Other Gods: On Science & American
Social Thought. Johns Hopkins.

Rosenberg, Claude N.
xRosenberg, Claude N.
The Common Sense Way to Stock Market
Profits. NAL.
Stock Market Primer. Warner Bks.

Rosenberg, Daniel, 1953-
xRosenberg, Daniel.
Mary Brown: From Harper's Ferry to
California. Am Inst Marxist.

Rosenberg, David A.
xRosenberg, David A.
ed. Marcos & Martial Law in the Philippines.
Cornell U Pr.
Rosenberg, E. see Rosenberg, Emily S.

Rosenberg, Edgar.
xRosenberg, Edgar.
From Shylock to Svengali: Jewish Stereotypes
in English Fiction. Stanford U Pr.

Rosenberg, Eleanor.
xRosenberg, Eleanor.
Leicester, Patron of Letters. Octagon.

Rosenberg, Emily S.
xRosenberg, E.
Postwar America: Readings & Reminiscences.
P-H.

Rosenberg, Hans, 1904-
xRosenberg, Hans.
Bureaucracy, Aristocracy & Autocracy: The
Prussian Experience, 1660-1815. Beacon Pr.
Bureaucracy, Aristocracy & Autocracy: The
Prussian Experience, 1660-1815. Harvard U
Pr.

Rosenberg, Harold.
xRosenberg, Harold.
Barnett Newman. Abrams.
The De-Definition of Art. Macmillan.
Discovering the Present: Three Decades in Art,
Culture, & Politics. U of Chicago Pr.

Rosenberg, Henry J.
xRosenberg, Henry J.
Projects in Clerical Record Keeping. SW Pub.

Rosenberg, Israel.
xRosenberg, Israel.
Shay Agnon's World of Mystery & Allegory:
An Analysis of Iddo & 'Aynam. Dorrance.
Rosenberg, J. see Rosenberg, Jack M.
Rosenberg, J. F. see Rosenberg, Jay F.

Rosenberg, Jack, 1932-
xRosenberg, Jack.
Total Orgasm. Random.

Rosenberg, Jack M.
xRosenberg, J.
Prescriber's Guide to Drug Interactions. Med
Economics.

Rosenberg, Jakob, 1893-
xRosenberg, Jakob.

Great Draughtsmen from Pisanello to Picasso.
Har-Row.
Great Draughtsmen from Pisanello to Picasso.
Harvard U Pr.

Rosenberg, James L.
xRosenberg, James L.
A Primer of Kinetics. AMS Pr.
Rosenberg, Jay. see Rosenberg, Jay F.
Rosenberg, Jay F.
xRosenberg, J. F.
Linguistic Representation. Kluwer Boston.
xRosenberg, Jay.
The Practice of Philosophy: A Handbook for
Beginners. P-H.
xRosenberg, Jay F.
Readings in the Philosophy of Language. P-H.
Rosenberg, Jerome L. see Rosenberg, Jerome Laib.
Rosenberg, Jerome Laib, 1921-
xRosenberg, Jerome L.
Schaum's Outline of College Chemistry.
McGraw.
Rosenberg, Jerome R.
xRosenberg, Jerome R.
Managing Your Own Money. Newsweek.
Rosenberg, Jerry M. see Rosenberg, Jerry Martin.
Rosenberg, Jerry Martin.
xRosenberg, Jerry M.
Dictionary of Business & Management. Wiley.
Rosenberg, Kenyon C.
xRosenberg, Kenyon C.
Media Equipment: A Guide & Dictionary. Libs
Unl.
Rosenberg, L. see Rosenberg, Larry J.
Rosenberg, Larry J.
xRosenberg, L.
Marketing. P-H.
Rosenberg, Magda.
xRosenberg, Magda.
Sixty-Plus & Fit Again: Exercises for Older
Men & Women. M Evans.
Rosenberg, Marshall B.
xRosenberg, Marshall B.
Diagnostic Teaching. Spec Child.
Rosenberg, Marvin.
xRosenberg, Marvin.
The Masks of King Lear. U of Cal Pr.
The Masks of Macbeth. U of Cal Pr.
Rosenberg, Maurice, 19189
xRosenberg, Maurice.
Pretrial Conference & Effective Justice: A
Controlled Test in Personal Injury Litigation.
Columbia U Pr.
Rosenberg, Morris.
xRosenberg, Morris.
Conceiving the Self. Basic.
Logic of Survey Analysis. Basic.
Society & the Adolescent Self-Image. Princeton
U Pr.
Rosenberg, Norman J., 1930-
xRosenberg, Norman J.
ed. North American Droughts. Westview.
Rosenberg, Peter D.
xRosenberg, Peter D.
Patent Law Fundamentals. Boardman.
Rosenberg, Philip. see Rosenberg, Phillip.
Rosenberg, Phillip.
xRosenberg, Philip.
Point Blank. Avon.
Point Blank. G&D.
Rosenberg, R. M. see Rosenberg, Reinhardt Mathias.
Rosenberg, R. Robert. see Rosenberg, Reuben Robert.
Rosenberg, Reinhardt Mathias.
xRosenberg, R. M.
Analytical Dynamics of Discrete Systems.
Plenum Pub.
Rosenberg, Reuben Robert.
xRosenberg, R. Robert.

Business & the Law. McGraw.
Business Mathematics. McGraw.
Business Mathematics. McGraw.
College Business Law. McGraw.
College Mathematics for Accounting &
Business Administration. McGraw.
Rosenberg, Roger N.
xRosenberg, Roger N.
ed. Neurology. Grune.
Rosenberg, Sidney, 1939-
xRosenberg, Sidney.
Any Dog Named Papageno Rosenberg Must
Be a Little Bit of All Right!. Chateau Pub.
Rosenberg, Stuart.
xRosenberg, Stuart.
When the Bough Breaks. T Y Crowell.
Rosenberg, Stuart E.
xRosenberg, Stuart E.
More Loves Than One: The Bible Confronts
Psychiatry. Ungar.
Rosenberg, William G.
xRosenberg, William G.
Liberals in the Russian Revolution: The
Constitutional Democratic Party, 1917-1921.
Princeton U Pr.
Rosenberger, Francis C. see Rosenberger, Francis
Coleman.
Rosenberger, Francis Coleman, 1915-
xRosenberger, Francis C.
An Alphabet. U Pr of Va.
Rosenberger, Homer T. see Rosenberger, Homer Tope.
Rosenberger, Homer Tope, 1908-
xRosenberger, Homer T.
Adventures & Philosophy of a Pennsylvania
Dutchman: An Autobiography in a Broad
Setting. Rose Hill.
Grassroots Philosophy for the Modern Mind.
Rose Hill.
Rosenberger, Joseph.
xRosenberger, Joseph.
The Mato Grosso Horror. Pinnacle Bks.
Nightmare in Algeria. Pinnacle Bks.
Vengeance of the Golden Hawk. Pinnacle Bks.
Rosenberger, Noah B. see Rosenberger, Noah Bryan.
Rosenberger, Noah Bryan, 1881-
xRosenberger, Noah B.
The Place of the Elementary Calculus in the
Senior High School Mathematics. AMS Pr.
Rosenberry, Edward H.
xRosenberry, Edward H.
Melville. Routledge & Kegan.
Melville & the Comic Spirit. Octagon.
Rosenblatt, Bernard A. see Rosenblatt, Bernard Abraham.
Rosenblatt, Bernard Abraham, 1886-
xRosenblatt, Bernard A.
The American Bridge to the Israel
Commonwealth. Greenwood.
Rosenblatt, Jack.
xRosenblatt, Jack.
Direct & Alternating Current Machinery.
McGraw.
Rosenblatt, Jon, 1947-
xRosenblatt, Jon.
Sylvia Plath: The Poetry of Initiation. U of NC
Pr.
Rosenblatt, Louise M. see Rosenblatt, Louise Michelle.
Rosenblatt, Louise Michelle.
xRosenblatt, Louise M.
The Reader, the Text, the Poem: The
Transactional Theory of the Literary Work. S
Ill U Pr.
Rosenblatt, Murray.
xRosenblatt, Murray.
Markov Processes: Structure & Asymptotic
Behavior. Springer-Verlag.
Random Processes. Springer-Verlag.
Rosenblatt, Paul C.
xRosenblatt, Paul C.

Grief & Mourning in Cross-Cultural
Perspective. HRAFP.
Rosenblatt, S. Bernard.
xRosenblatt, S. Bernard.
Communication in Business. P-H.
Modern Business: A Systems Approach. HM.
Rosenblatt, Samuel M.
xRosenblatt, Samuel M.
ed. Technology & Economic Development: A
Realistic Perspective. Westview.
Rosenblatt, Suzanne.
xRosenblatt, Suzanne.
Everyone Is Going Somewhere. Macmillan.
Rosenbloom, David H.
xRosenbloom, David H.
Federal Equal Employment Opportunity:
Politics & Public Personnel Administration.
Praeger.
Federal Service & the Constitution: The
Development of the Public Employment
Relationship. Cornell U Pr.
Rosenbloom, Jerry. see Rosenbloom, Jerry S.
Rosenbloom, Jerry S.
xRosenbloom, Jerry.
A Case Study in Risk Management. P-H.
xRosenbloom, Jerry S.
Automobile Liability Claims: Insurance
Company Philosophies & Practices. Irwin.
Rosenbloom, Joseph.
xRosenbloom, Joseph.
Bananas Don't Grow on Trees: A Guide to
Popular Misconceptions. Sterling.
Consumer Complaint Guide 1979. Macmillan
Info.
Consumer Protection Guide, 1978. Macmillan
Info.
Daffy Dictionary: Funabridged Definitions
from Aardvark to Zuider Zee. Sterling.
Doctor Knock-Knock's Official Knock-Knock
Dictionary. Sterling.
Gigantic Joke Book. Sterling.
Silly Verse (and Even Worse). Sterling.
Twist These on Your Tongue. Elsevier-Nelson.
Rosenbloom, Joseph R.
xRosenbloom, Joseph R.
Conversion to Judaism: From the Biblical
Period to the Present. Ktav.
Rosenblueth, Emilio, 1926-
xRosenblueth, Emilio.
ed. Design of Earthquake Resistant Structures.
Halsted Pr.
Rosenblum, Art. see Rosenblum, Arthur.
Rosenblum, Arthur.
xRosenblum, Art.
The Natural Birth Control Book. Aquarian Res.
Rosenblum, Davida, 1927-
xRosenblum, Davida.
Relatives. Dial.
Rosenblum, Estelle. see Rosenblum, Estelle H.
Rosenblum, Estelle H.
xRosenblum, Estelle.
Fundamentals of Hearing for Health
Professionals. Little.
Rosenblum, Marc.
xRosenblum, Marc.
Economics of the Consumer. Lerner Pubns.
How a Market Economy Works. Lerner Pubns.
Stock Market. Lerner Pubns.
Rosenblum, Martin J.
xRosenblum, Martin J.
Home. Membrane Pr.
Rosenblum, Mort.
xRosenblum, Mort.
Coups & Earthquakes: Reporting the World for
America. Har-Row.
Rosenblum, Myron.
xRosenblum, Myron.

Chemistry of the Iron Group Metallocenes:
Ferrocene, Ruthenocene, Osmocene. Krieger.
Rosenblum, Robert.
xRosenblum, Robert.
Cubism & Twentieth Century Art. Abrams.
Cubism & Twentieth Century Art. P-H.
Rosenblum, Robert. see Rosenblum, Robert J.
Rosenblum, Robert J.
xRosenblum, Robert.
The Sweetheart Deal. Ballantine.
Rosenblum, Victor G.
xRosenblum, Victor G.
ed. Cases on Constitutional Law: Political
Roles of the Supreme Court. Dorsey.
Rosenbrock, H. H.
xRosenbrock, H. H.
Computer-Aided Control System Design. Acad
Pr.
Rosenfeld, A. see Rosenfeld, Azriel.
Rosenfeld, Alvin H. see Rosenfeld, Alvin Hirsch.
Rosenfeld, Alvin Hirsch.
xRosenfeld, Alvin H.
ed. Confronting the Holocaust: The Impact of
Elie Wiesel. Ind U Pr.
Double Dying: Reflections on Holocaust
Literature. Ind U Pr.
Rosenfeld, Azriel.
xRosenfeld, A.
ed. Digital Picture Analysis. Springer-Verlag.
xRosenfeld, Azriel.
An Introduction to Algebraic Structures.
Holden-Day.
Picture Languages: Formal Models for Picture
Recognition. Acad Pr.
Rosenfeld, Erwin. see Rosenfeld, Erwin M.
Rosenfeld, Erwin M.
xRosenfeld, Erwin.
Afro Asian Culture Studies. Barron.
Rosenfeld, Jeffrey P.
xRosenfeld, Jeffrey P.
The Legacy of Aging: Inheritance &
Disinheritance in Social Perspective. Ablex
Pub.
Rosenfeld, Lawrence. see Rosenfeld, Lawrence B.
Rosenfeld, Lawrence B.
xRosenfeld, Lawrence.
Human Interaction in the Small Group Setting.
Merrill.
Rosenfeld, Marthe.
xRosenfeld, Marthe.
Edmond Jaloux: The Evolution of a Novelist.
Philos Lib.
Rosenfeld, Megan.
xRosenfeld, Megan.
Journalism & the New Woman. Watts.
Rosenfeld, Morris, 1862-1923
xRosenfeld, Morris.
Songs from the Ghetto. Irvington.
Rosenfeld, Paul, 1890-1946
xRosenfeld, Paul.
By Way of Art: Criticisms of Music, Literature,
Painting, Sculpture & the Dance. Arno.
Discoveries of a Music Critic. Scholarly.
Discoveries of a Music Critic. Vienna Hse.
Men Seen: Twenty Four Modern Authors.
Arno.
Musical Chronicle, 1917-1923. Arno.
Rosenfeld, Sam.
xRosenfeld, Sam.
Story of Coins. Harvey.
Rosenfeld, Sybil. see Rosenfeld, Sybil Marion.
Rosenfeld, Sybil Marion, 1903-
xRosenfeld, Sybil.
Strolling Players & Drama in the Provinces,
1660-1765. Octagon.
Rosenfels, Paul.
xRosenfels, Paul.

Homosexuality: The Psychology of the Creative
Process. Libra.
Love & Power: The Psychology of
Interpersonal Creativity. Libra.
Psychoanalysis & Civilization. Libra.
Rosenfield, Arthur T.
xRosenfield, Arthur T.
ed. Diagnostic Imaging in Renal Disease. ACC.
Rosenfield, Claire.
xRosenfield, Claire.
Paradise of Snakes: An Archetypal Analysis of
Conrad's Political Novels. U of Chicago Pr.
Rosenfield, Coleman R., 1923-
xRosenfield, Coleman R.
Law of Franchising. Lawyers Co-Op.
Rosenfield, James.
xRosenfield, James.
The Lion & the Lily. Dodd.
Rosenfield, John M.
xRosenfield, John M.
The Dynastic Arts of the Kushans. U of Cal
Pr.
Rosenfield, Lawrence. see Rosenfield, Lawrence William.
Rosenfield, Lawrence William.
xRosenfield, Lawrence.
The Communicative Experience. Allyn.
Rosenfield, Leonora. see Rosenfield, Leonora Davidson
(Cohen).
Rosenfield, Leonora Davidson (Cohen), 1909-
xRosenfield, Leonora.
From Beast Machine to Man Machine: Animal
Soul in French Letters from Descartes to La
Mettrie. Octagon.
Rosenfield, Richard E., 1915-
xRosenfield, Richard E.
Immunohematology Syllabus. Thieme-Stratton.
Rosengarten, A. see Rosengarten, Albert.
Rosengarten, Albert, b. 1809
xRosengarten, A.
A Handbook of Architectural Styles.
Longwood Pr.
Rosengarten, Frank, 1927-
xRosengarten, Frank.
Vasco Pratolini: The Development of a Social
Novelist. S Ill U Pr.
Rosenhan, D. see Rosenhan, David.
Rosenhan, David.
xRosenhan, D.
ed. Theory & Research in Abnormal
Psychology. HR&W.
Rosenheim, Edward W.
xRosenheim, Edward W.
Swift & the Satirist's Art. U of Chicago Pr.
Rosenheim, Margaret K. see Rosenheim, Margaret
Keeney.
Rosenheim, Margaret Keeney.
xRosenheim, Margaret K.
ed. Pursuing Justice for the Child. U of
Chicago Pr.
Rosenkrantz, Barbara G. see Rosenkrantz, Barbara
Gutmann.
Rosenkrantz, Barbara Gutmann.
xRosenkrantz, Barbara G.
Public Health & the State: Changing Views in
Massachusetts, 1842-1936. Harvard U Pr.
Rosenkranz, Friedrich.
xRosenkranz, Friedrich.
An Introduction to Corporate Modeling. Duke.
Rosenkranz, Samuel.
xRosenkranz, Samuel.
Meaning in Your Life. Philos Lib.
Rosenlof, George W. see Rosenlof, George Walter.
Rosenlof, George Walter, 1891-
xRosenlof, George W.
Library Facilities in Teacher-Training
Institutions. AMS Pr.
Rosenman, Martin F.
xRosenman, Martin F.

Loving Styles: A Guide for Increasing
Intimacy. P-H.
Rosenman, Samuel I. see Rosenman, Samuel Irving.
Rosenman, Samuel Irving, 1896-
xRosenman, Samuel I.
Working with Roosevelt. Da Capo.
Rosenmeyer, Thomas G.
xRosenmeyer, Thomas G.
The Green Cabinet: Theocritus & the European
Pastoral Lyric. U of Cal Pr.
Rosenmuller, J. see Rosenmuller, Joachim.
Rosenmuller, Joachim, 1940-
xRosenmuller, J.
Extreme Games & Their Solutions.
Springer-Verlag.
Rosenne, Shabtai.
xRosenne, Shabtai.
ed. League of Nations Committee of Experts
for the Progressive Codification of
International Law. Oceana.
ed. League of Nations Conference for the
Codification of International Law (1930).
Oceana.
The World Court: What It Is, How It Works.
Oceana.
Rosenof, Theodore.
xRosenof, Theodore.
Dogma, Depression, and the New Deal: The
Debate of Political Leaders Over Economic
Recovery. Kennikat.
Rosenquist, Carl M. see Rosenquist, Carl Martin.
Rosenquist, Carl Martin.
xRosenquist, Carl M.
Delinquency in Three Cultures. U of Tex Pr.
Rosenqvist, Terkel.
xRosenqvist, Terkel.
Principles of Extractive Metallurgy. McGraw.
Rosenstein, Solomon N. see Rosenstein, Solomon
Nathan.
Rosenstein, Solomon Nathan.
xRosenstein, Solomon N.
Dentistry in Cerebral Palsy & Related
Handicapping Conditions. C C Thomas.
Rosenstein-Rodan, P. N.
xRosenstein-Rodan, P. N.
ed. Capital Formation & Economic
Development. Allen Unwin.
Rosenstiel, Annette, 1911-
xRosenstiel, Annette.
Education & Anthropology: An Annotated
Bibliography. Garland Pub.
Rosenstiel, Leonie.
xRosenstiel, Leonie.
The Life & Works of Lili Boulanger. Fairleigh
Dickinson.
Rosenstock, Gershon G. see Rosenstock, Gershon
George.
Rosenstock, Gershon George, 1918-
xRosenstock, Gershon G.
Toward a New Morality. Philos Lib.
Rosenstock-Huessy, Eugen, 1888-
xRosenstock-Huessy, Eugen.
I Am an Impure Thinker. Argo Bks.
Multiformity of Man. Argo Bks.
Speech & Reality. Argo Bks.
Rosenstone, Robert A.
xRosenstone, Robert A.
Protest from the Right. Glencoe.
Rosenthal, Alan, 1932-
xRosenthal, Alan.
Legislative Performance in the States:
Explorations of Committee Behavior. Free Pr.
Rosenthal, Albert H. see Rosenthal, Albert Harold.
Rosenthal, Albert Harold, 1914-
xRosenthal, Albert H.
ed. Public Science Policy & Administration. U
of NM Pr.
Rosenthal, D. see Rosenthal, David.
Rosenthal, Daniel.
xRosenthal, Daniel.

Introduction to Properties of Materials. Van
  Nos Reinhold.
Rosenthal, David, 1945-
  xRosenthal, D.
    Genetic Theory & Abnormal Behavior.
      McGraw.
  xRosenthal, David H.
    Eyes on the Street. Barlenmir.
Rosenthal, David. see Rosenthal, David M.
Rosenthal, David H. see Rosenthal, David.
Rosenthal, David M.
  xRosenthal, David.
    Materialism & the Mind-Body Problem. P-H.
Rosenthal, Donald B., 1937-
  xRosenthal, Donald B.
    The Expansive Elite: District Politics & State
      Policy-Making in India. U of Cal Pr.
    ed. Urban Revitalization. Sage.
Rosenthal, Felix, 1924-
  xRosenthal, Felix.
    The Paper Air Force Training Manual.
      Celestial Arts.
Rosenthal, Franz, 1914-
  xRosenthal, Franz.
    The Classical Heritage in Islam. U of Cal Pr.
Rosenthal, Gertrude.
  xRosenthal, Gertrude.
    From El Greco to Pollock: Early & Late
      Works by European & American Artists.
      Baltimore Mus.
Rosenthal, Gilbert S.
  xRosenthal, Gilbert S.
    The Many Faces of Judaism. Behrman.
Rosenthal, Glenda G. see Rosenthal, Glenda Goldstone.
Rosenthal, Glenda Goldstone.
  xRosenthal, Glenda G.
    The Men Behind the Decisions: Cases in
      European Policy-Making. Lexington Bks.
Rosenthal, Harold. see Rosenthal, Harold D.
Rosenthal, Harold D.
  xRosenthal, Harold.
    ed. The Concise Oxford Dictionary of Opera.
      Oxford U Pr.
  xRosenthal, Harold D.
    Great Singers of Today. Arno.
Rosenthal, Joel T. see Rosenthal, Joel Thomas.
Rosenthal, Joel Thomas, 1934-
  xRosenthal, Joel T.
    Angles, Angels & Conquerors, 400-1154.
      Knopf.
Rosenthal, M. L. see Rosenthal, Macha Louis.
Rosenthal, Macha Louis.
  xRosenthal, M. L.
    Exploring Poetry. Macmillan.
Rosenthal, Michael, 1937-
  xRosenthal, Michael.
    Virginia Woolf. Columbia U Pr.
Rosenthal, Murray P.
  xRosenthal, Murray P.
    How to Select & Use Hi-Fi & Stereo
      Amplifiers. Hayden.
    How to Select & Use Hi-Fi & Stereo
      Equipment. Hayden.
    How to Select & Use Loudspeakers &
      Enclosures. Hayden.
    How to Select & Use Record Players. Hayden.
    Mini-Micro Soldering & Wire Wrapping.
      Hayden.
    Understanding Integrated Circuits. Hayden.
Rosenthal, R. see Rosenthal, Robert.
Rosenthal, Robert.
  xRosenthal, R.
    ed. Artifact in Behavioral Research. Acad Pr.
  xRosenthal, Robert.

Primer of Methods for the Behavioral Sciences.
  Wiley.
    Pygmalion in the Classroom: Teacher
      Expectation & Pupil's Intellectual
      Development. HR&W.
    Sensitivity to Nonverbal Communication: The
      Pons Test. Johns Hopkins.
    ed. Skill in Nonverbal Communication:
      Individual Differences. Oelgeschlager.
Rosenthal, Steven T.
  xRosenthal, Steven T.
    The Politics of Dependency: Urban Reform in
      Istanbul. Greenwood.
Rosenthal, Stuart.
  xRosenthal, Stuart.
    The Cinema of Federico Fellini. A S Barnes.
Rosenthal, Sylvia A.
  xRosenthal, Sylvia A.
    Soap Box Derby Racing. Lothrop.
Rosenthal, Ted. L.
  xRosenthal, Ted L.
    Social Learning & Cognition. Acad Pr.
Rosenthall, Leonard.
  xRosenthall, Leonard.
    The Application of Radioiodinated Rose Bengal
      & Colloidal Radiogold in the Detection of
      Hepatobiliary Disease. Green.
Rosenus, Alan, 1940-
  xRosenus, Alan.
    Devil Stories: (Modern Man in Search of a
      Resort). Urion Pr Oreg.
Rosenwaike, Ira, 1936-
  xRosenwaike, Ira.
    Population History of New York City.
      Syracuse U Pr.
Rosenwald, Henry M.
  xRosenwald, Henry M.
    ed. Age of Romanticism. Ungar.
Rosenzweig, Franz, 1886-1929
  xRosenzweig, Franz.
    Star of Redemption. Beacon Pr.
Rosenzweig, Norman, 1924-
  xRosenzweig, Norman.
    Community Mental Health Programs in
      England: An American View. Wayne St U
      Pr.
    ed. Sex Education of the Health Professional:
      A Curriculum Guide. Grune.
Rosenzweig, Saul, 1907-
  xRosenzweig, Saul.
    Aggressive Behavior & the Rosenzweig
      Picture-Frustration Study. Praeger.
Rosewall, Ken.
  xRosewall, Ken.
    Play Tennis with Rosewall. Wilshire.
Rosewater, Victor, 1871-1940
  xRosewater, Victor.
    History of Cooperative News-Gathering in the
      United States. Johnson Repr.
    Special Assessments: A Study in Municipal
      Finance. AMS Pr.
Rosichan, R. H. see Rosichan, Richard H.
Rosichan, Richard H.
  xRosichan, R. H.
    Stamps & Coins. Libs Unl.
Rosie, A. M. see Rosie, Aeneas Murdoch.
Rosie, Aeneas Murdoch.
  xRosie, A. M.
    Information & Communication Theory.
      Gordon.
    Information & Communication Theory. Van
      Nos Reinhold.
Rosignoli, Guido.
  xRosignoli, Guido.
    Army Badges & Insignia Since 1945. Sterling.
    Ribbons of Orders, Decorations, and Medals.
      Arco.
Rosin, Jacob.
  xRosin, Jacob.

In God's Image. Philos Lib.
Rosinski, Richard R.
  xRosinski, Richard R.
    The Development of Visual Perception.
      Goodyear.
Roskamm, H. see Roskamm, Helmut.
Roskamm, Helmut.
  xRoskamm, H.
    Coronary Heart Surgery: A Rehabilitation
      Measure. Springer-Verlag.
Roskamp, Karl W.
  xRoskamp, Karl W.
    Capital Formation in West Germany. Wayne St
      U Pr.
Roskies, Diane K.
  xRoskies, Diane K.
    The Shtetl Book. Ktav.
Roskin, Michael, 1939-
  xRoskin, Michael.
    Other Governments of Europe: Sweden, Spain,
      Italy, Yugoslavia, E. Germany. P-H.
Roskos, Roland. see Roskos, Roland R.
Roskos, Roland R.
  xRoskos, Roland.
    Problem Solving in Physical Chemistry. West
      Pub.
Roslavleva, Natalia. see Roslavleva, Natalia Petrovna.
Roslavleva, Natalia Petrovna.
  xRoslavleva, Natalia.
    Era of the Russian Ballet. Da Capo.
Rosler, H. J. see Rosler, Hans Jurgen.
Rosler, Hans Jurgen.
  xRosler, H. J.
    Geochemical Tables. Elsevier.
Rosler, Lee.
  xRosler, Lee.
    Opportunities in Life Insurance Sales. Farnswth
      Pub.
    Opportunities in Life Insurance Sales. Natl
      Textbk.
Rosman, Abraham.
  xRosman, Abraham.
    Feasting with Mine Enemy: Rank & Exchange
      Among Northwest Coast Societies. Columbia
      U Pr.
Rosmond, Babette.
  xRosmond, Babette.
    Monarch. Berkley Pub.
Rosner, Bernard.
  xRosner, Bernard.
    Inside the World of Miniatures & Dollhouses:
      A Comprehensive Guide to Collecting &
      Creating. McKay.
Rosner, F. see Rosner, Fred.
Rosner, Fred.
  xRosner, F.
    Medicine in the Bible & the Talmud: Selections
      from Classical Jewish Sources. Ktav.
Rosner, Jerome.
  xRosner, Jerome.
    Helping Children Overcome Learning
      Difficulties: A Step-by-Step Guide for Parents
      & Teachers. Walker & Co.
Rosner, Joseph, 1922-
  xRosner, Joseph.
    The Story of the Writings. Behrman.
Rosner, Paul.
  xRosner, Paul.
    Days & Nights for Making Love: Sexual
      Timing with Astrology. Vulcan Bks.
Rosner, Stanley.
  xRosner, Stanley.
    The Creative Expression. North River.
    The Marriage Gap. McGraw.
Rosolack, Mary N. see Rosolack, Mary Nichols.
Rosolack, Mary Nichols.
  xRosolack, Mary N.

Speech Improvement in Early Childhood
Through Auditory Awareness &
Discrimination. Interstate.

Rosow, Eugene.
xRosow, Eugene.
Born to Lose: The Gangster Film in America.
Oxford U Pr.

Rosow, Irving.
xRosow, Irving.
Socialization to Old Age. U of Cal Pr.

Ross, Alan O.
xRoss, Alan O.
Learning Disability: The Unrealized Potential.
McGraw.
Practice of Clinical Child Psychology. Grune.
Psychological Disorders of Children: A
Behavioral Approach to Theory, Research &
Therapy. McGraw.
Psychological Disorders of Children: A
Behavioral Approach to Theory, Research &
Therapy. McGraw.

Ross, Alan S. see Ross, Alan Strode Campbell.

Ross, Alan Strode Campbell.
xRoss, Alan S.
Essentials of Anglo-Saxon Grammar. Folcroft.

Ross, Alec.
xRoss, Alec.
Talking Is Speech. Macmillan.

Ross, Alf, 1899-
xRoss, Alf.
On Guilt, Responsibility & Punishment. U of
Cal Pr.
On Law & Justice. U of Cal Pr.

Ross, Angus, 1927-
xRoss, Angus.
The Ampurias Exchange. Walker & Co.
The Burgos Contract. Walker & Co.

Ross, Anne, Ph. D.
xRoss, Anne.
The Folklore of the Scottish Highlands.
Rowman.
Pagan Celtic Britain: Studies in Iconography &
Tradition. Columbia U Pr.

Ross, Arnold.
xRoss, Arnold.
Wonders of Barnacles. Dodd.

Ross, Bernard H., 1934-
xRoss, Bernard H.
ed. Urban Management: A Guide to
Information Sources. Gale.

Ross, Betty.
xRoss, Betty.
How to Beat the High Cost of Travel. S&S.
How to Beat the High Cost of Travel. US
News & World.

Ross, Carmen F.
xRoss, Carmen F.
Personal & Vocational Relationships in
Practical Nursing. Lippincott.

Ross, Charlotte, 1921-
xRoss, Charlotte.
Who Is the Minister's Wife?: A Search for
Personal Fulfillment. Westminster.

Ross, Clarissa.
xRoss, Clarissa.
China Shadow. Avon.

Ross, Clay C. see Ross, Clay Campbell.

Ross, Clay Campbell, 1892-1947
xRoss, Clay C.
The Relation Between Grade School Record &
High School Achievement: A Study of the
Diagnostic Value of Individual Record Cards.
AMS Pr.

Ross, Corinne M. see Ross, Corinne Madden.

Ross, Corinne Madden.
xRoss, Corinne M.
The New England Guest House Book. East
Woods.

Ross, D. W. see Ross, Denman Waldo.

Ross, Dana.
xRoss, Dana.
Demon of the Darkness. PB.
The Raven and the Phantom. PB.

Ross, Dave.
xRoss, Dave.
A Book of Hugs. T Y Crowell.

Ross, David.
xRoss, David.
ed. Illustrated Treasury of Poetry for Children.
G&D.

Ross, David. see Ross, David A.

Ross, David A., 1936-
xRoss, David A.
Introduction to Oceanography. P-H.
xRoss, David A.
Introduction to Oceanography. P-H.

Ross, Denman W. see Ross, Denman Waldo.

Ross, Denman Waldo, 1853-1935
xRoss, D. W.
On Drawing & Painting. AMS Pr.
xRoss, Denman W.
Early History of Landholding Among the
Germans. B Franklin.

Ross, Dorothy, 1936-
xRoss, Dorothy.
G. Stanley Hall: The Psychologist As Prophet.
U of Chicago Pr.

Ross, Douglas N.
xRoss, Douglas N.
Partners in Agroeconomic Development.
Conference Bd.

Ross, E. see Ross, Edward Denison.

Ross, E. Denison. see Ross, Edward Denison.

Ross, Earle D. see Ross, Earle Dudley.

Ross, Earle Dudley, 1885-
xRoss, Earle D.
Liberal Republican Movement. AMS Pr.
The Liberal Republican Movement. U of Wash
Pr.

Ross, Edward A. see Ross, Edward Alsworth.

Ross, Edward Alsworth.
xRoss, Edward A.
Sin & Society: An Analysis of Latter-Day
Iniquity. Peter Smith.
Social Trend. Arno.
Standing Room Only?. Arno.

Ross, Edward Denison, Sir, 1871-1940
xRoss, E.
This English Language. R West.
xRoss, E. Denison.
This English Language. Gale.

Ross, Ernest C. see Ross, Ernest Carson.

Ross, Ernest Carson.
xRoss, Ernest C.
Development of the English Sea Novel from
Defoe to Conrad. Folcroft.

Ross, Eulalie S. see Ross, Eulalie Steinmetz.

Ross, Eulalie Steinmetz.
xRoss, Eulalie S.
ed. Lost Half-Hour: A Collection of Stories.
HarBraceJ.

Ross, Eva J. see Ross, Eva Jeany.

Ross, Eva Jeany, 1903-
xRoss, Eva J.
Living in Society. Glencoe.

Ross, Fran.
xRoss, Fran.
Oreo. Greyfalcon Hse.

Ross, Frances. see Ross, Frances J.

Ross, Frances J.
xRoss, Frances.
Some Special Times: Selected Poems.
Pygmalion Pr.

Ross, Frank.
xRoss, Frank.
Dead Runner. Atheneum.
Dead Runner. Fawcett.

Ross, Frank. see Ross, Frank Xavier.

Ross, Frank Xavier, 1914-
xRoss, Frank.
Car Racing Against the Clock: The Story of
the World Land Speed Record. Lothrop.
Flying Paper Airplane Models. Lothrop.
Racing Cars & Great Races. Lothrop.
Space Science & You. Lothrop.
World of Engineering. Lothrop.
World of Power & Energy. Lothrop.

Ross, G. Max. see Ross, George Maxim.

Ross, George Maxim.
xRoss, G. Max.
When Lucy Went Away. Dutton.

Ross, Gregory A.
xRoss, Gregory A.
Grounds for Grammar. U Pr of Amer.

Ross, H. H. see Ross, Herbert Holdsworth.

Ross, Harry.
xRoss, Harry.
Utopias Old & New. Folcroft.

Ross, Herbert H. see Ross, Herbert Holdsworth.

Ross, Herbert Holdsworth, 1908-
xRoss, H. H.
Textbook of Entomology. Wiley.
xRoss, Herbert H.
Understanding Evolution. P-H.

Ross, Ian S. see Ross, Lan Simpson.

Ross, Irwin.
xRoss, Irwin.
The Loneliest Campaign: The Truman Victory
of 1948. Greenwood.

Ross, Ishbel, 1897-
xRoss, Ishbel.
An American Family: The Tafts, 1678 to 1964.
Greenwood.
First Lady of the South: The Life of Mrs.
Jefferson Davis. Greenwood.

Ross, J. M. see Ross, Jean Mary

Ross, Jack C.
xRoss, Jack C.
An Assembly of Good Fellows: Voluntary
Associations in History. Greenwood.

Ross, James B. see Ross, James Bruce.

Ross, James Bruce.
xRoss, James B.
ed. Portable Medieval Reader. Penguin.

Ross, James R.
xRoss, James R.
How to Buy a Car. St Martin.

Ross, Janet S.
xRoss, Janet S.
Foundations of Anatomy & Physiology.
Churchill.

Ross, Jean Mary.
xRoss, J. M.
A Critical Appraisal of Comprehensive
Education. Humanities.

Ross, Jessica.
xRoss, Jessica.
illus. Ms. Klondike. Viking Pr.

Ross, Joan.
xRoss, Joan.
Existentialism of Alberto Moravia. S Ill U Pr.

Ross, Joel E.
xRoss, Joel E.
Modern Management & Information Systems.
Reston.

Ross, John B.
xRoss, John B.
The Economic System of Mexico. Cal Inst Intl
St.

Ross, John D. see Ross, John Dawson.

Ross, John Dawson, 1853-1939
xRoss, John D.
Burns Handbook. AMS Pr.
Story of the Kilmarnock Burns. AMS Pr.

Ross, John E. see Ross, John Elliot.

Ross, John Elliot, 1884-1946
xRoss, John E.

Truths to Live by. Arno.
Ross, Josephine.
  xRoss, Josephine.
    The Tudors: England's Golden Age. Putnam.
Ross, K. A. see Ross, Kenneth A.
Ross, Kenneth A.
  xRoss, K. A.
    Elementary Analysis: The Theory of Calculus.
      Springer-Verlag.
Ross, Lan Simpson.
  xRoss, Ian S.
    Lord Kames & the Scotland of His Day.
      Oxford U Pr.
Ross, Laura.
  xRoss, Laura.
    Finger Puppets: Easy to Make, Fun to Use.
      Lothrop.
    Mask-Making with Pantomime & Stories from
      American History. Lothrop.
Ross, Leonard Q.
  xRoss, Leonard Q.
    Education of Hyman Kaplan. HarBraceJ.
Ross, Lewis.
  xRoss, Lewis.
    Extra-Marital Relationships. Kendall-Hunt.
Ross, Lillian.
  xRoss, Lillian.
    Moments with Chaplin. Dodd.
Ross, Louis.
  xRoss, Louis.
    In the Peanut Butter Colony. Dutton.
Ross, Malcolm H. see Ross, Malcolm Harrison.
Ross, Malcolm Harrison, 1895-1965
  xRoss, Malcolm H.
    All Manner of Men. Greenwood.
Ross, Marc H. see Ross, Marc Howard.
Ross, Marc Howard.
  xRoss, Marc H.
    Grass Roots in an African City: Political
      Behavior in Nairobi. MIT Pr.
Ross, Marianne.
  xRoss, Marianne.
    Good-Bye, Atlantis. Elsevier-Nelson.
Ross, Marilyn.
  xRoss, Marilyn.
    Awake to Terror. Popular Lib.
    The Curse of Black Charlie. Popular Lib.
    Delta Flame. Popular Lib.
    Fog Island Horror. Popular Lib.
    A Garden of Ghosts. Popular Lib.
    Passion Cargo. Popular Lib.
    Twice Dead. Popular Lib.
Ross, Marilyn H. see Ross, Marilyn Heimberg.
Ross, Marilyn Heimberg.
  xRoss, Marilyn H.
    Creative Loafing: A Shoestring Guide to New
      Leisure Fun. Comm Creat.
Ross, Mark.
  xRoss, Mark.
    Principles of Aural Rehabilitation. Bobbs.
Ross, Martin.
  xRoss, Martin.
    Music & James Joyce. Folcroft.

Ross, Martin H., 1918-
  xRoss, Martin H.
    Marrano. Branden.

Ross, Martin J.
  xRoss, Martin J.
    Handbook of Everyday Law. Fawcett.
    Handbook of Everyday Law. Har-Row.

Ross, Michael.
  xRoss, Michael.
    Banners of the King: The War of the Vendee,
      1793. Hippocrene Bks.
    Bougainville. Gordon-Cremonesi.
    Cross the Great Desert. Gordon-Cremonesi.
Ross, Mitchell S.
  xRoss, Mitchell S.

Literary Politicians. Doubleday.
Ross, Opal. see Ross, Opal Lambert.
Ross, Opal Lambert, 1906-
  xRoss, Opal.
    Fields & Pine Trees. Ye Galleon.
Ross, P. W. see Ross, Philip W.
Ross, Pat.
  xRoss, Pat.
    M & M & the Haunted House Game.
      Pantheon.
    Meet M & M. Pantheon.
Ross, Philip.
  xRoss, Philip.
    Government as a Source of Union Power: The
      Role of Public Policy in Collective
      Bargaining. Brown U Pr.
Ross, Philip W.
  xRoss, P. W.
    Clinical Bacteriology. Churchill.
Ross, R. see Ross, Raymond Samuel.
Ross, R. B.
  xRoss, R. B.
    Cleft Lip & Palate. Krieger.
Ross, R. T. see Ross, Robert Thomas.
Ross, Ralph. see Ross, Ralph Gilbert.
Ross, Ralph Gilbert.
  xRoss, Ralph.
    ed. Thomas Hobbes in His Time. U of Minn
      Pr.
Ross, Ramon. see Ross, Ramon Royal.
Ross, Ramon R. see Ross, Ramon Royal.
Ross, Ramon Royal.
  xRoss, Ramon.
    Storyteller. Merrill.
  xRoss, Ramon R.
    Storyteller. Merrill.
Ross, Raymond S. see Ross, Raymond Samuel.
Ross, Raymond Samuel, 1925-
  xRoss, R.
    Essentials of Speech Communication. P-H.
  xRoss, Raymond S.
    Speech Communication: Fundamentals &
      Practice. P-H.
Ross, Richard D.
  xRoss, Richard D.
    Air Pollution & Industry. Van Nos Reinhold.
Ross, Robert. see Ross, Robert Baldwin.
Ross, Robert B. see Ross, Robert Baldwin.
Ross, Robert Baldwin.
  xRoss, Robert.
    Aubrey Beardsley. Folcroft.
  xRoss, Robert B.
    Aubrey Beardsley. R West.
Ross, Robert H.
  xRoss, Robert H.
    Georgian Revolt: Rise & Fall of a Poetic Ideal,
      1910-1922. S Ill U Pr.
Ross, Robert H. see Ross, Robert Horace.
Ross, Robert Horace.
  xRoss, Robert H.
    Treasures of Tutankhamun in Needlepoint.
      Morrow.
Ross, Robert R. see Ross, Robert Robertson.
Ross, Robert Robertson.
  xRoss, Robert R.
    Self-Mutilation. Lexington Bks.
Ross, Robert S., 1940-
  xRoss, Robert S.
    American National Government: An
      Introduction to Political Institutions. Rand.
Ross, Robert Thomas, 1924-
  xRoss, R. T.
    How to Examine the Nervous System:
      Techniques & Methods. C C Thomas.
Ross, Robert W.
  xRoss, Robert W.

So It Was True: The American Protestant Press
  & the Nazi Persecution of the Jews. U of
  Minn Pr.
Ross, Rodger J.
  xRoss, Rodger J.
    Color Film for Color Television. Hastings.
Ross, Ronald G.
  xRoss, Ronald G.
    Data Base Systems: Design, Implementation, &
      Management. Am Mgmt.
Ross, Sam, 1912-
  xRoss, Sam.
    Ready for the Tiger. FS&G.
Ross, Sheldon. see Ross, Sheldon M.
Ross, Sheldon M.
  xRoss, Sheldon.
    A First Course in Probability. Macmillan.
  xRoss, Sheldon M.
    Applied Probability Models with Optimization
      Applications. Holden-Day.
    Introduction to Probability Models. Acad Pr.
Ross, Shepley L.
  xRoss, Shepley L.
    Differential Equations. Wiley.
Ross, Shirley.
  xRoss, Shirley.
    Fasting. Ballantine.
    Fasting. St Martin.
Ross, Sidney. see Ross, Sidney D.
Ross, Sidney D.
  xRoss, Sidney.
    Anodic Oxidation. Acad Pr.
Ross, Sinclair.
  xRoss, Sinclair.
    As for Me & My House. U of Nebr Pr.
Ross, Stanley R. see Ross, Stanley Ralph.
Ross, Stanley Ralph.
  xRoss, Stanley R.
    Speak When You Hear the Beep. Price Stern.
Ross, Stanley Robert.
  xRoss, Stanley R.
    ed. Latin America in Transition: Problems in
      Training & Research. State U NY Pr.
Ross, Stephen D. see Ross, Stephen David.
Ross, Stephen David.
  xRoss, Stephen D.
    In Pursuit of Moral Value. Freeman C.
    Literature & Philosophy: An Analysis of the
      Philosophical Novel. Irvington.
    Moral Decision: An Introduction to Ethics.
      Freeman C.
    Transition to an Ordinal Metaphysics. State U
      NY Pr.
Ross, Stephen V.
  xRoss, Stephen V.
    Spelling Made Simple. Doubleday.
Ross, Steven. see Ross, Steven T.
Ross, Steven T.
  xRoss, Steven.
    From Flintlock to Rifle: Infantry Tactics,
      1740-1866. Fairleigh Dickinson.
  xRoss, Steven T.
    ed. The French Revolution: Conflict or
      Continuity. Krieger.
    Quest for Victory: French Military Strategy,
      1792-1799. A S Barnes.
Ross, Thomas W. see Ross, Thomas Wynne.
Ross, Thomas Wynne, 1923-
  xRoss, Thomas W.
    Chaucer's Bawdy. Dutton.
Ross, Timothy A.
  xRoss, Timothy A.
    Chiang Kuei. Twayne.
Ross, Tony.
  xRoss, Tony.
    illus. Hugo & the Man Who Stole Colors.
      Follett.
Ross, Walter.
  xRoss, Walter.

Coast to Coast. S&S.
Ross, Walter. *see* Ross, Walter Sanford.
Ross, Walter Sanford, 1916-
xRoss, Walter.
Immortal. S&S.
Ross, Wilda. *see* Ross, Wilda S.
Ross, Wilda S.
xRoss, Wilda.
Can You Find the Animal?. Coward.
Ross, William D. *see* Ross, William David.
Ross, William David, Sir, 1877-
xRoss, William D.
Plato's Theory of Ideas. Greenwood.
Ross, William M., 1945-
xRoss, William M.
Oil Pollution As an International Problem: A
Study of Puget Sound & the Strait of
Georgia. U of Wash Pr.
Ross Russell, R. W.
xRoss Russell, R. W.
Cerebral Arterial Disease. Churchill.
Rossabi, Morris.
xRossabi, Morris.
China & Inner Asia: From 1368 to the Present
Day. Universe.
Rossano, A. T.
xRossano, A. T.
Air Pollution Control: Guidebook for
Management. McGraw.
Rossant, Colette.
xRossant, Colette.
A Mostly French Food Processor Cookbook.
NAL.
Rossdale, Peter. *see* Rossdale, Peter D.
Rossdale, Peter D.
xRossdale, Peter.
Horse Ailments Explained. Arco.
Rossel, Seymour.
xRossel, Seymour.
When a Jew Seeks Wisdom: The Sayings of the
Fathers. Behrman.
Rosselli, John.
xRosselli, John.
Lord William Bentinck: The Making of a
Liberal Imperialist, 1774-1839. U of Cal Pr.
Rosser, Barkley J. *see* Rosser, John Barkley.
Rosser, J. Barkley. *see* Rosser, John Barkley.
Rosser, James M.
xRosser, James M.
An Analysis of Health Care Delivery. Krieger.
Rosser, John B. *see* Rosser, John Barkley.
Rosser, John Barkley, 1907-
xRosser, Barkley J.
Simplified Independence Proofs: Boolean
Valued Models of Set Theory. Acad Pr.
xRosser, J. Barkley.
Many-Valued Logics. Greenwood.
xRosser, John B.
Logic for Mathematicians. Chelsea Pub.
Rossetti, Christina. *see* Rossetti, Christina Georgina.
Rossetti, Christina G. *see* Rossetti, Christina Georgina.
Rossetti, Christina Georgina.
xRossetti, Christina.
Goblin Market. Stonehill Pub Co.
Goblin Market. Dutton.
xRossetti, Christina G.
Maude: Prose & Verse. Shoe String.
Rossetti, Dante G. *see* Rossetti, Dante Gabriel.
Rossetti, Dante Gabriel, 1828-1882
xRossetti, Dante G.
The Ballad of Jan Van Hunks. Folcroft.
Rossetti, W. M. *see* Rossetti, William Michael.
Rossetti, William M. *see* Rossetti, William Michael.
Rossetti, William Michael, 1829-1919
xRossetti, W. M.
The Diary of W. M. Rossetti 1870-1873.
Oxford U Pr.
xRossetti, William M.

American Poems. AMS Pr.
American Poems. R West.
Bibliography of the Works of Dante Gabriel
Rossetti. AMS Pr.
Bibliography of the Works of Dante Gabriel
Rossetti. Folcroft.
ed. Humorous Poems. AMS Pr.
ed. Humorous Poems. R West.
Life of John Keats. AMS Pr.
Life of John Keats. Folcroft.
Lives of Famous Poets. AMS Pr.
Lives of Famous Poets. Arden Lib.
Lives of Famous Poets. Darby Bks.
Lives of Famous Poets. Folcroft.
Memoir of Shelley. AMS Pr.
A Memoir of Shelley. Arden Lib.
Memoir of Shelley. Folcroft.
Notes on the Royal Academy Exhibition, 1868.
AMS Pr.
Swinburne's Poems & Ballads: A Criticism.
AMS Pr.
Rossi, Alfred.
xRossi, Alfred.
Astonish Us in the Morning: Tyrone Guthrie
Remembered. Merrimack Bk Serv.
Astonish Us in the Morning: Tyrone Guthrie
Remembered. Wayne St U Pr.
Rossi, Bruno.
xRossi, Bruno.
A Dirty Way to Die. Nordon Pubns.
Rossi, Claude J. De. *see* De Rossi, Claude J.
Rossi, Ernest L. *see* Rossi, Ernest Lawrence.
Rossi, Ernest Lawrence.
xRossi, Ernest L.
Dreams & the Growth of Personality:
Expanding Awareness in Psychotherapy.
Pergamon.
Rossi, I. *see* Rossi, Ino.
Rossi, Ino.
xRossi, I.
Anthropology Full Circle. HR&W.
xRossi, Ino.
People in Culture: A Survey of Cultural
Anthropology. Praeger.
ed. The Unconscious in Culture: The
Structuralism of Claude Levi-Strauss in
Perspective. Dutton.
Rossi, John P.
xRossi, John P.
The Transformation of the British Liberal
Party: A Study of the Tactics of the Liberal
Opposition, 1874-1880. Am Philos.
Rossi, Paul A.
xRossi, Paul A.
Art of the Old West: From the Collection of
the Gilcrease Institute. Knopf.
Rossi, Peter H. *see* Rossi, Peter Henry.
Rossi, Peter Henry.
xRossi, Peter H.
Evaluation: A Systematic Approach. Sage.
Reforming Public Welfare: A Critique of the
Negative Income Tax Experiment. Russell
Sage.
Why Families Move. Sage.
Rossi, Vinio.
xRossi, Vinio.
Andre Gide. Columbia U Pr.
Rossi-Landi, Ferruccio.
xRossi-Landi, Ferruccio.
Ideologies of Linguistic Relativity. Mouton.
Linguistics & Economics. Mouton.
Rossides, Daniel. *see* Rossides, Daniel W.
Rossides, Daniel W., 1925-
xRossides, Daniel.
The History & Nature of Sociological Theory.
HM.
xRossides, Daniel W.
The American Class System: An Introduction
to Social Stratification. U Pr of Amer.
Rossie, Jonathan G. *see* Rossie, Jonathan Gregory.

Rossie, Jonathan Gregory.
xRossie, Jonathan G.
The Politics of Command in the American
Revolution. Syracuse U Pr.
Rossignol, James E. Le. *see* Le Rossignol, James E.
Rossignol, Lois J. *see* Rossignol, Lois Josephine.
Rossignol, Lois Josephine, 1916-
xRossignol, Lois J.
The Relationships Among Hearing Acuity,
Speech Production, & Reading Performance
in Grades 1a, 1b, & 2a. AMS Pr.
Rossiter, Charles M.
xRossiter, Charles M.
Communicating Personally: A Theory of
Interpersonal Communication and Human
Relationships. Bobbs.
Rossiter, Clare.
xRossiter, Clare.
Anne of Summer Ho. Ace Bks.
Anne of Summer Ho. St Martin.
The White Rose. St Martin.
Rossiter, Clinton. *see* Rossiter, Clinton Lawrence.
Rossiter, Clinton L. *see* Rossiter, Clinton Lawrence.
Rossiter, Clinton Lawrence, 1917-1970
xRossiter, Clinton.
First American Revolution: The American
Colonies on the Eve of Independence.
HarBraceJ.
Parties & Politics in America. Cornell U Pr.
Political Thought of the American Revolution.
HarBraceJ.
The Supreme Court & the Commander in
Chief. Cornell U Pr.
Supreme Court & the Commander in Chief. Da
Capo.
xRossiter, Clinton L.
Constitutional Dictatorship: Crisis Government
in the Modern Democracies. Greenwood.
Rossiter, John.
xRossiter, John.
The Deadly Gold. Popular Lib.
The Man Who Came Back. HM.
Rosskopf, Myron F. *see* Rosskopf, Myron Frederick.
Rosskopf, Myron Frederick.
xRosskopf, Myron F.
ed. Children's Mathematical Concepts: Six
Piagetian Studies in Mathematical Education.
Tchrs Coll.
Rossman, Charles.
xRossman, Charles.
ed. Mario Vargas Llosa: A Collection of
Critical Essays. U of Tex Pr.
Rossman, George, 1885-
xRossman, George.
ed. Advocacy & the King's English. Michie.
Rossman, Isadore. *see* Rossman, Isadore J.
Rossman, Isadore J., 1913-
xRossman, Isadore.
ed. Clinical Geriatrics. Lippincott.
Rossman, Michael.
xRossman, Michael.
Learning Without a Teacher. Phi Delta Kappa.
Rossman, Parker, 1919-
xRossman, Parker.
After Punishment What?: Discipline &
Reconciliation. Collins Pubs.
Hospice: Creating New Models of Care for the
Terminally Ill. Follett.
Rossman, Wendell E.
xRossman, Wendell E.
The Effective Architect. P-H.
Rossmann, P. *see* Rossmann, Pavel.
Rossmann, Pavel.
xRossmann, P.
Rejection Nephropathy. Elsevier.
Rossner, Judith.
xRossner, Judith.

Attachments. PB.
Attachments. S&S.
Looking for Mr. Goodbar. S&S.
Looking for Mr. Goodbar. PB.
Nine Months in the Life of an Old Maid.
Popular Lib.
Rossum, R. A. see Rossum, Ralph A.
Rossum, Ralph A., 1946-
xRossum, R. A.
The Politics of the Criminal Justice System: An
Organizational Analysis. Dekker.
Rost, Thomas L.
xRost, Thomas L.
Botany: A Brief Introduction to Plant Biology.
Wiley.
Rostand, Claude.
xRostand, Claude.
French Music Today. Da Capo.
Rostand, Edmond. see Rostand, Edmund.
Rostand, Edmund, 1868-1918
xRostand, Edmond.
Cyrano De Bergerac: A Heroic Comedy in
Five Acts. Oxford U Pr.
Cyrano De Bergerac: An Heroic Comedy in
Five Acts. R West.
Rostand, Jean, 1894-
xRostand, Jean.
The Substance of Man. Greenwood.
Rosten, Leo. see Rosten, Leo Calvin.
Rosten, Leo Calvin, 1908-
xRosten, Leo.
People I Have Loved, Known or Admired.
McGraw.
The Power of Positive Nonsense. McGraw.
Silky!: A Detective Story. Har-Row.
Rosten, Norman, 1914-
xRosten, Norman.
Return Again, Traveler. AMS Pr.
Selected Poems. Braziller.
Rostenberg, Leona.
xRostenberg, Leona.
Old & Rare: Thirty Years in the Book
Business. Allanheld & Schram.
Roston, Murray.
xRoston, Murray.
Milton & the Baroque. U of Pittsburgh Pr.
The Soul of Wit: A Study of John Donne.
Oxford U Pr.
Rostov, Mara.
xRostov, Mara.
Night Hunt. Putnam.
Rostovtsev, Mikhail. see Rostovtsev, Mikhail Ivanovich.
Rostovtsev, Mikhail I. see Rostovtsev, Mikhail Ivanovich.
Rostovtsev, Mikhail Ivanovich, 1870-1952
xRostovtsev, Mikhail.
History of the Ancient World. Greenwood.
xRostovtsev, Mikhail I.
Caravan Cities. AMS Pr.
Dura-Europos & Its Art. AMS Pr.
Rostow, Eugene V. see Rostow, Eugene Victor.
Rostow, Eugene Victor, 1913-
xRostow, Eugene V.
The Ideal in Law. U of Chicago Pr.
Law, Power, & the Pursuit of Peace. U of Nebr
Pr.
Rostow, W. W. see Rostow, Walt Whitman.
Rostow, Walt Whitman, 1916-
xRostow, W. W.
Politics & the Stages of Growth. Cambridge U
Pr.
The World Economy: History & Prospect. U of
Tex Pr.
Roszak, Theodore, 1933-
xRoszak, Theodore.
Where the Wasteland Ends: Politics &
Transcendence in Post-Industrial Society.
Doubleday.
Rota, Gian Carlo.
xRota, Gian-Carlo.

ed. Studies in Algebraic Topology. Acad Pr.
ed. Studies in Analysis. Acad Pr.
Rota, Gian-Carlo, 1932-
xRota, Gian-Carlo.
ed. Studies in Algebra & Number Theory.
Acad Pr.
Rota, Gian-Carlo. see Rota, Gian Carlo.
Rotar, Peter P.
xRotar, Peter P.
Grasses of Hawaii. U Pr of Hawaii.
Rotberg, Robert I.
xRotberg, Robert I.
Africa & Its Explorers: Motives, Methods, &
Impact. Harvard U Pr.
Christian Missionaries & the Creation of
Northern Rhodesia, 1880-1924. Princeton U
Pr.
ed. Conflict & Compromise in South Africa.
Lexington Bks.
Rotella, Guy L.
xRotella, Guy L.
E. E. Cummings: A Reference Guide. G K
Hall.
Rotenberg, Mordechai.
xRotenberg, Mordechai.
Damnation & Deviance: The Protestant Ethic
& the Spirit of Failure. Free Pr.
Rotenstreich. see Rotenstreich, Nathan.
Rotenstreich, Nathan, 1914-
xRotenstreich.
Theory & Practice. Kluwer Boston.
Roth, A. E. see Roth, Alvin E.
Roth, Alexander, 1919-
xRoth, Alexander.
ed. Allergy in the World: A Guide for
Physicians & Travelers. U Pr of Hawaii.
Roth, Alvin E., 1951-
xRoth, A. E.
Axiomatic Models of Bargaining.
Springer-Verlag.
Roth, Arnold, 1929-
xRoth, Arnold.
illus. A Comick Book of Sports. Scribner.
Roth, Arthur. see Roth, Arthur J.
Roth, Arthur J., 1925-
xRoth, Arthur.
The Iceberg Hermit. Schol Bk Serv.
Iceberg Hermit. Schol Bk Serv.
Two for Survival. Scribner.
You & Your Bicycle. Dandelion Pr.
The Yucky Monster. Dandelion Pr.
Roth, Audrey. see Roth, Audrey J.
Roth, Audrey J.
xRoth, Audrey.
Words People Use. Winthrop.
Roth, Bernhard A.
xRoth, Bernhard A.
The Complete Beginner's Guide to Archery.
Doubleday.
The Complete Beginner's Guide to Canoeing.
Doubleday.
The Complete Beginner's Guide to
Motorcycling. Doubleday.
Roth, Cecil, 1899-1970
xRoth, Cecil.
ed. The Concise Jewish Encyclopedia. NAL.
Dead Sea Scrolls: A New Historical Approach.
Norton.
A History of the Jews: From Earliest Times
Through the Six Day War. Schocken.
History of the Jews in Venice. Schocken.
A History of the Marranos. Arno.
A History of the Marranos. Hermon.
A History of the Marranos. Schocken.
Last Florentine Republic, 1527-1530. Russell.
Spanish Inquisition. Norton.
Roth, Charlene D. see Roth, Charlene Davis.
Roth, Charlene Davis, 1945-
xRoth, Charlene D.

The Art of Making Cloth Toys. Chilton.
The Art of Making Puppets & Marionettes.
Chilton.
Making Original Dolls of Composition, Bisque
& Porcelain. Crown.
Roth, Charles, 1916-
xRoth, Charles.
A New Way of Thinking. Unity Bks.
Roth, Charles. see Roth, Charles Edmund.
Roth, Charles B.
xRoth, Charles B.
Secrets of Closing Sales. P-H.
Roth, Charles E. see Roth, Charles Edmund.
Roth, Charles Edmund.
xRoth, Charles.
Then There Were None. A-W.
xRoth, Charles E.
The Farm Book. Har-Row.
Roth, Charles H.
xRoth, Charles H.
Fundamentals of Logic Design. West Pub.
Roth, David. see Roth, David F.
Roth, David F.
xRoth, David.
The Comparative Study of Politics. P-H.
Roth, Dennis M., 1943-
xRoth, Dennis M.
The Friar Estates of the Philippines. U of NM
Pr.
Roth, G. D. see Roth, Gunter Dietmar.
Roth, Gerhard, 1942-
xRoth, Gerhard.
Winterreise. FS&G.
Roth, Guenther.
xRoth, Guenther.
Max Weber's Vision of History: Ethics &
Methods. U of Cal Pr.
Roth, Gunter Dietmar.
xRoth, G. D.
ed. Astronomy: A Handbook. Springer-Verlag.
Roth, Henry.
xRoth, Henry.
Call It Sleep. Avon.
Call It Sleep. Avon.
Call It Sleep. Cooper Sq.
Roth, Holly.
xRoth, Holly.
Content Assignment. S&S.
Crimson in the Purple. S&S.
Roth, Hy.
xRoth, Hy.
The Little People. Everest Hse.
Roth, J. Paul. see Roth, John Paul.
Roth, Jane. see Roth, June Spiewak.
Roth, John K.
xRoth, John K.
A Consuming Fire: Encounters with Elie
Wiesel & the Holocaust. John Knox.
Roth, John Paul, 1922-
xRoth, J. Paul.
Computer Logic, Testing & Verification.
Computer Sci.
Roth, Jordan.
xRoth, Jordan.
Officer Survival: Arrest & Control. Davis Pub
Co.
Roth, Joseph, 1894-1939
xRoth, Joseph.
The Radetzky March. Overlook Pr.
Roth, June. see Roth, June Spiewak.
Roth, June S. see Roth, June Spiewak.
Roth, June Spiewak.
xRoth, Jane.
Freeze & Please Home Freezer Cookbook. Fell.
xRoth, June.

June Roth's Thousand Calorie Cook Book.
Arco.
Low-Cholesterol Jewish Cookery: The
Unsaturated Fat Way. Arco.
The Troubled Tummy Cookbook. Contemp
Bks.
xRoth, June S.
The Troubled Tummy Cookbook. G K Hall.
Roth, L. O. see Roth, Lawrence O.
Roth, Lawrence O.
xRoth, L. O.
An Introduction to Agricultural Engineering.
AVI.
Roth, Leland M.
xRoth, Leland M.
The Architecture of McKim, Mead & White,
1870-1920: A Building List. Garland Pub.
A Concise History of American Architecture.
Har-Row.
Roth, Leon, 1896-1963
xRoth, Leon.
Descartes' Discourse on Method. Folcroft.
Spinoza. Hyperion Conn.
Roth, Lloyd J. see Roth, Lloyd Joseph.
Roth, Lloyd Joseph.
xRoth, Lloyd J.
ed. Autoradiography of Diffusible Substances.
Acad Pr.
Roth, Martin.
xRoth, Martin.
Comedy & America: The Lost World of
Washington Irving. Kennikat.
Roth, Oscar.
xRoth, Oscar.
Heart Attack: A Question & Answer Book.
Contemp Bks.
Heart Attack: A Question & Answer Book.
Lippincott.
Roth, Philip.
xRoth, Philip.
The Ghost Writer. Fawcett.
The Ghost Writer. FS&G.
The Ghost Writer. G K Hall.
Goodbye Columbus. Bantam.
Letting Go. Random.
Portnoy's Complaint. Bantam.
Portnoy's Complaint. Random.
The Professor of Desire. Bantam.
The Professor of Desire. FS&G.
Reading Myself & Others. FS&G.
When She Was Good. Random.
xRoth, Philip M.
Goodbye, Columbus. HM.
Roth, Philip M. see Roth, Philip.
Roth, Richard, 1904-
xRoth, Richard.
Your Future in Architecture. Rosen Pr.
Roth, Robert J.
xRoth, Robert J.
ed. God Knowable & Unknowable. Fordham.
ed. Person & Community: A Philosophical
Exploration. Fordham.
Roth, Robert M.
xRoth, Robert M.
Underachieving Students & Guidance. HM.
Roth, Sanford H. see Roth, Sanford Harold.
Roth, Sanford Harold, 1934-
xRoth, Sanford H.
New Directions in Arthritis Therapy. PSG Pub.
Roth, Sid.
xRoth, Sid.
Something for Nothing. Logos.
Roth, Walter. see Roth, Walter Edmund.
Roth, Walter Edmund, 1861?-1933
xRoth, Walter.
Games, Sports & Amusements. Arno.
Rothafel, Roxy, 1909-
xRothafel, Roxy.

Roxy's Ski Guide to New England. East
Woods.
Rothbard, Murray. see Rothbard, Murray Newton.
Rothbard, Murray N. see Rothbard, Murray Newton.
Rothbard, Murray Newton, 1926-
xRothbard, Murray.
For a New Liberty: The Libertarian Manifesto.
Macmillan.
xRothbard, Murray N.
America's Great Depression. Inst Humane.
Conceived in Liberty. Arlington Hse.
Power & Market: Government & the Economy.
Inst Humane.
Rothbart, Harold A.
xRothbart, Harold A.
Cybernetic Creativity. Speller.
Mechanical Design & Systems Handbook.
McGraw.
Rothberg, Abraham.
xRothberg, Abraham.
Aleksandr Solzhenitsyn: The Major Novels.
Cornell U Pr.
Rothberg, Robert R.
xRothberg, Robert R.
ed. Corporate Strategy & Product Innovation.
Free Pr.
Rothblat, George H.
xRothblat, George H.
ed. Growth, Nutrition & Metabolism of Cells
in Culture. Acad Pr.
Rothblatt, Ben.
xRothblatt, Ben.
ed. Changing Perspectives on Man. U of
Chicago Pr.
Rothblatt, Donald N.
xRothblat, Donald N.
ed. National Policy for Urban & Regional
Development. Lexington Bks.
Rothchild, Sylvia, 1923-
xRothchild, Sylvia.
Sunshine & Salt. S&S.
Rothel, David, 1936-
xRothel, David.
Who Was That Masked Man: The Story of the
Lone Ranger. A S Barnes.
Rothenberg, Albert.
xRothenberg, Albert.
The Creativity Question. Duke.
The Emerging Goddess: The Creative Process
in Art, Science, & Other Fields. U of
Chicago Pr.
Rothenberg, Dianne.
xRothenberg, Dianne.
Compiled by Directory of Educational
Programs for Adults Who Work with
Children. Natl Assn Child.
Rothenberg, G. B.
xRothenberg, G. B.
Glass Technology-Recent Developments.
Noyes.
Paint Additives: Recent Developments. Noyes.
Refractory Materials. Noyes.
Rothenberg, Gunther E. see Rothenberg, Gunther Erich.
Rothenberg, Gunther Erich, 1923-
xRothenberg, Gunther E.
The Army of Francis Joseph. Purdue.
The Art of Warfare in the Age of Napoleon.
Ind U Pr.
Rothenberg, Jerome, 1924-
xRothenberg, Jerome.

Approach to the Welfare Analysis of
Intertemporal Resource Allocation. Intl
Pubns Serv.
ed. A Big Jewish Book: Poems & Other Visions
of the Jews from Tribal Times to the Present.
Doubleday.
Esther K Comes to America. Unicorn Pr.
The Measurement of Social Welfare.
Greenwood.
Revolution of the Word: A New Gathering of
American Avant Garde Poetry, 1914-1945.
Continuum.
Rothenberg, Mira.
xRothenberg, Mira.
Children with Emerald Eyes: Histories of
Extraordinary Boys & Girls. Dial.
Rothenberg, Polly.
xRothenberg, Polly.
The Complete Book of Ceramic Art. Crown.
Complete Book of Creative Glass Art. Crown.
Rothenberg, Robert E.
xRothenberg, Robert E.
The Complete Book of Breast Care. Ballantine.
Rothenberg, Ronald I., 1936-
xRothenberg, Ronald I.
Finite Mathematics. Wiley.
Rothenberg, Thomas J.
xRothenberg, Thomas J.
Efficient Estimation with A Priori Information.
Yale U Pr.
Rothenstein, John. see Rothenstein, John Knewstub
Maurice.
Rothenstein, John Knewstub Maurice, Sir, 1901-
xRothenstein, John.
ed. Stanley Spencer the Man: Correspondence
& Reminiscences. Ohio U Pr.
Turner. Braziller.
Rothenstein, William
xRothenstein, William.
Imperfect Encounter: Letters of William
Rothenstein & Rabindranath Tagore,
1911-1941. Harvard U Pr.
Rothfield, Lawrence I., 1927-
xRothfield, Lawrence I.
ed. Structure & Function of Biological
Membranes. Acad Pr.
Rothfleisch, Sheldon.
xRothfleisch, Sheldon.
The No-Nonsense Guide to Cosmetic Surgery.
G&D.
Rothkopf, Carol. see Rothkopf, Carol Zeman.
Rothkopf, Carol Z. see Rothkopf, Carol Zeman.

Rothkopf, Carol Zeman.

xRothkopf, Carol.
Austria. Watts.
The Common Market: Uniting the European
Community. Watts.

xRothkopf, Carol Z.
East Europe. Watts.
The Opening of the Suez Canal, November,
1869: A Water Gateway Joins East & West.
Watts.

Rothman, Daniel A.
xRothman, Daniel A.
The Professional Nurse & the Law. Little.
Rothman, David J.
xRothman, David J.
The Discovery of the Asylum: Social Order &
Disorder in the New Republic. Little.
ed. The Family. Arno.
Rothman, G.
xRothman, G.
Riddle of Cruelty. Philos Lib.
Rothman, J. see Rothman, Jack.
Rothman, Jack.
xRothman, J.

Promoting Innovation & Change in Organizations & Communities: A Planning Manual. Wiley.
Research Development in the Human Services: Toward a Systematic Methodology of Applied Social Science. P-H.
xRothman, Jack.
Using Research in Organizations: A Guide to Successful Application. Sage.

Rothman, Joel.
xRothman, Joel.
At Last to the Ocean: The Story of the Endless Cycle of Water. Macmillan.
How to Play Drums. A Whitman.
Secrets with Ciphers & Codes. Macmillan.
Secrets with Ciphers & Codes. Macmillan.
Which One Is Different?. Doubleday.

Rothman, John, 1924-
xRothman, John.
Origin & Development of Dramatic Criticism in the New York Times 1851-1880. Arno.
Rothman, Milton. see Rothman, Milton A.

Rothman, Milton A.
xRothman, Milton.
Energy & the Future. Watts.
xRothman, Milton A.
Discovering the Natural Laws: The Experimental Basis of Physics. Doubleday.

Rothman, Raymond C., 1922-
xRothman, Raymond C.
Notary Public Practices & Glossary. Natl Notary.

Rothman, Stanley.
xRothman, Stanley.
European Society & Politics: Britain, France & Germany. West Pub.
Soviet Politics & Society. West Pub.

Rothney, John.
xRothney, John.
ed. Brittany Affair & the Crisis of the Ancien Regime. Oxford U Pr.

Rothrock, George A.
xRothrock, George A.
The Huguenots: A Biography of a Minority. Nelson-Hall.

Rothschild, Donald P.
xRothschild, Donald P.
Consumer Protection: Text & Materials. Anderson Pub Co.
Rothschild, Edward F. see Rothschild, Edward Francis.

Rothschild, Edward Francis.
xRothschild, Edward F.
The Meaning of Unintelligibility in Modern Art. Oriole Edns.

Rothschild, Emma, 1948-
xRothschild, Emma.
Paradise Lost: The Decline of the Auto-Industrial Age. Random.
Paradise Lost: The Decline of the Auto-Industrial Age. Random.

Rothschild, Fritz.
xRothschild, Fritz.
The Lost Tradition in Music: Rhythm & Tempo in J. S. Bach's Time. Hyperion Conn.

Rothschild, Henry.
xRothschild, Henry.
ed. Human Diseases Caused by Viruses: Recent Developments. Oxford U Pr.

Rothschild, Joseph.
xRothschild, Joseph.
East Central Europe Between the Two World Wars. U of Wash Pr.
Rothschild, Kurt W. see Rothschild, Kurt Wilhelm.

Rothschild, Kurt Wilhelm.
xRothschild, Kurt W.
Theory of Wages. Kelley.

Rothschild, Lincoln, 1902-
xRothschild, Lincoln.

Forms & Their Meaning in Western Art. A S Barnes.
Rothschild, Marcus A. see Rothschild, Marcus Adolphus.

Rothschild, Marcus Adolphus.
xRothschild, Marcus A.
ed. Plasma Protein Metabolism: Regulation of Synthesis, Distribution & Degradation. Acad Pr.

Rothschild, William E.
xRothschild, William E.
Putting It All Together: A Guide to Strategic Thinking. Am Mgmt.
Strategic Alternatives: Selection, Development & Implementation. Am Mgmt.
Rothschuh, Karl E. see Rothschuh, Karl Ed.

Rothschuh, Karl Ed.
xRothschuh, Karl E.
History of Physiology. Krieger.

Rothstein, Arthur, 1915-
xRothstein, Arthur.
Photojournalism. Amphoto.

Rothstein, Eric.
xRothstein, Eric.
Restoration Tragedy: Form & the Process of Change. Greenwood.
Systems of Order & Inquiry in Later Eighteenth-Century Fiction. U of Cal Pr.

Rothstein, Margaret.
xRothstein, Margaret.
And Other Foolish Questions I Have Answered. Arbor Pubns.

Rothstein, Michael F.
xRothstein, Michael F.
Guide to the Design of Real-Time Systems. Krieger.

Rothstein, Robert L.
xRothstein, Robert L.
Alliances & Small Powers. Columbia U Pr.
Global Bargaining: UNCTAD & the Quest for a New International Economic Order. Princeton U Pr.

Rothwell, Evelyn.
xRothwell, Evelyn.
Oboe Technique. Oxford U Pr.
Rothwell, Kenneth S. see Rothwell, Kenneth Sprague.

Rothwell, Kenneth Sprague.
xRothwell, Kenneth S.
Questions of Rhetoric & Usage. Little.

Rothwell, Norman V.
xRothwell, Norman V.
Human Genetics. P-H.
Understanding Genetics. Oxford U Pr.

Rothwell, Roy.
xRothwell, Roy.
Intro. by Technical Change & Employment. St Martin.

Rotman, Joseph J., 1934-
xRotman, Joseph J.
An Introduction to Homological Algebra. Acad Pr.
Notes on Homological Algebras. Van Nos Reinhold.
The Theory of Groups: An Introduction. Allyn.

Rotondi, Cesar J.
xRotondi, Cesar J.
Grand Obese. St Martin.

Rotramel, Denny D.
xRotramel, Denny D.
Improving Your Accounting Practice. P-H.

Rottenberg, Isaac C.
xRottenberg, Isaac C.
The Promise & the Presence: Toward a Theology of the Kingdom of God. Eerdmans.

Rottenberg, Simon.
xRottenberg, Simon.
ed. The Economics of Medical Malpractice. Am Enterprise.

Rotter, Julian B.
xRotter, Julian B.

Clinical Psychology. P-H.
Personality. Scott F.

Rotzoll, Kim B.
xRotzoll, Kim B.
Advertising in Contemporary Society: Perspectives Toward Understanding. Grid Pub.
Roucek, Joseph S. see Roucek, Joseph Slabey.

Roucek, Joseph Slabey, 1902-
xRoucek, Joseph S.
Balkan Politics: International Relations in No Man's Land. Greenwood.
Capital Punishment. SamHar Pr.
ed. Challenge of Science Education. Arno.
Contemporary Political Ideologies. Philos Lib.
ed. Contemporary Sociology. Greenwood.
Contemporary Sociology. Philos Lib.
Czechs & the Slovaks in America. Lerner Pubns.
Negro Impact on Western Civilization. Philos Lib.
Sociology: An Introduction. Rowman.
ed. Sociology of Crime. Greenwood.
Teaching of History. Philos Lib.

Roud, Richard.
xRoud, Richard.
ed. Cinema: A Critical Dictionary, the Major Film-Makers. Viking Pr.

Rouder, Susan.
xRouder, Susan.
American Politics: Playing the Game. HM.
Roudiez, Leon S. see Roudiez, Leon Samuel.

Roudiez, Leon Samuel, 1917-
xRoudiez, Leon S.
French Fiction Today: A New Direction. Rutgers U Pr.

Roueche, Berton, 1911-
xRoueche, Berton.
Feral. PB.
The Last Enemy. Har-Row.
The Last Enemy. PB.

Roueche, John E.
xRoueche, John E.
Overcoming Learning Problems: A Guide to Developmental Education in College. Jossey-Bass.

Roueche, Nelda W.
xRoueche, Nelda W.
Fundamentals of Business Mathematics. P-H.

Rouge et Noir.
xRouge Et Noir.
Gambling World. Gale.

Roughgarden, Jonathan.
xRoughgarden, Jonathan.
Theory of Population Genetics & Evolutionary Ecology: An Introduction. Macmillan.

Roughsey, Dick.
xRoughsey, Dick.
illus. The Giant Devil-Dingo. Macmillan.

Rougier, Harry.
xRougier, Harry.
Getting Started: A Preface to Writing. Norton.
Rouillard, Clarence D. see Rouillard, Clarence Dana.

Rouillard, Clarence Dana, 1904-
xRouillard, Clarence D.
The Turk in French History, Thought & Literature, 1520-1660. AMS Pr.

Roukes, Nicholas.
xRoukes, Nicholas.
Classroom Craft Manual. Pitman Learning.
Masters of Wood Sculpture. Watson-Guptill.
Roulet, E. see Roulet, Eddy.

Roulet, Eddy.
xRoulet, E.
Linguistic Theory, Linguistic Description & Language Teaching. Longman.
Roumasset, J. A. see Roumasset, James A.

Roumasset, James A.
xRoumasset, J. A.

Rice & Risk: Decision-Making Among Low
    Income Farmers. Elsevier.
Round, Horace. *see* Round, John Horace.
Round, John H. *see* Round, John Horace.
Round, John Horace, 1854-1928
    xRound, Horace.
        Peerage & Pedigree: Studies in Peerage Law &
            Family History. Biblio Dist.
        Studies in Peerage & Family History. Biblio
            Dist.
    xRound, John H.
        Feudal England: Historical Studies on the
            Eleventh & Twelfth Centuries. Greenwood.
        Geoffrey De Mandeville: A Study of the
            Anarchy. B Franklin.
        Peerage & Pedigree: Studies in Peerage Law &
            Family History. Genealog Pub.
        Studies in Peerage & Family History. Genealog
            Pub.
Round Table on Transport Economics, 34th, Paris, 1976.
    xReport of Round Table, European Conference of
        Ministers of Transport on Transport Economics,
        34th, Paris, May 6-7, 1976.
        Psychological Determinants of User Behavior:
            Proceedings. OECD.
Rounds, Glen, 1906-
    xRounds, Glen.
        illus. The Cowboy Trade. Holiday.
        The Day the Circus Came to Lone Tree. Dell.
        The Day the Circus Came to Lone Tree.
            Holiday.
        illus. Lone Muskrat. Holiday.
        illus. Mr. Yowder, the Peripatetic Sign Painter:
            Three Tall Tales. Holiday.
        Once We Had a Horse. Holiday.
        illus. The Prairie Schooners. Holiday.
        illus. Stolen Pony. Holiday.
        Whitey & the Wild Horse. Dell.
        illus. Whitey & the Wild Horse. Holiday.
        illus. Whitey Ropes & Rides. Holiday.
Rounsefell, George A. *see* Rounsefell, George Armytage.
Rounsefell, George Armytage, 1905-
    xRounsefell, George A.
        Ecology Utilization & Management of Marine
            Fisheries. Mosby.
Rountree, Thomas J.
    xRountree, Thomas J.
        ed. Critics on Emerson. U of Miami Pr.
        ed. Critics on Hawthorne. U of Miami Pr.
        ed. Critics on Melville. U of Miami Pr.
        This Mighty Sum of Things: Wordsworth's
            Theme of Benevolent Necessity. U of Ala Pr.
Rourke, C. P. *see* Rourke, Colin P.
Rourke, Colin P.
    xRourke, C. P.
        Introduction to Piecewise-Linear Topology.
            Springer-Verlag.
Rourke, Francis E. *see* Rourke, Francis Edward.
Rourke, Francis Edward, 1922-
    xRourke, Francis E.
        Bureaucracy & Foreign Policy. Johns Hopkins.
        Bureaucracy, Politics, & Public Policy. Little.
Rous, S. N. *see* Rous, Stephen N.
Rous, Stephen N.
    xRous, S. N.
        Understanding Urology. S Karger.
Rousculp. *see* Rousculp, Charles G.
Rousculp, Charles G.
    xRousculp.
        Chalk Dust on My Shoulder. Merrill.
Rouse, C. C.
    xRouse, C. C.
        Montana Bullwhacker. Pacific Pr Pub Assn.
Rouse, Hunter.
    xRouse, Hunter.
        ed. Advanced Mechanics of Fluids. Krieger.
        Elementary Mechanics of Fluids. Dover.
Rouse, Irving, 1913-
    xRouse, Irving.

Prehistory in Haiti: A Study in Method.
    HRAFP.
Rouse, John E.
    xRouse, John E.
        Cattle of North America. U of Okla Pr.
        The Criollo: Spanish Cattle in the Americas. U
            of Okla Pr.
        World Cattle. U of Okla Pr.
Rouse, John E. *see* Rouse, John Edward.
Rouse, John Edward, 1942-
    xRouse, John E.
        ed. Urban Housing--Public & Private: A Guide
            to Information Sources. Gale.
Rouse, Park. *see* Rouse, Parke.
Rouse, Parke, 1915-
    xRouse, Park.
        Beautiful Virginia. Beautiful Am.
    xRouse, Parke.
        Richmond in Color. Hastings.
Rouse, Ruth.
    xRouse, Ruth.
        ed. History of the Ecumenical Movement: 1517
            to 1948. Westminster.
Rouse, Sue H.
    xRouse, Sue H.
        Calculations in Pharmacy. Lippincott.
Rouse, W. H. *see* Rouse, William Henry Denham.
Rouse, William H. *see* Rouse, William Henry Denham.
Rouse, William Henry Denham, 1863-1950
    xRouse, W. H.
        Gods, Heroes & Men of Ancient Greece.
            NAL.
    xRouse, William H.
        Homer. Folcroft.
Rousey, Clyde L.
    xRousey, Clyde L.
        Psychiatric Assessment by Speech & Hearing
            Behavior. C C Thomas.
Roush, John H.
    xRoush, John H.
        Successfully Fishing Lake Tahoe. J H Roush.
Rousmaniere, John.
    xRousmaniere, John.
        A Glossary of Modern Sailing Terms. Dodd.
Roussas, George G.
    xRoussas, George G.
        A First Course in Mathematical Statistics.
            A-W.
Rousseas, Stephen. *see* Rousseas, Stephen William.
Rousseas, Stephen William.
    xRousseas, Stephen.
        Monetary Theory. Knopf.
Rousseau, G. S. *see* Rousseau, George Sebastian.
Rousseau, George Sebastian.
    xRousseau, G. S.
        Organic Form: The Life of an Idea. Routledge
            & Kegan.
Rousseau, Jean J. *see* Rousseau, Jean Jacques.
Rousseau, Jean Jacques.
    xRousseau, Jean J.
        Reveries of the Solitary Walker. Penguin.
    xRousseau, Jean-Jacques.
        Confessions. French & Eur.
        Confessions. Larousse.
        Confessions. Penguin.
        Du Contrat Social. French & Eur.
        Du contrat social. Larousse.
        Du Contrat Social. Oxford U Pr.
        Emile: Or, Education. Dutton.
        First & Second Discourses. St Martin.
        The Government of Poland. Bobbs.
        The Reveries of a Solitary. B Franklin.
        The Reveries of the Solitary Walker. NYU Pr.
Rousseau, Jean-Jacques. *see* Rousseau, Jean Jacques.
Rousseau, M. *see* Rousseau, Madeleine Gandeix.
Rousseau, Madeleine Gandeix.
    xRousseau, M.
        Problems in Optics. Pergamon.
Rousseau, Philip.
    xRousseau, Phillip.

Ascetics, Authority, & the Church in the Age
    of Jerome & Cassian. Oxford U Pr.
Rousseau, Phillip. *see* Rousseau, Philip.
Roussel, Hubert.
    xRoussel, Hubert.
        The Houston Symphony Orchestra 1913-1971.
            U of Tex Pr.
Roussel, Raymond, 1877-1933
    xRoussel, Raymond.
        How I Wrote Certain of My Books. SUN.
Rout, Leslie B.
    xRout, Leslie B.
        Politics of the Chaco Peace Conference,
            1935-1939. U of Tex Pr.
Routh, Francis.
    xRouth, Francis.
        Stravinsky. Littlefield.
Routh, Guy.
    xRouth, Guy.
        The Origin of Economic Ideas. M E Sharpe.
        The Origin of Economic Ideas. Random.
Routh, Harold V. *see* Routh, Harold Victor.
Routh, Harold Victor, 1878-1951
    xRouth, Harold V.
        English Literature & Ideas in the Twentieth
            Century: An Inquiry into Present Difficulties
            & Future Prospects. Russell.
        God, Man & Epic Poetry: A Study in
            Comparative Literature. Greenwood.
Routh, Joseph I.
    xRouth, Joseph I.
        Experiments in Organic & Biochemistry.
            HR&W.
Routh, Joseph I. *see* Routh, Joseph Isaac.
Routh, Joseph Isaac.
    xRouth, Joseph I.
        A Brief Introduction to General, Organic
            Biochemistry. HR&W.
        Introduction to Biochemistry. HR&W.
Routh, Thomas A.
    xRouth, Thomas A.
        Choosing a Nursing Home: The Problems &
            Their Solutions. C C Thomas.
Routley, Erik.
    xRoutley, Erik.
        Church Music & the Christian & Faith. Hope
            Pub.
        Conversion. Fortress.
        The English Carol. Greenwood.
        Exploring the Psalms. Westminster.
        The Musical Wesleys. Greenwood.
        Twentieth Century Church Music. Oxford U
            Pr.
Routt, Ed. *see* Routt, Edd.
Routt, Edd.
    xRoutt, Ed.
        Dimensions of Broadcast Editorializing. TAB
            Bks.
    xRoutt, Edd.
        Business of Radio Broadcasting. TAB Bks.
        Radio Format Conundrum. Hastings.
Roux, George, 1914-
    xRoux, Georges.
        Ancient Iraq. Penguin.
Roux, Georges. *see* Roux, George.
Roven, Milton D.
    xRoven, Milton D.
        Non-Disabling Surgical Rehabilitation of the
            Forefoot. Green.
Rovere, Ernest W.
    xRovere, Ernest W.
        Contract Bridge Complete: A Comprehensive
            Text & Reference Book for Everyone, from
            Beginner to Expert. S&S.
Rovin, Jeff.
    xRovin, Jeff.

The Fabulous Fantasy Films. A S Barnes.
The Fantasy Almanac. Dutton.
The Films of Charlton Heston. Citadel Pr.
The Films of Charlton Heston. Lyle Stuart.
Mars!. Corwin.

Rovinski, Samuel.
xRovinski, Samuel.
Cultural Policy in Costa Rica. Unipub.

Row, John.
xRow, John.
Historie of the Kirk of Scotland. AMS Pr.

Rowan, Frances P. see Rowan, Frances Power.

Rowan, Frances Power, 1938-
xRowan, Frances P.
Chronically-Distressed Client: A Model for
Intervention in the Community. Mosby.

Rowan, Hester.
xRowan, Hester.
Alpine Encounter. Scribner.

Rowan, John.
xRowan, John.
Ordinary Ecstasy: Humanistic Psychology in
Action. Routledge & Kegan.

Rowan, Richard L.
xRowan, Richard L.
ed. Readings in Labor Economics & Labor
Relations. Irwin.

Rowan, Robert L.
xRowan, Robert L.
The Gay Health Guide. Little.

Rowan, Roy.
xRowan, Roy.
The Four Days of Mayaguez. Norton.

Rowan, Stephen A., 1928-
xRowan, Stephen A.
They Wouldn't Let Us Die: The Prisoners of
War Tell Their Story. Jonathan David.

Rowan-Robinson, Michael.
xRowan-Robinson, Michael.
Cosmic Landscape: Voyages Back Along the
Photon's Track. Oxford U Pr.

Rowat, Donald C. see Rowat, Donald Cameron.

Rowat, Donald Cameron.
xRowat, Donald C.
ed. Ombudsman: Citizen's Defender. U of
Toronto Pr.

Rowatt, G. Wade. see Rowatt, Wade.

Rowatt, Wade.
xRowatt, G. Wade.
The Two-Career Marriage. Westminster.

Rowbotham, John Frederick, 1859-1925
xRowbotham, John R.
Troubadours & Courts of Love. Gale.

Rowbotham, John R. see Rowbotham, John Frederick.

Rowbotham, Sheila.
xRowbotham, Sheila.
Women Resistance & Revolution: A History of
Women & Revolution in the Modern World.
Pantheon.
Women, Resistance & Revolution: A History of
Women & Revolution in the Modern World.
Random.

Rowe, Albert. see Rowe, Albert Holmes.
Rowe, Albert F. see Rowe, Albert Percival.
Rowe, Albert H. see Rowe, Albert Holmes.

Rowe, Albert Holmes.
xRowe, Albert.
jt. auth. Food Allergy, Its Manifestations &
Control, & the Elimination Diets - a
Compendium: With Important Consideration
of Inhalant, Drug, & Infectant Allergy. C C
Thomas.
xRowe, Albert H.
Food Allergy, Its Manifestations & Control, &
the Elimination Diets - a Compendium: With
Important Consideration of Inhalant, Drug, &
Infectant Allergy. C C Thomas.

Rowe, Albert Percival.
xRowe, Albert F.

If the Gown Fits. Intl Schol Bk Serv.

Rowe, Alick.
xRowe, Alick.
Boy at the Commercial. Merrimack Bk Serv.

Rowe, C. J.
xRowe, Christopher.
An Introduction to Greek Ethics. B&N.

Rowe, Chandler W.
xRowe, Chandler W.
Effigy Mound Culture of Wisconsin.
Greenwood.

Rowe, Christopher. see Rowe, C. J.

Rowe, Clarence J.
xRowe, Clarence J.
An Outline of Psychiatry. Wm C Brown.

Rowe, Colin.
xRowe, Colin.
Collage City. MIT Pr.
The Mathematics of the Ideal Villa & Other
Essays. MIT Pr.

Rowe, David N. see Rowe, David Nelson.

Rowe, David Nelson, 1905-
xRowe, David N.
Informal "Diplomatic Relations": The Case of
Japan & the Republic of China, 1972-1974.
Shoe String.
Modern China: A Brief History. Van Nos
Reinhold.

Rowe, Eleanor, 1934-
xRowe, Eleanor.
Hamlet: A Window on Russia. NYU Pr.

Rowe, G. S. see Rowe, Gail Stuart.
Rowe, G. W. scc Rowe, Geoffrey W.

Rowe, Gail Stuart, 1936-
xRowe, G. S.
Thomas McKean: The Shaping of an American
Republicanism. Colo Assoc.

Rowe, Geoffrey W.
xRowe, G. W.
Principles of Industrial Metalworking
Processes. Crane-Russak Co.

Rowe, George E., 1947-
xRowe, George E.
Thomas Middleton & the New Comedy
Tradition. U of Nebr Pr.

Rowe, H. E. see Rowe, Harrison E.

Rowe, Harrison E.
xRowe, H. E.
Signals & Noise in Communication Systems.
Van Nos Reinhold.

Rowe, Jack.
xRowe, Jack.
Inyo-Sierra Passage. McGraw.

Rowe, James E.
xRowe, James E.
ed. Coal Surface Mining Impacts of
Reclamation. Westview.

Rowe, James N., 1938-
xRowe, James N.
The Judas Squad. Little.

Rowe, Jeanne A.
xRowe, Jeanne A.
Album of Martin Luther King Jr. Watts.

Rowe, John.
xRowe, John.
The Aswan Solution. Doubleday.
The Chocolate Crucifix. David & Charles.

Rowe, John L.
xRowe, John L.
Typewriting Drills for Speed & Accuracy.
McGraw.

Rowe, John W. see Rowe, John Wilkinson Foster.

Rowe, John Wilkinson Foster, 1897-
xRowe, John W.
Primary Commodities in International Trade.
Cambridge U Pr.

Rowe, Joseph E. see Rowe, Joseph Everett.

Rowe, Joseph Everett, 1927-
xRowe, Joseph E.

Nonlinear Electron-Wave Interaction
Phenomena. Acad Pr.

Rowe, K. L. see Rowe, Kenneth L.

Rowe, Kenneth L.
xRowe, K. L.
Communications in Marketing. McGraw.
xRowe, Kenneth L.
Communications in Marketing. McGraw.

Rowe, Nicholas.
xRowe, Nicholas.
Fair Penitent. U of Nebr Pr.

Rowe, R. E. see Rowe, Roy Edward.

Rowe, Robert, 1902-
xRowe, Robert.
Adam Silver 1765-1795. Merrimack Bk Serv.

Rowe, Roy Edward.
xRowe, R. E.
Concrete Bridge Design. Burgess-Intl Ideas.

Rowe, Royle C.
xRowe, Royle C.
Geology of Our Western National Parks &
Monuments. Binford.

Rowe, W. W. see Rowe, William Woodin.

Rowe, William, 1941-
xRowe, William.
Flora & Fauna Design Fantasies. Dover.
Flora & Fauna Design Fantasies. Peter Smith.

Rowe, William D., 1930-
xRowe, William D.
An Anatomy of Risk. Wiley.

Rowe, William L.
xRowe, William L.
The Cosmological Argument. Princeton U Pr.
Religious Symbols & God: A Philosophical
Study of Tillich's Theology. U of Chicago Pr.

Rowe, William Woodin.
xRowe, W. W.
Nabokov & Others: Patterns in Russian
Literature. Ardis Pubs.

Rowell, Chester H. see Rowell, Chester Harvey.

Rowell, Chester Harvey, 1867-1948
xRowell, Chester H.
A Historical & Legal Digest of All the
Contested Election Cases in the House of
Representatives of the U.S. from the 1st to
the 56th Congress, 1789-1901. Greenwood.

Rowell, Galen. see Rowell, Galen A.

Rowell, Galen A.
xRowell, Galen.
High & Wild: A Mountaineer's World. Sierra.
In the Throne Room of the Mountain Gods.
Sierra.

Rowell, George
xRowell, George.
Late Victorian Plays, 1890-1914. Oxford U Pr.
Queen Victoria Goes to the Theatre.
Merrimack Bk Serv.

Rowell, Lois.
xRowell, Lois.
American Organ Music on Records. Organ Lit.

Rowell, Margit.
xRowell, Margit.
Ad Reinhardt & Color. S R Guggenheim.
The Planar Dimension: Europe, 1912-1932. S
R Guggenheim.

Rowen, B. see Rowen, Betty.

Rowen, Betty.
xRowen, B.
The Children We See: An Observational
Approach to Child Study. HR&W.

Rowen, Herbert H. see Rowen, Herbert Harvey.

Rowen, Herbert Harvey.
xRowen, Herbert H.

ed. Early Modern Europe: A Book of Source Readings. AHM Pub.
ed. From Absolutism to Revolution: 1648-1848. Macmillan.
History of Early Modern Europe, 1500-1815. Bobbs.
The Low Countries in Early Modern Times. Walker & Co.

Rowen, Lilian.
xRowen, Lilian.
The Working Woman's Body Book. Rawson Wade.

Rowen, Louis H. *see* Rowen, Louis Halle.

Rowen, Louis Halle.
xRowen, Louis H.
Polynomial Identities in Ring Theory. Acad Pr.

Rowen, R. *see* Rowen, Ruth Halle.
Rowen, Ruth H. *see* Rowen, Ruth Halle.

Rowen, Ruth Halle.
xRowen, R.
Music Through Sources & Documents. P-H.
xRowen, Ruth H.
Early Chamber Music. Da Capo.

Roweton, William E.
xRoweton, William E.
ed. Revitalizing Educational Psychology: Readings in Method & Substance. Nelson-Hall.

Rowland, A. Westley, 1915-
xRowland, A. Westley.
ed. Handbook of Institutional Advancement: A Practical Guide to College & University Relations, Fund Raising, Alumni Relations, Government Relations, Publications, & Executive Management for Continued Advancement. Jossey-Bass.

Rowland, Albert L. *see* Rowland, Albert Lindsay.

Rowland, Albert Lindsay.
xRowland, Albert L.
Studies in English Commerce & Exploration in the Reign of Elizabeth. B Franklin.

Rowland, Arthur R. *see* Rowland, Arthur Ray.

Rowland, Arthur Ray, 1930-
xRowland, Arthur R.
Catalog & Cataloging. Shoe String.
The Librarian & Reference Service. Shoe String.

Rowland, Benjamin.
xRowland, Benjamin.
Ancient Art from Afghanistan: Treasures of the Kabul Museum. Arno.
The Art & Architecture of India: Buddhist-Hindu-Jain. Penguin.
Cave to Renaissance. Little.

Rowland, Benjamin M.
xRowland, Benjamin M.
ed. Balance of Power or Hegemony: The Interwar Monetary System. NYU Pr.

Rowland, Beryl.
xRowland, Beryl.
Animals with Human Faces: A Guide to Animal Symbolism. U of Tenn Pr.
ed. Companion to Chaucer Studies. Oxford U Pr.

Rowland, John, 1923-
xRowland, John.
A History of Sino-Indian Relations: Hostile Co-Existence. Krieger.

Rowland, John T. *see* Rowland, John Tilghman.

Rowland, John Tilghman, 1888-
xRowland, John T.
North to Baffin Land. Seven Seas.

Rowland, Mary F.
xRowland, Mary F.
Pasternak's "Doctor Zhivago". S Ill U Pr.

Rowland, May.
xRowland, May.
Dare to Believe. Unity Bks.

Rowland, Peter, 1938-
xRowland, Peter.

David Lloyd George: A Biography. Macmillan.

Rowland, Tom.
xRowland, Tom.
Restoring & Renovating Antique Furniture. Transatlantic.
Restoring & Renovating Antique Furniture. Van Nos Reinhold.

Rowlands, John J., 1892-
xRowlands, John J.
Cache Lake Country: Life in the North Woods. Norton.

Rowlett, Elsebet S. *see* Rowlett, Elsebet Sander-Jrgensen.

Rowlett, Elsebet Sander-Jrgensen.
xRowlett, Elsebet S.
Neolithic Levels on the Titelberg, Luxembourg. Mus Anthro Mo.

Rowley, Anthony.
xRowley, Anthony.
ed. The Barons of European Industry. Holmes & Meier.

Rowley, C. D. *see* Rowley, Charles Dunford.
Rowley, Charles D. *see* Rowley, Charles Dunford.

Rowley, Charles Dunford.
xRowley, C. D.
The Politics of Educational Planning in Developing Countries. Unipub.
xRowley, Charles D.
The Australians in German New Guinea, 1914-1921. Intl Schol Bk Serv.
A Matter of Justice. Bks Australia.

Rowley, Charles K. *see* Rowley, Charles Kershaw.

Rowley, Charles Kershaw.
xRowley, Charles K.
Readings in Industrial Economics. Crane-Russak Co.

Rowley, H. H. *see* Rowley, Harold Henry.
Rowley, Harold H. *see* Rowley, Harold Henry.

Rowley, Harold Henry, 1890-
xRowley, H. H.
Job. Attic Pr.
Rediscovery of the Old Testament. Attic Pr.
xRowley, Harold H.
Prophecy & Religion in Ancient China & Israel. Allenson.
Re-Discovery of the Old Testament. Arno.

Rowley, J. E.
xRowley, J. E.
The Dissemination of Information. Westview.

Rowley, Samuel, d. 1633?
xRowley, Samuel.
When You See Me You Know Me. AMS Pr.

Rowlinson, J. S. *see* Rowlinson, John Shipley.

Rowlinson, John Shipley.
xRowlinson, J. S.
The Perfect Gas. Pergamon.

Rowntree, B. Seebohm. *see* Rowntree, Benjamin Seebohm.

Rowntree, Benjamin Seebohm, 1871-1954
xRowntree, B. Seebohm.
The Human Factor in Business. Arno.

Rowntree, Derek.
xRowntree, Derek.
Educational Technology in Curriculum Development. Har-Row.

Rowntree, Lester.
xRowntree, Lester.
Hardy Californians. Peregrine Smith.

Rowse, A. L. *see* Rowse, Alfred Leslie.
Rowse, Alfred. *see* Rowse, Alfred Leslie.
Rowse, Alfred L. *see* Rowse, Alfred Leslie.

Rowse, Alfred Leslie, 1903-
xRowse, A. L.
The Byrons & the Trevanions. St Martin.
A Cornish Childhood: Autobiography of a Cornishman. Potter.
On History: A Study of Present Tendencies. Folcroft.
xRowse, Alfred.
Queen Elizabeth & Her Subjects. Arno.
xRowse, Alfred L.

Appeasement: A Study in Political Decline, 1933-34. Norton.
On History: A Study of Present Tendencies. Arden Lib.

Rowsome, Frank.
xRowsome, Frank.
The Bright & Glowing Place. Greene.

Roxborough, Ian.
xRoxborough, Ian.
Chile: The State & Revolution. Holmes & Meier.
Theories of Under Development. Humanities.

Roxburgh, Nigel.
xRoxburgh, Nigel.
Policy Responses to Resource Depletion: A Case of Mercury. Jai Pr.

Roxe, Linda A.
xRoxe, Linda A.
Personnel Management for the Smaller Company: A Hands-on Manual. Am Mgmt.

Roy. *see* Roy, Archie E.
Roy, Alexander Le. *see* Le Roy, Alexander.

Roy, Andrew.
xRoy, Andrew.
A History of the Coal Miners of the United States: From the Development of the Mines to the Close of the Anthracite Strike of 1902, Including a Brief Sketch of Early British Miners. Greenwood.

Roy, Archie E.
xRoy.
Orbital Motion. Heyden.

Roy, Basanta K. *see* Roy, Basanta Koomar.

Roy, Basanta Koomar.
xRoy, Basanta K.
Rabindranath Tagore, the Man & His Poetry. R West.

Roy, Beth.
xRoy, Beth.
Bullock Carts & Motor Bikes: Ancient India on a New Road. Atheneum.

Roy, Cal.
xRoy, Cal.
illus. The Legend & the Storm. FS&G.
illus. The Painter of Miracles. FS&G.

Roy, Callista.
xRoy, Callista.
Introduction to Nursing: An Adaptation Model. P-H.

Roy, Claude C.
xRoy.
Pediatric Clinical Gastroenterology. Mosby.

Roy, Dilip K. *see* Roy, Dilip Kumar.

Roy, Dilip Kumar, 1939 (June 20)-
xRoy, Dilip K.
Tunnelling & Negative Resistance Phenomena in P-N Junctions. Pergamon.

Roy, Doreen.
xRoy, Doreen.
Champagne Decorating on a Beer Budget. Stein & Day.

Roy, E. P. *see* Roy, Ewell Paul.

Roy, Emil.
xRoy, Emil.
British Drama Since Shaw. S Ill U Pr.
Christopher Fry. S Ill U Pr.

Roy, Ewell P. *see* Roy, Ewell Paul.

Roy, Ewell Paul.
xRoy, E. P.
Cooperatives: Development, Principles & Management. Interstate.
xRoy, Ewell P.
Collective Bargaining in Agriculture. Interstate.
Contract Farming & Economic Integration. Interstate.
Economics: Applications to Agriculture & Agribusiness. Interstate.
Exploring Agribusiness. Interstate.

Roy, Frederick H. *see* Roy, Frederick Hampton.

Roy, Frederick Hampton.
  xRoy, Frederick H.
    Ocular Differential Diagnosis. Lea & Febiger.
Roy, Gaylord C. Le. *see* Le Roy, Gaylord C.
Roy, George R. *see* Roy, George Ross.
Roy, George Ross, 1924-
  xRoy, George R.
    tr. & ed. Twelve Modern French Canadian
      Poets. Greenwood.
Roy, Girish Chandra.
  xRoy, Girish Chandra.
    Indian Culture: The Tradition of Non-Violence
      & Social Change in India. South Asia Bks.
Roy, J. H. *see* Roy, James Henry Barstow.
Roy, James A. *see* Roy, James Alexander.
Roy, James Alexander, 1884-
  xRoy, James A.
    Cowper & His Poetry. AMS Pr.
    Cowper & His Poetry. Folcroft.
Roy, James Henry Barstow.
  xRoy, J. H.
    The Calf. Butterworths.
Roy, K. P. *see* Roy, Kali Pada.
Roy, Kali Pada, 1925-
  xRoy, K. P.
    Introduction to Heat Engines. Asia.
Roy, Kristina.
  xRoy, Kristina.
    The Heiress. Good News.
Roy, M. N. *see* Roy, Manabendra Nath.
Roy, M. P. *see* Roy, Mahendra Prakash.
Roy, Mahendra Prakash, 1923-
  xRoy, M. P.
    Origin, Growth, & Suppression of the Pindaris.
      Intl Pubns Serv.
    Origin Growth & Suppression of the Pindaris.
      Verry.
Roy, Manabendra N. *see* Roy, Manabendra Nath.
Roy, Manabendra Nath, 1893-1954
  xRoy, M. N.
    Revolution & Counter-Revolution in China.
      Gordon Pr.
  xRoy, Manabendra N.
    Revolution & Counter-Revolution in China.
      Hyperion Conn.
Roy, Probir.
  xRoy, Probir.
    Theory of Lepton-Hadron Processes at High
      Energies: Partons, Scale Invariance &
      Light-Cone Physics. Oxford U Pr.
Roy, Ramashray.
  xRoy, Ramashray.
    The Uncertain Verdict: A Study of the 1969
      Elections in Four Indian States. U of Cal Pr.
Roy, Robert H.
  xRoy, Robert H.
    The Administrative Process. Johns Hopkins.
    The Cultures of Management. Johns Hopkins.
Roy, Robert L.
  xRoy, Robert L.
    Underground Houses: How to Build a
      Low-Cost Home. Sterling.
Roy, Ron.
  xRoy, Ron.
    Awful Thursday. Pantheon.
    Three Ducks Went Wandering. Schol Bk Serv.
    Three Ducks Went Wandering. HM.
Roy, S. C. *see* Roy, Sarat Chandra.
Roy, S. N. *see* Roy, Samarendra Nath.
Roy, Samarendra Nath.
  xRoy, S. N.
    Analysis & Design of Certain Quantitative
      Multiresponse Experiments. Pergamon.
Roy, Sandra.
  xRoy, Sandra.
    Josephine Tey. Twayne.
Roy, Sarat Chandra, Rai Bahadur, 1871-1942
  xRoy, S. C.

Mundas & Their Country. Asia.
Roy, Subodh.
  xRoy, Subodh.
    ed. Communism in India: Unpublished
      Documents, 1925-1934. South Asia Bks.
Roy, Willy.
  xRoy, Willy.
    Coaching Winning Soccer. Contemp Bks.
Roy-Burman, P.
  xRoy-Burman, P.
    Analogues of Nucleic Acid Components:
      Mechanisms of Action. Springer-Verlag.
Royal Aeronautical Society. *see* Royal Aeronautical
Society, London.
Royal Aeronautical Society, London.
  xRoyal Aeronautical Society.
    A List of the Books, Periodicals & Pamphlets
      in the Library of the Royal Aeronautical
      Society: With Which Is Incorporated the
      Institution of Aeronautical Engineers. Arno.
Royal Automobile Club.
  xRoyal Automobile Club.
    RAC Castles, Historic Houses, Gardens &
      Other Places of Interest Open to the Public.
      British Bk Ctr.
    Rac Continental Handbook & Guide to
      Western Europe. British Bk Ctr.
    RAC Guide & Handbook to Britain 1975.
      British Bk Ctr.
    Rac Guide to Scandinavia & Eastern Europe.
      British Bk Ctr.
    RAC Guide to Touring in Ireland. British Bk
      Ctr.
    Rac Restaurant Guide & London Information.
      British Bk Ctr.
Royal Barry Will Associates.
  xRoyal Barry Wills Associates.
    More Houses for Good Living. Architectural.
Royal Barry Wills Associates. *see* Royal Barry Will
  Associates.
Royal, Brian James.
  xRoyal, Brian James.
    Enemies. Nordon Pubns.
Royal College of Physicians of London.
  xRoyal College of Physicians of London.
    Smoking & Health Now. Lippincott.
  xTheRoyal College of Physicians.
    Proceedings. State Mutual Bk.
Royal Commission Upon The Duties Of The
  Metropolitan Police. *see* Great Britain. Royal
  Commission Upon the Duties of the Metropolitan
  Police.
Royal Commonwealth Society.
  xRoyal Commonwealth Society, London.
    Subject Catalogue of the Royal Commonwealth
      Society. G K Hall.
Royal Commonwealth Society, London. *see* Royal
  Commonwealth Society.
Royal Geographical Society. *see* Royal Geographical
  Society, London.
Royal Geographical Society, London.
  xRoyal Geographical Society.
    The Country of Turkomans, an Anthology of
      Exploration. Humanities.
Royal Institute of Internatinal Affairs. *see* Royal Institute
  of International Affairs.
Royal Institute of International Affairs.
  xRoyal Institute of Internatinal Affairs.
    Atlantic Alliance: NATO's Role in the Free
      World. Greenwood.
  xRoyal Institute of International Affairs.

Balkan States, One: Economic. Johnson Repr.
Britain in Western Europe: WEU & the
  Atlantic Alliance. Greenwood.
British Foreign Policy: Some Relevant
  Documents, January, 1950 - April, 1955.
  Greenwood.
Documents of International Affairs, 1958.
  Oxford U Pr.
Documents on International Affairs, 1962.
  Oxford U Pr.
Great Britain & Palestine 1915-1945. Hyperion
  Conn.
Index to Periodical Articles, Nineteen Fifty to
  Nineteen Sixty-Four. G K Hall.
Index to Periodical Articles, Nineteen Sixty
  Five to Nineteen Seventy-Two. G K Hall.
International Gold Problem. Johnson Repr.
Monetary Policy & the Depression. Johnson
  Repr.
Nationalism. Kelley.
Problem of International Investment. Kelley.
Reports on Nationalism by a Study Group of
  Members of the Royal Institute of
  International Affairs: Proceedings. Biblio
  Dist.
South-Eastern Europe. Johnson Repr.
Unemployment, an International Problem: A
  Report. Johnson Repr.
World Agriculture: An International Survey.
  Johnson Repr.
xTheRoyal Institute of International Affairs,
London.
  Index to Periodical Articles, Nineteen
    Seventy-Three to Nineteen Seventy-Eight, in
    the Library of the Royal Institute of
    International Affairs. G K Hall.
**Royal Institute of International Affairs. Information
Dept.**
  xRoyal Institute Of International Affairs
  Information Department.
    Baltic States: A Survey of the Political &
      Economic Structure & the Foreign Relations
      of Estonia, Latvia & Lithuania. Greenwood.
    Great Britain & Egypt: 1914-1951. Greenwood.
Royal Institute of Naval Architects.
  xRoyal Institution of Naval Architects.
    ed. Prevention & Control of Fires in Ships. Intl
      Schol Bk Serv.
Royal Institution of Naval Architects. *see* Royal Institute
  of Naval Architects.
Royal Irish Academy. *see* Royal Irish Academy, Dublin.
**Royal Irish Academy Conference on Numerical Analysis,
Dublin, 1972.**
  xRoyal Irish Academy, Conference, 1972.
    Topics in Numerical Analysis: Proceedings.
      Acad Pr.
Royal Irish Academy, Conference, 1972. *see* Royal Irish
  Academy Conference on Numerical Analysis, Dublin,
  1972.
Royal Irish Academy, Dublin.
  xRoyal Irish Academy.
    Todd Lecture Series. AMS Pr.
Royal, Robert F.
  xRoyal, Robert F.
    The Gentle Art of Interviewing &
      Interrogation: A Professional Manual &
      Guide. P-H.
Royal, Rosamond.
  xRoyal, Rosamond.
    Rapture. Popular Lib.
Royal Society. *see* Royal Society of London.
**Royal Society of Literature of the United Kingdom,
London.**
  xFellows of the Royal Society of Literature of the
  U.K.

The Eighteen-Eighties, Essays. Core Collection.
The Eighteen-Seventies, Essays. Core Collection.
The Eighteen-Sixties, Essays. Core Collection.
xRoyal Society of Literature of the United Kingdom.
    The Eighteen Eighties: Essays by Fellows of the Royal Society of Literature. Somerset Pub.
xRoyal Society of Literature, United Kingdom.
    Essays by Divers Hands. Core Collection.
Royal Society of Literature, United Kingdom. see Royal Society of Literature of the United Kingdom, London.
Royal Society of London.
    xRoyal Society.
        Assessment of Sublethal Effects of Pollutants in the Sea. Scholium Intl.
        Influenza: Proceedings. Scholium Intl.
        The Middle Atmosphere As Observed from Baloons, Rockets & Satellites. Scholium Intl..
        Selected Lectures. Acad Pr.
    xRoyal Society of London.
        Long-Term Hazards from Environmental Chemicals. Scholium Intl.
        The Terrestrial Ecology of Aldabra. Scholium Intl.
        Theoretical & Practical Aspects of Uranium Geology. Scholium Intl.
    xRoyal Society of London Publications.
        Mineralogy: Towards the Twenty-First Century. Scholium Intl.
        Technologies for Rural Health. Scholium Intl.
Royal Society of London Publications. see Royal Society of London.
Royal Society of London. Study Group on Pollution in the Atmosphere.
    xRoyal Society of London, Study Group on Pollution in the Atmosphere, 1977.
        Pathways of Pollutants in the Atmosphere. Scholium Intl.
Royal United Services Institute. see Royal United Services Institute for Defense Studies.
Royal United Services Institute for Defense Studies.
    xRoyal United Services Institute.
        ed. Ten Years of Terrorism: Collected Views. Crane-Russak Co.
    xRoyal United Services Institute for Defence Studies, London.
        ed. International Weapon Developments: A Survey of Current Developments in Weapons Systems. Presidio Pr.
        ed. Rusi & Brassey's Defence Yearbook, 1977-78. Westview.
    xTheRoyal United Services Institute for Defence Studies.
        ed. International Weapon Developments: A Survey of Current Developments in Weapon Systems. Pergamon.
Royall, Vanessa.
    xRoyall, Vanessa.
        Flames of Desire. Dell.
Royce, Anya P. see Royce, Anya Peterson.
Royce, Anya Peterson.
    xRoyce, Anya P.
        Anthropology of Dance. Ind U Pr.
Royce, Charles C.
    xRoyce, Charles C.
        ed. Indian Land Cessions in the United States. Arno.
Royce, James E.
    xRoyce, James E.
        Personality & Mental Health. Glencoe.
Royce, Joseph.
    xRoyce, Joseph.
        Surface Anatomy. Davis Co.
Royce, Josiah, 1855-1916
    xRoyce, Josiah.

California, from the Conquest in 1846 to the Second Vigilance Committee in San Francisco, 1856: A Study of American Character. AMS Pr.
Conception of Immortality. Greenwood.
Conception of Immortality. Scholarly.
The Feud of Oakfield Creek: A Novel of California Life. Irvington.
The Feud of Oakfield Creek: A Novel of California Life. Johnson Repr.
Hope of the Great Community. Arno.
Letters of Josiah Royce. U of Chicago Pr.
Principles of Logic. Citadel Pr.
Problem of Christianity. U of Chicago Pr.
Race Questions, Provincialism, & Other American Problems. Arno.
The Religious Philosophy of Josiah Royce. Greenwood.
World & the Individual. Peter Smith.
Royce, Kenneth.
    xRoyce, Kenneth.
        The Masterpiece Affair. Avon.
        The Masterpiece Affair. S&S.
        ed. The Third Arm. McGraw.
        The Woodcutter Operation. S&S.
Royce, Patrick M.
    xRoyce, Patrick M.
        Sailing Illustrated: The Sailor's Bible Since '56. Western Marine Ent.
Royce, Samuel.
    xRoyce, Samuel.
        Deterioration & Race Education with Practical Application to the Condition of the People & Industry. Arno.
Royce, Sarah. see Royce, Sarah Bayliss.
Royce, Sarah Bayliss.
    xRoyce, Sarah.
        A Frontier Lady: Recollections of the Gold Rush & Early California. U of Nebr Pr.
Royden, H. L.
    xRoyden, H. L.
        Real Analysis. Macmillan.
Royer, James M.
    xRoyer, James M.
        Psychology of Learning: Educational Applications. Wiley.
Royer, King.
    xRoyer, King.
        Applied Field Surveying. Wiley.
        Desk Book for Construction Superintendents. P-H.
Royer, Pierre, 1917-
    xRoyer, Pierre.
        Pediatric Nephrology. Saunders.
Roylance, William H.
    xRoylance, William H.
        Complete Book of Insults, Boasts & Riddles. P-H.
Roys, R. L. see Roys, Ralph Loveland.
Roys, Ralph L. see Roys, Ralph Loveland.
Roys, Ralph Loveland, 1879-1965
    xRoys, R. L.
        The Indian Background of Colonial Yucatan. Gordon Pr.
    xRoys, Ralph L.
        The Ethno-Botany of the Maya. Inst Study Human.
Royston, Michael.
    xRoyston, Michael G.
        Pollution Prevention Pays. Pergamon.
Royston, Michael G. see Royston, Michael.
Rozanov, Iurii Anatolevich.
    xRozanov, Y. A.
        Probability Theory: A Concise Course. Dover.
Rozanov, Vasilii V. see Rozanov, Vasilii Vasilevich.
Rozanov, Vasilii Vasilevich.
    xRozanov, Vasilii V.
        Solitaria. Greenwood.
Rozanov, Y. A. see Rozanov, Iurii Anatolevich.

Rozanski, Mordechai.
    xRozanski, Mordechai.
        ed. Records of the Department of State Relating to the Internal Affairs of China, 1910-1929: A Descriptive Guide & Subject Index to Microcopy No. 329. Scholarly Res Inc.
Rozantsev, E. G., 1931-
    xRozantsev, E. G.
        Free Nitroxyl Radicals. Plenum Pub.
Rozenberg, Grzegorz.
    xRozenberg, Grzegorz.
        The Mathematical Theory of L Systems. Acad Pr.
Rozewicz, Tadeusz.
    xRozewicz, Tadeusz.
        The Survivor & Other Poems. Princeton U Pr.
Rozman, Deborah.
    xRozman, Deborah.
        Meditation for Children. PB.
    xRozman, Deborah A.
        Meditation for Children. Celestial Arts.
Rozman, Deborah A. see Rozman, Deborah.
Rozwenc, Edwin C. see Rozwenc, Edwin Charles.
Rozwenc, Edwin Charles, 1915-
    xRozwenc, Edwin C.
        ed. Causes of the American Civil War. Heath.
        Cooperatives Come to America: The History of the Protective Union Store Movement 1845-1867. Porcupine Pr.
Ruark, Robert, 1915-1965
    xRuark, Robert.
        Honey Badger. Fawcett.
Ruark, Robert. see Ruark, Robert Chester.
Ruark, Robert Chester, 1915-1965
    xRuark, Robert.
        Something of Value. PB.
Rubado, Clarence A. see Rubado, Clarence Arthur.
Rubado, Clarence Arthur, 1886-
    xRubado, Clarence A.
        Problems of the City School Superintendent in the Field of Arithmetic. AMS Pr.
Rubano, Judith.
    xRubano, Judith.
        Culture & Behavior in Hawaii: An Annotated Bibliography. U Pr of Hawaii.
Rubbra, Benedict.
    xRubbra, Benedict.
        Painting Children. Taplinger.
Rubel, Arthur J.
    xRubel, Arthur J.
        Across the Tracks: Mexican-Americans in a Texas City. U of Tex Pr.
Rubel, Fred N.
    xRubel, Fred N.
        Incineration of Solid Wastes. Noyes.
Rubel, Stanley M.
    xRubel, Stanley M.
        Intro. by & ed. Guide to Selling a Business. Capital Pub Corp.
        Intro. by & ed. Guide to Venture Capital Sources. Capital Pub Corp.
Ruben, Ann G.
    xRuben, Ann G.
        Our Teachers Are Crying: A Positive Approach to Solving Classroom Problems. Mss Info.
Ruben, Brent. see Ruben, Brent D.
Ruben, Brent D.
    xRuben, Brent.
        General Systems Theory & Human Communication. Hayden.
        Human Communication Handbook: Simulations & Games. Hayden.
    xRuben, Brent D.
        Human Communication Handbook: Simulations & Games. Hayden.
Ruben, Harvey L.
    xRuben, Harvey L.
        C.I.-Crisis Intervention. Popular Lib.
Ruben, M. see Ruben, Montague.

Ruben, Margarete.
    xRuben, Margarete.
        Parent Guidance in the Nursery School. Intl
          Univs Pr.
Ruben, Montague.
    xRuben, M.
        Contact Lens Practice: Visual, Therapeutic &
          Prosthetic. Macmillan.
    xRuben, Montague.
        Soft Contact Lenses: Clinical & Applied
          Technology. Wiley.
Ruben, Samuel.
    xRuben, Samuel.
        The Founders of Electrochemistry. Dorrance.
Rubens, Bernice.
    xRubens, Bernice.
        I Sent a Letter to My Love. St Martin.
Rubens, Horatio S. *see* Rubens, Horatio Seymour.
Rubens, Horatio Seymour, 1869-1941
    xRubens, Horatio S.
        Liberty, the Story of Cuba. AMS Pr.
Rubens, Peter P. *see* Rubens, Peter Paul.
Rubens, Peter Paul.
    xRubens, Peter P.
        Rubens. G&D.
Rubenstein, E. *see* Rubenstein, Edward.
Rubenstein, Edward, 1924-
    xRubenstein, E.
        Intensive Medical Care. McGraw.
        ed. Scientific American Medicine. Sci Am Illus
          Lib.
Rubenstein, Harvey M.
    xRubenstein, Harvey M.
        Central City Malls. Wiley.
        A Guide to Site & Environmental Planning.
          Wiley.
Rubenstein, James M.
    xRubenstein, James M.
        The French New Towns. Johns Hopkins.
Rubenstein, Jill.
    xRubenstein, Jill.
        ed. Sir Walter Scott: A Reference Guide. G K
          Hall.
Rubenstein, Richard L.
    xRubenstein, Richard L.
        My Brother Paul. Har-Row.
Rubenstein, Roberta, 1944-
    xRubenstein, Roberta.
        The Novelistic Vision of Doris Lessing:
          Breaking the Forms of Consciousness. U of
          Ill Pr.
Rubenstone, Jessie.
    xRubenstone, Jessie.
        Crochet for Beginners. Lippincott.
Rubey, Harry.
    xRubey, Harry.
        Construction & Professional Management: An
          Introduction. U of Okla Pr.
Rubiao, Murilo.
    xRubiao, Murilo.
        The Ex-Magician & Other Stories. Har-Row.
Rubin. *see* Rubin, Stanford E.
Rubin, A. J. *see* Rubin, Alan J.
Rubin, Alan J.
    xRubin, A. J.
        Aqueous-Environmental Chemistry of Metals.
          Ann Arbor Science.
    xRubin, Alan J.
        ed. Chemistry of Wastewater Technology. Ann
          Arbor Science.
Rubin, Arnold. *see* Rubin, Arnold D.
Rubin, Arnold D.
    xRubin, Arnold.
        The Leukemia Cell. CRC Pr.
Rubin, Arnold P., 1946-
    xRubin, Arnold P.
        The Evil That Men Do: The Story of the
          Nazis. Messner.
Rubin, Barry, 1941-
    xRubin, Barry.

How Others Report Us: America in the
        Foreign Press. Sage.
Rubin, Barry M.
    xRubin, Barry M.
        Human Rights & U. S. Foreign Policy.
          Westview.
Rubin, Bernard.
    xRubin, Bernard.
        Media, Politics, & Democracy. Oxford U Pr.
        ed. Questioning Media Ethics. Praeger.
Rubin, Bob.
    xRubin, Bob.
        All-Stars of the NFL. Random.
        Little Men of the NFL. Random.
Rubin, C. *see* Rubin, Charles J.
Rubin, Charles. *see* Rubin, Charles R.

Rubin, Charles J.
    xRubin, C.
        Junk Food. Dell.

Rubin, Charles R.
    xRubin, Charles.
        The Log of Rubin the Sailor. Intl Pub Co.

Rubin, Cynthia.

    xRubin, Cynthia.
        Shaker Miniature Furniture. Van Nos
          Reinhold.

Rubin, Dorothy.
    xRubin, Dorothy.
        Teaching Elementary Language Arts. HR&W.
Rubin, Edmund J. *see* Rubin, Edmund Joseph.
Rubin, Edmund Joseph.
    xRubin, Edmund J.
        Abstract Functioning in the Blind. Am Foun
          Blind.
Rubin, H. *see* Rubin, Harold.
Rubin, H. Ted, 1926-
    xRubin, H. Ted.
        The Courts: Fulcrum of the Justice System.
          Goodyear.
        Juvenile Justice: Policy Practice & Law.
          Goodyear.
Rubin, Harold, 1927-
    xRubin, H.
        Pensions & Employee Mobility in the Public
          Service. Kraus Repr.
Rubin, Harold. *see* Rubin, Harold Irving.
Rubin, Harold Irving, 1927-
    xRubin, Harold.
        The Ulcer Diet Cookbook. M Evans.
Rubin, Irvin I., 1919-
    xRubin, Irvin I.
        Injection Molding: Theory & Practice. Wiley.
Rubin, Irwin. *see* Rubin, Irwin M.
Rubin, Irwin M.
    xRubin, Irwin.
        Improving the Coordination of Care: A
          Program for Health Team Development.
          Ballinger Pub.

Rubin, James M.
    xRubin, James M.
        ed. Practical Points in Allergy. Med Exam.

Rubin, Jeffrey, 1949-

    xRubin, Jeffrey.
        Economics, Mental Health, & the Law.
          Lexington Bks.

Rubin, Jerome.

    xRubin, Jerome.

        jt. auth. Guide to Massachusetts Museums,
          Historic Houses & Points of Interest.
          Emporium Pubns.

Rubin, Jerry.
    xRubin, Jerry.
        Growing (Up) at Thirty-Seven. M Evans.
Rubin, Joan S. *see* Rubin, Joan Shelley.
Rubin, Joan Shelley, 1947-
    xRubin, Joan S.
        Constance Rourke & American Culture. U of
          NC Pr.
Rubin, Joseph J. *see* Rubin, Joseph Jay.
Rubin, Joseph Jay, 1912-
    xRubin, Joseph J.
        The Historic Whitman. Pa St U Pr.
Rubin, Judith A. *see* Rubin, Judith Aron.
Rubin, Judith Aron.
    xRubin, Judith A.
        Child Art Therapy: Understanding & Helping
          Children Grow Through Art. Van Nos
          Reinhold.
Rubin, Ken.
    xRubin, Ken.
        Drop Coin Here. Crown.
Rubin, L. *see* Rubin, Leroy.
Rubin, Leonard G.
    xRubin, Leonard G.
        The World of Fashion: An Introduction.
          Har-Row.
Rubin, Leroy.
    xRubin, L.
        Optometry Handbook. Butterworths.
Rubin, Lillian. *see* Rubin, Lillian B.
Rubin, Lillian B.
    xRubin, Lillian.
        Busing & Backlash: White Against White in an
          Urban School District. U of Cal Pr.
        Worlds of Pain: Life in the Working Class
          Family. Basic.
    xRubin, Lillian B.
        Women of a Certain Age: The Midlife Search
          for Self. Har-Row.
        Worlds of Pain: Life in the Working Class
          Family. Basic.
Rubin, Lionel F.
    xRubin, Lionel F.
        Pref. by Atlas of Veterinary Ophthalmoscopy.
          Lea & Febiger.
Rubin, Louis. *see* Rubin, Louis J.
Rubin, Louis D. *see* Rubin, Louis Decimus.
Rubin, Louis Decimus, 1923-
    xRubin, Louis D.
        ed. The American South: Portrait of a Culture.
          La State U Pr.
        ed. Experience of America: A Book of
          Readings. Macmillan.
        The Literary South. Wiley.
        ed. Southern Renascence: The Literature of the
          Modern South. Johns Hopkins.
        ed. Thomas Wolfe: A Collection of Critical
          Essays. P-H.
Rubin, Louis J.
    xRubin, Louis.
        The In-Service Education of Teachers: Trends,
          Processes & Prescriptions. Allyn.
    xRubin, Louis J.
        Critical Issues in Educational Policy: An
          Administrator's Overview. Allyn.
        Facts & Feelings in the Classroom. Walker &
          Co.
Rubin, Lucille S.
    xRubin, Lucille S.
        ed. Movement for the Actor. Drama Bk.
Rubin, Melvin L.
    xRubin, Melvin L.
        Fundamentals of Visual Science. C C Thomas.
        Optics for Clinicians. Triad Pub FL.
        Studies in Physiological Optics. C C Thomas.
Rubin, Mitchell I.
    xRubin, Mitchell I.
        Pediatric Nephrology. Williams & Wilkins.
Rubin, Morton, 1923-
    xRubin, Morton.

Canoeing & Kayaking. McGraw.
Ruck, Wolfgang E. *see* Ruck, Wolf.
Ruck-Pauquet, Gina.
  xRuck-Pauquet, Gina.
    Mumble Bear. Putnam.
Rucker, Bryce W.
  xRucker, Bryce W.
    First Freedom. S Ill U Pr.
Rucker, Rudolf V. *see* Rucker, Rudolf V. B.
Rucker, Rudolf V. B., 1946-
  xRucker, Rudolf V.
    Geometry, Relativity & the Fourth Dimension.
      Dover.
  xRucker, Rudolf v. B.
    Geometry, Relativity & the Fourth Dimension.
      Gannon.
Ruckman, Ivy.
  xRuckman, Ivy.
    Melba the Brain. Westminster.
Rudd, Dale F.
  xRudd, Dale F.
    Process Synthesis. P-H.
    Strategy of Process Engineering. Wiley.
Rudd, Ernest.
  xRudd, Ernest.
    The Highest Education: A Study of Graduate
      Education in Britain. Routledge & Kegan.
Rudd, Margaret, 1925-
  xRudd, Margaret.
    Organiz'd Innocence: The Story of Blake's
      Prophetic Books. Folcroft.
    Organiz'd Innocence: The Story of Blake's
      Prophetic Books. Greenwood.
Rudd, Walter G.
  xRudd, Walter G.
    Assembly Language Programming & the IBM
      360 & 370 Computers. P-H.
The Rudder.
  xRudder Editors.
    Good Sailing: An Illustrated Course on Sailing.
      McKay.
Rudder Editors. *see* The Rudder.
Rudder, Robert S.
  xRudder, Robert S.
    Compiled by The Literature of Spain in English
      Translation: A Bibliography. Ungar.
Rudder, Virgina. *see* Rudder, Virginia L.
Rudder, Virginia L., 1941-
  xRudder, Virgina.
    The Gallows Lord. Blair.
Ruddick, Sara.
  xRuddick, Sara.
    ed. Working It Out: 23 Women Writers,
      Artists, Scientists, & Scholars Talk About
      Their Lives & Work. Pantheon.
Ruddle, Kenneth.
  xRuddle, Kenneth.
    ed. Latin American Political Statistics: A
      Supplement to the Statistical Abstract of
      Latin America. UCLA Lat Am Ctr.
    Palm Sago: A Tropical Starch from Marginal
      Lands. U Pr of Hawaii.
Ruddock, E. C. *see* Ruddock, Ted.
Ruddock, Ted, 1930-
  xRuddock, E. C.
    Arch Bridges & Their Builders, 1735-1835.
      Cambridge U Pr.
Rude, George. *see* Rude, George F E.
Rude, George F E.
  xRude, George.
    Revolutionary Europe 1783-1815. Har-Row.
Rudeen, Kenneth.
  xRudeen, Kenneth.
    Muhammad Ali. T Y Crowell.
Rudelius, William.
  xRudelius, William.
    Introduction to Contemporary Business.
      HarBraceJ.
Rudell, Fredrica.
  xRudell, Fredrica.

Consumer Food Selection & Nutrition
  Information. Praeger.
Rudenko, O. V. *see* Rudenko, Oleg Vladimirovich.
Rudenko, Oleg Vladimirovich.
  xRudenko, O. V.
    ed. Theoretical Foundations of Nonlinear
      Acoustics. Plenum Pub.
Rudenstine, David.
  xRudenstine, David.
    The Rights of Ex-Offenders. Avon.
Rudestam, Kjell. *see* Rudestam, Kjell Erik.
Rudestam, Kjell Erik.
  xRudestam, Kjell.
    Methods of Self-Change: An ABC Primer.
      Brooks-Cole.
Rudhyar, Dane, 1895-
  xRudhyar, Dane.
    The Astrological Houses: The Spectrum of
      Individual Experience. Doubleday.
    Astrological Mandala: The Cycle of
      Transformations & Its 360 Symbolic Phases.
      Random.
    Astrological Triptych. ASI Pubs Inc.
    Astrology & the Modern Psyche: An
      Astrologer Looks at Depth Psychology.
      CRCS Pubns WA.
    Culture, Crisis & Creativity. Theos Pub Hse.
    New Mansions for New Men. Hunter Hse.
    Person-Centered Astrology. ASI Pubs Inc.
    Planetarization of Consciousness. ASI Pubs Inc.
Rudin, Harry R. *see* Rudin, Harry Rudolph.
Rudin, Harry Rudolph, 1898-
  xRudin, Harry R.
    Armistice 1918. Shoe String.
Rudin, M. E. *see* Rudin, Mary Ellen.
Rudin, Mary Ellen.
  xRudin, M. E.
    Lectures on Set Theoretic Topology. Am Math.
Rudin, Walter, 1921-
  xRudin, Walter.
    Function Theory in Polydiscs.
      Benjamin-Cummings.
    Lectures on the Edge-of-the-Wedge Theorem.
      Am Math.
    Principles of Mathematical Analysis. McGraw.
    Real & Complex Analysis. McGraw.
Rudkin, Margaret.
  xRudkin, Margaret.
    Margaret Rudkin Pepperidge Farm Cookbook.
      Atheneum.
Rudley, Stephen.
  xRudley, Stephen.
    The Abominable Snowcreature. Watts.
    Psychic Detectives. Watts.
Rudloe, Jack.
  xRudloe, Jack.
    The Living Dock at Panacea. Knopf.
    Time of the Turtle. Knopf.
    Time of the Turtle. Penguin.
Rudner, Ruth.
  xRudner, Ruth.
    Off & Walking: A Hiker's Guide to American
      Places. HR&W.
Rudnick, Milton L.
  xRudnick, Milton L.
    Christian Ethics for Today: An Evangelical
      Approach. Baker Bk.
Rudnik, Charles.
  xRudnik, Charles.
    Deep Clouds. Horizon.
Rudnitsky, Charles P.
  xRudnitsky, Charles P.
    How to Fight Industrial Larceny & Pilferage.
      Pilot Bks.
Rudoff, Alvin.
  xRudoff, Alvin.
    Work Furlough & the County Jail. C C
      Thomas.
Rudoff, Harvey.
  xRudoff, Harvey.

illus. Practically Complete Guide to Almost
  Real Musical Instruments for Nearly
  Everyone. Lerner Pubns.
Rudofsky, Bernard, 1905-
  xRudofsky, Bernard.
    The Unfashionable Human Body. Doubleday.
Rudolf, Kathleen B. *see* Rudolf, Kathleen Brady.
Rudolf, Kathleen Brady, 1907-
  xRudolf, Kathleen B.
    The Effect of Reading Instruction on
      Achievement in Eighth Grade Social Studies.
      AMS Pr.
Rudolf, Max.
  xRudolf, Max.
    The Grammar of Conducting: A Practical
      Guide to Baton Technique & Orchestral
      Interpretation. Schirmer Bks.
Rudolph, Frederick.
  xRudolph, Frederick.
    Curriculum: A History of the American
      Undergraduate Course of Study Since 1636.
      Jossey-Bass.
Rudolph, Lee.
  xRudolph, Lee.
    The Country Changes. Alicejamesbooks.
    Curses, & Songs & Poems. Alicejamesbooks.
Rudolph, Nancy.
  xRudolph, Nancy.
    Workyards-Playgrounds Planned for
      Adventure. Tchrs Coll.
Rudolph, Robert S.
  xRudolph, Robert S.
    Wood County Place Names. U of Wis Pr.
Rudolph, Ross.
  xRudolph, Ross.
    Skin Grafting. Little.
Rudolph, Susanne H. *see* Rudolph, Susanne Hoeber.
Rudolph, Susanne Hoeber.

  xRudolph, Susanne H.
    Education & Politics in India: Studies in
      Organization, Society & Policy. Harvard U
      Pr.
Rudolph, Wilma, 1940-
  xRudolph, Wilma.
    Wilma Rudolph on Track. Wanderer Bks.
Rudorff, Ray. *see* Rudorff, Raymond.
Rudorff, Raymond.
  xRudorff, Ray.
    The Venice Plot. Berkley Pub.
  xRudorff, Raymond.
    The Dracula Archives. Arbor Hse.
    The Venice Plot. Berkley Pub.
Rudowski, Victor A. *see* Rudowski, Victor Anthony.
Rudowski, Victor Anthony, 1924-
  xRudowski, Victor A.
    Lessing's "Aesthetica in Nuce": An Analysis of
      the May 26, 1769, Letter to Nicolai. U of
      NC Pr.
Rudowski, Witold.
  xRudowski, Witold.
    Burn Therapy & Research. Johns Hopkins.
Rudoy, Dean W. *see* Rudoy, Dean William.
Rudoy, Dean William.
  xRudoy, Dean W.
    Armed & Alone: The American Security
      Dilemma. Braziller.
Rudwick, Bernard. *see* Rudwick, Bernard H.
Rudwick, Bernard H.
  xRudwick, Bernard.
    Solving Management Problems: A Systems
      Approach to Planning & Control. Wiley.
  xRudwick, Bernard H.
    Systems Analysis for Effective Planning:
      Principles & Cases. Wiley.
Rudwick, Elliot. *see* Rudwick, Elliott M.

Rudwick, Elliott M.
 xRudwick, Elliot.
  Race Riot at East St. Louis, July 2, 1917.
   Atheneum.
 xRudwick, Elliott M.
  Race Riot at East St. Louis, July 2, 1917. S Ill
   U Pr.
Rudwin, Maximilian. *see* Rudwin, Maximilian Josef.
Rudwin, Maximilian J. *see* Rudwin, Maximilian Josef.
Rudwin, Maximilian Josef, 1885-
 xRudwin, Maximilian.
  The Devil in Legend & Literature. Open Court.
 xRudwin, Maximilian J.
  Devil in Legend & Literature. AMS Pr.
Rudy, Ann.
 xRudy, Ann.
  Mom Spelled Backwards Is Tired. Bobbs.
Rudy, Jack R.
 xRudy, Jack R.
  Archeological Survey of Western Utah. AMS
   Pr.
Rue, James. *see* Rue, James J.
Rue, James J.
 xRue, James.
  Daddy's Girl, Mama's Boy. NAL.
 xRue, James J.
  A Catechism for Divorced Catholics.
   Franciscan Herald.
  Daddy's Girl, Mama's Boy. Bobbs.
  Limbo World of the Divorced. Franciscan
   Herald.
Rue, John E.
 xRue, John E.
  Mao Tse-tung in Opposition, 1927-1935.
   Stanford U Pr.
Rue, Leonard L. *see* Rue, Leonard Lee.
Rue, Leonard Lee.
 xRue, Leonard L.
  World of the Red Fox. Lippincott.
  World of the White-Tailed Deer. Lippincott.
Rue, Leslie W.
 xRue, Leslie W.
  Management: Theory & Application. Irwin.
Rueckert, William H. *see* Rueckert, William Howe.
Rueckert, William Howe, 1926-
 xRueckert, William H.
  ed. Critical Responses to Kenneth Burke,
   1924-1966. U of Minn Pr.
  Glenway Wescott. Coll & U Pr.
Ruef, John. *see* Ruef, John Samuel.
Ruef, John Samuel.
 xRuef, John.
  Paul's First Letter to Corinth. Westminster.
Rueff, Jacques.
 xRueff, Jacques.
  The Gods & the Kings: A Glance at Creative
   Power. Macmillan.
Ruege, Klaus.
 xRuege, Klaus.
  Contemporary Soccer. Contemp Bks.
Ruehlmann, William, 1946-
 xRuehlmann, William.
  Stalking the Feature Story. Writers Digest.
Ruelens, Charles L. *see* Ruelens, Charles Louis.
Ruelens, Charles Louis, 1820-1890
 xRuelens, Charles L.
  Annales Plantiniennes Depuis la Fondation de
   l'Imprimerie Plantinienne a Anvers Jusqu'a
   la Mort De Chr. Plantin. B Franklin.
Ruelle, David.
 xRuelle, David.
  Thermodynamic Formalism: The Mathematical
   Structures of Classical Equilibrium Statistical
   Mechanics. A-W.
Ruesch, Jurgen.
 xRuesch, Jurgen.

  Nonverbal Communication: Notes on the
   Visual Perception of Human Relations. U of
   Cal Pr.
  Therapeutic Communication. Norton.
Rueschhoff, Phil H.
 xRueschhoff, Phil H.
  Teaching Art in the Elementary School:
   Enhancing Visual Perception. Wiley.
Ruether, Rosemary. *see* Ruether, Rosemary Radford.
Ruether, Rosemary R. *see* Ruether, Rosemary Radford.
Ruether, Rosemary Radford.
 xRuether, Rosemary.
  Faith & Fratricide: The Theological Roots of
   Anti-Semitism. Seabury.
 xRuether, Rosemary R.
  The Radical Kingdom: The Western
   Experience of Messianic Hope. Paulist Pr.
Rufer, Josef, 1893-
 xRufer, Joseph.
  Composition with Twelve Notes Related Only
   to One Another. Greenwood.
Rufer, Joseph. *see* Rufer, Josef.
Ruff, Howard J.
 xRuff, Howard J.
  How to Prosper During the Coming Bad Years.
   Times Bks.
  How to Prosper During the Coming Bad Years.
   Warner Bks.
Ruff, Peter.
 xRuff, Peter.
  Olivia Newton-John. Music Sales.
Ruffhead, Owen, 1723-1769
 xRuffhead, Owen.
  Life of Alexander Pope. Adler.
Ruffin, Thomas, 1787-1870
 xRuffin, Thomas.
  Papers of Thomas Ruffin. AMS Pr.
Ruffner, Frederick G.
 xRuffner, Frederick G.
  ed. Code Names Dictionary: A Guide to Code
   Names, Slang, Nicknames, Journalese, &
   Similar Terms. Gale.
Ruffner, James. *see* Ruffner, James A.
Ruffner, James A.
 xRuffner, James.
  ed. The Weather Almanac. Avon.
Ruge, Daniel.
 xRuge, Daniel.
  ed. Spinal Disorders: Diagnosis & Treatment.
   Lea & Febiger.
Ruge, Friederich. *see* Ruge, Friedrich.
Ruge, Friedrich.
 xRuge, Friederich.
  Soviets As Naval Opponents. Naval Inst Pr.
Rugg, Dean S.
 xRugg, Dean S.
  Spatial Foundations of Urbanism. Wm C
   Brown.
Rugg, Harold O. *see* Rugg, Harold Ordway.
Rugg, Harold Ordway, 1886-1960
 xRugg, Harold O.
  Teacher of Teachers: Frontiers of Theory &
   Practice in Teacher Education. Greenwood.
Ruggiero, G.
 xRuggiero, G.
  Radiological Exploration of the Ventricles &
   Subarachnoid Space. Springer-Verlag.
Ruggiero, Guido, 1944-
 xRuggiero, Guido.
  Violence in Early Renaissance Venice. Rutgers
   U Pr.
Ruggiers, Paul G.
 xRuggiers, Paul G.
  Florence in the Age of Dante. U of Okla Pr.
Ruggles, Eugene.
 xRuggles, Eugene.
  The Lifeguard in the Snow. U of Pittsburgh Pr.
Rugh, Roberts.
 xRugh, Roberts.

  From Conception to Birth: The Drama of
   Life's Beginnings. Har-Row.
Rugh, William A.
 xRugh, William A.
  The Arab Press: News Media & Political
   Process in the Arab World. Syracuse U Pr.
Rugman, Alan M.
 xRugman, Alan M.
  Multinationals in Canada: Theory,
   Performance, Economic Impact. Kluwer
   Boston.
Rugoff, Milton A. *see* Rugoff, Milton Allan.
Rugoff, Milton Allan, 1913-
 xRugoff, Milton A.
  Donne's Imagery: A Study in Creative Sources.
   Russell.
Ruhe, Robert V., 1918-
 xRuhe, Robert V.
  Quaternary Landscapes in Iowa. Iowa St U Pr.
Ruhen, Olaf.
 xRuhen, Olaf.
  Corcoran's the Name. FS&G.
Ruhnau, Helena E. *see* Ruhnau, Helena Elizabeth.
Ruhnau, Helena Elizabeth.
 xRuhnau, Helena E.
  Journeys into the Fifth Dimension. Colleasius
   Pr.
Ruigh, Robert E., 1925-
 xRuigh, Robert E.
  Parliament of 1624: Politics & Foreign Policy.
   Harvard U Pr.
Ruitenbeek, Hendrick M. *see* Ruitenbeek, Hendrik
 Marinus.
Ruitenbeek, Hendrik. *see* Ruitenbeek, Hendrik M.
Ruitenbeek, Hendrik M.
 xRuitenbeek, Hendrik.
  Psychotherapy: What It's All About. Avon.
Ruitenbeek, Hendrik M *see* Ruitenbeek, Hendrik
 Marinus.
Ruitenbeek, Hendrik Marinus, 1928-
 xRuitenbeek, Hendrick M.
  First Freudians. Aronson.
 xRuitenbeek, Hendrik.
  ed. Freud As We Knew Him. Wayne St U Pr.
 xRuitenbeek, Hendrik M.
  Freud & America. Macmillan.
 xRuitenbeek, Henrik M.
  Freud As We Knew Him. Wayne St U Pr.
Ruitenbeek, Henrik M. *see* Ruitenbeek, Hendrik Marinus.
Ruiz, Juan.
 xRuiz, Juan.
  Libro de Buen Amor. Princeton U Pr.
Ruiz, Ramon E. *see* Ruiz, Ramon Eduardo.
Ruiz, Ramon Eduardo.
 xRuiz, Ramon E.
  Cuba: The Making of a Revolution. Norton.
Rukert, Norman G., 1915-
 xRukert, Norman G.
  The Fells Point Story. Bodine.
  Historic Canton: Baltimore's Industrial
   Heartland & Its People. Bodine.
Rukeyser, Louis.
 xRukeyser, Louis.
  How to Make Money in Wall Street.
   Doubleday.
  How to Make Money in Wall Street.
   Doubleday.
Rukeyser, Muriel, 1913-
 xRukeyser, Muriel.
  The Collected Poems of Muriel Rukeyser.
   McGraw.
  Life of Poetry. Kraus Repr.
  The Life of Poetry. Morrow.
  Theory of Flight. AMS Pr.
Ruland, Richard, 1932-
 xRuland, Richard.
  America in Modern European Literature: From
   Image to Metaphor. NYU Pr.
Rule, Ann.
 xRule, Ann.

Beautiful Seattle. Beautiful Am.
Rule, James B., 1943-
    xRule, James B.
        Private Lives & Public Surveillance: Social
            Control in the Computer Age. Schocken.
Rule, Jane.
    xRule, Jane.
        The Desert of the Heart. Arno.
Ruley, M. J. *see* Ruley, Morris J.
Ruley, Morris J.
    xRuley, M. J.
        Projects in General Metalwork. McKnight.
Rulfo, Juan.
    xRulfo, Juan.
        Burning Plain & Other Stories. U of Tex Pr.
Rumaker, Michael, 1932-
    xRumaker, Michael.
        A Day & a Night at the Baths. Grey Fox.
Rumbelow, Donald.
    xRumbelow, Donald.
        The Complete Jack the Ripper. NAL.
Rumbold, Algernon, Sir.
    xRumbold, Algernon.
        Watershed in India 1914-1922. Humanities.
Rummel, R. J. *see* Rummel, Rudolph J.
Rummel, Rudolph J.
    xRummel, R. J.
        Field Theory Evolving. Sage.
        National Attributes & Behavior. Sage.
        Peace Endangered: The Reality of Detente.
            Sage.
    xRummel, Rudolph J.
        Applied Factor Analysis. Northwestern U Pr.
        Dimensions of Nations. Sage.
Rumney, Jay.
    xRumney, Jay.
        Probation & Social Adjustment. Greenwood.
Rumpf, Betty.
    xRumpf, Betty.
        Papier Mache. Lerner Pubns.
Rumpf, Howard A.
    xRumpf, Howard A.
        Corporate Liquidations for the Lawyer &
            Accountant. P-H.
Rumsey, Marian.
    xRumsey, Marian.
        Carolina Hurricane. Morrow.
        Carolina Hurricane. Schol Bk Serv.
        Danger on Shadow Mountain. Morrow.
        Devil's Doorstep. Morrow.
        Lost in the Desert. Morrow.
Runcie, John F.
    xRuncie, John F.
        Experiencing Social Research. Dorsey.
Runciman, S. *see* Runciman, Steven.
Runciman, Steven, 1903-
    xRunciman, S.
        The Byzantine Theocracy. Cambridge U Pr.
    xRunciman, Steven.
        Byzantine Civilization. St Martin.
        History of the Crusades. Cambridge U Pr.
        Last Byzantine Renaissance. Cambridge U Pr.
Runciman, Walter G. *see* Runciman, Walter Garrison.
Runciman, Walter Garrison, Hon, 1934-
    xRunciman, Walter G.
        A Critique of Max Weber's Philosophy of
            Social Science. Cambridge U Pr.
Runcorn, S K.
    xRuncorn, S. K.
        ed. Continental Drift. Acad Pr.
Rund, Hanno.
    xRund, Hanno.
        The Hamilton-Jacobi Theory in the Calculus of
            Variations: Its Role in Mathematics Theory &
            Application. Krieger.
Rundell, Walter, 1928-
    xRundell, Walter.

Early Texas Oil: A Photographic History,
    1866-1936. Tex A&M Univ Pr.
Military Money: A Fiscal History of the U.S.
    Army Overseas in World War II. Tex A&M
    Univ Pr.
Rundle, Anne.
    xRundle, Anne.
        Grey Ghyll. St Martin.
Rundle, Bede.
    xRundle, Bede.
        Perception, Sensation & Verification. Oxford U
            Pr.
Runeberg, J. L. *see* Runeberg, Johan Ludvig.
Runeberg, Johan Ludvig.
    xRuneberg, J. L.
        Tales of Ensign Stal. Am Scandinavian.
Runes, Dagobert D. *see* Runes, Dagobert David.
Runes, Dagobert David, 1902-
    xRunes, Dagobert D.
        ed. Concise Dictionary of Judaism. Greenwood.
        Dictionary of Philosophy. Littlefield.
        ed. Dictionary of Philosophy. Philos Lib.
        Letters to My God. Philos Lib.
        Letters to My Teacher. Philos Lib.
        ed. Lost Legends of Israel. Philos Lib.
        ed. Twentieth Century Philosophy: Living
            Schools of Thought. Greenwood.
Runge, Edith A. *see* Runge, Edith Amelia.
Runge, Edith Amelia, 1916-
    xRunge, Edith A.
        Primitivism & Related Ideas in Sturm und
            Drang Literature. Russell.
Runk, Wesley T.
    xRunk, Wesley T.
        Object Lessons for Christian Growth. Baker
            Bk.
Runkel, Philip. *see* Runkel, Philip Julian.
Runkel, Philip Julian.
    xRunkel, Philip.
        ed. The Changing College Classroom.
            Jossey-Bass.
Runkel, Phillip M.
    xRunkel, Phillip M.
        Alfred Lunt & Lynn Fontanne: A Bibliography.
            Carroll Coll.
Runkle, Gerald.
    xRunkle, Gerald.
        A History of Western Political Theory. Wiley.
Runner's World.
    xRunner's World.
        ed. The Runner's Diet: New & Revised.
            Anderson World.
    xRunner's World Editors.
        Age of the Runner. Anderson World.
        Athlete's Feet. Anderson World.
        Beginning Running. Anderson World.
        The Complete Runner. Anderson World.
        ed. The Complete Woman Runner. Anderson
            World.
        The Female Runner. Anderson World.
        Guide to Sprinting. Anderson World.
        ed. New Exercises for Runners. Anderson
            World.
        ed. New Guide to Distance Running. Anderson
            World.
        New Views of Speed Training. Anderson
            World.
        Practical Running Psychology. Anderson
            World.
        Racing Techniques. Anderson World.
        Runner's Training Guide. Anderson World.
        Runner's World Training Diary. Anderson
            World.
        Running After Forty. Anderson World.
        Running with the Elements. Anderson World.
        Young Runner. Anderson World.
    xRunner's World Magazine Editors.
        Running After Forty. Anderson World.
Runner's World Editors. *see* Runner's World.
Runner's World Magazine Editors. *see* Runner's World.

Running Press.
    xRunning Press.
        ed. The Scrabble Trade Mark Crossword
            Games Scorebook. Running Pr.
Runquist, Olaf A. *see* Runquist, Olaf Allan.
Runquist, Olaf Allan.
    xRunquist, Olaf A.
        Chemical Principles: A Introductory
            Programmed Text. Burgess.
Runte, Alfred, 1947-
    xRunte, Alfred.
        National Parks: The American Experience. U
            of Nebr Pr.
Runyan, John W., 1924-
    xRunyan, John W.
        Primary Care Guide. Har-Row.
Runyan, Paul.
    xRunyan, Paul.
        The Short Way to Lower Scoring. Golf Digest
            Bks.
Runyon, John H.
    xRunyon, John H.
        ed. Source Book of American Presidential
            Campaign & Election Statistics, 1948-1968.
            Ungar.
Runyon, Poke.
    xRunyon, Poke.
        Night Jump--Cuba. BJ Pub Group.
Runyon, R. *see* Runyon, Richard P.
Runyon, Richard P.
    xRunyon, R.
        Fundamentals of Behavioral Statistics. A-W.
    xRunyon, Richard P.
        Descriptive Statistics: A Contemporary
            Approach. A-W.
        Fundamentals of Behavioral Statistics. A-W.
        Inferential Statistics: A Contemporary
            Approach. A-W.
        Nonparametric Statistics: A Contemporary
            Approach. A-W.
Ruocchio, Albert C.
    xRuocchio, Albert C.
        Track Layout & Accessory Manual for Lionel
            Trains. MDK Inc.
Ruoff, James E.
    xRuoff, James E.
        Crowell's Handbook of Elizabethan & Stuart
            Literature. T Y Crowell.
Rupen, Robert. *see* Rupen, Robert Arthur.
Rupen, Robert Arthur, 1922-
    xRupen, Robert.
        How Mongolia Is Really Ruled: A Political
            History of the Mongolian People's Republic
            1900-1978. Hoover Inst Pr.
Ruperti, Alexander, 1913-
    xRuperti, Alexander.
        Cycles of Becoming: The Planetary Pattern of
            Growth. CRCS Pubns WA.
Rupley, William E.
    xRupley, William H.
        Reading Diagnosis & Remediation: A Primer
            for Classroom & Clinic. Rand.
Rupley, William H. *see* Rupley, William E.
Rupp, E. G. *see* Rupp, Ernest Gordon.
Rupp, Ernest Gordon.
    xRupp, E. G.
        ed. Martin Luther. St Martin.
    xRupp, Gordon.
        Thomas More: The King's Good Servant.
            Collins Pubs.
Rupp, George.
    xRupp, George.
        Beyond Existentialism & Zen: Religion in a
            Pluralistic World. Oxford U Pr.
        Culture-Protestantism: German Liberal
            Theology at the Turn of the Twentieth
            Century. Scholars Pr Ca.
Rupp, Gordon. *see* Rupp, Ernest Gordon.
Rupp, Israel D. *see* Rupp, Israel Daniel.

Rupp, Israel Daniel, 1803-1878
xRupp, Israel D.
History of Northampton, Lehigh, Monroe, Carbon, & Schuylkill Counties. Arno.

Rupp, Richard H.
xRupp, Richard H.
Celebration in Postwar American Fiction. U of Miami Pr.
ed. Critics on Whitman. U of Miami Pr.

Ruppe, Harry O.
xRuppe, Harry O.
Introduction to Astronautics. Acad Pr.

Ruppel, Gregg, 1948-
xRuppel, Gregg.
Manual of Pulmonary Function Testing. Mosby.

Ruppert, Donna, 1943-
xRuppert, Donna.
illus. The Dragon's Path. Dawne-Leigh.

Ruppli, Michel.
xRuppli, Michel.
Compiled by Atlantic Records: A Discography. Greenwood.
Compiled by The Prestige Label: A Discography. Greenwood.
The Savoy Label: A Discography. Greenwood.

Rusalem, Herbert.
xRusalem, Herbert.
ed. Contemporary Vocational Rehabilitation. NYU Pr.
Coping with the Unseen Environment: An Introduction to the Vocational Rehabilitation of Blind Persons. Tchrs Coll.
Guiding the Physically Handicapped College Student. Tchrs Coll.

Rusbuldt, Richard E.
xRusbuldt, Richard E.
Key Steps in Local Church Planning. Judson.

Rusch, William G.
xRusch, William G.
ed. The Trinitarian Controversy. Fortress.

Rusche, Georg.
xRusche, Georg.
Punishment & Social Structure. Russell.

Rusco, Elmer R.
xRusco, Elmer R.
Good Time Coming?: Black Nevadans in the Nineteenth Century. Greenwood.

Ruse, Michael.
xRuse, Michael.
The Darwinian Revolution: Science Red in Tooth & Claw. U of Chicago Pr.

Rush, Anne K. *see* Rush, Anne Kent.

Rush, Anne Kent, 1945-
xRush, Anne K.
The Basic Back Book. Moon Bks.
The Basic Back Book. Summit Bks.
Getting Clear Body Work for Women. Bookworks.
Moon, Moon. Moon Bks.
Moon, Moon. Random.

Rush, Beverly.
xRush, Beverly.
Stitch with Style. Madrona Pubs.

Rush, Cathy.
xRush, Cathy.
Women's Basketball. Dutton.

Rush, George E. *see* Rush, George Eugene.

Rush, George Eugene 1932-
xRush, George E.
Dictionary of Criminal Justice. Holbrook.

Rush, Harold M. *see* Rush, Harold M. F.

Rush, Harold M. F.
xRush, Harold M.
Organization Development: A Reconnaissance. Conference Bd.

Rush, James, 1786-1869
xRush, James.

The Collected Works of James Rush. M&S Pr.

Rush, Myron.
xRush, Myron.
How Communist States Change Their Rulers. Cornell U Pr.
Political Succession in the U.S.S.R.. Columbia U Pr.

Rush, Sarah.
xRush, Sarah.
Hucket-A-Bucket Again. Lerner Pubns.

Rushby, Nicholas J. *see* Rushby, Nicholas John.

Rushby, Nicholas John.
xRushby, Nicholas J.
Computers in the Teaching Process. Halsted Pr.

Rushdoony, R. J. *see* Rushdoony, Rousas John.
Rushdoony, Rousas. *see* Rushdoony, Rousas John.
Rushdoony, Rousas J. *see* Rushdoony, Rousas John.

Rushdoony, Rousas John.
xRushdoony, R. J.
Politics of Guilt & Pity. Presby & Reformed.
xRushdoony, Rousas.
Freud. Presby & Reformed.
xRushdoony, Rousas J.
Van Til. Presby & Reformed.

Rushforth, Peter, 1945-
xRushforth, Peter.
Kindergarten. Knopf.

Rushing, Jane (Gilmore).
xRushing, Jane G.
Against the Moon. Avon.
Tamzen. Popular Lib.
Walnut Grove. Avon.

Rushing, Jane G. *see* Rushing, Jane Gilmore.

Rushing, Jane Gilmore.
xRushing, Jane G.
The Raincrow. Avon.
The Raincrow. G K Hall.

Rushing, T. Benny.
xRushing, T. Benny.
Topological Embeddings. Acad Pr.

Rushing, William A.
xRushing, William A.
Class, Culture, and Alienation: A Study of Farmers & Farm Workers. Heath.
ed. Deviant Behavior & Social Process. Rand.

Rushmer, Robert F. *see* Rushmer, Robert Frazer.

Rushmer, Robert Frazer, 1914-
xRushmer, Robert F.
Cardiovascular Dynamics. Saunders.
Medical Engineering: Projections for Health Care Delivery. Acad Pr.

Rushmore, Helen.
xRushmore, Helen.
Cowboy Joe of the Circle S. HarBraceJ.
Old Billy Solves a Mystery. Garrard.

Rushmore, Robert.
xRushmore, Robert.
If My Love Leaves Me. PB.
Life of George Gershwin. Macmillan.

Rushmore, Stephen.
xRushmore, Stephen.
The Valuation of Hotels & Motels. Am Inst Real Estate Appraisers.

Rusho, W. L., 1928-
xRusho, W. L.
Powell's Canyon Voyage. Filter.

Rushton, William F. *see* Rushton, William Faulkner.

Rushton, William Faulkner.
xRushton, William F.
The Cajuns: From Acadia to Louisiana. FS&G.

Rusinoff, S. E. *see* Rusinoff, Samuel Eugene.

Rusinoff, Samuel Eugene, 1894-
xRusinoff, S. E.
Mathematics for Industry. Am Technical.

Rusinov, V. S. *see* Rusinov, Vladimir Sergeevich.

Rusinov, Vladimir Sergeevich.
xRusinov, V. S.

ed. The Dominant Focus: Electrophysiological Investigations. Plenum Pub.

Rusk, C. E. *see* Rusk, Claude Ewing.

Rusk, Claude Ewing, 1871-
xRusk, C. E.
Tales of a Western Mountaineer. Mountaineers.

Rusk, Ralph L. *see* Rusk, Ralph Leslie.

Rusk, Ralph Leslie, 1888-1962
xRusk, Ralph L.
The Literature of the Middle Western Frontier. Greenwood.

Rusk, Robert R. *see* Rusk, Robert Robertson.

Rusk, Robert Robertson, 1879-
xRusk, Robert R.
Doctrines of the Great Educators. St Martin.

Rusk, Rogers D., 1892-
xRusk, Rogers D.
Atoms, Men & Stars: A Survey of the Latest Developments of Physical Science & Their Relation to Life. Arno.

Ruskay, Sophie.
xRuskay, Sophie.
Horsecars & Cobblestones. A S Barnes.

Ruskin, Ariane.
xRuskin, Ariane.
Art of the High Renaissance. McGraw.
History in Art. Watts.
Nineteenth Century Art. McGraw.

Ruskin, John, 1819-1900
xRuskin, John.
Fors Clavigera, Letters to the Workmen & Labourers of Great Britain. Greenwood.
The Gulf of Years: Letters from John Ruskin to Kathleen Olander. Greenwood.
Letters of John Ruskin to Lord & Lady Mount-Temple. Ohio St U Pr.
Munera Pulveris: Six Essays on the Elements of Political Economy. Greenwood.
The Nature of Gothic: A Chapter from the Stones of Venice. Garland Pub.

Ruskowski, Leo F. *see* Ruskowski, Leo Francis.

Ruskowski, Leo Francis, 1907-
xRuskowski, Leo F.
French Emigre Priests in the United States (1791-1815). AMS Pr.

Russ, Charles V. *see* Russ, Charles V. J.

Russ, Charles V. J.
xRuss, Charles V.
Historical German Phonology & Morphology. Oxford U Pr.

Russ, Joanna.
xRuss, Joanna.
And Chaos Died. Ace Bks.
And Chaos Died. Berkley Pub.
And Chaos Died. Gregg.
The Female Man. Gregg.
Kittatinny: A Tale of Magic. Daughters.
Picnic on Paradise. Berkley Pub.
The Two of Them. Berkley Pub.

Russ, Lavinia.
xRuss, Lavinia.
Alec's Sand Castle. Har-Row.
The April Age. Atheneum.

Russek, H. *see* Russek, Henry I.

Russek, Henry I.
xRussek, H.
Cardiovascular Therapy: The Art & the Science. Krieger.

Russel, Robert R. *see* Russel, Robert Royal.

Russel, Robert Royal, 1890-
xRussel, Robert R.
Critical Studies in Antebellum Sectionalism: Essays in American Political & Economic History. Greenwood.

Russel, Valerie.
xRussel, Valerie.
Judging Horses & Ponies. Transatlantic.

Russell, A. G. *see* Russell, Alan Gladney.
Russell, A. J. *see* Russell, Andrew Joseph.
Russell, A. P. *see* Russell, Addison Peale.

Russell, Addison P. *see* Russell, Addison Peale.
Russell, Addison Peale, 1826-1912
  xRussell, A. P.
    Library Notes. R West.
  xRussell, Addison P.
    Library Notes. Arno.
Russell, Alan Gladney.
  xRussell, A. G.
    Colour, Race & Empire. Kennikat.
Russell, Andrew Joseph.
  xRussell, A. J.
    The Devalino Caper. Ballantine.
Russell, Andy, 1915-
  xRussell, Andy.
    Andy Russell's Adventures with Wild Animals.
     Knopf.
    Grizzly Country. Knopf.
    Horns in the High Country. Knopf.
Russell, Arthur J. *see* Russell, Arthur James.
Russell, Arthur James.
  xRussell, Arthur J.
    Their Religion. Arno.

**Russell, Bertrand Arthur William Russell, 3d Earl,
1872-1970**

  xRussell, B.
    If I Could Preach Just Once. Arno.
  xRussell, Bertrand.
    Atheism: Collected Essays, 1943-1949. Arno.
    Authority & the Individual. Allen Unwin.
    Authority & the Individual. AMS Pr.
    Autobiography of Bertrand Russell. Allen
     Unwin.
    Autobiography of Bertrand Russell: 1872-1914.
     Allen Unwin.
    Autobiography of Bertrand Russell: 1914-1944.
     Allen Unwin.
    Common Sense & Nuclear Warfare. AMS Pr.
    Common Sense & Nuclear Warfare. S&S.
    German Social Democracy. S&S.

    Human Society in Ethics & Politics. Allen
     Unwin.

    The Impact of Science on Society. Allen
     Unwin.
    Impact of Science on Society. AMS Pr.
    An Inquiry into Meaning & Truth. Allen
     Unwin.

    Inquiry into Meaning & Truth. Humanities.
    Marriage & Morals. Liveright.
    Our Knowledge of the External World.
     Humanities.

    An Outline of Philosophy. Allen Unwin.
    Outline of Philosophy. NAL.
    The Practice & Theory of Bolshevism. Allen
     Unwin.
    Principles of Mathematics. Norton.

    Religion & Science. Oxford U Pr.

  xRussell, Betrand.
    Unarmed Victory. Allen Unwin.

Russell, Bill. *see* Russell, William Felton.
Russell, C. A. *see* Russell, Colin Archibald.
Russell, C. R. *see* Russell, Charles Roberts.
Russell, C. V.
  xRussell, C. V.
    Post O-Level Studies in Modern Languages.
     Pergamon.
Russell, Carl P. *see* Russell, Carl Parcher.
Russell, Carl Parcher, 1894-1967
  xRussell, Carl P.
    Firearms, Traps & Tools of the Mountain Men.
     U of NM Pr.
Russell, Charles, 1893-
  xRussell, Charles.

    The Improvement of the City Elementary
     School Teacher in Service. AMS Pr.
Russell, Charles E. *see* Russell, Charles Edward.
Russell, Charles Edward, 1860-1941
  xRussell, Charles E.
    American Orchestra & Theodore Thomas.
     Greenwood.
    The Greatest Trust in the World. Arno.
Russell, Charles Roberts, 1914-
  xRussell, C. R.
    Reactor Safeguards. Pergamon.
Russell, Clifford S.
  xRussell, Clifford S.
    Steel Production: Processes, Products, &
     Residuals. Johns Hopkins.
Russell, Colin Archibald.
  xRussell, C. A.
    History of Valency. Humanities.
Russell, D. H. *see* Russell, Diane H.
Russell, David H. *see* Russell, David Harris.
Russell, David Harris, 1906-1965
  xRussell, David H.
    Characteristics of Good & Poor Spellers: A
     Diagnostic Study. AMS Pr.
Russell, David L. *see* Russell, David Lawson.
Russell, David Lawson, 1921-
  xRussell, David L.
    Optimization Theory. Benjamin-Cummings.
Russell, Diane H.
  xRussell, D. H.
    Polyamines As Biochemical Markers of Normal
     & Malignant Growth. Raven.
Russell, Don, 1946-
  xRussell, Don.
    Bowling Now. A S Barnes.
Russell, Donald B. *see* Russell, Donald Bert.
Russell, Donald Bert, 1899-
  xRussell, Donald B.
    Lives & Legends of Buffalo Bill. U of Okla Pr.
Russell, Donald E.
  xRussell, Donald E.
    Chiroptera & Dermoptera of the French Early
     Eocene. U of Cal Pr.
Russell, Doug.
  xRussell, Doug.
    Contemporary Platform Tennis. Contemp Bks.
Russell, Douglas A.
  xRussell, Douglas A.
    Intro. by & ed. An Anthology of Austrian
     Drama. Fairleigh Dickinson.
    Theatrical Style: A Visual Approach to the
     Theatre. Mayfield Pub.
Russell, E. W. *see* Russell, Sir Edward John.
Russell, Edward J. *see* Russell, Edward John.
Russell, Edward John, Sir, 1872-1965
  xRussell, Edward J.
    World Population & World Food Supplies.
     Greenwood.
Russell, Edward R. *see* Russell, Edward Richard Russell.
Russell, Edward Richard Russell.
  xRussell, Edward R.
    Ibsen on His Merits. Haskell.
    Ibsen on His Merits. Kennikat.
Russell, Elbert W.
  xRussell, Elbert W.
    Assessment of Brain Damage: A
     Neuropsychological Key Approach. Wiley.
Russell, Elfleda.
  xRussell, Elfleda.
    Off-Loom Weaving: A Basic Manual. Little.
Russell, Elmer B. *see* Russell, Elmer Beecher.
Russell, Elmer Beecher, 1885-
  xRussell, Elmer B.
    Review of American Colonial Legislation by
     the King in Council. Octagon.
Russell, Eric, fl. 1970-
  xRussell, Eric.
    Astrology & Prediction. Citadel Pr.
Russell, Frances Theresa Peet, 1873-1936
  xRussell, Francis T.

    One Word More on Browning. Folcroft.
Russell, Francis, 1910-
  xRussell, Francis.
    The President-Makers: From Mark Hanna to
     Joseph P. Kennedy. Little.
    World of Durer. Time-Life.
    World of Durer. Silver.
Russell, Francis. *see* Russell, Franklin.
Russell, Francis T. *see* Russell, Frances Theresa Peet.
Russell, Frank A. *see* Russell, Frank Alden.
Russell, Frank Alden, 1908-
  xRussell, Frank A.
    American Pilgrimage. Arno.
Russell, Frank M. *see* Russell, Frank Marion.
Russell, Frank Marion, 1886-
  xRussell, Frank M.
    Theories of International Relations. Arno.
Russell, Franklin.
  xRussell, Francis.
    The Okefenokee Swamp. Silver.
  xRussell, Franklin.
    Honeybees. Knopf.
    The Okefenokee Swamp. Time-Life.
Russell, Frederic. *see* Russell, Frederic Arthur.
Russell, Frederic Arthur, 1886-
  xRussell, Frederic.
    Textbook of Salesmanship. McGraw.
Russell, G. *see* Russell, Gerald.
Russell, G. E.
  xRussell, Gordon E.
    Plant Breeding for Pest & Disease Resistance.
     Butterworths.
Russell, G. Hugh. *see* Russell, George Hugh.
Russell, G. K. *see* Russell, George K.
Russell, Gene.
  xRussell, Gene.
    A Concordance to the Poems of Edward
     Taylor. IHS-PDS.
Russell, George Hugh.
  xRussell, G. Hugh.
    Human Behavior in Business. P-H.
Russell, George K.
  xRussell, G. K.
    Marihuana Today: A Compilation of Medical
     Findings for the Layman. Pergamon.
  xRussell, George K.
    Marihuana Today: A Compilation of Medical
     Findings for the Layman. Myrin Institute.
Russell, George W. *see* Russell, George William Erskine.
Russell, George W. E. *see* Russell, George William
  Erskine.
Russell, George William Erskine, 1853-1919
  xRussell, George W.
    Sydney Smith. Arden Lib.
  xRussell, George W. E.
    Afterthoughts. Arno.
    Half-Lengths. Arno.
    Portraits of the Seventies. Arno.
    Sydney Smith. Arden Lib.
    Sydney Smith. Folcroft.
    Sydney Smith. Gale.
Russell, Gerald.
  xRussell, G.
    Chemical Analysis in Photography. Focal Pr.
Russell, Gordon E. *see* Russell, G. E.
Russell, H. D. *see* Russell, Henry D.
Russell, Harold E.
  xRussell, Harold E.
    Understanding Human Behavior for Effective
     Police Work. Basic.
Russell, Harry K. *see* Russell, Harry Kitsun.
Russell, Harry Kitsun.
  xRussell, Harry K.
    ed. Literature in English. Arno.
Russell, Helen, 1930-
  xRussell, Helen.
    Pediatric Drugs & Nursing Intervention.
     McGraw.
Russell, Helen R. *see* Russell, Helen Ross.

Russell, Helen Ross, 1915-
  xRussell, Helen R.
      Foraging for Dinner: Collecting & Cooking
        Wild Foods. Elsevier-Nelson.
Russell, Henry D.
  xRussell, H. D.
      Notes on Methods for the Narcotization,
        Killing, Fixation, & Preservation of Marine
        Organisms. Marine Bio.
Russell, Howard S.
  xRussell, Howard S.
      A Long, Deep Furrow: Three Centuries of
        Farming in New England. U Pr of New Eng.
Russell, J. S. see Russell, John Samuel.
Russell, Jack, 1928-
  xRussell, Jack.
      Nelson & the Hamiltons. S&S.
Russell, James, 1948-
  xRussell, James.
      The Acquisition of Knowledge. St Martin.
Russell, James D.
  xRussell, James D.
      The Audio-Tutorial System. Educ Tech Pubns.
Russell, James E. see Russell, James Earl.
Russell, James Earl.
  xRussell, James E.
      ed. National Policies for Education, Health &
        Social Services. Russell.
Russell, Jeffrey B. see Russell, Jeffrey Burton.
Russell, Jeffrey Burton.
  xRussell, Jeffrey B.
      The Devil: Perceptions of Evil from Antiquity
        to Primitive Christianity. Cornell U Pr.
      Dissent & Reform in the Early Middle Ages.
        AMS Pr.
Russell, Joan.
  xRussell, Joan.
      Creative Movement & Dance for Children.
        Plays.
      The Woman's Day Book of Soft Toys & Dolls.
        S&S.
      The Woman's Day Book of Soft Toys & Dolls.
        S&S.
Russell, Joe W.
  xRussell, Joe W.
      Economic Disincentives for Energy
        Conservation. Ballinger Pub.
Russell, John.
  xRussell, John.
      The Book of Seamanship. Ziff-Davis Pub.
      Francis Bacon. Oxford U Pr.
      Where the Pavement Ends. Arno.
      World of Matisse. Time-Life.
      World of Matisse. Silver.
Russell, John. see Russell, John David.
Russell, John B. see Russell, John Blair.
Russell, John Blair, 1929-
  xRussell, John B.
      General Chemistry. McGraw.
Russell, John David.
  xRussell, John.
      Style in Modern British Fiction: Studies in
        Joyce, Lawrence, Forster, Lewis & Green.
        Johns Hopkins.
Russell, John H. see Russell, John Henderson.
Russell, John Henderson, 1884-
  xRussell, John H.
      The Free Negro in Virginia, 1619-1865. AMS
        Pr.
      The Free Negro in Virginia, 1619-1865. Dover.
      Free Negro in Virginia, 1619-1865. Negro U
        Pr.
      Free Negro in Virginia 1619-1865. Peter Smith.
Russell, John M., 1903-
  xRussell, John M.
      Giving & Taking: Across the Foundation Desk.
        Tchrs Coll.
Russell, John R.
  xRussell, John R.

Cases in Urban Management. MIT Pr.
Russell, John R. see Russell, John Robert.
Russell, John Robert.
  xRussell, John R.
      TA. PB.
Russell, John Samuel.
  xRussell, J. S.
      Soil Factors in Crop Production in a Semi-Arid
        Environment. U of Queensland Pr.
Russell, Joseph P.
  xRussell, Joseph P.
      Sharing Our Biblical Story: A Guide to Using
        Liturgical Readings As the Core of Church &
        Family Education. Winston Pr.
Russell, Josiah C. see Russell, Josiah Cox.
Russell, Josiah Cox, 1900-
  xRussell, Josiah C.
      Twelfth Century Studies. AMS Pr.
Russell, Leonard.
  xRussell, Leonard.
      Parody Party. Arden Lib.
      ed. Parody Party. Kennikat.
Russell, Letty M.
  xRussell, Letty M.
      ed. The Liberating Word: A Guide to
        Non-Sexist Interpretation of the Bible.
        Westminster.
Russell, Louise. see Russell, Louise B.
Russell, Louise B.
  xRussell, Louise.
      Technology in Hospitals: Medical Advances &
        Their Diffusion. Brookings.
Russell, Marjorie.
  xRussell, Marjorie H.
      Handbook of Christian Meditation. Devin.
Russell, Marjorie H. see Russell, Marjorie.
Russell, Maud.
  xRussell, Maud.
      Detective's Wife. Speller.
Russell, Morris C. see Russell, Morris Craw.
Russell, Morris Craw, 1840-
  xRussell, Morris C.
      Uncle Dudley's Odd Hours; Western Sketches,
        Indian Trail Echoes. Irvington.
Russell, Naomi.
  xRussell, Naomi.
      Light from the Valley. Herald Hse.
Russell, Nelson V. see Russell, Nelson Vance.
Russell, Nelson Vance, 1895-1951
  xRussell, Nelson V.
      The British Regime in Michigan & the Old
        North-West 1760-1796. Porcupine Pr.
Russell, Norman. see Russell, Norman H.
Russell, Norman H.
  xRussell, Norman.
      Introduction to Plant Science: A Humanistic &
        Ecological Approach. West Pub.
Russell, O. Ruth. see Russell, Olive Ruth.
Russell, Oland D.
  xRussell, Oland D.
      House of Mitsui. Greenwood.
Russell, Olive Ruth.
  xRussell, O. Ruth.
      Freedom to Die: Moral & Legal Aspects of
        Euthanasia. Human Sci Pr.
Russell, Pamela R. see Russell, Pamela Redford.
Russell, Pamela Redford.
  xRussell, Pamela R.
      The Woman Who Loved John Wilkes Booth.
        BJ Pub Group.
      The Woman Who Loved John Wilkes Booth.
        Putnam.
Russell, Peter, 1946-
  xRussell, Peter.
      The Brain Book. Dutton.
Russell, Phil R.
  xRussell, Phil R.
      Quack Doctor. Branch-Smith.
Russell, Ray.
  xRussell, Ray.

Case Against Satan. Astor-Honor.
Russell, Richard.
  xRussell, Richard.
      Reunion. Belmont-Tower.
Russell, Richard J.
  xRussell, Richard J.
      Glossary of Terms Used in Fluvial, Deltaic &
        Coastal Morphology & Processes. La State U
        Pr.
Russell, Robert, 1924-
  xRussell, Robert.
      Act of Loving. Vanguard.
Russell, Rosalind.
  xRussell, Rosalind.
      Life Is a Banquet. Ace Bks.
Russell Sage Foundation. see Russell Sage Foundation,
  New York.
Russell Sage Foundation, New York.
  xRussell Sage Foundation.
      San Francisco Relief Survey. Milford Hse.
Russell, Sheldon N.
  xRussell, Sheldon N.
      An Interdisciplinary Approach to Reading &
        Mathematics. Acad Therapy.
Russell, Sir Edward John.
  xRussell, E. W.
      Soil Conditions & Plant Growth. Longman.
Russell, Solveig. see Russell, Solveig Paulson.
Russell, Solveig P. see Russell, Solveig Paulson.
Russell, Solveig Paulson.
  xRussell, Solveig.
      From Footpaths to Freeways: The Story of
        Roads. Enslow Pubs.
  xRussell, Solveig P.
      The Mushmen. Dodd.
  xRussell, Solveig Pavlson.
      Four Legged Helpers. Broadman.
Russell, Solveig Pavlson. see Russell, Solveig Paulson.
Russell, T. Fraser. see Russell, T. W. F.
Russell, T. W. F.
  xRussell, T. Fraser.
      Introduction to Chemical Engineering Analysis.
        Wiley.
Russell, Terry.
  xRussell, Terry.
      On the Loose. Ballantine.
      On the Loose. Sierra.
Russell, Thomas, 1944-
  xRussell, Thomas.
      The Economics of Bank Credit Cards. Praeger.
Russell, Vera.
  xRussell, Vera.
      Friendly Workers Visit Larry. Denison.
Russell, Vivian.
  xRussell, Vivian.
      The History of Unicef. Viking Pr.
Russell, W. Clark. see Russell, William Clark.
Russell, W. Ritchie. see Russell, William Ritchie.
Russell, William Clark, 1844-1911
  xRussell, W. Clark.
      The Frozen Pirate. Arno.
Russell, William Felton.
  xRussell, Bill.
      Second Wind: The Memoirs of an Opinionated
        Man. Random.
Russell, William O. see Russell, William Oldnall.
Russell, William Oldnall, 1785-1833
  xRussell, William O.
      A Treatise on Crimes & Misdemeanors.
        Garland Pub.
Russell, William Ritchie.
  xRussell, W. Ritchie.
      Explaining the Brain. Oxford U Pr.
Russell-Hunter, W. D., 1926-
  xRussell-Hunter, W. D.
      A Life of Invertebrates. Macmillan.
Russell-Wood, A. J. R., 1939-
  xRussell-Wood, A. J. R.

ed. From Colony to Nation: Essays on the Independence of Brazil. Johns Hopkins.

Russett, Bruce M.
xRussett, Bruce M.
Community & Contention: Britain & America in the Twentieth Century. MIT Pr.
No Clear & Present Danger: A Skeptical View of the United States Entry into World War 2. Har-Row.
ed. Peace, War & Numbers. Sage.
Power & Community in World Politics. W H Freeman.
World Handbook of Political & Social Indicators. Greenwood.

Russett, Cynthia E. *see* Russett, Cynthia Eagle.

Russett, Cynthia Eagle.
xRussett, Cynthia E.
Darwin in America: The Intellectual Response, 1865-1912. W H Freeman.

Russo, Monica.
xRusso, Monica.
The Complete Book of Bird Houses & Feeders. Sterling.

Russo, Ronald A.
xRusso, Ronald A.
Plant Galls of the California Region. Boxwood.

Russo, Susan.
xRusso, Susan.
Compiled by The Moon's the North Wind's Cooky: Night Poems. Lothrop.

Russo, William.
xRusso, William.
Composing for the Jazz Orchestra. U of Chicago Pr.

Russon. *see* Russon, Allien R.

Russon, Allien R.
xRusson.
Personality Development for Business. SW Pub.

Rust, B. *see* Rust, Bert W.

Rust, Bert W.
xRust, B.
Mathematical Programming & the Numerical Solution of Linear Equations. Elsevier.

Rust, Brian. *see* Rust, Brian A. L.

Rust, Brian A. L., 1922-
xRust, Brian.
Compiled by Discography of Historical Records on Cylinders & 78s'. Greenwood.

Rust, Edgar.
xRust, Edgar.
No Growth: Impacts on Metropolitan Areas. Lexington Bks.

Rust, H. Lee.
xRust, H. Lee.
Jobsearch: The Complete Manual for Job Seekers. Am Mgmt.

Rustaveli, Shota, fl. 1190
xRustaveli, Shota.
The Lord of the Panther-Skin. State U NY Pr.

Rustow, Dankwart A.
xRustow, Dankwart A.
OPEC: Success & Prospects. NYU Pr.
Politics of Compromise: A Study of Parties & Cabinet Government in Sweden. Greenwood.

Rusz, Joe.
xRusz, Joe.
Porsche Sport 72. Norton.
Porsche Sport 73. Norton.

Rutan, J. *see* Rutan, Jackie.

Rutan, Jackie.
xRutan, J.
The Perfect Fit: Easy Pattern Alterations. P-H.

Rutan, Patricia M. *see* Rutan, Patricia McGeehan.

Rutan, Patricia McGeehan.
xRutan, Patricia M.
Career Education & English. HM.

Ruth, John. *see* Ruth, John L.

Ruth, John L.
xRuth, John.

A Quiet & Peaceable Life. Good Bks PA.

Ruth, Kent.
xRuth, Kent.
Oklahoma Travel Handbook. U of Okla Pr.

Rutherford, Andrew.
xRutherford, Andrew.
Byron: A Critical Study. Stanford U Pr.
The Literature of War: Five Studies in Heroic Virtue. B&N.
Standards Relating to Corrections Administration. Ballinger Pub.

Rutherford, Daniel E. *see* Rutherford, Daniel Edwin.

Rutherford, Daniel Edwin, 1906-
xRutherford, Daniel E.
Introduction to Lattice Theory. Hafner.
Substitutional Analysis. Hafner.

Rutherford, Noel.
xRutherford, Noel.
ed. Friendly Islands: A History of Tonga. Oxford U Pr.

Rutherford, Phillip R.
xRutherford, Phillip R.
Dictionary of Maine Place-Names. Wheelwright.

Rutherford, Robert B.
xRutherford, Robert B.
Teachers & Parents: A Guide to Interaction & Cooperation. Allyn.
ed. Vascular Surgery. Saunders.

Rutherford, William E.
xRutherford, William E.
Modern English. HarBraceJ.

Ruthven, K. K.
xRuthven, K. K.
A Guide to Ezra Pound's "Personae" 1926. U of Cal Pr.

Rutkevich, M. N. *see* Rutkevich, Mikhail Nikolaevich.

Rutkevich, Mikhail Nikolaevich.
xRutkevich, M. N.
ed. The Career Plans of Youth. M E Sharpe.

Rutkowski, Edwin H.
xRutkowski, Edwin H.
Politics of Military Aviation Procurement, 1926-1934: A Study in the Political Assertion of Consensual Values. Ohio St U Pr.

Rutkowski, George B.
xRutkowski, George B.
Fundamentals of Digital Electronics: A Laboratory Text. P-H.
Handbook of Integrated-Circuit Operational Amplifiers. P-H.
Solid State Electronics. Bobbs.

Rutland, Jonathan.
xRutland, Jonathan.
Human Body. Watts.
Plant Kingdom. Watts.
See Inside an Ancient Greek Town. Watts.
See Inside an Oil Rig & Tanker. Watts.

Rutland, Robert A. *see* Rutland, Robert Allen.

Rutland, Robert Allen, 1922-
xRutland, Robert A.
The Democrats from Jefferson to Carter. La State U Pr.

Rutland, William R. *see* Rutland, William Rutland.

Rutland, William Rutland.
xRutland, William R.
Thomas Hardy: A Study of His Writings & Their Background. Russell.

Rutledge, Samuel A. *see* Rutledge, Samuel Albert.

Rutledge, Samuel Albert, 1888-1941
xRutledge, Samuel A.
The Development of Guiding Principles for the Administration of Teachers Colleges & Normal Schools. AMS Pr.

Rutledge, Sarah, 1782-1855
xRutledge, Sarah.
The Carolina Housewife. U of SC Pr.

Rutledge, Thomas F.
xRutledge, Thomas F.

Acetylenes & Allenes: Addition, Cyclization & Polymerization Reactions. Van Nos Reinhold.
Acetylenic Compounds: Preparation & Substitution Reactions. Van Nos Reinhold.

Rutledge, Wiley, 1894-1949
xRutledge, Wiley.
Declaration of Legal Faith. Da Capo.

Rutledge, William A.
xRutledge, William A.
Introduction to Algebra for College Students. P-H.

Rutman, Darrett B. *see* Rutman, Darrett Bruce.

Rutman, Darrett Bruce.
xRutman, Darrett B.
American Puritanism: Faith & Practice. Norton.
ed. The Great Awakening: Event & Exegesis. Krieger.

Rutman, Leonard.
xRutman, Leonard S.
Evaluation Research Methods: A Basic Guide. Sage.

Rutman, Leonard S. *see* Rutman, Leonard.

Rutsala, Vern.
xRutsala, Vern.
The New Life. Trask Hse Bks.
Paragraphs. Columbia U Pr.

Rutstein, David D.
xRutstein, David D.
Coming Revolution in Medicine. MIT Pr.

Rutstrum, Calvin.
xRutstrum, Calvin.
Chips from a Wilderness Log. Stein & Day.
North American Canoe Country. Macmillan.
Once Upon a Wilderness. Macmillan.

Rutt, Richard.
xRutt, Richard.
The Bamboo Grove: An Introduction to Sijo. U of Cal Pr.

Ruttan, Vernon W.
xRuttan, Vernon W.
The Economic Demand for Irrigated Acreage: New Methodology & Some Preliminary Projections 1954-1980. Johns Hopkins.

Rutten, M. G. *see* Rutten, Martin Gerard.

Rutten, Martin Gerard.
xRutten, M. G.
The Geology of Western Europe. Elsevier.

Ruttenberg, Stanley H.
xRuttenberg, Stanley H.
The Federal-State Employment Service: A Critique. Johns Hopkins.

Ruttencutter, Helen D. *see* Ruttencutter, Helen Drees.

Ruttencutter, Helen Drees.
xRuttencutter, Helen D.
Pianist's Progress. T Y Crowell.

Rutter, F. R. *see* Rutter, Frank Roy.
Rutter, Frank R. *see* Rutter, Frank Roy.

Rutter, Frank Roy, 1874-1926
xRutter, F. R.
South American Trade of Baltimore. Johnson Repr.
xRutter, Frank R.
South American Trade of Baltimore. AMS Pr.

Rutter, Michael.
xRutter, Michael.
Changing Youth in a Changing Society: Patterns of Adolescent Development & Disorder. Harvard U Pr.
Fifteen Thousand Hours: Secondary Schools & Their Effects on Children. Harvard U Pr.

Ruttle, Lee, 1909-
xRuttle, Lee.
The Private War of Dr. Yamada. SF Bk Co.

Ruttner, Franz, 1882-1961
xRuttner, Franz.
Fundamentals of Limnology. U of Toronto Pr.

Rutz, Viola.
xRutz, Viola.

Little Tree & His Wish. Concordia.
Ruud, Josephine B. *see* Ruud, Josephine Bartow.
Ruud, Josephine Bartow.
  xRuud, Josephine B.
    Adult Education for Home & Family Life.
    Wiley.
Ruud, Martin B. *see* Ruud, Martin Bronn.
Ruud, Martin Bronn, 1885-1941
  xRuud, Martin B.
    Thomas Chaucer. AMS Pr.
Ruuth, Marianne.
  xRuuth, Marianne.
    Journey into Fear. Belmont-Tower.
Ruutz-Rees, Carolina. *see* Ruutz-Rees, Caroline.
Ruutz-Rees, Caroline, 1865-
  xRuutz-Rees, Carolina.
    Charles De Sainte-Marthe. AMS Pr.
Ruwet, Jean Claude.
  xRuwet, Jean-Claude.
    Introduction to Ethology: The Biology of
    Behavior. Intl Univs Pr.
Ruwet, Jean-Claude. *see* Ruwet, Jean Claude.
Ruwet, Nicolas.
  xRuwet, Nicolas.
    Problems in French Syntax: Transformational -
    Generative Studies. Longman.
Ruxton, George F. *see* Ruxton, George Frederick
  Augustus.
Ruxton, George Frederick Augustus, 1820-1848
  xRuxton, George F.
    Adventures in Mexico & the Rocky Mountains.
    Rio Grande.
    Life in the Far West. U of Okla Pr.
Ruzek, Shcryl B. *see* Ruzek, Sheryl Burt.
Ruzek, Sheryl Burt.
  xRuzek, Sheryl B.
    The Women's Health Movement: Feminist
    Alternatives to Medical Control. Praeger.
Ruzicho, Andrew J.
  xRuzicho, Andrew J.
    Civil Rights Litigation: An Investigation,
    Preparation & Trial Manual with 1979
    Supplement. Anderson Pub Co.
Ruzicka, J. *see* Ruzicka, Jaromir.
Ruzicka, Jaromir.
  xRuzicka, J.
    Substoichiometry in Radiochemical Analysis.
    Pergamon.
Ruzicka, William J.
  xRuzicka, William J.
    The Nightmare of Success: The Fallacy of the
    Super-Success Dream. Peninsula Pubns.
Rweyemamu, J. F.
  xRweyemamu, Justinian.
    Underdevelopment & Industrialization in
    Tanzania: A Study of Perverse Capitalist
    Industrial Development. Oxford U Pr.
Rweyemamu, Justinian. *see* Rweyemamu, J. F.
Ryall, R. W.
  xRyall, R. W.
    Mechanisms of Drug Action on the Nervous
    System. Cambridge U Pr.
Ryalls, Alan.
  xRyalls, Alan.
    Modern Camping. David & Charles.
Ryals, Clyde de L., 1928-
  xRyals, Clyde de L.
    Browning's Later Poetry, 1871-1889. Cornell U
    Pr.
Ryan. *see* Ryan, Frank L.
Ryan, Adrian.
  xRyan, Adrian.
    Still Life Painting Techniques. David &
    Charles.
Ryan, Allan J.
  xRyan, Allan J.
    The Physician & Sportsmedicine Guide to
    Running. McGraw.
Ryan, Bob.
  xRyan, Bob.

Celtics Pride: The Rebuilding of Boston's
    World Championship Basketball Team. Little.
Ryan, Bruce P.
  xRyan, Bruce P.
    Programmed Therapy for Stuttering in Children
    & Adults. C C Thomas.
Ryan, Chales C.
  xRyan, Charles C.
    Starry Messenger: The Best of Galileo. St
    Martin.
Ryan, Charles C. *see* Ryan, Chales C.
Ryan, Charles W. *see* Ryan, Charles William.
Ryan, Charles William, 1932-
  xRyan, Charles W.
    Spelling for Adults. Wiley.
Ryan, Cheli D. *see* Ryan, Cheli Duran.
Ryan, Cheli Duran.
  xRyan, Cheli D.
    Hildilid's Night. Macmillan.
    Hildilid's Night. Macmillan.
    Paz. Macmillan.
Ryan, Cornelius.
  xRyan, Cornelius.
    A Bridge Too Far. Popular Lib.
    A Bridge Too Far. S&S.
    The Last Battle. Popular Lib.
    Last Battle. S&S.
    Longest Day: June 6, 1944. S&S.
    A Private Battle. S&S.
Ryan, Craig, 1953-
  xRyan, Craig A.
    Beautiful New Mexico. Beautiful Am.
Ryan, Craig A. *see* Ryan, Craig.
Ryan, D. *see* Ryan, Daniel L.
Ryan, Daniel L., 1941-
  xRyan, D.
    Computer Aided Graphics & Design. Dekker.
Ryan, Desmond.
  xRyan, Desmond.
    Helix. Norton.
    The Sword of Light, from the Four Masters to
    Douglas Hyde, 1636-1938. Folcroft.
Ryan, Frank.
  xRyan, Frank.
    Discus. Viking Pr.
    Gymnastics for Girls. Penguin.
    Gymnastics for Girls. Viking Pr.
Ryan, Frank L.
  xRyan.
    The Social Studies Sourcebook: Ideas for
    Teaching in the Elementary & Middle
    School. Allyn.
Ryan, George E.
  xRyan, George E.
    Botolph of Boston. Chris Mass.
Ryan, James J. *see* Ryan, James Raymond.
Ryan, James Raymond, 1936-
  xRyan, James J.
    Orthopedic Surgery. Med Exam.
Ryan, Jeremy.
  xRyan, Jeremy.
    Electronic Assembly. Reston.
Ryan, John, 1921-
  xRyan, John.
    Pugwash in the Pacific. S G Phillips.
    Remembering How We Stood: Bohemian
    Dublin at the Mid-Century. Taplinger.
Ryan, John A. *see* Ryan, John Augustine.
Ryan, John Augustine, 1868-1945
  xRyan, John A.
    Declining Liberty, & Other Papers. Arno.
    Questions of the Day. Arno.
  xRyan, John Augustine
    Declining Liberty & Other Papers. Da Capo.
Ryan, John J. *see* Ryan, John Joseph.
Ryan, John Joseph.
  xRyan, John J.

The Nature, Structure, & Function of the
    Church in William of Ockham. Scholars Pr
    Ca.
Ryan, Kate, 1857-
  xRyan, Kate.
    Old Boston Museum Days. Scholarly.
Ryan, Kathleen.
  xRyan, Kathleen.
    Burnside, a Community: A Photographic
    History of Portland's Skid Row. Coast to
    Coast.
Ryan, Kenneth.
  xRyan, Kenneth.
    ed. The Catholic Digest Christmas Book.
    Carillon Bks.
    ed. The Truest Story. Carillon Bks.
Ryan, Kevin.
  xRyan, Kevin.
    ed. Biting the Apple: Accounts of First Year
    Teachers. Longman.
    ed. Don't Smile Until Christmas: Accounts of
    the First Year of Teaching. U of Chicago Pr.
    Kaleidoscope: Readings in Education. HM.
    ed. Teacher Education. U of Chicago Pr.
    Those Who Can, Teach. HM.
Ryan, Marah E. *see* Ryan, Marah Ellis (Martin).
Ryan, Marah Ellis (Martin), 1860?-1934
  xRyan, Marah E.
    Druid Path. Arno.
Ryan, Marleigh G. *see* Ryan, Marleigh Grayer.
Ryan, Marleigh Grayer.
  xRyan, Marleigh G.
    The Development of Realism in the Fiction of
    Tsubouchi Shoyo. U of Wash Pr.
Ryan, Mary P.
  xRyan, Mary P.
    Womanhood in America: From Colonial Times
    to the Present. New Viewpoints.
    Womanhood in America: From Colonial Times
    to the Present. Watts.
Ryan, Michael, 1937-
  xRyan, Michael.
    The Organization of Soviet Medical Care.
    Biblio Dist.
Ryan, Michael P.
  xRyan, Michael R.
    Homogeneous Relativistic Cosmologies.
    Princeton U Pr.
Ryan, Michael R. *see* Ryan, Michael P.
Ryan, Nolan.
  xRyan, Nolan.
    Pitching & Hitting. P-H.
Ryan, Paul B.
  xRyan, Paul B.
    The Panama Canal Controversy: U. S.
    Diplomacy & Defense Interests. Hoover Inst
    Pr.
Ryan, Peter, 1939-
  xRyan, Peter.
    Solar System. Viking Pr.
Ryan, Peter J.
  xRyan, Peter J.
    Options: Theory & Practice. Lexington Bks.
Ryan, Roderick T.
  xRyan, Roderick T.
    A History of Motion Picture Color
    Technology. Focal Pr.
Ryan, Sheila A.
  xRyan, Sheila A.
    Handbook of Practical Pharmacology. Mosby.
  xRyan, Shelia A.
    Handbook of Practical Pharmacology. Mosby.
Ryan, Shelia A. *see* Ryan, Sheila A.
Ryan, T. Antoinette.
  xRyan, T. Antoinette.
    Guidance Services: A Systems Approach to
    Organization & Administration. Interstate.
Ryan, Thomas, 1827-1903
  xRyan, Thomas.

Recollections of an Old Musician. Da Capo.
Ryan, Tom K.
xRyan, Tom K.
Tumbleweeds. Fawcett.
Ryan, W. Carson. *see* Ryan, Will Carson.
Ryan, W. J. *see* Ryan, William James Louden.
Ryan, Will Carson, 1885-
xRyan, W. Carson.
Studies in Early Graduate Education. Arno.
Ryan, William.
xRyan, William.
ed. Distress in the City: Essays on the Design
& Administration of Urban Mental Health
Services. UPBS.
The White House: An Architectural History.
McGraw.
Ryan, William James Louden.
xRyan, W. J.
Price Theory. St Martin.
Ryan, William R. *see* Ryan, William Redmond.
Ryan, William Redmond, 1791-1855
xRyan, William R.
Personal Adventures in Upper & Lower
California, in 1848-9. Arno.
Ryans, David G. *see* Ryans, David Garriott.
Ryans, David Garriott, 1909-
xRyans, David G.
Characteristics of Teachers: Their Description,
Comparison & Appraisal. ACE.
Ryavec, Karl W.
xRyavec, Karl W.
Implementation of Soviet Economic Reforms:
Political, Organizational & Social Processes.
Praeger.
ed. Soviet Society & the Communist Party. U
of Mass Pr.
Ryback, Ralph S.
xRyback, Ralph S.
The Problem Oriented Record in Psychiatry &
Mental Health Care. Grune.
Rybak, B. *see* Rybak, Boris.
Rybak, Boris.
xRybak, B.
Principles of Zoophysiology. Pergamon.
Rybczynski, T. M.
xRybczynski, T. M.
ed. The Economics of the Oil Crisis. Holmes &
Meier.
Rybicki, George B.
xRybicki, George B.
Radiative Processes in Astrophysics. Wiley.
Rybicki, Stephen.
xRybicki, Stephen A.
Abbreviations: A Reverse Guide to Standard &
Generally Accepted Abbreviated Forms.
Pierian.
Rybicki, Stephen A. *see* Rybicki, Stephen.
Rycaut, Paul, Sir, 1628-1700
xRycaut, Paul.
Present State of the Ottoman Empire. Arno.
Rychlak, Joseph F.
xRychlak, Joseph F.
Discovering Free Will & Personal
Responsibility. Oxford U Pr.
The Psychology of Rigorous Humanism. Wiley.
Rychtera, M. *see* Rychtera, Miroslav.
Rychtera, Miroslav.
xRychtera, M.
Deterioration of Electrical Equipment in
Adverse Environments. Davey.
Ryck, Francis.
xRyck, Francis.
Undesirable Company. Stein & Day.
Ryckman, John.
xRyckman, John.
Ginger's Upstairs Pet. Garrard.
Rycroft, Charles.
xRycroft, Charles.

A Critical Dictionary of Psychoanalysis.
Littlefield.
Imagination & Reality. Intl Univs Pr.
The Innocence of Dreams. Pantheon.
Rydberg, Ernie.
xRydberg, Ernie.
Footsy. G K Hall.
Rydberg, Per A. *see* Rydberg, Per Axel.
Rydberg, Per Axel, 1860-1931
xRydberg, Per A.
Flora of the Prairies & Plains of Central North
America. Dover.
Flora of the Prairies & Plains of Central North
America. Hafner.
Ryden, Elihu D. *see* Ryden, Elihu Daniel.
Ryden, Elihu Daniel.
xRyden, Elihu D.
Federal Fertility in the Stream of Commerce.
Mss Info.
Ryden, Hope.
xRyden, Hope.
America's Last Wild Horses. Dutton.
illus. The Little Deer of the Florida Keys.
Putnam.
Mustangs: A Return to the Wild. Penguin.
Ryder, Edward J., 1929-
xRyder, Edward J.
Leafy Salad Vegetables. AVI.
Ryder, F. G. *see* Ryder, Frank Glessner.
Ryder, Frank Glessner.
xRyder, F. G.
Lebendige Literatur: Deutsches Lesebuch Fur
Anfanger. HM.
Ryder, Joanne.
xRyder, Joanne.
Fireflies. Har-Row.
Simon Underground. Har-Row.
Snail in the Woods. Har-Row.
Ryder, John D. *see* Ryder, John Douglas.
Ryder, John Douglas, 1907-
xRyder, John D.
Introduction to Circuit Analysis. P-H.
Ryder, Rowland.
xRyder, Rowland.
Ravenstein: Portrait of a German General.
Hippocrene Bks.
Ryder, Verdene.
xRyder, Verdene.
Contemporary Living. Goodheart.
Rydholm, Sven A., 1923-
xRydholm, Sven A.
Pulping Processes. Wiley.
Rydjord, John.
xRydjord, John.
Foreign Interest in the Independence of New
Spain: An Introduction to the War for
Independence. Russell.
A History of Fairmount College. Regents Pr
KS.
Rye, Bjorn R. *see* Rye, Bjorn Robinson.
Rye, Bjorn Robinson.
xRye, Bjorn R.
The Expatriate. Bobbs.
Rye, Walter, 1843-1929
xRye, Walter.
Chaucer: A Norfolk Man. Folcroft.
Ryerson, A. E. *see* Ryerson, Adolphus Egerton.
Ryerson, Adolphus Egerton, 1803-1882
xRyerson, A. E.
Loyalists of America and Their Times,
1620-1816. Haskell.
Ryerson, Michael.
xRyerson, Mike.
Acoustic Troubleshooting of Audio Systems.
Reston.
Ryerson, Mike. *see* Ryerson, Michael.
Ryf, Robert S. *see* Ryf, Robert Stanley.
Ryf, Robert Stanley, 1918-
xRyf, Robert S.

Joseph Conrad. Columbia U Pr.
Ryglewicz, Hilary.
xRyglewicz, Hilary.
Working Couples: How to Cope with Two Jobs
& One Home. Sovereign Bks.
Ryken, Leland.
xRyken, Leland.
The Literature of the Bible. Zondervan.
Rykwert, Joseph, 1926-
xRykwert, Joseph.
The Idea of a Town: The Anthropology of
Urban Form in Rome, Italy & the Ancient
World. Princeton U Pr.
Ryland, Frederick, 1854-1902
xRyland, Frederick.
Chronological Outlines of English Literature. B
Franklin.
Chronological Outlines of English Literature.
Folcroft.
Chronological Outlines of English Literature.
Gale.
Chronological Outlines of English Literature. R
West.
Rylander, Paul N. *see* Rylander, Paul Nels.
Rylander, Paul Nels, 1920-
xRylander, Paul N.
Catalytic Hydrogenation Over Platinum
Metals. Acad Pr.
Rylands, G. W. *see* Rylands, George Humphrey
Wolfestan.
Rylands, George Humphrey Wolfestan, 1902-
xRylands, G. W.
Words & Poetry. AMS Pr.
Words & Poetry. R West.
Ryle, Gilbert, 1900-
xRyle, Gilbert.
Concept of Mind. B&N.
Dilemmas. Cambridge U Pr.
On Thinking. Rowman.
Rymer, Marilyn P.
xRymer, Marilyn P.
Medicaid Eligibility: Problems & Solutions.
Westview.
Ryrie, Charles. *see* Ryrie, Charles Caldwell.
Ryrie, Charles C. *see* Ryrie, Charles Caldwell.
Ryrie, Charles Caldwell, 1925-
xRyrie, Charles.
Survey of Bible Doctrine. Moody.
xRyrie, Charles C.
Balancing the Christian Life. Moody.
Dispensationalism Today. Moody.
Holy Spirit. Moody.
Revelation. Moody.
Rys, P. *see* Rys, Paul.
Rys, Paul.
xRys, P.
Fundamentals of the Chemistry & Application
of Dyes. Wiley.
Ryser, Darcy.
xRyser, Darcy.
ed. CAPStan: Poems by CAPS Poetry Fellows
1970-1975. Pub Ctr Cult Res.
Ryser, Herbert J. *see* Ryser, Herbert John.
Ryser, Herbert John.
xRyser, Herbert J.
Combinatorial Mathematics. Math Assn.
Ryssel, Fritz H. *see* Ryssel, Fritz Heinrich.
Ryssel, Fritz Heinrich, 1914-
xRyssel, Fritz H.
Thomas Wolfe. Ungar.
Rysten, Felix S. *see* Rysten, Felix S. A.
Rysten, Felix S. A.
xRysten, Felix S.
False Prophets in the Fiction of Camus,
Dostoevsky, Melville, & Others. U of Miami
Pr.
Ryzin, Lani van. *see* Van Ryzin, Lani.
S. S. Stewart Banjo Company. *see* Stewart, (S.S.) (Firm).
SAA State & Local Records Committee. *see* Society of

American Archivists. State and Local Records
Committee.
Saab, Ann P. *see* Saab, Ann Pottinger.
Saab, Ann Pottinger, 1934-
xSaab, Ann P.
The Origins of the Crimean Alliance. U Pr of
Va.
Saalheimer, Harriet, 1915-
xSaalheimer, Harriet.
Super Treasury of Valuable Things You Can
Get Free or for Next to Nothing. P-H.
Saalman, Howard.
xSaalman, Howard.
Medieval Cities. Braziller.
Saarinen, Thomas. *see* Saarinen, Thomas Frederick.
Saarinen, Thomas F. *see* Saarinen, Thomas Frederick.
Saarinen, Thomas Frederick.
xSaarinen, Thomas.
Environmental Planning: Perception &
Behavior. HM.
xSaarinen, Thomas F.
Perception of the Drought Hazard on the
Great Plains. U Chicago Dept Geog.
Saaty, Thomas L.
xSaaty, Thomas L.
The Four-Color Problem: Assaults & Conquest.
McGraw.
Sabaneev, Leonid. *see* Sabaneev, Leonid Leonidovich.
Sabaneev, Leonid Leonidovich, 1881-
xSabaneev, Leonid.
Music for the Films. Arno.
Sabaroff, Rose. *see* Sabaroff, Rose Epstein.
Sabaroff, Rose Epstein.
xSabaroff, Rose.
The Open Classroom: A Practical Guide for
the Teacher of the Elementary Grades.
Scarecrow.
Sabatier, Auguste, 1839-1901
xSabatier, Auguste.
Outlines of a Philosophy of Religion Based on
Psychology & History. Folcroft.
Sabatini, Rafael.
xSabatini, Rafael.
Captain Blood. Larlin Corp.
Master-at-Arms. Ballantine.
The Sea-Hawk. Ballantine.
Sea Hawk. Larlin Corp.
xSabatini, Raphael.
Captain Blood Returns. Am Repr-Rivercity Pr.
Sabatini, Raphael. *see* Sabatini, Rafael.
Sabatino, David A.
xSabatino, David A.
ed. Describing Learner Characteristics of
Handicapped Children & Youth. Grune.
Intervention Strategies for Specialized
Secondary Education. Allyn.
Specialized Education in Today's Secondary
Schools. Allyn.
Sabbagha, Rudy E.
xSabbagha, Rudy E.
Ultrasound in High-Risk Obstetrics. Lea &
Febiger.
Sabbath, Dan.
xSabbath, Dan.
End Product: The First Taboo. Urizen Bks.
Sabin, Francene.
xSabin, Francene.
Dogs of America. Putnam.
Perfect Pets. Putnam.
Women Who Win. Dell.
Women Who Win. Random.
Sabin, Lou. *see* Sabin, Louis.
Sabin, Louis.
xSabin, Lou.
Hot Shots of Pro Basketball. Random.
Stars of Pro Basketball. Random.
xSabin, Louis.
The Fabulous Dr. J: All-Time All-Star. Putnam.
Sabin, Margery, 1940-
xSabin, Margery.

English Romanticism & the French Tradition.
Harvard U Pr.
Sabin, William A.
xSabin, William A.
The Gregg Reference Manual. McGraw.
Sabine, George H. *see* Sabine, George Holland.
Sabine, George Holland, 1880-1961
xSabine, George H.
History of Political Theory. HR&W.
Sabine, Paul E. *see* Sabine, Paul Earls.
Sabine, Paul Earls, 1879-
xSabine, Paul E.
Atoms, Men, & God. Ed Res Inst.
Sabins, Floyd F.
xSabins, Floyd F.
Remote Sensing: Principles & Interpretation. W
H Freeman.
Sable, M. H. *see* Sable, Martin Howard.
Sable, Martin H. *see* Sable, Martin Howard.
Sable, Martin Howard.
xSable, M. H.
Latin American Jewry: A Research Guide.
Ktav.
xSable, Martin H.
Latin American Studies in the Non-Western
World & Eastern Europe: A Bibliography on
Latin America in the Languages of Africa,
Asia, the Middle East, & Eastern Europe.
Scarecrow.
Sabloff, Jeremy A.
xSabloff, Jeremy A.
ed. Ancient Civilization & Trade. U of NM Pr.
Sablosky, Irving L.
xSablosky, Irving L.
American Music. U of Chicago Pr.
Sabnis, Gajanan M.
xSabnis, Gajanan M.
ed. Handbook of Composite Construction
Engineering. Van Nos Reinhold.
Sabock, Ralph J.
xSabock, Ralph J.
The Coach. HR&W.
Sabrosky, Judith A.
xSabrosky, Judith A.
From Rationality to Liberation: The Evolution
of Feminist Ideology. Greenwood.
Sabsovich, Katharine.
xSabsovich, Katherine.
Adventures in Idealism: A Personal Record of
the Life of Professor Sabsovich. Arno.
Sabsovich, Katherine. *see* Sabsovich, Katharine.
Sacchetti, Franco, ca. 1330-ca. 1400
xSacchetti, Franco.
Tales from Sacchetti. Hyperion Conn.
Saccio, Peter.
xSaccio, Peter.
Court Comedies of John Lyly: A Study in
Allegorical Dramaturgy. Princeton U Pr.
Sacco, Nicola.
xSacco, Nicola.
Letters of Sacco & Vanzetti. Octagon.
Saccomanno, Geno, 1915-
xSaccomanno, Geno.
Diagnostic Pulmonary Cytology. Am Soc
Clinical.
Sachar, A. L. *see* Sachar, Abram Leon.
Sachar, Abram L.
xSachar, Abram L.
Course of Our Times. Dell.
The Course of Our Times. Knopf.
Sachar, Abram L. *see* Sachar, Abram Leon.
Sachar, Abram Leon, 1899-
xSachar, A. L.
History of the Jews. Knopf.
xSachar, Abram L.
A Host at Last. Little.
Sachar, Edward J.
xSachar, Edward J.
ed. Topics in Psychoendocrinology. Grune.
Sachar, Howard. *see* Sachar, Howard Morley.

Sachar, Howard M. *see* Sachar, Howard Morley.
Sachar, Howard Morley, 1928-
xSachar, Howard.
The Man on the Camel. Times Bks.
xSachar, Howard M.
Course of Modern Jewish History. Dell.
A History of Israel: From the Rise of Zionism
to Our Time. Knopf.
Sachar, Louis.
xSachar, Louis.
Sideways Stories from Wayside School. Follett.
Sacharow, Stanley.
xSacharow, Stanley.
Packaging Regulations. AVI.
Sacher, Jack.
xSacher, Jack.
The Art of Sound: An Introduction to Music.
P-H.
Sachs, Abraham S. *see* Sachs, Abraham Simchah.
Sachs, Abraham Simchah, 1879-1931
xSachs, Abraham S.
Worlds That Passed. Arno.
Sachs, Curt, 1881-1959
xSachs, Curt.
Our Musical Heritage: A Short History of
Music. Greenwood.
Sachs, Edwin. *see* Sachs, Edwin Thomas.
Sachs, Edwin Thomas, d. 1910
xSachs, Edwin.
Sleight of Hand: A Practical Manual of
Legerdemain for Amateurs & Others. Dover.
Sachs, Hans.
xSachs, Hans.
Book of Trades (Standebuch). Dover.
The Book of Trades (Standebuch). Peter Smith.
Sachs, Ignacy.
xSachs, Ignacy.
Studies in Political Economy of Development.
Pergamon.
Sachs, Julius von.
xSachs, Julius von.
History of Botany, 1530-1860. Russell.
Sachs, Margaret.
xSachs, Margaret.
Celestial Passengers: UFOs & Space Travel.
Penguin.
Sachs, Marilyn.
xSachs, Marilyn.
Amy & Laura. Doubleday.
Bus Ride. Dutton.
A December Tale. Doubleday.
Dorrie's Book. Doubleday.
Marv. Doubleday.
A Summer's Lease. Dutton.
The Truth About Mary Rose. Doubleday.
Truth About Mary Rose. Dell.
Sachs, Mendel.
xSachs, Mendel.
The Field Concept in Contemporary Science. C
C Thomas.
Sachs, Murray, 1924-
xSachs, Murray.
Career of Alphonse Daudet: A Critical Study.
Harvard U Pr.
Sachs, R. K. *see* Sachs, Rainer Kurt.
Sachs, Rainer Kurt.
xSachs, R. K.
General Relativity for Mathematicians.
Springer-Verlag.
Sachs, Robert G. *see* Sachs, Robert Green.
Sachs, Robert Green.
xSachs, Robert G.
ed. National Energy Issues: How Do We
Decide?: Plutonium As a Test Case. Ballinger
Pub.
Sachse, William L. *see* Sachse, William Lewis.
Sachse, William Lewis, 1912-
xSachse, William L.

Restoration England, 1660-1689. Cambridge U
Pr.
Sack, James J., 1944-
xSack, James J.
The Grenvillites, 1801-29: Party Politics &
Factionalism in the Age of Pitt & Liverpool.
U of Ill Pr.
Sacker, R. J. *see* Sacker, Robert J.
Sacker, Robert J.
xSacker, R. J.
Lifting Properties in Skew-Product Flows with
Applications to Differential Equations. Am
Math.
Sackett, Joseph F.
xSackett, Joseph F.
ed. New Techniques in Myelography.
Har-Row.
Sackett, S. J. *see* Sackett, Samuel John.
Sackett, Samuel John.
xSackett, S. J.
Cowboys & the Songs They Sang. A-W.
Sackheim, George I.
xSackheim, George I.
Chemistry for the Health Sciences. Macmillan.
Introduction to Chemistry for Biology
Students. Ed Methods.
A Programmed Approach to the Circulatory
System. Stipes.
Sackheim, Gertrude.
xSackheim, Gertrude.
The Practice of Clinical Casework. Human Sci
Pr.
Sacks, Ed.
xSacks, Ed.
Chicago Tenant's Handbook. Har-Row.
Sacks, Karen.
xSacks, Karen.
Sisters & Wives: The Past & Future of Sexual
Equality. Greenwood.
Sacks, Michael P. *see* Sacks, Michael Paul.
Sacks, Michael Paul.
xSacks, Michael P.
Women's Work in Soviet Russia: Continuity in
the Midst of Change. Praeger.
Sacks, Oliver W.
xSacks, Oliver W.
Awakenings. Random.
Sacks, Paul M.
xSacks, Paul M.
The Donegal Mafia: An Irish Political
Machine. Yale U Pr.
Sacks, R. D. *see* Sacks, Richard D.
Sacks, Richard D.
xSacks, R. D.
Simplified Circuit Analysis: Digital Analog
Logic. Dekker.
Sacks, Seymour.
xSacks, Seymour.
The Syracuse Black Community, 1970: A
Comparative Study. Syracuse U Cont Ed.
Sacks, Sheldon, 1930-
xSacks, Sheldon.
Fiction & the Shape of Belief: A Study of
Henry Fielding - with Glances at Swift,
Johnson, & Richardson. U of Chicago Pr.
ed. On Metaphor. U of Chicago Pr.
Sackville-West, Edward, Hon, 1901-1965
xSackville-West, Edward.
Inclinations. Folcroft.
Sackville-West, V. *see* Sackville-West, Victoria Mary.
Sackville-West, Victoria M. *see* Sackville-West, Victoria
Mary.
Sackville-West, Victoria Mary.
xSackville-West, V.
V. Sackville-West's Garden Book. Atheneum.
V. Sackville-West's Garden Book. Merrimack
Bk Serv.
xSackville-West, Victoria M.

Country Notes. Arno.
Saczalski, K.
xSaczalski, K. J.
ed. Measurement & Prediction of Structural &
Biodynamic Crash-Impact Response. ASME.
Saczalski, K. J. *see* Saczalski, K.
Sadat, Anwar, 1918-
xSadat, Anwar.
In Search of Identity: An Autobiography.
Har-Row.
xSadat, Anwar El.
In Search of Identity: An Autobiography.
Har-Row.
Sadat, Anwar El. *see* Sadat, Anwar.
Saddhatissa, H.
xSaddhatissa, H.
The Buddha's Way. Braziller.
Buddhist Ethics: Essence of Buddhism.
Braziller.
Sadhu, M. *see* Sadhu, Mouni.
Sadhu, Mouni.
xSadhu, M.
Concentration: A Guide to Mental Mastery.
Wilshire.
Sadhu, S. L. *see* Sadhu, Shyam Lal.
Sadhu, Shyam Lal, 1917-
xSadhu, S. L.
Folk Tales from Kashmir. Asia.
Sadick, Tamah L.
xSadick, Tamah L.
ed. Genetic Diseases & Developmental
Disabilities: Aspects of Detection &
Prevention. Westview.
Sadker, Myra.
xSadker, Myra P.
Teachers Make the Difference: An
Introduction to Education. Har-Row.
Sadker, Myra P. *see* Sadker, Myra.
Sadleir, M. *see* Sadleir, Michael.
Sadleir, Michael, 1888-1957
xSadleir, M.
Excursions in Victorian Bibliography. Dawson
Pub.
xSadleir, Michael.
Excursions in Victorian Bibliography. Folcroft.
ed. Trollope: A Commentary. Darby Bks.
Trollope: A Commentary. Octagon.
Trollope: A Commentary. R West.
Sadler, A. L. *see* Sadler, Arthur Lindsay.
Sadler, Arthur L. *see* Sadler, Arthur Lindsay.
Sadler, Arthur Lindsay, 1882-
xSadler, A. L.
Cha-No-Yu: The Japanese Tea Ceremony. C E
Tuttle.
xSadler, Arthur L.
The Maker of Modern Japan: The Life of
Tokugawa Ieyasu. AMS Pr.
Sadler, Ella J. *see* Sadler, Ella Jo.
Sadler, Ella Jo.
xSadler, Ella J.
Murder in the Afternoon. Zondervan.
Sadler, J. D. *see* Sadler, Jefferson Davis.
Sadler, James C.
xSadler, James C.
Average Cloudiness in the Tropics from
Satellite Observations. U Pr of Hawaii.
Sadler, Jefferson Davis, 1921-
xSadler, J. D.
Modern Latin. U of Okla Pr.
Sadler, John. *see* Sadler, John Edward.
Sadler, John Edward.
xSadler, John.
Concepts in Primary Education: Foundations
for the Child-Centered Classroom. Schocken.
Sadler, John M., 1930-
xSadler, John M.

How to Heat Your Home Without Going
Broke: Build Yourself an Amazing Stainless
Steel Wood Stove. J M Sadler.
Sadler, Lynn.
xSadler, Lynn.
Thomas Carew. G K Hall.
Thomas Carew. Twayne.
Sadler, Michael E. *see* Sadler, Michael Ernest.
Sadler, Michael Ernest, Sir, 1861-1943
xSadler, Michael E.
ed. Arts of West Africa (Excluding Music).
Arno.
Sadler, William A. *see* Sadler, William Alan.
Sadler, William Alan.
xSadler, William A.
Existence & Love: A New Approach in
Existential Phenomenology. Scribner.
Sadoff, Ira.
xSadoff, Ira.
Palm Reading in Winter. HM.
Sadoff, Robert L.
xSadoff, Robert L.
Forensic Psychiatry: A Practical Guide for
Lawyers & Psychiatrists. C C Thomas.
Sadoul, Georges.
xSadoul, Georges.
Dictionary of Film Makers. U of Cal Pr.
Dictionary of Films. U of Cal Pr.
French Film. Arno.
Sadoun, Roland.
xSadoun, Roland.
Drinking in French Culture. Coll & U Pr.
Drinking in French Culture. Rutgers Ctr
Alcohol.
Sadoveanu, Mihail, 1880-1961
xSadoveanu, Mihail.
The Mud-Hut Dwellers. Irvington.
Sadow, Joseph.
xSadow, Joseph.
Coins & Medals of the Vatican. S J Durst.
Sadowski, Karen.
xSadowski, Karen.
Where's Hodgey?. Creative Ed.
Saeger, Glen.
xSaeger, Glen.
String Designs. Sterling.
Safar, Peter.
xSafar, Peter.
Public Health Aspects of Critical Care
Medicine & Anesthesiology. Davis Co.
Safarian, A. E.
xSafarian, A. E.
Foreign Ownership of Canadian Industry. U of
Toronto Pr.
Safer, Arnold E.
xSafer, Arnold E.
International Oil Policy. Lexington Bks.
Safer, Daniel J.
xSafer, Daniel J.
Hyperactive Children: Diagnosis &
Management. Univ Park.
Saff, Donald.
xSaff, Donald.
Printmaking: History & Process. HR&W.
Screenprinting: History & Process. HR&W.
Saffady, William, 1944-
xSaffady, William.
Computer-Output Microfilm: Its Library
Applications. ALA.
Saffell, David C., 1941-
xSaffell, David C.
American Government: Reform in the
Post-Watergate Era. Winthrop.
Safford, E. L. *see* Safford, Edward L.
Safford, Ed. *see* Safford, Edward L.
Safford, Edward I. *see* Safford, Edward L.
Safford, Edward L.
xSafford, E. L.

CBers' Handy Manual of Base Stations. TAB
Bks.
CBer's Handy Manual of SSB. TAB Bks.
Radio Control Manual: Systems, Circuits,
Construction. TAB Bks.
xSafford, Ed.
Aviation Electronics Handbook. TAB Bks.
xSafford, Edward I.
Model Radio Control. TAB Bks.
xSafford, Edward L.
Advanced Radio Control. TAB Bks.
The Complete Microcomputer Systems
Handbook. TAB Bks.
Flying Model Airplanes & Helicopters by
Radio Control. TAB Bks.
Handbook of Marine Electronic & Electrical
Systems. TAB Bks.
Safford, Philip L.
xSafford, Philip L.
Developmental Intervention with Young
Physically Handicapped Children. C C
Thomas.
Safilios-Rothschild, Constantina, 1934-
xSafilios-Rothschild, Constantina.
Love, Sex & Sex Roles. P-H.
ed. Toward a Sociology of Women. Wiley.
Safran, Nadav.
xSafran, Nadav.
Egypt in Search of Political Community: An
Analysis of the Intellectual & Political
Evolution of Egypt, 1804-1952. Harvard U
Pr.
Safran, Rose.
xSafran, Rose.
Don't Go Dancing Mother. Tide Bk Pub Co.
Safran, William.
xSafran, William.
French Polity. Longman.
Safrit, Margaret J., 1935-
xSafrit, Margaret J.
Evaluation in Physical Education. P-H.
Sagamore Computer Conference, Aug. 20-23, 1974. see
Sagamore Computer Conference, 3d, Raguette Lake,
N.Y., 1974.
**Sagamore Computer Conference, 3d, Raguette Lake,
N.Y., 1974.**
xSagamore Computer Conference, Aug. 20-23,
1974.
Parallel Processing: Proceedings.
Springer-Verlag.
Sagan, Carl, 1934-
xSagan, Carl.
Broca's Brain: Reflections on the Romance of
Science. Random.
The Cosmic Connection: An Extraterrestrial
Perspective. Doubleday.
The Dragons of Eden. Ballantine.
The Dragons of Eden. Random.
Sagan, Eli.
xSagan, Eli.
Cannibalism: Human Aggression & Cultural
Form. Har-Row.
The Lust to Annihilate: A Psychoanalytic
Study of Violence in Ancient Greek Culture.
Psychohistory Pr.
Sagan, Leonard A.
xSagan, Leonard A.
ed. Human & Ecologic Effects of Nuclear
Power Plants. C C Thomas.
Sagar, Benjamin.
xSagar, Benjamin.
Sonnets of Robert Browning. Folcroft.
Sagar, K. see Sagar, Keith M.
Sagar, Keith M.
xSagar, K.
The Art of D. H. Lawrence. Cambridge U Pr.
The Art of Ted Hughes. Cambridge U Pr.
xSagar, Keith M.

The Life of D. H. Lawrence. Pantheon.
Sagarin, Edward, 1913-
xSagarin, Edward.
Anatomy of Dirty Words. Lyle Stuart.
ed. Deviance & Social Change. Sage.
Odd Man In: Societies of Deviants in America.
New Viewpoints.
Structure & Ideology in an Association of
Deviants. Arno.
Sagasti, Francisco R.
xSagasti, Francisco R.
Technology, Planning & Self-Reliant
Development: A Latin American View.
Praeger.
Sage, A. P. see Sage, Andrew P.
Sage, Alison.
xSage, Alison.
Ogre's Banquet. Doubleday.
Sage, Andrew P.
xSage, A. P.
Systems Engineering: Methodology &
Applications. Wiley.
xSage, Andrew P.
Estimation Theory with Applications to
Communications & Control. Krieger.
Linear Systems Control. Intl Schol Bk Serv.
Optimum Systems Control. P-H.
System Identification. Acad Pr.
ed. Systems Engineering: Methodology &
Applications. Inst Electrical.
Sage, Edwin R.
xSage, Edwin R.
Fun & Games with the Computer. Entelek.
Problem Solving with the Computer. Entelek.
Sage, George H. see Sage, George Harvey.
Sage, George Harvey.
xSage, George H
Introduction to Motor Behavior: A
Neuro-Psychological Approach. A-W.
Sport & American Society: Selected Readings.
A-W.
Sage, James.
xSage, James D.
The Boy & the Dove. Workman Pub.
Sage, James D. see Sage, James.
Sage, Laurent Le. see Le Sage, Laurent.
Sage, Leland L. see Sage, Leland Livingston.
Sage, Leland Livingston, 1899-
xSage, Leland L.
A History of Iowa. Iowa St U Pr.
Sage, Michael M.
xSage, Michael M.
Cyprian. Greeno Hadden.
Cyprian. Phila Patristic.
Sagebeer, Josephine. see Sagebeer, Josephine Evans.
Sagebeer, Josephine Evans.
xSagebeer, Josephine.
Maternal Health Nursing Review. Arco.
Sagel, Stuart S.
xSagel, Stuart S.
Special Procedures in Chest Radiology.
Saunders.
Sagendorph, Robb. see Sagendorph, Robb Hansell.
Sagendorph, Robb Hansell.
xSagendorph, Robb.
ed. That New England. Yankee Bks.
Sager, Clifford J.
xSager, Clifford J.
Intimate Partners: Hidden Patterns in Love
Relationships. McGraw.
Progress in Group & Family Therapy.
Brunner-Mazel.
Sager, Ruth.
xSager, Ruth.
Cytoplasmic Genes & Organelles. Acad Pr.
Saggerson, E. see Saggerson, E. P.
Saggerson, E. P.
xSaggerson, E.

Identification Tables for Minerals in Thin
Sections. Longman.
Saggs, H. W. see Saggs, H. W. F.
Saggs, H. W. F.
xSaggs, H. W.
The Encounter with the Divine in
Mesopotamia & Israel. Humanities.
Sagola, Mario. see Sagola, Mario J.
Sagola, Mario J.
xSagola, Mario.
The Manacle. Macmillan.
xSagola, Mario J.
The Naked Bishop. Coward.
Sagstetter, Karen.
xSagstetter, Karen.
Lobbying. Watts.
Saha, G. B. see Saha, Gopal B.
Saha, Gopal B.
xSaha, G. B.
Fundamentals of Nuclear Pharmacy.
Springer-Verlag.
Sahade, J.
xSahade, J.
Interacting Binary Stars. Pergamon.
Sahadi, Lou.
xSahadi, Lou.
Year of the Yankees. Contemp Bks.
Sahai, Bhagwant, 1929-
xSahai, Bhagwant.
Iconography of Minor Hindu & Buddhist
Deities. South Asia Bks.
Sahakian, William. see Sahakian, William S.
Sahakian, William S.
xSahakian, William.
Plato. Twayne.
xSahakian, William S.
Ideas of the Great Philosophers. Har-Row.
ed. Learning: Systems, Models, & Theories.
Rand.
ed. Psychology of Personality: Readings in
Theory. Rand.
Psychopathology Today: The Current Status of
Abnormal Psychology. Peacock Pubs.
ed. Psychotherapy & Counseling: Techniques in
Intervention. Rand.
Sahay, Arun.
xSahay, Arun.
Sociological Analysis. Routledge & Kegan.
Sahgal, Nayantara. see Sahgal, Nayantara Pandit.
Sahgal, Nayantara Pandit, 1927-
xSahgal, Nayantara.
Indira Gandhi's Emergence & Style. Carolina
Acad Pr.
Sahlein, Stephen.
xSahlein, Stephen.
The Affirmative Action Handbook: Dealing
with Day-to-Day Supervisory Problems. Exec
Ent.
Sahlins, Marshall. see Sahlins, Marshall David.
Sahlins, Marshall D. see Sahlins, Marshall David.
Sahlins, Marshall David.
xSahlins, Marshall.
Stone Age Economics. Aldine Pub.
xSahlins, Marshall D.
ed. Evolution & Culture. U of Mich Pr.
Sahlstrom, John W. see Sahlstrom, John Wesley.
Sahlstrom, John Wesley, 1894-
xSahlstrom, John W.
Some Code Controls of School Building
Construction in American Cities: An
Evaluation of Certain Building Code
Requirements. AMS Pr.
Said, Abdul. see Said, Abdul Aziz.
Said, Abdul A. see Said, Abdul Aziz.
Said, Abdul Aziz.
xSaid, Abdul.
Human Rights & World Order. Transaction
Bks.
xSaid, Abdul A.

ed. Ethnicity & U. S. Foreign Policy. Praeger.
ed. Ethnicity in an International Context.
    Transaction Bks.
ed. Human Rights & World Order. Praeger.
Said, Edward W.
    xSaid, Edward W.
    Orientalism. Pantheon.
    Orientalism. Random.
Said, Kamal el-Dien.
    xSaid, Kamal el-Dien.
    A Budgeting Model for an Institution of Higher
        Education. U of Tex Busn Res.
Saidi, F. *see* Saidi, Farrokh.
Saidi, Farrokh.
    xSaidi, F.
    Surgery of Hydatid Disease. Saunders.
Saidman, Lawrence J.
    xSaidman, Lawrence J.
    Monitoring in Anesthesia. Wiley.
Saiger, Lydia.
    xSaiger, Lydia.
    The Junk Food Cookbook. BJ Pub Group.
Saijo, Albert.
    xSaijo, Albert.
    The Backpacker. One Hund One Prods.
Saikal, Amin, 1951-
    xSaikal, Amin.
    The Rise & Fall of the Shah. Princeton U Pr.
Saikia, P. C. *see* Saikia, Paban Chandra.
Saikia, Paban Chandra, 1932-
    xSaikia, P. C.
    The Dibongiyas: Social & Religious Life of a
        Priestly Community. South Asia Bks.
Sailaja, P.
    xSailaja, P.
    Experimental Studies of the Differential Effect
        in Life Setting. Parapsych Foun.
Saine, Thomas P.
    xSaine, Thomas P.
    Georg Forster. Twayne.
Saini, B. Singh. *see* Saini, Balwant Singh.
Saini, Balwant Singh.
    xSaini, B. Singh.
    Architecture in Tropical Australia. Wittenborn.
Sainsbury, Isobel S.
    xSainsbury, Isobel S.
    The Milk Free & Milk & Egg Free Cookbook.
        Arco.
Sainsbury, John S.
    xSainsbury, John S.
    Dictionary of Musicians from the Earliest
        Times. Scholarly.
Sainsbury, Mark. *see* Sainsbury, Richard Mark.
Sainsbury, Richard Mark.
    xSainsbury, Mark.
    Russell. Routledge & Kegan.
Saint, Avice M. *see* Saint, Avice Marion.
Saint, Avice Marion.
    xSaint, Avice M.
    Learning at Work: Human Resources &
        Organizational Development. Nelson-Hall.
St. Clair, Alexandrine N.
    xSt. Clair, Alexandrine N.
    The Image of the Turk in Europe. Metro Mus
        Art.
St. Clair, Elizabeth.
    xSt. Clair, Elizabeth.
    Stonehaven. NAL.
St. Clair, Leonard.
    xSt. Clair, Leonard.
    Obsessions. S&S.
    The Seadon Fortune. Berkley Pub.
    The Seadon Fortune. S&S.
St. Claire, Jessica.
    xSt. Claire, Jessica.
    Cerissa. Nordon Pubns.
St. Cyres, Stafford Harry Northcote, Viscount, 1869-
    xSt. Cyres, Viscount.

Francois De Fenelon. Kennikat.
St. Cyres, Viscount. *see* St. Cyres, Stafford Harry
    Northcote.
St. Vincent, Edna Millay. *see* Millay, Edna St. Vincent.
Saint-Evremond, Charles De. *see* Saint-Evremond,
    Charles De Marguetel De Saint-Denis.
**Saint-Evremond, Charles de Marguetel de Saint-Denis,
    Seigneur De, 1613?-1703**
    xSaint-Evremond, Charles De.
    The Letters of Saint Evremond. Arno.
St. George, George.
    xSt. George, George.
    Soviet Deserts & Mountains. Silver.
    Soviet Deserts & Mountains. Time-Life.
St. George, Judith.
    xSt. George, Judith.
    The Amazing Voyage of the New Orleans.
        Putnam.
    The Halloween Pumpkin Smasher. Putnam.
    The Halo Wind. Putnam.
    Mystery at St. Martin's. Putnam.
St. James, Blakely.
    xSt. James, Blakely.
    Christina's Hunger. Playboy Pbks.
    Song for Christina. Playboy Pbks.
St. John, David, 1949-
    xSt. John, David.
    Hush. HM.
St. John, Glory.
    xSt. John, Glory.
    How to Count Like a Martian. Walck.
St. John, Patricia. *see* St. John, Patricia Mary.
St. John, Patricia Mary, 1920-
    xSt. John, Patricia.
    The Secret at Pheasant Cottage. Moody.
St. John, Wylly F. *see* St. John, Wylly Folk.
St. John, Wylly Folk.
    xSt. John, Wylly F.
    The Christmas Tree Mystery. Avon.
    The Ghost Next Door. PB.
    The Ghost Next Door. Archway.
    Ghost Next Door. Har-Row.
    Uncle Robert's Secret. Avon.
    Uncle Robert's Secret. Viking Pr.
St. John-Stevas, Norman.
    xSt. John-Stevas, Norman.
    Obscenity & the Law. Da Capo.
St. Johns, Adela R. *see* St. Johns, Adela (Rogers).
St. Johns, Adela (Rogers).
    xSt. Johns, Adela R.
    Final Verdict. NAL.
St. Johns Hospital Staff. *see* St. Johns Hospital,
    Springfield, Ill.
St. John's Hospital, Springfield, Ill.
    xSt. Johns Hospital Staff.
    The Administrative Manual of Saint Johns
        Hospital: Springfield, Illinois. Cath Health.
St. Johnston, Thomas R. *see* St. Johnston, Thomas
    Reginald.
St. Johnston, Thomas Reginald, Sir, 1881-1950
    xSt. Johnston, Thomas R.
    From a Colonial Governor's Notebook. Negro
        U Pr.
St. Joseph Medical Center.
    xSt. Joseph Medical Center.
    Obstetrical Procedure Manual: Delivery Suite,
        Nursery, Post Partum. Cath Health.
St. Louis. Board of Education.
    xSt. Louis Board Of Education.
    Missouri: The Simplified Constitution.
        McGraw.
St. Louis. Public Library.
    xSt. Louis Public Library.
    Heraldry Index of the St. Louis Public Library.
        G K Hall.
Saint-Marcoux. *see* Saint-Marcoux, Jeanne.
Saint-Marcoux, Jeanne, 1920-
    xSaint-Marcoux.
    Light. Vanguard.
St. Marie, Satenig S.

xSt. Marie, Satenig S.
    Homes Are for People. Wiley.
St. Mary's Hospital Medical Center (Madison, Wisc.).
    xSt. Mary's Medical Center Staff.
    Clinical Laboratory Manual. Cath Health.
St. Mary's Medical Center Staff. *see* St. Mary'S Hospital
    Medical Center (Madison, Wisc.).
Saint-Saens, C. *see* Saint-Saens, Camille.
Saint-Saens, Camille, 1835-1921
    xSaint-Saens, C.
    Musical Memories. AMS Pr.
    xSaint-Saens, Camille.
    Musical Memories. Da Capo.
    Musical Memories. Scholarly.
    Outspoken Essays on Music. Arno.
    Outspoken Essays on Music. Greenwood.
    Outspoken Essays on Music. Scholarly.
St. Sauver, Dennis.
    xSt. Sauver, Dennis.
    Montana Adventure. EMC.
    Pro Fever. EMC.
    Ride to Remember. EMC.
    The Tough Decision. Creative Ed.
    The Two That Count. Creative Ed.
Saint-Simon. *see* Saint-Simon, Claude Henri.
Saint-Simon, Claude H. *see* Saint-Simon, Claude Henri.
Saint-Simon, Claude Henri.
    xSaint-Simon.
    The Political Thought of Saint-Simon. Oxford
        U Pr.
    xSaint-Simon, Claude H.
    Selected Writings. Hyperion Conn.
St. Tamara.
    xSt. Tamara.
    illus. Asian Crafts. Lion.
Sainte-Beuve, Charles A. *see* Sainte-Beuve, Charles
    Augustin.
Sainte-Beuve, Charles Augustin.
    xSainte-Beuve, Charles A.
    Literary Criticism of Sainte-Beuve. U of Nebr
        Pr.
    Portraits of Men. Arno.
Saintsbury, George.
    xSaintsbury, George.
    East India Slavery. Biblio Dist.
    East India Slavery. Humanities.
Saintsbury, George E. *see* Saintsbury, George Edward
    Bateman.
Saintsbury, George Edward Bateman, 1845-1933
    xSaintsbury, George E.
    The English Novel. AMS Pr.
    English Novel. Folcroft.
    The English Novel. Norwood Edns.
    English Novel. Scholarly.
    Flourishing of Romance & the Rise of
        Allegory. Folcroft.
    Historical Novel. Folcroft.
    History of Elizabethan Literature. Folcroft.
    History of Elizabethan Literature. Russell.
    Later Nineteenth Century. Folcroft.
    Matthew Arnold. Russell.
    The Peace of the Augustans: A Survey of
        Eighteenth Century Literature As a Place of
        Rest & Refreshment. Russell.
    Prefaces & Essays. Arno.
    Prefaces & Essays. Greenwood.
Sainty, J. C. *see* Sainty, John Christopher.
Sainty, John Christopher.
    xSainty, J. C.
    Intro. by & ed. Officials of the Boards of Trade
        1660-1870. Humanities.
Saisselin, Remy G. *see* Saisselin, Remy Gilbert.
Saisselin, Remy Gilbert, 1925-
    xSaisselin, Remy G.

The Literary Enterprise in Eighteenth Century
France. Wayne St U Pr.
Taste in Eighteenth Century France: Critical
Reflections on the Origins of Aesthetics, or
An Apology for Amateurs. Syracuse U Pr.
Saito, Shiro.
xSaito, Shiro.
Filipinos Overseas: A Bibliography. Ctr
Migration.
Saitoti, Ole. *see* Saitoti, Tepilit Ole.
Saitoti, Tepilit Ole.
xSaitoti, Ole.
Maasai. Abrams.
Sajer, Guy.
xSajer, Guy.
Forgotten Soldier. Har-Row.
Sajkovic, Miriam. *see* Sajkovic, Miriam Taylor.
Sajkovic, Miriam Taylor.
xSajkovic, Miriam.
F. M. Dostoevsky: His Image of Man. U of Pa
Pr.
Sakall, Dan.
xSakall, Dan.
Love & Evil: From a Probation Officer's
Casebook. Little.
Sakamoto, Nobuko.
xSakamoto, Nobuko.
The People's Republic of China Cookbook.
Random.
Sakharov, Andrei D. *see* Sakharov, Andrei Dmitrievich.
Sakharov, Andrei Dmitrievich, 1921-
xSakharov, Andrei D.
Alarm & Hope. Random.
My Country & the World. Random.
Progress, Coexistence & Intellectual Freedom.
Norton.
Saklatvala, Beram.
xSaklatvala, Beram.
The Christian Island. Fairleigh Dickinson.
Origins of the English People. Taplinger.
Saklatwalla, Jamshedji E. *see* Saklatwalla, Jamshedji
Edulji.
Saklatwalla, Jamshedji Edulji.
xSaklatwalla, Jamshedji E.
Omar Khayyam As a Mystic. Folcroft.
Sakmyster, Thomas L.
xSakmyster, Thomas L.
Hungary, the Great Powers, & the Danubian
Crisis, 1936-1939. U of Ga Pr.
Sakoian, Frances.
xSakoian, Frances.
The Astrologer's Handbook. Har-Row.
The Astrology of Human Relationships.
Har-Row.
Predictive Astrology: Understanding Transits
As the Key to the Future. Har-Row.
Sakol, Jeanne. *see* Sakol, Jeannie.
Sakol, Jeannie.
xSakol, Jeanne.
Flora Sweet. Ballantine.
Sakolski, Aaron M. *see* Sakolski, Aaron Morton.
Sakolski, Aaron Morton, 1880-1955
xSakolski, Aaron M.
Principles of Investment. Arno.
Saks, S. *see* Saks, Stanislaw.
Saks, Stanislaw.
xSaks, S.
Analytic Functions. Elsevier.
Sakurai, J. J. *see* Sakurai, Jun John.
Sakurai, Jun John, 1933-
xSakurai, J. J.
Advanced Quantum Mechanics. A-W.
Currents & Mesons. U of Chicago Pr.
Sala, Darlene.
xSala, Darlene.
Bugs, Floods, & Fried Rice: One Mom's
Journal. Baker Bk.
Sala, Harold J.
xSala, Harold J.

They Shall Be One Flesh. Accent Bks.
Salacuse, Jeswald. *see* Salacuse, Jeswald W.
Salacuse, Jeswald W.
xSalacuse, Jeswald.
Introduction to Law in French Speaking Africa.
Michie.
Salad, Mohamed K. *see* Salad, Mohamed Khalief.
Salad, Mohamed Khalief.
xSalad, Mohamed K.
ed. Somalia: A Bibliographical Survey.
Greenwood.
Saladino, Tom.
xSaladino, Tom.
Pistol Pete Maravich: The Louisiana Purchase.
Strode.
Salaman, R. A.
xSalaman, R. A.
Dictionary of Tools Used in the Woodworking
& Allied Trades c. 1700-1970. Scribner.
Salamon, George.
xSalamon, George.
Arnold Zweig. Twayne.
Salamon, M. B. *see* Salamon, Myron Ben.
Salamon, Myron Ben, 1939-
xSalamon, M. B.
ed. Physics of Superionic Conductors.
Springer-Verlag.
Salant, Walter S.
xSalant, Walter S.
Import Liberalization & Employment: The
Effects of Unilateral Reductions in U.S.
Import Barriers. Brookings.
Salas, Luis.
xSalas, Luis.
Social Control & Deviance in Cuba. Praeger.
Salas, Rafael M.
xSalas, Rafael M
People: An International Choice, the
Multilateral Approach to Population.
Pergamon.
Salas, S. L. *see* Salas, Saturnino L.
Salas, Saturnino L.
xSalas, S. L.
Calculus: One & Several Variables. Wiley.
Precalculus: A Short Course. Wiley.
xSalas, Saturnino L.
Calculus: One & Several Variables. Wiley.
Precalculus. Wiley.
Salat, Barbara.
xSalat, Barbara.
ed. Well-Being. Doubleday.
Salazar, Adolfo, 1890-1958
xSalazar, Adolfo.
Music in Our Time: Trends in Music Since the
Romantic Era. Greenwood.
Salazar, Andres C., 1942-
xSalazar, Andres C.
ed. Digital Signal Computers & Processors. Inst
Electrical.
Salazar, Hector.
xSalazar, Hector.
Social Security & the Spanish-Speaking. R & E
Res Assoc.
Salcedo, Ernesto E.
xSalcedo, Ernesto E.
Atlas of Echocardiography. Saunders.
Saldich, Anne. *see* Saldich, Anne Rawley.
Saldich, Anne Rawley.
xSaldich, Anne.
Electronic Democracy: Television's Impact on
the American Political Process. Praeger.
Sale, J. Russell. *see* Sale, John Russell.
Sale, John Russell, 1945-
xSale, J. Russell.
Filippino Lippi's Strozzi Chapel in Santa Maria
Novella. Garland Pub.
Sale, Kirkpatrick.
xSale, Kirkpatrick.

Power Shift: The Rise of the Southern Rim &
Its Challenge to the Eastern Establishment.
Random.
Power Shift: The Rise of the Southern Rim &
Its Challenge to the Eastern Establishment.
Random.
Sale, Larry. *see* Sale, Larry L.
Sale, Larry L.
xSale, Larry.
Environmental Education in the Elementary
School. HR&W.
xSale, Larry L.
Introduction to Middle School Teaching.
Merrill.
xSale, Lee.
Environmental Education in the Elementary
School. HR&W.
Sale, Lee. *see* Sale, Larry L.
Sale, Randall D.
xSale, Randall D.
American Expansion: A Book of Maps. U of
Nebr Pr.
Sale, Richard, 1911-
xSale, Richard.
The White Buffalo. S&S.
Sale, Richard. *see* Sale, Richard T.
Sale, Richard T., 1939-
xSale, Richard.
The Sword & the Power of Gold: The Shah - a
Critical Biography. Paddington.
Sale, Roger.
xSale, Roger.
Fairy Tales & After: From Snow White to E.
B. White. Harvard U Pr.
On Not Being Good Enough: Writings of a
Working Critic. Oxford U Pr.
On Writing. Random.
Saleh, Adel A. *see* Saleh, Adel A. M.
Saleh, Adel A. M.
xSaleh, Adel A.
Theory of Resistive Mixers. MIT Pr.
Saleilles, Raymond, 1855-1912
xSaleilles, Raymond.
Individualization of Punishment. Patterson
Smith.
Salemme, Lucia A.
xSalemme, Lucia A.
Color Exercises for the Painter.
Watson-Guptill.
Salera, Virgil, 1913-
xSalera, Virgil.
Exchange Control & the Argentine Market.
AMS Pr.
Salerni. *see* Salerni, O. Leroy.
Salerni, O. Leroy, 1936-
xSalerni.
Natural & Synthetic Organic Medicinal
Compounds. Mosby.
Salerno, Nan F.
xSalerno, Nan F.
Shaman's Daughter. P-H.
Salert, B. *see* Salert, Barbara.
Salert, Barbara.
xSalert, B.
Revolutions & Revolutionaries: Four Theories.
Elsevier.
Sales, Bruce D. *see* Sales, Bruce Dennis.
Sales, Bruce Dennis.
xSales, Bruce D.
ed. The Criminal Justice System. Plenum Pub.
Sales, David.
xSales, David.
Suzuki 80-370cc RM Series Singles, 1975-77:
Service, Repair, Performance. Clymer Pubns.
Saletan, Eugene J.
xSaletan, Eugene J.
Theoretical Mechanics. Wiley.
Saletore, B. A. *see* Saletore, Bhasker Anand.
Saletore, Bhasker Anand.
xSaletore, B. A.

Ancient Indian Political Thought &
Institutions. Asia.
Salgado, Maria A. *see* Salgado, Maria Antonia.
Salgado, Maria Antonia.
xSalgado, Maria A.
Rafael Arevalo Martinez. Twayne.
Salibi, Kamal S. *see* Salibi, Kamal Suleiman.
Salibi, Kamal Suleiman, 1929-
xSalibi, Kamal S.
The Modern History of Lebanon. Caravan Bks.
The Modern History of Lebanon. Greenwood.
Syria Under Islam: Empire on Trial, 634-1097.
Caravan Bks.
Saliers, Don E., 1937-
xSaliers, Don E.
The Soul in Paraphrase: Prayer & the Religious
Affections. Seabury.
Salinas, Pedro, 1892-1951
xSalinas, Pedro.
Reality & the Poet in Spanish Poetry.
Greenwood.
Reality & the Poet in Spanish Poetry. Johns
Hopkins.
Saling, Ann.
xSaling, Ann.
The Carrot Cookbook. Pacific Search.
Rhubarb Renaissance: A Cookbook. Pacific
Search.
Salinger, Herman, 1905-
xSalinger, Herman.
ed. Twentieth-Century German Verse. Arno.
Salinger, J. D. *see* Salinger, Jerome David.
Salinger, Jerome David, 1919-
xSalinger, J. D.
The Catcher in the Rye. Little.
The Catcher in the Rye. Bantam.
Franny & Zooey. Bantam.
Nine Stories. Little.
Nine Stories. Bantam.
Salisbury, Allen, 1947-
xSalisbury, Allen.
The Civil War & the American System:
America's Battle with Britain 1860-76.
Campaigner.
Salinger, Wendy.
xSalinger, Wendy.
Folly River. Dutton.
Salisbury, Carola.
xSalisbury, Carola.
Dark Inheritance. Fawcett.
The Pride of the Trevallions. Fawcett.
The Winter Bride. Doubleday.
The Winter Bride. Fawcett.
Salisbury, Frank B.
xSalisbury, Frank B.
The Creation. Deseret Bk.
ed. Plant Physiology. Wadsworth Pub.
Salisbury, Harrison. *see* Salisbury, Harrison Evans.
Salisbury, Harrison E. *see* Salisbury, Harrison Evans.
Salisbury, Harrison Evans, 1908-
xSalisbury, Harrison.
The Unknown War. Bantam.
xSalisbury, Harrison E.
Orbit of China. Har-Row.
Salisbury, J. Kenneth.
xSalisbury, J. Kenneth.
Steam Turbines & Their Cycles. Krieger.
Salisbury, John.
xSalisbury, John.
The Baby Sitters. Atheneum.
Salisbury, Robert H. *see* Salisbury, Robert Holt.
Salisbury, Robert Holt, 1930-
xSalisbury, Robert H.
Citizen Participation in the Public Schools.
Lexington Bks.
Salisbury, Roger E.
xSalisbury, Roger E.

Burns of the Upper Extremity. Saunders.
Salisbury, William T. *see* Salisbury, William Tallmadge.
Salisbury, William Tallmadge.
xSalisbury, William T.
ed. Spain in the 1970s: Economics, Social
Structure, Foreign Policy. Praeger.
Salk, Lee, 1926-
xSalk, Lee.
Dear Dr. Salk: Answers to Your Questions
About Your Family. Har-Row.
How to Raise a Human Being: A Parents'
Guide to Emotional Health from Infancy
Through Adolescence. Random.
What Every Child Would Like Parents to
Know About Divorce. Har-Row.
What Every Child Would Like Parents to
Know About Divorce. Warner Bks.
Salkever, David. *see* Salkever, David S.
Salkever, David S.
xSalkever, David.
Hospital Sector Inflation. Lexington Bks.
Salkey, Andrew.
xSalkey, Andrew.
Hurricane. Oxford U Pr.
Salkin, Harvey M.
xSalkin, Harvey M.
Integer Programming. A-W.
Sall, Millard. *see* Sall, Millard J.
Sall, Millard J.
xSall, Millard.
Faith, Psychology & Christian Maturity.
Zondervan.
Sallee, Annie (Jenkins).
xSallee, Annie J.
Torchbearers in Honan. Arno.
Sallee, Annie J. *see* Sallee, Annie (Jenkins).
Sallee, James, d. 1975
xSallee, James.
History of Evangelistic Hymnody. Baker Bk.
Sallenave, Jean Paul, 1943-
xSallenave, Jean-Paul.
Experience Analysis in Industrial Planning.
Lexington Bks.
Sallenave, Jean-Paul. *see* Sallenave, Jean Paul.
Salley, Ruth E. *see* Salley, Ruth Esther.
Salley, Ruth Esther, 1902-
xSalley, Ruth E.
Some Factors Affecting the Supply of &
Demand for Pre-School Teachers in New
York City. AMS Pr.
Salli, Il'ya V. *see* Salli, Ilia Vasilevich.
Salli, Ilia Vasilevich.
xSalli, Il'ya V.
Structure Formation in Alloys. Plenum Pub.
Sallis, Susan.
xSallis, Susan.
A Time for Everything. Har-Row.
Sally, Paul J.
xSally, Paul J.
Analytic Continuation of the Irreducible
Unitary Representations of the Universal
Covering Group of Sl(2,R). Am Math.
Salm, Thomas J. Vander. *see* Vander Salm, Thomas J.
Salm, Walter G.
xSalm, Walter G.
Cassette Tape Recorders-How They Work-Care
& Repair. TAB Bks.
Tape Recording for Fun & Profit. TAB Bks.
Salmon, Charles G.
xSalmon, Charles G.
Steel Structures: Design & Behavior. Har-Row.
Salmon, E. T. *see* Salmon, Edward Togo.
Salmon, Edward Togo.
xSalmon, E. T.
A History of the Roman World from 30 B.C.
to A.D. 138. Methuen Inc.
Salmon, H. M. *see* Salmon, Maynard Hubbard.
Salmon, Jill.
xSalmon, Jill.

The Goatkeeper's Guide. Dairy Goat.
Salmon, Lucy M. *see* Salmon, Lucy Maynard.
Salmon, Lucy Maynard, 1853-1927
xSalmon, Lucy M.
Domestic Service. Arno.
Salmon, Margaret B. *see* Salmon, Margaret Belais.
Salmon, Margaret Belais.
xSalmon, Margaret B.
ed. Enjoying Your Restricted Diet. C C
Thomas.
Joy of Breastfeeding. Techkits.
A Professional Dietitian's Natural Fiber Diet.
P-H.
Salmon, Maynard Hubbard, 1945-
xSalmon, H. M.
photos by Gazehounds & Coursing. North Star.
Salmon, P. R. *see* Salmon, Paul Raymond.
Salmon, Paul Raymond.
xSalmon, P. R.
Fibre-Optic Endoscopy. Grune.
Salmon, Vivian.
xSalmon, Vivian.
The Works of Francis Lodwick: A Study of His
Writings in the Intellectual Context of the
Seventeenth Century. Longman.
Salmon, Wesley C.
xSalmon, Wesley C.
Logic. P-H.
Space, Time, & Motion: A Philosophical
Introduction. U of Minn Pr.
Salmona, M.
xSalmona, M.
ed. Insolubilized Enzymes. Raven.
Salmonson, R. F. *see* Salmonson, Roland Frank.
Salmonson, Roland Frank.
xSalmonson, R. F.
A Survey of Basic Accounting. Irwin.
Salny, Roslyn W.
xSalny, Roslyn W.
Hobby Collections A-Z. T Y Crowell.
Saloma, John S.
xSaloma, John S.
Parties: The Real Opportunity for Effective
Citizen Politics. Knopf.
Salomaa, Arto.
xSalomaa, Arto.
Formal Languages. Acad Pr.
Salomon, Erich.
xSalomon, Erich.
illus. Erich Salomon. Aperture.
Salop, L. J. *see* Salop, Lazar' Iosifovich.
Salop, Lazar' Iosifovich.
xSalop, L. J.
Precambrian of the Northern Hemisphere.
Elsevier.
Saloutos, Theodore.
xSaloutos, Theodore.
Greeks in the United States. Harvard U Pr.
Salpeter, Harry.
xSalpeter, Harry.
Dr. Johnson & Mr. Boswell. Folcroft.
Salser, Carl S. *see* Salser, Carl Walter.
Salser, Carl Walter.
xSalser, Carl S.
A Tyrant in Cap & Gown. Natl Book.
Salsini, Barbara.
xSalsini, Barbara.
Susan B. Anthony, a Crusader for Women's
Rights. SamHar Pr.
Salsini, Paul.
xSalsini, Paul.
Cole Porter, Twentieth Century Composer of
Popular Songs. SamHar Pr.
Frank Lloyd Wright: The Architectural Genius
of the Twentieth Century. SamHar Pr.
Salt, George.
xSalt, George.

Cellular Defence Reactions of Insects.
Cambridge U Pr.
Salt, Henry S. *see* Salt, Henry Stephens.
Salt, Henry Stephens, 1851-1939
xSalt, Henry S.
Life of Henry David Thoreau. Haskell.
Salter, Arthur. *see* Salter, Arthur Salter.
Salter, Arthur Salter, Baron, 1881-
xSalter, Arthur.
World's Economic Crisis, & the Way of
Escape. Arno.
Salter, Christopher L.
xSalter, Christopher L.
San Francisco's Chinatown: How Chinese a
Town?. R & E Res Assoc.
Salter, Frederick M. *see* Salter, Frederick Millet.
Salter, Frederick Millet, 1895-
xSalter, Frederick M.
Mediaeval Drama in Chester. Russell.
Salter, James.
xSalter, James.
Light Years. Random.
Solo Faces. Little.
Solo Faces. Penguin.
Salter, John R.
xSalter, John R.
The Jackson Mississippi: An American
Chronicle of Struggle & Schism. Exposition.
Salter, John T. *see* Salter, John Thomas.
Salter, John Thomas, 1898-
xSalter, John T.
The American Politician. Greenwood.
xSalter, John Thomas.
Public Men in & Out of Office. Da Capo.
Salter, Kenneth. *see* Salter, Kenneth W.
Salter, Kenneth W.
xSalter, Kenneth.
The Pentagon Papers Trial. Editorial Justa.
Salter, P. J. *see* Salter, Patrick Jeremy.
Salter, Patrick Jeremy.
xSalter, P. J.
ed. Know & Grow Vegetables. Oxford U Pr.
Salter, R. H. *see* Salter, Robin Hugh.
Salter, R. J. *see* Salter, Richard J.
Salter, Richard J.
xSalter, R. J.
Highway Traffic Analysis & Design. A-W.
Salter, Robin Hugh.
xSalter, R. H.
Common Gastroenterological Problems. Year
Bk Med.
Salter, W. E. *see* Salter, W. E. G.
Salter, W. E. G.
xSalter, W. E.
Productivity & Technical Change. Cambridge
U Pr.
Saltman, Avrom.
xSaltman, Avrom.
Theobald Archbishop of Canterbury.
Greenwood.
Saltman, David.
xSaltman, David.
Paper Basics: Forestry, Manufacture, Selection,
Purchasing, Mathematics & Metrics,
Recycling. Van Nos Reinhold.
Saltman, Jules.
xSaltman, Jules.
Abortion Today. C C Thomas.
Saltman, William M., 1917-
xSaltman, William M.
ed. The Stereo Rubbers. Wiley.
Saltmarsh, H. F. *see* Saltmarsh, Herbert Francis.
Saltmarsh, Herbert Francis, 1881-
xSaltmarsh, H. F.
Evidence of Personal Survival from Cross
Correspondences. Arno.
Foreknowledge. Arno.
Salton, Gerard.
xSalton, Gerard.

Dynamic Information & Library Processing.
P-H.
Salton, Milton R. *see* Salton, Milton R. J.
Salton, Milton R. J.
xSalton, Milton R.
Bacterial Cell Wall. Elsevier.
Saltonstall, Maxine. *see* Saltonstall, Maxine J.
Saltonstall, Maxine J.
xSaltonstall, Maxine.
In Lieu of. C E Tuttle.
Saltus, Edgar. *see* Saltus, Edgar Evertson.
Saltus, Edgar Everston, 1855-1921
xSaltus, Edgar.
Lords of the Ghostland: A History of the Ideal.
AMS Pr.
Saltus, Edgar Evertson, 1855-1921
xSaltus, Edgar.
Balzac. AMS Pr.
Facts in the Curious Case of H. Hyrtl, Esq.
AMS Pr.
Gardens of Aphrodite. AMS Pr.
Ghost Girl. AMS Pr.
Historia Amoris: A History of Love Ancient &
Modern. AMS Pr.
Imperial Orgy: An Account of the Tsars from
the First to the Last. AMS Pr.
Love & Lore. AMS Pr.
Monster. AMS Pr.
Paliser Case. AMS Pr.
Perfume of Eros: A Fifth Avenue Incident.
AMS Pr.
Pomps of Satan. AMS Pr.
Purple & Fine Women. AMS Pr.
Vanity Square: A Story of Fifth Avenue Life.
AMS Pr.
When Dreams Come True: A Story of
Emotional Life. AMS Pr.
Saltykov, Mikhail E. *see* Saltykov, Mikhail Evgrafovich.
Saltykov, Mikhail Evgrafovich, 1826-1889
xSaltykov, Mikhail E.
Fables. Greenwood.
Saltz, Daniel.
xSaltz, Daniel.
A Short Calculus: An Applied Approach.
Goodyear.
Saltz, Eli.
xSaltz, Eli.
The Cognitive Bases of Human Learning.
Dorsey.
Saltzman, Marvin L.
xSaltzman, Marvin L.
Eurail Guide: How to Travel Europe & All the
World by Train 1981. Eurail Guide.
Salukvadze, M. *see* Salukvadze, Mindiia Evgenevich.
Salukvadze, Mindiia Evgenevich.
xSalukvadze, M.
Vector-Valued Optimization Problems in
Control Theory. Acad Pr.
Salunkhe, D. K.
xSalunkhe, D. K.
Storage, Processing & Nutritional Quality of
Fruits & Vegetables. CRC Pr.
Salus, Naomi Panush.
xCassells.
Compiled by Cassell's Italian Dictionary:
Italian-English, English-Italian. Macmillan.
xSalus, Naomi Panush.
My Daddy's Mustache. Doubleday.
Salus, Peter H.
xSalus, Peter H.
Linguistics. Bobbs.
Salustri, Carlo A. *see* Salustri, Carlo Alberto.
Salustri, Carlo Alberto.
xSalustri, Carlo A.
Roman Satirical Poems & Their Translation.
Greenwood.
Salvadori, M. *see* Salvadori, Massimo.
Salvadori, Mario. *see* Salvadori, Mario George.
Salvadori, Mario George.
xSalvadori, Mario.

Structural Design in Architecture. P-H.
Salvadori, Massimo.
xSalvadori, M.
Cavour & the Unification of Italy. Krieger.
xSalvadori, Massimo.
The Liberal Heresy: Origins & Historical
Development. St Martin.
NATO: A Twentieth Century Community of
Nations. Peter Smith.
Salvany, Don F. Sarda y. *see* Sarda y Salvany, Don F.
Salvati, M. J.
xSalvati, M. J.
Build Your Own High-Quality, Low-Cost Test
Equipment. Hayden.
How to Custom Design Your Solid-State
Equipment. Hayden.
TV Antennas & Signal Distribution Systems.
Sams.
Salvato, Joseph A.
xSalvato, Joseph A.
Environmental Engineering & Sanitation.
Wiley.
Salvatore, Dominick.
xSalvatore, Dominick.
Schaum's Outline of Principles of Economics.
McGraw.
Salvatore, Paul J. *see* Salvatore, Paul John.
Salvatore, Paul John, 1895-
xSalvatore, Paul J.
Favart's Unpublished Plays: The Rise of the
Popular Comic Opera. AMS Pr.
Salvemini, Gaetano.
xSalvemini, Gaetano.
The Fascist Dictatorship in Italy. Fertig.
Under the Axe of Fascism. Citadel Pr.
Under the Axe of Fascism. Fertig.
Salvia, John.
xSalvia, John.
Assessment in Special & Remedial Education.
HM.
Salvo, Louis J. De. *see* De Salvo, Louis J.
Salwak, Dale.
xSalwak, Dale.
John Braine & John Wain: A Reference Guide.
G K Hall.
Salway, Peter.
xSalway, Peter.
Frontier People of Roman Britain. Cambridge
U Pr.
Salyer, Pauline A.
xSalyer, Pauline A.
Great Artists of China Decoration. Salyer.
Salyers, Paul, 1929-
xSalyers, Paul.
The Passing Day. Windy Row.
Salz, Kay.
xSalz, Kay.
ed. Craft Films: An Index of International
Films on Crafts. Neal-Schuman.
Salzano, Francisco M.
xSalzano, Francisco M.
Problems in Human Biology: A Study of
Brazilian Populations. Wayne St U Pr.
Salzberg, Doris T. *see* Salzberg, Doris Thorner.
Salzberg, Doris Thorner.
xSalzberg, Doris T.
Raggedy Granny Stories. Bobbs.
Salzer, F. *see* Salzer, Felix.
Salzer, Felix.
xSalzer, F.
Counterpoint in Composition: The Study of
Voice Leading. McGraw.
xSalzer, Felix.
Structural Hearing: Tonal Coherence in Music.
Dover.
Salzman, Jack.
xSalzman, Jack.
ed. Theodore Dreiser: The Critical Reception.
B Franklin.
Salzman, Leo. *see* Salzman, Leon.

Salzman, Leon.
xSalzman, Leo.
Modern Concepts of Psychoanalysis. Philos Lib.
xSalzman, Leon.
Developments in Psychoanalysis. Grune.
Salzman, Louis F. see Salzman, Louis Francis.
Salzman, Louis Francis, 1878-
xSalzman, Louis F.
England in Tudor Times: An Account of Its Social Life & Industries. Russell.
Salzman, Yuri.
xSalzman, Yuri.
Hope You're Feeling Better. Har-Row.
Salzmann, J. A. see Salzmann, Jacob Amos.
Salzmann, Jacob Amos.
xSalzmann, J. A.
Orthodontics in Daily Practice. Lippincott.
Samaan, Sadek H.
xSamaan, Sadek H.
Fears & Worries of Nigerian Igbo Secondary School Students: An Empirical Psychocultural Study. Ohio U Ctr Intl.
Samaha, Joel.
xSamaha, Joel B.
Law & Order in Historical Perspective: The Case of Elizabethan Essex. Acad Pr.
Samaha, Joel B. see Samaha, Joel.
Samal, Babrubahan.
xSamal, Babrubahan.
Transcription of the Eukaryotic Genome. Eden Med Res.
Samaras, Demetrios G.
xSamaras, Demetrios G.
Theory of Ion Flow Dynamics.. Dover.
Samaras, T. see Samaras, Thomas T.
Samaras, Thomas T.
xSamaras, T.
Engineering Graphics Desk Book. P-H.
xSamaras, Thomas T.
Fundamentals of Configuration Management. Wiley.
Industrial Manager's Desk Handbook. P-H.
Sambrook, James.
xSambrook, James.
Intro. by Pre-Raphaelitism: A Collection of Critical Essays. U of Chicago Pr.
Samek, R. A.
xSamek, Robert A.
The Legal Point of View. Philos Lib.
Samek, Robert A. see Samek, R. A.
Samelson, Hans, 1916-
xSamelson, Hans.
Introduction to Linear Algebra. Wiley.
Sames, James W. see Sames, James Walter.
Sames, James Walter, 1921-
xSames, James W.
Pref. by & Compiled by Index of Kentucky & Virginia Maps, 1562 to 1900. Kentucky Hist.
Samet, Philip.
xSamet, Philip.
ed. Cardiac Pacing. Grune.
Sametz, Arnold W.
xSametz, Arnold W.
ed. Financial Development & Economic Growth: The Economic Consequences of Underdeveloped Capital Markets. NYU Pr.
Samis, H. V. see Samis, Harvey V.
Samis, Harvey V.
xSamis, H. V.
ed. Aging & Biological Rhythms. Plenum Pub.
Samitz, M. H.
xSamitz, M. H.
Cutaneous Lesions of the Lower Extremities. Lippincott.
Samkange, Stanlake. see Samkange, Stanlake John Thompson.
Samkange, Stanlake John Thompson, 1922-
xSamkange, Stanlake.

The Year of the Uprising. Heinemann Ed.
Samli, A. Coskun.
xSamli, A. Coskun.
Marketing & Distribution Systems in Eastern Europe. Praeger.
Sammartino, Peter, 1904-
xSammartino, Peter.
A History of Higher Education in New Jersey. A S Barnes.
I Dreamed a College. A S Barnes.
Of Castles & Colleges: Notes toward an Autobiography. A S Barnes.
Sammon, Rick.
xSammon, Rick.
Minolta SRT's. Amphoto.
Minolta XD's. Amphoto.
Minolta XG's. Amphoto.
Sammons, David.
xSammons, David.
The Marriage Option. Beacon Pr.
Sammons, Jeffrey L.
xSammons, Jeffrey L.
Literary Sociology & Practical Criticism: An Inquiry. Ind U Pr.
Sammons, Martha C., 1949-
xSammons, Martha C.
A Guide Through Narnia. Shaw Pubs.
Samoiloff, Louise C. see Samoiloff, Louise Cripps.
Samoiloff, Louise Cripps.
xSamoiloff, Louise C.
Portrait of Puerto Rico. Schenkman.
Samora, Julian.
xSamora, Julian.
Gunpowder Justice: A Reassessment of the Texas Rangers. U of Notre Dame Pr.
A History of the Mexican-American People. U of Notre Dame Pr.
Samovar, Larry. see Samovar, Larry A.
Samovar, Larry A.
xSamovar, Larry.
Oral Communication: Message & Response. Wm C Brown.
Sampath, G.
xSampath, G.
Stochastic Models for Spike Trains of Single Neurons. Springer-Verlag.
Samperi, Frank.
xSamperi, Frank.
Branches. SBD.
Infinitesimals. SBD.
Of Light. SBD.
Samph, Thomas.
xSamph, Thomas.
ed. Evaluation in Medical Education: Past, Present, Future. Ballinger Pub.
Sampierre, Martin.
xSampierre, Martin.
Deborah. A S Barnes.
Samples, Gordon.
xSamples, Gordon.
The Drama Scholars' Index to Plays & Filmscripts: A Guide to Plays & Filmscripts in Selected Anthologies, Series & Periodicals. Scarecrow.
How to Locate Reviews of Plays & Films: A Bibliography of Criticism from the Beginnings to the Present. Scarecrow.
Sampson, Alden, 1853-1925
xSampson, Alden.
Studies in Milton & an Essay on Poetry. AMS Pr.
Sampson, Anthony.
xSampson, Anthony.
The Arms Bazaar: From Lebanon to Lockheed. Bantam.
Sampson, Edward C.
xSampson, Edward C.
E. B. White. Twayne.
Sampson, Fay.
xSampson, Fay.

Watch on Patterick Fell. Greenwillow.
Sampson, Geoffrey.
xSampson, Geoffrey.
Liberty & Language. Oxford U Pr.
Sampson, George, 1873-1950
xSampson, George.
ed. Nineteenth Century Essays. Arno.
Sampson, H. Grant.
xSampson, H. Grant.
The Anglican Tradition in Eighteenth Century Verse. Mouton.
Sampson, Henry, 1841-1891
xSampson, Henry.
History of Advertising from the Earliest Times. Gale.
Sampson, J. R. see Sampson, Jeffrey R.
Sampson, Jeffrey R., 1942-
xSampson, J. R.
Adaptive Information Processing: An Introductory Survey. Springer-Verlag.
Sampson, Olive. see Sampson, Olive C.
Sampson, Olive C.
xSampson, Olive.
Remedial Education. Routledge & Kegan.
Sampson, Patricia.
xSampson, Patricia.
A Star to Steer by: Success Through Positive Experiencing. Fell.
Sampson, Roy. see Sampson, Roy J.
Sampson, Roy J.
xSampson, Roy.
Domestic Transportation: Practice, Theory, & Policy. HM.
Sampson, William, 1764-1836
xSampson, William.
The Catholic Question in America. Da Capo.
Sampurnanand, 1891-
xSampurnanand.
Memories & Reflections. Asia.
Samra, C. S. see Samra, Chattar Singh.
Samra, Chattar Singh.
xSamra, C. S.
India & Anglo-Soviet Relations. Asia.
Sams, Eric.
xSams, Eric.
Brahms Songs. U of Wash Pr.
Sams, Henry W.
xSams, Henry W.
ed. Autobiography of Brook Farm. Peter Smith.
Sams (Howard W.) and Company, Inc., Indianapolis.
xHoward W. Sams Editorial Staff.
CB Radio. Sams.
Color-TV Field Service Guide. Sams.
Color TV Training Manual. Sams.
Dictionary of Audio & Hi-Fi. Sams.
Semiconductor Replacement Guide. Sams.
Sams (Howard W.) and Company, Inc., Indianapolis. Engineering Staff.
xHoward W. Sams Engineering Staff.
Photofact Television Course. Sams.
Reference Data for Radio Engineers. Sams.
Transistor Specifications Manual. Sams.
Transistor Substitution Handbook. Sams.
Tube Substitution Handbook. Sams.
xTheHoward W. Sams Engineering Staff.
Semiconductor General Purpose Replacements. Sams.
Samson, Jack.
xSamson, Jack.
Successful Outdoor Writing. Writers Digest.
Samson, Jim.
xSamson, Jim.
Music in Transition: A Study of Tonal Expansion & Atonality, 1900-1920. Norton.
Samson, Joan, 1937-
xSamson, Joan.
The Auctioneer. S&S.
Samsonov, G. V. see Samsonov, Grigorii Valentinovich.
Samsonov, Gregory V. see Samsonov, Grigorii Valentinovich.

Samsonov, Grigorii Valentinovich.
  xSamsonov, G. V.
    A Configurational Model of Matter. Plenum
      Pub.
    Germanides. Plenum Pub.
    Germanides. Primary.
    ed. Refractory Carbides. Plenum Pub.
    ed. Refractory Transition Metal Compounds:
      High Temperature Cermets. Acad Pr.
  xSamsonov, Gregory V.
    The Oxide Handbook. IFI Plenum.
Samter, Max, 1908-
  xSamter, Max.
    ed. Immunological Diseases. Little.
Samuda, Ronald J.
  xSamuda, Ronald J.
    Psychological Testing of American Minorities:
      Issues & Consequences. Har-Row.
Samuel, Claude.
  xSamuel, Claude.
    Prokofiev. Vienna Hse.
Samuel, Edwin., Hon
  xSamuel, Edwin.
    The Structure of Society in Israel. Peter Smith.
Samuel, Herbert L. *see* Samuel, Herbert Louis Samuel.
Samuel, Herbert Louis Samuel, Viscount, 1870-1963
  xSamuel, Herbert L.
    A Century's Changes of Outlook. AMS Pr.
    In Search of Reality. Arno.
Samuel, Irene, 1915-
  xSamuel, Irene.
    Plato & Milton. Cornell U Pr.
Samuel, John. *see* Samuel, John R.
Samuel, John R.
  xSamuel, John.
    Ski-Wise. Allen Unwin.
Samuel, Maurice, 1895-1972
  xSamuel, Maurice.
    Certain People of the Book. UAHC.
    Gentleman & the Jew. Behrman.
    The Gentleman & the Jew. Greenwood.
    Prince of the Ghetto. Schocken.
Samuel, Richard. *see* Samuel, Richard H.
Samuel, Richard H.
  xSamuel, Richard.
    Expressionism in German Life, Literature &
      the Theatre, 1910-24. Saifer.
Samuel, William, 1944-
  xSamuel, William.
    Melody of the Woodcutter & the King: The
      Account of an Awakening. Seed Center.
  xSamuel, William S.
    Contemporary Social Psychology: An
      Introduction. P-H.
Samuel, William S. *see* Samuel, William.
Samuels, Carl.
  xSamuels, Carl.
    Freakout: The Drug Nightmare at Home.
      Ashley Bks.
Samuels, Charles.
  xSamuels, Charles.
    Once Upon a Stage: The Merry World of
      Vaudeville. Dodd.
Samuels, Charles E.
  xSamuels, Charles E.
    Thomas Bailey Aldrich. Coll & U Pr.
Samuels, Charles T. *see* Samuels, Charles Thomas.
Samuels, Charles Thomas, 1936-1974
  xSamuels, Charles T.
    Mastering the Film & Other Essays. U of Tenn
      Pr.
Samuels, Ernest, 1903-
  xSamuels, Ernest.
    Bernard Berenson: The Making of a
      Connoisseur. Harvard U Pr.
Samuels, Frank G. *see* Samuels, Frank George.
Samuels, Frank George.
  xSamuels, Frank G.

    The Negro Tavern: A Microcosm of Slum Life.
      R & E Res Assoc.
Samuels, Gertrude.
  xSamuels, Gertrude.
    Adam's Daughter. NAL.
    Adam's Daughter. T Y Crowell.
    Of David & Eva: A Love Story. NAL.
Samuels, M. L. *see* Samuels, Michael Louis.
Samuels, Michael A. *see* Samuels, Michael Anthony.
Samuels, Michael Anthony.
  xSamuels, Michael A.
    Africa & the West. Westview.
Samuels, Michael Louis.
  xSamuels, M. L.
    Linguistic Evolution with Special Reference to
      English. Cambridge U Pr.
Samuels, Mike.
  xSamuels, Mike.
    The Well Baby Book. Summit Bks.
Samuels, Mimi.
  xSamuels, Mimi.
    The Complete Handbook of Peer Counseling.
      Fiesta Pub.
Samuels, Peggy.
  xSamuels, Peggy.
    The Illustrated Biographical Encyclopedia of
      Artists of the American West. Doubleday.
Samuels, Shirley C.
  xSamuels, Shirley C.
    Enhancing Self-Concept in Early Childhood:
      Theory & Practice. Human Sci Pr.
Samuels, Warren J., 1933-
  xSamuels, Warren J.
    Pareto on Policy. Elsevier.
Samuelson, David. *see* Samuelson, David W.
Samuelson, David W.
  xSamuelson, David.
    Motion Picture Camera Techniques. Focal Pr.
Samuelson, Paul A. *see* Samuelson, Paul Anthony.
Samuelson, Paul Anthony, 1915-
  xSamuelson, Paul A.
    Economics. McGraw.
    Economics. McGraw.
    Foundations of Economic Analysis. Atheneum.
    Readings in Economics. McGraw.
San Francisco Cancer Symposium, 10th, 1974.
  xAnnual West Coast Cancer Symposium, 10th, San
    Francisco, Calif., September 1974.
    Primary Bone Cancer: the Multidiscipline
      Disease: Proceedings. S Karger.
San Francisco Cancer Symposium, 11th, San Francisco,
  Calif., November, 1975. *see* San Fransisco Cancer
  Symposium, 11th, 1975.
San Fransisco Cancer Symposium, 11th, 1975.
  xSan Francisco Cancer Symposium, 11th, San
    Francisco, Calif., November, 1975.
    Breast Cancer-Its Impact on the Patient,
      Family, & Community: Proceedings. S
      Karger.
San Juan, Epifanio, 1938-
  xSan Juan, Epifanio.
    The Art of Oscar Wilde. Greenwood.
San Pietro, Anthony. *see* San Pietro, Anthony Gordan.
San Pietro, Anthony Gordan.
  xSan Pietro, Anthony.
    ed. Regulatory Mechanisms for Protein
      Synthesis in Mammalian Cells. Acad Pr.
Sanadi, D. R.
  xSanadi, D. Rao.
    ed. Chemical Mechanisms in Bioenergetics. Am
      Chemical.
  xSanadi, R. D.
    ed. Current Topics in Bioenergetics. Acad Pr.
  xSanadi, Rao.
    ed. Current Topics in Bioenergetics. Acad Pr.
  xSanadi, S. Rao.
    Current Topics in Bioenergetics. Acad Pr.
Sanadi, D. Rao. *see* Sanadi, D. R.
Sanadi, R. D. *see* Sanadi, D. R.
Sanadi, Rao. *see* Sanadi, D. R.

Sanadi, S. Rao. *see* Sanadi, D. R.
Sanborn, Franklin B. *see* Sanborn, Franklin Benjamin.
Sanborn, Franklin Benjamin, 1831-1917
  xSanborn, Franklin B.
    ed. Life of Henry David Thoreau, Including
      Many Essays Hitherto Unpublished & Some
      Accounts of His Family & Friends. Gale.
    Personality of Emerson. Folcroft.
    Personality of Emerson. Haskell.
Sanborn, William. *see* Sanborn, William B.
Sanborn, William B.
  xSanborn, William.
    Oddities of the Mineral World. Van Nos
      Reinhold.
  xSanborn, William B.
    Handbook of Crystal & Mineral Collecting.
      Gembooks.
Sanchez, George I. *see* Sanchez, George Isidore.
Sanchez, George Isidore, 1906-
  xSanchez, George I.
    Development of Higher Education in Mexico.
      Greenwood.
    Materials Relating to the Education of
      Spanish-Speaking People in the United States.
      Greenwood.
Sanchez, John.
  xSanchez, John.
    Slash & Thrust. Paladin Ent.
Sanchez, Jose.
  xSanchez, Jose.
    ed. Nineteenth Century Spanish Verse.
      Irvington.
Sanchez, Jose M. *see* Sanchez, Jose Mariano.
Sanchez, Jose Mariano, 1932-
  xSanchez, Jose M.
    Anticlericalism; A Brief History. U of Notre
      Dame Pr.
Sanchez, Nellie. *see* Sanchez, Nellie Van De Grift.
Sanchez, Nellie Van de Grift, 1856-1935
  xSanchez, Nellie.
    Spanish Arcadia. Arno.
Sanchez, Pedro A., 1940-
  xSanchez, Pedro A.
    Properties & Management of Soils in the
      Tropics. Wiley.
Sanchez, Sonia, 1935-
  xSanchez, Sonia.
    Love Poems. Okpaku Communications.
Sanchez, Tony.
  xSanchez, Tony.
    illus. Up & Down with the Rolling Stones.
      Morrow.
    Up & Down with the Rolling Stones. NAL.
Sanchez Reyes, Carmen.
  xSanchez Reyes, Carmen.
    Carlos Fuentes y "La Region Mas
      Transparente". U of PR Pr.
Sanchez-Saavedra, E. M.
  xSanchez-Saavedra, E. M.
    Compiled by A Guide to Virginia Military
      Organizations in the American Revolution,
      1774-1787. VA State Lib.
Sancho, Ignatius.
  xSancho, Ignatius.
    Letters of the Late Ignatius Sancho, an African.
      Arno.
Sancho, Pedro.
  xSancho, Pedro.
    Account of the Conquest of Peru. Kraus Repr.
    An Account of the Conquest of Peru.
      Longwood Pr.
Sancton, Pamela.
  xSancton, Pamela.
    ed. French Recipes North Americans Love
      Best. Tundra Bks.
Sand, George.
  xSand, George.

Indiana. Academy Chi Ltd.
Indiana. Fertig.
Indiana. French & Eur.
Lelia. Ind U Pr.
Leone Leoni. Academy Chi Ltd.
Leone Leoni. French & Eur.
Letters of George Sand. AMS Pr.
Letters of George Sand. Gordon Pr.
Mauprat. Academy Chi Ltd.
Mauprat. Da Capo.
Mauprat. French & Eur.
My Life. Har-Row.
My Life. Har-Row.
She & He. Academy Chi Ltd.
xSand, Georges.
Indiana. French & Eur.
Lelia. French & Eur.
Sand, George X., 1915-
xSand, George X.
The Complete Beginner's Guide to Fishing.
Doubleday.
Sand, Georges. *see* Sand, George.
Sand, L. B. *see* Sand, Leonard B.
Sand, Leonard B.
xSand, L. B.
ed. Natural Zeolites: Occurrence, Properties,
Use. Pergamon.
Sand, Maurice, 1823-1889
xSand, Maurice.
History of the Harlequinade. Arno.
Sandage, Allan.
xSandage, Allan.
The Hubble Atlas of Galaxies. Carnegie Inst.
Sandall, Tony.
xSandall, Tony.
Horse Breaking. Intl Pubns Serv.
Sandars, N. K. *see* Sandars, Nancy K.
Sandars, Nancy. *see* Sandars, Nancy K.
Sandars, Nancy K.
xSandars, N. K.
Prehistoric Art in Europe. Viking Pr.
xSandars, Nancy.
tr. Epic of Gilgamesh. Penguin.
Sandbach, F. H.
xSandbach, F. H.
The Comic Theatre of Greece & Rome.
Norton.
The Stoics. Norton.
Sandbach, Francis.
xSandbach, Francis.
Environment, Ideology & Policy. Allanheld.
Sandberg, Inger.
xSandberg, Inger.
Boy with Many Houses. Delacorte.
Let's Play Desert. Delacorte.
Little Ghost Godfrey. Delacorte.
Where Does All That Smoke Come from?.
Delacorte.
Sandberg, K. *see* Sandberg, Karl C.
Sandberg, Karl C.
xSandberg, K.
Creative English: The Basics for
Comprehension & Expression. P-H.
xSandberg, Karl C.
At the Crossroads of Faith & Reason: An
Essay on Pierre Bayle. U of Ariz Pr.
Trouble, Trouble, Trouble. Carolrhoda Bks.
Sandborn, E. B. *see* Sandborn, Edmund B.
Sandborn, Edmund B.
xSandborn, E. B.
Light & Electron Microscopy of Cells &
Tissues: An Atlas for Students in Biology &
Medicine. Acad Pr.
Sandbrook, R. *see* Sandbrook, Richard.
Sandbrook, Richard.
xSandbrook, R.
Proletarians & African Capitalism: The Kenyan
Case, 1960-1972. Cambridge U Pr.
Sandburg, Carl, 1878-1967
xSandburg, Carl.

Abe Lincoln Grows Up. HarBraceJ.
Abe Lincoln Grows up. HarBraceJ.
American Songbag. HarBraceJ.
Complete Poems of Carl Sandburg. HarBraceJ.
Early Moon. HarBraceJ.
Early Moon. HarBraceJ.
Honey & Salt. HarBraceJ.
Honey & Salt. HarBraceJ.
Letters of Carl Sandburg. HarBraceJ.
People, Yes. HarBraceJ.
Sandburg, Don.
xSandburg, Don.
Legal Guide to Mother Goose. Price Stern.
Sandburg, Helga.
xSandburg, Helga.
Children & Lovers: Fifteen Stories. HarBraceJ.
Sandeen, Arthur.
xSandeen, Arthur.
Undergraduate Education: Conflict & Change.
Lexington Bks.
Sandeen, Ernest R. *see* Sandeen, Ernest Robert.
Sandeen, Ernest Robert.
xSandeen, Ernest R.
ed. American Religion & Philosophy: A Guide
to Information Sources. Gale.
Roots of Fundamentalism: British & American
Millenarianism 1800-1930. Baker Bk.
Sandels, Stina.
xSandels, Stina.
Children in Traffic. Intl Pubns Serv.
Sanden, John H. *see* Sanden, John Howard.
Sanden, John Howard.
xSanden, John H.
Painting the Head in Oil. Watson-Guptill.
Sander, August.
xSander, August.
illus. August Sander. Aperture.
Sander, David.
xSander, David.
Orchids & Their Cultivation. Sterling.
Sander, David M.
xSander, David M.
Wood Engraving: An Adventure in
Printmaking. Viking Pr.
Sander, K. F. *see* Sander, Kenneth Frederick.
Sander, Kenneth Frederick.
xSander, K. F.
Transmission & Propagation of Electromagnetic
Waves. Cambridge U Pr.
Sander, Reinhard W.
xSander, Reinhard W.
ed. From Trinidad: An Anthology of Early
West Indian Writing. Holmes & Meier.
Sandercock, Leonie, 1949-
xSandercock, Leonie.
Cities for Sale: Property, Politics & Urban
Planning in Australia. Intl Schol Bk Serv.
Sanderlin, George. *see* Sanderlin, George William.
Sanderlin, George William, 1915-
xSanderlin, George.
A Hoop to the Barrel: The Making of the
American Constitution. Coward.
Mark Twain: As Others Saw Him. Coward.
Sanderlin, Owenita.
xSanderlin, Owenita.
Gifted Children: How to Identify & Teach
Them. A S Barnes.
Sanderlin, Walter S., 1920-
xSanderlin, Walter S.
The Great National Project: A History of the
Chesapeake & Ohio Canal. AMS Pr.
The Great National Project: A History of the
Chesapeake and Ohio Canal. Arno.
Sanders. *see* Sanders, Roger C.
Sanders, Charles R. *see* Sanders, Charles Richard.
Sanders, Charles Richard, 1904-
xSanders, Charles R.

Coleridge & the Broad Church Movement:
Studies in S. T. Coleridge, Dr. Arnold of
Rugby, J. C. Hare, Thomas Carlyle & F. D.
Maurice. Russell.
Strachey Family, 1588-1932: Their Writings &
Literary Associations. Greenwood.
Sanders, D. G. *see* Sanders, Donald G.
Sanders, Daniel S.
xSanders, Daniel S.
Impact of Reform Movements on Social Policy
Change: The Case of Social Insurance. Intl
Schol Bk Serv.
Sanders, David, 1950-
xSanders, David.
Patterns of Political Instability. St Martin.
The Queen Sends for Mrs. Chadwick. St
Martin.
Sanders, Derek A.
xSanders, Derek A.
Auditory Perception of Speech: An
Introduction to Principles & Problems. P-H.
Aural Rehabilitation. P-H.
Sanders, Donald G., 1899-
xSanders, D. G.
The Brasspounder. Dutton.
Sanders, Donald H.
xSanders, Donald H.
Computers & Management in a Changing
Society. McGraw.
Computers in Business. McGraw.
Statistics: A Fresh Approach. McGraw.
Statistics: A Fresh Approach. McGraw.
Sanders, E. P.
xSanders, E. P.
Paul & Palestinian Judaism: A Comparison of
Patterns of Religion. Fortress.
Sanders, Ed.
xSanders, Ed.
ed. Tales of Beatnik Glory. Stonehill Pub Co.
Sanders, G. D. *see* Sanders, Gerald De Witt.
Sanders, Gerald De Witt.
xSanders, G. D.
Chief Modern Poets of Britain & America.
Macmillan.
Sanders, Herbert H.
xSanders, Herbert H.
Glazes for Special Effects. Watson-Guptill.
World of Japanese Ceramics. Kodansha.
Sanders, Howard L.
xSanders, Howard L.
Cephalocarida: Functional Morphology, Larval
Development, Comparative External
Anatomy. Shoe String.
Sanders, I. T. *see* Sanders, Irwin Taylor.
Sanders, Irwin T. *see* Sanders, Irwin Taylor.
Sanders, Irwin Taylor, 1909-
xSanders, I. T.
The Community: An Introduction to a Social
System. Wiley.
xSanders, Irwin T.
photos by Balkan Village. Greenwood.
Sanders, J. M. *see* Sanders, John Howard.
Sanders, J. Oswald. *see* Sanders, John Oswald.
Sanders, Jack P. *see* Sanders, Jack Palmer.
Sanders, Jack Palmer, 1943-
xSanders, Jack P.
The Category of H - Modules Over a
Spectrum. Am Math.
Sanders, Jack T.
xSanders, Jack T.
Ethics in the New Testament: Change &
Development. Fortress.
Sanders, James A., 1927-
xSanders, James A.
Torah & Canon. Fortress.
Sanders, James W.
xSanders, James W.

Education of an Urban Minority: Catholics in Chicago 1833-1965. Oxford U Pr.

Sanders, Jane, 1940-
xSanders, Jane.
Cold War on the Campus: Academic Freedom at the University of Washington, 1946-64. U of Wash Pr.

Sanders, Jennings B. see Sanders, Jennings Bryan.

Sanders, Jennings Bryan, 1901-
xSanders, Jennings B.
Early American History, 1492-1789: Political, Social, Economic. Scholarly.
Evolution of Executive Departments of the Continental Congress, 1774-1789. Peter Smith.
Historical Interpretations & American Historianship. Kent St U Pr.
Presidency of the Continental Congress 1774-89: A Study in American Institutional History. Peter Smith.

Sanders, John Howard.
xSanders, J. M.
The Velocity of Light. Pergamon.

Sanders, John Oswald, 1902-
xSanders, J. Oswald.
Holy Spirit & His Gifts. Zondervan.
People Just Like Us. Moody.
Prayer Power Unlimited. Moody.
Prayer Power Unlimited. World Wide Pubs.

Sanders, John T.
xSanders, John T.
The Ethical Argument Against Government. U Pr of Amer.

Sanders, Julia E. see Sanders, Julia Elma.

Sanders, Julia Elma, 1844-
xSanders, Julia E.
Tatting Patterns. Dover.

Sanders, Lawrence, 1920-
xSanders, Lawrence.
The Marlow Chronicles. Berkley Pub.
Marlow Chronicles. Putnam.
The Pleasures of Helen. Berkley Pub.
The Tangent Factor. Berkley Pub.
The Tangent Factor. Putnam.
The Tangent Objective. Berkley Pub.
The Tangent Objective. Putnam.

Sanders, Leonard.
xSanders, Leonard.
The Hamlet Ultimatum. Scribner.
The Hamlet Warning. Warner Bks.

Sanders, Lloyd. see Sanders, Lloyd Charles.
Sanders, Lloyd C. see Sanders, Lloyd Charles.

Sanders, Lloyd Charles, 1857-
xSanders, Lloyd.
Holland House Circle. Arno.
The Holland House Circle. R West.
xSanders, Lloyd C.
Celebrities of the Century: Being a Dictionary of Men & Women of the Nineteenth Century. Gale.
Life of Richard Brinsley Sheridan. Folcroft.

Sanders, Lois J. see Sanders, Lois Joan.

Sanders, Lois Joan.
xSanders, Lois J.
Procedure Guides for Evaluation of Speech & Language Disorders in Children. Interstate.

Sanders, Marion.
xSanders, Marion.
Clinical Assessment of Learning Problems: Model, Process & Remedial Planning. Allyn.

Sanders, Marion K.
xSanders, Marion K.
Dorothy Thompson: A Legend in Her Time. Avon.

Sanders, N. see Sanders, Norman.

Sanders, Norman.
xSanders, N.

The Corporate Computer: How to Live with an Ecological Intrusion. McGraw.

Sanders, Norris M.
xSanders, Norris M.
Classroom Questions: What Kinds?. Har-Row.

Sanders, Paul A. see Sanders, Paul Amsdon.

Sanders, Paul Amsdon, 1913-
xSanders, Paul A.
Handbook of Aerosol Technology. Van Nos Reinhold.

Sanders, R. J. see Sanders, Richard J.
Sanders, Richard. see Sanders, Richard J.

Sanders, Richard J.
xSanders, R. J.
The Anatomy of Skiing. Random.
xSanders, Richard.
Anatomy of Skiing. Golden Bell.
xSanders, Richard J.
Carcinoids of the Gastrointestinal Tract. C C Thomas.

Sanders, Roger C.
xSanders.
Principles & Practice of Ultrasonography in Obstetrics & Gynecology. ACC.

Sanders, Ron.
xSanders, Ron.
Broadcasting in Guyana. Routledge & Kegan.

Sanders, Ronald.
xSanders, Ronald.
Lost Tribes & Promised Lands: The Origins of American Racism. Little.

Sanders, Sol. see Sanders, Sol W.

Sanders, Sol W.
xSanders, Sol.
Honda: The Man & His Machines. Little.

Sanders, Steven.
xSanders, Steven.
The Meaning of Life: Questions, Answers & Analysis. P-H.

Sanders, Thomas E. see Sanders, Thomas Edward.

Sanders, Thomas Edward.
xSanders, Thomas E.
Literature of the American Indian. Glencoe.

Sanders, William. see Sanders, William B.

Sanders, William B.
xSanders, William.
jt. auth. Criminal Justice: Situations & Decisions. HR&W.
xSanders, William B.
Detective Work: A Study of Criminal Investigations. Free Pr.

Sanders, William B. see Sanders, William Baxter.

Sanders, William Baxter, 1942-
xSanders, William B.
Guide to Inflatable Canoes & Kayaks. Anderson World.

Sanders, William T.
xSanders, William T.
The Basin of Mexico: Ecological Processes in the Evolution of a Civilization. Acad Pr.

Sanderson, Edgar, d. 1907
xSanderson, Edgar.
Africa in the Nineteenth Century. Metro Bks.
Africa in the Nineteenth Century. Negro U Pr.
Great Britain in Modern Africa. Negro U Pr.

Sanderson, Fred H. see Sanderson, Fred Hugo.

Sanderson, Fred Hugo.
xSanderson, Fred H.
Food Trends & Prospects in India. Brookings.

Sanderson, Glen C.
xSanderson, Glen C.
ed. Management of Migratory Shore & Upland Game Birds in North America. U of Nebr Pr.

Sanderson, J. D. see Sanderson, James Dean.

Sanderson, James Dean, 1925-
xSanderson, J. D.
How to Stop Worrying About Your Kids. Norton.

Sanderson, R. Thomas. see Sanderson, Robert Thomas.

Sanderson, Richard G.
xSanderson, Richard G.
ed. Cardiac Patient: A Comprehensive Approach. Saunders.

Sanderson, Robert Thomas, 1912-
xSanderson, R. Thomas.
Principles of Chemistry. Krieger.

Sanderson, William E. see Sanderson, William Elwood.

Sanderson, William Elwood, 1903-
xSanderson, William E.
Nez Perce Buffalo Horse. Caxton.

Sandford, C. T.
xSandford, C. T.
An Annual Wealth Tax. Holmes & Meier.

Sandford, Frank W, 1862-1948
xSandford, Frank W.
Art of War for the Christian Soldier. Kingdom.
The Golden Light Upon the Two Americas. Kingdom.

Sandford, J. C. see Sandford, John Cecil.

Sandford, Jeremy.
xSandford, Jeremy.
Cathy Come Home. Merrimack Bk Serv.
Edna the Inebriate Woman. Merrimack Bk Serv.

Sandford, John, 1944-
xSandford, John.
The Mass Media of the German Speaking Countries. Iowa St U Pr.

Sandford, John. see Sandford, John Loren.

Sandford, John Cecil.
xSandford, J. C.
The Domestic Rabbit. Halsted Pr.

Sandford, John Loren.
xSandford, John.
Restoring the Christian Family. Logos.

Sandford, Lettice.
xSandford, Lettice.
Straw Work & Corn Dollies. Viking Pr.

Sandford, Rick.
xSandford, Rick.
Heroes Die Young. Belmont-Tower.

Sandhu, Harjit S.
xSandhu, Harjit S.
Modern Corrections: The Offenders, Therapies & Community Reintegration. C C Thomas.

Sandhu, Swaran S.
xSandhu, Swaran S.
Nonviolence in Indian Religious Thought & Political Action. Dorrance.

Sandia Laboratories.
xSandia Laboratories.
Passive Solar Buildings: A Compilation of Data & Results. Solar Energy Info.

Sandifer, D. V. see Sandifer, Durward Valdamir.
Sandifer, Durward V. see Sandifer, Durward Valdamir.

Sandifer, Durward Valdamir, 1900-
xSandifer, D. V.
Evidence Before International Tribunals. Kraus Repr.
xSandifer, Durward V.
Evidence Before International Tribunals. U Pr of Va.

Sandiford, Keith A. see Sandiford, Keith A. P.

Sandiford, Keith A. P., 1936-
xSandiford, Keith A.
Great Britain & the Schleswig-Holstein Question 1848-64: A Study in Diplomacy, Politics & Public Opinion. U of Toronto Pr.

Sandiford, Ralph, 1693-1733
xSandiford, Ralph.
Brief Examination of the Practice of the Times. Arno.

Sandige, Richard. see Sandige, Richard S.

Sandige, Richard S.
xSandige, Richard.
Digital Concepts Using Standard Integrated Circuits. McGraw.

Sandler, Irving, 1925-
xSandler, Irving.

The Triumph of American Painting: A History
of Abstract Expressionism. Har-Row.
Sandler, J. J.
xSandler, Joseph.
The Patient & the Analyst: The Basis of the
Psychoanalytic Process. Intl Univs Pr.
Sandler, Joseph. see Sandler, J. J.
Sandler, Martin. see Sandler, Martin W.
Sandler, Martin W.
xSandler, Martin.
As New Englanders Played. Globe Pequot.
xSandler, Martin W.
The People Make a Nation. Allyn.
The People Make a Nation. Allyn.
The Story of American Photography: An
Illustrated History for Young People. Little.
This Was Connecticut: Images of a Vanished
World. Little.
This Was New England: Images of a Vanished
Past. NYGS.
Sandler, Merton.
xSandler, Merton.
ed. Mental Illness in Pregnancy & the
Puerperium. Oxford U Pr.
ed. Psychopharmacology of Aggression. Raven.
Sandler, Richard.
xSandler, Richard.
Daily Management of Youth - Onset Diabetes
Mellitus: An Integrated Guide for Patients &
Physicians. C C Thomas.
Sandler, Stanley R.
xSandler, Stanley R.
Organic Functional Group Preparations. Acad
Pr.
Polymer Syntheses. Acad Pr.
Sandler, Todd.
xSandler, Todd.
The Political Economy of Public Goods &
International Cooperation. U of Denver Intl.
Sandman, Peter. see Sandman, Peter M.
Sandman, Peter M.
xSandman, Peter.
Students & the Law. Macmillan.
Unabashed Career Guide. Macmillan.
xSandman, Peter M.
Media: An Introductory Analysis of American
Mass Communication. P-H.
xSandman, Peter S.
Media Casebook: An Introductory Reader in
American Mass Communications. P-H.
Sandman, Peter S. see Sandman, Peter M.
Sandmel, Samuel.
xSandmel, Samuel.
Anti-Semitism in the New Testament?.
Fortress.
Enjoyment of Scripture: The Law, the
Prophets, & the Writings. Oxford U Pr.
The Genius of Paul: A Study in History.
Fortress.
Philo of Alexandria: An Introduction. Oxford
U Pr.
When a Jew & Christian Marry. Fortress.
Sandmeyer, Elmer C. see Sandmeyer, Elmer Clarence.
Sandmeyer, Elmer Clarence, 1888-
xSandmeyer, Elmer C.
The Anti-Chinese Movement in California. U
of Ill Pr.
Sandon, Henry.
xSandon, Henry.
Coffee Pots & Teapots for the Collector. Arco.
Sandor, Bela I. see Sandor, Bela Imre.
Sandor, Bela Imre.
xSandor, Bela I.
Fundamentals of Cyclic Stress & Strain. U of
Wis Pr.
Strength of Materials. P-H.
Sandoz. see Sandoz, Ellis.
Sandoz, Ellis, 1931-
xSandoz.

Conceived in Liberty: American Individual
Rights Today. Duxbury Pr.
Sandoz, Mari, 1907-
xSandoz, Mari.
The Buffalo Hunters: The Story of the Hide
Men. U of Nebr Pr.
Cheyenne Autumn. Avon.
Cheyenne Autumn. Hastings.
Crazy Horse, the Strange Man of the Oglalas:
A Biography. U of Nebr Pr.
Horsecatcher. Westminster.
These Were the Sioux. Hastings.
These Were the Sioux. Dell.
Sandperl, Ira.
xSandperl, Ira.
A Little Kinder. Sci & Behavior.
Sandrea, Rafael.
xSandrea, Rafael.
Dynamics of Petroleum Reservoirs Under Gas
Injection. Gulf Pub.
Sandretto, Peter C.
xSandretto, Peter C.
The Economic Management of Research &
Engineering. Krieger.
Sandreuter, William O.
xSandreuter, William O.
Whitewater Canoeing. Follett.
Whitewater Canoeing. Winchester Pr.
Sandritter, W. see Sandritter, Walter.
Sandritter, Walter.
xSandritter, W.
Color Atlas & Textbook of Macropathology.
Year Bk Med.
Sandroff, Ronni.
xSandroff, Ronni.
Fighting Back. BJ Pub Group.
Fighting Back. Knopf.
Sandrow, Nahma.
xSandrow, Nahma.
Vagabond Stars: A World History of Yiddish
Theater. Har-Row.
Sandry, Esther.
xSandry, Esther.
Typewriting Office Practice Set. Pitman
Learning.
Sands, Donald E., 1929-
xSands, Donald E.
Introduction to Crystallography.
Benjamin-Cummings.
Sands, Frederick.
xSands, Frederick.
The Divine Garbo. G&D.
Sands, Gary.
xSands, Gary.
Housing Turnover & Housing Policy: Case
Studies of Vacancy Chains in New York
State. Praeger.
Sands, Harry.
xSands, Harry.
The Epilepsy Fact Book. Davis Co.
The Epilepsy Fact Book. Scribner.
Sands, Leo G.
xSands, Leo G.
CB Radio. A S Barnes.
CB Radio Accessories. Sams.
CB Radio Servicing Guide. Sams.
CBers' How-to Book. Hayden.
Easy Way to Service Radio Receivers. TAB
Bks.
Installing T.V. & FM Antennas. TAB Bks.
Most Often Asked Questions & Answers
About Amateur Radio. Hayden.
Questions & Answers About CB Operations.
Sams.
Questions & Answers About CB Radio Repair.
Sams.
Sound Systems Installers Handbook. Sams.
Sands, P. C. see Sands, Percy Cooper.
Sands, Percy C. see Sands, Percy Cooper.

Sands, Percy Cooper.
xSands, P. C.
Literary Genius of the New Testament. R
West.
xSands, Percy C.
The Client Princes of the Roman Empire
Under the Republic. Arno.
Literary Genius of the New Testament.
Greenwood.
Literary Genius of the Old Testament. Folcroft.
Sands, Pierre N. see Sands, Pierre Norman.
Sands, Pierre Norman.
xSands, Pierre N.
A Historical Study of the Academy of Motion
Picture Arts & Sciences, 1927-1947. Arno.
Sandstrom, Alan. see Sandstrom, Alan R.
Sandstrom, Alan R.
xSandstrom, Alan.
Image of Disease: Medical Practices of Nahua
Indians of the Huasteca. Mus Anthro Mo.
Sandved, Kjell. see Sandved, Kjell Bloch.
Sandved, Kjell Bloch.
xSandved, Kjell.
Insect Magic. Penguin.
Sandys, John E. see Sandys, John Edwin.
Sandys, John Edwin, Sir, 1844-1922
xSandys, John E.
History of Classical Scholarship. Hafner.
Sandywell, B. see Sandywell, Barry.
Sandywell, Barry.
xSandywell, B.
Problems of Reflexivity & Dialectics in
Sociological Inquiry: Language Theorizing
Difference. Routledge & Kegan.
Sandzen, S. C. see Sandzen, Sigurd Carl.
Sandzen, Sigurd Carl, 1932-
xSandzen, S. C.
Atlas of Wrist & Hand Fractures. PSG Pub.
Sanes, Samuel.
xSanes, Samuel.
A Physician Faces Cancer in Himself. State U
NY Pr.
Sanford, Adrian B.
xSanford, Adrian B.
Using English: Grammar & Writing Skills.
HarBraceJ.
Sanford, Aubrey. see Sanford, Aubrey C.
Sanford, Aubrey C.
xSanford, Aubrey.
Human Relations: The Theory & Practice of
Organizational Behavior. Merrill.
Sanford, Bob.
xSanford, Bob.
Riding the Dirt. Norton.
Sanford, Charles L, 1920-
xSanford, Charles L.
The Quest for Paradise: Europe & the
American Moral Imagination. AMS Pr.
Sanford, Charlotte.
xSanford, Charlotte.
Second Sight: A Miraculous Story of Vision
Regained. M Evans.
Sanford, David, 1943-
xSanford, David.
Who Put the Con in Consumer?. Liveright.
Sanford, Don.
xSanford, Don.
Prayers for Every Occasion. Zondervan.
Sanford, George B.
xSanford, George B.
Fighting Rebels & Redskins: Experiences in
Army Life of Colonel George B. Sanford,
1861-1892. U of Okla Pr.
Sanford, Harb. see Sanford, Herb.
Sanford, Herb.
xSanford, Harb.
Tommy & Jimmy: The Dorsey Years. Da
Capo.
Sanford, John L. see Sanford, John Langton.

Sanford, John Langton.
xSanford, John L.
Great Governing Families of England. Arno.
Sanford, Nevitt.
xSanford, Nevitt.
Where Colleges Fail: A Study of the Student
As a Person. Jossey-Bass.
xSanford, Nevitt R.
ed. College & Character. Montaigne.
Sanford, Nevitt R. see Sanford, Nevitt.
Sanford, Trent E. see Sanford, Trent Elwood.
Sanford, Trent Elwood, 1897-
xSanford, Trent E.
The Architecture of the Southwest: Indian,
Spanish, American. Greenwood.
Sanford, Vera, 1891-
xSanford, Vera.
The History & Significance of Certain Standard
Problems in Algebra. AMS Pr.
Sanger, C. P. see Sanger, Charles Percy.
Sanger, Charles Percy.
xSanger, C. P.
Structure of Wuthering Heights. Folcroft.
Sanger, Elliott. see Sanger, Elliott M.
Sanger, Elliott M.
xSanger, Elliott.
Rebel in Radio: The Story of WQXR. Hastings.
Sanger, Margaret, 1879-1966
xSanger, Margaret.
Margaret Sanger: An Autobiography. Dover.
Sanger, Mary B. see Sanger, Mary Bryna.
Sanger, Mary Bryna.
xSanger, Mary B.
Welfare of the Poor. Acad Pr.
Sanger, Richard H. see Sanger, Richard Harlakenden.
Sanger, Richard Harlakenden, 1905-
xSanger, Richard H.
Arabian Peninsula. Arno.
Where the Jordan Flows. Mid East Inst.
Sangharakshita. see Sangharakshita, Bhikshu.
Sangharakshita, Bhikshu, 1925-
xSangharakshita.
Survey of Buddhism. Shambhala Pubns.
SanGiovanni, Lucinda.
xSanGiovanni, Lucinda F.
Ex-Nuns: A Study of Emergent Role Passage.
Ablex Pub.
SanGiovanni, Lucinda F. see Sangiovanni, Lucinda.
Sangiuliano. see Sangiuliano, Iris.
Sangiuliano, Iris.
xSangiuliano.
In Her Time. Morrow.
xSangiuliano, Iris.
In Her Time. Morrow.
Sankey, Alice.
xSankey, Alice.
Hit the Bike Trail. A Whitman.
Sankey, Benjamin.
xSankey, Benjamin.
A Companion to William Carlos Williams'
Paterson. U of Cal Pr.
Sankey, Ira D. see Sankey, Ira David.
Sankey, Ira David, 1840-1908
xSankey, Ira D.
My Life & the Story of the Gospel Hymns &
of Sacred Songs & Solos. AMS Pr.
Sankhdher, M. M., 1930-
xSankhdher, M. M.
Reflections on Indian Politics. Intl Pubns Serv.
Sankoff, David.
xSankoff, David.
ed. Linguistic Variation: Models & Methods.
Acad Pr.
Sankoff, Gillian.
xSankoff, Gillian.
The Social Life of Language. U of Pa Pr.
Sannebeck, Norvelle.
xSannebeck, Norvelle.

All About Living in Hawaii. Pacific Bks.
Sannella, Lucia.
xSannella, Lucia.
The Female Pentecost. Ashley Bks.
Sanner, A. E. see Sanner, A. Elwood.
Sanner, A. Elwood.
xSanner, A. E.
Exploring Christian Education. Beacon Hill.
Sanness, Palmer.
xSanness, Palmer.
Incomparable Paul. Branden.
Sannwald, Rolf.
xSannwald, Rolf.
Economic Integration: Theoretical Assumptions
and Consequences of European Unification.
Greenwood.
Sano, Chie.
xSano, Chie.
Changing Values of the Japanese Family.
Greenwood.
Sansom, George. see Sansom, George Bailey.
Sansom, George Bailey, Sir, 1883-
xSansom, George.
A History of Japan to 1334. Stanford U Pr.
A History of Japan, 1334-1615. Stanford U Pr.
A History of Japan, 1615-1867. Stanford U Pr.
Sansom, Robert L.
xSansom, Robert L.
Economics of Insurgency in the Mekong Delta
of Vietnam. MIT Pr.
Sansom, William, 1912-
xSansom, William.
The Icicle & the Sun. Greenwood.
The Stories of William Sansom. Arno.
Sansone, G. see Sansone, Giovanni.
Sansone, Giovanni, 1888-
xSansone, G.
Orthogonal Functions. Krieger.
Sant, M. E. see Sant, Morgan.
Sant, Morgan.
xSant, M. E.
Industrial Movement & Regional Development:
The British Case. Pergamon.
Santa, Beauel M.
xSanta, Beauel M.
How to Use the Library. Pacific Bks.
**Santa Fe Conference on Radiation Effects in
Semiconductors.**
xConference On Radiation Effects In
Semiconductors - Sante Fe.
Radiation Effects in Semiconductors:
Proceedings. Plenum Pub.
Santayana, George, 1863-1952
xSantayana, George.
Character & Opinion in the United States.
Norton.
Dominations & Powers: Reflections on Liberty,
Society & Government. Kelley.
Egotism in German Philosophy. Haskell.
The Genteel Tradition at Bay. Haskell.
George Santayana's America: Essays on
Literature & Culture. U of Ill Pr.
The Idea of Christ in the Gospels: Or, God in
Man, a Critical Essay. AMS Pr.
Little Essays Drawn from the Writings of
George Santayana. Arno.
Lucifer. Irvington.
The Poet's Testament: Poems & Two Plays.
AMS Pr.
The Realm of Essence: Book First of "Realms
of Being". Greenwood.
The Realm of Matter: Book Second of "Realms
of Being". Greenwood.
Realms of Being. Cooper Sq.
Some Turns of Thought in Modern Philosophy:
Five Essays. Arno.
Sonnets & Other Verses. Folcroft.
Sante, Daniel P.
xSante, Daniel P.

Automatic Control System Technology. P-H.
Santee, Ross, 1889-
xSantee, Ross.
Cowboy. U of Nebr Pr.
Lost Pony Tracks. U of Nebr Pr.
Men & Horses. U of Nebr Pr.
Santillana, Giorgio De. see De Santillana, Giorgio.
Santis, Zerlina De. see De Santis, Zerlina.
Santmyer, Helen H. see Santmyer, Helen Hooven.
Santmyer, Helen Hooven, 1895-
xSantmyer, Helen H.
Ohio Town. Ohio St U Pr.
Santo, Charles P. De. see De Santo, Charles P.
Santomauro, Mary, 1935-
xSantomauro, Mary.
The Rest of the Afternoon Was Watermelon.
Ashley Bks.
Santoni, Ronald E.
xSantoni, Ronald E.
ed. Religious Language & the Problem of
Religious Knowledge. Ind U Pr.
Santos, Bienvenido N.
xSantos, Bienvenido N.
Scent of Apples: A Collection of Stories. U of
Wash Pr.
Santos, Harry G.
xSantos, Harry G.
How to Attack & Defeat the Zone Defenses in
Basketball. P-H.
Santos, Joyce A. Dos. see Dos Santos, Joyce A.
Santos, Miguel A.
xSantos, Miguel A.
ed. Readings in Biology & Man. Mss Info.
Santos-Dumont, Alberto, 1873-1932
xSantos-Dumont, Alberto.
My Airships: The Story of My Life. Dover.
My Airships: The Story of My Life. Peter
Smith.
Santoz, Montague.
xSantoz, Montague.
The World Monetary Catastrophe & the
Explosion of the Next International
Conflagration. Inst Econ Pol.
Sants, John.
xSants, John.
ed. Developmental Psychology & Society. St
Martin.
Santucci, James A.
xSantucci, James A.
An Outline of Vedic Literature. Scholars Pr Ca.
Santucho, Oscar J. see Santucho, Oscar Jose.
Santucho, Oscar Jose.
xSantucho, Oscar J.
George Gordon, Lord Byron: A
Comprehensive Bibliography of Secondary
Materials in English, 1807-1974. Scarecrow.
Sanuki, Matao.
xSanuki, Matao.
Alps. Kodansha.
Sanwal, B. D. see Sanwal, Bhairava Dat.
Sanwal, Bhairava Dat, 1917-
xSanwal, B. D.
Nepal & the East India Company. Asia.
Sanzotta, Donald.
xSanzotta, Donald.
Manager's Guide to Interpersonal Relations.
Am Mgmt.
Saperstein, Arlyne B.
xSaperstein, Arlyne B.
Introduction to Nursing Practice. Davis Co.
Saphier, M. see Saphier, Michael.
Saphier, Michael.
xSaphier, M.
Office Planning & Design. McGraw.
Sapin, Burton M.
xSapin, Burton M.
Contemporary American Foreign & Military
Policy. Scott F.
Sapio, Rodolfo De. see De Sapio, Rodolfo.

Sapir, Edward.
  xSapir, Edward.
    Native Accounts of Nootka Ethnography.
      AMS Pr.
    Navaho Texts. AMS Pr.
Sapir, J. David.
  xSapir, J. David.
    ed. The Social Use of Metaphor: Essays on the
      Anthropology of Rhetoric. U of Pa Pr.
Sapir, Richard.
  xSapir, Richard.
    Brain Drain. Pinnacle Bks.
    Child's Play. Pinnacle Bks.
    Deadly Seeds. Pinnacle Bks.
    Murder Ward. Pinnacle Bks.
  xSapir, Richard B.
    The Far Arena. Seaview Bks.
Sapir, Richard B. *see* Sapir, Richard.
Saporita, Jay.
  xSaporita, Jay.
    Pourin It All Out. Citadel Pr.
Saposs, David J. *see* Saposs, David Joseph.
Saposs, David Joseph.
  xSaposs, David J.
    Communism in American Politics. Pub Aff Pr.
Sappe, Arthur.
  xSappe, Arthur.
    Of Dust & Sparrows. NYU Pr.
Sapriel, J.
  xSapriel, J.
    Acousto-Optics. Wiley.
Sarachek, Joseph, 1892-
  xSarachek, Joseph.
    The Doctrine of the Messiah in Medieval
      Jewish Literature. Hermon.
Saracino, Dan. *see* Saracino, Daniel H.
Saracino, Daniel H., 1947-
  xSaracino, Dan.
    Abstract Algebra: A First Course. A-W.
Sarafino, Edward P.
  xSarafino, Edward P.
    Child & Adolescent Development. Scott F.
Sarason, I. G. *see* Sarason, Irwin G.
Sarason, Irwin G.
  xSarason, I. G.
    Abnormal Psychology: Problem of Maladaptive
      Behavior. P-H.
  xSarason, Irwin G.
    Abnormal Psychology: The Problem of
      Maladaptive Behavior. P-H.
    A Guide for Foster Parents. Human Sci Pr.
    Personality: An Objective Approach. Wiley.
    ed. Test Anxiety: Theory, Research, &
      Applications. L Erlbaum Assocs.
Sarason, Seymour B. *see* Sarason, Seymour Bernard.
Sarason, Seymour Bernard, 1919-
  xSarason, Seymour B.
    Clinical Interaction with Special Reference to
      the Rorschach. Greenwood.
    The Creation of Settings & the Future
      Societies. Jossey-Bass.
    Educational Handicap, Public Policy, & Social
      History: A Broadened Perspective on Mental
      Retardation. Free Pr.
    Work, Aging, & Social Change: Professionals &
      the One Life-One Career Imperative. Free Pr.
Saraydarian, H.
  xSaraydarian, Haroutiun.
    Cosmos in Man. Aqua Educ.
Saraydarian, Haroutiun. *see* Saraydarian, H.
Sarbaugh, L. E.
  xSarbaugh, L. E.
    Intercultural Communication. Hayden.
  xSarbaugh, Larry E.
    Teaching Speech Communication. Merrill.
Sarbaugh, Larry E. *see* Sarbaugh, L. E.
Sarbin, Theodore R.
  xAdelson, Daniel.

    ed. Challenges to the Criminal Justice System:
      The Perspectives of Community Psychology.
      Human Sci Pr.
  xSarbin, Theodore R.
    Hypnosis: A Social Psychological Analysis of
      Influence Communication. Irvington.
Sard, Arthur.
  xSard, Arthur.
    Linear Approximation. Am Math.
Sard, R. D., 1915-
  xSard, Robert D.
    Relativistic Mechanics: Special Relativity &
      Classical Particle Dynamics.
      Benjamin-Cummings.
Sard, Robert D. *see* Sard, R. D.
Sarda y Salvany, Don F. *see* Sarda y Salvany, Felix.
Sarda y Salvany, Felix.
  xSarda y Salvany, Don F.
    What Is Liberalism?. TAN Bks Pubs.
  xSarda y Salvany, Felix.
    What Is Liberalism?. Tan Bks Pubs.
Sardell, William.
  xSardell, William.
    Encyclopedia of Corporate Meetings, Minutes
      & Resolutions. P-H.
Sareil, Jean.
  xSareil, Jean.
    Au Jour le Jour: A French Review. P-H.
Saretsky, Lorelle.
  xSaretsky, Lorelle.
    ed. Integrating Ego Psychology & Object
      Relations Theory: Psychoanalytic
      Perspectives on Psychopathology.
      Kendall-Hunt.
Saretsky, Ted, 1932-
  xSaretsky, Theodore.
    Active Techniques & Group Psychotherapy.
      Aronson.
Saretsky, Theodore. *see* Saretsky, Ted.
Sarett, Morton R.
  xSarett, Morton R.
    The Jewelry in Your Life. Nelson-Hall.
Sarfatti, Magali.
  xSarfatti, Magali.
    Spanish Bureaucratic-Patrimonialism in
      America. U of Cal Intl St.
Sarff, Laura.
  xSarff, Laura.
    Symmography: Linear Thread Design. Davis
      Mass.
Sargant, William. *see* Sargant, William Walters.
Sargant, William L. *see* Sargant, William Lucas.
Sargant, William Lucas, 1809-1889
  xSargant, William L.
    Economy of the Labouring Classes. Kelley.
Sargant, William Walters.
  xSargant, William.
    ed. Introduction to Physical Methods of
      Treatment in Psychiatry. Aronson.
Sargeant, J A, 1903-
  xSargeant, J. A.
    Sumo: The Sport & the Tradition. C E Tuttle.
Sargeant, Winthrop, 1903-
  xSargeant, Winthrop.
    Listening to Music. Greenwood.
Sargeaunt, George M. *see* Sargeaunt, George Montague.
Sargeaunt, George Montague, d. 1934
  xSargeaunt, George M.
    Classical Studies. Kennikat.
Sargent, Arthur J. *see* Sargent, Arthur John.
Sargent, Arthur John, 1871-1947
  xSargent, Arthur J.
    Economic Policy of Colbert. B Franklin.
Sargent, Charles S., 1936-
  xSargent, Charles S.
    The Spatial Evolution of Greater Buenos Aires,
      Argentina, 1870-1930. ASU Lat Am St.
Sargent, Daniel, 1890-
  xSargent, Daniel.

    Thomas More. Arno.
Sargent, David R.
  xSargent, David R.
    Stock Market Profits & Higher Income for
      You. S&S.
Sargent, Eileen E.
  xSargent, Eileen E.
    How to Read a Book. Intl Reading.
Sargent, Epes, 1813-1880
  xSargent, Epes.
    Peculiar: A Tale of the Great Transition. Arno.
Sargent, Fitzwilliam, 1820-1889
  xSargent, Fitzwilliam.
    England, the United States & the Southern
      Confederacy. Negro U Pr.
Sargent, Helen D. *see* Sargent, Helen Durham.
Sargent, Helen Durham.
  xSargent, Helen D.
    Prediction in Psychotherapy Research: A
      Method for the Transformation of Clinical
      Judgments into Testable Hypotheses. Intl
      Univs Pr.
Sargent, J. *see* Sargent, John.
Sargent, John, Sir, 1888-
  xSargent, J.
    Society, Schools & Progress in India.
      Pergamon.
Sargent, Lyman T. *see* Sargent, Lyman Tower.
Sargent, Lyman Tower, 1940-
  xSargent, Lyman T.
    Contemporary Political Ideologies: A
      Comparative Analysis. Dorsey.
Sargent, Mary G. *see* Sargent, Mary Gay.
Sargent, Mary Gay.
  xSargent, Mary G.
    The Complete Pembroke Welsh Corgi. Howell
      Bk.
Sargent, Pamela.
  xSargent, Pamela.
    ed. More Women of Wonder: Science Fiction
      Novelettes by Women About Women.
      Random.
    The Sudden Star. Fawcett.
Sargent, Patricia.
  xSargent, Patricia.
    Mortal Encounter. Avon.
Sargent, Robert L.
  xSargent, Robert L.
    Automobile Sheet Metal Repair. Chilton.
Sargent, Sarah.
  xSargent, Sarah.
    Edward Troy & the Witch Cat. Follett.
Sargent, Theodore D., 1936-
  xSargent, Theodore D.
    Legion of Night: The Underwing Moths. U of
      Mass Pr.
Sargent, Thomas. *see* Sargent, Thomas J.
Sargent, Thomas J.
  xSargent, Thomas.
    Macroeconomic Theory. Acad Pr.
Sargent, Walter, 1868-
  xSargent, Walter.
    Enjoyment & Use of Color. Dover.
    Enjoyment & Use of Color. Peter Smith.
Sargent, Winthrop, 1825-1870
  xSargent, Winthrop.
    The Loyalist Poetry of the Revolution.
      Longwood Pr.
Sargious, Michael. *see* Sargious, Michel.
Sargious, Michel.
  xSargious, Michael.
    Pavements & Surfacings for Highways &
      Airports. Halsted Pr.
Sarin, L. N.
  xSarin, L. N.
    Indira Gandhi: A Political Biography. Intl
      Pubns Serv.
Sarin, Prem S.
  xSarin, Prem S.

ed. Inhibitors of DNA & RNA Polymerases.
Pergamon.
Sario, L. *see* Sario, Leo.
Sario, Leo.
xSario, L.
Capacity Functions. Springer-Verlag.
Classification Theory of Riemann Surfaces.
Springer-Verlag.
Sariola, Mauri.
xSariola, Mauri.
The Torvick Affair. Popular Lib.
Sariola, Sakari.
xSariola, Sakari.
Power & Resistance: The Colonial Heritage in
Latin America. Cornell U Pr.
The Puerto Rican Dilemma. Kennikat.
Sarkadi, K. *see* Sarkadi, Karoly.
Sarkadi, Karoly.
xSarkadi, K.
Mathematical Methods of Statistical Quality
Control. Acad Pr.
Sarkanen, K. V.
xSarkanen, K. V.
Lignins: Occurrence, Formation, Structure &
Reactions. Wiley.
Sarkar, Jadunath, Sir, 1870-1958
xSarkar, Jadunath.
Fall of the Mughal Empire. AMS Pr.
Sarkar, N. K.
xSarkar, Nihar.
ed. Foreign Investment & Economic
Development in Asia. South Asia Bks.
Sarkar, Nihar. *see* Sarkar, N. K.
Sarkesian. *see* Sarkesian, Sam Charles.
Sarkesian, Sam C. *see* Sarkesian, Sam Charles.
Sarkesian, Sam Charles.
xSarkesian.
Revolutionary Guerrilla Warfare. McGraw.
xSarkesian, Sam C.
The Professional Army Officer in a Changing
Society. Nelson-Hall.
ed. Revolutionary Guerrilla Warfare. Precedent
Pub.
Sarkissian, Adele.
xSarkissian, Adele.
ed. Children's Authors & Illustrators: An Index
to Biographical Dictionaries. Gale.
Writers for Young Adults: Biographies Master
Index. Gale.
Sarma, Mulukutla S., 1938-
xSarma, Mulukutla S.
Synchronous Machines: Their Theory, Stability,
& Excitation Systems. Gordon.
Sarmiento de Gamboa, Pedro, 1532?-1608?
xSarmiento De Gamboa, Pedro.
Narratives of the Voyages of Pedro Sarmiento
De Gamboa to the Straits of Magellan. B
Franklin.
Sarnat, Harvey B.
xSarnat, Harvey B.
Evolution of the Nervous System. Oxford U
Pr.
Sarnat, Marshall.
xSarnat, Marshall S.
ed. International Finance & Trade. Ballinger
Pub.
Sarnat, Marshall S. *see* Sarnat, Marshall.
Sarner, Stanley F.
xSarner, Stanley R.
Propellant Chemistry. Van Nos Reinhold.
Sarner, Stanley R. *see* Sarner, Stanley F.
Sarnoff. *see* Sarnoff, Irving.
Sarnoff, Charles.
xSarnoff, Charles.
Latency. Aronson.
Sarnoff, Irving, 1922-
xSarnoff.
Society with Tears. Citadel Pr.
Sarnoff, Jane.
xSarnoff, Jane.

A Chess Book. Scribner.
The Code & Cipher Book. Scribner.
A Great Bicycle Book. Scribner.
I Know! a Riddle Book. Scribner.
If You Were Really Superstitious. Scribner.
Monster Riddle Book. Scribner.
Space: A Fact & Riddle Book. Scribner.
Take Warning!: A Book of Superstitions.
Scribner.
Saroff, Jerome R. *see* Saroff, Jerome Ronald.
Saroff, Jerome Ronald.
xSaroff, Jerome R.
Survey Manual for Comprehensive Urban
Planning: The Use of Opinion Surveys &
Sampling Techniques in the Planning Process.
U of Wash Pr.
Sarolea, Charles, 1870-1953
xSarolea, Charles.
The French Renascence. Dynamic Learn Cor
Corp.
French Renascence. Kennikat.
The French Renascence. Norwood Edns.
Sarotte, Georges Michel, 1939-
xSarotte, Georges-Michel.
Like a Brother, Like a Lover: Male
Homosexuality in the American Novel &
Theatre from Herman Melville to James
Baldwin. Doubleday.
Sarotte, Georges-Michel. *see* Sarotte, Georges Michel.
Saroyan, Aram.
xSaroyan, Aram.
Genesis Angels: The Saga of Lew Welch & the
Beat Generation. Morrow.
The Street: An Autobiographical Novel.
Bookstore Pr.
Saroyan, William, 1908-
xSaroyan, William.
Chance Meetings. Norton.
Inhale & Exhale. Arno.
Places Where I've Done Time. Dell.
Sarri, Domenico. *see* Sarri, Dommenico.
Sarri, Dommenico.
xSarri, Domenico.
Arsace. Garland Pub.
Sarris, Andrew.
xSarris, Andrew.
American Cinema: Directors & Directions:
1929-1968. Dutton.
The Primal Screen: Essays on Film & Related
Subjects. S&S.
Sarshik, Steve. *see* Sarshik, Steven.
Sarshik, Steven.
xSarshik, Steve.
Without a Lawyer. NAL.
Sartain, John, 1808-1897
xSartain, John.
Reminiscences of a Very Old Man. Arno.
Sarti, Dennis A.
xSarti, Dennis A.
Diagnostic Ultrasound: Text & Cases. G K
Hall.
Sarti, Roland, 1937-
xSarti, Roland.
Fascism & the Industrial Leadership in Italy,
1919-1940: A Study in the Expansion of
Private Power Under Fascism. U of Cal Pr.
Sartin, Janet.
xSartin, Janet.
Janet Sartin on Beautiful Skin. Doubleday.
Sarton, George, 1884-
xSarton, George.
Ancient Science & Modern Civilization. U of
Nebr Pr.

Sarton, Mary. *see* Sarton, May.
Sarton, May, 1912-
xSarton, Mary.
Journal of a Solitude. G K Hall.
xSarton, May.

Collected Poems: 1930-1973. Norton.
Faithful Are the Wounds. Norton.

The Fur Person. NAL.
The Fur Person. Norton.
The Fur Person. G K Hall.
The House by the Sea: A Journal. Norton.
I Knew a Phoenix: Sketches for an
Autobiography. Norton.
Journal of a Solitude. Norton.
Journal of a Solitude, 1970-1971. Norton.
Plant Dreaming Deep. Norton.
Punch's Secret. Har-Row.
A Shower of Summer Days. Norton.
A World of Light: Portraits & Celebrations.
Norton.

Sarton, May. *see* Sarton, Mary.
Sartorelli, A. C. *see* Sartorelli, Alan Clayton.
Sartorelli, Alan Clayton.
xSartorelli, A. C.
ed. Antineoplastic & Immunosuppressive
Agents. Springer-Verlag.
Sartori, Giovanni, 1924-
xSartori, Giovanni.
Democratic Theory. Greenwood.
Democratic Theory. Liberty Fund.
Parties & Party Systems: A Framework for
Analysis. Cambridge U Pr.
Sartorius, Ina. *see* Sartorius, Ina (Craig).
Sartorius, Ina (Craig), 1892-
xSartorius, Ina.
Generalization in Spelling: A Study of Various
Bases of Generalization in Teaching Spelling.
AMS Pr.
Sartre. *see* Sartre, Jean Paul.
Sartre, Jean Paul, 1905-
xSartre.
Psychology of Imagination. Citadel Pr.
xSartre, Jean Paul.
The Psychology of Imagination. Greenwood.
xSartre, Jean-Paul.
The Age of Reason. Random.
Anti-Semite & Jew. Schocken.
Existential Psychoanalysis. Regnery-Gateway.
Existentialism & Human Emotions. Citadel Pr.
Existentialism & Human Emotions. Philos Lib.
Existentialism & Humanism. Haskell.
The Ghost of Stalin. Braziller.
Literary Essays. Citadel Pr.
Literary Essays. Philos Lib.
Literature & Existentialism. Citadel Pr.
Nausea. Bentley.
Nausea. New Directions.
No Exit & Three Other Plays. Random.
Psychology of Imagination. Lyle Stuart.
Troubled Sleep. Random.
The Words. Fawcett.
Sartre, Jean-Paul. *see* Sartre, Jean Paul.
Sarvetnick, Harold A., 1929-
xSarvetnick, Harold A.
Plastisols & Organosols. Van Nos Reinhold.
Polyvinyl Chloride. Krieger.
Sarvig, Ole, 1921-
xSarvig, Ole.
Late Day. Curbstone.
Sarvis, Betty.
xSarvis, Betty.
The Abortion Controversy. Columbia U Pr.
SAS Institute.
xSAS Institute Inc.
SAS-GRAPH User's Guide, 1980 Edition. SAS
Inst.
ed. SAS Views: Statistics, 1980 Edition. SAS
Inst.
ed. Sas Views, 1980 Edition. SAS Inst.
SAS Institute Inc. *see* Sas Institute.
Sasamori, Junzo
xSasamori, Junzo.

This Is Kendo: The Art of Japanese Fencing. C
E Tuttle.

Sasek, Lawrence A.
xSasek, Lawrence A.
Literary Temper of the English Puritans.
Greenwood.

Sasek, M. see Sasek, Miroslav.

Sasek, Miroslav.
xSasek, M.
illus. This Is New York. Macmillan.
illus. This Is San Francisco. Macmillan.
illus. This Is Washington, D.C.. Macmillan.
xSasek, Miroslav.
illus. This Is Australia. Macmillan.
illus. This Is Cape Kennedy. Macmillan.
This Is Edinburgh. Macmillan.
This Is Greece. Macmillan.
illus. This Is Historic Britain. Macmillan.
This Is Hong Kong. Macmillan.
This Is Ireland. Macmillan.
This Is Israel. Macmillan.
This Is London. Macmillan.
illus. This Is New York. Macmillan.
This Is Rome. Macmillan.
illus. This Is San Francisco. Macmillan.
illus. This Is Texas. Macmillan.
This Is Venice. Macmillan.
illus. This Is Washington, D. C. Macmillan.

Saslow, Helen.
xSaslow, Helen.
Arctic Summer. Barlenmir.

Sasmor, Jeanette L. see Sasmor, Jeannette L.

Sasmor, Jeannette L.
xSasmor, Jeanette L.
Childbirth Education: A Nursing Perspective.
Wiley.

Saso, Michael R.
xSaso, Michael R.
Taoism & the Rite of Cosmic Renewal. Wash
St U Pr.

Sass, C. Joseph.
xSass, C. Joseph.
COBOL Programming & Applications. Allyn.

Sass, Lorna J.
xSass, Lorna J.
Dinner with Tom Jones: Eighteenth-Century
Cookery Adapted for the Modern Kitchen.
Metro Mus Art.

Sasse, Christoph, 1930-
xSasse, Christoph.
Decision Making in the European Community.
Praeger.

Sasse, H. C.
xSasse, H. C.
Compiled by Cassell's Concise German-English
English-German Dictionary. Macmillan.

Sassouni, Viken.
xSassouni, Viken.
Diagnosis & Treatment of Dento-Facial
Abnormalities. C C Thomas.
Orthodontics in Dental Practice. Mosby.

Sastri, P. S.
xSastri, P. S.
Indian Idealism: Epistemology & Ontology.
South Asia Bks.

Satake, I. see Satake, Ichir O.

Satake, Ichir O.
xSatake, I.
Classification Theory of Semi-Simple Algebraic
Groups. Dekker.
Linear Algebra. Dekker.

Sataloff, Joseph.
xSataloff, Joseph.
Hearing Loss. Lippincott.

Satchidananda, Swami. see Satchidananda.

**Satellite Symposium on the Clinical Pharmacology of
Serotonin, Helsinki, 1975.**
xSymposium on the Clinical Pharmacology of
Serotonin, Satellite, Helsinki, July 1975.

Clinical Pharmacology of Serotonin:
Proceedings. S Karger.

Satchidananda, Swami.
xSatchidananda, Swami.
Integral Yoga - Hatha. HR&W.

Sathe, Vijay.
xSathe, Vijay.
Controllership in Divisionalized Firms:
Structure, Evaluation, & Development. Am
Mgmt.

Sather, Mike R.
xSather, Mike R.
Cancer Chemotherapeutic Agents: Handbook
of Clinical Data. G K Hall.

Sathre, Freda S.
xSathre, Freda S.
Let's Talk: An Introduction to Interpersonal
Communication. Scott F.

Satin, Mark. see Satin, Mark Ivor.

Satin, Mark Ivor, 1946-
xSatin, Mark.
New Age Politics: Healing Self & Society. Dell.

Satir, Virginia. see Satir, Virginia M.

Satir, Virginia M.
xSatir, Virginia.
Peoplemaking. Sci & Behavior.

Satkowski, Leon. see Satkowski, Leon George.

Satkowski, Leon George, 1947-
xSatkowski, Leon.
Studies on Vasari's Architecture. Garland Pub.

Sato, Gordon.
xSato, Gordon.
ed. Hormones & Cell Culture. Cold Spring
Harbor.

Sato, Shosuke, 1859-
xSato, Shosuke.
History of the Land Question in the United
States. AMS Pr.
History of the Land Question in the United
States. Johnson Repr.

Satow, Ernest M. see Satow, Ernest Mason.

Satow, Ernest Mason, Sir, 1843-1929
xSatow, Ernest M.
Diplomat in Japan. AMS Pr.

Satprakashananda, Swami.
xSatprakashananda, Swami.
The Goal & the Way: The Vedantic Approach
to Life's Problems. Vedanta Soc St Louis.
Hinduism & Christianity: Jesus Christ & His
Teachings in the Light of Vedanta. Vedanta
Soc St Louis.
Meditation: Its Process, Practice, &
Culmination. Vedanta Soc St Louis.
Swami Vivekananda's Contribution to the
Present Age. Vedanta Soc St Louis.

Satprakashananda, Swami. see Satprakashananda.

Satre, Elizabeth D. see Satre, Elizabeth Dahl.

Satre, Elizabeth Dahl.
xSatre, Elizabeth D.
The Story of Ellen: How Love Transforms a
Troubled Child. Augsburg.

Satterfield, Archie.
xSatterfield, Archie.
After the Gold Rush. Lippincott.
Alaska Bush Pilots in the Float Country.
Superior Pub.
Backroads of Washington. Rand.
Exploring the Yukon River. Mountaineers.
The Lewis & Clark Trail. Stackpole.
The Seattle Guidebook. Writing.

Satterlee, W. W.
xSatterlee, W. W.
Looking Backward & What I Saw. Arno.

Satterthwaite, Edwin H., 1943-
xSatterthwaite, Edwin H.
Source Language Debugging Tools. Garland
Pub.

Sattgast, Charles R. see Sattgast, Charles Richard.

Sattgast, Charles Richard, 1899-
xSattgast, Charles R.

The Administration of College & University
Endowments. AMS Pr.

Sattinger, D. H. see Sattinger, David H.

Sattinger, David H.
xSattinger, D. H.
Group Theoretic Methods in Bifurcation
Theory. Springer-Verlag.

Sattler, Helen R. see Sattler, Helen Roney.

Sattler, Helen Roney.
xSattler, Helen R.
The Eggless Cookbook. A S Barnes.
Nature's Weather Forecasters. Elsevier-Nelson.

Sattler, Henry V., 1917-
xSattler, Henry V.
Sex Is Alive & Well & Flourishing Among
Christians. Our Sunday Visitor.

Sattler, Jerome M.
xSattler, Jerome M.
Assessment of Children's Intelligence. HR&W.

Sattler, Rolf.
xSattler, Rolf.
Organogenesis of Flowers: Photographic
Text-Atlas. U of Toronto Pr.

Sattler, William M.
xSattler, William M.
Discussion & Conference. P-H.

Saturday Review.
xSaturday Review.
Writing for Love or Money. Arno.

Satyanarayana. see Satyanarayana, M.

Satyanarayana, M., 1928-
xSatyanarayana.
Positively Ordered Semi Groups. Dekker.

Satyaprakash.
xSatyaprakash.
ed. Gujarat: A Select Bibliography. South Asia
Bks.

Satz, Mario.
xSatz, Mario.
Sol. Doubleday.

Satz, Ronald N.
xSatz, Ronald N.
American Indian Policy in the Jacksonian Era.
U of Nebr Pr.

Sauber, S. Richard.
xSauber, S. Richard.
Preventive Educational Intervention for Mental
Health. Ballinger Pub.

Sauber, William J.
xSauber, William J.
The Fourth Kingdom. Aquari Corp.

Saucier, Walter J.
xSaucier, Walter J.
Principles of Meteorological Analysis. U of
Chicago Pr.

Saucier, Weems A. see Saucier, Weems Aurelius.

Saucier, Weems Aurelius.
xSaucier, Weems A.
Toward Humanistic Teaching in High School.
Heath.

Saucy, Robert L.
xSaucy, Robert L.
The Bible: Breathed from God. Victor Bks.
The Church in God's Program. Moody.

Sauer, Carl O. see Sauer, Carl Ortwin.

Sauer, Carl Ortwin, 1889-
xSauer, Carl O.
Colima of New Spain in the Sixteenth Century.
Greenwood.
The Early Spanish Main. U of Cal Pr.
Geography of the Ozark Highland of Missouri.
AMS Pr.
Geography of the Ozark Highland of Missouri.
Greenwood.
Northern Mists. Turtle Isl Foun.
Northern Mists. U of Cal Pr.
The Road to Cibola. AMS Pr.

Sauer, Gordon C.
xSauer, Gordon C.

Manual of Skin Diseases. Lippincott.

Sauer, Herbert I.
xSauer, Herbert I.
Geographic Patterns in the Risk of Dying &
Associated Factors United States, 1968-1972.
Natl Ctr Health Stats.

Sauer, Jonathan D.
xSauer, Jonathan D.
Coastal Plant Geography of Mauritius. La State
U Pr.
Geographic Reconnaissance of Seashore
Vegetation Along the Mexican Gulf Coast.
La State U Pr.

Sauerbier, Charles L.
xSauerbier, Charles L.
Marine Cargo Operations. Wiley.

Saul, Frank P.
xSaul, Frank P.
The Human Skeletal Remains of Altar De
Sacrificios: An Osteobiographic Analysis.
Peabody Harvard.

Saul, George B. see Saul, George Brandon.

Saul, George Brandon, 1901-
xSaul, George B.
Daniel Corkery. Bucknell U Pr.

Saul, John.
xSaul, John.
Punish the Sinners. Dell.

Saul, Leon J. see Saul, Leon Joseph.

Saul, Leon Joseph, 1901-
xSaul, Leon J.
The Childhood Emotional Pattern & Corey
Jones: A Psychoanalytic Biography. Van Nos
Reinhold.
The Childhood Emotional Pattern & Human
Hostility. Van Nos Reinhold.
The Childhood Emotional Pattern & Maturity.
Van Nos Reinhold.
The Childhood Emotional Pattern &
Psychodynamic Therapy. Van Nos Reinhold.
The Childhood Emotional Pattern in Marriage.
Van Nos Reinhold.
The Childhood Emotional Pattern: The Key to
Personality, Its Disorders & Therapy. Van
Nos Reinhold.

Saul, LouElla R. see Saul, Louella Rankin.

Saul, Louella Rankin.
xSaul, LouElla R.
Evidence for the Origin of the Mactridae
(Bivalvia) in the Cretaceous. U of Cal Pr.

Saul, Martha R. see Saul, Martha Roper.

Saul, Martha Roper.
xSaul, Martha R.
God Sees a Beautiful You. Broadman.

Saulaitis, Marija.
xSaulaitis, Marija.
And You. Manyland.

Saulez, William H. see Saulez, William Hely.

Saulez, William Hely.
xSaulez, William H.
The Romance of the Hebrew Language.
Folcroft.

Saulnier, Raymond J. see Saulnier, Raymond Joseph.

Saulnier, Raymond Joseph, 1908-
xSaulnier, Raymond J.
Strategy of Economic Policy. Fordham.

Saulson, Scott B.
xSaulson, Scott B.
Institutionalized Language Planning:
Documents & Analysis of the Revival of
Hebrew. Mouton.

Saum, Lewis O.
xSaum, Lewis O.
The Fur Trader & the Indian. U of Wash Pr.

Saunders, A. N. see Saunders, A. N. W.

Saunders, A. N. W.
xSaunders, A. N.
Greek Political Oratory. Penguin.

Saunders, Albert C. see Saunders, Albert C. W.

Saunders, Albert C. W.
xSaunders, Albert C.
Working with the Oscilloscope. TAB Bks.

Saunders, Beatrice.
xSaunders, Beatrice.
Portraits of Genius. Transatlantic.

Saunders, Blanche.
xSaunders, Blanche.
The Complete Book of Dog Obedience. Howell
Bk.
How to Trim, Groom & Show Your Dog.
Howell Bk.

Saunders, Bruce T.
xSaunders, Bruce T.
ed. Approaches with Emotionally Disturbed
Children. Exposition.

Saunders, C. T. see Saunders, Christopher Thomas.

Saunders, Christopher. see Saunders, Christopher C.

Saunders, Christopher C.
xSaunders, Christopher.
ed. Black Leaders in Southern African History.
Heinemann Ed.

Saunders, Christopher Thomas.
xSaunders, C. T.
ed. Industrial Policies & Technology Transfers
Between East & West. Springer-Verlag.

Saunders, D. S. see Saunders, David Stanley.

Saunders, David C. see Saunders, David Stanley.

Saunders, David Stanley, 1935-
xSaunders, D. S.
Insect Clocks. Pergamon.
xSaunders, David C.
An Introduction to Biological Rhythms.
Halsted Pr.

Saunders, E. Dale. see Saunders, Ernest Dale.

Saunders, Edith.
xSaunders, Edith
Hundred Days. Norton.

Saunders, Ernest Dale.
xSaunders, E. Dale.
Mudra: A Study of Symbolic Gestures in
Japanese Buddhist Sculpture. Princeton U Pr.

Saunders, Franklin F. see Saunders, Franklin Fay.

Saunders, Franklin Fay.
xSaunders, Franklin F.
Attitudes Toward Handicapped Persons: A
Study of the Differential Effects of Fine
Variables. R & E Res Assoc.

Saunders, Frederick, 1807-1902
xSaunders, Frederick.
The Story of Some Famous Books. Arno.
The Story of Some Famous Books. R West.

Saunders, George H., 1940-
xSaunders, George H.
Dynamics of Helicopter Flight. Wiley.

Saunders, Henry S. see Saunders, Henry Scholey.

Saunders, Henry Scholey, 1864-
xSaunders, Henry S.
ed. Parodies on Walt Whitman. AMS Pr.

Saunders, Hilary Aidan St. George, 1898-1951
xSaunders, Hillary S.
Per Ardua: The Rise of British Air Power
1911-1939. Arno.

Saunders, Hillary S. see Saunders, Hilary Aidan St.
George.

Saunders, Hilliard.
xSaunders, Hilliard.
The Complete Travel Guide to China. Hwong
Pub.

Saunders, J. H. see Saunders, James H.

Saunders, J. J. see Saunders, John Joseph.

Saunders, James H.
xSaunders, J. H.
Careers in Industrial Research & Development.
Dekker.

Saunders, Jason L. see Saunders, Jason Lewis.

Saunders, Jason Lewis.
xSaunders, Jason L.

ed. Greek & Roman Philosophy After
Aristotle. Free Pr.

Saunders, Jeraldine.
xSaunders, Jeraldine.
The Complete Guide to a Successful Cruise.
Contemp Bks.

Saunders, John Joseph, 1910-
xSaunders, J. J.
A History of Medieval Islam. Routledge &
Kegan.
The History of the Mongol Conquests.
Routledge & Kegan.

Saunders, John T. see Saunders, John Turk.

Saunders, John Turk.
xSaunders, John T.
Private-Language Problem: A Philosophical
Dialogue. Phila Bk Co.

Saunders, John W. see Saunders, John Warren.

Saunders, John Warren, 1919-
xSaunders, John W.
Patterns & Principles of Animal Development.
Macmillan.

Saunders, L. Z. see Saunders, Leon Z.

Saunders, Landon B.
xSaunders, Landon B.
The Power of Receiving. Bibl Res Pr.

Saunders, Laura.
xSaunders, Laura.
Strange Exile. Bouregy.

Saunders, Leon Z.
xSaunders, L. Z.
Ophthalmic Pathology of Animals: An Atlas &
Reference Book. S Karger.

Saunders, Michael.
xSaunders, Michael.
Developments in English Teaching.
Humanities.

Saunders, O. Elfrida
xSaunders, O. Elfrida.
History of English Art in the Middle Ages.
Arno.

Saunders, P. F. see Saunders, Philip Frederick.

Saunders, Philip Frederick.
xSaunders, P. F.
Bridge with a Perfect Partner. Barclay Bridge.

Saunders, Richard, 1947-
xSaunders, Richard.
Collecting & Restoring Wicker Furniture.
Crown.
The Railroad Mergers & the Coming of
Conrail. Greenwood.

Saunders, Rubie.
xSaunders, Rubie.
Baby Sitting: A Concise Guide. Archway.
Baby-Sitting: A Concise Guide. PB.
Calling All Girls Party Book. Schol Bk Serv.
The Franklin Watts Concise Guide to
Babysitting. Watts.
The Franklin Watts Concise Guide to Good
Grooming for Boys. Watts.
Quick & Easy House Keeping!. Watts.
xSaunders, Rudie.
Good Grooming for Girls. Watts.

Saunders, Rudie. see Saunders, Rubie.

Saunders, Susan.
xSaunders, Susan.
Wale's Tale. Viking Pr.

Saunders, W. L. see Saunders, Wilfred Leonard.

Saunders, Wilfred Leonard.
xSaunders, W. L.
ed. British Librarianship Today. Gaylord Prof
Pubns.

Saunders, William H.
xSaunders, William H.
Atlas of Ear Surgery. Mosby.

Sauneron, Serge.
xSauneron, Serge.
The Priests of Ancient Egypt. Grove.

Saurat, Denis, 1890-1958
xSaurat, Denis.

Gods of the People. Folcroft.
Modern French Literature 1870-1940.
Kennikat.

Sauser, Jean.
　xSauser, Jean.
　　Racquetball Strategy. Contemp Bks.
　　Teaching Your Child Racquetball. Contemp
　　　Bks.

Sauvageau, Juan.
　xSauvageau, Juan.
　　Stories That Must Not Die. Oasis Pr.
　　Stories That Must Not Die. Oasis Pr.
Sauvain, Walter H. see Sauvain, Walter Howard.
Sauvain, Walter Howard, 1904-
　xSauvain, Walter H.
　　A Study of the Opinions of Certain
　　　Professional & Non-Professional Groups
　　　Regarding Homogeneous or Ability
　　　Grouping. AMS Pr.
Sauve, Mary J. see Sauve, Mary Jane.
Sauve, Mary Jane.
　xSauve, Mary J.
　　Concepts & Skills in Physical Assessment.
　　　Saunders.
Sauver, Dennis St. see St. Sauver, Dennis.
Sava, Samuel G. see Sava, Samuel George.
Sava, Samuel George, 1931-
　xSava, Samuel G.
　　Learning Through Discovery for Young
　　　Children. McGraw.
Savage, Audrey.
　xSavage, Audrey.
　　Straight Talk. Stanwix.
Savage, C. Wade.
　xSavage, C. Wade.
　　The Measurement of Sensation: A Critique of
　　　Perceptual Psychophysics. U of Cal Pr.
Savage, D. see Savage, Derek S.
Savage, D. S. see Savage, Derek S.
Savage, Dean.
　xSavage, Dean.
　　Founders, Heirs, & Managers: French
　　　Industrial Leadership in Transition. Sage.
Savage, Derek S.
　xSavage, D.
　　The Personal Principle: Studies in Modern
　　　Poetry. Gordon Pr.
　xSavage, D. S.
　　Withered Branch: Six Studies in the Modern
　　　Novel. Folcroft.
　xSavage, Derek S.
　　The Personal Principle: Studies in Modern
　　　Poetry. Arden Lib.
　　Withered Branch: Six Studies in the Modern
　　　Novel. Core Collection.
Savage, Donald T.
　xSavage, Donald T.
　　Money & Banking. Wiley.
Savage, Elizabeth.
　xSavage, Elizabeth.
　　The Girls from the Five Great Valleys. G K
　　　Hall.
　　The Girls from the Five Great Valleys. Little.
　　Last Night at the Ritz. Popular Lib.
　　Willow Wood. Berkley Pub.
　　Willowwood. G K Hall.
Savage, Ernest A. see Savage, Ernest Albert.
Savage, Ernest Albert, 1877-1966
　xSavage, Ernest A.
　　Story of Libraries & Book Collecting. B
　　　Franklin.
　　Story of Libraries & Book Collecting. R West.
Savage, Frederick G.
　xSavage, Frederick G.
　　The Flora & Folklore of Shakespeare. AMS Pr.
Savage, George, 1909-
　xSavage, George.
　　Antique Collector's Handbook. Intl Pubns
　　　Serv.
Savage, J. E. see Savage, John E.

Savage, Jessie D.
　xSavage, Jessie D.
　　Professional Furniture Refinishing for the
　　　Amateur. Arco.
　　Professional Furniture Refinishing for the
　　　Amateur. Har-Row.
Savage, John E., 1939-
　xSavage, J. E.
　　The Complexity of Computing. Wiley.
Savage, John F.
　xSavage, John F.
　　Teaching Reading to Children with Special
　　　Needs. Allyn.
Savage, Leonard J.
　xSavage, Leonard J.
　　The Foundations of Statistics. Dover.
Savage, Marion D. see Savage, Marion Dutton.
Savage, Marion Dutton, 1888-
　xSavage, Marion D.
　　Industrial Unionism in America. Arno.
Savage, Mary.
　xSavage, Mary.
　　Addicted to Suicide: A Woman Struggling to
　　　Live. Schenkman.
Savage, Mildred. see Savage, Mildred (Spitz).
Savage, Mildred (Spitz), 1919-
　xSavage, Mildred.
　　Great Fall. S&S.
Savage, Thomas.
　xSavage, Thomas.
　　I Heard My Sister Speak My Name. G K Hall.
　　I Heard My Sister Speak My Name. Little.
Savage, Thomas G.
　xSavage, Thomas G.
　　And Now a Word from Our Creator. Loyola.
Savage, W. see Savage, William.
Savage, William, 1770-1843
　xSavage, W.
　　A Dictionary of the Art of Printing. Intl Pubns
　　　Serv.
　xSavage, William.
　　Dictionary of the Art of Printing. B Franklin.
Savage, William S. see Savage, William Sherman.
Savage, William Sherman.
　xSavage, William S.
　　Controversy Over the Distribution of Abolition
　　　Literature 1830-1860. Greenwood.
Savage, William W.
　xSavage, William W.
　　The Cherokee Strip Live Stock Association:
　　　Federal Regulation & the Cattleman's Last
　　　Frontier. U of Mo Pr.
　　The Cowboy Hero: His Image in American
　　　History & Culture. U of Okla Pr.
　　ed. Indian Life: Transforming an American
　　　Myth. U of Okla Pr.
Savala, Refugio.
　xSavala, Refugio.
　　The Autobiography of a Yaqui Poet. U of Ariz
　　　Pr.
Savannah Unit, Georgia Writers' Project, Work Projects.
　see Writers' Program. Georgia.
Savant, C. J.
　xSavant, C. J.
　　Control System Design. McGraw.
Savarese, Julia.
　xSavarese, Julia.
　　Final Proof. Norton.
Savarin, Julian J. see Savarin, Julian Jay.
Savarin, Julian Jay.
　xSavarin, Julian J.
　　The Archives of Haven. St Martin.
　　Beyond the Outer Mirr. St Martin.
Savas, E. S.
　xSavas, E. S.
　　The Organization & Efficiency of Solid Waste
　　　Collection. Lexington Bks.
Savasini, Jose A. see Savasini, Jose Augusto Arantes.
Savasini, Jose Augusto Arantes.
　xSavasini, Jose A.

Export Promotion: The Case of Brazil. Praeger.
Savchenko, Vladimir. see Savchenko, Vladimir Ivanovich.
Savchenko, Vladimir Ivanovich, 1933-
　xSavchenko, Vladimir.
　　Self-Discovery. Macmillan.
　　Self-Discovery. Macmillan.
Savell, Isabelle K. see Savell, Isabelle Keating.
Savell, Isabelle Keating, 1905-
　xSavell, Isabelle K.
　　Ladies Lib: How Rockland Women Got the
　　　Vote. Rockland County Hist.
Savelle, Mac. see Savelle, Max.
Savelle, Max.
　xSavelle, Mac.
　　History of Colonial America. HR&W.
Saveskie, Peter N.
　xSaveskie, Peter N.
　　Radio Propagation Handbook. TAB Bks.
Saveson, John E.
　xSaveson, John E.
　　Conrad, the Later Moralist. Humanities.
Saveth, Edward N. see Saveth, Edward Norman.
Saveth, Edward Norman, 1915-
　xSaveth, Edward N.
　　American History & the Social Sciences. Free
　　　Pr.
Savicevic, Dusan. see Savicevic, Dusan M.
Savicevic, Dusan M.
　xSavicevic, Dusan.
　　The System of Adult Education in Yugoslavia.
　　　Syracuse U Cont Ed.
Savigny, Friedrich K. Von. see Savigny, Friedrich Karl
　von.
Savigny, Friedrich Karl von, 1779-1861
　xSavigny, Friedrich K. Von.
　　Von Savigny's Treatise on Possession: Or the
　　　Jus Possessionis of the Civil Law. Hyperion
　　　Conn.
Savile, A. H.
　xSavile, A. H.
　　Extension in Rural Communities: A Manual for
　　　Agricultural & Home Extension Workers.
　　　Oxford U Pr.
Saville, Florence R. see Saville, Florence Rogers.
Saville, Florence Rogers.
　xSaville, Florence R.
　　Real Food for Your Baby. S&S.
Saville, Lloyd B. see Saville, Lloyd Blackstone.
Saville, Lloyd Blackstone, 1913-
　xSaville, Lloyd B.
　　Regional Economic Development in Italy.
　　　Duke.
Saville-Troike, Muriel.
　xSaville-Troike, Muriel.
　　A Guide to Culture in the Classroom. Natl
　　　Clearinghse Bilingual Ed.
Savin, Maynard, 1921-
　xSavin, Maynard.
　　Thomas William Robertson: His Plays &
　　　Stagecraft. Brown U Pr.
Savinkov, B. V. see Savinkov, Boris Viktorovich.
Savinkov, Boris Viktorovich, 1879-1925
　xSavinkov, B. V.
　　Memoirs of a Terrorist. Kraus Repr.
Savinskii, Igor D. see Savinskii, Igor' Dmitrievich.
Savinskii, Igor' Dmitrievich.
　xSavinskii, Igor D.
　　Probability Tables for Locating Elliptical
　　　Underground Masses with a Rectangular
　　　Grid. IFI Plenum.
Savitch, H. V.
　xSavitch, H. V.
　　Urban Policy & the Exterior City: Federal,
　　　State & Corporate Policies. Pergamon.
Savitskii, E. M. see Savitskii, Evgenii Mikhailovich.
Savitskii, Evgenii Mikhailovich.
　xSavitskii, E. M.
　　Superconducting Materials. Plenum Pub.
Savitt, Sam.
　xSavitt, Sam.

Around the World with Horses. Dial.

Savitt, Todd L., 1943-
xSavitt, Todd L.
Medicine & Slavery: The Diseases & Health Care of Blacks in Antebellum Virginia. U of Ill Pr.

Savitz, Harriet M. *see* Savitz, Harriet May.

Savitz, Harriet May.
xSavitz, Harriet M.
The Lionhearted. NAL.
The Lionhearted. John Day.
On the Move. Avon.
Wheelchair Champions: A History of Wheelchair Sports. John Day.

Savitz, Leonard D.
xSavitz, Leonard D.
Crime in Society. Wiley.
Delinquency & Migration. R & E Res Assoc.
Dilemmas in Criminology. McGraw.

Savonarola, Gerolamo. *see* Savonarola, Girolamo Maria Francesco Matteo.

Savonarola, Girolamo Maria Francesco Matteo.
xSavonarola, Gerolamo.
Liberty & Tyranny in the Government of Men. Am Classical Coll Pr.

Savory, Jerold.
xSavory, Jerold J.
Caged Light. Judson.
The Vanity Fair Gallery: A Collector's Guide to the Caricatures. A S Barnes.
The Vanity Fair Gallery: A Collector's Guide to the Caricatures. Art Alliance.

Savory, Jerold J. *see* Savory, Jerold.

Savory, Teo.
xSavory, Teo.
A Childhood. Unicorn Pr.
A Childhood. G K Hall.
A Clutch of Fables. Unicorn Pr.
Stonecrop: The Country I Remember. Unicorn Pr.

Savoy, Gene.
xSavoy, Gene.
Project X: The Search for the Secrets of Immortality. Bobbs.

Sawada, Hideo.
xSawada, Hideo.
Thermodynamics of Polymerization. Dekker.

Saward, E. W. *see* Saward, Ernest W.

Saward, Ernest W.
xSaward, E. W.
ed. The Regionalization of Personal Health Services. N Watson.

Sawer, Geoffrey.
xSawer, Geoffrey.
Australian Federalism in the Courts. Intl Schol Bk Serv.
Australian Government Today. Intl Schol Bk Serv.
Federation Under Strain: Australia 1972-1975. Intl Schol Bk Serv.
Guide to Australian Law for Journalists, Authors, Printers & Publishers. Intl Schol Bk Serv.
Law in Society. Oxford U Pr.

Sawhill, John C.
xSawhill, John C.
Energy Conservation & Public Policy. P-H.

Sawicki, Stanislaw J., 1919-
xSawicki, Stanislaw J.
Soviet Land & Housing Law: A Historical & Comparative Study. Praeger.

Sawin, Margaret M.
xSawin, Margaret M.
Family Enrichment with Family Clusters. Judson.

Sawmill Clinic, 1st, Portland, Feb. 1973. *see* Sawmill Clinic, 1st, Portland, Oregon, 1973.

Sawmill Clinic, 1st, Portland, Oregon, 1973.
xSawmill Clinic, 1st, Portland, Feb. 1973.

Modern Sawmill Techniques Vol. 1: Proceedings. Miller Freeman.

Sawmill and Plywood Clinic Business Management Workshop, Portland, Oregon, 1976.
xMiller Freeman Publications, Inc.
Business Management for Sawmills & Plywood Mills. Miller Freeman.

Sawyer, Charles H.
xSawyer, Charles H.
ed. Steroid Hormones & Brain Function. U of Cal Pr.

Sawyer, Donald J.
xSawyer, Donald J.
They Came to Sacandaga: The Story of Godfrey Shew: Fish House Patriot. Prospect.

Sawyer, Donald T.
xSawyer, Donald T.
Experimental Electrochemistry for Chemists. Wiley.

Sawyer, George. *see* Sawyer, George C.

Sawyer, George C.
xSawyer, George.
Business & Society: Managing Corporate Social Impact. HM.

Sawyer, George S.
xSawyer, George S.
Southern Institutes: Or, an Inquiry into the Origin & Early Prevalence of Slavery & the Slave Trade. Arno.
Southern Institutes: Or, an Inquiry into the Origin & Early Prevalence of Slavery & the Slave Trade. Negro U Pr.

Sawyer, J. O. *see* Sawyer, Jesse O.

Sawyer, Jesse.
xSawyer, Jesse.
Studies in American Indian Languages. U of Cal Pr.

Sawyer, Jesse O.
xSawyer, J. O.
English-Wappo Vocabulary. U of Cal Pr.

Sawyer, John F. *see* Sawyer, John F. A.

Sawyer, John F. A.
xSawyer, John F.
A Modern Introduction to Biblical Hebrew. Routledge & Kegan.

Sawyer, Malcolm C.
xSawyer, Malcolm C.
Theories of the Firm. St Martin.

Sawyer, P. H.
xSawyer, P. H.
From Roman Britain to Norman England. St Martin.
ed. Medieval Settlement: Continuity & Change. Crane-Russak Co.

Sawyer, Paul.
xSawyer, Paul.
There Once Was a Book of Limericks. Raintree Pubs.

Sawyer, Philip L.
xSawyer, Philip L.
Sudden Insurrection: Twelve Short Stories. P Sawyer.

Sawyer, Ruth, 1880-
xSawyer, Ruth.
Journey Cake, Ho!. Penguin.
Journey Cake, Ho!. Viking Pr.

Sawyer, W. W. *see* Sawyer, Walter Warwick.

Sawyer, Walter Warwick, 1911-
xSawyer, W. W.
A Concrete Approach to Abstract Algebra. Dover.
A First Look at Numerical Functional Analysis. Oxford U Pr.

Sax, Gilbert.
xSax, Gilbert.

Foundations of Educational Research. P-H.
Principles of Educational & Psychological Measurement & Evaluation. Wadsworth Pub.
Principles of Educational Measurement & Evaluation. Wadsworth Pub.

Sax, N. Irving. *see* Sax, Newton Irving.

Sax, Newton Irving.
xSax, N. Irving.
Dangerous Properties of Industrial Materials. Van Nos Reinhold.
Industrial Pollution. Van Nos Reinhold.

Sax, Saville.
xSax, Saville.
Reality Games. Popular Lib.

Saxe, R. F. *see* Saxe, Raymond Frederick.

Saxe, Raymond Frederick.
xSaxe, R. F.
High Speed Photography. Focal Pr.

Saxe, Richard. *see* Saxe, Richard W.

Saxe, Richard W.
xSaxe, Richard.
Opening the Schools: Alternative Ways of Learning. McCutchan.

Saxelby, F. Outwin.
xSaxelby, F. Outwin.
A Thomas Hardy Dictionary: The Characters & Scenes of the Novels & Poems Alphabetically Arranged & Described. Greenwood.

Saxena, S. K. *see* Saxena, Surendra Kumar.

Saxena, Surendra Kumar.
xSaxena, S. K.
ed. Energetics of Geological Processes. Springer-Verlag.
Thermodynamics of Rock-Forming Crystalline Solutions. Springer-Verlag.

Saxman, Ethel J. *see* Saxman, Ethel Julia.

Saxman, Ethel Julia, 1890-
xSaxman, Ethel J.
Students' Use in Leisure Time of Activities Learned in Physical Education in State Teachers College. AMS Pr.

Saxon, Burt.
xSaxon, Burt.
Modern Human Sexuality. HM.

Saxon, Charles. *see* Saxon, Charles D.

Saxon, Charles D.
xSaxon, Charles.
One Man's Fancy. Dodd.

Saxon, James A.
xSaxon, James A.
Cobol: A Self-Instructional Manual. P-H.

Saxon, Lyle, 1891-1946
xSaxon, Lyle.
Children of Strangers. Mockingbird Bks.

Saxon, Sue V.
xSaxon, Sue V.
Physical Change & Aging: A Guide for the Helping Professions. Tiresias Pr.

Saxton, Alexander. *see* Saxton, Alexander Plaisted.

Saxton, Alexander Plaisted.
xSaxton, Alexander.
The Indispensable Enemy: Labor & the Anti-Chinese Movement in California. U of Cal Pr.

Saxton, Andrew, 1942-
xSaxton, Andrew.
The Universal Symbolism of Love in Dramatic Representative Forms. Gloucester Art.

Saxton, Dean.
xSaxton, Dean.
Legends & Lore of the Papago & Pima Indians. U of Ariz Pr.

Saxton, Dolores F.
xSaxton, Dolores F.

Evolutionary Survey of the Plant Kingdom.
Wadsworth Pub.

Scaglia, Gustina.
    xScaglia, Gustina.
        A Translation of Vitruvius & Copies of Late
        Antique Drawings in Buonaccorso Ghiberti's
        Zibaldone. Am Philos.

Scagnetti, Jack.
    xScagnetti, Jack.
        The Joy of Walking. Wilshire.
        The Laurel & Hardy Scrapbook. Jonathan
        David.
        The Life & Loves of Gable. Jonathan David.

Scalapino, Robert A.
    xScalapino, Robert A.
        Asia & the Road Ahead: Issues for the Major
        Powers. U of Cal Pr.
        The Foreign Policy of Modern Japan. U of Cal
        Pr.
        Parties & Politics in Contemporary Japan. U of
        Cal Pr.

Scales, John W.
    xScales, John W.
        ed. Air Quality Instrumentation. Instru Soc.

Scalia, Joni L. *see* Scalia, Joni Lynn.

Scalia, Joni Lynn.
    xScalia, Joni L.
        The Cutting Edge. McGraw.

Scalia, S. Eugene. *see* Scalia, Samuel Eugene.

Scalia, Samuel Eugene, 1903-
    xScalia, S. Eugene.
        Luigi Capuana & His Times. S F Vanni.

Scalingi, Paula.
    xScalingi, Paula.
        The European Parliament: The Three-Decade
        Search for a United Europe. Greenwood.

Scally, Robert J.
    xScally, Robert J.
        The Origins of the Lloyd George Coalition:
        The Politics of Social Imperialism,
        1900-1918. Princeton U Pr.

Scalzo, Frank.
    xScalzo, Frank.
        A Computer Approach to Introductory College
        Mathematics. Van Nos Reinhold.

Scalzo, Joe.
    xScalzo, Joe.
        The Bobby Unser Story. Doubleday.

Scammon, John H.
    xScammon, John H.
        Living with the Psalms. Judson.

Scammon, Richard M.
    xScammon, Richard M.
        The Real Majority. Coward.

Scanlan, Betsey.
    xScanlan, Betsey.
        ed. The Family Bible Study Book. Revell.

Scanlan, Burt. *see* Scanlan, Burt K.

Scanlan, Burt K.
    xScanlan, Burt.
        Management & Organizational Behavior.
        Wiley.

Scanlan, Michael.
    xScanlan, Michael.
        Inner Healing. Paulist Pr.

Scanlan, Tom, 1937-
    xScanlan, Tom.
        Family, Drama, & American Dreams.
        Greenwood.

Scanlon, A. Clark.
    xScanlon, Clark.
        Hope in the Ruins. Broadman.

Scanlon, Clark. *see* Scanlon, A. Clark.

Scanlon, David G.
    xScanlon, David G.
        ed. Problems & Prospects in International
        Education. Tchrs Coll.

Scanlon, John. *see* Scanlon, John Joseph.

Scanlon, John Joseph.
    xScanlon, John.

How to Plan a College Program for Older
People. Acad Educ Dev.
How to Plan a College Program for Older
People. Interbk Inc.

Scanlon, Robert. *see* Scanlon, Robert A.

Scanlon, Robert A.
    xScanlon, Robert.
        ed. Law Enforcement Bible. Follett.

Scannell, Vernon.
    xScannell, Vernon.
        Not Without Glory: Poets of the Second World
        War. Biblio Dist.

Scanzoni, John. *see* Scanzoni, John H.

Scanzoni, John H., 1935-
    xScanzoni, John.
        Love & Negotiate: Creative Conflict in
        Marriage. Word Bks.
        Opportunity & the Family. Free Pr.

Scanzoni, Letha.
    xScanzoni, Letha.
        All We're Meant to Be: A Biblical Approach
        to Women's Liberation. Word Bks.
        Men, Women, & Change: A Sociology of
        Marriage & Family. McGraw.

Scapa, Ted.
    xScapa, Ted.
        Venice in November. Barron.

Scarborough, Dorothy, 1878-1935
    xScarborough, Dorothy.
        Can't Get a Red Bird. AMS Pr.
        The Wind. U of Tex Pr.

Scarborough, James B. *see* Scarborough, James Blaine.

Scarborough, James Blaine, 1885-
    xScarborough, James B.
        Gyroscope, Theory & Applications. Krieger.

Scarborough, John.
    xScarborough, John.
        Facets of Hellenic Life. HM.

Scarborough, Ruth, 1904-
    xScarborough, Ruth.
        Opposition to Slavery in Georgia Prior to 1860.
        Negro U Pr.

Scarborough, William K. *see* Scarborough, William
Kauffman.

Scarborough, William Kauffman.
    xScarborough, William K.
        Overseer: Plantation Management in the Old
        South. La State U Pr.

Scarf, Herbert. *see* Scarf, Herbert E.

Scarf, Herbert E.
    xScarf, Herbert.
        The Computation of Economic Equilibria. Yale
        U Pr.

Scarf, Maggi.
    xScarf, Maggi.
        Meet Benjamin Franklin. Random.

Scarf, Maggie, 1932-
    xScarf, Maggie.
        Unfinished Business: Pressure Points in the
        Lives of Women. Doubleday.

Scarfe, Herbert.
    xScarfe, Herbert.
        Crafts in Polyester Resin. Watson-Guptill.

Scargill, D. I. *see* Scargill, David Ian.

Scargill, David Ian.
    xScargill, D. I.
        The Form of Cities. St Martin.

Scaringi, Louis T.
    xScaringi, Louis T.
        A Guide to Money for College. Anchorage.

Scarne, John.
    xScarne, John.
        Scarne on Dice. Crown.
        Scarne on Dice. Stackpole.
        Scarne's Guide to Modern Poker. S&S.

Scarpa, Antonio.
    xScarpa, Antonio.

ed. Calcium Transport & Cell Function. NY
Acad Sci.

Scarpa, Ioannis S.
    xScarpa, Ioannis S.
        ed. Sourcebook on Food & Nutrition. Marquis.

Scarpelli, Emile M.
    xScarpelli, Emile M.
        ed. Pulmonary Disease of the Fetus, Newborn
        & Child. Lea & Febiger.
        ed. Pulmonary Physiology of the Fetus,
        Newborn & Child. Lea & Febiger.

Scarpellini, Bruno.
    xScarpellini, Bruno.
        Proof Theory & Intuitionistic Systems.
        Springer-Verlag.

Scarpitti, Frank. *see* Scarpitti, Frank R.

Scarpitti, Frank R.
    xScarpitti, Frank.
        Social Problems. HR&W.
    xScarpitti, Frank R.
        Social Problems. HR&W.

Scarron, Paul, 1610-1660
    xScarron, Paul.
        Comical Romance. Arno.
        Innocent Adultery & Other Short Novels.
        Arno.

Scarrow, Howard A.
    xScarrow, Howard A.
        Higher Public Service of the Commonwealth of
        Australia. Duke.

Scarry, Huck.
    xScarry, Huck.
        Huck Scarry's Steam Train Journey. Philomel.

Scarry, Patricia M.
    xScarry, Patricia M.
        Sweet Smell of Christmas. Western Pub.

Scarry, Richard.
    xScarry, Richard.
        The Bunny Book. Western Pub.
        The Bunny Book. Western Pub.
        Early Bird. Random.
        illus. Early Words. Random.
        The Funniest Storybook Ever. Random.
        illus. Great Big Car & Truck Book. Western
        Pub.
        illus. In My Town. Western Pub.
        illus. Learn to Count. Western Pub.
        More Adventures of Tinker & Tanker.
        Doubleday.
        Richard Scarry's Animal Nursery Tales.
        Western Pub.
        illus. Richard Scarry's Best Counting Book
        Ever. Random.
        illus. Richard Scarry's Best First Book Ever.
        Random.
        illus. Richard Scarry's Best Stories Ever.
        Western Pub.
        Richard Scarry's Busiest People Ever. Random.
        Richard Scarry's Cars & Trucks & Things That
        Go. Western Pub.
        illus. Richard Scarry's Color Book. Random.
        illus. Richard Scarry's Great Big Air Book.
        Random.
        Richard Scarry's Great Big Mystery Book.
        Random.
        illus. Richard Scarry's Great Big Schoolhouse.
        Random.
        illus. Richard Scarry's Hop Aboard, Here We
        Go. Western Pub.
        Richard Scarry's Lowly Worm Sniffy Book.
        Random.
        Richard Scarry's Please & Thank You Book.
        Random.
        Richard Scarry's Postman Pig & His Busy
        Neighbors. Random.

Scarth, John.
    xScarth, John.

Schaeffer, Susan Fromberg.
  xSchaeffer, Susan.
    Time in Its Flight. PB.
  xSchaeffer, Susan F.
    Falling. Macmillan.
    Falling. NAL.
    Rhymes & Runes of the Toad. Macmillan.
  xSchaeffer, Susan Fromberg.
    Time in Its Flight. Doubleday.
Schaeftler, Michael A.
  xSchaeftler, Michael A.
    The Liabilities of Office: Indemnification &
      Insurance of Corporate Officers & Directors.
      Little.
Schaenman, Philip S.
  xSchaenman, Philip S.
    Measuring Fire Protection Productivity in
      Local Government. Natl Fire Prot.
    Measuring Impacts of Land Development: An
      Initial Approach. Urban Inst.
Schaeppi, Mary.
  xSchaeppi, Mary.
    The Tale of the Magic Bread. Scroll Pr.
Schaevitz, Robert C.
  xSchaevitz, Robert C.
    Handbook of Federal Assistance: Financing,
      Grants, Technical Aids. Warren.
Schafer, Edward. see Schafer, Edward H.
Schafer, Edward H.
  xSchafer, Edward.
    Ancient China. Silver.
  xSchafer, Edward H.
    Ancient China. Time-Life.
    The Divine Woman: Dragon Ladies & Rain
      Maidens in T'ang Literature. N Point Pr.
    The Divine Woman: Dragon Ladies & Rain
      Maidens in T'ang Literature. U of Cal Pr.
    Pacing the Void: T'ang Approaches to the
      Stars. U of Cal Pr.
    Tu Wan's Stone Catalogue of Cloudy Forest: A
      Commentary & Synopsis. U of Cal Pr.
Schafer, Harald.
  xSchafer, Harald.
    Chemical Transport Reactions. Acad Pr.
Schafer, Heinrich.
  xSchafer, Heinrich.
    Principles of Egyptian Art. Oxford U Pr.
Schafer, Mike.
  xSchafer, Mike.
    ed. Classic Articles from Model Railroader.
      Kalmbach.
Schafer, R. Murray.
  xSchafer, R. Murray.
    The Tuning of the World. Knopf.
Schafer, Raymond.
  xSchafer, Raymond.
    Compiled by Greet God in the Morning.
      Vision Hse.
Schafer, Robert.
  xSchafer, Robert.
    The Suburbanization of Multifamily Housing.
      Lexington Bks.
Schafer, Roy.
  xSchafer, Roy.
    Aspects of Internalization. Intl Univs Pr.
Schafer, Stephen.
  xSchafer, Stephen.
    Compensation & Restitution to Victims of
      Crime. Patterson Smith.
    Introduction to Criminology. Reston.
    Readings in Contemporary Criminology.
      Reston.
Schafer, Walt. see Schafer, Walter E.
Schafer, Walter E., 1939-
  xSchafer, Walt.
    Stress, Distress & Growth. Intl Dialogue Pr.
Schaff, Adam.
  xSchaff, Adam.

    History & Truth. Pergamon.
    Marxism & the Human Individual. McGraw.
Schaff, David.
  xSchaff, David.
    Moon by Day. Four Seasons Foun.
Schaff, Philip.
  xSchaff, Phillip.
    History of the Christian Church. Church
      History.
    History of the Christian Church. Kregel.
Schaff, Phillip. see Schaff, Philip.
Schaffer, Albert, 1927-
  xSchaffer, Albert.
    Understanding Social Problems. Merrill.
Schaffer, Alexander J.
  xSchaffer, Alexander J.
    Diseases of the Newborn. Saunders.
Schaffer, Juan J. see Schaffer, Juan Jorge.
Schaffer, Juan Jorge.
  xSchaffer, Juan J.
    Geometry of Spheres in Normed Spaces.
      Dekker.
Schaffer, Kay F.
  xSchaffer, Kay F.
    Sex-Role Issues in Mental Health. A-W.
Schaffer, Ulrich, 1942-
  xSchaffer, Ulrich.
    A Growing Love: Meditations on Marriage &
      Commitment. Har-Row.
    A Growing Love: Meditations on Marriage and
      Commitment. Har-Row.
    Love Reaches Out: Meditations for People in
      Love. Har-Row.
Schaffer, W. A. see Schaffer, William A.
Schaffer, William A.
  xSchaffer, W. A.
    On the Use of Input-Output Models for
      Regional Planning. Kluwer Boston.
Schaffert, Arthur.
  xSchaffert, Arthur.
    illus. The Aquanauts. Coward.
Schaffner, Fenton.
  xSchaffner, Fenton.
    ed. The Liver & Its Diseases. Thieme-Stratton.
Schaffner, Nicholas, 1953-
  xSchaffner, Nicholas.
    The Boys from Liverpool. Methuen Inc.
Schagrin, Morton L.
  xSchagrin, Morton L.
    The Language of Logic: A Self-Instruction
      Text. Random.
Schaick, John Van. see Van Schaick, John.
Schaie, Klaus Warner, 1928-
  xSchaie, Warner K.
    Developmental Human Behavior Genetics:
      Nature-Nurture Redefined. Lexington Bks.
Schaie, Warner K. see Schaie, Klaus Warner.
Schakel, Peter J.
  xSchakel, Peter J.
    ed. Longing for a Form: Essays on the Fiction
      of C. S. Lewis. Baker Bk.
    ed. The Longing for a Form: Essays on the
      Fiction of C. S. Lewis. Kent St U Pr.
    Reading with the Heart: The Way into Narnia.
      Eerdmans.
Schall, Lawrence D.
  xSchall, Lawrence D.
    Introduction to Financial Management.
      McGraw.
    Introduction to Financial Management.
      McGraw.
Schaller, Friedrich.
  xSchaller, Friedrich.
    Soil Animals. U of Mich Pr.
    Soil Animals. U of Mich Pr.
Schaller, George. see Schaller, George B.
Schaller, George B.
  xSchaller, George.
    Wonders of Lions. Dodd.
  xSchaller, George B.

    Deer & the Tiger: A Study of Wildlife in India.
      U of Chicago Pr.
    Golden Shadows, Flying Hooves. Dell.
    Golden Shadows, Flying Hooves. Knopf.
    Stones of Silence: Journeys in the Himalaya.
      Viking Pr.
Schaller, Lyle E.
  xSchaller, Lyle E.
    Assimilating New Members. Abingdon.
    Creative Church Administration. Abingdon.
    Effective Church Planning. Abingdon.
    Local Church Looks to the Future. Abingdon.
    The Multiple Staff & the Larger Church.
      Abingdon.
    Parish Planning. Abingdon.
    The Pastor & the People: Building a New
      Partnership for Effective Ministry. Abingdon.
    Survival Tactics in the Parish. Abingdon.
    Understanding Tomorrow. Abingdon.
Schaller, Michael, 1947-
  xSchaller, Michael.
    The United States & China in the Twentieth
      Century. Oxford U Pr.
Schallert, William F.
  xSchallert, William F.
    Programming in FORTRAN. A-W.
Schalm, O. W. see Schalm, Oscar William.
Schalm, Oscar William.
  xSchalm, O. W.
    Bovine Mastitis. Lea & Febiger.
Schama, Simon.
  xSchama, Simon.
    Patriots & Liberators: Revolution in the
      Netherlands, 1780-1813. Knopf.
    Two Rothschilds & the Land of Israel. Knopf.
Schanda, E. see Schanda, Erwin.
Schanda, Erwin.
  xSchanda, E.
    ed. Remote Sensing for Environmental
      Sciences. Springer-Verlag.
Schandel, Terry K.
  xSchandel, Terry K.
    Tax Tactics for Teachers. Communication Skill.
Schane, Sanford A.
  xSchane, Sanford A.
    Generative Phonology. P-H.
Schank, Roger C.
  xSchank, Roger C.
    ed. Computer Models of Thought & Language.
      W H Freeman.
Schanne, Otto F.
  xSchanne, Otto F.
    Impedance Measurements in Biological Cells.
      Wiley.
Schantz, Maria E.
  xSchantz, Maria E.
    ed. Reading in American Schools: A Guide to
      Information Sources. Gale.
Schantz, William T.
  xSchantz, William T.
    Essentials of Business Law. Glencoe.
Schanz, Holly L. see Schanz, Holly Lee.
Schanz, Holly Lee.
  xSchanz, Holly L.
    Greek Sculptural Groups: Archaic & Classical.
      Garland Pub.
Schanzer, Ernest.
  xSchanzer, Ernest.
    The Problem Plays of Shakespeare: A Study of
      Julius Caesar, Measure for Measure, Antony
      & Cleopatra. Schocken.
Schaper, W. A. see Schaper, William August.
Schaper, William August, 1869-
  xSchaper, W. A.
    Sectionalism & Representation in South
      Carolina. Da Capo.
Schapera, Isaac, 1905-
  xSchapera, Isaac.

tr. Praise-Poems of Tswana Chiefs. Oxford U Pr.

Schapero, Max.
xSchapero, Max.
Amblyopia. Chilton.

Schapiro, Boris.
xSchapiro, Boris.
Bridge Analysis. Cornerstone.
Bridge Analysis. G K Hall.
Bridge Analysis. Sterling.

Schapiro, J. Salwyn. *see* Schapiro, Jacob Salwyn.

Schapiro, Jacob Salwyn, 1879-
xSchapiro, J. Salwyn.
Condorcet & the Rise of Liberalism. Octagon.

Schapiro, Leonard. *see* Schapiro, Leonard Bertram.

Schapiro, Leonard Bertram, 1908-
xSchapiro, Leonard.
The Government & Politics of the Soviet Union. Random.

Schapiro, R. L. *see* Schapiro, Rolf L.

Schapiro, Rolf L.
xSchapiro, R. L.
Clinical Radiology of the Pediatric Abdomen Gastrointestinal Tract. Univ Park.

Schapiro, Steve.
xSchapiro, Steve.
The Movie Poster Book. Dutton.

Schapper, Beatrice.
xSchapper, Beatrice.
ed. How to Make Money Writing Magazine Articles. Arco.

Schappes, Morris U. *see* Schappes, Morris Urman.

Schappes, Morris Urman, 1907-
xSchappes, Morris U.
ed. A Documentary History of the Jews in the United States, 1654-1875. Schocken.

Schapsmeier, Edward L.
xSchapsmeier, Edward L.
Encyclopedia of American Agricultural History. Greenwood.
Ezra Taft Benson & the Politics of Agriculture: The Eisenhower Years, 1953-61. Interstate.

Schara, Ron.
xSchara, Ron.
Muskie Mania. Contemp Bks.

Schardein, James L.
xSchardein, James L.
Drugs As Teratogens. CRC Pr.

Scharf, Aaron.
xScharf, Aaron.
Art & Photography. Penguin.

Scharf, Bella.
xScharf, Bella.
Illustrated Patchwork Crochet: Contemporary Granny Squares for Clothing & Home Decorating. Butterick Pub.

Scharf, Charles A.
xScharf, Charles A.
Acquisitions, Mergers, Sales & Takeovers: A Handbook with Forms. P-H.

Scharf, John Thomas, 1843-1898
xScharf, Thomas J.
History of Maryland from the Earliest Period to the Present Day. Gale.

Scharf, Lois.
xScharf, Lois.
To Work & to Wed: Female Employment, Feminism, & the Great Depression. Greenwood.

Scharf, Peter.
xScharf, Peter.
Growing up Moral: Dilemmas for Intermediate Grades. Winston Pr.

Scharf, Thomas J. *see* Scharf, John Thomas.

Scharff, B. *see* Scharff, Robert.

Scharff, Robert.
xScharff, B.
Refrigeration, Air-Conditioning, Range & Oven Servicing. McGraw.
xScharff, Robert.

The Complete Book of Home Remodeling. McGraw.
The Complete Book of Home Workshop Tools. McGraw.
Complete Book of Wood Finishing. McGraw.
Ice Hockey Rules in Pictures. G&D.
Successful Putting It All Together. Structures Pub.

Scharlemann, Martin H. *see* Scharlemann, Martin Henry.

Scharlemann, Martin Henry, 1910-
xScharlemann, Martin H.
Qumran & Corinth. Coll & U Pr.

Scharlemann, Robert P.
xScharlemann, Robert P.
Reflection & Doubt in the Thought of Paul Tillich. Yale U Pr.

Scharp, Hal.
xScharp, Hal.
Answers to Your Questions About Sharks. Naturegraph.
Freshwater Angler's Clinic. S&S.

Schary, Dore.
xSchary, Dore.
Case History of a Movie. Garland Pub.
Heyday: An Autobiography. Little.

Schatt, Stanley.
xSchatt, Stanley.
Understanding Modern American Literature: Cultural & Historical Perspectives. Intl Schol Bk Serv.

Schatten, Robert, 1911-
xSchatten, Robert.
Theory of Cross-Spaces. Kraus Repr.

Schattner, Regina.
xSchattner, Regina.
Early Childhood Curriculum for Multiply Handicapped Children. T Y Crowell.

Schattschneider, E. E. *see* Schattschneider, Elmer Eric.

Schattschneider, Elmer E. *see* Schattschneider, Elmer Eric.

Schattschneider, Elmer Eric, 1892-
xSchattschneider, E. E.
Party Government. Greenwood.
xSchattschneider, Elmer E.
Two Hundred Million Americans in Search of a Government. HR&W.

Schatz, Elihu A.
xSchatz, Elihu A.
Proof of the Accuracy of the Bible. Jonathan David.

Schatz, Letta.
xSchatz, Letta.
Banji's Magic Wheel. Follett.

Schatz, Sayre P.
xSchatz, Sayre P.
Nigerian Capitalism. U of Cal Pr.

Schatzberg, Michael C. *see* Schatzberg, Michael G.

Schatzberg, Michael G.
xSchatzberg, Michael C.
Politics & Class in Zaire: Bureaucracy, Business, & Beer in Lisala. Holmes & Meier.

Schatzman, E. L. *see* Schatzman, Evry L.

Schatzman, Evry L.
xSchatzman, E. L.
Structure of the Universe. McGraw.

Schauber, Ellen.
xSchauber, Ellen.
The Syntax & Semantics of Questions in Navajo. Garland Pub.

Schauensee, R. Meyer De. *see* De Schauensee, R. Meyer.

Schauer, Frederick F.
xSchauer, Frederick F.
The Law of Obscenity. BNA.

Schauer, William H., 1943-
xSchauer, William H.
The Politics of Space: A Comparison of the Soviet & American Space Programs. Holmes & Meier.

Schauffler, Robert H. *see* Schauffler, Robert Haven.

Schauffler, Robert Haven, 1879-1945
xSchauffler, Robert H.
Musical Amateur: A Book on the Human Side of Music. Arno.
The Musical Amateur: A Book on the Human Side of Music. Scholarly.

Schaum, Konrad.
xSchaum, Konrad.
ed. Deutsche Lyrik. Norton.

Schaumann, B. *see* Schaumann, Blanka.

Schaumann, Blanka.
xSchaumann, B.
Dermatoglyphics in Medical Disorders. Springer-Verlag.

Schaupp, Dietrich L.
xSchaupp, Dietrich L.
A Cross-Cultural Study of a Multinational Company: Attitudinal Responses to Participative Management. Praeger.

Schaupp, Wilhelm.
xSchaupp, Wilhelm.
External Walls: Cladding, Thermal Insulation, Dampproofing. Transatlantic.

Scheader, Catherine.
xScheader, Catherine.
Mary Cassatt. Childrens.

Scheaffer, R. L. *see* Scheaffer, Richard L.

Scheaffer, Richard L.
xScheaffer, R. L.
Introduction to Probability: Theory & Applications. Duxbury Pr.
xScheaffer, Richard L.
Elementary Survey Sampling. Duxbury Pr.

Schebesta, Paul, 1887-1967
xSchebesta, Paul.
Among Congo Pigmies. AMS Pr.

Schechter, Betty.
xSchechter, Betty.
Dreyfus Affair: A National Scandal. HM.

Schechter, Daniel S.
xSchechter, Daniel S.
Agenda for Continuing Education: A Challenge to Health Care Institutions. Hosp Res & Educ.

Schechter, Ruth L. *see* Schechter, Ruth Lisa.

Schechter, Ruth Lisa.
xSchechter, Ruth L.
Offshore. Barlenmir.
Suddenly Thunder. Barlenmir.

Schechter, Solomon, 1847-1915
xSchechter, Solomon.
Studies in Judaism. Arno.
Studies in Judaism. Atheneum.

Schechtman, Joseph B., 1891-1970
xSchechtman, Joseph B.
European Population Transfers, 1939-1945. Russell.
Postwar Population Transfers in Europe, 1945-1955. U of Pa Pr.

Schecter, Jerrold.
xSchecter, Jerrold.
An American Family in Moscow. Little.

Scheele, Adele M.
xScheele, Adele M.
Skills for Success: A Guide to the Top. Morrow.

Scheele, Godfrey.
xScheele, Godfrey.
The Prince Consort. Two Continents.

Scheer, Arnold H.
xScheer, Arnold H.
Approved Practices in Fruit & Vine Production. Interstate.

Scheer, Bradley T. *see* Scheer, Bradley Titus.

Scheer, Bradley Titus, 1914-
xScheer, Bradley T.
Animal Physiology. Krieger.

Scheer, Cynthia.
xScheer, Cynthia.

Bravo! Italian Cooking. Owlswood Prods.
German Home Cooking. Owlswood Prods.
Scheer, Gladys E., 1914-
xScheer, Gladys E.
The Church Library: Tips & tools. Bethany Pr.
Scheer, Julian.
xScheer, Julian.
Rain Makes Applesauce. Holiday.
Scheerenberger, R. C.
xScheerenberger, R. C.
Deinstitutionalization & Institutional Reform. C
C Thomas.
Scheerer, Penelope. see Scheerer, R. Penelope.
Scheerer, R. Penelope.
xScheerer, Penelope.
The Traveling Runner's Guide: Where to Run
in 21 Cities Around the U. S.. Dutton.
Scheffe, Henry, 1907-
xScheffe, Henry.
Analysis of Variance. Wiley.
Scheffer, Victor. see Scheffer, Victor B.
Scheffer, Victor B.
xScheffer, Victor.
Natural History of Marine Mammals. Scribner.
xScheffer, Victor B.
Adventures of a Zoologist. Scribner.
Little Calf. Scribner.
Scheffler, H. W. see Scheffler, Harold W.
Scheffler, Harold W.
xScheffler, H. W.
Australian Kin Classification. Cambridge U Pr.
Scheffler, Israel.
xScheffler, Israel.
The Anatomy of Inquiry: Philosophical Studies
in the Theory of Science. Hackett Pub.
Reason & Teaching. Bobbs.
Reason & Teaching. Irvington.
Scheflen, A. see Scheflen, Albert E.
Scheflen, Albert. see Scheflen, Albert E.
Scheflen, Albert E.
xScheflen, A.
ed. How Behavior Means. Gordon.
xScheflen, Albert.
How Behavior Means. Aronson.
xScheflen, Albert E.
Communicational Structure: Analysis of
Psychotherapy Transaction. Ind U Pr.
Schefler, William C.
xSchefler, William C.
Statistics for the Biological Sciences. A-W.
Scheib, Ida.
xScheib, Ida.
The First Book of Food. Watts.
Scheibe, E. see Scheibe, Erhard.
Scheibe, Erhard.
xScheibe, E.
The Logical Analysis of Quantum Mechanics.
Pergamon.
Scheibel, M. Barbara.
xScheibel, M. Barbara.
Noise: The Unseen Enemy. Pendulum Pr.
Scheick, William J.
xScheick, William J.
Critical Essays on Jonathan Edwards. G K
Hall.
Guide to Seventeenth Century American
Poetry. G K Hall.
Scheidegger, A. see Scheidegger, Adrian E.
Scheidegger, Adrian E., 1925-
xScheidegger, A.
Foundations of Geophysics. Elsevier.
xScheidegger, Adrian E.
Theoretical Geomorphology. Springer-Verlag.
xScheidegger, Adrien E.
Principles of Geodynamics. Springer-Verlag.
Scheidegger, Adrien E. see Scheidegger, Adrian E.
Scheidel, Thomas M. see Scheidel, Thomas Maynard.
Scheidel, Thomas Maynard.
xScheidel, Thomas M.

Discussing & Deciding: A Deskbook for Group
Leaders & Members. Macmillan.
Speech Communication & Human Interaction.
Scott F.
Scheidlinger, Saul, 1918-
xScheidlinger, Saul.
Psychoanalysis & Group Behavior: A Study of
Freudian Group Psychology. Greenwood.
Scheidt, David L.
xScheidt, David L.
Getting to Know Your Bible. Fortress.
Scheie, Harold G.
xScheie, Harold G.
Textbook of Ophthalmology. Saunders.
Scheier, Michael.
xScheier, Michael.
The Whole Mirth Catalog. Watts.
Schein, Clarance J. see Schein, Clarence J.
Schein, Clarence J.
xSchein, Clarance J.
Surgeon at Work. Stein & Day.
xSchein, Clarence J.
Surgeon at Work. Stein & Day.
Schein, Edgar H.
xSchein, Edgar H.
Career Dynamics: Matching Individual &
Organizational Needs. A-W.
Organizational Psychology. P-H.
Process Consultation: Its Role in Organization
Development. A-W.
Scheiner, Irwin.
xScheiner, Irwin.
Christian Converts & Social Protest in Meiji
Japan. U of Cal Pr.
Scheingold, Stuart A.
xScheingold, Stuart A.
The Politics of Rights: Lawyers, Public Policy
& Political Change. Yale U Pr.
Scheinman, Lawrence.
xScheinman, Lawrence.
Atomic Energy Policy in France Under the
Fourth Republic. Princeton U Pr.
Scheinman, Martin F.
xScheinman, Martin F.
Evidence & Proof in Arbitration. NY Sch
Indus Rel.
Scheinmann, F., 1933-
xScheinmann, F.
An Introduction to Spectroscopic Methods for
the Identification of Organic Compounds.
Pergamon.
Scheler, Max. see Scheler, Max Ferdinand.
Scheler, Max F. see Scheler, Max Ferdinand.
Scheler, Max Ferdinand, 1874-1928
xScheler, Max.
Formalism in Ethics & Non-Formal Ethics of
Values: A New Attempt Toward the
Foundation of an Ethical Personalism.
Northwestern U Pr.
Problems of a Sociology of Knowledge.
Routledge & Kegan.
xScheler, Max F.
On the Eternal in Man. Shoe String.
Schelkle, Karl H. see Schelkle, Karl Hermann.
Schelkle, Karl Hermann.
xSchelkle, Karl H.
The Spirit & the Bride: Woman in the Bible.
Liturgical Pr.
Schell, Edward.
xSchell, Edward.
photos by Tennessee. Graphic Arts Ctr.
Schell, Erwin H. see Schell, Erwin Haskell.
Schell, Erwin Haskell, 1889-1965
xSchell, Erwin H.
The Technique of Executive Control. Arno.
Schell, F. see Schell, Frank R.
Schell, Frank R.
xSchell, F.

Practical Problems in Mathematics--Metric
System. Delmar.
xSchell, Frank R.
Industrial Welding Procedures. Delmar.
Practical Problems in Mathematics for Welders.
Delmar.
Schell, Hal B.
xSchell, Hal B.
ed. Reader on the Library Building. IHS-PDS.
Schell, Herbert S. see Schell, Herbert Samuel.
Schell, Herbert Samuel, 1899-
xSchell, Herbert S.
History of South Dakota. U of Nebr Pr.
Schell, Jessie.
xSchell, Jessie.
Sudina. Avon.
Schell, Leo M.
xSchell, Leo M.
Fundamentals of Decoding for Teachers. Rand.
Schell, Mildred.
xSchell, Mildred.
Adapted by The Tiniest Christmas Star.
Judson.
Retold by A Tower Too Tall. Judson.
Schell, Orville.
xSchell, Orville.
Brown. Random.
In the People's Republic: An American's
First-Hand View of Living & Working in
China. Random.
Schellenberg, James A., 1932-
xSchellenberg, James A.
Masters of Social Psychology: Freud, Mead,
Lewin & Skinner. Oxford U Pr.
Masters of Social Psychology: Freud, Mead,
Lewin, & Skinner. Oxford U Pr.
Schellenberg, T. R. see Schellenberg, Theodore R.
Schellenberg, Theodore R., 1903-
xSchellenberg, T. R.
Modern Archives: Principles & Techniques. U
of Chicago Pr.
Scheller, William.
xScheller, William.
Successful Home Greenhouses. Structures Pub.
Schellhase, Kenneth C.
xSchellhase, Kenneth C.
Tacitus in Renaissance Political Thought. U of
Chicago Pr.
Schellie, Don, 1932-
xSchellie, Don.
Maybe Next Summer. Schol Bk Serv.
Schelling, F. W. see Schelling, Friedrich Wilhelm Joseph
Von.
Schelling, Felix. see Schelling, Felix Emmanuel.
Schelling, Felix E. see Schelling, Felix Emmanuel.
Schelling, Felix Emmanuel, 1858-1945
xSchelling, Felix.
English Lyric. Kennikat.
xSchelling, Felix E.
English Chronicle Play: A Study in the Popular
Historical Literature Environing Shakespeare.
B Franklin.
English Drama. AMS Pr.
English Literature During the Lifetime of
Shakespeare. Russell.
The English Lyric. Somerset Pub.
Foreign Influences in Elizabethan Plays. AMS
Pr.
ed. Typical Elizabethan Plays. Arno.
Schelling, Friedrich. see Schelling, Friedrich Wilhelm
Joseph Von.
Schelling, Friedrich Wilhelm Joseph von.
xSchelling, F. W.
System of Transcendental Idealism (1800). U
Pr of Va.
xSchelling, Friedrich.
On University Studies. Ohio U Pr.
Schelling, T. C. see Schelling, Thomas C.
Schelling, Thomas C.
xSchelling, T. C.

First Century of Italian Humanism. Haskell.
First Century of Italian Humanism. Russell.
History of Florence: From the Founding of the
City Through the Renaissance. Ungar.
History of the Balkan Peninsula: From the
Earliest Times to the Present Day. Arno.
Medici. Peter Smith.

Schevill, James. *see* Schevill, James Erwin.

Schevill, James Erwin, 1920-
xSchevill, James.
The Buddhist Car & Other Characters.
Swallow.
The Mayan Poems. SBD.
Stalingrad Elegies. Swallow.

Schevill, Rudolph, 1874-1946
xSchevill, Rudolph.
Cervantes. R West.

Schewe, Charles D.
xSchewe, Charles D.
Marketing: Concepts & Applications. McGraw.
ed. Marketing Information Systems: Selected
Readings. Am Mktg.

Schey, Harry M. *see* Schey, Harry Moritz.

Schey, Harry Moritz, 1930-
xSchey, Harry M.
Div, Grad, Curl & All That: An Informal Text
on Vector Calculus. Norton.

Schiamberg, Lawrence B.
xSchiamberg, Lawrence B.
Adolescent Alienation. Merrill.

Schiavo, Giovanni. *see* Schiavo, Giovanni Ermenegildo.

Schiavo, Giovanni Ermenegildo, 1898-
xSchiavo, Giovanni.
Four Centuries of Italian-American History.
Vigo Pr.

Schiavone, Giuseppe.
xSchiavone, Giuseppe.
The Institutions of Comecon. Holmes & Meier.

Schick, Alice.
xSchick, Alice.
The Peregrine Falcons. Dial.
Santaberry & the Snard. Bookstore Pr.
Santaberry & the Snard. Lippincott.

Schick, Allen.
xSchick, Allen.
Budget Innovation in the States. Brookings.

Schick, Edwin A.
xSchick, Edwin A.
Revelation-the Last Book of the Bible. Fortress.

Schick, Eleanor, 1942-
xSchick, Eleanor.
Andy. Macmillan.
City Green. Macmillan.
illus. City in Summer. Macmillan.
City in the Summer. Macmillan.
illus. City in the Winter. Macmillan.
illus. City in the Winter. Macmillan.
illus. City Sun. Macmillan.
illus. Home Alone. Dial.
I'm Going to the Ocean. Macmillan.
illus. Little School at Cottonwood Corners.
Har-Row.
Neighborhood Knight. Greenwillow.
illus. One Summer Night. Greenwillow.
illus. Peggy's New Brother. Macmillan.
illus. Summer at the Sea. Greenwillow.

Schick, James. *see* Schick, Jim.

Schick, Jim.
xSchick, James.
Civilized Tent Camping. Barron.

Schick, Kurt.
xSchick, Kurt.
Introduction to Electricity. McGraw.

Schick, M. *see* Schick, Martin J.

Schick, Martin. *see* Schick, Martin J.

Schick, Martin J.
xSchick, M.
ed. Nonionic Surfactants. Dekker.
xSchick, Martin.

---

ed. Surface Characteristics of Fibers & Textiles.
Dekker.

Schick, Marvin.
xSchick, Marvin.
Learned Hand's Court. Greenwood.

Schick, Richard P.
xSchick, Richard P.
The Public Interest in Government Labor
Relations. Ballinger Pub.

Schickedanz, H. Ruth.
xSchickedanz, H. Ruth.
Restorative Nursing in a General Hospital. C C
Thomas.

Schickel, Richard.
xSchickel, Richard.
Another I, Another You: A Love Story for the
Once Married. Har-Row.
The World of Carnegie Hall. Greenwood.
World of Goya. Time-Life.
World of Goya. Silver.
The World of Tennis. Random.

Schickele, Peter.
xSchickele, Peter.
The Definitive Biography of P. D. Q. Bach.
Random.

Schieck, Paul.
xSchieck, Paul.
Trolleys of Lower Delaware Valley,
Pennsylvania. Cox.

Schieffelin, Edward L.
xSchieffelin, Edward L.
The Sorrow of the Lonely & the Burning of the
Dancers. St Martin.

Schiel, Jacob H. *see* Schiel, Jacob Heinrich Wilhelm.

Schiel, Jacob Heinrich Wilhelm, 1813-
xSchiel, Jacob H.
Journey Through the Rocky Mountains & the
Humboldt Mountains to the Pacific Ocean. U
of Okla Pr.

Schier, Norma.
xSchier, Norma.
The Anagram Detectives. Mysterious Pr.

Schier, Steven E.
xSchier, Steven E.
The Rules & the Game: Democratic National
Convention Delegate Selection in Iowa &
Wisconsin. U Pr of Amer.

Schiesel, Jane.
xSchiesel, Jane.
The Otis Redding Story. Doubleday.

Schiesl, Martin. *see* Schiesl, Martin J.

Schiesl, Martin J.
xSchiesl, Martin.
The Politics of Efficiency: Municipal
Administration & Reform in America,
1880-1920. U of Cal Pr.

Schievella, P. S., 1914-
xSchievella, Pat S.
Critical Analysis: Language & Its Functions.
Humanities.

Schievella, Pat S. *see* Schievella, P. S.

Schiff, Barry. *see* Schiff, Barry J.

Schiff, Barry J.
xSchiff, Barry.
The Vatican Target. Fawcett.
The Vatican Target. St Martin.

Schiff, Eric, 1901-
xSchiff, Eric.
Inflation & the Earning Power of Depreciable
Assets. Am Enterprise.
Value-Added Taxation in Europe. Am
Enterprise.

Schiff, Gert.
xSchiff, Gert.
Images of Horror & Fantasy. Abrams.

Schiff, Hilda.
xSchiff, Hilda.
ed. Contemporary Approaches to English
Studies. B&N.

Schiff, Jacqui L. *see* Schiff, Jacqui Lee.

Schiff, Jacqui Lee.
xSchiff, Jacqui L.
Cathexis Reader: Transactional Analysis
Treatment of Psychosis. Har-Row.

Schiff, Leon, 1901-
xSchiff, Leon.
ed. Diseases of the Liver. Lippincott.

Schiff, Leonard I. *see* Schiff, Leonard Isaac.

Schiff, Leonard Isaac, 1915-
xSchiff, Leonard I.
Quantum Mechanics. McGraw.

Schiff, Lillian.
xSchiff, Lillian.
Getting Started in Film-Making. Sterling.

Schiff, Martin M., 1922-
xSchiff, Martin M.
Doctor Schiff's Miracle Weight-Loss Guide.
P-H.

Schiff, Michael.
xSchiff, Michael.
Accounting Reporting Problems: Interim
Reporting. Finan Exec.

Schiff, William.
xSchiff, William.
Perception: An Applied Approach. HM.

Schiffer, Don.
xSchiffer, Don.
The First Book of Basketball. Watts.
Football Rules in Pictures. G&D.
xSchiffer, Donald.
First Book of Basketball. Watts.

Schiffer, Donald. *see* Schiffer, Don.

Schiffer, Irvine.
xSchiffer, Irvine.
Charisma: A Psychoanalytic Look at Mass
Society. Free Pr.
Charisma: A Psychoanalytic Look at Mass
Society. U of Toronto Pr.

Schiffer, Margaret B. *see* Schiffer, Margaret Berwind.

Schiffer, Margaret Berwind.
xSchiffer, Margaret B.
Chester County, Pennsylvania Inventories.
Schiffer.
Historical Needlework of Pennsylvania.
Schiffer.

Schiffer, Mortimer.
xSchiffer, Mortimer.
The Therapeutic Play Group. Grune.

Schiffer, Peter B. *see* Schiffer, Peter Berwind.

Schiffer, Peter Berwind.
xSchiffer, Peter B.
The Chester County Historical Society.
Schiffer.

Schiffer, Stephen R.
xSchiffer, Stephen R.
Meaning. Oxford U Pr.

Schifferes, Justus J.
xSchifferes, Justus J.
The Family Medical Encyclopedia. PB.

Schiffman, Steve.
xSchiffman, Steve.
Once a Thief. Revell.

Schiffrin, Harold Z.
xSchiffrin, Harold Z.
Sun Yat-sen & the Origins of the Chinese
Revolution. U of Cal Pr.

Schild, Erich, 1917-
xSchild, Erich.
Structural Failure in Residential Buildings.
Halsted Pr.

Schildknecht, C. E. *see* Schildknecht, Calvin Everett.

Schildknecht, Calvin Everett.
xSchildknecht, C. E.
ed. Polymerization Processes. Wiley.

Schildkrout, Enid.
xSchildkrout, Enid.
People of the Zongo: The Transformation of
Ethnic Identities in Ghana. Cambridge U Pr.

Schildt, John W.
xSchildt, John W.

Drums Along the Antietam. McClain.
Schill, Gottfried.
xSchill, Gottfried.
Catenanes, Rotaxanes & Knots. Acad Pr.
Schill, William J. see Schill, William John.
Schill, William John.
xSchill, William J.
Career Choice & Career Preparation. Interstate.
Schillebeeckx, E. see Schillebeeckx, Edward Cornelis
Florentius.
Schillebeeckx, Edward. see Schillebeeckx, Edward
Cornelis Florentius.
Schillebeeckx, Edward Cornelis Florentius, 1914-
xSchillebeeckx, E.
ed. Truth & Certainty. Seabury.
xSchillebeeckx, Edward.
Jesus: An Experiment in Christology. Seabury.
ed. Problem of Eschatology. Paulist Pr.
Schiller, A. Arthur, 1902-
xSchiller, A. Arthur.
Foreign Law Classification in the Columbia
University Law Library. Oceana.
Schiller, B. R. see Schiller, Bradley R.
Schiller, Bradley. see Schiller, Bradley R.
Schiller, Bradley R., 1943-
xSchiller, B. R.
The Economics of Poverty & Discrimination.
P-H.
xSchiller, Bradley.
The Economy Today. Random.
xSchiller, Bradley R,
Economics of Poverty & Discrimination. P-H.
Schiller, Craig, 1951-
xSchiller, Craig.
The Guilty Conscience of a Conservative.
Arlington Hse.
Schiller, Don.
xSchiller, Donald.
CATV Program Origination & Production.
TAB Bks.
Schiller, Donald. see Schiller, Don.
Schiller, F. C. see Schiller, Ferdinand Canning Scott.
Schiller, Ferdinand C. see Schiller, Ferdinand Canning
Scott.
Schiller, Ferdinand Canning Scott, 1864-1937
xSchiller, F. C.
Studies in Humanism. Century Bookbindery.
xSchiller, Ferdinand C.
Formal Logic, a Scientific & Social Problem.
AMS Pr.
Our Human Truths. AMS Pr.
Riddles of the Sphinx: A Study in the
Philosophy of Humanism. Greenwood.
Studies in Humanism. Arno.
Studies in Humanism. Greenwood.
Schiller, Herbert I., 1919-
xSchiller, Herbert I.
Communication & Cultural Domination. M E
Sharpe.
Communication & Cultural Domination.
Pantheon.
Mass Communications & American Empire.
Beacon Pr.
Mass Communications & American Empire.
Kelley.
ed. Super-State: Readings in the
Military-Industrial Complex. U of Ill Pr.
Schiller, Mayer.
xSchiller, Mayer.
The Road Back: A Discovery of Judaism
Without Embellishments. Feldheim.
Schiller, Patricia.
xSchiller, Patricia.
Creative Approach to Sex Education &
Counseling. Follett.
Schilling, Bernard N. see Schilling, Bernard Nicholas.
Schilling, Bernard Nicholas.
xSchilling, Bernard N.

Human Dignity & the Great Victorians. Shoe
String.
Schilling, O. F. see Schilling, Otto Franz Georg.
Schilling, Otto Franz Georg, 1911-
xSchilling, O. F.
Theory of Valuations. Am Math.
Schilling, S. Paul. see Schilling, Sylvester Paul.
Schilling, Sylvester Paul, 1904-
xSchilling, S. Paul.
God & Human Anguish. Abingdon.
Schillinger, Frances.
xSchillinger, Frances.
Joseph Schillinger:: A Memoir. Da Capo.
Schimke, Joel.
xSchimke, Joel.
Approximate Solution of Plane Orthotropic
Elasticity Problems. Mgmt Info Serv.
Schimke, R. Neil, 1935-
xSchimke, R. Neil.
Genetics & Cancer in Man. Churchill.
Schimmel, David.
xSchimmel, David.
The Civil Rights of Students. Har-Row.
Schimmel, Nancy.
xSchimmel, Nancy.
Just Enough to Make a Story: A Sourcebook
for Storytelling. Sisters Choice.
Schimmel, Paul. see Schimmel, Paul R.
Schimmel, Paul R.
xSchimmel, Paul.
Transfer RNA: Structure, Properties &
Recognition. Cold Spring Harbor.
Schindeler, F. F.
xSchindeler, Fred F.
Responsible Government in Ontario. U of
Toronto Pr.
Schindeler, Fred F. see Schindeler, F. F.
Schindler, George.
xSchindler, George.
Presto!: Magic for the Beginner. Reiss Pub.
Schipf, Robert G.
xSchipf, Robert G.
Automotive Repair & Maintenance. Libs Unl.
Home Repair & Improvement. Libs Unl.
Outdoor Recreation. Libs Unl.
Schipper, I. A.
xSchipper, I. A.
Lecture Outline of Preventive Veterinary
Medicine for Animal Science Students.
Burgess.
Schipper, Jakob, 1842-1915
xSchipper, Jakob.
History of English Versification. AMS Pr.
Schirmer, Walter F. see Schirmer, Walter Franz.
Schirmer, Walter Franz, 1888-
xSchirmer, Walter F.
John Lydgate: A Study in the Culture of the
XVth Century. Greenwood.
Schiro, Michael.
xSchiro, Michael.
Curriculum for Better Schools: The Great
Ideological Debate. Educ Tech Pubns.
Schirokauer, Conrad.
xSchirokauer, Conrad.
A Brief History of Chinese & Japanese
Civilizations. HarBraceJ.
Schisgal, Murray, 1926-
xSchisgal, Murray.
Days & Nights of a French Horn Player. Little.
Schlachter, Gail. see Schlachter, Gail A.
Schlachter, Gail A.
xSchlachter, Gail.
Library Science Dissertations 1925-1972: An
Annotated Bibliography. Libs Unl.
Schlack, Beverly Ann.
xSchlack, Beverly Ann.
Continuing Presences: Virginia Woolf's Use of
Literary Allusion. Pa St U Pr.
Schlaegel, T. F.
xSchlaegel, T. F.

Ocular Histoplasmosis. Grune.
Ocular Toxoplasmosis & Pars Planitis. Grune.
Schlafly, Phyllis.
xSchlafly, Phyllis.
A Choice Not an Echo. Pere Marquette.
The Power of the Positive Woman. Arlington
Hse.
Schlagheck, James L.
xSchlagheck, James L.
The Political, Economic, & Labor Climate in
Mexico. Indus Res Unit-Wharton.
Schlaich, Joan.
xSchlaich, Joan.
ed. Dance: The Art of Production. Mosby.
Schlaifer, Robert.
xSchlaifer, Robert.
Analysis of Decisions Under Uncertainty.
Krieger.
Computer Programs for Elementary Decision
Analysis. Harvard Busn.
Introduction to Statistics for Business
Decisions. McGraw.
Schlatter, Richard B. see Schlatter, Richard Bulger.
Schlatter, Richard Bulger, 1912-
xSchlatter, Richard B.
Private Property: The History of an Idea.
Russell.
Schlauch, Margaret, 1898-
xSchlauch, Margaret.
Chaucer's Constance & Accused Queens.
Gordian.
English Medieval Literature & Its Social
Foundations. Cooper Sq.
English Medieval Literature & Its Social
Foundations. Gordon Pr.
Medieval Narrative: A Book of Translations.
Gordian.
Studies in Language & Literature in Honour of
Margaret Schlauch. Russell.
Schlayer, Mary E. see Schlayer, Mary Elizabeth.
Schlayer, Mary Elizabeth.
xSchlayer, Mary E.
How to Be a Financially Secure Woman.
Ballantine.
How to Be a Financially Secure Woman.
Rawson Wade.
Schlebecker, John T.
xSchlebecker, John T.
Cattle Raising on the Plains, 1900-1961. U of
Nebr Pr.
Whereby We Thrive: A History of American
Farming 1607-1972. Iowa St U Pr.
Schlee, Ann.
xSchlee, Ann.
Guns of Darkness. Atheneum.
Schlee, Susan.
xSchlee, Susan.
On Almost Any Wind: The Saga of the
Oceanographic Research Vessel "Atlantis".
Cornell U Pr.
Schlehofer, Jo.
xSchlehofer, Jo.
Joy in Parenting: Parenting Skills with
Pre-Schoolers Through Adolescents. Paulist
Pr.
Schlei, Barbara L. see Schlei, Barbara Lindemann.
Schlei, Barbara Lindemann.
xSchlei, Barbara L.
Employment Discrimination Law: 1979
Supplement. BNA.
Schleicher, Edythe Hembroff. see Hembroff-Schleicher,
Edythe.
Schleicher, Robert. see Schleicher, Robert H.
Schleicher, Robert H.
xSchleicher, Robert.

Building & Flying Model Aircraft. Chilton.
Building Plastic Models. Kalmbach.
Building Plastic Railroad Models. Kalmbach.
Model Car Racing. Chilton.
Model Car, Truck & Motorcycle Handbook.
Chilton.
Tyco Model Railroad Manual. Chilton.
Schleiden, M. J. see Schleiden, Matthias Jacob.
Schleiden, Matthias Jacob, 1804-1881
xSchleiden, M. J.
Principles of Scientific Botany: Or Botany As
an Inductive Science. Kraus Repr.
Schleier, Curt, 1944-
xSchleier, Curt.
You'd Better Not Tell. Westminster.
Schleier, Louis M. see Schleier, Louis Martin.
Schleier, Louis Martin, 1894-
xSchleier, Louis M.
Problems in the Training of Certain
Special-Class Teachers. AMS Pr.
Schleiermacher, Friedrich. see Schleiermacher, Friedrich
Ernst Daniel.
Schleiermacher, Friedrich Ernst Daniel, 1768-1834
xSchleiermacher, Friedrich.
The Life of Jesus. Fortress.
Schleifer, Abdullah.
xSchleifer, Abdullah.
The Fall of Jerusalem. Monthly Rev.
Schleifer, James T., 1942-
xSchleifer, James T.
The Making of Tocqueville's "Democracy in
America". U of NC Pr.
Schlein, Miriam.
xSchlein, Miriam.
Antarctica: The Great White Continent.
Hastings.
Giraffe: The Silent Giant. Schol Bk Serv.
The Girl Who Would Rather Climb Trees.
HarBraceJ.
I, Tut: The Boy Who Became Pharaoh. Schol
Bk Serv.
Lucky Porcupine!. Schol Bk Serv.
On the Track of the Mystery Animal: The
Story of the Discovery of the Okapi. Schol
Bk Serv.
Snake Fights, Rabbit Fights, & More: A Book
About Animal Fighting. Crown.
What's Wrong with Being a Skunk?. Schol Bk
Serv.
Schleiner, Winfried.
xSchleiner, Winfried.
Imagery of John Donne's Sermons. Brown U
Pr.
Schleman, Hilton R. see Schleman, Milton R.
Schleman, Milton R.
xSchleman, Hilton R.
Rhythm on Record. Greenwood.
Schlemm, Betty L.
xSchlemm, Betty L.
Painting with Light. Watson-Guptill.
Schlemmer. see Schlemmer, Richard M.
Schlemmer, Oskar, 1888-1943
xSchlemmer, Oskar.
The Letters & Diaries of Oskar Schlemmer.
Columbia U Pr.
Schlemmer, Richard M.
xSchlemmer.
Handbook of Advertising Art Production. P-H.
Schlereth, Hewitt.
xSchlereth, Hewitt.
Commonsense Celestial Navigation. Contemp
Bks.
Commonsense Sailboat Buying. Contemp Bks.
Schlesinger, Arthur M. see Schlesinger, Arthur Meier.
Schlesinger, Arthur Meier.
xSchlesinger, Arthur M.

Congress & the Presidency: Their Role in
Modern Times. Am Enterprise.
Intro. by Congress Investigates: A Documented
History, 1792-1974. Chelsea Hse.
ed. History of American Presidential Elections.
Chelsea Hse.
Imperial Presidency. HM.
The Imperial Presidency. Popular Lib.
In Retrospect: The History of a Historian.
HarBraceJ.
Learning How to Behave: A Historical Study of
American Etiquette Books. Cooper Sq.
Prelude to Independence: The Newspaper War
on Britain, 1764-1776. Greenwood.
Schlesinger, Benjamin.
xSchlesinger, Benjamin.
ed. Family Planning in Canada: A Source
Book. U of Toronto Pr.
ed. The One Parent Family: Perspectives &
Annotated Bibliography. U of Toronto Pr.
Schlesinger, Benno, M.D.
xSchlesinger, Benno.
Higher Cerebral Functions & Their Clinical
Disorders: The Organic Basis of Psychology
& Psychiatry. Grune.
Schlesinger, G.
xSchlesinger, G.
Confirmation & Confirmability. Oxford U Pr.
Schlesinger, George N.
xSchlesinger, George N.
Aspects of Time. Hackett Pub.
Schlesinger, Hilde S.
xSchlesinger, Hilde S.
Sound & Sign: Childhood Deafness & Mental
Health. U of Cal Pr.
Schlesinger, I. M.
xSchlesinger, I. M.
Production & Comprehension of Utterances.
Halsted Pr.
Schlesinger, Marian Cannon.
xSchlesinger, Marian Cannon.
Snatched from Oblivion: A Cambridge Memoir.
Little.
Schlesinger, R. W. see Schlesinger, Robert Walter.
Schlesinger, Robert Walter, 1913-
xSchlesinger, R. W.
Dengue Viruses. Springer-Verlag.
Schlesinger, Rudolf.
xSchlesinger, Rudolf.
Federalism in Central & Eastern Europe.
Greenwood.
History of the Communist Party of USSR: Past
& Present. South Asia Bks.
Schlesinger, Steven. see Schlesinger, Steven R.
Schlesinger, Steven R.
xSchlesinger, Steven.
Exclusionary Injustice: The Problem of Illegally
Obtained Evidence. Dekker.
Schlichting, Hermann.
xSchlichting, Hermann.
Boundary Layer Theory. McGraw.
xSchlichting, Hermann T.
Aerodynamics of the Airplane. McGraw.
Schlichting, Hermann T. see Schlichting, Hermann.
Schlichting, Marvin.
xSchlichting, Marvin.
Basic Algebra. Van Nos Reinhold.
Schlick, M. see Schlick, Moritz.
Schlick, Moritz, 1882-1936
xSchlick, M.
General Theory of Knowledge. Springer-Verlag.
Schliephake, Konrad.
xSchliephake, Konrad.
Oil & Regional Development: Examples from
Algeria & Tunisia. Praeger.
Schlight, John.
xSchlight, John.

Monarchs & Mercenaries: A Reappraisal of the
Importance of Knight Service in Norman &
Early Angevin England. NYU Pr.
Schlink, Basilea.
xSchlink, M. Basilea.
Repentance - the Joy-Filled Life. Zondervan.
Schlink, Edmund, 1903-
xSchlink, Edmund.
The Doctrine of Baptism. Concordia.
Schlink, F. J. see Schlink, Frederick John.
Schlink, Frederick John, 1891-
xSchlink, F. J.
Eat, Drink & Be Wary. Arno.
Schlink, M. Basilea. see Schlink, Basilea.
Schlittler, Emil, 1906-
xSchlittler, Emil.
ed. Antihypertensive Agents. Acad Pr.
Schloming, Gordon C. see Schloming, Gordon Clark.
Schloming, Gordon Clark.
xSchloming, Gordon C.
Father to Son: Thoughts to Live by. Vanguard.
Schloss, Joseph D.
xSchloss, Joseph D.
Evidence & Its Legal Aspects. Merrill.
Schlossberg, Allan.
xSchlossberg, Allan.
Adult Tooth Movement in General Dentistry.
Saunders.
Schlossberg, Dan.
xSchlossberg, Dan.
The Baseball Catalogue. Jonathan David.
Schlossberg, Leon.
xSchlossberg, Leon.
ed. Johns Hopkins Atlas of Human Functional
Anatomy. Johns Hopkins.
Schlossberg, Nancy K.
xSchlossberg, Nancy K
Counseling Adults. Brooks-Cole.
Schlossberg, Stephen I.
xSchlossberg, Stephen I.
Organizing & the Law. BNA.
Schlossman, Steven L.
xSchlossman, Steven L.
Love & the American Delinquent: The Theory
& Practice of "Progressive" Juvenile Justice,
1825-1920. U of Chicago Pr.
Schlote, Werner.
xSchlote, Werner.
British Overseas Trade from 1700 to the
1930's. Greenwood.
Schlozman, Kay L. see Schlozman, Kay Lehman.
Schlozman, Kay Lehman.
xSchlozman, Kay L.
Injury to Insult: Unemployment, Class, &
Political Response. Harvard U Pr.
Schlueter, June.
xSchlueter, June.
Metafictional Characters in Modern Drama.
Columbia U Pr.
Schluger, Saul.
xSchluger, Saul.
Periodontal Disease: Basic Phenomena, Clinical
Management, & Occlusal & Restorative
Interrelationships. Lea & Febiger.
Schlundt, Christena L.
xSchlundt, Christena L.
ed. Professional Appearances of Ruth St. Denis
& Ted Shawn: A Chronology & an Index of
Dances 1906-1932. NY Pub Lib.
ed. Professional Appearances of Ted Shawn &
His Men Dancers: A Chronology & an Index
of Dances 1933-1940. NY Pub Lib.
Schluntz, Roger. see Schluntz, Roger L.
Schluntz, Roger L.
xSchluntz, Roger.
ed. Architecture Schools in North America:
Members & Affiliates of the ACSA.
Petersons Guides.
Schluter, William C. see Schluter, William Charles.

Schluter, William Charles, 1890-1932
  xSchluter, William C.
    Pre-War Business Cycle, 1907-1914. AMS Pr.
Schmalenberg, Claudia.
  xSchmalenberg, Claudia.
    Coping with Reality Shock: The Voices of
      Experience. Nursing Res.
Schmalensee, Richard.
  xSchmalensee, Richard.
    The Control of Natural Monopolies. Lexington
      Bks.
Schmalstieg, William R.
  xSchmalstieg, William R.
    Indo-European Linguistics: A New Synthesis.
      Pa St U Pr.
Schmalz, Larry C.
  xSchmalz, Larry C.
    Computer Glossary for Students & Teachers. T
      Y Crowell.
Schmandt-Besserat, Denise.
  xSchmandt-Besserat, Denise.
    ed. Early Technologies. Undena Pubns.
Schmeckebier. see Schmeckebier, Laurence Frederick.
Schmeckebier, Laurence E. see Schmeckebier, Laurence
  Eli.
Schmeckebier, Laurence Eli, 1906-
  xSchmeckebier, Laurence E.
    A Handbook of Italian Renaissance Painting.
      AMS Pr.
    Modern Mexican Art. Greenwood.
Schmeckebier, Laurence F. see Schmeckebier, Laurence
  Frederick.
Schmeckebier, Laurence Frederick.
  xSchmeckebier.
    Catalogue & Index of Publications of the
      Hayden, King, Powell & Wheeler Surveys.
      Da Capo.
  xSchmeckebier, Laurence F.
    The Bureau of Foreign & Domestic Commerce:
      Its History, Activities & Organization. AMS
      Pr.
    The Bureau of Internal Revenue: Its History,
      Activities & Organization. AMS Pr.
    The Bureau of Prohibition: Its History,
      Activities & Organization. AMS Pr.
    Congressional Apportionment. Greenwood.
    The Customs Service: Its History, Activities &
      Organization. AMS Pr.
    The Federal Radio Commission: Its History,
      Activities & Organization. AMS Pr.
    The Government Printing Office: Its History,
      Activities & Organization. AMS Pr.
    History of the Know-Nothing Party in
      Maryland. AMS Pr.
    The Public Health Service: Its History,
      Activities & Organization. AMS Pr.
Schmeidler, Gertrude R. see Schmeidler, Gertrude Raffel.
Schmeidler, Gertrude Raffel.
  xSchmeidler, Gertrude R.
    ed. Parapsychology: Its Relation to Physics,
      Biology, Psychology, & Psychiatry.
      Scarecrow.
Schmeling, Gareth L.
  xSchmeling, Gareth L.
    Chariton. Twayne.
Schmemann, Alexander, 1921-
  xSchmemann, Alexander.
    Historical Road of Eastern Orthodoxy. St
      Vladimirs.
    Introduction to Liturgical Theology. St
      Vladimirs.
    Of Water & the Spirit: A Liturgical Study of
      Baptism. St Vladimirs.
    ed. Ultimate Questions: An Anthology of
      Modern Russian Religious Thought. St
      Vladimirs.
Schmerling, Hilda L.
  xSchmerling, Hilda L.

Finger of God: Religious Thought & Themes in
  Literature from Chaucer to Kafka. Gordon
  Pr.
Schmerling, Susan F., 1946-
  xSchmerling, Susan F.
    Aspects of English Sentence Stress. U of Tex
      Pr.
Schmertz, Herbert, 1930-
  xSchmertz, Herbert.
    Corporations & the First Amendment. Am
      Mgmt.
    The Takeover. S&S.
Schmetterer, L. see Schmetterer, Leopold.
Schmetterer, Leopold, 1919-
  xSchmetterer, L.
    Introduction to Mathematical Statistics.
      Springer-Verlag.
Schmid, A. Allan.
  xSchmid, A. Allan.
    Converting Land from Rural to Urban Uses.
      Johns Hopkins.
Schmid, A. Allan. see Schmid, Alfred Allan.
Schmid, Alfred Allan, 1935-
  xSchmid, A. Allan.
    Property, Power & Public Choice: An Inquiry
      into Law & Economics. Praeger.
Schmid, Calvin F. see Schmid, Calvin Fisher.
Schmid, Calvin Fisher.
  xSchmid, Calvin F.
    Handbook of Graphic Presentation. Wiley.
    Social Trends in Seattle. Greenwood.
Schmid, Georg.
  xSchmid, Georg.
    Principles of Integral Science of Religion.
      Mouton.
Schmid, Hermann, 1925-
  xSchmid, Hermann.
    Decimal Computation. Wiley.
Schmid, Loren C. see Schmid, Loren Clark.
Schmid, Loren Clark, 1931-
  xSchmid, Loren C.
    Critical Assemblies & Reactor Research.
      Krieger.
Schmid, Rex E.
  xSchmid, Rex E.
    Contemporary Issues in Special Education.
      McGraw.
Schmid, Richard, 1934-
  xSchmid, Richard.
    Richard Schmid Paints the Figure: Advanced
      Techniques in Oil. Watson-Guptill.
Schmiderer, Dorothy.
  xSchmiderer, Dorothy.
    illus. Alphabeast Book: An Abecedarium.
      HR&W.
Schmidgall, Gary, 1945-
  xSchmidgall, Gary.
    Literature As Opera. Oxford U Pr.
    Literature As Opera. Oxford U Pr.
Schmidhauser, John. see Schmidhauser, John Richard.
Schmidhauser, John R. see Schmidhauser, John Richard.
Schmidhauser, John Richard.
  xSchmidhauser, John.
    The Supreme Court & Congress: Conflict &
      Interaction, 1945-1968. Free Pr.
  xSchmidhauser, John R.
    Judges & Justices: The Federal Appellate
      Judiciary. Little.
    The Supreme Court As Final Arbiter in
      Federal-State Relations, 1789-1957.
      Greenwood.
Schmidhofer, E. see Schmidhofer, Ernst.
Schmidhofer, Ernst, 1911-
  xSchmidhofer, E.
    Cerebral Training: An Application of Clinical
      Neurophysiology. Hafner.
Schmidman, John.
  xSchmidman, John.
    Unions in Post-Industrial Society. Pa St U Pr.
Schmidt. see Schmidt, Roger.

Schmidt, Anthony J.
  xSchmidt, Anthony J.
    Cellular Biology of Vertebrate Regeneration &
      Repair. U of Chicago Pr.
Schmidt, Arno.
  xSchmidt, Arno B.
    Notes from the Chef's Desk. CBI Pub.
Schmidt, Arno B. see Schmidt, Arno.
Schmidt, Arthur W. see Schmidt, Arthur Warren.
Schmidt, Arthur Warren, 1897-
  xSchmidt, Arthur W.
    Development of a State's Minimum
      Educational Program. AMS Pr.
Schmidt, Benno C.
  xSchmidt, Benno C.
    Freedom of the Press Vs. Public Access.
      Praeger.
Schmidt, Bob.
  xSchmidt, Bob.
    Great Fishing Close to Chicago. Contemp Bks.
Schmidt, Carl T. see Schmidt, Carl Theodore.
Schmidt, Carl Theodore.
  xSchmidt, Carl T.
    The Corporate State in Action: Italy Under
      Fascism. Russell.
Schmidt, Ernst G., 1931-
  xSchmidt, Ernst G.
    Choose to Win!. Abingdon.
Schmidt, Folke. see Schmidt, Folke Fredrik.
Schmidt, Folke Fredrik, 1909-
  xSchmidt, Folke.
    Law & Industrial Relations in Sweden.
      Rothman.
Schmidt, Frances.
  xSchmidt, Frances.
    ed. Public Relations in Health & Welfare.
      Columbia U Pr.
Schmidt, George, 1926-
  xSchmidt, George.
    Physics of High Temperature Plasmas. Acad
      Pr.
Schmidt, George P. see Schmidt, George Paul.
Schmidt, George Paul, 1894-
  xSchmidt, George P.
    The Liberal Arts College: A Chapter in
      American Cultural History. Greenwood.
Schmidt, Gerald D.
  xSchmidt, Gerald D.
    Foundations of Parasitology. Mosby.
    ed. Problems in Systematics of Parasites. Univ
      Park.
Schmidt, Glen H. see Schmidt, Glen Henry.
Schmidt, Glen Henry.
  xSchmidt, Glen H.
    Principles of Dairy Science. W H Freeman.
Schmidt, H. J. see Schmidt, Heinz-Jurgen.
Schmidt, Heinz-Jurgen, 1948-
  xSchmidt, H. J.
    Axiomatic Characterization of Physical
      Geometry. Springer-Verlag.
Schmidt, Herman.
  xSchmidt, Herman.
    ed. Prayer & Community. Seabury.
Schmidt, Herman. see Schmidt, Herman A. P.
Schmidt, Herman A. P.
  xSchmidt, Herman.
    ed. The Liturgical Experience of Faith.
      Seabury.
    ed. Liturgy in Transition. Seabury.
    Liturgy, Self-Expression of the Church.
      Seabury.
    ed. Politics & Liturgy. Seabury.
Schmidt, Hubert G. see Schmidt, Hubert Glasgow.
Schmidt, Hubert Glasgow, 1905-
  xSchmidt, Hubert G.
    Agriculture in New Jersey: A Three Hundred
      Year History. Rutgers U Pr.
Schmidt, Hugo, 1929-
  xSchmidt, Hugo.

Nikolaus Lenau. Irvington.
Schmidt, J. E. see Schmidt, Jacob Edward.
Schmidt, J. H. see Schmidt, Jay H.
Schmidt, J. William. see Schmidt, Joseph William.
Schmidt, Jacob Edward, 1903-
xSchmidt, J. E.
Analyzer of Medical-Biological Words: A
Clarifying Dissection of Medical
Terminology, Showing How It Works, for
Medics, Paramedics, Students, & Visitors
from Foreign Countries. C C Thomas.
English Idioms & Americanisms for Foreign
Students, Professionals & Physicians. C C
Thomas.
English Word Power for Physicians & Other
Professionals: A Vigorous & Cultured
Vocabulary. C C Thomas.
Paramedical Dictionary: A Practical Dictionary
for the Semi-Medical & Ancillary Medical
Professions. C C Thomas.
Structural Units of Medical & Biological
Terms: A Convenient Guide, in English, to
the Roots, Stems, Prefixes, Suffixes, & Other
Combining Forms Which Are the Building
Blocks of Medical & Related Scientific
Words. C C Thomas.
Schmidt, Janet.
xSchmidt, Janet.
Demystifying Parole. Lexington Bks.
Schmidt, Jay H.
xSchmidt, J. H.
Getting Along: How to Be Happy with
Yourself & Others. Putnam.
Schmidt, Joseph William.
xSchmidt, J. William.
Mathematical Foundations for Management
Science & Systems Analysis. Acad Pr.
Schmidt, Karl A.
xSchmidt, Karl A.
Easy Ways to Enlarge Your German
Vocabulary. Dover.
Schmidt, Margaret F. see Schmidt, Margaret Fox.
Schmidt, Margaret Fox.
xSchmidt, Margaret F.
Passion's Child: The Extraordinary Life of Jane
Digby. Har-Row.
Schmidt, Nancy J.
xSchmidt, Nancy J.
Children's Books on Africa & Their Authors:
An Annotated Bibliography. Holmes &
Meier.
Schmidt, Paul F., 1947-
xSchmidt, Paul F.
Coping with Difficult People. Westminster.
Schmidt, Paul F. see Schmidt, Paul Frank.
Schmidt, Paul Frank, 1915-
xSchmidt, Paul F.
Fuel Oil Manual. Indus Pr.
Schmidt, Paul Frederic, 1925-
xSchmidt, Paul F.
Perception & Cosmology in Whitehead's
Philosophy. Rutgers U Pr.
Schmidt, Peter, 1947-
xSchmidt, Peter.
Econometrics. Dekker.
Schmidt, Peter R.
xSchmidt, Peter R.
Historical Archaeology: A Structural Approach
in an African Culture. Greenwood.
Schmidt, R. F. see Schmidt, Robert F.
Schmidt, Robert F.
xSchmidt, R. F.
Fundamentals of Neurophysiology.
Springer-Verlag.
ed. Fundamentals of Sensory Physiology.
Springer-Verlag.
Schmidt, Roger, 1931-
xSchmidt.

Exploring Religion. Duxbury Pr.
Schmidt, Stanley.
xSchmidt, Stanley.
Newton & the Quasi-Apple. Popular Lib.
Newton & the Quasi-Apple. Ultramarine Pub.
Schmidt, Steffen W.
xSchmidt, Steffen W.
Friends, Followers & Factions: A Reader in
Political Clientelism. U of Cal Pr.
ed. Soldiers in Politics. Geron-X.
Schmidt, Victor E.
xSchmidt, Victor E.
Teaching Science with Everyday Things.
McGraw.
Schmidt, W. see Schmidt, Wilhelm.
Schmidt, W. M. see Schmidt, Wolfgang M.
Schmidt, Wilhelm, 1868-1954
xSchmidt, W.
The Origin & Growth of Religion: Facts &
Theories. Cooper Sq.
Schmidt, Wolfgang M.
xSchmidt, W. M.
Diophantine Approximation. Springer-Verlag.
Schmidt-Brummer, Horst.
xSchmidt-Brummer, Horst.
Venice, California: An Urban Fantasy. Viking
Pr.
Schmidt-Nielsen, Knut. see Schmidt-Nielsen, Knut
Stortebecker.
Schmidt-Nielsen, Knut Stortebecker, 1915-
xSchmidt-Nielsen, Knut.
Animal Physiology. Cambridge U Pr.
Animal Physiology. P-H.
Schmidtke, John R.
xSchmidtke, Jon R.
ed. Immunology for the Practicing Physician.
Plenum Pub.
Schmidtke, Jon R. see Schmidtke, John R.
Schmiedeck, Raoul A.
xSchmiedeck, Raoul A.
The Personal Sphere Model. Grune.
Schmicdicke. see Schmiedicke, Robert E.
Schmiedicke, Robert E.
xSchmiedicke.
Principles of Cost Accounting. SW Pub.
Schminke, C. W. see Schminke, Clarence W.
Schminke, Clarence W.
xSchminke, C. W.
Teaching the Child Mathematics. HR&W.
Schmirler, Otto.
xSchmirler, Otto.
The Art of Wrought Metalwork for House &
Garden. Architectural.
Art of Wrought Metalwork for House &
Garden. Hastings.
Schmitt, Abraham.
xSchmitt, Abraham.
The Art of Listening with Love. Word Bks.
Dialogue with Death. Word Bks.
Schmitt, Bernadotte E. see Schmitt, Bernadotte Everly.
Schmitt, Bernadotte Everly, 1886-1969
xSchmitt, Bernadotte E.
The Coming of the War, 1914. Fertig.
England & Germany, 1740-1914. Fertig.
Schmitt, Bernard. see Schmitt, Bernard A.
Schmitt, Bernard A., 1948-
xSchmitt, Bernard.
Protein, Calories & Development: Nutritional
Variables in the Economics of Developing
Nations. Westview.
Schmitt, Carl, 1888-
xSchmitt, Carl.
The Concept of the Political. Rutgers U Pr.
Schmitt, Cecilia.
xSchmitt, Cecilia.
Rapport & Success: Human Relations in Music
Education. Dorrance.
Schmitt, Conrad J.
xSchmitt, Conrad J.

Let's Speak Spanish. McGraw.
Schaum's Outline of Spanish Grammar.
McGraw.
Schmitt, F. O. see Schmitt, Francis Otto.
Schmitt, Francis O. see Schmitt, Francis Otto.
Schmitt, Francis Otto.
xSchmitt, F. O.
ed. Functional Linkage in Biomolecular
Systems. Raven.
xSchmitt, Francis O.
ed. The Neurosciences: Fourth Study Program.
MIT Pr.
Schmitt, Francis P.
xSchmitt, Francis P.
Church Music Transgressed: Reflections on
Reform. Seabury.
Schmitt, Gladys, 1909-
xSchmitt, Gladys.
The Godforgotten. HarBraceJ.
Sonnets for an Analyst. HarBraceJ.
Schmitt, Hans A.
xSchmitt, Hans A.
European Union: From Hitler to De Gaulle.
Van Nos Reinhold.
Schmitt, Raymond L., 1936-
xSchmitt, Raymond L.
The Reference Other Orientation: An
Extension of the Reference Group Concept. S
Ill U Pr.
Schmitt, Richard, 1927-
xSchmitt, Richard.
Martin Heidegger on Being Human: An
Introduction to Sein und Zeit. Peter Smith.
Schmitt, Robert C.
xSchmitt, Robert C.
Demographic Statistics of Hawaii, 1778-1965.
U Pr of Hawaii.
Historical Statistics of Hawaii. U Pr of Hawaii.
Schmitter, Philippe C.
xSchmitter, Philippe C.
Autonomy or Dependence As Regional
Integration Outcomes: Central America. U of
Cal Intl St.
Schmitthoff, Clive. see Schmitthoff, Clive Maximilian.
Schmitthoff, Clive Maximilian.
xSchmitthoff, Clive.
International Commercial Arbitration. Oceana.
Schmitz, Dennis, 1937-
xSchmitz, Dennis.
Goodwill, Inc. Ecco Pr.
String. Ecco Pr.
Schmitz, Dorothy C. see Schmitz, Dorothy Childers.
Schmitz, Dorothy Childers.
xSchmitz, Dorothy C.
Dorothy Hamill: Skate to Victory. Crestwood
Hse.
The Fabulous Frisbee. Crestwood Hse.
Schmitz, Ettore, 1861-1928
xSchmitz, Ettore.
Confessions of Zeno. Greenwood.
Schmitz, Homer. see Schmitz, Homer H.
Schmitz, Homer H.
xSchmitz, Homer.
Hospital Information Systems. Aspen Systems.
Schmitz, James H., 1911-
xSchmitz, James H.
Pride of Monsters. Macmillan.
A Pride of Monsters. Macmillan.
Schmitz, Mark.
xSchmitz, Mark.
Economic Analysis of Antebellum Sugar
Plantations in Louisiana. Arno.
Schmoe, Floyd. see Schmoe, Floyd Wilfred.
Schmoe, Floyd Wilfred, 1895-
xSchmoe, Floyd.
A Year in Paradise. Mountaineers.
Schmorleitz, Morton S.
xSchmorleitz, Morton S.
Castles in Japan. C E Tuttle.
Schmuck, Richard. see Schmuck, Richard A.

Schmuck, Richard A.
  xSchmuck, Richard.
    Problem Solving to Improve Classroom
      Learning. SRA.
  xSchmuck, Richard A.
    Group Processes in the Classroom. Wm C
      Brown.
    A Humanistic Psychology of Education:
      Making the School Everybody's House.
      Mayfield Pub.
Schmutz, Ervin M.
  xSchmutz, Ervin M.
    Plants That Poison: An Illustrated Guide for
      the American Southwest. Northland.
Schmutzler, Robert.
  xSchmutzler, Robert.
    Art Nouveau. Abrams.
Schnabel, Artur, 1882-1951
  xSchnabel, Artur.
    Music & the Line of Most Resistance. Da
      Capo.
Schnacke, Dick.
  xSchnacke, Dick.
    American Folk Toys: How to Make Them.
      Penguin.
Schnackenburg, Rudolf, 1914-
  xSchnackenburg, Rudolf.
    The Gospel According to St. John. Seabury.
    Present & Future: Modern Aspects of New
      Testament Theology. U of Notre Dame Pr.
  xSchnackenburg, Rudolph.
    Church in the New Testament. Seabury.
Schnackenburg, Rudolph. see Schnackenburg, Rudolf.
Schnall, David. see Schnall, David J.
Schnall, David J.
  xSchnall, David.
    Radical Dissent in Contemporary Israeli
      Politics: Cracks in the Wall. Praeger.
Schnall, Maxine.
  xSchnall, Maxine.
    The Broadbelters. M Evans.
Schneck, Stephen.
  xSchneck, Stephen.
    Complete Home Medical Guide for Cats. G K
      Hall.
    Complete Home Medical Guide for Cats. Stein
      & Day.
    Complete Home Medical Guide for Dogs. G K
      Hall.
    The Complete Home Medical Guide for Dogs.
      Stein & Day.
Schnee, Heinrich, 1871-1949
  xSchnee, Heinrich.
    German Colonization Past & Future: The Truth
      About the German Colonies. Kennikat.
Schnee, Jerome E.
  xSchnee, Jerome E.
    The Progress of Management: Process &
      Behavior in a Changing Environment. P-H.
Schneebaum, Tobias.
  xSchneebaum, Tobias.
    Wild Man. Viking Pr.
Schneeberger, Pierre Francis.
  xSchneeberger, Pierre-F.
    Chinese Jades & Other Hardstones. Routledge
      & Kegan.
Schneeberger, Pierre-F. see Schneeberger, Pierre Francis.
Schneede, Uwe M.
  xSchneede, Uwe M.
    Max Ernst. Oxford U Pr.
    Surrealism. Abrams.
Schneerer, W. F. see Schneerer, William F.
Schneerer, William F.
  xSchneerer, W. F.
    Programmed Graphics. McGraw.
Schneewind, J. B. see Schneewind, Jerome B.
Schneewind, Jerome B., 1930-
  xSchneewind, J. B.

Sidgwick's Ethics & Victorian Moral
  Philosophy. Oxford U Pr.
Schneewind, John H.
  xSchneewind, John H.
    Medical & Surgical Emergencies. Year Bk
      Med.
Schneid, Hayyim.
  xSchneid, Hayyim.
    ed. The Family. Jewish Pubn.
    ed. Marriage. Jewish Pubn.
Schneider. see Schneider, Mark.
Schneider, Allen M.
  xSchneider, Allen M.
    An Introduction to Physiological Psychology.
      Random.
Schneider, Anne.
  xSchneider, Anne.
    The Climber's Sourcebook. Doubleday.
Schneider, Arnold E. see Schneider, Arnold Edward.
Schneider, Arnold Edward.
  xSchneider, Arnold E.
    Understanding Business Law. McGraw.
Schneider, Ben R. see Schneider, Ben Ross.
Schneider, Ben Ross, 1920-
  xSchneider, Ben R.
    The Ethos of Restoration Comedy. U of Ill Pr.
    Compiled by Index to the London Stage,
      1660-1800. S Ill U Pr.
Schneider, Camille.
  xSchneider, Camille.
    Alsace. French & Eur.
Schneider, Clarence E.
  xSchneider, Clarence E.
    Syntax & Style. Chandler & Sharp.
Schneider, Daniel E. see Schneider, Daniel Edward.
Schneider, Daniel Edward, 1907-
  xSchneider, Daniel E.
    The Psychoanalyst & the Artist. Humanities.
Schneider, Daniel J., 1927-
  xSchneider, Daniel J.
    The Crystal Cage: Adventures of the
      Imagination in the Fiction of Henry James.
      Regents KS.
    Symbolism: The Manichean Vision: A Study in
      the Art of James, Conrad, Woolf & Stevens.
      U of Nebr Pr.
Schneider, David J.
  xSchneider, David J.
    Person Perception. A-W.
Schneider, David M. see Schneider, David Moses.
Schneider, David Moses.
  xSchneider, David M.
    History of Public Welfare in New York State:
      1609-1866. Patterson Smith.
Schneider, David Murray, 1918-
  xSchneider, David M.
    American Kinship: A Cultural Account. U of
      Chicago Pr.
    Class Differences in American Kinship. Univ
      Microfilms.
    ed. Matrilineal Kinship. U of Cal Pr.
Schneider, Dee.
  xSchneider, Dee.
    Avons Award Bottles, Gifts & Prizes. Avons
      Res.
Schneider, Diana J. see Schneider, Diana Johnson.
Schneider, Diana Johnson.
  xSchneider, Diana J.
    ed. Proteins of the Nervous System. Raven.
Schneider, E. L. see Schneider, Edward L.
Schneider, E. V. see Schneider, Eugene V.
Schneider, Earl, 1922-
  xSchneider, Earl.
    All About Aquariums. TFH Pubns.
Schneider, Edward L.
  xSchneider, E. L.
    ed. The Genetics of Aging. Plenum Pub.
  xSchneider, Edward L.

    ed. The Aging Reproductive System. Raven.
Schneider, Elisabeth Wintersteen, 1897-
  xSchneider, Elizabeth W.
    T. S. Eliot: The Pattern in the Carpet. U of Cal
      Pr.
Schneider, Elizabeth W. see Schneider, Elisabeth
  Wintersteen.
Schneider, Eugene V.
  xSchneider, E. V.
    Industrial Sociology: The Social Relations of
      Industry & the Community. McGraw.
Schneider, Franz.
  xSchneider, Franz.
    tr. Last Letters from Stalingrad. Greenwood.
Schneider, G. W. see Schneider, Gerhard W.
Schneider, Gerhard W.
  xSchneider, G. W.
    Export-Import Financing: A Practical Guide.
      Ronald Pr.
Schneider, H. G. see Schneider, Helmut Gunther.
Schneider, Hans J., 1935-
  xSchneider, Hans J.
    Flying to Be Free. World Wide OR.
Schneider, Harold K.
  xSchneider, Harold K.
    Livestock & Equality in East Africa: The
      Economic Basis for Social Structure. Ind U
      Pr.
Schneider, Harriet. see Schneider, Harriet L.
Schneider, Harriet L.
  xSchneider, Harriet.
    Evaluation of Nursing Competence. Little.
Schneider, Helmut Gunther.
  xSchneider, H. G.
    Advances in Epitaxy & Endotaxy: Selected
      Chemical Problems. Elsevier.
Schneider, Herbert W. see Schneider, Herbert Wallace.
Schneider, Herbert Wallace, 1892-
  xSchneider, Herbert W.
    The Fascist Government of Italy. Greenwood.
    A History of American Philosophy. Columbia
      U Pr.
    Morals for Mankind. U of Mo Pr.
Schneider, Herman, 1905-
  xSchneider, Herman.
    How Scientists Find Out: About Matter, Time,
      Space, & Energy. McGraw.
Schneider, Isidor, 1896-
  xSchneider, Isidor.
    ed. The Enlightenment: The Culture of the
      Eighteenth Century. Braziller.
Schneider, Jane.
  xSchneider, Jane.
    Culture & Political Economy in Western Sicily.
      Acad Pr.
Schneider, Jason, 1942-
  xSchneider, Jason.
    Complete Guide to Woodburning Stoves.
      Cornerstone.
Schneider, Jerrold E.
  xSchneider, Jerrold E.
    Ideological Coalitions in Congress. Greenwood.
Schneider, John. see Schneider, John Hoke.
Schneider, John Hoke.
  xSchneider, John.
    ed. Survey of Commercially Available
      Computer-Readable Bibliographic Data Bases.
      Am Soc Info Sci.
Schneider, Kenneth R.
  xSchneider, Kenneth R.

Autokind vs Mankind: An Analysis of
Tyranny, a Proposal for Rebellion, a Plan for
Reconstruction. Schocken.
On the Nature of Cities: Toward Enduring &
Creative Human Environments. Jossey-Bass.
Schneider, L. see Schneider, Louis.
Schneider, Leo.
xSchneider, Leo.
Long Life to You: Modern Medicine at Work.
HarBraceJ.
Schneider, Louis, 1915-
xSchneider, L.
ed. The Idea of Culture in the Social Sciences.
Cambridge U Pr.
xSchneider, Louis.
The Freudian Psychology & Veblen's Social
Theory. Greenwood.
The Sociological Way of Looking at the World.
McGraw.
Schneider, Mark, 1950-
xSchneider, Mark.
The Best from the Bottle. Music Sales.
Schneider, Nina, 1913-
xSchneider, Nina.
The Woman Who Lived in a Prologue. HM.
Schneider, Pierre.
xSchneider, Pierre.
World of Manet. Time-Life.
World of Manet. Silver.
World of Watteau. Time-Life.
World of Watteau. Silver.
Schneider, R. see Schneider, Robert R.
Schneider, Raymond K.
xSchneider, Raymond K.
Systematic Commercial Refrigeration Service.
Busn News.
Schneider, Richard C., 1929-
xSchneider, Richard C.
Crafts of the North American Indians: A
Craftsman's Manual. Van Nos Reinhold.
Schneider, Robert R.
xSchneider, R.
Reinforced Masonry Design. P-H.
Schneider, Ronald M.
xSchneider, Ronald M.
Communism in Guatemala. Octagon.
Schneider, Stephen H. see Schneider, Stephen Henry.
Schneider, Stephen Henry.
xSchneider, Stephen H.
The Genesis Strategy: Climate & Global
Survival. Plenum Pub.
Schneider, Wolf, 1925-
xSchneider, Wolf.
Babylon Is Everywhere: The City As Man's
Fate. Greenwood.
Schneiderman, Beth K. see Schneiderman, Beth Kline.
Schneiderman, Beth Kline.
xSchneiderman, Beth K.
ed. By & About Women: An Anthology of
Short Fiction. HarBraceJ.
Schneiders, Alexander A. see Schneiders, Alexander
Aloysius.
Schneiders, Alexander Aloysius.
xSchneiders, Alexander A.
Personality Development & Adjustment in
Adolescence. Glencoe.
Schneirla, T. C. see Schneirla, Theodore Christian.
Schneirla, Theodore Christian.
xSchneirla, T. C.
Army Ants: A Study in Social Organization. W
H Freeman.
Schnell, Donald E., 1936-
xSchnell, Donald E.
Carnivorous Plants of the United States &
Canada. Blair.
Schneller, Donald P.
xSchneller, Donald P.

The Prisoner's Family: A Study of the Effects
of Imprisonment on the Families of Prisoners.
R & E Res Assoc.
Schnepf, Max.
xSchnepf, Max.
ed. Farmland, Food & the Future. Soil
Conservation.
Schnepper, Jeff A.
xSchnepper, Jeff A.
Inside IRS: How Internal Revenue Works (You
Over). Stein & Day.
Schnessel, S. Michael.
xSchnessel, S. Michael.
Icart. Potter.
Schnittkind, Henry T. see Schnittkind, Henry Thomas.
Schnittkind, Henry Thomas.
xSchnittkind, Henry T.
Living Biographies of Great Poets. Arno.
Schnitzer, M.
xSchnitzer, M.
ed. Soil Organic Matter. Elsevier.
Schnitzer, Martin.
xSchnitzer, Martin.
Contemporary Government & Business
Relations. Rand.
The Swedish Investment Reserve: A Device for
Economic Stabilization?. Am Enterprise.
Schnitzler, Arthur, 1862-1931
xSchnitzler, Arthur.
Casanova's Homecoming. AMS Pr.
Daybreak. AMS Pr.
Dr. Graesler. AMS Pr.
Flight into Darkness. AMS Pr.
The Little Comedy & Other Stories. Ungar.
Little Novels. AMS Pr.
Professor Bernhardi. AMS Pr.
Some Day Peace Will Return: Notes on War &
Peace. Ungar.
Schnurr, William.
xSchnurr, William.
Johnnie Death. PB.
Schob, David E., 1941-
xSchob, David E.
Hired Hands & Plowboys: Farm Labor in the
Midwest, 1815-60. U of Ill Pr.
Schoch, Hank. see Schoch, Henry A.
Schoch, Henry A.
xSchoch, Hank.
Theodore Roosevelt: The Story Behind the
Scenery. K C Pubns.
Schochet, Sydney S.
xSchochet, Sydney S.
Essentials of Neuropathology. ACC.
Schock, A. Clyde.
xSchock, A. Clyde.
Analytic Geometry & an Introduction to
Calculus. P-H.
Schock, Edson I.
xSchock, Edson J.
How to Build Small Boats. A S Barnes.
Schock, Edson J. see Schock, Edson I.
Schoder, Judith.
xSchoder, Judith.
Brotherhood of Pirates. Messner.
Schoder, Raymond. see Schoder, Raymond V.
Schoder, Raymond V., 1916-
xSchoder, Raymond.
Masterpieces of Greek Art. Ares.
Schoen, Carol.
xSchoen, Carol.
The Writing Experience. Little.
Schoen, Douglas E., D. Phil
xSchoen, Douglas E.
Enoch Powell & the Powellites. St Martin.
Schoen, Elin.
xSchoen, Elin.
Tales of an All-Night Town. HarBraceJ.
Schoen, Juliet P.
xSchoen, Juliet P.

Silents to Sound: A History of the Movies.
Schol Bk Serv.
Schoen, Linda. see Schoen, Linda Allen.
Schoen, Linda A. see Schoen, Linda Allen.
Schoen, Linda Allen.
xSchoen, Linda.
ed. The AMA Book of Skin & Hair Care.
Avon.
xSchoen, Linda A.
ed. The AMA Book of Skin & Hair Care.
Lippincott.
Schoen, Sterling H. see Schoen, Sterling Harry.
Schoen, Sterling Harry.
xSchoen, Sterling H.
Cases in Collective Bargaining & Industrial
Relations: A Decisional Approach. Irwin.
Schoenbaum, David.
xSchoenbaum, David.
Hitler's Social Revolution: Class & Status in
Nazi Germany 1933-1939. Norton.
Schoenberg, B. Mark, 1928-
xSchoenberg, B. Mark.
ed. Bereavement Counseling: A
Multidisciplinary Handbook. Greenwood.
Schoenberg, B. S. see Schoenberg, Bruce S.
Schoenberg, Bernard.
xSchoenberg, Bernard.
Anticipatory Grief. Columbia U Pr.
ed. Psychosocial Aspects of Terminal Care.
Columbia U Pr.
Schoenberg, Bruce S., 1942-
xSchoenberg, B. S.
Multiple Primary Malignant Neoplasms: The
Connecticut Experience, 1935-1964.
Springer-Verlag.
xSchoenberg, Bruce S.
ed. Neurological Epidemiology. Principles &
Clinical Applications. Raven.
Schoenberg, I. J.
xSchoenberg, I. J.
ed. Approximations with Special Emphasis on
Spline Functions: Proceedings. Acad Pr.
Schoenberg, Robert J., 1933-
xSchoenberg, Robert J.
Art of Being a Boss: Inside Intelligence from
Top-Level Business Leaders & Young
Executives on the Move. Lippincott.
Schoenberg, Sandra. see Schoenberg, Sandra Perlman.
Schoenberg, Sandra Perlman.
xSchoenberg, Sandra.
Neighborhoods That Work: Sources for
Viability in the Inner City. Rutgers U Pr.
Schoenberger, Dale T.
xSchoenberger, Dale T.
Gunfighters. Caxton.
Schoenberner, Franz, 1892-
xSchoenberner, Franz.
Confessions of a European Intellectual.
Macmillan.
Schoener, Allon.
xSchoener, Allon.
Portal to America: The Lower East Side,
1870-1925. HR&W.
Schoenfeld, C. G. see Schoenfeld, Charles George.
Schoenfeld, Charles George.
xSchoenfeld, C. G.
Psychoanalysis & the Law. C C Thomas.
Schoenfeld, Clarence A. see Schoenfeld, Clarence Albert.
Schoenfeld, Clarence Albert.
xSchoenfeld, Clarence A.
American University in Summer. U of Wis Pr.
xSchoenfeld, Clay.
Down Wisconsin Sideroads. Tamarack Pr.
Schoenfeld, Clay. see Schoenfeld, Clarence Albert.
Schoenfeld, Jo-Ann, 1932-
xSchoenfeld, Jo-Ann.
The Ready Aim Cookbook. Hopkinson.
Schoenfield, Leslie J.
xSchoenfield, Leslie J.

Diseases of the Gallbladder & Biliary System. Wiley.

Schoenherr, John.
xSchoenherr, John.
The Barn. Little.

Schoenhof, Jacob, 1839-1903
xSchoenhof, Jacob.
The Economy of High Wages. Garland Pub.

Schoenstein, Ralph, 1933-
xSchoenstein, Ralph.
Citizen Paul: A Story of Father & Son. FS&G.

Schoenwald, Richard L., 1927-
xSchoenwald, Richard L.
ed. Nineteenth Century Thought: The Discovery of Change. Peter Smith.

Schoffeniels, E. *see* Schoffeniels, Ernest.

Schoffeniels, Ernest.
xSchoffeniels, E.
Anti-Chance. Pergamon.

Schofield, B. B. *see* Schofield, Brian Betham.

Schofield, Brian Betham, 1895-
xSchofield, B. B.
The Attack on Taranto. Naval Inst Pr.

Schofield, Heather.
xSchofield, Heather.
Flower Painting Techniques. Larousse.

Schofield, Maria.
xSchofield, Maria.
ed. Decorative Art & Modern Interiors 1977. Van Nos Reinhold.
ed. Decorative Art & Modern Interiors 1978. Van Nos Reinhold.

Schofield, Robert E.
xSchofield, Robert E.
Mechanism & Materialism: British Natural Philosophy in the Age of Reason. Princeton U Pr.

Schofield, Sue.
xSchofield, Sue.
Development & the Problems of Village Nutrition. Allanheld.
Development & the Problems of Village Nutrition. Biblio Dist.

Schofield, W. *see* Schofield, Wilfred.

Schofield, Wilfred.
xSchofield, W.
Engineering Surveying. Butterworths.

Schofield, William H. *see* Schofield, William Henry.

Schofield, William Henry, 1870-1920
xSchofield, William H.
English Literature, from the Norman Conquest to Chaucer. Greenwood.
English Literature from the Norman Conquest to Chaucer. Haskell.
English Literature from the Norman Conquest to Chaucer. Phaeton.

Scholder, Fritz, 1937-
xScholder, Fritz.
Indian Kitsch: The Use & Misuse of Indian Images. Northland.

Scholefield, Alan.
xScholefield, Alan.
The Alpha Raid. Morrow.
Point of Honour. Ballantine.
Point of Honour. Morrow.
Venom. Morrow.
Venom. Popular Lib.

Scholefield, Guy H. *see* Scholefield, Guy Hardy.

Scholefield, Guy Hardy, 1877-1963
xScholefield, Guy H.
Notable New Zealand Statesmen: Twelve Prime Ministers. Arno.

Scholem, Gershom. *see* Scholem, Gershom Gerhard.

Scholem, Gershom Gerhard, 1897-
xScholem, Gershom.
On Jews & Judaism in Crisis: Selected Essays. Schocken.

Scholes, France V. *see* Scholes, France Vinton.

Scholes, France Vinton.
xScholes, France V.

Maya Chontal Indians of Acalan-Tixchel: A Contribution to the History & Ethnography of the Yucatan Peninsula. U of Okla Pr.
Troublous Times in New Mexico, 1659-1670. AMS Pr.

Scholes, Percy A. *see* Scholes, Percy Alfred.

Scholes, Percy Alfred.
xScholes, Percy A.
Concise Oxford Dictionary of Music. Oxford U Pr.
Great Dr. Burney: His Life, His Travels, His Works, His Family & His Friends. Greenwood.
Great Dr. Burney: His Life, His Travels, His Works, His Family & His Friends. R West.
The Life & Activities of Sir John Hawkins: Musician, Magistrate & Friend of Johnson. Da Capo.
Oxford Companion to Music. Oxford U Pr.
Puritans & Music in England & New England: A Contribution to the Cultural History of 2 Nations. Oxford U Pr.

Scholes, Robert. *see* Scholes, Robert E.

Scholes, Robert E.
xScholes, Robert.
Fabulation & Metafiction. U of Ill Pr.
Nature of Narrative. Oxford U Pr.
ed. Some Modern Writers: Essays & Fiction by Conrad, Dinesen, Lawrence, Orwell, Faulkner & Ellison. Oxford U Pr.
Structural Fabulation: An Essay on Fiction of the Future. U of Notre Dame Pr.
Structuralism in Literature: An Introduction. Yale U Pr.

Scholes, Samuel. *see* Scholes, Samuel Ray.

Scholes, Samuel R. *see* Scholes, Samuel Ray.

Scholes, Samuel Ray.
xScholes, Samuel.
Modern Glass Practice. CBI Pub.
xScholes, Samuel R.
Opportunities in Ceramic Engineering. Natl Textbk.

Scholl, Geraldine T.
xScholl, Geraldine T.
Measures of Psychological, Vocational, & Educational Functioning in the Blind & Visually Handicapped. Am Foun Blind.

Scholl, Inge, 1922-
xScholl, Inge.
Students Against Tyranny: The Resistance of the White Rose, Munich, 1942-1943. Columbia U Pr.

Schollander, Don.
xSchollander, Don.
Inside Swimming. Contemp Bks.

Schollhammer, Hans.
xSchollhammer, Hans.
Entrepreneurship & Small Business Management. Wiley.

Scholz, Jackson. *see* Scholz, Jackson Volney.

Scholz, Jackson Volney.
xScholz, Jackson.
Backfield Blues. Morrow.

Scholz, William.
xScholz, William.
Profitable Hotel-Motel Management. P-H.

Schon, Isabel.
xSchon, Isabel.
A Hispanic Heritage: A Guide to Juvenile Books About Hispanic People & Cultures. Scarecrow.

Schonberg, Harold C.
xSchonberg, Harold C.

Chamber & Solo Instrument Music. Greenwood.
The Collector's Chopin & Schumann. Greenwood.
Great Conductors. S&S.
The Great Conductors. S&S.
Great Pianists. S&S.
Lives of the Great Composers. Norton.

Schonborg, Virginia.
xSchonborg, Virginia.
illus. Subway Swinger. Morrow.

Schonborn, Karl L.
xSchonborn, Karl L.
Dealing with Violence: The Challenge Faced by Police & Other Peacekeepers. C C Thomas.

Schondorf, Hubert.
xSchondorf, Hubert.
Aspiration Cytology of the Breast. Saunders.

Schonell, Fred J. *see* Schonell, Fred Joyce.

Schonell, Fred Joyce.
xSchonell, Fred J.
Psychology & Teaching of Reading. Philos Lib.

Schoner, Bertram.
xSchoner, Bertram.
Marketing Research: A Short Course for Professionals. Wiley.

Schonfeld, William R., 1942-
xSchonfeld, William R.
Obedience & Revolt: French Behavior Toward Authority. Sage.

Schonfeldt, N. *see* Schonfeldt, Nikolaus.

Schonfeldt, Nikolaus.
xSchonfeldt, N.
Surface Active Ethylene Oxide Adducts. Pergamon.

Schonfield, Hugh J. *see* Schonfield, Hugh Joseph.

Schonfield, Hugh Joseph, 1901-
xSchonfield, Hugh J.
The Politics of God. Univ of Trees.
Popular Dictionary of Judaism. Citadel Pr.

Schonzeler, Hans Hubert.
xSchonzeler, Hans-Hubert.
Bruckner. Merrimack Bk Serv.
Bruckner. Vienna Hse.

Schonzeler, Hans-Hubert. *see* Schonzeler, Hans Hubert.

School Library Manpower Project.
xSchool Library Manpower Project.
Occupational Definitions for School Library Media Personnel. ALA.

School of Oriental & African Studies, University of London. *see* London. University. School of Oriental and African Studies.

Schoolcraft, Henry R. *see* Schoolcraft, Henry Rowe.

Schoolcraft, Henry Rowe.
xSchoolcraft, Henry R.
ed. Fire Plume: Legends of the American Indians. Dial.
Historical & Statistical Information Respecting the History, Condition & Prospects of the Indian Tribes of the United States. AMS Pr.
Notes on the Iroquois: Or, Contributions to the Statistics, Aboriginal History, Antiquities & General Ethnology of Western New York. Kraus Repr.
Personal Memoirs of a Residence of Thirty Years with the Indian Tribes on the American Frontiers: With Brief Notices of Passing Events, Facts & Opinions, A.D. 1812 to A.D. 1842. AMS Pr.
Personal Memoirs of a Residence of Thirty Years with the Indian Tribes on the American Frontiers: 1812-1842. Arno.
Summary Narrative of an Exploratory Expedition to the Sources of the Mississippi River, in 1820. Kraus Repr.

Schoolcraft, Mary H. *see* Schoolcraft, Mary Howard.

Schoolcraft, Mary Howard.
xSchoolcraft, Mary H.

Plantation Life: The Narratives of Mrs. Henry
Rowe Schoolcraft. Negro U Pr.
Schoolfield, George C.
xSchoolfield, George C.
ed. German Lyric of the Baroque in English
Translation. AMS Pr.
tr. & ed. Swedo-Finnish Short Stories. Am
Scandinavian.
Schools Council. *see* Great Britain. Schools Council.
Schools Council History 13-16 Project. *see* Great Britain.
Schools Council. History 13-16 Project.
Schools Councils History 13-16 Project. *see* Great
Britain. Schools Council. History 13-16 Project.
Schoon, Louise. *see* Schoon, Louise Sherman.
Schoon, Louise Sherman.
xSchoon, Louise.
The Complete Pork Cook Book. Stein & Day.
Schoonmaker, Ann.
xSchoonmaker, Ann.
Me, Myself & I: Every Woman's Journey to
Her Self. Har-Row.
Schoonmaker, Paul D.
xSchoonmaker, Paul D.
The Prison Connection: A Lay Ministry Behind
Bars. Judson.
Schoonover, Thomas D. *see* Schoonover, Thomas David.
Schoonover, Thomas David, 1936-
xSchoonover, Thomas D.
Dollars Over Dominion: The Triumph of
Liberalism in Mexican-United States
Relations, 1861-1867. La State U Pr.
Schoop, Trudi.
xSchoop, Trudi.
Won't You Join the Dance?: A Dancer's Essay
into the Treatment of Psychosis. Mayfield
Pub.
Schoor, Gene.
xSchoor, Gene.
Billy Martin. Doubleday.
Football's Greatest Coach: Vince Lombardi.
Doubleday.
Joe Dimaggio: A Biography. Doubleday.
The Story of Yogi Berra. Doubleday.
Schopenhauer, Arthur, 1788-1860
xSchopenhauer, Arthur.
On the Basis of Morality. Bobbs.
Parerga & Paralipomena: Short Philosophical
Essays. Oxford U Pr.
Studies in Pessimism. Scholarly.
World As Will & Representation. Dover.
World As Will & Representation. Peter Smith.
Schopf, Thomas J. *see* Schopf, Thomas J. M.
Schopf, Thomas J. M.
xSchopf, Thomas J.
Paleoceanography. Harvard U Pr.
Schopler, Eric.
xSchopler, Eric.
ed. Psychopathology & Child Development:
Research & Treatment. Plenum Pub.
Schor, Lynda.
xSchor, Lynda.
True Love & Real Romance. Coward.
Schor, Sandra.
xSchor, Sandra.
The Random House Guide to Basic Writing.
Random.
Schor, Stanley S.
xSchor, Stanley S.
The Capital Product Ratio & Size of
Establishment for Manufacturing Industries.
Arno.
Schorer, Mark, 1908-
xSchorer, Mark.
ed. Story: A Critical Anthology. P-H.
Schorger, Arlie W. *see* Schorger, Arlie William.
Schorger, Arlie William, 1884-1972
xSchorger, Arlie W.
The Passenger Pigeon: Its Natural History &
Extinction. U of Okla Pr.
Schorr, A. E. *see* Schorr, Alan Edward.

Schorr, Alan E. *see* Schorr, Alan Edward.
Schorr, Alan Edward.
xSchorr, A. E.
Government Documents in the Library
Literature. Pierian.
xSchorr, Alan E.
ed. Directory of Special Libraries in Alaska.
SLA.
Schorr, Daniel.
xSchorr, Daniel.
Clearing the Air. Berkley Pub.
Schorr, Justin, 1928-
xSchorr, Justin.
Toward the Transformation of Art. Fairleigh
Dickinson.
Schorr, Philip.
xSchorr, Philip.
Planned Relocation. Lexington Bks.
Schorsch, Anita.
xSchorsch, Anita.
The Art of the Weaver. Universe.
Images of Childhood: An Illustrated Social
History. Mayflower Bks.
Schorske, Carl E.
xSchorske, Carl E.
Fin-De-Siecle Vienna: Politics & Culture.
Knopf.
Fin-De-Siecle Vienna: Politics & Culture.
Random.
German Social Democracy, 1905-1917: The
Development of the Great Schism. Russell.
Schott, Brian, 1944-
xSchott, Brian.
Riskm: A Player's Manual. Ga St U Busn Pub.
Schott, Joseph L.
xSchott, Joseph L.
No Left Turns. Ballantine.
Schottelius, Byron A.
xSchottelius, Byron A.
Textbook of Physiology. Mosby.
Schottenfeld, David.
xSchottenfeld, David.
ed. Cancer Epidemiology & Prevention:
Current Concepts. C C Thomas.
Schotter, Roni.
xSchotter, Roni.
A Matter of Time. Philomel.
Schottroff, Luise.
xSchottroff, Luise.
Essays on the Love Commandment. Fortress.
Schouler, James, 1839-1920
xSchouler, James.
Historical Briefs: With a Biography. Arno.
Schowalter, William R. *see* Schowalter, William
Raymond.
Schowalter, William Raymond, 1929-
xSchowalter, William R.
Mechanics of Non-Newtonian Fluids.
Pergamon.
Schrade, Hubert, 1900-
xSchrade, Hubert.
German Romantic Painting. Abrams.
Schrade, Leo, 1903-1964
xSchrade, Leo.
Bach: The Conflict Between the Sacred & the
Secular. Da Capo.
Schrader, Frederick F. *see* Schrader, Frederick Franklin.
Schrader, Frederick Franklin, 1857-
xSchrader, Frederick F.
The Germans in the Making of America.
Haskell.
Schrader, Lee F.
xSchrader, Lee F.
Farmers Cooperatives & Federal Income Taxes.
Ballinger Pub.
Schrader, Paul. *see* Schrader, Paul J.
Schrader, Paul J.
xSchrader, Paul.

Guidelines for Family Care Home Operators.
Springer Pub.
Schrader, Robert W. *see* Schrader, Robert William.
Schrader, Robert William.
xSchrader, Robert W.
The Nature of Theological Argument: A Study
of Paul Tillich. Scholars Pr Ca.
Schraff, Anne. *see* Schraff, Anne E.
Schraff, Anne E.
xSchraff, Anne.
Adventures of Peter & Paul: Acts of the
Apostles for the Young. Liguori Pubns.
Christians Courageous. Concordia.
Faith of the Presidents. Concordia.
Tecumseh. Dillon.
Schraff, Francis.
xSchraff, Francis.
jt. auth. Adventures of Peter & Paul: Acts of
the Apostles for the Young. Liguori Pubns.
Schrag, Calvin O.
xSchrag, Calvin O.
Existence & Freedom: Towards an Ontology of
Human Finitude. Northwestern U Pr.
Experience & Being: Prolegomena to a Future
Ontology. Northwestern U Pr.
Schrag, Peter.
xSchrag, Peter.
Mind Control. Dell.
Mind Control. Pantheon.
Schram, Joseph. *see* Schram, Joseph F.
Schram, Joseph F.
xSchram, Joseph.
Successful Bathrooms. Structures Pub.
Successful Children's Rooms. Structures Pub.
xSchram, Joseph F.
Finding & Fixing the Older Home Structures
Pub.
Improving the Outside of Your Home.
Structures Pub.
Successful Home Additions. Structures Pub.
Schram, Stuart R.
xSchram, Stuart R.
Mao Tse-Tung. S&S.
Schramm, Carl J.
xSchramm, Carl J.
ed. Alcoholism & Its Treatment in Industry.
Johns Hopkins.
Schramm, G. M. *see* Schramm, Gene Moshe.
Schramm, Gene Moshe, 1929-
xSchramm, G. M.
The Graphemes of Tiberian Hebrew. U of Cal
Pr.
Schramm, Gunter.
xSchramm, Gunter.
The Role of Low-Cost Power in Economic
Development: A Case Study; Alaska. Arno.
Schramm, John.
xSchramm, John.
Things That Make for Peace: A Personal
Search for a New Way of Life. Augsburg.
Schramm, Sarah S. *see* Schramm, Sarah Slavin.
Schramm, Sarah Slavin, 1942-
xSchramm, Sarah S.
Plow Women Rather Than Reapers: An
Intellectual History of Feminism in the
United States. Scarecrow.
Schramm, Wilbur. *see* Schramm, Wilbur Lang.
Schramm, Wilbur Lang, 1907-
xSchramm, Wilbur.
Men, Messages & Media: A Look at Human
Communication. Har-Row.
xSchramm, Wilbur Lang.
The People Look at Educational Television: A
Report of Nine Representative ETV Stations.
Greenwood.
Schran, Peter.
xSchran, Peter.

The Development of Chinese Agriculture, 1950-1959. U of Ill Pr.
Guerrilla Economy: The Development of the Shensi Kansu Ninghsia Border Region, 1937-1945. State U NY Pr.

Schrank, Jeffrey.
xSchrank, Jeffrey.
Deception Detection: An Educator's Guide to the Art of Insight. Beacon Pr.
The Guide to Short Films. Hayden.
Teaching Human Beings: 101 Subversive Activities for the Classroom. Beacon Pr.
Understanding Mass Media. Amphoto.

Schraufnagel, Noel.
xSchraufnagel, Noel.
From Apology to Protest: The Black American Novel. Everett-Edwards.

Schreck, Everett M.
xSchreck, Everett M.
Principles & Styles of Acting. A-W.

Schrecker, John E.
xSchrecker, John E.
Imperialism & Chinese Nationalism: Germany in Shantung. Harvard U Pr.

Schrecker, Paul, 1889-
xSchrecker, Paul.
Work & History: An Essay on the Structure of Civilization. Peter Smith.

Schreiber, Angela M.
xSchreiber, Angela M.
ed. Marriage & Family in a World of Change. Ave Maria.

Schreiber, Carol T. see Schreiber, Carol Tropp.

Schreiber, Carol Tropp.
xSchreiber, Carol T.
Changing Places: Men & Women in Transitional Occupations. MIT Pr.

Schreiber, Elizabeth A. see Schreiber, Elizabeth Anne.
Schreiber, Elizabeth Ann. see Schreiber, Elizabeth Anne.

Schreiber, Elizabeth Anne.
xSchreiber, Elizabeth A.
Wonders of Terns. Dodd.
xSchreiber, Elizabeth Ann.
Wonders of Sea Gulls. Dodd.

Schreiber, Flora R. see Schreiber, Flora Rheta.

Schreiber, Flora Rheta.
xSchreiber, Flora R.
Sybil. Warner Bks.

Schreiber, George. see Schreiber, Georges.

Schreiber, Georges, 1904-
xSchreiber, George.
ed. Portraits & Self-Portraits. Arno.

Schreiber, Harvey K.
xSchreiber, Harvey K.
The Eagle & the Sword. Popular Lib.

Schreiber, Hermann.
xSchreiber, Hermann.
Vanished Cities. Knopf.

Schreiber, Irving.
xSchreiber, Irving.
ed. Automatic Tax Planner. Panel Pubs.
ed. How to Handle Tax Audits, Requests for Rulings, Fraud Cases & Other Procedures Before the IRS. Panel Pubs.
ed. How to Plan for Tax Savings in Real Estate Transactions. Panel Pubs.

Schreiber, Jan. see Schreiber, Jan Edward.

Schreiber, Jan Edward, 1941-
xSchreiber, Jan.
The Ultimate Weapon: Terrorists & the World Order. Morrow.

Schreiber, Joanne.
xSchreiber, Joanne.
Sewing to Decorate Your Home. Doubleday.

Schreiber, Linda.
xSchreiber, Linda.
Marathon Mom: The Wife & Mother Running Book. HM.

Schreiber, Mary L.
xSchreiber, Mary L.

Women's Gymnastics. Goodyear.

Schreiber, Melvyn H.
xSchreiber, Melvyn H.
Indications & Alternatives in X-Ray Diagnosis: A Guide to the Effective Employment of Roentgenologic Studies in the Solution of Diagnostic Problems. C C Thomas.

Schreiber, Meyer.
xSchreiber, Meyer.
ed. Social Work & Mental Retardation. T Y Crowell.

Schreiber, Vernon R.
xSchreiber, Vernon R.
Wrestling with God: Messages for Lent & Easter on the Life of Jacob. Augsburg.

Schreiber, W. G.
xSchreiber, W. G.
A Bullet or a Rope. Bouregy.
Massacre at Fort Caid. Bouregy.

Schreier, Konrad F.
xSchreier, Konrad F.
Remington Rolling Block Firearms. Pioneer Pr.

Schreiner, Olive, 1855-1920
xSchreiner, Olive.
From Man to Man or Perhaps Only ..... Arden Lib.
From Man to Man or Perhaps Only.... R West.
Letters of Olive Schreiner 1876-1920.. Hyperion Conn.
Undine. Johnson Repr.
Undine. R West.

Schreiner, Samuel A.
xSchreiner, Samuel A.
Pleasant Places. Arbor Hse.
Pleasant Places. Fawcett.
Thine Is the Glory. Arbor Hse.

Schreiner, Samuel A. see Schreiner, Samuel Agnew.

Schreiner, Samuel Agnew.
xSchreiner, Samuel A.
The Condensed World of the Reader's Digest. Stein & Day.

Schrenk, William G., 1910-
xSchrenk, William G.
Analytical Atomic Spectroscopy. Plenum Pub.

Schretlen, M. J. see Schretlen, Martinus Joseph Antonius Maria.

Schretlen, Martinus Joseph Antonius Maria, 1890-
xSchretlen, M. J.
Dutch & Flemish Woodcuts of the Fifteenth Century. Hacker.

Schriber, T. J. see Schriber, Thomas J.

Schriber, Thomas J., 1935-
xSchriber, T. J.
Simulation Using GPSS. Wiley.
xSchriber, Thomas J.
Fundamentals of Flowcharting. Krieger.

Schrieber, Albert N.
xSchrieber, Albert N.
Defense Procurement & Small Business: A Survey of Practices & Opinions of Small Business Firms Selling to Defense Programs. U of Wash Pr.

Schrier, Robert W.
xSchrier, Robert W.
ed. Renal & Electrolyte Disorders. Little.

Schroder, David.
xSchroder, David.
Engagement in the Mirror: Hairdressers & Their Work. R & E Res Assoc.

Schroder, K. see Schroder, Klaus.

Schroder, Klaus, 1928-
xSchroder, K.
ed. Electronic, Magnetic & Thermal Properties of Solid Materials. Dekker.

Schroder, William. see Schroder, William E.

Schroder, William E.
xSchroder, William.
illus. Pea Soup & Sea Serpents. Lothrop.

Schroeder, Albert H.
xSchroeder, Albert H.

Archeological Excavations at Willow Beach, Arizona, 1950. AMS Pr.

Schroeder, Eileen.
xSchroeder, Eileen.
Going to the Dogs. Crown.

Schroeder, Gertrude G.
xSchroeder, Gertrude G.
The Growth of Major Steel Companies: 1900-1950. AMS Pr.

Schroeder, H. E. see Schroeder, Hubert Ernst.

Schroeder, Hubert Ernst.
xSchroeder, H. E.
Fine Structure of the Developing Epithelial Attachment of Human Teeth. S Karger.

Schroeder, Janet E.
xSchroeder, Janet E.
Dialogue with the Other: Martin Buber & the Quaker Experience. Pendle Hill.

Schroeder, Joseph J.
xSchroeder, Joseph J.
ed. Gun Collector's Digest. Follett.

Schroeder, M. J. see Schroeder, Mary Juliana.

Schroeder, Mary Juliana, Sister.
xSchroeder, M. J.
Mary-Verse in "Meistergesang". AMS Pr.

Schroeder, Oliver.
xSchroeder, Oliver C.
ed. Dental Jurisprudence: A Handbook of Practical Law. PSG Pub.

Schroeder, Oliver C. see Schroeder, Oliver.

Schroeder, Paul W.
xSchroeder, Paul W.
Austria, Great Britain, & the Crimean War: The Destruction of the European Concert. Cornell U Pr.

Schroeder, Rosella J.
xSchroeder, Rosella J.
It's Not Really Magic: Microwave Cooking for Young People. Dillon.

Schroeder, Theodore A. see Schroeder, Theodore Albert.

Schroeder, Theodore Albert, 1864-1953
xSchroeder, Theodore A.
Free Speech for Radicals. B Franklin.

Schroeder, Warren L. see Schroeder, Warren Lee.

Schroeder, Warren Lee, 1939-
xSchroeder, Warren L.
ed. Soils in Construction. Wiley.

Schroeder, William L. see Schroeder, William Lawrence.

Schroeder, William Lawrence.
xSchroeder, William L.
Oliver Wendell Holmes: An Appreciation. Folcroft.

Schroeppel, Tom.
xSchroeppel, Tom.
The Bare Bones Camera Course for Film & Video. Schroeppel.

Schroeter, Leonard.
xSchroeter, Leonard.
The Last Exodus. U of Wash Pr.
The Last Exodus. Universe.

Schroth, Raymond A.
xSchroth, Raymond A.
The Eagle & Brooklyn: A Community Newspaper, 1841-1955. Greenwood.

Schroyer, Trent.
xSchroyer, Trent.
The Critique of Domination: The Origins & Development of Critical Theory. Beacon Pr.
The Critique of Domination: The Origins & Development of Critical Theory. Braziller.

Schrut, Albert.
xSchrut, Albert H.
Are You Listening, Doctor?. Nelson-Hall.

Schrut, Albert H. see Schrut, Albert.
Schryver, Alice. see Schryver, Alice Stinnett.

Schryver, Alice Stinnett, 1911-
xSchryver, Alice.
French Cooking for Beginners. Dodd.

Schubel, J. R.
xSchubel, Jerry R.

ed. Power Plant Entrainment: A Biological
Assessment. Acad Pr.
Schubel, Jerry R. *see* Schubel, J. R.
Schubert, Delwyn G.
xSchubert, Delwyn G.
Improving the Reading Program. Wm C
Brown.
Schubert, Earl D., 1916-
xSchubert, Earl D.
ed. Psychological Acoustics. DH&R.
Schubert, Franz P. *see* Schubert, Franz Peter.
Schubert, Franz Peter.
xSchubert, Franz P.
Franz Schubert's Letters & Other Writings.
Arno.
Franz Schubert's Letters & Other Writings.
Greenwood.
Schubert, Glendon. *see* Schubert, Glendon A.
Schubert, Glendon A.
xSchubert, Glendon.
Human Jurisprudence: Public Law As Political
Science. U Pr of Hawaii.
xSchubert, Glendon A.
The Presidency in the Courts. Da Capo.
Schubert, Kurt, 1923-
xSchubert, Kurt.
Dead Sea Community: Its Origin & Teachings.
Greenwood.
Schubert, Maxwell.
xSchubert, Maxwell.
A Primer on Connective Tissue Biochemistry.
Lea & Febiger.
Schubert, Ruth L.
xSchubert, Ruth L.
The Camper's Cookbook. Little.
Schubert, Walter J.
xSchubert, Walter J.
Lignin Biochemistry. Acad Pr.
Schuchat, Theodor.
xSchuchat, Theodor.
Planning the Rest of Your Life. Phi Delta
Kappa.
Schuchhardt, Walter Herwig, 1900-
xSchuchhardt, Walter-Herwig.
Greek Art. Universe.
Schuchhardt, Walter-Herwig. *see* Schuchhardt, Walter
Herwig.
Schuckman, Terry.
xSchuckman, Terry.
Aging Is Not for Sissies. Westminster.
Schuell, Hildred.
xSchuell, Hildred.
Differential Diagnosis of Aphasia with the
Minnesota Test. U of Minn Pr.
Schueller, Wolfgang, 1934-
xSchueller, Wolfgang.
High-Rise Building Structures. Wiley.
Schuett, Virginia. *see* Schuett, Virginia E.
Schuett, Virginia E., 1947-
xSchuett, Virginia.
ed. Low Protein Cookery for Phenylketonuria.
U of Wis Pr.
Schuettinger, Robert. *see* Schuettinger, Robert Lindsay.
Schuettinger, Robert Lindsay, 1936-
xSchuettinger, Robert.
Lord Acton: Historian of Liberty. Open Court.
Schug, Charles, 1945-
xSchug, Charles.
The Romantic Genesis of the Modern Novel.
U of Pittsburgh Pr.
Schug, John. *see* Schug, John A.
Schug, John A.
xSchug, John.
Padre Pio. Our Sunday Visitor.
Schuh, Fred. *see* Schuh, Frederik.
Schuh, Frederik, 1875-
xSchuh, Fred.

The Master Book of Mathematical Recreations.
Peter Smith.
Schuh, Nita.
xSchuh, Nita.
After Winter, Spring. Logos.
Schuhardt, Vernon T.
xSchuhardt, Vernon T.
Pathogenic Microbiology: The Biology &
Prevention of Selected Bacterial, Fungal,
Rickettsial, & Viral Diseases of Clinical
Importance. Lippincott.
Schuhmacher, W. W.
xSchuhmacher, W. W.
Cybernetic Aspects of Language. Mouton.
Schuknecht, Harold F. *see* Schuknecht, Harold Frederich.
Schuknecht, Harold Frederich, 1917-
xSchuknecht, Harold F.
Pathology of the Ear. Harvard U Pr.
Stapedectomy. Little.
Schul, Bill.
xSchul, Bill.
The Psychic Power of Pyramids. Fawcett.
Pyramids & the Second Reality. Fawcett.
Schul, Bill D.
xSchul, Bill D.
How to Be an Effective Group Leader.
Nelson-Hall.
Schulberg, Budd.
xSchulberg, Budd.
Swan Watch. Delacorte.
What Makes Sammy Run?. Bentley.
What Makes Sammy Run?. Penguin.
Schulberg, Herbert C.
xSchulberg, Herbert C.
ed. Developments in Human Services. Human
Sci Pr.
ed. The Evaluator & Management. Sage.
ed. Program Evaluation in the Health Fields.
Human Sci Pr.
Schuld, Frank P.
xSchuld, Frank P.
The Simple Squeeze in Bridge. Sterling.
Schulder, Diane.
xSchulder, Diane.
Abortion Rap. McGraw.
Schuler, Edgar A. *see* Schuler, Edgar Albert.
Schuler, Edgar Albert.
xSchuler, Edgar A.
Public Opinion & Constitution Making in
Pakistan 1958-1962. Mich St U Pr.
ed. Readings in Sociology. Har-Row.
Schuler, Elizabeth.
xSchuler, Elizabeth.
German Cookery. Crown.
Schuler, Elizabeth. *see* Schuler, Elizabeth Meriwether.
Schuler, Elizabeth M. *see* Schuler, Elizabeth Meriwether.
Schuler, Elizabeth Meriwether.
xSchuler, Elizabeth.
Raising Puppies for Pleasure & Profit.
Macmillan.
xSchuler, Elizabeth M.
The Dog Lover's Answer Book. S&S.
Schuler, Frederic.
xSchuler, Frederic.
Flameworking: Glassmaking for the Craftsman.
Chilton.
xSchuler, Frederic W.
Glassforming: Glassmaking for the Craftsman.
Chilton.
Schuler, Frederic W. *see* Schuler, Frederic.
Schuler, Randall S.
xSchuler, Randall S.
Case Problems in Management. West Pub.
Schuler, S. *see* Schuler, Stanley.
Schuler, Stanley.
xSchuler, S.

How to Design, Build & Maintain Your
Swimming Pool. Macmillan.
xSchuler, Stanley.
The Complete Book of Closets & Storage. M
Evans.
The Gardener's Basic Book of Trees & Shrubs.
S&S.
Handyman's Guide to Home Remodeling.
Reston.
The Homeowner's Minimum-Maintenance
Manual. M Evans.
How to Build Fences, Gates & Walls.
Macmillan.
How to Build Fences, Gates & Walls.
Macmillan.
How to Design & Build a Fireplace.
Macmillan.
How to Design & Build a Fireplace.
Macmillan.
How to Design, Build & Maintain Your
Swimming Pool. Macmillan.
Planning & Planting the Small Garden Plot: A
Practical Guide. Dial.
Schulitz, K. P. *see* Schulitz, Klaus-Peter.
Schulitz, Klaus-Peter.
xSchulitz, K. P.
ed. Late Reconstructions of Injured Ligaments
of the Knee. Springer-Verlag.
Schulke, Flip.
xSchulke, Flip.
ed. Martin Luther King, Jr.: A
Documentary...Montgomery to Memphis.
Norton.
Underwater Photography for Everyone. P-H.
Schull, Diantha D. *see* Schull, Diantha Dow.
Schull, Diantha Dow.
xSchull, Diantha D.
Landmarks of Otsego County. Syracuse U Pr.
Schull, Joseph.
xSchull, Joseph.
The Great Scot: A Biography of Donald
Gordon. McGill-Queens U Pr.
Schuller, Gunther.
xSchuller, Gunther.
Horn Technique. Oxford U Pr.
Schuller, Robert. *see* Schuller, Robert Harold.
Schuller, Robert H.
xSchuller, Robert H.
Peace of Mind Through Possibility Thinking.
BJ Pub Group.
Peace of Mind Through Possibility Thinking.
Doubleday.
Schuller, Robert H. *see* Schuller, Robert Harold.
Schuller, Robert Harold.
xSchuller, Robert.
Power Ideas for a Happy Family. Pillar Bks.
xSchuller, Robert H.
The Greatest Possibility Thinker That Ever
Lived. Revell.
Power Ideas for a Happy Family. Revell.
Reach Out for a New Life. Dutton.
Reach Out for New Life. Bantam.
Schulman. *see* Schulman, Eveline D.
Schulman, Arnold.
xSchulman, Arnold.
Baba. PB.
Schulman, Elias.
xSchulman, Elias.
A History of Jewish Education in the Soviet
Union, 1918-1948. Ktav.
Schulman, Eveline D., 1919-
xSchulman.
Focus on the Retarded Adult: Programs &
Services. Mosby.
Schulman, Grace.
xSchulman, Grace.
Burn Down the Icons: Poems. Princeton U Pr.
Schulman, Janet.
xSchulman, Janet.

Camp Kee Wee's Secret Weapon. Greenwillow.
The Great Big Dummy. Greenwillow.
The Nutcracker. Dutton.
Schulman, Jerome L.
xSchulman, Jerome L.
The Child with Cancer: Clinical Approaches to
Psychosocial Care - Research in Psychosocial
Aspects. C C Thomas.
Coping with Tragedy: Successfully Facing the
Problem of a Seriously Ill Child. Follett.
Schulman, L. M.
xSchulman, L. M.
ed. Loners: Short Stories About the Young &
Alienated. Macmillan.
xSchulman, Lester M.
Frwd. by Loners: Short Stories About the
Young & Alienated. Macmillan.
Schulman, Lester M. *see* Schulman, L. M.
Schulman, Martin.
xSchulman, Martin Bud.
The Professional's Investment Guide: How to
Multiply the Profits from Your Practice.
Acropolis.
Schulman, Martin Bud. *see* Schulman, Martin.
Schulman, Michael.
xSchulman, Michael.
ed. Contemporary Scenes for Student Actors.
Penguin.
Schulmerich, Alma.
xSchulmerich, Alma A.
Josie Pearl. Nevada Pubns.
Schulmerich, Alma A. *see* Schulmerich, Alma.
Schult, Joachim.
xSchult, Joachim.
Curious Boating Inventions. Taplinger.
Curious Yachting Inventions. Taplinger.
Schulte, Henry F.
xSchulte, Henry F.
The Spanish Press, 1470-1966: Print, Power &
Politics. U of Ill Pr.
Schulte, Renee K.
xSchulte, Renee K.
ed. The Young Nixon: An Oral Inquiry. CSUF
Oral Hist.
Schulten, Adolf, 1870-1960
xSchulten, Adolf.
Geschichte Von Numantia. Arno.
Schultes, Richard E. *see* Schultes, Richard Evans.
Schultes, Richard Evans.
xSchultes, Richard E.
The Botany & Chemistry of Hallucinogens. C
C Thomas.
Hallucinogenic Plants. Western Pub.
Schulthess, Emil.
xSchulthess, Emil.
Africa. S&S.
Schults, Raymond L.
xSchults, Raymond L.
Crusader in Babylon: W.T. Stead & the "Pall
Mall Gazette". U of Nebr Pr.
Schultz, Alfred P. *see* Schultz, Alfred Paul Karl Eduard.
Schultz, Alfred Paul Karl Eduard, 1878-
xSchultz, Alfred P.
Race or Mongrel. Gordon Pr.
Schultz, Arnold.
xSchultz, Arnold.
A Theory of Consciousness. Philos Lib.
Schultz, Barbara. *see* Schultz, Barbara A.
Schultz, Barbara A.
xSchultz, Barbara.
ed. Bicycles & Bicycling: A Guide to
Information Sources. Gale.
Schultz, D. O. *see* Schultz, Donald O.
Schultz, D. R. *see* Schultz, Duane R.
Schultz, Donald. *see* Schultz, Donald O.
Schultz, Donald O., 1939-
xSchultz, D. O.
The Subversive. C C Thomas.
xSchultz, Donald.

Principles of Physical Security. Gulf Pub.
xSchultz, Donald O.
Criminal Investigation Techniques. Gulf Pub.
Critical Issues in Criminal Justice. C C
Thomas.
ed. Modern Police Administration. Gulf Pub.
Police Pursuit Driving Handbook. Gulf Pub.
Schultz, Duane. *see* Schultz, Duane P.
Schultz, Duane P.
xSchultz, Duane.
Growth Psychology: Models of the Healthy
Personality. Van Nos Reinhold.
Theories of Personality. Brooks-Cole.
Wake Island. Playboy Pbks.
xSchultz, Duane P.
Psychology & Industry Today. Macmillan.
Schultz, Duane R.
xSchultz, D. R.
The Complement System. S Karger.
Schultz, George J.
xSchultz, George J.
ed. Foreign Trade Marketplace. Gale.
Schultz, Gwen. *see* Schultz, Gwen M.
Schultz, Gwen M.
xSchultz, Gwen.
Ice Age Lost. Reading Gems.
Icebergs & Their Voyages. Morrow.
Schultz, Harold J. *see* Schultz, Harold John.
Schultz, Harold John.
xSchultz, Harold J.
History of England. Har-Row.
Schultz, Harry D.
xSchultz, Harry D.
Financial Tactics & Terms for the Sophisticated
International Investor. Har-Row.
Schultz, Henry, 1893-1938
xSchultz, Henry.
Theory & Measurement of Demand. U of
Chicago Pr.
Schultz, J. S. *see* Schultz, Jon S.
Schultz, James W. *see* Schultz, James Willard.
Schultz, James Willard.
xSchultz, James W.
Floating on the Missouri. U of Okla Pr.
Schultz, John J.
xSchultz, John J.
Understanding & Using Radio Communications
Receivers. TAB Bks.
Schultz, Jon S.
xSchultz, J. S.
Comparative Statutory Sources. W S Hein.
Schultz, Lawrence. *see* Schultz, Lawrence E.
Schultz, Lawrence E.
xSchultz, Lawrence.
How to Repair CB Radios. McGraw.
Schultz, Leroy G.
xSchultz, Leroy G.
Rape Victimology. C C Thomas.
Schultz, Louis C.
xSchultz, Louis C.
Operative Dentistry. Lea & Febiger.
Schultz, Mort J. *see* Schultz, Morton J.
Schultz, Morton J.
xSchultz, Mort J.
How to Fix It. McGraw.
xSchultz, Morton J.
How to Fix It. McGraw.
Schultz, Neil, 1952-
xSchultz, Neil.
The Complete Book of Safe Moped Operation
& Repair. Doubleday.
Complete Guide to Motorcycle Repair &
Maintenance. Arco.
The Complete Guide to Motorcycle Repair &
Maintenance. Doubleday.
Schultz, Peter H., 1944-
xSchultz, Peter H.

Moon Morphology: Interpretations Based on
Lunar Orbiter Photography. U of Tex Pr.
Schultz, Richard C. *see* Schultz, Richard Carlton.
Schultz, Richard Carlton, 1927-
xSchultz, Richard C.
Facial Injuries. Year Bk Med.
ed. Outpatient Surgery. Lea & Febiger.
Schultz, Richard J.
xSchultz, Richard J.
Christian's Mission. Concordia.
Schultz, Robert E.
xSchultz, Robert E.
Life Insurance Housing Projects. Irwin.
Schultz, Samuel J.
xSchultz, Samuel J.
The Gospel of Moses. Moody.
Schultz, Stanley K.
xSchultz, Stanley K.
The Culture Factory: Boston Public Schools,
1789-1860. Oxford U Pr.
Schultz, Theodore D. *see* Schultz, Theodore David.
Schultz, Theodore David, 1929-
xSchultz, Theodore D.
Quantum Field Theory & the Many-Body
Problem. Gordon.
Schultz, Theodore W. *see* Schultz, Theodore William.
Schultz, Theodore William.
xSchultz, Theodore W.
ed. Distortions of Agricultural Incentives. Ind
U Pr.
Economic Value of Education. Columbia U Pr.
ed. Food for the World. Arno.
Schultz, William E. *see* Schultz, William Eben.
Schultz, William Eben.
xSchultz, William E.
Gay's Beggar's Opera: Its Content, History &
Influence. Elliots Bks.
Gay's Beggar's Opera: Its Content, History &
Influence. Russell.
Schultze, Charles L.
xSchultze, Charles L.
National Income Analysis. P-H.
Schultze, Russell S.
xSchultze, Russell S.
How Many Mountains?. Broadman.
Schulz, Ann.
xSchulz, Ann.
Local Politics & Nation-States: Case Studies in
Politics & Policy. ABC-Clio.
Schulz, Bruno, 1892-1942
xSchulz, Bruno.
Sanatorium Under the Sign of the Hourglass.
Walker & Co.
The Street of Crocodiles. Penguin.
Schulz, Charles. *see* Schulz, Charles M.
Schulz, Charles M.
xSchulz, Charles.
Summers Fly, Winters Walk. Fawcett.
Summers Fly, Winters Walk. HR&W.
There's No Time for Love, Charlie Brown.
NAL.
xSchulz, Charles M.

Id & the Regulatory Principles of Mental
Functioning. Intl Univs Pr.
Schur, Sylvia.
xSchur, Sylvia.
The Tappan Creative Cookbook for Microwave
Ovens & Ranges. HR&W.
The Tappan Creative Cookbook for Microwave
Ovens & Ranges. NAL.
Schure, Edouard, 1841-1929
xSchure, Edouard.
The Great Initiates: A Study of the Secret
History of Religions. Har-Row.
xSchure, Edward.
From Sphinx to Christ: An Occult History.
Multimedia.
Schure, Edward. see Schure, Edouard.
Schurer, Emil, 1844-1910
xSchurer, Emil.
The Literature of the Jewish People in the
Time of Jesus. Schocken.
Schurle, A. W. see Schurle, Arlo W.
Schurle, Arlo W.
xSchurle, A. W.
Topics in Topology. Elsevier.
Schurman, Dewey, 1943-
xSchurman, Dewey.
Athletic Fitness: The Athlete's Guide to
Training & Conditioning. Atheneum.
Schurman, Donald M.
xSchurman, Donald M.
Education of a Navy: The Development of
British Naval Strategic Thought, 1867-1914.
U of Chicago Pr.
Schurman, Nona.
xSchurman, Nona.
Modern Dance Fundamentals. Macmillan.
Schurmann, Franz. see Schurmann, Herbert Franz.
Schurmann, Herbert Franz.
xSchurmann, Franz.
Ideology & Organization in Communist China.
U of Cal Pr.
The Logic of World Power: An Inquiry into
the Origins, Currents & Contradictions of
World Politics. Pantheon.
Schurz, Carl.
xSchurz, Carl.
Charles Sumner: An Essay. Greenwood.
Speeches, Correspondence & Political Papers of
Carl Schurz. Negro U Pr.
Schusky, Ernest L. see Schusky, Ernest Lester.
Schusky, Ernest Lester, 1931-
xSchusky, Ernest L.
The Forgotten Sioux: An Ethnohistory of the
Lower Brule Reservation. Nelson-Hall.
ed. Political Organization of Native North
Americans. U Pr of Amer.
Variation in Kinship. HR&W.
Schussheim, Morton J.
xSchussheim, Morton J.
Toward a New Housing Policy: The Legacy of
the Sixties. Comm Econ Dev.
Schuster, Arthur, Sir, 1851-1934
xSchuster, Arthur.
The Progress of Physics During 33 Years,
1875-1908. Arno.
Schuster, Ilsa. see Schuster, Ilsa M. Glazer.
Schuster, Ilsa M. Glazer.
xSchuster, Ilsa.
The New Women of Lusaka. Mayfield Pub.
Schuster, Marie, 1936-
xSchuster, Marie.
The Library-Centered Approach to Learning.
Etc Pubns.
Schuster, Mary I.
xSchuster, Mary I.
Creative Responses for Composition. Random.
Schuster, Mel.
xSchuster, Mel.

The Contemporary Greek Cinema. Scarecrow.
Schuster, Peter.
xSchuster, Peter.
The Hydrogen Bond: Recent Developments in
Theory & Experiments. Elsevier.
Schutte, K. see Schutte, Kurt.
Schutte, Kurt.
xSchutte, K.
Proof Theory. Springer-Verlag.
Schutz, Albert J., 1936-
xSchutz, Albert J.
Nguna Grammar. U Pr of Hawaii.
Schutz, Alfred.
xSchutz, Alfred.
The Structures of the Life-World.
Northwestern U Pr.
Schutz, Barry. see Schutz, Barry M.
Schutz, Barry M.
xSchutz, Barry.
Natives & Settlers: A Comparative Analysis of
the Politics of Opposition & Mobilization in
Northern Ireland & Rhodesia. U of Denver
Intl.
Schutz, Howard. see Schutz, Howard G.
Schutz, Howard G.
xSchutz, Howard.
Lifestyles & Consumer Behavior of Older
Americans. Praeger.
Schutz, J. H. see Schutz, John Howard.
Schutz, John Howard.
xSchutz, J. H.
Paul & the Anatomy of Apostolic Authority.
Cambridge U Pr.
Schutz, Susan P. see Schutz, Susan Polis.
Schutz, Susan Polis.
xSchutz, Susan P.
Come into the Mountains, Dear Friend. Blue
Mtn Pr CO.
Peace Flows from the Sky. Blue Mtn Pr CO.
Schutz, Walter E.
xSchutz, Walter E.
Getting Started in Candlemaking. Macmillan.
Schutz, Will. see Schutz, William C.
Schutz, William C.
xSchutz, Will.
Leaders of Schools: FIRO Theory Applied to
Administrators. Univ Assocs.
Schutze, Alfred, 1903-1972
xSchutze, Alfred.
Enigma of Evil. St George Bk Serv.
Schutze, Gertrude.
xSchutze, Gertrude.
Documentation Source Book. Scarecrow.
Information & Library Science Source Book:
Supplement to Documentation Source Book.
Scarecrow.
Schuyler, George. see Schuyler, George W.
Schuyler, George W.
xSchuyler, George.
Hunger in a Land of Plenty. Schenkman.
Schuyler, James.
xSchuyler, James.
What's for Dinner?. Black Sparrow.
Schuyler, Keith C.
xSchuyler, Keith C.
Getting Your Start in Flyrod Fishing. McKay.
Schuyler, Philippa. see Schuyler, Philippa Duke.
Schuyler, Philippa Duke.
xSchuyler, Philippa.
Who Killed the Congo ?. Devin.
Schuyler, R. L. see Schuyler, Robert Livingston.
Schuyler, Robert L., 1947-
xSchuyler, Robert L.
ed. Archaeological Perspectives on Ethnicity in
America: Afro-American & Asian American
Culture History. Baywood Pub.
ed. Historical Archaeology: A Guide to
Substantive & Theoretical Contributions.
Baywood Pub.
Schuyler, Robert L. see Schuyler, Robert Livingston.

Schuyler, Robert Livingston, 1883-
xSchuyler, R. L.
British Constitutional History Since 1832. Peter
Smith.
xSchuyler, Robert L.
Parliament & the British Empire: Some
Constitutional Controversies Concerning
Imperial Legislative Jurisdiction. AMS Pr.
Schwab, Adolf J.
xSchwab, Adolf J.
High-Voltage Measurement Techniques. MIT
Pr.
Schwab, Arnold. see Schwab, Arnold T.
Schwab, Arnold T.
xSchwab, Arnold.
A Matter of Life & Death: Vital Biographical
Facts About Selected American Artists.
Garland Pub.
Schwab, Joseph J. see Schwab, Joseph Jackson.
Schwab, Joseph Jackson, 1909-
xSchwab, Joseph J.
College Curriculum & Student Protest. U of
Chicago Pr.
Schwab, Peter, 1940-
xSchwab, Peter.
Decision-Making in Ethiopia: A Study of the
Political Process. Fairleigh Dickinson.
Haile Selassie I: Ethiopia's Lion of Judah.
Nelson-Hall.
Schwabe, Calvin W.
xSchwabe, Calvin W.
Cattle, Priests, & Progress in Medicine. U of
Minn Pr.
Unmentionable Cuisine. U Pr of Va.
Schwalb, Marvin N.
xSchwalb, Marvin N.
ed. Genetics & Morphogenesis in the
Basidiomycetes. Acad Pr.
Schwaller de Lubicz, R. A.
xSchwaller de Lubicz, R. A.
Symbol & the Symbolic: Egypt, Science & the
Evolution of Consciousness. Autumn Pr.
Schwamm, Ellen.
xSchwamm, Ellen.
Adjacent Lives. Avon.
Adjacent Lives. Knopf.
Schwandt, Mary, b. 1848
xSchwandt, Mary.
Captivity of Mary Schwandt. Ye Galleon.
Schwantes, Carlos A., 1945-
xSchwantes, Carlos A.
Radical Heritage: Labor, Socialism, & Reform
in Washington & British Columbia,
1885-1917. U of Wash Pr.
Schwantes, Dave.
xSchwantes, Dave.
Taming Your TV & Other Media. Southern
Pub.
Schwarcz, Henry P., 1933-
xSchwarcz, Henry P.
Pre-Cretaceous Sedimentation &
Metamorphism in the Winchester Area:
Northern Peninsular Ranges, California. Geol
Soc.
Schwartz, A. M. see Schwartz, Anthony Max.
Schwartz, Abba P.
xSchwartz, Abba P.
Open Society. S&S.
Schwartz, Al.
xSchwartz, Alvan R.
Travel--at Its Best!. Branden.
Schwartz, Allan B.
xSchwartz, Allan B.
Nephrology for the Practicing Physician.
Grune.
Schwartz, Alvan R. see Schwartz, Al.
Schwartz, Alvin, 1916-
xSchwartz, Alvin.

Rainy Day Book. Trident.
The Rainy Day Book. S&S.
Stores. Macmillan.
Schwartz, Andrew J.
xSchwartz, Andrew J.
America & the Russo-Finnish War.
Greenwood.
Schwartz, Anthony Max.
xSchwartz, A. M.
Surface Active Agents & Detergents. Krieger.
Schwartz, Arthur. *see* Schwartz, Arthur N.
Schwartz, Arthur N.
xSchwartz, Arthur.
Survival Handbook for Children of Aging
Parents. Follett.
xSchwartz, Arthur N.
Introduction to Gerontology. HR&W.
Professional Obligations & Approaches to the
Aged. C C Thomas.
Schwartz, Arthur R.
xSchwartz, Arthur.
Cooking in a Small Kitchen. Little.
Schwartz, Barry, 1938-
xSchwartz, Barry.
ed. The Changing Face of the Suburbs. U of
Chicago Pr.
Queuing & Waiting: Studies in the Social
Organization of Access & Delay. U of
Chicago Pr.
Schwartz, Barry. *see* Schwartz, Barry N.
Schwartz, Barry N.
xSchwartz, Barry.
ed. Human Connection & the New Media.
P-H.
Psychology of Learning & Behavior. Norton.
Schwartz, Benjamin I.
xSchwartz, Benjamin I.
Chinese Communism & the Rise of Mao.
Harvard U Pr.
Schwartz, Benjamin I. *see* Schwartz, Benjamin Isadore.
Schwartz, Benjamin Isadore, 1916-
xSchwartz, Benjamin I.
In Search of Wealth & Power: Yen Fu & the
West. Harvard U Pr.
Schwartz, Bernard, 1923-
xSchwartz, Bernard.
American Constitutional Law. Greenwood.
A Basic History of the U.S. Supreme Court.
Krieger.
A Commentary on the Constitution of the
United States. Rothman.
Constitutional Law: A Textbook. Macmillan.
Compiled by The Economic Regulation of
Business & Industry: A Legislative History of
U.S. Regulatory Agencies. Bowker.
From Confederation to Nation: The American
Constitution, 1835-1877. Johns Hopkins.
The Great Rights of Mankind: A History of
the American Bill of Rights. Oxford U Pr.
The Professor & the Commissions. Greenwood.
Reins of Power: A Constitutional History of
the United States. Hill & Wang.
Schwartz, Bertram.
xSchwartz, Bertram.
ed. Measurement Techniques for Thin Films.
Johnson Repr.
Schwartz, Charles.
xSchwartz, Charles.
Cole Porter: A Biography. Da Capo.
Cole Porter: A Biography. Dial.
Gershwin, His Life & Music. Da Capo.
A Modern Interpretation of Judaism: Faith
Through Reason. Schocken.
Schwartz, David J. *see* Schwartz, David Joseph.
Schwartz, David Joseph.
xSchwartz, David J.
Marketing Today: A Basic Approach.
HarBraceJ.
Schwartz, Eduard, 1858-1940
xSchwartz, Eduard.

Ethik der Griechen. Arno.
Schwartz, Elias, 1935-
xSchwartz, Elias.
ed. Hemoglobinopathies in Children. PSG Pub.
Schwartz, Elizabeth. *see* Schwartz, Elizabeth Reeder.
Schwartz, Elizabeth Reeder.
xSchwartz, Elizabeth.
When Flying Animals Are Babies. Holiday.
Schwartz, Elliot S. *see* Schwartz, Elliott S.
Schwartz, Elliott S.
xSchwartz, Elliot S.
The Symphonies of Ralph Vaughan Williams.
U of Mass Pr.
Schwartz, Eugene. *see* Schwartz, Eugene M.
Schwartz, Eugene M.
xSchwartz, Eugene.
How to Double Your Child's Grades in School.
Fell.
xSchwartz, Eugene M.
How to Double Your Child's Grades in School.
B&N.
Schwartz, Florence.
xSchwartz, Florence.
A Cross Cultural Encounter: A
Non-Traditional Approach to Social Work
Education. R & E Res Assoc.
Schwartz, Fred.
xSchwartz, Fred.
Psychoanalytic Model of Attention & Learning.
Intl Univs Pr.
Schwartz, Gary.
xSchwartz, Gary.
Sect Ideologies & Social Status. U of Chicago
Pr.
Schwartz, George I.
xSchwartz, George I.
Food Chains & Ecosystems: Ecology for Young
Experimenters. Doubleday.
Schwartz, George R.
xSchwartz, George R.
Principles & Practice of Emergency Medicine.
Saunders.
Schwartz, Harry, 1919-
xSchwartz, Harry.
China. Atheneum.
Planning for the Lower East Side. Irvington.
Schwartz, Harry W. *see* Schwartz, Harry Wayne.
Schwartz, Harry Wayne.
xSchwartz, Harry W.
Story of Musical Instruments, from Shepherd's
Pipe to Symphony. Arno.
Schwartz, Harvey.
xSchwartz, Harvey.
The March Inland: Origins of the ILWU
Warehouse Division, 1934-1938. U Cal LA
Indus Rel.
Schwartz, Harwood M. *see* Schwartz, Harwood Muzzy.
Schwartz, Harwood Muzzy, 1881-
xSchwartz, Harwood M.
Improvement in the Maintenance of Public
School Buildings. AMS Pr.
Schwartz, Helene. *see* Schwartz, Helene E.
Schwartz, Helene E.
xSchwartz, Helene.
Lawyering. FS&G.
Schwartz, Herman M. *see* Schwartz, Herman Meyer.
Schwartz, Herman Meyer, 1911-
xSchwartz, Herman M.
Introduction to Special Relativity. Krieger.
Schwartz, Hillel, 1948-
xSchwartz, Hillel.
The French Prophets: The History of a
Millenarian Group in Eighteenth-Century
England. U of Cal Pr.
Schwartz, Howard.
xSchwartz, Howard.
Qualitative Sociology: A Method to the
Madness. Free Pr.
Schwartz, Howard D.
xSchwartz, Howard D.

Dominant Issues in Medical Sociology. A-W.
Schwartz, Jacob T.
xSchwartz, Jacob T.
Differential Geometry & Topology. Gordon.
Lectures on the Mathematical Method in
Analytical Economics. Gordon.
Nonlinear Functional Analysis. Gordon.
Theory of Money. Gordon.
Schwartz, Joe.
xSchwartz, Joe.
Einstein for Beginners. Pantheon.
Schwartz, Jonathan, 1938-
xSchwartz, Jonathan.
Distant Stations. Avon.
Distant Stations. Doubleday.
Schwartz, Joseph, 1910-
xSchwartz, Joseph.
Don't Ever Retire but Do It Early & Often.
Farnswth Pub.
Schwartz, Judy I.
xSchwartz, Judy J.
Teaching the Linguistically Diverse. NY St
Eng Coun.
Schwartz, Judy J. *see* Schwartz, Judy I.
Schwartz, Jules J., 1932-
xSchwartz, Jules J.
Corporate Policy: A Casebook. P-H.
Schwartz, Julius.
xSchwartz, Julius.
Earthwatch: Space-Time Investigations with a
Globe. McGraw.
Schwartz, L. *see* Schwartz, Lawrence H.
Schwartz, Laura.
xSchwartz, Laura.
How to Get a Glamour Job. Times Bks.
Schwartz, Laurent.
xSchwartz, Laurent.
Application of Distributions to the Theory of
Elementary Particles in Quantum Mechanics.
Gordon.
Mathematics for the Physical Sciences. A-W.
Schwartz, Lawrence H.
xSchwartz, L.
Psychodynamics of Patient Care. P-H.
Schwartz, Lazar M.
xSchwartz, Lazar M.
Compendium of Immunology. Van Nos
Reinhold.
xSchwartz, Lazarm.
Compendium of Immunology. Educ Medical.
Schwartz, Lazarm. *see* Schwartz, Lazar M.
Schwartz, Leland. *see* Schwartz, Leland P.
Schwartz, Leland P.
xSchwartz, Leland.
Survey of Electronics. Merrill.
Schwartz, Lita L. *see* Schwartz, Lita Linzer.
Schwartz, Lita Linzer.
xSchwartz, Lita L.
American Education: A Problem-Centered
Approach. U Pr of Amer.
Schwartz, Lynne S. *see* Schwartz, Lynne Sharon.
Schwartz, Lynne Sharon.
xSchwartz, Lynne S.
Rough Strife. Har-Row.
Schwartz, M. *see* Schwartz, Michael A.
Schwartz, M. M. *see* Schwartz, Mel M.
Schwartz, Martin.
xSchwartz, Martin.
Advanced Class Radio Amateur License Guide.
AMECO.
Amateur Radio Novice Class Theory Course.
Ameco.
Amateur Radio Theory Course. AMECO.
Commercial Radio Operator Theory Course.
AMECO.
General Class Radio Amateur License Guide.
AMECO.
Radio Electronics Made Simple. AMECO.
Schwartz, Martin F., 1936-
xSchwartz, Martin F.

Stuttering Solved. Lippincott.

Schwartz, Maurice L.
xSchwartz, Maurice L.
ed. Barrier Islands. Acad Pr.

Schwartz, Max, 1922-
xSchwartz, Max.
Civil Engineering for the Plant Engineer. Krieger.

Schwartz, Mel M.
xSchwartz, M. M.
Metals Joining Manual. McGraw.
xSchwartz, Mel M.
Modern Metal Joining Techniques. Wiley.

Schwartz, Melvin, 1932-
xSchwartz, Melvin.
Principles of Electrodynamics. McGraw.

Schwartz, Michael, 1942-
xSchwartz, Michael.
Radical Protest & Social Structure: The Southern Farmer's Alliance & Cotton Tenancy, 1880-1890. Acad Pr.

Schwartz, Michael A., 1930-
xSchwartz, M.
ed. Prescription Drugs in Short Supply: Case Histories. Dekker.

Schwartz, Mildred A.
xSchwartz, Mildred A.
Politics & Territory: The Sociology of Regional Persistence in Canada. McGill-Queens U Pr.

Schwartz, Mischa.
xSchwartz, Mischa.
Communication Systems & Techniques. McGraw.
Information Transmission, Modulation & Noise: A Unified Approach. McGraw.

Schwartz, Mortimer. *see* Schwartz, Mortimer D.

Schwartz, Mortimer D.
xSchwartz, Mortimer.
Environmental Law: A Guide to Information Sources. Gale.
xSchwartz, Mortimer D.
ed. Space Law Perspectives: Commentaries Based on Volumes 1-15 (1957-1972) of the Colloquia on the Law of Outer Space. Rothman.

Schwartz, Morton.
xSchwartz, Morton.
The Foreign Policy of the USSR: Domestic Factors. Dickenson.
Soviet Perceptions of the United States. U of Cal Pr.

Schwartz, Murray M.
xSchwartz, Murray M.
ed. Representing Shakespeare: New Psychoanalytic Essays. Johns Hopkins.

Schwartz, Nancy B.
xSchwartz, Nancy B.
Compiled by Historic American Buildings Survey, District of Columbia Catalog,. U Pr of Va.

Schwartz, Narda L. *see* Schwartz, Narda Lacey.

Schwartz, Narda Lacey, 1948-
xSchwartz, Narda L.
Articles on Women Writers, 1960-1975: A Bibliography. ABC-Clio.

Schwartz, Peter J.
xSchwartz, Peter J.
ed. Neural Mechanisms in Cardiac Arrhythmias. Raven.

Schwartz, R. S. *see* Schwartz, Robert S.

Schwartz, Randall.
xSchwartz, Randall.
Carnivorous Plants. Avon.

Schwartz, Richard B.
xSchwartz, Richard B.
Boswell's Johnson: A Preface to the "Life". U of Wis Pr.

Schwartz, Robert J.
xSchwartz, Robert J.

Complete Dictionary of Abbreviations. T Y Crowell.

Schwartz, Robert S.
xSchwartz, R. S.
ed. Immunological Aspects of Neoplasia. S Karger.
xSchwartz, Robert S.
ed. Progress in Clinical Immunology. Grune.

Schwartz, Ronald, 1937-
xSchwartz, Ronald.
Jose Maria Gironella. Twayne.

Schwartz, Sheila.
xSchwartz, Sheila.
Growing up Guilty. Pantheon.
Teaching Adolescent Literature: A Humanistic Approach. Hayden.

Schwartz, Sidney, 1930-
xSchwartz, Sidney.
Housing Careers. P-H.

Schwartz, Steven, 1942-
xSchwartz, Steven.
The Book of Waters. A & W Pubs.

Schwartz, Stuart B.
xSchwartz, Stuart B.
Sovereignty & Society in Colonial Brazil: The High Court of Bahia & Its Judges, 1609-1751. U of Cal Pr.

Schwartz, Susan.
xSchwartz, Susan.
Cascade Companion. Pacific Search.

Schwartz, Thomas.
xSchwartz, Thomas.
The Art of Logical Reasoning. Random.

Schwartz, Tony.
xSchwartz, Tony.
The Responsive Chord. Doubleday.

Schwartz, William.
xSchwartz, William.
ed. Practice of Group Work. Columbia U Pr.

Schwartzberg, Joseph E.
xSchwartzberg, Joseph E.
ed. A Historical Atlas of South Asia. U of Chicago Pr.

Schwartzman, David.
xSchwartzman, David.
Innovation in the Pharmaceutical Industry. Johns Hopkins.

Schwartzman, Paulette.
xSchwartzman, Paulette.
Collector's Guide to European & American Art Pottery. Collector Bks.

Schwartzman, Sylvan D. *see* Schwartzman, Sylvan David.

Schwartzman, Sylvan David.
xSchwartzman, Sylvan D.
Elements of Financial Analysis. Van Nos Reinhold.
Reform Judaism - Then & Now. UAHC.

Schwarz, Alfred.
xSchwarz, Alfred.
From Buchner to Beckett: Dramatic Theory & the Modes of Tragic Drama. Ohio U Pr.

Schwarz, Berthold E. *see* Schwarz, Berthold Eric.

Schwarz, Berthold Eric, 1924-
xSchwarz, Berthold E.
Psychic-Nexus: Psychic Phenomena in Psychiatry & Everyday Life. Van Nos Reinhold.

Schwarz, Boris, 1906-
xSchwarz, Boris.
Music & Musical Life in Soviet Russia: 1917-1970. Norton.

Schwarz, Daniel R.
xSchwarz, Daniel R.
Disraeli's Fiction. B&N.

Schwarz, Edward W., 1929-
xSchwarz, Edward W.
How to Use Interest Rate Futures Contracts. Dow Jones-Irwin.

Schwarz, Egon, 1922-
xSchwarz, Egon.

Joseph von Eichendorff. Twayne.

Schwarz, Hans, 1939-
xSchwarz, Hans.
On the Way to the Future: A Christian View of Eschatology in the Light of Current Trends in Religion, Philosophy, & Science. Augsburg.
Our Cosmic Journey: Christian Anthropology in the Light of Current Trends in the Sciences, Philosophy,& Theology. Augsburg.

Schwarz, Henry F. *see* Schwarz, Henry Frederick.

Schwarz, Henry Frederick.
xSchwarz, Henry F.
The Imperial Privy Council in the Seventeenth Century. Greenwood.

Schwarz, Henry G., 1928-
xSchwarz, Henry G.
ed. Mongolian Short Stories. West Wash Univ.

Schwarz, Jack.
xSchwarz, Jack.
The Path of Action. Dutton.

Schwarz, Meier, 1926-
xSchwarz, Meir.
A Guide to Commercial Hydroponics. Intl Schol Bk Serv.

Schwarz, Meir. *see* Schwarz, Meier.

Schwarz, Ralph. *see* Schwarz, Ralph J.

Schwarz, Ralph J.
xSchwarz, Ralph.
Linear Systems. McGraw.

Schwarz, Ted, 1945-
xSchwarz, Ted.
Beginner's Guide to Coin Collecting. Doubleday.

Schwarz, Ted. *see* Schwarz, Theodore.

Schwarz, Theodore.
xSchwarz, Ted.
Coins As Living History. Arco.
A History of United States Coinage. A S Barnes.
How to Be a Freelance Photographer. Contemp Bks.
How to Make Money with Your Camera. H P Bks.
How to Start a Professional Photography Business. Contemp Bks.

Schwarz, Urs, 1905-
xSchwarz, Urs.
Confrontation & Intervention in the Modern World. Oceana.

Schwarz-Bart, Andre, 1928-
xSchwarz-Bart, Andre.
The Last of the Just. Atheneum.
The Last of the Just. Bentley.

Schwarzenbach, G. *see* Schwarzenbach, Gerold.

Schwarzenbach, Gerold.
xSchwarzenbach, G.
Complexometric Titrations. Methuen Inc.

Schwarzenberg, Adolph.
xSchwarzenberg, Adolph.
Prince Felix Zu Schwarzenberg: Prime Minister of Austria, 1848-1852. AMS Pr.

Schwarzenberger, Georg, 1908-
xSchwarzenberger, Georg.
The Dynamics of International Law. Rothman.
The Inductive Approach to International Law. Oceana.

Schwarzenegger, Arnold.
xSchwarzenegger, Arnold.
Arnold: The Education of a Body Builder. S&S.
Arnold: The Education of a Bodybuilder. PB.
Arnold's Bodyshaping for Women. S&S.

Schwarzrock, Shirley P. *see* Schwarzrock, Shirley Pratt.

Schwarzrock, Shirley Pratt.
xSchwarzrock, Shirley P.
Effective Medical Assisting. Wm C Brown.

Schwarzschild, Bettina.
xSchwarzschild, Bettina.

Scientific Personnel Office. *see* National Research
Council. Office of Scientific Personnel.

Scifres, Bill, 1925-
xScifres, Bill.
Indiana Outdoors: A Guide to Fishing,
Hunting, & Wild Crops. Ind U Pr.

Scigliano, R. *see* Scigliano, Robert G.

Scigliano, Robert. *see* Scigliano, Robert G.

Scigliano, Robert G.
xScigliano, R.
Supreme Court & the Presidency. Free Pr.
xScigliano, Robert.
South Vietnam: Nation Under Stress.
Greenwood.

Scimecca, Joseph.
xScimecca, Joseph.
Education & Society. HR&W.
xScimecca, Joseph A.
The Sociological Theory of C. Wright Mills.
Kennikat.

Scimecca, Joseph A. *see* Scimecca, Joseph.

Scioletti, Daniel C.
xScioletti, Daniel C.
Legal Decisions for CPA's & Business People.
Kendall-Hunt.

Scithers, George. *see* Scithers, George H.

Scithers, George H., 1929-
xScithers, George.
ed. Isaac Asimov's Masters of Science Fiction.
Dial.
xScithers, George H.
ed. Isaac Asimov's Masters of Science Fiction.
Davis Pubns.

Sciulli, Paul W.
xSciulli, Paul W.
An Introduction to Mendelian Genetics &
Gene Action. Burgess.

Sclar, D. *see* Sclar, Deanna.

Sclar, Deanna.
xSclar, D.
Auto Repair for Dummies. McGraw.

Sclare, Donald.
xSclare, Donald.
Beaux-Arts Estates: A Guide to the
Architecture of Long Island. Viking Pr.

Sclater, William L. *see* Sclater, William Lutley.

Sclater, William Lutley.
xSclater, William L.
The Geography of Mammals. Arno.

Scobey, Joan.
xScobey, Joan.
Celebrity Needlepoint. Dial.
The First Easy-to-See Needlepoint Workbook.
Rawson Wade.
Gifts from Your Garden. Bobbs.
xScobey, Joan M.
Short Rations: Confessions of a Cranky Calorie
Counter. HR&W.

Scobey, Joan M. *see* Scobey, Joan.

Scobie, G. E. *see* Scobie, Geoffrey E. W.

Scobie, Geoffrey E. W.
xScobie, G. E.
Psychology of Religion. Halsted Pr.

Scobie, James R., 1929-
xScobie, James R.
Argentina: A City & a Nation. Oxford U Pr.
Revolution on the Pampas: A Social History of
Argentine Wheat. U of Tex Pr.

Scoggin, Margaret C. *see* Scoggin, Margaret Clara.

Scoggin, Margaret Clara, 1905-
xScoggin, Margaret C.
ed. Edge of Danger: True Stories of Adventure.
Knopf.
ed. More Chucklebait: Funny Stories for
Everyone. Knopf.

Scoles, Eugene F.
xScoles, Eugene F.

Problems & Materials on Decedents' Estates &
Trusts. Little.

Scollard, Clinton, 1860-1932
xScollard, Clinton.
Ballads of American Bravery. Arno.

Scollon, Ronald, 1939-
xScollon, Ronald.
Conversations with a One Year Old: A Case
Study of the Developmental Foundation of
Syntax. U Pr of Hawaii.
Linguistic Convergence: An Ethnography of
Speaking at Fort Chipewyan, Alberta. Acad
Pr.

Sconce, J. S. *see* Sconce, James S.

Sconce, James S.
xSconce, J. S.
Chlorine: Its Manufacture, Properties & Uses.
Krieger.

Scontras, Charles A. *see* Scontras, Charles Andrew.

Scontras, Charles Andrew, 1929-
xScontras, Charles A.
Organized Labor & Labor Politics in Maine,
1880-1890. U Maine Orono.

Scopick, David, 1944-
xScopick, David.
The Gum Bichromate Book: Contemporary
Methods for Photographic Printmaking. Light
Impressions.

Scopp, Irwin W. *see* Scopp, Irwin Walter.

Scopp, Irwin Walter, 1909-
xScopp, Irwin W.
Oral Medicine: A Clinical Approach with Basic
Science Correlation. Mosby.

Scoppettone, Sandra.
xScoppettone, Sandra.
The Late Great Me. Putnam.
Some Unknown Person. Putnam.
Such Nice People. Putnam.
Trying Hard to Hear You. Har-Row.
Trying Hard to Hear You. Bantam.

Scorer, R. S. *see* Scorer, Richard Segar.

Scorer, Richard Segar, 1919-
xScorer, R. S.
Air Pollution. Pergamon.
The Clever Moron. Routledge & Kegan.
A Colour Guide to Clouds. Pergamon.

Scoresby, William, 1789-1857
xScoresby, William.
American Factories & Their Female
Operatives: With an Appeal on Behalf of the
British Factory Population & Suggestions for
the Improvement of Their Condition. B
Franklin.

Scortia, Thomas N.
xScortia, Thomas N.
The Gold Crew. Warner Bks.
The Nightmare Factor. Doubleday.

Scorza, Manuel.
xScorza, Manuel.
Drums for Rancas. Har-Row.

Scorza, Thomas J., 1948-
xScorza, Thomas J.
In the Time Before Steamships: Billy Budd, the
Limits of Politics, & Modernity. N Ill U Pr.

Scot, Reginald, 1538?-1599
xScot, Reginald.
The Discoverie of Witchcraft. Dover.
The Discoverie of Witchcraft. Walter J
Johnson.

Scotland. Treaties. *see* Scotland. Treaties, Etc.

Scotland. Treaties, Etc.
xScotland. Treaties.
Treaty of Union of Scotland & England.
Greenwood.

Scott. *see* Scott, Dr.

Scott, A. *see* Scott, Austin.

Scott, A. C. *see* Scott, Adolphe Clarence.

Scott, A. F. *see* Scott, Arthur Finley.

Scott, Adolphe C. *see* Scott, Adolphe Clarence.

Scott, Adolphe Clarence, 1909-
xScott, A. C.
Puppet Theatre of Japan. C E Tuttle.
The Theatre in Asia. Macmillan.
xScott, Adolphe C.
The Classical Theatre of China. Greenwood.

Scott, Alice.
xScott, Alice.
Ask Alice Scott About Small Animal Pets.
Arco.
How to Raise & Train a Pekingese. TFH
Pubns.

Scott, Allan W.
xScott, Allan W.
Cooling of Electronic Equipment. Wiley.

Scott, Andrew M. *see* Scott, Andrew MacKay.

Scott, Andrew MacKay.
xScott, Andrew M.
Politics, U.S.A.: Cases on the American
Democratic Process. Macmillan.

Scott, Ann H. *see* Scott, Ann Herbert.

Scott, Ann Herbert.
xScott, Ann H.
Census, U. S. A.: Fact Finding for the
American People, 1790-1970. HM.
On Mother's Lap. McGraw.

Scott, Antonia.
xScott, Antonia.
Falcon's Island. PB.

Scott, Arthur Finley.
xScott, A. F.
The Early Hanoverian Age: 1714-1760
Commentaries of an Era. Biblio Dist.

Scott, Arthur L. *see* Scott, Arthur Lincoln.

Scott, Arthur Lincoln, 1914-
xScott, Arthur L.
ed. Mark Twain: Selected Criticism. SMU
Press.

Scott, Austin, 1848-1922
xScott, A.
Influence of the Proprietors in Founding the
State of New Jersey. Johnson Repr.
xScott, Austin.
The Influence of the Proprietors in Founding
the State of New Jersey. AMS Pr.

Scott, Austin W. *see* Scott, Austin Wakeman.

Scott, Austin Wakeman, 1884-
xScott, Austin W.
Abridgment of The Law of Trusts. Little.
Cases & Other Materials on Civil Procedure.
Little.
The Law of Trusts. Little.

Scott, Bill. *see* Scott, William Neville.

Scott, C. R. *see* Scott, Charles Robin.

Scott, Carole E. *see* Scott, Carole Elizabeth.

Scott, Carole Elizabeth.
xScott, Carole E.
Your Financial Plan: A Consumer's Guide.
Har-Row.

Scott, Cecil W. *see* Scott, Cecil Winfield.

Scott, Cecil Winfield, 1905-
xScott, Cecil W.
Indefinite Teacher Tenure: A Critical Study of
the Historical, Legal, Operative &
Comparative Aspects. AMS Pr.
ed. Public Education Under Criticism. Arno.

Scott, Charles R.
xScott, Charles R.
Tempomatic IV: A Management Simulation.
HM.

Scott, Charles Robin.
xScott, C. R.
ed. Developments in Soil Mechanics.
Burgess-Intl Ideas.

Scott, Charles T.
xScott, Charles T.
ed. Readings for the History of the English
Language. Irvington.

Scott, Chris, 1945-
xScott, Chris.

To Catch a Spy. Penguin.
Scott, Claudia D. *see* Scott, Claudia Devita.
Scott, Claudia Devita.
xScott, Claudia D.
Forecasting Local Government Spending.
Urban Inst.
Scott, Clifford H.
xScott, Clifford H.
Lester Frank Ward. Twayne.
Scott, Cyril. *see* Scott, Cyril Meir.
Scott, Cyril Meir, 1879-
xScott, Cyril.
Music, Its Secret Influence Throughout the
Ages. Gordon Pr.
Scott, D. F. *see* Scott, David F.
Scott, D. R., 1887-1954
xScott.
The Cultural Significance of Accounts. Scholars
Bk.
xScott, D. R.
Cultural Significance of Accounts. Lucas.
Scott, David F., 1942-
xScott, D. F.
Cases in Finance. P-H.
Scott, David L. *see* Scott, David Logan.
Scott, David Logan, 1942-
xScott, David L.
Financing the Growth of Electric Utilities.
Praeger.
Traveling & Camping in the National Park
Areas: Eastern States. Globe Pequot.
Traveling & Camping in the National Park
Areas: Western States. Globe Pequot.
Scott, Dixon, 1881-1915
xScott, Dixon.
Men of Letters. Folcroft.
Men of Letters. Scholarly.
Scott, Donald F.
xScott, Donald F.
About Epilepsy. Intl Univs Pr
Scott, Donald M.
xScott, Donald M.
From Office to Profession: The New England
Ministry, 1750-1850. U of Pa Pr.
Scott, Douglas, 1926-
xScott, Douglas.
Operation Artemis. Ballantine.
Operation Artemis. Bobbs.
The Spoils of War. Coward.
Scott, Dr, 1887-1954
xScott.
Theory of Accounts. Arno.
Scott, Dru.
xScott, Dru.
How to Put More Time in Your Life. Rawson
Wade.
Scott, Ed.
xScott, Ed.
Honda Odyssey: 1977-1979
Service-Repair-Performance. Clymer Pubns.
Scott, Edward M.
xScott, Edward M.
The Adolescent Gap: Research Findings on
Drug Using & Non-Drug Using Teens. C C
Thomas.
Scott, Eileen. *see* Scott, Eileen P.
Scott, Eileen P.
xScott, Eileen.
ed. Can't Your Child See?. Univ Park.
Scott, Emmett J. *see* Scott, Emmett Jay.
Scott, Emmett Jay, 1873-1957
xScott, Emmett J.
Negro Migration During the War. Arno.
Scott, Ernest, Sir, 1868-1939
xScott, Ernest.
ed. Australian Discovery. Johnson Repr.
Scott, Ernest F. *see* Scott, Ernest Findlay.
Scott, Ernest Findlay, 1868-1954
xScott, Ernest F.

Paul's Epistle to the Romans. Greenwood.
Scott, Evelyn, 1893-
xScott, Evelyn.
The Narrow House. Arno.
On William Faulkner's the Sound & the Fury.
Folcroft.
Scott, Fred N. *see* Scott, Fred Newton.
Scott, Fred Newton, 1860-1931
xScott, Fred N.
The Fred Newton Scott Anniversary Papers.
Arden Lib.
Fred Newton Scott Anniversary Papers.
Folcroft.
Scott, G. *see* Scott, Gerald.
Scott, Gary I. *see* Scott, Gary L.
Scott, Gary L., 1937-
xScott, Gary I.
Chinese Treaties: The Post-Revolutionary
Restoration of International Law and Order.
Oceana.
Scott, Gavin, 1950-
xScott, Gavin.
Hot Pursuit. St Martin.
Scott, Geoffrey, 1885-1929
xScott, Geoffrey.
The Architecture of Humanism: A Study in the
History of Taste. Norton.
The Architecture of Humanism: A Study in the
History of Taste. Peter Smith.
Scott, Geoffrey A. *see* Scott, Geoffrey A. J.
Scott, Geoffrey A. J.
xScott, Geoffrey A.
Grassland Development in the Gran Pajonal of
Eastern Peru: A Study of Soil-Vegetation
Nutrient Systems. Univ Microfilms.
Scott, George G. *see* Scott, George Gilbert.
Scott, George Gilbert, Sir, 1811-1878
xScott, George G.
Personal & Professional Recollections. Da
Capo.
Scott, George R. *see* Scott, George Ryley.
Scott, George Ryley, 1886-
xScott, George R.
The History of Corporal Punishment: A Survey
of Flagellation in Its Historical,
Anthropological & Sociological Aspects.
Gale.
A History of Prostitution from Antiquity to the
Present Day. AMS Pr.
Scott, Gerald.
xScott, G.
Atmospheric Oxidation & Antioxidants.
Elsevier.
Scott, Geraldine.
xScott, Geraldine.
Prevalence of Chronic Conditions of the
Genitourinary, Nervous, Endocrine,
Metabolic and Blood and Blood-Forming
Systems, and of Other Selected Chronic
Conditions: United States, 1973. Natl Ctr
Health Stats.
Scott, Gini G. *see* Scott, Gini Graham.
Scott, Gini Graham.
xScott, Gini G.
Cult & Countercult: A Study of a Spiritual
Growth Group & a Witchcraft Order.
Greenwood.
Scott, Gwendolyn D.
xScott, Gwendolyn D.
Learning, Feeling, Doing: Designing Creative
Learning Experiences for Elementary Health
Education. P-H.
On Becoming a Health Educator. Wm C
Brown.
Scott, Harold G. *see* Scott, Harold George.
Scott, Harold George.
xScott, Harold G.
Lelia: The Compleat Ballerina. Pelican.
Scott, Harold R. *see* Scott, Harold Richard.

Scott, Harold Richard.
xScott, Harold R.
From Inside Scotland Yard. Macmillan.
Scott, Harriet. *see* Scott, Harriet Fast.
Scott, Harriet Fast.
xScott, Harriet.
The Armed Forces of the USSR. Westview.
Scott, Harry A. *see* Scott, Harry Alexander.
Scott, Harry Alexander, 1894-
xScott, Harry A.
Personnel Study of Directors of Physical
Education for Men in Colleges &
Universities. AMS Pr.
Scott, Hugh, 1885-
xScott, Hugh.
In the High Yemen. AMS Pr.
Scott, J. *see* Scott, James.
Scott, J. I. *see* Scott, John Irving E.
Scott, J. M. *see* Scott, James Maurice.
Scott, Jack, 1942-
xScott, Jack.
Athletic Revolution. Free Pr.
Bill Walton: On the Road with the Portland
Trail Blazers. T Y Crowell.
Scott, Jack B., 1928-
xScott, Jack B.
Gods Plan Unfolded. Tyndale.
Scott, Jack D. *see* Scott, Jack Denton.
Scott, Jack Denton.
xScott, Jack D.
The Book of the Goat. Putnam.
Canada Geese. Putnam.
City of Birds & Beasts: Behind the Scenes at
the Bronx Zoo. Putnam.
Discovering the American Stork. HarBraceJ.
Discovering the Mysterious Egret. HarBraceJ.
The Gulls of Smuttynose Island. Putnam.
Little Dogs of the Prairie. Putnam
Return of the Buffalo. Putnam.
The Submarine Bird. Putnam.
The Survivors: Enduring Animals of North
America. HarBraceJ.
That Wonderful Pelican. Putnam.
Scott, Jack S.
xScott, Jack S.
A Clutch of Vipers. Har-Row.
Scott, James, 1938-
xScott, J.
Palaeontology: An Introduction. Heinman.
xScott, James.
Palaeontology: An Introduction. Taplinger.
Scott, James. *see* Scott, James S.
Scott, James B. *see* Scott, James Brown.
Scott, James Brown, 1866-1943
xScott, James B.
Law, the State, & the International
Community. AMS Pr.
Law, the State & the International Community.
Greenwood.
Scott, James C.
xScott, James C.
The Moral Economy of the Peasant: Rebellion
& Subsistence in Southeast Asia. Yale U Pr.
Scott, James D. *see* Scott, James Dacon.
Scott, James Dacon.
xScott, James D.
Cable Television: Strategy for Penetrating Key
Urban Markets. U Mich Busn Div Res.
Educating Asian Students for Business Careers.
U Mich Busn Div Res.
Scott, James H. *see* Scott, James Henderson.
Scott, James Henderson.
xScott, James H.
Introduction to Dental Anatomy. Churchill.
Scott, James Maurice.
xScott, J. M.
Icebound: Journeys to the Northwest Sea.
Gordon-Cremonesi.
Scott, James S.
xScott, James.

ed. Immunology of Human Reproduction.
Grune.
Scott, Jeannette.
xScott, Jeannette.
ed. Membrane & Ultrafiltration Technology:
Recent Advances. Noyes.
Scott, Jody.
xScott, Jody.
Passing for Human. DAW Bks.
Scott, John, 1820-1907
xScott, John.
Lost Principle: Or, the Sectional Equilibrium:
How It Was Created - How Destroyed - How
It May Be Restored. Negro U Pr.
Scott, John. *see* Scott, John P.
Scott, John A. *see* Scott, John Adams.
Scott, John Adams, 1867-1947
xScott, John A.
Homer & His Influence. Cooper Sq.
Scott, John Anthony, 1916-
xScott, John A.
Fanny Kemble's America. T Y Crowell.
Trumpet of a Prophecy: Revolutionary America
1763-1783. Knopf.
Scott, John D. *see* Scott, John Dick.
Scott, John Dick, 1917-
xScott, John D.
Pretty Penny. HarBraceJ.
Scott, John Irving E.
xScott, J. I.
ed. Getting the Most Out of High School.
Oceana.
Scott, John M. *see* Scott, John Martin.
Scott, John Martin, 1913-
xScott, J.
Everyday Living Approach to Teaching
Elementary Science. P-H.
xScott, John M.
Adventures in Science. Loyola.
Countdown to Encounter: Von Braun & the
Astronauts. Our Sunday Visitor.
The Last Word in Lonesome Is Me. Our
Sunday Visitor.
Scott, John P.
xScott, John.
Corporations, Classes & Capitalism. St Martin.
Scott, John P. *see* Scott, John Paul.
Scott, John Paul, 1909-
xScott, John P.
Aggression. U of Chicago Pr.
Animal Behavior. U of Chicago Pr.
Scott, John S., 1915-
xScott, John S.
Dictionary of Building. Penguin.
Scott, Kenneth.
xScott, Kenneth.
Abstracts from the Pennsylvania Gazette,
1748-1755. Genealog Pub.
Counterfeiting in Colonial New York. Am
Numismatic.
Counterfeiting in Colonial Pennsylvania. Am
Numismatic.
Counterfeiting in Colonial Rhode Island. RI
Hist Soc.
Denizations, Naturalizations & Oaths of
Allegiance in Colonial New York. Genealog
Pub.
The Imperial Cult Under the Flavians. Arno.
New York Alien Residents, 1825-1848.
Genealog Pub.
Scott, Latayne C. *see* Scott, Latayne Colvett.
Scott, Latayne Colvett, 1952-
xScott, Latayne C.
The Mormon Mirage. Zondervan.
Scott, Lou P. *see* Scott, Lou Peveto.
Scott, Lou Peveto.
xScott, Lou P.
Self Instruction & Review in Nursing.
Macmillan.
Scott, Louise B. *see* Scott, Louise Binder.

Scott, Louise Binder.
xScott, Louise B.
Learning Time with Language Experiences for
Young Children. McGraw.
Rhymes for Fingers & Flannelboards. McGraw.
Scott, M. F. *see* Scott, Maurice Fitzgerald.
Scott, M. Gladys. *see* Scott, Myrtle Gladys.
Scott, Marcia.
xScott, Marcia.
Daring Sea Captains. Lerner Pubns.
Scott, Maria L. *see* Scott, Maria Luisa.
Scott, Maria Luisa.
xScott, Maria L.
Cook Like a Peasant, Eat Like a King. Follett.
Scott, Mariana.
xScott, Mariana.
ed. The Heliand. AMS Pr.
Scott, Marvin. *see* Scott, Marvin B.
Scott, Marvin B.
xScott, Marvin.
The Essential Profession: Contemporary Issues
in Education. Greylock Pubs.
Scott, Maurice. *see* Scott, Maurice Fitzgerald.
Scott, Maurice Fitzgerald.
xScott, M. F.
Project Appraisal in Practice: The
Little-Mirrlees Method Applied in Kenya.
Holmes & Meier.
xScott, Maurice.
Can We Get Back to Full Employment?.
Holmes & Meier.
Scott, Michael, 1924-
xScott, Michael.
The Crafts Business Encyclopedia: Marketing,
Management, & Money. HarBraceJ.
The Record of Singing. Holmes & Meier.
The Record of Singing. Scribner.
Scott, Michael R.
xScott, Michael R.
How I Find Stocks That Double in a Year.
Windsor.
Scott, Myrtle Gladys, 1905-
xScott, M. Gladys.
Analysis of Human Motion: A Textbook in
Kinesiology. Irvington.
Scott, Naomi.
xScott, Naomi.
Heart Throbs: The Best of DC Romance
Comics. S&S.
Scott, Natalie V. *see* Scott, Natalie Vivian.
Scott, Natalie Vivian.
xScott, Natalie V.
Gourmet's Guide to New Orleans. Pelican.
Scott, Nathan A.
xScott, Nathan A.
ed. Climate of Faith in Modern Literature.
Allenson.
Mirrors of Man in Existentialism. Abingdon.
Mirrors of Man in Existentialism. Abingdon.
Reinhold Niebuhr. U of Minn Pr.
Scott, Niki.
xScott, Niki.
The Working Woman: A Handbook. Andrews
& McMeel.
Scott, P. J. M. *see* Scott, Peter James Malcolm.
Scott, Patrick G. *see* Scott, Patrick Greig.
Scott, Patrick Greig.
xScott, Patrick G.
The Early Editions of Arthur Hugh Clough.
Garland Pub.
Scott, Paul, 1920-
xScott, Paul.
The Raj Quartet. Morrow.
Staying on. Avon.
Staying on. Morrow.
The Towers of Silence. Avon.
The Towers of Silence. Morrow.
Scott, Peter, 1946-
xScott, Peter.

Strategies for Postsecondary Education.
Halsted Pr.
The Thames & Hudson Manual of
Metalworking. Thames Hudson.
Scott, Peter D. *see* Scott, Peter Dale.
Scott, Peter Dale.
xScott, Peter D.
The Assassinations: Dallas & Beyond - a Guide
to Coverups & Investigations. Random.
Crime & Cover-Up: The CIA, Mafia, & the
Dallas-Watergate Connection. Ramparts.
Scott, Peter James Malcolm.
xScott, P. J. M.
Reality & Comic Confidence in Charles
Dickens. B&N.
Scott Polar Research Institute. *see* Scott Polar Research
Institute, Cambridge, England. Library.
**Scott Polar Research Institute, Cambridge, England.
Library.**
xScott Polar Researcch Institute.
The Library Catalogue of the Scott Polar
Research Institute. G K Hall.
Scott, R. A. *see* Scott, Robert A.
Scott, R. B. *see* Scott, Robert Balgarnie Young.
Scott, R. P. *see* Scott, Raymond Peter William.
Scott, Ralph W.
xScott, Ralph W.
A New Look at Biblical Crime. Nelson-Hall.
Scott, Ray G.
xScott, Ray G.
How to Build Your Own Underground Home.
TAB Bks.
Scott, Raymond Peter William, 1924-
xScott, R. P.
Liquid Chromatography Detectors. Elsevier.
Scott, Robert A.
xScott, R. A.
Why Sociology Does Not Apply: A Study of
the Use of Sociology in Public Policy.
Elsevier.
Scott, Robert Balgarnie Young, 1899-
xScott, R. B.
Relevance of the Prophets. Macmillan.
Scott, Robert E. *see* Scott, Robert Edwin.
Scott, Robert Edwin.
xScott, Robert E.
ed. Latin American Modernization Problems:
Case Studies in the Crises of Change. U of Ill
Pr.
Scott, Robert G. *see* Scott, Robert Gillam.
Scott, Robert Gillam.
xScott, Robert G.
Design Fundamentals. Krieger.
Design Fundamentals. McGraw.
Scott, Robert H. *see* Scott, Robert Haney.
Scott, Robert Haney.
xScott, Robert H.
Problems in National Income Analysis &
Forecasting. Scott F.
Scott, Robert J., 1937-
xScott, Robert J.
Fiberglass Boat Design & Construction. De
Graff.
Scott, Robert L. *see* Scott, Robert Lee.
Scott, Robert Lee, 1908-
xScott, Robert L.
God Is My Co-Pilot. Ballantine.
Compiled by The Rhetoric of Black Power.
Greenwood.
Scott, Ronald F.
xScott, Ronald F.
Soil Mechanics & Engineering. McGraw.
Scott, Roy V. *see* Scott, Roy Vernon.
Scott, Roy Vernon.
xScott, Roy V.

The Public Career of Cully A. Cobb: A Study
in Agricultural Leadership. U Pr of Miss.
The Reluctant Farmer: The Rise of Agricultural
Extension to 1914. U of Ill Pr.
Scott, Ruth K.
xScott, Ruth K.
Parties in Crisis: Party Politics in America.
Wiley.
Scott, S. P. *see* Scott, Samuel Parsons.
Scott, Samuel F.
xScott, Samuel F.
The Response of the Royal Army to the
French Revolution: The Role & Development
of the Line Army, 1793-1878. Oxford U Pr.
Scott, Samuel P. *see* Scott, Samuel Parsons.
Scott, Samuel Parsons, 1846-1929
xScott, S. P.
History of the Moorish Empire in Europe.
Gordon Pr.
xScott, Samuel P.
History of the Moorish Empire in Europe.
AMS Pr.
Scott, Sarah. *see* Scott, Sarah Robinson.
Scott, Sarah Robinson, 1723-1795
xScott, Sarah.
The History of Cornelia, 1750. Garland Pub.
Scott, Stanley.
xScott, Stanley.
Governing California's Coast. Inst Gov Stud
Berk.
Scott, Temple, 1864-1939
xScott, Temple.
Lord Chesterfield & His Letters to His Sons.
Folcroft.
Scott, Thomas Cyril, 1907-
xScott, Tom.
Obedience & Security Training for Dogs. Arco.
Scott, Tom. *see* Scott, Thomas Cyril.
Scott, Toni.
xScott, Toni.
The Complete Book of Stuffedwork. HM.
Scott, Virgil.
xScott, Virgil.
Studies in the Short Story. HR&W.
Walk-in. PB.
Walk-in. S&S.
Scott, W. B. *see* Scott, William Benson.
Scott, Waldron.
xScott, Waldron.
Karl Barth's Theology of Mission.
Inter-Varsity.
Scott, Walter, Sir, Bart, 1771-1832
xScott, Walter.
Antiquary. Dutton.
Catalogue of the Library at Abbotsford. AMS
Pr.
Guy Mannering. Dutton.
Letters of Sir Walter Scott. AMS Pr.
The Letters of Sir Walter Scott & Charles
Kirkpatrick Sharpe to Robert Chambers.
Folcroft.
Letters on Demonology & Witchcraft. Gordon
Pr.
Letters on Demonology & Witchcraft. R West.
Life of John Dryden. U of Nebr Pr.
The Prefaces to the Waverley Novels. U of
Nebr Pr.
Quentin Durward. Airmont.
Scott, Walter D. *see* Scott, Walter Dill.
Scott, Walter Dill, 1869-1955
xScott, Walter D.
The Psychology of Advertising. Arno.
Scott, William A., 1920-
xScott, William A.
ed. Sources of Protestant Theology. Glencoe.
Scott, William B., 1945-
xScott, William B.

In Pursuit of Happiness: American Conceptions
of Property, from the Seventeenth to the
Twentieth Century. Ind U Pr.
Scott, William Benson.
xScott, W. B.
Chicago Letter & Other Parodies. Ardis Pubs.
Scott, William Beverley, 1917-
xScott, W. B.
Freshwater Fishes of Eastern Canada. U of
Toronto Pr.
Scott, William C. *see* Scott, William G.
Scott, William E. *see* Scott, William Evans.
Scott, William Evans.
xScott, William E.
Alliance Against Hitler: The Origins of the
Franco-Soviet Pact. Duke.
Scott, William F. *see* Scott, William Fontaine.
Scott, William Fontaine, 1919-
xScott, William F.
Soviet Sources of Military Doctrine & Strategy.
Crane-Russak Co.
Scott, William G.
xScott, William C.
Organizational America. HM.
xScott, William G.
Organization Theory: A Structural &
Behavioral Analysis. Irwin.
Organizational America. HM.
Scott, William Neville.
xScott, Bill.
Boori. Oxford U Pr.
Scott, William R. *see* Scott, William Robert.
Scott, William Robert, 1868-1940
xScott, William R.
Adam Smith As Student & Professor. Kelley.
Scott, William T. *see* Scott, William Thompson.
Scott, William Thompson, 1866-
xScott, William T.
Chesterton & Other Essays. Folcroft.
Scott, Winfield T. *see* Scott, Winfield Townley.
Scott, Winfield Townley, 1910-1968
xScott, Winfield T.
Change of Weather. Greenwood.
Dirty Hand: Literary Notebooks of Winfield
Townley Scott. U of Tex Pr.
xScott, Winfield Townley.
The Dark Sister. NYU Pr.
Scott, Zelma.
xScott, Zelma.
History of Coryell County, Texas. Tex St Hist
Assn.
Scott-James, R. A. *see* Scott-James, Rolfe Arnold.
Scott-James, Rolfe A. *see* Scott-James, Rolfe Arnold.
Scott-James, Rolfe Arnold, 1878-
xScott-James, R. A.
Personality in Literature 1913-1931. Folcroft.
xScott-James, Rolfe A.
Personality in Literature. Arno.
Scott-Maxwell, Florida. *see* Scott-Maxwell, Florida (Pier).
Scott-Maxwell, Florida (Pier), 1884-
xScott-Maxwell, Florida.
Measure of My Days. Knopf.
The Measure of My Days. Penguin.
Scott-Moncrieff, C. K. *see* Scott-Moncrieff, Charles
Kenneth.
Scott-Moncrieff, Charles Kenneth, 1889-1930
xScott-Moncrieff, C. K.
ed. Marcel Proust: An English Tribute. Haskell.
Scott-Stokes, Henry, 1938-
xScott-Stokes, Henry.
The Life & Death of Yukio Mishima. FS&G.
Scottish Council for Research in Education.
xScottish Council For Research In Education.
Study of Fifteen-Year-Olds. Verry.
Scovel, Myra.
xScovel, Myra.
In Clover. Westminster.
Scovil, Elisabeth Robinson, 1849-
xScovil, Elizabeth R.

Prayers for Girls. Nelson.
Scovil, Elizabeth R. *see* Scovil, Elisabeth Robinson.
Scoville, John. *see* Scoville, John Watson.
Scoville, John Watson.
xScoville, John.
ed. Fact & Fancy in the T. N. E. C.
Monographs: Reviews of the 43 Monographs
Issued by the Temporary National Economic
Committee. Arno.

Scranton, Pierce E.
xScranton, Pierce E.
Practical Techniques in Venipuncture. Williams
& Wilkins.

Scranton, Robert L. *see* Scranton, Robert Lorentz.

Scranton, Robert Lorentz, 1912-
xScranton, Robert L.
Greek Architecture. Braziller.

Screech, M. A. *see* Screech, Michael Andrew.

Screech, Michael Andrew.
xScreech, M. A.
Rabelais. Cornell U Pr.
Scriabine, Alexander.
xScriabine, Alexander.
ed. The Pharmacology of Antihypertensive
Drugs. Raven.
Scriber, Kent.
xScriber, Kent.
Relevant Topics in Athletic Training.
Mouvement Pubns.
Scribner, Ginger.
xScribner, Ginger.
The Quick & Easy Microwave Oven
Cookbook. Cornerstone.
Scripps, Edward W. *see* Scripps, Edward Wyllis.
Scripps, Edward Wyllis, 1854-1926
xScripps, Edward W.
Damned Old Crank: A Self-Portrait of E. W.
Scripps Drawn from His Unpublished
Writings. Greenwood.
Scripps, John L. *see* Scripps, John Locke.
Scripps, John Locke, 1818-1866
xScripps, John L.
Life of Abraham Lincoln. Greenwood.
Scriptural Rosary Center.
xChristianica Center.
Scriptural Rosary. Christianica.
Scriven, Michael.
xScriven, Michael.
Primary Philosophy. McGraw.
Reasoning. McGraw.
Scrivener, Frederick H. *see* Scrivener, Frederick Henry
Ambrose.
Scrivener, Frederick Henry Ambrose, 1813-1891
xScrivener, Frederick H.
Bezae Codex Cantabrigiensis: Being an Exact
Copy, in Ordinary Type of the Celebrated
Uncial Graeco-Latin Manuscript of the Four
Gospels & Acts of the Apostles. Pickwick.
Scrivenor, Patrick, 1943-
xScrivenor, Patrick.
In Praise of Male Chauvinism. David &
Charles.
Scriver, Bob.
xScriver, Bob.
An Honest Try. Lowell Pr.
Scriver, Charles R.
xScriver, Charles R.
Amino Acid Metabolism & Its Disorders.
Saunders.
Scroggie, W. Graham. *see* Scroggie, William Graham.
Scroggie, William Graham, 1877-1958
xScroggie, W. Graham.
Studies in Philemon. Kregel.
Tested by Temptation. Kregel.
Scroggins, Daniel C.
xScroggins, Daniel C.

Concordance of Jose Hernandez Martin Fierro. U of Mo Pr.

Scroggs, James. *see* Scroggs, James R.

Scroggs, James R.
  xScroggs, James.
    Letting Love in. P-H.

Scroggs, Robin.
  xScroggs, Robin.
    Paul for a New Day. Fortress.

Scroggs, William O. *see* Scroggs, William Oscar.

Scroggs, William Oscar, 1879-
  xScroggs, William O.
    Filibusters & Financiers: The Story of William Walker & His Associates. Russell.

Scrope, George Julius Duncombe Poulett, 1797-1876
  xScrope, George P.
    The Geology & Extinct Volcanos of the Central France. Arno.

Scrope, George P. *see* Scrope, George Julius Duncombe Poulett.

Scruggs, C. G. *see* Scruggs, Charles G.

Scruggs, Charles G.
  xScruggs, C. G.
    The Peaceful Atom & the Deadly Fly. Jenkins.

Scrugham, Mary, 1885-
  xScrugham, Mary.
    The Peaceable Americans of 1860-1861: A Study in Public Opinion. Octagon.

Scruton, Roger.
  xScruton, Roger.
    The Aesthetics of Architecture. Princeton U Pr.

Scrutton, Thomas E. *see* Scrutton, Thomas Edward.

Scrutton, Thomas Edward, Sir, 1856-1934
  xScrutton, Thomas E.
    Commons & Common Fields: The History & Policy of the Laws Relating to Commons & Enclosures in England. B Franklin.

Scudder, Horace E. *see* Scudder, Horace Elisha.

Scudder, Horace Elisha, 1838-1902
  xScudder, Horace E.
    Men & Letters: Essays in Characterization & Criticism. Arno.
    Noah Webster. Arden Lib.
    Noah Webster. Chelsea Hse.
    Noah Webster. Folcroft.

Scudder, Kenyon J. *see* Scudder, Kenyon Judson.

Scudder, Kenyon Judson, 1890-
  xScudder, Kenyon J.
    Prisoners Are People. Greenwood.

Scudder, Ralph E.
  xScudder, Ralph E.
    Custer Country. Binford.

Scudder, Vida D. *see* Scudder, Vida Dutton.

Scudder, Vida Dutton, 1861-1954
  xScudder, Vida D.
    Life of the Spirit in the Modern English Poets. Arno.

Scull, Andrew. *see* Scull, Andrew T.

Scull, Andrew T.
  xScull, Andrew.
    Museums of Madness: The Social Organization of Insanity in Nineteenth Century England. St Martin.

Scullard, H. H. *see* Scullard, Howard Hayes.

Scullard, Howard H. *see* Scullard, Howard Hayes.

Scullard, Howard Hayes, 1903-
  xScullard, H. H.
    Roman Britain: Outpost of the Empire. Thames Hudson.
  xScullard, Howard H.
    Etruscan Cities & Rome. Cornell U Pr.

Scully, Alice.
  xScully, Alice.
    Fun in Bed. S&S.

Scully, J C.
  xScully, J. C.
    The Fundamentals of Corrosion. Pergamon.

Scully, Vincent. *see* Scully, Vincent Joseph.

Scully, Vincent Joseph, 1920-
  xScully, Vincent.
    Frank Lloyd Wright. Braziller.
    Pueblo: Mountain, Village, Dance. Viking Pr.

Sculthorpe, William J. *see* Sculthorpe, William L.

Sculthorpe, William L.
  xSculthorpe, William J.
    Design of High Pressure Steam & High Temperature Water Plants. Indus Pr.

Scupham, Peter, 1933-
  xScupham, Peter.
    The Hinterland. Oxford U Pr.

Scurlock, R. G. *see* Scurlock, Ralph Geoffrey.

Scurlock, Ralph Geoffrey.
  xScurlock, R. G.
    Low Temperature Behaviour of Solids. Routledge & Kegan.

Seaberg, Dorothy I.
  xSeaberg, Dorothy I.
    The Four Faces of Teaching: The Role of the Teacher in Humanizing Education. Goodyear.

Seabrook, Jeremy, 1939-
  xSeabrook, Jeremy.
    Mother & Son. Pantheon.
    What Went Wrong: Why Hasn't Having More Made People Happier. Pantheon.

Seabrook, Peter.
  xSeabrook, Peter.
    Rand McNally Book of the Garden. Rand.

Seabrook, Steven.
  xSeabrook, Steven.
    The Official Mork & Mindy Scrapbook. PB.

Seabrooke, Brenda.
  xSeabrooke, Brenda.
    Home Is Where They Take You in. Morrow.

Seabury, David, 1885-1960
  xSeabury, David.
    Art of Selfishness. Cornerstone.
    Art of Selfishness. PB.

Seabury, Samuel, Bp, 1729-1796
  xSeabury, Samuel.
    Letters of a Westchester Farmer, 1774-1775. Da Capo.

Seabury, William M. *see* Seabury, William Marston.

Seabury, William Marston, 1878-1949
  xSeabury, William M.
    The Public & the Motion Picture Industry. Ozer.

Seager, Allan.
  xSeager, Allan.
    Death of Anger. Astor-Honor.

Seager, Elizabeth.
  xSeager, Elizabeth.
    ed. The Countryman Book of Village Trades & Crafts. David & Charles.

Seager, Henry R. *see* Seager, Henry Rogers.

Seager, Henry Rogers.
  xSeager, Henry R.
    Trust & Corporation Problems. Arno.

Seager, Robert, 1924-
  xSeager, Robert.
    Alfred Thayer Mahan: The Man & His Letters. Naval Inst Pr.

Seagrave, Charles E. *see* Seagrave, Charles Edwin.

Seagrave, Charles Edwin.
  xSeagrave, Charles E.
    The Southern Negro Agricultural Worker: 1850-1870. Arno.

Seagraves, Margaret C.
  xSeagraves, Margaret C.
    Move to Learn: Lesson Plans for Elementary Physical Education. Hunter NC.

Seagren, Dan. *see* Seagren, Daniel.

Seagren, Daniel.
  xSeagren, Dan.
    The Parables. Tyndale.

Seagull, Louis M.
  xSeagull, Louis M.

Southern Republicanism 1940-1972. Halsted Pr.

Seale, Bobby, 1936-
  xSeale, Bobby.
    A Lonely Rage: The Autobiography of Bobby Seale. Times Bks.

Seale, Ervin.
  xSeale, Ervin.
    Take off from Within. Har-Row.

Seale, J. N.
  xSeale, J. N.
    Questions & Answers on Diesel Engines. Hayden.

Seale, M. S. *see* Seale, Morris S.

Seale, Morris S.
  xSeale, M. S.
    Qur'an & Bible: Studies in Interpretation & Dialogue. Biblio Dist.

Seale, William.
  xSeale, William.
    Recreating the Historic House Interior. AASLH.

Sealey, L. G. *see* Sealey, L. G. W.

Sealey, L. G. W.
  xSealey, L. G.
    Communication & Learning in the Primary School. Schocken.
  xSealey, Leonard G.
    Communication & Learning in the Primary School. Humanities.

Sealey, Leonard.
  xSealey, Leonard.
    Children's Writing: An Approach for the Primary Grades. Intl Reading.

Sealey, Leonard G. *see* Sealey, L. G. W.

Seals, Monroe, 1867-
  xSeals, Monroe.
    History of White County Tennessee. Reprint.

Sealtest. *see* Sealtest, Inc. Sealtest Laboratory Kitchen, New York.

Sealtest, Inc. Sealtest Laboratory Kitchen, New York.
  xSealtest.
    Great Cooking with Dairy Products. Benjamin Co.

Sealts, Merton M.
  xSealts, Merton M.
    The Early Lives of Melville: Nineteenth-Century Biographical Sketches & Their Authors. U of Wis Pr.
    ed. Emerson's Nature: Origin, Growth, Meaning. S Ill U Pr.
    Melville As Lecturer. Folcroft.
    Melville's Reading: A Check-List of Books Owned & Borrowed. U of Wis Pr.

Sealy, Adrienne.
  xSealy, Adrienne.
    And Even a Child Shall Lead Them. Vantage.

Sealy, Shirley.
  xSealy, Shirley.
    Forever After. Deseret Bk.

Seaman, Barbara.
  xSeaman, Barbara.
    Free & Female: The Sex Life of the Contemporary Woman. Fawcett.

Seaman, Kenneth.
  xSeaman, Kenneth.
    The Complete Chub Angler. David & Charles.

Seaman, N. G. *see* Seaman, Norma Gilm.

Seaman, Norma Gilm, 1873-
  xSeaman, N. G.
    Indian Relics of the Pacific Northwest. Binford.

Seaman, Sylvia S.
  xSeaman, Sylvia S.
    How to Be a Jewish Grandmother. Doubleday.

Seamands, John T.
  xSeamands, John T.
    On Tiptoe with Joy. Baker Bk.

Seamon, David.
  xSeamon, David.

A Geography of the Life World: Movement,
　　Rest & Encounter. St Martin.
Seamon, John G., 1943-
　　xSeamon, John G.
　　　Memory & Cognition: An Introduction. Oxford
　　　　U Pr.
Searcy, Margaret Z. *see* Searcy, Margaret Zehmer.
Searcy, Margaret Zehmer.
　　xSearcy, Margaret Z.
　　　Alli Gator Gets a Bump on His Nose. Portals
　　　　Pr.
　　　Ikwa of the Temple Mounds. U of Ala Pr.
Searcy, Ronald L.
　　xSearcy, Ronald L.
　　　Diagnostic Biochemistry. McGraw.
Searle, Charles E., 1922-
　　xSearle, Charles E.
　　　ed. Chemical Carcinogens. Am Chemical.
Searle, Chris.
　　xSearle, Chris.
　　　The Forsaken Lover: White Words & Black
　　　　People. Routledge & Kegan.
Searle, G. W. *see* Searle, Graham William.
Searle, Graham William.
　　xSearle, G. W.
　　　The Counter Reformation. Rowman.
Searle, Humphrey.
　　xSearle, Humphrey.
　　　Twentieth-Century Counterpoint: A Guide for
　　　　Students. Hyperion Conn.
Searle, Pauline.
　　xSearle, Pauline.
　　　Dawn Over Oman. Allen Unwin.
Searle, S. R. *see* Searle, Shayle R.
Searle, Shayle R.
　　xSearle, S. R.
　　　Linear Models. Wiley.
　　　Matrix Algebra for Business & Economics.
　　　　Wiley.
　　　Matrix Algebra for the Biological Sciences.
　　　　Including Applications in Statistics. Wiley.
Searles, Aysel.
　　xSearles, Aysel.
　　　ed. Guide to Financial Aids for Students in
　　　　Arts & Sciences for Graduate & Professional
　　　　Study. Arco.
Searles, Baird.
　　xSearles, Baird.
　　　A Reader's Guide to Science Fiction. Avon.
　　　Reader's Guide to Science Fiction. Facts on
　　　　File.
Searls, Evelyn F.
　　xSearls, Evelyn F.
　　　How to Use WISC Scores in Reading
　　　　Diagnosis. Intl Reading.
Searls, Hank. *see* Searls, Henry.
Searls, Henry.
　　xSearls, Hank.
　　　Pentagon. PB.
Sears, Clara E. *see* Sears, Clara Endicott.
Sears, Clara Endicott, 1863-
　　xSears, Clara E.
　　　Compiled by Bronson Alcott's Fruitlands.
　　　　Porcupine Pr.
　　　Gleanings from Old Shaker Journals. Hyperion
　　　　Conn.
Sears, D. W.
　　xSears, D. W.
　　　The Nature & Origin of Meteorites. Oxford U
　　　　Pr.
Sears, Donald A.
　　xSears, Donald A.
　　　The Discipline of English: A Guide to Literary
　　　　Research. Greenwood.
Sears, Francis W. *see* Sears, Francis Weston.
Sears, Francis Weston.
　　xSears, Francis W.
　　　College Physics. A-W.
　　　Mechanics, Wave Motion & Heat. A-W.
Sears, Joan N. *see* Sears, Joan Niles.

Sears, Joan Niles.
　　xSears, Joan N.
　　　The First One Hundred Years of Town
　　　　Planning in Georgia. Cherokee.
Sears, Joel L.
　　xSears, Joel L.
　　　Optimization Techniques in Fortran. McGraw.
　　　Optimization Techniques in Fortran. Petrocelli.
Sears, John V. *see* Sears, John Van der Zee.
Sears, John Van der Zee, 1835-
　　xSears, John V.
　　　My Friends at Brook Farm. AMS Pr.
Sears, Lorenzo, 1838-1916
　　xSears, Lorenzo.
　　　American Literature in the Colonial & National
　　　　Periods. B Franklin.
　　　American Literature in the Colonial & National
　　　　Periods. R West.
Sears, Louis M. *see* Sears, Louis Martin.
Sears, Louis Martin, 1883-
　　xSears, Louis M.
　　　George Washington & the French Revolution.
　　　　Greenwood.
Sears, Paul B. *see* Sears, Paul Bigelow.
Sears, Paul Bigelow, 1891-
　　xSears, Paul B.
　　　Deserts on the March. U of Okla Pr.
　　　This Is Our World. U of Okla Pr.
Sears, Pauline S. *see* Sears, Pauline Snedden.
Sears, Pauline Snedden.
　　xSears, Pauline S.
　　　ed. Intellectual Development. McCutchan.
Sears, Robert R. *see* Sears, Robert Richardson.
Sears, Robert Richardson.
　　xSears, Robert R.
　　　Identification & Child Rearing. Stanford U Pr.
　　　Patterns of Child Rearing. Stanford U Pr.
Sears, Ruth M. *see* Sears, Ruth McCarthy.
Sears, Ruth McCarthy.
　　xSears, Ruth M.
　　　In the Shadow of the Tower. Nordon Pubns.
　　　A Lonely Place. Nordon Pubns.
　　　Port of No Return. Manor Bks.
　　　The Solitary Heart. Bouregy.
　　xSears, Ruth McCarthy.
　　　Dr. Sara's Vigil. Bouregy.
Sears, Stephen. *see* Sears, Stephen W.
Sears, Stephen W.
　　xSears, Stephen.
　　　Hometown U.S.A.. S&S.
　　xSears, Stephen W.
　　　The American Heritage History of the
　　　　Automobile in America. Am Heritage.
　　　The American Heritage History of the
　　　　Automobile in America. S&S.
　　　Hometown U. S. A. Am Heritage.
Sears, William. *see* Sears, William B.
Sears, William B.
　　xSears, William.
　　　Release the Sun. Baha'i.
Seary, E. R.
　　xSeary, E. R.
　　　Place Names of the Avalon Peninsula of the
　　　　Island of Newfoundland. U of Toronto Pr.
Seashore, Carl E. *see* Seashore, Carl Emil.
Seashore, Carl Emil.
　　xSeashore, Carl E.
　　　Psychology of Music. Dover.
　　　Psychology of Music. Peter Smith.
Seashore, Marjorie J.
　　xSeashore, Marjorie J.
　　　Prisoner Education: Project Newgate & Other
　　　　College Programs.. Praeger.
Seashore, Stanley E. *see* Seashore, Stanley Emanuel.
Seashore, Stanley Emanuel, 1915-
　　xSeashore, Stanley E.
　　　Group Cohesiveness in the Industrial Work
　　　　Group. Arno.
Seasoltz, R. Kevin.
　　xSeasoltz, R. Kevin.

　　　New Liturgy, New Laws. Liturgical Pr.
Seaton, Alexander A. *see* Seaton, Alexander Adam.
Seattle Art Museum.
　　xSeattle Art Museum.
　　　Guy Anderson. U of Wash Pr.
　　　Johsel Namkung: An Artist's View of Nature.
　　　　U of Wash Pr.
Seattle City Light. *see* Seattle Dept. of Lighting.
Seattle Dept. of Lighting.
　　xSeattle City Light.
　　　Power Generation Alternatives. Cone-Heiden.
Seaton, Albert, 1921-
　　xSeaton, Albert.
　　　The Crimean War: A Russian Chronicle. St
　　　　Martin.
　　　The Soviet Army. Hippocrene Bks.
Seaton, Alexander Adam.
　　xSeaton, Alexander A.
　　　The Theory of Toleration Under the Later
　　　　Stuarts. Octagon.
Seaton, Paul.
　　xSeaton, Paul.
　　　Waterskiing. Merrimack Bk Serv.
Seaton, S. Lee.
　　xSeaton, S. Lee.
　　　ed. Political Anthropology: The State of the
　　　　Art. Mouton.
Seaver, Henry L. *see* Seaver, Henry Latimer.
Seaver, Henry Latimer.
　　xSeaver, Henry L.
　　　Great Revolt in Castile: A Study of the
　　　　Comunero Movement of 1520-1521.
　　　　Octagon.
Seaver, Judith W.
　　xSeaver, Judith W.
　　　Careers with Young Children: Making Your
　　　　Decision. Natl Assn Child Ed.
Seaver, Paul S.
　　xSeaver, Paul S.
　　　The Puritan Lectureships: The Politics of
　　　　Religious Dissent, 1560-1662. Stanford U Pr.
Seaward, M. R. *see* Seaward, M. R. D.
Seaward, M. R. D.
　　xSeaward, M. R.
　　　ed. Lichen Ecology. Acad Pr.
Seawell, L. Vann. *see* Seawell, Lloyd Vann.
Seawell, Lloyd Vann, 1930-
　　xSeawell, L. Vann.
　　　Hospital Financial Accounting Theory &
　　　　Practice. Hospital Finan.
　　　Introduction to Hospital Accounting. Hospital
　　　　Finan.
Seay, Albert.
　　xSeay, Albert.
　　　Music in the Medieval World. P-H.
Seay, James.
　　xSeay, James.
　　　Let Not Your Hart. Columbia U Pr.
Sebald, H. *see* Sebald, Hans.
Sebald, Hans.
　　xSebald, H.
　　　Witchcraft: The Heritage of a Heresy. Elsevier.
　　xSebald, Hans.
　　　Adolescence: A Social Psychological Analysis.
　　　　P-H.
Sebastian, Margaret.
　　xSebastian, Margaret.
　　　Bow Street Brangle. Popular Lib.
　　　Bow Street Gentleman. Popular Lib.
　　　Courtship of Colonel Crowne. Popular Lib.
　　　Her Knight on a Barge. Popular Lib.
　　　Lord Dedringham's Divorce. Popular Lib.
　　　Lord Orlando's Protegee. Berkley Pub.
　　　The Poor Relation. Popular Lib.
Sebeok, Thomas A. *see* Sebeok, Thomas Albert.
Sebeok, Thomas Albert, 1920-
　　xSebeok, Thomas A.

The Sign & Its Masters. U of Tex Pr.
ed. Speaking of Apes: A Critical Anthology of Two-Way Communication with Man. Plenum Pub.
ed. Speech Surrogates: Drum & Whistle Systems. Mouton.
Seber, G. A. *see* Seber, George Arthur Frederick.
Seber, George Arthur Frederick.
xSeber, G. A.
The Estimation of Animal Abundance & Related Parameters. Hafner.
Linear Regression Analysis. Wiley.
Sebesky, Don.
xSebesky, Donald.
The Contemporary Arranger. Alfred Pub.
Sebesky, Donald. *see* Sebesky, Don.
Sebesta, Sam. *see* Sebesta, Sam Leaton.
Sebesta, Sam L. *see* Sebesta, Sam Leaton.
Sebesta, Sam Leaton.
xSebesta, Sam.
The First R: Readings on Teaching Reading. SRA.
xSebesta, Sam L.
Literature for Thursday's Child. SRA.
Sebestyen, Gyula, 1921-
xSebestyen, Gyula.
Lightweight Building Construction. Halsted Pr.
Sebestyen, Ouida.
xSebestyen, Ouida.
Words by Heart. Bantam.
Words by Heart. Little.
Sebold, Russell P., 1928-
xSebold, Russell P.
Colonel Don Jose Cadalso. Irvington.
Seccombe, Thomas.
xSeccombe, Thomas.
The Age of Shakespeare. Folcroft.
Sechehaye, M. A. *see* Sechehaye, Marguerite Albert.
Sechehaye, Marguerite Albert, 1887-
xSechehaye, M. A.
Symbolic Realization: A New Method of Psychotherapy Applied to a Case of Schizophrenia. Intl Univs Pr.
Sechenov, Ivan M. *see* Sechenov, Ivan Mikhailovich.
Sechenov, Ivan Mikhailovich, 1829-1905
xSechenov, Ivan M.
Reflexes of the Brain. MIT Pr.
Seckinger, Donald S.
xSeckinger, Donald S.
A Problems Approach to Foundations of Education. Wiley.
Secombe, Harry.
xSecombe, Harry.
Goon for Lunch. St Martin.
Second International Symposium. *see* International Symposium on Psoriasis, 2d, Stanford University, 1976.
Second Zero Gravity Symposium-Los Angeles-1963. *see* American Astronautical Society.
Secondi, John J.
xSecondi, John J.
For People Who Make Love: A Doctor's Guide to Sexual Health. Taplinger.
Secor, Jane.
xSecor, Jane.
Patient Care in Respiratory Problems. Saunders.
Secord, Paul F.
xSecord, Paul F.
Understanding Social Life: An Introduction to Social Psychology. McGraw.
Sectional Committee on Protective Equipment. *see* National Fire Protection Association. Sectional Committee on Protective Equipment for Fire Fighters.
Seculoff, James. *see* Seculoff, James F.
Seculoff, James F.
xSeculoff, James.
God & the Teenager. Our Sunday Visitor.
Sedano, H. O. *see* Sedano, Heddie O.

Sedano, Heddie O.
xSedano, H. O.
Oral Manifestations of Inherited Disorders. Butterworths.
Sedding, John. *see* Sedding, John Dando.
Sedding, John Dando, 1838-1891
xSedding, John.
Art & Handicraft. Garland Pub.
Seddon, George.
xSeddon, George.
Natural Food Book. Rand.
The Pocket Guide to Indoor Plants. S&S.
Seddon, Herbert, Sir.
xSeddon, Herbert.
Surgical Disorders of Peripheral Nerves. Churchill.
Seder, John.
xSeder, John.
Getting It Together: Black Businessmen in America. HarBraceJ.
Sedgefield, Walter J. *see* Sedgefield, Walter John.
Sedgefield, Walter John, 1866-1945
xSedgefield, Walter J.
Anglo-Saxon Book of Verse & Prose. AMS Pr.
Sedgewick, Robert, 1946-
xSedgewick, Robert.
Quicksort. Garland Pub.
Sedgwick, Alexander C. *see* Sedgwick, Alexander Cameron.
Sedgwick, Alexander Cameron, 1901-
xSedgwick, Alexander C.
Ralliement in French Politics, 1890-1898. Harvard U Pr.
Sedgwick, Anne D. *see* Sedgwick, Anne Douglas.
Sedgwick, Anne Douglas, 1873-1935
xSedgwick, Anne D.
Adrienne Toner: A Novel. Scholarly.
Sedgwick, Catharine Maria, 1789-1867
xSedgwick, Catherine M.
Hope Leslie: Or Early Times in the Massachusetts. Somerset Pub.
Sedgwick, Catherine M. *see* Sedgwick, Catharine Maria.
Sedgwick, Ellery, 1872-1960
xSedgwick, Ellery.
Thomas Paine. Folcroft.
Sedgwick, Henry D. *see* Sedgwick, Henry Dwight.
Sedgwick, Henry Dwight, 1861-1957
xSedgwick, Henry D.
Alfred De Musset (1810-1857). Folcroft.
Horace: A Biography. Russell.
In Praise of Gentlemen. Arno.
Sedgwick, John P.
xSedgwick, John P.
Art Appreciation Made Simple. Doubleday.
Rhythms of Western Art. Scarecrow.
Sedgwick, Kate.
xSedgwick, Kate.
Children in Art. HR&W.
Sedgwick, Michael.
xSedgwick, Michael.
Passenger Cars: 1924-42. Macmillan.
Sedgwick, Paulita.
xSedgwick, Paulita.
illus. Circus ABC. HR&W.
Sedgwick, Robert P.
xSedgwick, Robert P.
Cerebral Degenerations in Childhood. Med Exam.
Sedgwick, Theodore, 1780-1839
xSedgwick, Theodore.
Public & Private Economy. Arno.
Sedlacek, William E.
xSedlacek, William E.
Racism in American Education: A Model for Change. Nelson-Hall.
Sedra, Adel S.
xSedra, Adel S.

Filter Theory & Design: Active & Passive. Intl Schol Bk Serv.
Sedriks, A. John.
xSedriks, A. John.
Corrosion of Stainless Steels. Wiley.
Sedway Cooke (Firm).
xSedway-Cooke.
Land & the Environment: Planning in California Today. W Kaufmann.
Sedway-Cooke. *see* Sedway Cooke (Firm).
Sedwick, Angie, 1925-
xSedwick, Angie.
Synergy. Windy Row.
See, Carolyn.
xSee, Carolyn.
Mothers, Daughters. PB.
See, Henri. *see* See, Henri Eugene.
See, Henri E. *see* See, Henri Eugene.
See, Henri Eugene, 1864-1936
xSee, Henri.
Economic Interpretation of History. Kelley.
Modern Capitalism: Its Origin & Evolution. Kelley.
xSee, Henri E.
Economic Interpretation of History. B Franklin.
See, Margielea S. *see* See, Margielea Stonestreet.
See, Margielea Stonestreet, 1911-
xSee, Margielea S.
Noon Shouts. McClain.
Seeber, Edward D. *see* Seeber, Edward Derbyshire.
Seeber, Edward Derbyshire, 1904-
xSeeber, Edward D.
Anti-Slavery Opinion in France During the Second Half of the Eighteenth Century. Negro U Pr.
Seeber, Louise C. *see* Seeber, Louise Combes.
Seeber, Louise Combes.
xSeeber, Louise C.
George Elbert Burr, 1859-1939: Catalogue Raisonne & Guide to the Etched Works. Northland.
Seed, David.
xSeed, David.
Stream Runner. Schol Bk Serv.
Seed, Jenny.
xSeed, Jenny.
The Bushman's Dream: African Tales of the Creation. Bradbury Pr.
The Great Thirst. Bradbury Pr.
Seed, Philip.
xSeed, Philip.
The Expansion of Social Work in Britain. Routledge & Kegan.
Seedor, Marie M.
xSeedor, Marie M.
Therapy with Oxygen & Other Gases: A Programmed Unit in Fundamentals of Nursing. Lippincott.
Seeds, H. *see* Seeds, Harice L.
Seeds, Harice L.
xSeeds, H.
Fortran IV for Business & General Applications. Wiley.
Seeds, Nicholas M. *see* Seeds, Nicholas W.
Seeds, Nicholas W.
xSeeds, Nicholas M.
ed. Cell Aggregation & Adhesion. Mss Info.
Seefeldt, Carol.
xSeefeldt, Carol.
ed. Curriculum for the Preschool-Primary Child: A Review of the Research. Merrill.
Teaching Young Children. P-H.
Seeger, Charles. *see* Seeger, Charles Louis.
Seeger, Charles Louis, 1886-
xSeeger, Charles.
Studies in Musicology, 1935-1975. U of Cal Pr.
Seeger, Elizabeth.
xSeeger, Elizabeth.

Eastern Religions. T Y Crowell.
Seeger, Pete. *see* Seeger, Peter.
Seeger, Peter.
xSeeger, Pete.
The Foolish Frog. Macmillan.
The Incompleat Folksinger. S&S.
Seeger, W. *see* Seeger, Wolfgang.
Seeger, Wolfgang.
xSeeger, W.
Atlas of Topographical Anatomy of the Brain
& Surrounding Structures for Neurosurgeons,
Neuroradiologists, & Neuropathologists.
Springer-Verlag.
Seehafer, M. E.
xSeehafer, M. E.
Development & Manufacture of Sterilized Milk
Concentrate. Unipub.
Seel, David J. *see* Seel, David John.
Seel, David John, 1925-
xSeel, David J.
Challenge & Crisis in Missionary Medicine.
William Carey Lib.
Seele, Hermann.
xSeele, Hermann.
The Cypress & Other Writings of a German
Pioneer in Texas. U of Tex Pr.
Seeley, J. R. *see* Seeley, John Robert.
Seeley, John R. *see* Seeley, John Robert.
Seeley, John Robert, Sir, 1834-1895
xSeeley, J. R.
The Growth of British Policy: A Historical
Essay. Scholarly.
xSeeley, John R.
Expansion of England. U of Chicago Pr.
Life & Times of Stein: Or Germany & Prussia
in the Napoleonic Age. Haskell.
Seeley, Robert T.
xSeeley, Robert T.
Calculus of One & Several Variables. Scott F.
Seeley, Vernon D.
xSeeley, Vernon D.
Activities in Ceramics. McKnight.
Seelhammer, Ruth.
xSeelhammer, Ruth.
Hopkins Collected at Gonzaga. Loyola.
Seelig, Michael. *see* Seelig, Michael Y.
Seelig, Michael Y.
xSeelig, Michael.
The Architecture of Self-Help Communities.
McGraw.
xSeelig, Michael Y.
The Architecture of Self Help Communities.
McGraw.
Seely, Charles. *see* Seely, Charles Sherlock.
Seely, Charles Sherlock, 1892-
xSeely, Charles.
Essentials of Modern Materialism. Philos Lib.
Seely, Edward D.
xSeely, Edward D.
Teaching Early Adolescents Creatively: A
Manual for Church School Teachers.
Westminster.
Seely, Samuel, 1909-
xSeely, Samuel.
Introduction to Engineering Systems.
Pergamon.
Seelye, John. *see* Seelye, John D.
Seelye, John D.
xSeelye, John.
True Adventures of Huckleberry Finn. S&S.
xSeelye, John D.
True Adventures of Huckleberry Finn.
Northwestern U Pr.
Seeman, Ernest, 1886-
xSeeman, Ernest.
American Gold. Avon.
American Gold. Dial.
Seers, Dudley.
xSeers, Dudley.

ed. Cuba, the Economic & Social Revolution.
Greenwood.
ed. Underdeveloped Europe: Studies in
Core-Periphery Relations. Humanities.
Seese, Ethel. *see* Seese, Ethel Gray.
Seese, Ethel Gray.
xSeese, Ethel.
Psychic Hinge. Golden Quill.
Seese, William S.
xSeese, William S.
In Preparation for College Chemistry. P-H.
Seesholtz, Anna G. *see* Seesholtz, Anna Groh.
Seesholtz, Anna Groh, 1883-
xSeesholtz, Anna G.
Friends of God: Practical Mystics of the
Fourteenth Century. AMS Pr.
Seever, R.
xSeever, R.
Mopeds. Harvey.
Seevers, James A.
xSeevers, James A.
Space. Raintree Child.
Sefton, Catherine.
xSefton, Catherine.
In a Blue Velvet Dress. Har-Row.
In a Blue Velvet Dress. Har-Row.
Segal, Alan.
xSegal, Alan F.
Two Powers in Heaven: Early Rabbinic
Reports About Christianity & Gnosticism.
Humanities.
Segal, Alan F. *see* Segal, Alan.
Segal, Bernard L.
xSegal, Bernard L.
Auscultation of the Heart. Grune.
Segal, Brenda L. *see* Segal, Brenda Lesley.
Segal, Brenda Lesley.
xSegal, Brenda L.
Aliya! A Love Story. St Martin.
Segal, David.
xSegal, David.
ed. The Economics of Neighborhood. Acad Pr.
Segal, David R.
xSegal, David R.
Society & Politics: Uniformity & Diversity in
Modern Democracy. Scott F.
Segal, Erich. *see* Segal, Erich W.
Segal, Erich W.
xSegal, Erich.
Oliver's Story. Avon.
Oliver's Story. G K Hall.
Oliver's Story. Har-Row.
Segal, Harold. *see* Segal, Harold L.
Segal, Harold L.
xSegal, Harold.
ed. Protein Turnover & Lysosome Function.
Acad Pr.
Segal, I. E. *see* Segal, Irving Ezra.
Segal, Irving Ezra.
xSegal, I. E.
Mathematical Problems of Relativistic Physics.
Am Math.
Segal, Jerry.
xSegal, Jerry.
One on One. Warner Bks.
Segal, Joyce.
xSegal, Joyce.
It's Time to Go to Bed. Doubleday.
Segal, Judith A.
xSegal, Judith A.
Food for the Hungry: The Reluctant Society.
Johns Hopkins.
Segal, M. H. *see* Segal, Moses Hirsch.
Segal, Maybelle.
xSegal, Maybelle.
Reflexology. Whitmore.
Reflexology. Wilshire.
Segal, Moses Hirsch, 1877-
xSegal, M. H.

A Grammar of Mishnaic Hebrew. Oxford U Pr.
Segal, Patrick, 1948-
xSegal, Patrick.
The Man Who Walked in His Head. Morrow.
Segal, Rebecca, 1915-
xSegal, Rebecca.
Got No Time to Fool Around: A Motivation
Program for Education. Westminster.
Segal, Ronald, 1932-
xSegal, Ronald.
African Profiles. Peter Smith.
Leon Trotsky. Pantheon.
Segalen, Victor.
xSegalen, Victor.
The Great Statuary of China. U of Chicago Pr.
Rene Leys. O'Hara.
Stelae. SBD.
Segall, Ascher. *see* Segall, Ascher J.
Segall, Ascher J.
xSegall, Ascher.
Systematic Course Design for the Health
Fields. Wiley.
Segall, J. B. *see* Segall, Jacob Bernard.
Segall, J. Peter.
xSegall, J. Peter.
ed. Student Political Involvement in the
1970's. Kennikat.
Segall, Jacob B. *see* Segall, Jacob Bernard.
Segall, Jacob Bernard, 1866-
xSegall, J. B.
Corneille & the Spanish Drama. Gordon Pr.
xSegall, Jacob B.
Corneille & the Spanish Drama. AMS Pr.
Segall, Marshall H.
xSegall, Marshall H.
Cross-Cultural Psychology: Human Behavior in
Global Perspective. Brooks-Cole.
Influence of Culture on Visual Perception.
Bobbs.
Segallis, William, 1939-
xSegallis, William.
Guide to Electronic Components. CBI Pub.
Segan, Ann, 1949-
xSegan, Anne.
illus. One Meter Max. P-H.
Segan, Anne. *see* Segan, Ann.
Segar, William, Sir, d. 1633
xSegar, William.
The Booke of Honor & Armes & Honor
Military & Civil. Schol Facsimiles.
Segel, Yonny.
xSegel, Yonny.
Drafting Made Simple. Doubleday.
Seger, Gerhart H. *see* Seger, Gerhart Heinrich.
Seger, Gerhart Heinrich, 1896-
xSeger, Gerhart H.
Germany. Fideler.
Seger, Imogen.
xSeger, Imogen.
Sociology for the Modern Mind. Macmillan.
Segerberg, Osborn.
xSegerberg, Osborn.
Living with Death. Dutton.
Segerlind, Larry J., 1937-
xSegerlind, Larry J.
Applied Finite Element Analysis. Wiley.
Segler, Franklin M.
xSegler, Franklin M.
Broadman Minister's Manual. Broadman.
Theology of Church & Ministry. Broadman.
Segraves, Kelly L.
xSegraves, Kelly L.
Deadly Delusion. Beta Bk.
Delicate Deception. Beta Bk.
A Double Minded Man. Beta Bk.
Lolly. Beta Bk.
Segre, Beniamino.
xSegre, Beniamino.

Some Properties of Differentiable Varieties &
Transformations: With Special Reference to
the Analytic & Algebraic Cases.
Springer-Verlag.

Segre, Cesare.
xSegre, Cesare.
Structures & Time: Narration, Poetry, Models.
U of Chicago Pr.

Segre, Emilio.
xSegre, Emilio.
Enrico Fermi, Physicist. U of Chicago Pr.

Segre, Roberto.
xSegre, Roberto.
ed. Latin America in Its Architecture. Holmes
& Meier.

Seguin, C. Alberto.
xSeguin, C. Alberto.
Introduction to Psychosomatic Medicine. Intl
Univs Pr.

Seguin, Edward, 1812-1880
xSeguin, Edward.
Idiocy & Its Treatment by the Physiological
Method. Kelley.

Segundo, Jean L. *see* Segundo, Juan Luis.

Segundo, Juan L. *see* Segundo, Juan Luis.

Segundo, Juan Luis.
xSegundo, Jean L.
Grace & the Human Condition. Orbis Bks.
xSegundo, Juan L.
Evolution & Guilt. Orbis Bks.
The Liberation of Theology. Orbis Bks.
Our Idea of God. Orbis Bks.
Theology for Artisans of a New Humanity.
Orbis Bks.

Segura, Pancho.
xSegura, Pancho.
Pancho Segura's Championship Strategy: How
to Play Winning Tennis. McGraw.

Segy, Ladislas.
xSegy, Ladislas.
African Sculpture. Dover.
African Sculpture. Peter Smith.
African Sculpture Speaks. Da Capo.
Masks of Black Africa. Dover.
Masks of Black Africa. Peter Smith.

Sehested, Ove H.
xSehested, Ove H.
Better & Better. Uranus Pub.

Sehgal, S. *see* Sehgal, Sudarshan K.

Sehgal, Sudarshan K., 1936-
xSehgal, S.
Topics in Group Rings. Dekker.

Sehnert, Keith W.
xSehnert, Keith W.
How to Be Your Own Doctor - Sometimes.
G&D.

Seibels, Gren.
xSeibels, Gren.
A Gaggle of One. Soaring Symposia.

Seibert, Joseph C.
xSeibert, Joseph C.
Concepts of Marketing Management. Har-Row.

Seibutsugaku Fokenkyujo, Tokyo.
xBiological Laboratory, Imperial Household.
ed. The Crabs of Sagami Bay: Collected by His
Majesty the Emperor of Japan. U Pr of
Hawaii.

Seid, Robert.
xSeid, Robert.
Applied Problems for Fundamentals of
Three-Dimensional Descriptive Geometry.
HarBraceJ.

Seide, Diane.
xSeide, Diane.
Careers in Medical Science. Elsevier-Nelson.
Looking Good: The Everything Guide to
Health, Beauty & Modeling. Elsevier-Nelson.

Seide, Katharine.
xSeide, Katharine.

ed. The Paul Felix Warburg Union Catalog of
Arbitration: A Selective Bibliography &
Subject Index of Peaceful Dispute Settlement
Procedures - Commercial, International,
Labor. Rowman.

Seide, Michael.
xSeide, Michael.
The Common Thread: A Book of Stories.
Arno.

Seidel, Alison P.
xSeidel, Alison P.
Compiled by Literary Criticism & Authors'
Biographies: An Annotated Index. Scarecrow.

Seidel, Frederick, 1936-
xSeidel, Frederick.
Sunrise. Penguin.
Sunrise. Viking Pr.

Seidel, George J. *see* Seidel, George Joseph.

Seidel, George Joseph, 1932-
xSeidel, George J.
Crisis of Creativity. U of Notre Dame Pr.
Martin Heidegger & the Pre-Socratics: An
Introduction to His Thought. U of Nebr Pr.

Seidel, L. E. *see* Seidel, Leon E.

Seidel, Leon E.
xSeidel, L. E.
Applied Textile Marketing. Textile Bk.

Seidel, Michael. *see* Seidel, Michael A.

Seidel, Michael A.
xSeidel, Michael.
ed. Homer to Brecht: The European Epic &
Dramatic Traditions. Yale U Pr.

Seidelman, James E.
xSeidelman, James E.
Creating Mosaics. Macmillan.
Creating with Paint. Macmillan.
Creating with Papier-Mache. Macmillan.
Creating with Wood. Macmillan.

Seiden, Hank.
xSeiden, Hank.
Advertising Pure & Simple. Am Mgmt.

Seidenberg, Robert.
xSeidenberg, Robert.
Marriage in Life & Literature. Philos Lib.

Seidensticker, Edward G., 1921-
xSeidensticker, Edward G.
Genji Days. Kodansha.

Seidensticker, O. *see* Seidensticker, Oswald.

Seidensticker, Oswald.
xSeidensticker, O.
First Century of German Printing in America,
1728-1830. Kraus Repr.

Seidl-Hohenveldern, I. *see* Seidl-Hohenveldern, Ignaz.

Seidl-Hohenveldern, Ignaz.
xSeidl-Hohenveldern, I.
American-Austrian Private International Law.
Oceana.

Seidler, Edouard.
xSeidler, Edouard.
Let's Call It Fiesta: An Auto-Biography of
Ford's Project Bobcat. Aztex.

Seidler, Rosalie.
xSeidler, Rosalie.
illus. Panda Cake. Schol Bk Serv.

Seidler, Tor.
xSeidler, Tor.
Dulcimer Boy. Viking Pr.

Seidlin, Joseph, 1892-
xSeidlin, Joseph.
Critical Study of the Teaching of Elementary
College Mathematics. AMS Pr.

Seidman, Ann. *see* Seidman, Ann Willcox.

Seidman, Ann Willcox, 1926-
xSeidman, Ann.
ed. Natural Resources & National Welfare: The
Case of Copper. Praeger.
South Africa & U. S. Multinational
Corporations. Lawrence Hill.

Seidman, Harold.
xSeidman, Harold.

Politics, Position & Power: The Dynamics of
Federal Organization. Oxford U Pr.

Seidman, Hillel.
xSeidman, Hillel.
The Glory of the Jewish Holidays. Shengold.

Seidman, Hugh, 1940-
xSeidman, Hugh.
Collecting Evidence. Yale U Pr.

Seidman, Laurence. *see* Seidman, Laurence Ivan.

Seidman, Laurence I. *see* Seidman, Laurence Ivan.

Seidman, Laurence Ivan, 1925-
xSeidman, Laurence.
The Fools of '49: The California Gold Rush,
1848-1856. Knopf.
xSeidman, Laurence I.
Once in the Saddle: The Cowboy's Frontier.
Knopf.

Seidman, Laurence S.
xSeidman, Laurence S.
The Design of Federal Employment Programs.
Lexington Bks.

Seidman, Robert. *see* Seidman, Robert J.

Seidman, Robert J.
xSeidman, Robert.
Bucks County Idyll. S&S.
One Smart Indian. Putnam.
xSeidman, Robert J.
One Smart Indian. Overlook Pr.

Seidman, Steve.
xSeidman, Steve.
ed. The Film Career of Billy Wilder. G K Hall.
The Film Career of Billy Wilder. Redgrave Pub
Co.
The Film Career of Billy Wilder. Two
Continents.

Seif, Elliott.
xSeif, Elliott.
Teaching Significant Social Studies in the
Elementary School. Rand.

Seifert, Anne.
xSeifert, Anne.
His, Mine, & Ours: A Guide to Keeping
Marriage from Ruining a Perfectly Good
Relationship. Macmillan.

Seifert, Elizabeth, 1897-
xSeifert, Elizabeth.

Army Doctor. Amereon Ltd.
Bright Banners. Amereon Ltd.
The Bright Coin. Amereon Ltd.
Bright Scalpel. Amereon Ltd.
A Certain Doctor French. Amereon Ltd.
Doctor at the Crossroads. Amereon Ltd.
Doctor Comes to Bayard. Amereon Ltd.
The Doctor Disagrees. Amereon Ltd.
Doctor Ellison's Decision. Amereon Ltd.
A Doctor for Blue Jay Cove. Amereon Ltd.
A Doctor in the Family. Amereon Ltd.
Dr. Jeremy's Wife. Amereon Ltd.
The Doctor Makes a Choice. Amereon Ltd.
Doctor of Mercy. Amereon Ltd.
Doctor on Trial. Amereon Ltd.
The Doctor Takes a Wife. Amereon Ltd.
Dr. Tuck. Dodd.
Doctor with a Mission. Amereon Ltd.
The Doctor's Affair. Dodd.
The Doctor's Bride. Amereon Ltd.
The Doctor's Desperate Hour. Dodd.
The Doctor's Desperate Hour. NAL.
The Doctor's Husband. Amereon Ltd.
Doctors on Eden Place. NAL.
The Doctor's Promise. Dodd.
The Doctor's Strange Secret. Amereon Ltd.
The Doctors Were Brothers. Dodd.
The Doctors Were Brothers. G K Hall.
Dusty Spring. Amereon Ltd.
Girl Intern. Amereon Ltd.
A Great Day. Amereon Ltd.
Hillbilly Doctor. Amereon Ltd.
Homecoming. Amereon Ltd.
The Honor of Dr. Shelton. Amereon Ltd.
Hospital Zone. Amereon Ltd.
Legacy for a Doctor. Amereon Ltd.
Love Calls the Doctor. Amereon Ltd.
Lucinda Marries the Doctor. Amereon Ltd.
Marriage for Three. Amereon Ltd.
Old Doc. Amereon Ltd.
Orchard Hill. Amereon Ltd.
Ordeal of Three Doctors. Amereon Ltd.
Pay the Doctor. Amereon Ltd.
Rebel Doctor. Dodd.
The Strange Loyalty of Dr. Carlisle. Amereon
    Ltd.
Substitute Doctor. Amereon Ltd.
Surgeon in Charge. Amereon Ltd.
Take Three Doctors. Amereon Ltd.
Two Doctors & a Girl. Dodd.
Two Doctors & a Girl. NAL.
When Doctors Marry. Amereon Ltd.
Seifert, Shirley, 1889-
    xSeifert, Shirley.
    The Turquoise Trail. Am Repr-Rivercity Pr.
Seifert, William W.
    xSeifert, William W.
    ed. Energy & Development: A Case Study.
        MIT Pr.
Seigel, Jerrold. see Seigel, Jerrold E.
Seigel, Jerrold E.
    xSeigel, Jerrold.
    Marx's Fate: The Shape of a Life. Princeton U
        Pr.
Seigfried, Charlene H. see Seigfried, Charlene Haddock.
Seigfried, Charlene Haddock, 1943-
    xSeigfried, Charlene H.
    Chaos & Context: A Study in William James.
        Ohio U Pr.
Seignobos, Charles, 1854-1942
    xSeignobos, Charles.
    The Evolution of the French People. Octagon.
Seike, Kiyosi, 1918-
    xSeike, Kiyosi.
    The Art of Japanese Joinery. Weatherhill.
Seiler, John.
    xSeiler, John.

ed. Southern Africa Since the Portuguese Coup.
    Westview.
Seiler, Karl.
    xSeiler, Karl.
    Introduction to Systems Cost Effectiveness.
        Krieger.
Seilhamer, George O. see Seilhamer, George Overcash.
Seilhamer, George Overcash, 1839-1916
    xSeilhamer, George O.
    History of the American Theatre. Arno.
    History of the American Theatre. Greenwood.
    History of the American Theatre. Haskell.
    History of the American Theatre 1888-1891.
        Scholarly.
Sein, Kenneth.
    xSein, Kenneth.
    The Great Po Sein: A Chronicle of the
        Burmese Theater. Greenwood.
Seippel, R. G. see Seippel, Robert G.
Seippel, Robert G.
    xSeippel, R. G.
    Fundamentals of Electricity: Basics of
        Electricity, Electronics, Controls &
        Computers. Am Technical.
Seiss, Joseph. see Seiss, Joseph Augustus.
Seiss, Joseph A. see Seiss, Joseph Augustus.
Seiss, Joseph Augustus, 1823-1904
    xSeiss, Joseph.
    The Gospel in the Stars. Gordon Pr.
    The Great Pyramid: A Miracle in Stone.
        Multimedia.
    xSeiss, Joseph A.
    The Gospel in the Stars. Kregel.
Seitel, Peter.
    xSeitel, Peter.
    See So That We May See: Performances &
        Interpretations of Traditional Tales from
        Tanzania. Ind U Pr.
Seiter, Richard P.
    xSeiter, Richard P.
    Evaluation Research As a Feedback
        Mechanism for Criminal Justice Policy
        Making: A Critical Analysis. R & E Res
        Assoc.
Seiter, William J., 1953-
    xSeiter, William J.
    Studies in Niuean Syntax. Garland Pub.
Seitz, Don C. see Seitz, Don Carlos.
Seitz, Don Carlos, 1862-1935
    xSeitz, Don C.
    Also Rans: Great Men Who Missed Making
        the Presidential Goal. Arno.
    Artemus Ward (Charles Farrar Browne): A
        Biography & Bibliography. Beekman Pubs.
    Dreadful Decade: Detailing Some Phases in the
        History of the United States from
        Reconstruction to Resumption, 1869-1879.
        Greenwood.
    Joseph Pulitzer, His Life & Letters. AMS Pr.
    Under the Black Flag. Gale.
Seitz, Neil, 1943-
    xSeitz, Neil E.
    Financial Analysis: A Programmed Approach.
        Reston.
Seitz, Neil E. see Seitz, Neil.
Seitz, Nick.
    xSeitz, Nick.
    Superstars of Golf. Golf Digest Bks.
Seitz, Steven T. see Seitz, Steven Thomas.
Seitz, Steven Thomas, 1947-
    xSeitz, Steven T.
    Bureaucracy Policy & the Public. Mosby.
Seitz, William C. see Seitz, William Chapin.
Seitz, William Chapin.
    xSeitz, William C.
    The Sixties: Art in the Age of Aquarius.
        Braziller.
Seixas, Judith S.
    xSeixas, Judith S.

Living with a Parent Who Drinks Too Much.
    Greenwillow.
Sejourne, Laurette.
    xSejourne, Laurette.
    Burning Water: Thought & Religion in Ancient
        Mexico. Shambhala Pubns.
Seki, Keigo, 1899-
    xSeki, Keigo.
    ed. Folktales of Japan. U of Chicago Pr.
Sekiguchi, Sueo.
    xSekiguchi, Sueo.
    Japanese Direct Foreign Investment. Allanheld.
Sekine, Tatsuya.
    xSekine, Tatsuya.
    Solvent Extraction Chemistry. Dekker.
Seklemian, M.
    xSeklemian, M.
    Sek Says. Retail Report.
Sela, Michael.
    xSela, Michael.
    ed. The Antigens. Acad Pr.
Sela, Owen.
    xSela, Owen.
    An Exchange of Eagles. Pantheon.
    The Petrograd Consignment. Dell.
    The Petrograd Consignment. Dial.
Selame, Elinor.
    xSelame, Elinor.
    Developing a Corporate Identity: How to Stand
        Out in the Crowd. Lebhar Friedman.
Selber, Lillian (Perlstein), 1894-
    xSelber, Lillian P.
    A Little Quiet Dreaming, a Little Time to
        Think. Pacesetter Pr.
Selber, Lillian P. see Selber, Lillian (Perlstein).
Selberg, Charles A.
    xSelberg, Charles A.
    Foil. A-W.
Selbo, M. L. see Selbo, Magnus Leonard.
Selbo, Magnus Leonard, 1901-
    xSelbo, M. L.
    Adhesive Bonding of Wood. Sterling.
Selby, Donald J. see Selby, Donald Joseph.
Selby, Donald Joseph.
    xSelby, Donald J.
    Toward the Understanding of St. Paul. P-H.
Selby, Hubert.
    xSelby, Hubert.
    The Demon. NAL.
    Last Exit to Brooklyn. Ballantine.
    Last Exit to Brooklyn. Grove.
    Requiem for a Dream. Playboy Pbks.
Selby, Peter H.
    xSelby, Peter H.
    Geometry & Trigonometry for Calculus. Wiley.
    Practical Algebra. Wiley.
    Using Graphs & Tables. Wiley.
Selby, Robin. see Selby, Robin C.
Selby, Robin C.
    xSelby, Robin.
    The Principle of Reserve in the Writings of
        John Henry, Cardinal Newman. Oxford U Pr.
Selby, Thomas G. see Selby, Thomas Gunn.
Selby, Thomas Gunn, 1846-1910
    xSelby, Thomas G.
    Theology of Modern Fiction. Folcroft.
Selby-Bigge, L. A. see Selby-Bigge, Lewis Amherst.
Selby-Bigge, Lewis Amherst, Bart, Sir
    xSelby-Bigge, L. A.
    ed. British Moralists: Being Selections from
        Writers Principally of the Eighteenth
        Century. Irvington.
Selcamm, George.
    xSelcamm, George.
    Fifty-Seventh Street. Norton.
    Night Is for Music. Norton.
Selcher, Wayne A., 1942-
    xSelcher, Wayne A.

The Afro-Asian Dimension of Brazilian Foreign
Policy. U Presses Fla.
Selden, Bernice.
xSelden, Bernice.
The Body-Mind Book: Nine Ways to
Awareness. Messner.
Selden, John.
xSelden, John.
Table Talk. R West.
Table-Talk. Saifer.
Selden, Mark.
xSelden, Mark.
ed. People's Republic of China: A
Documentary History of Revolutionary
Change. Monthly Rev.
Selden, Samuel, 1899-
xSelden, Samuel.
First Steps in Acting. Irvington.
Stage in Action. S Ill U Pr.
Stage Scenery & Lighting. P-H.
ed. Theatre Double Game. U of NC Pr.
Seldes, G. *see* Seldes, George.
Seldes, George, 1890-
xSeldes, G.
Freedom of the Press. Da Capo.
xSeldes, George.
Even the Gods Can't Change History. Lyle
Stuart.
Seldes, Gilbert. *see* Seldes, Gilbert Vivian.
Seldes, Gilbert V. *see* Seldes, Gilbert Vivian.
Seldes, Gilbert Vivian, 1893-
xSeldes, Gilbert.
An Hour with the Movies & the Talkies. Arno.
xSeldes, Gilbert V.
Great Audience. Greenwood.
Seldes, Lee.
xSeldes, Lee.
The Legacy of Mark Rothko. HR&W.
The Legacy of Mark Rothko. Penguin.
Seldes, Marian.
xSeldes, Marian.
The Bright Lights: A Theatre Life. HM.
Seldin, Joseph J.
xSeldin, Joseph J.
The Golden Fleece: Selling the Good Life to
Americans. Arno.
Seldin, Maury, 1931-
xSeldin, Maury.
ed. The Real Estate Handbook. Dow
Jones-Irwin.
Real Estate Investment for Profit Through
Appreciation. Reston.
Real Estate Investment Strategies. Wiley.
You Can Profit from Real Estate Appreciation.
Reston.
Seldon, M. Robert.
xSeldon, Robert.
Life Cycle Costing: A Better Method for
Government Procurement. Westview.
Seldon, Robert. *see* Seldon, M. Robert.
Selekman, Benjamin M. *see* Selekman, Benjamin Morris.
Selekman, Benjamin Morris, 1893-1962
xSelekman, Benjamin M.
Problems in Labor Relations. McGraw.
Self, Carolyn S. *see* Self, Carolyn Shealy.
Self, Carolyn Shealy.
xSelf, Carolyn S.
Learning to Pray. Word Bks.
Self, Charles. *see* Self, Charles R.
Self, Charles R.
xSelf, Charles.
How to Build Your Own Vacation Home. TAB
Bks.
xSelf, Charles R.

The Brazer's Handbook. Sterling.
Building Your Own Home. Reston.
Do-It-Yourselfer's Guide to Chainsaw Use &
Repair. TAB Bks.
Western Horsemanship. Winchester Pr.
Wood Heating Handbook. TAB Bks.
Working with Plywood, Including
Indoor-Outdoor Projects. TAB Bks.
Self, Huber.
xSelf, Huber.
Environment & Man in Kansas: A
Geographical Analysis. Regents Pr KS.
Self, Margaret C. *see* Self, Margaret Cabell.
Self, Margaret Cabell.
xSelf, Margaret C.
American Quarter Horse in Pictures. Wilshire.
Complete Book of Horses & Ponies. McGraw.
The Horseman's Encyclopedia. Arco.
Hunter in Pictures. Wilshire.
The Nature of the Horse. Arco.
The Problem Horse & the Problem Horseman.
Arco.
Self, Robert T.
xSelf, Robert T.
Barrett Wendell. Twayne.
Self-Realisation Fellowship.
xSelf-Realization Fellowship.
Paramahansa Yogananda: In Memoriam. Self
Realization.
Rajarsi Janakananda: A Great Western Yogi.
Self Realization.
Self-Realization Fellowship. *see* Self-Realisation
Fellowship.
Selfe, Lorna.
xSelfe, Lorna.
Nadia: A Case of Extraordinary Drawing
Ability in an Autistic Child. HarBraceJ.
NADIA: Case of Extraordinary Drawing
Ability in an Autistic Child. Acad Pr.
Selfridge, Oliver.
xSelfridge, Oliver.
All About Mud. A-W.
Selfridge, Oliver. *see* Selfridge, Oliver G.
Selfridge, Oliver G.
xSelfridge, Oliver.
Trouble with Dragons. A-W.
Selfridge-Field, Eleanor.
xSelfridge-Field, Eleanor.
Venetian Instrumental Music from Gabrieli to
Vivaldi. Biblio Dist.
Selig, Elaine B. *see* Selig, Elaine Booth.
Selig, Elaine Booth.
xSelig, Elaine B.
Demon Summer. PB.
Mariner's End. PB.
Seliger, Howard H. *see* Seliger, Howard Harold.
Seliger, Howard Harold.
xSeliger, Howard H.
Light: Physical & Biological Action. Acad Pr.
Seliger, M.
xSeliger, Martin.
Ideology & Politics. Free Pr.
Seliger, Martin. *see* Seliger, M.
Seligman, Charles G. *see* Seligman, Charles Gabriel.
Seligman, Charles Gabriel.
xSeligman, Charles G.
The Melanesians of British New Guinea. AMS
Pr.
Seligman, G. B.
xSeligman, George.
Rational Methods in Lie Algebras. Dekker.
Seligman, George. *see* Seligman, G. B.
Seligman, Milton.
xSeligman, Milton.

ed. Counselor Education & Supervision:
Readings in Theory, Practice, & Research. C
C Thomas.
Group Counseling & Group Psychotherapy
with Rehabilitation Clients. C C Thomas.
Strategies for Helping Parents of Exceptional
Children: A Guide for Teachers. Free Pr.
Seligsohn, D. *see* Seligsohn, Daniel.
Seligsohn, Daniel.
xSeligsohn, D.
Analysis of Species-Specific Molar Adaptations
in Strepsirhine Primates. S Karger.
Seligson, Marcia.
xSeligson, Marcia.
Cosmopolitan's Super Diets & Exercise Guide.
Avon.
Options: A Personal Expedition Through the
Sexual Frontier. Random.
Seligson, Mitchell A.
xSeligson, Mitchell A.
Peasants of Costa Rica & the Development of
Agrarian Capitalism. U of Wis Pr.
ed. Politics & the Poor. Holmes & Meier.
Seligson, Tom.
xSeligson, Tom.
Stalking. Everest Hse.
Stalking. NAL.
Selikoff, Irving. *see* Selikoff, Irving J.
Selikoff, Irving J.
xSelikoff, Irving.
Asbestos & Disease. Acad Pr.
xSelikoff, Irving J.
ed. Health Hazards of Asbestos Exposure. NY
Acad Sci.
Selin, Iuan. *see* Selin, Ivan.
Selin, Ivan.
xSelin, Iuan.
Detection Theory. Princeton U Pr.
Selincourt, Ernest De. *see* De Selincourt, Ernest.
Selinko, Annemarie.
xSelinko, Annemarie.
Desiree. Morrow.
Selko, Daniel. *see* Selko, Daniel Theodore.
Selko, Daniel Theodore.
xSelko, Daniel.
The Federal Financial System. Da Capo.
Sell, Irene L.
xSell, Irene L.
Dying & Death: An Annotated Bibliography.
Tiresias Pr.
Sell, Kenneth D.
xSell, Kenneth D.
ed. Divorce in the United States, Canada, &
Great Britain: A Guide to Information
Sources. Gale.
Sell, Stewart.
xSell, Stewart.

Immunology, Immunopathology & Immunity.
Har-Row.

Sellari, Dot.

xSellari, Dot.
jt. auth. Official Price Guide to Bottles, Old &
New. Hse of Collectibles.

Sellars, Roy W. *see* Sellars, Roy Wood.
Sellars, Roy Wood, 1880-
xSellars, Roy W.
Critical Realism: A Study of the Nature &
Conditions of Knowledge. Russell.
Evolutionary Naturalism. Russell.
Sellars, Wilfred.
xSellars, Wilfrid.
ed. Readings in Ethical Theory. P-H.
Sellars, Wilfrid. *see* Sellars, Wilfred.
Selle, Erwin S. *see* Selle, Erwin Stevenson.
Selle, Erwin Stevenson, 1887-
xSelle, Erwin S.

The Organization & Activities of the National Education Association: A Case Study in Educational Sociology. AMS Pr.

Selleck, Jack.
xSelleck, Jack.
Faces. Davis Mass.

Selleck, R. J. *see* Selleck, Richard Joseph Wheeler.

Selleck, Richard Joseph Wheeler.
xSelleck, R. J.
English Primary Education & the Progressives: 1914-1939. Routledge & Kegan.

Sellen, Jane B.
xSellen, Jane B.
How Your Government Works. Monarch Pr.

Sellers, C. G. *see* Sellers, Charles Grier.

Sellers, Charles. *see* Sellers, Charles Grier.

Sellers, Charles C. *see* Sellers, Charles Coleman.

Sellers, Charles Coleman, 1903-
xSellers, Charles C.
Dickinson College: A History. Columbia U Pr.

Sellers, Charles Grier.
xSellers, C. G.
As It Happened: A History of the United States. McGraw.
xSellers, Charles.
Synopsis of American History. Rand.

Sellers, Con.
xSellers, Con.
Marilee. PB.
Sweet Caroline. PB.

Sellers, Gene. *see* Sellers, Gene R.

Sellers, Gene R.
xSellers, Gene.
Understanding Algebra & Trigonometry. Merrill.
xSellers, Gene R.
Understanding College Algebra. Merrill.

Sellers, L. *see* Sellers, Leslie.

Sellers, Leonard. *see* Sellers, Leonard L.

Sellers, Leonard L.
xSellers, Leonard.
Mass Media Issues: Articles & Commentaries. P-H.

Sellers, Leslie.
xSellers, L.
Cooking with Love. Pergamon.
The Simple Subs Book. Pergamon.

Sellery, G. C. *see* Sellery, George Clarke.

Sellery, George Clarke.
xSellery, G. C.
Medieval Foundations of Western Civilization. Haskell.

Selley, Richard C., 1939-
xSelley, Richard C.
Ancient Sedimentary Environments. Cornell U Pr.

Sellin, David.
xSellin, David.
The First Pose. Norton.

Sellin, Donald F., 1934-
xSellin, Donald F.
Mental Retardation: Nature, Needs, & Advocacy. Allyn.

Sellin, Eric, 1933-
xSellin, Eric.
Dramatic Concepts of Antonin Artaud. U of Chicago Pr.
The Inner Game of Soccer. Anderson World.

Sellin, Johan Thorsten.
xSellin, Thorsten.
ed. Delinquency: Selected Studies. Krieger.
The Measurement of Delinquency. Patterson Smith.
The Penalty of Death. Sage.

Sellin, Thorsten. *see* Sellin, Johan Thorsten.

Sells, Elijah W. *see* Sells, Elijah Watt.

Sells, Elijah Watt, 1858-1924
xSells, Elijah W.

The Natural Business Year & Thirteen Other Themes. Arno.

Sells, James. *see* Sells, James William.

Sells, James William.
xSells, James.
Partner with the Living Lord. Upper Room.

Sells, S. B. *see* Sells, Saul B.

Sells, Saul B., 1913-
xSells, S. B.
Human Functioning in Longitudinal Perspective: Studies of Normal & Psychopathic Populations. Williams & Wilkins.

Sells, William.
xSells, William.
Remarks on the Condition of the Slaves in the Island of Jamaica. Humanities.

Sellwood, Arthur. *see* Sellwood, Arthur V.

Sellwood, Arthur V.
xSellwood, Arthur.
The Victorian Railway Murders. David & Charles.

Selman, Edythea G. *see* Selman, Edythea Ginis.

Selman, Edythea Ginis.
xSelman, Edythea G.
School & Me. HR&W.

Selman, Joseph.
xSelman, Joseph.
Fundamentals of X-Ray & Radium Physics. C C Thomas.

Selmier, Dean.
xSelmier, Dean.
Blow Away. Viking Pr.

Selsam. *see* Selsam, Millicent E.

Selsam, J. Paul. *see* Selsam, John Paul.

Selsam, John Paul, 1898-1950
xSelsam, J. Paul.
Pennsylvania Constitution of 1776: A Study in Revolutionary Democracy. Octagon.

Selsam, Millicent. *see* Selsam, Millicent Ellis.

Selsam, Millicent (Ellis).
xSelsam.
A First Look at Fish. Schol Bk Serv.
A First Look at Leaves. Schol Bk Serv.
A First Look at Mammals. Schol Bk Serv.

A First Look at Snakes, Lizards & Other Reptiles. Schol Bk Serv.
xSelsam, Millicent.
All Kinds of Babies. Schol Bk Serv.
A First Look at Animals Without Backbones. Walker & Co.
A First Look at Fish. Walker & Co.
A First Look at Monkeys & Apes. Walker & Co.
A First Look at Sharks. Walker & Co.
A First Look at the World of Plants. Walker & Co.
How Kittens Grow. Schol Bk Serv.
How Kittens Grow. Schol Bk Serv.
Play with Plants. Morrow.
Tyrannosaurus Rex. Har-Row.
xSelsam, Millicent E.
The Apple & Other Fruits. Morrow.
Bulbs, Corms & Such. Morrow.
Egg to Chick. Har-Row.
A First Look at Animals with Backbones. Walker & Co.
A First Look at Birds. Walker & Co.
A First Look at Flowers. Walker & Co.
A First Look at Frogs, Toads & Salamanders. Walker & Co.
A First Look at Insects. Walker & Co.
ed. A First Look at Leaves. Walker & Co.
First Look at Mammals. Walker & Co..

A First Look at Snakes, Lizards & Other Reptiles. Walker & Co.

A First Look at Whales. Walker & Co.

Greg's Microscope. Har-Row.
How Animals Tell Time. Morrow.

How to Grow House Plants. Morrow.

Maple Tree. Morrow.
More Potatoes!. Har-Row.
Peanut. Morrow.

The Plants We Eat. Morrow.

Play with Seeds. Morrow.
Play with Trees. Morrow.

Popcorn. Morrow.
Questions & Answers About Ants. Schol Bk Serv.
Vegetables from Stems & Leaves. Morrow.
When an Animal Grows. Har-Row.

Selsam, Millicent E. *see* Selsam, Millicent (Ellis).

Selss, Albert M. *see* Selss, Albert Maximilian.

Selss, Albert Maximilian.
xSelss, Albert M.
A Critical Outline of the Literature of Germany. Arno.

Seltman, Charles. *see* Seltman, Charles Theodore.

Seltman, Charles T. *see* Seltman, Charles Theodore.

Seltman, Charles Theodore, 1886-1957
xSeltman, Charles.
Athens: Its History & Coinage Before the Persian Invasion. Ares.
xSeltman, Charles T.
Women in Antiquity. Hyperion Conn.

Seltz, David. *see* Seltz, David D.

Seltz, David D.
xSeltz, David.
Food Service Marketing & Promotion. Lebhar Friedman.
xSeltz, David D.
How to Prepare Effective Business Program Blueprints: A Management Handbook. A-W.
Industrial Selling: Gateway to the Million Dollar Sale!. McGraw.

Seltz-Petrash, Ann.
xSeltz-Petrash, Ann.
Compiled by AAAS Science Film Catalog. Bowker.

Seltzer, Charles A. *see* Seltzer, Charles Alden.

Seltzer, Charles Alden, 1875-1942
xSeltzer, Charles A.
Arizona Jim. Amereon Ltd.
Clear the Trail. Amereon Ltd.
Ferguson's Trail. Belmont-Tower.
The Gentleman from Virginia. Amereon Ltd.
Gone North. Amereon Ltd.
Lonesome Ranch. Amereon Ltd.

Seltzer, David.
xSeltzer, David.
The Omen. NAL.
Prophecy. Ballantine.

Seltzer, Leon E.
xSeltzer, Leon E.
Exemptions & Fair Use in Copyright: The Exclusive Rights Tensions in the 1976 Copyright Act. Harvard U Pr.

Seltzer, William.
xSeltzer, William.
Demographic Data Collection: A Summary of Experience. Population Coun.

Selvi, A. M. *see* Selvi, Arthur Mark.

Selvi, Arthur Mark, 1912-
xSelvi, A. M.

Folklore of Other Lands: Folk Tales, Proverbs, Songs, Rhymes & Games of Italy, France, the Hispanic World & Germany. S F Vanni.

Selvin, David F.
xSelvin, David F.
Champions of Labor. Abelard.

Selwood, P. W. see Selwood, Pierce Wilson.

Selwood, Pierce W. see Selwood, Pierce Wilson.

Selwood, Pierce Wilson, 1905-
xSelwood, P. W.
Chemisorption & Magnetization. Acad Pr.
xSelwood, Pierce W.
Adsorption & Collective Paramagnetism. Acad Pr.

Selwyn, Francis.
xSelwyn, Francis.
Cracksman on Velvet. Stein & Day.
Sergeant Verity & the Blood Royal. Stein & Day.

Selye, H. see Selye, Hans.

Selye, Hans, 1907-
xSelye, H.
Experimental Cardiovascular Diseases. Springer-Verlag.
Hormones & Resistance. Springer-Verlag.
Stress in Health and Disease. Butterworths.
xSelye, Hans.
Calciphylaxis. U of Chicago Pr.
The Stress of My Life: A Scientist's Memoirs. Van Nos Reinhold.
Stress Without Distress. Lippincott.
Stress Without Distress. NAL.

Selz, Jean.
xSelz, Jean.
Gustave Moreau. Crown.
Matisse. Crown.
Turner. Crown.

Selz, Peter.
xSelz, Peter.
German Expressionist Painting. U of Cal Pr.

Selzer, Joae. see Selzer, Joae Graham.

Selzer, Joae Graham, 1926-
xSelzer, Joae.
When Children Ask About Sex: A Guide for Parents. Beacon Pr.

Selzer, Richard.
xSelzer, Richard.
Confessions of a Knife. S&S.

Selznick, Gene.
xSelznick, Gene.
Inside Volleyball. Contemp Bks.

Selznick, Gertrude Jaeger.
xSelznick, Gertude J.
The Tenacity of Prejudice: Anti-Semitism in Contemporary America. Greenwood.

Selznick, Gertude J. see Selznick, Gertrude Jaeger.

Selznick, Philip.
xSelznick, Philip.
Law, Society, & Industrial Justice. Transaction Bks.
Leadership in Administration: A Sociological Interpretation. Har-Row.

Semat, H. see Semat, Henry.

Semat, Henry, 1900-
xSemat, H.
Fundamentals of Physics. HR&W.

Semel, Vicki G. see Semel, Vicki Granet.

Semel, Vicki Granet.
xSemel, Vicki G.
At the Grass Roots in the Garden State: Reform & Regular Democrats in New Jersey. Fairleigh Dickinson.

Semenko, Irina M. see Semenko, Irina Mikhailovna.

Semenko, Irina Mikhailovna.
xSemenko, Irina M.
Vasily Zhukovsky. Twayne.

Semenow, Robert W. see Semenow, Robert William.

Semenow, Robert William, 1897-
xSemenow, Robert W.

Questions & Answers on Real Estate. P-H.

Seminar on Canadian-American Relations, University of Windsor.
xUniversity of Windsor Seminar on Canadian-American Relations, 8th Annual, 1966.
International Megalopolis. U of Toronto Pr.

Seminar on Differential Equations & Dynamical Systems, 2nd, 1969. see Seminar on Differential Equations and Dynamical Systems, 2d, University of Maryland, 1969.

Seminar on Differential Equations and Dynamical Systems, 2d, University of Maryland, 1969.
xSeminar on Differential Equations & Dynamical Systems, 2nd, 1969.
Proceedings. Springer-Verlag.

Seminar on Economic & Legal Aspects of Transfrontier Pollution, August 1972. see Seminar on Economic and Legal Aspects of Transfrontier Pollution, Paris, 1972.

Seminar on Economic and Legal Aspects of Transfrontier Pollution, Paris, 1972.
xSeminar on Economic & Legal Aspects of Transfrontier Pollution, August 1972.
Problems in Transfrontier Pollution: Proceedings. OECD.

Seminar on Engineering Equipment for Founderies and Advanced Methods of Producing Such Equipment, Geneva, 1977.
xSeminar on Engineering Equipment for Foundries & Advanced Methods of Producing Such Equipment, Geneva, 1977.
Engineering Equipment for Foundries: Proceedings. Pergamon.

Seminar on Leadership & Political Institutions in India. see Seminar on Leadership and Political Institutions in India, University of California, Berkeley, 1956.

Seminar on Leadership and Political Institutions in India, University of California, Berkeley, 1956.
xSeminar on Leadership & Political Institutions in India.
Leadership & Political Institutions in India: Proceedings. Greenwood.

Seminar on Synoptic Analysis & Forecasting in the Tropics of Asia & the Southwest Pacific, Singapore, Dec. 1970. see Seminar on Synoptic Analysis and Forecasting in the Tropics of Asia and South-West Pacific, Singapore, 1970.

Seminar on Synoptic Analysis and Forecasting in the Tropics of Asia and South-West Pacific, Singapore, 1970.
xSeminar on Synoptic Analysis & Forecasting in the Tropics of Asia & the Southwest Pacific, Singapore, Dec. 1970.
Proceedings. Unipub.

Seminar on the Acquisition of Latin American Library Materials, 2d, University of Texas, 1957.
xSeminar on the Acquisitions of Latin American Library Materials, Austin.
Final Report. Greenwood.

Seminar on the Acquisitions of Latin American Library Materials, Austin. see Seminar on the Acquisition of Latin American Library Materials, 2d, University of Texas, 1957.

Semler, Isabel P. see Semler, Isabel Parker.

Semler, Isabel Parker.
xSemler, Isabel P.
Horatio Parker: A Memoir for His Grandchildren, Compiled from Letters & Papers. AMS Pr.

Semm, K.
xSemm, K.
Atlas of Gynecologic Laparoscopy & Hysteroscopy. Saunders.

Semmes, Raphael, 1890-1952
xSemmes, Raphael.
Crime & Punishment in Early Maryland. Patterson Smith.

Semmingsen, Ingrid, 1910-
xSemmingsen, Ingrid.

Norway to America: A History of the Migration. U of Minn Pr.

Semmler, Clement.
xSemmler, Clement.
Douglas Stewart. Twayne.

Semonche, John E., 1933-
xSemonche, John E.
Charting the Future: The Supreme Court Responds to a Changing Society, 1890-1920. Greenwood.

Semones, Hattie, 1891-1969
xSemones, Hattie.
Duel with Destiny. Commonwealth Pr.

Sempangi, F. Kefa.
xSempangi, F. Kefa.
A Distant Grief. Regal.

Semper, Karl. see Semper, Karl Gottfried.

Semper, Karl Gottfried, 1832-1893
xSemper, Karl.
Animal Life As Affected by the Natural Conditions of Existence. Arno.

Semple, Campbell.
xSemple, Campbell.
Primary Management of Hand Injuries. Year Bk Med.

Semple, Ellen C. see Semple, Ellen Churchill.

Semple, Ellen Churchill.
xSemple, Ellen C.
American History & Its Geographic Conditions. Russell.
Influences of Geographic Environment on the Basis of Ratzel's System of Anthropo-Geography. Russell.

Semprevivo, Philip C.
xSemprevivo, Philip C.
Systems Analysis: Definition Process & Design. SRA.

Semrad, Alice. see Semrad, Alice M.

Semrad, Alice M., 1929-
xSemrad, Alice.
Comprehensive Review for Medical Technologists. Mosby.

Sen, Amartya K. see Sen, Amartya Kumar.

Sen, Amartya Kumar.
xSen, Amartya K.
Choice of Techniques: An Aspect of the Theory of Planned Economic Development. Kelley.

Sen, Bandhudas.
xSen, Bandhudas.
The Green Revolution in India: A Perspective. Halsted Pr.

Sen, Jyoti P. see Sen, Jyoti Prakash.

Sen, Jyoti Prakash.
xSen, Jyoti P.
The Progress of T. S. Eliot As Poet & Critic. Havertown Bks.
The Progress of T. S. Eliot As Poet & Critic. Humanities.
The Progress of T. S. Eliot As Poet & Critic. Norwood Edns.

Sen, K. M. see Sen, Kshitimohan.

Sen, Kshitimohan.
xSen, K. M.
Hinduism. Gannon.
xSen, Kshitimohan M.
Hinduism. Penguin.

Sen, Kshitimohan M. see Sen, Kshitimohan.

Sen, Ramendra K. see Sen, Ramendra Kumar.

Sen, Ramendra Kumar.
xSen, Ramendra K.
A Brief Introduction to a Comparative Study of Greek & Indian Poetics & Aesthetics. Folcroft.

Sen, Soshitsu.
xSen, Soshitsu.
Chado: The Japanese Way of Tea. Weatherhill.

Sen, S. P. see Sen, Siba Pada.

Sen, Siba Pada.
xSen, S. P.

Historians & Historiography in Modern India. Intl Pubns Serv.

Sen, Sudhir.
  xSen, Sudhir.
    Reaping the Green Revolution: Food & Jobs for All. Orbis Bks.
    A Richer Harvest: New Horizons for Developing Countries. Orbis Bks.

Sen, Sukomal, 1934-
  xSen, Sukomal.
    Working Class of India: History of Emergence & Movement, 1930-1970. South Asia Bks.

Senate Committee On The District Of Columbia. *see* United States. Congress. Senate. Committee on the District of Columbia.

Sencourt, Robert, 1890-
  xSencourt, Robert.
    India in English Literature. R West.

Sendak, Maurice.
  xSendak, Maurice.
    illus. Chicken Soup with Rice: A Book of Months. Schol Bk Serv.
    illus. Higglety Pigglety Pop: Or, There Must Be More to Life. Har-Row.
    illus. In the Night Kitchen. Har-Row.
    illus. Sign on Rosie's Door. Har-Row.
    illus. Where the Wild Things Are. Har-Row.

Sendrey, Alfred, 1884-
  xSendrey, Alfred.
    Music in the Social & Religious Life of Antiquity. Fairleigh Dickinson.

Seneca. *see* Seneca, Lucius Annaeus.

Seneca, Joseph J.
  xSeneca, Joseph J.
    Environmental Economics. P-H.

Seneca, Lucius Annaeus.
  xSeneca.
    Medea. Bobbs.
    Medea. Oxford U Pr.

Senechal, Marjorie.
  xSenechal, Marjorie.
    ed. Patterns of Symmetry. U of Mass Pr.

Senefelder, Alois, 1771-1834
  xSenefelder, Alois.
    A Complete Course of Lithography. Da Capo.

Seneviratne, H. L., 1934-
  xSeneviratne, H. L.
    Rituals of the Kandyan State. Cambridge U Pr.

Seney, Edgar F.
  xSeney, Edgar F.
    Gregarian Invasion. Wake-Brook.

Senghor, L. S. *see* Senghor, Leopold Sedar.

Senghor, Leopold Sedar.
  xSenghor, L. S.
    Nocturnes. Heinemann Ed.

Sengupta, Arjun.
  xSengupta, Arjun.
    ed. Commodities, Finance & Trade: Issues in the North-South Negotiations. Greenwood.

Sengupta, N. K. *see* Sengupta, Nitish K.

Sengupta, Nitish K., 1934-
  xSengupta, N. K.
    Corporate Management in India. Intl Bk Dist.

Senich, Peter R.
  xSenich, Peter R.
    Pictorial History of U.S. Sniping. Paladin Ent.

Senior, C. M.
  xSenior, C. M.
    A Nation of Pirates: English Piracy in Its Heyday, 1603-1640. Crane-Russak Co.

Senior, Nassau W. *see* Senior, Nassau William.

Senior, Nassau William.
  xSenior, Nassau W.
    Industrial Efficiency & Social Economy. Arno.
    Outline of the Science of Political Economy. Kelley.

Senn, Alfred.
  xSenn, Alfred.

Lithuanian Dialectology. Johnson Repr.

Senn, Frank C.
  xSenn, Frank C.
    The Pastor As Worship Leader: A Manual for Corporate Worship. Augsburg.

Senn, James A.
  xSenn, James A.
    Information Systems in Management. Wadsworth Pub.

Senn, Milton J. *see* Senn, Milton J. E.

Senn, Milton J. E., 1902-
  xSenn, Milton J.
    Speaking Out for America's Children. Yale U Pr.

Senna, Carl, 1944-
  xSenna, Carl.
    ed. The Fallacy of I. Q.. Okpaku Communications.

Senna, Joseph J.
  xSenna, Joseph J.
    Introduction to Criminal Justice. West Pub.

Senne, Rene Le. *see* Le Senne, Rene.

Sennett, Richard, 1943-
  xSennett, Richard.
    Authority. Knopf.
    ed. Classic Essays on the Culture of Cities. P-H.
    The Fall of Public Man. Knopf.
    Families Against the City: Middle Class Homes of Industrial Chicago, 1872-1890. Harvard U Pr.
    Families Against the City: Middle Class Homes of Industrial Chicago, 1872-1890. Random.

Sennett, Ted.
  xSennett, Ted.
    Masters of Menace: Greenstreet & Lorre. Dutton.

Sennewald, Charles A., 1931-
  xSennewald, Charles A.
    Effective Security Management. Butterworths.

Sennholz, Hans F.
  xSennholz, Hans F.
    ed. Gold Is Money. Greenwood.

Senning, Alexander.
  xSenning, Alexander.
    ed. Sulfur in Organic & Inorganic Chemistry. Dekker.

Sensabaugh, George. *see* Sensabaugh, George Frank.

Sensabaugh, George F. *see* Sensabaugh, George Frank.

Sensabaugh, George Frank, 1906-
  xSensabaugh, George.
    Milton in Early America. Gordian.
    That Grand Whig Milton. Arno.
  xSensabaugh, George F.
    That Grand Whig, Milton. AMS Pr.

Sensat, Julius, 1947-
  xSensat, Julius.
    Habermas & Marxism: An Appraisal. Sage.

Sensoir, Jean Jacques.
  xSensoir, Jean-Jacques.
    The Ninth Decade: Secret Plans for the Coming Communist Takeovers. Exposition.

Sensoir, Jean-Jacques. *see* Sensoir, Jean Jacques.

Sentell, R. Perry. *see* Sentell, Robert Perry.

Sentell, Robert Perry.
  xSentell, R. Perry.
    Studies in Georgia Local Government Law. Michie.

Senter, Isaac, 1753?-1799
  xSenter, Isaac.
    Journal of Isaac Senter. Arno.

Senter, R. J.
  xSenter, R. J.
    Psychology: The Exploration of Human Behavior. Scott F.

Senter, Ruth. *see* Senter, Ruth Hollinger.

Senter, Ruth Hollinger, 1944-
  xSenter, Ruth.

So You're the Pastor's Wife. Zondervan.

Senungetuk, Joseph E.
  xSenungetuk, Joseph E.
    Give or Take a Century: An Eskimo Chronicle. Indian Hist Pr.

Seoane, Rhoda (Low).
  xSeoane, Rhoda L.
    Whole Armor. Speller.

Seoane, Rhoda L. *see* Seoane, Rhoda (Low).

Seppa, D. A. *see* Seppa, Dale Allan.

Seppa, Dale A. *see* Seppa, Dale Allan.

Seppa, Dale Allan.
  xSeppa, D. A.
    Paraguayan Paper Money. Obol Intl.
  xSeppa, Dale A.
    The Paper Money of Brasil. Obol Intl.

Seppa, Heikki.
  xSeppa, Heikki.
    Form Emphasis for Metalsmiths. Kent St U Pr.

Sequoia, Anna.
  xSequoia, Anna.
    Backpacking on a Budget. Penguin.

Ser-Vo-Tel Institute.
  xSer-Vo-Tel Institute.
    Dishwashing Procedures. CBI Pub.
    Host-Hostess. CBI Pub.
    Salad Preparation. CBI Pub.
    Sandwich Preparation. CBI Pub.
    Waiter-Waitress. CBI Pub.
  xSer-Vol-Tel Institute.
    Breakfast Preparation. CBI Pub.
    Busing Attendant. CBI Pub.
    Cashiering. CBI Pub.
    Cleaning & Sanitation. CBI Pub.
    Counter Service. CBI Pub.
    Customer-Employee Relationship. CBI Pub.
    Food Care & Food Storage. CBI Pub.
    Foodservice Safety. CBI Pub.
    Foodservice Vocabulary. CBI Pub.
    Fry Cooking. CBI Pub.
    Grill Cooking. CBI Pub.
    Kitchen Sanitation. CBI Pub.
    Luncheon Cooking. CBI Pub.

Ser-Vol-Tel Institute. *see* Ser-Vo-Tel Institute.

Serafetinides, E. A.
  xSerafetinides, E. A.
    Methods of Biobehavioral Research. Grune.

Seraphin, B. O.
  xSeraphin, B. O.
    Optical Properties of Solids: New Developments. Elsevier.
    ed. Solar Energy Conversion: Solid-State Physics Aspects. Springer-Verlag.

Serb, Ann T. *see* Serb, Ann Toland.

Serb, Ann Toland.
  xSerb, Ann T.
    The Mother-in-Law. Carillon Bks.
  xSerb, Ann Toland.
    Stop the World-Our Gerbils Are Loose. Doubleday.

Serban, George.
  xSerban, George.
    ed. Animal Models in Human Psychobiology. Plenum Pub.
    ed. Cognitive Defects in the Development of Mental Illness. Brunner-Mazel.

Serbein, Oscar N, 1919-
  xSerbein, Oscar N.
    Educational Activities of Business. ACE.

Serebrennikov, George N. *see* Serebrennikov, Georgii Nikolaevich.

Serebrennikov, Georgii Nikolaevich.
  xSerebrennikov, George N.
    Position of Women in the U.S.S.R. Arno.

Serebriakoff, Victor.
  xSerebriakoff, Victor.
    How Intelligent Are You?. NAL.

Seredy, Kate.
  xSeredy, Kate.

illus. Good Master. Viking Pr.
The White Stag. Penguin.
illus. White Stag. Viking Pr.

Sereno, Kenneth K.
xSereno, Kenneth K.
ed. Foundations of Communication Theory.
Har-Row.

Serenyi, Peter, 1931-
xSerenyi, Peter.
ed. Le Corbusier in Perspective. P-H.

Serfaty, Simon.
xSerfaty, Simon.
ed. The Foreign Policies of the French Left.
Westview.
France, DeGaulle, & Europe: The Policy of the
Fourth & Fifth Republics Toward the
Continent. Johns Hopkins.

Serge, Victor, 1890-1947
xSerge, Victor.
From Lenin to Stalin. Monad Pr.

Sergeant, Howard, 1914-
xSergeant, Howard.
ed. The Two Continents Book of Childrens
Verse. Two Continents.

Sergeant, John, 1939-
xSergeant, John.
Frank Lloyd Wright's Usonian Houses: The
Case for Organic Architecture.
Watson-Guptill.

Sergeant, Philip W. *see* Sergeant, Philip Walsingham.

Sergeant, Philip Walsingham.
xSergeant, Philip W.
Championship Chess. Dover.
Dominant Women. Arno.

Sergiovanni, Thomas. *see* Sergiovanni, Thomas J.

Sergiovanni, Thomas J.
xSergiovanni, Thomas.
Supervision: Human Perspectives. McGraw.
xSergiovanni, Thomas J.
Educational & Organizational Leadership in
Elementary Schools. P-H.
The New School Executive: A Theory of
Administration. Har-Row.

Serif, Med.
xSerif, Med.
How to Manage Yourself. Fell.

Serizawa, K. *see* Serizawa, Katsusuke.

Serizawa, Katsusuke, 1915-
xSerizawa, K.
Tsubo: Vital Points Oriental Therapy. Wehman.
xSerizawa, Katsusuke.
Tsubo: Vital Points for Oriental Therapy. Japan
Pubns.

Serjeantson, Mary S. *see* Serjeantson, Mary Sidney.

Serjeantson, Mary Sidney, 1896-
xSerjeantson, Mary S.
A History of Foreign Words in English. Arden
Lib.

Serle, Geoffrey.
xSerle, Geoffrey.
Golden Age: A History of the Colony of
Victoria, 1851-1861. Intl Schol Bk Serv.

Serlin, Florence R. *see* Serlin, Florence Rhyn.

Serlin, Florence Rhyn.
xSerlin, Florence R.
Living with Yourself, Living with Others: A
Woman's Guide. P-H.

Serling, Robert. *see* Serling, Robert J.

Serling, Robert J.
xSerling, Robert.
McDermott's Sky. PB.
McDermott's Sky. Stein & Day.
xSerling, Robert J.
From the Captain to the Colonel: An Informal
History of Eastern Airlines. Dial.
McDermott's Sky. Laurel Group.
The Presidents Plane Is Missing. Dell.
President's Plane Is Missing. Doubleday.
Wings. Dial.

Seroff, Victor I. *see* Seroff, Victor Ilyitch.

Seroff, Victor Ilyitch.
xSeroff, Victor I.
Dmitri Shostakovich: The Life & Background
of a Soviet Composer. Scholarly.
Rachmaninoff. Arno.

Seronde, Joseph.
xSeronde, Joseph.
ed. Nine Classic French Plays. Heath.

Serow, William J.
xSerow, William J.
The Population of Virginia: Past, Present &
Future. U Pr of Va.

Serpa Pinto, Alexandre A. *see* Serpa Pinto, Alexandre
Alberto da Rocha de.

**Serpa Pinto, Alexandre Alberto da Rocha de,
1846-1900**
xSerpa Pinto, Alexandre A.
How I Crossed Africa, from the Atlantic to the
Indian Ocean, Through Unknown Countries.
Johnson Repr.

Serraillier, Ian.
xSerraillier, Ian.
Silver Sword. S G Phillips.
Suppose You Met a Witch. Little.

Serrano, Miguel, 1917-
xSerrano, Miguel.
C. G. Jung & Hermann Hesse: A Record of
Two Friendships. Schocken.
The Ultimate Flower. Schocken.

Serre, J. *see* Serre, Jean Pierre.

Serre, Jean Pierre.
xSerre, J.
A Course in Arithmetic. Springer-Verlag.

Serron, Luis A.
xSerron, Luis A.
Scarcity, Exploitation, & Poverty: Malthus &
Marx in Mexico. U of Okla Pr.

Servadio, Gaia.
xServadio, Gaia.
Melinda. FS&G.
A Siberian Encounter. FS&G.

Servan-Schreiber, J. J. *see* Servan-Schreiber, Jean
Jacques.

Servan-Schreiber, Jean Jacques.
xServan-Schreiber, J. J.
American Challenge. Avon.
xServan-Schreiber, Jean-J.
The American Challenge. Atheneum.

Servan-Schreiber, Jean-J. *see* Servan-Schreiber, Jean
Jacques.

Serve, M. Paul.
xServe, M. Paul.
A Step-by-Step Approach to Elementary
Organic Synthesis. Ann Arbor Science.

Serven, James Edsall, 1899-
xServen, Jamese.
Rare & Valuable Antique Arms. Pioneer Pr.

Serven, Jamese. *see* Serven, James Edsall.

Servey, Richard E.
xServey, Richard E.
Teacher Talk: The Knack of Asking Questions.
Pitman Learning.

Servi, Vera, 1932-
xServi, Vera.
Gourmet Dictionary. Camaro Pub.

Service, Elman R. *see* Service, Elman Rogers.

Service, Elman Rogers, 1915-
xService, Elman R.
The Hunters. P-H.
Origins of the State & Civilization: The Process
of Cultural Evolution. Norton.
Profiles in Ethnology. Har-Row.

Service, Robert. *see* Service, Robert William.

Service, Robert William, 1874-1958
xService, Robert.

Later Collected Verse. Dodd.
More Collected Verse. Dodd.
More Selected Verse of Robert Service. Dodd.
The Song of the Campfire. Dodd.

Service, William, 1930-
xService, William.
Owl. Penguin.
xService, William S.
Owl. Knopf.

Service, William S. *see* Service, William.

Serviss, Garrett P. *see* Serviss, Garrett Putman.

Serviss, Garrett Putman, 1851-1929
xServiss, Garrett P.
Columbus of Space. Hyperion Conn.

Servodidio, Mirella D. *see* Servodidio, Mirella
D'Ambrosio.

Servodidio, Mirella D'Ambrosio.
xServodidio, Mirella D.
The Quest for Harmony: The Dialectics of
Communication in the Poetry of Eugenio
Florit. Society Sp & Sp-Am.

Serwadda, W. Moses.
xSerwadda, W. Moses.
Songs & Stories from Uganda. T Y Crowell.

Sesame Street.
xSesame Street.
Alphabet Book. Random.
Big Bird's Busy Book. Random.
Big Bird's Rhyming Book. Random.
Cookie Monster, Where Are You?. Random.
Cookie Monster's Book of Cookie Shapes.
Western Pub.
Counting Book. Random.
Grover's Super Surprise Book. Random.
In & Out: A Book of Pop-up Opposites.
Random.
The King on a Swing. Random.
More Posters from Sesame Street. Random.
The Sesame Street Mother Goose. Random.
The Sesame Street Postcard Book. Random.
Sherlock Hemlock: Great Twiddlebug Mystery.
Western Pub.
Who Am I?. Western Pub.
Who Are the People in Your Neighborhood?.
Random.
Your Friends from Sesame Street. Random.
xStreet Sesame.
Up & Down Book Starring Ernie & Bert.
Western Pub.

Seshadri, K.
xSeshadri, K.
Agricultural Administration in Andhra Pradesh:
A Study of the Process of Implementation of
Intensive Agricultural Development
Programmes. InterCulture.

Seshadri, S. R., 1925-
xSeshadri, S. R.
Fundamentals of Transmission Lines &
Electromagnetic Fields. A-W.

Seskin, Jane.
xSeskin, Jane.
Getting My Head Straight. Price Stern.
Older Women-Younger Men. Doubleday.

Sessa, Anne D. *see* Sessa, Anne Dzamba.

Sessa, Anne Dzamba.
xSessa, Anne D.
Richard Wagner & the English. Fairleigh
Dickinson.

Sessions, Bruce.
xSessions, Bruce.
The Complete Dog Training Manual. TAB Bks.
Dog Owner's Medical Manual. TAB Bks.
How to Train a Watchdog. TAB Bks.

Sessions, Keith.
xSessions, Keith.
Fixin up Your Van on a Budget. TAB Bks.
Vanner's How-to Guide to Murals, Painting &
Pinstriping. TAB Bks.

Sessions, Ken. *see* Sessions, Ken W.

Severs, Jonathan Burke.
  xSevers, J. Burke.
    Literary Relationships of Chaucer's Clerkes
    Tale. Shoe String.
Severs, Vesta N. *see* Severs, Vesta-Nadine.
Severs, Vesta-Nadine.
  xSevers, Vesta N.
    Lucinda. Concordia.
Severson, Charmaine.
  xSeverson, Charmaine.
    The I Hate Camp Book. Tobey Pub.
Severy, Lawrence J.
  xSevery, Lawrence J.
    A Contemporary Introduction to Social
    Psychology. McGraw.
Sevin, Dieter.
  xSevin, Dieter H.
    Zur Diskussion: A Modern Approach to
    German Conversation. Har-Row.
Sevin, Dieter H. *see* Sevin, Dieter.
Sevin, Leonce J.
  xSevin, Leonce J.
    Field-Effect Transistors. McGraw.
Sewall, Hannah R. *see* Sewall, Hannah Robie.
Sewall, Hannah Robie, 1861-
  xSewall, Hannah R.
    Theory of Value Before Adam Smith. Kelley.
Sewall, Richard B. *see* Sewall, Richard Benson.
Sewall, Richard Benson.
  xSewall, Richard B.
    The Vision of Tragedy. Yale U Pr.
Sewall, Samuel, 1652-1730
  xSewall, Samuel.
    Diary of Samuel Sewall, 1674-1729. Arno.
Seward, Charles.
  xSeward, Charles.
    Bedside Diagnosis. Churchill.
Seward, Desmond, 1935-
  xSeward, Desmond.
    Eleanor of Aquitaine. Times Bks.
Sewell, Albert.
  xSewell, Albert.
    The Observer's Book of Soccer. Scribner.
Sewell, Elizabeth, 1919-
  xSewell, Elizabeth.
    Field of Nonsense. Folcroft.
    The Structure of Poetry. Folcroft.
Sewell, James P. *see* Sewell, James Patrick.
Sewell, James Patrick.
  xSewell, James P.
    Functionalism & World Politics: A Study Based
    on United Nations Programs Financing
    Economic Development. Princeton U Pr.
Sewell, Richard. *see* Sewell, Richard H.
Sewell, Richard H.
  xSewell, Richard.
    Ballots for Freedom: Antislavery Politics in the
    United States, 1837-1860. Norton.
  xSewell, Richard H.
    Ballots for Freedom: Antislavery Politics in the
    United States 1837-1860. Oxford U Pr.
Sewell, William H.
  xSewell, William H.
    Coronary Disease Management: Coronary,
    Arteriography, Nitrates, & the Triple Pedicle
    Operation. Green.
Sewell, William H. *see* Sewell, William Hamilton.
Sewell, William Hamilton.
  xSewell, William H.
    Education, Occupation, and Earnings:
    Achievement in the Early Career. Acad Pr.
Sewell, Winifred.
  xSewell, Winifred.
    Guide to Drug Information. Drug Intl Pubns.
    ed. Reader in Medical Librarianship. IHS-PDS.
Sewid, James.
  xSewid, James.

    Guests Never Leave Hungry: The
    Autobiography of James Sewid, a Kwakiutl
    Indian. Yale U Pr.
Sewill, Louise.
  xSewill, Louise.
    Science on Stage: Four Plays: Ecology,
    Nutrition, Metrics, Matter & Energy.
    Monkey Sisters.
Sewny, Vahan D. *see* Sewny, Vahan Dicran.
Sewny, Vahan Dicran, 1903-
  xSewny, Vahan D.
    Social Theory of James Mark Baldwin. Kelley.
Sewter, A. C.
  xSewter, A. Charles.
    The Stained Glass of William Morris & His
    Circle: A Catalogue. Yale U Pr.
Sewter, A. Charles. *see* Sewter, A. C.
Sexton. *see* Sexton, William P.
Sexton, Anne.
  xSexton, Anne.
    The Awful Rowing Toward God. HM.
    The Death Notebooks. HM.
    Love Poems. HM.
Sexton, Linda G. *see* Sexton, Linda Gray.
Sexton, Linda Gray, 1953-
  xSexton, Linda G.
    Between Two Worlds: Young Women in Crisis.
    Morrow.
Sexton, Patricia C. *see* Sexton, Patricia Cayo.
Sexton, Patricia Cayo.
  xSexton, Patricia C.
    American School: A Sociological Analysis.
    P-H.
Sexton, Thomas. *see* Sexton, Thomas G.
Sexton, Thomas G.
  xSexton, Thomas.
    Can Intelligence Be Taught?. Phi Delta Kappa.
Sexton, Virginia S. *see* Sexton, Virginia Staudt.
Sexton, Virginia Staudt.
  xSexton, Virginia S.
    ed. Psychology Around the World.
    Brooks-Cole.
Sexton, William P.
  xSexton.
    Organization Theories. Merrill.
Sey, Katalin B.
  xSey, Katalin B.
    Coins & Medals. Intl Pubns Serv.
Seybolt, Peter J.
  xSeybolt, Peter J.
    ed. Language Reform in China: Documents &
    Commentary. M E Sharpe.
    ed. Revolutionary Education in China:
    Documents & Commentary. M E Sharpe.
Seybolt, Robert F. *see* Seybolt, Robert Francis.
Seybolt, Robert Francis, 1888-1951
  xSeybolt, Robert F.
    Apprenticeship & Apprenticeship Education in
    Colonial New England & New York. AMS
    Pr.
    Apprenticeship & Apprenticeship Education in
    Colonial New England, & New York. Arno.
    Evening School in Colonial America. Arno.
    Private Schools of Colonial Boston. Arno.
    Private Schools of Colonial Boston. Elliots Bks.
    Private Schools of Colonial Boston.
    Greenwood.
    Public Schools of Colonial Boston. Arno.
Seyd, Ernest, 1833-1881
  xSeyd, Ernest.
    Bullion & Foreign Exchanges Theoretically &
    Practically Considered: A Defence of the
    Double Evaluation with Special Reference to
    the Proposed System of Universal Coinage.
    Arno.
Seyfarth, Shaw, Fairweather & Geraldson. *see* Seyfarth,
  Shaw, Fairweather and Geraldson.
Seyfarth, Shaw, Fairweather and Geraldson.
  xSeyfarth, Shaw, Fairweather & Geraldson.

    Labor Relations & the Law in Belgium & the
    United States. U Mich Busn Div Res.
    Labor Relations & the Law in France & the
    United States. U Mich Busn Div Res.
    Labor Relations & the Law in Italy & the
    United States. U Mich Busn Div Res.
    Labor Relations & the Law in the United
    Kingdom & the United States. U Mich Busn
    Div Res.
    Labor Relations & the Law in West Germany
    & the United States. U Mich Busn Div Res.
Seyfert, Carl K.
  xSeyfert, Carl K.
    Earth History & Plate Tectonics: An
    Introduction to Historical Geology. Har-Row.
Seyferth, D. *see* Seyferth, Dietmar.
Seyferth, Dietmar.
  xSeyferth, D.
    ed. Organometallic Chemistry Reviews: Annual
    Surveys - Silicon, Tin, Lead. Elsevier.
Seyler, Athene.
  xSeyler, Athene.
    Craft of Comedy. Theatre Arts.
Seyler, Dorothy U.
  xSeyler, Dorothy U.
    Thinking for Writing. SRA.
Seymour, Charles, 1885-
  xSeymour, Charles.
    American Diplomacy During the World War.
    Greenwood.
    American Diplomacy During the World War.
    Shoe String.
    American Neutrality, 1914-1917: Essays on the
    Causes of American Intervention in the
    World War. Shoe String.
Seymour, Flora W. *see* Seymour, Flora Warren Smith.
Seymour, Flora Warren Smith, 1888-1948
  xSeymour, Flora W.
    Indian Agents of the Old Frontier. Kraus Repr.
    Indian Agents of the Old Frontier. Octagon.
    Story of the Red Man. Arno.
Seymour, Frederick. *see* Seymour, Frederick H. A.
Seymour, Frederick H. A.
  xSeymour, Frederick.
    Siena & Her Artists. Longwood Pr.
Seymour, Gabriel, 1958-
  xSeymour, Gabriel.
    Concord Hymn. Lime Rock Pr.
Seymour, Gerald.
  xSeymour, Gerald.
    The Glory Boys. Fawcett.
    The Glory Boys. Random.
    Kingfisher. Avon.
    Kingfisher. Summit Bks.
Seymour, Harold J. *see* Seymour, Harold James.
Seymour, Harold James, 1894-
  xSeymour, Harold J.
    Designs for Fund-Raising: Principles, Patterns,
    Techniques. McGraw.
Seymour, Janette.
  xSeymour, Janette.
    Purity's Passion. PB.
Seymour, John, 1914-
  xSeymour, John.
    The Countryside Explained. Merrimack Bk
    Serv.
    The Fat of the Land: Family Farming on Five
    Acres. Schocken.
    The Self-Sufficient Gardener: A Complete
    Guide to Growing & Preserving All Your
    Own Food. Doubleday.
Seymour, Miranda.
  xSeymour, Miranda.
    Count Manfred. Popular Lib.
    The Goddess. Berkley Pub.
    The Goddess. Coward.
Seymour, Raymond B. *see* Seymour, Raymond Benedict.
Seymour, Raymond Benedict, 1912-
  xSeymour, Raymond B.

Humanistic Psychology. P-H.

Shaffer, Kenneth R.
xShaffer, Kenneth R.
Decision Making: A Seminar in Public Library
Management. Shoe String.

Shaffer, Louis R. *see* Shaffer, Louis Richard.

Shaffer, Louis Richard.
xShaffer, Louis R.
Critical-Path Method. McGraw.

Shaffer, Ray, 1929-
xShaffer, Ray.
A Guide to Places on the Colorado Prairie.
Pruett.

Shaffer, Sam. *see* Shaffer, Samuel.

Shaffer, Samuel.
xShaffer, Sam.
On & off the Floor. Newsweek.

Shaffer, Susan E.
xShaffer, Susan E.
ed. Guide to Book Publishing Courses:
Academic & Professional Programs. Petersons
Guides.

Shaffer, William R.
xShaffer, William R.
Computer Simulations of Voting Behavior.
Oxford U Pr.

Shafirov, P. P. *see* Shafirov, Petr Pavlovich.

Shafirov, Petr Pavlovich.
xShafirov, P. P.
A Discourse Concerning the Just Causes of the
War Between Sweden & Russia, 1700-1721.
Oceana.

Shaftan, Gerald W.
xShaftan, Gerald W.
Quick Reference to Surgical Emergencies.
Lippincott.

Shaftel, Oscar.
xShaftel, Oscar.
An Understanding of the Buddha. Schocken.

Shafton, Anthony.
xShafton, Anthony.
Conditions of Awareness: Subjective Factors in
the Social Adaptations of Man & Other
Primates. Riverstone.

Shagass, Charles.
xShagass, Charles.
Evoked Brain Potentials in Psychiatry. Plenum
Pub.

Shah, Douglas.
xShah, Douglas.
The Meditators. Logos.

Shah, Giri R. *see* Shah, Giriraj.

Shah, Giriraj, 1940-
xShah, Giri R.
India Rediscovered. South Asia Bks.

Shah, Idries, Saved, 1924-
xShah, Idries.
Reflections. Penguin.
Subtleties of the Inimitable Mulla Nasrudin.
Dutton.
Sufis. Doubleday.
Thinkers of the East. Penguin.

Shah, M. J. *see* Shah, Manesh J.

Shah, Manesh J., 1932-
xShah, M. J.
Engineering Simulation Using Small Scientific
Computers. P-H.

Shaha, Rishikesh.
xShaha, Rishikesh.
Nepali Politics: Retrospect & Prospect. Oxford
U Pr.

Shahan, Robert W.
xShahan, Robert W.
ed. Spinoza: New Perspectives. U of Okla Pr.

Shahine, Y. A.
xShahine, Y. A.
The Arab Contribution to Medicine. Longman.

Shahrani, M. Nazif Mohib, 1945-
xShahrani, M. Nazif Mohib.

The Kirghiz & Wakhi of Afghanistan:
Adaptation to Closed Frontiers. U of Wash
Pr.

Shahshahani, S., 1942-
xShahshahani, S.
A New Mathematical Framework for the Study
of Linkage & Selection. Am Math.

Shai, Aron.
xShai, Aron.
The Origins of the War in the East: Britain,
China & Japan, 1937-39. Biblio Dist.

Shain, Henry.
xShain, Henry.
Legal First Aid. T Y Crowell.

Shain, Martin.
xShain, Martin.
Employee Assistance Programs: Philosophy,
Theory, & Practice. Lexington Bks.

Shain, Merle.
xShain, Merle.
When Lovers Are Friends. Bantam.
When Lovers Are Friends. Lippincott.

Shain, Russell E. *see* Shain, Russell Earl.

Shain, Russell Earl.
xShain, Russell E.
An Analysis of Motion Pictures About War
Released by American Film Industry,
1939-1970. Arno.

Shainberg, Lawrence, 1936-
xShainberg, Lawrence.
Brain Surgeon: An Intimate View of His
World. Lippincott.

Shairp, J. C. *see* Shairp, John Campbell.

Shairp, John C. *see* Shairp, John Campbell.

Shairp, John Campbell, 1819-1885
xShairp, J. C.
Studies in Poetry & Philosophy. Kennikat.
Studies in Poetry & Philosophy. R West.
xShairp, John C.
Aspects of Poetry: Being Lectures Delivered at
Oxford. Arno.

Shakers.
xShakers.
A Collection of Millennial Hymns Adapted to
the Present Order of the Church. AMS Pr.
Testimonies in the Life, Character, Revelations,
& Doctrines of Mother Ann Lee. AMS Pr.

Shakespeare. *see* Shakespeare, William.

Shakespeare Association. *see* Shakespeare Association,
London.

Shakespeare Association, London.
xShakespeare Association.
Series of Papers on Shakespeare & the Theatre.
Folcroft.

Shakespeare, William, 1564-1616
xShakespeare.
Julius Caesar. Raintree Pubs.
xShakespeare, William.

All's Well That Ends Well. Cambridge U Pr.
All's Well That Ends Well. Methuen Inc.
All's Well That Ends Well. NAL.
All's Well That Ends Well. Penguin.
All's Well That Ends Well. Wiley.
All's Well That Ends Well. Airmont.
All's Well That Ends Well. PB.
Antony & Cleopatra. Aurora Pubs.
Antony & Cleopatra. Cambridge U Pr.
Antony & Cleopatra. Methuen Inc.
Antony & Cleopatra. Oxford U Pr.
Antony & Cleopatra. Penguin.
Antony & Cleopatra. Plays.
Antony & Cleopatra. Wiley.
Antony & Cleopatra. Airmont.
Antony & Cleopatra. PB.
As You Like It. Cambridge U Pr.
As You Like It. Mayflower Bks.
As You Like It. Methuen Inc.
As You Like It. Modern Lang.
As You Like It. NAL.
As You Like It. Oxford U Pr.
As You Like It. Penguin.
As You Like It. Plays.
As You Like It. Wiley.
As You Like It. Airmont.
As You Like It. PB.
Comedy of Errors. Cambridge U Pr.
Comedy of Errors. Methuen Inc.
Comedy of Errors. NAL.
The Comedy of Errors. PB.
Comedy of Errors. Penguin.
Comedy of Errors. Wiley.
Comedy of Errors. Airmont.
Complete Works. Oxford U Pr.
Complete Works. Somerset Pub.
Coriolanus. Cambridge U Pr.
Coriolanus. Methuen Inc.
Coriolanus. NAL.
Coriolanus. Penguin.
Coriolanus. Airmont.
Coriolanus. PB.
Cymbeline. Cambridge U Pr.
Cymbeline. Methuen Inc.
Cymbeline. NAL.
Cymbeline. Oxford U Pr.
Cymbeline. Penguin.
Cymbeline. PB.
Hamlet. Aurora Pubs.
Hamlet. Cambridge U Pr.
Hamlet. Dover.
Hamlet. NAL.
Hamlet. Paddington.
Hamlet. Peter Smith.
Hamlet. Wiley.
Hamlet. Plays.
Hamlet. Norton.
Hamlet. Penguin.
Hamlet. AHM Pub.
Hamlet. Hayden.
Hamlet. Airmont.
Hamlet. PB.
Henry VIII. Mayflower Bks.
Henry VIII. Wiley.
Julius Caesar. Cambridge U Pr.
Julius Caesar. Mayflower Bks.
Julius Caesar. Methuen Inc.
Julius Caesar. NAL.
Julius Caesar. PB.
Julius Caesar. Wiley.
Julius Caesar. Airmont.
Julius Caesar. Penguin.
Julius Caesar. Plays.
Julius Caesar. Hayden.
Love's Labour's Lost. Cambridge U Pr.
Love's Labour's Lost. Methuen Inc.
Loves Labours Lost. PB.
Love's Labour's Lost. Wiley.
Measure for Measure. Cambridge U Pr.
Measure for Measure. Mayflower Bks.

Measure for Measure. Methuen Inc.
Measure for Measure. Modern Lang.
Measure for Measure. NAL.
Measure for Measure. Oxford U Pr.
Measure for Measure. Penguin.
Measure for Measure. Wiley.
Measure for Measure. Yale U Pr.
Measure for Measure. PB.
Measure for Measure: Concordance to the Text
  of the First Folio. Oxford U Pr.
Midsummer Nights' Dream. Abaris Bks.
Midsummer Night's Dream. Cambridge U Pr.
Midsummer Night's Dream. NAL.
Midsummer-Night's Dream. Oxford U Pr.
A Midsummer Night's Dream. Viking Pr.
Midsummer Night's Dream. Wiley.
Midsummer Night's Dream. Penguin.
Midsummer Night's Dream. Plays.
Midsummer Night's Dream. Airmont.
A Midsummer Night's Dream. PB.
Much Ado About Nothing. AMS Pr.
Much Ado About Nothing. Cambridge U Pr.
Much Ado About Nothing. Dover.
Much Ado About Nothing. NAL.
Much Ado About Nothing. Penguin.
Much Ado About Nothing. Peter Smith.
Much Ado About Nothing. Wiley.
Much Ado About Nothing. AHM Pub.
Much Ado About Nothing. Airmont.
Much Ado About Nothing. PB.
Much Ado About Nothing: Concordance to the
  Text of the First Quarto of 1600. Oxford U
  Pr.
Othello. Cambridge U Pr.
Othello. Dover.
Othello. Methuen Inc.
Othello. NAL.
Othello. Oxford U Pr.
Othello. Peter Smith.
Othello. Plays.
Othello. Wiley.
Othello. Penguin.
Othello. AHM Pub.
Othello. Airmont.
Othello 1622. Oxford U Pr.
Pericles. Cambridge U Pr.
Pericles. Methuen Inc.
Pericles. PB.
Pericles. Penguin.
Pericles. Wiley.
Richard II. Mayflower Bks.
Richard II. Wiley.
Richard III. Wiley.
Richard the Third. AMS Pr.
Richard Third. Cambridge U Pr.
Richard Third. NAL.
Richard Third. Oxford U Pr.
Richard Third. Penguin.
Richard Third. Airmont.
Richard Third. PB.
Romeo & Juliet. Cambridge U Pr.
Romeo & Juliet. Mayflower Bks.
Romeo & Juliet. Methuen Inc.
Romeo & Juliet. NAL.
Romeo & Juliet. Oxford U Pr.
Romeo & Juliet. Penguin.
Romeo & Juliet. Plays.
Romeo & Juliet. Wiley.
Romeo & Juliet. Raintree Pubs.
Romeo & Juliet. Schol Bk Serv.
Romeo & Juliet. Airmont.
Sonnets. Cambridge U Pr.
Sonnets. Dufour.
Sonnets. Dutton.
Sonnets. NAL.
The Sonnets. St Martin.
The Sonnets. Wiley.
Sonnets. Penguin.
Sonnets. AHM Pub.
The Sonnets of William Shakespeare. Arden

Lib.
Taming of the Shrew. AMS Pr.
Taming of the Shrew. Cambridge U Pr.
Taming of the Shrew. NAL.
Taming of the Shrew. Penguin.
Taming of the Shrew. Wiley.
Taming of the Shrew. Airmont.
Taming of the Shrew. PB.
Taming of the Shrew: A Concordance to the
  Text of the First Folio. Oxford U Pr.
Troilus & Cressida. Cambridge U Pr.
Troilus & Cressida. NAL.
Troilus & Cressida. Penguin.
Troilus & Cressida. Wiley.
Troilus & Cressida. AHM Pub.
Troilus & Cressida. PB.
Twelfth Night. Cambridge U Pr.
Twelfth Night. Mayflower Bks.
Twelfth Night. Methuen Inc.
Twelfth Night. NAL.
Twelfth Night. Penguin.
Twelfth Night. Wiley.
Twelfth Night. Plays.
Twelfth Night. Airmont.
Twelfth Night: A Concordance to the Text of
  the First Folio. Oxford U Pr.
Two Gentlemen of Verona. Cambridge U Pr.
The Two Gentlemen of Verona. Methuen Inc.
Two Gentlemen of Verona. Penguin.
Two Gentlemen of Verona. Penguin.
Two Gentlemen of Verona. Wiley.
Two Gentlemen of Verona. PB.
Two Gentlemen of Verona: Concordance to the
  Text of the First Folio. Oxford U Pr.
jt. auth. Two Noble Kinsmen. AMS Pr.
jt. auth. The Two Noble Kinsmen. U of Nebr
  Pr.
The Two Noble Kinsmen. Wiley
Works of Shakespeare. AMS Pr.
Works of William Shakespeare. AMS Pr.

Shakhnovich, A. R.
  xShakhnovich, A. R.
    The Brain & Regulation of Eye Movement.
    Plenum Pub.
Shakibi, G. Jami. *see* Shakibi, Jami G.
Shakibi, Jami G.
  xShakibi, G. Jami.
    ed. Cardiology Review. Med Exam.
Shaklee, Forrest C. *see* Shaklee, Forrest Clell.
Shaklee, Forrest Clell.
  xShaklee, Forrest C.
    Reflections on a Philosophy. Benjamin Co.
Shakman, Robert.
  xShakman, Robert.
    Where You Live May Be Hazardous to Your
    Health. Stein & Day.
Shakow, David, 1901-
  xShakow, David.
    Adaptation in Schizophrenia: The Theory of
    Segmental Set. Wiley.
Shale, Richard, 1947-
  xShale, Richard.
    ed. Academy Awards: An Ungar Reference
    Index. Ungar.
Shallenberger, R. S.
  xShallenberger, R. S.
    Sugar Chemistry. AVI.
Shalvey, Thomas, 1937-
  xShalvey, Thomas.
    Claude Levi-Strauss: Social Psychotherapy &
    the Collective Unconscious. U of Mass Pr.
Shama, Avraham.
  xShama, Avraham.
    Marketing in a Slow Growth Economy: The
    Impact of Stagflation on Consumer
    Psychology. Praeger.
Shamburger, Page.
  xShamburger, Page.
    Classic Monoplanes. TAB Bks.
Shames, I. *see* Shames, Irving Herman.

Shames, Irving H. *see* Shames, Irving Herman.
Shames, Irving Herman, 1923-
  xShames, I.
    Engineering Mechanics. P-H.
  xShames, Irving H.
    Introduction to Solid Mechanics. P-H.
    Mechanics of Fluids. McGraw.
Shamkovich, Leonid. *see* Shamkovich, Leonid
  Aleksandrovich.
Shamkovich, Leonid Aleksandrovich.
  xShamkovich, Leonid.
    The Modern Chess Sacrifice. McKay.
Shampine, Lawrence F.
  xShampine, Lawrence F.
    Computer Solution of Ordinary Differential
    Equations: The Initial Value Problem. W H
    Freeman.
Shamsie, Jalal. *see* Shamsie, S. J.
Shamsie, S. J.
  xShamsie, Jalal.
    ed. New Directions in Children's Mental
    Health. Spectrum Pub.
Shanahan, P. *see* Shanahan, Patrick.
Shanahan, Patrick.
  xShanahan, P.
    The Atiyah-Singer Index Theorem: An
    Introduction. Springer-Verlag.
Shanahan, William F.
  xShanahan, William F.
    International Student Guide to United States
    Colleges & Universities. Monarch Pr.
Shanahan, William O. *see* Shanahan, William Oswald.
Shanahan, William Oswald, 1913-
  xShanahan, William O.
    Prussian Military Reforms, 1786-1813. AMS
    Pr.
Shanas, Ethel.
  xShanas, Ethel.
    ed. Family, Bureaucracy, & the Elderly. Duke.
Shand, R. T. *see* Shand, Richard Tregurtha.
Shand, Richard Tregurtha.
  xShand, R. T.
    ed. Agricultural Development in Asia. U of Cal
    Pr.
    ed. International Aid: Some Political,
    Administrative, & Technical Realities. Bks
    Australia.
Shands, William E.
  xShands, William E.
    Federal Resource Lands & Their Neighbors.
    Conservation Foun.
Shane, Harold D.
  xShane, Harold D.
    Mathematics for Business Applications. Merrill.
Shane, Harold G. *see* Shane, Harold Gray.
Shane, Harold Gray.
  xShane, Harold G.
    ed. Classroom-Relevant Research in the
    Language Arts. Assn Supervision.
Shane, Jay.
  xShane, Jay F.
    On the Color TV Service Bench. TAB Bks.
Shane, Jay F. *see* Shane, Jay.
Shane, Ruth.
  xShane, Ruth.
    The New Baby. Western Pub.
Shaner, Richard C.
  xShaner, Richard C.
    ed. Peregrine Anthology. Wampeter Pr.
Shaner, W. W. *see* Shaner, Willis W.
Shaner, Willis W.
  xShaner, W. W.
    Project Planning for Developing Economies.
    Praeger.
Shanet, Howard.
  xShanet, Howard.
    Learn to Read Music. Merrimack Bk Serv.
    Learn to Read Music. S&S.
Shange, Ntozake.
  xShange, Ntozake.

For Colored Girls Who Have Considered
  Suicide-When the Rainbow Is Enuf. Bantam.
For Colored Girls Who Have Considered
  Suicide When the Rainbow Is Enuf: A
  Choreopoem. Macmillan.
Shangold, Jules.
  xShangold, Jules.
    Opportunities in a Podiatry Career. Natl
    Textbk.
Shank, Alan, 1936-
  xShank, Alan.
    American Politics, Policies & Priorities. Allyn.
    Political Power & the Urban Crisis. Holbrook.
Shank, Dorothy E. *see* Shank, Dorothy Esther.
Shank, Dorothy Esther, 1890-
  xShank, Dorothy E.
    Guide to Modern Meals. McGraw.
Shank, W. H. *see* Shank, William H.
Shank, William H.
  xShank, W. H.
    Amazing Pennsylvania Canals. Am Canal &
    Transport.
    Historic Bridges of Pennsylvania. Am Canal &
    Transport.
    Indian Trails to Superhighways. Am Canal &
    Transport.
Shankland, Craig.
  xShankland, Craig.
    The Golfer's Stroke Saving Handbook. Little.
    The Golfer's Stroke-Saving Handbook. NAL.
  xShankland, Dale.
    jt. auth. The Golfer's Stroke-Saving Handbook.
    NAL.
Shankland, Dale. *see* Shankland, Craig.
Shankman, Florence. *see* Shankman, Florence Vogel.
Shankman, Florence Vogel.
  xShankman, Florence.
    Games & Activities to Reinforce Reading
    Skills. Mss Info.
Shanks, Ann Z. *see* Shanks, Ann Zane.
Shanks, Ann Zane, 1927-
  xShanks, Ann Z.
    photos by About Garbage & Stuff. Viking Pr.
Shanks, Bob.
  xShanks, Bob.
    The Cool Fire: How to Make It in Television.
    Norton.
    The Cool Fire: How to Make It in Television.
    Random.
Shanks, Daniel, 1917-
  xShanks, Daniel.
    Solved & Unsolved Problems in Number
    Theory. Chelsea Pub.
Shanks, Edward, 1892-1953
  xShanks, Edward B.
    Edgar Allan Poe. Folcroft.
Shanks, Edward B. *see* Shanks, Edward.
Shanks, M. *see* Shanks, Merrill E.
Shanks, M. E. *see* Shanks, Merrill E.
Shanks, Merrill. *see* Shanks, Merrill E.
Shanks, Merrill E.
  xShanks, M.
    Pre-Calculus Mathematics. A-W.
  xShanks, M. E.
    Calculus, Analytic Geometry, Elementary
    Functions. HR&W.
  xShanks, Merrill.
    Pre-Calculus Mathematics. A-W.
Shanks, Michael, 1927-
  xShanks, Michael.
    European Social Policy, Today & Tomorrow.
    Pergamon.
Shanks, Ralph C.
  xShanks, Ralph C.
    Lighthouses & Lifeboats on the Redwood
    Coast. Costano.
Shanmugam, K. Sam.
  xShanmugam, K. Sam.

Digital & Analog Communication Systems.
  Wiley.
Shannon, Alexander H. *see* Shannon, Alexander Harvey.
Shannon, Alexander Harvey, 1869-
  xShannon, Alexander H.
    Racial Integrity & Other Features of the Negro
    Problem. Arno.
Shannon, David. *see* Shannon, David A.
Shannon, David A.
  xShannon, David.
    ed. Great Depression. Peter Smith.
  xShannon, David A.
    The Decline of American Communism: A
    History of the Communist Party of the
    United States Since 1945. Chatham Bkseller.
    ed. Great Depression. P-H.
Shannon, Dell.
  xShannon, Dell.
    Deuces Wild. Morrow.
    Deuces Wild. PB.
Shannon, Doris.
  xShannon, Doris.
    Beyond the Shining Mountains. Fawcett.
    Beyond the Shining Mountains. St Martin.
    Cain's Daughters. Fawcett.
    Cain's Daughters. St Martin.
Shannon, Ellen. *see* Shannon, Ellen C.
Shannon, Ellen C.
  xShannon, Ellen.
    The Expectant Mother's Guide to Happy
    Eating. A S Barnes.
Shannon, Foster H., 1930-
  xShannon, Foster H.
    The Growth Crisis in the American Church: A
    Presbyterian Case Study. William Carey Lib.
Shannon, Francis John.
  xShannon, John.
    Business Taxes in State & Local Governments.
    Kraus Repr.
Shannon, Harper.
  xShannon, Harper.
    Trumpets in the Morning. Broadman.
Shannon, James. *see* Shannon, James P.
Shannon, James P.
  xShannon, James.
    Catholic Colonization on the Western Frontier.
    Arno.
Shannon, John. *see* Shannon, Francis John.
Shannon, Mary L. *see* Shannon, Mary Lee.
Shannon, Mary Lee.
  xShannon, Mary L.
    The Map Abstract of Criminal Justice
    Information: Alabama. U of Ala Pr.
Shannon, Robert E., 1932-
  xShannon, Robert E.
    Systems Simulation: The Art & Science. P-H.
Shannon, Thomas A. *see* Shannon, Thomas Anthony.
Shannon, Thomas Anthony.
  xShannon, Thomas A.
    An Introduction to Bioethics. Paulist Pr.
Shannon, William V.
  xShannon, William V.
    American Irish. Macmillan.
Shanor, Charles A.
  xShanor, Charles A.
    Military Law in a Nutshell. West Pub.
Shanor, Donald. *see* Shanor, Donald R.
Shanor, Donald R.
  xShanor, Donald.
    The Soviet Triangle. St Martin.
Shantz, Homer L. *see* Shantz, Homer Leroy.
Shantz, Homer Leroy.
  xShantz, Homer L.
    Vegetation & Soils of Africa. AMS Pr.
Shao, Stephen. *see* Shao, Stephen Pinyee.
Shao, Stephen P. *see* Shao, Stephen Pinyee.
Shao, Stephen Pinyee, 1924-
  xShao, Stephen.
    Statistics for Business & Economics. Merrill.
  xShao, Stephen P.

Essentials of Business Statistics. Merrill.
    ed. Mathematics for Management & Finance.
    SW Pub.
Shapcott, Thomas. *see* Shapcott, Thomas W.
Shapcott, Thomas W.
  xShapcott, Thomas.
    Selected Poems. U of Queensland Pr.
Shapin, Betty.
  xShapin, Betty.
    ed. Education in Parapsychology: Proceedings,
    International Conference, San Francisco,
    1975. Parapsych Foun.
Shapiro, Amy, 1943-
  xShapiro, Amy.
    Sun Signs: The Stars in Your Life. Raintree
    Pubs.
Shapiro, Andrew O.
  xShapiro, Andrew O.
    Media Access: Your Rights to Express Your
    Views on Radio & Television. Little.
Shapiro, Arthur K.
  xShapiro, Arthur K.
    ed. Gilles de la Tourette Syndrome. Raven.
Shapiro, Barbara S.
  xShapiro, Barbara S.
    Camille Pissarro: The Impressionist Printmaker.
    Mus Fine Arts Boston.
Shapiro, Barry A.
  xShapiro, Barry A.
    Clinical Application of Blood Gases. Year Bk
    Med.
    Clinical Application of Respiratory Care. Year
    Bk Med.
Shapiro, Cecile.
  xShapiro, Cecile.
    Fine Prints: Collecting, Buying & Selling.
    Har-Row.
Shapiro, Charles.
  xShapiro, Charles.
    ed. Twelve Original Essays on Great American
    Novels. Wayne St U Pr.
    ed. Twelve Original Essays on Great English
    Novels. Wayne St U Pr.
Shapiro, David, 1947-
  xShapiro, David.
    Lateness: A Book of Poems. Overlook Pr.
    The Page-Turner. Liveright.
Shapiro, Edward, 1920-
  xShapiro, Edward.
    Understanding Money. HarBraceJ.
Shapiro, Eileen C.
  xShapiro, Eileen C.
    Becoming a Physician: Development of Values
    & Attitudes in Medicine. Ballinger Pub.
Shapiro, Eli, 1916-
  xShapiro, Eli.
    Credit Union Development in Wisconsin. AMS
    Pr.
Shapiro, Gilbert, 1934-
  xShapiro, Gilbert.
    Physics Without Math: A Descriptive
    Introduction. P-H.
Shapiro, Harry L. *see* Shapiro, Harry Lionel.
Shapiro, Harry Lionel, 1902-
  xShapiro, Harry L.
    Aspects of Culture. Arno.
    Migration & Environment. Arno.
    Peking Man. S&S.
    Pitcairn Islanders. S&S.
Shapiro, Harvey, 1937-
  xShapiro, Harvey.
    Faster Than Sound. A S Barnes.
    Lauds & Nightsounds. SUN.
Shapiro, Howard I., 1932-
  xShapiro, Howard I.
    Cranes & Derricks. McGraw.
Shapiro, Irwin.
  xShapiro, Irwin.

Dan McCann & His Fast Sooner Hound.
  Garrard.
Darwin & the Enchanted Isles. Coward.
The Gift of Magic Sleep: Early Experiments in
  Anesthesia. Coward.
Gretchen & the White Steed. Garrard.
The Hungry Ghost Mystery. Garrard.
Joe Magarac & His U. S. A. Citizen Papers. U
  of Pittsburghh Pr.
Paul Bunyan Tricks a Dragon. Garrard.

Shapiro, Jacob, 1925-
  xShapiro, Jacob.
  Radiation Protection: A Guide for Scientists &
    Physicians. Harvard U Pr.
Shapiro, Jeremy F., 1939-
  xShapiro, Jeremy F.
  Mathematical Programming: Structures &
    Algorithms. Wiley.
Shapiro, Jerrold L. see Shapiro, Jerrold Lee.
Shapiro, Jerrold Lee.
  xShapiro, Jerrold L.
  Methods of Group Psychotherapy &
    Encounter: A Tradition of Innovation.
    Peacock Pubs.
Shapiro, Jim.
  xShapiro, Jim.
  On the Road: The Marathon. Crown.
Shapiro, Jon E.
  xShapiro, Jon E.
  ed. Using Literature & Poetry Affectively. Intl
    Reading.
Shapiro, Karl. see Shapiro, Karl Jay.
Shapiro, Karl J. see Shapiro, Karl Jay.
Shapiro, Karl Jay, 1913-
  xShapiro, Karl.
  Adult Book Store. Random.
  English Prosody & Modern Poetry. Folcroft.
  xShapiro, Karl J.
  Prosody Handbook. Har-Row.
Shapiro, Kenneth. see Shapiro, Kenneth Joel.
Shapiro, Kenneth Joel.
  xShapiro, Kenneth.
  The Experience of Introversion: An Integration
    of Phenomenological Empirical & Jungian
    Approaches. Duke.
Shapiro, Louis, 1941-
  xShapiro, Louis W.
  Introduction to Abstract Algebra. McGraw.
Shapiro, Louis W. see Shapiro, Louis.
Shapiro, Mark, 1922-
  xShapiro, Mark.
  The Sociobiology of Homo Sapiens. Pinecrest
    Fund.
Shapiro, Martin. see Shapiro, Martin M.
Shapiro, Martin M.
  xShapiro, Martin.
  The Politics of Constitutional Law. Winthrop.
Shapiro, Max. see Shapiro, Max S.
Shapiro, Max S.
  xShapiro, Max.
  Mathematics Encyclopedia: A Made Simple
    Book. Doubleday.
  xShapiro, Max S.
  ed. The Cadillac Modern Encyclopedia.
    Cadillac.
  ed. Mythologies of the World: A Concise
    Encyclopedia. Doubleday.
Shapiro, Michael, 1938-
  xShapiro, Michael.
  Children of the Revels: The Boy Companies of
    Shakespeare's Time and Their Plays.
    Columbia U Pr.
Shapiro, Milton. see Shapiro, Milton J.
Shapiro, Milton J.
  xShapiro, Milton.
  Undersea Raiders: U. S. Submarines in World
    War II. McKay.
  xShapiro, Milton J.

Pro Quarterbacks. Messner.
Shapiro, Nat.
  xShapiro, Nat.
  ed. Encyclopedia of Quotations About Music.
    Doubleday.
Shapiro, Neal.
  xShapiro, Neal.
  The World of Horseback Riding. Atheneum.
Shapiro, Norman. see Shapiro, Norman R.
Shapiro, Norman R.
  xShapiro, Norman.
  ed. Negritude: Black Poetry from Africa & the
    Caribbean. October.
  xShapiro, Norman R.
  tr. The Comedy of Eros: Medieval French
    Guides to the Art of Love. U of Ill Pr.
Shapiro, Robert H.
  xShapiro, Robert H.
  ed. Exercises in Organic Spectroscopy. HR&W.
Shapiro, Sam.
  xShapiro, Sam.
  Infant, Perinatal, Maternal, & Childhood
    Mortality in the United States. Harvard U Pr.
Shapiro, Samuel.
  xShapiro, Samuel.
  Richard Henry Dana, Jr. Mich St U Pr.
Shapiro, Stephen.
  xShapiro, Stephen.
  Feeling Safe: Making Space for the Self. P-H.
Shapiro, Stephen. see Shapiro, Steve.
Shapiro, Steve.
  xShapiro, Stephen.
  Trusting Yourself: Psychotherapy As a
    Beginning. P-H.
Shapiro, Stuart C. see Shapiro, Stuart Charles.
Shapiro, Stuart Charles.
  xShapiro, Stuart C.
  Techniques of Artificial Intelligence. D Van
    Nostrand.
Shapiro, T. see Shapiro, Theda.
Shapiro, Theda.
  xShapiro, T.
  Painters & Politics: The European Avant-Garde
    & Society, 1900-1925. Elsevier.
Shapiro, Theodore.
  xShapiro, Theodore.
  Clinical Psycholinguistics. Plenum Pub.
Shapiro, Warren.
  xShapiro, Warren.
  Social Organization in Aboriginal Australia. St
    Martin.
Shapiro, Yonathan.
  xShapiro, Yonathan.
  Leadership of the American Zionist
    Organization, 1897-1930. U of Ill Pr.
Shaplen, Robert, 1917-
  xShaplen, Robert.
  A Turning Wheel: Three Decades of the Asian
    Revolution As Witnessed by a Correspondent
    for The New Yorker. Random.
Shapley, Harlow, 1885-
  xShapley, Harlow.
  Galaxies. Atheneum.
  Galaxies. Harvard U Pr.
Shapley, Rufus E. see Shapley, Rufus Edmonds.
Shapley, Rufus Edmonds, 1840-1906
  xShapley, Rufus E.
  Solid for Mulhooly: A Political Satire. Arno.
Shapo, Marshall S., 1936-
  xShapo, Marshall S.
  The Duty to Act: Tort Law, Power, & Public
    Policy. U of Tex Pr.
Shapp, Martha.
  xShapp, Martha.

Let's Find Out About Animals of Long Ago.
  Watts.
Let's Find Out About Babies. Watts.
Let's Find Out About Birds. Watts.
Let's Find Out About Cavemen. Watts.
Let's Find Out About Daniel Boone. Watts.
Let's Find Out About Fall. Watts.
Let's Find Out About Firemen. Watts.
Let's Find Out About Houses. Watts.
Let's Find Out About Safety. Watts.
Let's Find Out About Snakes. Watts.
Let's Find Out About Spring. Watts.
Let's Find Out About Thanksgiving. Watts.
Let's Find Out About the Moon. Watts.
Let's Find Out About the Sun. Watts.
Let's Find Out About Trees, Arbor Day.
  Watts.
Let's Find Out About Water. Watts.
Let's Find Out About Winter. Watts.
Sharar, Abdul H. see Sharar, Abdul Halim.
Sharar, Abdul Halim.
  xSharar, Abdul H.
  Lucknow: The Last Phase of an Oriental
    Culture. Westview.
**Share Working Conference on Data Base Management
  Systems, 2d, Montreal, Quebec, 1976.**
  xShare Working Conference on Data Base
    Management Systems, 2nd, Canada, 1977.
  The ANSI-SPARC DBMS Model: Proceedings.
    Elsevier.
Sharer, Robert. see Sharer, Robert J.
Sharer, Robert J.
  xSharer, Robert.
  ed. The Prehistory of Chalchuapa, El Salvador.
    U of Pa Pr.
  xSharer, Robert J.
  Fundamentals of Archaeology.
    Benjamin-Cummings.
Sharkansky, Ira.
  xSharkansky, Ira.
  Public Administration: Policy-Making in
    Government Agencies. Rand.
  Wither the State?: Politics & Public Enterprise
    in Three Countries. Chatham Hse Pubs.
Sharkey, Robert. see Sharkey, Robert P.
Sharkey, Robert P.
  xSharkey, Robert.
  Money, Class, & Party: An Economic Study of
    Civil War & Reconstruction. Johns Hopkins.
  xSharkey, Robert P.
  Money, Class, & Party: An Economic Study of
    Civil War & Reconstruction. AMS Pr.
Sharma, B. L. see Sharma, Brij Lal.
Sharma, Baldev R. see Sharma, Baldev Raj.
Sharma, Baldev Raj, 1939-
  xSharma, Baldev R.
  Indian Industrial Worker: Issues in Perspective.
    Intl Bk Dist.
Sharma, Brij Lal, 1906-
  xSharma, B. L.
  Pakistan-China Axis. Asia.
Sharma, G. D. see Sharma, Ghanshyam Datt.
Sharma, Ghanshyam Datt, 1931-
  xSharma, G. D.
  The Alaskan Shelf. Springer-Verlag.
Sharma, Jagdish S. see Sharma, Jagdish Saran.
Sharma, Jagdish Saran, 1924-
  xSharma, Jagdish S.
  India's Minorities: A Bibliographical Study.
    Advent Bk.
  India's Minorities: A Bibliographical Study.
    Verry.
  Substance of Library Science. Asia.
Sharma, K. D. see Sharma, Kashinath Datta.
Sharma, Kashinath Datta, 1922-
  xSharma, K. D.
  Fundamentals of Machine Design. Asia.
Sharma, Miriam, 1941-
  xSharma, Miriam.

The Politics of Inequality: Competition &
Control in an Indian Village. U Pr of Hawaii.
Sharma, P. *see* Sharma, Parmananda.
Sharma, P. Vallabh.
xSharma, P.
Geophysical Methods in Geology. Elsevier.
Sharma, Parmananda, 1924-
xSharma, P.
Men & Mules on a Mission of Democracy.
Asia.
Sharma, Partap.
xSharma, Partap.
The Surangini Tales. HarBraceJ.
Sharma, Ram. *see* Sharma, Shri Ram.
Sharma, Rameshwar K.
xSharma, Rameshwar K.
ed. Endocrine Control in Neoplasia. Raven.
Sharma, Shri Ram, Professor of Political Science.
xSharma, Ram.
Indian Foreign Policy: Annual Survey 1974.
Intl Pubns Serv.
xSharma, Shri Ram.
Indian Foreign Policy: Annual Survey. Intl
Pubns Serv.
Sharman, Julian.
xSharman, Julian.
Cursory History of Swearing. B Franklin.
Sharmat, Majorie W. *see* Sharmat, Marjorie Weinman.
Sharmat, Marjorie. *see* Sharmat, Marjorie Weinman.
Sharmat, Marjorie M. *see* Sharmat, Marjorie Weinman.
Sharmat, Marjorie W. *see* Sharmat, Marjorie Weinman.
Sharmat, Marjorie Weinman.
xSharmat, Majorie W.
Say Hello, Vanessa. Holiday.
xSharmat, Marjorie.
Mooch the Messy Meets Prudence the Neat.
Coward.
xSharmat, Marjorie M.
Taking Care of Melvin. Holiday.
xSharmat, Marjorie W.
Burton & Dudley. Holiday.
Burton & Dudley. Avon.
Edgemont. Coward.
Edgemont. Coward.
Gladys Told Me to Meet Her Here. Har-Row.
Goodnight, Andrew, Goodnight, Craig.
Har-Row.
Griselda's New Year. Macmillan.
Hot Thirsty Day. Macmillan.
I Am Not a Pest. Dutton.
I Don't Care. Macmillan.
I Want Mama. Har-Row.
I'm Not Oscar's Friend Anymore. Dutton.
I'm Terrific. Holiday.
I'm Terrific. Schol Bk Serv.
Mr. Jameson & Mr. Phillips. Har-Row.
Mooch the Messy. Har-Row.
Nate the Great. Coward.
Nate the Great. Dell.
Nate the Great & the Lost List. Coward.
Nate the Great & the Phony Clue. Coward.
Nate the Great & the Sticky Case. Coward.
Nate the Great Goes Undercover. Dell.
Nate the Great Goes Undercover. Coward.
Octavia Told Me a Secret. Schol Bk Serv.
Scarlet Monster Lives Here. Har-Row.
Sometimes Mama & Papa Fight. Har-Row.
Sophie & Gussie. Macmillan.
Sophie and Gussie. Macmillan.
Thornton the Worrier. Holiday.
The Trip & Other Sophie & Gussie Stories.
Macmillan.
What Are We Going to Do About Andrew?.
Macmillan.
xSharmat, Marjorie Weinman.
Uncle Boris & Maude. Doubleday.
Sharmat, Mitchell.
xSharmat, Mitchell.
Gregory, the Terrible Eater. Schol Bk Serv.
Sharon, Richard. *see* Sharon, Richard K.

Sharon, Richard K.
xSharon, Richard.
Diary of a Lover. Warner Bks.
xSharon, Richard K.
Diary of a Lover. Warner Bks.
Sharon, Ruth.
xSharon, Ruth.
Arts & Crafts the Year Round. United Syn Bk.
Sharp, Andrew.
xSharp, Andrew.
Discovery of Australia. Oxford U Pr.
Sharp, Ansel M. *see* Sharp, Ansel Miree.
Sharp, Ansel Miree.
xSharp, Ansel M.
Public Finance: The Economics of Government
Revenues & Expenditures. West Pub.
Sharp, Archibald, 1862-1934
xSharp, Archibald.
Bicycles & Tricycles: An Elementary Treatise
on Their Design & Construction. MIT Pr.
Sharp, Cecil. *see* Sharp, Cecil James.
Sharp, Cecil James.
xSharp, Cecil.
Compiled by Cecil Sharp's Collection of
English Folk Songs. Oxford U Pr.
Sharp, David, 1840-1922
xSharp, David.
Looking Inside Exciting Places. Rand.
Looking Inside Ships Through the Ages. Rand.
Sharp, Dolph.
xSharp, Dolph.
I'm O.K., You're Not So Hot. Price Stern.
Sharp, Duane. *see* Sharp, Duane E.
Sharp, Duane E.
xSharp, Duane.
Handbook of Interactive Computer Terminals.
Reston.
Sharp, Ed.
xSharp, Ed.
The Old House Handbook for Chicago &
Suburbs. Chicago Review.
Sharp, Elizabeth N.
xSharp, Elizabeth N.
Simple Machines & How They Work. Random.
Sharp, Evelyn.
xSharp, Evelyn.
Thinking Is Child's Play. Avon.
Sharp, F. A. *see* Sharp, Florence A.
Sharp, Florence A., 1913-
xSharp, F. A.
These Kids Don't Count. Acad Therapy.
Sharp, Gene.
xSharp, Gene.
The Politics of Nonviolent Action. Porter
Sargent.
Sharp, Harold S.
xSharp, Harold S.
Footnotes to World History: A Bibliographic
Source Book. Scarecrow.
Handbook of Geographical Nicknames.
Scarecrow.
Sharp, Lauriston.
xSharp, Lauriston.
Bang Chan: Social History of a Rural
Community in Thailand. Cornell U Pr.
Sharp, Lloyd B. *see* Sharp, Lloyd Burgess.
Sharp, Lloyd Burgess, 1895-
xSharp, Lloyd B.
Education & the Summer Camp: An
Experiment. AMS Pr.
Sharp, Margery, 1905-
xSharp, Margery.
The Faithful Servants. Little.
The Innocents. Little.
The Stone of Chastity. AMS Pr.
Summer Visits. Little.
The Turret. Dell.
The Turret. Little.
Sharp, Marilyn.
xSharp, Marilyn.

Sunflower. Fawcett.
Sunflower. Marek.
Sharp, R. F. *see* Sharp, Robert Farquharson.
Sharp, R. Farquharson. *see* Sharp, Robert Farquharson.
Sharp, Robert Farquharson, 1864-1945
xSharp, R. F.
A Dictionary of English Authors. Folcroft.
xSharp, R. Farquharson.
A Dictionary of English Authors. Longwood
Pr.
Sharp, Robert L. *see* Sharp, Robert Lathrop.
Sharp, Robert Lathrop.
xSharp, Robert L.
From Donne to Dryden: The Revolt Against
Metaphysical Poetry. Octagon.
From Donne to Dryden: The Revolt Against
Metaphysical Poetry. Somerset Pub.
Sharp, Ronald A.
xSharp, Ronald A.
Keats, Skepticism, & the Religion of Beauty. U
of Ga Pr.
Sharp, U. S. *see* Sharp, Ulysses S. Grant.
Sharp, Ulysses S. Grant, 1906-
xSharp, U. S.
Strategy for Defeat: Vietnam in Retrospect.
Presidio Pr.
Sharp, Vicki F.
xSharp, Vicki F.
Statistics for the Social Sciences. Little.
Sharp, W. *see* Sharp, William.
Sharp, Walter R. *see* Sharp, Walter Rice.
Sharp, Walter Rice, 1896-
xSharp, Walter R.
Field Administration in the United Nations
System: The Conduct of International
Economic & Social Programs. Greenwood.
Sharp, Watson.
xSharp, Watson.
The Catholic & the Jewish Approach to Sex &
Their Relative Influence Upon the Cultural
Character of Our Society. Am Classical Coll
Pr.
Sharp, William, 1855-1905
xSharp, W.
ed. Studies & Appreciations. Arno.
xSharp, William.
Gypsy Christ, & Other Tales. Arno.
Life & Letters of Joseph Severn. AMS Pr.
Life & Letters of Joseph Severn. Folcroft.
Life of Percy Bysshe Shelley. Folcroft.
Life of Percy Bysshe Shelley. Kennikat.
The Sin-Eater, & Other Tales & Episodes.
Arno.
Studies & Appreciations. Arno.
Sharpe, Anthony N.
xSharpe, Anthony N.
Mechanizing Microbiology. C C Thomas.
Sharpe, Charles K. *see* Sharpe, Charles Kirkpatrick.
Sharpe, Charles Kirkpatrick.
xSharpe, Charles K.
Historical Account of the Belief in Witchcraft
in Scotland. Gale.
Sharpe, D. W. *see* Sharpe, David William.
Sharpe, David J.
xSharpe, David J.
Cases & Materials on Law & Medicine. West
Pub.
Sharpe, David William.
xSharpe, D. W.
Injective Modules. Cambridge U Pr.
Sharpe, Deborah T.
xSharpe, Deborah T.
The Psychology of Color & Design. Littlefield.
The Psychology of Color & Design.
Nelson-Hall.
Sharpe, Ella F. *see* Sharpe, Ella Freeman.
Sharpe, Ella Freeman, 1875-1947
xSharpe, Ella F.
Dream Analysis. Brunner-Mazel.
xSharpe, Ella Freeman.

Collected Papers on Psycho-Analysis.
Brunner-Mazel.
Sharpe, Grant W. *see* Sharpe, Grant William.
Sharpe, Grant William.
xSharpe, Grant W.
Introduction to Forestry. McGraw.
Sharpe, Kenneth Evan.
xSharpe, Kenneth Evan.
Peasant Politics: Struggle in a Dominican
Village. Johns Hopkins.
Sharpe, Kevin.
xSharpe, Kevin.
ed. Faction & Parliament: Essays in Early
Stuart History. Oxford U Pr.
Sharpe, L. J. *see* Sharpe, Laurence James.
Sharpe, Laurence James.
xSharpe, L. J.
ed. Decentralist Trends in Western
Democracies. Sage.
Sharpe, Robert.
xSharpe, Robert.
The Success Factor. Warner Bks.
xSharpe, Robert F.
The Planned Giving Idea Book. Nelson.
Sharpe, Robert F. *see* Sharpe, Robert.
Sharpe, Robert J.
xSharpe, Robert J.
The Law of Habeas Corpus. Oxford U Pr.
Sharpe, Tom.
xSharpe, Tom.
The Great Pursuit. Har-Row.
The Wilt Alternative. St Martin.
Sharpe, W. F. *see* Sharpe, William F.
Sharpe, William, 1724-1783
xSharpe, William.
A Dissertation Upon Genius. Schol Facsimiles.
Sharpe, William F.
xSharpe, W. F.
Portfolio Theory & Capital Markets. McGraw.
xSharpe, William F.
BASIC: An Introduction to Computer
Programming Using the BASIC Language.
Free Pr.
Economics of Computers. Columbia U Pr.
Introduction to Managerial Economics.
Columbia U Pr.
Sharpless, F. Parvin.
xSharpless, F. Parvin.
Romanticism: A Literary Perspective. Hayden.
Symbol & Myth in Modern Literature. Hayden.
Sharpless, John B. *see* Sharpless, John Burk.
Sharpless, John Burk.
xSharpless, John B.
City Growth in the United States, England &
Wales, 1820-1861: The Effects of Location,
Size & Economic Structure on Interurban
Variations in Demographic Growth. Arno.
Sharpless, Richard.
xSharpless, Richard E.
Gaitan of Colombia: A Political Biography. U
of Pittsburgh Pr.
Sharpless, Richard E. *see* Sharpless, Richard.
Sharpton, Robert. *see* Sharpton, Robert E.
Sharpton, Robert E.
xSharpton, Robert.
String Art: Step-by-Step. Chilton.
Sharrer, Harvey L.
xSharrer, Harvey L.
The Legendary History of Britain in Lope
Garcia De Salazar's Libro De las
Bienandanzas e Fortunas. U of Pa Pr.
Sharretts, Richard W.
xSharretts, Richard W.
Command Voice. Stackpole.
Sharrock, Floyd W.
xSharrock, Floyd W.

Prehistoric Occupation Patterns in Southwest
Wyoming & Cultural Relationships with the
Great Basin & Plains Culture Areas. AMS Pr.
Sharrock, J. T. R.
xSharrock, J. T. R.
Rare Birds in Britain & Ireland. Buteo.
Sharry, John J.
xSharry, John J.
Complete Denture Prosthodontics. McGraw.
Sharvy, Robert.
xSharvy, Robert.
Logic: An Outline. Littlefield.
Shattuck, Charles H. *see* Shattuck, Charles Harlen.
Shattuck, Charles Harlen, 1910-
xShattuck, Charles H.
The Hamlet of Edwin Booth. U of Ill Pr.
Shattuck, Louise F.
xShattuck, Louise F.
From Riches to Bitches (And a Cadillac for
Your Vet): Being a Mirthful Recounting of
the Carry-on Kennel Chronicles. Howell Bk.
Shattuck, Roger.
xShattuck, Roger.
Marcel Proust. Penguin.
Shattuck, Ruth R.
xShattuck, Ruth R.
Creative Cooking without Wheat, Milk & Eggs.
A S Barnes.
Shatz, Stephen S.
xShatz, Stephen S.
Profinite Groups, Arithmetic, & Geometry.
Princeton U Pr.
Shauers, Margaret.
xShauers, Margaret.
Dark Knight. Bouregy.
Shave, David W., 1931-
xShave, David W.
Communication Breakdown: Cause & Cure
Green.
The Therapeutic Listener. Krieger.
Shavelson, Melville, 1917-
xShavelson, Melvin.
Lualda. Arbor Hse.
Shavelson, Melvin. *see* Shavelson, Melville.
Shaver, James P.
xShaver, James P.
ed. Building Rationales for Citizenship
Education. Coun Soc Studies.
Shaver, Kelly. *see* Shaver, Kelly G.
Shaver, Kelly G., 1941-
xShaver, Kelly.
An Introduction to Attribution Processes.
Winthrop.
xShaver, Kelly G.
Principles of Social Psychology. Winthrop.
Shaw, A. *see* Shaw, Albert.
Shaw, Alan C., 1937-
xShaw, Alan C.
Logical Design of Operating Systems. P-H.
Shaw, Albert, 1857-1947
xShaw, A.
Cooperation in the Northwest. Johnson Repr.
xShaw, Albert.
Icaria, a Chapter in the History of
Communism. AMS Pr.
Shaw, Arch W. *see* Shaw, Arch Wilkinson.
Shaw, Arch Wilkinson, 1876-
xShaw, Arch W.
An Approach to Business Problems. Hive Pub.
Some Problems in Market Distribution:
Illustrating the Application of a Basic
Philosophy of Business. Harvard U Pr.
Shaw, Arnold.
xShaw, Arnold.
Honkers & Shouters: The Golden Years of
Rhythm & Blues. Macmillan.
Shaw, B. L. *see* Shaw, Bernard Leslie.
Shaw, Barnabas.
xShaw, Barnabas.

Memorials of South Africa. Negro U Pr.
Memorials of South Africa. Verry.
Shaw, Bernard. *see* Shaw, George Bernard.
Shaw, Bernard Leslie.
xShaw, B. L.
Inorganic Hydrides. Pergamon.
Shaw, Bob.
xShaw, Bob.
Cosmic Kaleidoscope. Dell.
Cosmic Kaleidoscope. Doubleday.
Medusa's Children. Dell.
Medusa's Children. Doubleday.
Orbitsville. Ace Bks.
Shaw, Bradley A.
xShaw, Bradley A.
Compiled by Latin American Literature in
English Translation: An Annotated
Bibliography. NYU Pr.
Shaw, Catherine M.
xShaw, Catherine M.
Richard Brome. Twayne.
Shaw, Clifford R. *see* Shaw, Clifford Robe.
Shaw, Clifford Robe.
xShaw, Clifford R.
Brothers in Crime. Arden Lib.
Brothers in Crime. U of Chicago Pr.
Shaw, D.
xShaw, D.
ed. Atomic Diffusion in Semiconductors.
Plenum Pub.
Shaw, D. J. *see* Shaw, Duncan J.
Shaw, David, 1943-
xShaw, David.
Journalism Today: A Changing Press for a
Changing America. Har-Row.
The Levy Caper. Macmillan.
Shaw, Derek.
xShaw, Derek.
Fourier Transform N.M.R. Spectroscopy.
Elsevier.
Shaw, Duncan J.
xShaw, D. J.
Introduction to Colloid & Surface Chemistry.
Butterworths.
Shaw, Earl L. *see* Shaw, L. Earl.
Shaw, Edward S. *see* Shaw, Edward Stone.
Shaw, Edward Stone.
xShaw, Edward S.
Financial Deepening in Economic
Development. Oxford U Pr.
Shaw, Evelyn. *see* Shaw, Evelyn S.
Shaw, Evelyn S.
xShaw, Evelyn.
Fish Out of School. Har-Row.
Sea Otters. Har-Row.
Shaw, Frederic. *see* Shaw, Frederic Joseph.
Shaw, Frederic Joseph, 1883-
xShaw, Frederic.
Little Railways of the World. Howell-North.
Shaw, George B. *see* Shaw, George Bernard.
Shaw, George Bernard.
xShaw, Bernard.
The Great Composers: Reviews &
Bombardments. U of Cal Pr.
How to Become a Musical Critic. Da Capo.
The Rationalization of Russia. Greenwood.
xShaw, George B.

Arms & the Man. Bobbs.
Arms & the Man. Penguin.
Caesar & Cleopatra. Penguin.
Caesar & Cleopatra. Airmont.
Caesar & Cleopatra: A History. AHM Pub.
Cashel Byron's Profession. Penguin.
Crime of Imprisonment. Greenwood.
Dramatic Criticism: 1895-98; a Selection by
  John F. Matthews. Greenwood.
ed. Fabian Essays in Socialism. Peter Smith.
Flyleaves. W Thomas Taylor.
The Perfect Wagnerite: A Commentary on the
  Niblung's Ring. Dover.
Perfect Wagnerite: A Commentary on the
  Niblung's Ring. Peter Smith.
Prefaces by Bernard Shaw. Scholarly.

Shaw, Gerald.
xShaw, Gerald.
  Some Beginnings: The Cape Times 1876-1910.
    Oxford U Pr.

Shaw, Harry, 1905-
xShaw, Harry.
  Better Jobs Through Better Speech. Littlefield.
  A Complete Course in Freshman English.
    Har-Row.
  Concise Dictionary of Literary Terms.
    McGraw.
  Dictionary of Literary Terms. McGraw.
  Dictionary of Problem Words & Expressions.
    McGraw.
  Punctuate It Right!. B&N.
  Punctuate It Right. Har-Row.
  Spell It Right!. B&N.
  Spell It Right. Har-Row.

Shaw, Henry, 1800-1873
xShaw, Henry.
  The Encyclopedia of Ornament. St Martin.
Shaw, Henry W. see Shaw, Henry Wheeler.

Shaw, Henry Wheeler.
xShaw, Henry W.
  Uncle Sam's Uncle Josh: Or, Josh Billings on
    Practically Everything, Distilled from Josh's
    Rum & Tansy New England Wit by Donald
    Day. Greenwood.

Shaw, Irwin, 1913-
xShaw, Irwin.
  Evening in Byzantium. Delacorte.
  Evening in Byzantium. Dell.
  Love on a Dark Street. Dell.
  Nightwork. Delacorte.
  Nightwork. Dell.
  Paris Paris. Dell.
  Rich Man, Poor Man. Delacorte.
  Rich Man, Poor Man. Dell.
  The Top of the Hill. Delacorte.
  Top of the Hill. Dell.
Shaw, J. see Shaw, John.
Shaw, James H. see Shaw, James Headon.

Shaw, James Headon.
xShaw, James H.
  Textbook of Oral Biology. Saunders.

Shaw, John, 1931-
xShaw, J.
  Reactor Operation. Pergamon.
xShaw, John.
  Red Army Resurgent. Time-Life.
Shaw, John C. see Shaw, John Clark.

Shaw, John Clark, 1933-
xShaw, John C.
  The Quality-Productivity Connection in
    Service-Sector Management. Van Nos
    Reinhold.
Shaw, John E. see Shaw, John E. B.

Shaw, John E. B.
xShaw, John E.
  Professional Guide to Commodity Speculation.
    P-H.

Shaw, Kerry.
xShaw, Kerry.

Swamp Angel. Aurora Pubs.

Shaw, L. Earl.
xShaw, Earl L.
  Readings on the American Political System.
    Heath.
xShaw, L. Earl.
  Modern Competing Ideologies. Heath.
Shaw, Leroy R. see Shaw, Leroy Robert.

Shaw, Leroy Robert.
xShaw, Leroy R.
  ed. German Theater Today: A Symposium. U
    of Tex Pr.

Shaw, Luci.
xShaw, Luci.
  Listen to the Green. Shaw Pubs.
Shaw, M. see Shaw, Marvin E.
Shaw, M. P. see Shaw, Melvin P.

Shaw, Malcolm.
xShaw, Malcolm.
  Anglo-American Democracy. Humanities.
Shaw, Margaret F. see Shaw, Margaret Fay.

Shaw, Margaret Fay.
xShaw, Margaret F.
  Folksongs & Folklore of South Uist. Oxford U
    Pr.
Shaw, Martin. see Shaw, Martin Fallas.

Shaw, Martin Fallas.
xShaw, Martin.
  ed. National Anthems of the World. Arco.

Shaw, Marvin E.
xShaw, M.
  Group Dynamics: The Psychology of Small
    Group Behavior. McGraw.

Shaw, Melvin P.
xShaw, M. P.
  The Gunn-Hilsum Effect. Acad Pr.
Shaw, Merville C. see Shaw, Merville Charles.

Shaw, Merville Charles, 1925-
xShaw, Merville C.
  Function of Theory in Guidance Programs.
    HM.

Shaw, Nathan C.
xShaw, Nathan C.
  ed. Administration of Continuing Education: A
    Guide for Administrators. Natl Assn Con
    Adult Ed.

Shaw, O'Wendell.
xShaw, O'Wendell.
  Greater Need Below. AMS Pr.
Shaw, Patick W. see Shaw, Patrick W.

Shaw, Patrick W.
xShaw, Patick W.
  Literature: A College Anthology. HM.

Shaw, Peter, 1936-
xShaw, Peter.
  The Character of John Adams. Norton.
  The Character of John Adams. U of NC Pr.

Shaw, Richard.
xShaw, Richard.
  Call Me Al Raft. Elsevier-Nelson.
  ed. The Cat Book. Warne.
  ed. The Frog Book. Warne.

Shaw, Richard J.
xShaw, Richard J.
  Field Guide to the Vascular Plants of Grand
    Teton National Park & Teton County,
    Wyoming. Utah St U Pr.
Shaw, Robert B. see Shaw, Robert Burns.

Shaw, Robert Burns, 1947-
xShaw, Robert B.
  In Witness. SBD.
Shaw, Robert W. see Shaw, Robert Wilson.

Shaw, Robert Wilson, 1897-
xShaw, Robert W.
  Some Aspects of Self-Insight As Found in
    Students of a Two-Year Normal School.
    AMS Pr.
Shaw, Russell. see Shaw, Russell B.

Shaw, Russell B.
xShaw, Russell.

Church & State: A Novel of Politics & Power.
  Our Sunday Visitor.
Shaw, S. J. see Shaw, Stanford Jay.

Shaw, Sharon, 1937-
xShaw, Sharon.
  Auctions. Blair.

Shaw, Simeon.
xShaw, Simeon.
  History of the Staffordshire Potteries.
    Weinstock.

Shaw, Stanford Jay.
xShaw, S. J.
  History of the Ottoman Empire & Modern
    Turkey. Cambridge U Pr.

Shaw, Thurstan.
xShaw, Thurstan.
  Igbo-Ukwu: An Account of Archaeological
    Discoveries in Eastern Nigeria. Northwestern
    U Pr.

Shaw, Timothy M.
xShaw, Timothy M.
  Dependence & Underdevelopment: The
    Development & Foreign Policies of Zambia.
    Ohio U Ctr Intl.
  ed. The Politics of Africa: Dependence &
    Development. Holmes & Meier.
Shaw, W. D. see Shaw, William David.
Shaw, W. S. see Shaw, William.
Shaw, Warren C. see Shaw, Warren Choate.

Shaw, Warren Choate, 1887-
xShaw, Warren C.
  History of American Oratory. Folcroft.
  History of American Oratory. R West.

Shaw, William.
xShaw, W. S.
  Tun Razak: His Life & Times. Longman.
xShaw, William.
  Golden Dreams & Waking Realities. Arno.
Shaw, William A. see Shaw, William Arthur.

Shaw, William Arthur, 1865-1943
xShaw, William A.
  History of Currency, 1251-1894. Kelley.
  A History of the English Church During the
    Civil Wars & Under the Commonwealth,
    1640-1660. B Franklin.

Shaw, William David.
xShaw, W. D.
  Dialectical Temper: The Rhetorical Art of
    Robert Browning. Cornell U Pr.

Shaw, William H., 1948-
xShaw, William H.
  Marx's Theory of History. Stanford U Pr.

Shaw-Kennedy, Ronald.
xShaw-Kennedy, Ronald.
  Venice Rediscovered. A S Barnes.
  Venice Rediscovered. Art Alliance.

Shawcross, William.
xShawcross, William.
  Dubcek. S&S.

Shawn, Ted, 1891-1972
xShawn, Ted.
  Dance We Must. Haskell.
  One Thousand & One Night Stands. Da Capo.

Shawver, Donald L.
xShawver, Donald L.
  ed. Marketing Doctoral Dissertation Abstracts,
    1974-75. Am Mktg.

Shay, Frank, 1888-
xShay, Frank.
  ed. A Treasury of Plays for Women. Core
    Collection.

Shay, Gene.
xShay, Gene.
  Gene Shay's Secrets of Magic Revealed: 15
    Amazing Mind Boggling Tricks You Can
    Master in Minutes. Running Pr.

Shay, Philip W.
xShay, Philip W.

The Need for a Unified Discipline of
Management. Am Mgmt.
Shay, Robert P. see Shay, Robert Paul.
Shay, Robert Paul, 1947-
xShay, Robert P.
British Rearmament in the Thirties: Politics &
Profits. Princeton U Pr.
Shay, Sunny.
xShay, Sunny.
How to Raise & Train an Afghan. TFH Pubns.
Shayer, David.
xShayer, David.
The Teaching of English in Schools 1900-1970.
Routledge & Kegan.
Shayne, Neil T., 1932-
xShayne, Neil T.
The Paralegal Profession: A Career Guide.
Oceana.
Shcharansky, Avital.
xShcharansky, Avital.
Next Year in Jerusalem. Morrow.
Shea, Edward J.
xShea, Edward J.
Ethical Decisions in Physical Education &
Sport. C C Thomas.
Shea, George.
xShea, George.
Big Bad Ernie. Creative Ed.
I Died Here. Childrens.
Nightmare Nina. Creative Ed.
Spiders. EMC.
Shea, John.
xShea, John.
The Challenge of Jesus. Doubleday.
Stories of God: An Unauthorized Biography.
Thomas More.
Shea, John D. see Shea, John Dawson Gilmary.
Shea, John Dawson Gilmary, 1824-1892
xShea, John D.
History of the Catholic Missions Among the
Indian Tribes of the United States,
1529-1854. AMS Pr.
xShea, John G.
History of the Catholic Missions Among the
Indian Tribes of the United States,
1529-1854. Arno.
Shea, John G. see Shea, John Dawson Gilmary.
Shea, John Gerald.
xShea, John G.
Antique Country Furniture of North America.
Van Nos Reinhold.
Colonial Furniture Making for Everybody. Van
Nos Reinhold.
Shea, Richard F.
xShea, Richard F.
Amplifier Handbook. McGraw.
Shea, Robert.
xShea, Robert J.
The Eye in the Pyramid. Dell.
Leviathan. Dell.
Shea, Robert J. see Shea, Robert.
Shea, William R.
xShea, William R.
ed. Contemporary Issues in Political
Philosophy. N Watson.
Galileo's Intellectual Revolution: Middle
Period, 1610-1632. N Watson.
ed. Values & the Quality of Life. N Watson.
Sheaffer, Louis.
xSheaffer, Louis.
O'Neill, Son & Artist. Little.
O'Neill, Son & Playwright. Little.
Sheagren, John N.
xSheagren, John N.
Financial Advice for Physicians. C C Thomas.
Sheahan, D. F. see Sheahan, Desmond F.
Sheahan, Desmond. see Sheahan, Desmond F.
Sheahan, Desmond F.
xSheahan, D. F.

Modern Crystal & Mechanical Filters. Wiley.
xSheahan, Desmond.
ed. Modern Crystal & Mechanical Filters. Inst
Electrical.
Sheahan, John.
xSheahan, John.
Promotion & Control of Industry in Postwar
France. Harvard U Pr.
Sheaks, Barclay.
xSheaks, Barclay.
Drawing & Painting the Natural Environment.
Davis Mass.
Shealy, C. Norman.
xShealy, C. Norman.
Occult Medicine Can Save Your Life: A
Modern Doctor Looks at Unconventional
Healing. Dial.
Pain Game. Celestial Arts.
Sheard, Wendy S. see Sheard, Wendy Stedman.
Sheard, Wendy Stedman.
xSheard, Wendy S.
ed. Collaboration in Italian Renaissance Art.
Yale U Pr.
Shearer, John.
xShearer, John.
Billy Jo Jive & the Case of the Missing
Pigeons. Dell.
Billy Jo Jive, Super Private Eye: The Case of
the Missing Ten Speed Bike. Delacorte.
illus. Little Man in the Family. Delacorte.
Shearer, Marshall L.
xShearer, Marshall L.
Rapping About Sex. Har-Row.
Shearer, William M.
xShearer, William M.
Illustrated Speech Anatomy. C C Thomas.
Shearin, Hubert G. see Shearin, Hubert Gibson.
Shearin, Hubert Gibson.
xShearin, Hubert G.
A Syllabus of Kentucky Folk-Songs. Folcroft.
Shears, F. S. see Shears, Frederick Sidney.
Shears, Frederick Sidney.
xShears, F. S.
Froissart, Chronicler & Poet. Folcroft.
Shears, Lambert A. see Shears, Lambert Armour.
Shears, Lambert Armour, 1890-
xShears, Lambert A.
Influence of Walter Scott on the Novels of
Theodor Fontane. AMS Pr.
Shears, Loyda M.
xShears, Loyda M.
Games in Education & Development. C C
Thomas.
Shears, Sarah.
xShears, Sarah.
Annie Parsons. Merrimack Bk Serv.
Courage in Parting. Merrimack Bk Serv.
Courage in War. Merrimack Bk Serv.
Louise. Merrimack Bk Serv.
Louise's Daughters. Merrimack Bk Serv.
Louise's Inheritance. Merrimack Bk Serv.
Other People's Children. Merrimack Bk Serv.
Sheavyn, P. see Sheavyn, Phoebe Anne Beale.
Sheavyn, Phoebe. see Sheavyn, Phoebe Anne Beale.
Sheavyn, Phoebe Anne Beale.
xSheavyn, P.
The Literary Profession in the Elizabethan
Age. State Mutual Bk.
xSheavyn, Phoebe.
Literary Profession in the Elizabethan Age.
Haskell.
Shebar, Sharon S. see Shebar, Sharon Sigmond.
Shebar, Sharon Sigmond.
xShebar, Sharon S.
The Mysterious World of Honeybees. Messner.
Shebbeare, John, 1709-1788
xShebbeare, John.

The History of the Excellence & Decline of the
Constitution, Religion, Laws, Manners, &
Genius of the Sumatrans, 1763. Garland Pub.
The Marriage Act. Garland Pub.
Sheckley, Robert, 1928-
xSheckley, Robert.
Crompton Divided. Bantam.
Crompton Divided. HR&W.
Shecter, Ben.
xShecter, Ben.
illus. Conrad's Castle. Har-Row.
Game for Demons. Har-Row.
illus. The River Witches. Har-Row.
illus. Someplace Else. Har-Row.
illus. Stone House Stories. Har-Row.
illus. A Summer Secret. Har-Row.
The Whistling Whirligig. Har-Row.
Shedd, Charles W. see Shedd, Charlie W.
Shedd, Charlie. see Shedd, Charlie W.
Shedd, Charlie W.
xShedd, Charles W.
Grandparents: Then God Created
Grandparents & It Was Very Good.
Doubleday.
xShedd, Charlie.
Celebration in the Bedroom. Word Bks.
xShedd, Charlie W.
The Exciting Church: Where People Really
Pray. Word Bks.
Grandparents: Then God Created
Grandparents & It Was Very Good.
Doubleday.
How to Develop a Praying Church. Abingdon.
How to Develop a Tithing Church. Abingdon.
Letters to Karen: On Keeping Love in
Marriage. Avon.
Letters to Karen: On Keeping Love In
Marriage. Abingdon.
Letters to Philip: On How to Treat a Woman.
Doubleday.
Stork Is Dead. Pillar Bks.
The Stork Is Dead. Word Bks.
Talk to Me. Pillar Bks.
Talk to Me!. Revell.
Shedd, W. G. see Shedd, William Greenough Thayer.
Shedd, William Greenough Thayer, 1820-1894
xShedd, W. G.
Sermons to the Natural Man. Banner of Truth.
Shedenhelm, W. R. C.
xShedenhelm, W. R. C.
The Backpacker's Guide. Anderson World.
Shedlock, Marie L., 1854-1935
xShedlock, Marie L.
The Art of the Story-Teller. Dover.
Sheean, Vincent, 1899-
xSheean, Vincent.
First & Last Love. Greenwood.
Orpheus at Eighty. Greenwood.
Sheed, F. see Sheed, Francis Joseph.
Sheed, F. J. see Sheed, Francis Joseph.
Sheed, Francis J. see Sheed, Francis Joseph.
Sheed, Francis Joseph, 1897-
xSheed, F.
The Lord's Prayer: The Prayer of Jesus.
Seabury.
xSheed, F. J.
Death into Life: A Conversation. Arena
Lettres.
Our Hearts Are Restless: The Prayer of St.
Augustine. Seabury.
Theology & Sanity. Our Sunday Visitor.
xSheed, Francis J.
Sidelights on the Catholic Revival. Arno.
Sheed, Wilfrid.
xSheed, Wilfrid.
The Good Word & Other Words. Penguin.
People Will Always Be Kind. FS&G.
Transatlantic Blues. Avon.

Sheehan, Angela.
  xSheehan, Angela.
    The Beaver. Watts.
    The Butterfly. Watts.
    ed. Discovering Nature. Raintree Child.
    The Otter. Watts.
Sheehan, Denza C. *see* Sheehan, Dezna C.
Sheehan, Dezna C.
  xSheehan, Denza C.
    Theory & Practice of Histotechnology. Mosby.
Sheehan, George.
  xSheehan, George.
    Encyclopedia of Athletic Medicine. Anderson
      World.
Sheehan, James J.
  xSheehan, James J.
    Career of Lujo Brentano: A Study of
      Liberalism & Social Reform in Imperial
      Germany. U of Chicago Pr.
    German Liberalism in the Nineteenth Century.
      U of Chicago Pr.
Sheehan, John F. *see* Sheehan, John F. X.
Sheehan, John F. X.
  xSheehan, John F.
    On Becoming Whole in Christ: An
      Interpretation of the Spiritual Exercises.
      Loyola.
Sheehan, Larry.
  xSheehan, Larry.
    ed. The Whole Golf Catalog. Atheneum.
Sheehan, Peter W.
  xSheehan, Peter W.
    ed. The Function & Nature of Imagery. Acad
      Pr.
Sheehan, Robert.
  xSheehan, Robert.
    Introduction to Police Administration: A
      Systems & Behavioral Approach with Case
      Studies. A-W.
Sheehan, Susan.
  xSheehan, Susan.
    A Prison & a Prisoner. HM.
Sheehan, Thomas John.
  xSheehan, Tom.
    Orchid Genera Illustrated. Van Nos Reinhold.
Sheehan, Tom. *see* Sheehan, Thomas John.
Sheehy, Emma D. *see* Sheehy, Emma Dickson.
Sheehy, Emma Dickson.
  xSheehy, Emma D.
    Children Discover Music & Dance. Tchrs Coll.
    Fives & Sixes Go to School. Greenwood.
Sheehy, Eugene P. *see* Sheehy, Eugene Paul.
Sheehy, Eugene Paul.
  xSheehy, Eugene P.
    ed. Guide to Reference Books. ALA.
Sheeler, Willard D. *see* Sheeler, Willard de Mont.
Sheeler, Willard de Mont.
  xSheeler, Willard D.
    Grammar & Drillbook. English Lang.
    Grammar & Drillbook. Oxford U Pr.
Sheen, Fulton J. *see* Sheen, Fulton John.
Sheen, Fulton John, Bp, 1895-
  xSheen, Fulton J.
    Children & Parents. S&S.
    Cross & the Crisis. Arno.
    Life of Christ. Doubleday.
    Lift up Your Heart. Doubleday.
    Moods & Truths. Kennikat.
    Moral Universe: A Preface to Christian Living.
      Arno.
    Old Errors & New Labels. Kennikat.
    Peace of Soul. Doubleday.
    Power of Love. Doubleday.
    The World's First Love. Doubleday.
    The World's Great Love: The Prayer of the
      Rosary. Seabury.
Sheen, Jack H.
  xSheen, Jack H.

    Aesthetic Rhinoplasty. Mosby.
Sheeran, James. *see* Sheeran, James J.
Sheeran, James J.
  xSheeran, James.
    How to Skyrocket Your Income: The
      Businessman's Guide to Making Money. Fell.
Sheerin, John B.
  xSheerin, John B.
    Peace, War & the Young Catholic. Paulist Pr.
Sheet Metal & Air Conditioning Contractors National
  Association. *see* Sheet Metal and Air Conditioning
  Contractors' National Association.
**Sheet Metal and Air Conditioning Contractors' National
  Association.**
  xSheet Metal & Air Conditioning Contractors
    National Association.
    Fundamentals of Solar Heating: A
      Correspondence Course. Solar Energy Info.
Sheets, Boyd. *see* Sheets, Boyd V.
Sheets, Boyd V.
  xSheets, Boyd.
    Anatomy & Physiology of the Speech
      Mechanism. Bobbs.
Sheets, Herman E.
  xSheets, Herman E.
    ed. Hydronautics. Acad Pr.
Sheets, Payson D.
  xSheets, Payson D.
    ed. Volcanic Activity & Human Ecology. Acad
      Pr.
Sheetz, Ann K. *see* Sheetz, Ann Kindig.
Sheetz, Ann Kindig.
  xSheetz, Ann K.
    Born Again but Still Wet Behind the Ears.
      Christian Herald.
Sheff, Alexander L.
  xSheff, Alexander L.
    Bookkeeping Made Easy. Har-Row.
    How to Write Letters for All Occasions.
      Doubleday.
Sheffer, Gabriel.
  xSheffer, Gabriel.
    Dynamics of Conflict: A Re-Examination of
      the Arab-Israel Conflict. Humanities.
Sheffield, Charles.
  xSheffield, Charles.
    The Web Between the Worlds. Ace Bks.
Sheffield, Edward F. *see* Sheffield, Edward Fletcher.
Sheffield, Edward Fletcher, 1912-
  xSheffield, Edward F.
    ed. Teaching in the Universities: No One Way.
      McGill-Queens U Pr.
Sheffield, James R.
  xSheffield, James R.
    Education in Kenya: An Historical Study.
      Tchrs Coll.
    Non-Formal Education in African
      Development. Interbk Inc.
Sheffield, Janet. *see* Sheffield, Janet N.
Sheffield, Janet N.
  xSheffield, Janet.
    Not Just Sugar & Spice. Morrow.
Sheffield, John.
  xSheffield, John.
    Plasma Scattering of Electromagnetic
      Radiation. Acad Pr.
Sheffield, John B. *see* Sheffield, John Baker Holroyd, 1st
  Earl of.
Sheffield, John Baker Holroyd, 1st Earl of, 1735-18212
  xSheffield, John B.
    Observations on the Commerce of American
      States. Kelley.
Sheffield, Margaret.
  xSheffield, Margaret.
    Where Do Babies Come from?. Knopf.
Sheffield, Robert.
  xSheffield, Robert.
    ed. The Ice Skating Book. Universe.
Sheffy, Lester F. *see* Sheffy, Lester Fields.

Sheffy, Lester Fields.
  xSheffy, Lester F.
    Francklyn Land & Cattle Company: A
      Panhandle Enterprise, 1882-1957. U of Tex
      Pr.
Shefrin, Bruce M.
  xShefrin, Bruce M.
    The Future of U. S. Politics in an Age of
      Economic Limits. Westview.
Sheftel, Chuck.
  xSheftel, Chuck.
    Contemporary Racquetball. Contemp Bks.
Shefter, Harry.
  xShefter, Harry.
    How to Prepare Talks & Oral Reports. PB.
Sheikh, Bilquis.
  xSheikh, Bilquis.
    I Dared to Call Him Father. Chosen Bks Pub.
Sheil, Mary. *see* Sheil, Mary Leonora Woulfe.
Sheil, Mary Leonora Woulfe, Lady.
  xSheil, Mary.
    Glimpses of Life & Manners in Persia. Arno.
Sheiner, Ben, 1925-
  xSheiner, Ben.
    Intellectual Mysticism. Philos Lib.
Sheinwold, Alfred, 1911-
  xSheinwold, Alfred.
    Bridge Play. Cornerstone.
    Duplicate Bridge. Dover.
    Duplicate Bridge. Gannon.
    First Book of Bridge. Har-Row.
    First Book of Bridge. Merrimack Bk Serv.
Shelbourne, Cecily.
  xShelbourne, Cecily.
    Stage of Love. Berkley Pub.
Shelby, David S.
  xShelby, David S.
    Anterior Restoration, Fixed Bridgework, &
      Esthetics. C C Thomas.
Shelden, M. Gene. *see* Shelden, Martha Gene.
Shelden, Martha Gene.
  xShelden, M. Gene.
    Design Through Draping. Burgess.
Sheldon, Aure.
  xSheldon, Aure.
    Fit for a King. Carolrhoda Bks.
    Of Cobblers & Kings. Schol Bk Serv.
Sheldon, Charles. *see* Sheldon, Charles Monroe.
Sheldon, Charles H.
  xSheldon, Charles H.
    Politicians, Judges, & the People: A Study in
      Citizens' Participation. Greenwood.
Sheldon, Charles L. *see* Sheldon, Charles Monroe.
Sheldon, Charles M. *see* Sheldon, Charles Monroe.
Sheldon, Charles Monroe, 1857-1946
  xSheldon, Charles.
    In His Steps. BJ Pub Group.
    In His Steps. Revell.
    In His Steps. Zondervan.
  xSheldon, Charles L.
    In His Steps. Whitaker Hse.
  xSheldon, Charles M.
    In His Steps. Baker Bk.
    In His Steps. Broadman.
    In His Steps. G&D.
    In His Steps. Good News.
    In His Steps. Keats.
    In His Steps. Moody.
    In His Steps. Zondervan.
Sheldon, Eleanor B. *see* Sheldon, Eleanor Harriet
  (Bernert).
Sheldon, Eleanor Harriet (Bernert).
  xSheldon, Eleanor B.
    ed. Indicators of Social Change: Concepts &
      Measurements. Russell Sage.
Sheldon, G. W. *see* Sheldon, George William.
Sheldon, George William, 1843-1914
  xSheldon, G. W.
    Hours with Art & Artists. Garland Pub.
Sheldon, Henry D. *see* Sheldon, Henry Davidson.

Sheldon, Henry Davidson, 1874-1948
  xSheldon, Henry D.
    Student Life & Customs. Arno.
Sheldon, Margaret R. see Sheldon, Margaret Rothery.
Sheldon, Margaret Rothery.
  xSheldon, Margaret R.
    Clipping Your Poodle. Arco.
    Poodles. Arco.
Sheldon, Mary. see Sheldon, Mary (French).
Sheldon, Mary (French), 1847-1936
  xSheldon, Mary.
    Sultan to Sultan: Adventures Among the Masai
      & Other Tribes of East Africa. Arno.
Sheldon, Oliver.
  xSheldon, Oliver.
    The Philosophy of Management. Arno.
Sheldon, Robert. see Sheldon, Robert A.
Sheldon, Robert A.
  xSheldon, Robert.
    Roadside Geology of Texas. Mountain Pr.
Sheldon, Roger.
  xSheldon, Roger.
    Opportunities in Carpentry Careers. Natl
      Textbk.
Sheldon, Roy.
  xSheldon, Roy.
    Consumer Engineering: A New Technique for
      Prosperity. Arno.
Sheldon, Sidney.
  xSheldon, Sidney.
    The Other Side of Midnight. Dell.
    The Other Side of Midnight. Morrow.
    A Stranger in the Mirror. Morrow.
    A Stranger in the Mirror. Warner Bks.
Sheldon, Stephen. see Sheldon, Stephen H.
Sheldon, Stephen H.
  xSheldon, Stephen.
    Pediatric Differential Diagnosis: A
      Problem-Oriented Approach. Raven.
Sheldon, Walt. see Sheldon, Walter J.
Sheldon, Walter J.
  xSheldon, Walt.
    Enjoy Japan: A Personal & Highly Unofficial
      Guide. C E Tuttle.
Sheldon, William. see Sheldon, William D.
Sheldon, William D.
  xSheldon, William.
    Where It's At. Allyn.
  xSheldon, William D.
    Arrivals & Departures. Allyn.
    At Home. Allyn.
    Finding the Way. Allyn.
    From the Top. Allyn.
    Our School. Allyn.
    Out of Sight. Allyn.
    Over & Out. Allyn.
    Play It Again. Allyn.
    Prime Time. Allyn.
    Story Caravan. Allyn.
Sheldon, William Du Bose.
  xSheldon, William.
    Populism in the Old Dominion: Virginia Farm
      Politics, 1885-1900. Peter Smith.
Sheldon, William Herbert.
  xSheldon, William.
    Varieties of Delinquent Youth. Hafner.
    Varieties of Temperament: A Psychology of
      Constitutional Differences. Hafner.
Sheldon, Wilmon H. see Sheldon, Wilmon Henry.
Sheldon, Wilmon Henry, 1875-
  xSheldon, Wilmon H.
    God & Polarity: A Synthesis of Philosophies.
      Greenwood.
Sheldon-Williams, Miles.
  xSheldon-Williams, Miles.
    The Power of Ula. Arno.
Sheldrake, P. see Sheldrake, Peter.
Sheldrake, Peter.
  xSheldrake, P.

    Accountability in Higher Education. Allen
      Unwin.
Sheleff, Leon S. see Sheleff, Leon Shaskolsky.
Sheleff, Leon Shaskolsky.
  xSheleff, Leon S.
    The Bystander: Behavior, Law & Ethics.
      Lexington Bks.
Shelford, Victor E. see Shelford, Victor Ernest.
Shelford, Victor Ernest, 1877-
  xShelford, Victor E.
    The Ecology of North America. U of Ill Pr.
Shell, Adeline G. see Shell, Adeline Garner.
Shell, Adeline Garner.
  xShell, Adeline G.
    Brown Bagging It: The Lunch Box Idea Book.
      Sovereign Bks.
    Working Parent Food Book. Cornerstone.
    Working Parent Food Book. S&S.
Shell, Marc.
  xShell, Marc.
    The Economy of Literature. Johns Hopkins.
Shell, Susan M. see Shell, Susan Meld.
Shell, Susan Meld, 1948-
  xShell, Susan M.
    The Rights of Reason: A Study of Kant's
      Philosophy & Politics. U of Toronto Pr.
Shellabarger, Samuel, 1888-1954
  xShellabarger, Samuel.
    Lord Chesterfield & His World. Biblo.
Shelley, Bruce L. see Shelley, Bruce Leon.
Shelley, Bruce Leon, 1927-
  xShelley, Bruce L.
    Four Marks of a Total Christian. Victor Bks.
Shelley, Henry C. see Shelley, Henry Charles.
Shelley, Henry Charles.
  xShelley, Henry C.
    Life & Letters of Edward Young. Scholarly.
Shelley, Mary. see Shelley, Mary Wollstonecraft
  (Godwin).
Shelley, Mary V. see Shelley, Mary Virginia.
Shelley, Mary Virginia.
  xShelley, Mary V.
    Dr. Ed: The Story of General Edward Hand.
      Sutter House.
Shelley, Mary W. see Shelley, Mary Wollstonecraft
  (Godwin).
Shelley, Mary Wollstonecraft (Godwin), 1797-1851
  xShelley, Mary.
    Frankenstein. Dell.
    Frankenstein. Dutton.
    Frankenstein. PB.
    Frankenstein. Delacorte.
    Frankenstein. Western Pub.
    Frankenstein. Pendulum Pr.
    Frankenstein. Airmont.
    Frankenstein. Bantam.
    Frankenstein. Schol Bk Serv.
    Last Man. U of Nebr Pr.
  xShelley, Mary W.
    Frankenstein. NAL.
    Frankenstein: Or, the Modern Prometheus.
      Macmillan.
    The Letters of Mary W. Shelley (Mostly
      Unpublished). Folcroft.
Shelley, Percy B. see Shelley, Percy Bysshe.
Shelley, Percy Bysshe, 1792-1822
  xShelley, Percy B.
    An Address to the Irish People. AMS Pr.
    Cenci. Bobbs.
    Cenci: A Tragedy in Five Acts. Phaeton.
    A Defence of Poetry & a Letter to Lord
      Ellenborough. Folcroft.
    Letters from Percy Bysshe Shelley to Jane
      Clairmont.. Folcroft.
    New Shelley Letters. Hyperion Conn.
    On the Vegetable System of Diet. Folcroft.
    A Proposal for Putting Reform to the Vote
      Throughout the Kingdom. AMS Pr.
Shelley Society, London. see Shelly Society, London.

Shelley Society London Publications. see Shelly Society,
  London.
Shelley Society's London Publications. see Shelly
  Society, London.
Shelly, Judith A. see Shelly, Judith Allen.
Shelly, Maynard. see Shelly, Maynard Wolfe.
Shelly, Maynard W. see Shelly, Maynard Wolfe.
Shelly Society, London.
  xShelley Society, London.
    Publications. AMS Pr.
  xShelley Society London Publications.
    The Mask of Anarchy: Written on the
      Occasion of the Massacre of Manchester.
      AMS Pr.
    The Shelley Society's Papers: Papers Read
      Before the Society & Abstracts of Any Not
      Fully Reported. AMS Pr.
  xShelley Society's London Publications.
    Note-Book of the Shelley Society. AMS Pr.
Shelly, Gary B.
  xShelly, Gary B.
    DOS Job Control for Assembler Language
      Programmers. Anaheim Pub Co.
    DOS Job Control for Cobol Programmers.
      Anaheim Pub Co.
    Introduction to Computer Programming ANSI
      Cobol. Anaheim Pub Co.
    Introduction to Computers & Data Processing.
      Anaheim Pub Co.
    Introduction to Flowcharting & Computer
      Programming Logic. Anaheim Pub Co.
    OS Job Control Language. Anaheim Pub Co.
Shelly, Judith Allen.
  xShelly, Judith A.
    Caring in Crisis: Bible Studies for Helping
      People. Inter-Varsity.
Shelly, Maynard Wolfe, 1928-
  xShelly, Maynard.
    How to Be Happy, Happier, Happiest.
      Chatham Sq.
  xShelly, Maynard W.
    ed. Analyses of Satisfaction. Mss Info.
Shelnutt, Eve, 1943-
  xShelnutt, Eve.
    The Love Child. Black Sparrow.
Shelton, Austin J.
  xShelton, Austin J.
    ed. African Assertion: A Critical Anthology of
      African Literature. Odyssey Pr.
    Igbo-Igala Borderland: Religion & Social
      Control in Indigenous African Colonialism.
      State U NY Pr.
Shelton, Baker O.
  xShelton, Baker O.
    Teaching & Guiding the Slow Learner. P-H.
Shelton, Barbara.
  xShelton, Barbara.
    Woody. Christian Herald.
Shelton, Brenda K. see Shelton, Brenda Kurtz.
Shelton, Brenda Kurtz.
  xShelton, Brenda K.
    Reformers in Search of Yesterday: Buffalo in
      the 1890's. State U NY Pr.
Shelton, Gene.
  xShelton, Gene.
    Track of the Snake. Belmont-Tower.
Shelton, Herbert M. see Shelton, Herbert McGolphin.
Shelton, Herbert McGolphin, 1895-
  xShelton, Herbert M.
    Fasting for Renewal of Life. Natural Hygiene.
Shelton, Jay, 1942-
  xShelton, Jay W.
    Wood Heat Safety. Garden Way Pub.
Shelton, Jay W. see Shelton, Jay.
Shelton, John S.
  xShelton, John S.
    Geology Illustrated. W H Freeman.
Shelton, Richard, 1933-
  xShelton, Richard.

The Bus to Veracruz. U of Pittsburgh Pr.
Of All the Dirty Words. U of Pittsburgh Pr.
Shelton, Wilma Loy, 1889-
xShelton, Wilma Loy.
Checklist of New Mexico Publications,
1850-1953. U of NM Pr.
Shemel, Sidney.
xShemel, Sidney.
More About This Business of Music.
Watson-Guptill.
This Business of Music. Watson-Guptill.
This Business of Music. Watson-Guptill.
Shemin, Margaretha.
xShemin, Margaretha.
Mrs. Herring. Lothrop.
Shen. see Shen, Jerome T. Y.
Shen, Benjamin S. see Shen, Benjamin Shih Ping.
Shen, Benjamin Shih Ping.
xShen, Benjamin S.
ed. Spallation Nuclear Reactions & Their
Applications. Kluwer Boston.
Shen, Hsieh W. see Shen, Hsieh Wen.
Shen, Hsieh Wen.
xShen, Hsieh W.
Modeling of Rivers. Wiley.
Shen, Jerome T. Y., 1918-
xShen.
Clinical Practice of Adolescent Medicine.
ACC.
Shen, T. H. see Shen, Tsung-Han.
Shen, Tsung-Han, 1895-
xShen, T. H.
Agricultural Resources of China. Cornell U Pr.
Shen, Y. R. see Shen, Yuen-Ron.
Shen, Yuen-Ron.
xShen, Y. R.
ed. Nonlinear Infrared Generation.
Springer-Verlag.
Shenk, Al.
xShenk, Al.
Calculus & Analytic Geometry. Goodyear.
xShenk, Norman A.
Calculus & Analytic Geometry. Goodyear.
Shenk, Norman A. see Shenk, Al.
Shenkel, James D. see Shenkel, James Donald.
Shenkel, James Donald.
xShenkel, James D.
Chronology & Recensional Development in the
Greek Text of Kings. Harvard U Pr.
Shenkel, William M. see Shenkel, William Monroe.
Shenkel, William Monroe, 1923-
xShenkel, William M.
Marketing Real Estate. P-H.
Modern Real Estate Management. McGraw.
Shenker, Israel.
xShenker, Israel.
Noshing Is Sacred. Bobbs.
Shenkman, Richard.
xShenkman, Richard.
One Night Stands with American History:
Odd, Amusing, & Little-Known Incidents.
Morrow.
Shennan, J. H.
xShennan, J. H.
Philippe, Duke of Orleans: Regent of France,
1715-1723. Thames Hudson.
Shenoy, G. K.
xShenoy, G. K.
ed. Mossbauer Isomer Shifts. Elsevier.
Shenstone, William.
xShenstone, William.
The Letters of William Shenstone. AMS Pr.
Shenton, James. see Shenton, James Patrick.
Shenton, James P. see Shenton, James Patrick.
Shenton, James Patrick.
xShenton, James.
ed. Free Enterprise Forever: Scientific
American in the 19th Century. Images
Graphiques.
xShenton, James P.

ed. Ethnic Groups in American Life. Arno.
Shepard, Anna O. see Shepard, Anna Osler.
Shepard, Anna Osler, 1903-
xShepard, Anna O.
Ceramics for the Archaeologist. Carnegie Inst.
Shepard, Edward M. see Shepard, Edward Morse.
Shepard, Edward Morse, 1850-1911
xShepard, Edward M.
Martin Van Buren. AMS Pr.
Martin Van Buren. Chelsea Hse.
Shepard, Francis. see Shepard, Francis Parker.
Shepard, Francis P. see Shepard, Francis Parker.
Shepard, Francis Parker, 1897-
xShepard, Francis.
Submarine Canyons & Other Sea Valleys.
Krieger.
xShepard, Francis P.
Earth Beneath the Sea. Atheneum.
The Earth Beneath the Sea. Johns Hopkins.
Submarine Geology. Har-Row.
Shepard, George H. see Shepard, George Hugh.
Shepard, George Hugh, 1870-
xShepard, George H.
The Application of Efficiency Principles. Hive
Pub.
Shepard, J. M. see Shepard, Jon M.
Shepard, Jon M.
xShepard, J. M.
Sociology & Social Problems: A Conceptual
Approach. P-H.
xShepard, Jon M.
Automation & Alienation: A Study of Office &
Factory Workers. MIT Pr.
Shepard, Judith.
xShepard, Judith.
Seascapes. Permanent Pr.
Seascapes. Watts.
Shepard, Lawrence.
xShepard, Lawrence.
The Securities Brokerage Industry: Nonprice
Competition & Noncompetitive Pricing.
Lexington Bks.
Shepard, Leslie.
xShepard, Leslie.
ed. The Dracula Book of Great Vampire
Stories. BJ Pub Group.
ed. The Dracula Book of Great Vampire
Stories. Citadel Pr.
History of Street Literature: The Story of
Broadside Ballads, Chapbooks, Proclamations,
News-Sheets, Etc.. Gale.
How to Protect Yourself Against Black Magic
& Witchcraft. Citadel Pr.
Shepard, Marion L.
xShepard, Marion L.
Introduction to Energy Technology. Ann Arbor
Science.
Shepard, Mark, 1950-
xShepard, Mark.
How to Love Your Flute: A Guide to Flutes &
Flute-Playing. Panjandrum.
Shepard, Martin, 1934-
xShepard, Martin.
The Do-It-Yourself Psychotherapy Book.
Dutton.
The Do-It-Yourself Psychotherapy Book.
Permanent Pr.
Marathon 16. PB.
A Question of Values. Dutton.
Shepard, Odell, 1884-1967
xShepard, Odell.
The Lore of the Unicorn. Allen Unwin.
The Lore of the Unicorn. Har-Row.
Pedlar's Progress: The Life of Bronson Alcott.
Greenwood.
Shepard, Paul.
xShepard, Paul.

ed. Subversive Science: Essays Toward an
Ecology of Man. HM.
Shepard, Priscilla.
xShepard, Priscilla.
ed. God Is Love. Gibson.
Shepard, Robert S. see Shepard, Robert Stanley.
Shepard, Robert Stanley, 1927-
xShepard, Robert S.
Human Physiology Examination Review. Arco.
Shepard, Thomas.
xShepard, Thomas.
Works. AMS Pr.
Shepard, Thomas H.
xShepard, Thomas H.
Catalog of Teratogenic Agents. Johns Hopkins.
Shepard, Tim.
xShepard, Tim.
Peaches Point. T Y Crowell.
Shepardson, Mary.
xShepardson, Mary.
The Navajo Mountain Community: Social
Organization & Kinship Terminology. U of
Cal Pr.
Shephard, Esther.
xShephard, Esther.
Oriental Tale & a Romantic Poet. Pacific Rim
Res.
Shephard, G. C. see Shephard, Geoffrey Colin.
Shephard, Geoffrey Colin.
xShephard, G. C.
Vector Spaces of Finite Dimension. Halsted Pr.
Shephard, R. J. see Shephard, Roy J.
Shephard, Ronald W. see Shephard, Ronald William.
Shephard, Ronald William.
xShephard, Ronald W.
Theory of Cost & Production Functions.
Princeton U Pr.
Shephard, Roy J.
xShephard, R. J.
Human Physiological Work Capacity.
Cambridge U Pr.
xShephard, Roy J.
Endurance Fitness. U of Toronto Pr.
The Fit Athlete. Oxford U Pr.
Men at Work: Applications of Ergonomics to
Performance & Design. C C Thomas.
Shepherd, D. G.
xShepherd, Dennis G.
Principles of Turbomachinery. Macmillan.
Shepherd, David L. see Shepherd, David Leroy.
Shepherd, David Leroy, 1921-
xShepherd, David L.
Comprehensive High School Reading Methods.
Merrill.
Shepherd, Dennis G. see Shepherd, D G.
Shepherd, Elizabeth.
xShepherd, Elizabeth.
Arms of the Sea: Our Vital Estuaries. Lothrop.
Discoveries of Esteban the Black. Dodd.
Shepherd, Geoffrey S. see Shepherd, Geoffrey Seddon.
Shepherd, Geoffrey Seddon, 1898-
xShepherd, Geoffrey S.
Agricultural Price Analysis. Iowa St U Pr.
Farm Policy: New Directions. Iowa St U Pr.
Shepherd, George W.
xShepherd, George W.
Anti-Apartheid: Transnational Conflict &
Western Policy in the Liberation of South
Africa. Greenwood.
Shepherd, Gordon M.
xShepherd, Gordon M.
The Synaptic Organization of the Brain.
Oxford U Pr.
Shepherd, Henry E. see Shepherd, Henry Elliot.
Shepherd, Henry Elliot, 1844-1929
xShepherd, Henry E.
A Commentary Upon Tennyson's in
Memoriam. Folcroft.
Shepherd, J. see Shepherd, John.

Shepherd, J. Barrie.
  xShepherd, J. Barrie.
    Diary of Daily Prayer. Augsburg.
Shepherd, J. T. see Shepherd, John Thompson.
Shepherd, Jack.
  xShepherd, Jack.
    The Adams Chronicles: Four Generations of
      Greatness. Little.
    The Politics of Starvation. Carnegie Endow.
Shepherd, Jean.
  xShepherd, Jean.
    The Ferrari in the Bedroom. Dodd.
Shepherd, John.
  xShepherd, J.
    Higher Electrical Engineering. Soccer.
Shepherd, John T. see Shepherd, John Thompson.
Shepherd, John Thompson.
  xShepherd, J. T.
    ed. The Human Cardiovascular System: Facts
      & Concepts. Raven.
  xShepherd, John T.
    Veins & Their Control. Saunders.
Shepherd, Margaret.
  xShepherd, Margaret.
    Learning Calligraphy: A Book of Lettering,
      Design & History. Macmillan.
Shepherd, Massey H. see Shepherd, Massey Hamilton.
Shepherd, Massey Hamilton, 1913-
  xShepherd, Massey H.
    Companion of Prayer for Daily Living.
      Morehouse.
    The Psalms in Christian Worship: A Practical
      Guide. Augsburg.
Shepherd, Robert H. see Shepherd, Robert Henry
  Wishart.
Shepherd, Robert Henry Wishart, 1888-
  xShepherd, Robert H.
    Lovedale & Literature for the Bantu: A Brief
      History & a Forecast Negro U Pr.
Shepherd, Robert P. see Shepherd, Robert Perry.
Shepherd, Robert Perry, 1867-
  xShepherd, Robert P.
    Turgot & the Six Edicts. AMS Pr.
    Turgot & the Six Edicts. B Franklin.
Shepherd, Roy E.
  xShepherd, Roy E.
    History of the Rose. E M Coleman Ent.
Shepherd, W.
  xShepherd, W.
    Energy Flow & Power Factor in Nonsinusoidal
      Circuits. Cambridge U Pr.
Shepherd, W. E.
  xShepherd, W. Ernest.
    The Dublin & South Eastern Railway. David &
      Charles.
Shepherd, W. Ernest. see Shepherd, W. E.
Shepherd, Walter.
  xShepherd, Walter.
    Textiles. John Day.
Shepherd, William, 1824-
  xShepherd, William.
    Prairie Experiences in Handling Cattle &
      Sheep. Arno.
Shepherd, William C.
  xShepherd, William C.
    Symbolical Consciousness: A Commentary on
      Love's Body. Scholars Pr Ca.
Shepherd, William G.
  xShepherd, William G.
    The Economics of Industrial Organization.
      P-H.
    ed. Public Enterprise: Economic Analysis of
      Theory & Practice. Lexington Bks.
    Public Policies Toward Business. Irwin.
    ed. Public Policies Toward Business: Readings
      & Cases. Irwin.
Shepherd, William R. see Shepherd, William Robert.
Shepherd, William Robert, 1871-1934
  xShepherd, William R.

    History of Proprietary Government in
      Pennsylvania. AMS Pr.
    Story of New Amsterdam. Friedman.
Shepler, Frederic J. see Shepler, Frederic Joseph.
Shepler, Frederic Joseph.
  xShepler, Frederic J.
    Creatures Within: Imaginary Beings in the
      Work of Henri Michaux. Physsardt.
Sheppard , P. M. see Sheppard, Philip Macdonald.
Sheppard, Alfred Tresidder, 1871-1947
  xSheppard, Alfred T.
    Art & Practice of Historical Fiction. Folcroft.
Sheppard, Harold L.
  xSheppard, Harold L.
    ed. Poverty & Wealth in America. New
      Viewpoints.
Sheppard, J. T. see Sheppard, John Tresidder.
Sheppard, John Tresidder, 1881-
  xSheppard, J. T.
    Aeschylus & Sophocles: Their Work &
      Influence. Cooper Sq.
    Greek Tragedy. Folcroft.
    Pattern of the Iliad. Haskell.
Sheppard, Joseph, 1930-
  xSheppard, Joseph.
    Anatomy: A Complete Guide for Artists.
      Watson-Guptill.
    Drawing the Female Figure. Watson-Guptill.
    Drawing the Male Figure. Watson-Guptill.
    Learning from the Old Masters.
      Watson-Guptill.
Sheppard, Mary.
  xSheppard, Mary.
    All Angels Cry. Moore Pub Co.
Sheppard, Philip M. see Sheppard, Philip MacDonald.
Sheppard, Philip MacDonald.
  xSheppard , P. M.
    ed. Practical Genetics. Halsted Pr.
  xSheppard, Philip M.
    Natural Selection & Heredity. Humanities.
Sheppard, Sally.
  xSheppard, Sally.
    The First Book of Brazil. Watts.
    Indians of the Eastern Woodlands. Watts.
    Indians of the Plains. Watts.
Sheppard, Thomas F.
  xSheppard, Thomas F.
    Lourmarin in the Eighteenth Century: A Study
      of a French Village. Johns Hopkins.
Sheppard, W. J. see Sheppard, William John Limmer.
Sheppard, W. L. see Sheppard, William John Limmer.
Sheppard, William C.
  xSheppard, William C.
    Child Behavior: Learning & Development.
      Rand.
    Teaching Social Behavior to Young Children.
      Res Press.
Sheppard, William John Limmer, 1861-
  xSheppard, W. J.
    Great Hymns & Their Stories. Gordon Pr.
  xSheppard, W. L.
    Great Hymns & Their Stories. Chr Lit.
Shepperson, W. see Shepperson, Wilbur Stanley.
Shepperson, Wilbur S. see Shepperson, Wilbur Stanley.
Shepperson, Wilbur Stanley.
  xShepperson, W.
    Questions from the Past. U of Nev Pr.
  xShepperson, Wilbur S.
    Restless Strangers: Nevada's Immigrants &
      Their Interpreters. U of Nev Pr.
Sheps, Mindel C.
  xSheps, Mindel C.
    Mathematical Models of Conception & Birth.
      U of Chicago Pr.
Shepsle, Kenneth A.
  xShepsle, Kenneth A.

    The Giant Jigsaw Puzzle: Democratic
      Committee Assignments in the Modern
      House. U of Chicago Pr.
Sheptock, Joanne.
  xSheptock, Joanne.
    Our Growing Family. Logos.
Sher, Barbara.
  xSher, Barbara.
    Wishcraft: How to Get What You Really Want.
      Viking Pr.
Sher, Gerson. see Sher, Gerson S.
Sher, Gerson S., 1947-
  xSher, Gerson.
    ed. Marxist Humanism & Praxis. Prometheus
      Bks.
  xSher, Gerson S.
    Praxis: Marxist Criticism & Dissent in Socialist
      Yugoslavia. Ind U Pr.
Shera, Frank H. see Shera, Frank Henry.
Shera, Frank Henry, 1882-
  xShera, Frank H.
    Amateur in Music. Arno.
Shera, Jesse H. see Shera, Jesse Hauk.
Shera, Jesse Hauk, 1903-
  xShera, Jesse H.
    Foundations of the Public Library: The Origins
      of the Public Library Movement in New
      England, 1629-1855. Shoe String.
    Sociological Foundations of Librarianship. Asia.
Sherard, James L.
  xSherard, James L.
    Earth & Earth-Rock Dams: Engineering
      Problems of Design & Construction. Wiley.
Sheras, Peter L.
  xSheras, Peter L.
    Clinical Psychology: A Social Psychological
      Approach. Van Nos Reinhold.
Sheraton, Mimi.
  xSheraton, Mimi.
    From My Mother's Kitchen: Recipes &
      Reminiscences. Har-Row.
Sherbet, G. V. see Sherbet, Gajanan V.
Sherbet, Gajanan V.
  xSherbet, G. V.
    ed. Neoplasia & Cell Differentiation. S Karger.
Sherbiny, Naiem A.
  xSherbiny, Naiem A.
    Arab Oil: Impact on Arab Countries & Global
      Implications. Praeger.
Sherbo, Arthur, 1918-
  xSherbo, Arthur.
    English Poetic Diction from Chaucer to
      Wordsworth. Mich St U Pr.
Sherbourne, Julia F. see Sherbourne, Julia Florence.
Sherbourne, Julia Florence.
  xSherbourne, Julia F.
    Toward Reading Comprehension. Heath.
Sherburn, George. see Sherburn, George Wiley.
Sherburn, George W. see Sherburn, George Wiley.
Sherburn, George Wiley, 1884-
  xSherburn, George.
    Early Career of Alexander Pope. Oxford U Pr.
  xSherburn, George W.
    Early Career of Alexander Pope. Russell.
Sherburne, Andrew, 1765-1831
  xSherburne, Andrew.
    Memoirs of Andrew Sherburne: A Pensioner of
      the Navy of the Revolution. Arno.
Sherburne, Zoa.
  xSherburne, Zoa.
    Almost April. Morrow.
    Girl in the Mirror. Morrow.
    The Girl Who Knew Tomorrow. Morrow.
    Leslie. Morrow.
Shere, Waris.
  xShere, Waris.
    ed. In Search of Peace. Exposition.
Sherer, Michael L.
  xSherer, Michael L.

Stories for Special Days: Messages for Children
on the Lesser Festivals. Augsburg.
Sherer, R. J. see Sherer, Ray J.
Sherer, Ray J.
xSherer, R. J.
Twelve Short Novels. HR&W.
Sherer, Robert G.
xSherer, Robert G.
Subordination or Liberation?: The Development
& Conflicting Theories of Black Education in
Nineteenth Century Alabama. U of Ala Pr.
Shereshefsky, Pauline M.
xShereshefsky, Pauline M.
Psychological Aspects of a First Pregnancy &
Early Postnatal Adaptation. Raven.
Sherfan, Andrew D. see Sherfan, Andrew Dib.
Sherfan, Andrew Dib.
xSherfan, Andrew D.
A Third Treasury of Kahlil Gibran. Citadel Pr.
Sherfey, Florence. see Sherfey, Florence E.
Sherfey, Florence E., 1920-
xSherfey, Florence.
Eastern Washington's Vanished Gristmills &
the Men Who Ran Them. Ye Galleon.
Sherfey, Mary J. see Sherfey, Mary Jane.
Sherfey, Mary Jane, 1933-
xSherfey, Mary J.
The Nature & Evolution of Female Sexuality.
Random.
Sheridan, Anne M. see Sheridan, Anne Marie.
Sheridan, Anne Marie.
xSheridan, Anne M.
The Far off Rhapsody. PB.
xSheridan, Anne-Marie.
The Far-off Rhapsody. S&S.
Sheridan, Anne-Marie.
xSheridan, Anne-Marie.
Summoned to Darkness. S&S.
Sheridan, Anne-Marie. see Sheridan, Anne Marie.
Sheridan, C. L. see Sheridan, Charles L.
Sheridan, Charles. see Sheridan, Charles L.
Sheridan, Charles L., 1937-
xSheridan, C. L.
Fundamentals of Experimental Psychology.
HR&W.
xSheridan, Charles.
Methods in Experimental Psychology. HR&W.
Sheridan, James. see Sheridan, James Francis.
Sheridan, James E.
xSheridan, James E.
China in Disintegration: The Republican Era in
Chinese History, 1912-1949. Free Pr.
Chinese Warlord: The Career of Feng
Yu-hsiang. Stanford U Pr.
Sheridan, James Francis, 1927-
xSheridan, James.
Once More from the Middle: A Philosophical
Anthropology. Ohio U Pr.
Sheridan, John D. see Sheridan, John Desmond.
Sheridan, John Desmond, 1903-
xSheridan, John D.
The Hungry Sheep: Catholic Doctrine Restated
Against Contemporary Attacks. Arlington
Hse.
Sheridan, Kathleen, 1939-
xSheridan, Kathleen.
Living with Divorce. Thomas More.
Sheridan, Lionel A. see Sheridan, Lionel Astor.
Sheridan, Lionel Astor.
xSheridan, Lionel A.
The Constitution of Malaysia. Oceana.
Sheridan, Philip G.
xSheridan, Philip G.
Fund Raising for the Small Organization. M
Evans.
Sheridan, Thomas, 1719-1788
xSheridan, Thomas.
Course of Lectures on Elocution. Arno.
Sherif, Carolyn W.
xSherif, Carolyn W.

ed. Attitude, Ego-Involvement, & Change.
Greenwood.
Orientation in Social Psychology. Har-Row.
Sherif, June L. see Sherif, June Lowry.
Sherif, June Lowry.
xSherif, June L.
Careers in Foreign Languages: A Handbook.
Regents Pub.
Sherif, Mohamed A. see Sherif, Mohamed Ahmed.
Sherif, Mohamed Ahmed.
xSherif, Mohamed A.
Ghazali's Theory of Virtue. State U NY Pr.
Sheringham, George.
xSheringham, George.
Design in the Theatre. Arno.
Sherlock, Patti.
xSherlock, Patti.
Alone on the Mountain: Sheepherding in the
American West. Doubleday.
Sherlock, Robert.
xSherlock, Robert.
Industrial Archaeology of Staffordshire. David
& Charles.
Sherlock, Sheila.
xSherlock, Sheila.
Color Atlas of Liver Disease. Year Bk Med.
Sherman, Alan.
xSherman, Alan.
Basic Concepts of Chemistry. HM.
The Elements of Life: Approach to Chemistry
for the Health Sciences. P-H.
Sherman, C. Neil. see Sherman, Charles Neil.
Sherman, Charles Neil.
xSherman, C. Neil.
Educational Information Center: An
Introduction. Tinnon-Brown.
Sherman, D. R.
xSherman, D. R.
The Lion's Paw. Doubleday.
Sherman, Dan.
xSherman, Dan.
King Jaguar. Arbor Hse.
King Jaguar. Fawcett.
Riddle. Arbor Hse.
Riddle. Fawcett.
Swann. Arbor Hse.
Swann. Fawcett.
Sherman, Emalene.
xSherman, Emalene.
Student Journalist & Free-Lance Writing.
Rosen Pr.
Sherman, Eric.
xSherman, Eric.
Directing the Film: Film Directors on Their
Art. Little.
Sherman, F. D. see Sherman, Frank Dempster.
Sherman, Frank Dempster.
xSherman, F. D.
Little Folk Lyrics. Arno.
Sherman, Frederic F. see Sherman, Frederic Fairchild.
Sherman, Frederic Fairchild, 1874-1940
xSherman, Frederic F.
Early American Portraiture. Arno.
Sherman, G W.
xSherman, G. W.
The Chemists & Other Poems. Cobra Pr.
Sherman, Geraldine.
xSherman, Geraldine.
Animals with Pouches: The Marsupials.
Holiday.
Sherman, Harold. see Sherman, Harold Morrow.
Sherman, Harold Morrow, 1898-
xSherman, Harold.
How to Foresee & Control Your Future.
Fawcett.
How to Make ESP Work for You. Fawcett.
How to Use the Power of Prayer. Anthony.
How to Use the Power of Prayer. R Collier.
Sherman, Howard J.
xSherman, Howard J.

The Soviet Economy. Little.
Stagflation: A Radical Theory of
Unemployment & Inflation. Har-Row.
Sherman, Ivan.
xSherman, Ivan.
illus. I Am a Giant. HarBraceJ.
I Do Not Like It When My Friend comes to
Visit. HarBraceJ.
Sherman, J. Gilmour. see Sherman, John Gilmour.
Sherman, James E.
xSherman, James E.
Ghost Towns & Mining Camps of New
Mexico. U of Okla Pr.
Ghost Towns of Arizona. U of Okla Pr.
Sherman, James R.
xSherman, James R.
How to Overcome a Bad Back. Pathway Bks.
Sherman, Jane, 1908-
xSherman, Jane.
The Drama of Denishawn Dance. Columbia U
Pr.
Sherman, Jerry.
xSherman, Jerry.
Woman Power in Textile & Apparel Sales.
Fairchild.
Sherman, John Gilmour.
xSherman, J. Gilmour.
The Personalized System of Instruction. Educ
Tech Pubns.
Sherman, John K.
xSherman, John K.
Music & Maestros: The Story of the
Minneapolis Symphony Orchestra. U of Minn
Pr.
Sherman, Jory.
xSherman, Jory.
Hellfire Trail. Nordon Pubns.
Sherman, Julia A. see Sherman, Julia Ann.
Sherman, Julia Ann, 1934-
xSherman, Julia A.
Sex-Related Cognitive Differences: An Essay
Theory & Evidence. C C Thomas.
Sherman, Laura Beth, 1951-
xSherman, Laura M.
Fires on the Mountain: The Macedonian
Revolutionary Movement & the Kidnapping
of Ellen Stone. East Eur Quarterly.
Sherman, Laura M. see Sherman, Laura Beth.
Sherman, Lewis, 1896-
xSherman, Lewis M.
The Secret Wind. Valkyrie Pr.
Sherman, Lewis M. see Sherman, Lewis.
Sherman, Lila.
xSherman, Lila.
Art Museums of America: A Guide to
Collections in the United States & Canada.
Morrow.
Sherman, Margaret R.
xSherman, Margaret R.
California's Amazing Agriculture. Pacific Bks.
Sherman, Mark.
xSherman, Mark.
Afterplay. Stein & Day.
Sherman, Michael I.
xSherman, Michael I.
ed. Concepts in Mammalian Embryogensis.
MIT Pr.
Sherman, Murray H. see Sherman, Murray Herbert.
Sherman, Murray Herbert, 1922-
xSherman, Murray H.
Psychoanalysis & Old Vienna: Freud, Reik,
Schnitzler, Kraus. Human Sci Pr.
Sherman, Robert R.
xSherman, Robert R.
ed. Understanding History of Education.
Schenkman.
Sherman, Roger, 1930-
xSherman, Roger.

The Economics of Industry. Little.
Sherman, Steve.
 xSherman, Steve.
  Appalachian Odyssey: Walking the Trail from
   Georgia to Maine. Greene.
Sherman, Stuart P. *see* Sherman, Stuart Pratt.
Sherman, Stuart Pratt, 1881-1926
 xSherman, Stuart P.
  Americans. R West.
  Americans. Scholarly.
  Matthew Arnold, How to Know Him. Shoe
   String.
  On Contemporary Literature. AMS Pr.
  On Contemporary Literature. Arno.
  On Contemporary Literature. R West.
  Significance of Sinclair Lewis. Folcroft.
Sherman, Thomas M.
 xSherman, Thomas M.
  Individually Responsive Instruction. Educ Tech
   Pubns.
Sherman, William L.
 xSherman, William L.
  Forced Native Labor in Sixteenth-Century
   Central America. U of Nebr Pr.
Sherman, William R. *see* Sherman, William Roderick.
Sherman, William Roderick.
 xSherman, William R.
  The Diplomatic & Commercial Relations of the
   United States & Chile, 1820-1914. Russell.
Shermer, Carl L. *see* Shermer, Carl Louis.
Shermer, Carl Louis, 1910-
 xShermer, Carl L.
  Design in Structural Steel. Krieger.
Shero, Fred.
 xShero, Fred.
  Hockey for the Coach, the Player & the Fan
   3&3.
Sherover, Charles M.
 xSherover, Charles M.
  ed. The Human Experience of Time: The
   Development of Its Philosophic Meaning.
   NYU Pr.
Sherr, Sol.
 xSherr, Sol.
  Electronic Displays. Wiley.
 xSherr, Solomon.
  ed. Fundamentals of Display System Design.
   Wiley.
Sherr, Solomon. *see* Sherr, Sol.
Sherrard, O. A. *see* Sherrard, Owen Aubrey.
Sherrard, Owen A. *see* Sherrard, Owen Aubrey.
Sherrard, Owen Aubrey, 1887-1962
 xSherrard, O. A.
  A Life of John Wilkes. Arno.
 xSherrard, Owen A.
  Freedom from Fear: The Slave & His
   Emancipation. Greenwood.
  A Life of John Wilkes. Arno.
  Life of John Wilkes. R West.
  Lord Chatham: A War Minister in the Making.
   Greenwood.
  Lord Chatham & America. Greenwood.
  Lord Chatham: Pitt & the Seven Years' War.
   Greenwood.
Sherrard, Peter.
 xSherrard, Philip.
  The Wound of Greece: Studies in
   Neo-Hellenism. St Martin.
Sherrard, Philip.
 xSherrard, Philip.
  Byzantium. Silver.
Sherrard, Philip. *see* Sherrard, Peter.
Sherrer, Charles W.
 xSherrer, Charles W.
  Ethical & Professional Standards for Academic
   Psychologists & Counsellors. C C Thomas.
Sherrill, Claudine.
 xSherrill, Claudine.

Adapted Physical Education & Recreation: A
 Multidisciplinary Approach. Wm C Brown.
Creative Arts for the Severely Handicapped. C
 C Thomas.
Sherrill, John. *see* Sherrill, John L.
Sherrill, John L.
 xSherrill, John.
  They Speak with Other Tongues. Revell.
Sherrill, Kenneth S.
 xSherrill, Kenneth S.
  Power, Policy, & Participation: An Introduction
   to American Government. Har-Row.
Sherrill, Lewis J. *see* Sherrill, Lewis Joseph.
Sherrill, Lewis Joseph, 1892-
 xSherrill, Lewis J.
  Struggle of the Soul. Macmillan.
Sherrill, Robert.
 xSherrill, Robert.
  Governing America: An Introduction.
   HarBraceJ.
  Why They Call It Politics: A Guide to
   America's Government. HarBraceJ.
Sherrill, W. A. *see* Sherrill, Wallace A.
Sherrill, Wallace A.
 xSherrill, W. A.
  An Anthology of I Ching. Routledge & Kegan.
Sherrington, C. E. *see* Sherrington, Charles Ely Rose.
Sherrington, Charles E. *see* Sherrington, Charles Ely
 Rose.
Sherrington, Charles Ely Rose, 1897-
 xSherrington, C. E.
  Hundred Years of Inland Transport,
   1830-1933. Biblio Dist.
 xSherrington, Charles E.
  Hundred Years of Inland Transport 1830-1933.
   Kelley.
Sherrod, John.
 xSherrod, John.
  ed. Information Systems & Networks: Eleventh
   Annual Symposium. Greenwood.
  ed. Reader in Science Information. IHS-PDS.
Sherrod, Kathryn.
 xSherrod, Kathryn.
  Infancy. Brooks-Cole.
Sherron, R. H. *see* Sherron, Ronald H.
Sherron, Ronald H.
 xSherron, R. H.
  ed. Introduction to Educational Gerontology.
   Hemisphere Pub.
Sherry, John H. *see* Sherry, John Harold.
Sherry, John Harold.
 xSherry, John H.
  The Laws of Innkeepers: For Hotels, Motels,
   Restaurants & Clubs. Cornell U Pr.
Sherry, Michael S., 1945-
 xSherry, Michael S.
  Preparing for the Next War: American Plans
   for Postwar Defense, 1941-45. Yale U Pr.
Sherry, Norman.
 xSherry, Norman.
  Charlotte & Emily Bronte. Arco.
  Conrad & His World. Scribner.
  ed. Conrad: The Critical Heritage. Routledge &
   Kegan.
  Conrad's Eastern World. Cambridge U Pr.
  Conrad's Western World. Cambridge U Pr.
Sherry, Patrick.
 xSherry, Patrick J.
  Religion, Truth & Language-Games. B&N.
Sherry, Patrick J. *see* Sherry, Patrick.
Shershin, Anthony C. *see* Shershin, Anthony Connors.
Shershin, Anthony Connors.
 xShershin, Anthony C.
  Introduction to Topological Semigroups. Univ
   Microfilms.
Sherson, Erroll. *see* Sherson, Erroll Henry Stuart.
Sherson, Erroll Henry Stuart, 1858-
 xSherson, Erroll.

London's Lost Theatres of the Nineteenth
 Century. Arno.
Shertzer, Bruce.
 xShertzer, Bruce.
  Career Planning: Freedom to Choose. HM.
  Fundamentals of Guidance. HM.
  Fundamentals of Individual Appraisal:
   Assessment Techniques for Counselors. HM.
 xShertzer, Bruce E.
  Fundamentals of Counseling. HM.
  Fundamentals of Guidance. HM.
Shertzer, Bruce E. *see* Shertzer, Bruce.
Sherudi, Edwina.
 xSherudi, Edwina.
  Grandma Strikes Back. Fell.
Shervatov, V. G.
 xShervatov, V. G.
  Hyperbolic Functions. Heath.
Sherwani, H. K. *see* Sherwani, Haroon Khan.
Sherwani, Haroon K. *see* Sherwani, Haroon Khan.
Sherwani, Haroon Khan.
 xSherwani, H. K.
  Studies in Muslim Political Thought &
   Administration. Kazi Pubns.
 xSherwani, Haroon K.
  Studies in Muslim Political Thought &
   Administration. Porcupine Pr.
Sherwen, Douglas S.
 xSherwen, Douglas S.
  The Persian Corridor: The Little-Known Story
   of the Signal Corps in the Middle East
   During World War II. Exposition.
Sherwig, John M., 1923-
 xSherwig, John M.
  Guineas & Gunpowder: British Foreign Aid in
   the Wars with France, 1793-1815. Harvard U
   Pr.
Sherwin, Martin J.
 xSherwin, Martin J.
  A World Destroyed: The Atomic Bomb & the
   Grand Alliance. Knopf.
  A World Destroyed: The Atomic Bomb & the
   Grand Alliance. Random.
Sherwin, Oscar, 1902-
 xSherwin, Oscar.
  Prophet of Liberty: The Life & Times of
   Wendell Phillips. Greenwood.
Sherwin, Paul S., 1946-
 xSherwin, Paul S.
  Precious Bane: Collins & the Miltonic Legacy.
   U of Tex Pr.
Sherwin-White, A. N. *see* Sherwin-White, Adrian
 Nicholas.
Sherwin-White, Adrian N. *see* Sherwin-White, Adrian
 Nicolas.
Sherwin-White, Adrian Nicholas.
 xSherwin-White, A. N.
  Roman Society & Roman Law in the New
   Testament. Baker Bk.
 xSherwin-White, Adrian N.
  Racial Prejudice in Imperial Rome. Cambridge
   U Pr.
Sherwood, Arthur W., 1927-
 xSherwood, Arthur W.
  Understanding the Chesapeake: A Layman's
   Guide. Cornell Maritime.
Sherwood, Gerald E.
 xSherwood, Gerald E.
  How to Select and Renovate an Older House.
   Dover.
  How to Select & Renovate an Older House.
   Peter Smith.
Sherwood, Hugh C.
 xSherwood, Hugh C.

How Corporate & Municipal Debt Is Rated:
An Inside Look at Standard & Poor's Rating
System. Wiley.
How to Invest in Bonds. McGraw.
How to Invest in Bonds. Walker & Co.
Sherwood, John M.
xSherwood, John M.
Georges Mandel & the Third Republic.
Stanford U Pr.
Sherwood, John N. *see* Sherwood, John Neil.
Sherwood, John Neil.
xSherwood, John N.
The Plastically Crystalline State:
Orientationally-Disordered Crystals. Wiley.
Sherwood, Margaret P. *see* Sherwood, Margaret Pollock.
Sherwood, Margaret Pollock, 1864-1955
xSherwood, Margaret P.
Dryden's Dramatic Theory & Practice. Russell.
Princess Pourquoi. Arno.
Undercurrents of Influence in English
Romantic Poetry. AMS Pr.
Undercurrents of Influence in English
Romantic Poetry. Arno.
Sherwood, Mary. *see* Sherwood, Mary Martha Butt.
Sherwood, Mary Martha Butt, 1775-1851
xSherwood, Mary.
The History of the Fairchild Family. Garland
Pub.
Sherwood, Michael.
xSherwood, Michael.
Logic of Explanation in Psychoanalysis. Acad
Pr.
Sherwood, Nancy. *see* Sherwood, Nancy M.
Sherwood, Nancy M.
xSherwood, Nancy.
A Stereotaxic Atlas of the Developing Rat
Brain. U of Cal Pr.
Sherwood, Roy.
xSherwood, Roy.
The Court of Oliver Cromwell. Rowman.
Sherwood, Ruth. *see* Sherwood, Ruth F.
Sherwood, Ruth F.
xSherwood, Ruth.
Homes, Today & Tomorrow. Bennett Co.
Sherwood, T. K. *see* Sherwood, Thomas Kilgore.
Sherwood, Thomas Kilgore.
xSherwood, T. K.
Mass Transfer. McGraw.
Sherwood, Valarie.
xSherwood, Valerie.
This Loving Torment. Warner Bks.
Sherwood, Valerie. *see* Sherwood, Valarie.
Shesgreen, Sean, 1939-
xShesgreen, Sean.
Literary Portraits in the Novels of Henry
Fielding. N Ill U Pr.
Sheskin, Arlene.
xSheskin, Arlene.
Cryonics: A Sociology of Death &
Bereavement. Halsted Pr.
Shestack, Melvin.
xShestack, Melvin.
Country Music Encyclopedia. T Y Crowell.
Shestov, Lev, 1866-1938
xShestov, Lev.
Athens & Jerusalem. Ohio U Pr.
Dostoevsky, Tolstoy & Nietzsche. Ohio U Pr.
In Job's Balances: On the Sources of the
Eternal Truths. Ohio U Pr.
Shetter, Janette.
xShetter, Janette.
Rhythms of the Ecosystem. Pendle Hill.
Shevelov, George Y.
xShevelov, George Y.
ed. Reader in the History of the Eastern Slavic
Languages: Russian, Belorussian, Ukranian.
Columbia U Pr.
Shevelson, Joseph F.
xShevelson, Joseph F.

Roller Skating. Harvey.
Shevin, David, 1951-
xShevin, David.
The Stop Book. Konglomerati.
Shewan, Cynthia M.
xShewan, Cynthia M.
ed. Speech & Language Disorders: Selected
Readings. Har-Row.
Shewan, Rodney.
xShewan, Rodney.
Oscar Wilde: Art & Egotism. B&N.
Shewbridge, Edythe.
xShewbridge, Edythe A.
Portraits of Poverty. Norton.
Shewbridge, Edythe A. *see* Shewbridge, Edythe.
Shewmake, Georgia M.
xShewmake, Georgia M.
Balcony of Evil. Bouregy.
Shewmon, Paul G.
xShewmon, Paul G.
Diffusion in Solids. McGraw.
Shibata, Shingo, 1930-
xShibata, Shingo.
Lessons of the Vietnam War: Philosophical
Considerations on the Vietnam Revolution.
Humanities.
Shibayama, Zenkei, 1894-
xShibayama, Zenkei.
Flower Does Not Talk: Zen Essays. C E
Tuttle.
Shibel, Elaine. *see* Shibel, Elaine M.
Shibel, Elaine M.
xShibel, Elaine.
Respiratory Emergencies. Mosby.
Shibles, Warren. *see* Shibles, Warren A.
Shibles, Warren A.
xShibles, Warren.
Rational Love. Language Pr.
Time: A Critical Analysis for Children.
Language Pr.
Shibley, David.
xShibley, David.
A Charismatic Truce. Nelson.
Shibutani, Tamotsu, 1920-
xShibutani, Tamotsu.
The Derelicts of Company K: A Sociological
Study of Demoralization. U of Cal Pr.
Improvised News: A Sociological Study of
Rumor. Bobbs.
Improvised News: A Sociological Study of
Rumor. Irvington.
Shichor, David.
xShichor, David.
ed. Critical Issues in Juvenile Delinquency.
Lexington Bks.
Shichor, Y. *see* Shichor, Yitzhak.
Shichor, Yitzhak.
xShichor, Y.
The Middle East in China's Foreign Policy:
1949-1977. Cambridge U Pr.
Shick, Tom W.
xShick, Tom W.
Behold the Promised Land: A History of
Afro-American Settler Society in 19th
Century Liberia.. Johns Hopkins.
Shidle, Norman G. *see* Shidle, Norman Glass.
Shidle, Norman Glass, 1895-
xShidle, Norman G.
Art of Successful Communication: Business &
Personal Achievement Through Written
Communication. McGraw.
Shiel, M. P. *see* Shiel, Matthew Phipps.
Shiel, Matthew P. *see* Shiel, Matthew Phipps.
Shiel, Matthew Phipps, 1865-1947
xShiel, M. P.

The Lord of the Sea. Arno.
Prince Zaleski & Cummings King Monk.
Arkham.
The Purple Cloud. Buccaneer Bks.
The Purple Cloud. Gregg.
xShiel, Matthew P.
Prince Zaleski. Arno.
Shields, Frederic. *see* Shields, Frederic James.
Shields, Frederic James.
xShields, Frederic.
Life & Letters of Frederic Shields. AMS Pr.
Shields, J.
xShields, J.
Adhesive Bonding. Oxford U Pr.
Adhesives Handbook. Butterworths.
Shields, James J.
xShields, James J.
The Crisis in Education Is Outside the
Classroom. Phi Delta Kappa.
Shields, John P. *see* Shields, John Potter.
Shields, John Potter.
xShields, John P.
Introduction to Radio Astronomy. Sams.
Shields, Joseph D. *see* Shields, Joseph Dunbar.
Shields, Joseph Dunbar, 1820-1886
xShields, Joseph D.
The Life & Times of Seargent Smith Prentiss.
Arno.
Shields, Mike.
xShields, Mike.
A Taste of Rabbit Tracks: Expedition into a
Frozen Wilderness. Exposition.
Shields, Robert W. *see* Shields, Robert Wylie.
Shields, Robert Wylie, 1919-
xShields, Robert W.
Cure of Delinquents: The Treatment of
Maladjustment. Intl Univs Pr.
Shields, Roger E. *see* Shields, Roger Elwood.
Shields, Roger Elwood.
xShields, Roger E.
Economic Growth with Price Deflation,
1873-1896. Arno.
Shields, Thomas W.
xShields, Thomas W.
Bronchial Carcinoma. C C Thomas.
ed. General Thoracic Surgery. Lea & Febiger.
Shiels, Archibald Williamson, 1878-
xShiels, Archie W.
The Purchase of Alaska. Intl Schol Bk Serv.
Shiels, Archie W. *see* Shiels, Archibald Williamson.
Shiels, Frederick L.
xShiels, Frederick L.
America, Okinawa, & Japan: Case Studies for
Foreign Policy Theory. U Pr of Amer.
Shiels, Tony.
xShiels, Tony.
Entertaining with "ESP". David & Charles.
Entertaining with ESP. Wilshire.
Shiels, William E. *see* Shiels, William Eugene.
Shiels, William Eugene, 1897-
xShiels, William E.
Gonzalo De Tapia, 1561-1594: Founder of the
First Permanent Jesuit Mission in North
America. Greenwood.
Shierman, Gail.
xShierman, Gail.
Total Woman's Fitness Guide. Anderson
World.
Shiffert, Edith. *see* Shiffert, Edith (Marcombe).
Shiffert, Edith (Marcombe).
xShiffert, Edith.
tr. Anthology of Modern Japanese Poetry. C E
Tuttle.
Shiffrin, Nancy.
xShiffrin, Nancy.
Acupressure. Major Bks.
Shifreen, Lawrence J., 1948-
xShifreen, Lawrence J.

Henry Miller: A Bibliography of Secondary
Sources. Scarecrow.
Shiga, Naoya, 1883-1971
xShiga, Naoya.
A Dark Night's Passing. Kodansha.
Shigley, Joseph E. *see* Shigley, Joseph Edward.
Shigley, Joseph Edward.
xShigley, Joseph E.
Applied Mechanics of Materials. McGraw.
Dynamic Analysis of Machines. McGraw.
Mechanical Engineering Design. McGraw.
Mechanical Engineering Design. McGraw.
Shih, Vincent Y. *see* Shih, Vincent Yu-Chung.
Shih, Vincent Yu-Chung, 1902-
xShih, Vincent Y.
The Taiping Ideology: Its Sources,
Interpretations & Influences. U of Wash Pr.
Shillaber, Benjamin P. *see* Shillaber, Benjamin Penhallow.
Shillaber, Benjamin Penhallow, 1814-1890
xShillaber, Benjamin P.
Life & Sayings of Mrs. Partington. Irvington.
Shiller, Jack G.
xShiller, Jack G.
Childhood Injury: A Common Sense Approach.
Stein & Day.
Shilling, C. W. *see* Shilling, Charles Wesley.
Shilling, Charles W. *see* Shilling, Charles Wesley.
Shilling, Charles Wesley.
xShilling, C. W.
An Annotated Bibliography on Diving &
Submarine Medicine. Gordon.
xShilling, Charles W.
Radiation: Use & Control in Industrial
Application. Grune.
ed. The Underwater Handbook: A Guide to
Physiology & Performance for the Engineer.
Plenum Pub.
Shilling, N. A.
xShilling, N A
Doing Business in Saudi Arabia & the Arab
Gulf States. Inter-Crescent.
Shiloh, Ailon.
xShiloh, Ailon.
ed. Ethnic Groups of America; Their
Morbidity, Mortality & Behavior Disorders,
Vol. 2: The Blacks. C C Thomas.
Shils, Edward. *see* Shils, Edward Albert.
Shils, Edward A. *see* Shils, Edward Albert.
Shils, Edward Albert, 1911-
xShils, Edward.
Center & Periphery: Essays in
Macro-Sociology. U of Chicago Pr.
xShils, Edward A.
The Torment of Secrecy: The Background &
Consequences of American Security Policies.
S Ill U Pr.
Shils, Maurice E. *see* Shils, Maurice Edward.
Shils, Maurice Edward.
xShils, Maurice E.
ed. Modern Nutrition in Health & Disease. Lea
& Febiger.
Shilt, Bernard A. *see* Shilt, Bernard Abdil.
Shilt, Bernard Abdil.
xShilt, Bernard A.
Business Principles & Management. SW Pub.
Shimaguchi, Mitsuaki, 1942-
xShimaguchi, Mitsuaki.
Marketing Channels in Japan. Univ Microfilms.
Shimahara, Mobuo. *see* Shimahara, Nobuo.
Shimahara, Nobuo.
xShimahara, Mobuo.
Adaptation & Education in Japan. Praeger.
Shiman, D. A. *see* Shiman, David A.
Shiman, David A.
xShiman, D. A.
Teachers on Individualization: The Way We
Do It. McGraw.
Shimanoff, Susan B.
xShimanoff, Susan B.

Communication Rules: Theory & Research.
Sage.
Shimazaki, Toson, 1872-1943
xShimazaki, Toson.
The Family. Intl Schol Bk Serv.
Shimazaki, Toson. *see* Shimazaki, Toson. '
Shimberg, Elaine F. *see* Shimberg, Elaine Fantle.
Shimberg, Elaine Fantle, 1937-
xShimberg, Elaine F.
How to Be a Successful Housewife-Writer.
Writers Digest.
Shimek, William J.
xShimek, William J.
The Celsius Thermometer. Lerner Pubns.
The Gram. Lerner Pubns.
The Liter. Lerner Pubns.
Shimer. *see* Shimer, Genevieve.
Shimer, Genevieve.
xShimer.
Drawing Children. G&D.
Shimer, John A.
xShimer, John A.
This Sculptured Earth: The Landscape of
America. Columbia U Pr.
Shimin, Symeon, 1902-
xShimin, Symeon.
illus. I Wish There Were Two of Me. Warne.
A Special Birthday. McGraw.
Shimkin, Demitri Boris.
xShimkin, Demitri.
Extended Family in Black Societies. Beresford
Bk Serv.
Shimkin, Demitri. *see* Shimkin, Demitri Boris.
Shimoda, K. *see* Shimoda, K Oichi.
Shimoda, Koichi.
xShimoda, K.
ed. High-Resolution Laser Spectroscopy.
Springer-Verlag.
Shin, Kilman.
xShin, Kilman.
Death Penalty & Crime: Empirical Studies. Ctr
Econ Analysis.
Inflation, Stock Price, & Housing Cost:
Empirical Studies. Ctr Econ Analysis.
Shinagel, Michael.
xShinagel, Michael.
ed. A Concordance to the Poems of Jonathan
Swift. Cornell U Pr.
Shinar, David.
xShinar, David.
Psychology on the Road: The Human Factor in
Traffic Safety. Wiley.
Shinbrot, M. *see* Shinbrot, Marvin.
Shinbrot, Marvin.
xShinbrot, M.
Lectures on Fluid Mechanics. Gordon.
Shine, Frances.
xShine, Frances L.
Johnny Noon. Dodd.
Shine, Frances L. *see* Shine, Frances.
Shine, Hill.
xShine, Hill.
Booker Memorial Studies: Eight Essays on
Victorian Literature in Memory of John
Manning Booker, 1881-1948. Folcroft.
Booker Memorial Studies: Eight Essays on
Victorian Literature in Memory of John
Manning Booker, 1881-1948. Russell.
Carlyle's Fusion of Poetry, History & Religion
by 1834. Kennikat.
Shine, Ian.
xShine, Ian B.
Thomas Hunt Morgan: Pioneer of Genetics. U
Pr of Ky.
Shine, Ian B. *see* Shine, Ian.
Shineberg, D. *see* Shineberg, Dorothy Lois.
Shineberg, Dorothy Lois.
xShineberg, D.

They Came for Sandalwood: A Study of the
Sandalwood Trade in the South-West Pacific,
1830-1865. Intl Schol Bk Serv.
Shinebourne, Elliot A.
xShinebourne, Elliot A.
Current Paediatric Cardiology. Oxford U Pr.
Shingle, Frank.
xShingle, Frank.
Room with No Number: A Novel. Exposition.
Shingleton, John D.
xShingleton, John D.
Trout, the Whole Trout, & Nothing but the
Trout: Solemnly Sworn Testimony on
America's No. 1 Gamefish & How to Hook
Him. Winchester Pr.
Shinn, C. H. *see* Shinn, Charles Howard.
Shinn, Charles H. *see* Shinn, Charles Howard.
Shinn, Charles Howard, 1852-1924
xShinn, C. H.
Cooperation on the Pacific Coast. Johnson
Repr.
xShinn, Charles H.
Cooperation on the Pacific Coast. AMS Pr.
Shinn, Glen C.
xShinn, Glen C.
Working in Agricultural Mechanics. McGraw.
Shinn, Larry D., 1942-
xShinn, Larry D.
Two Sacred Worlds: Experience & Structure in
the World's Religions. Abingdon.
Shinners, Stanley M.
xShinners, Stanley M.
A Guide to Systems Engineering &
Management. Lexington Bks.
Modern Control, System Theory &
Application. A-W.
Shinnie, Margaret
xShinnie, Margaret.
Ancient African Kingdoms. NAL.
Shinnie, P. L.
xShinnie, P. L.
African Iron Age. Oxford U Pr.
Shinoda. *see* Shinoda, Kozo.
Shinoda, Kozo, 1926-
xShinoda.
ed. Principles of Solution & Solubility. Dekker.
Shinskey, F. Greg.
xShinskey, F. Greg.
Distillation Control: For Productivity & Energy
Conservation. McGraw.
Shintri, Sarojini.
xShintri, Sarojini.
Woman in Shakespeare. Folcroft.
Shipes, Ellen A.
xShipes, Ellen A.
Sexual Counseling for Ostomates: A Resource
Book for Health Care Professionals. C C
Thomas.
Shipherd, Jacob R.
xShipherd, Jacob R.
History of the Oberlin-Wellington Rescue. Da
Capo.
History of the Oberlin-Wellington Rescue.
Negro U Pr.
Shiplett, June. *see* Shiplett, June Lund.
Shiplett, June Lund.
xShiplett, June.
The Raging Winds of Heaven. NAL.
Shiplett, Paul D.
xShiplett, Paul D.
Bags of Bones. Broken Whisker.
Shipley, Gertrude T. *see* Shipley, Gertrude Tyson.
Shipley, Gertrude Tyson, 1888-
xShipley, Gertrude T.
Evaluation of Guided Study & Small-Group
Discussion in a Normal School. AMS Pr.
Shipley, Joseph T. *see* Shipley, Joseph Twadell.
Shipley, Joseph Twadell, 1893-
xShipley, Joseph T.

Art of Eugene O'Neill. Folcroft.
Dictionary of Early English. Littlefield.
Dictionary of Word Origins. Greenwood.
Dictionary of Word Origins. Littlefield.
Guide to Great Plays. Pub Aff Pr.
Literary Isms. Folcroft.
ed. Modern French Poetry: An Anthology.
Arno.

Shipley, Peter.
xShipley, Peter.
Revolutionaries in Modern Britain. Merrimack
Bk Serv.
Revolutionaries in Modern Britain.
Transatlantic.

Shipley, R. Bruce. *see* Shipley, Randall Bruce.

Shipley, Randall Bruce, 1913-
xShipley, R. Bruce.
Introduction to Matrices & Power Systems.
Wiley.

Shipley, Thorne.
xShipley, Thorne.
Sensory Integration in Children: Evoked
Potentials & Intersensory Functions in
Pediatrics & Psychology. C C Thomas.

Shipman, Carl.
xShipman, Carl.
How to Select & Use Nikon & Nikkormat SLR
Cameras. H P Bks.
Understanding Photography. H P Bks.

Shipman, George A. *see* Shipman, George Anderson.

Shipman, George Anderson, 1903-
xShipman, George A.
Designing Program Action - Against Urban
Poverty. U of Ala Pr.

Shipman, Harry L.
xShipman, Harry L.
The Restless Universe: An Introduction to
Astronomy. HM.

Shipman, Helen.
xShipman, Helen.
Any Teacher Can: A Systematic Approach to
Behavior Management & Positive Teaching.
Loyola.

Shipman, Homer D. *see* Shipman, Homer David.

Shipman, Homer David.
xShipman, Homer D.
Historical Models & the Anticipation of the
Future. Inst Econ Pol.

Shipman, James T.
xShipman, James T.
An Introduction to Physical Science. Heath.

Shipman, Louis E. *see* Shipman, Louis Evan.

Shipman, Louis Evan, 1869-1933
xShipman, Louis E.
Predicaments. Arno.

Shipman, M. D.
xShipman, M. D.
Sociology of the School. Humanities.

Shipman, Natalie.
xShipman, Natalie.
Once Upon a Summer. Assoc Bk.

Shipman, William D.
xShipman, William D.
An Inquiry into the High Cost of Electricity in
New England. Columbia U Pr.

Shipp, Albert M. *see* Shipp, Albert Micajah.

Shipp, Albert Micajah, 1819-1887
xShipp, Albert M.
The History of Methodism in South Carolina.
Reprint.

Shipp, Nelson. *see* Shipp, Nelson Mclester.

Shipp, Nelson McLester, 1892-
xShipp, Nelson.
A Vagabond Newsman. Cherokee.

Shipp, Ralph D.
xShipp, Ralph D.
Practical Selling. HM.

Shipp, Ralph D. *see* Shipp, Ralph Danforth.

Shipp, Ralph Danforth, 1925-
xShipp, Ralph D.

Retail Merchandising: Principles &
Applications. HM.

Shippen, J. M. *see* Shippen, John Matthew.

Shippen, John Matthew.
xShippen, J. M.
Basic Farm Machinery. Pergamon.

Shippey, T. A.
xShippey, T. A.
Beowulf. Charles River Bks.
Old English Verse. Humanities.

Shipps, Fred C.
xShipps, Fred C.
Anatomical Exercises in Computerized
Tomography Body Scanning. C C Thomas.

Shipton, Clifford K. *see* Shipton, Clifford Kenyon.

Shipton, Clifford Kenyon.
xShipton, Clifford K.
ed. National Index of American Imprints
Through 1800: The Short-Title Evans. Am
Antiquarian.

Shipway, George, 1908-
xShipway, George.
Free Lance. HarBraceJ.
The Paladin. HarBraceJ.

Shipway, V. C. *see* Shipway, Verna (Cook).

Shipway, Verna (Cook).
xShipway, V. C.
Decorative Design in Mexican Homes.
Hastings.
xShipway, Verna C.
Decorative Design in Mexican Homes.
Architectural.
Houses of Mexico: Origins & Traditions.
Architectural.
Houses of Mexico: Origins & Traditions.
Hastings.

Shipway, Verna C. *see* Shipway, Verna (Cook).

Shirakawa, Yoshikazu, 1935-
xShirakawa, Yoshikazu.
photos by The Himalayas. Abrams.

Shircliffe, Arnold, 1880-1952
xShircliffe, Arnold.
The Edgewater Sandwich & Hors D'oeuvres
Book. Dover.

Shire, Ellen.
xShire, Ellen.
illus. Adventures of Miss Bigley & Her Little
Store. Walker & Co.

Shire, Helena. *see* Shire, Helena Mennie.

Shire, Helena Mennie.
xShire, Helena.
A Preface to Spenser. Longman.

Shire, J. G. M.
xShire, John G.
Genetic Variation in Hormone Systems. CRC
Pr.

Shire, John G. *see* Shire, J. G. M.

Shirer, William. *see* Shirer, William Lawrence.

Shirer, William L. *see* Shirer, William Lawrence.

Shirer, William Lawrence, 1904-
xShirer, William.
Collapse of the Third Republic: An Inquiry
into the Fall of France in 1940. S&S.
xShirer, William L.
The Berlin Diary: The Journal of a Foreign
Correspondent, 1934-1941. Penguin.
The Challenge of Scandinavia: Norway,
Sweden, Denmark, & Finland in Our Time.
Greenwood.

Shires, David B.
xShires, David B.
Computer Technology in the Health Sciences.
C C Thomas.
Family Medicine: A Guidebook for
Practitioners of the Art. McGraw.

Shires, G. Thomas. *see* Shires, George Thomas.

Shires, George Thomas, 1925-
xShires, G. Thomas.

ed. Care of the Trauma Patient. McGraw.

Shires, H. Bess.
xShires, H. Bess.
Adventures in Pennsylvania. Penns Valley.

Shirk, George H.
xShirk, George H.
Oklahoma Place Names. U of Okla Pr.

Shirley. *see* Shirley, Isabel M.

Shirley, Frances A. *see* Shirley, Frances Ann.

Shirley, Frances Ann.
xShirley, Frances A.
Swearing & Perjury in Shakespeare's Plays.
Allen Unwin.

Shirley, Glenn.
xShirley, Glenn.
Last of the Real Badmen: Henry Starr. U of
Nebr Pr.
Law West of Fort Smith: A History of Frontier
Justice in the Indian Territory, 1834-1896. U
of Nebr Pr.
Pawnee Bill: A Biography of Major Gordon W.
Lillie. U of Nebr Pr.
Temple Houston: Lawyer with a Gun. U of
Okla Pr.

Shirley, Hale F. *see* Shirley, Hale Foreman.

Shirley, Hale Foreman, M.d, 1901-
xShirley, Hale F.
Pediatric Psychiatry. Harvard U Pr.

Shirley, Hardy L. *see* Shirley, Hardy Lomax.

Shirley, Hardy Lomax, 1900-
xShirley, Hardy L.
Forestry & Its Career Opportunities. McGraw.

Shirley, Isabel M.
xShirley.
A User's Guide to Diagnostic Ultrasound. Univ
Park.

Shirley, John, 1890-1967
xShirley, John.
Richard Hooker & Contemporary Political
Ideas. Hyperion Conn.

Shirley, John. M. *see* Shirley, John Major.

Shirley, John Major, 1831-1887
xShirley, John. M.
Dartmouth College Causes & the Supreme
Court of the United States. Da Capo.

Shirley, Thelma H.
xShirley, Thelma H.
Success Guide to Exciting Fashion Shows.
Fashion Imprints.

Shirreffs, Gordon D.
xShirreffs, Gordon D.
Arizona Justice. Belmont-Tower.
The Brave Rifles. Nordon Pubns.
Enemy Seas. Westminster.
Last Man Alive. Belmont Tower.
Legend of the Damned. Fawcett.
The Proud Gun. Belmont-Tower.

Shirts, Morris A.
xShirts, Morris A.
Call It Right!: Umpiring in the Little League.
Sterling.

Shishkin, J. K.
xShishkin, J. K.
The Palace of the Governors. Museum NM Pr.

Shissler, Barbara. *see* Shissler, Barbara Johnson.

Shissler, Barbara Johnson.
xShissler, Barbara.
Worker in Art. Lerner Pubns.

Shively, W. *see* Shively, W. Phillips.

Shively, W. Phillips, 1942-
xShively, W.
Craft of Political Research: A Primer. P-H.
xShively, W. Phillips.
The Craft of Political Research. P-H.

Shivers, Alfred S.
xShivers, Alfred S.
Maxwell Anderson. Twayne.

Shivers, Jay S. *see* Shivers, Jay Sanford.

Shivers, Jay Sanford, 1930-
xShivers, Jay S.

Essentials of Recreational Services. Lea &
Febiger.
Planning Recreational Places. Fairleigh
Dickinson.
Recreational Service for the Aging. Lea &
Febiger.
Therapeutic & Adapted Recreational Services.
Lea & Febiger.

Shivji, I. G.
xShivji, Issa G.
Class Struggles in Tanzania. Monthly Rev.
Shivji, Issa G. see Shivji, I. G.
Shklar, G. see Shklar, Gerald.
Shklar, Gerald.
xShklar, G.
Oral Manifestations of Systemic Disease.
Butterworths.
Shlaim, A. see Shlaim, Avi.
Shlaim, Avi.
xShlaim, A.
The EEC & Eastern Europe. Cambridge U Pr.
ed. The EEC & the Mediterranean Countries.
Cambridge U Pr.
Shlakman, Vera, 1909-
xShlakman, Vera.
Economic History of a Factory Town: A Study
of Chicopee, Massachusetts. Octagon.
Shloss, Carol.
xShloss, Carol.
Flannery O'Connor's Dark Comedies: The
Limits of Inference. La State U Pr.
Shneidman, Edwin S.
xShneidman, Edwin S.
ed. Death: Current Perspectives. Aronson.
ed. Death: Current Perspectives. Mayfield Pub.
The Deaths of Man. Times Bks.
Psychology of Suicide. Aronson.
ed. Suicidology: Contemporary Developments.
Grune
ed. Thematic Test Analysis. Grune.
Voices of Death. Har-Row.
Shnider, Sol M.
xShnider, Sol M.
Anesthesia for Obstetrics. Williams & Wilkins.
ed. Obstetrical Anesthesia: Current Concepts &
Practice. Krieger.
Shock, Nathan W. see Shock, Nathan Wetheril.
Shock, Nathan Wetheril.
xShock, Nathan W.
Classified Bibliography of Gerontology &
Geriatrics. Kraus Repr.
Shockley, Ann A. see Shockley, Ann Allen.
Shockley, Ann Allen.
xShockley, Ann A.
ed. Living Black American Authors: A
Biographical Directory. Bowker.
Shockley, John S. see Shockley, John Staples.
Shockley, John Staples, 1944-
xShockley, John S.
Chicano Revolt in a Texas Town. U of Notre
Dame Pr.
Shockley, Martin.
xShockley, Martin S.
The Richmond Stage, 1784-1812. U Pr of Va.
Shockley, Martin S. see Shockley, Martin.
Shockley, Norman.
xShockley, Normman.
Back from the Edge. Upper Room.
Shockley, Normman. see Shockley, Norman.
Shoden, Rebecca. see Shoden, Rebecca J.
Shoden, Rebecca J.
xShoden, Rebecca.
Fundamentals of Clinical Nutrition. McGraw.
Shoebridge, Marjorie.
xShoebridge, Marjorie.
Ranleigh Court. Doubleday.
Shoemaker, Charles C. see Shoemaker, Charles Chalmers.
Shoemaker, Charles Chalmers, 1860-
xShoemaker, Charles C.

Compiled by Humorous Dialogues & Dramas:
A Collection of the Rarest, Brightest, Most
Mirth Producing Dialogues Ever Published.
Arno.
Shoemaker, David. see Shoemaker, David P.
Shoemaker, David M., 1940-
xShoemaker, David M.
Principles & Procedures of Multiple Matrix
Sampling. Ballinger Pub.
Shoemaker, David P.
xShoemaker, David.
Experiments in Physical Chemistry. McGraw.
Shoemaker, Helen. see Shoemaker, Helen Smith.
Shoemaker, Helen S. see Shoemaker, Helen Smith.
Shoemaker, Helen Smith.
xShoemaker, Helen.
Prayer & Evangelism. Word Bks.
xShoemaker, Helen S.
The Exploding Mystery of Prayer. Seabury.
Shoemaker, Kathryn. see Shoemaker, Kathryn E.
Shoemaker, Kathryn E.
xShoemaker, Kathryn.
Creative Christmas: Simple Crafts from Many
Lands. Winston Pr.
Shoemaker, Lynn.
xShoemaker, Lynn.
Curses & Blessings. SBD.
Shoemaker, Richard W. see Shoemaker, Richard Warren.
Shoemaker, Richard Warren, 1918-
xShoemaker, Richard W.
Perfect Numbers. NCTM.
Shoemaker, William C.
xShoemaker, William C.
Fluid-Electrolyte Therapy in Acute Illness.
Year Bk Med.
Shoemaker, William H. see Shoemaker, William
Hutchinson.
Shoemaker, William Hutchinson, 1902-
xShoemaker, William H.
The Multiple Stage in Spain During the
Fifteenth & Sixteenth Centuries. Greenwood.
Shoenfelt, Joseph F.
xShoenfelt, Joseph F.
Designing & Making Handwrought Jewelry.
McGraw.
Shogan, Robert.
xShogan, Robert.
Promises to Keep: Carter's First 100 Days. T
Y Crowell.
Shohat, J. A. see Shohat, James Alexander.
Shohat, James Alexander.
xShohat, J. A.
Problem of Moments. Am Math.
Shohet, J. L. see Shohet, Juda Leon.
Shohet, Juda Leon, 1937-
xShohet, J. L.
Plasma State. Acad Pr.
Sholevar , G. Pirooz. see Sholevar, G. Pirooz.
Sholevar, G. Pirooz.
xSholevar , G. Pirooz.
Changing Sexual Values & the Family. C C
Thomas.
xSholevar, Pirooz.
ed. Treatment of Emotional Disorders in
Children & Adolescents. Spectrum Pub.
Sholevar, Pirooz. see Sholevar, G. Pirooz.
Sholinsky, Jane.
xSholinsky, Jane.
The Challenge of Skiing. Watts.
Peanut Parade. Messner.
Sholl, Betsy.
xSholl, Betsy.
Appalachian Winter. Alicejamesbooks.
Changing Faces. Alicejamesbooks.
Sholl, Donald A. see Sholl, Donald Arthur.
Sholl, Donald Arthur.
xSholl, Donald A.
Organization of the Cerebral Cortex. Hafner.
Sholto-Douglas, Nora I.
xSholto-Douglas, Nora I.

Synopses of English Fiction. Folcroft.
Shomon, Joseph James, 1914-
xShomon, Joseph James.
Open Land for Urban America: Acquisition,
Safekeeping, & Use. Johns Hopkins.
Shone, Richard.
xShone, Richard.
The Post-Impressionists. Mayflower Bks.
Shonfield, Andrew.
xShonfield, Andrew.
Modern Capitalism: The Changing Balance of
Public & Private Power. Oxford U Pr.
Shonle, John I.
xShonle, John I.
Environmental Applications of General
Physics. A-W.
Shonnard, Frederic.
xShonnard, Frederic.
History of Westchester County, New York,
from Its Earliest Settlement to the Year
1900. Harbor Hill Bks.
Shontz, F. C. see Shontz, Franklin C.
Shontz, Franklin C.
xShontz, F. C.
Perceptual & Cognitive Aspects of Body
Experience. Acad Pr.
xShontz, Franklin C.
The Psychological Aspects of Physical Illness &
Disability. Macmillan.
Shook, L. K. see Shook, Laurence K.
Shook, Laurence K.
xShook, L. K.
Catholic Post-Secondary Education in
English-Speaking Canada: A History. U of
Toronto Pr.
Shook, Robert. see Shook, Robert L.
Shook, Robert L., 1938-
xShook, Robert.
Total Commitment. Fell.
xShook, Robert L.
The Entrepreneurs: Twelve Who Took Risks &
Succeeded. Har-Row.
Winning Images. Macmillan.
Winning Images. PB.
Shooman, Martin L.
xShooman, Martin L.
Probabilistic Reliability: An Engineering
Approach. McGraw.
Shopen, Timothy.
xShopen, Timothy.
Languages & Their Speakers. Winthrop.
Languages & Their Status. Winthrop.
Shopland, A. J.
xShopland, A. J.
Refer to Occupational Therapy. Churchill.
Shoppee, Charles W., 1904-
xShoppee, Charles W.
ed. Excited States of Matter. Tex Tech Pr.
Shopsin, Baron.
xShopsin, Baron.
ed. Manic Illness. Raven.
Shor, Elizabeth N. see Shor, Elizabeth Noble.
Shor, Elizabeth Noble.
xShor, Elizabeth N.
Dinner in the Morning: A Collection of
Breakfast & Brunch Recipes. Rand-Tofua.
Fossils & Flies: The Life of a Compleat
Scientist, Samuel Wendell Williston
1851-1918. U of Okla Pr.
Scripps Institution of Oceanography: Probing
the Oceans, 1936-1976. Rand-Tofua.
Shore, Anne.
xShore, Anne.
Whispers of the Heart. Dell.
Shore, Barry.
xShore, Barry.
Operations Management. McGraw.
Shore, Bernard, 1896-
xShore, Bernard.

Orchestra Speaks. Arno.
Sixteen Symphonies. Hyperion Conn.
Shore, Dinah, 1920-
xShore, Dinah.
Someone's in the Kitchen with Dinah.
Doubleday.
Shore, Jane, 1947-
xShore, Jane.
Eye Level. U of Mass Pr.
Shore, William I.
xShore, William I.
Fact-Finding in the Maintenance of
International Peace. Oceana.
Shore, William T. see Shore, William Teignmouth.
Shore, William Teignmouth, 1865-1932
xShore, William T.
Charles Dickens. Norwood Edns.
Shore, Wilma.
xShore, Wilma.
Who in the Zoo?. Lippincott.
Shores, David L.
xShores, David L.
ed. Papers in Language Variation: Samla-Ads
Collection. U of Ala Pr.
Shores, Louis, 1904-
xShores, Louis.
Library Education. Libs Unl.
Mark Hopkins' Log & Other Essays. Shoe
String.
Reference As the Promotion of Free Inquiry.
Libs Unl.
Shorey, H. H. see Shorey, Harry H.
Shorey, Harry H.
xShorey, H. H.
Animal Communication by Pheromones. Acad
Pr.
Chemical Control of Insect Behavior: Theory &
Application. Wiley.
Shorr, Joseph E.
xShorr, Joseph E.
Psycho-Imagination Therapy. Thieme-Stratton.
Psychotherapy Through Imagery.
Thieme-Stratton.
Shorrock, William I., 1941-
xShorrock, William I.
French Imperialism in the Middle East: The
Failure of Policy in Syria & Lebanon,
1900-1914. U of Wis Pr.
Short, Andrew.
xShort, Andrew.
Lightweight Concrete. Intl Ideas.
Short, Anthony.
xShort, Anthony.
The Communist Insurrection in Malaya
1948-1960. Crane-Russak Co.
Short, Ernest. see Short, Ernest Henry.
Short, Ernest Henry, 1875-1959
xShort, Ernest.
Fifty Years of Vaudeville. Greenwood.
Theatrical Cavalcade. Kennikat.
Theatrical Cavalcade. R West.
Short Hills Garden Club.
xShort Hills Garden Club.
Down to Earth Gardening. Scribner.
Short, J. R. see Short, John R.
Short, James F.
xShort, James F.
ed. Collective Violence. Am Acad Pol Soc Sci.
Short, James F. see Short, James F. Jr.
Short, James F., Jr.
xShort, James F.
Group Process & Gang Delinquency. U of
Chicago Pr.
Short, John R.
xShort, J. R.
Urban Data Sources. Butterworths.
Short, K. see Short, Kenneth L.
Short, Kenneth. see Short, Kenneth R. M.
Short, Kenneth L.
xShort, K.

Microprocessors & Programmed Logic. P-H.
Short, Kenneth R. M.
xShort, Kenneth.
The Dynamite War: Irish-American Bombers in
Victorian Britain. Humanities.
Short, Lloyd M. see Short, Lloyd Milton.
Short, Lloyd Milton, 1897-
xShort, Lloyd M.
The Bureau of Navigation: Its History,
Activities & Organization. AMS Pr.
Steamboat-Inspection Service: Its History,
Activities & Organization. AMS Pr.
Short, Luke.
xShort, Luke.
Brand of Empire. Dell.
The Some-Day Country. Bantam.
Short, Michael.
xShort, Michael.
Gustav Holst,1874-1934: A Centenary
Documentation. Rowman.
Short, Nicholas M.
xShort, Nicholas M.
Planetary Geology. P-H.
Short, Philip.
xShort, Philip.
Banda. Routledge & Kegan.
Short, Robert L.
xShort, Robert L.
The Parables of Peanuts. Fawcett.
Parables of Peanuts. Har-Row.
Short, Roy H. see Short, Roy Hunter.
Short, Roy Hunter, Bp, 1902-
xShort, Roy H.
Methodism in Kentucky. Academy Bks.
Short, Vaughn.
xShort, Vaughn T.
Raging River - Lonely Trail: Tales Told by the
Campfires Glow. Two Horses.
Short, Vaughn T. see Short, Vaughn.
Short, William A. see Short, William Harrison.
Short, William Harrison, 1868-1935
xShort, William A.
A Generation of Motion Pictures. Garland Pub.
Shortall, Leonard. see Shortall, Leonard W.
Shortall, Leonard W.
xShortall, Leonard.
A Little Toad to the Rescue. Western Pub.
Shorter, Aylward.
xShorter, Aylward.
African Christian Spirituality. Orbis Bks.
African Christian Theology: Adaptation or
Incarnation?. Orbis Bks.
East African Societies. Routledge & Kegan.
Prayer in the Religious Traditions of Africa.
Oxford U Pr.
Shorter, Clement K. see Shorter, Clement King.
Shorter, Clement King, 1857-1926
xShorter, Clement K.
Charlotte Bronte & Her Circle. Gale.
Charlotte Bronte & Her Circle. Greenwood.
Charlotte Bronte & Her Circle. R West.
Shorter, E. see Shorter, Edward.
Shorter, Edward.
xShorter, E.
Strikes in France, 1930-1968. Cambridge U Pr.
xShorter, Edward.
The Historian & the Computer: A Practical
Guide. Norton.
Shortney, Joan R. see Shortney, Joan Ranson.
Shortney, Joan Ranson.
xShortney, Joan R.
How to Live on Nothing. PB.
Shortridge, Lillie.
xShortridge, Lillie M.
Introduction to Nursing Practice. McGraw.
Shortridge, Lillie M. see Shortridge, Lillie.
Shostak, Arthur B.
xShostak, Arthur B.

Blue Collar Stress. A-W.
Our Sociological Eye: Personal Essays on
Society & Culture. Alfred Pub.
Privilege in America: An End to Inequality?.
P-H.
Shostakovich, Dmitri. see Shostakovich, Dmitrii
Dmitrievich.
Shostakovich, Dmitrii Dmitrievich.
xShostakovich, Dmitri.
Testimony: The Memoirs of Dmitri
Shostakovich. Har-Row.
Shostakovskii, M. F. see Shostakovskii, Mikhail
Fedorovich.
Shostakovskii, Mikhail Fedorovich.
xShostakovskii, M. F.
The Chemistry of Diacetylenes. Halsted Pr.
Shosteck, Patti.
xShosteck, Patti.
A Lexicon of Jewish Cooking. Contemp Bks.
Shosteck, Robert, 1910-
xShosteck, Robert.
Camper's Park Guide: Where to Camp, What
to Do in 888 Parks, Forests & Other
Recreation Areas from Maine to Florida.
EPM Pubns.
Shostrom, Everett L.
xShostrom, Everett L.
Actualizing Therapy: Foundations for a
Scientific Ethic. EDITS Pubs.
Shotwell, B. M.
xShotwell, Berenice M.
Getting Better Acquainted with Your Bible.
Shadwold.
Shotwell, Berenice M. see Shotwell, B. M.
Shotwell, James T. see Shotwell, James Thomson.
Shotwell, James Thomson.
xShotwell, James T.
Lessons on Security & Disarmament from the
History of the League of Nations.
Greenwood.
On the Rim of the Abyss. Garland Pub.
The Story of Ancient History. Columbia U Pr.
Turkey at the Straits: A Short History. Arno.
Shouksmith, George.
xShouksmith, George.
Assessment Through Interviewing. Pergamon.
Shouldice, Robert G.
xShouldice, Robert G.
Medical Group Practice & Health Maintenance
Organizations. Info Resources.
Shoumatoff, Alex.
xShoumatoff, Alex.
Florida Ramble. Har-Row.
Shoup, Barbara J.
xShoup, Barbara J.
Living & Learning for Credit. Phi Delta Kappa.
Shoup, Carl S. see Shoup, Carl Sumner.
Shoup, Carl Summner, 1902-
xShoup, Carl S.
Federal Estate & Gift Taxes. Greenwood.
Shoup, Carl Sumner.
xShoup, Carl S.
ed. Fiscal Harmonization in Common Markets.
Columbia U Pr.
Shoup, Donald C.
xShoup, Donald C.
Program Budgeting for Urban Police Services:
With Special Reference to Los Angeles.
Irvington.
Shoup, Laurence H.
xShoup, Laurence H.
Imperial Brain Trust: The Council on Foreign
Relations & the United States Foreign Policy.
Monthly Rev.
Shoup, Paul.
xShoup, Paul.
Communism & the Yugoslav National
Question. Columbia U Pr.
Shoup, T. see Shoup, Terry E.

Shoup, Terry E., 1944-
xShoup, T.
Practical Guide to Computer Methods for Engineers. P-H.
Shourds, Thomas.
xShourds, Thomas.
History & Genealogy of Fenwick's Colony. Genealog Pub.
Shout, Howard F. see Shout, Howard Franklin.
Shout, Howard Franklin.
xShout, Howard F.
Start Supervising. BNA.
Shover, John L.
xShover, John L.
Cornbelt Rebellion: The Farmers' Holiday Association. U of Ill Pr.
First Majority - Last Minority: The Transforming of Rural Life in America. N Ill U Pr.
Shover, Neal.
xShover, Neal.
A Sociology of American Corrections. Dorsey.
Showalter, Dennis E.
xShowalter, Dennis E.
Railroads & Rifles: Soldiers, Technology & Unification of Germany. Shoe String.
Showalter, Elaine.
xShowalter, Elaine.
ed. These Modern Women: Autobiographies of Women in the Twenties. Feminist Pr.
Women's Liberation & Literature. HarBraceJ.
Showalter, English.
xShowalter, English.
The Evolution of the French Novel, 1641-1782. Princeton U Pr.
Showalter, Grace I.
xShowalter, Grace I.
The Music Books of Ruebush & Kieffer, 1866-1942: A Bibliography. U Pr of Va.
Showalter, Mary E. see Showalter, Mary Emma.
Showalter, Mary Emma, 1913-
xShowalter, Mary E.
Mennonite Community Cookbook: Favorite Family Recipes. Herald Pr.
Showell, Ellen H. see Showell, Ellen Harvey.
Showell, Ellen Harvey.
xShowell, Ellen H.
The Ghost of Tillie Jean Cassaway. Schol Bk Serv.
Showerman, Grant, 1870-1935
xShowerman, Grant.
The Great Mother of the Gods. Gordon Pr.
Horace & His Influence. Cooper Sq.
Showers, Norman. see Showers, Norman E.
Showers, Norman E.
xShowers, Norman.
Bowling. Goodyear.
xShowers, Norman E.
Bowling. Goodyear.
Showers, Paul.
xShowers, Paul.
Baby Starts to Grow. T Y Crowell.
Follow Your Nose. T Y Crowell.
How You Talk. T Y Crowell.
How You Talk. T Y Crowell.
Indian Festivals. T Y Crowell.
Listening Walk. T Y Crowell.
Me & My Family Tree. T Y Crowell.
The Moon Walker. Doubleday.
Use Your Brain. T Y Crowell.
Where Does the Garbage Go?. T Y Crowell.
Showers, Victor, 1910-
xShowers, Victor.
World Facts & Figures: A Unique, Authoritative Collection of Comparative Information About Cities, Countries, & Geographic Features of the World. Wiley.
Showler, Brian.
xShowler, Brian.

The Public Employment Service. Longman.
Shows, Charles, 1912-
xShows, Charles.
Walt: Backstage Adventures with Walt Disney. Comm Creat.
Walt: Backstage Adventures with Walt Disney. Windsong.
Shrader, Robert L.
xShrader, Robert L.
Electronic Communication. McGraw.
Electronic Communication. McGraw.
Practice Tests for Radiotelephone Licenses. McGraw.
Shrader, Stephen.
xShrader, Stephen.
Leaving by the Closet Door. SBD.
Shreffler, Philip A.
xShreffler, Philip A.
The H. P. Lovecraft Companion. Greenwood.
Shreve, R. Norris. see Shreve, Randolph Norris.
Shreve, Randolph Norris.
xShreve, R. Norris.
Chemical Process Industries. McGraw.
Shreve, Susan.
xShreve, Susan.
The Nightmares of Geranium Street. Avon.
The Nightmares of Geranium Street. Knopf.
Shreve, Susan R. see Shreve, Susan Richards.
Shreve, Susan Richards.
xShreve, Susan R.
Children of Power. Berkley Pub.
Children of Power. Macmillan.
Shri Ram Centre for Industrial Relations and Human Resources.
xShri Ram Centre for Industrial Relations, New Delhi.
Human Problems of Shift Work. Intl Pubns Serv.
Shriberg, Linda K.
xShriberg, Linda K.
Kids in the Kitchen. Wanderer Bks.
Shrimali, K. L. see Shrimali, Kalulal.
Shrimali, Kalulal, 1909-
xShrimali, K. L.
Prospects for Democracy in India. S Ill U Pr.
Shriner, Ralph. see Shriner, Ralph Lloyd.
Shriner, Ralph Lloyd, 1899-
xShriner, Ralph.
The Systematic Identification of Organic Compounds: A Laboratory Manual. Wiley.
Shriver, Donald W.
xShriver, Donald W.
ed. Medicine & Religion: Strategies of Care. U of Pittsburgh Pr.
Rich Man Poor Man. John Knox.
Shriver, Harry C. see Shriver, Harry Clair.
Shriver, Harry Clair, 1904-
xShriver, Harry C.
The Government Lawyer: Essays on Men, Books, & the Law. Fox Hills.
Shriver, J. Nicholas.
xShriver, Nicholas.
ed. How-to-Live-&-Die-with Maryland Probate. Gulf Pub.
Shriver, Nicholas. see Shriver, J. Nicholas.
Shriver, William P. see Shriver, William Payne.
Shriver, William Payne, 1872-
xShriver, William P.
Immigrant Forces: Factors in the New Democracy. Ozer.
Shroff, Homai J., 1926-
xShroff, Homai J.
The Eighteenth Century Novel: The Idea of the Gentleman. Humanities.
Shrope, Wayne A. see Shrope, Wayne Austin.
Shrope, Wayne Austin.
xShrope, Wayne A.

Experiences in Communication. HarBraceJ.
Speaking & Listening: A Contemporary Approach. HarBraceJ.
Shryock, Clifford.
xShryock, Clifford.
How to Raise & Train a Chow Chow. TFH Pubns.
Shryock, R. H. see Shryock, Richard Harrison.
Shryock, Richard H. see Shryock, Richard Harrison.
Shryock, Richard Harrison, 1893-1972
xShryock, R. H.
The Development of Modern Medicine: An Interpretation of the Social & Scientific Factors Involved. U of Wis Pr.
xShryock, Richard H.
American Medical Research Past & Present. Arno.
Georgia & the Union in 1850. AMS Pr.
Medicine & Society in America: 1660-1860. Cornell U Pr.
Medicine in America: Historical Essays. Johns Hopkins.
xShryock, Richard Harrison.
National Tuberculosis Association 1904-1954: A Study of the Voluntary Health Movement in the United States. Arno.
Shtasel, Philip, 1925-
xShtasel, Philip.
Speak to Me in Nuclear Medicine. Har-Row.
Shtern, V. Y. see Shtern, Vladimir Iakovlevich.
Shtern, Vladimir Iakovlevich.
xShtern, V. Y.
The Gas-Phase Oxidation of Hydrocarbons. Pergamon.
Shtipelman, Boris A., 1938-
xShtipelman, Boris A.
Design & Manufacture of Hypoid Gears. Wiley.
Shu, Austin C. see Shu, Austin C. W.
Shu, Austin C. W.
xShu, Austin C.
ed. Modern Chinese Authors: A List of Pseudonyms. Chinese Materials.
Shub, David, 1887-1973
xShub, David.
Lenin: A Biography. Penguin.
Shub, Elizabeth.
xShub, Elizabeth.
The Adventures of Little Mouk. Macmillan.
Shubik, Martin.
xShubik, Martin.
Games for Society, Business and War: Towards a Theory of Gaming. Elsevier.
The Uses & Methods of Gaming. Elsevier.
Shuell, Thomas J.
xShuell, Thomas J.
Learning & Instruction. Brooks-Cole.
Shuffelton, Frank, 1940-
xShuffelton, Frank.
Thomas Hooker, 1586-1647. Princeton U Pr.
Shuffstall, R. M.
xShuffstall, Richard M.
The Hospital Laboratory: Modern Concepts of Management, Operations, & Finance. Mosby.
Shuffstall, Richard M. see Shuffstall, R. M.
Shuford, Wade H.
xShuford, Wade H.
The Aortic Arch & Its Malformations: With Emphasis on the Angiographic Features. C C Thomas.
Shugar, G. J. see Shugar, Gershon J.
Shugar, Gershon J., 1918-
xShugar, G. J.
Arithmetic: A Practical Approach. Glencoe.
xShugar, Gershon J.
How to Get into Medical & Dental School. Arco.
xShugar, Gershon L.

How to Get into Medical & Dental School.
Arco.
Shugar, Gershon L. *see* Shugar, Gershon J.
Shugg, Roger W. *see* Shugg, Roger Wallace.
Shugg, Roger Wallace.
xShugg, Roger W.
Origins of Class Struggle in Louisiana: A Social
History of White Farmers & Laborers During
Slavery & After, 1840-1875. La State U Pr.
Shukla, Satyendra R. *see* Shukla, Satyendra R.
Shukla, Satyendra R., 1929-
xShukla, Satyendra R.
Sikkim: The Story of Integration. Verry.
Shukman, A. *see* Shukman, Ann.
Shukman, Ann.
xShukman, A.
Literature & Semiotics: A Study of the
Writings of Yu. M. Lotman. Elsevier.
Shukri, Ahmed, 1892-
xShukri, Ahmed.
Muhammedan Law of Marriage & Divorce.
AMS Pr.
Shuler, J. L. *see* Shuler, John Lewis.
Shuler, John Lewis, 1887-
xShuler, J. L.
Give Your Guilt Away. Pacific Pr Pub Assn.
Link of Love. Pacific Pr Pub Assn.
Shulevitz, Uri, 1935-
xShulevitz, Uri.
illus. Dawn. FS&G.
illus. Oh What a Noise. Macmillan.
illus. One Monday Morning. Scribner.
illus. Rain Rain Rivers. FS&G.
tr. Soldier & Tsar in the Forest: A Russian
Tale. FS&G.
Shull, Peg.
xShull, Peg.
photos by Children of Appalachia. Messner.
Shulman, Abraham.
xShulman, Abraham.
Coming Home to Zion: A Pictorial History of
Pre-Israel Palestine. Doubleday.
Shulman, Arnold. *see* Shulman, Arnold Roy.
Shulman, Arnold Roy.
xShulman, Arnold.
Optical Data Processing. Wiley.
Shulman, David.
xShulman, David.
An Annotated Bibliography of Cryptography.
Garland Pub.
Shulman, David D. *see* Shulman, David Dean.
Shulman, David Dean, 1949-
xShulman, David D.
Tamil Temple Myths: Sacrifice & Divine
Marriage in the South Indian Saiva Tradition.
Princeton U Pr.
Shulman, Frank J. *see* Shulman, Frank Joseph.
Shulman, Frank Joseph, 1943-
xShulman, Frank J.
Doctoral Dissertations on South Asia,
1966-1970: An Annotated Bibliography
Covering North America, Europe, &
Australia. Ctr S&SE Asian.
Shulman, H. G.
xShulman, Harvey G.
Presentation Rate, Retention Interval, &
Encoding in Short-Term Recognition
Memory for Homonyms, Synonyms, &
Identical Words. Mgmt Info Serv.
Shulman, Harvey G. *see* Shulman, H. G.
Shulman, Irving.
xShulman, Irving.
Cry Tough. PB.
Valentino. PB.
Shulman, Joel J., 1926-
xShulman, Joel J.
How to Get Published in Business-Professional
Journals. Am Mgmt.
Shulman, Martha. *see* Shulman, Martha Rose.
Shulman, Martha R. *see* Shulman, Martha Rose.

Shulman, Martha Rose.
xShulman, Martha.
The Vegetarian Feast. Har-Row.
xShulman, Martha R.
The Vegetarian Feast. Har-Row.
Shulman, Max, 1919-
xShulman, Max.
Barefoot Boy with Cheek. AMS Pr.
Barefoot Boy with Cheek. Doubleday.
Shulman, Morton.
xShulman, Morton.
Anyone Can Make Big Money Buying Art.
Macmillan.
Shulman, Sandra.
xShulman, Sandra.
Nightmare. Macmillan.
Shultz, George P. *see* Shultz, George Pratt.
Shultz, George Pratt.
xShultz, George P.
Economic Policy Beyond the Headlines.
Norton.
Leaders & Followers in an Age of Ambiguity.
NYU Pr.
Shultz, William J. *see* Shultz, William John.
Shultz, William John, 1902-1970
xShultz, William J.
Humane Movement in the United States,
1910-1922. AMS Pr.
Shulvass, Moses A. *see* Shulvass, Moses Avigdor.
Shulvass, Moses Avigdor, 1909-
xShulvass, Moses A.
From East to West: The Westward Migration
of Jews from Eastern Europe During the
Seventeenth & Eighteenth Centuries. Wayne
St U Pr.
Shumaker, Arthur W. *see* Shumaker, Arthur Wesley.
Shumaker, Arthur Wesley, 1913-
xShumaker, Arthur W.
A History of Indiana Literature: With
Emphasis on the Authors of Imaginative
Works Who Commenced Writing Prior to
World War II. Ind U Pr.
Shumaker, Virginia O.
xShumaker, Virginia O.
The Alaska Pipeline. Messner.
Shumaker, Wayne.
xShumaker, Wayne.
Approach to Poetry. P-H.
The Occult Sciences in the Renaissance: A
Study in Intellectual Patterns. U of Cal Pr.
Shuman, Larry J.
xShuman, Larry J.
ed. Operations Research in Health Care: A
Critical Analysis. Johns Hopkins.
Shuman, R. Baird. *see* Shuman, Robert Baird.
Shuman, Robert Baird.
xShuman, R. Baird.
Clifford Odets. Coll & U Pr.
ed. Galaxy of Black Writing. Moore Pub Co.
Questions English Teachers Ask. Hayden.
Shuman, Samuel I.
xShuman, Samuel I.
American Law: An Introductory Survey of
Some Principles, Cases & Text. Wayne St U
Pr.
ed. Law & Disorder: The Legitimation of
Direct Action As an Instrument of Social
Policy. Wayne St U Pr.
Legal Positivism: Its Scope & Limitations.
Wayne St U Pr.
Psychosurgery & the Medical Control of
Violence: Autonomy & Deviance. Wayne St
U Pr.
Shumway, Asahel A. *see* Shumway, Asahel Adams.
Shumway, Asahel Adams, 1833-
xShumway, Asahel A.
Genealogy of the Shumway Family in the
United States of America. Shumway.
Shumway, Nina P. *see* Shumway, Nina Paul.

Shumway, Nina Paul.
xShumway, Nina P.
Your Desert & Mine. ETC Pubns.
Shumway, Stanley.
xShumway, Stanley.
Harmony & Ear Training at the Keyboard. Wm
C Brown.
Shunaman, Fred.
xShunaman, Fred.
How to Use Test Instruments in Electronics
Servicing. TAB Bks.
Shupp, Paul F. *see* Shupp, Paul Frederick.
Shupp, Paul Frederick, 1890-
xShupp, Paul F.
European Powers & the Near Eastern
Question, 1806-1807. AMS Pr.
The European Powers & the Near Eastern
Question: 1806-1807. R S Barnes.
Shura, Mary F. *see* Shura, Mary Francis.
Shura, Mary Francis.
xShura, Mary F.
The Barkley Street Six-Pack. Dodd.
Chester. Dodd.
The Gray Ghosts of Taylor Ridge. Schol Bk
Serv.
The Gray Ghosts of Taylor Ridge. Dodd.
Mister Wolf & Me. Dodd.
Riddle of Raven's Gulch. Dodd.
Shure, Myrna B.
xShure, Myrna B.
Problem-Solving Techniques in Childrearing.
Jossey-Bass.
Shurter, Edwin. *see* Shurter, Edwin Du Bois.
Shurter, Edwin Du Bois.
xShurter, Edwin.
ed. Masterpieces of Modern Verse. Granger
Bk.
Shurter, Robert L. *see* Shurter, Robert Lefevre.
Shurter, Robert Lefevre, 1907-
xShurter, Robert L.
The Utopian Novel in America, 1865-1900.
AMS Pr.
Shurtleff, Forrest E.
xShurtleff, Forrest E.
Children's Radiographic Technic. Lea &
Febiger.
Shurtleff, Harold R. *see* Shurtleff, Harold Robert.
Shurtleff, Harold Robert.
xShurtleff, Harold R.
The Log-Cabin Myth: A Study of the Early
Dwellings of the English Colonists in North
America. Peter Smith.
Shurtleff, Michael.
xShurtleff, Michael.
Audition: Everything an Actor Needs to Know
to Get the Part. Walker & Co.
Shurtleff, William.
xShurtleff, William.
The Book of Tempeh. Har-Row.
The Book of Tempeh. Har-Row.
The Book of Tofu. Autumn Pr.
The Book of Tofu. Ballantine.
Shuster, Carl N. *see* Shuster, Carl Nathaniel.
Shuster, Carl Nathaniel, 1890-
xShuster, Carl N.
A Study of the Problems in Teaching the Slide
Rule. AMS Pr.
Shuster, George N. *see* Shuster, George Nauman.
Shuster, George Nauman, 1894-
xShuster, George N.

Catholic Education in a Changing World. U of
   Notre Dame Pr.
Catholic Spirit in Modern English Literature.
   Arno.
The English Ode from Milton to Keats. Peter
   Smith.
The English Ode from Milton to Keats.
   Somerset Pub.
ed. Freedom & Authority in the West. U of
   Notre Dame Pr.
Hill of Happiness. Arno.
Religion Behind the Iron Curtain. Greenwood.
Shuster, M. R. *see* Shuster, Milan Robert.
Shuster, Milan Robert.
   xShuster, M. R.
   The Public International Law of Money.
      Oxford U Pr.
Shuster, Sam.
   xShuster, Sam.
   Dermatology in Internal Medicine. Oxford U
      Pr.
Shuster, William M. *see* Shuster, William Morgan.
Shuster, William Morgan, 1877-1960
   xShuster, William M.
   Strangling of Persia: Story of the European
      Diplomacy & Oriental Intrigue That Resulted
      in the Denationalization of Twelve Million
      Mohammedans, a Personal Narrative.
      Greenwood.
Shusterman, David.
   xShusterman, David.
   C. P. Snow. Twayne.
   Quest for Certitude in E. M. Forster's Fiction.
      Haskell.
Shute, Henry. *see* Shute, Henry Augustus.
Shute, Henry A. *see* Shute, Henry Augustine.
Shute, Henry Augustine.
   xShute, Henry A.
   Brite & Fair. Bauhan.
Shute, Henry Augustus.
   xShute, Henry.
   The Real Diary of a Real Boy. Bauhan.
Shute, Richard, 1849-1886
   xShute, Richard.
   On the History of the Process by Which the
      Aristotelian Writings Arrived at Their
      Present Form. Arno.
Shute, Wilfrid E., 1907-
   xShute, Wilfrid E.
   Your Child & Vitamin E. Keats.
Shuter, Robert.
   xShuter, Robert.
   Understanding Misunderstandings: Exploring
      Interpersonal Communication. Har-Row.
Shutler, Richard.
   xShutler, Richard.
   Oceanic Prehistory. Benjamin-Cummings.
Shutt, R. P.
   xShutt, R. P.
   ed. Bubble & Spark Chambers: Principles &
      Use. Acad Pr.
Shuttle, Penelope, 1947-
   xShuttle, Penelope.
   Rainsplitter in the Zodiac Garden. Longship
      Pr.
Shuttleworth, F. K. *see* Shuttleworth, Frank Kayley.
Shuttleworth, Floyd S. *see* Shuttleworth, Floyd Stephen.
Shuttleworth, Floyd Stephen.
   xShuttleworth, Floyd S.
   Non-Flowering Plants. Western Pub.
   Orchids. Western Pub.
Shuttleworth, Frank K. *see* Shuttleworth, Frank Kayley.
Shuttleworth, Frank Kayley, 1899-
   xShuttleworth, F. K.
   Adolescent Period: A Graphic Atlas. Kraus
      Repr.
   xShuttleworth, Frank K.

Adolescent Period: A Graphic & Pictorial
   Atlas. Kraus Repr.
Shuy, Roger W.
   xShuy, Roger W.
   ed. Linguistic Theory: What Can It Say About
      Reading?. Intl Reading.
   The Northern-Midland Dialect Boundary in
      Illinois. U of Ala Pr.
   ed. Some New Directions in Linguistics.
      Georgetown U Pr.
Shy, DeWitt M.
   xShy, DeWitt M.
   Live Smart-Die Smarter. Strode.
Shy, John. *see* Shy, John W.
Shy, John W.
   xShy, John.
   A People Numerous & Armed: Reflections on
      the Military Struggle for American
      Independence. Oxford U Pr.
   A People Numerous & Armed: Reflections on
      the Military Struggle for American
      Independence. Oxford U Pr.
   Toward Lexington: The Role of the British
      Army in the Coming of the American
      Revolution. Princeton U Pr.
Shye, Samuel.
   xShye, Samuel.
   ed. Theory Construction & Data Analysis in
      the Behavioral Sciences. Jossey-Bass.
Shyer, Marlene F. *see* Shyer, Marlene Fanta.
Shyer, Marlene Fanta.
   xShyer, Marlene F.
   My Brother, the Thief. Scribner.
   Never Trust a Handsome Man. Coward.
Siau, John F.
   xSiau, John F.
   Flow in Wood. Syracuse U Pr.
Sibbett, Ed.
   xSibbett, Ed.
   Peasant Designs for Artists & Craftsmen.
      Dover.
   Peasant Designs for Artists & Craftsmen. Peter
      Smith.
   Stained Glass Pattern Book: 88 Designs for
      Workable Projects. Peter Smith.
Siberell, Anne.
   xSiberell, Anne.
   Houses: Shelters from Prehistoric Times to
      Today. HR&W.
Sibley, Agnes M. *see* Sibley, Agnes Marie.
Sibley, Agnes Marie, 1914-
   xSibley, Agnes M.
   Alexander Pope's Prestige in America
      1725-1835. Folcroft.
Sibley, Celestine.
   xSibley, Celestine.
   Day by Day with Celestine Sibley. Doubleday.
   Jincey. S&S.
Sibley, Elbridge.
   xSibley, Elbridge.
   Differential Mortality in Tennessee, 1917-1928.
      Negro U Pr.
Sibley, Gertrude M. *see* Sibley, Gertrude Marian.
Sibley, Gertrude Marian, 1892-
   xSibley, Gertrude M.
   Compiled by Lost Plays & Masques,
      1500-1642. Russell.
Sibley, Marilyn M. *see* Sibley, Marilyn Mcadams.
Sibley, Marilyn McAdams.
   xSibley, Marilyn M.
   Port of Houston: A History. U of Tex Pr.
Sibley, Mulford Q. *see* Sibley, Mulford Quickert.
Sibley, Mulford Quickert.
   xSibley, Mulford Q.
   Conscription of Conscience: The American
      State & the Conscientious Objector, 1940-47.
      Johnson Repr.
Sibley, Susan.
   xSibley, Susan.

Woodsmoke. Avon.
Woodsmoke. Blair.
Sibley, William F.
   xSibley, William F.
   The Shiga Hero. U of Chicago Pr.
Sibmacher, Johan. *see* Sibmacher, Johann.
Sibmacher, Johann, d. 1611
   xSibmacher, Johan.
   illus. Baroque Charted Designs for Needlework.
      Dover.
Sibson, Robert E. *see* Sibson, Robert Earl.
Sibson, Robert Earl, 1925-
   xSibson, Robert E.
   Increasing Employee Productivity. Am Mgmt.
Sibthorpe, A. B. *see* Sibthorpe, A. B. C.
Sibthorpe, A. B. C.
   xSibthorpe, A. B.
   History of Sierra Leone. Biblio Dist.
Sicard, Clara.
   xSicard, Clara.
   The Ghost: A Legend. Arno.
Sicard, Gerald L.
   xSicard, Gerald L.
   Sociology for Our Times. Scott F.
Sices, David.
   xSices, David.
   Theater of Solitude: The Drama of Alfred de
      Musset. U Pr of New Eng.
Sichel, Peter M. *see* Sichel, Peter M. F.
Sichel, Peter M. F.
   xSichel, Peter M.
   Which Wine?: The Wine Drinker's Buying
      Guide. Har-Row.
Sichel, Werner.
   xSichel, Werner.
   ed. Economic Advice & Executive Policy:
      Recommendations from Past Members of the
      Council of Economic Advisers. Praeger.
Sicher, Harry, 1889-
   xSicher, Harry.
   Oral Anatomy. Mosby.
Sicilia, Gail.
   xSicilia, Gail.
   Compiled by Hollywood Squares. Popular Lib.
Sickels, Eleanor M. *see* Sickels, Eleanor Maria.
Sickels, Eleanor Maria, 1894-
   xSickels, Eleanor M.
   In Calico & Crinoline: True Stories of
      American Women, 1608-1865. Arno.
Sickels, Robert J.
   xSickels, Robert J.
   The Presidency: An Introduction. P-H.
   Race, Marriage, & the Law. U of NM Pr.
Sicker, Philip.
   xSicker, Philip.
   Love & the Quest for Identity in the Fiction of
      Henry James. Princeton U Pr.
Sickle, Dirck Van. *see* Van Sickle, Dirck.
Sickman, Laurence. *see* Sickman, Laurence C. S.
Sickman, Laurence C. S.
   xSickman, Laurence.
   Art & Architecture of China. Penguin.
Siddall, James. *see* Siddall, James N.
Siddall, James N.
   xSiddall, James.
   Analytical Decision Making in Engineering
      Design. P-H.
Sidders, P. A.
   xSidders, Peter.
   A Guide to World Screw Threads. Indus Pr.
Sidders, Peter. *see* Sidders, P. A.
Siddiqui, Nafis A. *see* Siddiqui, Nafis Ahmad.
Siddiqui, Nafis Ahmad, 1935-
   xSiddiqui, Nafis A.
   Population Geography of Muslims in India.
      Verry.
Siddons, Anne R. *see* Siddons, Anne Rivers.
Siddons, Anne Rivers.
   xSiddons, Anne R.

The House Next Door. S&S.
Siddons, H. *see* Siddons, Harold.
Siddons, Harold.
　xSiddons, H.
　　Cardiac Pacemakers. C C Thomas.
Sidebotham, R. *see* Sidebotham, Roy.
Sidebotham, Roy.
　xSidebotham, R.
　　Accounting for Industrial Management.
　　Pergamon.
Sidel, Ruth.
　xSidel, Ruth.
　　Urban Survival: The World of Working-Class
　　Women. Beacon Pr.
Sider, J. W., 1941-
　xSider, J. W.
　　The Troublesome Raigne of John King of
　　England. Garland Pub.
Sider, Ronald J.
　xSider, Ronald J.
　　Christ & Violence. Herald Pr.
　　Rich Christians in an Age of Hunger: A
　　Biblical Study. Inter-Varsity.
　　Rich Christians in an Age of Hunger: A
　　Biblical Study. Paulist Pr.
Sidgwick, Frank.
　xSidgwick, Frank.
　　The Ballad. Folcroft.
　　ed. Ballads & Lyrics of Love. Longwood Pr.
　　ed. Legendary Ballads. Longwood Pr.
　　Sources & Analogues of a Midsummer Night's
　　Dream. AMS Pr.
　　Sources & Analogues of a Midsummer Night's
　　Dream. Folcroft.
Sidis, Boris.
　xSidis, Boris.
　　Multiple Personality: Experimental
　　Investigation into the Nature of Human
　　Individuality. Greenwood.
Sidman, Richard L.
　xSidman, Richard L.
　　Atlas of the Mouse Brain & Spinal Cord.
　　Harvard U Pr.
Sidney, Algernon, 1622-1683
　xSidney, Algernon.
　　Discourses Concerning Government. Arno.
Sidney, Philip.
　xSidney, Philip.
　　Complete Poems of Sir Philip Sidney. Arno.
　　Countess of Pembroke's Arcadia. Oxford U Pr.
Sidorova, Vera F. *see* Sidorova, Vera Fedorovna.
Sidorova, Vera Fedorovna.
　xSidorova, Vera F.
　　The Postnatal Growth & Restoration of
　　Internal Organs in Vertebrates. PSG Pub.
Sidorsky, David.
　xSidorsky, David.
　　Intro. by & ed. Essays on Human Rights:
　　Contemporary Issues & Jewish Perspectives.
　　Jewish Pubn.
Sidowski, Joseph B., 1925-
　xSidowski, Joseph B.
　　Experimental Methods & Instrumentation in
　　Psychology. McGraw.
Siebenschuh, William R.
　xSiebenschuh, William R.
　　Form & Purpose in Boswell's Biographical
　　Works. U of Cal Pr.
Sieber, J. E. *see* Sieber, Joan E.
Sieber, Joan E.
　xSieber, J. E.
　　Anxiety, Learning, & Instruction. Halsted Pr.
Sieber, Roy.
　xSieber, Roy.
　　African Furniture & Household Objects. Ind U
　　Pr.
Siebert, Horst.
　xSiebert, Horst.

The Political Economy of Environmental
　Protection. Jai Pr.
　ed. Regional Environmental Policy: The
　Economic Issues. NYU Pr.
Siebert, Wilbur H. *see* Siebert, Wilbur Henry.
Siebert, Wilbur Henry, 1866-1961
　xSiebert, Wilbur H.
　　The Legacy of the American Revolution to the
　　British West Indies & Bahamas: A Chapter
　　Out of the History of the American Loyalists.
　　Irvington.
　　Loyalists in East Florida, 1774-1785: The Most
　　Important Documents Pertaining Thereto....
　　Irvington.
　　Loyalists of Pennsylvania. Irvington.
　　Underground Railroad from Slavery to
　　Freedom. Arno.
　　The Underground Railroad from Slavery to
　　Freedom. Peter Smith.
　　Underground Railroad from Slavery to
　　Freedom. Russell.
Siebring, B. Richard.
　xSiebring, B. Richard.
　　General Chemistry. Wadsworth Pub.
Sieburth, John M. *see* Sieburth, John Mcneill.
Sieburth, John McNeill.
　xSieburth, John M.
　　Sea Microbes. Oxford U Pr.
Sieburth, Richard.
　xSieburth, Richard.
　　Instigations: Ezra Pound & Remy De
　　Gourmont. Harvard U Pr.
Siedel, George J.
　xSiedel, George J.
　　Real Estate Law. West Pub.
Siedentop, Daryl.
　xSiedentop, Daryl.
　　Physical Education: Introductory Analysis. Wm
　　C Brown.
Siegal, Harvey A.
　xSiegal, Harvey A.
　　Outposts of the Forgotten: Socially Terminal
　　People in Slum Hotels & Single Room
　　Occupancy Tenements. Transaction Bks.
Siegal, Lewis J.
　xSiegal, Lewis J.
　　Forensic Medicine: Courtroom Applications to
　　Legal Principles. Grune.
Siegal, Mordecai.
　xSiegal, Mordecai.
　　Good Dog, Bad Dog. HR&W.
　　Good Dog, Bad Dog. NAL.
　xSiegal, Mordecai.
　　The Good Dog Book: Loving Care. Macmillan.
Siegal, Mordecal. *see* Siegal, Mordecai.
Siegal, Sanford.
　xSiegal, Sanford.
　　Dr. Siegal's Natural Fiber Cookbook. Dial.
　　Dr. Siegal's Natural Fiber Permanent
　　Weight-Loss Diet. Dial.
Siegan, Bernard. *see* Siegan, Bernard H.
Siegan, Bernard H.
　xSiegan, Bernard.
　　Other People's Property. Lexington Bks.
　xSiegan, Bernard H.
　　The Interaction of Economics & the Law.
　　Lexington Bks.
　　Regulation, Economics, & the Law. Lexington
　　Bks.
Siegel, Abraham J.
　xSiegel, Abraham J.
　　ed. Impact of Computers on Collective
　　Bargaining. MIT Pr.
Siegel, Arthur. *see* Siegel, Arthur I.
Siegel, Arthur I.
　xSiegel, Arthur.
　　Puerto Ricans in Philadelphia. Arno.
　xSiegel, Arthur I.

Professional Police-Human Relations Training.
　C C Thomas.
Siegel, Beatrice.
　xSiegel, Beatrice.
　　Indians of the Woodland Before & After the
　　Pilgrims. Walker & Co.
Siegel, Benjamin, 1914-
　xSiegel, Benjamin.
　　The Adventures of Richard O'Boy. Lippincott
　　& Crowell.
　　This Healing Passion. PB.
Siegel, Benjamin M.
　xSiegel, Benjamin M.
　　ed. Modern Developments in Electron
　　Microscopy. Acad Pr.
Siegel, Brian.
　xSiegel, Brian.
　　How to Succeed in Law School. Barron.
Siegel, Carl L. *see* Siegel, Carl Ludwig.
Siegel, Carl Ludwig.
　xSiegel, Carl L.
　　Lectures on Celestial Mechanics.
　　Springer-Verlag.
Siegel, Curt, 1911-
　xSiegel, Curt.
　　Structure & Form in Modern Architecture.
　　Krieger.
Siegel, Dorothy.
　xSiegel, Dorothy.
　　Topics in English Morphology. Garland Pub.
Siegel, Edward T.
　xSiegel, Edward T.
　　Endocrine Diseases of the Dog. Lea & Febiger.
Siegel, Eli, 1902-
　xSiegel, Eli.
　　Children's Guide to Parents & Other Matters:
　　Little Essays for Children & Others.
　　Definition.
　　Damned Welcome: Aesthetic Realism Maxims.
　　Definition.
　　The Frances Sanders Lesson & Two Related
　　Works. Definition.
　　Hot Afternoons Have Been in Montana:
　　Poems. Definition.
　　The Opposites Class: Aesthetic Realism Class
　　on Opposites. Aesthetic Realism.
Siegel, Ernest.
　xSiegel, Ernest.
　　Creating Instructional Sequences. Acad
　　Therapy.
　　The Exceptional Child Grows Up: Guidelines
　　for Understanding & Helping the Brain
　　Injured Adolescent & Young Adult. Dutton.
Siegel, Frederic R.
　xSiegel, Frederic R.
　　Applied Geochemistry. Wiley.
Siegel, Gilbert B.
　xSiegel, Gilbert B.
　　Breaking with Orthodoxy in Public
　　Administration. U Pr of Amer.
Siegel, H. H. *see* Siegel, Harvey H.
Siegel, Harry.
　xSiegel, Herbert.
　　A Guide to Business Principles & Practices for
　　Interior Designers. Watson-Guptill.
Siegel, Harvey H.
　xSiegel, H. H.
　　Alcohol Detoxification Programs: Treatment
　　Instead of Jail. C C Thomas.
Siegel, Herbert. *see* Siegel, Harry.
Siegel, Irving H. *see* Siegel, Irving Herbert.
Siegel, Irving Herbert.
　xSiegel, Irving H.
　　Company Productivity: Measurement for
　　Improvement. Upjohn Inst.
Siegel, James T.
　xSiegel, James T.

Shadow & Sound: The Historical Thought of a
Sumatran People. U of Chicago Pr.

Siegel, Laurence.
xSiegel, Laurence.
Psychology in Industrial Organizations. Irwin.

Siegel, Lee.
xSiegel, Lee.
Sacred & Profane Dimensions of Love in
Indian Traditions As Exemplified in the
Gitagovind of Jayadeva. Oxford U Pr.

Siegel, Linda.
xSiegel, Linda.
Caspar David Friedrich & the Age of German
Romanticism. Branden.

Siegel, Marcia B.
xSiegel, Marcia B.
The Shapes of Change: Images of American
Dance. HM.

Siegel, Mark R. see Siegel, Mark Richard.
Siegel, Mark Richard.
xSiegel, Mark R.
Pynchon: Creative Paranoia in "Gravity's
Rainbow. Kennikat.

Siegel, Michael H.
xSiegel, Michael H.
ed. Psychological Research: The Inside Story.
Har-Row.

Siegel, Murray J.
xSiegel, Murray J.
Think Thin. Eriksson.

Siegel, Paul.
xSiegel, Paul.
Strategic Planning of Management Information
Systems. Van Nos Reinhold.

Siegel, Paul N.
xSiegel, Paul N.
ed. His Infinite Variety: Major Shakespearean
Criticism Since Johnson. Arno.

Siegel, R. see Siegel, Robert.
Siegel, R. K. see Siegel, Ronald K.
Siegel, Richard L.
xSiegel, Richard L.
Comparing Public Policies: United States,
Soviet Union & Europe. Dorsey.

Siegel, Robert.
xSiegel, R.
Thermal Radiation Heat Transfer. McGraw.
xSiegel, Robert.
Thermal Radiation Heat Transfer. McGraw.

Siegel, Ronald K.
xSiegel, R. K.
ed. Hallucinations: Behavior, Experience, &
Theory. Wiley.

Siegel, S. see Siegel, Seymour.
Siegel, Seymour.
xSiegel, S.
ed. Conservative Judaism & Jewish Law. Ktav.

Siegel, Sidney.
xSiegel, Sidney.
Bargaining & Group Decision Making:
Experiments in Bilateral Monopoly.
Greenwood.
Nonparametric Statistics for the Behavioral
Sciences. McGraw.

Siegel, Steven A. see Siegel, Steven W.
Siegel, Steven W., 1946-
xSiegel, Steven A.
Compiled by Archival Resources. K G Saur.

Siegel, William L. see Siegel, William Laird.
Siegel, William Laird.
xSiegel, William L.
How to Run a Successful Restaurant. Wiley.

Siegele, H. H. see Siegele, Herman Hugo.
Siegele, Herman Hugo, 1883-
xSiegele, H. H.
Cabinets & Built-Ins. Sterling.
Carpentry. Craftsman.

Siegelman, Stanley S.
xSiegelman, Stanley S.

ed. Pulmonary System: Practical Approaches to
Pulmonary Diagnosis. Grune.

Siegener, Ray.
xSiegener, Ray.
Staying in the Game: How to Keep Young &
Active. HM.

Siegfried, Andre, 1875-1959
xSiegfried, Andre.
The Mediterranean. Hyperion Conn.
Switzerland, a Democratic Way of Life.
Hyperion Conn.
Tableau Politique De la France De L'ouest
Sous la Troisieme Republique: The Political
Map of Western France Under the Third
Republic. Arno.

Siegler, Bobbie, 1937-
xSiegler, Bobbie.
The Psychic Cookbook. Celestial Arts.

Siegler, Miriam.
xSiegler, Miriam.
Patienthood: The Art of Being a Responsible
Patient. Macmillan.

Siegler, Susan.
xSiegler, Susan.
Needlework Patterns from the Metropolitan
Museum of Art. NYGS.

Siegman, Aron W. see Siegman, Aron Wolfe.
Siegman, Aron Wolfe.
xSiegman, Aron W.
ed. Nonverbal Behavior & Communication.
Halsted Pr.
ed. Of Speech & Time: Temporal Speech
Patterns in Interpersonal Context. Halsted Pr.

Siegmeister, Elie, 1909-
xSiegmeister, Elie.
Music & Society. Haskell.

Siegmund, Georg, 1903-
xSiegmund, Georg.
Buddhism & Christianity: A Preface to
Dialogue. U of Ala Pr.

Sielaff, Theodore J.
xSielaff, Theodore J.
Introduction to Business: American Enterprise
in Action. Wadsworth Pub.

Sieller, William V. see Sieller, William Vincent.
Sieller, William Vincent.
xSieller, William V.
Gather Back the Dream. Golden Quill.
Green Water for a Granite Valley. Golden
Quill.

Siemaszko, Frederick.
xSiemaszko, Frederick.
Computing in Clinical Laboratories. Wiley.

Siemens, Georg, 1882-
xSiemens, Georg.
History of the House of Siemens. Arno.

Sienkiewicz, Henryk.
xSienkiewicz, Henryk.
Pan Michael, an Historical Novel of Poland,
the Ukraine, & Turkey. Greenwood.

Sienko, Michell J.
xSienko, Michell J.
Chemistry. McGraw.
Chemistry. McGraw.
Chemistry: Principles & Properties. McGraw.
Experimental Chemistry. McGraw.

Sierra-Franco, Miriam.
xSierra-Franco, Miriam.
Therapeutic Communication in Nursing.
McGraw.

Siever, Raymond.
xSiever, Raymond.
Commentary by Energy & Environment:
Readings from Scientific American. W H
Freeman.

Sievers, Allen M. see Sievers, Allen Morris.
Sievers, Allen Morris, 1918-
xSievers, Allen M.

Revolution, Evolution, & the Economic Order.
Greenwood.

Sievers, Eduard, 1850-1932
xSievers, Eduard.
Old English Grammar. AMS Pr.
Old English Grammar. Greenwood.
Old English Grammar. Scholarly.

Sievers, W. David. see Sievers, Wieder David.
Sievers, Wieder David, 1919-
xSievers, W. David.
Directing for the Theatre. Wm C Brown.

Sievert, Norman W.
xSievert, Norman W.
Career Education & Industrial Education. HM.

Siff, Elliott J.
xSiff, Elliott J.
Engineering Approach to Gyroscopic
Instruments. Speller.

Sifferlen, Thomas P.
xSifferlen, Thomas P.
Digital Electronics with Engineering
Applications. P-H.

Sifneos, P. E. see Sifneos, Peter E.
Sifneos, Peter E.
xSifneos, P. E.
Short-Term Dynamic Psychotherapy:
Evaluation & Technique. Plenum Pub.
xSifneos, Peter E.
Ascent from Chaos: A Psychosomatic Case
Study. Harvard U Pr.

Sigafoos, Robert A. see Sigafoos, Robert Alan.
Sigafoos, Robert Alan, 1923-
xSigafoos, Robert A.
Cotton Row to Beale Street: A Business
History of Memphis. Memphis St Univ.

Sigal, I. M. see Sigal, Israel Michael.
Sigal, Israel Michael, 1945-
xSigal, I. M.
Mathematical Foundations of Quantum
Scattering Theory for Multiparticle Systems.
Am Math.

Sigel, Efrem.
xSigel, Efrem.
Crisis!: The Taxpayer Revolt & Your Kids'
Schools. Knowledge Indus.
ed. Videotext: The Coming Revolution in
Home-Office Information Retrieval.
Knowledge Indus.

Sigerist, Henry E. see Sigerist, Henry Ernest.
Sigerist, Henry Ernest, 1891-1957
xSigerist, Henry E.
Civilization & Disease. U of Chicago Pr.
Great Doctors: A Biographical History of
Medicine. Arno.

Sigford, Ann, 1950-
xSigford, Ann.
Eight Words for Thirsty. Dillon.

Siggia, Sidney.
xSiggia, Sidney.
ed. Instrumental Methods of Organic
Functional Group Analysis. Wiley.
Quantitative Organic Analysis via Functional
Groups. Wiley.

Siggins, Maggie.
xSiggins, Maggie.
Guide to Eastern Ski Resorts. McGraw.

Sightler, Verna W.
xSightler, Verna W.
Reach for the Stars. Bouregy.

Sigler, Jay A.
xSigler, Jay A.
American Rights Policies. Dorsey.
Double Jeopardy: The Development of a Legal
& Social Policy. Cornell U Pr.
The Legal Sources of Public Policy. Lexington
Bks.

Sigler, L. E.
xSigler, L. E.

Algebra. Springer-Verlag.
Exercises in Set Theory. Springer-Verlag.
Sigmund, Paul. *see* Sigmund, Paul E.
Sigmund, Paul E.
xSigmund, Paul.
Natural Law in Political Thought. Winthrop.
xSigmund, Paul E.
The Overthrow of Allende & the Politics of
Chile, 1964-1976. U of Pittsburgh Pr.
Signoret, Simone, 1921-
xSignoret, Simone.
Nostalgia Isn't What It Used to Be. Har-Row.
Nostalgia Isn't What It Used to Be. Penguin.
Signs of the Times.
xSigns of the Times Editorial Staff.
ed. Crane Safety & Operation. Signs of Times.
Signs of the Times Editorial Staff. *see* Signs of the Times.
Sigworth, Oliver. *see* Sigworth, Oliver F.
Sigworth, Oliver F.
xSigworth, Oliver.
Nature's Sternest Painter: Five Essays on the
Poetry of George Crabbe. U of Ariz Pr.
Sih, Paul K. T. *see* Sih, Paul Kwang Tsien.
Sih, Paul Kwang Tsien.
xSih, Paul K. T.
ed. Nationalist China During the Sino-Japanese
War, 1937-1945. Exposition.
Sihler, E. G. *see* Sihler, Ernest Gottlieb.
Sihler, Ernest Gottlieb, 1853-1942
xSihler, E. G.
A Complete Lexicon of the Latinity of
Caesar's Gallic War. Humanities.
Sijben, J. J.
xSijben, J. J.
Money & Economic Growth. Kluwer Boston.
Sik, Ota, 1919-
xSik, Ota.
Plan & Market Under Socialism. M E Sharpe.
The Third Way: Marxist-Leninist Theory &
Modern Industrial Society. M E Sharpe.
Sikes, Edward E. *see* Sikes, Edward Ernest.
Sikes, Edward Ernest, 1867-1940
xSikes, Edward E.
The Greek View of Poetry. Hyperion Conn.
Lucretius, Poet & Philosopher. Russell.
Roman Poetry. Hyperion Conn.
Sikes, S. K. *see* Sikes, Sylvia K.
Sikes, Sylvia K.
xSikes, S. K.
Natural History of the African Elephant.
Elsevier.
Sikes, Walter W.
xSikes, Walter W.
Renewing Higher Education from Within: A
Guide for Campus Change Teams.
Jossey-Bass.
Sikking, Robert P.
xSikking, Robert P.
Light for Our Age. Unity Bks.
A Matter of Life & Death. De Vorss.
Siklossy, Laurent.
xSiklossy, Laurent.
Let's Talk Lisp. P-H.
Sikora, Joseph J. *see* Sikora, Joseph John.
Sikora, Joseph John.
xSikora, Joseph J.
Inquiry into Being. Loyola.
Sikora, R. I. *see* Sikora, Richard I.
Sikora, Richard I.
xSikora, R. I.
ed. Obligations to Future Generations. Temple
U Pr.
Sikorski, R. *see* Sikorski, Roman.
Sikorski, Roman.
xSikorski, R.
Boolean Algebras. Springer-Verlag.
Sikorsky, Robert.
xSikorsky, Robert.

How to Get More Miles per Gallon. St Martin.
Sikula, Andrew F.
xSikula, Andrew F.
Personnel Administration & Human Resources
Management. Wiley.
Personnel Management: A Short Course for
Professionals. Wiley.
Silas, A. E.
xSilas, A. E.
The Panorama Egg. DAW Bks.
Silber, Bettina.
xSilber, Bettina.
ed. New Perspectives on the International Oil
Supply. Americans Energy Ind.
Silber, Irwin, 1925-
xSilber, Irwin.
Songs of Independence. Stackpole.
Silber, Joan.
xSilber, Joan.
Household Words. Viking Pr.
Silber, Sherman. *see* Silber, Sherman J.
Silber, Sherman J.
xSilber, Sherman.
Microsurgery. Williams & Wilkins.
xSilber, Sherman J.
How to Get Pregnant. Scribner.
Silberberg, Norman E.
xSilberberg, Norman E.
ed. Who Speaks for the Child?. C C Thomas.
Silberer, H. *see* Silberer, Herbert.
Silberer, Herbert, 1882-1922
xSilberer, H.
Problems of Mysticism & Its Symbolism.
Weiser.
Silberg, Moshe, 1900-
xSilberg, Moshe.
Talmudic Law & the Modern State. United Syn
Bk.
Silberling, E. *see* Silberling, Edouard.
Silberling, Edouard.
xSilberling, E.
Dictionnaire De Sociologie Phalansterienne:
Guide Des Oeuvres Completes De Charles
Fourier. B Franklin.
Silberling, N. J. *see* Silberling, Norman John.
Silberling, Norman John, 1928-
xSilberling, N. J.
Age Relationships of the Golconda Thrust
Fault, Sonoma Range, North-Central Nevada.
Geol Soc.
Pre-Tertiary Stratigraphy & Structure of
Northwestern Nevada. Geol Soc.
Silberman, Charles. *see* Silberman, Charles E.
Silberman, Charles E., 1925-
xSilberman, Charles.
Crisis in Black & White. Random.
xSilberman, Charles E.
Criminal Violence, Criminal Justice. Random.
Crisis in Black & White. Random.
Crisis in the Classroom: The Remaking in
American Education. Random.
ed. The Open Classroom Reader. Random.
ed. The Open Classroom Reader. Random.
Silberman, Melvin L.
xSilberman, Melvin L.
ed. The Psychology of Open Teaching &
Learning: An Inquiry Approach. Little.
ed. Real Learning: A Sourcebook for Teachers.
Little.
Silberner, Edmund.
xSilberner, Edmund.
Problem of War in Nineteenth Century
Economic Thought. Garland Pub.
Silberschlag, Eisig, 1903-
xSilberschlag, Eisig.
From Renaissance to Renaissance: Hebrew
Literature 1492-1967. Ktav.
Silberstang, Edwin, 1930-
xSilberstang, Edwin.

How to Gamble & Win. Cornerstone.
How to Gamble & Win. Watts.
Playboy's Book of Games. Wideview Bks.
Snake Eyes. Dutton.
Snake Eyes. PB.
Winning Casino Craps. McKay.
Silbey, Joel H.
xSilbey, Joel H.
ed. National Development & Sectional Crisis,
1815-1860. Phila Bk Co.
A Respectable Minority: The Democratic Party
in the Civil War Era, 1860-1868. Norton.
Silburn, P. A. *see* Silburn, Percy Arthur Baxter.
Silburn, Percy Arthur Baxter, 1874-
xSilburn, P. A.
Governance of Empire. Kennikat.
Silcock, Arnold, 1889-
xSilcock, Arnold.
Introduction to Chinese Art & History.
Greenwood.
Silcock, T. H.
xSilcock, Thomas H.
Commonwealth Economy in Southeast Asia.
Duke.
Southeast Asian University: A Comparative
Account of Some Development Problems.
Duke.
Silcock, Thomas H. *see* Silcock, T. H.
Silcox, Claris E. *see* Silcox, Claris Edwin.
Silcox, Claris Edwin.
xSilcox, Claris E.
Catholics, Jews, & Protestants: A Study of
Relationships in the United States & Canada.
Greenwood.
Siler, Lari F. *see* Siler, Lari Field.
Siler, Lari Field.
xSiler, Lari F.
Adrienne's House. HR&W.
Silfen, Martin E.
xSilfen, Martin E.
Counseling Clients in the Entertainment
Industry, 1979. PLI.
Silfen, Paul Harrison, 1936-
xSilfen, Paul Harrison.
The Influence of the Mongols of Russia: A
Dimensional History. Exposition.
Siliconix, Inc. *see* Siliconix Incorporated.
Siliconix Incorporated.
xSiliconix, Inc.
Designing with Field Effect Transistors.
McGraw.
Silitch, Clarissa M.
xSilitch, Clarissa M.
ed. The Forgotten Art of Making Old
Fashioned Jellies, Jams, Preserves, Conserves,
Marmalades, Butters, Honeys & Leathers.
Yankee Bks.
Silj, Alessandro, 1935-
xSilj, Alessandro.
Never Again Without a Rifle!: The Origins of
Italian Terrorism. Karz Pub.
Siljander, Raymond P.
xSiljander, Raymond P.
Applied Police & Fire Photography. C C
Thomas.
Applied Surveillance Photography. C C
Thomas.
Fundamentals of Physical Surveillance: A
Guide for Uniformed & Plainclothes
Personnel. C C Thomas.
Silk, Dennis, 1928-
xSilk, Dennis.
The Punished Land. Penguin.
The Punished Land. Viking Pr.
Silk, John.
xSilk, John.
Statistical Concepts in Geography. Allen
Unwin.
Silk, Joseph, 1942-
xSilk, Joseph.

The Big Bang: The Creation & Evolution of the
Universe. W H Freeman.
Silk, Leonard.
xSilk, Leonard.
The Economists. Avon.
The Economists. Basic.
Silk, Leonard S. see Silk, Leonard Solomon.
Silk, Leonard Solomon, 1918-
xSilk, Leonard S.
Veblen: A Play in Three Acts. Kelley.
Silkin, Jon.
xSilkin, Jon.
Amana Grass. Columbia U Pr.
Silko, Leslie M. see Silko, Leslie Marmon.
Silko, Leslie Marmon.
xSilko, Leslie M.
Ceremony. Viking Pr.
Ceremony. NAL.
Sill, Edward R. see Sill, Edward Rowland.
Sill, Edward Rowland, 1841-1887
xSill, Edward R.
The Prose of Edward Rowland Sill: With an
Introduction Comprising Some Familiar
Letters. R West.
Sill, Hal. see Sill, Harold D.
Sill, Harold D.
xSill, Hal.
Misbehavin' with Fats: A Toby Bradley
Adventure. A-W.
Sill, Sterling W.
xSill, Sterling W.
Christmas Sermons. Deseret Bk.
The Nine Lives of Sterling W. Sill: An
Autobiography. Horizon Utah.
Principles, Promises & Powers. Deseret Bk.
Sill, Webster H., 1916-
xSill, Webster H.
The Plant Protection Discipline: Problems &
Possible Developmental Strategies. Allanheld.
The Plant Protection Discipline: Problems &
Possible Developmental Strategies. Halsted
Pr.
Sillers, Florence W. see Sillers, Florence Warfield.
Sillers, Florence Warfield.
xSillers, Florence W.
Compiled by History of Bolivar
County,Mississippi. Reprint.
Silliman, Benjamin, 1779-1864
xSilliman, Benjamin.
A Journal of Travels in England, Holland, &
Scotland, & of Two Passages Over the
Atlantic in the Years 1805 & 1806. Arno.
Silliman, Ron. see Silliman, Ronald.
Silliman, Ronald, 1946-
xSilliman, Ron.
Ketjak. SBD.
Sillitoe, Alan.
xSillitoe, Alan.
Loneliness of the Long-Distance Runner.
Knopf.
Loneliness of the Long-Distance Runner. NAL.
The Widower's Son. Har-Row.
The Widower's Son. Har-Row.
Sillitoe, Paul.
xSillitoe, Paul.
Give & Take: Exchange in Wola Society. St
Martin.
Sills, Barbara. see Sills, Barbara Wilcox.
Sills, Barbara Wilcox.
xSills, Barbara.
The Mother-to-Mother Baby Care Book.
Camaro Pub.
Silman, Roberta.
xSilman, Roberta.
Boundaries: A Novel. Little.
Somebody Else's Child. Dell.
Somebody Else's Child. Warne.
Silnitsky, Frantisek.
xSilnitsky, Frantizek.

ed. Communism & Eastern Europe: A
Collection of Essays. Karz Pub.
Silnitsky, Frantizek. see Silnitsky, Frantisek.
Silone, Ignazio, 1900-
xSilone, Ignazio.
Bread & Wine. NAL.
Silva, John W.
xSilva, John W.
ed. An Introduction to Crime & Justice. Mss
Info.
Silva, Jose.
xSilva, Jose.
The Silva Mind Control Method. PB.
The Silva Mind Control Method. S&S.
Silva, Ruth C. see Silva, Ruth Caridad.
Silva, Ruth Caridad, 1920-
xSilva, Ruth C.
Presidential Succession. Greenwood.
Silvanie, Haig, 1898-
xSilvanie, Haig.
Responsibility of States for Acts of
Unsuccessful Insurgent Governments. AMS
Pr.
Silvaroli, Nicholas J.
xSilvaroli, Nicholas J.
Classroom Reading Inventory. Wm C Brown.
Silvennoinen, P.
xSilvennoinen, P.
Reactor Core Fuel Management. Pergamon.
Silver, Alain.
xSilver, Alain.
Film Noir: An Encyclopedic Reference to the
American Style. Overlook Pr.
Robert Aldrich: A Guide to References &
Resources. G K Hall.
Silver, Alice M. see Silver, Alice Moolten.
Silver, Alice Moolten.
xSilver, Alice M.
There Must Be Beauty Too. Philos Lib.
Silver, Caroline, 1938-
xSilver, Caroline.
Classic Lives: The Education of a Racehorse.
HarBraceJ.
Silver, George. see Silver, George A.
Silver, George A.
xSilver, George.
Family Medical Care: A Design for Health
Maintenance. Ballinger Pub.
Silver, Gerald A.
xSilver, Gerald A.
Data Processing for Business. HarBraceJ.
Introduction to Systems Analysis. P-H.
Simplified FORTRAN IV Programming.
HarBraceJ.
The Social Impact of Computers. HarBraceJ.
Silver, Harold.
xSilver, Harold.
English Education & the Radicals, 1780-1850.
Routledge & Kegan.
Silver, Howard. see Silver, Howard F.
Silver, Howard A., 1946-
xSilver, Howard A.
Mathematics: Contemporary Topics &
Applications. P-H.
Silver, Howard F.
xSilver, Howard.
Introduction to Engineering Thermodynamics.
West Pub.
Silver, Isidore, 1934-
xSilver, Isidore.
Law & Economics. Lerner Pubns.
Silver, J. A. see Silver, John Archer.
Silver, James W. see Silver, James Wesley.
Silver, James Wesley, 1907-
xSilver, James W.
Confederate Morale & Church Propaganda.
Norton.
Confederate Morale & Church Propaganda.
Peter Smith.
Silver, John A. see Silver, John Archer.

Silver, John Archer, d. 1916
xSilver, J. A.
Provisional Government of Maryland:
1774-1777. Johnson Repr.
xSilver, John A.
The Provisional Government of Maryland
(1774-1777). AMS Pr.
Silver, Nathan.
xSilver, Nathan.
Lost New York. Schocken.
Silver, Pamela.
xSilver, Pamela.
The Education of the Poor: The History of a
National School 1824-1974. Routledge &
Kegan.
Silver, Rae.
xSilver, Rae.
Intro. by Hormones & Reproductive Behavior:
Readings from Scientific American. W H
Freeman.
ed. Parental Behavior in Birds. Acad Pr.
Silver, Sylvia, 1942-
xSilver, Sylvia.
Anaerobic Bacteriology for the Clinical
Laboratory. Mosby.
Silverberg, Robert.
xSilverberg, Robert.
ed. The Aliens: Seven Stories of Science
Fiction. Elsevier-Nelson.
ed. The Androids Are Coming: Seven Stories
of Science Fiction. Elsevier-Nelson.
Auk, the Dodo, & the Oryx: Vanished &
Vanishing Creatures. T Y Crowell.
ed. Best of New Dimensions. PB.
The Book of Skulls. Berkley Pub.
Capricorn Games. Donning Co.
Clocks for the Ages; How Scientists Date the
Past. Macmillan.
Collision Course. Ace Bks.
ed. Deep Space: Eight Stories of Science
Fiction. Elsevier-Nelson.
Downward to the Earth. Berkley Pub.
Dying Inside. Ballantine.
The Edge of Space: Three Original Novellas of
Science Fiction. Elsevier-Nelson.
ed. Galactic Dreamers: Science Fiction As
Visionary Literature. Random.
Ghost Towns of the American West. T Y
Crowell.
ed. The Infinite Web: Eight Stories of Science
Fiction. Dial.
Lord Valentine's Castle. Har-Row.
ed. Mutants: Eleven Stories of Science Fiction.
Elsevier-Nelson.
Next Stop the Stars. Ace Bks.
Nightwings. Avon.
The Silent Invaders. Ace Bks.
Stepsons of Terra. Ace Bks.
The Stochastic Man. Fawcett.
Thorns. Ballantine.
Those Who Watch. NAL.
A Time of Changes. Berkley Pub.
ed. Trips in Time: Nine Stories of Science
Fiction. Elsevier-Nelson.
Unfamiliar Territory. Berkley Pub.
Silverberg, S. G.
xSilverberg, Steven G.
Estrogens & Cancer. Wiley.
Surgical Pathology of the Uterus. Wiley.
Silverberg, Steven G. see Silverberg, S. G.
Silverman, Al.
xSilverman, Al.
Foster & Laurie. Little.
Foster & Laurie. Popular Lib.
Silverman, Alan S.
xSilverman, Alan S.
Handbook of Chinese for Mathematicians.
IEAS Ctr Chinese Stud.
Silverman, Bertram.
xSilverman, Bertram.

The Worker in Post-Industrial Capitalism: Liberal & Radical Responses. Free Pr.

Silverman, Burt, 1928-
  xSilverman, Burt.
    Painting People. Watson-Guptill.

Silverman, David.
  xSilverman, David.
    The Material Word: Some Theories of Language & Its Limits. Routledge & Kegan.
    Reading Castaneda: A Prologue to the Social Sciences. Routledge & Kegan.

Silverman, Eliot N.
  xSilverman, Eliot N.
    Statistics: A Common Sense Approach. Prindle.

Silverman, Herb.
  xSilverman, Herb.
    Complex Variables. HM.

Silverman, Hugh.
  xSilverman, Hugh.
    Piaget, Philosophy & the Human Sciences. Humanities.

Silverman, I. see Silverman, Irwin.

Silverman, Irwin.
  xSilverman, I.
    Human Subject in the Psychological Laboratory. Pergamon.

Silverman, Jerry.
  xSilverman, Jerry.
    How to Play the Guitar. Doubleday.

Silverman, Kenneth.
  xSilverman, Kenneth.
    ed. Colonial American Poetry. Hafner.

Silverman, Leslie.
  xSilverman, Leslie.
    Particle Size Analysis in Industrial Hygiene. Acad Pr.

Silverman, Meyer M.
  xSilverman, Meyer M.
    Occlusion in Prosthodontics & in the Natural Dentition. Mutual.

Silverman, R. see Silverman, Rhoda.

Silverman, Rhoda.
  xSilverman, R.
    ed. Radiation Therapy with Heavy Particles & Fast Electrons. Noyes.

Silverman, Richard A.
  xSilverman, Richard A.
    Complex Analysis with Applications. P-H.

Silverman, Robert E.
  xSilverman, R.
    Essentials of Psychology. P-H.
  xSilverman, Robert E.
    Psychology. P-H.

Silverman, Sanford L.
  xSilverman, Sanford L.
    Theory of Relationships. Philos Lib.

Silverman, William A.
  xSilverman, William A.
    Retrolental Fibroplasia: A Modern Parable. Grune.

Silverman, William B.
  xSilverman, William B.
    Rabbinic Wisdom & Jewish Values. UAHC.

Silvern, Leonard C. see Silvern, Leonard Charles.

Silvern, Leonard Charles, 1919-
  xSilvern, Leonard C.
    Fundamentals of Teaching Machine & Programmed Learning Systems. Ed & Training.
    Fundamentals of Teaching Machine & Programmed Learning Systems Guide. Ed & Training.

Silvers, William L.
  xSilvers, William L.
    I Filed Bankruptcy & I'm Glad I Did. Bryden.

Silverstein, Alvin.
  xSilverstein, Alvin.
    Aging. Watts.
    Alcoholism. Lippincott.
    Allergies. Lippincott.
    Apples: All About Them. P-H.
    Cancer. John Day.
    Conquest of Death. Macmillan.
    Diabetes: The Sugar Disease. Lippincott.
    Digestive System: How Living Creatures Use Food. P-H.
    Endocrine System: Hormones in the Living World. P-H.
    The Genetics Explosion. Schol Bk Serv.
    Guinea Pigs, All About Them. Lothrop.
    Human Anatomy & Physiology. Wiley.
    Muscular System: How Living Creatures Move. P-H.
    Potatoes: All About Them. P-H.
    The World of Bionics. Methuen Inc.

Silverstein, Charles.
  xSilverstein, Charles.
    A Family Matter: A Parent's Guide to Homosexuality. McGraw.

Silverstein, Harvey. see Silverstein, Harvey B.

Silverstein, Harvey B.
  xSilverstein, Harvey.
    Superships & Nation-States: The Transnational Politics of the Intergovernmental Maritime Consultative Organization. Westview.

Silverstein, Josef.
  xSilverstein, Josef.
    Burmese Politics: The Dilemma of National Unity. Rutgers U Pr.

Silverstein, Lee M.
  xSilverstein, Lee M.
    Consider the Alternative. CompCare.

Silverstein, M. L. see Silverstein, Martin L.

Silverstein, Martin L., 1939-
  xSilverstein, M. L.
    Boundary Theory for Symmetric Markov Processes. Springer-Verlag.
    Symmetric Markov Processes. Springer-Verlag.

Silverstein, Max.
  xSilverstein, Max.
    Psychiatric Aftercare: Planning for Community Mental Health Service. U of Pa Pr.

Silverstein, Mel.
  xSilverstein, Mel.
    Side Effects. Doubleday.
  xSilverstein, Melvin J.
    Conspiracy of Silence. Doubleday.

Silverstein, Melvin J. see Silverstein, Mel.

Silverstein, Mira.
  xSilverstein, Mira.
    Bargello Plus. Scribner.

Silverstein, Shel.
  xSilverstein, Shel.
    illus. Giving Tree. Har-Row.

Silverstone. see Silverstone, Lou.

Silverstone, Lou.
  xSilverstone.
    Politically Mad. Warner Bks.

Silverstone, Marilyn.
  xSilverstone, Marilyn.
    Bala: Child of India. Hastings.

Silverstone, Trevor.
  xSilverstone, Trevor.
    Drug Treatment in Psychiatry. Routledge & Kegan.

Silvert, Kalman H.
  xSilvert, Kalman H.
    ed. Discussion at Bellagio: The Political Alternatives of Development. Am U Field.
    Education, Values & the Possibilities for Social Change in Chile. Inst Study Human.

Silverthorne. see Silverthorne, L. C.

Silverthorne, Elizabeth.
  xSilverthorne, Elizabeth.
    I, Heracles. Abingdon.

Silverthorne, L. C.
  xSilverthorne.
    The British Foot Guards: A Bibliography. Hope Farm.

Silvester, Hans. see Silvester, Hans Walter.

Silvester, Hans Walter.
  xSilvester, Hans.
    Horses of the Camargue. Penguin.

Silvette, Herbert.
  xSilvette, Herbert.
    Doctor on the Stage: Medicine & Medical Men in Seventeenth-Century England. U of Tenn Pr.

Silvia, M. T. see Silvia, Manuel T.

Silvia, Manuel T.
  xSilvia, M. T.
    Deconvolution of Geophysical Time Series in the Exploration of Oil & Natural Gas. Elsevier.

Silvian, Leonore.
  xSilvian, Leonore.
    Understanding Diabetes. Monarch Pr.

Silving, Helen.
  xSilving, Helen.
    Criminal Justice. W S Hein.

Silvis, Craig.
  xSilvis, Craig.
    Rat Stew. HM.

Silvius, G. Harold. see Silvius, George Harold.

Silvius, George Harold.
  xSilvius, G. Harold.
    Planning & Organizing Instruction. McKnight.
    Teaching Successfully in Industrial Education. McKnight.

Silvoso, Joseph A. see Silvoso, Joseph Anton.

Silvoso, Joseph Anton.
  xSilvoso, Joseph A.
    Auditing. SW Pub.

Sim, Stephen K.
  xSim, Stephen K.
    Medicinal Plant Alkaloids: An Introduction for Pharmacy Students. U of Toronto Pr.

Simak, Clifford D., 1904-
  xSimak, Clifford D.
    All Flesh Is Grass. Avon.
    The Fellowship of the Talisman. Ballantine.
    Mastodonia. Ballantine.
    Out of Their Minds. Berkley Pub.
    They Walked Like Men. Avon.
    The Trouble with Tycho. Ace Bks.

Simckes, Seymour.
  xSimckes, Seymour.
    The Comatose Kids. Fiction Coll.

Simcox, Carroll E. see Simcox, Carroll Eugene.

Simcox, Carroll Eugene, 1912-
  xSimcox, Carroll E.
    Notes to the Overworld. Seabury.

Sime, James, 1843-1895
  xSime, James.
    Life of Johann Wolfgang Goethe. Kennikat.
    Life of Johann Wolfgang Goethe. R West.

Simenon, Georges, 1903-
  xSimenon, Georges.

The Accomplices. HarBraceJ.
African Trio: Talatala, Tropic Moon, Aboard
   the Aquitaine. HarBraceJ.
The Cat. HarBraceJ.
Disappearance of Odile. HarBraceJ.
Family Lie. HarBraceJ.
The Glass Cage. HarBraceJ.
Maigret & the Killer. HarBraceJ.
Maigret & the Man on the Bench. HarBraceJ.
Maigret & the Toy Village. HarBraceJ.
Maigret & the Wine Merchant. HarBraceJ.
Maigret in Exile. HarBraceJ.
Maigret Sets a Trap. HarBraceJ.
Maigret's Rival. HarBraceJ.
Monsieur Monde Vanishes. HarBraceJ.
The Night Club. HarBraceJ.
Sunday. HarBraceJ.
The Venice Train. HarBraceJ.
When I Was Old. HarBraceJ.
The White Horse Inn. HarBraceJ.

Simeon, Michel.
   xSimeon, Michel.
   Freud: The Psychoanalytic Adventure. HR&W.
Simeon, Richard.
   xSimeon, Richard.
   Federal-Provincial Diplomacy: The Making of
      Recent Policy in Canada. U of Toronto Pr.
Simic, Charles, 1938-
   xSimic, Charles.
   Charon's Cosmology. Braziller.
Simini, Joseph Peter.
   xSimini, Joseph Peter.
   Accounting Made Simple. Doubleday.
Simkin, James. see Simkin, James Solomon.
Simkin, James Solomon, 1919-
   xSimkin, James.
   Gestalt Therapy Mini Lectures. Celestial Arts.
Simkin, William E.
   xSimkin, William E.
   Mediation & the Dynamics of Collective
      Bargaining. BNA.
Simkins, Francis B. see Simkins, Francis Butler.
Simkins, Francis Butler, 1898-
   xSimkins, Francis B.
   Everlasting South. La State U Pr.
   A History of the South. Random.
Simkovich, Marcellus.
   xSimkovich, Marcellus.
   The Approaching Maximal Leadership Conflict
      for Domination of the World. Inst Econ Pol.
Simmel, Edward C.
   xSimmel, Edward G.
   ed. Early Experiences & Early Behavior:
      Implications for Social Development. Acad
      Pr.
Simmel, Edward G. see Simmel, Edward C.
Simmel, Georg, 1858-1918
   xSimmel, Georg.
   Essays on Interpretation in Social Science.
      Rowman.
   The Problems of the Philosophy of History: An
      Epistemological Essay. Free Pr.
   Sociology of Religion. Arno.
Simmel, Johannes M. see Simmel, Johannes Mario.
Simmel, Johannes Mario.
   xSimmel, Johannes M.
   Caesar Code. Popular Lib.
   The Cain Conspiracy. Popular Lib.
   I Confess. Popular Lib.
Simmen, Edward.
   xSimmen, Edward.
   ed. Pain & Promise: The Chicano Today. NAL.
Simmonds, James D.
   xSimmonds, James D.
   Masques of God: Form & Theme in the Poetry
      of Henry Vaughan. U of Pittsburgh Pr.
Simmonds, N. W. see Simmonds, Norman Willison.
Simmonds, Norman Willison, 1922-
   xSimmonds, N. W.

ed. Evolution of Crop Plants. Longman.
   Principles of Crop Improvement. Longman.
Simmons, Alan F.
   xSimmons, Alan F.
   Potted Orchards: Growing Fruit in Small
      Spaces. David & Charles.
Simmons, Alan John, 1950-
   xSimmons, John A.
   Moral Principles & Political Obligations.
      Princeton U Pr.
Simmons, Anthony.
   xSimmons, Anthony.
   The Optimists of Nine Elms. Pantheon.
Simmons, Bill.
   xSimmons, Bill.
   Money-Saving Answers to Your Car Care
      Questions. TAB Bks.
Simmons, Bob.
   xSimmons, Bob.
   Crepes & Omelets. Nitty Gritty.
Simmons, Charles W.
   xSimmons, Charles W.
   Afro-American History. Merrill.
Simmons College, Boston. School of Library Science.
   xSimmons College, Boston School of Library
      Science.
   Books & Publishing, 1956. Arno.
Simmons, D. M. see Simmons, Donald M.
Simmons, Donald C.
   xSimmons, Donald C.
   Extralinguistic Usages of Tonality in Efik
      Folklore. U of Ala Pr.
Simmons, Donald M.
   xSimmons, D. M.
   Nonlinear Programming for Operations
      Research. P-H.
   xSimmons, Donald M.
   Linear Programming for Operations Research.
      Holden-Day.
Simmons, Edgar.
   xSimmons, Edgar.
   Driving to Biloxi: Poems. La State U Pr.
Simmons, Ernest J. see Simmons, Ernest Joseph.
Simmons, Ernest Joseph, 1903-
   xSimmons, Ernest J.
   Chekhov: A Biography. U of Chicago Pr.
   English Literature & Culture in Russia,
      1553-1840. Octagon.
   Feodor Dostoevsky. Columbia U Pr.
   Outline of Modern Russian Literature:
      1880-1940. Greenwood.
   Pushkin. Peter Smith.
Simmons, George B., 1940-
   xSimmons, George B.
   The Indian Investment in Family Planning.
      Population Coun.
Simmons, Harold E. see Simmons, Harold Ernest.
Simmons, Harold Ernest, 1915-
   xSimmons, Harold E.
   The Psychoendocrine Aspects of Epilepsy. Gen
      Welfare.
   Work Relief to Rehabilitation. Gen Welfare.
Simmons, Harvey G.
   xSimmons, Harvey G.
   French Socialists in Search of a Role,
      1956-1967. Cornell U Pr.
Simmons, Jack, 1915-
   xSimmons, Jack.
   Southey. Kennikat.
   Southey. R West.
Simmons, James R. see Simmons, James Robert.
Simmons, James Robert.
   xSimmons, James R.
   Quest for Ethics. Philos Lib.
Simmons, James W. see Simmons, James William.
Simmons, James William, 1919-1976
   xSimmons, James W.

Relationship of Esteem Values with Intelligence
   Quotient & Grade Point Averages. R & E
   Res Assoc.
Simmons, Jeffrey.
   xSimmons, Jeffrey.
   Lucky Fellow. St Martin.
Simmons, John, 1938-
   xSimmons, John.
   ed. Cocoa Production: Economic & Botanical
      Perspectives. Praeger.
Simmons, John A. see Simmons, Alan John.
Simmons, John S. see Simmons, John Stephen.
Simmons, John Stephen.
   xSimmons, John S.
   Decisions About the Teaching of English.
      Allyn.
Simmons, Marc.
   xSimmons, Marc.
   The Little Lion of the Southwest: A Life of
      Manuel Antonio Chaves. Swallow.
Simmons, Mary K. see Simmons, Mary Kay.
Simmons, Mary Kay.
   xSimmons, Mary K.
   Cameron Hill. PB.
   The Year of the Rooster. PB.
Simmons, Max.
   xSimmons, Max.
   Dyes & Dyeing. Van Nos Reinhold.
Simmons, Merle. see Simmons, Merle Edwin.
Simmons, Merle E. see Simmons, Merle Edwin.
Simmons, Merle Edwin, 1918-
   xSimmons, Merle.
   Folklore Bibliography for 1973. Res Ctr Lang
      Semiotic.
   xSimmons, Merle E.
   Folklore Bibliography for 1974. Res Ctr Lang
      Semiotic.
   Folklore Bibliography for 1975. Inst Study
      Human.
Simmons, Ozzie G.
   xSimmons, Ozzie G.
   Anglo-Americans & Mexican Americans in
      South Texas. Arno.
Simmons, Patricia A.
   xSimmons, Patricia A.
   Guess What, God!. Broadman.
Simmons, Patricia W. see Simmons, Patricia Worth.
Simmons, Patricia Worth.
   xSimmons, Patricia W.
   photos by The President & Her Sweet Old
      Ladies: A Chronicle of the Burton Senior
      Citizens. Branden.
Simmons, Paul D.
   xSimmons, Paul D.
   ed. Issues in Christian Ethics. Broadman.
Simmons, Paula.
   xSimmons, Paula.
   The Green Tomato Cookbook. Pacific Search.
   The Handspinner's Guide to Selling. Pacific
      Search.
   Raising Sheep the Modern Way. Garden Way
      Pub.
   Spinning & Weaving with Wool. Pacific Search.
Simmons, Peter J.
   xSimmons, Peter J.
   Choice & Demand. Halsted Pr.
Simmons, Richard E.
   xSimmons, Richard E.
   Managing Behavioral Processes: Applications of
      Theory & Research. AHM Pub.
Simmons, Robert A.
   xSimmons, Robert A.
   Fighting to Live & to Be. Chris Mass.
   Leadership for the New Frontier. Chris Mass.
Simmons, Robert H. see Simmons, Robert Harrison.
Simmons, Robert Harrison.
   xSimmons, Robert H.

Public Administration: Values, Policy, &
Change. Alfred Pub.

Simmons, Robert R.
xSimmons, Robert R.
The Strained Alliance: Peking, P'yongyang,
Moscow & the Politics of the Korean Civil
War. Free Pr.

Simmons, Roger A.
xSimmons, Roger A.
Palca & Pucara: A Study of the Effects of
Revolution on Two Bolivian Haciendas. U of
Cal Pr.

Simmons, Seymour.
xSimmons, Seymour.
Drawing: The Creative Process. P-H.

Simmons, Steven J.
xSimmons, Steven J.
The Fairness Doctrine & the Media. U of Cal
Pr.

Simmons, Virginia M. *see* Simmons, Virginia Mcconnell.

Simmons, Virginia McConnell, 1928-
xSimmons, Virginia M.
San Luis Valley: The Land of the Six-Armed
Cross. Pruett.

Simmons, Walt. *see* Simmons, Walter J.

Simmons, Walter J.
xSimmons, Walt.
Lapstrake Boatbuilding. Intl Marine.
xSimmons, Walter J.
Lapstrake Boatbuilding. Intl Marine.

Simms, Brigitte S. *see* Simms, Brigitte Schermer.

Simms, Brigitte Schermer, 1936-
xSimms, Brigitte S.
German-American Cookery: A Bilingual Guide.
C E Tuttle.

Simms, D. J. *see* Simms, David John.

Simms, David John.
xSimms, D. J.
Lectures on Geometric Quantization.
Springer-Verlag.

Simms, Henry H. *see* Simms, Henry Harrison.

Simms, Henry Harrison, 1896-
xSimms, Henry H.
A Decade of Sectional Controversy,
1851-1861. Greenwood.

Simms, James R.
xSimms, James R.
Measure of Knowledge. Philos Lib.

Simms, W. Gilmore. *see* Simms, William Gilmore.
Simms, William G. *see* Simms, William Gilmore.

Simms, William Gilmore, 1806-1870
xSimms, W. Gilmore.
Border Beagles: A Tale of Mississippi. AMS Pr.
Guy Rivers: A Tale of Georgia. AMS Pr.
Mellichampe: A Legend of the Santee. AMS
Pr.
Southward Ho: A Spell of Sunshine. AMS Pr.
xSimms, William G.
The Life of Francis Marion. Arno.
Martin Faber: The Story of a Criminal; &
Other Tales. Arno.
Mellichampe: A Legend of the Santee. Reprint.

Simo, Connie.
xSimo, Connie.
Sandtiquity. Taplinger.

Simon. *see* Simon, Herbert Alexander.

Simon, Alexander.
xSimon, Alexander.
ed. Aging in Modern Society. Am Psychiatric.

Simon, Andre L. *see* Simon, Andre Louis.

Simon, Andre Louis.
xSimon, Andre L.
Dictionary of Gastronomy. Overlook Pr.
How to Make Wines & Cordials. Peter Smith.
Mushroom Recipes. Dover.

Simon, Andrew L.
xSimon, Andrew L.
Energy Resources. Pergamon.

Simon, Anne W.
xSimon, Anne W.

The Thin Edge. Avon.
The Thin Edge: Coast & Man in Crisis.
Har-Row.

Simon, Arthur, 1930-
xSimon, Arthur.
Bread for the World. Eerdmans.
Bread for the World. Paulist Pr.

Simon, Arthur. *see* Simon, Arthur R.

Simon, Arthur B.
xSimon, Arthur B.
Algebra & Trigonometry with Analytic
Geometry. W H Freeman.

Simon, Arthur R.
xSimon, Arthur.
Faces of Poverty. Macmillan.

Simon, Barry.
xSimon, Barry.
Functional Integration & Quantum Physics.
Acad Pr.
Quantum Mechanics for Hamiltonians Defined
As Quadratic Forms. Princeton U Pr.
Trace Ideals & Their Applications. Cambridge
U Pr.

Simon, Bennett, 1933-
xSimon, Bennett.
Mind & Madness in Ancient Greece: The
Classical Roots of Modern Psychiatry.
Cornell U Pr.

Simon, Bernard.
xSimon, Bernard.
ed. Simon's Directory of Theatrical Materials,
Services & Information. Package Publ.

Simon, Bert.
xSimon, Bert.
Ham Radio Incentive Licensing Guide. TAB
Bks.

Simon, Carly.
xSimon, Carly.
The Carly Simon Complete. Knopf.

Simon, Claude.
xSimon, Claude.
Histoire. Braziller.
The Palace. Braziller.

Simon, Dyanne. *see* Simon, Dyanne Asimow.

Simon, Dyanne Asimow.
xSimon, Dyanne.
The Barter Book. Dutton.

Simon, Edith, 1917-
xSimon, Edith.
Reformation. Time-Life.
Reformation. Silver.

Simon, G. *see* Simon, George.

Simon, George.
xSimon, G.
Principles of Bone X-Ray Diagnosis.
Butterworths.
Principles of Chest X-Ray Diagnosis.
Butterworths.

Simon, George T. *see* Simon, George Thomas.

Simon, George Thomas.
xSimon, George T.
The Best of the Music Makers. Doubleday.
Feeling of Jazz. S&S.

Simon, Gerhard.
xSimon, Gerhard.
Church, State & Opposition in U. S. S. R.. U of
Cal Pr.

Simon, Harold A.
xSimon, Harold A.
A Student's Introduction to Engineering
Design. Pergamon.

Simon, Herbert Alexander, 1916-
xSimon.
Models of Thought. Yale U Pr.

Simon, Hilda.
xSimon, Hilda.

Chameleons & Other Quick-Change Artists.
Dodd.
The Courtship of Birds. Dodd.
illus. Frogs & Toads of the World. Lippincott.
Strange Breeding Habits of Aquarium Fish.
Dodd.
Wonders of Hummingbirds. Dodd.

Simon, Howard. *see* Simon, Mina Lewiton.

Simon, Irene.
xSimon, Irene.
ed. Neo-Classical Criticism, 1660-1800. U of
SC Pr.

Simon, Joan.
xSimon, Joan.
Education & Society in Tudor England.
Cambridge U Pr.

Simon, John.
xSimon, John.
Filth-Diseases & Their Prevention. Arno.

Simon, John. *see* Simon, John Ivan.
Simon, John A. *see* Simon, John Allsebrook Simon, 1st
Viscount.

Simon, John Allsebrook Simon, 1st Viscount, 1873-1954
xSimon, John A.
Comments & Criticisms. Kennikat.

Simon, John G.
xSimon, John G.
The Ethical Investor: Universities & Corporate
Responsibility. Yale U Pr.

Simon, John Ivan.
xSimon, John.
Uneasy Stages: A Chronicle of the New York
Theater, 1963-1973. Random.

Simon, John K.
xSimon, John K.
ed. Modern French Criticism: From Proust &
Valery to Structuralism. U of Chicago Pr.

Simon, Julian. *see* Simon, Julian Lincoln.
Simon, Julian L. *see* Simon, Julian Lincoln.

Simon, Julian Lincoln, 1932-
xSimon, Julian.
Applied Managerial Economics. P-H.
xSimon, Julian L.
The Economics of Population Growth.
Princeton U Pr.

Simon, Kate.
xSimon, Kate.
England's Green & Pleasant Land. Knopf.

Simon, Leon.
xSimon, Leon.
Awakening Palestine. Hyperion Conn.
Studies in Jewish Nationalism. Hyperion Conn.

Simon, Linda, 1946-
xSimon, Linda.
Thornton Wilder-His World. Doubleday.

Simon, Marcia L.
xSimon, Marica L.
A Special Gift. HarBraceJ.

Simon, Marica L. *see* Simon, Marcia L.

Simon, Matthew, 1921-1968
xSimon, Matthew.
Cyclical Fluctuations & International Capital
Movements of the U. S.: 1865-1897. Arno.

Simon, Michael.
xSimon, Michael.
First Lessons in Black & White Photography.
HR&W.

Simon, Michael A.
xSimon, Michael A.
Matter of Life: Philosophical Problems of
Biology. Yale U Pr.

Simon, Michael S.
xSimon, Michael S.
Construction Contracts & Claims. McGraw.

Simon, Myron.
xSimon, Myron.
The Georgian Poetic. U of Cal Pr.

Simon, Neil.
xSimon, Neil.
The Collected Plays of Neil Simon. Avon.
Collected Plays of Neil Simon. Random.
The Comedy of Neil Simon. Avon.
Comedy of Neil Simon. Random.
Last of the Red Hot Lovers. Random.
Odd Couple. Random.

Simon, Norma.
xSimon, Norma.
Go Away, Warts!. A Whitman.
How Do I Feel. A Whitman.
I Know What I Like. A Whitman.
I Was So Mad!. A Whitman.
I'm Busy, Too. A Whitman.
Our First Sukkah. United Syn Bk.
Simhat Torah. United Syn Bk.
We Remember Philip. A Whitman.

Simon, Paul, 1928-
xSimon, Paul.
Lincoln's Preparation for Greatness: The
Illinois Legislative Years. U of Ill Pr.

Simon, Pedro.
xSimon, Pedro.
Expedition of Pedro De Ursua & Lope De
Aguirre in Search of El Dorado & Omagua in
1560. B Franklin

Simon, Peter, 1947-
xSimon, Peter.
Decent Exposures. Wingbow Pr.

Simon, Philip J. see Simon, Philip Jerome.
Simon, Philip Jerome, 1901-
xSimon, Philip J.
Cleft Roots. Priam Pr.

Simon, Raymond.
xSimon, Raymond.
Public Relations: Concepts & Practices. Grid
Pub.
Public Relations Management: Cases &
Simulations. Grid Pub.
Publicity & Public Relations Work Text. Grid
Pub.

Simon, Reeva S.
xSimon, Reeva S.
The Modern Middle East: A Guide to
Research Tools in the Social Sciences.
Westview.

Simon, Rita J. see Simon, Rita James.
Simon, Rita James.
xSimon, Rita J.
ed. As We Saw the Thirties: Essays on Social
& Political Movements of a Decade. U of Ill
Pr.
The Jury: Its Role in American Society.
Lexington Bks.

Simon, Roger D.
xSimon, Roger D.
The City-Building Process: Housing & Services
in New Milwaukee Neighborhoods. Am
Philos.

Simon, Seymour.
xSimon, Seymour.

About the Food You Eat. McGraw.
About Your Lungs. McGraw.
Animal Fact & Animal Fable. Crown.
Animals in Your Neighborhood. Walker & Co.
A Building on Your Street. Holiday.
Creatures from Lost Worlds. Lippincott.
illus. Danger from Below: Earthquakes - Past,
Present, & Future. Schol Bk Serv.
Deadly Ants. Schol Bk Serv.
Discovering What Earthworms Do. McGraw.
Discovering What Gerbils Do. McGraw.
Discovering What Puppies Do. McGraw.
Everything Moves. Walker & Co.
Exploring Fields & Lots: Easy Science Projects.
Garrard.
Finding Out with Your Senses. McGraw.
From Shore to Ocean Floor: How Life Survives
in the Sea. Watts.
The Long View into Space. Crown.
Look to the Night Sky: An Introduction to
Star Watching. Viking Pr.
Look to the Night Sky: An Introduction to
Star Watching. Penguin.
Meet the Giant Snakes. Walker & Co.
The Optical Illusion Book. Schol Bk Serv.
Paper Airplane Book. Penguin.
The Paper Airplane Book. Viking Pr.
Projects with Air. Watts.
Projects with Plants. Watts.
Space Monsters: From Movies, TV & Books.
Lippincott.
Strange Mysteries from Around the World.
Schol Bk Serv.
Tropical Saltwater Aquariums: How to Set
Them up & Keep Them Going. Viking Pr.

Simon, Sheldon. see Simon, Sheldon W.
Simon, Sheldon W., 1937-
xSimon, Sheldon.
Asian Neutralism & the U.S. Policy. Am
Enterprise.
xSimon, Sheldon W.
ed. The Military & Security in the Third
World: Domestic & International Impacts.
Westview.

Simon, Sidney B.
xSimon, Sidney B.
ed. Degrading the Grading Myths: A Primer of
Alternatives to Grades & Marks. Assn
Supervision.
Developing Values with Exceptional Children.
P-H.
Readings in Values Clarification. Winston Pr.

Simon, Ted, 1931-
xSimon, Ted.
Jupiter's Travels. Doubleday.

Simon, Ulrich. see Simon, Ulrich E.
Simon, Ulrich E.
xSimon, Ulrich.
A Theology of Auschwitz: The Christian Faith
& the Problem of Evil. John Knox.

Simon, Walter M. see Simon, Walter Michael.
Simon, Walter Michael, 1922-
xSimon, Walter M.
The Failure of the Prussian Reform Movement,
1807-1819. Fertig.

Simon, William, 1927-
xSimon, William.
Mathematical Magic. Scribner.
Mathematical Techniques for Biology &
Medicine. MIT Pr.

Simon, William. see Simon, William E.
Simon, William E., 1927-
xSimon, William.
A Time for Truth. Berkley Pub.
xSimon, William E.
A Time for Truth. McGraw.
A Time for Truth. Readers Digest Pr.

Simon, William H.
xSimon, William H.

ed. The Human Joint in Health & Disease. U
of Pa Pr.

Simon, William J. see Simon, William John.
Simon, William John.
xSimon, William J.
Clinical Dental Assisting. Har-Row.

Simon, Yves. see Simon, Yves Rene Marie.
Simon, Yves R. see Simon, Yves Rene Marie.
Simon, Yves Rene Marie.
xSimon, Yves.
Freedom & Community. Fordham.
Freedom of Choice. Fordham.
A General Theory of Authority. U of Notre
Dame Pr.
Great Dialogue of Nature & Space. Magi Bks.
Work, Society, & Culture. Fordham.
xSimon, Yves R.
A General Theory of Authority. Greenwood.

Simon, Zeno.
xSimon, Zeno.
Quantum Biochemistry & Specific Interactions.
Intl Schol Bk Serv.

Simond, Ada D. see Simond, Ada Deblanc.
Simond, Ada Deblanc.
xSimond, Ada D.
Let's Pretend: Mae Dee & Her Family Join the
Juneteenth Celebration. Stevenson Pr.

Simonds, A. P.
xSimonds, A. P.
Karl Mannheim's Sociology of Knowledge.
Oxford U Pr.

Simonds, Frank H. see Simonds, Frank Herbert.
Simonds, Frank Herbert, 1878-1936
xSimonds, Frank H.
They Won the War. Arno.

Simonds, H. R. see Simonds, Herbert Rumsey.
Simonds, Herbert Rumsey, 1887-
xSimonds, H. R.
A Concise Guide to Plastics. Krieger.

Simonds, Thomas C., 1833?-1857
xSimonds, Thomas C.
History of South Boston. Arno.

Simone, Andre, 1893-
xSimone, Andre.
Men of Europe. Arno.

Simonet, Andre.
xSimonet, Andre.
Apostles for Our Time: Thoughts on Apostolic
Spirituality. Alba.

Simonov, Konstantin M. see Simonov, Konstantin
Mikhailovich.
Simonov, Konstantin Mikhailovich, 1915-
xSimonov, Konstantin M.
Living & the Dead. Greenwood.

Simons, A. M. see Simons, Algie Martin.
Simons, Algie Martin, 1870-1950
xSimons, A. M.
The American Farmer. Arno.

Simons, Daryl B.
xSimons, Daryl B.
Sediment Transport Technology. WRP.

Simons, Elwyn L.
xSimons, Elwyn L.
Primate Evolution: An Introduction to Man's
Place in Nature. Macmillan.

Simons, George F.
xSimons, George F.
Journal for Life: Discovering Faith and Values
Through Journal Keeping - Theology from
Experience. ACTA Found.

Simons, Gustave.
xSimons, Gustave.
Coping with Crisis. Macmillan.

Simons, Harry.
xSimons, Harry.
Intermediate Accounting Standard Volume. SW
Pub.

Simons, Henry C. see Simons, Henry Calvert.
Simons, Henry Calvert, 1899-1946
xSimons, Henry C.

Economic Policy for a Free Society. U of
 Chicago Pr.
 Personal Income Taxation: The Definition of
 Income As a Problem of Fiscal Policy. U of
 Chicago Pr.
Simons, Howard.
 xSimons, Howard.
 ed. The Media & Business. Random.
 Simons' List Book. S&S.
Simons, J. B.
 xSimons, J. B.
 Arnold Bennett & His Novels: A Critical
 Study. Folcroft.
Simons, J. H. *see* Simons, Joseph H.
Simons, Joseph. *see* Simons, Joseph B.
Simons, Joseph B.
 xSimons, Joseph.
 Living Together: Communication in the
 Unmarried Relationship. Nelson-Hall.
 The Search for Self: An Introduction to
 Personal Social Adjustment. Heath.
Simons, Joseph H, 1897-
 xSimons, J. H.
 ed. Fluorine Chemistry. Acad Pr.
 xSimons, Joseph H.
 Structure of Science. Philos Lib.
Simons, Richard C.
 xSimons, Richard C.
 ed. Understanding Human Behavior in Health
 & Illness. Williams & Wilkins.
Simons, S.
 xSimons, S.
 Vector Analysis for Mathematicians, Scientists
 & Engineers. Pergamon.
Simonsen, Clifford E.
 xSimonsen, Clifford E.
 Juvenile Justice in America. Glencoe.
Simonsen, Sigurd J. *see* Simonsen, Sigurd Jay.
Simonsen, Sigurd Jay, 1891-
 xSimonsen, Sigurd J.
 The Brush Coyotes. Arno.
Simonsohn, S. *see* Simonsohn, Shelomo.
Simonsohn, Shelomo.
 xSimonsohn, S.
 History of the Jews in the Duchy of Mantua.
 Ktav.
Simonson, Ernst.
 xSimonson, Ernst.
 Psychological Aspects & Physiological
 Correlates of Work & Fatigue. C C Thomas.
Simonson, Harold P. *see* Simonson, Harold Peter.
Simonson, Harold Peter, 1926-
 xSimonson, Harold P.
 Francis Grierson. Coll & U Pr.
 ed. Quartet: A Book of Stories, Plays, Poems,
 & Critical Essays. Har-Row.
 Trio: A Book of Stories, Plays, & Poems.
 Har-Row.
Simonson, Lee, 1888-
 xSimonson, Lee.
 The Stage Is Set. Arno.
 Stage Is Set. Theatre Arts.
 ed. Theatre Art. Cooper Sq.
Simonson, Ray W. *see* Simonson, Roy Walter.
Simonson, Roy Walter.
 xSimonson, Ray W.
 ed. Non-Agricultural Applications of Soil
 Surveys. Elsevier.
Simont, Marc.
 xSimont, Marc.
 A Child's Eye View of the World. Delacorte.
Simonton, Carl. *see* Simonton, Oscar Carl.
Simonton, Oscar Carl.
 xSimonton, Carl.
 Getting Well Again: A Step-by-Step Self-Help
 Guide to Overcoming Cancer for Patients &
 Their Families. J P Tarcher.
Simonyi, K. *see* Simonyi, Karoly.
Simonyi, Karoly.
 xSimonyi, K.

Foundations of Electrical Engineering.
 Pergamon.
Simos, Bertha G.
 xSimos, Bertha G.
 A Time to Grieve: Loss As a Universal Human
 Experience. Family Serv.
Simper, Robert.
 xSimper, Robert.
 Gaff Sail. Intl Pubns Serv.
 Gaff Sail. Naval Inst Pr.
Simpkin, Richard.
 xSimpkin, Richard.
 Cruising Yachtsman's Troubleshooter. Barrie &
 Jenkins.
Simpkins, C. O. *see* Simpkins, Cuthbert Ormond.
Simpkins, Cuthbert Ormond, 1947-
 xSimpkins, C. O.
 Coltrane: A Biography. Herndon Hse.
Simpson, A. W. *see* Simpson, Alfred William Brian.
Simpson, Alan.
 xSimpson, Alan.
 Puritanism in Old & New England. U of
 Chicago Pr.
Simpson, Alfred William Brian.
 xSimpson, A. W.
 A History of the Common Law of Contract:
 The Rise of the Action of Assumpsit. Oxford
 U Pr.
Simpson, Antony E.
 xSimpson, Antony E.
 Guide to Library Research in Public
 Administration. Ctr Productive Public.
Simpson, B. *see* Simpson, Brian.
Simpson, Benjamin R. *see* Simpson, Benjamin Roy.
Simpson, Benjamin Roy, 1877-
 xSimpson, Benjamin R.
 Correlations of Mental Abilities. AMS Pr.
Simpson, Bertram L. *see* Simpson, Bertram Lenox.
Simpson, Bertram Lenox, 1877-1930
 xSimpson, Bertram L.
 Indiscreet Letters from Peking. Arno.
Simpson, Bessie C. *see* Simpson, Bessie Chenault.
Simpson, Bessie Chenault.
 xSimpson, Bessie C.
 Stuttering Therapy: A Guide for the Speech
 Clinician. Interstate.
Simpson, Brian.
 xSimpson, B.
 Geological Maps. Pergamon.
Simpson, Cuthbert A. *see* Simpson, Cuthbert Aikman.
Simpson, Cuthbert Aikman, 1892-1969
 xSimpson, Cuthbert A.
 Revelation & Response in the Old Testament.
 AMS Pr.
Simpson, D. P.
 xSimpson, D. P.
 Compiled by Cassell's Concise Latin-English,
 English-Latin Dictionary.. Macmillan.
Simpson, D. P. *see* Simpson, Donald Penistan.
Simpson, David, 1951-
 xSimpson, David.
 Irony & Authority in Romantic Poetry.
 Rowman.
Simpson, Dick. *see* Simpson, Dick W.
Simpson, Dick W.
 xSimpson, Dick.
 Strategies for Change: How to Make the
 American Political Dream Work. Swallow.
 Who Rules: An Introduction to the Study of
 Politics. Swallow.
Simpson, Donald Penistan.
 xSimpson, D. P.
 ed. Cassell's Latin Dictionary: Latin-English,
 English-Latin. Macmillan.
Simpson, Eileen. *see* Simpson, Eileen B.
Simpson, Eileen B.
 xSimpson, Eileen.

The Maze. S&S.
 Reversals: A Personal Account of Victory Over
 Dyslexia. HM.
Simpson, Elizabeth. *see* Simpson, Elizabeth Leonie.
Simpson, Elizabeth Leonie.
 xSimpson, Elizabeth.
 Humanistic Education: An Interpretation.
 Ballinger Pub.
Simpson, Frederick A. *see* Simpson, Frederick Arthur.
Simpson, Frederick Arthur, 1883-
 xSimpson, Frederick A.
 Louis Napoleon & the Recovery of France.
 Greenwood.
Simpson, George. *see* Simpson, George E.
Simpson, George E.
 xSimpson, George.
 Ghostboat. Dell.
 xSimpson, George E.
 Thin Air. Dell.
Simpson, George E. *see* Simpson, George Eaton.
Simpson, George Eaton.
 xSimpson, George E.
 Racial & Cultural Minorities: An Analysis of
 Prejudice & Discrimination. Har-Row.
Simpson, George G. *see* Simpson, George Gaylord.
Simpson, George Gaylord, 1902-
 xSimpson, George G.
 Concession to the Improbable: An
 Unconventional Autobiography. Yale U Pr.
 Meaning of Evolution: A Study of the History
 of Life & of Its Significance for Man. Yale U
 Pr.
 Penguins: Past & Present, Here & There. Yale
 U Pr.
 Principles of Animal Taxonomy. Columbia U
 Pr.
 This View of Life: The World of an
 Evolutionist. HarBraceJ.
Simpson, I. M. *see* Simpson, Ian Morven.
Simpson, Ian Morven, 1922-
 xSimpson, I. M.
 Fieldwork in Geology. Allen Unwin.
Simpson, J. L. *see* Simpson, Joe Leigh.
Simpson, Jacqueline.
 xSimpson, Jacqueline.
 ed. Icelandic Folktales & Legends. U of Cal Pr.
 tr. Legends of Icelandic Magicians. Rowman.
 The Viking World. St Martin.
Simpson, James C.
 xSimpson, James C.
 Fishes of Idaho. U Pr of Idaho.
Simpson, James H. *see* Simpson, James Hervey.
Simpson, James Hervey.
 xSimpson, James H.
 Navaho Expedition: Journal of a Military
 Reconnaissance from Santa Fe, New Mexico,
 to the Navaho Country, Made in 1849. U of
 Okla Pr.
Simpson, Janice. *see* Simpson, Janice Claire.
Simpson, Janice Claire.
 xSimpson, Janice.
 Andrew Young: A Matter of Choice. EMC.
 Ray Kroc: Big Mac Man. EMC.
 Sylvester Stallone: Going the Distance. EMC.
Simpson, Jean, 1942-
 xSimpson, Jean.
 Shisha Mirror Embroidery: A Contemporary
 Approach. Van Nos Reinhold.
Simpson, Joe Leigh.
 xSimpson, J. L.
 ed. Disorders of Sexual Differentiation:
 Etiology & Clinical Delineation. Acad Pr.
Simpson, John E. *see* Simpson, John Eddins.
Simpson, John Eddins.
 xSimpson, John E.
 Compiled by Georgia History: A Bibliography.
 Scarecrow.
Simpson, John F. *see* Simpson, John Frederick.
Simpson, John Frederick.
 xSimpson, John F.

Clinical Evaluation of the Nervous System.
Little.
Simpson, Kemper, 1893-
xSimpson, Kemper.
Economics for the Accountant. Arno.
Simpson, L. L. *see* Simpson, Lance L.
Simpson, Lance L.
xSimpson, L. L.
ed. Drug Treatment of Mental Disorders.
Raven.
Simpson, Lewis P.
xSimpson, Lewis P.
The Dispossessed Garden: Pastoral & History
in Southern Literature. U of Ga Pr.
Simpson, Louis. *see* Simpson, Louis Aston Marantz.
Simpson, Louis Aston Marantz, 1923-
xSimpson, Louis.
An Introduction to Poetry. St. Martin.
A Revolution in Taste: Studies of Dylan
Thomas, Allen Ginsberg, Sylvia Plath, &
Robert Lowell. Macmillan.
Simpson, Margarete, 1888-
xSimpson, Margarete.
Parent Preferences of Young Children. AMS
Pr.
Simpson, Marianna S. *see* Simpson, Marianna Shreve.
Simpson, Marianna Shreve, 1949-
xSimpson, Marianna S.
The Illustration of an Epic: The Earliest
Shahnama Manuscripts. Garland Pub.
Simpson, Michael A.
xSimpson, Michael A.
ed. Clinical Psycholinguistics. Irvington.
Simpson, Penny.
xSimpson, Penny.
The Japanese Pottery Handbook. Kodansha.
Simpson, Percy, 1865-1962
xSimpson, Percy.
Proof-Reading in the Sixteenth, Seventeenth &
Eighteenth Centuries. Folcroft.
Proof-Reading in the Sixteenth, Seventeenth, &
Eighteenth Centuries. Oxford U Pr.
Studies in Elizabethan Drama. Folcroft.
Simpson, R. Hope.
xSimpson, R. Hope.
Catalogue of the Ships in Homer's Iliad.
Oxford U Pr.
Simpson, Ray H. *see* Simpson, Ray Hamill.
Simpson, Ray Hamill, 1907-
xSimpson, Ray H.
A Study of Those Who Influence & of Those
Who Are Influenced in a Discussion. AMS
Pr.
Simpson, Richard, 1931-
xSimpson, Richard.
Ooti. Celestial Arts.
Simpson, Robert. *see* Simpson, Robert Wilfred Levick.
Simpson, Robert W. *see* Simpson, Robert Wilfred Levick.
Simpson, Robert Wilfred Levick, 1921-
xSimpson, Robert.
ed. Symphony. Penguin.
xSimpson, Robert W.
Carl Nielsen, Symphonist, 1865-1931.
Hyperion Conn.
Simpson, Rosemary, 1942-
xSimpson, Rosemary.
The Seven Hills of Paradise. Doubleday.
Simpson, Ruth, 1926-
xSimpson, Ruth.
From the Closet to the Courts: The Lesbian
Transition. Penguin.
Simpson, Thomas. *see* Simpson, Thomas D.
Simpson, Thomas D., 1942-
xSimpson, Thomas.
Money, Banking & Economic Analysis. P-H.
xSimpson, Thomas D.
Money, Banking & Economic Analysis. P-H.
Simpson, W. K. *see* Simpson, William Kelly.
Simpson, William, 1823-1899
xSimpson, William.

The Jonah Legend: A Suggestion of
Interpretation. Gale.
Simpson, William K. *see* Simpson, William Kelly.
Simpson, William Kelly.
xSimpson, W. K.
tr. The Literature of Ancient Egypt: An
Anthology of Stories, Instructions, & Poetry.
Yale U Pr.
xSimpson, William K.
ed. The Literature of Ancient Egypt: An
Anthology of Stories, Instructions, & Poetry.
Yale U Pr.
Sims, Benjamin T.
xSims, Benjamin T.
Fundamentals of Topology. Macmillan.
Sims, Chester T. *see* Sims, Chester Thomas.
Sims, Chester Thomas.
xSims, Chester T.
ed. The Superalloys. Wiley.
Sims Conference of Epidemiology, Alta, Utah, 1974.
xSIMS Conference on Epidemiology, Alta, Utah,
July 8-12, 1974.
Proceedings. Soc Indus-Appl Math.
SIMS Conference on Epidemiology, Alta, Utah, July
8-12, 1974. *see* Sims Conference of Epidemiology,
Alta, Utah, 1974.
Sims, Dorothy D.
xSims, Dorothy D.
The Food Processor Cookbook. Music Sales.
Sims, Edward R.
xSims, Edward R.
A Season with the Savior: Meditations on
Mark. Seabury.
Sims, J. Marion. *see* Sims, James Marion.
Sims, J. Taylor.
xSims, J. Taylor.
Marketing Channels: Systems & Strategies.
Har-Row.
Sims, James H.
xSims, James H.
Dramatic Uses of Biblical Allusions in Marlowe
& Shakespeare. U Presses Fla.
Sims, James Marion, 1813-1883
xSims, J. Marion.
Story of My Life. Da Capo.
Sims, Janet, 1945-
xSims, Janet L.
Compiled by The Progress of Afro-American
Women: A Selected Bibliography & Resource
Guide. Greenwood.
Sims, Janet L. *see* Sims, Janet.
Sims, John A.
xSims, John A.
Animals in the American Economy. Iowa St U
Pr.
Sims, John H.
xSims, John H.
ed. Human Behavior & the Environment
Interactions Between Man & His Physical
World. Maaroufa Pr.
Sims, Judy.
xSims, Judy.
Intro. by & ed. Puppets for Dreaming &
Scheming: A Puppet Source Book. Early
Stages.
Sims, Naomi, 1949-
xSims, Naomi.
How to Be a Top Model. Doubleday.
Sims, Newell L. *see* Sims, Newell Leroy.
Sims, Newell Leroy, 1878-
xSims, Newell L.
Hoosier Village: A Sociological Study with
Special Reference to Social Causation. AMS
Pr.
Sims, Patsy.
xSims, Patsy.
Cleveland Benjamin's Dead. Dutton.
Simsova, S. *see* Simsova, Silva.
Simsova, Silva.
xSimsova, S.

Handbook of Comparative Librarianship. Shoe
String.
ed. Lenin, Krupskaia & Libraries. Shoe String.
ed. Nicholas Rubakin & Bibliopsychology. Shoe
String.
Sinai, I. Robert.
xSinai, I. Robert.
The Decadence of the Modern World.
Schenkman.
Sinanian, Sylva. *see* Sinanian, Sylvia.
Sinanian, Sylvia.
xSinanian, Sylva.
ed. Eastern Europe in the 1970's. Irvington.
Sinanoglu, Oktay.
xSinanoglu, Oktay.
Sigma Molecular Orbital Theory. Yale U Pr.
Sinclair, A. M. *see* Sinclair, Allan M.
Sinclair, Allan M.
xSinclair, A. M.
Automatic Continuity of Linear Operators.
Cambridge U Pr.
Sinclair, Andrew.
xSinclair, Andrew.
Adventures in the Skin Trade. New Directions.
Breaking of Bumbo. S&S.
John Ford. Dial.
My Friend Judas. S&S.
Project. S&S.
Sinclair, B. *see* Sinclair, Bruce.
Sinclair, Bruce.
xSinclair, B.
ed. Let Us Be Honest & Modest: Technology
& Society in Canadian History. Oxford U Pr.
Sinclair, Catherine, 1800-1864
xSinclair, Catherine.
Holiday House. Garland Pub.
Sinclair, David.
xSinclair, David.
Edgar Allan Poe. Rowman.
Sinclair, David. *see* Sinclair, David Cecil.
Sinclair, David Cecil.
xSinclair, David.
Human Growth After Birth. Oxford U Pr.
Sinclair, Dorothy.
xSinclair, Dorothy.
Administration of the Small Public Library.
ALA.
Sinclair, I. *see* Sinclair, Ian Robertson.
Sinclair, Ian Robertson.
xSinclair, I.
Master Stereo Cassette Recording. Hayden.
Sinclair, James.
xSinclair, James.
Warrior Queen. Berkley Pub.
Warrior Queen. St Martin.
Sinclair, James E.
xSinclair, James E.
How the Experts Buy & Sell Gold Bullion,
Gold Stocks & Gold Coins. Arlington Hse.
Sinclair, John L., 1902-
xSinclair, John L.
In Time of Harvest. U of NM Pr.
Sinclair, Keith.
xSinclair, Keith.
Looking Back: A Photographic History of New
Zealand. Oxford U Pr.
Sinclair, Keith V. *see* Sinclair, Keith Val.
Sinclair, Keith Val.
xSinclair, Keith V.
Compiled by French Devotional Texts of the
Middle Ages: A Bibliographic Manuscript
Guide. Greenwood.
Sinclair, Louis.
xSinclair, Louis.
Leon Trotsky: A Bibliography. Hoover Inst Pr.
Sinclair, May.
xSinclair, May.

Intercessor, & Other Stories. Arno.
Tales Told by Simpson. Arno.

Sinclair, Michael.
xSinclair, Michael.
The Dollar Covenant. Norton.
The Masterplayers. Norton.

Sinclair, T. A. *see* Sinclair, Thomas Alan.

Sinclair, Thomas Alan, 1899-
xSinclair, T. A.
A History of Greek Political Thought.
Routledge & Kegan.

Sinclair, Upton. *see* Sinclair, Upton Beall.

Sinclair, Upton B. *see* Sinclair, Upton Beall.

Sinclair, Upton Beall, 1878-1968
xSinclair, Upton.
Boston: A Documentary Novel of the
Sacco-Vanzetti Case. Bentley.
Sylvia: A Novel. Scholarly.
xSinclair, Upton B.
Goose-Step: A Study of American Education.
AMS Pr.
King Coal: A Novel. AMS Pr.
Little Steel. AMS Pr.
Money Writes. Scholarly.

Sinclair, William A. *see* Sinclair, William Angus.

Sinclair, William Angus, 1905-
xSinclair, William A.
Socialism & the Individual: Notes on Joining
the Labour Party. Greenwood.

Sinden, J. A.
xSinden, J. A.
Unpriced Values: Decisions Without Market
Prices. Wiley.

Sinden, Margaret. *see* Sinden, Margaret J.

Sinden, Margaret J., 1915-
xSinden, Margaret.
Gerhart Hauptmann: The Prose Plays. Russell.

Sindermann, Carl J.
xSindermann, Carl J.
ed. Disease Diagnosis & Control in North
American Marine Aquaculture. Elsevier.

Sindler, Allan P.
xSindler, Allan P.
Bakke, DeFunis & Minority Admissions: The
Quest for Equal Opportunity. Longman.
ed. Change in the Contemporary South. Duke.
Political Parties in the United States. St
Martin.
Unchosen Presidents: The Vice-President &
Other Frustrations of Presidential Succession.
U of Cal Pr.

Siney, Marion C.
xSiney, Marion C.
The Allied Blockade of Germany: 1914-1916.
Greenwood.

Sinfield, A. *see* Sinfield, Alan.

Sinfield, Alan.
xSinfield, A.
Dramatic Monologue. Methuen Inc.

Sing, Charles F.
xSing, Charles F.
ed. Genetic Analysis of Common Diseases:
Applications to Predictive Factors in
Coronary Disease Proceedings, Workshop
Snowbird Utah, August 1978. A R Liss.

Singapore (City). University. Library.
xUniversity Of Singapore Library.
Catalogue of the Singapore-Malaysia
Collection. G K Hall.

Singelmann, Jay.
xSingelmann, Jay.
Business Programming Logic: A Structured
Approach. P-H.

Singer, Aaron.
xSinger, Aaron.
ed. Campaign Speeches of American
Presidential Candidates, 1928-1972. Ungar.

Singer, Andrew.
xSinger, Andrew.

The Backyard Poultry Book. Arco.

Singer, Armand. *see* Singer, Armand Edwards.

Singer, Armand Edwards, 1914-
xSinger, Armand.
Paul Bourget. Twayne.

Singer, Benjamin D., 1931-
xSinger, Benjamin D.
Racial Factors in Psychiatric Intervention. R &
E Res Assoc.

Singer, Bernard M. *see* Singer, Bertrand B.

Singer, Bertrand B.
xSinger, Bernard M.
Mathematics for Industrial Careers. McGraw.

Singer, Brett.
xSinger, Brett.
The Petting Zoo. S&S.

Singer, Caroline.
xSinger, Caroline.
Boomba Lives in Africa. Arno.

Singer, Charles G. *see* Singer, Charles Gregg.

Singer, Charles Gregg, 1910-
xSinger, Charles G.
South Carolina in the Confederation. Porcupine
Pr.

Singer, Charles J. *see* Singer, Charles Joseph.

Singer, Charles Joseph, 1876-1960
xSinger, Charles J.
Greek Biology & Greek Medicine. AMS Pr.

Singer, Dorothy. *see* Singer, Dorothy G.

Singer, Dorothy G.
xSinger, Dorothy.
A Piaget Primer: How a Child Thinks. NAL.
xSinger, Dorothy G.
ed. A Piaget Primer: How a Child Thinks. Intl
Univs Pr.

Singer, Edgar A. *see* Singer, Edgar Arthur.

Singer, Edgar Arthur, Jr.
xSinger, Edgar A.
Experience & Reflection. U of Pa Pr.
Mind As Behavior & Studies in Empirical
Idealism. AMS Pr.

Singer, Ferdinand L. *see* Singer, Ferdinand Leon.

Singer, Ferdinand Leon, 1907-
xSinger, Ferdinand L.
Strength of Materials. Har-Row.

Singer, Frederick.
xSinger, Frederick.
ed. Paget's Disease of Bone. Plenum Pub.

Singer, Frieda.
xSinger, Frieda.
ed. Daughters in High School: An Anthology
of Their Work. Daughters.

Singer, H. W. *see* Singer, Hans Wolfgang.

Singer, Hans W. *see* Singer, Hans Wolfgang.

Singer, Hans Wolfgang.
xSinger, H. W.
The Strategy of International Development:
Essays in the Economics of Backwardness. M
E Sharpe.
xSinger, Hans W.
Rich & Poor Countries. Johns Hopkins.

Singer, Harry.
xSinger, Harry.
ed. Theoretical Models & Processes of
Reading. Intl Reading.

Singer, I. J. *see* Singer, Israel Joshua.

Singer, I. M. *see* Singer, Isadore Manuel.

Singer, Irving.
xSinger, Irving.
The Goals of Human Sexuality. Schocken.

Singer, Isaac B. *see* Singer, Isaac Bashevis.

Singer, Isaac Bashevis.
xSinger, Isaac B.

Alone in the Wild Forest. FS&G.
A Day of Pleasure: Stories of a Boy Growing
up in Warsaw. FS&G.
Enemies: A Love Story. Fawcett.
Enemies, a Love Story. FS&G.
The Family Moskat. Fawcett.
In My Father's Court. Fawcett.
In My Father's Court. FS&G.
The Manor. Avon.
Nobel Lecture. FS&G.
Old Love. FS&G.
Shosha. Fawcett.
Shosha. FS&G.
Shosha. G K Hall.
The Spinoza of Market Street. Fawcett.
The Spinoza of Market Street. FS&G.
A Tale of Three Wishes. FS&G.
When Shlemiel Went to Warsaw & Other
Stories. FS&G.
xSinger, Isaac Bashevis.
A Little Boy in Search of God: Mysticism in a
Personal Light. Doubleday.

Singer, Isadore Manuel.
xSinger, I. M.
Lecture Notes on Elementary Topology &
Geometry. Springer-Verlag.

Singer, Israel Joshua, 1893-1944

xSinger, I. J.
Family Carnovsky. Vanguard.
Of a World That Is No More. Vanguard.

Singer, Jerome. *see* Singer, Jerome L.

Singer, Jerome L.
xSinger, Jerome.
The Inner World of Daydreaming. Har-Row.
xSinger, Jerome L.
The Child's World of Make-Believe:
Experimental Studies of Imaginative Play.
Acad Pr.
Imagery & Daydream Methods in
Psychotherapy & Behavior Modification.
Acad Pr.
Mind Play: The Creative Uses of Fantasy. P-H.

Singer, Joe, 1923-
xSinger, Joe.
How to Paint Figures in Pastel.
Watson-Guptill.
How to Paint Portraits in Pastel.
Watson-Guptill.
Painting Women's Portraits. Watson-Guptill.

Singer, Julia.
xSinger, Julia.
Impressions: A Trip to the German Democratic
Republic. Atheneum.

Singer, June. *see* Singer, June K.

Singer, June K.
xSinger, June.
Androgyny: Toward a New Theory of
Sexuality. Doubleday.

Singer, K. *see* Singer, Karam.

Singer, Karam.
xSinger, K.
The Prognosis of Narcotic Addiction.
Butterworths.

Singer, Lester. *see* Singer, Lester C.

Singer, Lester C.
xSinger, Lester.
Sociology: A Student's Introduction. U Pr of
Amer.

Singer, Linda R.
xSinger, Linda R.
Standards Relating to Dispositions. Ballinger
Pub.

Singer, Marcus G. *see* Singer, Marcus George.

Singer, Marcus George, 1926-
xSinger, Marcus G.

Generalization in Ethics: An Essay in the Logic of Ethics, with the Rudiments of a System of Moral Philosophy. Atheneum.
Generalization in Ethics: An Essay in the Logic of Ethics with the Rudiments of a System of Moral Philosophy. Russell.

Singer, Marilyn.
xSinger, Marilyn.
The Dog Who Insisted He Wasn't. Dutton.
No Applause, Please. Dutton.

Singer, Peter.
xSinger, Peter.
Marx. Hill & Wang.
Practical Ethics. Cambridge U Pr.

Singer, R. see Singer, Rolf.

Singer, Richard G.
xSinger, Richard G.
Just Deserts: Sentencing Based on Equality & Desert. Ballinger Pub.

Singer, Robert D.
xSinger, Robert D.
Psychological Development in Children. HR&W.

Singer, Robert N.
xSinger, Robert N.
Motor Learning & Human Performance: An Application to Motor & Movement Behaviors. Macmillan.
ed. Psychomotor Domain: Movement Behaviors. Lea & Febiger.
ed. Readings in Motor Learning. Lea & Febiger.
Teaching Physical Education: A Systems Approach. HM.

Singer, Rolf.
xSinger, R.
The Agaricales in Modern Taxonomy. Lubrecht & Cramer.

Singer, S. F. see Singer, Siegfried Fred.
Singer, S. Fred. see Singer, Siegfried Fred.

Singer, Sam, 1944-
xSinger, Sam.
Human Genetics: An Introduction to the Principles of Heredity. W H Freeman.

Singer, Samuel L.
xSinger, Samuel L.
The Student Journalist & Reviewing the Performing Arts. Rosen Pr.

Singer, Sarah.
xSinger, Sarah.
After the Beginning. Bauhan.

Singer, Siegfried Fred, 1924-
xSinger, S. F.
ed. The Changing Global Environment. Kluwer Boston.
xSinger, S. Fred.
Intro. by Energy: Readings from Scientific American. W H Freeman.
ed. Torques & Attitude Sensing in Earth Satellites. Acad Pr.

Singer, Stanley, 1925-
xSinger, Stanley.
The Nature of Ball Lightning. Plenum Pub.

Singer, Walter.
xSinger, Walter.
Pharmacy Review. Arco.

Singh, B. N. see Singh, Baij Nath.

Singh, Baij Nath, 1914-
xSingh, B. N.
Pathogenic & Non-Pathogenic Amoebae. Halsted Pr.

Singh, Baljit, 1929-
xSingh, Baljit.
Indian Foreign Policy: An Analysis. Asia.

Singh, Bhawani, 1935-
xSingh, Bhawani.
Council of States in India: A Structural & Functional Profile. Intl Pubns Serv.

Singh, D. Bright. see Singh, David Bright.

Singh, David Bright, 1917-
xSingh, D. Bright.
Inflationary Price Trends in India Since 1939. Asia.

Singh, Dharam Jit.
xSingh, Dharamjit.
Indian Cookery. Penguin.

Singh, Dharamjit. see Singh, Dharam Jit.

Singh, Diwakar P. see Singh, Diwakar Prasad.

Singh, Diwakar Prasad.
xSingh, Diwakar P.
American Attitude Towards Indian Nationalist Movement. South Asia Bks.

Singh, Jagjit.
xSingh, Jagjit.
Great Ideas & Theories of Modern Cosmology. Dover.
Great Ideas & Theories of Modern Cosmology. Peter Smith.
Great Ideas in Information Theory, Language & Cybernetics. Dover.
Great Ideas of Operations Research. Dover.
Great Ideas of Operations Research. Peter Smith.

Singh, Jyoti S. see Singh, Jyoti Shankar.

Singh, Jyoti Shankar.
xSingh, Jyoti S.
World Population Policies. Praeger.

Singh, K. Rajendra.
xSingh, K. Rajendra.
Politics of the Indian Ocean. Verry.

Singh, Karan, Sadri-i-riyasat of Jammu and Kashmir, 1931-
xSingh, Karan.
Towards a New India. Intl Bk Dist.

Singh, Khushwant.
xSingh, Khushwant.
I Shall Not Hear the Nightingale. Greenwood.

Singh, Lalita P. see Singh, Lalita Prasad.

Singh, Lalita Prasad.
xSingh, Lalita P.
Politics of Economic Cooperation in Asia: A Study of Asian International Organizations. U of Mo Pr.

Singh, M. M. see Singh, Madan Mohan.
Singh, M. Mohan. see Singh, Madan Mohan.

Singh, Madan Mohan.
xSingh, M. M.
Life in North-Eastern India in Pre-Mauryan Times: With Special References to 600 B.C. to 325 B.C. Orient Bk Dist.
xSingh, M. Mohan.
Life in North-Eastern India in Pre-Mauryan Times: With Special Reference to C.600b.C.-325b.C.. Verry.

Singh, R. John. see Singh, Roopnarine John.

Singh, Roderick P.
xSingh, Roderick P.
Anatomy of Hearing & Speech. Oxford U Pr.

Singh, Roopnarine John, 1932-
xSingh, R. John.
French Diplomacy in the Caribbean & the American Revolution. Exposition.

Singh, S. see Singh, Sadanand.
Singh, S. P. see Singh, Shish Pal.

Singh, Sadanand.
xSingh, S.
Distinctive Features: Theory & Validation. Univ Park.

Singh Saini, B. see Saini, B. Singh.
Singh, Sarva D. see Singh, Sarva Daman.

Singh, Sarva Daman.
xSingh, Sarva D.
Polyandry in Ancient India. Advent Bk.

Singh, Shamsher.
xSingh, Shamsher.

Coffee, Tea, & Cocoa: Market Prospects & Development Lending. Johns Hopkins.

Singh, Shish Pal, 1931-
xSingh, S. P.
Centre-State Relations in Agricultural Development. Advent Bk.

Singh, Tarlok, 1913-
xSingh, Tarlok.
India's Development Experience. St Martin.

Singh, Vijai P.
xSingh, Vijai P.
Caste, Class & Democracy: Changes in a Stratification System. Schenkman.

Singhal, D. P. see Singhal, Damodar P.

Singhal, Damodar P.
xSinghal, D. P.
India & World Civilization. Mich St U Pr.
xSinghal, Damodar P.
Pakistan. P-H.

Singhal, Radhey L. see Singhal, Radhey Lal.

Singhal, Radhey Lal.
xSinghal, Radhey L.
ed. Lead Toxicity. Urban & S.

Singhal, Ramash. see Singhal, Ramesh P.

Singhal, Ramesh P.
xSinghal, Ramash.
The Home Plumber's Bible. TAB Bks.

Singham, A. W.
xSingham, A. W.
ed. The Nonaligned Movement in World Politics. Lawrence Hill.

Singletary, Ernest E.
xSingletary, Ernest E.
Law Briefs on Litigation & the Rights of Exceptional Children, Youth, & Adults. U Pr of Amer.

Singletary, Otis A.
xSingletary, Otis A.
Negro Militia & Reconstruction. U of Tex Pr.

Singletary, W. E. see Singletary, Wilson E.

Singletary, Wilson E.
xSingletary, W. E.
ANS COBOL: A Pragmatic Approach. McGraw.

Singleton, Charles S. see Singleton, Charles Southward.

Singleton, Charles Southward, 1909-
xSingleton, Charles S.
Dante's Commedia: Elements of Structure. Johns Hopkins.
Journey to Beatrice. Johns Hopkins.

Singleton, Edward B.
xSingleton, Edward B.
Radiology of the Alimentary Tract in Infants & Children. Saunders.

Singleton, Esther, d. 1930
xSingleton, Esther.
Dutch New York. Arno.
Orchestra & Its Instruments. Gordon Pr.
The Orchestra & Its Instruments. Longwood Pr.
Story of the White House. Arno.

Singleton, Fred. see Singleton, Frederick Bernard.

Singleton, Frederick Bernard.
xSingleton, Fred.
Twentieth Century Yugoslavia. Columbia U Pr.

Singleton, George M. see Singleton, George Michael.

Singleton, George Michael.
xSingleton, George M.
Adventures with Aeneas. St Martin.

Singleton, Gregory H., 1940-
xSingleton, Gregory H.
Religion in the City of Angels: American Protestant Culture & Urbanization, Los Angeles, 1850-1930. Univ Microfilms.

Singleton, Marvin K. see Singleton, Marvin Kenneth.

Singleton, Marvin Kenneth.
xSingleton, Marvin K.

H. L. Mencken & the American Mercury
Adventure. Duke.
Singleton, Mary Ann.
xSingleton, Mary Ann.
Life After Marriage: Divorce As a New
Beginning. Stein & Day.
Singleton, Paul.
xSingleton, Paul.
Dictionary of Microbiology. Wiley.
Sinha, Amarendra Nath, 1913-
xSinha, Amarendro N.
Law of Citizenship & Aliens in India. Asia.
Sinha, Amarendro N. *see* Sinha, Amarendra Nath.
Sinha, Jai B. *see* Sinha, Jai Ballabha Prasad.
Sinha, Jai Ballabha Prasad.
xSinha, Jai B.
Some Problems of Public Sector Organizations.
Intl Pubns Serv.
Sinha, P. B. *see* Sinha, Prem Bahadur.
Sinha, Prem Bahadur, 1939-
xSinha, P. B.
Indian National Liberation Movement &
Russia: 1905-1917. Verry.
Sinha, R. *see* Sinha, Radha.
Sinha, Radha.
xSinha, R.
Income Distribution, Growth & Basic Needs in
India. Biblio Dist.
xSinha, Radha.
ed. The World Food Problem: Consensus &
Conflict. Pergamon.
Sinha, Raghuvir.
xSinha, Raghuvir.
Religion & Culture of North-Eastern India.
South Asia Bks.
Sinha, Sasadhar.
xSinha, Sasadhar.
Indian Independence in Perspective. Asia.
Sinick, Daniel.
xSinick, Daniel.
Occupational Information & Guidance. HM.
Sink, John D.
xSink, John D.
ed. The Control of Metabolism. Pa St U Pr.
Sinkankas, John.
xSinkankas, John.
Gemstones of North America. Van Nos
Reinhold.
Prospecting for Gemstones & Minerals. Van
Nos Reinhold.
Van Nostrand's Standard Catalog of Gems.
Van Nos Reinhold.
Sinkey, Joseph F.
xSinkey, Joseph F.
Problem & Failed Institutions in the
Commercial Banking Industry. Jai Pr.
Sinkler, Lorraine.
xSinkler, Lorraine.
The Alchemy of Awareness. Har-Row.
Sinnecker, Herbert.
xSinnecker, Herbert.
General Epidemiology. Wiley.
Sinnema, William, 1937-
xSinnema, William.
Electronic Transmission Technology: Lines,
Waves & Antennas. P-H.
Sinnes, A. Cort.
xSinnes, A. Cort.
All About Fertilizers, Soils & Water. Ortho.
Sinnett, Alfred P. *see* Sinnett, Alfred Percy.
Sinnett, Alfred Percy, 1840-1921
xSinnett, Alfred P.
ed. Incidents in the Life of Madame Blavatsky.
Arno.
Sinnett, E. Robert. *see* Sinnett, Earle Robert.
Sinnett, Earle Robert.
xSinnett, E. Robert.
Crisis Services for Campus & Community: A
Handbook for the Volunteer. C C Thomas.
Sinnigen, William G. *see* Sinnigen, William Gurnee.

Sinnigen, William Gurnee.
xSinnigen, William G.
A History of Rome to A.D. 565. Macmillan.
Sinning, Wayne E.
xSinning, Wayne E.
Experiments & Demonstrations in Exercise
Physiology. HR&W.
Sinopoulos, Takis.
xSinopoulos, Takis.
Landscape of Death: The Selected Poems of
Takis Sinopoulos. Ohio St U Pr.
Sinor, Denis.
xSinor, Denis.
History of Hungary. Greenwood.
Sinor, John.
xSinor, John.
Finsterhall of San Pasqual. Joyce Pr.
Ghosts of Cabrillo Lighthouse. Joyce Pr.
Sinski, James T. *see* Sinski, James Thomas.
Sinski, James Thomas, 1927-
xSinski, James T.
Dermatophytes in Human Skin, Hair & Nails.
C C Thomas.
Siohan, Robert, 1894-
xSiohan, Robert.
Stravinsky. Vienna Hse.
Sion, Abraham.
xSion, Abraham.
Prostitution & the Law. Merrimack Bk Serv.
Sion, M. *see* Sion, Maurice.
Sion, Maurice.
xSion, M.
A Theory of Semigroup Valued Measures.
Springer-Verlag.
Siotis, Dino. *see* Siotis, Dinos.
Siotis, Dinos.
xSiotis, Dino.
ed. Twenty Contemporary Greek Poets. Wire
Pr.
Siou, Lily.
xSiou, Lily.
Chi-Kung: The Art of Mastering the Unseen
Life Force. C E Tuttle.
Sipe, C. Hale. *see* Sipe, Chester Hale.
Sipe, Chester Hale, 1880-
xSipe, C. Hale.
Fort Ligonier & Its Times. Arno.
Siple, Patricia.
xSiple, Patricia.
ed. Understanding Language Through Sign
Language Research. Acad Pr.
Siporin, Max.
xSiporin, Max.
Introduction to Social Work Practice.
Macmillan.
Siposs, George. *see* Siposs, George C.
Siposs, George C.
xSiposs, George.
RC Modeler's Handbook of Gliders &
Sailplanes. TAB Bks.
Sippl, Charles. *see* Sippl, Charles J.
Sippl, Charles J.
xSippl, Charles.
Computer Power for the Small Business. P-H.
xSippl, Charles J.
Computer Dictionary. Bobbs.
Computer Dictionary. Sams.
Computer Dictionary & Handbook. Bobbs.
Computer Dictionary & Handbook. Sams.
Data Communications Dictionary. Van Nos
Reinhold.
Sipple, Horace. *see* Sipple, Horace Lawson.
Sipple, Horace Lawson.
xSipple, Horace.
ed. Sugars in Nutrition. Acad Pr.
SIPRI. *see* Stockholm International Peace Research
Institute.
Sir Thomas Beecham Society.
xSir Thomas Beecham Society.

Sir Thomas Beecham Discography. Greenwood.
Siracusa, Carl.
xSiracusa, Carl.
A Mechanical People: Perceptions of the
Industrial Order in Massachusetts,
1815-1880. Columbia U Pr.
Siracusa, Joseph M.
xSiracusa, Joseph M.
The Impact of the Cold War: Reconsiderations.
Kennikat.
Sirageldin, Ismail Abdel-Hamid.
xSirageldin, Ismail Abdel-Hamid.
Non-Market Components of National Income.
U of Mich Soc Res.
Sirc, Ljubo.
xSirc, Ljubo.
The Yugoslav Economy Under
Self-Management. St Martin.
Sircar, D. C. *see* Sircar, Dineschandra.
Sircar, Dineschandra.
xSircar, D. C.
Some Epigraphical Records of the Medieval
Period from Eastern India. South Asia Bks.
Sire, Glen.
xSire, Glen.
Deathmakers. S&S.
Sire, James W.
xSire, James W.
How to Read Slowly: A Christian Guide to
Reading with the Mind. Inter-Varsity.
Siren, Osvald, 1879-
xSiren, Osvald.
Chinese Painting: Leading Masters &
Principles. Hacker.
Giotto & Some of His Followers. Hacker.
History of Early Chinese Art. Hacker.
A History of Later Chinese Painting. Hacker.
Sirica, John J.
xSirica, John J.
To Set the Record Straight: The Break-In, the
Tapes, the Conspirators, the Pardon. NAL.
To Set the Record Straight: The Break-in, the
Tapes, the Conspirators, the Pardon. Norton.
Sirota, David.
xSirota, David.
Essentials of Real Estate Finance. Real Estate
Ed Co.
Sirota, N. N. *see* Sirota, Nikolai Nikolaevich.
Sirota, Nikolai Nikolaevich.
xSirota, N. N.
ed. Chemical Bonds in Semiconductors &
Thermodynamics. Plenum Pub.
Sirrocco, Alvin.
xSirrocco, Alvin.
Inpatient Health Facilities As Reported in the
1973 MFI Survey. Natl Ctr Health Stats.
Sisam, Kenneth.
xSisam, Kenneth.
Cynewulf & His Poetry. Folcroft.
Sisco, F. T. *see* Sisco, Frank Thayer.
Sisco, Frank Thayer.
xSisco, F. T.
Columbium & Tantalum. Krieger.
Sisemore, John T.
xSisemore, John T.
Rejoice, You're a Sunday School Teacher.
Broadman.
Siskind, Charles S. *see* Siskind, Charles Seymour.
Siskind, Charles Seymour, 1897-
xSiskind, Charles S.
Direct-Current Machinery. McGraw.
Sisley, Nick.
xSisley, Nick.
Deer Hunting Across North America. Freshet
Pr.
Grouse & Woodcock: An Upland Hunter's
Book. Stackpole.
Sisson, C. H. *see* Sisson, Charles Hubert.
Sisson, C. J. *see* Sisson, Charles Jasper.

Sisson, Charles Hubert, 1914-
xSisson, C. H.
In the Trojan Ditch: Collected Poems &
Selected Translations. Persea Bks.
Sisson, Charles J. see Sisson, Charles Jasper.
Sisson, Charles Jasper, 1885-1966
xSisson, C. J.
Lost Plays of Shakespeare's Age. R West.
xSisson, Charles J.
Lost Plays of Shakespeare's Age. Biblio Dist.
Thomas Lodge & Other Elizabethans. Octagon.
Sisson, Joseph A., 1930-
xSisson, Joseph A.
The Bare Facts of General Pathology.
Lippincott.
Handbook of Clinical Pathology. Lippincott.
Sisson, Richard.
xSisson, Richard.
The Congress Party in Rajasthan: Political
Integration & Institution-Building in an
Indian State. U of Cal Pr.
Training for Evangelism. Moody.
Sisson, Roger L.
xSisson, Roger L.
Computer Applications: A Short Course for
Non-EDP Managers. Wiley.
Sissons, Michael.
xSissons, Michael.
ed. Age of Austerity. Greenwood.
Sissors, Jack Z. see Sissors, Jack Zanville.
Sissors, Jack Zanville.
xSissors, Jack Z.
Advertising Media Planning. Crain Bks.
Sit, Amy. see Sit, Amy Wang.
Sit, Amy Wang.
xSit, Amy.
The Rib. New Leaf.
Sitaram, K. S.
nSitaram, K. S.
Foundations of Intercultural Communication.
Merrill.
Sitchin, Zecharia.
xSitchin, Zecharia.
The Twelfth Planet. Avon.
The Twelfth Planet. Stein & Day.
Sitenko, A. G. see Sitenko, Aleksei Grigorevich.
Sitenko, Aleksei Grigor'Evich.
xSitenko, A. G.
Lectures in Scattering Theory. Pergamon.
Lectures on the Theory of the Nucleus.
Pergamon.
Sites, P. see Sites, Paul.
Sites, Paul, 1926-
xSites, P.
Control & Constraint: An Introduction to
Sociology. Macmillan.
Sitney, P. Adams.
xSitney, P. Adams.
ed. The Avant-Garde Film: A Reader of
Theory & Criticism. NYU Pr.
Visionary Film: The American Avant-Garde
1943-1978. Oxford U Pr.
Visionary Film: The American Avant-Garde
1943-1978. Oxford U Pr.
Sitomer, Mindel.
xSitomer, Mindel.
Circles. T Y Crowell.
How Did Numbers Begin?. T Y Crowell.
Spirals. T Y Crowell.
Sitte, Camillo, 1843-1903
xSitte, Camillo.
The Art of Building Cities: City Building
According to Its Artistic Fundamentals.
Hyperion Conn.
Sittig, M. see Sittig, Marshall.
Sittig, Marshall.
xSittig, M.

Automotive Pollution Control Catalysts &
Devices. Noyes.
Detergent Manufacture Including Zeolite
Builders & Other New Materials. Noyes.
Fertilizer Industry: Processes, Pollution Control
& Energy Conservation. Noyes.
Handbook of Catalyst Manufacture. Noyes.
Hazardous & Toxic Effects of Industrial
Chemicals. Noyes.
How to Remove Pollutants & Toxic Materials
from Air & Water: A Practical Guide. Noyes.
Particulates & Fine Dust Removal: Processes &
Equipment. Noyes.
Pharmaceutical Manufacturing Encyclopedia.
Noyes.
Pollution Control in the Asbestos, Cement,
Glass & Allied Mineral Industries. Noyes.
Pollution Control in the Organic Chemical
Industry. Noyes.
Pollution Control in the Plastics & Rubber
Industry. Noyes.
Pollution Detection & Monitoring Handbook.
Noyes.
Practical Techniques for Saving Energy in the
Chemical, Petroleum & Metals Industries.
Noyes.
Pulp & Paper Manufacture: Energy
Conservation & Pollution Prevention. Noyes.
xSittig, Marshall.
ed. Geophysical & Geochemical Techniques for
Exploration of Hydrocarbons & Minerals.
Noyes.
Incineration of Industrial Hazardous Wastes &
Sludges. Noyes.
Landfill Disposal of Hazardous Wastes &
Sludges. Noyes.
Nitrogen in Industry. Van Nos Reinhold.
Sittler, Joseph.
xSittler, Joseph.
Ecology of Faith. Fortress.
Sitwell, Edith, Dame, 1887-1964
xSitwell, Edith.
Aspects of Modern Poetry. Arno.
Bath. Greenwood.
Bath. Hyperion Conn.
Collected Poems. Vanguard.
English Eccentrics. Vanguard.
I Live Under a Black Sun: A Novel.
Greenwood.
Music & Ceremonies. Vanguard.
Sitwell, Osbert, Sir, Bart, 1892-1969
xSitwell, Osbert.
The Collected Satires & Poems of Osbert
Sitwell. AMS Pr.
England Reclaimed, & Other Poems.
Greenwood.
Great Morning. Greenwood.
Laughter in the Next Room. Greenwood.
Penny Foolish: A Book of Tirades &
Panegyrics. Arno.
Pound Wise. Arno.
Triple Fugue. Arno.
Sitwell, S. see Sitwell, Sacheverell.
Sitwell, Sacheverell, 1897-
xSitwell, S.
Liszt. Gordon Pr.
xSitwell, Sacheverell.
Arabesque & Honeycomb. Arno.
Collected Poems. AMS Pr.
Liszt. Dover.
Selected Poems. AMS Pr.
Southern Baroque Art: A Study of Painting,
Architecture & Music in Italy & Spain of the
17th & 18th Centuries. Arno.
Thirteenth Caesar & Other Poems. Folcroft.
Siu, Ralph G. see Siu, Ralph Gun Hoy.

Siu, Ralph Gun Hoy, 1917-
xSiu, Ralph G.
The Craft of Power. Wiley.
Tao of Science: An Essay on Western
Knowledge & Eastern Wisdom. MIT Pr.
Sivachev, Nikolai V. see Sivachev, Nikolai Vasilevich.
Sivachev, Nikolai Vasilevich.
xSivachev, Nikolai V.
Russia & the United States. U of Chicago Pr.
Sivaramamurti, C.
xSivaramamurti, C.
The Art of India. Abrams.
Sivazlian, B. D.
xSivazlian, B. D.
Optimization Techniques in Operations
Research. P-H.
Sive, Helen. see Sive, Helen R.
Sive, Helen R.
xSive, Helen.
Music's Connecticut Yankee: An Introduction
to the Life and Music of Charles Ives.
Atheneum.
Sive, Mary R. see Sive, Mary Robinson.
Sive, Mary Robinson, 1928-
xSive, Mary R.
ed. Environmental Legislation: A Sourcebook.
Praeger.
Siven, C. H. see Siven, Claes-Henric.
Siven, Claes-Henric, 1940-
xSiven, C. H.
A Study in the Theory of Inflation &
Unemployment. Elsevier.
Sivetz, Michael.
xSivetz, Michael.
Coffee Technology. AVI.
Sivin, Irving.
xSivin, Irving.
Contraception & Fertility Change in the
International Postpartum Program. Population
Coun.
Sixth International Gas Bearing Symposium. see
International Gas Bearing Symposium, 6th, University
of Southampton, 1974.
Sizemore, Chris C. see Sizemore, Chris Costner.
Sizemore, Chris Costner.
xSizemore, Chris C.
I'm Eve. BJ Pub Group.
Sizemore, Michael. see Sizemore, Michael M.
Sizemore, Michael M.
xSizemore, Michael.
Energy Planning for Buildings. Am Inst Arch.
Sizer, Theodore, 1892-1967
xSizer, Theodore.
Aspects of the Social History of America.
Arno.
Sizer, Theodore R.
xSizer, Theodore R.
Age of the Academies. Tchrs Coll.
Places for Learning, Places for Joy:
Speculations on American School Reform.
Harvard U Pr.
Sjahrir, Soetan, 1909-1966
xSjahrir, Soetan.
Out of Exile. Greenwood.
xSjahrir, Sutan.
Our Struggle. Cornell Mod Indo.
Sjahrir, Sutan. see Sjahrir, Soetan.
Sjo, John.
xSjo, John.
Economics for Agriculturalists: A Beginning
Text in Agricultural Economics. Grid Pub.
Sjoback, H. see Sjoback, Hans.
Sjoback, Hans.
xSjoback, H.
Psychoanalytic Theory of Defensive Processes.
Halsted Pr.
Sjoberg, Gideon.
xSjoberg, Gideon.

ed. Ethics, Politics, & Social Research.
Schenkman.
Sjoman, Vilgot.
xSjoman, Vilgot.
Diary with Ingmar Bergman. Karoma.
Sjowall, Maj.
xSjowall, Maj.
The Abominable Man. Random.
The Laughing Policeman. Random.
Murder at the Savoy. Random.
Skaggs, Merrill M. *see* Skaggs, Merrill Maguire.
Skaggs, Merrill Maguire.
xSkaggs, Merrill M.
The Folk of Southern Fiction. U of Ga Pr.
Skala, John J.
xSkala, John J.
Dad & His Teenagers. Dghtrs St Paul.
Skalka, Patricia.
xSkalka, Patricia.
A Complete Guide to Skiing in the Midwest.
Contemp Bks.
Skard, Sigmund, 1903-
xSkard, Sigmund.
American Myth & the European Mind:
American Studies in Europe, 1776-1960. U of
Pa Pr.
Skarin, Annalee.
xSkarin, Annalee.
Secrets of Eternity. De Vorss.
Skarmeta, Antonio.
xSkarmeta, Antonio.
Chileno!. Morrow.
Skeat, W. W. *see* Skeat, Walter William.
Skeat, Walter W. *see* Skeat, Walter William.
Skeat, Walter William, 1835-1912
xSkeat, W. W.
Evolution of the Canterbury Tales. Gordon Pr.
xSkeat, Walter W.
ed. Concise Etymological Dictionary of the
English Language. Oxford U Pr.
English Dialects from the Eighth Century to
the Present Day. Folcroft.
English Dialects from the Eighth Century to
the Present Day. Kraus Repr.
Evolution of Canterbury Tales. Haskell.
Glossarial Index to the Works of Geoffrey
Chaucer. Folcroft.
Sked, Alan.
xSked, Alan.
Post-War Britain: A Political History. B&N.
Skeel, Dorothy. *see* Skeel, Dorothy J.
Skeel, Dorothy J.
xSkeel, Dorothy.
The Challenge of Teaching Social Studies in
the Elementary School. Goodyear.
Skeet, Muriel. *see* Skeet, Muriel H.
Skeet, Muriel H.
xSkeet, Muriel.
ed. Health Auxiliaries & the Health Team.
Biblio Dist.
Skehan, Everett M.
xSkehan, Everett M.
A Bullet for Georgie. HM.
A Bullet for Georgie. Popular Lib.
Skeist, Irving.
xSkeist, Irving.
ed. Handbook of Adhesives. Krieger.
ed. Handbook of Adhesives. Van Nos
Reinhold.
Plastics in Building. Van Nos Reinhold.
Skelley, Ester G. *see* Skelley, Esther G.
Skelley, Esther G.
xSkelley, Ester G.
Medications & Mathematics for the Nurse.
Delmar.
Skelly, Madge.
xSkelly, Madge.
Glossectomee Speech Rehabilitation. C C
Thomas.
Skelton, C. I. *see* Skelton, Clement Lister.

Skelton, Clement Lister, 1919-
xSkelton, C. I.
The Regiment. Dell.
Skelton, Eugene.
xSkelton, Eugene.
Meet the Prophets. Broadman.
Skelton, Marvin L.
xSkelton, Marvin L.
Memoirs of a World War II Pilot. Military Aff
Aero.
Skelton, R. A. *see* Skelton, Raleigh Ashlin.
Skelton, Raleigh Ashlin.
xSkelton, R. A.
Maps: A Historical Survey of Their Study &
Collecting. U of Chicago Pr.
Skemp, A. R. *see* Skemp, Arthur Rowland.
Skemp, Arthur Rowland, 1882-1918
xSkemp, A. R.
Francis Bacon. Kennikat.
Skene, Reg.
xSkene, Reg.
The Cuchulain Plays of W. B. Yeats: A Study.
Columbia U Pr.
Skerman, V. B. *see* Skerman, V. B. D.
Skerman, V. B. D.
xSkerman, V. B.
ed. Abstracts of Microbiological Methods.
Wiley.
Sketchley, Rose E. *see* Sketchley, Rose Esther Dorothea.
Sketchley, Rose Esther Dorothea, 1875-
xSketchley, Rose E.
English Book-Illustration of To-Day:
Appreciations of the Work of Living English
Illustrators with Lists of Their Books. Gale.
Ski Magazine.
xSki Magazine Editors.
Ski Magazine's Encyclopedia of Skiing.
Har-Row.
Ski Magazine's Expert Tips for Better Skiing.
Har-Row.
Skier's Handbook. Har-Row.
Ski Magazine Editors. *see* Ski Magazine.
Skidelsky, Robert. *see* Skidelsky, Robert Jacob
Alexander.
Skidelsky, Robert Jacob Alexander, 1939-
xSkidelsky, Robert.
ed. The End of the Keynesian Era: Essays on
the Disintegration of the Keynesian Political
Economy. Holmes & Meier.
Skidmore, Max J.
xSkidmore, Max J.
American Government: A Brief Introduction.
St Martin.
Medicare & the American Rhetoric of
Reconciliation. U of Ala Pr.
Skidmore, R. A. *see* Skidmore, Rex Austin.
Skidmore, Rex A. *see* Skidmore, Rex Austin.
Skidmore, Rex Austin.
xSkidmore, R. A.
Introduction to Social Work. P-H.
xSkidmore, Rex A.
Marriage: Much More Than a Dream. Deseret
Bk.
Skidmore, William.
xSkidmore, William L.
Theoretical Thinking in Sociology. Cambridge
U Pr.
Skidmore, William L. *see* Skidmore, William.
Skiles, Marlin.
xSkiles, Marlin.
Music Scoring for TV & Motion Pictures. TAB
Bks.
Skillen, Charles R.
xSkillen, Charles R.
American Police Handgun Training. C C
Thomas.
Skilling, H. Gordon. *see* Skilling, Harold Gordon.
Skilling, H. H. *see* Skilling, Hugh Hildreth.
Skilling, Harold Gordon.
xSkilling, H. Gordon.

Communism National & International: Eastern
Europe After Stalin. U of Toronto Pr.
Czechoslovakia's Interrupted Revolution.
Princeton U Pr.
Skilling, Hugh H. *see* Skilling, Hugh Hildreth.
Skilling, Hugh Hildreth, 1905-
xSkilling, H. H.
Fundamentals of Electric Waves. Krieger.
xSkilling, Hugh H.
Electromechanics: A First Course in
Electromechanical Energy Conversion.
Krieger.
Skillman, John J. *see* Skillman, John Joakim.
Skillman, John Joakim.
xSkillman, John J.
ed. Intensive Care. Little.
Skinner, B. *see* Skinner, Brian J.
Skinner, B. F. *see* Skinner, Burrhus Frederic.
Skinner, Betty L. *see* Skinner, Betty Lee.
Skinner, Betty Lee.
xSkinner, Betty L.
Daws: The Story of Dawson Trotman, Founder
of the Navigators. Zondervan.
Skinner, Brian J., 1928-
xSkinner, B.
Earth Resources. P-H.
Skinner, Burrhus Frederic, 1904-
xSkinner, B. F.
About Behaviorism. Knopf.
About Behaviorism. Random.
Contingencies of Reinforcement: A Theoretical
Analysis. P-H.
Particulars of My Life. Knopf.
Reflections on Behaviorism & Society. P-H.
Skinner, Charles M. *see* Skinner, Charles Montgomery.
Skinner, Charles Montgomery, 1852-1907
xSkinner, Charles M.
American Myths & Legends. Gale.
Skinner, Charles R. *see* Skinner, Charles Rufus.
Skinner, Charles Rufus, 1844-1928
xSkinner, Charles R.
Arbor Day Manual: An Aid in Preparing
Programs for Arbor Day Exercises. Arno.
ed. The Bright Side: The Book of Good Cheer.
Arno.
Skinner, Craig.
xSkinner, Craig.
Teaching Ministry of the Pulpit: Its History,
Theology, Psychology & Practice for Today.
Baker Bk.
Skinner, Frank.
xSkinner, Frank.
Underscore. Criterion Mus.
Skinner, Gilbert H.
xSkinner, Gilbert H.
Principles of Supervision in Law Enforcement
Agencies. C C Thomas.
Skinner, Gordon.
xSkinner, Gordon B.
Introduction to Chemical Kinetics. Acad Pr.
Skinner, Gordon B. *see* Skinner, Gordon.
Skinner, Henry D. *see* Skinner, Henry Devenish.
Skinner, Henry Devenish, 1887-
xSkinner, Henry D.
Comparatively Speaking: Studies in Pacific
Material Culture. Intl Pubns Serv.
Skinner, Hubert M. *see* Skinner, Hubert Marshall.
Skinner, Hubert Marshall, 1855-1916
xSkinner, Hubert M.
The Story of the Letters & Figures. Gale.
Skinner, Louise.
xSkinner, Louise.
Motor Development in the Preschool Years. C
C Thomas.
Skinner, Orten C.
xSkinner, Orten C.
Introduction to Diagnostic Microbiology.
Bobbs.
Skinner, Paul H.
xSkinner, Paul H.

Speech, Language & Hearing: Normal
Processes & Disorders. A-W.
Skinner, R. N. *see* Skinner, Richard N.

Skinner, Richard.
xSkinner, Richard.
Kate the Skate. Carson Pr.

Skinner, Richard D. *see* Skinner, Richard Dana.

Skinner, Richard Dana, 1893-1941
xSkinner, Richard D.
Eugene O'Neill: A Poet's Quest. Russell.

Skinner, Richard N.
xSkinner, R. N.
Launching New Products in Competitive
Markets. Intl Pubns Serv.

Skinner, Thomas. *see* Skinner, Tom.

Skinner, Tom, 1942-
xSkinner, Thomas.
How Black Is the Gospel?. Pillar Bks.
xSkinner, Tom.
How Black Is the Gospel?. Holman.
If Christ Is the Answer, What Are the
Questions?. Zondervan.

Skinner, Wickham.
xSkinner, Wickham.
Manufacturing in the Corporate Strategy.
Wiley.

Skipper, G. C.
xSkipper, G. C.
Ghost in the Church. Childrens.
The Ghosts at Manor House. Childrens.
Night in the Attic. Childrens.

Skitt, Jack. *see* Skitt, John.

Skitt, John.
xSkitt, Jack.
Waste Disposal Management & Practice.
Halsted Pr.

Sklar, Dusty.
xSklar, Dusty.
Gods & Beasts: The Nazis & the Occult. T Y
Crowell.

Sklar, Kathryn K. *see* Sklar, Kathryn Kish.

Sklar, Kathryn Kish.
xSklar, Kathryn K.
Catharine Beecher: A Study in American
Domesticity. Norton.
Catharine Beecher: A Study in American
Domesticity. Yale U Pr.

Sklar, Lawrence.
xSklar, Lawrence.
Space, Time, & Spacetime. U of Cal Pr.

Sklar, Maurice.
xSklar, Maurice.
How Children Learn to Speak. Western Psych.

Sklar, Morty.
xSklar, Morty.
ed. The Actualist Anthology. Spirit That
Moves.

Sklar, Richard L.
xSklar, Richard L.
Corporate Power in an African State: The
Political Impact of Multinational Mining
Companies in Zambia. U of Cal Pr.

Sklar, Robert.
xSklar, Robert.
ed. The Plastic Age. Braziller.

Sklare, Marshall, 1921-
xSklare, Marshall.
America's Jews. Random.
Jewish Identity on the Suburban Frontier: A
Study of Group Survival in the Open Society.
U of Chicago Pr.
Not Quite at Home: How an American Jewish
Community Lives with Itself & Its Neighbors.
Am Jewish Comm.

Sklarew, Myra.
xSklarew, Myra.
From the Backyard of the Diaspora. Dryad Pr.

Sklorz, Martin.
xSklorz, Martin.

Table Tennis. Charles River Bks.
Table Tennis. Sterling.

Skoda, J. *see* Skoda, Jan.

Skoda, Jan.
xSkoda, J.
ed. Antimetabolites in Biochemistry, Biology &
Medicine: Proceedings, Prague, 1978.
Pergamon.

Skoggard, Bruno.
xSkoggard, Bruno.
China Hand. Dodd.

Skoglund, Elizabeth.
xSkoglund, Elizabeth.
Beyond Loneliness. Doubleday.
Loving Begins with Me. Har-Row.

Skoglund, John E.
xSkoglund, John E.
Manual of Worship. Judson.

Skogsbergh, Helga.
xSkogsbergh, Helga.
Songs of Pilgrimage. Covenant.

Skold, Betty W. *see* Skold, Betty Westrom.

Skold, Betty Westrom.
xSkold, Betty W.
Lord, I Have a Question: Story Devotions for
Girls. Augsburg.

Skolem, Thoralf, 1887-
xSkolem, Thoralf A.
Abstract Set Theory. U of Notre Dame Pr.

Skolem, Thoralf A. *see* Skolem, Thoralf.

Skolnick, Arlene. *see* Skolnick, Arlene S.

Skolnick, Arlene S.
xSkolnick, Arlene.
Family in Transition: Rethinking Marriage,
Sexuality, Child Rearing, & Family
Organization. Little.

Skolnick, Jerome. *see* Skolnick, Jerome H.

Skolnick, Jerome H.
xSkolnick, Jerome.
House of Cards: Legalization & Control of
Casino Gambling. Little.
xSkolnick, Jerome H.
ed. Crisis in American Institutions. Little.

Skolnik, Merrill I. *see* Skolnik, Merrill Ivan.

Skolnik, Merrill Ivan, 1927-
xSkolnik, Merrill I.
Introduction to Radar Systems. McGraw.
Introduction to Radar Systems. McGraw.

Skolnik, Peter L.
xSkolnik, Peter L.
Fads: America's Crazes, Fevers & Fancies from
the 1890s to the 1970s. T Y Crowell.

Skolsky, Mindy W. *see* Skolsky, Mindy Warshaw.

Skolsky, Mindy Warshaw.
xSkolsky, Mindy W.
Carnival & Kopeck & More About Hannah.
Har-Row.
The Whistling Teakettle & Other Stories About
Hannah. Har-Row.

Skoog, Douglas A. *see* Skoog, Douglas Arvid.

Skoog, Douglas Arvid.
xSkoog, Douglas A.
Analytical Chemistry. HR&W.
Fundamentals of Analytical Chemistry.
HR&W.

Skordas, Gust.
xSkordas, Gust.
The Early Settlers of Maryland: An Index of
Names of Immigrants Compiled from
Records of Land Patents 1633-1680, in the
Hall of Records, Annapolis, Maryland.
Genealog Pub.

Skorpen, Liesel M. *see* Skorpen, Liesel Moak.

Skorpen, Liesel Moak.
xSkorpen, Liesel M.

All the Lassies. Dial.
His Mother's Dog. Har-Row.
Old Arthur. Har-Row.
Outside My Window. Har-Row.
That Mean Man. Har-Row.

Skousen, Max B. *see* Skousen, Max Bentley.

Skousen, Max Bentley, 1921-
xSkousen, Max B.
Christianity & est. De Vorss.

Skousen, Royal.
xSkousen, Royal.
Substantive Evidence in Phonology: The
Evidence from Finnish & French. Mouton.

Skousen, W. Cleon. *see* Skousen, Willard Cleon.

Skousen, Willard Cleon, 1913-
xSkousen, W. Cleon.
The Fourth Thousand Years. Bookcraft Inc.
The Third Thousand Years. Bookcraft Inc.

Skovholt, Thomas M.
xSkovholt, Thomas M.
ed. Counseling Men. Brooks-Cole.

Skowronski, Marjory, 1948-
xSkowronski, Marjory.
Abortion & Alternatives. Les Femmes Pub.

Skrade, Carl.
xSkrade, Carl.
God & the Grotesque. Westminster.

Skrapek, Wayne A.
xSkrapek, Wayne A.
Mathematical Dictionary for Economics &
Business Administration. Allyn.

Skrebneski, Victor.
xSkrebneski, Victor.
Skrebneski Portraits: A Matter of Record.
Doubleday.

Skrine, Peter. *see* Skrine, Peter N.

Skrine, Peter N.
xSkrine, Peter.
The Baroque: Literature & Culture in
Seventeenth Century Europe. Holmes &
Meier.

Skrupskelis, Alina.
xSkrupskelis, Alina.
ed. Lithuanian Writers in the West: An
Anthology. Lithuanian Lib.

Skrzynecki, Peter, 1945-
xSkrzynecki, Peter.
Immigrant Chronicle. U of Queensland Pr.

Skubik, Stephen J.
xSkubik, Stephen J.
ed. Handbook of Humor by Famous Politicians.
Acropolis.

Skudrzyk, Eugen, 1913-
xSkudrzyk, Eugen.
Simple & Complex Vibratory Systems. Pa St U
Pr.

Skurnik, W. A. *see* Skurnik, W. A. E.

Skurnik, W. A. E.
xSkurnik, W. A.
The Foreign Policy of Senegal. Northwestern U
Pr.

Skurzynski, Gloria.
xSkurzynski, Gloria.
Honest Andrew. HarBraceJ.
In a Bottle with a Cork on Top. Dodd.
Martin by Himself. HM.
The Poltergeist of Jason Morey. Dodd.
What Happened in Hamelin. Schol Bk Serv.

Skutch, Alexander F. *see* Skutch, Alexander Frank.

Skutch, Alexander Frank., 1904-
xSkutch, Alexander F.
The Imperative Call: A Naturalist's Quest in
Temperate & Tropical America. U Presses
Fla.
The Life of the Hummingbird. Crown.

Skvorecky, Josef.
xSkvorecky, Josef.

The Bass Saxophone. Knopf.
Skwire, David.
xSkwire, David.
Student's Book of College English. Glencoe.
Writing with a Thesis: A Rhetoric & Reader.
HR&W.
Sky, Gino.
xSky, Gino.
Appaloosa Rising: The Legend of the Cowboy
Buddha. Doubleday.
Skynner, A. C. see Skynner, A. C. Robin.
Skynner, A. C. Robin.
xSkynner, A. C.
Systems of Family & Marital Psychotherapy.
Brunner-Mazel.
Slaatte, Howard A.
xSlaatte, Howard A.
Time & Its End: A Comparative Existential
Interpretation of Time & Eschatology. U Pr
of Amer.
Slaatte, Howard A. see Slaatte, Howard Alexander.
Slaatte, Howard Alexander.
xSlaatte, Howard A.
Fire in the Brand: An Introduction to the
Creative Work & Theology of John Wesley.
Exposition.
Slabaugh, Wendell H.
xSlabaugh, Wendell H.
College Physical Science. P-H.
Slaby, Andrew E. see Slaby, Andrew Edmund.
Slaby, Andrew Edmund.
xSlaby, Andrew E.
Dementia in the Presenium. C C Thomas.
Slack, A. V. see Slack, Archie Vivian.
Slack, Archie Vivian.
xSlack, A. V.
ed. Ammonia. Dekker.
Slack, Claudia.
xSlack, Claudia.
Outrageous Fortune. NAL.
Slack, John M. see Slack, John Madison.
Slack, John Madison.
xSlack, John M.
Actinomyces, Filamentous Bacteria: Biology &
Pathogenicity. Burgess.
Slack, Kenneth.
xSlack, Kenneth.
The United Reformed Church. Pergamon.
Slack, Walter.
xSlack, Walter H.
The Grim Science: The Struggle for Power.
Kennikat.
Slack, Walter H. see Slack, Walter.
Sladden, Susan.
xSladden, Susan.
Psychiatric Nursing in the Community: A
Study of the Working Situation. Churchill.
Slade, Herbert. see Slade, Herbert Edwin William.
Slade, Herbert Edwin William.
xSlade, Herbert.
Exploration into Contemplative Prayer. Paulist
Pr.
Slade, Jack.
xSlade, Jack.
Blood Knife. Nordon Pubns.
Canyon Kill. Nordon Pubns.
Cattle Baron. Belmont Tower.
Honcho. Nordon Pubns.
The Man from Tombstone & Gunfight at
Ringo Junction. Belmont-Tower.
Slade, P. see Slade, Philip E.
Slade, P. E. see Slade, Philip E.
Slade, Philip E., 1929-
xSlade, P.
ed. Thermal Characterization Techniques.
Dekker.
xSlade, P. E.
ed. Polymer Molecular Weights. Dekker.
Sladek, John. see Sladek, John Thomas.

Sladek, John Thomas.
xSladek, John.
Black Aura. Walker & Co.
The Muller-Fokker Effect. PB.
Slaga, Thomas J.
xSlaga, Thomas J.
ed. Mechanisms of Tumor Promotion &
Cocarcinogenesis. Raven.
Slagle, Kenneth C. see Slagle, Kenneth Chester.
Slagle, Kenneth Chester, 1905-
xSlagle, Kenneth C.
English Country Squire As Depicted in English
Prose Fiction from 1740. Octagon.
Slama, K.
xSlama, K.
Insect Hormones & Bioanalogues.
Springer-Verlag.
Slama-Cazacu, T. see Slama-Cazacu, Tatiana.
Slama-Cazacu, Tatiana.
xSlama-Cazacu, T.
Dialogue in Children. Mouton.
xSlama-Cazacu, Tatiana.
Introduction to Psycholinguistics. Mouton.
Slanger, Elissa.
xSlanger, Elissa.
ed. Ski Woman's Way. Summit Bks.
Slate. see Slate, William G.
Slate, William G.
xSlate.
Disorders of Female Urethra & Urinary
Incontinence. Williams & Wilkins.
Slater. see Slater, Harry.
Slater, Abby.
xSlater, Abby.
In Search of Margaret Fuller: A Biography.
Delacorte.
Slater, Charles C., 1939-1978
xSlater, Charles C.
Easing Transition in Southern Africa: New
Techniques for Policy Planning. Westview.
Slater, Eliot.
xSlater, Eliot.
Genetics of Mental Disorders. Oxford U Pr.
Slater, Frank.
xSlater, Frank.
ed. Cost Reduction for Special Libraries and
Information Centers. Am Soc Info Sci.
Slater, Gilbert, 1864-1938
xSlater, Gilbert.
English Peasantry & the Enclosure of Common
Fields. Kelley.
Slater, Harry.
xSlater.
Basic Plumbing. Delmar.
xSlater, Harry.
Basic Plumbing. Van Nos Reinhold.
Slater, J. see Slater, Jeffrey.
Slater, J. H. see Slater, John Herbert.
Slater, J. Herbert. see Slater, John Herbert.
Slater, Jeffrey, 1947-
xSlater, J.
Practical Accounting Procedures. P-H.
Slater, John C. see Slater, John Clarke.
Slater, John Clarke, 1900-1976
xSlater, John C.
The Calculation of Molecular Orbitals. Wiley.
Quantum Theory of Matter. Krieger.
Solid State & Molecular Theory: A Scientific
Biography. Wiley.
Slater, John Herbert, 1854-1921
xSlater, J. H.
Early Editions: A Bibliographical Survey of the
Works of Some Popular Modern Authors.
Folcroft.
xSlater, J. Herbert.
How to Collect Books. R West.
Slater, Kitty.
xSlater, Kitty.

Hunt Country of America. Arco.
Slater, Leslie G.
xSlater, Leslie G.
Secrets of Making Wine from Fruits & Berries.
Terry Pub.
Slater, Lucy J. see Slater, Lucy Joan.
Slater, Lucy Joan.
xSlater, Lucy J.
More Fortran Programs for Economists.
Cambridge U Pr.
Slater, Mariam.
xSlater, Mariam K.
The Caribbean Family: Legitimacy in
Martinique. St Martin.
Slater, Mariam K. see Slater, Mariam.
Slater, Nigel, 1944-
xSlater, Nigel.
Falcon. Atheneum.
Slater, Noel B. see Slater, Noel Bryan.
Slater, Noel Bryan.
xSlater, Noel B.
Theory of Unimolecular Reactions. Cornell U
Pr.
Slater, Peter G. see Slater, Peter Gregg.
Slater, Peter Gregg, 1940-
xSlater, Peter G.
Children in the New England Mind: In Death
& in Life. Shoe String.
Slater, Phil.
xSlater, Phil.
Origin & Significance of the Frankfurt School:
A Marxist Perspective. Routledge & Kegan.
Slater, Philip.
xSlater, Philip.
Earthwalk. Doubleday.
Slater, Philip. see Slater, Philip Elliot.
Slater, Philip Elliot.
xSlater, Philip.
Footholds: Understanding the Shifting Family
& Sexual Tensions in Our Culture. Beacon
Pr.
The Pursuit of Loneliness: American Culture at
the Breaking Point. Beacon Pr.
Wealth Addiction. Dutton.
Slater, Robert H. see Slater, Robert Henry Lawson.
Slater, Robert Henry Lawson.
xSlater, Robert H.
World Religions & World Community.
Columbia U Pr.
Slater, S. D., 1927-
xSlater, S. D.
The Strategy of Cash: A Liquidity Approach to
Maximizing the Company's Profits. Wiley.
Slater, Scott.
xSlater, Scott.
Exits: Dying Words & Last Moments. Dutton.
Slater, Victor Wallace.
xSlater, Wallace.
Simplified Course in Hatha Yoga. Theos Pub
Hse.
Slater, Wallace. see Slater, Victor Wallace.
Slatoff, Walter J. see Slatoff, Walter Jacob.
Slatoff, Walter Jacob, 1922-
xSlatoff, Walter J.
Quest for Failure: A Study of William
Faulkner. Greenwood.
Slattery, John C. see Slattery, John Charles.
Slattery, John Charles, 1932-
xSlattery, John C.
Momentum, Energy & Mass Transfer in
Continua. Krieger.
Slattery, Thomas C.
xSlattery, Thomas C.
Percy Grainger: The Inveterate Innovator.
Instrumental Co.
Slatzer, Robert F.
xSlatzer, Robert F.

The Life & Curious Death of Marilyn Monroe.
Pinnacle Bks.
Slaughter, Carolyn.
xSlaughter, Carolyn.
Relations. PB.
Relations. Van Nos Reinhold.

Slaughter, Frank. see Slaughter, Frank Gill.
Slaughter, Frank G. see Slaughter, Frank Gill.
Slaughter, Frank Gill, 1908-
xSlaughter, Frank.
The Mapmaker. PB.
A Touch of Glory. PB.
xSlaughter, Frank G.
Buccaneer Surgeon. PB.
Code Five. PB.
Countdown. PB.
Darien Venture. PB.
Daybreak. PB.
The Deadly Lady of Madagascar. PB.
Devil's Harvest. PB.
Doctors' Wives. PB.
East Side General. Am Repr-Rivercity Pr.
East Side General. PB.
Flight from Natchez. PB.
Galileans. PB.

In a Dark Garden. Am Repr-Rivercity Pr.
In a Dark Garden. PB.
Passionate Rebel. Doubleday.

Plague Ship. PB.
Spencer Brade, M.D.. Am Repr-Rivercity Pr.
Stonewall Brigade. Doubleday.

The Stonewall Brigade. PB.
That None Should Die. Am Repr-Rivercity Pr.
That None Should Die. PB.

Slaughter, Jean, 1924-
xSlaughter, Jean.
Pony Care. Knopf.
Slaughter, Stella. see Slaughter, Stella (Stillson).
Slaughter, Stella (Stillson).
xSlaughter, Stella.
Educable Mentally Retarded Child & His
Teacher. AHM Pub.
Slaven, Anthony.
xSlaven, Anthony.
Development of the West of Scotland.
Routledge & Kegan.
Slavens, Thomas P., 1928-
xSlavens, Thomas P.
Informational Interviews & Questions.
Scarecrow.
Slavicek, John J.
xSlavicek, John J.
The Simplified Guide to Personal Bankruptcy.
Crown.
Slavin, Albert.
xSlavin, Albert.
Financial Accounting: A Basic Approach.
Dryden Pr.
Slavin, Arthur J.
xSlavin, Arthur J.
ed. Tudor Men & Institutions: Studies in
English Law & Government. La State U Pr.
Slavin, Morris.
xSlavin, Morris.
Atomic Absorption Spectroscopy. Wiley.
Emission Spectrochemical Analysis. Krieger.
Slavin, Neal.
xSlavin, Neal.
Portugal. Lustrum Pr.
When Two or More Are Gathered Together.
FS&G.
Slavitt, David R., 1935-
xSlavitt, David R.

Child's Play. La State U Pr.
Slavkin, Harold C.
xSlavkin, Harold C.
ed. Cellular Induction. Mss Info.
ed. Developmental Aspects of Oral Biology.
Acad Pr.
Developmental Craniofacial Biology. Lea &
Febiger.
Slavson, S. R. see Slavson, Samuel Richard.
Slavson, Samuel Richard, 1891-
xSlavson, S. R.
ed. Fields of Group Psychotherapy. Intl Univs
Pr.
Group Psychotherapies for Children: A
Textbook. Intl Univs Pr.
Introduction to Group Therapy. Intl Univs Pr.
ed. Practice of Group Therapy. Intl Univs Pr.
Textbook in Analytic Group Psychotherapy.
Intl Univs Pr.
Slawecki, Leon M. see Slawecki, Leon M. S.
Slawecki, Leon M. S.
xSlawecki, Leon M.
French Policy Towards the Chinese in
Madagascar. Shoe String.
Slawson, John, 1896-
xSlawson, John.
Delinquent Boy: A Socio-Psychological Study.
Russell.
Unequal Americans: Practices & Politics of
Intergroup Relations. Greenwood.
Slaymaker, S. R.
xSlaymaker, S. R.
Simplified Fly Fishing. Har-Row.
Slaymaker, Thomas.
xSlaymaker, Thomas.
Power Volleyball. HR&W,
Slayter, Elizabeth M.
xSlayter, Elizabeth M.
Optical Methods in Biology. Krieger.
Slayton, Mariette P. see Slayton, Mariette Paine.
Slayton, Mariette Paine.
xSlayton, Mariette P.
Early American Decorating Techniques:
Step-by-Step Directions for Mastering
Traditional Crafts. Macmillan.
Slayton, Philip.
xSlayton, Philip.
The Professions & Public Policy. U of Toronto
Pr.
Slayton, William L.
xSlayton, William L.
Social Trends: Their Impact on the Public
Service. Intl Personnel Mgmt.
Sleath, Eleanor.
xSleath, Eleanor.
Nocturnal Minstrel: Or, the Spirit of the Wood.
Arno.
Sleator, William.
xSleator, William.
Among the Dolls. Dutton.
House of Stairs. Dutton.
House of Stairs. Avon.
Into the Dream. Dutton.
Once, Said Darlene. Dutton.
Sleeman, John F.
xSleeman, John F.
Economic Crisis: A Christian Perspective.
Allenson.
Sleeman, W. H. see Sleeman, William Henry.
Sleeman, William Henry.
xSleeman, W. H.
Rambles & Recollections of an Indian Official.
Oxford U Pr.
Sleeper, Harold R. see Sleeper, Harold Reeve.
Sleeper, Harold Reeve, 1893-1960
xSleeper, Harold R.

Building Planning & Design Standards for
Architects, Engineers, Designers, Consultants,
Building Committees, Draftsman & Students.
Wiley.
Sleeth, Ronald E. see Sleeth, Ronald Eugene.
Sleeth, Ronald Eugene.
xSleeth, Ronald E.
Look Who's Talking: A Guide for Lay
Speakers in the Church. Abingdon.
Sleigh, M. A.
xSleigh, M. A.
ed. Cilia & Flagella. Acad Pr.
Sleight, Jack.
xSleight, Jack.
The Home Book of Smoke Cooking, Meat,
Fish & Game. BJ Pub Group.
Home Book of Smoke-Cooking Meat, Fish &
Game. Stackpole.
Sleisenger, Lenore.
xSleisenger, Lenore.
Guidebook for the Volunteer Reading Teacher.
C B Slack.
Guidebook for the Volunteer Reading Teacher.
Tchrs Coll.
Slepian, Jan. see Slepian, Janice B.
Slepian, Janice B.
xSlepian, Jan.
The Alfred Summer. Macmillan.
The Hungry Thing. Schol Bk Serv.
Slepian, Paul.
xSlepian, Paul.
Mathematical Foundations of Network
Analysis. Springer-Verlag.
Slesinger, Tess, 1905-1945
xSlesinger, Tess.
On Being Told That Her Second Husband Has
Taken His First Lover, & Other Stories.
Times Bks.
Slessarev, Helga.
xSlessarev, Helga.
Eduard Morike. Irvington.
Slesser, Malcolm.
xSlesser, Malcolm.
Energy in the Economy. St Martin.
Sletten, Harvey. see Sletten, Harvey M.
Sletten, Harvey M., 1912-
xSletten, Harvey.
Growing up on Bald Hill Creek. Iowa St U Pr.
Slezak, Walter, 1902-
xSlezak, Walter.
My Stomach Goes Traveling. Doubleday.
Slichter, C. P. see Slichter, Charles P.
Slichter, Charles P.
xSlichter, C. P.
Principles of Magnetic Resonance.
Springer-Verlag.
Slichter, Sumner. see Slichter, Sumner Huber.
Slichter, Sumner H. see Slichter, Sumner Huber.
Slichter, Sumner Huber, 1892-1959
xSlichter, Sumner.
The American Economy: Its Problems &
Prospects. Greenwood.
xSlichter, Sumner H.
The Impact of Collective Bargaining on
Management. Brookings.
Slide, Anthony.
xSlide, Anthony.
Aspects of American Film History Prior to
1920. Scarecrow.
Early American Cinema. A S Barnes.
Films on Film History. Scarecrow.
The Idols of Silence. A S Barnes.
Slifkin, Michael A.
xSlifkin, Michael A.
Charge Transfer Interactions of Biomolecules.
Acad Pr.
Slijper, E. J. see Slijper, Everhard Johannes.
Slijper, Everhard Johannes.
xSlijper, E. J.

Whales. Cornell U Pr.
Slimmer Magazine.
    xSlimmer Magazine.
        ed. Let's Start to Slim. Intl Pubns Serv.
    xSlimmer Magazine Editorial Staff.
        ed. Let's Start to Slim. Beekman Pubs.
Slimmer Magazine Editorial Staff. *see* Slimmer Magazine.
Slisenko, A. O.
    xSlisenko, A. O.
        ed. Studies in Constructive Mathematics &
            Mathematical Logic. Plenum Pub.
Slivka, Rose.
    xSlivka, Rose.
        ed. Crafts of the Modern World. Horizon.
Sloan, A. *see* Sloan, Allyn.
Sloan, A. W. *see* Sloan, Archibald Walker.
Sloan, Alfred P. *see* Sloan, Alfred Pritchard.
Sloan, Alfred Pritchard.
    xSloan, Alfred P.
        Adventures of a White-Collar Man. Arno.
Sloan, Allan K.
    xSloan, Allan K.
        Citizen Participation in Transportation
            Planning: The Boston Experience. Ballinger
            Pub.
Sloan, Allyn.
    xSloan, A.
        Dog & Man: The Story of a Friendship. Arno.
Sloan, Archibald Walker.
    xSloan, A. W.
        Man in Extreme Environments. C C Thomas.
Sloan, Bernard.
    xSloan, Bernard.
        The Best Friend You'll Ever Have. Crown.
Sloan, Douglas.
    xSloan, Douglas.
        Education & Values. Tchrs Coll.
Sloan, Eugene B.
    xSloan, Eugene B.
        South Carolina: A Journalist & His State.
            Lewis-Sloan.
Sloan, Frank. *see* Sloan, Frank A.
Sloan, Frank A.
    xSloan, Frank.
        Private Physicians & Public Programs.
            Lexington Bks.
    xSloan, Frank A.
        Access to Ambulatory Care & the U. S.
            Economy. Lexington Bks.
        Hospital Labor Markets: Analysis of Wages &
            Work Force Composition. Lexington Bks.
Sloan, Harold S. *see* Sloan, Harold Stephenson.
Sloan, Harold Stephenson.
    xSloan, Harold S.
        Dictionary of Economics. B&N.
Sloan, Irving J.
    xSloan, Irving J.
        Environment & the Law. Oceana.
        Living Together:: Unmarrieds & the Law.
            Oceana.
Sloan, John.
    xSloan, John.
        Gist of Art: Principles & Practise Expounded
            in the Classroom & Studio. Peter Smith.
Sloan, Kathleen L. *see* Sloan, Kathleen Lewis.
Sloan, Kathleen Lewis.
    xSloan, Kathleen L.
        ed. Nothing But The Best Southern Recipes:
            With Metric Working Equivalents.
            Lewis-Sloan.
Sloan, M. E. *see* Sloan, Martha E.
**Sloan-Kettering Institute for Cancer Research, New
    York.**
    xMemorial Sloan-Kettering Cancer Center.
        Guidelines for Comprehensive Nursing Care in
            Cancer. Springer Pub.
Sloan, Martha E.
    xSloan, M. E.

Computer Hardware & Organization. SRA.
Sloane, Albert E.
    xSloane, Albert E.
        Manual of Refraction. Little.
Sloane, Alvin, 1901-
    xSloane, Alvin.
        Engineering Kinematics. Peter Smith.
Sloane, Bruce, 1935-
    xSloane, Bruce.
        Cavers, Caves, & Caving. Rutgers U Pr.
Sloane, David E. *see* Sloane, David E. E.
Sloane, David E. E., 1943-
    xSloane, David E.
        Mark Twain As a Literary Comedian. La State
            U Pr.
Sloane, Eric.
    xSloane, Eric.
        Age of Barns. T Y Crowell.
        Cracker Barrel. T Y Crowell.
        I Remember America. Ballantine.
        I Remember America. T Y Crowell.
        The Legacy. T Y Crowell.
        Look at the Sky & Tell the Weather. Dutton.
        Look at the Sky & Tell the Weather. T Y
            Crowell.
        A Museum of Early American Tools.
            Ballantine.
        Museum of Early American Tools. T Y
            Crowell.
        Our Vanishing Landscape. Ballantine.
        Recollections in Black & White. Ballantine.
        Recollections in Black & White. T Y Crowell.
        Return to Taos: A Sketchbook of Roadside
            Americana. T Y Crowell.
        Reverence for Wood. Ballantine.
        Reverence for Wood. T Y Crowell.
Sloane, Ethel.
    xSloane, Ethel.
        Biology of Women. Wiley.
Sloane, Eugene A.
    xSloane, Eugene A.
        The Complete Book of Locks, Keys, Burglar &
            Smoke Alarms, & Other Security Devices.
            Morrow.
        The Complete Book of Locks, Keys, Burglar &
            Smoke Alarms & Other Security Devices.
            NAL.
Sloane, Eugene H. *see* Sloane, Eugene Hulse.
Sloane, Eugene Hulse, 1902-
    xSloane, Eugene H.
        Psychology for Living. Owl Pr.
Sloane, Eunice.
    xSloane, Eunice M.
        Illustrating Fashion. Har-Row.
Sloane, Eunice M. *see* Sloane, Eunice.
Sloane, Howard N. *see* Sloane, Howard Norman.
Sloane, Howard Norman, 1932-
    xSloane, Howard N.
        Classroom Management: Remediation &
            Prevention. Wiley.
        The Good Kid Book: A Manual for Parents.
            NAL.
        A Guide to Motivating Learners. Educ Tech
            Pubns.
        Structured Teaching: A Design for Classroom
            Management & Instruction. Res Press.
Sloane, Irving.
    xSloane, Irving.
        Guitar Repair: A Manual of Repair for Guitars
            & Fretted Instruments. Dutton.
Sloane, Joseph C.
    xSloane, Joseph C.
        French Painting Between the Past &
            Present: Artists, Critics, & Traditions from
            1848 to 1870. Princeton U Pr.
Sloane, Leonard.
    xSloane, Leonard.

The Anatomy of the Floor: The Trillion Dollar
            Market at the New York Stock Exchange.
            Doubleday.
Sloane, Nathan H.
    xSloane, Nathan H.
        Review of Biochemistry. Macmillan.
Sloane, R. Bruce. *see* Sloane, Robert Bruce.
Sloane, Randy.
    xSloane, Randy.
        Traveler's Guide to Running in Major
            American Cities. Stackpole.
Sloane, Robert Bruce.
    xSloane, R. Bruce.
        A General Guide to Abortion. Nelson-Hall.
Sloane, Robert M.
    xSloane, Robert M.
        A Guide to Health Facilities: Personnel and
            Management. Mosby.
Sloane, Sheila B.
    xSloane, Sheila B.
        The Medical Word Book: A Spelling &
            Vocabulary Guide to Medical Transcription.
            Saunders.
Sloane, William. *see* Sloane, William Milligan.
Sloane, William M. *see* Sloane, William Milligan.
Sloane, William Milligan.
    xSloane, William.
        The Craft of Writing. Norton.
    xSloane, William M.
        The French War & the Revolution. Irvington.
        The French War & the Revolution. Norwood
            Edns.
        Life of Napoleon Bonaparte. AMS Pr.
Sloat, Clarence.
    xSloat, Clarence.
        Introduction to Phonology. P-H.
Slobin, Dan I. *see* Slobin, Dan Isaac.
Slobin, Dan Isaac, 1939-
    xSlobin, Dan I.
        Psycholinguistics. Scott F.
Slobin, Mark.
    xSlobin, Mark.
        Music in the Culture of Northern Afghanistan.
            U of Ariz Pr.
Slobodin, Richard, 1915-
    xSlobodin, Richard.
        W. H. R. Rivers. Columbia U Pr.
Slobodkin, Florence.
    xSlobodkin, Florence.
        Cowboy Twins. Vanguard.
Slobodkin, Louis, 1903-
    xSlobodkin, Louis.
        Amiable Giant. Vanguard.
        Excuse Me! Certainly!. Vanguard.
        illus. First Book of Drawing. Watts.
        Good Place to Hide. Macmillan.
        Late Cuckoo. Vanguard.
        Melvin the Moose Child. Vanguard.
        illus. Moon Blossom & the Golden Penny.
            Vanguard.
        Nomi & the Lovely Animals. Vanguard.
        illus. Polka-Dot Goat. Macmillan.
        illus. Read About the Policeman. Watts.
        illus. The Space Ship in the Park. Macmillan.
        illus. Space Ship Returns to the Apple Tree.
            Macmillan.
        illus. Space Ship Under the Apple Tree.
            Macmillan.
        illus. Space Ship Under the Apple Tree.
            Macmillan.
        Spaceship Returns to the Apple Tree.
            Macmillan.
Slobodkin, Marvin.
    xSlobodkin, Marvin.
        Inside Dope. Dutton.
Slobodkina, Esphyr, 1908-
    xSlobodkina, Esphyr.
        illus. Billy, the Condominium Cat. A-W.
Slocum, Elliott L.
    xSlocum, Elliott L.

Atlanta Distributors, Inc.: Time-Sharing
Financial Accounting Modules. Ga St U Busn
Pub.
Slocum, Walter. see Slocum, Walter L.
Slocum, Walter L.
xSlocum, Walter.
Occupational Careers: A Sociological
Perspective. Beresford Bk Serv.
Slom, Stanley H.
xSlom, Stanley H.
How to Sell Furniture. Fairchild.
Sloma, Richard S.
xSloma, Richard S.
How to Measure Managerial Performance. Free
Pr.
Sloman, Aaron.
xSloman, Aaron.
The Computer Revolution in Philosophy:
Philosophy, Science & Models of Mind.
Humanities.
Sloman, Martyn.
xSloman, Martyn.
Socialising Public Ownership. Humanities.
Slonaker, David F.
xSlonaker, David F.
Teenagers Ahead. Nelson-Hall.
Slone, Verna M. see Slone, Verna Mae.
Slone, Verna Mae, 1914-
xSlone, Verna M.
What My Heart Wants to Tell. Har-Row.
What My Heart Wants to Tell. New Republic.
Slonim, I. Ya. see Slonim, Izrail Iakovlevich.
Slonim, Izrail Iakovlevich.
xSlonim, I. Ya.
The NMR of Polymers. Plenum Pub.
Slonim, Marc.
xSlonim, Marc
From Chekhov to the Revolution: Russian
Literature, 1900-1917. Oxford U Pr.
Slonim, N. Balfour.
xSlonim, N. Balfour.
Respiratory Physiology. Mosby.
Slonimsky, Nicholas. see Slonimsky, Nicolas.
Slonimsky, Nicolas, 1894-
xSlonimsky, Nicholas.
Music Since 1900. Scribner.
xSlonimsky, Nicolas.
Music of Latin America. Da Capo.
The Road to Music. Da Capo.
The Road to Music. Peter Smith.
A Thing or Two About Music. Greenwood.
Slonneger, J. C.
xSlonneger, J. C.
Dynagraph Analysis of Sucker Rod Pumping.
Gulf Pub.
Sloop, Joe. see Sloop, Joseph G.
Sloop, Joseph G.
xSloop, Joe.
Advanced Color Television Servicing. Sams.
Sloot, William.
xSloot, William.
Solid State Servicing. Sams.
Slosar, John A.
xSlosar, John A.
Prisonization, Friendship & Leadership.
Lexington Bks.
Slosberg, Michael. see Slosberg, Mike.
Slosberg, Mike.
xSlosberg, Michael.
The August Strangers. Dial.
Sloshberg, Willard.
xSloshberg, Willard.
Contemporary Society. West Pub.
Sloss, Hattie (Hecht).
xSloss, Hattie H.

Certain Poets of Importance: Victorian Verse
Chosen for Comparison. Arden Lib.
Compiled by Certain Poets of Importance:
Victorian Verse Chosen for Comparison.
Arno.
Sloss, Hattie H. see Sloss, Hattie (Hecht).
Sloss, Leon.
xSloss, Leon.
NATO Reform: Prospects & Priorities. Sage.
Sloss, V.
xSloss, V.
Handbook of Bovine Obstetrics. Williams &
Wilkins.
Slosser, Bob.
xSlosser, Bob.
Miracle in Darien. Logos.
Slosson, Annie (Trumbull), 1838-1926
xSlosson, Annie T.
Local Colorist. Arno.
Slosson, Annie T. see Slosson, Annie (Trumbull).
Slosson, Edwin E. see Slosson, Edwin Emery.
Slosson, Edwin Emery, 1865-1929
xSlosson, Edwin E.
Great American Universities. Arno.
Slosson, P. W. see Slosson, Preston William.
Slosson, Preston W. see Slosson, Preston William.
Slosson, Preston William, 1892-
xSlosson, P. W.
The Decline of the Chartist Movement. AMS
Pr.
xSlosson, Preston W.
Decline of the Chartist Movement. Biblio Dist.
Slote, Alfred.
xSlote, Alfred.
The Hotshot. Dell.
The Hotshot. Watts.
Love & Tennis. Macmillan.
Matt Gargan's Boy. Avon.
Matt Gargan's Boy. Lippincott.
My Father, the Coach. Avon.
My Trip to Alpha I. Avon.
Stranger on the Ball Club. Dell.
Strangers & Comrades. S&S.
Slotnikoff, Will.
xSlotnikoff, Will.
First Time I Live: A Romantic Book About the
Writing of a Book & the Birth of a Writer.
Manch Lane.
Slovenko, Ralph.
xSlovenko, Ralph.
Psychiatry & Law. Little.
Slowinski, Emil J.
xSlowinski, Emil J.
Qualitative Analysis & the Properties of Ions in
Aqueous Solution. HR&W.
Sloyan, Gerard S. see Sloyan, Gerard Stephen.
Sloyan, Gerard Stephen, 1919-
xSloyan, Gerard S.
Christ the Lord. Doubleday.
Commentary on the New Lectionary. Paulist
Pr.
Sloyer, Clifford W.
xSloyer, Clifford W.
Algebra & Its Applications: A Problem Solving
Approach. A-W.
Slurzberg, Morris.
xSlurzberg, Morris.
Essentials of Communication Electronics.
McGraw.
Slusher, Harold S. see Slusher, Harold Schultz.
Slusher, Harold Schultz.
xSlusher, Harold S.
Critique of Radiometric Dating. CLP Pubs.
Slusser, George E. see Slusser, George Edgar.
Slusser, George Edgar.
xSlusser, George E.

The Bradbury Chronicles. Borgo Pr.
The Delany Intersection: Samuel R. Delany
Considered As a Writer of Semi-Precious
Words. Borgo Pr.
The Farthest Shores of Ursula K. le Guin.
Borgo Pr.
Frank Herbert: Prophet of Dune. Borgo Pr.
I. Asimov: The Foundations of His Science
Fiction. Borgo Pr.
The Space Odysseys of Arthur C. Clarke.
Borgo Pr.
Slusser, Gerald H.
xSlusser, Gerald H.
A Christian Look at Secular Society.
Westminster.
Sluzas, Raymond.
xSluzas, Raymond.
A Graphic Guide to Industrialized Building
Elements. CBI Pub.
Sluzki, Carlos E.
xSluzki, Carlos E.
ed. Double Bind: The Foundation of the
Communicational Approach to the Family.
Grune.
Sly, Michael R. see Sly, R. Michael.
Sly, R. Michael.
xSly, Michael R.
Pediatric Allergy. Med Exam.
Slyke, Helen Van. see Van Slyke, Helen.
Slyke, Lyman P. Van. see Van Slyke, Lyman P.
Smail, D. J. see Smail, David John.
Smail, David John.
xSmail, D. J.
Psychotherapy: A Personal Approach. Biblio
Dist.
Smail, Thomas. see Smail, Thomas A.
Smail, Thomas A., 1928-
xSmail, Thomas.
The Reflected Glory: The Spirit in Christ &
Christians. Eerdmans.
Smailes, Arthur E.
xSmailes, Arthur E.
Geography of Towns. Humanities.
Smal-Stocki, Roman.
xSmal-Stocki, Roman.
The Captive Nations: Nationalism of the
Non-Russian Nations in the Soviet Union.
Coll & U Pr.
Smale, Gerald G.
xSmale, Gerald G.
Prophecy, Behaviour & Change: An
Examination of Self-Fulfilling Prophecies in
Helping Relationships. Routledge & Kegan.
Small, Albion W. see Small, Albion Woodbury.
Small, Albion Woodbury, 1854-1926
xSmall, Albion W.
The Meaning of Social Science. Johnson Repr.
Origins of Sociology. Russell.
Small, Christopher.
xSmall, Christopher.
Mary Shelley's Frankenstein: Tracing the
Myth. U of Pittsburgh Pr.
Small, Dwight H. see Small, Dwight Hervey.
Small, Dwight Hervey.
xSmall, Dwight H.
How Should I Love You?. Har-Row.
The Right to Remarry. Revell.
Small, Howard I.
xSmall, Howard I.
Monty's Pal. TBW Bks.
Small, HyDee.
xSmall, HyDee.
The Complete Bed Building Book. TAB Bks.
Small, Ian.
xSmall, Ian.
The Aesthetes: A Sourcebook. Routledge &
Kegan.
Small, John, 1828-1886
xSmall, John.

ed. English Metrical Homilies from
Manuscripts of the Fourteenth Century. AMS
Pr.

Small, Leonard, 1913-
xSmall, Leonard.
The Briefer Psychotherapies. Brunner Mazel.

Small, Marvin, 1899-
xSmall, Marvin.
Special Diet Cook Book. Dutton.

Small, Melvin.
xSmall, Melvin.
ed. Public Opinion & Historians:
Interdisciplinary Perspectives. Wayne St U
Pr.

Small, Miriam R. *see* Small, Miriam Rossiter.

Small, Miriam Rossiter.
xSmall, Miriam R.
Oliver Wendell Holmes. Coll & U Pr.
Oliver Wendell Holmes. Twayne.

Small, Norman J. *see* Small, Norman Jerome.

Small, Norman Jerome, 1907-
xSmall, Norman J.
Some Presidential Interpretations of the
Presidency. AMS Pr.
Some Presidential Interpretations of the
Presidency. Da Capo.

Small, Samuel, 1920-
xSmall, Samuel.
Starting a Business After Fifty. Pilot Bks.

Small, Walter H. *see* Small, Walter Herbert.

Small, Walter Herbert, 1856-1909
xSmall, Walter H.
Early New England Schools. Arno.

Small, William J.
xSmall, William J.
Political Power & the Press. Norton.

Smaller War Plants Corporation.
xU. S. Smaller War Plants Corporation.
Economic Concentration & World War II.
Johnson Repr.

Smalley, Beryl.
xSmalley, Beryl.
Historians in the Middle Ages. Scribner.
Study of the Bible in the Middle Ages. U of
Notre Dame Pr.

Smalley, Eugene V. *see* Smalley, Eugene Virgil.

Smalley, Eugene Virgil, 1841-1899
xSmalley, Eugene V.
History of the Northern Pacific Railroad. Arno.

Smalley, Peter, 1943-
xSmalley, Peter.
Trove. Norton.

Smalley, Ruth E. *see* Smalley, Ruth Elizabeth.

Smalley, Ruth Elizabeth.
xSmalley, Ruth E.
Theory for Social Work Practice. Columbia U
Pr.

Smalley, Stephen B.
xSmalley, Stephen B.
The Cincinnati, Georgetown & Portsmouth
Railroad. Trolley Talk.

Smalley, William A. *see* Smalley, William Allen.

Smalley, William Allen.
xSmalley, William A.
ed. Readings in Missionary Anthropology II.
William Carey.

Smallman, Kirk.
xSmallman, Kirk.
Creative Film Making. Macmillan.

Smallwood, Charles A., 1912-
xSmallwood, Charles A.
The White Front Cars of San Francisco.
Interurban.

Smallwood, Frank.
xSmallwood, Frank.
Free & Independent. Greene.
Greater London: The Politics of Metropolitan
Reform. Irvington.

Smallwood, Richard D.
xSmallwood, Richard D.

Decision Structure for Teaching Machines.
MIT Pr.

Smallwood, W. L. *see* Smallwood, William L.

Smallwood, William L.
xSmallwood, W. L.
Life Science. McGraw.
xSmallwood, William L.
Life Science. McGraw.

Smallwood, William M. *see* Smallwood, William Martin.

Smallwood, William Martin, 1873-
xSmallwood, William M.
Natural History & the American Mind. AMS
Pr.

Smaridge, Norah.
xSmaridge, Norah.
Choosing Your Retirement Hobby. Dodd.
Famous Literary Teams for Young People.
Dodd.
The Mystery at Greystone Hall. Dodd.
Only Silly People Waste. Abingdon.
Raggedy Andy: The I Can Do It, You Can Do
It Book. Western Pub.
The Story of Cake. Abingdon.

Smart, Alastair, 1922-
xSmart, Alastair.
The Dawn of Italian Painting, 1250-1400.
Cornell U Pr.
Renaissance & Mannerism in Italy. HarBraceJ.
Renaissance & Mannerism in Northern Europe
& Spain. HarBraceJ.

Smart, Barry.
xSmart, Barry.
Sociology, Phenomenology & Marxian
Analysis: A Critical Discussion of the Theory
& Practice of a Science of Society. Routledge
& Kegan.

Smart, Bath C. *see* Smart, Bath Charles.

Smart, Bath Charles.
xSmart, Bath C.
Dialect of the English Gypsies. Gale.

Smart, Carol.
xSmart, Carol.
Women, Sexuality & Social Control. Routledge
& Kegan.

Smart, D. R.
xSmart, D. R.
Fixed Point Theorems. Cambridge U Pr.

Smart, Don.
xSmart, Don.
Federal Aid to Australian Schools. U of
Queensland Pr.

Smart, George. *see* Smart, George Thomas.

Smart, George Thomas.
xSmart, George.
Leaves from the Journals of Sir George Smart.
Da Capo.

Smart, James D.
xSmart, James D.
ABC's of Christian Faith. Westminster.
Doorway to a New Age: A Study of Paul's
Letter to the Romans. Westminster.
History & Theology in Second Isaiah: A
Commentary on Isaiah 35, 40-66.
Westminster.
The Past, Present, & Future of Biblical
Theology. Westminster.
Strange Silence of the Bible in the Church: A
Study in Hermeneutics. Westminster.
Teaching Ministry of the Church: An
Examination of Basic Principles of Christian
Education. Westminster.

Smart, James R.
xSmart, James R.
Modern Geometries. Brooks-Cole.

Smart, John J. *see* Smart, John Jamieson Carswell.

Smart, John Jamieson Carswell, 1920-
xSmart, John J.
ed. Problems of Space & Time. Macmillan.

Smart, L. Edwin. *see* Smart, Louis Edwin.

Smart, Louis Edwin.
xSmart, L. Edwin.
Practical Rules for Graphic Presentation of
Business Statistics. Ohio St U Admin Sci.

Smart, Ninian, 1927-
xSmart, Ninian.
The Long Search. Little.
Religious Experience of Mankind. Scribner.

Smart, Patricia.
xSmart, Patricia.
Thinking & Reasoning. Shoe String.

Smart, Russell. *see* Smart, Russell Cook.

Smart, Russell Cook.
xSmart, Russell.
Readings in Child Development &
Relationships. Macmillan.

Smart, William, 1853-1915
xSmart, William.
A Disciple of Plato: A Critical Study of John
Ruskin. Folcroft.
Economic Annals of the Nineteenth Century.
Kelley.
ed. Eight Modern Essayists. St Martin.

Smart, William M. *see* Smart, William Marshall.

Smart, William Marshall, 1889-
xSmart, William M.
Riddle of the Universe. Halsted Pr.

Smartt, J.
xSmartt, J.
Tropical Pulses. Longman.

Smath, Jerry.
xSmath, Jerry.
illus. But No Elephants. Parents.

Smathers, George H. *see* Smathers, George Henry.

Smathers, George Henry, 1854-
xSmathers, George H.
The History of Land Titles in Western North
Carolina. Arno.

Smeaton, B. Hunter. *see* Smeaton, Barnston Hunter.

Smeaton, Barnston Hunter, 1915-
xSmeaton, B. Hunter.
Lexical Expansion Due to Technical Change:
As Illustrated by the Arabic of Al Hasa,
Saudi Arabia. Res Ctr Lang Semiotic.

Smeaton, George, 1814-1889
xSmeaton, George.
The Doctrine of the Holy Spirit. Banner of
Truth.

Smeaton, Oliphant. *see* Smeaton, William Henry
Oliphant.

Smeaton, R. W. *see* Smeaton, Robert W.

Smeaton, Robert W.
xSmeaton, R. W.
Switchgear & Control Handbook. McGraw.

Smeaton, William H. *see* Smeaton, William Henry
Oliphant.

Smeaton, William Henry Oliphant, 1856-1914
xSmeaton, Oliphant.
Longfellow & His Poetry. Folcroft.
xSmeaton, William H.
ed. Longfellow & His Poetry. AMS Pr.

Smedley, Agnes, 1890-1950
xSmedley, Agnes.
China's Red Army Marches. Hyperion-Conn.
Chinese Destinies: Sketches of Present-Day
China. Hyperion-Conn.
Daughter of Earth. Feminist Pr.
The Great Road: The Life & Times of Chu
Teh. Monthly Rev.
Portraits of Chinese Women in Revolution.
Feminist Pr.

Smedley, Jonathan, 1671-1729
xSmedley, Jonathan.
Gulliveriana. Gordon Pr.

Smedley, Robert C. *see* Smedley, Robert Clemens.

Smedley, Robert Clemens, 1832-1883
xSmedley, Robert C.

History of the Underground Railroad in
Chester & the Neighboring Counties of
Pennsylvania. Arno.
History of the Underground Railroad in
Chester & the Neighboring Counties of
Pennsylvania. Negro U Pr.
Smellie, Kingsley B. see Smellie, Kingsley Bryce.
Smellie, Kingsley Bryce, 1897-
xSmellie, Kingsley B.
A Hundred Years of English Government.
AMS Pr.
Smelser, Marshall.
xSmelser, Marshall.
American History at a Glance. B&N.
American History at a Glance. Har-Row.
The Life That Ruth Built: A Biography. Times
Bks.
Smelser, Neil J.
xSmelser, Neil J.
ed. Public Higher Education in California. U of
Cal Pr.
ed. Sociology: An Introduction. Wiley.
The Sociology of Economic Life. P-H.
ed. Themes of Work & Love in Adulthood.
Harvard U Pr.
Theory of Collective Behavior. Free Pr.
Smerk, George M.
xSmerk, George M.
ed. Readings in Urban Transportation. Ind U
Pr.
Smernoff, Richard. see Smernoff, Richard A.
Smernoff, Richard A.
xSmernoff, Richard.
Andre Chenier. Twayne.
Smet, Robin De. see De Smet, Robin.
Smeyak, G. Paul.
xSmeyak, G. Paul.
Broadcast News Writing. Grid Pub.
Smiddy, F. G. see Smiddy, Francis Geoffrey.
Smiddy, Francis Geoffrey.
xSmiddy, F. G.
The Investigation of the Surgical Patient.
Lippincott.
Smidt, Christine.
xSmidt, Christine.
An Acquaintance with Grief. Herald Hse.
Smigel, Edwin O. see Smigel, Erwin Orson.
Smigel, Erwin O. see Smigel, Erwin Orson.
Smigel, Erwin Orson.
xSmigel, Edwin O.
ed. Work & Leisure: A Contemporary Social
Problem. Coll & U Pr.
xSmigel, Erwin O.
Crimes Against Bureaucracy. Van Nos
Reinhold.
Smigel, Irwin.
xSmigel, Irwin.
Dental Health, Dental Beauty. M Evans.
Smil, Vaclav.
xSmil, Vaclav.
China's Energy:: Achievements, Problems,
Prospects. Praeger.
Smilansky, Moshe.
xSmilansky, Moshe.
The Gifted Disadvantaged: A Ten Year
Longitudinal Study of Compensatory
Education in Israel. Gordon.
Smiley, Albert K. see Smiley, Albert Keith.
Smiley, Albert Keith, 1944-
xSmiley, Albert K.
Competitive Bidding Under Uncertainty: The
Case of Offshore Oil. Ballinger Pub.
Smiley, David. see Smiley, David L.
Smiley, David L., 1921-
xSmiley, David.
Lion of White Hall: The Life of Cassius M.
Clay (1810-1903). Peter Smith.
Smiley, Jane.
xSmiley, Jane.

Barn Blind. Har-Row.
Smiley, Nixon, 1911-
xSmiley, Nixon.
Crowder Tales. E A Seemann.
Florida: Land of Images. E A Seemann.
Tropical Planting & Gardening for South
Florida & the West Indies. U of Miami Pr.
Smiley, Sam, 1931-
xSmiley, Sam.
Drama of Attack: Didactic Plays of the
American Depression. U of Mo Pr.
Smiley, Virginia.
xSmiley, Virginia.
Liza Hunt, Pediatric Nurse. Bouregy.
Smillie, I. S.
xSmillie, I. S.
Diseases of the Knee Joint. Churchill.
Injuries of the Knee Joint. Churchill.
Smirnov, M. M. see Smirnov, Modest Mikhailovich.
Smirnov, Modest Mikhailovich.
xSmirnov, M. M.
Equations of Mixed Type. Am Math.
Smirnov, V. I. see Smirnov, Vladimir Ivanovich.
Smirnov, Vladimir Ivanovich, 1887-
xSmirnov, V. I.
ed. Linear Operators & Operator Equations.
Plenum Pub.
Smit, Erasmus.
xSmit, Erasmus.
Diary of Erasmus Smit. Verry.
Smith. see Smith, Rodney.
Smith, A. C. see Smith, Anthony Charles H.
Smith, A. Delafield. see Smith, Arthur Delafield.
Smith, A. H. see Smith, Arthur Henderson.
Smith, A. Hassell, 1926-
xSmith, A. Hassell.
County & Court: Government & Politics in
Norfolk 1558-1603. Oxford U Pr.
Smith, A. L. see Smith, Albert Lee.
Smith, A. Ledyard. see Smith, Augustus Ledyard.
Smith, A. Merriman, 1913-1970
xSmith, Merriman.
A President's Odyssey. Greenwood.
Smith, A. Robert. see Smith, Arthur Robert.
Smith, A. W. see Smith, Archibald William.
Smith, Abbot E. see Smith, Abbot Emerson.
Smith, Abbot Emerson.
xSmith, Abbot E.
Colonists in Bondage: White Servitude &
Convict Labor in America, 1607-1776.
Norton.
Smith, Abbott P.
xSmith, Abbott P.
Complete Guide to Selling Intangibles. P-H.
Smith, Adam.
xSmith, Adam.
An Inquiry into the Nature & Causes of the
Wealth of Nations. Oxford U Pr.
An Inquiry into the Nature & Causes of the
Wealth of Nations. U of Chicago Pr.
Lectures on Jurisprudence. Oxford U Pr.
Lectures on Rhetoric & Belles Lettres. S Ill U
Pr.
The Theory of Moral Sentiments. Liberty
Fund.
The Theory of Moral Sentiments. Oxford U Pr.
Smith, Agnes, 1906-
xSmith, Agnes.
An Edge of the Forest. McClain.
Smith, Alan, 1925 (Oct. 31)-
xSmith, Alan.
ed. Country Life International Dictionary of
Clocks. Putnam.
Getting Started in Treasure Hunting. Stackpole.
Working with Horses. David & Charles.
Smith, Alan G. see Smith, Alan Gordon Rae.
Smith, Alan Gordon Rae.
xSmith, Alan G.

ed. The Reign of James VI & I. St Martin.
Smith, Albert A., 1935-
xSmith, Albert A.
The Coupling of External Electromagnetic
Fields to Transmission Lines. Wiley.
Smith, Albert B. see Smith, Albert Brewster.
Smith, Albert Brewster, 1930-
xSmith, Albert B.
Ideal & Reality in the Fictional Narratives of
Theophile Gautier. U Presses Fla.
Smith, Albert Lee, 1924-
xSmith, A. L.
ed. Analysis of Silicones. Wiley.
Smith, Alden W. see Smith, Alden Wallace.
Smith, Alden Wallace, 1914-
xSmith, Alden W.
Participation in Organizations: A Study of
Columbia College Alumni. AMS Pr.
Smith, Alexander, 1830?-1867
xSmith, Alexander.
Dreamthorp: A Book of Essays Written in the
Country. Arno.
Smith, Alexander B.
xSmith, Alexander B.
Introduction to Probation & Parole. West Pub.
Some Sins Are Not Crimes: A Plea for Reform
of the Criminal Law. New Viewpoints.
Smith, Alfred G. see Smith, Alfred Goud.
Smith, Alfred Goud, 1921-
xSmith, Alfred G.
Cognitive Styles in Law Schools. U of Tex Pr.
Smith, Alice E. see Smith, Alice Elizabeth.
Smith, Alice Elizabeth, 1896-
xSmith, Alice E.
George Smith's Money: A Scottish Investor in
America. State Hist Soc Wis.
Smith, Alice K. see Smith, Alice Kimball.
Smith, Alice Kimball.
xSmith, Alice K.
Peril & a Hope: The Scientists' Movement in
America, 1945-47. MIT Pr.
Peril & a Hope: The Scientists' Movement in
America, 1945-47. U of Chicago Pr.
Smith, Alice L. see Smith, Alice Lorraine.
Smith, Alice Lorraine, 1920-
xSmith, Alice L.
Microbiology & Pathology. Mosby.
Principles of Microbiology. Mosby.
Smith, Allen W. see Smith, Allen William.
Smith, Allen William.
xSmith, Allen W.
Understanding Inflation & Unemployment.
Nelson-Hall.
Smith, Alpheus. see Smith, Alpheus Wilson.
Smith, Alpheus Wilson.
xSmith, Alpheus.
Elements of Physics. McGraw.
Smith, Alson. see Smith, Alson Jesse.
Smith, Alson Jesse.
xSmith, Alson.
The Psychic Source Book. Assoc Bk.
Smith, Ann, 1927-
xSmith, Ann.
Stretch!. Acropolis.
The Tummy Trimmer Primer. G&D.
Smith, Ann P.
xSmith, Ann P.
ed. Orthopedic Nursing. Med Exam.
Smith, Anna H.
xSmith, Anna H.
Africana Byways. Munger Africana Lib.
Smith, Anne.
xSmith, Anne.
ed. The Art of Emily Bronte. B&N.
ed. The Art of Malcolm Lowry. B&N.
ed. Lawrence & Women. B&N.
ed. The Novels of Thomas Hardy. B&N.
Smith, Anne M. see Smith, Anne Marie.
Smith, Anne Marie.
xSmith, Anne M.

Play for Convalescent Children in Hospitals & at Home. A S Barnes.

Smith, Anne Milne, 1900-
xSmith, Anne M.
Ethnography of the Northern Utes. Museum NM Pr.

Smith, Annette. *see* Smith, Annette Klein.

Smith, Annette Klein.
xSmith, Annette.
Terror in Cairo. HarBraceJ.

Smith, Anthony, 1938-
xSmith, Anthony.
ed. The British Press Since the War. Rowman.
Goodbye Gutenberg: The Newspaper Revolution of the 1980's. Oxford U Pr.
The Human Pedigree. McGraw.
The Newspaper: An International History. Thames Hudson.
Television & Political Life: Studies of Six European Countries. St Martin.

Smith, Anthony Charles H.
xSmith, A. C.
Paper Voices: The Popular Press & Social Change, 1935-1965. Rowman.

Smith, Anthony D.
xSmith, Anthony D.
Nationalism in the Twentieth Century. NYU Pr.

Smith, Anthony D. *see* Smith, Anthony Douglas.

Smith, Anthony Douglas, 1933-
xSmith, Anthony D.
The Concept of Social Change: A Critique of the Functionalist Theory of Social Change. Routledge & Kegan.
Nationalist Movements. St Martin.

Smith, Archibald William.
xSmith, A. W.
A Gardener's Dictionary of Plant Names: A Handbook on the Origin & Meaning of Some Plant Names. St Martin.

Smith, Arlo I., 1911-
xSmith, Arlo I.
A Guide to Wildflowers of the Mid-South: West Tennessee into Central Arkansas & South Through Alabama & into East Texas. Memphis St Univ.

Smith, Arthur A. *see* Smith, Arthur Allen.

Smith, Arthur Allen, 1924-
xSmith, Arthur A.
Rachel. Morehouse.

Smith, Arthur C. *see* Smith, Arthur Cosslett.

Smith, Arthur Cosslett, 1852-1926
xSmith, Arthur C.
Monk & the Dancer. Arno.

Smith, Arthur Delafield.
xSmith, A. Delafield.
The Right to Life. Coll & U Pr.

Smith, Arthur H. *see* Smith, Arthur Henderson.

Smith, Arthur Henderson, 1845-1932
xSmith, A. H.
Chinese Characteristics. Biblio Dist.
xSmith, Arthur H.
China in Convulsion. AMS Pr.
China in Convulsion. Biblio Dist.
Chinese Characteristics. Kennikat.
Chinese Characteristics. Norwood Edns.

Smith, Arthur L. *see* Smith, Arthur Lionel.

Smith, Arthur Lionel.
xSmith, Arthur L.
Church & State in the Middle Ages. Biblio Dist.

Smith, Arthur Robert.
xSmith, A. Robert.
An American Rape: A True Account of the Giles-Johnson Case. New Republic.

Smith, Audley L. *see* Smith, Audley Lawrence.

Smith, Audley Lawrence, 1899-1954
xSmith, Audley L.

Richard Hurd's Letters on Chivalry & Romance. Folcroft.

Smith, Augustus H.
xSmith, Augustus H.
Economics for Our Times. McGraw.

Smith, Augustus Ledyard, 1901-
xSmith, A. Ledyard.
Excavations at Altar De Sacrificios: Architecture, Settlement, Burials & Caches. Peabody Harvard.

Smith, B. H. *see* Smith, Brandes H.

Smith, B. L. *see* Smith, Bobby L.

Smith, B. O. *see* Smith, Bunnie Othanel.

Smith, Bailey E.
xSmith, Bailey E.
Real Christianity. Broadman.

Smith, Barbara H. *see* Smith, Barbara Herrnstein.

Smith, Barbara Herrnstein.
xSmith, Barbara H.
On the Margins of Discourse: The Relation of Literature to Language. U of Chicago Pr.

Smith, Barbara L. *see* Smith, Barbara Leigh.

Smith, Barbara Leigh.
xSmith, Barbara L.
Political Research Methods: Foundations & Techniques. HM.

Smith, Bardwell L., 1925-
xSmith, Bardwell L.
ed. Religion & Legitimation of Power in Sri Lanka. Anima Bks.

Smith, Beatrice S.
xSmith, Beatrice S.
The Case of the Lost Dogs. Carolrhoda Bks.
The Case of the Missing Bills. Carolrhoda Bks.
Don't Mention Moon to Me. Elsevier-Nelson.
The Fish Creek Mystery. Carolrhoda Bks.
From Peanuts to President. Raintree Pubs.
The Ghost in the Park. Carolrhoda Bks.
Proudest Horse on the Prairie. Lerner Pubns.

Smith, Ben.
xSmith, Ben.
Gunpowder Valley. Assoc Bk.

Smith, Ben B.
xSmith, Ben B.
How to Use the Magic of Self-Cybernetics. Littlefield.

Smith, Bernard. *see* Smith, Bernard William.

Smith, Bernard T., 1938-
xSmith, Bernard T.
Focus Forecasting: Computer Techniques for Inventory Control. CBI Pub.

Smith, Bernard William.
xSmith, Bernard.
European Vision & the South Pacific, 1768-1850: A Study in the History of Art & Ideas. Oxford U Pr.

Smith, Bert K. *see* Smith, Bert Kruger.

Smith, Bert Kruger, 1915-
xSmith, Bert K.
Aging in America. Beacon Pr.
The Pursuit of Dignity: New Living Alternatives for the Elderly. Beacon Pr.

Smith, Bertha.
xSmith, Bertha.
Go Home & Tell. Broadman.

Smith, Betty J.
xSmith, Betty J.
Fundamentals of Anesthesia Care. Mosby.

Smith, Bobby L.
xSmith, B. L.
O'Casey's Satiric Vision. Kent.St U Pr.

Smith, Bradford, 1909-1964
xSmith, Bradford.
Dear Gift of Life: A Man's Encounter with Death. Pendle Hill.

Smith, Bradley.
xSmith, Bradley.

The Emergency Book: You Can Save a Life. S&S.

Smith, Bradley F.
xSmith, Bradley F.
Adolf Hitler: His Family, Childhood, & Youth. Hoover Inst Pr.
Operation Sunrise: The Secret Surrender. Basic.
Reaching Judgment at Nuremburg. Basic.

Smith, Brandes H.
xSmith, B. H.
Bridged Aromatic Compounds. Acad Pr.

Smith, Brendan.
xSmith, Brendan.
Brendan's Leather Book. Outer Straubville.

Smith, Brian.
xSmith, Brian.
Memory. Humanities.

Smith, Brian. *see* Smith, Brian C.

Smith, Brian C.
xSmith, Brian.
Administering Britain. Biblio Dist.

Smith, Bruce D.
xSmith, Bruce D.
ed. Mississippian Settlement Patterns. Acad Pr.
Prehistoric Patterns of Human Behavior: A Case Study in the Mississippi Valley. Acad Pr.

Smith, Bruce L. *see* Smith, Bruce L. R.

Smith, Bruce L. R.
xSmith, Bruce L.
ed. Dilemma of Accountability in Modern Government: Independence Versus Control. St Martin.

Smith, Bryan C.
xSmith, Bryan C.
Community Health: An Epidemiological Approach. Macmillan.

Smith, Budford Don, 1925-
xSmith, Buford D.
Design of Equilibrium Stage Processes. McGraw.

Smith, Buford D. *see* Smith, Budford Don.

Smith, Bunnie Othanel.
xSmith, B. O.
ed. Socialization & Schooling: The Basics of Reform. Phi Delta Kappa.

Smith, C. A. *see* Smith, Catherine A.

Smith, C. Alphonso. *see* Smith, Charles Alphonso.

Smith, C. E. *see* Smith, Charles Edgar.

Smith, C. Fox. *see* Smith, Cicely Fox.

Smith, C. Ray.
xSmith, C. Ray.
The American Endless Weekend. Am Inst Arch.
Supermannerism: New Attitudes in Post-Modern Architecture. Dutton.

Smith, C. W. *see* Smith, Charles William.

Smith, Carl. *see* Smith, Carl Bernard.

Smith, Carl B. *see* Smith, Carl Bernard.

Smith, Carl Bernard.
xSmith, Carl.
Getting People to Read: Volunteer Programs That Work. Delacorte.
xSmith, Carl B.
ed. Parents & Reading. Intl Reading.
Reading Activities for Middle & Secondary Schools: A Handbook for Teachers. HR&W.

Smith, Carlyle S. *see* Smith, Carlyle Shreeve.

Smith, Carlyle Shreeve.
xSmith, Carlyle S.
The Archaeology of Coastal New York. AMS Pr.

Smith, Carol A.
xSmith, Carol A.
ed. Regional Analysis. Acad Pr.

Smith, Carol H.
xSmith, Carol H.

T. S. Eliot's Dramatic Theory & Practice:
From Sweeney Agonistes to the Elder
Statesman. Gordian.

Smith, Catherine A.
xSmith, C. A.
ed. Handbook of Auditory & Vestibular
Research Methods. C C Thomas.

Smith, Cecil. *see* Smith, Cecil Michener.

Smith, Cecil Michener, 1906-
xSmith, Cecil.
Worlds of Music. Greenwood.

Smith, Charles A. *see* Smith, Charles Alonzo.

Smith, Charles Alonzo, 1895-
xSmith, Charles A.
Some Relationships Existing in School
Expenditure Among Florida Counties. AMS
Pr.

Smith, Charles Alphonso, 1864-1924
xSmith, C. Alphonso.
Edgar Allan Poe: How to Know Him. Folcroft.
Repetition & Parallelism in English Verse: A
Study in the Technique of Poetry. Folcroft.

Smith, Charles D. *see* Smith, Charles Daniel.

Smith, Charles Daniel.
xSmith, Charles D.
The Early Career of Lord North the Prime
Minister, 1754-1770. Fairleigh Dickinson.

Smith, Charles Edgar.
xSmith, C. E.
ed. Foundations of Guidance & Counseling:
Multidisciplinary Readings. Lippincott.

Smith, Charles G. *see* Smith, Charles George.

Smith, Charles George, 1891-
xSmith, Charles G.
Spenser's Theory of Friendship. AMS Pr.
Spenser's Theory of Friendship. Folcroft.

Smith, Charles H. *see* Smith, Charles Henry.

Smith, Charles Henry, 1826-1903
xSmith, Charles H.
Farm & the Fireside: Sketches of Domestic
Life In War & Peace. Scholarly.

Smith, Charles K. *see* Smith, Charles Kay.

Smith, Charles Kay.
xSmith, Charles K.
Styles & Structures: Alternative Approaches to
College Writing. Norton.

Smith, Charles M. *see* Smith, Charles Merrill.

Smith, Charles Merrill.
xSmith, Charles M.
Reverend Randollph & the Avenging Angel.
Putnam.

Smith, Charles O., 1920-
xSmith, Charles O.
Introduction to Reliability in Design. McGraw.

Smith, Charles P.
xSmith, Charles P.
ed. Achievement-Related Motives in Children.
Russell Sage.

Smith, Charles W. *see* Smith, Charles William.

Smith, Charles William, 1940-
xSmith, C. W.
Country Music. Ballantine.
Country Music. FS&G.
The Thin Men of Haddam. Avon.
xSmith, Charles W.
A Critique of Sociological Reasoning: An Essay
in Philosophical Sociology. Rowman.

Smith, Charlotte W. *see* Smith, Charlotte Watkins.

Smith, Charlotte Watkins.
xSmith, Charlotte W.
Carl Becker: On History & the Climate of
Opinion. S Ill U Pr.

Smith, Chester M.
xSmith, Chester M.
American Philatelic Periodicals. Am Philatelic.

Smith, Christine.
xSmith, Christine.
The Baptistery of Pisa. Garland Pub.

Smith, Christopher.
xSmith, Christopher.

FTC Trade Regulation: Advertising,
Rulemaking, & New Consumer Protection.
PLI.

Smith, Christopher J.
xSmith, Christopher J.
Geography & Mental Health. Assn Am
Geographers.

Smith, Chuck, 1927-
xSmith, Chuck.
End Times. Word for Today.
What the World Is Coming to. Word for
Today.

Smith, Cicely Fox.
xSmith, C. Fox.
Valiant Sailor. S G Phillips.

Smith, Clarissa R.
xSmith, Clarissa R.
A Workbook in Auditory Training for Adults:
With a Special Section on the
Institutionalized Geriatric Patient. C C
Thomas.

Smith, Clark Ashton, 1893-
xSmith, C. A.
Abominations of Yondo. Wehman.

Smith, Clifford N. *see* Smith, Clifford Neal.

Smith, Clifford Neal.
xSmith, Clifford N.
Encyclopedia of German-American
Genealogical Research. Bowker.
Federal Land Series: A Calendar of Archival
Materials on the Land Patents Issued by the
United States Government, with Subject,
Tract, & Name Indexes, 1810 to 1814. ALA.

Smith, Clifford T. *see* Smith, Clifford Thorpe.

Smith, Clifford Thorpe.
xSmith, Clifford T.
An Historical Geography of Western Europe
Before 1800. Longman.

Smith, Clodus R.
xSmith, Clodus R.
Planning & Paying Your Way to College.
Macmillan.

Smith, Clyde. *see* Smith, Clyde H.

Smith, Clyde H.
xSmith, Clyde.
photos by Pennsylvania. Graphic Arts Ctr.

Smith, Coho, 1826-1914
xSmith, Coho.
jt. auth. Cohographs. Branch-Smith.

Smith, Colin.
xSmith, Colin.
Contemporary French Philosophy: A Study in
Norms & Values. Greenwood.

Smith, Colin L.
xSmith, Colin L.
The Embassy of Sir William White of
Constantinople 1886-1891. Greenwood.

Smith, Cordwainer.
xSmith, Cordwainer.
Norstrilia. Ballantine.
Quest of the Three Worlds. Ballantine.
Space Lords. BJ Pub Group.

Smith, Courtland L.
xSmith, Courtland L.
Salmon Fishers of the Columbia. Oreg St U Pr.

Smith, Craig. *see* Smith, Craig W.

Smith, Craig B.
xSmith, Craig B.
ed. Efficient Electricity Use: A Reference Book
on Energy Management for Engineers,
Architects, Planners, & Managers. Pergamon.

Smith, Craig W.
xSmith, Craig.
Getting Grants. Har-Row.

Smith, Culver H.
xSmith, Culver H.

The Press, Politics, & Patronage: The American
Government's Use of Newspapers,
1789-1875. U of Ga Pr.

Smith, Curt.
xSmith, Curt.
America's Dizzy Dean. Bethany Pr.

Smith, Cushing.
xSmith, Cushing.
I Can Heal Myself & I Will. Fell.

Smith, Cynthia S.
xSmith, Cynthia S.
How to Get Big Results from a Small
Advertising Budget. Dutton.

Smith, Cyril S. *see* Smith, Cyril Stanley.

Smith, Cyril Stanley, 1903-
xSmith, Cyril S.
From Art to Science: Seventy-Two Objects
Illustrating the Nature of Discovery. MIT Pr.
ed. Sources for the History of the Science of
Steel, 1532-1786. MIT Pr.

Smith, D. H. *see* Smith, David Howard.

Smith, D. Moody. *see* Smith, Dwight Moody.

Smith, D. N. *see* Smith, Duncan N.

Smith, Dale.
xSmith, Dale.
Forage Management in the North.
Kendall-Hunt.

Smith, Daniel M. *see* Smith, Daniel Malloy.

Smith, Daniel Malloy, 1922-
xSmith, Daniel M.
Aftermath of War: Bainbridge Colby &
Wilsonian Diplomacy. Am Philos.
American Diplomatic Experience. HM.

Smith, Darrell H. *see* Smith, Darrell Hevenor.

Smith, Darrell Hevenor.
xSmith, Darrell H.
The Bureau of Education: Its History,
Activities & Organization. AMS Pr.
The Forest Service: Its History, Activities &
Organization. AMS Pr.
The Office of the Supervising Architect of
Treasury: Its History, Activities &
Organization. AMS Pr.
The Panama Canal: Its History, Activities &
Organization. AMS Pr.

Smith, Datus C. *see* Smith, Datus Clifford.

Smith, Datus Clifford.
xSmith, Datus C.
A Guide to Book Publishing. Bowker.

Smith, Dave. *see* Smith, David Jeddie.

Smith, David. *see* Smith, David J.

Smith, David B. *see* Smith, David Beach.

Smith, David Beach.
xSmith, David B.
Systems Engineering & Management. A-W.

Smith, David C. *see* Smith, David Clayton.

Smith, David Clayton, 1929-
xSmith, David C.
A History of Lumbering in Maine, 1861-1960.
U Maine Orono.

Smith, David E., 1936-
xSmith, David E.
Prairie Liberalism: The Liberal Party in
Saskatchewan, 1905-1971. U of Toronto Pr.

Smith, David E. *see* Smith, David Elvin.

Smith, David Elvin, 1939-
xSmith, David E.
Amphetamine Use, Misuse & Abuse. G K Hall.

Smith, David Eugene, 1860-1944
xSmith, David E.
History of Mathematics. Peter Smith.

Smith, David G.
xSmith, David G.
Convention & the Constitution: Political Ideas
of the Founding Fathers. St Martin.

Smith, David H., 1921-
xSmith, David H.
Remember the Good Times. Broadman.

Smith, David Howard.
xSmith, D. H.

Confucius. Scribner.
Smith, David J., 1938-
  xSmith, David.
    Socialist Propaganda in the Twentieth-Century
     British Novel. Rowman.
Smith, David Jeddie, 1942-
  xSmith, Dave.
    The Fisherman's Whore. Ohio U Pr.
Smith, David L. see Smith, David Larmer.
Smith, David Larmer.
  xSmith, David L.
    Little Railways of South-West Scotland. Kelley.
Smith, David M.
  xSmith, David M.
    ed. Sociolinguistics in Cross-Cultural Analysis.
     Georgetown U Pr.
Smith, David M. see Smith, David N.
Smith, David Marshall, 1936-
  xSmith, David M.
    Human Geography: A Welfare Approach. St
     Martin.
Smith, David N., 1952-
  xSmith, David M.
    Who Rules the Universities?: An Essay in Class
     Analysis. Monthly Rev.
  xSmith, David N.
    Who Rules the Universities?: An Essay in Class
     Analysis. Monthly Rev.
Smith, David S. see Smith, David Spencer.
Smith, David Spencer.
  xSmith, David S.
    Muscle. Acad Pr.
Smith, David W.
  xSmith, David W.
    ed. The Biologic Ages of Man: From
     Conception Through Old Age. Saunders.
    Growth & Its Disorders: Basics & Standards,
     Approach & Classifications, Growth
     Deficiency Disorders, Growth Excess
     Disorders, Obesity. Saunders.
    ed. Introduction to Clinical Pediatrics.
     Saunders.
    Mothering Your Unborn Baby. Saunders.
Smith, Deboyd L.
  xSmith, DeBoyd L.
    A Guide to Marine Coastal Plankton & Marine
     Invertebrate Larvae. Kendall-Hunt.
Smith, Delbert D.
  xSmith, Delbert D.
    Space Stations: International Law & Policy.
     Westview.
Smith, Demaris C.
  xSmith, Demaris C.
    Starting & Operating a Clipping Service. Pilot
     Bks.
Smith, Dennis, 1940-
  xSmith, Dennis.
    The Final Fire. NAL.
Smith, Don, 1926-
  xSmith, Don.
    The Baja Run: Racing Fury. Troll Assocs.
    How Sports Began. Watts.
Smith, Donald. see Smith, Donald G.
Smith, Donald E. see Smith, Donald E P.
Smith, Donald E P.
  xSmith, Donald E.
    Learning to Learn. HarBraceJ.
Smith, Donald Eugene, 1927-
  xSmith, Donald E.
    India As a Secular State. Princeton U Pr.
    Religion & Politics in Burma. Princeton U Pr.
Smith, Donald G.
  xSmith, Donald.
    How to Cure Yourself of Positive Thinking. E
     A Seemann.
  xSmith, Donald G.

How to Cure Yourself of Positive Thinking.
  PB.
Smith, Donald R., 1939-
  xSmith, Donald R.
    Variational Methods in Optimization. P-H.
Smith, Donald R. see Smith, Donald Ridgeway.
Smith, Donald Ridgeway, 1909-
  xSmith, Donald R.
    General Urology. Lange.
Smith, Donnal V. see Smith, Donnal Vore.
Smith, Donnal Vore, 1901-
  xSmith, Donnal V.
    Chase & Civil War Politics. Arno.
Smith, Doris B. see Smith, Doris Buchanan.
Smith, Doris Buchanan.
  xSmith, Doris B.
    Dreams & Drummers. T Y Crowell.
    A Taste of Blackberries. T Y Crowell.
    Taste of Blackberries. Schol Bk Serv.
  xSmith, Doris Buchanan.
    Tough Chauncey. Morrow.
Smith, Dorothy, 1922-
  xSmith, Dorothy.
    In Our Own Interest: A Handbook for the
     Citizen Lobbyist in State Legislatures.
     Madrona Pubs.
Smith, Dorothy L.
  xSmith, Dorothy L.
    Medication Guide for Patient Counseling. Lea
     & Febiger.
Smith, Dorothy V. see Smith, Dorothy Valentine.
Smith, Dorothy Valentine.
  xSmith, Dorothy V.
    This Was Staten Island. Staten Island.
Smith, Doug. see Smith, Douglas W.
Smith, Douglas. see Smith, Douglas Henry.
Smith, Douglas Henry.
  xSmith, Douglas.
    Hotel & Restaurant Design. Intl Schol Bk Serv.
Smith, Douglas W.
  xSmith, Doug.
    Europe by Rail & Backpack. D Smith.
Smith, Duane A.
  xSmith, Duane A.
    Colorado Mining: A Photographic History. U
     of Nm Pr.
Smith, Duncan N.
  xSmith, D. N.
    A Forgotten Sector: The Training of Ancillary
     Staff in Hospitals. Pergamon.
Smith, Dwight L. see Smith, Dwight la Vern.
Smith, Dwight La Vern, 1918-
  xSmith, Dwight L.
    ed. The American & Canadian West: A
     Bibliography. ABC-Clio.
    ed. Indians of the United States & Canada: A
     Bibliography. ABC-Clio.
Smith, Dwight Moody.
  xSmith, D. Moody.
    Interpreting the Gospels for Preaching.
     Fortress.
Smith, E . E. see Smith, E. E.
Smith, E. B. see Smith, Elbert B.
Smith, E. Baldwin. see Smith, Earl Baldwin.
Smith, E. D.
  xSmith, E. D.
    Battle for Burma. David & Charles.
  xSmith, Eric D.
    Battle for Burma. Holmes & Meier.
Smith, E. Durham.
  xSmith, E. Durham.
    Spina Bifida & the Total Care of Spinal
     Myelomeningocele. C C Thomas.
Smith, E. E.
  xSmith, E . E.
    Galactic Patrol. BJ Pub Group.
  xSmith, E. E.

Gray Lensman. BJ Pub Group.
  xSmith, Edward E.
    Triplanetary. BJ Pub Group.
Smith, E. E. see Smith, Edward E.
Smith, E. Lester. see Smith, Ernest Lester.
Smith, E. Newbold. see Smith, Edgar Newbold.
Smith, Earl Baldwin, 1888-1956
  xSmith, E. Baldwin.
    Architectural Symbolism of Imperial Rome &
     the Middle Ages. Hacker.
Smith, Edgar F. see Smith, Edgar Fahs.
Smith, Edgar Fahs, 1854-1928
  xSmith, Edgar F.
    Chemistry in America: Chapters from the
     History of the Science in the United States.
     Arno.
Smith, Edgar Newbold.
  xSmith, E. Newbold.
    Down Denmark Strait. Little.
Smith, Edith K.
  xSmith, Edith K.
    How to Raise & Train a Great Pyrenees. TFH
     Pubns.
Smith, Edward, 1839-1919
  xSmith, Edward.
    The Life of Sir Joseph Banks. Arno.
Smith, Edward B. see Smith, Edward Brinton.
Smith, Edward Brinton.
  xSmith, Edward B.
    Gemcutting: A Lapidary Handbook. P-H.
Smith, Edward C. see Smith, Edward Conrad.
Smith, Edward Conrad, 1891-
  xSmith, Edward C.
    Borderland in the Civil War. AMS Pr.
    Borderland in the Civil War. Arno.
    Dictionary of American Politics. B&N.
    Dictionary of American Politics. Har-Row.
Smith, Edward E.
  xSmith, E. E.
    First Lensman. BJ Pub Group.
    Spacehounds of IPC. BJ Pub Group.
  xSmith, Edward E.
    Subspace Explorers. Canaveral.
Smith, Edward E. see Smith, E. E.
Smith, Edward O.
  xSmith, Edward O.
    Crown & Commonwealth: A Study in the
     Official Elizabethan Doctrine of the Prince.
     Am Philos.
Smith, Edward W. see Smith, Edward W. L.
Smith, Edward W. L., 1942-
  xSmith, Edward W.
    ed. The Growing Edge of Gestalt Therapy.
     Brunner-Mazel.
Smith, Edwin. see Smith, Edwin H.
Smith, Edwin H.
  xSmith, Edwin.
    Literacy Education for Adolescents & Adults:
     A Teacher's Resource Book. Boyd & Fraser.
  xSmith, Edwin H.
    Teaching Reading to Adults. Monarch Pr.
Smith, Edwin W. see Smith, Edwin William.
Smith, Edwin William.
  xSmith, Edwin W.
    Ila-Speaking Peoples of Northern Rhodesia.
     Univ Bks.
Smith, Egerton.
  xSmith, Egerton.
    Principles of English Metre. Greenwood.
Smith, Elbert B.
  xSmith, E. B.
    The Presidency of James Buchanan. Regents Pr
     KS.
  xSmith, Elbert B.
    Francis Preston Blair. Free Pr.
Smith, Elise C.
  xSmith, Elise C.

ed. Effects of Melting & Processing Variables
on Mechanical Properties of Steels, Series
MPC-6. ASME.
ed. Properties of Steel Weldments for Elevated
Temperature Pressure Containment
Applications: MPC-9. ASME.
Smith, Gerald B. *see* Smith, Gerald Birney.
Smith, Gerald Birney.
xSmith, Gerald B.
ed. Religious Thought in the Last
Quarter-Century. Arno.
Smith, Gerald W.
xSmith, Gerald W.
ed. Engineering Economy: Analysis of Capital
Expenditures. Iowa St U Pr.
Smith, Gerald W. *see* Smith, Gerald Walker.
Smith, Gerald Walker.
xSmith, Gerald W.
Couple Therapy. Macmillan.
Smith, Gerard.
xSmith, Gerard.
Freedom in Molina. Loyola.
A Trio of Talks. Marquette.
Truth That Frees. Marquette.
Smith, Gilbert.
xSmith, Gilbert.
Social Work & the Sociology of Organizations.
Routledge & Kegan.
Smith, Godfrey, 1926-
xSmith, Godfrey.
Caviare. Coward.
Smith, Goldwin, 1823-1910
xSmith, Goldwin.
Cowper. AMS Pr.
Cowper. Folcroft.
Life of Jane Austen. Folcroft.
Smith, Goldwin. *see* Smith, Goldwin Albert.
Smith, Goldwin Albert.
xSmith, Goldwin.
ed. The Professor & the Public: The Role of
the Scholar in the Modern World. Wayne St
U Pr.
Smith, Gordon R. *see* Smith, Gordon Ross.
Smith, Gordon Ross.
xSmith, Gordon R.
ed. Classified Shakespeare Bibliography,
1936-1958. Pa St U Pr.
Smith, Gordon S.
xSmith, Gordon S.
One Man & His Sea. Hastings.
Smith, Grafton E. *see* Smith, Grafton Elliot.
Smith, Grafton Elliot, Sir, 1871-1937
xSmith, G. Elliot.
Diffusion of Culture. Kennikat.
xSmith, Grafton E.
Ancient Egyptians & the Origin of Civilization.
Arno.
Smith, Grahame.
xSmith, Grahame.
Dickens, Money & Society. U of Cal Pr.
Smith, Guy V.
xSmith, Guy V.
Master Guide to Real Estate Valuation. P-H.
Smith, H. *see* Smith, Hillas.
Smith, H. Allen. *see* Smith, Harry Allen.
Smith, H. M. *see* Smith, Howard Michael.
Smith, H. Maynard. *see* Smith, Herbert Maynard.
Smith, H. Maynard. *see* Smith, Herbert Maynard.
Smith, H. Shelton. *see* Smith, Hilrie Shelton.
Smith, Halbert C.
xSmith, Halbert C.
Real Estate & Urban Development. Irwin.
Smith, Hannah (Whitall), 1832-1911
xSmith, Hannah W.
Christian's Secret of a Happy Life. Revell.
Smith, Hannah W. *see* Smith, Hannah (Whitall).
Smith, Harlan I. *see* Smith, Harlan Ingersoll.
Smith, Harlan Ingersoll, 1872-1940
xSmith, Harlan I.

Archaeology of the Gulf of Georgia & Puget
Sound. AMS Pr.
Archaeology of the Thompson River Region,
British Columbia. AMS Pr.
Cairns of British Columbia & Washington.
AMS Pr.
Smith, Harmon L., 1930-
xSmith, Harmon L.
Ethics & the New Medicine. Abingdon.
Smith, Harold. *see* Smith, Harold T.
Smith, Harold E. *see* Smith, Harold Eugene.
Smith, Harold Eugene, 1916-
xSmith, Harold E.
Historical & Cultural Dictionary of Thailand.
Scarecrow.
Smith, Harold T.
xSmith, Harold.
The Administrative Manager. SRA.
Smith, Harold W. *see* Smith, Harold William.
Smith, Harold William.
xSmith, Harold W.
Approximate Analysis of Randomly Excited
Non-Linear Controls. MIT Pr.
Smith, Harriet L.
xSmith, Harriet L.
Academic Sketches. S S S Pub Co.
Smith, Harris P. *see* Smith, Harris Pearson.
Smith, Harris Pearson, 1891-
xSmith, Harris P.
Farm Machinery & Equipment. McGraw.
Smith, Harry Allen.
xSmith, H. Allen.
Don't Get Perconel with a Chicken. Stein &
Day.
The Life & Legend of Gene Fowler. Morrow.
Smith, Harry P. *see* Smith, Harry Pearse.
Smith, Harry Pearse, 1885-
xSmith, Harry P.
Business Administration of a City School
System. AMS Pr.
Smith, Harvey A. *see* Smith, Harvey Arthur.
Smith, Harvey Arthur, 1889-
xSmith, Harvey A.
Economy in Public School Fire Insurance.
AMS Pr.
Smith, Harvey G. *see* Smith, Hervey Garrett.
Smith, Helen (Vandervort).
xSmith, Helen V.
How to Know the Non-Gilled Fleshy Fungi.
Wm C Brown.
Smith, Helen A. *see* Smith, Helen Ainslie.
Smith, Helen Ainslie.
xSmith, Helen A.
One Hundred Famous Americans. Arno.
Smith, Helen K. *see* Smith, Helen Krebs.
Smith, Helen Krebs.
xSmith, Helen K.
The Presumptuous Dreamers: A Sociological
History of the Life & Times of Abigail Scott
Duniway, 1834-1871. S S S Pub Co.
Smith, Helen V. *see* Smith, Helen (Vandervort).
Smith, Henry C. *see* Smith, Henry Clay.
Smith, Henry Clay, 1913-
xSmith, Henry C.
Personality Development. McGraw.
Smith, Henry L. *see* Smith, Henry Lester.
Smith, Henry Lee, 1913-
xSmith, Henry L.
Linguistic Science & the Teaching of English.
Harvard U Pr.
Smith, Henry Lester, 1876-
xSmith, Henry L.
Survey of a Public School System. AMS Pr.
Smith, Henry N. *see* Smith, Henry Nash.
Smith, Henry Nash.
xSmith, Henry N.

ed. Mark Twain: A Collection of Critical
Essays. P-H.
Mark Twain: The Development of a Writer.
Atheneum.
Mark Twain: The Development of a Writer.
Harvard U Pr.
Smith, Herbert F.
xSmith, Herbert F.
How to Get What You Want from God. Our
Sunday Visitor.
Sexual Inversion: The Questions-with Catholic
Answers. Dghtrs St Paul.
Smith, Herbert F. *see* Smith, Herbert Franklin.
Smith, Herbert Franklin.
xSmith, Herbert F.
Richard Watson Gilder. Irvington.
Smith, Herbert H.
xSmith, Herbert H.
The Citizen's Guide to Planning. Planners Pr.
Smith, Herbert Maynard, 1869-1949
xSmith, H. Maynard.
Pre-Reformation England. Arden Lib.
xSmith, H. Maynard.
Pre-Reformation England. Russell.
Smith, Herman W., 1943-
xSmith, Herman W.
Strategies of Social Research: The
Methodological Imagination. P-H.
Smith, Hervey G. *see* Smith, Hervey Garrett.
Smith, Hervey Garrett.
xSmith, Harvey G.
The Arts of the Sailor. B&N.
xSmith, Hervey G.
Marlinspike Sailor. De Graff.
Smith, Hilary D. *see* Smith, Hilary Dansey.
Smith, Hilary Dansey.
xSmith, Hilary D.
Preaching in the Spanish Golden Age: A Study
of Some Preachers of the Reign of Philip III.
Oxford U Pr.
Smith, Hillas.
xSmith, H.
ed. Antibiotics in Clinical Practice. Univ Park.
Smith, Hilrie Shelton, 1893-
xSmith, H. Shelton.
In His Image, but: Racism in Southern
Religion, 1780-1910. Duke.
Smith, Holland M. *see* Smith, Holland McTyeire.
Smith, Holland McTyeire.
xSmith, Holland M.
Coral & Brass. Zenger Pub.
Smith, Horace W. *see* Smith, Horace Wemyss.
Smith, Horace Wemyss, 1825-1891
xSmith, Horace W.
Life & Correspondence of the Rev. William
Smith, D.D.. Arno.
Smith, Horatio. *see* Smith, Horatio Elwin.
Smith, Horatio E. *see* Smith, Horatio Elwin.
Smith, Horatio Elwin, 1886-1946
xSmith, Horatio.
Masters of French Literature. Arno.
xSmith, Horatio E.
Literary Criticism of Pierre Bayle. B Franklin.
Smith, Howard. *see* Smith, Howard Everett.
Smith, Howard E. *see* Smith, Howard Everett.
Smith, Howard Everett.
xSmith, Howard.
The Animal Olympics. Doubleday.
xSmith, Howard E.
The Complete Beginner's Guide to Mountain
Climbing. Doubleday.
Giant Animals. Doubleday.
Play with the Sun. McGraw.
Play with the Wind. McGraw.
Smith, Howard M. *see* Smith, Howard Michael.
Smith, Howard Michael.
xSmith, H. M.
ed. Holographic Recording Materials.
Springer-Verlag.
xSmith, Howard M.

Principles of Holography. Wiley.
Smith, Huron H. *see* Smith, Huron Herbert.
Smith, Huron Herbert, 1883-1933
  xSmith, Huron H.
    Ethnobotany of the Menomini Indians.
      Greenwood.
Smith, Huston.
  xSmith, Huston.
    Forgotten Truth: The Primordial Tradition.
      Har-Row.
    Forgotten Truth: The Primordial Tradition.
      Har-Row.
    The Purposes of Higher Education.
      Greenwood.
    Religions of Man. Har-Row.
    Religions of Man. Har-Row.
    Religions of Man. Har-Row.
Smith, I. Evelyn.
  xSmith, I. Evelyn.
    ed. Readings in Adoption. Philos Lib.
Smith, I. MacFarlane. *see* Smith, Ian Macfarlane.
Smith, Ian Macfarlane.
  xSmith, I. MacFarlane.
    Spatial Ability: Its Educational & Social
      Significance. EDITS Pubs.
  xSmith, MacFarlane I.
    Spatial Ability: Its Educational & Social
      Significance. EDITS Pubs.
Smith, Ian W. *see* Smith, Ian W. M.
Smith, Ian W. M.
  xSmith, Ian W.
    Kinetics & Dynamics of Elementary Gas
      Reactions. Butterworths.
Smith, Irving H.
  xSmith, Irving H.
    ed. Trotsky. P-H.
Smith, Ivan.
  xSmith, Ivan.
    Death of a Wombat. David & Charles.
Smith, Ivor.
  xSmith, Ivor.
    Chromatographic & Electrophoretic
      Techniques. Year Bk Med.
Smith, J. C. *see* Smith, Joseph C.
Smith, J. Gray. *see* Smith, James Gray.
Smith, J. Harold, 1910-
  xSmith, J. Harold.
    Fast Your Way to Health. Nelson.
Smith, J. Lawton. *see* Smith, Joseph J. Lawton.
Smith, J. M. *see* Smith, Joe Mauk.
Smith, J. Maynard. *see* Smith, John Maynard.
Smith, J. Richard. *see* Smith, John Richard.
Smith, Jack. *see* Smith, Jack Clifford.
Smith, Jack Clifford, 1916-
  xSmith, Jack.
    Spend All Your Kisses, Mr. Smith. McGraw.
Smith, Jack L.
  xSmith, Jack L.
    Accounting for Financial Statement
      Presentation. McGraw.
Smith, James.
  xSmith, James.
    Rejected Addresses: Or, the New Theatrum
      Poetarum. R West.
Smith, James. *see* Smith, James Atkinson.
Smith, James A.
  xSmith, James A.
    Classroom Organization for the Language Arts.
      Peacock Pubs.
    Creative Teaching of Reading in the
      Elementary School. Allyn.
    Word Music & Word Magic: Children's
      Literature Methods. Allyn.
Smith, James A. *see* Smith, James Atkinson.
Smith, James Atkinson, 1928-
  xSmith, James.
    Rapists Beware. Green.
  xSmith, James A.
    Rapists Beware. Macmillan.
Smith, James B. *see* Smith, James Bernard.

Smith, James Bernard, 1918-
  xSmith, James B.
    Business Law in California. General Educ.
Smith, James C. *see* Smith, James Cruickshanks.
Smith, James Cruickshanks, 1867-1949
  xSmith, James C.
    Some Characteristics of Scots Literature.
      Folcroft.
Smith, James E. *see* Smith, James Eugene.
Smith, James Eugene, 1905-
  xSmith, James E.
    One Hundred Years of Hartford's Courant,
      from Colonial Times Through the Civil War.
      Shoe String.
Smith, James F. *see* Smith, James Francis.
Smith, James Francis.
  xSmith, James F.
    Chrysanthemums. Hippocrene Bks.
Smith, James Gray, 1797-1875
  xSmith, J. Gray.
    A Brief Historical, Statistical & Descriptive
      Review of East Tennessee, United States of
      America. Reprint.
Smith, James H. *see* Smith, James Henry.
Smith, James Henry, 1884-
  xSmith, James H.
    Legal Limitations on Bonds & Taxation for
      Public School Buildings. AMS Pr.
Smith, James L. *see* Smith, James Leslie.
Smith, James Leslie.
  xSmith, James L.
    Melodrama. Methuen Inc.
Smith, James M. *see* Smith, James Morton.
Smith, James Morton.
  xSmith, James M.
    Freedom's Fetters: The Alien & Sedition Laws
      & American Civil Liberties. Cornell U Pr.
    ed. Seventeenth-Century America: Essays in
      Colonial History. Greenwood.
    ed. Seventeenth-Century America: Essays in
      Colonial History. Norton.
Smith, James P.
  xSmith, James P.
    ed. Female Labor Supply: Theory &
      Estimation. Princeton U Pr.
    Sociology & Nursing. Churchill.
Smith, James W. *see* Smith, James Woodruff.
Smith, James Woodruff.
  xSmith, James W.
    The Loner. BJ Pub Group.
Smith, Jane I.
  xSmith, Jane I.
    ed. Women in Contemporary Muslim Societies.
      Bucknell U Pr.
Smith, Janet, 1912-
  xSmith, Janet.
    Mark Twain on Man & Beast. Lawrence Hill.
Smith, Janet. *see* Smith, Janet Lynne.
Smith, Janet A. *see* Smith, Janet Adam.
Smith, Janet Adam.
  xSmith, Janet A.
    John Buchan & His World. Scribner.
Smith, Janet Lynne, 1944-
  xSmith, Janet.
    An Annotated Bibliography of & About
      Ernesto Cardenal. ASU Lat Am St.
Smith, Janet M.
  xSmith, Janet M.
    The French Background of Middle Scots
      Literature. Folcroft.
Smith, Jay H.
  xSmith, Jay H.

Fiery Tennis Star: Jimmy Connors. Creative
      Ed.
    Fran Tarkenton. Creative Ed.
    The Infielders. Creative Ed.
    Meet the Infielders. Creative Ed.
    Meet the Managers. Creative Ed.
    Meet the Pitchers. Creative Ed.
    The Pitchers. Creative Ed.
Smith, Jean De Mouth, 1949-
  xSmith, Jean F.
    Horse Markings & Coloration. A S Barnes.
Smith, Jean Edward.
  xSmith, Jean Edward.
    The Defense of Berlin. Johns Hopkins.
Smith, Jean F. *see* Smith, Jean De Mouth.
Smith, Jean L. *see* Smith, Jean Louise.
Smith, Jean Louise.
  xSmith, Jean L.
    Take More Joy. St Marys.
Smith, Jean R. *see* Smith, Jean Reeder.
Smith, Jean Reeder.
  xSmith, Jean R.
    Essentials of World History. Barron.
Smith, Jewell E. *see* Smith, Jewell Ellen.
Smith, Jewell Ellen.
  xSmith, Jewell E.
    Great Jehoshaphat & Gully Dirt!. Blair.
Smith, Jim, 1920-
  xSmith, Jim.
    illus. The Frog Band & Durrington Dormouse.
      Little.
    The Frog Band & the Mystery of Lion Castle.
      Little.
    illus. The Frog Band & the Mystery of Lion
      Castle. Little.
Smith, Joan, 1938-
  xSmith, Joan.
    Aurora. Walker & Co.
    Dame Durden's Daughter. Fawcett.
    Dame Durden's Daughter. Walker & Co.
    Imprudent Lady. Fawcett.
    Imprudent Lady. Walker & Co.
    Imprudent Lady. G K Hall.
    The Talk of the Town. Fawcett.
    Talk of the Town. Walker & Co.
    Talk of the Town. G K Hall.
Smith, JoAnn K. *see* Smith, Joann Kelley.
Smith, Joann Kelley.
  xSmith, JoAnn K.
    Free Fall. Judson.
Smith, Joe M. *see* Smith, Joe Mauk.
Smith, Joe Mauk, 1916-
  xSmith, J. M.
    Introduction to Chemical Engineering
      Thermodynamics. McGraw.
  xSmith, Joe M.
    Chemical Engineering Kinetics. McGraw.
  xSmith, Joseph M.
    Chemical Engineering Kinetics. McGraw.
Smith, Joel.
  xSmith, Joel.
    ed. Legislatures in Development: Dynamics of
      Change in New & Old States. Duke.
Smith, John, 1924-
  xSmith, John.
    The Arts Betrayed. Universe.
    ed. My Kind of Verse. Macmillan.
    Select Discourses. Schol Facsimiles.
Smith, John. *see* Smith, John Upham Murray.
Smith, John C. *see* Smith, John Chabot.
Smith, John Chabot.
  xSmith, John C.
    Alger Hiss: The True Story. Penguin.
Smith, John E. *see* Smith, John Edwin.
Smith, John Edwin.
  xSmith, John E.

Experience & God. Oxford U Pr.
Experience & God. Oxford U Pr.
Purpose & Thought: The Meaning of
  Pragmatism. Yale U Pr.
Reason & God: Encounters of Philosophy with
  Religion. Greenwood.
Religion & Empiricism. Marquette.
Spirit of American Philosophy. Oxford U Pr.

Smith, John F., 1939-
xSmith, John F.
  Compiled by A Critical Bibliography of
    Building Conservation: Historic Towns,
    Buildings, Their Furnishings & Fittings.
    Merrimack Bk Serv.
Smith, John H. *see* Smith, John Harrington.
Smith, John Harrington.
xSmith, John H.
  The Gay Couple in Restoration Comedy.
    Octagon.
Smith, John Holland.
xSmith, John H.
  Death of Classical Paganism. Scribner.
Smith, John I.
xSmith, John I.
  Modern Operational Circuit Design. Wiley.
Smith, John L., 1935-
xSmith.
  Ground Ladder Operations. R J Brady.
Smith, John M. *see* Smith, John Merlin Powis.
Smith, John Maynard, 1920-
xSmith, J. Maynard.
  The Evolution of Sex. Cambridge U Pr.
  Mathematical Ideas in Biology. Cambridge U
    Pr.
xSmith, John M.
  The Theory of Evolution. Penguin.
Smith, John Merlin Powis, 1866-1932
xSmith, John M.
  The Origin & History of Hebrew Law.
    Hyperion Conn.
  Prophets & Their Times. U of Chicago Pr.
Smith, John Richard.
xSmith, J. Richard.
  Focke-Wulf. Arco.
Smith, John Upham Murray, 1933-
xSmith, John.
  Computer Simulation Models. Hafner.
Smith, Jon M., 1938-
xSmith, Jon M.
  Financial Analysis & Business Decisions on the
    Pocket Calculator. Wiley.
Smith, Joseph, 1945-
xSmith, Joseph.
  Illusions of Conflict: Anglo-American
    Diplomacy Toward Latin America,
    1865-1896. U of Pittsburgh Pr.
Smith, Joseph C.
xSmith, J. C.
  Legal Obligation. U of Toronto Pr.
Smith, Joseph F. *see* Smith, Joseph Fielding.
Smith, Joseph Fielding, 1876-
xSmith, Joseph F.
  Answers to Gospel Questions. Deseret Bk.
Smith, Joseph Francis.
xSmith, Joseph F.
  Pediatric Neuropathology. McGraw.
Smith, Joseph H., 1927-
xSmith, Joseph H.
  ed. The Literary Freud: Mechanisms of
    Defense & the Poetic Will. Yale U Pr.
  Psychiatry & the Humanities. Yale U Pr.
Smith, Joseph J. Lawton, 1929-
xSmith, J. Lawton.
  ed. Neuro-Ophthalmology Focus, 1980.
    Masson Pub.
Smith, Joseph M. *see* Smith, Joe Mauk.
Smith, Josephine M. *see* Smith, Josephine Metcalfe.
Smith, Josephine Metcalfe.
xSmith, Josephine M.

Chronology of Librarianship. Scarecrow.
Smith, Joyce M. *see* Smith, Joyce Marie.
Smith, Joyce Marie.
xSmith, Joyce M.
  Coping with Life & Its Problems. Tyndale.
Smith, Judith M.
xSmith, Judith M.
  Child Management: A Program for Parents &
    Teachers. Res Press.
Smith, Julian. *see* Smith, Julian W.
Smith, Julian W.
xSmith, Julian.
  Outdoor Education. P-H.
Smith, Justin. *see* Smith, Justin Harvey.
Smith, Justin H. *see* Smith, Justin Harvey.
Smith, Justin Harvey, 1857-1930
xSmith, Justin.
  Our Struggle for the Fourteenth Colony:
    Canada & the American Revolution. Da
    Capo.
xSmith, Justin H.
  The Annexation of Texas. AMS Pr.
Smith, K. *see* Smith, Keith.
Smith, K. M. *see* Smith, Kenneth Manley.
Smith, Karl J.
xSmith, Karl J.
  Beginning Algebra for College Students.
    Brooks-Cole.
  College Algebra. Brooks-Cole.
  Finite Mathematics: A Discrete Approach.
    Scott F.
  Introduction to Symbolic Logic. Brooks-Cole.
  The Nature of Modern Mathematics.
    Brooks-Cole.
  Precalculus Mathematics: A Functional
    Approach. Brooks-Cole.
  Trigonometry for College Students.
    Brooks-Cole.
Smith, Kathryn. *see* Smith, Kathryn Johnson.
Smith, Kathryn Johnson.
xSmith, Kathryn.
  Hey Kids, Stay Well-Feel Good. Pacific Pr Pub
    Assn.
Smith, Kay N. *see* Smith, Kay Nolte.
Smith, Kay Nolte.
xSmith, Kay N.
  The Watcher. Coward.
Smith, Keith.
xSmith, K.
  Human Adjustment to Flood Hazard.
    Longman.
xSmith, Keith.
  Practical Silver-Smithing & Jewelry. Van Nos
    Reinhold.
  Principles of Applied Climatology. Halsted Pr.
Smith, Keith V.
xSmith, Keith V.
  Essentials of Investing. Irwin.
  Guide to Working Capital Management.
    McGraw.
  Readings on the Management of Working
    Capital. West Pub.
Smith, Kenneth H.
xSmith, Kenneth H.
  American Economic History. Lerner Pubns.
  Money & Banking. Lerner Pubns.
  Taxes. Lerner Pubns.
Smith, Kenneth M. *see* Smith, Kenneth Manley.
Smith, Kenneth Manley, 1892-
xSmith, K. M.
  Plant Viruses. Methuen Inc.
  Textbook of Plant Virus Diseases. Acad Pr.
xSmith, Kenneth M.
  Insect Virology. Acad Pr.
Smith, L. *see* Smith, Louis De Spain.
Smith, L. R. *see* Smith, Leila R.
Smith, Larry.
xSmith, L.

Lectures on the Eilenberg-Moore Spectral
  Sequence. Springer-Verlag.
Smith, Larry E.
xSmith, Larry E.
  English for Cross-Cultural Communication. St
    Martin.
Smith, Laura L. *see* Smith, Laura Lee W.
Smith, Laura Lee W.
xSmith, Laura L.
  Food Service Science. AVI.
Smith, Lawrence B. *see* Smith, Lawrence Berk.
Smith, Lawrence Berk.
xSmith, Lawrence B.
  Postwar Canadian Housing & Residential
    Mortgage Markets & the Role of
    Government. U of Toronto Pr.
Smith, Lee L.
xSmith, L.
  Practical Approach to the Nongraded
    Elementary School. P-H.
xSmith, Lee L.
  Teaching in a Nongraded School. P-H.
Smith, Leila R., 1928-
xSmith, L. R.
  English for Careers. Wiley.
xSmith, Leila R.
  English for Careers. Wiley.
Smith, Lendon. *see* Smith, Lendon H.
Smith, Lendon H., 1921-
xSmith, L.
  The Children's Doctor. P-H.
xSmith, Lendon.
  The Children's Doctor. P-H.
  The Encyclopedia of Baby & Child Care. P-H.
  Feed Your Kids Right: Dr. Smith's Program
    for Your Child's Total Health. McGraw.
  Improving Your Child's Behavior Chemistry.
    P-H.
  Improving Your Child's Behavior Chemistry.
    PB.
xSmith, Lendon H.
  The Encyclopedia of Baby & Child Care.
    Warner Bks.
Smith, Leona W. *see* Smith, Leona Woodring.
Smith, Leona Woodring.
xSmith, Leona W.
  The Forgotten Art of Flower Cookery.
    Har-Row.
Smith, LeRoi. *see* Smith, Leroi Tex.
Smith, LeRoi Tex.
xSmith, LeRoi.
  How to Fix Up Old Cars. Dodd.
  How to Fix up Old Cars. Dodd.
xSmith, Leroy.
  Money-Savers' Do-It-Yourself Car Repair.
    Macmillan.
Smith, Leroy. *see* Smith, Leroi Tex.
Smith, Lillian. *see* Smith, Lillian Eugenia.
Smith, Lillian Eugenia, 1897-
xSmith, Lillian.
  Our Faces, Our Words. Norton.
Smith, Logan P. *see* Smith, Logan Pearsall.
Smith, Logan Pearsall, 1865-1946
xSmith, Logan P.
  Fine Writing. Folcroft.
  Four Words: Romantic Originality, Creative,
    Genius. Folcroft.
  Prospects of Literature. Folcroft.
  Reperusals & Re-Collections. Arno.
Smith, Lou.
xSmith, Lou.
  The Fourth Man. NAL.
  Master Plot. Playboy Pbks.
  Master Plot. St Martin.
Smith, Louis, 1905-
xSmith, Louis.
  American Democracy & Military Power. Arno.
Smith, Louis. *see* Smith, Louis De Spain.
Smith, Louis De Spain, 1910-
xSmith, L.

The Pathogenic Anaerobic Bacteria. C C
    Thomas.
    xSmith, Louis.
        Botulism: The Organism, Its Toxins, the
        Disease. C C Thomas.
Smith, Lucia B.
    xSmith, Lucia B.
        My Mom Got a Job. HR&W.
        A Special Kind of Sister. HR&W.
Smith, Lydia A. *see* Smith, Lydia Averell Hurd.
Smith, Lydia Averell Hurd.
    xSmith, Lydia A.
        Activity & Experience: Sources of English
        Informal Education. Agathon.
Smith, Lyman B.
    xSmith, Lyman B.
        Bromelioideae (Bromeliaceae). NY Botanical.
Smith, Lynn S.
    xSmith, Lynn S.
        A Practical Approach to Serials Cataloging. Jai
        Pr.
Smith, Lynwood S.
    xSmith, Lynwood S.
        Living Shores of the Pacific Northwest. Pacific
        Search.
Smith, M. Brewster. *see* Smith, Mahlon Brewster.
Smith, M. Daniel. *see* Smith, Maurice Daniel.
Smith, M. Estellie, 1935-
    xSmith, M. Estellie.
        Those Who Live from the Sea: A Study in
        Maritime Anthropology. West Pub.
Smith, M. G. *see* Smith, Michael Garfield.
Smith, Mabel S. *see* Smith, Mabell Shippie (Clarke).
Smith, Mabell Shippie (Clarke), 1864-1942
    xSmith, Mabel S.
        Studies in Dickens. Haskell.
        Studies in Dickens. R West.
Smith, MacFarlane I. *see* Smith, Ian Macfarlane.
Smith, Macklin, 1944-
    xSmith, Macklin.
        Prudentius 'psychomachia': A Reexamination.
        Princeton U Pr.
Smith, Mahlon Brewster, 1919-
    xSmith, M. Brewster.
        Humanizing Social Psychology. Jossey-Bass.
Smith, Malcolm, 1938-
    xSmith, Malcolm.
        How I Learned to Meditate. Logos.
Smith, Margaret, 1884-
    xSmith, Margaret.
        An Early Mystic of Baghdad: A Study of the
        Life & Teaching of Harith b. Asad
        al-Muhasibi, A.D. 781-A.D. 857. AMS Pr.
Smith, Margaret R. *see* Smith, Margaret Ruth.
Smith, Margaret Ruth, 1902-
    xSmith, Margaret R.
        Student Aid: Bases of Selection of Students to
        Whom Loans, Scholarships & Fellowships
        Are Awarded in a Graduate School of
        Education. AMS Pr.
Smith, Marian W. *see* Smith, Marian Wesley.
Smith, Marian Wesley, 1907-1961
    xSmith, Marian W.
        Indians of the Urban Northwest. AMS Pr.
        Puyallup-Nisqually. AMS Pr.
Smith, Marilyn A. *see* Smith, Marilynn A.
Smith, Marilynn A.
    xSmith, Marilyn A.
        Christmas Programs for Church Groups. Baker
        Bk.
Smith, Marion B. *see* Smith, Marion Bodwell.
Smith, Marion Bodwell, 1912-
    xSmith, Marion B.
        Dualities in Shakespeare. U of Toronto Pr.
        Marlowe's Imagery & the Marlowe Canon.
        Arden Lib.
        Marlowe's Imagery & the Marlowe Canon.
        Folcroft.
Smith, Marion H. *see* Smith, Marion Hagens.

Smith, Marion Hagens.
    xSmith, Marion H.
        Families Around the World. Fideler.
        Our Earth. Fideler.
Smith, Mark, 1935-
    xSmith, Mark.
        The Death of the Detective. Avon.
        The Delphinium Girl. Har-Row.
        The Moon Lamp. Avon.
        The Moon Lamp. Knopf.
Smith, Martin, 1942-
    xSmith, Martin C.
        Nightwing. BJ Pub Group.
Smith, Martin C. *see* Smith, Martin.
Smith, Martin R., 1934-
    xSmith, Martin R.
        I Hate to See a Manager Cry: How to Prevent
        the Litany of Management from Fouling up
        Your Career. A-W.
        Qualitysense: Organizational Approaches to
        Improving Product Quality & Service. Am
        Mgmt.
Smith, Mary P. *see* Smith, Mary Prudence (Wells).
Smith, Mary Prudence (Wells), 1840-1930
    xSmith, Mary P.
        Boy Captive of Old Deerfield. Am
        Repr-Rivercity Pr.
Smith, Matthew H. *see* Smith, Matthew Hale.
Smith, Matthew Hale, 1810-1879
    xSmith, Matthew H.
        Bulls & Bears of New York: With the Crisis of
        1873, & the Cause. Arno.
Smith, Maurice Daniel.
    xSmith, M. Daniel.
        Educational Psychology & Its Classroom
        Applications. Allyn.
Smith, Maury.
    xSmith, Maury.
        A Practical Guide to Value Clarification. Univ
        Assocs.
Smith, Max, 1905-
    xSmith, Max.
        Relationship Between Item Validity & Test
        Validity. AMS Pr.
Smith, Meredith, 1871-
    xSmith, Meredith.
        Education & the Integration of Behavior. AMS
        Pr.
Smith, Merriman. *see* Smith, A. Merriman.
Smith, Michael Garfield.
    xSmith, M. G.
        Corporations & Society: Social Anthropology
        of Collective Action. Beresford Bk Serv.
Smith, Michael M.
    xSmith, Michael M.
        The Mexicans in Oklahoma. U of Okla Pr.
        The Real Expedicion Maritima De la Vacuna
        in New Spain & Guatemala. Am Philos.
Smith, Michael P.
    xSmith, Michael P.
        American Politics & Public Policy. Random.
        The City & Social Theory. St Martin.
Smith, Michael R. *see* Smith, Michael Robert.
Smith, Michael Robert.
    xSmith, Michael R.
        Law & the North Carolina Teacher. Interstate.
Smith, Mickey. *see* Smith, Mickey C.
Smith, Mickey C.
    xSmith, Mickey.
        Handbook of Institutional Pharmacy Practice.
        Williams & Wilkins.
    xSmith, Mickey C.
        Principles of Pharmaceutical Marketing. Lea &
        Febiger.
Smith, Mildred N. *see* Smith, Mildred Nelson.
Smith, Mildred Nelson.
    xSmith, Mildred N.
        Word of Wisdom Helps--Food. Herald Hse.
Smith, Mortimer. *see* Smith, Mortimer Brewster.
Smith, Mortimer B. *see* Smith, Mortimer Brewster.

Smith, Mortimer Brewster, 1906-
    xSmith, Mortimer.
        Life of Ole Bull. Greenwood.
    xSmith, Mortimer B.
        Diminished Mind: A Study of Planned
        Mediocrity in Our Public Schools.
        Greenwood.
Smith, Morton, 1915-
    xSmith, Morton.
        Ancient Greeks. Cornell U Pr.
        Clement of Alexandria, & a Secret Gospel of
        Mark. Harvard U Pr.
Smith, Munroe, 1854-1926
    xSmith, Munroe.
        The Development of European Law. Hyperion
        Conn.
Smith, Myron J.
    xSmith, Myron J.
        Cloak & Dagger Bibliography: An Annotated
        Guide to Spy Fiction, 1937-1975. Scarecrow.
        Navies in the American Revolution: A
        Bibliography. Scarecrow.
        World War I in the Air: A Bibliography &
        Chronology. Scarecrow.
Smith, N. *see* Smith, Nila Banton.
Smith, N. D. *see* Smith, Norman David.
Smith, Nancy. *see* Smith, Nancy Woollcott.
Smith, Nancy A.
    xSmith, Nancy A.
        Old Furniture: Understanding the Craftsman's
        Art. Bobbs.
        Old Furniture: Understanding the Craftsman's
        Art. Little.
Smith, Nancy R.
    xSmith, Nancy R.
        ed. Symbolic Functioning in Childhood.
        Halsted Pr.
Smith, Nancy Woollcott.
    xSmith, Nancy.
        Jason the Lobsterman. Tashmoo.
Smith, Nathan J., 1921-
    xSmith, Nathan J.
        Food for Sport. Bull Pub.
Smith, Nathaniel B.
    xSmith, Nathaniel B.
        ed. The Expansion & Transformations of
        Courtly Literature. U of Ga Pr.
Smith, Neil.
    xSmith, Neil.
        Modern Linguistics: The Results of Chomsky's
        Revolution. Ind U Pr.
Smith, Nila Banton.
    xSmith, N.
        Reading Instruction for Today's Children. P-H.
Smith, Noel T.
    xSmith, Noel T.
        CBer's Factbook. Hayden.
Smith, Norman. *see* Smith, Norman F.
Smith, Norman David.
    xSmith, N. D.
        Discovering Flight. Dufour.
Smith, Norman F.
    xSmith, Norman.
        If It Shines, Clangs & Bends, Its Metal.
        Coward.
        Space: What's Out There. Coward.
        Sunpower. Coward.
    xSmith, Norman F.
        Gliding, Soaring, & Skysailing. Messner.
Smith, Norman F. *see* Smith, Norman Foster.
Smith, Norman Foster, 1914-
    xSmith, Norman F.
        Michigan Trees Worth Knowing. Hillsdale
        Educ.
Smith, Norman L. *see* Smith, Norman Lewis.
Smith, Norman Lewis.
    xSmith, Norman L.
        The Return of Billy the Kid. Coward.
Smith, Ora, 1900-
    xSmith, Ora.

Potatoes: Production, Storing, Processing. AVI.
Smith, Oscar E. *see* Smith, Oscar Edmund.
Smith, Oscar Edmund, 1919-
xSmith, Oscar E.
Yankee Diplomacy: U. S. Intervention in
Argentina. Greenwood.
Smith, P. *see* Smith, Paul.
Smith, P. D. *see* Smith, Percy De Willard.
Smith, P. J. *see* Smith, Peter John.
Smith, Page.
xSmith, Page.
The Chicken Book. Little.
Smith, Parker F., 1943-
xSmith, Parker F.
Exile's Odyssey: The Memoirs of an American
Deserter. A S Barnes.
Smith, Patricia. *see* Smith, Patricia R.
Smith, Patricia R.
xSmith, Patricia.
Antique Collector's Dolls: Second Series.
Collector Bks.
Modern Collector's Dolls. Collector Bks.
xSmith, Patricia R.
Modern Collector's Dolls. Crown.
Smith, Patrick D., 1927-
xSmith, Patrick D.
Forever Island: A Novel. Norton.
Smith, Patrick Hall. *see* Hall-Smith, Patrick.
Smith, Patti.
xSmith, Patti.
Babel. Berkley Pub.
Babel. Putnam.
Smith, Pattie S. *see* Smith, Pattie Sherwood.
Smith, Pattie Sherwood.
xSmith, Pattie S.
Joseph Pulitzer, Giant of Journalism. SamHar
Pr.
Smith, Paul, 1937-
xSmith, P.
ed. The Historian & Film. Cambridge U Pr.
Smith, Paul F., 1919-
xSmith, Paul F.
Money & Financial Intermediation: The
Theory & Structure of Financial Systems.
P-H.
Smith, Paul H. *see* Smith, Paul Hubert.
Smith, Paul Hubert, 1931-
xSmith, Paul H.
Loyalists & Redcoats: A Study in British
Revolutionary Policy. Norton.
Loyalists & Redcoats: A Study in British
Revolutionary Policy. U of NC Pr.
Smith, Pauline C. *see* Smith, Pauline Coggeshall.
Smith, Pauline Coggeshall, 1908-
xSmith, Pauline C.
Brush Fire!. Westminster.
Smith, Peggy B.
xSmith, Peggy B.
Adolescent Pregnancy: Perspectives for the
Health Professional. G K Hall.
Smith, Percy D. *see* Smith, Percy De Willard.
Smith, Percy de Willard, 1900-
xSmith, P. D.
Modern Marine Electricity & Electronics.
Cornell Maritime.
xSmith, Percy D.
Deck Machinery. Cornell Maritime.
Smith, Peter. *see* Smith, Peter F.
Smith, Peter C. *see* Smith, Peter Charles.
Smith, Peter Charles, 1940-
xSmith, Peter C.
The Great Ships Pass: British Battleships at
War 1939-45. Naval Inst Pr.
Smith, Peter F.
xSmith, Peter.
Protecting the Consumer: An Economic &
Legal Analysis. Biblio Dist.
Smith, Peter H.
xSmith, Peter H.

Argentina & the Failure of Democracy:
Conflict Among the Political Elites,
1904-1955. U of Wis Pr.
Labyrinths of Power: Political Recruitment in
Twentieth-Century Mexico. Princeton U Pr.
Smith, Peter H. *see* Smith, Peter H. K.
Smith, Peter H. K.
xSmith, Peter H.
Upgrading Lecture Rooms. Burgess-Intl Ideas.
Smith, Peter John.
xSmith, P. J.
ed. The Prairie Provinces. U of Toronto Pr.
Smith, Peter L.
xSmith, Peter L.
A Pictorial History of Canal Craft. David &
Charles.
Smith, Philip C. *see* Smith, Philip Chadwick Foster.
Smith, Philip Chadwick Foster.
xSmith, Philip C.
Fired by Manley Zeal: A Naval Fiasco of the
American Revolution. Peabody Mus Salem.
The Frigate Essex Papers: Building the Salem
Frigate, 1798-1799. Peabody Mus Salem.
Smith, Philip G.
xSmith, Philip G.
ed. Theories of Value & Problems of
Education. U of Ill Pr.
Smith, Philip H. *see* Smith, Philip Hubert.
Smith, Philip Henry, 1842-
xSmith, Philip H.
Legends of the Shawangunk (Shon-Gum) & Its
Environs. Syracuse U Pr.
Smith, Philip Hubert, 1906-
xSmith, Philip H.
The Design & Tuning of Competition Engines.
Bentley.
Smith, Preserved, 1880-1941
xSmith, Preserved.
History of Modern Culture. Peter Smith.
Smith, R. *see* Smith, Rixey.
Smith, R. C. *see* Smith, Ronald C.
Smith, R. E. *see* Smith, Robert E. F.
Smith, R. F. *see* Smith, Ray F.
Smith, R. F. I.
xSmith, R. E.
ed. Public Service Inquiries in Australia. U of
Queensland Pr.
Smith, R. Harris. *see* Smith, Richard Harris.
Smith, R. Nelson. *see* Smith, Robert Nelson.
Smith, Ralph A. *see* Smith, Ralph Alexander.
Smith, Ralph Alexander.
xSmith, Ralph A.
ed. Aesthetic Concepts & Education. U of Ill
Pr.
ed. Aesthetics & Problems of Education. U of
Ill Pr.
ed. Regaining Educational Leadership: Critical
Essays on PBTE-CBTE, Behavioral
Objectives, & Accountability. Krieger.
Smith, Ralph E. *see* Smith, Ralph Ely.
Smith, Ralph Ely.
xSmith, Ralph E.
ed. The Subtle Revolution: Women at Work.
Urban Inst.
Smith, Ralph J. *see* Smith, Ralph Judson.
Smith, Ralph Judson.
xSmith, Ralph J.
Engineering As a Career. McGraw.
Smith, Ralph L. *see* Smith, Ralph Lee.
Smith, Ralph Lee, 1927-
xSmith, Ralph L.
The Tarnished Badge. Arno.
Smith, Raoul N.
xSmith, Raoul N.
Probabilistic Performance Models of Language.
Mouton.
Smith, Ray, 1915-
xSmith, Ray.

The Deer on the Freeway. Dakota Pr.
The Greening Tree. Kirk Pr.
The Long Slide. Atheneum.
October Rain. Kirk Pr.
Permanent Fires: Reviews of Poetry 1958-1973.
Scarecrow.
Smith, Ray. *see* Smith, Raymond Kenneth.
Smith, Ray F.
xSmith, R. F.
ed. Annual Review of Entomology. Annual
Reviews.
Smith, Raymond J.
xSmith, Raymond J.
Charles Churchill. Twayne.
Smith, Raymond Kenneth.
xSmith, Ray.
The Long Dive. Atheneum.
Smith, Richard.
xSmith, Richard.
The Bronx Diet. Workman Pub.
The Dieter's Guide to Weight Loss During
Sex. Workman Pub.
Smith, Richard E. *see* Smith, Richard Edwin.
Smith, Richard Edwin.
xSmith, Richard E.
The Failure of the Roman Republic. Arno.
Failure of the Roman Republic. Russell.
Smith, Richard Eugene.
xSmith, Richard E.
Richard Aldington. Twayne.
Smith, Richard F. *see* Smith, Richard Furnald.
Smith, Richard Furnald.
xSmith, Richard F.
Chemistry for the Million. Scribner.
Smith, Richard Harris, 1946-
xSmith, R. Harris.
OSS: The Secret History of America's First
Central Intelligence Agency. U of Cal Pr.
Smith, Richard J.
xSmith, Richard J.
Practice FCC-Type Exams for Radio-Telephone
Operator's License--3rd Class. Hayden.
Practice FCC-Type Exams for Radiotelephone
Operator's License-1st Class. Hayden.
Practice FCC-Type Exams for Radiotelephone
Operator's License-2nd Class. Hayden.
Smith, Richard J. *see* Smith, Richard John.
Smith, Richard John.
xSmith, Richard J.
Teaching Children to Read. A-W.
Teaching Reading in the Middle Grades. A-W.
Smith, Richard P., 1949-
xSmith, Richard P.
Deer Hunting. Stackpole.
Smith, Richard T. *see* Smith, Richard Thomas.
Smith, Richard Thomas.
xSmith, Richard T.
ed. Immune Surveillance. Acad Pr.
Smith, Rixey.
xSmith, R.
Carter Glass: A Biography. Da Capo.
Smith, Robb.
xSmith, Robb.
Amphoto Guide to Filters. Amphoto.
Smith, Robert.
xSmith, Robert.
By Any Means Necessary: The Revolutionary
Struggle at San Francisco State. Jossey-Bass.
Hiking Hawaii: The Big Island. Wilderness Pr.
Hiking Kauai: The Garden Isle. Wilderness Pr.
Hit Hard! Throw Hard!: The Secrets of Power
Baseball. Little.
Massachusetts Colony. Macmillan.
Smith, Robert. *see* Smith, Robert Mcneil.
Smith, Robert A. *see* Smith, Robert Arthur.
Smith, Robert Arthur.
xSmith, Robert A.

The Fox Trap. Fawcett.
Prey. Fawcett.
Smith, Robert B. see Smith, Robert Baer.
Smith, Robert Baer.
xSmith, Robert B.
ed. Cenozoic Tectonics & Regional Geophysics
of Western Cordillera. Geol Soc.
Smith, Robert Boyer.
xSmith, Robert B.
ed. Complications of Urologic Surgery:
Prevention & Management. Saunders.
Smith, Robert E. see Smith, Robert Ellis.
Smith, Robert E. F.
xSmith, R. E.
Enserfment of the Russian Peasantry.
Cambridge U Pr.
xSmith, R. F.
Peasant Farming in Muscovy. Cambridge U Pr.
Smith, Robert Edward, 1943-
xSmith.
Fundamentals of Oral Interpretation. SRA.
Smith, Robert Elijah, 1911-
xSmith, Robert E.
Discovering BASIC: A Problem Solving
Approach. Hayden.
Smith, Robert Ellis.
xSmith, Robert E.
Compilation of State & Federal Privacy Laws.
Privacy Journal.
Privacy: How to Protect What's Left of It.
Doubleday.
xSmith, Robert Ellis.
Privacy: How to Protect What's Left of It.
Doubleday.
Smith, Robert Ernest, 1879-
xSmith, Robert E.
Forging & Welding. McKnight.
Patternmaking & Founding. McKnight.
Smith, Robert F. see Smith, Robert Freeman.
Smith, Robert Freeman, 1930-
xSmith, Robert F.
Background to Revolution: The Development
of Modern Cuba. Krieger.
Smith, Robert H. see Smith, Robert Hudson.
Smith, Robert Hudson, 1910-
xSmith, Robert H.
Pathological Physiology for the
Anesthesiologist. C C Thomas.
Smith, Robert J. see Smith, Robert Joseph.
Smith, Robert John, 1927-
xSmith, Robert J.
Ancestor Worship in Contemporary Japan.
Stanford U Pr.
Smith, Robert Joseph, 1931-
xSmith, Robert J.
ed. The Psychopath in Society. Acad Pr.
Smith, Robert K. see Smith, Robert Kimmel.
Smith, Robert Kimmel.
xSmith, Robert K.
Chocolate Fever. Dell.
Sadie Shapiro, Matchmaker. G K Hall.
Sadie Shapiro, Matchmaker. S&S.
Smith, Robert L. see Smith, Robert Leonard.
Smith, Robert Leo.
xSmith, Robert L.
Ecology & Field Biology. Har-Row.
ed. The Ecology of Man: An Ecosystem
Approach. Har-Row.
Smith, Robert Leonard.
xSmith, Robert L.
Counseling Couples in Groups: A Manual for
Improving Troubled Relationships. C C
Thomas.
Smith, Robert M.
xSmith, Robert M.
The Exceptional Child: A Functional
Approach. McGraw.
Smith, Robert M. see Smith, Robert Metcalf.
Smith, Robert McNeil.
xSmith, Robert.

Introduction to Mental Retardation. McGraw.
Teacher Diagnosis of Educational Difficulties.
Merrill.
xSmith, Robert M.
Evaluating Educational Environments. Merrill.
Smith, Robert Metcalf, 1886-1952
xSmith, Robert M.
The Variant Issues of Shakespeare's Second
Folio & Milton's First Published English
Poem. Folcroft.
Smith, Robert Moors, 1912-
xSmith, Robert M.
Anesthesia for Infants & Children. Mosby.
Smith, Robert Nelson.
xSmith, R. Nelson.
Solving General Chemistry Problems. W H
Freeman.
Smith, Robert R. see Smith, Robert Ray.
Smith, Robert Ray.
xSmith, Robert R.
Essentials of Neurosurgery. Lippincott.
Smith, Robert S. see Smith, Robert Sidney.
Smith, Robert Sellers.
xSmith, Robert S.
Alabama Law for the Layman. Strode.
Lawyer's Model Letter Book. P-H.
Smith, Robert Sidney, 1904-1969
xSmith, Robert S.
The Spanish Guild Merchant: A History of the
Consulado, 1250-1700. Octagon.
Smith, Robert Sydney.
xSmith, Robert S.
The Lagos Consulate, 1851-1861. U of Cal Pr.
Smith, Robert T., 1932-
xSmith, Robert.
Instrument Flying Guide. TAB Bks.
xSmith, Robert T.
How to Fly Lightplanes. TAB Bks.
Smith, Robert T. see Smith, Robert Tighe.
Smith, Robert Tighe, 1926-
xSmith, Robert T.
Put Them in Cages. Creative Ed.
White Buses Can Fly. Creative Ed.
Smith, Robert V., 1942-
xSmith, Robert V.
Development & Management of Research
Groups: A Guide for University Researchers.
U of Tex Pr.
Smith, Robert W.
xSmith, Robert W.
Hsing-I: Chinese Mind-Body Boxing.
Kodansha.
Secrets of Shaolin Temple Boxing. C E Tuttle.
Smith, Robert W. see Smith, Robert Wayne.
Smith, Robert Wayne, 1903-
xSmith, Robert W.
The Coeur d'Alene Mining War of 1892: A
Case Study of an Industrial Dispute. Peter
Smith.
Smith, Robertson. see Smith, Robinson.
Smith, Robinson, 1876-
xSmith, Robertson.
The Life of Cervantes. Haskell.
xSmith, Robinson.
The Life of Cervantes. Folcroft.
Smith, Rodney.
xSmith.
Surgery of the Gall Bladder & Bile Ducts.
Butterworths.
Smith, Roger, M.D.
xSmith, Roger.
Biochemical Disorders of the Skeleton.
Butterworths.
Smith, Roger M.
xSmith, Roger M.
ed. Southeast Asia: Documents of Political
Development & Change. Cornell U Pr.
Smith, Roland. see Smith, Rowland.
Smith, Roland A.
xSmith, Roland A.

Before You Build Your Church. Broadman.
Smith, Ronald. see Smith, Ronald C.
Smith, Ronald C.
xSmith, R. C.
Materials of Construction. McGraw.
Principles & Practices of Heavy Construction.
P-H.
xSmith, Ronald.
Principles & Practices of Light Construction.
P-H.
xSmith, Ronald C.
Materials of Construction. McGraw.
Principles & Practices of Light Construction.
P-H.
Smith, Ronald E. see Smith, Ronald Edward.
Smith, Ronald Edward.
xSmith, Ronald E.
Psychology: The Frontiers of Behavior.
Har-Row.
Smith, Ronald G. see Smith, Ronald Gregor.
Smith, Ronald Gregor.
xSmith, Ronald G.
Martin Buber. John Knox.
Smith, Ronald W. see Smith, Ronald Wayne.
Smith, Ronald Wayne.
xSmith, Ronald W.
Sociology: An Introduction. St Martin.
Smith, Rowland, 1938-
xSmith, Roland.
ed. Exile & Tradition: Studies in African &
Caribbean Literature. Holmes & Meier.
Smith, Russell E.
xSmith.
Electricity for Refrigeration, Heating & Air
Conditioning. Duxbury Pr.
Smith, Russell E. see Smith, Russell Eugene.
Smith, Russell Eugene.
xSmith, Russell E.
American Social Welfare Institutions. Wiley.
Smith, Ruth S.
xSmith, Ruth S.
Cataloging Made Easy: How to Organize Your
Congregation's Library. Seabury.
Smith, S. S. see Smith, Samuel Stephenson.
Smith, S. Stephenson. see Smith, Samuel Stephenson.
Smith, Sally L. see Smith, Sally Liberman.
Smith, Sally Liberman.
xSmith, Sally L.
No Easy Answers: Teaching the Learning
Disabled Child. Winthrop.
Smith, Samuel, 1720-1776
xSmith, Samuel.
History of the Colony of Nova-Caesaria or
New Jersey. Reprint.
Ideas of the Great Educators. B&N.
Read It Right, & Remember What You Read.
Har-Row.
Smith, Samuel S. see Smith, Samuel Stelle.
Smith, Samuel Stelle.
xSmith, Samuel S.
Fight for the Delaware, 1777. Freneau.
Smith, Samuel Stephenson, 1897-1961
xSmith, S. S.
Craft of the Critic. Arno.
The Craft of the Critic. R West.
xSmith, S. Stephenson.
How to Double Your Vocabulary. T Y Crowell.
Smith, Seba, 1792-1868
xSmith, Seba.
Letters Written During the President's Tour
'Down East'. Arno.
Smith, Shea.
xSmith, Shea.
Strategies in Business. Ronald Pr.
Smith, Sherwood. see Smith, F. Sherwood.
Smith, Shirley. see Smith, Shirley M.
Smith, Shirley M.
xSmith, Shirley.

ed. Reference Book Review Index, 1970-1972. Pierian.

Smith, Sophie S. *see* Smith, Sophie Shilleto.

Smith, Sophie Shilleto.
xSmith, Sophie S.
Dean Swift. Folcroft.

Smith, Stan.
xSmith, Stan.
Inside Tennis. Contemp Bks.
Pass the Ammunition. Manor Bks.
Stan Smith's Six Tennis Basics. Atheneum.

Smith, Stanley A. De. *see* De Smith, Stanley A.

Smith, Stephen, 1823-1922
xSmith, Stephen.
Doctor in Medicine & Other Papers on
Professional Subjects. Arno.

Smith, Steve, 1941-
xSmith, Steve.
Fly the Biggest Piece Back. Mountain Pr.

Smith, Steven B. *see* Smith, Steven Bradley.

Smith, Steven Bradley.
xSmith, Steven B.
Meaning & Negation. Mouton.

Smith, Stevenson.
xSmith, Stevenson.
General Psychology in Terms of Behavior.
Johnson Repr.

Smith, Susy.
xSmith, Susy.
Confessions of a Psychic. Macmillan.
Do We Live After Death?. Manor Bks.
Mediumship of Mrs. Leonard. Univ Bks.

Smith, Sydney, 1912-
xSmith, Sydney.
The Survivor. St Martin.

Smith, T. Alexander, 1936-
xSmith, T. Alexander.
Comparative Policy Process. ABC-Clio.

Smith, T. C. *see* Smith, Thomas C.
Smith, T. Lynn. *see* Smith, Thomas Lynn.
Smith, T. Roger. *see* Smith, Thomas Roger.
Smith, Terrence L. *see* Smith, Terrence Lore.

Smith, Terrence Lore.
xSmith, Terrence L.
The Money War. Atheneum.

Smith, Thelma E.
xSmith, Thelma E.
Guide to the Municipal Government of the
City of New York. Law-Arts.

Smith, Theodore A., 1905-
xSmith, Theodore A.
Dynamic Business Strategy: The Art of
Planning for Success. McGraw.

Smith, Theodore C. *see* Smith, Theodore Clarke.

Smith, Theodore Clarke, 1870-1960
xSmith, Theodore C.
Liberty & Free Soil Parties in the Northwest.
Arno.
Liberty & Free-Soil Parties in the Northwest.
Russell.
Parties & Slavery, 1850-1859. Haskell.

Smith, Thomas. *see* Smith, Thomas H.

Smith, Thomas C.
xSmith, T. C.
Introduction to Digital Computer Plotting.
Gordon.

Smith, Thomas C. *see* Smith, Thomas Carlyle.

Smith, Thomas Carlyle.
xSmith, Thomas C.
The Agrarian Origins of Modern Japan.
Stanford U Pr.

Smith, Thomas E., 1937-
xSmith, Thomas E.
Industrial Energy Management for Cost
Reduction. Ann Arbor Science.

Smith, Thomas H., 1936-
xSmith, Thomas.
ed. The Ohio Reader. Eerdmans.
xSmith, Thomas H.

The Mapping of Ohio. Kent St U Pr.

Smith, Thomas L. *see* Smith, Thomas Lynn.

Smith, Thomas Lynn.
xSmith, T. Lynn.
Colombia: Social Structure & the Process of
Development. U Presses Fla.
Demography: Principles & Methods. Alfred
Pub.
Latin American Population Studies. U Presses
Fla.
Process of Rural Development in Latin
America. U Presses Fla.
The Race Between Population & Food Supply
in Latin America. U of NM Pr.
xSmith, Thomas L.
Brazil, Portrait of Half a Continent.
Greenwood.

Smith, Thomas Roger, 1830-1903
xSmith, T. Roger.
Architecture, Gothic & Renaissance. Longwood
Pr.

Smith, Thomas V. *see* Smith, Thomas Vernor.

Smith, Thomas Vernor, 1890-1964
xSmith, Thomas V.
Creative Sceptics: In Defense of the Liberal
Temper. Arno.
Foundations of Democracy: Series of Debates.
Arno.

Smith, Thurman L.
xSmith, Thurman L.
Investors Can Beat Inflation. Liberty Pub.

Smith, Timothy L. *see* Smith, Timothy Lawrence.

Smith, Timothy Lawrence, 1924-
xSmith, Timothy L.
Revivalism & Social Reform: American
Protestantism on the Eve of the Civil War.
Peter Smith.

Smith, Tony, 1942-
xSmith, Tony.
The French Stake in Algeria, 1945-1962.
Cornell U Pr.

Smith, U. S.
xSmith, U. S.
Up a Tree with Mark Twain: An Oracular
Opus Exposing a Literary Hoax So
Horrendous May God Have Mercy on the
First Amendment. Shondo-Shando.

Smith, V. Kerry. *see* Smith, Vincent Kerry.
Smith, V. L. *see* Smith, Vernon L.

Smith, Valene L.
xSmith, Valene L.
ed. Hosts & Guests: The Anthropology of
Tourism. U of Pa Pr.

Smith, Verity, 1939-
xSmith, Verity.
Ramon del Valle-Inclan. Twayne.

Smith, Vernon. *see* Smith, Vernon H.

Smith, Vernon H.
xSmith, Vernon.
Optional Alternative Public Schools. Phi Delta
Kappa.
What the People Think About Their Schools:
Gallup's Findings. Phi Delta Kappa.

Smith, Vernon L.
xSmith, V. L.
ed. Economics of Natural & Environmental
Resources. Gordon.

Smith, Vernon M.
xSmith.
North Carolina: A Reader. Paladin Hse.

Smith, Vian.
xSmith, Vian.
Portrait of Dartmoor. Intl Pubns Serv.
Tall & Proud. Archway.
Tall & Proud. PB.

Smith, Vincent Kerry, 1945-
xSmith, V. Kerry.

Economic Consequences of Air Pollution.
Ballinger Pub.
Structure & Properties of a Wilderness Travel
Simulator: An Application to the Spanish
Peaks Area. Johns Hopkins.

Smith, Vivian. *see* Smith, Vivian Brian.

Smith, Vivian Brian.
xSmith, Vivian.
Vance & Nettie Palmer. Twayne.

Smith, Voncile M.
xSmith, Voncile M.
Communication for Health Professionals.
Lippincott.

Smith, W. *see* Smith, Wilbur A.

Smith, W. Allen.
xSmith, W. Allen.
Elementary Numerical Analysis. Har-Row.

Smith, W. G. *see* Smith, William Glyn.
Smith, W. H. *see* Smith, Warren Hunting.
Smith, W. W. *see* Smith, William Wright.
Smith, W. Wright. *see* Smith, William Wright.

Smith, Waldemar R., 1943-
xSmith, Waldemar R.
The Fiesta System and Economic Change.
Columbia U Pr.

Smith, Wallace, 1888?-1937
xSmith, Wallace.
Are You Decent?. Arno.
The Little Tigress: Tales Out of the Dust of
Mexico. Arno.

Smith, Wallace F. *see* Smith, Wallace Francis.

Smith, Wallace Francis, 1926-
xSmith, Wallace F.
Housing: The Social & Economic Elements. U
of Cal Pr.

Smith, Walter B. *see* Smith, Walter Buckingham.

Smith, Walter Buckingham.
xSmith, Walter B.
Economic Aspects of the Second Bank of the
United States. Greenwood.
Fluctuations in American Business, 1790-1860.
Russell.

Smith, Walter Thomas.
xSmith.
ed. Recent Advances in Neuropathology.
Churchill.

Smith, Ward D.
xSmith, Ward D.
Chinese Banknotes. Shirjieh Pubs.

Smith, Warren B.
xSmith, Warren B.
White Servitude in Colonial South Carolina. U
of SC Pr.

Smith, Warren Hunting, 1905-
xSmith, W. H.
Architecture in English Fiction. Shoe String.

Smith, Watson, 1897-
xSmith, Watson.
Painted Ceramics of the Western Mound at
Awatovi. Peabody Harvard.
Prehistoric Kivas of Antelope Mesa,
Northeastern Arizona. Peabody Harvard.

Smith, Wesley D., 1930-
xSmith, Wesley D.
The Hippocratic Tradition. Cornell U Pr.

Smith, Whitney.
xSmith, Whitney.
The Flag Book of the United States. Morrow.
Flags & Arms Across the World. McGraw.

Smith, Wilbur.
xSmith, Wilbur.
Eagle in the Sky. Doubleday.

Smith, Wilbur. *see* Smith, Wilbur A.

Smith, Wilbur A.
xSmith, W.
The Sunbird. Doubleday.
The Sunbird. NAL.
xSmith, Wilbur.

Cry Wolf. Dell.
Cry Wolf. Doubleday.
The Eye of the Tiger. Doubleday.
Hungry As the Sea. Doubleday.
A Sparrow Falls. Doubleday.

Smith, Wilfred, 1903-1955
xSmith, Wilfred.
A Historical Introduction to the Economic
Geography of Great Britain. Westview.

Smith, Wilfred C. see Smith, Wilfred Cantwell.

Smith, Wilfred Cantwell, 1916-
xSmith, Wilfred C.
Faith & Belief. Princeton U Pr.

Smith, Willard. see Smith, Willard Mallalieu.

Smith, Willard Mallalieu, 1888-1959
xSmith, Willard.
Nature of Comedy. Folcroft.

Smith, Willard S.
xSmith, Willard S.
Animals, Birds & Plants of the Bible.
Abingdon.

Smith, William.
xSmith, William.
ed. Dictionary of Christian Antiquities: Being a
Continuation of the Dictionary of the Bible.
Kraus Repr.
ed. Dictionary of Christian Biography,
Literature, Sects & Doctrines. AMS Pr.
ed. Dictionary of Christian Biography,
Literature, Sects & Doctrines: Being a
Continuation of the Dictionary of the Bible.
Kraus Repr.
Dictionary of Greek & Roman Antiquities.
Longwood Pr.
ed. Dictionary of Greek & Roman Biography &
Mythology. AMS Pr.
ed. Dictionary of Greek & Roman Geography.
AMS Pr.
A General Idea of the College of Mirania.
Johnson Repr.
The History of the Post Office in British North
America, 1639-1870. Octagon.
History of the Province of New York. Harvard
U Pr.

Smith, William A. see Smith, William Anton.

Smith, William Anton, 1880-
xSmith, William A.
Ancient Education. Greenwood.

Smith, William B. see Smith, William Benjamin.

Smith, William Benjamin, 1850-1934
xSmith, William B.
Color Line: A Brief in Behalf of the Unborn.
Arno.
Color Line: A Brief in Behalf of the Unborn.
Negro U Pr.

Smith, William C. see Smith, William Carlson.

Smith, William Carlson, 1883-
xSmith, William C.
Americans in Process: A Study of Our Citizens
of Oriental Ancestry. Arno.

Smith, William D. see Smith, William David.

Smith, William David.
xSmith, William D.
Minority Issues in Mental Health. A-W.

Smith, William E. see Smith, William Ernest.

Smith, William Ernest, 1892-
xSmith, William E.
Francis Preston Blair Family in Politics. Da
Capo.

Smith, William F. see Smith, William Frank.

Smith, William Frank.
xSmith, William F.
From Thought to Theme: A Rhetoric & Reader
for College English. HarBraceJ.
Rhetoric for Today. HarBraceJ.

Smith, William G. see Smith, William Gardner.

Smith, William Gardner, 1926-
xSmith, William G.

Anger at Innocence. Chatham Bkseller.
Last of the Conquerors. Chatham Bkseller.
South Street. Chatham Bkseller.

Smith, William Glyn, 1905-
xSmith, W. G.
Gardening for Food. Scribner.

Smith, William J. see Smith, William Jay.

Smith, William Jay.
xSmith, William J.
The Pirate Book. Delacorte.

Smith, William K. see Smith, William Kay.

Smith, William Kay, 1920-
xSmith, William K.
Analytic Geometry. Macmillan.
Calculus with Analytic Geometry. Macmillan.

Smith, William O. see Smith, William O'Daniel.

Smith, William O'Daniel.
xSmith, William O.
Food Services. McGraw.

Smith, William R. see Smith, William Robertson.

Smith, William Robertson.
xSmith, William R.
Kinship & Marriage in Early Arabia. AMS Pr.

Smith, William Roy, 1876-1938
xSmith, William R.
Nationalism & Reform in India. Kennikat.

Smith, William Rudolph, 1787-1868
xSmith, William R.
Observations on the Wisconsin Territory. Arno.

Smith, William S. see Smith, William Stevenson.

Smith, William Stevenson.
xSmith, William S.
History of Egyptian Sculpture & Painting in
the Old Kingdom. Hacker.

Smith, William Wright.
xSmith, W. W.
The Genus Primula. Lubrecht & Cramer.
nSmith, W. Wright.
The Genus Primula. Intl Schol Bk Serv.

Smith, Willie.
xSmith, Willie.
Music on My Mind: The Memoirs of an
American Pianist. Da Capo.

Smith, Willy.
xSmith, W.
Problems in Modern Physics. Gordon.

Smith, Wilson, 1897-
xSmith, Wilson.
ed. Mechanisms of Virus Infection. Acad Pr.

Smith, Woodruff D.
xSmith, Woodruff D.
The German Colonial Empire. U of NC Pr.

Smith, Zay N.
xSmith, Zay N.
The Mirage. Random.

Smither, Effie B.
xSmither, Effie B.
Gregg Medical Shorthand Manual &
Dictionary. McGraw.

Smitherman, Geneva.
xSmitherman, Geneva.
Talkin and Testifyin: The Language of Black
America. HM.

Smithers, A. J., 1919-
xSmithers, A. J.
Toby: A Real-Life Ripping Yarn.
Gordon-Cremonesi.

Smithers, W. D. see Smithers, Wilfred Dudley.

Smithers, Wilfred Dudley, 1895-
xSmithers, W. D.
Chronicles of the Big Bend: A Photographic
Memoir of Life on the Border. Madrona Pr.

Smithies, Frank, 1912-
xSmithies, Frank.
Integral Equations. Cambridge U Pr.

Smithline, Arnold.
xSmithline, Arnold.
Natural Religion in American Literature. Coll
& U Pr.

Smithson, E. W. see Smithson, Edward Walter.

Smithson, Edward Walter.
xSmithson, E. W.
Baconian Essays. Kennikat.

Smithsonian Institute. see Smithsonian Institution.

Smithsonian Institution.
xSmithsonian Institute.
A Zoo for All Seasons: The Smithsonian
Animal World. Norton.
xSmithsonian Institution.
The American Land: The Smithsonian Book of
the American Environment. Norton.
Educational & Federal Laboratory-University
Relationships: Symposium Held at the
Museum of History & Technology
Smithsonian Institution, October 29-31.
Arno.
Every Four Years: The American Presidency.
Norton.
Knowledge Among Men. S&S.
The Thomas Eakins Collection of the
Hirshhorn Museum & Sculpture Garden. U
of Chicago Pr.
xSmithsonian Institution, Washington, D. C.
Dictionary Catalog of the Library of the Freer
Gallery of Art. G K Hall.
Index to Grass Species. G K Hall.
xU. S. House of Representatives, 55th Congress,
2nd Session, Doc. No. 575, Pt. 3.
Annual Report of the Board of Regents of the
Smithsonian Institution Showing the
Operation, Expenditures & Condition of the
Institution for the Year Ending June 30,
1897: A Memorial of George Brown Goode
Together with a Selection of His Papers on
Museums & on the History of Science in
America. Arno.

**Smithsonian Instituion. National Collection of Fine
Arts.**
xSmithsonian Institution, National Collection of
Fine Arts (NCFA).
Images of an Era: The American Poster
1945-1975. MIT Pr.

Smithsonian Institution, National Collection of Fine Arts
(NCFA). see Smithsonian Instituion. National
Collection of Fine Arts.

Smithsonian Institution, Washington, D. C. see
Smithsonian Institution.

Smock, David R.
xSmock, David R.
Conflict & Control in an African Trade Union:
A Study of the Nigerian Coal Miner's Union.
Hoover Inst Pr.
Cultural & Political Aspects of Rural
Transformation: A Case Study of Eastern
Nigeria. Irvington.
The Politics of Pluralism: A Comparative Study
of Lebanon and Ghana. Elsevier.

Smock, Martha.
xSmock, Martha.
Halfway up the Mountain. Unity Bks.
Meet It with Faith. Unity Bks.
Turning Points. Unity Bks.

Smoke, Jim.
xSmoke, Jim.
Growing Through Divorce. Bantam.
Growing Through Divorce. Harvest Hse.

Smolansky, Oles M.
xSmolansky, Oles M.
The Soviet Union & the Arab East Under
Khrushchev. Bucknell U Pr.

Smolders, P. L. L.
xSmolders, Peter L.
Soviets in Space. Taplinger.

Smolders, Peter L. see Smolders, P. L. L.

Smolensky, Jack.
xSmolensky, Jack.

A Guide to Child Growth & Development.
   Kendall-Hunt.
Principles of School Health. Heath.
Smolira, M.
   xSmolira, M.
      Analysis of Tall Buildings by the Force
         Displacement Method. Halsted Pr.
Smoll, Frank L.
   xSmoll, Frank L.
      ed. Psychological Perspectives in Youth Sports.
         Halsted Pr.
Smoller, Sanford J.
   xSmoller, Sanford J.
      Adrift Among Geniuses: Robert McAlmon,
         Writer & Publisher of the Twenties. Pa St U
         Pr.
Smollett, Tobias. *see* Smollett, Tobias George.
Smollett, Tobias George, 1721-1771
   xSmollett, Tobias.
      The Adventures of Roderick Random. Oxford
         U Pr.
      Letters of Tobias Smollett. Oxford U Pr.
Smoodin, Roberta, 1952-
   xSmoodin, Roberta.
      Ursus Major. Knopf.
Smooha, Sammy.
   xSmooha, Sammy.
      Israel: Pluralism & Conflict. U of Cal Pr.
Smookler, Helene V.
   xSmookler, Helene V.
      Economic Integration in New Communities:
         An Evaluation of Factors Affecting Policies
         & Implementation. Ballinger Pub.
Smoot, Dan.
   xSmoot, Dan.
      The Business End of Government. Western
         Islands.
Smorto, M. P. *see* Smorto, Mario P.
Smorto, Mario P.
   xSmorto, M. P.
      Clinical Electroneurography: An Introduction
         to Nerve Conduction Tests. Williams &
         Wilkins.
   xSmorto, Mario P.
      Neuromotor Examination of the Limbs: A
         Photographic Atlas. Williams & Wilkins.
Smothermon, Ron, 1943-
   xSmothermon, Ron.
      Winning Through Enlightenment. Context
         Pubns.
Smoyak, Shirley.
   xSmoyak, Shirley.
      ed. The Psychiatric Nurse As a Family
         Therapist. Wiley.
Smucker, Barbara. *see* Smucker, Barbara Claassen.
Smucker, Barbara Claassen.
   xSmucker, Barbara.
      Days of Terror. Herald Pr.
Smucker, Jesse N.
   xSmucker, Jesse N.
      Look to Your Faith. Faith & Life.
Smullyan, R. M. *see* Smullyan, Raymond M.
Smullyan, Raymond. *see* Smullyan, Raymond M.
Smullyan, Raymond M.
   xSmullyan, R. M.
      First-Order Logic. Springer-Verlag.
   xSmullyan, Raymond.
      The Chess Mysteries of Sherlock Holmes.
         Knopf.
      This Book Needs No Title: A Budget of Living
         Paradoxes. P-H.
   xSmullyan, Raymond M.
      The Tao Is Silent. Har-Row.
Smyer, Richard I., 1935-
   xSmyer, Richard I.
      Primal Dream & Primal Crime: Orwell's
         Development As a Psychological Novelist. U
         of Mo Pr.
Smykla, John O. *see* Smykla, John Ortiz.

Smykla, John Ortiz.
   xSmykla, John O.
      Coed Prison. Human Sci Pr.
Smyly, John.
   xSmyly, John.
      The Totem Poles of Skedans. U of Wash Pr.
Smyth, Alfred P.
   xSmyth, Alfred P.
      Scandinavian York & Dublin: The History &
         Archaeology of the Two Related Viking
         Kingdoms. Humanities.
Smyth, D. H. *see* Smyth, David Henry.
Smyth, David Henry, 1908-
   xSmyth, D. H.
      Alternatives to Animal Experiments. Biblio
         Dist.
Smyth, Henry D. *see* Smyth, Henry De Wolf.
Smyth, Henry De Wolf, 1898-
   xSmyth, Henry D.
      Atomic Energy for Military Purposes: The
         Official Report on the Development of the
         Atomic Bomb Under the Auspices of the
         United States Government, 1940-1945. Da
         Capo.
Smyth, Herbert W. *see* Smyth, Herbert Weir.
Smyth, Herbert Weir, 1857-1937
   xSmyth, Herbert W.
      Aeschylean Tragedy. AMS Pr.
      Aeschylean Tragedy. Biblo.
      Aeschylean Tragedy. Gordon Pr.
      ed. Greek Melic Poets. Biblo.
Smyth, J. D. *see* Smyth, James Desmond.
Smyth, James Desmond.
   xSmyth, J. D.
      Introduction to Animal Parasitology. Krieger.
Smyth, James E. *see* Smyth, James Everil.
Smyth, James Everil.
   xSmyth, James E.
      Law & Business Administration in Canada.
         P-H.
Smyth, John. *see* Smyth, John George.
Smyth, John George, Sir, Bart, 1893-
   xSmyth, John.
      Leadership in Battle 1914-1918. Hippocrene
         Bks.
Smyth, John P. *see* Smyth, John Paterson.
Smyth, John Paterson, d. 1932
   xSmyth, John P.
      How We Got Our Bible. Folcroft.
Smyth, Paul, 1944-
   xSmyth, Paul.
      Conversions. U of Ga Pr.
Smyth, Pete.
   xSmyth, Peter R.
      A Guide to Marine Photography. Norton.
Smyth, Peter R. *see* Smyth, Pete.
Smyth, W. *see* Smyth, William.
Smyth, William, 1765-1849
   xSmyth, W.
      Lectures on the History of the French
         Revolution. AMS Pr.
Smythe. *see* Smythe, Reginald.
Smythe, R. H. *see* Smythe, Reginald Harrison.
Smythe, Reginald.
   xSmythe.
      Live It Up Andy Capp. Fawcett.
      None of Your Lip, Andy Capp!. Fawcett.
      Take a Bow, Andy Capp. Fawcett.
Smythe, Reginald H. *see* Smythe, Reginald Harrison.
Smythe, Reginald Harrison.
   xSmythe, R. H.
      Breeding & Rearing of Dogs. Arco.
   xSmythe, Reginald H.
      Private Life of the Dog: Does It Think. Arco.
Smythe, William E. *see* Smythe, William Ellsworth.
Smythe, William Ellsworth, 1861-1922
   xSmythe, William E.
      Conquest of Arid America. U of Wash Pr.
Snaith, Norman H. *see* Snaith, Norman Henry.

Snaith, Norman Henry, 1898-
   xSnaith, Norman H.
      The Distinctive Ideas of the Old Testament.
         Schocken.
Snape, W. H. *see* Snape, Wilfrid Handley.
Snape, Wilfrid Handley.
   xSnape, W. H.
      How to Find Out About Local Government.
         Pergamon.
Snapper, Isidore.
   xSnapper, Isidore.
      Chinese Lessons to Western Medicine: A
         Contribution to Geographical Medicine from
         the Clinics of Peiping. Grune.
Snavely, Tipton R. *see* Snavely, Tipton Ray.
Snavely, Tipton Ray, 1890-
   xSnavely, Tipton R.
      George Tucker As Political Economist. U Pr of
         Va.
Snavely, William P.
   xSnavely, William P.
      Theory of Economic Systems: Capitalism,
         Socialism, Corporatism. Merrill.
Snawder, Kenneth D., 1934-
   xSnawder, Kenneth D.
      Handbook of Clinical Pedodontics. Mosby.
Snead, R. E. *see* Snead, Rodman E.
Snead, Rodman E.
   xSnead, R. E.
      Atlas of World Physical Features. Wiley.
      World Atlas of Geomorphic Features. Krieger.
Snead, Sam. *see* Snead, Samuel.
Snead, Samuel.
   xSnead, Sam.
      Golf Begins at Forty. Dial.
      Golf Begins at Forty. G K Hall.
Sneath, E. Hershey. *see* Sneath, Elias Hershey.
Sneath, Elias Hershey, 1857-1935
   xSneath, E. Hershey.
      Wordsworth, Poet of Nature & Poet of Man.
         Kennikat.
Sneddon, I. N. *see* Sneddon, Ian Naismith.
Sneddon, Ian Naismith.
   xSneddon, I. N.
      ed. Encyclopedic Dictionary of Mathematics
         for Engineers. Pergamon.
Snee, Joseph M.
   xSnee, Joseph M.
      Status of Forces Agreements & Criminal
         Jurisdiction. Oceana.
Sneed, J. D. *see* Sneed, Joseph D.
Sneed, Joseph D.
   xSneed, J. D.
      The Logical Structure of Mathematical Physics.
         Kluwer Boston.
   xSneed, Joseph D.
      The Logical Structure of Mathematical Physics.
         Kluwer Boston.
Sneed, Marcy C. *see* Sneed, Marcy Cavanagh.
Sneed, Marcy Cavanagh, 1928-
   xSneed, Marcy C.
      Human Life: Our Legacy & Our Challenge.
         McGraw.
Sneeden, R. P. *see* Sneeden, R. P. A.
Sneeden, R. P. A.
   xSneeden, R. P.
      Organochromium Compounds. Acad Pr.
Sneersohn, Haym Z. *see* Sneersohn, Hyam Zvee.
Sneersohn, Hyam Zvee, 1834-1882?
   xSneersohn, Haym Z.
      Palestine & Roumania: A Description of the
         Holy Land & the Past & Present State of
         Roumania & the Roumanian Jews. Arno.
Snelgrove, Alfred K. *see* Snelgrove, Alfred Kitchener.
Snelgrove, Alfred Kitchener, 1902-
   xSnelgrove, Alfred K.
      Opportunities in Geology & Geological
         Engineering. Natl Textbk.
Snell, Daniel C.
   xSnell, Daniel C.

A Workbook of Cuneiform Signs. Undena
Pubns.
Snell, David, 1942-
xSnell, David.
Lights, Camera...Murder. St Martin.
Snell, Edwin M. see Snell, Edwin Marion.
Snell, Edwin Marion.
xSnell, Edwin M.
Modern Fables of Henry James. Russell.
Snell, F. J. see Snell, Frederick John.
Snell, Frank.
xSnell, Frank.
How to Stand up & Speak Well in Business.
Cornerstone.
How to Win the Meeting. Dutton.
Snell, Frank M. see Snell, Fred M.
Snell, Fred M.
xSnell, Frank M.
ed. Progress in Theoretical Biology. Acad Pr.
Snell, Frederick J. see Snell, Frederick John.
Snell, Frederick John, 1862-
xSnell, F. J.
The Fourteenth Century. Folcroft.
xSnell, Frederick J.
Age of Chaucer. Folcroft.
Age of Chaucer: 1346-1400. AMS Pr.
The Customs of Old England. Folcroft.
Snell, J. Laurie. see Snell, James Laurie.
Snell, James Laurie.
xSnell, J. Laurie.
Introduction to Probability Theory with
Computing. P-H.
Snell, John L.
xSnell, John L.
Nazi Revolution: Hitler's Dictatorship & the
German Nation. Heath.
Snell, Richard S.
xSnell, Richard S.
Atlas of Clinical Anatomy. Little.
An Atlas of Normal Radiographic Anatomy.
Little.
Clinical Anatomy for Medical Students. Little.
Gross Anatomy Dissector: A Companion for
the Atlas of Clinical Anatomy. Little.
Sneller, Anne G. see Sneller, Anne Gertrude.
Sneller, Anne Gertrude, 1883-
xSneller, Anne G.
Vanished World. Syracuse U Pr.
Snellgrove, David L.
xSnellgrove, David L.
The Cultural Heritage of Ladakh. Great
Eastern.
The Cultural History of Tibet. Great Eastern.
ed. The Nine Ways of Bon: Excerpts from
Gzi-brjid. Great Eastern.
Snelling. see Snelling, Henry Hunt.
Snelling, Henry Hunt, 1816-1897
xSnelling.
History & Practice of the Art of Photography.
Morgan.
Snelling, Laurence, 1933-
xSnelling, Laurence.
Long Shadows. Norton.
Sneve, Virginia D. see Sneve, Virginia Driving Hawk.
Sneve, Virginia Driving Hawk.
xSneve, Virginia D.
ed. South Dakota Geographic Names. Brevet
Pr.
When Thunders Spoke. Holiday.
Sniatycki, J. see Sniatycki, Jedrzej.
Sniatycki, Jedrzej.
xSniatycki, J.
Geometric Quantization & Quantum
Mechanics. Springer-Verlag.
Snider, Clyde F. see Snider, Clyde Frank.
Snider, Clyde Frank, 1904-
xSnider, Clyde F.

Local Government in Rural America.
Greenwood.
Snider, Delbert A.
xSnider, Delbert A.
Introduction to International Economics. Irwin.
Snider, H. Wayne. see Snider, Harold Wayne.
Snider, Harold Wayne.
xSnider, H. Wayne.
Life Insurance Investment in Commercial Real
Estate. Irwin.
Snider, Nancy.
xSnider, Nancy.
Soybean (Protein) Recipe Ideas. Arc Bks.
Sniderman, Paul M.
xSniderman, Paul M.
Personality & Democratic Politics. U of Cal Pr.
Sniff, William F.
xSniff, William F.
A Curriculum for the Mentally Retarded
Young Adult. C C Thomas.
Snipes, Katherine, 1922-
xSnipes, Katherine.
Robert Graves. Ungar.
Snitslaar, Louis. see Snitslaar, Louise.
Snitslaar, Louise.
xSnitslaar, Louis.
Sidelights of Robert Browning's the Ring & the
Book. Haskell.
Sidelights of Robert Browning's the Ring & the
Book. R West.
xSnitslaar, Louise.
Sidelights on Robert Browning's "the Ring &
the Book". Folcroft.
Snizek, William E.
xSnizek, William E.
ed. Contemporary Issues in Theory &
Research: A Metasociological Perspective.
Greenwood.
Snodgrass, A. M. see Snodgrass, Anthony M.
Snodgrass, Anthony M.
xSnodgrass, A. M.
Arms & Armour of the Greeks. Cornell U Pr.
Snodgrass, Jon.
xSnodgrass, Jon.
ed. For Men Against Sexism: A Book of
Readings. Times Change.
Snodgrass, Milton M. see Snodgrass, Milton Moore.
Snodgrass, Milton Moore.
xSnodgrass, Milton M.
Agriculture, Economics & Resource
Management. P-H.
Snodgrass, Robert E. see Snodgrass, Robert Evans.
Snodgrass, Robert Evans, 1875-
xSnodgrass, Robert E.
Anatomy of the Honey Bee. Comstock.
Snodgrass, W. D. see Snodgrass, William De Witt.
Snodgrass, Wilfred.
xSnodgrass, Wilfred.
Fundamentals of Family Practice. Davis Co.
Snodgrass, William De Witt, 1926-
xSnodgrass, W. D.
The Fuhrer Bunker: A Cycle of Poems in
Progress. Boa Edns.
Snoek, Johan M.
xSnoek, Johan M.
Grey Book: A Collection of Protests Against
Anti-Semitism & the Persecution of Jews
Issued by Non-Roman Catholic Churches &
Church Leaders During Hitler's Rule.
Humanities.
Snook, Barbara.
xSnook, Barbara.
Costumes for Children. Branford.
Needlework Stitches. Crown.
Puppets. Branford.
Snook, I. A.
xSnook, I. A.
Indoctrination & Education. Routledge &
Kegan.
Snook, Patricia K. see Snook, Patrick K.

Snook, Patrick K.
xSnook, Patricia K.
Fishing the Great Lakes. Contemp Bks.
Snopek, Albert M. see Snopek, Albert Michael.
Snopek, Albert Michael, 1942-
xSnopek, Albert M.
Fundamentals of Special Radiographic
Procedures. McGraw.
Snortum, John R.
xSnortum, John R.
ed. Criminal Justice: Allies & Adversaries.
Palisades Pub.
Snouffer, Gary H.
xSnouffer, Gary H.
Health Insurance Agent. Arco.
Life Insurance Agent. Arco.
Snover, Stephen. see Snover, Stephen L.
Snover, Stephen L.
xSnover, Stephen.
How to Program Your Programmable
Calculator. P-H.
Snow, A. J. see Snow, Adolph Judah.
Snow, Adolph Judah, 1894-
xSnow, A. J.
Matter & Gravity in Newton's Physical
Philosophy. Arno.
Snow, C. P. see Snow, Charles Percy.
Snow, Charles Percy, Baron Snow, 1905-
xSnow, C. P.
A Coat of Varnish. Scribner.
Death Under Sail. Garland Pub.
The Homecoming. Scribner.
In Their Wisdom. Scribner.
The Light & the Dark. Scribner.
The Masters. Scribner.
The Realists. Scribner.
Strangers & Brothers. Scribner.
Snow, Dean R., 1940-
xSnow, Dean R.
Native American Prehistory: A Critical
Bibliography. Ind U Pr.
Snow, Edgar, 1905-1972
xSnow, Edgar.
ed. Living China: Modern Chinese Short
Stories. Hyperion Conn.
Random Notes on Red China, 1936-1945.
Harvard U Pr.
Snow, Edward A.
xSnow, Edward A.
A Study of Vermeer. U of Cal Pr.
Snow, Edward R. see Snow, Edward Rowe.
Snow, Edward Rowe.
xSnow, Edward R.
Adventures, Blizzards & Coastal Calamities.
Dodd.
Marine Mysteries & Dramatic Disasters of
New England. Dodd.
Tales of Terror & Tragedy. Dodd.
Snow, James B.
xSnow, James B.
ed. Controversy in Otolaryngology. Saunders.
An Introduction to Otorhinolaryngology. Year
Bk Med.
Snow, Jimmy.
xSnow, Jimmy.
I Cannot Go Back. Logos.
Snow, John H. see Snow, John Howland.
Snow, John Howland.
xSnow, John H.
The Turning of the Tides. Long Hse.
Snow, Karen, 1923-
xSnow, Karen.
Wonders. Penguin.
Wonders. Viking Pr.
Snow, Keith R.
xSnow, Keith R.
Arachnids. Columbia U Pr.
Insects & Disease. Krieger.
Snow, Laurence H., 1932-
xSnow, Laurence H.

Contemporary Psychiatry. Year Bk Med.
Snow, Marshall S. *see* Snow, Marshall Solomon.
Snow, Marshall Solomon, 1842-1916
  xSnow, Marshall S.
    The City Government of Saint-Louis. AMS Pr.
    The City Government of Saint Louis. Johnson
      Repr.
Snow, Peter G.
  xSnow, Peter G.
    Political Forces in Argentina. Praeger.
Snow, Richard. *see* Snow, Richard F.
Snow, Richard F.
  xSnow, Richard.
    The Funny Place. O'Hara.
Snow, Royall H. *see* Snow, Royall Henderson.
Snow, Royall Henderson, 1898-
  xSnow, Royall H.
    Thomas Lovell Beddoes: Eccentric & Poet.
      Folcroft.
Snow, Vernon F.
  xSnow, Vernon F.
    Parliament in Elizabethan England: John
      Hooker's "Order & Usage". Yale U Pr.
Snow, Wilbert, 1884-
  xSnow, Wilbert.
    Codline's Child: The Autobiography of Wilbert
      Snow. Columbia U Pr.
Snowden, James.
  xSnowden, James.
    Folk Dress of Europe. Mayflower Bks.
Snowden, John B. *see* Snowden, John Baptist.
Snowden, John Baptist.
  xSnowden, John B.
    From Whence Cometh. Vantage.
Snowden, Obed L.
  xSnowden, Obed L.
    Profitable Farm Marketing. P-H.
Snowman, Daniel.
  xSnowman, Daniel.
    ed. If I Had Been...: Ten Historical Fantasies.
      Rowman.
Snyder, Agnes, 1885-
  xSnyder, Agnes.
    Dauntless Women in Childhood Education,
      1856-1931. ACEI.
Snyder, Al.
  xSnyder, Al.
    Lightplane Construction & Repair. TAB Bks.
Snyder, Alice D. *see* Snyder, Alice Dorothea.
Snyder, Alice Dorothea.
  xSnyder, Alice D.
    Coleridge on Logic & Learning: With
      Selections from the Unpublished Manuscripts.
      Folcroft.
    Critical Principle of the Reconciliation of
      Opposites As Employed by Coleridge.
      Folcroft.
Snyder, Carl, 1869-1946
  xSnyder, Carl.
    Capitalism the Creator: The Economic
      Foundations of Modern Industrial Society.
      Arno.
Snyder, Carl D. *see* Snyder, Carl Dean.
Snyder, Carl Dean.
  xSnyder, Carl D.
    White-Collar Workers & the UAW. U of Ill Pr.
Snyder, Carl H.
  xSnyder, Carl H.
    Introduction to Modern Organic Chemistry.
      Har-Row.
Snyder, Carol.
  xSnyder, Carol.
    Ike & Mama & the Block Wedding. Coward.
    Ike & Mama & the Once-a-Year Suit. Coward.
Snyder, Charles M. *see* Snyder, Charles Mccool.
Snyder, Charles McCool.
  xSnyder, Charles M.

Red & White on the New York Frontier: A
  Struggle for Survival, Insights from the
  Papers of Erastus Granger, Indian Agent,
  1807-1819. Harbor Hill Bks.
Snyder, Charles R.
  xSnyder, Charles R.
    Alcohol & the Jews: A Cultural Study of
      Drinking & Sobriety. S Ill U Pr.
Snyder, D. Paul, 1933-
  xSnyder, Paul D.
    Toward One Science: The Convergence of
      Traditions. St Martin.
Snyder, Donald L. *see* Snyder, Donald Lee.
Snyder, Donald Lee.
  xSnyder, Donald L.
    Random Point Processes. Wiley.
Snyder, Edward. *see* Snyder, Edward Douglas.
Snyder, Edward Douglas, 1889-
  xSnyder, Edward.
    Hypnotic Poetry: A Study of Trance-Inducing
      Technique in Certain Poetry & Its Literary
      Significance. Gordon Pr.
Snyder, Eugene E.
  xSnyder, Eugene E.
    Portland Names & Neighborhoods: Their
      Historic Origins. Binford.
Snyder, Franklyn B. *see* Snyder, Franklyn Bliss.
Snyder, Franklyn Bliss, 1884-1958
  xSnyder, Franklyn B.
    Life of Robert Burns. Shoe String.
Snyder, Gary.
  xSnyder, Gary.
    Back Country. New Directions.
    He Who Hunted Birds in His Father's Village:
      The Dimensions of a Haida Myth. Grey Fox.
    The Real Work: Interviews & Talks. New
      Directions.
    Regarding Wave. New Directions.
Snyder, Gerald S.
  xSnyder, Gerald S.
    Are There Alien Beings?: The Story of UFOs.
      Messner.
    In the Footsteps of Lewis & Clark. Natl Geog.
    Is There a Loch Ness Monster?. Wanderer Bks.
    Let's Talk About Computers. Jonathan David.
    The Right to Be Informed: Censorship in the
      United States. Messner.
    The Right to Be Let Alone: Privacy in the
      United States. Messner.
Snyder, Glenn H. *see* Snyder, Glenn Herald.
Snyder, Glenn Herald.
  xSnyder, Glenn H.
    Deterrence & Defense: Toward a Theory of
      National Security. Greenwood.
Snyder, Harold E. *see* Snyder, Harold Elam.
Snyder, Harold Elam, 1907-
  xSnyder, Harold E.
    Educational Inbreeding. AMS Pr.
Snyder, Helen I. *see* Snyder, Helen Irene.
Snyder, Helen Irene, 1922-
  xSnyder, Helen I.
    Contemporary Educational Psychology: Some
      Models Applied to the School Setting.
      Krieger.
Snyder, Howard A.
  xSnyder, Howard A.
    The Community of the King. Inter-Varsity.
Snyder, James C.
  xSnyder, James C.
    Fiscal Management & Planning in Local
      Government. Lexington Bks.
    ed. Introduction to Architecture. McGraw.
Snyder, John.
  xSnyder, John.
    Commercial Artists Handbook. Watson-Guptill.
Snyder, John P. *see* Snyder, John Parr.
Snyder, John Parr, 1926-
  xSnyder, John P.

The Mapping of New Jersey: The Men & the
  Art. Rutgers U Pr.
Snyder, L. *see* Snyder, Louis Leo.
Snyder, L. L. *see* Snyder, Louis Leo.
Snyder, L. R. *see* Snyder, Lloyd R.
Snyder, Laurence H. *see* Snyder, Laurence Hasbrouck.
Snyder, Laurence Hasbrouck, 1901-
  xSnyder, Laurence H.
    Principles of Heredity. Heath.
Snyder, Le Moyne, 1898-
  xSnyder, LeMoyne.
    Homicide Investigation: Practical Information
      for Coroners, Police Officers, & Other
      Investigators. C C Thomas.
Snyder, LeMoyne. *see* Snyder, le Moyne.
Snyder, Leon C.
  xSnyder, Leon C.
    Gardening in the Upper Midwest. U of Minn
      Pr.
    Trees & Shrubs for Northern Gardens. U of
      Minn Pr.
Snyder, Leslie.
  xSnyder, Leslie.
    Gold & Black Gold: Basic Value Investing for
      the New Economic Era. Exposition.
Snyder, Llewellyn R.
  xSnyder, Llewellyn R.
    Computational Arithmetic. McGraw.
    Essential Business Mathematics. McGraw.
Snyder, Lloyd R.
  xSnyder, L. R.
    Introduction to Modern Liquid
      Chromatography. Wiley.
    Principles of Adsorption Chromatography: The
      Separation of Nonionic Organic Compounds.
      Dekker.
Snyder, Louis.
  xSnyder, Louis.
    Community of Sound: Boston Symphony & Its
      World of Players. Beacon Pr.
Snyder, Louis B. *see* Snyder, Louis Leo.
Snyder, Louis L. *see* Snyder, Louis Leo.
Snyder, Louis Leo, 1907-
  xSnyder, L.
    ed. Frederick the Great. P-H.
  xSnyder, L. L.
    The Age of Reason. Peter Smith.
    The World in the Twentieth Century. Peter
      Smith.
  xSnyder, Louis B.
    ed. The Imperialism Reader: Documents &
      Readings on Modern Expansionism.
      Kennikat.
  xSnyder, Louis L.
    The Age of Reason. Krieger.
    Age of Reason. Van Nos Reinhold.
    ed. Documents of German History.
      Greenwood.
    Fifty Major Documents of the Nineteenth
      Century. Krieger.
    ed. Fifty Major Documents of the Twentieth
      Century. Van Nos Reinhold.
    The First Book of the Soviet Union. Watts.
    ed. Historic Documents of World War I.
      Greenwood.
    The World in the Twentieth Century. Krieger.
Snyder, Paul D. *see* Snyder, D. Paul.
Snyder, Raymond A. *see* Snyder, Raymond Albert.
Snyder, Raymond Albert.
  xSnyder, Raymond A.
    Professional Preparation in Health, Physical
      Education, & Recreation. Greenwood.
Snyder, Richard V.
  xSnyder, Richard V.
    Color Creations in Buttercream. Exposition.
    Decorating Cakes for Fun & Profit. Exposition.
Snyder, Robert.
  xSnyder, Robert.

Buckminster Fuller: An Autobiographical
Monologue Scenario. St Martin.

Snyder, Robert L.
xSnyder, Robert L.
Pare Lorentz & the Documentary Film. U of
Okla Pr.

Snyder, Ross.
xSnyder, Ross.
On Becoming Human. Abingdon.
ed. Openings into Ministry. Exploration Pr.

Snyder, Solomon H., 1938-
xSnyder, Solomon H.
Biological Aspects of Mental Disorder. Oxford
U Pr.
Opiate Receptor Mechanisms: Neurochemical
& Neurophysiological Processes in Opiate
Drug Action & Addiction. MIT Pr.
Uses of Marijuana. Oxford U Pr.

Snyder, Susan.
xSnyder, Susan.
The Comic Matrix of Shakespeare's Tragedies:
Romeo & Juliet, Hamlet, Othello & King
Lear. Princeton U Pr.

Snyder, Zilpha. *see* Snyder, Zilpha Keatley.
Snyder, Zilpha K. *see* Snyder, Zilpha Keatley.
Snyder, Zilpha Keatley.
xSnyder, Zilpha.
And All Between. Atheneum.
xSnyder, Zilpha K.
Changeling. Atheneum.
Changeling. Atheneum.
Egypt Game. Atheneum.
Egypt Game. Atheneum.
Eyes in the Fishbowl. Atheneum.
The Princess & the Giants. Atheneum.
The Truth About Stone Hollow. Atheneum.
Truth About Stone Hollow. Atheneum.
Velvet Room. Atheneum.
The Velvet Room. Atheneum.

Soal, Samuel G. *see* Soal, Samuel George.
Soal, Samuel George.
xSoal, Samuel G.
Modern Experiments in Telepathy. Greenwood.

Soames, Mary.
xSoames, Mary.
Clementine Churchill: The Biography of a
Marriage. HM.

Soares, Mario.
xSoares, Mario.
Portugal's Struggle for Liberty. Allen Unwin.

Soaring Society of America.
xSoaring Society of America.
American Soaring Handbook. Aviation.

Sobchack, Thomas.
xSobchack, Thomas.
An Introduction to Film. Little.

Sobchack, Vivian C. *see* Sobchack, Vivian Carol.

Sobchack, Vivian Carol.
xSobchack, Vivian C.
The Limits of Infinity: The American Science
Fiction Film. A S Barnes.

Sobel. *see* Sobel, Herbert S.

Sobel, Brian, 1954-
xSobel, Brian.
Illustrated Guide to Fast Pitch Softball.
Anderson World.

Sobel, David. *see* Sobel, David Stuart.
Sobel, David J. *see* Sobel, David Stuart.

Sobel, David Stuart.
xSobel, David.
Ways of Health: Holistic Approaches to
Ancient & Contemporary Medicine.
HarBraceJ.
xSobel, David J.
Ways of Health: Holistic Approaches to

Ancient & Contemporary Medicine.
HarBraceJ.

Sobel, Eli.
xSobel, Eli.
ed. Liebesspiele. Oxford U Pr.

Sobel, Frances. *see* Sobel, Frances (Selkin).
Sobel, Frances (Selkin), 1888-
xSobel, Frances.
Teacher's Marks & Objective Tests As Indices
of School Adjustment. AMS Pr.

Sobel, Herbert S.
xSobel.
Introduction to Digital Computer Design. A-W.

Sobel, Irwin Philip.
xSobel, Irwin Philip.
Dr. Monte Cristo. Doubleday.

Sobel, Lester. *see* Sobel, Lester A.
Sobel, Lester A.
xSobel, Lester.
ed. Castro's Cuba in the 1970's. Facts on File.
Peacemaking in the Middle East. Facts on File.
ed. Political Terrorism. Facts on File.
xSobel, Lester A.
ed. Cancer & the Environment. Facts on File.
ed. Chile & Allende. Facts on File.
ed. Consumer Protection. Facts on File.
ed. Corruption in Business. Facts on File.
ed. Great American Tax Revolt. Facts on File.
Medical Science & the Law: The Life & Death
Controversy. Facts on File.
ed. Palestinian Impasse: Arab Guerrillas &
International Terror. Facts on File.
ed. Political Terrorism. Facts on File.
ed. Pornography, Obscenity & the Law. Facts
on File.
Post-Watergate Morality. Facts on File.

Sobel, Max. *see* Sobel, Max A.
Sobel, Max A.
xSobel, Max.
Teaching Mathematics: A Source Book for
Aids, Activities, & Strategies. P-H.

Sobel, Mechal.
xSobel, Mechal.
Trabelin' on: The Slave Journey to an
Afro-Baptist Faith. Greenwood.

Sobel, Robert, 1931 (Feb. 19)-
xSobel, Robert.
For Want of a Nail: If Burgoyne Had Won at
Saratoga. Macmillan.
Great Bull Market: Wall Street in the 1920's.
Norton.
Inside Wall Street: Continuity & Change in the
Financial District. Norton.
Panic on Wall Street: A History of America's
Financial Disasters. Macmillan.
They Satisfy: The Cigarette in American Life.
Doubleday.

Sobelman, I. I. *see* Sobelman, Igor Ilich.
Sobelman, Igor Ilich.
xSobelman, I. I.
Atomic Spectra & Radiative Transitions.
Springer-Verlag.

Sober, Elliot.
xSober, Elliott.
Simplicity. Oxford U Pr.

Sober, Elliott. *see* Sober, Elliot.
Sobey, Francine.
xSobey, Francine.
ed. Changing Roles in Social Work Practice.
Temple U Pr.
Nonprofessional Revolution in Mental Health.
Columbia U Pr.

Sobieszek, Robert. *see* Sobieszek, Robert A.
Sobieszek, Robert A.
xSobieszek, Robert.
Spirit of Fact: The Daguerreotypes of
Southworth & Hawes, 1843-1862. Godine.

Sobin, Dennis P.
xSobin, Dennis P.

Future of the American Suburbs: Survival or
Extinction. Kennikat.

Sobin, Gustaf.
xSobin, Gustaf.
The Tale of the Yellow Triangle. Braziller.

Soble, Alan.
xSoble, Alan.
ed. Philosophy of Sex: Contemporary Readings.
Littlefield.
ed. Philosophy of Sex: Contemporary Readings.
Rowman.

Soble, Ronald L.
xSoble, Ronald L.
Whatever Became of Free Enterprise?. NAL.

Sobol, Donald. *see* Sobol, Donald J.
Sobol, Donald J., 1924-
xSobol, Donald.
Encyclopedia Brown Gets His Man. Bantam.
Encyclopedia Brown Keeps the Peace. Bantam.
xSobol, Donald J.
ed. The Best Animal Stories of Science Fiction
& Fantasy. Warne.
Encyclopedia Brown & the Case of the Dead
Eagles. Elsevier-Nelson.
Encyclopedia Brown & the Case of the Dead
Eagles. Schol Bk Serv.
Encyclopedia Brown & the Case of the
Midnight Visitor. Bantam.
Encyclopedia Brown & the Case of the
Midnight Visitor. Elsevier-Nelson.
Encyclopedia Brown Boy Detective. Bantam.
Encyclopedia Brown Carries on. Schol Bk Serv.
Encyclopedia Brown Finds the Clues.
Elsevier-Nelson.
Encyclopedia Brown Finds the Clues. Bantam.
Encyclopedia Brown Gets His Man.
Elsevier-Nelson.
Encyclopedia Brown Keeps the Peace.
Elsevier-Nelson.
Encyclopedia Brown Lends a Hand.
Elsevier-Nelson.
Encyclopedia Brown Solves Them All.
Elsevier-Nelson.
Encyclopedia Brown Solves Them All. Schol
Bk Serv.
Encyclopedia Brown's Record Book of Weird
& Wonderful Facts. Delacorte.
True Sea Adventures. Elsevier-Nelson.

Sobol, Evelyn G.
xSobol, Evelyn G.
Family Nursing: A Study Guide. Mosby.

Sobol, Harriet L. *see* Sobol, Harriet Langsam.
Sobol, Harriet Langsam.
xSobol, Harriet L.
Cosmo's Restaurant. Macmillan.
My Brother Steven Is Retarded. Macmillan.
My Other-Mother, My Other-Father.
Macmillan.

Sobol, I. M. *see* Sobol, Ilia Meerovich.
Sobol, Ilia Meerovich.
xSobol, I. M.
The Monte Carlo Method. U of Chicago Pr.

Sobol, Rose.
xSobol, Rose.
Woman Chief. Dell.
Woman Chief. Dial.

Sobolev, Sergei L. *see* Sobolev, Sergei L'Vovich.
Sobolev, Sergei L' vovich, 1908-
xSobolev, Sergei L.
tr. Applications of Functional Analysis in
Mathematical Physics. Am Math.

Sobolev, V. V. *see* Sobolev, Viktor Viktorovich.
Sobolev, Viktor Viktorovich.
xSobolev, V. V.
Light Scattering in Planetary Atmospheres.
Pergamon.

Sobosan, Jeffrey G., 1946-
xSobosan, Jeffrey G.

Imbalances in Development: The Indonesian Experience. Ohio U Ctr Intl.

Sofer, Cyril.
xSofer, Cyril.
Organizations in Theory & Practice. Basic.

Soffer, Reba N.
xSoffer, Reba N.
Ethics & Society in England: The Revolution in the Social Sciences, 1870-1914. U of Cal Pr.

Softly, Barbara.
xSoftly, Barbara.
The Queens of England. Stein & Day.

Sogeri Senior High School. Expressive Arts Department.
xStudents, Expressive Arts Dept., Sogeri National High School, Papua New Guinea.
Pukari-Voices of Papua New Guinea. Rand-Tofua.

Soggin, J. Alberto.
xSoggin, J. Alberto.
Joshua, a Commentary. Westminster.

Sohl, Jerry.
xSohl, Jerry.
Lemon Eaters. S&S.

Sohl, Robert.
xSohl, Robert.
ed. Gospel According to Zen: Beyond the Death of God. NAL.

Sohn-Rethel, Alfred, 1899-
xSohn-Rethel, Alfred.
Intellectual & Manual Labour: A Critique of Epistemology. Humanities.

Sohner, Charles P.
xSohner, Charles P.
American Government & Politics Today. Scott F.
California Government & Politics Today. Scott F.
The People's Power: American Government & Politics Today. Scott F.

Soisson, Harold E.
xSoisson, Harold E.
Instrumentation in Industry. Wiley.

Soja, Edward W.
xSoja, Edward W.
Geography of Modernization in Kenya: A Spatial Analysis of Social, Economic, & Political Growth. Syracuse U Pr.

Sokel, Walter H. see Sokel, Walter Herbert.

Sokel, Walter Herbert, 1917-
xSokel, Walter H.
Franz Kafka. Columbia U Pr.

Sokol, David M.
xSokol, David M.
American Architecture & Art: A Guide to Information Sources. Gale.

Sokol, Ronald P.
xSokol, Ronald P.
Federal Habeas Corpus. Michie.
Law Abiding Policeman. Michie.

Sokolnikoff, Ivan S. see Sokolnikoff, Ivan Stephen.

Sokolnikoff, Ivan Stephen, 1901-
xSokolnikoff, Ivan S.
Mathematical Theory of Elasticity. McGraw.

Sokoloff, B. see Sokoloff, Boris.

Sokoloff, B. A.
xSokoloff, B. A.
Saul Bellow: A Comprehensive Bibliography. Folcroft.

Sokoloff, Boris.
xSokoloff, B.
Carcinoid & Serotonin. Springer-Verlag.

Sokoloff, Kiril.
xSokoloff, Kiril.
The Thinking Investor's Guide to the Stock Market. McGraw.

Sokoloff, L. see Sokoloff, Leon.

Sokoloff, Leon, 1919-
xSokoloff, L.

The Joints & Synovial Fluid. Acad Pr.
xSokoloff, Leon.
ed. The Joints & Synovial Fluid. Acad Pr.

Sokoloff, Louis.
xSokoloff, Louis.
ed. Regulatory Biochemistry in Neural Tissues. MIT Pr.

Sokolow, Leonid, 1922-
xSokolow, Leonid.
A Dual Ether Universe: Introducing a New Unified Field Theory. Exposition.

Sokolow, Maurice.
xSokolow, Maurice.
Clinical Cardiology. Lange.

Sola, Carla De. see De Sola, Carla.

Sola, Ralph De. see De Sola, Ralph.

Solan, Miriam.
xSolan, Miriam.
Seductions. Barlenmir.

Solar Age.
xSolar Age Magazine.
ed. The Solar Age Resource Book: A Complete Guidebook for the Consumer to Harnessing the Power of Solar Energy, in Depth & up-to-Date. SolarVision.
xSolar Age Magazine Editors.
ed. Solar Age Catalog: A Guide to Solar Energy Knowledge & Materials. SolarVision.

Solar Age Magazine. see Solar Age.

Solar Age Magazine Editors. see Solar Age.

Solar Cooling & Heating Forum, Dec. 13-15, 1976, Miami Beach. see Solar Cooling and Heating Forum, Miami Beach, Florida, 1976.

Solar Cooling and Heating Forum, Miami Beach, Florida, 1976.
xSolar Cooling & Heating Forum, Dec. 13-15, 1976, Miami Beach.
Solar Cooling & Heating: Architectural, Engineering & Legal Aspects, Proceedings. Hemisphere Pub.

Solar Energy & Conservation Symposium-Workshop, Miami Beach, Florida, 1978. see Solar Energy and Conservation Symposium, Miami Beach, Florida, 1978.

Solar Energy and Conservation Symposium, Miami Beach, Florida, 1978.
xSolar Energy & Conservation Symposium-Workshop, Miami Beach, Florida, 1978.
Solar Energy & Conservation: Technology, Commercialization, Utilization: Proceedings. Pergamon.

Solar Energy Group, Los Alamos Scientific Laboratory. see United States. Argonne National Laboratory, Lemont, Illinois. Solar Energy Group.

Solar Energy Research Institute.
xSolar Energy Research Institute.
Fuel from Farms. Solar Energy Info.
Solar Energy Technical Training Directory. Solar Energy Info.

Solarex Corporation.
xSolarex Corporation.
Guide to Solar Electricity. Solar Energy Info.

Solberg, Carl, 1915-
xSolberg, Carl.
Conquest of the Skies: A History of Commercial Aviation in America. Little.

Solberg, Carl E.
xSolberg, Carl E.
Oil & Nationalism in Argentina: A History. Stanford U Pr.

Solberg, Curtis B.
xSolberg, Curtis B.
A People's Heritage: Patterns in United States History. Wiley.

Solbrig, Otto T. see Solbrig, Otto Thomas.

Solbrig, Otto Thomas.
xSolbrig, Otto T.

Introduction to Population Biology & Evolution. A-W.
ed. Topics in Plant Population Biology. Columbia U Pr.

Soldo, Betty L. see Soldo, Betty Lougaris.

Soldo, Betty Lougaris.
xSoldo, Betty L.
The Inside-Out Beauty Book. Revell.

Soldo, John J.
xSoldo, John J.
Delano in America & Other Early Poems. Pearl Pr.

Soldofsky. see Soldofsky, Robert M.

Soldofsky, Robert M.
xSoldofsky.
Financial Management. SW Pub.

Soldon, Norbert C.
xSoldon, Norbert C.
Women in British Trade Unions 1874-1976. Rowman.

Solerti, Angelo, 1865-1907
xSolerti, Angelo.
Musica, Ballo E Drammatica Alla Corte Medicea Dal 1600 Al 1637. Arno.

Solheim, B. see Solheim, Bjrn.

Solheim, Bjrn.
xSolheim, B.
Cell Wall Biochemistry Related to Specificity in Host-Plant Pathogen Interactions. Universitet.

Solian, Alexandru.
xSolian, Alexandru.
Theory of Modules. Wiley.

Solinger, Dorothy J.
xSolinger, Dorothy J.
Regional Government & Political Integration in Southwest China, 1949-1954: A Case Study. U of Cal Pr.

Solis y Rivadeneyra, Antonio de, 1610-1686
xSolis Y Rivadeneyra, Antonio De.
The History of the Conquest of Mexico by the Spaniards. AMS Pr.

Soll, D.
xSoll, Dieter.
ed. Transfer RNA: Biological Aspects. Cold Spring Harbor.

Soll, Dieter. see Soll, D.

Soll, Ivan.
xSoll, Ivan.
Introduction to Hegel's Metaphysics. U of Chicago Pr.

Solla , Price, Derek J. De. see Price, Derek J.

Solla, Price, Derek De. see Price, Derek de Solla.

Sollberger, Edmond.
xSollberger, Edmond.
Business & Administrative Correspondence Under the Kings of Ur. J J Augustin.

Solle, Dorothee.
xSolle, Dorothee.
Revolutionary Patience. Orbis Bks.

Soller, J. Theodore. see Soller, Theodore.

Soller, Theodore.
xSoller, J. Theodore.
ed. Cathode Ray Tube Displays. Dover.

Sollers, Philippe, 1936-
xSollers, Philippe.
The Park. Red Dust.

Sollinger, C. see Sollinger, Charles.

Sollinger, Charles.
xSollinger, C.
String Class Publications in the United States, 1851-1951. Info Coord.

Solly, Edward, 1819-1886
xSolly, Edward.
ed. Index of Hereditary English, Scottish, & Irish Titles of Honour. Genealog Pub.

Solman, Joseph, 1909-
xSolman, Joseph.

The Monotypes of Joseph Solman. Da Capo.
Solmon, Lewis C.
xSolmon, Lewis C.
Capital Formation by Expenditures on Formal
Education: 1880 & 1890. Arno.
College As a Training Ground for Jobs.
Praeger.
Solmsen, Friedrich, 1904-
xSolmsen, Friedrich.
Intellectual Experiments of the Greek
Enlightenment. Princeton U Pr.
Solo, Dan X.
xSolo, Dan X.
ed. Sans Serif Display Alphabets: 100
Complete Fonts. Dover.
Solo, Robert A.
xSolo, Robert A.
Economic Organizations & Social Systems.
Bobbs.
Economic Organizations & Social Systems.
Irvington.
ed. Inducing Technological Change for
Economic Growth & Development. Mich St
U Pr.
Organizing Science for Technology Transfer in
Economic Development. Mich St U Pr.
Solodovnikov, A. S. *see* Solodovnikov, Aleksandr
Samuilovich.
Solodovnikov, Aleksandr Samuilovich.
xSolodovnikov, A. S.
Systems of Linear Inequalities. U of Chicago
Pr.
Solomon, Arthur P.
xSolomon, Arthur P.
ed. The Prospective City: Economic,
Population, Energy, & Environmental
Developments Shaping Our Cities & Suburbs.
MIT Pr.
Solomon, Barbara H.
xSolomon, Barbara H.
ed. Ain't We Got Fun: Essays, Lyrics, &
Stories of the Twenties. NAL.
Solomon, Barbara M. *see* Solomon, Barbara Miller.
Solomon, Barbara Miller.
xSolomon, Barbara M.
Ancestors & Immigrants: A Changing New
England Tradition. U of Chicago Pr.
Solomon, Brad.
xSolomon, Brad.
The Gone Man. Avon.
The Gone Man. Random.
Jake & Katie. Dial.
The Open Shadow. Avon.
Solomon, Carl. *see* Solomon, Carl W.
Solomon, Carl W.
xSolomon, Carl.
More Mishaps. City Lights.
Solomon, Charles R.
xSolomon, Charles R.
Counseling with the Mind of Christ: The
Dynamics of Spirituotherapy. Revell.
Solomon, Charmaine.
xSolomon, Charmaine.
Chinese Diet Cookbook. McGraw.
The Complete Asian Cookbook. McGraw.
Solomon, D. *see* Solomon, David Henry.
Solomon, D. H. *see* Solomon, David Henry.
Solomon, David. *see* Solomon, David Harris.
Solomon, David Harris.
xSolomon, David.
Inside the Australian Parliament. Allen Unwin.
Solomon, David Henry.
xSolomon, D.
ed. Step-Growth Polymerizations. Dekker.
xSolomon, D. H.
The Chemistry of Organic Film Formers.
Krieger.
Solomon, Eric.
xSolomon, Eric.

Stephen Crane in England: A Portrait of the
Artist. Ohio St U Pr.
Solomon, Ezra.
xSolomon, Ezra.
The Anxious Economy. SF Bk Co.
The Anxious Economy. W H Freeman.
An Introduction to Financial Management.
Goodyear.
Theory of Financial Management. Columbia U
Pr.
Solomon, Frederick, 1899-
xSolomon, Frederick.
Critique of Modern Art. New English Art.
Solomon, Gail E.
xSolomon, Gail E.
Clinical Management of Seizures: A Guide for
the Physician. Saunders.
Solomon, Hannah.
xSolomon, Hannah.
Bake Bread. Lippincott.
Solomon, Harry M.
xSolomon, Harry M.
Sir Richard Blackmore. Twayne.
Solomon, Hassim M., 1934-
xSolomon, Hassim M.
Community Corrections. Holbrook.
Solomon, Herbert.
xSolomon, Herbert.
ed. Studies in Item Analysis & Prediction.
Stanford U Pr.
Solomon, Jack.
xSolomon, Jack.
Cracklin Bread & Asfidity: Folk Recipes &
Remedies. U of Ala Pr.
Solomon, Jon, 1950-
xSolomon, Jon.
The Ancient World in the Cinema. A S Barnes.
Solomon, Kenneth Ira.
xSolomon, Kenneth L.
Profitable Restaurant Management. P-H.
Solomon, Kenneth L. *see* Solomon, Kenneth Ira.
Solomon, Larry.
xSolomon, Larry.
The Caddis & the Angler. Stackpole.
ed. The Complete Book of Modern Fly
Fishing. Follett.
Solomon, Lawrence.
xSolomon, Lawrence.
College Board Achievement Test: Biology.
Arco.
The Conserver Solution. Doubleday.
Solomon, Lawrence M. *see* Solomon, Lawrence Marvin.
Solomon, Lawrence Marvin.
xSolomon, Lawrence M.
Adolescent Dermatology. Saunders.
Neonatal Dermatology. Saunders.
Solomon, Leslie.
xSolomon, Leslie.
Getting Involved with Your Own Computer: A
Guide for Beginners. Enslow Pubs.
Solomon, Lewis D.
xSolomon, Lewis D.
Multinational Corporations & the Emerging
World Order. Kennikat.
Solomon, Margaret C.
xSolomon, Margaret C.
Eternal Geomater: The Sexual Universe of
"Finnegans Wake". S Ill U Pr.
Solomon, Maynard.
xSolomon, Maynard.
Beethoven. Schirmer Bks.
Solomon, Neil.
xSolomon, Neil.
Dr. Solomon's High Health Diet & Exercise
Plan: How to Make Cholesterol Work for
You. Putnam.
Doctor Solomon's Proven Master Plan for
Total Body Fitness & Maintenance. Putnam.
Family Therapy & Social Change. Irvington.
Solomon, Pearl C. *see* Solomon, Pearl Chesler.

Solomon, Pearl Chesler.
xSolomon, Pearl C.
Dickens & Melville in Their Time. Columbia U
Pr.
Solomon, Philip.
xSolomon, Philip H.
The Life After Birth: Imagery in Samuel
Beckett's Trilogy. Romance.
Solomon, Philip H. *see* Solomon, Philip.
Solomon, Richard H., 1937-
xSolomon, Richard H.
Mao's Revolution & the Chinese Political
Culture. U of Cal Pr.
A Revolution Is Not a Dinner Party: A Feast
of Images of the Maoist Transformation of
China. Doubleday.
Solomon, Robert C.
xSolomon, Robert C.
The Passions. Doubleday.
Solomon, Ruth F. *see* Solomon, Ruth Freeman.
Solomon, Ruth Freeman.
xSolomon, Ruth F.
The Eagle & the Dove. BJ Pub Group.
The Eagle & the Dove. PB.
Solomon, Shirl.
xSolomon, Shirl.
How to Really Know Yourself Through Your
Handwriting. Taplinger.
Solomon, Stanley J.
xSolomon, Stanley J.
ed. The Classic Cinema: Essays in Criticism.
HarBraceJ.
The Film Idea. HarBraceJ.
Solomon, Susan G. *see* Solomon, Susan Gross.
Solomon, Susan Gross.
xSolomon, Susan G.
Soviet Agrarian Debate: A Controversy in
Social Science, 1923-1929. Westview.
Solomons, David.
xSolomons, David.
The Cost of Physicians' & Certain Paramedical
Services in New York Municipal Hospitals.
Irwin.
Solomons, G. L.
xSolomons, G. L.
Materials & Methods in Fermentation. Acad
Pr.
Solomons, T. Graham. *see* Solomons, T. W. Graham.
Solomons, T. W. Graham.
xSolomons, T. Graham.
Solutions Manual for Organic Chemistry.
Wiley.
xSolomons, T. W. Graham.
Organic Chemistry. Wiley.
Solomos, Alexes.
xSolomos, Alexis.
The Living Aristophanes. U of Mich Pr.
Solomos, Alexis. *see* Solomos, Alex Es.
Solotaroff, Robert.
xSolotaroff, Robert.
Down Mailer's Way. U of Ill Pr.
Solow, Robert M.
xSolow, Robert M.
Growth Theory: An Exposition. Oxford U Pr.
Solso, Robert L.
xSolso, Robert L.
Cognitive Psychology. HarBraceJ.
ed. Theories in Cognitive Psychology: The
Loyola Symposium. Halsted Pr.
Soltau, Henry W., 1805-1875
xSoltau, Henry W.
Holy Vessels & Furniture of the Tabernacle.
Kregel.
Tabernacle, Priesthood & the Offerings. Kregel.
Soltis, Andrew.
xSoltis, Andrew.
The Art of Defense in Chess. McKay.
Soltow, Lee.
xSoltow, Lee.

Men & Wealth in the United States,
1850-1870. Yale U Pr.
Patterns of Wealthholding in Wisconsin Since
1850. U of Wis Pr.
Soltow, Martha J. *see* Soltow, Martha Jane.
Soltow, Martha Jane.
xSoltow, Martha J.
American Women & the Labor Movement,
1825-1974: An Annotated Bibliography.
Scarecrow.
Solution Mining Symposium, Dallas, 1974.
xSymposium on Solution Mining, 1974.
Proceedings. Soc Mining Eng.
Solvay Conference on Physics. *see* Solvay Conference on
Physics, 15th, Brussels, 1970.
Solvay Conference on Physics, 15th, Brussels, 1970.
xSolvay Conference on Physics.
Symmetry Properties of Nuclei. Gordon.
Solve, Norma D. *see* Solve, Norma Dobie.
Solve, Norma Dobie, 1890-
xSolve, Norma D.
Stuart Politics in Chapman's Tragedy of
Chabot. Haskell.
xSolve, Norma Dobie.
Stuart Politics in Chapman's Tragedy of
Chabot. R West.
Solymar, L. *see* Solymar, Laszlo.
Solymar, Laszlo.
xSolymar, L.
Lectures on Electromagnetic Theory: A Short
Course for Engineers. Oxford U Pr.
Solymosi, F.
xSolymosi, F.
Structure & Stability of Salts of Halogen
Oxyacids in the Solid Phase. Wiley.
Solzhenitsyn, Aleksandr. *see* Solzhenitsyn, Aleksandr
Isaevich.
Solzhenitsyn, Aleksandr I. *see* Solzhenitsyn, Aleksandr
Isaevich.
Solzhenitsyn, Aleksandr Isaevich, 1910-
xSolzhenitsyn, Aleksandr.
Candle in the Wind. U of Minn Pr.
Detente: Prospects for Democracy &
Dictatorship. Transaction Bks.
xSolzhenitsyn, Aleksandr I.
Cancer Ward. Dial.
xSolzhenitsyn, Alexander.
August 1914. Bantam.
August 1914. FS&G.
Cancer Ward. Bantam.
Cancer Ward. FS&G.
The First Circle. Bantam.
Nobel Lecture. FS&G.
Stories & Prose Poems. FS&G.
xSolzhenitsyn, Alexandr I.
First Circle. Har-Row.
Solzhenitsyn, Alexander. *see* Solzhenitsyn, Aleksandr
Isaevich.
Solzhenitsyn, Alexandr I. *see* Solzhenitsyn, Aleksandr
Isaevich.
Soma, John T.
xSoma, John T.
The Computer Industry: An Economic-Legal
Analysis of Its Technology & Growth.
Lexington Bks.
Sombart, Werner, 1863-1941
xSombart, Werner.
Socialism & the Social Movement. Kelley.
Somekh, Emile.
xSomekh, Emile.
Allergy & Your Child. Har-Row.
Somer, John. *see* Somer, John L.
Somer, John L.
xSomer, John.
Literary Experience: Public & Private Voices.
Scott F.
Somerfield, Elizabeth.
xSomerfield, Elizabeth.
The Boxer. Arco.
Somers, Gerald G. *see* Somers, Gerald George.

Somers, Gerald George.
xSomers, Gerald G.
ed. Retraining the Unemployed. U of Wis Pr.
Somers, Grover T. *see* Somers, Grover Thomas.
Somers, Grover Thomas, 1888-
xSomers, Grover T.
Pedagogical Prognosis: Predicting the Success
of Prospective Teachers. AMS Pr.
Somers, Herman M. *see* Somers, Herman Miles.
Somers, Herman Miles.
xSomers, Herman M.
Doctors, Patients, & Health Insurance: The
Organization & Financing of Medical Care.
Brookings.
Presidential Agency: OWMR, the Office of
War Mobilization & Reconversion.
Greenwood.
Somers, Robert, 1822-1891
xSomers, Robert.
The Southern States Since the War, 1870-71.
Arno.
The Southern States Since the War, 1870-71. U
of Ala Pr.
Somerset, J. A. *see* Somerset, J. A. B.
Somerset, J. A. B.
xSomerset, J. A.
ed. Four Tudor Interludes. Humanities.
Somerset, Rose.
xSomerset, Rose.
The Highwayman's Lady. Berkley Pub.
Somervell, D. C. *see* Somervell, David Churchill.
Somervell, David C. *see* Somervell, David Churchill.
Somervell, David Churchill, 1885-
xSomervell, D. C.
English Thought in the Nineteenth Century. R
West.
xSomervell, David C.
English Thought in the Nineteenth Century.
Greenwood.
Somerville, Christopher.
xSomerville, Christopher.
Walking Old Railways. David & Charles.
Somerville, Edith Anna Oenone.
xSomerville, Edith O.
The Real Charlotte. Intl Pubns Serv.
Somerville, Edith O. *see* Somerville, Edith Anna Oenone.
Somerville, Mary. *see* Somerville, Mary Fairfax.
Somerville, Mary Fairfax, 1780-1872
xSomerville, Mary.
Personal Recollections, from Early Life to Old
Age, of Mary Somerville. AMS Pr.
Somerville, Robert, 1940-
xSomerville, Robert.
Pope Alexander III & the Council of Tours
(1163): A Study of Ecclesiastical Politics &
Institutions in the Twelfth Century. U of Cal
Pr.
Somerville, Rose M.
xSomerville, Rose M.
Introduction to Family Life & Sex Education.
P-H.
Somfai, Laszlo.
xSomfai, Laszlo.
Joseph Haydn: His Life in Contemporary
Pictures. Taplinger.
Somit, Albert.
xSomit, Albert.
Development of American Political Science:
From Burgess to Behavioralism. Irvington.
Somjee, A. H. *see* Somjee, Abdulkarim Husseinbhoy.
Somjee, Abdulkarim Husseinbhoy.
xSomjee, A. H.
Political Theory of John Dewey. Tchrs Coll.
Sommar, H. G. *see* Sommar, Helen G.
Sommar, Helen G.
xSommar, H. G.
A Brief Guide to Sources of Fiber & Textile
Information. Textile Bk.
xSommar, Helen G.

A Brief Guide to Sources of Fiber & Textile
Information. Info Resources.
Sommer, Alfred, 1942-
xSommer, Alfred.
Epidemiology & Statistics for the
Ophthalmologist. Oxford U Pr.
Sommer, Barbara B. *see* Sommer, Barbara Baker.
Sommer, Barbara Baker, 1938-
xSommer, Barbara B.
Puberty & Adolescence. Oxford U Pr.
Sommer, Elyse.
xSommer, Elyse.
The Bread Dough Craft Book. Lothrop.
Designing with Cutouts: The Art of
Decoupage. Lothrop.
How to Make Money in the
Antiques-&-Collectibles Business. HM.
A Patchwork, Applique, & Quilting Primer.
Lothrop.
Sommer, H. Oskar. *see* Sommer, Heinrich Oskar.
Sommer, Heinrich Oskar, 1861-
xSommer, H. Oskar.
ed. Vulgate Version of the Arthurian
Romances. AMS Pr.
Sommer, Robert.
xSommer, Robert.
The End of Imprisonment. Oxford U Pr.
Sidewalk Fossils. Walker & Co.
Sommerfeld, Ray M. *see* Sommerfeld, Raynard M.
Sommerfeld, Raynard M.
xSommerfeld, Ray M.
The Dow Jones-Irwin Guide to Tax Planning.
Dow Jones-Irwin.
Federal Taxes & Management Decisions. Irwin.
An Introduction to Taxation. HarBraceJ.
Sommerfeldt, John R.
xSommerfeldt, John R.
ed. Cistercian Ideals & Reality. Cistercian
Pubns.
Sommerhoff, G.
xSommerhoff, Gerd.
Logic of the Living Brain. Wiley.
Sommerhoff, Gerd. *see* Sommerhoff, G.
Sommerich, Otto C.
xSommerich, Otto C.
Foreign Law: A Guide to Pleading & Proof.
Oceana.
Sommers, Justine.
xSommers, Justine.
Courageous Beauty. Ace Bks.
Sommerville, C. John. *see* Sommerville, Charles John.
Sommerville, Charles John, 1938-
xSommerville, C. John.
Popular Religion in Restoration England. U
Presses Fla.
Somogyi, J. C. *see* Somogyi, Johann Carl.
Somogyi, Johann Carl.
xSomogyi, J. C.
ed. Solution of Nutritional Problems: The
Contribution of Producers, Distributors &
Nutritionists. S Karger.
Sondheimer, E. *see* Sondheimer, Ernest.
Sondheimer, Ernest.
xSondheimer, E.
ed. Chemical Ecology. Acad Pr.
Sondley, Forster Alexander, 1857-1931
xSondley, Foster A.
A History of Buncombe County, North
Carolina. Reprint.
Sondley, Foster A. *see* Sondley, Forster Alexander.
Sone, Monica. *see* Sone, Monica Itoi.
Sone, Monica Itoi, 1919-
xSone, Monica.
Nisei Daughter. U of Wash Pr.
Sonenblum, Sidney.
xSonenblum, Sidney.

How Cities Provide Services: An Evaluation of
Alternative Delivery Structures. Ballinger
Pub.

Song, Bang-Song.
xSong, Bang-Song.
An Annotated Bibliography of Korean Music.
Asian Music Pub.

Song, Choan-Seng, 1929-
xSong, Choan-Seng.
Third-Eye Theology: Theology in Formation in
Asian Settings. Orbis Bks.

Song, Joseph, 1927-
xSong, Joseph.
Pathology of Sickle Cell Disease. C C Thomas.

Songe, Alice H.
xSonge, Alice H.
American Universities & Colleges: A
Dictionary of Name Changes. Scarecrow.

Soni, Atmaram H.
xSoni, Atmaram H.
Mechanism Synthesis & Analysis. McGraw.

Soni, R. L.
xSoni, R. L.
The Only Way to Deliverance. Great Eastern.

Sonneborn, Ruth A.
xSonneborn, Ruth A.
Friday Night Is Papa Night. Viking Pr.
I Love Gram. Viking Pr.
Question & Answer Book of Everyday Science.
Random.

Sonnenberg, G. J. see Sonnenberg, Gerrit Jacobus.

Sonnenberg, Gerrit Jacobus, 1903-
xSonnenberg, G. J.
Radar & Electronic Navigation. Butterworths.

Sonnenblick, E. see Sonnenblick, Edmund H.

Sonnenblick, Edmund H.
xSonnenblick, E.
ed. Exercise & Heart Disease. Grune.

Sonnenschmidt, Frederic H.
xSonnenschmidt, Fredric H.
The Professional Chef's Art of Garde Manger.
CBI Pub.

Sonnenschmidt, Fredric H. see Sonnenschmidt, Frederic
H.

Sonnichsen, C. L. see Sonnichsen, Charles Leland.

Sonnichsen, Charles Leland, 1901-
xSonnichsen, C. L.
From Hopalong to Hud: Thoughts on Western
Fiction. Tex A&M Univ Pr.
The Grave of John Wesley Hardin: Three
Essays on Grassroots History. Tex A&M
Univ Pr.
Outlaw: Bill Mitchell, Alias Baldy Russell: His
Life & Times. Swallow.

Sonquist, John A.
xSonquist, John A.
Multivariate Model Building: The Validation of
a Search Strategy. U of Mich Soc Res.
Survey & Opinion Research: Procedures for
Processing & Analysis. P-H.

Sontag, Alan.
xSontag, Alan.
The Bridge Bum: My Life & Play. Morrow.

Sontag, E. D. see Sontag, Eduardo D.

Sontag, Eduardo D.
xSontag, E. D.
Polynomial Response Maps. Springer-Verlag.

Sontag, Frederick.
xSontag, Frederick.
Existentialist Prolegomena: To a Future
Metaphysics. U of Chicago Pr.
God & America's Future. McGrath.
A Kierkegaard Handbook. John Knox.
Love Beyond Pain: Mysticism Within
Christianity. Paulist Pr.
What Can God Do?. Abingdon.

Sontag, Lester W. see Sontag, Lester Warren.

Sontag, Lester Warren.
xSontag, Lester W.

Fetal Heart Rate As a Behavioral Indicator.
Kraus Repr.

Sontag, Raymond J. see Sontag, Raymond James.

Sontag, Raymond James, 1897-
xSontag, Raymond J.
Broken World, 1919-1939. Har-Row.
xSontag, Raymond V.
A Broken World. Har-Row.

Sontag, Raymond V. see Sontag, Raymond James.

Sontag, Susan.
xSontag, Susan.
The Benefactor. Dell.
The Benefactor. FS&G.
ed. Death Kit. Dell.
Death Kit. FS&G.
I, Etcetera. FS&G.
I, Etcetera. Random.
Illness As Metaphor. FS&G.
Illness As Metaphor. Random.
ed. On Photography. Dell.
On Photography. FS&G.
Styles of Radical Will. Dell.
Styles of Radical Will. FS&G.

Sontheimer, Kurt.
xSontheimer, Kurt.
The Government & Politics of East Germany.
St Martin.
Government & Politics of West Germany.
Humanities.

Sontheimer, Stanley.
xSontheimer, Stanley.
Taxi Passengers Sertem: New York City
Edition. Bradley David Assocs.

Sonyel, S. R. see Sonyel, Salahi Ramsdan.

Sonyel, Salahi Ramsdan, 1932-
xSonyel, S. R.
Turkish Diplomacy, 1918-1923: Mustafa Kemal
& the Turkish National Movement. Sage.

Soo, Chee, 1919-
xSoo, Chee.
The Chinese Art of Kai Men.
Gordon-Cremonesi.

Soong, T. T.
xSoong, T. T.
Random Differential Equations in Science &
Engineering. Acad Pr.

Soons, Alan.
xSoons, Alan.
Alonso De Castillo Solorzano. Twayne.

Soothill, Keith.
xSoothill, Keith.
The Prisoner's Release: A Study of the
Employment of Ex-Prisoners. Allen Unwin.

Soothill, W. E. see Soothill, William Edward.

Soothill, William Edward.
xSoothill, W. E.
tr. The Lotus of the Wonderful Law: Or the
Lotus Gospel - Saddharma Pundarika Sutra
Miao-fa Lien Hua Ching. Rowman.

Sootin, Harry.
xSootin, Harry.
Gregor Mendel: Father of the Science of
Genetics. Vanguard.

Soper. see Soper, Michael R.

Soper, Alexander C. see Soper, Alexander Coburn.

Soper, Alexander Coburn, 1904-
xSoper, Alexander C.
The Evolution of Buddhist Architecture in
Japan. Hacker.

Soper, Davison E., 1943-
xSoper, Davison E.
Classical Field Theory. Wiley.

Soper, Edmund Davison, 1876-1961
xSoper, Edward D.
Racism, a World Issue. Negro U Pr.

Soper, Edward D. see Soper, Edmund Davison.

Soper, Michael R.
xSoper.

Guidelines to Chronic Care: A Team
Approach. R J Brady.

Sopher, Charles D.
xSopher, Charles D.
Soils & Soil Management. Reston.

Sopher, David E.
xSopher, David E.
ed. Exploration of India: Geographical
Perspectives on Society & Culture. Cornell U
Pr.

Sopher, Irvin M.
xSopher, Irvin M.
Forensic Dentistry. C C Thomas.

Sophian, J. see Sophian, John.

Sophian, John.
xSophian, J.
Pregnancy Nephropathy. Butterworths.

Sophocles.
xSophocles.
Ajax. Arno.
The Antigone. Allen Unwin.
Antigone. Cambridge U Pr.
Antigone. French & Eur.
Antigone. Har-Row.
Antigone. Oxford U Pr.
Electra: A Tragedy. AMS Pr.
Oedipus the King. Oxford U Pr.
Oedipus the King. U of Minn Pr.
Oedipus the King. PB.

Soppe, Dale.
xSoppe, Dale.
By Their Fruits You Shall Know Them. De
Vorss.

Sorabji, Richard.
xSorabji, Richard.
Aristotle on Memory. Brown U Pr.
Necessity, Cause & Blame: Perspectives on
Aristotle's Theory. Cornell U Pr.

Sorani, Giuliano.
xSorani, Giuliano.
Introduction to Real & Complex Manifolds.
Gordon.

Sorauf, Francis Joseph, 1928-
xSorauf, Frank J.
Party Politics in America. Little.

Sorauf, Frank J. see Sorauf, Francis Joseph.

Sorden, L. G. see Sorden, Leland George.

Sorden, Leland George.
xSorden, L. G.
I Am the Mississippi. Stanton & Lee.

Sordillo, Donald A., 1939-
xSordillo, Donald A.
The Programmer's ANSI COBOL Reference
Manual. P-H.

Sorel, Albert, 1842-1906
xSorel, Albert.
The Eastern Question in the Eighteenth
Century: The Partition of Poland & the
Treaty of Kainardji. Fertig.
Montesquieu. Kennikat.

Sorel, Edward, 1929-
xSorel, Edward.
Superpen: The Cartoons & Caricatures of
Edward Sorel. Random.

Sorel, George. see Sorel, Georges.

Sorel, Georges, 1847-1922
xSorel, George.
Reflections on Violence. Macmillan.
xSorel, Georges.
From Georges Sorel: Essays in Socialism &
Philosophy. Oxford U Pr.
The Illusions of Progress. U of Cal Pr.
Introduction a l'economie moderne. AMS Pr.
Reflections on Violence. AMS Pr.
Reflections on Violence. Peter Smith.

Sorell, Walter, 1905-
xSorell, Walter.

ed. Dance Has Many Faces. Columbia U Pr.
Hanya Holm: The Biography of an Artist.
  Columbia U Pr.
Story of the Human Hand. Bobbs.

Sorensen, Chris.
  xSorensen, Chris.
  Antique Airplanes. Scribner.
Sorensen, Jacki.
  xSorensen, Jacki.
  Aerobic Dancing. Rawson Wade.
Sorensen, Karen C. *see* Sorensen, Karen Creason.
Sorensen, Karen Creason.
  xSorensen, Karen C.
  Basic Nursing: A Psychophysiologic Approach.
    Saunders.
Sorensen, Virginia. *see* Sorensen, Virginia Eggertsen.
Sorensen, Virginia Eggertsen, 1912-
  xSorensen, Virginia.
  Friends of the Road. Atheneum.
  Lotte's Locket. HarBraceJ.
Sorenson, Gary.
  xSorenson, Gary W.
  Income Changes & Labor Force Participation.
    Oreg St U Pr.
Sorenson, Gary W. *see* Sorenson, Gary.
Sorenson, Herbert, 1898-
  xSorenson, Herbert.
  Psychology for Living. McGraw.
  Psychology in Education. McGraw.
Sorenson, Robert J. *see* Sorenson, Robert James.
Sorenson, Robert James.
  xSorenson, Robert J.
  Design for Accessibility. McGraw.
Sorenson, Virginia M.
  xSorenson, Virginia M.
  The Student Teacher's Handbook. Learning
    Pubns.
Sorin, Gerald, 1940-
  xSorin, Gerald.
  Abolitionism: A New Perspective. HR&W.
  Abolitionism: A New Perspective. Praeger.
Sorine, Daniel S.
  xSorine, Daniel S.
  Dancershoes. Knopf.
Sorkin, Alan. *see* Sorkin, Alan L.
Sorkin, Alan L.
  xSorkin, Alan.
  The Economics of the Postal System:
    Alternatives & Reform. Lexington Bks.
  xSorkin, Alan L.
  American Indians & Federal Aid. Brookings.
Sorley, W. R. *see* Sorley, William Ritchie.
Sorley, William Ritchie, 1855-1935
  xSorley, W. R.
  A History of British Philosophy to 1900.
    Greenwood.
Sorochan, Walter D.
  xSorochan, Walter D.
  Teaching Elementary Health Science. A-W.
  Teaching Secondary Health Science. Wiley.
Sorokin, Boris, 1922-
  xSorokin, Boris.
  Tolstoy in Prerevolutionary Russian Criticism.
    Ohio St U Pr.
Sorokin, Pitirim. *see* Sorokin, Pitirim Aleksandrovich.
Sorokin, Pitirim A. *see* Sorokin, Pitirim Aleksandrovich.
Sorokin, Pitirim Aleksandrovich, 1889-
  xSorokin, Pitirim.
  Fads & Foibles in Modern Sociology & Related
    Sciences. Greenwood.
  xSorokin, Pitirim A.

Altruistic Love: A Study of American Good
  Neighbors & Christian Saints. Kraus Repr.
American Sex Revolution. Porter Sargent.
Hunger As a Factor in Human Affairs. U
  Presses Fla.
A Long Journey: The Autobiography of Pitirim
  A. Sorokin. Coll & U Pr.
Society, Culture & Personality: Their Structure
  & Dynamics. a System of General Sociology.
  Cooper Sq.
Sociological Theories of Today. Arno.
Sorosky, Arthur D.
  xSorosky, Arthur D.
  The Adoption Triangle: The Effects of the
    Sealed Record on Adoptees, Birth Parents, &
    Adoptive Parents. Doubleday.
Sorrels, William W. *see* Sorrels, William Wright.
Sorrels, William Wright.
  xSorrels, William W.
  The Maroon Bulldogs: Mississippi State
    Football. Strode.
  Memphis' Greatest Debate: A Question of
    Water. Memphis St Univ.
Sorrentino, Anthony.
  xSorrentino, Anthony.
  How to Organize the Neighborhood for
    Delinquency Prevention. Human Sci Pr.
  Organizing Against Crime: Redeveloping the
    Neighborhood. Human Sci Pr.
Sorrentino, Gilbert.
  xSorrentino, Gilbert.
  Imaginative Qualities of Actual Things. SBD.
  The Orangery. U of Tex Pr.
  Steelwork. SBD.
  White Sail. Black Sparrow.
Sorrentino, Joseph. *see* Sorrentino, Joseph N.
Sorrentino, Joseph N.
  xSorrentino, Joseph.
  Moral Revolution. Manor Bks.
Sors, L. *see* Sors, Laszlo.
Sors, Laszlo.
  xSors, L.
  Fatigue Design of Machine Components.
    Pergamon.
Sorsby, A. *see* Sorsby, Arnold.
Sorsby, Arnold, 1900-
  xSorsby, A.
  Clinical Genetics. Butterworths.
  Diseases of the Fundus Oculi. Butterworths.
Sorum, C. Harvey. *see* Sorum, Clarence Harvey.
Sorum, Clarence Harvey, 1899-
  xSorum, C. Harvey.
  How to Solve General Chemistry Problems.
    P-H.
Sorum, Paul C. *see* Sorum, Paul Clay.
Sorum, Paul Clay, 1943-
  xSorum, Paul C.
  Intellectuals & Decolonization in France. U of
    NC Pr.
Sosa, Ernest.
  xSosa, Ernest.
  ed. Causation & Conditionals. Oxford U Pr.
Sosin, Jack M.
  xSosin, Jack M.
  Agents & Merchants: British Colonial Policy &
    the Origins of the American Revolution,
    1763-1775. U of Nebr Pr.
  ed. Opening of the West. U of SC Pr.
  The Revolutionary Frontier, 1763-1783. U of
    NM Pr.
Sosin, Mark.
  xSosin, Mark.
  Practical Black Bass Fishing. Crown.
  Practical Light Tackle Fishing. Doubleday.
Sosna, Morton.
  xSosna, Morton.
  In Search of the Silent South: Southern
    Liberals & the Race Issue. Columbia U Pr.
Sosne, Michael.
  xSosne, Michael.

Handbook of Adapted Physical Education
  Equipment & Its Use. C C Thomas.
Sosnoff, Martin T.
  xSosnoff, Martin T.
  Humble on Wall Street. Arlington Hse.
Soth, Lauren. *see* Soth, Lauren K.
Soth, Lauren K.
  xSoth, Lauren.
  Farm Trouble. Greenwood.
Sotheran, Charles, 1847-1902
  xSotheran, Charles.
  Horace Greeley & Other Pioneers of American
    Socialism. Hyperion Conn.
Soto, Benigno.
  xSoto, Benigno.
  Radiographic Anatomy of the Coronary
    Arteries: An Atlas. Futura Pub.
Soto, Gary.
  xSoto, Gary.
  The Tale of Sunlight. U of Pittsburgh Pr.
Soto, Osvaldo N.
  xSoto, Osvaldo N.
  Repaso De Gramatica. HarBraceJ.
Soubiran, Andre, 1910-
  xSoubiran, Andre.
  Open Letter to a Woman of Today. Heineman.
Soucek, Branko.
  xSoucek, Branko.
  Computers in Neurobiology & Behavior. Wiley.
Soucheray, Joe.
  xSoucheray, Joe.
  Bruce Jenner. Creative Ed.
  Fred Lynn. Creative Ed.
  Walter Payton. Creative Ed.
Souckova, Milada, 1899-
  xSouckova, Milada.
  Literary Satellite. Czechoslovak-Russian
    Literary Relations. U of Chicago Pr.
Souerwine, Andrew H.
  xSouerwine, Andrew H.
  Career Strategies: Planning for Personal
    Achievement. Am Mgmt.
Soule, Gardner.
  xSoule, Gardner.
  The Maybe Monsters. Putnam.
  Men Who Dared the Sea: The Ocean
    Adventures of the Ancient Mariners. T Y
    Crowell.
Soule, George, 1834-1926
  xSoule, George.
  Soule's New Science & Practice of Accounts.
    Arno.
  ed. The Theatre of the Mind. P-H.
Soule, George. *see* Soule, George Henry.
Soule, George H. *see* Soule, George Henry.
Soule, George Henry, 1887-
  xSoule, George.
  A Planned Society. Quality Lib.
  xSoule, George H.
  Ideas of the Great Economists. NAL.
  The Planned Society. Peter Smith.
Soulen, Richard N., 1933-
  xSoulen, Richard N.
  Handbook of Biblical Criticism. John Knox.
Soulsby, E. J. *see* Soulsby, E. J. L.
Soulsby, E. J. L.
  xSoulsby, E. J.
  ed. Immunity to Animal Parasites. Acad Pr.
Sound Research Laboratories.
  xSound Research Laboratories.
  Basic Vibration Control. Methuen Inc.
  Practical Building Acoustics. Methuen Inc.
Souper. *see* Souper, Patrick C.
Souper, Patrick C.
  xSouper.
  About to Teach: An Introduction to Method in
    Teaching. Routledge & Kegan.
Source Inc.
  xTheSource Collective.

Organizing for Health Care: A Tool for
Change. Beacon Pr.
Sourek, Otakar.
xSourek, Otakar.
The Chamber Music of Antonin Dvorak.
Greenwood.
The Orchestral Works of Antonin Dvorak.
Greenwood.
Sourirajan, S.
xSourirajan, S.
Reverse Osmosis. Acad Pr.
Soustelle, Jacques, 1912-
xSoustelle, Jacques.
Daily Life of the Aztecs on the Eve of the
Spanish Conquest. Stanford U Pr.
Soutar, George, 1864-1939
xSoutar, George.
Nature in Greek Poetry, Studies Partly
Comparative. Johnson Repr.
South Africa - Commissioner On Native Grievances
Inquiry. *see* South Africa. Commissioner on Native
Grievances Inquiry.
**South Africa. Commissioner on Native Grievances
Inquiry.**
xSouth Africa - Commissioner On Native
Grievances Inquiry.
Report of the Native Grievances Inquiry,
1913-1914. Negro U Pr.
South African Native Races Committee, London.
xSouth African Native Races Committee.
ed. South African Natives, Their Progress &
Present Condition. Negro U Pr.
South Atlantic Modern Language Association.
xSouth Atlantic Modern Language Association.
South Atlantic Studies for Sturgis E. Leavitt.
Arno.
The South Atlantic Quarterly.
xSouth Atlantic Quarterly.
Fifty Years of the South Atlantic Quarterly.
Arno.
South East Regional Computer Conference, 1st. *see*
Southeast Asia Regional Computer Conference, 1st.,
Singapore, 1976.
South, G. F.
xSouth, G. F.
Boolean Algebra & It's Uses. Van Nos
Reinhold.
South, Grace.
xSouth, Grace.
Merrie. Doubleday.
South Kensington Museum, London.
xSouth Kensington Museum, London.
First Proofs of the Universal Catalogue of
Books on Art. B Franklin.
South Penn School Study Council.
xSouth Penn School Study Council.
Developing Staff Attitudes in Junior High
Schools. Interstate.
Muslim Heartlands. Interstate.
Southall, Ivan.
xSouthall, Ivan.
Ash Road. Greenwillow.
Fly West. Macmillan.
Hills End. Macmillan.
A Journey of Discovery: On Writing for
Children. Macmillan.
King of the Sticks. Greenwillow.
Matt & Jo. Macmillan.
Southall, Raymond.
xSouthall, Raymond.
The Courtly Maker: An Essay on the Poetry of
Wyatt & His Contemporaries. Biblio Dist.
Southam, B. C.
xSoutham, B. C.
Guide to the Selected Poems of T. S. Eliot.
HarBraceJ.
Southampton Conf. on Short-Run Econometric Models of
UK Economy. *see* Southampton Conference on Short
Run Econometric Models of the U.K. Economy,
University of Southampton, 1969.

**Southampton Conference on Short Run Econometric
Models of the U.K. Economy, University of
Southampton, 1969.**
xSouthampton Conf. on Short-Run Econometric
Models of UK Economy.
Econometric Study of the UK: Proceedings.
Kelley.
Southard, Samuel.
xSouthard, Samuel.
Religious Inquiry: An Introduction to the Why
& How. Abingdon.
**Southeast Asia Regional Computer Conference, 1st.,
Singapore, 1976.**
xSouth East Regional Computer Conference, 1st.
SEARCC 76: Proceedings. Elsevier.
Southeast Asia Sawmill Seminar, 1st, Singapore, 1975.
xSoutheast Asia Sawmill Seminar, 1st,Singapore,
June 1975.
Sawmill Techniques for Southeast Asia:
Proceedings. Miller Freeman.
Southeast Asia Sawmill Seminar, 1st,Singapore, June
1975. *see* Southeast Asia Sawmill Seminar, 1st,
Singapore, 1975.
Southerland, Ellease, 1943-
xSoutherland, Ellease.
Let the Lion Eat Straw. NAL.
Let the Lion Eat Straw. Scribner.
Let the Lion Eat Straw. G K Hall.
Southern California Research Council.
xSouthern California Research Council.
The Air of Southern California: How Clean &
at What Price?. Econ Res Ctr.
Dignity or Despair: The Economics of Aging in
Southern California. Econ Res Ctr.
Southern Education Reporting Service.
xSouthern Education Reporting Service.
With All Deliberate Speed:
Segregation-Desegregation in Southern
Schools. Negro U Pr.
Southern, Eileen.
xSouthern, Eileen.
Music of Black Americans: A History. Norton.
ed. Readings in Black American Music.
Norton.
Southern, Richard.
xSouthern, Richard.
The Staging of Plays Before Shakespeare.
Theatre Arts.
**Southern Society for the Promotion of the Study of
Race Conditions and Problems in the South.**
xSouthern Society For The Promotion Of The
Study Of Race Conditions And Problems In The
South.
Race Problems of the South. Negro U Pr.
Southern Sociological Congress.
xSouthern Sociological Congress.
Call of the New South: Addresses Delivered at
the Southern Sociological Congress. Negro U
Pr.
Democracy in Earnest. Negro U Pr.
Southerne, Thomas.
xSoutherne, Thomas.
Oroonoko. U of Nebr Pr.
Southey, Robert.
xSouthey, Robert.
Chronicle of the Cid. R West.
History of Brazil. B Franklin.
History of Brazil. Greenwood.
Southey's Life of Nelson. AMS Pr.
Southward, A. J.
xSouthward, Alan J.
Life on the Sea-Shore. Harvard U Pr.
Southward, Alan J. *see* Southward, A. J.
Southwell Cathedral.
xSouthwell Cathedral.
Visitations & Memorials of Southwell Minister.
Johnson Repr.
Southwell, Eugene A.
xSouthwell, Eugene A.

Personality: Readings in Theory & Research.
Brooks-Cole.
Southwell, Robert, 1561?-1595
xSouthwell, Robert.
Complete Poems of Robert Southwell. AMS Pr.
Marie Magdalens Funeral Teares. Schol
Facsimiles.
Two Letters & Short Rules of a Good Life.
Folger Bks.
Southwell, Samuel B.
xSouthwell, Samuel B.
Quest for Eros: Browning & "Fifine". U Pr of
Ky.
Southwell, Sheila.
xSouthwell, Sheila.
Painting China & Porcelain. Sterling.
Southwest Educational Development Laboratory.
xSouthwest Educational Development Laboratory.
Bilingual Continuous Progress Mathematics.
NELP.
Bilingual Early Childhood Program:
Supplementary Activities: Level II. NELP.
Bilingual Kindergarten Program. NELP.
Concepts & Language. NELP.
Paso a Paso. NELP.
Southwick, Arthur F.
xSouthwick, Arthur F.
The Law of Hospital & Health Care
Administration. Health Admin Pr.
Southwick, Charles H.
xSouthwick, Charles H.
Ecology & the Quality of Our Environment.
Van Nos Reinhold.
Southwick, F. Townsend. *see* Southwick, Frank
Townsend.
Southwick, Frank Townsend.
xSouthwick, F. Townsend.
Steps to Oratory: A School Speaker. Arno.
Southwick, Marcia.
xSouthwick, Marcia.
Build with Adobe. Swallow.
Southworth, Constant, 1894-
xSouthworth, Constant.
The French Colonial Venture. Arno.
Southworth, Franklin. *see* Southworth, Franklin C.
Southworth, Franklin C.
xSouthworth, Franklin.
Student's Hindi-Urdu Reference Manual. U of
Ariz Pr.
xSouthworth, Franklin C.
Foundations of Linguistics. Free Pr.
Southworth, Herbert R. *see* Southworth, Herbert
Rutledge.
Southworth, Herbert Rutledge.
xSouthworth, Herbert R.
Guernica! Guernica!: A Study of Journalism,
Diplomacy, Propaganda, & History. U of Cal
Pr.
Southworth, James A. *see* Southworth, James Granville.
Southworth, James G. *see* Southworth, James Granville.
Southworth, James Granville, 1896-
xSouthworth, James A.
More Modern American Poets. Folcroft.
xSouthworth, James G.
More Modern American Poets. Arno.
The Prosody of Chaucer & His Followers:
Supplementary Chapters to "Verses of
Cadence". Greenwood.
Some Modern American Poets. Arno.
Southworth, Susan.
xSouthworth, Susan.
Ornamental Ironwork: An Illustrated Guide to
Its Design, History & Use in American
Architecture. Godine.
Souvarine, Boris.
xSouvarine, Boris.
Stalin: A Critical Survey of Bolshevism. Arno.
Stalin: A Critical Survey of Bolshevism.
Octagon.
Souviney. *see* Souviney, Randall.

Souviney, Randall.
xSouviney.
Mathmatters: Developing Computational Skills with Developmental Sequences. Goodyear.

Sovern, M. I. *see* Sovern, Michael I.
Sovern, Michael I.
xSovern, M. I.
Legal Restraints on Racial Discrimination in Employment. Kraus Repr.
Sovik, E. A.
xSovik, Edward A.
Architecture for Worship. Augsburg.
Sovik, Edward A. *see* Sovik, E. A.
Sovold, Pamela.
xSovold, Pamela.
Market Notebook. Madrona Pubs.
Soward, Frederic H. *see* Soward, Frederic Hubert.
Soward, Frederic Hubert.
xSoward, Frederic H.
Canada & the United Nations. Greenwood.
Sowell, Ellis. *see* Sowell, Ellis Mast.
Sowell, Ellis Mast.
xSowell, Ellis.
The Evolution of the Theories & Techniques of Standard Costs. U of Ala Pr.
Sowell, Thomas, 1930-
xSowell, Thomas.
Affirmative Action Reconsidered: Was It Necessary in Academia?. Am Enterprise.
Classical Economics Reconsidered. Princeton U Pr.
ed. Essays & Data on American Ethnic Groups. Urban Inst.
Knowledge & Decisions. Basic.
Race & Economics. Longman.
Sowers, Miriam.
xSowers, Miriam.
Parables from Paradise. Branden.
Sowls, Lyle K.
xSowls, Lyle K.
Prairie Ducks: A Study of Their Behavior, Ecology & Management. U of Nebr Pr.
Sox, Harold C.
xSox, Harold C.
ed. Carbohydrate Moieties of Immunoglobulin. Mss Info.
Soyer, Abraham.
xSoyer, Abraham.
Adventures of Yemima & Other Stories. Viking Pr.
Soyer, Raphael, 1899-
xSoyer, Raphael.
Diary of an Artist. New Republic.
Soyinka, Wole.
xSoyinka, Wole.
The Bacchae of Euripides: A Communion Rite. Norton.
Collected Plays. Oxford U Pr.
A Shuttle in the Crypt. Hill & Wang.
Sozialdemokratische Partei Deutschlands.
xSozialdemokratische Partei Deutschlands.
Protokoll der Verhandlungen Des Parteitages. Greenwood.
Space Electronics, Los Angeles, 1965.
xSpace Electronics Symposium - Los Angeles - 1965.
Space Electronics Symposium: Proceedings. Am Astronaut.
Space Electronics Symposium - Los Angeles - 1965. *see* Space Electronics, Los Angeles, 1965.
Space Science Board. *see* National Research Council. Panel on Planetary Astronomy.
Spache, Evelyn B.
xSpache, Evelyn B.
Reading Activities for Child Involvement. Allyn.
Spache, George D. *see* Spache, George Daniel.
Spache, George Daniel.
xSpache, George D.

Art of Efficient Reading. Macmillan.
Diagnosing & Correcting Reading Disabilities. Allyn.
Good Reading for Poor Readers. Garrard.
Good Reading for the Disadvantaged Reader: Multi-Ethnic Resources. Garrard.
Spackman, Robert R.
xSpackman, Robert R.
Conditioning for Baseball: Pre-Season, Regular Season & Off-Season. C C Thomas.
Conditioning for Football: Pre-Season, Regular Season & Off-Season. C C Thomas.
Exercise in the Office: Easy Ways to Better Health & Firmer Figures. S Ill U Pr.
Spackman, W. M. *see* Spackman, William Mode.
Spackman, William Mode, 1905-
xSpackman, W. M.
An Armful of Warm Girl. Knopf.
Spacks, Barry.
xSpacks, Barry.
Imagining a Unicorn. U of Ga Pr.
Spacks, Patricia. *see* Spacks, Patricia Ann (Meyer).
Spacks, Patricia Ann (Meyer).
xSpacks, Patricia.
ed. Late Augustan Poetry. Irvington.
Spada, James.
xSpada, James.
Captain & Tennille. Creative Ed.
The Films of Robert Redford. Citadel Pr.
Spadoni, Adriana.
xSpadoni, Adriana.
Not All Rivers. AMS Pr.
Spady, Richard H., 1952-
xSpady, Richard H.
Econometric Estimation of Cost Functions for the Regulated Transportation Industries. Garland Pub.
Spaet, Theodore H.
xSpaet, Theodore H.
ed. Progress in Hemostasis & Thrombosis. Grune.
ed. Progress on Hemostasis & Thrombosis. Grune.
Spaeth, Adolph, 1839-1910
xSpaeth, Adolph.
Charles Porterfield Krauth. Arno.
Spaeth, Harold J.
xSpaeth, Harold J.
Introduction to Supreme Court Decision Making. Har-Row.
Supreme Court Policy Making: Explanation & Prediction. W H Freeman.
Spaeth, J. Duncan. *see* Spaeth, John Duncan Ernst.
Spaeth, John Duncan Ernst, 1868-1954
xSpaeth, J. Duncan.
tr. Old English Poetry. Gordian.
Spaeth, Sigmund. *see* Spaeth, Sigmund Gottfried.
Spaeth, Sigmund G. *see* Spaeth, Sigmund Gottfried.
Spaeth, Sigmund Gottfried, 1885-1965
xSpaeth, Sigmund.
Fifty Years with Music. Greenwood.
Read'em & Weep: The Songs You Forgot to Remember. Da Capo.
Weep Some More, My Lady. Da Capo.
xSpaeth, Sigmund G.
At Home with Music. Arno.
The Common Sense of Music. Greenwood.
Great Symphonies: How to Recognize & Remember Them. Greenwood.
Spaethling, Robert.
xSpaethling, Robert.
ed. Reader in German Literature. Oxford U Pr.
Spain, August O., 1907-
xSpain, August O.
Political Theory of John C. Calhoun. Octagon.
Spain, Barry.
xSpain, Barry.

Functions of Mathematical Physics. Van Nos Reinhold.
Spain, David H.
xSpain, David H.
ed. The Human Experience: Readings in Sociocultural Anthropology. Dorsey.
Spain, Hensley.
xSpain, Hensley.
The Avocado Cookbook. Creative Arts Bk.
Spain, Rufus B.
xSpain, Rufus B.
At Ease in Zion: A Social History of Southern Baptists, 1865-1900. Vanderbilt U Pr.
Spainhower, James I.
xSpainhower, James I.
Pulpit, Pew & Politics. Bethany Pr.
Spalding, Eugenia (Kennedy).
xSpalding, Eugenia K.
Professional Nursing: Foundations, Perspectives & Relationships. Lippincott.
Spalding, Eugenia K. *see* Spalding, Eugenia (Kennedy).
Spalding, Henry D.
xSpalding, Henry D.
Encyclopedia of Black Folklore & Humor. Jonathan David.
The Nixon Nobody Knows. Jonathan David.
Spalding, Hobart.
xSpalding, Hobart A.
Organized Labor in Latin America: Historical Case Studies of Workers in Dependent Societies. NYU Pr.
Spalding, Hobart A. *see* Spalding, Hobart.
Spalding, J. Howard. *see* Spalding, John Howard.
Spalding, John Howard.
xSpalding, J. Howard.
Introduction to Swedenborg's Religious Thought. Swedenborg.
Spalding, John L. *see* Spalding, John Lancaster.
Spalding, John Lancaster, Abp, 1840-1916
xSpalding, John L.
Opportunity, & Other Essays & Addresses. Arno.
Spalding, Phinizy.
xSpalding, Phinizy.
Oglethorpe in America. U of Chicago Pr.
Spalding, Walter R. *see* Spalding, Walter Raymond.
Spalding, Walter Raymond, 1865-1962
xSpalding, Walter R.
Music at Harvard: A Historical Review of Men & Events. Da Capo.
Spalek, John M.
xSpalek, John M.
German Expressionism in the Fine Arts: A Bibliography. Hennessey.
Guide to the Archival Materials of the German-Speaking Emigration to the United States After 1933: Verzeichnis der Quellen und Materialien der Deutschspragen Emigration in den U. S. A. Seit 1933. U Pr of Va.
Spande, Norma.
xSpande, Norma.
Your Guide to Successful Home Bible Studies. Nelson.
Spangler, Charles W.
xSpangler, Charles W.
Organic Chemistry: A Brief Contemporary Perspective. P-H.
Spangler, Earl.
xSpangler, Earl.
Negro in America. Lerner Pubns.
Spangler, Merlin G. *see* Spangler, Merlin Grant.
Spangler, Merlin Grant.
xSpangler, Merlin G.
Soil Engineering. Har-Row.
Spanier, David.
xSpanier, David.
Total Poker. S&S.
Spanier, Edwin H. *see* Spanier, Edwin Henry.

Spanier, Edwin Henry, 1921-
 xSpanier, Edwin H.
  Algebraic Topology. McGraw.
Spanier, Graham B.
 xSpanier, Graham B.
  Human Sexuality in a Changing Society.
  Burgess.
Spanier, Jerome.
 xSpanier, Jerome.
  Monte Carlo Principles & Neutron Transport
  Problems. A-W.
Spanier, John. see Spanier, John W.
Spanier, John W.
 xSpanier, John.
  American Foreign Policy Since World War II.
  HR&W.
  How American Foreign Policy Is Made.
  Krieger.
 xSpanier, John W.
  Truman-MacArthur Controversy & the Korean
  War. Norton.
Spann, J. Richard. see Spann, John Richard.
Spann, John Richard, 1891-
 xSpann, J. Richard.
  ed. Christian Faith & Secularism. Kennikat.
Spann, Meno, 1903-
 xSpann, Meno.
  Franz Kafka. Twayne.
Spann, Nancie.
 xSpann, Nancie.
  The Last Meal on Earth. Cal Living Bks.
Spann, Othmar. see Spann, Othmar.
Spann, Othmar, 1878-1950
 xSpann, Othman.
  The History of Economics. Arno.
Spann, R. N.
 xSpann, R. N.
  Government Administration in Australia. Allen
  Unwin.
Spann, Robert M.
 xSpann, Robert M.
  The Supply of Natural Resources: The Case of
  Oil & Natural Gas. Arno.
Spanos, William V.
 xSpanos, William V.
  Christian Tradition in Modern British Verse
  Drama: The Poetics of Sacramental Time.
  Rutgers U Pr.
  ed. Martin Heidegger & the Question of
  Literature: Toward a Postmodern Literary
  Hermeneutics. Ind U Pr.
Spanuth, Jurgen.
 xSpanuth, Jurgen.
  Atlantis of the North. Van Nos Reinhold.
Sparano, Vin. see Sparano, Vin T.
Sparano, Vin T.
 xSparano, Vin.
  Complete Outdoors Encyclopedia. Har-Row.
 xSparano, Vin T.
  ed. The American Fisherman's Fresh & Salt
  Water Guide. Follett.
  ed. The American Fisherman's Fresh & Salt
  Water Guide. Winchester Pr.
  The Complete Outdoors Encyclopedia.
  Har-Row.
Sparberg, Marshall, 1936-
 xSparberg, Marshall.
  Ileostomy Care. C C Thomas.
Sparer, Fred.
 xSparer, Fred.
  How to Build Recreational Vehicle Parks.
  Trail-R.
Spargo, Emma J. see Spargo, Emma Jane Marie.
Spargo, Emma Jane Marie, Sister.
 xSpargo, Emma J.
  The Category of the Aesthetic in the
  Philosophy of Saint Bonaventure. Franciscan
  Inst.
Spargo, John, 1876-1966
 xSpargo, John.

 Early American Pottery & China. C E Tuttle.
 The Potters & Potteries of Bennington. Peter
 Smith.
Spark, Muriel.
 xSpark, Muriel.
  The Abbess of Crewe. Penguin.
  The Hothouse by the East River. Penguin.
  Not to Disturb. Penguin.
  Prime of Miss Jean Brodie. Dell.
  Prime of Miss Jean Brodie. Lippincott.
  The Takeover. Penguin.
  Territorial Rights. Coward.
Sparke, William.
 xSparke, William.
  Doublespeak: Language for Sale. Har-Row.
Sparkes, Roy.
 xSparkes, Roy.
  Painting Without a Brush. David & Charles.
Sparkes, Vernone M., 1938-
 xSparkes, Vernone M.
  Theological Enterprise. Herald Hse.
Sparkia, Roy.
 xSparkia, Roy.
  The Dirty Rotten Truth. NAL.
Sparkman, Brandon.
 xSparkman, Brandon.
  Preparing Your Preschooler for Reading: A
  Book of Games. Schocken.
Sparkman, G. Temp. see Sparkman, Temp.
Sparkman, Temp.
 xSparkman, G. Temp.
  Writing Your Own Worship Materials. Judson.
Sparks, Beatrice. see Sparks, Beatrice Mathews.
Sparks, Beatrice Mathews.
 xSparks, Beatrice.
  ed. Jay's Journal. Times Bks.
Sparks, Donald B.
 xSparks, Donald B.
  Administrative Improvement Methods. Gulf
  Pub.
Sparks, Edwin E. see Sparks, Edwin Erle.
Sparks, Edwin Erle, 1860-1924
 xSparks, Edwin E.
  National Development, 1877-1885. Scholarly.
Sparks, F. E. see Sparks, Francis Edgar.
Sparks, Francis E. see Sparks, Francis Edgar.
Sparks, Francis Edgar.
 xSparks, F. E.
  Causes of the Maryland Revolution of 1689.
  Johnson Repr.
 xSparks, Francis E.
  Causes of the Maryland Revolution of 1689.
  AMS Pr.
Sparks, Howard.
 xSparks, Howard.
  Amazing Mail Order Business & How to
  Succeed in It. Fell.
Sparks, J. E.
 xSparks, J. E.
  Read Right: Comprehension Power. Glencoe.
  Reading for Power & Flexibility. Glencoe.
Sparks, James A. see Sparks, James Allen.
Sparks, James Allen, 1933-
 xSparks, James A.
  Potshots at the Preacher. Abingdon.
Sparks, John.
 xSparks, John.
  Owls: Their Natural & Unnatural History.
  Taplinger.
Sparling, Edward J. see Sparling, Edward James.
Sparling, Edward James, 1896-
 xSparling, Edward J.
  Do College Students Choose Vocations
  Wisely?. AMS Pr.
Sparling, S. R. see Sparling, Shirley Ray.
Sparling, Shirley Ray.
 xSparling, S. R.
  Botany: A Laboratory Manual. Macmillan.
Sparling, Wayne. see Sparling, Wayne C.

Sparling, Wayne C.
 xSparling, Wayne.
  Southern Idaho Ghost Towns. Caxton.
Sparnon, Norman. see Sparnon, Norman J.
Sparnon, Norman J.
 xSparnon, Norman.
  A Guide to Japanese Flower Arrangement. C E
  Tuttle.
Sparrow, Geoffrey.
 xSparrow, Geoffrey.
  Foxes & Physic. J A Allen.
Sparrow, Gregory S. see Sparrow, Gregory Scott.
Sparrow, Gregory Scott.
 xSparrow, Gregory S.
  Lucid Dreaming: Dawning of the Clear
  Light-Based on the Edgar Cayce Readings.
  ARE Pr.
Sparrow, Jane.
 xSparrow, Jane.
  Diary of a Delinquent Episode. Routledge &
  Kegan.
  Diary of a Student Social Worker. Routledge &
  Kegan.
Sparrow, John. see Sparrow, John Hanbury Angus.
Sparrow, John Hanbury Angus, 1906-
 xSparrow, John.
  Half Lines & Repetitions in Virgil. Garland
  Pub.
  Independent Essays. Greenwood.
Sparrow, W. Keats. see Sparrow, Wendall Keats.
Sparrow, Wendall Keats.
 xSparrow, W. Keats.
  The Practical Craft: Readings for Business &
  Technical Writers. HM.
Spartanburg Unit of the S.C. Writers' Program. see
 Writers' Program. North Carolina.
Spater, George.
 xSpater, George.
  A Marriage of True Minds: An Intimate
  Portrait of Leonard & Virginia Woolf.
  HarBraceJ.
Spatz, Don.
 xSpatz, Donald.
  A Few Kind Words. Bodine.
Spatz, Donald. see Spatz, Don.
Spatz, Jonas, 1935-
 xSpatz, Jonas.
  Hollywood in Fiction: Some Versions of the
  American Myth. Mouton.
Spatz, Lois.
 xSpatz, Lois S.
  Aristophanes. Twayne.
Spatz, Lois S. see Spatz, Lois.
Spaulding, C. E.
 xSpaulding, C. E.
  The Complete Care of Orphaned or
  Abandoned Baby Animals. Rodale Pr Inc.
Spaulding, E. Wilder. see Spaulding, Ernest Wilder.
Spaulding, Edith R. see Spaulding, Edith Rogers.
Spaulding, Edith Rogers, 1881-
 xSpaulding, Edith R.
  Experimental Study of Psychopathic
  Delinquent Women. Patterson Smith.
Spaulding, Ernest Wilder, 1899-
 xSpaulding, E. Wilder.
  Ambassadors Ordinary & Extraordinary. Pub
  Aff Pr.
Spaulding, Robert K. see Spaulding, Robert Kilgurn.
Spaulding, Robert Kilgurn, 1898
 xSpaulding, Robert K.
  How Spanish Grew. Peter Smith.
  How Spanish Grew. U of Cal Pr.
Spaulding, Seth.
 xSpaulding, Seth.
  The World's Students in the United States: A
  Review & Evaluation of Research on Foreign
  Students. Praeger.
Speads, Carola H.
 xSpeads, Carola H.

Breathing: The ABCs. Har-Row.
Breathing: The ABC's. Har-Row.
Speaight, George.
xSpeaight, George.
History of the English Toy Theatre. Plays.
Speaight, Robert, 1904-
xSpeaight, Robert.
Life of Hilaire Belloc. Arno.
Spear, Athena T. see Spear, Athena Tacha.
Spear, Athena Tacha.
xSpear, Athena T.
Brancusi's Birds. NYU Pr.
Spear, Mary E. see Spear, Mary Eleanor.
Spear, Mary Eleanor.
xSpear, Mary E.
Practical Charting Techniques. McGraw.
Spear, Norman E.
xSpear, Norman E.
ed. Ontogeny of Learning & Memory. Halsted
Pr.
The Processing of Memories: Forgetting &
Retention. Halsted Pr.
Spear, Percival. see Spear, Thomas George Percival.
Spear, Richard E., 1940-
xSpear, Richard E.
Caravaggio & His Followers. Har-Row.
Spear, Roberta.
xSpear, Roberta.
Silks. HR&W.
Spear, Thomas George Percival.
xSpear, Percival.
India: A Modern History. U of Mich Pr.
Spear, Victor I. see Spear, Victor Irwin.
Spear, Victor Irwin.
xSpear, Victor I.
Sports Illustrated Racquetball. Lippincott.
Speare, Elizabeth G. see Speare, Elizabeth George.
Speare, Elizabeth George.
xSpeare, Elizabeth G.
The Bronze Bow. HM.
Bronze Bow. HM.
Calico Captive. HM.
Spearing, A. C.
xSpearing, A. C.
Medieval Dream-Poetry. Cambridge U Pr.
Spearman, Charles. see Spearman, Charles Edward.
Spearman, Charles E. see Spearman, Charles Edward.
Spearman, Charles Edward, 1863-1945
xSpearman, Charles.
The Nature of "Intelligence" & the Principles of
Cognition. Arno.
xSpearman, Charles E.
Abilities of Man, Their Nature &
Measurement. AMS Pr.
Spearman, Frank H.
xSpearman, Frank H.
Whispering Smith. Nordon Pubns.
Spearritt, Peter.
xSpearritt, Peter.
ed. Australian Popular Culture. Allen Unwin.
Spears, Betty. see Spears, Betty Mary.
Spears, Betty Mary.
xSpears, Betty.
History of Sport & Physical Activity in the
United States. Wm C. Brown.
Spears, Charleszine (Wood).
xSpears, Charleszine W.
How to Wear Colors: With Emphasis on Dark
Skins. Burgess.
Spears, Charleszine W. see Spears, Charleszine (Wood).
Spears, Harold, 1902-
xSpears, Harold.
Principles of Teaching. Greenwood.
Spears, Jack, 1919-
xSpears, Jack.
The Civil War on the Screen & Other Essays.
A S Barnes.
Spears, John R. see Spears, John Randolph.
Spears, John Randolph, 1850-1936
xSpears, John R.

Illustrated Sketches of Death Valley & Other
Borax Deserts of the Pacific Coast. Sagebrush
Pr.
Stories of the Sea. Arno.
Spears, Monroe K. see Spears, Monroe Kirklyndorf.
Spears, Monroe Kirklyndorf.
xSpears, Monroe K.
The Levitator & Other Poems. Pilgrim Pr.
Spears, W. H.
xSpears, W. H.
Constantine's Triumph: A Tale of the Era of
the Martyrs. Spears.
Greek Fire: The Fabulous Secret Weapon That
Saved Europe. Spears.
Speas, Jan C. see Speas, Jan Cox.
Speas, Jan Cox.
xSpeas, Jan C.
Bride of the Machugh. Avon.
The Growing Season. Avon.
Speca, Bob.
xSpeca, Bob.
The Great Falling Domino Book. Warner Bks.
Specht, Harry.
xSpecht, Harry.
Integrating Social Work Methods. Allen
Unwin.
Special Collections Department. see Merril Library.
Special Collections Dept.
Special Commission on Investigation of the Judicial
System, Commonwealth of Massachusetts. see
Massachusetts. Special Commission on Investigation of
the Judicial System.
Special Committee, New York City Bar Association. see
Association of the Bar of the City of New York.
Committee on the Medical Expert Testimony Project.
Special Committee of the Senate to Investigate Organized
Crime in Interstate Commerce. see United States.
Congress. Senate. Special Committee to Investigate
Organized Crime in Interstate Commerce.
Special Committee on Campus Tensions.
xSpecial Committee on Campus Tensions.
Campus Tensions: Analysis &
Recommendations. ACE.
Special Grand Jury, Commonwealth of Pennsylvania. see
Philadelphia Co., Grand Jury.
**Special Libraries Associations. Networking Committee.
Guidelines Subcommittee.**
xGuidelines Subcommittee, SLA Networking
Committee.
Getting into Networking: Guidelines for
Special Libraries. SLA.
Speck, Frank G. see Speck, Frank Gouldsmith.
Speck, Frank Gouldsmith, 1881-1950
xSpeck, Frank G.
Catawba Texts. AMS Pr.
Creek Indians of Taskigi Town. Kraus Repr.
Naskapi: The Savage Hunters of the Labrador
Peninsula. U of Okla Pr.
Penobscot Man: The Life History of a Forest
Tribe in Maine. Octagon.
Speck, Ross V.
xSpeck, Ross V.
Family Networks. Pantheon.
Specter, Gerald. see Specter, Gerald A.
Specter, Gerald A.
xSpecter, Gerald.
ed. Crisis Intervention. Human Sci Pr.
Spector, Ivar, 1898-
xSpector, Ivar.
The Soviet Union & the Muslim World,
1917-1958. U of Wash Pr.
Spector, Jack J.
xSpector, Jack J.
The Aesthetics of Freud: A Study in
Psychoanalysis & Art. McGraw.
xSpector, Jack L.
The Murals of Eugene Delacroix at
Saint-Sulpice. NYU Pr.
Spector, Jack L. see Spector, Jack J.

Spector, Lee C.
xSpector, Lee C.
Applying Macroeconomic Principles: A Student
Guide to Analyzing Economic News.
Har-Row.
Spector, Malcolm.
xSpector, Malcom.
Constructing Social Problems.
Benjamin-Cummings.
Spector, Malcom. see Spector, Malcolm.
Spector, Marjorie.
xSpector, Marjorie.
Pencil to Press: How This Book Came to Be.
Lothrop.
Spector, Marshall, 1936-
xSpector, Marshall.
Concepts of Reduction in Physical Science.
Temple U Pr.
Spector, Rachel E., 1940-
xSpector, Rachel E.
Cultural Diversity in Health & Illness. ACC.
Spector, Robert D. see Spector, Robert Donald.
Spector, Robert Donald.
xSpector, Robert D.
Arthur Murphy. Twayne.
Par Lagerkvist. Twayne.
Spector, Ronald.
xSpector, Ronald.
Admiral of the New Empire: The Life &
Career of George Dewey. La State U Pr.
Spector, Samuel I. see Spector, Samuel Ira.
Spector, Samuel Ira.
xSpector, Samuel I.
Municipal & County Zoning in a Changing
Urban Environment. Ga St U Busn Pub.
Spector, Sheshannah. see Spector, Shoshannah.
Spector, Shoshannah.
xSpector, Sheshannah.
Five Young Heroes of Israel. Shengold.
Spector, W. G. see Spector, Walter Graham.
Spector, Walter Graham.
xSpector, W. G.
An Introduction to General Pathology.
Churchill.
Spectorsky, Auguste C., 1910-
xSpectorsky, Auguste C.
ed. College Years. Arno.
Spectre, Peter H.
xSpectre, Peter H.
The Barbie Doll House. Van Nos Reinhold.
Spedding, D. J.
xSpedding, D. J.
Air Pollution. Oxford U Pr.
Speech Association of America.
xSpeech Association Of America.
History & Criticism of American Public
Address. Russell.
Speed, Harold, 1873-
xSpeed, Harold.
The Practice & Science of Drawing. Dover.
The Practice & Science of Drawing. Peter
Smith.
Speer, Eugene E. see Speer, Eugene R.
Speer, Eugene R.
xSpeer, Eugene E.
Generalized Feynman Amplitudes. Princeton U
Pr.
Speer, Frederic.
xSpeer, Frederic.
Allergy & Immunology in Children. C C
Thomas.
Allergy of the Nervous System. C C Thomas.
Food Allergy. PSG Pub.
Speer, Michael L.
xSpeer, Michael L.
A Complete Guide to the Christian's Budget.
Broadman.
Put Your Best Foot Forward. Broadman.
Speer, Robert E. see Speer, Robert Elliott.

Speer, Robert Elliott, 1867-1947
xSpeer, Robert E.
Race & Race Relations: A Christian View of
Human Contacts. Negro U Pr.
Some Great Leaders in the World Movement.
Arno.
Speers, Rex W.
xSpeers, Rex W.
Group Therapy in Childhood Psychosis. U of
NC Pr.
Speerstra, Karen.
xSpeerstra, Karen.
Let's Go Jesus. Concordia.
Speeth, Kathleen R. see Speeth, Kathleen Riordan.
Speeth, Kathleen Riordan, 1937-
xSpeeth, Kathleen R.
The Gurdjieff Work. And-or Pr.
The Gurdjieff Work. PB.
Speier, Hans.
xSpeier, Hans.
Force & Folly: Essays on Foreign Affairs & the
History of Ideas. MIT Pr.
Speier, Matthew.
xSpeier, Matthew.
How to Observe Face to Face Communication:
A Sociological Introduction. Goodyear.
Speiser, Stuart M.
xSpeiser, Stuart M.
Attorney's Fees. Lawyers Co-Op.
Speke, John H. see Speke, John Hanning.
Speke, John Hanning, 1827-1864
xSpeke, John H.
Journal of the Discovery of the Source of the
Nile. Dutton.
Journal of the Discovery of the Source of the
Nile. Greenwood.
Spell, Jefferson R. see Spell, Jefferson Rea.
Spell, Jefferson Rea, 1886-
xSpell, Jefferson R.
Contemporary Spanish-American Fiction.
Biblo.
Spellman, Norman W., 1928-
xSpellman, Norman W.
Growing a Soul: The Story of A. Frank Smith.
SMU Press.
Speltz, Alexander.
xSpeltz, Alexander.
Styles of Ornament. Dover.
Styles of Ornament. Peter Smith.
Spence, Alexander. see Spence, Alexander P.
Spence, Alexander P.
xSpence, Alexander.
Human Anatomy & Physiology.
Benjamin-Cummings.
Spence, Dale W.
xSpence, Dale W.
Essentials of Kinesiology: A Laboratory
Manual. Lea & Febiger.
Spence, Eleanor.
xSpence, Eleanor.
The Devil Hole. Lothrop.
The Nothing Place. Har-Row.
Spence, Jack.
xSpence, Jack.
Search for Justice: Neighborhood Courts in
Allende's Chile. Westview.
Spence, Janet T. see Spence, Janet Taylor.
Spence, Janet Taylor.
xSpence, Janet T.
Masculinity & Femininity: Their Psychological
Dimensions, Correlates & Antecedents. U of
Tex Pr.
Spence, Jeffery. see Spence, Jeoffry.
Spence, Jeoffry.
xSpence, Jeffery.
Victorian & Edwardian Railway Travel. David
& Charles.
Spence, Jonathan. see Spence, Jonathan D.
Spence, Jonathan D.
xSpence, Jonathan.

The Death of Woman Wang. Penguin.
The Death of Woman Wang. Viking Pr.
Spence, Joseph.
xSpence, Joseph.
Anecdotes, Observations & Characters of
Books & Men: Collected from the
Conversation of Mr. Pope & Other Eminent
Persons of His Time. S Ill U Pr.
Letters from the Grand Tour. McGill-Queens
U Pr.
Polymetis. Garland Pub.
Spence, L. see Spence, Lewis.
Spence, Larry D.
xSpence, Larry D.
The Politics of Social Knowledge. Pa St U Pr.
Spence, Lewis, 1874-1955
xSpence, L.
A Dictionary of Medieval Romance &
Romance Writers. Gordon Pr.
xSpence, Lewis.
British Fairy Origins. Folcroft.
Dictionary of Medieval Romance & Romance
Writers. Longwood Pr.
The History of Atlantis. Citadel Pr.
History of Atlantis. Univ Bks.
The Outlines of Mythology. Folcroft.
Popol Vuh: Mythic & Heroic Sagas of the
Kiches of Central America. AMS Pr.
Spence, Peter, 1944-
xSpence, Peter.
Some of Our Best Friends Are Animals: The
Story of a Wildlife Park. St Martin.
Spence, Ralph B. see Spence, Ralph Beckett.
Spence, Ralph Beckett, 1901-
xSpence, Ralph B.
The Improvement of College Marking Systems.
AMS Pr.
Spence, Robert.
xSpence, Robert.
Linear Active Networks. Wiley.
Spence, William P. see Spence, William Perkins.
Spence, William Perkins, 1925-
xSpence, William P.
Architecture: Design-Engineering-Drawing.
McKnight.
Spencer, A. J. see Spencer, Anthony James Merrill.
Spencer, Albert. see Spencer, Albert G.
Spencer, Albert G.
xSpencer, Albert.
Wood & Wood Products. Merrill.
Spencer, Anna G. see Spencer, Anna Garlin.
Spencer, Anna Garlin, 1851-1931
xSpencer, Anna G.
The Family & Its Members. Hyperion Conn.
Spencer, Anthony James Merrill.
xSpencer, A. J.
Engineering Mathematics. Van Nos Reinhold.
Spencer, Arthur.
xSpencer, Arthur.
Gotland. David & Charles.
Spencer, Baldwin.
xSpencer, Baldwin.
Across Australia. AMS Pr.
Native Tribes of Central Australia. Humanities.
Spencer, Benjamin T. see Spencer, Benjamin Townley.
Spencer, Benjamin Townley.
xSpencer, Benjamin T.
Quest for Nationality: An American Literary
Campaign. Syracuse U Pr.
Spencer, Charles.
xSpencer, Charles.
The World of Serge Diaghilev. Merrimack Bk
Serv.
The World of Serge Diaghilev. Penguin.
The World of Serge Diaghilev. Viking Pr.
Spencer, Chauncey E., 1906-
xSpencer, Chauncey E.
Who Is Chauncey Spencer?. Broadside.
Spencer, D. A. see Spencer, Douglas Arthur.

Spencer, Dale R.
xSpencer, Dale R.
Law for the Newsman. Lucas.
Spencer, David E. see Spencer, David Ellsworth.
Spencer, David Ellsworth.
xSpencer, David E.
Local Government in Wisconsin. AMS Pr.
Local Government in Wisconsin. Johnson
Repr.
Spencer, Donald. see Spencer, Donald D.
Spencer, Donald D.
xSpencer, Donald.
Computers in Action: How Computers Work.
Hayden.
Problems for Computer Solution. Hayden.
Sixty Challenging Problems with BASIC
Solutions. Hayden.
xSpencer, Donald D.
Computer Dictionary. Camelot Pub.
Computer Dictionary for Everyone. Scribner.
The Computer Quiz Book. Camelot Pub.
Computer Science Mathematics. Merrill.
FORTRAN Programming. Camelot Pub.
Fun with Computers & Basic. Camelot Pub.
Fundamentals of Digital Computers. Sams.
Game Playing with BASIC. Hayden.
Game Playing with Computers. Hayden.
Guide to BASIC Programming. A-W.
Introduction to Information Processing. Merrill.
Problem Solving with FORTRAN.. P-H.
A Quick Look at Basic. Camelot Pub.
The Story of Computers. Camelot Pub.
Using Basic in the Classroom. Camelot Pub.
Spencer, Donald S., 1945-
xSpencer, Donald S.
Louis Kossuth & Young America: A Study of
Sectionalism & Foreign Policy, 1848-1852. U
of Mo Pr.
Spencer, Douglas Arthur, 1901-
xSpencer, D. A.
Focal Dictionary of Photographic Technologies.
Focal Pr.
Spencer, Elizabeth.
xSpencer, Elizabeth.
This Crooked Way. McGraw.
Spencer, Elma D. see Spencer, Elma Dill (Russell).
Spencer, Elma Dill (Russell).
xSpencer, Elma D.
Green Russell & Gold. U of Tex Pr.
Spencer, Francis M.
xSpencer, Francis M.
The Color Atlas of Intestinal Parasites. C C
Thomas.
Spencer, Harold, 1920-
xSpencer, Harold.
ed. Readings in Art History. Scribner.
Spencer, Hazelton, 1893-1944
xSpencer, Hazelton.
British Literature. Heath.
Spencer, Henry R. see Spencer, Henry Russell.
Spencer, Henry Russell, 1879-
xSpencer, Henry R.
Government & Politics of Italy. AMS Pr.
Spencer, Herbert, 1820-1903
xSpencer, Herbert.
Education-Intellectual, Moral & Physical.
Norwood Edns.
The Evolution of Society: Selections from
Herbert Spencer's "Principles of Sociology".
U of Chicago Pr.
First Principles. Greenwood.
Intro. By The Principles of Ethics. Liberty
Fund.
The Principles of Psychology. Longwood Pr.
The Principles of Sociology. Greenwood.
Various Fragments. Arno.
Spencer, J. E. see Spencer, Joseph Earle.
Spencer, James H.
xSpencer, James H.

The Hospital Emergency Department. C C
Thomas.
Spencer, Joseph Earle.
xSpencer, J. E.
ed. Day Tours in & Around Los Angeles.
Pacific Bks.
Spencer, Metta, 1931-
xSpencer, Metta.
Foundations of Modern Sociology. P-H.
xSpencer, Netta.
Foundations of Modern Sociology. P-H.
Spencer, Mike.
xSpencer, Mike.
The Ultimate Soup Book. Celestial Arts.
Spencer, Milton H.
xSpencer, Milton H.
Contemporary Macroeconomics. Worth.
Contemporary Microeconomics. Worth.
Spencer, Netta. *see* Spencer, Metta.
Spencer, Peter L. *see* Spencer, Peter Lincoln.
Spencer, Peter Lincoln, 1893-
xSpencer, Peter L.
Reading Reading. Alpha Iota.
Spencer, Peter S.
xSpencer, Peter S.
Experimental & Clinical Neurotoxicology.
Williams & Wilkins.
Spencer, Richard P.
xSpencer, Richard P.
ed. Therapy in Nuclear Medicine. Grune.
Spencer, Robert F.
xSpencer, Robert F.
The Native Americans: Ethnology &
Backgrounds of the North American Indians.
Har-Row.
The North Alaskan Eskimo: A Study in
Ecology and Society. Dover.
The North Alaskan Eskimo: A Study in
Ecology & Society. Scholarly.
ed. Religion & Change in Contemporary Asia.
U of Minn Pr.
Spencer, Robert L.
xSpencer, Robert L.
The Performance of the Best Investment
Advisory Services. Odd John.
Spencer, Roberta T.
xSpencer, Roberta T.
Patient Care in Endocrine Problems. Saunders.
Spencer, Ross H.
xSpencer, Ross H.
The Dada Caper. Avon.
Spencer, Ruth.
xSpencer, Ruth.
Aircraft Woodwork. TAB Bks.
Spencer, Samuel R.
xSpencer, Samuel R.
Booker T. Washington & the Negro's Place in
American Life. Little.
Spencer, Scott.
xSpencer, Scott.
Endless Love. Knopf.
Spencer, Sharon.
xSpencer, Sharon.
Collage of Dreams: The Writings of Anais Nin.
Swallow.
Space, Time & Structure in the Modern Novel.
NYU Pr.
Space, Time & Structure in the Modern Novel.
Swallow.
Spencer, Stanley.
xSpencer, Stanley.
Stanley Spencer the Man: Correspondence &
Reminiscences. Ohio U Pr.
Spencer, Terence. *see* Spencer, Terence John Bew.
Spencer, Terence J. *see* Spencer, Terence John Bew.
Spencer, Terence John Bew, 1915-
xSpencer, Terence.
Fair Greece, Sad Relic: Literary Philhellenism
from Shakespeare to Byron. Scholarly.
xSpencer, Terence J.

Fair Greece, Sad Relic: Literary PhilHellenism
from Shakespeare to Byron. Octagon.
Spencer, Theodore, 1902-1949
xSpencer, Theodore.
Death & Elizabethan Tragedy: A Study of
Convention & Opinion in the Elizabethan
Drama. Somerset Pub.
Spencer, William.
xSpencer, William.
Algiers in the Age of the Corsairs. U of Okla
Pr.
Spencer, Zane.
xSpencer, Zane.
Branded Runaway. Westminster.
Cry of the Wolf. Westminster.
Spencer-Brown, G.
xSpencer-Brown, G.
Laws of Form. Dutton.
Spender, John A. *see* Spender, John Alfred.
Spender, John Alfred, 1862-1942
xSpender, John A.
Men & Things. Arno.
Spender, Stephen, 1909-
xSpender, Stephen.
ed. Choice of English Romantic Poetry. Arno.
The Creative Element: A Study of Vision,
Despair, & Orthodoxy Among Some Modern
Writers. Arno.
Destructive Element: A Study of Modern
Writers & Beliefs. Folcroft.
European Witness. Greenwood.
Learning Laughter. Greenwood.
Life & the Poet. Folcroft.
Life & the Poet. Haskell.
T. S. Eliot. Penguin.
Spengemann, William C.
xSpengemann, William C.
The Adventurous Muse: The Poetics of
American Fiction, 1789-1900. Yale U Pr.
The Forms of Autobiography: Episodes in the
History of a Literary Genre. Yale U Pr.
Spengler, Joseph J. *see* Spengler, Joseph John.
Spengler, Joseph John, 1902-
xSpengler, Joseph J.
Facing Zero Population Growth: Reactions &
Interpretations, Past & Present. Duke.
France Faces Depopulation. Greenwood.
Indian Economic Thought: A Preface to Its
History. Duke.
Origins of Economic Thought & Justice. S Ill
U Pr.
Population & America's Future. W H Freeman.
Spengler, Oswald, 1880-1936
xSpengler, Oswald.
The Decline of the West. Knopf.
Spens, Janet, 1876-
xSpens, Janet.
Spenser's Faerie Queene: An Interpretation.
Russell.
Spenser, Edmund.
xSpenser, Edmund.
The Faerie Queene. Biblio Dist.
Faerie Queene. Oxford U Pr.
Works of Edmund Spenser. AMS Pr.
Sperakis, Nicholas, 1943-
xSperakis, Nick.
Woodcuts. Smyrna.
Sperakis, Nick. *see* Sperakis, Nicholas.
Speranza, Gino. *see* Speranza, Gino Charles.
Speranza, Gino Charles, 1872-1927
xSperanza, Gino.
Race or Nation: Conflict of Divided Loyalties.
Arno.
Sperber, Al.
xSperber, Al.
Out of Sight: Ten Stories of Victory Over
Blindness. Little.
Sperber, D. *see* Sperber, Dan.
Sperber, Dan.
xSperber, D.

Rethinking Symbolism. Cambridge U Pr.
Sperber, G. H. *see* Sperber, Geoffrey H.
Sperber, Geoffrey H.
xSperber, G. H.
Craniofacial Embryology. Year Bk Med.
Sperber, Manes, 1905-
xSperber, Manes.
Achilles Heel. Kennikat.
Sperber, Murray. *see* Sperber, Murray A.
Sperber, Murray A.
xSperber, Murray.
ed. And I Remember Spain: A Spanish Civil
War Anthology. Macmillan.
ed. Arthur Koestler: A Collection of Critical
Essays. P-H.
Literature & Politics. Hayden.
Sperber, Paula.
xSperber, Paula.
Inside Bowling for Women. Contemp Bks.
Sperber, Philip.
xSperber, Philip.
The Science of Business Negotiation. Pilot Bks.
Spergel, Irving.
xSpergel, Irving.
Racketville, Slumtown, Haulburg: An
Exploratory Study of Delinquent Subcultures.
U of Chicago Pr.
Sperisen, Francis J, 1900-
xSperisen, Francis J.
Art of the Lapidary. Glencoe.
Sperle, Diana H. *see* Sperle, Diana Henryetta.
Sperle, Diana Henryetta, 1889-
xSperle, Diana H.
Case Method Technique in Professional
Training: A Survey of the Use of Case
Studies As a Method of Instruction in
Selected Fields, & a Study of Its Application
in a Teachers College. AMS Pr.
Sperlich, Norbert.
xSperlich, Norbert.
Guatemalan Backstrap Weaving. U of Okla Pr.
Sperling, A. P. *see* Sperling, Abraham Paul.
Sperling, Abraham Paul, 1912-
xSperling, A. P.
Arithmetic Made Simple. Doubleday.
How to Make Psychology Work for You.
Fawcett.
Psychology Made Simple. Doubleday.
Sperling, Melitta.
xSperling, Melitta.
Psychosomatic Disorders in Childhood.
Aronson.
Sperling, Susan K. *see* Sperling, Susan Kelz.
Sperling, Susan Kelz.
xSperling, Susan K.
Poplollies & Bellibones: A Celebration of Lost
Words. Potter.
Spero, Herbert, 1908-
xSpero, Herbert.
Money & Banking. Har-Row.
Spero, James.
xSpero, James.
The Great Sights of New York: A
Photographic Guide. Dover.
ed. North American Mammals: A Photographic
Album for Artists & Designers. Dover.
Spero, Joan E. *see* Spero, Joan Edelman.
Spero, Joan Edelman.
xSpero, Joan E.
The Politics of International Economic
Relations. St Martin.
Spero, Moshe H. *see* Spero, Moshe Halevi.
Spero, Moshe Halevi.
xSpero, Moshe H.
Judaism & Psychology: Halakhic Perspectives.
Ktav.
Spero, Sterling D. *see* Spero, Sterling Denhard.
Spero, Sterling Denhard, 1896-
xSpero, Sterling D.

The Family That Changed: A Child's Book About Divorce. Crown.

Spilken, Aron.
xSpilken, Aron.
Burning Moon. Playboy Pbks.

Spillane, Frank Morrison, 1918-
xSpillane, Mickey.
The Long Wait. NAL.
My Gun Is Quick. NAL.
One Lonely Night. NAL.
Twisted Thing. NAL.
Vengeance Is Mine. NAL.

Spillane, John.
xSpillane, John.
TV Field & Bench Servicer's Handbook. TAB Bks.
Spillane, John D. see Spillane, John David.

Spillane, John David.
xSpillane, John D.
Atlas of Clinical Neurology. Oxford U Pr.
ed. Tropical Neurology. Oxford U Pr.

Spillane, Mickey.
xSpillane, Mickey.
Day of the Guns. NAL.
Deep. NAL.
Girl Hunters. NAL.
Spillane, Mickey. see Spillane, Frank Morrison.

Spiller, Earl A.
xSpiller, Earl A.
Financial Accounting: Basic Concepts. Irwin.

Spiller, David.
xSpiller, David.
Book Selection: An Introduction to Principles & Practice. Shoe String.
Spiller, Earl A. see Spiller.

Spiller, Gene A.
xSpiller, Gene A.
ed. Fiber in Human Nutrition. Plenum Pub.
Spiller, Robert E. see Spiller, Robert Ernest.

Spiller, Robert Ernest, 1896-
xSpiller, Robert E.
The American in England During the First Half Century of Independence. Porcupine Pr.
Cycle of American Literature: An Essay in Historical Criticism. Macmillan.
Spillman, Jane S. see Spillman, Jane Shadel.

Spillman, Jane Shadel.
xSpillman, Jane S.
Cut & Engraved Glass of Corning, 1868-1940. Corning.

Spilsbury, Richard.
xSpilsbury, Richard.
Providence Lost: A Critique of Darwinism. Oxford U Pr.

Spindler, Arthur.
xSpindler, Arthur.
Public Welfare. Human Sci Pr.
Spindler, George D. see Spindler, George Dearborn.

Spindler, George Dearborn.
xSpindler, George D.
ed. The Making of Psychological Anthropology. U of Cal Pr.

Spinell, Michael R.
xSpinell, Michael R.
A Clinical Guide to Soft Contact Lenses. Chilton.

Spinelli, Donald C.
xSpinelli, Donald C.
ed. A Concordance to Marivaux's Comedies in Prose. Univ Microfilms.

Spinelli, Joseph S.
xSpinelli, Joseph S.
Drugs in Veterinary Practice. Mosby.
Spingarn, J. E. see Spingarn, Joel Elias.
Spingarn, Joel E. see Spingarn, Joel Elias.

Spingarn, Joel Elias, 1875-1939
xSpingarn, J. E.
A History of Literary Criticism in the Renaissance. R West.
xSpingarn, Joel E.

ed. Critical Essays of the Seventeenth Century. Ind U Pr.
History of Literary Criticism in the Renaissance. Greenwood.
Spink, John S. see Spink, John Stephenson.

Spink, John Stephenson.
xSpink, John S.
French Free-Thought from Gassendi to Voltaire. Greenwood.
Spink, Wesley W. see Spink, Wesley William.

Spink, Wesley William, 1904-
xSpink, Wesley W.
Nature of Brucellosis. U of Minn Pr.

Spinka, Matthew, 1890-
xSpinka, Matthew.
Christian Thought: From Erasmus to Berdyaev. Greenwood.
Spinks, J. W. see Spinks, John William Tranter.

Spinks, John William Tranter.
xSpinks, J. W.
ed. An Introduction to Radiation Chemistry. Wiley.
Spinnanger, Ruthe. see Spinnanger, Ruthe T.

Spinnanger, Ruthe T.
xSpinnanger, Ruthe.
Better Than Divorce. Logos.

Spinner, Stephanie.
xSpinner, Stephanie.
ed. Feminine Plural: Stories by Women About Growing up. Macmillan.
Spinner, T. J. see Spinner, Thomas J.

Spinner, Thomas J.
xSpinner, T. J.
George Joachim Goschen: The Transformation of a Victorian Liberal. Cambridge U Pr.

Spino, Dyveke.
xSpino, Dyveke.
New Age Training for Fitness & Health. Grove.
Spinrad. see Spinrad, Leonard.
Spinrad, L. see Spinrad, Leonard.

Spinrad, Leonard.
xSpinrad.
Speaker's Lifetime Library. P-H.
xSpinrad, L.
Instant Almanac of Events, Anniversaries, Observances, Quotations & Birthdays for Every Day of the Year. P-H.

Spinrad, Norman.
xSpinrad, Norman.
Agent of Chaos. Popular Lib.
The Men in the Jungle. Nordon Pubns.
Songs from the Stars. S&S.
A World Between. BJ Pub Group.

Spira, Michael.
xSpira, Michael.
How to Lose Weight Without Really Dieting. Penguin.

Spirer, Louis Ziegler.
xSpirer, Louise.
This Is the Miniature Schnauzer. TFH Pubns.
Spirer, Louise. see Spirer, Louis Ziegler.
Spirer, Louise Z. see Spirer, Louise Ziegler.

Spirer, Louise Ziegler.
xSpirer, Louise Z.
This Is the Pomeranian. TFH Pubns.

Spirn, Jeffrey R.
xSpirn, Jeffrey R.
Program Behavior: Models & Measurements. Elsevier.

Spiro, Herbert J.
xSpiro, Herbert J.
Responsibility in Government: Theory & Practice. Van Nos Reinhold.

Spiro, Herbert T.
xSpiro, Herbert T.

Finance for the Nonfinancial Manager. Wiley.
Financial Planning for the Independent Professional. Wiley.

Spiro, Howard M.
xSpiro, Howard M.
Clinical Gastroenterology. Macmillan.

Spiro, Melford E.
xSpiro, Melford E.
Burmese Supernaturalism. Inst Study Human.
Gender & Culture: Kibbutz Women Revisited. Schocken.

Spiro, Stanley R.
xSpiro, Stanley R.
Amnesia-Analgesia Techniques in Dentistry. C C Thomas.

Spiro, Thomas G.
xSpiro, Thomas G.
Environmental Issues in Chemical Perspective. State U NY Pr.
ed. Nucleic Acid-Metal Ion Interactions. Wiley.
Spirt, Diana. see Spirt, Diana L.

Spirt, Diana L.
xSpirt, Diana.
Pref. by Introducing More Books: A Guide to the Middle Grades. Bowker.
xSpirt, Diana L.
Library-Media Manual. Wilson.

Spittler, Russell P.
xSpittler, Russell P.
The Church. Gospel Pub.
The Corinthian Correspondence. Gospel Pub.
God the Father. Gospel Pub.

Spitz, A. Edward.
xSpitz, A. Edward.
Retailing: Case Problems. Grid Pub.
xSpitz, E.
Retailing. P H.
xSpitz, Edward A.
Product Planning. Van Nos Reinhold.
Spitz, E. see Spitz, A. Edward.
Spitz, Edward A. see Spitz, A. Edward.
Spitz, Lewis W. see Spitz, Lewis William.

Spitz, Lewis William.
xSpitz, Lewis W.
ed. Discord, Dialogue, & Concord: Studies in the Lutheran Reformation's Formula of Concord. Fortress.
The Northern Renaissance. P-H.

Spitz, Mark.
xSpitz, Mark.
The Mark Spitz Complete Book of Swimming. T Y Crowell.
Spitz, Rene A. see Spitz, Rene Arpad.

Spitz, Rene Arpad, 1887-
xSpitz, Rene A.
First Year of Life: A Psychoanalytic Study of Normal & Deviant Development of Object Relations. Intl Univs Pr.
Genetic Field Theory of Ego Formation: Its Implications for Pathology. Intl Univs Pr.
No & Yes: On the Genesis of Human Communication. Intl Univs Pr.
Spitz, Robert S. see Spitz, Robert Stephen.

Spitz, Robert Stephen.
xSpitz, Robert S.
Barefoot in Babylon: The Creation of the Woodstock Music Festival, 1969. Viking Pr.

Spitz, Werner U.
xSpitz, Werner U.
ed. Medicolegal Investigation of Death: Guidelines for the Application of Pathology to Crime Investigation. C C Thomas.

Spitzbart, Abraham.
xSpitzbart, Abraham.
Analytic Geometry. Scott F.
Calculus with Analytic Geometry. Scott F.
College Algebra. A-W.

Spitzberg, Irving J.
xSpitzberg, Irving R.

ed. Exchange of Expertise: The Counterpart
System in the New International Order.
Westview.
Spitzberg, Irving R. *see* Spitzberg, Irving J.
Spitzer, Alan B. *see* Spitzer, Alan Barrie.
Spitzer, Alan Barrie, 1925-
xSpitzer, Alan B.
Old Hatreds & Young Hopes: The French
Carbonari Against the Bourbon Restoration.
Harvard U Pr.
Revolutionary Theories of Louis-Auguste
Blanqui. AMS Pr.
Spitzer, Dan.
xSpitzer, Dan.
Wanderlust: Overland Through Asia & Africa.
Marek.
Spitzer, Leo, 1939-
xSpitzer, Leo.
The Creoles of Sierra Leone: Responses to
Colonialism, 1870-1945. U of Wis Pr.
Spitzer, Lyman, 1914-
xSpitzer, Lyman.
Diffuse Matter in Space. Wiley.
Spitzer, Mary E.
xSpitzer, Mary E.
A Renal Failure Diet Manual Utilizing the
Food Exchange System. C C Thomas.
Spitzer, Robert L.
xSpitzer, Robert L.
ed. Critical Issues in Psychiatric Diagnosis.
Raven.
Spivack, Charlotte.
xSpivack, Charlotte.
The Comedy of Evil & Shakespeare's Stage.
Fairleigh Dickinson.
Spivack, Julius.
xSpivack, Julius.
What You Should Know About Labor
Relations. Oceana.
Spivak, Jerry L.
xSpivak, Jerry L.
Manual of Clinical Problems in Internal
Medicine: Annotated with Key References.
Little.
Spivak, John L. *see* Spivak, John Louis.
Spivak, John Louis, 1897-
xSpivak, John L.
Georgia Nigger. Patterson Smith.
Spivak, Michael.
xSpivak, Michael.
Calculus. Publish or Perish.
Calculus on Manifolds: A Modern Approach to
Classical Theorems of Advanced Calculus.
Benjamin-Cummings.
A Comprehensive Introduction to Differential
Geometry. Publish or Perish.
Spivey, R. A. *see* Spivey, Robert A.
Spivey, Richard L.
xSpivey, Richard L.
Maria. Northland.
Spivey, Robert A.
xSpivey, R. A.
Anatomy of the New Testament: A Guide to
Its Structure & Meaning. Macmillan.
Splaver, Bernard R.
xSplaver, Bernard R.
Successful Catering. CBI Pub.
Splaver, Sarah.
xSplaver, Sarah.
Career Choices in Psychology. Messner.
Nontraditional Careers for Women. Messner.
Nontraditional College Routes to Careers.
Messner.
Splittstoesser, Walter E.
xSplittstoesser, Walter E.
Vegetable Growing Handbook. AVI.
Spock, Benjamin. *see* Spock, Benjamin McLane.
Spock, Benjamin M. *see* Spock, Benjamin McLane.
Spock, Benjamin McLane, 1903-
xSpock, Benjamin.

Baby & Child Care. Dutton.
Baby & Child Care. PB.
Baby & Child Care. PB.
xSpock, Benjamin M.
The Problems of Parents. Greenwood.
Spoczynska, Joy D. *see* Spoczynska, Joy O. I.
Spoczynska, Joy O. I.
xSpoczynska, Joy D.
The World of the Wasp. Crane-Russak Co.
Spodek, Bernard.
xSpodek, Bernard.
Early Childhood Education. P-H.
ed. Studies in Open Education. Agathon.
Teaching in the Early Years. P-H.
ed. Teaching Practices: Reexamining
Assumptions. Natl Assn Child Ed.
Spodick, David. *see* Spodick, David H.
Spodick, David H.
xSpodick, David.
ed. Pericardial Diseases. Davis Co.
Spoehr, Alexander, 1913-
xSpoehr, Alexander.
ed. Maritime Adaptations: Essays on
Contemporary Fishing Communities. U of
Pittsburgh Pr.
Spoehr, Florence M. *see* Spoehr, Florence Mann.
Spoehr, Florence Mann.
xSpoehr, Florence M.
White Falcon: The House of Godeffroy & Its
Commercial & Scientific Role in the Pacific.
Pacific Bks.
Spoehr, Herman A. *see* Spoehr, Herman Augustus.
Spoehr, Herman Augustus, 1885-1954
xSpoehr, Herman A.
The Carbohydrate Economy of Cacti. Johnson
Repr.
Spohler, Albert A. *see* Spohler, Albert A. C.
Spohler, Albert A. C.
xSpohler, Albert A.
Stock Market & Me: An Independent
Approach to Wall Street. A A Spohler.
Spohn. *see* Spohn, Robert F.
Spohn, Robert F.
xSpohn.
Retailing. Reston.
Spohr, Louis, 1784-1859
xSpohr, Louis.
Autobiography. Da Capo.
Spolsky, Bernard.
xSpolsky, Bernard.
ed. Case Studies in Bilingual Education.
Newbury Hse.
Spong, John S. *see* Spong, John Shelby.
Spong, John Shelby.
xSpong, John S.
The Easter Moment. Seabury.
The Living Commandments. Seabury.
This Hebrew Lord. Seabury.
Sponheim, Paul R.
xSponheim, Paul R.
Faith & Process: The Significance of Process
Thought for Christian Faith. Augsburg.
Sponseller, Doris.
xSponseller, Doris.
ed. Play As a Learning Medium. Natl Assn
Child Ed.
Sponsored by the Center for Blood Research. *see* Center
for Blood Research.
Spooner, John D.
xSpooner, John D.
Smart People: A User's Guide to the Experts.
Little.
Spooner, Lysander.
xSpooner, Lysander.
The Collected Works of Lysander Spooner.
M&S Pr.
Unconstitutionality of Slavery. B Franklin.
Spooner, Robert B., 1920-
xSpooner, Robert B.

Hospital Electrical Safety Simplified. Instru
Soc.
Spooner, Robert D. *see* Spooner, Robert Donald.
Spooner, Robert Donald.
xSpooner, Robert D.
Response of Natural Gas & Crude Oil
Exploration & Discovery to Economic
Incentives. Arno.
Spore, Keith.
xSpore, Keith.
Death of a Scavenger. Belmont-Tower.
Sporn, Philip.
xSporn, Philip.
Energy in an Age of Limited Availability &
Delimited Applicability. Pergamon.
Sporting News.
xSporting News Staff.
ed. Daguerreotypes. Sporting News.
Sporting News Staff. *see* Sporting News.
Sports Illustrated. *see* Sports Illustrated (Chicago).
Sports Illustrated (Chicago).
xSports Illustrated.
Golf Lessons from Great Pros. P-H.
xSports Illustrated Editors.
Sports Illustrated Baseball. Lippincott.
Sports Illustrated Basketball. Lippincott.
Sports Illustrated Book of Track & Field:
Running Events. Lippincott.
Sports Illustrated Dog Training. Lippincott.
Sports Illustrated Golf. Lippincott.
Sports Illustrated Horseback Riding. Lippincott.
Sports Illustrated Ice Hockey. Lippincott.
Sports Illustrated Skiing. Lippincott.
Sports Illustrated Skin Diving & Snorkeling.
Lippincott.
Sports Illustrated Small Boat Sailing.
Lippincott.
Sports Illustrated Squash. Lippincott.
Sports Illustrated Swimming & Diving.
Lippincott.
Sports Illustrated Editors. *see* Sports Illustrated
(Chicago).
Sposito, V. A., 1936-
xSposito, Vincent A.
Linear & Nonlinear Programming. Iowa St U
Pr.
Sposito, Vincent A. *see* Sposito, V. A.
Spoto, Donald, 1941-
xSpoto, Donald.
Camerado: Hollywood & the American Man.
NAL.
Spotte, Stephen. *see* Spotte, Stephen H.
Spotte, Stephen H.
xSpotte, Stephen.
Marine Aquarium Keeping: The Science,
Animals & Art. Wiley.
Seawater Aquariums: The Captive
Environment. Wiley.
Spottiswood, John, Abp. of St. Andrews, 1565-1639
xSpottiswood, John.
History of the Church of Scotland. AMS Pr.
Spottiswoode, J.
xSpottiswoode, J.
Moorland Gamekeeper. David & Charles.
Spottiswoode, Raymond, 1913-
xSpottiswoode, Raymond.
A Grammar of the Film: An Analysis of Film
Technique. U of Cal Pr.
Spotts, Frederic.
xSpotts, Frederic.
The Churches & Politics in Germany.
Columbia U Pr.
Spotts, James V.
xSpotts, James V.
Cocaine Users: A Representative Case
Approach. Free Pr.
Spotts, M. F. *see* Spotts, Merhyle Franklin.
Spotts, Merhyle Franklin, 1895-
xSpotts, M. F.

Quasielastic Neutron Scattering for the
Investigation of Diffusive Motions in Solids
& Liquids. Springer-Verlag.
Springer, Tonny Albert, 1926-
xSpringer, T. A.
Jordan Algebras & Algebraic Groups.
Springer-Verlag.
Sprinkle, Patricia H. see Sprinkle, Patricia Houck.
Sprinkle, Patricia Houck.
xSprinkle, Patricia H.
Hunger: Understanding the Crisis Through
Games, Dramas, & Songs. John Knox.
Sprinthall, Norman A., 1931-
xSprinthall, Norman A.
Guidance for Human Growth. Van Nos
Reinhold.
ed. Value Development As the Aim of
Education. Character Res.
Sprinthall, Richard C.
xSprinthall, Richard C.
Educational Psychology: A Developmental
Approach. A-W.
Spritz, Kenneth, 1948-
xSpritz, Kenneth.
Theatrical Evolution: 1776-1976. Pub Ctr Cult
Res.
Sproul, Barbara C.
xSproul, Barbara C.
Primal Myths: Creating the World. Har-Row.
Sproule, J. Michael.
xSproule, J. Michael.
Argument: Language & Its Influence. McGraw.
Sproull, Lee.
xSproull, Lee.
Organizing an Anarchy: Belief, Bureaucracy, &
Politics in the National Institute of
Education. U of Chicago Pr.
Sprouse, Robert T. see Sprouse, Robert Thomas.
Sprouse, Robert Thomas.
xSprouse, Robert T.
The Essentials of Financial Statement Analysis.
A-W.
Sprout, Harold. see Sprout, Harold Hance.
Sprout, Harold Hance.
xSprout, Harold.
The Context of Environmental Politics:
Unfinished Business for America's Third
Century. U Pr of Ky.
Toward a Politics of the Planet Earth. Van Nos
Reinhold.
Sprowls, Joseph B. see Sprowls, Joseph Barnett.
Sprowls, Joseph Barnett.
xSprowls, Joseph B.
ed. Prescription Pharmacy: Dosage Formulation
& Pharmaceutical Adjuncts. Lippincott.
Spruce, Richard, 1817-1893
xSpruce, Richard.
Notes of a Botanist on the Amazon & Andes.
Johnson Repr.
Spruch, Grace M. see Spruch, Grace Marmor.
Spruch, Grace Marmor.
xSpruch, Grace M.
The Ubiquitous Atom. Scribner.
Spruill, Julia C. see Spruill, Julia Cherry.
Spruill, Julia Cherry.
xSpruill, Julia C.
Women's Life and Work in the Southern
Colonies. Norton.
Women's Life & Work in the Southern
Colonies. Russell.
Spruill, Stephen G. see Spruill, Steven G.
Spruill, Steven G.
xSpruill, Stephen G.
The Psychopath Plague. Dell.
xSpruill, Steven G.
The Psychopath Plague. Doubleday.
Sprung, Barbara.
xSprung, Barbara.

Non-Sexist Education for Young Children: A
Practical Guide. Schol Bk Serv.
Non-Sexist Education for Young Children: A
Practical Guide. Women's Action.
Sprung, Mervyn.
xSprung, Mervyn.
ed. The Question of Being: East-West
Perspectives. Pa St U Pr.
Sprunger, Keith L.
xSprunger, Keith L.
The Learned Doctor William Ames: Dutch
Backgrounds of English & American
Puritanism. U of Ill Pr.
Sprunt, Alexander.
xSprunt, Alexander.
Carolina Low Country Impressions. Devin.
South Carolina Bird Life. U of SC Pr.
Sprunt, James, 1846-1924
xSprunt, James.
Chronicles of the Cape Fear River, 1660-1916.
Reprint.
Tales & Traditions of the Lower Cape Fear:
1661-1896. Reprint.
Spufford, Margaret.
xSpufford, Margaret.
Contrasting Communities: English Villagers in
the Sixteenth & Seventeenth Centuries.
Cambridge U Pr.
Spulber, Nicholas. see Spulber, Nicolas.
Spulber, Nicolas.
xSpulber, Nicholas.
Organizational Alternatives in Soviet-Type
Economies. Cambridge U Pr.
xSpulber, Nicolas.
The Economics of Communist Eastern Europe.
Greenwood.
Quantitative Economic Policy & Planning:
Theory & Models of Economic Control.
Norton.
Socialist Management & Planning: Topics in
Comparative Socialist Economics. Ind U Pr.
Spunt, Georges.
xSpunt, Georges.
The Step-by-Step Chinese Cookbook. T Y
Crowell.
Spurgeon, C. H.
xSpurgeon, Charles H.
Christ's Glorious Achievements. Baker Bk.
Passion & Death of Christ. Eerdmans.
Twelve Sermons on Conversion. Baker Bk.
Twelve Sermons on Repentance. Baker Bk.
Twelve Sermons on Various Subjects. Baker
Bk.
Spurgeon, C. H. see Spurgeon, Charles Haddon.
Spurgeon, Caroline. see Spurgeon, Caroline Frances
Eleanor.
Spurgeon, Caroline F. see Spurgeon, Caroline Frances
Eleanor.
Spurgeon, Caroline Frances Eleanor, 1869-1942
xSpurgeon, Caroline.
Leading Motives in the Imagery of
Shakespeare's Tragedies. Haskell.
xSpurgeon, Caroline F.
Five Hundred Years of Chaucer Criticism &
Allusion, 1357-1900. Russell.
Leading Motives in the Imagery of
Shakespeare's Tragedies. Folcroft.
Spurgeon, Charles H. see Spurgeon, Charles Haddon.
Spurgeon, Charles Haddon, 1834-1892
xSpurgeon, C. H.
According to Promise. Pilgrim Pubns.
Twelve Sermons on Holiness. Reiner.
xSpurgeon, Charles H.
Lectures to My Students. Baker Bk.
Lectures to My Students. Zondervan.
Twelve Sermons on the Holy Spirit. Baker Bk.
Spurlin, P. M. see Spurlin, Paul Merrill.
Spurlin, Paul Merrill, 1902-
xSpurlin, P. M.

Montesquieu in America: 1760-1801. Octagon.
Spurlock, Clark.
xSpurlock, Clark.
Education & the Supreme Court. Greenwood.
Spurr, Stephen H. see Spurr, Stephen Hopkins.
Spurr, Stephen Hopkins.
xSpurr, Stephen H.
American Forest Policy in Development. U of
Wash Pr.
Forest Ecology. Wiley.
Spurrier, Robert L.
xSpurrier, Robert L.
Inexpensive Justice: Self Representation in the
Small Claims Court. Kennikat.
Spurzheim, Johann C. see Spurzheim, Johann Gaspar.
Spurzheim, Johann Gaspar, 1776-1832
xSpurzheim, Johann C.
Observations on the Deranged Manifestations
of the Mind, or Insanity. Schol Facsimiles.
Spyker, John H. see Spyker, John Howland.
Spyker, John Howland.
xSpyker, John H.
Little Lives. Avon.
xSpyker, John Howland.
Little Lives. G&D.
Spykman, E. C. see Spykman, Elizabeth Choate.
Spykman, Elizabeth C. see Spykman, Elizabeth Choate.
Spykman, Elizabeth Choate.
xSpykman, E. C.
Edie on the Warpath. HarBraceJ.
xSpykman, Elizabeth C.
Lemon & a Star. HarBraceJ.
Spyridakis, Stylianos.
xSpyridakis, Stylianos.
Ptolemaic Itanos & Hellenistic Crete. U of Cal
Pr.
Squadrito, Kathleen. see Squadrito, Kathleen M.
Squadrito, Kathleen M.
xSquadrito, Kathleen.
John Locke. Twayne.
Squibb, Betsy.
xSquibb, Betty.
Family Day Care: How to Provide It in the
Home. Harvard Common Pr.
Squibb, Betty. see Squibb, Betsy.
Squibb, G. D. see Squibb, George Drewry.
Squibb, George Drewry, 1906-
xSquibb, G. D.
Doctors' Commons: A History of the College
of Advocates & Doctors of Law. Oxford U
Pr.
Squibb, Robert.
xSquibb, Robert.
The Gardener's Calendar for South Carolina,
Georgia, & North Carolina. U of Ga Pr.
Squier, Ephraim G. see Squier, Ephraim George.
Squier, Ephraim George, 1821-1888
xSquier, Ephraim G.
Nicaragua, Its People, Scenery, Monuments,
Resources, Condition & Proposed Canal.
AMS Pr.
Squire, Charles.
xSquire, Charles.
Celtic Myth & Legend. Newcastle Pub.
Celtic Myth & Legend, Poetry & Romance.
Borgo Pr.
Celtic Myth & Legend, Poetry and Romance.
Longwood Pr.
Squire, David.
xSquire, David.
Wheels. Lerner Pubns.
Squire, Enid.
xSquire, Enid.
Introducing Systems Design. A-W.
Squire, James R.
xSquire, James R.

High School English Instruction Today: The
National Study of High School English
Programs. Irvington.
Responses of Adolescents while Reading Four
Short Stories. NCTE.
Squire, John C. see Squire, John Collings.
Squire, John Collings, Sir, 1884-1958
xSquire, John C.
Outside Eden. Arno.
Squire Law Library.
xUniversity of Cambridge, Squire Law Library.
Catalogue of International Law. Oceana.
Law Catalogue. Oceana.
Squire, Robin.
xSquire, Robin.
Portrait of Barbara. St Martin.
Squires, Dick.
xSquires, Dick.
The Other Racquet Sports. McGraw.
The Other Racquet Sports. McGraw.
Squires, Dick. see Squires, Richard S.
Squires, Eric.
xSquires, Eric.
Pit Pony Heroes. David & Charles.
Squires, James Radcliffe, 1917-
xSquires, Radcliffe.
Frederic Prokosch. Coll & U Pr.
Frederic Prokosch. Irvington.
Squires, Michael.
xSquires, Michael.
The Pastoral Novel: Studies in George Eliot,
Thomas Hardy, & D. H.Lawrence. U Pr of
Va.
Squires, Radcliffe. see Squires, James Radcliffe.
Squires, Richard C. see Squires, Richard S.
Squires, Richard S.
xSquires, Dick.
How to Play Platform Tennis. McGraw.
xSquires, Richard C.
How to Play Platform Tennis. Davin.
SRA Data Processing & Curriculum Group. see Sra
Data-Processing Curriculum Group.
Sra Data-Processing Curriculum Group.
xSRA Data Processing & Curriculum Group.
Case Study in Business System Design. SRA.
Sreenivasan, K. see Sreenivasan, Kasturiswami.
Sreenivasan, Kasturiswami, 1917-
xSreenivasan, K.
Productivity & Social Environment. Asia.
Srejovic, Dragoslav.
xSrejovic, Dragoslav.
Museums of Yugoslavia. Newsweek.
Sreniawski, R. W.
xSreniawski, R. W.
ed. Readings in Geography. Mss Info.
Srere, Paul A.
xSrere, Paul A.
ed. Microenvironments & Metabolic
Compartmentation. Acad Pr.
Sri Ram, N. see Sri Ram, Nilakanta.
Sri Ram, Nilakanta.
xSri Ram, N.
Approach to Reality. Theos Pub Hse.
Thoughts for Aspirants. Theos Pub Hse.
Thoughts for Aspirants. Theos Pub Hse.
Srikantaiah, Taverekere.
xSrikantaiah, Taverekere.
Introduction to Quantitative Research Methods
for Librarians. Headway Pubns.
Srinath, M. D.
xSrinath, M. D.
An Introduction to Statistical Signal Processing
with Applications. Wiley.
Srinivas, M. N. see Srinivas, Mysore Narasimhachar.
Srinivas, Mysore N. see Srinivas, Mysore Narasimhachar.
Srinivas, Mysore Narasimhachar.
xSrinivas, M. N.
The Remembered Village. U of Cal Pr.
xSrinivas, Mysore N.

ed. India's Villages. Asia.
Marriage & Family in Mysore. AMS Pr.
Srinivasa Iyengar, K. R.
xSrinivasa Iyengar, K. R.
Gerard Manley Hopkins: The Man & the Poet.
Folcroft.
Srinivasan, R. see Srinivasan, Rangaswamy.
Srinivasan, Rangaswamy.
xSrinivasan, R.
ed. Organic Photochemical Syntheses. Krieger.
Srinivasan, S. K. see Srinivasan, S. Kidambi.
Srinivasan, S. Kidambi.
xSrinivasan, S. K.
Stochastic Point Processes & Their
Applications. Hafner.
Stochastic Processes. McGraw.
Srivastava, Jane J. see Srivastava, Jane Jonas.
Srivastava, Jane Jonas.
xSrivastava, Jane J.
Area. T Y Crowell.
Averages. T Y Crowell.
Computers. T Y Crowell.
Number Families. T Y Crowell.
Spaces, Shapes, & Sizes. T Y Crowell.
Srivastava, M. S. see Srivastava, Muni Shanker.
Srivastava, Muni Shanker.
xSrivastava, M. S.
An Introduction to Multivariate Statistics.
Elsevier.
Srivastava, Nagendra. see Srivastava, Nagendra Mohan
Prasad.
Srivastava, Nagendra Mohan Prasad, 1941-
xSrivastava, Nagendra.
Growth of Nationalism in India: Effects of
International Events. Intl Pubns Serv.
Srivastava, Probodh K.
xSrivastava, Probodh K.
Basic Genetics for Health Professionals. PSG
Pub.
Sroka, Barbara.
xSroka, Barbara.
One Is a Whole Number. Victor Bks.
Sroka, Kazimierz A.
xSroka, Kazimierz A.
The Syntax of English Phrasal Verbs. Mouton.
Srouji, Jacque, 1944-
xSrouji, Jacque.
Critical Mass: Nuclear Power, the Alternative
to Energy Famine. Aurora Pubs.
Staaks, Walter, 1917-
xStaaks, Walter.
French Verb Usage: A Direct Approach for
American Students. Scott F.
Staal, J. F.
xStaal, J. F.
A Reader on the Sanskrit Grammarians. MIT
Pr.
Staar, Richard F. see Staar, Richard Felix.
Staar, Richard Felix.
xStaar, Richard F.
ed. Aspects of Modern Communism. U of SC
Pr.
Communist Regimes in Eastern Europe.
Hoover Inst Pr.
Staats, Arthur W.
xStaats, Arthur W.
Learning, Language, & Cognition: Theory,
Research, & Method for the Study of Human
Behavior & Its Development. Irvington.
Staats Bibliotech Preussischer Kulturbesitz Berlin. see
Staats Biblioteck Preussischer Kulturbesitz.
Staats Biblioteck Preussischer Kulturbesitz.
xStaats Bibliotech Preussischer Kulturbesitz Berlin.
ed. Union List of German Language Serials. K
G Saur.
xStaats Bibliothek Preussischer Kulturbesitz.
ed. Union List of Serials in Libraries of W.
Germany. K G Saur.
xStaatsbibliothek Preussischer Kulturbesitz.

ed. Bibliographische Berichte - Bibliographical
Bulletin. Intl Pubns Serv.
Staats Bibliothek Preussischer Kulturbesitz. see Staats
Biblioteck Preussischer Kulturbesitz.
Staatsbibliothek Preussischer Kulturbesitz. see Staats
Biblioteck Preussischer Kulturbesitz.
Stabb, Martin S.
xStabb, Martin S.
Jorge Luis Borges. St Martin.
Jorge Luis Borges. Twayne.
Stabiner, Karen.
xStabiner, Karen.
Limited Engagements. Playboy Pbks.
Limited Engagements. Seaview Bks.
Stableford, Brian M.
xStableford, Brian M.
Balance of Power. DAW Bks.
The City of the Sun. DAW Bks.
A Clash of Symbols: The Triumph of James
Blish. Borgo Pr.
Critical Threshold. DAW Bks.
The Mysteries of Modern Science. Littlefield.
The Mysteries of Modern Science. Routledge
& Kegan.
The Realms of Tartarus. DAW Bks.
Stables, Mira.
xStables, Mira.
Honey-Pot. Fawcett.
Stabley, Fred . W. see Stabley, Fred W.
Stabley, Fred W.
xStabley, Fred . W.
The Spartans: A Story of Michigan State
Football. Strode.
Stace, C.
xStace, C.
Stilus Artifex. Cambridge U Pr.
Stace, C. A. see Stace, Clive A.
Stace, Clive A.
xStace, C. A.
ed. Hybridization & the Flora of the British
Isles. Acad Pr.
Stacey, Barrie.
xStacey, Barrie.
Political Socialization in Western Society: An
Analysis from a Life-Span Perspective. St
Martin.
Psychology & Social Structure. Methuen Inc.
Stacey, Frank. see Stacey, Frank A.
Stacey, Frank A.
xStacey, Frank.
British Government 1966 to 1975: Years of
Reform. Oxford U Pr.
Stacey, John, fl. 1964-
xStacey, John.
John Wyclif & Reform. AMS Pr.
Stacey, W. H. see Stacey, Weston M.
Stacey, Weston M.
xStacey, W. H.
Space-Time Nuclear Reactor Kinetics. Acad Pr.
xStacey, Weston M.
Variational Methods in Nuclear Reactor
Physics. Acad Pr.
Stachowicz, Jim.
xStachowicz, Jim.
Diver's Guide to Florida & the Florida Keys.
Windward Pub.
Stachura, Peter. see Stachura, Peter D.
Stachura, Peter D.
xStachura, Peter.
ed. The Shaping of the Nazi State. B&N.
xStachura, Peter D.
Nazi Youth in the Weimar Republic.
ABC-Clio.
Stack, Carol B.
xStack, Carol B.
All Our Kin: Strategies for Survival in a Black
Community. Har-Row.
Stack, H. Graham. see Stack, Hugh Graham.
Stack, Hugh Graham.
xStack, H. Graham.

The Palmar Fascia. Churchill.

Stack, John F.
  xStack, John F.
    International Conflict in an American City:
      Boston's Irish, Italians & Jews, 1935-1944.
      Greenwood.

Stack, Louise.
  xStack, Louise.
    Torment to Triumph in Southern Africa.
      Friend Pr.

Stack, Robert.
  xStack, Robert.
    Straight Shooting. Macmillan.

Stacy, Gardner W. *see* Stacy, Gardner Wesley.

Stacy, Gardner Wesley, 1921-
  xStacy, Gardner W.
    Organic Chemistry: A Background for the Life
      Sciences. Har-Row.

Stacy, James, 1830-1912
  xStacy, James.
    History & Published Records of the Midway
      Congregational Church, Liberty County,
      Georgia. Reprint.

Stade, George.
  xStade, George.
    Confessions of a Ladykiller. Norton.

Stadelman, William J.
  xStadelman, William J.
    Egg Science & Technology. AVI.

Stadler, John.
  xStadler, John.
    Cat at Bat. Dutton.

Stadter, Philip A.
  xStadter, Philip A.
    Arrian of Nicomedia. U of NC Pr.
    The Speeches in Thucydides: A Collection of
      Original Studies with a Bibliography. U of
      NC Pr.

Stadtfeld, Curtis K., 1935-
  xStadtfeld, Curtis K.
    The Whitetail Deer: A Year's Cycle. Dial.

Stadtler, Bea.
  xStadtler, Bea.
    The Holocaust: A History of Courage &
      Resistance. Behrman.

Stael-Holstein, Anne L. *see* Stael-Holstein, Anne Louise
  Germaine Necker.

**Stael-Holstein, Anne Louise Germaine Necker, Baronne
De, 1766-1817**
  xStael-Holstein, Anne L.
    Reflections on Suicide. AMS Pr.

Staff of Eastman Kodak Co.,. *see* Eastman Kodak
  Company.

Staff of the Federal Architecture Project. *see* Federal
  Architecture Project.

Staff of the McGraw-Hill Encyclopedia of Science &
  Technology. *see* McGraw-Hill Encyclopedia of
  Science and Technology.

Staff of the Survey Research Center. *see* Michigan.
  University. Survey Research Center.

Stafford, Barbara. *see* Stafford, Barbara Maria.

Stafford, Barbara Maria, 1941-
  xStafford, Barbara.
    Symbol & Myth: Humbert De Superville's
      Essay on Absolute Signs in Art. U Delaware
      Pr.

Stafford, Caroline.
  xStafford, Caroline.
    The Honour of Ravensholme. S&S.
    The House by Exmoor. Fawcett.
    The House of Exmoor. S&S.

Stafford, Clayton.
  xStafford, Clayton.
    The Swan & the Eagle & Other Poems. SBD.

Stafford, Eugene C.
  xStafford, Eugene C.
    Modern Industrial Ceramics. Bobbs.

Stafford, Howard A.
  xStafford, Howard A.

Principles of Industrial Facility Location.
    Conway Pubns.

Stafford, Jean.
  xStafford, Jean.
    Boston Adventure. HarBraceJ.

Stafford, John, 1917-
  xStafford, John.
    Literary Criticism of Young America: A Study
      in the Relationship of Politics & Literature,
      1837-1850. Russell.

Stafford, L. W. *see* Stafford, L. W. T.

Stafford, L. W. T.
  xStafford, L. W.
    The Modern Economy: A Theoretical Debate
      & Its Practical Implications. Longman.

Stafford, Linley M.
  xStafford, Linley M.
    One Man's Family: A Single Father & His
      Children. Random.

Stafford, Maureen.
  xStafford, Maureen.
    An Illustrated Dictionary of Ornament. St
      Martin.

Stafford, Tim.
  xStafford, Tim.
    Do You Sometimes Feel Like a Nobody?.
      Zondervan.
    ed. The Trouble with Parents: How to Make
      Peace with Yours. Zondervan.

Stafford, William. *see* Stafford, William Edgar.

Stafford, William Edgar, 1914-
  xStafford, William.
    Someday, Maybe. Har-Row.
    Stories That Could Be True: New & Collected
      Poems. Har-Row.

Stafford-Clark, David.
  xStafford-Clark, David.
    Psychiatry for Students. Allen Unwin.

Stafleu, Frans A. *see* Stafleu, Frans Antonie.

Stafleu, Frans Antonie.
  xStafleu, Frans A.
    Taxonomic Literature: A Selective Guide to
      Botanical Publications with Dates,
      Commentaries & Types. Intl Pubns Serv.

Stage, Sarah.
  xStage, Sarah.
    Female Complaints: Lydia Pinkham & the
      Business of Women's Medicine. Norton.

Stagg, Frank, 1911-
  xStagg, Frank.
    The Holy Spirit Today. Broadman.

Stagg, Glenn W.
  xStagg, Glenn W.
    Computer Methods in Power System Analysis.
      McGraw.

Stagner, Lloyd E., 1923-
  xStagner, Lloyd E.
    Steam Locomotives of the Frisco Line. Pruett.

Stagner, Ross, 1909-
  xStagner, Ross.
    Psychology of Personality. McGraw.
    Psychology of Union-Management Relations.
      Brooks-Cole.

Stahl, Dona. *see* Stahl, Dona Kofod.

Stahl, Dona Kofod.
  xStahl, Dona.
    Individualized Teaching in the Elementary
      Schools. P-H.

Stahl, Franklin W.
  xStahl, Franklin W.
    Genetic Recombination: Thinking About It in
      Phage & Fungi. W H Freeman.
    Mechanics of Inheritance. P-H.

Stahl, Fred A.
  xStahl, Fred A.
    Reverse Dictionary of the Spanish Language. U
      of Ill Pr.

Stahl, Hilda. *see* Stahl, Hildaann.

Stahl, Hildaann.
  xStahl, Hilda.

Elizabeth Gail & the Mystery at the Johnson
    Farm. Tyndale.

Stahl, Jaspar J. *see* Stahl, Jasper J.

Stahl, Jasper J, 1886-
  xStahl, Jaspar J.
    History of Old Broadbay & Waldoboro.
      Wheelwright.

Stahl, Nancy, 1937-
  xStahl, Nancy.
    If It's Raining, This Must Be the Weekend.
      Andrews & McMeel.
    If It's Raining This Must Be the Weekend.
      Berkley Pub.

Stahl, Norman.
  xStahl, Norman.
    The Assault on Mavis A. Popular Lib.
    The Assault on Mavis A.. Random.

Stahl, O. Glenn. *see* Stahl, Oscar Glenn.

Stahl, Oscar Glenn.
  xStahl, O. Glenn.
    Frontier Mother. Chris Mass.
    The Personnel Job of Government Managers.
      Intl Personnel Mgmt.
    Public Personnel Administration. Har-Row.

Stahl, Sidney M.
  xStahl, Sidney M.
    Reading & Understanding Applied Statistics: A
      Self-Learning Approach. Mosby.

Stahl, William H. *see* Stahl, William Harris.

Stahl, William Harris.
  xStahl, William H.
    Martianus Capella & the Seven Liberal Arts.
      Columbia U Pr.

Stahl, William M.
  xStahl, William M.
    Supportive Care of the Surgical Patient. Grune.

Stahls, Paul. *see* Stahls, Paul F.

Stahls, Paul F.
  xStahls, Paul.
    Plantation Homes of the Lafourche Country.
      Pelican.
    Plantation Homes of the Teche Country.
      Pelican.

Stahr, H. M.
  xStahr, H. M.
    ed. Analytical Toxicology Methods Manual.
      Iowa St U Pr.

Stainback, Berry.
  xStainback, Berry.
    Pro Football Heroes of Today. Random.

Stainback, Susan B. *see* Stainback, Susan Bray.

Stainback, Susan Bray.
  xStainback, Susan B.
    Classroom Discipline: A Positive Approach. C
      C Thomas.
  xStainback, William C.
    jt. auth. Classroom Discipline: A Positive
      Approach. C C Thomas.

Stainback, William C.
  xStainback, William C.
    Establishing a Token Economy in the
      Classroom. Merrill.

Stainback, William C. *see* Stainback, Susan Bray.

Stainer, Cecie.
  xStainer, Cecie.
    Dictionary of Violin Makers. Longwood Pr.

Staines, David, 1946-
  xStaines, David.
    Intro. by Canadian Imagination: Dimensions of
      a Literary Culture. Harvard U Pr.

Stainton, J. D. *see* Stainton, J. D. A.

Stainton, J. D. A.
  xStainton, J. D.
    Forests of Nepal. Hafner.

Stair, Ralph M.
  xStair, Ralph M.
    Production & Operations Management: A
      Self-Correcting Approach. Allyn.

Stairs, Denis.
  xStairs, Denis.

The Diplomacy of Constraint: Canada, the Korean War, & the United States. U of Toronto Pr.

Stakgold, Ivar.
  xStakgold, Ivar.
    Green's Functions & Boundary Value Problems. Wiley.
Stakman, E. C. *see* Stakman, Elvin Charles.
Stakman, Elvin Charles.
  xStakman, E. C.
    Campaigns Against Hunger. Harvard U Pr.
Staley, Allen.
  xStaley, Allen.
    The Pre-Raphaelite Landscape. Oxford U Pr.
Staley, Eugene, 1906-
  xStaley, Eugene.
    Raw Materials in Peace & War. Arno.
Staley, Thomas F.
  xStaley, Thomas F.
    ed. Approaches to Joyce's Portrait: Ten Essays. U of Pittsburgh Pr.
    ed. James Joyce Today: Essays on the Major Works. Greenwood.
Stalin, Iosif, 1879-1953
  xStalin, Iosif.
    The October Revolution: A Collection of Articles & Speeches. AMS Pr.
  xStalin, Joseph.
    Great Patriotic War of the Soviet Union. Greenwood.
    Leninism: Selected Writings. Greenwood.
Stalin, Joseph. *see* Stalin, Iosif.
Stalker, James, 1848-1927
  xStalker, James M.
    Life of St. Paul. Revell.
Stalker, James M. *see* Stalker, James.
Stallard, John.
  xStallard, John.
    Four in a Wild Place. Norton.
Stallings, Barbara.
  xStallings, Barbara.
    Class Conflict & Economic Development in Chile, 1958-1973. Stanford U Pr.
Stallings, John. *see* Stallings, John Robert.
Stallings, John Robert, 1935-
  xStallings, John.
    Group Theory & Three-Dimensional Manifolds. Yale U Pr.
Stallings, Penny.
  xStallings, Penny.
    Flesh & Fantasy. St Martin.
Stallknecht, Newton P. *see* Stallknecht, Newton Phelps.
Stallknecht, Newton Phelps, 1906-
  xStallknecht, Newton P.
    George Santayana. U of Minn Pr.
    Strange Seas of Thought: Studies in William Wordsworth's Philosophy of Man & Nature. Greenwood.
Stallman, R. W. *see* Stallman, Robert Wooster.
Stallman, Robert W. *see* Stallman, Robert Wooster.
Stallman, Robert Wooster, 1911-
  xStallman, R. W.
    The Houses That James Built and Other Literary Studies. Ohio U Pr.
    Stephen Crane: A Critical Bibliography. Iowa St U Pr.
  xStallman, Robert W.
    ed. The Critic's Notebook. Greenwood.
Stallworth, Anne N. *see* Stallworth, Anne Nall.
Stallworth, Anne Nall.
  xStallworth, Anne N.
    Where the Bright Lights Shine. Vanguard.
  xStallworth, Anne Nall.
    Where the Bright Lights Shine. Popular Lib.
Stallworth, Lyn.
  xStallworth, Lyn.
    Woman's Day Snack Cookbook. Macmillan.
Stallworthy, E. A. *see* Stallworthy, Ernest A.
Stallworthy, Ernest A.
  xStallworthy, E. A.

Control of Investment in New Manufacturing Facilities. Beekman Pubs.
Stallworthy, Jon.
  xStallworthy, Jon.
    A Familiar Tree. Oxford U Pr.
    ed. The Penguin Book of Love Poetry. Penguin.
Stalvey, Lois M. *see* Stalvey, Lois Mark.
Stalvey, Lois Mark.
  xStalvey, Lois M.
    The Education of a Wasp. Morrow.
Stam, James H., 1937-
  xStam, James H.
    Inquiries into the Origin of Language: The Fate of a Question. Har-Row.
Stamaty, Mark. *see* Stamaty, Mark Alan.
Stamaty, Mark A. *see* Stamaty, Mark Alan.
Stamaty, Mark Alan.
  xStamaty, Mark.
    illus. Who Needs Donuts?. Dial.
  xStamaty, Mark A.
    Who Needs Donuts?. Dial.
Stambaugh, Joan, 1932-
  xStambaugh, Joan.
    Nietzsche's Thought of Eternal Return. Johns Hopkins.
Stambler, Irwin.
  xStambler, Irwin.
    Catfish Hunter: The Three-Million Dollar Arm. Putnam.
    Encyclopedia of Pop, Rock & Soul. St Martin.
    Ocean Liners of the Air. Putnam.
    Racing the Sprint Cars. Putnam.
Stambolian, George.
  xStambolian, George.
    ed. Homosexualities & French Literature: Cultural Contexts, Critical Texts. Cornell U Pr.
    Marcel Proust & the Creative Encounter. U of Chicago Pr.
Stambuk, George.
  xStambuk, George.
    American Military Forces Abroad: Their Impact on the Western State System. Ohio St U Pr.
Stamm, A. J. *see* Stamm, Alfred Joaquim.
Stamm, Alfred Joaquim, 1897-
  xStamm, A. J.
    Wood & Cellulose Science. Wiley.
Stamm, Douglas R.
  xStamm, Douglas R.
    Under Water: The Northern Lakes. U of Wis Pr.
Stamm, Laura.
  xStamm, Laura.
    ed. Power Skating the Hockey Way. Dutton.
Stamm, Mildred.
  xStamm, Millie.
    Meditation Moments for Women. Zondervan.
Stamm, Millie. *see* Stamm, Mildred.
Stammbach, U.
  xStammbach, U.
    Homology in Group Theory. Springer-Verlag.
Stammler, Rudolf, 1856-1938
  xStammler, Rudolf.
    Theory of Justice. Kelley.
    Theory of Justice. Rothman.
Stamp, Don.
    Challenge of Archery. Intl Pubns Serv.
    The Challenge of Archery. Transatlantic.
Stamp, E. *see* Stamp, Edward.
Stamp, Edward.
  xStamp, E.
    International Auditing Standards. P-H.
Stamp, Elizabeth.
  xStamp, Elizabeth.
    ed. Growing Out of Poverty. Oxford U Pr.
Stamp, L. Dudley. *see* Stamp, Laurence Dudley.

Stamp, Laurence Dudley, 1898-
  xStamp, L. Dudley.
    Asia: A Regional & Economic Geography. Methuen Inc.
Stampe, David, 1938-
  xStampe, David.
    A Dissertation on Natural Phonology. Garland Pub.
Stamper, Alva W. *see* Stamper, Alva Walker.
Stamper, Alva Walker.
  xStamper, Alva W.
    A History of the Teaching of Elementary Geometry. AMS Pr.
Stamper, B. Maxwell, 1947-
  xStamper, B. Maxwell.
    Population & Planning in Developing Nations: A Review of Sixty Development Plans for the 1970s. Population Coun.
Stamper, Eugene.
  xStamper, Eugene.
    Mechanical Engineering & Economics & Ethics for Professional Engineering Examinations. Hayden.
Stampfle, Felice.
  xStampfle, Felice.
    Compiled by Drawings from the Collection of Lore & Rudolf Heinemann. Pierpont Morgan.
Stampp, Kenneth M. *see* Stampp, Kenneth Milton.
Stampp, Kenneth Milton.
  xStampp, Kenneth M.
    And the War Came: The North and the Secession Crisis, 1860-1861. Greenwood.
    And the War Came: The North & the Secession Crisis, 1860-1861. La State U Pr.
    ed. The Causes of the Civil War. P-H.
    ed. Causes of the Civil War. Peter Smith.
    Indiana Politics During the Civil War. Ind U Pr.
    The Southern Road to Appomattox. Tex Western.
Stamps, Ellen. *see* Stamps, Ellen De Kroon.
Stamps, Ellen D. *see* Stamps, Ellen De Kroon.
Stamps, Ellen De Kroon, 1940-
  xStamps, Ellen.
    My Years with Corrie. Revell.
  xStamps, Ellen D.
    My Years with Corrie. G K Hall.
Stan-Padilla, Viento, 1945-
  xStan-Padilla, Viento.
    Dream Feather. Dawne-Leigh.
Stanard, Mary Mann Page (Newton), 1865-1929
  xStanard, Mary N.
    Colonial Virginia: Its People & Customs. Gale.
Stanard, Mary N. *see* Stanard, Mary Mann Page (Newton).
Stanat, Donald F.
  xStanat, Donald F.
    Discrete Mathematics in Computer Science. P-H.
Stanback, Thomas M.
  xStanback, Thomas M.
    Understanding the Service Economy: Employment, Productivity, Location. Johns Hopkins.
Stanbury, C. M.
  xStanbury, C. M.
    Anti-Matter. Dustbooks.
Stanbury, David.
  xStanbury, David.
    Living World. Macmillan.
Stanchfield, Jo M.
  xStanchfield, Jo M.
    Horizons. HM.
    Paces. HM.
    Patterns. HM.
Stancu, Zaharia.
  xStancu, Zaharia.
    Barefoot. Irvington.
Stancyk, Stephen E.
  xStancyk, Stephen E.

ed. Reproductive Ecology of Marine
Invertebrates. U of SC Pr.
Standard Education Corporation. *see* Standard
Educational Corporation.
Standard Educational Corporation.
xStandard Education Corporation.
New Standard Encyclopedia. Standard Ed..
Standard, Stella.
xStandard, Stella.
Our Daily Bread. Berkley Pub.
Stella Standard's Soup Book. Taplinger.
**Standard Symposium on Mathematical Methods in the
Social Sciences, Stanford University, 1959.**
xFirst Stanford Symposium.
Mathematical Methods in the Social Sciences,
1959: Proceedings. Stanford U Pr.
Standing Conference on Library Materials on Africa.
xStanding Conference on Library Materials on
Africa.
Periodicals from Africa: A Bibliography &
Union List of Periodicals Published in Africa.
G K Hall.
Standing, E. M. *see* Standing, E. Mortimer.
Standing, E. Mortimer.
xStanding, E. M.
The Montessori Revolution in Education.
Schocken.
Standish, Thomas A., 1941-
xStandish, Thomas A.
A Data Definition Facility for Programming
Languages. Garland Pub.
Data Structure Techniques. A-W.
Standl, Hans, 1926-
xStandl, Hans.
Pistol Shooting As a Sport. Crown.
Standley, Fred L.
xStandley, Fred L.
Stopford Brooke. Twayne.
Standley, K J.
xStandley, K. J.
Oxide Magnetic Materials. Oxford U Pr.
Standley, P. *see* Standley, Paul Carpenter.
Standley, Paul Carpenter, 1884-1963
xStandley, P.
Trees & Shrubs of Mexico. Gordon Pr.
Stands in Timber, John.
xStands In Timber, John.
Cheyenne Memories. U of Nebr Pr.
Cheyenne Memories. Yale U Pr.
Stanek, Muriel. *see* Stanek, Muriel Novella.
Stanek, Muriel Novella.
xStanek, Muriel.
Growl When You Say R. A Whitman.
Left, Right, Left, Right. A Whitman.
One, Two, Three for Fun. A Whitman.
Stanerson, Lavon.
xStanerson, Lavon.
Creative Stitchery. Lerner Pubns.
Stanescu, Dan C.
xStanescu, Dan C.
Early Detection of Chronic Bronchitis &
Pulmonary Emphysema. Lippincott.
Stanfield, Ron.
xStanfield, Ron.
The Economic Surplus & Neo-Marxism.
Lexington Bks.
Stanford, A. L. *see* Stanford, Augustus L.
Stanford, Ann.
xStanford, Ann.
The Descent. SBD.
Stanford Arms Control Group.
xStanford Arms Control Group.
International Arms Control: Issues &
Agreements. Stanford U Pr.
Stanford, Augustus L., 1931-
xStanford, A. L.
Foundations of Biophysics. Acad Pr.
Stanford, Barbara D. *see* Stanford, Barbara Dodds.
Stanford, Barbara Dodds.
xStanford, Barbara D.

I, Too, Sing America: Black Voices in
American Literature. Hayden.
Stanford, Charles V. *see* Stanford, Charles Villiers.
Stanford, Charles Villiers, Sir, 1852-1924
xStanford, Charles V.
Studies & Memories. Longwood Pr.
Stanford, Donald E., 1913-
xStanford, Donald E.
In the Classic Mode: The Achievement of
Robert Bridges. U Delaware Pr.
Stanford, Gene.
xStanford, Gene.
Human Interaction in Education. Allyn.
Learning Discussion Skills Through Games.
Schol Bk Serv.
Stanford, Melvin J., 1932-
xStanford, Melvin J.
Management Policy. P-H.
Stanford, Miles. *see* Stanford, Miles J.
Stanford, Miles J.
xStanford, Miles.
Abide Above: A Guide to Spiritual Growth.
Zondervan.
Stanford, Quentin. *see* Stanford, Quentin H.
Stanford, Quentin H.
xStanford, Quentin.
ed. The World's Population: Problems of
Growth. Oxford U Pr.
xStanford, Quentin H.
Geography: A Study of Its Elements. Oxford U
Pr.
Stanford, Ray.
xStanford, Ray.
Socorro "Saucer" in a Pentagon Pantry.
Blueapple Bks.
Stanford Research Institute.
xStanford Research Institute.
Jicarilla Apache Tribe of the Jicarilla Indian
Reservation in New Mexico, 1849-1870:
Historical & Documentary Evidence.
Clearwater Pub.
Solar Energy in America's Future. Solar
Energy Info.
Stanford University.
xStanford University.
Stanford Studies in History, Economics &
Political Science. AMS Pr.
Stanford Studies in Language & Literature.
AMS Pr.
Stanford University. Dramatists' Alliance.
xStanford University Dramatists' Alliance.
Plays of the Southern Americas. Arno.
**Stanford University. Hoover Institution on War,
Revolution and Peace.**
xHoover Institution Staff.
Archival & Manuscript Materials at the Hoover
Institution on War, Revolution & Peace: A
Checklist of Major Collections. Hoover Inst
Pr.
xStanford University, Hoover Institution on War,
Revolution & Peace.

Catalog of the Arabic Collection. G K Hall.
Catalog of the Chinese Collection. G K Hall.
Catalog of the Chinese Collection First
Supplement. G K Hall.
The Catalog of the Chinese Collection: Second
Supplement. G K Hall.
Catalog of the Japanese Collection. G K Hall.
Catalog of the Japanese Collection, First
Supplement. G K Hall.
Catalog of the Japanese Collection: Second
Supplement. G K Hall.
Catalog of the Turkish & Persian Collections.
G K Hall.
Catalog of the Western Language Collection. G
K Hall.
Catalog of the Western Language Collections,
First Supplement. G K Hall.
The Catalog of the Western Language
Collections: Second Supplement. G K Hall.
Catalogs of the Western Language Serials &
Newspaper Collection. G K Hall.
Stanford University. School of Letters.
xStanford University, School of Letters.
Stanford Studies in Language & Literature
1941: Fiftieth Anniversary of the Founding of
Stanford University. Arno.
Stanford, W. Bedell. *see* Stanford, William Bedell.
Stanford, William Bedell.
xStanford, W. Bedell.
Enemies of Poetry. Routledge & Kegan.
Stanforth, Deidre. *see* Stanforth, Deirdre.
Stanforth, Deirdre.
xStanforth, Deidre.
Buying & Renovating a House in the City: A
Practical Guide. Knopf.
xStanforth, Deirdre.
Romantic New Orleans. Penguin.
Stang, Alan.
xStang, Alan.
The Highest Virtue. Western Islands.
Stang, Joanne.
xStang, JoAnne.
Shadows on the Sceptered Isle. Crown.
Stang, Sondra J.
xStang, Sondra J.
Ford Madox Ford. Ungar.
Stange, Douglas C.
xStange, Douglas C.
Patterns of Antislavery Among American
Unitarians, 1831-1860. Fairleigh Dickinson.
Stange, G. Robert. *see* Stange, George Robert.
Stange, George Robert, 1919-
xStange, G. Robert.
Matthew Arnold: The Poet As Humanist.
Gordian.
Stangel, John J., 1941-
xStangel, John J.
Fertility & Conception: An Essential Guide for
Childless Couples. Facts on File.
Fertility & Conception: An Essential Guide for
Childless Couples. NAL.
Fertility & Conception: An Essential Guide for
Childless Couples. Paddington.
Stanger, Frank B. *see* Stanger, Frank Bateman.
Stanger, Frank Bateman.
xStanger, Frank B.
God's Healing Community. Abingdon.
Stanger, Margaret A.
xStanger, Margaret A.
That Quail, Robert. Fawcett.
That Quail, Robert. Lippincott.
Stangler, Sharon. *see* Stangler, Sharon R.
Stangler, Sharon R.
xStangler, Sharon.
Screening Growth & Development of Preschool
Children: A Guide for Test Selection.
McGraw.
Stangos, Nikos.
xStangos, Nikos.

Greek Phrase Book. Penguin.
Greek Phrase Book. Peter Smith.
Stangvik, Gunnar.
xStangvik, Gunnar.
Self-Concept & School Segregation.
Humanities.
Stanhope, Henry.
xStanhope, Henry.
The Soldiers: An Anatomy of the British
Army. David & Charles.
Stanhope, Philip H. see Stanhope, Philip Henry Stanhope,
5th Earl.
Stanhope, Philip Henry Stanhope, 5th Earl, 1805-1875
xStanhope, Philip H.
Life of the Right Honourable William Pitt.
AMS Pr.
Staniar, William.
xStaniar, William.
ed. Plant Engineering Handbook. McGraw.
Stanier, Roger. see Stanier, Roger Y.
Stanier, Roger Y.
xStanier, Roger.
Introduction to the Microbial World. P-H.
Staniforth, A. R.
xStaniforth, A. R.
Cereal Straw. Oxford U Pr.
Staniforth, Maxwell.
xStaniforth, Maxwell.
tr. Early Christian Writings: The Apostolic
Fathers. Penguin.
Stanislaw, Richard J.
xStanislaw, Richard J.
Intro. by A Checklist of Four-Shape
Shape-Note Tunebooks. Inst Am Music.
Stanislawczyk, Irene E.
xStanislawczyk, Irene E.
Creativity in the Language Classroom.
Newbury Hse.
Stanislawski, Dan.
xStanislawski, Dan.
Anatomy of Eleven Towns in Michoacan.
Greenwood.
Individuality of Portugal: A Study in
Historical-Political Geography. Greenwood.
Stankiewicz, W. J.
xStankiewicz, W. J.
ed. In Defense of Sovereignty. Oxford U Pr.
Stanley, Autumn.
xStanley, Autumn.
Asparagus: The Sparrowgrass Cookbook.
Pacific Search.
Stanley, Carleton. see Stanley, Carleton Wellesley.
Stanley, Carleton Wellesley, 1886-1971
xStanley, Carleton.
Matthew Arnold. Folcroft.
xStanley, Carlton W.
Matthew Arnold. R West.
Stanley, Carlton W. see Stanley, Carleton Wellesley.
Stanley, Charles J.
xStanley, Charles J.
ed. Maine Moments in New York. Pittore
Euforico.
Stanley, David M.
xStanley, David M.
Apostolic Church in the New Testament.
Paulist Pr.
Stanley, David T.
xStanley, David T.
Changing Administrations: The 1961 & 1964
Transitions in Six Departments. Brookings.
The Higher Civil Service: An Evaluation of
Federal Personnel Practices. Brookings.
Men Who Govern: A Biographical Profile of
Federal Political Executives. Brookings.
Prisoners Among Us: The Problem of Parole.
Brookings.
Stanley, Del. see Stanley, Delmar S.
Stanley, Delmar S.
xStanley, Del.

Practical Accounting. Goodyear.
xStanley, Delmar S.
Practical Accounting. Goodyear.
Stanley, Dorothy E. see Stanley, Dorothy Evelyn.
Stanley, Dorothy Evelyn, 1909-
xStanley, Dorothy E.
How to Live Creatively. Donning Co.
Stanley Gibbons Ltd. see Gibbons (Stanley) Ltd.,
London.
Stanley, H. Eugene. see Stanley, Harry Eugene.
Stanley, Harry Eugene.
xStanley, H. Eugene.
Introduction to Phase Transitions & Critical
Phenomena. Oxford U Pr.
Stanley, Henry M. see Stanley, Henry Morton.
Stanley, Henry Morton, Sir, 1841-1904
xStanley, Henry M.
My Kalulu, Prince, King, & Slave: A Story of
Central Africa. Negro U Pr.
Story of Emin's Rescue As Told in Stanley's
Letters. Negro U Pr.
Stanley, J. A.
xStanley, J. A.
From CB to Ham Beginner. Sams.
Stanley, Linda.
xStanley, Linda.
Close-up on Composition. Wadsworth Pub.
xStanley, Linda C.
The Foreign Critical Reputation of F. Scott
Fitzgerald: An Analysis & Annotated
Bibliography. Greenwood.
Stanley, Linda C. see Stanley, Linda.
Stanley, Michael.
xStanley, Michael.
The Boomerang Conspiracy. Avon.
The Swiss Conspiracy. Avon.
Stanley, Peter W.
xStanley, Peter W.
A Nation in the Making: The Philippines & the
United States, 1899-1921. Harvard U Pr.
Stanley, R. C. see Stanley, Reginald Cyril.
Stanley, Reginald Cyril.
xStanley, R. C.
Applied Physical Techniques. Crane-Russak
Co.
Stanley, Richard. see Stanley, Richard P.
Stanley, Richard P., 1944-
xStanley, Richard.
Ordered Structures & Partitions. Am Math.
Stanley, Robert H.
xStanley, Robert H.
The Media Environment: Mass
Communications in American Society.
Hastings.
Stanley, Sam. see Stanley, Samuel L.
Stanley, Samuel L.
xStanley, Sam.
ed. American Indian Economic Development.
Beresford Bk Serv.
Stanley, William D.
xStanley, William D.
Digital Signal Processing. Reston.
Stanley, William O. see Stanley, William Oliver.
Stanley, William Oliver, 1903-
xStanley, William O.
Education & Social Integration. Tchrs Coll.
Stanley, William T.
xStanley, William T.
Compiled by Broadway in the West End: An
Index of Reviews of the American Theatre in
London, 1950-1975. Greenwood.
Stanlis, Peter J. see Stanlis, Peter James.
Stanlis, Peter James, 1920-
xStanlis, Peter J.
Edmund Burke & the Natural Law. U of Mich
Pr.
Stannard, David E.
xStannard, David E.

The Puritan Way of Death: A Study in
Religion, Culture & Social Change. Oxford U
Pr.
The Puritan Way of Death: A Study in
Religion, Culture, & Social Change. Oxford U
Pr.
Shrinking History: On Freud & the Failure of
Psychohistory. Oxford U Pr.
Stannard, Una, 1927-
xStannard, Una.
Mrs Man. Germainbooks.
Stanner, W. E. see Stanner, W. E. H.
Stanner, W. E. H.
xStanner, W. E.
The South Seas in Transition: A Study of
Post-War Rehabilitation & Reconstruction in
Three British Pacific Dependencies. AMS Pr.
Stansberger, Richard, 1950-
xStansberger, Richard.
The Glass Hat. La State U Pr.
Stansbury, Donald L.
xStansbury, Donald L.
Impact: Short Stories for Pleasure. P-H.
Stansky, Peter.
xStansky, Peter.
ed. Churchill: A Profile. Hill & Wang.
Journey to the Frontier: Two Roads to the
Spanish Civil War. Norton.
Stanton, Ann M.
xStanton, Ann M.
When Mothers Go to Jail. Lexington Bks.
Stanton, Elizabeth.
xStanton, Elizabeth.
Sometimes I Like to Cry. A Whitman.
Stanton, Elizabeth (Cady), 1815-1902
xStanton, Elizabeth C.
Eighty Years & More Reminiscences,
1815-1897. Schocken.
ed. History of Woman Suffrage. Arno.
History of Woman Suffrage. Hacker.
Stanton, Elizabeth C. see Stanton, Elizabeth (Cady).
Stanton, Esther.
xStanton, Esther.
Clients Come Last: Volunteers & Welfare
Organizations. Sage.
Stanton, J. R. see Stanton, John R.
Stanton, John R., 1923-
xStanton, J. R.
Theory & Practice of Propellers from Auxiliary
Sailboats. Cornell Maritime.
Stanton, Maura. see Stanton, Mavra.
Stanton, Mavra.
xStanton, Maura.
Molly Companion. Avon.
Stanton, Mildred B. see Stanton, Mildred Bacon.
Stanton, Mildred Bacon, 1899-
xStanton, Mildred B.
Mechanical Ability of Deaf Children. AMS Pr.
Stanton, Phoebe B.
xStanton, Phoebe B.
The Gothic Revival & American Church
Architecture: An Episode in Taste,
1840-1856. Johns Hopkins.
Stanton, R. E. see Stanton, Ronald Ernest.
Stanton, R. L.
xStanton, R. L.
Ore Petrology. McGraw.
Stanton, Robert B. see Stanton, Robert Brewster.
Stanton, Robert Brewster.
xStanton, Robert B.
The Hoskaninni Papers, Mining in Glen
Canyon, 1897-1902. AMS Pr.
Stanton, Robert L. see Stanton, Robert Livingston.
Stanton, Robert Livingston, 1810-1885
xStanton, Robert L.
The Church & the Rebellion. Arno.
Stanton, Ronald Ernest.
xStanton, R. E.

Analytical Methods for Use in Geochemical Exploration. Halsted Pr.

Stanton, Royal.
xStanton, Royal.
The Dynamic Choral Conductor. Shawnee Pr.
Steps to Singing for Voice Classes. Wadsworth Pub.

Stanton, Theodore, 1851-1925
xStanton, Theodore.
ed. Reminiscences of Rosa Bonheur. Hacker.
Stanton, William. see Stanton, William Ragan.
Stanton, William R. see Stanton, William Ragan.

Stanton, William Ragan.
xStanton, William.
The Great United States Exploring Expedition of 1838-1842. U of Cal Pr.
The Leopard's Spots: Scientific Attitudes Toward Race in America, Eighteen Fifteen to Eighteen Fifty-Nine. Univ Place.
xStanton, William R.
Leopard's Spots: Scientific Attitudes Toward Race in America, 1815-1859. U of Chicago Pr.

Stanway, Andrew.
xStanway, Andrew.
Taking the Rough with the Smooth: Dietary Fibre & Your Health - a New Medical Breakthrough. Intl Schol Bk Serv.
Stanwood, Donald. see Stanwood, Donald A.

Stanwood, Donald A.
xStanwood, Donald.
The Memory of Eva Ryker. Dell.
xStanwood, Donald A.
The Memory of Eva Ryker. Coward.

Stanwood, Edward, 1841-1923
xStanwood, Edward.
American Tariff Controversies in the Nineteenth Century. Garland Pub.
History of the Presidency. Kelley.

Stanyer, Jeffrey.
xStanyer, Jeffrey.
County Government in England & Wales. Humanities.
Understanding Local Government. Biblio Dist.

Stanyon, Ellis.
xStanyon, Ellis.
Card Tricks for Everyone. Emerson.
Stapledon, Olaf. see Stapledon, William Olaf.
Stapledon, W. Olaf. see Stapledon, William Olaf.

Stapledon, William Olaf, 1886-1950
xStapledon, Olaf.
Last Men in London. Gregg.
Odd John & Sirius: Two Science-Fiction Novels. Peter Smith.
xStapledon, W. Olaf.
Darkness & the Light. Hyperion Conn.
Staples, Frederick. see Staples, Frederick Stanley.

Staples, Frederick Stanley, 1891-
xStaples, Frederick.
Auditing Manual. Counting Hse.
The Monthly Financial Statements. Counting Hse.
Standardized Audit Working Papers. Counting Hse.

Staples, I. Ezra.
xStaples, I. Ezra.
Impact of Decentralization on Curriculum: Selected Viewpoints. Assn Supervision.
Staples, M. P. see Staples, Michael P.

Staples, Michael P.
xStaples, M. P.
White Crane Gung-Fu. Wehman.
Staples, R. see Staples, Robert.

Staples, Robert.
xStaples, R.
Introduction to Black Sociology. McGraw.

Stapleton, Alfred.
xStapleton, Alfred.
All About the Merry Tales of Gotham. Folcroft.

Stapleton, Jean.
xStapleton, Jean.
Equal Dating. Abingdon.

Stapleton, John, fl. 1971-
xStapleton, John.
ed. Marketing Handbook. Herman Pub.
Stapleton, Richard J. see Stapleton, Richard John.

Stapleton, Richard John, 1940-
xStapleton, Richard J.
De-Gaming Teaching & Learning: How to Motivate Learners & Invite OKness. Effect Learning GA.
Stapleton, Ruth C. see Stapleton, Ruth Carter.

Stapleton, Ruth Carter.
xStapleton, Ruth C.
Brother Billy. Har-Row.
The Experience of Inner Healing. G K Hall.
The Gift of Inner Healing. Word Bks.
In His Footsteps: The Healing Ministry of Jesus, Then & Now. Har-Row.
Stapleton, W. Vaughan. see Stapleton, William Vaughan.

Stapleton, William Vaughan.
xStapleton, W. Vaughan.
In Defense of Youth: A Study of the Role of Counsel in American Juvenile Courts. Russell Sage.

Stapley, Ray.
xStapley, Ray.
The Car Owner's Handbook. Doubleday.

Stapp, William B.
xStapp, William B.
ed. Environmental Education: A Guide to Information Sources. Gale.

Stappenbeck, Herb.
xStappenbeck, Herb.
Compiled by A Catalogue of the Joseph Hergesheimer Collection at the University of Texas. U of Tex Hum Res.

Staquet, Maurice.
xStaquet, Maurice J.
ed. Randomized Trials in Cancer: A Critical Review by Sites. Raven.
Staquet, Maurice J. see Staquet, Maurice.

Star, Cima.
xStar, Cima.
Understanding Headaches. Monarch Pr.

Star, Steven H.
xStar, Steven H.
Problems in Marketing. McGraw.

Starbird, Kaye.
xStarbird, Kaye.
The Covered Bridge House & Other Poems. Schol Bk Serv.

Starbuck, Alma J.
xStarbuck, Alma J.
Complete Irish Wolfhound. Howell Bk.

Starbuck, George, 1931-
xStarbuck, George.
Desperate Measures. Godine.

Starch, Daniel, 1883-
xStarch, Daniel.
Advertising Principles. Arno.

Starchild, Adam.
xStarchild, Adam.
How to Develop & Manage a Successful Condominium. Bks Business.
It's Your Money: A Consumers Guide to Credit. Bks Business.
Starchild & Holahan's Seafood Cookbook. Pacific Search.
Tax Havens for Corporations. Gulf Pub.
Tax Havens: What They Are & What They Can Do for the Shrewd Investor. Arlington Hse.
Starcke, Carl N. see Starcke, Carl Nicolai.

Starcke, Carl Nicolai, 1858-1926
xStarcke, Carl N.
The Primitive Family in Its Origin & Development. U of Chicago Pr.

Starcke, Walter.
xStarcke, Walter.
This Double Thread. Attic Pr.
Ultimate Revolution. Har-Row.
xStarcke, Walter A.
The Gospel of Relativity. Har-Row.
Starcke, Walter A. see Starcke, Walter.
Stare, Frederick J. see Stare, Fredrick John.
Stare, Fredrick J. see Stare, Fredrick John.

Stare, Fredrick John.
xStare, Frederick J.
Living Nutrition. Wiley.
xStare, Fredrick J.
Eat OK Feel OK!: Food Facts & Your Health. Chris Mass.

Stark, Barbara L.
xStark, Barbara L.
ed. Prehistoric Coastal Adaptations: The Economy & Ecology of Maritime Middle America. Acad Pr.
Stark, David C. see Stark, David C. C.

Stark, David C. C.
xStark, David C.
ed. Practical Points in Anesthesiology. Med Exam.
Stark, Francis R. see Stark, Francis Raymond.

Stark, Francis Raymond, 1877-
xStark, Francis R.
Abolition of Privateering, & the Declaration of Paris. AMS Pr.

Stark, Freya.
xStark, Freya.
A Peak in Darien. Transatlantic.

Stark, Harold M., 1939-
xStark, Harold M.
An Introduction to Number Theory. MIT Pr.
Stark, J. P. see Stark, John Paul.
Stark, James H. see Stark, James Henry.

Stark, James Henry.
xStark, James H.
Loyalists of Massachusetts & the Other Side of the American Revolution. Kelley.

Stark, Joan S.
xStark, Joan S.
The Many Faces of Educational Consumerism. Lexington Bks.

Stark, John O.
xStark, John O.
Almanac of British & American Literature. Libs Unl.
The Literature of Exhaustion: Borges, Nabokov & Barth.. Duke.
Pynchon's Fictions: Thomas Pynchon & the Literature of Information. Ohio U Pr.

Stark, John Paul, 1938-
xStark, J. P.
Solid State Diffusion. Krieger.

Stark, Norman.
xStark, Norman.
The Formula Book. Andrews & McMeel.
The Formula Book. Avon.

Stark, Peter A.
xStark, Peter A.
Introduction to Numerical Methods. Macmillan.

Stark, Stephen L.
xStark, Stephen L.
Conducting Community Surveys. Pendell Pub.

Stark, Thomas.
xStark, Thomas.
Distribution of Personal Income in the United Kingdom, 1949-1963. Cambridge U Pr.

Stark, Werner, 1909-
xStark, Werner.

Sociology of Knowledge: An Essay in Aid of a
Deeper Understanding of the History of
Ideas. Humanities.

Starkes, M. Thomas.
xStarkes, M. Thomas.
Confronting Popular Cults. Broadman.
Starkey, Marion L. *see* Starkey, Marion Lena.
Starkey, Marion Lena.
xStarkey, Marion L.
Cherokee Nation. Russell.
Devil in Massachusetts: A Modern Inquiry into
the Salem Witch Trials. Peter Smith.
Starkey, Otis P. *see* Starkey, Otis Paul.
Starkey, Otis Paul.
xStarkey, Otis P.
The Anglo-American Realm. McGraw.
Starkie, Enid.
xStarkie, Enid.
Arthur Rimbaud. Greenwood.
Arthur Rimbaud. New Directions.
From Gautier to Eliot: The Influence of France
on English Literature, 1851-1939. Scholarly.
Starkie, Walter. *see* Starkie, Walter Fitzwilliam.
Starkie, Walter Fitzwilliam, 1894-
xStarkie, Walter.
Luigi Pirandello, 1867-1936. U of Cal Pr.
Starkman, Ernest S.
xStarkman, Ernest S.
ed. Combustion-Generated Air Pollution.
Plenum Pub.
Starkman, Miriam. *see* Starkman, Miriam (Kosh).
Starkman, Miriam (Kosh).
xStarkman, Miriam.
Swift's Satire on Learning in 'A Tale of a
Tub'. Octagon.
Starks, Charles. *see* Starks, Charles M.
Starks, Charles M.
xStarks, Charles.
Free Radical Telomerization. Acad Pr.
Starks, Michael.
xStarks, Michael.
Marijuana Potency. And-or Pr.
Starling, Alfred, 1928-
xStarling, Alfred.
Enjoying Indiana Birds. Ind U Pr.
Starling, Grover.
xStarling, Grover.
The Politics & Economics of Public Policy: An
Introductory Analysis with Cases. Dorsey.
Starling, Thomas.
xStarling, Thomas.
The Garlic Kid. Spindrift.
Starobin, Joseph R. *see* Starobin, Joseph Robert.
Starobin, Joseph Robert, 1913-
xStarobin, Joseph R.
American Communism in Crisis, 1943-1957.
Harvard U Pr.
American Communism in Crisis, 1943-1957. U
of Cal Pr.
Starobin, Robert S.
xStarobin, Robert S.
ed. Denmark Vesey: The Slave Conspiracy of
1822. P-H.
Industrial Slavery in the Old South. Oxford U
Pr.
Industrial Slavery in the Old South. Oxford U
Pr.
Starr, Bernard D.
xStarr, Bernard D.
Human Development & Behavior: Psychology
in Nursing. Springer Pub.
Starr, C. *see* Starr, Chauncey.
Starr, Chauncey.
xStarr, C.
Current Issues in Energy. Pergamon.
Starr, Chester G., 1914-
xStarr, Chester G.

Ancient Greeks. Oxford U Pr.
Ancient Romans. Oxford U Pr.
The Economic & Social Growth of Early
Greece, 800-500 B. C.. Oxford U Pr.
A History of the Ancient World. Oxford U Pr.
Starr, David E., 1940-
xStarr, David E.
Entity & Existence: An Ontological
Investigation of Aristotle & Heidegger. B
Franklin.
Starr, Douglas P.
xStarr, Douglas P.
How to Handle Speechwriting Assignments.
Pilot Bks.
Starr, Edward.
xStarr, Edward.
What You Should Know About Public
Relations. Oceana.
Starr, Fred.
xStarr, Fred.
Climb the Highest Mountain. Chris Mass.
Gifts from the Hill. Chris Mass.
Of These Hills and Us. Chris Mass.
Starr, Frederick, 1858-1933
xStarr, Frederick.
American Indians. AMS Pr.
In Indian Mexico: A Narrative of Travel &
Labor. AMS Pr.
Truth About the Congo: The Chicago Tribune
Articles. Negro U Pr.
Starr, G. *see* Starr, Graeme.
Starr, G. A. *see* Starr, George A.
Starr, George A.
xStarr, G. A.
Defoe & Casuistry. Princeton U Pr.
xStarr, George A.
Defoe & Spiritual Autobiography. Gordian.
Starr, George R. *see* Starr, George Ross.
Starr, George Ross.
xStarr, George R.
How to Make Working Decoys. Winchester Pr.
Starr, Graeme.
xStarr, G.
Political Parties in Australia. Heinemann Ed.
Starr, Herbert W. *see* Starr, Herbert Willmarth.
Starr, Herbert Willmarth, 1916-
xStarr, Herbert W.
Gray, As a Literary Critic. Folcroft.
Starr, J. Barton. *see* Starr, Joseph Barton.
Starr, John B. *see* Starr, John Bryan.
Starr, John Bryan.
xStarr, John B.
Continuing the Revolution: The Political
Thought of Mao. Princeton U Pr.
Ideology & Culture: An Introduction to the
Dialectic of Contemporary Chinese Politics.
Har-Row.
Post-Liberation Works of Mao Zedong: A
Bibliography & Index. IEAS Ctr Chinese
Stud.
Starr, Joseph Barton, 1945-
xStarr, J. Barton.
Tories, Dons, & Rebels: The American
Revolution in British West Florida. U Presses
Fla.
Starr, Kevin.
xStarr, Kevin.
Americans & the California Dream. Oxford U
Pr.
Starr, Martin K. *see* Starr, Martin Kenneth.
Starr, Martin Kenneth, 1927-
xStarr, Martin K.
Operations Management. P-H.
The Practice of Management Science. P-H.
Systems Management of Operations. P-H.
Starr, Philip C.
xStarr, Philip C.

Economics: Principles in Action. Wadsworth
Pub.
Starr, Raymond.
xStarr, Raymond.
ed. Race, Prejudice & the Origins of Slavery in
America. Schenkman.
Starr, Roger.
xStarr, Roger.
Housing & the Money Market. Basic.
Starr, S. Frederick.
xStarr, S. Frederick.
Decentralization and Self-Government in
Russia, 1830-1870. Princeton U Pr.
Melnikov: Solo Architect in a Mass Society.
Princeton U Pr.
Starr, Stephen Z.
xStarr, Stephen Z.
Colonel Grenfell's Wars: The Life of a Soldier
of Fortune. La State U Pr.
Starr, William T. *see* Starr, William Thomas.
Starr, William Thomas, 1910-
xStarr, William T.
Critical Bibliography of the Published Writings
of Romain Rolland. AMS Pr.
Starratt, Alfred B.
xStarratt, Alfred B.
Your Self, My Self & the Self of the Universe.
Stemmer Hse.
Starratt, Patricia E.
xStarratt, Patricia E.
The Natural Gas Shortage & the Congress. Am
Enterprise.
Starrett, Vincent, 1886-
xStarrett, Vincent.
Bookman's Holiday: The Private Satisfactions
of an Incurable Collector. Arno.
Buried Caesars: Essays in Literary
Appreciation. Arno.
Private Life of Sherlock Holmes. AMS Pr.
Private Life of Sherlock Holmes. Haskell.
The Private Life of Sherlock Holmes. Pinnacle
Bks.
Stary, J. *see* Stary, Jiri.
Stary, Jiri.
xStary, J.
ed. Critical Evaluation of Equilibrium
Constants Involving Hydroxyquinoline & Its
Metal Chelates: Critical Evaluation of
Equilibrium Constants in Solutions: Pt. A:
Stability Constants of Metal Complexes.
Pergamon.
Stary, P. *see* Stary, Petr.
Stary, Petr.
xStary, P.
ed. Aphid Parasites of the Central Asian Area.
Kluwer Boston.
Stasheff, Christopher.
xStasheff, Christopher.
A Wizard in Bedlam. DAW Bks.
A Wizard in Bedlam. Doubleday.
Stasheff, J. *see* Stasheff, James.
Stasheff, James.
xStasheff, J.
H-Spaces from a Homotopy Point of View.
Springer-Verlag.
Stassinopoulos, Arianna, 1950-
xStassinopoulos, Arianna.
After Reason. Stein & Day.
State Industrial Dirctories Corp. *see* State Industrial
Directories Corp.
State Industrial Directories. *see* State Industrial
Directories Corp.
State Industrial Directories Corp.
xState Industrial Dirctories Corp.
New Jersey State Industrial Directory, 1978.
State Indus Dir.
xState Industrial Directories.
Nebraska State Industrial Directory, 1980.
State Indus Dir.
xState Industrial Directories Corp.

Alabama State Industrial Directory, 1979. State Indus Dir.

Arizona State Industrial Directory, 1980. State Indus Dir.

Arkansas State Industrial Directory, 1980. State Indus Dir.

Connecticut State Industrial Directory, 1979. State Indus Dir.

Delaware State Industrial Directory, 1979-1980. State Indus Dir.

Delaware State Industrial Directory, 1980. State Indus Dir.

Florida State Industrial Directory, 1979. State Indus Dir.

Florida State Industrial Directory 1980. State Indus Dir.

Georgia State Industrial Directory, 1978. State Indus Dir.

Georgia State Industrial Directory, 1980. State Indus Dir.

Indiana State Industrial Directory, 1980. State Indus Dir.

Kentucky State Industrial Dirctory, 1979. State Indus Dir.

Louisiana State Industrial Directory, 1979. State Indus Dir.

Maine State Industrial Directory 1977. State Indus Dir.

Maine State Industrial Directory, 1979. State Indus Dir.

Maryland State Industrial Directory, 1978. State Indus Dir.

Maryland State Industrial Directory, 1979. State Indus Dir.

Maryland State Industrial Directory 1980. State Indus Dir.

Massachusetts State Industrial Directory, 1978. State Indus Dir.

Michigan State Industrial Directory, 1980. State Indus Dir.

Minnesota State Industrial Directory, 1980. State Indus Dir.

Mississippi State Industrial Directory, 1979. State Indus Dir.

Montana State Industrial Directory, 1980. State Indus Dir.

Nevada State Industrial Directory, 1980. State Indus Dir.

New Hampshire State Industrial Directory 1978-79. State Indus Dir.

New Jersey Industrial Directory 1980. State Indus Dir.

New Mexico State Industrial Directory 1980. State Indus Dir.

New York State Industrial Directory, 1979. State Indus Dir.

New York State Industrial Directory, 1980. State Indus Dir.

North Carolina State Industrial Directory, 1980. State Indus Dir.

North Dakota State Industrial Directory, 1980. State Indus Dir.

Oklahoma State Industrial Directory 1981. State Indus Dir.

Oregon State Industrial Directory, 1980. State Indus Dir.

Pennsylvania State Industrial Directory, 1979. State Indus Dir.

Rhode Island State Industrial Directory, 1980-81. State Indus Dir.

South Carolina State Directory, 1980. State Indus Dir.

South Carolina State Industrial Directory, 1979. State Indus Dir.

South Dakota State Industrial Directory, 1980. State Indus Dir.

Tennessee State Industrial Directory, 1979. State Indus Dir.

ed. Utah State Industrial Directory, 1980-81. State Indus Dir.

Vermont State Industrial Directory 1978-79. State Indus Dir.

Virginia State Industrial Directory, 1979. State Indus Dir.

Washington State Industrial Directory, 1981. State Indus Dir.

West Virginia State Industrial Directory, 1980-81. State Indus Dir.

Wisconsin State Industrial Directory, 1980. State Indus Dir.

xState Industrial Directories Corporation.
Massachusetts State Industrial Directory, 1979. State Indus Dir.

New Hampshire State Industrial Directory, 1980-81. State Indus Dir.

New Jersey State Industrial Directory, 1979. State Indus Dir.

Ohio Manufacturers Guide, 1980. State Indus Dir.

Vermont State Industrial Directory, 1980-81. State Indus Dir.

xState Industrial Directory Corp.
Alabama State Industrial Directory, 1978. State Indus Dir.

Kansas State Industrial Directory, 1980. State Indus Dir.

North Carolina State Industrial Directory, 1978. State Indus Dir.

State Industrial Directories Corporation. *see* State Industrial Directories Corp.

State Industrial Directory Corp. *see* State Industrial Directories Corp.

State of California. *see* California.

State of New Jersey Governor's Select Commission on Civil Disorder. *see* New Jersey. Governor'S Select Commission on Civil Disorder.

Staten, Hi W. *see* Staten, Hi Williamson.

Staten, Hi Williamson, 1895-
xStaten, Hi W.
Grasses & Grassland Farming. Devin.

Statham, Daphne.
xStatham, Daphne.
Radicals in Social Work. Routledge & Kegan.

Statham, Frances P. *see* Statham, Frances Patton.

Statham, Frances Patton.
xStatham, Frances P.
Flame of New Orleans. Fawcett.

Statham, Francis R. *see* Statham, Francis Reginald.

Statham, Francis Reginald.
xStatham, Francis R.
South Africa As It Is. Negro U Pr.

Statham, Ian.
xStatham, Ian.
Earth Surface Sediment Transport. Oxford U Pr.

Stationery Office (Great Britain). *see* Great Britain. Stationery Office.

Statistical Office of the United Nations. *see* United Nations. Statistical Office.

Statistics Canada. *see* Canada. Statistics Canada.

Statler, Oliver.
xStatler, Oliver.
Modern Japanese Prints: An Art Reborn. C E Tuttle.

Staton, Knofel.
xStaton, Knofel.
How to Know the Will of God. Standard Pub.

Staton, Thomas F. *see* Staton, Thomas Felix.

Staton, Thomas Felix.
xStaton, Thomas F.
How to Study. Am Guidance.

Statsky, William P.
xStatsky, William P.
Domestic Relations: Law & Skills. West Pub.

Statt, David A., 1942-
xStatt, David A.
Psychology: Making Sense. Har-Row.

Staub, George E.
xStaub, George E.

The Para-Professional in the Treatment of Alcoholism: A New Profession. C C Thomas.

Staubach, Roger.
xStaubach, Roger.
Staubach: First Down, Lifetime to Go. Word Bks.

Staubus, George J.
xStaubus, George J.
Activity Costing & Input-Output Accounting. Irwin.

A Theory of Accounting to Investors. Scholars Bk.

Staudacher, Joseph M.
xStaudacher, Joseph M.
Laymen Proclaim the Word. Franciscan Herald.

Staude, J. R. *see* Staude, John Raphael.

Staude, John Raphael.
xStaude, J. R.
Max Scheler, 1874-1928: An Intellectual Portrait. Free Pr.

Stauderman, Al. *see* Stauderman, Albert P.

Stauderman, Albert P.
xStauderman, Al.
Forty Proven Ways to a Successful Church. Abingdon.

Stauffer, D. A. *see* Stauffer, Donald Alfred.

Stauffer, Donald A. *see* Stauffer, Donald Alfred.

Stauffer, Donald Alfred, 1902-1952
xStauffer, D. A.
The Golden Nightingale: Essays on Some Principles of Poetry in the Lyrics of William Butler Yeats. Hafner.

The Intent of the Critic. Peter Smith.
xStauffer, Donald A.
Nature of Poetry. Peter Smith.

Stauffer, Russell G.
xStauffer, Russell G.
Diagnosis, Correction, & Prevention of Reading Disabilities. Har-Row.

Directing the Reading-Thinking Process. Har-Row.

The Language-Experience Approach to the Teaching of Reading. Har-Row.

Teaching Critical Reading at the Primary Level. Intl Reading.

Staum, Martin S.
xStaum, Martin S.
Cabanis: Enlightenment & Medical Philosophy in the French Revolution. Princeton U Pr.

Stave, Bruce M.
xStave, Bruce M.
ed. Socialism & the Cities. Kennikat.

Stave, Uwe, 1923-
xStave, Uwe.
Perinatal Physiology. Plenum Pub.

Staveley, A. L.
xStaveley, A. L.
Memories of Gurdjieff. Two Rivers.

Staveley, E. S.
xStaveley, E. S.
Greek & Roman Voting & Elections. Cornell U Pr.

Stavely, Keith W.
xStavely, Keith W.
The Politics of Milton's Prose Style. Yale U Pr.

Staves, Susan, 1942-
xStaves, Susan.
Players' Scepters: Fictions of Authority in the Restoration. U of Nebr Pr.

Stavis, Benedict.
xStavis, Benedict.
The Politics of Agricultural Mechanization in China. Cornell U Pr.

Stavrianos, L. S. *see* Stavrianos, Leften Stavros.

Stavrianos, Leften S. *see* Stavrianos, Leften Stavros.

Stavrianos, Leften Stavros.
xStavrianos, L. S.

The Balkans: 1815-1914. Krieger.
The Promise of the Coming Dark Age. W H
Freeman.
xStavrianos, Leften S.
A Global History. Allyn.
A Global History of Man. Allyn.
Stavrou, C. N. see Stavrou, Constantine Nicholas.
Stavrou, Constantine Nicholas, 1923-
xStavrou, C. N.
Whitman & Nietzsche: A Comparative Study
of Their Thought. AMS Pr.
Staynes, Jill.
xStaynes, Jill.
Out of That World. Merrimack Bk Serv.
Stead, Christina.
xStead, Christina.
A Christina Stead Reader. Random.
For Love Alone. HarBraceJ.
House of All Nations. Avon.
The Little Hotel. Avon.
Stead, Evelyn. see Stead, Evelyn S.
Stead, Evelyn S.
xStead, Evelyn.
Low-Fat Cookery. McGraw.
xStead, Evelyn S.
Low-Fat Cookery. Arc Bks.
Low-Fat Cookery. McGraw.
Stead, G. C. see Stead, George Christopher.
Stead, George Christopher.
xStead, G. C.
Divine Substance. Oxford U Pr.
Stead, Philip J. see Stead, Philip John.
Stead, Philip John.
xStead, Philip J.
ed. Pioneers in Policing. Patterson Smith.
Stead, Robert J. see Stead, Robert James Campbell.
Stead, Robert James Campbell, 1880-1959
xStead, Robert J.
The Homesteaders. U of Toronto Pr.
Stead, W. T. see Stead, William Thomas.
Stead, William T. see Stead, William Thomas.
Stead, William Thomas, 1849-1912
xStead, W. T.
The Americanization of the World: The Trend
of the Twentieth Century. Gordon Pr.
Borderland: A Casebook of True Supernatural
Stories. Univ Bks.
xStead, William T.
Chicago To-Day: Or, the Labour War in
America. Arno.
Steadman, Henry J.
xSteadman, Henry J.
Beating a Rap?: Defendants Found
Incompetent to Stand Trial. U of Chicago Pr.
Steadman, John. see Steadman, John M.
Steadman, John M.
xSteadman, John.
Nature into Myth: Medieval & Renaissance
Moral Symbols. Duquesne.
Steadman, P. see Steadman, Philip.
Steadman, Philip.
xSteadman, P.
Energy, Environment & Building. Cambridge U
Pr.
Steadman, Ralph.
xSteadman, Ralph.
Dogs Bodies. Paddington.
Dogs Bodies. Transatlantic.
Sigmund Freud. Paddington.
Sigmund Freud. S&S.
Steahr, Thomas E.
xSteahr, Thomas E.
North Carolina's Changing Population.
Carolina Pop Ctr.
Steakley, Douglas, 1944-
xSteakley, Douglas.
Holloware Techniques. Watson-Guptill.
Steakley, James D.
xSteakley, James D.

The Homosexual Emancipation Movement in
Germany. Arno.
Stealey, Sydnor L. see Stealey, Sydnor Lorenzo.
Stealey, Sydnor Lorenzo.
xStealey, Sydnor L.
ed. A Baptist Treasury. Arno.
Steamer, Robert J.
xSteamer, Robert J.
The Supreme Court in Crisis: A History of
Conflict. U of Mass Pr.
Stean, Michael.
xStean, Michael.
Simple Chess. Merrimack Bk Serv.
Steane, J. B.
xSteane, J. B.
Grand Tradition: Seventy Years of Singing on
Record, 1900-1970. Scribner.
Marlowe: A Critical Study. Cambridge U Pr.
Stearn, Colin W. see Stearn, Colin William.
Stearn, Colin William.
xStearn, Colin W.
Geological Evolution of North America. Wiley.
Stearn, Jess.
xStearn, Jess.
Dr. Thompson's New Way for You to Cure
Your Aching Back. Doubleday.
The Grapevine. Manor Bks.
A Matter of Immortality: Dramatic Evidence
of Survival. NAL.
xStearn, Jesse.
A Prophet in His Own Country: The Story of
the Young Edgar Cayce. G K Hall.
Stearn, Jesse. see Stearn, Jess.
Stearn, William T. see Stearn, William Thomas.
Stearn, William Thomas, 1911-
xStearn, William T.
Botanical Latin: History, Grammar, Syntax,
Terminology & Vocabulary. Hafner.
Stearns, F. see Stearns, Frank Preston.
Stearns, Frank P. see Stearns, Frank Preston.
Stearns, Frank Preston, 1846-1917
xStearns, F.
Life & Genius of Nathaniel Hawthorne.
Folcroft.
xStearns, Frank P.
Cambridge Sketches. Arno.
Stearns, Henry P. see Stearns, Henry Putnam.
Stearns, Henry Putnam, 1828-
xStearns, Henry P.
Insanity: Its Causes & Prevention. Arno.
Stearns, Marshall. see Stearns, Marshall Winslow.
Stearns, Marshall Winslow.
xStearns, Marshall.
Jazz Dance: The Story of American Vernacular
Dance. Schirmer Bks.
Stearns, Monroe.
xStearns, Monroe.
Mark Twain. Watts.
Story of New England. Random.
Stearns, Pamela.
xStearns, Pamela.
The Fool & the Dancing Bear. Little.
The Mechanical Doll. HM.
Stearns, Peter N.
xStearns, Peter N.

Be a Man!: Males in Modern Society. Holmes
& Meier.
European Society in Upheaval: Social History
Since 1750. Macmillan.
The Face of Europe. Forum Pr MO.
Lives of Labor: Work in a Maturing Industrial
Society. Holmes & Meier.
Old Age in European Society: The Case of
France. Holmes & Meier.
Paths to Authority: The Middle Class & the
Industrial Labor Force in France, 1820-48. U
of Ill Pr.
ed. Workers in the Industrial Revolution:
Recent Studies of Labor in the United States
& Europe. Transaction Bks.
Stearns, Philip. see Stearns, Philip Olcott.
Stearns, Philip Olcott.
xStearns, Philip.
How to Make Model Soldiers. Arco.
Stearns, Sam D. see Stearns, Samuel D.
Stearns, Samuel D.
xStearns, Sam D.
Digital Signal Analysis. Hayden.
Stearns, William. see Stearns, William F.
Stearns, William F.
xStearns, William.
ed. The Canoeist's Catalog. Intl Marine.
Stebbing, L. see Stebbing, Lionel.
Stebbing, Lionel.
xStebbing, L.
Dictionary of the Occult Sciences. Krishna Pr.
Stebbing, William, 1832-1926
xStebbing, William.
Some Verdicts of History Reviewed. Norwood
Edns.
Stebbings, H. see Stebbings, Howard.
Stebbings, Howard.
xStebbings, H.
Cell Motility. Longman.
Stebbins, G. Ledyard. see Stebbins, George Ledyard.
Stebbins, Genevieve.
xStebbins, Genevieve.
The Delsarte System of Expression. Dance
Horiz.
Stebbins, George L. see Stebbins, George Ledyard.
Stebbins, George Ledyard, 1906-
xStebbins, G. Ledyard.
Processes of Organic Evolution. P-H.
xStebbins, George L.
Variations & Evolution in Plants. Columbia U
Pr.
Stebbins, Giles B. see Stebbins, Giles Badger.
Stebbins, Giles Badger, 1817-1900
xStebbins, Giles B.
Facts & Opinions Touching the Real Origin,
Character & Influence of the American
Colonization Society. Negro U Pr.
Stebbins, Ray.
xStebbins, Ray.
Cold-Weather Camping. Contemp Bks.
Stebbins, Robert A., 1938-
xStebbins, Robert A.
Amateurs: On the Margin Between Work &
Leisure. Sage.
Commitment to Deviance: The
Nonprofessional Criminal in the Community.
Greenwood.
Stebbins, Robert C. see Stebbins, Robert Cyril.
Stebbins, Robert Cyril, 1915-
xStebbins, Robert C.
Amphibians & Reptiles of California. U of Cal
Pr.
Amphibians of Western North America. U of
Cal Pr.
Teaching & Research in the California Desert.
Inst Gov Stud Berk.
Stebbins, Theodore E.
xStebbins, Theodore E.

The Life & Works of Martin Johnson Heade. Yale U Pr.

Stecher, P. G. see Stecher, Paul G.

Stecher, Paul G.
 xStecher, P. G.
  ed. Industrial & Institutional Waste Heat Recovery. Noyes.
 xStecher, Paul G.
  ed. New Dental Materials. Noyes.

Steckel, Richard J.
 xSteckel, Richard J.
  Diagnosis & Staging of Cancer: A Radiologic Approach. Saunders.

Steckel, Robert C.
 xSteckel, Robert C.
  Profitable Telephone Sales Operations. Arco.

Stecker, Elinor. see Stecker, Elinor H.

Stecker, Elinor H.
 xStecker, Elinor.
  The Master Handbook of Still & Movie Titling for Amateur & Professional. TAB Bks.

Stecker, Margaret L. see Stecker, Margaret Loomis.

Stecker, Margaret Loomis, 1885-
 xStecker, Margaret L.
  Intercity Differences in Costs of Living in March, 1935 - 59 Cities. Da Capo.

Stedman, Edmund C. see Stedman, Edmund Clarence.

Stedman, Edmund Clarence, 1833-1908
 xStedman, Edmund C.
  Edgar Allan Poe. Folcroft.
  Genius & Other Essays. Kennikat.
  The Nature & Elements of Poetry. Arden Lib.
  The Nature & Elements of Poetry. Gloucester Art.
  Nature & Elements of Poetry. R West.
  Nature & Elements of Poetry. Russell.

Stedman, James M.
 xStedman, James M.
  Clinical Studies in Behavior Therapy with Children, Adolescents, & Their Families. C C Thomas.

Stedman, M. see Stedman, Murray Salisbury.

Stedman, Murray Salisbury, 1917-
 xStedman, M.
  State & Local Governments. Winthrop.

Stedman, Myrtle.
 xStedman, Myrtle.
  Adobe Architecture. Sunstone Pr.

Stedman, Preston, 1923-
 xStedman, Preston.
  The Symphony. P-H.

Stedman, Ray C.
 xStedman, Ray C.
  Authentic Christianity. Word Bks.
  Understanding Man. Word Bks.

Stedman, Raymond William.
 xStedman, William.
  Guide to Public Speaking. P-H.

Stedman, William. see Stedman, Raymond William.

Stedmond, John M.
 xStedmond, John M.
  Comic Art of Laurence Sterne: Convention & Innovation in "Tristram Shandy" & "A Sentimental Journey". U of Toronto Pr.

Stedwell, Paki.
 xStedwell, Paki.
  Vaulting: Gymnastics on Horseback. Wanderer Bks.
  Vaulting: Gymnastics on Horseback. Messner.

Steed, Ernest H. J.
 xSteed, Ernest H. J.
  Two Be One. Logos.

Steedman, Ian.
 xSteedman, Ian.

  ed. Fundamental Issues in Trade Theory. St Martin.
  Marx After Sraffa. Schocken.
  Trade Amongst Growing Economies. Cambridge U Pr.

Steedman, Marguerite C. see Steedman, Marguerite Couturier.

Steedman, Marguerite Couturier.
 xSteedman, Marguerite C.
  South Carolina Colony. Macmillan.

Steeds, J. W. see Steeds, John Wickham.

Steeds, John Wickham.
 xSteeds, J. W.
  Introduction to Anisotropic Elasticity Theory of Dislocations. Oxford U Pr.

Steefel, Lawrence D.
 xSteefel, Lawrence D.
  The Position of Duchamp's Glass in the Development of His Art. Garland Pub.

Steeg, Clarence L. Ver. see Ver Steeg, Clarence L.

Steegmuller, Francis, 1906-
 xSteegmuller, Francis.
  Silence at Salerno: A Comedy of Intrigue. HR&W.

Steel, Danielle.
 xSteel, Danielle.
  Passion's Promise. Dell.
  Season of Passion. Dell.

Steel, E. W. see Steel, Ernest William.

Steel, Edward M., Jr
 xSteel, Edward M.
  T. Butler King of Georgia. U of Ga Pr.

Steel, Eric M., 1904-
 xSteel, Eric M.
  Diderot's Imagery: A Study of a Literary Personality. Haskell.

Steel, Ernest William.
 xSteel, E. W.
  Water Supply & Sewerage. McGraw.

Steel, Robert G. see Steel, Robert George Douglas.

Steel, Robert George Douglas.
 xSteel, Robert G.
  Introduction to Statistics. McGraw.
  Principles & Procedures of Statistics: A Biometrical Approach. McGraw.

Steel, Rodney.
 xSteel, Rodney.
  The Encyclopedia of Pre-Historic Life. McGraw.

Steel, Ronald.
 xSteel, Ronald.
  ed. North Africa. Wilson.
  Pax Americana. Penguin.

Steele, Alexander.
 xSteele, Alexander.
  How to Spy on the U. S.. Arlington Hse.

Steele, Arthur R. see Steele, Arthur Robert.

Steele, Arthur Robert.
 xSteele, Arthur R.
  Flowers for the King: The Expedition of Ruiz & Pavon & the Flora of Peru. Duke.

Steele, Charles. see Steele, Charles Hutchins.

Steele, Charles Hutchins, 1932-
 xSteele, Charles.
  Guide to Fire Fighter Qualifications Training Programs. Natl Fire Prot.

Steele, Colin.
 xSteele, Colin.
  ed. Steady-State, Zero Growth & the Academic Library: A Collection of Essays. Shoe String.

Steele, D. R. see Steele, Dennis R.

Steele, Dennis R.
 xSteele, D. R.
  An Introduction to Elementary Computer & Compiler Design. Elsevier.

Steele, Earl L.
 xSteele, Earl L.
  Optical Lasers in Electronics. Krieger.

Steele, Eliza R.
 xSteele, Eliza R.

  A Summer Journey in the West. Arno.

Steele, Elizabeth.
 xSteele, Elizabeth.
  Hugh Walpole. Irvington.

Steele, F. I. see Steele, Fritz.

Steele, Fritz.
 xSteele, F. I.
  Open Organization: The Impact of Secrecy & Disclosure on People & Organizations. A-W.
 xSteele, Fritz.
  The Feel of the Work Place: Understanding & Improving Organization Climate. A-W.

Steele, Gerald L.
 xSteele, Gerald L.
  Exploring the World of Plastics. McKnight.

Steele, J. G. see Steele, John Gladstone.

Steele, James W. see Steele, James William.

Steele, James William, 1840-1905
 xSteele, James W.
  Frontier Army Sketches. U of NM Pr.

Steele, Joan.
 xSteele, Joan.
  Captain Mayne Reid. Twayne.

Steele, John Gladstone.
 xSteele, J. G.
  Conrad Martens in Queensland: The Frontier Travels of a Colonial Artist. U of Queensland Pr.

Steele, John H.
 xSteele, John H.
  The Structure of Marine Ecosystems. Harvard U Pr.

Steele, Jonathan.
 xSteele, Jonathan.
  Inside East Germany: The State That Came in from the Cold. Urizen Bks.

Steele, Lowell. see Steele, Lowell W.

Steele, Lowell W.
 xSteele, Lowell.
  Innovation in Big Business. Elsevier.

Steele, Mary Q.
 xSteele, Mary Q.
  The First of the Penguins. Macmillan.
  Journey Outside. Penguin.
  The True Men. Greenwillow.
  Wish, Come True. Schol Bk Serv.
  Wish, Come True. Greenwillow.

Steele, Max.
 xSteele, Max.
  Seasonal Jobs on Land & Sea. Har-Row.

Steele, Pauline F.
 xSteele, Pauline F.
  ed. Dental Specialties for the Dental Hygienist. Lea & Febiger.
  ed. Dimensions of Dental Hygiene. Lea & Febiger.
  ed. Review of Dental Hygiene: Questions & Answers. Lea & Febiger.

Steele, Richard.
 xSteele, Richard.
  The Conscious Lovers. U of Nebr Pr.
  Correspondence of Richard Steele. Oxford U Pr.
  Richard Steele. Greenwood.

Steele, Richard W.
 xSteele, Richard W.
  The First Offensive, 1942: Roosevelt, Marshall & the Making of American Strategy. Ind U Pr.

Steele, Robert M. see Steele, Robert Mccurdy.

Steele, Robert McCurdy, 1882-
 xSteele, Robert M.
  Study of Teacher Training in Vermont. AMS Pr.

Steele, Shirley.
 xSteele, Shirley.
  Educational Evaluation in Nursing. C B Slack.
 xSteele, Shirley M.
  Values Clarification in Nursing. ACC.

Steele, Shirley M. see Steele, Shirley.

Steele, Wilbur D. *see* Steele, Wilbur Daniel.
Steele, Wilbur Daniel, 1886-1970
  xSteele, Wilbur D.
    Full Cargo: More Stories. Greenwood.
Steele, William A. *see* Steele, William Arthur.
Steele, William Arthur, 1930-
  xSteele, William A.
    The Interaction of Gases with Solid Surfaces.
    Pergamon.
Steele, William O, 1917-
  xSteele, William O.
    Andy Jackson's Water Well. HarBraceJ.
    The Cherokee Crown of Tannassy. Blair.
    Daniel Boone's Echo. HarBraceJ.
    Davy Crockett's Earthquake. HarBraceJ.
    Flaming Arrows. HarBraceJ.
    Flaming Arrows. HarBraceJ.
    Lone Hunt. HarBraceJ.
    The Lone Hunt. HarBraceJ.
    The Magic Amulet. HarBraceJ.
    Perilous Road. HarBraceJ.
    The Perilous Road. HarBraceJ.
    The War Party. HarBraceJ.
    The War Party. HarBraceJ.
Steelman, Robert.
  xSteelman, Robert.
    Apache Wells. Ballantine.
Steelman, Robert J.
  xSteelman, Robert J.
    The Great Yellowstone Steamboat Race.
    Doubleday.
    Surgeon to the Sioux. Doubleday.
Steen, David.
  xSteen, David.
    Canadian Pilot's Fitness Manual. Delacorte.
Steen, Edwin B. *see* Steen, Edwin Benzel.
Steen, Edwin Benzel.
  xSteen, Edwin B.
    Dictionary of Biology. B&N.
Steen, Frederick H. *see* Steen, Frederick Henry.
Steen, Frederick Henry.
  xSteen, Frederick H.
    Analytic Geometry. Wiley.
Steen, Herman, 1893-
  xSteen, Herman.
    Flour Milling in America. Greenwood.
Steen, John W. *see* Steen, John Warren.
Steen, John Warren.
  xSteen, John W.
    Enlarge Your World. Broadman.
Steen, L. A. *see* Steen, Lynn A.
Steen, Lynn A.
  xSteen, L. A.
    Counterexamples in Topology. Springer-Verlag.
Steenbrink, P. A.
  xSteenbrink, P. A.
    Optimization of Transport Networks. Wiley.
Steene, Birgitta.
  xSteene, Birgitta.
    Greatest Fire: A Study of August Strindberg. S
    Ill U Pr.
    Ingmar Bergman. St Martin.
Steenrod, N. E. *see* Steenrod, Norman Earl.
Steenrod, Norman Earl, 1910-
  xSteenrod, N. E.
    Topology of Fibre Bundles. Princeton U Pr.
Steensma, Robert C., 1930-
  xSteensma, Robert C.
    Dr. John Arbuthnot. G K Hall.
    Dr. John Arbuthnot. Twayne.
Steenstrup, Johannes C. *see* Steenstrup, Johannes
  Christoffer Hagemann Reinhardt.
**Steenstrup, Johannes Christoffer Hagemann Reinhardt,
1844-1935**
  xSteenstrup, Johannes C.
    Medieval Popular Ballad. U of Wash Pr.
Steenwyk, Elizabeth. *see* Van Steenwyk, Elizabeth.
Steenwyk, Elizabeth Van. *see* Van Steenwyk, Elizabeth.
Steer, A. G. *see* Steer, Alfred Gilbert.
Steer, Alfred G. *see* Steer, Alfred Gilbert.

Steer, Alfred Gilbert, 1913-
  xSteer, A. G.
    Goethe's Science in the Structure of the
    Wanderjahre. U of Ga Pr.
  xSteer, Alfred G.
    Goethe's Social Philosophy As Revealed in
    "Campagne in Frankreich" & "Belagerlung
    Von Mainz". AMS Pr.
Steere, Daniel C.
  xSteere, Daniel C.
    I Am - I Can. Revell.
    I Am, I Can. Pillar Bks.
Steere, Douglas V. *see* Steere, Douglas Van.
Steere, Douglas Van, 1901-
  xSteere, Douglas V.
    On Being Present Where You Are. Pendle Hill.
    Prayer & Worship. Friends United.
Steere, Edward.
  xSteere, Edward.
    Swahili Exercises. Oxford U Pr.
Steers, J. A. *see* Steers, James Alfred.
Steers, James A. *see* Steers, James Alfred.
Steers, James Alfred, 1899-
  xSteers, J. A.
    ed. Applied Coastal Geomorphology. MIT Pr.
    The Coastline of Scotland. Cambridge U Pr.
    ed. Introduction to Coastline Development.
    MIT Pr.
  xSteers, James A.
    Coast of England & Wales in Pictures.
    Cambridge U Pr.
Steers, Richard M.
  xSteers, Richard M.
    Motivation & Work Behavior. McGraw.
    Organizational Effectiveness: A Behavioral
    View. Goodyear.
Steeves, Harrison R. *see* Steeves, Harrison Ross.
Steeves, Harrison Ross, 1881-
  xSteeves, Harrison R.
    Learned Societies & English Literary
    Scholarship in Great Britain & the United
    States. AMS Pr.
Steeves, Paul. *see* Steeves, Paul D.
Steeves, Paul D.
  xSteeves, Paul.
    Getting to Know Your Faith. Inter-Varsity.
Steeves, Taylor A.
  xSteeves, Taylor A.
    Patterns in Plant Development. P-H.
Stefan-Gruenfeldt, Paul.
  xStefan-Gruenfeldt, Paul.
    Anton Dvorak. Scholarly.
Stefani, S. *see* Stefani, Stefano S.
Stefani, Stefano S.
  xStefani, S.
    Mathematics for Technologists in Radiology,
    Nuclear Medicine & Radiation Therapy.
    Mosby.
Stefansson, Vilhjalmur, 1879-1962
  xStefansson, Vilhjalmur.
    Adventures in Error. Gale.
Steffen, Randy, 1917-
  xSteffen, Randy.
    The Horse Soldier. U of Okla Pr.
Steffens, H. J. *see* Steffens, Henry John.
Steffens, Henry J. *see* Steffens, Henry John.
Steffens, Henry John.
  xSteffens, H. J.
    James Prescott Joule & the Concept of Energy.
    N Watson.
  xSteffens, Henry J.
    The Development of Newtonian Optics in
    England. N Watson.
Steffens, Joseph L. *see* Steffens, Joseph Lincoln.
Steffens, Joseph Lincoln, 1866-1936
  xSteffens, Joseph L.
    The Struggle for Self-Government. Johnson
    Repr.
  xSteffens, Lincoln.

    Autobiography of Lincoln Steffens. HarBraceJ.
    The Letters of Lincoln Steffens. Greenwood.
Steffens, Lincoln. *see* Steffens, Joseph Lincoln.
Steffensmeier, Darrell J.
  xSteffensmeier, Darrell J.
    Examining Deviance Experimentally: Selected
    Readings. Alfred Pub.
Stefferud, Alfred.
  xStefferud, Alfred.
    Wonders of Seeds. HarBraceJ.
    The Wonders of Seeds. HarBraceJ.
Steffl, Bernita. *see* Steffl, Bernita M.
Steffl, Bernita M.
  xSteffl, Bernita.
    Discharge Planning Handbook. C B Slack.
Stefflre, Buford.
  xStefflre, Buford.
    Function of Counseling Theory. HM.
    jt. auth. Theories of Counseling. McGraw.
Steffy, Robert.
  xSteffy, Robert.
    The Captain Cook Cookbook. Determined
    Prods.
Stegeman, John F.
  xStegeman, John F.
    These Men She Gave: Civil War Diary of
    Athens, Georgia. U of Ga Pr.
Stegeman, Wilson, 1897-
  xStegeman, Wilson.
    Medical Terms Simplified. West Pub.
Stegenga, J.
  xStegenga, J.
    Greek-English Analytical Concordance of the
    Greek-English New Testament. Hellenes.
Steglich, W. G.
  xSteglich, W. G.
    American Social Problems: An Institutional
    View. Goodyear.
Stegman, Michael A.
  xStegman, Michael A.
    Nonmetropolitan Urban Housing: An
    Economic Analysis of Problems & Policies.
    Ballinger Pub.
Stegmuller, Wolfgang.
  xStegmuller, Wolfgang.
    ed. Collected Papers on Epistemology,
    Philosophy of Science & History of
    Philosophy. Kluwer Boston.
Stegner, Wallace. *see* Stegner, Wallace Earle.
Stegner, Wallace Earl, 1909-
  xStegner, Wallace.
    Angle of Repose. Doubleday.
    Angle of Repose. Fawcett.
Stegner, Wallace Earle, 1909-
  xStegner, Wallace.
    All the Little Live Things. U of Nebr Pr.
    Gathering of Zion: The Story of the Mormon
    Trail. McGraw.
    ed. Great American Short Stories. Dell.
    Recapitulation. Doubleday.
    Recapitulation. Fawcett.
    The Spectator Bird. Doubleday.
    The Spectator Bird. G K Hall.
    The Spectator Bird. U of Nebr Pr.
Stehbens, William E. *see* Stehbens, Williams E.
Stehbens, Williams E.
  xStehbens, William E.
    Hemodynamics & the Blood Vessel Wall. C C
    Thomas.
Stehling, Kurt R.
  xStehling, Kurt R.
    Computers & You. NAL.
Stehman, J. Warren. *see* Stehman, Jonas Warren.
Stehman, Jonas Warren, 1887-
  xStehman, J. Warren.
    Financial History of the American Telephone
    & Telegraph Company. Kelley.
Stehsel, Donald L.
  xStehsel, Donald L.

Hunting the California Black Bear. Stehsel.

Steichen, Edward, 1879-1973
  xSteichen, Edward.
    photos by Edward Steichen. Aperture.
    Life in Photography. Doubleday.
Steidel, Robert F., 1926-
  xSteidel, Robert F.
    An Introduction to Mechanical Vibrations.
      Wiley.
Steidl, Rose E.
  xSteidl, Rose E.
    Work in the Home. Wiley.
Steig, Irwin, 1901-
  xSteig, Irwin.
    Common Sense in Poker. Cornerstone.
    Play Gin to Win. Cornerstone.
Steig, Michael, 1936-
  xSteig, Michael.
    Dickens & Phiz. Ind U Pr.
Steig, William, 1907-
  xSteig, William.
    Abel's Island. Bantam.
    illus. Abel's Island. FS&G.
    illus. The Amazing Bone. FS&G.
    The Amazing Bone. Penguin.
    illus. Amos & Boris. FS&G.
    Amos & Boris. Penguin.
    C D B!. S&S.
    illus. Caleb & Kate. FS&G.
    Caleb & Kate. Schol Bk Serv.
    illus. Dominic. FS&G.
    illus. The Real Thief. FS&G.
    The Rejected Lovers. Dover.
    Sylvester & the Magic Pebble. S&S.
Steigel, A. *see* Steigel, Alois.
Steigel, Alois.
  xSteigel, A.
    Dynamic NMR Spectroscopy. Springer-Verlag.
Steiger, Arnald, 1896-
  xSteiger, Arnaldo.
    Origin & Spread of Oriental Words in
      European Languages. S F Vanni.
Steiger, Arnaldo. *see* Steiger, Arnald.
Steiger, Brad.
  xSteiger, Brad.
    Gods of Aquarius: UFO's & the
      Transformation of Man. HarBraceJ.
    The Hypnotist. Dell.
    Medicine Talk: A Guide to Walking in Balance
      & Surviving on the Earth Mother.
      Doubleday.
    Other Lives. Esoteric Pubns.
    Valentino. Manor Bks.
    Worlds Before Our Own. Putnam.
Steiger, George N. *see* Steiger, George Nye.
Steiger, George Nye, 1883-
  xSteiger, George N.
    China & the Occident: The Origin &
      Development of the Boxer Movement.
      Russell.
Steiger, H. *see* Steiger, Heinhard.
Steiger, Heinhard.
  xSteiger, H.
    Law & Practice Relating to Pollution Control
      in the Federal Republic of Germany. Nichols
      Pub.
Steigerwald, Robert, 1925-
  xSteigerwald, Robert.
    Anti-Communist Myths in Left Disguise. Intl
      Pub Co.
Steigleman, Walter A. *see* Steigleman, Walter Allan.
Steigleman, Walter Allan, 1907-
  xSteigleman, Walter A.
    Newspaperman & the Law. Greenwood.
Steiglitz, Kenneth, 1939-
  xSteiglitz, Kenneth.
    An Introduction to Discrete Systems. Wiley.
Steila, Donal. *see* Steila, Donald.
Steila, Donald, 1939-
  xSteila, Donal.

Geography of Soils: Formation, Distribution &
  Management. P-H.
Steiman, Harvey.
  xSteiman, Harvey.
    Great Recipes from San Francisco: Favorite
      Dishes from the City's Leading Restaurants.
      J P Tarcher.
Steimle, Edmund A.
  xSteimle, Edmund A.
    Preaching the Story. Fortress.
Stein. *see* Stein, Edwin I.
Stein, Aaron Marc, 1906-
  xStein, Aaron Marc.
    Chill Factor. Doubleday.
    The Rolling Heads. Doubleday.
Stein, Allen F.
  xStein, Allen F.
    The Southern Experience in Short Fiction.
      Scott F.
Stein, Arnold. *see* Stein, Arnold Sidney.
Stein, Arnold Sidney, 1915-
  xStein, Arnold.
    The Art of Presence: The Poet & Paradise
      Lost. U of Cal Pr.
    George Herbert's Lyrics. Johns Hopkins.
Stein, Ben. *see* Stein, Benjamin.
Stein, Benjamin, 1944-
  xStein, Ben.
    The View from Sunset Boulevard: America As
      Brought to You by the People Who Make
      Television. Doubleday.
  xStein, Benjamin.
    Dreemz. Ballantine.
Stein, Bruno, 1930-
  xStein, Bruno.
    Social Security & Pensions in Transition:
      Understanding the American Retirement
      System. Free Pr.
    Work & Welfare in Britain & the U. S. A..
      Halsted Pr.
Stein, Charles.
  xStein, Charles.
    ed. Critical Materials Problems in Energy
      Production. Acad Pr.
Stein, Charlotte M. *see* Stein, Charlotte Markman.
Stein, Charlotte Markman.
  xStein, Charlotte M.
    Dialogues in a Cave. Double M Pr.
Stein, Clarence S.
  xStein, Clarence S.
    Toward New Towns for America. MIT Pr.
Stein, Donald G.
  xStein, Donald G.
    Learning & Memory. Macmillan.
Stein, E. M. *see* Stein, Elias M.
Stein, Edwin.
  xStein, Edwin I.
    First Course in Fundamentals of Mathematics.
      Allyn.
Stein, Edwin I.
  xStein.
    Basic Mathematics for College Students. Allyn.
  xStein, Edwin I.
    Fundamentals of Mathematics. Allyn.
Stein, Edwin I. *see* Stein, Edwin.
Stein, Elias M., 1931-
  xStein, E. M.
    Boundary Behavior of Holomorphic Functions
      of Several Complex Variables. Princeton U
      Pr.
  xStein, Elias M.
    Introduction to Fourier Analysis on Euclidean
      Spaces. Princeton U Pr.
Stein, Elizabeth P.
  xStein, Elizabeth P.
    David Garrick, Dramatist. Arno.
    David Garrick, Dramatist. Kraus Repr.
Stein, Erwin, 1885-1958
  xStein, Erwin.

Orpheus in New Guises. Hyperion Conn.

Stein, George H., 1934-
  xStein, George H.
    ed. Hitler. P-H.
Stein, Gertrude, 1874-1946
  xStein, Gertrude.
    Alphabets & Birthdays. Arno.
    Autobiography of Alice B. Toklas. Peter Smith.
    Autobiography of Alice B. Toklas. Random.
    Fernhurst, Q. E. D., and Other Early Writings.
      Liveright.
    Geography & Plays. Haskell.
    Gertrude Stein on Picasso. Liveright.
    How to Write. Dover.
    How to Write. Peter Smith.
    How to Write. Sherry Urie.
    How to Write. Ultramarine Pub.
    Lectures in America. Random.
    Lucy Church Amiably. Ultramarine Pub.
    Matisse, Picasso & Gertrude Stein, with Two
      Shorter Stories. Ultramarine Pub.
    Paris, France. Liveright.
    A Primer for the Gradual Understanding of
      Gertrude Stein. Black Sparrow.
Stein, Guenther.
  xStein, Guenther.
    The Challenge of Red China. Da Capo.
Stein, Harold A.
  xStein, Harold A.
    Ophthalmic Assistant: Fundamentals & Clinical
      Practice. Mosby.
Stein, Harvey.
  xStein, Harvey.
    Parallels: A Look at Twins. Dutton.
Stein, Herbert.
  xStein, Herbert.
    Economic Planning & the Improvement of
      Economic Policy. Am Enterprise.
    Fiscal Revolution in America. U of Chicago Pr.
Stein, Howard F.
  xStein, Howard F.
    The Ethnic Imperative: Examining the New
      White Ethnic Movement. Pa St U Pr.
Stein, J. Stewart.
  xStein, J. Stewart.
    Construction Glossary: An Encyclopedic
      Reference & Manual. Wiley.
Stein, Jack M. *see* Stein, Jack Madison.
Stein, Jack Madison.
  xStein, Jack M.
    Richard Wagner & the Synthesis of the Arts.
      Greenwood.
Stein, Jay W. *see* Stein, Jay Wobith.
Stein, Jay Wobith, 1920-
  xStein, Jay W.
    Mass Media, Education, & a Better Society.
      Nelson-Hall.
    ed. Public Communications & Liberal-General
      Education in High School & College.
      Interstate.
Stein, Jeff.
  xStein, Jeff.
    The Who. Stein & Day.
Stein, Jerome L.
  xStein, Jerome L.
    Money & Capacity Growth. Columbia U Pr.
Stein, Joe.
  xStein, Joe.
    Don Coryell Win with Honor. Joyce Pr.
Stein, Joseph, 1910-
  xStein, Joseph.
    Making Life Meaningful. Nelson-Hall.
Stein, Leon, 1910-
  xStein, Leon.

Anthology of Musical Forms. Summy.
Out of the Sweatshop: The Struggle for
Industrial Democracy. Times Bks.
ed. The Pullman Strike. Arno.
ed. Religion, Reform & Revolution: Labor
Panaceas in the Nineteenth Century. Arno.
Stein, Leonard J. *see* Stein, Leonard Jacques.
Stein, Leonard Jacques, 1887-
xStein, Leonard J.
Balfour Declaration. S&S.
Stein, Lincoln D. *see* Stein, Lincoln David.
Stein, Lincoln David.
xStein, Lincoln D.
Family Games. Macmillan.
Family Games. Macmillan.
Stein, Louis, 1917-
xStein, Louis.
Beyond Death & Exile: The Spanish
Republicans in France, 1939-1955. Harvard
U Pr.
Stein, M. Aurel. *see* Stein, Mark Aurel.
Stein, M. L. *see* Stein, Meyer L.
Stein, Marc A. *see* Stein, Mark Aurel.
Stein, Mark. *see* Stein, Mark L.
Stein, Mark Aurel, Sir, 1862-1943
xStein, M. Aurel.
Ancient Khotan: Detailed Report of
Archaeological Explorations in Chinese
Turkestan. Hacker.
xStein, Marc A.
On Alexander's Track in the Indus: Personal
Narrative of the Explorations on the
North-West Frontier of India. Arno.
Stein, Mark L.
xStein, Mark.
Good & Bad Feelings. Morrow.
Stein, Maurice R.
xStein, Maurice R.
Eclipse of Community: An Interpretation of
American Studies. Princeton U Pr.
Stein, Meyer L.
xStein, M. L.
Reporting Today: The Newswriter's Handbook.
Cornerstone.
Stein, Morris I. *see* Stein, Morris Isaac.
Stein, Morris Isaac, 1921-
xStein, Morris I.
ed. Contemporary Psychotherapies. Free Pr.
Personality Measures in Admissions:
Antecedent & Personality Factors as
Predictors of College Success. College Bd.
Stein, Peter J.
xStein, Peter J.
The Family: Functions, Conflicts & Symbols.
A-W.
Stein, Philip.
xStein, Philip.
Graphical Analysis: Understanding Graphs &
Curves in Technology. Hayden.
Stein, R. B.
xStein, R. B.
ed. Control of Posture & Locomotion. Plenum
Pub.
Stein, R. Conrad.
xStein, R. Conrad.
The Story of Arlington National Cemetery.
Childrens.
The Story of D-Day. Childrens.
The Story of Ellis Island. Childrens.
The Story of the Battle for Iwo Jima.
Childrens.
The Story of the Battle of the Bulge. Childrens.
The Story of the Golden Spike. Childrens.
The Story of the Homestead Act. Childrens.
The Story of the Smithsonian Institution.
Childrens.
The Story of the U.S.S. Arizona. Childrens.
Stein, Ralph, 1909-
xStein, Ralph.

The Greatest Cars. S&S.
Stein, Rita.
xStein, Rita.
A Literary Tour Guide to the United States:
South & Southwest. Morrow.
Stein, Rita F.
xStein, Rita F.
Disturbed Youth & Ethnic Family Patterns.
State U NY Pr.
Stein, Robert. *see* Stein, Robert Louis.
Stein, Robert G.
xStein, Robert G.
Mathematics: An Exploratory Approach.
McGraw.
Stein, Robert Louis.
xStein, Robert.
The French Slave Trade in the Eighteenth
Century: An Old Regime Business. U of Wis
Pr.
Stein, Sandra K. *see* Stein, Sandra Kovacs.
Stein, Sandra Kovacs.
xStein, Sandra K.
Instant Numerology: Charting Your Roadmap
to the Future. Har-Row.
Stein, Sara. *see* Stein, Sara Bonnett.
Stein, Sara B. *see* Stein, Sara Bonnett.
Stein, Sara Bonnett.
xStein, Sara.
The Science Book. Workman Pub.
xStein, Sara B.
A Child Goes to School. Doubleday.
Child Goes to School. Doubleday.
A Family Dollhouse. Viking Pr.
Stein, Sarah K. *see* Stein, Sarah Kisch.
Stein, Sarah Kisch.
xStein, Sarah K.
ed. Leaders in Israel: Thumb-Nail Sketches of
the Officers of the First Provisional
Government. Arno.
Stein, Sherman K.
xStein, Sherman K.
Calculus & Analytic Geometry. McGraw.
Calculus: in the First Three Dimensions.
McGraw.
Stein, Sol.
xStein, Sol.
The Childkeeper. HarBraceJ.
Other People. Dell.
Other People. HarBraceJ.
The Resort. Morrow.
Stein, Stanley J.
xStein, Stanley J.
Colonial Heritage of Latin America: Essays on
Economic Dependence in Perspective.
Oxford U Pr.
Stein, Theodore J.
xStein, Theodore J.
Children in Foster Homes: Achieving
Continuity of Care. Praeger.
Stein, Toby.
xStein, Toby.
Getting Together. Atheneum.
Stein, Walter, 1924-
xStein, Walter.
Criticism As Dialogue. Cambridge U Pr.
Stein, Walter J.
xStein, Walter J.
California & the Dust Bowl Migration.
Greenwood.
Stein, William W.
xStein, William W.
Hualcan: Life in the Highlands of Peru.
Greenwood.
Stein, Zena.
xStein, Zena.
Famine & Human Development: The Dutch
Hunger Winter 1944-1945. Oxford U Pr.
Steinaker, Norman.
xSteinaker, Norman.

The Experiential Taxonomy: A New Approach
to Teaching & Learning. Acad Pr.
Steinbach, Marten.
xSteinbach, Marten.
Medical Palmistry: Health & Character in the
Hand. Univ Bks.
Steinbacher, John. *see* Steinbacher, John A.
Steinbacher, John A., 1925-
xSteinbacher, John.
The Child Seducers. Educator Pubns.
Steinbeck, John. *see* Steinbeck, John Ernst.
Steinbeck, John Ernst, 1902-
xSteinbeck, John.
Burning Bright: A Play in Story Form.
Penguin.
Cannery Row. Viking Pr.
A Cup of Gold. Penguin.
East of Eden. Bantam.
East of Eden. Penguin.
East of Eden. Viking Pr.
The Grapes of Wrath. Penguin.
Grapes of Wrath. Viking Pr.
In Dubious Battle. Penguin.
In Touch. Knopf.
Long Valley. Bantam.
Once There Was a War. Penguin.
The Pearl. Viking Pr.
The Portable Steinbeck. Penguin.
Portable Steinbeck. Viking Pr.
Steinbeck: A Life in Letters. Penguin.
Sweet Thursday. Penguin.
Tortilla Flat. Penguin.
Tortilla Flat. Viking Pr.
Travels with Charley: In Search of America.
Viking Pr.
The Wayward Bus. Penguin.
Steinberg. *see* Steinberg, Saul.
Steinberg, Alfred, 1917-
xSteinberg, Alfred.
The Bosses. NAL.
Steinberg, Barbara.
xSteinberg, Barbara.
Who Keeps America Clean?. Random.
Steinberg, Bernard D.
xSteinberg, Bernard D.
Principles of Aperture & Array System Design:
Including Random & Adaptive Arrays. Wiley.
Steinberg, Charles S. *see* Steinberg, Charles Side.
Steinberg, Charles Side, 1913-
xSteinberg, Charles S.
The Communicative Arts: An Introduction to
Mass Media. Hastings.
The Information Establishment: Our
Government & the Media. Hastings.
The Mass Communicators: Public Relations,
Public Opinion, & Mass Media. Greenwood.
ed. Mass Media & Communication. Hastings.
Steinberg, David.
xSteinberg, David.
Computational Matrix Algebra. McGraw.
Fatherjournal: Five Years of Awakening to
Fatherhood. Times Change.
Steinberg, David J. *see* Steinberg, David Joel.
Steinberg, David Joel.
xSteinberg, David J.
In Search of Southeast Asia: A Modern
History. Praeger.
Steinberg, Erwin R. *see* Steinberg, Erwin Ray.
Steinberg, Erwin Ray.
xSteinberg, Erwin R.
The Stream of Consciousness & Beyond in
Ulysses. U of Pittsburgh Pr.
ed. Stream-of-Consciousness Technique in the
Modern Novel. Kennikat.
Steinberg, Fannie.
xSteinberg, Fannie.
Birthday in Kishinev. Jewish Pubn.
Steinberg, Ffranz U. *see* Steinberg, Franz U.
Steinberg, Franz U., 1913-
xSteinberg, Ffranz U.

The Immobilized Patient. Plenum Pub.
Steinberg, Ira S.
  xSteinberg, Ira S.
    Population & Frustration. Ohio St U Pr.
    Ralph Barton Perry on Education for
      Democracy. Ohio St U Pr.
Steinberg, Isaac. *see* Steinberg, Isaac Nachman.
Steinberg, Isaac Nachman, 1888-1957
  xSteinberg, Isaac.
    Spiridonova, Revolutionary Terrorist. Arno.
Steinberg, J. Leonard. *see* Steinberg, Jay Leonard.
Steinberg, Jay Leonard, 1930-
  xSteinberg, J. Leonard.
    ed. Counselor As an Applied Behavioral
      Scientist. Mss Info.
Steinberg, Joseph.
  xSteinberg, Joseph.
    Estimating for the Building Trades. Am
      Technical.
Steinberg, Joseph L.
  xSteinberg, Joseph L.
    Camper's Favorite Campgrounds: The East
      Coast, from Maine to Florida. Dial.
Steinberg, Jules.
  xSteinberg, Jules.
    Customers Don't Bite: Selling with Confidence.
      Fairchild.
Steinberg, Leo, 1920-
  xSteinberg, Leo.
    Other Criteria: Confrontations with Twentieth
      Century Art. Oxford U Pr.
    Other Criteria: Confrontations with
      Twentieth-Century Art. Oxford U Pr.
Steinberg, Peter.
  xSteinberg, Peter.
    Play Bridge in Four Hours. G&D.
Steinberg, Phil. *see* Steinberg, Phillip Orso.
Steinberg, Phillip Orso.
  xSteinberg, Phil.
    Aquariums. Lerner Pubns.
Steinberg, R. *see* Steinberg, Robert.
Steinberg, Rafael.
  xSteinberg, Rafael.
    Cooking of Japan. Time-Life.
    Cooking of Japan. Silver.
    Pacific & Southeast Asian Cooking. Time-Life.
    Pacific & Southeast Asian Cooking. Silver.
    Return to the Philippines. Silver.
    The Return to the Philippines. Time-Life.
Steinberg, Robert, 1922-
  xSteinberg, R.
    Conjugacy Classes in Algebraic Groups.
      Springer-Verlag.
Steinberg, Ronald M.
  xSteinberg, Ronald M.
    Fra Girolamo Savonarola, Florentine Art &
      Renaissance Historiography. Ohio U Pr.
Steinberg, S. H. *see* Steinberg, Sifgrid Henry.
Steinberg, Salme H. *see* Steinberg, Salme Harju.
Steinberg, Salme Harju, 1940-
  xSteinberg, Salme H.
    Reformer in the Marketplace: Edward W. Bok
      & the Ladies' Home Journal. La State U Pr.
Steinberg, Saul.
  xSteinberg.
    The Inspector. Penguin.
  xSteinberg, Saul.
    The Inspector. Viking Pr.
    The Passport. Random.
    The Passport. Random.
Steinberg, Sheila.
  xSteinberg, Sheila.
    Rhode Island: An Historical Guide. RI Pubns
      Soc.
Steinberg, Sifgrid Henry, 1899-
  xSteinberg, S. H.
    Five Hundred Years of Printing. Penguin.
Steinberg, Theodore L.
  xSteinberg, Theodore L.

Mendele Mocher Seforim. Twayne.
Steinberger, G. *see* Steinberger, Georg.
Steinberger, Georg, 1865-1904
  xSteinberger, G.
    In the Footprints of the Lamb. Bethany Fell.
Steinbock, B. *see* Steinbock, Bonnie.
Steinbock, Bonnie.
  xSteinbock, B.
    Killing & Letting Die. P-H.
Steinbrecher, Edwin C.
  xSteinbrecher, Edwin C.
    The Inner Guide Meditation. Blue Feather.
Steinbrocker, Otto.
  xSteinbrocker, Otto.
    Aspiration & Injection Therapy in Arthritis &
      Musculoskeletal Disorders: A Handbook on
      Technique & Management. Har-Row.
Steinbruckner, Bruno F. *see* Steinbruckner, Bruno
  Friedrich.
Steinbruckner, Bruno Friedrich.
  xSteinbruckner, Bruno F.
    Ludwig Thoma. Twayne.
Steinbrueck, Victor.
  xSteinbrueck, Victor.
    Market Sketchbook. U of Wash Pr.
Steinbrunner, Chris.
  xSteinbrunner, Chris.
    Encyclopedia of Mystery & Detection.
      McGraw.
Steincrohn, Peter J. *see* Steincrohn, Peter Joseph.
Steincrohn, Peter Joseph, 1899-
  xSteincrohn, Peter J.
    Ask Dr. Steincrohn: What You Always Wanted
      to Ask Your Doctor & Didn't. Acropolis.
    Low Blood Sugar. NAL.
Steindl, J. *see* Steindl, Joseph.
Steindl, Josef. *see* Steindl, Joseph.
Steindl, Joseph.
  xSteindl, J.
    Maturity & Stagnation in American Capitalism.
      Monthly Rev.
  xSteindl, Josef.
    Maturity & Stagnation in American Capitalism.
      Monthly Rev.
Steindler, R. A.
  xSteindler, R. A.
    Reloader's Guide. Follett.
  xSteindler, Robert A.
    Home Gunsmithing Digest. Follett.
Steindler, R. A. *see* Steindler, R. A
Steindler, Robert A. *see* Steindler, R. A.
Steindorff, Georg.
  xSteindorff, George.
    When Egypt Ruled the East. U of Chicago Pr.
Steindorff, George. *see* Steindorff, Georg.
Steiner, B. C. *see* Steiner, Bernard Christian.
Steiner, Barbara. *see* Steiner, Barbara A.
Steiner, Barbara A.
  xSteiner, Barbara.
    Biography of a Bengal Tiger. Putnam.
Steiner, Bernard C. *see* Steiner, Bernard Christian.
Steiner, Bernard Christian, 1867-1926
  xSteiner, B. C.
    History of Slavery in Connecticut. Johnson
      Repr.
    The History of University Education in
      Maryland. Johnson Repr.
  xSteiner, Bernard C.

Descriptions of Maryland. AMS Pr.
History of Slavery in Connecticut. AMS Pr.
The History of University Education in
  Maryland. AMS Pr.
Life & Administration of Sir Robert Eden.
  AMS Pr.
The Life & Correspondence of James
  McHenry. Arno.
Life of Reverdy Johnson. Russell.
Life of Roger Brooke Taney, Chief Justice of
  the United States Supreme Court.
  Greenwood.
Maryland During the English Civil Wars. AMS
  Pr.
Maryland Under the Commonwealth: A
  Chronicle of the Years 1649-1658. AMS Pr.
  xSteiner, Bernhard C.
    Life & Administration of Sir Robert Eden.
      Johnson Repr.
Steiner, Bernhard C. *see* Steiner, Bernard Christian.
Steiner, Charlotte.
  xSteiner, Charlotte.
    illus. Hungry Book. Knopf.
    illus. Let Her Dance. Lothrop.
    Little Train That Saved the Day. Wonder.
Steiner, Claude, 1935-
  xSteiner, Claude M.
    Healing Alcoholism. Grove.
Steiner, Claude M. *see* Steiner, Claude.
Steiner, Edward A. *see* Steiner, Edward Alfred.
Steiner, Edward Alfred, 1866-1956
  xSteiner, Edward A.
    Broken Wall: Stories of the Mingling Folk.
      Arno.
    From Alien to Citizen. Arno.
    On the Trail of the Immigrant. Arno.
Steiner, Elizabeth.
  xSteiner, Elizabeth.
    Education & American Culture. Macmillan.
Steiner, Florence.
  xSteiner, Florence.
    ed. Performing with Objectives. Newbury Hse.
Steiner, Gary A. *see* Steiner, Gary Albert.
Steiner, Gary Albert.
  xSteiner, Gary A.
    ed. Creative Organization. U of Chicago Pr.
Steiner, George, 1929-
  xSteiner, George.
    After Babel: Aspects of Language &
      Translation. Oxford U Pr.
    After Babel: Aspects of Language &
      Translation. Oxford U Pr.
    The Death of Tragedy. Oxford U Pr.
    Extraterritorial: Papers on Literature & the
      Language Revolution. Atheneum.
    Martin Heidegger. Penguin.
    Martin Heidegger. Viking Pr.
    On Difficulty & Other Essays. Oxford U Pr.
Steiner, George A. *see* Steiner, George Albert.
Steiner, George Albert.
  xSteiner, George A.
    Business, Government & Society: A Managerial
      Perspective. Random.
    Industrial Project Management. Interbk Inc.
    Strategic Planning: What Every Manager Must
      Know. Free Pr.
Steiner, Gerald M.
  xSteiner, Gerald M.
    Intro. by Home for Sale by Owner. Ana-Doug
      Pub.
    Home for Sale by Owner. Dutton.
Steiner, Gilbert Y. *see* Steiner, Gilbert Yale.
Steiner, Gilbert Yale.
  xSteiner, Gilbert Y.
    The Children's Cause. Brookings.
Steiner, H. Arthur, 1905-
  xSteiner, H. Arthur.
    Government in Fascist Italy. Greenwood.
Steiner, Irene H. *see* Steiner, Irene Hunter.

Steiner, Irene Hunter.
xSteiner, Irene H.
The Year Growing Ancient. St Martin.
Steiner, Jean Francois, 1938-
xSteiner, Jean-Francis.
Treblinka. NAL.
Steiner, Jean-Francis. *see* Steiner, Jean Francois.
Steiner, Jesse F. *see* Steiner, Jesse Frederick.
Steiner, Jesse Frederick, 1880-
xSteiner, Jesse F.
The Japanese Invasion. Arno.
North Carolina Chain Gang: A Study of
County Convict Road Work. Negro U Pr.
Steiner, John M. *see* Steiner, John Michael.
Steiner, John Michael, 1928-
xSteiner, John M.
Power Politics & Social Change in National
Socialist Germany: A Process of Escalation
into Mass Destruction. Mouton.
Steiner, Jorg.
xSteiner, Jorg.
Rabbit Island. HarBraceJ.
Steiner, Jurg.
xSteiner, Jurg.
A Theory of Political Decision Modes:
Intraparty Decision Making in Switzerland. U
of NC Pr.
Steiner, Kurt.
xSteiner, Kurt.
Local Government in Japan. Stanford U Pr.
Steiner, Lee R. *see* Steiner, Lee Rabinowitz.
Steiner, Lee Rabinowitz, 1901-
xSteiner, Lee R.
Psychic Self-Healing for Psychological
Problems. P-H.
Steiner, Mark.
xSteiner, Mark.
Mathematical Knowledge. Cornell U Pr.
Steiner, Peter O. *see* Steiner, Peter Otto.
Steiner, Peter Otto, 1922-
xSteiner, Peter O.
Workable Competition in the Radio
Broadcasting Industry. Arno.
Steiner, Robert, 1948-
xSteiner, Robert.
Bathers. New Directions.
Steiner, Robert B.
xSteiner, Robert B.
Oral Surgery & Anesthesia. Saunders.
Steiner, Robert F.
xSteiner, Robert F.
The Chemical Foundations of Molecular
Biology. Krieger.
ed. Excited States of Proteins & Nucleic Acids.
Plenum Pub.
Steiner, Rudolf.
xSteiner, Rudolf.
Calendar of the Soul. Anthroposophic.
The Christ Impulse & the Development of Ego
Consciousness. Anthroposophic.
Christianity As a Mystical Fact & the
Mysteries of Antiquity. Multimedia.
Christianity As Mystical Fact & the Mysteries
of Antiquity. Anthroposophic.
Goethe's Conception of the World. Haskell.
Occult Signs & Symbols. Anthroposophic.
Outline of Occult Science. Anthroposophic.
Reincarnation & Immortality. Har-Row.
Steiner, Stan. *see* Steiner, Stanley.
Steiner, Stanley.
xSteiner, Stan.
The Vanishing White Man. Har-Row.
The Vanishing White Man. Har-Row.
Steiner, Wendy, 1949-
xSteiner, Wendy.
Exact Resemblance to Exact Resemblance: The
Literary Portraiture of Gertrude Stein. Yale
U Pr.
Steiner, Zara. *see* Steiner, Zara S.

Steiner, Zara S.
xSteiner, Zara.
Britain & the Origins of the First World War.
St Martin.
xSteiner, Zara S.
Foreign Office & Foreign Policy 1898-1914.
Cambridge U Pr.
Steinfatt, Thomas. *see* Steinfatt, Thomas M.
Steinfatt, Thomas M., 1941-
xSteinfatt, Thomas.
Human Communication: An Interpersonal
Introduction. Bobbs.
Steinfeldt, Cecilia.
xSteinfeldt, Cecilia.
The Onderdonks: A Family of Texas Painters.
Trinity U Pr.
Steingraber, Jack.
xSteingraber, Jack.
FORTRAN Fundamentals: A Short Course.
Hayden.
Steingress, Fred M. *see* Steingress, Frederick M.
Steingress, Frederick M.
xSteingress, Fred M.
Low Pressure Boilers. Am Technical.
Steinhardt, J. *see* Steinhardt, Jacinto.
Steinhardt, Jacinto.
xSteinhardt, J.
Multiple Equilibria in Proteins. Acad Pr.
Steinhart, Edward I.
xSteinhart, Edward I.
Conflict & Collaboration: The Kingdoms of
Western Uganda, 1890 - 1907. Princeton U
Pr.
Steinhauer, Harry, 1905-
xSteinhauer, Harry.
tr. Twelve German Novellas. U of Cal Pr.
Steinhaus, Edward A. *see* Steinhaus, Edward Arthur.
Steinhaus, Edward Arthur, 1914-1969
xSteinhaus, Edward A.
Disease in a Minor Chord: Being a
Semihistorical & Semibiographical Account of
a Period in Science When One Could Be
Happily Yet Seriously Concerned with the
Diseases of Lowly Animals Without
Backbones, Especially the Insects. Ohio St U
Pr.
Insect Microbiology: An Account of the
Microbes Associated with Insects & Ticks.
Hafner.
ed. Insect Pathology: An Advanced Treatise.
Acad Pr.
Steinhaus, Hugo, 1887-
xSteinhaus, Hugo.
Mathematical Snapshots. Oxford U Pr.
Steinherz, H. A.
xSteinherz, H. A.
Handbook of High Vacuum Engineering.
Krieger.
Steinhoff, Dan.
xSteinhoff, Dan.
The World of Business. McGraw.
Steinhoff, Ernst A.
xSteinhoff, Ernst A.
ed. Organizing Space Activities for World
Needs. Pergamon.
Steinhoff, Patricia G.
xSteinhoff, Patricia G.
Abortion Politics: The Hawaii Experience. U Pr
of Hawaii.
Steinhoff, Richard. *see* Steinhoff, Richard L.
Steinhoff, Richard L.
xSteinhoff, Richard.
Arithmetic. McGraw.
Steinhoff, William. *see* Steinhoff, William R.
Steinhoff, William R.
xSteinhoff, William.
George Orwell & the Origins of 1984. U of
Mich Pr.
Steinitz, Carl.
xSteinitz, Carl.

Systems Analysis Model of Urbanization &
Change: An Experiment in Interdisciplinary
Education. MIT Pr.
Steinitz, Paul.
xSteinitz, Paul.
Bach's Passions. Scribner.
Steinkraus, William.
xSteinkraus, William.
Riding & Jumping. Doubleday.
Steinman, D. B. *see* Steinman, David Barnard.
Steinman, David B. *see* Steinman, David Barnard.
Steinman, David Barnard, 1886-1960
xSteinman, D. B.
Songs of a Bridge Builder. InterCulture.
xSteinman, David B.
The Builders of the Bridge: The Story of John
Roebling & His Son. Arno.
Steinman, Michael.
xSteinman, Michael.
Energy & Environmental Issues: The Making &
Implementation of Public Policy Issues.
Lexington Bks.
Steinmark, Freddie.
xSteinmark, Freddie.
I Play to Win. Little.
Steinmetz, Charles P. *see* Steinmetz, Charles Proteus.
Steinmetz, Charles Proteus.
xSteinmetz, Charles P.
Lectures in Electrical Engineering. Dover.
Lectures on Electrical Engineering. Dover.
Steinmetz, Lawrence L.
xSteinmetz, Lawrence L.
Art & Skill of Delegation. A-W.
First-Line Management: Approaching
Supervision Effectively. Business Pubns.
Human Relations: People & Work. Har-Row.
Steinmetz, Leon.
xSteinmetz, Leon.
Clocks in the Woods. Har-Row.
Steinmetz, Richard H.
xSteinmetz, Richard H.
This Was Harrisburg: A Photographic History.
Stackpole.
Steinmetz, Suzanne K.
xSteinmetz, Suzanne K.
Cycle of Violence: Assertive, Aggressive, &
Abusive Family Interation. Praeger.
Steinzor, Bernard.
xSteinzor, Bernard.
When Parents Divorce: A New Approach to
New Relationships. Pantheon.
Steiss, Alan W. *see* Steiss, Alan Walter.
Steiss, Alan Walter.
xSteiss, Alan W.
Dynamic Change & the Urban Ghetto.
Lexington Bks.
Local Government Finance: Capital Facilities
Planning & Debt Administration in Local
Government. Lexington Bks.
Public Budgeting & Management. Lexington
Bks.
Steitz, Edward S.
xSteitz, Edward S.
Illustrated Basketball Rules. Doubleday.
Stekl, William. *see* Stekl, William F.
Stekl, William F.
xStekl, William.
The Connecticut River. Columbia U Pr.
Stekler, H. O. *see* Stekler, Herman O.
Stekler, Herman O.
xStekler, H. O.
The Structure & Performance of the Aerospace
Industry. U of Cal Pr.
Steklov Institute of Mathematics, Academy of Sciences,
U S S R, Vol. 132. *see* International Conference on
Number Theory, Moscow, 1971.
Steklov Institute of Mathematics, No. 112. *see*
Akademiia Nauk Sssr. Matematicheskii Institut.
Stell, P. M. *see* Stell, Philip Michael.

Stell, Philip Michael.
  xStell, P. M.
    Head & Neck Surgery. Lippincott.
Stella, Antonio, 1868-1927
  xStella, Antonio.
    Some Aspects of Italian Immigration to the
     United States. Arno.
Stellman, Jeanne M., 1947-
  xStellman, Jeanne M.
    Women's Work, Women's Health: Myths &
     Realities. Pantheon.
    Work Is Dangerous to Your Health: A
     Handbook of Health Hazards in the
     Workplace & What You Can Do About
     Them. Pantheon.
Steltzer, Ulli.
  xSteltzer, Ulli.
    Indian Artists at Work. U of Wash Pr.
Stelzer, Dick.
  xStelzer, Dick.
    The Star Treatment. Bobbs.
    Star Treatment. NAL.
Stelzig, Eugene L.
  xStelzig, Eugene L.
    All Shades of Consciousness: Wordsworth's
     Poetry & the Self in Time. Mouton.
Stelzle, Charles, 1869-1941
  xStelzle, Charles.
    A Son of the Bowery: The Life Story of an
     East Side American. Arno.
Stem, Carl H.
  xStem, Carl H.
    ed. Eurocurrencies & the International
     Monetary System. Am Enterprise.
Stem, Thad.
  xStem, Thad.
    Thad Stem's Ark. Moore Pub Co.
    Thad Stem's First Reader. Moore Pub Co.
Stember, C. H. see Stember, Charles Herbert.
Stember, Charles Herbert, 1916-
  xStember, C. H.
    Sexual Racism: The Emotional Barrier to an
     Integrated Society. Elsevier.
Stemp, Isay.
  xStemp, Isay.
    ed. Corporate Growth Strategies. Am Mgmt.
Stenberg, Odin K.
  xStenberg, Odin K.
    A Church Without Walls. Bethany Fell.
  xStenberg, Odink.
    Pref. by A Church Without Walls. Bethany
     Fell.
Stenberg, Odink. see Stenberg, Odin K.
Stenchever, Morton A., 1931-
  xStenchever, Morton A.
    Human Cytogenetics: A Workbook in
     Reproductive Biology. Year Bk Med.
Stendahl, Brita. see Stendahl, Brita K.
Stendahl, Brita K.
  xStendahl, Brita.
    Sabbatical Reflections: The Ten
     Commandments in a New Day. Fortress.
Stenesh, J., 1927-
  xStenesh, J.
    Dictionary of Biochemistry. Wiley.
Stenger, Erich, 1878-
  xStenger, Erich.
    The History of Photography. Arno.
Stenhagen, E.
  xStenhagen, E.
    ed. Registry of Mass Spectral Data. Wiley.
Stenholm, Anne.
  xStenholm, Anne.
    Travel Agency: A How-to-Do-It Manual for
     Starting One of Your Own. Freelance Pubns.
Stenquist, John L. see Stenquist, John Langdon.
Stenquist, John Langdon, 1885-1952
  xStenquist, John L.
    Measurements of Mechanical Ability. AMS Pr.
Stensland, Anna L. see Stensland, Anna Lee.

Stensland, Anna Lee.
  xStensland, Anna L.
    Literature by & About the American Indian:
     An Annotated Bibliography. NCTE.
Stensvold, Mike.
  xStensvold, Mike.
    ed. Increasing Film Speed. Petersen Pub.
Stent, Gunther S. see Stent, Gunther Siegmund.
Stent, Gunther Siegmund, 1924-
  xStent, Gunther S.
    Paradoxes of Progress. W H Freeman.
Stenton, Doris M. see Stenton, Doris Mary Parsons.
Stenton, Doris Mary Parsons, Lady.
  xStenton, Doris M.
    English Society in the Early Middle Ages.
     Penguin.
    English Society in the Early Middle Ages,
     1066-1307. Gannon.
    The English Woman in History. Schocken.
Stenton, F. M. see Stenton, Frank Merry.
Stenton, Frank. see Stenton, Frank Merry.
Stenton, Frank M. see Stenton, Frank Merry.
Stenton, Frank Merry, Sir, 1880-
  xStenton, F. M.
    Anglo-Saxon England. Gordon Pr.
  xStenton, Frank.
    Anglo-Saxon England. Oxford U Pr.
  xStenton, Frank M.
    The First Century of English Feudalism,
     1066-1166. Greenwood.
Stenz, Anita M. see Stenz, Anita Maria.
Stenz, Anita Maria.
  xStenz, Anita M.
    Edward Albee: The Poet of Loss. Mouton.
Stepanoff, A. J. see Stepanoff, Alexey Joakim.
Stepanoff, Alexey Joakim.
  xStepanoff, A. J.
    Centrifugal & Axial Flow Pumps: Theory,
     Design & Application. Wiley.
Stepelevich, Lawrence S., 1930-
  xStepelevich, Lawrence S.
    Intro. by & ed. The Capitalist Reader.
     Arlington Hse.
Stephan. see Stephan, Karl.
Stephan, Karl.
  xStephan.
    Viscosity of Dense Fluids. Plenum Pub.
Stephan, Leslie.
  xStephan, Leslie.
    Murder R.F.D.. Scribner.
Stephan, Walter G.
  xStephan, Walter G.
    ed. School Desegregation: Past, Present, &
     Future. Plenum Pub.
Stephanides, Marios, 1945-
  xStephanides, Marios.
    The Greeks in Detroit: Authoritarianism - a
     Critical Analysis of Greek Culture,
     Personality, Attitudes & Behavior. R & E Res
     Assoc.
Stephen.
  xStephen.
    Caravan. Bookworks.
Stephen, James, 1758-1832
  xStephen, James.
    Crisis of the Sugar Colonies: Or, an Enquiry
     into the Objects & Probable Effects of the
     French Expedition to the West Indies. Negro
     U Pr.
Stephen, James F. see Stephen, James Fitzjames.
Stephen, James Fitzjames, Bart., Sir, 1829-1894
  xStephen, James F.
    Liberty, Equality, Fraternity. Cambridge U Pr.
Stephen, Leslie. see Stephen, Leslie.
Stephen, Leslie, Sir, 1832-1904
  xStephen, Lesie.
    Some Early Impressions. R West.
  xStephen, Leslie.

    English Utilitarians. Kelley.
    George Eliot. AMS Pr.
    George Eliot. R West.
    History of English Thought in the Eighteenth
     Century. Peter Smith.
    Hours in a Library. Gordon Pr.
    Hours in a Library. Johnson Repr.
    Hours in a Library. Scholarly.
    Robert Louis Stevenson: An Essay. R West.
    Selected Writings in British Intellectual
     History. U of Chicago Pr.
    Some Early Impressions. B Franklin.
    Swift. AMS Pr.
    Swift. Arden Lib.
    Swift. Darby Bks.
    Swift. Folcroft.
Stephens. see Stephens, Lester D.
Stephens, A. see Stephens, Anthony R.
Stephens, Alan. see Stephens, Alan Archer.
Stephens, Alan Archer, 1925-
  xStephens, Alan.
    White River Poems: Conversations,
     Pronouncements, Testimony, Recollections &
     Mediations on the Subject of the White River
     Massacre, Sept. 29, 1879. Swallow.
Stephens, Anthony R.
  xStephens, A.
    Rainer Maria Rilke's Gedichte an Die Nacht:
     An Essay in Interpretation. Cambridge U Pr.
Stephens, Charles A. see Stephens, Charles Asbury.
Stephens, Charles Asbury, 1844-1931
  xStephens, Charles A.
    My Folks in Maine. Arno.
Stephens, Fran C. see Stephens, Fran Carlock.
Stephens, Fran Carlock.
  xStephens, Fran C.
    Compiled by The Hartley Coleridge Letters: A
     Calendar & Index. U of Tex Hum Res.
Stephens, Frank F. see Stephens, Frank Fletcher.
Stephens, Frank Fletcher.
  xStephens, Frank F.
    History of the University of Missouri. U of Mo
     Pr.
Stephens, Frederick J. see Stephens, Frederick John.
Stephens, Frederick John, 1877-
  xStephens, Frederick J.
    A Collector's Pictorial Book of Bayonets.
     Hippocrene Bks.
Stephens, Gwen J.
  xStephens, Gwen J.
    Pathophysiology for Health Practitioners.
     Macmillan.
Stephens, H. A. see Stephens, Homer A.
Stephens, Henry L. see Stephens, Henry Louis.
Stephens, Henry Louis, 1824-1882
  xStephens, Henry L.
    illus. Frog He Would A-Wooing Go. Walker &
     Co.
Stephens, Henry M. see Stephens, Henry Morse.
Stephens, Henry Morse, 1857-1919
  xStephens, Henry M.
    Story of Portugal. AMS Pr.
    The Story of Portugal. Gordon Pr.
Stephens, Homer A.
  xStephens, H. A.
    Poisonous Plants of the Central United States.
     Regents Pr Ks.
  xStephens, Homer A.
    Woody Plants of the North Central Plains.
     Regents Pr KS.
Stephens, J. S. see Stephens, John Stewart.
Stephens, James.
  xStephens, James.

Deirdre. Arden Lib.
Deirdre. Macmillan.
Francis Bacon & the Style of Science. U of
    Chicago Pr.
The Insurrection in Dublin. Humanities.
Mary, Mary. Arden Lib.
Mary, Mary. Scholarly.
Stephens, John. see Stephens, John Lloyd.
Stephens, John L. see Stephens, John Lloyd.
Stephens, John Lloyd, 1805-1852
    xStephens, John.
    Incidents of Travel in Central America,
        Chiapas & Yucatan. Dover.
    xStephens, John L.
    Incidents of Travel in Central America,
        Chiapas, & Yucatan. Peter Smith.
    Incidents of Travel in Egypt, Arabia Petraea &
        the Holy Land. U of Okla Pr.
Stephens, John M. see Stephens, John Mortimer.
Stephens, John Mortimer, 1901-
    xStephens, John M.
    Influence of Different Stimuli Upon Preceding
        Bonds: An Examination of the Law of Effect.
        AMS Pr.
Stephens, John Stewart.
    xStephens, J. S.
    A Revised Classification of the Blennioid
        Fishes of the American Family Chaenopsidae.
        U of Cal Pr.
Stephens, John W.
    xStephens, John W.
    Understanding Diabetes. Touchstone Pr Ore.
Stephens, Julius H. see Stephens, Julius Harold.
Stephens, Julius Harold.
    xStephens, Julius H.
    The Churches & the Kingdom. Greenwood.
Stephens, L. see Stephens, Lillian S.
Stephens, Lester D.
    xStephens.
    Probing the Past: A Guide to the Study &
        Teaching of History. Allyn.
    xStephens, Lester D.
    Historiography: A Bibliography. Scarecrow.
Stephens, Lillian S.
    xStephens, L.
    The Teachers Guide to Open Education.
        HR&W.
Stephens, Mark.
    xStephens, Mark.
    Three Mile Island. Random.
Stephens, Martha.
    xStephens, Martha.
    Cast a Wistful Eye. Macmillan.
Stephens, Meic.
    xStephens, Meic.
    Linguistic Minorities in Western Europe. Intl
        Learn Syst.
Stephens, Michael D. see Stephens, Michael Dawson.
Stephens, Michael Dawson.
    xStephens, Michael D.
    ed. Higher Education Alternatives. Longman.
Stephens, Otis H., 1936-
    xStephens, Otis H.
    The Supreme Court & Confessions of Guilt. U
        of Tenn Pr.
Stephens, Peter J. see Stephens, Peter John.
Stephens, Peter John.
    xStephens, Peter J.
    The Story of Fire Fighting. Harvey.
Stephens, Richard B.
    xStephens, Richard B.
    Federal Estate & Gift Taxation. Warren.
Stephens, Robert. see Stephens, Robert T.
Stephens, Robert Henry, 1920-
    xStephens, Robert.
    The Arabs' New Frontier. Westview.
Stephens, Robert T.
    xStephens, Robert.

Worktext in Intermediate Algebra. West Pub.
Stephens, Roger B.
    xStephens, Roger B.
    Arteries & Veins of the Human Brain. C C
        Thomas.
Stephens, Thomas. see Stephens, Thomas M.
Stephens, Thomas A. see Stephens, Thomas Arthur.
Stephens, Thomas Arthur, 1852-1925
    xStephens, Thomas A.
    Contribution to the Bibliography of the Bank of
        England. Kelley.
Stephens, Thomas M.
    xStephens, Thomas.
    Implementing Behavioral Approaches in
        Elementary & Secondary Schools. Merrill.
    xStephens, Thomas M.
    Directive Teaching of Children with Learning
        & Behavioral Handicaps. Merrill.
Stephens, Trent D. see Stephens, Trent Dee.
Stephens, Trent Dee.
    xStephens, Trent D.
    Atlas of Human Embryology. Macmillan.
Stephens, W. D. see Stephens, W. Peter.
Stephens, W. Peter.
    xStephens, W. D.
    Holy Spirit in the Theology of Martin Bucer.
        Cambridge U Pr.
Stephens, William. see Stephens, William M.
Stephens, William M.
    xStephens, William.
    Life in the Tidepool. McGraw.
Stephens, William N.
    xStephens, William N.
    Our Children Should Be Working. C C
        Thomas.
Stephens, Wilson.
    xStephens, Wilson.
    Field Bedside Book. David & Charles.
Stephenson. see Stephenson, George E.
Stephenson, Andrew, 1856-1927
    xStephenson, Andrew.
    Public Lands & Agrarian Laws of the Roman
        Republic. AMS Pr.
    Public Lands & Agrarian Laws of the Roman
        Republic. Johnson Repr.
Stephenson, Carl, 1886-
    xStephenson, Carl.
    Mediaeval Feudalism. Cornell U Pr.
Stephenson, E. M. see Stephenson, Ethel M.
Stephenson, Ethel M.
    xStephenson, E. M.
    T. S. Eliot & the Lay Reader. Folcroft.
    T. S. Eliot & the Lay Reader. Gordon Pr.
    xStephenson, Ethel M.
    T. S. Eliot & the Lay Reader. Haskell.
Stephenson, F. Douglas.
    xStephenson, F. Douglas.
    Gestalt Therapy Primer: Introductory Readings
        in Gestalt Therapy. C C Thomas.
Stephenson, F. Richard. see Stephenson, Francis Richard.
Stephenson, Francis Richard.
    xStephenson, F. Richard.
    Applications of Early Astronomical Records.
        Oxford U Pr.
Stephenson, G. T. see Stephenson, Gilbert Thomas.
Stephenson, Geoffrey M.
    xStephenson, Geoffrey M.
    Development of Conscience. Humanities.
    Industrial Relations: A Social Psychological
        Approach. Wiley.
Stephenson, George E.
    xStephenson.
    Power Technology. Delmar.
Stephenson, George M. see Stephenson, George
Malcolm.
Stephenson, George Malcolm, 1883-
    xStephenson, George M.

The Puritan Heritage. Greenwood.
Religious Aspects of Swedish Immigration: A
    Study of Immigrant Churches. Arno.
Stephenson, Gilbert T. see Stephenson, Gilbert Thomas.
Stephenson, Gilbert Thomas, 1884-
    xStephenson, G. T.
    Race Distinctions in American Law. Gordon
        Pr.
    xStephenson, Gilbert T.
    Race Distinctions in American Law. AMS Pr.
    Race Distinctions in American Law. Arno.
    Race Distinctions in American Law. Johnson
        Repr.
    Race Distinctions in American Law. Negro U
        Pr.
Stephenson, Hugh E.
    xStephenson, Hugh E.
    Immediate Care of the Acutely Ill & Injured.
        Mosby.
Stephenson, James H., 1919-
    xStephenson, James H.
    A Doctor's Guide to Helping Yourself with
        Homeopathic Remedies. Formur Intl.
    A Doctor's Guide to Helping Yourself with
        Homeopathic Remedies. P-H.
Stephenson, John R.
    xStephenson, John R.
    ed. Molecular Biology of RNA Tumor Viruses.
        Acad Pr.
Stephenson, Ralph.
    xStephenson, Ralph.
    Cinema As Art. Penguin.
Stephenson, Reginald J. see Stephenson, Reginald Joseph.
Stephenson, Reginald Joseph.
    xStephenson, Reginald J.
    Exploring in Physics: A New Outlook on
        Problems in Physics. U of Chicago Pr.
Stephenson, Richard M. see Stephenson, Richard
Montgomery.
Stephenson, Richard Montgomery.
    xStephenson, Richard M.
    The Complete Book of Ballroom Dancing.
        Doubleday.
Stephenson, Robert L. see Stephenson, Robert Lloyd.
Stephenson, Robert Lloyd.
    xStephenson, Robert L.
    The Accokeek Creek Site: A Middle Atlantic
        Seaboard Culture Sequence. U Mich Mus
        Anthro.
Stephenson, Sue H.
    xStephenson, Sue H.
    Rustic Furniture. Van Nos Reinhold.
Stephenson, Wendell H. see Stephenson, Wendell
Holmes.
Stephenson, Wendell Holmes, 1899-1970
    xStephenson, Wendell H.
    Alexander Porter, Whig Planter of Old
        Louisiana. Da Capo.
    South Lives in History: Southern Historians &
        Their Legacy. Negro U Pr.
Stephenson, William.
    xStephenson, William.
    Play Theory of Mass Communication. U of
        Chicago Pr.
Stepto, Robert B.
    xStepto, Robert B.
    From Behind the Veil: A Study of
        Afro-American Narrative. U of Ill Pr.
Steptoe, John, 1950-
    xSteptoe, John.
    illus. Marcia. Viking Pr.
    Stevie. Har-Row.
    xSteptoe, John L.
    illus. Stevie. Har-Row.
Steptoe, John L. see Steptoe, John.
Steranko, J. see Steranko, James.
Steranko, James.
    xSteranko, J.

The Steranko History of the Comics. Crown.

Sterba, James P.
xSterba, James P.
Justice: Alternative Political Perspectives. Wadsworth Pub.

Sterkx, H. E.
xSterkx, H. E.
Free Negro in Ante-Bellum Louisiana, 1724-1860. Fairleigh Dickinson.
Partners in Rebellion: Alabama Women in the Civil War. Fairleigh Dickinson.

Sterling, Christopher. *see* Sterling, Christopher H.

Sterling, Christopher H.
xSterling, Christopher.
The Mass Media: Aspen Institute Guide to Communication Industry Trends. Aspen Inst Human.

Sterling, Dorothy, 1913-
xSterling, Dorothy.
Black Foremothers: Three Lives. Feminist Pr.
Fall Is Here. Natural Hist.
The Outer Lands: A Natural History Guide to Cape Cod, Martha's Vineyard, Nantucket, Block Island, & Long Island. Norton.

Sterling, E. M.
xSterling, E. M.
The South Cascades: The Gifford Pinchot National Forest. Mountaineers.
Trips & Trails, 1. Mountaineers.
Trips & Trails, 2. Mountaineers.

Sterling, George, 1869-1926
xSterling, George.
Sonnets to Craig. AMS Pr.
Truth. AMS Pr.

Sterling, Philip.
xSterling, Philip.
Four Took Freedom: The Lives of Harriet Tubman, Frederick Douglass, Robert Small, & Blanche K. Bruce. Doubleday.

Sterling Publishing Company Editors. *see* Sterling Publishing Company, Inc.

Sterling Publishing Company, Inc.
xEditorial Staff.
ed. Ivory Coast - in Pictures. Sterling.
xSterling Publishing Company Editors.
Spain in Pictures. Sterling.
Switzerland in Pictures. Sterling.

Sterling, Richard W.
xSterling, Richard W.
Ethics in a World of Power: The Political Ideas of Friedrich Meinecke. Princeton U Pr.

Sterling, Robert R.
xSterling, Robert R.
ed. Accounting for a Simplified Firm Owning Depreciable Assets: Seventeen Essays & a Synthesis Based on a Common Case. Scholars Bk.
ed. Asset Valuation & Income Determination: A Consideration of the Alternatives. Scholars Bk.
Theory of Measurement of Enterprise Income. Scholars Bk.

Sterling, Theodor D.
xSterling, Theodor D.
Computers & the Life Sciences. Columbia U Pr.

Sterman, M. B.
xSterman, M. B.
Brain Development & Behavior. Acad Pr.

Stermole, Franklin J.
xStermole, Franklin J.
Economic Evaluation & Investment Decision Methods. Invest Eval.

Stern. *see* Stern, Lawrence.

Stern, Aaron.
xStern, Aaron.
The Naked Truth: Observations of an Iconoclast. Renaissance Pub.

Stern, Arthur C. *see* Stern, Arthur Cecil.

Stern, Arthur Cecil.
xStern, Arthur C.
Fundamentals of Air Pollution. Acad Pr.

Stern, Benjamin J., 1899-
xStern, Benjamin J.
Opportunities in Drafting Today. Natl Textbk.

Stern, Bernhard J. *see* Stern, Bernhard Joseph.

Stern, Bernhard Joseph, 1894-1956
xStern, Bernhard J.
Lewis Henry Morgan, Social Evolutionist. Russell.
Lummi Indians of Northwest Washington. AMS Pr.
ed. Understanding the Russians: A Study of Soviet Life & Culture. Arno.

Stern, Clarence A. *see* Stern, Clarence Ames.

Stern, Clarence Ames.
xStern, Clarence A.
Protectionist Republicanism: Republican Tariff Policy in the McKinley Period. Stern.
Resurgent Republicanism: The Handiwork of Hanna. Stern.

Stern, Curt, 1902-
xStern, Curt.
Genetic Mosaics & Other Essays. Harvard U Pr.
Principles of Human Genetics. W H Freeman.

Stern, D. Nordlinger. *see* Stern, Duke Nordlinger.

Stern, David. *see* Stern, David H.

Stern, David H.
xStern, David.
Surfing Guide to Southern California. Mntn & Sea.

Stern, Don.
xStern, Don.
Backgammon. Watts.
xStern, Donald.
Backgammon: A Quick Course in Winning Play. Cornerstone.

Stern, Donald. *see* Stern, Don.

Stern, Duke Nordlinger.
xStern, D. Nordlinger.
Cases in Labor Law. Grid Pub.

Stern, E. Mark.
xStern, E. Mark.
Psychotheology. Paulist Pr.

Stern, Elizabeth G. *see* Stern, Elizabeth Gertrude (Levin).

Stern, Elizabeth Gertrude (Levin), 1890-
xStern, Elizabeth G.
I Am a Woman & a Jew. Arno.

Stern, Ellen.
xStern, Ellen P.
ed. The Limits of Military Intervention. Sage.

Stern, Ellen P. *see* Stern, Ellen.

Stern Family Fund. *see* Edgar Stern Family Fund.

Stern, Fritz. *see* Stern, Fritz Richard.

Stern, Fritz Richard, 1926-
xStern, Fritz.
Gold & Iron: Bismarck, Bleichroder & the Building of the German Empire. Knopf.
ed. The Varieties of History: From Voltaire to the Present. Random.

Stern, Gerald M. *see* Stern, Gerald Malcolm.

Stern, Gerald Malcolm.
xStern, Gerald M.
ed. The Clinical Uses of Levodopa. Univ Park.

Stern, Geraldine.
xStern, Geraldine.
Israeli Women Speak Out. Lippincott.

Stern, Gladys B. *see* Stern, Gladys Bronwyn.

Stern, Gladys Bronwyn.
xStern, Gladys B.
Dogs in an Omnibus. Arno.

Stern, Henry R.
xStern, Henry R.
A Handbook of English-German Idioms & Useful Expressions. HarBraceJ.

Stern, Herman I. *see* Stern, Herman Isidore.

Stern, Herman Isidore, 1854-
xStern, Herman I.
The Gods of Our Fathers: A Study of Saxon Mythology. Longwood Pr.

Stern, J. David. *see* Stern, Julius David.

Stern, J. P. *see* Stern, Joseph Peter.

Stern, J. T. *see* Stern, Jack T.

Stern, Jack T.
xStern, J. T.
Functional Myology of the Hip & Thigh of Cebid Monkeys & Its Implications for the Evolution of Erect Posture. S Karger.

Stern, James L.
xStern, James L.
Final-Offer Arbitration: The Effects on Public Safety Employee Bargaining. Lexington Bks.

Stern, Jane.
xStern, Jane.
Auto Ads. Random.
Friendly Relations. Random.
Roadfood. Random.

Stern, Josef.
xStern, Jossi.
People of the Book: An Artistic Exploration of the Bible. Collins Pubs.

Stern, Joseph J.
xStern, Joseph J.
Growth & Development in Pakistan, 1955-1969. Harvard U Intl Aff.

Stern, Joseph Peter.
xStern, J. P.
Friedrich Nietzsche. Penguin.
Hitler: The Fuhrer & the People. U of Cal Pr.
Idylls & Realities: Studies in Nineteenth-Century German Literature. Ungar.
On Realism. Routledge & Kegan.
A Study of Nietzsche. Cambridge U Pr.

Stern, Jossi. *see* Stern, Josef.

Stern, Julius David, 1886-
xStern, J. David.
Memoirs of a Maverick Publisher. S&S.

Stern, K. *see* Stern, Klaus.

Stern, Kingsley R. *see* Stern, Kingsley Rowland.

Stern, Kingsley Rowland.
xStern, Kingsley R.
Introductory Plant Biology. Wm C Brown.

Stern, Klaus.
xStern, K.
Genetics of Forest Ecosystems. Springer-Verlag.

Stern, Lawrence, 1935-
xStern.
Stage Management: A Guidebook of Practical Techniques. Allyn.
xStern, Lawrence.
School & Community Theater Management: A Handbook for Survival. Allyn.

Stern, Leo.
xStern, Leo.
Intensive Care of the Newborn II. Masson Pub.

Stern, Louis W.
xStern, Louis W.
Marketing Channels. P-H.

Stern, M. H. *see* Stern, Malcolm H.

Stern, Madeleine. *see* Stern, Madeleine Bettina.

Stern, Madeleine B. *see* Stern, Madeleine Bettina.

Stern, Madeleine Bettina, 1912-
xStern, Madeleine.
Life of Margaret Fuller. Haskell.
xStern, Madeleine B.
Pantarch: A Biography of Stephen Pearl Andrews. U of Tex Pr.
Purple Passage: Life of Mrs Frank Leslie. U of Okla Pr.
xStern, Madeline B.
Louisa May Alcott. U of Okla Pr.

Stern, Madeline B. *see* Stern, Madeleine Bettina.

Stern, Malcolm H.
xStern, M. H.

Chopping Wood, Carrying Water. Padma.
Continuum: An Autobiography at Thirty.
Padma.
Stetson, Damon.
xStetson, Damon.
Starting Over. Macmillan.
Stetson, Joe.
xStetson, Joe.
Hunting with Flushing Dogs. TFH Pubns.
Hunting with Pointing Dogs. TFH Pubns.
Stetson Mid-Winter Trial Seminar, 2nd, Miami Beach, Fla.
xStetson University.
Trial Techniques. Trans-Media Pub.
Stetson, Patricia C.
xStetson, Patricia C.
ed. The Psychology of Learning & Teaching.
Mss Info.
Stetson University. *see* Stetson Mid-Winter Trial
Seminar, 2nd, Miami Beach, Fla.
Stetter, H. J. *see* Stetter, Hans J.
Stetter, Hans J., 1930-
xStetter, H. J.
Analysis of Discretization Methods for
Ordinary Differential Equations.
Springer-Verlag.
Stettler, H. *see* Stettler, Howard F.
Stettler, Howard F.
xStettler, H.
Auditing Principles. P-H.
xStettler, Howard F.
Systems-Based Independent Audits. P-H.
Stettner, N. *see* Stettner, Nora.
Stettner, Nora.
xStettner, N.
Productivity, Bargaining & Industrial Change.
Pergamon.
Steuck, Jeanine.
xSteuck, Jeanine.
Good Morning Judy!. Augsburg.
Steudel, Ralf, 1937-
xSteudel, Ralf.
Chemistry of the Non-Metals: With an
Introduction to Atomic Structure and
Chemical Bonding. De Gruyter.
Steuding, Bob.
xSteuding, Bob.
Gary Snyder. Twayne.
Steuer, Aron, 1898-
xSteuer, Aron.
Aesop in the Courts. Law-Arts.
Steuernagel, Gertrude A.
xSteuernagel, Gertrude A.
Political Philosophy As Therapy: Marcuse
Reconsidered. Greenwood.
Steven, Hugh.
xSteven, Hugh.
The Man with the Noisy Heart. Moody.
Stevens, A. *see* Stevens, Andrew J.
Stevens, Andrew J.
xStevens, A.
Troubleshooting & Repairing Automotive
Electronic Ignition Systems. Reston.
Stevens, Barbara C. *see* Stevens, Barbara Christine.
Stevens, Barbara Christine.
xStevens, Barbara C.
Marriage & Fertility of Women Suffering from
Schizophrenia or Affective Disorders. Oxford
U Pr.
Stevens, Barbara J., 1946-
xStevens, Barbara J.
Handbook of Municipal Waste Management
Systems: Planning & Practice. Van Nos
Reinhold.
Nursing Theory: Analysis, Application,
Evaluation. Little.
Stevens, Beulah F. *see* Stevens, Beulah Fern.
Stevens, Beulah Fern, 1937-
xStevens, Beulah F.

Dear Georgia. Southern Pub.
Stevens, Bob, 1923-
xStevens, Bob.
More There I Was. Aero.
Stevens, Bob C.
xStevens, Bob C.
The Collector's Book of Snuff Bottles.
Weatherhill.
Stevens, Carl M.
xStevens, Carl M.
Strategy & Collective Bargaining Negotiation.
Greenwood.
Stevens, Carla.
xStevens, Carla.
Hooray for Pig!. HM.
How to Make Possum's Honey Bread. HM.
Insect Pets: Catching & Caring for Them.
Greenwillow.
Stories from a Snowy Meadow. HM.
Trouble for Lucy. HM.
Stevens, Carolyn B.
xStevens, Carolyn B.
Special Needs of Long-Term Patients.
Lippincott.
Stevens, Charles E. *see* Stevens, Charles Emery.
Stevens, Charles Emery, 1815-1893
xStevens, Charles E.
Anthony Burns: A History. Corner Hse.
Stevens, Chris.
xStevens, Chris.
Fastest Machines. Raintree Child.
Stevens, Christopher.
xStevens, Christopher.
The Soviet Union & Black Africa. Holmes &
Meier.
Stevens, Clifford. *see* Stevens, Clifford J.
Stevens, Clifford J.
xStevens, Clifford.
Portraits of Faith. Our Sunday Visitor.
Wild Dogs of Chongdo. Our Sunday Visitor.
Stevens, David, 1933-
xStevens, David.
White for Danger. Stein & Day.
Stevens, David H. *see* Stevens, David Harrison.
Stevens, David Harrison, 1884-
xStevens, David H.
Party Politics & English Journalism,
1702-1742. Russell.
Stevens, Denis.
xStevens, Denis.
ed. The Penguin Book of English Madrigals for
Four Voices. Penguin.
Stevens, Denis. *see* Stevens, Denis William.
Stevens, Denis William, 1922-
xStevens, Denis.
ed. History of Song. Norton.
Monteverdi: Sacred, Secular & Occasional
Music. Fairleigh Dickinson.
Stevens, Eden V. *see* Stevens, Eden Vale.
Stevens, Eden Vale.
xStevens, Eden V.
Buffalo Bill. Putnam.
Stevens, Edward, 1928-
xStevens, Edward.
Business Ethics. Paulist Pr.
The Morals Game. Paulist Pr.
The Religion Game American Style. Paulist Pr.
Stevens, Evelyn P.
xStevens, Evelyn P.
Protest & Response in Mexico. MIT Pr.
Stevens, Floyd A.
xStevens, Floyd A.
Complete Course in Electronic Piano Tuning.
Nelson-Hall.
Complete Course in Professional Piano Tuning,
Repair & Rebuilding. Nelson-Hall.
Stevens, Franklin.
xStevens, Franklin.

Dance As Life: A Season with American Ballet
Theatre. Har-Row.
Stevens, G. Melvin. *see* Stevens, Grant Melvin.
Stevens, G. T. *see* Stevens, Gladstone Taylor.
Stevens, George E.
xStevens, George E.
Law & the Student Press. Iowa St U Pr.
Stevens, George L.
xStevens, George L.
Case for Early Reading. Green.
Stevens, Georgiana G.
xStevens, Georgiana G.
Jordan River Partition. Hoover Inst Pr.
Stevens, Gigs.
xStevens, Gigs.
Free-Form Bargello. Scribner.
Stevens, Gladstone Taylor, 1930-
xStevens, G. T.
Economic & Financial Analysis of Capital
Investments. Wiley.
Stevens, Grant Melvin, 1926-
xStevens, G. Melvin.
The Female Reproductive System. Year Bk
Med.
Stevens, Harvey.
xStevens, Harvey.
The Southern Almanac. Hammond Inc.
Stevens, Henry, 1819-1886
xStevens, Henry.
Historical & Geographical Notes on the
Earliest Discoveries in America 1453-1869. B
Franklin.
Historical Nuggets: Bibliotheca Americana or a
Descriptive Account of My Collection of
Rare Books Relating to America. B Franklin.
Stevens, Holly. *see* Stevens, Holly Bright.
Stevens, Holly Bright.
xStevens, Holly.
Souvenirs & Prophecies: The Young Wallace
Stevens. Knopf.
Stevens, J. E. *see* Stevens, John E.
Stevens, James S. *see* Stevens, James Stacy.
Stevens, James Stacy, 1864-1940
xStevens, James S.
Quotations & References in Charles Dickens.
Folcroft.
Stevens, John E, 1921-
xStevens, J. E.
ed. Music & Poetry in the Early Tudor Court.
Cambridge U Pr.
Stevens, Joseph H.
xStevens, Joseph H.
Administering Early Childhood Education
Programs. Little.
Stevens, Joseph L.
xStevens, Joseph L.
Impact of Federal Legislation & Programs on
Private Land in Urban & Metropolitan
Development. Irvington.
Stevens, Karl K., 1939-
xStevens, Karl K.
Statics & Strength of Materials. P-H.
Stevens, Kim.
xStevens, Kim.
The Bee Gees: A Photo-Bio. BJ Pub Group.
Stevens, L. Robert. *see* Stevens, Lewell Robert.
Stevens, Laura J.
xStevens, Laura J.
How to Feed Your Hyperactive Child.
Doubleday.
How to Improve Your Child's Behavior
Through Diet. Doubleday.
Stevens, Laurence.
xStevens, Laurence.

Stevens, Leonard A.
xStevens, Leonard A.
Guide to Buying, Selling & Starting a Travel
Agency. Chicago Review.
Guide to Buying, Selling & Starting a Travel
Agency. Merton Hse.
The Travel Agency Personnel Manual. Merton
Hse.

Stevens, Leonard A.
xStevens, Leonard A.
Explorers of the Brain. Knopf.
How a Law Is Made: The Story of a Bill
Against Air-Pollution. T Y Crowell.

Stevens, Lewell Robert.
xStevens, L. Robert.
Charles Darwin. Twayne.

Stevens, Lucile V. *see* Stevens, Lucile Vernon.

Stevens, Lucile Vernon.
xStevens, Lucile V.
Joni of Storm Hill. Bouregy.

Stevens, Malcolm P., 1934-
xStevens, Malcolm P.
Polymer Chemistry: An Introduction. A-W.

Stevens, Margaret.
xStevens, Margaret.
When Grandpa Died. Childrens.

Stevens, Marion K. *see* Stevens, Marion Keith.

Stevens, Marion Keith.
xStevens, Marion K.
The Practical Nurse in Supervisory Roles.
Saunders.

Stevens, Mark, 1947-
xStevens, Mark.
How to Pyramid Small Business Ventures into
a Personal Fortune. P-H.
How to Run Your Own Business Successfully.
Monarch Pr.
Leveraged Finance: How to Raise & Invest
Cash. P-H.

Stevens, Martin.
xStevens, Martin.
ed. Old English Literature: Twenty-Two
Analytical Essays. U of Nebr Pr.

Stevens, Mary O. *see* Stevens, Mary Otis.

Stevens, Mary Otis.
xStevens, Mary O.
World of Variation. MIT Pr.

Stevens, Matthew.
xStevens, Matthew.
Comprehensive Review for the Radiologic
Technologist. Mosby.

Stevens, Norman D.
xStevens, Norman D.
Library Humor: A Bibliothecal Miscellany to
1970. Scarecrow.

Stevens, Patricia B. *see* Stevens, Patricia Bunning.

Stevens, Patricia Bunning.
xStevens, Patricia B.
God Save Ireland!: The Irish Conflict in the
Twentieth Century. Macmillan.
Merry Christmas!: A History of the Holiday.
Macmillan.

Stevens, Paul M.
xStevens, Paul M.
Gathered Gold. Word Bks.

Stevens, Peter S.
xStevens, Peter S.
Patterns in Nature. Little.

Stevens, R. T.
xStevens, R. T.
The Summer Day Is Done. Warner Bks.

Stevens, Richard P., 1931-
xStevens, Richard P.
Historical Dictionary of the Republic of
Botswana. Scarecrow.

Stevens, Robert. *see* Stevens, Robert Bocking.

Stevens, Robert Bocking.
xStevens, Robert.
Law & Politics: The House of Lords As a
Judicial Body, 1800-1976. U of NC Pr.

Stevens, Robert D. *see* Stevens, Robert David.

Stevens, Robert David.
xStevens, Robert D.
ed. Reader in Documents of International
Organizations. IHS-PDS.

Stevens, Roger, Sir, 1906-
xStevens, Roger.
The Land of the Great Sophy. Intl Pubns Serv.
The Land of the Great Sophy. Taplinger.

Stevens, Roger T., 1927-
xStevens, Roger T.
Operational Test & Evaluation: A Systems
Engineering Process. Wiley.

Stevens, Rosemary.
xStevens, Rosemary.
American Medicine & the Public Interest. Yale
U Pr.

Stevens, Russell B., 1915-
xStevens, Russell B.
Plant Disease. Wiley.

Stevens, S. K. *see* Stevens, Sylvester Kirby.

Stevens, Shane.
xStevens, Shane.
By Reason of Insanity. Dell.
By Reason of Insanity. S&S.
Rat Pack. PB.

Stevens, Suzanne H., 1938-
xStevens, Suzanne H.
The Learning Disabled Child: Ways That
Parents Can Help. Blair.

Stevens, Sylvester K. *see* Stevens, Sylvester Kirby.

Stevens, Sylvester Kirby, 1904-
xStevens, S. K.
Pennsylvania Colony. Macmillan.
xStevens, Sylvester K.
American Expansion in Hawaii, 1842-1898.
Russell.

Stevens, Wallace, 1879-1955.
xStevens, Wallace.
The Palm at the End of the Mind: Selected
Poems & a Play. Knopf.
The Palm at the End of the Mind: Selected
Poems & a Play. Random.

Stevens, William K.
xStevens, William K.
Illinois Estate Administration. Little.

Stevens, William O. *see* Stevens, William Oliver.

Stevens, William Oliver, 1878-
xStevens, William O.
Famous American Statesmen. Dodd.
Footsteps to Freedom. Dodd.

Stevens, William W. *see* Stevens, William Wilson.

Stevens, William Wilson.
xStevens, William W.
Doctrines of the Christian Religion. Broadman.
A Guide for New Testament Study. Broadman.
A Guide for Old Testament Study. Broadman.

Stevenson. *see* Stevenson, Roger E.

Stevenson, Adlai E.
xStevenson, Adlai E.
Call to Greatness. Atheneum.

Stevenson, Anne, 1933 (jan. 3)-
xStevenson, Anne.
Correspondences: A Family History in Letters.
Columbia U Pr.
Enough of Green. Oxford U Pr.
Mask of Treason. Putnam.
Reversals. Columbia U Pr.

Stevenson, Arthur F.
xStevenson, Arthur F.
Tables of Scattering Functions for
Heterodisperse Systems. Wayne St U Pr.

Stevenson, Arthur L. *see* Stevenson, Arthur Linwood.

Stevenson, Arthur Linwood, 1891-
xStevenson, Arthur L.
Story of Southern Hymnology. AMS Pr.

Stevenson, Burton E. *see* Stevenson, Burton Egbert.

Stevenson, Burton Egbert, 1872-
xStevenson, Burton E.
ed. Home Book of Verse for Young Folks.
HR&W.

Stevenson, Charles. *see* Stevenson, Charles Leslie.

Stevenson, Charles Leslie, 1908-
xStevenson, Charles.
Ethics & Language. AMS Pr.

Stevenson, D. E.
xStevenson, D. E.
Celia's House. HR&W.
Still Glides the Stream. HR&W.

Stevenson, D. E. *see* Stevenson, Dorothy Emily.

Stevenson, David L. *see* Stevenson, David Lloyd.

Stevenson, David Lloyd, 1910-
xStevenson, David L.
Love-Game Comedy. AMS Pr.

Stevenson, Dorothy Emily, 1892-1973.
xStevenson, D. E.
Baker's Daughter. Ace Bks.
The Baker's Daughter. G K Hall.
Gerald & Elizabeth. Ace Bks.
Green Money. Ace Bks.
Listening Valley. Ace Bks.
Mrs. Tim Carries on. G K Hall.
Mrs. Tim Flies Home. G K Hall.
Mrs. Tim Gets a Job. G K Hall.
The Young Clementina. Ace Bks.

Stevenson, Drew.
xStevenson, Drew.
Ballad of Penelope Lou... & Me. Crossing Pr.

Stevenson, Dwight E. *see* Stevenson, Dwight Eshelman.

Stevenson, Dwight Eshelman, 1906-
xStevenson, Dwight E.
Monday's God. Bethany Pr.

Stevenson, E. J. *see* Stevenson, Edward J.

Stevenson, Edward J.
xStevenson, E. J.
Extractive Metallurgy: Recent Advances
Noyes.

Stevenson, Florence.
xStevenson, Florence.
The Curse of the Concullens. NAL.
Dark Encounter. NAL.
Dark Odyssey. NAL.

Stevenson, Forrest F. *see* Stevenson, Forrest Frederick.

Stevenson, Forrest Frederick.
xStevenson, Forrest F.
Plant Anatomy. Wiley.

Stevenson, Francis S. *see* Stevenson, Francis Seymour.

Stevenson, Francis Seymour, 1862-
xStevenson, Francis S.
History of Montenegro. Arno.

Stevenson, Frederick W.
xStevenson, Frederick W.
Projective Planes. W H Freeman.

Stevenson, George A.
xStevenson, George A.
Graphic Arts Encyclopedia. McGraw.

Stevenson, Harold W. *see* Stevenson, Harold William.

Stevenson, Harold William, 1924-
xStevenson, Harold W.
Children's Learning. P-H.

Stevenson, Ian.
xStevenson, Ian.
Diagnostic Interview. Har-Row.
Twenty Cases Suggestive of Reincarnation. U
Pr of Va.

Stevenson, J. *see* Stevenson, James.

Stevenson, James, Lecturer.
xStevenson, J.
The Catacombs: Rediscovered Monuments of
Early Christianity. Thames Hudson.
xStevenson, James.
Clams Can't Sing. Greenwillow.
Could Be Worse!. Penguin.
illus. Could Be Worse!. Greenwillow.
Howard. Greenwillow.
Let's Boogie!. Dodd.
illus. Monty. Schol Bk Serv.
illus. Monty. Greenwillow.

Stevenson, James. *see* Stevenson, James Perry.

Stevenson, James P. *see* Stevenson, James Perry.

Stevenson, James Perry.
    xStevenson, James.
        Grumman F-14 "Tomcat". Aero.
    xStevenson, James P.
        McDonnell Douglas F-15 "Eagle". Aero.

Stevenson, Janet.
    xStevenson, Janet.
        Montgomery Bus Boycott, December, 1955:
        American Blacks Demand an End to
        Segregation. Watts.
        Women's Rights. Watts.

Stevenson, John, 1946-
    xStevenson, John.
        ed. London in the Age of Reform. Biblio Dist.

Stevenson, John R. *see* Stevenson, John Reese.

Stevenson, John Reese.
    xStevenson, John R.
        Chilean Popular Front. Greenwood.

Stevenson, Joseph, 1806-1895
    xStevenson, Joseph.
        ed. Life & Death of King James the First of
        Scotland. AMS Pr.

Stevenson, Lionel, 1902-
    xStevenson, Lionel.
        Dr. Quicksilver: The Life of Charles Lever.
        Russell.
        The English Novel: A Panorama. Greenwood.
        The Pre-Raphaelite Poets. Norton.
        The Pre-Raphaelite Poets. U of NC Pr.

Stevenson, Merritt R.
    xStevenson, Merritt R.
        A Marine Atlas of the Pacific Coastal Waters
        of South America. U of Cal Pr.

Stevenson, Nancy, 1916-
    xStevenson, Nancy.
        The Natural Way to Reading: A How-to
        Method for Parents of Slow Learners,
        Dyslexic, & Learning Disabled Children.
        Little.

Stevenson, Noel. *see* Stevenson, Noel C.

Stevenson, Noel C.
    xStevenson, Noel.
        How to Build a More Lucrative Law Practice.
        P-H.

Stevenson, Richard. *see* Stevenson, Richard A.

Stevenson, Richard A., 1938-
    xStevenson, Richard.
        Fundamentals of Finance. McGraw.
    xStevenson, Richard A.
        Fundamentals of Investments. West Pub.

Stevenson, Robert.
    xStevenson, Robert.
        Christmas Music from Baroque Mexico. U of
        Cal Pr.

Stevenson, Robert. *see* Stevenson, Robert Murrell.

Stevenson, Robert A.
    xStevenson, Robert A.
        The Complete Book of Salt-Water Aquariums:
        How to Equip & Maintain Your Marine
        Aquarium & Understand Its Ecology. T Y
        Crowell.

Stevenson, Robert F.
    xStevenson, Robert F.
        Population & Political Systems in Tropical
        Africa. Columbia U Pr.

Stevenson, Robert L. *see* Stevenson, Robert Louis.

Stevenson, Robert Louis, 1850-1894
    xStevenson, Robert L.

A Child's Garden of Verses. Biblio Dist.
A Child's Garden of Verses. Platt.
A Child's Garden of Verses. Random.
Child's Garden of Verses. G&D.
Child's Garden of Verses. Western Pub.
A Child's Garden of Verses. Green Tiger.
Child's Garden of Verses. Scribner.
Child's Garden of Verses. Airmont.
Child's Garden of Verses. Penguin.
Dr. Jekyll & Mr. Hyde & the Suicide Club.
    Hippocrene Bks.
The Dynamiter. Arno.
Master of Ballantrae. Airmont.
Memories & Portraits. Scholarly.
Selections from a Child's Garden of Verses.
    Dandelion Pr.
The Touchstone. Greenwillow.
The Works of Robert Louis Stevenson. AMS
    Pr.
xStevenson, Robert Louis.
    A Child's Garden of Verses. Pr Tuscany.
    The Works of Robert Louis Stevenson. R West.

Stevenson, Robert M. *see* Stevenson, Robert Murrell.

Stevenson, Robert Murrell.
    xStevenson, Robert.
        Protestant Church Music in America: A Short
        Survey of Men & Movements from 1564 to
        the Present. Norton.
        Spanish Cathedral Music in the Golden Age.
        Greenwood.
        Spanish Music in the Age of Columbus.
        Hyperion Conn.
    xStevenson, Robert M.
        Patterns of Protestant Church Music. Duke.

Stevenson, Robert P. *see* Stevenson, Robert Presley.

Stevenson, Robert Presley.
    xStevenson, Robert P.
        How to Build & Buy Cabinets for the Modern
        Kitchen. Arco.

Stevenson, Roger E., 1940-
    xStevenson.
        The Fetus & Newly Born Infant: Influences of
        the Prenatal Environment. Mosby.

Stevenson, Thomas G. *see* Stevenson, Thomas George.

Stevenson, Thomas George, 1809 or 1894
    xStevenson, Thomas G.
        Choice Old Scottish Ballads. Charles River
        Bks.

Stevenson, Thomas H. *see* Stevenson, Thomas Hulbert.

Stevenson, Thomas Hulbert, 1919-
    xStevenson, Thomas H.
        Politics & Government. Littlefield.

Stevenson, Victor.
    xStevenson, Victor.
        ed. The Music Makers. Abrams.

Stevenson, Violet. *see* Stevenson, Violet W.

Stevenson, Violet W.
    xStevenson, Violet.
        Grow & Cook: Making the Most of Food from
        Your Garden. David & Charles.

Stevenson, William, 1925-
    xStevenson, William.
        Bushbabies. HM.

Stevenson, William B. *see* Stevenson, William Barron.

Stevenson, William Barron, 1869-
    xStevenson, William B.
        Grammar of Palestinian Jewish Aramaic.
        Oxford U Pr.

Stevenson, William J.
    xStevenson, William J.
        Business Statistics: Concepts & Applications.
        Har-Row.

Stevensville Historical Society.
    xStevensville Historical Society.
        Montana Genesis. Mountain Pr.

Stever, Donald W., 1944-
    xStever, Donald W.

        Seabrook & the Nuclear Regulatory
        Commission: The Licensing of a Nuclear
        Power Plant. U Pr of New En.

Stever, James A., 1943-
    xStever, James A.
        Diversity & Order in State & Local Politics. U
        of SC Pr.

Stevick, Daniel. *see* Stevick, Daniel B.

Stevick, Daniel B.
    xStevick, Daniel.
        Canon Law: A Handbook. Seabury.

Stevick, Earl W.
    xStevick, Earl W.
        Teaching Languages: A Way & Ways.
        Newbury Hse.

Stevick, P. *see* Stevick, Philip.

Stevick, Philip.
    xStevick, P.
        Anti-Story: An Anthology of Experimental
        Fiction. Free Pr.
    xStevick, Philip.
        Chapter in Fiction: Theories of Narrative
        Division. Syracuse U Pr.
        ed. Theory of the Novel. Free Pr.

Steward, Austin, 1794-1860
    xSteward, Austin.
        Twenty-Two Years a Slave, & Forty Years a
        Freeman. Negro U Pr.

Steward, Barbara.
    xSteward, Barbara.
        Evermore. Morrow.
        The Lincoln Diddle. Morrow.

Steward, F. C. *see* Steward, Frederick Campion.
Steward, Frederick C. *see* Steward, Frederick Campion.

Steward, Frederick Campion.
    xSteward, F. C.
        Plants, Chemicals & Growth. Acad Pr.
    xSteward, Frederick C.
        About Plants: Topics in Plant Biology. A-W.

Steward, Hal D.
    xSteward, Hal D.
        Money Making Secrets of the Millionaires.
        P-H.
        Money Making Secrets of the Millionaires.
        P-H.
        Successful Writers Guide. P-H.

Steward, J. W.
    xSteward, J. W.
        Tailed Amphibians of Europe. Taplinger.

Steward, John, 1918-
    xSteward, John S.
        The Game Plan for Handicapping Harness
        Races. Vantage.

Steward, John S. *see* Steward, John.
Steward, Julian. *see* Steward, Julian Haynes.
Steward, Julian H. *see* Steward, Julian Haynes.

Steward, Julian Haynes.
    xSteward, Julian.
        Evolution & Ecology: Essays on Social
        Transformation. U of Ill Pr.
    xSteward, Julian H.
        Theory of Culture Change: The Methodology
        of Multilinear Evolution. U of Ill Pr.

Steward, T. G. *see* Steward, Theophilus Gould.

Steward, Theophilus Gould, 1843-1924 or 5
    xSteward, T. G.
        Colored Regulars in the United States Army.
        Arno.

Stewart. *see* Stewart, Ray E.

Stewart, A. C.
    xStewart, A. C.
        Dark Dove. S G Phillips.
        Ossian House. S G Phillips.
        Silas & Con. Atheneum.

Stewart, Allegra.
    xStewart, Allegra.
        Gertrude Stein & the Present. Harvard U Pr.

Stewart, Ann H. *see* Stewart, Ann Harleman.

Stewart, Ann Harleman.
    xStewart, Ann H.

Graphic Representation of Models in Linguistic
Theory. Ind U Pr.

Stewart, Basil, 1880-
xStewart, Basil.
A Guide to Japanese Prints & Their Subject
Matter. Dover.

Stewart, Bob.
xStewart, Bob.
Pagan Imagery in English Folksong.
Humanities.

Stewart, Bob R.
xStewart, Robert.
Leadership for Agricultural Industry. McGraw.

Stewart, Bryce M. see Stewart, Bryce Morrison.

Stewart, Bryce Morrison, 1883-1956
xStewart, Bryce M.
Canadian Labor Laws & the Treaty. AMS Pr.

Stewart, Charles D. see Stewart, Charles David.

Stewart, Charles David, 1868-
xStewart, Charles D.
Some Textual Difficulties in Shakespeare. AMS
Pr.

Stewart, Charles F.
xStewart, Charles F.
Economy of Morocco, 1912-1962. Harvard U
Pr.

Stewart, Charles T., 1922-
xStewart, Charles T.
Air Pollution, Human Health, & Public Policy.
Lexington Bks.
Low-Wage Workers in an Affluent Society.
Nelson-Hall.

Stewart, Charles W. see Stewart, Charles William.

Stewart, Charles William.
xStewart, Charles W.
The Minister As Family Counselor. Abingdon.
Person & Profession: Career Development in
the Ministry. Abingdon.

Stewart, D. see Stewart, David.

Stewart, Darryl.
xStewart, Darryl.
Point Pelee: Canada's Deep South. Wayne St
U Pr.

Stewart, David, 1938-
xStewart, D.
Exploring the Philosophy of Religion. P-H.

Stewart, Desmond.
xStewart, Desmond.
The Vampire of Mons. Avon.

Stewart, Desmond. see Stewart, Desmond Stirling.

Stewart, Desmond Stirling.
xStewart, Desmond.
Mecca. Newsweek.
Pyramids & Sphinx. Newsweek.

Stewart, Diana.
xStewart, Diana.
Adapted by Romeo & Juliet. Raintree Pubs.

Stewart, Don. see Stewart, Don K.

Stewart, Don K.
xStewart, Don.
Instruction As a Humanizing Science. Slate
Servs.

Stewart, Douglas, 1914-
xStewart, Douglas.
The Ark of God: Studies in Five Modern
Novelists. (James Joyce, Aldous Huxley,
Rose Macaulay, Joyce Cary). Folcroft.
The Ark of God: Studies in Five Modern
Novelists: James Joyce Aldous Huxley, Rose
Macauley, Joyce Cary. R West.

Stewart, Dwight.
xStewart, Dwight.
Western Horsemanship & Equitation. Arco.

Stewart, Edgar I. see Stewart, Edgar Irving.

Stewart, Edgar Irving.
xStewart, Edgar I.
Custer's Luck. U of Okla Pr.

Stewart, Edward, 1938-
xStewart, Edward.

Ballerina. Berkley Pub.
Ballerina. Doubleday.
Launch. NAL.

Stewart, Edward T. see Stewart, Edward Turlington.

Stewart, Edward Turlington.
xStewart, Edward T.
An Atlas of Endoscopic Retrograde
Cholangiopancreatography. Mosby.

Stewart, Elbert W.
xStewart, Elbert W.
The Human Bond: Introduction to Social
Psychology. Wiley.
Introduction to Sociology. McGraw.
Introduction to Sociology. McGraw.
The Troubled Land: Social Problems in
Modern America. McGraw.

Stewart, Elinore (Pruitt), 1878-
xStewart, Elinore P.
Letters of a Woman Homesteader. U of Nebr
Pr.

Stewart, Elinore P. see Stewart, Elinore (Pruitt).

Stewart, Ernest I. see Stewart, Ernest Israel.

Stewart, Ernest Israel.
xStewart, Ernest I.
Rehabilitation of the Drunken Driver: A
Corrective Course in Phoenix, Arizona for
Persons Convicted of Driving Under the
Influence of Alcohol. Tchrs Coll.

Stewart, Estelle M. see Stewart, Estelle May.

Stewart, Estelle May, 1887-1938
xStewart, Estelle M.
The Cost of American Almshouses. Arno.

Stewart, F. H. see Stewart, Felicia Hance.

Stewart, Felicia Hance.
xStewart, F. H.
My Body, My Health: The Concerned
Woman's Guide to Gynecology. Wiley.

Stewart, Frank.
xStewart, Frank.
ed. Poetry Hawaii: A Contemporary
Anthology. U Pr of Hawaii.

Stewart, Frank H., 1873-1948
xStewart, Frank H.
History of the First United States Mint.
Quarterman.
Notes on Old Gloucester County, New Jersey.
Genealog Pub.

Stewart, Frank H. see Stewart, Frank Henderson.

Stewart, Frank Henderson.
xStewart, Frank H.
Fundamentals of Age-Group Systems. Acad Pr.

Stewart, Frank M. see Stewart, Frank Moore.

Stewart, Frank Moore, 1917-
xStewart, Frank M.
Introduction to Linear Algebra. Krieger.

Stewart, Fred M. see Stewart, Fred Mustard.

Stewart, Fred Mustard, 1932-
xStewart, Fred M.
A Rage Against Heaven. Fawcett.
A Rage Against Heaven. Viking Pr.

Stewart, G. W. see Stewart, Gilbert W.

Stewart, Garrett.
xStewart, Garrett.
Dickens & the Trials of Imagination. Harvard
U Pr.

Stewart, George. see Stewart, George R.

Stewart, George R.
xStewart, George.
Earth Abides. Fawcett.
xStewart, George R.
Earth Abides. Hermes.

Stewart, George R. see Stewart, George Rippey.

Stewart, George Rippey, 1895-
xStewart, George R.

American Given Names: Their Origin &
History in the Context of the English
Language. Oxford U Pr.
American Place-Names: A Concise & Selective
Dictionary for the Continental United States
of America. Oxford U Pr.
American Ways of Life. Russell.
California Trail: An Epic with Many Heroes.
McGraw.

Stewart, Gilbert W.
xStewart, G. W.
Introduction to Matrix Computations. Acad Pr.

Stewart, Gordon.
xStewart, Gordon.
A People Highly Favoured of God: The Nova
Scotia Yankees & the American Revolution.
Shoe String.

Stewart, Gordon M. see Stewart, Gordon Mcnett.

Stewart, Gordon McNett.
xStewart, Gordon M.
The Literary Contributions of Christoph Daniel
Ebeling. Humanities.

Stewart, Gordon W.
xStewart, Gordon W.
Everybody's Fitness Book: A Simple, Safe &
Sane Approach to Personal Fitness.
Doubleday.

Stewart, Harold.
xStewart, Harold.
Chime of Windbells: A Year of Japanese Haiku
in English Verse. C E Tuttle.

Stewart, Harry L.
xStewart, Harry L.
ABC's of Hydraulic Circuits. Sams.
Hydraulics for off-the Road Equipment. Audel.
Pumps. Audel.

Stewart, Helen H. see Stewart, Helen Hinton.

Stewart, Helen Hinton.
xStewart, Helen H.
The Supernatural in Shakespeare. Folcroft.

Stewart, Hilary.
xStewart, Hilary.
Indian Fishing: Early Methods on the
Northwest Coast. U of Wash Pr.
Looking at Indian Art of the Northwest Coast.
U of Wash Pr.

Stewart, Hugh H. see Stewart, Hugh Henry.

Stewart, Hugh Henry, 1881-1954
xStewart, Hugh H.
Comparative Study of the Concentration &
Regular Plans of Organization in the Senior
High School. AMS Pr.

Stewart, I. N. see Stewart, Ian.

Stewart, Ian.
xStewart, I. N.
Algebraic Number Theory. Methuen Inc.
xStewart, Ian.
The Foundations of Mathematics. Oxford U Pr.
The Peking Payoff. Macmillan.

Stewart, Irvin. see Stewart, Irwin.

Stewart, Irwin, 1899-
xStewart, Irvin.
Organizing Scientific Research for War: The
Administrative History of the Office of
Scientific Research & Development. Arno.

Stewart, J. A. see Stewart, John Alexander.
Stewart, J. D. see Stewart, Jimmie D.
Stewart, J. E. see Stewart, James E.
Stewart, J. H. see Stewart, John Hall.
Stewart, J. I. see Stewart, John Innes Mackintosh.
Stewart, J. I. M. see Stewart, John Innes Mackintosh.
Stewart, J. M. see Stewart, John M.

Stewart, Jack C.
xStewart, Jack C.
Counseling Parents of Exceptional Children.
Merrill.
ed. Counseling Parents of Exceptional
Children. Mss Info.

Stewart, James E., 1927-
xStewart, J. E.

Infrared Spectroscopy: Experimental Methods
& Techniques. Dekker.
Stewart, James H.
xStewart, James H.
How to Skip Rope Like a Champ. Jym Ent.
Stewart, James I. see Stewart, James Innes.
Stewart, James Innes, Q.C.
xStewart, James I.
Real Estate Appraisal in a Nutshell: A
Restatement & Simplification of Theory &
Practice. U of Toronto Pr.
Stewart, James S. see Stewart, James Stuart.
Stewart, James Stuart, 1896-
xStewart, James S.
Faith to Proclaim. Baker Bk.
The Life & Teaching of Jesus Christ.
Abingdon.
Stewart, Jimmie D.
xStewart, J. D.
VHF Radio Propagation. Sams.
Stewart, John. see Stewart, John Benjamin.
Stewart, John A. see Stewart, John Alexander.
Stewart, John Alexander, 1846-1933
xStewart, J. A.
Notes on the Nicomachean Ethics of Aristotle.
Arno.
xStewart, John A.
Plato's Doctrine of Ideas. Folcroft.
Stewart, John B. see Stewart, John Benjamin.
Stewart, John Benjamin, 1924-
xStewart, John.
The Canadian House of Commons: Procedure
and Reform. McGill-Queens U Pr.
xStewart, John B.
The Moral & Political Philosophy of David
Hume. Greenwood.
Stewart, John C. see Stewart, John Craig.
Stewart, John Craig.
xStewart, John C.
Governors of Alabama. Pelican.
Stewart, John Hall, 1904-
xStewart, J. H.
The Restoration Era in France 1814-1830.
Peter Smith.
Stewart, John I. see Stewart, John Innes Mackintosh.
Stewart, John Innes Mackintosh, 1906-
xStewart, J. I.
The Gaudy. Norton.
Joseph Conrad. Dodd.
Thomas Hardy: A Critical Biography. Dodd.
xStewart, J. I. M.
A Memorial Service. Norton.
xStewart, John I.
Appleby on Ararat. Greenwood.
Stewart, John M.
xStewart, J. M.
Non-Equilibrium Relativistic Kinetic Theory.
Springer-Verlag.
Stewart, John W., 1945-
xStewart, John W.
How to Make Your Own Solar Electricity.
TAB Bks.
Stewart, Karen R. see Stewart, Karen Robb.
Stewart, Karen Robb.
xStewart, Karen R.
ed. Adolescent Sexuality & Teenage Pregnancy:
A Selected, Annotated Bibliography with
Summary Forewords. Carolina Pop Ctr.
Stewart, Kenneth.
xStewart, Kenneth.
A Background to Racing. J A Allen.
Stewart, Lawrence D. see Stewart, Lawrence Delbert.
Stewart, Lawrence Delbert, 1926-
xStewart, Lawrence D.
Paul Bowles: The Illumination of North Africa.
S Ill U Pr.
Stewart, Linda.
xStewart, Linda.

Panic on Page One. Delacorte.
Panic on Page One. Dell.
Stewart, Lowell O., 1895-
xStewart, Lowell O.
Public Land Surveys. Arno.
Stewart, Madeau.
xStewart, Madeau.
The Music Lover's Guide to the Instruments of
the Orchestra. Van Nos Reinhold.
Stewart, Margaret M.
xStewart, Margaret M.
Amphibians of Malawi. State U NY Pr.
Stewart, Marie M, 1899-
xStewart, Marie M.
Business English & Communication. McGraw.
College English & Communication. McGraw.
Stewart, Marjabelle. see Stewart, Marjabelle Young.
Stewart, Marjabelle Y. see Stewart, Marjabelle Young.
Stewart, Marjabelle Young.
xStewart, Marjabelle.
Executive Etiquette. St Martin.
xStewart, Marjabelle Y.
The New Etiquette Guide to Getting Married
Again. St Martin.
Stewart, Marjorie, 1925-
xStewart, Marjorie.
Women in Neighborhood Evangelism. Gospel
Pub.
Stewart, Mark A.
xStewart, Mark A.
Raising a Hyperactive Child. Har-Row.
Stewart, Mary, 1916-
xStewart, Mary.
Airs Above the Ground. Fawcett.
The Crystal Cave. Fawcett.
The Crystal Cave. Morrow.
The Hollow Hills. Fawcett.
The Hollow Hills. Morrow.
The Last Enchantment. Fawcett.
The Last Enchantment. Morrow.
The Little Broomstick. Morrow.
Ludo & the Star Horse. Morrow.
The Moon-Spinners. Fawcett.
My Brother Michael. Fawcett.
My Brother Michael. Morrow.
My Brother Michael. Watts.
Nine Coaches Waiting. Fawcett.
Nine Coaches Waiting. Morrow.
This Rough Magic. Fawcett.
This Rough Magic. Morrow.
Touch Not the Cat. Fawcett.
Touch Not the Cat. G K Hall.
Touch Not the Cat. Morrow.
Stewart, Maxwell S. see Stewart, Maxwell Slutz.
Stewart, Maxwell Slutz, 1900-
xStewart, Maxwell S.
Building for Peace at Home & Abroad. Arno.
Stewart, Michael, 1933-
xStewart, Michael.
The Jekyll & Hyde Years: Politics & Economic
Policy Since 1964. Rowman.
Stewart, Michael M.
xStewart, Michael M.
Ecologic Determinants of Health Problems.
Springer Pub.
Stewart, N. see Stewart, Norman R.
Stewart, Norman R., 1931-
xStewart, N.
Systematic Counseling. P-H.
Stewart, P. R.
xStewart, P. R.
ed. The Ribonucleic Acids. Springer-Verlag.
Stewart, Pamela, 1946-
xStewart, Pamela.
Half-Tones. Maguey Pr.
Stewart, Philip D.
xStewart, Philip D.

Political Power in the Soviet Union: A Study
of Decision-Making in Stalingrad. Bobbs.
Political Power in the Soviet Union: A Study
of Decision-Making in Stalingrad. Irvington.
Stewart, Phyllis L.
xStewart, Phyllis L.
ed. Varieties of Work Experience: The Social
Control of Occupational Groups & Roles.
Halsted Pr.
Stewart, R. A. see Stewart, Robert A.
Stewart, Ramona, 1922-
xStewart, Ramona.
Sixth Sense. Delacorte.
Sixth Sense. Dell.
Stewart, Ray E.
xStewart.
Oral Facial Genetics. Mosby.
Stewart, Regina.
xStewart, Regina.
Bottles. Western Pub.
Stoneware. Western Pub.
Stewart, Robert. see Stewart, Robert Mackenzie.
Stewart, Robert A.
xStewart, R. A.
Person - Perception & Stereotyping. Lexington
Bks.
Person-Perception & Stereotyping. Lexington
Bks.
Stewart, Robert Mackenzie.
xStewart, Robert.
Politics of Protection: Lord Derby & the
Protectionist Party, 1841-1852. Cambridge U
Pr.
Stewart, Roderick.
xStewart, Roderick.
Bethune. Shoe String.
Stewart, Ronald.
xStewart, Ronald.
Improving Energy Efficiency in Buildings. State
U NY Pr.
Stewart, Rosemary.
xStewart, Rosemary.
How Computers Affect Management. MIT Pr.
Stewart, (S.S.) (Firm).
xS. S. Stewart Banjo Company.
S. S. Stewart's Extra Fine Banjos. Mih.
Stewart, Susan.
xStewart, Susan.
Nonsense: Aspects of Intertextuality in
Folklore & Literature. Johns Hopkins.
Stewart, Suzanne.
xStewart, Suzanne.
Parent Alone. Word Bks.
Stewart, T. D. see Stewart, Thomas Dale.
Stewart, Thomas C.
xStewart, Thomas C .
Vanilmandelic Acid & Catecholamine
Determinations. Am Soc Clinical.
Stewart, Thomas Dale, 1901-
xStewart, T. D.
The People of America. Scribner.
Stewart, V. Lorne.
xStewart, V. Lorne.
ed. The Changing Faces of Juvenile Justice.
NYU Pr.
Intro. by Justice & Troubled Children Around
the World. NYU Pr.
Stewart, W. D. see Stewart, William Duncan Patterson.
Stewart, W. E. see Stewart, William E.
Stewart, W. Grant. see Stewart, William Grant.
Stewart, Watt.
xStewart, Watt.
Builders of Latin America. Arno.
Chinese Bondage in Peru: A History of the
Chinese Coolie in Peru, 1849-1874.
Greenwood.
Stewart, William A. see Stewart, William Alexander
Campbell.
Stewart, William Alexander Campbell, 1915-
xStewart, William A.

Progressives & Radicals in English Education, 1750-1970. Kelley.

Stewart, William Duncan Patterson.
xStewart, W. D.
ed. Nitrogen Fixation by Free-Living Micro-Organisms. Cambridge U Pr.
Nitrogen Fixation in Plants. Humanities.

Stewart, William E.
xStewart, W. E.
The Interferon System. Springer-Verlag.

Stewart, William Grant.
xStewart, W. Grant.
The Popular Superstitions & Festive Amusements of the Highlanders of Scotland. R West.

Stewartson, K.
xStewartson, K.
Theory of Laminar Boundary Layers in Compressible Fluids. Oxford U Pr.

Stewig. *see* Stewig, John W.

Stewig, John W.
xStewig.
Exploring Language with Children. Merrill.

Steyaert, Thomas A.
xSteyaert, Thomas A.
Life & Patterns of Order. McGraw.

Steyermark, Al, 1904-
xSteyermark, Al.
Quantitative Organic Microanalysis. Acad Pr.

Steyermark, Julian A. *see* Steyermark, Julian Alfred.

Steyermark, Julian Alfred, 1909-
xSteyermark, Julian A.
Flora of Missouri. Iowa St U Pr.

Steyskal, G. C. *see* Steyskal, George C.

Steyskal, George C.
xSteyskal, G. C.
Taxonomy of North American Flies of the Genus Limnia (Diptera: Sciomyzidae). U of Cal Pr.

Stiansen, Peder, 1879-
xStiansen, Peder.
History of the Norwegian Baptists in America. Arno.

Stibbert, Frederic.
xStibbert, Frederic.
Civil & Military Clothing in Europe: From the First to the Eighteenth Century. Arno.

Stibitz, E. Earle. *see* Stibitz, Edward Earle.

Stibitz, Edward Earle, 1909-
xStibitz, E. Earle.
ed. Illinois Poets: A Selection. S Ill U Pr.

Sticca, Sandro.
xSticca, Sandro.
ed. The Medieval Drama. State U NY Pr.

Stich, Rodney.
xStich, Rodney.
ed. The Unfriendly Skies: An Aviation Watergate. Diablo West Pr.

Stick, David.
xStick, David.
Cape Hatteras Seashore. McNally.

Stick, David. *see* Stick, David.

Stick, David, 1919-
xStick, David.
Outer Banks of North Carolina, 1584-1958. U of NC Pr.

Stickgold, Bob.
xStickgold, Bob.
Gloryhits. Ballantine.

Stickley, Gustav.
xStickley, Gustav.
The Best of Craftsman Homes. Peregrine Smith.
Craftsman Homes: Architecture & Furnishings of the American Arts & Crafts Movement. Dover.

Stickney, Dorothy.
xStickney, Dorothy.

Openings & Closings. Doubleday.

Stickney, John, 1946-
xStickney, John.
Self-Made: Braving an Independent Career in a Corporate Age. Putnam.

Stickney, Robert R.
xStickney, Robert R.
Principles of Warmwater Aquaculture. Wiley.

Stickney, Trumbull, 1874-1904
xStickney, Trumbull.
Dramatic Verses. Irvington.

Stickter, Jim.
xStickter, Jim.
Allende & the Saga of Chile. Hemisphere Hse.
Long Road South, Long Road North. Hemisphere Hse.
Three Magic Words. Hemisphere Hse.

Stieber, Carolyn.
xStieber, Carolyn.
Politics of Change in Michigan. Mich St U Pr.

Stieber, Jack. *see* Stieber, Jack W.

Stieber, Jack W, 1919-
xStieber, Jack.
Steel Industry Wage Structure: A Study of the Joint Union-Management Job Evaluation Program in the Basic Steel Industry. Harvard U Pr.

Stiefbold, Annette E.
xStiefbold, Annette E.
The French Communist Party in Transition: PCF-CPSU Relations & the Challenge to Soviet Authority. Praeger.

Stiefel, E. L. *see* Stiefel, Eduard L.

Stiefel, Eduard L., 1909-
xStiefel, E. L.
Introduction to Numerical Mathematics. Acad Pr
Linear & Regular Celestial Mechanics: Perturbed Two-Body Motion, Numerical Methods, Canonical Theory. Springer-Verlag.

Stiegeler, Stella E.
xStiegeler, Stella E.
A Dictionary of Earth Sciences. Universe.

Stieglitz, Harold.
xStieglitz, Harold.
Chief Executive & His Job. Conference Bd.

Stiehm, E. Richard.
xStiehm, E. Richard.
Immunologic Disorders in Infants & Children. Saunders.

Stienon, Elaine.
xStienon, Elaine.
Utah Spring. Herald Hse.

Stieper, Donald R.
xStieper, Donald R.
Dimensions of Psychotherapy: An Experimental & Clinical Approach. Irvington.

Stierlin, Helm.
xStierlin, Helm.
The First Interview with the Family. Brunner-Mazel.

Stifel, Laurence D. *see* Stifel, Laurence Davis.

Stifel, Laurence Davis.
xStifel, Laurence D.
Textile Industry: A Case Study of Industrial Development in the Philippines. Cornell SE Asia.

Stigler, George J. *see* Stigler, George Joseph.

Stigler, George Joseph, 1911-
xStigler, George J.
Capital & Rates of Return in Manufacturing Industries. Arno.
The Citizen & the State: Essays on Regulation. U of Chicago Pr.
Theory of Price. Macmillan.

Stigler, Robert, 1921-
xStigler, Robert.

Varieties of Culture in the Old World. St Martin.

Stigler, Stephen M.
xStigler, Stephen M.
ed. American Contributions to Mathematical Statistics in the Nineteenth Century: An Original Anthology. Arno.

Stigum, Marcia. *see* Stigum, Marcia L.

Stigum, Marcia L.
xStigum, Marcia.
The Money Market: Myth, Reality & Practice. Dow Jones-Irwin.

Stiles, David. *see* Stiles, David R.

Stiles, David R.
xStiles, David.
Easy-to-Make Children's Furniture. Pantheon.

Stiles, Deirdre.
xStiles, Deirdre.
Dangerford. Belmont-Tower.
Rakehell. Nordon Pubns.
Tara. Nordon Pubns.
That Collison Woman. Nordon Pubns.

Stiles, Karl A. *see* Stiles, Karl Amos.

Stiles, Karl Amos, 1897-1968
xStiles, Karl A.
Handbook of Histology. McGraw.

Stiles, Lindley J. *see* Stiles, Lindley Joseph.

Stiles, Lindley Joseph.
xStiles, Lindley J.
ed. Morality Examined: Guidelines for Teachers. Princeton Bk Co.

Stiles, Martha B. *see* Stiles, Martha Bennett.

Stiles, Martha Bennett.
xStiles, Martha B.
The Star in the Forest: A Mystery of the Dark Ages. Schol Bk Serv
Tana & the Useless Monkey. Elsevier-Nelson.

Stiles, Norman.
xStiles, Norman.
Grover & the Everything in the Whole Wide World Museum. Random.

Stiles, Tom.
xStiles, Tom.
Calculate to Save. Odin Pr.

Still, Henry.
xStill, Henry.
Surviving the Male Mid-Life Crisis. T Y Crowell.

Still, Jack W.
xStill, Jack W.
A Guide to Managerial Accounting in Small Companies. Arno.

Still, James, 1812-1885
xStill, James.
Early Recollections & Life of Dr. James Still. Arno.
Early Recollections & Life of Dr. James Still, 1812-1885. Rutgers U Pr.
Pattern of a Man & Other Stories. Gnomon Pr.

Still, Richard R. *see* Still, Richard Ralph.

Still, Richard Ralph.
xStill, Richard R.
Essentials of Marketing. P-H.

Still, William, 1821-1902
xStill, William.
Underground Railroad. Arno.
Underground Railroad. Johnson Chi.

Stille, John K. *see* Stille, John Kenneth.

Stille, John Kenneth.
xStille, John K.
Condensation Monomers. Krieger.

Stiller, Calvin R.
xStiller, Calvin R.
ed. Immunologic Monitoring of the Transplant Patient. Grune.

Stiller, Richard.
xStiller, Richard.

Broken Promises: The Strange History of the Fourteenth Amendment. Random.

The Love Bugs: A Natural History of the V.D.'s. Elsevier-Nelson.

Queen of Populists: The Story of Mary Elizabeth Lease. T Y Crowell.

Your Body Is Trying to Tell You Something: How to Understand Its Signals & Respond to Its Needs. HarBraceJ.

Stilling, Roger, 1938-
xStilling, Roger.
Love & Death in Renaissance Tragedy. La State U Pr.

Stillinger, Elizabeth.
xStillinger, Elizabeth.
Antiques Guide to Decorative Arts in America 1600-1875. Dutton.

Stillinger, Jack.
xStillinger, Jack.
Hoodwinking of Madeline & Other Essays on Keats's Poems. U of Ill Pr.
The Texts of Keat's Poems. Harvard U Pr.

Stillman, Clark. see Stillman, Clark Ezra Clark Stillman.

Stillman, Clark Ezra Clark Stillman.
xStillman, Clark.
Spanish at Sight. Ungar.

Stillman, Damie.
xStillman, Damie.
The Decorative Work of Robert Adam. Transatlantic.

Stillman, David M.
xStillman, David M.
Comunicando: A First Course in Spanish. Heath.

Stillman, Irwin. see Stillman, Irwin Maxwell.

Stillman, Irwin M. see Stillman, Irwin Maxwell.

Stillman, Irwin Maxwell.
xStillman, Irwin.
Doctor's Quick Weight Loss Diet. P-H.
xStillman, Irwin M.
Doctor's Quick Inches-off Diet. Dell.

Stillman, N. J. see Stillman, William James.

Stillman, Norman A., 1945-
xStillman, Norman A.
The Jews of Arab Lands: A History & Source Book. Jewish Pubn.

Stillman, Peter. see Stillman, Peter R.

Stillman, Peter R.
xStillman, Peter.
Improving Your Camera Handling. SamHar Pr.
Stained Glass for the Amateur. SamHar Pr.
xStillman, Peter R.
Introduction to Myth. Hayden.

Stillman, R. C. see Stillman, Richard C.

Stillman, Richard. see Stillman, Richard Joseph.

Stillman, Richard C.
xStillman, R. C.
ed. The Psychopharmacology of Hallucinogens. Pergamon.

Stillman, Richard J.
xStillman, Richard J.
The Rise of the City Manager: A Public Professional in Local Government. U of NM Pr.

Stillman, Richard J. see Stillman, Richard Joseph.

Stillman, Richard Joseph, 1917-
xStillman, Richard.
Guide to Personal Finance: A Lifetime Program of Money Management. P-H.
Personal Finance Guide & Workbook: A Managerial Approach to Successful Household Record Keeping. Pelican.
Public Administration: Concepts & Cases. HM.
xStillman, Richard J.
Moneywise: The Prentice-Hall Book of Personal Money Management. P-H.
Public Administration: Concepts & Cases. HM.

Stillman, Richard M., 1947-
xStillman, Richard M.

General Surgery: Review & Assessment. ACC.

Stillman, William James, 1828-1901
xStillman, N. J.
The Coinage of the Greeks. Obol Intl.

Stillman, Yedida K. see Stillman, Yedida Kalfon.

Stillman, Yedida Kalfon.
xStillman, Yedida K.
Palestinian Costume & Jewelry. U of NM Pr.

Stillwell, Margaret B. see Stillwell, Margaret Bingham.

Stillwell, Margaret Bingham, 1887-
xStillwell, Margaret B.
The Awakening Interest in Science During the First Century of Printing, 1450-1550. U Pr of Va.

Stillwell, Richard.
xStillwell, Richard.
ed. The Princeton Encyclopedia of Classical Sites. Princeton U Pr.

Stilman, Leon.
xStilman, Leon.
Graded Readings in Russian History: The Formation of the Russian State. Columbia U Pr.

Stilwell, Anne.
xStilwell, Anne.
The Child Who Walks Alone: Case Studies of Rejection in the Schools. U of Tex Pr.

Stilwell, Hart, 1902-
xStilwell, Hart.
Border City. AMS Pr.

Stimler, Saul.
xStimler, Saul.
Data Processing Systems: Their Performance Evaluation, Measurement & Improvement. Stimler Assoc.

Stimmel, Barry, 1939-
xStimmel, Barry.
Cardiovascular Effects of Mood-Altering Drugs. Raven.

Stimpson, George W. see Stimpson, George William.

Stimpson, George William, 1896-
xStimpson, George W.
Popular Questions Answered. Gale.

Stimson, Edward W.
xStimson, Edward W.
Renewal in Christ: As the Celtic Church Led "The Way". Vantage.

Stimson, Frank J. see Stimson, John Francis.

Stimson, H. L. see Stimson, Henry Lewis.

Stimson, Henry L. see Stimson, Henry Lewis.

Stimson, Henry Lewis.
xStimson, H. L.
American Policy in Nicaragua. AMS Pr.
xStimson, Henry L.
American Policy in Nicaragua. Arno.
American Policy in Nicaragua. Scholarly.
On Active Service in Peace & War. Octagon.

Stimson, Hugh M.
xStimson, Hugh M.
One Thousand Chinese Characters with Literary Glosses. Far Eastern Pubns.

Stimson, John Francis, 1883-
xStimson, Frank J.
ed. Songs & Tales of the Sea Kings: Interpretations of Oral Literature of Polynesia. Peabody Mus Salem.

Stimson, Michael J.
xStimson, Mike.
Stimson's Rally Factors. TAB Bks.

Stimson, Mike. see Stimson, Michael J.

Stimson, Russell. see Stimson, Russell L.

Stimson, Russell L.
xStimson, Russell.
Opportunities in Opticianry Today. Natl Textbk.

Stinchcomb, James. see Stinchcomb, James D.

Stinchcomb, James D.
xStinchcomb, James.

Opportunities in Law Enforcement & Related Careers. Natl Textbk.

Stinchcombe, Arthur L.
xStinchcombe, Arthur L.
Constructing Social Theories. HarBraceJ.
Theoretical Methods in Social History. Acad Pr.

Stinchcombe, William C.
xStinchcombe, William C.
American Revolution & the French Alliance. Syracuse U Pr.

Stine, Bob. see Stine, Jovial Bob.

Stine, G. Harry. see Stine, George Harry.

Stine, George Harry, 1928-
xStine, G. Harry.
Shuttle into Space: A Ride in America's Space Transportation System. Follett.

Stine, Jovial B. see Stine, Jovial Bob.

Stine, Jovial Bob.
xStine, Bob.
How to Be Funny: An Extremely Silly Guidebook. Bantam.
The Pigs' Book of World Records. Random.
xStine, Jovial B.
How to Be Funny: An Extremely Silly Guidebook. Dutton.

Stine, William R.
xStine, William R.
Chemistry for the Consumer. Allyn.

Stineman, Esther.
xStineman, Esther.
Women's Studies: A Recommended Core Bibliography. Libs Unl.

Stinetorf, Louise A.
xStinetorf, Louise A.
White Witch Doctor. Westminster.

Stinnett, Caskie.
xStinnett, Caskie.
Grand & Private Pleasures. Little.

Stinnett, Nick.
xStinnett, Nick.
ed. Building Family Strengths: Blueprints for Action. U of Nebr Pr.
The Family & Alternate Life-Styles. Nelson-Hall.
Relationships in Marriage & Family. Macmillan.

Stinson, Robert, 1941-
xStinson, Robert.
Lincoln Steffens. Ungar.

Stiny, George.
xStiny, George.
Algorithmic Aesthetics: Computer Models for Criticism & Design in the Arts. U of Cal Pr.

Stipanovich, Joseph, 1946-
xStipanovich, Joseph.
The South Slavs in Utah: A Social History. R & E Res Assoc.
The South Slavs in Utah: A Social History. Ragusan Pr.

Stipe, Gordon J. see Stipe, J. Gordon.

Stipe, J. Gordon.
xStipe, Gordon J.
The Development of Physical Theories. Krieger.

Stirk, S. D. see Stirk, Samuel Dickinson.

Stirk, Samuel Dickinson.
xStirk, S. D.
The Prussian Spirit: A Survey of German Literature & Politics, 1914-1940. Gordon Pr.
Prussian Spirit: A Survey of German Literature & Politics 1914-1940. Kennikat.

Stirling, Brents, 1904-
xStirling, Brents.
Populace in Shakespeare. AMS Pr.

Stirling, J. see Stirling, James.

Stirling, James, 1805-1883
xStirling, J.
Letters from the Slave States. Kraus Repr.
xStirling, James.

Letters from the Slave States. Negro U Pr.
Stirling, Jessica.
xStirling, Jessica.
The Dark Pasture. Ballantine.
The Dark Pasture. St Martin.
Stirling, Leader.
xStirling, Leader.
Tanzanian Doctor. McGill-Queens U Pr.
Stirling, Monica, 1916-
xStirling, Monica.
A Screen of Time: A Study of Luchino
Visconti. HarBraceJ.
Stirling, Nora. see Stirling, Nora B.
Stirling, Nora B., 1900-
xStirling, Nora.
Who Wrote the Modern Classics. T Y Crowell.
Stirling, Patrick J. see Stirling, Patrick James.
Stirling, Patrick James, 1809-1891
xStirling, Patrick J.
Australian & Californian Gold Discoveries &
Their Probable Consequences. Greenwood.
Stirton, Paul.
xStirton, Paul.
Renaissance Painting. Mayflower Bks.
Stirton, R. A. see Stirton, Ruben Arthur.
Stirton, Ruben Arthur.
xStirton, R. A.
Australian Tertiary Deposits Containing
Terrestrial Mammals. U of Cal Pr.
Stites, Francis N.
xStites, Francis N.
Private Interest & Public Gain: The Dartmouth
College Case, 1819. U of Mass Pr.
Stites, Richard.
xStites, Richard.
The Women's Liberation Movement in Russia:
Feminism, Nihilism, & Bolshevism,
1860-1930. Princeton U Pr.
Stites, Sara H. see Stites, Sara Henry.
Stites, Sara Henry, 1877-
xStites, Sara H.
Economics of the Iroquois. AMS Pr.
Stith, William, 1707-1755
xStith, William.
History of the First Discovery & Settlement of
Virginia. Johnson Repr.
History of the First Discovery & Settlement of
Virginia. Reprint.
Stivers, Richard.
xStivers, Richard.
A Hair of the Dog: Irish Drinking & American
Stereotype. Pa St U Pr.
Stiverson, Gregory A.
xStiverson, Gregory A.
Poverty in a Land of Plenty: Tenancy in
Eighteenth-Century Maryland. Johns
Hopkins.
Stobart, Mabel A. see Stobart, Mabel Annie (Boulton).
Stobart, Mabel Annie (Boulton), 1862-1954
xStobart, Mabel A.
Torchbearers of Spiritualism. Kennikat.
Stobbs, John.
xStobbs, John.
Anatomy of Golf: Technique & Tactic.
Emerson.
Tackle Golf. Soccer.
Stobbs, William.
xStobbs, William.
Retold by & illus. The Hare & the Frogs: An
Aesop Fable. Merrimack Bk Serv.
Stock, Brian.
xStock, Brian.
ed. Medieval Latin Lyrics. Godine.
Stock, Dennis.
xStock, Dennis.
Circle of Seasons. Viking Pr.
James Dean Revisited. Penguin.
Stock, F. Patricia. see Stock, F. Patricia Pechanec.
Stock, F. Patricia Pechanec.
xStock, F. Patricia.

Personal Safety & Defense for Women.
Burgess.
Stock, Garfield R.
xStock, Garfield R.
Professional Real Estate Brokerage: A Guide
for Real Estate Executives. Dow Jones-Irwin.
Stock, Irvin, 1920-
xStock, Irvin.
Mary McCarthy. U of Minn Pr.
Stock, J. T. see Stock, John Thomas.
Stock, John Thomas, 1911-
xStock, J. T.
Amperometric Titrations. Krieger.
Stock, Noel.
xStock, Noel.
Life of Ezra Pound. Pantheon.
Stock, R. see Stock, Ralph.
Stock, Ralph.
xStock, R.
Chromatographic Methods. Methuen Inc.
Stock, S. George. see Stock, St. George William Joseph.
Stock, St. George. see Stock, St. George William Joseph.
Stock, St. George William Joseph, 1850-
xStock, S. George.
Stoicism. Arno.
xStock, St. George.
Stoicism. Kennikat.
Stockard, James.
xStockard, James G.
Rethinking People Management: A New Look
at the Human Resources Function. Am
Mgmt.
Stockard, James G.
xStockard, James G.
Career Development & Job Training: A
Manager's Handbook. Am Mgmt.
Stockard, James G. see Stockard, James.
Stockbridge, Grant.
xStockbridge, Grant.
Death & the Spider. PB.
Hordes of the Red Butcher. PB.
Stocker, Claudell S.
xStocker, Claudell S.
Listening for the Visually Impaired: A
Teaching Manual. C C Thomas.
Stockham, John D.
xStockham, John J.
Particle Size Analysis. Ann Arbor Science.
Stockham, John J. see Stockham, John D.
Stockham, Peter.
xStockham, Peter.
ed. Chapbook ABC's: Reprints of Five Rare &
Charming Early Juveniles. Dover.
ed. Chapbook Riddles: Reprints of Six Rare &
Charming Early Juveniles. Dover.
ed. Little Book of Early American Crafts and
Trades. Dover.
Little Book of Early American Crafts &
Trades. Peter Smith.
Stockhammer, M. see Stockhammer, Morris.
Stockhammer, Morris.
xStockhammer, M.
ed. Thomas Aquinas Dictionary. Philos Lib.
xStockhammer, Morris.
ed. Plato Dictionary. Philos Lib.
Stockholm International Peace Research Institute.
xSIPRI.

Anti-Personnel Weapons. Crane-Russak Co.
Arms Control: A Survey & Appraisal of
Multilateral Agreements. Crane-Russak Co.
Chemical Weapons: Destruction & Conversion.
Crane-Russak Co.
Internationalization to Prevent the Spread of
Nuclear Weapons. Crane-Russak Co.
Outer Space: Battlefield of the Future.
Crane-Russak Co.
Postures for Non-Proliferation. Crane-Russak
Co.
Strategic Disarmament: Verification & National
Security. Crane-Russak Co.
Tactical Nuclear Weapons: European
Perspectives. Crane-Russak Co.
Weapons of Mass Destruction & the
Environment. Crane-Russak Co.
World Armaments & Disarmament: SIPRI
Yearbook 1980. Crane-Russak Co.
World Armaments & Disarmament: SIPRI
Yearbooks 1968-1979 Cumulative Index.
Crane-Russak Co.
xStockholm International Peace Research Institute.
Armaments & Disarmament in the Nuclear
Age: A Handbook. Humanities.
The Arms Trade Registers. MIT Pr.
Arms Trade with the Third World. Humanities.
Arms Trade with the 3rd World. Holmes &
Meier.
Chemical Disarmament: New Weapons for
Old. Humanities.
Chemical Disarmament: Some Problems of
Verification. Humanities.
Communications Satellites. Humanities.
Ecological Consequences of the Second
Indochina War. Humanities.
Incendiary Weapons. MIT Pr.
The Law of War & Dubious Weapons.
Humanities.
The Near-Nuclear Countries & the Npt.
Humanities.
The Nuclear Age. MIT Pr.
Oil & Security. Humanities.
Problem of Chemical & Biological Warfare: A
Study of the Historical, Technical, Military,
Legal & Political Aspects of CBW, & Possible
Disarmament Measures. Humanities.
S I P R I Yearbook of World Armaments &
Disarmament 1972. Humanities.
S I P R I Yearbook of World Armaments &
Disarmaments 1968-69. Humanities.
S I P R I Yearbook of World Armaments &
Disarmaments, 1969-70. Humanities.
Safeguards Against Nuclear Proliferation. MIT
Pr.
Southern Africa: The Escalation of a Conflict.
Praeger.
Tactical & Strategic Antisubmarine Warfare.
MIT Pr.
World Armament and Disarmament: SIPRI
Yearbook 1976. MIT Pr.
World Armaments & Disarmament: SIPRI
Yearbook 1975. MIT Pr.
World Armaments & Disarmaments: SIPRI
Yearbook, 1974. MIT Pr.
Yearbook of World Armament & Disarmament.
Humanities.
xStockholm International Peach Research Institute.
Medical Protection Against Chemical Warfare
Agents. Humanities.
xStolkholm.
Arms Trade with the Third World. Penguin.
xTheStockholm International Peace Research
Institute.
Resources Devoted to Military Research &
Development: An International Comparison.
Humanities.
Stockholm International Peach Research Institute. see
Stockholm International Peace Research Institute.

Stocking, George W., 1928-
    xStocking, George W.
        Race, Culture & Evolution: Essays in the
            History of Anthropology. Free Pr.
Stocking, George W. see Stocking, George Ward.
Stocking, George Ward.
    xStocking, George W.
        Monopoly & Free Enterprise. Greenwood.
Stockley, Violet A. see Stockley, Violet Annie Alice.
Stockley, Violet Annie Alice.
    xStockley, Violet A.
        German Literature As Known in England,
            1750-1830. Kennikat.
        German Literature As Known in England
            1750-1830. Scholars Ref Lib.
Stocks, J. L. see Stocks, John Leofric.
Stocks, John L. see Stocks, John Leofric.
Stocks, John Leofric, 1882-1937
    xStocks, J. L.
        Morality & Purpose. Schocken.
    xStocks, John L.
        Aristotelianism. Cooper Sq.
        Reason & Intuition & Other Essays. Arno.
Stocksmeier, U. see Stocksmeier, Uwe.
Stocksmeier, Uwe.
    xStocksmeier, U.
        ed. Psychological Approach to the
            Rehabilitation of Coronary Patients.
            Springer-Verlag.
Stockton, Doris S. see Stockton, Doris Skillman.
Stockton, Doris Skillman.
    xStockton, Doris S.
        Essential College Algebra. HM.
        Essential Precalculus. HM.
        Essential Trigonometry. HM.
Stockton, Frank R. see Stockton, Frank Richard.
Stockton, Frank Richard, 1834-1902
    xStockton, Frank R.
        Buccaneers & Pirates of Our Coasts.
            Macmillan.
        Buccaneers & Pirates of Our Coasts.
            Macmillan.
Stockton, John R. see Stockton, John Robert.
Stockton, John Robert.
    xStockton, John R.
        Introduction to Business & Economic Statistics.
            SW Pub.
Stockton, William.
    xStockton, William.
        Altered Destinies. Doubleday.
        Altered Destinies. NAL.
Stockum, Hilda Van. see Van Stockum, Hilda.
Stockwell, Edward G.
    xStockwell, Edward G.
        Population & People. New Viewpoints.
Stockwell, J. see Stockwell, John.
Stockwell, John.
    xStockwell, J.
        How to Be a Fix-It Genius Using 7 Simple
            Tools. McGraw.
    xStockwell, John.
        In Search of Enemies: A CIA Story. Norton.
Stockwell, L. T. see Stockwell, la Tourette.
Stockwell, La Tourette.
    xStockwell, L. T.
        Dublin Theatres & Theatre Customs,
            1637-1820. Arno.
Stockwell, Richard E.
    xStockwell, Richard E.
        The Stockwell Guide for Technical &
            Vocational Writing. Benjamin-Cummings.
Stockwell, Robert P.
    xStockwell, Robert P.
        Foundations of Syntactic Theory. P-H.
        Grammatical Structures of English & Spanish.
            U of Chicago Pr.
Stoddard, Alan.
    xStoddard, Alan.

Back-Relief from Pain. Arco.
Stoddard, Alexandra.
    xStoddard, Alexandra.
        Style for Living: How to Make Where You
            Live You. Doubleday.
Stoddard, Charles H. see Stoddard, Charles Hatch.
Stoddard, Charles Hatch, 1912-
    xStoddard, Charles H.
        Essentials of Forestry Practice. Wiley.
Stoddard, Edward.
    xStoddard, Edward.
        The First Book of Magic. Avon.
        The First Book of Magic. Watts.
Stoddard, Elizabeth D. see Stoddard, Elizabeth Drew
    (Barstow).
Stoddard, Elizabeth Drew (Barstow), 1823-1902
    xStoddard, Elizabeth D.
        Two Men: A Novel. Johnson Repr.
Stoddard, Ellwyn R., 1927-
    xStoddard, Ellwyn R.
        Conceptual Models of Human Behavior in
            Disaster. Tex Western.
Stoddard, Francis H. see Stoddard, Francis Hovey.
Stoddard, Francis Hovey, 1847-1936
    xStoddard, Francis H.
        Evolution of the English Novel. Haskell.
Stoddard, Francis R. see Stoddard, Francis Russell.
Stoddard, Francis Russell, 1877-
    xStoddard, Francis R.
        The Truth About the Pilgrims. Genealog Pub.
Stoddard, George D. see Stoddard, George Dinsmore.
Stoddard, George Dinsmore, 1897-
    xStoddard, George D.
        The Outlook for American Education. S Ill U
            Pr.
Stoddard, Henry L. see Stoddard, Henry Luther.
Stoddard, Henry Luther, 1861-1947
    xStoddard, Henry L.
        As I Knew Them: Presidents & Politics from
            Grant to Coolidge. Kennikat.
Stoddard, Herbert L.
    xStoddard, Herbert L.
        Memoirs of a Naturalist. U of Okla Pr.
Stoddard, Hope.
    xStoddard, Hope.
        Famous American Women. T Y Crowell.
Stoddard, Richard.
    xStoddard, Richard.
        ed. Stage Scenery, Machinery, & Lighting: A
            Guide to Information Sources. Gale.
Stoddard, Richard H. see Stoddard, Richard Henry.
Stoddard, Richard Henry, 1825-1903
    xStoddard, Richard H.
        The Life of Washington Irving. Folcroft.
        Personal Recollections of Lamb, Hazlitt, &
            Others. R West.
Stoddard, Sandol.
    xStoddard, Sandol.
        The Hospice Movement: A Better Way of
            Caring for the Dying. Stein & Day.
Stoddard, Theodore L. see Stoddard, Theodore Lothrop.
Stoddard, Theodore Lothrop, 1883-1950
    xStoddard, Theodore L.
        French Revolution in San Domingo. Negro U
            Pr.
Stoddard, William O. see Stoddard, William Osborn.
Stoddard, William Osborn, 1835-1925
    xStoddard, William O.
        Men of Business. Arno.
Stoddart, Brigitte.
    xStoddart, Brigitte.
        Papercutting. Taplinger.
Stoddart, D. M. see Stoddart, David Michael.
Stoddart, David Michael.
    xStoddart, D. M.
        ed. Ecology of Small Mammals. Methuen Inc.
Stoddart, L. A. see Stoddart, Laurence Alexander.
Stoddart, Laurence Alexander.
    xStoddart, L. A.

Range Management. McGraw.
Stoddart, William.
    xStoddart, William.
        Sufism: The Mystical Doctrines & Methods of
            Islam. Weiser.
Stodelle, Ernestine.
    xStodelle, Ernestine.
        The Dance Technique of Doris Humphrey &
            Its Creative Potential. Princeton Bk Co.
Stodola, Jiri.
    xStodola, Jiri.
        Encyclopedia of Water Plants. TFH Pubns.
Stoeber, Edward A.
    xStoeber, Edward A.
        Tax & Fringe Benefit Planning for Professional
            Corporations. Natl Underwriter.
Stoebuck, William B.
    xStoebuck, William B.
        Nontrespassory Takings in Eminent Domain.
            Michie.
Stoecker, W F.
    xStoecker, W. F.
        Refrigeration & Air Conditioning. McGraw.
Stoecker, W. F. see Stoecker, Wilbert F.
Stoecker, Wilbert F.
    xStoecker, W. F.
        Design of Thermal Systems. McGraw.
        Using SI Units (Standard International Metric)
            in Heating, Air Conditioning, &
            Refrigeration. Busn News.
Stoeckle, Bernard. see Stoeckle, Bernhard.
Stoeckle, Bernhard.
    xStoeckle, Bernard.
        ed. The Concise Dictionary of Christian Ethics.
            Seabury.
Stoeffler, Ernest F. see Stoeffler, F. Ernest.
Stoeffler, F. Ernest.
    xStoeffler, Ernest F.
        Continental Pietism & Early American
            Christianity. Eerdmans.
Stoehr, Taylor, 1931-
    xStoehr, Taylor.
        Free Love in America: A Documentary
            History. AMS Pr.
        Nay-Saying in Concord: Emerson, Alcott &
            Thoreau. Shoe String.
Stoel, Thomas B.
    xStoel, Thomas B.
        Fluorocarbon Regulation: An International
            Comparison. Lexington Bks.
Stoer, J. see Stoer, Josef.
Stoer, Josef.
    xStoer, J.
        Introduction to Numerical Analysis.
            Springer-Verlag.
Stoessinger, John G. see Stoessinger, John George.
Stoessinger, John George.
    xStoessinger, John G.
        Crusaders & Pragmatists: Movers of Modern
            American Foreign Policy. Norton.
        Refugee & the World Community. U of Minn
            Pr.
Stoesz, Samuel J.
    xStoesz, Samuel S.
        Life Is for Growth. Chr Pubns.
Stoesz, Samuel S. see Stoesz, Samuel J.
Stoetzer, O. Carlos, 1921-
    xStoetzer, O. Carlos.
        The Scholastic Roots of the Spanish American
            Revolution. Fordham.
Stoever, William K. see Stoever, William K. B.
Stoever, William K. B., 1941-
    xStoever, William K.
        A Faire & Easie Way to Heaven: Covenant
            Theology & Antinomianism in Early
            Massachusetts. Columbia U Pr.
Stoff, Michael B.
    xStoff, Michael B.

Oil, War & American Security: The Search for
a National Policy on Foreign Oil, 1941-1947.
Yale U Pr.

Stoff, Sheldon.
xStoff, Sheldon P.
The Pumpkin Quest. Chris Mass.
Stoff, Sheldon P. *see* Stoff, Sheldon.

Stoffle, Carla.
xStoffle, Carla.
Materials & Methods for Political Science
Research. Neal-Schuman.

Stogdill, Ralph M. *see* Stogdill, Ralph Melvin.

Stogdill, Ralph Melvin, 1904-
xStogdill, Ralph M.
Handbook of Leadership: A Survey of Theory
& Research. Free Pr.
ed. Leader Behavior: Its Description &
Measurement. Ohio St U Admin Sci.
Leadership & Role Expectations. Ohio St U
Admin Sci.
Predictive Study of Administrative Work
Patterns. Ohio St U Admin Sci.

Stohlman, Robert F.
xStohlman, Robert F.
The Powerless Position: The Commanding
General of the Army of the United States,
1864-1903. Military Aff Aero.

Stoianovich, Traian.
xStoianovich, Traian.
French Historical Method: The "Annales"
Paradigm. Cornell U Pr.

Stoil, Michael J. *see* Stoil, Michael Jon.

Stoil, Michael Jon, 1950-
xStoil, Michael J.
Cinema Beyond the Danube: The Camera &
Politics. Scarecrow.

Stojkovic, Alexander.
xStojkovic, Alexander.
ed. The Living Matter. Maxima.

Stoker, Bram, 1847-1912
xStoker, Bram.
Dracula. Dell.
Dracula. Doubleday.
Dracula. Merrimack Bk Serv.
Dracula. Modern Lib.
Dracula. Penguin.
Dracula. Putnam.
Dracula. NAL.
Dracula. Delacorte.
Dracula. G&D.
Dracula. Pendulum Pr.
Dracula. Airmont.
Dracula. Schol Bk Serv.
Personal Reminiscences of Henry Irving.
Greenwood.
Under the Sunset. Borgo Pr.
Under the Sunset. Newcastle Pub.

Stoker, Howard W., 1925-
xStoker, Howard W.
Automated Data Processing in Testing. HM.

Stoker, J. J. *see* Stoker, James Johnston.

Stoker, James Johnston, 1905-
xStoker, J. J.
Nonlinear Elasticity. Gordon.

Stokes, Aldwyn. *see* Stokes, Aldwyn B.

Stokes, Aldwyn B.
xStokes, Aldwyn.
ed. Psychiatry in Transition: 1966-1967. U of
Toronto Pr.

Stokes, Anson. *see* Stokes, Anson Phelps.

Stokes, Anson Phelps.
xStokes, Anson.
Church & State in the United States.
Greenwood.

Stokes, Arch. *see* Stokes, Arch Y.

Stokes, Arch Y.
xStokes, Arch.

The Equal Opportunity Handbook for Hotels,
Restaurants & Institutions. CBI Pub.

Stokes, Bruce.
xStokes, Bruce.
Filling the Family Planning Gap. Worldwatch
Inst.
Local Responses to Global Problems: A Key to
Meeting Basic Human Needs. Worldwatch
Inst.
Worker Participation: Productivity & the
Quality of Work Life. Worldwatch Inst.

Stokes, Charles J.
xStokes, Charles J.
Economics for Managers. McGraw.
Housing Market Performance in the United
States. Praeger.

Stokes, Donald W.
xStokes, Donald W.
A Guide to Nature in Winter: Northeast &
North Central North America. Little.
A Guide to the Behavior of Common Birds.
Little.

Stokes, Durward T.
xStokes, Durward T.
The History of Dillon County, South Carolina.
U of SC Pr.

Stokes, E. Joan. *see* Stokes, Elizabeth Joan.
Stokes, E. T. *see* Stokes, Eric.

Stokes, Elizabeth Joan.
xStokes, E. Joan.
Clinical Bacteriology. Year Bk Med.

Stokes, Eric.
xStokes, E. T.
The Peasant & the Raj: Studies in Agrarian
Society & Peasant Rebellion in Colonial
India. Cambridge U Pr.

Stokes, Gale, 1933-
xStokes, Gale.
Legitimacy Through Liberalism: Vladimir
Jovanovic & the Transformation of Serbian
Politics. U of Wash Pr.

Stokes, George G. *see* Stokes, George Gabriel.

Stokes, George Gabriel.
xStokes, George G.
Mathematical & Physical Papers. Johnson
Repr.
Memoir & Scientific Correspondence of the
Late Sir George Gabriel Stokes. Johnson
Repr.

Stokes, George S. *see* Stokes, George Stewart.

Stokes, George Stewart.
xStokes, George S.
Agnes Repplier, Lady of Letters. Greenwood.

Stokes, Gordon.
xStokes, Gordon.
Toy Making in Wood. Transatlantic.

Stokes, Houston H.
xStokes, Houston H.
Unemployment & Adjustment in the Labor
Market: A Comparison Between the Regional
& National Responses. U Chicago Dept
Geog.

Stokes, Jack.
xStokes, Jack.
illus. Let's Be Nature's Friend!. McKay.
Let's Make a Tent. McKay.
Let's Make Stilts. Walck.

Stokes, Judy F. *see* Stokes, Judy Ford.

Stokes, Judy Ford.
xStokes, Judy F.
Cost-Effective Quality Food Service: An
Institutional Guide. Aspen Systems.

Stokes, McNeill.
xStokes, McNeill.
Labor Law in Contractors' Language. McGraw.

Stokes, Michael C.
xStokes, Michael C.
One & Many in Presocratic Philosophy.
Harvard U Pr.

Stokes, P. *see* Stokes, Peter G.

Stokes, Peter. *see* Stokes, Peter G.

Stokes, Peter G.
xStokes, P.
A Guide to Sports Medicine. Longman.
xStokes, Peter.
ed. A Guide to Sports Medicine. Churchill.

Stokes, Terry.
xStokes, Terry.
Life in These United States. St Luke TN.

Stokes, Vernon L.
xStokes, Vernon L.
Manufacturing Materials. Merrill.
Manufacturing Processes. Merrill.

Stokes, William L. *see* Stokes, William Lee.

Stokes, William Lee, 1915-
xStokes, William L.
Essentials of Earth History: An Introduction to
Historical Geology. P-H.

Stokes, William N.
xStokes, William N.
Oil Mill on the Texas Plains: A Study in
Agricultural Cooperation. Tex A&M Univ Pr.

Stokes, William S. *see* Stokes, William Sylvane.

Stokes, William Sylvane.
xStokes, William S.
Honduras: An Area Study in Government.
Greenwood.

Stokesbury, Leon.
xStokesbury, Leon.
Often in Different Landscapes. U of Tex Pr.

Stokey, Edith.
xStokey, Edith.
A Primer for Policy Analysis. Norton.

Stokoe, W. C. *see* Stokoe, William C.
Stokoe, W. J. *see* Stokoe, William John.

Stokoe, William C.
xStokoe, W. C.
A Dictionary of American Sign Language on
Linguistic Principles. Linstok Pr.
xStokoe, William C.
Dictionary of American Sign Language on
Linguistic Principles. Linstok Pr.

Stokoe, William John.
xStokoe, W. J.
The Observer's Book of Butterflies. Scribner.

Stokols, Daniel.
xStokols, Daniel.
ed. Readings in Environmental Psychology.
Mss Info.

Stolarsky, Kenneth B.
xStolarsky, Kenneth B.
Algebraic Numbers & Diophantine
Approximation. Dekker.

Stolberg, Benjamin, 1891-1951
xStolberg, Benjamin.
Story of the CIO. Arno.

Stoler, Mark A.
xStoler, Mark A.
The Politics of the Second Front: American
Military Planning & Diplomacy in Coalition
Warfare, 1941-1943. Greenwood.

Stolkholm. *see* Stockholm International Peace Research
Institute.

Stoll, Basil A. *see* Stoll, Basil Arnold.

Stoll, Basil Arnold.
xStoll, Basil A.
ed. Host Defence in Breast Cancer. Year Bk
Med.

Stoll, Elmer E. *see* Stoll, Elmer Edgar.

Stoll, Elmer Edgar, 1874-1959
xStoll, Elmer E.
Falstaff. Folcroft.
Hamlet: An Historical & Comparative Study.
Somerset Pub.
Hamlet the Man. Folcroft.

Stoll, Jerry.
xStoll, Jerry.
ed. I Am a Lover. Pacific Coast.

Stoll, R. R. *see* Stoll, Robert Roth.
Stoll, Robert R. *see* Stoll, Robert Roth.

Stoll, Robert Roth.
  xStoll, R. R.
    Linear Algebra. Acad Pr.
  xStoll, Robert R.
    Linear Algebra. Acad Pr.
Stoll, W. see Stoll, Wilhelm.
Stoll, Wilhelm.
  xStoll, W.
    Value Distribution of Holomorphic Maps into
      Compact Complex Manifolds.
      Springer-Verlag.
    Value Distribution on Parabolic Spaces.
      Springer-Verlag.
Stolle, C. see Stolle, Carlton.
Stolle, Carlton.
  xStolle, C.
    Auditing of Computer-Generated Accounts: A
      Simulation. McGraw.
Stoller, David S.
  xStoller, David S.
    Operations Research: Process & Strategy. U of
      Cal Pr.
Stoller, Leo.
  xStoller, Leo.
    After Walden: Thoreau's Changing Views on
      Economic Man. Stanford U Pr.
Stoller, Nathan.
  xStoller, Nathan.
    Supervision & the Improvement of Instruction.
      Educ Tech Pubns.
Stoller, Robert. see Stoller, Robert J.
Stoller, Robert J.
  xStoller, Robert.
    Sexual Excitement: Dynamics of Erotic Life.
      Pantheon.
Stollerman, Gene H.
  xStollerman, Gene H.
    Rheumatic Fever & Streptococcal Infection.
      Grune.
Stolnitz, Jerome.
  xStolnitz, Jerome.
    ed. Aesthetics. Macmillan.
Stoloff, Carolyn.
  xStoloff, Carolyn.
    Stepping Out. Unicorn Pr.
Stolovitch, Harold D.
  xStolovitch, Harold D.
    Audiovisual Training Modules. Educ Tech
      Pubns.
    Frame Games. Educ Tech Pubns.
Stolpe, Hjalmar, 1841-1905
  xStolpe, Hjalmar.
    Amazon Indian Designs from Brazilian &
      Guianan Wood Carvings. Dover.
    Amazon Indian Designs from Brazilian &
      Guianan Wood Carvings. Peter Smith.
Stolten, Jane H. see Stolten, Jane Henry.
Stolten, Jane Henry.
  xStolten, Jane H.
    The Geriatric Aide. Little.
Stoltenberg, Carl. see Stoltenberg, Carl H.
Stoltenberg, Carl H.
  xStoltenberg, Carl.
    Planning Research for Resource Decisions.
      Iowa St U Pr.
Stoltenberg, Donald.
  xStoltenberg, Donald.
    Collagraph Printmaking. Davis Mass.
Stoltman, James B., 1935-
  xStoltman, James B.
    Groton Plantation: An Archaeological Study of
      a South Carolina Locality. Peabody Harvard.
    The Laurel Culture in Minnesota. Minn Hist.
Stoltzfus, Ben. see Stoltzfus, Ben Frank.
Stoltzfus, Ben Frank, 1927-
  xStoltzfus, Ben.
    Gide & Hemingway: Rebels Against God.
      Kennikat.
    Gide's Eagles. S Ill U Pr.
Stolz, Lois H. see Stolz, Lois Hayden (Meek).

Stolz, Lois Hayden. see Stolz, Lois Hayden (Meek).
Stolz, Lois Hayden (Meek).
  xStolz, Lois H.
    Father Relations of War-Born Children: The
      Effect of Postwar Adjustment of Fathers on
      the Behavior & Personality of First Children
      Born While Fathers Were at War.
      Greenwood.
  xStolz, Lois Hayden.
    A Study of Learning & Retention in Young
      Children. AMS Pr.
Stolz, Lois M. see Stolz, Lois Meek.
Stolz, Lois Meek.
  xStolz, Lois M.
    Influences on Parent Behavior. Stanford U Pr.
Stolz, Mary. see Stolz, Mary Slattery.
Stolz, Mary Slattery, 1920-
  xStolz, Mary.
    Bully of Barkham Street. Har-Row.
    Bully of Barkham Street. Dell.
    By the Highway Home. Har-Row.
    Dragons of the Queen. Har-Row.
    Ferris Wheel. Har-Row.
    Ferris Wheel. Har-Row.
    Go & Catch a Flying Fish. Har-Row.
    Hospital Zone. Har-Row.

    Leap Before You Look. Dell.
    Leap Before You Look. Har-Row.

    Maximilian's World. Har-Row.
    Noonday Friends. Har-Row.
    Noonday Friends. Har-Row.
    Pray Love, Remember. Har-Row.

    Ready or Not. Har-Row.
    Who Wants Music on Monday. Har-Row.
    Wonderful Terrible Time. Har-Row.
Stolz, Matthew. see Stolz, Matthew F.
Stolz, Matthew F.
  xStolz, Matthew.
    Politics of the New Left. Glencoe.
Stolzenberg, Mark.
  xStolzenberg, Mark.
    Exploring Mime. Sterling.
Stombaugh, Ray M. see Stombaugh, Ray Merton.
Stombaugh, Ray Merton, 1893-
  xStombaugh, Ray M.
    Survey of the Movements Culminating in
      Industrial Arts Education in Secondary
      Schools. AMS Pr.
Stomberg, A. A. see Stomberg, Andrew Adin.
Stomberg, Andrew A. see Stomberg, Andrew Adin.
Stomberg, Andrew Adin, 1871-
  xStomberg, A. A.
    History of Sweden. Kraus Repr.
  xStomberg, Andrew A.
    History of Sweden. AMS Pr.
Stommel, Henry. see Stommel, Henry M.
Stommel, Henry M.
  xStommel, Henry.
    Oceanographic Atlases: A Guide to Their
      Geographic Coverage & Contents. Woods
      Hole.
Stonaker, Frances B. see Stonaker, Frances Benson.
Stonaker, Frances Benson.
  xStonaker, Frances B.
    Famous Mathematicians. Lippincott.
Stone, A. Harris.
  xStone, A. Harris.
    Last Free Bird. P-H.
Stone, Alan, 1931-
  xStone, Alan.
    Economic Regulation & the Public Interest:
      The Federal Trade Commission in Theory &
      Practice. Cornell U Pr.
Stone, Alan. see Stone, Alan A.
Stone, Alan A.
  xStone, Alan.

    Abnormal Personality Through Literature. P-H.
Stone, Albert E.
  xStone, Albert E.
    Innocent Eye: Childhood in Mark Twain's
      Imagination. Shoe String.
Stone, Andy.
  xStone, Andy.
    Song of the Kingdom. Doubleday.
Stone, Archie A. see Stone, Archie Augustus.
Stone, Archie Augustus, 1893-
  xStone, Archie A.
    Careers in Agribusiness & Industry. Interstate.
Stone, Arlene.
  xStone, Arlene.
    The Women's House. Allegany Mtn Pr.
Stone, Ben.
  xStone, Ben.
    Clipping & Grooming Your Spaniel & Setter.
      Arco.
Stone, Bernard.
  xStone, Bernard.
    The Charge of the Mouse Brigade. Pantheon.
Stone, Bob, fl. 1947-
  xStone, Bob.
    Successful Direct Marketing Methods. Crain
      Bks.
Stone, C. see Stone, Clarence Nathan.
Stone, Calvin P. see Stone, Calvin Perry.
Stone, Calvin Perry, 1892-1954
  xStone, Calvin P.
    ed. Comparative Psychology. Greenwood.
Stone, Christopher. see Stone, Christopher Reynolds.
Stone, Christopher D.
  xStone, Christopher D.
    Where the Law Ends: Social Control of
      Corporate Behavior. Har-Row.
Stone, Christopher Reynolds, 1882-1965
  xStone, Christopher.
    Parody. Folcroft.
Stone, Clarence Nathan.
  xStone, C.
    Urban Policy & Politics in a Bureaucratic Age.
      P-H.
Stone, Cliff W. see Stone, Cliff Winfield.
Stone, Cliff Winfield, 1874-
  xStone, Cliff W.
    Arithmetical Abilities & Some Factors
      Determining Them. AMS Pr.
    Standardized Reasoning Tests in Arithmetic &
      How to Utilize Them. AMS Pr.
Stone, D. A. see Stone, David A.
Stone, Dave. see Stone, David Ulric.
Stone, David. see Stone, David Ulric.
Stone, David A.
  xStone, D. A.
    Stratified Polyhedra. Springer-Verlag.
Stone, David Ulric, 1927-
  xStone, Dave.
    How to Sell New Homes & Condominiums.
      McGraw.
  xStone, David.
    How to Sell New Homes & Condominiums.
      McGraw.
Stone, Donald. see Stone, Donald Ralph.
Stone, Donald Ralph.
  xStone, Donald.
    Orthopaedic Physician's Assistant Techniques.
      Bobbs.
Stone, Doris. see Stone, Doris Zemurray.
Stone, Doris Zemurray, 1909-
  xStone, Doris.
    Pre-Columbian Man in Costa Rica. Peabody
      Harvard.
Stone, E. see Stone, Eric.
Stone, Edward, 1913-
  xStone, Edward.

Certain Morbidness: A View of American
Literature. S Ill U Pr.
ed. What Was Naturalism?: Materials for an
Answer. P-H.
Stone, Elaine M. see Stone, Elaine Murray.
Stone, Elaine Murray.
xStone, Elaine M.
Pedro Menendez de Aviles & the Founding of
St. Augustine. Kenedy.
Stone, Elizabeth. see Stone, Elizabeth W.
Stone, Elizabeth W., 1918-
xStone, E.
Model Continuing Education Recognition
System in Library & Information Science. K
G Saur.
xStone, Elizabeth.
Continuing Library Education As Viewed in
Relation to Other Continuing Professional
Education Movements. Am Soc Info Sci.
xStone, Elizabeth W.
ed. American Library Development: 1600 -
1899. Wilson.
Factors Related to the Professional
Development of Librarians. Scarecrow.
Stone, Elna.
xStone, Elna.
How to Choose Your Work. Glencoe.
How to Get a Job. Glencoe.
Stone, Eric, 1892-
xStone, E.
Medicine Among the American Indians.
Hafner.
xStone, Eric P.
Medicine Among the American Indians. AMS
Pr.
Stone, Eric P. see Stone, Eric.
Stone, Ferdinand Fairflax, 1908-
xStone, Ferdinand F.
Handbook of Law Study. Little.
Stone, Ferdinand F. see Stone, Ferdinand Fairflax.
Stone, Frank A.
xStone, Frank A.
Scots & Scotch Irish in Connecticut: A
History. World Educ Proj.
Stone, Frederick H. see Stone, Frederick Hope.
Stone, Frederick Hope.
xStone, Frederick H.
Child Psychiatry for Students. Churchill.
Stone, Gary K.
xStone, Gary K.
Personal & Business Estate Planning: Selected
Readings. Mich St U Busn.
Stone, Geoffrey.
xStone, Geoffrey.
Melville. Octagon.
Stone, George K.
xStone, George K.
More Science Projects You Can Do. P-H.
Stone, Gregory. see Stone, Gregory V.
Stone, Gregory B.
xStone, Gregory B.
ed. In the Spirit of Enterprise from the Rolex
Awards. W H Freeman.
Stone, Gregory V.
xStone, Gregory.
Prospecting for Lode Gold. Dorrance.
Stone, Harlan F. see Stone, Harlan Fiske.
Stone, Harlan Fiske, 1872-1946
xStone, Harlan F.
Law & Its Administration. AMS Pr.
Stone, Harold. see Stone, Harold S.
Stone, Harold S., 1938-
xStone, Harold.
Introduction to Computer Organization & Data
Structures. McGraw.
xStone, Harold S.

Discrete Mathematical Structures & Their
Applications. SRA.
Introduction to Computer Architecture. SRA.
Stone, Harris, 1934-
xStone, Harris.
Workbook of an Unsuccessful Architect.
Monthly Rev.
Stone, Helen D.
xStone, Helen D.
Creating a Foster Parent-Agency Handbook.
Child Welfare.
Stone, Howard W.

xStone, Howard W.
Crisis Counseling. Fortress.
Suicide & Grief. Fortress.
ed. Using Behavioral Methods in Pastoral
Counseling. Fortress.
Stone, I. F. see Stone, Isidor F.
Stone, Irving.
xStone, Irving.
Adversary in the House. Doubleday.
Adversary in the House. NAL.
Agony & the Ecstasy. NAL.
Agony & the Ecstasy. Doubleday.
The Greek Treasure: A Biographical Novel of
Henry & Sophia Schliemann. Doubleday.
Love Is Eternal. NAL.
Love Is Eternal. Doubleday.
The Passionate Journey. Doubleday.
The Passionate Journey. NAL.
They Also Ran. Doubleday.
They Also Ran. NAL.
Stone, Isidor F., 1907-
xStone, I. F.
Underground to Palestine. Pantheon.
Stone, James C. see Stone, James Champion.
Stone, James Champion, 1916-
xStone, James C.
Breakthrough in Teacher Education.
Jossey-Bass.
ed. Portraits of the American University:
1890-1910. Jossey-Bass.
Teachers for the Disadvantaged. Jossey-Bass.
Stone, James M. see Stone, James Martin.
Stone, James Martin.
xStone, James M.
One Way for Wall Street: A View of the
Future of the Securities Industry. Little.
Stone, Jeremy J.
xStone, Jeremy J.
Strategic Persuasion: Arms Limitations
Through Dialogue. Columbia U Pr.
Stone, Joe.
xStone, Joe.
The Master's Book of Pool & Billiards. Crown.
Stone, John F.
xStone, John F.
Plant Modification for More Efficient Water
Use. Elsevier.
Stone, Jonathan.
xStone, Jonathan.
English Silver of the Eighteenth Century.
October.
Stone, Josephine R. see Stone, Josephine Rector.
Stone, Josephine Rector.
xStone, Josephine R.
Green Is for Galanx. Atheneum.
Praise All the Moons of Morning. Atheneum.
Those Who Fall from the Sun. Atheneum.
Stone, Judith.
xStone, Judith.
In the Jaws of Death. Raintree Pubs.
Minutes to Live. Raintree Pubs.
Stone, Julius, 1907-
xStone, Julius.

Conflict Through Consensus: United Nations
Approaches to Aggression. Johns Hopkins.
Human Law & Human Justice. Stanford U Pr.
Legal System & Lawyers' Reasonings. Stanford
U Pr.
Of Law & Nations: Between Power Politics &
Human Hopes. W S Hein.
Stone, Kurt.
xStone, Kurt.
Music Notation in the Twentieth Century: A
Practical Guidebook. Norton.
Stone, L. Joseph. see Stone, Lawrence Joseph.
Stone, Lawrence.
xStone, Lawrence.
The Causes of the English Revolution.
Har-Row.
Crisis of the Aristocracy, 1558-1641. Oxford U
Pr.
Stone, Lawrence Joseph.
xStone, L. Joseph.
Childhood & Adolescence: A Psychology of
the Growing Person. Random.
Stone, Leslie F.
xStone, Leslie F.
Out of the Void. Bouregy.
Stone, Lilly C.
xStone, Lilly C.
English Sports & Recreations. Folger Bks.
Stone, M. H. see Stone, Marshall Harvey.
Stone, Marshall Harvey, 1903-
xStone, M. H.
Linear Transformations in Hilbert Space &
Their Applications to Analysis. Am Math.
Stone, Martha, 1898-
xStone, Martha.
At the Sign of Midnight: The Conchcros
Dance Cult of Mexico. U of Ariz Pr.
Stone, Melville E. see Stone, Melville Elijah.
Stone, Melville Elijah, 1848-1929
xStone, Melville E.
Fifty Years a Journalist. Arno.
Fifty Years a Journalist. Greenwood.
Stone, Merlin.
xStone, Merlin.
Marketing & Economics. St Martin.
Product Planning: An Integrated Approach.
Halsted Pr.
When God Was a Woman. Dial.
When God Was a Woman. HarBraceJ.
Stone, Mike.
xStone, Mike.
Mopedaller's Handy Manual. TAB Bks.
Stone, Morris, 1912-
xStone, Morris.
Labor-Management Contracts at Work:
Analysis of Awards Reported by the
American Arbitration Association.
Greenwood.
Stone, Nancy.
xStone, Nancy.
Wooden River. Eerdmans.
Stone, Norman.
xStone, Norman.
The Eastern Front, 1914-1917. Scribner.
Hitler. Little.
Stone, P. A.
xStone, P. A.
Structure, Size & Costs of Urban Settlements.
Cambridge U Pr.
Stone, Peter.
xStone, Peter.
Gravel Pit Angling. David & Charles.
Stone, Philip J.
xStone, Philip J.
General Inquirer: A Computer Approach to
Content Analysis. MIT Pr.
Stone, Ralph A.
xStone, Ralph A.

ed. Wilson & the League of Nations: Why
America's Rejection. Krieger.

Stone, Richard G., 1937-
xStone, Richard G.
A Brittle Sword: The Kentucky Militia,
1776-1912. U Pr of Ky.

Stone, Robert.
xStone, Robert.
Dog Soldiers. Ballantine.
Dog Soldiers. HM.

Stone, Robert B.
xStone, Robert B.
The Power of Miracle Metaphysics. P-H.

Stone, Ronald H.
xStone, Ronald H.
Paul Tillich's Radical Social Thought. John
Knox.
Realism & Hope. U Pr of Amer.

Stone, Russell A., 1944-
xStone, Russell A.
ed. OPEC & the Middle East: The Impact of
Oil on Societal Development. Praeger.

Stone, Ruth.
xStone, Ruth.
Cheap: New Poems & Ballads. HarBraceJ.
Cheap: New Poems & Ballads. HarBraceJ.
Topography & Other Poems. HarBraceJ.

Stone, Ruth M.
xStone, Ruth M.
African Music & Oral Data: A Catalog of Field
Recordings, 1902-1975. Ind U Pr.

Stone, Scott C. *see* Stone, Scott C. S.

Stone, Scott C. S., 1932-
xStone, Scott C.
Pearl Harbor: The Way It Was--December 7,
1941. Island Her.
Spies. St Martin.

Stone, Thomas E., 1923-
xStone, Thomas E.
Organizing & Operating Special Classes for
Emotionally Disturbed Elementary School
Children. P-H.

Stone, Victor J., 1921-
xStone, Victor J.
Civil Liberties & Civil Rights. U of Ill Pr.

Stone, W. Clement, 1902-
xStone, W. Clement.
Success System That Never Fails. P-H.
The Success System That Never Fails. PB.

Stone, Wilfred. *see* Stone, Wilfred Healey.

Stone, Wilfred Healey, 1917-
xStone, Wilfred.
Religion & Art of William Hale White (Mark
Rutherford). R West.

Stone, William.
xStone, William D.
Earth Moving Machines. Raintree Pubs.

Stone, William D. *see* Stone, William.

Stone, William F.
xStone, William F.
The Psychology of Politics. Free Pr.

Stone, William J.
xStone, William J.
Sports Conditioning & Weight Training:
Programs for Athletic Competition. Allyn.

Stone, William L. *see* Stone, William Leete.

Stone, William Leete, 1835-1908
xStone, William L.
Ballads & Poems Relating to the Burgoyne
Campaign. Kennikat.
ed. Letters of Brunswick & Hessian Officers
During the American Revolution. Da Capo.

Stone, Williard E., 1910-
xStone, Williard E.
ed. Theory Formulations. U Presses Fla.

Stone, Witmer.
xStone, Witmer.

The Plants of Southern New Jersey.
Quarterman.

Stonecipher, Harry W.
xStonecipher, Harry W.
Editorial & Persuasive Writing: Opinion
Functions of the News Media. Hastings.
The Mass Media & the Law in Illinois. S Ill U
Pr.

Stonehill, Charles A. *see* Stonehill, Charles Archibald.

Stonehill, Charles Archibald.
xStonehill, Charles A.
Anonyma & Pseudonyma. Longwood Pr.

Stonehouse, Bernard.
xStonehouse, Bernard.
Bears. Raintree Pubs.
A Closer Look at Reptiles. Watts.
A Closer Look at Whales & Dolphins. Watts.
ed. Evolutionary Ecology. Univ Park.
Penguins. McGraw.

Stoneley, Jack.
xStoneley, Jack.
Cauldron of Hell: Tunguska. S&S.
Scruffy. Random.

Stoneman, William E., 1939-
xStoneman, William E.
A History of the Economic Analysis of the
Great Depression in America. Garland Pub.

Stonequist, Everett V.
xStonequist, Everett V.
Marginal Man: A Study in Personality &
Culture Conflict. Russell.

Stoner, Carol.
xStoner, Carol H.
ed. Producing Your Own Power: How to Make
Nature's Energy Sources Work for You.
Random.
Producing Your Own Power: How to Make
Nature's Energy Sources Work for You.
Rodale Pr Inc.

Stoner, Carol H. *see* Stoner, Carol.

Stoner, Carroll.
xStoner, Carroll.
All Gods Children: The Cult Experience -
Salvation or Slavery?. Penguin.

Stoneridge, M. A.
xStoneridge, M. A.
A Dog of Your Own. Doubleday.
Horse of Your Own. Doubleday.

Stones, E.
xStones, Edgar.
Psychopedagogy: Psychological Theory & the
Practice of Teaching. Methuen Inc.

Stones, Edgar. *see* Stones, E.

Stonier, A. W. *see* Stonier, Alfred William.

Stonier, Alfred William.
xStonier, A. W.
A Textbook of Economic Theory. Longman.

Stonum, Gary L. *see* Stonum, Gary Lee.

Stonum, Gary Lee.
xStonum, Gary L.
Faulkner's Career: An Internal Literary
History. Cornell U Pr.

Stoodley, Bartlett H.
xStoodley, Bartlett H.
ed. Society & Self: A Reader in Social
Psychology. Free Pr.

Stookey, Robert W., 1917-
xStookey, Robert W.
America & the Arab States: An Uneasy
Encounter. Wiley.

Stoop, Dave. *see* Stoop, David A.

Stoop, David A.
xStoop, Dave.
The Total(ed) Parent: (Hope for Parents
Caught in the Struggle). Harvest Hse.

Stoops, John A.
xStoops, John A.
Religious Values in Education. Interstate.

Stoppard, Miriam.
xStoppard, Miriam.

Dr. Miriam Stoppard's Book of Baby Care.
Atheneum.

Stoppard, Tom.
xStoppard, Tom.
Dirty Linen & New-Found-Land. Grove.
Dirty Linen & New-Found-Land. Grove.
Enter a Free Man. Grove.
Lord Malquist & Mr Moon. Grove.

Stopple, Libby.
xStopple, Libby.
A Box of Peppermints. Am Univ Artforms.
Song for All Seasons. Am Univ Artforms.

Storaska, Frederic, 1942
xStoraska, Frederic.
How to Say No to a Rapist - and Survive.
Warner Bks.
How to Say No to a Rapist & Survive.
Random.

Storer, Douglas.
xStorer, Douglas.
Amazing but True. S&S.

Storer, Norman W.
xStorer, Norman W.
Focus on Society: An Introduction to
Sociology. A-W.

Storer, Tracy I. *see* Storer, Tracy Irwin.

Storer, Tracy Irwin.
xStorer, Tracy I.
California Grizzly. U of Nebr Pr.
General Zoology. McGraw.
Sierra Nevada Natural History: An Illustrated
Handbook. U of Cal Pr.

Storey, David, 1933-
xStorey, David.
Pasmore. Avon.

Storey, Del.
xStorey, Del.
Collision Course. Logos.

Storey, Edward.
xStorey, Edward.
Portrait of the Fen Country. Intl Pubns Serv.

Storey, G. A. *see* Storey, George Adolphus.

Storey, George Adolphus, 1834-1919
xStorey, G. A.
The Theory & Practice of Perspective. Arno.

Storey, Gladys.
xStorey, Gladys.
Dickens & Daughter. Haskell.

Storey, Joyce.
xStorey, Joyce.
The Thames & Hudson Manual of Dyes &
Fabrics. Thames Hudson.

Storey, Margaret.
xStorey, Margaret.
Ask Me No Questions. Dutton.
The Double Wizard. Merrimack Bk Serv.
The Family Tree. Elsevier-Nelson.

Storey, Mark.
xStorey, Mark.
Poetry & Humour from Cowper to Clough.
Rowman.

Storey, Mary R. *see* Storey, Mary Rose.

Storey, Mary Rose.
xStorey, Mary R.
Mona Lisas. Abrams.

Storey, Moorfield, 1845-1929
xStorey, Moorfield.
Charles Sumner. AMS Pr.
Charles Sumner. Chelsea Hse.
Charles Sumner. Russell.
The Conquest of the Philippines by the United
States, 1898-1925. Arno.

Stork, C. W. *see* Stork, Charles Wharton.

Stork, Charles W. *see* Stork, Charles Wharton.

Stork, Charles Wharton, 1881-
xStork, C. W.
Anthology of Swedish Lyrics. Gordon Pr.
xStork, Charles W.

ed. Anthology of Norwegian Lyrics. Arno.

Storm, George, 1923-
xStorm, George.
Managing the Occupational Education Laboratory. Prakken.

Storm, Margaret.
xStorm, Margaret.
Home Maid Spanish. Crown.
Home Maid Spanish Cookbook. Crown.

Stormen, Win.
xStormen, Win.
Popular Piano Self-Taught. Arco.

Storms, Edmund K. *see* Storms, Edmund Kugler.

Storms, Edmund Kugler, 1931-
xStorms, Edmund K.
Refractory Carbides. Acad Pr.

Storms, Godfrid.
xStorms, Godfrid.
Anglo-Saxon Magic. Folcroft.
xStorms, Godfried.
Anglo-Saxon Magic. Gordon Pr.

Storms, Godfried. *see* Storms, Godfrid.

Storr, Catherine.
xStorr, Catherine.
Lucy. P-H.
Winter's End. Har-Row.

Storrer, William A. *see* Storrer, William Allin.

Storrer, William Allin.
xStorrer, William A.
The Architecture of Frank Lloyd Wright: A Complete Catalog. MIT Pr.

Storrs, Ronald, Sir, 1881-1955
xStorrs, Ronald.
Memoirs of Sir Ronald Storrs. AMS Pr.
The Memoirs of Sir Ronald Storrs. Arno.

Storry, George Richard, 1913-
xStorry, Richard.
Japan & the Decline of the West in Asia. St Martin

Storry, Richard.
xStorry, Richard.
History of Modern Japan. Penguin.

Storry, Richard. *see* Storry, George Richard.

Story, Alfred I. *see* Story, Alfred Thomas.

Story, Alfred T. *see* Story, Alfred Thomas.

Story, Alfred Thomas, 1842-1934
xStory, Alfred I.
The Story of Photography. Light Impressions.
xStory, Alfred T.
The Story of Photography. Arden Lib.

Story, Bettie W. *see* Story, Bettie Wilson.

Story, Bettie Wilson.
xStory, Bettie W.
Summer of Jubilee. Cook.

Story, Donna K. *see* Story, Donna Ketchum.

Story, Donna Ketchum, 1932-
xStory, Donna K.
Principles & Practices of Nursing Care. McGraw.

Story, Joseph, 1779-1845
xStory, Joseph.
Commentaries on Equity Jurisprudence, As Administered in England & America. Arno.

Story, Norah.
xStory, Norah.
Oxford Companion to Canadian History & Literature. Oxford U Pr.

Story, Ronald.
xStory, Ronald.
The Space Gods Revealed: A Close Look at the Theories of Erich Von Daniken. Har-Row.
xStory, Ronald D.
ed. The Encyclopedia of UFOs. Doubleday.
ed. The Encyclopedia of UFOs. Doubleday.

Story, Ronald D. *see* Story, Ronald.

Story, Russell M. *see* Story, Russell McCulloch.

Story, Russell McCulloch, 1883-1942
xStory, Russell M.

The American Municipal Executive. Johnson Repr.

Storz, Johannes.
xStorz, Johannes.
Chlamydia & Chlamydia-Induced Diseases. C C Thomas.

Stott, John R. *see* Stott, John R. W.

Stott, John R. W.
xStott, John R.
Baptism & Fullness: The Work of the Holy Spirit Today. Inter-Varsity.
Down to Earth: Studies in Christianity & Culture. Eerdmans.
ed. The Gospel & Culture. William Carey Lib.

Stott, William, 1940-
xStott, William.
Documentary Expression & Thirties America. Oxford U Pr.
Documentary Expression & Thirties America. Oxford U Pr.

Stotz, Gustaf.
xStotz, Gustaf.
Film und Foto. Arno.

Stoudt, John J. *see* Stoudt, John Joseph.

Stoudt, John Joseph, 1911-
xStoudt, John J.
Sunbonnets & Shoofly Pies: Pennsylvania Dutch Cultural History. A S Barnes.

Stouffer, Samuel A. *see* Stouffer, Samuel Andrews.

Stouffer, Samuel Andrews, 1900-
xStouffer, Samuel A.
Measurement & Prediction. Peter Smith.

Stourzh, Gerald.
xStourzh, Gerald.
Readings in American Democracy. Oxford U Pr.

Stout, David F.
xStout, David F.
Handbook of Microcircuit Design & Application. McGraw.

Stout, George L. *see* Stout, George Leslie.

Stout, George Leslie.
xStout, George L.
The Care of Pictures. Dover.

Stout, James H.
xStout, James H.
Backpacking with Small Children. T Y Crowell.

Stout, Janis P.
xStout, Janis P.
Sodoms in Eden: The City in American Fiction Before 1860. Greenwood.

Stout, John E. *see* Stout, John Elbert.

Stout, John Elbert, 1867-1942
xStout, John E.
Development of High-School Curricula in the North Central States from 1860-1918. Arno.

Stout, Neil R.
xStout, Neil R.
The Perfect Crisis: The Beginning of the Revolutionary War. NYU Pr.

Stout, Rex.
xStout, Rex.
The Broken Vase. BJ Pub Group.
Double for Death. BJ Pub Group.
A Family Affair. G K Hall.
A Family Affair. Viking Pr.
The Final Deduction. Bantam.
The Hand in the Glove. BJ Pub Group.
The League of Frightened Men. BJ Pub Group.
The Nero Wolfe Cookbook. Viking Pr.
Over My Dead Body. BJ Pub Group.

Stout, Russell, 1932-
xStout, Russell.
Management or Control?:: The Organizational Challenge. Ind U Pr.
Organizations, Management, & Control: An Annotated Bibliography. Ind U Pr.

Stout, Wesley W. *see* Stout, Wesley Winans.

Stout, Wesley Winans, 1890-
xStout, Wesley W.

Tanks Are Mighty Fine Things. Paladin Ent.
Tanks Are Mighty Fine Things. Sycamore Island.

Stout, William B. *see* Stout, William Bushnell.

Stout, William Bushnell, 1880-
xStout, William B.
So Away I Went!. Arno.

Stout, William F.
xStout, William F.
Almost Sure Convergence. Acad Pr.

Stoutamire, Albert.
xStoutamire, Albert.
Music of the Old South: Colony to Confederacy. Fairleigh Dickinson.

Stoutenburg, Adrien.
xStoutenburg, Adrien.
American Tall Tales. Penguin.
American Tall Tales. Viking Pr.
Greenwich Mean Time. U of Utah Pr.
Where to Now, Blue?. Schol Bk Serv.

Stoutenburgh, John L. *see* Stoutenburgh, John Leeds.

Stoutenburgh, John Leeds, 1921-
xStoutenburgh, John L.
ed. Dictionary of Arts & Crafts. Philos Lib.

Stovall, Floyd, 1896-
xStovall, Floyd.
Desire & Restraint in Shelley. Haskell.
Desire & Restraint in Shelley. Scholarly.
The Foreground of 'Leaves of Grass'. U Pr of Va.

Stove, D. C. *see* Stove, David C.

Stove, David C.
xStove, D. C.
Probability & Hume's Inductive Scepticism. Oxford U Pr.

Stovel, John A.
xStovel, John A.
Canada in the World Economy. Harvard U Pr.

Stover, John F.
xStover, John F.
American Railroads. U of Chicago Pr.

Stover, Leon E.
xStover, Leon E.
The Cultural Ecology of Chinese Civilization: Peasants & Elites in the Last of the Agrarian States. Universe.
Stonehenge: The Indo-European Heritage. Nelson-Hall.

Stover, Marjorie F. *see* Stover, Marjorie Filley.

Stover, Marjorie Filley.
xStover, Marjorie F.
Chad & the Elephant Engine. Atheneum.

Stover, Webster. *see* Stover, Webster Schultz.

Stover, Webster S. *see* Stover, Webster Schultz.

Stover, Webster Schultz, 1902-
xStover, Webster.
How to Become a College President. Am Librarians.
xStover, Webster S.
Alumni Stimulation by the American College President. AMS Pr.

Stow, John, 1525-1605
xStow, John.
Survey of London. Dutton.

Stow, K. R. *see* Stow, Kenneth R.

Stow, Kenneth R.
xStow, K. R.
Catholic Thought & Papal Jewry Policy: 1553-1593. Ktav.

Stowe, A. Monroe. *see* Stowe, Ancel Roy Monroe.

Stowe, Ancel R. *see* Stowe, Ancel Roy Monroe.

Stowe, Ancel Roy Monroe, 1882-1952
xStowe, A. Monroe.
English Grammar Schools in the Reign of Queen Elizabeth. Folcroft.
xStowe, Ancel R.
English Grammar Schools in the Reign of Queen Elizabeth. AMS Pr.

Stowe, Aurelia.
xStowe, Aurelia.

ed. Love Will Come: Stories of Romance.
Random.

Stowe, Harriet B. *see* Stowe, Harriet Elizabeth (Beecher).
Stowe, Harriet Beecher. *see* Stowe, Harriet Elizabeth
(Beecher).

Stowe, Harriet Elizabeth (Beecher), 1811-1896

xStowe, Harriet B.
Chimney-Corner. Arno.
The Pearl of Orr's Island. Irvington.
Pearl of Orr's Island. Scholarly.
Pearl of Orr's Island. Stowe-Day.
Uncle Tom's Cabin. Brown Bk.
Uncle Tom's Cabin. Dutton.
Uncle Tom's Cabin. Har-Row.
Uncle Tom's Cabin. Hippocrene Bks.
Uncle Tom's Cabin. HM.
Uncle Tom's Cabin. Macmillan.
Uncle Tom's Cabin. Braziller.
Uncle Tom's Cabin. Coward.
Uncle Tom's Cabin. Airmont.
Uncle Tom's Cabin. PB.
xStowe, Harriet Beecher.
Uncle Tom's Cabin. NAL.

Stowe, James L.
xStowe, James L.
Winter Stalk. PB.
Winter Stalk. S&S.

Stowe, Keith S., 1943-
xStowe, Keith S.
Ocean Science. Wiley.

Stowe, Leland, 1899-
xStowe, Leland.
Crusoe of Lonesome Lake. Random.

Stowe, Noel J.
xStowe, Noel J.
California Government: The Challenge of
Change. Glencoe.

Stowe, Richard S.
xStowe, Richard S.
Alexandre Dumas, Pere. Twayne.
Stowell, Charles J. *see* Stowell, Charles Jacob.

Stowell, Charles Jacob, 1883-
xStowell, Charles J.
The Journeymen Tailors' Union of America: A
Study in Trade Union Policy. Johnson Repr.
Stowell, John C. *see* Stowell, John Charles.

Stowell, John Charles, 1938-
xStowell, John C.
Carbanions in Organic Synthesis. Wiley.
Stowell, Robert F. *see* Stowell, Robert Frederick.

Stowell, Robert Frederick, 1920-
xStowell, Robert F.
Thoreau Gazetteer. Princeton U Pr.
Stowell, Roy S. *see* Stowell, Roy Sherman.

Stowell, Roy Sherman.
xStowell, Roy S.
The Significance of the Ring & the Book.
Folcroft.

Stowers, Carlton.
xStowers, Carlton.
Profiles of Christian Athletes Who Became...the
Overcomers. Word Bks.

Stowitschek, Joseph J.
xStowitschek, Joseph J.
Instructional Materials for Exceptional
Children: Selection, Management &
Adaptation. Aspen Systems.

Stoy, Joseph.
xStoy, Joseph.
Denotational Semantics: The Scott-Strachey
Approach to the Programming Language
Theory. MIT Pr.

Straayer, John A.
xStraayer, John A.

American Government, Policy &
Non-Decisions. Merrill.
American State & Local Government. Merrill.
Introduction to American Government &
Policy. Merrill.
Strachan, C. *see* Strachan, Charles.
Strachan, C. J. *see* Strachan, Colin John Logan.

Strachan, Charles.
xStrachan, C.
The Theory of Beta-Decay. Pergamon.

Strachan, Colin John Logan.
xStrachan, C. J.
ed. Surgical Sepsis. Grune.
Strachan, R. H. *see* Strachan, Robert Harvey.

Strachan, Robert Harvey, 1873-
xStrachan, R. H.
Soul of Modern Poetry. Kennikat.
Strachan-Davidson, James L. *see* Strachan-Davidson,
James Leigh.

Strachan-Davidson, James Leigh, 1843-1916
xStrachan-Davidson, James L.
Cicero & the Fall of the Roman Republic.
AMS Pr.
Cicero & the Fall of the Roman Republic.
Arno.

Strache, Wolf, 1910-
xStrache, Wolf.
Forms & Patterns in Nature. Pantheon.
xStrache, Wolfe.
Forms & Patterns in Nature. Saifer.
Strache, Wolfe. *see* Strache, Wolf.

Strachey, Alix.
xStrachey, Alix.
Unconscious Motives of War: A
Psychoanalytical Contribution. Verry.
Strachey, Giles L. *see* Strachey, Giles Lytton.

Strachey, Giles Lytton, 1880-1932
xStrachey, Giles L.
Characters & Commentaries. Greenwood.
xStrachey, Lytton.
Literary Essays. HarBraceJ.
Pope. Folcroft.
Queen Victoria. HarBraceJ.
Queen Victoria. HarBraceJ.

Strachey, John.
xStrachey, John.
India, Its Administration & Progress. AMS Pr.
Literature & Dialectical Materialism. Haskell.
Strachey, Lytton. *see* Strachey, Giles Lytton.
Strachey, Marjorie. *see* Strachey, Marjorie Colvile.

Strachey, Marjorie Colvile.
xStrachey, Marjorie.
The Fathers Without Theology. Braziller.

Strack, Jay.
xStrack, Jay.
Drugs & Drinking: The All American Cop-Out.
Nelson.

Stradley, William E.
xStradley, William E.
Administrator's Guide to an Individualized
Performance Results Curriculum. Ctr Appl
Res.
Supervising Student Teachers. Interstate.

Straeten, Edmund Sebastian Joseph Van Der, 1855-1934
xStraeten, Edmund Van Der.
History of the Violoncello, the Viol Da Gamba,
Their Precursors & Collateral Instruments.
AMS Pr.
Straeten, Edmund Van Der. *see* Straeten, Edmund
Sebastian Joseph Van Der.
Straetz, Ralph A. *see* Straetz, Ralph Arthur.

Straetz, Ralph Arthur.
xStraetz, Ralph A.
P.R. Politics in Cincinnati: Thirty-Two Years of
City Government Through Professional
Representation. NYU Pr.

Strage, Mark.
xStrage, Mark.

The Durable Fig Leaf: A Historical, Cultural,
Medical, Social, Literary, & Iconographic
Account of Man's Relations with His Penis.
Morrow.
Strahan, J. Dermot. *see* Strahan, Joseph Dermot.

Strahan, Joseph Dermot.
xStrahan, J. Dermot.
Color Atlas of Periodontology. Year Bk Med.
Strahan, Richard D. *see* Strahan, Richard Dobbs.

Strahan, Richard Dobbs, 1927-
xStrahan, Richard D.
Courts & the Schools. Prof Educ Pubn.

Strahler, Arthur N. *see* Strahler, Arthur Newell.

Strahler, Arthur Newell, 1918-

xStrahler, Arthur N.
The Earth Sciences. Har-Row.
Elements of Physical Geography. Wiley.

Geography & Man's Environment. Wiley.
Geologist's View of Cape Cod. Natural Hist.
Principles of Earth Science. Har-Row.

Straight, Henry Stephen, 1943-

xStraight, Stephen H.
The Acquisition of Maya Phonology: Variation
in Yucatec Child Language. Garland Pub.

Straight, Michael. *see* Straight, Michael Whitney.

Straight, Michael Whitney.
xStraight, Michael.
Trial by Television & Other Encounters. Devon
Pr.
Straight, Stephen H. *see* Straight, Henry Stephen.
Strain. *see* Strain, James J.

Strain, Barbara.
xStrain, Barbara.
Communication Skills. A-W.

Strain, James J.
xStrain.
Psychological Care of the Medically Ill: A
Primer in Liaison Psychiatry. ACC.

Strain, Lucille B.
xStrain, Lucille B.
Accountability in Reading Instruction. Merrill.

Strain, Phillip S.
xStrain, Phillip S.
Teaching Exceptional Children: Assessing &
Modifying Social Behavior. Acad Pr.
Strain, Samuel F. *see* Strain, Samuel Frederick.

Strain, Samuel Frederick, 1895-
xStrain, Samuel F.
From the Nolichucky to Memphis:
Reminiscences of a Tennessee Doctor.
Memphis St Univ.
Strain, Virginia S. *see* Strain, Virginia Safford.

Strain, Virginia Safford.
xStrain, Virginia S.
A Place of Your Own. McGraw.

Strait, Paul, 1940-
xStrait, Paul.
Cologne in the Twelfth Century. U Presses Fla.

Strait, Raymond.
xStrait, Raymond.
Star Babies. St Martin.
Strait, Treva A. *see* Strait, Treva Adams.

Strait, Treva Adams, 1909-
xStrait, Treva A.
The Price of Free Land. Lippincott.
Strakhov, N. M. *see* Strakhov, Nikolai Mikhailovich.

Strakhov, Nikolai Mikhailovich, 1900-
xStrakhov, N. M.
Principles of Lithogenesis. Plenum Pub.
Strakhovsky, Leonid I. *see* Strakhovsky, Leonid Ivan.

Strakhovsky, Leonid Ivan, 1898-1963
xStrakhovsky, Leonid I.

Craftsmen of the Word: Three Poets of
Modern Russia Gumilyov, Akhmatova,
Mandelstam. Greenwood.
Strand, Helen. *see* Strand, Helen R.
Strand, Helen R.
xStrand, Helen.
An Illustrated Guide to Medical Terminology.
Krieger.
Strand, Marcella M.
xStrand, Marcella M.
Clinical Laboratory Tests: A Manual for
Nurses. Mosby.
Strand, Mark, 1934-
xStrand, Mark.
ed. Contemporary American Poets: American
Poetry Since 1940. NAL.
The Late Hour. Atheneum.
The Monument. Ecco Pr.
Strand, Paul.
xStrand, Paul.
Ghana: An African Portrait. Aperture.
Strand, Thomas, 1944-
xStrand, Thomas.
Questions to Brecht. Thorp Springs.
Strandberg, Carl H.
xStrandberg, Carl H.
Aerial Discovery Manual. Wiley.
Strandness, D. E.
xStrandness, D. E.
Collateral Circulation in Clinical Surgery.
Saunders.
Strang, Barbara M. *see* Strang, Barbara M. H.
Strang, Barbara M. H.
xStrang, Barbara M.
ed. A History of English. Methuen Inc.
Strang, Celia.
xStrang, Celia.
Foster Mary McGraw
Strang, Clara. *see* Strang, Clara Weatherwax.
Strang, Clara Weatherwax.
xStrang, Clara.
Marching! Marching!. AMS Pr.
Strang, G. *see* Strang, William Gilbert.

Strang, Lewis. *see* Strang, Lewis Clinton.
Strang, Lewis Clinton, 1869-1935
xStrang, Lewis.
Celebrated Comedians of Light Opera &
Musical Comedy in America. Somerset Pub.
Strang, Paul D.
xStrang, Paul D.
The Complete Great Pyrenees. Howell Bk.
Strang, Ruth. *see* Strang, Ruth May.
Strang, Ruth M. *see* Strang, Ruth May.
Strang, Ruth May, 1895-
xStrang, Ruth.
Reading Diagnosis & Remediation. Intl
Reading.
ed. Understanding & Helping the Retarded
Reader. U of Ariz Pr.
xStrang, Ruth M.
Subject Matter in Health Education: An
Analysis & Evaluation of the Contents of
Some Courses of Study & Textbooks Dealing
with Health & Suggestions for Using Such an
Analysis. AMS Pr.
Strang, W. Gilbert. *see* Strang, William Gilbert.
Strang, William Gilbert.
xStrang, G.
An Analysis of the Finite Element Method.
P-H.
xStrang, Gilbert.
Linear Algebra & Its Applications. Acad Pr.
xStrang, W. Gilbert.
Linear Algebra & Its Applications. Acad Pr.
Strange, Edw. F. *see* Strange, Edward Fairbrother.
Strange, Edward Fairbrother, 1862-1929
xStrange, Edw. F.

Hokusai, the Old Man Mad with Painting..
Folcroft.
Strange, Maureen.
xStrange, Maureen.
Beginners. Doubleday.
Strange, Richard Le. *see* Le Strange, Richard.
Stranger, Joyce.
xStranger, Joyce.
The Fox at Drummers' Darkness. FS&G.
Stranges, Frank E.
xStranges, Frank E.
Stranger at the Pentagon. Intl Evang.
Stranks, C. J. *see* Stranks, Charles James.
Stranks, Charles James.
xStranks, C. J.
The Life & Writings of Jeremy Taylor.
Folcroft.
Stranks, D. R.
xStranks, D. R.
Chemistry: A Structural View. Cambridge U
Pr.
Stransky, Jan.
xStransky, Jan.
East Wind Over Prague. Greenwood.
Strassels, Paul N.
xStrassels, Paul N.
All You Need to Know About the IRS.
Random.
Strasser, Alex. *see* Strasser, Alexander.
Strasser, Alexander.
xStrasser, Alex.
The Work of the Science Film Maker. Focal
Pr.
The Work of the Science Film Maker.
Hastings.
Strasser, Daniel.
xStrasser, Daniel.
The Finances of Europe. Praeger.
Strasser, Federico.
xStrasser, Federico.
Functional Design of Metal Stampings. SME.
Strasser, Hermann, 1941-
xStrasser, Hermann.
The Normative Structure of Sociology:
Conservative & Emancipatory Themes in
Social Thought. Routledge & Kegan.
Strasser, Marland K. *see* Strasser, Marland Keith.
Strasser, Marland Keith, 1915-
xStrasser, Marland K.
Fundamentals of Safety Education. Macmillan.
Strassmann, W. Paul. *see* Strassmann, Wolfgang Paul.
Strassmann, Wolfgang Paul, 1926-
xStrassmann, W. Paul.
Housing & Building Technology in Developing
Countries. Mich St U Busn.
Strate, Jeffrey T.
xStrate, Jeffrey T.
Post-Military Coup Strategy in Uganda: Amin's
Early Attempts to Consolidate Political
Support in Africa. Ohio U Ctr Intl.
Stratemeyer, Florence B. *see* Stratemeyer, Florence
Barbara.
Stratemeyer, Florence Barbara, 1900-
xStratemeyer, Florence B.
Effective Use of Curriculum Materials: Study
of Units Relating to the Curriculum to Be
Included in the Professional Preparation of
Elementary Teachers. AMS Pr.
Stratemeyer Syndicate.
xStratemeyer Syndicate.
Nancy Drew & the Hardy Boys Meet Dracula.
G&D.
Stratford, Alan H.
xStratford, H. Alan.
Air Transport Economics in the Supersonic
Era. St Martin.
Stratford, H. Alan. *see* Stratford, Alan H.
Stratford, Philip.
xStratford, Philip.

Faith & Fiction: Creative Process in Greene &
Mauriac. U of Notre Dame Pr.
Stratford, William D., 1909-
xStratford, William D.
Some Restrictions & Limitations to the Free
Interstate Movement of Teachers. AMS Pr.
Stratman, Carl J. *see* Stratman, Carl Joseph.
Stratman, Carl Joseph, 1917-1972
xStratman, Carl J.
Britain's Theatrical Periodicals, 1720-1967: A
Bibliography. NY Pub Lib.
Dramatic Play Lists: 1591-1963. NY Pub Lib.
Restoration & Eighteenth-Century Theatre
Research: Bibliographical Guide, 1900-1968.
S Ill U Pr.
Stratmann, Franz H. *see* Stratmann, Franz Heinrich.
Stratmann, Franz Heinrich.
xStratmann, Franz H.
A Supplement of the Dictionary of the English
Language of the XII, XIII, XIV, & XV
Centuries. R West.
Stratonovich, R L.
xStratonovich, R. L.
Topics in the Theory of Random Noise.
Gordon.
Stratton, Clarence, 1880-1951
xStratton, Clarence.
Handbook of English. Gale.
Stratton, Dorothy C. *see* Stratton, Dorothy Constance.
Stratton, Dorothy Constance, 1899-
xStratton, Dorothy C.
Problems of Students in a Graduate School of
Education. AMS Pr.
Stratton, R. B. *see* Stratton, Royal B.
Stratton, Royal B., d. 1875
xStratton, R. B.
Captivity of the Oatman Girls. Irvington.
Straub, Peter.
xStraub, Peter.
Ghost Story. Coward.
Ghost Story. PB.
If You Could See Me Now. Coward.
If You Could See Me Now. PB.
Marriages. PB.
Straub, William F., 1926-
xStraub, William F.
The Lifetime Sports-Oriented Physical
Education Program. P-H.
Strauch, Larry, 1947-
xStrauch, Larry.
Coaching Football's Double Slot Attack. P-H.
Strauch, Michael J.
xStrauch, Michael J.
Pharmacology of Respiratory Therapy
Medications. Year Bk Med.
Straughn, James H. *see* Straughn, James Henry.
Straughn, James Henry, Bp, 1877-
xStraughn, James H.
Inside Methodist Union. Abingdon.
Straus, Bernard.
xStraus, Bernard.
The Maladies of Marcel Proust. Holmes &
Meier.
Straus, E. W. *see* Straus, Erwin Walter Maximilian.
Straus, Erwin Walter Maximilian.
xStraus, E. W.
Psychiatry & Philosophy. Springer-Verlag.
Straus, Franklin.
xStraus, Franklin.
Destructive David. Concordia.
Straus, Hal.
xStraus, Hal.
ed. The Gymnastics Guide. Anderson World.
Roller Skating Guide. Anderson World.
Straus, Hannah A. *see* Straus, Hannah Alice.
Straus, Hannah Alice.
xStraus, Hannah A.

Attitude of the Congress of Vienna Toward
Nationalism in Germany, Italy, & Poland.
AMS Pr.
Straus, Murray A. *see* Straus, Murray Arnold.
Straus, Murray Arnold, 1926-
xStraus, Murray A.
Family Measurement Techniques: Abstracts of
Published Instruments, 1935-1975. U of Minn
Pr.
Sociological Analysis: An Empirical Approach
Through Replication. Har-Row.
Straus, Oscar S. *see* Straus, Oscar Solomon.
Straus, Oscar Solomon, 1850-1926
xStraus, Oscar S.
American Spirit. Arno.
Straus, Robert.
xStraus, Robert.
Drinking in College. Greenwood.
Strausfeld, N. J. *see* Strausfeld, Nicholas James.
Strausfeld, Nicholas James, 1942-
xStrausfeld, N. J.
Atlas of an Insect Brain. Springer-Verlag.
Strauss, Anselm. *see* Strauss, Anselm L.
Strauss, Anselm A. *see* Strauss, Anselm L.
Strauss, Anselm L.
xStrauss, Anselm.
Images of the American City. Transaction Bks.
Negotiations: Varieties, Contexts, Processes &
Social Order. Jossey-Bass.
xStrauss, Anselm A.
Chronic Illness & the Quality of Life. Mosby.
xStrauss, Anselm L.
Professions, Work & Careers. Transaction Bks.
ed. Where Medicine Fails. Transaction Bks.
Strauss, Botho, 1944-
xStrauss, Botho.
Devotion. FS&G.
Strauss, C. T.
xStrauss, C. T.
Buddha & His Doctrine. Kennikat.
Strauss, David, 1937-
xStrauss, David.
Menace in the West: The Rise of French
Anti-Americanism in Modern Times.
Greenwood.
Strauss, David F. *see* Strauss, David Friedrich.
Strauss, David Friedrich, 1808-1874
xStrauss, David F.
The Christ of Faith & the Jesus of History: A
Critique of Schleiermacher's the Life of
Jesus. Fortress.
The Life of Jesus Critically Examined. Fortress.
Life of Jesus Critically Examined. Scholarly.
Strauss, H. William. *see* Strauss, Harry William.
Strauss, Harry William.
xStrauss, H. William.
An Atlas of Cardiovascular Nuclear Medicine:
Selected Case Studies. Mosby.
Cardiovascular Nuclear Medicine. Mosby.
Strauss, K.
xStrauss, K.
Applied Science in the Casting of Metals.
Pergamon.
Strauss, Larry. *see* Strauss, Lawrence.
Strauss, Lawrence.
xStrauss, Larry.
Opportunities for Retailers Selling Telephones
& Related Products. Telecom Lib.
Strauss, Lehman.
xStrauss, Lehman.
Demons, Yes - but Thank God for Good
Angels. Loizeaux.
End of This Present World. Zondervan.
Strauss, Leo.
xStrauss, Leo.

The Argument & the Action of Plato's Laws.
U of Chicago Pr.
The City & Man. U of Chicago Pr.
ed. History of Political Philosophy. Rand.
Natural Right & History. U of Chicago Pr.
Persecution & the Art of Writing. Greenwood.
Political Philosophy: Six Essays. Pegasus.
Socrates & Aristophanes. U of Chicago Pr.
Spinoza's Critique of Religion. Schocken.
Thoughts on Machiavelli. U of Chicago Pr.
Strauss, Maurice B. *see* Strauss, Maurice Benjamin.
Strauss, Maurice Benjamin, 1904-
xStrauss, Maurice B.
ed. Familiar Medical Quotations. Little.
Strauss, Richard H.
xStrauss, Richard H.
ed. Diving Medicine. Grune.
Strauss, Richard L.
xStrauss, Richard L.
Confident Children & How They Grow..
Tyndale.
Marriage Is for Love. Tyndale.
Strauss, Steven.
xStrauss, Steven.
The Pharmacist & the Law. Williams &
Wilkins.
Strauss, Victor.
xStrauss, Victor.
Graphic Arts Management. Bowker.
The Printing Industry: An Introduction to Its
Many Branches, Processes & Products.
Bowker.
Strauss, Walter A.
xStrauss, Walter A.
Descent & Return: The Orphic Theme in
Modern Literature. Harvard U Pr.
Strauss, Werner.
xStrauss, Werner.
Air Pollution Control. Wiley.
Straussman, Jeffrey D., 1945-
xStraussman, Jeffrey D.
The Limits of Technocratic Politics.
Transaction Bks.
Strausz-Hupe, Robert, 1903-
xStrausz-Hupe, Robert.
Geopolitics: The Struggle for Space & Power.
Arno.
Stravinskas, Peter M. *see* Stravinskas, Peter M. J.
Stravinskas, Peter M. J.
xStravinskas, Peter M.
The Church After the Council: A Primer for
Adults. Alba.
Stravinsky, Vera.
xStravinsky, Vera.
Fantastic Cities & Other Paintings. Godine.
Straw Dog.
xStraw Dog.
The Art of Ragtime Guitar. Schirmer Bks.
Improvising Blues Guitar. Schirmer Bks.
Improvising Rock Guitar. Schirmer Bks.
Slide Guitar. Schirmer Bks.
Strawson, P. F.
xStrawson, P. F.
Introduction to Logical Theory. Methuen Inc.
Strax, Philip.
xStrax; Philip.
Early Detection: Breast Cancer Is Curable.
NAL.
Strayer, George D. *see* Strayer, George Drayton.
Strayer, George Drayton, 1906-
xStrayer, George D.
Centralizing Tendencies in the Administration
of Public Education: A Study of Legislation
for Schools in North Carolina, Maryland, &
New York Since 1900. AMS Pr.
City School Expenditures: Variability &
Interrelations of the Principal Items. AMS Pr.
Strayer, J. R. *see* Strayer, Joseph Reese.
Strayer, Joseph R. *see* Strayer, Joseph Reese.

Strayer, Joseph Reese, 1904-
xStrayer, J. R.
Administration of Normandy Under Saint
Louis. Kraus Repr.
xStrayer, Joseph R.
Administration of Normandy Under Saint
Louis. AMS Pr.
Albigensian Crusades. Dial.
Feudalism. Krieger.
Mainstream of Civilization. HarBraceJ.
On the Medieval Origins of the Modern State.
Princeton U Pr.
The Reign of Philip the Fair. Princeton U Pr.
Studies in Early French Taxation. Greenwood.
Strayer, Martha.
xStrayer, Martha.
The D. A. R.: An Informal History.
Greenwood.
Strean, Herbert S.
xStrean, Herbert S.
Clinical Social Work: Theory & Practice. Free
Pr.
Crucial Issues in Psychotherapy. Scarecrow.
The Experience of Psychotherapy: A
Practitioner's Manual. Scarecrow.
Personality Theory & Social Work Practice.
Scarecrow.
The Social Worker As Psychotherapist.
Scarecrow.
xStrean, Herbet S.
Psychoanalytic Theory & Social Work Practice.
Free Pr.
Strean, Herbet S. *see* Strean, Herbert S.
Streater, Jack W.
xStreater, Jack W.
How to Use Integrated Circuit Logic Elements.
Sams.
Streatfeild, Noel.
xStreatfeild, Noel.
First Book of England. Watts.
First Book of the Opera. Watts.
The Thames: London's River. Garrard.
Streatfeild, Richard A. *see* Streatfeild, Richard
Alexander.
Streatfeild, Richard Alexander, 1866-1919
xStreatfeild, Richard A.
Handel. Greenwood.
Masters of Italian Music. Arno.
Strebel, Ralph F. *see* Strebel, Ralph Frederick.
Strebel, Ralph Frederick, 1894-
xStrebel, Ralph F.
The Nature of the Supervision of
Student-Teaching in Universities Using
Cooperating Public High Schools & Some
Conditioning Factors. AMS Pr.
Street, A. Edmund. *see* Street, Arthur Edmund.
Street, Alfred B. *see* Street, Alfred Billings.
Street, Alfred Billings, 1811?-1881
xStreet, Alfred B.
Woods & Waters: Or, the Saranacs & Racket.
Harbor Hill Bks.
Street, Arthur Edmund, 1855-
xStreet, A. Edmund.
Memoir of George Edmund Street, R. A.
1824-1881. Arno.
Street, Cecil J. *see* Street, Cecil John Charles.
Street, Cecil John Charles, 1884-
xStreet, Cecil J.
President Masaryk. Arno.
Street, David.
xStreet, David.
ed. Innovation in Mass Education. Krieger.
The Welfare Industry: Functionaries &
Recipients in Public Aid. Sage.
Street, Don. *see* Street, Donald.
Street, Donald.
xStreet, Don.

Reptiles of Northern & Central Europe. David & Charles.

Street, Donald M.
xStreet, Donald M.
A Cruising Guide to the Lesser Antilles. Norton.
The Ocean Sailing Yacht. Norton.
Seawise. Norton.

Street, G. S. *see* Street, George Slythe.

Street, George Slythe, 1867-1936
xStreet, G. S.
Autobiography of a Boy. Garland Pub.

Street, H. *see* Street, Harry.

Street, H. E. *see* Street, Herbert Edward.

Street, Harry.
xStreet, H.
Governmental Liability: A Comparative Study. Shoe String.

Street, Herbert Edward.
xStreet, H. E.
Plant Metabolism. Pergamon.
ed. Plant Tissue & Cell Culture. U of Cal Pr.

Street, James. *see* Street, James Howell.

Street, James H. *see* Street, James Harry.

Street, James Harry.
xStreet, James H.
ed. Technological Progress in Latin America: The Prospects for Overcoming Dependency. Westview.

Street, James Howell, 1903-1954
xStreet, James.
Good-Bye My Lady. Archway.
Good-Bye, My Lady. Lippincott.
Goodbye My Lady. PB.

Street, Philip, 1915-
xStreet, Philip.
Animal Migration & Navigation. Scribner.
Animal Partners & Parasites. Taplinger.
Animal Reproduction. Taplinger.
Animal Weapons. Taplinger.

Street, Robert L.
xStreet, Robert L.
The Analysis & Solution of Partial Differential Equations. Brooks-Cole.

Street, Roy F. *see* Street, Roy Frink.

Street, Roy Frink, 1898-
xStreet, Roy F.
Gestalt Completion Test: A Study of a Cross-Section of Intellect. AMS Pr.

Street Sesame. *see* Sesame Street.

Streeten, Paul.
xStreeten, Paul.
The Limits of Development Research. Pergamon.

Streeter, Sebastian F. *see* Streeter, Sebastian Ferris.

Streeter, Sebastian Ferris, 1810-1864
xStreeter, Sebastian F.
Papers Relating to the Early History of Maryland. AMS Pr.
Papers Relating to the Early History of Maryland. Arno.

Streeter, Tal.
xStreeter, Tal.
The Art of the Japanese Kite. Weatherhill.

Streeter, Victor L. *see* Streeter, Victor Lyle.

Streeter, Victor Lyle, 1909-
xStreeter, Victor L.
Fluid Mechanics. McGraw.

Streetman, B. *see* Streetman, Ben G.

Streetman, Ben G.
xStreetman, B.
Solid State Electronic Devices. P-H.

Streets, R. B. *see* Streets, Rubert Burley.

Streets, Rubert Burley.
xStreets, R. B.
Diseases of the Cultivated Plants of the Southwest. U of Ariz Pr.

Strehlow, H. *see* Strehlow, Hans.

Strehlow, Hans.
xStrehlow, H.

Fundamentals of Chemical Relaxation. Verlag Chemie.

Strehlow, Roger A.
xStrehlow, Roger A.
Fundamentals of Combustion. Krieger.

Streib, Gordon F. *see* Streib, Gordon Franklin.

Streib, Gordon Franklin.
xStreib, Gordon F.
Retirement in American Society: Impact & Process. Cornell U Pr.

Streightoff, Frank H. *see* Streightoff, Frank Hatch.

Streightoff, Frank Hatch, 1886-1935
xStreightoff, Frank H.
Distribution of Incomes in the United States. AMS Pr.

Streiker, Lowell D.
xStreiker, Lowell D.
The Cults Are Coming. Abingdon.

Streitwieser, Andrew.
xStreitwieser, Andrew.
Introduction to Organic Chemistry. Macmillan.

Strelka, Joseph, 1927-
xStrelka, Joseph P.
ed. Literary Criticism & Myth. Pa St U Pr.
ed. Literary Criticism & Psychology. Pa St U Pr.
ed. Literary Criticism & Sociology. Pa St U Pr.
ed. Patterns of Literary Style. Pa St U Pr.
ed. The Personality of the Critic. Pa St U Pr.
ed. Problems of Literary Evaluation. Pa St U Pr.
ed. Protest-Form-Tradition: Essays on German Exile Literature. U of Ala Pr.
ed. Theories of Literary Genre. Pa St U Pr.

Strelka, Joseph P. *see* Strelka, Joseph.

Stremler, Ferrel G.
xStremler, Ferrel G.
Introduction to Communication Systems. A W.

Stren, Patti.
xStren, Patti.
Hug Me. Har-Row.
illus. There's a Rainbow in My Closet. Har-Row.

Stren, Richard E.
xStren, Richard E.
Housing the Urban Poor in Africa: Policy, Politics, & Bureaucracy in Mombasa. U of Cal Intl St.

Streng. *see* Streng, Frederick J.

Streng, Alice. *see* Streng, Alice H.

Streng, Alice H.
xStreng, Alice.
Syntax, Speech & Hearing: Applied Linguistics for Teachers of Children with Language & Hearing Disabilities. Grune.

Streng, Frederick J.
xStreng.
Understanding Religious Life. Duxbury Pr.
xStreng, Frederick J.
Understanding Religious Life. Dickenson.

Streng, William D.
xStreng, William D.
Faith for Today: A Brief Outline of Christian Thought. Augsburg.

Stresau, Hermann, 1894-1964
xStresau, Hermann.
Thornton Wilder. Ungar.

Stresau, Marion.
xStresau, Marion.
Canoeing the Boundary Waters: The Account of One Family's Explorations. Signpost Bk Pub.

Strete, Craig.
xStrete, Craig K.
Paint Your Face on a Drowning in the River. Greenwillow.
xStrete, Craig Kee.
When Grandfather Journeys into Winter. Greenwillow.

Strete, Craig K. *see* Strete, Craig.

Strete, Craig Kee. *see* Strete, Craig.

Stretton, H. *see* Stretton, Hugh.

Stretton, Hesba, 1832-1911
xStretton, Hesba.
Little Meg's Children. Johnson Repr.

Stretton, Hugh.
xStretton, H.
Capitalism, Socialism and the Environment. Cambridge U Pr.
xStretton, Hugh.
Urban Planning in Rich & Poor Countries. Oxford U Pr.

Strevens, Peter.
xStrevens, Peter D.
ed. Five Inaugural Lectures. Oxford U Pr.

Strevens, Peter D. *see* Strevens, Peter.

Stribling, Mary Lou.
xStribling, Mary Lou.
Crafts from North American Indian Arts: Techniques, Designs & Contemporary Applications. Crown.

Stribling, T. S.
xStribling, T. S.
Store. Larlin Corp.

Stribling, T. S. *see* Stribling, Thomas Sigismund.

Stribling, Thomas Sigismund, 1881-1965
xStribling, T. S.
Clues of the Caribbees: Being Certain Criminal Investigations of Henry Poggioli, Ph. D.. Dover.
Forge. Scholarly.

Strich, Fritz, 1882-1963
xStrich, Fritz.
Goethe & World Literature. Greenwood.
Goethe & World Literature. Kennikat.

Strick, Anne.
xStrick, Anne.
Injustice for All. Putnam.

Strick, J. C.
xStrick, John C.
Canadian Public Finance. HR&W.

Strick, John C. *see* Strick, J. C.

Strickberger, Monroe W.
xStrickberger, Monroe W.
Genetics. Macmillan.

Strickland, A. G., 1925-
xStrickland, A. G.
How to Get Action: Key to Successful Management. P-H.

Strickland, Arvarh E.
xStrickland, Arvarh E.
History of the Chicago Urban League. U of Ill Pr.

Strickland, G. *see* Strickland, Geoffrey.

Strickland, Geoffrey.
xStrickland, G.
Stendhal: The Education of a Novelist. Cambridge U Pr.

Strickland, Glenn G., 1917-
xStrickland, Glenn G.
Genesis Revisited: A Revolutionary New Solution to the Mystery of Man's Origins. Dial.

Strickland, Reba C. *see* Strickland, Reba Carolyn.

Strickland, Reba Carolyn, 1904-
xStrickland, Reba C.
Religion & the State in Georgia in the Eighteenth Century. AMS Pr.

Strickland, Rennard.
xStrickland, Rennard.
Fire & the Spirits: Cherokee Law from Clan to Court. U of Okla Pr.
How to Get into Law School. Dutton.
The Indians in Oklahoma. U of Okla Pr.

Strickland, Ruth G. *see* Strickland, Ruth Gertrude.

Strickland, Ruth Gertrude, 1898-
xStrickland, Ruth G.

A Study of the Possibilities of Graphs As a
   Means of Instruction in the First Four
   Grades of the Elementary School. AMS Pr.
Strickland, Stephen P. *see* Strickland, Stephen Parks.
Strickland, Stephen Parks.
   xStrickland, Stephen P.
   Politics, Science, & Dread Disease: A Short
      History of the United States Medical
      Research Policy. Harvard U Pr.
Strickland, Walter G., 1850-1928
   xStrickland, Walter G.
   Dictionary of Irish Artists. Biblio Dist.
Strickland, Winifred G. *see* Strickland, Winifred Gibson.
Strickland, Winifred Gibson.
   xStrickland, Winifred G.
   Expert Obedience Training for Dogs.
      Macmillan.
   The German Shepherd Today. Macmillan.
   Obedience Class Instruction for Dogs: The
      Trainer's Manual. Macmillan.
Strickler, Timothy L.
   xStrickler, Timothy L.
   Functional Osteology & Myology of the
      Shoulder in the Chiroptera. S Karger.
Stride, G. T.
   xStride, G. T.
   Peoples & Empires of West Africa: West Africa
      in History 1000-1800. Holmes & Meier.
Striebel, C. *see* Striebel, Charlotte.
Striebel, Charlotte, 1929-
   xStriebel, C.
   Optimal Control of Discrete Time Stochastic
      Systems. Springer-Verlag.
Strieder, W. C. *see* Strieder, William.
Strieder, William.
   xStrieder, W. C.
   Variational Methods Applied to Problems of
      Diffusion & Reaction. Springer-Verlag.
Striganov, A. R. *see* Striganov, Arkadii Romanovich.
Striganov, Arkadii Romanovich.
   xStriganov, A. R.
   Tables of Spectral Lines of Neutral & Ionized
      Atoms. IFI Plenum.
Strik, J. J. *see* Strik, J. J. T. W. A.
Strik, J. J. T. W. A.
   xStrik, J. J.
   ed. Chemical Porphyria in Man. Elsevier.
Strike, Kenneth A.
   xStrike, Kenneth A.
   ed. Ethics & Educational Policy. Routledge &
      Kegan.
Striker, Fran.
   xStriker, Fran.
   The Lone Ranger & the Gold Robbery.
      Pinnacle Bks.
Striker, Fran. *see* Striker, Francis Hamilton.
Striker, Francis Hamilton, 1903-1962
   xStriker, Fran.
   The Lone Ranger & the Mystery Ranch. Am
      Repr-Rivercity Pr.
   The Lone Ranger & the Mystery Ranch.
      Pinnacle Bks.
   The Lone Ranger in Wild Horse Canyon. Am
      Repr-Rivercity Pr.
Striker, John. *see* Striker, John M.
Striker, John M.
   xStriker, John.
   Power Plays: How to Deal Like a Lawyer in
      Person-to-Person Confrontations & Get Your
      Rights. Rawson Wade.
   xStriker, John M.
   Super Threats: How to Sound Like a Lawyer &
      Get Your Rights on Your Own. Rawson
      Wade.
Strindberg, A. *see* Strindberg, August.
Strindberg, August.
   xStrindberg, A.
   Natives of Hemso. Am Scandinavian.
   xStrindberg, August.

By the Open Sea. Haskell.
The Confession of a Fool. Haskell.
The Dance of Death. Norton.
A Dream Play & Four Chamber Plays. Norton.
A Dream Play & Four Chamber Plays. U of
   Wash Pr.
Eight Expressionist Plays. NYU Pr.
Fair Haven & Foul Strand. Haskell.
Gustav Adolf. U of Wash Pr.
Historical Miniatures. Arno.
The Natives of Hemso. Liveright.
Open Letters to the Intimate Theater. U of
   Wash Pr.
The People of Hemso. Greenwood.
Pre-Inferno Plays: The Father, Lady Julie,
   Creditors, the Stronger, the Bond. Norton.
Pre-Inferno Plays: The Father, Lady Julie,
   Creditors, The Stronger, The Bond. U of
   Wash Pr.
The Vasa Trilogy: Master Olof, Gustav Vasa,
   Erik XIV. U of Wash Pr.
World Historical Plays. Am Scandinavian.
Striner, Herbert E.
   xStriner, Herbert E.
   An Analysis of the Bituminous Coal Industry
      in Terms of Total Energy Supply & a
      Synthetic Oil Program. Arno.
Stringer, Arthur J. *see* Stringer, Arthur John Arbuthnott.
Stringer, Arthur John Arbuthnott, 1874-1950
   xStringer, Arthur J.
   Loom of Destiny. Arno.
Stringer, L. *see* Stringer, Leslie.
Stringer, Leslie.
   xStringer, L.
   Teach Yourself German Reader. McKay.
Stringer, Michael, 1924-
   xStringer, Michael.
   Identification Guide to Cage & Aviary Birds.
      Arco.
Stringfellow, William.
   xStringfellow, William.
   Conscience & Obedience: The Politics of
      Romans 13 & Revelation 13 in the Light of
      the Second Coming. Word Bks.
   An Ethic for Christians & Other Aliens in a
      Strange Land. Word Bks.
Stripling, George W. *see* Stripling, George William
   Frederick.
Stripling, George William Frederick.
   xStripling, George W.
   The Ottoman Turks & the Arabs 1511-1574.
      Porcupine Pr.
Strippel, Dick.
   xStrippel, Dick.
   Amelia Earhart: The Myth & the Reality.
      Exposition.
Strober, Gerald.
   xStrober, Gerald.
   Billy Graham: His Life & Faith. PB.
Strober, Gerald S.
   xStrober, Gerald S.
   Graham: A Day in Billy's Life. Doubleday.
   Graham: A Day in Billy's Life. G K Hall.
Strobl, W. *see* Strobl, Walter M.
Strobl, Walter M., 1921-
   xStrobl, W.
   Crime Prevention Through Physical Security.
      Dekker.
Strobos, Robert.
   xStrobos, Robert.
   Treading Water. La State U Pr.
Strode, Hudson, 1892-
   xStrode, Hudson.
   Ultimates in the Far East: Travels in the Orient
      & India. HarBraceJ.
Strodt, Walter. *see* Strodt, Walter Charles.
Strodt, Walter Charles.
   xStrodt, Walter.

Principal Solutions of Ordinary Differential
   Equations in the Complex Domain. Am
   Math.
Stroebel, Leslie.
   xStroebel, Leslie.
   Dictionary of Contemporary Photography.
      Morgan.
Stroh, Guy W.
   xStroh, Guy W.
   American Ethical Thought. Nelson-Hall.
Strohecker, H. F. *see* Strohecker, Henry Frederick.
Strohecker, Henry Frederick.
   xStrohecker, H. F.
   The Grasshoppers of California (Orthoptera:
      Acridoidea). U of Cal Pr.
Strohmeier, W. *see* Strohmeier, Walter.
Strohmeier, Walter.
   xStrohmeier, W.
   Variable Stars. Pergamon.
Stroll, Avrum, 1921-
   xStroll, Avrum.
   ed. Epistemology: New Essays in the Theory of
      Knowledge. Greenwood.
   Introduction to Philosophy. HR&W.
Strom. *see* Strom, Robert D.
Strom, Maryalls G., 1946-
   xStrom, Maryalls G.
   Library Services to the Blind & Physically
      Handicapped. Scarecrow.
Strom, Robert D.
   xStrom.
   Teaching in the Slum School. Merrill.
   xStrom, Robert D.
   Growing Together: Parent & Child
      Development. Brooks-Cole.
   Parent & Child in Fiction. Brooks-Cole.
Stroman, Duane F.
   xStroman, Duane F.
   The Medical Establishment & Social
      Responsibility. Kennikat.
   The Quick Knife: Unnecessary Surgery U.S.A..
      Kennikat.
Stroman, J. H.
   xStroman, James H.
   Secretary's Manual. NAL.
Stroman, James H. *see* Stroman, J. H.
Stromberg, Ann.
   xStromberg, Ann H.
   ed. Women Working: Theories & Facts in
      Perspective. Mayfield Pub.
Stromberg, Ann H. *see* Stromberg, Ann.
Stromberg, Roland N., 1916-
   xStromberg, Roland N.
   After Everything: Western Intellectual History
      Since 1945. St Martin.
   Europe in the Twentieth Century. P-H.
   European Intellectual History Since 1789. P-H.
   An Intellectual History of Modern Europe.
      P-H.
Strome, Marshall.
   xStrome, Marshall.
   ed. Differential Diagnosis in Pediatric
      Otolaryngology. Little.
Strommen, Merton P.
   xStrommen, Merton P.
   Five Cries of Youth. Har-Row.
Stronach, David.
   xStronach, David.
   Pasargadae: A Report on the Excavations
      Conducted by the British Institute of Persian
      Studies from 1961 to 1963. Oxford U Pr.
Strong. *see* Strong, Merle Edward.
Strong, Ann L. *see* Strong, Ann Louise.
Strong, Ann Louise.
   xStrong, Ann L.
   Land Banking: European Reality, American
      Prospect. Johns Hopkins.
   Private Property & the Public Interest: The
      Brandywine Experience. Johns Hopkins.
Strong, Augustus H. *see* Strong, Augustus Hopkins.

Strong, Augustus Hopkins, 1836-1921
  xStrong, Augustus H.
     American Poets & Their Theology. Arno.
Strong, Bethany.
  xStrong, Bethany.
     First Love. BJ Pub Group.
     First Love. Parable Pr.
Strong, Bryan.
  xStrong, Bryan.
     Human Sexuality: Essentials. West Pub.
  xStrong, F. Bryan.
     The Marriage & Family Experience: A Text
        with Readings. West Pub.
Strong, Donald S. see Strong, Donald Stuart.
Strong, Donald Stuart.
  xStrong, Donald S.
     Organized Anti-Semitism in America: The Rise
        of Group Prejudice During the Decade
        1930-1940. Greenwood.
Strong, Emory. see Strong, Emory M.
Strong, Emory M.
  xStrong, Emory.
     Stone Age in the Great Basin. Binford.
     Stone Age on the Columbia River. Binford.
Strong, Eugenie. see Strong, Eugenie (Sellers).
Strong, Eugenie (Sellers).
  xStrong, Eugenie.
     Art in Ancient Rome. Greenwood.
Strong, F. Bryan. see Strong, Bryan.
Strong, J. P. see Strong, Jack Perry.
Strong, Jack Perry, 1928-
  xStrong, J. P.
     ed. Atherosclerosis in Primates. S Karger.
Strong, Josiah, 1847-1916
  xStrong, Josiah.
     Twentieth Century City. Arno.
Strong, June.
  xStrong, June.
     Where Are We Running?. Southern Pub.
Strong, Kendrick.
  xStrong, Kendrick.
     All the Master's Men. Christian Herald.
Strong, L. A. see Strong, Leonard Alfred George.
Strong, Leah A.
  xStrong, Leah A.
     Joseph Hopkins Twichell: Mark Twain's Friend
        & Pastor. U of Ga Pr.
Strong, Leonard Alfred George, 1896-1958
  xStrong, L. A.
     Personal Remarks. Folcroft.
Strong, Margaret K. see Strong, Margaret Kirkpatrick.
Strong, Margaret Kirkpatrick.
  xStrong, Margaret K.
     Public Welfare Administration in Canada.
        Patterson Smith.
Strong, Merle Edward.
  xStrong.
     Industrial, Labor & Community Relations.
        Delmar.
Strong, Roy. see Strong, Roy C.
Strong, Roy C.
  xStrong, Roy.
     Mary, Queen of Scots. Stein & Day.
Strong, S. J. see Strong, Stuart James.
Strong, Stuart James.
  xStrong, S. J.
     The Placenta in Twin Pregnancy. Pergamon.
Strong, W. E. see Strong, William Emerson.
Strong, William B.
  xStrong, William B.
     Atherosclerosis: Its Pediatric Aspects. Grune.
     An Introduction to Pediatric Cardiology. C C
        Thomas.
Strong, William D. see Strong, William Duncan.
Strong, William Duncan, 1899-1962
  xStrong, William D.

     Aboriginal Society in Southern California.
        Kraus Repr.
     Aboriginal Society in Southern California.
        Malki Mus Pr.
Strong, William Emerson, 1840-1891
  xStrong, W. E.
     Trip to the Yellowstone National Park in July,
        August, & September, 1875. U of Okla Pr.
Strongman, K. T.
  xStrongman, K. T.
     The Psychology of Emotion. Wiley.
Strony, Madeline S.
  xStrony, Madeline S.
     Refresher Course in Gregg Shorthand.
        McGraw.
Stroock, D. W. see Stroock, Daniel W.
Stroock, Daniel W.
  xStroock, D. W.
     Multi-Dimensional Diffusion Processes.
        Springer-Verlag.
Strooker, J. R. see Strooker, Jan R.
Strooker, Jan R.
  xStrooker, J. R.
     Introduction to Categories, Homological
        Algebra & Sheaf Cohomology. Cambridge U
        Pr.
Stroop, Juergen, 1895-
  xStroop, Jurgen.
     The Stroop Report: The Jewish Quarter of
        Warsaw Is No More!. Pantheon.
Stroop, Jurgen. see Stroop, Juergen.
Stroot, Violet R.
  xStroot, Violet R.
     Fluids & Electrolytes: A Practical Approach.
        Davis Co.
Strope, Nancy.
  xStrope, Nancy
     Cattle Country Cook Book: Basic Recipes East
        of the Cascades. Binford.
Stropus, Judith. see Stropus, Judith V.
Stropus, Judith V.
  xStropus, Judith.
     Stropus Guide to Auto Race Timing & Scoring.
        TAB Bks.
Strose, Susanne.
  xStrose, Susanne.
     Candle-Making. Sterling.
Stross, Brian.
  xStross, Brian.
     Pref. by Love in the Armpit: Tzeltal Tales of
        Love, Murder & Cannibalism. Mus Anthro
        Mo.
     The Origin & Evolution of Language. Wm C
        Brown.
Strother, Edward S.
  xStrother, Edward S.
     Effective Speaker. HM.
Strother, Elsie W.
  xStrother, Elsie W.
     Follow Through to Love. Bouregy.
Strother, Horatio T.
  xStrother, Horatio T.
     The Underground Railroad in Connecticut.
        Columbia U Pr.
Stroud, A. see Stroud, A. H.
Stroud, A. H.
  xStroud, A.
     Approximate Calculation of Multiple Integrals.
        P-H.
Stroud, Barry.
  xStroud, Barry.
     Hume. Routledge & Kegan.
Stroud, John.
  xStroud, John.
     European Transport Aircraft Since 1910. Aero.
Stroud, Parry. see Stroud, Parry Edmund.
Stroud, Parry Edmund, 1917-
  xStroud, Parry.

     Stephen Vincent Benet. Coll & U Pr.
     Stephen Vincent Benet. Twayne.
Stroud, Ronald. see Stroud, Ronald S.
Stroud, Ronald S.
  xStroud, Ronald.
     The Axones & Kyrbeis of Drakon & Solon. U
        of Cal Pr.
Strout, Alan M. see Strout, Alan Mayne.
Strout, Alan Mayne.
  xStrout, Alan M.
     Technological Change & United States Energy
        Consumption, 1939-1954. Arno.
Strout, Cushing.
  xStrout, Cushing.
     Pragmatic Revolt in American History: Carl
        Becker & Charles Beard. Cornell U Pr.
     The Pragmatic Revolt in American History:
        Carl Becker & Charles Beard. Greenwood.
Stroyen, William B.
  xStroyen, William B.
     Communist Russia & the Russian Orthodox
        Church 1943-1962. Intl Schol Bk Serv.
Struble, Mildred C. see Struble, Mildred Clara.
Struble, Mildred Clara, 1894-
  xStruble, Mildred C.
     Johnson Handbook. Folcroft.
Struble, Raimond A.
  xStruble, Raimond A.
     Nonlinear Differential Equations. Krieger.
     Nonlinear Differential Equations. McGraw.
Struckmeyer, O. K. see Struckmeyer, Otto Keith.
Struckmeyer, Otto Keith.
  xStruckmeyer, O. K.
     Croce & Literary Criticism. Folcroft.
Structural Optimization Symposium. see Structural
  Optimization Symposium, New York, 1974.
Structural Optimization Symposium, New York, 1974.
  xStructural Optimization Symposium.
     AMD: Proceedings. ASME.
Struening, Elmer L. see Struening, Elmer Louis.
Struening, Elmer Louis.
  xStruening, Elmer L.
     Handbook of Evaluation Research. Sage.
Struever, Stuart.
  xStruever, Stuart.
     Koster: Americans in Search of Their
        Prehistoric Past. NAL.
     ed. Prehistoric Agriculture. Natural Hist.
Strugatski, A. see Strugatski, Arkadi.
Strugatski, Arkadi.
  xStrugatski, A.
     The Final Circle of Paradise. DAW Bks.
  xStrugatski, Arkadi.
     Monday Begins on Saturday. DAW Bks.
Struhl, Paula R. see Struhl, Paula Rothenberg.
Struhl, Paula Rothenberg.
  xStruhl, Paula R.
     ed. Philosophy Now: An Introductory Reader.
        Random.
Struik, Dirk J. see Struik, Dirk Jan.
Struik, Dirk Jan, 1894-
  xStruik, Dirk J.
     Concise History of Mathematics. Dover.
Struk, D. S.
  xStruk, D. S.
     A Study of Vasyl' Stefanyk: The Pain at the
        Heart of Existence. Ukrainian Acad.
Strum, Philippa.
  xStrum, Philippa.
     The Supreme Court & Political Questions': A
        Study in Judicial Evasion. U of Ala Pr.
  xStrum, Phillippa.
     Presidential Power & American Democracy.
        Goodyear.
Strum, Phillippa. see Strum, Philippa.
Strumpel, Burkhard.
  xStrumpel, Burkhard.

ed. Economic Means for Human Needs: Social
    Indicators of Well-Being & Discontent. U of
    Mich Soc Res.
Strung, Norman.
    xStrung, Norman.
        Complete Hunter's Catalog. Lippincott.
        The Encyclopedia of Knives. Lippincott.
        Fishing the Headwaters of the Missouri.
          Mountain Pr.
        Spin-Fishing: The System That Does It All.
          Stein & Day.
        Whitewater!. Macmillan.
        Whitewater!. Macmillan.
Strunk, William.
    xStrunk, William, Jr.
        The Elements of Style. Macmillan.
Strunk, William, Jr. *see* Strunk, William.
Strupp, Hans H.
    xStrupp, Hans H.
        Introduction to Freud & Modern
          Psychoanalysis. Barron.
Struther, Jan.
    xStruther, Jan.
        Mrs. Miniver. HarBraceJ.
Struthers, Sally.
    xStruthers, Sally.
        Sally Struthers' Natural Beauty Book.
          Doubleday.
Strutt, Edward C.
    xStrutt, Edward C.
        Fra Filippo Lippi. AMS Pr.
        Fra Filippo Lippi. Scholarly.
Stryk, Lucien.
    xStryk, Lucien.
        Awakening. Swallow.
        Notes for a Guidebook. AMS Pr.
Stryker, Lloyd P. *see* Stryker, Lloyd Paul.
Stryker, Lloyd Paul, 1885-
    xStryker, Lloyd P.
        Andrew Johnson: A Study in Courage.
          Scholarly.
Stryker, Ruth. *see* Stryker, Ruth Perin.
Stryker, Ruth Perin.
    xStryker, Ruth.
        Rehabilitative Aspects of Acute & Chronic
          Nursing Care. Saunders.
Stuart. *see* Stuart, Frank P.
Stuart, Ann. *see* Stuart, Anne.
Stuart, Anna. *see* Stuart, Anna Maude.
Stuart, Anna Maude.
    xStuart, Anna.
        Bread Plates & Platters. Wallace-Homestead.
Stuart, Anne.
    xStuart, Ann.
        Cameron's Landing. Dell.
Stuart, Darwin G.
    xStuart, Darwin G.
        Systematic Urban Planning. Praeger.
Stuart, Diana.
    xStuart, Diane.
        Destiny's Bride. Berkley Pub.
Stuart, Diane. *see* Stuart, Diana.
Stuart, Dorothy M. *see* Stuart, Dorothy Margaret.
Stuart, Dorothy Margaret.
    xStuart, Dorothy M.
        Boy Through the Ages. Gale.
        The Boy Through the Ages. Norwood Edns.
        Horace Walpole. Folcroft.
Stuart, Francis, 1902-
    xStuart, Francis.
        A Hole in the Head. Longship Pr.
Stuart, Frank P.
    xStuart.
        Immunological Tolerance & Enhancement.
          Univ Park.
Stuart, Frederic. *see* Stuart, Fredric.
Stuart, Frederick. *see* Stuart, Fredric.
Stuart, Fredric.
    xStuart, Frederic.

The Effects of Television on the Motion
    Picture & Radio Industries. Arno.
    xStuart, Frederick.
        Fortran Programming. Wiley.
    xStuart, Fredric.
        Introduction to Standard COBOL
          Programming. HarBraceJ.
Stuart, Gene S.
    xStuart, Gene S.
        Secrets from the Past. Natl Geog.
Stuart, Jesse, 1907-
    xStuart, Jesse.
        Head O' W-Hollow. U Pr of Ky.
        Head O'w-Hollow. Arno.
        If I Were Seventeen Again & Other Essays.
          Archer Edns.
        The Kingdom Within: A Spiritual
          Autobiography. McGraw.
        Lost Sandstones & Lonely Skies & Other
          Essays. Archer Edns.
        Men of the Mountains. U Pr of Ky.
        Old Ben. McGraw.
        Penny's Worth of Character. McGraw.
        A Ride with Huey the Engineer. Landfall Pr.
    xStuart, Jessie.
        Taps for Private Tussie. Mockingbird Bks.
Stuart, Jessie. *see* Stuart, Jesse.
Stuart, John, 1749-1823
    xStuart, John.
        Memoir of Indian Wars & Other Occurrences.
          McClain.
Stuart, Lyle.
    xStuart, Lyle.
        Mary Louise. Citadel Pr.
Stuart, M. *see* Stuart, Moses.
Stuart, M. S. *see* Stuart, Merah Steven.
Stuart, Malcolm.
    xStuart, Malcolm.
        ed. The Encyclopedia of Herbs & Herbalism.
          G&D.
Stuart, Merah Steven, 1878-
    xStuart, M. S.
        An Economic Detour: A History of Insurance
          in the Lives of American Negroes. Johnson
          Repr.
Stuart, Micheline.
    xStuart, Micheline.
        The Tarot Path to Self-Development.
          Shambhala Pubns.
Stuart, Moses, 1780-1852
    xStuart, M.
        Conscience & the Constitution: With Remarks
          on the Recent Speech of the Hon. Daniel
          Webster in the Senate of the United States
          on the Subject of Slavery. Arno.
Stuart, Paul, 1943-
    xStuart, Paul.
        The Indian Office: Growth & Development of
          an American Institution, 1865-1900. Univ
          Microfilms.
Stuart, R. D.
    xStuart, R. D.
        Introduction to Fourier Analysis. Methuen Inc.
Stuart, Reginald C.
    xStuart, Reginald C.
        The Half-Way Pacifist: Thomas Jefferson's
          View of War. U of Toronto Pr.
Stuart, Richard B.
    xStuart, Richard B.
        Act Thin, Stay Thin: New Ways to Lose
          Weight & Keep It off. Norton.
Stuart, Ruth. *see* Stuart, Ruth (McEnery).
Stuart, Ruth (McEnery), 1856-1917
    xStuart, Ruth.
        Aunt Amity's Silver Wedding, & Other Stories.
          Arno.
    xStuart, Ruth M.

A Golden Wedding, & Other Tales. Mss Info.
A Golden Wedding & Other Tales. Somerset
    Pub.
Stuart, Ruth M. *see* Stuart, Ruth (McEnery).
Stuart, Sandra L. *see* Stuart, Sandra Lee.
Stuart, Sandra Lee.
    xStuart, Sandra L.
        The Pink Palace: Behind Closed Doors at the
          Beverly Hills Hotel. Lyle Stuart.
Stuart, Simon, 1930-
    xStuart, Simon.
        New Phoenix Wings: Reparation in Literature.
          Routledge & Kegan.
Stuart, V. A.
    xStuart, V. A.
        The Cannons of Lucknow. Pinnacle Bks.
Stuart, W. J.
    xStuart, W. J.
        Forbidden Planet. Gregg.
Stuart-Harris, Charles H. *see* Stuart-Harris, Charles
    Herbert.
Stuart-Harris, Charles Herbert.
    xStuart-Harris, Charles H.
        Influenza: The Viruses & the Disease. Psg Pub.
Stuart-Kotze, R.
    xStuart-Kotze, Robin.
        Introduction to Organizational Behavior: A
          Situational Approach. Reston.
Stuart-Kotze, Robin. *see* Stuart-Kotze, R.
Stub, Holger R. *see* Stub, Holger Richard.
Stub, Holger Richard.
    xStub, Holger R.
        Sociology of Education: A Sourcebook. Dorsey.
Stubberud, Allen R.
    xStubberud, Allen R.
        Analysis & Synthesis of Linear Time-Variable
          Systems. U of Cal Pr.
Stubbes, Phillip.
    xStubbes, Phillip.
        The Anatomie of Abuses. Walter J Johnson.
Stubblebine, James H.
    xStubblebine, James H.
        Duccio Di Buoninsegna & His School.
          Princeton U Pr.
Stubbs, Charles W. *see* Stubbs, Charles William.
Stubbs, Charles William, Bp. of Truro, 1845-1912
    xStubbs, Charles W.
        Charles Kingsley & the Christian Social
          Movement. AMS Pr.
        The Christ of English Poetry. Folcroft.
Stubbs, George.
    xStubbs, George.
        The Anatomy of the Horse. Dover.
        The Anatomy of the Horse. Peter Smith.
        Anatomy of the Horse. Saifer.
Stubbs, Jean, 1926-
    xStubbs, Jean.
        By Our Beginnings. NAL.
        By Our Beginnings. St Martin.
        Dear Laura. Stein & Day.
        The Golden Crucible. G K Hall.
        The Golden Crucible. Stein & Day.
        Painted Face. Stein & Day.
Stubbs, Joanna.
    xStubbs, Joanna.
        Hannah. Andre Deutsch.
Stubbs, John C. *see* Stubbs, John Caldwell.
Stubbs, John Caldwell.
    xStubbs, John C.
        ed. Federico Fellini: A Guide to References &
          Resources. G K Hall.
Stubbs, Marcia.
    xStubbs, Marcia.
        The Little, Brown Reader. Little.
Stubbs, Michael.
    xStubbs, Michael.

ed. Explorations in Classroom Observation. Wiley.

Language & Literacy: The Sociolinguistics of Reading & Writing. Routledge & Kegan.

Stubbs, William.
xStubbs, William.
ed. The Constitutional History of England. U of Chicago Pr.
Germany in the Early Middle Ages, 476-1250. AMS Pr.
Germany in the Early Middle Ages, 476-1250. Fertig.
Germany in the Later Middle Ages, 1200-1500. AMS Pr.
Germany in the Later Middle Ages, 1200-1500. Fertig.
Historical Introductions to the Rolls Series. Haskell.

Stubenrauch, Bob.
xStubenrauch, Bob.
Where Freedom Grew. Dodd.

Stuchlik, Milan.
xStuchlik, Milan.
Life on a Half Share: Mechanisms of Social Recruitment Among the Mapuche of Southern Chile. St Martin.

Stuckenschmidt, H. H. *see* Stuckenschmidt, Hans Heinz.
Stuckenschmidt, Hans H. *see* Stuckenschmidt, Hans Heinz.

Stuckenschmidt, Hans Heinz, 1901-
xStuckenschmidt, H. H.
Arnold Schoenberg. Schirmer Bks.
Twentieth Century Music. McGraw.
xStuckenschmidt, Hans H.
Arnold Schoenberg. Greenwood.

Stuckey, Gilbert B.
xStuckey, Gilbert B.
Evidence for the Law Enforcement Officer. McGraw.
Procedures in the Justice System. Merrill.

Stuckey, Ronald L.
xStuckey, Ronald L.
Intro. by Development of Botany in Selected Regions of North America Before 1900: An Original Anthology. Arno.

Stuckey, W. J. *see* Stuckey, William Joseph.

Stuckey, William Joseph.
xStuckey, W. J.
Caroline Gordon. Twayne.
The Pulitzer Prize Novels: A Critical Backward Look. U of Okla Pr.

Stucki, Margaret E.
xStucki, Margaret E.
The Revolutionary Mission of Modern Art: Or Crud and Other Essays on Art. Birds' Meadow Pub.

Student X.
xStudent X.
Professors & Other Inmates. Arlington Hse.

Students, Expressive Arts Dept., Sogeri National High School, Papua New Guinea. *see* Sogeri Senior High School. Expressive Arts Department.

Studley, Vance.
xStudley, Vance.
The Art & Craft of Handmade Paper. Van Nos Reinhold.
Left-Handed Calligraphy. Van Nos Reinhold.
Making Artist's Tools. Van Nos Reinhold.
The Woodworker's Book of Wooden Toys: How to Make Toys That Whirr, Bob & Make Musical Sounds. Van Nos Reinhold.

Studt, Ward B.
xStudt, Ward B.
Medicine in the Intermountain West: A History of Health Care in Rural Areas of the West. Olympus Pub Co.

Study Commission on Pharmacy.
xTheStudy Commission on Pharmacy.

Pharmacists for the Future. Health Admin Pr.

Study Commission on Undergraduate Education and the Education of Teachers.
xStudy Commission on Undergraduate Education & the Education of Teachers.
Teacher Education in the United States: The Responsibility Gap. U of Nebr Pr.

Stueart, Robert D.
xStueart, Robert D.
Library Management. Libs Unl.

Stuebe, Charles.
xStuebe, Charles.
ed. A Directory of Resources for Aging, Gerontology, & Retirement. Minn Scholarly.

Stuebe, Isabel C. *see* Stuebe, Isabel Combs.

Stuebe, Isabel Combs, 1943-
xStuebe, Isabel C.
The Life & Works of William Hodges. Garland Pub.

Stuempfle, Herman G.
xStuempfle, Herman G.
Preaching Law & Gospel. Fortress.

Stuenkel, Omar.
xStuenkel, Omar.
We Are One in the Spirit: How to Receive & Use the Holy Spirit's Gifts. Augsburg.

Stuenkel, Walter W., 1912-
xStuenkel, Walter W.
Books of the Old Testament. Concordia.

Stuhlmacher, Peter.
xStuhlmacher, Peter.
Historical Criticism & Theological Interpretation of Scripture: Towards a Hermeneutic of Concent. Fortress.

Stuhlmueller, Carroll.
xStuhlmueller, Carroll.
The Psalms. Franciscan Herald.
Thirsting for the Lord: Essays in Biblical Spirituality. Alba.
Thirsting for the Lord: Essays in Biblical Spirituality. Doubleday.

Stuhr, Walter M.
xStuhr, Walter M.
The Public Style: A Study of the Community Participation of Protestant Ministers. Ctr Sci Study.

Stull, Dalene W. *see* Stull, Dalene Workman.

Stull, Dalene Workman.
xStull, Dalene W.
Spatter of Pearls. Golden Quill.

Stull, Sally.
xStull, Sally.
What You Can Do with a Horse. A S Barnes.

Stultz, Newell M. *see* Stultz, Newell Maynard.

Stultz, Newell Maynard.
xStultz, Newell M.
Afrikaner Politics in South Africa, 1934-1948. U of Cal Pr.

Stumbo, C. R. *see* Stumbo, Charles Raymond.

Stumbo, Charles Raymond, 1914-
xStumbo, C. R.
Thermobacteriology in Food Processing. Acad Pr.

Stumm, Erwin C. *see* Stumm, Erwin Charles.

Stumm, Erwin Charles, 1908-
xStumm, Erwin C.
Silurian & Devonian Corals of the Falls of the Ohio. Geol Soc.

Stumm, W. *see* Stumm, Werner.

Stumm, Werner.
xStumm, W.
Aquatic Chemistry: Introduction Emphasizing Chemical Equalibria in Natural Waters. Wiley.
xStumm, Werner.
Aquatic Chemistry: An Introduction Emphasizing Chemical Equilibria in Natural Waters. Wiley.

Stumme, John R., 1942-
xStumme, John R.

Socialism in Theological Perspective: A Study of Paul Tillich, 1918-1933. Scholars Pr Ca.

Stumpf, Harry P.
xStumpf, Harry P.
Community Politics & Legal Services: The Other Side of the Law. Sage.

Stumpf, Samuel E. *see* Stumpf, Samuel Enoch.

Stumpf, Samuel Enoch, 1918-
xStumpf, Samuel E.
Democratic Manifesto: The Impact of Dynamic Christianity Upon Public Life & Government. Vanderbilt U Pr.
Elements of Philosophy: An Introduction. McGraw.

Stumphauzer, Jerome S.
xStumphauzer, Jerome S.
Progress in Behavior Therapy with Delinquents. C C Thomas.

Stunkard, Albert J., 1922-
xStunkard, Albert J.
I Almost Feel Thin. Bull Pub.
The Pain of Obesity. Bull Pub.

Stupak, Ronald J.
xStupak, Ronald J.
Understanding Political Science: The Arena of Power. Alfred Pub.

Stuper, Andrew J.
xStuper, Andrew J.
Computer Assisted Studies of Chemical Structure & Biological Function. Wiley.

Stupka, Arthur.
xStupka, Arthur.
Notes on the Birds of Great Smoky Mountains National Park. U of Tenn Pr.

Stupochenko, Evgenii Vladimirovich.
xStupochenko, Y. V.
Relaxation in Shock Waves. Springer-Verlag.

Stupochenko, Y. V. *see* Stupochenko, Evgenii Vladimirovich.

Sturcken, H. Tracy.
xSturcken, H. Tracy.
Don Juan Manuel. Twayne.

Sturdevant, Clifford. *see* Sturdevant, Clifford M.

Sturdevant, Clifford M.
xSturdevant, Clifford.
Art & Science of Operative Dentistry. McGraw.

Sturdivant, F. D. *see* Sturdivant, Frederick D.

Sturdivant, Frederick D.
xSturdivant, F. D.
Ghetto Marketplace. Free Pr.

Sturdy, David.
xSturdy, David.
Historic Monuments of England & Wales. Biblio Dist.

Sturdza, Michel.
xSturdza, Michel.
Suicide of Europe: Memoirs of Prince Michel Sturdza. Western Islands.

Sturgeon, Kelso.
xSturgeon, Kelso.
Guide to Sports Betting. NAL.

Sturgeon, Theodore.
xSturgeon, Theodore.
The Cosmic Rape. Gregg.
Cosmic Rape. PB.
The Dreaming Jewels. Amereon Ltd.
More Than Human. Garland Pub.
Starshine. BJ Pub Group.
Sturgeon in Orbit. BJ Pub Group.
A Touch of Strange. DAW Bks.

Sturges, Lena. *see* Sturges, Lena E.

Sturges, Lena E.
xSturges, Lena.
ed. Preserving Foods. Oxmoor Hse.

Sturges, Patricia P. *see* Sturges, Patricia Patterson.

Sturges, Patricia Patterson, 1930-
xSturges, Patricia P.

The Endless Chain of Nature: Experiment at
  Hubbard Brook. Westminster.
Sturgess, Rosemary.
  xSturgess, Rosemary.
  The Baby Book. David & Charles.
Sturgis, Alice F. *see* Sturgis, Alice Fleenor.
Sturgis, Alice Fleenor.
  xSturgis, Alice F.
  Learning Parliamentary Procedure. McGraw.
Sturgis, Margie.
  xSturgis, Margie.
  Let the Record Show: Memoirs of a Parole
    Board Member. Exposition.
Sturgis, Russell.
  xSturgis, Russell.
  Annotated Bibliography of Fine Art. Longwood
    Pr.
  European Architecture: A Historical Study.
    Longwood Pr.
Sturkie, P. D. *see* Sturkie, Paul D.
Sturkie, Paul D.
  xSturkie, P. D.
  ed. Avian Physiology. Springer-Verlag.
Sturm, Mary M. *see* Sturm, Mary Mark.
Sturm, Mary Mark.
  xSturm, Mary M.
  Guide to Modern Clothing. McGraw.
Sturmthal, Adolf. *see* Sturmthal, Adolf Fox.
Sturmthal, Adolf Fox.
  xSturmthal, Adolf.
  ed. White-Collar Trade Unions: Contemporary
    Developments in Industrialized Societies. U
    of Ill Pr.
Sturrock, John.
  xSturrock, John.
  Paper Tigers: The Ideal Fictions of Jorge Luis
    Borges. Oxford U Pr.
Stursberg, Peter.
  xStursberg, Peter.
  Lester Pearson & the Dream of Unity.
    Doubleday.
Sturtevant, Alfred H. *see* Sturtevant, Alfred Henry.
Sturtevant, Alfred Henry.
  xSturtevant, Alfred H.
  Introduction to Genetics. Dover.
Sturtevant, David R. *see* Sturtevant, David Reeves.
Sturtevant, David Reeves.
  xSturtevant, David R.
  Popular Uprisings in the Philippines. Cornell U
    Pr.
Sturtevant, E. H. *see* Sturtevant, Edgar Howard.
Sturtevant, Edgar H. *see* Sturtevant, Edgar Howard.
Sturtevant, Edgar Howard, 1875-1952
  xSturtevant, E. H.
  The Pronunciation of Greek & Latin. Ares.
  xSturtevant, Edgar H.
  An Introduction to Linguistic Science. AMS
    Pr.
  The Pronunciation of Greek & Latin.
    Greenwood.
Sturtevant, Sarah M. *see* Sturtevant, Sarah Martha.
Sturtevant, Sarah Martha.
  xSturtevant, Sarah M.
  A Personnel Study of Deans of Girls in High
    Schools. AMS Pr.
  A Personnel Study of Deans of Women in
    Teachers Colleges & Normal Schools. AMS
    Pr.
Stuteville, John R.
  xStuteville, John R.
  Marketing in a Consumer-Oriented Society.
    Wadsworth Pub.
Stutley, Margaret, 1917-
  xStutley, Margaret.
  Ancient Indian Magic & Folklore: An
    Introduction. Great Eastern.
Stutts, Ann.
  xStutts, Ann.

Women's Basketball. Goodyear.
Stutz, Robert M.
  xStutz, Robert M.
  ed. Exploring Behavior & Experience: Readings
    in General Psychology. P-H.
Stwertka, Eve.
  xStwertka, Eve.
  Marijuana. Watts.
  Steel Mill. Watts.
Styan, J. L.
  xStyan, J. L.
  Chekhov in Performance: A Commentary of
    the Major Plays. Cambridge U Pr.
  Dark Comedy: The Development of Modern
    Comic Tragedy. Cambridge U Pr.
  Drama, Stage & Audience. Cambridge U Pr.
  Dramatic Experience. Cambridge U Pr.
Stych, F. S. *see* Stych, Franklin Samuel.
Stych, Franklin Samuel, 1916-
  xStych, F. S.
  How to Find Out About Italy. Pergamon.
Stycos, J. Mayone.
  xStycos, J. Mayone.
  ed. Clinics, Contraception & Communication:
    Evaluation Studies of Family Planning
    Programs in Four Latin American Countries.
    Irvington.
Styers, John.
  xStyers, John.
  Cold Steel. Paladin Ent.
Stykolt, Stefan.
  xStykolt, Stefan.
  Economic Analysis & Combines Policy: A
    Study of Intervention into the Canadian
    Market for Tires. U of Toronto Pr.
Styne, Dorothy Van. *see* Van Alstyne, Dorothy.
Styron, William.
  xStyron, William.
  Confessions of Nat Turner. NAL.
  Confessions of Nat Turner. Random.
  In the Clap Shack & the Long March. NAL.
  Lie Down in Darkness. NAL.
  Long March. Random.
  Sophie's Choice. Bantam.
  Sophie's Choice. Random.
Suares, J. C. *see* Suares, Jean-Claude.
Suares, Jean-Claude.
  xSuares, J. C.
  Literary Cat. Berkley Pub.
  Literary Cat. Berkley Pub.
  The Literary Dog. Berkley Pub.
  xSuares, Jean-Claude.
  The Illustrated Cat. Crown.
Subba Rao, T. V. *see* Subba Rao, Tirupasoor Venkata.
Subba Rao, Tirupasoor Venkata, 1891-1958
  xSubba Rao, T. V,
  Studies in Indian Music. Asia.
Subercaseaux, Benjamin, 1902-
  xSubercaseaux, Benjamin.
  Chile, A Geographic Extravaganza. Hafner.
Subitzky, Seymour.
  xSubitzky, Seymour.
  ed. Geology of Selected Areas in New Jersey
    & Eastern Pennsylvania & Guidebook of
    Excursions. Rutgers U Pr.
Subotnick, Steven I.
  xSubotnick, Steven I.
  Cures for Common Running Injuries. Anderson
    World.
Subramani.
  xSubramani.
  ed. The Indo-Fijian Experience. U of
    Queensland Pr.
Subramaniam, K.
  xSubramaniam, K.
  Brahmin Priest of Tamil Nadu. Halsted Pr.
Succop, Margaret P. *see* Succop, Margaret Phillips.
Succop, Margaret Phillips, 1914-
  xSuccop, Margaret P.

Twenty-Four Sonnets & Other Poems. Windy
  Row.
Suchar, Elizabeth W.
  xSuchar, Elizabeth W.
  Financial Aid Guide for College. Monarch Pr.
Suchenwirth, Richard, 1896-
  xSuchenwirth, Richard.
  Command and Leadership in the German Air
    Force. Arno.
  Historical Turning Points in the German Air
    Force War Effort. Arno.
  Pocket Book of Clinical Neurology. Year Bk
    Med.
Sucher, Harry V.
  xSucher, Harry V.
  Simplified Boatbuilding: The V-Bottom Boat.
    Norton.
Suchet, J. P. *see* Suchet, Jacques Paul.
Suchet, Jacques Paul, 1923-
  xSuchet, J. P.
  Crystal Chemistry & Semiconduction in
    Transition Metal Binary Compounds. Acad
    Pr.
Suchlicki, Jaime.
  xSuchlicki, Jaime.
  ed. Cuba, Castro, & Revolution. U of Miami
    Pr.
Suchman, Edward A. *see* Suchman, Edward Allen.
Suchman, Edward Allen.
  xSuchman, Edward A.
  Evaluative Research: Principles & Practice in
    Public Service & Social Action Programs.
    Russell Sage.
Suckling, Norman.
  xSuckling, Norman.
  Faure. Greenwood.
  Faure. Hyperion Conn.
  Paul Valery & the Civilized Mind. Greenwood.
Suckow, Miriam P.
  xSuckow, Miriam P.
  Social Welfare & Health Expenditures in New
    York City: A Comparison of Expenditures for
    Social Welfare & Organized Health Services
    & the Sources of Their Financing. Comm
    Coun Great NY.
Suckow, Ruth, 1892-1960
  xSuckow, Ruth.
  Country People. Arno.
  Some Others & Myself: Seven Stories & a
    Memoir. Greenwood.
Suda, J. *see* Suda, Jyoti Prasad.
Suda, Jyoti Prasad.
  xSuda, J.
  Religions in India: A Study of Their Essential
    Unity. Humanities.
Sudakov, N. *see* Sudakov, V. N.
Sudakov, V. N.
  xSudakov, N.
  Geometric Problems in the Theory of
    Infinite-Dimensional Probability
    Distributions, V. Am Math.
Sudan Law Reports: Civil Cases.
  xFaculty of Law, University of Khartoum.
  Sudan Law Reports, 1900-1940. Oceana.
Sudarshan, E. C. *see* Sudarshan, E. C. G.
Sudarshan, E. C. G.
  xSudarshan, E. C.
  Classical Dynamics: A Modern Perspective.
    Wiley.
  ed. The Past Decade in Particle Theory.
    Gordon.

Suddick, Tom.
  xSuddick, Tom.
  A Few Good Men. Avon.

Sudduth, Thomas D. *see* Sudduth, Tom.

Sudduth, Tom.

xSudduth, Thomas D.
  Northern Colorado Ski Tours. Touchstone Pr
  Ore.

xSudduth, Tom.
  Colorado Front Range Ski Tours. Touchstone
  Pr Ore.

Sudilovsky, A. see Sudilovsky, Abraham.
Sudilovsky, Abraham.
  xSudilovsky, A.
    ed. Predictability in Psychopharmacology:
    Preclinical & Clinical Correlations. Raven.

Sudman, Seymour.
  xSudman, Seymour.
    Applied Sampling. Acad Pr.
    Consumer Panels, 1980. Am Mktg.
    Response Effects in Surveys: A Review &
    Synthesis. NORC.

Sudnow, David.
  xSudnow, David.
    Passing On: The Social Organization of Dying.
    P-H.
    Talk's Body: A Meditation Between Two
    Keyboards. Knopf.
    Talk's Body: A Meditation Between Two
    Keyboards. Penguin.

Sudworth, George B. see Sudworth, George Bishop.
Sudworth, George Bishop, 1862-1927
  xSudworth, George B.
    Forest Trees of the Pacific Slope. Dover.
    Forest Trees of the Pacific Slope. Peter Smith.

Suchsdorf, Adie.
  xSuehsdorf, Adie.
    The Great American Baseball Scrapbook.
    Random.

Sueltz, Arthur F. see Sueltz, Arthur Fay.
Sueltz, Arthur Fay
  xSueltz, Arthur F.
    Deeper into John's Gospel. Har-Row.

Suen, Ching Y.
  xSuen, Ching Y.
    Computational Analysis of Mandarin.
    Birkhauser.

Suenens, Leon-Joseph.
  xSuenens, Leon-Joseph.
    Charismatic Renewal & Social Action: A
    Dialogue. Servant.

Suetin, A. S.
  xSuetin, A. S.
    Modern Chess Opening Theory. Pergamon.

Suetonius Tranquillus, C.
  xSuetonius Tranquillus, C.
    History of Twelve Caesars. AMS Pr.

Sueur, Meridel Le. see Le Sueur, Meridel.
Suffern, Arthur E. see Suffern, Arthur Elliott.
Suffern, Arthur Elliott, 1878-1959
  xSuffern, Arthur E.
    Conciliation & Arbitration in the Coal Industry
    of America. AMS Pr.

Suffet, I. H.
  xSuffet, I. H.
    Fate of Pollutants in the Air & Water
    Environments. Wiley.

Sufrin, Sidney C., 1910-
  xSufrin, Sidney C.
    Management of Business Ethics. Kennikat.

Sugano, Satoru.
  xSugano, Satoru.
    Multiplets of Transition-Metal Ions in Crystals.
    Acad Pr.

Sugar, Andrew.
  xSugar, Andrew.
    The Complete Tent Book. Contemp Bks.

Sugar, Bert R. see Sugar, Bert Randolph.
Sugar, Bert Randolph.
  xSugar, Bert R.

  Hit the Sign & Win a Free Suit of Clothes
  from Harry Finklestein. Contemp Bks.
  The Sports Collectors Bible. Bobbs.

Sugar, Max.
  xSugar, Max.
    ed. Female Adolescent Development.
    Brunner-Mazel.

Sugar, Peter F.
  xSugar, Peter F.
    Industrialization of Bosnia-Hercegovina,
    1878-1918. U of Wash Pr.

Sugarman, B. see Sugarman, Barry.
Sugarman, Barry, 1939-
  xSugarman, B.
    Daytop Village: A Therapeutic Community.
    HR&W.

Sugden, Edward H. see Sugden, Edward Holdsworth.
Sugden, Edward Holdsworth, 1854-1935
  xSugden, Edward H.
    Topographical Dictionary to the Works of
    Shakespeare & His Fellow Dramatists. Adler.

Sugden, H. W. see Sugden, Herbert Wilfred.
Sugden, Herbert W. see Sugden, Herbert Wilfred.
Sugden, Herbert Wilfred, 1891-
  xSugden, H. W.
    Grammar of Spenser's "Faerie Queene". Kraus
    Repr.
  xSugden, Herbert W.
    The Grammar of Spenser's Faerie Queene.
    Folcroft.

Sugerman, A. Arthur.
  xSugerman, A. Arthur.
    ed. Expanding Dimensions of Consciousness.
    Springer Pub.

Sugerman, Shirley.
  xSugerman, Shirley.
    ed. The Evolution of Consciousness: Studies in
    Polarity. Columbia U Pr.

Sugg, Richard P.
  xSugg, Richard P.
    Appreciating Poetry. HM.

Suggs, George G., 1929-
  xSuggs, George G.
    Colorado's War on Militant Unionism: James
    H. Peabody & the Western Federation of
    Miners. Wayne St U Pr.

Suggs, James C.
  xSuggs, James C.
    ed. This We Believe. Bethany Pr.

Sugimoto, Howard H. see Sugimoto, Howard Hiroshi.
Sugimoto, Howard Hiroshi.
  xSugimoto, Howard H.
    Japanese Immigration, the Vancouver Riots &
    Canadian Diplomacy. Arno.

Sugita, Yutaka. see Sugita, Yutake.
Sugita, Yutake, 1930-
  xSugita, Yutaka.
    The Flower Family. McGraw.

Suhadolnik, R. J. see Suhadolnik, Robert J.
Suhadolnik, Robert J., 1925-
  xSuhadolnik, R. J.
    Nucleosides As Biological Probes. Wiley.

Suhl, Yuri, 1908-
  xSuhl, Yuri.
    An Album of the Jews in America. Watts.
    The Purim Goat. Schol Bk Serv.
    Simon Boom Gives a Wedding. Schol Bk Serv.
    tr. & ed. They Fought Back: The Story of the
    Jewish Resistance in Nazi Europe. Schocken.
    Uncle Misha's Partisans. Schol Bk Serv.

Suib, Leonard.
  xSuib, Leonard.
    Marionettes, Onstage!. Har-Row.

Suid, Lawrence. see Suid, Lawrence H.
Suid, Lawrence H.
  xSuid, Lawrence.
    Guts & Glory: Great American War Movies.
    A-W.

Suinn, Richard M.
  xSuinn, Richard M.

  Fundamentals of Behavior Pathology. Wiley.
    ed. Innovative Medical-Psychiatric Therapies.
    Univ Park.

Sukenick, Ronald.
  xSukenick, Ronald.
    Long Talking Bad Conditions Blues. Fiction
    Coll.

Sukhwal, B. L., 1929-
  xSukhwal, Bheru L.
    South Asia: A Systematic Geographic
    Bibliography. Scarecrow.

Sukhwal, Bheru L. see Sukhwal, B. L.
Suksdorf, Henry F. see Suksdorf, Henry Ferdinand.
Suksdorf, Henry Ferdinand, 1843-
  xSuksdorf, Henry F.
    Our Race Problems. Arno.

Suleiman, E. N. see Suleiman, Ezra N.
Suleiman, Ezra N., 1941-
  xSuleiman, E. N.
    Politics, Power & Bureaucracy in France: The
    Administrative Elite. Princeton U Pr.

Suleiman, Michael W.
  xSuleiman, Michael W.
    Political Parties in Lebanon: The Challenge of
    a Fragmented Political Culture. Cornell U Pr.

Sulentic, Jack W.
  xSulentic, Jack W.
    The Revised New General Catalogue of
    Nonstellar Astronomical Objects. U of Ariz
    Pr.

Sulik, Boleslaw.
  xSulik, Boleslaw.
    A Change of Tack: The Making of "the
    Shadow Line". Ny Zoetrope.

Sulivan, G. L. see Sulivan, George Lydiard.
Sulivan, George Lydiard.
  xSulivan, G. L.
    Dhow Chasing in Zanzibar Waters & on the
    Eastern Coast of Africa. Biblio Dist.

Sullenger, Thomas E. see Sullenger, Thomas Earl.
Sullenger, Thomas Earl, 1893-
  xSullenger, Thomas E.
    Neglected Areas in Family Living. Chris Mass.

Sullens, Idelle.
  xSullens, Idelle.
    ed. The Whole Idea Catalog: College Writing
    Projects. Phila Bk Co.

Sullerot, Evelyn. see Sullerot, Evelyne.
Sullerot, Evelyne.
  xSullerot, Evelyn.
    Women on Love: Eight Centuries of Feminine
    Writing. Doubleday.

Sullins, S. E., 1940-
  xSullins, S. E.
    Complete Book of Multiple Defenses in
    Football. P-H.

Sullins, Walter L.
  xSullins, Walter L.
    Matrix Algebra for Statistical Applications.
    Interstate.

Sullivan Assoc. see Sullivan Associates.
Sullivan Associates.
  xSullivan Assoc.

Comprehension Readers. Behavioral Res.
I Can Read. Behavioral Res.
Instructional Objectives & Teacher's Guide.
Behavioral Res.
M. W. Sullivan Stories. Behavioral Res.
Reading Readiness Readers. Behavioral Res.
Reading Vocabulary. Behavioral Res..
Short Short Stories. Behavioral Res.
Sullivan Basal Mathematics Program.
Behavioral Res.
Sullivan Fun Readers. Behavioral Res.
Sullivan Reading Plays. Behavioral Res.
Sullivan Reading Program. Behavioral Res.
Sullivan Topic Readers. Behavioral Res.
Supervisor's Manual for Amanecer. Behavioral
Res.
Teacher's Enrichment Activities Guide.
Behavioral Res.
xSullivan Associates.
Math Word Problems. Behavioral Res.
Programmed Reading, Ser. 1. McGraw.
Read & Think Storybook Series. McGraw.
Sullivan, Barry J. see Sullivan, Barry James.
Sullivan, Barry James.
xSullivan, Barry J.
Industrialization in the Building Industry. Van
Nos Reinhold.
Sullivan, C. Stephan. see Sullivan, C. Stephen.
Sullivan, C. Stephen.
xSullivan, C. Stephan.
ed. Readings in Sacramental Theology. P-H.
Sullivan, Charles W. see Sullivan, Charles William.
Sullivan, Charles William, 1944-
xSullivan, Charles W.
As Tomorrow Becomes Today. P-H.
Sullivan, Clara K. see Sullivan, Clara Katherine.
Sullivan, Clara Katherine, 1916-
xSullivan, Clara K.
Tax on Value Added. Columbia U Pr.
Sullivan, D. J. see Sullivan, Daniel James.
Sullivan, Daniel J. see Sullivan, Daniel James.
Sullivan, Daniel James, 1909-
xSullivan, D. J.
Fundamentals of Logic. McGraw.
xSullivan, Daniel J.
Introduction to Philosophy. Glencoe.
Sullivan, Denis. see Sullivan, Denis G.
Sullivan, Denis G.
xSullivan, Denis.
Explorations in Convention Decision Making:
The Democratic Party in the 1970s. W H
Freeman.
xSullivan, Denis G.
The Politics of Representation: The Democratic
Convention 1972. St Martin.
Sullivan, Dennis. see Sullivan, Dennis C.
Sullivan, Dennis C.
xSullivan, Dennis.
The Mask of Love: Corrections in America -
Toward a Mutual Aid Alternative. Kennikat.
Sullivan, Dorothy D.
xSullivan, Dorothy D.
Teaching Reading Through Motor Learning. C
C Thomas.
Sullivan, Edmund B.
xSullivan, Edmund P.
Collecting Political Americana. Crown.
Sullivan, Edmund P. see Sullivan, Edmund B.
Sullivan, Edward D. see Sullivan, Edward Dean.
Sullivan, Edward Daniel, 1913-
xSullivan, Edward D.
Maupassant the Novelist. Greenwood.
Sullivan, Edward Dean, 1888-1938
xSullivan, Edward D.
Rattling the Cup on Chicago Crime. Arno.
Sullivan, Eileen.
xSullivan, Eileen.
Arthur Ford Speaks from Beyond. O'Hara.
Sullivan, Eileen. see Sullivan, Eileen A.

Sullivan, Eileen A.
xSullivan, Eileen.
Thomas Davis. Bucknell U Pr.
Sullivan, Eleanor.
xSullivan, Eleanor.
ed. Alfred Hitchcock's Tales to Make Your
Blood Run Cold. Davis Pubns.
ed. Alfred Hitchcock's Tales to Scare You
Stiff. Davis Pubns.
Sullivan, Eugene T.
xSullivan, Eugene T.
ed. Beautiful Bridal Cakes the Wilton Way.
Wilton.
ed. Discover the Fun of Cake Decorating.
Wilton.
Sullivan, F. R. see Sullivan, Frank R.
Sullivan, Frank C., 1900-
xSullivan, Frank C.
Crisis of Confidence: Utilities, Public Relations
& Credibility. Phoenix Pub.
Sullivan, Frank R.
xSullivan, F. R.
Lower Tertiary Nannoplankton from the
California Coast Ranges. U of Cal Pr.
Sullivan, George, 1927-
xSullivan, George.
Better Roller Skating for Boys & Girls. Dodd.
Better Volleyball for Girls. Dodd.
By Chance a Winner: The History of Lotteries.
Dodd.
Complete Guide to Softball. Fleet.
Dave Cowens: A Biography. Doubleday.
Do-It-Yourself Moving. Macmillan.
Dollar Squeeze - & How to Beat It. Macmillan.
Fell's Teen Age Guide to Skin & Scuba
Diving. Fell.
Football. Follett.
Guide to Badminton. Fleet.
Home Run!. Dodd.
How Do They Package It?. Westminster.
How Do They Run It?. Westminster.
How Does It Get There?. Westminster.
Linebacker!. Dodd.
Modern Olympic Superstars. Dodd.
More How Do They Make It. Westminster.
The Picture History of the Boston Red Sox.
Bobbs.
Plants to Grow Indoors. Follett.
Pro Football & the Running Back. Dodd.
Pro Football's Greatest Upsets. Garrard.
Pro Football's Kicking Game. Dodd.
Pro Football's Passing Game. Dodd.
Queens of the Court. Dodd.
The Supercarriers. Dodd.
This Is Pro Basketball. Dodd.
This Is Pro Football. Dodd.
This Is Pro Hockey. Dodd.
This Is Pro Soccer. Dodd.
Understanding Architecture. Warne.
Understanding Photography. Cornerstone.
Understanding Photography. Warne.
Sullivan, Harry S. see Sullivan, Harry Stack.
Sullivan, Harry Stack, 1892-1949
xSullivan, Harry S.
Clinical Studies in Psychiatry. Norton.
Conceptions of Modern Psychiatry. Norton.
Fusion of Psychiatry & Social Science. Norton.
Psychiatric Interview. Norton.
Sullivan, J. P. see Sullivan, John Patrick.
Sullivan, J. W. see Sullivan, John William Navin.
Sullivan, James, 1744-1808
xSullivan, James.
The History of Land Titles in Massachusetts.
Arno.
History of the District of Maine. Maine St
Mus.
Sullivan, James. see Sullivan, James A.
Sullivan, James A., 1937-
xSullivan, James.

Fluid Power: Theory & Applications. Reston.
xSullivan, James A.
Fundamentals of Fluid Mechanics. Reston.
Sullivan, Jeremiah J.
xSullivan, Jeremiah J.
Foreign Investment in the U. S. Fishing
Industry. Lexington Bks.
Pacific Basin Enterprise & the Changing Law
of the Sea. Lexington Bks.
Sullivan, Jerry.
xSullivan, Jerry.
Hiking Trails in the Midwest. Contemp Bks.
Hiking Trails in the Southern Mountains.
Contemp Bks.
Sullivan, Jessie P.
xSullivan, Jessie P.
Exciting Object Lessons & Ideas for Children's
Sermons. Baker Bk.
Object Lessons & Stories for the Children's
Church. Baker Bk.
Sullivan, John, 1904-
xSullivan, John.
G. K. Chesterton: A Bibliography. Greenwood.
Sullivan, John C. see Sullivan, John Cavanaugh.
Sullivan, John Cavanaugh, 1904-
xSullivan, John C.
A Study of the Social Attitudes & Information
on Public Problems of Women Teachers in
Secondary Schools. AMS Pr.
Sullivan, John J. see Sullivan, John Joseph.
Sullivan, John Joseph.
xSullivan, John J.
ed. Explorations in Urban Land Economics.
Lincoln Inst Land.
Sullivan, John L.
xSullivan, John L.
Introduction to Police Science. McGraw.
Sullivan, John L. see Sullivan, John Lawrence.
Sullivan, John Lawrence.
xSullivan, John L.
Multiple Indicators: An Introduction. Sage.
Sullivan, John Patrick.
xSullivan, J. P.
Propertius: A Critical Introduction. Cambridge
U Pr.
Sullivan, John W. see Sullivan, John Wadsworth William.
Sullivan, John Wadsworth William, 1901-
xSullivan, John W.
Story of Metals. Iowa St U Pr.
Sullivan, John William Navin, 1886-1937
xSullivan, J. W.
Limitations of Science. Kelley.
Sullivan, Joseph P.
xSullivan, Joseph P.
Partnerships & Taxes: A Practical Guide. Panel
Pubs.
Sullivan, Katharine.
xSullivan, Katharine.
Girls on Parole. Greenwood.
Sullivan, Kathleen E.
xSullivan, Kathleen E.
Paragraph Practice: Writing the Paragraph &
the Short Composition. Macmillan.
Sullivan, Kaye, 1921-
xSullivan, Kaye.
Films for, by & About Women. Scarecrow.
Sullivan, Kevin.
xSullivan, Kevin.
Oscar Wilde. Columbia U Pr.
Sullivan, Linda. see Sullivan, Linda E.
Sullivan, Linda E.
xSullivan, Linda.
ed. Encyclopedia of Governmental Advisory
Organizations. Gale.
Sullivan, Louis H., 1856-1924
xSullivan, Louis H.
Kindergarten Chats & Other Writings.
Wittenborn.
Sullivan, M. W. see Sullivan, Maurice W.
Sullivan, Margaret. see Sullivan, Margaret Walker.

Sullivan, Margaret W. see Sullivan, Margaret Walker.
Sullivan, Margaret Walker, 1922-
  xSullivan, Margaret.
    Living with Epilepsy. Caroline Hse.
  xSullivan, Margaret W.
    Living with Epilepsy. Nellen Pub.
Sullivan, Marianna P.
  xSullivan, Marianna P.
    France's Vietnam Policy: A Study in
    French-American Relations. Greenwood.
Sullivan, Mark, 1874-1952
  xSullivan, Mark.
    Our Times. Scribner.
Sullivan, Mary B. see Sullivan, Mary Beth.
Sullivan, Mary Beth.
  xSullivan, Mary B.
    Feeling Free. A-W.
Sullivan, Mary R. see Sullivan, Mary Rose.
Sullivan, Mary Rose.
  xSullivan, Mary R.
    Browning's Voices in The Ring & the Book: A
    Study of Method & Meaning. U of Toronto
    Pr.
Sullivan, Mary W.
  xSullivan, Mary W.
    Brian-Foot-in-the-Mouth. Elsevier-Nelson.
    What's This About Pete?. Elsevier-Nelson.
Sullivan, Maurice W.
  xSullivan, M. W.
    A Programmed Introduction to the Game of
    Chess. Behavioral Res.
    The Programmed Method for Learning to Play
    Chess. Times Bks.
Sullivan, Michael, 1916-
  xSullivan, Michael.
    The Arts of China. U of Cal Pr.
    The Cave Temples of Maichishan. U of Cal Pr.
    Symbols of Eternity: The Art of Landscape
    Painting in China. Stanford U Pr.
Sullivan, Nora.
  xSullivan, Nora.
    Dinosaurs. Watts.
Sullivan, Peggy, 1929-
  xSullivan, Peggy.
    Carl H. Milam & the American Library
    Association. Wilson.
    Opportunities in Library & Information
    Science. Natl Textbk.
    Problems in School Media Management.
    Bowker.
Sullivan, Richard E. see Sullivan, Richard Eugene.
Sullivan, Richard Eugene, 1921-
  xSullivan, Richard E.
    Aix-La-Chapelle in the Age of Charlemagne. U
    of Okla Pr.
Sullivan, Robert J. see Sullivan, Robert Joseph.
Sullivan, Robert Joseph, 1940-
  xSullivan, Robert J.
    Medical Record & Index Systems for
    Community Practice. Ballinger Pub.
Sullivan, Robert L. see Sullivan, Robert Lee.
Sullivan, Robert Lee.
  xSullivan, Robert L.
    Power System Planning. McGraw.
Sullivan, Roger J., 1928-
  xSullivan, Roger J.
    Morality & the Good Life: A Commentary on
    Aristotle's "Nicomachean Ethics". Memphis
    St Univ.
Sullivan, Rosemary.
  xSullivan, Rosemary.
    Theodore Roethke: The Garden Master. U of
    Wash Pr.
Sullivan, Teresa A., 1949-
  xSullivan, Teresa A.
    Marginal Workers, Marginal Jobs: The
    Underutilization of American Workers. U of
    Tex Pr.
Sullivan, Tim. see Sullivan, Tim D.

Sullivan, Tim D.
  xSullivan, Tim.
    Glitter Street. Rawson Wade.
Sullivan, Tom.
  xSullivan, Tom.
    If You Could See What I Hear. Har-Row.
    If You Could See What I Hear. NAL.
Sullivan, Walter, 1924-
  xSullivan, Walter.
    Death by Melancholy: Essays on Modern
    Southern Fiction. La State U Pr.
Sullivan, William A. see Sullivan, William Arnold.
Sullivan, William Arnold, 1920-
  xSullivan, William A.
    The Industrial Worker in Pennsylvania,
    1800-1840. Johnson Repr.
Sullivan, William C.
  xSullivan, William C.
    The Bureau: My Thirty Years in Hoover's FBI.
    Norton.
Sullivan, William F. see Sullivan, William G.
Sullivan, William G.
  xSullivan, William F.
    Fundamentals of Forecasting. Reston.
Sulloway, Alison G.
  xSulloway, Alison G.
    Gerard Manley Hopkins & the Victorian
    Temper. Columbia U Pr.
Sulloway, Frank J.
  xSulloway, Frank J.
    Freud, Biologist of the Mind: Beyond the
    Psychoanalytic Legend. Basic.
Sulman, F. G. see Sulman, Felix Gad.
Sulman, Felix G. see Sulman, Felix Gad.
Sulman, Felix Gad, 1907-
  xSulman, F. G.
    Hypothalamic Control of Lactation.
    Springer-Verlag.
  xSulman, Felix G.
    The Effect of Air Ionization, Electric Fields,
    Atmospherics & Other Electric Phenomena
    on Man & Animal. C C Thomas.
Sulnick, Robert H., 1943-
  xSulnick, Robert H.
    Civil Litigation & the Police: A Method of
    Communication. C C Thomas.
Sultan, Paul E.
  xSultan, Paul E.
    The Disenchanted Unionist. Greenwood.
Sultan, William J.
  xSultan, William J.
    Practical Baking. AVI.
Sultz, Harry A.
  xSultz, Harry A.
    Long-Term Childhood Illness. U of Pittsburgh
    Pr.
Sulzberger, C. L. see Sulzberger, Cyrus Leo.
Sulzberger, Cyrus Leo, 1912-
  xSulzberger, C. L.
    The Coldest War: Russia's Game in China.
    HarBraceJ.
    Fall of Eagles. Crown.
    Postscript with a Chinese Accent: Memoirs &
    Diaries, 1972-73. Macmillan.
Sulzby, James F. see Sulzby, James Frederick.
Sulzby, James Frederick, 1905-
  xSulzby, James F.
    Historic Alabama Hotels & Resorts. U of Ala
    Pr.
Sumichrast, Michael.
  xSumichrast, Michael.
    Opportunities in Building Construction. Natl
    Textbk.
Sumler, David E.
  xSumler, David E.
    A History of Europe in the Twentieth Century.
    Dorsey.
Summer, Charles E. see Summer, Charles Edgar.
Summer, Charles Edgar.
  xSummer, Charles E.

    Strategic Behavior in Business & Government.
    Little.
Summer, Claire.
  xSummer, Claire.
    The Affordable Computer: Microcomputer
    Applications in Business & Industry. Am
    Mgmt.
**Summer Conference on International Law, 5th, Cornell
University, 1964.**
  xSummer Conference on International Law,
    Cornell Law School, 5th, June 18-20, 1964.
    Human Rights: Protection of the Individual
    Under International Law, Proceedings.
    Rothman.
**Summer Institute in Theoretical Physics, Centro de
Investigacion y de Estudios Avanzados del IPN,
1973.**
  xTheSummer Institute in Theoretical Physics,
    Mexico City, 1973.
    Particles, Quantum Fields & Statistical
    Mechanics: Proceedings. Springer-Verlag.
**Summer School on Topological Vector Spaces,
Universite Libre de Bruxelles, 1972.**
  xSummer School on Topological Vector Spaces.
    Proceedings. Springer-Verlag.
**Summer Workshop on Invariant Imbedding, University
of Southern California, 1970.**
  xSummer Workshop on Invariant Imbedding -
    University of Southern California - Jun-Aug,
    1970.
    Proceedings. Springer-Verlag.
Summerall, C. P. see Summerall, Charles P.
Summerall, Charles P.
  xSummerall, C. P.
    Monitoring Heart Rhythm. Wiley.
Summerhayes, Martha, 1846-1911
  xSummerhayes, Martha.
    Vanished Arizona: Recollections of an Army
    Life of a New England Woman. Rio Grande.
    Vanished Arizona: Recollections of the Army
    Life of a New England Woman. U of Nebr
    Pr.
Summerhayes, R. S. see Summerhays, Reginald Sherriff.
Summerhays, Reginald S. see Summerhays, Reginald
Sherriff.
Summerhays, Reginald Sherriff, 1881-
  xSummerhays, R. S.
    The Observer's Book of Horses & Ponies.
    Scribner.
    The Problem Horse. J A Allen.
  xSummerhays, Reginald S.
    The Arabian Horse. Arco.
    Arabian Horse. Wilshire.
    Problem Horse. Arco.
Summers, Anthony.
  xSummers, Anthony.
    Conspiracy. McGraw.
    The File on the Tsar. BJ Pub Group.
Summers, Claude J.
  xSummers, Claude J.
    Ben Jonson. Twayne.
Summers, Donald B. see Summers, Donald Balch.
Summers, Donald Balch, 1902-
  xSummers, Donald B.
    The Chemistry Handbook. Prindle.
    Chemistry Handbook. Ind Sch Pr.
Summers, Dorothy.
  xSummers, Dorothy.
    East Coast Floods. David & Charles.
Summers, Edward L.
  xSummers, Edward L.
    An Introduction to Accounting for Decision
    Making & Control. Irwin.
Summers, Francis M. see Summers, Francis Marion.
Summers, Francis Marion.
  xSummers, Francis M.
    Review of the Mite Family Cheyletidae. U of
    Cal Pr.
Summers, Gene F., 1936-
  xSummers, Gene F.

ed. Industrial Invasion of NonMetropolitan
America: A Quarter Century of Experience.
Praeger.
ed. Nonmetropolitan Industrial Growth &
Community Change. Lexington Bks.
Summers, Gerald.
xSummers, Gerald.
An African Bestiary. S&S.
Summers, Harrison B. *see* Summers, Harrison Boyd.
Summers, Harrison Boyd.
xSummers, Harrison B.
Broadcasting & the Public. Wadsworth Pub.
How to Debate: A Textbook for Beginners.
Wilson.
ed. Thirty-Year History of Programs Carried
on National Radio Networks in the United
States, 1926-1956. Arno.
Summers, James L.
xSummers, James L.
Long Ride Home. Westminster.
Summers, Jo An.
xSummers, JoAn.
Fruitbasket Friends. Logos.
Summers, JoAn. *see* Summers, Jo An.
Summers, Lewis P. *see* Summers, Lewis Preston.
Summers, Lewis Preston, 1868-1943
xSummers, Lewis P.
Annals of Southwest Virginia, 1769-1800.
Genealog Pub.
Summers, M. *see* Summers, Montague.
Summers, M. J. *see* Summers, Marcia J.
Summers, Marcia J.
xSummers, M. J.
ed. Our Chemical Culture: Drug Use & Misuse.
Stash.
Summers, Marvin. *see* Summers, Marvin R.
Summers, Marvin R.
xSummers, Marvin.
Law & Order in a Democratic Society. Merrill.
Summers, Montague, 1880-1948
xSummers, M.
Popular History of Witchcraft. Wehman.
xSummers, Montague.
The Geography of Witchcraft. Citadel Pr.
The Geography of Witchcraft. Routledge &
Kegan.
History of Witchcraft & Demonology.
Routledge & Kegan.
History of Witchcraft & Demonology. Univ
Bks.
Summers, Ray.
xSummers, Ray.
Essentials of New Testament Greek.
Broadman.
Life Beyond. Broadman.
Summers, Robert E. *see* Summers, Robert Edward.
Summers, Robert Edward, 1918- ed
xSummers, Robert E.
ed. America's Weapons of Psychological
Warfare. Arno.
Summers, True.
xSummers, True.
Poppy. Avon.
Summerson, John. *see* Summerson, John Newenham.
Summerson, John Newenham, Sir, 1904-
xSummerson, John.
The Architecture of Victorian London. U Pr of
Va.
Georgian London. MIT Pr.
Georgian London. Penguin.
Summerton, Margaret.
xSummerton, Margaret.
A Dark & Secret Place. Avon.
The Ghost Flowers. Ace Bks.
Sumner, B. H. *see* Sumner, Benedict Humphrey.
Sumner, Benedict Humphrey, 1893-1951
xSumner, B. H.
Tsardom & Imperialism in the Far East &
Middle East, 1880-1914. Shoe String.
Sumner, Michael. *see* Sumner, Michael T.

Sumner, Michael T.
xSumner, Michael.
The Dollars & Sense of Hospital Malpractice
Insurance. Abt Assoc.
Sumner, Robert L. *see* Sumner, Robert Leslie.
Sumner, Robert Leslie, 1922-
xSumner, Robert L.
Armstrongism: The Worldwide Church of God
Examined in the Searching Light of
Scripture. Bibl Evang Pr.
Sumner, W. Dayton, 1926-
xSumner, W. Dayton.
Breaking Your Horse's Bad Habits. A S
Barnes.
Breaking Your Horse's Bad Habits. Wilshire.
Sumner, William. *see* Sumner, William Leslie.
Sumner, William G. *see* Sumner, William Graham.
Sumner, William Graham, 1840-1910
xSumner, William G.
Andrew Jackson. AMS Pr.
Andrew Jackson. Chelsea Hse.
Andrew Jackson As a Public Man: What He
Was, What Chances He Had, & What He
Did with Them. Greenwood.
Challenge of Facts & Other Essays. AMS Pr.
Earth-Hunger & Other Essays. Arno.
Earth-Hunger & Other Essays. Transaction
Bks.
Financier & the Finances of the American
Revolution. B Franklin.
Financier & the Finances of the American
Revolution. Kelley.
Folkways & Mores. Schocken.
Forgotten Man's Almanac: Rations of
Common Sense from William Graham
Sumner. Greenwood.
What Social Classes Owe to Each Other. Arno.
What Social Classes Owe to Each Other.
Caxton.
Sumner, William L. *see* Sumner, William Leslie.
Sumner, William Leslie, 1904-1973
xSumner, William.
The Organ: Its Evolution, Principles of
Construction & Use. Scholarly.
xSumner, William L.
The Organ: Its Evolution, Principles of
Construction & Use. St Martin.
Sumners, Cecil L. *see* Sumners, Cecil Lamar.
Sumners, Cecil Lamar, 1920-
xSumners, Cecil L.
Governors of Mississippi. Pelican.
Sumowski, Werner.
xSumowski, Werner.
The Drawings of the Rembrandt School. Abaris
Bks.
Sumption, Jonathan.
xSumption, Jonathan.
The Albigensian Crusade. Merrimack Bk Serv.
Sumption, Lois L. *see* Sumption, Lois Lintner.
Sumption, Lois Lintner.
xSumption, Lois L.
Around-the-World Cooky Book. Dover.
Sumrall, Lester. *see* Sumrall, Lester Frank.
Sumrall, Lester Frank, 1913-
xSumrall, Lester.
Demons: The Answer Book. Nelson.
Miracles Don't Just Happen. Logos.
Sumrall, Raymond O.
xSumrall, Raymond O.
Map Abstract of Crime & Requests for Police
Services: Birmingham Alabama, 1975. U of
Ala Pr.
The Map Abstract of Trends in Calls for Police
Service: Birmingham, Alabama, 1975-1976. U
of Ala Pr.
Sumrall, Velma.
xSumrall, Velma.

Telling the Story of the Local Church: The
Who, What, When, Where & Why of
Communication. Seabury.
Sun, Kungtu C., 1895-
xSun, Kungtu C.
Economic Development of Manchuria in the
First Half of the Twentieth Century. Harvard
U Pr.
Sunagel, Lois A.
xSunagel, Lois A.
The Amethyst Quest. Bouregy.
Sund, Robert, 1929-
xSund, Robert.
Bunch Grass. U of Wash Pr.
Sund, Robert B.
xSund, Robert B.
Teaching Science by Inquiry in the Secondary
School. Merrill.
The Sunday Times, London.
xSunday Times, London.
Seven Deadly Sins. Arno.
Sundberg, Elmer W.
xSundberg, Elmer W.
Building Trades Blueprint Reading. Am
Technical.
Sundberg, Norman D.
xSundberg, Norman D.
The Assessment of Persons. P-H.
Sundberg, Richard J., 1938-
xSundberg, Richard J.
Chemistry of Indoles. Acad Pr.
Sundberg-Weitman, B. *see* Sundberg-Weitman, Brita.
Sundberg-Weitman, Brita, 1934-
xSundberg-Weitman, B.
Discrimination on Grounds of Nationality:
Free Movement of Workers of Freedom of
Establishment Under the EEC Treaty.
Elsevier.
Sundby, Per, 1926-
xSundby, Per.
Alcoholism & Mortality. Rutgers Ctr Alcohol.
Sundemo, Herbert, 1926-
xSundemo, Herbert.
Revell's Dictionary of Bible Times. Revell.
Sunder, John E. *see* Sunder, John Edward.
Sunder, John Edward.
xSunder, John E.
Fur Trade on the Upper Missouri, 1840-1865.
U of Okla Pr.
Sunderland, Sydney.
xSunderland, Sydney.
Nerves & Nerve Injuries. Churchill.
Sunderlin, Sylvia.
xSunderlin, Sylvia.
Antrim's Orange. Scribner.
ed. The Most Enabling Environment:
Education Is for All Children. ACEI.
Sundkler, Bengt G. *see* Sundkler, Bengt Gustaf Malcolm.
Sundkler, Bengt Gustaf Malcolm, 1909-
xSundkler, Bengt G.
Bantu Prophets in South Africa. Oxford U Pr.
Sundquist, Eric J.
xSundquist, Eric J.
Home As Found: Authority & Genealogy in
Nineteenth Century American Literature.
Johns Hopkins.
Sundquist, James L.
xSundquist, James L.
Dispersing Population: What America Can
Learn from Europe. Brookings.
Dynamics of the Party System: Alignment &
Realignment of Political Parties in the United
States. Brookings.
Politics & Policy: The Eisenhower, Kennedy, &
Johnson Years. Brookings.
Sundsfjord, J. A.
xSundsfjord, J. A.
ed. Progesterone Physiology. Mss Info.
Sundstrom, Donald W. *see* Sundstrom, Donald William.

Sundstrom, Donald William.
  xSundstrom, Donald W.
    Wastewater Treatment. P-H.
Sundstrom, Lars, 1927-
  xSundstrom, Lars.
    The Exchange Economy of Pre Colonial
    Tropical Africa. St Martin.
Sundwall, Johannes, 1877-
  xSundwall, Johannes.
    Abhandlungen Zur Geschichte Des
    Ausgehenden Romertums. Arno.
Sung, Betty L. *see* Sung, Betty Lee.
Sung, Betty Lee.
  xSung, Betty L.
    An Album of Chinese Americans. Watts.
    The Chinese in America. Macmillan.
  xSung, Betty Lee.
    A Survey of Chinese-American Manpower &
    Employment. Praeger.
Sung, Z. D.
  xSung, Z. D.
    The Symbols of Yi-King: Or the Symbols of
    the Chinese Logic of Changes. Chinese
    Materials.
Sunnucks, Anne.
  xSunnucks, Anne.
    Encyclopaedia of Chess. St Martin.
Sunseri, Alvin. *see* Sunseri, Alvin R.
Sunseri, Alvin R.
  xSunseri, Alvin.
    Seeds of Discord: New Mexico in the
    Aftermath of the American Conquest,
    1846-1861. Nelson-Hall.
Sunset.

  xSunset Editors.
    Add-a-Room. Sunset-Lane.
    African Violets. Sunset-Lane.
    Alaska. Sunset-Lane.

    Alaska: Travel Guide. Sunset-Lane.
    Arizona: Travel Guide. Sunset-Lane.
    Australia. Sunset-Lane.

    Back Roads of California. Sunset-Lane.
    Barbecue Cook Book. Sunset-Lane.
    Basic Carpentry Illustrated. Sunset-Lane.

    Basic Gardening Illustrated. Sunset-Lane.
    Basic Home Repairs Illustrated. Sunset-Lane.
    Basic Home Wiring Illustrated. Sunset-Lane.
    Basic Plumbing Illustrated. Sunset-Lane.
    Bathrooms. Sunset-Lane.
    Bathrooms: Planning & Remodeling.
    Sunset-Lane.
    Beautiful California. Sunset-Lane.
    Beautiful Hawaii. Sunset-Lane.
    Beautiful Northwest. Sunset-Lane.
    Bedrooms. Sunset-Lane.
    Bonsai. Sunset-Lane.
    Bookshelves & Cabinets. Sunset-Lane.
    Breads. Sunset-Lane.
    Breakfast & Brunch. Sunset-Lane.
    Building Barbecues. Sunset-Lane.
    Bulbs: How to Grow. Sunset-Lane.
    Cabins & Vacation Houses. Sunset-Lane.
    Cactus & Succulents. Sunset-Lane.
    California Coast. Sunset-Lane.
    Casserole Book. Sunset-Lane.
    Casserole Cook Book. Sunset-Lane.
    Children's Crafts. Sunset-Lane.
    Children's Rooms & Play Yards. Sunset-Lane.
    Chinese Cook Book. Sunset-Lane.
    Convection Oven Cook Book. Sunset-Lane.
    Cooking for Two. Sunset-Lane.
    Crochet. Sunset-Lane.
    Curtains, Draperies & Shades. Sunset-Lane.
    Decks: How to Build. Sunset-Lane.
    Desert Gardening. Sunset-Lane.
    Desserts Cook Book. Sunset-Lane.
    Europe: Discovery Trips. Sunset-Lane.

    Family Rooms, Dens & Studios. Sunset-Lane.
    Favorite Recipes. Sunset-Lane.
    Fences & Gates. Sunset-Lane.
    Fireplaces. Sunset-Lane.
    Fireplaces: How to Build. Sunset-Lane.
    Food Processor Cook Book. Sunset-Lane.
    ed. French Cook Book. Sunset-Lane.
    Furniture: Easy-to-Make. Sunset-Lane.
    Furniture Finishing & Refinishing. Sunset-Lane.
    Furniture Upholstery. Sunset-Lane.
    Furniture Upholstery & Repair. Sunset-Lane.
    Garden & Patio Building Book. Sunset-Lane.
    Garden Pools, Fountains & Waterfalls.
    Sunset-Lane.
    Gardening in Containers. Sunset-Lane.
    Ghost Towns of the West. Sunset-Lane.
    Gold Rush Country. Sunset-Lane.
    Greenhouse Gardening. Sunset-Lane.
    Ground Beef. Sunset-Lane.
    Hawaii: Travel Guide. Sunset-Lane.
    Herbs: How to Grow. Sunset-Lane.
    Home Canning. Sunset-Lane.
    ed. Homeowner's Guide to Wood Stoves.
    Sunset-Lane.
    Hors d'oeuvres. Sunset-Lane.
    Hot Tubs, Spas & Home Saunas. Sunset-Lane.
    House Plants. Sunset-Lane.
    Indoor Plants: Decorating with. Sunset-Lane.
    Insulation & Weatherstripping. Sunset-Lane.
    Islands of the South Pacific. Sunset-Lane.
    Italian Cookbook. Sunset-Lane.
    Kitchens: Planning & Remodeling.
    Sunset-Lane.
    Knitting. Sunset-Lane.
    Landscaping & Garden Remodeling.
    Sunset-Lane.
    ed. Macrame. Sunset-Lane.
    Mexican Cook Book. Sunset-Lane.
    Mexico: Travel Guide. Sunset-Lane.
    Microwave Cook Book. Sunset-Lane.
    National Parks of the West. Sunset-Lane.
    Needlepoint. Sunset-Lane.
    New Zealand. Sunset-Lane.
    Northern California. Sunset-Lane.
    Northern California: Travel Guide.
    Sunset-Lane.
    Orchids: How to Grow. Sunset-Lane.
    Oregon: Travel Guides. Sunset-Lane.
    ed. The Orient. Sunset-Lane.
    Oriental Cook Book. Sunset-Lane.
    Outdoor Furniture. Sunset-Lane.
    Paneling, Painting & Wallpapering.
    Sunset-Lane.
    Pasta Cook Book. Sunset-Lane.
    Patio Roofs. Sunset-Lane.
    Patios & Decks. Sunset-Lane.
    Picture Framing & Wall Display. Sunset-Lane.
    Pillows: How to Make. Sunset-Lane.
    Planning Your New Home. Sunset-Lane.
    ed. Plant Containers You Can Make.
    Sunset-Lane.
    Pruning Handbook. Sunset-Lane.
    Quilting & Patchwork. Sunset-Lane.
    Remodeling Your Home. Sunset-Lane.
    Roses: How to Grow. Sunset-Lane.
    Salads: Favorite Recipes. Sunset-Lane.
    San Francisco. Sunset-Lane.
    Seafood Cook Book. Sunset-Lane.
    ed. Slipcovers & Bedspreads. Sunset-Lane.
    Small-Space Gardens. Sunset-Lane.
    Soft Toys & Dolls. Sunset-Lane.
    Solar Heating & Cooling: Homeowner's Guide.
    Sunset-Lane.
    Soups & Stews. Sunset-Lane.
    Southeast Asia: Travel Guide. Sunset-Lane.
    Southern California: Travel Guide.
    Sunset-Lane.
    Storage. Sunset-Lane.
    Swimming Pools. Sunset-Lane.
    ed. Tables & Chairs: Easy to Make.

    Sunset-Lane.
    Things to Make for Children. Sunset-Lane.
    Tile: Remodeling. Sunset-Lane.
    Vegetable Gardening. Sunset-Lane.
    Vegetables Cookbook. Sunset-Lane.
    Walks, Walls, & Patio Floors. Sunset-Lane.
    Washington: Travel Guide. Sunset-Lane.
    Western Garden Book: Sunset New.
    Sunset-Lane.
    Wine Country. Sunset-Lane.
    Wine Country: California. Sunset-Lane.
    Wok Cook Book. Sunset-Lane.
    Woodcarving Techniques & Projects.
    Sunset-Lane.
    ed. Woodworking Projects. Sunset-Lane.

Sunset Editors. *see* Sunset.

Sunshine, John.
  xSunshine, John.
    How to Enjoy Your Retirement. Am Mgmt.
Suntharalingam, R.
  xSuntharalingam, R.
    Politics & Nationalist Awakening in South
    India, 1852-1891. U of Ariz Pr.
Suny, Roger G. *see* Suny, Ronald Grigor.
Suny, Ronald Grigor.
  xSuny, Roger G.
    Baku Commune, 1917-1918: Class &
    Nationality in the Russian Revolution.
    Princeton U Pr.
Super, Donald E. *see* Super, Donald Edwin.
Super, Donald Edwin.
  xSuper, Donald E.
    Appraising Vocational Fitness: By Means of
    Psychological Tests. Har-Row.
    Computer-Assisted Counseling. Tchrs Coll.
    Opportunities in Psychology Careers Today
    Natl Tontblu
Superior, Irving.
  xSuperior, Irving.
    Superior Limericks. Ashley Bks.
Suppe, Frederick.
  xSuppe, Frederick.
    ed. The Structure of Scientific Theories. U of
    Ill Pr.
Suppes, P. *see* Suppes, Patrick Colonel.
Suppes, Patrick. *see* Suppes, Patrick Colonel.
Suppes, Patrick Colonel, 1922-
  xSuppes, P.
    ed. Space, Time & Geometry. Kluwer Boston.
  xSuppes, Patrick.
    Axiomatic Set Theory. Dover.
    Introduction to Logic. Van Nos Reinhold.
    ed. Logic & Probability in Quantum
    Mechanics. Kluwer Boston.
    Markov Learning Models for Multiperson
    Interactions. Stanford U Pr.
Supraner, Robyn.
  xSupraner, Robyn.
    Giggly-Wiggly, Snickety-Snick. Schol Bk Serv.
    Sam Sunday & the Strange Disappearance of
    Chester Cats. Parents.
    Think About It, You Might Learn Something.
    HM.
Supreme Commander for Allied Powers. *see* Supreme
  Commander for the Allied Powers.
Supreme Commander for the Allied Powers.
  xSupreme Commander for Allied Powers.
    Political Reorientation of Japan 1945-1948.
    Scholarly.
Supreme Commander for the Allied Powers. Government
Section.
  xSupreme Commander For The Allied Powers -
  Government Section.
    Political Reorientation of Japan, September
    1945 to September 1948: Report.
    Greenwood.
Suprunenko, D. A. *see* Suprunenko, Dmitrii Alekseevich.
Suprunenko, Dmitri A. *see* Suprunenko, Dmitrii
  Alekseevich.

Suprunenko, Dmitrii Alekseevich.
  xSuprunenko, D. A.
      Matrix Groups. Am Math.
  xSuprunenko, Dmitri A.
      Commutative Matrices. Acad Pr.
Sur, Mary, 1911-
  xSur, Mary.
      Collective Bargaining: A Comparative Study of
      Developments in India & Other Countries.
      Asia.
Suran, Bernard G.
  xSuran, Bernard G.
      Oddballs: The Social Maverick & the
      Dynamics of Individuality. Nelson-Hall.
Surburg, Raymond F., 1909-
  xSurburg, Raymond F.
      How Dependable Is the Bible. Holman.
Suret-Canale, Jean.
  xSuret-Canale, Jean.
      French Colonialism in Tropical Africa,
      1900-1945. Universe.
Surette, Dick, 1935-
  xSurette, Dick.
      Trout & Salmon Fly Index. Stackpole.
Surette, Leon.
  xSurette, Leon.
      A Light from Eleusis: A Study of Ezra Pound's
      Cantos. Oxford U Pr.
Surge, Frank.
  xSurge, Frank.
      Famous Spies. Lerner Pubns.
Surghnor, M. F., b. 1833
  xSurghnor, M. F.
      Uncle Tom of the Old South: A Story of the
      South in Reconstruction Days. Arno.
Surles, Richard H.
  xSurles, Richard H.
      ed. Legal Periodical Management Data. W S
      Hein.
Surrey, M. J. see Surrey, M. J. C.
Surrey, M. J. C.
  xSurrey, M. J.
      The Analysis & Forecasting of the British
      Economy. Cambridge U Pr.
      An Introduction to Econometrics. Oxford U
      Pr.
Surtees, Robert, 1779-1834
  xSurtees, Robert.
      The History & Antiquities of the County
      Palatine of Durham. Rowman.
Surtees, Virginia.
  xSurtees, Virginia.
      The Paintings & Drawings of Dante Gabriel
      Rossetti (1828-1882): A Catalogue Raisonne.
      Oxford U Pr.
Surwillo, Walter W.
  xSurwillo, Walter W.
      Experimental Design in Psychiatry: Research
      Methods for Clinical Practice. Grune.
Suryadinata, Leo.
  xSuryadinata, Leo.
      The Pre-World War II Peranakan Chinese
      Press of Java: A Preliminary Survey. Ohio U
      Ctr Intl.
Susann, Jacqueline.
  xSusann, Jacqueline.
      Love Machine. Bantam.
      Love Machine. S&S.
      Once Is Not Enough. Bantam.
      Once Is Not Enough. Morrow.
      Valley of the Dolls. Bantam.
Suschitzky, H.
  xSuschitzky, H.
      ed. Polychloroaromatic Compounds. Plenum
      Pub.
Suschitzky, Wolfgang.
  xSuschitzky, Wolfgang.
      Brendan of Ireland. Hastings.
Suskind, Richard.
  xSuskind, Richard.

      By Bullet, Bomb & Dagger: The Story of
      Anarchism. Macmillan.
Suslov, Aleksandr, 1950-
  xSuslov, Alexander.
      Loosestrife City. Ardis Pubs.
Suslov, Alexander. see Suslov, Aleksandr.
Susser, Mervyn. see Susser, Mervyn W.
Susser, Mervyn W.
  xSusser, Mervyn.
      Causal Thinking in the Health Sciences:
      Concepts & Strategies of Epidemiology.
      Oxford U Pr.
  xSusser, Mervyn W.
      Sociology in Medicine. Oxford U Pr.
Susser, Samuel M. see Susser, Samuel S.
Susser, Samuel S.
  xSusser, Samuel M.
      The Truth About Selling. NAL.
  xSusser, Samuel S.
      The Truth About Selling. Eriksson.
Susskind, Charles.
  xSusskind, Charles.
      Understanding Technology. Johns Hopkins.
Sussman. see Sussman, Aaron.
Sussman, Aaron.
  xSussman.
      The Magic of Walking. S&S.
  xSussman, Aaron.
      The Amateur Photographer's Handbook. T Y
      Crowell.
      The Magic of Walking. S&S.
Sussman, Art.
  xSussman, Art.
      Handmade Hot Water Systems. Garcia River.
      Handmade Hot Water Systems. Vermont
      Crossroads.
Sussman, Carl.
  xSussman, Carl.
      ed. Planning the Fourth Migration: The
      Neglected Vision of the Regional Planning
      Association of America. MIT Pr.

Sussman, Gerald J. see Sussman, Gerald Jay.

Sussman, Gerald Jay.
  xSussman, Gerald J.
      A Computer Model of Skill Acquisition.
      Elsevier.

Sussman, Henry.
  xSussman, Henry.
      Franz Kafka: Geometrician of Metaphor. Coda
      Pr.
Sussman, Herbert L.
  xSussman, Herbert L.
      Fact into Figure: Typology in Carlyle, Ruskin,
      & the Pre-Raphaelite Brotherhood. Ohio St U
      Pr.

Sussman, Irving.

  xSussman, Irving.
      This Train Is Bound for Glory. Franciscan
      Herald.
Sussman, Leon N., 1907-
  xSussman, Leon N.
      Paternity Testing by Blood Grouping. C C
      Thomas.
Sussman, Leonard D. see Sussman, Leonard R.
Sussman, Leonard R.
  xSussman, Leonard D.
      Mass News Media & the Third World
      Challenge. Sage.
Sussman, Lyle.
  xSussman, Lyle.
      Communication for Supervisors & Managers.
      Alfred Pub.
Sussman, Marvin B.
  xSussman, Marvin B.

      ed. Author's Guide to Journals in Sociology &
      Related Fields. Haworth Pr.
      Marriage & the Family: Current Critical Issues.
      Haworth Pr.
      ed. Sourcebook in Marriage & the Family. HM.
Sussman, Robert W., 1941-
  xSussman, Robert W.
      Primate Ecology: Problem Oriented Field
      Studies. Wiley.
Sussmann, Leila. see Sussmann, Leila Aline.
Sussmann, Leila Aline, 1922-
  xSussmann, Leila.
      Tales Out of School: Implementing
      Organizational Change in the Elementary
      Grades. Temple U Pr.
Sutak, Ken, 1948-
  xSutak, Ken.
      The Great Motion Picture Soundtrack
      Robbery: An Analysis of Copyright
      Protection. Shoe String.
Sutch, William B. see Sutch, William Ball.
Sutch, William Ball, 1904-
  xSutch, William B.
      Price Fixing in New Zealand. AMS Pr.
Sutcliff, Rosemary.
  xSutcliff, Rosemary.
      The Chronicles of Robin Hood. Oxford U Pr.
      Song for a Dark Queen. T Y Crowell.
      Sun Horse, Moon Horse. Dutton.
Sutcliffe, Peter. see Sutcliffe, Peter H.
Sutcliffe, Peter H.
  xSutcliffe, Peter.
      The Oxford University Press: An Informal
      History. Oxford U Pr.
Sutcliffe, Sheila.
  xSutcliffe, Sheila.
      Martello Towers. Fairleigh Dickinson.
Suter, David W. see Suter, David Winston.
Suter, David Winston.
  xSuter, David W.
      Tradition & Composition in the Parables of
      Enoch. Scholars Pr Ca.
Sutermeister. see Sutermeister, Robert A.
Sutermeister, Robert A.
  xSutermeister.
      People & Productivity. McGraw.
Suters, Everett T. see Suters, Everett Thomas.
Suters, Everett Thomas.
  xSuters, Everett T.
      Succeed in Spite of Yourself. Dutton.
      Succeed in Spite of Yourself. Van Nos
      Reinhold.
Sutherland, Alexander, 1852-1902
  xSutherland, Alexander.
      The Origin & Growth of the Moral Instinct.
      Arno.
Sutherland, Anne.
  xSutherland, Anne.
      Gypsies: The Hidden Americans. Free Pr.
Sutherland, Audrey, 1921-
  xSutherland, Audrey.
      Paddling My Own Canoe. U Pr of Hawaii.
Sutherland, Donald, 1915-
  xSutherland, Donald.
      Gertrude Stein: A Biography of Her Work.
      Greenwood.
      On, Romanticism. NYU Pr.
Sutherland, Donald W.
  xSutherland, Donald W.
      The Assize of Novel Disseisin. Oxford U Pr.
Sutherland, Douglas.
  xSutherland, Douglas.
      The English Gentleman's Child. Viking Pr.
Sutherland, Edwin H. see Sutherland, Edwin Hardin.
Sutherland, Edwin Hardin.
  xSutherland, Edwin H.

Criminology. Har-Row.
On Analyzing Crime. U of Chicago Pr.
ed. Prisons of Tomorrow. Arno.
Twenty Thousand Homeless Men: A Study of
Unemployed Men in the Chicago Shelters.
Arno.

Sutherland, Elizabeth, 1946-
xSutherland, Elizabeth.
Mouth of the Whale. Mudborn.

Sutherland, George, 1862-1942
xSutherland, George.
Constitutional Power & World Affairs. Johnson
Repr.

Sutherland, Ivan E. *see* Sutherland, Ivan Edward.

Sutherland, Ivan Edward, 1938-
xSutherland, Ivan E.
Sketchpad: A Man-Machine Graphical
Communication System. Garland Pub.

Sutherland, J. A. *see* Sutherland, John.
Sutherland, J. G. *see* Sutherland, John Georgeson.
Sutherland, J. R. *see* Sutherland, James Runcieman.
Sutherland, James. *see* Sutherland, James Runcieman.
Sutherland, James R. *see* Sutherland, James Runcieman.

Sutherland, James Runcieman, 1900-
xSutherland, J. R.
Wordsworth & Pope. Folcroft.
xSutherland, James.
Medium of Poetry. Folcroft.
ed. The Oxford Book of Literary Anecdotes.
Oxford U Pr.
ed. The Oxford Book of Literary Anecdotes.
PB.
The Oxford Book of Literary Anecdotes. S&S.
Restoration Tragedies. Oxford U Pr.
xSutherland, James R.
Background for Queen Anne. Folcroft.
The English Critic. Folcroft.
English Literature of the Late Seventeenth
Century. Oxford U Pr.

Sutherland, John, 1903-
xSutherland, J. A.
Fiction & the Fiction Industry. Humanities.
xSutherland, John.
Thackeray at Work. Humanities.

Sutherland, John D. *see* Sutherland, John Derg.

Sutherland, John Derg.
xSutherland, John D.
ed. Psychoanalysis & Contemporary Thought.
Arno.

Sutherland, John Georgeson.
xSutherland, J. G.
At Sea with Joseph Conrad. Folcroft.
At Sea with Joseph Conrad. Haskell.

Sutherland, John W.
xSutherland, John W.
Administrative Decision Making: Extending
the Bounds of Rationality. Van Nos
Reinhold.
Systems: Analysis, Administration &
Architecture. Van Nos Reinhold.

Sutherland, Mary E. *see* Sutherland, Mary Ethel.

Sutherland, Mary Ethel, 1889-
xSutherland, Mary E.
One-Step Problem Patterns & Their Relation to
Problem Solving in Arithmetic. AMS Pr.

Sutherland, N. S. *see* Sutherland, Norman Stuart.
Sutherland, Nicola M. *see* Sutherland, Nicola Mary.

Sutherland, Nicola Mary.
xSutherland, Nicola M.
The French Secretaries of State in the Age of
Catherine De Medici. Greenwood.

Sutherland, Norman Stuart.
xSutherland, N. S.
Breakdown. NAL.
Breakdown. Stein & Day.
Mechanisms of Animal Discrimination &
Learning. Acad Pr.
ed. Tutorial Essays in Psychology: A Guide to
Recent Advances. Halsted Pr.

Sutherland, Robert L. *see* Sutherland, Robert Lee.

Sutherland, Robert Lee.
xSutherland, Robert L.
Color, Class, & Personality. Greenwood.

Sutherland, Stella H. *see* Sutherland, Stella Helen.

Sutherland, Stella Helen.
xSutherland, Stella H.
Population Distribution in Colonial America.
AMS Pr.

Sutherland, Stewart R.
xSutherland, Stewart R.
Atheism & the Rejection of God:
Contemporary Philosophy & "The Brothers
Karamazov". Biblio Dist.

Sutherland, Wilson A. *see* Sutherland, Wilson Alexander.

Sutherland, Wilson Alexander.
xSutherland, Wilson A.
Introduction to Metric & Topological Spaces.
Oxford U Pr.

Sutherland, Zena.
xSutherland, Zena.
ed. The Best in Children's Books: The
University of Chicago Guide to Children's
Literature, 1966-72. U of Chicago Pr.

Sutphen, Dick. *see* Sutphen, Richard.

Sutphen, Richard.
xSutphen, Dick.
Deep Breath of Yesterday. Valley Sun.

Sutphin, Florence E.
xSutphin, Florence E.
Autobiography by Chucky Woodchuck. Chris
Mass.

Sutphin, Stanley T.
xSutphin, Stanley T.
Options in Contemporary Theology. U Pr of
Amer.

Sutter, Robert G.
xSutter, Robert G.
China-Watch: Toward Sino-American
Reconciliation. Johns Hopkins.
Chinese Foreign Policy After the Cultural
Revolution: 1966-1977. Westview.

Suttie, John W., 1934-
xSuttie, John W.
Introduction to Biochemistry. HR&W.

Sutton, Albert A. *see* Sutton, Albert Alton.

Sutton, Albert Alton, 1906-
xSutton, Albert A.
Design & Makeup of the Newspaper.
Greenwood.
Education for Journalism in the United States
from Its Beginning to 1940. AMS Pr.

Sutton, Ann.
xSutton, Ann.
Appalachian Trail: Wilderness on the Doorstep.
Lippincott.
Life of the Desert. McGraw.
The Pacific Crest Trail: Escape to the
Wilderness. Lippincott.
Tablet Weaving. Branford.
Wildlife of the Forests. Abrams.

Sutton, Antony C.
xSutton, Antony C.
Trilaterals Over Washington. August Corp.

Sutton, C. J. *see* Sutton, Clive Julian.

Sutton, Carole.
xSutton, Carole.
Psychology for Social Workers & Counsellors:
An Introduction. Routledge & Kegan.

Sutton, Clive Julian.
xSutton, C. J.
Economics & Corporate Strategy. Cambridge U
Pr.

Sutton, Dana F. *see* Sutton, Dana Ferrin.

Sutton, Dana Ferrin.
xSutton, Dana F.
Self & Society in Aristophanes. U Pr of Amer.

Sutton, David, 1917-
xSutton, David.

Radiology for Medical Students. Churchill.

Sutton, Eve.
xSutton, Eve.
My Cat Likes to Hide in Boxes. Schol Bk Serv.

Sutton, Felix.
xSutton, Felix.
Sons of Liberty. Messner.

Sutton, George M. *see* Sutton, George Miksch.

Sutton, George Miksch, 1898-
xSutton, George M.
Bird Student: An Autobiography. U of Tex Pr.
Fifty Common Birds of Oklahoma & the
Southern Great Plains. U of Okla Pr.
Portraits of Mexican Birds: Fifty Selected
Paintings. U of Okla Pr.

Sutton, Graham, 1892-
xSutton, Graham.
Some Contemporary Dramatists. Kennikat.
Some Contemporary Dramatists. R West.

Sutton, H. Eldon. *see* Sutton, Harry Eldon.

Sutton, Harry Eldon.
xSutton, H. Eldon.
Mutagenic Effects of Environmental
Contaminants. Acad Pr.

Sutton, Hilton.
xSutton, Hilton.
The Mid-East Peace Puzzle. Nelson.

Sutton, Imre, 1928-
xSutton, Imre.
Indian Land Tenure: Bibliographical Essays & a
Guide to the Literature. Clearwater Pub.

Sutton, Jane.
xSutton, Jane.
What Should a Hippo Wear?. HM.

Sutton, Jefferson.
xSutton, Jefferson.
Cassady. St Martin.

Sutton, Margaret.
xSutton, Margaret.
The Clue of the Stone Lantern. Amereon Ltd.
Palace Wagon Family: A True Story of the
Donner Party. Knopf.
The Rainbow Riddle. Amereon Ltd.
The Spirit of Fog Island. Amereon Ltd.
The Vanishing Shadow. Amereon Ltd.

Sutton, Max K. *see* Sutton, Max Keith.

Sutton, Max Keith.
xSutton, Max K.
R. D. Blackmore. Twayne.

Sutton, N. G. *see* Sutton, Neville G.

Sutton, Neville G.
xSutton, N. G.
Injuries of the Spinal Cord: Management of
Paraplegia & Tetraplegia. Butterworths.

Sutton, Oliver G. *see* Sutton, Oliver Graham.

Sutton, Oliver Graham, Sir.
xSutton, Oliver G.
Challenge of the Atmosphere. Greenwood.

Sutton, Richard L. *see* Sutton, Richard Lightburn.

Sutton, Richard Lightburn.
xSutton, Richard L.
The Practitioners' Dermatology. Yorke Med.

Sutton, Robert P.
xSutton, Robert P.
The Prairie State: A Documentary History of
Illinois. Eerdmans.

Sutton, Roberta (Briggs).
xSutton, Roberta B.
Speech Index: An Index to Collections of
World Famous Orations & Speeches for
Various Occasions; Supplement 1966 to 1970.
Scarecrow.

Sutton, Roberta B. *see* Sutton, Roberta (Briggs).

Sutton, Walter.
xSutton, Walter.
American Free Verse: The Modern Revolution
on Poetry. New Directions.
Modern American Criticism. Greenwood.

Sutton, Walter. *see* Sutton, Walter E.

Sutton, Walter E.
    xSutton, Walter.
        ed. Modern Criticism: Theory & Practice.
            Irvington.
Sutton, William A. see Sutton, William Alfred.
Sutton, William Alfred, 1915-
    xSutton, William A.
        Carl Sandburg Remembered. Scarecrow.
Sutton, William Francis.
    xSutton, Willie.
        Where the Money Was. Ballantine.
Sutton, Willie. see Sutton, William Francis.
Sutton-Smith, Brian.
    xSutton-Smith, Brian.
        The Games of the Americas: A Book of
            Readings. Arno.
        Play & Learning. Halsted Pr.
Sutulov, Alexander.
    xSutulov, Alexander.
        Copper Porphyries. Miller Freeman.
Suval, Stanley.
    xSuval, Stanley.
        The Anschluss Question in the Weimar Era: A
            Study of Nationalism in Germany & Austria,
            1918-1932. Johns Hopkins.
Suvin, Darko.
    xSuvin, Darko.
        ed. H. G. Wells & Modern Science Fiction.
            Bucknell U Pr.
Suwa, Nozomi.
    xSuwa, Nozomi.
        Pref. by Psychophysiological Studies of
            Emotion & Mental Disorders. Igaku-Shoin.
Suydam, Marilyn N.
    xSuydam, Marilyn N.
        Classroom Ideas from Research on
            Computational Skills. NCTM.
Suzuki, David T.
    xSuzuki, David T.
        An Introduction to Genetic Analysis. W H
            Freeman.
Suzuki, Yoshio, 1931-
    xSuzuki, Yoshio.
        Money & Banking Contemporary Japan: The
            Theoretical Setting & Its Application. Yale U
            Pr.
Svalastoga, Kaare.
    xSvalastoga, Kaare.
        Prestige, Class & Mobility. Arno.
Svarlien, Oscar.
    xSvarlien, Oscar.
        Eastern Greenland Case in Historical
            Perspective. U Presses Fla.
Svarovsky. see Svarovsky, Ladislav.
Svarovsky, Ladislav.
    xSvarovsky.
        Solid Liquid Separation. Butterworths.
Svehla, G.
    xSvehla, Gyula.
        Automatic Potentiometric Titrations.
            Pergamon.
Svehla, Gyula. see Svehla, G.
Sveinson, Kelly. see Sveinson, Kelly M.
Sveinson, Kelly M.
    xSveinson, Kelly.
        Learning to Live with Cancer. St Martin.
Svejgaard, A. see Svejgaard, Arne.
Svejgaard, Arne.
    xSvejgaard, A.
        The HLA System: An Introductory Survey. S
            Karger.
Svelto, Orazio.
    xSvelto, Orazio.
        Principles of Lasers. Plenum Pub.
Svendgaard, N. A.
    xSvendgaard, N. A.

        Regenerative Properties of Central Monoamine
            Neurons: Studies in the Adult Rat Using
            Cerebral Iris Implants As Targets.
            Springer-Verlag.
Svennas, Elsie.
    xSvennas, Elsie.
        Handbook of Lettering for Stitchers. Van Nos
            Reinhold.
Svensson, Lennart, 1942-
    xSvensson, Lennart.
        Study Skill & Learning. Humanities.

Sverdrup, H. see Sverdrup, Harald Ulrik.

Sverdrup, Harald U. see Sverdrup, Harald Ulrik.

Sverdrup, Harald Ulrik, 1888-1957

    xSverdrup, H.
        Oceans: Their Physics, Chemistry & General
            Biology. P-H.

    xSverdrup, Harald U.
        Among the Tundra People. Scripps Inst Ocean.

Sverstiuk, Ievhen.
    xSverstiuk, Ievhen.
        Clandestine Essays. Ukrainian Acad.
Sveshnikov, A. A. see Sveshnikov, Aram Arutiunovich.
Sveshnikov, Aram Arutiunovich.
    xSveshnikov, A. A.
        Problems in Probability Theory, Mathematical
            Statistics & Theory of Random Functions.
            Dover.
Svestka, Z. see Svestka, Zdenek.
Svestka, Zdenek.
    xSvestka, Z.
        Solar Flares. Kluwer Boston.
Svet, Darii Iakovlevich.
    xSvet, Darii Y.
        Thermal Radiation: Metals, Semiconductors,
            Ceramics, Partly Transparent Bodies, &
            Films. Plenum Pub.
Svet, Darii Y. see Svet, Darii Iakovlevich.
Svidine, Nicholas. see Svidine, Nicolas.
Svidine, Nicolas.
    xSvidine, Nicholas.
        Cossack Gold: The Secret of the White Army
            Treasure. Little.
Svitak, Ivan.
    xSvitak, Ivan.
        Czechoslovak Experiment, 1968-1969.
            Columbia U Pr.
Svoboda, W. see Svoboda, William B.
Svoboda, William B.
    xSvoboda, W.
        Learning About Epilepsy. Univ Park.
Swabey, William C. see Swabey, William Curtis.
Swabey, William Curtis, 1894-
    xSwabey, William C.
        Ethical Theory: From Hobbes to Kant.
            Greenwood.
Swadley, Elizabeth.
    xSwadley, Elizabeth.
        Christmas at Home. Broadman.
Swados, Elizabeth.
    xSwados, Elizabeth.
        The Girl with the Incredible Feeling. Persea
            Bks.
        Lullaby. Har-Row.
Swados, Harvey.
    xSwados, Harvey.
        Nights in the Gardens of Brooklyn. Arno.
        On the Line. Dell.
        A Radical's America. Greenwood.
Swaim, Joseph C. see Swaim, Joseph Carter.
Swaim, Joseph Carter, 1904-
    xSwaim, Joseph C.
        Answers to Your Questions About the Bible.
            Vanguard.
Swaim, Lawrence.
    xSwaim, Lawrence.

        The Killing. HR&W.
Swaiman, Kenneth F.
    xSwaiman, Kenneth F.
        Pediatric Neuromuscular Diseases. Mosby.
Swain, Dwight V.
    xSwain, Dwight V.
        Film Scriptwriting: A Practical Manual.
            Hastings.
Swain, F. M. see Swain, Frederick Morrill.
Swain, Frederick M. see Swain, Frederick Morrill.
Swain, Frederick Morrill, 1916-
    xSwain, F. M.
        ed. Stratigraphic Micropaleontology of Atlantic
            Basin & Borderlands. Elsevier.
    xSwain, Frederick M.
        Non-Marine Organic Geochemistry. Cambridge
            U Pr.
        Ostracoda from the Gulf of California. Geol
            Soc.
Swain, James E. see Swain, James Edgar.
Swain, James Edgar, 1897-
    xSwain, James E.
        The Struggle for the Control of the
            Mediterranean Prior to 1848: A Study in
            Anglo-French Relations. Russell.
Swain, Martha.
    xSwain, Martha H.
        Pat Harrison: The New Deal Years. U Pr of
            Miss.
Swain, Martha H. see Swain, Martha.
Swain, Philip H.
    xSwain, Philip H.
        Remote Sensing: The Quantitative Approach.
            McGraw.
Swales, M. see Swales, Martin.
Swales, Martin.
    xSwales, M.
        The German Novelle. Princeton U Pr.
Swalin, Richard A.
    xSwalin, Richard A.
        Thermodynamics of Solids. Wiley.
Swallow, Alan.
    xSwallow, Alan.
        ed. Anchor in the Sea: An Anthology of
            Psychological Fiction. Swallow.
        Editor's Essays of Two Decades. Swallow.
Swallow, Jay.
    xSwallow, Jay.
        Pony Care. Allen Unwin.
Swallow, Norman.
    xSwallow, Norman.
        Eisenstein: A Documentary Portrait. Dutton.
Swalls, Fred. see Swalls, J. Fred.
Swalls, J. Fred.
    xSwalls, Fred.
        Legal Rights & Responsibilities of Indiana
            Teachers. Interstate.
Swalm, Charles M.
    xSwalm, Charles M.
        ed. Chemistry of Food Packaging. Am
            Chemical.
Swamy, N. V. see Swamy, Nyayapathi Venkata Vykuntha
    Jagannadha.
Swamy, Nyayapathi Venkata Vykuntha Jagannadha.
    xSwamy, N. V.
        Group Theory Made Easy for Scientists &
            Engineers. Wiley.
Swan, Abraham.
    xSwan, Abraham.
        British Architect. Da Capo.
Swan, Dale E. see Swan, Dale Evans.
Swan, Dale Evans.
    xSwan, Dale E.
        The Structure & Profitability of the Antebellum
            Rice Industry: 1859. Arno.
Swan, George W., 1938-
    xSwan, George W.

Some Current Mathematical Topics in Cancer
Research. Univ Microfilms.
Swan, Helena.
xSwan, Helena.
Girls' Christian Names: Their History,
Meaning & Association. C E Tuttle.
Swan, Howard, 1906-
xSwan, Howard.
Music in the Southwest, 1825-1950. Da Capo.
Swan, J. M. see Swan, John Melvin.
Swan, James G. see Swan, James Gilchrist.
Swan, James Gilchrist.
xSwan, James G.
The Northwest Coast: Or, Three Years'
Residence in Washington Territory. U of
Wash Pr.
Swan, John Melvin.
xSwan, J. M.
Organometallics in Organic Synthesis. Methuen
Inc.
Swan, Jon.
xSwan, Jon.
A Door to the Forest: Poems. Random.
Swan, Kenneth G.
xSwan, Kenneth G.
Gunshot Wounds: Pathophysiology &
Management. PSG Pub.
Swan, L. Alex. see Swan, Llewelyn Alex.
Swan, Lester A.
xSwan, Lester A.
The Common Insects of North America.
Har-Row.
Swan, Llewelyn Alex, 1938-
xSwan, L. Alex.
The Politics of Riot Behavior. U Pr of Amer.
Swan, Richard G.
xSwan, Richard G.
Theory of Sheaves. U of Chicago Pr.
Swan, Robert O.
xSwan, Robert O.
Munshi Premchand of Lamhi Village. Duke.
Swan, Sara.
xSwan, Sara K.
Home-Made Baby Toys. HM.
Swan, Sara K. see Swan, Sara.
Swan, Susan B. see Swan, Susan Burrows.
Swan, Susan Burrows.
xSwan, Susan B.
Plain & Fancy: American Women & Their
Needlework, 1700-1850. HR&W.
Swanberg, Annette.
xSwanberg, Annette.
Glad Rags: L. A. Directory to Chic on a
Shoestring. Chronicle Bks.
Swanberg, W. A., 1907-
xSwanberg, W. A.
Dreiser. Scribner.
Swancara, Frank.
xSwancara, Frank.
Obstruction of Justice by Religion: A Treatise
on Religious Barbarities of the Common Law,
& a Review of Judicial Oppressions of the
Non-Religious in the U.S.. Da Capo.
Swanda, John R.
xSwanda, John R.
Organizational Behavior: Systems &
Applications. Alfred Pub.
Swanekamp, Joan.
xSwanekamp, Joan.
Diamonds & Rust: A Bibliography &
Discography on Joan Baez. Pierian.
Swaney, Richard A.
xSwaney, Richard A.
Out of Darkness Light. Pacific Pr Pub Assn.
Swanfeldt, Andrew.
xSwanfeldt, Andrew.
Crossword Puzzle Dictionary. T Y Crowell.
Swanholm, Marx, 1941-
xSwanholm, Marx.

Alexander Ramsey & the Politics of Survival.
Minn Hist.
Swann, Peter C.
xSwann, Peter C.
A Concise History of Japanese Art. Kodansha.
Swann, Thomas B. see Swann, Thomas Burnett.
Swann, Thomas Burnett.
xSwann, Thomas B.
The Tournament of Thorns. Ace Bks.
Wonder & Whimsy: The Fantastic World of
Christina Rossetti. M Jones.
Swansea, Charleen.
xSwansea, Charleen.
ed. Love Stories by New Women. Avon.
ed. Love Stories by New Women. Red Clay.
Swanson, Alfred B., 1923-
xSwanson, Alfred B.
Flexible Implant Resection Arthroplasty in the
Hand & Extremities. Mosby.
Swanson, B. E. see Swanson, Bert E.
Swanson, B. Marian. see Swanson, Bernice Marian.
Swanson, Bernice Marian.
xSwanson, B. Marian.
Understanding Exceptional Children & Youth:
An Introduction to Special Education. Rand.
Swanson, Bert E.
xSwanson, B. E.
Discovering the Community. Halsted Pr.
Swanson, Bessie R.
xSwanson, Bessie R.
Music in the Education of Children.
Wadsworth Pub.
Swanson, Burton E.
xSwanson, Burton E.
Regional Agricultural Production Programs.
Training & Design Strategies. Intl
Development.
Swanson, C. R. see Swanson, Charles R.
Swanson, Carl B. see Swanson, Carl P.
Swanson, Carl P.
xSwanson, Carl B.
Cytogenetics: The Chromosome in Division,
Inheritance, & Evolution. P-H.
xSwanson, Carl P.
The Cell. P-H.
The Natural History of Man. P-H.
Swanson, Charles R.
xSwanson, C. R.
Criminal Investigation. Goodyear.
xSwanson, Charles R.
Criminal Investigation. Goodyear.
Swanson, Cheryl. see Swanson, Cheryl G.
Swanson, Cheryl G.
xSwanson, Cheryl.
A Question of Height Revisited: Assaults on
Police. Univ OK Gov Res.
Swanson, Donald F.
xSwanson, Donald F.
Origins of Hamilton's Fiscal Policies. U Presses
Fla.
Swanson, Ernst W. see Swanson, Ernst Werner.
Swanson, Ernst Werner.
xSwanson, Ernst W.
ed. Public Education in the South Today &
Tomorrow: A Statistical Survey. Greenwood.
Swanson, Evadene Adele Burris, 1911-
xSwanson, Evadene B.
Fort Collins Yesterdays. E Swanson.
Swanson, Evadene B. see Swanson, Evadene Adele
Burris.
Swanson, Frederick J. see Swanson, Frederick John.
Swanson, Frederick John, 1910-
xSwanson, Frederick J.
Music Teaching in the Junior High & the
Middle School. P-H.
Swanson, Gerald. see Swanson, Gerald L.

Swanson, Gerald L.
xSwanson, Gerald.
ed. Psychology Book Guide: 1974. G K Hall.
Swanson, Gordon I. see Swanson, Gordon Ira.
Swanson, Gordon Ira.
xSwanson, Gordon I.
ed. Manpower Research & Labor Economics.
Sage.
Swanson, H. Lee.
xSwanson, H. Lee.
Teaching Strategies for Children in Conflict:
Curriculum, Methods & Materials. Mosby.
Swanson, Leslie C. see Swanson, Leslie Charles.
Swanson, Leslie Charles, 1905-
xSwanson, Leslie C.
Canals of Mid-America. Swanson.
Swanson, Richard, 1940-
xSwanson, Richard.
For Your Information: A Guide to Writing
Reports. P-H.
Swanson, Roger M.
xSwanson, Roger M.
ed. The Freshman Writes. Odyssey Pr.
Swanston, Hamish. see Swanston, Hamish F. G.
Swanston, Hamish F. G., 1933-
xSwanston, Hamish.
In Defence of Opera. Penguin.
Swanstrom, Roy.
xSwanstrom, Roy.
History in the Making: An Introduction to the
Study of the Past. Inter-Varsity.
Swanton, John R. see Swanton, John Reed.
Swanton, John Reed, 1873-1958
xSwanton, John R.
Contributions to the Ethnology of the Haida.
AMS Pr.
Early History of the Creek Indians & Their
Neighbors. Johnson Rpt.
Early History of the Creek Indians & Their
Neighbors. Scholarly.
Haida Texts--Masset Dialect. AMS Pr.
Haida Texts & Myths: Skidegate Dialect.
Johnson Repr.
Indian Tribes of the Lower Mississippi Valley
& Adjacent Coast of the Gulf of Mexico.
Johnson Repr.
Indian Tribes of the Lower Mississippi Valley
& Adjacent Coast of the Gulf of Mexico.
Scholarly.
Indian Tribes of Washington, Oregon & Idaho.
Ye Galleon.
Indians of the Southeastern United States.
Greenwood.
The Indians' of the Southeastern United
States'. Scholarly.
Indians of the Southeastern United States.
Smithsonian.
A Structural & Lexical Comparison of the
Tunica, Chitimacha & Atakapa Languages.
Scholarly.
Swanton, Michael. see Swanton, Michael James.
Swanton, Michael James.
xSwanton, Michael.
ed. Beowulf. B&N.
Exploring Early Britain. Charles River Bks.
Swanwick, Keith.
xSwanwick, Keith.
A Basis for Music Education. Humanities.
Swarbrick, Brian, 1929-
xSwarbrick, Brian.
The Duffer's Guide to Bogey Golf. P-H.
Sward, Keith, 1904-
xSward, Keith.
Legend of Henry Ford. Atheneum.
Legend of Henry Ford. Russell.
Sward, Robert, 1933-
xSward, Robert.
Horgbortom Stringbottom, I Am Yours, You
Are History. Soft Pr.
Swarthout, Glendon. see Swarthout, Glendon Fred.

Swarthout, Glendon Fred.
 xSwarthout, Glendon.
  Luck & Pluck. Doubleday.
  The Melodeon. G K Hall.
  The Melodeon. PB.
  Skeletons. Doubleday.
  Whichaway. Random.

Swartley, David W. see Swartley, David Warren.

Swartley, David Warren.

 xSwartley, David W.
  My Friend, My Brother. Herald Pr.

Swartout, Robert R., 1946-
 xSwartout, Robert R.
  Mandarins, Gunboats, & Power Politics: Owen
   Nickerson Denny & International Rivalries in
   Korea. U Pr of Hawaii.

Swartz, B. K.
 xSwartz, B. K.
  Klamath Basin Petroglyphs. Ballena Pr.

Swartz, Clarence L. see Swartz, Clarence Lee.

Swartz, Clarence Lee.
 xSwartz, Clarence L.
  What Is Mutualism. Gordon Pr.

Swartz, Clifford E.
 xSwartz, Clifford E.
  The Fundamental Particles. A-W.
  Used Math for the First Two Years of College
   Science. P-H.

Swartz, Marc J.
 xSwartz, Marc J.
  Anthropology: Perspective on Humanity.
   Wiley.
  Culture: The Anthropological Perspective.
   Wiley.

Swartz, Melvin J. see Swartz, Melvin Jay.

Swartz, Melvin Jay.
 xSwartz, Melvin J.
  Don't Die Broke!: A Guide to Secure
   Retirement. Dutton.
  Don't Die Broke!: A Guide to Secure
   Retirement. Macmillan.

Swartz, Richard.
 xSwartz, Richard.
  Writing & Rewriting Sentences. P-H.

Swartz, Robert J.
 xSwartz, Robert J.
  ed. Perceiving, Sensing & Knowing: A Book of
   Readings from Twentieth-Century Sources in
   the Philosophy of Perception. U of Cal Pr.

Swartz, Ronald M.
 xSwartz, Ronald M.
  Knowledge & Fallibilism: Essays on Improving
   Education. NYU Pr.

Swartzburg, Susan G., 1938-
 xSwartzburg, Susan G.
  Preserving Library Materials: A Manual.
   Scarecrow.

Swartzlander, Earl E.
 xSwartzlander, Earl E.
  Computer Design Development: Principal
   Papers. Hayden.

Swarzenski, Hanns, 1903-
 xSwarzenski, Hanns.
  Monuments of Romanesque Art: The Art of
   Church Treasures in North-Western Europe.
   U of Chicago Pr.

Swayne, James C. see Swayne, James Colin.

Swayne, James Colin.
 xSwayne, James C.
  A Concise Glossary of Geographical Terms.
   Greenwood.

Swayne, Sam. see Swayne, Samuel F.

Swayne, Samuel F.
 xSwayne, Sam.
  Great-Grandfather in the Honey Tree. Viking
   Pr.

Swayze, John C. see Swayze, John Cameron.

Swayze, John Cameron.
 xSwayze, John C.
  The Art of Living. Playboy Pbks.

Swayze, Nathan L.
 xSwayze, Nathan L.
  Engraved Powder Horns of the French &
   Indian War & Revolutionary War Era. Gun
   Hill.

Swayzee, Cleon O. see Swayzee, Cleon Oliphant.

Swayzee, Cleon Oliphant, 1903-
 xSwayzee, Cleon O.
  Contempt of Court in Labor Injunction Cases.
   AMS Pr.

Swazey, Judith P.
 xSwazey, Judith P.
  Reflexes & Motor Integration: Sherrington's
   Concept of Integrative Action. Harvard U Pr.

Swearer, Donald K., 1934-
 xSwearer, Donald K.
  ed. Buddhism. Argus Comm.

Swearer, Harvey. see Swearer, Harvey F.

Swearer, Harvey F.
 xSwearer, Harvey.
  General Electric Monochrome TV Service
   Manual. TAB Bks.
  Pulse & Switching Circuits. TAB Bks.
 xSwearer, Harvey F.
  Commercial FCC License Handbook. TAB
   Bks.
  Installing & Servicing Electronic Protective
   Systems. TAB Bks.
  Modern Manual & Guide for TV Servicing.
   P-H.

Swearingen, Arthur Rodger, 1923-
 xSwearingen, Rodger.
  ed. Leaders of the Communist World. Free Pr.
  The Soviet Union & Postwar Japan: Escalating
   Challenge & Response. Hoover Inst Pr.

Swearingen, James E., 1939-
 xSwearingen, James E.
  Reflexivity in "Tristram Shandy: An Essay in
   Phenomenological Criticism. Yale U Pr.

Swearingen, Martha.
 xSwearingen, Martha.
  If Anything. Elsevier-Nelson.

Swearingen, Rodger. see Swearingen, Arthur Rodger.

Sweat, Clifford H.
 xSweat, Clifford H.
  ed. Early Adolescent Competencies. Interstate.

Sweat, Lynn.
 xSweat, Lynn.
  illus. The Wonderful Hunting Dog. Macmillan.

Sweazey, George E. see Sweazey, George Edgar.

Sweazey, George Edgar, 1905-
 xSweazey, George E.
  The Church As Evangelist. Har-Row.
  Preaching the Good News. P-H.

Swedenberg, H. T. see Swedenberg, Hugh Thomas.

Swedenberg, Hugh T. see Swedenberg, Hugh Thomas.

Swedenberg, Hugh Thomas, 1906-
 xSwedenberg, H. T.
  ed. England in the Restoration & Early
   Eighteenth Century: Essays on Culture &
   Society. U of Cal Pr.
 xSwedenberg, Hugh T.
  The Theory of the Epic in England 1650-1800.
   Russell.

Swedenborg, Emanuel.
 xSwedenborg, Emanuel.
  Four Doctrines. Swedenborg.
  Swedenborg's Journal of Dreams. Swedenborg.

Sweedler, Moss E.
 xSweedler, Moss E.
  Hopf Algebras. Benjamin-Cummings.

Sweeney, Charles. see Sweeney, R. Charles H.

Sweeney, Dennis M.
 xSweeney, Dennis M.

  Practice Manual for Social Security Claims.
   PLI.

Sweeney, Gerard M.
 xSweeney, Gerard M.
  Melville's Use of Classical Mythology.
   Humanities.

Sweeney, James J. see Sweeney, James Johnson.

Sweeney, James Johnson, 1900-
 xSweeney, James J.
  ed. African Sculpture. Princeton U Pr.
  Marc Chagall. Arno.

Sweeney, Karen O. see Sweeney, Karen O'Connor.

Sweeney, Karen O'Connor.
 xSweeney, Karen O.
  How to Make Money. Watts.
  Improve Your Love Life. Major Bks.
  Nature Runs Wild: True Disaster Stories.
   Watts.

Sweeney, R. Charles H.
 xSweeney, Charles.
  Naturalist in the Sudan. Taplinger.

Sweeney, Stephen B. see Sweeney, Stephen Binnington.

Sweeney, Stephen Binnington.
 xSweeney, Stephen B.
  Education for Administrative Careers in
   Government Service. Greenwood.

Sweeney, Thomas. see Sweeney, Thomas John.

Sweeney, Thomas J. see Sweeney, Thomas John.

Sweeney, Thomas John, 1936-
 xSweeney, Thomas.
  Adlerian Counseling. Accel Devel.
 xSweeney, Thomas J.
  Adlerian Counseling. HM.

Sweeney, W. Allison. see Sweeney, William Allison.

Sweeney, William Allison, 1851-
 xSweeney, W. Allison.
  History of the American Negro in the Great
   World War: His Splendid Record in the
   Battle Zones of Europe Including a Resume
   of His Past Services to His Country. Negro U
   Pr.

Sweeny, Allen.
 xSweeny, Allen.
  Accounting Fundamentals for Non-Financial
   Executives. Am Mgmt.
  Budgeting Fundamentals for Nonfinancial
   Executives. Am Mgmt.
  Roi Basics for Nonfinancial Executives. Am
   Mgmt.

Sweet, Charles F. see Sweet, Charles Filkins.

Sweet, Charles Filkins, 1854 or 5-1927
 xSweet, Charles F.
  Champion of the Cross. AMS Pr.

Sweet, Donald H.
 xSweet, Donald H.
  The Modern Employment Function. A-W.

Sweet, Henry, 1845-1912
 xSweet, Henry.
  The History of Language. Folcroft.
  The Practical Study of Languages: A Guide for
   Teachers & Learners. Oxford U Pr.
  Student's Dictionary of Anglo-Saxon. Oxford
   U Pr.

Sweet, J. P. see Sweet, John Philip McMurdo.

Sweet, John Philip McMurdo.
 xSweet, J. P.
  Revelation. Westminster.

Sweet, Louise E. see Sweet, Louise Elizabeth.

Sweet, Louise Elizabeth.
 xSweet, Louise E.
  ed. The Central Middle East: A Handbook of
   Anthropology & Published Research.
   HRAFP.

Sweet, Muriel.
 xSweet, Muriel.
  Common Edible & Useful Plants of the East &
   Midwest. Naturegraph.

Sweet, Paul R. see Sweet, Paul Robinson.

Sweet, Paul Robinson, 1907-
 xSweet, Paul R.

Friedrich Von Gentz, Defender of the Old
Order. Greenwood.

Sweet, Waldo E.
xSweet, Waldo E.
Latin: A Structural Approach. U of Mich Pr.
Sweet, William W. *see* Sweet, William Warren.
Sweet, William Warren, 1881-
xSweet, William W.
Religion in Colonial America. Cooper Sq.
Story of Religion in America. Baker Bk.
Sweeting, George, 1924-
xSweeting, George.
How to Be a Chalk Artist. Zondervan.
How to Solve Conflicts. Moody.
Sweetland, Ben.
xSweetland, Ben.
I Will. Wilshire.
Sweets, John F., 1945-
xSweets, John F.
The Politics of Resistance in France,
1940-1944: A History of the Mouvements
Unis De la Resistance. N Ill U Pr.
Sweetser, Thomas P.
xSweetser, Thomas P.
The Catholic Parish: Shifting Membership in a
Changing Church. Ctr Sci Study.
Sweetser, Wesley D.
xSweetser, Wesley D.
Ralph Hodgson: A Bibliography. Garland Pub.
Sweetwood, Hannelore.
xSweetwood, Hannelore.
Nursing in the Intensive Respiratory Care Unit.
Springer Pub.
The Patient in the Coronary Care Unit.
Springer Pub.
Sweezy, Paul M. *see* Sweezy, Paul Marlor.
Sweezy, Paul Marlor, 1910-
xSweezy, Paul M.
Modern Capitalism & Other Essays. Monthly
Rev.
Monopoly & Competition in the English Coal
Trade: 1550-1850. Greenwood.
On the Transition to Socialism. Monthly Rev.
Sweigard, Lulu E.
xSweigard, Lulu E.
Human Movement Potential: Its Ideokinetic
Facilitation. Har-Row.
Swell, Lila.
xSwell, Lila.
Success: You Can Make It Happen. BJ Pub
Group.
Sweningson, Sally.
xSweningson, Sally.
Indoor Gardening. Lerner Pubns.
Swensen, Clifford. *see* Swensen, Clifford H.
Swensen, Clifford H.
xSwensen, Clifford.
Approach to Case Conceptualization. HM.
xSwensen, Clifford H.
Introduction to Interpersonal Relations. Scott
F.
Swenson, Allan A.
xSwenson, Allan A.
Plan Your Own Landscape. G&D.
Swenson, Esther J. *see* Swenson, Esther Jeanette.
Swenson, Esther Jeanette, 1907-
xSwenson, Esther J.
Teaching Mathematics to Children. Macmillan.
Swenson, Leland.
xSwenson, Leland C.
Theories of Learning: Traditional Perspectives -
Contemporary Development. Wadsworth
Pub.
Swenson, Leland C. *see* Swenson, Leland.
Swenson, Loyd S.
xSwenson, Loyd S.

The Ethereal Aether: A History of the
Michelson-Morley-Miller Aether-Drift
Experiments, 1880-1930. U of Tex Pr.
Swenson, Peggye.
xSwenson, Peggye.
The Double M Factor. Double M Pr.
Swerdloff, Peter.
xSwerdloff, Peter.
Men & Women. Time-Life.
Men & Women. Silver.
Swerdlow, Irving.
xSwerdlow, Irving.
The Public Administration of Economic
Development. Praeger.
Swerdlow, Joel.
xSwerdlow, Joel.
Code Z. Putnam.
Swerdlow, R. *see* Swerdlow, Robert M.
Swerdlow, Robert M.
xSwerdlow, R.
Introduction to Graphic Arts. Am Technical.
Swern, Daniel, 1916-
xSwern, Daniel.
ed. Organic Peroxides. Krieger.
Swesnik, Richard H.
xSwesnik, Richard H.
Acquiring & Developing Income Producing
Real Estate. Reston.
Swetnam, Evelyn.
xSwetnam, Evelyn.
Yes, My Darling Daughter. Harvey.
Swetnam, George.
xSwetnam, George.
A Guidebook to Historic Western
Pennsylvania. U of Pittsburgh Pr.
Swezey, Robert L.
xSwezey, Robert L.
Arthritis. Rational Therapy & Rehabilitation.
Saunders.
Swiderska, Barbara.
xSwiderska, Barbara.
illus. The Fisherman's Bride. Scroll Pr.
Swidler, Ann, 1944-
xSwidler, Ann.
Organization Without Authority: Dilemmas of
Social Control in Free Schools. Harvard U
Pr.
Swidler, Gerald.
xSwidler, Gerald.
Handbook of Drug Interactions. Wiley.
Swidler, Leonard. *see* Swidler, Leonard J.
Swidler, Leonard J.
xSwidler, Leonard J.
Biblical Affirmations of Woman. Westminster.
Swiercinsky, Dennis.
xSwiercinsky, Dennis.
Manual for the Adult Neuropsychological
Evaluation. C C Thomas.
Swierenga, Robert P.
xSwierenga, Robert P.
Acres for Cents: Delinquent Tax Auctions in
Frontier Iowa. Greenwood.
Swieringa, Robert J.
xSwieringa, Robert J.
Some Effects of Participative Budgeting on
Managerial Behavior. Natl Assn Accts.
Swieson, Eddy.
xSwieson, Eddy.
When the Angels Laughed. Logos.
Swift, Ernest H. *see* Swift, Ernest Haywood.
Swift, Ernest Haywood.
xSwift, Ernest H.
Quantitative Measurements & Chemical
Equilibria. W H Freeman.
Swift, Hildegarde H. *see* Swift, Hildegarde Hoyt.
Swift, Hildegarde Hoyt.
xSwift, Hildegarde H.

Little Red Lighthouse & the Great Gray
Bridge. HarBraceJ.
The Little Red Lighthouse & the Great Gray
Bridge. HarBraceJ.
Swift, Joan Louise (Woodcock), 1919-
xSwift, Joan W.
Human Services Career Programs & the
Community College. Am Assn Comm Jr
Coll.
Swift, Joan W. *see* Swift, Joan Louise (Woodcock).
Swift, Jonathan, 1667-1745
xSwift, Jonathan.
Gulliver's Travels. Biblio Dist.
Gulliver's Travels. Bobbs.
Gulliver's Travels. Dell.
Gulliver's Travels. Dutton.
Gulliver's Travels. HM.
Gulliver's Travels. Oxford U Pr.
Gulliver's Travels. Penguin.
Gulliver's Travels. Schol Facsimiles.
Gulliver's Travels. St Martin.
Gulliver's Travels. NAL.
Gulliver's Travels. G&D.
Gulliver's Travels. Pendulum Pr.
Gulliver's Travels. Raintree Child.
Gulliver's Travels. Macmillan.
Gulliver's Travels. PB.
Gulliver's Travels. Airmont.
Gulliver's Travels. Norton.
Gulliver's Travels. AMSCO Sch.
The Letters of Jonathan Swift to Charles Ford.
AMS Pr.
The Letters of Jonathan Swift to Charles Ford.
Arden Lib.
Portable Swift. Penguin.
The Prose Works of Jonathan Swift. AMS Pr.
Prose Works of Jonathan Swift. B&N
Swift, Lloyd H., 1920-
xSwift, Lloyd H.
Botanical Classifications: A Comparison of
Eight Systems of Angiosperm Classification.
Shoe String.
Swift, Marshall S.
xSwift, Marshall S.
Alternative Teaching Strategies: Helping
Behaviorally Troubled Children Achieve. Res
Press.
Swift, Mary G. *see* Swift, Mary Grace.
Swift, Mary Grace.
xSwift, Mary G.
Art of the Dance in the U.S.S.R. U of Notre
Dame Pr.
Belles & Beaux on Their Toes: Dancing Stars
in Young America. U Pr of Amer.
A Loftier Flight: The Life & Accomplishments
of Charles Louis Didelot, Balletmaster.
Columbia U Pr.
Swift, Mildred. *see* Swift, Mildred G.
Swift, Mildred G.
xSwift, Mildred.
Looking at Cooking: Favorite Deep South
Recipes. Pelican.
Swift, William. *see* Swift, William Clement.
Swift, William Clement.
xSwift, William.
Principles of Finite Mathematics. P-H.
Swift, Zephaniah, 1759-1823
xSwift, Zephaniah.
A System of the Laws of the State of
Connecticut. Arno.
Swigart, Rob.
xSwigart, Rob.
The Time Trip. HM.
Swiger, Elinor P. *see* Swiger, Elinor Porter.
Swiger, Elinor Porter.
xSwiger, Elinor P.
Europe for Young Travelers. Bobbs.
xSwiger, Elinor Porter.
Careers in the Legal Profession. Watts.
Swigert, Victoria. *see* Swigert, Victoria Lynn.

Swigert, Victoria L. see Swigert, Victoria Lynn.
Swigert, Victoria Lynn.
  xSwigert, Victoria.
    Murder, Inequality, & the Law: Differential
      Treatment & the Legal Process. Lexington
      Bks.
  xSwigert, Victoria L.
    The Substance of Social Deviance. Alfred Pub.
Swiggart, Peter.
  xSwiggart, Peter.
    Art of Faulkner's Novels. U of Tex Pr.
Swihart, Judson J.
  xSwihart, Judson J.
    How Do You Say "I Love You?". Inter-Varsity.
Swihart, Phillip J.
  xSwihart, Phillip J.
    The Edge of Death. Inter-Varsity.
Swihart, Stephen. see Swihart, Stephen D.
Swihart, Stephen D.
  xSwihart, Stephen.
    Angels in Heaven & Earth. Logos.
Swihart, Thomas L., 1929-
  xSwihart, Thomas L.
    Journey Through the Universe: An
      Introduction to Astronomy. HM.
Swinburne, A. C. see Swinburne, Algernon Charles.
Swinburne, Algernon. see Swinburne, Algernon Charles.
Swinburne, Algernon C. see Swinburne, Algernon
  Charles.
Swinburne, Algernon Charles, 1837-1909
  xSwinburne, A. C.
    Ballads from the English Border. Gordon Pr.
  xSwinburne, Algernon.
    A Study of Victor Hugo. Folcroft.
  xSwinburne, Algernon C.
    Ballads of the English Border. Folcroft.
    Contemporaries of Shakespeare. Folcroft.
    George Chapman: A Critical Essay. Arden Lib.
    George Chapman: A Critical Essay. Darby Bks.
    George Chapman: A Critical Essay. Folcroft.
    Note on Charlotte Bronte. Folcroft.
    Note on Charlotte Bronte. Haskell.
    Study of Victor Hugo. Kennikat.
Swinburne, Herbert.
  xSwinburne, Herbert.
    Design Cost Analysis for Architects &
      Engineers. McGraw.
Swinburne, Laurence.
  xSwinburne, Laurence.
    America's First Football Game. Silver.
    The Deadly Diamonds. Raintree Pubs.
    Riders on the Wind. Raintree Pubs.
Swinburne, Richard.
  xSwinburne, Richard.
    The Coherence of Theism. Oxford U Pr.
Swindells, R. see Swindells, Robert.
Swindells, Robert.
  xSwindells, R.
    The Very Special Baby. P-H.
  xSwindells, Robert.
    When Darkness Comes. Morrow.
Swindle. see Swindle, Robert E.
Swindle, Robert E.
  xSwindle.
    Fundamentals of Modern Business. Wadsworth
      Pub.
  xSwindle, Robert E.
    The Business Communicator. P-H.
    Business Math Basics. Wadsworth Pub.
Swindler, Daris R. see Swindler, Daris Ray.
Swindler, Daris Ray.
  xSwindler, Daris R.
    A Racial Study of the West Nakanai. Univ
      Mus of U PA.
Swindler, William F. see Swindler, William Finley.
Swindler, William Finley.
  xSwindler, William F.
    The Constitution & Chief Justice Marshall.
      Dodd.
    Problems of Law in Journalism. Greenwood.

Swindoll, Charles R.
  xSwindoll, Charles R.
    Killing Giants, Pulling Thorns. Multnomah.

    Strike the Original Match. Multnomah.

Swinehart, James. see Swinehart, James S.

Swinehart, James S., 1929-
  xSwinehart, James.
    Organic Chemistry: An Experimental
      Approach. P-H.
Swinfen, D. B.
  xSwinfen, D. B.
    Imperial Control of Colonial Legislation,
      1813-1865: A Study of British Policy
      Towards Colonial Legislative Powers. Oxford
      U Pr.
Swingle, Paul G.
  xSwingle, Paul G.
    ed. Structure of Conflict. Acad Pr.
Swinnerton, Emily.
  xSwinnerton, Emily.
    George Eliot, Her Early Home. Folcroft.
Swinnerton, Frank. see Swinnerton, Frank Arthur.
Swinnerton, Frank A. see Swinnerton, Frank Arthur.
Swinnerton, Frank Arthur, 1884-
  xSwinnerton, Frank.
    Arnold Bennett: A Last Word. Doubleday.
    Reflections from a Village. David & Charles.
    Some Achieve Greatness. G K Hall.
  xSwinnerton, Frank A.
    Authors & the Book Trade. Arno.
    Authors & the Book Trade. R West.
    The Reviewing & Criticism of Books. Folcroft.
Swinnerton-Dyer, H. P. see Swinnerton-Dyer, H. P. F.
Swinnerton-Dyer, H. P. F.
  xSwinnerton-Dyer, H. P.
    Analytic Theory of Abelian Varieties.
      Cambridge U Pr.
Swint, Henry L. see Swint, Henry Lee.
Swint, Henry Lee.
  xSwint, Henry L.
    Northern Teacher in the South, 1862-1870.
      Octagon.
Swinton, W. E. see Swinton, William Elgin.
Swinton, William Elgin, 1900-
  xSwinton, W. E.
    Dinosaurs. Sabbot-Natural Hist Bks.
Swire, J. see Swire, Joseph.
Swire, Joseph, 1903-
  xSwire, J.
    Albania: The Rise of a Kingdom. Arno.
Swischuk, Leonard. see Swischuk, Leonard E.
Swischuk, Leonard E., 1937-
  xSwischuk, Leonard.
    Plain Film Interpretation in Congenital Heart
      Disease. Williams & Wilkins.
  xSwischuk, Leonard E.
    Radiology of the Newborn & Young Infant.
      Williams & Wilkins.
Swisher, Carl B. see Swisher, Carl Brent.
Swisher, Carl Brent, 1897-
  xSwisher, Carl B.
    American Constitutional Development.
      Greenwood.
    Stephen J. Field: Craftsman of the Law.
      Irvington.
    Stephen J. Field: Craftsman of the Law. U of
      Chicago Pr.
    The Supreme Court in Modern Role.
      Greenwood.
    The Taney Period, 1835-64. Macmillan.
  xSwisher, Carl Brent.
    The Supreme Court in Modern Role. NYU Pr.
Swisher, Doug.
  xSwisher, Doug.
    Fly Fishing Strategy. Crown.
Swisher, George M.
  xSwisher, George M.

    Introduction to Linear Systems Analysis. Intl
      Schol Bk Serv.
Swisher, Robert D. see Swisher, Robert Donald.
Swisher, Robert Donald, 1910-
  xSwisher, Robert D.
    Surfactant Biodegradation. Dekker.
Swisshelm, Jane G. see Swisshelm, Jane Grey (Cannon).
Swisshelm, Jane Grey (Cannon), 1815-1884
  xSwisshelm, Jane G.
    Half a Century. Hacker.
Switkin, Abraham.
  xSwitkin, Abraham.
    Hand Lettering Today. Har-Row.
Switzer, David K., 1925-
  xSwitzer, David K.
    Pastor, Preacher, Person: Developing a Pastoral
      Ministry in Depth. Abingdon.
Switzer, Ellen. see Switzer, Ellen Eichenwald.
Switzer, Ellen Eichenwald.
  xSwitzer, Ellen.
    How Democracy Failed. Atheneum.
Switzer, R. M. see Switzer, Robert M.
Switzer, Robert M., 1940-
  xSwitzer, R. M.
    Algebraic Topology-Homotopy & Homology.
      Springer-Verlag.
Switzerland. Constitution.
  xSwitzerland. Constitution.
    Federal Constitution of Switzerland.
      Greenwood.
Switzler, William F., 1819-1906
  xSwitzler, William F.
    Switzler's Illustrated History of Missouri, from
      1541-1877. Arno.
Swokowski, Earl W. see Swokowski, Earl William.
Swokowski, Earl William, 1926-
  xSwokowski, Earl W.
    Algebra & Trigonometry with Analytic
      Geometry. Prindle.
    Calculus with Analytic Geometry. Prindle.
    Functions & Graphs. Prindle.
    Fundamentals of Algebra & Trigonometry.
      Prindle.
    Fundamentals of College Algebra. Prindle.
    Fundamentals of Trigonometry. Prindle.
    A Precalculus Course in Algebra &
      Trigonometry. Prindle.
Swomley, J. see Swomley, John M.
Swomley, John M., 1915-
  xSwomley, J.
    Liberation Ethics. Macmillan.
  xSwomley, John M.
    Liberation Ethics. Macmillan.
Swonger, Alvin K.
  xSwonger, Alvin K.
    Drugs & Therapy: A Psychotherapist's
      Handbook of Psychotropic Drugs. Little.
Sworder, David.
  xSworder, David D.
    Optimal Adaptive Control Systems. Acad Pr.
Sworder, David D. see Sworder, David.
Swords, Peter D. see Swords, Peter Del.
Swords, Peter Del.
  xSwords, Peter D.
    The Costs and Resources of Legal Education:
      A Study in the Management of Educational
      Resources. Columbia U Pr.
Swyer, P. R. see Swyer, Paul R.
Swyer, Paul R.
  xSwyer, P. R.
    The Intensive Care of the Newly Born:
      Physiological Principles & Practice. S Karger.
Sybenga, J. see Sybenga, Jacob.
Sybenga, Jacob, 1926-
  xSybenga, J.
    General Cytogenetics. Elsevier.
    Meiotic-Configurations. Springer-Verlag.
Sychev, V. V. see Sychev, Viacheslav Vladimirovich.
Sychev, Viacheslav Vladimirovich.
  xSychev, V. V.

Complex Thermodynamic Systems. Plenum
Pub.
Sychra, Vaclar. *see* Sychra, Vaclav.
Sychra, Vaclav.
xSychra, Vaclar.
Atomic Fluorescence Spectroscopy. Van Nos
Reinhold.
Sydenham, C. *see* Sydenham, Charles Edward Poulett
Thomson.
Sydenham, Charles Edward Poulett Thomson.
xSydenham, C.
Letters from Lord Sydenham, Governor
General of Canada, 1839-41, to Lord John
Russell. Kelley.
Sydenham, Edward. *see* Sydenham, Edward Allen.
Sydenham, Edward A. *see* Sydenham, Edward Allen.
Sydenham, Edward Allen.
xSydenham, Edward.
The Coinage of the Roman Republic. S J
Durst.
xSydenham, Edward A.
The Coinage of the Roman Republic. Arno.
Sydenham, M. J.
xSydenham, M. J.
The First French Republic, 1792-1804. U of
Cal Pr.
The Girondins. Greenwood.
Sydney Category Theory Seminar 1972-1973.
xTheSidney Category Theory Seminar, 1972-1973.
Category Seminar: Proceedings.
Springer-Verlag.
Sydney Library of New South Wales. Mitchell Library.
xMitchell Library, Sydney.
Bibliography of Captain James Cook,
Circumnavigator. B Franklin.
xMitchell Library, the Library of New South
Wales. (Sydney, Australia).
Dictionary Catalog of Printed Books. G K Hall.
Sydnor, Charles S. *see* Sydnor, Charles Sackett.
Sydnor, Charles Sackett, 1898-
nSydnor, Charles S.
Gentleman of the Old Natchez Region,
Benjamin L. C. Wailes. Negro U Pr.
Sydnor, Charles W.
xSydnor, Charles W.
Soldiers of Destruction: The SS Death's Head
Division,. Princeton U Pr.
Syed, Anwar H. *see* Syed, Anwar Hussain.
Syed, Anwar Hussain, 1926-
xSyed, Anwar H.
China & Pakistan: Diplomacy of an Entente
Cordiale. U of Mass Pr.
Syers, W. E. *see* Syers, William Edward.
Syers, William. *see* Syers, William Edward.
Syers, William Edward, 1914-
xSyers, W. E.
The Backroads of Texas. Pacesetter Pr.
Off the Beaten Trail. Texian.
xSyers, William.
The Devil Gun. Popular Lib.
Sykes, Christopher, 1907-
xSykes, Christopher.
Evelyn Waugh: A Biography. Little.
Sykes, Christopher S. *see* Sykes, Christopher Simon.
Sykes, Christopher Simon, 1948-
xSykes, Christopher S.
The Golden Age of the Country House.
Mayflower Bks.
The Visitor's Book: A Family Album. Putnam.
Sykes, Gresham M.
xSykes, Gresham M.
Crime & Society. Random.
Society of Captives: A Study of a Maximum
Security Prison. Princeton U Pr.
Sykes, Jane.
xSykes, Jane.
ed. Designing Against Vandalism. Van Nos
Reinhold.
Sykes, Mark, Sir, Bart, 1879-1919
xSykes, Mark.

The Caliphs' Last Heritage. Arno.
Sykes, Norman, 1897-1961
xSykes, Norman.
The English Religious Tradition: Sketches of
Its Influence on Church, State & Society.
Hyperion Conn.
Sykes, P. M. *see* Sykes, Percy Molesworth.
Sykes, Percy M. *see* Sykes, Percy Molesworth.
Sykes, Percy Molesworth, Sir, 1867-1945
xSykes, P. M.
ed. The Glory of the Shia World. Arno.
xSykes, Percy M.
A History of Afghanistan. AMS Pr.
xSykes, Perry.
A History of Persia. Gordon Pr.
Sykes, Perry. *see* Sykes, Percy Molesworth.
Sykes, Stephen.
xSykes, Stephen.
Friedrich Schleiermacher. John Knox.
Sylvester, Anthony, Pseud.
xSylvester, Anthony.
Tunisia. Dufour.
Sylvester, Harry, 1908-
xSylvester, Harry.
Moon Gaffney. Arno.
Sylvester, Herbert M. *see* Sylvester, Herbert Milton.
Sylvester, Herbert Milton, 1849-
xSylvester, Herbert M.
Indian Wars of New England. Arno.
Sylvester, Natalie. *see* Sylvester, Natalie G.
Sylvester, Natalie G.
xSylvester, Natalie.
The Home-Baking Cookbook. G&D.
Sylvester, Nathaniel B. *see* Sylvester, Nathaniel Bartlett.
Sylvester, Nathaniel Bartlett, 1825-1894
xSylvester, Nathaniel B.
Historical Sketches of Northern New York &
the Adirondack Wilderness. Including
Traditions of the Indians, Early Explorers,
Pioneer Settlers, Hermit Hunters. Harbor Hill
Bks.
Sylvester, Richard S. *see* Sylvester, Richard Standish.
Sylvester, Richard Standish.
xSylvester, Richard S.
ed. The Anchor Anthology of Sixteenth
Century Verse. Peter Smith.
Sylvester, Sawyer F.
xSylvester, Sawyer F.
Prison Homicide. Halsted Pr.
Sylvester, William.
xSylvester, William.
Curses, Omens, Prayers. Ashland Poetry.
Sylvia, J. Gerin.
xSylvia, J. Gerin.
Cast Metals Technology. A-W.
Sylwester, Roland.
xSylwester, Roland.
Teaching Bible Stories More Effectively with
Puppets. Concordia.
Syme, Charlotte U.
xSyme, Charlotte U.
Love Is...Jelly on the Bread. Accent Bks.
Syme, Eric.
xSyme, Eric.
History of SDA Church-State Relations in the
United States. Pacific Pr Pub Assn.
Syme, G. J.
xSyme, G. J.
Social Structure in Farm Animals. Elsevier.
Syme, Ronald, 1910-
xSyme, Ronald.
Fur Trader of the North: The Story of Pierre
de la Verendrye. Morrow.
History in Ovid. Oxford U Pr.
Osceola, Seminole Leader. Morrow.
Toussaint, the Black Liberator. Morrow.
Symes, Ken M.
xSymes, Ken M.

Composing the Essay: Prewriting, Shaping, &
Revising. Har-Row.
xSymes, Kenneth M.
Two Voices: Writing About Literature. HM.
Symes, Kenneth M. *see* Symes, Ken M.
Symington, Thomas A. *see* Symington, Thomas
Alexander.
Symington, Thomas Alexander, 1883-
xSymington, Thomas A.
Religious Liberals & Conservatives: A
Comparison of Those Who Are Liberal in
Their Religious Thinking & Those Who Are
Conservative. AMS Pr.
Symmons, C. R. *see* Symmons, Clive Ralph.
Symmons, Clive Ralph.
xSymmons, C. R.
The Maritime Zones of Islands in International
Law. Kluwer Boston.
Symmons-Symonolewicz, Konstantin, 1909-
xSymmons-Symonolewicz, Konstantin.
Nationalist Movements: A Comparative View.
Maplewood.
Symon, James D. *see* Symon, James David.
Symon, James David.
xSymon, James D.
Byron in Perspective. Folcroft.
Symon, Keith R.
xSymon, Keith R.
Mechanics. A-W.
Symonds, Charles, Sir, 1890-
xSymonds, Charles.
Studies in Neurology. Oxford U Pr.
Symonds, Craig L.
xSymonds, Craig L.
Navalists & Antinavalists: The Naval Policy
Debate in the United States, 1785-1827. U
Delaware Pr.
Symonds, Curtis W.
xSymonds, Curtis W.
Basic Financial Management. Am Mgmt.
Symonds, Emily M. *see* Symonds, Emily Morse.
Symonds, Emily Morse, d. 1936
xSymonds, Emily M.
Little Memoirs of the Nineteenth Century.
Arno.
Symonds, John A. *see* Symonds, John Addington.
Symonds, John Addington, 1840-1893
xSymonds, John A.
Giovanni Boccaccio As Man & Author. AMS
Pr.
Many Moods: A Volume of Verse. Scholarly.
Symonds, Percival M. *see* Symonds, Percival Mallon.
Symonds, Percival Mallon.
xSymonds, Percival M.
Dynamics of Human Adjustment. Greenwood.
Ego & the Self. Greenwood.
From Adolescent to Adult. Greenwood.
Special Disability in Algebra. AMS Pr.
Symonds, Richard, 1918-
xSymonds, Richard.
British & Their Successors: A Study in the
Development of the Government Services in
the New States. Northwestern U Pr.
Symons, A. J. *see* Symons, Alphonse James Albert.
Symons, Alphonse James Albert, 1900-1941
xSymons, A. J.
An Anthology of Nineties' Verse. Folcroft.
An Anthology of Nineties' Verse. Scholarly.
Symons, Arthur, 1865-1945
xSymons, Arthur.

Charles Baudelaire: A Study. Folcroft.
Charles Baudelaire: A Study. R West.
Collected Works of Arthur Symons. AMS Pr.
Dramatis Personae. Arno.
Notes on Joseph Conrad: with Some
    Unpublished Letters. Arno.
Notes on Joseph Conrad with Some
    Unpublished Letters. Folcroft.
Notes on Joseph Conrad, with Some
    Unpublished Letters. Kelly.
Study of Oscar Wilde. Folcroft.
Study of Walter Pater. Folcroft.
The Symbolist Movement in Literature. AMS
    Pr.
Symbolist Movement in Literature. Dutton.
Symbolist Movement in Literature. Haskell.

Symons, Donald, 1942-
xSymons, Donald.
The Evolution of Human Sexuality. Oxford U
    Pr.
Play & Aggression: A Study of Rhesus
    Monkeys. Columbia U Pr.

Symons, Geraldine.
xSymons, Geraldine.
Crocuses Were Over, Hitler Was Dead.
    Lippincott.
Workhouse Child. Macmillan.

Symons, Julian, 1912-
xSymons, Julian.
The Blackheath Poisonings: A Victorian
    Murder Mystery. Har-Row.
The Blackheath Poisonings: A Victorian
    Murder Mystery. Penguin.
Bland Beginning. Har-Row.
The Color of Murder. Har-Row.
The Thirties: A Dream Revolved. Greenwood.

Symons, Leslie.
xSymons, Leslie.
Agricultural Geography. Westview.

**Symposia Angiologica Santoriana, 4th, Fribourg and
Nyon, Switzerland, 1972.**
xSymposia Angiologica Santoriana, 4th
    International Symposium, Fribourg-Nyon, 1972.
    Clinical Pharmacology: Flavonoids & Vascular
        Wall, Proceedings. S Karger.
Symposia in Applied Mathematics. see Symposium in
    Applied Mathematics, 20th, University of Montana,
    Misssoula, 1973.
Symposia in Applied Mathematics - New York - 1965.
    see Symposium in Applied Mathematics, 18th, 1965.
Symposia in Applied Mathematics - Santa Monica Calif -
    1953. see Symposium in Applied Mathematics, 6th,
    Santa Monica City College, 1953.
Symposia In Applied Mathematics - 17th - New York -
    1964. see Symposium in Applied Mathematics, 17th,
    New York, 1964.
Symposia in Applied Mathematics-Ann Arbor-1949. see
    Symposium in Applied Mathematics, 3d, University of
    Michigan, 1949.
Symposia in Applied Mathematics-Atlantic City &
    Chicago-1962. see Symposium in Applied
    Mathematics, 15th, Chicago and Atlantic City, 1962.
Symposia in Applied Mathematics-Cambridge,
    Mass.-1948. see Symposium in Applied Mathematics,
    2d, Massachusetts Institute of Technology, 1948.
Symposia in Applied Mathematics-Carnegie Institute of
    Technology-1952. see Symposium in Applied
    Mathematics, 5th, Carnegie Institute of Technology,
    1952.
Symposia in Applied Mathematics-Chicago-1956. see
    Symposium in Applied Mathematics, 8th, University
    of Chicago, 1956.
Symposia in Applied Mathematics-New York-1957. see
    Symposium in Applied Mathematics, 9th, New York
    University, 1957.
Symposia in Pure Mathematics - Berkeley, Calif. - 1971.
    see Symposium in Pure Mathematics, University of
    California at Berkeley, 1971.
Symposia in Pure Mathematics - St. Louis, 1972. see

Symposium in Pure Mathematics, St. Louis University,
    1972.
Symposia in Pure Mathematics - Stanford, Calif., 1973.
    see Symposium in Pure Mathematics, Stanford
    University, 1973.
Symposia in Pure Mathematics, Humboldt State
    University, Arcata, Calif., July 29-August 16, 1974.
    see Symposium in Pure Mathematics, Humboldt State
    University, 1974.
Symposia in Pure Mathematics, Vol. 26. see Symposium
    in Pure Mathematics, Williams College, 1972.
Symposia in Pure Mathematics-Boulder, 1965. see
    Symposium in Pure Mathematics, 9th, University of
    Colorado, 1965.
Symposia in Pure Mathematics-Chicago-1968. see
    Symposium on Nonlinear Functional Analysis,
    Chicago, 1968.
Symposia in Pure Mathematics-Los Angeles-1968. see
    Symposium in Pure Mathematics, University of
    California, los Angeles, 1968.
Symposia in Pure Mathematics-Madison, Wis.-1970. see
    Symposium in Pure Mathematics, University of
    Wisconsin, April 14-16, 1970.
Symposia in Pure Mathematics-New York-1968. see
    Symposium in Pure Mathematics, New York, 1968.
Symposia in Pure Mathematics-Northern Illinois Univ.,
    May 1974. see Symposium in Pure Mathematics,
    Northern Illinois University, 1974.
Symposia in Pure Mathematics-Pasadena-1963. see
    Symposium on Recent Developments in the Theory of
    Numbers, California Institute of Technology, 1963.
Symposia in Pure Mathematics-San Diego-1966. see
    Symposium in Pure Mathematics, University of
    California, San Diego, 1966.
Symposia in Pure Mathematics-Seattle-1961. see
    Symposium on Convexity, University of Washington,
    1961.
Symposia in Pure Mathematics-Tempe, Ariz.-1960. see
    Symposium in Pure Mathematics, 3d, University of
    Arizona, 1960.
Symposia on Special Functions & Wave Propagation,
    Washingtion, D.C., 1969. see Symposium on Special
    Functions, Washington, D.C., 1969.
Symposium. see Symposium on Isotope Ratios As
    Pollutant Source and Behavior Indicators, Vienna,
    1974.
Symposium - 3rd - Madison - 1970. see International
    Symposium on Polarization Phenomena in Nuclear
    Reactions, 3d, University of Wisconsin, 1970.
Symposium, Bloomington, Oct., 1970. see Symposium on
    Bioenergetics, Bloomington, Indiana, 1970.
Symposium by the New York University Medical Center
    & the National Foundation-March of Dimes, New
    York City, Mar. 1975. see Symposium on Infections
    of the Fetus and the Newborn Infant, New York,
    1975.
Symposium, Campione, Sept 1973. see International
    Symposium on Milk and Lactation, Campione
    D'Italia, 1973.
Symposium, Cornell University, Ithaca, New York, Oct.
    1974. see Symposium on Insects, Science, and Society,
    Cornell University, 1974.
Symposium, Dundee, 1974. see Symposium on Spectral
    Theory and Differential Equations, University of
    Dundee, 1974.
Symposium Held at the University of Sussex, Falmer,
    Sussex, Sept. 1971. see Symposium on Photographic
    Processing, University of Sussex, 1971.
Symposium Herrenalb - Germany - September 8-12 1969.
    see Iutam-Symposium on Instability of Continuous
    Systems, Herrenalb, Germany, 1969.
Symposium in Applied Mathematics, Durham, N.C.
xSociety for Industrial & Applied
    Mathematics-American Mathematical Society
    Symposia-N.C.-April, 1968.
    Numerical Solution of Field Problems in
        Continuum Physics: Proceedings. Am Math.
Symposium in Applied Mathematics, New York, 1969.
xSociety for Industrial & Applied

Mathematics-American Mathematical Society
    Symposia-New York-April, 1969.
    Mathematical Aspects of Electrical Network
        Analysis: Proceedings. Am Math.
Symposium in Applied Mathematics, New York, 1971.
xSociety for Industrial & Applied
    Mathematics-American Mathematical Society
    Symposia-New York-April, 1971.
    Mathematical Aspects of Statistical Mechanics:
        Proceedings. Am Math.
Symposium in Applied Mathematics, New York, 1974.
xSociety for Industrial & Applied
    Mathematics-American Mathematical Society
    Symposia-New York-April, 1974.
    Mathematical Aspects of Chemical &
        Biochemical Problems & Quantum
        Chemistry: Proceedings. Am Math.
**Symposium in Applied Mathematics, 2d, Massachusetts
Institute of Technology, 1948.**
xSymposia in Applied Mathematics-Cambridge,
    Mass.-1948.
    Electromagnetic Theory: Proceedings. Am
        Math.
**Symposium in Applied Mathematics, 3d, University of
Michigan, 1949.**
xSymposia in Applied Mathematics-Ann
    Arbor-1949.
    Elasticity: Proceedings. Am Math.
**Symposium in Applied Mathematics, 5th, Carnegie
Institute of Technology, 1952.**
xSymposia in Applied Mathematics-Carnegie
    Institute of Technology-1952.
    Wave Motion & Vibration Theory:
        Proceedings. Am Math.
**Symposium in Applied Mathematics, 6th, Santa Monica
City College, 1953.**
xSymposia in Applied Mathematics - Santa Monica
    Calif - 1953.
    Numerical Analysis: Proceedings. Am Math.
**Symposium in Applied Mathematics, 8th, University of
Chicago, 1956.**
xSymposia in Applied Mathematics-Chicago-1956.
    Calculus of Variations & Its Applications:
        Proceedings. Am Math.
**Symposium in Applied Mathematics, 9th, New York
University, 1957.**
xSymposia in Applied Mathematics-New
    York-1957.
    Applied Probability: Proceedings. Am Math.
**Symposium in Applied Mathematics, 10th, Columbia
University. 1958.**
xSymposia in Applied Mathematics-New
    York-1958.
    Combinatorial Analysis: Proceedings. Am
        Math.
**Symposium in Applied Mathematics, 11th, New York,
1959.**
xSymposia in Applied Mathematics-New
    York-1959.
    Nuclear Reactor Theory: Proceedings. Am
        Math.
**Symposium in Applied Mathematics, 13th, New York,
1960.**
xSymposia in Applied Mathematics - New York -
    1960.
    Structure of Language & Its Mathematical
        Aspects: Proceedings. Am Math.
xSymposia in Applied Mathematics-New
    York-1960.
    Hydrodynamic Instability: Proceedings. Am
        Math.
**Symposium in Applied Mathematics, 14th, New York,
1961.**
xSymposia in Applied Mathematics-New
    York-1961.

Mathematical Problems in the Biological
Sciences: Proceedings. Am Math.

**Symposium in Applied Mathematics, 15th, Chicago and
Atlantic City, 1962.**
xSymposia in Applied Mathematics-Atlantic City
& Chicago-1962.
Experimental Arithmetic, High Speed
Computing & Mathematics: Proceedings. Am
Math.

**Symposium in Applied Mathematics, 16th, New York,
1963.**
xSymposia in Applied Mathematics-New
York-1963.
Stochastic Processes in Mathematical Physics
& Engineering: Proceedings. Am Math.

**Symposium in Applied Mathematics, 17th, New York,
1964.**
xSymposia In Applied Mathematics - 17th - New
York - 1964.
Applications of Nonlinear Partial Differential
Equations in the Mathematical Physics:
Proceedings. Am Math.

Symposium in Applied Mathematics, 18th, 1965.
xSymposia in Applied Mathematics - New York -
1965.
Magneto-Fluid & Plasma Dynamics:
Proceedings. Am Math.

**Symposium in Applied Mathematics, 20th, University of
Montana, Misssoula, 1973.**
xSymposia in Applied Mathematics.
The Influence of Computing on Mathematical
Research & Education. Am Math.

Symposium in Cambridge, Mass, June 17-21, 1974. see
Symposium on Buckling of Structures, Harvard
University, 1974.

Symposium in Pure Mathematics - Berkeley - 1968. see
Symposium in Pure Mathematics, University of
California at Berkeley, 1968.

Symposium in Pure Mathematics - Chicago - 1966. see
Symposium in Pure Mathematics, 10th, University of
Chicago, 1966.

Symposium in Pure Mathematics - Monterey Calif -
1959. see Symposium in Pure Mathematics, 2d,
Monterey, California, 1959.

**Symposium in Pure Mathematics, Humboldt State
University, 1974.**
xSymposia in Pure Mathematics, Humboldt State
University, Arcata, Calif., July 29-August 16,
1974.
Algebraic Geometry-Arcata 1974: Proceedings.
Am Math.

Symposium in Pure Mathematics, New York, 1968.
xSymposia in Pure Mathematics-New York-1968.
Applications of Categorical Algebra:
Proceedings. Am Math.

**Symposium in Pure Mathematics, Northern Illinois
University, 1974.**
xSymposia in Pure Mathematics-Northern Illinois
Univ., May 1974.
Mathematical Developments Arising from the
Hilbert Problems: Proceedings. Am Math.

**Symposium in Pure Mathematics, St. Louis University,
1972.**
xSymposia in Pure Mathematics - St. Louis, 1972.
Analytic Number Theory: Proceedings. Am
Math.

**Symposium in Pure Mathematics, Stanford University,
1973.**
xSymposia in Pure Mathematics - Stanford, Calif.,
1973.
Differential Geometry, Pts 1-2: Vol. 27. Am
Math.

**Symposium in Pure Mathematics, University of
California at Berkeley, 1968.**
xSymposium in Pure Mathematics - Berkeley -
1968.

Global Analysis. Am Math.

**Symposium in Pure Mathematics, University of
California at Berkeley, 1971.**
xSymposia in Pure Mathematics - Berkeley, Calif. -
1971.
Partial Differential Equations: Proceedings. Am
Math.

**Symposium in Pure Mathematics, University of
California, Los Angeles, 1967.**
xSymposia in Pure Mathematics-Los Angeles-July,
1967.
Axiomatic Set Theory. Am Math.

**Symposium in Pure Mathematics, University of
California, Los Angeles, 1968.**
xSymposia in Pure Mathematics-Los Angeles-1968.
Combinatorics. Am Math.

**Symposium in Pure Mathematics, University of
California, San Diego, 1966.**
xSymposia in Pure Mathematics-San Diego-1966.
Entire Functions & Related Parts of Analysis:
Proceedings. Am Math.

**Symposium in Pure Mathematics, University of
Wisconsin, April 14-16, 1970.**
xSymposia in Pure Mathematics-Madison,
Wis.-1970.
Representation Theory of Finite Groups &
Related Topics: Proceedings. Am Math.

**Symposium in Pure Mathematics, University of
Wisconsin, June 29-July 17, 1970.**
xSymposia in Pure Mathematics-Madison,
Wisconsin-1970.
Algebraic Topology: Proceedings. Am Math.

**Symposium in Pure Mathematics, Williams College,
1972.**
xSymposia in Pure Mathematics, Vol. 26.
Harmonic Analysis on Homogeneous Spaces:
Proceedings. Am Math.

Symposium in Pure Mathematics, 1st, New York, 1959.
xSymposia in Pure Mathematics-New York-1959.
Finite Groups: Proceedings. Am Math.

**Symposium in Pure Mathematics, 2d, Monterey,
California, 1959.**
xSymposium in Pure Mathematics - Monterey
Calif - 1959.
Lattice Theory: Proceedings. Am Math.

**Symposium in Pure Mathematics, 3d, University of
Arizona, 1960.**
xSymposia in Pure Mathematics-Tempe,
Ariz-1960.
Differential Geometry: Proceedings. Am Math.

Symposium in Pure Mathematics, 5th, New York, 1961.
xSymposia in Pure Mathematics-New York-1961.
Recursive Function Theory: Proceedings. Am
Math.

**Symposium in Pure Mathematics, 9th, University of
Colorado, 1965.**
xSymposia in Pure Mathematics-Boulder, 1965.
Algebraic Groups & Discontinous Subgroups:
Proceedings. Am Math.

**Symposium in Pure Mathematics, 10th, University of
Chicago, 1966.**
xSymposium in Pure Mathematics - Chicago -
1966.
Singular Integrals: Proceedings. Am Math.

Symposium In The Philosophy Of Mind - Wayne State
University - 1962. see Wayne State University
Symposium on the Philosophy of Mind, 1962.

Symposium, Knoxville, July 15-19, 1974. see Symposium
on Dynamic Studies with Radioisotopes in Clinical
Medicine and Research, Knoxville, 1974.

Symposium Lausanne, Switzerland Aug. 16 to 20 1976.
see Herbette Symposium on Species Concept
Hymenomycetes, University of Lausanne, 1976.

Symposium, Liblice-Prague - 1970. see Symposium on
Immunogenetics of the H-2 System, Liblice,
Czechoslovak Republic, 1970.

Symposium, Lyndon Baines Johnson Library. see
Symposium on Education, Lyndon Baines Johnson
Library, 1972.

Symposium, Michigan, 1965. see Symposium on the

Fluid Mechanics of Internal Flow, Warren, Michigan,
1965.

Symposium, New Delhi, October 1978. see Symposium
on Recent Advances in Reproduction and Regulation
of Fertility, New Delhi, India, 1978.

Symposium, New York, 1960. see Symposium on Lunar
Flight, New York, 1960.

Symposium of International Union of Theoretical &
Applied Mechanics, Brussels, Belgium, 1973. see
Symposium on the Photoelastic Effect and Its
Applications, Brussels, 1973.

Symposium of Limnology of Shallow Waters, 1973. see
Symposium on Limonology of Shallow Waters,
Tihany, Hungary, 1973.

Symposium of National Libraries, Vienna, 1958. see
Symposium on National Libraries in Europe, Vienna,
1958.

Symposium of the Birth Defects Institute of the New
York State Dept. of Health, Second, October, 1971.
see Symposium on Heredity and Society, Albany,
New York, 1971.

Symposium Of The Entymological Society Of America -
Atlantic City - 1960. see Symposium on Biological
Transmission of Disease Agents, Atlantic City, 1960.

Symposium of the Group of European Nutritionists, 9th,
Chianciano, 1970. see Group of European
Nutritionists.

Symposium of the International Society for the Study of
Behavioral Development, University of Nijmegen, the
Netherlands, July, 1971. see International Society for
the Study of Behavioral Development.

Symposium of the Ophthalmic Microsurgery Study
Group, 2nd, Buergenstock, 1968. see Ophthalmic
Microsurgery Study Group.

**Symposium on Adaptive Economics, University of
Wisconsin, Madison, 1974.**
xSymposium, University of Wisconsin, Madison,
October, 1974.
Adaptive Economic Models: Proceedings. Acad
Pr.

Symposium on Alcoholism, Amsterdam, 1978.
xSymposium on Alcoholism, Amsterdam, May
1978.
Alcoholism, a Multidisciplinary Approach. S
Karger.

Symposium on Alcoholism, Amsterdam, May 1978. see
Symposium on Alcoholism, Amsterdam, 1978.

Symposium on Algebraic Topology. see Symposium on
Algebraic Topology, Seattle, 1971.

Symposium on Algebraic Topology, Seattle, 1971.
xSymposium on Algebraic Topology.
Proceedings. Springer-Verlag.

**Symposium on Anticholinergic Drugs and Brain
Functions in Animals and Man, 6th, Washington,
D.C., 1966.**
xSymposium on Anticholinergic Drugs & Brain
Functions in Animals & Man - 6th - Washington
D. C., 1968.
Anticholingeric Drugs & Brain Functions in
Animals & Man. Elsevier.

**Symposium on Automatic Demonstration, Versailles,
1968.**
xSymposium on Automatic Demonstration,
Versailles, 1968.
Proceedings. Springer-Verlag.

**Symposium on Beneficial Modifications of the Marine
Environment, Washington, D.C., 1968.**
xNational Academy of Sciences, Division of Earth
Sciences.
Beneficial Modifications of the Marine
Environment. Natl Acad Pr.

Symposium on Biochemistry & Biophysics of
Mitochondrial Membranes. see International
Symposium on Biochemistry and Biophysics of
Mitochondrial Membranes, Bressanone, 1971.

Symposium on Biochemistry & Physiology of Visual

Pigments, Bochum Univ., Germany, 1972. *see* Symposium on the Biochemistry and Physiology of Visual Pigments, Bochum, 1972.

Symposium on Biological Transmission of Disease Agents, Atlantic City, 1960.
　　xSymposium Of The Entymological Society Of America - Atlantic City - 1960.
　　　　Biological Transmission of Disease Agents: Proceedings. Acad Pr.

Symposium on Bioenergetics, Bloomington, Indiana, 1970.
　　xSymposium, Bloomington, Oct., 1970.
　　　　Horizons of Bioenergetics: Proceedings. Acad Pr.

Symposium on Biophysics and Physiology of Biological Transport, Frascati, 1965.
　　xSymposium on Biophysics & Physiology of Biological Transport, Frascati, 1965.
　　　　Proceedings. Springer-Verlag.

Symposium on Body Surface Mapping of Cardiac Fields, Burlington, Vermont, 1972.
　　xSymposium on Body Surface Mapping of Cardiac Fields, Burlington, Vermont, 1972.
　　　　Body Surface Mapping of Cardiac Fields: Proceedings. S Karger.

Symposium on Buckling of Structures, Harvard University, 1974.
　　xSymposium in Cambridge, Mass, June 17-21, 1974.
　　　　Buckling of Structures. Springer-Verlag.

Symposium on Business Taxation, Wayne State University, 1964.
　　xBusiness Taxation Symposium.
　　　　Effects of the Corporation Income Tax: Papers Presented at the Symposium on Business Taxation. Wayne St U Pr.

Symposium on Cerebral Gliomas, University of Chicago, 1974.
　　xSymposium on Cerebral Gliomas, University of Chicago, May 18-19, 1974.
　　　　Gliomas - Current Concepts in Biology, Diagnosis, & Therapy: Proceedings. Springer-Verlag.

Symposium on Chemical Reactions in Urban Atmospheres, Warren, Michigan, 1969.
　　xSymposium, Warren, Michigan, 1969.
　　　　Chemical Reactions in the Urban Atmosphere: Proceedings. Elsevier.

Symposium on Classical & Quantum Mechanical Aspects of Heavy Ion Collisions, Max-Planck-Institut Fuer. Kernphysik, Heidelberg, Oct 2-5, 1974. *see* Symposium on Classical and Quantum Mechanical Aspects of Heavy Ion Collisions, Max-Planck-Institut Fur Kernphysik, 1974.

Symposium on Classical and Quantum Mechanical Aspects of Heavy Ion Collisions, Max-Planck-Institut Fur Kernphysik, 1974.
　　xSymposium on Classical & Quantum Mechanical Aspects of Heavy Ion Collisions, Max-Planck-Institut Fuer. Kernphysik, Heidelberg, Oct 2-5, 1974.
　　　　Proceedings. Springer-Verlag.

Symposium on Comparative Leukemia Research, 7th International, Copenhagen, October, 1975. *see* International Symposium on Comparative Leukemia Research, 7th, Copenhagen, 1975.

Symposium on Comparative Pathology of the Heart, Boston, 1973.
　　xSymposium on Comparative Pathology of the Heart, Boston, Sept. 1973.
　　　　Comparative Pathology of the Heart: Proceedings. S Karger.

Symposium on Computers in Algebra and Number Theory, New York, 1970.
　　xSociety for Industrial & Applied Mathematics - American Mathematical Society Symposia - New

York - March, 1971.
　　　　Computers in Algebra & Number Theory: Proceedings. Am Math.

Symposium on Convexity, University of Washington, 1961.
　　xSymposia in Pure Mathematics-Seattle-1961.
　　　　Convexity: Proceedings. Am Math.

Symposium on Cosmochemistry, Cambridge Massachusetts, 1972.
　　xSymposium on Cosmochemistry, Cambridge, Mass., Aug. 1972.
　　　　Cosmochemistry: Proceedings. Kluwer Boston.

Symposium on Dynamic Aspects of Speech Perception, Eindhoven, 1975.
　　xSymposium on Dynamic Aspects of Speech Perception Held at I.P.O.,Eindhoven, the Netherlands,Aug.4-6,1975.
　　　　Structure & Process in Speech Perception: Proceedings. Springer-Verlag.

Symposium on Dynamic Studies with Radioisotopes in Clinical Medicine and Research, Knoxville, 1974.
　　xSymposium, Knoxville, July 15-19, 1974.
　　　　Dynamic Studies with Radioisotopes in Medicine 1974, Vol. II: Proceedings. Unipub.

Symposium on Education, Lyndon Baines Johnson Library, 1972.
　　xSymposium, Lyndon Baines Johnson Library.
　　　　Educating a Nation-a Symposium on Education: Proceedings. LBJ Sch Public Affairs.
　　　　Equal Opportunity in the United States-a Symposium on Education: Proceedings. LBJ Sch Public Affairs.

Symposium on Electromagnetic Distance Measurement, Oxford University, 1965.
　　xSymposium, Oxford, Sept. 1965.
　　　　Electromagnetic Distance Measurement: Proceedings. U of Toronto Pr.

Symposium on Energy Metabolism, 3d, Troon, Scotland, 1964.
　　xSymposium On Energy Metabolism - 3rd - Troon Scotland - 1964.
　　　　Energy Metabolism: Proceedings. Acad Pr.

Symposium On Energy Metabolism - 3rd - Troon Scotland - 1964. *see* Symposium on Energy Metabolism, 3d, Troon, Scotland, 1964.

Symposium on Equality of Opportunity in Employment in Theamerican Region, Panama, 1973.
　　xRegional Symposium, Panama, 1973.
　　　　Equality of Opportunity in Employment in the American Region: Problems & Policies Report & Documents. Intl Labour Office.

Symposium on Ergodic Theory, New Orleans, 1961.
　　xSymposium On Ergodic Theory - New Orleans - 1961.
　　　　Ergodic Theory: Proceedings. Acad Pr.

Symposium On Ergodic Theory - New Orleans - 1961. *see* Symposium on Ergodic Theory, New Orleans, 1961.

Symposium on Exact Philosophy, 1st, Montreal, 1971.
　　xSymposium on Exact Philosophy, 1st, Montreal, 1971.
　　　　Exact Philosophy, Problems, Tools, Goals: Proceedings. Kluwer Boston.

Symposium on Feedback and Dynamic Control of Plasmas, Princeton, N.J., 1970.
　　xAIP Conference, Princeton, 1970.
　　　　Feedback & Dynamic Control of Plasmas: Proceedings. Am Inst Physics.
　　xSociety for Industrial & Applied Mathematics - American Mathematical Society Symposia - New York, April, 1967.
　　　　Transport Theory: Proceedings. Am Math.

Symposium on Field Instruments, London, 1973.
　　xBritish Geotechnical Society.
　　　　Field Instrumentation in Geotechnical Engineering. Halsted Pr.

Symposium on Gastric Secretion, Frankfurt-Am-Main, 1971.

xSymposium on Gastric Secretion, Frankfurt Am Main, 1971.
　　　　Gastric Secretion. Acad Pr.

Symposium on General Topology and Its Relations to Modern Analysis and Algebra, 2nd, Prague, 1966.
　　xSymposium on General Topology & Its Relations to Modern Analysis and Algebra - 2nd - Prague - 1967.
　　　　Proceedings. Acad Pr.

Symposium on General Topology & Its Relations to Modern Analysis and Algebra - 2nd - Prague - 1967. *see* Symposium on General Topology and Its Relations to Modern Analysis and Algebra, 2nd, Prague, 1966.

Symposium on Hepato-Gastroenterology, 1st, University Hospital Center of Nice, 1972.
　　xSymposium on Hepato-Gastroenterology of the University Hospital Center of Nice, 1st, August 1972.
　　　　Treatment of Small Bowel Diseases: Proceedings. S Karger.

Symposium on Heredity and Society, Albany, New York, 1971.
　　xSymposium of the Birth Defects Institute of the New York State Dept. of Health, Second, October, 1971.
　　　　Heredity & Society. Acad Pr.

Symposium on High-Energy Electrons, Montreux, 1964. *see* Symposium on High Energy Electrons, Montreux, Switzerland, 1964.

Symposium on High Energy Electrons, Montreux, Switzerland, 1964.
　　xSymposium on High-Energy Electrons, Montreux, 1964.
　　　　Proceedings. Springer-Verlag.

Symposium on Hormones & Cell Regulation (INSERM), 1st, le Bischenberg, Bischoffsheim, France Sept. 27-30, 1976. *see* Inserm European Symposium on Hormones and Cell Regulation.

Symposium on Icthygenetics, 1st. *see* Ichthyological Symposium on Genetics and Mutagenesis, Neuherberg, Germany, 1972.

Symposium on Immunogenetics of the H-2 System, Liblice, Czechoslovak Republic, 1970.
　　xSymposium, Liblice-Prague - 1970.
　　　　Immunogenetics of the H-2 System: Proceedings. S Karger.

Symposium on Infections of the Fetus and the Newborn Infant, New York, 1975.
　　xSymposium by the New York University Medical Center & the National Foundation-March of Dimes, New York City, Mar. 1975.
　　　　Infections of the Fetus & the Newborn Infant: Proceedings. A R Liss.

Symposium On Informational Macromolecules - Rutgers University - 1962. *see* Symposium on Information Macromolecules, Rutgers University, 1962.

Symposium on Information Macromolecules, Rutgers University, 1962.
　　xSymposium On Informational Macromolecules - Rutgers University - 1962.
　　　　Informational Macromolecules: Proceedings. Acad Pr.

Symposium on Insects, Science, and Society, Cornell University, 1974.
　　xSymposium, Cornell University, Ithaca, New York, Oct. 1974.
　　　　Insects, Science, & Society: Proceedings. Acad Pr.

Symposium on Insulin Action, Toronto, 1971.
　　xSymposium on Insulin Action, Toronto, 1971.
　　　　Insulin Action: Proceedings. Acad Pr.

Symposium on Ionizing Radiation for Sterilization of Medical Products and Biological Tissues, Bombay, 1974.
　　xSymposium on Ionizing Radiation for Sterilization of Medical Products & Biological Tissues, Bombay, Dec 9-13, 1974.

Radiosterilization of Medical Products, 1974:
Proceedings. Unipub.

Symposium on Isotope Ratios As Pollutant Source and Behavior Indicators, Vienna, 1974.
xSymposium.
Isotope Ratios As Pollutant Source & Behavior Indicators: Proceedings. Unipub.

Symposium on Little Magazine, Library of Congress, 1965. see United States. Library of Congress. Reference Department.

Symposium on Limonology of Shallow Waters, Tihany, Hungary, 1973.
xSymposium of Limnology of Shallow Waters, 1973.
Limnology of Shallow Water: Proceedings. Intl Pubns Serv.

Symposium on Lunar Flight, New York, 1960.
xSymposium, New York, 1960.
Lunar Exploration & Spacecraft Systems: Proceedings. AM Astronaut.

Symposium on Manned Lunar Flight, Denver, 1961. see Symposium on Manned Lunar Flight, 1961.

Symposium on Manned Lunar Flight, 1961.
xSymposium on Manned Lunar Flight, Denver, 1961.
Manned Lunar Flight. Am Astronaut.

Symposium on Mathematical Foundations of Computer Science, 3d, Jadwisin, Poland, 1974.
xSymposium, 3rd, Jadwisin, June 17-22, 1974.
Mathematical Foundations of Computer Science. Springer-Verlag.

Symposium on Meson-, Photo-, & Electroproduction at Low & Intermediate Energies, Bonn, 1970. see Symposium on Meson-, Photo-, and Electroproduction at Low and Intermediate Energies, Bonn, 1970.

Symposium on Meson-, Photo-, and Electroproduction at Low and Intermediate Energies, Bonn, 1970.
xSymposium on Meson-, Photo-, & Electroproduction at Low & Intermediate Energies, Bonn, 1970.
Proceedings. Springer-Verlag.

Symposium on Modern Anesthetic Agents, 1st, Hamburg, Nov. 9-10, 1973. see European Symposium on Modern Anesthetic Agents, 1st, Hamburg, 1973.

Symposium on Muscular Dystrophy, Jerusalem, Israel, 1976.
xSymposium on Muscular Dystrophy, Jerusalem 1976.
Muscular Dystrophy 1976: Proceedings. S Karger.

Symposium on Myocardial Infarction, Palm Springs, Califo Rnia, 1977.
xSymposium, Palm Springs, Calif., March 1977.
Myocardial Infarction in the Spectrum of Ischemic Heart Disease: Proceedings. S Karger.

Symposium on National Libraries in Europe, Vienna, 1958.
xSymposium of National Libraries, Vienna, 1958.
National Libraries: Their Problems & Prospects. Unipub.

Symposium on Natriuretic Hormone, Czechoslovakia, June, 1969. see Symposium on Natriuretic Hormone, Smolenice Castle, 1969.

Symposium on Natriuretic Hormone, Smolenice Castle, 1969.
xSymposium on Natriuretic Hormone, Czechoslovakia, June, 1969.
Regulation of Body Fluid Volumes by the Kidney: Proceedings. S Karger.

Symposium on Neoplastic & Reconstructive Problems of the Female Breast, Vol. 7. see Symposium on Neoplastic and Reconstructive Problems of the Female Breast, Memorial Sloan-Kettering Cancer Center, 1972.

Symposium on Neoplastic and Reconstructive Problems of the Female Breast, Memorial Sloan-Kettering Cancer Center, 1972.
xSymposium on Neoplastic & Reconstructive Problems of the Female Breast, Vol. 7. Proceedings. Mosby.

Symposium on Nephrology, 3rd, Hannover, June 1975. see International Symposium on Nephrology.

Symposium on Nephrology, 6th, Hannover, May 1978. see International Symposium on Nephrology.

Symposium on Neuroglia, Berlin, 1966.
xSymposium on Neuroglia, 12th Meeting, Berlin, 1966.
Proceedings. Springer-Verlag.

Symposium on Neuroglia, 12th Meeting, Berlin, 1966. see Symposium on Neuroglia, Berlin, 1966.

Symposium on Nonlinear Elasticity, University of Wisconsin-Madison, 1973.
xSymposium on Nonlinear Elasticity, University of Wisconsin, April, 1973.
Nonlinear Elasticity: Proceedings. Acad Pr.

Symposium on Nonlinear Functional Analysis, Chicago, 1968.
xSymposia in Pure Mathematics-Chicago-1968.
Nonlinear Functional Analysis. Am Math.

Symposium on Nonlinear Functional Analysis, Madison, Wis., 1971.
xMRC Symposium-1971.
Contributions to Nonlinear Functional Analysis: Proceedings. Acad Pr.

Symposium on Non-Well-Posed Problems and Logarithmic Convexity, Heriot-Watt University, 1972.
xSymposium on Non-Well-Posed Problems & Logarithmic Convexity, Edinburgh, 1972.
Proceedings. Springer-Verlag.

Symposium on Ocular Pharmacology and Therapeutics, New Orleans 1970.
xNew Orleans Academy of Ophthalmology - 18th Symposium.
Symposium on Ocular Pharmacology & Therapeutics. Mosby.

Symposium on Optimization & Stability Problems in Continuum Mechanics, los Angeles, 1971. see Symposium on Optimization and Stability Problems in Continuum Mechanics, los Angeles, 1971.

Symposium on Optimization and Stability Problems in Continuum Mechanics, los Angeles, 1971.
xSymposium on Optimization & Stability Problems in Continuum Mechanics, los Angeles, 1971.
Proceedings. Springer-Verlag.

Symposium on Optimization in Structural Design, Warsaw, 1973.
xSymposium Warsaw, Aug. 21-24, 1973.
Optimization in Structural Design. Springer-Verlag.

Symposium on Optimazition, Nice, 1969.
xSymposium on Optimization, Nice, 1969.
Proceedings. Springer-Verlag.

Symposium on Optimization, Nice, 1969. see Symposium on Optimazition, Nice, 1969.

Symposium on Ordinary Differential Equations, Minneapolis, 1972.
xSymposium on Ordinary Differential Equations, Minneapolis, May, 1972.
Proceedings. Springer-Verlag.

Symposium on Pathology of Axons & Axonal Flow, Vienna, 1970. see Symposium on Pathology of Axons and Axonal Flow, Vienna, 1970.

Symposium on Pathology of Axons and Axonal Flow, Vienna, 1970.
xSymposium on Pathology of Axons & Axonal Flow, Vienna, 1970.
Proceedings. Springer-Verlag.

Symposium on Photographic Gelatin - 2nd, Trinity College, Cambridge, 1970. see Symposium on Photographic Gelatin, 2nd, Trinity College, Cambridge, England, 1970.

Symposium on Photographic Gelatin, 2nd, Trinity College, Cambridge, England, 1970.
xSymposium on Photographic Gelatin - 2nd, Trinity College, Cambridge, 1970.
Photographic Gelatin: Proceedings. Acad Pr.

Symposium on Photographic Processing, University of Sussex, 1971.
xSymposium Held at the University of Sussex, Falmer, Sussex, Sept. 1971.
Photographic Processing: Proceedings. Acad Pr.

Symposium on Probability Methods in Analysis, Loutraki, Greece, 1966.
xSymposium On Probability Methods In Analysis - Loutraki - Greece - 1966.
Proceedings. Springer-Verlag.

Symposium on Protein Structure. see International Symposium on Protein Structure and Crystallography, Madras, 1963.

Symposium on Psychophysiological Aspects of Space Flight,brooks Air Force Base, Texas, 1960.
xSymposium on Psychophysiological Aspects of Space Flight, Brooks Air Force Base, Texas, 1960.
Proceedings. Columbia U Pr.

Symposium on Pulmonary Circulation, Prague, 1969. see International Symposium on Pulmonary Circulation, Prague, 1969.

Symposium on Quantum, Chemistry, & Biochemistry, 8th, Jerusalem, April 1975. see Jerusalem Symposium on Quantum Chemistry and Biochemistry, 8th, 1975.

Symposium on Race & Race Relations. see Symposium on Race and Race Relations, London, 1959.

Symposium on Race and Race Relations, London, 1959.
xSymposium on Race & Race Relations.
Man, Race, & Darwin: Papers. Greenwood.

Symposium on Recent Advances in Reproduction and Regulation of Fertility, New Delhi, India, 1978.
xSymposium, New Delhi, October 1978.
Recent Advances in Reproduction & Regulation of Fertility: Proceedings. Elsevier.

Symposium on Recent Developments in the Theory of Numbers, California Institute of Technology, 1963.
xSymposia in Pure Mathematics-Pasadena-1963.
Theory of Numbers: Proceedings. Am Math.

Symposium on Reconstruction of the Auricle, Charlottesville, Virginia, 1973.
xSymposium on Reconstruction of the Auricle. Proceedings. Mosby.

Symposium on Relaxation Methods in Relation to Molecular Structure, Aberystwyth, 1965.
xSymposium On Relaxation Methods In Relation To Molecular Structure - Aberystwyth - 1965.
Molecular Relaxation Processes: Proceedings. Acad Pr.

Symposium on Satellite Dynamics, 4th, Sao Paulo, Brazil, 1974.
xCOSPAR-IAU-IUTAM Symposium, Sao Paulo, Brazil, June 19-21, 1974.
Satellite Dynamics. Springer-Verlag.

Symposium On Scientific Satellites. see Symposium on Scientific Satellites-Mission and Design, Philadelphia, 1962.

Symposium on Scientific Satellites-Mission and Design, Philadelphia, 1962.
xSymposium On Scientific Satellites.
Scientific Satellites. Am Astronaut.

Symposium on Several Complex Variables, Park City, Utah, 1970.
xSymposium On Several Complex Variables - Park City - Utah - 1970.
Proceedings. Springer-Verlag.

Symposium on Solution Mining, 1974. see Solution Mining Symposium, Dallas, 1974.

Symposium on Special Functions, Washington, D.C., 1969.
xSymposia on Special Functions & Wave Propagation, Washington, D.C., 1969.

The United Nations Secretariat. Greenwood.
Syrett, Harold C. *see* Syrett, Harold Coffin.
Syrett, Harold Coffin, 1913-
  xSyrett, Harold C.
    Andrew Jackson: His Contribution to the
     American Tradition. Greenwood.
    City of Brooklyn, 1865-1898: A Political
     History. AMS Pr.
Syrkin, Marie, 1900-
  xSyrkin, Marie.
    The State of the Jews. New Republic.
Syski. *see* Syski, R.
Syski, R., 1924-
  xSyski.
    Random Processes: A First Look. Dekker.
Systems Symposium - 3rd - Case Western Reserve
  University, Institute of Technology. *see* Systems
  Symposium, 3d, Case Institute of Technology, 1966.
Systems Symposium - 4th - Case Western Reserve
  University, Institute of Technology. *see* Systems
  Symposium, 4th, Case Western Reserve University,
  1968.
Systems Symposium, 3d, Case Institute of Technology,
1966.
  xSystems Symposium - 3rd - Case Western
    Reserve University, Institute of Technology.
    Systems Theory & Biology: Proceedings.
    Springer-Verlag.
Systems Symposium, 4th, Case Western Reserve
University, 1968.
  xSystems Symposium - 4th - Case Western Reserve
    University, Institute of Technology.
    Theoretical Approaches to Non-Numerical
    Problem Solving: Proceedings.
    Springer-Verlag.
Syvrud, Donald E. *see* Syvrud, Donald Eugene.
Syvrud, Donald Eugene, 1924-
  xSyvrud, Donald E.
    Foundations of Brazilian Economic Growth.
    Hoover Inst Pr.
Szabo, Denis, 1929-
  xSzabo, Denis.
    Criminology & Crime Policy. Lexington Bks.
    ed. Offenders & Corrections. Praeger.
Szabo, M. E.
  xSzabo, M. E.
    Algebra of Proofs. Elsevier.
Szabo, Marc.
  xSzabo, Marc.
    Drawing File for Architects, Illustrators, &
    Designers. Van Nos Reinhold.
Szabo, Tamas.
  xSzabo, Tamas.
    Boy on the Rooftop. Peter Smith.
Szabo, Zoltan, 1928-
  xSzabo, Zoltan.
    Creative Watercolor Techniques.
    Watson-Guptill.
Szabolcsi, Bence, 1899-
  xSzabolcsi, Bence.
    The Twilight of Ferenc Liszt. Branden.
Szacki, Jerzy.
  xSzacki, Jerzy.
    History of Sociological Thought. Greenwood.
Szajkowski, Z. *see* Szajkowski, Zosa.
Szajkowski, Zosa, 1911-
  xSzajkowski, Z.
    An Illustrated Sourcebook of Russian
    Antisemitism 1881-1977. Ktav.
Szalay, F. S. *see* Szalay, Frederick S.
Szalay, Frederick S.
  xSzalay, F. S.
    ed. Approaches to Primate Paleobiology. S
    Karger.
Szanto, George H., 1940-
  xSzanto, George H.
    Theater & Propaganda. U of Tex Pr.
Szarejko, Francis.
  xSzarejko, Francis W.

How to Manage Yourself & Others. Logos.
Szarejko, Francis W. *see* Szarejko, Francis.
Szarski, J. *see* Szarski, Jacek.
Szarski, Jacek.
  xSzarski, J.
    Differential Inequalities. Hafner.
  xSzarski, Jacek.
    Differential Inequalities. Intl Pubns Serv.
Szasz, Suzanne.
  xSzasz, Suzanne.
    Child Photography Simplified. Amphoto.
    Silent Miaow: A Manual for Kittens, Strays &
    Homeless Cats. Crown.
    The Unspoken Language of Children. Norton.
Szasz, Thomas. *see* Szasz, Thomas Stephen.
Szasz, Thomas S. *see* Szasz, Thomas Stephen.
Szasz, Thomas Stephen, 1920-
  xSzasz, Thomas.
    The Theology of Medicine: The Political -
    Philosophical Foundations of Medical Ethics.
    La State U Pr.
  xSzasz, Thomas S.
    Ethics of Psychoanalysis: The Theory &
    Method of Autonomous Psychotherapy.
    Basic.
    Psychiatric Justice. Greenwood.
Szathmary, Louis.
  xSzathmary, Louis.
    Chef's Secret Cook Book. Times Bks.
Szatmary, David, 1951-
  xSzatmary, David P.
    Shays' Rebellion: The Making of an Agrarian
    Insurrection. U of Mass Pr.
Szatmary, David P. *see* Szatmary, David.
Szczepanski, Jan, 1913-
  xSzczepanski, Jan.
    Higher Education in Eastern Europe. Interbk
    Inc.
Sze, William C., 1927-
  xSze, William S.
    ed. Human Life Cycle. Aronson.
Sze, William S. *see* Sze, William C.
Szebehely, Victor G. *see* Szebehely, Victor Goyzo.
Szebehely, Victor Goyzo, 1921-
  xSzebehely, Victor G.
    Theory of Orbits in the Restricted Problem of
    Three Bodies. Acad Pr.
Szebenyi, Emil. *see* Szebenyi, Emil S.
Szebenyi, Emil S., 1920-
  xSzebenyi, Emil.
    Atlas of Macaca Mulatta. Fairleigh Dickinson.
  xSzebenyi, Emil S.
    Atlas of Developmental Embryology. Fairleigh
    Dickinson.
Szechter, Szymon.
  xSzechter, Szymon.
    Bridge on Ice. Merrimack Bk Serv.
Szechy, K. *see* Szechy, Karoly.
Szechy, Karoly.
  xSzechy, K.
    Foundation Engineering: Soil Exploration &
    Spread Foundations. Intl Pubns Serv.
Szecsko, Tamas.
  xSzecsko, Tamas.
    Communication Policies in Hungary. Unipub.
Szego, Gabor, 1895-
  xSzego, Gabor.
    Orthogonal Polynomials. Am Math.
Szekely, E. *see* Szekely, Endre.
Szekely, Endre.
  xSzekely, E.
    Functional Laws of Psychodynamics.
    Springer-Verlag.
Szekely, Julian.
  xSzekely, Julian.
    Rate Phenomena in Process Metallurgy. Wiley.
Szekely, Maria.
  xSzekely, Maria.

From DNA to Protein: The Transfer of
  Genetic Information. Halsted Pr.
Szekeres, Cyndy.
  xSzekeres, Cyndy.
    Long Ago. McGraw.
Szemak, J.
  xSzemak, J.
    Living History of Hungary. Danubian.
Szent-Gyorgyi, Albert, 1893-
  xSzent-Gyorgyi, Albert.
    Crazy Ape. Philos Lib.
    Introduction to a Submolecular Biology. Acad
    Pr.
    The Living State & Cancer. Dekker.
Szentirmai, George.
  xSzentirmai, George.
    ed. Computer Aided Filter Design. Inst
    Electrical.
    ed. Computer-Aided Filter Design. Wiley.
Szeplaki, Joseph.
  xSzeplaki, Joseph.
    The Hungarians in America 1583-1974: A
    Chronology & Fact Book. Oceana.
Szigethy, Marion. *see* Szigethy, Marion C.
Szigethy, Marion C.
  xSzigethy, Marion.
    Maurice Falcolm Tauber: A Biobibliography
    1934-1973. Scarecrow.
Szigeti, Joseph, 1892-1973
  xSzigeti, Joseph.
    Szigeti on the Violin. Dover.
    With Strings Attached: Reminiscences &
    Reflections. Da Capo.
Szilassy, Sander. *see* Szilassy, Sandor.
Szilassy, Sandor.
  xSzilassy, Sander.
    Revolutionary Hungary 1918-1921. Danubian.
Szklarski, L. *see* Szklarski, Ludger M.
Szklarski, Ludger M.
  xSzklarski, L.
    Underground Electric Haulage. Pergamon.
Szladits, Charles, 1911-
  xSzladits, Charles.
    Guide to Foreign Legal Materials: French,
    German, Swiss. Oceana.
Szladits, Lola L.
  xSzladits, Lola L.
    Owen D. Young, Book Collector. NY Pub Lib.
Szokolay, S. V.
  xSzokolay, S. V.
    Solar Energy & Building. Halsted Pr.
Szporluk, Roman.
  xSzporluk, Roman.
    ed. The Influence of East Europe & the Soviet
    West on the USSR. Praeger.
Sztompka, Piotr.
  xSztompka, Piotr.
    Sociological Dilemmas: Toward a Dialectic
    Paradigm. Acad Pr.
Szucs, E. *see* Szucs, Ervin.
Szucs, Ervin.
  xSzucs, E.
    Similitude & Modelling. Elsevier.
Szulc, Tad.
  xSzulc, Tad.
    The Energy Crisis. Watts.
    The Energy Crisis. Watts.
Szulec, Jeanette A.
  xSzulec, Jeannette.
    Syllabus for the Surgeon's Secretary. Medical
    Arts.
Szulec, Jeannette. *see* Szulec, Jeanette A.
Szuprowicz, Bohdan O.
  xSzuprowicz, Bohdan O.
    Doing Business with People's Republic of
    China: Industries & Markets. Wiley.
Szurek, S. A. *see* Szurek, Stanislaus Andrew.
Szurek, Stanislaus Andrew.
  xSzurek, S. A.

ed. Antisocial Child: His Family & His
   Community. Sci & Behavior.

ed. Inpatient Care for the Psychotic Child. Sci
   & Behavior.

ed. Psychosomatic Disorders & Mental
   Retardation in Children. Sci & Behavior.

Szwarc, Michael.
   xSzwarc, Michael.
      Carbanions Living Polymers & Electron
      Transfer Processes. Krieger.

Szweda, Ralph A.

   xSzweda, Ralph A.
      Information Processing Management. Van Nos
      Reinhold.

Szykitka, Walter.
   xSzykitka, Walter.
      ed. How to Be Your Own Boss: The Complete
      Handbook for Starting & Running a Small
      Business. NAL.

Szyliowicz, Joseph S.
   xSzyliowicz, Joseph S.
      Education & Modernization in the Middle
      East. Cornell U Pr.
      ed. The Energy Crisis & U. S. Foreign Policy.
      Praeger.

Szymanski. *see* Szymanski, Albert.

Szymanski, Albert, 1941-
   xSzymanski.
      The Capitalist State & the Politics of Class.
      Winthrop.

Szymanski, Herman A.
   xSzymanski, Herman A.
      Infrared Band Handbook. IFI Plenum.

Ta'Unga.
   xTa'unga.
      Works of Ta'unga: Records of a Polynesian
      Traveller in the South Seas, 1833-1896. U Pr
      of Hawaii.

Taaffe, James G.
   xTaaffe, James G.
      Abraham Cowley. Irvington.
      Reading English Poetry. Free Pr.

Tab Books.
   xTab Books Editorial Staff.
      Master Transistor IC Diode Substitution
      Handbook. TAB Bks.
   xTab Editional Staff.
      Concrete & Masonry. TAB Bks.
   xTAB Editorial Staff.

Airline for Montgomery Ward Color T.V.
   Service Manual. TAB Bks.
ed. CB Radio Schematic-Servicing Manual.
   TAB Bks.
ed. CBer's Handy Atlas-Dictionary. TAB Bks.
ed. CBer's Handy Manual. TAB Bks.
ed. Home Audio System Schematic-Servicing
   Manual. TAB Bks.
Japanese Consumer Electronics
   Schematic-Servicing Manual. TAB Bks.
Japanese Monochrome TV Service Manual:
   Hitachi, Panasonic, Sharp. TAB Bks.
Master Transistor Substitution Handbook. TAB
   Bks.
Master Tube Substitution Handbook. TAB Bks.
Popular Tube-Transistor Substitution Guide.
   TAB Bks.
Practical Home Construction-Carpentry
   Handbook. TAB Bks.
RCA Color T.V. Manual. TAB Bks.
RCA Color TV Schematic Servicing Manual.
   TAB Bks.
Sears Color T. V. Service Manual. TAB Bks.
Toshiba Color TV. TAB Bks.
xTAB Staff.
   ed. RCA Color T.V. Schematic-Servicing
   Manual. TAB Bks.
Tab Books Editorial Staff. *see* Tab Books.
Tab Editional Staff. *see* Tab Books.
TAB Editorial Staff. *see* Tab Books.
TAB Staff. *see* Tab Books.
Taba, Hilda, 1902-
   xTaba, Hilda.
      Curriculum Development: Theory & Practice.
      HarBraceJ.
Tabachnick, Norman.
   xTabachnick, Norman.
      Accident or Suicide: Destruction by
      Automobile. C C Thomas.
Taback, Simms.
   xTaback, Simms.
      Joseph Had a Little Overcoat. Random.
Tabak, Daniel.
   xTabak, Daniel.
      Optimal Control by Mathematical
      Programming. SRL Pub Co.
Tabarly, Eric.
   xTabarly, Eric.
      Ocean Racing. Norton.
Tabasz, Thomas F.
   xTabasz, Thomas F.
      Toward an Economics of Prisons. Lexington
      Bks.
Tabb, William K.
   xTabb, William K.
      ed. Marxism & the Metropolis: New
      Perspectives in Urban Political Economy.
      Oxford U Pr.
Tabberer, Frank. *see* Tabberer, Frank Leonard.
Tabberer, Frank Leonard.
   xTabberer, Frank.
      Mathematics for Technicians. Butterworths.
Tabeling, Ernst.
   xTabeling, Ernst.
      Mater Larum: Zum Wesen der Larenreligion.
      Arno.
Taber, Anthony.
   xTaber, Anthony.
      Cats' Eyes. Dutton.

Taber, Ben-Zion, 1927-
   xTaber, Ben-Zion.
      Manual of Gynecologic & Obstetric
      Emergencies. Saunders.

Taber, Gladys. *see* Taber, Gladys Bagg.

Taber, Gladys (Bagg), 1899-
   xTaber, Gladys.
      Another Path. Lippincott.

Conversations with Amber. G K Hall.
Conversations with Amber. Lippincott.
Taber, Margaret R.
   xTaber, Margaret R.
      Electric Circuit Analysis. HM.
Tabery, Julia J. *see* Tabery, Julia Jordan.
Tabery, Julia Jordan.
   xTabery, Julia J.
      Communicating in Spanish for Medical
      Personnel. Little.
Tabler, Dave.
   xTabler, Dave.
      VW Bodywork. Clymer Pubns.
Tabor, D. *see* Tabor, David.
Tabor, David.
   xTabor, D.
      Gases, Liquids & Solids. Cambridge U Pr.
Tabor, Margaret.
   xTabor, Margaret.
      The Baker's Daughter. Coward.
Tabor, Pauline, 1905-
   xTabor, Pauline.
      Pauline's. Fawcett.
Tabor, Rowland W.
   xTabor, Rowland W.
      Guide to the Geology of Olympic National
      Park. U of Wash Pr.
Tabori, Paul, 1908-
   xTabori, Paul.
      Companions of the Unseen. Univ Bks.
Taborsky, Edward.
   xTaborsky, Edward.
      Communist Penetration of the Third World.
      Speller.
Tabouis, Genevieve. *see* Tabouis, Genevieve R.
Tabouis, Genevieve R., 1892-
   xTabouis, Genevieve.
      They Called Me Cassandra. Da Capo.
Tacchi, Derek.
   xTacchi, Derek.
      Ovarian Gynaecology. Saunders.
Tacey, William S. *see* Tacey, William Sanford.
Tacey, William Sanford.
   xTacey, William S.
      Business & Professional Speaking. Wm C
      Brown.
Tachau, Mary K. *see* Tachau, Mary K. Bonsteel.
Tachau, Mary K. Bonsteel, 1926-
   xTachau, Mary K.
      Federal Courts in the Early Republic:
      Kentucky, 1789-1816. Princeton U Pr.
Tachdjian, Mihran O.
   xTachdjian, Mihran O.
      Pediatric Orthopedics. Saunders.
Tache, J. *see* Tache, Jean.
Tache, Jean.
   xTache, J.
      ed. Cancer, Stress, & Death. Plenum Pub.
Tacitus. *see* Tacitus, Cornelius.
Tacitus, Cornelius.
   xTacitus.
      Annals of Imperial Rome. Penguin.
      The Histories. Penguin.
Tackett, T. *see* Tackett, Tim.
Tackett, Tim.
   xTackett, T.
      Hsing-I Kung-Fu. Wehman.
   xTackett, Tim.
      Hsing-I Kung-Fu. Ohara Pubns.
Tadmor, Joshua.
   xTadmor, S.
      Silent Warriors. Macmillan.
Tadmor, S. *see* Tadmor, Joshua.
Tadmor, Zehev.
   xTadmor, Zehev.
      Engineering Principles of Plasticating
      Extrusion. Krieger.
      Principles of Polymer Processing. Wiley.
Tadokoro, Hiroyuki, 1920-
   xTadokoro, Hiroyuki.

Structure of Crystalline Polymers. Wiley.

Taege, Marlys, 1928-
xTaege, Marlys.
And God Gave Women Talents!. Concordia.

Taetzsch, Lyn.
xTaetzsch, Lyn.
Opening Your Own Retail Store. Contemp Bks.
Practical Accounting for Small Business. Van Nos Reinhold.
Taking Charge on the Job: Techniques for Assertive Management. Exec Ent.

Taeuber, Conrad.
xTaeuber, Conrad.
The Changing Population of the United States. Russell.

Tafel, Edgar.
xTafel, Edgar.
Apprentice to Genius: Years with Frank Lloyd Wright. McGraw.

Taff, Charles A. see Taff, Charles Albert.

Taff, Charles Albert, 1916-
xTaff, Charles A.
Commercial Motor Transportation. Cornell Maritime.

Taft, Donald. see Taft, Donald Reed.

Taft, Donald R. see Taft, Donald Reed.

Taft, Donald Reed.
xTaft, Donald.
Two Portuguese Communities in New England. Arno.
xTaft, Donald R.
Criminology. Macmillan.
Two Portuguese Communities in New England. AMS Pr.

Taft, Edna.
xTaft, Edna.
Puritan in Voodoo-Land. Gale.

Taft, Frances B.
xTaft, Frances B.
Answering the Call. Judson.

Taft, Henry W. see Taft, Henry Waters.

Taft, Henry Waters, 1859-1945
xTaft, Henry W.
Opinions, Literary & Otherwise. Arno.

Taft, Jessie, 1882-1960
xTaft, Jessie.
Dynamics of Therapy in a Controlled Relationship. Peter Smith.

Taft, William H. see Taft, William Howard.

Taft, William Howard, Pres. U.S., 1857-1930
xTaft, William H.
Ethics in Service. Kennikat.
Newspapers As Tools for Historians. Lucas.
The Physical, Political & International Value of the Panama Canal. Inst Econ Pol.
Present Day Problems: A Collection of Addresses Delivered on Various Occasions. Arno.
World Peace: A Written Debate Between William Howard Taft & William Jennings Bryan. Ozer.

Tafuri, Manfredo.
xTafuri, Manfredo.
Architecture & Utopia: Design & Capitalist Development. MIT Pr.
Modern Architecture. Abrams.

Tagatz, Glenn E.
xTagatz, Glenn E.
Child Development & Individually Guided Education. A-W.

Tager, Mark.
xTager, Mark.
Whole Person Health Care. Victoria Hse.

Taggard, Genevieve, 1894-1948
xTaggard, Genevieve.
Life & Mind of Emily Dickinson. Cooper Sq.

Taggart, Dorothy T., 1917-
xTaggart, Dorothy T.

A Guide to Sources in Educational Media & Technology. Scarecrow.

Taggart, Herbert F. see Taggart, Herbert Francis.

Taggart, Herbert Francis, 1898-
xTaggart, Herbert F.
Cost Justification. Univ Microfilms.

Taggart, John, 1942-
xTaggart, John.
Dodeka. Membrane Pr.
The Pyramid Is a Pure Crystal. SBD.

Taggart, Robert, 1945-
xTaggart, Robert.
The Prison of Unemployment: Manpower Programs for Offenders. Johns Hopkins.

Tagliacozzo, Rhoda.
xTagliacozzo, Rhoda.
Saving Graces. St Martin.

Tagliaferri, Louis E.
xTagliaferri, Louis E.
Successful Supervision. Wiley.

Tagliavia, Sheila.
xTagliavia, Sheila.
An Arrangement for Life. Har-Row.

Tagliere, Daniel A.
xTagliere, Daniel A.
The Participative Prince: Techniques for Developing Your Organization & Improving Its Performance. ODS Pubns.

Tagnon, Henri J.
xTagnon, Henri J.
ed. Controversies in Cancer: Design of Trials & Treatment. Masson Pub.

Tagore, Rabindranath, Sir, 1861-1941
xTagore, Rabindranath.
Fireflies. Macmillan.
Fireflies. Macmillan.
The Housewarming, & Other Selected Writings. Greenwood.
The Later Poems of Rabindranath Tagore. T Y Crowell.
Mashi, & Other Stories. Arno.

Tagore, Rathindranath, 1888-1961
xTagore, Rathindranath.
On the Edges of the Time. Greenwood.

Tahtinen, Dale R.
xTahtinen, Dale R.
The Arab-Israeli Military Balance Today. Am Enterprise.
Arms in the Persian Gulf. Am Enterprise.
National Security Challenges to Saudi Arabia. Am Enterprise.

Taibleson, M. H., 1929-
xTaibleson, M. H.
Fourier Analysis on Local Fields. Princeton U Pr.

Taichert, Louise C.
xTaichert, Louise C.
Childhood Learning, Behavior & the Family. Human Sci Pr.

Taillandier, Yvon.
xTaillandier, Yvon.
Corot. Crown.

Taine, H. see Taine, Hippolyte Adolphe.

Taine, H. A. see Taine, Hippolyte Adolphe.

Taine, Hippolyte A. see Taine, Hippolyte Adolphe.

Taine, Hippolyte Adolphe, 1828-1893
xTaine, H.
Lectures on Art. Dynamic Learn.
xTaine, H. A.
History of English Literature. R West.
xTaine, Hippolyte A.

The Ancient Regime. Peter Smith.
Balzac, a Critical Study. Arden Lib.
History of English Literature. R West.
History of English Literature. Somerset Pub.
Lectures on Art. AMS Pr.
Lectures on Art. R West.
Lectures on Art. Scholarly.
Taine's Notes on England. Arno.

Tainiter, M., 1936-
xTainiter, Melvin.
The Art & Science of Decision Making. Timetable Pr.

Tainiter, Melvin. see Tainiter, M.

Taira, Koji, 1926-
xTaira, Koji.
Economic Development & the Labor Market in Japan. Columbia U Pr.

Tairas, J. N. see Tairas, J. N. B.

Tairas, J. N. B.
xTairas, J. N.
Indonesia: A Bibliography of Bibliographies. Oleander Pr.

Tait, A.
xTait, J.
Principles of Auto-Body Repairing & Repainting. P-H.

Tait, Alan A.
xTait, Alan A.
The Taxation of Personal Wealth. U of Ill Pr.

Tait, Cornelia D. see Tait, Cornelia Damian.

Tait, Cornelia Damian.
xTait, Cornelia D.
Art in Its Fourth Dimension. Philos Lib.

Tait, Elaine.
xTait, Elaine.
Best Restaurants Philadelphia & Environs. One Hund One Prods

Tait, J. see Tait, A.

Tait, James A.
xTait, James A.
Descriptive Cataloguing: A Student's Introduction to the Anglo-American Cataloguins Rules, 1967. Shoe String.

Tait, Joseph W. see Tait, Joseph Wilfrid.

Tait, Joseph Wilfrid, 1896-
xTait, Joseph W.
Some Aspects of the Effect of the Dominant American Culture Upon Children of Italian-Born Parents. AMS Pr.
Some Aspects of the Effect of the Dominant American Culture Upon Children of Italian Born Parents. Kelley.

Tait, M. E. see Tait, Margaret Evelyn.

Tait, Margaret Evelyn.
xTait, M. E.
Horses & Ponies: Their Care & Management for Owners & Riders. Arco.

Taiwo, Oladele.
xTaiwo, Oladele.
Culture & the Nigerian Novel. St Martin.

Takacs, James A.
xTakacs, James A.
Your Mind Can Drive You Crazy. Delphi Info.

Takacs, Lajos.
xTakacs, Lajos.
Combinatorial Methods in the Theory of Stochastic Processes. Krieger.

Takada, K Oin, 1924-
xTakada, Koin.
Spirit of Buddhism Today. Heian Intl.

Takada, Koin. see Takada, K Oin.

Takahashi, A. S. see Takahashi, Shinji.

Takahashi, M. see Takahashi, Matsumasa.

Takahashi, Matsumasa.
xTakahashi, M.
Atlas of Vertebral Angiography. Univ Park.

Takahashi, Naohiro, 1939-
xTakahashi, Naohiro.

Journey Through Africa. Kodansha.
Takahashi, Shinji, 1912-
xTakahashi, A. S.
Atlas of Axial Transverse Tomography & Its
Clinical Application. Springer-Verlag.
Takahashi, Y. *see* Takahashi, Yasundo.
Takahashi, Yasundo.
xTakahashi, Y.
Control & Dynamic Systems. A-W.
Takahashi, Yasushi.
xTakahashi, Y.
An Introduction to Field Quantization.
Pergamon.
Takaki, Masayoshi, 1864-
xTakaki, Masayoshi.
The History of Japanese Paper Currency
(1868-1890). AMS Pr.
Takaki, Ronald T., 1939-
xTakaki, Ronald T.
Iron Cages: Race & Culture in
Nineteenth-Century America. Knopf.
Takakusu, J. *see* Takakusu, Junjiro.
Takakusu, Janjiro. *see* Takakusu, Junjiro.
Takakusu, Junjiro.
xTakakusu, J.
Essentials of Buddhist Philosophy. Orient Bk
Dist.
xTakakusu, Janjiro.
The Essentials of Buddhist Philosophy. South
Asia Bks.
xTakakusu, Junjiro.
The Essentials of Buddhist Philosophy.
Greenwood.
Essentials of Buddhist Philosophy. Verry.
Takakusu, Junjiro. *see* Takakusu, Junjir O.
Takamura, Kotaro, 1883-1956.
xTakamura, Kotaro.
Chieko & Other Poems of Takamura Kotaro. U
Pr of Hawaii.
Takamura, Kotaro. *see* Takamura, Kotaro.
Takamura, S. *see* Takamura, Shinji.
Takamura, Shinji.
xTakamura, S.
Software Design for Electronic Switching
Systems. Inst Elect Eng.
Takashima, Shizuye.
xTakashima, Shizuye.
A Child in Prison Camp. Morrow.
Takaya, Ted T., 1927-
xTakaya, Ted T.
tr. Modern Japanese Drama: An Anthology.
Columbia U Pr.
Takayama, A. *see* Takayama, Akira.
Takayama, Akira, 1932-
xTakayama, A.
Mathematical Economics. HR&W.
Takesian, Sarkis A. *see* Takesian, Sarkis Armen.
Takesian, Sarkis Armen.
xTakesian, Sarkis A.
A Comparative Study of the
Mexican-American Graduate & Dropout. R
& E Res Assoc.
Takeuchi, H. *see* Takeuchi, Hitoshi.
Takeuchi, Hitoshi.
xTakeuchi, H.
Debate About the Earth: An Approach to
Geophysics Through Analysis of Continental
Drift. Freeman C.
Takeuchi, Kenji, 1932-
xTakeuchi, Kenji.
Tropical Hardwood Trade in the Asia-Pacific
Region. Johns Hopkins.
Takeuti, Gaisi, 1926-
xTakeuti, Gaisi.
Two Applications of Logic to Mathematics.
Princeton U Pr.
Takizawa, Matsuyo, 1898-
xTakizawa, Matsuyo.

Penetration of Money Economy in Japan & Its
Effects Upon Social & Political Institutions.
AMS Pr.
Taktsis, Costas, 1927-
xTaktsis, Costas.
Third Wedding. Red Dust.
Talal, N. *see* Talal, Norman.
Talal, Norman.
xTalal, N.
ed. Autoimmunity: Genetic, Immunologic &
Virologic & Clinical Aspects. Acad Pr.
Talamo, Joe.
xTalamo, Joseph.
Developing a Championship Football Program.
P-H.
Talamo, Joseph. *see* Talamo, Joe.
Talamonti, Leo.
xTalamonti, Leo.
Forbidden Universe: Mysteries of the Psychic
World. Stein & Day.
Talarzyk, W. Wayne.
xTalarzyk, W. Wayne.
Cases for Analysis in Marketing. Dryden Pr.
Talbert, E. Gene.
xTalbert, Gene.
Individualized Instruction: A Book of Readings.
Merrill.
Talbert, Gene. *see* Talbert, E. Gene.
Talbitzer, Bill.
xTalbitzer, W. M.
Too Much Blood. Vantage.
Talbitzer, W. M. *see* Talbitzer, Bill.
Talbot, Allan. *see* Talbot, Allan R.
Talbot, Allan R.
xTalbot, Allan.
Power Along the Hudson: The Storm King
Case & the Birth of Environmentalism.
Dutton.
Talbot, Carol.
xTalbot, Carol.
For This I Was Born. Moody.
Talbot, Charlene J. *see* Talbot, Charlene Joy.
Talbot, Charlene Joy.
xTalbot, Charlene J.
The Great Rat Island Adventure. Atheneum.
A Home with Aunt Florry. Atheneum.
An Orphan for Nebraska. Atheneum.
Talbot, Daniel.
xTalbot, Daniel.
ed. Film: An Anthology. U of Cal Pr.
Talbot, Gordon.
xTalbot, Gordon G.
Overcoming Materialism. Herald Pr.
Talbot, Gordon G. *see* Talbot, Gordon.
Talbot, Michael.
xTalbot, Michael.
Vivaldi. Biblio Dist.
Talbot, Nathan B. *see* Talbot, Nathan Bill.
Talbot, Nathan Bill, 1909-
xTalbot, Nathan B.
ed. Raising Children in Modern America: What
Parents & Society Should Be Doing for Their
Children. Little.
Talbot, Percy A. *see* Talbot, Percy Amaury.
Talbot, Percy Amaury, 1877-1945
xTalbot, Percy A.
In the Shadow of the Bush. AMS Pr.
In the Shadow of the Bush. Negro U Pr.
Some Nigerian Fertility Cults. Biblio Dist.
Talbot, Phillips.
xTalbot, Phillips.
South Asia in the World Today. AMS Pr.
Talbot, Ross B.
xTalbot, Ross B.
The Chicken War: An International Trade
Conflict Between the United States & the
European Economic Community, 1961-1964.
Iowa St U Pr.
Talbot, Samuel A. *see* Talbot, Samuel Armstrong.

Talbot, Samuel Armstrong.
xTalbot, Samuel A.
Systems Physiology. Wiley.
Talbot, Theodore, d. 1862
xTalbot, Theodore.
Soldier in the West: Letters of Theodore Talbot
During His Services in California, Mexico, &
Oregon, 1845-53. U of Okla Pr.
Talbot, Toby.
xTalbot, Toby.
A Book About My Mother. FS&G.
A Bucketful of Moon. Lothrop.
Tales from Count Lucanor. Dial.
The World of the Child: Clinical & Cultural
Studies from Birth to Adolescence. Aronson.
Talbot, W. H. *see* Talbot, William Henry Fox.
Talbot, William Henry Fox, 1800-1877
xTalbot, W. H.
Pencil of Nature. Da Capo.
Talbot-Booth, E. C. *see* Talbot-Booth, Eric Charles.
Talbot-Booth, E. G. *see* Talbot-Booth, Eric Charles.
Talbot-Booth, Eric Charles.
xTalbot-Booth, E. C.
Talbot-Booth's Merchant Ships. Nichols Pub.
xTalbot-Booth, E. G.
ed. Talbot-Booth's Merchant Ships. Nichols
Pub.
Talbott, David N.
xTalbott, David N.
The Saturn Myth. Doubleday.
Talbott, J. H. *see* Talbott, John Harold.
Talbott, John A.
xTalbott, John A.
The Death of the Asylum: A Critical Study of
State Hospital Management, Services & Care.
Grune.
Talbott, John E.
xTalbott, John E.
Politics of Educational Reform in France,
1918-1940. Princeton U Pr.
Talbott, John H. *see* Talbott, John Harold.
Talbott, John Harold, 1902-
xTalbott, J. H.
ed. Clinical Rheumatology. Elsevier.
xTalbott, John H.
Gout & Uric Acid Metabolism.
Thieme-Stratton.
Talbott, Strobe.
xTalbott, Strobe.
Endgame: The Inside Story of Salt II.
Har-Row.
Talburt, W. F. *see* Talburt, William F.
Talburt, William F.
xTalburt, W. F.
ed. Potato Processing. AVI.
Talcott, Sebastian V. *see* Talcott, Sebastian Visscher.
Talcott, Sebastian Visscher, b. 1812
xTalcott, Sebastian V.
Genealogical Notes of New York & New
England Families. Genealog Pub.
Talese, Gay.
xTalese, Gay.
Honor Thy Father. Fawcett.
Thy Neighbor's Wife. Doubleday.
Talhouk, Abdul M. *see* Talhouk, Abdul Mon'Im S.
Talhouk, Abdul Mon'Im S.
xTalhouk, Abdul M.
Insects & Mites Injurious to Crops in Middle
Eastern Countries. Intl Pubns Serv.
Taliaferro, Harden E., 1818?-1875
xTaliaferro, Harden E.
Fisher's River, North Carolina: Scenes &
Characters. Arno.
Taliaferro, Margaret.
xTaliaferro, Margaret.

Do You Ever Have Questions Like These?. Doubleday.
The Real Reason for Christmas: Letters to Children for the Twelve Nights of Christmas. Doubleday.

Taliaferro, William H. *see* Taliaferro, William Hay.

Taliaferro, William Hay, 1895-
xTaliaferro, William H.
ed. Medicine & the War. Arno.

The Talisman.
xTalisman Editors.
Western Sampler: Nine Contemporary Poets, Anthology. Talisman.

Talisman Editors. *see* The Talisman.

Talkington, P. C. *see* Talkington, Perry C.

Talkington, Perry C.
xTalkington, P. C.
ed. Evolving Concepts in Psychiatry. Grune.

Tall, Lambert.
xTall, Lambert.
Structural Steel Design. Wiley.

Tallach, John.
xTallach, John.
God Made Them Great. Banner of Truth.

Talland, George A.
xTalland, George A.
Deranged Memory: A Psychonomic Study of the Amnesic Syndrome. Acad Pr.

Tallant, Robert, 1909-
xTallant, Robert.
Louisiana Purchase. Random.

Tallarida, R. J. *see* Tallarida, Ronald J.

Tallarida, Ronald J.
xTallarida, R. J.
Dose-Response Relation in Pharmacology. Springer-Verlag.

Tallberg, Martin.
xTallberg, Martin.
Don Pellam: An Investigation into His Murder. Popular Lib.

Tallcott, Emogene.
xTallcott, Emogene.
Glacier Tracks. Lothrop.

Tallent, Norman, 1921-
xTallent, Norman.
Psychological Report Writing. P-H.
Report Writing in Special Education. P-H.

Talleur, Richard. *see* Talleur, Richard W.

Talleur, Richard W.
xTalleur, Richard.
Mastering the Art of Fly-Tying. Stackpole.
xTalleur, Richard W.
Fly Fishing for Trout: A Guide for Adult Beginners. Winchester Pr.

Talley, David.
xTalley, David.
Basic Telephone Switching Systems. Hayden.

Tallmadge, Benjamin, 1754-1835
xTallmadge, Benjamin.
Memoir of Colonel Benjamin Tallmadge. Arno.

Tallman. *see* Tallman, Drew.

Tallman, Drew.
xTallman.
Complete Guide to Football's Option Attacks. P-H.
xTallman, Drew.
Directory of Football Defenses: Successful Defenses & How to Attack Them. P-H.
Football Coach's Guide to High-Scoring Passing Offense. P-H.
How to Coach Football's Attacking Defenses. P-H.

Tallman, Frank.
xTallman, Frank.
Flying the Old Planes. Doubleday.

Tallman, Irving.
xTallman, Irving.

Passion, Action, & Politics: A Perspective on Social Problems & Social-Problem Solving. W H Freeman.

Tallon, Robert, 1939-
xTallon, Robert.
illus. Little Cloud. Parents.
illus. Worm Story. HR&W.

Tally, Ted.
xTally, Ted.
Hooters: A Play in Two Acts. Dramatists Play.

Talmadge, Marian.
xTalmadge, Marian.
Barney Ford, Black Baron. Dodd.
Colorado Hi-Ways & By-Ways: A Comprehensive Guide to Picturesque Trails & Tours. Pruett.

Talmage, Frank.
xTalmage, Frank.
Disputation & Dialogue: Readings in the Jewish Christian Encounter. Ktav.

Talmage, Harriet.
xTalmage, Harriet.
Statistics As a Tool for Educational Practitioners. McCutchan.
ed. Systems of Individualized Education. McCutchan.

Talmage, Thomas. *see* Talmage, Thomas De Witt.

Talmage, Thomas De Witt, 1832-1902
xTalmage, Thomas.
Talmage on Palestine: Series of Sermons. Arno.

Talman, James J. *see* Talman, James John.

Talman, James John, 1904-
xTalman, James J.
ed. Loyalist Narratives from Upper Canada. Greenwood.

Talmon, J. L. *see* Talmon, Jacob Leib.

Talmon, Jacob Leib, 1916-
xTalmon, J. L.
Origins of Totalitarian Democracy. Norton.

Talmor, Ezra.
xTalmor, Ezra.
Descartes & Hume. Pergamon.

Taloumis, George.
xTaloumis, George.
House Plants for Five Exposures. NAL.

Talpalar, Morris.
xTalpalar, Morris.
Sociology of Colonial Virginia. Philos Lib.
Sociology of the Bay Colony. Philos Lib.

Talpe, J. *see* Talpe, Jan.

Talpe, Jan.
xTalpe, J.
Theory of Experiments in Paramagnetic Resonance. Pergamon.

Talwani, Manik.
xTalwani, Manik.
ed. Deep Drilling Results in the Atlantic Ocean: Ocean Crust. Am Geophysical.

Talwar, Bhagat R. *see* Talwar, Bhagat Ram.

Talwar, Bhagat Ram, 1908-
xTalwar, Bhagat R.
The Talwars of Pathan Land & Subhas Chandra's Great Escape. South Asia Bks.

Tamari, M. *see* Tamari, Meir.

Tamari, Meir.
xTamari, M.
Financial Ratios: Analysis & Prediction. Merrimack Bk Serv.

Tambiah, S. J.
xTambiah, S. J.
Buddhism & the Spirit Cults in Northeast Thailand. Cambridge U Pr.

Tamedly, Elisabeth L.
xTamedly, Elisabeth L.
Socialism & International Economic Order. Caxton.

Tamir, Lois M., 1954-
xTamir, Lois M.

Communication & the Aging Process: Interaction Throughout the Life Cycle. Pergamon.

Tamir, T.
xTamir, T.
ed. Integrated Optics. Springer-Verlag.

Tamir, Vicki.
xTamir, Vicki.
Bulgaria & Her Jews: The History of a Dubious Symbiosis. Hermon.

Tammadge, A. *see* Tammadge, Alan.

Tammadge, Alan.
xTammadge, A.
A Parents' Guide to School Mathematics. Cambridge U Pr.

Tammelo, I. *see* Tammelo, Ilmar.

Tammelo, Ilmar, 1917-
xTammelo, I.
Modern Logic in the Service of Law. Springer-Verlag.

Tammi, O.
xTammi, O.
Extremum Problems for Bounded Univalent Functions. Springer-Verlag.

Tamney, Joseph B.
xTamney, Joseph B.
Solidarity in a Slum. Halsted Pr.
Solidarity in a Slum. Schenkman.

Tampion, John.
xTampion, John.
Dangerous Plants. Universe.

Tamuno, T. N. *see* Tamuno, Tekena N.

Tamuno, Tekena N.
xTamuno, T. N.
Pref. by The Evolution of the Nigerian State: The Southern Phase, 1898-1914. Humanities.

Tan, Chester C.
nTan, Chester C.
Boxer Catastrophe. Norton.
Boxer Catastrophe. Octagon.

Tanagras, A. *see* Tanagras, Angelos.

Tanagras, Angelos.
xTanagras, A.
Psychophysical Elements in Parapsychological Traditions. Parapsych Foun.

Tanaka, Beatrice.
xTanaka, Beatrice.
illus. The Tortoise & the Sword: A Vietnamese Legend. Lothrop.

Tanaka, Jack, 1943-
xTanaka, Jack.
Classroom Management: A Guide for the School Consultant. C C Thomas.

Tancred, Peter.
xTancred, Peter.
Athletic Throwing. Merrimack Bk Serv.

Tancredi, Laurence R.
xTancredi, Laurence R.
Legal Issues in Psychiatric Care. Har-Row.

Tandberg-Hanssen. *see* Tandberg-Hanssen, Einar.

Tandberg-Hanssen, Einar.
xTandberg-Hanssen.
Solar Prominences. Kluwer Boston.

Tandon, B. G.
xTandon, B. G.
The Imagery of Lord Byron's Plays. Humanities.

Tandon, J. N.
xTandon, J. N.
Solar Radiations & the Earth. College Mktg Grp.

Taneja, Nawal K.
xTaneja, Nawal K.
U. S. Airfreight Industry. Lexington Bks.

Tanenbaum, A. *see* Tanenbaum, Andrew S.

Tanenbaum, Andrew S., 1944-
xTanenbaum, A.
Structured Computer Organization. P-H.

Tanenbaum, Jan K. *see* Tanenbaum, Jan Karl.

Tanenbaum, Jan Karl, 1936-
    xTanenbaum, Jan K.
        France & the Arab Middle East, 1914-1920.
        Am Philos.
Tanenbaum, Robert.
    xTanenbaum, Robert.
        Badge of the Assassin. Dutton.
Tanford, Charles, 1921-
    xTanford, Charles.
        The Hydrophobic Effect: Formation of Micelles
        & Biological Membranes. Wiley.
Tang, Roger Y. see Tang, Roger Y. W.
Tang, Roger Y. W.
    xTang, Roger Y.
        Transfer Pricing Practices in the United States
        & Japan. Praeger.
Tangerman, E. J. see Tangerman, Elmer John.
Tangerman, Elmer J. see Tangerman, Elmer John.
Tangerman, Elmer John, 1907-
    xTangerman, E. J.
        Design & Figure Carving. Peter Smith.
        The Modern Book of Whittling &
        Woodcarving. McGraw.
        Whittling & Woodcarving. Gannon.
    xTangerman, Elmer J.
        Design & Figure Carving. Dover.
        Whittling & Woodcarving. Dover.
Tangye, Derek, 1912-
    xTangye, Derek.
        Somewhere a Cat Is Waiting. Delacorte.
Taniguchi, Kazuko.
    xTaniguchi, Kazuko.
        Monster Mary, Mischief Maker. McGraw.
Tanikawa, K. see Tanikawa, Ky Uichi.
Tanikawa, Ky Uichi.
    xTanikawa, K.
        Ultrastructural Aspects of the Liver & Its
        Disorders. Springer-Verlag.
    xTanikawa, Kyuichi.
        Ultrastructural Aspects of the Liver & Its
        Disorders. Igaku-Shoin.
Tanikawa, Kyuichi. see Tanikawa, Ky Uichi.
Tanizaki, Junichir O, 1886-1965
    xTanizaki, Junichiro.
        In Praise of Shadows. Leetes Isl.
Tanizaki, Junichiro. see Tanizaki, Junichir O.
Tank, Kurt L. see Tank, Kurt Lothar.
Tank, Kurt Lothar, 1910-
    xTank, Kurt L.
        Gunter Grass. Ungar.
Tank, Ronald W. see Tank, Ronald Warren.
Tank, Ronald Warren.
    xTank, Ronald W.
        ed. Focus on Environmental Geology: A
        Collection of Case Histories & Readings from
        Original Sources. Oxford U Pr.
Tanksley, Perry.
    xTanksley, Perry.
        Come Share the Joy. Revell.
        For the Good Times. Allgood Bks.
        Friend Gift. Allgood Bks.
        Friend Gift. Revell.
Tannahill, R. Neal.
    xTannahill, R. Neal.
        The Communist Parties of Western Europe: A
        Comparative Study. Greenwood.
Tannahill, Reay.
    xTannahill, Reay.
        Food in History. Stein & Day.
        Sex in History. Stein & Day.
Tannehill, Robert C.
    xTannehill, Robert C.
        The Sword of His Mouth. Fortress.
Tanneholz, Clifton D. see Tanneholz, Clifton David.
Tanneholz, Clifton David.
    xTanneholz, Clifton D.
        Gold, Inflation, the Middle East & the Lost
        Zionist Cause. Inst Econ Pol.
Tannen, Jack.
    xTannen, Jack.

How to Identify & Collect American First
        Editions: A Guidebook. Arco.
Tannenbaum. see Tannenbaum, Steven R.
Tannenbaum, Beulah.
    xTannenbaum, Beulah.
        Understanding Sound. McGraw.
Tannenbaum, Edward R.
    xTannenbaum, Edward R.
        ed. Modern Italy: A Topical History Since
        1861. NYU Pr.
Tannenbaum, Frank, 1893-1969
    xTannenbaum, Frank.
        Darker Phases of the South. Negro U Pr.
        Peace by Revolution: An Interpretation of
        Mexico. Arno.
Tannenbaum, Percy H.
    xTannenbaum, Percy H.
        ed. The Entertainment Functions of Television.
        L Erlbaum Assocs.
Tannenbaum, R. see Tannenbaum, Robert.
Tannenbaum, Robert.
    xTannenbaum, R.
        Leadership & Organization: A Behavioral
        Science Approach. McGraw.
Tannenbaum, Steven R., 1937-
    xTannenbaum.
        Nutritional & Safety Aspects of Food
        Processing. Dekker.
Tanner, Adrian.
    xTanner, Adrian.
        Bringing Home Animals: Religious Ideology &
        Mode of Production of the Mistassini Cree
        Hunters. St Martin.
Tanner, Clara L. see Tanner, Clara Lee.
Tanner, Clara Lee.
    xTanner, Clara L.
        Prehistoric Southwestern Craft Arts. U of Ariz
        Pr.
Tanner, Daniel.
    xTanner, Daniel.
        Curriculum Development: Theory into Practice.
        Macmillan.
        Using Behavioral Objectives in the Classroom.
        Macmillan.
Tanner, Donna M.
    xTanner, Donna M.
        The Lesbian Couple. Lexington Bks.
Tanner, Helen H. see Tanner, Helen Hornbeck.
Tanner, Helen Hornbeck.
    xTanner, Helen H.
        The Ojibwas: A Critical Bibliography. Ind U
        Pr.
Tanner, Henry.
    xTanner, Henry.
        Martyrdom of Lovejoy: An Account of the
        Life, Trials, & Perils of Rev. Elijah P.
        Lovejoy. Kelley.
Tanner, James T. see Tanner, James Taylor.
Tanner, James Taylor.
    xTanner, James T.
        Guide to the Study of Animal Populations. U
        of Tenn Pr.
Tanner, Jerald.
    xTanner, Jerald.
        Changing World of Mormonism. Moody.
Tanner, L. N. see Tanner, Laurel N.
Tanner, Laurel N.
    xTanner, L. N.
        Classroom Discipline for Effective Teaching &
        Learning. HR&W.
Tanner, Ogden.
    xTanner, Ogden.
        Garden Construction. Silver.
        Garden Construction. Time-Life.
        Rock & Water Gardens. Silver.
        Rock & Water Gardens. Time-Life.
        Stress. Time-Life.
        Stress. Silver.
Tanner, Paul.
    xTanner, Paul.

A Study of Jazz. Wm C Brown.
Tanner, Robert G.
    xTanner, Robert G.
        Stonewall in the Valley: Thomas J. Stonewall
        Jackson's Shenandoah Valley Campaign
        Spring 1862. Doubleday.
Tanner, Tony.
    xTanner, Tony.
        Adultery in the Novel: Contract &
        Transgression. Johns Hopkins.
        City of Words: American Fiction, 1950-1970.
        Har-Row.
Tanous, Helen N. see Tanous, Helen Nicol.
Tanous, Helen Nicol, 1917-
    xTanous, Helen N.
        Designing Dress Patterns. Bennett Co.
Tanous, Peter.
    xTanous, Peter.
        The Wheat Killing. Doubleday.
Tanquary, A. C.
    xTanquary, Charles.
        ed. Controlled Release of Biologically Active
        Agents. Plenum Pub.
Tanquary, Charles. see Tanquary, A. C.
Tansil, Rebecca C. see Tansil, Rebecca Catherine.
Tansil, Rebecca Catherine, 1900-
    xTansil, Rebecca C.
        Contributions of a Cumulative Personnel
        Records to a Teacher-Education Program As
        Evidenced by Their Use at the State
        Teachers College at Towson, Md. AMS Pr.
Tansill, Charles C. see Tansill, Charles Callan.
Tansill, Charles Callan, 1890-
    xTansill, Charles C.
        Back Door to War: The Roosevelt Foreign
        Policy 1933-1941. Greenwood.
        Purchase of the Danish West Indies.
        Greenwood.
        The Purchase of the Danish West Indies. Peter
        Smith.
Tansley, A. E.
    xTansley, A. E.
        Reading & Remedial Reading. Humanities.
Tansley, David V.
    xTansley, David V.
        Subtle Body: Essence & Shadow. Thames
        Hudson.
Tanton, John, 1934-
    xTanton, John H.
        Rethinking Immigration Policy. F A I R.
Tanton, John H. see Tanton, John.
Tanur, Judilh M. see Tanur, Judith M.
Tanur, Judith M.
    xTanur, Judilh M.
        ed. Statistics: A Guide to Business &
        Economics. Holden-Day.
    xTanur, Judith M.
        ed. Statistics: A Guide to Political & Social
        Issues. Holden-Day.
        ed. Statistics: A Guide to the Unknown.
        Holden-Day.
Tanyzer, Harold.
    xTanyzer, Harold.
        ed. Reading, Children's Books & Our
        Pluralistic Society. Intl Reading.
Tanz, Ralph D.
    xTanz, Ralph D.
        ed. Factors Influencing Myocardial
        Contractility. Acad Pr.
Tanzer, Michael.
    xTanzer, Michael.
        The Energy Crisis: World Struggle for Power &
        Wealth. Monthly Rev.
Tanzi, Vito.
    xTanzi, Vito.
        The Individual Income Tax & Economic
        Growth: An International Comparison,
        France, Germany, Italy, Japan, United
        Kingdom, United States. Johns Hopkins.
Tao, D. C. see Tao, Deh Chang.

Tao, Deh Chang, 1925-
xTao, D. C.
Fundamentals of Applied Kinematics. A-W.
Tapasyananda, Swami.
xTapasyananda, Swami.
Swami Ramakrishnananda: The Apostle of Sri
Ramakrishna to the South. Vedanta Pr.
Tape, Henry A. see Tape, Henry Aaron.
Tape, Henry Aaron, 1889-
xTape, Henry A.
Factors Affecting Turnover of Teachers of the
One-Room Rural Schools of Michigan. AMS
Pr.
Taper, Bernard.
xTaper, Bernard.
Arts in Boston. Harvard U Pr.
Tapia, Richard A.
xTapia, Richard A.
Nonparametric Probability Density Estimation.
Johns Hopkins.
Taplin, Oliver. see Taplin, Oliver Paul.
Taplin, Oliver Paul.
xTaplin, Oliver.
Greek Tragedy in Action. U of Cal Pr.
Tapp, June L. see Tapp, June Louin.
Tapp, June Louin.
xTapp, June L.
Ambivalent America: A Psycho-Political
Dialogue. Glencoe.
Tapp, Robert B.
xTapp, Robert B.
Religion Among the Unitarian Universalists:
Converts in the Step Father's House. Acad
Pr.
Tappan, Lewis, 1788-1873
xTappan, Lewis.
Life of Arthur Tappan. Arno.
Life of Arthur Tappan. Negro U Pr.
Tappan, Mel.
xTappan, Mel.
ed. A Guide to Handmade Knives & the
Official Directory of the Knifemaker's Guild.
Janus Pr.
Tappan, Paul W. see Tappan, Paul Wilbur.
Tappan, Paul Wilbur.
xTappan, Paul W.
Crime, Justice & Correction. McGraw.
Delinquent Girls in Court: A Study of the
Wayward Minor Court of New York.
Patterson Smith.
Tappan, William T., 1943-
xTappan, William T.
The Real Estate Acquisition Handbook:
Money-Making Techniques for the Serious
Investor. P-H.
Tapper, Colin.
xTapper, Colin.
Computer Law. Longman.
Tapper, Oliver.
xTapper, Oliver.
Armstrong Whitworth Aircraft Since 1913.
Merrimack Bk Serv.
Tar, Zoltan.
xTar, Zolton.
The Frankfurt School: The Critical Theories of
Max Horkheimer & Theoder W. Adorno.
Wiley.
Tar, Zolton. see Tar, Zoltan.
Tarachow, Sidney.
xTarachow, Sidney.
Introduction to Psychotherapy. Intl Univs Pr.
Tarasov, K I. see Tarasov, Konstantin Ivoanovich.
Tarasov, Konstantin Ivoanovich.
xTarasov, K I.
The Spectroscope. Heyden.
Taraval, Sigismundo, 1700-1763
xTaraval, Sigismundo.

Indian Uprising in Lower California,
1734-1737. AMS Pr.
Indian Uprising in Lower California 1734-1737.
Arno.
Tarbell, Ida. see Tarbell, Ida Minerva.
Tarbell, Ida M. see Tarbell, Ida Minerva.
Tarbell, Ida Minerva, 1857-1944
xTarbell, Ida.
Nationalizing of Business: 1878-1898. New
Viewpoints.
xTarbell, Ida M.
Life of Elbert H. Gary: The Story of Steel.
Greenwood.
Tarbuck, Edward. see Tarbuck, Edward J.
Tarbuck, Edward J.
xTarbuck, Edward.
Earth Science. Merrill.
Tarczan, Constance.
xTarczan, Constance.
An Educator's Guide to Psychological Tests:
Descriptions & Classroom Implications. C C
Thomas.
Tarde, Gabriel. see Tarde, Gabriel de.
Tarde, Gabriel de, 1843-1904
xTarde, Gabriel.
Penal Philosophy. Patterson Smith.
Underground Man. Hyperion Conn.
Tardiff, Olive, 1916-
xTardiff, Olive.
How to Live Happily with Your Retired
Husband. Pilot Bks.
Tardy, Mary T.
xTardy, Mary T.
ed. The Living Female Writers of the South.
Gale.
Tari, Mel.
xTari, Mel.
Gentle Breeze of Jesus. New Leaf.
Like a Mighty Wind. New Leaf.
Tarica, Ralph, 1922-
xTarica, Ralph.
Imagery in the Novels of Andre Malraux.
Fairleigh Dickinson.
Tarjan, Armen C. see Tarjan, Armen Charles.
Tarjan, Armen Charles, 1920-
xTarjan, Armen C.
Check List of Plant & Soil Nematodes: A
Nomenclatorial Compilation. U Presses Fla.
Tarkington, Booth, 1869-1946
xTarkington, Booth.
The Conquest of Canaan. Irvington.
Gentleman from Indiana. AMS Pr.
Gentleman from Indiana. Scholarly.
In the Arena: Stories of Political Life. Mss
Info.
In the Arena: Stories of Political Life. Somerset
Pub.
On Plays, Playwrights & Playgoers: Selections
from the Letters of Booth Tarkington.
Princeton Lib.
Tarleton, Banastre, Sir, Bart, 1754-1833
xTarleton, Banastre.
History of the Campaigns of 1780 & 1781 in
the Southern Provinces of North America.
Reprint.
Tarling, D. H. see Tarling, Donald Harvey.
Tarling, Donald Harvey.
xTarling, D. H.
ed. Evolution of the Earth's Crust. Acad Pr.
Tarling, Nicholas.
xTarling, Nicholas.
Imperial Britain in South-East Asia. Oxford U
Pr.
Sulu & Sabah: A Study of the British Policy
Towards the Philippines & North Borneo
from the Late Eighteenth Century. Oxford U
Pr.
Tarn, W. W. see Tarn, William Woodthorpe.
Tarn, William W. see Tarn, William Woodthorpe.

Tarn, William Woodthorpe, 1869-
xTarn, W. W.
Alexander the Great. Beacon Pr.
Alexander the Great. Cambridge U Pr.
xTarn, William W.
Antigonos Gonatas. Oxford U Pr.
Tarnopol, L. see Tarnopol, Lester.
Tarnopol, Lester.
xTarnopol, L.
ed. Reading Disabilities: An International
Perspective. Univ Park.
xTarnopol, Lester.
ed. Brain Function & Reading Disabilities.
Univ Park.
Learning Disabilities: Introduction to
Educational & Medical Management. C C
Thomas.
ed. Learning Disorders in Children: Diagnosis,
Medication, Education. Little.
Tarpey, Lawrence X.
xTarpey, Lawrence X.
A Preface to Marketing Management. Business
Pubns.
Tarpley, Fred.
xTarpley, Fred A.
From Blinky to Blue-John: A Word Atlas of
Northeast Texas. University Pr.
Tarpley, Fred A. see Tarpley, Fred.
Tarpy, Roger. see Tarpy, Roger M.
Tarpy, Roger M.
xTarpy, Roger.
Readings in Learning & Memory. Scott F.
xTarpy, Roger M.
Foundations of Learning & Memory. Scott F.
Tarr, David W.
xTarr, David W.
American Strategy in the Nuclear Age.
Macmillan.
Tarr, Herbert.
xTarr, Herbert.
So Help Me God!. Bantam.
So Help Me God!. Times Bks.
Tarr, Rodger L.
xTarr, Rodger L.
Thomas Carlyle: A Bibliography of
English-Language Criticism, 1824-1974. U Pr
of Va.
Tarr, Yvonne Y. see Tarr, Yvonne Young.
Tarr, Yvonne Young.
xTarr, Yvonne Y.
The Complete Outdoor Cookbook. Times Bks.
The Great Food Processor Cookbook. Random.
The Super-Easy Step-by-Step Book of Special
Breads. Random.
Tarrant, John J. see Tarrant, John J.
Tarrant, John. see Tarrant, John J.
Tarrant, John J.
xTarrant, John J.
Drucker: The Man Who Invented the
Corporate Society. CBI Pub.
xTarrant, John.
How to Negotiate a Raise. PB.
xTarrant, John J.
Drucker: The Man Who Invented the
Corporate Society. Warner Bks.
How to Negotiate a Raise. Van Nos Reinhold.
Tarrants, Thomas A.
xTarrants, Thomas A.
The Conversion of a Klansman: The Story of a
Former Ku Klux Klan Terrorist. Doubleday.
Tarrants, William E. see Tarrants, William Eugene.
Tarrants, William Eugene.
xTarrants, William E.
ed. Dictionary of Terms Used in the Safety
Profession. ASSE.
Tarschys, Daniel, 1943-
xTarschys, Daniel.

The Soviet Political Agenda: Problems &
Priorities 1950-1970. M E Sharpe.
Tarski, Alfred.
xTarski, Alfred.
Introduction to Logic & to the Methodology of
Deductive Sciences. Oxford U Pr.
Tart, Charles T., 1937-
xTart, Charles T.
Altered States of Consciousness: A Book of
Readings. Wiley.
The Application of Learning Theory to ESP
Performance. Parapsych Foun.
Learning to Use Extrasensory Perception. U of
Chicago Pr.
On Being Stoned: A Psychological Study of
Marijuana Intoxication. Sci & Behavior.
PSI: Scientific Studies of the Psychic Realm.
Dutton.
Tarter, Ralph E.
xTarter, Ralph E.
ed. Alcoholism: Interdisciplinary Approaches to
an Enduring Problem. A-W.
Taruc, Luis, 1913-
xTaruc, Luis.
Born of the People. Greenwood.
Tarver, John C. *see* Tarver, John Charles.
Tarver, John Charles, 1854-1926
xTarver, John C.
Gustave Flaubert As Seen in His Works &
Correspondence. R West.
Tasaki, Hanama.
xTasaki, Hanama.
Long the Imperial Way. Greenwood.
Tasch, Paul.
xTasch, Paul.
Paleobiology of the Invertebrates: Data
Retrieval from the Fossil Record. Wiley.
Taschdjian, Claire.
xTaschdjian, Claire.
The Peking Man Is Missing. Har-Row.
Tashjian, Dickran.
xTashjian, Dickran.
Memorials for Children of Change: The Art of
Early New England Stonecarving. Columbia
U Pr.
Tashkin, Donald P.
xTashkin, Donald P.
Guide to Pulmonary Medicine. Grune.
Tashman, Leonard J.
xTashman, Leonard J.
The Ways & Means of Statistics. HarBraceJ.
Task Force on Alternative Books in Print.
xTask Force on Alternatives in Print of the Social
Responsibilities Round Table of the American
Library Association.
Alternatives in Print: An International Catalog
of Books, Pamphlets, Periodicals &
Audiovisual Materials. Neal-Schuman.
Task Force on Alternatives in Print of the Social
Responsibilities Round Table of the American Library
Association. *see* Task Force on Alternative Books in
Print.
Task Force on Education & Employment. *see* Task Force
on Education and Employment (U.S.).
Task Force on Education and Employment (U.S.).
xTask Force on Education & Employment.
Education for Employment. Acropolis.
Task Force on Legalized Gambling.
xTask Force on Legalized Gambling.
Easy Money. Kraus Repr.
Task Force '74.
xTask Force, 1974.
The Adolescent, Other Citizens, & Their High
Schools. McGraw.
Task Force, 1974. *see* Task Force '74.
Tasker, James.
xTasker, James.
African Treehouse. Harvey.
Tasman, William.
xTasman, William.

Disorders of the Peripheral Fundus. Har-Row.
Tassel, Charles E. Van. *see* Van Tassel, Charles E.
Tassel, D. Van. *see* Van Tassel, D.
Tassel, Dennis Van. *see* Van Tassel, Dennis.
Tassell, Paul, 1934-
xTassell, Paul.
Sweeter Than Honey. Reg Baptist.
Tassin, Myron.
xTassin, Myron.
The Bacchus. Pelican.
Fifty Years at the Grand Ole' Opry. Pelican.
Tasso, Torquato, 1544-1595
xTasso, Torquato.
Discourses on the Heroic Poem. Oxford U Pr.
Tassoul, Jean-Louis.
xTassoul, Jean-Louis.
Theory of Rotating Stars. Princeton U Pr.
Tasto, Donald L.
xTasto, Donald L.
Spare the Couch: Self-Change for Self
Improvement. P-H.
Tatar, Maria M., 1945-
xTatar, Maria M.
Spellbound: Studies on Mesmerism &
Literature. Princeton U Pr.
Tatarkiewicz. *see* Tatarkiewicz, Wadysaw.
Tatarkiewicz, Wadysaw, 1886-
xTatarkiewicz.
Analysis of Happiness. Kluwer Boston.
Tate, Allen, 1899-
xTate, Allen.
Collected Poems 1919-1976. FS&G.
Fathers. Swallow.
The Fathers & Other Fiction. La State U Pr.
Reactionary Essays on Poetry & Ideas. Arno.
Reason in Madness: Critical Essays. Arno.
ed. Southern Vanguard. Arno.
Stonewall Jackson: The Good Soldier. U of
Mich Pr.
Tate, Carole.
xTate, Carole.
Rhymes & Ballads of London. Scroll Pr.
Tate, Curtis E.
xTate, Curtis E.
The Complete Guide to Your Own Business.
Dow Jones-Irwin.
Successful Small Business Management.
Business Pubns.
Tate Gallery, London.
xTate Gallery-London.
Art Books: An Annotated List Based on an
Exhibition at the Tate Gallery-Autumn 1968.
Intl Pubns Serv.
Tate Gallery-London. *see* Tate Gallery, London.
Tate, Gary.
xTate, Gary.
From Discovery to Style. Winthrop.
Tate, George W.
xTate, George W.
Principles of Quantitative Perimetry: Testing &
Interpreting the Visual Field. Grune.
Tate, James, 1943-
xTate, James.
The Lost Pilot. AMS Pr.
Riven Doggeries. Ecco Pr.
Torches. Unicorn Pr.
Tate, Joan.
xTate, Joan.
Grandpa & My Sister Bee. Childrens.
Tate, Lucius Eugene, 1879-
xTate, Luke E.
History of Pickens County. Reprint.
Tate, Luke E. *see* Tate, Lucius Eugene.
Tate, M. *see* Tate, Mildred Bertha (Thurow).
Tate, Merze, 1905-
xTate, Merze.
Disarmament Illusion: The Movement for a
Limitation of Armaments to 1907. Russell.
Tate, Mildred. *see* Tate, Mildred Bertha (Thurow).

Tate, Mildred Bertha (Thurow).
xTate, M.
Family Clothing. Textile Bk.
xTate, Mildred.
Home Economics As a Profession. McGraw.
xTate, Mildred T.
Family Clothing. Wiley.
Tate, Mildred T. *see* Tate, Mildred Bertha (Thurow).
Tate, Sharon L. *see* Tate, Sharon Lee.
Tate, Sharon Lee.
xTate, Sharon L.
Inside Fashion Design. Har-Row.
Tatham, John, fl. 1632-1664
xTatham, John.
Dramatic Works of John Tatham. Arno.
Tatlow, Peter.
xTatlow, Peter.
The World of Gymnastics. Atheneum.
Tatsch, J. H.
xTatsch, J. H.
Copper Deposits: Origin, Evolution, & Present
Characteristics. Tatsch.
The Earth's Tectonosphere: Its Past
Development & Present Behavior. Tatsch.
Geothermal Deposits: Origin, Evolution, &
Present Characteristics. Tatsch.
Gold Deposits: Origin, Evolution, and Present
Characteristics. Tatsch.
Tatsuoka, Maurice M.
xTatsuoka, Maurice M.
Multivariate Analysis: Techniques for
Educational & Psychological Research.
Wiley.
Tatter, Henry.
xTatter, Henry W.
The Preferential Treatment of the Actual
Settler in the Primary Disposition of the
Vacant Lands in the United States to 1841.
Arno.
Tatter, Henry W. *see* Tatter, Henry.
Tattersall, Bob. *see* Tattersall, Robert.
Tattersall, G. H.
xTattersall, G. H.
The Workability of Concrete. Scholium Intl.
Tattersall, Ian.
xTattersall, Ian T.
ed. Lemur Biology. Plenum Pub.
Tattersall, Ian T. *see* Tattersall, Ian.
Tattersall, Jill.
xTattersall, Jill.
Damnation Reef. Fawcett.
Damnation Reef. Morrow.
Tattersall, Robert.
xTattersall, Bob.
Decorating. Transatlantic.
Tatum, Charles M.
xTatum, Charles M.
A Selected & Annotated Bibliography of
Chicano Studies. Society Sp & Sp-Am.
Tatum, Elbert L. *see* Tatum, Elbert Lee.
Tatum, Elbert Lee.
xTatum, Elbert L.
The Changed Political Thought of the Negro,
1915-1940. Greenwood.
Tatum, Georgia L. *see* Tatum, Georgia Lee.
Tatum, Georgia Lee.
xTatum, Georgia L.
Disloyalty in the Confederacy. AMS Pr.
Tatum, Jack.
xTatum, Jack.
They Call Me Assassin. Everest Hse.
Tatum, James.
xTatum, James.
Apuleius & the Golden Ass. Cornell U Pr.
Tatum, Lawrie.
xTatum, Lawrie.
Our Red Brothers & the Peace Policy of
President Ulysses S. Grant. U of Nebr Pr.
Taub, A. H. *see* Taub, Abraham Haskel.

Taub, Abraham Haskel.
  xTaub, A. H.
    ed. Studies in Applied Mathematics. Math
      Assn.
Taub, Herbert.
  xTaub, Herbert.
    Principles of Communication Systems.
      McGraw.
Taub, William. *see* Taub, William L.
Taub, William L.
  xTaub, William.
    Forces of Power. G&D.
Taube, E. Louis. *see* Taube, Edward Louis.
Taube, Edward Louis.
  xTaube, E. Louis.
    Food Allergy & the Allergic Patient: A Simple
      Review of Problems Encountered by the
      Recently Diagnosed Patient. C C Thomas.
Taube, Mortimer, 1910-
  xTaube, Mortimer.
    Computers & Common Sense: The Myth of
      Thinking Machines. Columbia U Pr.
Tauber, Catherine A.
  xTauber, Catherine A.
    Taxonomy & Biology of the Lacewing Genus
      Meleoma (Neuroptera: Chrysopidae). U of
      Cal Pr.
Tauber, Gerald E.
  xTauber, Gerald E.
    ed. Albert Einstein's Theory of General
      Relativity. Crown.
Tauber, Herbert, 1912-
  xTauber, Herbert.
    Franz Kafka: An Interpretation of His Works.
      Haskell.
Tauber, Peter.
  xTauber, Peter.
    The Last Best Hope. Ballantine.
Taubes, Frederic, 1900-
  xTaubes, Frederic.
    Acrylic Painting for the Beginner.
      Watson-Guptill.
    Anatomy for Artists. G&D.
    Oil Painting for the Beginner. Watson-Guptill.
    Painter's Dictionary of Materials & Methods.
      Watson-Guptill.
    The Quickest Way to Draw Well. Penguin.
Taubman, Bryna.
  xTaubman, Bryna.
    How to Become an Assertive Woman. PB.
Taubman, Howard. *see* Taubman, Hyman Howard.
Taubman, Hyman Howard, 1907-
  xTaubman, Howard.
    Music on My Beat: An Intimate Volume of
      Shop Talk. Greenwood.
Taubman, Joseph.
  xTaubman, Joseph.
    Copyright & Antitrust. Fed Legal Pubn.
    The Joint Venture & Tax Classification. Fed
      Legal Pubn.
    Performing Arts Management & Law.
      Law-Arts.
Taubman, Paul.
  xTaubman, Paul.
    Higher Education & Earnings: College As an
      Investment & a Screening Device. Natl Bur
      Econ Res.
Tauchert, T. R., 1935-
  xTauchert, T. R.
    Energy Principles in Structural Mechanics.
      McGraw.
Taus, Esther (Rogoff), 1914-
  xTaus, Esther R.
    Central Banking Functions of the United States
      Treasury, 1789-1941. Russell.
Taus, Esther R. *see* Taus, Esther (Rogoff).
Taussig, Frank W. *see* Taussig, Frank William.
Taussig, Frank William, 1859-1940
  xTaussig, Frank W.

    Silver Situation in the United States. Arno.
    Silver Situation in the United States.
      Greenwood.
    Some Aspects of the Tariff Question: An
      Examination of the Development of
      American Industries Under Protection. AMS
      Pr.
Taussig, Helen B. *see* Taussig, Helen Brooke.
Taussig, Helen Brooke, 1898-
  xTaussig, Helen B.
    Congenital Malformations of the Heart.
      Harvard U Pr.
Tavard, George H. *see* Tavard, Georges Henri.
Tavard, Georges H. *see* Tavard, Georges Henri.
Tavard, Georges Henri, 1922-
  xTavard, George H.
    Holy Writ or Holy Church: The Crisis of the
      Protestant Reformation. Greenwood.
    The Inner Life: Foundations of Christian
      Mysticism. Paulist Pr.
  xTavard, Georges H.
    Two Centuries of Ecumenism. Greenwood.
Tave, Stuart M.
  xTave, Stuart M.
    Some Words of Jane Austen. U of Chicago Pr.
Tavel, Charles. *see* Tavel, Charles H.
Tavel, Charles H.
  xTavel, Charles.
    The Third Industrial Age: Strategy for Business
      Survival. Pergamon.
Tavel, David.
  xTavel, David.
    Church-State Issues in Education. Phi Delta
      Kappa.
Tavel, Morton E.
  xTavel, Morton E.
    Clinical Phonocardiography & External Pulse
      Recording. Year Bk Med.
Taveras, Juan M.
  xTaveras, Juan M.
    Normal Neuroradiology: & Atlas of the Skull,
      Sinuses & Facial Bones. Year Bk Med.
Taves, Isabella.
  xTaves, Isabella.
    True Ghost Stories. Watts.
Tavolga, William N., 1922-
  xTavolga, William N.
    ed. Sound Production in Fishes. Acad Pr.
Tavris, Carol.
  xTavris, Carol.
    The Longest War: Sex Differences in
      Perspective. HarBraceJ.
Tavuchis, Nicholas.
  xTavuchis, Nicholas.
    The Family Through Literature. McGraw.
Tawadros, Milad A.
  xTawadros, Milad A.
    Basic Statistics & Probability for Business &
      Economic Decisions. Kendall-Hunt.
Tawes, W. I. *see* Tawes, William I.
Tawes, William I.
  xTawes, W. I.
    Creative Bird Carving. Cornell Maritime.
    Creative Sculpture. Cornell Maritime.
Tawil, Raymonda.
  xTawil, Raymonda H.
    My Home, My Prison. HR&W.
Tawil, Raymonda H. *see* Tawil, Raymonda.
Tawney, R. H. *see* Tawney, Richard Henry.
Tawney, Richard H. *see* Tawney, Richard Henry.
Tawney, Richard Henry, 1880-
  xTawney, R. H.
    Agrarian Problem in the Sixteenth Century.
      Gannon.
  xTawney, Richard H.

    Acquisitive Society. HarBraceJ.
    British Labor Movement. Greenwood.
    Business & Politics Under James I: Lionel
      Cranfield As Merchant & Minister. Russell.
Tax, Herman R.
  xTax, Herman R.
    Podopediatrics. Williams & Wilkins.
Tax Institute.
  xTax Institute.
    Curbing Inflation Through Taxation. Arno.
Tax, Sol.
  xTax, Sol.
    ed. Horizons of Anthropology. Aldine Pub.
Taxay, Don.
  xTaxay, Don.
    Illustrated History of U. S. Commemorative
      Coinage. Arco.
Taybi, Hooshang, 1919-
  xTaybi, Hooshang.
    Radiology of Syndromes. Year Bk Med.
Tayler, Edward W. *see* Tayler, Edward William.
Tayler, Edward William.
  xTayler, Edward W.
    Nature & Art in Renaissance Literature.
      Columbia U Pr.
Tayler, R. J. *see* Tayler, Roger John.
Tayler, Roger John.
  xTayler, R. J.
    Astrophysics. Benjamin-Cummings.
    Galaxies: Structure & Evolution. Crane-Russak
      Co.
    The Origin of the Chemical Elements. Crane
      Russak Co.
Taylor. *see* Taylor, Harvey M.
Taylor, A. *see* Taylor, Anita.
Taylor, A. A. *see* Taylor, Alrutheus Ambush.
Taylor, A. E. *see* Taylor, Alfred Edward.
Taylor, A. J. *see* Taylor, Alan John Percivale.
Taylor, Alan J. *see* Taylor, Alan John Percivale.
Taylor, Alan John Percivale, 1906-
  xTaylor, A. J.
    Germany's First Bid for Colonies, 1884-1885:
      A Move in Bismarck's European Policy.
      Norton.
    Germany's First Bid for Colonies, 1884-1885:
      A Move in Bismarck's European Policy.
      Shoe String.
    The Habsburg Monarchy, 1809-1918: A
      History of the Austrian Empire &
      Austria-Hungary. U of Chicago Pr.
    How Wars Begin. Atheneum.
    Origins of the Second World War. Atheneum.
  xTaylor, Alan J.
    From Sarajevo to Potsdam. HarBraceJ.
    Origins of the Second World War. Fawcett.
    Struggle for Mastery in Europe: 1848-1918.
      Oxford U Pr.
    Struggle for Mastery in Europe, 1848-1918.
      Oxford U Pr.
Taylor, Albert B. *see* Taylor, Albert Booth.
Taylor, Albert Booth.
  xTaylor, Albert B.
    An Introduction to Medieval Romance.
      Folcroft
Taylor, Albert J.
  xTaylor, Albert J.
    Passing Your Biennial Flight Review. TAB Bks.
Taylor, Alfred E. *see* Taylor, Alfred Edward.
Taylor, Alfred Edward, 1869-1945
  xTaylor, A. E.
    David Hume & the Miraculous. Folcroft.
    Socrates. Greenwood.
    Socrates. R West.
  xTaylor, Alfred E.
    Plato. Arno.
    Socrates. Hyperion Conn.
    Thomas Hobbes. Kennikat.
Taylor, Alison, 1927-
  xTaylor, Alison.

Off Stage & On: An Introduction to Youth Drama. Pergamon.
Taylor, Alrutheus A. *see* Taylor, Alrutheus Ambush.
Taylor, Alrutheus Ambush.
xTaylor, A. A.
Negro in the Reconstruction of Virginia. Russell.
xTaylor, Alrutheus A.
The Negro in Tennessee, 1865-1880. Reprint.
Taylor, Andrew, 1940-
xTaylor, Andrew.
Ice Fishing. U of Queensland Pr.
Taylor, Angus E. *see* Taylor, Angus Ellis.
Taylor, Angus Ellis, 1911-
xTaylor, Angus E.
Advanced Calculus. Wiley.
Taylor, Anita, 1935-
xTaylor, A.
Speaking in Public. P-H.
xTaylor, Anita.
Communicating. P-H.
Couples: The Art of Staying Together. Acropolis.
Taylor, Anya.
xTaylor, Anya.
Magic & English Romanticism. U of Ga Pr.
Taylor, Archer, 1890-
xTaylor, Archer.
Annotated Collection of Mongolian Riddles. Am Philos.
Literary History of Meistergesang. Kraus Repr.
The Literary Riddle Before 1600. Greenwood.
Problems in German Literary History of the Fifteenth & Sixteenth Centuries. Kraus Repr.
Taylor, Arnold H.
xTaylor, Arnold H.
American Diplomacy & the Narcotics Traffic, 1900-1939: A Study in International Humanitarian Reform. Duke.
Taylor, Arthur J. *see* Taylor, Arthur John.
Taylor, Arthur John.
xTaylor, Arthur J.
ed. The Standard of Living in Britain in the Industrial Revolution. Methuen Inc.
Taylor, B. *see* Taylor, Bernard.
Taylor, Barbara J.
xTaylor, Barbara J.
Dear Mom & Dad: Parents & the Preschooler. Brigham.
When I Do, I Learn: A Guide to Creative Planning for Teachers & Parents of Preschool Children. Brigham.
Taylor, Barry, 1936-
xTaylor, Barry.
The Parents' Guide to Education. David & Charles.
Taylor, Bayard, 1825-1878
xTaylor, Bayard.
Dramatic Works of Bayard Taylor. Scholarly.
The Echo Club. Irvington.
A Journey to Central Africa: Or, Life & Landscapes from Egypt to the Negro Kingdoms of the White Nile. Darby Bks.
Studies in German Literature. Arden Lib.
xTaylor, Baynard.
Studies in German Literature. Arno.
Taylor, Baynard. *see* Taylor, Bayard.
Taylor, Benjamin.
xTaylor, Benjamin.
Storyology: Essays in Folk-Lore, Sea-Lore, & Plant-Lore. Folcroft.
Storyology: Essays in Folklore, Sea-Lore, & Plant-Lore. Gordon Pr.
Taylor, Bernard.
xTaylor, B.
ed. Corporate Strategy & Planning. Halsted Pr.
xTaylor, Bernard.

The Godsend. Avon.
Sweetheart, Sweetheart. Ballantine.
Sweetheart, Sweetheart. St Martin.
Taylor, Blaine, 1933-
xTaylor, Blaine.
The Success Ethic & the Shattered American Dream. Acropolis.
Taylor, Bryce.
xTaylor, Bryce.
Olympic Gymnastics for Men & Women. P-H.
Taylor, C. *see* Taylor, Charles.
Taylor, Charles, 1931-
xTaylor, C.
Hegel & Modern Society. Cambridge U Pr.
xTaylor, Charles.
Explanation of Behaviour. Humanities.
Taylor, Charles. *see* Taylor, Charles Alfred.
Taylor, Charles A. *see* Taylor, Charles Alfred.
Taylor, Charles Alfred.
xTaylor, Charles.
Sounds of Music. Scribner.
xTaylor, Charles A.
Images: A Unified View of Diffraction & Image Formation with All Kinds of Radiation. Crane-Russak Co.
Taylor, Charles D.
xTaylor, Charles D.
Show of Force. St Martin.
Taylor, Charles L.
xTaylor, Charles L.
Marked Bible. Pacific Pr Pub Assn.
Taylor, Charles T. *see* Taylor, Charles Thomas.
Taylor, Charles Thomas, 1941-
xTaylor, Charles T.
The Values. Philos Lib.
Taylor, Christiana J., 1943-
xTaylor, Christiana J.
Futurism: Politics, Painting & Performance. Univ Microfilms.
Taylor, Christopher, 1935-
xTaylor, Christopher.
Roads & Tracks of Britain. Biblio Dist.
Taylor, Clara M. *see* Taylor, Clara Mae.
Taylor, Clara Mae.
xTaylor, Clara M.
ed. Annotated International Bibliography of Nutrition Education. Tchrs Coll.
Taylor, Clarence E.
xTaylor, Clarence E.
Mathematics for Nursing. Little.
Taylor, Clarence R.
xTaylor, Clarence R.
How to Be a Successful Inventor: Patenting, Protecting, Marketing & Selling Your Invention. Exposition.
Taylor, Coley B. *see* Taylor, Coley Banks.
Taylor, Coley Banks, 1899-
xTaylor, Coley B.
Mark Twain's Margins on Thackeray's "Swift". Folcroft.
Mark Twain's Margins on Thackeray's Swift. Haskell.
Taylor, Daniel M.
xTaylor, Daniel M.
Explanation & Meaning: An Introduction to Philosophy. Cambridge U Pr.
Taylor, David, 1945-
xTaylor, David.
Acting & the Stage. Allen Unwin.
Is There a Doctor in the Zoo?. Bantam.
Is There a Doctor in the Zoo. Lippincott.
Taylor, Dawson.
xTaylor, Dawson.
Inside Golf. Contemp Bks.
Taylor, Deems, 1885-1966
xTaylor, Deems.
Some Enchanted Evenings: The Story of Rodgers & Hammerstein. Greenwood.
Taylor, Demetria. *see* Taylor, Demetria M.

Taylor, Demetria M., 1903-
xTaylor, Demetria.
Apple Kitchen Cookbook. Popular Lib.
Taylor, Donald. *see* Taylor, Donald Lavor.
Taylor, Donald A. *see* Taylor, Donald Arthur.
Taylor, Donald Arthur, 1923-
xTaylor, Donald A.
Institution Building in Business Administration: The Brazilian Experience. Mich St U Busn.
Taylor, Donald H.
xTaylor, Donald H.
Auditing: Integrated Concepts & Procedures. Wiley.
Taylor, Donald Lavor, 1916-
xTaylor, Donald.
Human Sexual Development: Perspectives in Sex Education. AHM Pub.
Taylor, Donald S.
xTaylor, Donald S.
Thomas Chatterton's Art: Experiments in Imagined History. Princeton U Pr.
Taylor, Donna.
xTaylor, Donna.
ed. The Great Lakes Region in Children's Books: A Selected Annotated Bibliography. Green Oak Pr.
Taylor, Douglas.
xTaylor, Douglas.
True Black Man's History. Philos Lib.
Taylor, E. Stewart. *see* Taylor, Edward Stewart.
Taylor, Edith (Meyer), 1904-
xTaylor, Edith M.
Psychological Appraisal of Children with Cerebral Defects. Harvard U Pr.
Taylor, Edith M. *see* Taylor, Edith (Meyer).
Taylor, Edith Wharton, 1930-
xTaylor, Elizabeth W.
Money on the Hoof-Sometimes. Old Army.
Taylor, Edmond, 1908-
xTaylor, Edmond.
Awakening from History. Gambit.
Taylor, Edward S., 1943-
xTaylor, Edward S.
Dimensional Analysis for Engineers. Oxford U Pr.
Taylor, Edward Stewart, 1911-
xTaylor, E. Stewart.
Essentials of Gynecology. Lea & Febiger.
Taylor, Edwina.
xTaylor, Edwina.
Came a Dark Rider. PB.
Taylor, Elizabeth W. *see* Taylor, Edith Wharton.
Taylor, Estella R. *see* Taylor, Estella Ruth.
Taylor, Estella Ruth.
xTaylor, Estella R.
Modern Irish Writers: Cross Currents of Criticism. Greenwood.
Taylor, Eva G. *see* Taylor, Eva Germaine Rimington.
Taylor, Eva Germaine Rimington, 1879-
xTaylor, Eva G.
Tudor Geography, 1485-1583. Octagon.
Taylor, F. *see* Taylor, Howard F.
Taylor, F. K. *see* Taylor, Frederick Kraupl.
Taylor, F. Sherwood. *see* Taylor, Frank Sherwood.
Taylor, Florance (Walton).
xTaylor, Florance W.
From Texas to Illinois. Lerner Pubns.
Plane Ride. Lerner Pubns.
Where's Luis. Lerner Pubns.
Taylor, Florance W. *see* Taylor, Florance (Walton).
Taylor, Florence M. *see* Taylor, Florence Marian Tompkins.
Taylor, Florence Marian Tompkins, 1892-
xTaylor, Florence M.
As for Me & My Family. Word Bks.
You Don't Have to Be Old When You Grow Old. Logos.
Taylor, Frank S. *see* Taylor, Frank Sherwood.
Taylor, Frank Sherwood, 1897
xTaylor, F. Sherwood.

The Alchemists. Beekman Pubs.
xTaylor, Frank S.
A History of Industrial Chemistry. Arno.

Taylor, Frederick Kraupl.
xTaylor, F. K.
The Concepts of Illness, Disease & Morbus.
Cambridge U Pr.

Taylor, Frederick L. see Taylor, Frederick Lewis.

Taylor, Frederick Lewis.
xTaylor, Frederick L.
The Art of War in Italy, 1494-1529.
Greenwood.

Taylor, Frederick W. see Taylor, Frederick Winslow.

Taylor, Frederick Winslow, 1856-1915
xTaylor, Frederick W.
Principles of Scientific Management. Norton.

Taylor, G. see Taylor, Geoffrey.

Taylor, G. A. see Taylor, Giles Aldred.

Taylor, G. D. see Taylor, Gerald Douglas.

Taylor, G. Jeffrey, 1944-
xTaylor, G. Jeffrey.
A Close Look at the Moon. Dodd.

Taylor, G. R. see Taylor, George Robert Stirling.

Taylor, Geoff.
xTaylor, Geoff.
Court of Honor. S&S.

Taylor, Geoffrey, 1929-
xTaylor, G.
Immunology in Medical Practice. Saunders.

Taylor, George, Sir, 1904-
xTaylor, George.
Spiralian Embryology. Mss Info.

Taylor, George. see Taylor, George Edward.

Taylor, George E. see Taylor, George Edward.

Taylor, George Edward, 1905-
xTaylor, George.
Japanese Sponsored Regime in North China.
Garland Pub.
xTaylor, George E.
The Struggle for North China. AMS Pr.

Taylor, George H.
xTaylor, George.
The High School Stage Band. Rosen Pr.

Taylor, George R.
xTaylor, George R.
Educational Strategies & Services for
Exceptional Children. C C Thomas.

Taylor, George R. see Taylor, George Rogers.

Taylor, George Robert Stirling.
xTaylor, G. R.
Modern English Statesmen. Kennikat.
xTaylor, George R.
Leaders of Socialism: Past & Present. Arno.

Taylor, George Rogers, 1895-
xTaylor, George R.
Compiled by American Economic History
Before 1860. AHM Pub.
ed. Approaches to American Economic
History. U Pr of Va.

Taylor, Georgia E. see Taylor, Georgia Elizabeth.

Taylor, Georgia Elizabeth.
xTaylor, Georgia E.
The Infidel. St Martin.

Taylor, Gerald Douglas.
xTaylor, G. D.
Materials of Construction. Longman.

Taylor, Gertrude.
xTaylor, Gertrude.
America's Knitting Book. Scribner.

Taylor, Giles Aldred.
xTaylor, G. A.
Organic Chemistry for Students of Biology &
Medicine. Longman.

Taylor, Glen H. see Taylor, Glen Hearst.

Taylor, Glen Hearst, 1904-
xTaylor, Glen H.
The Way It Was with Me. Lyle Stuart.

Taylor, Glenhall, 1903-
xTaylor, Glenhall.

Before Television: The Radio Years. A S
Barnes.

Taylor, Gordon R. see Taylor, Gordon Rattray.

Taylor, Gordon Rattray.
xTaylor, Gordon R.
The Natural History of the Mind. Dutton.
The Natural History of the Mind. Penguin.

Taylor, Graham D., 1944-
xTaylor, Graham D.
The New Deal & American Indian Tribalism:
The Administration of the Indian
Reorganization Act, 1934-45. U of Nebr Pr.

Taylor, Grant, 1923-
xTaylor, Grant.
English Conversation Practice. McGraw.

Taylor, H. M. see Taylor, Harold Mccarter.

Taylor, Halsey P.
xTaylor, Halsey P.
ed. The Craft of the Essay. HarBraceJ.

Taylor, Harold, 1914-
xTaylor, Harold.
Students Without Teachers: The Crisis in the
University. S Ill U Pr.
The World As Teacher. S Ill U Pr.

Taylor, Harold McCarter.
xTaylor, H. M.
Anglo-Saxon Architecture. Cambridge U Pr.

Taylor, Harvey M.
xTaylor.
English & Japanese in Contrast. Regents Pub.

Taylor, Henry, 1942-
xTaylor, Henry.
An Afternoon of Pocket Billiards: Poems. U of
Utah Pr.
Horse Show at Midnight: Poems. La State U
Pr.

Taylor, Henry O. see Taylor, Henry Osborn.

Taylor, Henry Osborn, 1856-1941
xTaylor, Henry O.
Ancient Ideals: A Study of Intellectual &
Spiritual Growth from Early Times to
Establishment of Christianity. Ungar.
Freedom of the Mind in History. Greenwood.
A Layman's View of History. AMS Pr.

Taylor, Herb, 1942-
xTaylor, Herb.
Underwater with the Nikonos & Nikon
Systems. Amphoto.

Taylor, Hilary.
xTaylor, Hilary.
James McNeill Whistler. Putnam.

Taylor, Howard C. see Taylor, Howard Cromwell.

Taylor, Howard Cromwell, 1887-
xTaylor, Howard C.
Educational Significance of the Early Federal
Land Ordinances. AMS Pr.
Educational Significance of the Early Federal
Land Ordinances. Arno.

Taylor, Howard F.
xTaylor, F.
Foundry Engineering. Wiley.

Taylor, Howard F. see Taylor, Howard Francis.

Taylor, Howard Francis, 1939-
xTaylor, Howard F.
Balance in Small Groups. Krieger.

Taylor, Hugh.
xTaylor, Hugh.
History As a Science. Kennikat.

Taylor, Insup.
xTaylor, Insup.
Introduction to Psycholinguistics. HR&W.

Taylor, Irwin M., 1914-
xTaylor, Irwin M.
Law of Insurance. Oceana.

Taylor, J. C. see Taylor, John Clayton.

Taylor, J. G.
xTaylor, John G.
Special Relativity. Oxford U Pr.

Taylor, J. G. see Taylor, John Gerald.

Taylor, J. Golden.
xTaylor, J. Golden.
ed. Literature of the American West. HM.
Neighbor Thoreau's Critical Humor. Folcroft.

Taylor, J. Lee. see Taylor, James Lee.

Taylor, J. Orville. see Taylor, John Orville.

Taylor, J. Paul. see Taylor, Jesse Paul.

Taylor, Jack.
xTaylor, Jack.
The Economic Development of Poland,
1919-1950. Greenwood.

Taylor, Jack. see Taylor, Jack R.

Taylor, Jack R.
xTaylor, Jack.
One Home Under God. Broadman.
xTaylor, Jack R.
After the Spirit Comes. Broadman.
God's Miraculous Plan of Economy.
Broadman.
Prayer: Life's Limitless Reach. Broadman.

Taylor, James B. see Taylor, James Bentley.

Taylor, James Bentley.
xTaylor, James B.
Community Worker. Aronson.

Taylor, James L. see Taylor, James Lumpkin.

Taylor, James Lee, 1931-
xTaylor, J. Lee.
Growing Plants Indoors. Burgess.

Taylor, James Lumpkin, 1892-
xTaylor, James L.
A Portuguese-English Dictionary. Stanford U
Pr.

Taylor, James M. see Taylor, James Monroe.

Taylor, James Monroe, 1848-1916
xTaylor, James M.
Before Vassar Opened: A Contribution to the
History of the Higher Education of Women
in America. Arno.

Taylor, Jerome.
xTaylor, Jerome.
ed. Medieval English Drama: Essays Critical &
Contextual. U of Chicago Pr.

Taylor, Jesse Paul, Bp, 1895-
xTaylor, J. Paul.
Holiness the Finished Foundation. Light &
Life.

Taylor, Joan J.
xTaylor, Joan J.
Bronze Age Goldwork of the British Isles.
Cambridge U Pr.

Taylor, Joan W. see Taylor, Joan Winifred.

Taylor, Joan Winifred.
xTaylor, Joan W.
African Zoo in the Family: The Story of a
Game Ranger's Wife & Her Wild Orphan
Pets. Emerson.

Taylor, Joe G. see Taylor, Joe Gray.

Taylor, Joe Gray.
xTaylor, Joe G.
Louisiana Reconstructed, 1863-1877. La State
U Pr.
Negro Slavery in Louisiana. Negro U Pr.

Taylor, John, 1753-1824
xTaylor, John.
Construction Construed & Constitutions
Vindicated. Da Capo.
A History of Ten Baptist Churches, of Which
the Author Has Been Alternately a Member.
Arno.
Icon Painting. Mayflower Bks.
Introduction to Psychology. Kendall-Hunt.

Taylor, John. see Taylor, John Vernon.

Taylor, John B. see Taylor, John Bernard.

Taylor, John Bernard.
xTaylor, John B.
The World of Islam. Friend Pr.

Taylor, John C., 1947-
xTaylor, John G.

From Modernization to Modes of Production:
A Critique of the Sociologies of Development
& Underdevelopment. Humanities.

Taylor, John Clayton.
xTaylor, J. C.
Gauge Theories of Weak Interactions.
Cambridge U Pr.

Taylor, John G. see Taylor, John C.

Taylor, John Gerald, 1931-
xTaylor, J. G.
Quantum Mechanics: An Introduction. Allen
Unwin.
xTaylor, John.
Superminds. Warner Bks.

Taylor, John L. see Taylor, John Laverack.

Taylor, John Laverack.
xTaylor, John L.
Learning & the Simulation Game. Sage.

Taylor, John Orville, 1807-1890
xTaylor, J. Orville.
District School. Arno.

Taylor, John R., 1933-
xTaylor, John R.
How to Start & Succeed in a Business of Your
Own. Reston.

Taylor, John R. see Taylor, John Russell.

Taylor, John Russell.
xTaylor, John R.
Hitch: The Life & Times of Alfred Hitchcock.
Pantheon.
Penguin Dictionary of the Theatre. Penguin.

Taylor, John T. see Taylor, John Thomas.

Taylor, John Thomas, 1947-
xTaylor, John T.
Illustrated Guide to Abbreviations for Use in
Religious Studies. Seminary Pr.

Taylor, John V. see Taylor, John Vernon.

Taylor, John Vernon.
xTaylor, John.
Christianity & Politics in Africa. Greenwood.
xTaylor, John V.
Enough Is Enough: A Biblical Call for
Moderation in a Consumer Oriented
Societed. Augsburg.
The Go-Between God: The Holy Spirit & the
Christian Mission. Oxford U Pr.
The Growth of the Church in Buganda: An
Attempt at Understanding. Greenwood.

Taylor, John W. see Taylor, John Willaim Ransom.

Taylor, John William Ransom.
xTaylor, John W.
Civil Aircraft of the World. Intl Pubns Serv.
Civil Aircraft of the World. Scribner.
Military Aircraft of the World. Scribner.
Spies in the Sky. Scribner.

Taylor, Joseph L.
xTaylor, Joseph L.
Measure Algebras. Am Math.

Taylor, Joseph L. see Taylor, Joseph Leon.

Taylor, Joseph Leon.
xTaylor, Joseph L.
A Group Home for Adolescent Girls: Practice
& Research. Child Welfare.

Taylor, Joshua C. see Taylor, Joshua Charles.

Taylor, Joshua Charles, 1917-
xTaylor, Joshua C.
The Fine Arts in America. U of Chicago Pr.
Futurism. NYGS.
Learning to Look: A Handbook for the Visual
Arts. U of Chicago Pr.

Taylor, Joy.
xTaylor, Joy.

The Foundations of Maths in the Infant
School. Allen Unwin.
Organizing the Open Classroom: A Teacher's
Guide to the Integrated Day. Schocken.
Reading & Writing in the First School. Allen
Unwin.

Taylor, K. see Taylor, Karl K.

Taylor, Karl K.
xTaylor, K.
Stages in Writing. McGraw.

Taylor, Kathrine K. see Taylor, Kathrine Kressmann.

Taylor, Kathrine Kressmann.
xTaylor, Kathrine K.
Diary of Florence in the Flood. S&S.

Taylor, Kenneth J. W., 1939-
xTaylor, Kenneth J. W.
Atlas of Gray Scale Ultrasonography.
Churchill.
ed. Diagnostic Ultrasound in Gastrointestinal
Disease. Churchill.

Taylor, Kenneth N. see Taylor, Kenneth Nathaniel.

Taylor, Kenneth Nathaniel.
xTaylor, Kenneth N.
Devotions for the Children's Hour. Moody.
Stories for the Children's Hour. Moody.
Taylor's Bible Story Book. Tyndale.

Taylor, Kent.
xTaylor, Kent.
Driving Like the Sun. Vagabond Pr.

Taylor, Kit S. see Taylor, Kit Sims.

Taylor, Kit Sims.
xTaylor, Kit S.
Sugar & the Underdevelopment of
Northeastern Brazil, 1500-1970. U Presses
Fla.

Taylor, L. B.
xTaylor.
Emergency Squads. Watts.
xTaylor, L. B.
Rescue: True Stories of Heroism. Watts.
Rescue!: True Stories of Heroism. Archway.
Shoplifting. Watts.
Space Shuttle. T Y Crowell.

Taylor, L. E. see Taylor, Loree Elizabeth.

Taylor, L. J.
xTaylor, L. J.
ed. A Librarian's Handbook. Oryx Pr.

Taylor, L. O. see Taylor, Leslie Owen.

Taylor, Lance.
xTaylor, Lance.
Macro Models for Developing Countries.
McGraw.

Taylor, Lauriston S. see Taylor, Lauriston Sale.

Taylor, Lauriston Sale, 1902-
xTaylor, Lauriston S.
Radiation Protection Standards. CRC Pr.

Taylor, Lee.
xTaylor, Lee.
Pend Oreille Profiles. Ye Galleon.

Taylor, Lee. see Taylor, Miller Lee.

Taylor, Leslie Owen, 1889-
xTaylor, L. O.
American Secondary School. Irvington.

Taylor, Lily R. see Taylor, Lily Ross.

Taylor, Lily Ross, 1886-
xTaylor, Lily R.
The Divinity of the Roman Emperor. Arno.
The Divinity of the Roman Emperor.
Porcupine Pr.
Party Politics in the Age of Caesar. Peter
Smith.
Party Politics in the Age of Caesar. U of Cal
Pr.

Taylor, Lisa.
xTaylor, Lisa.
ed. Urban Open Spaces. Rizzoli Intl.

Taylor, Lloyd C., 1923-
xTaylor, Lloyd C.

Margaret Ayer Barnes. Twayne.
The Medical Profession & Social Reform. St
Martin.

Taylor, Loree Elizabeth.
xTaylor, L. E.
South African Libraries. Shoe String.

Taylor, Louie S.
xTaylor, Louie S.
Copper Enameling. A S Barnes.

Taylor, Louis.
xTaylor, Louis.
Ride Western: A Complete Guide to Western
Horsemanship. Har-Row.

Taylor, M. see Taylor, Michael.

Taylor, M. C. see Taylor, Martin C.

Taylor, Malcolm. see Taylor, Malcolm Gordon.

Taylor, Malcolm Gordon.
xTaylor, Malcolm.
Health Insurance & Canadian Public Policy:
The Seven Decisions That Created the
Canadian Health Insurance System.
McGill-Queens U Pr.

Taylor, Martin C.
xTaylor, M. C.
Gabriela Mistral's Religious Sensibility. U of
Cal Pr.

Taylor, Marvin J., 1921-
xTaylor, Marvin J.
Introduction to Christian Education. Abingdon.

Taylor, Mary A. see Taylor, Mary Ann.

Taylor, Mary Ann.
xTaylor, Mary A.
Bittersweet Love. NAL.
xTaylor, Mary Ann.
Capture My Love. NAL.

Taylor, Mary C. see Taylor, Mary Christine.

Taylor, Mary Christine.
xTaylor, Mary C.
A History of the Foundations of Catholicism in
Northern New York. US Cath Hist.

Taylor, Maxwell D. see Taylor, Maxwell Davenport.

Taylor, Maxwell Davenport, 1901-
xTaylor, Maxwell D.
Precarious Security. Norton.
Uncertain Trumpet. Greenwood.

Taylor, Michael.
xTaylor, M.
Anarchy & Cooperation. Wiley.

Taylor, Michael J. see Taylor, Michael John Haddrick.

Taylor, Michael John Haddrick.
xTaylor, Michael J.
Helicopters of the World. Intl Pubns Serv.
Helicopters of the World. Scribner.

Taylor, Mildred. see Taylor, Mildred D.

Taylor, Mildred D.
xTaylor, Mildred.
Song of the Trees. Dial.
Song of the Trees. Bantam.

Taylor, Mildred G.
xTaylor, Mildred G.
How to Write a Research Paper. Pacific Bks.

Taylor, Miller Lee, 1930-
xTaylor, Lee.
Idea People. Nelson-Hall.

Taylor, Monica. see Taylor, Monica Jean.

Taylor, Monica Jean.
xTaylor, Monica.
Progress & Problems in Moral Education.
Humanities.

Taylor, Morris F.
xTaylor, Morris F.
O. P. McMains & the Maxwell Land Grant
Conflict. U of Ariz Pr.

Taylor, Overton H.
xTaylor, Overton H.
Economics & Liberalism: Collected Papers.
Harvard U Pr.

Taylor, Paul. see Taylor, Paul L.

Taylor, Paul A.
xTaylor, Paul A.

Frederick Winslow Taylor: A Memorial
Volume. Hive Pub.
Scientific Management in American Industry.
Hive Pub.
Taylor, Sydney.
xTaylor, Sydney.
All-Of-A-Kind Family. Dell.
All-of-a-Kind Family. Follett.
All-Of-A-Kind Family Downtown. Dell.
All-of-a-Kind Family Downtown. Follett.
Dog Who Came to Dinner. Follett.
More All-of-a-Kind Family. Dell.
More All-Of-A-Kind Family. Follett.
Taylor, Telford.
xTaylor, Telford.
Courts of Terror: Soviet Criminal Justice &
Jewish Emigration. Knopf.
Courts of Terror: Soviet Criminal Justice &
Jewish Emigration. Random.
Grand Inquest: The Story of Congressional
Investigations. Da Capo.
Munich: The Price of Peace. Doubleday.
Munich: The Price of Peace. Random.
Two Studies in Constitutional Interpretation.
Ohio St U Pr.
Taylor, Theodore.
xTaylor, Theodore.
Air Raid Pearl Harbor: The Story of December
7, 1941. T Y Crowell.
The Cay. Avon.
Cay. Doubleday.
Jule: The Story of Composer Jule Styne.
Random.
Taylor, Thomas, 1576-1632
xTaylor, Thomas.
Christ Revealed. Schol Facsimiles.
Taylor, Thomas F.
xTaylor, Thomas F.
Thematic Catalog of the Works of Jeremiah
Clarke. Info Coord.
Taylor, Thomas J. see Taylor, Thomas James.
Taylor, Thomas James, 1921-
xTaylor, Thomas J.
Medical Mathematics. Bobbs.
Taylor, Thomas T. see Taylor, Thomas Tallott.
Taylor, Thomas Tallott.
xTaylor, Thomas T.
Mechanics: Classical & Quantum. Pergamon.
Taylor, Trevor.
xTaylor, Trevor.
ed. Approaches & Theory in International
Relations. Longman.
Taylor, V. see Taylor, Valerie.
Taylor, V. J. see Taylor, Victor John.
Taylor, Valerie.
xTaylor, V.
Love Image. Naiad Pr.
xTaylor, Valerie.
ed. Great Shark Stories. Har-Row.
Taylor, Vernon L. see Taylor, Vernon Lyle.
Taylor, Vernon Lyle, 1922-
xTaylor, Vernon L.
Art of Argument. Scarecrow.
Taylor, Victor John.
xTaylor, V. J.
How to Build Period Country Furniture. Stein
& Day.
Taylor, Virginia H.
xTaylor, Virginia H.
Franco-Texan Land Company. U of Tex Pr.
Taylor, W. A. see Taylor, William Arthur.
Taylor, W. D. see Taylor, William Duncan.
Taylor, W. I. see Taylor, William I.
Taylor, Walter F. see Taylor, Walter Fuller.
Taylor, Walter Fuller, 1900-
xTaylor, Walter F.
Economic Novel in America. Octagon.
Taylor, Walter S.
xTaylor, Walter S.

Home Winemaker's Handbook. Har-Row.
Taylor, Warren, 1903-
xTaylor, Warren.
Tudor Figures of Rhetoric. Language Pr.
Taylor, Welford D. see Taylor, Welford Dunaway.
Taylor, Welford Dunaway.
xTaylor, Welford D.
Amelie Rives (Princess Troubetzkoy). Twayne.
Taylor, William Arthur.
xTaylor, W. A.
Historical Fiction. Folcroft.
Taylor, William B.
xTaylor, William B.
Drinking, Homicide, & Rebellion in Colonial
Mexican Villages. Stanford U Pr.
Taylor, William C. see Taylor, William Cooke.
Taylor, William Charles.
xTaylor, William C.
A History of Clay County. Jenkins.
Taylor, William Cooke, 1800-1849
xTaylor, William C.
Modern British Plutarch: Or, Lives of Men
Distinguished in the Recent History of
England for Their Talents, Virtues, or
Achievements. Arno.
Taylor, William D. see Taylor, William Duncan.
Taylor, William Duncan.
xTaylor, W. D.
ed. Eighteenth Century Comedy. Oxford U Pr.
xTaylor, William D.
Jonathan Swift: A Critical Essay. R West.
Taylor, William I.
xTaylor, W. I.
ed. Oxidative Coupling of Phenols. Dekker.
Taylor, William L. see Taylor, William Leonhard.
Taylor, William Leonhard.
xTaylor, William L.
Productive Monopoly: The Effect of Railroad
Control on New England Coastal Steamship
Lines, 1870-1916. Brown U Pr.
Taylor, William M. see Taylor, William Mackergo.
Taylor, William Mackergo, 1829-1895
xTaylor, William M.
Parables of Our Saviour. Kregel.
Taylor, William R. see Taylor, William Robert.
Taylor, William Randolph, 1895-
xTaylor, William R.
Marine Algae of the Eastern Tropical &
Sub-Tropical Coasts of the Americas. U of
Mich Pr.
Taylor, William Robert, 1922-
xTaylor, William R.
Cavalier & Yankee: The Old South &
American National Character. Harvard U Pr.
Taylor-Robinson, D.
xTaylor-Robinson, D.
Varicella Virus. Springer-Verlag.
Taymor, Melvin L.
xTaymor, Melvin L.
Infertility. Grune.
Tazewell, Charles.
xTazewell, Charles.
Littlest Angel. Childrens.
The Littlest Angel. Ideals.
Tchernavin, Tatiana.
xTchernavin, Tatiana.
My Childhood in Siberia. Oxford U Pr.
Tchernia, P.
xTchernia, P.
Descriptive Regional Oceanography. Pergamon.
Tchernoff, J., 1873-
xTchernoff, J.
Associations et Societes Secretes Sous la
Deuxieme Republique, 1848-1851. AMS Pr.
Tchobanoglous, George.
xTchobanoglous, George.
Solid Wastes: Engineering Principles &
Management Issues. McGraw.
Tchurmin, Avrhum Y. see Tchurmin, Avrhum Yuhzov.

Tchurmin, Avrhum Yuhzov.
xTchurmin, Avrhum Y.
Meditations from an Exploration of the
Ultimate Mysteries. Chris Mass.
Te Linde, Richard W. see Te Linde, Richard Wesley.
Te Linde, Richard Wesley.
xTe Linde, Richard W.
Operative Gynecology. Lippincott.
Teachers & Writers Collaborative. see Teachers and
Writers Collaborative.
Teachers and Writers Collaborative.
xTeachers & Writers Collaborative.
ed. Five Tales of Adventure: Collection of
Novels by Children. Tchrs & Writers Coll.
Teachey, William G.
xTeachey, William G.
Learning Laboratories: Guide to Adoption &
Use. Educ Tech Pubns.
Teachman, Jay.
xTeachman, Jay.
The Impact of Family Planning Programs on
Fertility Rates: A Case Study of Four
Nations. Comm & Family.
Tead, Ordway, 1891-
xTead, Ordway.
Administration: Its Purpose & Performance.
Shoe String.
Instincts in Industry. Arno.
Teaff, Grant.
xTeaff, Grant.
I Believe. Word Bks.
Teaford, Jon C.
xTeaford, Jon C.
The Municipal Revolution in America: Origins
of Modern Urban Government, 1650-1825. U
of Chicago Pr.
Teagarden, Florence M. see Teagarden, Florence Mabel.
Teagarden, Florence Mabel, 1887-
xTeagarden, Florence M.
A Study of the Upper Limits of the
Development of Intelligence. AMS Pr.
Teague, Bob.
xTeague, Bob.
Letters to a Black Boy. Walker & Co.
Teague, Burton W.
xTeague, Burton W.
Extra Pay for Service Abroad. Conference Bd.
Financial Planning for Executives. Conference
Bd.
Teague, S. J. see Teague, Sydney John.
Teague, Sydney John.
xTeague, S. J.
Microform Librarianship. Butterworths.
Teal, Larry.
xTeal, Larry.
Art of Saxophone Playing. Summy.
Teale, Edwin W. see Teale, Edwin Way.
Teale, Edwin Way, 1899-
xTeale, Edwin W.
A Naturalist Buys an Old Farm. Dodd.
Teale, Ruth.
xTeale, Ruth.
ed. Colonial Eve: Sources on Women in
Australia, 1788-1914. Oxford U Pr.
Tear, Jim.
xTear, Jim.
Fed up with Fat. Revell.
Teasdale, Sara, 1884-1933
xTeasdale, Sara.
Compiled by The Answering Voice: Love
Lyrics by Women. Arno.
Collected Poems of Sara Teasdale. Macmillan.
Collected Poems of Sara Teasdale. Macmillan.
Tebbel, John. see Tebbel, John William.
Tebbel, John William, 1912-
xTebbel, John.

The Media in America. NAL.
Open Letter to Newspaper Readers. Heineman.
Opportunities in Journalism. Natl Textbk.
Opportunities in Publishing Careers. Natl
   Textbk.
Tebbutt, T. H. see Tebbutt, T. H. Y.
Tebbutt, T. H. Y.
   xTebbutt, T. H.
   Principles of Water Quality Control. Pergamon.
Tebeau, Charlton W.
   xTebeau, Charlton W.
   A History of Florida. U of Miami Pr.
Tec, Leon.
   xTec, Leon.
   The Fear of Success. NAL.
Tec, Nechama.
   xTec, Nechama.
   Grass Is Green in Suburbia: A Sociological
      Study of Adolescent Usage of Illicit Drugs.
      Libra.
**Technical Committee on the Peaceful Uses of Nuclear
   Explosions, Vienna, 1975.**
   xTechnical Committee, Vienna Jan. 20-24, 1975.
   Peaceful Nuclear Explosions - Four:
      Proceedings. Unipub.
Technical Committee, Vienna Jan. 20-24, 1975. see
   Technical Committee on the Peaceful Uses of Nuclear
   Explosions, Vienna, 1975.
Technomic Publishing Company, Stamford, Conn.
   xTechnomic Research Staff.
   Biomedical Electronics: Marketing Guide &
      Company Directory for Patient Care Systems
      & Laboratory Equipment. Technomic.
   Developments in Rigid Urethane Foam
      Technology. Technomic.
   Flexible Urethane Foam Technology.
      Technomic.
   International Patents Digest of Foamed
      Plastics: Guide to the Published Patent
      Literature for 1971-73. Technomic.
   Marketing Guide to the Pharmaceuticals
      Industry. Technomic.
   xTechnomic's Staff.
   ed. Cellular Plastics in Transportation.
      Technomic.
Technomic Research Staff. see Technomic Publishing
   Company, Stamford, Conn.
Technomic's Staff. see Technomic Publishing Company,
   Stamford, Conn.
Techo, Robert.
   xTecho, Robert.
   Data Communications: An Introduction to
      Concepts & Design. Plenum Pub.
Teck, Alan.
   xTeck, Alan.
   Mutual Savings Banks & Savings & Loan
      Associations: Aspects of Growth. Columbia U
      Pr.
Tedd, L. A.
   xTedd, L. A.
   Introduction to Computer-Based Library
      Systems. Heyden.
Tedder, Jake D.
   xTedder, Jake D.
   Practical Applications of Business Mathematics.
      Reston.
Tedeschi, David H.
   xTedeschi, David H.
   ed. Importance of Fundamental Principles in
      Drug Evaluation. Raven.
Tedeschi, F. P. see Tedeschi, Frank P.
Tedeschi, Frank P.
   xTedeschi, F. P.
   Solid State Electronics. Delmar.
   xTedeschi, Frank P.
   The Active Filter Handbook. TAB Bks.
   Digital Computers & Logic Circuits. Glencoe.
   Solid-State Electronics. Van Nos Reinhold.
Tedford, R. H. see Tedford, Richard H.

Tedford, Richard H.
   xTedford, R. H.
   A Review of the Macropodid Genus Sthenurus.
      U of Cal Pr.
Tedlock, Dennis, 1939-
   xTedlock, Dennis.
   tr. Finding the Center: Narrative Poetry of the
      Zuni Indians. U of Nebr Pr.
Tedrow, J. C. F.
   xTedrow, John C.
   Soils of the Polar Landscapes. Rutgers U Pr.
Tedrow, John C. see Tedrow, J. C. F.
Tedrow, Thomas. see Tedrow, Thomas L.
Tedrow, Thomas L.
   xTedrow, Thomas.
   Death at Chappaquiddick. Pelican.
   xTedrow, Thomas L.
   Death at Chappaquiddick. Green Hill.
Teensma, E.
   xTeensma, E.
   Solipsism & Induction. Humanities.
Teeple, Gary.
   xTeeple, Gary.
   ed. Capitalism & the National Question in
      Canada. U of Toronto Pr.
Teeple, Howard M. see Teeple, Howard Merle.
Teeple, Howard Merle, 1911-
   xTeeple, Howard M.
   The Literary Origin of the Gospel of John.
      REI.
   The Noah's Ark Nonsense. REI.
Teeter, Don E.
   xTeeter, Don E.
   The Acoustic Guitar: Adjustment, Care,
      Maintenance, & Repair. U of Okla Pr.
Teger, Allan I.
   xTeger, Allan I.
   Too Much Invested to Quit. Pergamon.
Teggart, Frederick J. see Teggart, Frederick John.
Teggart, Frederick John, 1870-1946
   xTeggart, Frederick J.
   Theory & Processes of History. Peter Smith.
   Theory & Processes of History. U of Cal Pr.
Tegner, Bruce.
   xTegner, Bruce.
   Aikido & Jiu Jitsu Holds & Locks. Thor.
   Bruce Tegner's Complete Book of Judo. Thor.
   Bruce Tegner's Complete Book of Jujitsu.
      Thor.
   Bruce Tegner's Complete Book of Karate.
      Bantam.
   Bruce Tegner's Complete Book of
      Self-Defense. Thor.
   Instant Self-Defense. G&D.
Tegoborski, Ludwik, 1792-1857
   xTegoborski, Ludwik.
   Commentaries on the Productive Forces of
      Russia. Johnson Repr.
Teibl, Margaret.
   xTeibl, Margaret.
   Davey Come Home. Har-Row.
Teicher, Morton I.
   xTeicher, Morton I.
   ed. Reaching the Aged: Social Services in
      Forty-Four Countries. Sage.
Teichert, Pedro C. see Teichert, Pedro C M.
Teichert, Pedro C. M.
   xTeichert, Pedro C.
   Economic Policy Revolution &
      Industrialization in Latin America.
      Greenwood.
Teilhard de Chardin, Pierre.
   xTeilhard De Chardin, Pierre.

Activation of Energy. HarBraceJ.
Activation of Energy. HarBraceJ.
Christianity & Evolution. HarBraceJ.
Divine Milieu: An Essay on the Interior Life.
   Har-Row.
Early Man in China. AMS Pr.
Future of Man. Har-Row.
The Heart of Matter. HarBraceJ.
The Heart of the Matter. HarBraceJ.
Human Energy. HarBraceJ.
Human Energy. HarBraceJ.
Let Me Explain. Har-Row.
Toward the Future. HarBraceJ.
Toward the Future. HarBraceJ.
Teit, James A. see Teit, James Alexander.
Teit, James Alexander, 1864-
   xTeit, James A.
   The Lillooet Indians. AMS Pr.
   The Shuswap. AMS Pr.
   The Thompson Indians of British Columbia.
      AMS Pr.
Teitler, Ger. see Teitler, Gerke.
Teitler, Gerke.
   xTeitler, Ger.
   The Genesis of the Professional Officers'
      Corps. Sage.
Teiwes, Frederick C.
   xTeiwes, Frederick C.
   Politics & Purges in China: Rectification & the
      Decline of Party Norms, 1950-1965. M E
      Sharpe.
Teixidor, Javier.
   xTeixidor, Javier.
   The Pagan God: Popular Religion in the
      Greco-Roman Near East. Princeton U Pr.
Tejera, Victorino.
   nTejera, Victorino.
   Art & Human Intelligence. Irvington.
Tel Aviv University Conference on Erythropoiesis, 1970.
   xTel Aviv University Conference on
      Erythropoiesis, July, 1970, Petah Tikva.
   Erythropoiesis: Regulatory Mechanisms &
      Developmental Aspects. Acad Pr.
Teleki, Geza.
   xTeleki, Geza.
   Aerial Apes: Gibbons of Asia. Coward.
   Goblin, a Wild Chimpanzee. Dutton.
   Leakey the Elder: A Chimpanzee & His
      Community. Dutton.
Teleki, Gloria R. see Teleki, Gloria Roth.
Teleki, Gloria Roth.
   xTeleki, Gloria R.
   Collecting Traditional American Basketry.
      Dutton.
Telemaque, Eleanor W. see Telemaque, Eleanor Wong.
Telemaque, Eleanor Wong.
   xTelemaque, Eleanor W.
   It's Crazy to Stay Chinese in Minnesota.
      Elsevier-Nelson.
Telfer, Dariel.
   xTelfer, Dariel.
   Corrupters. S&S.
   Guilty Ones. S&S.
Telfer, Elizabeth.
   xTelfer, Elizabeth.
   Happiness. St Martin.
Telford, Charles W. see Telford, Charles Witt.
Telford, Charles Witt.
   xTelford, Charles W.
   The Exceptional Individual. P-H.
Telford, Shirley, 1925-
   xTelford, Shirley.
   Economic & Political Peace. William & Rich.
   Workers Profit Sharing: The Riddle of History
      Solved. William & Rich.
Telford, W. M. see Telford, William Murray.
Telford, William Murray, 1917-
   xTelford, W. M.

Applied Geophysics. Cambridge U Pr.
Tellenbach, Gerd, 1903-
 xTellenbach, Gerd.
  Church, State & Christian Society at the Time
   of the Investiture Contest. Humanities.
Teller, Edward, 1908-
 xTeller, Edward.
  The Legacy of Hiroshima. Greenwood.
  jt. auth. Power & Security. Lexington Bks.
  Reluctant Revolutionary. U of Mo Pr.
Teller, Raphael.
 xTeller, Raphael.
  Woodwork: A Basic Manual. Little.
Teller, Robert, 1939-
 xTeller, Robert.
  Practical English for Adult Learners. Hendel.
Teller, Sandy.
 xTeller, Sandy.
  This Was Sex. Citadel Pr.
Teller, Walter M. *see* Teller, Walter Magnes.
Teller, Walter Magnes.
 xTeller, Walter M.
  Joshua Slocum. Rutgers U Pr.
Teller, Woolsey.
 xTeller, Woolsey.
  The Atheism of Astronomy: A Refutation of
   the Theory That the Universe Is Governed
   by Intelligence. Arno.
Tellier, Richard. *see* Tellier, Richard D.
Tellier, Richard D.
 xTellier, Richard.
  Operations Management: Fundamental
   Concepts & Methods. Har-Row.
Tellington, Wentworth. *see* Tellington, Wentworth
 Jordan.
Tellington, Wentworth Jordan.
 xTellington, Wentworth.
  Endurance & Competitive Trail Riding.
   Doubleday.
Telser, Lester G., 1931-
 xTelser, Lester G.
  Competition, Collusion, & Game Theory.
   Beresford Bk Serv.
  Economic Theory & the Core. U of Chicago
   Pr.
  Functional Analysis in Mathematical
   Economics: Optimization Over Infinite
   Horizons. U of Chicago Pr.
Temerlin, Maurice K.
 xTemerlin, Maurice K.
  Lucy: Growing up Human-A Chimpanzee
   Daughter in a Psychotherapist's Family. Sci
   & Behavior.
Temes, Gabor C.
 xTemes, Gabor C.
  ed. Modern Filter Theory & Design. Wiley.
Temes, Lloyd.
 xTemes, Lloyd.
  Schaum's Outline of Electronic
   Communication. McGraw.
Temes, Roberta.
 xTemes, Roberta.
  Living with an Empty Chair: A Guide Through
   Grief. Irvington.
Temkin, Owsei, 1902-
 xTemkin, Owsei.
  The Double Face of Janus & Other Essays in
   the History of Medicine. Johns Hopkins.
  The Falling Sickness: A History of Epilepsy
   from the Greeks to the Beginnings of
   Modern Neurology. Johns Hopkins.
  Respect for Life in Medicine, Philosophy, &
   the Law. Johns Hopkins.
Temkin, Sanford.
 xTemkin, Sanford.
  Handbook of Comprehensive Planning in
   Schools. Educ Tech Pubns.
Temkine, Raymond. *see* Temkine, Raymonde.
Temkine, Raymonde, 1911-
 xTemkine, Raymond.

Grotowski. Avon.
Temko, Allan.
 xTemko, Allan.
  Eero Saarinen. Braziller.
Temko, Florence.
 xTemko, Florence.
  Decoupage Crafts. Doubleday.
  Folk Crafts for World Friendship. Doubleday.
  Folk Crafts for World Friendship. US Comm
   Unicef.
  Paperworks. Bobbs.
Temperley, H. W. *see* Temperley, Harold William
 Vazeille.
Temperley, Harold W. *see* Temperley, Harold William
 Vazeille.
Temperley, Harold William Vazeille.
 xTemperley, H. W.
  History of Serbia. Fertig.
 xTemperley, Harold W.
  History of Serbia. AMS Pr.
  Life of Canning. Greenwood.
  Life of Canning. Haskell.
Tempest, N. R.
 xTempest, N. R.
  Teaching Clever Children, 7-11. Routledge &
   Kegan.
Tempest, W.
 xTempest, W.
  ed. Infrasound & Low Frequency Vibration.
   Acad Pr.
Temple, Charles L. *see* Temple, Charles Lindsay.
Temple, Charles Lindsay, 1871-
 xTemple, Charles L.
  Native Races & Their Rulers: Sketches &
   Studies of Official Life & Administrative
   Problems in Nigeria. Biblio Dist.
  Native Races & Their Rulers: Sketches &
   Studies of Official Life & Administrative
   Problems in Nigeria. Metro Bks.
Temple, Douglas M.
 xTemple, Douglas M.
  Real Estate Finance in California. Goodyear.
Temple, Ed.
 xTemple, Ed.
  Only the Pure in Heart Survive. Broadman.
Temple, Mary.
 xTemple, Mary.
  How to Start a Secretarial & Business Service.
   Pilot Bks.
Temple, Oliver P. *see* Temple, Oliver Perry.
Temple, Oliver Perry, 1820-1907
 xTemple, Oliver P.
  East Tennessee & the Civil War. Arno.
Temple, Philip.
 xTemple, Philip.
  Castles in the Air: Men & Mountains in New
   Zealand. Intl Pubns Serv.
  Patterns of Water: The Great Southern Lakes
   of New Zealand. Intl Pubns Serv.
Temple, Richard C. *see* Temple, Richard Carnac.
Temple, Richard Carnac, Sir, Bart, 1850-1931
 xTemple, Richard C.
  The Legends of the Panjab. Arno.
Temple, Ruth. *see* Temple, Ruth (Zabriskie).
Temple, Ruth (Zabriskie).
 xTemple, Ruth.
  Nathalie Sarraute. Columbia U Pr.
 xTemple, Ruth Z.
  ed. Modern British Literature. Ungar.
  Twentieth Century British Literature: A
   Reference Guide & Bibliography. Ungar.
Temple, Ruth Z. *see* Temple, Ruth (Zabriskie).
Temple, William, Abp. of Canterbury, 1881-1944
 xTemple, William.
  Christianity & Social Order. Seabury.
  The Genius of English Poetry. Folcroft.
  Hope of a New World. Arno.
Templeton, A. C. *see* Templeton, Alexander Campbell.
Templeton, Alexander Campbell.
 xTempleton, A. C.

  ed. Tumours in a Tropical Country: A Survey
   of Uganda (1964-1968). Springer-Verlag.
Templeton, George S. *see* Templeton, George Streator.
Templeton, George Streator, 1887-
 xTempleton, George S.
  Domestic Rabbit Production. Interstate.
Templeton, June.
 xTempleton, June.
  Tales of Singing Brook Hill. Chris Mass.
Templewood, Samuel. *see* Templewood, Samuel John
 Gurney Hoare 1st Viscount.
**Templewood, Samuel John Gurney Hoare 1st Viscount,
 1880-1959**
 xTemplewood, Samuel.
  Nine Troubled Years. Greenwood.
Templin, Mildred C.
 xTemplin, Mildred C.
  Certain Language Skills in Children: Their
   Development & Interrelationships. U of Minn
   Pr.
  The Development of Reasoning in Children
   with Normal & Defective Hearing.
   Greenwood.
Temtamy, Samia. *see* Temtamy, Samia A.
Temtamy, Samia A.
 xTemtamy, Samia.
  ed. Genetics of Hand Malformations. March of
   Dimes.
Ten Boom, Corrie.
 xTen Boom, Corrie.
  Corrie's Christmas Memories. Revell.
  Don't Wrestle, Just Nestle. Revell.
  Each New Day. G K Hall.
  Each New Day. Revell.
  Each New Day. World Wide Pubs.
  He Sets the Captive Free. Revell.
  In My Father's House. Revell.
  This Day Is the Lord's. Revell.
  A Tramp Finds a Home. Revell.
Ten Broek, Jacobus.
 xTen Broek, Jacobus.
  Family Law & the Poor: Essays. Greenwood.
Ten Hoor, Marten.
 xTen Hoor, Marten.
  Education for Privacy. U of Ala Pr.
Tenaza. *see* Tenaza, Richard.
Tenaza, Richard.
 xTenaza.
  Penguins. Watts.
Tencin, Claudine. *see* Tencin, Claudine Alexandrine
 Guerin De.
Tencin, Claudine Alexandrine Guerin de.
 xTencin, Claudine.
  The Siege of Calais. Garland Pub.
Tendler, Judith.
 xTendler, Judith.
  Inside Foreign Aid. Johns Hopkins.
Tenenbaum, Elizabeth B. *see* Tenenbaum, Elizabeth
 Brody.
Tenenbaum, Elizabeth Brody, 1944-
 xTenenbaum, Elizabeth B.
  The Problematic Self: Approaches to Identity
   in Stendhal, D.H. Lawrence, & Malraux.
   Harvard U Pr.
Tenenbaum, Joseph, 1887-
 xTenenbaum, Joseph.
  Race & Reich: The Story of an Epoch.
   Greenwood.
Tenenti, Alberto.
 xTenenti, Alberto.
  Piracy and the Decline of Venice, 1580-1615.
   U of Cal Pr.
Teng. *see* Teng, Ssu-Yu.
Teng, Ssu-Yu.
 xTeng.
  China's Response to the West: A Documentary
   Survey, 1839-1923. Harvard U Pr.
Teng, Wayne C. *see* Teng, Wayne Chi-Yu.
Teng, Wayne Chi-Yu, 1920-
 xTeng, Wayne C.

Foundation Design. P-H.
Tengbom, Mildred.
xTengbom, Mildred.
Fill My Cup, Lord: Meditations on Word
Pictures in the New Testament. Augsburg.
Compiled by Table Prayers: New Prayers, Old
Favorites, Songs, & Responses. Augsburg.
Tennant, Emma.
xTennant, Emma.
The Bad Sister. Avon.
The Bad Sister. Coward.
The Last of the Country House Murders.
Elsevier-Nelson.
Wild Nights. HarBraceJ.
Tennant, P. E. *see* Tennant, Philip Ernest.
Tennant, P. F. *see* Tennant, Peter Frank Dalrymple.
Tennant, Peter Frank Dalrymple.
xTennant, P. F.
Ibsen's Dramatic Technique. Humanities.
Tennant, Philip Ernest.
xTennant, P. E.
Theophile Gautier. Humanities.
Tenneco Oil Company. *see* Tenneco Oil Company,
Houston, Texas.
Tenneco Oil Company, Houston, Texas.
xTenneco Oil Company.
Operators Handbook. Gulf Pub.
Tennekes, H.
xTennekes, Hendrik.
First Course in Turbulence. MIT Pr.
Tennekes, Hendrik. *see* Tennekes, H.
Tennenbaum, Silvia.
xTennenbaum, Silvia.
Rachel, the Rabbi's Wife. Morrow.
Tennenhouse, Dan J.
xTennenhouse, Dan J.
Attorneys Medical Deskbook. Lawyers Co-Op.
Tennenhouse, Leonard, 1942-
xTennenhouse, Leonard.
ed. The Practice of Psychoanalytic Criticism.
Wayne St U Pr.
Tennessee State Library & Archives. *see* Tennessee. State
Library and Archives, Nashville.
Tennessee. State Library and Archives, Nashville.
xTennessee State Library & Archives.
Marriages from Early Tennessee Newspapers,
1794-1851. Southern Hist Pr.
Tennessee. University.
xUniversity Of Tennessee.
Library in the University: University of
Tennessee Library Lectures, 1949-1966. Shoe
String.
Tenney, Edward A. *see* Tenney, Edward Andrews.
Tenney, Edward Andrews, 1899-
xTenney, Edward A.
Thomas Lodge. Russell.
Tenney, Merrill C. *see* Tenney, Merrill Chapin.
Tenney, Merrill Chapin, 1904-
xTenney, Merrill C.
Galatians: The Charter of Christian Liberty.
Eerdmans.
Tenney, Thomas A. *see* Tenney, Thomas Asa.
Tenney, Thomas Asa.
xTenney, Thomas A.
Mark Twain: A Reference Guide. G K Hall.
Tennissen, A. *see* Tennissen, Anthony C.
Tennissen, Anthony C.
xTennissen, A.
Nature of Earth Materials. P-H.
xTennissen, Anthony C.
Colorful Mineral Identifier. Sterling.
Tennov, Dorothy.
xTennov, Dorothy.
Psychotherapy: The Hazardous Cure.
Doubleday.
Super Self: A Woman's Guide to
Self-Management. BJ Pub Group.
Super Self: A Woman's Guide to
Self-Management. T Y Crowell.
Tennyson, Alfred. *see* Tennyson, Alfred Tennyson.

Tennyson, Alfred L. *see* Tennyson, Alfred Tennyson.
Tennyson, Alfred Tennyson.
xTennyson, Alfred.
Idylls of the King. Airmont.
Works of Tennyson. Greenwood.
xTennyson, Alfred L.
In Memoriam, The Princess, & Maud. Folcroft.
Tenpas, Margaret.
xTenpas, Margaret L.
Bridge to Blue Hill. Carolrhoda Bks.
Tenpas, Margaret L. *see* Tenpas, Margaret.
Tentler, T. *see* Tentler, Thomas N.
Tentler, Thomas N., 1932-
xTentler, T.
Sin & Confession on the Eve of the
Reformation. Princeton U Pr.
Teodorescu, Radu.
xTeodorescu, Radu.
Kid Fitness. Seaview Bks.
Teodorsson, Sven-Tage.
xTeodorsson, Sven-Tage.
The Phonology of Attic in the Hellenistic
Period. Humanities.
The Phonology of Ptolemaic Koine.
Humanities.
TePaske, John J. *see* TePaske, John Jay.
TePaske, John Jay.
xTePaske, John J.
Governorship of Spanish Florida, 1700-1763.
Duke.
Teple, Edwin R.
xTeple, Edwin R.
Arbitration & Conflict Resolution. BNA.
Teplitz, Jerry.
xTeplitz, Jerry.
How to Relax & Enjoy.... Japan Pubns.
Tepper, Bette. *see* Tepper, Bette K.
Tepper, Bette K.
xTepper, Bette.
Mathematics for Retail Buying. Fairchild.
Tepper, I. *see* Tepper, Irving.
Tepper, Irving.
xTepper, I.
Solid State Devices. A-W.
Tepper, M. *see* Tepper, Marvin.
Tepper, Marvin.
xTepper, M.
Advanced & Extra Class Amateur License Q &
A Manual. Hayden.
xTepper, Marvin.
Quad Sound. Hayden.
Tepper, Michael.
xTepper, Michael.
ed. Immigrants to the Middle Colonies: A
Consolidation of Ship Passenger Lists &
Associated Data from the New York
Genealogical & Biographical Record.
Genealog Pub.
ed. Passengers to America: A Consolidation of
Ship Passenger Lists from the New England
Historical & Genealogical Register. Genealog
Pub.
Tepperman, Jean.
xTepperman, Jean.
Not Servants, Not Machines: Office Workers
Speak Out!. Beacon Pr.
Ter Engel, Jan. *see* Wengel, Jan Ter.
Terasaki, Gwen.
xTerasaki, Gwen.
Bridge to the Sun. U of NC Pr.
Terborgh, George. *see* Terborgh, George Willard.
Terborgh, George Willard.
xTerborgh, George.
Automation Hysteria. Norton.
Terhorst, Jerald F.
xTerHorst, Jerald F.

The Flying White House: The Story of Air
Force One. Coward.
Gerald Ford & the Future of the Presidency.
Okpaku Communications.
Terkel, Louis.
xTerkel, Studs.
Giants of Jazz. T Y Crowell.
Talking to Myself: A Memoir of My Times.
Pantheon.
Working: People Talk About What They Do
All Day & How They Feel About What They
Do. Pantheon.
Terkel, Studs. *see* Terkel, Louis.
Terletskii, Iakov Petrovich, 1912-
xTerletskii, Yakov P.
Paradoxes in the Theory of Relativity. Plenum
Pub.
Terletskii, Yakov P. *see* Terletskii, Iakov Petrovich.
Terlouw, Jan.
xTerlouw, Jan.
How to Become King. Hastings.
Terman, D., 1933-
xTerman, Douglas.
First Strike. PB.
First Strike. Scribner.
Terman, Douglas. *see* Terman, D.
Terman, Lewis M. *see* Terman, Lewis Madison.
Terman, Lewis Madison.
xTerman, Lewis M.
The Gifted Child Grows up: Twenty-Five
Years' Follow-up of a Superior Group.
Stanford U Pr.
The Measurement of Intelligence. Arno.
Termini, B. *see* Termini, Benedict A.
Termini, Benedict A.
xTermini, B.
Essentials of Echocardiography. Med
Economics.
Termini, Maria.
xTermini, Maria.
Silkscreening. P-H.
Ternay, Andrew L.
xTernay, Andrew L.
Contemporary Organic Chemistry. HR&W.
Ternberg, Jessie. *see* Ternberg, Jessie L.
Ternberg, Jessie L.
xTernberg, Jessie.
A Handbook for Pediatric Surgery. Williams &
Wilkins.
Terp, Pop-Top.
xTerp, Pop-Top.
Pop-Topping. Chilton.
Terpstra, P. *see* Terpstra, Pieter.
Terpstra, Pieter.
xTerpstra, P.
Crystallometry. Acad Pr.
Terrace, Vincent, 1948-
xTerrace, Vincent.
The Complete Encyclopedia of Television
Programs. A S Barnes.
Terrall, Robert.
xTerrall, Robert.
Sand Dollars. St Martin.
Terray, Emmanuel.
xTerray, Emmanuel.
Marxism & "Primitive" Societies: Two Studies.
Monthly Rev.
Terrell, John U. *see* Terrell, John Upton.
Terrell, John Upton, 1900-
xTerrell, John U.
American Indian Almanac. T Y Crowell.
The Arrow & the Cross. Capra Pr.
The Plains Apache. T Y Crowell.
Pueblos, Gods & Spaniards. Dial.
xTerrell, John Upton.
Indian Women of the Western Morning: Their
Life in Early America. Doubleday.
Terrell, Neil.
xTerrell, Neil.

Power Technique of Radio - T.V. Copywriting.
TAB Bks.

Terrell, Trevor J.
xTerrell, Trevor J.
An Introduction to Digital Filters. Halsted Pr.

Terres, John K.
xTerres, John K.
Songbirds in Your Garden. T Y Crowell.

Terrien, Samuel. *see* Terrien, Samuel L.

Terrien, Samuel L, 1911-
xTerrien, Samuel.
Golden Bible Atlas. Western Pub.

Terrill, Rose. *see* Terrill, Ross.

Terrill, Ross.
xTerrill, Rose.
Mao: A Biography. Har-Row.
xTerrill, Ross.
R. H. Tawney & His Times: Socialism As
Fellowship. Harvard U Pr.

Terrill, Tom E.
xTerrill, Tom E.
ed. Such As Us: Southern Voices of the
Thirties. Norton.
ed. Such As Us: Southern Voices of the
Thirties. U of NC Pr.
The Tariff, Politics, & American Foreign
Policy, 1874-1901. Greenwood.

Terris, Susan.
xTerris, Susan.
The Chicken Pox Papers. Dell.
The Chicken Pox Papers. Watts.
No Boys Allowed. Doubleday.
The Pencil Families. Greenwillow.
Tucker & the Horse Thief. Schol Bk Serv.
Two P's in a Pod. Greenwillow.

Terris, Virginia R.
xTerris, Virginia R.
ed. Woman in America: A Guide to
Information Sources. Gale.

Terry, Ann.
xTerry, Ann.
Children's Poetry Preferences: A National
Survey of Upper Elementary Grades. NCTE.

Terry, C. S. *see* Terry, Charles Sanford.

Terry, Charles E. *see* Terry, Charles Edward.

Terry, Charles Edward.
xTerry, Charles E.
Opium Problem. Patterson Smith.

Terry, Charles S. *see* Terry, Charles Sanford.

Terry, Charles Sanford, 1864-1936
xTerry, C. S.
Music of Bach: An Introduction. Peter Smith.
xTerry, Charles S.
Bach: A Biography. Scholarly.
Bach's Orchestra. Scholarly.
John Christian Bach. Greenwood.

Terry, Edward M.
xTerry, Edward M.
A Richard Wagner Dictionary. Greenwood.

Terry, George R. *see* Terry, George Robert.

Terry, George Robert.
xTerry, George R.
Principles of Management. Irwin.

Terry, Len.
xTerry, Len.
Racing Car Design & Development. Bentley.

Terry, Lindsay.
xTerry, Lindsay.
How to Build an Evangelistic Church Music
Program. Nelson.

Terry, Mary. *see* Terry, Mary C.

Terry, Mary C.
xTerry, Mary.
Homecraft. Soccer.

Terry, Patricia. *see* Terry, Patricia Ann.

Terry, Patricia Ann.
xTerry, Patricia.
jt. auth. Modern French Poetry: A Bilingual
Anthology. Columbia U Pr.

Terry, R. C. *see* Terry, Reginald Charles.

Terry, Reginald Charles, 1932-
xTerry, R. C.
Anthony Trollope: The Artist in Hiding.
Rowman.

Terry, Robert W.
xTerry, Robert W.
For Whites Only. Eerdmans.

Terry, W. D. *see* Terry, William D.

Terry, Walter.
xTerry, Walter.
Frontiers of Dance: The Life of Martha
Graham. T Y Crowell.
The King's Ballet Master: A Biography of
Denmark's August Bournonville. Dodd.

Terry, William D.
xTerry, W. D.
ed. Immunobiology & Immunotherapy of
Cancer. Elsevier.
xTerry, William D.
ed. Immunotherapy of Cancer: Present Status
of Trials in Man. Raven.

Tersine, Richard J.
xTersine, Richard J.
Materials Management & Inventory Systems.
Elsevier.
Problems & Models in Operations
Management. Grid Pub.

Terway, Vinodini.
xTerway, Vinodini.
East India Company & Russia. Verry.

Terzaghi, Karl, 1883-
xTerzaghi, Karl.
Theoretical Soil Mechanics. Wiley.

Terzi, M. *see* Terzi, Mario.

Terzi, Mario.
xTerzi, M.
Genetics & the Animal Cell. Wiley.

Teschner, Richard V.
xTeschner, Richard V.
ed. The Spanish & English of United States
Hispanos: A Critical, Annotated Linguistic
Bibliography. Ctr Appl Ling.

TeSelle, Sallie M. *see* TeSelle, Sallie McFague.

TeSelle, Sallie McFague.
xTeSelle, Sallie M.
Literature & the Christian Life. Yale U Pr.

Tesla Museum. *see* Belgrad, Muzej Nikole Tesle.

Tessier, Thomas.
xTessier, Thomas.
The Nightwalker. Atheneum.

Tessman, Lora Heims, 1928-
xTessman, Lora Heims.
Children of Parting Parents. Aronson.

Testa. *see* Testa, Bernard.

Testa, Bernard.
xTesta.
Principles of Organic Stereochemistry. Dekker.
xTesta, Bernard.
Drug Metabolism: Chemical & Biochemical
Aspects. Dekker.

Testa, Fulvio.
xTesta, Fulvio.
The Land Where the Ice Cream Grows.
Doubleday.
A Short Step. Mayflower Bks.

Tester, Sylvia R. *see* Tester, Sylvia Root.

Tester, Sylvia Root.
xTester, Sylvia R.
Carla-Too-Little. Childs World.
Frustrated. Childrens.
Frustrated. Childs World.
The Great Big Boat. Childs World.
Jealous. Childrens.
Jealous. Childs World.
The Loud-Noisy, Dirty-Grimy, Bad & Naughty
Twins: A Book of Synonyms. Childs World.
Magic Monsters Around the Year. Childs
World.
Magic Monsters Learn About Safety. Childs
World.
Magic Monsters Learn About Weather.
Childrens.
Magic Monsters Learn About Weather. Childs
World.
Melinda. Childs World.
One Unicorn: A Counting Book. Childs World.
The Parade of Shapes. Childs World.
Sad. Childrens.
Sad. Childs World.
Sandy's New Home. Childs World.
Sometimes I'm Afraid. Childs World.
That Big Bruno. Childs World.
We Laughed a Lot, My First Day of School.
Childs World.
What Is a Monster?. Childs World.
A World of Color. Childs World.

Tetel, Marcel.
xTetel, Marcel.
Montaigne. Twayne.

Tetelman, A. S.
xTetelman, A. S.
Fracture of Structural Materials. Wiley.

Tetens, Alfred, 1835-1909
xTetens, Alfred.
Among the Savages of the South Seas:
Memoirs of Micronesia, 1862-1868. Stanford
U Pr.

Teternikov, Fedor. *see* Teternikov, Fedor Kuzmich.

Teternikov, Fedor Kuzmich, 1863-1927
xTeternikov, Fedor.
The Created Legend. Greenwood.
The Old House & Other Tales. Greenwood.

Tether, Graham.
xTether, Graham.
The Hair Book. Random.
Skunk & Possum. HM.

Tetlow, Elizabeth M.
xTetlow, Elizabeth N.
Women & Ministry in the New Testament.
Paulist Pr.

Tetlow, Elizabeth N. *see* Tetlow, Elizabeth M.

Tetmajer, Kazimierz, 1865-1940
xTetmajer, Kazimierz P.
Tales of the Tatras. Greenwood.

Tetmajer, Kazimierz P. *see* Tetmajer, Kazimierz.

Teune, Henry.
xTeune, Henry.
The Developmental Logic of Social Systems.
Sage.

Tevis, Walter. *see* Tevis, Walter S.

Tevis, Walter S.
xTevis, Walter.
The Hustler. Avon.
The Hustler. Oxford U Pr.
Mockingbird. Bantam.
The Mockingbird. Doubleday.

Tevoedjre, Albert, 1929-
xTevoedjre, Albert.
Pan-Africanism in Action: An Account of the
UAM. Harvard U Intl Aff.

Tewari, Harish C., 1944-
xTewari, Harish C.
Understanding Personality & Motives of
Women Managers. Univ Microfilms.

Tewarson, Reginald P.
xTewarson, Reginald P.

Sparse Matrices. Acad Pr.

Tewary, I. N., 1937-
xTewary, I. N.
The Peace-Keeping Power of the United
Nations General Assembly. Verry.

Tewary, V. K.
xTewary, V. K.
Mechanics of Fibre Composites. Halsted Pr.

Tewksbury, Donald G. see Tewksbury, Donald George.

Tewksbury, Donald George, 1894-1958
xTewksbury, Donald G.
Founding of American Colleges & Universities
Before the Civil War with Particular
Reference to the Religious Influences Bearing
Upon the College Movement. AMS Pr.
Founding of American Colleges & Universities
Before the Civil War. Arno.

Texas A & M University Library. see Texas. A and M
University, College Station. Library.

Texas. A and M University, College Station. Library.
xTexas A & M University Library.
Energy Bibliography & Index. Gulf Pub.

Texas Instruments Incorporated.
xEngineering Staff of Texas Instruments.
The Linear Control Circuits Data Book. Tex
Instr Inc.
The M O S Memory Data Book for Design
Engineers, 1980. Tex Instr Inc.
The MDS Memory Data Book, 1980. Tex Instr
Inc.
The Optoelectronics Data Book for Design
Engineers. Tex Instr Inc.
xTheEngineering Staff of Texas Instruments.
The Bipolar Microcomputer Components Data
Book. Tex Instr Inc.
The Interface Circuits Data Book for Design
Engineers. Tex Instr Inc.

Texas Instruments Learning Center.
xTexas Instruments Learning Center.
Understanding Solid State Electronics. Tex
Instr Inc.
xTexas Instruments Learning Center Staff.
Sourcebook for Programmable Calculators. Tex
Instr Inc.

Texas Instruments Learning Center Staff. see Texas
Instruments Learning Center.

**Texas. Legislature. Penitentiary Investigating
Committee.**
xTexas, Penitentiary Investigating Committee.
A Record of Evidence & Statements Before the
Penitentiary Investigating Committee:
Appointed by the Thirty-Third Legislature of
Texas. Arno.

Texas, Penitentiary Investigating Committee. see Texas.
Legislature. Penitentiary Investigating Committee.

Texas Tech University.
xTexas Tech University.
Utilization of Solar Energy for Feedmill &
Irrigation Operations. Solar Energy Info.

Texas. University.
xUniversity of Texas.
Catalog of the Latin American Collection. G K
Hall.
Catalog of the Texas Collection in the Barker
Texas History Center. G K Hall.

Texas. University at Austin.
xUniversity of Texas, Austin.
Catalog of the Latin American Collection of
the University of Texas Library: Second
Supplement. G K Hall.

Texas. University at Austin. Library.
xUniversity of Texas Library, Austin.
Catalog of the Latin American Collection of
the University of Texas Library, First
Supplement. G K Hall.

Texas. University. College of Fine Arts.
xConference on Latin-American Fine Arts, Texas
University, College of Fine Arts.

Proceedings. Greenwood.

Texas. University. Institute of Latin American Studies.
xInstitute of Latin American Studies.
Latin American Research & Publications at the
University of Texas at Austin, 1893-1969. U
of Tex Pr.
xTexas University Institute of Latin American
Studies.
Basic Industries in Texas & Northern Mexico.
Greenwood.
Essays in Mexican History: The Charles
Wilson Hackett Memorial Volume.
Greenwood.
Political, Economic, & Social Problems of the
Latin-American Nations of Southern South
America. Greenwood.
Seventy-Five Years of Latin American
Research at the University of Texas, Masters
Thesis & Doctoral Dissertations, 1893-1958,
& Publications of Latin American Interest,
1941-1958. Greenwood.
Some Educational & Anthropological Aspects
of Latin-America. Greenwood.

Texon, Meyer, 1909-
xTexon, Meyer.
The Hemodynamic Basis of Atherosclerosis.
Hemisphere Pub.

Textbook Committee of Barbering. see Milady Publishing
Corporation, New York. Textbook Committee of
Barbering.

Textile World.
xTextile World.
Leaders in the Textile Industry. McGraw.

Textor, Robert B.
xTextor, Robert B.
Compiled by Cross-Cultural Summary.
HRAFP.
ed. Cultural Frontiers of the Peace Corps. MIT
Pr.
Failure in Japan: With Keystones for a Positive
Policy. Greenwood.

Tey, Josephine.
xTey, Josephine.
Brat Farrar. Bentley.
Brat Farrar. Berkley Pub.
Brat Farrar. Macmillan.
The Daughter of Time. Berkley Pub.
The Daughter of Time. PB.
The Franchise Affair. Bentley.
Franchise Affair. Berkley Pub.
The Franchise Affair. PB.

Teyler, Timothy. see Teyler, Timothy J.

Teyler, Timothy J.
xTeyler, Timothy.
ed. Behavioral Sciences: PreTest
Self-Assessment & Review. McGraw-Pretest.
xTeyler, Timothy J.
The Brain & Learning. Greylock Pubs.
A Primer of Psychobiology: Brain & Behavior.
W H Freeman.

Thabault, Roger, 1895-
xThabault, Roger.
Education & Change in a Village Community:
Mazieres-en-Gatine 1848-1914. Schocken.

Thacher, Alida. see Thacher, Alida M.

Thacher, Alida M.
xThacher, Alida.
Fastest Woman on Earth. Raintree Pubs.
Games for All Seasons. Raintree Pubs.
Perilous Journey to the Top. Raintree Pubs.

Thacker, Ronald. see Thacker, Ronald J.

Thacker, Ronald J., 1935-
xThacker, Ronald.
Accounting Principles. P-H.

Thacker, Ronald J. see Thacker, Ronald James.

Thacker, Ronald James.
xThacker, Ronald J.
Introduction to Modern Accounting. P-H.
Modern Management Accounting. Reston.

Thackeray, Andrew D. see Thackeray, Andrew David.

Thackeray, Andrew David.
xThackeray, Andrew D.
Astronomical Spectroscopy. Macmillan.

Thackeray, Kit.
xThackeray, Kit.
Counterflood. Morrow.

Thackeray, W. M. see Thackeray, William Makepeace.

Thackeray, William M. see Thackeray, William
Makepeace.

Thackeray, William Makepeace.
xThackeray, W. M.
Vanity Fair. HM.
xThackeray, William M.
The Book of Snobs. St Martin.
A Collection of Letters of W. M. Thackeray.
Folcroft.
Hitherto Unidentified Contributions of W. M.
Thackeray to "Punch". AMS Pr.
Vanity Fair. Dutton.
Vanity Fair. Merrimack Bk Serv.
Vanity Fair. Modern Lib.
Vanity Fair. NAL.
Vanity Fair. Penguin.
Vanity Fair. AMSCO Sch.
Vanity Fair. Airmont.

Thackray, Patricia.
xThackray, Patricia.
Big Bird Gets Lost. Western Pub.
Raggedy Ann at the Carnival. Western Pub.

Thadani, B. N. see Thadani, Bhagwan Nebhraj.

Thadani, Bhagwan Nebhraj.
xThadani, B. N.
Modern Methods in Structural Mechanics.
Asia.

Thaeler, C. S. see Thaeler, Charles S.

Thaeler, Charles S
xThaeler, C. S.
An Analysis of the Distribution of Pocket
Gopher Species in Northeastern California
(Genus Thomomys).. U of Cal Pr.

Thain, Richard J.
xThain, Richard J.
The Managers: Career Alternatives for the
College Educated. Coll Placement.

Thain, Wilbur S.
xThain, Wilbur S.
Normal & Handicapped Children: A Growth &
Development Primer for Parents &
Professionals. PSG Pub.

Thakur, Upendra.
xThakur, Upendra.
Introduction to Homicide in India: Ancient &
Early Medieval Period. South Asia Bks.

Thaler, George J. see Thaler, George Julius.

Thaler, George Julius, 1918-
xThaler, George J.
Design of Feedback Systems. Acad Pr.

Thaler, Malcolm S.
xThaler, Malcolm S.
Medical Immunology. Lippincott.

Thaler, Mike, 1936-
xThaler, Mike.
illus. Chocolate Marshmelephant Sundae.
Avon.
illus. The Chocolate Marshmelephant Sundae.
Watts.
How Far Will a Rubber Band Stretch?. Schol
Bk Serv.
There's a Hippopotamus Under My Bed. Avon.
There's a Hippopotamus Under My Bed.
Watts.

Thalmann, Marianne, 1888-
xThalmann, Marianne.
The Literary Sign Language of German
Romanticism. Wayne St U Pr.

Thalmann, William G., 1947-
xThalmann, William G.

Dramatic Art in Aeschylus's Seven Against
Thebes. Yale U Pr.

Thane, Elswyth.
xThane, Elswyth.
Dawn's Early Light. Dutton.
From This Day Forward. Amereon Ltd.
Letter to a Stranger. Amereon Ltd.
Light Heart. Amereon Ltd.
Lost General. Amereon Ltd.
This Was Tomorrow. Amereon Ltd.
Tryst. Amereon Ltd.

Thane, Pat.
xThane, Pat.
ed. The Origins of British Social Policy.
Rowman.

Thapar, Romila.
xThapar, Romila.
History of India. Penguin.

Tharaud, Ross, 1953-
xTharaud, Ross.
Openings. SBD.

Tharp, Charles Patrick.
xTharp, Patrick.
Pharmacy Management for Students &
Practitioners. Mosby.

Tharp, Constance. see Tharp, Constance P.

Tharp, Constance P.
xTharp, Constance.
Total Thanks. Logos.

Tharp, Edgar.
xTharp, Edgar.
The Starving Artist's Cookbook. McGraw.

Tharp, Patrick. see Tharp, Charles Patrick.

Tharpe, Jac.
xTharpe, Jac L.
ed. Elvis: Images & Fancies. U Pr of Miss.

Tharpe, Jac L. see Tharpe, Jac.

Thatcher, B. B. see Thatcher, Benjamin Bussey.

Thatcher, Benjamin Bussey, 1809-1840
xThatcher, B. B.
Indian Biography: Or an Historical Account of
Those Individuals Who Have Been
Distinguished Among the North American
Natives As Orators,Worriors,Statesmen &
Other Remarkable Characters. Rio Grande.

Thatcher, Floyd. see Thatcher, Floyd W.

Thatcher, Floyd W.
xThatcher, Floyd.
ed. The Miracle of Easter. Word Bks.

Thatcher, Maurice H. see Thatcher, Maurice Hudson.

Thatcher, Maurice Hudson, 1870-1973
xThatcher, Maurice H.
Autobiography in Poetry. Speller.

Thaxter, Celia. see Thaxter, Celia (Laighton).

Thaxter, Celia (Laighton), 1835-1894
xThaxter, Celia.
Stories & Poems for Children. Arno.

Thayer, Charles W. see Thayer, Charles Wheeler.

Thayer, Charles Wheeler, 1910-
xThayer, Charles W.
Diplomat. Greenwood.

Thayer, Eli.
xThayer, Eli.
A History of the Kansas Crusade. Arno.

Thayer, Ernest L. see Thayer, Ernest Lawrence.

Thayer, Ernest Lawrence.
xThayer, Ernest L.
Casey at the Bat. Dover.
Casey at the Bat. Peter Smith.
Casey at the Bat. P-H.

Thayer, George, 1933-
xThayer, George.
Who Shakes the Money Tree?: American
Campaign Financing Practices from 1789 to
the Present. S&S.

Thayer, H. Standish. see Thayer, Horace Standish.

Thayer, Horace S. see Thayer, Horace Standish.

Thayer, Horace Standish, 1923-
xThayer, H. Standish.

Meaning & Action: A Critical History of
Pragmatism. Hackett Pub.
xThayer, Horace S.
Logic of Pragmatism: An Examination of John
Dewey's Logic. Greenwood.

Thayer, James B. see Thayer, James Bradley.

Thayer, James Bradley, 1831-1902
xThayer, James B.
Legal Essays. Rothman.
Preliminary Treatise on Evidence at Common
Law. Kelley.
Preliminary Treatise on Evidence at Common
Law. Rothman.

Thayer, James S. see Thayer, James Stewart.

Thayer, James Stewart.
xThayer, James S.
The Earhart Betrayal. Putnam.

Thayer, Lee. see Thayer, Lee O.

Thayer, Lee O.
xThayer, Lee.
Compiled by Ethics, Morality & the Media:
Reflections of American Culture. Hastings.

Thayer, Marjorie.
xThayer, Marjorie.
The Christmas Strangers. Childrens.
The Valentine Box. Childrens.

Thayer, Mary R. see Thayer, Mary Rebecca.

Thayer, Mary Rebecca, 1887-
xThayer, Mary R.
Influence of Horace on the Chief English Poets
of the Nineteenth Century. Haskell.
Influence of Horace on the Chief English Poets
of the Nineteenth Century. Russell.

Thayer, Nancy, 1943-
xThayer, Nancy.
Stepping. Doubleday.

Thayer, Philip W. see Thayer, Philip Warren.

Thayer, Philip Warren.
xThayer, Philip W.
ed. Nationalism & Progress in Free Asia. Johns
Hopkins.
ed. Southeast Asia in the Coming World. Arno.

Thayer, T. A. see Thayer, Thomas A.

Thayer, Theodore. see Thayer, Theodore George.

Thayer, Theodore George, 1904-
xThayer, Theodore.
Pennsylvania Politics & the Growth of
Democracy: 1740-1776. Pa Hist & Mus.

Thayer, Thomas A.
xThayer, T. A.
ed. Software Reliability: A Study of Large
Project Reality. Elsevier.

Thayer, Vivian T. see Thayer, Vivian Trow.

Thayer, Vivian Trow, 1886-
xThayer, Vivian T.
Religion in Public Education. Greenwood.

Thayer, William R. see Thayer, William Roscoe.

Thayer, William Roscoe, 1859-1923
xThayer, William R.
The Art of Biography. Folcroft.
The Art of Biography. R West.

Thayer, William S. see Thayer, William Sydney.

Thayer, William Sydney, 1864-1932
xThayer, William S.
Osler, & Other Papers. Arno.

Thayne, Emma Lou.
xThayne, Emma Lou.
Once in Israel. Brigham.

Theal, George M. see Theal, George Mccall.

Theal, George Mccall, 1837-1919
xTheal, George M.
History of South Africa Under the
Administration of the Dutch East India
Company, 1652-1795. Negro U Pr.

The Art Institute of Chicago. see Chicago Art Institute.

Thebaud, Francois.
xThebaud, Francois.
Pele. Har-Row.

Thebaud, Jo.
xThebaud, Jo.
Less Than Angels. St Marys.

Theberge, James D. see Theberge, James Daniel.

Theberge, James Daniel.
xTheberge, James D.
The Soviet Presence in Latin America.
Crane-Russak Co.

Theberge, Leonard. see Theberge, Leonard J.

Theberge, Leonard J.
xTheberge, Leonard.
ed. The Judiciary in a Democratic Society.
Lexington Bks.

The Better Business Bureau. see Better Business Bureau of
Western New York, Inc.

The British Council. see Great Britain. British Council.

The British Sulphur Corp. Ltd. see British Sulphur
Corporation, Ltd.

The Center for Compliance Information. see Aspen
Systems Corporation. Center for Compliance
Information.

The Child Study Association. see Child Study Association
of America. Children's Book Committee.

The Child Study Association of America. see Child Study
Association of America. Children'S Book Committee.

The Corning Museum of Glass. see Corning, N.Y.
Museum of Glass.

The Department of Paintings in the Rijkmuseum. see
Amsterdam. Rijks-Museum.

The Editors of Gun Digest. see The Gun Digest.

The Editors of Time-Life Books. see Time-Life Books.

The Engineering Staff of Texas Instruments. see Texas
Instruments Incorporated.

The Fourth International Conference on the Origin of
Life, 1973, Invited Papers & Contributed Papers. see
International Conference on the Origin of Life, 4th,
Barcelona, 1973.

The Gordons. see Gordons, The.

The Hammond Staff. see Hammond (C. S.) and Company,
Inc.

The Howard W. Sams Engineering Staff. see Sams
(Howard W.) and Company, Inc., Indianapolis.
Engineering Staff.

Theil, H. see Theil, Henri.

Theil, Henri.
xTheil, H.
Applied Economic Forecasting. Elsevier.
System-Wide Explorations in International
Economics, Input-Output Analysis, &
Marketing Research. Elsevier.
xTheil, Henri.
Introduction to Econometrics. P-H.
Operations Research & Quantitative

Economics: An Elementary Introduction.
McGraw.
Principles of Econometrics. Wiley.
The System-Wide Approach to
Microeconomics. U of Chicago Pr.

Theilen, Gordon H.
xTheilen, Gordon H.
ed. Veterinary Cancer Medicine. Lea &
Febiger.

Theiler, K. see Theiler, Karl.

Theiler, Karl.
xTheiler, K.
The House Mouse: Development & Normal
Stages from Fertilization to 4 Weeks of Age.
Springer-Verlag.

Theiler, Max.
xTheiler, Max.
The Arthropod-Borne Viruses of Vertebrates:
An Account of the Rockefeller Foundation
Virus Program, 1951-1970. Yale U Pr.

The Institute of Graphic Designers. see Institute of
Graphic Designers, San Francisco.

Theis, Dan.
xTheis, Dan.
The Education of Steven Bell. Raintree Pubs.
xTheis, Daniel.
The Crescent & the Cross: The Early Crusades.
Elsevier-Nelson.

Theis, Daniel. see Theis, Dan.

Theisen, R. see Theisen, Roger.

Theisen, Roger.
xTheisen, R.
Quantitative Electron Microprobe Analysis.
Springer-Verlag.

Theisen, William W. see Theisen, William Walter.

Theisen, William Walter, 1886-
xTheisen, William W.
City Superintendent & the Board of Education.
AMS Pr.

Theissen, Gerd.
xTheissen, Gerd.
A Critical Faith: A Case for Religion. Fortress.
Sociology of Early Palestinian Christianity.
Fortress.

Thelen, Herbert A. see Thelen, Herbert Arnold.

Thelen, Herbert Arnold, 1913-
xThelen, Herbert A.
Classroom Grouping for Teachability. Krieger.
Dynamics of Groups at Work. U of Chicago
Pr.
Education & the Human Quest. U of Chicago
Pr.

Thelen, Judith.
xThelen, Judith.
Improving Reading in Science. Intl Reading.

The Library of Congress. see United States. Library of
Congress.

The Library of Congress & the Research Libraries of the
New York Public Library. see United States. Library
of Congress.

The Library of Congress & University of Texas Library

(Austin). see United States. Library of Congress.

Thelin, John R., 1947-
xThelin, John R.
The Cultivation of Ivy: A Saga of the College
in America. Schenkman.

Thelning, K. see Thelning, Karl-Erik.

Thelning, Karl-Erik, 1920-
xThelning, K.
Steel & Its Heat Treatment: Bofors Handbook.
Butterworths.

The London Times. see The Times, London.

Thelwell, Norman, 1923-
xThelwell, Norman.
illus. Leg at Each Corner: Thelwell's Complete
Guide to Equitation. Dutton.
Penelope. Dutton.
A Plank Bridge by a Pool. Scribner.
Thelwell Goes West. Dutton.
illus. Thelwell's Riding Academy. Dutton.

Themal, Joachim.
xThemal, Joachim.
A Contemporary Approach to Art Teaching.
Van Nos Reinhold.

The Metropolitan Museum of Art. see New York (City).
Metropolitan Museum of Art.

The Michie Co. see Michie Company, Charlottesville, Va.

The National Cash Register Company. see National Cash
Register Company, Dayton, Ohio.

The National Computing Centre Ltd. see National
Computing Centre Limited.

The New York Botanical Garden Library. see New York
(City). Botanical Garden. Library.

The New York Times. see New York Times   The

The New York Times Co. see New York Times
Company.

The New Yorker Magazine. see New Yorker The

Theng, B. K. see Theng, B. K. G.

Theng, B. K. G.
xTheng, B. K.
Formation & Properties of Clay-Polymer
Complexes. Elsevier.
xTheng, Benny K.
The Chemistry of Clay-Organic Reactions.
Halsted Pr.

Theng, Benny K. see Theng, B. K. G.

The Norwegian American Historical Association. see
Norwegian-American Historical Association.

Theobald, John.
xTheobald, John.
Wells Fargo in Arizona Territory. AZ Hist
Foun.

Theobald, Robert.
xTheobald, Robert.
An Alternative Future for America's Third
Century. Swallow.

Theobald, William F.
xTheobald, William F.

Evaluation of Recreation & Park Programs.
Wiley.

Theocaris, P. S. see Theocaris, Pericles S.

Theocaris, Pericles S.
xTheocaris, P. S.
Matrix Theory of Photoelasticity.
Springer-Verlag.

Theocritus.
xTheocritus.
Idylls of Theocritus. Arno.

Theodoracopulos, Taki, 1937-
xTheodoracopulos, Taki.
The Greek Upheaval: Kings, Demagogues &
Bayonets. Caratzas Bros.

Theodore, Louis.
xTheodore, Louis.
Industrial Air Pollution Control Equipment for
Particulates. CRC Pr.

Theodorson, George A.
xTheodorson, George A.
Modern Dictionary of Sociology. T Y Crowell.

Theoharis, Athan. see Theoharis, Athan G.

Theoharis, Athan G.
xTheoharis, Athan.
ed. The Truman Presidency: The Origins of the
Imperial Presidency & the National Security
State. E M Coleman Ent.

Theoharous, Anne.
xTheoharous, Anne.
Cooking & Baking the Greek Way. HR&W.

The Olyslager Organization. see Olyslager Organisation.

Theophilus.
xTheophilus.
On Divers Arts: The Foremost Medieval
Treatise on Painting, Glassmaking, &
Metalwork. Dover.

Theosophical Research Centre, London. see Theosophical
Research Centre. Medical Group.

Theosophical Research Centre. Medical Group.
xTheosophical Research Centre, London.
Mystery of Healing. Theos Pub Hse.

The Phillips Collection. see Phillips Collection,
Washington, D.C.

The Piscatagua Gardening Club. see Piscataqua Garden
Club.

The Princeton Center for Infancy. see Princeton Center
for Infancy and Early Childhood.

The Reading Laboratory. see Reading Laboratory, Inc.

The Research Libraries of New York Public Library. see
New York (City). Public Library. Research Libraries.

The Research Libraries of the New York Public Library.
see New York (City). Public Library. Research
Libraries.

Thermal Expansion Symposium, Corning, N.Y., 1971.
xAIP Conference, Corning, N.Y., 1971.
Thermal Expansion 1971: Proceedings. Am
Inst Physics.

Thernstrom, Stephan.
xThernstrom, Stephan.
The Other Bostonians: Poverty & Progress in
the American Metropolis, 1880-1970.
Harvard U Pr.
Poverty & Progress: Social Mobility in a
Nineteenth Century City. Atheneum.
Poverty & Progress: Social Mobility in a
Nineteenth Century City. Harvard U Pr.

The Rockefeller University & State University of New
York, Nov. 26-27, 1965. see Rockefeller University,
New York.

Theroux, Paul.
xTheroux, Paul.
The Family Arsenal. Ballantine.
The Family Arsenal. HM.
The Great Railway Bazaar: By Train Through
Asia. HM.
The Old Patagonian Express: By Train
Through the Americas. HM.

Theroux, Rosemary. see Theroux, Rosemary T.

Theroux, Rosemary T.
xTheroux, Rosemary.
The Care of Twin Children: A Common-Sense
Guide for Parents. Ctr Multiple Gestation.

The Royal College of Physicians. see Royal College of
Physicians of London.

Therrien, Vincent.
xTherrien, Vincent.
Reaching Out: Together, Through the Holy
Spirit. Exposition.

Thesen, Arne.
xThesen, Arne.
ed. Computer Methods in Operations Research.
Acad Pr.

The Source Collective. see Source Inc.

The Summer Institute in Theoretical Physics, Mexico
City, 1973. see Summer Institute in Theoretical
Physics, Centro De Investigacion y De Estudios
Avanzados Del Ipn, 1973.

The Technical Staff of the Machinability Data Center. see
Machinability Data Center.

The Territorial Bureau of Immigration. see New Mexico
(Ter.). Bureau of Immigration.

The Twentieth Century Fund Task Force Report for a
National News Council. see Twentieth Century Fund.

The Universal House of Justice Staff. see Universal House
of Justice.

Theus, Will. see Theus, Will H.

Theus, Will H.
xTheus, Will.
How to Detect & Collect Antique Porcelain &
Pottery. Knopf.

Thevenin. see Thevenin, Rene.

Thevenin, Rene, 1877-
xThevenin.
Animal Migration. Walker & Co.

The Walters Art Gallery. see Walters Art Gallery,
Baltimore.

Thiagarajan, Sivasailam.
xThiagarajan, Sivasailam.
Experiential Learning Packages. Educ Tech
Pubns.
Grouprograms. Educ Tech Pubns.
Instructional Simulation Games. Educ Tech
Pubns.
Protocol Packages. Educ Tech Pubns.
Tutoraids. Educ Tech Pubns.

Thiam, Doudou.
xThiam, Doudou.

The Foreign Policy of African States:
Ideological Bases, Present Realities, Future
Prospects. Greenwood.

Thias, Hans H.
xThias, Hans H.
Cost-Benefit Analysis in Education: A Case
Study of Kenya. Johns Hopkins.

Thibeault, Donald W.
xThibeault, Donald W.
Neonatal Pulmonary Care. A-W.

Thibodeau, Lynn.
xThibodeau, Lynn.
ed. Remember, Remember. Carillon Bks.

Thie, Paul R., 1938-
xThie, Paul R.
An Introduction to Linear Programming &
Game Theory. Wiley.

Thiele, Colin.
xThiele, Colin.
February Dragon. Har-Row.
Fire in the Stone. Har-Row.
The Hammerhead Light. Har-Row.
Storm Boy. Har-Row.

Thiele, Edwin R. see Thiele, Edwin Richard.

Thiele, Edwin Richard, 1895-
xThiele, Edwin R.
A Chronology of the Hebrew Kings.
Zondervan.

Thielsch, Helmut.
xThielsch, Helmut.
Defects & Failures in Pressure Vessels &
Piping. Krieger.

Thier, Herbert D.
xThier, Herbert D.
Teaching Elementary School Science: A
Laboratory Approach. Heath.

Thierauf, Robert J.
xThierauf, Robert J.
Decision Making Through Operations
Research. Wiley.
Distributed Processing Systems. P-H.
Management Auditing: A Questionnaire
Approach. Am Mgmt.
Systems Analysis & Design of Real-Time
Management Information Systems. P-H.

Thierens, A. E.
xThierens, A. E.
Astrology & the Tarot. Borgo Pr.
Astrology & the Tarot. Newcastle Pub.

Thiers, Adolphe, 1797-1877
xThiers, Louis A.
The History of the French Revolution. Arno.

Thiers, Harry. see Thiers, Harry Delbert.

Thiers, Harry Delbert, 1919-
xThiers, Harry.
California Mushrooms: A Field Guide to the
Boletes. Hafner.

Thiers, Louis A. see Thiers, Adolphe.

Thiessen, Del. see Thiessen, Delbert D.

Thiessen, Delbert D.
xThiessen, Del.
The Gerbil in Behavioral Investigations:
Mechanisms of Territoriality & Olfactory
Communication. U of Tex Pr.
xThiessen, Delbert D.
The Evolution and Chemistry of Aggression. C
C Thomas.

Thiessen, Frank.
xThiessen, Frank J.
Automotive Principles & Service. Reston.

Thiessen, Frank J. see Thiessen, Frank.

Thiessen, Henry C. see Thiessen, Henry Clarence.

Thiessen, Henry Clarence.
xThiessen, Henry C.
Lectures in Systematic Theology. Eerdmans.

Thiessen, John C. see Thiessen, John Caldwell.

Thiessen, John Caldwell.
xThiessen, John C.

Pastoring the Smaller Church. Zondervan.

Thigpen, Janet.
xThigpen, Janet.
Power Volleyball for Girls & Women. Wm C
Brown.

Thigpen, S. G. see Thigpen, Samuel Grady.

Thigpen, Samuel Grady.
xThigpen, S. G.
Work & Play in Grandpa's Day. Thigpen.

Thiher, Allen, 1941-
xThiher, Allen.
The Cinematic Muse: Critical Studies in the
History of French Cinema. U of Mo Pr.

Thijn, C. J. see Thijn, Cornelis Jacob Pieter.

Thijn, Cornelis Jacob Pieter, 1933-
xThijn, C. J.
Arthrography of the Knee Joint.
Springer-Verlag.

Thimann, Kenneth V. see Thimann, Kenneth Vivian.

Thimann, Kenneth Vivian, 1904-
xThimann, Kenneth V.
Hormone Action in the Whole Life of Plants.
U of Mass Pr.

Thimm, Alfred L.
xThimm, Alfred L.
Business Ideologies in the Reform-Progressive
Era, 1880-1914. U of Ala Pr.

Thimm, Carl A. see Thimm, Carl Albert.

Thimm, Carl Albert.
xThimm, Carl A.
Complete Bibliography of Fencing & Duelling.
Arno.

Thio, Alex.
xThio, Alex.
Deviant Behavior. HM.

Third International Kant Congress. see International Kant
Congress, 3d, University of Rochester, 1970.

Third Paris-Dauphine Conference on Money &
International Monetary Problems, March 28-30, 1974.
see Paris- Dauphine Conference on Money and
International Monetary Problems, 3d, 1974.

Third Symposium, New Orleans, Nov. 26-29, 1972. see
Nasw Professional Symposium of Social Work Practice
and Social Justice, 3d, New Orleans, 1972.

Thirion, Andre, 1907-
xThirion, Andre.
Revolutionaries Without Revolution.
Macmillan.

Thiroux, Jacques P.
xThiroux, Jacques P.
Ethics: Theory and Practice. Glencoe.

Thirsk, H. R. see Thirsk, Harold Reginald.

Thirsk, Harold Reginald.
xThirsk, H. R.
A Guide to the Study of Electrode Kinetics.
Acad Pr.

Thirsk, Joan.
xThirsk, Joan.
The Restoration. Longman.

Thirtieth Annual Meeting of the National Academy of
Arbitrators. see National Academy of Arbitrators.

Thirty-Seventh Annual Scientific Meeting of the
Committee on Problems of Drug Dependence Division
of Medical Sciences, National Research Council. see
National Research Council. Committee on Problems
of Drug Dependence.

This, Leslie E.
xThis, Leslie E.
A Guide to Effective Management: Practical
Applications from Behavioral Science. A-W.
The Small Meeting Planner. Gulf Pub.

Thistlethwaite, Frank.
xThistlethwaite, Frank.
Anglo-American Connection in the Early
Nineteenth Century. Russell.

Thoburn, John T.
xThoburn, John T.

Primary Commodity Exports & Economic
Development: Theory, Evidence, & a Study
of Malaysia. Wiley.

Thody, Philip. *see* Thody, Philip Malcolm Waller.

Thody, Philip Malcolm Waller, 1928-
xThody, Philip.
Huxley: A Biographical Introduction. Scribner.

Thole, Simeon, 1935-
xThole, Simeon.
Behind the Pine Curtain: Portraits of Peter
Prep. Liturgical Pr.

Tholfsen, Trygve. *see* Tholfsen, Trygve R.

Tholfsen, Trygve R.
xTholfsen, Trygve.
Working Class Radicalism in Mid-Victorian
England. Columbia U Pr.

Thollander, Earl.
xThollander, Earl.
jt. auth. Back Roads of Arizona. Northland.
Back Roads of New England. Potter.
Back Roads of Oregon. Potter.

Thom, A. *see* Thom, Alexander.

Thom, Alexander.
xThom, A.
Megalithic Remains in Britain & Brittany.
Oxford U Pr.
xThom, Alexander.
Megalithic Lunar Observatories. Oxford U Pr.
Megalithic Sites in Britain. Oxford U Pr.

Thom, Bruce G.
xThom, Bruce G.
Coastal & Fluvial Landforms: Horry & Marion
Counties, South Carolina. La State U Pr.

Thom, Douglas A. *see* Thom, Douglas Armour.

Thom, Douglas Armour, 1887-1951
xThom, Douglas A.
Everyday Problems of the Everyday Child.
Johnson Repr.

Thom, James A. *see* Thom, James Alexander.

Thom, James Alexander.
xThom, James A.
Spectator Sport. Avon.

Thoma, Helmut.
xThoma, Helmut.
Anorexia Nervosa. Intl Univs Pr.

Thoma, Kurt H. *see* Thoma, Kurt Hermann.

Thoma, Kurt Hermann, 1883-
xThoma, Kurt H.
Oral Surgery. Mosby.

Thoma, R. W. *see* Thoma, Richard W.

Thoma, Richard W.
xThoma, R. W.
ed. Industrial Microbiology. Acad Pr.

Thomae, Betty K. *see* Thomae, Betty Kennedy.

Thomae, Betty Kennedy.
xThomae, Betty K.
Legal Secretary's Desk Book-with Forms. P-H.

Thomae, H. *see* Thomae, Hans.

Thomae, Hans, 1915-
xThomae, H.
ed. Patterns of Aging: Findings from the Bonn
Longitudinal Study of Aging. S Karger.

Thoman, Evelyn B.
xThoman, Evelyn B.
ed. Origins of the Infant's Social
Responsiveness. Halsted Pr.

Thoman, Richard S.
xThoman, Richard S.
The Geography of Economic Activity.
McGraw.
The United States & Canada: Present & Future.
Merrill.

Thomann, Robert V.
xThomann, Robert V.
Systems Analysis & Water Quality
Management. McGraw.

Thomas. *see* Thomas, George Brinton.

Thomas, A. F. *see* Thomas, Alan Francis.

Thomas, A. R. B. *see* Thomas, Andrew Rowland
Benedick.

Thomas, Abraham V. *see* Thomas, Abraham Vazhayil.

Thomas, Abraham Vazhayil, 1934-
xThomas, Abraham V.
Christians in Secular India. Fairleigh
Dickinson.

Thomas, Alan Francis.
xThomas, A. F.
Calculational Methods of Interacting Arrays of
Fissile Material. Pergamon.

Thomas, Alexander, 1914-
xThomas, Alexander.
Behavioral Individuality in Early Childhood.
Greenwood.
Dynamics of Psychological Development.
Brunner-Mazel.
Racism & Psychiatry. Brunner-Mazel.
Racism & Psychiatry. Citadel Pr.

Thomas, Andrew Rowland Benedick.
xThomas, A. R. B.
Chess Techniques. Routledge & Kegan.

Thomas, Ann (Van Wynen).

xThomas, Ann V.

The Concept of Aggression in International
Law. SMU Press.

Legal Limits on the Use of Chemical &
Biological Weapons. SMU Press.

Non-Intervention: The Law & Its Import in the
Americas. SMU Press.

Thomas, Ann V. *see* Thomas, Ann (Van Wynen).

Thomas, Anna.
xThomas, Anna.
The Vegetarian Epicure. Knopf.
The Vegetarian Epicure. Random.

Thomas, Anthony.
xThomas, Anthony.
Things We Touch. Watts.

Thomas Aquinas, Saint.
xThomas Aquinas.
Commentary on the Posterior Analytics of
Aristotle. Magi Bks.

Thomas, Art, 1952-
xThomas, Art.
photos by Bicycling Is for Me. Lerner Pubns.
photos by Wrestling Is for Me. Lerner Pubns.

Thomas, Arthur L. *see* Thomas, Arthur Lawrence.

Thomas, Arthur Lawrence.
xThomas, Arthur L.
Financial Accounting: The Main Ideas.
Wadsworth Pub.

Thomas, B. J.
xThomas, B. J.
Home Where I Belong. Word Bks.

Thomas, Benjamin P. *see* Thomas, Benjamin Platt.

Thomas, Benjamin Platt, 1902-1956
xThomas, Benjamin P.
Abraham Lincoln: A Biography. Modern Lib.
Theodore Weld, Crusader for Freedom.
Octagon.

Thomas, Bill, 1934-
xThomas, Bill.
American Rivers: A Natural History. Norton.
Eastern Trips & Trails. Stackpole.
Natural Washington. HR&W.
The Swamp. Norton.

Thomas, Bob, 1922-
xThomas, Bob.

Bud and Lou: The Abbott & Costello Story.
Lippincott.
The One & Only Bing. Ace Bks.
Walt Disney: An American Original. S&S.

Thomas, Brian, 1912-
xThomas, Brian.
Geometry in Pictorial Composition. Routledge
& Kegan.

Thomas, C. G. *see* Thomas, Carol G.

Thomas, C. R. *see* Thomas, Claude Ray.

Thomas, Cal.
xThomas, Cal.
A Freedom Dream. Word Bks.

Thomas, Calvin, 1854-1919
xThomas, Calvin.
A History of German Literature. Gordon Pr.
History of German Literature. Kennikat.
A History of German Literature. Norwood
Edns.
Life & Works of Friedrich Schiller. AMS Pr.
Life & Works of Friedrich Schiller. R West.

Thomas, Carol G., 1938-
xThomas, C. G.
Homer's History: Mycenaean or Dark Age.
Peter Smith.
xThomas, Carol G.
ed. Homer's History: Mycenaean or Dark
Age?. Krieger.

Thomas, Champ.
xThomas, Champ.
How to Create a Super Boxer. Exposition.

Thomas, Charles L. *see* Thomas, Charles la Mar.

Thomas, Charles la Mar, 1905-
xThomas, Charles L.
Catalytic Processes & Proven Catalysts. Acad
Pr.

Thomas, Charles M. *see* Thomas, Charles Marion.

Thomas, Charles Marion, 1902-
xThomas, Charles M.
American Neutrality in 1793: A Study in
Cabinet Government. AMS Pr.

Thomas, Charles W. *see* Thomas, Charles Wellington.

Thomas, Charles Wellington.
xThomas, Charles W.
Prison Organization & Inmate Subcultures.
Bobbs.

Thomas, Clara.
xThomas, Clara.
Love & Work Enough: The Life of Anna
Jameson. U of Toronto Pr.

Thomas, Claude Ray.
xThomas, C. R.
Communities of the Mountain West: Early
Histories & Name Origins of Approximately
200 Western Cities & Towns. Vantage.

Thomas, Clive.
xThomas, Clive.
Soccer Referee: A Guide to Fitness &
Technique. Biblio Dist.

Thomas, Clive Y. *see* Thomas, Clive Yolande.

Thomas, Clive Yolande.
xThomas, Clive Y.
Dependence & Transformation: The Economics
of the Transition to Socialism. Monthly Rev.

Thomas, Craig.
xThomas, Craig.
Firefox. Bantam.
Firefox. G K Hall.
Firefox. HR&W.
Snow Falcon. HR&W.

Thomas, D. Babatunde.
xThomas, D. Babatunde.

Importing Technology into Africa: Foreign
Investment and the Supply of Technological
Innovations. Praeger.
ed. Integration of Science and Technology with
Development: Caribbean and Latin American
Problems in the Context of the United
Nations Conference on Science and
Technology for Development. Pergamon.
Thomas, D. T. *see* Thomas, David T.
Thomas, Darwin L.
xThomas, Darwin L.
Family Socialization & the Adolescent:
Determinants of Self Concept, Religiousity,
Conformity & Countercultural Values.
Lexington Bks.
Thomas, David, 1813-1894
xThomas, David.
Acts of the Apostles. Kregel.
Gospel of John. Kregel.
The Gospel of Matthew. Kregel.
ed. Underwater Adventure Stories. PB.
Thomas, David D.
xThomas, David D.
Chrau Grammar. U Pr of Hawaii.
Thomas, David H. *see* Thomas, David Hurst.
Thomas, David Hurst.
xThomas, David H.
Archaeology. HR&W.
Thomas, David M.
xThomas, David M.
ed. Christian Reflections on Human Sexuality.
Abbey.
When God Is at Home with Your Family.
Abbey.
Thomas, David M. *see* Thomas, David Michael.
Thomas, David Michael, 1938-
xThomas, David M.
ed. Marital Spirituality. Abbey.
Thomas, David O. *see* Thomas, David Oswald.
Thomas, David Oswald.
xThomas, David O.
The Honest Mind: The Thought & Work of
Richard Price. Oxford U Pr.
Thomas, David S. *see* Thomas, David St. John.
Thomas, David St. John.
xThomas, David S.
Getting Published. Har-Row.
Summer Saturdays in the West. David &
Charles.
xThomas, David St. John.
The Great Way West: The History & Romance
of the Great Western Railway's Route from
Paddington to Penzance. David & Charles.
Thomas, David T.
xThomas, D. T.
Engineering Electromagnetics. Pergamon.
Thomas, David Y. *see* Thomas, David Yancey.
Thomas, David Yancey, 1872-1943
xThomas, David Y.
History of Military Government in Newly
Acquired Territory of the United States.
AMS Pr.
Thomas, Denis.
xThomas, Denis.
The Face of Christ. Doubleday.
Thomas, Dian, 1945-
xThomas, Dian.
Roughing It Easy. Warner Bks.
Roughing It Easy, 2. Warner Bks.
Thomas, Diane.
xThomas, Diane.
The Worldwide Creative Ojo Book. Hunter
Ariz.
Thomas, Donald F.
xThomas, Donald F.
The Deacon in a Changing Church. Judson.
Thomas, Dorothy.
xThomas, Dorothy.

Home Place. U of Nebr Pr.
Thomas, Dylan, 1914-1953

xThomas, Dylan.

Adventures in the Skin Trade & Other Stories.
New Directions.

A Child's Christmas in Wales. Godine.
Child's Christmas in Wales. New Directions.

Collected Poems. New Directions.
The Death of the King's Canary. Penguin.

The Death of the King's Canary. Viking Pr.
Early Prose Writings. New Directions.

Portrait of the Artist As a Young Dog. New
Directions.
Quite Early One Morning. New Directions.

Under Milk Wood: A Play for Voices. New
Directions.

Thomas, E. *see* Thomas, Edward.
Thomas, E. Barrington. *see* Thomas, Edmund Barrington.
Thomas, E. W. *see* Thomas, Edward Wilfrid.
Thomas, Earl W., 1915-
xThomas, Earl W.
A Grammar of Spoken Brazilian Portuguese.
Vanderbilt U Pr.
Syntax of Spoken Brazilian Portuguese.
Vanderbilt U Pr.
Thomas, Ebenezer S. *see* Thomas, Ebenezer Smith.
Thomas, Ebenezer Smith, 1775-1845
xThomas, Ebenezer S.
Reminiscences of the Last Sixty-Five Years.
Arno.
Thomas, Edith.
xThomas, Edith.
Eve & the Others. Continent Edns.
Thomas, Edmund Barrington.
xThomas, E. Barrington.
ed. Papua New Guinea Education. Oxford U
Pr.
Thomas, Edrie.
xThomas, Edrie.
Teaching Music Appreciation Through
Listening Skill Training. P-H.
Thomas, Edward, 1878-1917
xThomas, E.
Maurice Maeterlinck. Haskell.
xThomas, Edward.
Algernon Charles Swinburne: A Critical Study.
Folcroft.
Last Sheaf: Essays. Arno.
Last Sheaf: Essays. Folcroft.
Literary Pilgrim in England. Arno.
Literary Pilgrim in England. Folcroft.
A Literary Pilgrim in England. Oxford U Pr.
Maurice Maeterlinck. Folcroft.
Richard Jefferies. Merrimack Bk Serv.

Thomas, Edward J. *see* Thomas, Edward Joseph.
Thomas, Edward Joseph, 1869-
xThomas, Edward J.
The History of Buddhist Thought. Routledge &
Kegan.
Thomas, Edward Wilfrid, 1940-
xThomas, E. W.
Excitation in Heavy Particle Collisions.
Krieger.
Thomas, Edwin J. *see* Thomas, Edwin John.
Thomas, Edwin John, 1927-
xThomas, Edwin J.
Marital Communication & Decision Making:
Analysis, Assessment, & Change. Free Pr.
Thomas, Elaine.
xThomas, Elaine.
A Grammatical Description of the Engenni
Language. Summer Inst Ling.
Thomas, Elbert D. *see* Thomas, Elbert Duncan.

Thomas, Elbert Duncan, 1883-1953
xThomas, Elbert D.
Chinese Political Thought: A Study Based
Upon the Theories of the Principal Thinkers
of the Chou Period. Greenwood.
Thomas, Ellen L. *see* Thomas, Ellen Lamar.
Thomas, Ellen Lamar.
xThomas, Ellen L.
Improving Reading in Every Class: A
Sourcebook for Teachers. Allyn.
Thomas, Emery.
xThomas, Emery.
Generalized Pontrjagin Cohomology Operations
& Rings with Divided Powers. Am Math.
Thomas, Emory M., 1939-
xThomas, Emory M.
Confederate State of Richmond: A Biography
of the Capital. U of Tex Pr.
Thomas, Erik, 1939-
xThomas, Erik.
The Lebesgue-Nikodym Theorem for Vector
Valued Radon Measures. Am Math.
Thomas, Estelle (Webb).
xThomas, Estelle W.
Gift of Laughter. Westminster.
Thomas, Estelle W. *see* Thomas, Estelle (Webb).
Thomas, Evan W. *see* Thomas, Evan Welling.
Thomas, Evan Welling.
xThomas, Evan W.
Brain-Injured Children: With Special Reference
to Doman-Delacato Methods of Treatment. C
C Thomas.
Thomas, Evelyn A.
xThomas, Evelyn A.
The Ladder up: Life After Retirement. Psych &
Consul Assocs.
Thomas, F. Richard.
xThomas, F. Richard.
Frog Praises Night: Poems with Commentary.
S Ill U Pr.
Thomas, G. *see* Thomas, George Isaiah.
Thomas, Gareth.
xThomas, Gareth.
Transmission Electron Microscopy of
Materials. Wiley.
Thomas, George B. *see* Thomas, George Brinton.
Thomas, George Brinton, 1914-
xThomas.
Infinite Series & Elementary Differential
Equations. A-W.
xThomas, George B.
Calculus. A-W.
Calculus & Analytic Geometry. A-W.
Thomas, George Isaiah.
xThomas, G.
Administrator's Guide to the Year Round
School. P-H.

Thomas, Gilbert Oliver, 1891-
xThomas, Gilbert.
Calm Weather: A Volume of Essays. Arno.
Thomas, Gordon.
xThomas, Gordon.
The Day the Bubble Burst: A Social History of
the Wall Street Crash of 1929. Penguin.
The Day the World Ended. Stein & Day.
Enola Gay. Stein & Day.
Guernica. Ballantine.
Guernica. Stein & Day.
Thomas, Gordon K. *see* Thomas, Gordon Kent.
Thomas, Gordon Kent, 1935-
xThomas, Gordon K.
Wordsworth's Dirge & Promise: Napoleon,
Wellington, & the Convention of Cintra. U of
Nebr Pr.
Thomas Graham Memorial Symposium. *see* Thomas
Graham Memorial Symposium, University of
Strathclyde, 1969.

Thomas Graham Memorial Symposium, University of Strathclyde, 1969.
    xThomas Graham Memorial Symposium.
        Diffusion Processes: Proceedings. Gordon.
Thomas, Graham S. *see* Thomas, Graham Stuart.
Thomas, Graham St. *see* Thomas, Graham Stuart.
Thomas, Graham Stuart.
    xThomas, Graham S.
        The Old Shrub Roses. Biblio Dist.
    xThomas, Graham St.
        The Old Shrub Roses. Biblio Dist.
Thomas Grey Bicentenary Conference, Carleton University, 1971.
    xPapers from the Thomas Gray Bicentenary
        Conference at Carleton University.
        Fearful Joy. McGill-Queens U Pr.
Thomas, Harrison C. *see* Thomas, Harrison Cook.
Thomas, Harrison Cook, 1888-1969
    xThomas, Harrison C.
        Return of the Democratic Party to Power in
            1884. AMS Pr.
Thomas, Harry E. *see* Thomas, Harry Elliot.
Thomas, Harry Elliot, 1902-
    xThomas, Harry E.
        Handbook of Automated Electronic Clinical
            Analysis. Reston.
Thomas, Heather. *see* Thomas, Heather Smith.
Thomas, Heather S. *see* Thomas, Heather Smith.
Thomas, Heather Smith.
    xThomas, Heather.
        Horses. Western Pub.
    xThomas, Heather S.
        The Wild Horse Controversy. A S Barnes.
Thomas, Helen. *see* Thomas, Helen Noble.
Thomas, Helen Noble.
    xThomas, Helen.
        Time & Again: Memoirs & Letters. Parson Dhs.
Thomas, Henry.
    xThomas, Henry.
        Living Adventures in Science. Arno.
Thomas, Henry H.
    xThomas, Henry H.
        The Engineering of Large Dams. Wiley.
Thomas, Hugh. *see* Thomas, Hugh Swynnerton.
Thomas, Hugh Swynnerton, 1931-
    xThomas, Hugh.
        Spanish Civil War. Har-Row.
Thomas, I. D. *see* Thomas, Isaac David Ellis.
Thomas, Ian.
    xThomas, Ian.
        The Dory: Philosophy & Practice. Bailey
            Pubns.
Thomas, Ianthe.
    xThomas, Ianthe.
        Hi, Mrs. Mallory!. Har-Row.
        Lordy, Aunt Hattie. Har-Row.
Thomas, Isaac David Ellis.
    xThomas, I. D.
        ed. The Golden Treasury of Puritan
            Quotations. Moody.
        A Word from the Wise. Moody.
Thomas, J. *see* Thomas, John A.
Thomas, J. A. *see* Thomas, Joseph Anthony Charles.
Thomas, J. Alan. *see* Thomas, James Alan.
Thomas, J. Andre.
    xThomas, J. Andre.
        ed. Organ Culture. Acad Pr.
Thomas, J. B.
    xThomas, J. B.
        Primary Photoprocesses in Biology. Elsevier.
Thomas, J. Moulton. *see* Thomas, James Moulton.
Thomas, J. W. *see* Thomas, John Wesley.
Thomas, James A., 1941-
    xThomas, James A.
        Symbolic Logic. Merrill.
Thomas, James Alan.
    xThomas, J. Alan.

The Productive School: A Systems Analysis
    Approach to Educational Administration.
    Krieger.
Thomas, James B. *see* Thomas, James Blake.
Thomas, James Blake.
    xThomas, James B.
        Introduction to Human Embryology. Lea &
            Febiger.
Thomas, James L.
    xThomas, James L.
        ed. Motivating Children & Young Adults to
            Read. Oryx Pr.
        Turning Kids on to Print Using Nonprint. Libs
            Unl.
Thomas, James Moulton, 1903-
    xThomas, J. Moulton.
        Prayer Power. Word Bks.
Thomas, James W.
    xThomas, James W.
        Finite Mathematics. Allyn.
Thomas, James W. *see* Thomas, James Walter.
Thomas, James Walter.
    xThomas, James W.
        History of Allegany County, Maryland.
            Regional.
Thomas, Joan G. *see* Thomas, Joan Gale.
Thomas, Joan Gale.
    xThomas, Joan G.
        illus. If Jesus Came to My House. Lothrop.
        illus. Where Is God. Lothrop.
Thomas, John, 1900-1932
    xThomas, John.
        Dry Martini: A Gentleman Turns to Love. S Ill
            U Pr.
        Leonardo Da Vinci. S G Phillips.
        The North British Railway. David & Charles.
        North British Railway. Kelley.
Thomas, John A.
    xThomas, J.
        Regulatory Mechanisms Affecting Gonadal
            Hormone Action: Advances in Sex Hormone
            Research. Univ Park.
        Synopsis of Endocrine Pharmacology. Univ
            Park.
Thomas, John B. *see* Thomas, John Bowman.
Thomas, John Bowman, 1925-
    xThomas, John B.
        An Introduction to Applied Probability &
            Random Processes. Krieger.
        Introduction to Statistical Communication
            Theory. Wiley.
Thomas, John C. *see* Thomas, John Carl.
Thomas, John Carl.
    xThomas, John C.
        ed. American & British Pewter: An Historical
            Survey. Universe.
Thomas, John H. *see* Thomas, John Hunter.
Thomas, John Hunter.
    xThomas, John H.
        Flora of the Santa Cruz Mountains of
            California: A Manual of the Vascular Plants.
            Stanford U Pr.
        Native Shrubs of the Sierra Nevada. U of Cal
            Pr.
Thomas, John I.
    xThomas, John I.
        Education for Communism: School & State in
            the People's Republic of Albania. Hoover
            Inst Pr.
Thomas, John W. *see* Thomas, John Wesley.
Thomas, John Wesley.
    xThomas, J. W.
        Intro. by The Legend of Duke Ernst. U of
            Nebr Pr.
    xThomas, John W.
        Medieval German Lyric Verse in English
            Translation. AMS Pr.
Thomas, Joseph A. *see* Thomas, Joseph Anthony Charles.
Thomas, Joseph Anthony Charles.
    xThomas, J. A.

Textbook of Roman Law. Elsevier.
    xThomas, Joseph A.
        Private International Law. Greenwood.
Thomas, Karen.
    xThomas, Karen.
        Good Thing... the Bad Thing. P-H.
Thomas, Kas.
    xThomas, Kas.
        Guide to Homebuilt Rotorcraft. TAB Bks.
Thomas, Kathleen.
    xThomas, Kathleen.
        West Country Cookery. David & Charles.
Thomas, Keith. *see* Thomas, Keith Vivian.
Thomas, Keith Vivian.
    xThomas, Keith.
        Religion & the Decline of Magic. Scribner.
Thomas, Kurt.
    xThomas, Kurt.
        Kurt Thomas on Gymnastics. S&S.
Thomas, L. C. *see* Thomas, Leslie Charles.
Thomas, L. J.
    xThomas, L. J.
        An Introduction to Mining: Exploration,
            Feasibility, Extraction, Rock Mechanics.
            Halsted Pr.
Thomas, Leslie, 1931-
    xThomas, Leslie.
        Bare Nell. St Martin.
        Ormerod's Landing. St Martin.
Thomas, Leslie Charles.
    xThomas, L. C.
        The Identification of Functional Groups in
            Organophosphorus Compounds. Acad Pr.
Thomas, Lewis, 1913-
    xThomas, Lewis.
        The Lives of a Cell: Notes of a Biology
            Watcher. Bantam
        The Lives of a Cell: Notes of a Biology
            Watcher. Penguin.
        Lives of a Cell: Notes of a Biology Watcher.
            Viking Pr.
        The Medusa & the Snail: More Notes of a
            Biology Watcher. Viking Pr.
Thomas, Lewis H. *see* Thomas, Lewis Herbert.
Thomas, Lewis Herbert, 1917-
    xThomas, Lewis H.
        The Renaissance of Canadian History: A
            Biography of A. L. Burt. U of Toronto Pr.
        The Struggle for Responsible Government in
            the North-West Territories 1870-97. U of
            Toronto Pr.
Thomas, Lewis V. *see* Thomas, Lewis Victor.
Thomas, Lewis Victor, 1914-1965
    xThomas, Lewis V.
        A Study of Naima. NYU Pr.
Thomas, Linda.
    xThomas, Linda.
        Meet the Centers. Creative Ed.
        Meet the Goalies. Creative Ed.
        Muhammad Ali. Creative Ed.
Thomas, Lindon. *see* Thomas, Lindon C.
Thomas, Lindon C., 1941-
    xThomas, Lindon.
        Fundamentals of Heat Transfer. P-H.
Thomas, Lloyd B. *see* Thomas, Lloyd Brewster.
Thomas, Lloyd Brewster, 1941-
    xThomas, Lloyd B.
        Money, Banking & Economic Activity. P-H.
Thomas, Lorenzo, 1944-
    xThomas, Lorenzo.
        Chances Are Few. Blue Wind.
Thomas, Lowell. *see* Thomas, Lowell Jackson.
Thomas, Lowell J. *see* Thomas, Lowell Jackson.
Thomas, Lowell Jackson, 1892-
    xThomas, Lowell.
        Good Evening Everybody: From Cripple Creek
            to Samarkand. Morrow.
        The Silent War in Tibet. Greenwood.
    xThomas, Lowell J.

These Men Shall Never Die. Arno.

Thomas, M. Donald.
xThomas, M. Donald.
Performance Evaluation of Educational
Personnel. Phi Delta Kappa.

Thomas, Marcel, 1917-
xThomas, Marcel.
The Golden Age: Manuscript Painting at the
Time of Jean, Duke of Berry. Braziller.

Thomas, Marlo.
xThomas, Marlo.
Free to Be . . . You & Me. McGraw.

Thomas, Mary. *see* Thomas, Mary (Hedger).

Thomas, Mary (Hedger), 1889-
xThomas, Mary.
Mary Thomas's Knitting Book. Peter Smith.
Mary Thomas's Knitting Book. Dover.

Thomas, Mary E. *see* Thomas, Mary Edith.

Thomas, Mary Edith.
xThomas, Mary.
Medieval Skepticism & Chaucer. William-F.
xThomas, Mary E.
Medieval Skepticism & Chaucer. Cooper Sq.

Thomas, Mary M. *see* Thomas, Mary Martha Hosford.

Thomas, Mary Martha Hosford.
xThomas, Mary M.
Southern Methodist University: Founding &
Early Years. SMU Press.

Thomas, Meirion.
xThomas, Meirion.
Aids to Postgraduate Surgery. Churchill.

Thomas, Merlin.
xThomas, Merlin.
Louis-Ferdinand Celine. New Directions.

Thomas, Michael F. *see* Thomas, Michael Frederic.

Thomas, Michael Frederic.
xThomas, Michael F.
Tropical Geomorphology: A Study of
Weathering & Land-Form Development in
Warm Climates. Halsted Pr.

Thomas, Minor W. *see* Thomas, Minor Wine.

Thomas, Minor Wine, 1890-1966
xThomas, Minor W.
Public School Plumbing Equipment. AMS Pr.

Thomas, Nigel.
xThomas, Nigel.
The French Foreign Legion. St Martin.

Thomas, Norman. *see* Thomas, Norman Mattoon.

Thomas, Norman C.
xThomas, Norman C.
Congress: Politics & Practice. Phila Bk Co.
Frwd. by & ed. The Institutionalized
Presidency. Oceana.

Thomas, Norman M. *see* Thomas, Norman Mattoon.

Thomas, Norman Mattoon, 1884-
xThomas, Norman.
Great Dissenters. Norton.
Socialist's Faith. Kennikat.
xThomas, Norman M.
The Prerequisites for Peace. Greenwood.

Thomas, P. D. *see* Thomas, Peter David Garner.

Thomas, P. G. *see* Thomas, Percy Goronwy.

Thomas, Paul G., 1928-
xThomas, Paul G.
Psychofeedback. P-H.

Thomas, Paul I.
xThomas, Paul I.
How to Estimate Building Losses &
Construction Costs. P-H.
xThomas, Paul J.
How to Estimate Building Losses &
Construction Costs. P-H.

Thomas, Paul J. *see* Thomas, Paul I.

Thomas, Payne E. *see* Thomas, Payne Edward Lloyd.

Thomas, Payne Edward Lloyd, 1919-
xThomas, Payne E.
Guide for Authors: Manuscript, Proof &
Illustration. C C Thomas.

Thomas, Percy G. *see* Thomas, Percy Goronwy.

Thomas, Percy Goronwy, 1875-
xThomas, P. G.
Aspects of Literary Theory & Practice,
1550-1870. Kennikat.
English Literature Before Chaucer. R West.
xThomas, Percy G.
Aspects of Literary Theory & Practice
1550-1870. Folcroft.
English Literature Before Chaucer. Folcroft.

Thomas, Peter David Garner.
xThomas, P. D.
British Politics & the Stamp Act Crisis: The
First Phase of the American Revolution
1763-1767. Oxford U Pr.

Thomas, Piri, 1928-
xThomas, Piri.
Down These Mean Streets. Knopf.
Down These Mean Streets. Random.
Stories from El Barrio. Knopf.
Stories from El Barrio. Avon.

Thomas, R. Murray. *see* Thomas, Robert Murray.

Thomas, R. T.
xThomas, R. T.
Britain & Vichy: The Dilemma of
Anglo-French Relations, 1940-42. St Martin.

Thomas, Ralph H., 1929-
xThomas, Ralph H.
Ultrasonics in Packaging & Plastics Fabrication.
CBI Pub.

Thomas, Reuen, 1840-1907
xThomas, Reuen.
Leaders of Thought in the Modern Church.
Arno.

Thomas, Richard, 1951-
xThomas, Richard.
In the Moment. Avon.

Thomas, Robert Louis, 1914-1952
xThomas.
A Manual of Time Study for Supervisors.
Columbia Graphs.

Thomas, Robert Murray.
xThomas, R. Murray.
Comparing Theories of Child Development.
Wadsworth Pub.
Decisions in Teaching Elementary Social
Studies. Wadsworth Pub.

Thomas, Robert P. *see* Thomas, Robert Paul.

Thomas, Robert Paul.
xThomas, Robert P.
An Analysis of the Pattern of Growth of the
Automobile Industry: 1895-1929. Arno.

Thomas, Rosamund. *see* Thomas, Rosamund M.

Thomas, Rosamund M.
xThomas, Rosamund.
The British Philosophy of Administration: A
Comparison of British & American Ideas
1900-1939. Longman.

Thomas, Rose F. *see* Thomas, Rose Fay.

Thomas, Rose Fay, 1852-1929
xThomas, Rose F.
Memoirs of Theodore Thomas. Arno.

Thomas, Ross, 1926-
xThomas, Ross.
The Backup Men. PB.
The Eighth Dwarf. Avon.
Eighth Dwarf. S&S.
If You Can't Be Good. PB.

Thomas, Roy. *see* Thomas, Roy Edwin.

Thomas, Roy Edwin.
xThomas, Roy.
ed. Insurance Information Sources. Gale.

Thomas, Ryan.
xThomas, Ryan.
Getting Real: Poems After est. Images Pr.

Thomas, S B.
xThomas, S. B.
Government & Administration in Communist
China. Greenwood.

Thomas, Sarah M.
xThomas, Sarah M.
A Guide to Sources of Consumer Information.
Info Resources.

Thomas, Sherry.
xThomas, Sherry.
Country Women: A Handbook for the New
Farmer. Doubleday.

Thomas, Sidney, 1915-
xThomas, Sidney.
ed. Images of Man: Selected Readings in Arts
& Ideas in Western Civilization. Irvington.

Thomas, Sidney. *see* Thomas, Sidney R.

Thomas, Sidney R.
xThomas, Sidney.
Styles for English Language: Developing
Techniques in Prose, Drama & Verse.
Sterling.

Thomas, Steve. *see* Thomas, Steven.

Thomas, Steven.
xThomas, Steve.
Backyard Livestock: How to Grow Meat for
Your Family. Scribner.
xThomas, Steven.
Backyard Livestock: How to Grow Meat for
Your Family. Countryman.

Thomas, T. P. *see* Thomas, Thaddeus Peter.

Thomas, Terry. *see* Thomas, Terry C.

Thomas, Terry C.
xThomas, Terry.
At Least We Were Married. Zondervan.

Thomas, Thaddeus P. *see* Thomas, Thaddeus Peter.

Thomas, Thaddeus Peter, 1867-1936
xThomas, T. P.
The City Government of Baltimore. Johnson
Repr.
xThomas, Thaddeus P.
The City Government of Baltimore. AMS Pr.

Thomas, Tony, 1927-
xThomas, Tony.
The Films of Marlon Brando. Citadel Pr.
The Films of the Forties. Citadel Pr.
The Great Adventure Films. Citadel Pr.
The Great Adventure Films. Lyle Stuart.
Music for the Movies. A S Barnes.

Thomas, Trace Yerkes, 1899-
xThomas, Tracy Y.
Concepts from Tensor Analysis & Differential
Geometry. Acad Pr.

Thomas, Tracy Y. *see* Thomas, Trace Yerkes.

Thomas, Tracy Yerkes, 1899-
xThomas, Tracy Y.
Plastic Flow & Fracture in Solids. Acad Pr.

Thomas, Virginia C. *see* Thomas, Virginia Castleton.

Thomas, Virginia Castleton.
xThomas, Virginia C.
Look Younger, Look Prettier: Beauty Through
Diet & Yoga Techniques. Rodale Pr Inc.

Thomas, W. A. *see* Thomas, William Arthur.

Thomas, W. Hugh. *see* Thomas, Walter Hugh.

Thomas, Walter Hugh.
xThomas, W. Hugh.
The Murder of Rudolf Hess. Har-Row.

Thomas, Walter R.
xThomas, Walter R.
From a Small Naval Observatory. Arno.

Thomas, Wayne. *see* Thomas, Wayne H.

Thomas, Wayne H.
xThomas, Wayne.
Bail Reform in America. U of Cal Pr.

Thomas, William, 1906 (apr. 14)-
xThomas, William.
Country in the Boy. Elsevier-Nelson.
History of Italy (1549). Folger Bks.

Thomas, William A.
xThomas, William A.
Overcoming Legal Uncertainties About Use of
Solar Energy Systems. Am Bar Foun.

Thomas, William Arthur.
xThomas, W. A.

The Finance of British Industry, 1918-1976.
Methuen Inc.
Provincial Stock Exchanges. Biblio Dist.
Thomas, William B. see Thomas, William Beach.
Thomas, William Beach, Sir, 1868-1957
xThomas, William B.
The Story of the Spectator, 1828-1928. Arno.
Thomas, William C., 1919-
xThomas, William C.
Renal Calculi: A Guide to Management. C C
Thomas.
Thomas, William E.
xThomas, William E.
The New Boy Is Blind. Messner.
So You Want to Be a Dancer. Messner.
Thomas, William I. see Thomas, William Isaac.
Thomas, William Isaac, 1863-1947
xThomas, William I.
The Unadjusted Girl: With Cases & Standpoint
for Behavior Analysis. Gannon.
Thomas, Z. V., Mrs
xThomas, Z. V.
History of Jefferson County. Reprint.
Thomas a Kempis, 1380-1471
xThomas a Kempis.
Imitation of Christ. Collins Pubs.
The Imitation of Christ. Doubleday.
Imitation of Christ. Doubleday.
Imitation of Christ. Glencoe.
Imitation of Christ. Moody.
The Imitation of Christ. Our Sunday Visitor.
Imitation of Christ. Penguin.
The Imitation of Christ. Templegate.
Of the Imitation of Christ. Keats.
Thomasen, Suzi.
xThomasen, Suzi.
A Faraway Whistle. Solo Pr.
Thomason, James C.
xThomason, James C.
Common Sense About Your Family Dollars.
Victor Bks.
Thomason, Richmond H.
xThomason, Richmond H.
Symbolic Logic: An Introduction. Macmillan.
Thomason, W. O. see Thomason, William O.
Thomason, William O.
xThomason, W. O.
The Life Givers. Broadman.
Thomen, Harold O. see Thomen, Harold Ordell.
Thomen, Harold Ordell.
xThomen, Harold O.
Compiled by Supplement to the Index of
Congressional Committee Hearings Prior to
January 3, 1935. Greenwood.
Thomis, Malcolm I.
xThomis, Malcolm I.
Politics & Society in Nottingham 1785-1835.
Kelley.
Responses to Industrialisation: The British
Experience, 1780-1850. Shoe String.
Thomison, Dennis, 1937-
xThomison, Dennis.
ed. Readings About Adolescent Literature.
Scarecrow.
Thomlinson, Ralph.
xThomlinson, Ralph.
Population Dynamics: Causes & Consequences
of World Demographic Change. Random.
Sociological Concepts & Research: Acquisition,
Analysis & Interpretation of Social
Information. Random.
Thomopoulos, N. see Thomopoulos, Nicholas T.
Thomopoulos, Nicholas T.
xThomopoulos, N.
Applied Forecasting Methods. P-H.
Thompson, Sir Edward Maunde, 1840-1929
xThompson, E. M.
Handbook of Greek & Latin Palaeography.
Ares.
Thompson. see Thompson, Laurence G.

Thompson , Silvanus P. see Thompson, Silvanus Phillips.
Thompson, A. see Thompson, Arthur A.
Thompson, A. Hamilton. see Thompson, Alexander
Hamilton.
Thompson, Alan R. see Thompson, Alan Reynolds.
Thompson, Alan Reynolds, 1897-
xThompson, Alan R.
Anatomy of Drama. Arno.
Thompson, Alexander Hamilton, 1873-1952
xThompson, A. Hamilton.
English Monasteries. Folcroft.
Thompson, Allan.
xThompson, Allan.
The Dynamics of the Industrial Revolution. St
Martin.
Thompson, Andrew D.
xThompson, Andrew D.
When Your Child Learns to Choose. Abbey.
Thompson, Ann, 1941-
xThompson, Ann.
The Organic Baby Food Book. Trident.
Thompson, Anne A. see Thompson, Anne Armstrong.
Thompson, Anne Armstrong.
xThompson, Anne A.
The Romanov Ransom. BJ Pub Group.
The Romanov Ransom. S&S.
Thompson, Arthur A., 1940-
xThompson, A.
Economics of the Firm: Theory & Practice.
P-H.
xThompson, Arthur A.
Economics of the Firm: Theory & Practice.
P-H.
Strategy Formulation & Implementation: Tasks
of the General Manager. Business Pubns.
Thompson, Arthur W. see Thompson, Arthur William.
Thompson, Arthur William.
xThompson, Arthur W.
The Uncertain Crusade: America & the Russian
Revolution of 1905. U of Mass Pr.
Thompson, B. W.
xThompson, B. W.
Africa: The Climatic Background. Oxford U Pr.
Thompson, Bard, 1925-
xThompson, Bard.
Liturgies of the Western Church. Collins Pubs.
ed. Liturgies of the Western Church. Fortress.
Thompson, Ben.
xThompson, Ben.
Outlaw Trail. Nordon Pubns.
Ride to Hell. Belmont-Tower.
Texas Hellion. Belmont-Tower.
Thompson, Brenda.
xThompson, Brenda.
Animal Attackers. Lerner Pubns.
The Children's Crusade. Lerner Pubns.
Famous Planes. Lerner Pubns.
Flags. Lerner Pubns.
Gold & Jewels. Lerner Pubns.
The Great Wall of China. Lerner Pubns.
Monkeys and Apes. Lerner Pubns.
Pirates. Lerner Pubns.
Spaceship Earth. Lerner Pubns.
The Story of Steel. Lerner Pubns.
Under the Sea. Lerner Pubns.
Thompson, Bruce. see Thompson, Bruce S.
Thompson, Bruce S.
xThompson, Bruce.
Syrup Trees. Walnut AZ.
Thompson, C. J. see Thompson, Charles John Samuel.
Thompson, Carey C.
xThompson, Carey C.
ed. Institutional Adjustment: A Challenge to a
Changing Economy. U of Tex Pr.
Thompson, Charles H. see Thompson, Charles Herbert.
Thompson, Charles Herbert.
xThompson, Charles H.
Fundamentals of Pipe Drafting. Wiley.
Thompson, Charles John Samuel, 1862-1943
xThompson, C. J.

Love, Marriage & Romance in Old London.
Gale.
Quacks of Old London. Gale.
Thompson, Charles L. see Thompson, Charles Lowell.
Thompson, Charles Lowell.
xThompson, Charles L.
Guidance Activities for Counselors & Teachers.
Brooks-Cole.
Thompson, Charles W. see Thompson, Charles Willis.
Thompson, Charles Willis, 1871-1946
xThompson, Charles W.
Presidents I've Known & Two Near Presidents.
Arno.
Thompson, D. see Thompson, Denys.
Thompson, D. L. see Thompson, Donald L.
Thompson, Daniel C. see Thompson, Daniel Calbert.
Thompson, Daniel Calbert.
xThompson, Daniel C.
Private Black Colleges at the Crossroads.
Greenwood.
Sociology of the Black Experience. Greenwood.
Thompson, David, 1938-
xThompson, David.
Dante's Epic Journeys. Johns Hopkins.
xThompson, David B.
ed. Idea of Rome: From Antiquity to the
Renaissance. U of NM Pr.
Thompson, David B. see Thompson, David.
Thompson, David M. see Thompson, David Michael.
Thompson, David Michael.
xThompson, David M.
ed. Nonconformity in the Nineteenth Century.
Routledge & Kegan.
Thompson, Dennis. see Thompson, Dennis L.
Thompson, Dennis L.
xThompson, Dennis.
Politics, Policy & Natural Resources. Free Pr.
Thompson, Denys, 1907-
xThompson, D.
The Uses of Poetry. Cambridge U Pr.
xThompson, Denys.
ed. Directions in the Teaching of English.
Cambridge U Pr.
ed. Discrimination & Popular Culture.
Heinemann Ed.
ed. Distant Voices: Poetry of the Preliterate.
Rowman.
Thompson, Donald L.
xThompson, D. L.
Retail Management Cases. Free Pr.
Thompson, Donald N.
xThompson, Donald N.
The Economics of Environmental Protection.
Winthrop.
Thompson, Donna F. see Thompson, Donna Fay.
Thompson, Donna Fay, 1882-
xThompson, Donna F.
Professional Solidarity Among the Teachers of
England. AMS Pr.
Thompson, Donnis Hazel.
xThompson, R.
ed. Prentice-Hall Physical Activities Handbook
for Women. P-H.
Thompson, Dorothy.
xThompson, Dorothy.
ed. Early Chartists. U of SC Pr.
Thompson, Dorothy (Burr), 1900-
xThompson, Dorothy B.
Ptolemaic Oinochoai & Portraits in Faience:
Aspects of the Ruler-Cult. Oxford U Pr.
Thompson, Dorothy B. see Thompson, Dorothy (Burr).
Thompson, Dr. Alex. see Stearn, Jess.
Thompson, E. A.
xThompson, E. A.
A History of Attila & the Huns. Greenwood.
Human Evolutionary Trees. Cambridge U Pr.
Thompson, E. Brad. see Thompson, Edward Bradbridge.
Thompson, E. M. see Thompson.
Thompson, E. P. see Thompson, Edward Palmer.
Thompson, E. V. see Thompson, Ernest Victor.

Thompson, Earl.
xThompson, Earl.
Tattoo. NAL.
Thompson, Edgar T. see Thompson, Edgar Tristram.
Thompson, Edgar Tristram, 1900-
xThompson, Edgar T.
Plantation Societies, Race Relations & the
South: The Regimentation of Populatons.
Duke.
Thompson, Edward. see Thompson, Edward John.
Thompson, Edward Bradbridge.
xThompson, E. Brad.
Steroid Receptors & the Management of
Cancer. CRC Pr.
Thompson, Edward J. see Thompson, Edward John.
Thompson, Edward John, 1886-1946
xThompson, Edward.
Rabindranath Tagore: Poet & Dramatist.
Haskell.
Rabindranath Tagore: Poet & Dramatist. R
West.
xThompson, Edward J.
The Other Side of the Medal. Greenwood.
Rabindranath Tagore: Poet & Dramatist.
Greenwood.
Thompson, Edward Palmer, 1924-
xThompson, E. P.
The Poverty of Theory & Other Essays.
Monthly Rev.
Thompson, Edward R. see Thompson, Edward Raymond.
Thompson, Edward Raymond, 1872-
xThompson, Edward R.
Portraits of the Nineties. Arno.
Uncensored Celebrities. Arno.
Thompson, Edward Theodore.
xThompson.
Anatomy for the Medical Record Librarian.
Physicians Rec.
Medical Science for Medical Record Personnel.
Physicians Rec.
Textbook & Guide to the Standard
Nomenclature of Diseases & Operations.
Physicians Rec.
Thompson, Eileen.
xThompson, Eileen.
The Golden Coyote. S&S.
Thompson, Elbert N. see Thompson, Elbert Nevius
Sebring.
Thompson, Elbert Nevius Sebring, 1877-
xThompson, Elbert N.
English Moral Plays. AMS Pr.
The English Moral Plays. Folcroft.
Literary Bypaths of the Renaissance. AMS Pr.
Literary Bypaths of the Renaissance. Arno.
Thompson, Eleanor D. see Thompson, Eleanor Dumont.
Thompson, Eleanor Dumont.
xThompson, Eleanor D.
Pediatrics for Practical Nurses. Saunders.
Thompson, Ella M.
xThompson, Ella M.
Textbook of Basic Nursing. Lippincott.
Thompson, Ellen. see Thompson, Ellen R.
Thompson, Ellen R.
xThompson, Ellen.
Teaching & Understanding Contemporary
Piano Music. Kjos.
Thompson, Enid T.
xThompson, Enid T.
Local History Collections: A Manual for
Librarians. AASLH.
Thompson, Era B. see Thompson, Era Bell.
Thompson, Era Bell.
xThompson, Era B.
American Daughter. U of Chicago Pr.
Thompson, Ernest Victor, 1931-
xThompson, E. V.
Chase the Wind. Coward.
Thompson, Estelle.
xThompson, Estelle.

Hunter in the Dark. Walker & Co.
Thompson, Eva M. see Thompson, Ewa Majewska.
Thompson, Ewa M. see Thompson, Ewa Majewska.
Thompson, Ewa Majewska, 1937-
xThompson, Eva M.
Witold Gombrowicz. G K Hall.
xThompson, Ewa M.
Witold Gombrowicz. Twayne.
Thompson, Faith.
xThompson, Faith.
First Century of Magna Carta: Why It
Persisted As a Document. Russell.
Thompson, Flora.
xThompson, Flora.
Still Glides the Stream. Oxford U Pr.
Thompson, Francis, 1859-1907
xThompson.
Hound of Heaven. Peter Pauper.
xThompson, Francis.
Hound of Heaven. Morehouse.
Literary Criticisms. Greenwood.
Poems of Francis Thompson. Greenwood.
Works of Francis Thompson. AMS Pr.
Thompson, Francis. see Thompson, Francis G.
Thompson, Francis G.
xThompson, Francis.
Highlands & Islands. Intl Pubns Serv.
The Uists & Barra. David & Charles.
Thompson, Francis H., 1930-
xThompson, Francis H.
The Frustration of Politics: Truman, Congress,
& the Loyalty Issue, 1945-1953. Fairleigh
Dickinson.
Thompson, Frank E.
xThompson, Frank E.
Diving, Cutting & Welding in Underwater
Salvage Operations. Cornell Maritime.
Thompson, Fred G. see Thompson, Fred Gilbert.
Thompson, Fred Gilbert, 1934-
xThompson, Fred G.
Aquatic Snails of the Family Hydrobiidae of
Peninsular Florida. U Presses Fla.
Thompson, G. R. see Thompson, Gary Richard.
Thompson, Gary Richard, 1937-
xThompson, G. R.
The Gothic Imagination: Essays in Dark
Romanticism. Wash St U Pr.
Thompson, George, 1804-1878
xThompson, George.
Letters & Addresses. Negro U Pr.
Thompson, George C.
xThompson, George C.
Text, Cases & Materials on Antitrust
Fundamentals. West Pub.
Thompson, George H.
xThompson, George H.
Arkansas & Reconstruction: The Influence of
Geography, Economics, & Personality.
Kennikat.
Thompson, Ginnie.
xThompson, Ginnie.
Favorite Illustrations from Children's Classics
in Counted Cross-Stitch. Dover.
Thompson, Godfrey, 1921-
xThompson, Godfrey.
Planning & Design of Library Buildings.
Nichols Pub.
Thompson, H. C. see Thompson, Herley Curry.
Thompson, H. Stanley. see Thompson, Herbert Stanley.
Thompson, Harwood. see Thompson, Marvin.
Thompson, Helen, 1897-
xThompson, Helen.
Experimental Study of the Beginning Reading
of Deaf Mutes. AMS Pr.
Thompson, Henry T. see Thompson, Henry Tazewell.
Thompson, Henry Tazewell, 1859-
xThompson, Henry T.

Ousting the Carpetbagger from South Carolina.
Negro U Pr.
Thompson, Herbert Stanley, 1932-
xThompson, H. Stanley.
Topics in Neuro-Ophthalmology. Williams &
Wilkins.
Thompson, Herley Curry.
xThompson, H. C.
Growing Flowers. Oxmoor Hse.
Thompson, Homer C. see Thompson, Homer Columbus.
Thompson, Homer Columbus.
xThompson, Homer C.
Vegetable Crops. McGraw.
Thompson, Howard. see Thompson, Howard Arthur.
Thompson, Howard Arthur, 1931-
xThompson, Howard.
Cases in Marketing Including Interviews with
Key Executives. Har-Row.
Thompson, Hugo W., 1900-
xThompson, Hugo W.
Love-Justice. Chris Mass.
Thompson, Ian B. see Thompson, Ian Bentley.
Thompson, Ian Bentley.
xThompson, Ian B.
The Lower Rhone & Marseille. Oxford U Pr.
The Paris Basin. Oxford U Pr.
Thompson, J. A. see Thompson, Joe Allen.
Thompson, J. Eric. see Thompson, John Eric Sidney.
Thompson, J. H.
xThompson, J. H.
Canadian Textiles. Textile Bk.
Thompson, J. M.
xThompson, J. M.
The French Revolution. Biblio Dist.
Thompson, J. M. see Thompson, J. M. T.
Thompson, J. M. T.
xThompson, J. M.
General Theory of Elastic Stability. Wiley.
Thompson, J. W. see Thompson, James Westfall.
Thompson, James.
xThompson, James.
A History of the Principles of Librarianship.
Shoe String.
An Introduction to a University Library
Administration. K G Saur.
An Introduction to University Library
Administration. Shoe String.
Thompson, James C. see Thompson, James Clay.
Thompson, James Clay, 1943-
xThompson, James C.
Rolling Thunder: Understanding Policy &
Program Failure. U of NC Pr.
Thompson, James M. see Thompson, James Matthew.
Thompson, James Matthew, 1878-1956
xThompson, James M.
ed. English Witnesses of the French
Revolution. Kennikat.
Louis Napoleon & the Second Empire. Norton.
Thompson, James Michael, 1908-
xThompson, James M.
Tabulation Typing. McGraw.
Thompson, James R.
xThompson, James R.
Leigh Hunt. Twayne.
Thompson, James S.
xThompson, James S.
Core Textbook of Anatomy. Lippincott.
Genetics in Medicine. Saunders.
Thompson, James W. see Thompson, James Westfall.
Thompson, James Westfall, 1869-1941
xThompson, J. W.
A History of Historical Writing. Peter Smith.
xThompson, James W.

Byways in Bookland. Arno.
Economic & Social History of Europe in the
Later Middle Ages, 1300-1530. Ungar.
ed. Literacy of the Laity in the Middle Ages. B
Franklin.
The Literacy of the Laity in the Middle Ages.
Johnson Repr.
Medieval Library. Hafner.

Thompson, Jean.
xThompson, Jean.
Brother of the Wolves. Morrow.
Don't Forget Michael. Morrow.
House of Tomorrow. Har-Row.
I'm Going to Run Away. Abingdon.

Thompson, Joan, 1943-
xThompson, Joan.
Marblehead. G K Hall.
Marblehead. St Martin.
Parker's Island. St Martin.

Thompson, Joe Allen.
xThompson, J. A.
Modern British Monarchy. St Martin.

Thompson, John, 1922-
xThompson, John.
Christ in Perspective: Christological
Perspectives in the Theology of Karl Barth.
Eerdmans.
Life of John Thompson, a Fugitive Slave.
Negro U Pr.
Thompson, John A. *see* Thompson, John Arthur.

Thompson, John Archie.
xThompson, John A.
Speaking & Understanding Spanish. HR&W.

Thompson, John Arthur, 1913-
xThompson, John A.
The Book of Jeremiah. Eerdmans.

Thompson, John D.
xThompson, John D.
Applied Health Services Research. Lexington
Bks.
The Hospital: A Social & Architectural
History. Yale U Pr.

Thompson, John Eric, 1898-
xThompson, J. Eric.
Maya Hieroglyphic Writing: An Introduction.
U of Okla Pr.

Thompson, John Eric Sidney, 1898-
xThompson, J. Eric.
Maya Archaeologist. U of Okla Pr.
Maya History & Religion. U of Okla Pr.
Thompson, John H. *see* Thompson, John Henry.

Thompson, John Henry, 1919-
xThompson, John H.
ed. Geography of New York State. Syracuse U
Pr.

Thompson, John W.
xThompson, John W.
An Authentic History of the Douglass
Monument. Arno.
Compiled by Index to Illustrations of the
Natural World: Where to Find Pictures of the
Living Things of North America. Gaylord
Prof Pubns.

Thompson, Joseph R.
xThompson, Joseph R.
Correlative Sectional Anatomy of the Head &
Neck: A Color Atlas. Mosby.

Thompson, June M.
xThompson, June M.
Clinical Manual of Health Assessment. Mosby.

Thompson, Kenneth, 1923-
xThompson, Kenneth.
Auguste Comte: The Foundation of Sociology.
Halsted Pr.
Thompson, Kenneth. *see* Thompson, Kenneth W.

Thompson, Kenneth W, 1921-
xThompson, Kenneth.
Ethics, Functionalism, & Power in International
Politics: The Crisis in Values. La State U Pr.
xThompson, Kenneth W.

American Diplomacy & Emergent Patterns.
NYU Pr.
Christian Ethics & the Dilemmas of Foreign
Policy. Duke.
Foreign Assistance: A View from the Private
Sector. U of Notre Dame Pr.
ed. Higher Education & Social Change:
Promising Experiments in Developing
Countries. Praeger.
ed. The Moral Imperatives of Human Rights: A
World Survey. U Pr of Amer.
Moral Issue in Statecraft: Twentieth-Century
Approaches & Problems. La State U Pr.
Understanding World Politics. U of Notre
Dame Pr.
ed. The Virginia Papers on the Presidency: The
White Burkett Miller Center Forums, 1980,
Part II. U Pr of Amer.

Thompson, Laura, 1905-
xThompson, Laura.
Fijian Frontier. Octagon.
Guam & Its People. Greenwood.

Thompson, Laurence G.
xThompson.
Chinese Religion: An Introduction. Duxbury
Pr.
xThompson, Laurence G.
Chinese Religion: An Introduction. Dickenson.
The Chinese Way in Religion. Dickenson.
Thompson, Lawrance R. *see* Thompson, Lawrance Roger.

Thompson, Lawrance Roger, 1906-
xThompson, Lawrance R.
Fire & Ice: The Art & Thought of Robert
Frost. Russell.
Thompson, Lawrence. *see* Thompson, Lawrence Sidney.
Thompson, Lawrence S. *see* Thompson, Lawrence
Sidney.

Thompson, Lawrence Sidney, 1916-
xThompson, Lawrence.
The Southern Black, Slave & Free: A
Bibliography of Anti- & Pro-Slavery Books &
Pamphlets of Social & Economic Conditions
in the Southern States from the Beginnings to
1950. Whitston Pub.
xThompson, Lawrence S.
Printing in Colonial Spanish America. Whitston
Pub.
Thompson, Leonard. *see* Thompson, Leonard Monteath.

Thompson, Leonard Monteath.
xThompson, Leonard.
ed. Change in Contemporary South Africa. U
of Cal Pr.
Southern African History Before 1900: A
Select Bibliography of Articles. Hoover Inst
Pr.
Survival in Two Worlds: Moshoeshoe of
Lesotho, 1786-1870. Oxford U Pr.

Thompson, Lida F.
xThompson, Lida F.
Sociology: Nurses & Their Patients in a
Modern Society. Mosby.

Thompson, Lloyd J.
xThompson, Lloyd J.
Reading Disability: Developmental Dyslexia. C
C Thomas.
Thompson, Louis M. *see* Thompson, Louis Milton.

Thompson, Louis Milton.
xThompson, Louis M.
Soils & Soil Fertility. McGraw.
Thompson, M. W. *see* Thompson, Michael Warwick.

Thompson, Margaret.
xThompson, Margaret.
The Agrinion Hoard. Am Numismatic.
Thompson, Marilou B. *see* Thompson, Marilou Bonham.

Thompson, Marilou Bonham.
xThompson, Marilou B.
Abiding Appalachia: Where Mountain & Atom
Meet. St Luke TN.
Thompson, Martha. *see* Thompson, Martha A.

Thompson, Martha A.
xThompson, Martha.
Shock Syndrome: Mechanisms &
Manifestations; Nursing Assessment
Intervention & Evaluation. A-W.
Thompson, Martin. *see* Thompson, Martin J.

Thompson, Martin J.
xThompson, Martin.
Antitrust & the Health Care Provider. Aspen
Systems.

Thompson, Marvin.
xThompson, Harwood.
Florida Real Estate. Reston.
Florida Real Estate Resource Book. Reston.

Thompson, Maurice, 1844-1901
xThompson, Maurice.
Alice of Old Vincennes. Irvington.
Hoosier Mosaics. Mss Info.
Hoosier Mosaics. Somerset Pub.
Stories of the Cherokee Hills. Arno.

Thompson, Michael Warwick.
xThompson, M. W.
Defects & Radiation Damage in Metals.
Cambridge U Pr.

Thompson, Morton.
xThompson, Morton.
The Cry & the Covenant. NAL.
Not As a Stranger. NAL.

Thompson, Neville.
xThompson, Neville.
Anti-Appeasers: Conservative Opposition to
Appeasement in the 1930's. Oxford U Pr.

Thompson, Norman J.
xThompson, Norman J.
Fire Behavior & Sprinklers. Natl Fire Prot.
Thompson, Olive R. *see* Thompson, Olive Ross.

Thompson, Olive Ross.
xThompson, Olive R.
That His Word Will Live. Philos Lib.

Thompson, Oscar, 1887-1945
xThompson, Oscar.
Debussy: Man & Artist. Dover.
How to Understand Music. Arno.
How to Understand Music. R West.
Thompson, P. A. *see* Thompson, Philip A.
Thompson, Paul. *see* Thompson, Paul Richard.

Thompson, Paul D.
xThompson, Paul D.
Gases & Plasmas. Lippincott.

Thompson, Paul Richard.
xThompson, Paul.
The Edwardians in Photographs. Holmes &
Meier.

Thompson, Philip A.
xThompson, P. A.
Compressible Fluid Dynamics. McGraw.
Thompson, R. *see* Thompson, Donnis Hazel.
Thompson, R. W. *see* Thompson, Reginald William.

Thompson, Ralph, 1904-
xThompson, Ralph.
American Literary Annuals & Gift Books,
1825-1865. Shoe String.
Thompson, Ray. *see* Thompson, Raymond.

Thompson, Raymond.
xThompson, Ray.
The Number to Call Is.... St Martin.

Thompson, Reginald William.
xThompson, R. W.
An Echo of Trumpets. Soccer.
Montgomery. Ballantine.

Thompson, Richard.
xThompson, Richard.
Race & Sport. Oxford U Pr.

Thompson, Richard A., 1930-
xThompson, Richard A.
Energizers for Reading Instruction. P-H.
Thompson, Richard A. *see* Thompson, Richard Arlen.

Thompson, Richard Allen.
xThompson, Richard A.

Psychology & Culture. Wm C Brown.

Thompson, Richard Arlen.
xThompson, Richard A.
ed. Critical Care of Neurologic &
Neurosurgical Emergencies. Raven.
ed. Neoplasia in the Central Nervous System.
Raven.
ed. Stroke. Raven.

Thompson, Richard B., 1939-
xThompson, Richard B.
College Algebra. Prindle.

Thompson, Richard E.
xThompson, Richard E.
Helping Hospital Trustees Understand
Physicians. Am Hospital.

Thompson, Richard F. *see* Thompson, Richard Frederick.

Thompson, Richard Frederick, 1930-
xThompson, Richard F.
Foundations of Physiological Psychology.
Har-Row.
Introduction to Physiological Psychology.
Har-Row.

Thompson, Robert. *see* Thompson, Robert Grainger Ker.

Thompson, Robert B.
xThompson, Robert B.
Systems Approach to Instruction. Shoe String.

Thompson, Robert C.
xThompson, Robert C.
Introduction to Linear Algebra. Scott F.

Thompson, Robert F. *see* Thompson, Robert Farris.

Thompson, Robert Farris.
xThompson, Robert F.
African Art in Motion: Icon & Act in the
Collection of Katherine Coryton White. U of
Cal Pr.

Thompson, Robert Grainger Ker, Sir, 1916-
xThompson, Robert.
Revolutionary War in World Strategy:
1945-1969. Taplinger.

Thompson, Robert S. *see* Thompson, Robert Sydney.

Thompson, Robert Sydney, 1892-
xThompson, Robert S.
Effectiveness of Modern Spelling Instruction.
AMS Pr.

Thompson, Roger, 1933-
xThompson, Roger.
Unfit for Modest Ears: A Study of
Pornographic, Obscene & Bawdy Works
Written or Published in England in the
Second Half of the Seventeenth Century.
Rowman.

Thompson, Roy A.
xThompson, Roy A.
Toward New Horizons. Free Church Pubns.

Thompson, Russel G. *see* Thompson, Russell G.

Thompson, Russell G.
xThompson, Russel G.
ed. The Cost of Clean Water in Ammonia,
Chlor-Alkali, & Ethylene Production. Gulf
Pub.
xThompson, Russell G.
The Cost of Electricity: Cheap Power Vs. a
Clean Environment. Gulf Pub.

Thompson, Samuel W. *see* Thompson, Samuel Wesley.

Thompson, Samuel Wesley.
xThompson, Samuel W.
The Pathology of Parenteral Nutrition with
Lipids. C C Thomas.

Thompson, Silvanus Phillips, 1851-1916
xThompson , Silvanus P.
The Life of Lord Kelvin. Chelsea Pub.

Thompson, Slason, 1849-1935
xThompson, Slason.
Eugene Field: A Study in Heredity &
Contradictions. Beekman Pubs.
Eugene Field: A Study in Heredity &
Contradictions. R West.

Thompson, Stith, 1885-
xThompson, Stith.

The Folktale. AMS Pr.
The Folktale. U of Cal Pr.
ed. Four Symposia on Folklore. Greenwood.
ed. One Hundred Favorite Folk Tales. Ind U
Pr.
The Oral Tales of India. Greenwood.

Thompson, Sylvia V. *see* Thompson, Sylvia Vaughn
Sheekman.

Thompson, Sylvia Vaughn Sheekman.
xThompson, Sylvia V.
The Budget Gourmet. Random.

Thompson, T. Philips. *see* Thompson, Thomas Phillips.
Thompson, T. W. *see* Thompson, Thomas William.

Thompson, Thomas, 1934-
xThompson, Thomas.
Serpentine. Dell.
Serpentine. Doubleday.

Thompson, Thomas Phillips.
xThompson, T. Philips.
The Politics of Labor. U of Toronto Pr.

Thompson, Thomas T.
xThompson, Thomas T.
A Practical Approach to Modern X-Ray
Equipment. Little.
Primer of Clinical Radiology. Little.

Thompson, Thomas W. *see* Thompson, Thomas William.

Thompson, Thomas William.
xThompson, T. W.
Wordsworth's Hawkshead. Oxford U Pr.
xThompson, Thomas W.
Banking Tomorrow: Managing Markets
Through Planning. Van Nos Reinhold.

Thompson, Travis. *see* Thompson, Travis I.

Thompson, Travis I.
xThompson, Travis.
ed. Reinforcement Schedules & Multioperant
Analysis. P-H.

Thompson, Valerie.
xThompson, Valerie.
Cannibal Soup: Tubbing with the Thompsons.
Chronicle Bks.

Thompson, Vance, 1863-1925
xThompson, Vance.
The Carnival of Destiny. Arno.

Thompson, Victor A. *see* Thompson, Victor Alexander.

Thompson, Victor Alexander.
xThompson, Victor A.
Bureaucracy & Innovation. U of Ala Pr.

Thompson, Victor H.
xThompson, Victor H.
Eudora Welty: A Reference Guide. G K Hall.

Thompson, Vincent B. *see* Thompson, Vincent Bakpetu.

Thompson, Vincent Bakpetu.
xThompson, Vincent B.
Africa & Unity: The Evolution of
Pan-Africanism. Humanities.

Thompson, Virginia. *see* Thompson, Virginia Mclean.
Thompson, Virginia M. *see* Thompson, Virginia Mclean.

Thompson, Virginia McLean, 1903-
xThompson, Virginia.
The French Pacific Islands: French Polynesia &
New Caledonia. U of Cal Pr.
Historical Dictionary of the People's Republic
of the Congo (Congo-Brazzaville). Scarecrow.
Postmortem on Malaya. Darby Bks.
Thailand: The New Siam. Paragon.
xThompson, Virginia M.
French Indo-China. Octagon.
French West Africa. Greenwood.

Thompson, Vivian L. *see* Thompson, Vivian Laubach.

Thompson, Vivian Laubach.
xThompson, Vivian L.
George Washington. Putnam.

Thompson, W. B.
xThompson, William B.
Introduction to Plasma Physics. Pergamon.

Thompson, W. H.
xThompson, W. H.

Chaucer & His Times. Arden Lib.
Chaucer & His Times. Folcroft.

Thompson, W. S. *see* Thompson, Warren Simpson.
Thompson, W. Scott. *see* Thompson, Willard Scott.
Thompson, Warren S. *see* Thompson, Warren Simpson.

Thompson, Warren Simpson, 1887-1950
xThompson, W. S.
Population Trends in the United States.
Gordon.
Population Trends in the United States. Kraus
Repr.
xThompson, Warren S.
Population & Peace in the Pacific. Arno.
Population & Progress in the Far East. U of
Chicago Pr.
Population: The Growth of Metropolitan
Districts in the United States, 1900-1940.
Arno.

Thompson, Wayne. *see* Thompson, Wayne N.

Thompson, Wayne N.
xThompson, Wayne.
Responsible & Effective Communication. HM.
xThompson, Wayne N.
The Process of Persuasion: Principles &
Readings. Har-Row.

Thompson, Wilbur R. *see* Thompson, Wilbur Richard.

Thompson, Wilbur Richard.
xThompson, Wilbur R.
An Econometric Model of Postwar State
Industrial Development. Greenwood.
A Preface to Urban Economics. Johns Hopkins.

Thompson, Willard Scott.
xThompson, W. S.
Unequal Partners: Philippine & Thai Relations
with the United States. Lexington Bks.
xThompson, W. Scott.
ed. The Lessons of Vietnam. Crane-Russak Co.

Thompson, William, 1775-1833
xThompson, William.
Inquiry into the Principles of the Distribution
of Wealth Most Conducive to Human
Happiness. Kelley.

Thompson, William. *see* Thompson, William W.

Thompson, William A.
xThompson, William A.
Modern Sports Officiating: A Practical Guide.
Wm C Brown.

Thompson, William B. *see* Thompson, W. B.
Thompson, William E. *see* Thompson, William Edward.

Thompson, William Edward.
xThompson, William E.
A Focus on the Role of the Internal Auditor:
The Foreign Corrupt Practices Act,
Management Representations on Control &
the Internal Auditor. Inst Inter Aud.

Thompson, William I. *see* Thompson, William Irwin.

Thompson, William Irwin.
xThompson, William I.
Evil & World Order. Har-Row.
Evil & World Order. Har-Row.

Thompson, William W., 1931-
xThompson, William.
Calculus with Applications in the Management
& Social Sciences. P-H.

Thompson, Zadock, 1796-1856
xThompson, Zadock.
Natural History of Vermont. C E Tuttle.

Thoms, William J. *see* Thoms, William John.

Thoms, William John, 1803-1885
xThoms, William J.
ed. Early English Prose Romances. AMS Pr.

Thomsen, Blaine C.
xThomsen, Blaine C.
The Ammonite. Herald Hse.

Thomsen, Moritz.
xThomsen, Moritz.
Farm on the River of Emeralds. HM.

Thomsen, R. J. *see* Thomsen, Russel J.

Thomsen, Robert.
xThomsen, Robert.

Carriage Trade. S&S.
Thomsen, Russel J.
xThomsen, R. J.
Latter Day Saints & the Sabbath. Pacific Pr
Pub Assn.
Thomsen, Vilhelm L. *see* Thomsen, Vilhelm Ludvig
Peter.
Thomsen, Vilhelm Ludvig Peter, 1842-1927
xThomsen, Vilhelm L.
Relations Between Ancient Russia &
Scandinavia & the Origin of the Russian
State. B Franklin.
Thomsett, Michael C.
xThomsett, Michael C.
Builder's Guide to Accounting. Craftsman.
Thomson, A. W. *see* Thomson, A. W. J.
Thomson, A. W. J.
xThomson, A. W.
Industrial Relations Act: A Review & Analysis.
Rothman.
Thomson, Charles M.
xThomson, Charles M.
Fundamentals of Electronics. P-H.
Mathematics for Electronics. P-H.
Thomson, Clara L. *see* Thomson, Clara Linklater.
Thomson, Clara Linklater.
xThomson, Clara L.
George Eliot. Folcroft.
Thomson, D. F. *see* Thomson, Douglas Ferguson Scott.
Thomson, David, 1912-
xThomson, David.
The Babeuf Plot: The Making of a Republican
Legend. Greenwood.
England in the Nineteenth Century. Penguin.
England in the Nineteenth Century,
1815-1914. Gannon.
England in the Twentieth Century. Penguin.
England in the Twentieth Century, 1914-63.
Gannon.
Europe Since Napoleon. Knopf.
Thomson, Derick. *see* Thomson, Derick S.
Thomson, Derick S.
xThomson, Derick.
An Introduction to Gaelic Poetry. St Martin.
xThomson, Derick S.
Gaelic Sources of Macpherson's Ossian.
Folcroft.
Thomson, Donald A.
xThomson, Donald A.
Reef Fishes of the Sea of Cortez: The Rocky
Shore Fishes of the Gulf of California. Wiley.
Thomson, Douglas Ferguson Scott.
xThomson, D. F.
ed. Catullus: A Critical Edition. U of NC Pr.
Thomson, Duncan.
xThomson, Duncan.
The Life & Art of George Jamesone. Oxford U
Pr.
Thomson, F. P. *see* Thomson, Francis Paul.
Thomson, Francis Paul.
xThomson, F. P.
Money in the Computer Age. Pergamon.
Thomson, Frank. *see* Thomson, Frank S.
Thomson, Frank S.
xThomson, Frank.
Ninety-Six Years in the Black Hills. Harlo Pr.
Thomson, H. Douglas. *see* Thomson, Henry Douglas.
Thomson, Henry Douglas.
xThomson, H. Douglas.
Masters of Mystery: A Study of the Detective
Story. Dover.
Masters of Mystery: A Study of the Detective
Story. Folcroft.
Thomson, J. A. *see* Thomson, James Alexander Kerr.
Thomson, J. Oliver. *see* Thomson, James Oliver.
Thomson, J. R. *see* Thomson, John Robson.
Thomson, James, 1822-1892
xThomson, James.

Collected Papers in Physics & Engineering.
AMS Pr.
Thomson, James A. *see* Thomson, James Alexander Kerr.
Thomson, James Alexander Kerr, 1879-1959
xThomson, J. A.
The Greek Tradition: Essays in the
Reconstruction of Ancient Thought. Century
Bookbindery.
xThomson, James A.
The Greek Tradition: Essays in the
Reconstruction of Ancient Thought. Arno.
Thomson, James C. *see* Thomson, James Claude.
Thomson, James Claude, 1931-
xThomson, James C.
While China Faced West: American Reformers
in Nationalist China, 1928-1937. Harvard U
Pr.
Thomson, James Oliver.
xThomson, J. Oliver.
History of Ancient Geography. Biblo.
Thomson, James W. *see* Thomson, James William.
Thomson, James William.
xThomson, James W.
An Introduction to the Fundamentals of
Financial Analysis for Business Students. U
Pr of Amer.
Thomson, Jean. *see* Thomson, Jean M.
Thomson, Jean M.
xThomson, Jean.
ed. Blood Coagulation & Haemostasis: A
Practical Guide. Churchill.
Thomson, John, 1871-
xThomson, John.
Francis Thompson; Poet & Mystic. Folcroft.
Thomson, John A. *see* Thomson, John Arthur.
Thomson, John Arthur.
xThomson, John A.
Riddles of Science. Arno.
Thomson, John Robson, 1910-
xThomson, J. R.
An Introduction to Seed Technology. Halsted
Pr.
Thomson, John S. *see* Thomson, John Seabury.
Thomson, John Seabury, 1921-
xThomson, John S.
Potomac White Water: A Guide to Safe
Canoeing Above Washington. Appalachian
Bks.
Thomson, John W. *see* Thomson, John Walter.
Thomson, John Walter, 1913-
xThomson, John W.
Lichens of the Alaskan Arctic Slope. U of
Toronto Pr.
Thomson, Joseph, 1858-1895
xThomson, Joseph.
Mungo Park & the Niger. Argosy.
Thomson, Judith J.
xThomson, Judith J.
Acts & Other Events. Cornell U Pr.
Thomson, June.
xThomson, June.
The Habit of Loving. Bantam.
The Habit of Loving. Doubleday.
A Question of Identity. Bantam.
Thomson, Malcolm M., 1908-
xThomson, Malcolm M.
The Beginning of the Long Dash: A History of
Timekeeping in Canada. U of Toronto Pr.
Thomson, P. *see* Thomson, Peggy.
Thomson, Peggy.
xThomson, P.
On Reading Palms. P-H.
xThomson, Peggy.
On Reading Palms. P-H.
Thomson, R. G. *see* Thomson, Reginald G.
Thomson, Reginald G.
xThomson, R. G.
General Veterinary Pathology. Saunders.
Thomson, Robert, 1943-
xThomson, Robert.

Natural Medicine. McGraw.
Thomson, Robert W., 1934-
xThomson, Robert W.
An Introduction to Classical Armenian.
Caravan Bks.
Thomson, Rosemary.
xThomson, Rosemary.
The Price of Liberty. Creation Hse.
Thomson, Ruth.
xThomson, Ruth.
Exciting Things to Make with Paper.
Lippincott.
Peabody All at Sea. Lothrop.
Peabody's First Case. Lothrop.
Thomson, Ruth G. *see* Thomson, Ruth Gibbons.
Thomson, Ruth Gibbons, 1872-1956
xThomson, Ruth G.
Index to Full-Length Plays: 1895-1925. Faxon.
Index to Full-Length Plays: 1926-1944. Faxon.
Thomson, Scott. *see* Thomson, Scott D.
Thomson, Scott D.
xThomson, Scott.
Guidelines for Improving SAT Scores. Natl
Assn Principals.
Thomson, Suzi P. *see* Thomson, Suzi Park.
Thomson, Suzi Park.
xThomson, Suzi P.
Suzi: The Korean Connection. Condor Pub Co.
Thomson, T. R. *see* Thomson, Theodore Radford.
Thomson, Theodore Radford, 1897-
xThomson, T. R.
A Catalogue of British Family Histories. C E
Tuttle.
Thomson, Thomas, 1773-1852
xThomson, Thomas.
The History of Chemistry. Arno.
Thomson, Virgil, 1896-
xThomson, Virgil.
Art of Judging Music. Greenwood.
Music, Right & Left. Greenwood.
Musical Scene. Greenwood.
Thomson, W. B. *see* Thomson, W. R.
Thomson, W. R.
xThomson, W. B.
In Dickens Street. Norwood Edns.
xThomson, W. R.
In Dickens Street. Folcroft.
In Dickens Street. Haskell.
Thomson, Watson.
xThomson, Watson.
Turning into Tomorrow. Philos Lib.
Thomson, William. *see* Thomson, William Ennis.
Thomson, William A. *see* Thomson, William Archibald
Robson.
Thomson, William Archibald Robson.
xThomson, William A.
A Change of Air: Climate & Health. Scribner.
Thomson, William Ennis.
xThomson, William.
Introduction to Music Reading: Concepts &
Applications. Wadsworth Pub.
Thomy, Al.
xThomy, Al.
The Ramblin' Wreck: A Story of Georgia Tech
Football. Strode.
Thonis, E. *see* Thonis, Eleanor.
Thonis, Eleanor.
xThonis, E.
Teaching Reading to Non-English Speakers.
Macmillan.
xThonis, Eleanor W.
Literacy for America's Spanish Speaking
Children. Intl Reading.
Thonis, Eleanor W. *see* Thonis, Eleanor.
Thonssen, Lester.
xThonssen, Lester.
Speech Criticism. Krieger.
Speech Criticism. Wiley.
Thorburn, David.
xThorburn, David.

Ancient Astronauts. Crestwood Hse.
The Great Goalies. Creative Ed.
The Loch Ness Monster. Crestwood Hse.
Meet the Defensive Linemen. Creative Ed.
Meet the Receivers. Creative Ed.
Monster Tales of Native Americans. Crestwood
    Hse.
UFOs. Crestwood Hse.
Thorne, J. O.
    xThorne, J. O.
        ed. Chambers Biographical Dictionary.
            Littlefield.
        ed. Chambers Biographical Dictionary. Two
            Continents.
Thorne, Jean W. *see* Thorne, Jean Wright.
Thorne, Jean Wright.
    xThorne, Jean W.
        Horse & Rider. Crestwood Hse.
Thorne, Martha C. *see* Thorne, Martha Covington.
Thorne, Martha Covington.
    xThorne, Martha C.
        Handling Your Own Dog--for Show Obedience
            & Field Trials. Doubleday.
Thorne, Nicola.
    xThorne, Nicola.
        A Woman Like Us. St Martin.
Thorne, Peter J.
    xThorne, Peter J.
        Practical Electronic Projects for Model
            Railroaders. Kalmbach.
Thorne-Thomsen, Kathleen.
    xThorne-Thomsen, Kathleen.
        Alice in Stitches. HR&W.
        Why the Cake Won't Rise & the Jelly Won't
            Set: A Complete Guide to Avoiding Kitchen
            Failures. A & W Pubs.
Thorner, Marvin E. *see* Thorner, Marvin Edward.
Thorner, Marvin Edward.
    nThorner, Marvin E.
        Convenience & Fast Food Handbook. AVI.
        Non-Alcoholic Food Service Beverage
            Handbook. AVI.
        Quality Control in Food Service. AVI.
Thornes, Barbara.
    xThornes, Barbara.
        Who Divorces?. Routledge & Kegan.
Thornley, Gail.
    xThornley, Gail.
        ed. Critical Path Analysis in Practice: Collected
            Papers on Project Control. Methuen Inc.
Thorns, David C.
    xThorns, David C.
        Quest for Community: Social Aspects of
            Residential Growth. Halsted Pr.
Thornton, A. P. *see* Thornton, Archibald Paton.
Thornton, Alice B.
    xThornton, Alice B.
        How Come You're Not Married. Chris Mass.
Thornton, Archibald Paton.
    xThornton, A. P.
        Imperialism in the Twentieth Century. U of
            Minn Pr.
Thornton, Billy M.
    xThornton, Billy M.
        An Introduction to Management Science:
            Quantitative Approach to Managerial
            Decisions. Merrill.
Thornton, Frances (Clabaugh).
    xThornton, Frances C.
        The French Element in Spenser's Poetical
            Works. Folcroft.
Thornton, Frances C. *see* Thornton, Frances (Clabaugh).
Thornton, Harrison R. *see* Thornton, Harrison Robertson.
Thornton, Harrison Robertson, 1858-
    xThornton, Harrison R.
        Among the Eskimos of Wales, Alaska: 1890-93.
            AMS Pr.
Thornton, Helene.
    xThornton, Helene.

Mistress from Martinique. Fawcett.
Thornton, Ian. *see* Thornton, Ian W. B.
Thornton, Ian W. B.
    xThornton, Ian.
        Darwin's Islands: A Natural History of the
            Galapagos. Natural Hist.
Thornton, J. Mills, 1943-
    xThornton, J. Mills.
        Politics & Power in a Slave Society: Alabama,
            1800-1860. La State U Pr.
Thornton, J. Quinn. *see* Thornton, Jessy Quinn.
Thornton, James W.
    xThornton, James W.
        The Community Junior College. Wiley.
Thornton, Jessy Quinn, 1810-1888
    xThornton, J. Quinn.
        Oregon & California in 1848. Arno.
Thornton, John W. *see* Thornton, John Wingate.
Thornton, John Wingate, 1818-1878
    xThornton, John W.
        ed. Pulpit of the American Revolution: Political
            Sermons of the Period of 1776. Da Capo.
Thornton, Judith.
    xThornton, Judith.
        ed. Economic Analysis of the Soviet-Type
            System. Cambridge U Pr.
Thornton, Mary A. *see* Thornton, Mary Ann.
Thornton, Mary Ann.
    xThornton, Mary A.
        Even Elvis. New Leaf.
Thornton, Pat.
    xThornton, Pat.
        Contemporary Cross-Country Skiing. Contemp
            Bks.
Thornton, Percy M. *see* Thornton, Percy Melville.
Thornton, Percy Melville, 1841-1918
    xThornton, Percy M.
        Brunswick Accession. Kennikat.
Thornton, R H.
    xThornton, R. H.
        British Shipping. Cambridge U Pr.
Thornton, Weldon.
    xThornton, Weldon.
        Allusions in Ulysses: An Annotated List. U of
            NC Pr.
        J. M. Synge & the Western Mind. B&N.
        J. M. Synge & the Western Mind. Humanities.
Thorold, C. A.
    xThorold, C. A.
        Diseases of Cocoa. Oxford U Pr.
Thoroton, Robert.
    xThoroton, Robert.
        The Antiquities of Nottinghamshire. Rowman.
Thoroughbred Owners & Breeders Assn. *see*
    Thoroughbred Owners and Breeders Association.
Thoroughbred Owners & Breeders Association. *see*
    Thoroughbred Owners and Breeders Association.
Thoroughbred Owners and Breeders Association.
    xBlood Horse.
        ed. Stallion Register, 1981. Thoroughbred Own
            & Breed.
    xBlood-Horse.
        ed. Principal Winners Abroad of 1979.
            Thoroughbred Own & Breed.
        ed. Sires of Runners of 1979. Thoroughbred
            Own & Breed.
        ed. Stakes Winners of 1979. Thoroughbred
            Own & Breed.
    xBlood-Horse-Thoroughbred Owners & Breeders
        Assn.
        ed. The Breeder's Guide for 1979.
            Thoroughbred Own & Breed.
    xTheThoroughbread Owners & Breeders
        Association.
        Sires of Runners of 1978: Supplement.
            Thoroughbred Own and Breed.
        Stakes Winners of 1978: Supplement.
            Thoroughbred Own and Breed.
    xThoroughbred Owners & Breeders Assn.

ed. Thoroughbred Broodmare Records, 1979:
    Annual. Thoroughbred Own & Breed.
Thoroughbreds of Nineteen Seventy-Nine.
    Thoroughbred Own and Breed.
xThoroughbred Owners & Breeders Association.
    Sires of Runners of 1979: Supplement to the
        Blood-Horse. Thoroughbred Own and Breed.
    Stakes Winners of 1979: Supplement to the
        Blood-Horse. Thoroughbred Own and Breed.
    Training Thoroughbred Horses. Thoroughbred
        Own and Breed.
xThe Throroughbred Owners & Breeders
    Association.
    A Supplement to the Blood-Horse: Stallion
        Register of 1978. Thoroughbred Own and
        Breed.
Thorp, Margaret. *see* Thorp, Margaret (Farrand).
Thorp, Margaret (Farrand), 1891-
    xThorp, Margaret.
        America at the Movies. Arno.
    xThorp, Margaret F.
        America at the Movies. Norwood Edns.
        Charles Kingsley, 1819-1875. Octagon.
        Literary Sculptors. Duke.
Thorp, Margaret F. *see* Thorp, Margaret (Farrand).
Thorp, Raymond W.
    xThorp, Raymond W.
        Crow Killer: The Saga of Liver-Eating Johnson.
            Ind U Pr.
Thorp, Robbin W., 1933-
    xThorp, Robbin W.
        Systematics & Ecology of Bees of the Subgenus
            Diandrena (Hymenoptera: Andrenidae). U of
            Cal Pr.
Thorp, Roderick.
    xThorp, Roderick.
        Nothing Lasts Forever. Norton.
Thorp, Rosemary.
    xThorp, Rosemary.
        ed. Inflation & Stabilisation in Latin America.
            Holmes & Meier.
Thorp, Willard, 1899-
    xThorp, Willard.
        American Writing in the Twentieth Century.
            Harvard U Pr.
        ed. Lives of Eighteen from Princeton. Arno.
        Triumph of Realism in Elizabethan Drama:
            1558-1612. Gordian.
Thorpe, Earl E.
    xThorpe, Earl E.
        The Central Theme of Black History.
            Greenwood.
        Eros & Freedom in Southern Life & Thought.
            Greenwood.
        The Old South: A Psychohistory. Greenwood.
Thorpe, Elliott R., 1897-
    xThorpe, Elliott R.
        East Wind, Rain: The Intimate Account of an
            Intelligence Officer in the Pacific 1939-49.
            Gambit.
Thorpe, Francis N. *see* Thorpe, Francis Newton.
Thorpe, Francis Newton, 1857-1926
    xThorpe, Francis N.
        Constitutional History of the United States. Da
            Capo.
Thorpe, J. *see* Thorpe, John A.
Thorpe, James. *see* Thorpe, James Ernest.
Thorpe, James Ernest, 1915-
    xThorpe, James.
        Principles of Textual Criticism. Huntington Lib.
        The Use of Manuscripts in Literary Research:
            Problems of Access & Literary Property
            Rights. Modern Lang.
Thorpe, John A.
    xThorpe, J.
        Elementary Topics in Differential Geometry.
            Springer-Verlag.
Thorpe, Lewis. *see* Thorpe, Lewis G. M.
Thorpe, Lewis G. M., 1913-
    xThorpe, Lewis.

Intro. by Two Lives of Charlemagne. Penguin.
Thorpe, Michael.
xThorpe, Michael.
Doris Lessing's Africa. Holmes & Meier.
Matthew Arnold. Arco.
Thorpe, Peter.
xThorpe, Peter.
Eighteenth-Century English Poetry.
Nelson-Hall.
Why Literature Is Bad for You. Nelson-Hall.
Thorpe, Sylvia.
xThorpe, Sylvia.
Fair Shine the Day. Fawcett.
Golden Panther. Fawcett.
The Silver Nightingale. Fawcett.
The Sword and the Shadow. Fawcett.
Tarrington Chase. Fawcett.
Thorpe, W. H. *see* Thorpe, William Homan.
Thorpe, William Homan, 1902-
xThorpe, W. H.
Purpose in a World of Chance: A Biologist's
View. Oxford U Pr.
Thorsby, E.
xThorsby, E.
Genetics of Human Histocompatibility
Antigens & Their Relation to Disease. Mss
Info.
Thorson, Esther.
xThorson, Esther.
ed. Simulation in Higher Education: Papers
from the Denison Simulation Center, Denison
University, Granville, Ohio. Exposition.
Thorson, Gunnar, 1906-1971
xThorson, Gunner.
Life in the Sea. McGraw.
Thorson, Gunner. *see* Thorson, Gunnar.
Thorsten, Geraldine.
xThorsten, Geraldine.
God Herself: The Feminine Roots of
Astrology. Doubleday.
Thorstensen, Thomas C., 1919-
xThorstensen, Thomas C.
Practical Leather Technology. Krieger.
Thorvall, Kerstin.
xThorvall, Kerstin.
And Leffe Was Instead of a Dad. Bradbury Pr.
Thorwald, Jurgen.
xThorwald, Jurgen.
Century of the Detective. HarBraceJ.
The Illusion: Soviet Soldiers in Hitler's Armies.
HarBraceJ.
Thosteson, George. *see* Thosteson, George C.
Thosteson, George C.
xThosteson, George.
The Everyday Medical Handbook. Fawcett.
Thouless, D. J.
xThouless, D. J.
The Quantum Mechanics of Many-Body
Systems. Acad Pr.
Thralls, Zoe A. *see* Thralls, Zoe Agnes.
Thralls, Zoe Agnes, 1888-
xThralls, Zoe A.
Teaching of Geography. Irvington.
Thrapp, Dan L.
xThrapp, Dan L.
General Crook & the Sierra Madre Adventure.
U of Okla Pr.
Thrasher, Crystal.
xThrasher, Crystal.
Between Dark & Daylight. Atheneum.
The Dark Didn't Catch Me. Atheneum.
The Dark Didn't Catch Me. Atheneum.
Thrasher, James M.
xThrasher, James M.
Effective Planning for Better School Buildings.
Pendell Pub.
Thrasher, Max B. *see* Thrasher, Max Bennett.
Thrasher, Max Bennett, 1860-1903
xThrasher, Max B.

Tuskegee: Its Story & Its Work. Arno.
Tuskegee: Its Story & Its Work. Negro U Pr.
Thrasher, W. E. *see* Thrasher, Wil E.
Thrasher, Wil E.
xThrasher, W. E.
Ballooning: A Pictorial Guide & World
Directory. Thrasher.
Threadgold, L. T.
xThreadgold, L. T.
The Ultrastructure of the Animal Cell.
Pergamon.
Threlkeld, James L.
xThrelkeld, James L.
Thermal Environmental Engineering. P-H.
Thresh, Christine.
xThresh, Christine.
Spinning with a Drop Spindle. Thresh Pubns.
Thresh, Robert.
xThresh, Robert.
An Introduction to Natural Dyeing. Thresh
Pubns.
Throckmorton, Burton H. *see* Throckmorton, Burton
Hamilton.
Throckmorton, Burton Hamilton, 1921-
xThrockmorton, Burton H.
Adopted in Love: Contemporary Studies in
Romans. Seabury.
Throop, P. A. *see* Throop, Palmer Allan.
Throop, Palmer A. *see* Throop, Palmer Allan.
Throop, Palmer Allan, 1902-
xThroop, P. A.
Criticism of the Crusade: A Study of Public
Opinion & Crusade Propaganda. Gordon Pr.
xThroop, Palmer A.
Criticism of the Crusade: A Study of Public
Opinion & Crusade Propaganda. Porcupine
Pr.
The Throroughbred Owners & Breeders Association. *see*
Thoroughbred Owners and Breeders Association.
Throsby, C. D.
xThrosby, D. C.
The Economics of the Performing Arts. St
Martin.
Throsby, D. C. *see* Throsby, C. D.
Thrower, Norman J. *see* Thrower, Norman Joseph
William.
Thrower, Norman Joseph William.
xThrower, Norman J.
ed. The Compleat Plattmaker: Essays on Chart,
Map, & Globe-Making in England in the
17th & 18th Centuries. U of Cal Pr.
Thrum, Thomas G. *see* Thrum, Thomas George.
Thrum, Thomas George, 1843-1932
xThrum, Thomas G.
More Hawaiian Folk Tales: A Collection of
Native Legends & Traditions. AMS Pr.
Thrush, John C.
xThrush, John C.
Japan's Economic Growth & Educational
Change: 1950-1970. EBHA Pr.
Thubron, Colin.
xThubron, Colin.
Istanbul. Silver.
Istanbul. Time-Life.
Thucydides.
xThucydides.
History of the Peloponnesian War. Dutton.
History of the Peloponnesian War. Oxford U
Pr.
The Peloponnesian War. Penguin.
The Speeches of Pericles. Ungar.
Thulstrup, Niels.
xThulstrup, Niels.
Pref. by Kierkegaard's Relation to Hegel.
Princeton U Pr.
Thum, Marcella.
xThum, Marcella.

Abbey Court. Doubleday.
Exploring Literary America. Atheneum.
Thunell, Lars H., 1948-
xThunell, Lars H.
Political Risks in International Business:
Investment Behavior of Multinationals.
Praeger.
Thung, Mady A.
xThung, Mady A.
The Precarious Organisation: Sociological
Explorations of the Church's Mission &
Structure. Mouton.
Thung, Yvonne.
xThung, Yvonne.
ed. Guide to Indonesian Serials 1945-70 in the
Cornell University Library. Cornell SE Asia.
Thurber, Clarence E.
xThurber, Clarence E.
Development Administration in Latin America.
Duke.
Thurber, James, 1894-
xThurber, James.
Further Fables for Our Time. S&S.
Further Fables for Our Time. S&S.
The Great Quillow. HarBraceJ.
Many Moons. HarBraceJ.
Many Moons. HarBraceJ.
My Life & Hard Times. Har-Row.
Thurber, Kenneth J.
xThurber, Kenneth J.
Distributed Processor Communication
Architecture. Lexington Bks.
Thurber, Packard.
xThurber, Packard.
jt. auth. Claims Medical Manual. Pacific Bks.
Thurber, Walter A.
xThurber, Walter A.
Exploring Earth Science. Allyn.
Exploring Life Science. Allyn.
Thurer, Georg.
xThurer, Georg.
Free & Swiss: The Story of Switzerland. U of
Miami Pr.
Thurlbeck. *see* Thurlbeck, William M.
Thurlbeck, William M.
xThurlbeck.
ed. The Lung: Structure, Function & Disease.
Williams & Wilkins.
xThurlbeck, William M.
Chronic Airflow Obstruction in Lung Disease.
Saunders.
Thurley, Geoffrey.
xThurley, Geoffrey.
The American Moment: American Poetry in
the Mid-Century. St Martin.
The Dickens Myth: Its Genesis & Structure. St
Martin.
Thurman, Howard, 1899-
xThurman, Howard.
Disciplines of the Spirit. Friends United.
The Growing Edge. Friends United.
Meditations of the Heart. Friends United.
Thurman, Judith.
xThurman, Judith.
I'd Like to Try a Monster' S Eye. Atheneum.
Lost & Found. Atheneum.
Thurman, S. David, 1941-
xThurman, S. David.
The Right of Access to Information from the
Government. Oceana.
Thurman, Wallace, 1902-1934
xThurman, Wallace.
Infants of the Spring. AMS Pr.
Infants of the Spring. Arno.
Infants of the Spring. S Ill U Pr.
Thurmond, Nancy M. *see* Thurmond, Nancy Moore.
Thurmond, Nancy Moore.
xThurmond, Nancy M.

Mother's Medicine. Morrow.

Thurnam, John, 1810-1873
xThurnam, John.
Observations & Essays on the Statistics of Insanity. Arno.

Thurow, Glen E.
xThurow, Glen E.
Abraham Lincoln & American Political Religion. State U NY Pr.

Thurow, Lester C.
xThurow, Lester C.
Generating Inequality: Mechanisms of Distribution in the U. S. Economy. Basic.
Poverty & Discrimination. Brookings.
The Zero-Sum Society: Distribution & the Possibilities for Economic Change. Basic.

Thurow, Raymond C.
xThurow, Raymond C.
Atlas of Orthodontic Principles. Mosby.
Edgewise Orthodontics. Mosby.

Thursfield, James R. see Thursfield, James Richard.

Thursfield, James Richard, Sir, 1840-1923
xThursfield, James R.
Peel. Arno.

Thurston, David B.
xThurston, David B.
Design for Flying. McGraw.

Thurston, Donald R.
xThurston, Donald R.
Teachers & Politics in Japan. Princeton U Pr.

Thurston, Edgar, 1855-1935
xThurston, Edgar.
Omens & Superstitions of Southern India. Folcroft.

Thurston, Frederick.
xThurston, Frederick.
Clarinet Technique. Oxford U Pr.

Thurston, Herbert, 1856-1939
xThurston, Herbert.
Ghosts & Poltergeists. Folcroft.

Thurston, Jarvis A.
xThurston, Jarvis A.
Reading Modern Short Stories. Scott F.

Thurston, Mark A.
xThurston, Mark A.
Experiments in a Search for God: The Edgar Cayce Path of Application. ARE Pr.

Thurston, Robert.
xThurston, Robert.
Alicia II. Putnam.

Thurston, Robert H. see Thurston, Robert Henry.

Thurston, Robert Henry, 1839-1903
xThurston, Robert H.
History of the Growth of the Steam-Engine. Kennikat.

Thurstone, Louis L. see Thurstone, Louis Leon.

Thurstone, Louis Leon, 1887-1955
xThurstone, Louis L.
Measurement of Values. U of Chicago Pr.
The Nature of Intelligence. Greenwood.

Thursz, Daniel.
xThursz, Daniel.
Meeting Human Needs: An Overview of Nine Countries. Sage.

Thwaite, Ann.
xThwaite, Ann.
Horrible Boy. Childrens.
The Poor Pigeon. Childrens.

Thwaite, Anthony.
xThwaite, Anthony.
Contemporary English Poetry: An Introduction. Arden Lib.
ed. Contemporary English Poetry: An Introduction. Dufour.
A Portion for Foxes. Oxford U Pr.
Twentieth Century English Poetry: An Introduction. B&N.

Thwaites, R. G. see Thwaites, Reuben Gold.
Thwaites, Reuben G. see Thwaites, Reuben Gold.

Thwaites, Reuben Gold, 1853-1913
xThwaites, R. G.
Frontier Defense on the Upper Ohio: 1777-1778. Kraus Repr.
xThwaites, Reuben G.
Daniel Boone. Arno.
France in America, 1497-1763. Greenwood.
France in America, 1497-1763. Haskell.
ed. Revolution on the Upper Ohio, 1775-1777. Kennikat.

Thwing, Annie H. see Thwing, Annie Haven.

Thwing, Annie Haven, 1851-
xThwing, Annie H.
Crooked & Narrow Streets of the Town of Boston, 1630-1822. Gale.

Thwing, Charles F. see Thwing, Charles Franklin.

Thwing, Charles Franklin, 1853-1937
xThwing, Charles F.
Guides, Philosophers & Friends: Studies of College Men. Arno.

Thygerson, A. L. see Thygerson, Alton L.

Thygerson, Alton L.
xThygerson, A. L.
Accidents & Disasters: Causes & Countermeasures. P-H.
xThygerson, Alton L.
Disaster Survival Handbook. Brigham.

Thyne, J. M. see Thyne, James Morrison.

Thyne, James Morrison.
xThyne, J. M.
The Principles of Examining. Halsted Pr.

Thyssen, Fritz.
xThyssen, Fritz.
I Paid Hitler. Kennikat.

Tibbett, Lawrence, 1896-1960
xTibbett, Lawrence.
The Glory Road. Arno.

Tibbetts, A. M.
xTibbetts, A. M.
Strategies of Rhetoric. Scott F.
Strategies of Rhetoric with Handbook. Scott F.
What's Happening to American English?. Scribner.

Tibbetts, Orlando L.
xTibbetts, Orlando L.
More Sidewalk Prayers. Judson.
The Work of the Church Trustee. Judson.

Tibble, Anne. see Tibble, Anne (Northgrave).

Tibble, Anne (Northgrave).
xTibble, Anne.
Greenhorn: A Twentieth-Century Childhood. Routledge & Kegan.

Tibbles, Thomas H. see Tibbles, Thomas Henry.

Tibbles, Thomas Henry, 1840-1928
xTibbles, Thomas H.
The Ponca Chiefs: An Account of the Trial of Standing Bear. U of Nebr Pr.

Tice, George A.
xTice, George A.
Paterson. Rutgers U Pr.

Ticer, James W.
xTicer, James W.
Radiographic Technique in Small Animal Practice. Saunders.

Tichenor, Tom.
xTichenor, Tom.
illus. Christmas Tree Crafts. Lippincott.

Tichy, Noel M.
xTichy, Noel M.
Organization Design for Primary Health Care: The Case of the Dr. Martin Luther King Jr. Health Center. Praeger.

Tickell, Crispin.
xTickell, Crispin.
Climatic Change & World Affairs. Harvard U Intl Aff.

Tickle, Phyllis.
xTickle, Phyllis.
The Story of Two Johns. St Luke TN.

Tickner, Frederick W. see Tickner, Frederick Windham.

Tickner, Frederick Windham.
xTickner, Frederick W.
Women in English Economic History. Hyperion Conn.

Ticknor, George, 1791-1871
xTicknor, George.
Life of William Hickling Prescott. R West.

Tidball, Harriet.
xTidball, Harriet.
Brocade. HTH Pubs.

Tider, David.
xTider, David.
Building Your Own Toys. A S Barnes.

Tidsworth, Floyd, 1932-
xTidsworth, Floyd.
Planting & Growing Missions. Moore Pub Co.

Tidwell, William D.
xTidwell, William D.
Common Fossil Plants of Western North America. Brigham.

Tidy, Bill, 1933-
xTidy, Bill.
The Great Eric Ackroyd Disaster. Merrimack Bk Serv.

Tiebout, Charles M. see Tiebout, Charles Mills.

Tiebout, Charles Mills, 1924-
xTiebout, Charles M.
The Community Economic Base Study. Comm Econ Dev.

Tieck, Johann L. see Tieck, Johann Ludwig.

Tieck, Johann Ludwig.
xTieck, Johann L.
Letters of Ludwig Tieck, Hitherto Unpublished, 1792-1853. Kraus Repr.

Tiede, Clayton H.
xTiede, Clayton H.
Practical Band Instrument Repair Manual. Wm C Brown.

Tiede, David L. see Tiede, David Lenz.

Tiede, David Lenz.
xTiede, David L.
The Charismatic Figure As Miracle Worker. Scholars Pr Ca.
Prophecy & History in Luke-Acts. Fortress.

Tiedeken, R. see Tiedeken, Robert.

Tiedeken, Robert.
xTiedeken, R.
Fibre Optics & Its Applications. Focal Pr.

Tiedeman, David V.
xTiedeman, David V.
Career Development: Designing Our Career Machines. Carroll Pr.
Career Development: Designing Our Career Machines. Character Res.

Tiedeman, Herman R.
xTiedeman, Herman R.
Fundamentals of Psychological & Educational Measurement. C C Thomas.

Tiedemann, Arthur. see Tiedemann, Arthur E.

Tiedemann, Arthur E.
xTiedemann, Arthur.
An Introduction to Japanese Civilization. Heath.
xTiedemann, Arthur E.
ed. An Introduction to Japanese Civilization. Columbia U Pr.

Tiedjens, V. A. see Tiedjens, Victor Alphons.

Tiedjens, Victor Alphons, 1895-
xTiedjens, V. A.
More Food from Soil Science: The Natural Chemistry of Lime in Agriculture. Exposition.

Tiedt, Iris M.
xTiedt, Iris M.
Exploring Books with Children. HM.

Tiedt, Pamela. see Tiedt, Pamela L.

Tiedt, Pamela L.
xTiedt, Pamela.

Essentials of Canine & Feline
Electrocardiography. Mosby.
Tilley, Nannie M. *see* Tilley, Nannie May.
Tilley, Nannie May, 1899-
xTilley, Nannie M.
The Bright-Tobacco Industry, 1860-1929. Arno.
Tilley, Patrick.
xTilley, Patrick.
Fade-Out. Morrow.
Tilley, Pauline.
xTilley, Pauline.
Art in the Education of Subnormal Children.
Beekman Pubs.
Tilley, Terrence W.
xTilley, Terrence W.
Talking of God: An Introduction to
Philosophical Analysis of Religious Language.
Paulist Pr.
Tilley, W. H. *see* Tilley, Wesley H.
Tilley, Wesley H.
xTilley, W. H.
Background of "The Princess Casamassima". U
Presses Fla.
Tillich, Hannah.
xTillich, Hannah.
From Place to Place: Travels with Paul Tillich,
Travels Without Paul Tillich. Stein & Day.
From Time to Time. Stein & Day.
Tillich, Paul, 1886-1965
xTillich, Paul.
Courage to Be. Yale U Pr.
Dynamics of Faith. Har-Row.
The Future of Religions. Greenwood.
A History of Christian Thought. S&S.
Systematic Theology. U of Chicago Pr.
Theology of Culture. Oxford U Pr.
World Situation. Fortress.
xTillich, Paul J.
Christianity & the Encounter of the World
Religions. Columbia U Pr.

Tillich, Paul J. *see* Tillich, Paul.

Tillich, Paul Johannes Oskar, 1886-
xTillich, Paul.
Eternal Now. Scribner.

Tilling, Meriel.
xTilling, Meriel.
The Observer's Book of Sewing. Scribner.

Tillinghast, B. S. *see* Tillinghast, Burette Stinson.

Tillinghast, Burette Stinson, 1930-
xTillinghast, B. S.
Bridge to Bonito Island. Dial.
Tillinghast, Joseph A. *see* Tillinghast, Joseph Alexander.
Tillinghast, Joseph Alexander.
xTillinghast, Joseph A.
Negro in Africa & America. Arno.
Negro in Africa & America. Negro U Pr.
Tillman, Albert. *see* Tillman, Albert A.
Tillman, Albert A.
xTillman, Albert.
The Program Book for Recreation
Professionals. Mayfield Pub.
Tillman, Barrett.
xTillman, Barrett.
The Dauntless Dive Bomber of World War
Two. Naval Inst Pr.
Tillman, Carolyn.
xTillman, Carolyn.
Life on Wheels. Crescent Pubns.
Tillman, David A.
xTillman, David A.
Wood As an Energy Resource. Acad Pr.
Tillotson, Geoffrey.
xTillotson, Geoffrey.
Augustan Studies. Greenwood.
Pope & Human Nature. Oxford U Pr.
Tillotson, Kathleen. *see* Tillotson, Kathleen Mary.

Tillotson, Kathleen Mary.
xTillotson, Kathleen.
Matthew Arnold & Carlyle. Folcroft.
Tilly, Charles.
xTilly, Charles.
From Mobilization to Revolution. A-W.
ed. Historical Studies of Changing Fertility.
Princeton U Pr.
Tilly, Richard.
xTilly, Richard.
Financial Institutions & Industrialization in the
Rhineland, 1815-1870. U of Wis Pr.
Tillyard, Eustace M. *see* Tillyard, Eustace Mandeville
Wetenhall.
Tillyard, Eustace Mandeville Wetenhall, 1889-1962
xTillyard, Eustace M.
The English Epic & Its Background.
Greenwood.
Tillyard, Henry J. *see* Tillyard, Henry Julius Wetenhall.
Tillyard, Henry Julius Wetenhall, 1881-
xTillyard, Henry J.
Byzantine Music & Hymnography. AMS Pr.
Tilman, H. W. *see* Tilman, Harold William.
Tilman, Harold William, 1898-
xTilman, H. W.
In Mischief's Wake. Transatlantic.
Tilmanis, Gundars A.
xTilmanis, Gundars A.
Advanced Tennis for Coaches, Teachers &
Players. Lea & Febiger.
Tilmann, Klemens, 1904-
xTilmann, Klemens.
The Practice of Meditation. Paulist Pr.
Tilson, John Q. *see* Tilson, John Quillan.
Tilson, John Quillan, 1866-
xTilson, John Q.
How to Conduct a Meeting. Oceana.
Tilson, Marie A. *see* Tilson, Marie Agnes.
Tilson, Marie Agnes, 1886-
xTilson, Marie A.
Problems of Preschool Children: A Basis for
Parental Education. AMS Pr.
Tilton, John E.
xTilton, John E.
The Future of Nonfuel Minerals. Brookings.
Tilton, John W. *see* Tilton, John Warren.
Tilton, John Warren, 1891-
xTilton, John W.
Relation Between Association & the Higher
Mental Processes. AMS Pr.
Tilton, John Wightman, 1928-
xTilton, John W.
Cosmic Satire in the Contemporary Novel.
Bucknell U Pr.
Tilton, Timothy A. *see* Tilton, Timothy Alan.
Tilton, Timothy Alan.
xTilton, Timothy A.
Nazism, Neo-Nazism, & the Peasantry. Ind U
Pr.
Timasheff, S. *see* Timasheff, Serge N.
Timasheff, S. N. *see* Timasheff, Serge N.
Timasheff, Serge. *see* Timasheff, Serge N.
Timasheff, Serge N.
xTimasheff, S.
ed. Subunits in Biological Systems. Dekker.
xTimasheff, S. N.
ed. Structure & Stability of Biological
Macromolecules. Dekker.
ed. Subunits in Biological Systems. Dekker.
xTimasheff, Serge.
ed. Subunits in Biological Systems. Dekker.
Timber Engineering Company.
xTimber Engineering Company.
Timber Design & Construction Handbook.
McGraw.
Timber Research and Development Association.
xT.R.A.D.A.
Timbers of the World. Longman.
Timberg, Thomas A., 1942-
xTimberg, Thomas A.

The Federal Executive: The President & the
Bureaucracy. Irvington.
Timberlake, Bob.
xTimberlake, Bob.
The World of Bob Timberlake. Oxmoor Hse.
Timberlake, Charles E.
xTimberlake, Charles E.
Detente: A Documentary Record. Praeger.
Timberlake, Henry, d. 1765
xTimberlake, Henry.
Memoirs of Lieut. Henry Timberlake. Arno.
Timberlake, James H.
xTimberlake, James H.
Prohibition & the Progressive Movement,
1900-1920. Atheneum.
Timberlake, Karen.
xTimberlake, Karen.
Chemistry. Har-Row.
Timberlake, P. H. *see* Timberlake, Philip Hunter.
Timberlake, Philip Hunter, 1883-
xTimberlake, P. H.
The North American Species of Heterosarus
Robertson (Hymenoptera, Apoidea). U of Cal
Pr.
Supplementary Studies on the Systematics of
the Genus Perdita (Hymenoptera:
Andrenidae). U of Cal Pr.
Timberlake, Richard H. *see* Timberlake, Richard Henry.
Timberlake, Richard Henry, 1922-
xTimberlake, Richard H.
The Origins of Central Banking in the United
States. Harvard U Pr.
Timbie, William H. *see* Timbie, William Henry.
Timbie, William Henry.
xTimbie, William H.
Essentials of Electricity. Wiley.
Time & Life Editors. *see* Time-Life Books.
Time Editors. *see* Time Inc.
Time Inc.
xTime Editors.
Live Them Again. S&S.

Time Life Bks Editors. *see* Time-Life Books.

Time Life Books. *see* Time-Life Books.

Time Life Books Editors. *see* Time-Life Books.

Time-Life Bks. *see* Time-Life Books.

Time-Life Bks. Editors. *see* Time-Life Books.

Time-Life Books.
xEditors of Time-Life Books.
Boutique Attire. Silver.
The Custom Look. Silver.
Exotic Styling. Silver.
Life Goes to the Movies. Silver.
Making Home Furnishings. Silver.
Novel Materials. Silver.
Seven Centuries of Art: Survey & Index. Silver.
Shortcuts to Elegance. Silver.
Traditional Favorites. Silver.
xTheEditors of Time-Life Books.
Classic Desserts. Time-Life.
xTime & Life Editors.
ed. New Living Spaces. Silver.
xTime Life Bks Editors.
The Boat. Silver.
Boat Handling. Silver.
Classic Techniques. Silver.
Creative Design. Silver.
Delicate Wear. Silver.
How Things Work in Your Home. Silver.
xTime Life Books.
ed. Basic Tailoring. Silver.
ed. The Classic Boat. Silver.

ed. The Community. Silver.

ed. Crime. Silver.

ed. Cruising. Silver.

ed. Cruising Grounds. Silver.

The End & the Myth. Time-Life.

The Gamblers. Time-Life.

ed. Life Before Man. Silver.

ed. Maintenance. Silver.

ed. Masonry. Silver.

ed. Offshore-Cruising Navigation Racing.
Silver.

ed. Paint & Wallpaper. Silver.

ed. Personal Touch. Silver.

ed. Plumbing. Silver.

ed. Racing. Silver.

ed. Restyling Your Wardrobe. Silver.

ed. Seamanship. Silver.

ed. Space & Storage. Silver.

ed. Weatherproofing. Silver.

xTime Life Books Editors.

Beavers & Other Pond Dwellers. Time-Life.

Floors & Stairways. Time-Life.

Kangaroos & Other Creatures from Down
Under. Time-Life.

Life in the Coral Reef. Time-Life.

ed. Songbirds. Time-Life.

The Time-Life Gardening Yearbook. Time-Life.

xTime-Life Bks.

ed. Pork. Time-Life.

ed. Walls & Ceilings. Time-Life.

xTime-Life Bks. Editors.

ed. The Best of Life. Silver.

xTime-Life Books.

ed. Beef & Veal. Time-Life.

ed. China-Burma-India. Time-Life.

ed. The Classic Boat. Time-Life.

ed. Decorating with Plants. Time-Life.

ed. Decorative Techniques. Silver.

Doors & Windows. Time-Life.

ed. Gardening Under Lights. Time-Life.

ed. Greenhouse Gardening. Time-Life.

ed. The Handy Boatman. Time-Life.

ed. Heating & Cooling. Time-Life.

ed. Heating & Cooling. Silver.

ed. Herbs. Time-Life.

ed. Home Security. Time-Life.

ed. Island Life. Time-Life.

Kitchens & Bathrooms. Silver.

ed. Kitchens & Bathrooms. Time-Life.

ed. Matthew Brady & His World. Time-Life.

ed. New Living Spaces. Time-Life.

ed. Photography Year: 1979. Time-Life.

ed. Poultry. Time-Life.

ed. The Ranchers. Time-Life.

ed. Soups. Time-Life.

The Time-Life American Regional Cookbook.
Little.

ed. Weatherproofing. Time-Life.

ed. Wild-Flower Gardening. Time-Life.

xTime-Life Books Editors.

Adding on. Time-Life.

Advertising Giveaways to Baskets. Silver.

American Painting, Nineteen Hundred to
Nineteen Seventy. Time-Life.

Beads to Boxes. Silver.

ed. Built-Ins. Time-Life.

Buttons to Chess Sets. Silver.

Cabins & Cottages. Time-Life.

Children's Books to Comics. Silver.

Cookbooks to Detective Fiction. Silver.

Dogs to Fishing Tackle. Silver.

Fish. Time-Life.

Folk Art to Horse-Drawn Carriages. Silver.

Guide to the Natural World & Index to the
Life Nature Library. Silver.

ed. How Things Work in Your Home. G&D.

Inkwells to Lace. Silver.

Lalique to Masks. Silver.

Matchsafes to Nursing Bottles. Silver.

Modern American Painting: 1900 - 1970.
Silver.

Oak Furniture to Pharmacist's Equipment.
Silver.

The Old House. Time-Life.

ed. Pest & Diseases. Time-Life.

Pewter to Quilts. Silver.

ed. Photography Year: 1980. Time-Life.

ed. Recreational Areas. Time-Life.

Salads. Time-Life.

Seven Centuries of Art. Time-Life.

Snacks & Sandwiches. Time-Life.

The Sporting Scene. Silver.

Sports Afloat. Silver.

This Fabulous Century. Silver.

The Time-Life Holiday Cookbook. Time-Life.

Vegetables. Time-Life.

Working with Wood. Time-Life.

xTime-Life Editors.

Birds of Field & Forest. Time-Life.

Community. Time-Life.

The Glory & Pageantry of Christmas.
Hammond Inc.

The Handy Boatman. Silver.

Outdoor Structures. Time-Life.

Roofs & Siding. Time-Life.

Time-Life Holiday Cookbook. Silver.

The Time-Life International Cookbook.
HR&W.

xTime-Life Staff.

ed. Life Goes to War: A Picture History of
World War II. Little.

Time-Life Books Editors. *see* Time-Life Books.

Time-Life Editors. *see* Time-Life Books.

Time-Life Staff. *see* Time-Life Books.

Time-Life Television.

xTime-Life Television.

Bears & Other Carnivores. Time-Life.

Birds of Field & Forest. Silver.

ed. Domestic Descendants. Time-Life.

Spider & Insects. Time-Life.

ed. Whales & Other Sea Animals. Time-Life.

Wild Herds. Time-Life.

xTime-Life Television Editors.

Animal Defenses. Time-Life.

Fishes of Lakes, Rivers & Oceans. Time-Life.

Life in Zoos & Preserves. Time-Life.

Rabbits & Other Small Mammals. Time-Life.

Time-Life Television Editors. *see* Time-Life Television.

The Times, London.

xLondon Sunday Times.

Suffer the Children: The Story of Thalidomide.
Viking Pr.

xLondon Times.

American Writing Today. Arno.

Fifty Years: Memories & Contrasts. Arno.

Modern Essays. Arno.

The New York Times Atlas of the World.
Times Bks.

Third Leaders, Reprinted from the Times.
Arno.

The Times Atlas of the World: Comprehensive
Edition. Times Bks.

xLondon Times Editors.

ed. Signs of the Times: A Selection of Comic
Signs from the "the Times Diary".
Transatlantic.

xTheLondon Times.

The Bible Today: Historical, Social, & Literary
Aspects of the Old & New Testaments.
Greenwood.

Timko, Michael, 1925-

xTimko, Michael.

Innocent Victorian: The Satiric Poetry of
Arthur Hugh Clough. Ohio U Pr.

Timlin, Mabel F. *see* Timlin, Mabel Frances.

Timlin, Mabel Frances.

xTimlin, Mabel F.

Keynesian Economics. U of Toronto Pr.

Timm, Neil H.

xTimm, Neil H.

Multivariate Analysis with Applications in
Education & Psychology. Brooks-Cole.

Timm, Paul R.

xTimm, Paul R.

Managerial Communication: A Finger on the
Pulse. P-H.

Timm, Richard W., 1923-

xTimm, Richard W.

A Revision of the Nematode Order
Desmoscolecida Filipjev, 1929. U of Cal Pr.

Timmer, C. Peter.

xTimmer, C. Peter.

The Choice of Technology in Developing
Countries: Some Cautionary Tales. Harvard
U Intl Aff.

Timmerman, Maurine.

xTimmerman, Maurine.

Guitar in the Classroom. Wm C Brown.

Timmermann, Tim.

xTimmermann, Tim.

Growing Up Alive: Humanistic Education for
the Pre-Teen. Irvington.

Strategies in Humanistic Education. Irvington.

Timmermans, Claire.

xTimmermans, Claire.

How to Teach Your Baby to Swim. Stein &
Day.

Timmermans, Felix, 1886-1947

xTimmermans, Felix.

The Perfect Joy of St. Francis. Doubleday.

Timmins, Alice.

xTimmins, Alice.

Patchwork Simplified. Arco.

Timmis, Gerald C.

xTimmis, Gerald C.

Cardiovascular Review. Williams & Wilkins.

Cardiovascular Review 1980. Williams &
Wilkins.

Timmis, John H.

xTimmis, John H.

Thine Is the Kingdom: The Trial for Treason of
Thomas Wentworth, Earl of Strafford, First
Minister of King Charles I, & the Last Hope
of the English Crown. U of Ala Pr.

Timmons. *see* Timmons, Virginia Gayheart.

Timmons, Myra B. *see* Timmons, Myra Bownds.

Timmons, Myra Bownds.

xTimmons, Myra B.

Tailoring Techniques. Interstate.

Timmons, Tim.

xTimmons, Tim.

Maximum Living in a Pressure Cooker World. Word Bks.

Maximum Marriage. Revell.

The Ultimate Lifestyle. Vision Hse.

Timmons, Virginia G. *see* Timmons, Virginia Gayheart.

Timmons, Virginia Gayheart.

xTimmons.

Designing & Making Mosaics. P-H.

xTimmons, Virginia G.

Art Materials, Techniques, Ideas: A Resource Book for Teachers. Davis Mass.

Painting in the School Program. Davis Mass.

Timmons, W. H. *see* Timmons, Wilbert H.

Timmons, Wilbert H.

xTimmons, W. H.

Tadeo Ortiz, Mexican Colonizer & Reformer. Tex Western.

Timmons, William, 1878-

xTimmons, William.

Twilight on the Range: Recollections of a Latterday Cowboy. U of Tex Pr.

Timmons, William M. *see* Timmons, William Murray.

Timmons, William Murray, 1906-

xTimmons, William M.

Decisions & Attitudes As Outcomes of the Discussion of a Social Problem. AMS Pr.

Timms, E. V. *see* Timms, Edward Vivian.

Timms, Edward Vivian, 1895-

xTimms, E. V.

They Came from the Sea. BJ Pub Group.

Timms, Moira.

xTimms, Moira.

Natural Sources: Vitamin B-17--Laetrile. Celestial Arts.

Timms, Noel.

xTimms, Noel.

Sociological Approach to Social Problems. Humanities.

ed. Talking About Welfare: Readings in Philosophy & Social Policy. Routledge & Kegan.

Timoshenko, S. P. *see* Timoshenko, Stephen.

Timoshenko, Stephen.

xTimoshenko, S. P.

Mechanics of Materials. Van Nos Reinhold.

xTimoshenko, Stephen P.

Theory of Elastic Stability. McGraw.

Theory of Elasticity. McGraw.

Theory of Plates & Shells. McGraw.

Timoshenko, Stephen P. *see* Timoshenko, Stephen.

Timoshenko, Vladimir P. *see* Timoshenko, Vladimir Prokopovich.

Timoshenko, Vladimir Prokopovich, 1885-

xTimoshenko, Vladimir P.

Agricultural Russia & the Wheat Problem. Johnson Repr.

The World's Sugar: Progress & Policy. Stanford U Pr.

Timpe, Eugene F.

xTimpe, Eugene F.

Thoreau Abroad: Twelve Bibliographical Essays. Shoe String.

Tinbergen, Jan, 1903-

xTinbergen, Jan.

The Design of Development. Johns Hopkins.

Dynamics of Business Cycles. U of Chicago Pr.

Statistical Testing of Business-Cycle Theories. Agathon.

Tinbergen, Nikalaas. *see* Tinbergen, Nikolaas.

Tinbergen, Niko. *see* Tinbergen, Nikolass.

Tinbergen, Nikolaas.

xTinbergen, Nikalaas.

Study of Instinct. Folcroft.

xTinbergen, Niko.

Animal Behavior. Silver.

Animal Behavior. Silver.

xTinbergen, Nikolaas.

Study of Instinct. Oxford U Pr.

Tinbergen, Nikolass, 1907-

xTinbergen, Niko.

Curious Naturalists. Natural Hist.

Tindale, Norman B. *see* Tindale, Norman Barnett.

Tindale, Norman Barnett, 1900-

xTindale, Norman B.

Aboriginal Tribes of Australia: Their Terrain, Environmental Controls, Distribution, Limits, & Proper Names. U of Cal Pr.

Tindall, George B. *see* Tindall, George Brown.

Tindall, George Brown.

xTindall, George B.

The Disruption of the Solid South. Norton.

The Disruption of the Solid South. U of Ga Pr.

ed. Populist Reader: Selections from the Works of American Populist Leaders. Peter Smith.

South Carolina Negroes, 1877-1900. U of SC Pr.

xTindall, Geroge Brown.

The Ethnic Southerners. La State U Pr.

Tindall, Geroge Brown. *see* Tindall, George Brown.

Tindall, Gillian.

xTindall, Gillian.

The Born Exile: George Gissing. HarBraceJ.

Tindall, Robert Emmett, 1934-

xTindall, Robert Emmett.

Multinational Enterprises: Legal & Management Structures & Interrelationship with Ownership, Control, Antitrust, Labor Taxation & Disclosure. Oceana.

Tindall, William Y. *see* Tindall, William York.

Tindall, William York, 1903-

xTindall, William Y.

D. H. Lawrence & Susan His Cow. Cooper Sq.

Literary Symbol. Ind U Pr.

Literary Symbol. Peter Smith.

A Readers Guide to Dylan Thomas. Octagon.

A Reader's Guide to James Joyce. Octagon.

Tinder, Glenn. *see* Tinder, Glenn E.

Tinder, Glenn E,

xTinder, Glenn.

Political Thinking: The Perennial Questions. Little.

Tiner, J. H. *see* Tiner, John Hudson.

Tiner, John Hudson.

xTiner, J. H.

When Science Fails. Baker Bk.

Ting, William S.

xTing, William S.

Determination of Pinus Species by Pollen Statistics. U of Cal Pr.

Tingley, Donald F. *see* Tingley, Donald Fred.

Tingley, Donald Fred, 1922-

xTingley, Donald F.

ed. Social History of the United States: A Guide to Information Sources. Gale.

The Structuring of a State: The History of Illinois, 1899-1928. U of Ill Pr.

Tingley, Katherine. *see* Tingley, Katherine Augusta Westcott.

Tingley, Katherine Augusta Westcott.

xTingley, Katherine.

The Wisdom of the Heart: Katherine Tingley Speaks. Point Loma Pub.

Tinic, Seha M.

xTinic, Seha M.

Investing in Securities: An Efficient Markets Approach. A-W.

Tinker, Chauncey B. *see* Tinker, Chauncey Brewster.

Tinker, Chauncey Brewster, 1876-1963

xTinker, Chauncey B.

Nature's Simple Plan: A Phase of Radical Thought in the Mid-Eighteenth Century. Gordian.

Tinker, Edward L. *see* Tinker, Edward Larocque.

Tinker, Edward Larocque.

xTinker, Edward L.

Horsemen of the Americas & the Literature They Inspired. U of Tex Pr.

Tinker, Hugh.

xTinker, Hugh.

The Banyan Tree: Overseas Emigrants from India, Pakistan & Bangladesh. Oxford U Pr.

Tinker, Miles A. *see* Tinker, Miles Albert.

Tinker, Miles Albert, 1893-

xTinker, Miles A.

Legibility of Print. Iowa St U Pr.

Preparing Your Child for Reading. McGraw.

Teaching Elementary Reading. P-H.

Tinkham, M. *see* Tinkham, Michael.

Tinkham, Michael.

xTinkham, M.

Superconductivity. Gordon.

xTinkham, Michael.

Group Theory & Quantum Mechanics. McGraw.

Introduction to Superconductivity. Krieger.

Tinkle, L. *see* Tinkle, Lon.

Tinkle, Lon.

xTinkle, L.

Cowboy Reader. McKay.

xTinkle, Lon.

Valiant Few: Crisis at the Alamo. Macmillan.

Tinsley, Ian J., 1929-

xTinsley, Ian J.

Chemical Concepts in Pollutant Behavior. Wiley.

Tinsley, Russell.

xTinsley, Russell.

All About Small-Game Hunting in America. Follett.

ed. All About Small Game Hunting in America. Winchester Pr.

Tint, Herbert, 1924-

xTint, Herbert.

French Foreign Policy Since the Second World War. St Martin.

Tinterow, Maurice M., 1917-

xTinterow, Maurice M.

Foundations of Hypnosis: From Mesmer to Freud. C C Thomas.

Tipei, Nicolae.

xTipei, Nicolae.

Theory of Lubrication: With Applications to Liquid & Gas-Film Lubrication. Stanford U Pr.

Tippens, Paul E.

xTippens, Paul E.

Applied Physics. McGraw.

Tipper, Harry, 1910-

xTipper, Harry.

The System & What You Can Do With It. Gambit.

Tippett, Alan. *see* Tippett, Alan Richard.

Tippett, Alan R. *see* Tippett, Alan Richard.

Tippett, Alan Richard.

xTippett, Alan.

Aspects of Pacific Ethnohistory. William Carey Lib.

xTippett, Alan R.

The Deep-Sea Canoe: The Story of Third World Missionaries in the South Pacific. William Carey Lib.

Solomon Islands Christianity: A Study in Growth & Obstruction. William Carey Lib.

Tippett, James S. *see* Tippett, James Sterling.

Tippett, James Sterling, 1885-1958

xTippett, James S.

Crickety-Cricket!: The Best-Loved Poems of James S. Tippett. Har-Row.

Tippo, Oswald.

xTippo, Oswald.

Humanistic Botany. Norton.

Tips, Charles, 1949-

xTips, Charles.

Frisbee by the Masters. Celestial Arts.

Tipton, C. *see* Tipton, Charles Leon.

Tipton, Charles Leon, 1932-

xTipton, C.

Love, Life & Laughter. Windy Row.
Tobias, Jerry V., 1929-
xTobias, Jerry V.
ed. Foundations of Modern Auditory Theory. Acad Pr.
Tobias, Marc W. *see* Tobias, Marc Weber.
Tobias, Marc Weber.
xTobias, Marc W.
Field Manual of Criminal Law & Police Procedure. C C Thomas.
Pre-Trial Criminal Procedure: A Survey of Constitutional Rights. C C Thomas.
Tobias, Michael.
xTobias, Michael C.
ed. The Mountain Spirit. Overlook Pr.
Tobias, Michael C. *see* Tobias, Michael.
Tobias, Phillip V.
xTobias, Phillip V.
Brain in Hominid Evolution. Columbia U Pr.
Tobias, Richard. *see* Tobias, Richard Clark.
Tobias, Richard C. *see* Tobias, Richard Clark.
Tobias, Richard Clark, 1925-
xTobias, Richard.
T. E. Brown. Twayne.
xTobias, Richard C.
The Art of James Thurber. Ohio U Pr.
Tobias, Sheila.
xTobias, Sheila.
Overcoming Math Anxiety. HM.
Overcoming Math Anxiety. Norton.
Tobias, Tobi.
xTobias, Tobi.
Arthur Mitchell. T Y Crowell.
A Day off. Putnam.
Maria Tallchief. T Y Crowell.
Marian Anderson. T Y Crowell.
The Quitting Deal. Viking Pr.
The Quitting Deal. Penguin
An Umbrella Named Umbrella. Knopf.
Tobin, Charles E. *see* Tobin, Charles Emil.
Tobin, Charles Emil.
xTobin, Charles E.
Human Anatomy. Bobbs.
Tobin, Gary A.
xTobin, Gary A.
ed. The Changing Structure of the City: What Happened to the Urban Crisis?. Sage.
Tobin, Helen M., 1922-
xTobin, Helen M.
The Process of Staff Development: Components for Change. Mosby.
Tobin, J. Raymond. *see* Tobin, Joseph Raymond.
Tobin, Joseph Raymond, 1885-
xTobin, J. Raymond.
Inside Music: Answers to 1001 Questions. Emerson.
Tobin, Kay.
xTobin, Kay.
The Gay Crusaders. Arno.
Tobin, Ronald W., 1936-
xTobin, Ronald W.
Racine & Seneca. U of NC Pr.
Tobler, Alfred.
xTobler, Alfred.
Geoffrey Chaucer's Influence on English Literature. AMS Pr.
Tobler, John.
xTobler, John.
Guitar Heroes. St Martin.
Toboldt, Bill. *see* Toboldt, William King.
Toboldt, William King, 1895-
xToboldt, Bill.
Auto Body Repairing & Repainting. Goodheart.
Diesel: Fundamentals Service & Repair. Goodheart.
Fix Your Chevrolet. Goodheart.
Tobolsky, Arthur V. *see* Tobolsky, Arthur Victor.
Tobolsky, Arthur Victor.
xTobolsky, Arthur V.

Polymer Science & Materials. Krieger.
Tocchini, John J.
xTocchini, John J.
ed. Restorative Dentistry. McGraw.
Tocci, Ronald J.
xTocci, Ronald J.
Digital Systems: Principles & Applications. P-H.
Fundamentals of Electronic Devices. Merrill.
Fundamentals of Pulse & Digital Circuits. Merrill.
Introduction to Electric Circuit Analysis. Merrill.
Microprocessors & Microcomputers: Hardware & Software. P-H.
Toch, Hans.
xToch, Hans.
Living in Prison: The Ecology of Survival. Free Pr.
Men in Crisis: Human Breakdowns in Prison. Beresford Bk Serv.
Peacekeeping: Police, Prisons & Violence. Lexington Bks.
Psychology of Crime & Criminal Justice. HR&W.
ed. Therapeutic Communities in Corrections. Praeger.
Todd, A. C. *see* Todd, Arthur Cecil.
Todd, Arthur Cecil.
xTodd, A. C.
The Industrial Archaeology of Cornwall. David & Charles.
Todd, Charles B. *see* Todd, Charles Burr.
Todd, Charles Burr, 1849-
xTodd, Charles B.
In Olde Massachusetts: Sketches of Old Times & Places During the Early Days of the Commonwealth. Gale.
Todd, Charles L.
xTodd, Charles L.
Alexander Bryan Johnson: Philosophical Banker. Syracuse U Pr.
Todd, David.
xTodd, David.
Experimental Organic Chemistry. P-H.
Todd, David K. *see* Todd, David Keith.
Todd, David Keith, 1923-
xTodd, David K.
Groundwater Hydrology. Wiley.
Todd, Emmanuel, 1951-
xTodd, Emmanuel.
The Final Fall: Essay on the Decomposition of the Soviet Sphere. Karz Pub.
Todd, Floyd.
xTodd, Floyd.
Good Morning, Lord: Devotions for Campers. Baker Bk.
Todd, Frank S.
xTodd, Frank S.
Waterfowl: Ducks, Geese & Swans of the World. HarBraceJ.
Todd, H. E. *see* Todd, Herbert Eatton.
Todd, Herbert Eatton.
xTodd, H. E.
George the Fire Engine. Childrens.
The Roundabout Horse. Childrens.
Todd, Ian.
xTodd, Ian.
Ghosts of the Assassins. E A Seemann.
Todd, James M. *see* Todd, James Maclean.
Todd, James Maclean.
xTodd, James M.
ed. Voices from the Past: A Classical Anthology for the Modern Reader.. Granger Bk.
Todd, Janet M., 1942-
xTodd, Janet M.

In Adam's Garden: A Study of John Clare's Pre-Asylum Poetry. U Presses Fla.
Todd, Larry.
xTodd, Larry.
illus. Tales of Fantasy. Troubador Pr.
Todd, Loreto.
xTodd, Loreto.
Some Day Been Dey: West African Pidgin Folktales. Routledge & Kegan.
Todd, M. J. *see* Todd, Michael J.
Todd, Michael J., 1947-
xTodd, M. J.
The Computation of Fixed Points & Applications. Springer-Verlag.
Todd, Robert M., 1897-
xTodd, Robert M.
Sopwith Camel Fighter Ace. AJAY Ent.
Todd, Terry.
xTodd, Terry.
Fitness for Athletes. Contemp Bks.
Inside Powerlifting. Contemp Bks.
Todd, William M. *see* Todd, William Mills.
Todd, William Mills.
xTodd, William M.
ed. Literature & Society in Imperial Russia, 1800-1914. Stanford U Pr.
Todisco, Paula J., 1950-
xTodisco, Paula J.
Boston's First Neighborhood: The North End. Boston Public Lib.
Todor, Dumitru N.
xTodor, Dumitru N.
Thermal Analysis of Minerals. Intl Schol Bk Serv.
Todorov, Tsvetan.
xTodorov, Tzvetan.
The Fantastic: A Structural Approach to a Literary Genre. Cornell U Pr.
The Fantastic: A Structural Approach to a Literary Genre. UPBS.
Todorov, Tzvetan. *see* Todorov, Tsvetan.
Toelken, Barre.
xToelken, Barre.
The Dynamics of Folklore. HM.
Toepffer, Iohannes. *see* Toepffer, Johannes.
Toepffer, Johannes.
xToepffer, Iohannes.
Attische Genealogie. Arno.
Toeplitz, Otto, 1881-1940
xToeplitz, Otto.
Calculus: A Genetic Approach. U of Chicago Pr.
Toff, Nancy.
xToff, Nancy.
Development of the Modern Flute. Taplinger.
Toffler, Alan. *see* Toffler, Alvin.
Toffler, Alvin.
xToffler, Alan.
The Third Wave. Morrow.
xToffler, Alvin.
Future Shock. Bantam.
Future Shock. Random.
ed. The Futurists. Random.
ed. Learning for Tomorrow: The Role of the Future in Education. Random.
ed. Learning for Tomorrow: The Role of the Future in Education. Random.
The Third Wave. Bantam.
Toga, Carl J.
xToga, Carl J.
Geriatric Dentistry: Clinical Application of Selected Biomedical & Psychosocial Topics. Lexington Bks.
Toglia, Michael P.
xToglia, Michael P.
Handbook of Semantic Word Norms. Halsted Pr.
Togliatti, Palmiro, 1893-1964
xTogliatti, Palmiro.

Lectures on Fascism. Intl Pub Co.
Tohei, Koichi, 1920-
    xTohei, Koichi.
        Ki in Daily Life. Japan Pubns.
Tohei, Koichi. see Tohei, Koichi.
Toit, Brian M. Du. see Du Toit, Brian M.
Tokes, Rudolf. see Tokes, Rudolf L.
Tokes, Rudolf L., 1935-
    xTokes, Rudolf.
        ed. Opposition in Eastern Europe. Johns
        Hopkins.
    xTokes, Rudolf L.
        ed. Dissent in the USSR: Politics, Ideology &
        People. Johns Hopkins U Pr.
    xTokes, Rudolph L.
        ed. Eurocommunism & Detente. NYU Pr.
Tokes, Rudolph L. see Tokes, Rudolf L.
Tokheim, Roger. see Tokheim, Roger L.
Tokheim, Roger L.
    xTokheim, Roger.
        Digital Electronics. McGraw.
    xTokheim, Roger L.
        Schaum's Outline of Digital Principles.
        McGraw.
Toklas, Alice B.
    xToklas, Alice B.
        Alice B. Toklas Cook Book. Doubleday.
Tokle, Art.
    xTokle, Art.
        The Complete Guide to Cross Country Skiing
        & Touring. HR&W.
        A Complete Guide to Cross-Country Skiing &
        Touring. Random.
Tokson, Elliot.
    xTokson, Elliot.
        Cavender's Balkan Quest. Fawcett.
    xTokson, Elliott.
        Desert Captive. Fawcett.
Tokson, Elliott. see Tokson, Elliot.
Tolan, Stephanie S.
    xTolan, Stephanie S.
        The Last of Eden. Warne.
        The Liberation of Tansy Warner. Scribner.
Toland, John.
    xToland, John.
        Adolf Hitler. Doubleday.
        A Collection of Several Pieces. Garland Pub.
        Dillinger Days. Random.
        The Flying Tigers. Dell.
        Flying Tigers. Random.
        Flying Tigers. Random.
        Letters to Serena. Garland Pub.
        Pantheisticon. Garland Pub.
Tolansky, S. see Tolansky, Samuel.
Tolansky, Samuel.
    xTolansky, S.
        Multiple Beam Interference Microscopy of
        Metals. Acad Pr.
        Multiple-Beam Interferometry of Surfaces &
        Films. Dover.
        Multiple-Beam Interferometry of Surfaces &
        Films. Peter Smith.
Tolbert, E. L.
    xTolbert, E. L.
        Counseling for Career Development. HM.
        Introduction to Counseling. McGraw.
        An Introduction to Guidance. Little.
Tolbert, Frank X.
    xTolbert, Frank X.
        A Bowl of Red. Doubleday.
        Day of San Jacinto. Jenkins.
Tolbert, Malcolm.
    xTolbert, Malcolm O.
        Good News from Matthew. Broadman.
Tolbert, Malcolm O. see Tolbert, Malcolm.
Toledano, Ralph De. see De Toledano, Ralph.
Toledo Museum of Art.
    xToledo Museum of Art Staff.

American Paintings in the Toledo Museum of
Art. Toledo Mus Art.
    xToledo Museum Staff.
        Toledo Museum of Art, American Paintings.
        Toledo Mus Art.
Toledo Museum of Art Staff. see Toledo Museum of Art.
Toledo Museum Staff. see Toledo Museum of Art.
Toledo, Romeo T.
    xToledo, Romeo T.
        Fundamentals of Food Process Engineering.
        AVI.
Toledo, S. A. see Toledo, Sue Ann.
Toledo, Sue Ann, 1940-
    xToledo, S. A.
        Tableau Systems for First Order Number
        Theory & Certain Higher Order Theories.
        Springer-Verlag.
Toles, E. B.
    xToles, E. B.
        A Layman Shares Jesus. Broadman.
Tolf, Robert W.
    xTolf, Robert W.
        Best Restaurants Florida's Gold Coast. One
        Hund One Prods.
        Country Inns of the Old South. One Hund One
        Prods.
Tolg, G. see Tolg, Gunther.
Tolg, Gunther.
    xTolg, G.
        Ultramicro Elemental Analysis. Krieger.
Tolis, George.
    xTolis, George.
        ed. Clinical Neuroendocrinology: A
        Pathophysiological Approach. Raven.
Toliver, Harold E.
    xToliver, Harold E.
        Pastoral Forms & Attitudes. U of Cal Pr.
Toliver, Raymond. see Toliver, Raymond F.
Toliver, Raymond F.
    xToliver, Raymond.
        Fighter Aces of the U. S. A.. Aero.
    xToliver, Raymond F.
        Fighter Aces of the Luftwaffe. Aero.
Tolkien, J. R. see Tolkien, John Ronald Reuel.
Tolkien, John Ronald Reuel, 1892-1973
    xTolkien, J. R.
        The Father Christmas Letters. HM.
        The Lord of the Rings. Fotonovel.
        The Lord of the Rings. HM.
        The Pictures of J. R. R. Tolkien. HM.
        Return of the King. Ballantine.
        Return of the King. HM.
        The Silmarillion. Ballantine.
        Silmarillion. HM.
        Two Towers. HM.
Toll, Nelly.
    xToll, Nelly.
        Without Surrender: Art of the Holocaust.
        Running Pr.
Toll, William.
    xToll, William.
        The Resurgence of Race: Black Social Theory
        from Reconstruction to the Pan-African
        Conferences. Temple U Pr.
Tolle, H. see Tolle, Henning.
Tolle, Henning.
    xTolle, H.
        Optimization Methods. Springer-Verlag.
Tolle, Jean B. see Tolle, Jean Bashor.
Tolle, Jean Bashor.
    xTolle, Jean B.
        The Great Pete Penney. Atheneum.
Tollenaere, J. P.
    xTollenaere, J. P.
        Atlas of the Three-Dimensional Structure of
        Drugs. Elsevier.
Toller, C. Van. see Van Toller, C.
Toller, Jane.
    xToller, Jane.

English Country Furniture. A S Barnes.
Turned Woodware for Collectors: Treen &
Other Objects. A S Barnes.
Tolles, Frederick B. see Tolles, Frederick Barnes.
Tolles, Frederick Barnes, 1915-
    xTolles, Frederick B.
        George Logan of Philadelphia. Arno.
Tolley, B. Stuart.
    xTolley, B. Stuart.
        Advertising & Marketing Research: A New
        Methodology. Nelson-Hall.
Tolley, George S.
    xTolley, George S.
        Urban Growth Policy in a Market Economy.
        Acad Pr.
Tolley, William P. see Tolley, William Pearson.
Tolley, William Pearson, 1900-
    xTolley, William P.
        Adventure of Learning. Syracuse U Pr.
Tolliver, Ruby C.
    xTolliver, Ruby C.
        The Summer of Decision. Broadman.
Tolman, Albert. see Tolman, Albert Harris.
Tolman, Albert H. see Tolman, Albert Harris.
Tolman, Albert Harris, 1856-1928
    xTolman, Albert.
        A View of the Views About Hamlet. Folcroft.
    xTolman, Albert H.
        Falstaff & Other Shakespearean Topics. AMS
        Pr.
        Falstaff & Other Shakespearean Topics.
        Folcroft.
Tolman, Edward C. see Tolman, Edward Chace.
Tolman, Edward Chace, 1886-1959
    xTolman, Edward C.
        Purposive Behavior in Animals & Men.
        Irvington.
Tolman, Newton F.
    xTolman, Newton F.
        North of Monadnock. Am Repr-Rivercity Pr.
        North of Monadnock. Bauhan.
        Our Loons Are Always Laughing. Am
        Repr-Rivercity Pr.
        Quick Tunes & Good Times. Bauhan.
Tolman, Richard C. see Tolman, Richard Chace.
Tolman, Richard Chace, 1881-1948
    xTolman, Richard C.
        The Principles of Statistical Mechanics. Dover.
Tolman, Ruth.
    xTolman, Ruth.
        Charm & Poise for Getting Ahead. Milady.
        Guide to Fashion Merchandise Knowledge.
        Milady.
        Guide to Fashion Merchandise Knowledge.
        Milady.
Tolnay, Charles De. see De Tolnay, Charles.
Toloudis, Constantin.
    xToloudis, Constantin.
        Jacques Audiberti. Twayne.
Tolson, Melvin. see Tolson, Melvin Beaunorus.
Tolson, Melvin B. see Tolson, Melvin Beaunorus.
Tolson, Melvin Beaunorus.
    xTolson, Melvin.
        Libretto for the Republic of Liberia. Macmillan.
    xTolson, Melvin B.
        A Gallery of Harlem Portraits. U of Mo Pr.
        Libretto for the Republic of Liberia. Twayne.
Tolstoi, Lev N. see Tolstoi, Lev Nikolaevich.
Tolstoi, Lev Nikolaevich.
    xTolstoi, Lev N.
        Complete Works of Count Tolstoy. AMS Pr.
Tolzmann, Don H. see Tolzmann, Don Heinrich.
Tolzmann, Don Heinrich, 1945-
    xTolzmann, Don H.
        German-American Literature. Scarecrow.
        German Americana: A Bibliography.
        Scarecrow.
Toma, Peter A.
    xToma, Peter A.

Politics in Hungary. W H Freeman.
Tomalin, Claire.
    xTomalin, Claire.
        The Life & Death of Mary Wollstonecraft. HarBraceJ.
        The Life & Death of Mary Wollstonecraft. NAL.
Tomalin, Ruth.
    xTomalin, Ruth.
        Gone Away. Merrimack Bk Serv.
Toman, W. *see* Toman, Walter.
Toman, Walter.
    xToman, W.
        An Introduction to Psychoanalytic Theory of Motivation. Pergamon.
Tomasi, S. M. *see* Tomasi, Silvano M.
Tomasi, Silvano M.
    xTomasi, S. M.
        ed. Italian-Americans & Religion: An Annotated Bibliography. Ctr Migration.
Tomasic, Roman.
    xTomasic, Roman.
        ed. Lawyers & the Community. Allen Unwin.
Tomat, Jean H. *see* Tomat, Jean Hunter.
Tomat, Jean Hunter.
    xTomat, Jean H.
        Learning Through Music for Special Children & Their Teachers. Merriam-Eddy.
Tomback, Richard S.
    xTomback, Richard S.
        A Comparative Semitic Lexicon of the Phoenician & Punic Languages. Scholars Pr Ca.
Tombes, A. S. *see* Tombes, Averett S.
Tombes, Averett S., 1932-
    xTombes, A. S.
        Introduction to Invertebrate Endocrinology. Acad Pr.
Tombs, M. *see* Tombs, M. P.
Tombs, M. P.
    xTombs, M.
        The Osmotic Pressure of Biological Macromolecules. Oxford U Pr.
Tomczak, Larry, 1949-
    xTomczak, Larry.
        Clap Your Hands!. Logos.
        Straightforward. Logos.
Tomek, William G.
    xTomek, William G.
        Agricultural Product Prices. Cornell U Pr.
Tomeski, Edward. *see* Tomeski, Edward Alexander.
Tomeski, Edward A. *see* Tomeski, Edward Alexander.
Tomeski, Edward Alexander.
    xTomeski, Edward.
        People-Oriented Computer Systems: The Computer in Crisis. Krieger.
    xTomeski, Edward A.
        Computer Revolution: The Executive & the New Information Technology. Macmillan.
        Fundamentals of Computers in Business: A Systems Approach. Holden-Day.
Tomie, Paola De. *see* De Paola, Tomie.
Tomikel, John.
    xTomikel, John.
        Edible Wild Plants of Pennsylvania & New York. Allegheny.
        A Summary of Earth Processes & Environments. Allegheny.
Tomkins, Calvin, 1925-
    xTomkins, Calvin.
        Off the Wall: The Art World of Our Time. Doubleday.
        World of Marcel Duchamp. Time-Life.
        World of Marcel Duchamp. Silver.
Tomkins, Mary E.
    xTomkins, Mary E.
        Ida M. Tarbell. Twayne.
Tomkins, William.
    xTomkins, William.

Indian Sign Language. Dover.
Indian Sign Language. Peter Smith.
Tomkis, Thomas. *see* Tomkis, Thomas, fl. 1604-1615.
Tomkis, Thomas, fl. 1604-1615.
    xTomkis, Thomas.
        Lingua. AMS Pr.
Tomlenov, A. D.
    xTomlenov, A. D.
        ed. Plastic Flow of Metals. Plenum Pub.
Tomlinson, Charles, 1927-
    xTomlinson, Charles.
        Dante, Beatrice & the Divine Comedy. Folcroft.
        In Black & White: The Graphics of Charles Tomlinson. Persea Bks.
        ed. Marianne Moore: A Collection of Critical Essays. P-H.
Tomlinson, Eustace W.
    xTomlinson, Eustace W.
        Administration of Decedents' Estates. P-H.
Tomlinson, Gerald, 1933-
    xTomlinson, Gerald.
        On a Field of Black. Caroline Hse.
        On a Field of Black. Nellen Pub.
Tomlinson, H. M. *see* Tomlinson, Henry Major.
Tomlinson, Henry J. *see* Tomlinson, Henry Major.
Tomlinson, Henry M. *see* Tomlinson, Henry Major.
Tomlinson, Henry Major, 1873-1958
    xTomlinson, H. M.
        Norman Douglas. Folcroft.
        Norman Douglas. Haskell.
        Out of Soundings. R West.
    xTomlinson, Henry J.
        Thomas Hardy. R West.
    xTomlinson, Henry M.
        Out of Soundings. Arno.
        Thomas Hardy. Folcroft.
        Thomas Hardy. Haskell.
Tomlinson, Hilda. *see* Tomlinson, Jill.
Tomlinson, James C. *see* Tomlinson, James Christopher.
Tomlinson, James Christopher.
    xTomlinson, James C.
        ed. Guide to Graduate Studies in Great Britain. Agathon.
Tomlinson, Jill.
    xTomlinson, Hilda.
        Hilda, the Hen Who Wouldn't Give up. HarBraceJ.
Tomlinson, John D.
    xTomlinson, John D.
        International Control of Radiocommunications. Arno.
Tomlinson, Kerry.
    xTomlinson, Kerry.
        Time Payment. Mudborn.
Tomlinson, R. A. *see* Tomlinson, Richard Allan.
Tomlinson, Richard Allan.
    xTomlinson, R. A.
        Argos & the Argolid: From the End of the Bronze Age to the Roman Occupation. Cornell U Pr.
        Greek Sanctuaries. St Martin.
Tomlinson-Keasey, Carol.
    xTomlinson-Keasey, Carol.
        Child's Eye View. St Martin.
Tommaso, Andrea Di. *see* Di Tommaso, Andrea.
Tomovic, R. *see* Tomovic, Rajko.
Tomovic, Rajko.
    xTomovic, R.
        General Sensitivity Theory. Elsevier.
    xTomovic, Rajko.
        High-Speed Analog Computers. Dover.
Tompert, Ann.
    xTompert, Ann.

Badger on His Own. Crown.
Charlotte & Charles. Crown.
Little Otter Remembers & Other Stories. Crown.
Three Foolish Tales. Crown.
Tompkins, Dorothy C. *see* Tompkins, Dorothy Louise (Campbell) Culver.
Tompkins, Dorothy Louise (Campbell) Culver.
    xTompkins, Dorothy C.
        Furlough from Prison. Inst Gov Stud Berk.
        The Prison & the Prisoner. Inst Gov Stud Berk.
        Strip Mining for Coal. Inst Gov Stud Berk.
Tompkins, E. Berkeley, 1935-
    xTompkins, E. Berkeley.
        Anti-Imperialism in the United States: The Great Debate, 1890-1920. U of Pa Pr.
Tompkins, Enoch. *see* Tompkins, Enoch H.
Tompkins, Enoch H.
    xTompkins, Enoch.
        Practical Beekeeping. Garden Way Pub.
Tompkins, Hamilton B. *see* Tompkins, Hamilton Bullock.
Tompkins, Hamilton Bullock, 1843-1921
    xTompkins, Hamilton B.
        Burr Bibliography: A List of Books Relating to Aaron Burr. AMS Pr.
        Burr Bibliography: A List of Books Relating to Aaron Burr. B Franklin.
Tompkins, Iverna.
    xTompkins, Iverna.
        How to Live with Kids & Enjoy It. Logos.
        The Worth of a Woman. Logos.
Tompkins, J. M. *see* Tompkins, Joyce Marjorie Sanxter.
Tompkins, Joyce. *see* Tompkins, Joyce Marjorie Sanxter.
Tompkins, Joyce Marjorie Sanxter.
    xTompkins, J. M.
        Popular Novel in England, 1770-1800. U of Nebr Pr.
    xTompkins, Joyce.
        The Popular Novel in England 1770-1800. Greenwood.
Tompkins, Peter.
    xTompkins, Peter.
        Secrets of the Great Pyramid. Har-Row.
Tompkins, Stuart R. *see* Tompkins, Stuart Ramsay.
Tompkins, Stuart Ramsay, 1886-
    xTompkins, Stuart R.
        The Triumph of Bolshevism: Revolution or Reaction?. U of Okla Pr.
Tomsich, John, 1935-
    xTomsich, John.
        A Genteel Endeavor: American Culture & Politics in the Gilded Age. Stanford U Pr.
Ton, Mary E. *see* Ton, Mary Ellen.
Ton, Mary Ellen.
    xTon, Mary E.
        For the Love of My Daughter. Cook.
Tondeur, Philippe.
    xTondeur, Philippe.
        Introduction to Lie Groups & Transformation Groups. Springer-Verlag.
Toner, Joseph M. *see* Toner, Joseph Meredith.
Toner, Joseph Meredith, 1825-1896
    xToner, Joseph M.
        Contributions to the Annals of Medical Progress & Medical Education in the United States Before & During the War of Independence. B Franklin.
Toney, Anthoney. *see* Toney, Anthony.
Toney, Anthony.
    xToney, Anthoney.
        Painting & Drawing: Discovering Your Own Visual Language. P-H.
    xToney, Anthony.
        Creative Painting & Drawing. Dover.
Toney, William T.
    xToney, William T.

A Descriptive Study of the Control of Illegal
Mexican Migration in the Southwestern U.S..
R & E Res Assoc.

Tong, Hsin-Min, 1947-
xTong, Hsin-Min.
Plant Location Decisions of Foreign
Manufacturing Investors in the U.S.. Univ
Microfilms.

Tong, L. S. see Tong, Long-Sun.

Tong, Long-Sun.
xTong, L. S.
Thermal Analysis of Pressurized Water
Reactors. Am Nuclear Soc.

Tongue, Ruth L.
xTongue, Ruth L.
The Chime Child: Or, Somerset Singers - Being
an Account of Some of Their Songs
Collected Over Sixty Years. Gale.

Tonkin, John.
xTonkin, John M.
Church & the Secular Order in Reformation
Thought. Columbia U Pr.

Tonkin, John M. see Tonkin, John.

Tonkin, Peter.
xTonkin, Peter.
Killer. Coward.
Killer. NAL.

Tonkinson, Robert.
xTonkinson, Robert.
The Mardudjara Aborigines: Living the Dream
in Australia's Desert. HR&W.

Tonne. see Tonne, Herbert Arthur.

Tonne, Herbert Arthur, 1902-
xTonne.
Principles of Business Education. McGraw.

Tonner, Leslie.
xTonner, Leslie.
Love Song. St Martin.

Tonnies, Ferdinand, 1855-1936
xTonnies, Ferdinand.
On Social Ideas & Ideologies. Har-Row.

Tonomura, Y. see Tonomura, Yuji.

Tonomura, Yuji.
xTonomura, Y.
Muscle Proteins, Muscle Contraction & Cation
Transport. Univ Park.

Toohey, Robert E.
xToohey, Robert E.
Liberty & Empire: British Radical Solutions to
the American Problem, 1774-1776. U Pr of
Ky.

Tooker, Dan.
xTooker, Dan.
Fiction: Interviews with Northern California
Novelists. HarBraceJ.
Fiction!: Interviews with Northern California
Novelists. W Kaufmann.

Tooker, Elisabeth. see Tooker, Elizabeth.

Tooker, Elizabeth.
xTooker, Elisabeth.
ed. Native North American Spirituality of the
Eastern Woodlands: Sacred Myths, Dreams,
Vision Speeches, Healing Formulas, Rituals &
Ceremonials. Paulist Pr.

Tooker, Elva.
xTooker, Elva.
Nathan Trotter: Philadelphia Merchant,
1787-1853. Arno.

Tooker, William W. see Tooker, William Wallace.

Tooker, William Wallace, 1848-1917
xTooker, William W.
The Indian Place-Names on Long Island &
Islands Adjacent with Their Probable
Significations. Kennikat.

Toole, John K. see Toole, John Kennedy.

Toole, John Kennedy, 1937-1969
xToole, John K.
A Confederacy of Dunces. La State U Pr.

Toole, K. Ross. see Toole, Kenneth Ross.

Toole, Kenneth Ross, 1920-
xToole, K. Ross.
Twentieth-Century Montana: A State of
Extremes. U of Okla Pr.

Tooley, Desmond F. see Tooley, Desmond Francis.

Tooley, Desmond Francis.
xTooley, Desmond F.
Production Control Systems & Records.
Beekman Pubs.

Tooley, R. V. see Tooley, Ronald Vere.

Tooley, Ronald Vere, 1898-
xTooley, R. V.
Maps & Mapmakers. Crown.
Tooley's Dictionary of Mapmakers. A R Liss.

Toomay, Pat.
xToomay, Pat.
The Crunch. Norton.

Toomer, Jean, 1894-1967
xToomer, Jean.
Cane. Liveright.

Toomey, Lee.
xToomey, Lee.
Down & Out. Intl Pubns Serv.

Toon, Peter, 1939-
xToon, Peter.
The Development of Doctrine in the Church.
Eerdmans.

Tooze, Ruth.
xTooze, Ruth.
Literature & Music As Resources for Social
Studies. Greenwood.

Topalis, Mary.
xTopalis, Mary.
Psychiatric Nursing. Mosby.

Topel, David G.
xTopel, David G.
ed. Pork Industry: Problems & Progress. Iowa
St U Pr.

Topel, John. see Topel, L. John.

Topel, L. John.
xTopel, John.
The Way to Peace: Liberation Through the
Bible. Orbis Bks.

Topete, Jose M. see Topete, Jose Manuel.

Topete, Jose Manuel.
xTopete, Jose M.
Working Bibliography of Brazilian Literature. U
Presses Fla.

Topliff, Samuel, 1789-1864
xTopliff, Samuel.
Topliff's Travels: Letters from Abroad in the
Years 1828 & 1829. Arno.

Toplin, Robert B. see Toplin, Robert Brent.

Toplin, Robert Brent, 1940-
xToplin, Robert B.
Abolition of Slavery in Brazil: 1880-1888.
Atheneum.
Unchallenged Violence: An American Ordeal.
Greenwood.

Topliss, Eda.
xTopliss, Eda.
Provision for the Disabled. Biblio Dist.

Topliss, W. S.
xTopliss, W. S.
The Optical Dispensing & Workshop Practice.
Butterworths.

**Topology Conference, Virginia Polytechnic Institute and
State University, 1973.**
xVirginia Polytechnic Institute & State University,
March 22-24, 1973.
Topology Conference: Proceedings.
Springer-Verlag.

Toponce, Alexander, 1839-1923
xToponce, Alexander.
Reminiscences of Alexander Toponce. U of
Okla Pr.

Toporek, Milton, 1920-
xToporek, Milton.
Basic Chemistry of Life. Mosby.

Topp, Dale, 1937-
xTopp, Dale.
Music in the Christian Community. Eerdmans.

Topper, Suzanne.
xTopper, Suzanne.
Astaire & Rogers. Nordon Pubns.
Doesn't Everyone...?. Nordon Pubns.
The Fruit Cookbook. Avon.

Topping, Aileen M. see Topping, Aileen Moore.

Topping, Aileen Moore.
xTopping, Aileen M.
Intro. by An Impartial Account of the Late
Expedition Against St. Augustine Under
General Oglethorpe. U Presses Fla.

Topping, Donald M.
xTopping, Donald M.
Chamorro-English Dictionary. U Pr of Hawaii.

Topping, Frank.
xTopping, Frank.
Lord of the Morning. Fortress.

Topsell, Edward.
xTopsell, Edward.
History of Four-Footed Beasts, & Serpents &
Insects. Da Capo.

Topsfield, L. T.
xTopsfield, L. T.
Troubadours & Love. Cambridge U Pr.

Torbert, Eugene C. see Torbert, Eugene Charles.

Torbert, Eugene Charles.
xTorbert, Eugene C.
Cervantes' Place-Names: A Lexicon.
Scarecrow.

Torbert, Floyd J. see Torbert, Floyd James.

Torbert, Floyd James.
xTorbert, Floyd J.
illus. Park Rangers & Game Wardens the
World Over. Hastings.

Torbert, Marianne.
xTorbert, Marianne.
Follow Me: A Handbook of Movement
Activities for Children. P-H.

Torbert, William R., 1944-
xTorbert, William R.
Creating a Community of Inquiry: Conflict,
Collaboration, Transformation. Wiley.

Torbet, Laura.
xTorbet, Laura.
The Complete Book of Mopeds. T Y Crowell.

Torbet, Robert G. see Torbet, Robert George.

Torbet, Robert George, 1912-
xTorbet, Robert G.
A History of the Baptists. Judson.

Torchio, Menico.
xTorchio, Menico.
The World Beneath the Sea. Crown.

Tord, Bijou Le. see Le Tord, Bijou.

Toren, Heller.
xToren, Heller.
For Love of a Painted Lady. PB.

Torgersen, Don A. see Torgersen, Don Arthur.

Torgersen, Don Arthur.
xTorgersen, Don A.
The Girl Who Tricked the Troll. Childrens.
The Scariest Night in Troll Forest. Childrens.
The Troll Who Lived in the Lake. Childrens.
The Troll Who Went to School. Childrens.

Torgersen, Eric, 1943-
xTorgersen, Eric.
At War with Friends. SBD.

Torgeson, Dewayne C. see Torgeson, Dewayne Clinton.

Torgeson, Dewayne Clinton, 1925-
xTorgeson, Dewayne C.
ed. Fungicides: An Advanced Treatise. Acad
Pr.

Torjesen, Hakon.
xTorjesen, Hakon.

The Househusband's World: Reflections of a
Former Diplomat-- at Home. The Garden.
Torkelson, Ted.
xTorkelson, Ted.
One Heart, One Vote. Pacific Pr Pub Assn.
Tormey, Alan.
xTormey, Alan.
Concept of Expression: A Study in
Philosophical Psychology & Aesthetics.
Princeton U Pr.
Tormey, John C.
xTormey, John C.
What's Cooking in the Priesthood?. Alba Bks.
Tornabene, Lyn.
xTornabene, Lyn.
Long Live the King: A Biography of Clark
Gable. Putnam.
Torneden, Roger L.
xTorneden, Roger L.
Foreign Disinvestment by U. S. Multinational
Corporations: With Eight Case Studies.
Praeger.
Torney, John A.
xTorney, John A.
Aquatic Instruction Coaching & Management.
Burgess.
Toro, Gelson.
xToro, Gelson.
Practical Clinical Chemistry. Little.
Toro, Vincent Del. see Del Toro, Vincent.
Torok, Lou.
xTorok, Lou.
Straight Talk from Prison: A Convict Reflects
on Youth, Crime & Society. Human Sci Pr.
The Strange World of Prison. Bobbs.
Toropov, N. A. see Toropov, Nikita Aleksandrovich.
Toropov, Nikita Aleksandrovich.
xToropov, N. A.
High-Temperature Chemistry of Silicate &
Other Oxide Systems. Plenum Pub.
Torrance, E. P. see Torrance, Ellis Paul.
Torrance, E. Paul. see Torrance, Ellis Paul.
Torrance, Ellis Paul.
xTorrance, E. P.
Gifted Children in the Classroom. Macmillan.
xTorrance, E. Paul.
Creative Learning & Teaching. Har-Row.
ed. Discovery & Nurturance of Giftedness in
the Culturally Different. Coun Exc Child.
Education & the Creative Potential. U of Minn
Pr.
Guiding Creative Talent. Krieger.
The Search for "Satori" & Creativity. Creat
Educ Found.
Torrance, John.
xTorrance, John.
Estrangement, Alienation, & Exploitation: A
Sociological Approach to Historical
Materialism. Columbia U Pr.
Torrance, Thomas. see Torrance, Thomas Forsyth.
Torrance, Thomas F. see Torrance, Thomas Forsyth.
Torrance, Thomas Forsyth.
xTorrance, Thomas.
Space Time & Resurrection. Eerdmans.
xTorrance, Thomas F.
Apocalypse Today. Attic Pr.
Calvin's Doctrine of Man. Greenwood.
God & Rationality. Oxford U Pr.
The Ground & Grammar of Theology. U Pr of
Va.
Space, Time & Incarnation. Oxford U Pr.
Theological Science. Oxford U Pr.
Torre, Betty L.
xTorre, Betty L.
Rice. Condor Pub Co.
Torre, Frank D.
xTorre, Frank D.
Woodworking for Kids. Doubleday.
Torrence, Frederic Ridgely, 1875-1950
xTorrence, Ridgely.

Story of John Hope. Arno.
Torrence, Ridgely. see Torrence, Frederic Ridgely.
Torrend, J.
xTorrend, J.
Specimens of Bantu Folk-Lore from Northern
Rhodesia. Kennikat.
Specimens of Bantu Folk-Lore from Northern
Rhodesia. Negro U Pr.
Specimens of Bantu Folklore from Northern
Rhodesia. Gordon Pr.
Torrens, Ian M. see Torrens, Ian Mcc.
Torrens, Ian McC.
xTorrens, Ian M.
Interatomic Potentials. Acad Pr.
Torrens, Paul R.
xTorrens, Paul R.
The American Health Care System: Issues &
Problems. Mosby.
Torres, Edwin.
xTorres, Edwin.
After Hours. Dial.
Q & A. Avon.
Torres, Elias L., 1878-
xTorres, Elias L.
Twenty Episodes in the Life of Pancho Villa.
Encino Pr.
Torres, Hazel O.
xTorres, Hazel O.
Modern Dental Assisting. Saunders.
Torres, Sergio.
xTorres, Sergio.
Theology in the Americas. Orbis Bks.
Torres, Tereska.
xTorres, Tereska.
Only Reason. S&S.
Torres, Victor.
xTorres, Victor.
Run of Tull Xtvol. Bethany Fell.
Torres-Reilly, Marta.
xTorres-Reilly, Morta.
Guide to Professional Organizations. Natl
Clearinghouse Bilingual Ed.
Torres-Reilly, Morta. see Torres-Reilly, Marta.
Torrey, Charles C. see Torrey, Charles Cutler.
Torrey, Charles Cutler, 1863-1956
xTorrey, Charles C.
Ezra Studies. Ktav.
Torrey, E. Fuller. see Torrey, Edwin Fuller.
Torrey, Edwin Fuller.
xTorrey, E. Fuller.
Community Health, & Mental Health Care
Delivery for North American Indians. Mss
Info.
The Death of Psychiatry. Penguin.
Torrey, John.
xTorrey, John.
Flora of North America. Hafner.
Torrey, John G.
xTorrey, John G.
Development in Flowering Plants. Macmillan.
Torrey, R. A. see Torrey, Reuben Archer.
Torrey, Reuben A. see Torrey, Reuben Archer.
Torrey, Reuben Archer, 1856-1928
xTorrey, R. A.
How to Bring Men to Christ. Bethany Fell.
How to Bring Men to Christ. Revell.
xTorrey, Reuben A.
How to Succeed in the Christian Life. Moody.
Torrey, S.
xTorrey, S.
ed. Sludge Disposal by Landspreading
Techniques. Noyes.
ed. Trace Contaminants from Coal. Noyes.
Torrington, Derek, 1931-
xTorrington, Derek.
Comparative Industrial Relations in Europe.
Greenwood.
Tors, Ivan.
xTors, Ivan.

My Life in the Wild. HM.
Torshen, K. P. see Torshen, Kay Pomerance.
Torshen, Kay Pomerance.
xTorshen, K. P.
The Mastery Approach to Competency - Based
Education. Acad Pr.
Tortora, Gerald. see Tortora, Gerard J.
Tortora, Gerard. see Tortora, Gerard J.
Tortora, Gerard J.
xTortora, Gerald.
Principles of Anatomy & Physiology. Har-Row.
xTortora, Gerard.
Principles of Human Anatomy. Har-Row.
Tortoriello, Thomas R.
xTortoriello, Thomas R.
Communication in the Organization: An
Applied Approach. McGraw.
Tory, G. see Tory, Geoffroy.
Tory, Geoffroy, 1480-1533
xTory, G.
ed. Champ Fleury. Kraus Repr.
xTory, Geoffroy.
Champ Fleury. Johnson Repr.
xTory, Geofroy.
Champ Fleury. Dover.
Champ Fleury. Peter Smith.
Tory, Geofroy. see Tory, Geoffroy.
Toscano, Mario.
xToscano, Mario.
Origins of the Pact of Steel. Johns Hopkins.
Toscano, N. C. see Toscano, Nick C.
Toscano, Nick C.
xToscano, N. C.
Pest Management Guide for Insects &
Nematodes of Cotton in California. Ag Sci
Pubns
Toscano, Vincent L.
xToscano, Vincent L.
Since Dallas: Images of John F. Kennedy in
Popular & Scholarly Literature, 1963-1973. R
& E Res Assoc.
Tosches, Nick.
xTosches, Nick.
Country: The Biggest Music in America. Dell.
Country: The Biggest Music in America. Stein
& Day.
Tosh, Dennis. see Tosh, Dennis S.
Tosh, Dennis O. see Tosh, Dennis S.
Tosh, Dennis S.
xTosh, Dennis.
Real Estate Principles for License Preparation.
Reston.
xTosh, Dennis O.
Real Estate Principles for License Preparation.
Reston.
Tosh, John.
xTosh, John.
Clan Leaders & Colonial Chiefs in Lango: The
Political History of an East African Stateless
Society, 1800-1939. Oxford U Pr.
Tosi, Francesco. see Tosi, Pietro Francesco.
Tosi, Henry L.
xTosi, Henry L.
ed. Organizational Behavior & Management: A
Contingency Approach. Wiley.
Readings in Management: Contingencies,
Structure & Process. Wiley.
Tosi, Pietro F. see Tosi, Pietro Francesco.
Tosi, Pietro Francesco.
xTosi, Francesco.
Observations on the Florid Song. Scholarly.
xTosi, Pietro F.
Observations on the Florid Song. Johnson
Repr.
Tosiello, Rosario J. see Tosiello, Rosario Joseph.
Tosiello, Rosario Joseph.
xTosiello, Rosario J.

The Birth & Early Years of the Bell Telephone
System, 1876-1880. Arno.

Toski, Bob.
xToski, Bob.
How to Become a Complete Golfer. Golf
Digest Bks.
The Touch System for Better Golf. Bantam.
The Touch System for Better Golf. Golf Digest
Bks.

Tosteson, D. C.
xTosteson, D. C.
ed. Membrane Transport Processes. Raven.

Totah, Khalil A. see Totah, Khalil Abdallah.

Totah, Khalil Abdallah, 1886-1955
xTotah, Khalil A.
Contribution of the Arabs to Education. AMS
Pr.

Toth, A. G.
xToth, A. G.
Legal Protection of Individuals in the European
Communities. Elsevier.

Totman, Conrad. see Totman, Conrad D.

Totman, Conrad D.
xTotman, Conrad.
Politics in the Tokugawa Bakufu, 1600-1843.
Harvard U Pr.

Totman, Jane.
xTotman, Jane.
The Murderess: A Psychosocial Study of
Criminal Homicide. R & E Res Assoc.

Totman, Richard.
xTotman, Richard.
Social Causes of Illness. Pantheon.

Toto, Patrick D., 1921-
xToto, Patrick D.
Pathology of the Oral Cavity. Am Soc Clinical.

Tottel, R. see Tottel, Richard.

Tottel, Richard.
xTottel, R.
Tottel's Miscellany, 1557-1587. Harvard U Pr.

Totten, George O. see Totten, George Oakley.

Totten, George Oakley, 1866-1939
xTotten, George O.
Maya Architecture. B Franklin.

Totten, Joseph G. see Totten, Joseph Gilbert.

Totten, Joseph Gilbert, 1788-1864
xTotten, Joseph G.
Report of General J. G. Totten, Chief
Engineer, on the Subject of National
Defenses. Arno.

Totten, W. Fred. see Totten, William Fred.

Totten, William Fred, 1905-
xTotten, W. Fred.
Power of Community Education. Pendell Pub.

Totterdell.
xTotterdell, Barry.
ed. Public Library Purpose: A Reader. Shoe
String.

Totterdell, Barry. see Totterdell.

Touche Ross & Co. see Touche Ross and Company.

Touche Ross and Company.
xTouche Ross & Co.
The Standard Manual of Accounting for
Shopping Centers. Urban Land.

Touchstone, Joseph C.
xTouchstone, Joseph C.
Practice of Thin Layer Chromatography. Wiley.
ed. Quantitative Thin Layer Chromatography.
Wiley.

Tougas, Gerard.
xTougas, Gerard.
History of French-Canadian Literature.
Greenwood.

Tough, Allen. see Tough, Allen M.

Tough, Allen M.
xTough, Allen.
Expand Your Life: A Pocket Book for Personal
Change. College Bd.

Tough, Joan.
xTough, Joan.

Development of Meaning: A Study of
Children's Use of Language. Allen Unwin.
The Development of Meaning: A Study of
Children's Use of Language. Halsted Pr.

Touliatos, John.
xTouliatos, John.
ed. Family & Human Development. Mss Info.

Toulmin, David.
xToulmin, David.
Straw into Gold: A Scots Miscellany. Intl
Pubns Serv.

Toulmin, Harry A. see Toulmin, Harry Aubrey.

Toulmin, Harry Aubrey, 1890-
xToulmin, Harry A.
The City Manager: A New Profession. Arno.

Toulmin, Stephen. see Toulmin, Stephen Edelston.

Toulmin, Stephen Edelston.
xToulmin, Stephen.
Foresight & Understanding: An Enquiry into
the Aims of Science. Har-Row.
An Introduction to Reasoning. Macmillan.
Uses of Argument. Cambridge U Pr.

Touloukian, Robert J.
xTouloukian, Robert J.
ed. Diagnosis & Early Management of Trauma
Emergencies: A Manual for the Emergency
Service. C C Thomas.

Toumanova, Nina A. see Toumanova, Nina Andronikova.

Toumanova, Nina Andronikova, Princess, 1888-
xToumanova, Nina A.
Anton Chekhov: The Voice of Twilight Russia.
Columbia U Pr.

Tourette, Jacquelin La. see La Tourrette, Jacqueline.

Tourgee, Albion W. see Tourgee, Albion Winegar.

Tourgee, Albion Winegar, 1838-1905
xTourgee, Albion W.
Hot Plowshares. Irvington.
Pactolus Prime. Irvington.

Tourism Education Corp. see Tourism Education
Corporation.

Tourism Education Corporation.
xTourism Education Corp.
A Hospitality Industry Guide for Writing &
Using Task Unit Job Descriptions. CBI Pub.
xTourism Education Corporation.
Wine Service Procedures. CBI Pub.

Tourneur. see Tourneur, Cyril.

Tourneur, Cyril.
xTourneur.
The Atheist's Tragedy. Norton.
The Revenger's Tragedy. Norton.
xTourneur, Cyril.
Revenger's Tragedy. U of Nebr Pr.

Tourney, Leonard D.
xTourney, Leonard D.
Joseph Hall. G K Hall.
Joseph Hall. Twayne.

Tournier, Paul.
xTournier, Paul.
The Adventure of Living. Har-Row.
Are You Nobody?. John Knox.
A Doctor's Casebook in the Light of the Bible.
Har-Row.
Meaning of Gifts. John Knox.
Meaning of Persons. Har-Row.
The Meaning of Persons. Har-Row.
Secrets. John Knox.
Secrets. Pillar Bks.
Strong & the Weak. Westminster.
The Whole Person in a Broken World.
Har-Row.

Tourrette, Jacqueline La. see La Tourrette, Jacqueline.

Tourtellot, Arthur B. see Tourtellot, Arthur Bernon.

Tourtellot, Arthur Bernon.
xTourtellot, Arthur B.
An Anatomy of American Politics: Innovation
Versus Conservatism. Greenwood.
Presidents on the Presidency. Russell.

Toussaint, Charmian E. see Toussaint, Charmian
Edwards.

Toussaint, Charmian Edwards.
xToussaint, Charmian E.
The Trusteeship System of the United Nations.
Greenwood.

Toussaint, Stanley D., 1928-
xToussaint, Stanley D.
Behold the King: A Study of Matthew.
Multnomah.

Touster, Alison, 1952-
xTouster, Alison.
The First Movement. Dragons Teeth.

Touster, Irwin.
xTouster, Irwin.
The Perez Arson Mystery. Dial.

Toutant, William H.
xToutant, William H.
Fundamental Concepts of Music. Wadsworth
Pub.

Touton, Frank C. see Touton, Frank Charles.

Touton, Frank Charles, 1880-1936
xTouton, Frank C.
Solving Geometric Originals. AMS Pr.

Touval, Saadia.
xTouval, Saadia.
The Boundary Politics of Independent Africa.
Harvard U Pr.

Tovar, Antonio.
xTovar, Antonio.
The Ancient Languages of Spain & Portugal. S
F Vanni.

Tovell, Harold M. see Tovell, Harold M. M.

Tovell, Harold M. M.
xTovell, Harold M.
Gynecologic Operations: As Performed by
Members of the Staff of Woman's Hospital,
St. Luke's Hospital Center, New York, New
York. Har-Row.

Tovey, Donald F. see Tovey, Donald Francis.

Tovey, Donald Francis, Sir, 1875-1940
xTovey, Donald F.
The Main Stream of Music & Other Essays.
AMS Pr.

Tovey, Doreen.
xTovey, Doreen.
Cats in the Belfry. Merrimack Bk Serv.
Donkey Work. Merrimack Bk Serv.
Double Trouble. Norton.
Life with Grandma. Merrimack Bk Serv.

Tovey, Duncan C. see Tovey, Duncan Crookes.

Tovey, Duncan Crookes.
xTovey, Duncan C.
Reviews & Essays in English Literature.
Kennikat.
Reviews & Essays in English Literature. R
West.

Tovias, Alfred.
xTovias, Alfred.
Tariff Preferences in Mediterranean Diplomacy.
St Martin.

Tower, Merrill E.
xTower, Merrill E.
Flight Facts for Private Pilots. Aero.

Tower, Samuel A.
xTower, Samuel A.
A Stamp Collector's History of the United
States. Messner.

Towers, John, 1836-1922
xTowers, John.
Dictionary-Catalogue of Operas & Operettas.
Da Capo.

Towers, T. D., 1914-
xTowers, T. D.
Practical Solid-State DC Power Supplies. TAB
Bks.
Towers' International OpAmp Linear-IC
Selector. TAB Bks.

Towle, Charlotte.
xTowle, Charlotte.

Common Human Needs. Natl Assn Soc Wkrs.

Towle, Judith W.
xTowle, Judith W.
Favorite Mexican Recipes. Pelican.

Towle, Tony, 1939-
xTowle, Tony.
Autobiography & Other Poems. SUN.

Towler, J. see Towler, John.

Towler, John, 1811-1889
xTowler, J.
Silver Sunbeam. Morgan.

Towler, Robert.
xTowler, Robert.
Homo Religiosus: Sociological Problems in the Study of Religion. St Martin.

Towles, Martin F.
xTowles, Martin F.
Practical Accounting Systems & Procedures. P-H.

Town Hall Inc. see Town Hall, Inc., New York.

Town Hall, Inc., New York.
xTown Hall Inc.
People in Your Life. Arno.

Town of Berne Bicentennial Commission. see Berne, N.Y. Bicentennial Commission.

Towne, Laura M. see Towne, Laura Matilda.

Towne, Laura Matilda.
xTowne, Laura M.
Letters & Diary of Laura M. Towne: Written from the Sea Islands of South Carolina, 1862-1884. Negro U Pr.

Towne, Mary.
xTowne, Mary.
The Glass Room. Archway.
Glass Room. PB.
Glass Room. FS&G.
Goldenrod. Atheneum.

Towne, Ruth. see Towne, Ruth Warner.

Towne, Ruth Warner, 1917-
xTowne, Ruth.
Senator William J. Stone & the Politics of Compromise. Kennikat.

Towner, W. Sibley. see Towner, Wayne Sibley.

Towner, Wayne Sibley.
xTowner, W. Sibley.
How God Deals with Evil. Westminster.

Townley, Helen M.
xTownley, Helen M.
Systems Analysis for Information Retrieval. Westview.

Townley, Rod.
xTownley, Rod.
The Early Poetry of William Carlos Williams. Cornell U Pr.

Towns, Elmer. see Towns, Elmer L.

Towns, Elmer J. see Towns, Elmer L.

Towns, Elmer L.
xTowns, Elmer.
Getting a Church Started in the Face of Insurmountable Odds with Limited Resources. Impact Tenn.
The Successful Sunday School & Teachers Guidebook. Creation Hse.
xTowns, Elmer J.
Successful Church Libraries. Baker Bk.
xTowns, Elmer L.
Evangelize Thru Christian Education. Evang Tchr.
History of Religious Educators. Baker Bk.
How to Grow an Effective Sunday School. Accent Bks.

Townsend, A. A. see Townsend, Albert Alan.

Townsend, Albert Alan.
xTownsend, A. A.
The Structure of Turbulent Shear Flow. Cambridge U Pr.

Townsend, Anita.
xTownsend, Anita.

The Kangaroo. Watts.

Townsend, Carl.
xTownsend, Carl.
How to Make Money with Your Micro-Computer. Robotics Pr.
How to Make Money with Your Microcomputer. Intl Schol Bk Serv.

Townsend, Carolynn E.
xTownsend, Carolynn E.
Nutrition & Diet Modifications. Delmar.

Townsend, Doris M. see Townsend, Doris Mcferran.

Townsend, Doris McFerran.
xTownsend, Doris M.
Diet Without Hunger. Larousse.

Townsend, Edward A. see Townsend, Edward Arthur.

Townsend, Edward Arthur.
xTownsend, Edward A.
Using Statistics in Classroom Instruction. Macmillan.

Townsend, Edward W. see Townsend, Edward Waterman.

Townsend, Edward Waterman, 1855-1942
xTownsend, Edward W.
A Daughter of the Tenements. Irvington.
Near a Whole City Full. Scholarly.

Townsend, Elinor.
xTownsend, Elinor.
illus. Sicily: A Sketch Book. Phoenix Pub.

Townsend, Elsie. see Townsend, Elsie Doig.

Townsend, Elsie D. see Townsend, Elsie Doig.

Townsend, Elsie Doig.
xTownsend, Elsie.
None to Give Away. Herald Hse.
xTownsend, Elsie D.
If You Would Learn...Go Teach. Herald Hse.

Townsend, George A. see Townsend, George Alfred.

Townsend, George Alfred, 1841-1914
xTownsend, George A.
Campaigns of a Non-Combatant. Arno.
Tales of the Chesapeake. Arno.

Townsend, H. E. see Townsend, Herbert Edward Routledge.

Townsend, Herbert Edward Routledge.
xTownsend, H. E.
Immigrant Pupils in England: The L. E. A. Response. Humanities.

Townsend, J. Ives. see Townsend, Joel Ives.

Townsend, James R. see Townsend, James Roger.

Townsend, James Roger.
xTownsend, James R.
Politics in China. Little.
The Revolutionization of Chinese Youth: A Study of Chung-Kuo Ch'ing-Nien. IEAS Ctr Chinese Stud.

Townsend, Janet.
xTownsend, Janet.
The Comic Book Mystery. Pantheon.

Townsend, Joel Ives.
xTownsend, J. Ives.
ed. Lectures in Biological Sciences. U of Tenn Pr.

Townsend, John, fl. 1977-
xTownsend, John.
Oman: The Making of a Modern State. St Martin.

Townsend, John R. see Townsend, John Rowe.

Townsend, John Rowe.
xTownsend, John R.

The Creatures. Lippincott.
Good-Bye to the Jungle. Dell.
Good-Bye to the Jungle. Lippincott.
Good Night, Prof, Dear. Lippincott.
Goodnight Prof Dear. Dell.
Noah's Castle. Dell.
Noah's Castle. Lippincott.
Pirate's Island. Lippincott.
A Sounding of Storytellers. Lippincott.
The Summer People. Dell.
The Summer People. Lippincott.
Trouble in the Jungle. Lippincott.
Trouble in the Jungle. Dell.

Townsend, Leah, 1889-
xTownsend, Leah.
South Carolina Baptists, 1670-1805. Church History.
South Carolina Baptists: 1670-1805. Genealog Pub.

Townsend, Marion E. see Townsend, Marion Ernest.

Townsend, Marion Ernest, 1889-
xTownsend, Marion E.
Administration of Student Personnel Services in Teacher-Training Institutions of the United States. AMS Pr.

Townsend, Mary E. see Townsend, Mary Evelyn.

Townsend, Mary Elizabeth.
xTownsend, Mary E.
Great Characters of Fiction. Folcroft.

Townsend, Mary Evelyn, 1884-
xTownsend, Mary E.
Origins of Modern German Colonialism, 1871-1885. Fertig.

Townsend, P. D. see Townsend, Peter David.

Townsend, Peter, 1914-
xTownsend, Peter.
Duel of Eagles. PD.
Duel of Eagles. S&S.

Townsend, Peter David.
xTownsend, P. D.
Colour Centres & Imperfections in Insulators & Semiconductors. Crane-Russak Co.

Townsend, Reginald T. see Townsend, Reginald Townsend.

Townsend, Reginald Townsend, 1890-
xTownsend, Reginald T.
This, That & the Other Thing. Arno.

Townsend, Sallie.
xTownsend, Sallie.
The Amateur Navigator's Handbook. T Y Crowell.

Townshend, George, 1876-1957
xTownshend, George.
Christ & Baha'u'llah. Baha'i.

Townsley, Ralph. see Townsley, Ralph R.

Townsley, Ralph R.
xTownsley, Ralph.
Passive Equalizer Design Data. TAB Bks.

Townsley, W. A.
xTownsley, W. A.
The Government of Tasmania. U of Queensland Pr.

Townson, Duncan. see Townson, William Duncan.

Townson, William Duncan.
xTownson, Duncan.
Famous Generals. Watts.

Toye, Clive.
xToye, Clive.
Soccer. Watts.

Toye, William.
xToye, William.
How Summer Came to Canada. Oxford U Pr.
ed. Supplement to the Oxford Companion to Canadian History & Literature. Oxford U Pr.

Toynbee. see Toynbee, Arnold Joseph.

Toynbee, Arnold. see Toynbee, Arnold Joseph.

Toynbee, Arnold J. see Toynbee, Arnold Joseph.

Toynbee, Arnold Joseph, 1889-
xToynbee.

Intro. by An Historian's Approach to Religion.
Oxford U Pr.
xToynbee, Arnold.
An Historian's Approach to Religion. Oxford
U Pr.
A Study of History. Oxford U Pr.
xToynbee, Arnold J.
Acquaintances. Oxford U Pr.
Change & Habit: The Challenge of Our Time.
Oxford U Pr.
Cities on the Move. Oxford U Pr.
Constantine Porphyrogenitus & His World.
Oxford U Pr.
Experiences. Oxford U Pr.
ed. The Initial Triumph of the Axis. Johnson
Repr.
Surviving the Future. Oxford U Pr.
Turkey. Greenwood.
Twelve Men of Action in Graeco-Roman
History. Arno.
Toynbee, J. M. *see* Toynbee, Jocelyn M. C.
Toynbee, Jocelyn M. C.
xToynbee, J. M.
Animals in Roman Life & Art. Cornell U Pr.
Toynbee, Paget J. *see* Toynbee, Paget Jackson.
Toynbee, Paget Jackson.
xToynbee, Paget J.
Dictionary of Proper Names & Notable
Matters in the Works of Dante. Oxford U Pr.
Toynbee, Philip.
xToynbee, Philip.
Barricades. Greenwood.
Prothalamium, a Cycle of the Holy Graal: A
Novel. Greenwood.
Toys 'n Things Training & Resource Center. *see* Toys 'n
Things Training and Resource Center.
Toys 'n Things Training and Resource Center.
xToys 'n Things Training & Resource Center.
Teachables from Trashables: Home-Made Toys
That Teach. Toys N Things.
Tozer, A. W. *see* Tozer, Aiden Wilson.
Tozer, Aiden Wilson, 1897-
xTozer, A. W.
The Divine Conquest. Revell.
Tozer, H. F. *see* Tozer, Henry Fanshawe.
Tozer, Henry Fanshawe, 1829-1916
xTozer, H. F.
An English Commentary on Dante's "Divina
Commedia". Cooper Sq.
An English Commentary on Dante's Divina
Commedia. R West.
Tozzer, Alfred M. *see* Tozzer, Alfred Marston.
Tozzer, Alfred Marston, 1877-1954
xTozzer, Alfred M.
A Comparative Study of the Mayas & the
Lacandones. AMS Pr.
Tozzi, Romano.
xTozzi, Romano.
Spencer Tracy. Brown Bk.
Trabasso, T. *see* Trabasso, Tom.
Trabasso, Tom.
xTrabasso, T.
Attention in Learning: Theory & Research.
Krieger.
Trabue, Marion R. *see* Trabue, Marion Rex.
Trabue, Marion Rex, 1890-1972
xTrabue, Marion R.
Completion-Test Language Scales. AMS Pr.
Tracey, Margot, 1907-
xTracey, Margot.
Red Rose. David & Charles.
Tracey, Michael.
xTracey, Michael.
The Production of Political Television.
Routledge & Kegan.
Tracey, William R.
xTracey, William R.

Designing Training & Development Systems.
Am Mgmt.
Tracht, Myron E.
xTracht, Myron E.
ed. Digestive System Basic Sciences. Med
Exam.
Trachtenberg, Alan.
xTrachtenberg, Alan.
Brooklyn Bridge: Fact & Symbol. U of Chicago
Pr.
ed. Democratic Vistas, 1860-1880. Braziller.
Trachtenberg, Inge.
xTrachtenberg, Inge.
My Daughter, My Son. Summit Bks.
Trachtenberg, Leo.
xTrachtenberg, Leo.
The Sponsor's Guide to Filmmaking.
Hopkinson.
Trachtenberg, Marc, 1946-
xTrachtenberg, Marc.
Reparation in World Politics: France &
European Economic Diplomacy, 1916-1923.
Columbia U Pr.
Trachtenberg, Marvin.
xTrachtenberg, Marvin.
The Statue of Liberty. Viking Pr.
Track & Field News Editorial Staff. *see* Track and Field
News.
Track & Field News Staff. *see* Track and Field News.
Track and Field News.
xTrack & Field News Editorial Staff.
ed. Olympic Images: 1976 Olympic Track &
Field. Tafnews.
xTrack & Field News Staff.
Olympic Track & Field. Tafnews.
Tracton, Ken.
xTracton, Ken.
Display Electronics. TAB Bks.
How to Build Your Own Working 16-Bit
Microcomputer. TAB Bks.
IC Function Locator. TAB Bks.
Integrated Circuits Guidebook. TAB Bks.
The Most Popular Subroutines in BASIC. TAB
Bks.
Programmer's Guide to LISP. TAB Bks.
Tracy, David.
xTracy, David.
Celebrating the Medieval Heritage: A Colloquy
on the Thought of Aquinas & Bonaventura. U
of Chicago Pr.
Tracy, Don, 1905-
xTracy, Don.
Crimson Is the Eastern Shore. Baronet.
Crimson Is the Eastern Shore. Charter Bks.
Death Calling Collect. PB.
High, Wide and Ransom. PB.
Last Boat Out of Cincinnati. Trident.
Tracy, Honor. *see* Tracy, Honor Lilbush Wingfield.
Tracy, Honor Lilbush Wingfield, 1915-
xTracy, Honor.
The Ballad of Castle Reef. Random.
Tracy, Jack, 1945-
xTracy, Jack W.
Conan Doyle & the Latter-Day Saints.
Gaslight.
Tracy, Jack W. *see* Tracy, Jack.
Tracy, James D.
xTracy, James D.
The Politics of Erasmus: A Pacifist Intellectual
& His Political Milieu. U of Toronto Pr.
Tracy, John A.
xTracy, John A.
Fundamentals of Financial Accounting. Wiley.
Fundamentals of Management Accounting.
Wiley.
How to Read a Financial Report: Wringing
Cash Flow & Other Vital Signs Out of the
Numbers. Wiley.
Tracy, John E. *see* Tracy, John Evarts.

Tracy, John Evarts, 1880-1959
xTracy, John E.
The Successful Practice of Law. Greenwood.
Tracy, Joseph, 1793?-1874
xTracy, Joseph.
The Great Awakening. Banner of Truth.
Tracy, Marian. *see* Tracy, Marian Coward.
Tracy, Marian Coward.
xTracy, Marian.
ed. Favorite American Regional Recipes. Peter
Smith.
Tracy, Robert, 1928-
xTracy, Robert.
Trollope's Later Novels. U of Cal Pr.
Tracy, Robert A. *see* Tracy, Robert Archer.
Tracy, Robert Archer, 1878-
xTracy, Robert A.
The Sword of Nemesis. AMS Pr.
Tracy, Roger S. *see* Tracy, Roger Sherman.
Tracy, Roger Sherman, 1841-1926
xTracy, Roger S.
The White Man's Burden: A Satirical Forecast.
Arno.
Tracy, Stephen V., 1941-
xTracy, Stephen V.
The Lettering of an Athenian Mason. Am Sch
Athens.
T.R.A.D.A. *see* Timber Research and Development
Association.

Tragatsch, Erwin.
xTragatsch, Erwin.
ed. The Complete Illustrated Encyclopedia of
the World's Motorcycles. HR&W.
Trager, Frank N.
xTrager, Frank N.
Burma: From Kingdom to Republic, a
Historical & Political Analysis. Greenwood.
ed. Communist China, 1949-1969: A
Twenty-Year Appraisal. NYU Pr.
Trager, William, 1910-
xTrager, William.
Symbiosis. Van Nos Reinhold.
Tragle, Henry I. *see* Tragle, Henry Irving.
Tragle, Henry Irving.
xTragle, Henry I.
Coxey's Army. Viking Pr.
Nat Turner's Slave Revolt 1831. Viking Pr.
Trahey, Jane.
xTrahey, Jane.
Life with Mother Superior. FS&G.
Trail, Florence, 1854-1944
xTrail, Florence.
A History of Italian Literature. Haskell.
A History of Italian Literature. R West.
Traill, H. D. *see* Traill, Henry Duff.
Traill, Henry D. *see* Traill, Henry Duff.
Traill, Henry Duff, 1842-1900
xTraill, H. D.
Sterne. AMS Pr.
Sterne. R West.
xTraill, Henry D.
Lord Strafford. Arno.
Train, John.
xTrain, John.
Compiled by Even More Remarkable Names.
Potter.
Traina, Richard P.
xTraina, Richard P.
American Diplomacy and the Spanish Civil
War. Greenwood.
Trainer, David.
xTrainer, David.
A Day in the Life of a TV News Reporter.
Troll Assocs.
Trainer, Orvel.
xTrainer, Orvel.

Deathroads: The Story of the Donut Shop
Murders. Pruett.
Ice Harvest. Pruett.
Training & Retraining Inc. *see* Training and Retraining,
Inc., New York.
Training and Retraining, Inc., New York.
xTraining & Retraining Inc.
Basic Electricity - Electronics. Bobbs.
Transistor Fundamentals. Bobbs.
Training System, Inc.
xTraining Systems Inc.
Simplified Transistor Theory. Hayden.
Training Systems Inc. *see* Training System, Inc.
Trainor, Jim.
xTrainor, Jim.
The Complete Baseball Play Book. Doubleday.
Trainor, Lynn. *see* Trainor, Lynn E. H.
Trainor, Lynn E. H.
xTrainor, Lynn.
From Physical Concept to Mathematical
Structure: An Introduction to Theoretical
Physics. U of Toronto Pr.
Traisman, Howard S.
xTraisman, Howard S.
Management of Juvenile Diabetes Mellitus.
Mosby.
Traister, John. *see* Traister, John E.
Traister, John E.
xTraister, John.
Practical Plumbing Drafting. Sams.
xTraister, John E.
Basic Gunsmithing. TAB Bks.
Construction Electrical Contracting. Wiley.
Do-It-Yourselfer's Guide to Modern
Energy-Efficient Heating & Cooling Systems.
TAB Bks.
Electrical Inspection Guidebook. Reston.
The First Book of Electronic Projects. TAB
Bks.
Handbook of Electrical Systems Design
Practices. Reston.
Handbook of Modern Electrical Wiring.
Reston.
How to Build Your Own Boat from Scratch.
TAB Bks.
Practical Electrical Measuring. Sams.
Traister, Robert.
xTraister, Robert J.
DC Power Supplies: Application & Theory.
Reston.
Traister, Robert J. *see* Traister, Robert.
Tralins, Robert.
xTralins, Robert.
Supernatural Warnings. Popular Lib.
Trammell, Robert, 1939-
xTrammell, Robert.
George Washington Trammell. Salt Lick.
Trani, Eugene P.
xTrani, Eugene P.
The Presidency of Warren G. Harding. Regents
Pr KS.
**Trans-Disciplinary Symposium on Philosophy and
Medicine, 1st, Galveston. 1974.**
xTrans-Disciplinary Symposium on Philosophy &
Medicine, 1st Galveston, May 9-11, 1974.
Evaluation & Explanation in the Biomedical
Sciences: Proceedings. Kluwer Boston.
Transistor Applications, Inc.
xGernsback Library Staff.
Handbook of Semiconductor Circuits. Tab Bks.
Transtromer, Tomas.
xTranstromer, Tomas.
Baltics. SBD.
Selected Poems. Ardis Pubs.
Tranter, John.
xTranter, John.
The Livin' Is Easy. Soccer.
Tranter, N. L.
xTranter, Neil L.

Population Since the Industrial Revolution: The
Case of England & Wales. Humanities.
Tranter, Neil L. *see* Tranter, N. L.
Trantham, Carla R. *see* Trantham, Carla Ross.
Trantham, Carla Ross.
xTrantham, Carla R.
Normal Language Development: The Key to
Diagnosis & Therapy for
Language-Disordered Children. Williams &
Wilkins.
Trap, Jack.
xTrap, Jack.
Roller Skating from Start to Finish. Penguin.
Trapp, Frank Anderson.
xTrapp, Frank Anderson.
The Attainment of Delacroix. Johns Hopkins.
Trapp, Maria A. *see* Trapp, Maria Augusta.
Trapp, Maria Augusta.
xTrapp, Maria A.
Story of the Trapp Family Singers. Lippincott.
xTrapp, Maria Augusta.
Story of the Trapp Family Singers. Doubleday.
Trask, David F.
xTrask, David F.
General Tasker Howard Bliss & the "Sessions
of the World," 1919. Am Philos.
Trask, Jonathan.
xTrask, Jonathan.
The Camp. Belmont-Tower.
Trask, Kate. *see* Trask, Kate (Nichols).
Trask, Kate (Nichols), 1853-1922
xTrask, Kate.
Lessons in Love. Arno.
Trattner, Ernest R. *see* Trattner, Ernest Robert.
Trattner, Ernest Robert, 1898-
xTrattner, Ernest R.
Architects of Ideas: The Story of the Great
Theories of Mankind. Greenwood.
Understanding the Talmud. Greenwood.
Trattner, Walter I.
xTrattner, Walter I.
From Poor Law to Welfare State: A History of
Social Welfare in America. Free Pr.
Homer Folks: Pioneer in Social Welfare.
Columbia U Pr.
Traub, Jack, 1936-
xTraub, Jack.
Accounting & Reporting Practices of Private
Foundations: A Critical Evaluation. Praeger.
Traub, Stuart H.
xTraub, Stuart H.
ed. Theories of Deviance. Peacock Pubs.
Traubel, Horace.
xTraubel, Horace.
In Re Walt Whitman. Arden Lib.
xTraubel, Horace L.
In Re Walt Whitman. Folcroft.
Traubel, Horace L. *see* Traubel, Horace.
Traugott, E. C. *see* Traugott, Elizabeth Closs.
Traugott, Elizabeth Closs.
xTraugott, E. C.
History of English Syntax: A Transformational
Approach to the History of English Sentence
Structure. HR&W.
Traugott, John.
xTraugott, John.
Tristram Shandy's World: Sterne's
Philosophical Rhetoric. Russell.
Trauner, Doris A.
xTrauner, Doris A.
Childhood Neurologic Problems: A Textbook
for Health Care Professionals. Year Bk Med.
Trauner, Michael.
xTrauner, Michael.
Gently by the Hand. PB.
Trautlein, J. *see* Trautlein, Joseph J.
Trautlein, Joseph J.
xTrautlein, J.

ed. Aerosols, Airways & Asthma. Spectrum
Pub.
Trautmann, Frederic.
xTrautmann, Frederic.
The Voice of Terror: A Biography of Johann
Most. Greenwood.
Travel, I.
xTravel, I.
Bitten by Britain: Enjoying England. Sutter
House.
Traven, B.
xTraven, B.
The Creation of the Sun & the Moon.
Lawrence Hill.
General from the Jungle. Hill & Wang.
March to the Monteria. Hill & Wang.
The Night Visitor & Other Stories. Hill &
Wang.
Treasure of Sierra Madre. NAL.
The Treasure of the Sierra Madre. Bentley.
Traven, Beatrice.
xTraven, Beatrice.
The Complete Book of Natural Cosmetics. PB.
The Complete Book of Natural Cosmetics.
S&S.
Travers, J. F. *see* Travers, John F.
Travers, John F.
xTravers, J. F.
The Growing Child: Introduction to Child
Development. Wiley.
xTravers, John F.
Educational Psychology. Har-Row.
Travers, Kenneth J.
xTravers, Kenneth J.
Mathematics Teaching. Har-Row.
Travers, Milton.
xTravers, Milton
Each Other's Victims. PB.
Travers, P. L. *see* Travers, Pamela L.
Travers, Pamela L., 1906-
xTravers, P. L.
Mary Poppins in the Kitchen: A Cookery Book
with a Story. HarBraceJ.
Mary Poppins in the Park. HarBraceJ.
Mary Poppins Opens the Door. HarBraceJ.
xTravers, Pamela L.
Friend Monkey. HarBraceJ.
Mary Poppins. HarBraceJ.
Mary Poppins. HarBraceJ.
Mary Poppins Comes Back. HarBraceJ.
Mary Poppins Comes Back. HarBraceJ.
Mary Poppins from A to Z. HarBraceJ.
Mary Poppins in the Park. HarBraceJ.
Mary Poppins Opens the Door. HarBraceJ.
Travers, Robert M. *see* Travers, Robert Morris William.
Travers, Robert Morris William, 1913-
xTravers, Robert M.
Essentials of Learning. Macmillan.
Introduction to Educational Research.
Macmillan.
Traversa, Vincenzo. *see* Traversa, Vincenzo Paolo.
Traversa, Vincenzo Paolo, 1923-
xTraversa, Vincenzo.
Parola E Pensiero: Introduzione Alla Lingua
Italiana Moderna. Har-Row.
Travis, Arthur E.
xTravis, Arthur E.
Where on Earth Is Heaven. Broadman.
Travis, Georgia.
xTravis, Georgia.
Chronic Illness in Children: Its Impact on
Child & Family. Stanford U Pr.
Travis, John W.
xTravis, John W.
Let's Tune Up. Travis.
Travis, Neal.
xTravis, Neal.
Manhattan. Berkley Pub.
Travis, William P. *see* Travis, William Penfield.

Travis, William Penfield.
xTravis, William P.
Theory of Trade & Protection. Harvard U Pr.
Traxel, David.
xTraxel, David.
An American Saga: The Life & Times of
Rockwell Kent. Har-Row.
Traylor, Ellen G. see Traylor, Ellen Gunderson.
Traylor, Ellen Gunderson.
xTraylor, Ellen G.
John, Son of Thunder. Tyndale.
Traylor, Joseph G., 1942-
xTraylor, Joseph G.
Physics of Stereo-Quad Sound. Iowa St U Pr.
Traynham, James. see Traynham, James G.
Traynham, James G.
xTraynham, James.
Organic Nomenclature: A Programmed
Introduction. P-H.
xTraynham, James G.
Organic Nomenclature: A Programmed
Introduction. P-H.
Traynor, Roger J.
xTraynor, Roger J.
Riddle of Harmless Error. Ohio St U Pr.
Treadgold, Donald W., 1922-
xTreadgold, Donald W.
Lenin & His Rivals: The Struggle for Russia's
Future 1898-1906. Greenwood.
Twentieth Century Russia. Rand.
Treadway, Charles. see Treadway, Charles F.
Treadway, Charles F.
xTreadway, Charles.
Fifty Character Stories. Broadman.
Trease, Geoffrey, 1909-
xTrease, Geoffrey.
Follow My Black Plume. Vanguard.
Silken Secret. Vanguard.
White Nights of St. Petersburg. Vanguard.
Treasure, G. R. see Treasure, Geoffrey Russell Richards.
Treasure, Geoffrey Russell Richards.
xTreasure, G. R.
Cardinal Richelieu and the Development of
Absolutism. St Martin.
Treat, Payson J. see Treat, Payson Jackson.
Treat, Payson Jackson, 1879-
xTreat, Payson J.
Diplomatic Relations Between the United
States & Japan, 1853-1905. Peter Smith.
National Land System, 1785-1820. Russell.
Treat, Roger. see Treat, Roger L.
Treat, Roger L.
xTreat, Roger.
ed. The Encyclopedia of Football. A S Barnes.
The Encyclopedia of Football. Doubleday.
Trebilcock, M. J.
xTrebilcock, M. J.
Debtor & Creditor: Cases, Notes & Materials.
U of Toronto Pr.
Treble, J. H. see Treble, James H.
Treble, James H.
xTreble, J. H.
Urban Poverty in Britain, 1830-1914. St
Martin.
Tree, Herbert B. see Tree, Herbert Beerbohm.
Tree, Herbert Beerbohm, Sir, 1853-1917
xTree, Herbert B.
Nothing Matters, & Other Stories. Arno.
Treece, Henry, 1911-1966
xTreece, Henry.
Dylan Thomas, "Dog Among the Fairies".
Folcroft.
How I See Apocalypse. AMS Pr.
Man with a Sword. Oxford U Pr.
Men of the Hills. S G Phillips.
Ride into Danger. S G Phillips.
Treece, Malra.
xTreece, Malra.

Communication for Business & the Professions.
Allyn.
Treese, Glenn J. Van. see Van Treese, Glenn J.
Trefil, J. S.
xTrefil, James S.
From Atoms to Quarks. Scribner.
Trefil, James S. see Trefil, J. S.
Trefousse, Hans L. see Trefousse, Hans Louis.
Trefousse, Hans Louis.
xTrefousse, Hans L.
The Causes of the Civil War: Institutional
Failure or Human Blunder?. Krieger.
Germany & American Neutrality, 1939-1941.
Octagon.
Impeachment of a President: Andrew Johnson,
the Blacks, & Reconstruction. U of Tenn Pr.
Trefzger, John D.
xTrefzger, John D.
Reading the Bible with Understanding: A
Guide for Beginners. Bethany Pr.
Tregarthen, Enys.
xTregarthen, Enys.
The Doll Who Came Alive. John Day.
Tregaskis, Richard. see Tregaskis, Richard William.
Tregaskis, Richard William, 1916-
xTregaskis, Richard.
Guadalcanal Diary. Random.
Tregear, Edward, 1846-1931
xTregear, Edward.
The Maori Race. AMS Pr.
Tregear, Mary.
xTregear, Mary.
Chinese Art. Oxford U Pr.
Tregear, T. R. see Tregear, Thomas R.
Tregear, Thomas R.
xTregear, T. R.
Economic Geography of China. Elsevier.
Tregenza, Peter.
xTregenza, Peter.
Design of Interior Circulation. Van Nos
Reinhold.
Tregonning, K. G.
xTregonning, Kennedy G.
Southeast Asia: A Critical Bibliography. U of
Ariz Pr.
Tregonning, Kennedy G. see Tregonning, K. G.
Treharne, R. F. see Treharne, Reginald Francis.
Treharne, Reginald Francis.
xTreharne, R. F.
ed. Documents of the Baronial Movement of
Reform & Rebellion, 1258-1267. Oxford U
Pr.
Treiman, Sam B.
xTreiman, Sam B.
Lectures on Current Algebra & Its
Applications. Princeton U Pr.
Trejo, Arnulfo D.
xTrejo, Arnulfo D.
ed. The Chicanos: As We See Ourselves. U of
Ariz Pr.
Trelawny, Edward J. see Trelawny, Edward John.
Trelawny, Edward John, 1792-1881
xTrelawny, Edward J.
Adventures of a Younger Son. AMS Pr.
Adventures of a Younger Son. Oxford U Pr.
Trelease, Allen W.
xTrelease, Allen W.
White Terror: The Ku Klux Klan Conspiracy &
Southern Reconstruction. Greenwood.
Trelease, Frank J., 1913-
xTrelease, Frank J.
Cases & Materials on Water Law. West Pub.
Trelease, Sam F. see Trelease, Sam Farlow.
Trelease, Sam Farlow, 1892-
xTrelease, Sam F.
How to Write Scientific & Technical Papers.
MIT Pr.
Trelease, W. see Trelease, William.
Trelease, William, 1857-1945
xTrelease, W.

Plant Materials of Decorative Gardening: The
Woody Plants. Peter Smith.
Tremain, Henry E. see Tremain, Henry Edwin.
Tremain, Henry Edwin, 1841-1910
xTremain, Henry E.
ed. Sectionalism Unmasked. Negro U Pr.
Tremain, Ruthven.
xTremain, Ruthven.
Fooling Around with Words. Greenwillow.
illus. My Friends: A Self-Portrait Autograph
Book. Macmillan.
illus. Teapot. Switcheroo, & Other Silly Word
Games. Greenwillow.
Tremaine, Howard M.
xTremaine, Howard M.
Audio Cyclopedia. Sams.
Tremayne, Peter.
xTremayne, Peter.
The Fires of Lan-Kern. St Martin.
The Revenge of Dracula. D M Grant.
The Revenge of Dracula. Walker & Co.
Tremblay, Bill.
xTremblay, Bill.
The Anarchist Heart. SBD.
Crying in the Cheap Seats. U of Mass Pr.
Tremblay, Edward. see Tremblay, Edward A.
Tremblay, Edward A.
xTremblay, Edward.
When You Go to Tonga. Dghtrs St Paul.
Tremblay, J. P. see Tremblay, Jean-Paul.
Tremblay, Jean P. see Tremblay, Jean-Paul.
Tremblay, Jean-Paul.
xTremblay, J. P.
Discrete Mathematical Structures with
Applications to Computer Science. McGraw.
xTremblay, Jean P.
Structured Fortran WATFIV-S Programming.
McGraw.
xTremblay, Jean-Paul.
Introduction to Computer Science: An
Algorithmic Approach. McGraw.
Tremblay, Suzanne, 1932-
xTremblay, Suzanne.
The Professional Skin Care Manual. P-H.
Treml, Vladimir G.
xTreml, Vladimir G.
ed. Soviet Economic Statistics. Duke.
Tremmel, William C.
xTremmel, William C.
Religion: What Is It?. HR&W.
Tremonte, Julia.
xTremonte, Julia.
The Devil's House. Pinnacle Bks.
Trench, R. C. see Trench, Richard Chenevix.
Trench, Richard. see Trench, Richard Chenevix.
Trench, Richard Chenevix, Abp. of Dublin, 1807-1886
xTrench, R. C.
Notes on the Parables of Our Lord. Baker Bk.
xTrench, Richard.
On the Study of Words. R West.
Trench, William F., 1931-
xTrench, William F.
Advanced Calculus. Har-Row.
Multivariable Calculus with Linear Algebra &
Series. Acad Pr.
Trenchard, John.
xTrenchard, John.
Cato's Letters: Or, Essays on Liberty, Civil &
Religious, & Other Important Subjects.
Russell.
Trend, John B. see Trend, John Brande.
Trend, John Brande, 1887-
xTrend, John B.
Lorca & the Spanish Poetic Tradition. Russell.
Origins of Modern Spain. Russell.
Trend, M. G.
xTrend, M. G.

Housing Allowances for the Poor: A Social
Experiment. Westview.

Trenerry, Walter N.
xTrenerry, Walter N.
Murder in Minnesota: A Collection of True
Cases. Minn Hist.

Trengove, Alan.
xTrengove, Alan.
ed. How to Play Tennis the Professional Way.
S&S.

Trenholm, Virginia C. *see* Trenholm, Virginia Cole.

Trenholm, Virginia Cole, 1902-
xTrenholm, Virginia C.
Arapahoes, Our People. U of Okla Pr.

Trenholme, Louise. *see* Trenholme, Louise (Irby).

Trenholme, Louise (Irby), 1890-
xTrenholme, Louise.
Ratification of the Federal Constitution in
North Carolina. AMS Pr.

Trensky, Paul. *see* Trensky, Paul I.

Trensky, Paul I.
xTrensky, Paul.
Czech Drama Since World War II. M E
Sharpe.

Trent, W. P. *see* Trent, William Peterfield.

Trent, William. *see* Trent, William

Trent, William P. *see* Trent, William Peterfield.

Trent, William, 1715-1787?
xTrent, William.
Journal of Captain William Trent from
Logstown to Pickawillany, A.D. 1752. Arno.

Trent, William Peterfield.
xTrent, W. P.
Great Writers of America. Folcroft.
xTrent, William P.
ed. Colonial Prose & Poetry. AMS Pr.
Daniel Defoe, How to Know Him. Phaeton.
English Culture in Virginia: A Study of the
Gilmer Letters & an Account of the English
Professors Obtained by Jefferson for the
University of Virginia. Johnson Repr.
Great Writers of America. Arden Lib.
A History of American Literature. Folcroft.
Longfellow, & Other Essays. Arno.

Trentin, J. J. *see* Trentin, John Joseph.

Trentin, John Joseph, 1918-
xTrentin, J. J.
ed. Oncogenesis & Natural Immunity in Syrian
Hamsters. S Karger.

Trepman, Paul.
xTrepman, Paul.
Among Men & Beasts. A S Barnes.

Trepp, Leo.
xTrepp, Leo.
The Complete Book of Jewish Observance.
Behrman.
The Complete Book of Jewish Observance.
Summit Bks.

Trescott, Martha M. *see* Trescott, Martha Moore.

Trescott, Martha Moore, 1941-
xTrescott, Martha M.
ed. Dynamos & Virgins Revisited: Women &
Technological Change in History: an
Anthology. Scarecrow.

Treseder, Neil.
xTreseder, Neil.
Magnolias. Merrimack Bk Serv.

Treshow, Michael.
xTreshow, Michael.
Environment & Plant Response. McGraw.
The Human Environment. McGraw.

Tress, Arthur.
xTress, Arthur.
The Dream Collector. Avon.
Theater of the Mind. Morgan.

Tresselt, Alvin. *see* Tresselt, Alvin R.

Tresselt, Alvin R.
xTresselt, Alvin.
Wonder-Fish from the Sea. Schol Bk Serv.
xTresselt, Alvin R.

Autumn Harvest. Lothrop.
Frog in the Well. Lothrop.
World in the Candy Egg. Lothrop.

Tressler, Donald K. *see* Tressler, Donald Kiteley.

Tressler, Donald Kiteley.
xTressler, Donald K.
Fruit & Vegetable Juice Processing Technology.
AVI.

Tretter, Steven A.
xTretter, Steven A.
Introduction to Discrete-Time Signal
Processing. Wiley.

Tretyak, Vladislav.
xTretyak, Vladislav.
The Hockey I Love. Lawrence Hill.

Treuer, Robert.
xTreuer, Robert.
Voyageur Country: A Park in the Wilderness.
U of Minn Pr.

Trevanian.
xTrevanian.
The Loo Sanction. Avon.
Shibumi. Ballantine.
Shibumi. Crown.

Trevelyan, George M. *see* Trevelyan, George Macaulay.

Trevelyan, George Macaulay, 1876-1962
xTrevelyan, George M.
Autobiography & Other Essays. Arno.
Autobiography & Other Essays. Folcroft.
England in the Age of Wycliffe. AMS Pr.
Garibaldi & the Thousand. AMS Pr.
Garibaldi & the Thousand. Folcroft.
Garibaldi's Defence of the Roman Republic,
1848-9. Greenwood.
A Layman's Love of Letters. Greenwood.
Life of John Bright. Greenwood.
Life of John Bright. R West.

Trevelyan, George O. *see* Trevelyan, George Otto.

Trevelyan, George Otto, Sir, Bart, 1838-1928
xTrevelyan, George O.
The Life & Letters of Lord Macaulay. Oxford
U Pr.
Marginal Notes by Lord Macaulay. Darby Bks.

Trevelyan, Humphrey, Baron Trevelyan, 1905-
xTrevelyan, Humphrey.
Public & Private. David & Charles.
xTrevelyan, Humphry.
Goethe & the Greeks. Octagon.

Trevelyan, Humphry. *see* Trevelyan, Humphrey.

Trevelyan, Julia.
xTrevelyan, Julia.
The Landsend Terror. NAL.

Trevelyan, Marie, 1853-
xTrevelyan, Marie.
Folk-Lore & Folk-Stories of Wales. Norwood
Edns.

Trevelyan, R. C. *see* Trevelyan, Robert Calverley.

Trevelyan, Raleigh.
xTrevelyan, Raleigh.
A Pre-Raphaelite Circle. Rowman.

Trevelyan, Robert Calverley, 1872-
xTrevelyan, R. C.
Thamyris: Is There a Future for Poetry?. Arden
Lib.

Trever, Albert A. *see* Trever, Albert Augustus.

Trever, Albert Augustus, 1874-1940
xTrever, Albert A.
A History of Greek Economic Thought.
Porcupine Pr.

Treverton, Gregory F.
xTreverton, Gregory F.
The Dollar Drain & American Forces in
Germany: Managing the Political Economics
of Alliance. Ohio U Pr.

Treves, Francois, 1930-
xTreves, Francois.

Linear Partial Differential Equations with
Constant Coefficients. Gordon.
Topological Vector Spaces, Distributions &
Kernels. Acad Pr.

Treves, Ralph.
xTreves, Ralph.
Early American Furniture You Can Build.
Arco.
How to Make Your Own Recreation & Hobby
Rooms. Har-Row.

Trevino, Elizabeth (Borton), 1904-
xTrevino, Elizabeth B.
I, Juan De Pareja. Dell.
xTrevino, Elizabeth B. De.
I, Juan De Pareja. FS&G.

Trevino, Elizabeth B. *see* Trevino, Elizabeth (Borton).

Trevino, Elizabeth B. De. *see* Trevino, Elizabeth
(Borton).

Trevino, Lee.
xTrevino, Lee.
Groove Your Golf Swing My Way. Atheneum.

Trevisick, Charles.
xTrevisick, Charles.
My Home Is a Zoo. Merrimack Bk Serv.

Trevithick, J. A. *see* Trevithick, James Anthony.

Trevithick, James Anthony.
xTrevithick, J. A.
The Economics of Inflation. Halsted Pr.

Trevor, Elleston.
xTrevor, Elleston.
Badger's Beech. Aurora Pubs.
Badger's Beech. Sherbourne.
Sweethallow Valley. Sherbourne.
The Theta Syndrome. Doubleday.
The Theta Syndrome. Fawcett.

Trevor, Meriol.
xTrevor, Meriol.
The Civil Prisoners. Dutton.
The Civil Prisoners. Fawcett.
Enemy at Home. PB.
The Fortunate Marriage. Fawcett.
The Fugitives. PB.
The Marked Man. PB.
The Wanton Fires. Dutton.

Trevor, William, 1928-
xTrevor, William.
Angels at the Ritz & Other Stories. Viking Pr.
Children of Dynmouth. Viking Pr.
Lovers of Their Time & Other Stories. Viking
Pr.

Trevor-Roper, H. R. *see* Trevor-Roper, Hugh Redwald.

Trevor-Roper, Hugh. *see* Trevor-Roper, Hugh Redwald.

Trevor-Roper, Hugh R. *see* Trevor-Roper, Hugh
Redwald.

Trevor-Roper, Hugh Redwald.
xTrevor-Roper, H. R.
Historical Essays. Gannon.
The Last Days of Hitler. Arden Lib.
Men & Events: Historical Essays. Octagon.
xTrevor-Roper, Hugh.
Hermit of Peking: The Hidden Life of Sir
Edmund Backhouse. Penguin.
Princes & Artists: Patronage & Ideology at
Four Habsburg Courts, 1517-1633. Har-Row.

xTrevor-Roper, Hugh R.
European Witch Craze in the Sixteenth &
Seventeenth Centuries & Other Essays.
Har-Row.
Last Days of Hitler. Macmillan.

Trew, Anthony. *see* Trew, Antony.

Trew, Antony, 1906-
xTrew, Anthony.
The Antonov Project. St Martin.
xTrew, Antony.
Death of a Supertanker. St Martin.
Ultimatum. St Martin.

Trewartha, Glen. *see* Trewartha, Glenn Thomas.

Trewartha, Glenn T. *see* Trewartha, Glenn Thomas.

Trewartha, Glenn Thomas, 1896-
  xTrewartha, Glen.
    The Earth's Problem Climates. U of Wis Pr.
  xTrewartha, Glenn T.
    Earth's Problem Climates. U of Wis Pr.
    Fundamentals of Physical Geography.
      McGraw.
    An Introduction to Climate. McGraw.
    Introduction to Climate. McGraw.
Trewatha, Robert L.
  xTrewatha, Robert L.
    Management: Functions & Behavior. Business
      Pubns.
Trewin, Ion.
  xTrewin, Ion.
    Journalism. David & Charles.
Trewin, J. C. see Trewin, John Courtenay.
Trewin, John C. see Trewin, John Courtenay.
Trewin, John Courtenay, 1908-
  xTrewin, J. C.
    The Edwardian Theatre. Rowman.
  xTrewin, John C.
    Going to Shakespeare. Allen Unwin.
Treybal, Robert E. see Treybal, Robert Ewald.
Treybal, Robert Ewald, 1915-
  xTreybal, Robert E.
    Mass Transfer Operations. McGraw.
Trezevant, D. H.
  xTrezevant, Daniel H.
    Letters to His Excellency Governor Manning
      on the Lunatic Asylum. Arno.
Trezevant, Daniel H. see Trezevant, D. H.
Triadu, Joan.
  xTriadu, Joan.
    Compiled by Anthology of Catalan Lyric
      Poetry. AMS Pr.
    Compiled by An Anthology of Catalan Lyric
      Poetry. Greenwood.
Triandis, Harry C. see Triandis, Harry Charalambos.
Triandis, Harry Charalambos, 1926-
  xTriandis, Harry C.
    ed. Analysis of Subjective Culture. Wiley.
    Attitude & Attitude Change. Wiley.
    ed. Variations in Black & White Perceptions of
      the Social Environment. U of Ill Pr.
Trias, Robert A.
  xTrias, Robert A.
    The Hand Is My Sword: A Karate Handbook.
      C E Tuttle.
Tribe, David. see Tribe, David H.
Tribe, David H.
  xTribe, David.
    President Charles Bradlaugh, MP. Shoe String.
    Questions of Censorship. St Martin.
Tribe, Ian.
  xTribe, Ian.
    The Plant Kingdom. G&D.
Tribe, Keith.
  xTribe, Keith.
    Land, Labour & Economic Discourse.
      Routledge & Kegan.
Tribe, Laurence H.
  xTribe, Lawrence H.
    ed. When Values Conflict: Essays on
      Environmental Analysis, Discourse and
      Decision. Ballinger Pub.
Tribe, Lawrence H. see Tribe, Laurence H.
Tribe, M. A. see Tribe, Michael A.
Tribe, Michael A.
  xTribe, M. A.
    Cell Membranes. Cambridge U Pr.
    Dynamic Aspects of Cells. Cambridge U Pr.
    Light Microscopy. Cambridge U Pr.
    Nerves & Muscle. Cambridge U Pr.
    Protein Synthesis. Cambridge U Pr.
  xTribe, Michael A.
    Case Studies in Genetics. Cambridge U Pr.
Trible, Phyllis.
  xTrible, Phyllis.

    God & the Rhetoric of Sexuality. Fortress.
Tribolet, J. see Tribolet, Jose Manuel.
Tribolet, Jose Manuel.
  xTribolet, J.
    Seismic Applications of Homomorphic Signal
      Processing. P-H.
Tricart, J. see Tricart, Jean.
Tricart, Jean.
  xTricart, J.
    An Introduction to Climatic Geomorphology.
      St Martin.
    Structural Geomorphology. Longman.
Trice, Harrison M. see Trice, Harrison Miller.
Trice, Harrison Miller, 1920-
  xTrice, Harrison M.
    Alcoholism in America. Krieger.
Triche, Charles W.
  xTriche, Charles W.
    Euthanasia Controversy, 1812-1974: A
      Bibliography with Select Annotations.
      Whitston Pub.
    The Sickle Cell Hemoglobinopathies: A
      Comprehensive Bibliography 1910-1972.
      Whitston Pub.
    The Sickle Cell Hemoglobinopathies: A
      Comprehensive Bibliography 1973-75.
      Whitston Pub.
Trick, Timothy N., 1939-
  xTrick, Timothy N.
    An Introduction to Circuit Analysis. Wiley.
Tricker, R. A. see Tricker, R. A. R.
Tricker, R. A. R.
  xTricker, R. A.
    Introduction to Meteorological Optics. Elsevier.
Triebel, Walter A.
  xTriebel, Walter A.
    Integrated Digital Electronics. P-H.
Trieste Symposium, 1968. see International Symposium
  on Contemporary Physics, Trieste, 1968.
Triffin, Robert.
  xTriffin, Robert.
    Europe & the Money Muddle: From
      Bilateralism to Near-Convertibility
      1947-1956. Greenwood.
    Monopolistic Competition & General
      Equilibrium Theory. Harvard U Pr.
Trifilo, S. Samuel. see Trifilo, Santo Samuel.
Trifilo, Santo Samuel, 1917-
  xTrifilo, S. Samuel.
    Maximilian & Carlota in Mexican Drama. Univ
      of Wis Latin Am.
Trigg, Emma G. see Trigg, Emma Gray (White).
Trigg, Emma Gray (White).
  xTrigg, Emma G.
    Paulownia Tree. Golden Quill.
Trigg, George L.
  xTrigg, George L.
    ed. Crucial Experiments in Modern Physics.
      Crane-Russak Co.
Trigg, R. see Trigg, Roger.
Trigg, Roger.
  xTrigg, R.
    Reason & Commitment. Cambridge U Pr.
Trigger, Bruce G.
  xTrigger, Bruce G.
    The Children of Aataentsic: A History of the
      Huron People to 1660. McGill-Queens U Pr.
    Late Nubian Settlement at Arminna West.
      Penn-Yale Expedit.
    The Late Nubian Settlement at Arminna West.
      Univ Mus of U PA.
Triggle, D. J.
  xTriggle, D. J.
    Chemical Aspects of the Autonomic Nervous
      System. Acad Pr.
    Chemical Pharmacology of the Synapse. Acad
      Pr.
    ed. Cholinergic Ligand Interactions. Acad Pr.
Trigoboff, Joe.
  xTrigoboff, Joseph.

    Abu. Lothrop.
    Streets. Windy Row.
Trigoboff, Joseph. see Trigoboff, Joe.
Trillin, Calvin.
  xTrillin, Calvin.
    Alice, Let's Eat: Further Adventures of a
      Happy Eater. Random.
    American Fried: Adventures of a Happy Eater.
      Random.
Trilling, Diana.
  xTrilling, Diana.
    Reviewing the Forties. HarBraceJ.
Trilling, Lionel, 1905-1975
  xTrilling, Lionel.
    Pref. by E. M. Forster. HarBraceJ.
    E. M. Forster. New Directions.
    The Liberal Imagination: Essays on Literature
      & Society. HarBraceJ.
    The Liberal Imagination: Essays on Literature
      & Society. Scribner.
    The Middle of the Journey. Avon.
    Intro. by The Middle of the Journey.
      HarBraceJ.
    The Middle of the Journey. Scribner.
    Of This Time, of That Place & Other Stories.
      HarBraceJ.
    Prefaces to the Experience of Literature.
      HarBraceJ.
    Pref. by Sincerity & Authenticity. HarBraceJ.
Trilling, Richard J.
  xTrilling, Richard J.
    Party Image & Electoral Behavior. Wiley.
Trim, J. L. see Trim, John L. M.
Trim, John L. M.
  xTrim, J. L.
    English Pronunciation Illustrated. Cambridge U
      Pr.
Trimble, Marshall.
  xTrimble, Marshall.
    Arizona: A Panoramic History of a Frontier
      State. Doubleday.

Trimingham, J. Spencer. see Trimingham, John Spencer.
Trimingham, John Spencer.
  xTrimingham, J. Spencer.
    Christianity Among the Arabs in Pre-Islamic
      Times. Longman.
    History of Islam in West Africa. Oxford U Pr.
    The Influence of Islam Upon Africa. Longman.
    Sufi Orders in Islam. Oxford U Pr.
    The Sufi Orders in Islam. Oxford U Pr.
Trimmer, Eric. see Trimmer, Eric J.
Trimmer, Eric J.
  xTrimmer, Eric.
    The First Seven Years. St Martin.
Trimmer, Joseph F.
  xTrimmer, Joseph F.
    ed. The National Book Awards for Fiction: An
      Index to the First Twenty-Five Years. G K
      Hall.
Trine, Ralph W. see Trine, Ralph Waldo.
Trine, Ralph Waldo, 1866-1958
  xTrine, Ralph W.
    In Tune with the Infinite. Bobbs.
    In Tune with the Infinite. Keats.
Trinkaus, J. P. see Trinkaus, John Philip.
Trinkaus, John Philip, 1918-
  xTrinkaus, J. P.
    Cells into Organs: The Forces That Shape the
      Embryo. P-H.
Trinkner, Charles L.
  xTrinkner, Charles L.
    ed. Teaching for Better Use of Libraries. Shoe
      String.
Trinks, W. see Trinks, Willibald.
Trinks, Willibald.
  xTrinks, W.
    Industrial Furnaces. Wiley.
Triola, Mario F.
  xTriola, Mario F.

Mathematics & the Modern World. Benjamin-Cummings.
A Survey of Mathematics. Benjamin-Cummings.

Tripathi, G. P. *see* Tripathi, Ganga Prasad.

Tripathi, Ganga Prasad, 1925-
xTripathi, G. P.
Indo-Afghan Relations, 1882 to 1907. Intl Pubns Serv.

Triplett, Frank.
xTriplett, Frank.
The Life, Times, & Treacherous Death of Jesse James. Nordon Pubns.
Life, Times & Treacherous Death of Jesse James. Swallow.

Tripodi, Tony.
xTripodi, Tony.
Assessment of Social Research: Guidelines for the Use of Research in Social Work & Social Science. Peacock Pubs.
Differential Social Program Evaluation. Peacock Pubs.
Uses & Abuses of Social Research in Social Work. Columbia U Pr.

Tripole, Martin R.
xTripole, Martin R.
The Jesus Event & Our Response. Alba.

Tripp, C. A.
xTripp, C. A.
Homosexual Matrix. McGraw.
Homosexual Matrix. NAL.

Tripp, Jenny.
xTripp, Jenny.
The Man Who Was Left for Dead. Raintree Pubs.
One Was Left Alive. Raintree Pubs.

Tripp, Wallace.
xTripp, Wallace.
A Great Big Ugly Man Came up & Tied His Horse to Me: A Book of Nonsense Verse. Little.
A Great Big Ugly Man Came Up & Tied His Horse to Me: A Book of Nonsense Verse. Little.

Trippett, Frank.
xTrippett, Frank.
The First Horsemen. Silver.

Triseliotis, J. B.
xTriseliotis, John.
In Search of Origins: The Experiences of Adopted People. Routledge & Kegan.

Triseliotis, J. P.
xTriseliotis, John.
ed. New Developments in Foster Care & Adoption. Routledge & Kegan.

Triseliotis, John. *see* Triseliotis, J. B.

Triska, Jan F.
xTriska, Jan F.
ed. Communist Party States: Comparative & International Studies. Bobbs.
ed. Constitutions of the Communist Party-States. Hoover Inst Pr.

Triston, H. U.
xTriston, H. U.
Men in Cages. Gale.

Tristram, W. Outram. *see* Tristram, William Outram.

Tristram, William Outram.
xTristram, W. Outram.
Coaching Days & Coaching Ways. Norwood Edns.

Tritton, Arthur S. *see* Tritton, Arthur Stanley.

Tritton, Arthur Stanley, 1881-
xTritton, Arthur S.
Teach Yourself Arabic. McKay.

Tritton, S. M.
xTritton, S. M.
Guide to Better Wine & Beer Making for Beginners. Dover.

Trivedi, R. D.
xTrivedi, R. D.

Compendious History of English Literature. Intl Bk Dist.
Compendious History of English Literature. Intl Pubns Serv.

Trivelpiece, Laurel.
xTrivelpiece, Laurel.
During Water Peaches. Lippincott.
Legless in Flight. Woolmer-Brotherson.

Trivers, J. *see* Trivers, James.

Trivers, James.
xTrivers, J.
I Can Stop Anytime I Want. P-H.
xTrivers, James.
Hamburger Heaven. Avon.
Hamburger Heaven. P-H.
I Can Stop Any Time I Want. Dell.

Trivett, Daphne. *see* Trivett, Daphne Harwood.

Trivett, Daphne Harwood.
xTrivett, Daphne.
Time for Clocks. T Y Crowell.

Trivett, John V.
xTrivett, John V.
Building Tables on Tables: A Book About Multiplication. T Y Crowell.

Trivieri, Lawrence A.
xTrivieri, Lawrence A.
Fundamental Concepts of Elementary Mathematics. Har-Row.

Trobisch, Ingrid. *see* Trobisch, Ingrid (Hult).

Trobisch, Ingrid (Hult).
xTrobisch, Ingrid.
On Our Way Rejoicing. Har-Row.

Trobisch, Walter.
xTrobisch, Walter.
I Married You. Har-Row.
Living with Unfulfilled Desires. Inter-Varsity.
Love Yourself: Self Acceptance & Depression. Inter-Varsity.

Trobridge, Gerry.
xTrobridge, Gerry.
Conversation with a World Voyager. McKay.
Conversation with a World Voyager. Seven Seas.

Troebst, Cord Christian, 1933-
xTroebst, Cord Christian.
The Art of Survival. Doubleday.

Troeger, Thomas H., 1945-
xTroeger, Thomas H.
Are You Saved?: Answers to the Awkward Question. Westminster.
Meditation: Escape to Reality. Westminster.
Rage! Reflect, Rejoice!: Praying with the Psalmists. Westminster.

Troelstra, A. S. *see* Troelstra, Anne Sjerp.

Troelstra, Anne Sjerp.
xTroelstra, A. S.
Choice Sequences: A Chapter of Intuitionistic Mathematics. Oxford U Pr.
Principles of Intuitionism. Springer-Verlag.

Troelstrup, Arch W. *see* Troelstrup, Archie William.
Troelstrup, Archibald. *see* Troelstrup, Archie William.

Troelstrup, Archie William, 1901-
xTroelstrup, Arch W.
The Consumer in American Society: Personal & Family Finance. McGraw.
xTroelstrup, Archibald.
The Consumer in American Society: Personal & Family Finance. McGraw.

Troeltsch, Ernst, 1865-1923
xTroeltsch, Ernst.
Absoluteness of Christianity & the History of Religions. John Knox.

Troise, Joe.
xTroise, Joe.
Cherries & Lemons: The Used-Car Buyer's Handbook. And Bks.

Troitsky, M. S.
xTroitsky, M. S.

Stiffened Plates: Bending, Stability & Vibrations. Elsevier.

Trojcak, Doris A.
xTrojcak, Doris A.
Science with Children. McGraw.

Troland, Leonard T. *see* Troland, Leonard Thompson.

Troland, Leonard Thompson, 1889-
xTroland, Leonard T.
Principles of Psychophysiology: A Survey of Modern Scientific Psychology. Greenwood.

Troll. *see* Troll, Lillian E.

Troll, Lillian E.
xTroll.
Looking Ahead: A Woman's Guide to the Problems & Joys of Growing Older. P-H.
xTroll, Lillian E.
Families in Later Life. Wadsworth Pub.

Trollope, A. *see* Trollope, Anthony.

Trollope, Anthony, 1815-1882
xTrollope, A.
North America. Dawson Pub.
xTrollope, Anthony.
Autobiography. Oxford U Pr.
An Autobiography. U of Cal Pr.
Barchester Towers. Dutton.
Barchester Towers. Merrimack Bk Serv.
Barchester Towers. NAL.
Barchester Towers. Oxford U Pr.
Can You Forgive Her?. Oxford U Pr.
Can You Forgive Her?. Penguin.
The Claverings. Dover.
The Claverings. Oxford U Pr.
Clergymen of the Church of England. Humanities.
Doctor Thorne. Oxford U Pr.
Duke's Children. Oxford U Pr.
The Eustace Diamonds. Lighthouse Pr NY.
The Eustace Diamonds. Oxford U Pr.
The Eustace Diamonds. Penguin.
Framley Parsonage. Dutton.
Framley Parsonage. Merrimack Bk Serv.
Framley Parsonage. Oxford U Pr.
The Last Chronicle of Barset. Dutton.
Last Chronicle of Barset. HM.
The Last Chronicle of Barset. Merrimack Bk Serv.
Last Chronicle of Barset. Oxford U Pr.
The Letters of Anthony Trollope. Greenwood.
North America. Kelley.
Prime Minister. Oxford U Pr.
Ralph the Heir. Dover.
Thackeray. AMS Pr.
Thackeray. Folcroft.
Thackeray. Gale.
The Tireless Traveler: Twenty Letters to the Liverpool Mercury. U of Cal Pr.
The Vicar of Bullhampton. Dover.
The Vicar of Bullhampton. Oxford U Pr.
Warden. Dutton.
Warden. Heinemann Ed.
The Warden. Merrimack Bk Serv.
Warden. Oxford U Pr.

Trollope, Henry M. *see* Trollope, Henry Merivale.

Trollope, Henry Merivale, b. 1846
xTrollope, Henry M.
The Life of Moliere. Arden Lib.
The Life of Moliere. Folcroft.

Trollope, Joanna.
xTrollope, Joanna.
Eliza Stanhope. Dell.
Eliza Stanhope. Dutton.
Mistaken Virtues. Dutton.

Tromba, A. J. *see* Tromba, Anthony.

Tromba, Anthony.
xTromba, A. J.
On the Number of Simply Connected Minimal Surfaces Spanning a Curve. Am Math.

Trombly, Catherine A. *see* Trombly, Catherine Anne.

Trombly, Catherine Anne.
xTrombly, Catherine A.

Occupational Therapy for Physical
Dysfunction. Williams & Wilkins.

Trompf, G. W.
xTrompf, G. W.
The Idea of Historical Recurrence in Western
Thought: From Antiquity to the Reformation.
U of Cal Pr.

Tronaas, Edward M.
xTronaas, Edward M.
Mathematics for Technicians. P-H.

Tronc, Keith. see Tronc, Keith Ernest.

Tronc, Keith Ernest.
xTronc, Keith.
Financial Management in School
Administration. U of Queensland Pr.
ed. A Principal's Workbook: Simulations of
School Administration. U of Queensland Pr.

Tronick, Edward.
xTronick, Edward.
Infant Curriculum: The Bromley-Heath Guide
to the Care of Infants in Groups. Media
Projects.

Tronzo, Raymond G.
xTronzo, Raymond G.
ed. Surgery of the Hip Joint. Lea & Febiger.

Trooboff, Peter D.
xTrooboff, Peter D.
ed. Law & Responsibility in Warfare: The
Vietnam Experience. U of NC Pr.

Tropman, John E.
xTropman, John E.
Essentials of Committee Management.
Nelson-Hall.
ed. Strategic Perspectives on Social Policy.
Pergamon.

Troppmann, R. see Troppmann, Robert.

Troppmann, Robert.
xTroppmann, R.
Football's Master Defense Guide. P-H.

Trosclair.
xTrosclair.
A Cajun Night Before Christmas. Pelican.

Trost, Barry M.
xTrost, Barry M.
Problems in Spectroscopy: Organic Structure
Determination by NMR, IR, UV & Mass
Spectra. Benjamin-Cummings.

Trost, Lucille W. see Trost, Lucille Wood.

Trost, Lucille Wood.
xTrost, Lucille W.
Lives & Deaths of a Meadow. Putnam.

Trotman, R. E. see Trotman, Robert Edward.

Trotman, Robert Edward.
xTrotman, R. E.
Technological Aids to Microbiology. Intl Ideas.

Trott, Lamarr B.
xTrott, Lamarr B.
Contributions to the Biology of Carapid Fishes
(Paracanthopterygii, Gadiformes). U of Cal
Pr.

Trott, Susan.
xTrott, Susan.
The Housewife & the Assassin. Avon.
The Housewife & the Assassin. St Martin.

Trotta, Maurice S.
xTrotta, Maurice S.
Arbitration of Labor-Management Disputes.
Am Mgmt.

Trotter, Alexander.
xTrotter, Alexander.
Observations on the Financial Position &
Credit of Such of the States of the North
American Union As Have Contracted Public
Debts. Kelley.

Trotter, Ann.
xTrotter, Ann.

Britain & East Asia, 1933 to 1937. Cambridge
U Pr.
ed. Continuing Revolution: China Since 1894.
Intl Pubns Serv.

Trotter, David, 1951-
xTrotter, David.
The Poetry of Abraham Cowley. Rowman.

Trottman, Rosemary W.
xTrottman, Rosemary W.
The History of Zephyrhills, 1821-1921.
Vantage.

Trotzer, James P., 1943-
xTrotzer, James P.
The Counselor & the Group: Integrating
Theory, Training & Practice. Brooks-Cole.

Trounce, J. R. see Trounce, John Reginald.

Trounce, John Reginald.
xTrounce, J. R.
Clinical Pharmacology for Nurses. Churchill.

Troup, Freda, 1911-
xTroup, Freda.
South Africa: An Historical Introduction. Intl
Pubns Serv.

Troupin, Rosalind H.
xTroupin, Rosalind H.
Diagnostic Radiology in Clinical Medicine.
Year Bk Med.

Trout, Charles H.
xTrout, Charles H.
Boston, the Great Depression, & the New
Deal. Oxford U Pr.

Troutman, Charles.
xTroutman, Charles.
Everything You Want to Know About the
Mission Field, but Are Afraid You Won't
Learn Until You Get There: Letters to a
Perspective Missionary. Inter-Varsity.

Trouton, Ruth.
xTrouton, Ruth.
Peasant Renaissance in Yugoslavia, 1900-1950.
Greenwood.

Trover, Ellen L. see Trover, Ellen Lloyd.

Trover, Ellen Lloyd.
xTrover, Ellen L.
ed. Chronology & Documentary Handbook of
the State of Alaska. Oceana.

Trow, George S. see Trow, George Swift.

Trow, George Swift.
xTrow, George S.
Meet Robert E. Lee. Random.

Trow, Micheal-Arthur, 1957-
xTrow, Mike.
The Pulse of '64: The Mersey Beat. Vantage.

Trow, Mike. see Trow, Micheal-Arthur.

Trow, William C. see Trow, William Clark.

Trow, William Clark, 1894-
xTrow, William C.
Educational Psychology. Greenwood.
xTrow, Wm. Clark.
Paths to Educational Reform. Educ Tech
Pubns.
ed. Psychological Foundations of Educational
Technology. Educ Tech Pubn.

Trow, Wm. Clark. see Trow, William Clark.

Trowbridge, C. L. see Trowbridge, Charles L.

Trowbridge, Charles L.
xTrowbridge, C. L.
The Theory & Practice of Pension Funding.
Irwin.

Trowbridge, Hoyt.
xTrowbridge, Hoyt.
From Dryden to Jane Austen: Essays on
English Critics & Writers, 1660-1818. U of
NM Pr.

Trowbridge, J. T. see Trowbridge, John Townsend.

Trowbridge, John, 1843-1923
xTrowbridge, John.
What Is Electricity. Arno.

Trowbridge, John T. see Trowbridge, John Townsend.

Trowbridge, John Townsend, 1827-1916
xTrowbridge, J. T.
South: A Tour of Its Battle Fields & Ruined
Cities. Arno.
xTrowbridge, John T.
Neighbor Jackwood. Irvington.

Troxell, George E. see Troxell, George Earl.

Troxell, George Earl.
xTroxell, George E.
Composition & Properties of Concrete.
McGraw.

Troxell, Hyla A.
xTroxell, Hyla A.
The Norman Davis Collection. Am
Numismatic.

Troxell, Mary D.
xTroxell, Mary D.
Retail Merchandising Mathematics: Principles
& Procedures. P-H.

Troy, Charles E., 1936-
xTroy, Charles E.
The Comic Intermezzo: A Study in the History
of Eighteenth-Century Italian Opera. Univ
Microfilms.

Troy, George.
xTroy, George.
Native to the Grain. HarBraceJ.

Troyat, Henri, 1911-
xTroyat, Henri.
Baroness. S&S.
Daily Life in Russia Under the Last Tsar.
Stanford U Pr.

Troyka, Lynn Q. see Troyka, Lynn Quitman.

Troyka, Lynn Quitman.
xTroyka, Lynn Q.
Steps in Composition. P-H.
Structured Reading. P-H.
Taking Action: Writing, Reading, Speaking &
Listening Through Simulation Games. P-H.

Truax, Carol.
xTruax, Carol.
Woman's Day Book of Salads. Dutton.

Trubo, Richard.
xTrubo, Richard.
How to Get a Good Night's Sleep. Little.

Truby, J. David.
xTruby, J. David.
Quiet Killers. Paladin Ent.

Trucchi, Lorenza.
xTrucchi, Lorenza.
Francis Bacon. Abrams.

Trucks, H. E.
xTrucks, H. E.
Designing for Economical Production. SME.

Trudeau, G. B., 1948-
xTrudeau, G. B.
As the Kid Goes for Broke. Bantam.
But the Pension Fund Was Just Sitting There.
Bantam.
Call Me When You Find America. Bantam.
The President Is a Lot Smarter Than You
Think. Popular Lib.
Stalking the Perfect Tan. HR&W.
A Tad Overweight, but Violet Eyes to Die for.
HR&W.
xTrudeau, Garry.
But the Pension Fund Was Just Sitting There.
HR&W.
But This War Had Such Promise. HR&W.
Call Me When You Find America. HR&W.
Guilty, Guilty, Guilty. HR&W.
The President Is a Lot Smarter Than You
Think. HR&W.
xTrudeau, Garry B.
As the Kid Goes for Broke. HR&W.

Trudeau, Garry. see Trudeau, G. B.

Trudeau, Garry B. see Trudeau, G. B.

Trudeau, Margaret, 1948-
xTrudeau, Margaret.

Beyond Reason. Paddington.
Beyond Reason. PB.
Trudeau, Pierre E. *see* Trudeau, Pierre Elliott.
Trudeau, Pierre Elliott.
xTrudeau, Pierre E.
Approaches to Politics. Oxford U Pr.
Trudeau, Richard J.
xTrudeau, Richard J.
Dots & Lines. Kent St U Pr.
Trudgill, P. *see* Trudgill, Peter.
Trudgill, Peter.
xTrudgill, P.
Sociolinguistic Patterns in British English. Univ
Park.
xTrudgill, Peter.
Sociolinguistics: An Introduction. Penguin.
Trudgill, S. T.
xTrudgill, Stephen A.
Soil & Vegetation Systems. Oxford U Pr.
Trudgill, Stephen A. *see* Trudgill, S. T.
Trudinger, P. A.
xTrudinger, P. A.
ed. Biogeochemical Cycling of
Mineral-Forming Elements. Elsevier.
True, Alfred C. *see* True, Alfred Charles.
True, Alfred Charles, 1853-1929
xTrue, Alfred C.
History of Agricultural Education in the United
States 1785-1925. Arno.
History of Agricultural Extension Work in the
United States 1785-1923. Arno.
True, Dan, 1924-
xTrue, Dan.
A Family of Eagles. Everest Hse.
Trueba, Henry T.
xTrueba, Henry T.
ed. Bilingual Multicultural Education & the
Professional: From Theory to Practice.
Newbury Hse.
Trueblood, Alan S.
xTrueblood, Alan S.
Experience and Artistic Expression in Lope De
Vega: The Making of la Dorotea. Harvard U
Pr.
Trueblood, Benjamin F. *see* Trueblood, Benjamin
Franklin.
Trueblood, Benjamin Franklin, 1847-1916
xTrueblood, Benjamin F.
Development of the Peace Idea & Other
Essays. Garland Pub.
The Development of the Peace Idea & Other
Essays. Ozer.
Trueblood, D. Elton. *see* Trueblood, David Elton.
Trueblood, David Elton, 1900-
xTrueblood, D. Elton.
People Called Quakers. Friends United.
xTrueblood, Elton.
The Humor of Christ. Har-Row.
The Incendiary Fellowship. Har-Row.
The Life We Prize. Word Bks.
Trueblood, Elton. *see* Trueblood, David Elton.
Trueblood, Paul G. *see* Trueblood, Paul Graham.
Trueblood, Paul Graham.
xTrueblood, Paul G.
Flowering of Byron's Genius: Studies in
Byron's Don Juan. Russell.
Lord Byron. Twayne.
Trueman, Richard. *see* Trueman, Richard E.
Trueman, Richard E.
xTrueman, Richard.
An Introduction to Quantitative Methods for
Decision Making. HR&W.
Truesdell, William G.
xTruesdell, William G.
Guide to the Wilderness Waterway of the
Everglades National Park. U of Miami Pr.
Truette, Everett E. *see* Truette, Everett Ellsworth.
Truette, Everett Ellsworth, 1861-1933
xTruette, Everett E.

Organ Registration: A Comprehensive Treatise
on the Distinctive Quality of Tone of Organ
Stops. Longwood Pr.
Truettner, William H.
xTruettner, William H.
The Natural Man Observed: A Study of
Catlin's Indian Gallery. Smithsonian.
Truffaut, Francois.
xTruffaut, Francois.
The Films in My Life. S&S.
The Films in My Life. S&S.
Hitchcock. S&S.
Truitt, Deborah.
xTruitt, Deborah.
ed. Dolphins & Porpoises: A Comprehensive,
Annotated Bibliography of the Smaller
Cetacea. Gale.
Truitt, Evelyn M. *see* Truitt, Evelyn Mack.
Truitt, Evelyn Mack, 1931-
xTruitt, Evelyn M.
Who Was Who on Screen. Bowker.
Trullinger, James W.
xTrullinger, James W.
The Complete Pug. Howell Bk.
Trullinger, James W. *see* Trullinger, James Walker.
Trullinger, James Walker.
xTrullinger, James W.
Village at War: An Account of Revolution in
Vietnam. Longman.
Truman, Ben C. *see* Truman, Benjamin Cummings.
Truman, Benjamin Cummings, 1835-1916
xTruman, Ben C.
History of the World's Fair: Being a Complete
& Authentic Description of the Columbian
Exposition, from Its Inception. Arno.
Truman, David B. *see* Truman, David Bicknell.
Truman, David Bicknell, 1913-
xTruman, David B.
Governmental Process: Political Interests &
Public Opinion. Knopf.
Truman, Harry S.
xTruman, Harry S.
The Truman Administration, Its Principles &
Practice. Greenwood.
Truman Speaks. Kraus Repr.
Truman, Ruth, 1931-
xTruman, Ruth.
Underground Manual for Ministers' Wives.
Abingdon.
Trumbo, Dalton, 1905-
xTrumbo, Dalton.
Johnny Got His Gun. Bantam.
Johnny Got His Gun. Lyle Stuart.
Night of the Aurochs. Viking Pr.
Trump, B. F. *see* Trump, Benjamin F.
Trump, Banjamin F. *see* Trump, Benjamin F.
Trump, Benjamin F.
xTrump, B. F.
Diagnostic Electron Microscopy. Wiley.
xTrump, Banjamin F.
Diagnostic Electron Microscopy. Wiley.
xTrump, Benjamin F.
ed. Pathobiology of Cell Membranes. Acad Pr.
Trump, J. Lloyd.
xTrump, J. Lloyd.
Secondary School Curriculum Improvement:
Meeting Challenges of the Times. Allyn.
Trumpler, Paul R. *see* Trumpler, Paul Robert.
Trumpler, Paul Robert.
xTrumpler, Paul R.
Design of Film Bearings. Macmillan.
Truscott, Alan. *see* Truscott, Alan F.
Truscott, Alan F.
xTruscott, Alan.
Teach Yourself Basic Bidding. Arco.
Truscott, Lucian K.
xTruscott, Lucian K.
The Complete Van Book. Crown.
Dress Gray. Fawcett.
Truscott, Lucian K. *see* Truscott, Lucian King.

Truscott, Lucian King.
xTruscott, Lucian K.
Command Missions. Arno.
Trusler, Ivan.
xTrusler, Ivan.
Functional Lessons in Singing. P-H.
Truss, Jan.
xTruss, Jan.
Bird at the Window. Har-Row.
Trussell, John R.
xTrussell, John R.
Introduction to Furniture Making. Sterling.
Trussler, Simon.
xTrussler, Simon.
Burlesque Plays of the Eighteenth Century.
Oxford U Pr.
Trusty, Francis M.
xTrusty, Francis M.
ed. Administering Human Resources: A
Behavioral Approach to Educational
Administration. McCutchan.
Trusty-Hiersche, Robin. *see* Trusty-Hiersche, Robin Lou.
Trusty-Hiersche, Robin Lou.
xTrusty-Hiersche, Robin.
Songs & Dances of the Woman Within.
Grossmont Pr.
Trutter, John T. *see* Trutter, John Thomas.
Trutter, John Thomas.
xTrutter, John T.
The Governor Takes a Bride: The Celebrated
Marriage of Cora English & John R. Tanner,
Governor of Illinois, 1897-1901. S Ill U Pr.
Truzzi, Marcello.
xTruzzi, Marcello.
Sociology & Everyday Life. P-H.
Sociology for Pleasure. P-H.
Tryon, Caroline M. *see* Tryon, Caroline McCann.
Tryon, Caroline McCann.
xTryon, Caroline M.
Evaluations of Adolescent Personality by
Adolescents. Kraus Repr.
Tryon, Rolla M. *see* Tryon, Rolla Milton.
Tryon, Rolla Milton, 1916-
xTryon, Rolla M.
The Ferns of Minnesota. U of Minn Pr.
Tryon, Thomas.
xTryon, Thomas.
Crowned Heads. Fawcett.
Crowned Heads. Knopf.
Other. Fawcett.
The Other. Knopf.
Trzebinski, Errol, 1936-
xTrzebinski, Errol.
Silence Will Speak: A Study of the Life of
Denys Finch Hatton & His Relationship with
Karen Blixen. U of Chicago Pr.
Trzyna, Thaddeus C.
xTrzyna, Thaddeus C.
ed. The California Handbook: A
Comprehensive Guide to Sources of Current
Information & Action. Cal Inst Public.
Population: An International Directory of
Organizations & Information Resources. Cal
Inst Public.
Tsai, Christiana.
xTsai, Christiana.
Christiana Tsai. Moody.
Tsang, Chiu-Sam. *see* Tsang, Chiu-Sam.
Tsang, Chiu-Sam, 1901-
xTsang , Chiu-Sam.
Society, Schools & Progress in China.
Pergamon.
Tsang, Wing-Sum.
xTsang, Wing-Sum.
Metabolic Activation of Polynuclear Aromatic
Hydrocarbons. Pergamon.
Tsanin, Mordecai, 1906-
xTsanin, Mordechai.
Artapanos Comes Home. A S Barnes.
Tsanin, Mordechai. *see* Tsanin, Mordecai.

Tsanoff, R. A. *see* Tsanoff, Radoslav Andrea.
Tsanoff, Radoslav A. *see* Tsanoff, Radoslav Andrea.
Tsanoff, Radoslav Andrea, 1887-
　　xTsanoff, R. A.
　　　　The Moral Ideals of Our Civilization. Gordon
　　　　　Pr.
　　xTsanoff, Radoslav A.
　　　　Moral Ideals of Our Civilization. Arno.
　　　　Worlds to Know: A Philosophy of Cosmic
　　　　　Perspectives. Humanities.
Tsao, Wen-Yen, 1908-
　　xTsao, Wen-Yen.
　　　　The Constitutional Structure of Modern China.
　　　　　Hyperion Conn.
Tschebotarioff, Gregory P. *see* Tschebotarioff, Gregory
　Porphyriewitch.
Tschebotarioff, Gregory Porphyriewitch, 1899-
　　xTschebotarioff, Gregory P.
　　　　Foundations, Retaining & Earth Structures:
　　　　　The Art of Design Construction & Its
　　　　　Scientific Basis in Soil Mechanics. McGraw.
Tschopik, Harry, 1915-1956
　　xTschopik, Harry.
　　　　Highland Communities of Central Peru: A
　　　　　Regional Survey. Greenwood.
Tschumi, Raymond.
　　xTschumi, Raymond.
　　　　Theory of Culture. NOK Pubs.
　　　　Thought in Twentieth-Century English Poetry.
　　　　　Folcroft.
Tse, Francis S. *see* Tse, Francis Sing.
Tse, Francis Sing.
　　xTse, Francis S.
　　　　Mechanical Vibrations: Theory & Applications.
　　　　　Allyn.
Tselementes, Nicholas, 1880-
　　xTselementes, Nicholas.
　　　　Greek Cookery. Divry.
Tseng, Charles C., 1932-
　　xTseng, Charles C.
　　　　Anatomical Studies of Flower & Fruit in
　　　　　Hydrocotyloideae (Umbelliferae). U of Cal
　　　　　Pr.
Tseng, Henry P.
　　xTseng, Henry P.
　　　　Law Schools of the World. W S Hein.
Tseng, Rosy.
　　xTseng, Rosy.
　　　　Chinese Cooking Made Easy. C E Tuttle.
Tsien, Tsuen-Hsuin.
　　xTsien, Tsuen-Hsuin.
　　　　ed. China: An Annotated Bibliography of
　　　　　Bibliographies. G K Hall.
Tsipis, Kosta.
　　xTsipis, Kosta.
　　　　The Future of the Sea-Based Deterrent. MIT
　　　　　Pr.
Tsirakis, Jack K.
　　xTsirakis, Jack K.
　　　　The Art of Jeet-Kung-Tao. Exposition.
Tsirpanlis, Constantine. *see* Tsirpanlis, Constantine N.
Tsirpanlis, Constantine N.
　　xTsirpanlis, Constantine.
　　　　Modern Greek Idiom & Phrase Book. Barron.
Tso, Lin, Security Analyst.
　　xTso, Lin.
　　　　How to Make Money in Listed Options. Fell.
　　　　How to Make Money Trading Listed Puts.
　　　　　Fell.
Tso, Shih K. *see* Tso, Shih Kan Sheldon.
Tso, Shih Kan Sheldon.
　　xTso, Shih K.
　　　　The Labor Movement in China. Hyperion
　　　　　Conn.
Tsokos, C. P. *see* Tsokos, Chris P.
Tsokos, Chris P.
　　xTsokos, C. P.
　　　　Random Integral Equations with Applications
　　　　　to Stochastic Systems. Springer-Verlag.
　　xTsokos, Chris P.

　　　　Random Integral Equations with Applications
　　　　　to Life Sciences & Engineering. Acad Pr.
Tsoukalis, L. *see* Tsoukalis, Loukas.
Tsoukalis, Loukas.
　　xTsoukalis, L.
　　　　Greece & the European Community. Renouf.
　　xTsoukalis, Loukas.
　　　　The Politics & Economics of European
　　　　　Monetary Integration. Allen Unwin.
Tsuchiya, Keiz O, 1924-
　　xTsuchiya, Keizo.
　　　　Productivity & Technological Progress in
　　　　　Japanese Agriculture. Intl Schol Bk Serv.
Tsuchiya, Keizo. *see* Tsuchiya, Keiz O.
Tsuchiya, T. *see* Tsuchiya, Takao.
Tsuchiya, Takao, 1896-
　　xTsuchiya, T.
　　　　An Economic History of Japan. Porcupine Pr.
Tsuda, Margaret.
　　xTsuda, Margaret.
　　　　Cry Love Aloud. Discovery Bks.
Tsuda, Noritake, 1883-
　　xTsuda, Noritake.
　　　　Handbook of Japanese Art. C E Tuttle.
Tsuji, J. *see* Tsuji, Jiro.
Tsuji, Jiro, 1927-
　　xTsuji, J.
　　　　Organic Synthesis with Palladium Compounds.
　　　　　Springer-Verlag.
Tsuji, K. *see* Tsuji, Kiyoshi.
Tsuji, Kiyoshi.
　　xTsuji, K.
　　　　ed. GLC & HPLC Determination of
　　　　　Therapeutic Agents. Dekker.
Tsuji, Masatsugu, 1894-1960
　　xTsuji, Masatugu.
　　　　Potential Theory in Modern Function Theory.
　　　　　Chelsea Pub.
Tsuji, Masatugu. *see* Tsuji, Masatsugu.
Tsukashima, Ronald T.
　　xTsukashima, Ronald T.
　　　　The Social & Psychological Correlates of Black
　　　　　Anti-Semitism. R & E Res Assoc.
Tsukui, J. *see* Tsukui, Jinkichi.
Tsukui, Jinkichi.
　　xTsukui, J.
　　　　Turnpike Optimality in Input-Output Systems:
　　　　　Theory & Application for Planning. Elsevier.
Tsurumi, Yoshi.
　　xTsurumi, Yoshi.
　　　　Japanese Business: A Research Guide with
　　　　　Annotated Bibliography. Praeger.
Tsvetaeva, M. *see* Tsvetaeva, Marina Ivanovna Efron.
Tsvetaeva, Marina. *see* Tsvetaeva, Marina Ivanovna
　Efron.
Tsvetaeva, Marina Ivanovna Efron, 1892-1941
　　xTsvetaeva, M.
　　　　The Demesne of Swans. Ardis Pubs.
　　xTsvetaeva, Marina.
　　　　A Captive Spirit: Selected Prose. Ardis Pubs.
Tsypkin, Iakov Zalmanovich.
　　xTsypkin, Ya. Z.
　　　　Adaptation & Learning in Automatic Systems.
　　　　　Acad Pr.
　　　　Foundations of the Theory of Learning
　　　　　Systems. Acad Pr.
Tsypkin, Ya. Z. *see* Tsypkin, Iakov Zalmanovich.
Tsytovich, N. A. *see* Tsytovich, Nikolai Aleksandrovich.
Tsytovich, Nikolai Aleksandrovich.
　　xTsytovich, N. A.
　　　　Mechanics of Frozen Ground. McGraw.
Tsytovich, V. N. *see* Tsytovich, Vadim Nikolaevich.
Tsytovich, Vadim Nikolaevich.
　　xTsytovich, V. N.
　　　　Nonlinear Effects in Plasma. Plenum Pub.
　　　　Theory of Turbulent Plasma. Plenum Pub.
Tu, Anthony T., 1930-
　　xTu, Anthony T.

　　　　Venoms: Chemistry & Molecular Biology.
　　　　　Wiley.
Tu, Wei-Ming.
　　xTu, Wei-Ming.
　　　　Neo-Confucian Thought in Action: Wang
　　　　　Yang-Ming's Youth. U of Cal Pr.
Tuan, I-Fu, 1930-
　　xTuan, Yi-Fu.
　　　　China. Beresford Bk Serv.
　　　　Landscapes of Fear. Pantheon.
　　　　Space & Place: The Perspective of Experience.
　　　　　U of Minn Pr.
Tuan, Yi-Fu. *see* Tuan, I-Fu.
Tubb, E. C.
　　xTubb, E. C.
　　　　Collision Course. Amereon Ltd.
Tubbs, D. B. *see* Tubbs, Douglas B.
Tubbs, Douglas B.
　　xTubbs, D. B.
　　　　Art & the Automobile. G&D.
Tubbs, Stewart L.
　　xTubbs, Stewart L.
　　　　Human Communication. Random.
　　　　Systems Approach to Small Group Interaction.
　　　　　A-W.
Tubby, Pamela.
　　xTubby, Pamela.
　　　　Working with Metal. T Y Crowell.
Tubesing, Richard. *see* Tubesing, Richard L.
Tubesing, Richard L.
　　xTubesing, Richard.
　　　　Architectural Preservation in the United States,
　　　　　1941-1975: A Bibliography of Federal, State,
　　　　　& Local Government Publications. Garland
　　　　　Pub.
Tubis, Manuel.
　　xTubis, Manuel.
　　　　Radiopharmacy. Wiley.
Tucci, Douglass S. *see* Tucci, Douglass Shand.
Tucci, Douglass Shand.
　　xTucci, Douglass S.
　　　　Church Building in Boston, 1720-1970: An
　　　　　Introduction to the Work of Ralph Adams
　　　　　Cram & the Boston Gothicists. First Am
　　　　　Bank.
　　　　Ralph Adams Cram, American Medievalist.
　　　　　Boston Public Lib.
Tucci, Giuseppe, 1894-
　　xTucci, Giuseppe.
　　　　The Religions of Tibet. U of Cal Pr.
Tucci, Niccolo, 1908-
　　xTucci, Niccolo.
　　　　The Sun & the Moon. Knopf.
Tuccille, Jerome.
　　xTuccille, Jerome.
　　　　Everything the Beginner Needs to Know to
　　　　　Invest Shrewdly. Arlington Hse.
　　　　Everything the Beginner Needs to Know to
　　　　　Invest Shrewdly. B&N.
　　　　Mind Over Money: Why Most People Lose
　　　　　Money in the Stock Market & How You Can
　　　　　Become a Winner. Morrow.
Tucek, S.
　　xTucek, S.
　　　　Acetylcholine Synthesis in Neurons. Methuen
　　　　　Inc.
Tuch, Barbara.
　　xTuch, Barbara.
　　　　How to Teach Children to Draw, Paint and
　　　　　Use Color.. P-H.
Tuchel, V., 1906-
　　xTuchel, V.
　　　　Non-Specific Mesenteric Lymphadenitis. S
　　　　　Karger.
Tuchman, Barbara. *see* Tuchman, Barbara (Wertheim).
Tuchman, Barbara (Wertheim).
　　xTuchman, Barbara.

The Guns of August. Bantam.
Stilwell & the American Experience in China
1911-1945. Bantam.
xTuchman, Barbara W.
Guns of August. Macmillan.
Stilwell & the American Experience in China,
1911-45. Macmillan.
Tuchman, Barbara W. *see* Tuchman, Barbara (Wertheim).
Tuchman, G. *see* Tuchman, Gaye.
Tuchman, Gaye.
xTuchman, G.
TV Establishment: Programming for Power &
Profit. P-H.
Tuck, Curt.
xTuck, Curt.
ed. The Fannie Mae Guide to Buying,
Financing & Selling Your Home. Doubleday.
Tuck, James A.
xTuck, James A.
Onondaga Iroquois Prehistory: A Study in
Settlement Archaeology. Syracuse U Pr.
Tuck, William P.
xTuck, William P.
Facing Grief & Death. Broadman.
ed. The Struggle for Meaning. Judson.
Tucker, Abraham, 1705-1774
xTucker, Abraham.
The Light of Nature Pursued. Garland Pub.
Tucker, Alfred R. *see* Tucker, Alfred Robert.
Tucker, Alfred Robert, Bp, 1849-1914
xTucker, Alfred R.
Eighteen Years in Uganda & East Africa.
Negro U Pr.
Tucker, Allen B.
xTucker, Allen B.
Programming Languages. McGraw.
Text Processing: Algorithms, Languages, &
Applications. Acad Pr.
Tucker, Clara, 1897-
xTucker, Clara.
A Study of Mothers' Practices & Children's
Activities in a Co-Operative Nursery School.
AMS Pr.
Tucker, David M., 1937-
xTucker, David M.
Lieutenant Lee of Beale Street. Vanderbilt U
Pr.
Tucker, Donald S. *see* Tucker, Donald Skeele.
Tucker, Donald Skeele, 1884-
xTucker, Donald S.
Evolution of People's Banks. AMS Pr.
Tucker, Earl.
xTucker, Earl.
Rambling Roses & Flying Bricks. Strode.
Tucker, Ephraim W.
xTucker, Ephraim W.
History of Oregon. Ye Galleon.
Tucker, Gene M.
xTucker, Gene M.
Form Criticism of the Old Testament. Fortress.
Tucker, George, 1775-1861
xTucker, George.
Progress of the United States in Population &
Wealth in Fifty Years, As Exhibited by the
Decennial Census. B Franklin.
Theory of Money & Banks Investigated.
Greenwood.
Theory of Money & Banks Investigated.
Kelley.
Tucker, Gilbert M. *see* Tucker, Gilbert Milligan.
Tucker, Gilbert Milligan, 1847-1932
xTucker, Gilbert M.
American English. Folcroft.
American English. Norwood Edns.
Tucker, Glenn.
xTucker, Glenn.
Lee & Longstreet at Gettysburg. Bobbs.
Tucker, Helen.
xTucker, Helen.

A Strange & Ill-Starred Marriage. Fawcett.
Tucker, Howard, 1928-
xTucker, Howard F.
Automatic Transmissions. Van Nos Reinhold.
Automatic Transmissions. Delmar.
Tucker, Howard F. *see* Tucker, Howard.
Tucker, Josiah, 1712-1799
xTucker, Josiah.
Four Tracts on Political & Commercial
Subjects. Kelley.
Tucker, Louis L. *see* Tucker, Louis Leonard.
Tucker, Louis Leonard, 1927-
xTucker, Louis L.
Puritan Protagonist: President Thomas Clap of
Yale College. U of NC Pr.
Tucker, Louise E. *see* Tucker, Louise Emery.
Tucker, Louise Emery, 1876-
xTucker, Louise E.
A Study of Problem Pupils. AMS Pr.
Tucker, Martin.
xTucker, Martin.
Africa in Modern Literature: A Survey of
Contemporary Writing in English. Ungar.
ed. Critical Temper: A Survey of Modern
Criticism on English & American Literature
from the Beginnings to the Twentieth
Century. Ungar.
Tucker, Mary E. *see* Tucker, Mary Eliza (Perine).
Tucker, Mary Eliza (Perine), 1838-
xTucker, Mary E.
Life of Mark M. Pomeroy. Arno.
Tucker, Michael R.
xTucker, Michael R.
The Church That Dared to Change. Tyndale.
Tucker, Nathaniel, 1750-1807
xTucker, Nathaniel.
The Complete Published Poems of Nathaniel
Tucker, Together with Columbinus. A Mask
(1783). Schol Facsimiles.
Tucker, Patsy M. *see* Tucker, Patsy McKimmon.
Tucker, Patsy McKimmon.
xTucker, Patsy M.
Carolina Treasures. Moore Pub Co.
Tucker, R. H. *see* Tucker, Roy Henry.
Tucker, Ray. *see* Tucker, Ray Thomas.
Tucker, Ray T. *see* Tucker, Ray Thomas.
Tucker, Ray Thomas.
xTucker, Ray.
Sons of the Wild Jackass. U of Wash Pr.
xTucker, Ray T.
Sons of the Wild Jackass. Arno.
Tucker, Richard N. *see* Tucker, Richard Neil.
Tucker, Richard Neil.
xTucker, Richard N.
The Organisation & Management of
Educational Technology. Biblio Dist.
Tucker, Richard P.
xTucker, Richard P.
Ranade & the Roots of Indian Nationalism. U
of Chicago Pr.
Tucker, Robert C.
xTucker, Robert C.
ed. Marx-Engels Reader. Norton.
Marxian Revolutionary Idea. Norton.
Stalin As Revolutionary, 1879-1929: A Study
in History & Personality. Norton.
Tucker, Robert W.
xTucker, Robert W.
The Inequality of Nations. Basic.
The Just War: A Study in Contemporary
American Doctrine. Greenwood.
The Radical Left & American Foreign Policy.
Johns Hopkins.
Tucker, Roy Henry, 1922-
xTucker, R. H.
Global Geophysics. Elsevier.
Tucker, Ruth.
xTucker, Ruth.

How to Set Your Own Neighborhood
Preschool. Arlington Hse.
Tucker, S. Marion. *see* Tucker, Samuel Marion.
Tucker, Samuel Marion.
xTucker, S. Marion.
Twenty-Five Modern Plays. R West.
Tucker, Spencer. *see* Tucker, Spencer A.
Tucker, Spencer A.
xTucker, Spencer.
Handbook of Business Formulas & Controls.
McGraw.
xTucker, Spencer A.
The Complete Machine-Hour Rate System for
Cost-Estimating & Pricing. P-H.
Tucker, St. George, 1752-1827
xTucker, St. George.
Dissertation on Slavery: With a Proposal for
the Gradual Abolition of It, in the State of
Virginia. Negro U Pr.
Tucker, Susan M. *see* Tucker, Susan Martin.
Tucker, Susan Martin, 1943-
xTucker, Susan M.
Patient Care Standards. Mosby.
Tucker, Tarvez.
xTucker, Tarvez.
Prepared Childbirth. Tobey Pub.
Tucker, W. E. *see* Tucker, William Eldon.
Tucker, Wallace A. *see* Tucker, Wallace H.
Tucker, Wallace H.
xTucker, Wallace A.
Radiation Processes in Astrophysics. MIT Pr.
Tucker, William Eldon.
xTucker, W. E.
Sportsmen & Their Injuries: Fitness, First Aid,
Treatment, & Rehabilitations. Transatlantic.
Tucker, William R., 1923-
xTucker, William R.
The Fascist Ego: A Political Biography of
Robert Brasillach. U of Cal Pr.
Tucker, Wilson, 1914-
xTucker, Wilson.
Ice & Iron. Ballantine.
The Lincoln Hunters. Ace Bks.
Tuckerman, H. T. *see* Tuckerman, Henry Theodore.
Tuckerman, Henry T. *see* Tuckerman, Henry Theodore.
Tuckerman, Henry Theodore, 1813-1871
xTuckerman, H. T.
Characteristics of Literature. R West.
xTuckerman, Henry T.
The Optimist. Johnson Repr.
Tuckerman, Joseph, 1778-1840
xTuckerman, Joseph.
On the Elevation of the Poor: A Selection from
His Reports As Minister at Large in Boston.
Arno.
Tuckett, David.
xTuckett, David.
ed. Basic Readings in Medical Sociology.
Methuen Inc.
Tuckey, John S. *see* Tuckey, John Sutton.
Tuckey, John Sutton, 1921-
xTuckey, John S.
Mark Twain & Little Satan: The Writing of
"the Mysterious Stranger". Greenwood.
Tuckman, Bruce W., 1938-
xTuckman, Bruce W.
Conducting Educational Research. HarBraceJ.
Evaluating Instructional Programs. Allyn.
Measuring Educational Outcomes:
Fundamentals of Testing. HarBraceJ.
Tuckman, Howard P.
xTuckman, Howard P.
Economics of the Rich. Random.
Publication, Teaching, & the Academic Reward
Structure. Lexington Bks.
Tuckman, Jacob, 1908-
xTuckman, Jacob.
Influence of Varying Amounts of Punishment
on Mental Connections. AMS Pr.
Tuckwell, W. *see* Tuckwell, William.

Tuckwell, William, 1829-1919
  xTuckwell, W.
    Chaucer. Folcroft.
    Spenser. Folcroft.
  xTuckwell, William.
    Chaucer. R West.
Tucson International Topical Conference on Nuclear Physics, University of Arizona, 1975.
  xTucson International Topical Conference on Nuclear Physics Held at the University of Arizona, Tucson, Jun 2-6, 1975.
    Effective Interactions & Operators in Nuclei: Proceedings. Springer-Verlag.
Tudge, Colin.
  xTudge, Colin.
    The Famine Business. St Martin.
Tudor, Andre. *see* Tudor, Andrew.

Tudor, Andrew, 1942-
  xTudor, Andre.
    Image & Influence: Studies in the Sociology of Film. St Martin.
Tudor, Bethany.
  xTudor, Bethany.
    Samuel's Treehouse. Philomel.

Tudor, Dean.

    Contemporary Popular Music. Libs Unl.

    Grass Roots Music. Libs Unl.

    Jazz. Libs Unl.

    Popular Music Periodicals Index: 1973. Scarecrow.

    Popular Music Periodicals Index, 1974. Scarecrow.

    Compiled by Popular Music Periodicals Index, 1975. Scarecrow.

    Popular Music Periodicals Index, 1976. Scarecrow.

Tudor, Tash. *see* Tudor, Tasha.
Tudor, Tasha.
  xTudor, Tash.
    illus. Corgiville Fair. T Y Crowell.
  xTudor, Tasha.
    Corgiville Fair. T Y Crowell.
    illus. Corgiville Fair. T Y Crowell.
    illus. First Graces. Walck.
    illus. First Poems of Childhood. Platt.
    illus. First Poems of Childhood. Platt.
    illus. First Prayers. Walck.
    illus. More Prayers. Walck.
    The Springs of Joy. Rand.
    illus. Take Joy: The Tasha Tudor Christmas Book. Philomel.
    illus. Tale for Easter. Walck.
    ed. Tasha Tudor's Bedtime Book. Platt.
Tudor, William, 1779-1830
  xTudor, William.
    Life of James Otis of Massachusetts. Da Capo.
Tuell, Anne K. *see* Tuell, Anne Kimball.
Tuell, Anne Kimball, 1876-
  xTuell, Anne K.
    Mrs. Meynell & Her Literary Generation. Scholarly.
Tuell, Jack M., 1923-
  xTuell, Jack M.
    The Organization of the United Methodist Church. Abingdon.
Tuer, Andrew W. *see* Tuer, Andrew White.
Tuer, Andrew White, 1838-1900
  xTuer, Andrew W.
    History of the Horn Book. Arno.
Tuerck, David G.
  xTuerck, David G.

    ed. The Political Economy of Advertising. Am Enterprise.
Tuffs, J Elsden.
  xTuffs, J. Elsden.
    Teach Yourself Magic. Emerson.
Tufnell, Edward C. *see* Tufnell, Edward Carleton.
Tufnell, Edward Carleton.
  xTufnell, Edward C.
    Character, Object & Effects of Trades' Unions: With Some Remarks on the Law Concerning Them. Arno.
Tufte, Edward R., 1942-
  xTufte, Edward R.
    Data Analysis for Politics & Policy. P-H.
    ed. The Quantitative Analysis of Social Problems. A-W.
Tufte, Virginia.
  xTufte, Virginia.
    ed. Changing Images of the Family. Yale U Pr.
Tugby, Donald. *see* Tugby, Donald John.
Tugby, Donald John, 1920-
  xTugby, Donald.
    Cultural Change & Identity: Mandailing Immigrants in West Malaysia. U of Queensland Pr.
Tuggle, Francis D.
  xTuggle, Francis D.
    How to Program a Computer (Using Fortran IV). Grid Pub.
    Organizational Processes. AHM Pub.
Tugwell, Franklin, 1942-
  xTugwell, Franklin.
    The Politics of Oil in Venezuela. Stanford U Pr.
Tugwell, Rexford G. *see* Tugwell, Rexford Guy.
Tugwell, Rexford Guy.
  xTugwell, Rexford G.
    Changing the Colonial Climate. Arno.
    A Chronicle of Jeopardy: 1945-1955. U of Chicago Pr.
    The Compromising of the Constitution. U of Notre Dame Pr.
    Economic Basis of Public Interest. Kelley.
    The Enlargement of the Presidency. Octagon.
    In Search of Roosevelt. Harvard U Pr.
    The Industrial Discipline & the Governmental Arts. Arno.
    Puerto Rican Public Papers of R. G. Tugwell, Governor. Arno.
Tuite, James. *see* Tuite, James J.
Tuite, James J.
  xTuite, James.
    How to Enjoy Sports on TV. TAB Bks.
Tuke, Daniel H. *see* Tuke, Daniel Hack.
Tuke, Daniel Hack, 1827-1895
  xTuke, Daniel H.
    A Dictionary of Psychological Medicine. Arno.
    The Insane in the United States & Canada. Arno.
Tuke, Diana R. *see* Tuke, Diana Rosemary.
Tuke, Diana Rosemary.
  xTuke, Diana R.
    Bit by Bit: A Guide to Equine Bits. Arco.
Tukey, John W. *see* Tukey, John Wilder.
Tukey, John Wilder, 1915-
  xTukey, John W.
    Exploratory Data Analysis. A-W.
Tulane Drama Review.
  xTulane Drama Review.
    Theatre in the Twentieth Century. Arno.
Tulane Tidelands Institute.
  xTulane Tidelands Institute.
    Proceedings. Claitors.
Tulane University, New Orleans. *see* Tulane University of Louisiana.
Tulane University of Louisiana.
  xTulane University, New Orleans.
    Catalog of the Latin American Library of the Tulane University Library. G K Hall.
  xTulant University, New Orleans.

    Catalog of the Latin American Library of the Tulane University Library: Third Supplement. G K Hall.
Tulant University, New Orleans. *see* Tulane University of Louisiana.
Tulchin, Joseph S., 1939-
  xTulchin, Joseph S.
    The Aftermath of War: World War I & U.S. Policy Toward Latin America. NYU Pr.
Tulchinsky, Dan.
  xTulchinsky, Dan.
    Maternal-Fetal Endocrinology. Saunders.
Tuleja, Thaddeus V.
  xTuleja, Thaddeus V.
    Twilight of the Sea Gods. Greenwood.
Tulipan, A. *see* Tulipan, Alan B.
Tulipan, Alan B.
  xTulipan, A.
    ed. Psychiatric Clinics in Transition. Brunner-Mazel.
  xTulipan, Alan B.
    Outpatient Psychiatry in the 1970's. Brunner-Mazel.
Tull, James E.
  xTull, James E.
    A History of Southern Baptist Landmarkism in the Light of Historical Baptist Ecclesiology: Doctoral Dissertation. Arno.
Tullar, Richard M., 1910-
  xTullar, Richard M.
    The Human Species: Its Nature, Evolution & Ecology. McGraw.
Tuller, Burl A.
  xTuller, Burl A.
    The Data Processing Operations Analysis Handbook with Forms. Today News.
Tullett, Tom.
  xTullett, Tom.
    Strictly Murder. St Martin.
Tulley, Walter J.
  xTulley, Walter J.
    Called to Teach: A Spiritual Guide for Teachers & Aides. Alba.
Tullis, F. LaMond, 1935-
  xTullis, F. LaMond.
    Lord & Peasant in Peru: A Paradigm of Political & Social Change. Harvard U Pr.
Tullis, James L.
  xTullis, James L.
    Clot. C C Thomas.
Tullo, Frank Di. *see* Di Tullo, Frank.
Tullock, Gordon.
  xTullock, Gordon.
    Logic of the Law. Basic.
    Organization of Inquiry. Duke.
    Toward a Mathematics of Politics. U of Mich Pr.
Tulloh, Bruce.
  xTulloh, Bruce.
    Natural Fitness. S&S.
Tully, Andrew, 1914-
  xTully, Andrew.
    When They Burned the White House. Ballantine.
    When They Burned the White House. S&S.
    White Tie & Dagger. PB.
Tully, Gerie.
  xTully, Gerie.
    France Especially for Women. Abelard.
Tully, Jim.
  xTully, Jim.
    A Dozen & One. Arno.
Tully, Marianne.
  xTully, Marianne.
    Dread Diseases. Watts.
    Facts About the Human Body. Watts.
  xTully, Mary A.
    jt. auth. Facts About the Human Body. Watts.
Tully, Marjorie F.
  xTully, Marjorie F.

An Annotated Bibliography of Spanish Folklore
in New Mexico & Southern Colorado. Arno.
Tully, Mary A. see Tully, Marianne.
Tulman, David.
xTulman, Victor D.
Going Home. Times Bks.
Tulman, Victor D. see Tulman, David.
Tulving, Endel.
xTulving, Endel.
ed. Organization of Memory. Acad Pr.
Tuma, D. T. see Tuma, David T.
Tuma, David T.
xTuma, D. T.
ed. Problem Solving & Education: Issues in
Teaching & Research. Halsted Pr.
xTuma, David T.
ed. Problem Solving & Education: Issues in
Teaching & Research. L Erlbaum Assocs.
Tuma, Elias H.
xTuma, Elias H.
The Economic Case for Palestine. St Martin.
Twenty-Six Centuries of Agrarian Reform: A
Comparative Analysis. U of Cal Pr.
Tuma, J. see Tuma, Jan J.
Tuma, Jan J.
xTuma, J.
Engineering Soil Mechanics. P-H.
xTuma, Jan J.
Dynamics. Quantum Pubs.
Tumblin, C. R., 1917-
xTumblin, Charles R.
Construction Cost Estimates. Wiley.
Tumblin, Charles R. see Tumblin, C. R.
Tumin, Melvin M. see Tumin, Melvin Marvin.
Tumin, Melvin Marvin, 1919-
xTumin, Melvin M.
Desegregation: Resistance & Readiness.
Princeton U Pr.
Tumulty, Joseph P. see Tumulty, Joseph Patrick.
Tumulty, Joseph Patrick, 1879-1954
xTumulty, Joseph P.
Woodrow Wilson As I Know Him. AMS Pr.
Woodrow Wilson As I Know Him. Scholarly.
Tumulty, Philip A.
xTumulty, Philip A.
The Effective Clinician: His Methods &
Approach to Diagnosis & Care. Saunders.
Tunell, George.
xTunell, George.
Thermodynamic Relations in Open Systems.
Univ Microfilms.
Tung, L. H. see Tung, Lu-Ho.
Tung, Lu-Ho, 1923-
xTung, L. H.
Fractionation of Synthetic Polymers: Principles
& Practices. Dekker.
Tung, S. T.
xTung, S. T.
One Small Dog. Dodd.
Tunink, Wilfrid.
xTunink, Wilfrid.
Jesus Is Lord. Doubleday.
Tunis, Edwin, 1897-
xTunis, Edwin.
illus. Chipmunks on the Doorstep. T Y
Crowell.
illus. Frontier Living. T Y Crowell.
illus. Indians. T Y Crowell.
illus. The Tavern at the Ferry. T Y Crowell.
illus. Wheels: A Pictorial History. T Y Crowell.
Tunis, John R.
xTunis, John R.
Silence Over Dunkerque. Morrow.
World Series. Bantam.
Tunis, John R. see Tunis, John Roberts.
Tunis, John Roberts, 1889-
xTunis, John R.
Go, Team, Go. Morrow.
Tunison, Joseph S. see Tunison, Joseph Salathiel.

Tunison, Joseph Salathiel, 1849-1916
xTunison, Joseph S.
Dramatic Traditions of the Dark Ages. B
Franklin.
Dramatic Traditions of the Dark Ages.
Folcroft.
Dramatic Traditions of the Dark Ages. R West.
Tunkin, G. I. see Tunkin, Grigorii Ivanovich.
Tunkin, Grigorii Ivanovich.
xTunkin, G. I.
Theory of International Law. Harvard U Pr.
Tunnard, C. see Tunnard, Christopher.
Tunnard, Christopher.
xTunnard, C.
The Modern American City. Peter Smith.
xTunnard, Christopher.
Modern American City. Van Nos Reinhold.
A World with a View: An Inquiry into the
Nature of Scenic Values. Yale U Pr.
Tunney, Christopher, 1924-
xTunney, Christopher.
Aircraft. Lerner Pubns.
Tunnicliffe, Charles. see Tunnicliffe, Charles Frederick.
Tunnicliffe, Charles Frederick, 1901-
xTunnicliffe, Charles.
A Sketchbook of Birds. HR&W.
Tunstall, Brian. see Tunstall, William Cuthbert Brian.
Tunstall, Jeremy.
xTunstall, Jeremy.
Journalists at Work: Specialist Correspondents;
Their News Organizations, News Sources, &
Competitor Colleagues. Sage.
The Media Are American. Columbia U Pr.
ed. The Open University Opens. U of Mass Pr.
Tunstall, William Cuthbert Brian, 1900-
xTunstall, Brian.
The Realities of Naval History. Arno.
Tuomela, R. see Tuomela, Raimo.
Tuomela, Raimo.
xTuomela, R.
Theoretical Concepts. Springer-Verlag.
xTuomela, Raimo.
ed. Dispositions. Kluwer Boston.
Tupling, George H. see Tupling, George Henry.
Tupling, George Henry, 1883-
xTupling, George H.
The Economic History of Rossendale. Johnson
Repr.
Tupper, E. Frank. see Tupper, Elgin Frank.
Tupper, Elgin Frank, 1941-
xTupper, E. Frank.
Theology of Wolfhart Pannenberg.
Westminster.
Tupper, Frederic A. see Tupper, Frederic Allison.
Tupper, Frederic Allison, 1858-
xTupper, Frederic A.
Moonshine: A Story of the Reconstruction
Period. Arno.
Tupper, Frederick, 1871-
xTupper, Frederick.
Types of Society in Medieval Literature. Biblo.
Types of Society in Medieval Literature.
Folcroft.
Types of Society in Medieval Literature.
Johnson Repr.
Turabian, Kate L.
xTurabian, Kate L.
Students Guide for Writing College Papers. U
of Chicago Pr.
Turan, P. see Turan, Pal.
Turan, Pal.
xTuran, P.
Topics in Number Theory. Elsevier.
Turbak, Albin F.
xTurbak, Albin F.
ed. Solvent Spun Rayon, Modified Cellulose
Fibers & Derivatives. Am Chemical.
Turban, Efraim.
xTurban, Efraim.

Fundamentals of Management Science.
Business Pubns.
ed. Readings in Management Science. Business
Pubns.
xTurban, Ephraim.
Cost Containment in Hospitals. Aspen Systems.
Turban, Ephraim. see Turban, Efraim.
Turbayne, A. A. see Turbayne, Albert Angus.
Turbayne, Albert Angus.
xTurbayne, A. A.
Monograms & Ciphers. Dover.
Monograms & Ciphers. Peter Smith.
Turberville, A. S. see Turberville, Arthur Stanley.
Turberville, Arthur Stanley, 1888-1945
xTurberville, A. S.
Spanish Inquisition. Shoe String.
Turbeville, Deborah, 1938-
xTurbeville, Deborah.
Wallflower. Congreve Pub.
Wallflower. S&S.
Turchi, Boone A.
xTurchi, Boone A.
The Demand for Children: The Economics of
Fertility in the United States. Ballinger Pub.
Turck, J. A. see Turck, J. A. V.
Turck, J. A. V.
xTurck, J. A.
Origin of Modern Calculating Machines. Arno.
Turco, Lewis.
xTurco, Lewis.
Awaken, Bells Falling: Poems, 1959-1967. U of
Mo Pr.
First Poems. Golden Quill.
Turco, Salvatore.
xTurco, Salvatore.
Sterile Dosage Forms: Their Preparation &
Clinical Application. Lea & Febiger.
Ture, Norman B.
xTure, Norman B.
Accelerated Depreciation in the United States,
1954-1960. Natl Bur Econ Res.
The Future of Private Pension Plans. Am
Enterprise.
Turek, Samuel L.
xTurek, Samuel L.
Orthopaedics: Principles & Their Application.
Lippincott.
Turekian, Karl K.
xTurekian, Karl K.
Oceans. P-H.
Turell, Ebenezer, 1702-1778
xTurell, Ebenezer.
The Life & Character of the Reverend
Benjamin Colman, D. D.. Schol Facsimiles.
Turetzky, Bertram, 1933-
xTuretzky, Bertram.
The Contemporary Contrabass. U of Cal Pr.
Turgenev, Ivan. see Turgenev, Ivan Sergeevich.
Turgenev, Ivan S. see Turgenev, Ivan Sergeevich.
Turgenev, Ivan Sergeevich, 1818-1883
xTurgenev, Ivan.
Fathers & Sons. Modern Lib.
Fathers & Sons. NAL.
Fathers & Sons. Penguin.
Fathers & Sons. Norton.
Fathers & Sons. AMSCO Sch.
Fathers & Sons. PB.
First Love. Penguin.
Home of the Gentry. Gannon.
Home of the Gentry. Penguin.
xTurgenev, Ivan S.
Desperate Character, Etc. Arno.
Dream Tales & Prose Poems. Arno.
Fathers & Sons. Airmont.
Memoirs of a Sportsman. Arno.
Torrents of Spring, Etc.. Arno.
Turgeon, A. J. see Turgeon, Alfred J.
Turgeon, Alfred J., 1943-
xTurgeon, A. J.

Turfgrass Management. Reston.
Turgot, A. Robert. *see* Turgot, Anne Robert Jacques.
**Turgot, Anne Robert Jacques, Baron De L'aulne,
1727-1781**
  xTurgot, A. Robert.
    Reflections on the Formation & the
    Distribution of Riches. Kelley.
Turk, Amos.
  xTurk, Amos.
    Introduction to Chemistry. Acad Pr.
Turk, Edward B. *see* Turk, Edward Baron.
Turk, Edward Baron.
  xTurk, Edward B.
    Baroque Fiction-Making: A Study of
    Gomberville's Polexandre. U of NC Pr.
Turk, J. L.
  xTurk, J. L.
    Immunology in Clinical Medicine. ACC.
Turk, Jonathan.
  xTurk, Jonathan.
    Ecosystems, Energy, Population. HR&W.
Turk, Laurel H. *see* Turk, Laurel Herbert.
Turk, Laurel Herbert, 1903-
  xTurk, Laurel H.
    Foundation Course in Spanish. Heath.
    Mastering Spanish. Heath.
Turkdogan, E. T.
  xTurkdogan, E. T.
    Physical Chemistry of High Temperature
    Technology. Acad Pr.
Turkevich, Ludmilla B. *see* Turkevich, Ludmilla Buketoff.
Turkevich, Ludmilla Buketoff.
  xTurkevich, Ludmilla B.
    Cervantes in Russia. Gordian.
Turki, Fawaz, 1940-
  xTurki, Fawaz.
    The Disinherited: Journal of a Palestinian
    Exile. Monthly Rev.
Turkin, Hy.
  xTurkin, Hy.
    The Official Encyclopedia of Baseball. A S
    Barnes.
    The Official Encyclopedia of Baseball.
    Doubleday.
Turkle, Brinton.
  xTurkle, Brinton.
    Deep in the Forest. Dutton.
    Rachel & Obadiah. Dutton.
Turkle, Sherry.
  xTurkle, Sherry.
    Psychoanalytic Politics: Freud's French
    Revolution. Basic.
Turley, Peter T.
  xTurley, Peter T.
    Peirce's Cosmology. Philos Lib.
Turnbull, Agnes (Sligh), 1888-
  xTurnbull, Agnes S.
    The Flowering. HM.
Turnbull, Agnes S. *see* Turnbull, Agnes Sligh.
Turnbull, Agnes Sligh, 1888-
  xTurnbull, Agnes S.
    The Richlands. Fawcett.
Turnbull, Andrew, 1921-
  xTurnbull, Andrew.
    Thomas Wolfe. S&S.
Turnbull, Ann.
  xTurnbull, Ann.
    The Frightened Forest. HM.
Turnbull, Colin. *see* Turnbull, Colin M.
Turnbull, Colin M.
  xTurnbull, Colin.
    Forest People. S&S.
  xTurnbull, Colin M.
    ed. Africa & Change. Phila Bk Co.
    Forest People. S&S.
    Lonely African. S&S.
Turnbull, D. E.
  xTurnbull, D. E.
    Fluid Power Engineering. Butterworths.
Turnbull, Eleanor L. *see* Turnbull, Eleanor Laurelle.

Turnbull, Eleanor Laurelle.
  xTurnbull, Eleanor L.
    tr. Contemporary Spanish Poetry: Selections
    from Ten Poets. Greenwood.
Turnbull, G. L. *see* Turnbull, Gerard L.
Turnbull, Gerard L.
  xTurnbull, G. L.
    Traffic & Transport: An Economic History of
    Pickfords. Allen Unwin.
Turnbull, H. Rutherford.
  xTurnbull, H. Rutherford.
    Law & the Mentally Handicapped in North
    Carolina. U of NC Inst Gov.
    North Carolina Primary & General Election
    Law & Procedure. U of NC Inst Gov.
Turnbull, Herbert Westren, 1885-1961
  xTurnbull, Herbert Westren.
    The Great Mathematicians. NYU Pr.
Turnbull, J. G. *see* Turnbull, John Gudert.
Turnbull, John G. *see* Turnbull, John Gudert.
Turnbull, John Gudert.
  xTurnbull, J. G.
    Economic & Social Security. Wiley.
  xTurnbull, John G.
    Economic & Social Security. Ronald Pr.
Turnbull, Patrick.
  xTurnbull, Patrick.
    Dordogne. David & Charles.
    The South of France. Hastings.
Turnbull, Ralph G. *see* Turnbull, Ralph G., Ed.
Turnbull, Ralph G., Ed.
  xTurnbull, Ralph G.
    ed. Baker's Dictionary of Practical Theology.
    Baker Bk.
Turnbull, Roderick.
  xTurnbull, Roderick.
    More Maple Hill Stories. Lowell Pr.
Turnbull, W. *see* Turnbull, William Robertson.
Turnbull, William Robertson.
  xTurnbull, W.
    Othello: A Critical Study. Gordon Pr.
Turnell, Martin.
  xTurnell, Martin.
    Art of French Fiction. New Directions.
    Classical Moment: Studies of Corneille,
    Moliere, & Racine. Greenwood.
Turner. *see* Turner, Charles F.
Turner, A. *see* Turner, Arlin.
Turner, A. Mason.
  xTurner, A. Mason.
    Inquiries in Chemistry. Allyn.
Turner, Alberta. *see* Turner, Alberta T.
Turner, Alberta T.
  xTurner, Alberta.
    ed. Poets Teaching: The Creative Process.
    Longman.
  xTurner, Alberta T.
    Learning to Count. U of Pittsburgh Pr.
    Lid & Spoon. U of Pittsburgh Pr.
    Need. Ashland Poetry.
Turner, Ann. *see* Turner, Ann Warren.
Turner, Ann Warren.
  xTurner, Ann.
    A Hunter Comes Home. Crown.
Turner, Anthony.
  xTurner, Anthony.
    Burgundy. David & Charles.
Turner, Arlin.
  xTurner, A.
    George W. Cable: A Biography. Peter Smith.
  xTurner, Arlin.
    George W. Cable: A Biography. La State U Pr.
Turner, Arthur R., 1895-
  xTurner, Arthur R.
    Frozen Blood: A Review of the Literature
    1949-1968. Gordon.
Turner, B. L. *see* Turner, Billie Lee.

Turner, Barry A.
  xTurner, Barry A.
    Man-Made Disasters. Crane-Russak Co.
Turner, Ben. *see* Turner, Ben C. A.
Turner, Ben C. A.
  xTurner, Ben.
    Growing Your Own Wine. Merrimack Bk Serv.
Turner, Billie Lee, 1925-
  xTurner, B. L.
    The Legumes of Texas. U of Tex Pr.
Turner, C. C. *see* Turner, Charles Cyril.
Turner, C. Donnell. *see* Turner, Clarence Donnell.
Turner, C. E. *see* Turner, Clair Elsmere.
Turner, Carl B.
  xTurner, Carl B.
    Analysis of Soviet Views on John Maynard
    Keynes. Duke.
Turner, Charles Cyril, 1870-
  xTurner, C. C.
    Old Flying Days. Arno.
Turner, Charles F.
  xTurner.
    Chemistry of Fire & Hazardous Materials.
    Allyn.
Turner, Clair Elsmere, 1890-
  xTurner, C. E.
    Personal & Community Health. Mosby.
Turner, Clarence Donnell, 1903-
  xTurner, C. Donnell.
    General Endocrinology. HR&W.
Turner, Darwin T., 1931-
  xTurner, Darwin T.
    Compiled by Afro-American Writers. AHM
    Pub.
    In a Minor Chord: Three Afro-American
    Writers & Their Search for Identity. S Ill U
    Pr.
    Theory & Practice in the Teaching of
    Literature by Afro-Americans. NCTE.
Turner, David R.
  xTurner, David R.
    Draftsman: Civil & Mechanical Engineering
    (All Grades). Arco.
Turner, David R. *see* Turner, David Reuben.
Turner, David Reuben.
  xTurner, David R.
    Civil Engineer, Senior & Supervising. Arco.
    Complete Guide to U.S. Civil Service Jobs.
    Arco.
    Detective Investigator. Arco.
    Homestudy Course for Civil Service Jobs.
    Arco.
    Law Enforcement Positions. Arco.
    Preliminary Arithmetic for the High School
    Equivalency Diploma Test. Arco.
    Preliminary Practice for the High School
    Equivalency Diploma Test. Arco.
Turner, Daymond.
  xTurner, Daymond.
    Gonzalo Fernandez de Oviedo y Valdes: An
    Annotated Bibliography. U of NC Pr.
Turner, Dean.
  xTurner, Dean.
    Commitment to Care: An Integrated
    Philosophy of Science, Education, &
    Religion. Devin.
    Krinkle Nose: A Prayer of Thanks. Devin.
Turner, Dennis C., 1948-
  xTurner, Dennis C.
    The Vampire Bat: A Field Study in Behavior &
    Ecology. Johns Hopkins.
Turner, Denys, 1942-
  xTurner, Denys.
    On the Philosophy of Karl Marx. Humanities.
Turner, Diane E.
  xTurner, Diane E.
    Understanding Your Horse's Lameness. Arco.
Turner, Dick, 1911-
  xTurner, Dick.

Sunrise on Mackenzie. Hancock Hse.
Turner, Dona.
  xTurner, Dona.
    My Cat Pearl. T Y Crowell.
Turner, Dorothea. *see* Turner, Dorothea Fletcher.
Turner, Dorothea Fletcher, 1905-
  xTurner, Dorothea.
    Handbook of Diet Therapy. U of Chicago Pr.
Turner, Dorothy B. *see* Turner, Dorothy Banker.
Turner, Dorothy Banker.
  xTurner, Dorothy B.
    Earn As You Learn Writing. Creative Pr.
Turner, E. S. *see* Turner, Ernest Sackville.
Turner, Edmund R. *see* Turner, Edward Raymond.
Turner, Edward R. *see* Turner, Edward Raymond.
Turner, Edward Raymond.
  xTurner, Edmund R.
    Negro in Pennsylvania: Slavery, Servitude,
      Freedom, 1639-1861. Negro U Pr.
  xTurner, Edward R.
    Cabinet Council of England in the Seventeenth
      & Eighteenth Centuries, 1622-1784. Russell.
    Negro in Pennsylvania: Slavery - Servitude -
      Freedom 1639-1861. Arno.
Turner, Elsa. *see* Turner, Elsa Mcfarland.
Turner, Elsa McFarland, 1909-
  xTurner, Elsa.
    Look High, Grow Tall. Nortex Pr.
Turner, Eric G. *see* Turner, Eric Gardiner.
Turner, Eric Gardiner.
  xTurner, Eric G.
    The Typology of the Early Codex. U of Pa Pr.
Turner, Ernest Sackville, 1909-
  xTurner, E. S.
    A History of Courting. State Mutual Bk.
Turner, Francis J.
  xTurner, Francis J.
    Igneous & Metamorphic Petrology. McGraw.
Turner, Francis J. *see* Turner, Francis Joseph.
Turner, Francis Joseph, 1929-
  xTurner, Francis J.
    Differential Diagnosis & Treatment in Social
      Work. Free Pr.
    ed. Social Work Treatment: Interlocking
      Theoretical Approaches. Free Pr.
Turner, Frederick, 1943-
  xTurner, Frederick.
    Counter-Terra. Christopher's Bks.
    A Double Shadow. Berkley Pub.
    A Double Shadow. Putnam.
Turner, Frederick. *see* Turner, Frederick W.
Turner, Frederick C.
  xTurner, Frederick C.
    Responsible Parenthood: Politics of Mexico's
      New Population Policies. Am Enterprise.
Turner, Frederick J. *see* Turner, Frederick Jackson.
Turner, Frederick Jackson, 1861-1932
  xTurner, Frederick J.
    Character & Influence of the Indian Trade in
      Wisconsin: A Study of the Trading Post As
      an Institution. B Franklin.
    The Character & Influence of the Indian Trade
      in Wisconsin: A Study of the Trading Post
      As an Institution. Johnson Repr.
    The Character & Influence of the Indian Trade
      in Wisconsin: A Study of the Trading Post
      As an Institution. U of Okla Pr.
    ed. Correspondence of the French Ministers to
      the United States, 1791-1797. Da Capo.
    The Frontier in American History. Krieger.
    The Significance of Sections in American
      History. Peter Smith.
    Significance of the Frontier in American
      History. Ungar.
Turner, Frederick W., 1937-
  xTurner, Frederick.
    Beyond Geography: The Western Spirit
      Against the Wilderness. Viking Pr.
  xTurner, Frederick W.

    ed. The Portable North American Indian
      Reader. Penguin.
    ed. The Portable North American Indian
      Reader. Viking Pr.
Turner, Geoffrey.
  xTurner, Geoffrey.
    Indians of North America. Sterling.
Turner, George.
  xTurner, George E.
    Human Monsters in the Cinema. A S Barnes.
Turner, George. *see* Turner, George Barton.
Turner, George Barton, 1922-
  xTurner, George.
    Narrow Gauge Nostalgia. Trans-Anglo.
Turner, George E. *see* Turner, George.
Turner, George K. *see* Turner, George Kibbe.
Turner, George Kibbe, 1869-
  xTurner, George K.
    Hagar's Hoard. U Pr of Ky.
Turner, Glen O. *see* Turner, Glenn O.
Turner, Glenn O.
  xTurner, Glen O.
    Cardiovascular Care Unit: A Guide for
      Planning & Operation. Wiley.
Turner, H. A. *see* Turner, H. A. B.
Turner, H. A. B.
  xTurner, H. A.
    Collector's Guide to Staffordshire Pottery
      Figures. Emerson.
    A Collector's Guide to Staffordshire Pottery
      Figures. Wallace-Homestead.
Turner, Harold W.
  xTurner, Harold W.
    Religious Innovation in Africa: Collected
      Essays on New Religious Movements. G K
      Hall.
Turner, Henry. *see* Turner, Henry A.
Turner, Henry A.
  xTurner, Henry.
    Government & Politics of California. McGraw.
Turner, Henry A. *see* Turner, Henry Ashby.
Turner, Henry Ashby.
  xTurner, H. A.
    Nazism & the Third Reich. New Viewpoints.
  xTurner, Henry A.
    ed. Reappraisals of Fascism. New Viewpoints.
    Stresemann & the Politics of the Weimar
      Republic. Greenwood.
Turner, Henry E. *see* Turner, Henry Ernest William.
Turner, Henry Ernest William, 1907-
  xTurner, Henry E.
    The Pattern of Christian Truth: A Study in the
      Relations Between Orthodoxy & Heresy in
      the Early Church. AMS Pr.
Turner, J. D. *see* Turner, John Derfel.
Turner, James, 1947-
  xTurner, James G.
    The Politics of Landscape: Rural Scenery &
      Society in English Poetry, 1630-1660.
      Harvard U Pr.
Turner, James E. *see* Turner, James Edward.
Turner, James Edward.
  xTurner, James E.
    Regeneration in Lower Vertebrates &
      Invertebrates. Mss Info.
Turner, James F.
  xTurner, James F.
    Fundamental Electronics. Merrill.
Turner, James G. *see* Turner, James.
Turner, Jeffrey S.
  xTurner, Jeffrey S.
    Contemporary Adulthood. HR&W.
Turner, John D. *see* Turner, John Derfel.
Turner, John Derfel.
  xTurner, J. D.
    ed. Education for the Professions. State Mutual
      Bk.
  xTurner, John D.

    ed. Education for the Professions. Standing
      Orders.
Turner, John E. *see* Turner, John Elliot.
Turner, John Elliot, 1917-
  xTurner, John E.
    Labour's Doorstep Politics in London. U of
      Minn Pr.
Turner, John H. *see* Turner, John Howard.
Turner, John Henry.
  xTurner, John H.
    Studies in Managerial Process & Organizational
      Behavior. Scott F.
Turner, John Howard.
  xTurner, John H.
    London, Brighton & South Coast Railway.
      David & Charles.
Turner, John K. *see* Turner, John Kenneth.
Turner, John Kenneth.
  xTurner, John K.
    Barbarous Mexico. U of Tex Pr.
Turner, Jonathan. *see* Turner, Jonathan H.
Turner, Jonathan H.
  xTurner, Jonathan.
    Sociology: Studying the Human System.
      Goodyear.
  xTurner, Jonathan H.
    American Society: Problems of Structure.
      Har-Row.
    Functionalism. Benjamin-Cummings.
    Inequality: Privilege & Poverty in America.
      Goodyear.
    Sociology: Studying the Human System.
      Goodyear.
    The Structure of Sociological Theory. Dorsey.
Turner, Julius.
  xTurner, Julius.
    Party & Constituency: Pressures on Congress.
      AMS Pr.
Turner, Keith.
  xTurner, Keith.
    North Wales Tramways. David & Charles.
Turner, Louis.
  xTurner, Louis.
    The Golden Hordes: International Tourism &
      the Pleasure Periphery. St Martin.
    Multinational Companies & the Third World.
      Hill & Wang.
Turner, Martha A. *see* Turner, Martha Anne.
Turner, Martha Anne.
  xTurner, Martha A.
    Richard Bennett Hubbard: An American Life.
      Shoal Creek Pub.
Turner, Mary Jane, 1923-
  xTurner, Mary Jane.
    Law in the Classroom: Activities & Resources.
      Soc Sci Ed.
Turner, Morrie.
  xTurner, Morrie.
    All God's Chillun Got Soul. Judson.
    Famous Black Americans. Judson.
Turner, Nancy J.
  xTurner, Nancy J.
    Wild Coffee & Tea Substitutes of Canada. U of
      Chicago Pr.
Turner, Nat.
  xTurner, Nat.
    The Confession, Trial & Execution of Nat
      Turner, the Negro Insurrectionist. AMS Pr.
Turner, Nathan W.
  xTurner, Nathan W.
    Effective Leadership in Small Groups. Judson.
Turner, Paul.
  xTurner, Paul.
    Clinical Pharmacology. Churchill.
Turner, Paul V.
  xTurner, Paul V.

The Education of le Corbusier. Garland Pub.

Turner, Pearl.
　xTurner, Pearl.
　　Index to Outdoor Sports, Games & Activities.
　　Faxon.

Turner, Percy M. *see* Turner, Percy Moore.

Turner, Percy Moore.
　xTurner, Percy M.
　　The Appreciation of Painting. Arno.

Turner, Peter P. *see* Turner, Peter Percival.

Turner, Peter Percival.
　xTurner, Peter P.
　　The Cardiovascular System. Churchill.

Turner, Philip.
　xTurner, Philip.
　　Devil's Nob. Elsevier-Nelson.
　xTurner, Phillip.
　　ed. Brian Wildsmith's Illustrated Bible Stories.
　　Watts.

Turner, Phillip. *see* Turner, Philip.

Turner, Priscilla.
　xTurner, Priscilla.
　　Captives of Endless Snow. Raintree Pubs.

Turner, R. Kerry.
　xTurner, R. Kerry.
　　Economics of Planning. St Martin.

Turner, Ralph B.
　xTurner, Ralph B.
　　Analytical Biochemistry of Insects. Elsevier.

Turner, Ralph H.
　xTurner, Ralph H.
　　Family Interaction. Wiley.

Turner, Richard.
　xTurner, Richard.
　　The Eye of the Needle: Toward Participatory
　　Democracy in South Africa. Orbis Bks.

Turner, Robert, 1915-
　xTurner, Robert.
　　Some of My Best Friends Are Writers but I
　　Wouldn't Want My Daughter to Marry One.
　　Sherbourne.

Turner, Robert. *see* Turner, Robert D.

Turner, Robert D.
　xTurner, Robert.
　　Vancouver Island Railroads. Golden West.

Turner, Rufus. *see* Turner, Rufus P.

Turner, Rufus P.
　xTurner, Rufus.
　　Impedance. TAB Bks.
　xTurner, Rufus P.
　　ABC's of Calculus. Sams.
　　ABC's of FETS. Sams.
　　ABC's of Integrated Circuits. Sams.
　　ABC's of Resistance & Resistors. Sams.
　　The Antenna Construction Handbook for Ham,
　　CB & SWL. TAB Bks.
　　FET Circuits. Sams.
　　Frequency & Its Measurement. Sams.
　　Getting Acquainted with the IC. Sams.
　　Illustrated Dictionary of Electronics. TAB Bks.
　　Solar Cells & Photocells. Bobbs.
　　ed. Solar Cells & Photocells. SAMS.

Turner, S. *see* Turner, Stephen.

Turner, Stephen.
　xTurner, S.
　　The Design of Organic Syntheses. Elsevier.

Turner, Stephen. *see* Turner, Stephen C.

Turner, Stephen C.
　xTurner, Stephen.
　　Our Noisy World. Messner.

Turner, Susan.
　xTurner, Susan.
　　Lost at Sea. Raintree Pubs.

Turner, Victor. *see* Turner, Victor Witter.

Turner, Victor Witter.
　xTurner, Victor.

The Forest of Symbols: Aspects of Ndembu
　Ritual. Cornell U Pr.
Revelation & Divination in Ndembu Ritual.
　Cornell U Pr.

Turner, W. B.
　xTurner, W. B.
　　Fungal Metabolites. Acad Pr.

Turner, Walter J. *see* Turner, Walter James.

Turner, Walter James, 1889-1946
　xTurner, Walter J.
　　Wagner. Greenwood.

Turner, Wayne C.
　xTurner, Wayne C.
　　Introduction to Industrial & Systems
　　Engineering. P-H.

Turner, William. *see* Turner, William W.

Turner, William C.
　xTurner, William C.
　　Handbook of Thermal Insulation Design
　　Economics for Pipes & Equipment. Krieger.

Turner, William O. *see* Turner, William Oliver.

Turner, William Oliver.
　xTurner, William O.
　　Call the Beast Thy Brother. Berkley Pub.
　　Mayberly's Kill. Berkley Pub.

Turner, William W.
　xTurner, William.
　　Power on the Right. Ramparts.

Turner Ettlinger, D. M.
　xTurner Ettlinger, D. M.
　　ed. Natural History Photography. Acad Pr.

Turney, Alfred W.
　xTurney, Alfred W.
　　Disaster at Moscow: Von Bock's Campaigns,
　　1941-1942. U of NM Pr.

Turney-High, Harry H. *see* Turney-High, Harry Holbert.

Turney-High, Harry Holbert, 1899-
　xTurney-High, Harry H.
　　Chateau-Gerard: The Life & Times of a
　　Walloon Village. U of SC Pr.
　　Primitive War: Its Practice & Concepts. U of
　　SC Pr.

Turnill, Reginald.
　xTurnill, Reginald.
　　The Observer's Book of Manned Spaceflight.
　　Scribner.
　　The Observer's Spaceflight Directory. Warne.

Turnock, David.
　xTurnock, David.
　　Eastern Europe. Westview.
　　The New Scotland. David & Charles.

Turns, Keith.
　xTurns, Keith.
　　The Independent Bus: An Historical Survey of
　　Some Independent Bus Operators. David &
　　Charles.

Turow, Joseph.
　xTurow, Joseph G.
　　Getting Books to Children: An Exploration of
　　Publisher-Market Relations. ALA.

Turow, Joseph G. *see* Turow, Joseph.

Turow, Rita.
　xTurow, Rita.
　　Daddy Doesn't Live Here Anymore.
　　Doubleday.

Turow, Scott.
　xTurow, Scott.
　　One "L". Putnam.

Turquet-Milnes, Gladys R. *see* Turquet-Milnes, Gladys
　Rosaleen.

Turquet-Milnes, Gladys Rosaleen.
　xTurquet-Milnes, Gladys R.
　　Some Modern French Writers: A Study in
　　Bergsonism. Arno.

Turrell, G. *see* Turrell, George.

Turrell, George.
　xTurrell, G.

Infrared & Raman Spectra of Crystals. Acad
　Pr.

Turro, Nicholas J., 1938-
　xTurro, Nicholas J.
　　Modern Molecular Photochemistry.
　　Benjamin-Cummings.

Turrou, Leon G.
　xTurrou, Leon G.
　　Nazi Spy Conspiracy in America. Arno.

Turska, Krystyna, 1933-
　xTurska, Krystyna.
　　illus. Tamara & the Sea Witch. Schol Bk Serv.
　　illus. The Woodcutter's Duck. Macmillan.

Turski, W. M. *see* Turski, Wadysaw.

Turski, Wadysaw.
　xTurski, W. M.
　　Computer Programming Methodology. Heyden.

Turtle, William J. *see* Turtle, William John.

Turtle, William John.
　xTurtle, William J.
　　Dr. Turtle's Babies. Popular Lib.

Turvey, Ralph.
　xTurvey, Ralph.
　　Economic Analysis & Public Enterprises. Allen
　　Unwin.
　　Economic Analysis & Public Enterprises.
　　Rowman.

Turville-Petre, Edward Oswald Gabriel.
　xTurville-Petre, Gabriel.
　　Origins of Icelandic Literature. Oxford U Pr.

Turville-Petre, Gabriel. *see* Turville-Petre, Edward
　Oswald Gabriel.

Turyn, Aleksander, 1900-
　xTuryn, Alexander.
　　Dated Greek Manuscripts of the Thirteenth &
　　Fourteenth Centuries in the Libraries of Italy.
　　U of Ill Pr.

Turyn, Alexander. *see* Turyn, Aleksander.

Tushman, Michael.
　xTushman, Michael.
　　Organizational Change: An Exploratory Study
　　& Case History. NY Sch Indus Rel.

Tuska, Jon.
　xTuska, Jon.
　　ed. Close up: The Contract Director.
　　Scarecrow.
　　The Films of Mae West. Citadel Pr.

Tuskegee Institute, Alabama, Dept. of Records &
　Research. *see* Tuskegee Institute. Dept. of Records
　and Research.

Tuskegee Institute. Dept. of Records and Research.
　xTuskegee Institute, Alabama, Dept. of Records &
　Research.
　　Pamphlets: 1949-1961. Kraus Repr.

Tussing, Lyle.
　xTussing, Lyle.
　　Psychology for Better Living. Wiley.

Tussman, Joseph.
　xTussman, Joseph.
　　Government & the Mind. Oxford U Pr.
　　Obligation & the Body Politic. Oxford U Pr.

Tustin, Frances.
　xTustin, Frances.
　　Autism & Childhood Psychosis. Aronson.

Tute, Richard C. *see* Tute, Richard Clifford.

Tute, Richard Clifford, Sir, 1874-
　xTute, Richard C.
　　After Materialism-What?. Arno.

Tutein, Peter, 1902-1949
　xTutein, Peter.
　　The Sealers. E M Coleman Ent.

Tuten, Edward G. *see* Tuten, Edward T.

Tuten, Edward T.
　xTuten, Edward G.
　　Guide to Selecting a Private School for Your
　　Child. Pilot Bks.

Tuten, Frederic.
　xTuten, Frederic.

Adventures of Mao on the Long March.
Citadel Pr.
Tutin, John R. see Tutin, John Ramsden.
Tutin, John Ramsden.
xTutin, John R.
Concordance to FitzGerald's Translation of the
Rubaiyat of Omar Khayyam. B Franklin.
Concordance to Fitzgerald's Translation of the
Rubaiyat of Omar Khayyam. Johnson Repr.
Wordsworth Dictionary of Persons & Places
with Familiar Quotations from His Works. B
Franklin.
The Wordsworth Dictionary of Persons &
Places with the Familiar Quotations from His
Works Including Index & a Chronologically
Arranged List of His Best Poems. Johnson
Repr.
Tutko, Thomas. see Tutko, Thomas A.
Tutko, Thomas A.
xTutko, Thomas.
Psychology of Coaching. Allyn.
Tutsch, Hans E. see Tutsch, Hans Emanuel.
Tutsch, Hans Emanuel, 1918-
xTutsch, Hans E.
Facets of Arab Nationalism. Wayne St U Pr.
Tutt, Clara. see Tutt, Clara Little.
Tutt, Clara Little.
xTutt, Clara.
Carl Schurz, Patriot. State Hist Soc Wis.
Tutt, Norman.
xTutt, Norman.
Care or Custody: Community Homes & the
Treatment of Delinquency. Agathon.
Tutt, Patricia.
xTutt, Patricia.
VNR Metric Handbook of Architectural
Standards. Van Nos Reinhold.
Tuttiett, Mary G. see Tuttiett, Mary Gleed.
Tuttiett, Mary Gleed, d. 1923
xTuttiett, Mary G.
World's Mercy. Arno.
Tuttle, Alva M.
xTuttle, Alva M.
Use of Statistical Techniques by Ohio
Manufacturers. Ohio St U Admin Sci.
Tuttle, Anthony.
xTuttle, Anthony.
The Catchers. Creative Ed.
Meet the Catchers. Creative Ed.
Steve Cauthen: Boy Jockey. Putnam.
Tuttle, Charles E.
xTuttle, Charles E.
Incredible Japan. C E Tuttle.
Tuttle, Herbert, 1846-1894
xTuttle, Herbert.
History of Prussia. AMS Pr.
Tuttle, Margaret W. see Tuttle, Margaret Wheaton.
Tuttle, Margaret Wheaton.
xTuttle, Margaret W.
The Crimson Cage. Tashmoo.
Tuttle, Michael D.
xTuttle, Michael D.
Practical Business Math: A Performance
Approach. Wm C Brown.
Tuttle, S. B. see Tuttle, Stanley B.
Tuttle, Stanley B.
xTuttle, S. B.
Mechanisms for Engineering Design. Krieger.
Tuttle, W. C. see Tuttle, Wilbur C.
Tuttle, Wilbur C., 1883-
xTuttle, W. C.
Renegade Sheriff. Bouregy.
Tuttle, William M., 1937-
xTuttle, William M.
Race Riot: Chicago in the Red Summer of
1919. Atheneum.
Tutuola, Amos.
xTutuola, Amos.

Palm-Wine Drinkard & His Dead Palm-Wine
Tapster in the Dead's Town. Greenwood.
Tuve, George L. see Tuve, George Lewis.
Tuve, George Lewis.
xTuve, George L.
Engineering Experimentation. McGraw.
Tuve, Richard L.
xTuve, Richard L.
Principles of Fire Protection Chemistry. Natl
Fire Prot.
Tuwiner, Sidney B. see Tuwiner, Sidney Bertram.
Tuwiner, Sidney Bertram, 1912-
xTuwiner, Sidney B.
Diffusion & Membrane Technology. Am
Chemical.
Tuzin, Donald F.
xTuzin, Donald F.
The Ilahita Arapesh: Dimensions of Unity. U
of Cal Pr.
TV Guide.
xT.V. Guide.
TV Guide Book of Crossword Puzzles. Popular
Lib.
Tver, David F.
xTver, David F.
Dictionary of Astronomy, Space &
Atmospheric Phenomena. Van Nos Reinhold.
The Petroleum Dictionary. Van Nos Reinhold.
Tveten, John L.
xTveten, John L.
Exploring the Bayous. McKay.
Twaddle, Andrew C., 1938-
xTwaddle, Andrew C.
Sickness Behavior & the Sick Role. G K Hall.
Sickness Behavior & the Sick Role.
Schenkman.
A Sociology of Health. Mosby.
Twain, Mark.
xTwain, Mark.
The Adventures of Huckleberry Finn. Andor
Pub.
Adventures of Huckleberry Finn. Bobbs.
Adventures of Huckleberry Finn. Dell.
The Adventures of Huckleberry Finn. G K
Hall.
Adventures of Huckleberry Finn. Har-Row.
Adventures of Huckleberry Finn. Har-Row.
Adventures of Huckleberry Finn. Har-Row.
Adventures of Huckleberry Finn. HR&W.
Adventures of Huckleberry Finn. Macmillan.
The Adventures of Huckleberry Finn.
Merrimack Bk Serv.
The Adventures of Huckleberry Finn. Penguin.
Adventures of Huckleberry Finn. NAL.
The Adventures of Huckleberry Finn. Penguin.
Adventures of Huckleberry Finn. G&D.
The Adventures of Huckleberry Finn. Airmont.
The Adventures of Huckleberry Finn. G&D.
Adventures of Huckleberry Finn. AMSCO Sch.
The Adventures of Huckleberry Finn. Bantam.
Adventures of Huckleberry Finn. Macmillan.
The Adventures of Huckleberry Finn. Schol Bk
Serv.
The Adventures of Huckleberry Finn. PB.
Adventures of Huckleberry Finn. HM.
The Adventures of Huckleberry Finn.
McDougal-Littell.
The Adventures of Huckleberry Finn. Regents
Pub.
Letters from the Earth. Har-Row.
Letters from the Earth. Har-Row.
Twark, Alan J. see Twark, Allan Joseph.
Twark, Allan Joseph.
xTwark, Alan J.
Security Analysis & Portfolio Management: A
Casebook. Holden-Day.
Twedt, Dik W. see Twedt, Dik Warren.
Twedt, Dik Warren.
xTwedt, Dik W.

ed. Personality Research in Marketing: A
Bibliography. Am Mktg.
Tweedie, Jill, 1936-
xTweedie, Jill.
In the Name of Love. Pantheon.
Tweedie, Michael. see Tweedie, Michael Willmer Forbes.
Tweedie, Michael Willmer Forbes, 1907-
xTweedie, Michael.
Atlas of Insects. T Y Crowell.
The World of Dinosaurs. Morrow.
Tweeten, Luther. see Tweeten, Luther G.
Tweeten, Luther G.
xTweeten, Luther.
Foundations of Farm Policy. U of Nebr Pr.
Twelvetrees, Harper, 1823-1881
xTwelvetrees, Harper.
The Story of the Life of John Anderson, the
Fugitive Slave. Arno.
Twentieth Century Fund, Inc. see Twentieth Century
Fund.
Twentieth Century Fund.
xThe Twentieth Century Fund.
Confronting Youth Crime: Report of the
Twentieth Century Fund Task Force on
Sentencing Policy Toward Young Offenders.
Holmes & Meier.
xThe Twentieth Century Fund Task Force Report
for a National News Council.
A Free & Responsive Press. Kraus Repr.
xTwentieth Century Fund, Inc.
Law Enforcement: The Federal Role, Report of
the Twentieth Century Fund Task Force on
the Law Enforcement Assistance
Administration. McGraw.
xTwentieth Century Fund.
Abuse on Wall Street: Conflicts of Interest in
the Securities Markets. Greenwood.
America's Needs & Resources: A New Survey.
Kraus Repr.
Commission on Campaign Costs in the
Electronic Era. Voters' Time. Kraus Repr.
Europe's Needs & Resources, Trends, &
Prospects in Eighteen Countries. Kraus Repr.
Labor & Government: An Investigation. Kraus
Repr.
Report on the Greeks: Findings of a Twentieth
Century Fund Team Which Surveyed
Conditions in 1947. Kraus Repr.
The Security Markets: Findings &
Recommendations of a Special Staff of the
Twentieth Century Fund. Arno.
Task Force on Governance of New Towns:
New Towns: laboratories for Democracy
Report. Kraus Repr.
xTwentieth Century Fund, Inc.
Building a Broader Market: Report of the
Twentieth Century Fund Task Force on the
Municipal Bond Market. McGraw.
Funds for the Future: Report of the Twentieth
Century Fund Task Force on College &
University Endowment Policy. McGraw.
Providing for Energy: Report of the Twentieth
Century Fund Task Force on United States
Energy Policy. McGraw.
Rights in Conflict: Report of the Twentieth
Century Fund Task Force on Justice,
Publicity & the First Amendment. McGraw.
**Twentieth Century Fund. Corporation Survey
Committee.**
xTwentieth Century Fund. Corporation Survey
Committee.
A Memorandum on the Problem of Big
Business. Kraus Repr.
Twentieth Century Fund, Inc. see Twentieth Century
Fund.
Twentieth Century Fund. Labor Committee.
xTwentieth Century Fund. Labor Committee.

Partners in Production: A Basis for
Labor-Management Understanding a Report
by the Labor Committee. Kraus Repr.
Trends in Collective Bargaining. Kraus Repr.

**Twentieth Century Fund. Task Force on Broadcasting
and the Legislature.**
xReport of the Twentieth Century Fund Task
Force on Broadcasting & the Legislature.
Openly Arrived at. Twentieth Fund.

**Twentieth Century Fund. Task Force on Community
Development Corporation.**
xTwentieth Century Fund. Task Force on
Community Development Corporations.
CDC's: New Hope for the Inner City. Kraus
Repr.

**Twentieth Century Fund. Task Force on Employment
Problems of Black Youth.**
xTwentieth Century Fund. Task Force on
Employment Problem of Black Youth.
The Job Crisis & Black Youth. Kraus Repr.

**Twentieth Century Fund. Task Force on Financing
Congressional Campaigns.**
xTwentieth Century Fund. Task Force on
Financing Congressional Campaigns.
Electing Congress: The Financial Dilemma.
Kraus Repr.

**Twentieth Century Fund. Task Force on International
Satellite Communications.**
xTwentieth Century Fund. Task Force on
International Satellite Communications.
Communicating by Satellite. Kraus Repr.
The Future of Satellite Communications:
Resources Management & the Needs of
Nations. Kraus Repr.

**Twentieth Century Fund. Task Force on Labor Disputes
in Public Employment.**
xTwentieth Century Fund Task Force on Labor
Disputes in Public Employment.
Pickets at City Hall. Kraus Repr.

**Twentieth Century Fund. Task Force on Municipal Bond
Credit Ratings.**
xTwentieth Century Fund. Task Force on
Municipal Bond Credit Ratings.
The Rating Game: Report of the Twentieth
Century Fund Task Force on Municipal Bond
Credit Ratings : Background Paper. Kraus
Repr.

**Twentieth Century Fund. Task Force on Performing
Arts Centers.**
xTwentieth Century Fund Task Force on
Performing Arts Centers.
Bricks, Mortar & the Performing Arts: A
Report. Kraus Repr.

Twersky, Isadore.
xTwersky, Isadore.
Rabad of Posquieres: A Twelfth-Century
Talmudist. Harvard U Pr.
Rabad of Posquieres: A Twelfth-Century
Talmudist. Jewish Pubn.
ed. Studies in Medieval Jewish History &
Literature. Harvard U Pr.

Tweton, D. Jerome.
xTweton, D. Jerome.
North Dakota: The Heritage of a People. N
Dak Inst.

Twiford, Rainer, 1952-
xTwiford, Rainor.
A Child with a Problem: A Guide to the
Psychological Disorders of Children. P-H.
Twiford, Rainor. see Twiford, Rainer.

Twight, Charlotte.
xTwight, Charlotte.
America's Emerging Fascist Economy.
Arlington Hse.

Twiname, Eric.
xTwiname, Eric.
Start to Win. Norton.
Twining, William. see Twining, William L.

Twining, William L.
xTwining, William.

How to Do Things with Rules: A Primer of
Interpretation. Rothman.

Twitchell, Mary.
xTwitchell, Mary.
Wood Energy: A Practical Guide to Heating
with Wood. Garden Way Pub.

Twitchell, Paul, 1908-
xTwitchell, Paul.
The ECK Vidya: The Ancient Science of
Prophecy. IWP Pub.
Eckankar Dictionary. IWP Pub.
Twitchell, Ralph E. see Twitchell, Ralph Emerson.

Twitchell, Ralph Emerson, 1859-1925
xTwitchell, Ralph E.
The Spanish Archives of New Mexico. AMS
Pr.
The Spanish Archives of New Mexico. Arno.
Twitchett, D. C. see Twitchett, Denis Crispin.

Twitchett, Denis Crispin.
xTwitchett, D. C.
Financial Administration Under the T'ang
Dynasty. Cambridge U Pr.

Twombly, Gerald H.
xTwombly, Gerald H.
A Superman for a Total Woman. Beta Bk.

Twomey, S.
xTwomey, S.
Atmospheric Aerosols. Elsevier.

Tworkov, Jack.
xTworkov, Jack.
The Camel Who Took a Walk. Dutton.

Twyman, Robert W, 1919-
xTwyman, Robert W.
History of Marshall Field & Co., 1852-1906.
Arno.

Tyabji, Badr- ud- din, 1907-
xTyabji, Badr-Ud-Din.
Chaff & Grain. Asia.

Tyack, David B.
xTyack, David B.
The One Best System: A History of American
Urban Education. Harvard U Pr.
Turning Points in American Educational
History. Wiley.

Tyagi, Sushila, 1943-
xTyagi, Sushila.
Indo Nepalese Relations: 1858-1914. South
Asia Bks.
Tybout, Richard A. see Tybout, Richard Alton.

Tybout, Richard Alton.
xTybout, Richard A.
Reactor Supply Industry. Ohio St U Admin
Sci.
Tye, R. P. see Tye, Ronald Phillip.

Tye, Ronald Phillip.
xTye, R. P.
ed. Thermal Conductivity. Acad Pr.
Tykac, J. see Tykac, Jan.

Tykac, Jan.
xTykac, J.
A Field Guide in Color to Plants. Mayflower
Bks.

Tyl, Noel, 1936-
xTyl, Noel.
Aspects & Houses in Analysis. Llewellyn
Pubns.
Astrological Counsel. Llewellyn Pubns.
The Expanded Present. Llewellyn Pubns.
Horoscope Construction. Llewellyn Pubns.
Integrated Transits. Llewellyn Pubns.
Prediction Techniques Synthesized. Llewellyn
Pubns.
Special Horoscope Dimensions. Llewellyn
Pubns.
Teaching & Study Guide to the Principles &
Practice of Astrology. Llewellyn Pubns.

Tyldesley, John R.
xTyldesley, John R.

An Introduction to Applied Thermodynamics
& Energy Conversion. Longman.

Tyldesley, W. R.
xTyldesley, W. R.
Oral Diagnosis. Pergamon.

Tyler, Anne.
xTyler, Anne.
Celestial Navigation. Knopf.
Celestial Navigation. Popular Lib.
The Clock Winder. Knopf.
The Clock Winder. Popular Lib.
Earthly Possessions. G K Hall.
Earthly Possessions. Knopf.
If Morning Ever Comes. Knopf.
If Morning Ever Comes. Popular Lib.
Morgan's Passing. Knopf.

Tyler, Daniel, b.1816
xTyler, Daniel.
A Concise History of the Mormon Battalion in
the Mexican War, 1846-1848. Rio Grande.
Tyler, David B. see Tyler, David Budlong.

Tyler, David Budlong, 1899-
xTyler, David B.
Steam Conquers the Atlantic. Arno.

Tyler, Edward.
xTyler, Edward.
Prayers in Celebration of the Turning Year.
Abingdon.
Tyler, Hamilton. see Tyler, Hamilton A.

Tyler, Hamilton A.
xTyler, Hamilton.
Organic Gardening Without Poisons. PB.
xTyler, Hamilton A.
Owls by Day & Night. Naturegraph.
Pueblo Animals & Myths. U of Okla Pr.
Pueblo Birds & Myths. U of Okla Pr.
Swallowtail Butterflies of North America.
Naturegraph.

Tyler, I. Keith, 1905-
xTyler, I. Keith.
Spelling As a Secondary Learning: The
Extension of Spelling Vocabularies with
Different Methods of Organizing & Teaching
the Social Studies. AMS Pr.

Tyler, J. Allen.
xTyler, J. Allen.
ed. A Concordance to the Fables & Tales of
Jean De la Fontaine. Cornell U Pr.
Tyler, J. E. see Tyler, J. E. A.

Tyler, J. E. A.
xTyler, J. E.
The New Tolkien Companion. Avon.
The New Tolkien Companion. St Martin.
The Tolkien Companion. St Martin.

Tyler, Jenny.
xTyler, Jenny.
Children's Book of the Seas. EMC.

Tyler, John E.
xTyler, J. E.
Measurements of Spectral Irradiance
Underwater. Gordon.
xTyler, John E.
ed. Light in the Sea. Acad Pr.
Tyler, Leona. see Tyler, Leona Elizabeth.
Tyler, Leona E. see Tyler, Leona Elizabeth.

Tyler, Leona Elizabeth, 1906-
xTyler, Leona.
Tests & Measurements. P-H.
xTyler, Leona E.
Individuality: Human Possibilities & Personal
Choice in the Psychological Development of
Men & Women. Jossey-Bass.
Psychology of Human Differences. P-H.
Tyler, Lyon G. see Tyler, Lyon Gardiner.

Tyler, Lyon Gardiner, 1853-1935
xTyler, Lyon G.
England in America, 1580-1652. Greenwood.
England in America, 1580-1652. Haskell.
Letters & Times of the Tylers. Da Capo.
Tyler, M. see Tyler, Moses Coit.

Tyler, Martin.
　　xTyler, Martin.
　　　　Skills & Tactics of Soccer. Arco.
Tyler, Moses C. *see* Tyler, Moses Coit.
Tyler, Moses Coit, 1835-1900
　　xTyler, M.
　　　　Patrick Henry. Gordon Pr.
　　xTyler, Moses C.
　　　　Literary History of the American Revolution. B
　　　　　Franklin.
　　　　Literary History of the American Revolution
　　　　　1763-1783. Ungar.
　　　　Patrick Henry. AMS Pr.
　　　　Patrick Henry. B Franklin.
　　　　Patrick Henry. Chelsea Hse.
　　　　Patrick Henry. Norwood Edns.
　　　　Patrick Henry. Cornell U Pr.
Tyler, O. Z. *see* Tyler, Orville Zelotes.
Tyler, Orville Zelotes, 1905-
　　xTyler, O. Z.
　　　　Osceola, Seminole Chief: An Unremembered
　　　　　Saga. Anna Pub.
Tyler, Parker.
　　xTyler, Parker.
　　　　The Hollywood Hallucination. S&S.
Tyler, Poyntz.
　　xTyler, Poyntz.
　　　　ed. Airways of America. Wilson.
　　　　ed. Securities, Exchanges & the SEC. Wilson.
Tyler, Ralph. *see* Tyler, Ralph Winfred.
Tyler, Ralph W. *see* Tyler, Ralph Winfred.
Tyler, Ralph Winfred.
　　xTyler, Ralph.
　　　　ed. From Youth to Constructive Adult Life:
　　　　　The Role of the Public School. McCutchan.
　　xTyler, Ralph W.
　　　　Crucial Issues in Testing. McCutchan.
　　　　Prospects for Research & Development in
　　　　　Education. McCutchan.
Tyler, Royall, 1757-1826
　　xTyler, Royall.
　　　　Contrast: A Comedy. B Franklin.
　　　　Contrast: A Comedy in Five Acts. AMS Pr.
　　　　Prose of Royall Tyler. C E Tuttle.
Tyler, W. T.
　　xTyler, W. T.
　　　　The Man Who Lost the War. Dial.
Tyler, William.
　　xTyler, William.
　　　　The Sociology of Educational Inequality.
　　　　　Methuen Inc.
Tyler, William R.
　　xTyler, William R.
　　　　Dijon & the Valois Dukes of Burgundy. U of
　　　　　Okla Pr.
Tylor, E. *see* Tylor, Edward Burnett.
Tylor, Edward Burnett, Sir, 1832-1917
　　xTylor, E.
　　　　Primitive Culture. Gordon Pr.
Tymchuk, Alexander J.
　　xTymchuk, Alexander J.
　　　　Parent & Family Therapy: An Integrative
　　　　　Approach to Family Interventions. Spectrum
　　　　　Pub.
Tymieniecka, Anna Teresa.
　　xTymieniecka, Anna-Teresa.
　　　　ed. The Crisis of Culture: Steps to Re-Open the
　　　　　Phenomenological Investigation of Man.
　　　　　Kluwer Boston.
Tymieniecka, Anna-Teresa. *see* Tymieniecka, Anna
　　Teresa.
Tymn, Marshall. *see* Tymn, Marshall B.
Tymn, Marshall B.
　　xTymn, Marshall.
　　　　ed. Fantasy Literature: A Core Collection &
　　　　　Reference Guide. Bowker.
　　xTymn, Mashall B.
　　　　The Year's Scholarship in Science Fiction &
　　　　　Fantasy: 1972-1975. Kent St U Pr.
Tymn, Mashall B. *see* Tymn, Marshall B.

Tynan, Kathleen.
　　xTynan, Kathleen.
　　　　Agatha. Ballantine.
Tyndale-Biscoe, Hugh.
　　xTyndale-Biscoe, Hugh.
　　　　Life of Marsupials. Univ Park.
Tyndall, John, 1820-1893
　　xTyndall, John.
　　　　Sound. Greenwood.
Tyndall, Robert E.
　　xTyndall, Robert E.
　　　　Musical Form. Greenwood.
Tyne, Claude H. Van. *see* Van Tyne, Claude H.
Tyne, Josselyn Van. *see* Van Tyne, Josselyn.
Tynianov, Iurii Nikolaevich, 1894-1943
　　xTynianov, Iurii N.
　　　　Death & Diplomacy in Persia. Hyperion Conn.
Tynianov, Iurii N. *see* Tynianov, Iurii Nikolaevich.
Tyran, Michael R.
　　xTyran, Michael R.
　　　　Computerized Accounting Methods &
　　　　　Controls. P-H.
Tyras, G. *see* Tyras, George.
Tyras, George.
　　xTyras, G.
　　　　Radiation & Propagation of Electromagnetic
　　　　　Waves. Acad Pr.
Tyre, Nedra.
　　xTyre, Nedra.
　　　　Hall of Death. S&S.
Tyrer, J. H. *see* Tyrer, John William Howard.
Tyrer, John William Howard.
　　xTyrer, J. H.
　　　　The Astute Physician: How to Think in
　　　　　Clinical Medicine. Elsevier.
Tyrner-Stastny, Gabrielle.
　　xTyrner-Stastny, Gabrielle.
　　　　The Gypsy in Northwest America. Wash St
　　　　　Hist Soc.
Tyrrell. *see* Tyrrell, William Blake.
Tyrrell, Bernard, 1933-
　　xTyrrell, Bernard.
　　　　Christotherapy: Healing Through
　　　　　Enlightenment. Seabury.
Tyrrell, G. N. *see* Tyrrell, George Nugent Merle.
Tyrrell, George Nugent Merle.
　　xTyrrell, G. N.
　　　　Homo Faber: A Study of Man's Mental
　　　　　Evolution. Greenwood.
Tyrrell, J. A. *see* Tyrrell, John Alfred.
Tyrrell, James W. *see* Tyrrell, James Williams.
Tyrrell, James Williams, 1863-1945
　　xTyrrell, James W.
　　　　Across the Sub-Arctics of Canada: A Journey
　　　　　of 3200 Miles by Canoe & Snowshoe
　　　　　Through the Hudson Bay Region. AMS Pr.
Tyrrell, John Alfred.
　　xTyrrell, J. A.
　　　　Generalized Clifford Parallelism. Cambridge U
　　　　　Pr.
Tyrrell, Joseph B. *see* Tyrrell, Joseph Burr.
Tyrrell, Joseph Burr, 1858-1957
　　xTyrrell, Joseph B.
　　　　ed. Documents Relating to the Early History of
　　　　　Hudson Bay. Greenwood.
Tyrrell, R. Emmett.
　　xTyrrell, R. Emmett.
　　　　The Future That Doesn't Work: Social
　　　　　Democracy's Failures in Britain. Doubleday.
Tyrrell, R. W. *see* Tyrrell, Robert.
Tyrrell, Robert.
　　xTyrrell, R. W.
　　　　The Work of the Television Journalist. Focal
　　　　　Pr.
Tyrrell, Thomas J., 1938-
　　xTyrrell, Thomas J.

　　　　Urgent Longings: Reflections on the
　　　　　Experience of Infatuation, Human Intimacy,
　　　　　& Contemplative Love. Affirmation.
Tyrrell, William Blake.
　　xTyrrell.
　　　　Medical Terminology for Medical Students. C
　　　　　C Thomas.
Tyrwhitt, Thomas, 1730-1786
　　xTyrwhitt, Thomas.
　　　　Observations & Conjectures Upon Some
　　　　　Passages of Shakespeare. AMS Pr.
Tysen, Frank J.
　　xTysen, Frank J.
　　　　District Administration in Metropolitan
　　　　　Calcutta. Asia.
Tysinger, D. S.
　　xTysinger, D. S.
　　　　The Clinical Physics & Physiology of Chronic
　　　　　Lung Disease, Inhalation Therapy, &
　　　　　Pulmonary Function Testing. C C Thomas.
Tyson, George E. *see* Tyson, George F.
Tyson, George F.
　　xTyson, George E.
　　　　Preliminary Report on Manuscript Materials in
　　　　　the British Archives Relating to the
　　　　　American Revolution in the West Indian
　　　　　Islands. Kraus Repr.
　　xTyson, George F.
　　　　Compiled by A Guide to Manuscript Sources
　　　　　in United States & West Indian Depositories
　　　　　Relating to the British West Indies During
　　　　　the Era of the American Revolution.
　　　　　Scholarly Res Inc.
　　　　ed. Toussaint L'Ouverture. P-H.
Tyson, Joseph B.
　　xTyson, Joseph B.
　　　　Synoptic Abstract. Biblical Res Assocs
Tyson, Mary C. *see* Tyson, Mary Catherine.
Tyson, Mary Catherine.
　　xTyson, Mary C.
　　　　Psychology of Successful Weight Control.
　　　　　Nelson-Hall.
Tytell, J. *see* Tytell, John.
Tytell, John.
　　xTytell, J.
　　　　ed. Affinities: A Short Story Anthology.
　　　　　Har-Row.
Tyus, Wyomia.
　　xTyus, Wyomia.
　　　　Inside Jogging for Women. Contemp Bks.
Tzagoloff, Alexander, 1937-
　　xTzagoloff, Alexandre.
　　　　ed. Membrane Biogenesis: Mitochondria,
　　　　　Chloroplasts & Bacteria. Plenum Pub.
Tzagoloff, Alexandre. *see* Tzagoloff, Alexander.
Tzannes, Nicolaos.
　　xTzannes, Nicolaos.
　　　　Backgammon Games & Strategies. A S Barnes.
Tzara, Tristan, 1896-1963
　　xTzara, Tristan.
　　　　Approximate Man & Other Writings. Wayne St
　　　　　U Pr.
U S Marine Corps. *see* United States. Marine Corps.
U. S.Census Office, 1880. *see* United States. Census
　　Office. 10th Census, 1880.
Ubbelohde, Carl.
　　xUbbelohde, Carl.
　　　　American Colonies & the British Empire,
　　　　　1607-1763. AHM Pub.
　　　　Colorado Reader. Pruett.
Ubelaker, Douglas H.
　　xUbelaker, Douglas H.
　　　　Human Skeletal Remains: Excavation, Analysis,
　　　　　Interpretation. Beresford Bk Serv.
　　　　Human Skeletal Remains: Excavation, Analysis,
　　　　　Interpretation. Taraxacum.
Ubell, Earl.
　　xUbell, Earl.

How to Save Your Life. HarBraceJ.

Ubicini, Jean Henri Abdolonyme, 1818-1884
xUbicini, M. A.
Letters on Turkey. Arno.

Ubicini, M. A. *see* Ubicini, Jean Henri Abdolonyme.

Uchelen, Rod Van. *see* Van Uchelen, Rod.

Uchendu, Victor C. *see* Uchendu, Victor Chikezie.

Uchendu, Victor Chikezie.
xUchendu, Victor C.
Igbo of Southeast Nigeria. HR&W.

Uchida, Yoshiko.
xUchida, Yoshiko.
Journey Home. Atheneum.
Promised Year. HarBraceJ.

U.C.L.A. Law Review.
xUCLA Law Review Staff.
Computerization of Government Files: What
Impact on the Individual?. Am Bar Foun.

UCLA Law Review Staff. *see* U.C.L.A. Law Review.

UCLA Moot Court Honors Program. *see* California.
University. University at los Angeles. Moot Court
Honors Program.

**U.C.L.A. Sociolinguistics Conference, Los Angeles and
Lake Arrowhead, Calif., 1964.**
xUCLA Sociolinguistics Conference, 1964.
Sociolinguistics: Proceedings. Mouton.

UCLA Sociolinguistics Conference, 1964. *see* U.C.L.A.
Sociolinguistics Conference, los Angeles and Lake
Arrowhead, Calif., 1964.

Udall, Morris K.
xUdall, Morris K.
Education of a Congressman: The Newsletters
of Morris K. Udall. Bobbs.

Udall, Nicholas.
xUdall, Nicholas.
Ralph Roister Doister. Octagon.

Udall, Stewart. *see* Udall, Stewart L.

Udall, Stewart L.
xUdall, Stewart.
The Energy Balloon. McGraw.

Uddgren, Carl Gustaf, 1865-1927
xUddgren, Gustaf.
Strindberg the Man. Haskell.

Uddgren, Gustaf. *see* Uddgren, Carl Gustaf.

Ude, Louis E. *see* Ude, Louis Eustache.

Ude, Louis Eustache.
xUde, Louis E.
The French Cook. Arco.

Udell, Jon G.
xUdell, Jon G.
The Economics of the American Newspaper.
Hastings.

Uden, Grant.
xUden, Grant.
Dictionary of Chivalry. T Y Crowell.
ed. Longman Illustrated Companion to World
History. Longman.

Uden, Peter C.
xUden, Peter C.
ed. Analytical Chemistry of Liquid Fuel
Sources: Tar Sands, Oil Shale, Coal &
Petroleum. Am Chemical.

Udenfriend, Sidney, 1918-
xUdenfriend, Sidney.
Fluorescence Assay in Biology & Medicine.
Acad Pr.

Udis, Bernard.
xUdis, Bernard.
From Guns to Butter: Technology
Organizations & Reduced Military Spending
in Western Europe. Ballinger Pub.

Udo, Reuben K.
xUdo, Reuben K.
A Comprehensive Geography of West Africa.
Holmes & Meier.
Geographical Regions of Nigeria. U of Cal Pr.

Udokang, Okon.
xUdokang, Okon.

Succession of New States to International
Treaties. Oceana.

Udolf, Roy.
xUdolf, Roy.
The College Instructor's Guide to Teaching &
Academia. Nelson-Hall.
Logic Design for Behavioral Scientists.
Nelson-Hall.

Udovitch, Abraham L.
xUdovitch, Abraham L.
Partnership & Profit in Medieval Islam.
Princeton U Pr.

Udry, J. R. *see* Udry, J. Richard.

Udry, J. Richard.
xUdry, J. R.
The Media & Family Planning. Ballinger Pub.
xUdry, Richard J.
The Media & Family Planning. Carolina Pop
Ctr.

Udry, Janice (May).
xUdry, Janice M.
Angie. Har-Row.
Glenda. Archway.
Glenda. PB.
Let's Be Enemies. Har-Row.
Let's Be Enemies. Schol Bk Serv.
Mary Jo's Grandmother. A Whitman.

Udry, Janice M. *see* Udry, Janice (May).

Udry, Janice May.
xUdry, Janice M.
Oh No, Cat!. Coward.
Sunflower Garden. Harvey.

Udry, Richard J. *see* Udry, J. Richard.

Udwadia, F. E. *see* Udwadia, Farokh E.

Udwadia, Farokh E.
xUdwadia, F. E.
Pulmonary Eosinophilia. S Karger.

Udy, Stanley H, 1928-
xUdy, Stanley H.
Organization of Work: A Comparative Analysis
of Production Among Nonindustrial Peoples.
HRAFP.

Uebele-Kallhardt, B. M.
xUebele-Kallhardt, B. M.
Human Oocytes & Their Chromosomes: An
Atlas. Springer-Verlag.

Ueda, Makato. *see* Ueda, Makoto.

Ueda, Makoto, 1931-
xUeda, Makato.
Compiled by Modern Japanese Haiku: An
Anthology. U of Toronto Pr.
xUeda, Makoto.
Modern Japanese Writers and the Nature of
Literature. Stanford U Pr.

Ueda, Y. *see* Ueda, Yasushi.

Ueda, Yasushi.
xUeda, Y.
ed. Current Research in Nephrology in Japan.
S Karger.

Uehara, Toyoaki.
xUehara, Toyoaki.
Fundamentals of Japanese. Ind U Pr.

Uelsmann, Jerry, 1934-
xUelsmann, Jerry.
Silver Meditations. Morgan.

Uffelman, Larry K.
xUffelman, Larry K.
Charles Kingsley. Twayne.

Ugarte, Manuel.
xUgarte, Manuel.
Destiny of a Continent. AMS Pr.

Ugural, A. C.
xUgural, A. C.
Advanced Strength & Applied Elasticity.
Elsevier.

Uhde, Wilhelm, 1874-1947
xUhde, Wilhelm.
Five Primitive Masters. Arno.

Uhl, Harold J.
xUhl, Harold J.

The Gospel for Children: Object Messages
from the Gospel of Mark. Augsburg.

Uhl, Kenneth P.
xUhl, Kenneth P.
Marketing Research: Information Systems &
Decision Making. Krieger.

Uhley, Herman N.
xUhley, Herman N.
Vector Electrocardiography. Lippincott.

Uhlig, Herbert H. *see* Uhlig, Herbert Henry.

Uhlig, Herbert Henry, 1907-
xUhlig, Herbert H.
Corrosion & Corrosion Control: An
Introduction to Corrosion Science &
Engineering. Wiley.

Uhlin, Donald M.
xUhlin, Donald M.
Art for Exceptional Children. Wm C Brown.

Uhlinger, Susan. *see* Uhlinger, Susan J.

Uhlinger, Susan J., 1942-
xUhlinger, Susan.
Soybean Cooking. Greene.

Uhlman, Fred.
xUhlman, Fred.
Reunion. FS&G.
Reunion. Penguin.

Uhlman, Thomas M.
xUhlman, Thomas M.
Racial Justice: Black Judges & Defendants in
an Urban Trial Court. Lexington Bks.

Uhlmann, Dietrich.
xUhlmann, Dietrich.
Hydrobiology: A Text for Engineers &
Scientists. Wiley.

Uhlmann, E. *see* Uhlmann, Erich.

Uhlmann, Erich, 1904-
xUhlmann, E.
Power Transmission by Direct Current.
Springer-Verlag.

Uhnak, Dorothy.
xUhnak, Dorothy.
The Bait. PB.

Uhr, Jonathan W.
xUhr, Jonathan W.
ed. Immunologic Intervention. Acad Pr.

Uhr, Leonard. *see* Uhr, Leonard Merrick.

Uhr, Leonard Merrick, 1927-
xUhr, Leonard.
Pattern Recognition, Learning & Thought:
Computer-Programmed Models of Higher
Mental Processes. P-H.

Uhran, Mark.
xUhran, Mark.
Solar Energy for the Northeast. Peregrine Pr.

Uhrbrock, Richard S. *see* Uhrbrock, Richard Stephen.

Uhrbrock, Richard Stephen, 1894-
xUhrbrock, Richard S.
Analysis of the Downey Will-Temperament
Tests. AMS Pr.

Uitti, Karl D.
xUitti, Karl D.
Linguistics & Literary Theory. Norton.
Story, Myth & Celebration in Old French
Narrative Poetry 1050-1200. Princeton U Pr.

Ukena, Ann S. *see* Ukena, Ann Seymour.

Ukena, Ann Seymour, 1940-
xUkena, Ann S.
Statistics Today. Har-Row.

Ukers, William H. *see* Ukers, William Harrison.

Ukers, William Harrison, 1873-1954
xUkers, William H.
All About Coffee. Gale.

Ulam, Adam B. *see* Ulam, Adam Bruno.

Ulam, Adam Bruno, 1922-
xUlam, Adam B.
A History of Soviet Russia. HR&W.
Ideologies & Illusions: Revolutionary Thought
from Herzen to Solzhenitsyn. Harvard U Pr.

Ulam, S. M. *see* Ulam, Stanislaw M.

Ulam, Stanislaw M.
  xUlam, S. M.
    Adventures of a Mathematician. Scribner.
Ulanoff, Stanley M.
  xUlanoff, Stanley M.
    Advertising in America: An Introduction to
      Persuasive Communication. Hastings.
Ulanov, Ann. see Ulanov, Ann Belford.
Ulanov, Ann Belford.
  xUlanov, Ann.
    Religion & the Unconscious. Westminster.
Ulanov, Barry.
  xUlanov, Barry.
    A Handbook of Jazz. Greenwood.
    A History of Jazz in America. Da Capo.
Ulbrich, Holley H.
  xUlbrich, Holley H.
    Managing Personal Finance. Business Pubns.
Ulc, Otto.
  xUlc, Otto.
    Politics in Czechoslovakia. W H Freeman.
Uldall, Robert.
  xUldall, Robert.
    Renal Nursing. Mosby.
Uldricks, Teddy J.
  xUldricks, Teddy J.
    Diplomacy & Ideology: The Origins of Soviet
      Foreign Relations, 1917-1930. Sage.
Ulene, Art.
  xUlene, Art.
    Help Yourself to Health: A Health Information
      & Services Directory. Putnam.
Ulett, George A. see Ulett, George Andrew.
Ulett, George Andrew.
  xUlett, George A.
    A Synopsis of Contemporary Psychiatry.
      Mosby.
ULI Research Division. see Urban Land Institute.
  Research Division.
Ulich, Robert, 1890-
  xUlich, Robert.
    ed. Education & the Idea of Mankind. U of
      Chicago Pr.
    Education of Nations: A Comparison in
      Historical Perspective. Harvard U Pr.
    Fundamentals of Democratic Education: An
      Introduction to Educational Philosophy.
      Norwood Edns.
    History of Religious Education: Documents &
      Interpretations from the Judaeo - Christian
      Tradition. NYU Pr.
    Progress or Disaster?: From the Bourgeois to
      the World Citizen. NYU Pr.
Ullendorff, Edward.
  xUllendorff, Edward.
    The Ethiopians: An Introduction to Country &
      People. Oxford U Pr.
Ullerich, Curtis.
  xUllerich, Curtis.
    Rural Employment & Manpower Problems in
      China. M E Sharpe.
Ullman, Berthold L. see Ullman, Berthold Louis.
Ullman, Berthold Louis, 1882-
  xUllman, Berthold L.
    Ancient Writing & Its Influence. Cooper Sq.
Ullman, Betty E.
  xUllman, Betty E.
    The Voluptuaries. Putnam.
Ullman, Edward L. see Ullman, Edward Louis.
Ullman, Edward Louis, 1912-
  xUllman, Edward L.
    American Commodity Flow: A Geographical
      Interpretation of Rail & Water Traffic Based
      on Principles of Spatial Interchange. U of
      Wash Pr.
Ullman, Gerald. see Ullman, Gerald H.
Ullman, Gerald H.
  xUllman, Gerald.

Ocean Freight Forwarder, the Exporter & the
  Law. Cornell Maritime.
Ullman, James M. see Ullman, James Michael.
Ullman, James Michael.
  xUllman, James M.
    Good Night Irene. S&S.
Ullman, James R. see Ullman, James Ramsey.
Ullman, James Ramsey, 1907-1971
  xUllman, James R.
    Banner in the Sky. Archway.
Ullman, Jeffrey D., 1942-
  xUllman, Jeffrey D.
    Principles of Database Systems. Computer Sci.
Ullman, Leslie.
  xUllman, Leslie.
    Natural Histories. Yale U Pr.
Ullman, Montague.
  xUllman, Montague.
    Working with Dreams. Delacorte.
    Working with Dreams. Dell.
Ullman, Pierre L., 1929-
  xUllman, Pierre L.
    Mariano De Larra & Spanish Political
      Rhetoric. U of Wis Pr.
Ullman, Shimon.
  xUllman, Shimon.
    The Interpretation of Visual Motion. MIT Pr.
Ullmann, J. R., 1936-
  xUllmann, J. R.
    Pattern Recognition Techniques. Crane-Russak
      Co.
Ullmann, John E.
  xUllmann, John E.
    ed. The Suburban Economic Network:
      Economic Activity, Resource Use, & the
      Great Sprawl. Praeger.
Ullmann, Liv.
  xUllmann, Liv.
    Changing. Bantam.
    Changing. Knopf.
Ullmann, Stephen.
  xUllmann, Stephen.
    The Image in the Modern French Novel: Gide,
      Alain-Fournier, Proust, Camus. Greenwood.
    Style in the French Novel. Biblio Dist.
Ullmann, Walter, 1910-
  xUllmann, Walter.
    Law & Politics in the Middle Ages: An
      Introduction to the Sources of Medieval
      Political Ideas. Cornell U Pr.
    The Origins of the Great Schism: A Study in
      Fourteenth-Century Ecclesiastical History.
      Shoe String.
Ullyot, James R.
  xUllyot, James R.
    Moneymaking in the Twin Cities Local
      Over-the-Counter Marketplace. Am Natl
      Pub.
Ullyot, Joan, 1940-
  xUllyot, Joan.
    Running Free: A Book for Women Runners &
      Their Friends. Putnam.
    Women's Running. Anderson World.
Ulman, Elinor.
  xUlman, Elinor.
    ed. Art Therapy: In Theory & Practice.
      Schocken.
    ed. Art Therapy Viewpoints. Schocken.
Ulmen, G. L.
  xUlmen, G. L.
    Science of Society: Toward an Understanding
      of the Life & Work of Karl August Wittfogel.
      Mouton.
Ulmer, Donald E.
  xUlmer, Donald E.
    Approved Practices in Raising & Handling
      Horses. Interstate.
Ulmer, Gregory L., 1944-
  xUlmer, Gregory L.

The Legend of Herostratus: Existential Envy in
  Rousseau & Unamuno. U Presses Fla.
Ulmer, Melville J. see Ulmer, Melville Jack.
Ulmer, Melville Jack, 1911-
  xUlmer, Melville J.
    The Economic Theory of Cost of Living Index
      Numbers. AMS Pr.
Ulrich, Celeste.
  xUlrich, Celeste.
    The Social Matrix of Physical Education.
      Greenwood.
Ulrich, Henri, 1925-
  xUlrich, Henri.
    Chemistry of Imidoyl Halides. Plenum Pub.
Ulrich, Homer, 1906-
  xUlrich, Homer.
    The Education of a Concert-Goer. Greenwood.
    History of Music & Musical Style. HarBraceJ.
    A Survey of Choral Music. HarBraceJ.
Ulrichs, Carl H. see Ulrichs, Carl Heinrich.
Ulrichs, Carl Heinrich, d. 1894
  xUlrichs, Carl H.
    Forschungen Uber das Ratsel der
      Mannmannlichen Liebe. Arno.
Ultan, Lloyd, 1929-
  xUltan, Lloyd.
    Music Theory: Problems & Practices in the
      Middle Ages & Renaissance. U of Minn Pr.
Ultimacc Systems, Inc.
  xUltimacc Systems Inc.
    System Three Sixty - Dos Console: A
      Self-Instructional Guide. P-H.
Ulyatt, Kenneth, 1920-
  xUlyatt, Kenneth.
    North Against the Sioux. Penguin.
Uman, Martin A.
  xUman, Martin A
    Introduction to Plasma Physics. McGraw.
    Understanding Lightning. Bek Tech.
Umans, Shelley.
  xUmans, Shelley.
    Designs for Reading Programs. Tchrs Coll.
Umen, Samuel.
  xUmen, Samuel.
    Nature of Judaism. Philos Lib.
Uminski, Sigmund H.
  xUminski, Sigmund H.
    Tales of Early Poland. Endurance.
Umphlett, Wiley L. see Umphlett, Wiley Lee.
Umphlett, Wiley Lee, 1931-
  xUmphlett, Wiley L.
    Mythmakers of the American Dream: The
      Nostalgic Vision in Popular Culture. A S
      Barnes.
Umstead, David A., 1942-
  xUmstead, David A.
    Investment Strategies for Doctors. P-H.
UNA-USA National Policy Panel. see Una-Usa National
  Policy Panel on the United Nations in the 1970'S.
**UNA-USA National Policy Panel on Science and
Technology in an Era of Interdependence.**
  xUNA-USA National Policy Panel.
    Science & Technology in an Era of
      Independence. UNA-USA.
**UNA-USA National Policy Panel on the United Nations
in the 1970's.**
  xUNA-USA National Policy Panel.
    The United Nations in the 1970's: A Strategy
      for a Unique Era in the Affairs of Nations.
      UNA-USA.
Unamuno y Jugo, Miguel de, 1864-1936
  xUnamuno y Jugo, Miguel De.
    Perplexities & Paradoxes. Greenwood.
Uncle Ben's Inc.
  xUncle Ben's Inc.
    Rice Cookery. H P Bks.
Underdown, David.
  xUnderdown, David.

Somerset in the Civil War & Interregnum. Shoe
String.
Underdown, G. W.
xUnderdown, G. W.
Practical Fire Precautions. Beekman Pubs.
Underhill, A. B. see Underhill, Anne Barbara.
Underhill, Anne B. see Underhill, Anne Barbara.
Underhill, Anne Barbara, 1920-
xUnderhill, A. B.
The Early Type Stars. Kluwer Boston.
xUnderhill, Anne B.
The Early Type Stars. Gordon.
Underhill, Evelyn, 1875-1941
xUnderhill, Evelyn.
The Essentials of Mysticism & Other Essays.
AMS Pr.
Practical Mysticism. Dutton.
Worship. Hyperion Conn.
Underhill, John G. see Underhill, John Garrett.
Underhill, John Garrett, 1876-
xUnderhill, John G.
Spanish Literature in the England of the
Tudors. AMS Pr.
Spanish Literature in the England of the
Tudors. Gordon Pr.
Underhill, Miriam.
xUnderhill, Miriam.
Give Me the Hills. Chatham Pr.
Underhill, Ralph.
xUnderhill, Ralph.
Occupational Values & Post-College Career
Change. NORC.
Underhill, Raymond A. see Underhill, Raymond Alden.
Underhill, Raymond Alden.
xUnderhill, Raymond A.
Laboratory Anatomy of the Frog. Wm C
Brown.
Underhill, Robert.
xUnderhill, Robert.
Turkish Grammar. MIT Pr.
Underhill, Robert G.
xUnderhill, Robert G.
Teaching Elementary School Mathematics.
Merrill.
Underhill, Ruth. see Underhill, Ruth Murray.
Underhill, Ruth M.
xUnderhill, Ruth.
First Penthouse Dwellers of America. Gannon.
Underhill, Ruth M. see Underhill, Ruth Murray.
Underhill, Ruth Murray, 1884-
xUnderhill, Ruth.
Papago Woman. HR&W.
Pueblo Crafts. Filter.
xUnderhill, Ruth M.
Indians of Southern California. AMS Pr.
Indians of the Pacific Northwest. AMS Pr.
Navajos. U of Okla Pr.
The Northern Paiute Indians of California &
Nevada. AMS Pr.
A Papago Calendar Record. AMS Pr.
Papago Indian Religion. AMS Pr.
The Papago Indians of Arizona & Their
Relatives the Pima. AMS Pr.
Pueblo Crafts. AMS Pr.
Underwager, Ralph C.
xUnderwager, Ralph C.
I Hurt Inside: A Christian Psychologist Helps
You Understand & Overcome Feelings of
Fear, Frustration, & Failure. Augsburg.
Underwood, Benton. see Underwood, Benton J.
Underwood, Benton J.
xUnderwood, Benton.
Experimentation in Psychology. Wiley.
xUnderwood, Benton J.
Psychological Research. P-H.
Underwood, Betty.
xUnderwood, Betty.
The Forge & the Forest. HM.
Tamarack Tree. HM.
Underwood, E. E. see Underwood, Erwin E.

Underwood, Erwin E., 1918-
xUnderwood, E. E.
Quantitative Stereology. A-W.
Underwood, G.
xUnderwood, G.
Attention & Memory. Pergamon.
Underwood, Jane H. see Underwood, Jane Hainline.
Underwood, Jane Hainline.
xUnderwood, Jane H.
Human Variation & Human Microevolution.
P-H.
Underwood, John, 1934-
xUnderwood, John.
The Death of an American Game: The Crisis
in Football. Little.
Underwood, Joseph H. see Underwood, Joseph Harding.
Underwood, Joseph Harding, 1874-
xUnderwood, Joseph H.
Distribution of Ownership. AMS Pr.
Underwood, Lamar.
xUnderwood, Lamar.
ed. Lamar Underwood's Bass Almanac.
Doubleday.
Underwood, Michael, 1916-
xUnderwood, Michael.
Anything but the Truth. St Martin.
A Clear Case of Suicide. St Martin.
The Fatal Trip. St Martin.
Murder with Malice. St Martin.
Smooth Justice. St Martin.
Victim of Circumstance. St Martin.
Underwood, Peter.
xUnderwood, Peter.
The Ghosts of Borley: Annals of the Haunted
Rectory. David & Charles.
Undset, Sigrid, 1882-1949
xUndset, Sigrid.
Happy Times in Norway. Greenwood.
Men, Women & Places. Arno.
Stages on the Road. Arno.
UNESCO. see United Nations Educational, Scientific
and Cultural Organization.
UNESCO-Asian Cultural Center. see Asian Cultural
Centre for Unesco.
Ungar, Frederick.
xUngar, Frederick.
ed. Handbook of Austrian Literature. Ungar.
ed. Practical Wisdom: A Treasury of
Aphorisms and Reflections from the German.
Ungar.
Ungar, Sanford J.
xUngar, Sanford J.
FBI. Little.
Unger. see Unger, Walter P.
Unger, Abraham.
xUnger, Abraham.
Glorious Obsession. Belmont-Tower.
Unger, Carl, 1878-1929
xUnger, Carl.
Principles of Spiritual Science. Anthroposophic.
Unger, E. A. see Unger, Elizabeth A.
Unger, Elizabeth A.
xUnger, E. A.
Computer Science Fundamentals: An
Algorithmic Approach Via Structured
Programming. Merrill.
Unger, F. see Unger, Felix.
Unger, Felix.
xUnger, F.
ed. Assisted Circulation. Springer-Verlag.
Unger, Frederic W. see Unger, Frederic William.
Unger, Frederic William.
xUnger, Frederic W.
The Authentic History of the War Between
Russia & Japan. Scholarly Res Inc.
Unger, H. G. see Unger, Hans-Georg.
Unger, Hans-Georg, 1926-
xUnger, H. G.

Introduction to Quantum Electronics.
Pergamon.
Planar Optical Waveguides & Fibres. Oxford U
Pr.
Unger, I. see Unger, Irwin.
Unger, Irwin.
xUnger, I.
Greenback Era: A Social & Political History of
American Finance, 1865-1879. Princeton U
Pr.
xUnger, Irwin.
These United States: The Questions of Our
Past. Little.
The Vulnerable Years: The United States,
1896-1917. NYU Pr.
Unger, June D.
xUnger, June D.
Ear, Nose & Throat Radiology. Saunders.
Unger, Leonard.
xUnger, Leonard.
Donne's Poetry & Modern Criticism. Russell.
T. S. Eliot. U of Minn Pr.
Unger, Maurice. see Unger, Maurice Albert.
Unger, Maurice Albert, 1917-
xUnger, Maurice.
How to Invest in Real Estate. McGraw.
Unger, Merrill. see Unger, Merrill Frederick.
Unger, Merrill F. see Unger, Merrill Frederick.
Unger, Merrill Frederick, 1909-
xUnger, Merrill.
Unger's Bible Dictionary. Moody.
Unger's Guide to the Bible. Tyndale.
xUnger, Merrill F.
Archaeology & the New Testament.
Zondervan.
Archeology & the Old Testament. Zondervan.
The Baptism & Gifts of the Holy Spirit.
Moody.
Principles of Expository Preaching. Zondervan.
Unger, Peter. see Unger, Peter K.
Unger, Peter K.
xUnger, Peter.
Ignorance: A Case for Scepticism. Oxford U
Pr.
Unger, Rhoda K. see Unger, Rhoda Kesler.
Unger, Rhoda Kesler.
xUnger, Rhoda K.
Female & Male: Psychological Perspectives.
Har-Row.
Unger, Richard, 1939-
xUnger, Richard.
Holderlin's Major Poetry: The Dialectics of
Unity. Ind U Pr.
Unger, Roberto M. see Unger, Roberto Mangabeira.
Unger, Roberto Mangabeira.
xUnger, Roberto M.
Law in Modern Society: Toward a Criticism of
Social Theory. Free Pr.
Unger, Walter P., 1939-
xUnger.
Hair Transplantation. Dekker.
xUnger, Walter P.
The Intelligent Man's Guide to Hair
Transplants & Other Methods of Hair
Replacement. Contemp Bks.
Ungerer, Tomi, 1931-
xUngerer, Tomi.
illus. I Am Papa Snap & These Are My
Favorite No Such Stories. Har-Row.
illus. Moon Man. Har-Row.
No Kiss for Mother. Dell.
illus. No Kiss for Mother. Har-Row.
Orlando the Brave Vulture. Har-Row.
Ungerleider, J. Thomas.
xUngerleider, J. Thomas.
ed. The Problems & Prospects of LSD. C C
Thomas.
Ungerman, Florence W. see Ungerman, Florence
Winship.

Ungerman, Florence Winship.
    xUngerman, Florence W.
        Centerville Shipmasters & Seafaring Days. W S
          Sullwold.

Ungnade, Herbert E. *see* Ungnade, Herbert Ernst.

Ungnade, Herbert Ernst, 1911-
    xUngnade, Herbert E.
        Guide to the New Mexico Mountains. U of
          NM Pr.

Ungrue, Dawn.
    xUngrue, Dawn.
        Conferencing in California: A Guide to
          Affordable Retreats & Centers. Impact Pubs
          Cal.

UNICEF. *see* United Nations. Children's Fund.

Union of American Hebrew Congregations.
    xUnion of American Hebrew Congregations.
        Spiritual Resistance: Art from the
          Concentration Camps 1940-1945. Jewish
          Pubn.

Union of Concerned Scientists.
    xTheUnion of Concerned Scientists.
        The Nuclear Fuel Cycle: A Survey of the
          Public Health, Environmental & National
          Security Aspects of Nuclear Power. MIT Pr.

Unione, Fototeca. *see* Fototeca Unione.

Unitas, John.
    xUnitas, John.
        Improving Health & Performance in the
          Athlete. P-H.
    xUnitas, Johnny.
        Pro Quarterback: My Own Story. S&S.

Unitas, Johnny. *see* Unitas, John.

United Empire Loyalist Centennial Committee, Toronto.
    xUnited Empire Loyalist Centennial Committee -
        Toronto.
        Old United Empire Loyalists List. Genealog
          Pub.
    xUnited Empire Loyalists Centennial Committee.
        The Centennial of the Settlement of Upper
          Canada by the United Empire Loyalists,
          1784-1884. Irvington.

United Empire Loyalists Centennial Committee. *see*
    United Empire Loyalist Centennial Committee,
    Toronto.

United Nations. Children's Fund.
    xUNICEF.
        Neglected Years: Early Childhood. US Comm
          UNICEF.

**United Nations. Economic Commission for Latin
America.**
    xEconomic Commission for Latin America.
        Development Problems in Latin America: An
          Analysis by the United Nations Economic
          Commission for Latin America. U of Tex Pr.

**United Nations Educational, Scientific and Cultural
Organization.**
    xUNESCO.
        The Conservation of Cities. St Martin.
        Cumulative Index to English Translations,
          1948-1968. G K Hall.
        Human Rights, Comments & Interpretations: A
          Symposium. Greenwood.
        The Influence of the Cinema on Children &
          Adolescents. Greenwood.
        International Directory of Adult Education.
          Greenwood.
        International Register of Current Team
          Research in the Social Sciences, 1950-1952.
          Greenwood.
        Interrelations of Cultures: Their Contribution to
          International Understanding. Greenwood.
        News Agencies, Their Structure & Operation.
          Greenwood.
        ed. La Pensee Scientifique: Interaction.
          Mouton.
        Planning Buildings & Facilities for Higher
          Education. DH&R.
        Press, Film, Radio. Arno.
        Race Concept, Results of an Inquiry.
          Greenwood.
        Race, Science, & Society. Columbia U Pr.
        Seven Hundred Science Experiments for
          Everyone. Doubleday.
        Teaching of Modern Languages. Greenwood.
        Television: A World Survey. Arno.
        Ten Years of Films on Ballet & Classical
          Dance, 1955-1965,Catalogue. Unipub.
        Trade Barriers to Knowledge: A Manual of
          Regulations Affecting Educational, Scientific
          & Cultural Materials. Greenwood.
        The University Teaching of Social Sciences.
          Sociology, Social Psychology, &
          Anthropology. Greenwood.
        Urbanization in Latin America. Columbia U Pr.
        ed. World Guide to Library Schools & Training
          Courses in Documentation. Shoe String.
        World Illiteracy at Mid-Century, a Statistical
          Study. Greenwood.

United Nations. Statistical Office.
    xStatistical Office of the United Nations.
        ed. World Trade Annual 1972. Walker & Co.

US - Italy Seminar on Variable Structure Systems, 2nd.
    see United States-Italy Seminar on Variable Structure
    Systems, 2nd, Corvallis, Oregon, 1974.

United States. Agricultural Research Service.
    xAgricultural Research Service of the U. S.
    Department of Agriculture.
        Common Weeds of the United States. Peter
          Smith.

United States. Alien Property Custodian.
    xU.S. Office of the Alien Property Custodian.
        Alien Property Custodian Report: A Detailed
          Report by the Alien Property Custodian of
          All Proceedings.. Arno.
        Annual Reports: March 11, 1942 to June 30,
          1943; for the Fiscal Year Ending June 30,
          1944; for the Fiscal Year Ending June 30,
          1945; for the Fiscal Year Ending June 30,
          1946.. Arno.

**United States. Argonne National Laboratory, Lemont,
Illinois. Solar Energy Group.**
    xSolar Energy Group, Los Alamos Scientific
    Laboratory.
        Passive Solar Heating & Cooling Conference &
          Workshop Proceedings, 1976. Solar Energy
          Info.

United States. Army.
    xU.S. Army.
        Advisor Handbook for Counterinsurgency:
          Field Manual 31-73. Paladin Ent.
        Basic Criminal Investigations. Paladin Ent.
        Boobytraps: FM 5-13. Paladin Ent.
        Civil Disturbances Handbook for Small Unit
          Leaders. Paladin Ent.
        Deal the First Deadly Blow. Paladin Ent.
        Physical Security. Paladin Ent.
        Stoner 63 Weapons Systems. Paladin Ent.

**United States. Board of Governors of the Federal
Reserve System.**
    xBoard of Governers, Federal Reserve System.
        All-Bank Statistics, United States, 1896-1955.
          Arno.

United States. Bureau of Corporations.
    xU. S. Department of Commerce & Labor.
        Report of the Commissioner of Corporations
          on the Petroleum Industry: Foreign Trade,
          Pt. 3. Arno.

United States. Bureau of Labor.
    xU.S. Bureau of Labor.
        Slums of Baltimore, Chicago, New York &
          Philadelphia. Negro U Pr.

United States. Bureau of Naval Personnel.
    xBureau of Naval Personnel.
        Basic Construction Techniques for Houses &
          Small Buildings Simply Explained. Peter
          Smith.
        Compiled by Basic Optics & Optical
          Instruments. Peter Smith.
        Digital Computer Basics. Peter Smith.
        Tools & Their Uses. Peter Smith.
    xU. S. Navy.
        Basic Electronics. Dover.
    xU. S. Navy (Bureau of Naval Personnel).
        Basic Data Processing. Dover.
        Basic Electricity. Dover.
        Basic Machines & How They Work. Dover.
        Basic Optics & Optical Instruments. Dover.
        Digital Computer Basics. Dover.
        Second-Level Basic Electronics. Dover.
        Tools & Their Uses. Dover.
    xU. S. Navy Bureau of Naval Personnel.
        Basic Construction Techniques for Houses &
          Small Buildings. Dover.
        Basic Electricity. Gannon.

United States. Bureau of the Census.
    xBureau Of The Census.
        ed. Government Dossier: An Inventory of
          Government Information About Individuals.
          Arno.
    xBureau of the Census, U.S. Department of
    Commerce.
        Housing Construction Statistics, 1889 to 1964.
          Arno.
    xU.S. Bureau of the Census, 1900.
        Abstract of the Fourteenth Census of the
          United States, 1920. Arno.
        Abstract of the Twelfth Census of the United
          States, 1900. Arno.
        Census of Population, 1950. Arno.
        Fifteenth Census of the United States, 1930.
          Arno.
        Nineteen-Seventy Census of Population:
          Characteristics of the Population, Part I,
          United States Summary. Arno.
        Population, Nineteen Sixty. Arno.
        Sixteenth Census of the United States, 1940.
          Arno.
        Thirteenth Census of the United States Taken
          in the Year 1910. Arno.

**United States Cabinet Committee on Opportunity for
the Spanish Speaking.**
    xU.S. Cabinet Committee on Opportunities for
    Spanish Speaking People.
        The Spanish Speaking in the United States: A
          Guide to Materials. Blaine Ethridge.

United States Cartridge Company.
    xU.S. Cartridge Company.

U.S. Cartridge Company Collection of
 Firearms. Sycamore Island.
United States. Census Office.
 xU.S. Census Office.
 Street & Electric Railways. Arno.
United States. Census Office. 1st Census, 1790.
 xU.S. Census Office, 1790.
 Return of the Whole Number Persons Within
  the Several Districts of the United States.
  Arno.
U.S. Census Office, 1790. *see* United States. Census
 Office. 1st Census, 1790.
U.S. Census Office, 1800. *see* United States. Census
 Office. 2nd Census, 1800.
U.S. Census Office, 1810. *see* United States. Census
 Office. 3rd Census, 1810.
U.S. Census Office, 1820. *see* United States. Census
 Office. 4th Census, 1820.
U.S. Census Office, 1830. *see* United States. Census
 Office. 5th Census, 1830.
U.S. Census Office, 1840. *see* United States. Census
 Office. 6th Census, 1840.
U.S. Census Office, 1850. *see* United States. Census
 Office. 7th Census, 1850.
U.S. Census Office, 1860. *see* United States. Census
 Office. 8th Census, 1860.
U. S. Census Office, 1870. *see* United States. Census
 Office. 9th Census, 1870.
U.S. Census Office, 1890. *see* United States. Census
 Office. 11th Census, 1890.
United States. Census Office. 2nd Census, 1800.
 xU.S. Census Office, 1800.
 Return of the Whole Number of Persons
  Within the Several Districts of the United
  States. Arno.
United States. Census Office. 3rd Census, 1810.
 xU.S. Census Office, 1810.
 Aggregate Amount of Each Description of
  Persons. Arno.
United States. Census Office. 4th Census, 1820.
 xU.S. Census Office, 1820.
 Census for 1820. Arno.
United States. Census Office. 5th Census, 1830.
 xU.S. Census Office, 1830.
 Abstract of the Returns of the Fifth Census.
  Arno.
United States. Census Office. 6th Census, 1840.
 xU.S. Census Office, 1840.
 Compendium of the Enumeration of the
  Inhabitants. Arno.
United States. Census Office. 7th Census, 1850.
 xU.S. Census Office, 1850.
 The Seventh Census of the United States.
  Arno.
United States. Census Office. 8th Census, 1860.
 xU.S. Census Office, 1860.
 Statistics of the United States. Arno.
United States. Census Office. 9th Census, 1870.
 xU. S. Census Office, 1870.
 A Compendium of the Ninth Census. Arno.
United States. Census Office. 10th Census, 1880.
 xU. S.Census Office, 1880.
 Compendium of the Tenth Census. Arno.
United States. Census Office. 11th Census, 1890.
 xU.S. Census Office, 1890.
 Abstract of the Eleventh Census. Arno.
United States. Central Inteligence Agency.
 xCentral Intelligence Agency.
 CIA Ammunition & Explosives Supply Catalog.
  Paladin Ent.
 CIA Explosives for Sabotage Manual. Paladin
  Ent.
 CIA Flaps & Seals Manual. Paladin Ent.
 CIA Special Weapons Supply Catalog. Paladin
  Ent.
United States. Children's Bureau.
 xU.S. Children's Bureau.
 Juvenile Courts at Work. AMS Pr.
United States. Commission on Campus Unrest.
 xCommission On Campus Unrest.

Report of the President's Commission on
 Campus Unrest. Avon.
U. S. Commissioner of Education. *see* United States.
 Office of Education. (Public Libraries).
United States Conference of Mayors.
 xU.S. Conference of Mayors.
 The Employee Assistance Programs: Toward a
  More Productive Work Force. Hazelden.
United States. Congress.
 xDepartment of Energy.
 Solar Heating & Cooling: Commercial Buildings
  Demonstration Project Summaries. Solar
  Energy Info.
 xU. S. Congress.
 American State Papers. Arno.
 U. S. Congress House: Report...Washington,
  1813. Garland Pub.
United States. Congress. House.
 xU. S. Congress, House of Representatives.
 The Overseas Private Investment Corporation:
  A Critical Analysis. Arno.
 Report of the Board of Fortifications or Other
  Defenses Appointed by the President of the
  U. S. Under the Provisions of the the Act of
  Congress, Approved March 3, 1885 & Plates
  to Accompany the Report. Arno.
 xU.S. House of Representatives.
 Affairs in the Late Insurrectionary States.
  Arno.
 California & New Mexico: Message from the
  President of the United States, January 21,
  1850. Arno.
 Digested Summary & Alphabetical List of
  Private Claims Which Have Been Presented
  to House of Rep. 1st-35th Congr.. Genealog
  Pub.
 The Existing Laws of the U. S. of a General &
  Permanent Character, & Relating to the
  Survey & Disposition of the Public Domain,
  December 1, 1880. Arno.
 Ku Klux Klan: 67th Congress, First Session,
  House Committee on Rules Hearings. Arno.
 Laws of the United States. Arno.
 Memphis Riots & Massacres: Report Submitted
  by E.B. Washburne, 39th Congress First
  Session, House Report No. 101. Arno.
 New Orleans Riots of July Thirtieth, Eighteen
  Sixty-Six: 39th Congress, Second Session,
  House Report No. 16. Arno.
 Small Business Problems in Urban Areas. Arno.
**United States. Congress. House. Committee on Banking
and Currency.**
 xCommittee on Banking & Currency, U. S. Senate,
  1934.
 Stock Exchange Practices. Arno.
 xCommittee On Banking And Currency - Staff
  Report.
 Growth of Unregistered Bank Holding
  Companies: Problems & Prospects. Arno.
 xU.S House Committee on Banking & Currency.
 Demonstration Cities Housing & Urban
  Development & Urban Mass Transit. Arno.
 xU. S. House of Representatives, Committee on
  Banking & Currency.
 Gold Panic Investigation. Arno.
**United States. Congress. House. Committee on Banking,
Currency and Housing.**
 xU. S. House Committee on Banking, Currency &
  Housing.
 The New York City Fiscal Crisis. Arno.
**United States. Congress. House. Committee on
Commerce.**
 xUnited States 27th Congress, 3rd Session, 1842.
 Report of Mr. Kennedy, of Maryland. Arno.
**United States. Congress. House. Committee on
Education and Labor. General Subcommittee on
Education.**
 xU. S. House of Representatives, Committee on
  Education & Labor, General Subcommittee on
  Education.

Bilingual Education Programs, Hearings. Arno.
**United States. Congress. House. Committee on
Government Operations.**
 xU.S. House Committee on Government
  Operations.
 Federal-State-Local Relations: Federal
  Grants-in Aid State & Local Officials. Arno.
**United States. Congress. House. Committee on Indian
Affairs.**
 xU. S. Congress. House. Commitee on Indian
  Affairs.
 Readjustment of Indian Affairs: Hearings. AMS
  Pr.
**United States. Congress. House. Committee on the
District of Columbia.**
 xUnited States, House of Representatives
  Committee on the District of Columbia.
 Investigation of the Metropolitan Police
  Department. Arno.
U. S. Congress, House of Representatives. *see* United
 States. Congress. House.
**United States. Congress. House. Select Committee on
Small Business.**
 xU. S. House of Representatives, Select Committee
  on Small Business.
 Problems of Small-Business Financing. Arno.
 Status of Small Business in Retail Trade
  (1948-1958). Arno.
**United States. Congress. House. Select Committee on
Small Business. Subcommittee No. 1.**
 xU. S. House of Representatives, Subcommittee
  No. 1 of the Select Committee on Small
  Business.
 Monopolistic & Unfair Trade Practices. Arno.
 Organization & Operation of the Small
  Business Administration. Arno.
 The Organization & Procedures of the Federal
  Regulatory Commissions & Agencies & Their
  Effect on Small Business. Arno.
**United States. Congress. House. Select Committee on
Small Business. Subcommittee. No. 2 on Government
Procurement and Economic Concentration.**
 xUnited States House of Representatives,
  Subcommittee No. 2 of the Select Committee on
  Small Business.
 Definition of "Small Business" Within Meaning
  of Small Business Act of 1953, As Amended.
  Arno.
**United States. Congress. House. Select Committee on
the Memphis Riots.**
 xUnited States 39th Congress, 1st Session,
  1865-1866 House.
 Memphis Riots & Massacres: House Report
  No. 101. Arno.
**United States. Congress. House. Select Committee on
the New Orleans Riots.**
 xUnited States 39th Congress, 2nd Session,
  1866-1867, House.
 Report of the Select Committee on the New
  Orleans Riots: House Report No. 16. Arno.
**United States. Congress. House. Select Committee to
Investigate the Interstate Migration of Destitute
Citizens.**
 xUnited States Congress, House Select Committee
  to Investigate Migration of Destitute Citizens.
 Interstate Migrations: A Report. Da Capo.
**United States. Congress. House. Special Committee on
Victor L. Berger Investigation.**
 xUnited States, 66th Congress, House of
  Representatives, 1st. Session.
 Case of Victor L. Berger of Wisconsin. Da
  Capo.
**United States. Congress. Joint Committee on
Reconstruction.**
 xU. S. 39th Congress 1st Session.

Report of the Joint Committee on
Reconstruction. Arno.
United States. Congress. Joint Committee on the Investigation of the Pearl Harbor Attack.
xU. S. Congress Joint Committee on the
Investigation of the Pearl Harbor Attack.
Investigation of the Pearl Harbor
Attack...Barkley Report. AMS Pr.
xUnited States, 79th Congress, 2nd Session.
Report of the Joint Committee on the
Investigation of the Pearl Harbor Attack. Da
Capo.
United States. Congress. Joint Select Committee on the Condition of Affairs in the Late Insurrectionary States.
xU. S. Congress. Report of the Joint Select
Committee to Inquire into the Condition of
Affairs in the Late Insurrectionary States.
Ku Klux Conspiracy Report. AMS Pr.
U. S. Congress. Report of the Joint Select Committee to
Inquire into the Condition of Affairs in the Late
Insurrectionary States. *see* United States. Congress.
Joint Select Committee on the Condition of Affairs in
the Late Insurrectionary States.
United States. Congress. Joint Special Committee to Inquire into the Condition of the Indian Tribes.
xU. S. Congress Joint Special Committee to
Inquire into the Condition of the Indian Tribes.
Condition of the Indian Tribes. Kraus Repr.
United States. Congress. Senate.
xU. S. Congress, Senate.
American Petroleum Interests in Foreign
Countries. Arno.
Committee on Foreign Regulations. Somerset
Pub.
Committee on the Judiciary-Juvenile
Delinquency. Somerset Pub.
Committee on Unemployment Problems.
Somerset Pub.
xU.S. Senate.
Invasion at Harper's Ferry: Report Submitted
by J. M. Mason, Select Committee, 36th
Congress, 1st Session, Rep. Com. No. 278.
Arno.
A National Plan for American Forestry. Arno.
The Western Range. Arno.
United States. Congress. Senate. Committee on Banking and Currency. Subcommittee on Small Business.
xU. S. Senate Subcommittee of the Committee on
Banking & Currency.
Credit Needs of Small Business. Arno.
United States. Congress. Senate. Committee on Education and Labor.
xCommittee on Education & Labor, U.S. Senate,
76th Congress, 3rd Session.
Violations of Free Speech & Rights of Labor:
Hearings Before a Subcommittee on
Education & Labor. Arno.
U. S. Congress,(Senate), Committee on Foreign
Relations. *see* United States. Congress. Senate.
Committee on Foreign Relations.
United States. Congress. Senate. Committee on Foreign Relations.
xU. S. Congress,(Senate), Committee on Foreign
Relations.
The United States & the Korean Problem
Documents, 1943-1953. AMS Pr.
United States. Congress. Senate. Committee on Government Operations.
xU.S. Senate Committee on Government
Operations.
Creative Federalism. Arno.
The Effect of Inflation & Recession on State &
Local Governments. Arno.
United States. Congress. Senate. Committee on Labor and Public Welfare.
xU. S. Senate, Committee on Labor & Public
Welfare.

Bilingual Education, Health, & Manpower
Programs. Arno.
Bilingual Educations. Arno.
United States. Congress. Senate. Committee on the District of Columbia.
xSenate Committee On The District Of Columbia.
Crime & Law Enforcement in the District of
Columbia: Hearings & Report. Arno.
xU. S. Senate Committee On The District Of
Columbia.
Women's Suffrage & the Police: Three Senate
Documents. Arno.
United States. Congress. Senate. Committee on the Judiciary.
xUnited States Senate Committee on the Judiciary,
75th Congress, 1st Session.
A Judge on Trial: Hearings on the Nomination
of George Harrold Carswell: Proceedings. Da
Capo.
Reorganization of the Federal Judiciary. Da
Capo.
U. S. Congress-Senate Library. *see* United States.
Congress. Senate. Library.
United States. Congress. Senate. Library.
xU. S. Congress-Senate Library.
Cumulative Index of Congressional Committee
Hearings (Not Confidential in Character)
from Eighty-Sixth Congress (January 7, 1959)
Through Eighty-Seventh Congress (January 3,
1963): Quadrennial Supplement. Greenwood.
xU. S. Senate Library.
ed. Index of Congressional Committee
Hearings Prior to January 3, 1935, in the U.
S. Senate Library. Kraus Repr.
United States. Congress. Senate. Select Committee on Equal Educational Opportunity.
xU. S. Congress, Senate Select Committee on
Equal Opportunity.
Toward Equal Educational Opportunity. AMS
Pr.
xUnites States Senate, Commitee on Equal
Educational Opportunity.
Equal Educational Opportunity for Puerto
Rican Children. Arno.
United States. Congress. Senate. Select Committee on Nutrition and Human Needs.
xU. S. Senate Select Committee on Nutrition &
Human Needs.
Eating in America. MIT Pr.
United States. Congress. Senate. Select Committee on Small Business. Subcommittee on Monopoly and Anticompetitive Activities.
xU. S. Senate, Subcommittee on Monopoly of the
Select Committee on Small Business.
Foreign Legislation Concerning Monopoly &
Cartel Practices. Arno.
United States. Congress. Senate. Special Committee to Investigate Organized Crime in Interstate Commerce.
xSpecial Committee of the Senate to Investigate
Organized Crime in Interstate Commerce.
Reports on Crime Investigation: 82nd
Congress,First Session, Senate Reports. Arno.
xU.S. Senate Special Committee to Investigate
Organized Crime in Interstate Commerce.
Reports on Crime Investigations: Vol. 6 of the
Senate Reports, 82d Congress, 1st Session,
Reports Nos. 141, 307, 725. Arno.
U. S. Constitution Sesquicentennial Commission. *see*
United States. Constitution Sesquincentennial
Commission.
United States. Constitution Sesquincentennial Commission.
xU. S. Constitution Sesquicentennial Commission.
History of the Formation of the Union Under
the Constitution with Liberty Documents &
Report of the Commission. Greenwood.
United States. Constitutional Convention, 1787.
xU. S. Constitutional Convention - 1787.

Debates in the Federal Convention of 1787,
Which Framed the Constitution of the United
States. Greenwood.
To Secure These Blessings: The Great Debates
of the Constitutional Convention of 1787.
Kraus Repr.
United States. Continental Congress.
xU. S. Continental Congress.
Secret Journals of the Acts & Proceedings of
Congress. Johnson Repr.
United States. Copyright Office.
xU. S. Copyright Office.
Copyright in Congress, 1789-1904. Greenwood.
Dramatic Compositions Copyrighted in the
United States, 1870-1916. Johnson Repr.
United States. Council of National Defence.
xU.S. Council of National Defense.
Woman in the War: A Bibliography. Zenger
Pub.
United States. Country Life Commission.
xCommission on Country Life.
Report of the Commission on Country Life.
Arno.
U. S. Delegation to the U N Conference on International
Organization. *see* United States. Delegation to the
United Nations Conference on International
Organization, San Francisco, 1945.
United States. Delegation to the United Nations Conference on International Organization, San Francisco, 1945.
xU. S. Delegation to the U N Conference on
International Organization.
Charter of the United Nations. Greenwood.
Report to the President on the Results of the
San Francisco Conference: 1945 Charter of
the United Nations. Scholarly.
U. S. Delegation to the U. N. Conference on
the International Organizations. Somerset
Pub.
U.S. Dept. of Agriculture. *see* United States. Department
of Agriculture.
U. S. Department of Agriculture Forest Service. *see*
United States. Forest Service.
United States. Department of Agriculture.
xU.S. Department of Agriculture.
Botany Subject Index. G K Hall.
Cheeses of the World. Dover.
Cheeses of the World. Peter Smith.
Climate & Man: Nineteen Forty-One Yearbook
of Agriculture, House Document No. 27,
77th Congress, 1st Session. Gale.
Common Weeds of the United States. Dover.
Complete Guide to Home Canning, Preserving
& Freezing. Dover.
Complete Guide to Home Canning, Preserving,
& Freezing. Peter Smith.
Dictionary Catalog of the National Agricultural
Library, 1862-1965. Rowman.
Growing Vegetables in the Home Garden.
Dover.
Handbook for the Home. Barron.
Handbook of Nutritional Contents of Foods.
Peter Smith.
Handbook of the Nutritional Contents of
Foods. Dover.
How to Buy Food for Economy & Quality.
Dover.
Yearbook of Agriculture, 1939: Food & Life;
Part 1: Human Nutrition. Arno.
Yearbook of Agriculture, 1940: Farmers in a
Changing World. Arno.
xU.S. Dept. of Agriculture.
Encyclopedia of Food & Nutrition. Sterling.
Small-Scale Alcohol Production. Solar Energy
Info.
Vacation Homes & Cabins: Sixteen Complete
Plans. Dover.
United States. Department of Agriculture. Agricultural Economics.

xU. S. Department of Agriculture Bureau of
Agricultural Economics Editors.
  Agricultural Economics Bibliography. Arno.
  Culture of Contemporary Rural Communities.
  Greenwood.
U. S. Dept of Agriculture, Soil Conservation Service. *see*
United States. Soil Conservation Service.
U. S. Dept. of Agriculture-Forest Service. *see* United
States. Forest Service.
U. S. Dept. of Agriculture-Soil Conservation Service &
Forest Service. *see* United States. Forest Service.

United States. Department of Commerce.
  xU. S. Department of Commerce.
  Catalogs of the Bureau of the Census Library,
  Washington, D. C.. G K Hall.
  NBS Metric Practice Guide & Style Manual.
  Am Metric.
  Statistics on American Business Abroad,
  1950-1975: An Original Anthology. Arno.
  U. S. Business Investments in Foreign
  Countries: A Supplement to the Survey of
  Current Business. Arno.
  U. S. Investments in the Latin American
  Economy. Arno.
  xU.S. Dept. of Commerce, Bureau of Foreign &
  Domestic Commerce.
  Investments in Latin America & the British
  West Indies.. Arno.
U. S. Department of Commerce & Labor. *see* United
States. Bureau of Corporations.
U.S. Dept. of Commerce, Bureau of Foreign & Domestic
Commerce. *see* United States. Department of
Commerce.

United States. Dept. of Commerce. Library.
  xU.S. Dept. of Commerce Library.
  Price Sources: Index of Commercial &
  Economic Publications Currently Received in
  the Libraries of the Dept. of Commerce
  Which Contain Current Market Commodity
  Prices. B Franklin.

United States. Dept. of Defense. Defense Supply
Management Agency.
  xDept. of Defense-Defense Supply Agency.
  Defense in-Plant Quality Assurance Program.
  Global Eng.
U. S. Department of Energy. *see* United States. Dept. of
Energy.

United States. Dept. of Energy.
  xDepartment of Energy.
  Fuels from Biomass Program: Program
  Summary. Solar Energy Info.
  Guide to Solar Energy Programs. Solar Energy
  Info.
  National Program for Solar Heating & Cooling
  of Buildings: Annual Report. Solar Energy
  Info.
  National Program Plan for Research &
  Development in Solar Heating & Cooling for
  Buildings, Agricultural, & Industrial
  Applications. Solar Energy Info.
  Solar Energy: A Status Report. Solar Energy
  Info.
  Solar Heating & Cooling: Research &
  Development Project Summaries. Solar
  Energy Info.
  Solar Thermal Power Systems: Annual
  Technical Progress Report. Solar Energy Info.
  Solar Thermal Power Systems Program:
  Program Summary. Solar Energy Info.
  Wind Energy Systems: Program Summary.
  Solar Energy Info.
  xDepartmnet of Energy.
  Photovoltaics Energy Systems: Program
  Summary. Solar Energy Info.
  xU. S. Department of Energy.
  Distributed Energy Systems in California's
  Future. Solar Energy Info.
  The Report of the Alcohol Fuels Policy

Review. Solar Energy Info.
  xU. S. Dept. of Energy.
  Solar Geothermal Electric & Storage Systems
  Program Summary Document. Solar Energy
  Info.
U. S. Dept. of Forestry. *see* United States. Forest
Products Laboratory, Madison, Wisconsin.

United States. Department of Health, Education, and
Welfare.
  xU. S. Department of Health, Education, &
  Welfare.
  Toward a Social Report. U of Mich Pr.
  Work in America: Report of a Special Task
  Force to the Secretary of Health, Education,
  & Welfare. MIT Pr.
  xU. S. Dept of Health, Education & Welfare,
  Public Health Service.
  Vital Statistics Rates in the United States:
  1940-1960. Arno.

United States. Department of Health, Education, and
Welfare. Library.
  xU. S. Department of Health, Education & Welfare
  Library.
  Basic Readings in Social Security. Greenwood.
U. S. Dept of Health, Education & Welfare, Public
Health Service. *see* United States. Department of
Health, Education, and Welfare.

United States. Dept. of Health, Education, and Welfare.
Secretary's Advisory Committee on Automated
Personal Data Systems.
  xU.S. Dept. of Health, Education, & Welfare,
  Advisory Committee on Automated Personal
  Data Systems.
  Records, Computers, & the Rights of Citizens.
  MIT Pr.

United States. Department of Health, Education, and
Welfare. Washington, D.C.
  xU. S. Department of Health, Education and
  Welfare Washington D. C.
  Author-Title Catalog of the Department
  Library. G K Hall.
  Subject Catalog of the Department Library. G
  K Hall.
  Subject Catalog of the Department Library:
  First Supplement. G K Hall.
U. S. Department of Housing & Urban Development. *see*
United States. Dept. of Housing and Urban
Development.

United States. Dept. of Housing and Urban
Development.
  xHousing & Urban Development Dept.
  Your Guide to Energy Saving Home
  Improvements. G&D.
  xU. S. Department of Housing & Urban
  Development.
  Dictionary Catalog of the United States
  Department of Housing & Urban
  Development Library & Information
  Division. G K Hall.
  The Energy-Wise Home Buyer: A Guide to
  Selecting an Energy Efficient Home. Solar
  Energy Info.
  How to Insulate Your Home & Save Fuel.
  Dover.
  How to Insulate Your Home & Save Fuel.
  Peter Smith.
  xU.S. Dept. of HUD.
  Energy Saving Home Improvements. Sterling.
  xU. S. Housing & Home Finance Agency.
  Application of Climatic Data to House Design.
  AMS Pr.
  What People Want When They Buy a House:

A Guide for Architects & Builders Based
  Principally on a Survey. Somerset Pub.
  xU.S.Department of Housing & Urban
  Development, Washington, D.C.
  Dictionary Catalog of the United States
  Department of Housing & Urban
  Development, Library & Information
  Division Second Suppl. G K Hall.
U.S. Dept. of HUD. *see* United States. Dept. of Housing
and Urban Development.

United States. Department of Justice.
  xUnited States, Department of Justice.
  Attorney General's Survey of Release
  Procedures, Vol. 2: Probation. Arno.
  Attorney General's Survey of Release
  Procedures, Vol. 4: Parole. Arno.
  Prejudice & Property, an Historic Brief Against
  Racial Convenants. Greenwood.

United States. Department of Labor.
  xBureau of Statistics, U.S. Dept. of Labor.
  Labor Unionism in American Agriculture.
  Arno.
  xU. S. Department of Labor.
  The American Workers' Fact Book.
  Greenwood.
  Farm Labor Fact Book. Greenwood.
  Jobs, Jobs, Jobs for the College Graduate.
  Barron.
  Migration of Workers. Da Capo.
  Occupational Outlook for Two Year College
  Graduates. Barron.
  xU. S. Department of Labor. Washington D. C.
  Catalog of the United States Department of
  Labor Library (Washington, D.C.). G K Hall.
U. S. Department Of Labor - Division Of Negro
Economics. *see* United States. Department of Labor.
Division of Negro Economics.

United States. Department of Labor. Division of Negro
Economics.
  xU. S. Department Of Labor - Division Of Negro
  Economics.
  Negro at Work During the World War &
  During Reconstruction. Negro U Pr.
  Negro Migration in 1916-1917 - Reports.
  Negro U Pr.
U. S. Department of Labor. Washington D. C. *see* United
States. Department of Labor.
U. S. Dept. of State. *see* United States. Department of
State.

United States. Department of State.
  xU. S. Department of State.
  Affairs in the Kongo. Negro U Pr.
  The China White Paper: August 1949. Stanford
  U Pr.
  The Conferences at Malta & Yalta, 1945.
  Greenwood.
  Congo Conference. Negro U Pr.
  The Diplomatic Correspondence of the United
  States of America: From the Signing of the
  Definitive Treaty of Peace, 10th Sept., 1783,
  to the Adoption of the Constitution, Mar. 4,
  1789. AMS Pr.
  A General Index to a Census of Pensioners for
  Revolutionary or Military Service, 1840.
  Genealog Pub.

Solar Collector Manufacturing Activity. Solar
Energy Info.
xFederal Energy Administration.
Guide to Energy Conservation in Agriculture.
Solar Energy Info.
A Guide to Energy Savings: For the Dairy
Farmer. Solar Energy Info.
A Guide to Energy Savings: For the Field
Crops Producer. Solar Energy Info.
A Guide to Energy Savings: For the Livestock
Producer. Solar Energy Info.
A Guide to Energy Savings: For the Orchard
Grower. Solar Energy Info.
A Guide to Energy Savings: For the Poultry
Producer. Solar Energy Info.
A Guide to Energy Savings: For the Vegetable
Producer. Solar Energy Info.
Wind Energy Conversion Systems
Manufacturing & Sales Activity. Solar Energy
Info.

United States. Federal Housing Administration.
xU. S. Federal Housing Administration.
The Structure & Growth of Residential
Neighborhoods in American Cities. Scholarly.

United States. Federal Trade Commission.
xFederal Trade Commission.
Report of the Federal Trade Commission on
the Radio Industry: In Response to House
Resolution 548, 67th Congress, Fourth
Session, December 1, 1923. Arno.
xFederal Trade Commission, United States.
Cooperative Marketing. Arno.
xU. S. Federal Trade Commission.
Chain Stores: Letters from the Chairman of the
Federal Trade Commission Transmitting in
Response to Senate Resolution No. 224.
Arno.
The International Petroleum Cartel. Arno.
Report of the Federal Trade Commission on
Foreign Ownership in the Petroleum
Industry.. Arno.

United States. Federal Works Agency.
xU. S. Federal Works Agency.
Final Report on the WPA Program, 1935-1943.
Greenwood.
Final Statistical Report of the Federal
Emergency Relief Administration. Da Capo.

**United States. Forest Products Laboratory, Madison,
Wisconsin.**
xU. S. Dept. of Forestry.
Encyclopedia of Wood. Sterling.

United States. Forest Service.
xU. S. Department of Agriculture Forest Service.
A Tree Hurts, Too. Scribner.
xU. S. Dept. of Agriculture-Forest Service.
Timber Resources for America's Future: Forest
Resource Report No. 14. Arno.
xU. S. Dept. of Agriculture-Soil Conservation
Service & Forest Service.
Headwaters Control & Use: A Summary of
Fundamental Principles & Their Application
in the Conservation & Utilization of Waters
& Soils Throughout Headwater Areas. Arno.
xUS Forest Service.
Encyclopedia of Wood. Sterling.

United States. General Accounting Office.
xU. S. General Accounting Office.
How the Internal Revenue Service Selects
Individual Income Tax Returns for Audit.
Bks Business.

United States. Geographic Board.
xUnited States Geographic Board.
Sixth Report of the United States Geographic
Board. Gale.

United States. Geographical Survey.
xU. S. Geographical Surveys.
Report Upon United States Geographical
Surveys West of the 100th Meridian: Incl.
Supplement. AMS Pr.
U. S. Geographical Surveys. see United States.

Geographical Survey.
**United States. George Washington Bicentennial
Commission.**
xU. S. George Washington Bicentennial
Commission.
The Music of George Washington's Time.
AMS Pr.
U.S House Committee on Banking & Currency. see
United States. Congress. House. Committee on
Banking and Currency.
U.S. House Committee on Government Operations. see
United States. Congress. House. Committee on
Government Operations.
U.S. House of Representatives. see United States.
Congress. House.
U. S. Housing & Home Finance Agency. see United
States. Dept. of Housing and Urban Development.
United States. Immigration Commission, 1907-1910.
xUnited States Immigration Commission.
Dictionary of Races or Peoples. Gale.
United States. Industrial Commission.
xUnited States Industrial Commission - 57th
Congress - 1st Session.
Reports. Greenwood.
Reports of the Industrial Commission on
Immigration Including Testimony, with
Review & Digest, & Special Reports on
Education Including Testimony with Review
& Digest. Arno.
United States. Internal Revenue Service.
xInternal Revenue Service.
ed. Nineteen Seventy-Eight U. S. Income Tax
Guide. DMR Pubns.
xU.S. Internal Revenue Service.
Confidential Official IRS Tax Audit Guide.
Arco.
**United States-Italy Seminar on Variable Structure
Systems, 2nd, Corvallis, Oregon, 1974.**
xUS - Italy Seminar on Variable Structure Systems,
2nd.
Variable Structure Systems with Application to
Economics & Biology: Proceedings.
Springer-Verlag.
**United States. Law Enforcement Assistance
Administration.**
xLaw Enforcement Assistance Administration.
National Crime Surveys: Cities Attitude
Sub-Sample, 1972-1975. ICPSR.
National Crime Surveys: Cities, 1972-1975.
ICPSR.
United States. Library of Congress.
xLibrary of Congress.
American Prints in the Library of Congress: A
Catalog of the Collection. Johns Hopkins.
Bibliographic Guide to Law. G K Hall.
Bibliography of the Catholic Church.
Merrimack Bk Serv.
Catalog of Brazilian Acquisitions of the Library
of Congress, 1964-1974. G K Hall.
Catalog of United States Census Publications:
1946-1972. Greenwood.
Charles Fenderich: Lithographer of American
Statesmen. U of Chicago Pr.
Charles Fenderich: Lithographer of American
Statesmen. U of Chicago Pr.
ed. Congressional Anthology: Favorite Poems
of Senators & Representatives. U Pr of Wash.
Library of Congress Author Catalog of Printed
Cards, Second Supplement, 1948-1952.
Rowman.
Library of Congress Catalog, Books: Subjects,
Quinquennial Edition, 1955-1959. Rowman.
Library of Congress Catalog of Printed Cards,
First Supplement, 1942-1947. Rowman.
Library of Congress Catalog of Printed Cards,
1898-1942. Rowman.
National Union Catalog, a Cumulative Author
List, 1953-57. Rowman.
National Union Catalog, 1956-1967. Rowman.
xLibrary of Congress, Washington, D. C.

Africa South of the Sahara: Index to Periodical
Literature, First Supplement. G K Hall.
Africa South of the Sahara: Index to Periodical
Literature, 1900-1970. G K Hall.
Catalog of Broadsides in the Rare Book
Division. G K Hall.
Far Eastern Languages Catalog. G K Hall.
Index to Latin American Legislation, First
Supplement, 1961-1965. G K Hall.
Index to Latin American Legislation, Second
Supplement. G K Hall.
Index to Latin American Legislation,
1950-1960. G K Hall.
Southeast Asia Subject Catalog. G K Hall.
xTheLibrary of Congress.
Bibliographic Guide to Law: Nineteen
Seventy-Eight. G K Hall.
xTheLibrary of Congress & the Research Libraries
of the New York Public Library.
Bibliographic Guide to Psychology: Nineteen
Seventy-Eight. G K Hall.
xTheLibrary of Congress & University of Texas
Library (Austin).
Bibliographic Guide to Latin American Studies:
1979. G K Hall.
xU. S. Library of Congress.
Catalogue of Opera Librettos Printed Before
1800. B Franklin.
Guide to the Official Publications of Other
American Republics: Washington, 1945-48.
Johnson Repr.
Statistical Bulletins: An Annotated
Bibliography of the General Statistical
Bulletins of Major Political Subdivisions of
the World. Greenwood.
Statistical Yearbooks: An Annotated
Bibliography of the General Statistical
Yearbooks of Major Political Subdivisions of
the World. Greenwood.
**United States. Library of Congress. Census Library
Project.**
xU. S. Library Of Congress - Census Library
Project.
Catalog of United States Census Publications,
1790-1945. Greenwood.
xU. S. Library of Congress Census Library Project.
Catalog of United States Census Publications,
1790-1945. B Franklin.
General Censuses & Vital Statistics in the
Americas: An Annotated Bibliography of the
Historical Censuses & Current Vital Statistics
of the 21 American Republics. Blaine
Ethridge.
National Censuses & Vital Statistics in Europe
1918-1939. B Franklin.
State Censuses. B Franklin.

U. S. Library of Congress Div. of Manuscripts. see
United States. Library of Congress. Manuscript
Division.
U. S. Library Of Congress-European Affairs Division. see
United States. Library of Congress. European Affairs
Division.
**United States. Library of Congress. European Affairs
Division.**
xU. S. Library Of Congress - European Affairs
Division.
Introduction to Europe: A Selective Guide to
Background Reading. Greenwood.
xU. S. Library Of Congress-European Affairs
Division.
Introduction to Africa: A Selective Guide to
Background Reading. Negro U Pr.
**United States. Library of Congress. General Reference
And Bibliography Division.**
xU. S. Library Of Congress - General Reference
And Bibliography Division.
Current National Bibliographies. Greenwood.
Guide to Bibliographic Tools for Research in
Foreign Affairs. Greenwood.

Iran: A Selected & Annotated Bibliography. Greenwood.
North & Northeast Africa: A Selected, Annotated List of Writings, 1951-1957. Greenwood.
xU. S. Library of Congress, General Reference & Bibliography Division.
Sixty American Poets, Eighteen Ninety-Six - Nineteen Fourty-Four. Gale.

United States. Library of Congress. Geography and Map Division.
xLibrary of Congress, Geography & Map Division (Washington, D. C.).
The Bibliography of Cartography, First Supplement. G K Hall.
xLibrary of Congress, Washington, D.C. Geography & Map Division.
The Bibliography of Cartography. G K Hall.

United States. Library of Congress. Information Systems Office.
xInformation Systems Office - Library Of Congress.
Format Recognition Process for MARC Records. ALA.

United States. Library of Congress. Legislative Reference Service.
xU. S. Library Of Congress - Legislative Reference Service.
Congress & the Monopoly Problem: Fifty-Six Years of Antitrust Development, 1900-1956. Greenwood.
Soviet Economic Growth: A Comparison with the United States. Greenwood.
Trends in Economic Growth: A Comparison of the Western Powers & the Soviet Bloc. Greenwood.
U. S. Foreign Aid: Its Purposes, Scope, Administration, & Related Information. Greenwood.
xU. S. Library of Congress Legislative Reference Service.
Proposed Amendments to the Constitution of the United States Introduced in Congress from Dec. 4, 1889 to July 2, 1926. Greenwood.
Provisions of Federal Law Held Unconstitutional by the Supreme Court of the United States. Greenwood.
xUnited States Senate Committee On The Judiciary - 89th Congress - 1st Session.
Internal Security & Subversion: Principal State Laws & Cases. Da Capo.

United States. Library of Congress. Manuscript Division.
xU. S. Library of Congress Div. of Manuscripts.
Calendar of the Correspondence of George Washington, Commander in Chief of the Continental Army with the Continental Congress. B Franklin.

United States. Library of Congress. Map Division.
xU. S. Library of Congress Map Division.
Civil War Maps: An Annotated Lists of Maps & Atlases in Map Collections of Library of Congress. Greenwood.
A List of Maps of America in the Library of Congress. B Franklin.

United States. Library of Congress. Music Division.
xU. S. Library of Congress Music Division.
African Music: A Brief Annotated Bibliography. Greenwood.
Bibliography of Latin American Folk Music. AMS Pr.
Catalogue of Opera Librettos Printed Before 1800. Johnson Repr.
U. S. Library Of Congress - Orientalia Division. see United States. Library of Congress. Orientalia Division.

United States. Library of Congress. Orientalia Division.
xU. S. Library Of Congress - Orientalia Division.

Arabian Peninsula: A Selected, Annotated List of Periodicals, Books & Articles in English. Greenwood.
Southeast Asia: An Annotated Bibliography of Selected Reference Sources. Greenwood.

United States. Library of Congress. Periodicals Division.
xU. S. Library Of Congress - Periodicals Division.
Check List of American Eighteenth Century Newspapers in the Library of Congress. Greenwood.

United States. Library of Congress. Processing Dept.
xU. S. Library Of Congress - Processing Department.
British Manuscripts Project: A Checklist of the Microfilm Prepared in England & Wales for the American Council of Learned Societies 1941-1945. Greenwood.

United States. Library of Congress. Reference Department.
xSymposium on Little Magazine, Library of Congress, 1965.
Little Magazine & Contemporary Literature. Modern Lang.
xU. S. Library Of Congress - Reference Department.
Indochina: A Bibliography of the Land & People. Greenwood.
Soviet Geography: A Bibliography. Greenwood.
xUnited States Library of Congress, Reference Dept.
Walt Whitman: A Catalogue Based Upon the Collection of the Library of Congress. Folcroft.

United States. Library of Congress. Science and Technology Division.
xLibrary of Congress, Science & Technology Div.
ed. Air Pollution Bibliography, Two Vols. in One. Kraus Repr.
xU. S. Library of Congress, Science & Technology Division.
Mainland China Organizations of Higher Learning in Science & Technology & Their Publications, a Selected Guide. AMS Pr.

United States. Library of Congress. Science Policy Research Division.
xU. S. Library of Congress. Science Policy Research Division, 95th Congress, 1st Session 1977.
State Legislature Use of Information Technology. Greenwood.

United States. Marine Corps.
xU S Marine Corps.
The Marine Corps Reserve. Scholarly.
xU. S. Marine Corps.
Guadalcanal Campaign. Greenwood.
History of the United States Marine Corps Reserve. Scholarly.
U. S. Marine Operations in Korea. Scholarly.
U. S. Military Academy. see United States. Military Academy, West Point.

United States. Military Academy, West Point.
xU. S. Military Academy.
Centennial of the United States Military Academy at West Point, New York, 1802-1902. Greenwood.

United States. Mutual Security Agency.
xU. S. Mutual Security Agency.
The Structure & Growth of the Italian Economy. Greenwood.

United States. Mutual Security Mission to China.
xU. S. Mutual Security Mission To China.
Economic Progress of Free China 1951-1958. Greenwood.

United States. National Archives.
xU. S. National Archives.
Handbook of Federal World War Agencies & Their Records, 1917-1921. Greenwood.
List of Documents Concerning the Negotiation of Ratified Indian Treaties: 1801-1869. Kraus Repr.

United States. National Bureau of Standards.

xNational Bureau of Standards.
Detector Sensitivity & Siting Requirements for Dwellings. Natl Fire Prot.
Detector Sensitivity & Siting Requirements for Dwellings: Phase 2. Natl Fire Prot.
The Results of a Round Robin Flat Plate Collector Test Program. Solar Energy Info.

United States. National Center for Health Statistics.
xNational Center for Health Statistics.
Health Manpower, a County & Metropolitan Area Data Book, 1972-1973. Natl Ctr Health Stats.
Hospitals: A County & Metropolitan Area Data Book, 1972. Natl Ctr Health Stats.
A Study of the Effect of Remuneration Upon Response in the Health & Nutrition Examination Survey. Natl Ctr Health Stats.

United States. National Commission on Food Marketing.
xU. S. National Commission on Food Marketing.
Food from Farmer to Consumer. Arno.
U.S. National Committee for Geochemistry, Div. of Earth Sciences. see National Research Council. Panel on Orientations for Geochemistry.

United States National Committee for the International Council for Building Research Studies and Documentation.
xU. S. National Committee for the International Council for Building Research, Studies & Documentation, National Research Council.
Modeling Techniques for Community Development. Natl Acad Pr.

United States National Committee for the International Hydrological Decade.
xU. S. National Committee for the International Hydrological Decade.
Advanced Concepts & Techniques in the Study of Snow & Ice Resources. Natl Acad Pr.

United States. National Committee on Vital and Health Statistics.
xNational Committee for Vital & Health Statistics.
The Analytical Potential of Nchs Data for Health Care Systems. Natl Ctr Health Stats.

United States. National Emergency Council.
xU. S. Emergency Council.
Report on Economic Conditions of the South. Da Capo.

United States. National Institute of Mental Health. Program Analysis and Evaluation Branch.
xNational Institute of Mental Health.
The Mental Health of the Child: Program Reports. Arno.
U. S. National Oceanic & Atmospheric Administration. see United States. National Oceanic and Atmospheric Administration.

United States. National Oceanic and Atmospheric Administration.
xOfficials of the National Oceanic & Atmospheric Administration.
Climates of the States. Water Info.
xU. S. National Oceanic & Atmospheric Administration.
The Complete Underwater Diving Manual. McKay.

United States. National Office of Vital Statistics.
xU. S. Public Health Service, Federal Security Agency, National Office of Vital Statistics.
Vital Statistics Rates in the United States: 1900-1940. Arno.

United States. National Resources Board. Land Planning Committee.
xLand Planning Committee, U.S. National Resources Board.
Report of the Land Planning Committee. Arno.

United States. National Resources Committee.
xU. S. National Resources Committee, May 1938.
Consumer Incomes in the United States. Da Capo.

The Problems of a Changing Population: Report of the Committee on Population Problems to the National Resources Committee. Arno.

Regional Factors in National Planning & Development. Da Capo.

Research: A National Resource. Arno.

The Structure of the American Economy. Da Capo.

United States. National Resources Committee. Science Committee.

xCongress, 75th, 1st Session, House Document No. 360.

Technological Trends & National Policy, Including the Social Implications of New Inventions: National Resources Committee, Report of the Subcommittee on Technology. Arno.

United States. National Resources Planning Board.

xUnited States National Resources Planning Board. Industrial Location & National Resources. Kraus Repr.

Security Work & Relief Policies. Da Capo.

United States. National Resources Planning Board. Public Works Committee.

xUnited States National Resources Planning Board, Public Works Committee.

The Economic Effects of the Public Works Expenditures, 1933-1938. Da Capo.

United States. National Science Foundation.

xU. S. National Science Foundation. Graduate Student Enrollment & Support in American Universities & Colleges 1954. Scholarly.

United States. National Water Commission.

xNational Water Commission. Water Policies for the Future. Water Info.

United States. Nautical Almanac Office.

xUnited States. Nautical Almanac Office. Sunrise & Sunset Tables for Key Cities & Weather Stations in the United States.. Gale.

U. S. Naval Institute. see United States Naval Institute, Annapolis.

United States Naval Institute, Annapolis.

xU. S. Naval Institute. Naval Regulations 1802. Naval Inst Pr. Space Atlas. Am Map.

United States. Naval Photographic Interpretation Center.

xU. S. Naval Photographic Interpretation Center. Antarctic Bibliography. Greenwood.

United States. Naval Training Command.

xU.S. Naval Training Command. Navigation. McKay.

U. S. Navy. see United States. Bureau of Naval Personnel.

U. S. Navy (Bureau of Naval Personnel). see United States. Bureau of Naval Personnel.

U. S. Navy Bureau of Naval Personnel. see United States. Bureau of Naval Personnel.

U. S. News & World Report. see U.S. News and World Report, Inc.

U.S. News & World Report Editors. see U.S. News and World Report, Inc.

United States. Office of Adviser on Negro Affairs.

xUnited States Office Of Adviser On Negro Affairs.

Urban Negro Worker in the United States, 1925-1936. Negro U Pr.

United States. Office of Business Economics.

xU. S. Office Of Business Economics.

Personal Income by States Since 1929: A Supplement to the Survey of Current Business. Greenwood.

Regional Trends in the United States Economy: A Supplement to the Survey of Current Business. Greenwood.

United States. Office of Education.

xU. S. Office of Education.

Accreditation in Higher Education. Greenwood.

Bibliography of Research Studies in Education, Nineteen Twenty-Six to Nineteen Forty. Gale.

Negro Education: A Study of the Private & Higher Schools for Colored People in the United States. Negro U Pr.

Survey of Negro Colleges & Universities. Negro U Pr.

United States. Office of Education. Bureau of Research.

xU. S. Office of Education, Bureau of Research. Interpretative Studies on Bilingual Education. Arno.

United States. Office of Education. Division of Higher Education.

xUnited States Office of Education, Division of Higher Education.

The College Presidency Nineteen Hundred-Nineteen Sixty: An Annotated Bibliography. Greenwood.

U. S. Office Of Education - Division Of International Education. see United States. Office of Education. Division of International Education.

United States. Office of Education. Division of International Education.

xU. S. Office Of Education - Division Of International Education.

Education in the USSR. Greenwood.

United States. Office of Education. (Public Libraries).

xU. S. Commissioner of Education.

Public Libraries in the United States of America: Their History, Condition & Management. Rowman.

United States. Office of Strategic Services.

xOffice Strategic Services.

O S S Sabotage & Demolition Manual. Paladin Ent.

xOfice of Strategic Services.

Locks, Picks & Clicks. Paladin Ent.

xU. S. Office Of Strategic Services.

ed. Assessment of Men: Selection of Personnel for the Office of Strategic Services. Johnson Repr.

U.S. Office of the Alien Property Custodian. see United States. Alien Property Custodian.

United States Pay Department. see United States. Pay Department (War Department).

United States. Pay Department (War Department).

xUnited States Pay Department. Pierce's Register. Genealog Pub.

United States. Pension Bureau.

xUnited States Pension Bureau.

List of Pensioners on the Roll January 1, 1883, with Added Tables of Contents. Genealog Pub.

Pensioners of Revolutionary War- Struck off the Roll. Genealog Pub.

United States. Post Office Department.

xU. S. Post Office Department.

Street Directory of the Principal Cities of the United States: Embracing Letter-Carrier Offices Established to April 30, 1908. Gale.

United States. President's Commission on Immigration and Naturalization.

xPresident's Commission On Immigration. Whom We Shall Welcome. Da Capo.

United States. President's Commission on Law Enforcement and Administration of Justice.

xPresident'S Commission On Law Enforcement And Administration Of Justice.

Task Force Report: The Police. Arno.

United States. President's Commission on the Health Needs of the Nation.

xPresident's Commission on the Health Needs of the Nation.

Building America's Health: A Report. Arno.

United States. President's Commission on the Status of Women.

xU.S. President's Commission on the Status of Women.

American Women: The Report. Zenger Pub.

United States. President's Committee for the White House Conference on Education.

xU. S. President's Committee For The White House Conference On Education.

Report to the President: Full Report. Greenwood.

United States. Public Health Service.

xU. S. Public Health Service.

Air Pollution in Donora: An Analysis of the Extreme Effects of Smog. Pergamon.

U. S. Public Health Service, Federal Security Agency, National Office of Vital Statistics. see United States. National Office of Vital Statistics.

United States. Public Lands Commission.

xU.S. House of Representatives, 46th Congress.

Report of the Public Lands Commission. Arno.

United States-Puerto Rico Commission on the Status of Puerto Rico.

xUnited States-Puerto Rico Commission on the Status of Puerto Rico.

Status of Puerto Rico. Arno.

United States Sanitary Commission.

xU. S. Sanitary Commission.

The Sanitary Commission of the U. S. Army, a Succinct Narrative of Its Works & Purposes. Arno.

United States. Selective Service System.

xU. S. Selective Service System.

Backgrounds of Selective Service. Arno.

U.S. Senate. see United States. Congress. Senate.

U.S. Senate Committee on Government Operations. see United States. Congress. Senate. Committee on Government Operations.

U. S. Senate, Committee on Labor & Public Welfare. see United States. Congress. Senate. Committee on Labor and Public Welfare.

U. S. Senate Committee On The District Of Columbia. see United States. Congress. Senate. Committee on the District of Columbia.

U.S. Senate, Juvenile Court of the District of Columbia. see District of Columbia. Juvenile Court.

U. S. Senate Library. see United States. Congress. Senate. Library.

U. S. Senate Select Committee on Nutrition & Human Needs. see United States. Congress. Senate. Select Committee on Nutrition and Human Needs.

U.S. Senate Special Committee to Investigate Organized Crime in Interstate Commerce. see United States. Congress. Senate. Special Committee to Investigate Organized Crime in Interstate Commerce.

U. S. Senate Subcommittee of the Committee on Banking & Currency. see United States. Congress. Senate. Committee on Banking and Currency. Subcommittee on Small Business.

U. S. Senate, Temporarary National Economic Committee. see United States. Temporary National Economic Committee.

United States. Small Business Administration.

xU.S. Small Business Administration.

Protect Your Business Against Crime. Sterling.

U. S. Smaller War Plants Corporation. see Smaller War Plants Corporation.

United States. Social Security Administration.

xSocial Security Administration.

Survey of Low Income Aged & Disabled, 1973-1975. ICPSR.

United States. Soil Conservation Service.

xU. S. Dept of Agriculture, Soil Conservation Service.

Drainage of Agricultural Land. Water Info.

University of California, Berkeley. *see* California. University, Berkeley.

University of California, Berkeley, Institute of Governmental Studies Library. *see* California. University. Institute of Governmental Studies Library.

University of California, Berkeley, Library. *see* California. University, Berkeley. Library.

University Of California Heller Committee For Research In Social Economics. *see* California. University. Heller Committee for Research in Social Economics.

University Of California Philosophical Union - 1932. *see* California. University. Philosophical Union.

University of Cambridge, Squire Law Library. *see* Squire Law Library.

University of Chicago. *see* Chicago. University.

University of Chicago - Graduate Library School - 35th Conference. *see* Chicago. University. Graduate Library School.

University of Cincinnati. *see* Cincinnati University.

University of Florida. *see* Florida. University, Gainesville.

University of Hawaii, Honolulu. *see* Hawaii. University, Honolulu.

University Of Illinois - English Dept. *see* Illinois. University. Department of English.

University of Illinois at Urbana-Champaign - Library. *see* Illinois. University at Urbana-Champaign. Library.

University of Iowa Hospitals & Clinic Staff. *see* Iowa. University Hospitals. Dept. of Nutrition.

University Of Kansas - Department Of English. *see* Kansas. University. Dept. of English.

University of London. *see* London. University.

University Of London - Institute Of Historical Research. *see* London. University. Institute of Historical Research.

University of London - School of Oriental & African Studies. *see* London. University. School of Oriental and African Studies.

University Of London - Warburg Institute Library. *see* London. University. Warburg Institute, Library.

University of London, Institute of Education. *see* London. University. Institute of Education.

University Of London Library. *see* London. University. Library.

University of Maryland Staff. *see* Maryland. University. Lower Division Chemistry Staff.

University of Miami Law Center & School of Medicine. *see* Medical Institute for Attorneys, 1st, Miami Beach, Florida, 1969.

University of Michigan. *see* Michigan. University.

University of Michigan, Ann Arbor. *see* Michigan. University.

University of Natal-Conference on Medical Education Durban - July 1964. *see* Conference on Medical Education, Pietermaritzburg, 1964.

University of Nebraska-Lincoln. Bureau of Business Research.
    xBureau of Business Research.
        ed. Health Care Cost Containment: The Managerial Approach. Bur Busn Res U Nebr.

University of North Carolina Division of the Humanities *see* North Carolina. University. Division of the Humanities.

University of North Carolina Woman's College Faculty. *see* North Carolina. University. Woman'S College, Greensboro.

University of Oklahoma Executive Planning Committee. *see* Oklahoma. University. Executive Planning Committee.

University of Oregon. *see* Oregon. University.

University Of Oxford. *see* Oxford. University.

University of Pennsylvania. *see* Pennsylvania. University.

University of Pennsylvania, Institute of Contemporary Art. *see* Pennsylvania. University. Institute of Contemporary Art.

University of Pittsburgh, Bureau of Business Research. *see* Pittsburgh. University. Bureau of Business Research.

University of Queensland, Department of Physics. *see* Queensland. University, Brisbane. Library.

University of Rhodesia. Library.
    xUniversity of Rhodesia Library.
        Catalog of the C. M. Doke Collection on African Languages. G K Hall.

University Of Singapore Library. *see* Singapore (City). University. Library.

University of Southern California Center for Health Services Research. *see* Los Angeles. University of Southern California. Center for Health Sciences Research.

University of Southern California, Los Angeles. *see* Los Angeles. University of Southern California.

University of Southern California,Los Angeles. *see* Los Angeles. University of Southern California.

University Of Tennessee. *see* Tennessee. University.

University of Texas. *see* Texas. University.

University of Texas, Austin. *see* Texas. University at Austin.

University of Texas Library, Austin. *see* Texas. University at Austin. Library.

University of Texas Medical Branch at Galveston.
    xMedical Branch of the University of Texas.
        The University of Texas Medical Branch at Galveston: A Seventy-Five Year History. U of Tex Pr.

University of Virginia Hospital Circle.
    xTheUniversity of Virginia Hospital Circle.
        The Monticello Cook Book. Dietz.

University Of Washington. *see* Washington (State) University.

University of Washington Libraries. *see* Washington (State) University. Library.

University of Windsor Seminar on Canadian-American Relations, 8th Annual, 1966. *see* Seminar on Canadian-American Relations, University of Windsor.

University of Wurzburg, Library. *see* Wurzburg. Universitat. Bibliothek.

Unkelbach, Kurt.
    xUnkelbach, Kurt.
        Both Ends of the Leash: Selecting & Training Your Dog. P-H.
        Catnip: Selecting & Training Your Cat. P-H.
        How to Make Money in Dogs. Dodd.
        How to Show Your Dog & Win. Watts.
        Uncle Charlie's Poodle. Dodd.

Unnerstad, Edith.
    xUnnerstad, Edith.
        Spettecake Holiday. Macmillan.

Unrau, John.
    xUnrau, John.
        Looking at Architecture with Ruskin. U of Toronto Pr.

Unruh, G. *see* Unruh, Glenys G.

Unruh, Glenys G.
    xUnruh, G.
        Innovations in Secondary Education. HR&W.
        Innovations in Secondary Education. Krieger.
    xUnruh, Glenys G.
        Responsive Curriculum Development: Theory & Action. McCutchan.

Unruh, John D. *see* Unruh, John David.

Unruh, John David, 1937-1976
    xUnruh, John D.
        The Plains Across: The Overland Emigrants & the Trans-Mississippi West, 1840-60. U of Ill Pr.

Unschuld, Paul. *see* Unschuld, Paul Ulrich.

Unschuld, Paul Ulrich, 1943-
    xUnschuld, Paul.
        Medical Ethics in Imperial China: A Study in Historical Anthropology. U of Cal Pr.

Unsworth, Mair.
    xUnsworth, Mair.
        Came a Stranger. Ace Bks.

Unterecker, John. *see* Unterecker, John Eugene.

Unterecker, John Eugene, 1922-
    xUnterecker, John.

Lawrence Durrell. Columbia U Pr.
        Reader's Guide to William Butler Yeats. Octagon.

Unterman, Lee D.
    xUnterman, Lee D.
        The Future of the United States Multinational Corporation. U Pr of Va.

Untermann, Richard.
    xUntermann, Richard.
        Principles & Practices of Grading, Drainage & Road Alignment: An Ecological Approach. Reston.

Untermeyer, Bryna. *see* Untermeyer, Bryna (Ivens).

Untermeyer, Bryna (Ivens).
    xUntermeyer, Bryna.
        ed. The Golden Treasury of Children's Literature. Western Pub.
        ed. Legendary Animals. Western Pub.
        ed. Old Friends & Lasting Favorites. Western Pub.

Untermeyer, Louis, 1885-1977
    xUntermeyer, Louis.
        A Galaxy of Verse. M Evans.
        ed. Golden Book of Fun & Nonsense. Western Pub.
        ed. The Golden Treasury of Poetry. Western Pub.
        ed. Love Sonnets. Crown.
        ed. Modern American & Modern British Poetry. HarBraceJ.
        ed. Modern American Poetry. HarBraceJ.
        ed. Modern British Poetry. HarBraceJ.
        ed. Paths of Poetry: Twenty-Five Poets & Their Poems. Delacorte.

Unthank, L. L.
    xUnthank, L. L.
        What You Should Know About Individual Retirement Accounts. Dow Jones-Irwin.

Unwin, Derick.
    xUnwin, Derick.
        ed. The Encyclopaedia of Educational Media Communications & Technology. Greenwood.

Unwin, G. *see* Unwin, George.

Unwin, George, 1870-1925
    xUnwin, G.
        Industrial Organization in the Sixteenth & Seventeenth Centuries. Biblio Dist.
    xUnwin, George.
        Industrial Organization in the Sixteenth & Seventeenth Centuries. Kelley.

Unwin, Philip.
    xUnwin, Philip.
        Travelling by Train in the Edwardian Age. Allen Unwin.

Unwin, Rayner.
    xUnwin, Rayner.
        The Defeat of John Hawkins: A Biography of His Third Slaving Voyage. Allen Unwin.

Unwin, Stanley.
    xUnwin, Stanley.
        Truth About Publishing. Allen Unwin.

Unzicker, Cecilia E. *see* Unzicker, Cecilia Elizabeth.

Unzicker, Cecilia Elizabeth, 1899-
    xUnzicker, Cecilia E.
        An Experimental Study of the Effect of the Use of the Typewriter on Beginning Reading. AMS Pr.

Upadhyaya, G. S.
    xUpadhyaya, G. S.
        Problems in Metallurgical Thermodynamics & Kinetics. Pergamon.

Updegraff, Clarence M. *see* Updegraff, Clarence Milton.

Updegraff, Clarence Milton, 1893-
    xUpdegraff, Clarence M.
        Arbitration & Labor Relations. BNA.

Updegraff, Harlan, 1874-
    xUpdegraff, Harlan.

The Origin of the Moving School in
  Massachusetts. AMS Pr.
Origin of the Moving School in Massachusetts.
  Arno.
Updike, Daniel B. *see* Updike, Daniel Berkeley.
Updike, Daniel Berkeley.
  xUpdike, Daniel B.
    Notes on the Merrymount Press & Its Work.
      Milford Hse.
Updike, John.
  xUpdike, John.
    Assorted Prose. Knopf.
    Centaur. Fawcett.
    Centaur. Knopf.
    The Coup. Fawcett.
    The Coup. Knopf.
    Couples. Fawcett.
    Couples. Knopf.
    A Month of Sundays. Fawcett.
    A Month of Sundays. Knopf.
    Museums & Women & Other Stories. Knopf.
    Of the Farm. Fawcett.
    Of the Farm. Knopf.
    Poorhouse Fair. Fawcett.
    The Poorhouse Fair. Knopf.
    Problems & Other Stories. Knopf.
    Rabbit Redux. Fawcett.
    Rabbit Run. Fawcett.
    Rabbit Run. Knopf.
Updyke, Frank A. *see* Updyke, Frank Arthur.
Updyke, Frank Arthur.
  xUpdyke, Frank A.
    The Diplomacy of the War of 1812. Peter
      Smith.
Upham, Elizabeth. *see* Upham, Elizabeth Norine.
Upham, Elizabeth Norine.
  xUpham, Elizabeth.
    Little Brown Bear. Platt.
Upham, Samuel C. *see* Upham, Samuel Curtis.
Upham, Samuel Curtis, 1819-1885
  xUpham, Samuel C.
    Notes of a Voyage to California Via Cape
      Horn, Together with Scenes in el Dorado, in
      the Years 1849-50. Arno.
Upham, Thomas C. *see* Upham, Thomas Cogswell.
Upham, Thomas Cogswell, 1799-1872
  xUpham, Thomas C.
    Outlines of Imperfect & Disordered Mental
      Action. Arno.
Uphaus, Robert W.
  xUphaus, Robert W.
    The Impossible Observer: Reason & the Reader
      in Eighteenth-Century Prose. U Pr of Ky.
Uphaus, Suzanne H. *see* Uphaus, Suzanne Henning.
Uphaus, Suzanne Henning, 1942-
  xUphaus, Suzanne H.
    John Updike. Ungar.
Upledger, John E., 1932-
  xUpledger, John E.
    An Osteopathic Doctor's Treasury of Health
      Secrets. P-H.
Uppal, J. S., 1927-
  xUppal, J. S.
    ed. India's Economic Problems: An Analytical
      Approach. St Martin.
  xUppal, Jogindar S.
    Economic Development in South Asia. St
      Martin.
Uppal, Jogindar S. *see* Uppal, J. S.
Upper, Dennis.
  xUpper, Dennis.
    ed. Covert Conditioning. Pergamon.
Uppvall, Axel J. *see* Uppvall, Axel Johan.
Uppvall, Axel Johan, 1872-
  xUppvall, Axel J.
    August Strindberg: A Psychoanalytic Study
      with Special Reference to the Oedipus
      Complex. Haskell.
Upshur, A. P. *see* Upshur, Abel Parker.

Upshur, Abel Parker, 1790-1844
  xUpshur, A. P.
    A Brief Enquiry into the True Nature &
      Character of Our Federal Government. Da
      Capo.
Upson, Lent D. *see* Upson, Lent Dayton.
Upson, Lent Dayton, 1886-1949
  xUpson, Lent D.
    Practice of Municipal Administration. Arno.
Upson, Norma.
  xUpson, Norma.
    The Crawfish Cookbook. Pacific Search.
    The Eggplant Cookbook. Pacific Search.
Upton, Anthony F.
  xUpton, Anthony F.
    Intro. by The Finnish Revolution. U of Minn
      Pr.
Upton, Arthur C., 1923-
  xUpton, Arthur C.
    Radiation Injury: Effects, Principles, &
      Perspectives. U of Chicago Pr.
Upton, Arvin.
  xUpton, Arvin.
    Lorenzino. Norton.
Upton, Charles, 1948-
  xUpton, Charles.
    Panic Grass. City Lights.
Upton, G. *see* Upton, Graham.
Upton, Graham, 1944-
  xUpton, G.
    ed. Physical & Creative Activities for the
      Mentally Handicapped. Cambridge U Pr.
Upton, Joe, 1946-
  xUpton, Joe.
    photos by Alaska Blues: A Fisherman's
      Journal. Alaska Northwest.
Upton, John, 1707-1760
  xUpton, John.
    Critical Observations on Shakespeare. AMS Pr.
    A Woodcarver's Primer. Sterling.
Upton, Joseph M.
  xUpton, Joseph M.
    History of Modern Iran: An Interpretation.
      Harvard U Pr.
Upton, M.
  xUpton, M.
    Agricultural Production Economics &
      Resource-Use. Oxford U Pr.
Upton, Mark.
  xUpton, Mark.
    Dark Summer. Coward.
    Dark Summer. PB.
    The Dream Lover. Coward.
    Dream Lover. PB.
Upton, Peter.
  xUpton, Peter.
    Green Hill Far Away. Ballantine.
    Green Hill Far Away. S&S.
Upton, Robert.
  xUpton, Robert.
    A Golden Fleecing. St Martin.
Uraguchi, Kenji.
  xUraguchi, Kenji.
    ed. Toxicology, Biochemistry & Pathology of
      Mycotoxins. Halsted Pr.
Ural, Oktay.
  xUral, Oktay.
    Construction of Lower-Cost Housing. Wiley.
URANTIA Foundation. *see* Urantia Foundation,
  Chicago.
URANTIA Foundation, Chicago.
  xURANTIA Foundation.
    URANTIA Book. URANTIA Foun.
Uram, Paul, 1926-
  xUram, Paul.
    The Complete Stretching Book. Anderson
      World.
Urbach, E. E. *see* Urbach, Efraim Elimelech.
Urbach, Efraim Elimelech, 1912-
  xUrbach, E. E.

    The Laws Regarding Slavery As a Source for
      Social History of the Period of the Second
      Temple, the Mishnah & Talmud. Arno.
Urbach, Reinhard, 1939-
  xUrbach, Reinhard.
    Arthur Schnitzler. Ungar.
Urban, G. R. *see* Urban, George R.
Urban, George R., 1921-
  xUrban, G. R.
    ed. Communist Reformation: Nationalism,
      Internationalism, & Change in the World
      Communist Movement. St Martin.
    ed. Detente. Universe.
    ed. Eurocommunism: Its Roots & Future in
      Italy & Elsewhere. Universe.
Urban, Glen. *see* Urban, Glen L.
Urban, Glen L.
  xUrban, Glen.
    Design & Marketing of New Products. P-H.
Urban Institute.
  xUrban Institute.
    ed. Struggle to Bring Technology to Cities.
      Urban Inst.
Urban Land Institute.
  xUrban Land Institute Editors.
    ed. Parking Requirements for Shopping
      Centers. Urban Land.
Urban Land Institute Editors. *see* Urban Land Institute.
**Urban Land Institute. Real Estate Financial Reporting
Committee.**
  xUrban Land Institute Real Estate Financial
    Reporting & Steering Committees.
    Real Estate Financial Reporting. Urban Land.
Urban Land Institute. Research Division.
  xULI Research Division.
    Effects of Regulations on Housing Costs: Two
      Case Studies. Urban Land.
    Joint Development: Making the Real
      Estate-Transit Connection. Urban Land.
    Large Scale Development: Benefits,
      Constraints, & State & Local Policy
      Incentives. Urban Land.
    New Opportunities, for Residential
      Development in Central Cities. Urban Land.
Urban, Linwood.
  xUrban, Linwood P.
    ed. The Power of God: Readings on
      Omnipotence & Evil. Oxford U Pr.
Urban, Linwood P. *see* Urban, Linwood.
Urban Technology Seminar. *see* Urban Technology
  Seminar. University of Texas at Austin, 1972.
**Urban Technology Seminar. University of Texas at
Austin, 1972.**
  xUrban Technology Seminar.
    Proceedings. LBJ Sch Public Affairs.
Urban, Wilbur M. *see* Urban, Wilbur Marshall.
Urban, Wilbur Marshall, 1873-
  xUrban, Wilbur M.
    The Intelligible World: Metaphysics & Value.
      AMS Pr.
    The Intelligible World: Metaphysics & Value.
      Greenwood.
Urbano, Paul.
  xUrbano, Paul D.
    The Marks of the Nails. Am Natl Pub.
Urbano, Paul D. *see* Urbano, Paul.
Urbanski, Edmund S. *see* Urbanski, Edmund Stefan.
Urbanski, Edmund Stefan.
  xUrbanski, Edmund S.
    Hispanic America & Its Civilizations: Spanish
      Americans & Anglo-Americans. U of Okla
      Pr.
Urbanski, J. *see* Urbanski, Jerzy.
Urbanski, Jerzy.
  xUrbanski, J.
    Handbook of Analysis of Synthetic Polymers &
      Plastics. Halsted Pr.
Urbanski, Marie M. *see* Urbanski, Marie Mitchell Olesen.
Urbanski, Marie Mitchell Olesen.
  xUrbanski, Marie M.

Margaret Fuller's Woman in the Nineteenth
Century: A Literary Study of Form &
Content, of Sources & Influence. Greenwood.

Urdang, Stephanie.
xUrdang, Stephanie.
Fighting Two Colonialisms: Women in
Guinea-Bissau. Monthly Rev.

Ure, Percy N. see Ure, Percy Neville.

Ure, Percy Neville, 1879-1950
xUre, Percy N.
Justinian & His Age. Greenwood.

Ure, Stellanie, 1943-
xUre, Stellanie.
Hawk Lady. Doubleday.

Uri, Pierre.
xUri, Pierre.
Development Without Dependence. Praeger.

Urick, R. J. see Urick, Robert J.

Urick, Robert J.
xUrick, R. J.
Principles of Underwater Sound. McGraw.

Uris, Auren.
xUris, Auren.
The Executive Deskbook. Van Nos Reinhold.
Executive Dissent: How to Say No & Win. Am
Mgmt.
Executive Interviewer's Deskbook. Gulf Pub.
Mastering the Art of Dictation. Gulf Pub.
Memos for Managers. T Y Crowell.

Uris, Leon. see Uris, Leon M.

Uris, Leon M., 1924-
xUris, Leon.
Angry Hills. Bantam.
Armageddon. Dell.
Armageddon. Doubleday.
Exodus. Doubleday.
Exodus. Bantam.

Uris, Norman B. see Uris, Norman Burton.

Uris, Norman Burton.
xUris, Norman B.
Doodle Book. Macmillan.

Urlsperger, Samuel, 1685-1772
xUrlsperger, Samuel.
Detailed Reports on the Salzburger Emigrants
Who Settled in America, 1736. U of Ga Pr.

Uroff, Margaret D. see Uroff, Margaret Dickie.

Uroff, Margaret Dickie.
xUroff, Margaret D.
Sylvia Plath & Ted Hughes. U of Ill Pr.

Urquhart, Clara.
xUrquhart, Clara.
ed. A Matter of Life. Greenwood.

Urquhart, Colin.
xUrquhart, Colin.
When the Spirit Comes. Bethany Fell.

Urquhart, Leonard C. see Urquhart, Leonard Church.

Urquhart, Leonard Church, 1886-
xUrquhart, Leonard C.
Civil Engineering Handbook. McGraw.

Urquidi, Victor L.
xUrquidi, Victor L.
Free Trade & Economic Integration in Latin
America: The Evolution of a Common
Market Policy. U of Cal Pr.

Urry, John.
xUrry, John.
Reference Groups & the Theory of Revolution.
Routledge & Kegan.

Ursic, Henry S.
xUrsic, Henry S.
Security Management Systems. C C Thomas.

Ursin, Holger.
xUrsin, Holger.
ed. Psychobiology of Stress: A Study of Coping
Men. Acad Pr.

Ursini, James.
xUrsini, James.
The Vampire Film. A S Barnes.

Urwick, Lyndall. see Urwick, Lyndall Fownes.

Urwick, Lyndall Fownes, 1891-
xUrwick, Lyndall.
Management of Tomorrow. Arno.

Urwick Technology Management, Ltd.
xUrwick Technology Management Ltd.
Environmental Impacts & Policies for the EEC
Tanning Industry. Intl Pubns Serv.

Urwin, G. C. see Urwin, George Glencairn.

Urwin, George Glencairn.
xUrwin, G. C.
ed. Humorists of the Eighteenth Century.
Transatlantic.

Urzidil, Johannes, 1896-
xUrzidil, Johannes.
There Goes Kafka. Wayne St U Pr.

U.S. News and World Report, Inc.
xU. S. News & World Report.
Communism & the New Left. Macmillan.
Social Security & Medicare - Simplified.
Macmillan.
U. S. on the Moon. Macmillan.
xU.S. News & World Report Editors.
The Family Register of Personal & Financial
Papers. S&S.
Famous Soviet Spies. S&S.
Plan Your Retirement Now So You Won't Be
Sorry Later. S&S.
Stocks, Bonds & Mutual Funds. S&S.
Teach Your Wife How to Be a Widow. S&S.
Two Hundred Years: A Bicentennial Illustrated
History of the United States. S&S.
What Everyone Needs to Know About Law.
S&S.
What Everyone Should Know About Credit.
S&S.
xU. S. News And World Report.
Good Things About the U. S. Today.
Macmillan.
Inflation Simplified. Macmillan.
Investments, Insurance, Wills - Simplified.
Macmillan.
U. S. on the Moon. Macmillan.

U.S.Department of Housing & Urban Development,
Washington, D.C. see United States. Dept. of Housing
and Urban Development.

Usdin, Gene. see Usdin, Gene L.

Usdin, Gene L.
xUsdin, Gene.
ed. Overview of the Psychotherapies.
Brunner-Mazel.
ed. Psychiatry in General Medical Practice.
McGraw.
xUsdin, Gene L.
Psychoneurosis & Schizophrenia. Lippincott.

Useem, Elizabeth. see Useem, Elizabeth L.

Useem, Elizabeth L.
xUseem, Elizabeth.
ed. The Education Establishment. P-H.

Useem, Michael.
xUseem, Michael.
Protest Movements in America. Bobbs.

Ushenko, Andrew P. see Ushenko, Andrew Paul.

Ushenko, Andrew Paul, 1901-
xUshenko, Andrew P.
Power & Events: An Essay on Dynamics in
Philosophy. Greenwood.

Usher, Abbot P. see Usher, Abbott Payson.

Usher, Abbott P. see Usher, Abbott Payson.

Usher, Abbott Payson, 1883-1965
xUsher, Abbot P.
The History of the Grain Trade in France,
1400-1710. Octagon.
xUsher, Abbott P.
Early History of Deposit Banking in
Mediterranean Europe. Russell.

Usher, Dan, 1934-
xUsher, Dan.

The Measurement of Economic Growth.
Columbia U Pr.
The Price Mechanism & the Meaning of
National Income Statistics. Greenwood.

Usher, George.
xUsher, George.
A Dictionary of Plants Used by Man. Hafner.

Usher, Gray.
xUsher, Gray.
The Graveyard Companion: Twenty Stories of
Fantasy & Terror. Elsevier-Nelson.

Usher, Stephen, 1931-
xUsher, Stephen.
Historians of Greece & Rome. Taplinger.

Usherwood, P. N. see Usherwood, Peter Norman Russell.

Usherwood, Peter Norman Russell.
xUsherwood, P. N.
Insect Muscle. Acad Pr.

Uslan, Michael.
xUslan, Michael.
Rock 'n Roll Trivia Quiz Book. S&S.
TV Trivia Quiz Book. Crown.

Uslaner, Eric M.
xUslaner, Eric M.
Patterns of Decision Making in State
Legislatures. Praeger.

Usoltseva, E. V.
xUsoltseva, E. V.
Surgery of Diseases & Injuries of the Hand.
Mosby.

Uspenskii, V. A. see Uspenskii, Vladimir Andreevich.

Uspenskii, Vladimir Andreevich.
xUspenskii, V. A.
Pascal's Triangle. U of Chicago Pr.

Uspensky, James V. see Uspensky, James Victor.

Uspensky, James Victor, 1883-
xUspensky, James V.
Theory of Equations. McGraw.

Ustinov, Peter.
xUstinov, Peter.
Dear Me. Little.
Dear Me. Penguin.

Utecht, Bob.
xUtecht, Bob.
This Is Gold Country. Piper.

Utley, Freda, 1898-
xUtley, Freda.
China Story. Constructive Action.

Utley, Jean.
xUtley, Jean.
What's Its Name?: A Guide to Speech &
Hearing Development. U of Ill Pr.

Utley, Robert M. see Utley, Robert Marshall.

Utley, Robert Marshall, 1929-
xUtley, Robert M.
Last Days of the Sioux Nation. Yale U Pr.

Utt, Richard. see Utt, Richard H.

Utt, Richard H.
xUtt, Richard.
Creation: Nature's Designs & Designer. Pacific
Pr Pub Assn.

Uttal, William R.
xUttal, William R.
The Psychobiology of Mind. Halsted Pr.

Utter, Robert P. see Utter, Robert Palfrey.

Utter, Robert Palfrey.
xUtter, Robert P.
Pamela's Daughters. Russell.
Pearls & Pepper. Arno.
Pearls & Pepper. Norwood Edns.

Utting, Francis A. see Utting, Francis Arthur James.

Utting, Francis Arthur James, 1905-
xUtting, Francis A.
The Story of Sierra Leone. Arno.

Uttley, Alison.
xUttley, Alison.

From Spring to Spring: Stories of the Four
Seasons. Merrimack Bk Serv.
Stories for Christmas. Merrimack Bk Serv.
Utton, Albert E., 1931-
xUtton, Albert E.
ed. National Petroleum Policy: A Critical
Review. U of NM Pr.
Intro. by & ed. Pollution & International
Boundaries: United States - Mexican
Environmental Problems. U of NM Pr.
Utton, M. A. *see* Utton, Michael A.
Utton, Michael A.
xUtton, M. A.
Diversification & Competition. Cambridge U
Pr.
Utz. *see* Utz, Lois.
Utz, Lois.
xUtz.
A Delightful Day with Bella Ballet. Oddo.
The Houndstooth Check. Oddo.
The Simple Pink Bubble That Ended the
Trouble with Jonathan Hubble. Oddo.
Utz, Peter.
xUtz, Peter.
Video User's Handbook. P-H.
Uvarov, E. B. *see* Uvarov, Eugene Boris.
Uvarov, Eugene Boris.
xUvarov, E. B.
Dictionary of Science. Penguin.
Uveges, Joseph A. *see* Uveges, Joseph Andrew.
Uveges, Joseph Andrew.
xUveges, Joseph A.
Cases in Public Administration: Narratives in
Administrative Problems. Allyn.
The Dimensions of Public Administration.
Allyn.
Uvezian, Sonia.
xUvezian, Sonia.
Cooking from the Caucasus. HarBraceJ.
The Cuisine of Armenia. Har-Row.
Uviller, H. Richard.
xUviller, H. Richard.
Processes of Criminal Justice: Adjudication.
West Pub.
The Processes of Criminal Justice: Investigation
& Adjudication. West Pub.
Processes of Criminal Justice: Investigation.
West Pub.
Uwechue, Raph.
xUwechue, Raph.
Reflections on the Nigerian Civil War: Facing
the Future. Holmes & Meier.
Uyehara, Cecil H.
xUyehara, Cecil H.
Leftwing Social Movements in Japan: An
Annotated Bibliography. Greenwood.
Uyehara, M.
xUyehara, Mitoshi.
Bruce Lee--Farewell, My Friend. Ohara Pubns.
Uyehara, Mitoshi. *see* Uyehara, M.
Uzgiris, Ina C.
xUzgiris, Ina C.
Assessment in Infancy: Ordinal Scales of
Psychological Development. U of Ill Pr.
Uznadze, Dmitrii N. *see* Uznadze, Dmitrii Nikolaevich.
Uznadze, Dmitrii Nikolaevich.
xUznadze, Dmitrii N.
Psychology of Set. Plenum Pub.
Uzoigwe, G. N.
xUzoigwe, G. N.
Britain & the Conquest of Africa: The Age of
Salisbury. U of Mich Pr.
Uzunoglu, Vasil.
xUzunoglu, Vasil.
Analysis & Design of Digital Systems. Gordon.
Vacandard, Elphege, 1849-1927
xVacandard, Elphege.

The Inquisition: A Critical & Historical Study
of the Coercive Power of the Church.
Richwood Pub.
Vacca, Roberto, 1927-
xVacca, Roberto.
Coming Dark Age. Doubleday.
Vachell, Horace A. *see* Vachell, Horace Annesley.
Vachell, Horace Annesley, 1861-1955
xVachell, Horace A.
Bunch Grass: A Chronicle of Life on a Cattle
Ranch. Arno.
Vachon, Brian, 1941-
xVachon, Brian.
Writing for Regional Publications. Writers
Digest.
Vacquier, V.
xVacquier, Victor.
Geomagnetism in Marine Geology. Elsevier.
Vacquier, Victor. *see* Vacquier, V.
Vacuum Metallurgy Conference, Pittsburgh, Pa., 1977.
xVacuum Metallurgy Conference, 1977.
Vacuum Metallurgy: Proceedings. Sci Pr.
xVan Valkenburgh, Nooger & Neville Inc.
Basic Electricity. Brolet.
Vacuum Metallurgy Conference, 1977. *see* Vacuum
Metallurgy Conference, Pittsburgh, Pa., 1977.
Vagaggini, Cipriano, 1909-
xVagaggini, Cipriano.
Canon of the Mass & Liturgical Reform. Alba.
Vagners, Juris.
xVagners, Juris.
ed. Oil on Puget Sound: An Interdisciplinary
Study in Systems Engineering. U of Wash Pr.
Vago, Robert M. *see* Vago, Robert Michael.
Vago, Robert Michael.
xVago, Robert M.
The Sound Pattern of Hungarian. Georgetown
U Pr.
Vahanian, Gabriel, 1927-
xVahanian, Gabriel.
No Other God. Braziller.
Vaid, Krishna B. *see* Vaid, Krishna Baldev.
Vaid, Krishna Baldev, 1927-
xVaid, Krishna B.
Steps in Darkness. InterCulture.
Steps in Darkness. Viking Pr.
Vaidon, Lawdom.
xVaidon, Lawdom.
Tangier: A Different Way. Scarecrow.
Vaidya, Karuna Kar, 1917-
xVaidya, Karuna Kar.
tr. Nepalese Short Stories. Gallery Pr.
Vail, Gladys E. *see* Vail, Gladys Ellen.
Vail, Gladys Ellen, 1902-
xVail, Gladys E.
Foods. HM.
Vail, Lauren O.
xVail, Lauren O.
Divorce: The Man's Complete Guide to
Winning. Sovereign Bks.
Vail, Priscilla L.
xVail, Priscilla L.
The World of the Gifted Child. Penguin.
The World of the Gifted Child. Walker & Co.
Vail, Van Horn.
xVail, Van Horn.
Modern German. HarBraceJ.
Vaillancourt, Raymond.
xVaillancourt, Raymond.
Toward a Renewal of Sacramental Theology.
Liturgical Pr.
Vailland, Roger.
xVailland, Roger.
Turn of the Wheel. Greenwood.
Vaillant, George C. *see* Vaillant, George Clapp.
Vaillant, George Clapp, 1901-1945
xVaillant, George C.
Indian Arts in North America. Cooper Sq.
Vaillant, George E.
xVaillant, George E.

Adaptation to Life. Little.
Vainshtein, Boris K. *see* Vainshtein, Boris
Konstantinovich.
Vainshtein, Boris Konstantinovich.
xVainshtein, Boris K.
Diffraction of X-Rays by Chain Molecules.
Elsevier.
Vairo, Philip D.
xVairo, Philip D.
Learning & Teaching in the Elementary
School. Scarecrow.
Vaisala, J. *see* Vaisala, Jussi.
Vaisala, Jussi.
xVaisala, J.
Lectures on N-Dimensional Quasiconformal
Mappings. Springer-Verlag.
Vaisman, Izu.
xVaisman, Izu.
Cohomology & Differential Forms. Dekker.
Vaisrub, S. *see* Vaisrub, Samuel.
Vaisrub, Samuel.
xVaisrub, S.
Medicine's Metaphors: Messages & Menaces.
Med Economics.
Vaitsos, Constantine V. *see* Vaitsos, Constantino V.
Vaitsos, Constantino V.
xVaitsos, Constantine V.
Intercountry Income Distribution &
Transnational Enterprises. Oxford U Pr.
Vajda, Albert, 1919-
xVajda, Albert.
Lend Me an Eye. Merrimack Bk Serv.
Vajda, Imre.
xVajda, Imre.
ed. Foreign Trade in a Planned Economy.
Cambridge U Pr.
Vajda, Mihaly.
xVajda, Mihaly.
Fascism As a Mass Movement. St Martin.
Vajda, Miklos.
xVajda, Miklos.
ed. & Intro. by & ed. Modern Hungarian
Poetry. Columbia U Pr.
Vajda, S.
xVajda, S.
Introduction to Linear Programming & the
Theory of Games. Methuen Inc.
Mathematics of Manpower Planning. Wiley.
Patterns & Configurations in Finite Spaces.
Hafner.
Probabilistic Programming. Acad Pr.
Vajk, J. Peter, 1942-
xVajk, J. Peter.
Doomsday Has Been Cancelled. Peace Pr.
Vakar, N. P. *see* Vakar, Nicholas P.
Vakar, Nicholas P.
xVakar, N. P.
Word Count of Spoken Russian: The Soviet
Usage. Ohio St U Pr.
Vakil, C. N. *see* Vakil, Chandulal Nagindas.
Vakil, Chandulal Nagindas.
xVakil, C. N.
Poverty & Planning. Greenwood.
Val Baker, Denys, 1917-
xVal Baker, Denys.
Face in the Mirror. Arkham.
Women Writing. St Martin.
Val, Miles P. Du. *see* Du Val, Miles P.
Valaskakis, Kimon, 1941-
xValaskakis, Kimon.
The Conserver Society: A Workable
Alternative for the Future. Har-Row.
Valdes, Joan.
xValdes, Joan.
ed. The Media Works. Pflaum-Standard.
Valdes, Mario J.
xValdes, Mario J.

Death in the Literature of Unamuno. U of Ill
Pr.
Valdes, Nelson P.
xValdes, Nelson P.
The Cuban Revolution: A Research-Study
Guide 1959-1969. U of NM Pr.
Valdes-Fallis, Guadalupe.
xValdes-Fallis, Guadalupe.
Spanish for the Spanish-Speaking: A
Descriptive Bibliography of Materials. NELP.
Valdman, Albert.
xValdman, Albert.
Drillbook of French Pronunciation. Har-Row.
Introduction to French Phonology &
Morphology. Newbury Hse.
Vale, Brenda.
xVale, Brenda.
The Autonomous House: Design & Planning
for Self Sufficiency. Universe.
Valencak, Hannelore.
xValencak, Hannelore.
A Tangled Web. Morrow.
When Half-Gods Go. Morrow.
Valency, Maurice. *see* Valency, Maurice Jacques.
Valency, Maurice J. *see* Valency, Maurice Jacques.
Valency, Maurice Jacques, 1903-
xValency, Maurice.
The End of the World: An Introduction to
Contemporary Drama. Oxford U Pr.
In Praise of Love: An Introduction to the
Love-Poetry of the Renaissance. Octagon.
xValency, Maurice J.
The Cart & the Trumpet: The Plays of George
Bernard Shaw. Oxford U Pr.
Valens, E. G.
xValens, E. G.
The Other Side of the Mountain. Warner Bks.
Valens, Evans G.
xValens, Evans G.
A Long Way up: The Story of Jill Kinmont.
Har-Row.
Valensi, Lucette.
xValensi, Lucette.
On the Eve of Colonialism: North Africa
Before the French Conquest 1790-1830.
Holmes & Meier.
Valenstein, Elliot S.
xValenstein, Elliot S.
Brain Stimulation & Motivation: Research &
Commentary. Scott F.
Valenta, Jiri.
xValenta, Jiri.
Soviet Intervention in Czechoslovakia, 1968:
Anatomy of a Decision. Johns Hopkins.
Valente, Cecilia M.
xValente, Cecilia M.
The Political, Economic, & Labor Climate in
Venezuela. Indus Res Unit-Wharton.
Valentine, Alan C. *see* Valentine, Alan Chester.
Valentine, Alan Chester, 1901-
xValentine, Alan C.
ed. Fathers to Sons: Advice Without Consent.
U of Okla Pr.
Valentine, Bettylou, 1937-
xValentine, Bettylou.
Hustling & Other Hard Work: Life Styles in
the Ghetto. Free Pr.
Valentine, Charles A.
xValentine, Charles A.
Culture & Poverty: Critique &
Counter-Proposals. U of Chicago Pr.
Valentine, D. H. *see* Valentine, David Henriques.
Valentine, David Henriques.
xValentine, D. H.
ed. Taxonomy, Phytogeography & Evolution.
Acad Pr.
Valentine, F. A. *see* Valentine, Frederick Albert.
Valentine, Foy.
xValentine, Foy.

Citizenship for Christians. Broadman.
Valentine, Frederick Albert, 1911-
xValentine, F. A.
Convex Sets. Krieger.
Valentine, G. H. *see* Valentine, Gordon Howard.
Valentine, Gordon Howard.
xValentine, G. H.
Chromosome Disorders: An Introduction for
Clinicians. Lippincott.
Valentine, James.
xValentine, James.
photos by North Carolina. Graphic Arts Ctr.
Valentine, James W.
xValentine, James W.
Evolutionary Paleoecology of the Marine
Biosphere. P-H.
Valentine, Jean.
xValentine, Jean.
The Messenger. FS&G.
Ordinary Things. FS&G.
Valentine, Jerome L.
xValentine, Jerome L.
Quantitative Techniques for Financial Analysis.
Irwin.
Valentine, John.
xValentine, John.
Puppies. Entwhistle Bks.
Valentine, Percy F. *see* Valentine, Percy Friars.
Valentine, Percy Friars, 1884-
xValentine, Percy F.
ed. Twentieth Century Education: Recent
Developments in American Education.
Greenwood.
Valentine, Tom.
xValentine, Tom.
The Great Pyramid: Man's Monument to Man.
Pinnacle Bks.
Inside Wrestling. Contemp Bks.
Psychic Surgery. PB.
Valentino, Lou.
xValentino, Lou.
The Films of Lana Turner. Citadel Pr.
Valenzuela, Luisa, 1938-
xValenzuela, Luisa.
Strange Things Happen Here: Twenty-Six Short
Stories & a Novel. HarBraceJ.
Valeriani, Richard.
xValeriani, Richard.
Travels with Henry. Berkley Pub.
Travels with Henry. HM.
Valery, Paul, 1871-1945
xValery, Paul.
Collected Works of Paul Valery. Princeton U
Pr.
Valery, Paul. *see* Valery, Paul Ambroise.
Valery, Paul Ambroise.
xValery, Paul.
Charmes ou Poemes. Humanities.
Valeton, E. M. *see* Valeton, Elsa M.
Valeton, Elsa M.
xValeton, E. M.
Dutch Costumes. Heinman.
Valett, Robert E.
xValett, Robert E.
Programming Learning Disabilities. Pitman
Learning.
Remediation of Learning Disabilities: A
Handbook of Psychoeducational Resource
Programs. Pitman Learning.
Valette, Jean Paul.
xValette, Jean-Paul.
Contacts: Langue et Culture Francaises. HM.
Valette, Jean-Paul. *see* Valette, Jean Paul.
Valette, Rebecca M.
xValette, Rebecca M.

Arthur de Gobineau & the Short Story. U of
NC Pr.
C'est de la Prose. HarBraceJ.
Lectures libres. HarBraceJ.
Modern Language Performance Objectives &
Individualization: A Handbook. HarBraceJ.
Vali, Ferenc. *see* Vali, Ferenc Albert.
Vali, Ferenc A. *see* Vali, Ferenc Albert.
Vali, Ferenc Albert.
xVali, Ferenc.
The Turkish Straits & NATO. Hoover Inst Pr.
xVali, Ferenc A.
Bridge across the Bosporus: The Foreign Policy
of Turkey. Johns Hopkins.
The Quest for a United Germany. Johns
Hopkins.
Valin, Jonathan.
xValin, Jonathan.
Lime Pit. Dodd.
Valkenberg, Phil Van. *see* Van Valkenberg, Phil.
Vallance, Elizabeth. *see* Vallance, Elizabeth M.
Vallance, Elizabeth M.
xVallance, Elizabeth.
Women in the House: A Study of Women
Members of Parliament. Humanities.
Vallance, H. A.
xVallance, H. A.
Highland Railway. Kelley.
Vallas, Leon, 1879-1956
xVallas, Leon.
Cesar Franck. Greenwood.
Claude Debussy, His Life & Works. Peter
Smith.
Valle, Stephen K.
xValle, Stephen K.
Alcoholism Counseling: Issues for an Emerging
Profession. C C Thomas.
Vallee, Jacques.
xVallee, Jacques.
Challenge to Science: The UFO Enigma.
Ballantine.

Vallejo, Cesar. *see* Vallejo, Cesar Abraham.

Vallejo, Cesar Abraham.
xVallejo, Cesar.
Cesar Vallejo: The Complete Posthumous
Poetry. U of Cal Pr.
Spain, Let This Cup Pass from Me. SBD.

Vallejo, Doris.

xVallejo, Doris.

The Boy Who Saved the Stars. O'Quinn
Studio.

Vallen, Jerome J.
xVallen, Jerome J.
Check in-Check Out: Principles of Effective
Front Office Management. Wm C Brown.
Vallens, Vivian M.
xVallens, Vivian M.
Working Women in Mexico During the
Porfiriato, 1880-1910. R & E Res Assoc.
Vallentin, Antonina, 1893-1957
xVallentin, Antonina.
This I Saw: The Life & Times of Goya.
Greenwood.
Vallentine, John F.
xVallentine, John F.
Range Development & Improvements.
Brigham.
Valletutti. *see* Valletutti, Peter J.
Valletutti, P. *see* Valletutti, Peter J.
Valletutti, Peter J.
xValletutti.
ed. Interdisciplinary Approaches to Human
Services. Univ Park.
xValletutti, P.

Individualizing Educational Objectives &
Programs: A Modular Approach. Univ Park.

Vallianatos, E. G.
xVallianatos, E. G.
Fear in the Countryside: The Control of
Agricultural Resources in the Poor Countries
by Non-Peasant Elites. Ballinger Pub.

Vallier, Ivan.
xVallier, Ivan.
ed. Comparative Methods in Sociology: Essays
on Trends & Applications. U of Cal Pr.

Vallieres, Pierre.
xVallieres, Pierre.
White Niggers of America: The Precocious
Autobiography of a Quebec Terrorist.
Monthly Rev.

Vallin, Jean.
xVallin, Jean.
Plant World. Sterling.

Vallins, G. H. *see* Vallins, George Henry.

Vallins, George Henry.
xVallins, G. H.
The Pattern of English. Westview.

Valmy, Christine.
xValmy, Christine.
Esthetics: The Keystone Guide to Skin Care.
Keystone Pubns.

Valois, Ninette de. *see* De Valois, Ninette.

Valticos, N. *see* Valticos, Nicolas.

Valticos, Nicolas.
xValticos, N.
International Labour Law. Kluwer Boston.

Valtin, Heinz.
xValtin, Heinz.
Renal Dysfunction: Mechanisms Involved in
Fluid & Solute Imbalance. Little.

Valyi, L. *see* Valyi, Laszlo.

Valyi, Laszlo.
xValyi, L.
Atom & Ion Sources. Wiley.

Vambe, Lawrence, 1917-
xVambe, Lawrence.
From Rhodesia to Zimbabwe. U of Pittsburgh
Pr.
An Ill-Fated People: Zimbabwe Before & After
Rhodes. U of Pittsburgh Pr.

Vambery, Armin, 1832-1913
xVambery, Arminius.
History of Bokhara. Arno.

Vambery, Arminius. *see* Vambery, Armin.

Vambery, Robert G., 1942-
xVambery, Robert G.
Capital Investment Control in the Air
Transport Industry. Oceana.

Van Abbe, Derek. *see* Van Abbe, Derek Maurice.

Van Abbe, Derek Maurice.
xVan Abbe, Derek.
Goethe: New Perspectives on a Writer & His
Time. Bucknell U Pr.

Van Allsburg, Chris.
xVan Allsburg, Chris.
The Garden of Abdul Gasazi. HM.

Van Alphen, Corry.
xVan Alphen, Corry.
Effective Use of House Plants. Emerson.

Van Alstyne, Dorothy, 1899-
xVan Alstyne, Dorothy.
The Environment of Three-Year Old Children:
Factors Related to Intelligence & Vocabulary
Tests. AMS Pr.
Play Behavior & Choice of Play Materials of
Pre-School Children. Arno.

Van Antwerp, William C. *see* Van Antwerp, William
Clarkson.

Van Antwerp, William Clarkson, 1867-1938
xVan Antwerp, William C.
A Collector's Comment on His First Editions
of the Works of Sir Walter Scott. Folcroft.
The Stock Exchange from Within. Arno.

Van Arsdell, Paul M. *see* Van Arsdell, Paul Marion.

Van Arsdell, Paul Marion, 1905-
xVan Arsdell, Paul M.
Corporation Finance: Policy, Planning,
Administration. Ronald Pr.

Van Ash, Cay.
xVan Ash, Cay.
Master of Villainy: A Biography of Sax
Rohmer. Bowling Green Univ.

Van Atta, Winfred.
xVan Atta, Winfred.
Adam Sleep. Doubleday.

Van Beek, Gus W. *see* Van Beek, Gus Willard.

Van Beek, Gus Willard, 1922-
xVan Beek, Gus W.
Hajar Bin Humeid: Investigations at a
Pre-Islamic Site in South Arabia. Johns
Hopkins.

Van Benthuysen, Robert F.
xVan Benthuysen, Robert F.
ed. Monmouth County, New Jersey: A
Bibliography of Published Works 1676-1973.
Ploughshare Pr.

Van Bruggen, Theodore, 1926-
xVan Bruggen, Theodore.
The Vascular Plants of South Dakota. Iowa St
U Pr.

Van Brunt, H. L., 1936-
xVan Brunt, H. L.
Indian Territory & Other Poems. The Smith.

Van Brunt, Henry.
xVan Brunt, Henry.
Architecture & Society: Selected Essays of
Henry Van Brunt. Harvard U Pr.

Van Brunt, LeRoy. *see* Van Brunt, LeRoy B.

Van Brunt, LeRoy B.
xVan Brunt, LeRoy.
Applied ECM. EW Eng.

Van Buren, Martin.
xVan Buren, Martin.
The Autobiography of Martin Van Buren. Da
Capo.

Van Buren, Martin, Pres. U. S. 1782-1862.
xVan Buren, Martin.
Inquiry into the Origin & Course of Political
Parties in the United States. Kelley.

Van Buren, Paul M. *see* Van Buren, Paul Matthews.

Van Buren, Paul Matthews, 1924-
xVan Buren, Paul M.
The Burden of Freedom: Americans and the
God of Israel. Seabury.
Discerning the Way: A Theology of the
Jewish-Christian Reality. Seabury.

Van Camp, Gena R.
xVan Camp, Gena R.
Kumeyaay Pottery: Paddle-&-Anvil Techniques
of Southern California. Ballena Pr.

Van Cise, Jerrold G.
xVan Cise, Jerrold G.
The Federal Antitrust Laws. Am Enterprise.
Understanding the Antitrust Laws. PLI.

Van Cise, Philip S. *see* Van Cise, Philip Sidney.

Van Cise, Philip Sidney, 1884-
xVan Cise, Philip S.
Fighting the Underworld. Greenwood.

Van Cleave, W. R. *see* Van Cleave, William R.

Van Cleave, William R.
xVan Cleave, W. R.
Tactical Nuclear Weapons: An Examination of
the Issues. Crane-Russak Co.

Van Cleef, E. *see* Van Cleef, Eugene.

Van Cleef, Eugene, 1887-
xVan Cleef, E.
Cities in Action. Pergamon.

Van Cortlandt, Philip.
xVan Cortlandt, Philip.
The Revolutionary War Memoir & Selected
Correspondence of Philip Van Cortlandt.
Sleepy Hollow.

Van Creveld, Martin L.
xVan Creveld, Martin L.

Hitler's Strategy 1940-1941: The Balkan Clue.
Cambridge U Pr.

Van Dahm, Thomas E. *see* Van Dahm, Thomas Edward.

Van Dahm, Thomas Edward, 1924-
xVan Dahm, Thomas E.
Money & Banking: An Introduction to the
Financial System. Heath.

Van Dalen, Deobold B, 1911-
xVan Dalen, Deobold B.
World History of Physical Education: Cultural,
Philosophical & Comparative. P-H.

Van De Kamp, Peter, 1901-
xVan De Kamp, Peter.
Principles of Astrometry: With Special
Emphasis on Long-Focus Photographic
Astrometry. W H Freeman.

Van De Linde, Gerald. *see* Van De Linde, Gerard.

Van De Linde, Gerard, 1840-
xVan De Linde, Gerald.
Reminiscences. Arno.

Van De Vate, Dwight, 1929-
xVan De Vate, Dwight.
ed. Persons, Privacy & Feeling: Essays in the
Philosophy of Mind. Memphis St Univ.

Van De Ven, Andrew H.
xVan De Ven, Andrew H.
Group Decision Making & Effectiveness: An
Experimental Study. Kent St U Pr.
Measuring & Assessing Organizations. Wiley.

Van De Voort, Alice M. *see* Van De Voort, Alice Maria.

Van De Voort, Alice Maria, 1884-
xVan De Voort, Alice M.
The Teaching of Science in Normal Schools &
Teachers Colleges. AMS Pr.

Van de Wetering, Jan. *see* Van De Wetering, Janwillem.

Van De Wetering, Janwillem.
xVan de Wetering, Jan
The Maine Massacre. PB.
xVan De Wetering, Janwillem.
Hugh Pine. HM.
The Maine Massacre. HM.
The Maine Massacre. G K Hall.

Van Deburg, William L.
xVan Deburg, William L.
The Slave Drivers: Black Agricultural Labor
Supervisors in the Antebellum South.
Greenwood.

Van Den Berghe, P. L. *see* Van Den Berghe, Pierre L.

Van Den Berghe, Pierre L.
xVan Den Berghe, P. L.
Human Family Systems: An Evolutionary
View. Elsevier.
xVan Den Berghe, Pierre L.
Inequality in the Peruvian Andes: Class &
Ethnicity in Cuzco. U of Mo Pr.
ed. The Liberal Dilemma in South Africa. St
Martin.
Power & Privilege at an African University.
Schenkman.
Race & Racism: A Comparative Perspective.
Wiley.

Van Den Bruck, Arthur Moeller. *see* Moeller Van Den
Bruck, Arthur.

Van Den Haag, Ernest.
xVan den Haag, Ernest.
Punishing Criminals: Concerning Very Old &
Painful Question. Basic.

Van Denburg, Joseph K. *see* Van Denburg, Joseph King.

Van Denburg, Joseph King, 1874-
xVan Denburg, Joseph K.
Causes of the Elimination of Students in Public
Secondary Schools of New York City. AMS
Pr.

Van Der Bent, A. J. *see* Van der Bent, Ans Joachim.

Van der Bent, Ans Joachim.
xVan Der Bent, A. J.
God So Loves the World: The Immaturity of
World Christianity. Orbis Bks.

Van Der Eyken, W. *see* Van der Eyken, Willem.

Van der Eyken, Willem.
xVan Der Eyken, W.
   ed. Learning & Earning: Aspects of Day -
     Release in Further Education. Humanities.
Van der Kloot, William G.
xVan der Kloot, William G.
   ed. Readings in Behavior. Irvington.
Van der Lingen, Gerrit J.
xVan Der Lingen, Gerrit J.
   ed. Diagenesis of Deep-Sea Biogenic
     Sediments. Acad Pr.
Van der Meer, Ron.
xVan Der Meer, Ron.
   jt. auth. Oh Lord!. Crown.
Van der Meid, Louise.
xVan Der Meid, Louise B.
   Siamese Cats. TFH Pubns.
Van Der Meid, Louise B. *see* Van der Meid, Louise.
Van Der Merwe, H. W. *see* Van der Merwe, Hendrik W.
Van der Merwe, Hendrik W.
xVan Der Merwe, H. W.
   The Future of the University in Southern
     Africa. St Martin.
xVan Der Merwe, Hendrik W.
   ed. African Perspectives on South Africa:
     Collection of Speeches, Articles &
     Doucuments. Hoover Inst Pr.
Van der Plank, J. E.
xVan Der Plank, J. E.
   Principles of Plant Infection. Acad Pr.
Van der Post, Laurens.
xVan Der Post, Laurens.
   African Cooking. Time-Life.
   African Cooking. Silver.
   A Far-off Place. HarBraceJ.
   A Far-off Place. Morrow.
   First Catch Your Eland. Morrow.
   The Lost World of the Kalahari. HarBraceJ.
   Venture to the Interior. Greenwood.
   Venture to the Interior. HarBraceJ.
Van Der Putte, S. C. *see* Van der Putte, S. C. J.
Van der Putte, S. C. J., 1940-
xVan Der Putte, S. C.
   The Development of the Lymphatic System in
     Man. Springer-Verlag.
Van der Reis, L. *see* Van der Reis, Leo.
Van der Reis, Leo.
xVan der Reis, L.
   ed. Immune Disorders. S Karger.
xVan der Reis, Leo.
   ed. The Esophagus. S Karger.
Van Der Straeten, Edmund. *see* Straeten, Edmund Van
Der.
Van der Veer, Judy.
xVan Der Veer, Judy.
   Higher Than the Arrow. Avon.
Van der Veur, Paul W.
xVan der Veur, Paul W.
   Freemasonry in Indonesia from Radermacher
     to Soekanto, 1762-1961. Ohio U Ctr Intl.
Van der Zee, Henri.
xVan der Zee, Henri.
   A Sweet & Alien Land: The Story of the
     Dutch in New York. Viking Pr.
Van der Ziel, Aldert, 1910-
xVan Der Ziel, Aldert.
   Noise in Measurements. Wiley.
   Nonlinear Electronic Circuits. Wiley.
   Solid State Physical Electronics. P-H.
Van Deusen, Edmund L.
xVan Deusen, Edward.
   What You Can Do About Baldness. Stein &
     Day.
Van Deusen, Edward. *see* Van Deusen, Edmund L.
Van Deusen, G. *see* Van Deusen, Glyndon Garlock.
Van Deusen, Glyndon G. *see* Van Deusen, Glyndon
Garlock.
Van Deusen, Glyndon Garlock, 1897-
xVan Deusen, G.

The Rise & Decline of Jacksonian Democracy.
   Krieger.
xVan Deusen, Glyndon G.
   The Life of Henry Clay. Greenwood.
Van Deusen, John G. *see* Van Deusen, John George.
Van Deusen, John George, 1890-
xVan Deusen, John G.
   Economic Bases of Disunion in South Carolina.
     AMS Pr.
Van Devanter, Ann C.
xVan Devanter, Ann C.
   Anywhere So Long As There Be Freedom:
     Charles Carroll of Carrollton, His Family &
     His Maryland. Baltimore Mus.
Van Doren, Carl. *see* Van Doren, Carl Clinton.
Van Doren, Carl C. *see* Van Doren, Carl Clinton.
Van Doren, Carl Clinton, 1885-1950
xVan Doren, Carl.
   Life of Thomas Love Peacock. Russell.
xVan Doren, Carl C.
   Many Minds. Greenwood.
   Swift. AMS Pr.
Van Doren, Carlton. *see* Van Doren, Carlton S.
Van Doren, Carlton S.
xVan Doren, Carlton.
   ed. Land & Leisure: Concepts & Methods in
     Outdoor Recreation. Maaroufa Pr.
Van Doren, Mark, 1894-
xVan Doren, Mark.
   Autobiography. Greenwood.
   Collected & New Poems: 1924-1963. Hill &
     Wang.
   Collected Stories. Hill & Wang.
   Nathaniel Hawthorne. Greenwood.
Van Dorn, Theodore.
xVan Dorn, Theodore.
   Drunks Diary. Philos Lib.
Van Dresser, Peter.
xVan Dresser, Peter.
   Homegrown Sundwellings. Lightning Tree.
Van Druten, John.
xVan Druten, John.
   I Am a Camera: A Play in Three Acts.
     Greenwood.
Van Dusen, William D.
xVan Dusen, William D.
   Planning for a Statewide Educational
     Information Center Network. College Bd.
Van Duyn, J.
xVan Duyn, J.
   Documentation Manual. Van Nos Reinhold.
Van Duzee, Mabel.
xVan Duzee, Mabel.
   A Medieval Romance of Friendship: Eger &
     Grime. B Franklin.
Van Duzer, Henry S. *see* Van Duzer, Henry Sayre.
Van Duzer, Henry Sayre, 1853-1928
xVan Duzer, Henry S.
   Thackeray Library. B Franklin.
Van Dyk, Fay B. *see* Van Dyk, Fay Blix.
Van Dyk, Fay Blix, 1951-
xVan Dyk, Fay B.
   His Touch Is Love. Southern Pub.
Van Dyke. *see* Van Dyke, Henry.
Van Dyke, Dick.
xVan Dyke, Dick.
   Faith, Hope & Hilarity. Doubleday.
   Faith, Hope, & Hilarity. Warner Bks.
Van Dyke, Henry, 1852-1933
xVan Dyke.
   Story of Other Wise Man. Peter Pauper.
xVan Dyke, Henry.
   Counsels by the Way. Arno.
   Dead Piano. FS&G.
   The Spirit of Christmas. Arden Lib.
Van Dyke, John C. *see* Van Dyke, John Charles.
Van Dyke, John Charles, 1856-1932
xVan Dyke, John C.

The Desert. Peregrine Smith.
   The Desert. R West.
Van Dyke, Paul, 1859-1933
xVan Dyke, Paul.
   Renascence Portraits. Arno.
Van Dyke, Vernon, 1912-
xVan Dyke, Vernon.
   Human Rights, the United States, & World
     Community. Oxford U Pr.
   Political Science: A Philosophical Analysis.
     Stanford U Pr.
Van Etten, Glen.
xVan Etten, Glen.
   The Severely & Profoundly Handicapped:
     Programs, Methods & Materials. Mosby.
Van Evera, Maxine.
xVan Evera, Maxine.
   Building Your Swing for Better Golf with Amy
     Alcott. A S Barnes.
Van Every, Dale, 1896-
xVan Every, Dale.
   Ark of Empire: The American Frontier,
     1784-1803. Arno.
   A Company of Heroes: The American Frontier,
     1775-1783. Arno.
   Disinherited: The Lost Birthright of the
     American Indian. Avon.
   The Final Challenge: The American Frontier,
     1804-1845. Arno.
   Forth to the Wilderness: The First American
     Frontier, 1754-1774. Arno.
Van Evrie, John H., 1814-1896
xVan Evrie, John H.
   Negroes & Negro Slavery: The First an Inferior
     Race, the Latter Its Normal Condition. Arno.
   White Supremacy & Negro Subordination: Or,
     Negroes, a Subordinate Race & So-Called
     Slavery Its Normal Condition. Negro U Pr.
Van Fleet, James. *see* Van Fleet, James K.
Van Fleet, James K.
xVan Fleet, James.
   How to Put Yourself Across with People. P-H.
   Power with People. P-H.
xVan Fleet, James K.
   Doctor Van Fleet's Amazing New "Non-Glue
     Food" Diet. P-H.
   Extraordinary Healing Secrets from a Doctor's
     Private Files. P-H.
   Van Fleet's Master Guide for Managers. P-H.
Van Fraassen, B. C. *see* Van Fraassen, Bastiaan C.
Van Fraassen, Bastiaan C., 1941-
xVan Fraassen, B. C.
   Formal Semantics & Logic. Macmillan.
Van Geel, Tyll.
xVan Geel, Tyll.
   Authority to Control the School Program.
     Lexington Bks.
Van Gelder. *see* Van Gelder, Arthur Pine.
Van Gelder, Arthur Pine.
xVan Gelder.
   History of the Explosives Industry in America.
     Arno.
Van Gelder, Dora, 1904-
xVan Gelder, Dora.
   The Real World of Fairies. Theos Pub Hse.
Van Gelder, Lydia.
xVan Gelder, Lydia.
   Ikat. Watson-Guptill.
Van Gelder, Patricia.
xVan Gelder, Patricia.
   Careers in the Insurance Industry. Watts.
Van Gerpen, Maurice.
xVan Gerpen, Maurice.
   Privileged Communication & the Press: The
     Citizen's Right to Know Versus the Law's
     Right to Confidential News Source Evidence.
     Greenwood.
Van Gigch, John P.
xVan Gigch, John P.

Applied General Systems Theory. Har-Row.
Using Systems Analysis to Implement
Cost-Effectiveness & Program Budgeting in
Education. Educ Tech Pubns.
Van Gulik, Robert.
xVan Gulik, Robert.
The Chinese Nail Murders. U of Chicago Pr.
Van Hattum, Rolland J. *see* Van Hattum, Rolland James.
Van Hattum, Rolland James, 1924-
xVan Hattum, Rolland J.
Clinical Speech in the Schools: Organization &
Management. C C Thomas.
Communication Disorders. Macmillan.
Developmental Language Programming for the
Retarded. Allyn.
Van Heijenoort, Jean, 1912-
xVan Heijenoort, Jean.
Frege & Godel: Two Fundamental Texts in
Mathematical Logic. Harvard U Pr.
ed. From Frege to Godel: A Source Book in
Mathematical Logic, 1879-1931. Harvard U
Pr.
Van Herk, Aritha.
xVan Herk, Aritha.
Judith. Little.
Van Heyningen, Christina.
xVan Heyningen, Christina.
Clarissa, Poetry & Morals. Arden Lib.
Clarissa, Poetry & Morals. R West.
Van Hise, Charles R. *see* Van Hise, Charles Richard.
Van Hise, Charles Richard, 1857-1918
xVan Hise, Charles R.
Concentration & Control: A Solution of the
Trust Problem in the United States. Arno.
Van Hoesen, Karl. *see* Van Hoesen, Karl Duane.
Van Hoesen, Karl Duane, 1900-
xVan Hoesen, Karl.
Handbook of Conducting. Irvington.
Van Hoesen, Walter H. *see* Van Hoesen, Walter
Hamilton.
Van Hoesen, Walter Hamilton, 1897-
xVan Hoesen, Walter H.
Crafts & Craftsmen of New Jersey. Fairleigh
Dickinson.
Early Taverns & Stagecoach Days in New
Jersey. Fairleigh Dickinson.
Van Hoose, William H.
xVan Hoose, William H.
Ethical & Legal Issues in Counseling &
Psychotherapy. Jossey-Bass.
Van Horn, Carl E.
xVan Horn, Carl E.
Policy Implementation in the Federal System:
National Goals & Local Implementors.
Lexington Bks.
Van Horn, James.
xVan Horn, James.
The Community Orchestra: A Handbook for
Conductors, Managers, & Boards.
Greenwood.
Van Horne, James C.
xVan Horne, James C.
Financial Management & Policy. P-H.
Financial Market Rates & Flows. P-H.
Function & Analysis of Capital Market Rates.
P-H.
Fundamentals of Financial Management. P-H.
Van House, Charles. *see* Van House, Charles L.
Van House, Charles L.
xVan House, Charles.
Accounting for Life Insurance Companies.
Irwin.
Van Houten, Franklyn B. *see* Van Houten, Franklyn
Bosworth.
Van Houten, Franklyn Bosworth, 1914-
xVan Houten, Franklyn B.
ed. Ancient Continental Deposits. Acad Pr.
Van Houten, Ron.
xVan Houten, Ron.

Learning Through Feedback: A Systematic
Approach for Improving Academic
Performance. Human Sci Pr.
Van Hove, M. A. *see* Van Hove, Michel Andre.
Van Hove, Michel Andre.
xVan Hove, M. A.
Surface Crystallography by LEED: Theory,
Computation & Structural Results.
Springer-Verlag.
Van Impe, Jack.
xVan Impe, Jack.
Israel's Final Holocaust. Nelson.
Van Iten, Richard J.
xVan Iten, Richard J.
ed. Problem of Universals. Irvington.
Van Kaam, Adrian. *see* Van Kaam, Adrian L.
Van Kaam, Adrian L.
xVan Kaam, Adrian.
The Art of Existential Counseling. Dimension
Bks.
xVan Kaam, Adrian L.
Existential Foundations of Psychology.
Duquesne.
Van Laan, Thomas F.
xVan Laan, Thomas F.
Idiom of Drama. Cornell U Pr.
Role Playing in Shakespeare. U of Toronto Pr.
Van Leeuwen, Jean.
xVan Leeuwen, Jean.
The Great Cheese Conspiracy. Dell.
The Great Christmas Kidnaping Caper. Dial.
Tales of Oliver Pig. Dial.
Van Liere, Edward J. *see* Van Liere, Edward Jerald.
Van Liere, Edward Jerald, 1896-
xVan Liere, Edward J.
Early Teachers in West Virginia University
School of Medicine, 1869-1922. McClain.
History of Medical Education in West Virginia.
McClain.
Medical & Other Essays. McClain.
Van Loan, Charles E. *see* Van Loan, Charles Emmett.
Van Loan, Charles Emmett, 1876-1919
xVan Loan, Charles E.
Lucky Seventh: Tales of the Big League. Arno.
Van Loon, Dirk.
xVan Loon, Dirk.
The Family Cow. Garden Way Pub.
Van Loon, Hendrik W. *see* Van Loon, Hendrik Willem.
Van Loon, Hendrik Willem, 1882-1944
xVan Loon, Hendrik W.
The Arts. Liveright.
The Story of Mankind. Liveright.
Van Loon, Jon C. *see* Van Loon, Jon Clement.
Van Loon, Jon Clement, 1937-
xVan Loon, Jon C.
ed. Analytical Atomic Absorption
Spectroscopy: Selected Methods. Acad Pr.
Van Lustbader, Eric.
xVan Lustbader, Eric.
The Sunset Warrior. Berkley Pub.
The Sunset Warrior. BJ Pub Group.
Van Maanen, J. *see* Van Maanen, John.
Van Maanen, John.
xVan Maanen, J.
Organizational Careers: Some New
Perspectives. Wiley.
Van Meter, C. H.
xVan Meter, C. H.
Principles of Police Interrogation. C C Thomas.
Van Meter, Eddy J.
xVan Meter, Eddy J.
ed. Theory Development & Educational
Administration. Mss Info.
Van Name, Willard G. *see* Van Name, Willard Gibbs.
Van Name, Willard Gibbs, 1872-
xVan Name, Willard G.
Vanishing Forest Reserves. Arno.
Van Namee, J. William.
xVan Namee, J. William.

Hopedale Tavern & What It Wrought. Arno.
Van Ness, H. C. *see* Van Ness, Hendrick C.
Van Ness, Hendrick C.
xVan Ness, H. C.
Understanding Thermodynamics. McGraw.
Van Ness, Peter.
xVan Ness, Peter.
Revolution & Chinese Foreign Policy: Peking's
Support for Wars of National Liberation. U
of Cal Pr.
Van Niel, Robert.
xVan Niel, Robert.
Survey of Historical Source Materials in Java &
Manila. U Pr of Hawaii.
Van Norman, Richard W.
xVan Norman, Richard W.
Experimental Biology. P-H.
Van O'Connor, William. *see* O'Connor, William Van.
Van Orden, M. D., 1921-
xVan Orden, M. D.
The Book of United States Navy Ships. Dodd.
Van Osdol, Bob.
xVan Osdol, Bob M.
ed. Special Education: A New Look. Mss Info.
Van Osdol, Bob M. *see* Van Osdol, Bob.
Van Osdol, William R.
xVan Osdol, William R.
An Introduction to Exceptional Children. Wm
C Brown.
Parents, Teachers, Kids. Mss Info.
Van Over, Raymond.
xVan Over, Raymond.
Total Meditation: Mind Control Techniques
from a Small Planet in Space. Macmillan.
Van Pelt, Ethel.
xVan Pelt, Ethel.
Silver Threads to Love. Bouregy.
Van Pelt, Sydney J. *see* Van Pelt, Sydney James.
Van Pelt, Sydney James, 1908-
xVan Pelt, Sydney J.
Secrets of Hypnotism. Wehman.
Secrets of Hypnotism. Wilshire.
Van Pool, Gerald M.
xVan Pool, Gerald M.
Improving Your Student Council. Natl Assn
Principals.
Van Ravenswaay, Charles.
xVan Ravenswaay, Charles.
A Nineteenth-Century Garden. Universe.

Van Ravensway, Charles. *see* Van Ravenswaay, Charles.

Van Rensselaer, Philip.

xVan Rensselaer, Phillip.

That Vanderbilt Woman. Playboy Pbks.

Van Rensselaer, Phillip. *see* Van Rensselaer, Philip.

Van Rijsbergen, C. J., 1943-

xVan Rijsbergen, C. J.
ed. Information Retrieval. Butterworths.
Van Riper, Charles. *see* Van Riper, Charles Gage.
Van Riper, Charles G. *see* Van Riper, Charles Gage.
Van Riper, Charles Gage, 1905-
xVan Riper, Charles.
A Career in Speech Pathology. P-H.
Nature of Stuttering. P-H.
xVan Riper, Charles G.
An Introduction to General American
Phonetics. Har-Row.
Van Riper, Guernsey.
xVan Riper, Guernsey.
Game of Basketball. Garrard.
Van Riper, Paul P.
xVan Riper, Paul P.
History of the United States Civil Service.
Greenwood.
Van Rjndt, Philippe, 1950-
xVan Rjndt, Philippe.

Blueprint. Putnam.
xVan Rjndt, Phillipe.
Blueprint. Berkley Pub.
Van Rjndt, Phillipe. see Van Rjndt, Philippe.
Van Roosbroeck, G. L. see Van Roosbroeck, Gustave Leopold.

Van Roosbroeck, Gustave Leopold, 1888-1936
xVan Roosbroeck, G. L.
Persian Letters Before Montesquieu. B Franklin.
Van Ryzin. see Van Ryzin, Lani.

Van Ryzin, Lani.
xVan Ryzin.
Cutting a Record in Nashville. Watts.
xVan Ryzin, Lani.
Disco. Watts.
Sidewalk Games. Raintree Pubs.

Van Schaack, Eric.
xVan Schaack, Eric.
Baroque Art in Italy. McGraw.

Van Schaick, John, 1873-
xVan Schaick, John.
Characters in Tales of a Wayside Inn. Haskell.

Van Seters, John.
xVan Seters, John.
Abraham in History & Tradition. Yale U Pr.

Van Sickle, Dirck.
xVan Sickle, Dirck.
Montana Gothic. Avon.
Montana Gothic. HarBraceJ.

Van Slyke, Helen, 1919-
xVan Slyke, Helen.
All Visitors Must Be Announced. Doubleday.
Always Is Not Forever. Popular Lib.
A Necessary Woman. Doubleday.
A Necessary Woman. Popular Lib.
No Love Lost. Lippincott.
The Rich & the Righteous. Popular Lib.

Van Slyke, Lyman P.
xVan Slyke, Lyman P.
Enemies & Friends: The United Front in Chinese Communist History. Stanford U Pr.

Van Steenwyk, Elizabeth.
xVan Steenwyk, Elizabeth.
Dorothy Hamill: Olympic Champion. Harvey.
Mystery at Beach Bay. Creative Ed.
Ride to Win. Creative Ed.
Rivals on Ice. A Whitman.

Van Stockum, Hilda, 1908-
xVan Stockum, Hilda.
The Borrowed House. FS&G.

Van Tassel, Charles E.
xVan Tassel, Charles E.
Analysis of Factors Influencing Retail Sales. Mich St U Busn.
Van Tassel, D. see Van Tassel, Dennie.
Van Tassel, David D. see Van Tassel, David Dirck.

Van Tassel, David Dirck, 1928-
xVan Tassel, David D.
ed. Aging, Death, & the Completion of Being. U of Pa Pr.

Van Tassel, Dennie, 1939-
xVan Tassel, D.
Computer Security Management. P-H.
ed. Computers, Computers, Computers: In Fiction & in Verse. Elsevier-Nelson.
xVan Tassel, Dennis.
The Compleat Computer. SRA.
Program Style, Design, Efficiency, Debugging & Testing. P-H.
Van Tassel, Dennis. see Van Tassel, Dennie.

Van Til, Cornelius, 1895-
xVan Til, Cornelius.

Case for Calvinism. Presby & Reformed.
Christian Theistic Ethics. Presby & Reformed.
Christian Theory of Knowledge. Presby & Reformed.
Christianity & Barthianism. Presby & Reformed.
Defense of the Faith. Presby & Reformed.

Van Til, William.
xVan Til, William.
Modern Education for the Junior High School Years. Bobbs.

Van Toller, C.
xVan Toller, C.
The Nervous Body: An Introduction to the Autonomic Nervous System & Behaviour. Wiley.
Van Treese, Glenn J. see Van Treese, Glenn Joseph.

Van Treese, Glenn Joseph.
xVan Treese, Glenn J.
D'Alembert & Frederick the Great: A Study of Their Relationship. Learned Pubns.
Van Tyne, Claude H. see Van Tyne, Claude Halstead.

Van Tyne, Claude Halstead, 1869-1930
xVan Tyne, Claude H.
The American Revolution. Norwood Edns.
England & America: Rivals in the American Revolution. Russell.
The Loyalists in the American Revolution. B Franklin.
The Loyalists in the American Revolution. Peter Smith.

Van Tyne, Josselyn.
xVan Tyne, Josselyn.
Fundamentals of Ornithology. Wiley.

Van Uchelen, Rod.
xVan Uchelen, Rod.
Say It with Pictures: Graphic Communication with Illustration. Van Nos Reinhold.
Van Valkenberg, Phil. see Van Valkenberg, Philip.

Van Valkenberg, Philip.
xVan Valkenberg, Phil.
More Wisconsin Bike Trips. Tamarack Pr.
Van Valkenburg, M. E. see Van Valkenburg, Mac Elwyn.

Van Valkenburg, Mac Elwyn.
xVan Valkenburg, M. E.
Introduction to Modern Network Synthesis. Wiley.
Van Valkenburgh, Nooger & Neville Inc. see Van Valkenburgh, Nooger and Neville, Inc., New York.

Van Valkenburgh, Nooger and Neville, Inc., New York.
xVan Valkenburgh, Nooger & Neville Inc.
Basic Electricity. Hayden.
Basic Electronic Circuits, British Edition. Brolet.
Basic Electronics. Brolet.
Basic Radar-British Edition. Brolet.
Basic Synchros & Servomechanisms, British Edition. Brolet.
Basic Television 1972, British Edition. Brolet.
Mastery Learning: Mastery Testing Introductory Packets. Brolet.

Van Vechten, Carl, 1880-1964
xVan Vechten, Carl.
Nigger Heaven. Octagon.
Sacred & Profane Memories. Arno.
Sacred & Profane Memories. Greenwood.
The Tattooed Countess. AMS Pr.

Van Veen, Ted.
xVan Veen, Ted.
Rhododendrons in America. Van Veen.

Van Velsen, J.
xVan Velsen, J.
The Politics of Kinship: A Study in Social Manipulation Among the Lakeside Tonga of Malawi. Humanities.

Van Vlack, Lawrence H.
xVan Vlack, Lawrence H.
Materials Science for Engineers. A-W.
A Textbook of Materials Technology. A-W.
Van Vleck, David. see Van Vleck, David B.

Van Vleck, David B.
xVan Vleck, David.
How & Why Not to Have That Baby. Eriksson.
Van Vleck, John H. see Van Vleck, John Hasbrouck.

Van Vleck, John Hasbrouck, 1899-
xVan Vleck, John H.
Theory of Electric & Magnetic Susceptibilities. Oxford U Pr.
Van Vogt, A. see Van Vogt, Alfred Elton.

Van Vogt, A. E.
xVan Vogt, A. E.
Away & Beyond. BJ Pub Group.
Earth Factor X. DAW Bks.
Renaissance. PB.
Rogue Ship. DAW Bks.
Supermind. DAW Bks.
Two-Hundred Million A.D.. Zebra.
The World of Null-A. Berkley Pub.
Van Vogt, A. E. see Van Vogt, Alfred Elton.

Van Vogt, Alfred Elton, 1912-
xVan Vogt, A.
Money Personality. P-H.
xVan Vogt, A. E.
Children of Tomorrow. Ace Bks.
The Weapon Makers. PB.
Van Voorhis, John S. see Van Voorhis, John Stogdell.

Van Voorhis, John Stogdell, 1823-
xVan Voorhis, John S.
The Old & New Monongahela. Genealog Pub.

Van Vuuren, Nancy, 1938-
xVan Vuuren, Nancy.
The Subversion of Women As Practiced by Churches, Witch-Hunters, & Other Sexists. Westminster.
Van Wagenen, Beulah. see Van Wagenen, Beulah (Clark).

Van Wagenen, Beulah (Clark), 1900-
xVan Wagenen, Beulah.
Extra-Curricular Activities in the Colleges of the United Lutheran Church in America: A Survey & Program. AMS Pr.

Van Wagenen, Gertrude.
xVan Wagenen, Gertrude.
Postnatal Development of the Ovary in Homo Sapiens & Macaca Mulatta & Induction of Ovulation in the Macaque. Yale U Pr.

Van Way, Charles W.
xVan Way, Charles W.
Surgical Skills in Patient Care. Mosby.
Van Wert, W. F. see Van Wert, William F.
Van Wert, William. see Van Wert, William F.

Van Wert, William F.
xVan Wert, W. F.
The Theory & Practice of the Cine-Roman. Arno.
xVan Wert, William.
The Film Career of Alain Robbe-Grillet. Redgrave Pub Co.
xVan Wert, William F.
The Film Career of Alain Robbe-Grillet. G K Hall.
The Film Career of Alain Robbe-Grillet. Two Continents.

Van Why, Joseph S.
xVan Why, Joseph S.
Nook Farm. Stowe-Day.

Van Winkle, Matthew, 1910-
xVan Winkle, Matthew.
Distillation. McGraw.

Van Woerkom, Dorothy.
xVan Woerkom, Dorothy.
Hidden Messages. Crown.
A Hundred Angels Singing. Concordia.
The Queen Who Couldn't Bake Gingerbread. Knopf.
xVan Woerkom, Dorothy O.
Abu Ali: Three Tales of the Middle East. Macmillan.
Van Woerkom, Dorothy O. see Van Woerkom, Dorothy.

Van World.
xVan World Editors.

Do-It-Yourselfer's Guide to Van Conversion. TAB Bks.

Super Vans. TAB Bks.

Van World Editors. *see* Van World.

Van Wormer, Joe.
xVan Wormer, Joe.
World of the American Elk. Lippincott.
World of the Canada Goose. Lippincott.
World of the Pronghorn. Lippincott.

Van Wormer, Katherine S.
xVan Wormer, Katherine S.
Sex Role Behavior in a Woman's Prison: An Ethological Analysis. R & E Res Assoc.

Van Wyck Mason, F.
xVan Wyck Mason, F.
Stars on the Sea. Berkley Pub.

Van Wyk, Helen.
xVan Wyk, Helen.
Acrylic Portrait Painting. Watson-Guptill.

Van Wyk Smith, M.
xVan Wyk Smith, M.
Drummer Hodge: The Poetry of the Anglo-Boer War, 1899-1902. Oxford U Pr.

Van Wylen, Gordon. *see* Van Wylen, Gordon John.

Van Wylen, Gordon J. *see* Van Wylen, Gordon John.

Van Wylen, Gordon John.
xVan Wylen, Gordon.
Thermodynamics. Wiley.
xVan Wylen, Gordon J.
Fundamentals of Classical Thermodynamics. Wiley.

Van Zandt, Roland.
xVan Zandt, Roland.
Chronicles of the Hudson: Three Centuries of Travelers' Accounts. Rutgers U Pr.

Van Zeggeren, F.
xVan Zeggeren, F.
Computation of Chemical Equilibria. Cambridge U Pr.

Van Zeller, Hubert, 1905-
xVan Zeller, Hubert.
Choice of God. Templegate.

Van Zile, Judy.
xVan Zile, Judy.
ed. Dance in Africa, Asia, & the Pacific: Selected Readings. Mss Info.

Van Zoost, Brenda.
xVan Zoost, Brenda L.
ed. Psychological Readings for the Dental Profession. Nelson-Hall.

Van Zoost, Brenda L. *see* Van Zoost, Brenda.

Van Zyl Slabbert, F. *see* Van Zyl Slabbert, Frederik.

Van Zyl Slabbert, Frederik.
xVan Zyl Slabbert, F.
South Africa's Options. St Martin.

Van-Loon, Antonia, 1940-
xVan-Loon, Antonia.
For Love & Honor. St Martin.
Katherine. St Martin.

Vanags, Patricia.
xVanags, Patricia.
Imperial Rome. Watts.

Vanasse, G. A. *see* Vanasse, George A.

Vanasse, George A.
xVanasse, G. A.
ed. Spectrometric Techniques. Acad Pr.

Vanberg, Bent. *see* Vanberg, Kent.

Vanberg, Kent.
xVanberg, Bent.
Of Norwegian Ways. Dillon.

Vanbreuseghem, R.
xVanbreuseghem, R.
Practical Guide to Medical & Veterinary Mycology. Masson Pub.

Vanbrugh. *see* Vanbrugh, John.

Vanbrugh, John.
xVanbrugh.
The Relapse. Norton.
xVanbrugh, John.

The Provoked Husband. U of Nebr Pr.
Relapse. U of Nebr Pr.

Vance, Adrian.
xVance, Adrian.
Audio Visual Production. Amphoto.
UFO's, the Eye & the Camera. Barlenmir.

Vance, Catherine S. *see* Vance, Catherine Stuart.

Vance, Catherine Stuart, 1885-
xVance, Catherine S.
The Girl Reserve Movement of the Young Women's Christian Association: An Analysis of the Educational Principles & Procedures Used Throughout Its History. AMS Pr.

Vance, Edward F., 1929-
xVance, Edward F.
Coupling to Shielded Cables. Wiley.

Vance, Elbridge P. *see* Vance, Elbridge Putnam.

Vance, Elbridge Putnam, 1915-
xVance, Elbridge P.
Introduction to Modern Mathematics. A-W.
Modern College Algebra. A-W.

Vance, Jack.
xVance, Jack.
The Eyes of the Overworld. Gregg.
Eyes of the Overworld. PB.
The Palace of Love. DAW Bks.
Star King. DAW Bks.
xVance, John.
Space Opera. DAW Bks.

Vance, Jack. *see* Vance, John Holbrook.

Vance, James E.
xVance, James E.
This Scene of Man: The Role & Structure of the City in the Geography of Western Civilization. Har-Row.

Vance, John. *see* Vance, Jack.

Vance, John Holbrook, 1916-
xVance, Jack.
The Best of Jack Vance. PB.
The Best of Jack Vance. Taplinger.
Marune: Alastor 933. Ballantine.
Maske: Thaery. Berkley Pub.
Maske: Thaery. Berkley Pub.
Maske: Thaery. Ultramarine Pub.

Vance, John T. *see* Vance, John Thomas.

Vance, John Thomas, 1884-1943
xVance, John T.
The Background of Hispanic-American Law: Legal Sources & Juridical Literature of Spain. Hyperion Conn.
A Guide to the Law & Legal Literature of Mexico. Gordon Pr.

Vance, Malcolm.
xVance, Malcolm.
The Complete Movie Quizbook. Sterling.

Vance, Mary. *see* Vance, Mary A.

Vance, Mary A.
xVance, Mary.
Books on Architecture: A Selected Bibliography. Vance Biblios.
Historical Society Architectural Publications: New York, North Carolina, & North Dakota. Vance Biblios.

Vance, Rupert B. *see* Vance, Rupert Bayless.

Vance, Rupert Bayless, 1899-
xVance, Rupert B.
Human Geography of the South: A Study in Regional Resources & Human Adequacy. Russell.

Vance, Samuel.
xVance, Samuel.
Courageous & the Proud. Norton.

Vance, Steve.
xVance, Steve.
Planet of the Gawfs. Nordon Pubns.

Vance, William E.
xVance, William E.
Drifter's Gold. Doubleday.

Vancil, Richard F.
xVancil, Richard F.

Financial Executive's Handbook. Dow Jones-Irwin.
Replacement Cost Accounting: Readings on Concepts, Uses & Methods. T Horton & Dghts.

Vancleemput, W. M. *see* Vancleemput, William M.

Vancleemput, William M., 1945-
xVancleemput, W. M.
Computer Aided Design of Digital Systems: A Bibliography, 1977-78. Computer Sci.

Vande Vere, E. K. *see* Vande Vere, Emmett K.

Vande Vere, Emmett K.
xVande Vere, E. K.
Rugged Heart. Southern Pub.

Vandeman, G. E. *see* Vandeman, George E.

Vandeman, George.
xVandeman, George.
Tying Down the Sun. Pacific Pr Pub Assn.

Vandeman, George. *see* Vandeman, George E.

Vandeman, George E.
xVandeman, G. E.
Psychic Roulette. Pacific Pr Pub Assn.
xVandeman, George.
How to Burn Your Candle. Pacific Pr Pub Assn.
How to Live with a Tiger. Pacific Pr Pub Assn.
Impersonation Game. Pacific Pr Pub Assn.

Vandenberg, Arthur H. *see* Vandenberg, Arthur Hendrick.

Vandenberg, Arthur Hendrick.
xVandenberg, Arthur H.
The Private Papers of Senator Vandenberg. Greenwood.

Vandenberg, Donald.
xVandenberg, Donald.
ed. Teaching & Learning. U of Ill Pr.
ed. Theory of Knowledge & Problems of Education. U of Ill Pr.

Vandenbergh, C. W.
xVandenbergh, C. W.
Sunbursts for the Spirit. Pine Row.

Vandenbosch, Amry.
xVandenbosch, Amry.
The Changing Face of Southeast Asia. U Pr of Ky.

VandenBroeck, G. *see* Vandenbroeck, Goldian.

Vandenbroeck, Goldian.
xVandenBroeck, G.
Less Is More: The Art of Voluntary Poverty. Har-Row.

Vander, A. J. *see* Vander, Arthur J.

Vander, Arthur J.
xVander, A. J.
Human Physiology: The Mechanisms of Body Function. McGraw.
xVander, Arthur J.
Renal Physiology. McGraw.

Vander, Karen D. Ven. *see* Vander Ven, Karen D.

Vander Molen, Robert.
xVander Molen, Robert.
Circumstances. Sumac Mich.

Vander Salm, Thomas J.
xVander Salm, Thomas J.
Atlas of Bedside Procedures. Little.

Vander Ven, Karen D. *see* Vander Ven, Karen Dahlberg.

Vander Ven, Karen Dahlberg.
xVander Ven, Karen D.
Home & Community Influences on Young Children. Delmar.

Vander Zanden, James W. *see* Vander Zanden, James Wilfrid.

Vander Zanden, James Wilfrid.
xVander Zanden, James W.
Sociology. Wiley.

Vanderbilt, Arthur T., 1888-1957
xVanderbilt, Arthur T.
The Challenge of Law Reform. Greenwood.
Changing Law: A Biography of Arthur T. Vanderbilt. Rutgers U Pr.

Vanderbilt, Byron M. *see* Vanderbilt, Byron Michael.

Vanderbilt, Byron Michael, 1906-
  xVanderbilt, Byron M.
    Thomas Edison, Chemist. Am Chemical.
Vanderbilt, Gloria, 1924-
  xVanderbilt, Gloria.
    Woman to Woman. Doubleday.
Vanderbilt, Kermit.
  xVanderbilt, Kermit.
    Charles Eliot Norton: Apostle of Culture in a
      Democracy. Harvard U Pr.
Vanderbilt, M. Daniel. *see* Vanderbilt, Mortimer Daniel.
Vanderbilt, Mortimer Daniel.
  xVanderbilt, M. Daniel.
    Matrix Structural Analysis. Quantum Pubs.
Vanderbilt University Hospital Dietary Staff. *see*
  Vanderbilt University, Nashville. Hospital.
Vanderbilt University, Nashville. Hospital.
  xVanderbilt University Hospital Dietary Staff.
    ed. Diet Manual. Vanderbilt U Pr.

Vandergraft, James S.
  xVandergraft, James S.
    Introduction to Numerical Computations. Acad
      Pr.

Vandergriff, Aola.
  xVandergriff, Aola.
    Daughters of the Southwind. Warner Bks.

    Daughters of the Wild Country. Warner Bks.
    House of the Dancing Dead. Warner Bks.
Vanderlip, Frank A. *see* Vanderlip, Frank Arthur.
Vanderlip, Frank Arthur, 1864-1937
  xVanderlip, Frank A.
    Business & Education. Arno.
Vandermeulen, Carl.
  xVandermeulen, Carl.
    Photography for Student Publications.
      Middleburg Pr.
Vanderpoel, John H. *see* Vanderpoel, John Henry.
Vanderpoel, John Henry, 1857-1911
  xVanderpoel, John H.
    Human Figure. Dover.
    The Human Figure. Gannon.
Vanderpoel, Sally.
  xVanderpoel, Sally.
    The Care & Feeding of Your Diabetic Child.
      Fell.
Vanderpool, James A.
  xVanderpool, James A.
    People in Pain: A Guide to Pastoral Care. C C
      Thomas.
Vanderveen, Bart H. *see* Vanderveen, Bart Harmannus.
Vanderveen, Bart Harmannus.
  xVanderveen, Bart H.
    The Observer's Army Vehicles Directory.
      Warne.
Vandervelde, Maryanne.
  xVandervelde, Maryanne.
    The Changing Life of the Corporate Wife.
      Atheneum.
    The Changing Life of the Corporate Wife.
      Warner Bks.
Vanderwerf, Calvin A. *see* Vanderwerf, Calvin Anthony.
Vanderwerf, Calvin Anthony, 1917-
  xVanderwerf, Calvin A.
    Acids, Bases & the Chemistry of the Covalent
      Bond. Van Nos Reinhold.
Vanderwerth, W. C.
  xVanderwerth, W. C.
    Indian Oratory: Famous Speeches by Noted
      Indian Chieftains. U of Okla Pr.
Vanderwood, Paul J.
  xVanderwood, Paul J.
    Night Riders of Reelfoot Lake. Memphis St
      Univ.
VanderZwaag, Harold. *see* VanderZwaag, Harold J.
VanderZwaag, Harold J.
  xVanderZwaag, Harold.

    Introduction to Sport Studies: From the
      Classroom to the Ball Park. Wm C Brown.
Vandeweghe, Ernest M.
  xVandeweghe, Ernest M.
    Growing with Sports: A Parent's Guide to the
      Young Athlete. P-H.
Vandiver, Frank E. *see* Vandiver, Frank Everson.
Vandiver, Frank Everson, 1925-
  xVandiver, Frank E.
    Rebel Brass: The Confederate Command
      System. Greenwood.
    The Southwest: South or West?. Tex A&M
      Univ Pr.
    Their Tattered Flags: The Epic of the
      Confederacy. Har-Row.
Vandivert, Rita.
  xVandivert, Rita.
    Understanding Animals As Pets. Warne.
Vanduyn, J. *see* Vanduyn, Julia.
Vanduyn, Julia, 1926-
  xVanduyn, J.
    Practical Systems & Procedures Manual.
      Reston.
Vandyne, William J. *see* Vandyne, William Johnson.
Vandyne, William Johnson.
  xVandyne, William J.
    Revels of Fancy. Arno.
Vane, John R.
  xVane, John R.
    ed. Prostacyclin. Raven.
Vane, Peter K.
  xVane, Peter K.
    Pebble People Pets & Things. Butterick Pub.
Vanecko, James J.
  xVanecko, James J.
    ed. Who Benefits from Federal Education
      Dollars?: The Development of ESEA Title I
      Allocation Policy. Abt Assoc.
Vanek, Jaroslav.
  xVanek, Jaroslav.
    General Equilibrium of International
      Discrimination: The Case of Customs Unions.
      Harvard U Pr.
    General Theory of Labor-Managed Market
      Economies. Cornell U Pr.
    Maximal Economic Growth: A Geometric
      Approach to Von Neumann's Growth Theory
      & the Turnpike Theorem. Cornell U Pr.
    Participatory Economy: An Evolutionary
      Hypothesis & a Strategy for Development.
      Cornell U Pr.
Vanek, Miroslav.
  xVanek, Miroslav.
    Psychology & the Superior Athlete. Macmillan.
Vanfossen, Beth E. *see* Vanfossen, Beth Ensminger.
Vanfossen, Beth Ensminger.
  xVanfossen, Beth E.
    The Structure of Social Inequality. Little.
Vangelisti, Paul.
  xVangelisti, Paul.
    Air. SBD.
Vangermeersch, Richard. *see* Vangermeersch, Richard G.
  J.
Vangermeersch, Richard G. J.
  xVangermeersch, Richard.
    Financial Reporting Techniques in 20 Industrial
      Companies Since 1861. Univ Microfilms.
Vanier, Jean, 1928-
  xVanier, Jean.
    Followers of Jesus. Paulist Pr.
Vanlandingham, K. E. *see* Vanlandingham, Kenneth Earl.
Vanlandingham, Kenneth Earl, 1920-
  xVanlandingham, K. E.
    Problems in Constitutional Law: A Symposium.
      Da Capo.
Vann, Edwin.
  xVann, Edwin G.
    Fundamentals of Biostatistics. Heath.
Vann, Edwin G. *see* Vann, Edwin.

Vann, Richard T.
  xVann, Richard T.
    ed. Century of Genius: European Thought
      1600-1700. P-H.
Vanneman, Peter.
  xVanneman, Peter.
    The Supreme Soviet: Politics & the Legislative
      Process in the Soviet Political System. Duke.
Vannier, Maryhelen.
  xVannier, Maryhelen.
    Individual & Team Sports for Girls & Women.
      HR&W.
    Teaching Health in Elementary Schools. Lea &
      Febiger.
    Teaching Physical Education in Elementary
      Schools. HR&W.
Vanocur, Edith.
  xVanocur, Edith.
    A Chicken in Every Pot. T Y Crowell.
Vansant, Carl.
  xVansant, Carl.
    Strategic Energy Supply & National Security.
      Irvington.
Vanselow, Ralf.
  xVanselow, Ralf.
    ed. Chemistry & Physics of Solid Surfaces.
      CRC Pr.
Vansina, Jan.
  xVansina, Jan.
    The Children of Woot: A History of the Kuba
      Peoples. U of Wis Pr.
Vansittart, Anthony.
  xVansittart, Anthony.
    The Dollar & the Implacable Compulsion of
      the Laws of History. Inst Econ Pol.
Vanstory, Burnette. *see* Vanstory, Burnette (Lightle).
Vanstory, Burnette (Lightle).
  xVanstory, Burnette.
    Georgia's Land of the Golden Isles. U of Ga
      Pr.
Vantine, Larry L.
  xVantine, Larry L.
    Teaching American Indian History: An
      Interdisciplinary Approach. R & E Res
      Assoc.
Vanton, Monte.
  xVanton, Monte.
    Marriage - Grounds for Divorce. S&S.
Vanuxem, Mary, 1881-
  xVanuxem, Mary.
    Education of Feeble-Minded Women. AMS Pr.
Vara, Albert C.
  xVara, Albert C.
    Food & Beverage Industries: A Bibliography &
      Guidebook. Gale.
Varble, Dale. *see* Varble, Dale L.
Varble, Dale L.
  xVarble, Dale.
    Cases in Marketing Management. Merrill.
Varco, Richard L. *see* Varco, Richard Lynn.
Varco, Richard Lynn.
  xVarco, Richard L.
    ed. Controversy in Surgery. Saunders.
Vardac, A. Nicholas.
  xVardac, A. Nicholas.
    Stage to Screen: Theatrical Method from
      Garrick to Griffith. Arno.
Vardaman, George T.
  xVardaman, George T.
    Communication in Modern Organizations.
      Wiley.
Vardamis, Alex A., 1934-
  xVardamis, Alex A.
    The Critical Reputation of Robinson Jeffers: A
      Bibliographical Study. Shoe String.
Vardin, Patricia. *see* Vardin, Patricia A.
Vardin, Patricia A.
  xVardin, Patricia.

ed. Children's Rights: Contemporary
Perspectives. Tchrs Coll.

Vardys, V. Stanley. *see* Vardys, Vytas Stanley.

Vardys, Vytas Stanley.
xVardys, V. Stanley.
ed. The Baltic States in Peace & War,
1917-1945. Pa St U Pr.
The Catholic Church, Dissent & Nationality in
Soviet Lithuania. East Eur Quarterly.

Varg, Paul A.
xVarg, Paul A.
The Closing of the Door: Sino-American
Relations, 1936-1946. Mich St U Pr.
Open Door Diplomat: The Life of W. W.
Rockhill. Greenwood.

Varga, Andrew C.
xVarga, Andrew C.
On Being Human: Principles of Ethics. Paulist
Pr.

Varga, Erugen. *see* Varga, Eugen.

Varga, Eugen, 1879-1964
xVarga, Erugen.
Twentieth Century Capitalism. Arno.

Varga, Judy.
xVarga, Judy.
illus. The Crow Who Came to Stay. Morrow.
illus. Once-a-Year Witch. Morrow.

Varga, Richard S.
xVarga, Richard S.
Matrix Iterative Analysis. P-H.

Vargas, Glenn.
xVargas, Glenn.
Descriptions of Gem Materials. Glenn Vargas.
Diagrams for Faceting. Glenn Vargas.

Vargas Llosa, Mario, 1936-
xVargas Llosa, Mario.
The Cubs & Other Stories. Har-Row.
The Time of the Hero. Har-Row.

Vargin, V V
xVargin, V. V.
Catalyzed Controlled Crystallization of Glasses
in the Lithium Aluminosilicate System.
Plenum Pub.

Vargus, Ione D.
xVargus, Ione D.
Revival of Ideology: The Afro-American
Society Movement. R & E Res Assoc.

Varketta, Ralph.
xVarketta, Ralph.
Gourmet Cooking Confidential. Exposition.

Varkey, Ouseph.
xVarkey, Ouseph.
At the Crossroads: Sino- Indian Border Dispute
& the Communist Party of India, 1959-1963.
South Asia Bks.

Varley, H. Paul.
xVarley, H. Paul.
Imperial Restoration in Medieval Japan.
Columbia U Pr.

Varley, John, 1947-
xVarley, John.
The Ophiuchi Hotline. Dell.
The Ophiuchi Hotline. Dial.
Titan. Berkley Pub.

Varma, Baidya N. *see* Varma, Baidya Nath.

Varma, Baidya Nath, 1921-
xVarma, Baidya N.
The Sociology & Politics of Development: A
Theoretical Study. Routledge & Kegan.

Varma, Monika.
xVarma, Monika.
Green Leaves & Gold. InterCulture.

Varma, Nirmal.
xVarma, Nirmal.
The Hill Station & Other Stories. InterCulture.

Varma, Ravi.
xVarma, Ravi.
Chemical Analysis by Microwave Rotational
Spectroscopy. Wiley.

Varma, V. P. *see* Varma, Vishwanath Prasad.

Varma, Vishwanath Prasad, 1924-
xVarma, V. P.
The Political Philosophy of Sri Aurobindo.
Orient Bk Dist.
The Political Philosophy of Sri Aurobindo.
Verry.

Varneke, B. V. *see* Varneke, Boris Vasilevich.

Varneke, Boris Vasilevich, 1874-
xVarneke, B. V.
History of the Russian Theatre: Seventeenth
Through Nineteenth Centuries. Hafner.

Varney, Glenn H.
xVarney, Glenn H.
Organization Development Approach to
Management Development. A-W.
Organization Development for Managers. A-W.

Varnusz, Egon.
xVarnusz, Egon.
Selected Games of Lajos Portisch. Arco.

Varriale, Philip.
xVarriale, Philip.
ed. Cardiac Pacing: A Concise Guide to
Clinical Practice. Lea & Febiger.

Vartanian, H. G.
xVartanian, H. G.
Honeymoon in a Taxicab. Harlo Pr.

Vartanian, Michael M.
xVartanian, Michael M.
The Computational Tools of Engineering. A-W.

Vas Dias, Robert.
xVas Dias, Robert.
Speech Acts & Happenings. Bobbs.

Vasari, Giorgio.
xVasari, Giorgio.
Artists of the Renaissance. Viking Pr.
Lives of the Most Eminent Painters, Sculptors
& Architects. AMS Pr.

Vasconcellos, John.
xVasconcellos, John.
A Liberating Vision: Politics for Growing
Humans. Impact Pubs Cal.

Vasey, George.
xVasey, George.
Illustrations of Eating: Displaying the
Omnivorous Character of Man & Exhibiting
the Natives of Various Countries at Feeding
Time, by a Beef-Eater. Grant Dahlstrom.

Vash, Carolyn L.
xVash, Carolyn L.
The Burnt-Out Administrator. Springer Pub.

Vasile, Albert J.
xVasile, Albert J.
Speak with Confidence: A Practical Guide.
Winthrop.

Vasiliev, Alexander A. *see* Vasiliev, Alexander
Alexandrovich.

Vasiliev, Alexander Alexandrovich, 1867-1953
xVasiliev, Alexander A.
History of the Byzantine Empire, 324-1453.
Peter Smith.
History of the Byzantine Empire, 324-1453. U
of Wis Pr.

Vasiliu, Emanuel.
xVasiliu, Emanuel.
Outline of a Semantic Theory of Kernel
Sentences. Mouton.

Vasiliu, Mircea.
xVasiliu, Mircea.
illus. A Day at the Beach. Random.
illus. Good Night, Sleep Tight Book. Western
Pub.
Once Upon a Pirate Ship. Western Pub.

Vasiloff, Mary Jean.
xVasiloff, Mary Jean.
Alone with Your Horse. Har-Row.

Vasquez, Librado K. *see* Vasquez, Librado Keno.

Vasquez, Librado Keno.
xVasquez, Librado K.

Regional Dictionary of Chicano Slang. Jenkins.

Vasquez, Richard.
xVasquez, Richard.
Chicano. Avon.

Vass, Winifred K. *see* Vass, Winifred Kellersberger.

Vass, Winifred Kellersberger.
xVass, Winifred K.
Thirty-One Banana Leaves. John Knox.

Vasseur, J. P. *see* Vasseur, Jean Pierre.

Vasseur, Jean Pierre.
xVasseur, J. P.
Properties & Applications of Transistors.
Pergamon.

Vassos, Basil H.
xVassos, Basil H.
Analog & Digital Electronics for Scientists.
Wiley.

Vassos, John, 1898-
xVassos, John.
Contempo, Phobia and Other Graphic
Interpretations. Dover.
Contempo, Phobia & Other Graphic
Interpretations. Peter Smith.

Vasta, Ross.
xVasta, Ross.
Studying Children: An Introduction to
Research Methods. W H Freeman.

Vasu, Ellen S. *see* Vasu, Ellen Storey.

Vasu, Ellen Storey.
xVasu, Ellen S.
An Introduction to Research & the Computer:
A Self-Instructional Package. U NC Inst Res
Soc Sci.

Vasu, Michael L. *see* Vasu, Michael Lee.

Vasu, Michael Lee.
xVasu, Michael L.
Politics & Planning: A National Study of
American Planners. U NC Pr.

Vasu, Srisa Chandra, Rai Bahadur, 1861-1918?
xVasu, Srisa Chandra.
A Catechism of Hindu Dharma. AMS Pr.

Vasudevan, M. *see* Vasudevan, Mullath.

Vasudevan, Mullath, 1927-
xVasudevan, M.
Criteria & Methods for Educational Research,
Reform & Planning. Vantage.

Vaswig, William L.
xVaswig, William L.
I Prayed, He Answered. Augsburg.

Vatcher, William H.
xVatcher, William H.
Panmunjom: The Story of the Korean Military
Armistice Negotiations. Greenwood.

Vatican Council Two. *see* Vatican Council, 2d,
1962-1965.

Vatican Council, 2d, 1962-1965.
xVatican Council Two.
Constitution on the Sacred Liturgy. Paulist Pr.
Declaration of Religious Freedom. Paulist Pr.
Declaration on Christian Education. Paulist Pr.
Declaration on the Relation of the Church to
Non-Christian Religions. Paulist Pr.
Decree on Ecumenism. Paulist Pr.
Decree on Priestly Training & Decree on the
Ministry & Life of Priests. Paulist Pr.
Decree on the Apostolate of the Laity. Paulist
Pr.
Decree on the Pastoral Office of Bishops.
Paulist Pr.
Decree on the Renewal of Religious Life.
Paulist Pr.

Vatikiotis, P. J. *see* Vatikiotis, Panayiotis J.

Vatikiotis, Panayiotis J., 1928-
xVatikiotis, P. J.
Greece: A Political Essay. Sage.
xVatikiotis, Panayiotis J.
The Egyptian Army in Politics: Pattern for
New Nations. Greenwood.

Vatter, Harold G.
xVatter, Harold G.

The Drive to Industrial Maturity: The U. S.
 Economy, 1860-1914. Greenwood.
Small Enterprise & Oligopoly. Arno.
Vatter, Paul A.
 xVatter, Paul A.
  Quantitative Methods in Management: Text &
   Cases. Irwin.
Vatter, William J. *see* Vatter, William Joseph.
Vatter, William Joseph, 1905-
 xVatter, William J.
  Accounting Measurements for Financial
   Reports. Irwin.
  The Fund Theory of Accounting & Its
   Implications for Financial Reports. Arno.
  Fund Theory of Accounting & Its Implications
   for Financial Reports. U of Chicago Pr.
Vaubel, George D.
 xVaubel, George D.
  Municipal Home Rule in Ohio. W S Hein.
Vaudrin, Bill.
 xVaudrin, Bill.
  Racing Alaskan Sled Dogs. Alaska Northwest.
Vaughan. *see* Vaughan, William.
Vaughan, B. W., 1921-
 xVaughan, B. W.
  Planning in Education. Cambridge U Pr.
Vaughan, Beatrice.
 xVaughan, Beatrice.
  Citrus Cooking. Greene.
  Real Old-Time Yankee Apple Cooking.
   Greene.
  Real Old-Time Yankee Maple Cooking.
   Greene.
  Store-Cheese Cooking. Greene.
Vaughan, Bill.
 xVaughan, Bill.
  Sorry I Stirred It. S&S.
Vaughan, C. E. *see* Vaughan, Charles Edwyn.
Vaughan, Carter A.
 xVaughan, Carter A.
  Fortress Fury. Popular Lib.
Vaughan, Charles Edwyn, 1854-1922
 xVaughan, C. E.
  ed. English Literary Criticism. Kennikat.
Vaughan, David, 1924-
 xVaughan, David.
  Frederick Ashton & His Ballets. Knopf.
Vaughan, Frances E.
 xVaughan, Frances E.
  Awakening Intuition. Doubleday.
Vaughan, Harold. *see* Vaughan, Harold Cecil.
Vaughan, Harold C. *see* Vaughan, Harold Cecil.
Vaughan, Harold Cecil.
 xVaughan, Harold.
  The Monroe Doctrine, 1823: A Landmark in
   American Foreign Policy. Watts.
 xVaughan, Harold C.
  Citizen Genet Affair: A Chapter in the
   Formation of American Foreign Policy.
   Watts.
  The Colony of Georgia. Watts.
Vaughan, Herbert M. *see* Vaughan, Herbert
 Millingchamp.
Vaughan, Herbert Millingchamp, 1870-1948
 xVaughan, Herbert M.
  From Anne to Victoria: Fourteen Biographical
   Studies Between 1702 & 1901. Kennikat.
Vaughan, Janet M. *see* Vaughan, Janet Maria.
Vaughan, Janet Maria.
 xVaughan, Janet M.
  The Effects of Irradiation on the Skeleton.
   Oxford U Pr.
Vaughan, Linda K. *see* Vaughan, Linda Kent.
Vaughan, Linda Kent.
 xVaughan, Linda K.
  Canoeing & Sailing. Wm C Brown.
Vaughan, P. *see* Vaughan, Percy.
Vaughan, Percy.
 xVaughan, P.

Early Shelley Pamphlets. Haskell.
Vaughan, Philip. *see* Vaughan, Philip H.
Vaughan, Philip H.
 xVaughan, Philip.
  The Truman Administration's Legacy for Black
   America. Mojave Bks.
Vaughan, Richard, 1927-
 xVaughan, Richard.
  ed. Post-War Integration in Europe. St Martin.
  Twentieth Century Europe: Paths to Unity.
   B&N.
  Valois Burgundy. Shoe String.
Vaughan, Robert, 1795-1868
 xVaughan, Robert.
  The Life & Opinions of John de Wycliffe, D.
   D.. AMS Pr.
  The Valkyrie Mandate. PB.
Vaughan, Roger.
 xVaughan, Roger.
  The Grand Gesture: Ted Turner, Mariner, &
   the America's Cup. Little.
Vaughan, Thomas, 1924-
 xVaughan, Thomas.
  The Bybee-Howell House on Sauvie Island:
   The Oregon Territorial Farmstead. Oreg Hist
   Soc.
  A Century of Portland Architecture. Oreg Hist
   Soc.
Vaughan, Walter R. *see* Vaughan, Walter Raleigh.
Vaughan, Walter Raleigh, 1848-
 xVaughan, Walter R.
  Vaughan's Freedmen's Pension Bill. Arno.
Vaughan, William, 1943-
 xVaughan.
  German Romanticism & English Art. Yale U
   Pr.
Vaughan Williams, Ursula.
 xVaughan Williams, Ursula.
  R. V. W.: A Biography of Ralph Vaughan
   Williams. Oxford U Pr.
Vaughn, Alan.
 xVaughn, Alan.
  Incredible Coincidence: The Baffling World of
   Synchronicity. NAL.
Vaughn, Ann.
 xVaughn, Ann.
  You Are What You Make Yourself. Seaview
   Bks.
Vaughn, Gwenyth R.
 xVaughn, Gwenyth R.
  Speech Facilitation: Extraoral & Intraoral
   Stimulation Technique for Improvement of
   Articulation Skills. C C Thomas.
Vaughn, Richard C.
 xVaughn, Richard C.
  Introduction to Industrial Engineering. Iowa St
   U Pr.
  Legal Aspects of Engineering. Kendall-Hunt.
  Quality Control. Iowa St U Pr.
Vaughn, Robert G.
 xVaughn, Robert G.
  Conflict-of-Interest Regulation in the Federal
   Executive Branch. Lexington Bks.
Vaughn, Ruth.
 xVaughn, Ruth.
  Celebrate with Words. Broadman.
  Even When I Cry. Moody.
  More Skits That Win. Zondervan.
  To Be a Graduate. Nelson.
  Write to Discover Yourself. Doubleday.
Vaughn, Stephen, 1947-
 xVaughn, Stephen L.
  Holding Fast the Inner Lines: Democracy,
   Nationalism, & the Committee on Public
   Information. U of NC Pr.
Vaughn, Stephen L. *see* Vaughn, Stephen.
Vaught, John, 1909-
 xVaught, John.

Rebel Coach: My Football Family. Memphis St
 Univ.
Vaught, Laud O. *see* Vaught, Laud Oswald.
Vaught, Laud Oswald, 1925-
 xVaught, Laud O.
  Focus on the Christian Family. Pathway Pr.
Vaupel, James W.
 xVaupel, James W.
  The World's Multinational Enterprises: A
   Sourcebook of Tables Based on a Study of
   the Largest U.S. & Non-U.S. Manufacturing
   Corporations. Harvard Busn.
Vaux, Kenneth.
 xVaux, Kenneth L.
  Will to Live-Will to Die: Ethics & the Search
   for a Good Death. Augsburg.
Vaux, Kenneth L. *see* Vaux, Kenneth.
Vaux, Robert. *see* Vaux, Roberts.
Vaux, Roberts, 1786-1836
 xVaux, Robert.
  Memoirs of the Life of Anthony Benezet. B
   Franklin.
Vauxhall Motors. *see* Vauxhall Motors, Ltd.
Vauxhall Motors, Ltd.
 xVauxhall Motors.
  Motor Car: The Inside Story. Soccer.
Vavra, Robert.
 xVavra, Robert.
  illus. Felipe the Bullfighter. HarBraceJ.
  Lion & Blue. Reynal.
  Such Is the Real Nature of Horses. Morrow.
Vayda, Andrew P. *see* Vayda, Andrew Peter.
Vayda, Andrew Peter.
 xVayda, Andrew P.
  ed. Environment & Cultural Behavior:
   Ecological Studies in Cultural Anthropology.
   U of Tex Pr.
Vaz, E. *see* Vaz, Edmund W.
Vaz, Edmund W.
 xVaz, E.
  Aspects of Deviance. P-H.
Vazakas, Byron.
 xVazakas, Byron.
  Nostalgias for a House of Cards: Poems.
   October.
Vazquez, D. *see* Vazquez, David.
Vazquez, David.
 xVazquez, D.
  Inhibitors of Protein Biosynthesis.
   Springer-Verlag.
Vazsonyi, Andrew.
 xVazsonyi, Andrew.
  Business Mathematics for Colleges. Irwin.
  Introduction to Data Processing. Irwin.
  Introduction to Electronic Data Processing.
   Irwin.
Vdovenko, V. M. *see* Vdovenko, Viktor Mikhailovich.
Vdovenko, Viktor Mikhailovich.
 xVdovenko, V. M.
  Analytical Chemistry of Radium. Halsted Pr.
Veall, Donald.
 xVeall, Donald.
  Popular Movement for Law Reform 1640-1660.
   Oxford U Pr.
Veaner, Allen B., 1929-
 xVeaner, Allen B.
  Studies in Micropublishing: 1853-1976.
   Microform Rev.
Veatch, H. C. *see* Veatch, Henry C.
Veatch, Henry. *see* Veatch, Henry Babcock.
Veatch, Henry B. *see* Veatch, Henry Babcock.
Veatch, Henry Babcock.
 xVeatch, Henry.
  Realism & Nominalism Revisited. Marquette.
 xVeatch, Henry B.

For an Ontology of Morals: A Critique of
Contemporary Ethical Theory. Northwestern
U Pr.
Rational Man: A Modern Interpretation of
Aristotelian Ethics. Ind U Pr.
Rational Man: A Modern Interpretation of
Aristotelian Ethics. Peter Smith.
Two Logics: The Conflict Between Classical &
Neo-Analytic Philosophy. Northwestern U
Pr.

Veatch, Henry C.
xVeatch, H. C.
Pulse & Switching Circuit Action. McGraw.
Pulse & Switching Circuit Measurements.
McGraw.

Veatch, Richard, 1926-
xVeatch, Richard.
Canada & the League of Nations. U of Toronto
Pr.

Veatch, Robert M.
xVeatch, Robert M.
Case Studies in Medical Ethics. Harvard U Pr.
Death, Dying, & the Biological Revolution:
Our Last Quest for Responsibility. Yale U Pr.
ed. Ethics and Health Policy. Ballinger Pub.
ed. Life Span: The Hastings Center Report on
Values & Life-Extending Technologies.
Har-Row.
Value-Freedom in Science & Technology: A
Study of the Importance of Religious, Ethical,
& Other Socio-Cultural Factors in Selected
Medical Decisions Regarding Birth Control.
Scholars Pr Ca.

Veazie, W. H.
xVeazie, Walter.
Marketing of Information Analysis Center
Products & Services. Am Soc Info Sci.
Veazie, Walter. *see* Veazie W H

Veblen, Thorstein, 1857-1929
xVeblen, Thorstein.
Theory of the Leisure Class. NAL.
The Theory of the Leisure Class. Penguin.
xVeblen, Thorstein B.
Higher Learning in America. Kelley.
Theory of Business Enterprise. Kelley.
Theory of the Leisure Class. Kelley.
Veblen, Thorstein B. *see* Veblen, Thorstein.

Vecellio, Cesare, 1530 (ca.)-1601
xVecellio, Cesare.
Vecellio's Renaissance Costume Book: All 500
Woodcut Illustrations from the Famous
Sixteenth-Century Compendium of World
Costume. Peter Smith.

Vecera, Miroslav.
xVecera, Miroslav.
Detection & Identification of Organic
Compounds. Plenum Pub.
Vecera, Miroslav. *see* Vecera, Miroslav.
Vechten, Carl Van. *see* Van Vechten, Carl.

Vedder, Alan C., 1912-
xVedder, Alan C.
Furniture of Spanish New Mexico. Sunstone
Pr.
Vedder, Clyde B. *see* Vedder, Clyde Bennett.

Vedder, Clyde Bennett.
xVedder, Clyde B.
The Delinquent Girl. C C Thomas.
Juvenile Offenders. C C Thomas.
Penology: A Realistic Approach. C C Thomas.
ed. Problems of the Middle-Aged. C C
Thomas.
Vedral, Joyce. *see* Vedral, Joyce L.

Vedral, Joyce L.
xVedral, Joyce.
A Literary Survey of the Bible. Logos.

Veech, James, 1808-1879
xVeech, James.

The Monongahela of Old: Or, Historical
Sketches of South-Western Pennsylvania to
the Year 1800. Genealog Pub.

Veeck, Bill.
xVeeck, Bill.
Thirty Tons a Day. Popular Lib.

Veenendaal, Cornelia.
xVeenendaal, Cornelia.
Green Shaded Lamps. Alicejamesbooks.
Veer, Judy Van Der. *see* Van Der Veer, Judy.

Veerathappa, K., 1930-
xVeerathappa, K.
British Conservative Party & Indian
Independence, 1930-1947. South Asia Bks.

Veglahn, Nancy.
xVeglahn, Nancy.
Coils, Magnets & Rings: Michael Faraday's
World. Coward.
Dance of the Planets: The Universe of Nicolaus
Copernicus. Coward.
Spider of Brooklyn Heights. Scribner.
The Vandals of Treason House. HM.

Vehanen, Kosti.
xVehanen, Kosti.
Marian Anderson, a Portrait. Greenwood.
Veibel, S. *see* Veibel, Stig.

Veibel, Stig, 1898-
xVeibel, S.
The Determination of Hydroxyl Groups. Acad
Pr.

Veiga, John F.
xVeiga, John F.
The Dynamics of Organization Theory:
Gaining a Macro Perspective. West Pub.
Veinott, Cyril G. *see* Veinott, Cyril George.

Veinott, Cyril George.
xVeinott, Cyril G.
Computer-Aided Design of Electric Machinery.
MIT Pr.

Veinus, Abraham.
xVeinus, Abraham.
Concerto. Dover.
Concerto. Peter Smith.

Veit, Fritz, 1907-
xVeit, Fritz.
Community College Library. Greenwood.

Veitch, Tom.
xVeitch, Tom.
The Luis Armed Story. Full Court NY.

Veith, Ilza.
xVeith, Ilza.
Hysteria: The History of a Disease. U of
Chicago Pr.

Veith, Richard.
xVeith, Richard.
Talk-Back TV: Two-Way Cable Television.
TAB Bks.

Veley, Charles, 1943-
xVeley, Charles.
Catching Up. M Evans.
Children of the Dark. Doubleday.
Veley, Victor F. *see* Veley, Victor F. C.

Veley, Victor F. C.
xVeley, Victor F.
Practical Electronics Math. TAB Bks.
Third Class FCC License Study Guide. TAB
Bks.

Velie, Alan R., 1937-
xVelie, Alan R.
American Indian Literature: An Anthology. U
of Okla Pr.

Velie, Lester.
xVelie, Lester.
Desperate Bargain: Why Jimmy Hoffa Had to
Die. Readers Digest Pr.

Velikhov, E. P.
xVelikhov, E. P.

ed. Science, Technology & the Future: Soviet
Scientists Analysis of the Problems of &
Prospects for the Development of Science &
Technology & Their Role in Society.
Pergamon.

Velikovsky, Immanuel.
xVelikovsky, Immanuel.
Earth in Upheaval. Doubleday.
Peoples of the Sea. Doubleday.
Worlds in Collision. Doubleday.
Worlds in Collision. PB.

Veliz, Claudio.
xVeliz, Claudio.
The Centralist Tradition of Latin America.
Princeton U Pr.
Vella, Walter F. *see* Vella, Walter Francis.

Vella, Walter Francis, 1924-
xVella, Walter F.
ed. Aspects of Vietnamese History. U Pr of
Hawaii.
Chaiyo! King Vajiravudh & the Development
of Thai Nationalism. U Pr of Hawaii.

Vellacott, Philip.
xVellacott, Philip.
Sophocles & Oedipus: A Study of Oedipus
Tyrannus with a New Translation. U of Mich
Pr.

Vellela, Tony.
xVellela, Tony.
Food Co-Ops for Small Groups. Workman Pub.

Vellutino, Frank R.
xVellutino, Frank R.
Dyslexia: Theory & Research. MIT Pr.
Velsen, J. Van. *see* Van Velsen, J.

Velthuijs, Max, 1923-
xVelthuijs, Max.
illus. The Painter & the Bird. A-W.

Veltri, John.
xVeltri, John.
Architectural Photography. Amphoto.

Velz, Clarence J.
xVelz, Clarence J.
Applied Stream Sanitation. Wiley.
Ven, Andrew H. Van de. *see* Van de Ven, Andrew H.
Venables, E. *see* Venables, Ethel Craig (Howell).

Venables, Edmund, 1819-1895
xVenables, Edmund.
Life of John Bunyan. Folcroft.

Venables, Ethel Craig (Howell), Lady.
xVenables, E.
Leaving School & Starting Work. Pergamon.

Venables, Peter, Sir, 1904-
xVenables, Peter.
Higher Education Developments: The
Technological Universities 1956-1976.
Merrimack Bk Serv.

Venancio Filho, Fernando.
xVenancio Filho, Fernando.
Introduction to Matrix Structural Theory in Its
Application to Civil & Aircraft Construction.
Ungar.

Vence, Celine.
xVence, Celine.
The Grand Masters of French Cuisine: Five
Centuries of Great Cooking. Putnam.
Venden, Morris. *see* Venden, Morris L.

Venden, Morris L.
xVenden, Morris.
From Exodus to Advent. Southern Pub.

Venditti, Arnaldo.
xVenditti, Arnaldo.
The Loggia del Capitaniato. Pa St U Pr.
Vendler, Helen H. *see* Vendler, Helen Hennessy.

Vendler, Helen Hennessy.
xVendler, Helen H.

The Little Kid's Americana Craft Book.
Taplinger.
The Little Kid's Craft Book. Taplinger.
The Little Kid's Four Seasons Craft Book.
Taplinger.

Vermeil, Edmond, 1878-
xVermeil, Edmond.
Germany's Three Reichs: Their History &
Culture. Norwood Edns.

Vermes, Geza.
xVermes, Geza.
The Dead Sea Scrolls: Qumran in Perspective.
Fortress.

Vermes, Jean C. *see* Vermes, Jean Campbell Pattison.

Vermes, Jean Campbell Pattison.
xVermes, Jean C.
Secretary's Guide to Dealing with People. P-H.

Vermeule, Cornelius. *see* Vermeule, Cornelius Clarkson.

Vermeule, Cornelius Clarkson.
xVermeule, Cornelius.
Greek & Roman Sculpture in Gold & Silver.
Mus Fine Arts Boston.

Vermeule, Emily.
xVermeule, Emily.
Aspects of Death in Early Greek Art & Poetry.
U of Cal Pr.
Greece in the Bronze Age. U of Chicago Pr.
xVermeule, Emily T.
Greece in the Bronze Age. U of Chicago Pr.

Vermeule, Emily T. *see* Vermeule, Emily.

Vermilye, Jerry.
xVermilye, Jerry.
Cary Grant. Brown Bk.
The Films of Charles Bronson. Citadel Pr.
The Films of Elizabeth Taylor. Citadel Pr.
The Great British Films. Citadel Pr.

Vernadakis, Antonia.
xVernadakis, Antonia.
ed. Drugs & the Developing Brain. Plenum
Pub.

Vernadsky, George, 1887-
xVernadsky, George.
Ancient Russia. Yale U Pr.
History of Russia. Yale U Pr.
The Origins of Russia. Greenwood.
Russian Historiography: A History. Nordland
Pub.

Vernam, Glenn R.
xVernam, Glenn R.
The Talking Rifle. Manor Bks.

Vernant, Jacques.
xVernant, Jacques.
Refugee in the Postwar World. Elliots Bks.

Vernazza, Marcelle.
xVernazza, Marcelle.
Music Plus: For the Young Child in Special
Education. Pruett.

Vernberg, F. John.

xVernberg, F. J.
jt. auth. Environmental Physiology of Marine
Animals. Springer-Verlag.
xVernberg, F. John.
ed. Pollution & Physiology of Marine
Organisms. Acad Pr.

Vernberg, W. B. *see* Vernberg, Winona B.
Vernberg, Winona. *see* Vernberg, Winona B.

Vernberg, Winona B.

xVernberg, W. B.
Environmental Physiology of Marine Animals.
Springer-Verlag.
xVernberg, Winona.
ed. Symbiosis in the Sea. U of SC Pr.
xVernberg, Winona B.
Marine Pollution: Functional Responses. Acad
Pr.
jt. ed. Pollution & Physiology of Marine
Organisms. Acad Pr.

Verne, Jules, 1828-1905
xVerne, Jules.
An Antarctic Mystery. Gregg.
Around the World in Eighty Days. Assoc Bk.
Around the World in Eighty Days. Biblio Dist.
Around the World in Eighty Days. Dell.
Around the World in Eighty Days. Pendulum
Pr.
Around the World in Eighty Days. Dodd.
Around the World in Eighty Days. Viking Pr.
Around the World in Eighty Days. Airmont.
For the Flag. Assoc Bk.
From the Earth to the Moon. Amereon Ltd.
From the Earth to the Moon. Biblio Dist.
From the Earth to the Moon. Airmont.
The Fur Country: Seventy Degrees North
Latitude. Amereon Ltd.
Journey to the Center of the Earth. Pendulum
Pr.
Journey to the Center of the Earth. Airmont.
A Journey to the Center of the Earth. Schol Bk
Serv.
Master of the World. Airmont.
Propeller Island. Assoc Bk.
Propeller Island. Beekman Pubs.
Twenty Thousand Leagues Under the Sea.
Biblio Dist.
Twenty Thousand Leagues Under the Sea.
Dutton.
Twenty Thousand Leagues Under the Sea.
NAL.
Twenty Thousand Leagues Under the Sea.
NAL.
Twenty-Thousand Leagues Under the Sea.
Pitman Learning.
Twenty Thousand Leagues Under the Sea.
Raintree Pubs.
Twenty Thousand Leagues Under the Sea.
Pendulum Pr.
Twenty Thousand Leagues Under the Sea.
AMSCO Sch.
Twenty Thousand Leagues Under the Sea.
Macmillan.
Twenty Thousand Leagues Under the Sea.
Airmont.
Twenty-Thousand Leagues Under the Sea.
Bantam.
Twenty Thousand Leagues Under the Sea. PB.

Verner, Bill.
xVerner, Bill.
Racquetball. Mayfield Pub.

Verner, Lawrence.
xVerner, Lawrence.
Mathematics for Health Practitioners: Basic
Concepts & Clinical Applications. Lippincott.

Verneuil, Louis, 1893-1952
xVerneuil, Louis.
The Fabulous Life of Sarah Bernhardt.
Greenwood.

Verney, Douglas V.
xVerney, Douglas V.
British Government & Politics: Life Without a
Declaration of Independence. Har-Row.

Verney, Michael. *see* Verney, Michael P.

Verney, Michael P.
xVerney, Michael.
Complete Amateur Boat Building. Intl Marine.

Verney, Peter, 1930-
xVerney, Peter.
Animals in Peril: Man's War Against Wildlife.
Brigham.
The Earthquake Handbook. Paddington.

Verney, Stephen.
xVerney, Stephen.
People & Cities. Revell.

Vernon, Arthur.
xVernon, Arthur.
The History & Romance of the Horse. Gale.

Vernon, Edward.
xVernon, Edward.

Practice Makes Perfect. St Martin.
Practice What You Preach. St Martin.

Vernon, Horace M. *see* Vernon, Horace Middleton.

Vernon, Horace Middleton, 1870-
xVernon, Horace M.
Industrial Fatigue & Efficiency. Arno.

Vernon, Ida (Stevenson) Weldon.
xVernon, Ida W.
Pedro De Valdivia, Conquistador of Chile.
Greenwood.

Vernon, Ida W. *see* Vernon, Ida (Stevenson) Weldon.
Vernon, Ivan. *see* Vernon, Ivan R.

Vernon, Ivan R.
xVernon, Ivan.
ed. The Pricing Function: A Pragmatic
Approach. Lexington Bks.
xVernon, Ivan R.
ed. Introduction to Manufacturing
Management. SME.
ed. Modern Aspects of Manufacturing
Management: Selected Readings. SME.
ed. Realistic Cost Estimating for
Manufacturing. SME.

Vernon, J. B. *see* Vernon, James B.

Vernon, Jack.
xVernon, Jack.
Macroeconomics. Dryden Pr.

Vernon, James B.
xVernon, J. B.
Linear Vibration Theory: Generalized
Properties & Numerical Methods. Krieger.

Vernon, John, 1943
xVernon, John.
Poetry & the Body. U of Ill Pr.

Vernon, John M. *see* Vernon, John Mitcham.

Vernon, John Mitcham, 1937-
xVernon, John M.
Public Investment Planning in Civilian Nuclear
Power. Duke.

Vernon, Louise A.
xVernon, Louise A.
Doctor in Rags. Herald Pr.
Ink on His Fingers. Herald Pr.

Vernon, M. D. *see* Vernon, Magdalen Dorothea.
Vernon, Magdalen D. *see* Vernon, Magdalen Dorothea.

Vernon, Magdalen Dorothea, 1901-
xVernon, M. D.
Further Study of Visual Perception. Hafner.
Reading & Its Difficulties: A Psychological
Study. Cambridge U Pr.
xVernon, Magdalen D.
Human Motivation. Cambridge U Pr.

Vernon, Philip E. *see* Vernon, Philip Ewart.

Vernon, Philip Ewart.
xVernon, Philip E.
Intelligence & Cultural Environment. Methuen
Inc.
The Structure of Human Abilities. Greenwood.

Vernon, R. *see* Vernon, Raymond.

Vernon, Raymond, 1913-
xVernon, R.
The Economic Environment of International
Business. P-H.
xVernon, Raymond.
Dilemma of Mexico's Development: The Roles
of the Private & Public Sectors. Harvard U
Pr.
The Economic & Political Consequences of
Multinational Enterprise: An Anthology.
Harvard Busn.
Economic Environment & International
Business. P-H.
ed. The Oil Crisis. Norton.
Storm Over the Multinationals: The Real
Issues. Harvard U Pr.

Vernon, Richard.
xVernon, Richard.

Commitment & Change: Georges Sorel & the
 Idea of Revolution. U of Toronto Pr.
Vernon, Walter M.
 xVernon, Walter M.
  Introductory Psychology. Rand.
Vernon, Walter N.
 xVernon, Walter N.
  Forever Building: The Life & Ministry of Paul
  E. Martin. SMU Press.
Vernon, William John Borlase-Warren-Venables.
 xVernon, William W.
  Readings on the Purgatorio of Dante. R West.
Vernon, William W. see Vernon, William John
 Borlase-Warren-Venables.
Verny, Thomas R.
 xVerny, Thomas R.
  Inside Groups: A Practical Guide to Encounter
  Groups & Group Therapy. McGraw.
Vero, Radu.
 xVero, Radu.
  Understanding Perspective. Van Nos Reinhold.
Veron, Enid.
 xVeron, Enid.
  ed. Humor in America: An Anthology.
  HarBraceJ.
Veronis, Andrew.
 xVeronis, Andrew.
  Integrated Circuit Fabrication Technology.
  Reston.
Verrall, Arthur W. see Verrall, Arthur Woollgar.
Verrall, Arthur Woollgar.
 xVerrall, Arthur W.
  Collected Studies in Greek & Latin
  Scholarship. Russell.
Verrall, John, 1908-
 xVerrall, John W.
  Fugue & Invention in Theory & Practice.
  Pacific Bks.
Verrall, John W. see Verrall, John.
Verran, Roger, 1916-
 xVerran, Roger.
  Can You Survive Your Escape?: Life on
  California's North Coast. Presidio Pr.
  The Fog & San Francisco. Pacific Bks.
Verrette, Joyce.
 xVerrette, Joyce.
  Dawn of Desire. Avon.
  Winged Priestess. Fawcett.
Verrier, Michelle.
 xVerrier, Michelle.
  Fantin-Latour. Crown.
  The Orientalists. Rizzoli Intl.
Verschueren, Karel.
 xVerschueren, Karel.
  Handbook of Environmental Data on Organic
  Chemicals. Van Nos Reinhold.
Verschuur, Gerrit. see Verschuur, Gerrit L.
Verschuur, Gerrit L., 1937-
 xVerschuur, Gerrit.
  Starscapes: Topics in Astronomy. Little.
 xVerschuur, Gerrit L.
  Cosmic Catastrophes. A-W.
Versenyi, Laszlo.
 xVersenyi, Laszlo.
  Socratic Humanism. Greenwood.
Versenyi, Lazslo. see Versenyi, Laszlo.
Versfeld, Marthinus.
 xVersfeld, Marthinus.
  Our Selves. Rowman.
Verstappen, H. see Verstappen, Herman Theodoor.
Verstappen, Herman Theodoor.
 xVerstappen, H.
  Remote Sensing in Geomorphology. Elsevier.
Versteegh, C. H. see Versteegh, C. H. M.
Versteegh, C. H. M.
 xVersteegh, C. H.
  Greek Elements in Arabic Linguistic Thinking.
  Humanities.
Vertes, A. see Vertes, Attila.

Vertes, Attila.
 xVertes, A.
  Mossbauer Spectroscopy. Elsevier.
Verwey, Gerlof, 1901-
 xVerwey, Gerlof.
  Economist's Handbook: A Manual of
  Statistical Sources. Gale.
Verwoerd, C. D. A.
 xVerwoerd, C. D. A.
  Cephalic Neural Crest & Placodes.
  Springer-Verlag.
Verwoerdt, Adriaan.
 xVerwoerdt, Adriaan.
  Communication with the Fatally Ill. C E
  Tuttle.
 xVerwoerdt, Adrian.
  Clinical Geropsychiatry. Williams & Wilkins.
Verwoerdt, Adrian. see Verwoerdt, Adriaan.
Very, Alice.
 xVery, Alice.
  How to Use Peat Moss. Branden.
Veryan, Patricia.
 xVeryan, Patricia.
  The Lord & the Gypsy. Fawcett.
  The Lord & the Gypsy. Walker & Co.
  Love's Duet. Fawcett.
  Mistress of Willowvale. Walker & Co.
Verzijl, J. J.
 xVerzijl, J. J.
  Production Planning & Information Systems.
  Halsted Pr.
Vesely, J. see Vesely, Josef.
Vesely, Josef.
 xVesely, J.
  Analysis with Ion-Selective Electrodes. Halsted
  Pr.
Vesenyi, Paul E., 1911-
 xVesenyi, Paul E.
  An Introduction to Periodical Bibliography.
  Pierian.
Veseth, Michael.
 xVeseth, Michael.
  Introductory Macroeconomics. Acad Pr.
Vesey, Godfrey. see Vesey, Godfrey Norman
 Agmondisham.
Vesey, Godfrey Norman Agmondisham.
 xVesey, Godfrey.
  Personal Identity: A Philosophical Analysis.
  Cornell U Pr.
  ed. Understanding Wittgenstein. Cornell U Pr.
  ed. Understanding Wittgenstein. St Martin.
Vesilind, P. Aarne.
 xVesilind, P. Aarne.
  Environmental Pollution & Control. Ann Arbor
  Science.
  Treatment & Disposal Wastewater Sludges.
  Ann Arbor Science.
Vesper, Carl H. see Vesper, Karl H.
Vesper, K. see Vesper, Karl H.
Vesper, Karl H.
 xVesper, Carl H.
  Engineers at Work: A Casebook. HM.
 xVesper, K.
  New Venture Strategies. P-H.
Vespucci, Amerigo.
 xVespucci, Amerigo.
  Letters of Amerigo Vespucci & Other
  Documents Illustrative of His Career. B
  Franklin.
Vess, David M.
 xVess, David M.
  Medical Revolution in France, 1789-1796. U
  Presses Fla.
Vessey, D. W. see Vessey, David.
Vessey, David.
 xVessey, D. W.
  Statius & the Thebaid. Cambridge U Pr.
Vest, Charles M.
 xVest, Charles M.

Holographic Interferometry. Wiley.
Vestal, David.
 xVestal, David.
  The Craft of Photography. Har-Row.
  The Craft of Photography. Har-Row.
Vester, Bertha H. see Vester, Bertha Hedges (Spafford).
Vester, Bertha Hedges (Spafford), 1878-
 xVester, Bertha H.
  Our Jerusalem: An American Family in the
  Holy City, 1881-1949. Arno.
Vesterman, William, 1942-
 xVesterman, William.
  Stylistic Life of Samuel Johnson. Rutgers U Pr.
Vestermark, Mary. see Vestermark, Mary J.
Vestermark, Mary J.
 xVestermark, Mary.
  Freedom Is an Inside Job. John Knox.
Vestermark, S. D.
 xVestermark, S. D.
  Controlling Crime in the School: A Complete
  Security Handbook for Administrators. P-H.
Vestly, Anne-Cath. see Vestly, Anne-Catharina.
Vestly, Anne-Catharina.
 xVestly, Anne-Cath.
  Aurora & Socrates. T Y Crowell.
Vethake, Henry, 1792-1866
 xVethake, Henry.
  Principles of Political Economy. Kelley.
Vetter, Bob.
 xVetter, Robert.
  Jesus Was a Single Adult. Cook.
Vetter, George, 1925-
 xVetter, George.
  Successful Civil Litigation: How to Win Your
  Case Before You Enter the Courtroom. P-H.
Vetter, Harold J.
 xVetter, Harold J.
  Introduction to Criminology. C C Thomas.
  The Nature of Crime. HR&W.
Vetter, Marjorie. see Vetter, Marjorie Meyn.
Vetter, Marjorie Meyn.
 xVetter, Marjorie.
  Questions Girls Ask. Dutton.
Vetter, Robert. see Vetter, Bob.
Vetterling-Braggin, Mary.
 xVetterling-Braggin, Mary.
  ed. Feminism & Philosophy. Littlefield.
  ed. Feminism & Philosophy. Rowman.
Vettorazzi, G.
 xVettorazzi, G.
  International Regulatory Aspects for Pesticide
  Chemicals. CRC Pr.
Vevers, Gwynne. see Vevers, Henry Gwynne.
Vevers, Henry Gwynne.
 xVevers, Gwynne.
  Fishes. McGraw.
  Octopus, Cuttlefish & Squid. McGraw.
  The Underwater World. St Martin.
Vexler, Robert I.
 xVexler, Robert I.
  Baltimore: A Chronological & Documentary
  History. Oceana.
  Cincinnati: A Chronological & Documentary
  History. Oceana.
  Cleveland: A Chronological & Documentary
  History. Oceana.
  Detroit: A Chronological & Documentary
  History. Oceana.
  Pittsburgh: A Chronological & Documentary
  History. Oceana.
Veysey, Laurence. see Veysey, Laurence R.
Veysey, Laurence R.
 xVeysey, Laurence.
  The Communal Experience: Anarchist &
  Mystical Communities in Twentieth Century
  America. U of Chicago Pr.
Vezzani, A. A.
 xVezzani, A. A.

Reading & Detailing Assembly Drawings: Dies. Prakken.

Vezzoli, Gary C., 1942-
    xVezzoli, Gary C.
        Superior Horsemanship: Learning & Teaching the English Hunt Seat. A S Barnes.

Viadiu, J. see Viadiu, Jose.

Viadiu, Jose.
    xViadiu, J.
        A Chronology of the Spanish Civil War & Its Origins. Revisionist Pr.

Vial, James L.
    xVial, James L.
        ed. Evolutionary Biology of the Anurans: Contemporary Research on Major Problems. U of Mo Pr.

Viallate, Achille, 1866-
    xViallate, Achille.
        Economic Imperialism & International Relations During the Last Fifty Years. Arno.

Viaud, Gaston, 1899-
    xViaud, Gaston.
        Intelligence, Its Evolution & Forms. Greenwood.

Viazzi, Alfredo.
    xViazzi, Alfredo.
        Alfredo Viazzi's Italian Cooking. Random.

Vice Commission Of Chicago. see Chicago. Vice Commission.

Vichas, Robert P.
    xVichas, Robert P.
        Handbook of Financial Mathematics, Formulas & Tables. P-H.

Vick, James W.
    xVick, James W.
        Homology Theory: An Introduction to Algebraic Topology. Acad Pr.

Vickerman, R. W. see Vickerman, Roger William.

Vickerman, Roger William.
    xVickerman, R. W.
        Spatial Economic Behavior: The Microeconomic Foundations of Urban & Transport Economics. St Martin.

Vickers, Betty J.
    xVickers, Betty J.
        Swimming. Wm C Brown.

Vickers, Douglas.
    xVickers, Douglas.
        Financial Markets in the Capitalist Process. U of Pa Pr.

Vickers, Frank D.
    xVickers, Frank D.
        FORTRAN IV: A Modern Approach. Kendall-Hunt.

Vickers, Hugh.
    xVickers, Hugh.
        Great Operatic Disasters. St Martin.

Vickers, Robert H. see Vickers, Robert Henry.

Vickers, Robert Henry.
    xVickers, Robert H.
        The Powers & Duties of Police Officers & Coroners. AMS Pr.

Vickers, V. C. see Vickers, Vincent Cartwright.

Vickers, Vincent C. see Vickers, Vincent Cartwright.

Vickers, Vincent Cartwright, 1879-1939
    xVickers, V. C.
        The Google Book. Oxford U Pr.
    xVickers, Vincent C.
        Economic Tribulation. Gordon Pr.

Vickery, Donald M.
    xVickery, Donald M.
        Lifeplan for Your Health. A-W.
        Take Care of Yourself: A Consumer's Guide to Medical Care. A-W.

Vickery, Florence E.
    xVickery, Florence E.

Creative Programming for Older Adults: A Leadership Training Guidebook. Follett.
Old & Growing: Conversations, Letters, Observations, & Reflections on Growing Old. C C Thomas.

Vickery, John B.
    xVickery, John B.
        The Literary Impact of The Golden Bough. Princeton U Pr.

Vickery, Robert L.
    xVickery, Robert L.
        Anthrophysical Form: Two Families & Their Neighborhood Environments. U Pr of Va.

Vickery, Walter N., 1921-
    xVickery, Walter N.
        Alexander Pushkin. Twayne.

Vickery, William E. see Vickery, William Edward.

Vickery, William Edward.
    xVickery, William E.
        The Economics of the Negro Migration: 1900-1960. Arno.

Vickrey, William S. see Vickrey, William Spencer.

Vickrey, William Spencer, 1914-
    xVickrey, William S.
        Agenda for Progressive Taxation. Kelley.

Victor, Edward, 1914-
    xVictor, Edward.
        Science for the Elementary School. Macmillan.

Victor, Jeffrey S.
    xVictor, Jeffrey S.
        Human Sexuality: A Social Psychological Approach. P-H.

Victor, Joan B. see Victor, Joan Berg.

Victor, Joan Berg.
    xVictor, Joan B.
        Tarantulas. Dodd.

Victor, Orville J. see Victor, Orville James.

Victor, Orville James, 1827-1910
    xVictor, Orville J.
        History of American Conspiracies: A Record of Treason, Insurrections, Rebellion in the United States of America, from 1760 to 1860. Arno.

Victoria & Albert Museum. see Victoria and Albert Museum, South Kensington.

Victoria & Albert Museum, London. see Victoria and Albert Museum, South Kensington.

Victoria And Albert Museum. see Victoria and Albert Museum, South Kensington.

Victoria and Albert Museum, South Kensington.
    xVictoria & Albert Museum.
        National Art Library Catalogue of Exhibition Catalogues. G K Hall.
    xVictoria & Albert Museum, London.
        National Art Library Catalogue, Author Catalog. G K Hall.
    xVictoria And Albert Museum.
        Carolian Fabrics. Textile Bk.
        William & Mary Fabrics. Textile Bk.

Vida, Ginny.
    xVida, Ginny.
        ed. Our Right to Love: A Lesbian Resource Book. P-H.

Vidal, Gore, 1925-
    xVidal, Gore.
        An Evening with Richard Nixon. Random.
        Great American Families. Norton.
        Homage to Daniel Shays: Collected Essays, 1952-1972. Random.
        Matters of Fact & of Fiction: Essays 1973-1976. Random.
        Matters of Fact & of Fiction: Essays, 1973-1976. Random.

Vidas del Trobadors. see Vidas Dels Trobadors.

Vidas Dels Trobadors.
    xVidas del Trobadors.

Biographies Des Troubadours: Textes Provencaux Des Treizieme et Quatorzieme Siecles. B Franklin.

Vidaver, Robert M.
    xVidaver, Robert M.
        Developments in Human Services Education & Manpower. Human Sci Pr.

Videofreex. see Videofreex (Organization).

Videofreex (Organization).
    xVideofreex.
        Spaghetti City Video Manual. Praeger.

Vidic, Branislav.
    xVidic, Branislav.
        Atlas of the Anatomy of the Ear. Saunders.

Vidler, A. R. see Vidler, Alexander Roper.

Vidler, Alexander Roper, 1899-
    xVidler, A. R.
        Soundings: Essays Concerning Christian Understanding. Cambridge U Pr.
        Variety of Catholic Modernists. Cambridge U Pr.

Vidler, Virginia, 1928-
    xVidler, Virginia.
        Sugar-Bush Antiques. A S Barnes.

Vidt, Donald G.
    xVidt, Donald G.
        Cleveland Clinic Cardiovascular Consultations. Davis Co.

Vidyakara.
    xVidyakara.
        Subhasitaratnakosa. Harvard U Pr.

Vidyarthi, L. P. see Vidyarthi, Lalita Prasad.

Vidyarthi, Lalita Prasad.
    xVidyarthi, L. P.
        The Sacred Complex of Kashi: A Microcosm of Indian Civilization. South Asia Bks.
        South Asian Culture: An Anthropological Perspective. South Asia Bks.

Viehe, H. G. see Viehe, Heinz Gunter.

Viehe, Heinz Gunter.
    xViehe, H. G.
        ed. Chemistry of Acetylenes. Dekker.

Vieira, Luandino, 1935-
    xVieira, Luandino.
        The Real Life of Domingos Xavier. Heinemann Ed.

Viemeister, August, 1893-
    xViemeister, August.
        An Architectural Journey Through Long Island. Kennikat.

Viemeister, Peter E.
    xViemeister, Peter E.
        The Lightning Book. MIT Pr.

Vier, Peter C.
    xVier, Peter C.
        Evidence & Its Function According to John Duns Scotus. Franciscan Inst.

Vierck, Robert K.
    xVierck, Robert K.
        Vibration Analysis. Har-Row.

Viereck. see Viereck, Phillip.

Viereck, George S. see Viereck, George Sylvester.

Viereck, George Sylvester, 1884-1962
    xViereck, George S.
        A Game of Love & Other Plays. Core Collection.
        The House of the Vampire. Arno.

Viereck, Peter R. see Viereck, Peter Robert Edwin.

Viereck, Peter Robert Edwin, 1916-
    xViereck, Peter R.
        Strike Through the Mask: New Lyrical Poems. Greenwood.

Viereck, Phillip.
    xViereck.
        The Summer I Was Lost. Schol Bk Serv.
    xViereck, Phillip.
        Summer I Was Lost. John Day.

Vierling, Anton F.
    xVierling, Anton F.

Computer Assisted Learning. Hafner.
Vierling, Ronald.
xVierling, Ronald.
The Prairie Rider Cantos. Dakota Pr.
Vierow, Duain W., 1935-
xVierow, Duain W.
On the Move with the Master: A Daily
Devotional Guide on World Mission. William
Carey Lib.
Viessman, Warren.
xViessman, Warren.
Introduction to Hydrology. Har-Row.
Vieth, W. R. *see* Vieth, Wolf R.
Vieth, Wolf R.
xVieth, W. R.
ed. Biochemical Engineering. NY Acad Sci.
Vietor, Karl, 1892-1951
xVietor, Karl.
Goethe the Poet. Russell.
Vietor, Richard H. *see* Vietor, Richard H. K.
Vietor, Richard H. K., 1945-
xVietor, Richard H.
Environmental Politics & the Coal Coalition.
Tex A&M Univ Pr.
Vigdorchik, Michael. *see* Vigdorchik, Michael E.
Vigdorchik, Michael E.
xVigdorchik, Michael.
Arctic Pleistocene History & the Development
of Submarine Permafrost. Westview.
Vigersky, Robert A.
xVigersky, Robert A.
Anorexia Nervosa. Raven.
Vigeveno, H. S.
xVigeveno, H. S.
Divorce & the Children. Regal.
The Group. Vision Hse.
Vigil, Maurilio.
xVigil, Maurilio E.
Los Patrones: Profiles of Hispanic Political
Leaders in New Mexico History. U Pr of
Amer.
xVigil, Maurillo E.
Los Patrones: Profiles of Hispanic Political
Leaders in New Mexico History. U Pr of
Amer.
Vigil, Maurilio E. *see* Vigil, Maurilio.
Vigil, Maurillo E. *see* Vigil, Maurilio.
Vigna, Judith.
xVigna, Judith.
illus. Couldn't We Have a Turtle Instead. A
Whitman.
ed. Everyone Goes As a Pumpkin. A Whitman.
Gregory's Stitches. A Whitman.
ed. The Hiding House. A Whitman.
illus. The Little Boy Who Loved Dirt &
Almost Became a Superslob. A Whitman.
Vigneras, Louis A. *see* Vigneras, Louis-Andre.
Vigneras, Louis-Andre, 1903-
xVigneras, Louis A.
The Discovery of South America & the
Andalusian Voyages. U of Chicago Pr.
Vignes, Jacques, 1921-
xVignes, Jacques.
The Rage to Survive. Morrow.
Vignola, Leonard.
xVignola, Leonard.
Strategic Divestment. Am Mgmt.
Vignoles, Charles B. *see* Vignoles, Charles Blacker.
Vignoles, Charles Blacker, 1793-1875
xVignoles, Charles B.
Observations Upon the Floridas. U Presses Fla.
Vignoles, Keith H.
xVignoles, Keith H.
Dick Burgess of Bosham. State Mutual Bk.
Vignone, Joseph A.
xVignone, Joseph A.
Collective Bargaining Procedures for Public
Library Employees. Scarecrow.
Vigor, P. H. *see* Vigor, Peter Hast.

Vigor, Peter Hast.
xVigor, P. H.
The Soviet View of War, Peace & Neutrality.
Routledge & Kegan.
Vigor, William, Mrs, 1699?-1783
xVigor, William.
Letters from Russia. Arno.
Vijn, Cornelius.
xVijn, Cornelius.
Cetshwayo's Dutchman: Being the Private
Journal of a White Trader in Zululand
During the British Invasion. Negro U Pr.
Viktorov, I. A. *see* Viktorov, Igor' Aleksandrovich.
Viktorov, Igor' Aleksandrovich.
xViktorov, I. A.
Rayleigh & Lamb Waves: Physical Theory &
Applications. Plenum Pub.
Vilain, Raymond.
xVilain, Raymond.
Plastic Surgery of the Hand & Pulp. Masson
Pub.
Vilakazi, Absolom.
xVilakazi, Absolom L.
Africa's Rough Road: Problems of Change &
Development. U Pr of Amer.
Vilakazi, Absolom L. *see* Vilakazi, Absolom.
Vilenkin, N. Ja. *see* Vilenkin, Naum Iakovlevich.
Vilenkin, Naum Iakovlevich.
xVilenkin, N. Ja.
Special Functions & the Theory of Group
Representations. Am Math.
Vilips, Vess V.
xVilips, Vess V.
Data Modem Selection & Evaluation Guide.
Artech Hse.
Villa, Silvio.
xVilla, Silvio.
Unbidden Guest. Arno.
Villacorta, Aurora S.
xVillacorta, Aurora S.
Charleston Anyone?. Interstate.
Step by Step to Ballroom Dancing. Interstate.
Villadsen, John.
xVilladsen, John.
Solution of Differential Equation Models for
Polynomial Approximation. P-H.
Villani, F. *see* Villani, Florence.
Villani, Florence, 1921-
xVillani, F.
ed. Rare Earth Technology & Applications.
Noyes.
Villani, S. *see* Villani, Stelio.
Villani, Stelio.
xVillani, S.
ed. Uranium Enrichment. Springer-Verlag.
Villano, Anthony.
xVillano, Anthony.
Brick Agent: Inside the Mafia for the FBI.
Times Bks.
Villano, Caesar.
xVillano, Caesar.
Food Service Management & Control: The
Profitable Approach. Lebhar Friedman.
Villard, Henry, 1835-1900
xVillard, Henry.
ed. Lincoln on the Eve of '61: A Journalist's
Story. Greenwood.
Villard, Leonie.
xVillard, Leonie.
The Influence of Keats on Tennyson &
Rossetti. Folcroft.
Villard, Oswald G. *see* Villard, Oswald Garrison.
Villard, Oswald Garrison, 1872-1949
xVillard, Oswald G.
Prophets True & False. Arno.
Some Newspapers & Newspapermen. Arno.
Villari, Luigi, 1876-
xVillari, Luigi.

The Fascist Experiment. AMS Pr.
The Liberation of Italy. Devin.
Villari, Pasquale, 1827-1917
xVillari, Pasquale.
Life & Times of Niccolo Machiavelli.
Greenwood.
Life & Times of Niccolo Machiavelli. R West.
Life & Times of Niccolo Machiavelli.
Scholarly.
Studies, Historical & Critical. Arno.
Villars, Elizabeth.
xVillars, Elizabeth.
The Rich Girl. PB.
The Very Best People. Coward.
Villas, James.
xVillas, James.
Gerard de Nerval: A Critical Bibliography,
1900 to 1967. U of Mo Pr.
Villasenor, David. *see* Villasenor, David V.
Villasenor, David V.
xVillasenor, David.
Tapestries in Sand: The Spirit of Indian
Sandpainting. Naturegraph.
Villastrigo, Robert.
xVillastrigo, Robert.
How to Repair Movie & Slide Projectors. TAB
Bks.
Villate, Jose T.
xVillate, Jose T.
Dictionary of Environmental Engineering &
Related Sciences. Ediciones.
Villaverde, Manuel M. *see* Villaverde, Manuel Maria.
Villaverde, Manuel Maria.
xVillaverde, Manuel M.
Ailments of Aging: From Symptom to
Treatment. Van Nos Reinhold.
Internal Medicine: Medical Examination
Manual. Van Nos Reinhold.
Pain: From Symptom to Treatment. Van Nos
Reinhold.
Villee, Claude A. *see* Villee, Claude Alvin.
Villee, Claude Alvin, 1917-
xVillee, Claude A.
General Zoology. HR&W.
Villee, Dorothy B.
xVillee, Dorothy B.
Human Endocrinology: A Developmental
Approach. Saunders.
Villegas, Joseph E. *see* Villegas, Joseph Eduardo.
Villegas, Joseph Eduardo.
xVillegas, Joseph E.
Brazil As a Model for Developing Countries.
Vantage.
Villiard, Paul.
xVilliard, Paul.
Collecting Stamps. NAL.
Collecting Stamps. Doubleday.
Gemstones & Minerals: A Guide for the
Amateur Collector & Cutter. Winchester Pr.
A Manual of Veneering. Dover.
A Manual of Veneering. Peter Smith.
Raising Small Animals for Fun & Profit.
Scribner.
Vilnay, Zev, 1900-
xVilnay, Zev.
The Guide to Israel. Intl Pubns Serv.
Legends of Galilee, Jordan & Sinai. Jewish
Pubn.
Legends of Jerusalem. Jewish Pubn.
Vinacke, W. Edgar. *see* Vinacke, William Edgar.
Vinacke, William Edgar, 1917-
xVinacke, W. Edgar.
The Psychology of Thinking. McGraw.
Vinal, Harold, 1891-
xVinal, Harold.
White April. AMS Pr.
Vincent, Carl.
xVincent, Carl.

ed. General Bibliography of Motion Pictures. Arno.

Vincent, Denis.
   xVincent, Denis.
      One-Year Courses in Colleges & Sixth Forms: A Report from the Sixteen Plus Education Unit. Humanities.
      Reading Tests in the Classroom. Humanities.

Vincent, E. R. *see* Vincent, Eric Reginald Pearce.

Vincent, Elizabeth L. *see* Vincent, Elizabeth Lee.

Vincent, Elizabeth Lee, 1897-
   xVincent, Elizabeth L.
      A Study of Intelligence Test Elements. AMS Pr.

Vincent, Eric R. *see* Vincent, Eric Reginald Pearce.

Vincent, Eric Reginald Pearce, 1894-
   xVincent, E. R.
      Gabriele Rossetti in England. Folcroft.
      Re-Reading the Divine Comedy. R West.
   xVincent, Eric R.
      Byron, Hobhouse & Foscolo: New Documents in the History of a Collaboration. Octagon.

Vincent, Felix, 1946-
   xVincent, Felix.
      Catlands: Pays Des Chats. Tundra Bks.

Vincent, Gillian.
   xVincent, Gillian.
      Writer's Favourite Recipes. St Martin.

Vincent, Henry.
   xVincent, Henry.
      Story of the Commonweal. Arno.

Vincent, Howard P. *see* Vincent, Howard Paton.

Vincent, Howard Paton, 1904-
   xVincent, Howard P.
      Daumier & His World. Northwestern U Pr.
      The Tailoring of Melville's White Jacket. Northwestern U Pr.

Vincent, Jack E. *see* Vincent, Jack Ernest.

Vincent, Jack Ernest.
   xVincent, Jack E.
      Factor Analysis in International Relations: Interpretation, Problem Areas, & an Application. U Presses Fla.

Vincent, Jean A. *see* Vincent, Jean Anne.

Vincent, Jean Anne.
   xVincent, Jean A.
      History of Art. Har-Row.

Vincent, Joan.
   xVincent, Joan.
      African Elite: The Big Men of a Small Town. Columbia U Pr.

Vincent, John H. *see* Vincent, John Heyl.

Vincent, John Heyl, Bp, 1832-1920
   xVincent, John H.
      Chautauqua Movement. Arno.

Vincent, John M. *see* Vincent, John Martin.

Vincent, John Martin, 1857-1939
   xVincent, John M.
      Aids to Historical Research. Arno.
      Costume & Conduct in the Laws of Basel, Bern & Zurich, 1370-1800. Greenwood.
      Historical Research: An Outline of Theory & Practice. B Franklin.
      Switzerland at the Beginning of the Sixteenth Century. AMS Pr.

Vincent, Leon H. *see* Vincent, Leon Henry.

Vincent, Leon Henry, 1859-1941
   xVincent, Leon H.
      American Literary Masters. Arno.

Vincent, R. J., 1943-
   xVincent, R. J.
      Nonintervention & International Order. Princeton U Pr.

Vinci, Leonardo.
   xVinci, Leonardo.
      Didone Abbandonata. Garland Pub.

Vincie, Joseph F.
   xVincie, Joseph F.

C. G. Jung & Analytical Psychology: A Comprehensive Bibliography. Garland Pub.

Vine, Aubrey R. *see* Vine, Aubrey Russell.

Vine, Aubrey Russell, 1900-
   xVine, Aubrey R.
      The Nestorian Churches. AMS Pr.

Vine, Louis L.
   xVine, Louis L.
      Breeding, Whelping & Natal Care of Dogs. Arco.
      Common Sense Book of Complete Cat Care. Morrow.
      Common Sense Book of Complete Cat Care. Popular Lib.

Vine, P. A. *see* Vine, Paul A. L.

Vine, Paul A. L.
   xVine, P. A.
      London's Lost Route to the Sea: An Historical Account of the Inland Navigations Which Linked the Thames to the English Channel. David & Charles.

Vine, Victor T. Le. *see* Le Vine, Victor T.

Vine, W. E. *see* Vine, William Edwy.

Vine, William Edwy.
   xVine, W. E.
      An Expository Dictionary of Old Testament Words. Revell.

Vineberg, Arthur. *see* Vineberg, Arthur Martin.

Vineberg, Arthur Martin, 1903-
   xVineberg, Arthur.
      How to Live with Your Heart: The Family Guide to Heart Health. Times Bks.

Vineberg, Solomon, 1884-
   xVineberg, Solomon.
      Provincial & Local Taxation in Canada. AMS Pr.

Viner, Jacob, 1892-1970
   xViner, Jacob.
      Canada's Balance of International Indebtedness: 1900-1913. Arno.
      Canada's Balance of International Indebtedness, 1900-1913: An Inductive Study in the Study of International Trade. Porcupine Pr.
      Religious Thought & Economic Society: Four Chapters of an Unfinished Work. Duke.

Vines, Alice G. *see* Vines, Alice Gilmore.

Vines, Alice Gilmore.
   xVines, Alice G.
      Neither Fire nor Steel: Sir Christopher Hatton. Nelson-Hall.

Vines, Jerry.
   xVines, Jerry.
      Fire in the Pulpit. Broadman.
      Great Events in the Life of Christ. Victor Bks.

Vines, Sherard, 1890-
   xVines, Sherard.
      Georgian Satirists. Folcroft.

Vinet, Alexander. *see* Vinet, Alexandre Rodolphe.

Vinet, Alexandre Rodolphe, 1797-1847
   xVinet, Alexander.
      History of French Literature in the Eighteenth Century. Kennikat.

Viney, Wayne.
   xViney, Wayne.
      ed. The History of Psychology: A Guide to Information Sources. Gale.

Vinge, Clarence L.
   xVinge, Clarence L.
      Economic Geography. Rowman.

Vinge, Joan D.
   xVinge, Joan D.
      The Snow Queen. Dial.

Vining, Donald, 1917-
   xVining, Donald.
      A Gay Diary 1933-1946. Pepys Pr.
      A Gay Diary: 1946-1954. Pepys Pr.

Vining, Elizabeth G. *see* Vining, Elizabeth Gray.

Vining, Elizabeth Gray, 1902-
   xVining, Elizabeth G.

Being Seventy: The Measure of a Year. Viking Pr.
      Flora: A Biography. Lippincott.
      World in Tune. Pendle Hill.

Vinnichenko, N. K. *see* Vinnichenko, Nikolai Konstantinovich.

Vinnichenko, Nikolai Konstantinovich.
   xVinnichenko, N. K.
      ed. Turbulence in the Free Atmosphere. Plenum Pub.

Vinograd, Julia, 1943-
   xVinograd, Julia.
      Revolution & Other Poems. SBD.

Vinogradoff, Paul.
   xVinogradoff, Paul.
      Common-Sense in Law. Arno.
      Growth of the Manor. Kelley.
      Outlines of Historical Jurisprudence. AMS Pr.
      Self-Government in Russia. Hyperion Conn.

Vinsant, Marielle. *see* Vinsant, Marielle Ortiz.

Vinsant, Marielle O. *see* Vinsant, Marielle Ortiz.

Vinsant, Marielle Ortiz.
   xVinsant, Marielle.
      Commonsense Approach to Coronary Care: A Program. Mosby.
   xVinsant, Marielle O.
      A Commonsense Approach to Coronary Care: A Program. Mosby.

Vinson, Donald E.
   xVinson, Donald E.
      The Environment of Industrial Marketing. Grid Pub.

Vinson, Jack R., 1929-
   xVinson, Jack R.
      Structural Mechanics: The Behavior of Plates & Shells. Wiley.

Vinson, James.
   xVinson, James.
      ed. Contemporary Dramatists. St Martin.

Vinton, Eleanor.
   xVinton, Eleanor.
      On the Contoocook. Bauhan.

Vinton, John.
   xVinton, John.
      ed. The Dictionary of Contemporary Music. Dutton.

Vinyard, Dale.
   xVinyard, Dale.
      Congress. Scribner.

Vinycomb, John.
   xVinycomb, John.
      Fictitious & Symbolic Creatures in Art with Special Reference to Their Use in British Heraldry. Gale.

Viola, Herman J.
   xViola, Herman J.
      The Indian Legacy of Charles Bird King. Smithsonian.

Viola, Richard H.
   xViola, Richard H.
      Organizations in a Changing Society: Administration & Human Values. HR&W.

Violett, Ellen.
   xViolett, Ellen.
      Double Take. Ballantine.

Violi, Paul.
   xVioli, Paul.
      In Baltic Circles. Kulchur Foun.

Viorst, Judith.
   xViorst, Judith.
      How Did I Get to Be Forty... & Other Atrocities. S&S.
      I'll Fix Anthony. Har-Row.
      Love & Guilt & the Meaning of Life, Etc.. S&S.
      People & Other Aggravations. NAL.
      Try It Again, Sam: Safety When You Walk. Lothrop.

Virajananda, Swami, 1874 or 5-1951
   xVirajananda, Swami.

Toward the Goal Supreme. Vedanta Pr.
Virajananda, Swami. *see* Virajananda.
Virch, C. *see* Virch, Claus.
Virch, Claus, 1927-
    xVirch, C.
        Francisco Goya. McGraw.
Virginia - General Assembly - Joint Comm. On The State
    Library. *see* Virginia. General Assembly. Joint
    Committee on the State Library.
Virginia Association of Legal Secretaries.
    xVirginia Association of Legal Secretaries.
        Handbook for Legal Secretaries in Virginia.
        Michie.
Virginia Company of London.
    xVirginia Company of London.
        The Records of the Virginia Company of
        London. AMS Pr.
        Three Charters of the Virginia Company of
        London: With Seven Related Documents,
        1606-1621. U Pr of Va.
    xVirginia Company of London, 1619-1624.
        Proceedings. AMS Pr.
Virginia Company of London, 1619-1624. *see* Virginia
    Company of London.
**Virginia. General Assembly. Joint Committee on the
    State Library.**
    xVirginia - General Assembly - Joint Comm. On
    The State Library.
        Colonial Records of Virginia. Genealog Pub.
Virginia Polytechnic Institute & State University, March
    22-24, 1973. *see* Topology Conference, Virginia
    Polytechnic Institute and State University, 1973.
Viri, Anne De. *see* De Viri, Anne.
Viscardi, Henry, 1912-
    xViscardi, Henry.
        Abilities Story. Eriksson.
        Give Us the Tools. Eriksson.
Viscione, Jerry. *see* Viscione, Jerry A.
Viscione, Jerry A.
    xViscione, Jerry.
        Cases in Financial Management. HM.
        Financial Analysis: Principles & Procedures.
        HM.
Visconti, A. *see* Visconti, Antoine.
Visconti, Antoine.
    xVisconti, A.
        Quantum Field Theory. Pergamon.
Viscott, David. *see* Viscott, David S.
Viscott, David S., 1938-
    xViscott, David.
        How to Live with Another Person. Arbor Hse.
        How to Live with Another Person. PB.
        Risking. PB.
        Risking. S&S.
    xViscott, David S.
        How to Live with Another Person. Arbor Hse.
Viscusi, W. Kip.
    xViscusi, W. Kip.
        Employment Hazards: An Investigation of
        Market Performance. Harvard U Pr.
        Welfare of the Elderly: An Economic Analysis
        & Policy Prescription. Wiley.
Viser, Festus J. *see* Viser, Festus Justin.
Viser, Festus Justin, 1920-
    xViser, Festus J.
        USSR in Today's World. Memphis St Univ.
Visher, Stephen S. *see* Visher, Stephen Sargent.
Visher, Stephen Sargent, 1887-1967
    xVisher, Stephen S.
        Climatic Laws: Ninety Generalizations with
        Numerous Corollaries As to the Graphic
        Distribution of Temperature, Wind, Moisture,
        Etc.. AMS Pr.
Visiak, E. H. *see* Visiak, Edward Harold.
Visiak, Edward Harold.
    xVisiak, E. H.
        Portent of Milton: Some Aspects of His
        Genius. Humanities.
Vising, Johan, 1855-1942
    xVising, Johan.

Anglo-Norman Language in Literature. Gordon
Pr.
Visscher, Martha O. *see* Visscher, Martha Orrico.
Visscher, Martha Orrico.
    xVisscher, Martha O.
        The Ideas of Chemistry. HarBraceJ.
Visscher, Maurice B. *see* Visscher, Maurice Bolkes.
Visscher, Maurice Bolkes, 1901-
    xVisscher, Maurice B.
        Ethical Constraints & Imperatives in Medical
        Research. C C Thomas.
        ed. Humanistic Perspectives in Medical Ethics.
        Prometheus Bks.
Visser, H. *see* Visser, Hans.
Visser, Hans, 1943-
    xVisser, H.
        The Quantity of Money. Halsted Pr.
Vistelius, Andrei Borisovich.
    xVistelius, Andrew B.
        Studies in Mathematical Geology. Plenum Pub.
Vistelius, Andrew B. *see* Vistelius, Andrei Borisovich.
**Visual Communications Conference, 3rd, New York,
    1958.**
    xArt Directors Club, 3rd Communications
    Conference, New York.
        Creativity: An Examination of the Creative
        Process. Arno.
**Visual Communications Conference, 4th, New York,
    1959.**
    xArt Directors Club, 4th Communications
    Conference, New York.
        Symbology: The Use of Symbols in Visual
        Communications. Arno.
Vita-Finzi, Claudio.
    xVita-Finzi, Claudio.
        Archaeological Sites in Their Setting. Thames
        Hudson.
Vital, David.
    xVital, David.
        The Inequality of States: A Study of the Small
        Power in International Relations. Greenwood.
        The Origins of Zionism. Oxford U Pr.
Vitale, Anthony J.
    xVitale, Anthony J.
        Spoken Swahili. Spoken Lang Serv.
Vitale, Barbara A. *see* Vitale, Barbara Ann.
Vitale, Barbara Ann.
    xVitale, Barbara A.
        A Problem Solving Approach to Nursing Care
        Plans: A Program. Mosby.
Vitale, Edmund.
    xVitale, Edmund.
        Building Regulations: A Self Help Guide for
        the Owner-Builder. Scribner.
Vitale, Frank, 1931-
    xVitale, Frank.
        Individualized Fitness Programs. P-H.
Vitale, Philip H.
    xVitale, Philip H.
        Catholic Literary Opinion of the Twentieth
        Century. Auxiliary U Pr.
Vitelli, James R., 1920-
    xVitelli, James R.
        Van Wyck Brooks. Coll & U Pr.
        Van Wyck Brooks. Twayne.
        Van Wyck Brooks: A Reference Guide. G K
        Hall.
Viterbi, A. *see* Viterbi, Andrew J.
Viterbi, Andrew J.
    xViterbi, A.
        Principles of Coherent Communication.
        McGraw.
    xViterbi, Andrew J.
        Principles of Digital Communication & Coding.
        McGraw.
Viteritti, Joseph P., 1946-
    xViteritti, Joseph P.

Bureaucracy & Social Justice: Allocation of
Jobs & Services to Minority Groups.
Kennikat.
Vithoulkas, George.
    xVithoulkas, George.
        Homeopathy: Medicine of the New Man. Arco.
        The Science of Homeopathy. Grove.
        The Science of Homeopathy. Grove.
Vito, Michael C. De. *see* De Vito, Michael C.
Vittorini, Domenico.
    xVittorini, Domenico.
        Drama of Luigi Pirandello. Russell.
        Modern Italian Novel. Russell.
Vitz, Evelyn B. *see* Vitz, Evelyn Birge.
Vitz, Evelyn Birge.
    xVitz, Evelyn B.
        The Crossroad of Intention's: A Study of
        Symbolic Expression in the Poetry of
        Francois Villon. Mouton.
Vitz, Paul C., 1935-
    xVitz, Paul C.
        Psychology As Religion: The Cult of
        Self-Worship. Eerdmans.
Vivante, Arturo.
    xVivante, Arturo.
        English Stories. Street Fiction.
        Run to the Waterfall. Scribner.
Vivante, Leone, 1887-
    xVivante, Leone.
        English Poetry & Its Contribution to the
        Knowledge of a Creative Principle. Folcroft.
        English Poetry & Its Contribution to the
        Knowledge of a Creative Principle. R West.
        Essays on Art & Ontology. U of Utah Pr.
Vivas, Eliseo.
    xVivas, Eliseo.
        Creation & Discovery: Essays in Criticism &
        Aesthetics. Arno.
        Two Roads to Ignorance: A QuasiBiography. S
        Ill U Pr.
Vivekananda.
    xVivekananda, Swami.
        Inspired Talks: My Master & Other Writings.
        Ramakrishna.
        Meditation & Its Methods According to Swami
        Vivekananda. Vedanta Pr.
Vivekananda, Swami. *see* Vivekananda.
Vivian, Charles H.
    xVivian, Charles H.
        English Composition. Har-Row.
Vivian, Herbert, 1865-
    xVivian, Herbert.
        Abyssinia: Through the Lion-Land to the Court
        of the Lion of Judah. Negro U Pr.
Vivian, John.
    xVivian, John.
        Building Stone Walls. Garden Way Pub.
        Wood Heat. Rodale Pr Inc.
Vivian, June.
    xVivian, June.
        Home Tanners' Handbook. Reed.
Vivian, R. Gwinn.
    xVivian, R. Gwinn.
        Wooden Ritual Artifacts from Chaco Canyon,
        New Mexico: The Chetro Ketl Collection. U
        of Ariz Pr.
Vivien, Renee.
    xVivien, Renee.
        At the Sweet Hour of Hand-in-Hand. Naiad Pr.
Vivona, Charles M.
    xVivona, Charles M.
        ed. The Meanings of Deviance. Mss Info.
Vizard, David.
    xVizard, David.
        How to Modify Your Mini. H P Bks.
        How to Rebuild Your 1.3, 1.6 & 2.0 OHC
        Ford. H P Bks.
Vizenor, Gerald. *see* Vizenor, Gerald Robert.
Vizenor, Gerald Robert, 1934-
    xVizenor, Gerald.

The Everlasting Sky: New Voices from the
People Named the Chippewa. Macmillan.
Wordarrows: Indians & Whites in the New Fur
Trade. U of Minn Pr.
Vizetelly, Ernest A. see Vizetelly, Ernest Alfred.
Vizetelly, Ernest Alfred.
xVizetelly, Ernest A.
Loves of the Poets. Folcroft.
Vizetelly, Francis Horace.
xVizetelly, Frank H.
Desk-Book of Idioms & Idiomatic Phrases in
English Speech & Literature. Gale.
Vizetelly, Frank H. see Vizetelly, Francis Horace.
Vlachos, Helen, 1911-
xVlachos, Helen.
House Arrest. Gambit.
Vlack, Don.
xVlack, Don.
Art Deco Architecture in New York,
1920-1940. Har-Row.
Vlack, Lawrence H. Van. see Van Vlack, Lawrence H.
Vlad, Roman, 1919-
xVlad, Roman.
Stravinsky. Oxford U Pr.
Vladeck, Bruce C.
xVladeck, Bruce C.
Unloving Care: The Nursing Home Tragedy.
Basic.
Vladimirtsov, Boris. see Vladimirtsov, Boris Iakovlevich.
Vladimirtsov, Boris Iakovlevich, 1884-1931
xVladimirtsov, Boris.
Life of Chingis-Khan. Arno.
Vlahos, Olivia.
xVlahos, Olivia.
Body, Ultimate Symbol. Lippincott.
Far Eastern Beginnings. Viking Pr.
Vlangas, Alex W.
xVlangas, Alex W.
Learning Centers & Individualized Reading in
Behavioral Terms. Mss Info.
Vlasto, A. P.
xVlasto, A. P.
Entry of the Slavs into Christendom: An
Introduction to the Medieval History of the
Slav. Cambridge U Pr.
Vlastos, Gregory.
xVlastos, Gregory.
ed. The Philosophy of Socrates: A Collection of
Critical Essays. U of Notre Dame Pr.
Plato's Universe. U of Wash Pr.
Vleck, David Van. see Van Vleck, David.
Vleck, John H. Van. see Van Vleck, John H.
Vlekke, Bernard H. see Vlekke, Bernard Hubertus Maria.
Vlekke, Bernard Hubertus Maria, 1899-
xVlekke, Bernard H.
The Story of the Dutch East Indies. AMS Pr.
Vliet, R. G., 1929-
xVliet, R. G.
Water & Stone: Poems. Random.
Vlodaver, Zeev.
xVlodaver, Zeev.
Coronary Arterial Variations in the Normal
Heart & in Congenital Heart Disease. Acad
Pr.
Vocke, William C.
xVocke, William C.
American Foreign Policy: An Analytical
Approach. Free Pr.
Vockings, John.
xVockings, John.
Goal. Harvey.
Vodar, Boris.
xVodar, Boris.
Some Aspects of Vacuum Ultraviolet Radiation
Physics. Pergamon.
Voe, Thomas De. see De Voe, Thomas F.
Voe, Thomas F. De. see De Voe, Thomas F.
Voegeli, V. Jacque.
xVoegeli, V. Jacque.

Free but Not Equal: The Midwest & the Negro
During the Civil War. U of Chicago Pr.
Voegelin, Byron D.
xVoegelin, Byron D.
South Florida's Vanished People: Travels in the
Homeland of Ancient Calusa. Island Pr.
Voegelin, Eric, 1901-
xVoegelin, Eric.
Anamnesis. U of Notre Dame Pr.
From Enlightenment to Revolution. Duke.
Plato. La State U Pr.
Voelckers, Ellen, 1952-
xVoelckers, Ellen.
Food for Fitness & Sports. Rosen Pr.
Girls' Guide to Menstruation. Rosen Pr.
Voelker, Francis.
xVoelker, Francis.
Mass Media: Forces in Our Society.
HarBraceJ.
xVoelker, Francis H.
ed. Mass Media: Forces in Our Society.
HarBraceJ.
Voelker, Francis H. see Voelker, Francis.
Vogau, Boris A. see Vogau, Boris Andreevich.
Vogau, Boris Andreevich, 1894-1937
xVogau, Boris A.
Tales of the Wilderness. Arno.
Vogel, A. I. see Vogel, Arthur Israel.
Vogel, Albert W.
xVogel, Albert W.
ed. Foundations of Education: A Social View.
U of NM Pr.
Vogel, Amos.
xVogel, Amos.
Film As a Subversive Art. Random.
Vogel, Arthur A. see Vogel, Arthur Anton.
Vogel, Arthur Anton.
xVogel, Arthur A.
The Power of His Resurrection: The Mystical
Life of Christians. Seabury.
Vogel, Arthur Israel.
xVogel, A. I.
ed. Vogel's Textbook of Macro & Semimicro
Qualitative Inorganic Analysis. Longman.
Vogel, Claude. see Vogel, Claude Lawrence.
Vogel, Claude Lawrence, Father, 1894-
xVogel, Claude.
The Capuchins in French Louisiana
(1722-1766). AMS Pr.
Vogel, David, 1947-
xVogel, David.
Lobbying the Corporation: Citizen Challenges
to Business Authority. Basic.
Vogel, Donald.
xVogel, Donald.
Aunt Clara: The Paintings of Clara McDonald
Williamson. Amon Carter.
Vogel, Erwin.
xVogel, Erwin.
illus. How to Succeed in Job-Search - When
Really Trying!. Copy-Write.
Vogel, Ezra F.
xVogel, Ezra F.
Canton Under Communism: Programs &
Politics in a Provincial Capital, 1949-1968.
Harvard U Pr.
Japan As Number One: Lessons for America.
Har-Row.
Japan As Number One: Lessons for America.
Harvard U Pr.
ed. Modern Japanese Organization &
Decision-Making. U of Cal Pr.
Vogel, F. see Vogel, Friedrich.
Vogel, Friedrich.
xVogel, F.
Human Genetics: Problems & Approaches.
Springer-Verlag.
Vogel, Harold.
xVogel, Harold.

Corporate Law Department Practice. P-H.
Vogel, Ilse Margret.
xVogel, Ilse-Margret.
illus. Farewell, Aunt Isabell. Har-Row.
illus. The Rainbow Dress & Other Tollush
Tales. Har-Row.
Vogel, Ilse-Margret. see Vogel, Ilse Margret.
Vogel, Jane.
xVogel, Jane.
Allegory in Dickens. U of Ala Pr.
Vogel, Joseph F.
xVogel, Joseph F.
Dante Gabriel Rossetti's Versecraft. U Presses
Fla.
Vogel, Lise.
xVogel, Lise.
The Column of Antoninus Pius. Harvard U Pr.
Vogel, M. see Vogel, Margarete.
Vogel, Margarete, 1946-
xVogel, M.
Postnatal Development of the Cat's Retina.
Springer-Verlag.
Vogel, Robert.
xVogel, Robert.
ed. A Breviate of British Diplomatic Blue
Books, 1919-1939. McGill-Queens U Pr.
Vogel, Rosemarie. see Vogel, Rosmarie.
Vogel, Rosmarie.
xVogel, Rosemarie.
Natural Proteinase Inhibitors. Acad Pr.
Vogel, Steven.
xVogel, Steven.
A Functional Bestiary: Laboratory Studies
About Living Systems. A-W.
Vogel, Susan A. see Vogel, Susan Ann.
Vogel, Susan Ann.
xVogel, Susan A.
Syntactic Abilities in Normal & Dyslexic
Children. Univ Park.
Vogel, Traugott.
xVogel, Traugott.
Under the SS Shadow. Broadman.
Vogel, Virgil J.
xVogel, Virgil J.
American Indian Medicine. U of Okla Pr.
This Country Was Ours: A Documentary
History of the American Indian. Har-Row.
This Country Was Ours: A Documentary
History of the American Indian. Har-Row.
Vogel, Werner. see Vogel, Werner Franz.
Vogel, Werner Franz, 1893-1970
xVogel, Werner.
The Exact Overwire Measurement of Screws,
Gears, Splines & Worms. Wayne St U Pr.
Vogeler, Ingolf.
xVogeler, Ingolf.
ed. Dialectics of Third World Development.
Allanheld.
Vogeli, Bruce R. see Vogeli, Bruce Ramon.
Vogeli, Bruce Ramon.
xVogeli, Bruce R.
Soviet Secondary Schools for the
Mathematically Talented. NCTM.
Vogelsinger, Hubert.
xVogelsinger, Hubert.
How to Star in Soccer. Schol Bk Serv.
Voges, Nettie A. see Voges, Nettie Allen.
Voges, Nettie Allen.
xVoges, Nettie A.
Old Alexandria: Where America's Past Is
Present. EPM Pubns.
Voget, F. see Voget, Fred W.
Voget, Fred W.
xVoget, F.
The History of Ethnology. HR&W.
Vogh, James.
xVogh, James.

Arachne Rising: The Search for the Thirteenth
Sign of the Zodiac. Dial.
The Cosmic Factor: Bioastrology & You.
Dodd.
Vogler. see Vogler, David J.
Vogler, David J.
xVogler.
The Politics of Congress. Allyn.
xVogler, David J.
The Third House: Conference Committees in
the United States Congress. Northwestern U
Pr.
Vogt, A. E. Van. see Van Vogt, A. E.
Vogt, A. Van. see Van Vogt, A.
Vogt, Bill.
xVogt, Bill.
How to Build a Better Outdoors: The Action
Manual for Fisherman, Hunters, Backpackers,
Hikers, Canoeists, Birders, & All Nature
Lovers. McKay.
Vogt, Douglas.
xVogt, Douglas.
Reality Revealed: The Theory of
Multidimensional Reality. Vector Assocs.
Vogt, Esther. see Vogt, Esther Loewen.
Vogt, Esther L. see Vogt, Esther Loewen.
Vogt, Esther Loewen.
xVogt, Esther.
Harvest Gold. Cook.
xVogt, Esther L.
Ann. Herald Pr.
Eight Wells of Elim. Herald Pr.
Turkey Red. Cook.
Vogt, Evon Z. see Vogt, Evon Zartman.
Vogt, Evon Zartman.
xVogt, Evon Z.
ed. People of Rimrock: A Study of Values in
Five Cultures. Atheneum.
ed. People of Rimrock: A Study of Values in
Five Cultures. Harvard U Pr.
Water Witching U. S. A.. U of Chicago Pr.
Vogt, Hannah.
xVogt, Hannah.
Burden of Guilt: A Short History of Germany,
1914-1945. Oxford U Pr.
Vogt, John.
xVogt, John.
Portuguese Rule on the Gold Coast,
1469-1682. U of Ga Pr.
Vogt, Joseph, 1895-
xVogt, Joseph.
Ancient Slavery & the Ideal of Man. Harvard
U Pr.
Vogt, P. R. see Vogt, Peter Richard.
Vogt, Paul, 1926-
xVogt, Paul.
The Blue Rider. Barron.
Expressionism: German Painting 1905-1920.
Abrams.
Vogt, Peter Richard, 1939-
xVogt, P. R.
Subduction of Aseismic Oceanic Ridges:
Effects on Shape, Seismicity & Other
Characteristics of Consuming Plate
Boundaries. Geol Soc.
Vogt, Richard J.
xVogt, Richard J.
Altering Course. Norton.
Altering Course. Sail Bks.
Vogt, Von O. see Vogt, Von Ogden.
Vogt, Von Ogden, 1879-
xVogt, Von O.
Art & Religion. Elliots Bks.
Vohora, S. B.
xVohora, S. B.
Animal Origin Drugs Used in Unani Medicine.
Advent Bk.
Vohs, John L.
xVohs, John L.

Audiences, Messages, Speakers: An
Introduction to Human Communication.
HarBraceJ.
Voight, Barry.
xVoight, Barry.
ed. Mechanics of Thrust Faults & Decollement.
Acad Pr.
Voight, Randall L.
xVoight, Randall L.
The Source: A Reference Guide to Information
& Resources. Intl Res Eval.
Voight, Virginia F. see Voight, Virginia Frances.
Voight, Virginia Frances.
xVoight, Virginia F.
Adventures of Hiawatha. Garrard.
Catamount. Macrae.
Patriots' Gold. Macrae.
Voigt, David Q. see Voigt, David Quentin.
Voigt, David Quentin.
xVoigt, David Q.
America Through Baseball. Nelson-Hall.
A Little League Journal. Bowling Green Univ.
Voigt, Ellen B. see Voigt, Ellen Bryant.
Voigt, Ellen Bryant, 1943-
xVoigt, Ellen B.
Claiming Kin. Columbia U Pr.
Voigt, Johan C. see Voigt, Johan Carel.
Voigt, Johan Carel.
xVoigt, Johan C.
Fifty Years of the History of the Republic in
South Africa, 1795-1845. Negro U Pr.
Voigt, William.
xVoigt, William.
Public Grazing Lands: Use & Misuse by
Industry & Government. Rutgers U Pr.
Voinovich, Vladimir, 1932-
xVoinovich, Vladimir.
The Life & Extraordinary Adventures of
Private Ivan Chonkin. FS&G.
Voit, Pal.
xVoit, Pal.
Old Hungarian Stove Tiles. Intl Pubns Serv.
Volbach, Walther R. see Volbach, Walther Richard.
Volbach, Walther Richard, 1897-
xVolbach, Walther R.
Problems of Opera Production. Shoe String.
Volcker, Paul A.
xVolcker, Paul A.
The Rediscovery of the Business Cycle. Free
Pr.
Vold, George B. see Vold, George Bryan.
Vold, George Bryan, 1896-
xVold, George B.
Theoretical Criminology. Oxford U Pr.
Voldben, A.
xVoldben, A.
After Nostradamus. Citadel Pr.
Volgyes, Ivan, 1936-
xVolgyes, Ivan.
Hungarian Soviet Republic, 1919: An
Evaluation & a Bibliography. Hoover Inst Pr.
ed. Hungary in Revolution, 1918-19: Nine
Essays. U of Nebr Pr.
The Liberated Female: Life, Work & Sex in
Socialist Hungary. Westview.
ed. Political Socialization in Eastern Europe: A
Comparative Framework. Praeger.
Volk, Bruno W.
xVolk, Bruno W.
ed. The Gangliosidoses. Plenum Pub.
Volk, Vic.
xVolk, Vic.
Aunty. Stemmer Hse.
Volk, Wesley. see Volk, Wesley A.
Volk, Wesley A.
xVolk, Wesley.
Essentials of Medical Microbiology. Lippincott.
xVolk, Wesley A.

Basic Microbiology. Lippincott.
Volk, William.
xVolk, William.
Applied Statistics for Engineers. Krieger.
Volkan, Vamik.
xVolkan, Vamik D.
Primitive Internalized Object Relations: A
Clinical Study of Schizophrenic, Borderline,
& Narcissistic Patients. Intl Univs Pr.
Volkan, Vamik D. see Volkan, Vamik.
Volkell, Randolph Z., 1950-
xVolkell, Randolph Z.
Quick Legal Terminology. Wiley.
Volker, Klaus, 1938-
xVolker, Klaus.
Brecht Chronicle. Continuum.
Volkmor, Cara B.
xVolkmor, Cara M.
Structuring the Classroom for Success. Merrill.
Volkmor, Cara M. see Volkmor, Cara B.
Volkoff, Victor. see Volkoff, Vladimir.
Volkoff, Vladimir.
xVolkoff, Victor.
Tchaikovsky: A Self-Portrait. Taplinger.
Volkomer, Walter E.
xVolkomer, Walter E.
American Government. P-H.
Volkov, Shulamit, 1942-
xVolkov, Shulamit.
The Rise of Popular Antimodernism in
Germany: The Urban Master Artisans,
1873-1896. Princeton U Pr.
Voll, John. see Voll, John Obert.
Voll, John Obert, 1936-
xVoll, John.
Historical Dictionary of the Sudan. Scarecrow.
Vollmann, Thomas E.
xVollmann, Thomas E.
Operations Management: A Systems
Model-Building Approach. A-W.
Vollmer, Ernst.
xVollmer, Ernst.
Encyclopaedia of Hydraulics, Soil &
Foundation Engineering. Elsevier.
Volney, C. F. see Volney, Constantin Francois Chassebuf.
**Volney, Constantin Francois Chassebuf, Comte De,
1757-1820**
xVolney, C. F.
A New Translation of Volney's Ruins. Garland
Pub.
Volpe, E. Peter. see Volpe, Erminio Peter.
Volpe, Edmond. see Volpe, Edmond Loris.
Volpe, Edmond L. see Volpe, Edmond Loris.
Volpe, Edmond Loris.
xVolpe, Edmond.
Reader's Guide to William Faulkner. FS&G.
xVolpe, Edmond L.
A Reader's Guide to William Faulkner.
Octagon.
Volpe, Erminio Peter.
xVolpe, E. Peter.
Human Heredity & Birth Defects. Pegasus.
Understanding Evolution. Wm C Brown.
xVolpe, Peter E.
Man, Nature, & Society: An Introduction to
Biology. Wm C Brown.
Volpe, John.
xVolpe, John.
Proceedings of a Conference on the Foreign
Tax Credit. Chamber Comm US.
Volpe, Peter E. see Volpe, Erminio Peter.
Volpe, Stanley U.
xVolpe, Stanley U.
This Is the Boxer. TFH Pubns.
Voltaire. see Voltaire, Francois Marie Arouet De.
Voltaire, Francois M. see Voltaire, Francois Marie
Arouet De.
Voltaire, Francois Marie Arouet De, 1694-1778
xVoltaire.

Letters Concerning the English Nation. B
Franklin.
xVoltaire, Francois M.
The Portable Voltaire. Penguin.
Volterra, Enrico.
xVolterra, Enrico.
Advanced Strength of Materials. P-H.
Voltmer, Edward F. *see* Voltmer, Edward Frank.
Voltmer, Edward Frank.
xVoltmer, Edward F.
The Organization & Administration of Physical
Education. P-H.
Voltz, Jeanne.
xVoltz, Jeanne.
The California Cookbook. Bobbs.
The Los Angeles Times Natural Foods
Cookbook. NAL.
Volwiler, Albert T. *see* Volwiler, Albert Tangeman.
Volwiler, Albert Tangeman, 1888-1957
xVolwiler, Albert T.
George Croghan & the Westward Movement,
1741-1782. AMS Pr.
Von , Helms, E. Freienmuth. *see* Freienmuth Von Helms,
E.
Von Arx, William S. *see* Von Arx, William Stelling.
Von Arx, William Stelling, 1916-
xVon Arx, William S.
An Introduction to Physical Oceanography.
A-W.
Von, Aue, Hartmann. *see* Hartmann Von Aue.
Von Beyme, Klaus.
xVon Beyme, Klaus.
German Political Studies. Sage.
Von Blum, Paul.
xVon Blum, Paul.
The Art of Social Conscience. Universe.
Von Bober, Wolffgang, 1923-
xVon Bober, Wolffgang.
The Carver Effect: A Paranormal Experience.
Stackpole.
Von Bonin, Gerhardt. *see* Bonin, Gerhardt Von.
Von Braun, Wernher.
xVon Braun, Wernher.
History of Rocketry & Space Travel. T Y
Crowell.
The Mars Project. U of Ill Pr.
New Worlds: Discoveries from Our Solar
System. Doubleday.
Von Canon, Claudia.
xVon Canon, Claudia.
The Moonclock. G K Hall.
The Moonclock. HM.
Von Damm, Helene.
xVon Damm, Helene.
Sincerely, Ronald Reagan. Berkley Pub.
Sincerely, Ronald Reagan. Green Hill.
Von Der Borch, C. C. *see* Von der Borch, Chris C.
Von der Borch, Chris C.
xVon Der Borch, C. C.
ed. Synthesis of Deep Sea Drilling Results in
the Indian Ocean. Elsevier.
Von der Mehden, Fred R.
xVon Der Mehden, Fred R.
Religion & Nationalism in Southeast Asia:
Burma, Indonesia, & the Philippines. U of
Wis Pr.
South East Asia 1930-1970: The Legacy of
Colonialism & Nationalism. Norton.
Von Der Osten, Hans. *see* Osten, Hans Von Der.
Von der Porten, Ronald P.
xVon Der Porten, Ronald P.
Introduction to Defensive Bidding. P-H.
Von Dollinger, Johann J. *see* Dollinger, Johann J. Von.
Von Eckardt, Wolf.
xVon Eckardt, Wolf.
Back to the Drawing Board: Planning for
Livable Cities. New Republic.
Von Ende, Richard C.
xVon Ende, Richard C.

Church Music: An International Bibliography.
Scarecrow.
Von Foerster, H. *see* Von Foerster, Heinz.
Von Foerster, Heinz.
xVon Foerster, H.
ed. Music by Computers. Krieger.
Von Frank, Albert J.
xVon Frank, Albert J.
Whittier: A Comprehensive Annotated
Bibliography. Garland Pub.
Von Furstenberg, Egon.
xVon Furstenberg, Egon.
The Power Look. Fawcett.
The Power Look. HR&W.
The Power Look at Home: Decorating for
Men. Morrow.
Von Furstenberg, George M.
xVon Furstenberg, George M.
Patterns of Racial Discrimination. Lexington
Bks.
Von Gnielinski, Stefan.
xVon Gnielinski, Stefan.
ed. Liberia in Maps. Holmes & Meier.
Von Goethe, Johann W. *see* Goethe, Johann W. Von.
Von Hagen, Victor W. *see* Von Hagen, Victor Wolfgang.
Von Hagen, Victor Wolfgang, 1908-
xVon Hagen, Victor W.
The Aztec & Maya Papermakers. Hacker.
Aztec: Man & Tribe. NAL.
The Germanic People in America. U of Okla
Pr.
The Jicaque (Torrupan) Indians of Honduras.
AMS Pr.
Realm of the Incas. NAL.
World of the Maya. NAL.
Von Hahmann, Gail, 1947-
xVon Hahmann, Gail.
Collaborative Programming for Nonformal
Education. Ctr Intl Ed U of MA.
Von Hallberg, Robert, 1946-
xVon Hallberg, Robert.
Charles Olson: The Scholar's Art. Harvard U
Pr.
Von Hefele, Karl J. *see* Hefele, Karl J.
Von Heider, W. M.
xVon Heider, W. M.
Compiled by And Then Take Hands.
Dawne-Leigh.
Von Hentig, Hans. *see* Hentig, Hans Von.
Von Herder, Johann G. *see* Herder, Johann G. Von.
Von Hildebrand, Alice J. *see* Von Hildebrand, Alice M.
(Jourdain).
Von Hildebrand, Alice M. (Jourdain).
xVon Hildebrand, Alice J.
Introduction to a Philosophy of Religion.
Franciscan Herald.
Von Hildebrand, Dietrich.
xVon Hildebrand, Dietrich.
Art of Living. Franciscan Herald.
Ethics. Franciscan Herald.
Von Hippel, Arndt.
xVon Hippel, Arndt.
A Manual of Thoracic Surgery. C C Thomas.
Von Hippel, Ursula.
xVon Hippel, Ursula.
illus. The Craziest Halloween. Coward.
Von Hirsch, Andrew.
xVon Hirsch, Andrew.
The Question of Parole: Retention, Reform or
Abolition?. Ballinger Pub.
Von Hofe, Harold. *see* Von Hofe, Harold H.
Von Hofe, Harold H.
xVon Hofe, Harold.
Perspektiven Zu Aktuellen Fragen. HR&W.
Von Hoffman, Nicholas.
xVon Hoffman, Nicholas.
Left at the Post. Times Bks.
Von Humboldt, Alexander. *see* Humboldt, Alexander
Von.

Von Karman, Theodore, 1881-
xVon Karman, Theodore.
Aerodynamics. McGraw.
Von Kleist, Heinrich. *see* Kleist, Heinrich von.
Von Liebig, Justus. *see* Liebig, Justus Von.
Von Maltitz, F. *see* Von Maltitz, Frances Willard.
Von Maltitz, Frances. *see* Von Maltitz, Frances Willard.
Von Maltitz, Frances Willard, 1913-
xVon Maltitz, F.
Living & Learning in Two Languages:
Bilingual-Bicultural Education in the U.S..
McGraw.
xVon Maltitz, Frances.
The Rhone: River of Contrasts. Garrard.
Von Mehren, Arthur T. *see* Von Mehren, Arthur Taylor.
Von Mehren, Arthur Taylor.
xVon Mehren, Arthur T.
ed. Law in Japan: The Legal Order in a
Changing Society. Harvard U Pr.
Von Mendelssohn, Felix, 1918-
xVon Mendelssohn, Felix.
This Is Psychiatry. Thieme-Stratton.
Von Mises, Ludwig, 1881-1973
xVon Mises, Ludwig.
The Anti-Capitalistic Mentality. Libertarian.
Human Action: A Treatise on Economics.
Contemp Bks.
On the Manipulation of Money & Credit. Free
Market.
Von Mises, Richard.
xVon Mises, Richard.
Fluid Dynamics. Springer-Verlag.
Von Mosenthal, Salomon R. *see* Mosenthal, Salomon R.
Von.
Von Neumann, John, 1903-1957
xVon Neumann, John.
Continuous Geometry. Princeton U Pr.
Von Neumann, Robert.
xVon Neumann, Robert.
Design & Creation of Jewelry. Chilton.
Von Philippsberg, Eugen Philippovich. *see* Philippovich
Von Philippsberg, Eugen.
Von Riekhoff, Harald, 1937-
xVon Riekhoff, Harald.
German-Polish Relations 1918-1933. Johns
Hopkins.
Von Sachs, Julius. *see* Sachs, Julius Von.
Von Savigny, Friedrich K. *see* Savigny, Friedrich K. Von.
Von Vorys, Karl.
xVon Vorys, Karl.
Democracy Without Consensus: Communalism
& Political Stability in Malaysia. Princeton U
Pr.
Von Wartburg, Ursula.
xVon Wartburg, Ursula.
illus. The Workshop Book of Knitting.
Atheneum.
Von Welanetz, Diana.
xVon Welanetz, Diana.
The Art of Buffet Entertaining. J P Tarcher.
Von Winning, Hasso.
xVon Winning, Hasso.
Pre-Columbian Art of Mexico & Central
America. Abrams.
Vonnegut, Kurt.
xVonnegut, Kurt.
Cat's Cradle. Delacorte.
Cat's Cradle. Dell.
Cat's Cradle. Dell.
Vontress, Clemmont E., 1929-
xVontress, Clemmont E.
Counseling Negroes. HM.
Vontver, Louis A.
xVontver, Louis A.
Differential Diagnosis in Gynecology. Arco.
Obstetrics & Gynecology Review. Arco.
Voorhees, Richard J. *see* Voorhees, Richard Joseph.
Voorhees, Richard Joseph, 1916-
xVoorhees, Richard J.

The Paradox of George Orwell. Purdue.
Voorheis, Frank L.
  xVoorheis, Frank L.
    Bank Administered Pooled Equity Funds for
    Employee Benefit Plans. Mich St U Busn.
Voorhis, Harold V. see Voorhis, Harold Van Buren.
Voorhis, Harold Van Buren, 1894-
  xVoorhis, Harold V.
    The Eastern Star: The Evolution from a Rite to
    an Order. Macoy Pub.
Voorhis, Horace J. see Voorhis, Horace Jeremiah.
Voorhis, Horace Jeremiah, 1901-
  xVoorhis, Horace J.
    Confessions of a Congressman. Greenwood.
  xVoorhis, Jerry.
    The Strange Case of Richard Milhous Nixon.
    Eriksson.
    The Strange Case of Richard Milhous Nixon.
    Popular Lib.
Voorhis, Jerry. see Voorhis, Horace Jeremiah.
Voorhis, John S. Van. see Van Voorhis, John S.
Voorhoeve, Jan.
  xVoorhoeve, Jan.
    ed. Creole Drum: An Anthology of Creole
    Literature in Surinam. Yale U Pr.
Vore, Nicholas De. see De Vore, Nicholas.
Voreadou, R. see Voreadou, Rodiani.
Voreadou, Rodiani.
  xVoreadou, R.
    Coherence & Non-Commutative Diagrams in
    Closed Categories. Am Math.
Vorndran, Barbara S. see Vorndran, Barbara Sethney.
Vorndran, Barbara Sethney.
  xVorndran, Barbara S.
    General Merchandise Retailing. McGraw.
Voroba, Barry.
  xVoroba, Barry.
    Experimenting in the Hearing & Speech
    Sciences: 1978. Starkey Labs.
Vorpahl, Ben M. see Vorpahl, Ben Merchant.
Vorpahl, Ben Merchant.
  xVorpahl, Ben M.
    Frederic Remington & the West: With the Eye
    of the Mind. U of Tex Pr.
Vorrath, Harry H.
  xVorrath, Harry H.
    Positive Peer Culture. Aldine Pub.
Vorreux, Damien.
  xVorreux, Damien.
    First Encounter with Francis of Assisi.
    Franciscan Herald.
Vorspan, Albert.
  xVorspan, Albert.
    I'm OK, You're a Pain in the Neck.
    Doubleday.
Vorys, Karl Von. see Von Vorys, Karl.
Vos, George A. De. see De Vos, George A.
Vos, Howard F. see Vos, Howard Frederic.
Vos, Howard Frederic, 1925-
  xVos, Howard F.
    Effective Bible Study. Zondervan.
    Mark: A Study Guide Commentary.
    Zondervan.
Vos, Johannes G.
  xVos, Johannes G.
    Christian Introduction to Religions of the
    World. Baker Bk.
Vos, K.
  xVos, K.
    The Church on the Hill: St. John's Parish,
    Wynberg. Verry.
Vose, Clement E.
  xVose, Clement E.
    A Guide to Library Sources in Political
    Science: American Government. Am
    Political.
Vose, P. B. see Vose, Peter B.
Vose, Peter B.
  xVose, P. B.

Introduction to Nuclear Techniques in
  Agronomy & Plant Biology. Pergamon.
Voss, Carl H. see Voss, Carl Hermann.
Voss, Carl Hermann.
  xVoss, Carl H.
    Rabbi & Minister: The Friendship of Stephen
    S. Wise & John Haynes Holmes. Prometheus
    Bks.
Voss, Gilbert L.
  xVoss, Gilbert L.
    Oceanography. Western Pub.
Voss, Thomas M., 1945-
  xVoss, Thomas M.
    Antique American Country Furniture: A Field
    Guide. Lippincott.
  xVoss, Tom.
    Bargain Hunter's Guide to Used Furniture.
    Dell.
Voss, Tom. see Voss, Thomas M.
Vossler, Karl, 1872-1949
  xVossler, Karl.
    The Spirit of Language in Civilization. AMS
    Pr.
Vossler, Otto, 1902-
  xVossler, Otto.
    Jefferson & the American Revolutionary Ideal.
    U Pr of Amer.
Votaw, Dow.
  xVotaw, Dow.
    The Corporate Dilemma: Traditional Values
    Versus Contemporary Problems. P-H.
    Legal Aspects of Business Administration. P-H.
Voth, Norma J. see Voth, Norma Jost.
Voth, Norma Jost.
  xVoth, Norma J.
    Festive Breads of Easter. Herald Pr.
Voto, Bernard A. De. see De Voto, Bernard A.
Vought, Dale G., 1937-
  xVought, Dale G.
    Protestants in Modern Spain: The Struggle for
    Religious Pluralism. William Carey Lib.
Voulet, Jacqueline.
  xVoulet, Jacqueline.
    Book of Happy Cats. S&S.
Voyce, Arthur.
  xVoyce, Arthur.
    Art & Architecture of Medieval Russia. U of
    Okla Pr.
Vrbova, G. see Vrbova, Gerta.
Vrbova, Gerta.
  xVrbova, G.
    Nerve-Muscle Interaction. Methuen Inc.
Vreden, Werner.
  xVreden, Werner.
    Curved Continuous Beams for Highway
    Bridges. Ungar.
Vree, Dale, 1944-
  xVree, Dale.
    On Synthesizing Marxism & Christianity.
    Wiley.
Vreeken, Elizabeth.
  xVreeken, Elizabeth.
    Boy Who Would Not Say His Name. Follett.
Vreeland, Hamilton, 1892-
  xVreeland, Hamilton.
    Twilight of Individual Liberty. Arno.
Vreeland, Herbert H. see Vreeland, Herbert Harold.
Vreeland, Herbert Harold, 1920-
  xVreeland, Herbert H.
    Mongol Community & Kinship Structure.
    Greenwood.
Vreeland, R. see Vreeland, Richard C.
Vreeland, Richard C.
  xVreeland, R.
    Become Financially Independent: An
    Investment Plan That Really Works. P-H.
Vreeland, Walter M.
  xVreeland, Walter M.

The Care & Feeding of Agents. Natl
  Underwriter.
Vrettos, Theodore.
  xVrettos, Theodore.
    Birds of Winter. HM.
Vreuls, Diane.
  xVreuls, Diane.
    Are We There Yet?. S&S.
    Sums: A Looking Game. Viking Pr.
Vriend, John.
  xVriend, John.
    ed. Counseling Effectively in Groups. Educ
    Tech Pubns.
Vries , J. De. see De Vries, J.
Vries, J. de. see Vries, Johannes De.
Vries, Jan De. see De Vries, Jan.
Vries, Johannes De.
  xVries, J. de.
    The Netherlands Economy in the Twentieth
    Century: An Examination of the Most
    Characteristic Feature in the Period
    1900-1970. Humanities.
Vries, L. De. see De Vries, L.
Vries, Peter De. see De Vries, Peter.
Vries, Romana De. see De Vries, Romana.
Vroom, Richard.
  xVroom, Richard.
    ed. Old New Brunswick: A Victorian Portrait.
    Oxford U Pr.
Vroom, Victor H. see Vroom, Victor Harold.
Vroom, Victor Harold.
  xVroom, Victor H.
    Leadership & Decision-Making. U of Pittsburgh
    Pr.
    Work & Motivation. Wiley.
Vrooman, Alan. see Vrooman, Alan H.
Vrooman, Alan H.
  xVrooman, Alan.
    Good Writing: An Informal Manual of Style.
    Atheneum.
Vucinich, Alexander. see Vucinich, Alexander S.
Vucinich, Alexander S., 1914-
  xVucinich, Alexander.
    Social Thought in Tsarist Russia: The Quest for
    a General Science of Society, 1861-1917. U
    of Chicago Pr.
Vucinich, Wayne S.
  xVucinich, Wayne S.
    ed. The Peasant in Nineteenth-Century Russia.
    Stanford U Pr.
Vulliamy, Graham.
  xVulliamy, Graham.
    ed. Pop Music in School. Cambridge U Pr.
Vuuren, Nancy Van. see Van Vuuren, Nancy.
Vye, George.
  xVye, George.
    Cooking with Grass. Two Continents.
Vyn, Kathleen.
  xVyn, Kathleen.
    The Prairie Community. Messner.
    Spring in the High Sierras. Messner.
Vyshinskii, Andrei I. see Vyshinskii, Andrei Ianuarevich.
Vyshinskii, Andrei Ianuarevich.
  xVyshinskii, Andrei I.
    ed. The Law of the Soviet State. Greenwood.
Vysny, P. see Vysny, Paul.
Vysny, Paul, 1944-
  xVysny, P.
    Neo-Slavism & the Czechs, 1898-1914.
    Cambridge U Pr.
Vyverberg, Henry.
  xVyverberg, Henry.
    The Living Tradition: Art, Music & Ideas in
    the Western World. HarBraceJ.
Wa Said, Dibing. see Wa Said, Dibinga.
Wa Said, Dibinga.
  xWa Said, Dibing.

Theosophies of Plato, Aristotle & Plotinus.
Philos Lib.

Waagenaar, Sam.
xWaagenaar, Sam.
The Pope's Jews. Open Court.

Waaland, J. Robert.
xWaaland, J. Robert.
Common Seaweeds of the Pacific Coast. Pacific
Search.

Waardenburg, Jacques. *see* Waardenburg, Jean Jacques.

Waardenburg, Jean Jacques.
xWaardenburg, Jacques.
Classical Approaches to the Study of Religion:
Aims, Methods & Theories of Research, Pt. 2
Bibliography. Mouton.

Waber, Bernard.
xWaber, Bernard.
illus. Anteater Named Arthur. HM.
illus. But Names Will Never Hurt Me. HM.
illus. Cheese. HM.
illus. Firefly Named Torchy. HM.
illus. Goodbye, Funny Dumpy-Lumpy. HM.
illus. I Was All Thumbs. HM.
illus. Lovable Lyle. HM.
illus. Nobody Is Perfick. HM.
Rich Cat, Poor Cat. Schol Bk Serv.
You're a Little Kid with a Big Heart. HM.

Wace, Alan J. *see* Wace, Alan John Bayard.

Wace, Alan John Bayard.
xWace, Alan J.
The Nomads of the Balkans: An Account of
Life & Customs Among the Vlachs of
Northern Pindus. Arno.

Wach, Joachim, 1898-1955
xWach, Joachim.
The Comparative Study of Religions. Columbia
U Pr.
Types of Religious Experience: Christian &
Non-Christian. U of Chicago Pr.
Understanding & Believing: Essays.
Greenwood.

Wachhaus, Gustav.
xWachhaus, Gustav.
Fundamental Classroom Music Skills: Theory
& Performing Techniques. HR&W.

Wachs, Bob. *see* Wachs, Robert.

Wachs, Martin.
xWachs, Martin.
Transportation for the Elderly: Changing
Lifestyles, Changing Needs. U of Cal Pr.

Wachs, Robert, 1923-
xWachs, Bob.
The Patterned Shuffle Attack: A New
Approach to Individual Excellence &
Balanced Team Play. P-H.

Wachs, William.
xWachs, William.
How Sales Managers Get Things Done. P-H.

Wachspress, Eugene L.
xWachspress, Eugene L.
A Rational Finite Element Basis. Acad Pr.

Wacht, Walter F.
xWacht, Walter F.
The Domestic Air Transportation Network of
the United States. U Chicago Dept Geog.

Wachtel, Howard M.
xWachtel, Howard M.
Workers' Management & Workers' Wages in
Yugoslavia: The Theory & Practice of
Participatory Socialism. Cornell U Pr.

Wachtel, Paul L., 1940-
xWachtel, Paul L.
Psychoanalysis & Behavior Therapy: Toward an
Integration. Basic.

Wackenheim, A. *see* Wackenheim, Auguste.

Wackenheim, Auguste.
xWackenheim, A.

Angiography of the Mesencephalon: Normal &
Pathological Findings. Springer-Verlag.
The Narrow Lumbar Canal: Radiologic Signs &
Surgery. Springer-Verlag.
The Veins of the Posterior Fossa: Normal &
Pathological Findings. Springer-Verlag.

Wackenroder, Wilhelm H. *see* Wackenroder, Wilhelm
Heinrich.

Wackenroder, Wilhelm Heinrich.
xWackenroder, Wilhelm H.
Outpourings of an Art-Loving Friar. Ungar.

Wacker, Peter O.
xWacker, Peter O.
The Musconetcong Valley of New Jersey: A
Historical Geography. Rutgers U Pr.

Wada, Takashi, 1938-
xWada, Takashi.
The Art of Making Jewelry. Van Nos
Reinhold.

Waddell, Alfred M. *see* Waddell, Alfred Moore.

Waddell, Alfred Moore, 1834-1912
xWaddell, Alfred M.
A Colonial Officer & His Times, 1754-1773: A
Biographical Sketch of Gen. Hugh Waddell of
North Carolina. Reprint.

Waddell, Gene.
xWaddell, Gene.
Indians of the South Carolina Lowcountry,
1562-1751. Reprint.

Waddell, Helen. *see* Waddell, Helen Jane.

Waddell, Helen Jane, 1889-1965
xWaddell, Helen.
Stories from Holy Writ. Greenwood.

Waddell, Jack O.
xWaddell, Jack O.
ed. The American Indian in Urban Society.
Little.
ed. Drinking Behavior Among Southwestern
Indians: An Anthropological Perspective. U
of Ariz Pr.
Papago Indians at Work. U of Ariz Pr.

Waddell, Joseph J.
xWaddell, Joseph J.
ed. Concrete Construction Handbook.
McGraw.
Practical Quality Control for Concrete. Krieger.

Waddell, L. Austine. *see* Waddell, Laurence Austine.

Waddell, Laurence Austine, 1854-1938
xWaddell, L. Austine.
Lhasa & Its Mysteries: With a Record of the
Expedition of 1903-1904. Arno.

Waddell, Roberta.
xWaddell, Roberta.
ed. The Art Nouveau Style in Jewelry,
Metalwork, Glass, Ceramics, Textiles,
Architecture & Furniture. Peter Smith.

Waddington, C. H. *see* Waddington, Conrad Hal.

Waddington, Conrad H. *see* Waddington, Conrad Hal.

Waddington, Conrad Hal, 1905-
xWaddington, C. H.
The Evolution of an Evolutionist. Cornell U Pr.
xWaddington, Conrad H.
Principles of Development & Differentiation.
Macmillan.

Waddington, Lawrence C.
xWaddington, Lawrence C.
Arrest, Search & Seizure. Glencoe.
Criminal Evidence. Glencoe.

Waddington, Miriam.
xWaddington, Miriam.
The Price of Gold. Oxford U Pr.

Waddington, Richard.
xWaddington, Richard.
Catching Salmon. David & Charles.

Waddington, Samuel, 1844-1923
xWaddington, Samuel.
Arthur Hugh Clough: A Monograph. R West.

Waddy, Broughton.
xWaddy, Broughton.

A Word or Two Before You Go. Norton.

Waddy, Charis.
xWaddy, Charis.
The Muslim Mind. Longman.

Waddy, Lawrence.
xWaddy, Lawrence.
Drama in Worship. Paulist Pr.

Wade, Alex.
xWade, Alex.
A Design & Construction Handbook for
Energy Saving Houses. Rodale Pr Inc.

Wade, Anne.
xWade, Anne.
A Promise Is for Keeping. Childrens.

Wade, Bonnie. *see* Wade, Bonnie C.

Wade, Bonnie C.
xWade, Bonnie.
Music in India: The Classical Traditions. P-H.

Wade, C. *see* Wade, Carlson.

Wade, Carlson.
xWade, C.
All Natural Pain Relievers. P-H.
xWade, Carlson.
Brand-Name Handbook of Protein, Calories &
Carbohydrates. P-H.
The Bread Book. Har-Row.
Fact-Book on Hypertension, High Blood
Pressure & Your Diet. Keats.
Floor Decorating. A S Barnes.
Great Hoaxes & Famous Imposters. Jonathan
David.
Natural & Folk Remedies. P-H.
Natural Hormones: The Secret of Youthful
Health. P-H.
Natural Way to Health Through Controlled
Fasting. Arc Bks.

Wade, David.
xWade, David.
Pattern in Islamic Art. Overlook Pr.

Wade, Francis C.
xWade, Francis C.
Teaching & Morality. Loyola.

Wade, Gladys I. *see* Wade, Gladys Irene.

Wade, Gladys Irene.
xWade, Gladys I.
Thomas Traherne. Octagon.

Wade, H. T. *see* Wade, Herbert Treadwell.

Wade, H. W. *see* Wade, Henry William Rawson.

Wade, Harlan.
xWade, Harlan.
Electricity. Raintree Pubs.
Gears. Raintree Pubs.
Heat. Raintree Pubs.
Ideas. Raintree Pubs.
The Lever. Raintree Pubs.
Oil. Raintree Pubs.
Reflection. Raintree Pubs.
Sand. Raintree Pubs.
Size. Raintree Pubs.
Sound. Raintree Pubs.
Speed. Raintree Pubs.
Springs. Raintree Pubs.
Strength. Raintree Pubs.
Time. Raintree Pubs.
Water. Raintree Pubs.
The Wheel. Raintree Pubs.
Wood. Raintree Pubs.

Wade, Henry William Rawson.
xWade, H. W.
Administrative Law. Oxford U Pr.

Wade, Herbert Treadwell.
xWade, H. T.
This Glorious Cause: The Adventures of Two
Company Officers in Washington's Army.
Princeton U Pr.

Wade, Ira O. *see* Wade, Ira Owen.

Wade, Ira Owen, 1896-
xWade, Ira O.

Clandestine Organization & Diffusion of
  Philosophic Ideas in France from 1700 to
  1750. Octagon.
Intellectual Development of Voltaire. Princeton
  U Pr.
Intellectual Origins of the French
  Enlightenment. Princeton U Pr.
Wade, John, 1788-1875
  xWade, John.
    History of the Middle & Working Classes.
      Kelley.
Wade, John T. see Wade, John Thomas.
Wade, John Thomas, 1891-
  xWade, John T.
    A Measurement of the Secondary School As a
      Part of the Pupil's Environment. AMS Pr.
Wade, John W. see Wade, John William.
Wade, John William, 1925-
  xWade, John W.
    Architecture, Problems, & Purposes:
      Architectural Design As a Basic
      Problem-Solving Process. Wiley.
Wade, L. L. see Wade, Larry L.
Wade, Larry L.
  xWade, L. L.
    The Economic Development of South Korea:
      The Political Economy of Success. Praeger.
Wade, Mason.
  xWade, Mason.
    ed. Canadian Dualism: Studies of
      French-English Relations. U of Toronto Pr.
Wade, Mildred.
  xWade, Mildred.
    Games for Fun. Broadman.
    Socials for All Occasions. Broadman.
Wade, Nicholas.
  xWade, Nicholas.
    The Ultimate Experiment: Man Made
      Evolution. Walker & Co.
Wade, Thomas L. see Wade, Thomas Leonard.
Wade, Thomas Leonard.
  xWade, Thomas L.
    Contemporary Analytic Geometry. Krieger.
    Fundamental Mathematics. McGraw.
Wade, Torlen L.
  xWade, Torlen L.
    Planning & Managing Rural Health Centers.
      Ballinger Pub.
Wadekin, Karl Eugen.
  xWadekin, Karl-Eugen.
    Agriculture in Eastern Europe & the Soviet
      Union: Comparative Studies. Allanheld.
    The Private Sector in Soviet Agriculture. U of
      Cal Pr.
Wadekin, Karl-Eugen. see Wadekin, Karl Eugen.
Wadepuhl, Walter, 1895-
  xWadepuhl, Walter.
    Goethe's Interest in the New World. Haskell.
Wadland, John H. see Wadland, John Henry.
Wadland, John Henry.
  xWadland, John H.
    Ernest Thompson Seton: Man in Nature & the
      Progressive Era, 1880-1915. Arno.
Wadlington, Warwick, 1938-
  xWadlington, Warwick.
    The Confidence Game in American Literature.
      Princeton U Pr.
Wadsworth, Alfred P.
  xWadsworth, Alfred P.
    Cotton Trade & Industrial Lancashire
      1600-1780. Kelley.
Wadsworth, Barry J.
  xWadsworth, Barry J.
    Piaget's Theory of Cognitive Development: An
      Introduction for Students of Psychology &
      Education. Longman.
Wadsworth, Bruce.
  xWadsworth, Bruce.

An Adirondack Sampler: Day Hikes for All
  Seasons. ADK Mtn Club.
Wadsworth, John W.
  xWadsworth, John W.
    Designs from Plant Forms. Universe.
Wadsworth, Michael. see Wadsworth, Michael Edwin
  John.
Wadsworth, Michael Edwin John.
  xWadsworth, Michael.
    The Roots of Delinquency: Infancy,
      Adolescence & Crime. B&N.
Waelbroeck, L. see Waelbroeck, Lucien.
Waelbroeck, Lucien.
  xWaelbroeck, L.
    Topological Vector Spaces & Algebras.
      Springer-Verlag.
Waelder, Robert.
  xWaelder, Robert.
    Progress & Revolution: A Study of the Issues
      of Our Age. Intl Univs Pr.
    Psychoanalytic Avenues to Art. Intl Univs Pr.
Waesche, James F.
  xWaesche, James F.
    Beautiful Maryland. Beautiful Am.
Waffle, Harvey W.
  xWaffle, Harvey W.
    Architectural Drawing. Glencoe.
Wagar, W. W. see Wagar, W. Warren.
Wagar, W. Warren.
  xWagar, W. W.
    World Views: A Study in Comparative History.
      HR&W.
  xWagar, W. Warren.
    Books in World History: A Guide for Teachers
      & Students. Ind U Pr.
    H. G. Wells & the World State. Arno.
    ed. Idea of Progress Since the Renaissance.
      Wiley.
    World Views: A Study in Comparative History.
      HR&W.
Wagel, Srinivas Ram.
  xWagel, Srinivas.
    Finance in China. Garland Pub.
Wagel, Srinvas. see Wagel, Srinivas Ram.
Wagemaker, Herbert.
  xWagemaker, Herbert.
    How Can I Understand My Kids?. Zondervan.
Wagenen, Beulah Van. see Van Wagenen, Beulah.
Wagenen, Gertrude Van. see Van Wagenen, Gertrude.
Wagener, Hans, 1940-
  xWagener, Hans.
    The German Baroque Novel. Twayne.
Wagenheim, Kal.
  xWagenheim, Kal.
    Clemente!. WSP.
Wagenknecht, Edward. see Wagenknecht, Edward
  Charles.
Wagenknecht, Edward C. see Wagenknecht, Edward
  Charles.
Wagenknecht, Edward Charles, 1900-
  xWagenknecht, Edward.
    Eve & Henry James: Portraits of Women &
      Girls in His Fiction. U of Okla Pr.
    Personality of Chaucer. U of Okla Pr.
    Personality of Milton. U of Okla Pr.
    The Personality of Shakespeare. U of Okla Pr.
  xWagenknecht, Edward C.

Ambassadors for Christ: Seven American
  Preachers. Oxford U Pr.
Dickens & the Scandalmongers: Essays in
  Criticism. U of Okla Pr.
Guide to Bernard Shaw. Russell.
Mark Twain: The Man & His Work. U of Okla
  Pr.
Preface to Literature. Kraus Repr.
Ralph Waldo Emerson: Portrait of a Balanced
  Soul. Oxford U Pr.
Utopia Americana. Folcroft.
Utopia Americana. R West.
Wagenvoord, James.
  xWagenvoord, James.
    Flying Kites. Macmillan.
Wagenvoort, C. A. see Wagenvoort, Cornelis Adriaan.
Wagenvoort, Cornelis Adriaan.
  xWagenvoort, C. A.
    Pathology of Pulmonary Hypertension. Wiley.
Wager, Paul W. see Wager, Paul Woodford.
Wager, Paul Woodford, 1893-
  xWager, Paul W.
    County Government Across the Nation.
      Greenwood.
Wager, Walter. see Wager, Walter H.
Wager, Walter H.
  xWager, Walter.
    Blue Leader. Arbor Hse.
Wager, William, fl. 1566
  xWager, William.
    Longer Thou Livest the More Fool Thou Art.
      AMS Pr.
Waggin, Chuck.
  xWaggin, Chuck.
    A Light-Hearted Look at the Desert. U of Ariz
      Pr.
Waggoner, Diana.
  xWaggoner, Diane.
    The Hills of Faraway: A Guide to Fantasy.
      Atheneum.
Waggoner, Diane. see Waggoner, Diana.
Waggoner, Hyatt H. see Waggoner, Hyatt Howe.
Waggoner, Hyatt Howe.
  xWaggoner, Hyatt H.
    The Presence of Hawthorne. La State U Pr.
Wagley, Charles, 1913-
  xWagley, Charles.
    Amazon Town: A Study of Man in the
      Tropics. Oxford U Pr.
    Introduction to Brazil. Columbia U Pr.
    Latin American Tradition: Essays on the Unity
      & the Diversity of Latin American Culture.
      Columbia U Pr.
    ed. Race & Class in Rural Brazil. Russell.
Wagman, G. H. see Wagman, Gerald H.
Wagman, Gerald H.
  xWagman, G. H.
    Chromatography of Antibiotics. Elsevier.
Wagn, Klaus, 1937-
  xWagn, Klaus.
    What Time Does. Caann Verlag.
Wagner, Arthur L. see Wagner, Arthur Lockwood.
Wagner, Arthur Lockwood, 1853-1905
  xWagner, Arthur L.
    The Campaign of Koniggratz: A Study of the
      Austro-Prussian Conflict in the Light of the
      American Civil War. Greenwood.
Wagner, C. Peter.
  xWagner, C. Peter.
    Defeat of the Bird God. William Carey Lib.
    Frontiers in Missionary Strategy. Moody.
    Our Kind of People: The Ethical Dimensions
      of Church Growth in America. John Knox.
    Unreached Peoples '79. Cook.
    Unreached Peoples '80. Cook.
    Your Church Can Be Healthy. Abingdon.
  xWagner, Peter C.

Stop the World I Want to Get on. William
Carey Lib.
Wagner, Charles, 1852-1918
xWagner, Charles.
My Impressions of America. Arno.
Wagner, Charles A. *see* Wagner, Charles Abraham.
Wagner, Charles Abraham, 1899-
xWagner, Charles A.
ed. Prize Poems, 1913-1929. Granger Bk.
Wagner, Charles R.
xWagner, Charles R.
The CPA & the Computer Fraud. Lexington
Bks.
Wagner, Charles U.
xWagner, Charles U.
The Pastor, His Life & Work. Reg Baptist.
Wagner, Edward W.
xWagner, Edward W.
The Literati Purges: Political Conflict in Early
Yi Korea. Harvard U Pr.
Wagner, Eva. *see* Wagner, Eva (Bond).
Wagner, Eva (Bond), 1903-
xWagner, Eva.
Reading & Ninth Grade Achievement. AMS
Pr.
Wagner, F. J. *see* Wagner, Frederick J.
Wagner, Frederic H.
xWagner, Frederic H.
Wildlife of the Deserts. Abrams.
Wagner, Frederick J.
xWagner, F. J.
J. H. Shorthouse. Twayne.
Wagner, Geoffrey. *see* Wagner, Geoffrey Atheling.
Wagner, Geoffrey Atheling.
xWagner, Geoffrey.
Five for Freedom: A Study of Feminism in
Fiction. Fairleigh Dickinson.
Wagner, H. J., 1943-
xWagner, H. J.
Cell Types & Connectivity Patterns in Mosaic
Retinas. Springer-Verlag.
Wagner, Harold A.
xWagner, Harold A.
As I Lived It: An Autobiographical History of
the YMCA of Los Angeles, 1925-1966. A H
Clark.
Wagner, Harvey M.
xWagner, Harvey M.
Principles of Management Science: With
Applications to Executive Decisions. P-H.
Principles of Operations Research: With
Applications to Managerial Decisions. P-H.
Wagner, Henry R. *see* Wagner, Henry Raup.
Wagner, Henry Raup, 1862-1957
xWagner, Henry R.
Spanish Explorations in the Strait of Juan De
Fuca. AMS Pr.
Wagner, James K., 1938-
xWagner, James K.
Ford Trucks Since 1905. Crestline.
Wagner, Johannes, 1908-
xWagner, Johannes.
ed. Reforming the Rites of Death. Paulist Pr.
Wagner, Jon.
xWagner, Jon.
ed. Images of Information: Still Photography in
the Social Sciences. Sage.
Wagner, Joseph F. *see* Wagner, Joseph Frederick.
Wagner, Joseph Frederick.
xWagner, Joseph F.
Band Scoring. McGraw.
Orchestration: A Practical Handbook.
McGraw.
Wagner, Karl E. *see* Wagner, Karl Edward.
Wagner, Karl Edward.
xWagner, Karl E.
Darkness Weaves. Warner Bks.
Death Angel's Shadow. Warner Bks.
Wagner, Kenneth C.
xWagner, Kenneth C.

Economic Development Manual. U Pr of Miss.
Wagner, Kurt.
xWagner, Kurt.
A Plastic Surgeon Answers Your Questions: A
Personal Consultation in Book Form. P-H.
xWagner, Kurt J.
Beauty by Design: A Complete Look at
Cosmetic Surgery. McGraw.
Wagner, Kurt J. *see* Wagner, Kurt.
Wagner, Lee.
xWagner, Lee.
How to Have Fun Making Easter Decorations.
Creative Ed.
How to Have Fun Making Holiday
Decorations. Creative Ed.
How to Have Fun Pressing Flowers. Creative
Ed.
How to Have Fun with Decoupage. Creative
Ed.
Wagner, Leopold, 1858-
xWagner, Leopold.
More About Names. Gale.
More About Names. R West.
Wagner, Linda. *see* Wagner, Linda Welshimer.
Wagner, Linda W. *see* Wagner, Linda Welshimer.
Wagner, Linda Welshimer.
xWagner, Linda.
American Modern: Essays in Fiction & Poetry.
Kennikat.
xWagner, Linda W.
Critical Essays on Joyce Carol Oates. G K
Hall.
Denise Levertov. Coll & U Pr.
Dos Passos: Artist As American. U of Tex Pr.
Wagner, Marsden.
xWagner, Marsden.
The Danish National Child Care System: A
Successful System As Model for the
Reconstruction of American Child Care.
Westview.
Wagner, Mary.
xWagner, Mary M.
ed. Care of the Burn-Injured Patient: A
Multidisciplinary Involvement. PSG Pub.
Wagner, Mary M. *see* Wagner, Mary.
Wagner, Peter C. *see* Wagner, C. Peter.
Wagner, Philip L. *see* Wagner, Philip Laurence.
Wagner, Philip Laurence, 1921-
xWagner, Philip L.
Human Use of the Earth. Free Pr.
Wagner, Ray.
xWagner, Ray.
American Combat Planes. Doubleday.
Wagner, Richard.
xWagner, Richard.
Correspondence of Wagner & Liszt.
Greenwood.
Correspondence of Wagner & Liszt. Haskell.
Family Letters of Richard Wagner. Vienna
Hse.
Letters of Richard Wagner: The Burrell
Collection. Vienna Hse.
Letters of Richard Wagner to Anton Pusinelli.
Vienna Hse.
Wagner, Richard E.
xWagner, Richard E.
Inheritance & the State: Tax Principles for a
Free & Prosperous Commonwealth. Am
Enterprise.
Wagner, Richard H., 1934-
xWagner, Richard H.
Environment & Man. Norton.
Wagner, Roy.
xWagner, Roy.
Curse of Souw: Principles of Daribi Clan
Definition & Alliance in New Guinea. U of
Chicago Pr.
Lethal Speech: Daribi Myth As Symbolic
Obviation. Cornell U Pr.
Wagner, S. M. *see* Wagner, Stanley M.

Wagner, Sharon.
xWagner, Sharon.
Love's Broken Promises. Berkley Pub.
Wagner, Stanley M.
xWagner, S. M.
ed. Traditions of the American Jew. Ktav.
Wagner, Thomas J.
xWagner, Thomas J.
Basic Security Training Manual. C C Thomas.
Wagner, Vern.
xWagner, Vern.
Suspension of Henry Adams: A Study of
Manner & Matter. Wayne St U Pr.
Wagner, W. *see* Wagner, Walter.
Wagner, Walter, 1927-
xWagner, W.
ed. Inorganic Titrimetric Analysis:
Contemporary Methods. Dekker.
xWagner, Walter.
God Squad. Doubleday.
Wagner, William L., 1936-
xWagner, William L.
New Move Forward in Europe: Growth
Patterns of German-Speaking Baptists in
Europe. William Carey Lib.
Wagner, Willis H.
xWagner, Willis H.
Woodworking. Goodheart.
Wagniere, G. H. *see* Wagniere, Georges Henry.
Wagniere, Georges Henry, 1933-
xWagniere, G. H.
Introduction to Elementary Molecular Orbital
Theory & to Semiempirical Methods.
Springer-Verlag.
Wagoner, David.
xWagoner, David.
Baby, Come on Inside. FS&G.
The Hanging Garden. Little.
Where Is My Wandering Boy Tonight?. FS&G.
Who Shall Be the Sun?: Poems Based on the
Lore, Legends, & Myths of Northwest Coast
& Plateau Indians. Ind U Pr.
Whole Hog. Little.
Wagoner, George. *see* Wagoner, George E.
Wagoner, George E.
xWagoner, George.
Restoring Antique Bottles. Wagoner.
Wagoner, Jay J., 1923-
xWagoner, Jay J.
Arizona Territory 1863-1912: A Political
History. U of Ariz Pr.
Early Arizona: Prehistory to Civil War. U of
Ariz Pr.
Wagoner, Jennings. *see* Wagoner, Jennings L.
Wagoner, Jennings L.
xWagoner, Jennings.
Thomas Jefferson & the Education of a New
Nation. Phi Delta Kappa.
Wagonseller, Bill R.
xWagonseller, Bill R.
You & Your Child: A Common Sense
Approach to Successful Parenting. Res Press.
Wagschal, Peter H.
xWagschal, Peter H.
ed. Learning Tomorrows: Commentaries on the
Future of Education. Praeger.
Wahl, Edward C. *see* Wahl, Edward F.
Wahl, Edward F.
xWahl, Edward C.
Geothermal Energy Utilization. Wiley.
Wahl, Jahn. *see* Wahl, Jan.
Wahl, Jan.
xWahl, Jahn.
Mooga Mega Mekki. O'Hara.
xWahl, Jan.

Abe Lincoln's Beard. Delacorte.
Carrot Nose. FS&G.
Christmas in the Forest. Macmillan.
Doctor Rabbit's Foundling. Pantheon.
Doctor Rabbit's Lost Scout. Pantheon.
Dracula's Cat. P-H.
Five in the Forest. Follett.
Follow Me Cried Bee. Crown.
Frankenstein's Dog. P-H.
Grandmother Told Me. Little.
Grandpa's Indian Summer. P-H.
Great-Grandmother Cat Tales. Dell.
Great-Grandmother Cat Tales. Pantheon.
How the Children Stopped the Wars. Avon.
How the Children Stopped the Wars. FS&G.
May Horses. Delacorte.
The Muffletumps Christmas Party. Follett.
The Muffletumps' Halloween Scare. Follett.
The Norman Rockwell Storybook. S&S.
The Norman Rockwell Storybook. S&S.
Old Hippo's Easter Egg. HarBraceJ.
Old Hippo's Easter Egg. HarBraceJ.
Sylvester Bear Overslept. Parents.

Wahl, John.
  xWahl, John.
    I Can Count the Petals of a Flower. NCTM.
Wahl, Nicholas.
  xWahl, Nicholas.
    The Fifth Republic: France's New Political
      System. Greenwood.
Wahl, Ralph.
  xWahl, Ralph.
    Come Wade the River. Superior Pub.
Wahlfeldt, Bette G. *see* Wahlfeldt, Bette Galman.
Wahlfeldt, Bette Galman.
  xWahlfeldt, Bette G.
    Successful Sandy Soil Gardening. TAB Bks.
Wahlman, Maude.
  xWahlman, Maude.
    Contemporary African Arts. Field Mus.
Wahlstrom, Ernest E. *see* Wahlstrom, Ernest Eugene.
Wahlstrom, Ernest Eugene, 1909-
  xWahlstrom, Ernest E.
    Optical Crystallography. Wiley.
Wai, Dunstan M.
  xWai, Dunstan M.
    Southern Sudan: The Problem of National
      Integration. Biblio Dist.
Waidson, H. M.
  xWaidson, H. M.
    German Short Stories. Cambridge U Pr.
    Jeremias Gotthelf: An Introduction to the
      Swiss Novelist. Greenwood.
    The Modern German Novel, 1945-1965.
      Oxford U Pr.
Waife-Goldberg, Marie.
  xWaife-Goldberg, Marie.
    My Father, Sholom Aleichem. S&S.
Wain, Harry, 1907-
  xWain, Harry.
    History of Preventive Medicine. C C Thomas.
Wain, John.
  xWain, John.
    Arnold Bennett. Columbia U Pr.
    ed. Contemporary Reviews of Romantic
      Poetry. Arno.
    Contemporary Reviews of Romantic Poetry.
      Folcroft.
    ed. Edmund Wilson: The Man & His Work.
      NYU Pr.
    The Pardoner's Tale. Viking Pr.
    Professing Poetry. Penguin.
    Professing Poetry. Viking Pr.
Wainerdi, R. E. *see* Wainerdi, Richard Elliott.
Wainerdi, Richard E. *see* Wainerdi, Richard Elliott.
Wainerdi, Richard Elliott, 1931-
  xWainerdi, R. E.
    Analytical Chemistry in Space. Pergamon.
  xWainerdi, Richard E.

    ed. Modern Methods of Geochemical Analysis.
      Plenum Pub.
Wainhouse, David W. *see* Wainhouse, David Walter.
Wainhouse, David Walter.
  xWainhouse, David W.
    Arms Control Agreements: Designs for
      Verification & Organization. Johns Hopkins.
Wainwright, Frederick T. *see* Wainwright, Frederick
  Threlfall.
Wainwright, Frederick Threlfall.
  xWainwright, Frederick T.
    Problem of the Picts. Greenwood.
Wainwright, Gordon R. *see* Wainwright, Gordon Ray.
Wainwright, Gordon Ray.
  xWainwright, Gordon R.
    How to Read for Speed & Comprehension.
      P-H.
Wainwright, Jeffrey.
  xWainwright, Jeffrey.
    Heart's Desire. Persea Bks.
Wainwright, John.
  xWainwright, John.
    Landscape with Violence. Berkley Pub.
Wainwright, Nicholas B.
  xWainwright, Nicholas B.
    History of the Philadelphia National Bank: A
      Century & a Half of Philadelphia Banking,
      1803-1953. Arno.
Wainwright, S. A. *see* Wainwright, Stephen A.
Wainwright, S. D. *see* Wainwright, Stanley D.
Wainwright, Stanley D., 1927-
  xWainwright, S. D.
    Control Mechanisms & Protein Synthesis.
      Columbia U Pr.
Wainwright, Stephen A., 1931-
  xWainwright, S. A.
    Mechanical Design in Organisms. Halsted Pr.
    Mechanical Design in Organisms. Krieger.
Waisbren, Burton. *see* Waisbren, Burton A.
Waisbren, Burton A.
  xWaisbren, Burton.
    The Family First Aid Handbook. G&D.
  xWaisbren, Burton A.
    Critical Care Manual: A Systems Approach
      Method. Med Exam.
Wait, John V.
  xWait, John V.
    Introduction to Operational & Amplifier
      Theory Applications. McGraw.
Wait, R. *see* Wait, R. A.
Wait, R. A.
  xWait, R.
    The Numerical Solution of Algebraic
      Equations. Wiley.
Wait, R. J. *see* Wait, R. J. C.
Wait, R. J. C.
  xWait, R. J.
    The Background to Shakespeare's Sonnets.
      Schocken.
Waite, Arthur E. *see* Waite, Arthur Edward.
Waite, Arthur Edward, 1857-1942
  xWaite, Arthur E.
    The Pictorial Key to the Tarot: Being
      Fragments of a Secret Tradition Under the
      Veil of Divination. Har-Row.
    The Quest of the Golden Stairs: A Mystery of
      Kinghood in Faerie. Borgo Pr.
Waite, John B. *see* Waite, John Barker.
Waite, John Barker, 1882-
  xWaite, John B.
    Criminal Law in Action. Arno.
Waite, Kathleen B. *see* Waite, Kathleen Barnette.
Waite, Kathleen Barnette.
  xWaite, Kathleen B.
    Educable Mentally Retarded Child: Guidance
      & Curriculum. C C Thomas.
Waite, Mitchell.
  xWaite, Mitchell.

    Computer Graphics Primer. Sams.
    Microcomputer Primer. Bobbs.
    Microcomputer Primer. Sams.
Waite, R. *see* Waite, Robert George Leeson.
Waite, Robert. *see* Waite, Robert George Leeson.
Waite, Robert G. *see* Waite, Robert George Leeson.
Waite, Robert George Leeson, 1919-
  xWaite, R.
    Hitler & Nazi Germany. HR&W.
  xWaite, Robert.
    The Psychopathic God: Adolf Hitler. NAL.
  xWaite, Robert G.
    Psychopathic God: Adolf Hitler. Basic.
    Vanguard of Nazism: The Free Corps
      Movement in Postwar Germany, 1918-1923.
      Harvard U Pr.
    Vanguard of Nazism: The Free Corps
      Movement in Postwar Germany, 1918-23.
      Norton.
Waite, Thomas D.
  xWaite, Thomas D.
    Mathematics of Environmental Processes.
      Lexington Bks.
Waite, Virginia.
  xWaite, Virginia.
    Austria. Hastings.
Waite, William M. *see* Waite, William McCastline.
Waite, William McCastline.
  xWaite, William M.
    Implementing Software for Non-Numeric
      Applications. P-H.
Waith, Eugene M.
  xWaith, Eugene M.
    Pattern of Tragicomedy in Beaumont &
      Fletcher. Shoe String.
Waitley, Douglas.
  xWaitley, Douglas.
    My Backyard: A Living World of Nature. D
      White.
    The Roads We Traveled: An Amusing History
      of the Automobile. Messner.
Waitz, Theodor, 1821-1864
  xWaitz, Theodor.
    Introduction to Anthropology. AMS Pr.
Waitzkin, Howard.
  xWaitzkin, Howard.
    Exploitation of Illness in Capitalist Society.
      Bobbs.
Waitzman, Daniel.
  xWaitzman, Daniel.
    The Art of Playing the Recorder. AMS Pr.
Wakatama, Pius.
  xWakatama, Pius.
    Independence for the Third World Church: An
      African's Perspective on Missionary Work.
      Inter-Varsity.
Wake, Arthur N.
  xWake, Arthur N.
    Companion to Hymnbook for Christian
      Worship. Bethany Pr.
Wake, C. Staniland. *see* Wake, Charles Staniland.
Wake, Charles S. *see* Wake, Charles Staniland.
Wake, Charles Staniland, 1835-1910
  xWake, C. Staniland.
    The Origin & Significance of the Great
      Pyramid. Wizards.
  xWake, Charles S.
    The Development of Marriage & Kinship. U of
      Chicago Pr.
Wake, W. C. *see* Wake, William Charles.
Wake, William Charles.
  xWake, W. C.
    ed. Developments in Adhesives. Burgess-Intl
      Ideas.
Wakefield. *see* Wakefield, Joyce.
Wakefield, B. J. *see* Wakefield, Basil John.
Wakefield, Basil John, 1934-
  xWakefield, B. J.

The Chemistry of Organolithium Compounds.
Pergamon.
Wakefield, Dan.
xWakefield, Dan.
Going All the Way. Delacorte.
Home Free. Delacorte.
Starting Over. Delacorte.
Starting Over. Dell.
Wakefield, David.
xWakefield, David.
Fragonard. Two Continents.
Wakefield, Edward Jerningham, 1820-1876
xWakefield, Jerningham E.
Adventure in New Zealand. Transatlantic.
Wakefield, Ernest H. see Wakefield, Ernest Henry.
Wakefield, Ernest Henry, 1915-
xWakefield, Ernest H.
The Consumer's Electric Car. Ann Arbor
Science.
Wakefield, George L.
xWakefield.
An Introduction to Photography. Morgan.
Wakefield, Herbert R. see Wakefield, Herbert Russell.
Wakefield, Herbert Russell, 1889-
xWakefield, Herbert R.
Ghost Stories. Arno.
Wakefield, James A., 1948-
xWakefield, James A.
Using Personality to Individualize Instruction.
EDITS Pubs.
Wakefield, Jerningham E. see Wakefield, Edward
Jerningham.
Wakefield, Joyce.
xWakefield.
From Where You Are. Childrens.
xWakefield, Joyce.
Ask a Silly Question. Childrens.
Wakefield, Robert A.
xWakefield, Robert A.
Thinking & Driving. Stanwix.
Wakefield, Ron.
xWakefield, Ron.
The New BMW Guide. TAB Bks.
Wakefield, Tom.
xWakefield, Tom.
Some Mothers I Know: Living with
Handicapped Children. Routledge & Kegan.
Special School. Routledge & Kegan.
Wakefield Washington Associates, Inc.
xWakefield Washington Associates, Inc.
Family Research: A Source Book, Analysis &
Guide to Federal Funding. Greenwood.
Wakeley, Cecil. see Wakeley, Cecil Pembrey Grey.
Wakeley, Cecil Pembrey Grey.
xWakeley, Cecil.
ed. The Faber Medical Dictionary. Lippincott.
Stomach Ulcers. Arc Bks.
Wakeman, Frederic, 1909-
xWakeman, Frederic.
Fault of the Apple. S&S.
Free Agent. S&S.
Wakeman, Frederic. see Wakeman, Frederic E.
Wakeman, Frederic E.
xWakeman, Frederic.
The Fall of Imperial China. Free Pr.
History & Will: Philosophical Perspectives of
Mao Tse-Tung's Thought. U of Cal Pr.
xWakeman, Frederic E.
Strangers at the Gate: Social Disorder in South
China, 1839-1861. U of Cal Pr.
Wakeman, R. see Wakeman, Richard J.
Wakeman, Richard J.
xWakeman, R.
Filtration Post-Treatment Processes. Elsevier.
Wakerly, John. see Wakerly, John F.
Wakerly, John F.
xWakerly, John.

Logic Design Projects Using Standard
Integrated Circuits. Wiley.
Wakil, Salih J., 1927-
xWakil, Salih J.
ed. Lipid Metabolism. Acad Pr.
Wakin. see Wakin, Edward.
Wakin, Edward.
xWakin.
De-Romanization of the American Catholic
Church. NAL.
xWakin, Edward.
The De-Romanization of the American
Catholic Church. Greenwood.
Wakita, Osamu A.
xWakita, Osamu A.
The Professional Practice of Architectural
Detailing. Wiley.
Wakoski, Diane.
xWakoski, Diane.
Cap of Darkness. Black Sparrow.
Dancing on the Grave of a Son of a Bitch.
Black Sparrow.
Greed. Black Sparrow.
Inside the Blood Factory. Doubleday.
Waksman, Byron H.
xWaksman, Byron H.
Atlas of Experimental Immunobiology &
Immunopathology. Yale U Pr.
Walbank, F. W. see Walbank, Frank William.
Walbank, Frank William.
xWalbank, F. W.
Polybius. U of Cal Pr.
Walbert, David F.
xWalbert, David F.
ed. Abortion, Society & the Law. UPBS.
Walch, Margaret.
xWalch, Margaret.
The Color Source Book. Scribner.
Walch, Timothy.
xWalch, Timothy.
Archives & Manuscripts: Security. Soc Am
Archivists.
Walchars, John.
xWalchars, John.
The Unfinished Mystery. Seabury.
Walcher, D. N. see Walcher, Dwain N.
Walcher, Dwain N.
xWalcher, D. N.
ed. Food, Man, & Society. Plenum Pub.
xWalcher, Dwain N.
ed. Mutations: Biology & Society. Masson Pub.
Walcot, Peter.
xWalcot, Peter.
Greek Drama in Its Theatrical & Social
Context. Verry.
Walcott, Charles.
xWalcott, Charles.
Simple Simulations: A Guide to the Design &
Use of Simulation Games in Teaching
Political Science. Am Political.
Walcott, Derek.
xWalcott, Derek.
Another Life. FS&G.
The Star-Apple Kingdom. FS&G.
Walcott, F. G. see Walcott, Fred G.
Walcott, Fred G.
xWalcott, F. G.
Origins of Culture & Anarchy: Matthew
Arnold & Popular Education in England. U
of Toronto Pr.
Walcott, Robert.
xWalcott, Robert.
English Politics in the Early Eighteenth
Century. Russell.
Walczak, Z. see Walczak, Zbigniew K.
Walczak, Zbigniew K.
xWalczak, Z.
Formation of Synthetic Fibers. Gordon.
Wald, G. see Wald, George.

Wald, George.
xWald, G.
Twenty-Six Afternoons of Biology: An
Introductory Laboratory Manual. A-W.
Wald, Karen.
xWald, Karen.
The Children of Che: Childcare & Education in
Cuba. Ramparts.
Wald, Lillian D., 1867-1940
xWald, Lillian D.
The House on Henry Street. Peter Smith.
Wald, Robert M.
xWald, Robert M.
Space, Time & Gravity: The Theory of the Big
Bang & Black Holes. U of Chicago Pr.
Waldberg, Patrick.
xWaldberg, Patrick.
Surrealism. Oxford U Pr.
Waldeland, Lynne.
xWaldeland, Lynne.
John Cheever. Twayne.
Walden, Amelia. see Walden, Amelia Elizabeth.
Walden, Amelia Elizabeth.
xWalden, Amelia.
Go, Phillips, Go!. Westminster.
Play Ball, McGill!. Westminster.
Valerie Valentine Is Missing. Westminster.
Where Is My Heart?. Westminster.
Where Was Everyone When Sabrina
Screamed?. Schol Bk Serv.
Where Was Everyone When Sabrina
Screamed?. Westminster.
Walden, Russell.
xWalden, Russell.
ed. The Open Hand: Essays on le Corbusier.
MIT Pr.
Waldenstrom, Jan G. see Waldenstrom, Jan Gosta.
Waldenstrom, Jan Gosta, 1906-
xWaldenstrom, Jan G.
Monoclonal & Polyclonal
Hypergammaglobulinemia: Clinical &
Biological Significance. Vanderbilt U Pr.
Paraneoplasia: Biological Signals in the
Diagnosis of Cancer. Wiley.
Walders, Joe.
xWalders, Joe.
World's Most Challenging TV Quiz.
Doubleday.
Waldersee, Alfred H. see Waldersee, Alfred Heinrich
Karl Ludwig.
Waldersee, Alfred Heinrich Karl Ludwig.
xWaldersee, Alfred H.
A Field-Marshal's Memoirs: From the Diary,
Correspondence, & Reminiscences of Alfred
Count Von Waldersee. Greenwood.
Waldheim, Kurt.
xWaldheim, Kurt.
Austrian Example. Macmillan.
Waldhorn, Arthur, 1918-
xWaldhorn, Arthur.
A Reader's Guide to Ernest Hemingway.
Octagon.
Waldman, Anne, 1945-
xWaldman, Anne.
ed. Baby Breakdown. Bobbs.
Life Notes. Bobbs.
ed. Talking Poetics from Naropa Institute:
Annals of the Jack Kerouac School of
Disembodied Poetics. Shambhala Pubns.
Waldman, Charles.
xWaldman, Charles.
Strategies of International Mass Retailers.
Praeger.
Waldman, Diane.
xWaldman, Diane.
Intro. by British Art Now: An American
Perspective-1980 Exxon International
Exhibition. S R Guggenheim.
Waldman, Frank, 1919-
xWaldman, Frank.

Walker, D. F. *see* Walker, Donald F.
Walker, Dale L.
xWalker, Dale L.
Death Was the Black Horse: The Story of
Rough Rider Buckey O'Neill. Madrona Pr.
Compiled by The Fiction of Jack London: A
Chronological Bibliography. Tex Western.
Walker, Daniel P. *see* Walker, Daniel Pickering.
Walker, Daniel Pickering.
xWalker, Daniel P.
Decline of Hell: Seventeenth-Century
Discussions of Eternal Torment. U of
Chicago Pr.
Walker, David A. *see* Walker, David Addison.
Walker, David Addison, 1941-
xWalker, David A.
Understanding Pictures: A Study in the Design
of Appropriate Visuals Materials for
Education in Developing Countries. Ctr Intl
Ed U of MA.
Walker, David Allan, 1941-
xWalker, David A.
Iron Frontier: The Discovery & Early
Development of Minnesota's Three Ranges.
Minn Hist.
Walker, David C.
xWalker, D. C.
ed. Origins of Optical Activity in Nature.
Elsevier.
Walker, David M.
xWalker, David M.
Principles of Scottish Private Law. Oxford U
Pr.
Walker, Deborah K. *see* Walker, Deborah Klein.
Walker, Deborah Klein.
xWalker, Deborah K.
Socioemotional Measures for Preschool &
Kindergarten Children: A Handbook.
Jossey-Bass.
Walker, Deward E.
xWalker, Deward E.
Indians of Idaho. U Pr of Idaho.
Walker, Diana.
xWalker, Diana.
The Hundred Thousand Dollar Farm. Abelard.
Mother Wants a Horse. Abelard.
Mother Wants a Horse. Har-Row.
The Year of the Horse. Abelard.
The Year of the Horse. Har-Row.
Walker, Donald F.
xWalker, D. F.
Bovine & Equine Urogenital Surgery. Lea &
Febiger.
Walker, Dorothea.
xWalker, Dorothea.
Sheila Kaye-Smith. Twayne.
Walker, E. F. *see* Walker, Edwin Francis.
Walker, Edmund M. *see* Walker, Edmund Murton.
Walker, Edmund Murton, 1877-
xWalker, Edmund M.
The Odonata of Canada & Alaska. U of
Toronto Pr.
Walker, Edward. *see* Walker, Edward Everett.
Walker, Edward Everett, 1900-
xWalker, Edward.
Readings in American Public Opinion. Krieger.
Walker, Edward L.
xWalker, Edward L.
Conditioning & Instrumental Learning.
Brooks-Cole.
Psychological Complexity & Preference: A
Hedgehog Theory of Behavior. Brooks-Cole.
Walker, Edwin Francis, 1872-
xWalker, E. F.
Five Prehistoric Archeological Sites in los
Angeles County, California. Southwest Mus.
Walker, Egbert H. *see* Walker, Egbert Hamilton.
Walker, Egbert Hamilton.
xWalker, Egbert H.

Flora of Okinawa & the Southern Ryukyu
Islands. Smithsonian.
Walker, Elinor.
xWalker, Elinor.
Compiled by Book Bait: Detailed Notes on
Adult Books Popular with Young People.
ALA.
Walker, Ernest.
xWalker, Ernest.
A History of Music in England. Da Capo.
Walker, Ernest W. *see* Walker, Ernest Winfield.
Walker, Ernest Winfield.
xWalker, Ernest W.
Financial Management of the Small Firm. P-H.
Walker, Ernestein.
xWalker, Ernestein.
Struggle for the Reform of Parliament
1853-1867. Vantage.
Walker, Evelyn, 1874-1953
xWalker, Evelyn.
A Study of the Traite des Indivisibles of Gilles
Persone de Roberval. AMS Pr.
Walker, Francis, 1870-1950
xWalker, Francis.
Double Taxation in the United States. AMS Pr.
Walker, Francis A. *see* Walker, Francis Amasa.
Walker, Francis Amasa, 1840-1897
xWalker, Francis A.
Discussions in Economics & Statistics. B
Franklin.
Discussions in Economics & Statistics. Kelley.
Land & Its Rent. Hyperion Conn.
Money. Kelley.
Walker, Franklin D. *see* Walker, Franklin Dickerson.
Walker, Franklin Dickerson, 1900-
xWalker, Franklin D.
Frank Norris. A Biography. Russell.
Walker, G. *see* Walker, Gregory Piers Mountford.
Walker, Gerald Bromhead.
xWalker, Gerald Bromhead.
Diffusions: Five Studies in Early History. Attic
Pr.
Walker, Granville T.
xWalker, Granville T.
Go Placidly Amid the Noise & Haste:
Meditations on the "Desiderata". Bethany Pr.
Walker, Gregory Piers Mountford.
xWalker, G.
Soviet Book Publishing Policy. Cambridge U
Pr.
Walker, Greta.
xWalker, Greta.
Living on Your Own. Watts.
Walker, H. K. *see* Walker, Henry Kenneth.
Walker, H. Thomas.
xWalker, H. Thomas.
Teaching Media Skills: An Instructional
Program for Elementary & Middle School
Students. Libs Unl.
Walker, Harold B. *see* Walker, Harold Blake.
Walker, Harold Blake.
xWalker, Harold B.
Days Demanding Courage. Rand.
Walker, Henry.
xWalker, Henry.
Illustrated Baseball Dictionary for Young
People. P-H.
Illustrated Baseball Dictionary for Young
People. Harvey.
Illustrated Hockey Dictionary for Young
People. P-H.
The Illustrated Hockey Dictionary for Young
People. Harvey.
Walker, Henry Kenneth.
xWalker, H. K.
Clinical Methods: The History, Physical, &
Laboratory Examinations. Butterworths.
xWalker, Kenneth.

ed. Applying the Problem-Oriented System.
Williams & Wilkins.
Walker, Henry M., 1947-
xWalker, Henry M.
Problems for Computer Solutions Using
BASIC. Winthrop.
Problems for Computer Solutions Using
Fortran. Winthrop.
Walker, Henry P. *see* Walker, Henry Pickering.
Walker, Henry Pickering.
xWalker, Henry P.
Historical Atlas of Arizona. U of Okla Pr.
Walker, Hill M.
xWalker, Hill M.
The Acting-Out Child: Coping with Classroom
Disruption. Allyn.
Walker, Hugh, 1855-1939
xWalker, Hugh.
The Age of Tennyson. Arno.
The Age of Tennyson. Folcroft.
Age of Tennyson. R West.
Age of Tennyson. Scholarly.
Army of Darkness. DAW Bks.
The English Essay & Essayists. AMS Pr.
The English Essay & Essayists. Arden Lib.
English Satire & Satirists. Octagon.
English Satire & Satirists. R West.
The Greater Victorian Poets. Folcroft.
jt. auth. Outlines of Victorian Literature.
Folcroft.
Walker, Irma.
xWalker, Irma.
The Lucifer Wine. Ballantine.
The Murdoch Legacy. Ballantine.
Walker, Irma. *see* Walker, Ira.
Walker, J. F. *see* Walker, Joseph Frederic.
Walker, J. N.
xWalker, J. N.
Attacking the King. Oxford U Pr.
Chess Openings for Juniors. Oxford U Pr.
First Steps in Chess. Oxford U Pr.
Walker, J. R.
xWalker, J. R.
The Sun Dance & Other Ceremonies of the
Oglala Division of the Teton Dakota. AMS
Pr.
Walker, J. W. *see* Walker, John William.
Walker, James B. *see* Walker, James Blaine.
Walker, James Blaine, 1864-
xWalker, James B.
Fifty Years of Rapid Transit 1864-1917. Arno.
Walker, James C. *see* Walker, James Callan Gray.
Walker, James Callan Gray.
xWalker, James C.
Evolution of the Atmosphere. Hafner.
Evolution of the Atmosphere. Macmillan.
Walker, James E. *see* Walker, James Edwin.
Walker, James Edwin.
xWalker, James E.
Behavior Modification: A Practical Approach
for Educators. Mosby.
Walker, James L.
xWalker, James L.
Economic Development & Black Employment
in the Nonmetropolitan South. U of Tex
Busn Res.
Walker, James W.
xWalker, James W.
The End of Mandatory Retirement:
Implications for Management. Wiley.
Walker, Jane.
xWalker, Jane.

Compiled by The Paddington Business
Traveller's Handbook: A Guide to South &
Central America & the Caribbean.
Paddington.
ed. The Paddington Business Traveller's
Handbook: A Guide to the Middle East.
Paddington.

Walker, Janet A., 1942-
xWalker, Janet A.
The Japanese Novel of the Meiji Period & the
Ideal of Individualism. Princeton U Pr.

Walker, Janie (Roxburgh).
xWalker, Janie R.
Stories of the Victorian Writers. Arno.

Walker, Janie R. *see* Walker, Janie (Roxburgh).

Walker, Jearl, 1945-
xWalker, Jearl.
The Flying Circus of Physics. Wiley.
Intro. by The Physics of Everyday Phenomena:
Readings from Scientific American. W H
Freeman.

Walker, Jim, 1935-
xWalker, Jim.
Key System Album. Interurban.

Walker, John C. *see* Walker, John Charles.

Walker, John Charles, 1893-
xWalker, John C.
Plant Pathology. McGraw.

Walker, John H. *see* Walker, John Herbert.

Walker, John Herbert.
xWalker, John H.
God's Living Room. Logos.

Walker, John William, 1859-
xWalker, J. W.
The True History of Robin Hood. Rowman.

Walker, Jonathan, 1799-1878
xWalker, Jonathan.
Branded Hand: Trial & Imprisonment of
Jonathan Walker. Arno.

Walker, Joseph Frederic, 1903-
xWalker, J. F.
Formaldehyde. Krieger.

Walker, Keith M., 1940-
xWalker, Keith M.
Applied Mechanics for Engineering
Technology. Reston.

Walker, Kenneth. *see* Walker, Henry Kenneth.
Walker, Kenneth F. *see* Walker, Kenneth Frederick.

Walker, Kenneth Frederick.
xWalker, Kenneth F.
Australian Industrial Relations Systems.
Harvard U Pr.

Walker, Larry.
xWalker, Larry.
State Legislative Control of Federal Aid Funds:
The Case of Oklahoma. Univ OK Gov Res.

Walker, Laurence C., 1924-
xWalker, Laurence C.
Ecology & Our Forests. A S Barnes.

Walker, Leila J.
xWalker, Leila J.
Fundamental Skills in Serology: Agglutination
Tests, Syphilis Serology, Flourescent Staining.
C C Thomas.

Walker, Lenore. *see* Walker, Lenore E.

Walker, Lenore E.
xWalker, Lenore.
The Battered Woman. Har-Row.
xWalker, Lenore E.
The Battered Woman. Har-Row.

Walker, Leo.
xWalker, Leo.
The Wonderful Era of the Great Dance Bands.
Doubleday.

Walker, Les.
xWalker, Les.
Designing Houses: An Illustrated Guide.
Overlook Pr.
Housebuilding for Children. Overlook Pr.
xWalker, Lester.

Designing Houses: An Illustrated Guide.
Overlook Pr.

Walker, Lester. *see* Walker, Les.

Walker, Louisa.
xWalker, Louisa.
Graded Lessons in Macrame, Knotting &
Netting. Dover.
Graded Lessons in Macrame, Knotting, &
Netting. Peter Smith.

Walker, Lucille.
xWalker, Lucille.
What to Do When You Pray. Logos.

Walker, Lucy.
xWalker, Lucy.
The Other Girl. Ballantine.

Walker, M. I. *see* Walker, Michael Ivan.
Walker, Mabel G. *see* Walker, Mabel Gregory.

Walker, Mabel Gregory.
xWalker, Mabel G.
Fenian Movement. R Myles.

Walker, Mabel L. *see* Walker, Mabel Louise.

Walker, Mabel Louise, 1898-
xWalker, Mabel L.
Business Enterprise & the City. Kraus Repr.

Walker, Mack.
xWalker, Mack.
Germany & the Emigration, 1816-1885.
Harvard U Pr.

Walker, Margaret, 1915-
xWalker, Margaret.
For My People. AMS Pr.
For My People. Arno.
How I Wrote Jubilee. Third World.
October Journey. Broadside.
Prophets for a New Day. Broadside.

Walker, Marshall.
xWalker, Marshall.
Robert Penn Warren: A Vision Earned. B&N.

Walker, Martin, 1947-
xWalker, Martin.
The Infiltrator. Dial.

Walker, Mary A. *see* Walker, Mary Alexander.

Walker, Mary Alexander.
xWalker, Mary A.
To Catch a Zombi. Atheneum.

Walker, Michael Ivan.
xWalker, M. I.
Amateur Photomicrography. Focal Pr.

Walker, Mildred, 1905-
xWalker, Mildred.
Southwest Corner. Watts.

Walker, Mitch, 1951-
xWalker, Mitchell.
Men Loving Men: A Gay Sex Guide &
Consciousness Book. Bookpeople.

Walker, Mitchell. *see* Walker, Mitch.

Walker, Mort.
xWalker, Mort.
Backstage at the Strips. A & W Pubs.

Walker, Morton.
xWalker, Morton.
Total Health. Cornerstone.

Walker, Nigel.
xWalker, Nigel.
Morale in the Civil Service: A Study of the
Desk Worker. Greenwood.

Walker, P. *see* Walker, Pamela.
Walker, P. L. *see* Walker, Peter L.

Walker, Pamela.
xWalker, P.
Twyla. P-H.
xWalker, Pamela.
Twyla. Berkley Pub.

Walker, Paul L.
xWalker, Paul L.
Courage for Crisis Living. Revell.
Understanding the Bible & Science. Pathway
Pr.

Walker, Peter, 1931-
xWalker, Peter.

Moral Choices: Memory, Desire, &
Imagination in Nineteenth-Century American
Abolition. La State U Pr.

Walker, Peter L.
xWalker, P. L.
An Introduction to Complex Analysis. Halsted
Pr.

Walker, Peter S.
xWalker, Peter S.
Human Joints & Their Artificial Replacements.
C C Thomas.

Walker, R. B. *see* Walker, Robin Berwick.
Walker, R. C. *see* Walker, Russell C.
Walker, R. J. *see* Walker, Robert John.
Walker, Ralph. *see* Walker, Ralph T.

Walker, Ralph T., 1931-
xWalker, Ralph.
Hobby Gunsmithing. Follett.

Walker, Richard. *see* Walker, Richard Stuart.
Walker, Richard L. *see* Walker, Richard Louis.

Walker, Richard Louis, 1922-
xWalker, Richard L.
Multi-State System of Ancient China.
Greenwood.

Walker, Richard Stuart.
xWalker, Richard.
The Shell Book of Angling. David & Charles.
Still Water Angling. David & Charles.

Walker, Robert E.
xWalker, Robert E.
Swing End Offense. P-H.

Walker, Robert John, 1909-
xWalker, R. J.
Algebraic Curves. Springer-Verlag.

Walker, Robert N.
xWalker, Robert N.
Psychology of the Youthful Offender. C C
Thomas.

Walker, Robert W.
xWalker, Robert W.
Sub-Zero. Belmont-Tower.

Walker, Robin Berwick.
xWalker, R. B.
The Newspaper Press in New South Wales
1803-1920. Intl Schol Bk Serv.

Walker, Rodger.
xWalker, Rodger.
Pump Selection: A Consulting Engineer's
Manual. Ann Arbor Science.

Walker, Ronald G.
xWalker, Ronald G.
Infernal Paradise: Mexico & the Modern
English Novel. U of Cal Pr.

Walker, Russell C.
xWalker, R. C.
The Stone Cech Compactification.
Springer-Verlag.

Walker, Samuel, 1942-
xWalker, Samuel E.
Popular Justice: A History of American
Criminal Justice. Oxford U Pr.

Walker, Samuel E. *see* Walker, Samuel.
Walker, Samuel H. *see* Walker, Samuel Hamilton.

Walker, Samuel Hamilton.
xWalker, Samuel H.
Samuel H. Walker's Account of the Mier
Expedition. Tex St Hist Assn.

Walker, Sheila S.
xWalker, Sheila S.
Ceremonial Spirit Possession in Africa &
Afro-America: Forms, Meanings &
Functional Significance for Individuals &
Social Groups. Humanities.

Walker, Sloan.
xWalker, Sloan.
The One & Only Crazy Car Book. Wanderer
Bks.

Walker, Stuart, d. 1941
xWalker, Stuart.

Portmanteau Plays. Core Collection.
Walker, Stuart. *see* Walker, Stuart H.
Walker, Stuart H.
    xWalker, Stuart.
      Tactics of Small Boat Racing. Norton.
    xWalker, Stuart H.
      Advanced Racing Tactics. Norton.
      Performance Advances in Small Boat Racing.
        Norton.
Walker, Sydney.
    xWalker, Sydney.
      Psychiatric Signs & Symptoms Due to Medical
        Problems. C C Thomas.
Walker, Terry. *see* Walker, Terry M.
Walker, Terry M., 1938-
    xWalker, Terry.
      Introduction to Computer Science: An
        Interdisciplinary Approach. Allyn.
    xWalker, Terry M.
      Fundamentals of Computer Science. Allyn.
      Fundamentals of FORTRAN Programming:
        With Watfor-Watfiv. Allyn.
Walker, Thomas G.
    xWalker.
      American Politics & the Constitution. Duxbury
        Pr.
Walker, Thomas W.
    xWalker, Thomas W.
      The Christian Democratic Movement in
        Nicaragua. U of Ariz Pr.
Walker, Timothy, 1806-1856
    xWalker, Timothy.
      Introduction to American Law. Da Capo.
Walker, Tom, 1935-
    xWalker, Tom.
      Fort Apache. Avon.
Walker, W. F. *see* Walker, William Francis.
Walker, Warren F. *see* Walker, Warren Franklin.
Walker, Warren Franklin.
    xWalker, Warren F.
      Vertebrate Dissection. HR&W.
Walker, Warren S.
    xWalker, Warren S.
      Plots & Characters in the Fiction of James
        Fenimore Cooper. Shoe String.
Walker, William, 1926-
    xWalker, William.
      Basic Facts. Philos Lib.
Walker, William B.
    xWalker, William B.
      Industrial Innovation & International Trading
        Performance. Jai Pr.
Walker, William F.
    xWalker, William F.
      Color Atlas of General Surgical Diagnosis.
        Year Bk Med.
Walker, William Francis.
    xWalker, W. F.
      A Guide to Industrial Hydraulics.
        Transatlantic.
Walker, Williston, 1860-1922
    xWalker, Williston.
      Great Men of the Christian Church. Arno.
Walker-Smith, Derek, Sir, Bart, 1910-
    xWalker-Smith, Derek.
      Protectionist Case in the 1840's. Kelley.
Walkley, A. B. *see* Walkley, Arthur Bingham.
Walkley, Arthur B. *see* Walkley, Arthur Bingham.
Walkley, Arthur Bingham, 1855-1926
    xWalkley, A. B.
      Pastiche & Prejudice. Folcroft.
    xWalkley, Arthur B.
      Drama & Life. Arno.
      More Prejudice. Arno.
      Pastiche & Prejudice. Arno.
      Still More Prejudice. Arno.
Walkley, Christina.
    xWalkley, Christina.

Crinolines & Crimping Irons: Victorian Clothes,
    How They Were Cleaned & Cared for.
    Humanities.
Walkowitz, Daniel J.
    xWalkowitz, Daniel J.
      Worker City, Company Town: Iron &
        Cotton-Worker Protest in Troy & Cohoes,
        New York, 1855-84. U of Ill Pr.
Walkup, Eunice.
    xWalkup, Eunice.
      The Race. S&S.
Wall, Alfred H.
    xWall, Alfred H.
      Artistic Landscape Photography. Arno.
Wall, Annie R. *see* Wall, Annie Russell.
Wall, Annie Russell.
    xWall, Annie R.
      Sordello's Story, Retold in Prose. Folcroft.
Wall, C. T. *see* Wall, Charles Terence Clegg.
Wall, Carol.
    xWall, Carol.
      Predication: A Study of Its Development.
        Mouton.
Wall, Charles Terence Clegg.
    xWall, C. T.
      A Geometric Introduction to Topology. A-W.
      Surgery on Compact Manifolds. Acad Pr.
Wall, David.
    xWall, David.
      Intro. by & ed. Chicago Essays in Economic
        Development. U of Chicago Pr.
Wall, E. J. *see* Wall, Edward John.
Wall, Edward John, 1860-1928
    xWall, E. J.
      History of Three Color Photography. Focal Pr.
Wall, Elizabeth S.
    xWall, Elizabeth S.
      Computer Alphabet Book. Bayshore Bks.
Wall, Florence E. *see* Wall, Florence Emeline.
Wall, Florence Emeline, 1893-
    xWall, Florence E.
      Aid to State Board Examinations in Beauty
        Culture. Sheridan.
Wall, H. S. *see* Wall, Hubert Stanley.
Wall, Hubert Stanley, 1902-
    xWall, H. S.
      Creative Mathematics. U of Tex Pr.
Wall, J. C. *see* Wall, James Charles.
Wall, J. Charles. *see* Wall, James Charles.
Wall, James Charles.
    xWall, J. C.
      Devils. Gordon Pr.
    xWall, J. Charles.
      Devils. Gale.
      Devils. Rowman.
Wall, James W.
    xWall, James W.
      Davie County: A Brief History. NC Archives.
Wall, Joseph F. *see* Wall, Joseph Frazier.
Wall, Joseph Frazier.
    xWall, Joseph F.
      Andrew Carnegie. Oxford U Pr.
Wall, Maggie.
    xWall, Maggie.
      Creative Needlepoint Borders. Scribner.
Wall, Robert. *see* Wall, Robert Eugene.
Wall, Robert Eugene.
    xWall, Robert.
      Introduction to Mathematical Linguistics. P-H.
Wall Street Journal. *see* Wall Street Journal (Firm).
Wall Street Journal (Firm).
    xWall Street Journal.
      ed. American Dynasties Today. Dow
        Jones-Irwin.
      ed. The Best of the Wall Street Journal. Dow
        Jones-Irwin.
Wall, W. D. *see* Wall, William Douglas.
Wall, William Douglas.
    xWall, W. D.

      ed. Psychological Services for Schools. NYU
        Pr.
      ed. Psychological Services for Schools. Unipub.
Wallace, Albert H.
    xWallace, Albert H.
      Guy de Maupassant. Twayne.
Wallace, Alfred R. *see* Wallace, Alfred Russel.
Wallace, Alfred Russel, 1823-1913
    xWallace, Alfred R.
      Darwinism: An Exposition of the Theory of
        Natural Selection, with Some of Its
        Applications. AMS Pr.
Wallace, Amy.
    xWallace, Amy.
      The Psychic Healing Book. Delacorte.
Wallace, Anthony F. *see* Wallace, Anthony F. C.
Wallace, Anthony F. C.
    xWallace, Anthony F.
      Death & Rebirth of the Seneca. Knopf.
      The Death & Rebirth of the Seneca. Random.
      Rockdale: The Growth of an American Village
        in the Early Industrial Revolution. Norton.
Wallace, Archer, 1884-
    xWallace, Archer.
      In Spite of All. Arno.
      Religious Faith of Great Men. Arno.
Wallace, Aubrey.
    xWallace, Aubrey.
      Natural Foods for the Trail. Vogelsang Pr.
Wallace, Barbara B. *see* Wallace, Barbara Brooks.
Wallace, Barbara Brooks.
    xWallace, Barbara B.
      The Contest Kid Strikes Again. Abingdon.
      Palmer Patch. Follett.
Wallace, Bill C.
    xWallace, Bill C.
      Education & the Drug Scene. Prof Educ Pubn
Wallace, Brenton G. *see* Wallace, Brenton Greene.
Wallace, Brenton Greene, 1891-
    xWallace, Brenton G.
      Patton & His Third Army. Greenwood.
Wallace, Bruce, 1920-
    xWallace, Bruce.
      Chromosomes, Giant Molecules, & Evolution.
        Norton.
      Topics in Population Genetics. Norton.
Wallace, Charles W. *see* Wallace, Charles William.
Wallace, Charles William, 1865-1932
    xWallace, Charles W.
      Evolution of the English Drama up to
        Shakespeare: With a History of the First
        Blackfriars Theatre. Kennikat.
Wallace, Cornelia, 1939-
    xWallace, Cornelia.
      C'nelia. Holman.
Wallace, Daisy.
    xWallace, Daisy.
      ed. Fairy Poems. Holiday.
      ed. Ghost Poems. Holiday.
      ed. Giant Poems. Holiday.
      ed. Monster Poems. Holiday.
Wallace, Daniel.
    xWallace, Daniel.
      Energy We Can Live with: Approaches to
        Energy That Are Easy on the Earth & Its
        People. Rodale Pr Inc.
Wallace, David D. *see* Wallace, David Duncan.
Wallace, David Duncan, 1874-1951
    xWallace, David D.
      South Carolina: A Short History, 1520-1948. U
        of SC Pr.
Wallace, Don.
    xWallace, Don.
      ed. The Future of International Economic
        Organizations. Praeger.
Wallace, Donald M. *see* Wallace, Donald Mackenzie.
Wallace, Donald Mackenzie, Sir, 1841-1919
    xWallace, Donald M.

Egypt & the Egyptian Question. Russell.
Wallace, Duane C.
　xWallace, Duane C.
　　Thermodynamics of Crystals. Wiley.
Wallace, E. *see* Wallace, Elizabeth.
Wallace, Edgar, 1875-1932
　xWallace, Edgar.
　　Again the Three Just Men. Arno.
Wallace, Edwin, 1848-1884
　xWallace, Edwin.
　　Compiled by Outlines of the Philosophy of
　　Aristotle. Arno.
Wallace, Elizabeth, 1866-1960
　xWallace, E.
　　Mark Twain & the Happy Island. Haskell.
　xWallace, Elizabeth.
　　Mark Twain & the Happy Island. Folcroft.
Wallace, Ernest.
　xWallace, Ernest.
　　Comanches, Lords of the South Plains. U of
　　Okla Pr.
　　The Howling of the Coyotes: Reconstruction
　　Efforts to Divide Texas. Tex A&M Univ Pr.
Wallace, Evelyn.
　xWallace, Evelyn.
　　Cake Decorating & Sugarcraft. Arco.
Wallace, Forrest.
　xWallace, Forrest.
　　The Game of Wine. B&N.
Wallace, George J. *see* Wallace, George John.
Wallace, George John, 1906-
　xWallace, George J.
　　My World of Birds: Memoirs of an
　　Ornithologist. Dorrance.
Wallace, Gerald.
　xWallace, Gerald.
　　Educational Assessment of Learning Problems:
　　Testing for Teaching. Allyn.
　xWallace, Gerald M.
　　Teaching Children with Learning Problems.
　　Merrill.
Wallace, Gerald M. *see* Wallace, Gerald.
Wallace, Helen M.
　xWallace, Helen M.
　　ed. Maternal & Child Health Practices:
　　Problems, Resources & Methods of Delivery.
　　C C Thomas.
Wallace, Henry A. *see* Wallace, Henry Agard.
Wallace, Henry Agard, 1888-1965
　xWallace, Henry A.
　　Democracy Reborn. Da Capo.
　　Toward World Peace. Greenwood.
　　Toward World Peace. R S Barnes.
Wallace, Henry C. *see* Wallace, Henry Cantwell.
Wallace, Henry Cantwell, 1866-1924
　xWallace, Henry C.
　　Our Debt & Duty to the Farmer. Arno.
Wallace-Homestead Book Co.
　xWallace-Homestead Book Co.
　　ed. Oak Furniture, Styles & Prices.
　　Wallace-Homestead.
Wallace, Ian.
　xWallace, Ian.
　　Heller's Leap. DAW Bks.
　　The World Asunder. DAW Bks.
Wallace, Irving.
　xWallace, Irving.
　　Chapman Report. NAL.
　　The Fabulous Originals: Lives of Extraordinary
　　People Who Inspired Memorable Characters
　　in Fiction. Kraus Repr.
　　The Pigeon Project. Bantam.
　　Pigeon Project. S&S.
　　Prize. NAL.
　　Twenty-Seventh Wife. NAL.
　　The Two: A Biography. S&S.
Wallace, J. G. *see* Wallace, John Gilbert.
Wallace, Jeanne.
　xWallace, Jeanne.

Really Ridiculous Rabbit Riddles. Schol Bk
　Serv.
Wallace, Joanne.
　xWallace, Joanne.
　　Image of Loveliness. Revell.
Wallace, John Gilbert.
　xWallace, J. G.
　　Intro. by Stages & Transition in Conceptual
　　Development: An Experimental Study.
　　Humanities.
Wallace, Judith. *see* Wallace, Judith Gytha.
Wallace, Judith Gytha, 1932-
　xWallace, Judith.
　　Memories of a Country Childhood. U of
　　Queensland Pr.
Wallace, Karl R. *see* Wallace, Karl Richards.
Wallace, Karl Richards, 1905-
　xWallace, Karl R.
　　Understanding Discourse: The Speech Act &
　　Rhetorical Action. La State U Pr.
Wallace, Lee A.
　xWallace, Lee A.
　　A Guide to Virginia Military Organizations,
　　1861-1865. Va Bk.
Wallace, M. J. *see* Wallace, Margaret Ann Jaeger.
Wallace, Malcolm W. *see* Wallace, Malcolm William.
Wallace, Malcolm William, 1873-
　xWallace, Malcolm W.
　　Life of Sir Philip Sidney. Octagon.
Wallace, Margaret Ann Jaeger.
　xWallace, M. J.
　　Handbook of Child Nursing Care. Wiley.
Wallace, Mary E. *see* Wallace, Mary Elaine.
Wallace, Mary Elaine.
　xWallace, Mary E.
　　Opera Scenes for Class & Stage. S Ill U Pr.
Wallace, Michael.
　xWallace, Michael.
　　ed. Terrorism. Arno.
Wallace, Michele.
　xWallace, Michele.
　　Black Macho & the Myth of the Superwoman.
　　Dial.
Wallace, Paul A. W.
　xWallace, Paul A. W.
　　Indian Paths of Pennsylvania. Pa Hist & Mus.
Wallace, Pearlena.
　xWallace, Pearlena S.
　　ed. Teaching Mathematics Through the
　　Multisensory Approach: A Research
　　Perspective in the Elementary School.
　　Dorrance.
Wallace, Pearlena S. *see* Wallace, Pearlena.
Wallace, Richard W., 1933-
　xWallace, Richard W.
　　The Etchings of Salvator Rosa. Princeton U Pr.
Wallace, Robert, 1697-1771
　xWallace, Robert.
　　Characteristics of the Present Political State of
　　Great Britain. Kelley.
　　Dissertation on the Numbers of Mankind in
　　Ancient & Modern Times. Kelley.
　　The Grand Canyon. Time-Life.
　　The Grand Canyon. Silver.
　　World of Rembrandt. Time-Life.
　　World of Rembrandt. Silver.
　　World of Van Gogh. Time-Life.
　　World of Van Gogh. Silver.
Wallace, Robert A. *see* Wallace, Robert Ardell.
Wallace, Robert Ardell, 1938-
　xWallace, Robert A.
　　Ecology & Evolution of Animal Behavior.
　　Goodyear.
　　The Genesis Factor. Morrow.
Wallace, Robert C. *see* Wallace, Robert Charles.
Wallace, Robert Charles, 1881-1955
　xWallace, Robert C.

　　ed. Some Great Men of Queen's. Arno.
Wallace, Robert K., 1944-

　xWallace, Robert K.
　　A Century of Music-Making: The Lives of
　　Josef & Rosina Lhevinne. Ind U Pr.
Wallace, Roberta.
　xWallace, Roberta.
　　Staff Manual for Teaching Patients About
　　Rheumatoid Arthritis. Am Hospital.
Wallace, Ronald.
　xWallace, Ronald.
　　The Last Laugh: Form & Affirmation in the
　　Contemporary American Comic Novel. U of
　　Mo Pr.
Wallace, Ruth A.
　xWallace, Ruth A.
　　Contemporary Sociological Theory. P-H.
Wallace, S. C. *see* Wallace, Schuyler Crawford.
Wallace, Sally F. *see* Wallace, Sally Foster.
Wallace, Sally Foster, 1938-
　xWallace, Sally F.
　　Practically Painless English. P-H.
Wallace, Samuel E.
　xWallace, Samuel E.
　　After Suicide. Wiley.
　　ed. Total Institutions. Transaction Bks.
Wallace, Schuyler Crawford, 1898-
　xWallace, S. C.
　　Federal Departmentalization: A Critique of
　　Theories of Organization. Greenwood.
Wallace, Susan J.
　xWallace, Susan J.
　　Bahamian Scene. Dorrance.
Wallace, Sylvia.
　xWallace, Sylvia.
　　Empress. Morrow.
　　The Fountains. Morrow.
Wallace, Victor L.
　xWallace, Victor L.
　　On the Representation of Markovian Systems
　　by Network Models. Mgmt Info Serv.
Wallace, W. E. *see* Wallace, William Edward.
Wallace, Walter L.
　xWallace, Walter L.
　　Logic of Science in Sociology. Aldine Pub.
　　ed. Sociological Theory: Aldine Pub.
　　Student Culture. NORC.
Wallace, Willard M.
　xWallace, Willard M.
　　Appeal to Arms: A Military History of the
　　American Revolution. Peter Smith.
　　Appeal to Arms: A Military History of the
　　American Revolution. Times Bks.
Wallace, William, 1844-1897
　xWallace, William.
　　Prolegomena to the Study of Hegel's
　　Philosophy, & Especially of His Logic.
　　Russell.
Wallace, William Edward, 1917-
　xWallace, W. E.
　　Rare Earth Intermetallics. Acad Pr.
Wallace, William S. *see* Wallace, William Stewart.
Wallace, William Stewart, 1884-
　xWallace, William S.
　　Dictionary of North American Authors
　　Deceased Before 1950. Gale.
　　ed. Documents Relating to the North West
　　Company. Greenwood.
Wallace-Crabbe, Chris.
　xWallace-Crabbe, Chris.
　　ed. Six Voices: Contemporary Australian Poets.
　　Greenwood.
Wallach, Carla.
　xWallach, Carlo.
　　The Reluctant Weekend Gardener. Macmillan.
Wallach, Carlo. *see* Wallach, Carla.
Wallach, D. F. *see* Wallach, Donald Francis Hoelzl.
Wallach, Donald Francis Hoelzl.
　xWallach, D. F.

Evolving Strategies & Tactics in Membrane
Research. Springer-Verlag.
ed. Membrane Anomalies of Tumor Cells. S
Karger.
Membrane Molecular Biology of Neoplastic
Cells. Elsevier.
Wallach, Luitpold.
xWallach, Luitpold.
Diplomatic Studies in Latin & Greek
Documents from the Carolingian Age.
Cornell U Pr.
Wallach, Mark I.
xWallach, Mark I.
Christopher Morley. Twayne.
Wallach, Michael. *see* Wallach, Michael A.
Wallach, Michael A.
xWallach, Michael.
Teaching All Children to Read. U of Chicago
Pr.
xWallach, Michael A.
Teaching All Children to Read. U of Chicago
Pr.
Wallach, N. *see* Wallach, Nolan R.
Wallach, Nolan R.
xWallach, N.
Symplectic Geometry & Fourier Analysis.
Math Sci Pr.
Wallach, Paul I.
xWallach, Paul I.
Reading Construction Drawings. McGraw.
Wallach, Theresa.
xWallach, Theresa.
Easy Motorcycle Riding. Sterling.
Wallack, F. Bradford, 1943-
xWallack, F. Bradford.
The Epochal Nature of Process in Whitehead's
Metaphysics. State U NY Pr.
Wallack, John L. *see* Wallack, John Lester.
Wallack, John Lester, 1820-1888
xWallack, John L.
Memories of Fifty Years. Somerset Pub.
xWallack, Lester.
Memories of Fifty Years. Arno.
Wallack, L. R. *see* Wallack, Louis Robert.
Wallack, Lester. *see* Wallack, John Lester.
Wallack, Louis Robert, 1919-
xWallack, L. R.
American Pistol & Revolver Design &
Performance. Winchester Pr.
American Rifle Design & Performance.
Winchester Pr.
American Shotgun Design & Performance.
Winchester Pr.
The Deer Rifle. Winchester Pr.
Wallant, Edward L. *see* Wallant, Edward Lewis.
Wallant, Edward Lewis, 1926-1962
xWallant, Edward L.
The Children at the Gate. HarBraceJ.
The Human Season. HarBraceJ.
The Pawnbroker. HarBraceJ.
Pawnbroker. Manor Bks.
Wallas, Graham, 1858-1932
xWallas, Graham.
Our Social Heritage. Arno.
Wallat, Cynthia.
xWallat, Cynthia.
Home-School-Community Interaction: What
We Know & Why We Don't Know More.
Merrill.
Wallbank, T. W. *see* Wallbank, Thomas Walter.
Wallbank, T. Walter. *see* Wallbank, Thomas Walter.
Wallbank, Thomas Walter, 1901-
xWallbank, T. W.
Contemporary Africa: Continent in Transition.
Krieger.
Documents on Modern Africa. Krieger.
xWallbank, T. Walter.
Civilization Past & Present. Scott F.
Wallechinsky, David.
xWallechinsky, David.

The People's Almanac. Doubleday.
People's Almanac. Morrow.
The People's Almanac Presents the Book of
Lists. Bantam.
Wallen, C. C. *see* Wallen, Carl Christian.
Wallen, Carl. *see* Wallen, Carl J.
Wallen, Carl Christian.
xWallen, C. C.
ed. Climates of Northern & Western Europe.
Elsevier.
Wallen, Carl J.
xWallen, Carl.
Competency in Teaching Reading. SRA.
Word Attack Skills in Reading. Merrill.
xWallen, Carl J.
Competency in Teaching Reading. SRA.
Effective Classroom Management. Allyn.
Wallen, Norman E.
xWallen, Norman E.
Educational Research: A Guide to the Process.
Wadsworth Pub.
Wallenberg, Hans.
xWallenberg, Hans.
Report on Democratic Institutions in Germany.
Greenwood.
Wallender, Harvey W.
xWallender, Harvey W.
Technology Transfer & Management in the
Developing Countries: Company Cases &
Policy Analysis in Brazil, Kenya, Korea,
Peru, & Tanzania. Ballinger Pub.
Wallendorf, Melanie.
xWallendorf, Melanie.
Readings in Consumer Behavior: Individuals,
Groups & Organizations. Wiley.
Wallenstein, Nehemiah, 1901-
xWallenstein, Nehemiah.
Character & Personality of Children from
Broken Homes. AMS Pr.
Waller, Adrian.
xWaller, Adrian.
Adrian Waller's Guide to Music. Littlefield.
Theatre on a Shoestring. Littlefield.
Waller County Historical Commission.
xWaller County Historical Survey Committee.
One Hundred One Heritage Homes. Nortex Pr.
Waller County Historical Survey Committee. *see* Waller
County Historical Commission.
Waller, Coy W. *see* Waller, Coy Webster.
Waller, Coy Webster, 1914-
xWaller, Coy W.
Marihuana: An Annotated Bibliography.
Macmillan Info.
Waller, G. F.
xWaller, G. F.
The Strong Necessity of Time: The Philosophy
of Time in Shakespeare & Elizabethan
Literature. Mouton.
Waller, George M. *see* Waller, George Macgregor.
Waller, George Macgregor, 1919-
xWaller, George M.
American Revolution in the West. Nelson-Hall.
ed. Puritanism in Early America. Heath.
Waller, Irene.
xWaller, Irene.
Textile Sculptures. Taplinger.
Waller, Irvin.
xWaller, Irvin.
Burglary: The Victim & the Public. U of
Toronto Pr.
xWaller, J. Irvin.
Men Released from Prison. U of Toronto Pr.
Waller, J. Irvin. *see* Waller, Irvin.
Waller, James F. *see* Waller, James Flint.
Waller, James Flint, 1887-
xWaller, James F.
Outside Demands & Pressures on the Public
Schools. AMS Pr.
Waller, Julian A., 1932-
xWaller, Julian A.

Medical Impairment to Driving. C C Thomas.
Waller, Leslie, 1923-
xWaller, Leslie.
The Brave & the Free. Delacorte.
The Brave & the Free. Dell.
Waller, Maurice.
xWaller, Maurice.
Fats Waller. Schirmer Bks.
Waller, R. A.
xWaller, R. A.
Building on Springs. Pergamon.
Waller, Robert A., 1931-
xWaller, Robert A.
Rainey of Illinois: A Political Biography,
1903-34. U of Ill Pr.
Waller, W. *see* Waller, Willard Walter.
Waller, Willard W. *see* Waller, Willard Walter.
Waller, Willard Walter, 1899-1945
xWaller, W.
Sociology of Teaching. Wiley.
xWaller, Willard W.
Sociology of Teaching. Russell.
Waller, William, 1898-
xWaller, William.
ed. Nashville in the 1890's. Vanderbilt U Pr.
ed. Nashville, 1900 to 1910. Vanderbilt U Pr.
Wallerstein, James S.
xWallerstein, James S.
The Outer Darkness. Aurelon.
Wallerstein, Judith S.
xWallerstein, Judith S.
Surviving the Breakup: How Children &
Parents Cope with Divorce. Basic.
Wallerstein, Robert. *see* Wallerstein, Robert S.
Wallerstein, Robert S.
xWallerstein, Robert.
Psychotherapy & Psychoanalysis:
Theory Practice Research. Intl Univ Pr.
Wallerstein, Ruth C. *see* Wallerstein, Ruth Coons.
Wallerstein, Ruth Coons, 1893-1958
xWallerstein, Ruth C.
Richard Crashaw: A Study in Style & Poetic
Development. Humanities.
Walley, B. H. *see* Walley, Brian Halford.
Walley, Brian Halford.
xWalley, B. H.
Office Administration Handbook. Beekman
Pubs.
Walley, Dean.
xWalley, Dean.
I Love You Because. Gibson.
Wallfesh, Henry M.
xWallfesh, Henry M.
The Effects of Extending the Mandatory
Retirement Age. Am Mgmt.
Wallich, Henry C. *see* Wallich, Henry Christopher.
Wallich, Henry Christopher, 1914-
xWallich, Henry C.
The Cost of Freedom: A New Look at
Capitalism. Greenwood.
Public Finance in a Developing Country: El
Salvador, a Case Study. Greenwood.
Wallick, Clair H.
xWallick, Clair H.
Looking for Ideas: A Display Manual for
Libraries & Bookstores. Scarecrow.
Wallin, Georg A. *see* Wallin, Georg August.
Wallin, Georg August.
xWallin, Georg A.
Travels in Arabia, 1845-1848. Oleander Pr.
Wallin, Marie L. *see* Wallin, Marie-Louise.
Wallin, Marie-Louise.
xWallin, Marie L.
Tangles. Dell.
xWallin, Marie-Louise.
Tangles. Delacorte.
Walling, William.
xWalling, William.
The World I Left Behind Me. St Martin.
xWalling, William A.

Mary Shelley. Twayne.
Walling, William. *see* Walling, William English.
Walling, William A. *see* Walling, William.
Walling, William E. *see* Walling, William English.
Walling, William English, 1877-1936
xWalling, William.
Whitman & Traubel. Haskell.
xWalling, William E.
American Labor & American Democracy.
Arno.
ed. Socialists & the War. Garland Pub.
Wallington, Neil.
xWallington, Neil.
Fireman: A Personal Account. David &
Charles.
Wallington, Nellie (Urner), 1847-1933
xWallington, Nellie U.
Historic Churches of America. Longwood Pr.
Wallington, Nellie U. *see* Wallington, Nellie (Urner).
Wallis, Charles L. *see* Wallis, Charles Langworthy.
Wallis, Charles Langworthy, 1921-
xWallis, Charles L.
American Epitaphs, Grave & Humorous.
Dover.
American Epitaphs Grave & Humorous. Peter
Smith.
ed. Complete Sourcebook for the Lord's
Supper. Baker Bk.
ed. Lenten-Easter Sourcebook. Baker Bk.
ed. Speaker's Illustrations for Special Days.
Baker Bk.
Wallis, George A.
xWallis, George A.
Cattle Kings of the Staked Plains. Wallis
Pubns.
Unforgettable Men of the West. Wallis Pubns.
Wallis, J. H.
xWallis, John.
Thinking About Retirement. Pergamon.
Wallis, Jim.
xWallis, Jim.
Agenda for Biblical People. Har-Row.
Wallis, John. *see* Wallis, J. H.
Wallis, Mieczysaw.
xWallis, Mieczyslaw.
Arts & Signs. Humanities.
Wallis, Mieczyslaw. *see* Wallis, Mieczysaw.
Wallis, P. *see* Wallis, Peter John.
Wallis, Peter John.
xWallis, P.
Newton & Newtoniana, 1642-1975: A
Bibliography. Dawson Pub.
Wallis, Roy.
xWallis, Roy.
ed. Marginal Medicine. Free Pr.
Salvation & Protest: Studies of Social &
Religious Movements. St Martin.
ed. Sectarianism: Analyses of Religious &
Non-Religious Sects. Halsted Pr.
Wallis, W. Allen. *see* Wallis, Wilson Allen.
Wallis, Wilson Allen.
xWallis, W. Allen.
An Overgoverned Society. Free Pr.
Wallis, Wilson D. *see* Wallis, Wilson Dallam.
Wallis, Wilson Dallam, 1886-1970
xWallis, Wilson D.
The Canadian Dakota. AMS Pr.
Wallman, Sandra.
xWallman, Sandra.
ed. Ethnicity at Work. Holmes & Meier.
ed. Perceptions of Development. Cambridge U
Pr.
Wallner, Alexandra.
xWallner, Alexandra.
The Adventures of Strawberry Shortcake &
Her Friends. Random.
Wallo, Olav. *see* Wallo, Olav O.
Wallo, Olav O.
xWallo, Olav.

Twilight Over the Wilderness. Denison.
Wallovits, Sonia. *see* Wallovits, Sonia Emily.
Wallovits, Sonia Emily.
xWallovits, Sonia.
Filipinos in California. R & E Res Assoc.
Wallower, Lucille.
xWallower, Lucille.
African American Workshop. Penns Valley.
Colonial Pennsylvania. Elsevier-Nelson.
ed. Pennsylvania: A Bicentennial Workshop.
Penns Valley.
The Pennsylvania Dutch. Penns Valley.
Wallrath, Matthew.
xWallrath, Matthew.
Excavations in the Tehuantepec Region ,
Mexico. Am Philos.
Walls, David S.
xWalls, David S.
ed. Appalachia in the Sixties: Decade of
Reawakening. U Pr of Ky.
Walls, Dwayne E.
xWalls, Dwayne E.
The Chickenbone Special. HarBraceJ.
Walls, Ian G. *see* Walls, Ian Gascoigne.
Walls, Ian Gascoigne.
xWalls, Ian G.
The Complete Book of Greenhouse Gardening.
Times Bks.
Walls, James.
xWalls, James.
Land, Man & Sand: Desertification & Its
Solution. Macmillan Info.
Walls, Madge T. *see* Walls, Madge Tennent.
Walls, Madge Tennent, 1943-
xWalls, Madge T.
A Guide to the Independent Schools of
Hawaii. Pr Pacifica.
Wallwork, J. F. *see* Wallwork, Jean Faraday.
Wallwork, Jean Faraday.
xWallwork, J. F.
Language & People. Heinemann Ed.
Walmsley, R. *see* Walmsley, Robert.
Walmsley, Robert.
xWalmsley, R.
Clinical Anatomy of the Heart. Churchill.
Walpole, Horace.
xWalpole, Horace.
Castle of Otranto. Macmillan.
Memoirs of the Reign of King George the
Third. Arno.
Memoirs of the Reign of King George Third.
AMS Pr.

Walpole, Hugh, Sir, 1884-1941
xWalpole, Hugh.
Anthony Trollope. Arno.
Anthony Trollope. Folcroft.
Apple Trees: Four Reminiscences. Folcroft.
The English Novel: Some Notes on Its
Evolution. Folcroft.
Joseph Conrad. Folcroft.
Joseph Conrad. Haskell.
Walpole, Jane.
xWalpole, Jane R.
A Writer's Guide: Easy Ground Rules for
Successful Written English. P-H.
Walpole, Jane R. *see* Walpole, Jane.
Walpole, Ronald E.
xWalpole, Ronald E.
Introduction to Statistics. Macmillan.
Probability & Statistics for Engineers &
Scientists. Macmillan.
Walpole, Spencer, Sir, 1839-1907
xWalpole, Spencer.
Life of Lord John Russell. Greenwood.
Life of Lord John Russell. Haskell.
Some Unpublished Letters of Horace Walpole.
Folcroft.

Walraven, Gail, 1949-
xWalraven, Gail.
Handbook of Emergency Drugs. R J Brady.
Manual of Advanced Prehospital Care. R J
Brady.
Walrond, Eric.
xWalrond, Eric.
Tropic Death. Macmillan.
Walrond-Skinner, Sue.
xWalrond-Skinner, Sue.
Family Therapy: The Treatment of Natural
Systems. Routledge & Kegan.
Walsberg, Glenn E.
xWalsberg, Glenn E.
The Ecology & Energetics of Contrasting
Social Systems in the Phainopepla. U of Cal
Pr.
Walser, Martin, 1927-
xWalser, Martin.
Runaway Horse. HR&W.
Walser, Richard. *see* Walser, Richard Gaither.
Walser, Richard Gaither, 1908-
xWalser, Richard.
Literary North Carolina: A Brief Historical
Survey. NC Archives.
ed. Tar Heel Laughter. U of NC Pr.
Thomas Wolfe Undergraduate. Duke.
Walsh, A. E.
xWalsh, A. E.
Competition Policy: European & International
Trends & Practices. St Martin.
Structure & Development of the Common
Market. Taplinger.
Walsh, Annmarie H. *see* Walsh, Annmarie Hauck.
Walsh, Annmarie Hauck.
xWalsh, Annmarie H.
The Public's Business: The Politics & Practices
of Government Corporations. MIT Pr.
The Public's Business: The Politics & Practices
of Government Corporations-A Twentieth
Century Fund Study. MIT Pr.
Walsh, Chad, 1914-
xWalsh, Chad.
Doors into Poetry. P-H.
From Utopia to Nightmare. Greenwood.
The Literary Legacy of C. S. Lewis. HarBraceJ.
The Literary Legacy of C. S. Lewis. HarBraceJ.
Nellie & Her Flying Crocodile. Har-Row.
Twice Ten: An Introduction to Poetry. Wiley.
Walsh, Christopher.
xWalsh, Christopher.
Enzymatic Reaction Mechanisms. W H
Freeman.
Walsh, Don, 1931-
xWalsh, Don.
ed. The Law of the Sea: Issues in Ocean
Resource Management. Praeger.
Walsh, Dorothy.
xWalsh, Dorothy.
Literature & Knowledge. Columbia U Pr.
Walsh, Edmund A. *see* Walsh, Edmund Aloysius.
Walsh, Edmund Aloysius.
xWalsh, Edmund A.
ed. History & Nature of International
Relations. Arno.
Walsh, Edward J. *see* Walsh, Edward Joseph.
Walsh, Edward Joseph, 1937-
xWalsh, Edward J.
ed. Dirty Work, Race, & Self Esteem. U of
Mich Inst Labor.
Walsh, Ellen S. *see* Walsh, Ellen Stoll.
Walsh, Ellen Stoll.
xWalsh, Ellen S.
Brunus & the New Bear. Doubleday.
Walsh, Faust C. De. *see* De Walsh, Faust C.
Walsh, Frank K.
xWalsh, Frank K.

Indian Battles Along the Rogue River: One of
America's Wild & Scenic Rivers.
Te-Cum-Tom.

Walsh, George, 1931-
xWalsh, George.
Public Enemies: The Mayor, the Mob, & the
Crime That Was. Norton.

Walsh, H. M. *see* Walsh, Harry M.

Walsh, Harry M.
xWalsh, H. M.
The Outlaw Gunner. Cornell Maritime.

Walsh, Huber M.
xWalsh, Huber M.
Introducing the Young Child to the Social
World. Macmillan.

Walsh, J. J. *see* Walsh, James Joseph.

Walsh, James, 1920-
xWalsh, James.
ed. Pre-Reformation English Spirituality.
Fordham.

Walsh, James J. *see* Walsh, James Joseph.

Walsh, James Joseph, 1865-1942
xWalsh, J. J.
American Jesuits. Gordon Pr.
The World's Debt to the Irish. Gordon Pr.
xWalsh, James J.
American Jesuits. Arno.
A Golden Treasury of Medieval Literature.
Folcroft.
Medieval Medicine. AMS Pr.
Compiled by These Splendid Priests. Arno.
Compiled by These Splendid Sisters. Arno.

Walsh, James M. *see* Walsh, James Morgan.

Walsh, James Morgan, 1897-
xWalsh, James M.
Vandals of the Void. Hyperion Conn.

Walsh, James P., 1937-
xWalsh, James P.
Ethnic Militancy: An Irish Catholic Prototype.
R & E Res Assoc.

Walsh, Jill P. *see* Paton Walsh, Jill.

Walsh, John. *see* Walsh, John Edward.

Walsh, John E.
xWalsh, John.
First Book of Physical Fitness. Watts.
First Book of the Olympic Games. Watts.
xWalsh, John E.
Intercultural Education in the Community of
Man. U Pr of Hawaii.

Walsh, John E. *see* Walsh, John Edward.

Walsh, John Edward, 1927-
xWalsh, John.
Management Tactics: Short Cases in
Operational Management. McGraw.
xWalsh, John E.
Rakes & Ruffians: The Underworld of
Georgian Dublin. Rowman.

Walsh, Joseph L. *see* Walsh, Joseph Leonard.

Walsh, Joseph Leonard, 1895-
xWalsh, Joseph L.
Location of Critical Points of Analytic &
Harmonic Functions. Am Math.

Walsh, Ken.
xWalsh, Ken.
Sometimes I Weep. Judson.

Walsh, Len.
xWalsh, Len.
Read Japanese Today. C E Tuttle.

Walsh, Loren.
xWalsh, Loren.
Coaching Winning Softball. Contemp Bks.
Contemporary Softball. Contemp Bks.

Walsh, M. M. B.
xWalsh, M. M. B.
The Four-Colored Hoop. Putnam.

Walsh, Margaret.
xWalsh, Margaret.

The Manufacturing Frontier: Pioneer Industry
in Antebellum Wisconsin 1830-1860. State
Hist Soc Wis.

Walsh, Marie A. *see* Walsh, Marie Andre.

Walsh, Marie Andre.
xWalsh, Marie A.
The Development of a Rationale for a Program
to Prepare Teachers for Spanish-Speaking
Children in the Bilingual-Bicultural
Elementary School. R & E Res Assoc.

Walsh, P. G. *see* Walsh, Patrick Gerard.

Walsh, Patrick Gerard.
xWalsh, P. G.
Livy: His Historical Aims & Methods.
Cambridge U Pr.

Walsh, Richard.
xWalsh, Richard.
Charleston's Sons of Liberty: A Study of the
Artisans, 1763-1789. U of SC Pr.

Walsh, Robert, 1784-1859
xWalsh, Robert.
Appeal from the Judgments of Great Britain
Respecting the United States of America.
Negro U Pr.

Walsh, Roger N.
xWalsh, Roger N.
ed. Beyond Ego: Transpersonal Dimensions in
Psychology. J P Tarcher.

Walsh, Ruth M.
xWalsh, Ruth M.
Compiled by Business Communications: An
Annotated Bibliography. Greenwood.
Compiled by Job Satisfaction & Motivation: An
Annotated Bibliography. Greenwood.

Walsh, Sheila.
xWalsh, Sheila.
The Incomparable Miss Brady. NAL

Walsh, Thomas, 1908-
xWalsh, Thomas.
Eye of the Needle. S&S.

Walsh, Timothy J.
xWalsh, Timothy J.
Protecting Your Business Against Espionage.
Am Mgmt.

Walsh, Townsend.
xWalsh, Townsend.
Career of Dion Boucicault. Arno.

Walsh, William, 1916-
xWalsh, William.
D. J. Enright: Poet of Humanism. Cambridge U
Pr.
Patrick White: Voss. Dynamic Learn Corp.
Patrick White's Fiction. Rowman.

Walsh, William D. *see* Walsh, William David.

Walsh, William David, 1935-
xWalsh, William D.
The Diffusion of Technological Change in the
Pennsylvania Pig Iron Industry: 1850-1870.
Arno.

Walsh, William H. *see* Walsh, William Henry.

Walsh, William Henry.
xWalsh, William H.
Introduction to Philosophy of History.
Humanities.

Walsh, William T. *see* Walsh, William Thomas.

Walsh, William Thomas, 1891-1949
xWalsh, William T.
Characters of the Inquisition. Kennikat.
xWalsh, William Thomas.
Our Lady of Fatima. Doubleday.

Walsky, Joan R., 1946-
xWalsky, Joan R.
The Well-Written Theme. Har-Row.

Walston, Marie.
xWalston, Marie.
These Were My Hills. Keats.

Walsworth, Nancy.
xWalsworth, Nancy.

Coping with School Age Motherhood. Rosen
Pr.

Walt Disley Studio. *see* Disney (Walt) Productions.
Walt Disney. *see* Disney (Walt) Productions.
Walt Disney Productions. *see* Disney (Walt) Productions.
Walt Disney Studio. *see* Disney (Walt) Productions.
Walt Disney Studios. *see* Disney (Walt) Productions.

Waltch, Lilla M.
xWaltch, Lilla M.
Cave of the Incas. Schol Bk Serv.

Walter, Bruno, 1876-1962
xWalter, Bruno.
Gustav Mahler. Da Capo.
Gustav Mahler. Vienna Hse.
Of Music & Music-Making. Norton.

Walter, Claire.
xWalter, Claire.
The Book of Winners. HarBraceJ.

Walter, D. *see* Walter, Don C.

Walter, Don C.
xWalter, D.
Men & Music in Western Culture. P-H.

Walter, Elizabeth.
xWalter, Elizabeth.
In the Mist & Other Uncanny Encounters.
Arkham.

Walter, Gerard, 1896-1974
xWalter, Gerard.
Nero. Greenwood.

Walter, Hartmut, 1940-
xWalter, Hartmut.
Eleonora's Falcon: Adaptations to Prey &
Habitat in a Social Raptor. U of Chicago Pr.

Walter, Heinrich, 1898-
xWalter, Heinrich.
Ecology of Tropical & Subtropical Vegetation.
Van Nos Reinhold.

Walter, J. *see* Walter, Joseph.

Walter, J. B. *see* Walter, John Brian.

Walter, John Brian.
xWalter, J. B.
General Pathology. Churchill.

Walter, Joseph, Physician.
xWalter, J.
Cancer & Radiotherapy: A Short Guide for
Nurses and Medical Students. Churchill.

Walter, M. R.
xWalter, M. R.
Stromatolites. Elsevier.

Walter, Marion.
xWalter, Marion.
Look at Annette. M Evans.

Walter, Marion I.
xWalter, Marion I.
Boxes, Squares, & Other Things: A Teacher's
Guide for a Unit in Informal Geometry.
NCTM.

Walter, Martin.
xWalter, Martin.
Gem Cutting Is Easy. Crown.
Gemstone Carving. Chilton.

Walter, Otis M.
xWalter, Otis M.
Speaking to Inform & Persuade. Macmillan.
Thinking & Speaking: A Guide to Intelligent
Oral Communication. Macmillan.

Walter, W. Grey. *see* Walter, William Grey.

Walter, William B. *see* Walter, William Goff.

Walter, William Goff.
xWalter, William B.
Introduction to Microbiology. Van Nos
Reinhold.

Walter, William Grey, 1910-
xWalter, W. Grey.
Living Brain. Norton.

Walter, Wolfgang, 1927-
xWalter, Wolfgang.

Differential & Integral Inequalities. Springer-Verlag.

Walters, A. A.
xWalters, A. A.
Introduction to Econometrics. Norton.
Noise & Prices. Oxford U Pr.
xWalters, Alan A.
The Economics of Road User Charges. Johns Hopkins.

Walters, Alan A. see Walters, A. A.

Walters Art Gallery, Baltimore.
xTheWalters Art Gallery.
Jewelry: Ancient to Modern. Viking Pr.

Walters, Barbara, 1931-
xWalters, Barbara.
How to Talk with Practically Anybody About Practically Anything. Dell.
How to Talk with Practically Anybody About Practically Anything. Doubleday.

Walters, Charles Glenn.
xWalters, Glenn.
Marketing Channels. Goodyear.

Walters, Donald N.
xWalters, Donald N.
Reader: An Introduction to Oral Interpretation. Odyssey Pr.

Walters, Dorothy, 1928-
xWalters, Dorothy.
Flannery O'Connor. Twayne.

Walters, Everett, 1915-
xWalters, Everett.
ed. Graduate Education Today. ACE.

Walters, Frederick C. see Walters, Frederick Charles.

Walters, Frederick Charles, 1889-
xWalters, Frederick C.
A Statistical Study of Certain Aspects of the Time Factor in Intelligence. AMS Pr.

Walters, Glenn. see Walters, Charles Glenn.

Walters, Gordon B.
xWalters, Gordon B.
The Significance of Diderot's "Essai sur le Merite et la Vertu". U of NC Pr.

Walters, Henry B. see Walters, Henry Beauchamp.

Walters, Henry Beauchamp, 1867-1944
xWalters, Henry B.
The Art of the Greeks. Arno.

Walters, Hugh.
xWalters, Hugh.
The Caves of Drach. Merrimack Bk Serv.
The Last Disaster. Merrimack Bk Serv.

Walters, L. D. see Walters, Lettice D'Oyly.

Walters, L. D'O. see Walters, Lettice D'Oyly.

Walters, Lettice D'Oyly, 1880-
xWalters, L. D.
An Anthology of Recent Poetry. Folcroft.
xWalters, L. D'O.
Compiled by Anthology of Recent Poetry. Arno.

Walters, R. H. see Walters, Rodri Havard.

Walters, Raymond, 1912-
xWalters, Raymond.
Alexander James Dallas, Lawyer-Politician-Financier. Da Capo.

Walters, Robert S., 1941-
xWalters, Robert S.
American & Soviet Aid: A Comparative Analysis. U of Pittsburgh Pr.

Walters, Rodri Havard.
xWalters, R. H.
The Economic & Business History of the South Wales Steam Coal Industry. Arno.

Walters, Ronald G.
xWalters, Ronald G.
The Antislavery Appeal: American Abolitionism After 1830. Johns Hopkins.

Walthall, Joe E.
xWalthall, Joe E.

Walthall, Wylie A.
xWalthall, Wylie A.
Getting into Business. Har-Row.

Waltham, J. E.
xWaltham, J. E.
North East England. Cambridge U Pr.

Walther, Tom.
xWalther, Tom.
illus. A Spider Might. Scribner.
A Spider Might. Sierra.

Waltner, James. see Waltner, James H.

Waltner, James H.
xWaltner, James.
This We Believe. Faith & Life.

Waltner, Willard.
xWaltner, Willard.
Hobbycraft for Juniors. Lantern.
Holiday Hobbycraft. Lantern.

Walton, Alan G.
xWalton, Alan G.
The Formation & Properties of Precipitates. Krieger.

Walton, Alan H. see Walton, Alan Hull.

Walton, Alan Hull.
xWalton, Alan H.
Open Grave. Taplinger.

Walton, Alice.
xWalton, Alice.
The Cult of Asklepios. Johnson Repr.

Walton, Anne.
xWalton, Anne.
Molecular & Crystal Structure Models. Halsted Pr.

Walton, Bryce, 1918-
xWalton, Bryce.
The Fire Trail. T Y Crowell.

Walton, Clyde C.
xWalton, Clyde C.
ed. Illinois Reader. N Ill U Pr.

Walton, Douglas.
xWalton, Douglas N.
On Defining Death: An Analytic Study of the Concept of Death in Philosophy & Medical Ethics. McGill-Queens U Pr.

Walton, Douglas N. see Walton, Douglas.

Walton, Edgar H. see Walton, Edgar Harris.

Walton, Edgar Harris.
xWalton, Edgar H.
Inner History of the National Convention of South Africa. Negro U Pr.

Walton, Gary M.
xWalton, Gary M.
Economic Issues in American History. Har-Row.

Walton, Hanes, 1941-
xWalton, Hanes.
Political Philosophy of Martin Luther King Jr. Negro U Pr.

Walton, Harold F. see Walton, Harold Frederick.

Walton, Harold Frederick.
xWalton, Harold F.
Modern Chemical Analysis & Instrumentation. Dekker.

Walton, Harry.
xWalton, Harry.
Home & Workshop Guide to Sharpening. Har-Row.
Home & Workshop Guide to Sharpening. Har-Row.
How to Build Your Cabin or Modern Vacation Home. Har-Row.

Walton, Izaak, 1593-1683
xWalton, Izaak.
The Compleat Angler. Biblio Dist.
Compleat Angler. Dutton.
Compleat Angler. Oxford U Pr.

Walton, J. D.
xWalton, Jesse D.

ed. Radome Engineering Handbook: Design & Principles. Dekker.

Walton, Jesse D. see Walton, J. D.

Walton, John, 1910-
xWalton, John.
Administration & Policy-Making in Education. Johns Hopkins.
Cities in Change: Studies on the Urban Condition. Allyn.

Walton, John H., 1952-
xWalton, John W.
Chronological Charts of the Old Testament. Zondervan.

Walton, John W. see Walton, John H.

Walton, Joseph S. see Walton, Joseph Solomon.

Walton, Joseph Solomon, d. 1912
xWalton, Joseph S.
Conrad Weiser & the Indian Policy of Colonial Pennsylvania. Arno.

Walton, Leslie B. see Walton, Leslie Bannister.

Walton, Leslie Bannister, 1895-
xWalton, Leslie B.
Perez Galdos & the Spanish Novel of the Nineteenth Century. Gordian.

Walton, Richard. see Walton, Richard J.

Walton, Richard J.
xWalton, Richard.
The Power of Oil: Economic, Social, Political. HM.

Walton, Stephen, 1945-
xWalton, Stephen.
No Transfer. Vanguard.

Walton, Thomas F.
xWalton, Thomas F.
Communications & Data Management. Wiley.

Walton, Todd.
xWalton, Todd.
Forgotten Impulses. S&S.
Inside Moves. NAL.

Walton, W. C. see Walton, William Clarence.

Walton, W. Robert, 1902-
xWalton, W. Robert.
The Retirement Decision: How the New Social Security & Retirement Age Laws Affect You. Andrews & McMeel.

Walton, William C. see Walton, William Clarence.

Walton, William Clarence.
xWalton, W. C.
Groundwater Resource Evaluation. McGraw.
xWalton, William C.
World of Water. Taplinger.

Waltrip, John R. see Waltrip, John Richard.

Waltrip, John Richard.
xWaltrip, John R.
Public Power During the Truman Administration. Arno.

Waltz, Alan K.
xWaltz, Alan K.
Images of the Future. Abingdon.

Waltz, J. R. see Waltz, Jon R.

Waltz, Jon R.
xWaltz, J. R.
Medical Jurisprudence. Macmillan.
xWaltz, Jon R.
Criminal Evidence. Nelson Hall.

Waltz, Julie, 1942-
xWaltz, Julie.
Food Habit Management. Northwest Learn.

Waltz, Kenneth N. see Waltz, Kenneth Neal.

Waltz, Kenneth Neal, 1924-
xWaltz, Kenneth N.
Theory of International Politics. A-W.

Walvin, James.
xWalvin, James.
Leisure & Society: 1830-1950. Longman.

Walvoord, John F.
xWalvoord, John F.

Cooking from Scratch: The Single Man's Guide to Making Out in the Kitchen. Ballantine.

Warburg, Gabriel.
xWarburg, Garbiel.
Islam, Nationalism & Communism in a Traditional Society: The Case of Sudan. Biblio Dist.

Warburg, Garbiel. *see* Warburg, Gabriel.

Warburg, Sandol S. *see* Warburg, Sandol Stoddard.

Warburg, Sandol Stoddard.
xWarburg, Sandol S.
Free. HM.
Growing Time. HM.
Hooray for Us. HM.
I Like You. HM.
On the Way Home. HM.

Warburton, Annie O. *see* Warburton, Annie Osborne.

Warburton, Annie Osborne.
xWarburton, Annie O.
Melody Writing & Analysis. Greenwood.

Warburton, Beatrice A.
xWarburton, Bee.
ed. The World of Irises. Am Iris.

Warburton, Bee. *see* Warburton, Beatrice A.

Warburton, Clark, 1896-
xWarburton, Clark.
Economic Results of Prohibition. AMS Pr.

Warburton, Geoffrey B. *see* Warburton, Geoffrey Barratt.

Warburton, Geoffrey Barratt, 1924-
xWarburton, Geoffrey B.
ed. Dynamical Behaviour of Structures. Pergamon.

Warburton, Irene P.
xWarburton, Irene P.
On the Verb in Modern Greek. Res Ctr Lang Semiotic.

Warburton, Minnie.
xWarburton, Minnie.
Mykonos. Coward.

Warburton, Robert.
xWarburton, Robert.
Eighteen Years in the Khyber, 1879-1898. Oxford U Pr.

Warcollier, Rene, 1876-
xWarcollier, Rene.
Experimental Telepathy. Arno.

Ward, A. B. *see* Ward, Arthur Barlett.

Ward, A. C. *see* Ward, Alfred Charles.

Ward, A. W. *see* Ward, Adolphus William.

Ward, Adolphous W. *see* Ward, Adolphus William.

Ward, Adolphus W. *see* Ward, Adolphus William.

Ward, Adolphus William.
xWard, A. W.
ed. Cambridge History of British Foreign Policy, 1783-1918. Octagon.
Chaucer. Dynamic Learn Corp.
Chaucer. R West.
xWard, Adolphous W.
Chaucer. Arden Lib.
xWard, Adolphus W.
Chaucer. AMS Pr.
Great Britain & Hanover: Some Aspects of the Personal Union. Haskell.
History of English Dramatic Literature to the Death of Queen Anne. Ungar.

Ward, Alan J.
xWard, Alan J.
Childhood Autism and Structural Therapy: Selected Papers on Early Childhood Autism. Nelson-Hall.

Ward, Albert.
xWard, Albert.
Book Production, Fiction, & the German Reading Public. Oxford U Pr.

Ward, Alfred C. *see* Ward, Alfred Charles.

Ward, Alfred Charles, 1891-
xWard, A. C.

Frolic & the Gentle: A Centenary Study of Charles Lamb. Folcroft.
Frolic & the Gentle: A Centenary Study of Charles Lamb. Kennikat.
Longman Companion to Twentieth Century Literature. Longman.
xWard, Alfred C.
Illustrated History of English Literature. Somerset Pub.
Twentieth-Century Literature: 1901-1940. Core Collection.

Ward, Allen M., 1942-
xWard, Allen M.
Marcus Crassus & the Late Roman Republic. U of Mo Pr.

Ward, Andrew.
xWard, Andrew.
Baby Bear & the Long Sleep. Little.

Ward, Arthur Barlett, 1879-
xWard, A. B.
Rajah's Servant. Cornell SE Asia.

Ward, Arthur S. *see* Ward, Arthur Sarsfield.

Ward, Arthur Sarsfield, 1883-1959
xWard, Arthur S.
Grey Face. Arno.

Ward, Barbara M. *see* Ward, Barbara McLean.

Ward, Barbara McLean.
xWard, Barbara M.
Silver in American Life: Selections from the Mabel Brady Garvan & Other Collections at Yale University. Am Fed Arts.

Ward, Benedicta, 1933-
xWard, Benedicta.
The Desert Christian: The Sayings of the Desert Fathers: the Alphabetical Collection. Macmillan.

Ward, Benjamin. *see* Ward, Benjamin N.

Ward, Benjamin N.
xWard, Benjamin.
The Ideal Worlds of Economics: Liberal, Radical & Conservative Economic Worldviews. Basic.

Ward, Bill. *see* Ward, William G.

Ward, Bill G. *see* Ward, William G.

Ward, Brice.
xWard, Brice.
Computer Technician's Handbook. TAB Bks.
Solid State Circuits Guide Book. TAB Bks.

Ward, Charles. *see* Ward, Charles A.

Ward, Charles A.
xWard, Charles.
Oracles of Nostradamus. Gordon Pr.

Ward, Charles E. *see* Ward, Charles Eugene.

Ward, Charles Eugene.
xWard, Charles E.
Life of John Dryden. U of NC Pr.

Ward, Charles R.
xWard, Charlie.
Silk Stockin Row. McClain.

Ward, Charlie. *see* Ward, Charles R.

Ward, Charlotte Berkley Reed, 1929-
xWard, Charlotte R.
This Blue Planet: Introduction to Physical Science. Little.

Ward, Charlotte R. *see* Ward, Charlotte Berkley Reed.

Ward, Clarence, 1884-
xWard, Clarence.
Mediaeval Church Vaulting. AMS Pr.

Ward, Colin.
xWard, Colin.
The Child in the City. Pantheon.
Streetwork: The Exploding School. Routledge & Kegan.
ed. Vandalism. Van Nos Reinhold.

Ward, Cyrenus O. *see* Ward, Cyrenus Osborne.

Ward, Cyrenus Osborne.
xWard, Cyrenus O.

Ancient Lowly: A History of the Ancient Working People from the Earliest Known Period to the Adoption of Christianity by Constantine. B Franklin.

Ward, D. C. *see* Ward, David C.

Ward, David, 1938-
xWard, David.
Cities & Immigrants: A Geography of Change in Nineteenth-Century America. Oxford U Pr.
ed. Geographic Perspectives on America's Past: Readings on the Historical Geography of the United States. Oxford U Pr.
Jonathan Swift: An Introductory Essay. Methuen Inc.

Ward, David C.
xWard, D. C.
ed. Replication of Mammalian Parvoviruses. Cold Spring Harbor.

Ward, David J.
xWard, David J.
Consumer Finance: The Consumer Experience. Irwin.

Ward, Diana V. *see* Ward, Diana Valiela.

Ward, Diana Valiela.
xWard, Diana V.
Biological Environmental Impact Studies: Theory & Methods. Acad Pr.

Ward, Don.
xWard, Don.
Cowboys & Cattle Country. Am Heritage.

Ward, Douglas Turner.
xWard, Douglas Turner.
Two Plays. Okpaku Communications.

Ward, Dwayne.
xWard, Dwayne.
Toward a Critical Political Economics: A Critique of Liberal & Radical Economic Thought. Goodyear.

Ward, E. P. *see* Ward, Edward Peter.

Ward, Edward Peter.
xWard, E. P.
The Dynamics of Planning. Pergamon.

Ward, Elizabeth S. *see* Ward, Elizabeth Stuart Phelps.

Ward, Elizabeth Stuart Phelps, 1844-1911
xWard, Elizabeth S.
A Lost Hero. Arno.
The Story of Avis. Arno.

Ward, Fay E.
xWard, Fay E.
Cowboy at Work: All About His Job & How He Does It. Hastings.

Ward, Florence E. *see* Ward, Florence Elizabeth.

Ward, Florence Elizabeth.
xWard, Florence E.
Montessori Method & the American School. Arno.

Ward, George W. *see* Ward, George Washington.

Ward, George Washington.
xWard, George W.
The Early Development of the Chesapeake & Ohio Canal Project. AMS Pr.
The Early Development of the Chesapeake & Ohio Canal Project. Johnson Repr.

Ward, Gray.
xWard, Gray.
ed. Integrated Optics & Optical Communications. Mss Info.
xWard, Grey.
ed. Integrated Optics & Optical Communications. Mss Info.

Ward, Grey. *see* Ward, Gray.

Ward, Harry M.
xWard, Harry M.
Duty, Honor or Country: General George Weedon & the American Revolution. Am Philos.

Ward, Herbert, 1863-1919
xWard, Herbert.

Five Years with the Congo Cannibals. Negro U Pr.

Ward, Howard L.
xWard, Howard L.
A Preventive Point of View. C C Thomas.

Ward, Ian, 1949-
xWard, Ian.
ed. Anatomy of the Motor Car. St Martin.
Athletics for Student & Coach. Intl Pubns Serv.
Athletics for Student & Coach. Transatlantic.

Ward, Ian M. *see* Ward, Ian Macmillan.

Ward, Ian Macmillan, 1928-
xWard, Ian M.
Mechanical Properties of Solid Polymers. Wiley.

Ward, J. *see* Ward, Joe H.

Ward, J. A. *see* Ward, Joseph Anthony.

Ward, J. Neville. *see* Ward, Joseph Neville.

Ward, James, 1851-1924
xWard, James.
Historic Ornament: Treatise on Decorative Art & Architectural Ornament. Longwood Pr.

Ward, James A. *see* Ward, James Arthur.

Ward, James Arthur, 1941-
xWard, James A.
That Man Haupt: A Biography of Herman Haupt. La State U Pr.

Ward, Joe H.
xWard, J.
Introduction to Linear Models. P-H.

Ward, John. *see* Ward, John L.

Ward, John L., 1930-
xWard, John.
The Arkansas Rockefeller. La State U Pr.

Ward, John T. *see* Ward, John Towers.

Ward, John Towers.
xWard, John T.
Chartism. Humanities.

Ward, Jonas.
xWard, Jonas.
Buchanan Calls the Shots. Fawcett.
Buchanan Gets Mad. Fawcett.
Buchanan on the Prod. Fawcett.
Buchanan Says No. Fawcett.
Buchanan Takes Over. Fawcett.
Buchanan's Big Showdown. Fawcett.
Buchanan's Gun. Fawcett.
Buchanan's Manhunt. Fawcett.
Buchanan's Revenge. Fawcett.
Buchanan's Siege. Fawcett.
Buchanan's Stolen Railway. Fawcett.
Buchanan's Texas Treasure. Fawcett.
Get Buchanan!. Fawcett.

Ward, Joseph Anthony, 1931-
xWard, J. A.
The Imagination of Disaster: Evil in the Fiction of Henry James. R West.

Ward, Joseph Neville.
xWard, J. Neville.
ed. Five for Sorrow Ten for Joy: A Consideration of the Rosary. Doubleday.

Ward, Keith, 1938-
xWard, Keith.
The Concept of God. St Martin.

Ward, Lester F. *see* Ward, Lester Frank.

Ward, Lester Frank, 1841-1913
xWard, Lester F.
Dynamic Sociology. Johnson Repr.
Intro. by Lester Frank Ward: Selections from His Work. Greenwood.
The Psychic Factors of Civilization. Johnson Repr.
Pure Sociology. Kelley.

Ward, Lynd. *see* Ward, Lynd Kendall.

Ward, Lynd Kendall, 1905-
xWard, Lynd.
God's Man: A Novel in Woodcuts. St Martin.

Ward, Martha C. *see* Ward, Martha Coonfield.

Ward, Martha Coonfield.
xWard, Martha C.

Them Children: A Study in Language Learning. Irvington.

Ward, Martha E. *see* Ward, Martha Eads.

Ward, Martha Eads.
xWard, Martha E.
Authors of Books for Young People. Scarecrow.
Illustrators of Books for Young People. Scarecrow.

Ward, Mary A. *see* Ward, Mary Alice.

Ward, Mary Alice.
xWard, Mary A.
How to Raise & Train a Beagle. TFH Pubns.

Ward, May A. *see* Ward, May Alden.

Ward, May Alden, 1853-1918
xWard, May A.
Prophets of the Nineteenth Century: Carlyle, Ruskin, Tolstoi. Folcroft.

Ward, Melanie.
xWard, Melanie.
Dreams to Come. BJ Pub Group.

Ward, Michael.
xWard, Michael.
The Measurement of Capital: The Methodology of Capital Stock Estimates in OECD Countries. OECD.

Ward (Montgomery) and Company.
xMontgomery Ward.
Catalogue & Buyers Guide Summer & Spring 1895: No. 57. Dover.
xMontgomery Ward & Co.
Catalogue & Buyer's Guide No. 57: Spring & Summer 1895. Peter Smith.

Ward, Nathaniel.
xWard, Nathaniel.
Simple Cobler of Aggawam in America. U of Nebr Pr.

Ward, Norman.
xWard, Norman.
Canadian House of Commons: Representation. U of Toronto Pr.
Public Purse: A Study in Canadian Democracy. U of Toronto Pr.

Ward, Patricia A., 1940-
xWard, Patricia A.
The Medievalism of Victor Hugo. Pa St U Pr.

Ward, Patricia D. *see* Ward, Patricia Dawson.

Ward, Patricia Dawson.
xWard, Patricia D.
The Threat of Peace: James F. Byrnes & the Council of Foreign Ministers, 1945-46. Kent St U Pr.

Ward, Patricia S.
xWard, Patricia S.
Learning Packets: New Approach to Individualizing Instruction. P-H.

Ward, Philip.
xWard, Philip.
Apuleius on Trial at Sabratha. Oleander Pr.
A Dictionary of Common Fallacies. Oleander Pr.
Garrity & Other Plays. Oleander Pr.
Maps on the Ceiling: Libyan Poems. Oleander Pr.
Touring Cyprus. Oleander Pr.

Ward, Ralph T.
xWard, Ralph T.
Pirates in History. York Pr.

Ward, Richard A. *see* Ward, Richard Alexander.

Ward, Richard Alexander, 1929-
xWard, Richard A.
Economics of Health Resources. A-W.

Ward, Richard F. *see* Ward, Richard Frederick.

Ward, Richard Frederick, 1923-
xWard, Richard F.
South & West of the Capitol Dome. Vantage.

Ward, Richard H.
xWard, Richard A.
Introduction to Criminal Investigation. A-W.

Ward, Richard J. *see* Ward, Richard Joseph.

Ward, Richard Joseph.
xWard, Richard J.
A Palestine State: A Rational Approach. Kennikat.

Ward, Ritchie R.
xWard, Ritchie R.
Living Clocks. Knopf.
Living Clocks. NAL.

Ward, Robert H.
xWard, Robert H.
The Complete Samoyed. Howell Bk.

Ward, Russell A.
xWard, Russell A.
The Aging Experience: An Introduction to Social Gerontology. Har-Row.

Ward, Samuel R. *see* Ward, Samuel Ringgold.

Ward, Samuel Ringgold, b. 1817
xWard, Samuel R.
Autobiography of a Fugitive Negro. Arno.
Autobiography of a Fugitive Negro. Johnson Chi.

Ward, Scott.
xWard, Scott.
How Children Learn to Buy: The Development of Consumer Information-Processing Skills. Sage.

Ward, T. S.
xWard, T. S.
The Measurement & Reform of Budgetary Policy. Heinemann Ed.

Ward, W. E. *see* Ward, William Ernest Frank.

Ward, Wilfrid P. *see* Ward, Wilfrid Philip.

Ward, Wilfrid Philip, 1856-1916
xWard, Wilfrid P.
Men & Matters. Arno.
Problems & Persons. Arno.

Ward, William B.
xWard, William B.
Toward Responsible Discipleship. John Knox.

Ward, William Ernest Frank, 1900-
xWard, W. E.
Government in West Africa. Allen Unwin.
A History of Ghana. Allen Unwin.

Ward, William G.
xWard, Bill.
The Student Journalist As Editor. Rosen Pr.
xWard, Bill G.
Student Journalist & Creative Writing. Rosen Pr.
xWard, William G.
Student Journalist & Designing the Opinion Pages. Rosen Pr.
Student Journalist & Editorial Leadership. Rosen Pr.
Student Journalist & Thinking Editorials. Rosen Pr.

Ward, William G. *see* Ward, William George.

Ward, William George, 1812-1882
xWard, William G.
The Ideal of a Christian Church Considered in Comparison with Existing Practice. AMS Pr.

Ward, William S. *see* Ward, William Smith.

Ward, William Smith, 1907-
xWard, William S.
British Periodicals & Newspapers, 1789-1832: A Bibliography of Secondary Sources. U Pr of Ky.
Literary Reviews in British Periodicals, 1821-1826: A Bibliography with a Supplementary List of General (Non-Review) Articles on Literary Subjects. Garland Pub.

Ward, Winifred. *see* Ward, Winifred Louise.

Ward, Winifred Louise, 1884-
xWard, Winifred.
Stories to Dramatize. Anchorage.

Ward-Harris, Joan.
xWard-Harris, Joan.
Creature Comforts. St Martin.

Wardale, E. E. *see* Wardale, Edith Elizabeth.

Wardale, Edith E. *see* Wardale, Edith Elizabeth.

Wardale, Edith Elizabeth.
　xWardale, E. E.
　　Chapters on Old English Literature. Folcroft.
　xWardale, Edith E.
　　Chapters on Old English Literature. Somerset
　　　Pub.
　　An Introduction to Middle English. AMS Pr.
Wardell, Sandra C.
　xWardell, Sandra C.
　　Acute Intervention: Nursing Process
　　　Throughout the Life Span. Reston.
Wardell, William M.
　xWardell, William M.
　　ed. Controlling the Use of Therapeutic Drugs:
　　　An International Comparison. Am Enterprise.
Warder, A. K. see Warder, Anthony Kennedy.
Warder, Anthony K. see Warder, Anthony Kennedy.
Warder, Anthony Kennedy.
　xWarder, A. K.
　　Outline of Indian Philosophy. Orient Bk Dist.
　xWarder, Anthony K.
　　Outline of Indian Philosophy. Intl Pubns Serv.
Wardhaugh, Ronald.
　xWardhaugh, Ronald.
　　Introduction to Linguistics. McGraw.
　　ed. A Survey of Applied Linguistics. U of Mich
　　　Pr.
Wardin, Albert W.
　xWardin, Albert W.
　　Baptist Atlas. Broadman.
Wardle, David.
　xWardle, David.
　　Education & Society in Nineteenth Century
　　　Nottingham. Cambridge U Pr.
Wardle, Robert A. see Wardle, Robert Arnold.
Wardle, Robert Arnold.
　xWardle, Robert A.
　　Advances in the Zoology of Tapeworms,
　　　1950-1970. U of Minn Pr.
Wardle, William L. see Wardle, William Lansdell.
Wardle, William Lansdell.
　xWardle, William L.
　　The History & Religion of Israel. Greenwood.
Wardley-Smith, J.
　xWardley-Smith, J.
　　The Prevention of Oil Pollution. Halsted Pr.
　　ed. The Prevention of Oil Pollution. State
　　　Mutual Bk.
Wardrop, James L.
　xWardrop, James L.
　　Standardized Testing in the Schools: Uses &
　　　Roles. Brooks-Cole.
Wardrop, Marjory S. see Wardrop, Marjory Scott.
Wardrop, Marjory Scott, 1869-1909
　xWardrop, Marjory S.
　　Georgian Folktales. AMS Pr.
Wardroper, John.
　xWardroper, John.
　　The Caricatures of George Cruikshank. Godine.
Wardropper, Bruce W.
　xWardropper, Bruce W.
　　ed. Spanish Poetry of the Golden Age.
　　　Irvington.
Wardwell, Douglas O.
　xWardwell, Douglas O.
　　Television Production Handbook. TAB Bks.
Ware. see Ware, George Whitaker.
Ware, Alan.
　xWare, Alan.
　　The Logic of Party Democracy. St Martin.
Ware, Caroline F. see Ware, Caroline Farrar.
Ware, Caroline Farrar.
　xWare, Caroline F.

　　The Cultural Approach to History. Gordon Pr.
　　The Early New England Cotton Manufacture:
　　　A Study in Industrial Beginnings. Johnson
　　　Repr.
　　Early New England Cotton Manufacture: A
　　　Study in Industrial Beginnings. Russell.
　　Greenwich Village, 1920-1930: A Comment on
　　　American Civilization in the Post-War Years.
　　　Octagon.
Ware, Ethel K. see Ware, Ethel Kime.
Ware, Ethel Kime, 1900-
　xWare, Ethel K.
　　Constitutional History of Georgia. AMS Pr.
Ware, George W. see Ware, George Whitaker.
Ware, George Whitaker, 1902-
　xWare.
　　Producing Vegetable Crops. Thomson Pub CA.
　xWare, George W.
　　German & Austrian Porcelain. Crown.
　　Producing Vegetable Crops. Interstate.
Ware, James E.
　xWare, James E.
　　The Price & Consumption of Water for
　　　Residential Use in Georgia. Ga St U Busn
　　　Pub.
Ware, Leon.
　xWare, Leon.
　　Delta Mystery. Westminster.
Ware, Linda J. see Ware, Linda Jacobs.
Ware, Linda Jacobs, 1943-
　xWare, Linda J.
　　God, Why Is She the Way She Is?. Concordia.
Ware, Mitchell.
　xWare, Mitchell.
　　Operational Handbook for Narcotic Law
　　　Enforcement Officers. C C Thomas.
Ware, Timothy, 1934-
　xWare, Timothy.
　　Orthodox Church. Penguin.
Wareham, John.
　xWareham, John.
　　Secrets of a Corporate Headhunter. Atheneum.
Wareing, P. F.
　xWareing, P. F.
　　The Control of Growth & Differentiation in
　　　Plants. Pergamon.
Wares, William A.
　xWares, William A.
　　The Theory of Dumping & American
　　　Commercial Policy. Lexington Bks.
Warfel, George H.
　xWarfel, George H.
　　Identification Technologies: Computer, Optical,
　　　& Chemical Aids to Personal ID. C C
　　　Thomas.
Warfel, Harry R. see Warfel, Harry Redcay.
Warfel, Harry Redcay.
　xWarfel, Harry R.
　　ed. American Local Color Stories. Cooper Sq.
　　American Novelists of Today. Greenwood.
Warfel, John H.
　xWarfel, John H.
　　The Extremities. Lea & Febiger.
Warfield, B. B. see Warfield, Benjamin Breckinridge.
Warfield, Benjamin B. see Warfield, Benjamin
　Breckinridge.
Warfield, Benjamin Breckinridge, 1851-1921
　xWarfield, B. B.
　　Faith & Life. Banner of Truth.
　xWarfield, Benjamin B.
　　Calvin & Augustine. Presby & Reformed.
　　Perfectionism. Presby & Reformed.
　　Person & Work of Christ. Presby & Reformed.
Warfield, John N.
　xWarfield, John N.
　　Societal Systems: Planning, Policy, &
　　　Complexity. Wiley.
Warfield, R. B. see Warfield, Robert B.
Warfield, Robert B., 1940-
　xWarfield, R. B.

　　Nilpotent Groups. Springer-Verlag.
Warford, Jeremy J.
　xWarford, Jeremy J.
　　Public Policy Toward General Aviation.
　　　Brookings.
Warga, J. see Warga, Jack.
Warga, Jack, 1922-
　xWarga, J.
　　Optimal Control of Differential & Functional
　　　Equations. Acad Pr.
Warga, Richard G.
　xWarga, Richard G.
　　Personal Awareness: A Psychology of
　　　Adjustment. HM.
Wargo, M. J.
　xWargo, Michael J.
　　ed. Achievement Testing of Disadvantaged &
　　　Minority Students for Educational Program
　　　Evaluation. CTB McGraw-Hill.
Wargo, Michael J. see Wargo, M. J.
Warham, Joyce.
　xWarham, Joyce.
　　Introduction to Administration for Social
　　　Workers. Humanities.
　　An Open Case: The Organisational Context of
　　　Social Work. Routledge & Kegan.
Warhol, Andy.
　xWarhol, Andy.
　　Andy Warhol's Exposures. G&D.
Waring, Edward S. see Waring, Edward Scott.
Waring, Edward Scott.
　xWaring, Edward S.
　　A Tour to Sheeraz by the Route of Kazroon &
　　　Feerozabad. Arno.
Waring, Ethel M. see Waring, Ethel May (Bushnell).
Waring, Ethel May (Bushnell), Mrs, 1888-
　xWaring, Ethel M.
　　The Relation Between Early Language Habits
　　　& Early Habits of Conduct Control. AMS Pr.
Waring, Janet.
　xWaring, Janet.
　　Early American Stencils on Walls & Furniture.
　　　Dover.
　　Early American Stencils on Walls & Furniture.
　　　Peter Smith.
Waring, Luther H. see Waring, Luther Hess.
Waring, Luther Hess, 1865-1941
　xWaring, Luther H.
　　Political Theories of Martin Luther. Kennikat.
Waring, Walter, 1917-
　xWaring, Walter.
　　Thomas Carlyle. Twayne.
Wark, Kenneth, 1927-
　xWark, Kenneth.
　　Thermodynamics. McGraw.
Wark, Robert R.
　xWark, Robert R.
　　Drawings from the Turner Shakespeare.
　　　Huntington Lib..
Warken, Philip W., 1935-
　xWarken, Philip W.
　　A History of the National Resources Planning
　　　Board, 1933-1943. Garland Pub.
Warkov, Seymour.
　xWarkov, Seymour.
　　Energy Policy in the United States: Social &
　　　Behavioral Dimensions. Praeger.
　　Graduate Student Finances, 1963: A Survey of
　　　Thirty-Seven Fields of Study. NORC.
　　Lawyers in the Making. Greenwood.
Warley, Thorald K. see Warley, Thorald Keith.
Warley, Thorald Keith.
　xWarley, Thorald K.
　　ed. Agricultural Producers & Their Markets.
　　　Kelley.
Warlick, Harold C.
　xWarlick, Harold C.
　　Conquering Loneliness. Word Bks.
Warmbrand, Max.
　xWarmbrand, Max.

How Thousands of My Arthritis Patients
Regained Their Health. Arc Bks.
How Thousands of My Arthritis Patients
Regained Their Health. P-H.
Overcoming Arthritis & Other Rheumatic
Diseases. Devin.

Warmbrunn, Werner.
xWarmbrunn, Werner.
The Dutch Under German Occupation,
1940-1945. Stanford U Pr.

Warmington, Eric H. *see* Warmington, Eric Herbert.

Warmington, Eric Herbert, 1898-
xWarmington, Eric H.
ed. Greek Geography. AMS Pr.

Warmke, Germaine L. *see* Warmke, Germaine le Clerc.

Warmke, Germaine Le Clerc.
xWarmke, Germaine L.
Caribbean Seashells: A Guide to the Marine
Mollusks of Puerto Rico & Other West
Indian Islands, Bermuda & the Lower Florida
Keys. Dover.

Warne, Frank J. *see* Warne, Frank Julian.

Warne, Frank Julian, 1874-
xWarne, Frank J.
The Immigrant Invasion. Ozer.
The Workers at War. AMS Pr.

Warnecke, Steven J. *see* Warnecke, Steven Joshua.

Warnecke, Steven Joshua.
xWarnecke, Steven J.
ed. Industrial Policies in Western Europe.
Praeger.

Warner, Aaron W.
xWarner, Aaron W.
ed. Environment of Change. Columbia U Pr.

Warner, Amos G. *see* Warner, Amos Griswold.

Warner, Amos Griswold, 1861-1900
xWarner, Amos G.
American Charities. Arno.
American Charities. Russell.

Warner, Anne R., 1928-
xWarner, Anne R.
ed. Innovations in Community Health Nursing:
Health Care Delivery in Shortage Areas.
Mosby.

Warner, Beverley E. *see* Warner, Beverley Ellison.

Warner, Beverley Ellison, 1855-1910
xWarner, Beverley E.
ed. Famous Introductions to Shakespeare's
Plays by the Notable Editors of the 18th
Century. B Franklin.

Warner, Bob.
xWarner, Robert.
Don't Blame the Fish. Winchester Pr.

Warner, Carmen G. *see* Warner, Carmen Germaine.

Warner, Carmen Germaine, 1941-
xWarner, Carmen G.
Rape & Sexual Assault: Management &
Intervention. Aspen Systems.

Warner, Charles D. *see* Warner, Charles Dudley.

Warner, Charles Dudley, 1829-1900
xWarner, Charles D.
A Little Journey in the World. Irvington.
A Little Journey in the World. Johnson Repr.
That Fortune. Irvington.
That Fortune. R West.
xWarner, Charles W.
A Little Journey in the World. R West.

Warner, Charles W. *see* Warner, Charles Dudley.

Warner, D. Michael.
xWarner, D. Michael.
Decision Making & Control for Health
Administration: The Management of
Quantitative Analysis. Health Admin Pr.
Exercises in Quantitative Techniques for
Hospital Planning & Control. Health Admin
Pr.

Warner, Deborah J. *see* Warner, Deborah Jean.

Warner, Deborah Jean.
xWarner, Deborah J.

The Sky Explored: Celestial Cartography,
1500-1800. A R Liss.

Warner, Dorothy D. *see* Warner, Dorothy Dunstedter.

Warner, Dorothy Dunstedter.
xWarner, Dorothy D.
Adapting American Antiques. Glencoe.

Warner, Ezra J.
xWarner, Ezra J.
Generals in Gray: Lives of the Confederate
Commanders. La State U Pr.

Warner, Frank.
xWarner, Frank.
ed. Readings in Controversial Issues in
Education of the Mentally Retarded. Mss
Info.

Warner, Frank M. *see* Warner, Frank Melville.

Warner, Frank Melville.
xWarner, Frank M.
Applied Descriptive Geometry. McGraw.

Warner, Frank W. *see* Warner, Frank Wilson.

Warner, Frank Wilson, 1938-
xWarner, Frank W.
Foundations of Differentiable Manifolds & Lie
Groups. Scott F.

Warner, Gertrude. *see* Warner, Gertrude Chandler.

Warner, Gertrude C. *see* Warner, Gertrude Chandler.

Warner, Gertrude Chandler, 1890-
xWarner, Gertrude.
Boxcar Children. A Whitman.
xWarner, Gertrude C.
Bus Station Mystery. A Whitman.
Caboose Mystery. A Whitman.
Houseboat Mystery. A Whitman.
Woodshed Mystery. A Whitman.

Warner, Henry J. *see* Warner, Henry James.

Warner, Henry James.
xWarner, Henry J.
Albigensian Heresy. Russell.

Warner, Homer R., 1922-
xWarner, Homer R.
Computer-Assisted Medical Decision-Making.
Acad Pr.

Warner, Horace E. *see* Warner, Horace Everett.

Warner, Horace Everett, 1839-1930
xWarner, Horace E.
The Ethics of Force. Ozer.

Warner, Irving R.
xWarner, Irving R.
The Art of Fund Raising. Har-Row.

Warner, Joan E. *see* Warner, Joan Elizabeth.

Warner, Joan Elizabeth.
xWarner, Joan E.
Business English for Careers. Reston.
xWarner, Joan Elizabeth.
Business Calculator Operations. Reston.

Warner, Ken, 1928-
xWarner, Ken.
The Practical Book of Guns. Winchester Pr.
The Practical Book of Knives. Winchester Pr.

Warner, Kenneth O. *see* Warner, Kenneth Oren.

Warner, Kenneth Oren.
xWarner, Kenneth O.
ed. Practical Guidelines to Public Pay
Administration. Intl Personnel Mgmt.
Public Management at the Bargaining Table.
Intl Personnel Mgmt.

Warner, Langdon, 1881-1955
xWarner, Langdon.
The Enduring Art of Japan. Grove.

Warner, Louis A.
xWarner, Louis A.
Stand up but Don't Get off. NELF Pr.

Warner, Lucille S. *see* Warner, Lucille Schulberg.

Warner, Lucille Schulberg.
xWarner, Lucille S.
From Slave to Abolitionist: The Life of William
Wells Brown. Dial.

Warner, Marina, 1946-
xWarner, Marina.

Alone of All Her Sex: The Myth & the Cult of
the Virgin Mary. Knopf.
Alone of All Her Sex: The Myth & the Cult of
the Virgin Mary. PB.
The Crack in the Teacup: Britain in the
Twentieth Century. HM.
In a Dark Wood. Knopf.

Warner, Mickey.
xWarner, Mickey.
Industrial Foodservice & Cafeteria
Management. CBI Pub.

Warner, Mignon.
xWarner, Mignon.
A Medium for Murder. Dell.

Warner, Oliver, 1903-
xWarner, Oliver.
The British Navy: A Concise History. Thames
Hudson.
Captain Marryat: A Rediscovery. Hyperion
Conn.

Warner, Peter O., 1937-
xWarner, Peter O.
Analysis of Air Pollutants. Wiley.

Warner, Philip.
xWarner, Philip.
The Soldier: His Daily Life Through the Ages.
Taplinger.

Warner, Ralph. *see* Warner, Ralph E.

Warner, Ralph E.
xWarner, Ralph.
Everybody's Guide to Small Claims Court.
A-W.
xWarner, Ralph E.
Protect Your Home with a Declaration of
Homestead. Nolo Pr.

Warner, Raynor. *see* Warner, Raynor M.

Warner, Raynor M.
xWarner, Raynor.
Business & Preservation: A Survey of Business
Conservation of Buildings & Neighborhoods.
Inform.
xWarner, Raynor M.
New Profits from Old Buildings: Private
Enterprise Approaches to Making
Preservation Pay. McGraw.

Warner, Rex, 1905-
xWarner, Rex.
Greek Philosophers. NAL.
The Stories of the Greeks. FS&G.

Warner, Richard, 1946-
xWarner, Richard.
Morality in Medicine: An Introduction to
Medical Ethics. Alfred Pub.

Warner, Robert. *see* Warner, Bob.

Warner, Sam B. *see* Warner, Sam Bass.

Warner, Sam Bass, 1889-
xWarner, Sam B.
Crime & Criminal Statistics in Boston. Arno.
ed. Planning for a Nation of Cities. MIT Pr.
Private City: Philadelphia in Three Periods of
Its Growth. U of Pa Pr.
Streetcar Suburbs: The Process of Growth in
Boston, 1870-1900. Harvard U Pr.

Warner, Sylvia T. *see* Warner, Sylvia Townsend.

Warner, Sylvia Townsend, 1893-
xWarner, Sylvia T.
The Barnards of Loseby. Popular Lib.
Mr. Fortune's Maggot. AMS Pr.

Warner, T. E. *see* Warner, Thomas E.

Warner, Thomas E.
xWarner, T. E.
An Annotated Bibliography of Woodwind
Instruction Books, 1600-1830. Info Coord.

Warner, W. Lloyd. *see* Warner, William Lloyd.

Warner, Wayne. *see* Warner, Wayne E.

Warner, Wayne E.
xWarner, Wayne.
Letters to Tony. Gospel Pub.
Warner, William, 1558?-1609
xWarner, William.
Albion's England. Adler.
Warner, William L. see Warner, William Lloyd.
Warner, William Lloyd, 1898-
xWarner, W. Lloyd.
American Life: Dream & Reality. U of Chicago Pr.
Occupational Mobility in American Business & Industry, 1928-1952. Arno.
The Status System of a Modern Community. Greenwood.
xWarner, William L.
Color & Human Nature: Negro Personality Development in a Northern City. Negro U Pr.
Democracy in Jonesville: A Study in Quality & Inequality. Greenwood.
Social Systems of American Ethnic Groups. Greenwood.
Warnier, Jean Dominique.
xWarnier, Jean-Dominique.
Program Modification. Kluwer Boston.
Warnier, Jean-Dominique. see Warnier, Jean Dominique.
Warnke, Mike.
xWarnke, Mike.
Hitchhiking on Hope Street. Doubleday.
Warnock, Geoffrey J. see Warnock, Geoffrey James
Warnock, Geoffrey James, 1923-
xWarnock, Geoffrey J.
Contemporary Moral Philosophy. St Martin.
Warnock, Mary.
xWarnock, Mary.
Ethics Since 1900. Oxford U Pr.
Existentialism. Oxford U Pr.
Imagination. U of Cal Pr.
Warnock, Robert.
xWarnock, Robert.
The World in Literature. Scott F.
Warr, P. see Warr, Peter Bryan.
Warr, Peter. see Warr, Peter Bryan.
Warr, Peter Bryan.
xWarr, P.
Personal Goals & Work Design. Wiley.
xWarr, Peter.
Developing Employee Relations. Renouf.
Warrack, John. see Warrack, John Hamilton.
Warrack, John Hamilton, 1928-
xWarrack, John.
Tchaikovsky Symphonies & Concertos. U of Wash Pr.
Warren, A. see Warren, Austin.
Warren, Ann.
xWarren, Ann.
Modern Guide to House Plants. M Evans.
Warren, Austin, 1899-
xWarren, A.
Alexander Pope As Critic & Humanist. Peter Smith.
Warren, Barbara, 1947-
xWarren, Barbara.
The Feminine Image in Literature. Hayden.
Warren, Beatrice, 1942-
xWarren, Beatrice.
Semantic Patterns of Noun-Noun Compounds. Humanities.
Warren, Bill.
xWarren, Bill.
Inflation & Wages in Underdeveloped Countries: India, Peru & Turkey, 1939-1960. Biblio Dist.
Warren, C. Henry. see Warren, Clarence Henry.
Warren, Carl.
xWarren, Carl.

From the Counter to the Bottom Line. Intl Schol Bk Serv.
Warren, Charles, 1868-1954
xWarren, Charles.
Bankruptcy in United States History. Da Capo.
California Perspectives: Four Leaders Look at the State of the State. Inst Gov Stud Berk.
Congress, the Constitution & the Supreme Court. Johnson Repr.
A History of the American Bar. Longwood Pr.
History of the Harvard Law School & of Early Legal Conditions in America. Da Capo.
The Supreme Court & Sovereign States. Da Capo.
Warren, Clarence Henry, 1895-
xWarren, C. Henry.
ed. Men Behind the Music. Kennikat.
Warren, David.
xWarren, David.
The Great Escaper. Raintree Child.
Natural Bone. SBD.
World According to Two Feathers. SBD.
Warren, David G.
xWarren, David G.
A Legal Guide for Rural Health Programs. Ballinger Pub.
Warren, Donald I.
xWarren, Donald I.
The Radical Center: Middle Americans & the Politics of Alienation. U of Notre Dame Pr.
Warren, Donald R., 1933-
xWarren, Donald R.
ed. History, Education, & Public Policy: Recovering the American Educational Past. McCutchan.
Warren, Dorothy Moody.
xWarren, Dorothy Moody.
ed. Anthology of Bells: The Bell Collectors' Treasury of Verses. Exposition.
Warren, Earl, 1891-1974
xWarren, Earl.
The Public Papers of Chief Justice Earl Warren. Greenwood.
Warren, Fintan B.
xWarren, Fintan B.
Vasco De Quiroga & His Pueblo-Hospitals of Santa Fe. AAFH.
Warren, Frank A.
xWarren, Frank A.
Liberals & Communism: The "Red Decade" Revisited. Greenwood.
Warren, Frederick E. see Warren, Frederick Edward.
Warren, Frederick Edward, 1842-1930
xWarren, Frederick E.
Liturgy & Ritual of the Ante-Nicene Church. AMS Pr.
Warren, G. Garry. see Warren, George Garry.
Warren, G. M.
xWarren, G. M.
Destiny's Children. PB.
Warren, Geoffrey.
xWarren, Geoffrey.
A Stitch in Time: Victorian & Edwardian Needlecraft. Taplinger.
Vanishing Street Furniture. David & Charles.
Warren, George Garry, 1948-
xWarren, G. Garry.
The Handicapped Librarian: A Study in Barriers. Scarecrow.
Warren, Harmoni.
xWarren, Harmoni.
A Legend Was Born. Ashley Bks.
Warren, Henry, 1794-1879
xWarren, Henry.
Artistic Anatomy of a Human Figure. Gloucester Art.
Warren, Howard C. see Warren, Howard Crosby.
Warren, Howard Crosby, 1867-1934
xWarren, Howard C.

A History of the Association Psychology. Johnson Repr.
Warren, James E. see Warren, James Edward.
Warren, James Edward, 1908-
xWarren, James E.
How to Write a Research Paper. Branden.
Warren, Janet.
xWarren, Janet.
A Feast of Scotland. Little.
Warren, Josiah, 1798-1874
xWarren, Josiah.
True Civilization, an Immediate Necessity, & the Last Ground of Hope for Mankind. B Franklin.
Warren, Kay B., 1947-
xWarren, Kay B.
The Symbolism of Subordination: Indian Identity in a Guatemalan Town. U of Tex Pr.
Warren, Kenneth.
xWarren, Kenneth.
North-East England. Oxford U Pr.
Warren, Kenneth S.
xWarren, Kenneth S.
ed. Geographic Medicine for the Practitioner: Algorithms in the Diagnosis & Management of Exotic Diseases. U of Chicago Pr.
Warren, L. see Warren, Lee.
Warren, Lee.
xWarren, L.
Dance of Africa: An Introduction. P-H.
xWarren, Lee.
Theater of Africa: An Introduction. P-H.
Warren, Louis A. see Warren, Louis Austin.
Warren, Louis Austin, 1885-
xWarren, Louis A.
Lincoln's Youth: Indiana Years, Seven to Twenty-One, 1816-1830. Greenwood.
Warren, Malcolm W.
xWarren, Malcom W.
Training for Results: A Systems Approach to the Development of Human Resources in Industry. A-W.
Warren, Malcom W. see Warren, Malcolm W.
Warren, Mary.
xWarren, Mary P.
Little Boat That Almost Sank. Concordia.
Warren, Mary P. see Warren, Mary Phraner.
Warren, Mary Phraner.
xWarren, Mary P.
Ghost Town for Sale. Westminster.
The Land of Christmas. Augsburg.
Warren, Mashuri L., 1940-
xWarren, Mashuri L.
Introductory Physics. W H Freeman.
Warren, Max, 1904-
xWarren, Max.
I Believe in the Great Commission. Eerdmans.
Warren, Michael.
xWarren, Michael.
photos by Appalachian Trail. Graphic Arts Ctr.
A Future for Youth Catechesis. Paulist Pr.
Warren, Mildred Evans.
xWarren, Mildred Evans.
Art of Southern Cooking. Doubleday.
Warren, Murray.
xWarren, Murray.
A Descriptive & Annotated Bibliography of Thomas Chatterton. Garland Pub.
Warren, Neil, 1905-
xWarren, Neil.
ed. Studies in Cross-Cultural Psychology. Acad Pr.
Warren, Patricia N. see Warren, Patricia Nell.
Warren, Patricia Nell.
xWarren, Patricia N.

The Beauty Queen. Bantam.
The Beauty Queen. Morrow.
The Fancy Dancer. Bantam.
The Fancy Dancer. Morrow.
The Front Runner. Bantam.
Warren, Paulette.
xWarren, Paulette.
Caliban's Castle. Berkley Pub.
Warren, Rachelle. *see* Warren, Rachelle B.
Warren, Rachelle B.
xWarren, Rachelle.
The Neighborhood Organizer's Handbook. U
of Notre Dame Pr.
Warren, Richard.
xWarren, Richard.
Compiled by Charles E. Ives: Discography.
Greenwood.
Warren, Rita M.
xWarren, Rita M.
Caring: Supporting Children's Growth. Natl
Assn Child Ed.
Warren, Robert P. *see* Warren, Robert Penn.
Warren, Robert Penn, 1905-
xWarren, Robert P.
All the King's Men. Random.
Circus in the Attic & Other Stories. HarBraceJ.
Democracy & Poetry. Harvard U Pr.
Night Rider. Random.
Who Speaks for the Negro. Random.
Warren, Roland L. *see* Warren, Roland Leslie.
Warren, Roland Leslie, 1915-
xWarren, Roland L.
The Community in America. Rand.
Studying Your Community. Free Pr.
Warren, Ruth.
xWarren, Ruth.
The First Book of Modern Greece. Watts.
First Book of the Arab World. Watts.
Modern Greece. Watts.
Warren, Samuel, 1807-1877
xWarren, Samuel.
Experiences of a Barrister & Confessions of an
Attorney. Arno.
Warren, Sidney, 1916-
xWarren, Sidney.
Farthest Frontier: The Pacific Northwest.
Kennikat.
Warren, Ted.
xWarren, Ted.
How to Make the Stock Market Make Money
for You. Sherbourne.
Warren, Thomas B.
xWarren, Thomas B.
ed. God Demands Doctrinal Preaching. Natl
Christian Pr.
Warren, W. L. *see* Warren, Wilfred Lewis.
Warren, Wilfred Lewis.
xWarren, W. L.
King John. U of Cal Pr.
Warrick, Patricia S.
xWarrick, Patricia S.
The Cybernetic Imagination in Science Fiction.
MIT Pr.
Warriner, Doreen, 1904-
xWarriner, Doreen.
ed. Contrasts in Emerging Societies: Readings
in the Social & Economic History of
South-Eastern Europe in the Nineteenth
Century. AMS Pr.
Warriner, Hope R.
xWarriner, Hope R.
Sights & Sounds of the City: Vistas y Sonidos
De la Ciudad. Blaine Ethridge.
Warring, R. H. *see* Warring, Ronald Horace.
Warring, Ronald Horace.
xWarring, R. H.
Modern Crystal Radios. TAB Bks.
Power Tools. Soccer.
Warshall, Peter.
xWarshall, Peter.

Septic Tank Practices. Doubleday.
Warshaw, Jerry.
xWarshaw, Jerry.
ed. The Funny Drawing Book. A Whitman.
Warshaw, Leon J.
xWarshaw, Leon J.
Managing Stress. A-W.
Warshaw, Thayer S., 1915-
xWarshaw, Thayer S.
Religion, Education, & the Supreme Court.
Abingdon.
Warshawsky, A. G., 1883-
xWarshawsky, Abel G.
Paris Unconquered. Wake-Brook.
Warshawsky, Abel G. *see* Warshawsky, A. G.
Warshofsky, Fred.
xWarshofsky, Fred.
Doomsday: The Science of Catastrophe. PB.
Warshow, Robert, 1917-1955
xWarshow, Robert.
Immediate Experience: Movies, Comics,
Theatre & Other Aspects of Popular Culture.
Atheneum.
Wartburg, Ursula Von. *see* Von Wartburg, Ursula.
Wartella, Ellen.
xWartella, Ellen.
ed. Children Communicating: Media &
Development of Thought, Speech,
Understanding. Sage.
Warth, Robert D.
xWarth, Robert D.
The Allies & the Russian Revolution from the
Fall of the Monarchy to the Peace of
Brest-Litovsk. Russell.
Leon Trotsky. Twayne.
Wartofsky, Marx W.
xWartofsky, Marx W.
Feuerbach. Cambridge U Pr.
Warton, Joseph, 1722-1800
xWarton, Joseph.
Odes on Various Subjects. Schol Facsimiles.
Warton, Thomas, 1728-1790
xWarton, Thomas.
History of English Poetry. Johnson Repr.
History of English Poetry. Somerset Pub.
Observations on the Fairy Queen of Spenser.
Greenwood.
Wartski, Maureen C. *see* Wartski, Maureen Crane.
Wartski, Maureen Crane.
xWartski, Maureen C.
A Boat to Nowhere. Westminster.
My Brother Is Special. NAL.
My Brother Is Special. Westminster.
Warwick, Alan R. *see* Warwick, Alan Ross.
Warwick, Alan Ross.
xWarwick, Alan R.
Let's Look at Castles. A Whitman.
Let's Look at Prehistoric Animals. A Whitman.
Warwick, Dolores.
xWarwick, Dolores.
Learn to Say Goodbye. FS&G.
Warwick, Donald. *see* Warwick, Donald P.
Warwick, Donald P.
xWarwick, Donald.
A Theory of Public Bureaucracy: Politics,
Personality, & Organization in the State
Department. Harvard U Pr.
xWarwick, Donald P.
A Theory of Public Bureaucracy: Politics,
Personality, & Organization in the State
Department. Harvard U Pr.
Warwick, E. J. *see* Warwick, Everett James.
Warwick, Everett James.
xWarwick, E. J.
Breeding & Improvement of Farm Animals.
McGraw.
Warwick, Helen.
xWarwick, Helen.

Complete Labrador Retriever. Howell Bk.
Warwick, Jack.
xWarwick, Jack.
Long Journey: Literary Themes of French
Canada. U of Toronto Pr.
Warwick, James. *see* Warwick, James S.
Warwick, James S.
xWarwick, James.
Beginning Jewelry. Scribner.
Warwick, Paul.
xWarwick, Paul.
The French Popular Front: A Legislative
Analysis. U of Chicago Pr.
Wasan, M. T.
xWasan, M. T.
Parametric Estimation. McGraw.
Stochastic Approximation. Cambridge U Pr.
Wasbauer, M. S. *see* Wasbauer, Marius S.
Wasbauer, Marius S.
xWasbauer, M. S.
Revision of the Male Wasps of the Genus
Brachycistis in America North of Mexico
(Hymenoptera: Tiphiidae). U of Cal Pr.
Wasby, Stephen L., 1937-
xWasby, Stephen L.
ed. Civil Liberties: Policy & Policy-Making.
Lexington Bks.
ed. Civil Liberties: Policy & Policy Making. S
Ill U Pr.
Continuity & Change: From the Warren Court
to the Burger Court. Goodyear.
Desegregation from Brown to Alexander: An
Exploration of Supreme Court Strategies. S
Ill U Pr.
Waschek, Carmen.
xWaschek, Carmen.
Inflation Fighter's Big Book: Beat the High
Cost of Operating Your Home. Reston.
Waser, Jurg.
xWaser, Jurg.
Chem One. McGraw.
Quantitative Chemistry: A Laboratory Text.
Benjamin-Cummings.
Washburn, A. *see* Washburn, Albert Lincoln.
Washburn, A. L. *see* Washburn, Albert Lincoln.
Washburn, Albert Lincoln, 1911-
xWashburn, A.
Periglacial Processes & Environments. St
Martin.
xWashburn, A. L.
Geocryology: A Survey of Periglacial Processes
& Environments. Halsted Pr.
Washburn, Bradford, 1910-
xWashburn, Bradford.
Tourist Guide to Mount McKinley. Alaska
Northwest.
Washburn, Charles.
xWashburn, Charles.
Come into My Parlor: A Biography of the
Aristocratic Everleigh Sisters of Chicago.
Arno.
Washburn, David E.
xWashburn, David E.
Ethnic Studies in Pennsylvania. U Ctr Intl St.
Washburn, Donald E.
xWashburn, Donald E.
ed. Coping with Increasing Complexity:
Implications of General Semantics & General
Systems. Gordon.
Washburn, Dorothy K. *see* Washburn, Dorothy Koster.
Washburn, Dorothy Koster.
xWashburn, Dorothy K.
A Symmetry Analysis of Upper Gila Area
Ceramic Design. Peabody Harvard.
Washburn, Henry B. *see* Washburn, Henry Bradford.
Washburn, Henry Bradford, 1869-1962
xWashburn, Henry B.
Men of Conviction. Arno.
Washburn, Sherwood L. *see* Washburn, Sherwood
Larned.

Washburn, Sherwood Larned.
xWashburn, Sherwood L.
Human Evolution: Biosocial Perspectives.
Benjamin-Cummings.
Washburn, Wilcomb E.
xWashburn, Wilcomb E.
The Governor & the Rebel: A History of
Bacon's Rebellion in Virginia. Norton.
The Indian in America. Har-Row.
The Indian in America. Har-Row.
Washburn, Winifred Y.
xWashburn, Winifred Y.
Vocational Mainstreaming. Acad Therapy.
Washburne, Chandler, 1924-
xWashburne, Chandler.
Primitive Drinking: A Study of the Uses &
Functions of Alcohol in Preliterate Societies.
Coll & U Pr.
Washburne, George A. see Washburne, George Adrian.
Washburne, George Adrian, 1884-1948
xWashburne, George A.
Imperial Control of the Administration of
Justice in the Thirteen American Colonies
1684-1776. AMS Pr.
Washington, Allyn J.
xWashington, Allyn J.
Essentials of Basic Mathematics.
Benjamin-Cummings.
Introduction to Algebra. Benjamin-Cummings.
Introduction to Geometry.
Benjamin-Cummings.
Plane Trigonometry. Benjamin-Cummings.
Washington, Booker T. see Washington, Booker
Taliaferro.
Washington, Booker Taliaferro, 1859?-1915
xWashington, Booker T.
Frederick Douglass. Argosy.
Frederick Douglass. Greenwood.
Frederick Douglass. Haskell.
Negro in Business. AMS Pr.
The Negro in Business. Johnson Repr.
Negro in Business. Metro Bks.
Negro in the South: His Economic Progress in
Relation to His Moral & Religious
Development. AMS Pr.
The Negro in the South: His Economic
Progress in Relation to His Moral &
Religious Development. Metro Bks.
Negro Problem: A Series of Articles by
Representative American Negroes of Today.
Arno.
Sowing & Reaping. Arno.
Story of My Life & Work. Negro U Pr.
The Story of the Negro: The Rise of the Race
from Slavery. Peter Smith.
ed. Tuskegee & Its People: Their Ideals &
Achievements. Arno.
ed. Tuskegee & Its People: Their Ideals &
Achievements. Negro U Pr.
Working with the Hands: Being a Sequel to up
from Slavery Covering the Author's
Experiences in Industrial Training at
Tuskegee. Arno.
Washington Consulting Group.
xWashington Consulting Group.
Uplift: What People Themselves Can Do.
Olympus Pub Co.
**Washington, D.C. Joint Library of the International
Monetary Fund and the International Bank for
Reconstruction and Development.**
xJoint Bank-Fund Library (Washington, D. C.).
Economics, Finance & Development: Subject
Headings Used in the Main Catalog of the
Joint Bank-Fund Library. G K Hall.
xJoint Bank-Fund Library, Washington, D. C.

Economics & Finance: Index to Periodical
Articles, Nineteen Forty-Seven to Nineteen
Seventy-One. Second Supplement. G K Hall.
Economics & Finance: Index to Periodical
Articles, 1947-1971. G K Hall.
Economics & Finance: Index to Periodical
Articles, 1947-1971, Joint Bank-Fund Library
(Washington, D.C.), First Supplement. G K
Hall.
Washington Researchers.
xWashington Researchers.
A Researcher's Guide to Washington: 1978
Edition. Wash Res.
Washington, Rosemary G.
xWashington, Rosemary G.
Gymnastics Is for Me. Lerner Pubns.
Washington (State) University.
xUniversity Of Washington.
Manual of Freshman English. Pacific Bks.
Washington (State) University. Library.
xUniversity of Washington Libraries.
The Dictionary Catalog of the Pacific
Northwest Collection of the University of
Washington Libraries, Seattle. G K Hall.
Washington University Department of Medicine. see
Washington University, St. Louis. Dept. of Medicine.
Washington University School of Medicine. see
Washington University, St. Louis. School of Medicine.
Washington University, St. Louis.
xWashington University, St. Louis.
Studies in Honor of Frederick W. Shipley, by
His Colleagues. Washington Univ. Studies NS
No. 14. Arno.
Washington University, St. Louis. Dept. of Medicine.
xWashington University Department of Medicine.
Manual of Medical Therapeutics. Little.
Washington University, St. Louis, Dept. of Political
Science. see Conference on Democracy in the Mid
20th Century, Washington University, 1958.
Washington University, St. Louis. School of Medicine.
xWashington University School of Medicine.
Manual of Medical Therapeutics. Little.
Washizu, Kyuichiro, 1921-
xWashizu, Kyuichiro.
Variational Methods in Elasticity & Plasticity.
Pergamon.

Washnis, George J.
xWashnis, George J.
Citizen Involvement in Crime Prevention.
Lexington Bks.
Municipal Decentralization & Neighborhood
Resources: Case Studies of Twelve Cities.
Irvington.
Washton, Andrew D.
xWashton, Andrew D.
What Happens Next?: Stories to Finish for
Intermediate Writers. Tchrs Coll.
Wasiolek, Edward.
xWasiolek, Edward.
Dostoevsky: The Major Fiction. MIT Pr.
Waskow, Arthur I.
xWaskow, Arthur I.
Godwrestling. Schocken.
Wasley, John.
xWasley, John.
A Guide to Hi-Fi. Transatlantic.
Wasmuth. see Wasmuth, Carl Erwin.
Wasmuth, Carl E. see Wasmuth, Carl Erwin.
Wasmuth, Carl Erwin, 1916-
xWasmuth.
jt. auth. Law & the Surgical Team. Krieger.
xWasmuth, Carl E.
Law for the Physician. Lea & Febiger.
Wasmuth, W. see Wasmuth, William J.
Wasmuth, William J.
xWasmuth, W.
Effective Supervision: Developing Your Skills
Through Critical Incidents. P-H.
Wason, Betty. see Wason, Elizabeth.

Wason, Elizabeth, 1912-
xWason, Betty.
The Art of Spanish Cooking. Cornerstone.
Art of Spanish Cooking. Doubleday.
Wason, Margaret O. see Wason, Margaret Ogilvie.
Wason, Margaret Ogilvie.
xWason, Margaret O.
Class Struggles in Ancient Greece. Fertig.
Wason, P. C. see Wason, Peter Cathcart.
Wason, Peter Cathcart.
xWason, P. C.
Psychology of Reasoning: Structure & Content.
Harvard U Pr.
Wasp, Edward J.
xWasp, Edward J.
Solid-Liquid Flow Slurry Pipeline
Transportation. Gulf Pub.
Wass, Alonzo.
xWass, Alonzo.
Data Book for Residential Contractors &
Estimators. Reston.
Estimating Residential Construction. P-H.
Wass, Hannelore.
xWass, Hannelore.
Humanistic Teacher Education: An Experiment
in Systematic Curriculum Innovation.
Publishers Consult.
Wasser, Edna.
xWasser, Edna.
Creative Approaches in Casework with the
Aging. Family Serv.
Wasserberger, Jonathan.
xWasserberger, Jonathan.
Advanced Paramedic Procedures: A Practical
Approach. Mosby.
Wasserman, Burton.
xWasserman, Burton.
Exploring the Visual Arts. Davis Mass.
Wasserman, Earl R. see Wasserman, Earl Reeves.
Wasserman, Earl Reeves, 1913-
xWasserman, Earl R.
ed. Aspects of the Eighteenth Century. Johns
Hopkins.
The Subtler Language: Critical Readings of
Neoclassic & Romantic Poems. Greenwood.
The Subtler Language: Critical Readings of
Neoclassic & Romantic Poems. Johns
Hopkins.
Wasserman, Fred W.
xWasserman, Fred W.
Building a Group Practice. C C Thomas.
Wasserman, Gary.
xWasserman, Gary.
The Basics of American Politics. Little.
Wasserman, Gerald S., 1937-
xWasserman, Gerald S.
Color Vision: An Historical Introduction.
Wiley.
Wasserman, Harry H.
xWasserman, Harry H.
ed. Singlet Oxygen. Acad Pr.
Wasserman, Harvey.
xWasserman, Harvey.
Energy War: Reports from the Front. Lawrence
Hill.
Wasserman, Martin.
xWasserman, Martin.
Dead Bodies Do Not Make a Good Bathroom
Deodorant: Deviant Communications As
Existential Allegories. Mandarin.
Wasserman, Paul.
xWasserman, Paul.

ed. Commodity Prices: A Source Book &
Index. Gale.
ed. Encyclopedia of Business Information
Sources. Gale.
ed. Ethnic Information Sources of the United
States: A Guide to Organizations, Agencies,
Foundations, Institutions, Media, Commercial
& Trade Bodies, Government Programs,
Research Institutes, Libraries & Museums,
Etc.. Gale.
ed. Learning Independently. Gale.
ed. Library Bibliographies & Indexes: A Subject
Guide to Resource Material Available from
Libraries, Information Centers, Library
Schools, & Library Associations in the U. S.
& Canada. Gale.
ed. Reader in Library Administration.
IHS-PDS.

Wasserman, Pauline.
xWasserman, Pauline.
Don't Ask Your Waiter. Stein & Day.
Guide to Fortified Wines. Cornerstone.
Wasserman, Robert H. see Wasserman, Robert Harry.
Wasserman, Robert Harry.
xWasserman, Robert H.
ed. Fundamental Topics in Relativistic Fluid
Mechanics & Magnetohydrodynamics:
Proceedings. Acad Pr.
Wasserman, Sheldon.
xWasserman, Sheldon.
White Wines of the World. Stein & Day.
Wassermann, Gerhard D.
xWassermann, Gerhard D.
Brains & Reasoning: Brain Science As a Basis
of Applied & Pure Philosophy. Shoe String.
Wassermann, Jacob. see Wassermann, Jakob.
Wassermann, Jakob, 1873-1934
xWassermann, Jacob.
Maurizius Case. Liveright.
Wasserstein, Bruce.
xWasserstein, Bruce.
Corporate Finance Law: A Guide for the
Executive. McGraw.
Wasserstein, Wendy.
xWasserstein, Wendy.
Uncommon Women & Others. Avon.
Wasserstrom, Richard. see Wasserstrom, Richard A.
Wasserstrom, Richard A.
xWasserstrom, Richard.
Philosophy & Social Issues: Five Studies. U of
Notre Dame Pr.
Today's Moral Problems. Macmillan.
xWasserstrom, Richard A.
Morality & the Law. Wadsworth Pub.
Wasserstrom, William.
xWasserstrom, William.
Legacy of Van Wyck Brooks: A Study of
Maladies & Motives. S Ill U Pr.
Van Wyck Brooks. U of Minn Pr.
Wasson, Chester R.
xWasson, Chester R.
Buying Behavior & Marketing Decisions.
Irvington.
Competition & Human Behavior. Irvington.
Dynamic Competitive Strategy & Product Life
Cycles. Austin Pr.
Strategy of Marketing Research. Irvington.
Wasson, George S. see Wasson, George Savary.
Wasson, George Savary, 1855-1932
xWasson, George S.
Home from Sea. Arno.
Wasson, John M.
xWasson, John M.
Subject & Structure: An Anthology for Writers.
Little.
Wasson, Valentina P. see Wasson, Valentina Pavlovna.
Wasson, Valentina Pavlovna.
xWasson, Valentina P.

The Chosen Baby. Lippincott.
Wastberg, Per.
xWastberg, Per.
ed. An Anthology of Modern Swedish
Literature. Cross Cult.
Wastell, C.
xWastell, Christopher.
ed. Cimetidine: The Westminster Hospital
Symposium. Churchill.
Wastell, Christopher. see Wastell, C.
Wat, Aleksander.
xWat, Alexander.
Mediterranean Poems. Ardis Pubs.
Wat, Alexander. see Wat, Aleksander.
Watanabe, Hitoshi, 1919-
xWatanabe, Hitoshi.
ed. Human Activity System: Its Spatiotemporal
Structure. Intl Schol Bk Serv.
Watanabe, Ruth T. see Watanabe, Ruth Taiko.
Watanabe, Ruth Taiko.
xWatanabe, Ruth T.
Introduction to Music Research. P-H.
Watanabe, Shigeo.
xWatanabe, Shigeo.
How Do I Put It on?. Philomel.
Watanabe, Yoshio.
xWatanabe, Yoshio.
ed. Cardiac Arrhythmias: Electrophysiologic
Basis for Clinical Interpretation. Grune.
Watanuki, Joji, 1931-
xWatanuki, Joji.
Politics in Postwar Japanese Society. Intl Schol
Bk Serv.

Water Research Centre.
xWater Research Enter.
Water Purification in the EEC. Pergamon.
Water Research Enter. see Water Research Centre.
Water Resources Center, University at Berkeley, Calif.
see California. University. Water Resources Centre.
Water Resources Scientific Information Center.
xWater Resources Scientific Information Center.
ed. Algae Abstracts. IFI Plenum.
Waterbury, John.
xWaterbury, John.
Egypt: Burdens of the Past, Options for the
Future. Ind U Pr.
Hydropolitics of the Nile Valley. Syracuse U
Pr.
North for the Trade: The Life & Times of a
Berber Merchant. U of Cal Pr.
Waterfield, Hermione.
xWaterfield, Hermoine.
Faberge Imperial Eggs & Other Fantasies.
Scribner.
Waterfield, Hermoine. see Waterfield, Hermione.
Waterford, Van.
xWaterford, Van.
All About Telephones. TAB Bks.
Buyer's Guide to Everything Electronic for the
Home. TAB Bks.
Radar Detector Handy Manual. TAB Bks.
Waterhouse, Ellis K. see Waterhouse, Ellis Kirkham.
Waterhouse, Ellis Kirkham, 1905-
xWaterhouse, Ellis K.
Painting in Britain: 1530-1790. Viking Pr.
Waterhouse, George R. see Waterhouse, George Robert.
Waterhouse, George Robert, 1810-1888
xWaterhouse, George R.
A Natural History of the Mammalia. Arno.
Waterhouse, Marian.
xWaterhouse, Marian.
Practical Mathematics in Allied Health: A
Textbook for the Medical Disciplines. Urban
& S.
Waterhouse, R. B. see Waterhouse, Robert Barry.
Waterhouse, Robert Barry, 1922-
xWaterhouse, R. B.
Fretting Corrosion. Pergamon.
Waterhouse, Shirley. see Waterhouse, Shirley A.

Waterhouse, Shirley A.
xWaterhouse, Shirley.
Word Processing Fundamentals. Har-Row.
Waterhouse, W. see Waterhouse, William C.
Waterhouse, William C.
xWaterhouse, W.
Introduction to Affine Group Schemes.
Springer-Verlag.
Waterloo, Stanley, 1846-1913
xWaterloo, Stanley.
Armageddon. Gregg.
The Story of Ab: A Tale of the Time of the
Cave Man. Arno.
Waterlow, Charlotte.
xWaterlow, Charlotte.
Superpowers & Victims: The Outlook for
World Community. P-H.
Waterman, Arthur. see Waterman, Arthur E.
Waterman, Arthur E., 1926-
xWaterman, Arthur.
Chronology of American Literary History.
Merrill.
xWaterman, Arthur E.
Susan Glaspell. Coll & U Pr.
Susan Glaspell. Irvington.
Waterman, Cary, 1942-
xWaterman, Cary.
The Salamander Migration & Other Poems. U
of Pittsburgh Pr.
Waterman, Charles. see Waterman, Charles F.
Waterman, Charles F.
xWaterman, Charles.
The Treasury of Sporting Guns. Random.
xWaterman, Charles F.
Modern Fresh & Salt Water Fly Fishing.
Macmillan.
The Practical Book of Trout Fishing. S&S.
Waterman, Leroy, 1875-
xWaterman, Leroy.
The Religion of Jesus: Christianity's Unclaimed
Heritage of Prophetic Religion. Greenwood.
Waterman, Philip F., 1895-
xWaterman, Philip F.
Story of Superstition. AMS Pr.
Waterman, T. T. see Waterman, Thomas Talbot.
Waterman, Thomas T. see Waterman, Thomas Tileston.
Waterman, Thomas Talbot, 1885-1936
xWaterman, T. T.
Notes on the Ethnology of the Indians of
Puget Sound. Mus Am Ind.
Waterman, Thomas Tileston.
xWaterman, Thomas T.
Domestic Colonial Architecture of Tidewater
Virginia. Da Capo.
Waterman, William R. see Waterman, William Randall.
Waterman, William Randall, 1892-
xWaterman, William R.
Frances Wright. AMS Pr.
Waterman, Willoughby C. see Waterman, Willoughby
Cyrus.
Waterman, Willoughby Cyrus, 1888-
xWaterman, Willoughby C.
Prostitution & Its Repression in New York
City, 1900-1931. AMS Pr.
Waters, Clara E. see Waters, Clara Erskine Clement.
Waters, Clara Erskine Clement, 1834-1916
xWaters, Clara E.
A Handbook of Legendary & Mythological
Art. Longwood Pr.
Waters, Ethel, 1900-
xWaters, Ethel.
His Eye Is on the Sparrow. BJ Pub Group.
His Eye Is on the Sparrow: An Autobiography.
Greenwood.
Waters, Eugene A. see Waters, Eugene Albertice.
Waters, Eugene Albertice, 1899-
xWaters, Eugene A.

A Study of the Application of an Educational
Theory to Science Instruction. AMS Pr.
Waters, Farl J.
xWaters, Farl J.
ABC's of Electronics. Sams.
Waters, Frank, 1902-
xWaters, Frank.
The Earp Brothers of Tombstone: The Story of
Mrs. Virgil Earp. U of Nebr Pr.
People of the Valley. Swallow.
Waters, John F. *see* Waters, John Frederick.
Waters, John Frederick, 1930-
xWaters, John F.
Carnivorous Plants. Watts.
Creatures of Darkness. Walker & Co.
Creatures of Darkness. Schol Bk Serv.
Crime Labs: The Science of Forensic Medicine.
Watts.
Exploring New England Shores: A
Beachcomber's Handbook. Stone Wall Pr.
Fishing. Watts.
Giant Sea Creatures, Real & Fantastic. Follett.
Green Turtle Mysteries. T Y Crowell.
Hungry Sharks. T Y Crowell.
A Jellyfish Is Not a Fish. T Y Crowell.
Marine Animal Collectors: How Creatures of
the Sea Contribute to Science & Our
Knowledge of Man. Hastings.
Maritime Careers. Watts.
Some Mammals Live in the Sea. Dodd.
Summer of the Seals. Warne.
Waters, John J., 1935-
xWaters, John J.
The Otis Family in Provincial & Revolutionary
Massachusetts. Norton.
Otis Family in Provincial & Revolutionary
Massachusetts. U of NC Pr.
Waters, Kathleen.
xWaters, Kathleen.
Medical Records in Health Information. Aspen
Systems.
Waters, Margaret R. *see* Waters, Margaret Ruth.
Waters, Margaret Ruth.
xWaters, Margaret R.
Revolutionary Soldiers Buried in Indiana, with
Supplement. Genealog Pub.
Waters, Thomas F.
xWaters, Thomas F.
The Streams & Rivers of Minnesota. U of
Minn Pr.
Waterson, A. P.
xWaterson, A. P.
An Introduction to the History of Virology.
Cambridge U Pr.
Wathen, James F., 1932-
xWathen, James F.
The Great Sacrilege. TAN Bks Pubs.
Wathen, Thomas W.
xWathen, Thomas W.
Security Subjects: An Officer's Guide to Plant
Protection. C C Thomas.
Watkin, Brian.
xWatkin, Brian.
The National Health Service: The First Phase
1948-1974 & After. Allen Unwin.
Watkin, David, 1941-
xWatkin, David.
English Architecture: A Concise History.
Oxford U Pr.
Morality & Architecture: The Development of
a Theme in Architectural History & Theory
from the Gothic Revival to the Modern
Movement. Oxford U Pr.
Watkin, Edward I. *see* Watkin, Edward Ingram.
Watkin, Edward Ingram, 1888-
xWatkin, Edward I.
Men & Tendencies. Arno.
Watkin, R. V.
xWatkin, R. V.

Computer Technology for Technicians &
Technician Engineers. Longman.
Watkins. *see* Watkins, Joel S.
Watkins, A. M. *see* Watkins, Arthur Martin.
Watkins, Arthur M. *see* Watkins, Arthur Martin.
Watkins, Arthur Martin, 1924-
xWatkins, A. M.
Buying Land: How to Profit from the Last
Great Land Boom. Times Bks.
How to Judge a House. Dutton.
xWatkins, Arthur M.
Building or Buying the High-Quality House at
Lowest Cost. Doubleday.
The New Complete Book of Home
Remodeling, Improvement, & Repair.
Scribner.
Watkins, Carleton E. *see* Watkins, Carleton Emmons.
Watkins, Carleton Emmons.
xWatkins, Carleton E.
Photographs of the Columbia River & Oregon.
Friends Photography.
Watkins, Derek.
xWatkins, Derek.
Wine & Beer Making. David & Charles.
Watkins, Ernest, 1902-
xWatkins, Ernest.
The Cautious Revolution: Britain Today &
Tomorrow. Greenwood.
Watkins, Evan, 1946-
xWatkins, Evan.
The Critical Act: Criticism & Community Yale
U Pr.
Watkins, Floyd C.
xWatkins, Floyd C.
Flesh & the Word: Eliot, Hemingway,
Faulkner. Vanderbilt U Pr.
In Time & Place: Some Origins of American
Fiction. U of Ga Pr.
Practical English Handbook. HM.
Watkins, George P. *see* Watkins, George Pendleton.
Watkins, George Pendleton, 1876-1933
xWatkins, George P.
Growth of Large Fortunes: A Study of
Economic Causes Affecting the Acquisition &
Distribution of Property. Kelley.
Watkins, Glenn. *see* Watkins, Glenn Elson.
Watkins, Glenn Elson, 1927-
xWatkins, Glenn.
Gesualdo: The Man & His Music. U of NC Pr.
Watkins, James, 1919-
xWatkins, James.
Back of Beyond. Cambrian.
Watkins, Jane.
xWatkins, Jane.
Family Affairs. PB.
Watkins, Joel S.
xWatkins.
Our Geological Environment. HR&W.
Watkins, John.
xWatkins, Ward.
Adverse Response to Intravenous Drugs.
Grune.
Watkins, John G. *see* Watkins, John Goodrich.
Watkins, John Goodrich, 1913-
xWatkins, John G.
Objective Measurement of Instrumental
Performance. AMS Pr.
Watkins, John H. *see* Watkins, John Henry.
Watkins, John Henry, 1928-
xWatkins, John H.
Arithmetic & Algebra. Har-Row.
Watkins, John V. *see* Watkins, John Vertrees.
Watkins, John Vertrees.
xWatkins, John V.
Florida Landscape Plants: Native & Exotic. U
Presses Fla.
Watkins, Morris, 1923-
xWatkins, Morris.

Literacy, Bible Reading & Church Growth
Through the Ages. William Carey Lib.
Watkins, Owen. *see* Watkins, Owen C.
Watkins, Owen C.
xWatkins, Owen.
The Puritan Experience: Studies in Spiritual
Autobiography. Schocken.
Watkins, Paul.
xWatkins, Paul.
My Life with Charles Manson. Bantam.
Watkins, R. P.
xWatkins, R. P.
Computer Problem Solving. Krieger.
Watkins, Renee N. *see* Watkins, Renee Neu.
Watkins, Renee Neu.
xWatkins, Renee N.
ed. Humanism & Liberty: Writings on Freedom
from Fifteenth-Century Florence. U of SC Pr.
Watkins, Robert N.
xWatkins, Robert N.
Petroleum Refinery Distillation. Gulf Pub.
Watkins, Ronald.
xWatkins, Ronald.
Hamlet. Rowman.
Watkins, Vernon. *see* Watkins, Vernon Phillips.
Watkins, Vernon Phillips, 1906-1967
xWatkins, Vernon.
Fidelities. New Directions.
I That Was Born in Wales: A New Selection
from the Poems of Vernon Watkins. Verry.
Watkins, Walter B. *see* Watkins, Walter Barker Critz.
Watkins, Walter Barker Critz, 1907-1957
xWatkins, Walter B.
Anatomy of Milton's Verse. Shoe String.
Perilous Balance: The Tragic Genius of Swift,
Johnson & Sterne. Somerset Pub.

Watkins, William J. *see* Watkins, William Jon.
Watkins, William Jon.
xWatkins, William J.
A Fair Advantage. P-H.
The Psychic Experiment Book. P-H.
Watlington, Frank.
xWatlington, Frank.
How to Build & Use Low Cost Hydrophones.
TAB Bks.
Watlington, Patricia.
xWatlington, Patricia.
The Partisan Spirit: Kentucky Politics,
1779-1792. U of NC Pr.
Watman, Mel. *see* Watman, Melvyn Francis.
Watman, Melvyn Francis.
xWatman, Mel.
The Encyclopaedia of Athletics. St Martin.
Watrous, James.
xWatrous, James.
Craft of Old Master Drawings. U of Wis Pr.
Watson, A. A. *see* Watson, Aldren Auld.
Watson, Alan.
xWatson, Alan.
The Law of Succession in the Later Roman
Republic. Oxford U Pr.
The Law of the Ancient Romans. SMU Press.
Watson, Alan D.
xWatson, Alan D.
Society in Colonial North Carolina. NC
Archives.
Watson, Aldren A. *see* Watson, Aldren Auld.
Watson, Aldren Auld, 1917-
xWatson, A. A.
illus. My Garden Grows. Viking Pr.
xWatson, Aldren A.
Country Furniture. NAL.
Country Furniture. T Y Crowell.
My Garden Grows. Viking Pr.
Watson, Alice E. *see* Watson, Alice Erwin.
Watson, Alice Erwin, 1887-
xWatson, Alice E.

Experimental Studies in the Psychology &
Pedagogy of Spelling. AMS Pr.
Watson, Andrew. *see* Watson, Andrew J.
Watson, Andrew J.
xWatson, Andrew.
Living in China. Littlefield.
Living in China. Rowman.
Watson, Andrew S.
xWatson, Andrew S.
Psychiatry for Lawyers. Intl Univs Pr.
Watson, Annita. *see* Watson, Annita B.
Watson, Annita B.
xWatson, Annita.
Care Planning: Chronic Problem - STAT
Solution. KP Med.
Watson, B. W. *see* Watson, Bernard William.
Watson, Barbara B. *see* Watson, Barbara Bellow.
Watson, Barbara Bellow.
xWatson, Barbara B.
Women's Studies: The Social Realities.
Har-Row.
Watson, Bernard William.
xWatson, B. W.
ed. Medical Imaging Techniques. Inst Elect
Eng.
Watson, Burton, 1925-
xWatson, Burton.
tr. Chinese Lyricism: Shih Poetry from the
Second to Twelfth Century. Columbia U Pr.
tr. Chinese Rhyme-Prose: Poems in the Fu
Form from the Han & Six Dynasties Period.
Columbia U Pr.
Early Chinese Literature. Columbia U Pr.
Watson, Charles E.
xWatson, Charles E.
Management Development Through Training.
A-W.
Watson, Charles S., 1931-
xWatson, Charles S.
Antebellum Charleston Dramatists. U of Ala
Pr.
Watson, Clarissa.
xWatson, Clarissa.
The Fourth Stage of Gainsborough Brown.
Penguin.
Watson, Clyde.
xWatson, Clyde.
Father Fox's Pennyrhymes. Schol Bk Serv.
Father Fox's Pennyrhymes. T Y Crowell.
Midnight Moon. Philomel.
Quips & Quirks. T Y Crowell.
Watson, David. *see* Watson, David C. K.
Watson, David C. *see* Watson, David Charles
Cuningham.
Watson, David C. K.
xWatson, David.
I Believe in Evangelism. Eerdmans.
xWatson, David C.
How to Win the War: Strategies for Spiritual
Conflict. Shaw Pubs.
Watson, David Charles Cuningham.
xWatson, David C.
The Great Brain Robbery. Moody.
Watson, David L., 1934-
xWatson, David.
Psychology: What It Is & How to Use It.
Har-Row.
Watson, Derek.
xWatson, Derek.
Bruckner. Biblio Dist.
Bruckner. Littlefield.
Watson, Donald, 1937-
xWatson, Donald.
Energy Conservation Through Building Design.
McGraw.
Watson, Donald A. *see* Watson, Donald Arthur.
Watson, Donald Arthur.
xWatson, Donald A.

Specifications Writing for Architects &
Engineers. McGraw.
Watson, Donald S. *see* Watson, Donald Stevenson.
Watson, Donald Stevenson, ed.
xWatson, Donald S.
Price Theory & Its Uses. HM.
ed. Price Theory in Action: A Book of
Readings. HM.
Watson, E. Lacon. *see* Watson, Edmund Henry Lacon.
Watson, Edmund Henry Lacon, 1865-1948
xWatson, E. Lacon.
Lectures on Dead Authors & Other Essays.
Folcroft.
Watson, Elizabeth. *see* Watson, Elizabeth G.
Watson, Elizabeth E. *see* Watson, Elizabeth Elaine.
Watson, Elizabeth Elaine.
xWatson, Elizabeth E.
God Made the Sea, the Sand, & Me.
Broadman.
Where Are You, God?. Broadman.
Watson, Elizabeth G.
xWatson, Elizabeth.
Guests of My Life. Celo Pr.
Watson, Ernest W. *see* Watson, Ernest William.
Watson, Ernest William, 1884-1969
xWatson, Ernest W.
Art of Pencil Drawing. Watson-Guptill.
Ernest W. Watson's Course in Pencil
Sketching: Four Books in One. Van Nos
Reinhold.
How to Use Creative Perspective. Van Nos
Reinhold.
Watson, Foster, 1860-1929
xWatson, Foster.
Old Grammar Schools. Biblio Dist.
Old Grammar Schools. Kelley.
Watson, Francis, 1907-
xWatson, Francis.
A Concise History of India. Scribner.
A Concise History of India. Thames Hudson.
Daniel Defoe. R West.
Watson, G. J. *see* Watson, George J.
Watson, G. N. *see* Watson, George Neville.
Watson, Geoffrey, 1942-
xWatson, Geoffrey.
The Nooriabad File. Scribner.
Watson, George, 1927-
xWatson, George.
Concise Cambridge Bibliography of English
Literature, 600-1950. Cambridge U Pr.
ed. Literary English Since Shakespeare. Oxford
U Pr.
Watson, George. *see* Watson, George Grimes.
Watson, George Grimes, 1927-
xWatson, George.
The Literary Critics: A Study of English
Descriptive Criticism. Biblio Dist.
Watson, George J.
xWatson, G. J.
Irish Identity & the Literary Revival: Synge,
Yeats, Joyce & O'Casey. B&N.
Watson, George Neville, 1886-
xWatson, G. N.
Complex Integration & Cauchy's Theorem.
Hafner.
Watson, Goodwin B. *see* Watson, Goodwin Barbour.
Watson, Goodwin Barbour, 1899-
xWatson, Goodwin B.
The Measurement of Fairmindedness. AMS Pr.
Watson, Graham, 1913-
xWatson, Graham.
Book Society. Atheneum.
Watson, Hugh J.
xWatson, Hugh J.
Computers for Business: A Managerial
Emphasis. Business Pubns.
Watson, J. N. *see* Watson, J. N. P.
Watson, J. N. P.
xWatson, J. N.

Captain General & Rebel Chief: The Life of
James, Duke of Monmouth. Allen Unwin.
ed. The World's Greatest Horse Stories.
Paddington.
Watson, J. Throck. *see* Watson, Jack Throck.
Watson, Jack M. *see* Watson, Jack Mclaurin.
Watson, Jack McLaurin, 1908-
xWatson, Jack M.
The Education of School Music Teachers for
Community Music Leadership. AMS Pr.
Watson, Jack Throck, 1939-
xWatson, J. Throck.
Introduction to Mass Spectrometry:
Biomedical, Environmental & Forensic
Applications. Raven.
Watson, James, 1936-
xWatson, James.
Liberal Studies in Further Education: An
Informal Survey. Humanities.
Watson, James Wreford.
xWatson, Wreford J.
A Social Geography of the United States.
Longman.
Watson, Jane W. *see* Watson, Jane Werner.
Watson, Jane Werner, 1915-
xWatson, Jane W.
Alternate Energy Sources. Watts.
The Case of the Semi-Human Beans. Coward.
Disney's Numbers Are Fun. Western Pub.
The Golden Book of the Mysterious. Western
Pub.
India Celebrates!. Garrard.
Parade of Soviet Holidays. Garrard.
The People's Republic of China: Red Star of
the East. Garrard.
Tanya & the Geese. Garrard.
Whales. Western Pub.
Watson, Jean, 1940-
xWatson, Jean.
Nursing: The Philosophy & Science of Caring.
Little.
The Pilgrim's Progress in Modern English.
Zondervan.
Watson, Jeannette E.
xWatson, Jeannette E.
Medical-Surgical Nursing & Related
Physiology. Saunders.
Watson, John, 1850-1907
xWatson, John.
Afterwards, & Other Stories. Arno.
Days of Auld Lang Syne. Arno.
The Philosophy of Kant Explained. Folcroft.
The Philosophy of Kant Explained. Garland
Pub.
The Philosophy of Kant Explained. Norwood
Edns.
Watson, John B. *see* Watson, John Broadus.
Watson, John Broadus, 1878-1958
xWatson, John B.
Psychological Care of Infant & Child. Arno.
Watson, John C.
xWatson, John C.
Patient Care & Special Procedures in
Radiologic Technology. Mosby.
Watson, L. S. *see* Watson, Luke S.
Watson, Lawrence.
xWatson, Lawrence.
In a Dark Time. Scribner.
Watson, Lewis.
xWatson, Lewis.
How to Build a Low-Cost House of Stone.
Stonehouse.
Watson, Lillian (Eichler), 1902-
xWatson, Lillian E.
ed. Light from Many Lamps. PB.
Light from Many Lamps. S&S.
Standard Book of Letter Writing & Correct
Social Forms. P-H.
Watson, Lillian E. *see* Watson, Lillian (Eichler).

Watson, Luke S.
xWatson, L. S.
Child Behavior Modification: A Manual for Teachers, Nurses & Parents. Pergamon.

Watson, Lyall.
xWatson, Lyall.
Gifts of Unknown Things. S&S.

Watson, Naomi.
xWatson, Naomi.
Energize with Isometric Quickies. Butterfly Pr.

Watson, Patrick.
xWatson, Patrick.
Alter Ego. Fawcett.
Alter Ego. Viking Pr.

Watson, Patty J. see Watson, Patty Jo.

Watson, Patty Jo.
xWatson, Patty J.
Archeology of the Mammoth Cave Area. Acad Pr.
xWatson, Patty Jo.
Archaeological Ethnography in Western Iran. U of Ariz Pr.

Watson, Paul B. see Watson, Paul Barron.

Watson, Paul Barron, 1861-1948
xWatson, Paul B.
Marcus Aurelius Antoninus. Arno.
Some Women of France. Arno.

Watson, Paul G.
xWatson, Paul G.
Using the Computer in Education: A Briefing for School Decision Makers. Educ Tech Pubns.

Watson, Pauline.
xWatson, Pauline.
Days with Daddy. P-H.
Surprise for Mother. P-H.
The Walking Coat. Walker & Co.
What Would You Do?. P-H.

Watson, Percy.
xWatson, Percy.
Building the Medieval Cathedrals. Lerner Pubns.

Watson, Richard A.
xWatson, Richard A.
Under Plowman's Floor. Zephyrus Pr.

Watson, Richard A. see Watson, Richard Abernathy.

Watson, Richard Abernathy, 1923-
xWatson, Richard A.
Promise & Performance of American Democracy. Wiley.

Watson, Robert.
xWatson, Robert.
Lily Lang. PB.
Lily Lang. St Martin.

Watson, Robert G. see Watson, Robert Grant.

Watson, Robert Grant.
xWatson, Robert G.
Spanish & Portuguese South America During the Colonial Period. Gordon Pr.

Watson, Robert I. see Watson, Robert Irving.

Watson, Robert Irving, 1909-
xWatson, Robert I.
Basic Writings in the History of Psychology. Oxford U Pr.
ed. The History of Psychology & the Behavioral Sciences: A Bibliographic Guide. Springer Pub.
Psychology of the Child & the Adolescent. Macmillan.
R. I. Watson's Selected Papers on the History of Psychology. U Pr of New Eng.

Watson, Ronald.
xWatson, Ronald.
The Twelfth Gun. Nordon Pubns.

Watson, Sara R. see Watson, Sara Ruth.

Watson, Sara Ruth.
xWatson, Sara R.

V. Sackville-West. Twayne.

Watson, Simon.
xWatson, Simon.
No Man's Land. Greenwillow.
The Partisan. Macmillan.

Watson, Thomas E. see Watson, Thomas Edward.

Watson, Thomas Edward, 1856-1922
xWatson, Thomas E.
The People's Party Campaign Book. Arno.

Watson, Tony J.
xWatson, Tony J.
The Personnel Managers: A Study in the Sociology of Work & Employment. Routledge & Kegan.

Watson, Virginia D. see Watson, Virginia Drew.

Watson, Virginia Drew.
xWatson, Virginia D.
Prehistory of the Eastern Highlands of New Guinea. U of Wash Pr.

Watson, W. E. see Watson, William Eric.

Watson, Walter A. see Watson, Walter Allen.

Watson, Walter Allen, 1867-1919
xWatson, Walter A.
Notes on Southside Virginia. Genealog Pub.

Watson, Wendy.
xWatson, Wendy.
illus. Lollipop. T Y Crowell.
Lollipop. Penguin.

Watson, Wilbur H.
xWatson, Wilbur H.
Human Aging & Dying: A Study in Sociocultural Gerontology. St Martin.

Watson, William, 1917-
xWatson, William.
Ancient Chinese Bronzes. Merrimack Bk Serv.
Style in the Arts of China. Penguin.

Watson, William Eric.
xWatson, W. E.
Cell Biology of Brain. Halsted Pr.
Cell Biology of Brain. Methuen Inc.

Watson, William H. see Watson, William Heriot.

Watson, William Heriot, 1899-
xWatson, William H.
Understanding Physics Today. Cambridge U Pr.

Watson, William R., 1887-1973
xWatson, William R.
Retrospective: Recollections of a Montreal Art Dealer. U of Toronto Pr.

Watson, Wreford J. see Watson, James Wreford.

Watt, Alan. see Watt, Alan Stewart.

Watt, Alan John, 1936-
xWatt, J.
Rational Moral Education. Intl Schol Bk Serv.

Watt, Alan Stewart, Sir, 1901-
xWatt, Alan.
Evolution of Australian Foreign Policy (1938-1965). Cambridge U Pr.

Watt, D. E. see Watt, Donald Elmslie Robertson.

Watt, Donald Elmslie Robertson.
xWatt, D. E.
A Biographical Dictionary of Scottish Graduates to A. D. 1410. Oxford U Pr.

Watt, Francis, 1849-1927
xWatt, Francis.
Canterbury Pilgrims & Their Ways. Folcroft.

Watt, George.
xWatt, George.
China Spy. Diane Bks.
China "Spy". Intl Pubns Serv.
A Dictionary of the Economic Products of India. Intl Pubns Serv.
A Dictionary of the Economic Products of India. Intl Schol Bk Serv.

Watt, George C.
xWatt, George C.
Accounting for the Multinational Corporation. Dow Jones-Irwin.

Watt, Harry, 1906-
xWatt, Henry.

Don't Look at the Camera. Merrimack Bk Serv.

Watt, Henry. see Watt, Harry.

Watt, Ian. see Watt, Ian P.

Watt, Ian P.
xWatt, Ian.
Conrad in the Nineteenth Century. U of Cal Pr.

Watt, J. see Watt, Alan John.

Watt, J. A. see Watt, John A.

Watt, James. see Watt, James W.

Watt, James W., 1843-1944
xWatt, James.
Journal of Mule Train Packing in Eastern Washington in the 1860's. Ye Galleon.

Watt, John A.
xWatt, J. A.
Church & the Two Nations in Medieval Ireland. Cambridge U Pr.

Watt, John R. see Watt, John Robertson.

Watt, John Robertson, 1934-
xWatt, John R.
The District Magistrate in Late Imperial China. Columbia U Pr.

Watt, Kenneth E. see Watt, Kenneth E. F.

Watt, Kenneth E. F., 1929-
xWatt, Kenneth E.
Principles of Environmental Science. McGraw.

Watt, Lauchlan M. see Watt, Lauchlan Maclean.

Watt, Lauchlan MacLean, 1867-
xWatt, Lauchlan M.
Douglas's "Aeneid". AMS Pr.
xWatt, Lauchland Maclean.
Thomas Carlyle. Folcroft.
xWatt, Laughlan M.
Attic & Elizabethan Tragedy. Kennikat.
Burns. Folcroft.

Watt, Lauchland Maclean. see Watt, Lauchlan Maclean.

Watt, Laughlan M. see Watt, Lauchlan Maclean.

Watt, Richard M, 1930-
xWatt, Richard M.
Dare Call It Treason. S&S.

Watt, Ruth.
xWatt, Ruth.
Love Unveiled. Bouregy.

Watt, William W. see Watt, William Whyte.

Watt, William Whyte, 1912-
xWatt, William W.
An American Rhetoric. HR&W.

Wattenberg, William W., 1911-
xWattenberg, William W.
Adolescent Years. HarBraceJ.
ed. All Men Are Created Equal. Wayne St U Pr.

Wattenmaker, Beverly. see Wattenmaker, Beverly S.

Wattenmaker, Beverly S.
xWattenmaker, Beverly.
A Guidebook for Teaching Foreign Language: Spanish, French, & German. Allyn.

Watters, Gary Z.
xWatters, Gary Z.
Modern Analysis & Control of Unsteady Flow in Pipelines. Ann Arbor Science.

Watters, Mary, 1896-
xWatters, Mary.
History of the Church in Venezuela, 1810-1930. AMS Pr.

Watters, Pat.
xWatters, Pat.
Climbing Jacob's Ladder: The Arrival of Negroes in Southern Politics. HarBraceJ.

Watters, Ron.
xWatters, Ron.
Ski Camping. Chronicle Bks.

Watters, Thomas, 1840-1901
xWatters, Thomas.
On Yuan Chwang's Travels in India 629-645 A. D.. AMS Pr.

Watters, William R.
xWatters, William R.

Formula Criticism & the Poetry of the Old
   Testament. De Gruyter.
Watterson, John S.
   xWatterson, John S.
   The Egypt-Israel Treaty & the Peace-War
      Prospects for the World. Inst Econ Pol.
Watterson, Joseph.
   xWatterson, Joseph.
   Architecture: A Short History. Norton.
Watts, A. G.
   xWatts, A. G.
   Diversity & Choice in Higher Education.
      Routledge & Kegan.
Watts, Alan. see Watts, Alan Wilson.
Watts, Alan W. see Watts, Alan Wilson.
Watts, Alan Wilson, 1915-
   xWatts, Alan.
   The Art of Contemplation. Pantheon.
   In My Own Way: An Autobiography.
      Pantheon.
   Meditation. BJ Pub Group.
   Tao: The Watercourse Way. Pantheon.
   xWatts, Alan W.
   The Book: On the Taboo Against Knowing
      Who You Are. Random.
   In My Own Way: An Autobiography. Random.
   Nature, Man & Woman. Random.
   Psychotherapy East & West. Random.
Watts, Anthony J. see Watts, Anthony John.
Watts, Anthony John.
   xWatts, Anthony J.
   Allied Submarines. Arco.
   Axis Submarines. Arco.
Watts, D. G. see Watts, David George.
Watts, David George.
   xWatts, D. G.
   The Learning of History. Routledge & Kegan.
Watts, Denis. see Watts, Denis Claude Vernon.
Watts, Denis Claude Vernon.
   xWatts, Denis.
   Tackle Athletics This Way. Soccer.
   Tackle Athletics This Way. Soccer.
Watts, Don.
   xWatts, Don.
   A Catalog of Operational Transfer Functions.
      Garland Pub.
Watts, Franklin.
   xWatts, Franklin.
   Corn. Childrens.
   Let's Find Out About Christmas. Watts.
   Let's Find Out About Easter. Watts.
   Oranges. Childrens.
   Rice. Childrens.
   Wheat. Childrens.
Watts, Harold H. see Watts, Harold Holliday.
Watts, Harold Holliday, 1906-
   xWatts, Harold H.
   Hound & Quarry. R West.
Watts, Harriet.
   xWatts, Harriet.
   How to Start Your Own Preschool Playgroup.
      Universe.
Watts, Henry E. see Watts, Henry Edward.
Watts, Henry Edward, 1826-1904
   xWatts, Henry E.
   Life of Miguel De Cervantes. Gale.
   Life of Miguel De Cervantes. R West.
Watts, John, 1926-
   xWatts, John.
   Teaching. David & Charles.
Watts, L. see Watts, Lynne.
Watts, Lisa.
   xWatts, Lisa.
   The Children's Book of the Earth. EMC.
Watts, Lynne.
   xWatts, L.
   Legibility in Children's Books: A Review of
      Research. Humanities.
Watts, Mabel.
   xWatts, Mabel.

Boy Who Listened to Everyone. Schol Bk Serv.
The Narrow Escapes of Solomon Smart. Schol
   Bk Serv.
While the Horses Galloped to London. Schol
   Bk Serv.
Watts, Marjorie-Ann.
   xWatts, Marjorie-Ann.
   illus. Crocodile Medicine. Warne.
Watts, Nelson B.
   xWatts, Nelson B.
   Practical Endocrine Diagnosis. Lea & Febiger.
Watts, Richard G., 1934-
   xWatts, Richard G.
   Straight Talk About Death with Young People.
      Westminster.
Watts, Robert A.
   xWatts, Robert A.
   Who Are Billy's Friends. Broadman.
Watts, V. Orval. see Watts, Vervon Orval.
Watts, Vervon Orval.
   xWatts, V. Orval.
   Politics vs. Prosperity. Pendell Pub.
Watts-Dunton, Theodore, 1832-1914
   xWatts-Dunton, Theodore.
   Old Familiar Faces. Arno.
Watzlawick, Paul.
   xWatzlawick, Paul.
   How Real Is Real?: Confusion, Disinformation,
      Communication. Random.
   ed. The Interactional View: Studies at the
      Mental Research Institute, Palo Alto,
      1965-1974. Norton.
Wauchope, Robert, 1909-
   xWauchope, Robert.
   They Found the Buried Cities: Exploration &
      Excavation in the American Tropics. U of
      Chicago Pr.
Waud, Roger N.
   xWaud, Roger N.
   Economics. Har-Row.
   Macroeconomics. Har-Row.
   Microeconomics. Har-Row.
Waud, Sydney P.
   xWaud, Sydney P.
   Cooking up a Storm. Chatham Sq.
Waugaman, Charles A.
   xWaugaman, Charles A.
   Cheyenne Artist: The Story of Richard West.
      Friend Pr.
Waugh, Albert E. see Waugh, Albert Edmund.
Waugh, Albert Edmund, 1902-
   xWaugh, Albert E.
   Sundials, Their Theory & Construction. Peter
      Smith.
Waugh, Alec, 1898-
   xWaugh, Alec.
   The Fatal Gift. Manor Bks.
Waugh, Arthur, 1866-1943
   xWaugh, Arthur.
   Alfred Lord Tennyson: A Study of His Life &
      Work. Arden Lib.
Waugh, Auberon.
   xWaugh, Auberon.
   Path of Dalliance. S&S.
Waugh, Carol A. see Waugh, Carol Ann.
Waugh, Carol Ann.
   xWaugh, Carol A.
   The Roller Skating: The Sport of a Lifetime.
      Macmillan.
Waugh, Coulton, 1896-
   xWaugh, Coulton.
   How to Paint with a Knife. Watson-Guptill.
Waugh, Evelyn. see Waugh, Evelyn Arthur St. John.
Waugh, Evelyn Arthur St. John, 1903-
   xWaugh, Evelyn.
   Decline & Fall. Little.
   The End of the Battle. Little.
   When the Going Was Good. Greenwood.
Waugh, Hal.
   xWaugh, Hal.

Fair Chase with Alaskan Guides. Alaska
   Northwest.
Waugh, Norah.
   xWaugh, Norah.
   Corsets & Crinolines. Theatre Arts.
   Cut of Men's Clothes: 1600-1900. Theatre
      Arts.
   Cut of Women's Clothes: 1600-1930. Theatre
      Arts.
Wauthier, Claude, 1923-
   xWauthier, Claude.
   The Literature & Thought of Modern Africa.
      Three Continents.
Wavell, Archibald P. see Wavell, Archibald Percival
   Wavell, 1st Earl Of.
**Wavell, Archibald Percival Wavell, 1st Earl Of,
   1883-1950**
   xWavell, Archibald P.
   Palestine Campaigns. Arno.
Wawn, William T.
   xWawn, William T.
   The South Sea Islanders & the Queensland
      Labour Trade. U Pr of Hawaii.
Wax, Judith.
   xWax, Judith.
   Starting in the Middle. HR&W.
Wax, Murray L. see Wax, Murray Lionel.
Wax, Murray Lionel.
   xWax, Murray L.
   ed. Federal Regulations: Ethical Issues & Social
      Research. Westview.
   Indian-Americans: Unity & Diversity. P-H.
Waxer, Peter H.
   xWaxer, Peter H.
   Nonverbal Aspects of Psychotherapy. Praeger.
Waxman, Chaim I. see Waxman, Chaim Isaac.
Waxman, Chaim Isaac.
   xWaxman, Chaim I.
   The Stigma of Poverty: A Critique of Poverty
      Theories & Policies. Pergamon.
Waxman, Meyer, 1884-
   xWaxman, Meyer.
   A History of Jewish Literature. A S Barnes.
Waxman, Stephanie, 1944-
   xWaxman, Stephanie.
   Growing Up-Feeling Good: A Child's
      Introduction to Sexuality. Panjandrum.
Way, Brian.
   xWay, Brian.
   Development Through Drama. Humanities.
Way, Charles W. Van. see Van Way, Charles W.
Way, Irene.
   xWay, Irene.
   Armada Quest. Zondervan.
Waybill, Marjorie. see Waybill, Marjorie Ann.
Waybill, Marjorie Ann.
   xWaybill, Marjorie.
   Chinese Eyes. Herald Pr.
Wayland, Francis, 1796-1865
   xWayland, Francis.
   Notes on the Principles & Practices of Baptist
      Churches. Arno.
Wayland, Sloan. see Wayland, Sloan Rigdon.
Wayland, Sloan Rigdon.
   xWayland, Sloan.
   The Educational Characteristics of the
      American People. Arno.
Wayman, Alex.
   xWayman, Alex.
   The Buddhist Tantras: Light on Indo-Tibetan
      Esotericism. Weiser.
Wayne, Bennett.
   xWayne, Bennett.

ed. The Founding Fathers. Garrard.

ed. Four Women of Courage. Garrard.

ed. Hockey Hotshots. Garrard.

ed. Indian Patriots of the Eastern Woodlands. Garrard.

ed. Indian Patriots of the Great West. Garrard.

Commentary by & ed. The Super Showmen. Garrard.

Commentaries by & ed. Women Who Dared to Be Different. Garrard.

ed. Women with a Cause. Garrard.

Wayne State University, Detroit, Dept. of English.
  xWayne State University English Department.
    Studies in Honor of John Wilcox. Arno.
Wayne State University English Department. *see* Wayne State University, Detroit, Dept. of English.
Wayne State University Symposium on the Philosophy of Mind, 1962.
  xSymposium In The Philosophy Of Mind - Wayne State University - 1962.
    Intentionality, Minds, & Perception. Arno.
Wayne, Stephen J.
  xWayne, Stephen J.
    The Legislative Presidency. Har-Row.
Wayper, C.L.
  xWayper, C. L.
    Political Thought. Philos Lib.
Wayson, Billy L.
  xWayson, Billy L.
    Local Jails: The New Correctional Dilemma. Lexington Bks.
Wead, Doug.
  xWead, Doug.
    The Compassionate Touch. Bethany Fell.
  xWead, Douglas.
    The Compassionate Touch. Bethany Fell.
Wead, Douglas. *see* Wead, Doug.
Wead, George.
  xWead, George.
    Buster Keaton & the Dynamics of Visual Wit. Arno.
    ed. The Film Career of Buster Keaton. G K Hall.
    The Film Career of Buster Keaton. Redgrave Pub Co.
    The Film Career of Buster Keaton. Two Continents.
Weakley, Clare.
  xWeakley, Clare.
    The Holy Spirit & Power. Logos.
  xWeakley, Clare G.
    Happiness Unlimited: John Wesley's Commentary on the Sermon on the Mount. Logos.
Weakley, Clare G. *see* Weakley, Clare.
Weal, Elke C.
  xWeal, Elke C.
    ed. Combat Aircraft of World War II. Macmillan.
Weales, Gerald C. *see* Weales, Gerald Clifford.
Weales, Gerald Clifford, 1925-
  xWeales, Gerald C.
    Religion in Modern English Drama. Greenwood.
Wearin, Otha D. *see* Wearin, Otha Donner.
Wearin, Otha Donner.
  xWearin, Otha D.
    Grass Grown Trails. Wallace-Homestead.
    I Remember Yesteryear. Wallace-Homestead.
Wearing, J. P.
  xWearing, J. P.
    American & British Theatrical Biography: A Directory. Scarecrow.
    The London Stage 1890-1899: A Calendar of Plays & Players. Scarecrow.
Weart, Edith L. *see* Weart, Edith Lucie.
Weart, Edith Lucie.
  xWeart, Edith L.

The Story of Your Bones. Coward.

The Story of Your Brain & Nerves. Coward.

The Story of Your Respiratory System. Coward.

The Story of Your Skin. Coward.
Weart, Spencer. *see* Weart, Spencer R.
Weart, Spencer R., 1942-
  xWeart, Spencer.
    Scientists in Power. Harvard U Pr.
Weatherburn, Charles E. *see* Weatherburn, Charles Ernest.
Weatherburn, Charles Ernest, 1884-
  xWeatherburn, Charles E.
    First Course in Mathematical Statistics. Cambridge U Pr.
Weatherby, Harold L., 1934-
  xWeatherby, Harold L.
    Cardinal Newman in His Age: His Place in English Theology & Literature. Vanderbilt U Pr.
Weatherby, W. J. *see* Weatherby, William J.
Weatherby, William J.
  xWeatherby, W. J.
    Conversations with Marilyn. Ballantine.
Weatherford, John W., 1924-
  xWeatherford, John W.
    Collective Bargaining & the Academic Librarian. Scarecrow.
Weatherford, Marion T.
  xWeatherford, Marion T.
    Arlington, Child of the Columbia. Oreg Hist Soc.
Weatherford, Richard M.
  xWeatherford, Richard M.
    ed. Stephen Crane: The Critical Heritage. Routledge & Kegan.
Weatherford, Willis D. *see* Weatherford, Willis Duke.
Weatherford, Willis Duke, 1875-1970
  xWeatherford, Willis D.
    Negro from Africa to America. Negro U Pr.
    Race Relations: Adjustment of Whites & Negroes in the United States. Negro U Pr.
Weatherhead, A. K. *see* Weatherhead, Andrew Kingsley.
Weatherhead, A. Kingsley. *see* Weatherhead, Andrew Kingsley.
Weatherhead, Andrew Kingsley, 1923-
  xWeatherhead, A. K.
    Stephen Spender & the Thirties. Bucknell U Pr.
  xWeatherhead, A. Kingsley.
    Leslie Weatherhead: A Personal Portrait. Abingdon.
    A Reading of Henry Green. U of Wash Pr.
Weatherhead, Leslie D. *see* Weatherhead, Leslie Dixon.
Weatherhead, Leslie Dixon, 1893-
  xWeatherhead, Leslie D.
    The Christian Agnostic. Abingdon.
    Life Begins at Death. Abingdon.
    A Private House of Prayer. Abingdon.
Weatherill, Lorna.
  xWeatherill, Lorna.
    Pottery Trade & North Staffordshire 1660-1760. Kelley.
Weatherley, Richard.
  xWeatherley, Richard A.
    Reforming Special Education: Policy Implementation from State Level to Street Level. MIT Pr.
Weatherley, Richard A. *see* Weatherley, Richard.
Weatherly, Tom, 1942-
  xWeatherly, Tom.
    Maumau American Cantos. Corinth Bks.
Weatherman, H. M. *see* Weatherman, Hazel Marie.
Weatherman, Hazel Marie, 1920-
  xWeatherman, H. M.
    Colored Glassware of the Depression Era 1970. Weatherman.
Weaver, Barbara N.
  xWeaver, Barbara N.

The Corporate Memory: A Profitable & Practical Approach to Information Management & Retention Systems. Krieger.

The Corporate Memory: A Profitable, Practical Approach to Information Management & Retention. Wiley.
Weaver, Bennett, 1892-
  xWeaver, Bennett.
    Prometheus Unbound. Shoe String.
    Toward the Understanding of Shelley. Octagon.
Weaver, Bertrand.
  xWeaver, Bertrand.
    His Cross in Your Life. Alba Bks.
Weaver, C. *see* Weaver, Constance.
Weaver, Constance.
  xWeaver, C.
    Psycholinguistics & Reading: From Process to Practice. Winthrop.
  xWeaver, Constance.
    Grammar for Teachers: Perspectives & Definitions. NCTE.
Weaver, Gerald L.
  xWeaver, Gerald L.
    Structural Detailing for Technicians. McGraw.
Weaver, Harriet E. *see* Weaver, Harriett E.
Weaver, Harriett E.
  xWeaver, Harriet E.
    Frosty: A Raccoon to Remember. PB.
  xWeaver, Harriett E.
    Adventures in the Redwoods. Chronicle Bks.
    Frosty: A Raccoon to Remember. Archway.
Weaver, J. E. *see* Weaver, John Ernest.
Weaver, Janet.
  xWeaver, Janet.
    Huggables: How to Make Large Stuffed Animals. Lorenz Pr.
Weaver, Jerry L.
  xWeaver, Jerry L.
    Conflict & Control in Health Care Administration. Sage.
Weaver, John C. *see* Weaver, John Carrier.
Weaver, John Carrier, 1915-
  xWeaver, John C.
    Byways to Hell: An Address to the Phi Beta Kappa Society, University of Wisconsin. U of Wis Pr.
Weaver, John D. *see* Weaver, John Downing.
Weaver, John Downing, 1912-
  xWeaver, John D.
    Brownsville Raid. Norton.
Weaver, John Ernest, 1884-
  xWeaver, J. E.
    Native Vegetation of Nebraska. U of Nebr Pr.
Weaver, P. R. *see* Weaver, Paul Richard Carey.
Weaver, Paul Richard Carey.
  xWeaver, P. R.
    Familia Caesaris: A Social Study of the Emperor's Freedmen & Slaves. Cambridge U Pr.
Weaver, Richard. *see* Weaver, Richard M.
Weaver, Richard L., 1941-
  xWeaver, Richard L.
    Understanding Interpersonal Communication. Scott F.
Weaver, Richard M, 1910-
  xWeaver, Richard.
    A Rhetoric & Composition Handbook. Morrow.
  xWeaver, Richard M.
    The Ethics of Rhetoric. Regnery-Gateway.
    Ideas Have Consequences. U of Chicago Pr.
Weaver, Rip.
  xWeaver, Rip.
    Modern Basic Drafting. Gulf Pub.
    Piper's Pocket Handbook. Gulf Pub.
    Process Piping Drafting. Gulf Pub.
  xWeaver, Rip B.
    Process Piping Design. Gulf Pub.
Weaver, Rip B. *see* Weaver, Rip.
Weaver, Robert C. *see* Weaver, Robert Clifton.

ed. Good Reading: A Guide for Serious
    Readers. Bowker.
Good Reading: A Guide for Serious Readers.
    NAL.
Weber, Karl.
    xWeber, Karl.
    Camargue: Soul of Wilderness. McKay.
    Camargue: The Soul of a Wilderness. Intl
        Pubns Serv.
Weber, Ken.
    xWeber, Ken.
    Canoeing Massachusetts, Rhode Island &
        Connecticut. NH Pub Co.
Weber, Kurt, 1909-
    xWeber, Kurt.
    Lucius Cary. AMS Pr.
Weber, Lenora (Mattingly), 1895-
    xWeber, Lenora M.
    Angel in Heavy Shoes: A Katie Rose Story. T
        Y Crowell.
    Bright Star Falls. T Y Crowell.
    Don't Call Me Katie Rose. T Y Crowell.
    How Long Is Always?. T Y Crowell.
    I Met a Boy I Used to Know. T Y Crowell.
    Meet the Malones. T Y Crowell.
Weber, Lenora M. *see* Weber, Lenora (Mattingly).
Weber, Lillian.
    xWeber, Lillian.
    The English Infant School & Informal
        Education. Workshop Ctr.
Weber, M. *see* Weber, Max.
Weber, Marianne. *see* Weber, Marianne Schnitger.
Weber, Marianne Schnitger, 1870-1954
    xWeber, Marianne.
    Max Weber: A Biography. Wiley.
Weber, Max, 1864-1920
    xWeber, M.
    Ancient Judaism. Free Pr.
    xWeber, Max.
    Critique of Stammler. Free Pr.
    Economy & Society: An Outline of Interpretive
        Sociology. U of Cal Pr.
    General Economic History. Transaction Bks.
    Max Weber on Universities: The Power of the
        State & the Dignity of the Academic Calling
        in Imperial Germany. U of Chicago Pr.
    Max Weber: The Interpretation of Social
        Reality. Schocken.
    Protestant Ethic & the Spirit of Capitalism.
        Scribner.
    Sociology of Religion. Beacon Pr.
Weber, Max M. *see* Weber, Max Maria.
Weber, Max Maria, Freiherr Von, 1822-1881
    xWeber, Max M.
    Carl Maria Von Weber, the Life of an Artist.
        Greenwood.
Weber, Michael. *see* Weber, Michael P.
Weber, Michael P.
    xWeber, Michael.
    The American City. West Pub.
Weber, Nancy, 1942-
    xWeber, Nancy.
    Lily, Where's Your Daddy?. Marek.
Weber, Neal A. *see* Weber, Neal Albert.
Weber, Neal Albert.
    xWeber, Neal A.
    Gardening Ants, the Attines. Am Philos.
Weber, Ralph E. *see* Weber, Ralph Edward.
Weber, Ralph Edward.
    xWeber, Ralph E.
    ed. From the Foreign Press: Two Centuries of
        American History. Krieger.
    United States Diplomatic Codes & Ciphers,
        1775-1938. Precedent Pub.
Weber, Robert L.
    xWeber, Robert L.
    College Physics. McGraw.
    Physics on Stamps. A S Barnes.
Weber, Samuel, 1940-
    xWeber, Samuel M.

Unwrapping Balzac: A Reading of "La Peau de
    Chagrin". U of Toronto Pr.
Weber, Samuel E. *see* Weber, Samuel Edwin.
Weber, Samuel Edwin, 1875-
    xWeber, Samuel E.
    Charity School Movement in Colonial
        Pennsylvania. Arno.
Weber, Samuel M. *see* Weber, Samuel.
Weber, Sarah A. *see* Weber, Sarah Appleton.
Weber, Sarah Appleton.
    xWeber, Sarah A.
    Theology & Poetry in the Middle English
        Lyric: A Study of Sacred History & Aesthetic
        Form. Ohio St U Pr.
Weber, Thad L.
    xWeber, Thad L.
    Alarm Systems & Theft Prevention.
        Butterworths.
Weber, Theodore R.
    xWeber, Theodore R.
    Foreign Policy Is Your Business. John Knox.
Weber, Thomas W., 1930-
    xWeber, Thomas W.
    An Introduction to Process Dynamics &
        Control. Wiley.
Weber, Timothy P.
    xWeber, Timothy P.
    The Future Explored. Victor Bks.
Weber, Tom, 1917-
    xWeber, Tom.
    All the Heroes Are Dead: The Ecology of John
        Steinbeck's Cannery Row. Ramparts.
Weber, William, 1940-
    xWeber, William.
    Music & the Middle Class: The Social
        Structure of Concert Life in London, Paris, &
        Vienna Between 1830 & 1848. Holmes &
        Meier.
Weber, William J.
    xWeber, William J.
    illus. Wild Orphan Friends. HR&W.
Webering, Damascene.
    xWebering, Damascene.
    Theory of Demonstration According to William
        Ockham. Franciscan Inst.
Webern, Anton. *see* Webern, Anton Von.
Webern, Anton Von, 1883-1945
    xWebern, Anton.
    The Path to the New Music. Eur-Am Music.
Weborg, John.
    xWeborg, John.
    Where Is It Written?: An Introductory,
        Annotated Bibliography in Spirituality.
        Franciscan Herald.
Webster. *see* Webster, John.
Webster, A. Blyth. *see* Webster, Adam Blyth.
Webster, Adam Blyth, 1882-1956
    xWebster, A. Blyth.
    George Saintsbury. Folcroft.
Webster, C. C. *see* Webster, Cyril Charles.
Webster, C. K. *see* Webster, Charles Kingsley.
Webster, Charles.
    xWebster, Charles.
    The Great Instauration: Science, Medicine &
        Reform 1626-1660. Holmes & Meier.
    ed. The Intellectual Revolution of the
        Seventeenth Century. Routledge & Kegan.
Webster, Charles. *see* Webster, Charles Kingsley.
Webster, Charles Kingsley, Sir, 1886-1961
    xWebster, C. K.
    Palmerston, Metternich & the European
        System: 1830-1841. Haskell.
    xWebster, Charles.
    Foreign Policy of Palmerston 1830-1841:
        Britain, the Liberal Movement & the Eastern
        Question. Humanities.
Webster, Cyril Charles.
    xWebster, C. C.
    Agriculture in the Tropics. Longman.
Webster, D. *see* Webster, Donald.

Webster, David, 1930-
    xWebster, David.
    How to Do a Science Project. Watts.
    Let's Find Out About Mosquitoes. Watts.
Webster, Donald.
    xWebster, D.
    ed. Beryllium Science & Technology. Plenum
        Pub.
Webster, Donald B. *see* Webster, Donald Blake.
Webster, Donald Blake.
    xWebster, Donald B.
    Decorated Stoneware Pottery of North
        America. C E Tuttle.
Webster, Donald E. *see* Webster, Donald Everett.
Webster, Donald Everett.
    xWebster, Donald E.
    The Turkey of Ataturk: Social Process in the
        Turkish Reformation. AMS Pr.
Webster, Elizabeth J.
    xWebster, Elizabeth J.
    Professional Approaches with Parents of
        Handicapped Children. C C Thomas.
Webster, Frederick. *see* Webster, Frederick E.
Webster, Frederick E.
    xWebster, Frederick.
    Organizational Buying Behavior. P-H.
    xWebster, Frederick E.
    Industrial Marketing Strategy. Ronald Pr.
    Marketing Communication: Modern
        Promotional Strategy. Wiley.
Webster, G. D. *see* Webster, Gary D.
Webster, Gary D.
    xWebster, G. D.
    Chester Through Derry Conodonts &
        Stratigraphy of Northern Clark & Southern
        Lincoln Counties, Nevada. U of Cal Pr.
Webster, Graham.
    xWebster, Graham.
    Practical Archaeology: An Introduction to
        Archaeological Field Work Excavations. St
        Martin.
Webster, Grant.
    xWebster, Grant.
    The Republic of Letters: A History of Postwar
        American Literary Opinion. Johns Hopkins.
Webster, Henry K. *see* Webster, Henry Kitchell.
Webster, Henry Kitchell, 1875-1932
    xWebster, Henry K.
    The Banker & the Bear: The Story of a Corner
        in Lard. Irvington.
    Who Is the Next. Garland Pub.
Webster, Hutton, 1875-1955
    xWebster, Hutton.
    Rest Days, the Christian Sunday, the Jewish
        Sabbath & Their Historical &
        Anthropological Prototypes. Gale.
    Taboo: A Sociological Study. Octagon.
Webster, J. B. *see* Webster, James Bertin.
Webster, James Bertin.
    xWebster, J. B.
    ed. Chronology, Migration & Drought in
        Interlacustrine Africa. Holmes & Meier.
Webster, Jan, 1924-
    xWebster, Jan.
    Beggarman's Country. St Martin.
    Colliers Row. Lippincott.
    Colliers Row. Warner Bks.
    Saturday City. St Martin.
Webster, Jay.
    xWebster, Jay.
    Auto Mechanics. Glencoe.
    Principles of Automatic Transmissions.
        Prakken.
Webster, Jean, 1876-1916
    xWebster, Jean.
    Dear Enemy. Gregg.
Webster, John, 1580?-1625?
    xWebster.

The Devil's Law Case. Norton.
The Duchess of Malfi. Norton.
The White Devil. Norton.
xWebster, John.
The Devil's Law-Case. U of Nebr Pr.
Duchess of Malfi. Hill & Wang.
Duchess of Malfi. Barron.
The Duchess of Malfi. AHM Pub.
Introduction to Fungi. Cambridge U Pr.
The White Devil. Johns Hopkins.
White Devil. U of Nebr Pr.
Webster, John C. see Webster, John C. B.
Webster, John C. B., 1935-
xWebster, John C.
The Christian Community & Change in
Nineteenth Century North India. South Asia
Bks.
Webster, John G.
xWebster, John G.
Medical Instrumentation: Application &
Design. HM.
Webster, John M.
xWebster, John M.
ed. Economic Nematology. Acad Pr.
Webster, Laura J. see Webster, Laura Josephine.
Webster, Laura Josephine.
xWebster, Laura J.
Operation of the Freedmen's Bureau in South
Carolina. Russell.
Webster, Murray.
xWebster, Murray.
Sources of Self Evaluation: A Formal Theory
of Significant Others & Social Influence.
Wiley.
Webster, Ned.
xWebster, Ned.
ed. Penny Crossword Puzzles. PB.
Webster, Nell.
xWebster, Nell.
Eating & Living the TM Way. PB.
Webster, Nesta. see Webster, Nesta Helen.
Webster, Nesta Helen.
xWebster, Nesta.
World Revolution: The Plot Against
Civilization. Gordon Pr.
Webster, Noah, 1758-1843
xWebster, Noah.
American Dictionary of the English Language.
Found Am Christ.
An American Selection of Lessons in Reading
& Speaking. Arno.
Collection of Papers on Political, Literary &
Moral Subjects. B Franklin.
Webster, Norman, 1941-
xWebster, Norman.
City People, City Life. EMC.
Posters & Pedicarts. EMC.
Stubborn Land. EMC.
Webster, Owen.
xWebster, Owen.
The Outward Journey. Bks Australia.
Webster, R.
xWebster, R.
Quantitative & Numerical Methods in Soil
Classification & Survey. Oxford U Pr.
Webster, Richard A, 1928-
xWebster, Richard A.
The Cross & the Fasces: Christian Democracy
and Fascism in Italy. Stanford U Pr.
Industrial Imperialism in Italy, 1908-1915. U of
Cal Pr.
Webster, Ronald C.
xWebster, Ronald C.
Hill Country Poems. McClain.
Webster, Thomas B. see Webster, Thomas Bertram
Lonsdale.
Webster, Thomas Bertram Lonsdale, 1905-
xWebster, Thomas B.

Art & Literature in Fourth Century Athens.
Greenwood.
Wechsberg, Joseph.
xWechsberg, Joseph.
Cooking of Vienna's Empire. Time-Life.
Cooking of Vienna's Empire. Silver.
The Danube. Newsweek.
In Leningrad. Doubleday.
Looking for a Bluebird. Greenwood.
Wechsler, Arnold.
xWechsler, Arnold.
Dr. Wechsler's New You Diet. Citadel Pr.
Wechsler, Harold. see Wechsler, Harold S.
Wechsler, Harold S., 1946-
xWechsler, Harold.
The Qualified Student: A History of Selective
College Admission in America. Wiley.
Wechsler, Henry.
xWechsler, Henry.
Explorations in Nursing Research. Human Sci
Pr.
ed. The Horizons of Health. Harvard U Pr.
ed. Social Work Research in the Human
Services. Human Sci Pr.
Wechsler, James. see Wechsler, James Arthur.
Wechsler, James A. see Wechsler, James Arthur.
Wechsler, James Arthur, 1915-
xWechsler, James.
Revolt on the Campus. U of Wash Pr.
xWechsler, James A.
Age of Suspicion. Greenwood.
Reflections of an Angry Middle-Aged Editor.
Arno.
Wechsler, Louis K.
xWechsler, Louis K.
College Entrance Examinations. B&N.
Wechter, Nell W. see Wechter, Nell Wise.
Wechter, Nell Wise.
xWechter, Nell W.
Swamp Girl. Blair.
Taffy of Torpedo Junction. Blair.
Weck, Thomas L., 1942-
xWeck, Thomas L.
Moving up Quickly: How to Use Executive
Job-Hunting Techniques to Land a Better
Job. Wiley.
Wecter, Dixon, 1906-1950
xWecter, Dixon.
When Johnny Comes Marching Home.
Greenwood.
Wedberg, Anders, 1913-
xWedberg, Anders.
Plato's Philosophy of Mathematics.
Greenwood.
Wedde, Ian.
xWedde, Ian.
Spells for Coming Out. Oxford U Pr.
Wedderburn, Dorothy.
xWedderburn, Dorothy.
ed. Poverty, Inequality & Class Structure.
Cambridge U Pr.
Worker's Attitudes & Technology. Cambridge
U Pr.
Wedding, Dan.
xWedding, Dan.
Great Cases in Psychotherapy. Peacock Pubs.
Weddle, Ferris.
xWeddle, Ferris.
Tall Like a Pine. A Whitman.
Weddle, Perry.
xWeddle, Perry.
Argument: A Guide to Critical Thinking.
McGraw.
Wedeck, H. E. see Wedeck, Harry Ezekiel.
Wedeck, Harry E. see Wedeck, Harry Ezekiel.
Wedeck, Harry Ezekiel, 1894-
xWedeck, H. E.

Dictionary of Astrology. Citadel Pr.
Dictionary of Astrology. Philos Lib.
Dictionary of Gypsy Life & Lore. Philos Lib.
ed. Dictionary of Pagan Religions. Philos Lib.
xWedeck, Harry E.
ed. Dictionary of Aphrodisiacs. Philos Lib.
Dictionary of Pagan Religions. Citadel Pr.
ed. Dictionary of Spiritualism. Philos Lib.
Triumph of Satan. Citadel Pr.
The Triumph of Satan. Univ Bks.
Wedekind, Frank.
xWedekind, Frank.
The Lulu Plays. Riverrun Texas.
Wedel, Leonard E.
xWedel, Leonard E.
Church Staff Administration: Practical
Approaches. Broadman.
Wedel, Waldo R. see Wedel, Waldo Rudolph.
Wedel, Waldo Rudolph, 1908-
xWedel, Waldo R.
Prehistoric Man on the Great Plains. U of Okla
Pr.
Wedemeyer, Karl E. see Wedemeyer, Karl Eric.
Wedemeyer, Karl Eric.
xWedemeyer, Karl E.
Interstate Natural Gas Supply & Intrastate
Market Behavior. Arno.
Wedepohl, K. H. see Wedepohl, Karl Hans.
Wedepohl, Karl Hans.
xWedepohl, K. H.
ed. Handbook of Geochemistry.
Springer-Verlag.
Wedertz, Bill.
xWedertz, Bill.
ed. Dictionary of Naval Abbreviations. Naval
Inst Pr.
Wedertz, Frank S.
xWedertz, Frank S.
Mono Diggings. Chalfant Pr.
Wedge, Eleanor F.
xWedge, Eleanor F.
ed. Nefertiti Graffiti: Comments on an
Exhibition. Bklyn Mus.
Wedgewood, Cicely Veronica, 1910-
xWedgewood, Cicily V.
Thirty Years War. Humanities.
Wedgewood, Cicily V. see Wedgewood, Cicely Veronica.
Wedgeworth, Ann.
xWedgeworth, Ann.
Magnificent Strangers. Gospel Pub.
Wedgeworth, Robert.
xWedgeworth, Robert.
ed. ALA World Encyclopedia of Library &
Information Services. ALA.
Wedgwood, Cicely V. see Wedgwood, Cicely Veronica.
Wedgwood, Cicely Veronica, 1910-
xWedgwood, Cicily V.
Richelieu & the French Monarchy. Macmillan.
World of Rubens. Time-Life.
Wedgwood, Henry A. see Wedgwood, Henry Allen.
Wedgwood, Henry Allen, 1799-1885
xWedgwood, Henry A.
People of the Potteries. Kelley.
Wedgwood, Josiah, 1899-1968
xWedgwood, Josiah.
Economics of Inheritance. Kennikat.
Wedmore, Frederick, Sir, 1844-1921
xWedmore, Frederick.
Life of Honore De Balzac. Folcroft.
Life of Honore De Balzac. Kennikat.
Weed, L. L. see Weed, Lawrence L.
Weed, Lawrence L.
xWeed, L. L.
ed. Implementing the Problem-Oriented
Medical Record. Med Communications.
Weed, Michael. see Weed, Michael R.
Weed, Michael R.
xWeed, Michael.

Letters of Paul to the Ephesians, Colossians, &
Philemon. Sweet.

Weed, Thurlow, 1797-1882
xWeed, Thurlow.
Life of Thurlow Weed. AMS Pr.

Weeden, Theodore J.
xWeeden, Theodore J.
Mark-Traditions in Conflict. Fortress.

Weeden, W. B. see Weeden, William Babcock.
Weeden, William B. see Weeden, William Babcock.

Weeden, William Babcock, 1834-1912
xWeeden, W. B.
Indian Money As a Factor in New England
Civilization. Gordon Pr.
Indian Money As a Factor in New England
Civilization. Johnson Repr.
xWeeden, William B.
Indian Money As a Factor in New England
Civilization. AMS Pr.

Weekes, Blanche E. see Weekes, Blanche Ethel.

Weekes, Blanche Ethel.
xWeekes, Blanche E.
The Influence of Meaning on Children's
Choices of Poetry. AMS Pr.

Weekes, Claire.
xWeekes, Claire.
Hope & Help for Your Nerves. Bantam.
Hope & Help for Your Nerves. Dutton.
Peace from Nervous Suffering. Bantam.
Peace from Nervous Suffering. Dutton.

Weekes, Richard V., 1924-
xWeekes, Richard V.
ed. Muslim Peoples: A World Ethnographic
Survey. Greenwood.

Weekley, Ernest, 1865-1954
xWeekley, Ernest.
Adjectives & Other Words. Arno.
Adjectives & Other Words. Folcroft.
More Words, Ancient & Modern. Arno.
Surnames. Folcroft.
Words Ancient & Modern. Folcroft.
Words & Names. Arno.

Weekley, Richard.
xWeekley, Richard.
The Adventures of Chet Blake - Plastic Man.
Crescent Pubns.

Weeks, Albert. see Weeks, Albert Loren.

Weeks, Albert Loren, 1923-
xWeeks, Albert.
The Troubled Detente. NYU Pr.

Weeks, David A.
xWeeks, David A.
ed. Human Resources: Toward Rational Policy
Planning. Conference Bd.
National Health Insurance & Corporate Benefit
Plans: An Interim Report. Conference Bd.
ed. Rethinking Employee Benefits
Assumptions. Conference Bd.

Weeks, Edward, 1898-
xWeeks, Edward.
Fresh Waters. Little.

Weeks, Helen F. see Weeks, Helen Foss.

Weeks, Helen Foss, 1883-
xWeeks, Helen F.
Factors Influencing the Choice of Courses by
Students in Certain Liberal Arts Colleges.
AMS Pr.

Weeks, Jim.
xWeeks, Jim.
The Sooners: A Story of Oklahoma Football.
Strode.

Weeks, John.
xWeeks, John.
Airborne Equipment: A History of Its
Development. Hippocrene Bks.
Pyramids. Cambridge U Pr.
The Pyramids. Lerner Pubns.

Weeks, John R. see Weeks, John Robert.

Weeks, John Robert, 1944-
xWeeks, John R.

Population: An Introduction to Concepts &
Issues. Wadsworth Pub.

Weeks, Kent M., 1937-
xWeeks, Kent M.
Frwd. by Ombudsmen Around the World: A
Comparative Chart. Inst Gov Stud Berk.

Weeks, Kent R.
xWeeks, Kent R.
Classic Christian Townsite at Arminna West.
Penn-Yale Expedit.
The Classic Christian Townsite at Arminna
West. Univ Mus of U PA.

Weeks, Morris.
xWeeks, Morris.
illus. The Last Wild Horse. HM.

Weeks, Nora.
xWeeks, Nora.
The Medical Discoveries of Edward Bach,
Physician. Keats.

Weeks, Philip E.
xWeeks, Philip E.
After You Receive Power. Morehouse.

Weeks, Raymond, 1863-1954
xWeeks, Raymond.
Hound-Tuner of Callaway. Arno.

Weeks, S. B. see Weeks, Stephen Beauregard.
Weeks, Stephen B. see Weeks, Stephen Beauregard.

Weeks, Stephen Beauregard, 1865-1918
xWeeks, S. B.
The Religious Development in the Province of
North Carolina. Johnson Repr.
xWeeks, Stephen B.
Church & State in North Carolina. AMS Pr.
Church & State in North Carolina. Johnson
Repr.
History of Public School Education in
Alabama. Negro U Pr.
The Religious Development in the Province of
North Carolina. AMS Pr.
Southern Quakers & Slavery: A Study in
Institutional History. AMS Pr.
Southern Quakers & Slavery: A Study in
Institutional History. Humanities.

Weeks, Thelma E.
xWeeks, Thelma E.
Born to Talk. Newbury Hse.

Weeks, Walter. see Weeks, Walter Leroy.

Weeks, Walter Leroy.
xWeeks, Walter.
Antenna Engineering. McGraw.

Weems, Benjamin. see Weems, Benjamin B.

Weems, Benjamin B.
xWeems, Benjamin.
Reform, Rebellion & the Heavenly Way. U of
Ariz Pr.

Weems, David B.
xWeems, David B.
How to Design, Build & Test Complete
Speaker Systems. TAB Bks.

Weems, John E. see Weems, John Edward.

Weems, John Edward.
xWeems, John E.
A Weekend in September. Tex A&M Univ Pr.
xWeems, John Edward.
The Tornado. Doubleday.

Weems, Mason L. see Weems, Mason Locke.

Weems, Mason Locke, 1759-1825
xWeems, Mason L.
Life of Washington. Harvard U Pr.

Weerts, Richard K.
xWeerts, Richard K.
ed. Original Manuscript Music for Wind &
Percussion Instruments. Music Ed.

Weese, Asa O. see Weese, Asa Orrin.

Weese, Asa Orrin, 1885-1955
xWeese, Asa O.
Animal Ecology of an Illinois Elm-Maple
Forest. Johnson Repr.

Weese, Samuel H., 1935-
xWeese, Samuel H.

Non-Admitted Insurance in the United States.
Irwin.

Wegbreit, Ben.
xWegbreit, Ben.
Studies in Extensible Programming Languages.
Garland Pub.

Wegelin, Christof, 1911-
xWegelin, Christof.
Image of Europe in Henry James. SMU Press.

Wegen, Ron. see Wegen, Ronald.

Wegen, Ronald.
xWegen, Ron.
illus. Where Can the Animals Go.
Greenwillow.

Wegener, A. see Wegener, Alfred Lothar.
Wegener, Alfred. see Wegener, Alfred Lothar.

Wegener, Alfred Lothar, 1880-1930
xWegener, A.
Origin of Continents & Oceans. Gordon Pr.
xWegener, Alfred.
Origin of Continents & Oceans. Dover.

Wegener, Charles.
xWegener, Charles.
Liberal Education & the Modern University. U
of Chicago Pr.

Wegener, Frank C. see Wegener, Frank Corliss.

Wegener, Frank Corliss, 1908-
xWegener, Frank C.
The Organic Philosophy of Education.
Greenwood.

Wegener, Maj-Greth.
xWegener, Maj-Greth.
American Cooking for Foreign Lands. North
Castle.

Wegner, Daniel M.
xWegner, Daniel M.
Implicit Psychology: An Introduction to Social
Cognition. Oxford U Pr.
ed. The Self in Social Psychology. Oxford U
Pr.

Wegner, Peter.
xWegner, Peter.
jt. ed. & ed. Research Directions in Software
Technology. MIT Pr.

Wegner, Robert. see Wegner, Robert E. C.

Wegner, Robert E. C.
xWegner, Robert.
Cases in Organizational & Administrative
Behavior. P-H.

Wehman, Paul.
xWehman, Paul H.
Curriculum Design for Severely & Profoundly
Handicapped. Human Sci Pr.

Wehman, Paul H. see Wehman, Paul.

Wehr, Hans.
xWehr, Hans.
A Dictionary of Modern Written Arabic.
Spoken Lang Serv.

Wehr, Paul.
xWehr, Paul.
Conflict Regulation. Westview.

Wehringer, Cameron K., 1924-
xWehringer, Cameron K.
Arbitration Precepts & Principles. Oceana.
When & How to Choose an Attorney. Oceana.

Wehrle, Edmund S.
xWehrle, Edmund S.
Britain, China & the Antimissionary Riots,
1891-1900. U of Minn Pr.

Wehrmaker, Suzanne. see Wehrmaker, Suzanne L.

Wehrmaker, Suzanne L.
xWehrmaker, Suzanne.
Case Studies in Neurological Nursing. Little.

Wehrum, Victoria.
xWehrum, Victoria.
The American Theatre. Watts.

Wei, C. C.
xWei, C. C.

The Precision Bidding System in Bridge.
    Dover.
Wei, James.
    xWei, James.
        The Structure of the Chemical Processing
            Industries: Function & Economics. McGraw.
Wei, Wen P. *see* Wei, Wen Pin.
Wei, Wen Pin, 1888-
    xWei, Wen P.
        Currency Problem in China. AMS Pr.
Weibel, Kathleen.
    xWeibel, Kathleen.
        ed. The Role of Women in Librarianship,
            1876-1976: The Entry, Advancement &
            Struggle for Equalization in One Profession.
            Oryx Pr.
Weich, I. Edward.
    xWeich, I. Edward.
        Real Estate. Har-Row.
Weichert, Charles K. *see* Weichert, Charles Kipp.
Weichert, Charles Kipp, 1902-
    xWeichert, Charles K.
        Anatomy of the Chordates. McGraw.
Weichlein, William J. *see* Weichlein, William Jesset.
Weichlein, William Jesset, 1917-
    xWeichlein, William J.
        A Checklist of American Music Periodicals,
            1850-1900. Info Coord.
Weichmann, Louis J.
    xWeichmann, Louis J.
        A True History of the Assassination of
            Abraham Lincoln & the Conspiracy of 1865.
            Knopf.
Weick, Carl. *see* Weick, Carl B.
Weick, Carl B.
    xWeick, Carl.
        Applied Electronics. McGraw.
Weick, Karl E.
    xWeick, Karl E.
        Social Psychology of Organizing. A-W.
Weidemann, Charles C. *see* Weidemann, Charles Conrad.
Weidemann, Charles Conrad, 1895-
    xWeidemann, Charles C.
        How to Construct the True-False Examination.
            AMS Pr.
Weidenaar, Dennis J.
    xWeidenaar, Dennis J.
        Economics: An Introduction to the World
            Around You. A-W.
Weidenbaum, Murray L.
    xWeidenbaum, Murray L.
        The Future of Business Regulation: Private
            Action & Public Demand. Am Mgmt.
        Government Credit Subsidies for Energy
            Development. Am Enterprise.
        Prospects for Reallocating Public Resources: A
            Study in Federal-State Fiscal Relations. Am
            Enterprise.
Weidenfeld, Sheila R. *see* Weidenfeld, Sheila Rabb.
Weidenfeld, Sheila Rabb.
    xWeidenfeld, Sheila R.
        First Lady's Lady: With the Fords at the
            White House. Putnam.
Weidenreich, Franz, 1873-1948
    xWeidenreich, Franz.
        Giant Early Man from Java & South China.
            AMS Pr.
Weidensee, Victor. *see* Weidensee, Victor J.
Weidensee, Victor J.
    xWeidensee, Victor.
        Instrumental Music in the Public Schools:
            Organization & Administration. Taplinger.
Weider, Joe.
    xWeider, Joe.
        The IFBB Album of Bodybuilding All-Stars.
            Dutton.
Weidhorn, Manfred, 1931-
    xWeidhorn, Manfred.

Sword & Pen: A Survey of the Writings of Sir
    Winston Churchill. U of NM Pr.
Weidman, Jerome, 1913-
    xWeidman, Jerome.
        A Family Fortune. PB.
        A Family Fortune. S&S.
        The Price Is Right. Manor Bks.
Weidmann, J. *see* Weidmann, Joachim.
Weidmann, Joachim.
    xWeidmann, J.
        Linear Operators in Hilbert Spaces.
            Springer-Verlag.
Weiers, Ronald M.
    xWeiers, Ronald M.
        Chilton's More-Miles-per Dollar Guide.
            Chilton.
Weierstrass, Karl T. *see* Weierstrass, Karl Theodor
    Wilhelm.
Weierstrass, Karl Theodor Wilhelm.
    xWeierstrass, Karl T.
        Mathematische Werke. Johnson Repr.
Weigall, Arthur. *see* Weigall, Arthur Edward Pearse
    Brome.
Weigall, Arthur E. *see* Weigall, Arthur Edward Pearse
    Brome.
Weigall, Arthur Edward Pearse Brome, 1880-1934
    xWeigall, Arthur.
        Ancient Egypt. R West.
        Glory of the Pharaohs. Kennikat.
        The Paganism in Our Christianity. Gordon Pr.
    xWeigall, Arthur E.
        Ancient Egypt. Folcroft.
        Personalities of Antiquity. Arno.
Weigand, George.
    xWeigand, George.
        How to Succeed in High School & Score High
            on College Entrance Examinations. Barron.
Weigand, Hermann J. *see* Weigand, Hermann John.
Weigand, Hermann John, 1892
    xWeigand, Hermann J.
        The Modern Ibsen: A Reconsideration. Arno.
        Thomas Mann's Novel, "Der Zauberberg": A
            Study. AMS Pr.
Weigand, J. *see* Weigand, James E.
Weigand, James E.
    xWeigand, J.
        ed. Implementing Teacher Competencies:
            Positive Approaches to Personalizing
            Education. P-H.
    xWeigand, James E.
        ed. Developing Teacher Competencies. P-H.
Weigel, John A.
    xWeigel, John A.
        Colin Wilson. Twayne.
        Lawrence Durrell. Dutton.
        Lawrence Durrell. Twayne.
Weigelin, E. *see* Weigelin, Erich.
Weigelin, Erich.
    xWeigelin, E.
        Ophthalmodynamometry. Hafner.
Weigelt, Curt H., 1883-
    xWeigelt, Curt H.
        Sienese Painting of the Trecento. Hacker.
Weiger, John G.
    xWeiger, John G.
        Cristobal De Virues. Twayne.
        The Individuated Self: Cervantes & the
            Emergence of the Individual. Ohio U Pr.
        The Valencian Dramatists of Spain's Golden
            Age. Twayne.
Weight, Harold O., 1911-
    xWeight, Harold O.
        Lost Mines of Death Valley. Calico Pr.
Weigle, Luther A. *see* Weigle, Luther Allan.
Weigle, Luther Allan, 1880-
    xWeigle, Luther A.

English New Testament from Tyndale to the
    Revised Standard Version. Greenwood.
The Glory Days: From the Life of Luther
    Allan Weigle. Friend Pr.
Weigle, Marta.
    xWeigle, Marta.
        Brothers of Light, Brothers of Blood: The
            Penitentes of the Southwest. U of NM Pr.
        A Penitente Bibliography. U of NM Pr.
Weigle, Oscar.
    xWeigle, Oscar.
        Jokes, Riddles, Funny Stories. G&D.
Weigle, Palmy, 1920-
    xWeigle, Palmy.
        Double Weave. Watson-Guptill.
Weigley, R. F. *see* Weigley, Russell Frank.
Weigley, Russell F. *see* Weigley, Russell Frank.
Weigley, Russell Frank.
    xWeigley, R. F.
        History of the United States Army. Macmillan.
    xWeigley, Russell F.
        ed. The American Military: Readings in the
            History of the Military in American Society.
            A-W.
        The American Way of War: A History of
            United States Military Strategy & Policy.
            Macmillan.
Weihaupt, John G.
    xWeihaupt, John G.
        Exploration of the Oceans: An Introduction to
            Oceanography. Macmillan.
Weihofen, Henry.
    xWeihofen, Henry.
        Legal Services & Community Mental Health
            Centers. Am Psychiatric.
        Legal Writing Style. West Pub.
        The Urge to Punish: New Approaches to the
            Problem of Mental Irresponsibility for Crime.
            Greenwood.
Weihs, Erika.
    xWeihs, Erika.
        Count the Cats. Doubleday.
Weihs, Thomas J. *see* Weihs, Thomas Johannes.
Weihs, Thomas Johannes.
    xWeihs, Thomas J.
        Children in Need of Special Care. Schocken.
Weik, Martin H.
    xWeik, Martin H.
        Standard Dictionary of Computers &
            Information Processing. Hayden.
Weik, Mary H. *see* Weik, Mary Hays.
Weik, Mary Hays.
    xWeik, Mary H.
        A House on Liberty Street. Atheneum.
Weil. *see* Weil, Lisl.
Weil, A. *see* Weil, Andre.
Weil, Andre.
    xWeil, A.
        Number Theory for Beginners. Springer-Verlag.
Weil, Andrew.
    xWeil, Andrew.
        The Natural Mind: A New Way of Looking at
            Drugs & the Higher Consciousness. HM.
Weil, Dorothy.
    xWeil, Dorothy.
        In Defense of Women: Susanna Rowson,
            1762-1824. Pa St U Pr.
Weil, Gordon L. *see* Weil, Gordon Lee.
Weil, Gordon Lee.
    xWeil, Gordon L.
        The Consumer's Guide to Banks. Stein & Day.
Weil, Lisl.
    xWeil.
        Candy Egg Bunny. Schol Bk Serv.
    xWeil, Lisl.

illus. The Candy Egg Bunny. Holiday.
illus. Chicken. Warne.
Donkey Head. Atheneum.
Esther. Atheneum.
illus. Fat Ernest. Schol Bk Serv.
illus. The Funny Old Bag. Schol Bk Serv.
Gertie & Gus. Schol Bk Serv.
illus. Gillie & the Flattering Fox. Atheneum.
illus. Hopping Knapsack. Macmillan.
illus. Melissa. Macmillan.
illus. Melissa's Friend Fabrizzio. Macmillan.
Ralphi Rhino. Walker & Co.
Weil, M. H. *see* Weil, Max Harry.
Weil, Mark. *see* Weil, Mark S.
Weil, Mark S.
xWeil, Mark.
The History & Decoration of the Ponte S.
Angelo. Pa St U Pr.
Weil, Max Harry.
xWeil, M. H.
Diagnosis & Treatment of Shock. Krieger.
Weil, Mildred. *see* Weil, Mildred W.
Weil, Mildred W.
xWeil, Mildred.
ed. The Sociology of the Arts. Interstate.
xWeil, Mildred W.
Marriage, the Family, & Society: Toward a
Sociology of Marriage & the Family.
Interstate.
Weil, Robert, d. 1906
xWeil, Robert.
The Legal Status of the Indian. AMS Pr.
Weil, Simone, 1909-1943
xWeil, Simone.
Gravity & Grace. Octagon.
Lectures on Philosophy. Cambridge U Pr.
Oppression & Liberty. U of Mass Pr.
Weil, William B.
xWeil, William B.
Fluid & Electrolyte Metabolism in Infants &
Children: A Unified Approach. Grune.
Weiland, Barbara.
xWeiland, Barbara.
The Picnic Cookbook. Butterick Pub.
Weiland, Robert. *see* Weiland, Robert G.
Weiland, Robert G.
xWeiland, Robert.
Geography in Living. Pruett.
Weilbacher, William M.
xWeilbacher, William M.
Marketing Management Cases: Planning &
Executing Marketing Strategy. Macmillan.
Weiler, Nicholas W.
xWeiler, Nicholas W.
Reality & Career Planning: A Guide for
Personal Growth. A-W.
Weiler, Philip. *see* Weiler, Philip G.
Weiler, Philip G.
xWeiler, Philip.
Adult Day Care: Community Work with the
Elderly. Springer Pub.
Weill, Alain.
xWeill, Alain.
Art Nouveau Postcards: The Posterist's
Postcards. Images Graphiques.
Weill, Francis Samuel, 1933-
xWeill, Francis W.
Ultrasonography of Digestive Diseases. Mosby.
Weill, Francis W. *see* Weill, Francis Samuel.
Weill, Herman.
xWeill, Herman N.
European Diplomatic History 1815-1914:
Documents & Interpretations. Exposition.
Weill, Herman N. *see* Weill, Herman.
Weills, Christopher.
xWeills, Christopher.

The Goodfellow Catalog of Wonderful Things:
Traditional & Contemporary Crafts. Berkley
Pub.
Weimann, Robert.
xWeimann, Robert.
Structure & Society in Literary History: Studies
in the History & Theory of Historical
Criticism. U Pr of Va.
Weimer, Arthur M. *see* Weimer, Arthur Martin.
Weimer, Arthur Martin.
xWeimer, Arthur M.
Real Estate. Wiley.
Weimer, W. B. *see* Weimer, Walter B.
Weimer, Walter B.
xWeimer, W. B.
ed. Cognition & the Symbolic Processes.
Halsted Pr.
Weimer, Wayne.
xWeimer, Wayne.
Arithmetic Readiness Inventory. Merrill.
Wein, Harold H.
xWein, Harold H.
Domestic Air Cargo: Its Prospects. Mich St U
Busn.
Optimal Staging & Phasing of Multi-Product
Capacity. Mich St U Busn.
Weinbaum, Batya.
xWeinbaum, Batya.
The Curious Courtship of Women's Liberation
& Socialism. South End Pr.
Weinbaum, Paul O. *see* Weinbaum, Paul Owen.
Weinbaum, Paul Owen, 1945-
xWeinbaum, Paul O.
Mobs & Demagogues: The New York
Response to Collective Violence in the Early
Nineteenth Century. Univ Microfilms.
Weinberg, Albert K. *see* Weinberg, Albert Katz.
Weinberg, Albert Katz.
xWeinberg, Albert K.
Manifest Destiny: A Study of Nationalist
Expansionism in American History. AMS Pr.
Manifest Destiny: A Study of Nationalist
Expansionism in American History. Times
Bks.
Weinberg, Arthur.
xWeinberg, Arthur.
ed. Passport to Utopia: Great Panaceas in
American History. Times Bks.
Weinberg, Bernard, 1909-
xWeinberg, Bernard.
Art of Jean Racine. U of Chicago Pr.
Critical Prefaces of the French Renaissance.
AMS Pr.
ed. French Poetry of the Renaissance. S Ill U
Pr.
A History of Literary Criticism in the Italian
Renaissance. U of Chicago Pr.
Weinberg, C. *see* Weinberg, Carl.
Weinberg, Carl.
xWeinberg, C.
Education & Social Problems. Free Pr.
xWeinberg, Carl.
Education Is a Shuck: How the Educational
System Is Failing Our Children. Morrow.
Weinberg, Elizabeth A. *see* Weinberg, Elizabeth Ann.
Weinberg, Elizabeth Ann.
xWeinberg, Elizabeth A.
The Development of Sociology in the Soviet
Union. Routledge & Kegan.
Weinberg, Eve.
xWeinberg, Eve.
Community Surveys with Local Talent: A
Handbook. NORC.
Weinberg, George. *see* Weinberg, George H.
Weinberg, George H.
xWeinberg, George.

The Action Approach: How Your Personality
Developed & How You Can Change It. St
Martin.
Self Creation. Avon.
Self Creation. St Martin.
Society & the Healthy Homosexual.
Doubleday.
Weinberg, Gerald M.
xWeinberg, Gerald M.
An Introduction to General Systems Thinking.
Wiley.
On the Design of Stable Systems. Wiley.
Psychology of Computer Programming. Van
Nos Reinhold.
Weinberg, H. Barbara. *see* Weinberg, Helene Barbara.
Weinberg, Harry L.
xWeinberg, Harry L.
Levels of Knowing & Existence: Studies in
General Semantics. Inst Gen Semantics.
Weinberg, Helene Barbara, 1942-
xWeinberg, H. Barbara.
The Decorative Work of John la Farge.
Garland Pub.
Weinberg, Henry.
xWeinberg, Henry.
ed. Abnormal Personalities: A Book of Case
Readings. Mss Info.
Weinberg, Herman. *see* Weinberg, Herman G.
Weinberg, Herman G.
xWeinberg, Herman.
The Lubitsch Touch: A Critical Study. Dover.
xWeinberg, Herman G.
Stroheim: A Pictorial Record of His Nine
Films. Dover.
Weinberg, Julia.
xWeinberg, Julia.
The Big Beautiful Book of Hors D'Oeuvres.
Butterick Pub.
Gourmet Bouquet. Butterick Pub.
Weinberg, Julius, 1922-
xWeinberg, Julius.
Edward Alsworth Ross & the Sociology of
Progressivism. State Hist Soc Wis.
Weinberg, Julius R. *see* Weinberg, Julius Rudolph.
Weinberg, Julius Rudolph, 1908-
xWeinberg, Julius R.
Abstraction, Relation, & Induction: Three
Essays in the History of Thought. U of Wis
Pr.
Ockham, Descartes, & Hume: Self Knowledge,
Substance, & Causality. U of Wis Pr.
Problems in Philosophical Inquiry. Irvington.
Weinberg, Kurt.
xWeinberg, Kurt.
On Gide's Promethee: Private Myth & Public
Mystification. Princeton U Pr.
Weinberg, Lee S.
xWeinberg, Lee S.
Law & Society: An Interdisciplinary
Introduction. U Pr of Amer.
Weinberg, Leonard B.
xWeinberg, Leonard B.
After Mussolini: Italian Neo-Fascism & the
Nature of Fascism. U Pr of Amer.
Weinberg, Meyer, 1920-
xWeinberg, Meyer.
ed. Education of the Minority Child: A
Comprehensive Bibliography of 10,000
Selected Entries. Integrated Ed Assoc.
Weinberg, Nathan.
xWeinberg, Nathan G.
Preservation in American Towns & Cities.
Westview.
Weinberg, Nathan G. *see* Weinberg, Nathan.
Weinberg, Norbert.
xWeinberg, Norbert.
Beyond the Wall. Bloch.
The Essential Torah. Bloch.
Weinberg, Paul.
xWeinberg, Paul J.

Weininger, Stephen J.
 xWeininger, S. J.
  Contemporary Organic Chemistry. HR&W.
Weinland, James D. *see* Weinland, James Davis.
Weinland, James Davis, 1894-
 xWeinland, James D.
  How to Improve Your Memory. B&N.
  How to Improve Your Memory. Har-Row.
  How to Study. Branden.
  How to Think Straight. Littlefield.
Weinmann, Karl, 1873-1929
 xWeinmann, Karl.
  History of Church Music. Greenwood.
Weinrach, Stephen G.
 xWeinrach, Stephen G.
  ed. How Career Choices Are Made. Mss Info.
Weinrauch, J. Donald.
 xWeinrauch, J. Donald.
  Applied Marketing Principles. P-H.
Weinreb, Lloyd L., 1936-
 xWeinreb, Lloyd L.
  Denial of Justice: Criminal Process in the
   United States. Free Pr.
Weinreich, Gabriel.
 xWeinreich, Gabriel.
  Notes for General Physics. Neo Pr.
Weinreich, Max, 1894-1969
 xWeinreich, Max.
  History of the Yiddish Language. Ktav.
  History of the Yiddish Language. U of Chicago
   Pr.
Weinreich, Uriel.
 xWeinreich, Uriel.
  Modern English-Yiddish, Yiddish-English
   Dictionary. McGraw.
  Modern English-Yiddish Yiddish-English
   Dictionary. Schocken.
  Modern English-Yiddish, Yiddish-English
   Dictionary. Yivo Inst.
  On Semantics. U of Pa Pr.
Weinrich, A. K. *see* Weinrich, A. K. H.
Weinrich, A. K. H., 1933-
 xWeinrich, A. K.
  African Farmers in Rhodesia: Old & New
   Peasant Communities in Karangaland. Oxford
   U Pr.
  Mucheke: Race, Status & Politics in a
   Rhodesian Community. Holmes & Meier.
Weinstein, Alan.
 xWeinstein, Alan.
  Lectures on Symplectic Manifolds. Am Math.
Weinstein, Allen.
 xWeinstein, Allen.
  ed. Origins of Modern America, 1860-1900.
   Phila Bk Co.
  Perjury: The Hiss-Chambers Case. Knopf.
  Perjury: The Hiss-Chambers Case. Random.
Weinstein, Alvin S., 1928-
 xWeinstein, Alvin S.
  Products Liability & the Reasonably Safe
   Product: A Guide for Management, Design &
   Marketing. Wiley.
Weinstein, Bernard L.
 xWeinstein, Bernard L.
  Regional Growth & Decline in the United
   States: The Rise of the Sunbelt & the Decline
   of the Northeast. Praeger.
Weinstein, Brian.
 xWeinstein, Brian.
  Gabon: Nation-Building on the Ogooue. MIT
   Pr.
Weinstein, Deena.
 xWeinstein, Deena.
  Bureaucratic Opposition: Challenging Abuses at
   the Workplace. Pergamon.
Weinstein, Florence.
 xWeinstein, Florence.

  Intro. by & ed. Crocheting Tablecloths &
   Placemats. Dover.
  ed. Crocheting Tablecloths & Placemats. Peter
   Smith.
Weinstein, Franklin B.
 xWeinstein, Franklin B.
  Indonesian Foreign Policy & the Dilemma of
   Dependence: From Sukarno to Soeharto.
   Cornell U Pr.
Weinstein, Fred.
 xWeinstein, Fred.
  Psychoanalytic Sociology: An Essay on the
   Interpretation of Historical Data & the
   Phenomena of Collective Behavior. Johns
   Hopkins.
Weinstein, Grace. *see* Weinstein, Grace W.
Weinstein, Grace W.
 xWeinstein, Grace.
  Life Plans: Looking Forward to Retirement.
   HR&W.
 xWeinstein, Grace W.
  Children & Money: A Guide for Parents.
   Schocken.
  Money of Your Own. Dutton.
  People Study People: The Story of Psychology.
   Dutton.
Weinstein, Jack B.
 xWeinstein, Jack B.
  Reform of Court Rule-Making Procedures.
   Ohio St U Pr.
Weinstein, James, 1926-
 xWeinstein, James.
  Ambiguous Legacy: The Left in American
   Politics. New Viewpoints.
Weinstein, Joshua.
 xWeinstein, Joshua.
  Buber & Humanistic Education. Philos Lib.
Weinstein, Leo.
 xWeinstein, Leo.
  Hippolyte Taine. Twayne.
Weinstein, Malcolm S., 1942-
 xWeinstein, Malcolm S.
  Health in the City: Environmental &
   Behavioral Influences. Pergamon.
Weinstein, Martin.
 xWeinstein, Martin.
  ed. Revolutionary Cuba in the World Arena.
   Inst Study Human.
Weinstein, Michael.
 xWeinstein, Michael.
  World of Jewel Stones. Sheridan.
Weinstein, Philip R.
 xWeinstein, Philip R.
  Lumbar Spondylosis: Diagnosis, Management
   & Surgical Treatment. Year Bk Med.
Weinstein, Robert A.
 xWeinstein, Robert A.
  Collection, Use, & Care of Historical
   Photographs. AASLH.
  Grays Harbor: 1885-1913. Penguin.
  Grays Harbor: 1885-1913. Viking Pr.
Weinstein, Warren.
 xWeinstein, Warren.
  ed. Chinese & Soviet Aid to Africa. Praeger.
  Historical Dictionary of Burundi. Scarecrow.
  ed. Soviet & Chinese Aid to African Nations.
   Praeger.
Weinstock, Herbert, 1905-
 xWeinstock, Herbert.
  Donizetti & the World of Opera in Italy, Paris
   & Vienna in the First Half of the Nineteenth
   Century. Octagon.
  Handel. Greenwood.
Weinstock, Stefan.
 xWeinstock, Stefan.
  Divus Julius. Oxford U Pr.
Weinstock, Stephen M. *see* Weinstock, Stephen Mark.
Weinstock, Stephen Mark.
 xWeinstock, Stephen M.

  A Decision-Oriented Manual of Retinoscopy. C
   C Thomas.
Weintraub, Andrew.
 xWeintraub, Andrew.
  ed. The Economic Growth Controversy. M E
   Sharpe.
Weintraub, Daniel J.
 xWeintraub, Daniel J.
  Perception. Brooks-Cole.
Weintraub, Hyman.
 xWeintraub, Hyman G.
  Andrew Furuseth, Emancipator of the Seamen.
   U of Cal Pr.
Weintraub, Hyman G. *see* Weintraub, Hyman.
Weintraub, Karl J. *see* Weintraub, Karl Joachim.
Weintraub, Karl Joachim, 1924-
 xWeintraub, Karl J.
  The Value of the Individual: Self &
   Circumstance in Autobiography. U of
   Chicago Pr.
Weintraub, Rodelle.
 xWeintraub, Rodelle.
  Fabian Feminist: Bernard Shaw and Woman.
   Pa St U Pr.
Weintraub, Ruth (Goldstein), 1905-
 xWeintraub, Ruth G.
  Government Corporations & State Law. AMS
   Pr.
Weintraub, Ruth G. *see* Weintraub, Ruth (Goldstein).
Weintraub, Sidney, 1914-
 xWeintraub, Sidney.
  A General Theory of the Price Level, Output,
   Income Distribution, & Economic Growth.
   Greenwood.
  ed. Income Inequality. Am Acad Pol Soc Sci.
  Price Theory. Greenwood.
Weintraub, Sol.
 xWeintraub, Sol.
  Introduction to Statistics. Univ Stat Tracts.
Weintraub, Stanley.
 xWeintraub, Stanley.
  ed. Directions in Literary Criticism:
   Contemporary Approaches to Literature. Pa
   St U Pr.
  The London Yankees: Portraits of American
   Writers & Artists in England, 1894-1914.
   HarBraceJ.
Weinwurm, George. *see* Weinwurm, George F.
Weinwurm, George F.
 xWeinwurm, George.
  On the Management of Computer
   Programming. Van Nos Reinhold.
Weir, A. J.
 xWeir, A. J.
  Lebesgue Integration & Measure. Cambridge U
   Pr.
Weir, A. J. *see* Weir, Alan J.
Weir, Alan J.
 xWeir, A. J.
  General Integration & Measure. Cambridge U
   Pr.
Weir, LaVada.
 xWeir, LaVada.
  Advanced Skateboarding: A Complete Guide to
   Skatepark Riding & Other Tips for the Better
   Skateboarder. Wanderer Bks.
  Breaking Point. Creative Ed.
  Chaotic Kitchen. Creative Ed.
  The Horse-Flambeau. Creative Ed.
  Laurie Loves a Horse. Creative Ed.
  A Long Distance. Creative Ed.
  Men!. Creative Ed.
  The Roller Skating Book. Messner.
Weir, Nancie MacCullough.
 xWeir, Nancy M.
  Silver Spoons. PB.
Weir, Nancy M. *see* Weir, Nancie MacCullough.
Weir, Sam.
 xWeir, Sam.

How We Made a Million Dollars Recycling
  Great Old Houses. Contemp Bks.
Weir, Thomas R.
  xWeir, Thomas R.
    Atlas of Winnipeg. U of Toronto Pr.
Weis, Ezra H. *see* Weis, Ezra Herman Franklin.
Weis, Ezra Herman Franklin, 1887-1948
  xWeis, Ezra H.
    The Music Preparation of Elementary Teachers
      in State Teachers Colleges. AMS Pr.
Weis, Frederick L. *see* Weis, Frederick Lewis.
Weis, Frederick Lewis, 1895-1966
  xWeis, Frederick L.
    The Colonial Clergy of Maryland, Delaware &
      Georgia. Genealog Pub.
    The Colonial Clergy of Virginia, North
      Carolina & South Carolina. Genealog Pub.
Weis, Norm. *see* Weis, Norman D.
Weis, Norman D.
  xWeis, Norm.
    The Starduster. P-H.
  xWeis, Norman D.
    Ghost Towns of the Northwest. Caxton.
Weis, P. *see* Weis, Paul.
Weis, Paul.
  xWeis, P.
    Nationality & Statelessness in International
      Law. Sijthoff & Noordhoff.
  xWeis, Paul.
    Nationality & Statelessness in International
      Law. Hyperion Conn.
Weisband, Edward, 1939-
  xWeisband, Edward.
    Turkish Foreign Policy, 1943-1945: Small State
      Diplomacy & Great Power Politics. Princeton
      U Pr.
Weisberg, Arthur.
  xWeisberg, Arthur.
    The Art of Wind Playing. Schirmer Bks.
Weisberg, Harold, 1913-
  xWeisberg, Harold.
    Post Mortem: JFK Assassination Cover-Up
      Smashed!. Weisberg.
    Whitewash: The Report on the Warren Report.
      Weisberg.
Weisberg, Herbert F.
  xWeisberg, Herbert F.
    An Introduction to Survey Research & Data
      Analysis. W H Freeman.
Weisberg, Richard C. *see* Weisberg, Richard Chadbourn.
Weisberg, Richard Chadbourn.
  xWeisberg, Richard C.
    The Politics of Crude Oil Pricing in the Middle
      East, 1970 - 1975: A Study in International
      Bargaining. U of Cal Intl St.
Weisberg, Robert W.
  xWeisberg, Robert W.
    Memory, Thought, & Behavior. Oxford U Pr.
Weisberger, Bernard A., 1922-
  xWeisberger, Bernard A.
    Booker T. Washington. NAL.
    The Dream Maker: William C. Durant,
      Founder of General Motors. Little.
    The Impact of Our Past: A History of the
      United States. McGraw.
    Pathways to the Present: A New History of the
      United States. Har-Row.
    They Gathered at the River: The Story of the
      Great Revivalists & Their Impact Upon
      Religion in America. Octagon.
    They Gathered at the River: The Story of the
      Great Revivalists & Their Impact Upon
      Religion in America. Times Bks.
Weisbord, Albert, 1900-
  xWeisbord, Albert.
    Passaic: The Story of a Struggle Against
      Starvation Wages & for the Right to
      Organize. AMS Pr.
Weisbord, M. *see* Weisbord, Marvin Ross.

Weisbord, Marvin Ross.
  xWeisbord, M.
    Improving Police Department Management
      Through Problem Solving Task Forces: A
      Case in Organization Development. A-W.
Weisbord, Robert G.
  xWeisbord, Robert G.
    Genocide?: Birth Control & the Black
      American. Greenwood.
Weisbord, Vera B. *see* Weisbord, Vera Buch.
Weisbord, Vera Buch, 1895-
  xWeisbord, Vera B.
    A Radical Life. Ind U Pr.
Weisbrod, Burton A. *see* Weisbrod, Burton Allen.
Weisbrod, Burton Allen, 1931-
  xWeisbrod, Burton A.
    Disease & Economic Development: The Impact
      of Parasitic Diseases in St. Lucia. U of Wis
      Pr.
    Public Interest Law: An Economic &
      Institutional Analysis. U of Cal Pr.
Weisbrod, Carol.
  xWeisbrod, Carol.
    The Boundaries of Utopia. Pantheon.
Weisbrot, Robert.
  xWeisbrot, Robert.
    The Jews of Argentina: From the Inquisition to
      Peron. Jewish Pubn.
Weisburd, Claudia.
  xWeisburd, Claudia.
    Raising Your Own Livestock. P-H.
Weisburg, Hilda K.
  xWeisburg, Hilda K.
    Elementary School Librarian's Almanac: A
      Complete Media Program for Every Month
      of the School Year. Ctr Appl Res.
Weise, Arthur J. *see* Weise, Arthur James.
Weise, Arthur James, 1838-1910 or 11
  xWeise, Arthur J.
    The Discoveries of America to the Year 1525.
      Milford Hse.
Weisel, Mindy.
  xWeisel, Mindy.
    The Rainbow Diet Book. Sovereign Bks.
Weiser, H. H. *see* Weiser, Harry Howard.
Weiser, Harry Howard.
  xWeiser, H. H.
    Practical Food Microbiology & Technology.
      AVI.
Weiser, Marjorie P. *see* Weiser, Marjorie P. K.
Weiser, Marjorie P. K.
  xWeiser, Marjorie P.
    ed. Ethnic America. Wilson.
Weisfeiler, B. *see* Weisfeiler, Boris.
Weisfeiler, Boris, 1941-
  xWeisfeiler, B.
    ed. On Construction & Identification of
      Graphs. Springer-Verlag.
Weisfelder, Richard F.
  xWeisfelder, Richard F.
    Defining National Purpose in Lesotho. Ohio U
      Ctr Intl
Weisgard, Leonard, 1916-
  xWeisgard, Leonard.
    My First Picture Book. G&D.
Weisgerber, Charles A., 1912-
  xWeisgerber, Charles A.
    Psychological Assessment of Candidates for a
      Religious Order. Loyola.
Weisgerber, Jean.
  xWeisgerber, Jean.
    Faulkner & Dostoevsky: Influence &
      Confluence. Ohio U Pr.
Weisgerber, Robert A.
  xWeisgerber, Robert A.
    A Special Educator's Guide to Vocational
      Training. C C Thomas.
Weisheipl, James A.
  xWeisheipl, James A.

Development of Physical Theory in the Middle
  Ages. U of Mich Pr.
Development of Physical Theory in the Middle
  Ages. U of Mich Pr.
Weisheit, Eldon.
  xWeisheit, Eldon.
    Excuse Me, Sir. Concordia.
Weisinger, Herbert.
  xWeisinger, Herbert.
    Agony & the Triumph: Papers on the Use &
      Abuse of Myth. Mich St U Pr.
Weisinger, Mort.
  xWeisinger, Mort.
    The Complete Alibi Handbook. Citadel Pr.
Weiskopf, Don.
  xWeiskopf, Donald C.
    A Guide to Recreation & Leisure. Allyn.
    How to Play Baseball. Sporting News.
Weiskopf, Donald C. *see* Weiskopf, Don.
Weiskopf, Herman.
  xWeiskopf, Herman.
    The Perfect Game. P-H.
Weisman, Avery D.
  xWeisman, Avery D.
    Coping with Cancer. McGraw.
    The Realization of Death: A Guide for the
      Psychological Autopsy. Aronson.
Weisman, Gisele.
  xWeisman, Gisele.
    The Winner's Way: A Transactional Analysis
      Guide for Living, Working, & Learning.
      Brooks-Cole.
Weisman, Herman M.
  xWeisman, Herman M.
    Information Systems, Services & Centers.
      Wiley.
Weismann, August, 1834-1914
  xWeismann, August.
    Evolution Theory. AMS Pr.
    Germ Plasm: A Theory of Heredity. AMS Pr.
Weiss. *see* Weiss, William.
Weiss , Edwin. *see* Weiss, Edwin.
Weiss, Ann E., 1943-
  xWeiss, Ann E.
    The American Congress. Messner.
    The American Presidency. Messner.
    Polls & Surveys: A Look at Public Opinion
      Research. Watts.
    The School on Madison Avenue: Advertising &
      What It Teaches. Dutton.
    What's That You Said. HarBraceJ.
Weiss, Carol H.
  xWeiss, Carol H.
    Evaluating Action Programs: Readings in
      Social Action & Education. Allyn.
    Introduction to Sample Surveys for
      Government Managers. Urban Inst.
    Using Social Research for Public
      Policy-Making. Lexington Bks.
Weiss, E. *see* Weiss, Edwin.
Weiss, Earle B.
  xWeiss, Earle B.
    ed. Bronchial Asthma: Mechanisms &
      Therapeutics. Little.
    Status Asthmaticus. Univ Park.
Weiss, Edith.
  xWeiss, E.
    Catering Handbook. Radio City.
  xWeiss, Edith.
    Catering Handbook. Hayden.
Weiss, Edoardo, 1889-
  xWeiss, Edoardo.
    Structure & Dynamics of the Human Mind.
      Grune.
Weiss, Edward.
  xWeiss, Edward.
    The Paprikas Weiss Hungarian Cookbook.
      Morrow.
Weiss, Edward C. *see* Weiss, Edward Craig.

Weiss, Edward Craig.
  xWeiss, Edward C.
    ed. The Many Faces of Information Science.
      Westview.
Weiss, Edwin.
  xWeiss , Edwin.
    Algebraic Number Theory. Chelsea Pub.
  xWeiss, E.
    Cohomology of Groups. Acad Pr.
  xWeiss, Edwin.
    First Course in Algebra & Number Theory.
      Acad Pr.
Weiss, Elizabeth. *see* Weiss, Elizabeth S.
Weiss, Elizabeth S.
  xWeiss, Elizabeth.
    The Gourmet's Low-Cholesterol Cookbook. BJ
      Pub Group.
Weiss, Ellen.
  xWeiss.
    Things to Make & Do for Christmas. Watts.
  xWeiss, Ellen.
    Millicent Maybe. Avon.
    illus. Millicent Maybe. Watts.
Weiss, G. H. *see* Weiss, Gloria Hooper.
Weiss, Gloria Hooper, 1928-
  xWeiss, G. H.
    Commercial Processing of Poultry. Noyes.
Weiss, H. *see* Weiss, Herbert.
Weiss, Harvey.
  xWeiss, Harvey.
    Ceramics, from Clay to Kiln. A-W.
    illus. How to Make Your Own Books. T Y
      Crowell.
    illus. How to Run a Railroad: Everything You
      Need to Know About Model Trains. T Y
      Crowell.
    illus. Model Buildings & How to Make Them.
      T Y Crowell.
    Paint, Brush & Palette. A-W.
    Sticks, Spools & Feathers. A-W.
    illus. Working with Cardboard & Paper. A-W.
Weiss, Helen G. *see* Weiss, Helen Ginandes.
Weiss, Helen Ginandes.
  xWeiss, Helen G.
    Home Is a Learning Place: A Parents Guide to
      Learning Disabilities. Little.
Weiss, Herbert, 1920-
  xWeiss, H.
    Structure & Application of Galvanomagnetic
      Devices. Pergamon.
Weiss, Herbert F.
  xWeiss, Herbert F.
    Political Protest in the Congo: The
      Parti-Solidaire Africain During the
      Independence Struggle. Princeton U Pr.
Weiss, Herman.
  xWeiss, Herman.
    Passion in the Wind. Popular Lib.
Weiss, Horace John.
  xWeiss, John.
    ed. The Origins of Modern Consciousness.
      Wayne St U Pr.
Weiss, Joan T. *see* Weiss, Joan Talmage.
Weiss, Joan Talmage.
  xWeiss, Joan T.
    Home for a Stranger. HarBraceJ.
Weiss, Johannes, 1863-1914
  xWeiss, Johannes.
    Earliest Christianity: A History of the Period
      A.D. 30-150. Peter Smith.
Weiss, John, 1944-
  xWeiss, John.

Advanced Bass Fishing. Follett.

The Whitetail Deer Hunter's Handbook.
  Winchester Pr.

Weiss, John. *see* Weiss, Horace John.

Weiss, Karel.
  xWeiss, Karl.
    ed. The Prison Experience: An Anthology.
      Delacorte.
    ed. Under the Mask: An Anthology About
      Prejudice in America. Delacorte.

Weiss, Karl. *see* Weiss, Karel.
Weiss, L. *see* Weiss, Lionel.

Weiss, Leatie.
  xWeiss, Leatie.
    Funny Feet. Avon.
    illus. Funny Feet. Watts.

Weiss, Leonard.
  xWeiss, Leonard.
    Pulmonary Metastasis. G K Hall.
Weiss, Leonard W.
  xWeiss, Leonard W.
    Case Studies in American Industry. Wiley.
    Economics & American Industry. Krieger.
    Economics & Society. Wiley.
Weiss, Lionel.
  xWeiss, L.
    Maximum Probability Estimators & Related
      Topics. Springer-Verlag.

Weiss, Louise, 1850-
  xWeiss, Louise.
    Access to the World: A Travel Guide for the
      Handicapped. Chatham Sq.

Weiss, Malcolm E.
  xWeiss, Malcolm E.
    Solomon Grundy, Born on Oneday: A Finite
      Arithmetic Puzzle. T Y Crowell.

Weiss, Marian.
  xWeiss, Marian.
    ed. Early Therapeutic, Social, & Vocational
      Problems in the Rehabilitation of Persons
      with Spinal Cord Injuries. Plenum Pub.

Weiss, Mark L.
  xWeiss, Mark L.
    Human Biology & Behavior: An
      Anthropological Perspective. Little.

Weiss, Melford S.
  xWeiss, Melford Stephen.
    Valley City: A Chinese Community in
      America. Schenkman.

Weiss, Melford Stephen. *see* Weiss, Melford S.
Weiss, N. A. *see* Weiss, Neil A.
Weiss, Nancy. *see* Weiss, Nancy Joan.
Weiss, Nancy Joan.
  xWeiss, Nancy.
    National Urban League, 1910-1940. Oxford U
      Pr.
Weiss, Nathan S.
  xWeiss, Nathan S.
    jt. ed. Practical Points in Allergy. Med Exam.
Weiss, Neil A.
  xWeiss, N. A.
    Finite Mathematics. Worth.
Weiss, Paul, 1901-
  xWeiss, Paul.

Cinematics. S Ill U Pr.
First Considerations: An Examination of
  Philosophical Evidence. S Ill U Pr.
God We Seek. S Ill U Pr.
History: Written & Lived. S Ill U Pr.
Nine Basic Arts. S Ill U Pr.
Our Public Life. S Ill U Pr.
Reality. S Ill U Pr.
Religion & Art. Marquette.
Right & Wrong: A Philosophical Dialogue
  Between Father & Son. S Ill U Pr.
World of Art. S Ill U Pr.
You, I, & the Others. S Ill U Pr.
Weiss, Peter, 1916-
  xWeiss, Peter.
    Persecution & Assassination of Jean-Paul
      Marat As Performed by the Inmates of the
      Asylum of Charenton Under the Direction of
      the Marquis De Sade. Atheneum.
    Simple Printmaking. Lothrop.
Weiss, Rita.
  xWeiss, Rita.
    Charted Monograms for Needlepoint &
      Cross-Stitch. Dover.
    Christmas Needlepoint Designs. Dover.
    ed. Crocheting Doilies. Dover.
    ed. Floral Doilies for Crocheting. Gannon.
    Needlepoint Designs After Illustrations by
      Beatrix Potter. Dover.
Weiss, Robert M. *see* Weiss, Robert Monroe.
Weiss, Robert Monroe, 1929-
  xWeiss, Robert M.
    ed. Conant Controversy in Teacher Education.
      Phila Bk Co.
Weiss, Robert S. *see* Weiss, Robert Stuart.
Weiss, Robert Stuart, 1925-
  xWeiss, Robert S.
    Going It Alone: The Family Life & Social
      Situation of the Single Parent. Basic.
    Marital Separation. Basic.
Weiss, Roberto.
  xWeiss, Roberto.
    Dawn of Humanism in Italy. Haskell.
Weiss, Ruth, 1928-
  xWeiss, Ruth.
    Desert Journal. Good Gay.
    Light & Other Poems. SF Arts & Letters.
    Single Out. DAurora Pr.
Weiss, Seymour N.
  xWeiss, Seymour N.
    How to Raise & Train a Lakeland Terrier. TFH
      Pubns.
Weiss, Susan A. *see* Weiss, Susan Archer Talley.
Weiss, Susan Archer. *see* Weiss, Susan Archer Talley.
Weiss, Susan Archer Talley, 1835-
  xWeiss, Susan A.
    The Home Life of Poe. Arden Lib.
  xWeiss, Susan Archer.
    The Home Life of Poe. Folcroft.
Weiss, Theodore. *see* Weiss, Theodore Russell.
Weiss, Theodore Russell, 1916-
  xWeiss, Theodore.
    Breath of Clowns & Kings: Shakespeare's Early
      Comedies & Histories. Atheneum.
    Gunsight. NYU Pr.
    Views & Spectacles: New & Selected Shorter
      Poems. Macmillan.
    World Before Us: Poems 1950-1970.
      Macmillan.
Weiss, Thomas G. *see* Weiss, Thomas George.
Weiss, Thomas George.
  xWeiss, Thomas G.
    The World Food Conference & Global Problem
      Solving. Praeger.
Weiss, Ulrich.
  xWeiss, Ulrich.
    Biosynthesis of Aromatic Compounds. Wiley.
Weiss, W. H., 1918-
  xWeiss, W. H.

The Art & Skill of Managing People. P-H.
Weiss, William.
　xWeiss.
　　Home Maintenance. Bennett Co.
Weissberg, Robert.
　xWeissberg, Robert.
　　Public Opinion & Popular Government. P-H.
　　Understanding American Government. HR&W.
Weissberger, Arnold.
　xWeissberger, Arnold.
　　Special Topics in Heterocyclic Chemistry.
　　　Wiley.
Weissbort, Daniel.
　xWeissbort, Daniel.
　　Soundings. Persea Bks.
Weisser, Michael. *see* Weisser, Michael R.
Weisser, Michael R.
　xWeisser, Michael.
　　Crime & Punishment in Early Modern Europe.
　　　Humanities.
　　The Peasants of the Montes: The Roots of
　　　Rural Rebellion in Spain. U of Chicago Pr.
Weissermel, K. *see* Weissermel, Klaus.
Weissermel, Klaus.
　xWeissermel, K.
　　Industrial Organic Chemistry: Important Raw
　　　Materials & Intermediates. Verlag Chemie.
Weissert. *see* Weissert, L. R.
Weissert, L. R.
　xWeissert.
　　Fabrication of Thorium Fuel Elements. Am
　　　Nuclear Soc.
Weissglass, Julian.
　xWeissglass, Julian.
　　Exploring Elementary Mathematics: A
　　　Small-Group Approach for Teaching. W H
　　　Freeman.
Weisskopf, Walter A.
　xWeisskopf, Walter A.
　　Alienation & Economics. Dell.
　　The Psychology of Economics. U of Chicago
　　　Pr.
Weissleder, Wolfgang, 1920-
　xWeissleder, Wolfgang.
　　ed. The Nomadic Alternative: Modes &
　　　Models of Interaction in the African-Asian
　　　Deserts & Steppes. Beresford Bk Serv.
Weissler, Arnold M.
　xWeissler, Arnold M.
　　ed. Noninvasive Cardiology. Grune.
Weissler, Paul.
　xWeissler, Paul.
　　Weekend Mechanic's Handbook: Complete
　　　Auto Repairs You Can Make. Arco.

Weissman, Cynthia.
　xWeissman, Cynthia.
　　Breakfast for Sammy. Schol Bk Serv.

Weissman, David. *see* Weissman, David Joel.
Weissman, David Joel.
　xWeissman, David.
　　Eternal Possibilities: A Neutral Ground for
　　　Meaning & Existence. S Ill U Pr.

Weissman, Myrna M.
　xWeissman, Myrna M.
　　The Depressed Woman: A Study of Social
　　　Relationships. U of Chicago Pr.

Weissman, Paul, 1932-
　xWeissman, Paul.
　　Lords of Power. Morrow.

Weissman, Rudolph L. *see* Weissman, Rudolph Leo.
Weissman, Rudolph Leo, 1900-
　xWeissman, Rudolph L.
　　Small Business & Venture Capital. Arno.
Weissman, Stephen R.
　xWeissman, Stephen R.

American Foreign Policy in the Congo,
　1960-1964. Cornell U Pr.
　xWeissman, Steve.
　　Trojan Horse: A Radical Look at Foreign Aid.
　　　Ramparts.
Weissman, Steve. *see* Weissman, Stephen R.
Weissmann, Adolf, 1873-1929
　xWeissmann, Adolf.
　　The Problems of Modern Music. Hyperion
　　　Conn.
Weissmann, Gerald.
　xWeissmann, Gerald.
　　ed. The Biological Revolution: Applications of
　　　Cell Biology to Public Welfare. Plenum Pub.
　　ed. Mediators of Inflammation. Plenum Pub.
Weisstub, David, 1944-
　xWeisstub, David N.
　　ed. Law & Psychiatry in the Canadian Context.
　　　Pergamon.
Weisstub, David N. *see* Weisstub, David.
Weisz, Frank B.
　xWeisz, Frank B.
　　SuperTrust. Farnswth Pub.
Weit, Erwin.
　xWeit, Erwin.
　　At the Red Summit: Interpreter Behind the
　　　Iron Curtain. Macmillan.
Weitenkampf, Frank, 1866-1962
　xWeitenkampf, Frank.
　　American Graphic Art. Gale.
　　American Graphic Art. Johnson Repr.
Weitz, C. *see* Weitz, Charles A.
Weitz, Charles A.
　xWeitz, C.
　　Introduction to Physical Anthropology &
　　　Archaeology. P-H.
Weitz, M. *see* Weitz, Morris.
Weitz, Morris.
　xWeitz, M.
　　Twentieth-Century Philosophy: The Analytic
　　　Tradition. Free Pr.
　xWeitz, Morris.
　　Hamlet & the Philosophy of Literary Criticism.
　　　U of Chicago Pr.
　　The Opening Mind: A Philosophical Study of
　　　Humanistic Concepts. U of Chicago Pr.
　　Problems in Aesthetics: An Introductory Book
　　　of Readings. Macmillan.
Weitz, R. *see* Weitz, Raanan.
Weitz, Raanan.
　xWeitz, R.
　　Agricultural Development, Planning &
　　　Implementation: Israel Case Study. Kluwer
　　　Boston.
Weitz, Shirley.
　xWeitz, Shirley.
　　Nonverbal Communication: Readings with
　　　Commentary. Oxford U Pr.
Weitzel, Eugene J.
　xWeitzel, Eugene J.
　　Contemporary Pastoral Counseling. Glencoe.
Weitzen, Hyman. *see* Weitzen, Hyman G.
Weitzen, Hyman G.
　xWeitzen, Hyman.
　　The Retirement Daybook. Chilton.
Weitzman, Cay.
　xWeitzman, Cay.
　　Distributed Micro Minicomputer Systems:
　　　Structure, Implementation & Application.
　　　P-H.
Weitzmann, C. F. *see* Weitzmann, Karl Friedrich.
Weitzmann, Karl Friedrich.
　xWeitzmann, C. F.
　　History of Pianoforte-Playing &
　　　Pianoforte-Literature. Da Capo.
Weitzmann, Kurt, 1904-
　xWeitzmann, Kurt.

Late Antique-Early Christian Painting.
　Braziller.
The Place of Book Illumination in Byzantine
　Art. Princeton U Pr.
Studies in Classical & Byzantine Manuscript
　Illumination. U of Chicago Pr.
Wekerle, Gerda R.
　xWekerle, Gerda R.
　　ed. New Space for Women. Westview.
Wekstein, Louis, 1917-
　xWekstein, Louis.
　　Handbook of Suicidology: Principles, Problems
　　　& Practice. Brunner-Mazel.
Welanetz, Diana Von. *see* Von Welanetz, Diana.
Welber, Robert.
　xWelber, Robert.
　　Frog, Frog, Frog. Pantheon.
　　Goodbye, Hello. Pantheon.
　　Song of the Seasons. Pantheon.
Welborn, David M., 1934-
　xWelborn, David M.
　　Governance of Federal Regulatory Agencies. U
　　　of Tenn Pr.
Welby, Earle T. *see* Welby, Thomas Earle.
Welby, T. Earle. *see* Welby, Thomas Earle.
Welby, Thomas Earle, 1881-1933
　xWelby, Earle T.
　　Arthur Symons: A Critical Study. Norwood
　　　Edns.
　xWelby, T. Earle.
　　Arthur Symons: A Critical Study. Folcroft.
　　A Popular History of English Poetry. Folcroft.
　　Popular History of English Poetry. Kennikat.
　　A Study of Swinburne. Folcroft.
Welch, Anthony.
　xWelch, Anthony.
　　Calligraphy in the Arts of the Muslim World.
　　　U of Tex Pr.
Welch, C. E. *see* Welch, Claude E.
Welch, Charles D.
　xWelch, Charles D.
　　Introduction to Soil Science in the Southeast.
　　　U of NC Pr.
Welch, Claude E.
　xWelch, C. E.
　　Manual of Lower Gastrointestinal Surgery.
　　　Springer-Verlag.
　xWelch, Claude E.
　　Polypoid Lesions of the Gastrointestinal Tract.
　　　Saunders.
Welch, Herbert, Bp, 1862-1969
　xWelch, Herbert.
　　Men of the Outposts: The Romance of the
　　　Modern Christian Movement. Arno.
Welch, Holmes.
　xWelch, Holmes.
　　Buddhism Under Mao. Harvard U Pr.
　xWelch, Holmes H.
　　Buddhist Revival in China. Harvard U Pr.
　　Practice of Chinese Buddhism, 1900-1950.
　　　Harvard U Pr.
Welch, Holmes H. *see* Welch, Holmes.
Welch, I. David. *see* Welch, Ira David.
Welch, Ira David.
　xWelch, I. David.
　　ed. Educational Accountability: A Humanistic
　　　Perspective. Publishers Consult.
Welch, James, 1940-
　xWelch, James.
　　The Death of Jim Loney. Har-Row.
Welch, June R. *see* Welch, June Rayfield.
Welch, June Rayfield, 1927-
　xWelch, June R.
　　The Glory That Was Texas. GLA Pr.
　　Going Great in the Lone Star State. GLA Pr.
　　Historic Sites of Texas. GLA Pr.
　　People & Places in the Texas Past. GLA Pr.
　　illus. The Texas Senator. GLA Pr.
Welch, Lew.
　xWelch, Lew.

I Remain: The Letters of Lew Welch with the
   Correspondence of His Friends. Grey Fox.
Welch, Mary S. see Welch, Mary Scott.
Welch, Mary Scott.
   xWelch, Mary S.
      The Family Wilderness Handbook. Ballantine.
      Networking: The Great New Way for Women
         to Get Ahead. HarBraceJ.
Welch, Reuben.
   xWelch, Reuben.
      We Really Do Need to Listen. Impact Tenn.
      When You Run Out of Fantastic-Persevere.
         Impact Tenn.
Welch, Richard E.
   xWelch, Richard E.
      Response to Imperialism: The United States &
         the Philippine-American War, 1899-1902. U
         of NC Pr.
Welch, Robert B., 1941-
   xWelch, Robert B.
      Perceptual Modification: Adapting to Altered
         Sensory Environments. Acad Pr.
Welch, Ronald, 1909-
   xWelch, Ronald.
      Knight Crusader. Oxford U Pr.
Welch, S. M. see Welch, Stephen M.
Welch, Sidney R., 1871-
   xWelch, Sidney R.
      Portuguese Rule & Spanish Crown in South
         Africa: 1581-1640. Verry.
Welch, Stephen M.
   xWelch, S. M.
      The Design of Biological Monitoring Systems
         for Pest Management. Halsted Pr.
Welch, Stuart C. see Welch, Stuart Cary.
Welch, Stuart Cary.
   xWelch, Stuart C.
      Imperial Mughal Painting. Braziller.
      Persian Painting: Five Royal Safavid
         Manuscripts of the Sixteenth Century.
         Braziller.
Welch, Susan.
   xWelch, Susan.
      ed. Legislative Reform & Public Policy.
         Praeger.
Welch, Theodore F.
   xWelch, Theodore F.
      Toshokan: Libraries in Japanese Society. ALA.
Welch, William A. see Welch, William Allen.
Welch, William Allen, 1923-
   xWelch, William A.
      Lightplane Propeller Design, Selection,
         Maintenance, & Repair. TAB Bks.
Welch, Winona H. see Welch, Winona Hazel.
Welch, Winona Hazel.
   xWelch, Winona H.
      Hookeriaceae. NY Botanical.
Welcher, Frank J. see Welcher, Frank Johnson.
Welcher, Frank Johnson.
   xWelcher, Frank J.
      Organic Reagents for Copper. Krieger.
Welcome, John, 1914-
   xWelcome, John.
      Bellary Bay. Atheneum.
      Grand National. S&S.
Welcomme, R. L.
   xWelcomme, Robin L.
      Fisheries Ecology of Floodplain Rivers.
         Longman.
Welcomme, Robin L. see Welcomme, R. L.
Weld, Eloise R.
   xWeld, Eloise R.
      Engagement. Random.
Weld, John, 1914-
   xWeld, John S.
      Meaning in Comedy: Studies in Elizabethan
         Romantic Comedy. State U NY Pr.
Weld, John S. see Weld, John.
Weld, Louis D. see Weld, Louis Dwight Harvell.

Weld, Louis Dwight Harvell, 1882-1946
   xWeld, Louis D.
      Private Freight Cars & American Railways.
         AMS Pr.
Weld, Ralph F. see Weld, Ralph Foster.
Weld, Ralph Foster, 1888-
   xWeld, Ralph F.
      Brooklyn Is America. AMS Pr.
Weld, Theodore D. see Weld, Theodore Dwight.
Weld, Theodore Dwight.
   xWeld, Theodore D.
      ed. American Slavery As It Is: Testimony of a
         Thousand Witnesses. Arno.
Weld, Wayne.
   xWeld, Wayne.
      World Directory of Theological Education by
         Extension. William Carey Lib.
Weld, William E. see Weld, William Ernest.
Weld, William Ernest, 1881-
   xWeld, William E.
      India's Demand for Transportation. AMS Pr.
Welding, Patsy R. see Welding, Patsy Ruth.
Welding, Patsy Ruth.
   xWelding, Patsy R.
      Let E.S.P. Work for You. Dial.
Weldon & Company. see Weldon and Company.
Weldon and Company.
   xWeldon & Company.
      Victorian Crochet. Peter Smith.
   xWeldon and Company.
      Victorian Crochet. Dover.
Weldon, Fay.
   xWeldon, Fay.
      Remember Me. Random.
      Words of Advice. Random.
Welfare Council, New York City. see Welfare Council of
   New York City.
Welfare Council of New York City.
   xWelfare Council, New York City.
      Puerto Ricans in New York City. Arno.
Welfeld, Irving H.
   xWelfeld, Irving H.
      America's Housing Problem: An Approach to
         Its Solution. Am Enterprise.
Welford, W. T.
   xWelford, W. T.
      The Optics of Nonimaging Concentrators:
         Light & Solar Energy. Acad Pr.
Welinder, Stig.
   xWelinder, Stig.
      The Mesolithic Stone Age of Eastern Middle
         Sweden. Humanities.
Welk. see Welk, Lawrence.
Welk, L. see Welk, Lawrence.
Welk, Lawrence.
   xWelk.
      My America, Your America. G K Hall.
   xWelk, L.
      My America, Your America. P-H.
      This I Believe. P-H.
   xWelk, Lawrence.
      Ah-One, Ah-Two!: Life with My Musical
         Family. Ballantine.
      This I Believe. G K Hall.
Welker, Carole E.
   xWelker, Carole E.
      Thoroughbred. Dreenan Pr.
Welker, David. see Welker, David Harold.
Welker, David Harold.
   xWelker, David.
      Theatrical Set Design: The Basic Techniques.
         Allyn.
Welker, Robert H. see Welker, Robert Henry.
Welker, Robert Henry.
   xWelker, Robert H.
      Natural Man: The Life of William Beebe. Ind
         U Pr.
Welkowitz, Walter, 1926-
   xWelkowitz, Walter.

Engineering Hemodynamics: With Application
   to Cardiac Assist Devices. Lexington Bks.
Welland, D. S. see Welland, D.S.R.
Welland, D.S.R.
   xWelland, D. S.
      ed. Pre-Raphaelites in Literature & Art. Arno.
Welland, Dennis. see Welland, Dennis Sydney Reginald.
Welland, Dennis Sydney Reginald.
   xWelland, Dennis.
      Mark Twain in England. Humanities.
Wellde, Kathryn.
   xWellde, Kathryn.
      Guess Who's in the Kitchen. Doubleday.
Wellek, Rene.
   xWellek, Rene.
      Confrontations: Studies in the Intellectual &
         Literary Relations Between Germany,
         England, & the U. S. During the 19th
         Century. Princeton U Pr.
      ed. Dostoevsky: A Collection of Critical
         Essays. P-H.
      The Literary Theory & Aesthetics of the
         Prague School. Mich Slavic Pubns.
      Theory of Literature. HarBraceJ.
Wellek, Susanne.
   xWellek, Susanne.
      Paul et Marie a l'Ecole. Ungar.
Weller, Charles.
   xWeller, Charles.
      How to Live with Hypoglycemia. BJ Pub
         Group.
Weller, George A. see Weller, George Anthony.
Weller, George Anthony, 1907-
   xWeller, George A.
      Clutch & Differential. Arno.
Weller, J. Marvin. see Weller, James Marvin.
Weller, James Marvin, 1899-
   xWeller, J. Marvin.
      Course of Evolution. McGraw.
Weller, John M.
   xWeller, John M.
      Fundamentals of Nephrology. Har-Row.
Weller, Leonard.
   xWeller, Leonard.
      Sociology in Israel. Greenwood.
Weller, Milton W. see Weller, Milton Webster.
Weller, Milton Webster.
   xWeller, Milton W.
      The Island Waterfowl. Iowa St U Pr.
Weller, Walter J.
   xWeller, Walter J.
      Assembly Level Programming for Small
         Computers. Lexington Bks.
Welles, Annette.
   xWelles, Annette.
      The Los Angeles Guidebook. Sherbourne.
Welles, E. R.
   xWelles, E. R.
      The Forgotten Legend of Sleepy Hollow.
         Learning Inc.
Welles, Elisabeth.
   xWelles, Elisabeth.
      Captain's Walk. PB.
   xWelles, Elizabeth.
      Fahnsworth Manor. PB.
Welles, Elizabeth. see Welles, Elisabeth.
Welles, Henry H. see Welles, Henry Hunter.
Welles, Henry Hunter, 1897-
   xWelles, Henry H.
      The Measurement of Certain Aspects of
         Personality Among Hard of Hearing Adults.
         AMS Pr.
Welles, Paul O. see Welles, Paul O'M.
Welles, Paul O'M., 1926-
   xWelles, Paul O.
      Project Lambda. Ashley Bks.
Welles, Sumner, 1892-
   xWelles, Sumner.

Where Are We Heading. Greenwood.

Wellesley, Kenneth.
xWellesley, Kenneth.
The Long Year A.D. 69. Westview.

Wellesz, Egon.
xWellesz, Egon.
Arnold Schonberg. Da Capo.
Arnold Schonberg. Greenwood.
History of Byzantine Music & Hymnography.
Oxford U Pr.

Welling, Richard, 1926-
xWelling, Richard.
Drawing with Markers. Watson-Guptill.

Wellisch, Hanan.
xWellisch, Hans.
ed. Nonbook Materials: A Bibliography of
Recent Publications. U of Md Lib Serv.
Wellisch, Hans. *see* Wellisch, Hanan.
Wellisch, J. B. *see* Wellisch, Jean B.

Wellisch, Jean B.
xWellisch, J. B.
ed. The Public Library & Federal Policy.
Greenwood.
Welliver, W. *see* Welliver, Warman.

Welliver, Warman, 1913-
xWelliver, W.
Character, Plot & Thought in Plato's
Timaeus-Critias. Humanities.

Wellman, Alice.
xWellman, Alice.
The White Sorceress. Putnam.

Wellman, Carl.
xWellman, Carl.
Challenge & Response: Justification in Ethics.
S Ill U Pr.
Morals & Ethics. Scott F.
Wellman, D. T. *see* Wellman, David T.

Wellman, David T.
xWellman, D. T.
ed. Portraits of White Racism. Cambridge U
Pr.
Wellman, Frederick L. *see* Wellman, Frederick Lovejoy.

Wellman, Frederick Lovejoy, 1897-
xWellman, Frederick L.
Dictionary of Tropical American Crops &
Their Diseases. Scarecrow.
Wellman, Manly W. *see* Wellman, Manly Wade.

Wellman, Manly Wade, 1905-
xWellman, Manly W.
The Old Gods Waken. Doubleday.
Wellman, Paul I. *see* Wellman, Paul Iselin.

Wellman, Paul Iselin, 1898-
xWellman, Paul I.
Greatest Cattle Drive. HM.

Wellmer, Albrecht.
xWellmer, Albrecht.
Critical Theory of Society. Continuum.
Wells, A. F. *see* Wells, Alexander Frank.

Wells, Alan, 1940-
xWells, Alan.
American Society: Problems & Dilemmas.
Goodyear.
ed. Mass Communications: A World View.
Mayfield Pub.
ed. Mass Media & Society. Mayfield Pub.

Wells, Alexander Frank.
xWells, A. F.
Structural Inorganic Chemistry. Oxford U Pr.
Third Dimension in Chemistry. Oxford U Pr.
Wells, Benjamin. *see* Wells, Benjamin Willis.

Wells, Benjamin Willis, 1856-1923
xWells, Benjamin.
Modern German Literature. Folcroft.
Wells, C. H. *see* Wells, Clifford H. J.

Wells, Camden.
xWells, Camden.
Improper Bostonian. Branden.

Wells, Carolyn, d. 1942
xWells, Carolyn.

ed. Nonsense Anthology. Arno.
Parody Anthology. Dover.
Parody Anthology. Gale.
A Parody Anthology. Gordon Pr.
Whimsey Anthology. Dover.
A Whimsey Anthology. Gale.

Wells, Charles E.
xWells, Charles E.
Neurology for Psychiatrists. Davis Co.

Wells, Claudia E.
xWells, Claudia E.
Whiskers, the Bank Mouse. Popcorn Pubs.

Wells, Clifford H. J.
xWells, C. H.
Introduction to Molecular Photochemistry.
Methuen Inc.

Wells, Damon.
xWells, Damon.
Stephen Douglas: The Last Years, 1857-1861.
U of Tex Pr.

Wells, Daniel A., 1943-
xWells, Daniel A.
The Literary Index to American Magazines:
1815-1865. Scarecrow.
Wells, David A. *see* Wells, David Ames.

Wells, David Ames, 1828-1898
xWells, David A.
Practical Economics: A Collection of Essays
Respecting Certain of the Recent Economic
Experiences of the United States.
Greenwood.

Wells, David F.
xWells, David F.
ed. Evangelicals: What They Believe, Who
They Are, Where They Are Changing. Baker
Bk.
The Search for Salvation. Inter-Varsity.

Wells, Ellen B.
xWells, Ellen B.
ed. Horsemanship: A Guide to Information
Sources. Gale.

Wells, Elmer E.
xWells, Elmer E.
The Mythical Negative Black Self Concept. R
& E Res Assoc.

Wells, Emma Helm Middleton, 1866-1945
xWells, Emma Middleton.
The History of Roane County, Tennessee
1801-1870. Regional.
Wells, Emma Middleton. *see* Wells, Emma Helm
Middleton.

Wells, F V.
xWells, V. F.
Cosmetics & the Skin. Krieger.

Wells, Frederick J.
xWells, Frederick J.
The Long-Run Availability of Phosphorus: A
Case Study in Mineral Resource Analysis.
Johns Hopkins.

Wells, G. L.
xWells, G. L.
Computation for Process Engineers. Intl Ideas.
Wells, Guy F. *see* Wells, Guy Fred.

Wells, Guy Fred, 1880-
xWells, Guy F.
Parish Education in Colonial Virginia. AMS Pr.
Parish Education in Colonial Virginia. Arno.
Wells, H. G. *see* Wells, Herbert George.
Wells, Henry W. *see* Wells, Henry Willis.

Wells, Henry Willis, 1895-
xWells, Henry W.
Introduction to Emily Dickinson. Hendricks
House.
Realm of Literature. Kennikat.
Wells, Herbert G. *see* Wells, Herbert George.

Wells, Herbert George, 1866-1946
xWells, H. G.

Crux Ansata: An Indictment of the Roman
Catholic Church. Arno.
First Men in the Moon. Airmont.
First Men in the Moon. Berkley Pub.
The Food of the Gods. Pendulum Pr.
Food of the Gods. Airmont.
Food of the Gods. Berkley Pub.
The Future in America. Arno.
Star Begotten. Manor Bks.
Things to Come. Gregg.
The Wonderful Visit. Arno.
Work, Wealth & Happiness of Mankind.
Greenwood.
xWells, Herbert G.
Floor Games. Arno.
Socialism & the Great State: Essays in
Construction. Arno.
Tales of Space & Time. Arno.
Thirty Strange Stories. Arno.
Twelve Stories & a Dream. Arno.
World Brain. Arno.
The World of William Clissold: A Novel at a
New Angle. Greenwood.

Wells, J. Gipson.
xWells, J. Gipson.
Contemporary Marriage: A Realistic Approach.
Macmillan.
Current Issues in Marriage & the Family.
Macmillan.
Wells, James M. *see* Wells, James Monroe.

Wells, James Monroe, b. 1838
xWells, James M.
Chisolm Massacre: A Picture of Home Rule in
Mississippi. Negro U Pr.

Wells, James R., 1932-
xWells, James R.
The Marching Band in Contemporary Music
Education. Interland Pub.

Wells, James S.
xWells, James S.
Plant Propagation Practices. Macmillan.

Wells, Joan, 1927-
xWells, Joan.
Downwind from Nobody. Garden Way Pub.
Wells, John E. *see* Wells, John Edwin.

Wells, John Edwin.
xWells, John E.
Manual of the Writings in Middle English:
1050-1400. Somerset Pub.

Wells, Joseph.
xWells, Joseph.
Studies in Herodotus. Arno.

Wells, Joyce, 1951-
xWells, Joyce.
The Cheese Stands Alone: Guide to Home
Cheesemaking. Hancock Hse.

Wells, Kenneth, 1927-
xWells, Kenneth.
Light & Electron Microscopic Studies of
Ascobolus Stercorarius: Aseus &
Ascosporeontogeny. U of Cal Pr.

Wells, Kenneth M.
xWells, Kenneth M.
Criminal Procedure & Trial Practice. P-H.

Wells, Louis T.
xWells, Louis T.
ed. The Product Life Cycle & International
Trade. Harvard Busn.
Wells, M. *see* Wells, Michael.
Wells, M. J. *see* Wells, Martin John.

Wells, Malcolm.
xWells, Malcolm.
How to Buy Solar Heating Without Getting
Burnt. Rodale Pr Inc.

Wells, Marian, 1931-
xWells, Marian.
When Love Is Not Enough. Bethany Fell.
Wells, Martin. *see* Wells, Martin John.

Wells, Martin John.
xWells, M. J.

Octopus: Physiology & Behaviour of an
Advanced Invertebrate. Methuen Inc.
xWells, Martin.
Lower Animals. McGraw.
Wells, Michael.
xWells, M.
Computing Systems Hardware. Cambridge U
Pr.
Wells, Peter, 1936-
xWells, Peter.
The American War of Independence. Holmes
& Meier.
Wells, Peter. see Wells, Peter R.
Wells, Peter N. see Wells, Peter Neil Temple.
Wells, Peter Neil Temple.
xWells, Peter N.
Ultrasonics in Clinical Diagnosis. Churchill.
Wells, Peter R.
xWells, Peter.
Linear Free Energy Relationships. Acad Pr.
Wells, R. A. see Wells, Ronald Allen.
Wells, R. O. see Wells, Raymond O'Neil.
Wells, Raymond O'Neil, 1940-
xWells, R. O.
Differential Analysis on Complex Manifolds.
Springer-Verlag.
Wells, Robert. see Wells, Robert W.
Wells, Robert V., 1943-
xWells, Robert V.
The Population of the British Colonies in
America Before 1776: A Survey of Census
Data. Princeton U Pr.
Wells, Robert W.
xWells, Robert.
This Is Milwaukee. Renaissance Bks.
xWells, Robert W.
Daylight in the Swamp. Doubleday.
Wells, Roger.
xWells, Roger.
Compiled by English-Eskimo &
Eskimo-English Vocabularies. AMS Pr.
Wells, Ronald A.
xWells, Ronald A.
Dictionaries & the Authoritarian Tradition: A
Study in English Usage & Lexicography.
Mouton.
Wells, Ronald Allen, 1942-
xWells, R. A.
Geophysics of Mars. Elsevier.
Wells, Rosemary.
xWells, Rosemary.
illus. Abdul. Dial.
illus. Don't Spill It Again, James. Dial.
illus. The Fog Comes on Little Pig Feet. Dial.
The Fog Comes on Little Pig Feet. Avon.
Leave Well Enough Alone. Dial.
Leave Well Enough Alone. Archway.
Leave Well Enough Alone. PB.
illus. Max's First Word. Dial.
illus. Max's Ride. Dial.
illus. Noisy Nora. Dial.
illus. Noisy Nora. Schol Bk Serv.
None of the Above. Dial.
Stanley & Rhoda. Dial.
illus. Unfortunately Harriet. Dial.
Wells, Stanley. see Wells, Stanley W.
Wells, Stanley W., 1930-
xWells, Stanley.
ed. English Drama (Excluding Shakespeare):
Select Bibliographical Guides. Oxford U Pr.
Shakespeare: The Writer & His Work. Scribner.
Wells, Ted. see Wells, Theodore Arthur.
Wells, Thelma. see Wells, Thelma J.
Wells, Thelma J.
xWells, Thelma.
Problems in Geriatric Nursing Care: A Study
of Nurses' Problems in Care of Old People in
Hospital. Churchill.
Wells, Theodore Arthur.
xWells, Ted.

Scientific Sailboat Racing. Dodd.
Wells, V. F. see Wells, F V.
Wells, Walter.
xWells, Walter.
Communications in Business. Wadsworth Pub.
Wells, William W.
xWells, William W.
ed. Cyclitols & Phosphoinositides. Acad Pr.
Wellstone, Paul D. see Wellstone, Paul David.
Wellstone, Paul David.
xWellstone, Paul D.
How the Rural Poor Got Power: Narrative of a
Grass-Roots Organizer: U of Mass Pr.
Wellwarth, George. see Wellwarth, George E.
Wellwarth, George E., 1932-
xWellwarth, George.
The Theater of Protest & Paradox:
Developments in Avant-Garde Drama. NYU
Pr.
xWellwarth, George E.
Spanish Underground Drama. Pa St U Pr.
Welmers, William E. see Welmers, William Everett.
Welmers, William Everett, 1916-
xWelmers, William E.
African Language Structures. U of Cal Pr.
Grammar of Vai. U of Cal Pr.
Wels, Byron. see Wels, Byron G.
Wels, Byron G.
xWels, Byron.
Fire & Theft Security Systems. TAB Bks.
Personal Computers: What They Are & How to
Use Them. P-H.
xWels, Byron G.
The Medicine Cabinet. Hammond Inc.
Welsch, Erwin K.
xWelsch, Erwin K.
Negro in the United States; A Research Guide.
Ind U Pr.
Welsch, Glenn A.
xWelsch, Glenn A.
Budgeting: Profit Planning & Control. P-H.
Cases in Profit Planning & Control. P-H.
Fundamentals of Financial Accounting. Irwin.
Intermediate Accounting. Irwin.
Welsch, J. R. see Welsch, Janice R.
Welsch, Janice R.
xWelsch, J. R.
Film Archetypes: Sisters, Mistresses, Mothers
& Daughters. Arno.
Welsch, Roger. see Welsch, Roger L.
Welsch, Roger L.
xWelsch, Roger.
Shingling the Fog & Other Plains Lies. U of
Nebr Pr.
xWelsch, Roger L.
Tall-Tale Postcards: A Pictorial History. A S
Barnes.
Welsch, Ulrich.
xWelsch, Ulrich.
Comparative Animal Cytology & Histology. U
of Wash Pr.
Welsch, Ulrike.
xWelsch, Ulrike.
World I Love to See. HM.
Welsh, George S. see Welsh, George Schlager.
Welsh, George Schlager.
xWelsh, George S.
Creativity & Intelligence: A Personality
Approach. U NC Inst Res Soc Sci.
Welsh, J. see Welsh, James.
Welsh, James.
xWelsh, J.
Introduction to Pascal. P-H.
Welsh, Ken.
xWelsh, Ken.
Hitch-Hiker's Guide to Europe. Stein & Day.
Welsh, Richard L.
xWelsh, Richard L.

ed. Foundations of Orientation & Mobility. Am
Foun Blind.
Welsh, Robert.
xWelsh, Robert.
Fishing Cartoon Book. David & Charles.
Welsh, Stanley L.
xWelsh, Stanley L.
Flowers of the Mountain Country. Brigham.
Welt, Bernard, 1952-
xWelt, Bernard.
Serenade. Z Pr.
Welter, Barbara.
xWelter, Barbara.
Dimity Convictions: The American Woman in
the Nineteenth Century. Ohio U Pr.
Welter, G. see Welter, Gerhard.
Welter, Gerhard.
xWelter, G.
Cleaning & Preservation of Coins & Medals. S
J Durst.
Welter, Paul, 1928-
xWelter, Paul.
How to Help a Friend. Tyndale.
Welter, Rush.
xWelter, Rush.
Popular Education & Democratic Thought in
America. Columbia U Pr.
Weltfish, Gene, 1902-
xWeltfish, Gene.
Caddoan Texts, Pawnee, South Band Dialect.
AMS Pr.
Weltner, K. see Weltner, Klaus.
Weltner, Klaus.
xWeltner, K.
The Measurement of Verbal Information in
Psychology & Education. Springer-Verlag.
Welton, David A.
xWelton, David A.
Children & Their World: Teaching Elementary
Social Studies. Rand.
Welty, Don A.
xWelty, Don A.
The Teacher Aide in the Instructional Team.
McGraw.
Welty, Eudora, 1909-
xWelty, Eudora.
A Curtain of Green & Other Stories.
HarBraceJ.
Delta Wedding. HarBraceJ.
The Eye of the Story: Selected Essays &
Reviews. Random.
Losing Battles. Random.
Losing Battles. Random.
The Optimist's Daughter. Random.
The Optimist's Daughter. Random.
Ponder Heart. HarBraceJ.
Ponder Heart. HarBraceJ.
Thirteen Stories. HarBraceJ.
Welty, James R.
xWelty, James R.
Fundamentals of Momentum, Heat & Mass
Transfer. Wiley.
Welwood, John, 1943-
xWelwood, John.
ed. The Meeting of the Ways. Explorations in
East-West Psychology. Schocken.
Welzel, Hans, 1904-
xWelzel, Hans.
Abhandlungen zum Strafrecht zur
Rechtsphilosophie. De Gruyter.
Wenburg, John.
xWenburg, John R.
The Personal Communication Process. Krieger.
Wenburg, John R. see Wenburg, John.
Wenckheim, Nicholas.
xWenckheim, Nicholas.
Image & Likeness: A Play in Three Acts.
Exposition.
Wende, S.
xWende, S.

Cerebral Magnification Angiography: Physical
Basis & Clinical Results. Springer-Verlag.

Wendel, Charles H.
xWendel, Charles H.
Encyclopedia of American Farm Tractors.
Crestline.

Wendel, T. M. *see* Wendel, Thomas M.

Wendel, Thomas M.
xWendel, T. M.
Introduction to Data Processing & Cobol.
McGraw.

Wendell, Barrett, 1855-1921
xWendell, Barrett.
English Composition. R West.
English Composition. Ungar.
A Literary History of America. Folcroft.
Literary History of America. Gale.
Literary History of America. Greenwood.
Literary History of America. Haskell.

Wender, Herbert, 1900-
xWender, Herbert.
Southern Commercial Conventions, 1837-1859.
AMS Pr.

Wender, Irving.
xWender, Irving.
ed. Organic Syntheses Via Metal Carbonyls.
Wiley.

Wendland, Michael F.
xWendland, Michael F.
The Arizona Project: How a Team of
Investigative Reporters Got Revenge on
Deadline. Andrews & McMeel.

Wendlandt, W. W. *see* Wendlandt, Wesley William.

Wendlandt, Wesley W. *see* Wendlandt, Wesley William.

Wendlandt, Wesley William.
xWendlandt, W. W.
Thermal Properties of Transition Metal
Ammine Complexes. Elsevier.
xWendlandt, Wesley W.
Thermal Methods of Analysis. Wiley.

Wendle, Bruce C.
xWendle, Bruce C.
ed. Engineering Guide to Plastics Plant Layout
& Machine Selection. Technomic.

Wendt, Albert, 1939-
xWendt, Albert.
Sons for the Return Home. Intl Pubns Serv.
Sons for the Return Home. Three Continents.

Wendt, Lloyd.
xWendt, Lloyd.
Chicago Tribune: The Rise of a Great
American Newspaper. Rand.

Wendt, N. *see* Wendt, Paul Francis.

Wendt, Paul Francis.
xWendt, N.
Real Estate Investment Analysis & Taxation.
McGraw.

Wengel, Jan ter.
xWengel, Jan Ter.
Allocation of Industry in the Andean Common
Market. Kluwer Boston.

Wenger, C. N. *see* Wenger, Christian Nat.

Wenger, Christian Nat, 1886-
xWenger, C. N.
Aesthetics of Robert Browning. Folcroft.

Wenger, J. C. *see* Wenger, John Christian.

Wenger, John Christian, 1910-
xWenger, J. C.
Disciples of Jesus. Herald Pr.
How Mennonites Came to Be. Herald Pr.

Wenger, Nanette K.
xWenger, Nanette K.
Cardiology for Nurses. McGraw.
Exercise & the Heart. Davis Co.
Rehabilitation of the Coronary Patient. Wiley.

Wenham, J. W. *see* Wenham, John William.

Wenham, John W. *see* Wenham, John William.

Wenham, John William.
xWenham, J. W.

Christ & the Bible. Inter-Varsity.
xWenham, John W.
The Goodness of God. Inter-Varsity.

Wenk, Arthur B.
xWenk, Arthur B.
Claude Debussy & the Poets. U of Cal Pr.

Wenk, Edward.
xWenk, Edward.
The Politics of the Ocean. U of Wash Pr.

Wenk, Ernst. *see* Wenk, Ernst A.

Wenk, Ernst A.
xWenk, Ernst.
ed. School Crime & Disruption. Intl Dialogue
Pr.

Wenk, Klaus.
xWenk, Klaus.
The Restoration of Thailand Under Rama I,
1782-1809. U of Ariz Pr.

Wenkam, Robert, 1920-
xWenkam, Robert.
Honolulu Is an Island. Rand.

Wenke, Robert J.
xWenke, Robert J.
Patterns in Prehistory: Mankind's First Three
Million Years. Oxford U Pr.

Wenley, Robert M. *see* Wenley, Robert Mark.

Wenley, Robert Mark, 1861-1929
xWenley, Robert M.
Stoicism & Its Influence. Cooper Sq.

Wenner, Lettie M. *see* Wenner, Lettie McSpadden.

Wenner, Lettie McSpadden.
xWenner, Lettie M.
One Environment Under Law: A Public Policy
Dilemma. Goodyear.

Wennerstrom, Mary H.
xWennerstrom, Mary H.
Anthology of Twentieth Century Music. P-H.

Wenninger, Magnus J.
xWenninger, Magnus J.
Spherical Models. Cambridge U Pr.

Wenrich, Ralph C.
xWenrich, Ralph C.
Leadership in Administration of Vocational &
Technical Education. Merrill.

Wensel, Louise. *see* Wensel, Louise O.

Wensel, Louise O.
xWensel, Louise.
Acupuncture for Americans. Reston.
Acupuncture in Medical Practice. Reston.

Wensinck, A. J. *see* Wensinck, Arent Jan.

Wensinck, Arent Jan, 1882-1939
xWensinck, A. J.
Muslim Creed: It's Genesis & Historical
Development. Biblio Dist.

Wensley, Frederick P. *see* Wensley, Frederick Porter.

Wensley, Frederick Porter, 1865-1949
xWensley, Frederick P.
Forty Years of Scotland Yard: The Record of a
Lifetime's Service in the Criminal
Investigation Department. Greenwood.

Went, Frits W. *see* Went, Frits Warmolt.

Went, Frits Warmolt.
xWent, Frits W.
Plants. Silver.

Wentinck, Charles.
xWentinck, Charles.
The Art Treasures of Europe. S&S.
Human Figure in Art from Prehistoric Times to
the Present Day. Livingston.

Wentink, Andrew M. *see* Wentink, Andrew Mark.

Wentink, Andrew Mark.
xWentink, Andrew M.
Balletomania: A Quizzical Potpourri of Ballet
Facts, Stars, Trivia, & Lore. Doubleday.

Wentworth, Felix. *see* Wentworth, Felix R. L.

Wentworth, Felix R. L.
xWentworth, Felix.

ed. Managing International Distribution. Am
Mgmt.

Wentworth, Frank L, 1866-1942
xWentworth, Frank L.
Aspen on the Roaring Fork. Sundance.

Wentworth, Harold.
xWentworth, Harold.
Dictionary of American Slang. T Y Crowell.

Wentworth, Patricia.
xWentworth, Patricia.
Silent Pool. Amereon Ltd.

Wentz, Anne C. *see* Wentz, Anne Colston.

Wentz, Anne Colston.
xWentz, Anne C.
Manual of Gynecologic Endocrinology &
Infertility. Williams & Wilkins.

Wentz, Frank M. *see* Wentz, Frank Meredith.

Wentz, Frank Meredith, 1917-
xWentz, Frank M.
Principles & Practice of Periodontics: With an
Atlas of Treatment. C C Thomas.

Wentz, Frederick K.
xWentz, Frederick K.
Getting into the Act: Opening up Lay Ministry
in the Weekday World. Abingdon.

Wentz, Walter B.
xWentz, Walter B.
Cases in Marketing Research. Har-Row.
Marketing. West Pub.
Marketing Research: Management, Methods, &
Cases. Har-Row.

Wentzel, Donat A. *see* Wentzel, Donat G.

Wentzel, Donat G.
xWentzel, Donat A.
ed. Plasma Instabilities in Astrophysics.
Gordon.

Wentzler, Rich.
xWentzler, Rich.
The Vitamin Book. Doubleday.
The Vitamin Book. St Martin.

Wenyon, Michael.
xWenyon, Michael.
Understanding Holography. Arco.

Wenz, W. *see* Wenz, Werner.

Wenz, Werner, 1926-
xWenz, W.
Abdominal Angiography. Springer-Verlag.

Wenzel, George L. *see* Wenzel, George Leonard.

Wenzel, George Leonard, 1902-
xWenzel, George L.
Wenzel's Menu Maker. Radio City.

Wepler, W. *see* Wepler, Wilhelm.

Wepler, Wilhelm.
xWepler, W.
Clinical Histopathology of the Liver: An Atlas.
Grune.

Wepman, Dennis.
xWepman, Dennis.
The Life: The Lore & Folk Poetry of the Black
Hustler. Holloway.
The Life: The Lore & Folk Poetry of the Black
Hustler. U of Pa Pr.

Weppner, Robert S.
xWeppner, Robert S.
ed. Street Ethnography: Selected Studies of
Crime & Drug Use in Natural Settings. Sage.

Werblowsky, Raphael J. *see* Werblowsky, Raphael
Jehudah Zwi.

Werblowsky, Raphael Jehudah Zwi, 1924-
xWerblowsky, Raphael J.
Lucifer & Prometheus: A Study of Milton's
Satan. AMS Pr.

Werbner, R. P.
xWerbner, R. P.
Regional Cults. Acad Pr.

Werbow, Stanley N. *see* Werbow, Stanley Newman.

Werbow, Stanley Newman.
xWerbow, Stanley N.

ed. Formal Aspects of Medieval German
Poetry: A Symposium. U of Tex Pr.
Were, G. S. *see* Were, Gideon S.
Were, Gideon. *see* Were, Gideon S.
Were, Gideon S.
xWere, G. S.
East Africa Through a Thousand Years: A
History of the Years A. D. 1000 to the
Present Day. Holmes & Meier.
xWere, Gideon.
A History of South Africa. Holmes & Meier.
Werge, John.
xWerge, John.
The Evolution of Photography. Arno.
Wergeland, Agnes M. *see* Wergeland, Agnes Mathilde.
Wergeland, Agnes Mathilde.
xWergeland, Agnes M.
Leaders in Norway, & Other Essays. Arno.
Wergin, Joseph P.
xWergin, Joseph P.
How to Win at Cribbage. Winchester Pr.
Werking, Richard H. *see* Werking, Richard Hume.
Werking, Richard Hume.
xWerking, Richard H.
The Master Architects: Building the United
States Foreign Service, 1890-1913. U Pr of
Ky.
Werkmeister, William H. *see* Werkmeister, William
Henry.
Werkmeister, William Henry.
xWerkmeister, William H.
ed. Reflections on Kant's Philosophy. U
Presses Fla.
Werlin, Herbert. *see* Werlin, Herbert H.
Werlin, Herbert H., 1932-
xWerlin, Herbert.
Governing an African City: A Study of
Nairobi. Holmes & Meier.
Wermer, J. *see* Wermer, John.
Wermer, John.
xWermer, J.
Banach Algebras & Several Complex Variables.
Springer-Verlag.
Potential Theory. Springer-Verlag.
Werne, Benjamin.
xWerne, Benjamin.
The Law & Practice of Public Employment
Labor Relations. Michie.
Wernecke, Herbert H. *see* Wernecke, Herbert Henry.
Wernecke, Herbert Henry, 1895-
xWernecke, Herbert H.
Celebrating Christmas Around the World.
Westminster.
Christmas Customs Around the World.
Westminster.
Werner, Alfred, 1911-
xWerner, Alfred.
Chagall. McGraw.
Degas Pastels. Watson-Guptill.
Inness Landscapes. Watson-Guptill.
Paul Gauguin. McGraw.
Werner, Alice, 1859-1935
xWerner, Alice.
Natives of British Central Africa. Negro U Pr.
Werner, Charles, 1928-
xWerner, Charles.
Reading to Learn: A Unit Approach. Reston.
Werner, Dietrich, 1937-
xWerner, Dietrich.
ed. The Biology of Diatoms. U of Cal Pr.
Werner, Don. *see* Werner, Donald L.
Werner, Donald L.
xWerner, Don.
Reflections of Winter. HR&W.
Werner, Emil A. *see* Werner, Emil Alphonse.
Werner, Emil Alphonse, 1866-1951
xWerner, Emil A.

Chemistry of Urea: The Theory of Its
Constitution, & of the Origin & Mode of Its
Formation in Living Organisms. Johnson
Repr.
Werner, Emmy E., 1929-
xWerner, Emmy E.
Cross-Cultural Child Development: A View
from the Planet Earth. Brooks-Cole.
Werner, Gerhard.
xWerner, Gerhard.
ed. Feature Extraction by Neurons & Behavior.
MIT Pr.
Werner, Heinz, 1890-
xWerner, Heinz.
Comparative Psychology of Mental
Development. Intl Univs Pr.
Werner, J. Paul.
xWerner, J. Paul.
Those Many-Splendored Faraway Places. J P
Werner.
Werner, Morris R. *see* Werner, Morris Robert.
Werner, Morris Robert, 1897-
xWerner, Morris R.
Brigham Young. Hyperion Conn.
Brigham Young. R West.
Privileged Characters. Arno.
Werner, Peter H.
xWerner, Peter H.
Inexpensive Physical Education Equipment for
Children. Burgess.
Learning Through Movement: Teaching
Cognitive Content Through Physical
Activities. Mosby.
Perceptual Motor Development Equipment:
Inexpensive Ideas & Activities. Wiley.
Werner, Raymond J.
xWerner, Raymond J.
Real Estate Closings. PLI.
Werner, Sarah. *see* Werner, Sarah S.
Werner, Sarah S.
xWerner, Sarah.
Atlas of Neonatal Electroencephalography.
Raven.
Wernick, Robert.
xWernick, Robert.
The Family. Silver.
The Family. Time-Life.
The Vikings. Silver.
The Vikings. Time-Life.
Wersba, Barbara.
xWersba, Barbara.
Dream Watcher. Atheneum.
Werskey, Gary.
xWerskey, Gary.
The Visible College: The Collective Biography
of British Scientific Socialists in the 1930's.
HR&W.
Werstein, Irving.
xWerstein, Irving.
Boxer Rebellion: Anti-Foreign Terror Seizes
China. Watts.
Civil War Sailor. Doubleday.
Cruise of the Essex: An Incident from the War
of 1812. Macrae.
Many Faces of the Civil War. Messner.
Strangled Voices: The Story of the Haymarket
Affair. Macmillan.
Wert, James E. *see* Wert, James Edward.
Wert, James Edward.
xWert, James E.
Financing Business Firms. Irwin.
Wert, W. F. Van. *see* Van Wert, W. F.
Wert, William F. Van. *see* Van Wert, William F.
Wert, William M. Van. *see* Van Wert, William.
Wertenbaker, Lael. *see* Wertenbaker, Lael Tucker.
Wertenbaker, Lael Tucker.
xWertenbaker, Lael.

World of Picasso. Time-Life.
World of Picasso. Silver.
Wertenbaker, Thomas J. *see* Wertenbaker, Thomas
Jefferson.
Wertenbaker, Thomas Jefferson, 1879-1966
xWertenbaker, Thomas J.
Father Knickerbocker Rebels: New York City
During the Revolution. Cooper Sq.
Planters of Colonial Virginia. Russell.
Torchbearer of the Revolution: The Story of
Bacon's Rebellion & Its Leader. Peter Smith.
Werth, Alexander, 1901-
xWerth, Alexander.
The De Gaulle Revolution. Greenwood.
Musical Uproar in Moscow. Greenwood.
The Twilight of France, 1933-1940. Fertig.
Werth, Kurt.
xWerth, Kurt.
Lazy Jack. Penguin.
illus. Lazy Jack. Viking Pr.
Wertham, Fredric, 1895-
xWertham, Fredric.
The World of Fanzines: A Special Form of
Communication. S Ill U Pr.
Wertheim, Alfred. *see* Wertheim, Alfred H.
Wertheim, Alfred H.
xWertheim, Alfred.
Natural Poisons in Natural Foods. Lyle Stuart.
Wertheim, Arthur F. *see* Wertheim, Arthur Frank.
Wertheim, Arthur Frank, 1935-
xWertheim, Arthur F.
Radio Comedy. Oxford U Pr.
Wertheim, W. F. *see* Wertheim, Willem Frederik.
Wertheim, Willem F. *see* Wertheim, Willem Frederik.
Wertheim, Willem Frederik, 1907-
xWertheim, W. F.
East-West Parallels: Sociological Approaches to
Modern Asia. Mouton.
xWertheim, Willem F.
Indonesian Society in Transition: A Study of
Social Change. Hyperion Conn.
Wertheimer, Max, 1880-1943
xWertheimer, Max.
Productive Thinking. Greenwood.
Wertheimer, Michael.
xWertheimer, Michael.
A Brief History of Psychology. HR&W.
Psychology & the Problems of Today. Scott F.
Wertheimer, Mildred S. *see* Wertheimer, Mildred Salz.
Wertheimer, Mildred Salz, 1896-
xWertheimer, Mildred S.
Pan-German League, 1890-1914. Octagon.
Wertheimer, Roger.
xWertheimer, Roger.
Significance of Sense: Meaning, Modality, &
Morality. Cornell U Pr.
Werthman, Michael. *see* Werthman, Michael S.
Werthman, Michael S.
xWerthman, Michael.
Self-Psyching: 35 Proven Techniques for
Overcoming Common Psychological
Problems. J P Tarcher.
Wertime, Theodore A.
xWertime, Theodore A.
Coming of the Age of Steel. U of Chicago Pr.
Wertsman, Vladimir, 1929-
xWertsman, Vladimir.
ed. The Romanians in America & Canada: A
Guide to Information Sources. Gale.
The Ukrainians in America: A Chronology &
Fact Book. Oceana.
Wertz, Richard W.
xWertz, Richard W.
Lying-in: A History of Childbirth in America.
Free Pr.
Lying-In: A History of Childbirth in America.
Schocken.
Wesberry, James P. *see* Wesberry, James Pickett.
Wesberry, James Pickett.
xWesberry, James P.

A Gossip's Story, & a Legendary Tale.
  Garland Pub.
A Tale of the Times. Garland Pub.
West, Jessamyn.
  xWest, Jessamyn.
  Cress Delahanty. Avon.
  Friendly Persuasion. HarBraceJ.
  The Friendly Persuasion. Penguin.
  The Massacre at Fall Creek. Fawcett.
  The Massacre at Fall Creek. HarBraceJ.
West, John, 1779?-1845
  xWest, John.
  Substance of a Journal During a Residence at
    the Red River Colony. Johnson Repr.
West, John B. see West, John Burnard.
West, John Burnard.
  xWest, John B.
  Pulmonary Pathophysiology: The Essentials.
    Williams & Wilkins.
West, John F. see West, John Foster.
West, John Foster, 1918-
  xWest, John F.
  Appalachian Dawn. Moore Pub Co.
  This Proud Land: The Blue Ridge Mountains.
    McNally.
West, Kenneth S.
  xWest, Kenneth S.
  The Captive Luftwaffe. Merrimack Bk Serv.
West, Leonard J. see West, Leonard Jordan.
West, Leonard Jordan, 1921-
  xWest, Leonard J.
  Modern College Typewriting: A Basic Course.
    HarBraceJ.
  Modern College Typewriting: A Complete
    Course. HarBraceJ.
  Modern College Typewriting: An Advanced
    Course. HarBraceJ.
West, Marion B.
  xWest, Marion B.
  No Turning Back. Broadman.
  Out of My Bondage. Broadman.
  Two of Everything but Me. Broadman.
West, Martin. see West, Martin Litchfield.
West, Martin Litchfield.
  xWest, Martin.
  Studies in Greek Elegy & Iambus. De Gruyter.
West, Max, 1870-1909
  xWest, Max.
  Inheritance Tax. AMS Pr.
West, Morris, 1916-
  xWest, Morris.
  The Navigator. Morrow.
  The Navigator. PB.
  xWest, Morris L.
  The Navigator. G K Hall.
West, Morris. see West, Morris L.
West, Morris L.
  xWest, Morris.
  The Devil's Advocate. PB.
  xWest, Morris L.
  The Devil's Advocate. Morrow.
West, Morris L. see West, Morris.
West, Nathanael, 1903-1940
  xWest, Nathanael.
  The Complete Works of Nathanael West.
    Octagon.
West, Norman D.
  xWest, Norman D.
  Psychiatry in Primary Care Medicine. Year Bk
    Med.
West, Paul, 1930-
  xWest, Paul.
  I'm Expecting to Live Quite Soon. Ultramarine
    Pub.
  Words for a Deaf Daughter. Har-Row.
  Words for a Deaf Daughter. NAL.
West, Ranyard, 1900-
  xWest, Ranyard.

Conscience & Society: A Study of the
    Psychological Prerequisites of Law & Order.
    Greenwood.
West, Rebecca, Pseud.
  xWest, Rebecca.
  Arnold Bennett Himself. Folcroft.
  The Thinking Reed. AMS Pr.
West, Richard S. see West, Richard Sedgewick.
West, Richard Sedgewick, 1902-
  xWest, Richard S.
  Admirals of American Empire: The Combined
    Story of George Dewey, Alfred Thayer
    Mahan, Winfield Scott Schley & William
    Thomas Sampson. Greenwood.
West, Robert C. see West, Robert Cooper.
West, Robert Cooper.
  xWest, Robert C.
  Cultural Geography of the Modern Tarascan
    Area. Greenwood.
  The Mining Community in Northern New
    Spain: The Parral Mining District. AMS Pr.
West, Robert Craig, 1947-
  xWest, Robert C.
  Banking Reform & Federal Reserve,
    1863-1923. Cornell U Pr.
West, Robert M.
  xWest, Robert M.
  Review of the North American Eocene &
    Oligocene Apatemyidae (Mammalia :
    Insectivora). Tex Tech Pr.
West, Serene, 1929-
  xWest, Serene.
  Very Practical Meditation. Donning Co.
West, Stanley A.
  xWest, Stanley A.
  The Chicano Experience. Westview.
West, Steven.
  xWest, Steven.
  How to Live to Be a 100 & Enjoy It!. AMW.
  The Power & Pleasure of Sex. AMW.
West, Theodora L.
  xWest, Theodora L.
  Continental Short Story: An Existential
    Approach. Odyssey Pr.
West, Thomas G., 1945-
  xWest, Thomas G.
  Plato's "Apology of Socrates": An
    Interpretation with a New Translation.
    Cornell U Pr.
West, Thomas R. see West, Thomas Reed.
West, Thomas Reed.
  xWest, Thomas R.
  Nature, Community, & Will: A Study in
    Literary & Social Thought. U of Mo Pr.
West, Tom.
  xWest, Tom.
  Payoff at Piute. Ace Bks.
West, Trudy.
  xWest, Trudy.
  Fireplace in the Home. David & Charles.
West, Uta.
  xWest, Uta.
  If Love Is the Answer, What Is the Question?.
    McGraw.
  If Love Is the Answer, What Is the Question?.
    PB.
West, Victor R. see West, Victor Royce.
West, Victor Royce.
  xWest, Victor R.
  Folklore in the Works of Mark Twain. Folcroft.
West Virginia Advocacy Seminar, 8th, Charleston, 1966.
  xWest Virginia Trial Lawyers Association.
  Trial Tactics. Trans-Media Pub.
West Virginia Trial Lawyers Association. see West
  Virginia Advocacy Seminar, 8th, Charleston, 1966.
West, Wallace.
  xWest, Wallace.
  Lords of Atlantis. Assoc Bk.
West, William R. see West, William Walter.

West, William Walter.
  xWest, William R.
  Exploring, Visualizing, Communicating: A
    Composition Text. P-H.
Westall, Robert.
  xWestall, Robert.
  Devil on the Road. Greenwillow.
Westbeau, Georges. see Westbeau, Georges H.
Westbeau, Georges H.
  xWestbeau, Georges.
  Little Tyke. Pacific Pr Pub Assn.
Westbrook, James. see Westbrook, James H.
Westbrook, James H.
  xWestbrook, James.
  Aim for a Job in Restaurants & Food Service.
    Rosen Pr.
  xWestbrook, James H.
  Aim for a Job in Restaurants & Food Service.
    Arco.
Westbrook, Perry. see Westbrook, Perry D.
Westbrook, Perry D.
  xWestbrook, Perry.
  Mary Wilkins Freeman. Coll & U Pr.
  xWestbrook, Perry D.
  Free Will & Determinism in American
    Literature. Fairleigh Dickinson.
  The Greatness of Man: An Essay on
    Dostoyevsky & Whitman. Fairleigh
    Dickinson.
  Mary Ellen Chase. Coll & U Pr.
  Mary Wilkins Freeman. Irvington.
Westbrook, Richard.
  xWestbrook, Richard.
  The Adulteress. Pelican.
Westby, David L., 1929-
  xWestby, David L.
  Clouded Vision: The Student Movement in the
    United States in the 1860's. Bucknell U Pr
Westcott, Alvin. see Westcott, Alvin M.
Westcott, Alvin M.
  xWestcott, Alvin.
  Fun with Timothy Triangle. Oddo.
  Word Bending with Aunt Sarah. Oddo.
  xWestcott, Alvin M.
  Creative Teaching of Mathematics in the
    Elementary School. Allyn.
Westcott, B. F. see Westcott, Brooke Foss.
Westcott, Brooke Foss, Bp. of Durham, 1825-1901
  xWestcott, B. F.
  On Some Points in Browning's View of Life.
    Folcroft.
Westcott, Cynthia, 1898-
  xWestcott, Cynthia.
  The Gardener's Bug Book. Doubleday.
Westcott, Edward N. see Westcott, Edward Noyes.
Westcott, Edward Noyes.
  xWestcott, Edward N.
  David Harum: A Story of American Life. R
    West.
Westcott, Jan.
  xWestcott, Jan.
  Captain Barney. Queens Hse.
Westcott, Jan. see Westcott, Jan Vlachos.
Westcott, Jan Vlachos, 1912-
  xWestcott, Jan.
  A Woman of Quality. Putnam.
Westcott, Linn. see Westcott, Linn Hanson.
Westcott, Linn Hanson, 1913-
  xWestcott, Linn.
  HO Railroad That Grows. Kalmbach.
  How to Build Model Railroad Benchwork.
    Kalmbach.
  How to Wire Your Model Railroad. Kalmbach.
  ed. Practical Guide to Model Railroading.
    Kalmbach.
Westerberg, A. W.
  xWesterberg, A. W.
  Process Flowsheeting. Cambridge U Pr.
Westerberg, Christine, 1950-
  xWesterberg, Christine.

The Cap That Mother Made. P-H.
illus. A Little Lion. P-H.
Westerby, Herbert.
xWesterby, Herbert.
History of Pianoforte Music. Da Capo.
Westerfield, H. Bradford, 1928-
xWesterfield, H. Bradford.
The Instruments of America's Foreign Policy.
Greenwood.
Westergaard, John. *see* Westergaard, John H.
Westergaard, John H.
xWestergaard, John.
Class in a Capitalist Society: A Study of
Contemporary Britain. Basic.
ed. Modern British Society: A Bibliography. St
Martin.
Westerhoff, John H.
xWesterhoff, John H.
ed. A Colloquy on Christian Education. Pilgrim
NY.
Inner Growth-Outer Change: An Educational
Guide to Church Renewal. Seabury.
Westerlund, Gunnar.
xWesterlund, Gunnar.
Organizational Myths. Har-Row.
Westerman, Maxine.
xWesterman, Maxine.
Intermediate Fashion Design & Water Color
Illustration. Fairchild.
Westermann, Claus.
xWestermann, Claus.
Blessing in the Bible & the Life of the Church.
Fortress.
Creation. Fortress.
God's Angels Need No Wings. Fortress.
The Promises to the Fathers: Studies on the
Patriarchal Narratives. Fortress.
Westermann, Diedrich, 1875-1956
xWestermann, Diedrich.
Africa & Christianity. AMS Pr.
Westermarck, Edward A. *see* Westermarck, Edward
Alexander.
Westermarck, Edward Alexander, 1862-1939
xWestermarck, Edward A.
Christianity & Morals. Arno.
Western Electric. *see* Western Electric Company, Inc.
Western Electric Company, Inc.
xWestern Electric.
Survival in the North. Wehman.
Western, J. R. *see* Western, John R.
Western, John R.
xWestern, J. R.
End of European Primacy, 1870-1945.
Humanities.
Western, John S. *see* Western, John Stuart.
Western, John Stuart.
xWestern, John S.
ed. Planning in Turbulent Environments. U of
Queensland Pr.
Western Resources Conference - 1964. *see* Western
Resources Conference, 10th, University of Colorado,
1964.
Western Resources Conference - 1966. *see* Western
Resources Conference, 8th, Colorado School of Mines,
1966.
Western Resources Conference - 1968. *see* Western
Resources Conference, 10th, Colorado State
University, 1968.
**Western Resources Conference, 3rd, Colorado State
University, 1961.**
xWestern Resources Conference, 3rd, Colorado
State University, 1961.
Land & Water: Planning for Economic Growth:
Proceedings. Greenwood.
**Western Resources Conference, 8th, Colorado School of
Mines, 1966.**
xWestern Resources Conference - 1966.

Natural Gas, Coal, Ground Water: Exploring
New Methods & Techniques in Resources
Research, Proceedings. Colo Assoc.
**Western Resources Conference, 10th, Colorado State
University, 1968.**
xWestern Resources Conference - 1968.
Public Land Policy: Proceedings. Colo Assoc.
**Western Resources Conference, 10th, University of
Colorado, 1964.**
xWestern Resources Conference - 1964.
New Horizons for Resources Research: Issues
& Methodology: Proceedings. Colo Assoc.
Western Writers of America.
xWestern Writers Of America.
Branded West: An Anthology. Arno.
Frontiers West. Arno.
Hoof Trails & Wagon Tracks: Stories of the
Western Trails by Members of the Western
Writers of America. Arno.
Hound Dogs & Others: A Collection of Stories.
Arno.
A Saddlebag of Tales: A Collection of Stories
by Members of the Western Writers of
America. Arno.
Spurs West. Arno.
Trails of the Iron Horse. Doubleday.
Water Trails West. Avon.
Water Trails West. Doubleday.
Wild Horse Roundup: A Collection of Stories
by Members of Western Writers of America.
Arno.
Wild Streets. Arno.
The Women Who Made the West. Doubleday.
Westerners, the Potomac Corral.
xPotomac Corral of the Westerners.
Great Western Indian Fights. U of Nebr Pr.
Westervelt, William D. *see* Westervelt, William Drake.
Westervelt, William Drake, 1849-1939
xWestervelt, William D.
Legends of Maui, a Demi God of Polynesia, &
of His Mother Hina. AMS Pr.
Westfall, Carroll. *see* Westfall, Carroll William.
Westfall, Carroll William.
xWestfall, Carroll.
In This Most Perfect Paradise: Alberti,
Nicholas V, and the Invention of Conscious
Urban Planning in Rome, 1447-55. Pa St U
Pr.
Westfall, Leon H. *see* Westfall, Leon Harvey.
Westfall, Leon Harvey, 1901-
xWestfall, Leon H.
A Study of Verbal Accompaniments to
Educational Motion Pictures. AMS Pr.
Westfall, Marty.
xWestfall, Marty.
The Handbook of Doll Repair & Restoration.
Crown.
Westin, Alan F.
xWestin, Alan F.
ed. Getting Angry Six Times a Week: A
Portfolio of Political Cartoons. Beacon Pr.
Individual Rights in the Corporation: A Reader
on Employee Rights. Pantheon.
ed. Information Technology in a Democracy.
Harvard U Pr.
Westin, Jeane.
xWestin, Jeane E.
Finding Your Roots: How Every American
Can Trace His Ancestors. J P Tarcher.
Finding Your Roots: How Every American
Can Trace His Ancestors, at Home &
Abroad. St Martin.
Westin, Jeane E. *see* Westin, Jeane.
Westing, Fred. *see* Westing, Frederick.
Westing, Frederick, 1903-
xWesting, Fred.
Penn Station: Its Tunnels & Side Rodders.
Superior Pub.
Westing, Howard J. *see* Westing, John Howard.
Westing, J. H. *see* Westing, John Howard.

Westing, John Howard.
xWesting, Howard J.
Modern Marketing Thought. Macmillan.
xWesting, J. H.
Purchasing Management: Materials in Motion.
Wiley.
Westinghouse. *see* Westinghouse Electric Corporation.
Westinghouse Electric Corporation.
xWestinghouse.
Cars & Car Equipment. Trolley Talk.
Westlake, Donald. *see* Westlake, Donald E.
Westlake, Donald E.
xWestlake, Donald.
I Gave at the Office. S&S.
xWestlake, Donald E.

Castle in the Air. M Evans.
Cops & Robbers. M Evans.

Dancing Aztecs. M Evans.
Enough. Fawcett.
Enough. M Evans.
Hot Rock. S&S.
I Gave at the Office. PB.
Nobody's Perfect. Fawcett.

Nobody's Perfect. M Evans.
Two Much. M Evans.

Westlake, G. *see* Westlake, George E.
Westlake, George E.
xWestlake, G.
ed. Automation & Management in the Clinical
Laboratory. Univ Park.
Westlake, H. D. *see* Westlake, Henry Dickinson.
Westlake, Harold.
xWestlake, Harold.
Cleft Palate. P-H.
Westlake, Henry Dickinson.
xWestlake, H. D.
Individuals in Thucydides. Cambridge U Pr.
Westland, Gordon.
xWestland, Gordon.
Current Crises of Psychology. Heinemann Ed.
Westland, Pamela.
xWestland, Pamela.
Decorating with Wild Flowers. Rodale Pr Inc.
Westman, Barbara.
xWestman, Barbara.
Anna's Magic Broom. HM.
Westman, Jack C.
xWestman, Jack C.
ed. Individual Differences in Children. Wiley.
Westman, Paul.
xWestman, Paul.
Alan Shepard: First American in Space. Dillon.
Ray Kroc: Mayor of McDonaldland. Dillon.
Walter Cronkite: The Most Trusted Man in
America. Dillon.
Westman, Robert S.
xWestman, Robert S.
ed. The Copernican Achievement. U of Cal Pr.
Westmoreland, W. C. *see* Westmoreland, William Childs.
Westmoreland, William Childs, 1914-
xWestmoreland, W. C.
A Soldier Reports. Dell.
Westmorland, Mildmay F. *see* Westmorland, Mildmay
Fane.
Westmorland, Mildmay Fane, Earl of, 1601-1666
xWestmorland, Mildmay F.
Otia Sacra. Schol Facsimiles.
Westoff, Charles F.
xWestoff, Charles F.
College Women & Fertility Values. Princeton
U Pr.
Family Growth in Metropolitan America.
Princeton U Pr.
Weston. *see* Weston, John Frederick.
Weston, Alan J.
xWeston, Alan J.

Communicative Disorders: An Appraisal. C C
   Thomas.
Weston, Corinne C. *see* Weston, Corinne Comstock.
Weston, Corinne Comstock.
   xWeston, Corinne C.
   English Constitutional Theory & the House of
      Lords. AMS Pr.
Weston, Edward.
   xWeston, Edward.
   Daybooks of Edward Weston. Aperture.
Weston, George F.
   xWeston, George F.
   Boston Ways: High, by, & Folk. Beacon Pr.
Weston, George M. *see* Weston, George Melville.
Weston, George Melville, 1816-1887
   xWeston, George M.
   Progress of Slavery in the United States. Arno.
   Progress of Slavery in the United States. Negro
      U Pr.
Weston, J. Fred. *see* Weston, John Frederick.
Weston, J. Frederick. *see* Weston, John Frederick.
Weston, Jessie L. *see* Weston, Jessie Laidlay.
Weston, Jessie Laidlay, 1850-1928
   xWeston, Jessie L.
   tr. Arthurian Romances Unrepresented in
      "Malory's Morte D'Arthur". AMS Pr.
   From Ritual to Romance. Doubleday.
   From Ritual to Romance. Peter Smith.
   Legend of Sir Gawain: Studies Upon Its
      Original Scope & Significance. AMS Pr.
   The Legend of Sir Gawain: Studies Upon Its
      Original Scope & Significance. R West.
   Legend of Sir Lancelot Du Lac: Studies Upon
      Its Origin, Development, & Position in the
      Arthurian Romantic Cycles. AMS Pr.
   tr. Legend of Sir Perceval: Studies Upon Its
      Origin, Development & Position in the
      Arthurian Cycle. AMS Pr.
   The Legends of the Wagner Drama: Studies in
      Mythology & Romance. Longwood Pr.
   The Quest of the Holy Grail. Gordon Pr.
   The Quest of the Holy Grail. Haskell.
Weston, John.
   xWeston, John.
   The Boy Who Sang the Birds. Scribner.
   Compiled by The Oxford Children's Dictionary
      in Colour. Oxford U Pr.
Weston, John Frederick.
   xWeston.
   Essentials of Managerial Finance. Dryden Pr.
   xWeston, J. Fred.
   Guide to International Financial Management.
      McGraw.
   xWeston, J. Frederick.
   ed. Defense-Space Market Research. MIT Pr.
Weston, Lee.
   xWeston, Lee.
   Body Rhythm: The Circadian Rhythms Within
      You. HarBraceJ.
Weston, Marybeth L. *see* Weston, Marybeth Little.
Weston, Marybeth Little.
   xWeston, Marybeth L.
   Decorating with Plants. Pantheon.
Weston, Michael.
   xWeston, Michael.
   Morality & the Self. NYU Pr.
Weston, P. *see* Weston, Paul B.
Weston, Paul. *see* Weston, Paul B.
Weston, Paul B.
   xWeston, P.
   Police Personnel Management. P-H.
   xWeston, Paul.
   Fundamentals of Evidence. P-H.
   xWeston, Paul B.

Administration of Justice. P-H.
   Combat Shooting for Police. C C Thomas.
   Criminal Investigation: Basic Perspectives. P-H.
   The Police Traffic Control Function. C C
      Thomas.
   Supervision in the Administration of Justice:
      Police, Corrections, Courts. C C Thomas.
Weston, Rubin F. *see* Weston, Rubin Francis.
Weston, Rubin Francis.
   xWeston, Rubin F.
   Racism in U. S. Imperialism: The Influence of
      Racial Assumptions on American Foreign
      Policy, 1893-1946. U of SC Pr.
Weston, Stephen F. *see* Weston, Stephen Francis.
Weston, Stephen Francis, 1855-1935
   xWeston, Stephen F.
   Principles of Justice in Taxation. AMS Pr.
Weston, W. J. *see* Weston, Windsor John.
Weston, William L.
   xWeston, William L.
   Practical Pediatric Dermatology. Little.
Weston, Windsor John.
   xWeston, W. J.
   Soft Tissues of the Extremities: A Radiologic
      Study of Rheumatic Disease. Springer-Verlag.
Westover, Frederick L. *see* Westover, Frederick Lowell.
Westover, Frederick Lowell, 1900-
   xWestover, Frederick L.
   Controlled Eye Movements Versus Practice
      Exercises in Reading. AMS Pr.
Westphal, Albert C. *see* Westphal, Albert Charles
   Frederick.
Westphal, Albert Charles Frederick, 1908-
   xWestphal, Albert C.
   House Committee on Foreign Affairs. AMS Pr.
Westphal, Clarence.
   xWestphal, Clarence.
   Mooney, the Pet Lion. Denison.
Westphal, E.
   xWestphal, E.
   Agricultural Systems in Ethiopia. Unipub.
Westphal, F. *see* Westphal, Fred A.
Westphal, Fred A.
   xWestphal, F.
   Art of Philosophy: An Introductory Reader.
      P-H.
   xWestphal, Fred A.
   Activity of Philosophy: A Concise
      Introduction. P-H.
Westphal, Frederick W. *see* Westphal, Frederick William.
Westphal, Frederick William, 1916-
   xWestphal, Frederick W.
   A Guide to Teaching Woodwinds. Wm C
      Brown.
Westphal, Merold.
   xWestphal, Merold.
   History & Truth in Hegel's Phenomenology.
      Humanities.
Westphal, U.
   xWestphal, U.
   Steroid-Protein Interactions. Springer-Verlag.
Westphall, Victor.
   xWestphall, Victor.
   Public Domain in New Mexico, 1854-1891. U
      of NM Pr.
   Thomas Benton Catron & His Era. U of Ariz
      Pr.
Westrate, E. V. *see* Westrate, Edwin Victor.
Westrate, Edwin Victor.
   xWestrate, E. V.
   Those Fatal Generals. Kennikat.
Westrich, Sal Alexander.
   xWestrich, Sal Alexander.
   The Ormee of Bordeaux: A Revolution during
      the Fronde. Johns Hopkins.
Westrup, J. A. *see* Westrup, Jack Allan.
Westrup, Jack. *see* Westrup, Jack Allan.
Westrup, Jack Allan, 1904-
   xWestrup, J. A.

Purcell. Littlefield.
   xWestrup, Jack.
   Purcell. Biblio Dist.
Westshore, Inc.
   xWestshore, Inc.
   Doing Business with the Russians. Praeger.
Westwood, J. N.
   xWestwood, J. N.
   Locomotive Designers in the Age of Steam.
      Fairleigh Dickinson.
Westwood, Jennifer.
   xWestwood, Jennifer.
   Stories of Charlemagne. S G Phillips.
Westwood, W. D. *see* Westwood, William Dickson.
Westwood, William Dickson.
   xWestwood, W. D.
   Tantalum Thin Films. Acad Pr.
Wetanson, Burt.
   xWetanson, Burt.
   The Hunters. Doubleday.
   The Hunters. Playboy Pbks.
Wetering, Jan Van de. *see* Van de Wetering, Jan.
Wetering, Janwillem Van De. *see* Van De Wetering,
   Janwillem.
Wetherbe, James C.
   xWetherbe, James C.
   Cases in Systems Design. West Pub.
Wetherbee, Winthrop, 1938-
   xWetherbee, Winthrop.
   Platonism & Poetry in the Twelfth Century:
      The Literary Influence of the School of
      Chartres. Princeton U Pr.
Wetherell, C. *see* Wetherell, Charles.
Wetherell, Charles, 1946-
   xWetherell, C.
   Etudes for Programmers. P-H.
Wetherell, June.
   xWetherell, June.
   Opal Street. Manor Bks.
Wetherill, P. M. *see* Wetherill, Peter Michael.
Wetherill, Peter Michael.
   xWetherill, P. M.
   The Literary Text: An Examination of Critical
      Methods. U of Cal Pr.
Wetmore, Alexander.
   xWetmore, Alexander.
   Song & Garden Birds of North America. Natl
      Geog.
Wetmore, Alphonso.
   xWetmore, Alphonso.
   Compiled by Gazetteer of the State of
      Missouri. Arno.
Wetmore, Thomas H. *see* Wetmore, Thomas Hall.
Wetmore, Thomas Hall, 1915-
   xWetmore, Thomas H.
   The Low-Central & Low-Back Vowels in the
      English of the Eastern United States. U of
      Ala Pr.
Wets, Roger J. *see* Wets, Roger J. B.
Wets, Roger J. B.
   xWets, Roger J.
   ed. Stochastic Systems: Modeling,
      Identification, and Optimization I-. Elsevier.
Wetterer, Margaret K.
   xWetterer, Margaret K.
   Patrick & the Fairy Thief. Atheneum.
Wetzel, Richard D.
   xWetzel, Richard D.
   Frontier Musicians on the Connoquenessing,
      Wabash & Ohio: A History of the Music &
      Musicians of George Rapp's Harmony
      Society (1805-1906). Ohio U Pr.
Wetzel, Robert G.
   xWetzel, Robert G.
   Limnology. Saunders.
Wetzsteon, Ross.
   xWetzsteon, Ross.

The Obie Winners: The Best of off-Broadway.
Doubleday.
Weule, Karl, 1864-1926
　xWeule, Karl.
　　Native Life in East Africa: The Results of an
　　Ethnological Research Expedition. Metro
　　Bks.
Wever, R. A. *see* Wever, Rutger A.
Wever, Rutger A.
　xWever, R. A.
　　The Circadian System of Man: Results of
　　Experiments Under Temporal Isolation.
　　Springer-Verlag.
Wevrick, L.
　xWevrick, L.
　　Applied Research in Public Personnel
　　Administration. Intl Personnel Mgmt.
Wewers, Gerd A.
　xWewers, Gerd S.
　　Geheimnis und Geheimhaltung Im
　　Rabbinischen Judentum. De Gruyter.
Wewers, Gerd S. *see* Wewers, Gerd A.
Wexler, David A.
　xWexler, David A.
　　Innovations in Client-Centered Therapy. Wiley.
Wexler, Harry J.
　xWexler, Harry J.
　　Housing & Local Government: A Research
　　Guide for Policymakers & Planners.
　　Lexington Bks.
Wexler, Kenneth.
　xWexler, Kenneth.
　　Formal Principles of Language Acquisition.
　　MIT Pr.
Wexler, Philip.
　xWexler, Philip.
　　The Sociology of Education: Beyond Equality.
　　Bobbs.
Wexler, Victor. *see* Wexler, Victor G.
Wexler, Victor G.
　xWexler, Victor.
　　David Hume & "The History of England". Am
　　Philos.
Wexley, Kenneth N.
　xWexley, Kenneth N.
　　ed. Organizational Behavior & Industrial
　　Psychology: Readings with Commentary.
　　Oxford U Pr.
Wexu, Mario, 1945-
　xWexu, Mario.
　　The Ear-Gateway to Balancing the Body: A
　　Modern Guide to Ear Acupuncture. ASI
　　Pubs Inc.
Weyand, Clint.
　xWeyand, Clint.
　　Thank You for Being. Weyand-Shaw.
Weyant, J.Thomas.
　xWeyant, J. Thomas.
　　Introduction to Agricultural Business &
　　Industry. Interstate.
Weydenthal, Jan B. de. *see* De Weydenthal, Jan B.
Weyer, Edward M. *see* Weyer, Edward Moffat.
Weyer, Edward Moffat, 1904-
　xWeyer, Edward M.
　　ed. Strangest Creatures on Earth. Sheridan.
Weygandt, Cornelius, 1871-1957
　xWeygandt, Cornelius.
　　Irish Plays & Playwrights. Greenwood.
Weygers, Alexander G.
　xWeygers, Alexander G.
　　Modern Blacksmith. Van Nos Reinhold.
　　The Recycling, Use, & Repair of Tools. Van
　　Nos Reinhold.
Weyl, Hermann, 1885-1955
　xWeyl, Hermann.

Concept of a Riemann Surface. A-W.
Symmetry. Princeton U Pr.
Theory of Groups & Quantum Mechanics.
Dover.
Weyl, Nathaniel, 1910-
　xWeyl, Nathaniel.
　　The Creative Elite in America. Pub Aff Pr.
Weymouth, Lally.
　xWeymouth, Lally.
　　America in 1876: The Way We Were. Random.
Weymouth, R. F. *see* Weymouth, Richard Francis.
Weymouth, Richard Francis, 1822-1902
　xWeymouth, R. F.
　　New Testament in Modern Speech. Kregel.
Weyrick, Robert C.
　xWeyrick, Robert C.
　　Fundamentals of Automatic Control. McGraw.
Wezel, Peter, 1941-
　xWezel, Peter.
　　illus. Good Bird. Har-Row.
Whale, H. A., 1921-
　xWhale, H. A.
　　Effects of Ionospheric Scattering on Very-Long
　　Distance Radio Communication. Plenum Pub.
Whalen, A. D. *see* Whalen, Anthony D.
Whalen, Anthony D.
　xWhalen, A. D.
　　Detection of Signals in Noise. Acad Pr.
Whalen, Doris H.
　xWhalen, Doris H.
　　The Secretary's Handbook. HarBraceJ.
Whalen, Joseph P.
　xWhalen, Joseph P.
　　Radiology of the Abdomen: Anatomic Basis.
　　Lea & Febiger.
Whalen, Philip.
　xWhalen, Philip.
　　Decompressions: Selected Poems. Grey Fox.
　　Off the Wall: Interviews with Philip Whalen.
　　Four Seasons Foun.
　　On Bear's Head. HarBraceJ.
Whalen, William J. *see* Whalen, William Joseph.
Whalen, William Joseph.
　xWhalen, William J.
　　Other Religions in a World of Change. Ave
　　Maria.
Whaler, James, 1889-
　xWhaler, James.
　　Counterpoint & Symbol: An Inquiry into the
　　Rhythm of Milton's Epic Style. Folcroft.
Whaley, Lucille F.
　xWhaley, Lucille F.
　　Nursing Care of Infants & Children. Mosby.
Whall, Hugh D.
　xWhall, Hugh P.
　　The Southern Cross: Australia's 1974
　　Challenge for America's Cup. Admiralty Pub
　　Hse.
Whall, Hugh P. *see* Whall, Hugh D.
Whalley, Joyce I. *see* Whalley, Joyce Irene.
Whalley, Joyce Irene.
　xWhalley, Joyce I.
　　Cobwebs to Catch Flies: Illustrated Books for
　　the Nursery & Schoolroom 1700-1900. U of
　　Cal Pr.
Whalon, Marion K.
　xWhalon, Marion K.
　　ed. Performing Arts Research: A Guide to
　　Information Sources. Gale.
Wharry, Rhoda. *see* Wharry, Rhoda E.
Wharry, Rhoda E.
　xWharry, Rhoda.
　　In Time & Space. Acad Therapy.
Wharton, Althea.
　xWharton, Althea.
　　White Ghost of Fenwick Hall. PB.
Wharton, Anne. *see* Wharton, Anne Hollingsworth.
Wharton, Anne H. *see* Wharton, Anne Hollingsworth.
Wharton, Anne Hollingsworth, 1845-1928
　xWharton, Anne.

Martha Washington. Reprint.
xWharton, Anne H.
　Colonial Days & Dames. Arno.
Wharton, Donald P.
　xWharton, Donald P.
　　ed. In the Trough of the Sea: Selected
　　American Sea-Deliverance Narratives,
　　1610-1766. Greenwood.
　　Richard Steere: Colonial Merchant Poet. Pa St
　　U Pr.
Wharton, Edith. *see* Wharton, Edith Newbold (Jones).
Wharton, Edith Newbold (Jones), 1862-1937
　xWharton, Edith.
　　The Custom of the Country. Scribner.
　　The Ghost Stories of Edith Wharton. Popular
　　Lib.
　　Ghost Stories of Edith Wharton. Scribner.
　　Greater Inclination. AMS Pr.
　　Greater Inclination. Folcroft.
　　Greater Inclination. Scholarly.
　　House of Mirth. NAL.
　　The House of Mirth. NYU Pr.
　　The House of Mirth. Queens Hse.
　　The House of Mirth. Scribner.
　　The Reef. Scribner.
　　Summer: A Novel. Scholarly.
　　Touchstone. AMS Pr.
　　Touchstone. Scholarly.
Wharton, James.
　xWharton, James.
　　Bounty of the Chesapeake: Fishing in Colonial
　　Virginia. U Pr of Va.
Wharton, John F. *see* Wharton, John Franklin.
Wharton, John Franklin, 1894-
　xWharton, John F.
　　Life Among the Playwrights: Being Mostly the
　　Story of the Playwrights Producing Co., Inc..
　　Times Bks.
Wharton, Mary E.
　xWharton, Mary E.
　　A Guide to the Wildflowers & Ferns of
　　Kentucky. U Pr of Ky.
Whatcom Museum of History & Art. *see* Whatcom
　Museum of History and Art.
Whatcom Museum of History and Art.
　xWhatcom Museum of History & Art.
　　Arts of a Vanished Era. U of Wash Pr.
　　Green Gold Harvest: A History of Logging &
　　Its Products. U of Wash Pr.
　　Whatcom Seascapes: The Influence of the Sea
　　on Whatcom County. U of Wash Pr.
Whately, Thomas.
　xWhately, Thomas.
　　Remarks on Some of the Characters of
　　Shakespere. AMS Pr.
Whatley, Arthur. *see* Whatley, Arthur A.
Whatley, Arthur A.
　xWhatley, Arthur.
　　Personnel Management in Action: Skill
　　Building Experiences. West Pub.
Whatley, Jo Ann.
　xWhatley, Jo Ann.
　　Banking & Finance Careers. Watts.
Whatmough, Joshua, 1897-1964
　xWhatmough, Joshua.
　　Foundations of Roman Italy. Haskell.
Whealon, John F.
　xWhealon, John F.
　　Living the Catholic Faith Today. Dghtrs St
　　Paul.
Wheare, K. C.
　xWheare, Kenneth C.
　　Lincoln. Macmillan.
Wheare, Kenneth C. *see* Wheare, Kenneth Clinton.
Wheare, Kenneth Clinton, Sir, 1907-
　xWheare, Kenneth C.

Government by Committee: An Essay on the British Constitution. Greenwood.
Legislatures. Oxford U Pr.
Modern Constitutions. Oxford U Pr.

Wheat, Ed.
xWheat, Ed.
Intended for Pleasure. Revell.

Wheat Flour Institute.
xWheat Flour Institute.
Winning Sandwiches for Menu Makers. CBI Pub.

Wheat, Harry G. *see* Wheat, Harry Grove.

Wheat, Harry Grove, 1890-
xWheat, Harry G.
The Relative Merits of Conventional & Imaginative Types of Problems in Arithmetic. AMS Pr.

Wheat, Leonard F.
xWheat, Leonard F.
Paul Tillich's Dialectical Humanism: Unmasking the God above God. Johns Hopkins.

Wheat, M. T. *see* Wheat, Marvin T.

Wheat, Margaret M.
xWheat, Margaret M.
Survival Arts of the Primitive Paiutes. U of Nev Pr.

Wheat, Marvin T.
xWheat, M. T.
Progress & Intelligence of Americans: Collateral Proof of Slavery, from the First to the Eleventh Chapter of Genesis, As Founded on Organic Law. Arno.

Wheat, Patte.
xWheat, Patte.
By Sanction of the Victim. Major Bks.
By Sanction of the Victim. Timely Bks.

Wheatcroft, John, 1925-
xWheatcroft, John.
Ofoti. A S Barnes.
Ordering Demons. A S Barnes.

Wheater, Paul. *see* Wheater, Paul R.

Wheater, Paul R.
xWheater, Paul.
ed. Functional Histology: A Text & Colour Atlas. Churchill.

Wheatley, David, 1919-
xWheatley, David.
ed. Stress & the Heart: Interactions of the Cardiovascular System, Behavioral State, & Psychotropic Drugs. Raven.

Wheatley, Dennis, 1897-
xWheatley, Dennis.
ed. A Century of Horror Stories. Arno.
The Devil Rides Out. Merrimack Bk Serv.
Murder off Miami. Mayflower Bks.

Wheatley, Edward W., 1936-
xWheatley, Edward W.
Values in Conflict: Contemporary Issues in Business & Society. Banyan Bks.

Wheatley, Henry B. *see* Wheatley, Henry Benjamin.

Wheatley, Henry Benjamin, 1838-1917
xWheatley, Henry B.
A Dictionary of Reduplicated Words in the English Language. Folcroft.
How to Form a Library. Arden Lib.
How to Form a Library. Folcroft.
Literary Blunders: A Chapter in the "History of Human Error". Arden Lib.

Wheatley, James H., 1929-
xWheatley, James M.
Patterns in Thackeray's Fiction. MIT Pr.

Wheatley, James M. *see* Wheatley, James H.

Wheatley, Katherine E. *see* Wheatley, Katherine Ernestine.

Wheatley, Katherine Ernestine.
xWheatley, Katherine E.
Racine & English Classicism. Greenwood.

Wheatley, Paul.
xWheatley, Paul.

From Court to Capital: A Tentative Interpretation of the Origins of the Japanese Urban Tradition. U of Chicago Pr.

Wheatley, Richard C.
xWheatley, Richard C.
Restoration of Antique & Classic Cars. Bentley.

Wheatley, Ronald.
xWheatley, Ronald.
Operation Sea Lion: German Plans for the Invasion of England, 1939-1942. Greenwood.

Wheatley, Vera.
xWheatley, Vera.
The Life & Work of Harriet Martineau. R West.

Wheaton, Christopher D.
xWheaton, Christopher D.
Compiled by Primary Cinema Resources: Index of Screen Plays, Interviews & Special Collections at the University of Southern California. G K Hall.

Wheaton, F. W. *see* Wheaton, Frederick Warner.

Wheaton, Frederick Warner, 1942-
xWheaton, F. W.
Aquacultural Engineering. Wiley.

Wheaton, Henry, 1785-1848
xWheaton, Henry.
Enquiry into the Validity of the British Claim to a Right of Visitation & Search of the American Vessels Suspected to Be Engaged in the African Slave-Trade. Negro U Pr.

Whedbee, Charles H. *see* Whedbee, Charles Harry.

Whedbee, Charles Harry.
xWhedbee, Charles H.
Outer Banks Mysteries & Seaside Stories. Blair.

Wheeler, Alwyne. *see* Wheeler, Alwyne C.

Wheeler, Alwyne C.
xWheeler, Alwyne.
Fishes of the British Isles & North-West Europe. Mich St U Pr.
xWheeler, Alwynne.
Fishes of the World: Illustrated Dictionary. Macmillan.

Wheeler, Alwynne. *see* Wheeler, Alwyne C.

Wheeler, Arthur L. *see* Wheeler, Arthur Leslie.

Wheeler, Arthur Leslie.
xWheeler, Arthur L.
Catullus & the Traditions of Ancient Poetry. U of Cal Pr.

Wheeler, B. E. *see* Wheeler, Bryan Edward John.

Wheeler, Benjamin I. *see* Wheeler, Benjamin Ide.

Wheeler, Benjamin Ide, 1854-1927
xWheeler, Benjamin I.
Analogy & the Scope of Its Application in Language. Johnson Repr.

Wheeler, Bryan Edward John.
xWheeler, B. E.
Introduction to Plant Diseases. Wiley.

Wheeler, Charles B.
xWheeler, Charles B.
Design of Poetry. Norton.

Wheeler, Charles F. *see* Wheeler, Charles Francis.

Wheeler, Charles Francis.
xWheeler, Charles F.
Classical Mythology in the Plays, Masques, & Poems of Ben Jonson. Kennikat.

Wheeler, Christopher, 1940-
xWheeler, Christopher.
White-Collar Power: Changing Patterns of Interest Group Behavior in Sweden. U of Ill Pr.

Wheeler, Cindy.
xWheeler, Cindy.
A Good Day, a Good Night. Lippincott.

Wheeler, D. G. *see* Wheeler, Gonzales.

Wheeler, Daniel D.
xWheeler, Daniel D.
A Practical Guide for Making Decisions. Free Pr.

Wheeler, David R.
xWheeler, David R.

Control Yourself. Nelson-Hall.

Wheeler, Douglas L.
xWheeler, Douglas L.
Angola. Greenwood.

Wheeler, E. Todd. *see* Wheeler, Edward Todd.

Wheeler, Edward Todd, 1906-
xWheeler, E. Todd.
Hospital Modernization & Expansion. McGraw.

Wheeler, Elmer. *see* Wheeler, Elmer Louis.

Wheeler, Elmer Louis, 1903-
xWheeler, Elmer.
How to Sell Yourself to Others. Cornerstone.

Wheeler, Geoffrey.
xWheeler, Geoffrey.
The Modern History of Soviet Central Asia. Greenwood.

Wheeler, George S. *see* Wheeler, George Shaw.

Wheeler, George Shaw.
xWheeler, George S.
The Human Face of Socialism: The Political Economy of Change in Czechoslovakia. Lawrence Hill.

Wheeler, Gerald E.
xWheeler, Gerald E.
Prelude to Pearl Harbor: The United States Navy & the Far East, 1921-1931. U of Mo Pr.

Wheeler, Gerald R.
xWheeler, Gerald R.
Counterdeterrence: A Report on Juvenile Sentencing & Effects of Prisonization. Nelson-Hall.

Wheeler, Gershon. *see* Wheeler, Gershon J.

Wheeler, Gershon J.
xWheeler, Gershon.
How to Repair Electrical Appliances. Reston.
Introduction to Microwaves. P-H.
xWheeler, Gershon J.
How to Repair Electrical Appliances. B&N.

Wheeler, Gonzales.
xWheeler, D. G.
Let's Speak English. McGraw.

Wheeler, H. *see* Wheeler, Harry.

Wheeler, Harry, 1919-
xWheeler, H.
Plant Pathogenesis. Springer-Verlag.

Wheeler, J. *see* Wheeler, Jesse H.

Wheeler, Jesse H.
xWheeler, J.
Regional Geography of the World. HR&W.

Wheeler, John H. *see* Wheeler, John Hill.

Wheeler, John Hill, 1806-1882
xWheeler, John H.
Reminiscences & Memoirs of North Carolina & Eminent North Carolinians. Genealog Pub.

Wheeler, Keith.
xWheeler, Keith.
The Road to Tokyo. Time-Life.

Wheeler, Ladd.
xWheeler, Ladd.
Interpersonal Influence. Allyn.

Wheeler, Lawrence.
xWheeler, Lawrence.
Orff & Kodaly Adapted for the Elementary School. Wm C Brown.

Wheeler, Margariete M. *see* Wheeler, Margariete Montague.

Wheeler, Margariete Montague.
xWheeler, Margariete M.
Mathematics Library: Elementary & Junior High School. NCTM.

Wheeler, Max.
xWheeler, Max.
Phonology of Catalan. Biblio Dist.

Wheeler, Michael, 1947-
xWheeler, Michael.

The Art of Allusion in Victorian Fiction. B&N.
Divided Children: A Legal Guide for
 Divorcing, Parents. Norton.
Lies, Damn Lies, & Statistics: The
 Manipulation of Public Opinion in America.
 Liveright.

Wheeler, Monroe.
 xWheeler, Monroe.
 Soutine. Arno.

Wheeler, Mortimer. see Wheeler, Robert Eric Mortimer.

Wheeler, Otis B.
 xWheeler, Otis B.
 Literary Career of Maurice Thompson. La
  State U Pr.

Wheeler, Penney E. see Wheeler, Penny Estes.

Wheeler, Penny Estes.
 xWheeler, Penney E.
 The Appearing. Southern Pub.

Wheeler, Richard.
 xWheeler, Richard.
 IWO. Lippincott & Crowell.
 The Siege of Vicksburg. T Y Crowell.

Wheeler, Richard A. see Wheeler, Richard Anson.

Wheeler, Richard Anson, 1817-
 xWheeler, Richard A.
 History of the Town of Stonington, County of
  New London, Connecticut, from Its First
  Settlement in 1649 to 1900. Verry.

Wheeler, Richard S.
 xWheeler, Richard S.
 Beneath the Blue Mountain. Doubleday.
 Bushwack. Doubleday.
 The Politics of Pakistan: A Constitutional
  Quest. Cornell U Pr.

Wheeler, Robert E. see Wheeler, Robert Eric Mortimer.

Wheeler, Robert Eric Mortimer, Sir, 1890-
 xWheeler, Mortimer.
 Indus Civilization. Cambridge U Pr.
 xWheeler, Robert E.
 Flames Over Persepolis: Turning-Point in
  History. Greenwood.

Wheeler, Ruric E.
 xWheeler, Ruric E.
 Modern Mathematics with Applications to
  Business & the Social Sciences. Brooks-Cole.

Wheeler, Russell C. see Wheeler, Russell Charles.

Wheeler, Russell Charles.
 xWheeler, Russell C.
 Atlas of Tooth Form. Saunders.
 Dental Anatomy, Physiology & Occlusion.
  Saunders.
 Pulp Cavities of the Permanent Teeth: An
  Anatomical Guide to Manipulative
  Endodontics. Saunders.

Wheeler, Sessions S.
 xWheeler, Sessions S.
 Desert Lake: The Story of Nevada's Pyramid
  Lake. Caxton.

Wheeler, Thomas G. see Wheeler, Thomas Gerald.

Wheeler, Thomas Gerald.
 xWheeler, Thomas G.
 All Men Tall. S G Phillips.
 Fanfare for the Stalwart. S G Phillips.

Wheeler, Tom.
 xWheeler, Tom.
 The Guitar Book: A Handbook for Electric &
  Acoustic Guitarists. Har-Row.

Wheeler, Tony.
 xWheeler, Tony.
 Across Asia on the Cheap. Hippocrene Bks.
 Papua New Guinea, a Travel Survival Kit.
  Hippocrene Bks.

Wheeler, W. H. see Wheeler, William H.

Wheeler, William.
 xWheeler, William.
 Wood Carving. Sterling.
 Woodcarving. Sterling.

Wheeler, William H.
 xWheeler, W. H.

Counterfeit!. Childrens.

Wheeler, William M. see Wheeler, William Morton.

Wheeler, William Morton, 1865-1937
 xWheeler, William M.
 Fungus-Growing Ants of North America.
  Dover.
 The Fungus-Growing Ants of North America.
  Peter Smith.

Wheeler-Bennett, J. W. see Wheeler-Bennett, John
 Wheeler.

Wheeler-Bennett, John. see Wheeler-Bennett, John
 Wheeler.

Wheeler-Bennett, John Wheeler, Sir, 1902-
 xWheeler-Bennett, J. W.
 Brest-Litovsk: The Forgotten Peace, March
  1918. Norton.
 Information on the Renunciation of War
  1927-1928. Kennikat.
 xWheeler-Bennett, John.
 Friends, Enemies & Sovereigns. St Martin.

Wheeley, B. Otto.
 xWheeley, B. Otto.
 God Can Work Through You. Judson.

Wheeling, Kenneth E. see Wheeling, Kenneth Edward.

Wheeling, Kenneth Edward.
 xWheeling, Kenneth E.
 Horse-Drawn Vehicles at the Shelburne
  Museum. Shelburne.

Wheelis, Allen, 1915-
 xWheelis, Allen.
 How People Change. Har-Row.
 On Not Knowing How to Live. Har-Row.
 On Not Knowing How to Live. Har-Row.
 Quest for Identity. Norton.

Wheelock, John H. see Wheelock, John Hall.

Wheelock, John Hall, 1886-
 xWheelock, John H.
 By Daylight & in Dream: New & Collected
  Poems, 1904-1970. Scribner.
 Dear Men & Women: New Poems. Scribner.
 This Blessed Earth: New & Selected Poems
  1927-1977. Scribner.

Wheelwright, E. L. see Wheelwright, Edward Lawrence.

Wheelwright, Edith G. see Wheelwright, Edith Grey.

Wheelwright, Edith Grey.
 xWheelwright, Edith G.
 Medicinal Plants & Their History. Dover.
 Medicinal Plants & Their History. Peter Smith.

Wheelwright, Edward Lawrence.
 xWheelwright, E. L.
 Chinese Road to Socialism: Economics of the
  Cultural Revolution. Monthly Rev.

Wheelwright, John, 1897-1940
 xWheelwright, John.
 Collected Poems of John Wheelwright. New
  Directions.

Wheelwright, Philip. see Wheelwright, Philip Ellis.

Wheelwright, Philip Ellis, 1901-
 xWheelwright, Philip.
 The Burning Fountain: A Study in the
  Language of Symbolism. Peter Smith.
 tr. & ed. Presocratics. Odyssey Pr.

Wheelwright, Steven C.
 xWheelwright, Steven C.
 Forecasting Methods for Management. Wiley.

Whelan, Elizabeth M.
 xWhelan, Elizabeth M.
 A Baby?...Maybe: A Guide to Making the
  Most Fateful Decision of Your Life. Bobbs.
 The Pregnancy Experience: The Psychology of
  Expectant Parenthood. Norton.
 Preventing Cancer. Norton.

Whelan, Gloria.
 xWhelan, Gloria.
 A Clearing in the Forest. Putnam.
 A Time to Keep Silent. Putnam.

Whelan, Kevin, Sister.
 xWhelan, Kevin.

Enthusiasm in English Poetry of the Eighteenth
 Century. Folcroft.

Whelan, Michael.
 xWhelan, Michael.
 Wonderworks: Science Fiction & Fantasy Art.
  Donning Co.

Whelpton, Eric.
 xWhelpton, Eric.
 Gastronomic Guide to Unknown France. Intl
  Pubns Serv.

Wherry, Joseph H.
 xWherry, Joseph H.
 Indian Masks & Myths of the West. T Y
  Crowell.
 The Totem Pole Indians. T Y Crowell.

Whetmore, Edward J. see Whetmore, Edward Jay.

Whetmore, Edward Jay.
 xWhetmore, Edward J.
 Mediamerica: Form, Content & Consequence
  of Mass Communication. Wadsworth Pub.

Whetten, Lawrence L.
 xWhetten, Lawrence L.
 Current Research in Comparative
  Communism:: An Analysis & Bibliographic
  Guide to the Soviet System. Praeger.

Whetzel, Herbert H. see Whetzel, Herbert Hice.

Whetzel, Herbert Hice, 1877-1944
 xWhetzel, Herbert H.
 An Outline of the History of Phytopathology.
  Arno.

Wheway, John, 1943-
 xWheway, John.
 The Green Table of Infinity. SBD.

Whewell, William, 1794-1866
 xWhewell, William.
 Mathematical Exposition of Some Doctrines of
  Political Economy. Kelley.

Whibley, Charles, 1859-1930
 xWhibley, Charles.
 Literary Portraits. Arno.
 Literary Portraits. Folcroft.
 Literary Studies. Arno.
 Literary Studies. Folcroft.
 Political Portraits. Folcroft.
 Political Portraits. Kennikat.
 Political Portraits, Second Series. Arno.
 Studies in Frankness. Folcroft.
 Studies in Frankness. Kennikat.

Whichcote, Benjamin, 1609-1683
 xWhichcote, Benjamin.
 The Works. Garland Pub.

Whicher, George F. see Whicher, George Frisbie.

Whicher, George Frisbie, 1889-1954
 xWhicher, George F.
 tr. The Goliard Poets: Medieval Latin Songs &
  Satires. Greenwood.

Whicher, Stephen. see Whicher, Stephen E.

Whicher, Stephen E.
 xWhicher, Stephen.
 ed. Twelve American Poets. Oxford U Pr.
 xWhicher, Stephen E.
 Freedom & Fate: An Inner Life of Ralph
  Waldo Emerson. U of Pa Pr.

Whiffen, Marcus.
 xWhiffen, Marcus.
 American Architecture Since 1780: A Guide to
  the Styles. MIT Pr.

Whillier, Austin.
 xWhillier, Austin.
 Solar Energy Collection & Its Utilization for
  House Heating. Arno.

Whimbey, Arthur.
 xWhimbey, Arthur.
 Intelligence Can Be Taught. Dutton.

Whinery, Leo H., 1926-
 xWhinery, Leo H.
 Predictive Sentencing: An Empirical
  Evaluation. Lexington Bks.

Whipkey, K. L. see Whipkey, Kenneth L.

Whipkey, Kenneth L.
    xWhipkey, K. L.
        The Power of Calculus. Wiley.
    xWhipkey, Kenneth L.
        Power of Mathematics: Applications to
            Management & the Social Sciences. Wiley.
        The Power of Mathematics: Applications to the
            Management & the Social Sciences. Wiley.
Whipple, A. B. *see* Whipple, Addison Beecher Colvin.
Whipple, Addison Beecher Colvin.
    xWhipple, A. B.
        The Clipper Ships. Time-Life.
        Fighting Sail. Time-Life.
        The Whalers. Time-Life.
Whipple, Chandler.
    xWhipple, Chandler.
        The Indian & the Whiteman in Massachusetts
            & Rhode Island. Berkshire Traveller.
Whipple, Dorothy V. *see* Whipple, Dorothy Vermilya.
Whipple, Dorothy Vermilya, 1900-
    xWhipple, Dorothy V.
        Dynamics of Development: Euthenic
            Pediatrics. McGraw.
Whipple, Edwin. *see* Whipple, Edwin Percy.
Whipple, Edwin P. *see* Whipple, Edwin Percy.
Whipple, Edwin Percy, 1819-1886
    xWhipple, Edwin.
        Literature & Life. Arno.
        Literature of the Age of Elizabeth. Arno.
    xWhipple, Edwin P.
        The Literature of the Age of Elizabeth.
            Folcroft.
Whipple, Fred L. *see* Whipple, Fred Lawrence.
Whipple, Fred Lawrence, 1906-
    xWhipple, Fred L.
        Earth, Moon, & Planets. Harvard U Pr.
Whipple, Gerald. *see* Whipple, Gerald H.
Whipple, Gerald H., 1923-
    xWhipple, Gerald.
        Acute Coronary Care. Little.
Whipple, J. B. *see* Whipple, James B.
Whipple, James B.
    xWhipple, J. B.
        Liberal Education Reconsidered: Reflections on
            Continuing Education for Contemporary
            Man. Syracuse U Cont Ed.
Whipple, L. *see* Whipple, Leon.
Whipple, Leon, 1882-
    xWhipple, L.
        Story of Civil Liberty in the United States. Da
            Capo.
    xWhipple, Leon.
        Story of Civil Liberty in the United States.
            Negro U Pr.
Whipple, M. A. *see* Whipple, Mary Anne.
Whipple, Mary Anne.
    xWhipple, M. A.
        The First Californians. Peek Pubns.
Whipple, Thomas K. *see* Whipple, Thomas King.
Whipple, Thomas King, 1890-1939
    xWhipple, Thomas K.
        Martial & English Epigram from Sir Thomas
            Wyatt to Ben Jonson. Phaeton.
Whipple, William, 1909-
    xWhipple, William J.
        Planning of Water Quality Systems. Lexington
            Bks.
Whipple, William J. *see* Whipple, William.
Whisenand, Paul M.
    xWhisenand, Paul M.
        Crime Prevention. Holbrook.
        Patrol Operations. P-H.
Whisenhunt, Donald W.
    xWhisenhunt, Donald W.
        ed. The Depression in the Southwest. Kennikat.
        The Environment & the American Experience:
            A Historian Looks at the Ecological Crisis.
            Kennikat.
Whishaw, Francis, 1804-1856
    xWhishaw, Francis.

        Railways of Great Britain & Ireland. Kelley.
Whisker, James B., 1939-
    xWhisker, James B.
        The Citizen Soldier & U. S. Military Policy.
            North River.
Whisman, Molly.
    xWhisman, Molly.
        My Hideout. Har-Row.
Whisnant, David E., 1938-
    xWhisnant, David E.
        Modernizing the Mountaineer: People, Power
            & Planning in Appalachia. B Franklin.
Whistler, Rex.
    xWhistler, Rex.
        AHA. HM.
Whistler, Roy L. *see* Whistler, Roy Lester.
Whistler, Roy Lester.
    xWhistler, Roy L.
        Guar: Agronomy, Production, Industrial Use, &
            Nutrition. Purdue.
Whiston, Thomas G., 1938-
    xWhiston, Tom.
        ed. The Uses & Abuses of Forecasting. Holmes
            & Meier.
Whiston, Tom. *see* Whiston, Thomas G.
Whiston, William, 1667-1752
    xWhiston, William.
        Astronomical Lectures. Johnson Repr.
Whitaker. *see* Whitaker, James H.
Whitaker, Albert C. *see* Whitaker, Albert Conser.
Whitaker, Albert Conser, 1877-
    xWhitaker, Albert C.
        History & Criticism of the Labor Theory of
            Value in English Political Economy. AMS Pr.
        History & Criticism of the Labor Theory of
            Value in English Political Economy. Kelley.
Whitaker, Arthur P. *see* Whitaker, Arthur Preston.
Whitaker, Arthur Preston, 1895-
    xWhitaker, Arthur P.
        Huancavelica Mercury Mine: A Contribution
            to the History of the Bourbon Renaissance in
            the Spanish Empire. Greenwood.
        ed. Latin America & the Enlightenment.
            Cornell U Pr.
        Spain & Defense of the West: Ally & Liability.
            Greenwood.
        Spanish-American Frontier, 1783-1795: The
            Westward Movement & the Spanish Retreat
            in the Mississippi Valley. U of Nebr Pr.
Whitaker, Ben. *see* Whitaker, Benjamin Charles George.
Whitaker, Benjamin Charles George.
    xWhitaker, Ben.
        Parks for People. Schocken.
        Police in Society. Methuen Inc.
Whitaker, D. S. *see* Whitaker, Dorothy Stock.
Whitaker, Dorothy Stock.
    xWhitaker, D. S.
        Psychotherapy Through the Group Process.
            Aldine Pub.
Whitaker, Haiganoosh.
    xWhitaker, Haiganoosh.
        ed. Studies in Neurolinguistics. Acad Pr.
Whitaker, Irwin.
    xWhitaker, Irwin.
        A Potter's Mexico. U of NM Pr.
Whitaker, J. R. *see* Whitaker, John R.
Whitaker, James H.
    xWhitaker.
        Agricultural Buildings & Structures. Reston.
Whitaker, James W.
    xWhitaker, James W.
        Feedlot Empire: Beef Cattle Feeding in Illinois
            & Iowa, 1840-1900. Iowa St U Pr.
Whitaker, John. *see* Whitaker, John F.
Whitaker, John C., 1926-
    xWhitaker, John C.

        Striking a Balance: Environment & Natural
            Resources Policy in the Nixon-Ford Years.
            Am Enterprise.
Whitaker, John F., 1936-
    xWhitaker, John.
        Personal Marriage Contract. OK Street.
Whitaker, John R.
    xWhitaker, J. R.
        Principles of Enzymology for the Food
            Sciences. Dekker.
    xWhitaker, John R.
        ed. Food Proteins. AVI.
Whitaker, Leo.
    xWhitaker, Leo.
        Return to Hawkeston Hall. Major Bks.
Whitaker, Reginald.
    xWhitaker, Reginald.
        The Government Party: Organizing &
            Financing the Liberal Party of Canada,
            1930-1958. U of Toronto Pr.
Whitaker, S. *see* Whitaker, Stephen.
Whitaker, S. F.
    xWhitaker, S. F.
        Night Sailing. Aztex.
Whitaker, Stephen.
    xWhitaker, S.
        Fundamental Principles of Heat Transfer.
            Pergamon.
Whitaker, Stephen P.
    xWhitaker, Stephen P.
        Imagination & Fancy in Nineteenth Century
            Literature. Folcroft.
Whitaker, Thomas.
    xWhitaker, Thomas.
        Design of Piled Foundations. Pergamon.
Whitaker, Thomas R.
    xWhitaker, Thomas R.
        Fields of Play in Modern Drama. Princeton U
            Pr.
        Swan & Shadow: Yeats's Dialogue with
            History. U of NC Pr.
Whitaker, Urban. *see* Whitaker, Urban George.
Whitaker, Urban George.
    xWhitaker, Urban.
        World & Ridgeway, South Carolina. U of SC
            Pr.
Whitbeck, Ray H. *see* Whitbeck, Ray Hughes.
Whitbeck, Ray Hughes.
    xWhitbeck, Ray H.
        Economic Geography of South America.
            Greenwood.
Whitbourne, Susan K. *see* Whitbourne, Susan Krauss.
Whitbourne, Susan Krauss.
    xWhitbourne, Susan K.
        Adult Development: The Differentiation of
            Experience. HR&W.
Whitby, Thomas. *see* Whitby, Thomas Joseph.
Whitby, Thomas Joseph.
    xWhitby, Thomas.
        Introduction to Soviet National Bibliography.
            Libs Unl.
Whitcomb, David K., 1942-
    xWhitcomb, David K.
        Externalities & Welfare. Columbia U Pr.
Whitcomb, Edward A.
    xWhitcomb, Edward A.
        Napoleon's Diplomatic Service. Duke.
Whitcomb, Helen.
    xWhitcomb, Helen.
        Charm: The Career Girls Guide to Business &
            Personal Success. McGraw.
Whitcomb, Ian, 1941-
    xWhitcomb, Ian.
        After the Ball. Penguin.
        After the Ball: Pop Music from Rag to Rock.
            S&S.
Whitcomb, John C. *see* Whitcomb, John Clement.
Whitcomb, John Clement, 1924-
    xWhitcomb, John C.

Esther, the Triumph of God's Sovereignty.
BMH Bks.
Solomon to the Exile: Studies in Kings &
Chronicles. Baker Bk.
Solomon to the Exile: Studies in Kings &
Chronicles. BMH Bks.
World That Perished. Baker Bk.
The World That Perished. BMH Bks.
Whitcomb, R. M. see Whitcomb, Richard M.
Whitcomb, Richard M.
xWhitcomb, R. M.
Non-Lead Antiknock Agents for Motor Fuels.
Noyes.
Whitcomb, Selden L. see Whitcomb, Selden Lincoln.
Whitcomb, Selden Lincoln, 1866-1930
xWhitcomb, Selden L.
Chronological Outlines of American Literature.
B Franklin.
Chronological Outlines of American Literature.
Folcroft.
Chronological Outlines of American Literature.
Gale.
Chronological Outlines of American Literature.
Gordon Pr.
Whitcraft, Leslie H. see Whitcraft, Leslie Harper.
Whitcraft, Leslie Harper, 1885-
xWhitcraft, Leslie H.
Some Influences of the Requirements &
Examinations of the College Entrance
Examination Board on Mathematics in
Secondary Schools in the United States.
AMS Pr.
White. see White, Elwyn Brooks.
White, A. D. see White, Andrew Dickson.
White, Alain C. see White, Alain Campbell.
White, Alain Campbell, 1880-
xWhite, Alain C.
The White King in Chess Strategy. Hippocrene
Bks.
White, Alan.
xWhite, Alan.
The Long Fuse. HarBraceJ.
The Long Midnight. HarBraceJ.
Ravenswyke. HM.
White, Andrew D. see White, Andrew Dickson.
White, Andrew Dickson, 1832-1918
xWhite, A. D.
European Schools of History & Politics.
Johnson Repr.
xWhite, Andrew D.
European Schools of History & Politics. AMS
Pr.
White, Anne T. see White, Anne Terry.
White, Anne Terry.
xWhite, Anne T.
All About Great Rivers of the World. Random.
All About Mountains & Mountaineering.
Random.
Human Cargo: The Story of the Atlantic Slave
Trade. Garrard.
ed. Of Beasts, Birds, & Men: Fables from
Three Lands. Garrard.
Prehistoric America. Random.
White, Anthony G.
xWhite, Anthony G.
Municipal Bonding & Taxation. Garland Pub.
Reforming Metropolitan Governments: A
Bibliography. Garland Pub.
White, Arthur. see White, Arthur S.
White, Arthur O., 1942-
xWhite, Arthur O.
Florida's Crisis in Public Education: Changing
Patterns of Leadership. U Presses Fla.
One Hundred Years of State Leadership in
Florida Public Education. Univ Microfilms.
White, Arthur S.
xWhite, Arthur.
Palaces of the People: A Social History of
Commercial Hospitality. Taplinger.
White, B. T. see White, Brian Terence.

White, Barbara A. see White, Barbara Anne.
White, Barbara Anne.
xWhite, Barbara A.
American Women Writers: An Annotated
Bibliography of Criticism. Garland Pub.
White, Barbara E. see White, Barbara Ehrlich.
White, Barbara Ehrlich.
xWhite, Barbara E.
ed. Impressionism in Perspective. P-H.
White, Barry B.
xWhite, Barry B.
Therapy in Acute Coronary Care. Year Bk
Med.
White, Benjamin V. see White, Benjamin Vroom.
White, Benjamin Vroom.
xWhite, Benjamin V.
The Excitement of Change: A Book of
Personal Growth. Seabury.
White, Bertha R. see White, Bertha Rothe.
White, Bertha Rothe.
xWhite, Bertha R.
Crimes & Penalties. Oceana.
Law of Buying & Selling. Oceana.
White, Betty, 1917-
xWhite, Betty.
Dancing Made Easy. Avon.
White, Brenda.
xWhite, Brenda.
The Literature & Study of Urban & Regional
Planning. Routledge & Kegan.
White, Brian Terence.
xWhite, B. T.
Tanks & Other Armored Fighting Vehicles
1942-1945. Macmillan.
Tanks & Other Tracked Vehicles in Service.
Sterling.
White, Burton L., 1929-
xWhite, Burton L.
The First Three Years of Life. Avon.
The First Three Years of Life. P-H.
White, C. C. see White, Charley C.
White, C. Langdon. see White, Charles Langdon.
White, Carl. see White, Carl Milton.
White, Carl Milton, 1903-
xWhite, Carl.
Historical Introduction to Library Education:
Problems & Progress to 1951. Scarecrow.
White, Carol, 1932-
xWhite, Carol.
Energy Potential: Toward a New
Electromagnetic Field Theory. Campaigner.
White, Carol H. see White, Carol Hellings.
White, Carol Hellings.
xWhite, Carol H.
Holding Hands: The Complete Guide to
Palmistry. Putnam.
White, Charles E. see White, Charles Edward.
White, Charles Edward.
xWhite, Charles E.
Fluorescence Analysis: A Practical Approach.
Dekker.
White, Charles Langdon, 1897-
xWhite, C. Langdon.
Regional Geography of Anglo-America. P-H.
White, Charley C.
xWhite, C. C.
No Quittin' Sense. U of Tex Pr.
White, Colin.
xWhite, Colin.
Edmund Dulac. Scribner.
White, D. see White, Denis.
White, Dan, 1943-
xWhite, Dan.
Play to Win: A Profile of Princeton Basketball
Coach Pete Carril. P-H.
White, David M. see White, David Manning.
White, David Manning.
xWhite, David M.

The Celluloid Weapon: Social Comment in the
American Film. Beacon Pr.
ed. Pop Culture in America. New Viewpoints.
White, Denis.
xWhite, D.
A Modern Introduction to Chemistry.
Pergamon.
White, Donald. see White, Donald Allen.
White, Donald Allen.
xWhite, Donald.
Questions & Answers on Maryland Real
Estate. Reston.
White, Donald W. see White, Donald Wallace.
White, Donald Wallace.
xWhite, Donald W.
A Village at War: Chatham, New Jersey, & the
American Revolution. Fairleigh Dickinson.
White, Douglas H., 1929-
xWhite, Douglas H.
Pope & the Context of Controversy: The
Manipulation of Ideas in an Essay on Man. U
of Chicago Pr.
White, E. B. see White, Elwyn Brooks.
White, Edgar.
xWhite, Edgar.
Children of Night. Lothrop.
The Crucificado: Two Plays. Morrow.
Omar at Christmas. Lothrop.
White, Edmund.
xWhite, Edmund.
The First Men. Silver.
The First Men. Time-Life.
Nocturnes for the King of Naples. Penguin.
Nocturnes for the King of Naples. St Martin.
White, Edwin. see White, Edwin C.
White, Edwin C.
xWhite, Edwin.
Acting & Stage Movement. Arco.
White, Edwin H. see White, Edwin Harold.
White, Edwin Harold.
xWhite, Edwin H.
Business Insurance. P-H.
White, Elijah.
xWhite, Elijah.
Exorcism As a Christian Ministry. Morehouse.
White, Ellen G. see White, Ellen Gould (Harmon).
White, Ellen Gould (Harmon), 1827-1915
xWhite, Ellen G.
Life at Its Best. Pacific Pr Pub Assn.
Thoughts from the Mount of Blessing. Pacific
Pr Pub Assn.
White, Elwyn B. see White, Elwyn Brooks.
White, Elwyn Brooks, 1899-
xWhite.
Charlotte's Web. Schol Bk Serv.
xWhite, E. B.
Charlotte's Web. Har-Row.
Charlotte's Web. Har-Row.
Essays of E. B. White. Har-Row.
Essays of E. B. White. Har-Row.
Letters of E. B. White. Har-Row.
Letters of E. B. White. Har-Row.
One Man's Meat. Har-Row.
One Man's Meat. Har-Row.
Stuart Little. Har-Row.
Stuart Little. Har-Row.
Trumpet of the Swan. Har-Row.
The Trumpet of the Swan. Har-Row.
xWhite, Elwyn B.
Quo Vadimus? or, the Case for the Bicycle.
Arno.
White, Emil H.
xWhite, Emil H.
Chemical Background for the Biological
Sciences. P-H.
White, Emmons E.
xWhite, Emmons E.

Appreciating India's Music: An Introduction, with an Emphasis on the Music of South India. Taplinger.

White, Eric W. *see* White, Eric Walter.

White, Eric Walter, 1905-
xWhite, Eric W.
Stravinsky: The Composer & His Works. U of Cal Pr.

White, Eugene E. *see* White, Eugene Edmond.

White, Eugene Edmond, 1919-
xWhite, Eugene E.
Practical Public Speaking. Macmillan.
Puritan Rhetoric: The Issue of Emotion in Religion. S Ill U Pr.
ed. Rhetoric in Transition: Studies in the Nature & Uses of Rhetoric. Pa St U Pr.

White, Florence M. *see* White, Florence Meiman.

White, Florence Meiman, 1910-
xWhite, Florence M.
Escape: The Life of Harry Houdini. Messner.

White, Frederick A. *see* White, Frederick Andrew.

White, Frederick Andrew, 1918-
xWhite, Frederick A.
Our Acoustic Environment. Wiley.

White, G. Edward.
xWhite, G. Edward.
The American Judicial Tradition: Profiles of Leading American Judges. Oxford U Pr.

White, George C. *see* White, George Clifford.

White, George Clifford.
xWhite, George C.
Disinfection of Wastewater & Water for Reuse. Van Nos Reinhold.
Handbook of Chlorination: For Potable Water, Waste Water, Cooling Water, Industrial Processes, & Swimming Pools. Van Nos Reinhold.

White, George E. *see* White, George Edward.

White, George Edward.
xWhite, George E.
Dental Caries: A Multifactorial Disease. C C Thomas.

White, George R., 1923-
xWhite, George R.
Concrete Technology. Delmar.
Concrete Technology. Van Nos Reinhold.

White, Gerald T. *see* White, Gerald Taylor.

White, Gerald Taylor, 1913-
xWhite, Gerald T.
Billions for Defense: Government Financing by the Defense Plant Corporation During World War II. U of Ala Pr.
Formative Years in the Far West: A History of Standard Oil Company of California & Predecessors Through 1919. Arno.

White, Gilbert F. *see* White, Gilbert Fowler.

White, Gilbert Fowler.
xWhite, Gilbert F.
Assessment of Research on Natural Hazards. MIT Pr.
Strategies of American Water Management. U of Mich Pr.

White, Gordon. *see* White, Gordon E.

White, Gordon E.
xWhite, Gordon.
John Caples: Adman. Crain Bks.

White, Graham J.
xWhite, Graham J.
FDR & the Press. U of Chicago Pr.

White, Guy K. *see* White, Guy Kendall.

White, Guy Kendall.
xWhite, Guy K.
Experimental Techniques in Low-Temperature Physics. Oxford U Pr.

White, Gwen.
xWhite, Gwen.

Perspective: A Guide for Artists, Architects & Designers. David & Charles.
Perspective: A Guide for Artists, Architects, & Designers. Watson-Guptill.

White, Harrison C.
xWhite, Harrison C.
Chains of Opportunity: System Models of Mobility in Organizations. Harvard U Pr.

White, Harry D. *see* White, Harry Dexter.

White, Harry Dexter, 1892-1948
xWhite, Harry D.
The French International Accounts: 1880-1913. Arno.

White, Harvey, 1938-
xWhite, Harvey.
Your Family Is Good for You. Berkley Pub.
Your Family Is Good for You. Random.

White, Harvey E. *see* White, Harvey Elliott.

White, Harvey Elliott, 1902-
xWhite, Harvey E.
Descriptive College Physics. Van Nos Reinhold.
Modern College Physics. Van Nos Reinhold.

White, Hayden V., 1928-
xWhite, Hayden V.
The Greco-Roman Tradition. Har-Row.

White, Helen (McCann).
xWhite, Helen M.
ed. Ho! for the Gold Fields: Northern Overland Wagon Trains of the 1860s. Minn Hist.

White, Helen C. *see* White, Helen Constance.

White, Helen Constance, 1896-1967
xWhite, Helen C.
Changing Styles in Literary Studies. Folcroft.
The Tudor Books of Private Devotion. Greenwood.

White, Helen M. *see* White, Helen (McCann).

White, Henry K. *see* White, Henry Kirke.

White, Henry Kirke, 1865-
xWhite, Henry K.
History of the Union Pacific Railway. Kelley.

White House Conference on Child Health and Protection.
xWhite House Conference on Child Health & Protection.
The Adolescent in the Family: A Study of Personality Development in the Home Environment. Arno.
Dependent & Neglected Children: Report of the Committee on Socially Handicapped; Dependency & Neglect. Arno.
The Home & the Child; Housing, Furnishing, Management, Income, Clothing. Arno.
Organization for the Care of Handicapped Children, National, State, Local. Arno.
The Young Child in the Home: A Survey of Three Thousand American Families. Arno.

White House Conference on Children in a Democracy, Washington, D.C., 1939-40.
xWhite House Conference on Children in a Democracy.
Final Report of the White House Conference on Children in a Democracy. Arno.

White, Howard, 1893-
xWhite, Howard.
Executive Influence in Determining Military Policy in the United States. Arno.

White, Howard A. *see* White, Howard Ashley.

White, Howard Ashley, 1913-
xWhite, Howard A.
Freedmen's Bureau in Louisiana. La State U Pr.

White, Irvin L., 1932-
xWhite, Irvin L.
Decision-Making for Space: Law & Politics in Air, Sea, & Outer Space. Purdue.
Law & Politics in Outer Space: A Bibliography. U of Ariz Pr.

White, J. B. *see* White, James Bernard.

White, J. P. *see* White, John Ponsford.

White, J. R. *see* White, James Richard Henry.

White, J. Roy.
xWhite, J. Roy.
Hill Country Revisited. Trinity U Pr.

White, J. Todd.
xWhite, J. Todd.
ed. Fighters for Independence: A Guide to Sources of Biographical Information on Soldiers & Sailors of the American Revolution. U of Chicago Pr.

White, James.
xWhite, James.
Monsters & Medics. Ballantine.

White, James B., 1938-
xWhite, James B.
The Legal Imagination: Studies in the Nature of Legal Thought & Expression. Little.

White, James Bernard.
xWhite, J. B.
Wastewater Engineering. Intl Schol Bk Serv.

White, James C. *see* White, James Clarke.

White, James Clarke.
xWhite, James C.
Pain & the Neurosurgeon: A Forty-Year Experience. C C Thomas.

White, James F.
xWhite, James F.
Christian Worship in Transition. Abingdon.
Introduction to Christian Worship. Abingdon.

White, James H. *see* White, James Harrison.

White, James Harrison, 1943-
xWhite, James H.
Pediatric Psychopharmacology: A Practical Guide to Clinical Application. Williams & Wilkins.

White, James J.
xWhite, James J.
Handbook of the Law Under the Uniform Commercial Code. West Pub.

White, James L.
xWhite, James L.
Divorce Proceedings. Dakota Pr.

White, James Richard Henry.
xWhite, J. R.
Successful Supervision. McGraw.

White, Jan. *see* White, Jan V.

White, Jan V., 1928-
xWhite, Jan.
The Graphic Idea Notebook. Watson-Guptill.
xWhite, Jan V.
Editing by Design: Word-&-Picture Communication for Editors & Designers. Bowker.

White, Jerry. *see* White, Jerry E.

White, Jerry E., 1937-
xWhite, Jerry.
Honesty, Morality, & Conscience. NavPress.

White, John. *see* White, John Warren.

White, John A.
xWhite, John A.
Analysis of Queueing Systems. Acad Pr.
Principles of Engineering Economic Analysis. Wiley.

White, John A. *see* White, John Albert.

White, John Albert.
xWhite, John A.
Siberian Intervention. Greenwood.

White, John Alexander, 1933-
xWhite, John A.
The Politics of Foreign Aid. St Martin.

White, John B. *see* White, John Bradley.

White, John Bradley, 1947-
xWhite, John B.
A Study of the Language of Love in the Song of Songs & Ancient Egyptian Poetry. Scholars Pr Ca.

White, John D. *see* White, John David.

White, John David, 1931-
  xWhite, John D.
    Analysis of Music. P-H.
White, John H.
  xWhite, John H.
    A History of the American Locomotive: Its
    Development, 1830-1880. Dover.
White, John H. *see* White, John Henry.
White, John Henry.
  xWhite, John H.
    History of the Phlogiston Theory. AMS Pr.
White, John I. *see* White, John Irwin.
White, John Irwin, 1902-
  xWhite, John I.
    Git Along Little Dogies: Songs & Songmakers
    of the American West. U of Ill Pr.
White, John K. *see* White, John Kennardh.
White, John Kennardh.
  xWhite, John K.
    Pottery Techniques of Native North America:
    An Introduction to Traditional Technology.
    U of Chicago Pr.
White, John Ponsford.
  xWhite, J. P.
    Towards a Compulsory Curriculum. Routledge
    & Kegan.
White, John T. *see* White, John Talbot.
White, John Talbot.
  xWhite, John T.
    A Countryman's Guide to the South East.
    Routledge & Kegan.
White, John Warren.
  xWhite, John.
    ed. Future Science: Life Energies & the Physics
    of Paranormal Phenomena. Doubleday.
    ed. Kundalini, Evolution & Enlightenment.
    Doubleday.
White, John Wesley.
  xWhite, John Wesley.
    Man from Krypton: The Gospel According to
    Superman. Bethany Fell.
White, Jon M. *see* White, Jon Manchip.
White, Jon Manchip.
  xWhite, Jon M.
    Everyday Life of the North American Indian.
    Holmes & Meier.
White, Joseph L.
  xWhite, Joseph L.
    The Limits of Trade Union Militancy: The
    Lancashire Textile Workers, 1910-1914.
    Greenwood.
White, Judy.
  xWhite, Judy.
    ed. Chile's Days of Terror: Eyewitness
    Accounts of the Military Coup. Path Pr NY.
White, K. D.
  xWhite, K. D.
    tr. Country Life in Classical Times. Cornell U
    Pr.
    Farm Equipment of the Roman World.
    Cambridge U Pr.
White, Katharine Sergeant Angell.
  xWhite, Katherine S.
    Onward & Upward in the Garden. FS&G.
White, Katherine S. *see* White, Katharine Sergeant
  Angell.
White, Kathleen.
  xWhite, Kathleen M.
    Adolescence. Brooks-Cole.
White, Kathleen M. *see* White, Kathleen.
White, L. P. *see* White, Leslie Paul.
White, Laurence B.
  xWhite, Laurence B.
    The Great Mysto... That's You. A-W.
    Science Games & Puzzles. A-W.
  xWhite, Lawrence B.
    The Trick Book. Doubleday.
White, Laurence J. *see* White, Lawrence J.
White, Lawrence B. *see* White, Laurence B.

White, Lawrence J.
  xWhite, Laurence J.
    Industrial Concentration & Economic Power in
    Pakistan. Princeton U Pr.
White, Leon S. *see* White, Leon Solomon.
White, Leon Solomon, 1919-
  xWhite, Leon S.
    Patriot for Liberty. Lippincott.
White, Leonard D. *see* White, Leonard Dupee.
White, Leonard Dupee, 1891-1958
  xWhite, Leonard D.
    City Manager. AMS Pr.
    City Manager. Greenwood.
    The Federalists: A Study in Administrative
    History. Greenwood.
White, Leslie A., 1900-1975
  xWhite, Leslie A.
    The Concept of Cultural Systems: A Key to
    Understanding Tribes & Nations. Columbia U
    Pr.
White, Leslie Paul.
  xWhite, L. P.
    Aerial Photography & Remote Sensing for Soil
    Survey. Oxford U Pr.
White, Lionel.
  xWhite, Lionel.
    Death of a City. Manor Bks.
    A Rich & Dangerous Game. Dale Books Inc.
White, Lynn. *see* White, Lynn Townsend.
White, Lynn T.
  xWhite, Lynn T.
    Careers in Shanghai: The Social Guidance of
    Personal Energies in a Developing Chinese
    City, 1949-1966. U of Cal Pr.
White, Lynn T. *see* White, Lynn Townsend.
White, Lynn Townsend, 1907-
  xWhite, Lynn.
    Medieval Religion & Technology: Collected
    Essays. U of Cal Pr.
    Medieval Technology & Social Change. Oxford
    U Pr.
  xWhite, Lynn T.
    ed. Frontiers of Knowledge in the Study of
    Man. Greenwood.
White, M. J. *see* White, Michael James Denham.
White, Mark.
  xWhite, Mark.
    Building the St. Pierre Dory. Intl Marine.
    Observer's Book of Jazz. Scribner.
White, Mary, 1869-
  xWhite, Mary.
    How to Do Bead Work. Peter Smith.
    How to Do Beadwork. Dover.
    How to Make Baskets. Gale.
    More Baskets & How to Make Them. Gale.
White, Mary L. *see* White, Mary Lou.
White, Mary Lou.
  xWhite, Mary L.
    Children's Literature: Criticism & Response.
    Merrill.
White, Melvin I. *see* White, Melvin Irvin.
White, Melvin Irvin.
  xWhite, Melvin I.
    Personal Income Tax Reduction in a Business
    Contraction. AMS Pr.
White, Michael James Denham, 1910-
  xWhite, M. J.
    Animal Cytology & Evolution. Cambridge U
    Pr.
White, Morton. *see* White, Morton Gabriel.
White, Morton G. *see* White, Morton Gabriel.
White, Morton Gabriel.
  xWhite, Morton.

    The Intellectual Versus the City: From Thomas
    Jefferson to Frank Lloyd Wright. Oxford U
    Pr.
    Pragmatism & the American Mind: Essays &
    Reviews in Philosophy & Intellectual History.
    Oxford U Pr.
    Pragmatism & the American Mind: Essays &
    Reviews in Philosophy & Intellectual History.
    Oxford U Pr.
    Social Thought in America: The Revolt Against
    Formalism. Oxford U Pr.
    Toward Reunion in Philosophy. Atheneum.
  xWhite, Morton G.
    Origin of Dewey's Instrumentalism. Octagon.
White, Nancy B. *see* White, Nancy Bean.
White, Nancy Bean.
  xWhite, Nancy B.
    Meet John F. Kennedy. Random.
White, Nelson C.
  xWhite, Nelson C.
    Abbott H. Thayer, Painter & Naturalist.
    Bauhan.
White, Newman I. *see* White, Newman Ivey.
White, Newman Ivey.
  xWhite, Newman I.
    An Anthology of Verse by American Negroes.
    Moore Pub Co.
White, Nicholas P.
  xWhite, Nicholas P.
    A Companion to Plato's Republic. Hackett
    Pub.
    Intro. by Plato on Knowledge & Reality.
    Hackett Pub.
White, Norval.
  xWhite, Norval.
    The Architecture Book. Knopf.
White, O. R. *see* White, Oran R.
White, Oran R.
  xWhite, O. R.
    ed. The Solar Output & Its Variation. Colo
    Assoc.
White, Osman. *see* White, Osmar.
White, Osmar.
  xWhite, Osman.
    Silent Reach. Scribner.
  xWhite, Osmar.
    Melbourne. Intl Pubns Serv.
    Melbourne for Everyone. David & Charles.
White, P. E. *see* White, Paul.
White, Patrick, 1912-
  xWhite, Patrick.
    The Aunt's Story. Avon.
    The Aunt's Story. Viking Pr.
    The Eye of the Storm. Avon.
    The Eye of the Storm. Viking Pr.
    A Fringe of Leaves. Avon.
    A Fringe of Leaves. Viking Pr.
    The Living & the Dead. AMS Pr.
    Riders in the Chariot. Avon.
    Riders in the Chariot. Viking Pr.
    The Twyborn Affair. Viking Pr.
White, Paul.
  xWhite, P. E.
    ed. The Geographical Impact of Migration.
    Longman.
  xWhite, Paul.
    Janet at School. T Y Crowell.
White, Paulette C., 1948-
  xWhite, Paulette C.
    Love Poem to a Black Junkie. Lotus.
White, Percival, 1887-1970
  xWhite, Percival.
    Advertising Research. Arno.
White, Peter R.
  xWhite, Peter R.
    Planning for Public Transport. Merrimack Bk
    Serv.
White, Philip D. *see* White, Phillip D.
White, Phillip D.
  xWhite, Philip D.

Decision Making in the Purchasing Process: A Report. Am Mgmt.

White, R. see White, Ruth Bennett.

White, R. E. see White, Robert Edwin.

White, R. J. see White, Reginald James.

White, R. S. see White, R. Stephen.

White, R. Stephen, 1920-
xWhite, R. S.
Space Physics. Gordon.

White, R. W. see White, Robert Winthrop.

White, Ralph K.
xWhite, Ralph K.
Autocracy & Democracy: An Experimental Inquiry. Greenwood.

White, Ray L. see White, Ray Lewis.

White, Ray Lewis.
xWhite, Ray L.
Gore Vidal. Coll & U Pr.
Gore Vidal. Twayne.

White, Reginald E. O.
xWhite, R. E.
Biblical Ethics. John Knox.
The Mind of Matthew. Westminster.

White, Reginald James.
xWhite, R. J.
Europe in the Eighteenth Century. St Martin.

White, Richard, 1947-
xWhite, Richard.
Land Use, Environment, & Social Change: The Shaping of Island County, Washington. U of Wash Pr.

White, Richard A. see White, Richard Alan.

White, Richard Alan, 1944-
xWhite, Richard A.
Paraguay's Autonomous Revolution, 1810-1840. U of NM Pr.

White, Rick.
xWhite, Rick.
The Complete Manual of Catamaran Racing. Dodd.

White, Robb, 1909-
xWhite, Robb.
Deathwatch. Dell.
Deathwatch. Doubleday.
Frogmen. Dell.
The Frogmen. Doubleday.
No Man's Land. Dell.

White, Robert Edwin, 1937-
xWhite, R. E.
Introduction to the Principles & Practice of Soil Science. Halsted Pr.

White, Robert G. see White, Robert Gordon.

White, Robert Gordon, 1924-
xWhite, Robert G.
Handbook of Industrial Infrared Analysis. Plenum Pub.

White, Robert I., 1937-
xWhite, Robert I.
Fundamentals of Vascular Radiology. Lea & Febiger.

White, Robert M., 1938-
xWhite, Robert M.
Quantum Theory of Magnetism. Krieger.

White, Robert R.
xWhite, Robert R.
Atlas of Pediatric Surgery. McGraw.

White, Robert W. see White, Robert Winthrop.

White, Robert Winthrop.
xWhite, R. W.
The Abnormal Personality. Wiley.
Case Workbook in Personality. HR&W.
The Enterprise of Living: A View of Personal Growth. HR&W.
xWhite, Robert W.
The Abnormal Personality. Wiley.
Ego & Reality in Psychoanalytic Theory: A Proposal Regarding the Independent Ego Energies. Intl Univs Pr.

White, Robin.
xWhite, Robin.

The Troll of Crazy Mule Camp. Dandelion Pr.

White, Roger.
xWhite, Roger.
In & Out of School: The ROSLA Community Education Project. Routledge & Kegan.

White, Ruth Bennett.
xWhite, R.
Food & Your Future. P-H.

White, Sheldon. see White, Shelton Harold.

White, Shelton Harold.
xWhite, Sheldon.
ed. Human Development in Today's World. Little.

White, Sidney H. see White, Sidney Howard.

White, Sidney Howard.
xWhite, Sidney H.
Sidney Howard. Twayne.

White, Simon.
xWhite, Simon.
Clear for Action!. St Martin.
The English Captain. St Martin.

White, Stanhope.
xWhite, Stanhope.
Dan Bana: The Memoirs of a Nigerian Official Heineman.

White, Stephen, 1945-
xWhite, Stephen.
Britain & the Bolshevik Revolution: A Study of the Politics of Diplomacy, 1920-24. Holmes & Meier.
Political Culture & Soviet Politics. St Martin.

White, Stephen D., 1945-
xWhite, Stephen D.
Sir Edward Coke & "The Grievances of the Commonwealth," 1621-1628. U of NC Pr.

White, Stephen S. see White, Stephen Solomon.

White, Stephen Solomon, 1890-
xWhite, Stephen S.
A Comparison of the Philosophies of F.C.S. Schiller & John Dewey. AMS Pr.

White, Suzanne, 1938-
xWhite, Suzanne.
Suzanne White's Book of Chinese Chance: What the Oriental Zodiac Can Tell You About Yourself & Your Future. M Evans.

White, T. C. see White, Thomas Cyril.

White, T. H. see White, Terence Hanbury.

White, Ted.
xWhite, Ted.
Forbidden World. Popular Lib.

White, Ted. see White, Ted E.

White, Ted E., 1912-
xWhite, Ted.
Club Operations & Management. CBI Pub.

White, Terence H. see White, Terence Hanbury.

White, Terence Hanbury, 1906-1964
xWhite, T. H.
Darkness at Pemberley. Dover.
Mistress Masham's Repose. Berkley Pub.
Mistress Masham's Repose. Gregg.
The Once & Future King. Berkley Pub.
illus. The Sword in the Stone. Putnam.
xWhite, Terence H.
The Once & Future King. Putnam.
Once & Future King. Berkley Pub.
The Sword in the Stone. Putnam.

White, Theodore. see White, Theodore Harold.

White, Theodore H. see White, Theodore Harold.

White, Theodore Harold, 1915-
xWhite, Theodore.
Breach of Faith: Fall of Richard Nixon. Atheneum.
xWhite, Theodore H.

Caesar at the Rubicon: A Play About Politics. Har-Row.
In Search of History: A Personal Adventure. Har-Row.

White, Thomas Cyril.
xWhite, T. C.
Orthodontics for Dental Students. Green.

White, Thomas T. see White, Thomas Taylor.

White, Thomas Taylor.
xWhite, Thomas T.
Liver, Bile Ducts & Pancreas. Grune.
Reoperative Gastrointestinal Surgery. Little.

White, Trumbull, 1868-1941
xWhite, Trumbull.
Puerto Rico & Its People. Arno.

White, V. see White, Virginia P.

White, V. P. see White, Virginia P.

White, Viola C. see White, Viola Chittenden.

White, Viola Chittenden, 1890-
xWhite, Viola C.
Horizons. AMS Pr.

White, Virginia P.
xWhite, V.
Grants for the Arts. Plenum Pub
xWhite, V. P.
Grants: How to Find Out About Them & What to Do Next. Plenum Pub.

White, W. Hale. see White, William Hale.

White, W. L.
xWhite, William L.
They Were Expendable. HarBraceJ.

White, Wain L.
xWhite, Wain L.
ed. Surgery: PreTest Self-Assessment & Review. McGraw-Pretest.

White, Wallace.
xWhite, Wallace.
One Dark Night. Watts.

White, Walter F. see White, Walter Francis.

White, Walter Francis, 1893-1955
xWhite, Walter F.
Fire in the Flint. Negro U Pr.
How Far the Promised Land?. AMS Pr.

White, William C. see White, William Charles.

White, William.
xWhite, William.
An Earthworm Is Born. Sterling.
Edge of the Ocean. Sterling.
Forest & Garden. Sterling.
A Frog Is Born. Sterling.
Inner Life of the House of Commons. Arno.
A Mosquito Is Born. Sterling.
Nathanael West: A Comprehensive Bibliography. Kent St U Pr.

White, William A. see White, William Allen.

White, William Alanson, 1870-1937
xWhite, William A.
Twentieth Century Psychiatry: Its Contribution to Man's Knowledge of Himself. Arno.
William Alanson White: The Autobiography of a Purpose. Arno.

White, William Allen, 1868-1944
xWhite, William A.
Autobiography of William Allen White. Macmillan.
A Certain Rich Man. Johnson Repr.
A Certain Rich Man. U Pr of Ky.
Court of Boyville. Arno.
In Our Town. Arno.
Masks in a Pageant. Greenwood.
Masks in a Pageant. Scholarly.
Politics: The Citizen's Business. Arno.
Puritan in Babylon: The Story of Calvin Coolidge. Peter Smith.
Stratagems & Spoils: Stories of Love & Politics. Johnson Repr.
Stratagems & Spoils: Stories of Love & Politics. Mss Info.

White, William C. see White, William Carter.

White, William Carter, 1882-
xWhite, William C.
    A History of Military Music in America.
    Greenwood.
White, William Chapman, 1903-1955
xWhite, William C.
    Adirondack Country. Knopf.
White, William Charles, Bp, 1873-1960
xWhite, Willam C.
    Chinese Jews: A Compilation of Matters
    Relating to the Jews of K'aifeng Fu.. U of
    Toronto Pr.
White, William D. see White, William Deacons.
White, William Deacons, 1945-
xWhite, William D.
    Public Health & Private Gain: The Economics
    of Licensing Clinical Laboratory Personnel.
    Maaroufa Pr.
White, William F., 1926-
xWhite, William F.
    Psychosocial Principles Applied to Classroom
    Teaching. McGraw.
White, William Hale.
xWhite, W. Hale.
    Description of the Wordsworth & Coleridge
    Manuscripts in the Possession of Mr. T.
    Norton Longman. Folcroft.
    An Examination of the Charge of Apostasy
    Against Wordsworth. Folcroft.
White, William J. see White, William Joseph.
White, William Joseph, 1926-
xWhite, William J.
    Airships for the Future. Sterling.
White, William L. see White, William Lindsay.
White, William Lindsay, 1900-1973
xWhite, William L.
    The Captives of Korea: An Unofficial White
    Paper on the Treatment of War Prisoners;
    Our Treatment of Theirs: Their Treatment of
    Ours. Greenwood.
White, William S. see White, William Spottswood.
White, William Spottswood, 1800-1873
xWhite, William S.
    The African Preacher: An Authentic Narrative.
    Arno.
White, Wilma L.
xWhite, Wilma L.
    Practical Automation for the Clinical
    Laboratory. Mosby.
Whitebread, Charles. see Whitebread, Charles H.
Whitebread, Charles H.
xWhitebread, Charles.
    Standards Relating to Transfer Between Courts.
    Ballinger Pub.
xWhitebread, Charles H.
    ed. Mass Production Justice & the
    Constitutional Ideal. U Pr of Va.
Whitechurch, Canon V. see Whitechurch, Victor
    Lawrence.
Whitechurch, Victor Lawrence, 1868-1933
xWhitechurch, Canon V.
    Stories of the Railway. Routledge & Kegan.
Whited. see Whited, N. W.
Whited, N. W.
xWhited.
    Automotive Oscilloscope. Delmar.
Whitehead, A. N. see Whitehead, Alfred North.
Whitehead, Albert C. see Whitehead, Albert Carlton.
Whitehead, Albert Carlton, 1875-
xWhitehead, Albert C.
    Standard Bearer: A Story of Army Life in the
    Time of Caesar. Biblo.
Whitehead, Alfred N. see Whitehead, Alfred North.
Whitehead, Alfred North, 1861-1947
xWhitehead, A. N.
    The Axioms of Descriptive Geometry. Hafner.
xWhitehead, Alfred N.

Adventures of Ideas. Free Pr.
Adventures of Ideas. Macmillan.
Concept of Nature. Cambridge U Pr.
Dialogues of Alfred North Whitehead.
    Greenwood.
Introduction to Mathematics. Oxford U Pr.
Nature & Life. Greenwood.
The Organisation of Thought, Educational &
    Scientific. Greenwood.
Principia Mathematica. Cambridge U Pr.
Religion in the Making. NAL.
Whitehead's American Essays in Social
    Philosophy. Greenwood.
Whitehead, Anthony, 1926-
xWhitehead, J. A.
    Psychiatric Disorders in Old Age: A Handbook
    for the Clinical Team. Springer Pub.
Whitehead, Barbara.
xWhitehead, Barbara.
    The Caretaker Wife. Berkley Pub.
    The Caretaker Wife. Doubleday.
xWhitehead, Barbara M.
    ed. The Wonderful Chirrionera & Other Tales
    from Mexican Folklore. Heidelberg Pubs.
Whitehead, Barbara M. see Whitehead, Barbara.
Whitehead, Evelyn E. see Whitehead, Evelyn Eaton.
Whitehead, Evelyn Eaton.
xWhitehead, Evelyn E.
    Christian Life Patterns: The Psychological
    Challenges & Religious Invitations of Adult
    Life. Doubleday.
Whitehead, G. see Whitehead, George William.
Whitehead, George William, 1918-
xWhitehead, G.
    Elements of Homotopy Theory.
    Springer-Verlag.
Whitehead, Hector F.
xWhitehead, Hector F.
    Cairn Terriers. Arco.
Whitehead, J. A. see Whitehead, Anthony.
Whitehead, James.
xWhitehead, James.
    Joiner. Avon.
Whitehead, James D.
xWhitehead, James D.
    ed. China & Christianity: Historical & Future
    Encounters. U of Notre Dame Pr.
Whitehead, K. D.
xWhitehead, K. D.
    The Need for the Magisterium of the Church.
    Franciscan Herald.
Whitehead, O. Z.
xWhitehead, O. Z.
    Some Early Baha'is of the West. Baha'i.
Whitehead, Raymond. see Whitehead, Raymond L.
Whitehead, Raymond L.
xWhitehead, Raymond.
    Love & Struggle in Mao's Thought. Orbis Bks.
Whitehead, Robert. see Whitehead, Robert J.
Whitehead, Robert J.
xWhitehead, Robert.
    First Book of Bears. Watts.
xWhitehead, Robert J.
    Rabbits & Hares. Watts.
Whitehead, T. P. see Whitehead, Thomas Patterson.
Whitehead, Thomas Patterson.
xWhitehead, T. P.
    Quality Control in Clinical Chemistry. Wiley.
Whitehill, Walter M. see Whitehill, Walter Muir.
Whitehill, Walter Muir.
xWhitehill, Walter M.

Arts in Early American History. U of NC Pr.
Boston in the Age of John Fitzgerald Kennedy.
    U of Okla Pr.
Boston: Portrait of a City. Barre.
Independent Historical Societies: An Enquiry
    into Their Research & Publication Functions
    & Their Financial Future. Harvard U Pr.
Massachusetts: A Pictorial History. Scribner.
Museum of Fine Arts, Boston: A Centennial
    History. Harvard U Pr.
Spanish Romanesque Architecture of the
    Eleventh Century. Oxford U Pr.
Whitehouse, David.
xWhitehouse, David.
    Archaeological Atlas of the World. W H
    Freeman.
Whitehouse, Donald. see Whitehouse, Donald S.
Whitehouse, Donald S.
xWhitehouse, Donald.
    Pray & Play: A Guide for Family Worship.
    Broadman.
Whitehouse, Gary E.
xWhitehouse, Gary E.
    Applied Operations Research: A Survey. Wiley.
    Systems Analysis & Design Using Network
    Techniques. P-H.
Whitehouse, Henry R. see Whitehouse, Henry Remsen.
Whitehouse, Henry Remsen, 1857-
xWhitehouse, Henry R.
    Life of Lamartine. Arno.
Whitehurst, Grover J.
xWhitehurst, Grover J.
    Child Behavior. HM.
    ed. The Functions of Language & Cognition.
    Acad Pr.
Whitehurst, Mary W. see Whitehurst, Mary Wood.
Whitehurst, Mary Wood, 1901-
xWhitehurst, Mary W.
    Integrated Lessons in Lipreading & Auditory
    Training. Alexander Graham.
Whiteley, C. H. see Whiteley, Charles Henry.
Whiteley, Charles Henry.
xWhiteley, C. H.
    Introduction to Metaphysics. Humanities.
Whiteley, John F., 1896-
xWhiteley, John F.
    Early Army Aviation: The Emerging Air
    Force. Military Aff Aero.
Whiteley, John M.
xWhiteley, John M.
    Approaches to Assertion Training.
    Brooks-Cole.
    Career Counseling. Brooks-Cole.
    The History of Counseling Psychology.
    Brooks-Cole.
    The Present & Future of Counseling
    Psychology. Brooks-Cole.
Whiteley, Paul.
xWhiteley, Paul.
    ed. Models of Political Economy. Sage.
Whitelock, Dorothy.
xWhitelock, Dorothy.
    tr. & ed. Anglo-Saxon Wills. AMS Pr.
Whitely, Roger.
xWhitely, Roger.
    Assess the IRS. Vantage.
Whiteman, Marjorie M. see Whiteman, Marjorie Millace.
Whiteman, Marjorie Millace.
xWhiteman, Marjorie M.
    Damages in International Law. Kraus Repr.
Whiteman, Maxwell.
xWhiteman, Maxwell.
    Copper for America: The Hendricks Family &
    a National Industry, 1755-1939. Rutgers U
    Pr.
    Gentlemen in Crisis: The First Century of the
    Union League of Philadelphia, 1862-1962.
    Union League PA.
Whitener. see Whitener, Jack R.

Meditation: Journey to the Self. S&S.

Whitman, John.
xWhitman, John.
The Best European Travel Tips: How to Save Money, Time & Trouble & Have a Great Trip!. Meadowbrook Pr.
The Psychic Power of Plants. NAL.
Starting from Scratch: A Guide to Indoor Gardening. NAL.
Starting from Scratch: A Guide to Indoor Gardening. Times Bks.
The Uncommon Guide to Europe. St Martin.
Whitman's off Season Travel Guide to Europe: Europe at Its Best from September to May. St Martin.

Whitman, Lawrence. *see* Whitman, Lawrence E.
Whitman, Lawrence E.
xWhitman, Lawrence.
Fire Prevention. Nelson-Hall.
xWhitman, Lawrence E.
Fire Safety in the Atomic Age. Nelson-Hall.

Whitman, Marina V. *see* Whitman, Marina Von Neumann.

Whitman, Marina Von Neumann.
xWhitman, Marina V.

Government Risk-Sharing in Foreign Investment. Princeton U Pr.

Reflections of Interdependence: Issues for Economic Theory & U. S. Policy. U of Pittsburgh Pr.

Whitman, Martin. *see* Whitman, Martin J.
Whitman, Martin J.
xWhitman, Martin.
The Aggressive Conservative Investor. Random.

Whitman, R. *see* Whitman, Ronald L.
Whitman, R. Douglas. *see* Whitman, Russell Douglas.
Whitman, R. L. *see* Whitman, Randal L.
Whitman, Randal L.
xWhitman, R. L.
English & English Linguistics. HR&W.

Whitman, Robert, 1936-
xWhitman, Robert.
Preparation for the Bar Examination. Monarch Pr.

Whitman, Roger C.
xWhitman, Roger C.
More First Aid for the Ailing House: Money-Saving Ways to Improve Your House & Property. McGraw.

Whitman, Ronald L.
xWhitman, R.
Chemistry Today. P-H.

Whitman, Russell Douglas.
xWhitman, R. Douglas.
Adjustment: The Development & Organization of Human Behavior. Oxford U Pr.

Whitman, Stephen F. *see* Whitman, Stephen French.
Whitman, Stephen French.
xWhitman, Stephen F.
Predestined: A Novel of New York Life. S Ill U Pr.

Whitman, Walt, 1819-1892
xWhitman, Walt.

Autobiographia: Or, The Story of a Life. Arden Lib.
Leaves of Grass. Adler.
Leaves of Grass. Doubleday.
Leaves of Grass. Eakins.
Leaves of Grass. NAL.
Leaves of Grass. Norton.
Leaves of Grass. Penguin.
Leaves of Grass. Peter Pauper.
Leaves of Grass. Cornell U Pr.
Leaves of Grass. Airmont.
Memoranda During the War & Death of Abraham Lincoln. Greenwood.
Overhead the Sun: Lines from Walt Whitman. FS&G.
Specimen Days. Godine.
Two Rivulets. Folcroft.
Two Rivulets. Norwood Edns.
Whitman & Rolleston: A Correspondence. Kraus Repr.

Whitman, William, 1900-
xWhitman, William.
Dog Corner Papers, Reprinted from the Piper. Arno.

Whitman, Willson.
xWhitman, Willson.
Bread & Circuses: A Study of Federal Theatre. Arno.

Whitmee, Jeanne.
xWhitmee, Jeanne.
A Lobster & a Lady. St Martin.

Whitmore. *see* Whitmore, Joanne Rand.
Whitmore, Dennis A. *see* Whitmore, Dennis Ainsworth.
Whitmore, Dennis Ainsworth.
xWhitmore, Dennis A.
Measurement & Control of Indirect Work. Intl Pubns Serv.

Whitmore, George, 1945-
xWhitmore, George.
The Confessions of Danny Slocum. St Martin.

Whitmore, Joanne Rand, 1938-
xWhitmore.
Giftedness, Conflict & Underachievement. Allyn.

Whitmore, Mary E. *see* Whitmore, Mary Ernestine.
Whitmore, Mary Ernestine, Sister.
xWhitmore, Mary E.
Medieval English Domestic Life & Amusements in the Works of Chaucer. Cooper Sq.

Whitmore, R. L. *see* Whitmore, Raymond Leslie.
Whitmore, Raymond Leslie.
xWhitmore, R. L.
Rheology of the Circulation. Pergamon.

Whitmore, T. C. *see* Whitmore, Timothy Charles.
Whitmore, Timothy Charles.
xWhitmore, T. C.
Tropical Rain Forests of the Far East. Oxford U Pr.

Whitnah, Dorothy L.
xWhitnah, Dorothy L.
Guide to the Golden Gate National Recreation Area. Wilderness.

Whitnall, Ernest S. *see* Whitnall, Samuel Ernest.
Whitnall, Samuel Ernest, 1876-1950
xWhitnall, Ernest S.
The Anatomy of the Human Orbit & Accessory Organs of Vision. Krieger.

Whitney, Adeline D. *see* Whitney, Adeline Dutton (Train).
Whitney, Adeline Dutton (Train), 1824-1906
xWhitney, Adeline D.
Homespun Yarns. Arno.

Whitney, Alma M. *see* Whitney, Alma Marshak.
Whitney, Alma Marshak.
xWhitney, Alma M.
Leave Herbert Alone. A-W.

Whitney, Annie W. *see* Whitney, Annie Weston.
Whitney, Annie Weston.
xWhitney, Annie W.

ed. Folk-Lore from Maryland. Kraus Repr.
Whitney, Bill, 1921-
xWhitney, Bill.
Drawings of Florence. Olivet.

Whitney, Charles A. *see* Whitney, Charles Allen.
Whitney, Charles Allen.
xWhitney, Charles A.
Whitney's Star Finder: A Field Guide to the Heavens. Knopf.

Whitney, Clara. *see* Whitney, Clara A.
Whitney, Clara A.
xWhitney, Clara.
Clara's Diary: An American Girl in Meiji Japan. Kodansha.

Whitney, David C.
xWhitney, David C.

Easy Book of Fractions. Watts.
The Easy Book of Numbers & Numerals. Watts.

The Easy Book of Sets. Watts.
First Book of Facts & How to Find Them Watts.

Let's Find Out About Milk. Watts.
Let's Find Out About Subtraction. Watts.

Whitney, E. L. *see* Whitney, Edson Leone.
Whitney, Edgar A.
xWhitney, Edgar A.
Complete Guide to Watercolor Painting. Watson-Guptill.

Whitney, Edson L. *see* Whitney, Edson Leone.
Whitney, Edson Leone, 1861-
xWhitney, E. L.
Government of the Colony of South Carolina. Johnson Repr.
xWhitney, Edson L.
Government of the Colony of South Carolina. AMS Pr.
Government of the Colony of South Carolina. Haskell.
Government of the Colony of South Carolina. Negro U Pr.

Whitney, Eleanor N.
xWhitney, Eleanor N.
Understanding Nutrition. West Pub.

Whitney, Frederick A. *see* Whitney, Frederick Adams.
Whitney, Frederick Adams, 1886-
xWhitney, Frederick A.
The Law of Modern Commercial Practices. Lawyers Co-Op.

Whitney, Frederick C.
xWhitney, Frederick C.
Mass Media & Mass Communications in Society. Wm C Brown.

Whitney, Geoffrey.
xWhitney, Geoffrey.
Choice of Emblemes. Arno.

Whitney, George D., 1918-
xWhitney, George D.
This Is the Beagle. TFH Pubns.

Whitney, Hassler.
xWhitney, Hassler.
Complex Analytic Varieties. A-W.
Geometric Integration Theory. Princeton U Pr.

Whitney, Janet. *see* Whitney, Janet (Payne).
Whitney, Janet (Payne), 1894-
xWhitney, Janet.
Abigail Adams. Greenwood.

Whitney, John R. *see* Whitney, John Raymond.
Whitney, John Raymond.
xWhitney, John R.
Religious Literature of the West. Augsburg.

Whitney, Leon. *see* Whitney, Leon Fradley.
Whitney, Leon F. *see* Whitney, Leon Fradley.
Whitney, Leon Fradley, 1894-
xWhitney, Leon.
First Aid for Pets. Vanguard.
xWhitney, Leon F.

The Complete Book of Cat Care. Doubleday.
Coon Hunter's Handbook. HR&W.
Dog Psychology: The Basis of Dog Training.
    Howell Bk.
How to Breed Dogs. Howell Bk.
The Natural Method of Dog Training. M
    Evans.

Whitney, Louisa (Goddard), 1819-1883
    xWhitney, Louise G.
    Burning of the Convent. Arno.
Whitney, Louise G. see Whitney, Louisa (Goddard).
Whitney, Mark S.
    xWhitney, Mark S.
    Critical Reactions & the Christian Element in
        the Poetry of Pierre de Ronsard. U of NC Pr.
Whitney Museum of American Art. see Whitney
    Museum of American Art, New York.
Whitney Museum of American Art (New York). see
    Whitney Museum of American Art, New York.
Whitney Museum of American Art, New York.
    xWhitney Museum of American Art.
    Selections from the Permanent Collection. U of
        Chicago Pr.
    xWhitney Museum of American Art (New York).
    Catalog of the Library of the Whitney Museum
        of American Art. G K Hall.

Whitney, Phyllis. see Whitney, Phyllis A.

Whitney, Phyllis A., 1903-
    xWhitney, Phyllis.
    Domino. G K Hall.
    Fire & the Gold. NAL.
    The Golden Unicorn. G K Hall.
    The Highest Dream. NAL.
    The Moonflower. Fawcett.
    Nobody Like Trina. NAL
    Turquoise Mask. Fawcett.
    xWhitney, Phyllis A.
    Columbella. Doubleday.
    Domino. Doubleday.
    The Glass Flame. Doubleday.
    The Glass Flame. Fawcett.
    The Glass Flame. G K Hall.
    The Golden Unicorn. Doubleday.
    The Golden Unicorn. Fawcett.
    Linda's Homecoming. NAL.
    Listen for the Whisperer. Doubleday.
    Listen for the Whisperer. Fawcett.
    A Long Time Coming. NAL.
    Lost Island. Doubleday.
    Lost Island. Fawcett.
    Quicksilver Pool. Fawcett.
    Secret of Emerald Star. G&D.
    The Secret of the Emerald Star. NAL.
    Secret of the Emerald Star. Westminster.
    Spindrift. Doubleday.
    Spindrift. Fawcett.
    Step to the Music. NAL.
    Step to the Music. T Y Crowell.
    The Stone Bull. Doubleday.
    The Stone Bull. Fawcett.
    The Stone Bull. G K Hall.
    The Turquoise Mask. Doubleday.
Whitney, Phyllis A. see Whitney, Phyllis Ayame.
Whitney, Phyllis Ayame, 1903-
    xWhitney, Phyllis A.
    Creole Holiday. NAL.
Whitney, Ronald G.
    xWhitney, Ronald G.
    The World of C. A. Stephens. Waynor.
Whitney, Stephen.
    xWhitney, Stephen.
    A Sierra Club Naturalist's Guide to the Sierra
        Nevada. Sierra.
Whitney, Thomas P.
    xWhitney, Thomas P.
    tr. Marko the Rich & Vasily the Unlucky.
        Macmillan.
Whitney, Thomas R. see Whitney, Thomas Richard.

Whitney, Thomas Richard, 1804-1858
    xWhitney, Thomas R.
    A Defence of the American Policy As Opposed
        to the Encroachments of Foreign Influence,
        & Especially to the Interference of the
        Papacy in the Political Interests & Affairs of
        the United States. Ozer.
Whitney, Victor P.
    xWhitney, Victor P.
    Trust Marketing Handbook. Bankers.
Whitney, William. see Whitney, William Dwight.
Whitney, William D. see Whitney, William Dwight.
Whitney, William Dwight, 1827-1894
    xWhitney, William.
    The Life & Growth of Language. R West.
    xWhitney, William D.
    Life & Growth of Language. Dover.
    Oriental & Linguistic Studies. Arno.
    Oriental & Linguistic Studies. Longwood Pr.
Whitridge, Arnold, 1891-
    xWhitridge, Arnold.
    Critical Ventures in Modern French Literature.
        Arno.
    Critical Ventures in Modern French Literature.
        Folcroft.
Whitsitt, William H. see Whitsitt, William Heth.
Whitsitt, William Heth, 1841-1911
    xWhitsitt, William H.
    A Question in Baptist History: Whether the
        Anabaptists in England Practiced Immersion
        Before the Year 1641?. Arno.
Whitson, Denton.
    xWhitson, Denton.
    For the Glory of Venice. Moore Pub Co.
Whitson, Gary L.
    xWhitson, Gary L.
    ed. Concepts in Radiation Cell Biology. Acad
        Pr.
Whitt, Peggy.
    xWhitt, Peggy.
    The Good Idea How to Save Money Book.
        TAB Bks.
Whittaker, David.
    xWhittaker, David.
    Stereochemistry & Mechanism. Oxford U Pr.
Whittaker, E. T. see Whittaker, Edmund Taylor.
Whittaker, Edmund T. see Whittaker, Edmund Taylor.
Whittaker, Edmund Taylor, Sir, 1873-1956
    xWhittaker, E. T.
    The Theory of Optical Instruments. Hafner.
    xWhittaker, Edmund T.
    From Euclid to Eddington: A Study of
        Conceptions of the External World. AMS Pr.
Whittaker, James B.
    xWhittaker, James B.
    Strategic Planning in a Rapidly Changing
        Environment. Lexington Bks.
Whittaker, James K.
    xWhittaker, James K.
    ed. Children Away from Home: A Sourcebook
        in Residential Treatment. Aldine Pub.
    Social Treatment: An Approach to
        Interpersonal Helping. Aldine Pub.
Whittaker, James O. see Whittaker, James Oliver.
Whittaker, James Oliver, 1927-
    xWhittaker, James O.
    Introduction to Psychology. HR&W.
Whittaker, Jerome.
    xWhittaker, Jerome.
    The Art of Writing As an Effective Instrument
        for the Development of a Rational Brain, the
        Ability to Think Straight, the Power of
        Convincing Expression & the Making of a
        Substantial Fortune Within the Course of a
        Few Years. Gloucester Art.
Whittaker, Kenneth.
    xWhittaker, Kenneth.
    Using Libraries. Philos Lib.
Whittaker, P. A. see Whittaker, Peter A.

Whittaker, Peter A.
    xWhittaker, P. A.
    Mitochondria: Structure, Function & Assembly.
        Longman.
Whittaker, Robert H. see Whittaker, Robert Harding.
Whittaker, Robert Harding, 1920-
    xWhittaker, Robert H.
    Classification of Natural Communities. Arno.
    Communities & Ecosystems. Macmillan.
Whittaker, William G. see Whittaker, William Gillies.
Whittaker, William Gillies, 1876-1944
    xWhittaker, William G.
    Collected Essays. Arno.
Whittam, J. R. see Whittam, John.
Whittam, John.
    xWhittam, J. R.
    The Politics of the Italian Army 1861-1918.
        Shoe String.
Whittemore, Edward.
    xWhittemore, Edward.
    Jerusalem Poker. Avon.
    Jerusalem Poker. HR&W.
    Quin's Shanghai Circus. Popular Lib.
Whittemore, Henry.
    xWhittemore, Henry.
    Genealogical Guide to the Early Settlers of
        America: With a Brief History of Those of
        the First Generation (Surnames Abby
        Through Prior). Genealog Pub.
Whittemore, L. H.
    xWhittemore, L. H.
    Peroff: The Man Who Knew Too Much.
        Ballantine.
    Peroff: The Man Who Knew Too Much.
        Morrow.
Whittemore, Lewis B. see Whittemore, Lewis Bliss.
Whittemore, Lewis Bliss, Bp.
    xWhittemore, Lewis B.
    The Church & Secular Education. Greenwood.
Whittemore, Margaret.
    xWhittemore, Margaret.
    Historic Kansas: A Centenary Sketchbook. AG
        Pr.
Whittemore, Reed, 1919-
    xWhittemore, Reed.
    Fifty Poems Fifty. U of Minn Pr.
    Little Magazines. U of Minn Pr.
Whittemore, Richard, 1918-
    xWhittemore, Richard.
    Nicholas Murray Butler & Public Education
        1862-1911. Tchrs Coll.
Whitten, Les, 1928-
    xWhitten, Les.
    Sometimes a Hero. Doubleday.
Whitten, Mary E.
    xWhitten, Mary E.
    Creative Pattern Practice: A New Approach to
        Writing. HarBraceJ.
Whitten, Norman E.
    xWhitten, Norman E.
    Class, Kinship, & Power in an Ecuadorian
        Town: The Negroes of San Lorenzo. Stanford
        U Pr.
Whitten, Robert H. see Whitten, Robert Harvey.
Whitten, Robert Harvey, 1873-1936
    xWhitten, Robert H.
    Public Administration in Massachusetts: The
        Relation of Central to Local Activity. AMS
        Pr.
Whitten, W. see Whitten, Wilfred.
Whitten, Wilfred, 1864-1942
    xWhitten, W.
    Daniel Defoe. Haskell.
    xWhitten, Wilfred.
    Daniel Defoe. Folcroft.
Whitten, Woodrow C., 1915-
    xWhitten, Woodrow C.

Criminal Syndicalism & the Law in California: 1919-1927. Am Philos.

Whittick, Arnold, 1898-
xWhittick, Arnold.
Encyclopedia of Urban Planning. Krieger.

Whittick, W. G.
xWhittick, W. G.
Canine Orthopedics. Lea & Febiger.

Whittier, J. G. see Whittier, John Greenleaf.

Whittier, John G. see Whittier, John Greenleaf.

Whittier, John Greenleaf, 1807-1892
xWhittier, J. G.
Whittier's Unknown Romance: Letters to Elizabeth Lloyd. Haskell.
xWhittier, John G.
Anti-Slavery Poems: Songs of Labor & Reform. Arno.
Leaves from Margaret Smith's Journal. Irvington.
The Letters of John Greenleaf Whittier. Harvard U Pr.
National Lyrics. Arno.
ed. Songs of Three Centuries. Arno.
Supernaturalism of New England. U of Okla Pr.

Whittingham, C. see Whittingham, Charles Percival.

Whittingham, Charles Percival.
xWhittingham, C.
The Mechanism of Photosynthesis. Univ Park.

Whittingham, Richard.
xWhittingham, Richard.
The Chicago Bears: An Illustrated History. Rand.

Whittington, H. G. see Whittington, Horace G.

Whittington, Herschel.
xWhittington, Herschel.
jt. auth. Step-by-Step Guide to Brake Servicing. TAB Bks.

Whittington, Horace G., 1929-
xWhittington, H. G.
Clinical Practice in Community Mental Health Centers. Intl Univs Pr.
Psychiatry on the College Campus. Intl Univs Pr.

Whittington, K. R.
xWhittington, K. R.
Oswald, the Silly Goose. Bradbury Pr.

Whittle, Amberys R.
xWhittle, Amberys R.
Trumbull Stickney. Bucknell U Pr.

Whittle, P. see Whittle, Peter.

Whittle, Peter.
xWhittle, P.
Probability. Wiley.

Whittlesey, Derwent S. see Whittlesey, Derwent Stainthorpe.

Whittlesey, Derwent Stainthorpe, 1890-1956
xWhittlesey, Derwent S.
The Earth & the State: A Study of Political Geography. Arno.

Whittock, Trevor.
xWhittock, Trevor.
Reading of the Canterbury Tales. Cambridge U Pr.

Whitton, John Boardman.
xWhitton, John G.
Propaganda Towards Disarmament in the War of Words. Oceana.

Whitton, John G. see Whitton, John Boardman.

Whittow, G. Causey, 1930-
xWhittow, G. Causey.
ed. Comparative Physiology of Thermoregulation. Acad Pr.

Whittredge, Worthington, 1820-1910
xWhittredge, Worthington.
Autobiography of Worthington Whittredge. Arno.

Whitwell, David.
xWhitwell, David.

ed. The College & University Band: An Anthology of Papers from the Conferences of the College Band Directors National Association, 1941-1975. Music Ed.

Whitworth, Geoffrey. see Whitworth, Geoffrey Arundel.

Whitworth, Geoffrey A. see Whitworth, Geoffrey Arundel.

Whitworth, Geoffrey Arundel, 1883-1951
xWhitworth, Geoffrey.
Art of Nijinsky. Arno.
Theatre in Action. Arno.
xWhitworth, Geoffrey A.
The Making of a National Theatre. Hyperion Conn.

Whitworth, William A. see Whitworth, William Allen.

Whitworth, William Allen, 1840-1905
xWhitworth, William A.
Choice & Chance with One Thousand Exercises. Hafner.
DCC Exercises: Including Hints for the Solution of All the Questions in "Choice & Chance". Hafner.

Who, Anthony.
xWho, Anthony.
Clickster Clackxter. Denlingers.

Whole Foods.
xWhole Foods Magazine Staff.
ed. Whole Foods, Natural Foods Guide. And-Or Pr.

Whole Foods Magazine Staff. see Whole Foods.

Wholey, Joseph S.
xWholey, Joseph S.
Federal Evaluation Policy: Analyzing the Effects of Public Programs. Urban Inst.

Whone, Herbert.
xWhone, Herbert.
Church, Monastery, Cathedral: A Guide to the Symbolism of the Christian Tradition. Enslow Pubs.
The Hidden Face of Music. Garden Studio.

Whorlow, R. W.
xWhorlow, R. W.
Rheological Techniques. Halsted Pr.

Why, Joseph S. Van. see Van Why, Joseph S.

Whybray, R. N.
xWhybray, R. N.
The Intellectual Tradition in the Old Testament. De Gruyter.

Whyburn, G. see Whyburn, Gordon Thomas.

Whyburn, Gordon T. see Whyburn, Gordon Thomas.

Whyburn, Gordon Thomas.
xWhyburn, G.
Dynamic Topology. Springer-Verlag.
xWhyburn, Gordon T.
Topological Analysis. Princeton U Pr.

Whynes, David K.
xWhynes, David K.
The Economics of Third World Military Expenditure. U of Tex Pr.

Whyte, Arthur J. see Whyte, Arthur James Beresford.

Whyte, Arthur James Beresford.
xWhyte, Arthur J.
Evolution of Modern Italy. Norton.

Whyte, Florence, 1892-
xWhyte, Florence.
The Dance of Death in Spain & Catalonia. Arno.
The Dance of Death in Spain & Catalonia. Gordon Pr.

Whyte, Frederic, 1867-1941
xWhyte, Frederic.
The Life of W. T. Stead. Arden Lib.
Life of W. T. Stead. Garland Pub.

Whyte, Karen C. see Whyte, Karen Cross.

Whyte, Karen Cross.
xWhyte, Karen C.
The Complete Yogurt Cookbook. Ballantine.

Whyte, L. L. see Whyte, Lancelot Law.

Whyte, Lancelot L. see Whyte, Lancelot Law.

Whyte, Lancelot Law, 1896-
xWhyte, L. L.
The Unconscious Before Freud. St Martin.
xWhyte, Lancelot L.
Accent on Form: An Anticipation of the Science of Tomorrow. Greenwood.
Focus & Diversions. Braziller.

Whyte, Martin K. see Whyte, Martin King.

Whyte, Martin King.
xWhyte, Martin K.
The Status of Women in Preindustrial Societies. Princeton U Pr.

Whyte, W. see Whyte, William Foote.

Whyte, William F. see Whyte, William Foote.

Whyte, William Foote, 1914-
xWhyte, W.
Power, Politics, & Progress: Social Change in Rural Peru. Elsevier.
xWhyte, William F.
Human Relations in the Restaurant Industry. Arno.
ed. Industry & Society. Greenwood.
Men at Work. Greenwood.
Money & Motivation: An Analysis of Incentives in Industry. Greenwood.
Organizing for Agricultural Development: Human Aspects in the Utilization of Science & Technology. Transaction Bks.
Toward an Integrated Theory of Development: Economic & Noneconomic Variables in Rural Development. NY Sch Indus Rel.

Whyte, William H. see Whyte, William Hollingsworth.

Whyte, William Hollingsworth.
xWhyte, William H.
Last Landscape. Doubleday.
Organization Man. S&S.
The Organization Man. S&S.

Wiarda, Howard. see Wiarda, Howard J.

Wiarda, Howard J.
xWiarda, Howard.
Latin American Politics & Development. HM.
xWiarda, Howard J.
ed. The Continuing Struggle for Democracy in Latin America. Westview.
Corporatism & Development: The Portuguese Experience. U of Mass Pr.
Critical Elections & Critical Coups: State, Society & the Military in the Processes of Latin American Development. Ohio U Ctr Intl.
Dictatorship & Development: The Methods of Control in Trujillo's Dominican Republic. U Presses Fla.
Dictatorship, Development & Disintegration: Politics & Social Change in the Dominican Republic. Univ Microfilms.
ed. Politics & Social Change in Latin America: The Distinct Tradition. U of Mass Pr.

Wiat, Philippa.
xWiat, Philippa.
Lion Without Claws. St Martin.

Wiatrowski, Claude A.
xWiatrowski, Claude A.
Logic Circuits & Microcomputer Systems. McGraw.

Wiberg, Hugh, 1933-
xWiberg, Hugh.
Backyard Vegetable Gardening for the Beginner. Exposition.

Wibking, Gladys.
xWibking, Gladys.
The Children & Other Poems. Golden Quill.

Wice, Paul B.
xWice, Paul B.
Criminal Lawyers: An Endangered Species. Sage.

Wick, Denis.
xWick, Denis.

Trombone Technique. Oxford U Pr.

Wick, John D., 1946-
xWick, John D.
Automatic Generation of Assemblers. Garland Pub.

Wicka, Donna K. see Wicka, Donna Konkel.

Wicka, Donna Konkel.
xWicka, Donna K.
Advice to Parents of a Cleft Palate Child. C C Thomas.

Wicke, Lothar.
xWicke, Lothar.
Atlas of Radiologic Anatomy. Urban & S.

Wickelgren, Wayne A., 1938-
xWickelgren, Wayne A.
Cognitive Psychology. P-H.
Learning & Memory. P-H.
xWickelgren, Wayne E.
How to Solve Problems: Elements of the Theory of Problems & Problem Solving. W H Freeman.

Wickelgren, Wayne E. see Wickelgren, Wayne A.

Wickens, James F.
xWickens, James F.
Colorado in the Great Depression. Garland Pub.

Wicker, Allan W.
xWicker, Allen W.
Introduction to Ecological Psychology. Brooks-Cole.

Wicker, Allen W. see Wicker, Allan W.

Wicker, Brian, 1929-
xWicker, Brian.
First the Political Kingdom: A Personal Appraisal of the Catholic Left in Britain. U of Notre Dame Pr.
The Story Shaped World: Fiction & Metaphysics: Some Variations on a Theme. U of Notre Dame Pr.
Toward a Contemporary Christianity. U of Notre Dame Pr.

Wicker, Ireene. see Wicker, Ireene Seaton.

Wicker, Ireene Seaton.
xWicker, Ireene.
How the Ocelots Got Their Spots. Lyle Stuart.

Wicker, K. see Wicker, Kevin.

Wicker, Kevin, 1953-
xWicker, K.
How to Play the Queen's Gambit, Exchange Variation. Hippocrene Bks.

Wicker, Tom.
xWicker, Tom.
On Press. Berkley Pub.
On Press. Viking Pr.

Wickersham, J. P. see Wickersham, James Pyle.

Wickersham, James Pyle, 1825-1893
xWickersham, J. P.
History of Education in Pennsylvania. Arno.

Wickes, Frances (Gillespy), 1875-
xWickes, Frances G.
The Inner World of Choice. P-H.

Wickes, Frances G. see Wickes, Frances (Gillespy).

Wickes, William E.
xWickes, William E.
Logic Design with Integrated Circuits. Wiley.

Wickham, Geoffrey. see Wickham, Geoffrey E.

Wickham, Geoffrey E.
xWickham, Geoffrey.
Rapid Perspective. Transatlantic.

Wickham, Glynne. see Wickham, Glynne William Gladstone.

Wickham, Glynne William Gladstone.
xWickham, Glynne.
The Medieval Theatre. St Martin.

Wickins, P. L., 1925-
xWickins, P. L.
The Industrial & Commercial Workers' Union of Africa. Oxford U Pr.

Wickiser, Ralph L. see Wickiser, Ralph Lewanda.

Wickiser, Ralph Lewanda, 1909-
xWickiser, Ralph L.
Introduction to Art Activities. Greenwood.

Wickman, Peter. see Wickman, Peter M.

Wickman, Peter M.
xWickman, Peter.
Readings in Criminology. Heath.
ed. Readings in Social Problems: Contemporary Perspectives. Har-Row.

Wickramasinghe, Priya.
xWickramasinghe, Priya.
Spicy & Delicious: Exotic & Tasty Recipes from India & Sri Lanka. Biblio Dist.

Wicks, Ch. B. see Wicks, Charles Beaumont.

Wicks, Charles Beaumont, 1907-
xWicks, Ch. B.
Charles-Guillaume Etienne, Dramatist & Publicist. Johnson Repr.

Wicks, Henry J.
xWicks, Henry J.
The Doctrine of God in the Jewish Apocryphal & Apocalyptic Literature. Ktav.

Wicks, Janis.
xWicks, Janis.
The Food Processor Cookbook. Nitty Gritty.

Wicks, Keith.
xWicks, Keith.
Stars & Planets. Watts.

Wicks, Robert.
xWicks, Robert G.
Society, Systems & Man: Selections for Reading & Composition. Wiley.

Wicks, Robert G. see Wicks, Robert.

Wicks, Robert J.
xWicks, Robert J.
Applied Psychology for Law Enforcement & Correction Officers. McGraw.
Counseling Strategies & Intervention Techniques for the Human Services. Har-Row.
Helping Others: Ways of Listening, Sharing & Counseling. Chilton.
Human Services: New Careers & Roles in the Helping Professions. C C Thomas.
International Corrections. Lexington Bks.
Practical Psychology of Leadership for Criminal Justice Officers: A Basic Programmed Text. C C Thomas.

Wicks, Walter, 1891-
xWicks, Walter.
Memories of the Skeena. Hancock Hse.

Wicksteed, Philip H. see Wicksteed, Philip Henry.

Wicksteed, Philip Henry, 1844-1927
xWicksteed, Philip H.
Dante & Aquinas. Haskell.
Four Lectures on Henrik Ibsen: Dealing Chiefly with His Metrical Works. Kennikat.

Wickstrom, Ralph L.
xWickstrom, Ralph L.
Fundamental Motor Patterns. Lea & Febiger.

Wickwar, W. Hardy. see Wickwar, William Hardy.

Wickwar, William Hardy.
xWickwar, W. Hardy.
Political Theory of Local Government. U of SC Pr.

Wickwire, Franklin B.
xWickwire, Franklin B.
British Subministers & Colonial America, 1763-1783. Princeton U Pr.

Widdicombe, J. see Widdicombe, J. G.

Widdicombe, J. G.
xWiddicombe, J.
ed. Respiratory Physiology. Univ Park.
xWiddicombe, J. G.
ed. Respiratory Pharmacology. Pergamon.

Widdows, Margharita. see Widdows, Margharita (Defries).

Widdows, Margharita (Defries).
xWiddows, Margharita.

English Literature. Kennikat.
English Literature. R West.

Widdowson, Gregory.
xWiddowson, Gregory C.
An Outline of Lay Sanctity. Our Sunday Visitor.

Widdowson, Gregory C. see Widdowson, Gregory.

Widdowson, H. G.
xWiddowson, H. G.
Explorations in Applied Linguistics. Oxford U Pr.
xWiddowson, Henry G.
Stylistics & the Teaching of Literature. Longman.

Widdowson, Henry G. see Widdowson, H. G.

Widener, Robert Q.
xWidener, Robert Q.
Attic of an Ignoramus. Courier Pr.

Widenor, William C.
xWidenor, William C.
Henry Cabot Lodge & the Search for an American Foreign Policy. U of Cal Pr.

Wider Opportunities for Women. Women's Work Force.
xWomen's Work Force.
National Directory of Women's Employment Programs: Who They Are; What They Do. WOW Inc.

Widgery, David.
xWidgery, David.
Health in Danger: The Crisis in the National Health Service. Shoe String.

Widick, B. J.
xWidick, B. J.
ed. Auto Work & Its Discontents. Johns Hopkins.

Widicus, Wilbur W.
xWidicus, Wilbur W.
Personal Investing. Irwin.

Widiss, Alan I., 1938-
xWidiss, Alan I.
ed. Arbitration: Commercial Disputes, Insurance, & Tort Claims. PLI.

Widmann, Frances K.
xWidmann, Frances K.
Clinical Interpretation of Laboratory Tests. Davis Co.
Pathobiology: How Disease Happens. Little.

Widmayer, Patricia A. see Widmayer, Patricia A. Heyndricks.

Widmayer, Patricia A. Heyndricks.
xWidmayer, Patricia A.
Spencer, the Smiling Sea Colt. Denison.

Widney, Gaylord G.
xWidney, Gaylord G.
Bunny Snowhite Visits Mr. McDougal's Garden. Grossmont Pr.

Widroe, Harvey J.
xWidroe, Harvey J.
Human Behavior & Brain Function. C C Thomas.

Widule, William.
xWidule, William.
Climber's Guide to Devil's Lake. U of Wis Pr.

Wiebe, Katie F. see Wiebe, Katie Funk.

Wiebe, Katie Funk.
xWiebe, Katie F.
Alone: A Widow's Search for Joy. Tyndale.
Day of Disaster. Herald Pr.

Wiebe, Robert H.
xWiebe, Robert H.
Businessmen & Reform: A Study of the Progressive Movement. Times Bks.

Wiebenson, Dora.
xWiebenson, Dora.
Sources of Greek Revival Architecture. Pa St U Pr.

Wiecek, William M., 1938-
xWiecek, William M.

Guarantee Clause of the U. S. Constitution.
Cornell U Pr.
The Sources of Antislavery Constitutionalism
in America, 1760-1848. Cornell U Pr.

Wiechmann, Ulrich E.
xWiechmann, Ulrich E.
Marketing Management in Multinational Firms:
The Consumer Packaged Goods Industry.
Praeger.

Wiecks, Tom.
xWiecks, Tom.
The Best Cookin' in the Country. Barleycorn.

Wied, George. *see* Wied, George L.

Wied, George L.
xWied, George.
Introduction to Quantitative Cytochemistry, 2.
Acad Pr.

Wiedel, Janine.
xWiedel, Janine.
Looking at Iran. Lippincott.

Wiedeman, George H.
xWiedeman, George H.
ed. Personality Development & Deviation: A
Textbook for Social Work. Intl Univs Pr.

Wiedemann, A. *see* Wiedemann, Alfred.

Wiedemann, Alfred, 1856-1936
xWiedemann, A.
Popular Literature in Ancient Egypt. Folcroft.

Wiedemer, John. *see* Wiedemer, John P.

Wiedemer, John P., 1918-
xWiedemer, John.
Real Estate Investment. Reston.
xWiedemer, John P.
Real Estate Finance. Reston.

Wiedenbach, Ernestine.
xWiedenbach, Ernestine.
Communication: Key to Effective Nursing.
Tiresias Pr.

Wieder, H. H., 1919-
xWieder, H. H.
Laboratory Notes on Electrical &
Galvano-Magnetic Measurements. Elsevier.

Wieder, Sol.
xWieder, Sol.
The Foundations of Quantum Theory. Acad Pr.

Wiederhold, Gio.
xWiederhold, Gio.
Database Design. McGraw.

Wiederholt, J. Lee.
xWiederholt, J. Lee.
The Resource Teacher: A Guide to Effective
Practices. Allyn.

Wiegel, Robert L.
xWiegel, Robert L.
Earthquake Engineering. P-H.
Oceanographical Engineering. P-H.

Wiegele. *see* Wiegele, Thomas C.

Wiegele, Thomas C.
xWiegele.
Biopolitics: Search for a More Human Political
Science. Westview.

Wieger, Leon, 1856-1933
xWieger, Leon.
History of the Religious Beliefs & Philosophical
Opinions in China from the Beginning to the
Present Time. Paragon.

Wiegerink, Ron. *see* Wiegerink, Ronald.

Wiegerink, Ronald.
xWiegerink, Ron.
ed. Developmental Disabilities: The D D
Movement. P H Brookes.

Wiegner, Kathleen.
xWiegner, Kathleen.
Country Western Breakdown. Crossing Pr.

Wieland, Christoph Martin.
xWieland, Christopher M.
Oberon: A Poetical Romance in Twelve Books.
Hyperion Conn.

Wieland, Christopher M. *see* Wieland, Christoph Martin.

Wieland, George F.
xWieland, George F.
Organizations: Behavior, Design, & Change.
Irwin.

Wielgus, Chuck.
xWielgus, Chuck.
The In-Your-Face Basketball Book. Everest
Hse.

Wieman, Harold.
xWieman, Harold.
Nature Walks on the San Luis Coast. Padre
Prods.

Wieman, Henry N. *see* Wieman, Henry Nelson.

Wieman, Henry Nelson.
xWieman, Henry N.
Normative Psychology of Religion. Greenwood.
Religious Experience & Scientific Method.
Greenwood.
Religious Experience & Scientific Method. S Ill
U Pr.

Wienandt, Elwyn A. *see* Wienandt, Elwyn Arthur.

Wienandt, Elwyn Arthur.
xWienandt, Elwyn A.
Anthem in England & America. Free Pr.

Wiener, Alexander S. *see* Wiener, Alexander Solomon.

Wiener, Alexander Solomon, 1907-
xWiener, Alexander S.
Rh-Hr Syllabus: The Types & Their
Applications. Grune.

Wiener, Daniel N.
xWiener, Daniel N.
Classroom Management & Discipline. Peacock
Pubs.

Wiener, H. *see* Wiener, Harold.

Wiener, Harold.
xWiener, H.
Eyes OK - I'm OK. Acad Therapy.

Wiener, Harvey.
xWiener, Harvey.
Creating Compositions. McGraw.
Reading Skills Handbook. HM.
xWiener, Harvey S.
Creating Compositions. McGraw.

Wiener, Harvey S. *see* Wiener, Harvey.

Wiener, Jerry M.
xWiener, Jerry M.
ed. Psychopharmacology in Childhood &
Adolescence. Basic.

Wiener, Leo, 1862-1939
xWiener, Leo.
The History of Yiddish Literature in the
Nineteenth Century. Hermon.

Wiener Library. *see* Wiener Library, London.

Wiener Library, London.
xWiener Library.
German Jewry: Its History, Life & Culture.
Greenwood.
On the Track of Tyranny. Arno.

Wiener, Lionel, 1879-1940
xWiener, Lionel.
Articulated Locomotives. Kalmbach.

Wiener, M. *see* Wiener, Matthew B.

Wiener, Matthew B.
xWiener, M.
Clinical Pharmacology & Therapeutics in
Nursing. McGraw.

Wiener, Norbert, 1894-
xWiener, Norbert.
Fourier Integral & Certain of Its Applications.
Dover.
God & Golem, Inc.: A Comment on Certain
Points Where Cybernetics Impinges on
Religion. MIT Pr.

Wiener, R. *see* Wiener, Robert A.

Wiener, Robert A.
xWiener, R.
Insolvency Accounting. McGraw.

Wienpahl, Paul.
xWienpahl, Paul.

The Matter of Zen: A brief account of Zazen.
NYU Pr.
The Radical Spinoza. NYU Pr.

Wier, Delight B. *see* Wier, Delight Bobilya.

Wier, Delight Bobilya.
xWier, Delight B.
Diary of the Farmer's Wife.
Wallace-Homestead.

Wier, Ester.
xWier, Ester.
Easy Does It. Vanguard.
Loner. McKay.

Wiernik, Peter, 1865-1936
xWiernik, Peter.
History of the Jews in America from the
Period of Discovery of the New World to the
Present Time. Greenwood.

Wiersbe, Warren. *see* Wiersbe, Warren W.

Wiersbe, Warren W.
xWiersbe, Warren.
His Name Is Wonderful. Tyndale.
xWiersbe, Warren W.
Be Ready. Victor Bks.
Meet Yourself in the Parables. Victor Bks.

Wiersma, William.
xWiersma, William.
Evaluation of Instruction in Individually
Guided Education. A-W.

Wierwille, Victor P. *see* Wierwille, Victor Paul.

Wierwille, Victor Paul.
xWierwille, Victor P.
Are the Dead Alive Now?. Am Christian.
Are the Dead Alive Now?. Devin.

Wierzbicki, Felix P. *see* Wierzbicki, Felix Paul.

Wierzbicki, Felix Paul, 1815-1860
xWierzbicki, Felix P.
California As It Is & As It May Be: Or a
Guide to the Gold Region. B Franklin.

Wieschhoff, Heinrich A. *see* Wieschhoff, Heinrich Albert.

Wieschhoff, Heinrich Albert, 1906-
xWieschhoff, Heinrich A.
Colonial Policies in Africa. Negro U Pr.

Wiese, Bennard R.
xWiese, Bennard R.
Everything You Need to Know to Stay
Married & Like It. Zondervan.

Wiesel, Elie, 1928-
xWiesel, Elie.
Four Hasidic Masters & Their Struggle Against
Melancholy. U of Notre Dame Pr.
A Jew Today. Random.
A Jew Today. Random.
Zalmen or the Madness of God. Random.

Wiesel, Elie. *see* Wiesel, Eliezer.

Wiesel, Eliezer.
xWiesel, Elie.
Legends of Our Time. Avon.
Night. Avon.
The Oath. Avon.
The Oath. Random.
One Generation After. Random.

Wiesel, Marion.
xWiesel, Marion.
tr. A Jew Today. Random.

Wieselberg, Helen.
xWieselberg, Helen.
The Lords of Dair. Putnam.

Wiesenthal, Eleanor.
xWiesenthal, Eleanor.
Let's Find Out About Eskimos. Watts.
Let's Find Out About Rivers. Watts.

Wiesner, Jerome B. *see* Wiesner, Jerome Bert.

Wiesner, Jerome Bert, 1915-
xWiesner, Jerome B.
Where Science & Politics Meet. McGraw.

Wiesner, William.
xWiesner, William.

Wilbur, Marguerite Knowlton (Eyer), 1889-
    xWilbur, Marguerite K.
        East India Company & the British Empire in
            the Far East. Russell.
Wilbur, Richard, 1921-
    xWilbur, Richard.
        Responses: Prose, Pieces, 1948-1976.
            HarBraceJ.
Wilbur, Richard. see Wilbur, J. Richard H.
Wilbur, Sibyl, 1871-1946
    xWilbur, Sibyl.
        Life of Mary Baker Eddy. Chr Science.
Wilburn, Michael D.
    xWilburn, Michael D.
        Optimizing Development Profits in Large Scale
            Real Estate Projects. Urban Land.
Wilby, C. B. see Wilby, Charles Bryan.
Wilby, Charles Bryan.
    xWilby, C. B.
        Concrete Shell Roofs. Halsted Pr.
Wilcken, Ulrich.
    xWilcken, Ulrich.
        Alexander the Great. Norton.
Wilcock, John.
    xWilcock, John.
        An Occult Guide to South America. Stein &
            Day.
        Traveling in Venezuela. Hippocrene Bks.
Wilcock, M. see Wilcock, Michael.
Wilcock, Michael.
    xWilcock, M.
        I Saw Heaven Opened: The Message of
            Revelation. Inter-Varsity.
Wilcox, C. J. see Wilcox, Charles J.
Wilcox, Charles J.
    xWilcox, C. J.
        ed. Large Dairy Herd Management. U Presses
            Fla.
Wilcox, Clair, 1898-
    xWilcox, Clair.
        A Charter for World Trade. Arno.
        Competition & Monopoly in American
            Industry. AMS Pr.
        Competition & Monopoly in American
            Industry. Greenwood.
        Economies of the World Today: Their
            Organization, Development & Performance.
            HarBraceJ.
        Toward Social Welfare: An Analysis of
            Programs & Proposals Attacking Poverty,
            Insecurity, & Inequality of Opportunity.
            Irwin.
Wilcox, Collin.
    xWilcox, Collin.
        Aftershock. BJ Pub Group.
        Long Way Down. BJ Pub Group.
        Power Plays. Random.
Wilcox, Daniel.
    xWilcox, Daniel.
        I'm My Mommy-I'm My Daddy. Western
            Pub.
Wilcox, Dennis J. see Wilcox, Dennis L.
Wilcox, Dennis L.
    xWilcox, Dennis J.
        Mass Media in Black Africa: Philosophy &
            Control. Praeger.
Wilcox, Desmond.
    xWilcox, Desmond.
        Americans. Delacorte.
Wilcox, Donald J.
    xWilcox, Donald J.
        Development of Florentine Humanist
            Historiography in the Fifteenth Century.
            Harvard U Pr.
Wilcox, Fred.
    xWilcox, Fred.
        ed. The Grass Roots: An Anti-Nuke
            Sourcebook. Crossing Pr.
Wilcox, Herbert, 1891-
    xWilcox, Herbert.

        Contrib. by Georgia Scribe: Selected Columns.
            Cherokee.
Wilcox, Howard.
    xWilcox, Howard.
        Bruce Moore: Notes Toward a Review of His
            Life & Art. Estate Bk.
Wilcox, John, 1887-
    xWilcox, John.
        Relation of Moliere to the Restoration
            Comedy. Arno.
Wilcox, Mary M., 1921-
    xWilcox, Mary M.
        Developmental Journey: A Guide to the
            Development of Logical & Moral Reasoning
            & Social Perspective. Abingdon.
Wilcox, Morris R, 1893-
    xWilcox, Morris R.
        Men & Mountains. Golden Quill.
Wilcox, Paul L.
    xWilcox, Paul L.
        Alaska & the Job. Branden.
Wilcox, R. see Wilcox, Ruth Turner.
Wilcox, R. Turner. see Wilcox, Ruth Turner.
Wilcox, Roger, 1934-
    xWilcox, Roger N.
        ed. Psychological Consequences of Being a
            Black American: A Source Book of Research
            by Black Psychologists. Wiley.
Wilcox, Roger N. see Wilcox, Roger.
Wilcox, Roger P.
    xWilcox, Roger P.
        Oral Reporting in Business & Industry. P-H.
Wilcox, Ruth Turner, 1888-
    xWilcox, R.
        Dictionary of Costume. David & Charles.
    xWilcox, R. Turner.
        Dictionary of Costume. Scribner.
        Five Centuries of American Costume. Scribner.
        Folk & Festival Costume of the World.
            Scribner.
Wilcox, Thomas W.
    xWilcox, Thomas W.
        The Anatomy of College English. Jossey-Bass.
Wilcox, Walter W. see Wilcox, Walter William.
Wilcox, Walter William.
    xWilcox, Walter W.
        Economics of American Agriculture. P-H.
        The Farmer in the Second World War. Da
            Capo.
Wilcox, Wayne. see Wilcox, Wayne Ayres.
Wilcox, Wayne A. see Wilcox, Wayne Ayres.
Wilcox, Wayne Ayres.
    xWilcox, Wayne.
        Asia & the International System. Winthrop.
    xWilcox, Wayne A.
        Pakistan: The Consolidation of a Nation.
            Columbia U Pr.
Wilcoxon, George D. see Wilcoxon, George Dent.
Wilcoxon, George Dent, 1913-
    xWilcoxon, George D.
        Athens Ascendant. Iowa St U Pr.
Wilcoxson, Kent H.
    xWilcoxson, Kent H.
        Angler's Guide to Freshwater Fishing in New
            England. Herman Pub.
Wilczak, Paul F.
    xWilczak, Paul F.
        ed. Parenting. Abbey.
Wilczynski, J. see Wilczynski, Jozef.
Wilczynski, Jozef, 1922-
    xWilczynski, J.
        Economics & Politics of East-West Trade.
            Beekman Pubs.
    xWilczynski, Jozef.
        The Multinationals & East-West Relations:
            Towards Transideological Collaboration.
            Westview.
Wild, J. P.
    xWild, J. P.

        Textile Manufacture in the Northern Roman
            Provinces. Cambridge U Pr.
Wild, John. see Wild, John Daniel.
Wild, John D. see Wild, John Daniel.
Wild, John Daniel, 1902-
    xWild, John.
        Plato's Modern Enemies & the Theory of
            Natural Law. U of Chicago Pr.
    xWild, John D.
        The Challenge of Existentialism. Greenwood.
Wild, Laura H. see Wild, Laura Hulda.
Wild, Laura Hulda, 1870-
    xWild, Laura H.
        Geographic Influences in Old Testament
            Masterpieces. Folcroft.
        Geographic Influences in Old Testament
            Masterpieces. R West.
Wild, Peter.
    xWild, Peter.
        Peligros. SBD.
Wild, R. see Wild, Ray.
Wild, R. A. see Wild, Ronald Arthur.
Wild, Ray.
    xWild, R.
        Mass Production Management: The Design &
            Operation of Production Flow-Line Systems.
            Wiley.
    xWild, Ray.
        Concepts for Operations Management. Wiley.
        Operations Management: A Policy Framework.
            Pergamon.
Wild, Robert, 1936-
    xWild, Robert.
        Enthusiasm in the Spirit. Ave Maria.
Wild, Robin.
    xWild, Robin.
        jt. auth. How Animals Work for Us. Enslow
            Pubs.
        Spot's Dogs & the Alley Cats. Lippincott.
Wild, Ronald Arthur.
    xWild, R. A.
        Social Stratification in Australia. Allen Unwin.
Wildavsky, Aaron.
    xWildavsky, Aaron.
        Dixon-Yates: A Study in Power Politics.
            Greenwood.
Wildavsky, Aaron. see Wildavsky, Aaron B.
Wildavsky, Aaron B.
    xWildavsky, Aaron.
        Budgeting: A Comparative Theory of
            Budgetary Processes. Little.
        The Politics of the Budgetary Process. Little.
        Speaking Truth to Power: The Art & Craft of
            Policy Analysis. Little.
Wildbur, Peter.
    xWildbur, Peter.
        International Trademark Design: A Handbook
            of Marks of Identity. Van Nos Reinhold.
Wilde, Douglas. see Wilde, Douglass J.
Wilde, Douglass. see Wilde, Douglass J.
Wilde, Douglass J.
    xWilde, Douglas.
        jt. auth. Foundations of Optimization. P-H.
    xWilde, Douglass.
        Foundations of Optimization. P-H.
    xWilde, Douglass J.
        Globally Optimal Design. Wiley.
Wilde, Jennifer.
    xWilde, Jennifer.
        Love's Tender Fury. Warner Bks.
Wilde, Johannes.
    xWilde, Johannes.
        Venetian Art from Bellini to Titian. Oxford U
            Pr.
Wilde, Larry.
    xWilde, Larry.

The Complete Book of Ethnic Humor. Corwin.
The Complete Book of Ethnic Humor. Pinnacle
Bks.
Wilde, Norman, 1867-1936
xWilde, Norman.
The Ethical Basis of the State. Hyperion Conn.
Wilde, Oscar.
xWilde, Oscar.
Ballad of Reading Gaol. Carrier Pigeon.
The Birthday of the Infanta. Viking Pr.
The Complete Shorter Fiction of Oscar Wilde.
Oxford U Pr.
De Profundis. Avon.
De Profundis & Other Writings. Penguin.
First Collected Edition of the Works of Oscar
Wilde. B&N.
The Happy Prince & Other Tales. Shambhala
Pubns.
Portable Oscar Wilde. Penguin.
Portable Oscar Wilde. Viking Pr.
Selected Letters of Oscar Wilde. Oxford U Pr.
Selected Letters of Oscar Wilde. Oxford U Pr.
The Selfish Giant. McGraw.
Selfish Giant. Methuen Inc.
The Soul of Man Under Socialism & Other
Essays. Peter Smith.
The Star Child: A Fairy Tale. Schol Bk Serv.
Works of Oscar Wilde. AMS Pr.
Works of Oscar Wilde. Collins Pubs.
Wilde, Percival, 1887-1953
xWilde, Percival.
Eight Comedies for Little Theatres. Core
Collection.
Wildenhain, Marguerite.
xWildenhain, Marguerite.
Pottery: Form & Expression. Pacific Bks.
Wilder, Alec.
xWilder, Alec.
American Popular Song: The Great Innovators,
1900-1950. Oxford U Pr.
American Popular Song: The Great Innovators,
1900-1950. Oxford U Pr.
Wilder, Amos N. see Wilder, Amos Niven.
Wilder, Amos Niven, 1895-
xWilder, Amos N.
Early Christian Rhetoric: The Language of the
Gospel. Harvard U Pr.
ed. Liberal Learning & Religion. Kennikat.
Theopoetic: Theology & the Religious
Imagination. Fortress.
Wilder, C. S. see Wilder, Charles S.
Wilder, Charles S.
xWilder, C. S.
Acute Conditions, Incidence & Associated
Disability, United States, July 1974-June
1975. Natl Ctr Health Stats.
Hospital & Surgical Insurance Coverage United
States 1974. Natl Ctr Health Stats.
Wilder, Cherry.
xWilder, Cherry.
The Luck of Brin's Five. PB.
The Luck of Brin's Five. Atheneum.
The Nearest Fire. Atheneum.
Wilder, Daniel W. see Wilder, Daniel Webster.
Wilder, Daniel Webster, 1832-1911
xWilder, Daniel W.
Annals of Kansas: 1541-1885. Arno.
Wilder, Edna, 1916-
xWilder, Edna.
Secrets of Eskimo Skin Sewing. Alaska
Northwest.
Wilder, G. see Wilder, George Durand.
Wilder, G. D. see Wilder, George Durand.
Wilder, George Durand.
xWilder, G.
Analysis of Chinese Characters. Krishna Pr.
xWilder, G. D.

Analysis of Chinese Characters. Chinese
Materials.
Analysis of Chinese Characters. Dover.
Wilder, Laura (Ingalls), 1867-1957
xWilder, Laura I.
By the Shores of Silver Lake. Har-Row.
Farmer Boy. Har-Row.
First Four Years. Har-Row.
Little House in the Big Woods. Har-Row.
Little House on the Prairie. Har-Row.
Little House on the Prairie. Har-Row.
Little Town on the Prairie. Har-Row.
The Long Winter. Har-Row.
On the Banks of Plum Creek. Har-Row.
On the Banks of Plum Creek. Har-Row.
These Happy Golden Years. Har-Row.
Wilder, Laura I. see Wilder, Laura (Ingalls).
Wilder, Leonard.
xWilder, Leonard.
Open Wide--It Won't Hurt. St Martin.
Wilder, Margaret G.
xWilder, Margaret G.
Black Assimilation in the Urban Environment:
The Impact of Migration & Mobility. R & E
Res Assoc.
Wilder, Mary H.
xWilder, Mary H.
Persons Hospitalized by Number of Episodes &
Days Hospitalized in a Year: United States,
1972. Natl Ctr Health Stats.
Wilder, Raymond L. see Wilder, Raymond Louis.
Wilder, Raymond Louis, 1896-
xWilder, Raymond L.
Topology of Manifolds. Am Math.
Wilder, Thornton. see Wilder, Thornton Niven.
Wilder, Thornton Niven, 1897-1975
xWilder, Thornton.
American Characteristics & Other Essays.
Har-Row.
The Bridge of San Luis Rey. Avon.
Bridge of San Luis Rey. Har-Row.
The Ides of March. Avon.
Theophilus North. Avon.
Theophilus North. Har-Row.
Wilder, Walter B. see Wilder, Walter Beebe.
Wilder, Walter Beebe, 1906-
xWilder, Walter B.
Bounty of the Wayside. Arno.
Wildermuth, K. see Wildermuth, Karl.
Wildermuth, Karl.
xWildermuth, K.
Cluster Representations of Nuclei.
Springer-Verlag.
Wilders, John.
xWilders, John.
The Lost Garden: A View of Shakespeare's
English & Roman History Plays. Rowman.
Wildes, Harry E. see Wildes, Harry Emerson.
Wildes, Harry Emerson, 1890-
xWildes, Harry E.
Anthony Wayne, Trouble Shooter of the
American Revolution. Greenwood.
xWildes, Henry.
Typhoon in Tokyo: The Occupation & Its
Aftermath. Octagon.
Wildes, Henry. see Wildes, Harry Emerson.
Wildgans, Friedrich.
xWildgans, Friedrick.
Anton Webern. October.
Wildgans, Friedrick. see Wildgans, Friedrich.
Wildhorn, Sorrel.
xWildhorn, Sorrell.
ed. How to Save Gasoline: Public Policy
Alternatives for the Automobile. Ballinger
Pub.
Wildhorn, Sorrell. see Wildhorn, Sorrel.
Wilding, L. A. see Wilding, Longworth Allen.
Wilding, Longworth Allen, 1902-
xWilding, L. A.

Greek for Beginners. Transatlantic.
Wilding, Michael.
xWilding, Michael.
ed. Marvell. Aurora Pubs.
Wilding, Peter.
xWilding, Peter.
Adventurers in the Eighteenth Century. Arno.
Wilding, Suzanne.
xWilding, Suzanne.
ed. Horse Tales. St Martin.
Wildlife Management Institute.
xWildlife Management Institute.
Big Game of North America. Stackpole.
Wildman, Allan K.
xWildman, Allan K.
The End of the Russian Imperial Army: The
Old Army & the Soldier's Revolt, March to
April 1917. Princeton U Pr.
Wildman, Eugene.
xWildman, Eugene.
ed. Anthology of Concretism. Swallow.
ed. Experiments in Prose. Swallow.
Montezuma's Ball. Swallow.
Wildman, M. S. see Wildman, Murray Shipley.
Wildman, Murray S. see Wildman, Murray Shipley.
Wildman, Murray Shipley, 1868-1930
xWildman, M. S.
Money Inflation in the United States: A Study
in Social Pathology. Gordon Pr.
xWildman, Murray S.
Money Inflation in the United States: A Study
in Social Pathology. Greenwood.
Wildridge, Thomas T. see Wildridge, Thomas Tindall.
Wildridge, Thomas Tindall.
xWildridge, Thomas T.
Grotesque in Church Art. Gale.
Wildschut, William.
xWildschut, William
Crow Indian Medicine Bundles. Mus Am Ind.
Wildsmith, Alan.
xWildsmith, Alan.
Northern Phantom. Andre Deutsch.
Wildsmith, Brian.
xWildsmith, Brian.
illus. The Lazy Bear. Watts.
The Little Wood Duck. Watts.
illus. The Owl & the Woodpecker. Watts.
Python's Party. Watts.
illus. The True Cross. Oxford U Pr.
illus. The True Cross. Watts.
illus. What the Moon Saw. Oxford U Pr.
Wildt, Al. see Wildt, Albert R.
Wildt, Albert R.
xWildt, Al.
Analysis of Covariance. Sage.
Wildung, Dietrich.
xWildung, Dietrich.
Egyptian Saints: Deification in Pharaonic
Egypt. NYU Pr.
Wile, Frederic William, 1873-1941
xWile, Frederick W.
ed. A Century of Industrial Progress. Arno.
Wile, Frederick W. see Wile, Frederic William.
Wileman, J. P.
xWileman, J. P.
Brazilian Exchange: The Study of an
Inconvertible Currency. Greenwood.
Wileman, Ralph E.
xWileman, Ralph E.
Exercises in Visual Thinking. Hastings.
Wilenski, R. H. see Wilenski, Reginald Howard.
Wilenski, Reginald Howard, 1887-
xWilenski, R. H.
French Painting. Peter Smith.
Wilensky, Harold L.
xWilensky, Harold L.
Organizational Intelligence: Knowledge &
Policy in Government & Industry. Basic.
Wilensky, Julius M.
xWilensky, Julius M.

Cape Cod: Where to Go, What to Do, How to
Do It. Wescott Cove.
Yachtsman's Guide to the Windward Islands.
Wescott Cove.
Wiles, Bertha H. *see* Wiles, Bertha Harris.
Wiles, Bertha Harris, 1896-
xWiles, Bertha H.
Fountains of Florentine Sculptors & Their
Followers from Donatello to Bernini. Hacker.
Wiles, Domini.
xWiles, Domini.
Death Flight. BJ Pub Group.
Wiles, Jon.
xWiles, Jon.
Planning Guidelines for Middle School
Education. Kendall-Hunt.
Wiles, Julian.
xWiles, Julian.
Tradd Street Follies. Tradd St Pr.
Wiles, Kimball.
xWiles, Kimball.
Supervision for Better Schools. P-H.
Wiles, M. *see* Wiles, Maurice.
Wiles, Maurice.
xWiles, M.
ed. Documents in Early Christian Thought.
Cambridge U Pr.
Wiles, Maurice. *see* Wiles, Maurice F.
Wiles, Maurice F.
xWiles, Maurice.
The Remaking of Christian Doctrine.
Westminster.
Wiles, P. *see* Wiles, Peter John De la Fosse.
Wiles, Paul.
xWiles, Paul.
ed. The Sociology of Crime & Delinquency:
The New Criminologies. B&N.
Wiles, Peter John de la Fosse.
xWiles, P.
ed. Prediction of Communist Economic
Performance. Cambridge U Pr.
Wiles, R. M. *see* Wiles, Roy McKeen.
Wiles, Roy McKeen.
xWiles, R. M.
Freshest Advices: Early Provincial Newspapers
in England. Ohio St U Pr.
Wiley & Sons Inc. *see* Wiley (John) and Sons, Inc.
Wiley, Autrey N. *see* Wiley, Autrey Nell.
Wiley, Autrey Nell, 1901-
xWiley, Autrey N.
ed. Rare Prologues & Epilogues 1642-1700.
Kennikat.
Wiley, B. I. *see* Wiley, Bell Irvin.
Wiley, Bell I. *see* Wiley, Bell Irvin.
Wiley, Bell Irvin, 1906-
xWiley, B. I.
Plain People of the Confederacy. Peter Smith.
xWiley, Bell I.
Common Soldier of the Civil War. Scribner.
ed. Slaves No More: Letters from Liberia,
1833-1869. U Pr of Ky.
Southern Negroes, 1861-1865. La State U Pr.
xWiley, Bell J.
Confederate Women. Greenwood.
Wiley, Bell J. *see* Wiley, Bell Irvin.
Wiley, Edwin, 1872-1924
xWiley, Edwin.
Study of the Supernatural in Three Plays of
Shakespeare. Folcroft.
Wiley, George E.
xWiley, George E.
Southern Plantation Stories & Sketches. Arno.
Wiley, Harvey W. *see* Wiley, Harvey Washington.
Wiley, Harvey Washington, 1844-1930
xWiley, Harvey W.
The History of a Crime Against the Food Law.
Arno.
Wiley, Jack.
xWiley, Jack.

Acrobatics Book. Anderson World.
The Bicycle Builder's Bible. TAB Bks.
Fiberglass Kit Boats. Follett.
Fiberglass Kit Boats. Intl Marine.
The Tumbling Book. McKay.
Wiley (John) and Sons, Inc.
xWiley & Sons Inc.
First One Hundred & Fifty Years: A History of
John Wiley & Sons Inc. Wiley.
Wiley, Leonard.
xWiley, Leonard.
Rare Wild Flowers of North America. L Wiley.
Wiley, Margaret L. *see* Wiley, Margaret Lenore.
Wiley, Margaret Lenore, 1908-
xWiley, Margaret L.
Subtle Knot: Creative Scepticism in
Seventeenth-Century England. Greenwood.
Wiley, Paul L.
xWiley, Paul L.
Conrad's Measure of Man. Gordian.
Wiley, Robert J.
xWiley, Robert J.
Real Estate Investment: Analysis & Strategy.
Ronald Pr.
Wiley, William L. *see* Wiley, William Leon.
Wiley, William Leon.
xWiley, William L.
The Early Public Theatre in France.
Greenwood.
Formal French. Harvard U Pr.
Gentleman of Renaissance France. Greenwood.
Wilf. *see* Wilf, Herbert S.
Wilf, H. S. *see* Wilf, Herbert S.
Wilf, Herbert S., 1931-
xWilf.
Programming for a Digital Computer in the
Fortran Language.. A-W.
xWilf, H. S.
Finite Sections of Some Classical Inequalities.
Springer-Verlag.
xWilf, Herbert S.
Mathematics for the Physical Sciences. Dover.
Wilford, D. Sykes.
xWilford, D. Sykes.
Monetary Policy & the Open Economy:
Mexico's Experience. Praeger.
Wilford, John N. *see* Wilford, John Noble.
Wilford, John Noble.
xWilford, John N.
ed. Scientists at Work: The Creative Process of
Scientific Research. Dodd.
Wilford, Lloyd A. *see* Wilford, Lloyd Alden.
Wilford, Lloyd Alden.
xWilford, Lloyd A.
Burial Mounds of Central Minnesota:
Excavation Reports. Minn Hist.
Burial Mounds of the Red River Headwaters.
Minn Hist.
Wilfred, Thomas, 1889-
xWilfred, Thomas.
Projected Scenery: A Technical Manual.
Drama Bk.
Wilgus, A. Curtis. *see* Wilgus, Alva Curtis.
Wilgus, Alva Curtis, 1897-
xWilgus, A. Curtis.
ed. Caribbean at Mid-Century. U Presses Fla.
ed. Caribbean: Its Economy. U Presses Fla.
ed. Caribbean: Its Political Problems. U Presses
Fla.
ed. Caribbean: Mexico Today. U Presses Fla.
ed. Caribbean: Natural Resources. U Presses
Fla.
Historical Atlas of Latin America: Political,
Geographic, Economic, Cultural. Cooper Sq.
Historiography of Latin America: A Guide to
Historical Writing, 1500-1800. Scarecrow.
Wilgus, Horace L. *see* Wilgus, Horace la Fayette.
Wilgus, Horace la Fayette, 1859-1935
xWilgus, Horace L.

A Study of the United States Steel Corporation
in Its Industrial & Legal Aspects. Arno.
Wilhelm, Gale, 1909-
xWilhelm, Gale.
Torchlight to Valhalla. Arno.
Wilhelm, Hellmut, 1905-
xWilhelm, Hellmut.
Change: Eight Lectures on the I Ching.
Princeton U Pr.
Wilhelm, J. *see* Wilhelm, Jochen.
Wilhelm, James J.
xWilhelm, James J.
Dante & Pound: The Epic of Judgement. Natl
Poet-Univ Me.
ed. Medieval Song: An Anthology of Hymns &
Lyrics. Dutton.
Wilhelm, Jochen, 1945-
xWilhelm, J.
Objectives & Multi-Objective Decision Making
Under Uncertainty. Springer-Verlag.
Wilhelm, Kate.
xWilhelm, Kate.
City of Cain. PB.
The Clewiston Test. FS&G.
The Clewiston Test. PB.
The Infinity Box: A Collection of Speculative
Fiction. Har-Row.
Margaret & I. PB.
More Bitter Than Death. S&S.
Somerset Dreams & Other Fictions. Har-Row.
Somerset Dreams & Other Fictions. Har-Row.
Wilhelm, L. W. *see* Wilhelm, Lewis Webb.
Wilhelm, Lewis Webb.
xWilhelm, L. W.
Local Institutions of Maryland. Johnson Repr.
Wilhelms, Christian.
xWilhelms, Christian.
Market & Marketing in the Federal Republic of
Germany: A Manual for Exporters from
Developing Countries. Intl Pubns Serv.
Wilhelms, Fred. *see* Wilhelms, Fred Theodore.
Wilhelms, Fred T. *see* Wilhelms, Fred Theodore.
Wilhelms, Fred Theodore, 1907-
xWilhelms, Fred.
What Should the Schools Teach?. Phi Delta
Kappa.
xWilhelms, Fred T.
Supervision in a New Key. Assn Supervision.
Wilhelmsen, Frederick D.
xWilhelmsen, Frederick D.
Christianity & Political Philosophy. U of Ga
Pr.
Wilhite, Bob. *see* Wilhite, Robert.
Wilhite, Robert.
xWilhite, Bob.
Standard Guide to U. S. Coin & Paper Money
Valuations. Krause Pubns.
xWilhite, Robert.
Standard Guide to U. S. Coin & Paper Money
Valuations. Krause Pubns.
Wilhoit, Francis M.
xWilhoit, Francis M.
The Politics of Massive Resistance. Braziller.
Quest for Equality in Freedom. Transaction
Bks.
Wilinsky, Harriet.
xWilinsky, Harriet.
Careers & Opportunities in Retailing. Natl Ret
Merch.
Wilk, Chester A.
xWilk, Chester A.
Chiropractic Speaks Out: A Reply to Medical
Propaganda, Bigotry & Ignorance. Wilk Pub.
Wilke, Arthur S.
xWilke, Arthur S.
The Hidden Professoriate: Credentialism,
Professionalism, & the Tenure Crisis.
Greenwood.
Wilken, Paul H.
xWilken, Paul H.

Foundations of Language: Talking & Reading
in Young Children. Oxford U Pr.

Wilkinson, Bertie, 1898-
xWilkinson, Bertie.
Later Middle Ages in England: 1216-1485.
Longman.

Wilkinson, Billy R.
xWilkinson, Billy R.
ed. Reader in Undergraduate Libraries.
IHS-PDS.

Wilkinson, Brenda. *see* Wilkinson, Brenda Scott.

Wilkinson, Brenda Scott.
xWilkinson, Brenda.
Ludell. Har-Row.
Ludell & Willie. Har-Row.
Ludell's New York Time. Har-Row.

Wilkinson, Burke, 1913-
xWilkinson, Burke.
Cry Sabotage: True Stories of 20th Century
Saboteurs. Dell.
Francis in All His Glory. FS&G.

Wilkinson, C. F. *see* Wilkinson, Christopher Foster.

Wilkinson, Catherine, 1941-
xWilkinson, Catherine.
The Hospital of Cardinal Tavera Toledo.
Garland Pub.

Wilkinson, Christopher Foster, 1938-
xWilkinson, C. F.
ed. Insecticide Biochemistry & Physiology.
Plenum Pub.

Wilkinson, David, 1943-1971
xWilkinson, David.
Cohesion & Conflict: Lessons from the Study
of Three-Party Interaction. St Martin.

Wilkinson, Endymion.
xWilkinson, Endymion.
The History of Imperial China: A Research
Guide. Harvard U Pr.
xWilkinson, Endymion P.
Studies in Chinese Price History. Garland Pub.

Wilkinson, Endymion P. *see* Wilkinson, Endymion.

Wilkinson, Ernest L.
xWilkinson, Ernest L.
Brigham Young University: A School of
Destiny. Brigham.

Wilkinson, Frederick. *see* Wilkinson, Frederick John.

Wilkinson, Frederick John, 1922-
xWilkinson, Frederick.
Antique Firearms. Presidio Pr.
Antique Firearms. Sterling.

Wilkinson, Gerald.
xWilkinson, Gerald.
Epitaph for the Elm. Merrimack Bk Serv.

Wilkinson, Herbert A. *see* Wilkinson, Herbert Arnold.

Wilkinson, Herbert Arnold, 1907-
xWilkinson, Herbert A.
The American Doctrine of State Succession.
AMS Pr.
The American Doctrine of State Succession.
Greenwood.

Wilkinson, J. F. *see* Wilkinson, John Frederick.

Wilkinson, J. Harvie, 1944-
xWilkinson, J. Harvie.
From Brown to Bakke: The Supreme Court &
School Integration 1954-1978. Oxford U Pr.

Wilkinson, James, 1757-1825
xWilkinson, James.
Memoirs of My Own Times. AMS Pr.

Wilkinson, James H. *see* Wilkinson, James Hardy.

Wilkinson, James Hardy.
xWilkinson, James H.
Algebraic Eigenvalue Problem. Oxford U Pr.

Wilkinson, Jean.
xWilkinson, Jean.
Flower Fabrications: Forty Hand Fashioned
Flowers to Create Including Silk Tulips,
Organdy Roses, Gingham Cornflowers and
Crepe Paper Daisies. Butterick Pub.

Wilkinson, John.
xWilkinson, John.

The Dynamic Programming of Human
Systems: A Social & Historical Analysis. Mss
Info.
Jerusalem Pilgrims Before the Crusades. Intl
Schol Bk Serv.

Wilkinson, John C. *see* Wilkinson, John C. M.

Wilkinson, John C. M., 1940-
xWilkinson, John C.
How to Buy, Sell & Hold Real Estate: A
Practical Tax Guide. P-H.

Wilkinson, John Frederick.
xWilkinson, J. F.
Introduction to Microbiology. Halsted Pr.

Wilkinson, Joseph W.
xWilkinson, Joseph W.
Accounting with the Computer: A Practice
Case and Simulation. Irwin.

Wilkinson, Jule.
xWilkinson, Jule.
Complete Book of Cooking Equipment. CBI
Pub.

Wilkinson, Karl.
xWilkinson, Karl.
Rewinding Small Motors. Transatlantic.

Wilkinson, L. P.
xWilkinson, L. P.
Golden Latin Artistry. Cambridge U Pr.

Wilkinson, Linda.
xWilkinson, Linda.
Peppermint Dreams. Harvest Hse.

Wilkinson, Marcia.
xWilkinson, Marcia.
Cervical Spondylosis: Its Early Diagnosis &
Treatment. Saunders.

Wilkinson, Marguerite. *see* Wilkinson, Marguerite Ogden
Bigelow.

Wilkinson, Marguerite Ogden Bigelow, 1883-1928
xWilkinson, Marguerite.
Compiled by Golden Songs of the Golden
State. Arno.
ed. Golden Songs of the Golden State. Granger
Bk.

Wilkinson, Norman B.
xWilkinson, Norman B.
E. I. du Pont, Botaniste: The Beginning of a
Tradition. U Pr of Va.
Papermaking in America. Eleutherian
Mills-Hagley.

Wilkinson, Paul.
xWilkinson, Paul.
Political Terrorism. Halsted Pr.

Wilkinson, Paul F.
xWilkinson, Paul F.
Environmental Impact of Outdoor Recreation
& Tourism: A Bibliography. Vance Biblios.

Wilkinson, Philip L.
xWilkinson.
Clinical Anesthesia: Case Selections from the
University of California, San Francisco.
Mosby.

Wilkinson, R. E. *see* Wilkinson, Robert E.

Wilkinson, Richard J. *see* Wilkinson, Richard James.

Wilkinson, Richard James, 1867-1941
xWilkinson, Richard J.
A History of the Penisular Malays, with
Chapters on Perak & Selangor. AMS Pr.

Wilkinson, Robert E.
xWilkinson, R. E.
How to Know the Weeds. Wm C Brown.

Wilkinson, Rupert.
xWilkinson, Rupert.
ed. Governing Elites: Studies in Training &
Selection. Oxford U Pr.
Prevention of Drinking Problems: Alcohol
Control & Cultural Influences. Oxford U Pr.

Wilkinson, Vivian C.
xWilkinson, Vivian C.

Therapeutic Media & Techniques of
Application: A Guide for Activities
Therapists. Van Nos Reinhold.

Wilkinson, Walter D.
xWilkinson, Walter D.
Properties of Refractory Metals. Am Nuclear
Soc.

Wilkinson-Latham, Christopher.
xWilkinson-Latham, Christopher.
Uniforms & Weapons of the Zulu War.
Hippocrene Bks.

Wilkinson-Latham, Robert.
xWilkinson-Latham, Robert.
Uniforms & Weapons of the Crimean War.
Hippocrene Bks.

Wilks, John, 1922-
xWilks, John.
Introduction to Liquid Helium. Oxford U Pr.
Properties of Liquid & Solid Helium. Oxford U
Pr.

Wilks, Yorick A. *see* Wilks, Yorick Alexander.

Wilks, Yorick Alexander.
xWilks, Yorick A.
Grammar, Meaning & the Machine Analysis of
Language. Routledge & Kegan.

Will, Frederic.
xWill, Frederic.
Flumen Historicum: Victor Cousin's Aesthetic
& Its Sources. U of NC Pr.
From a Year in Greece. U of Tex Pr.
Our Thousand Year Old Bodies: Selected
Poems. 1956-1976. U of Mass Pr.

Will, Frederick L.
xWill, Frederick L.
Induction & Justification: An Investigation of
Cartesian Procedure in the Philosophy of
Knowledge. Cornell U Pr.

Will, George F.
xWill, George F.
The Pursuit of Happiness & Other Sobering
Thoughts. Har-Row.
The Pursuit of Happiness, & Other Sobering
Thoughts. Har-Row.

Will, R. Ted.
xWill, R. Ted.
Retailing. Har-Row.

Will, Robert E. *see* Will, Robert Erwin.

Will, Robert Erwin.
xWill, Robert E.
ed. Poverty in Affluence: The Social, Political
& Economic Dimensions of Poverty in the
United States. HarBraceJ.

Will, Robin, 1948-
xWill, Robin.
Beautiful New York City. Beautiful Am.
Beautiful Ohio. Beautiful Am.
Beautiful Portland. Beautiful Am.

Will Rogers Cooperative Association. *see* Will Rogers
State Historic Park. Will Rogers Cooperative
Association.

**Will Rogers State Historic Park. Will Rogers
Cooperative Association.**
xWill Rogers Cooperative Association.
ed. Will Rogers Cookbook, Birthday
Centennial, 1879-1979. Palisades Pub.

Will, Thomas E.
xWill, Thomas E.
Telecommunications Structure & Management
in the Executive Branch of Government:
1900-1970. Westview.

Willame, Jean Claude.
xWillame, Jean-Claude.
Patrimonialism & Political Change in the
Congo. Stanford U Pr.

Willame, Jean-Claude. *see* Willame, Jean Claude.

Willan, T. S. *see* Willan, Thomas Stuart.

Willan, Thomas S. *see* Willan, Thomas Stuart.

Willan, Thomas Stuart.
xWillan, T. S.

The Inland Trade: Studies in English Internal
Trade in the Sixteenth & Seventeenth
Centuries. Rowman.
xWillan, Thomas S.
Early History of the Don Navigation. Kelley.
Early History of the Russia Company,
1553-1603. Kelley.
Eighteenth Century Shopkeeper, Abraham
Dent of Kirkby Stephen. Kelley.
English Coasting Trade 1600-1750. Kelley.
Muscovy Merchants of 1555. Kelley.
Studies in Elizabethan Foreign Trade. Kelley.
Willand, Lois.
xWilland, Lois.
Use-It-up Cookbook. Scribner.
Willard, Abbie. *see* Willard, Abbie F.
Willard, Abbie F.
xWillard, Abbie.
Wallace Stevens: A Poet & His Critics. ALA.
Willard, Barbara.
xWillard, Barbara.
The Country Maid. Greenwillow.
The Gardener's Grandchildren. McGraw.
Richleighs of Tantamount. HarBraceJ.
Willard, Dan E., 1948-
xWillard, Dan E.
Predicate-Oriented Database Search
Algorithms. Garland Pub.
Willard, Harold.
xWillard, Harold N.
Continuing Care in a Community Hospital.
Harvard U Pr.
Willard, Harold N. *see* Willard, Harold.
Willard, Hobart Hurd.
xWillard, Hobarth.
Instrumental Methods of Analysis, D Van
Nostrand.
Willard, Hobarth. *see* Willard, Hobart Hurd.
Willard, J. F. *see* Willard, James Field.
Willard, James Field, 1875-1946
xWillard, J. F.
ed. English Government at Work, 1327-1336.
Medieval Acad.
Willard, John W. *see* Willard, John Ware.
Willard, John Ware.
xWillard, John W.
Simon Willard & His Clocks. Dover.
Simon Willard & His Clocks. Peter Smith.
Willard, Margaret (Wheeler).
xWillard, Margaret W.
ed. Letters on the American Revolution
1774-1776. Kennikat.
Willard, Margaret W. *see* Willard, Margaret (Wheeler).
Willard, Mildred W. *see* Willard, Mildred Wilds.
Willard, Mildred Wilds.
xWillard, Mildred W.
The Ice Cream Cone. Follett.
Willard, Myra.
xWillard, Myra.
History of the White Australia Policy to 1920.
Biblio Dist.
History of the White Australia Policy to 1920.
Kelley.
Willard, Nancy.
xWillard, Nancy.
Childhood of the Magician. Liveright.
The Highest Hit. HarBraceJ.
Papa's Panda. HarBraceJ.
Simple Pictures Are Best. HarBraceJ.
Simple Pictures Are Best. HarBraceJ.
Willard, Samuel, 1640-1707
xWillard, Samuel.
Compleat Body of Divinity. Johnson Repr.
Willard, Stephen, 1941-
xWillard, Stephen.
Calculus & Its Applications. Prindle.
General Topology. A-W.
Willardson, Robert K.
xWillardson, Robert K.

Compound Semiconductors. Van Nos
Reinhold.
Willbanks, Ray.
xWillbanks, Ray.
Randolph Stow. Twayne.
Willcocks, M. P. *see* Willcocks, Mary Patricia.
Willcocks, Mary Patricia, 1869-
xWillcocks, M. P.
Bunyan Calling: A Voice from the Seventeenth
Century. Folcroft.
Bunyan Calling: A Voice from the Seventeenth
Century. R West.
A True-Born Englishman: Being the Life of
Henry Fielding. Folcroft.
Willcox, Donald. *see* Willcox, Donald J.
Willcox, Donald J., 1933-
xWillcox, Donald.
Modern Leather Design. Watson-Guptill.
Willcox, Sheila.
xWillcox, Sheila.
The Event Horse. Lippincott.
Willcox, Walter F. *see* Willcox, Walter Francis.
Willcox, Walter Francis, 1861-1964
xWillcox, Walter F.
Studies in American Demography. Russell.
Willcutt, J. Robert.
xWillcutt, J. Robert.
The Musical Instrument Collector. Bold
Strummer Ltd.
Willeby, Charles, 1865-
xWilleby, Charles.
Masters of English Music. Arno.
Masters of English Music. Longwood Pr.
Willeford, George.
xWilleford, George.
Cosmetic Surgery May Be for You. Knoll
Creek Pub.
Medical Word Finder. P-H.
Medical Word Finder. P-H.
Willeford, William.
xWilleford, William.
Fool & His Scepter: A Study in Clowns &
Jesters & Their Audience. Northwestern U
Pr.
Willems, Emilio.
xWillems, Emilio.
Latin American Culture: An Anthropological
Synthesis. Har-Row.
Willems, Jos L.
xWillems, Jos L.
ed. Cardiac Function & Aging. Mss Info.
Willems, Nicholas.
xWillems, Nicholas.
Structural Analysis for Engineers. McGraw.
Willemsen, Eleanor W. *see* Willemsen, Eleanor Walker.
Willemsen, Eleanor Walker, 1938-
xWillemsen, Eleanor W.
Understanding Statistical Reasoning: How to
Evaluate Research Literature in the
Behavioral Sciences. W H Freeman.
Willerding, Margaret. *see* Willerding, Margaret F.
Willerding, Margaret F.
xWillerding, Margaret.
The Business of Mathematics. Prindle.
xWillerding, Margaret F.
Algebra: A First Course for College Students.
Prindle.
College Algebra. Wiley.
College Algebra & Trigonometry. Wiley.
Modern Intermediate Algebra. Wiley.
xWillerding, Margret F.
A First Course in College Mathematics.
Prindle.
Willerding, Margret F. *see* Willerding, Margaret F.
Willerman, Lee, 1939-
xWillerman, Lee.

The Psychology of Individual & Group
Differences. W H Freeman.
ed. Readings About Individual & Group
Differences. W H Freeman.
Willerson, James T.
xWillerson, James T.
ed. Nuclear Cardiology. Davis Co.
Willett, Edward J.
xWillett, Edward J.
Modernizing the Little Red Schoolhouse: The
Economics of Improved Education. Educ
Tech Pubns.
Willett, John.
xWillett, John.
Art & Politics in the Weimar Period: The New
Sobriety, 1917-1933. Pantheon.
Theatre of Bertolt Brecht: A Study from Eight
Aspects. New Directions.
The Theatre of Erwin Piscator: Half a Century
of Politics in the Theatre. Holmes & Meier.
Willett, Joseph W.
xWillett, Joseph W.
The World Food Situation: Problems &
Prospects to 1985. Oceana.
Willett, Thomas. *see* Willett, Thomas D.
Willett, Thomas D.
xWillett, Thomas.
Floating Exchange Rates & International
Monetary Reform. Am Enterprise.
Willetts, R. F., 1915-
xWilletts, R. F.
Aristocratic Society in Ancient Crete.
Greenwood.
The Civilization of Ancient Crete. U of Cal Pr.
Cretan Cults & Festivals. Greenwood.
Willey, Austin, 1806-1896
xWilley, Austin.
History of the Anti-Slavery Cause in State &
Nation. Arno.
History of the Antislavery Cause in State &
Nation. Negro U Pr.
Willey, Basil, 1897-
xWilley, Basil.
Christianity, Past & Present. Hyperion Conn.
Coleridge on Imagination & Fancy. Folcroft.
More Nineteenth Century Studies: A Group of
Honest Doubters. Columbia U Pr.
Willey, E. L. *see* Willey, Ewart Lewis.
Willey, Ewart Lewis.
xWilley, E. L.
Some Commercial Autocodes: A Comparative
Study. Acad Pr.
Willey, Gordon R. *see* Willey, Gordon Randolph.
Willey, Gordon Randolph, 1913-
xWilley, Gordon R.
The Altar De Sacrificios Excavations: General
Summary & Conclusions. Peabody Harvard.
ed. Archaeological Researches in Retrospect.
Winthrop.
Archeology of the Florida Gulf Coast. AMS
Pr.
The Artifacts of Altar De Sacrificios. Peabody
Harvard.
A History of American Archaeology. W H
Freeman.
Pre-Columbian Archaeology: Readings from
Scientific American. W H Freeman.
Willey, Keith.
xWilley, Keith.
Assignment New Guinea. Intl Pubns Serv.
Willey, Thomas E., 1934-
xWilley, Thomas E.
Back to Kant: The Revival of Kantianism in
German Social & Historical Thought,
1860-1914. Wayne St U Pr.
William Andrews Clark Memorial Library-Los Angeles.
see California. University. University at los Angeles.
William Andrews Clark Memorial Library.

William Mackenzie Memorial Symposium, 3rd, Glasgow, 1974.
　　xWilliam Mackenzie Memorial Symposium.
　　　　Vision & Circulation: Proceedings. Mosby.
William O. Douglas Symposium, Fairhaven College, 1977. see Fairhaven College.
Williams, A. F. see Williams, Alan Francis.
Williams, A. L. see Williams, Arthur L.
Williams, Adele.
　　xWilliams, Adele.
　　　　Gracious Living: How to Enjoy Being a Woman. Arbor Hse.
Williams, Alan, 1935-
　　xWilliams, Alan.
　　　　The Widow's War. Rawson Wade.
Williams, Alan Francis, 1950-
　　xWilliams, A. F.
　　　　A Theoretical Approach to Inorganic Chemistry. Springer-Verlag.
Williams, Albert N. see Williams, Albert Nathaniel.
Williams, Albert Nathaniel, 1914-
　　xWilliams, Albert N.
　　　　Listening: A Collection of Critical Articles on Radio. Arno.
Williams, Alexander.
　　xWilliams, Alexander.
　　　　Aesop's Fables. Dandelion Pr.
　　　　Ali Baba & the Forty Thieves. Dandelion Pr.
Williams, Alexander Malcolm, 1858-
　　xWilliams, M. A.
　　　　Our Early Female Novelists & Other Essays. Folcroft.

Williams, Alfred, 1877-1930
　　xWilliams, Alfred.
　　　　Life in a Railway Factory. Kelley.

Williams, Alfred T. see Williams, Alfred Tuttle.
Williams, Alfred Tuttle, 1878-
　　xWilliams, Alfred T.
　　　　The Concept of Equality in the Writings of Rousseau, Bentham, & Kant. AMS Pr.
Williams, Alpheus S. see Williams, Alpheus Starkey.

Williams, Alpheus Starkey.
　　xWilliams, Alpheus S.
　　　　From the Cannon's Mouth: The Civil War Letters of General Alpheus S. Williams. Wayne St U Pr.

Williams, Ariadna Tyrkova.
　　xWilliams, Ariadne.
　　　　From Liberty to Brest-Litovsk: The First Year of the Russian Revolution. Hyperion Conn.
Williams, Ariadne. see Williams, Ariadna Tyrkova.
Williams, Arnold, 1907-
　　xWilliams, Arnold.
　　　　Drama of Medieval England. Mich St U Pr.
　　　　Flower on a Lowly Stalk: The Sixth Book of the Faerie Queene. Mich St U Pr.
Williams, Arthur B. see Williams, Arthur Bernard.
Williams, Arthur Bernard, 1940-
　　xWilliams, Arthur B.
　　　　Active Filter Design. Artech Hse.
Williams, Arthur L.
　　xWilliams, A. L.
　　　　Introduction to Chemistry. A-W.
　　xWilliams, Arthur L.
　　　　General Chemistry. A-W.
Williams, Aubrey L.
　　xWilliams, Aubrey L.
　　　　An Approach to Congreve. Yale U Pr.
Williams, B. A. see Williams, Bernard Arthur Owen.
Williams, B. J. see Williams, Bobby J.
Williams, Barbara.
　　xWilliams, Barbara.

Albert's Toothache. Dutton.
Breakthrough: Women in Politics. Walker & Co.
Brigham Young & Me, Clarissa. Doubleday.
Chester Chipmunk's Thanksgiving. Dutton.
Gary & the Very Terrible Monster. Childrens.
Guess Who's Coming to My Tea Party. HR&W.
Hello, Dandelions!. HR&W.
I Know a Salesperson. Putnam.
If He's My Brother. Harvey.
Twelve Steps to Better Exposition. Merrill.
Whatever Happened to Beverly Bigler's Birthday. HarBraceJ.
Whatever Happened to Beverly Bigler's Birthday. HarBraceJ.
Where Are You, Angela Von Hauptmann, Now That I Need You?. HR&W.
Williams, Basil, 1867-
　　xWilliams, Basil.
　　　　Carteret & Newcastle: A Contrast in Contemporaries. Biblio Dist.
　　　　Cecil Rhodes. Greenwood.
　　　　Life of William Pitt, Earl of Chatham. Octagon.
　　　　Stanhope: A Study in Eighteenth-Century War & Diplomacy. Greenwood.
Williams, Benjamin.
　　xWilliams, Benjamin.
　　　　Reducing Home Building Costs. Craftsman.
Williams, Benjamin B.
　　xWilliams, Benjamin B.
　　　　A Literary History of Alabama: The Nineteenth Century. Fairleigh Dickinson.
Williams, Benjamin H. see Williams, Benjamin Harrison.
Williams, Benjamin Harrison, 1889-
　　xWilliams, Benjamin H.
　　　　Economic Foreign Policy of the United States. Fertig.
Williams, Bernard Arthur Owen.
　　xWilliams, B. A.
　　　　Problems of the Self: Philosophical Papers, 1956-1972. Cambridge U Pr.
Williams, Blanche C. see Williams, Blanche Colton.
Williams, Blanche Colton, 1879-1944
　　xWilliams, Blanche C.
　　　　Gnomic Poetry in Anglo-Saxon. AMS Pr.
Williams, Bobby J.
　　xWilliams, B. J.
　　　　Evolution & Human Origins: An Introduction to Physical Anthropology. Har-Row.
Williams, Brad.
　　xWilliams, Brad.
　　　　Legendary Women of the West. McKay.
　　　　Lost Legends of the West. HR&W.
　　　　A Matter of Confidence. Popular Lib.
Williams, Brian.
　　xWilliams, Brian.
　　　　Aircraft. Watts.
　　　　Come to Russia. Watts.
　　　　Inventions & Discoveries. Watts.
Williams, C. Abdy. see Williams, Charles Francis Abdy.
Williams, C. B. see Williams, Carrington Bonsor.
Williams, C. F. see Williams, Charles Francis Abdy.
Williams, C. N.
　　xWilliams, C. N.
　　　　The Agronomy of the Major Tropical Crops. Oxford U Pr.
Williams, Carl E.
　　xWilliams, Carl E.
　　　　Choice-Challenge: Contemporary Readings in Marriage. Wm C Brown.
Williams, Carol T., 1935-
　　xWilliams, Carol T.
　　　　The Dream Beside Me: The Movies & the Children of the Forties. Fairleigh Dickinson.
　　　　Elements of Research: A Guide for Writers. Alfred Pub.
Williams, Carrington B. see Williams, Carrington Bonsor.
Williams, Carrington Bonsor, 1889-
　　xWilliams, C. B.

Style & Vocabulary: Numerical Studies. Hafner.
xWilliams, Carrington B.
　　Patterns in the Balance of Nature & Related Problems in Quantitative Ecology. Acad Pr.
Williams, Carroll L.
　　xWilliams, Carroll L.
　　　　Coach's Guide to Basketball's Simplified Shuffle. P-H.
Williams, Chancellor.
　　xWilliams, Chancellor.
　　　　The Raven. AMS Pr.
Williams, Charles, 1886-1945
　　xWilliams, Charles.
　　　　Greater Trumps. Eerdmans.
　　xWilliams, Charles W.
　　　　Bacon. Folcroft.
　　　　The Figure of Beatrice: A Study in Dante. Octagon.
　　　　Reason & Beauty in the Poetic Mind. Folcroft.
Williams, Charles F. see Williams, Charles Francis Abdy.
Williams, Charles Francis Abdy, 1855-1923
　　xWilliams, C. Abdy.
　　　　The Rhythm of Song. Longwood Pr.
　　　　Story of Notation. Gale.
　　　　The Story of Notation. Longwood Pr.
　　　　Story of Organ Music. Gale.
　　xWilliams, C. F.
　　　　The Story of the Organ. Gale.
　　xWilliams, Charles F.
　　　　Story of Notation. Greenwood.
　　　　Story of Notation. Haskell.
　　　　The Story of Organ Music. Arno.
Williams, Charles W. see Williams, Charles.
Williams, Charles Washington, 1896-
　　xWilliams, Charles W.
　　　　Creative Freedom. Speller.
　　　　Direction: The Essential Dimension. Speller.
Williams, Chester.
　　xWilliams, Chester.
　　　　Gable. Fleet.
　　　　Gable. NAL.
Williams, Claudette.
　　xWilliams, Claudette.
　　　　After the Storm. Fawcett.
　　　　Cassandra. Fawcett.
　　　　Sunday's Child. Fawcett.
Williams, Clifford, 1943-
　　xWilliams, Clifford.
　　　　Free Will & Determinism: A Dialogue. Hackett Pub.
Williams, Clinton.
　　xWilliams, Clinton.
　　　　This Little Room & Other Poems, 1945-1975. Talisman Research.
Williams, D. A. see Williams, David Alan.
Williams, D. F. see Williams, David Franklyn.
Williams, D. G. see Williams, Donald G.
Williams, D. S. see Williams, Denys Stephen Dodsley.
Williams, D. T. see Williams, Daniel T.
Williams, Daniel T.
　　xWilliams, D. T.
　　　　Compiled by Eight Negro Bibliographies. Kraus Repr.
Williams, David. see Williams, David L.
Williams, David Alan.
　　xWilliams, D. A.
　　　　Liquid Fuels. Pergamon.
Williams, David Franklyn.
　　xWilliams, D. F.
　　　　Materials in Clinical Dentistry. Oxford U Pr.
Williams, David G.
　　xWilliams, David G.
　　　　Cooperative Federalism in Employment Security: The Interstate Conference. U of Mich Inst Labor.
Williams, David J. see Williams, David John.
Williams, David John, 1937-
　　xWilliams, David J.

Polymer Science & Engineering. P-H.
Williams, David L.
xWilliams, David.
Faulkner's Women: The Myth & the Muse. McGill-Queens U Pr.
Williams, David R. *see* Williams, David Raymond.
Williams, David Raymond.
xWilliams, David R.
An Introduction to Bio-Inorganic Chemistry. C C Thomas.
Williams, DeAtna M.
xWilliams, DeAtna M.
Paper-Bag Puppets. Pitman Learning.
Williams, Denys Stephen Dodsley, 1897-
xWilliams, D. S.
ed. The Modern Diesel: Development & Design. Transatlantic.
Williams, Diane.
xWilliams, Diane.
Demons & Beasts in Art. Lerner Pubns.
Williams, Dick, 1931-
xWilliams, Dick.
Prayers for Today's Church. Augsburg.
Williams, Donald. *see* Williams, Donald R.
Williams, Donald C. *see* Williams, Donald Cary.
Williams, Donald Cary, 1899-
xWilliams, Donald C.
Ground of Induction. Russell.
Williams, Donald G.
xWilliams, D. G.
Thin Plate Design for In-Plane Loading. Halsted Pr.
Williams, Donald R.
xWilliams, Donald.
Basic Calculus with Applications. Wadsworth Pub.
Williams, Dorian.
xWilliams, Dorian.
Great Riding Schools of the World. Macmillan.
Williams, E. N. *see* Williams, E. Neville.
Williams, E. Neville.
xWilliams, E. N.
Eighteenth-Century Constitution: Documents & Commentary. Cambridge U Pr.
Williams, E. W. *see* Williams, Ed W.
Williams, Ed W.
xWilliams, E. W.
Modern Law Enforcement & Police Science. C C Thomas.
Williams, Edna R. *see* Williams, Edna Rees.
Williams, Edna Rees, 1899-
xWilliams, Edna R.
Conflict of Homonyms in English. Shoe String.
Williams, Edward A. *see* Williams, Edward Ainsworth.
Williams, Edward Ainsworth, 1907-
xWilliams, Edward A.
Federal Aid for Relief. AMS Pr.
Williams, Edward B. *see* Williams, Edward Bennett.
Williams, Edward Bennett.
xWilliams, Edward B.
One Man's Freedom. Atheneum.
Williams, Edward E. *see* Williams, Edward Ellerker.
Williams, Edward Ellerker, 1793-1822
xWilliams, Edward E.
Journal of Edward Ellerker Williams, Companion of Shelley & Byron in 1821 & 1822. Folcroft.
Williams, Edward I. *see* Williams, Edward Irwin Franklin.
Williams, Edward Irwin Franklin, 1886-
xWilliams, Edward I.
The Actual & Potential Use of Laboratory Schools in State Normal Schools & Teachers Colleges. AMS Pr.
Williams, Edward J.
xWilliams, Edward J.

Latin American Christian Democratic Parties. U of Tenn Pr.
Latin American Political Thought: A Developmental Perspective. U of Ariz Pr.
The Rebirth of the Mexican Petroleum Industry: Developmental Directions & Policy Implications. Lexington Bks.
Williams, Edward R. *see* Williams, Edward Roland.
Williams, Edward Roland.
xWilliams, Edward R.
Some Studies of Elizabethan Wales. Folcroft.
Williams, Elizabeth F. *see* Williams, Elizabeth Friar.
Williams, Elizabeth Friar.
xWilliams, Elizabeth F.
Notes of a Feminist Therapist. Dell.
Williams, Elsa S.
xWilliams, Elsa S.
Creative Canvas Work. Van Nos Reinhold.
The Joy of Stitching. Van Nos Reinhold.
Williams, Emmett.
xWilliams, Emmett.
An Anthology of Concrete Poetry. Ultramarine Pub.
Sweethearts. Ultramarine Pub.
Williams, Eric. *see* Williams, Eric Eustace.
Williams, Eric E. *see* Williams, Eric Eustace.
Williams, Eric Eustace, 1911-
xWilliams, Eric.
British Historians & the West Indies. Holmes & Meier.
From Columbus to Castro: The History of the Caribbean, 1492-1969. Har-Row.
History of the People of Trinidad & Tobago. Transatlantic.
Negro in the Caribbean. Haskell.
Negro in the Caribbean. Negro U Pr.
xWilliams, Eric E.
Capitalism & Slavery. Russell.
Williams, Ervin, 1933-
xWilliams, Ervin.
ed. Participative Management: Concepts, Theory, & Implementation. Ga St U Busn Pub.
Williams, Ethel L.
xWilliams, Ethel L.
Howard University Bibliography of African & Afro-American Religious Studies: With Locations in American Libraries. Scholarly Res Inc.
Williams, Evan.
xWilliams, Evan.
You Can Hit the Golf Ball Farther. Golf Digest Bks.
Williams, F. *see* Williams, Frederick.
Williams, Francis E. *see* Williams, Francis Edgar.
Williams, Francis Edgar.
xWilliams, Francis E.
The Vailala Madness & the Destruction of Native Ceremonies in the Gulf Division. AMS Pr.
Williams, Frederick.
xWilliams, F.
The Sounds of Children. P-H.
xWilliams, Frederick.
Explorations of the Linguistic Attitudes of Teachers. Newbury Hse.
Reasoning with Statistics. HR&W.
Williams, Gardner, 1895-
xWilliams, Gardner.
Humanistic Ethics. Philos Lib.
Williams, Gareth.
xWilliams, Gareth.
Computational Linear Algebra with Models. Allyn.
A Course in Linear Algebra. Gordon.
Finite Mathematics with Models. Allyn.
Williams, Gareth. *see* Williams, Gareth Howel.
Williams, Gareth Howel.
xWilliams, Gareth.

Practical Finite Mathematics. Allyn.
Williams, Gareth L.
xWilliams, Gareth.
The Academic Labour Market: Economic & Social Aspects of a Profession. Elsevier.
Williams, Garth.
xWilliams, Garth.
illus. Baby Animals. Western Pub.
Baby Farm Animals. Western Pub.
Baby Farm Animals. Western Pub.
illus. Rabbits' Wedding. Har-Row.
Williams, Gene B.
xWilliams, Gene B.
The Homeowner's Pest Extermination Handbook. Arco.
Williams, Geoffrey.
xWilliams, Geoffrey.
African Designs from Traditional Sources. Dover.
African Designs from Traditional Sources. Peter Smith.
Williams, George A. *see* Williams, George Abiah.
Williams, George Abiah, 1931-
xWilliams, George A.
Physical Science. McGraw.
Williams, George C. *see* Williams, George Christopher.
Williams, George Christopher, 1926-
xWilliams, George C.
Adaptation & Natural Selection: A Critique of Some Current Evolutionary Thought. Princeton U Pr.
Group Selection. Lieber-Atherton.
Williams, George H. *see* Williams, George Huntston.
Williams, George Huntston, 1914-
xWilliams, George H.
Radical Reformation. Westminster.
Williams, George M. *see* Williams, George Mason.
Williams, George Mason, 1940-
xWilliams, George M.
The Quest for Meaning of Svami Vivekananda: A Study of Religious Change. New Horizons.
Williams, George S. *see* Williams, George Scott.
Williams, George Scott, 1906-
xWilliams, George S.
Greenhouse Flowers & Bedding Plants for Agribusiness Studies. Interstate.
Williams, George W. *see* Williams, George Washington.
Williams, George Walton, 1922-
xWilliams, George W.
Image & Symbol in the Sacred Poetry of Richard Crashaw. U of SC Pr.
Williams, George Washington, 1849-1891
xWilliams, George W.
History of the Negro Race in America from 1619 to 1880. Arno.
History of the Negro Troops in the War of Rebellion 1861-65: Preceded by a Review of the Military Services of Negroes in Ancient & Modern Times. Humanities.
Williams, Gerald E.
xWilliams, Gerald E.
Practical Transistor Circuit Design & Analysis. McGraw.
Williams, Gerald E. *see* Williams, Gerald Earl.
Williams, Gerald Earl, 1931-
xWilliams, Gerald E.
Electronics for Everyone. SRA.
Williams, Gertrude. *see* Williams, Gertrude Joanne.
Williams, Gertrude Joanne.
xWilliams, Gertrude.
Traumatic Abuse & Neglect of Children. Johns Hopkins.
Williams, Gerwyn.
xWilliams, Gerwyn.
Tackle Rugger. Soccer.
Williams, Glyn.
xWilliams, Glyn.

ed. Social & Cultural Change in Contemporary
Wales. Routledge & Kegan.

Williams, Gordon.
xWilliams, Gordon.
The Duellist. PB.

Williams, Gordon. *see* Williams, Gordon Willis.

Williams, Gordon Willis.
xWilliams, Gordon.
Change & Decline: Roman Literature in the
Early Empire. U of Cal Pr.
Figures of Thought in Roman Poetry. Yale U
Pr.

Williams, Gurney.
xWilliams, Gurney.
Ghosts & Poltergeists. Watts.
True Escape & Survival Stories. Watts.
Twins. Watts.

Williams, Guy R.
xWilliams, Guy R.
Paint Now, Learn Later. Emerson.
Working with Leather. Emerson.
The World of Model Cars. Putnam.

Williams, Gwyn.
xWilliams, Gwyn.
Compiled by The Burning Tree: Poems from
the First Thousand Years of Welsh Verse.
Greenwood.

Williams, Gwyn A.
xWilliams, Gwyn A.
Goya & the Impossible Revolution. Pantheon.
The Search for Beulah Land: The Welsh & the
Atlantic Revolution. Holmes & Meier.

Williams, H. A. *see* Williams, Harry Abbott.

Williams, H. Lionel. *see* Williams, Henry Lionel.

Williams, Hank.
xWilliams, Hank.
Living Proof: An Autobiography. Putnam.

Williams, Harold. *see* Williams, Harold Herbert.

Williams, Harold Herbert, Sir, 1880-1964
xWilliams, Harold.
Modern English Writers: Being a Study of
Imaginative Literature 1890-1914. Folcroft.
Modern English Writers: Being a Study of
Imaginative Literature 1890-1914. Kennikat.
Text of Gulliver's Travels. Folcroft.

Williams, Harold S., 1898-
xWilliams, Harold S.
Foreigners in Mikadoland. C E Tuttle.

Williams, Harry Abbott.
xWilliams, H. A.
The True Wilderness. Collins Pubs.

Williams, Helen M. *see* Williams, Helen Maria.

Williams, Helen Maria, 1762-1827
xWilliams, Helen M.
Letters from France. Schol Facsimiles.

Williams, Henry Lionel.
xWilliams, H. Lionel.
Country Furniture of Early America. A S
Barnes.

Williams, Herbert L. *see* Williams, Herbert Lee.

Williams, Herbert Lee.
xWilliams, Herbert L.
No Room for Doubt. Broadman.

Williams, Howard D., 1909-
xWilliams, Howard D.
History of Colgate University. Van Nos
Reinhold.

Williams, Howel.
xWilliams, Howel.
Volcanology. Freeman C.
xWilliams, Howell.
The Sutter Buttes of California: A Study of
Plio-Pleistocene Volcanism. U of Cal Pr.

Williams, Howell. *see* Williams, Howel.

Williams, Hugo, 1942-
xWilliams, Hugo.
Some Sweet Day. Oxford U Pr.

Williams, Ioan M.
xWilliams, Ion M.

Thackeray. Arco.

Williams, Iolo. *see* Williams, Iolo Aneurin.

Williams, Iolo Aneurin, 1890-1962
xWilliams, Iolo.
English Folk-Song & Dance. Folcroft.

Williams, Ion M. *see* Williams, Ioan M.

Williams, J. *see* Williams, Jill.

Williams, J. B. *see* Williams, John Bickerton.

Williams, J. D. *see* Williams, John Daniel.

Williams, J. H. *see* Williams, John H.

Williams, J. R. *see* Williams, James Richard Mackenzie.

Williams, J. W. *see* Williams, John Warren.

Williams, Jack K. *see* Williams, Jack Kenny.

Williams, Jack Kenny, 1920-
xWilliams, Jack K.
Dueling in the Old South: Vignettes of Social
History. Tex A&M Univ Pr.

Williams, James R. *see* Williams, James Ralla.

Williams, James Ralla, 1930-
xWilliams, James R.
Canadian-United States Tariff & Canadian
Industry: A Multi-Sectoral Analysis. U of
Toronto Pr.

Williams, James Richard Mackenzie, 1923-
xWilliams, J. R.
Resources, Tariffs, & Trade: Ontario's Stake. U
of Toronto Pr.

Williams, Jay.
xWilliams, Jay.
A Bag Full of Nothing. Schol Bk Serv.
The Burglar Next Door. Schol Bk Serv.
The City Witch & the Country Witch.
Macmillan.
Danny Dunn & the Anti-Gravity Paint.
Archway.
Danny Dunn & the Anti-Gravity Paint.
McGraw.
Danny Dunn & the Automatic House.
Archway.
Danny Dunn & the Fossil Cave. Archway.
Danny Dunn & the Fossil Cave. McGraw.
Danny Dunn & the Heat Ray. Archway.
Danny Dunn & the Homework Machine.
Archway.
Danny Dunn & the Homework Machine.
McGraw.
Danny Dunn & the Smallifying Machine.
McGraw.
Danny Dunn & the Smallifying Machine.
Archway.
Danny Dunn & the Swamp Monster. Archway.
Danny Dunn & the Swamp Monster. McGraw.
Danny Dunn & the Universal Glue. Archway.
Danny Dunn & the Universal Glue. McGraw.
Danny Dunn & the Voice from Space.
Archway.
Danny Dunn & the Voice from Space.
McGraw.
Danny Dunn & the Weather Machine.
Archway.
Danny Dunn & the Weather Machine.
McGraw.
Danny Dunn, Invisible Boy. McGraw.
Danny Dunn, Invisible Boy. Archway.
Danny Dunn on the Ocean Floor. Archway.
Danny Dunn, Scientific Detective. McGraw.
Danny Dunn, Scientific Detective. Archway.
Danny Dunn, Time Traveler. Archway.
Danny Dunn, Time Traveler. McGraw.
Everyone Knows What a Dragon Looks Like.
Schol Bk Serv.
Forgetful Fred. Schol Bk Serv.
The Magic Grandfather. Schol Bk Serv.
One Big Wish. Macmillan.
Practical Princess. Schol Bk Serv.
The Practical Princess & Other Liberating
Fairy Tales. Schol Bk Serv.
The Reward Worth Having. Schol Bk Serv.
Silver Whistle. Parents.
The Surprising Things Maui Did. Schol Bk

Serv.

Williams, Jay G.
xWilliams, Jay G.
Understanding the Old Testament. Barron.

Williams, Jeanne.
xWilliams, Jeanne.
Daughter of the Sword. PB.

Williams, Jerold.
xWilliams, Jerold.
McKenzie Trails. Calapooya Bks.

Williams, Jerome, 1926-
xWilliams, Jerome.
Oceanographic Instrumentation. Naval Inst Pr.
Oceanography. Watts.
Science Puzzles. Watts.

Williams, Jerre S. *see* Williams, Jerre Stockton.

Williams, Jerre Stockton, 1916-
xWilliams, Jerre S.
Constitutional Analysis in a Nutshell. West
Pub.

Williams, Jerry J. *see* Williams, Jerry John.

Williams, Jerry John, 1931-
xWilliams, Jerry J.
Contemporary Astrology. Sherbourne.

Williams, Jesse L. *see* Williams, Jesse Lynch.

Williams, Jesse Lynch, 1871-1929
xWilliams, Jesse L.
Princeton Stories. Arno.

Williams, Jill.
xWilliams, J.
ed. Carbon Dioxide, Climate & Society:
Proceedings of an IIASA Workshop, Feb.
1978. Pergamon.

Williams, John, 1908-
xWilliams, John.
Atlas of Weapons & War. T Y Crowell.
Early Spanish Manuscript Illumination.
Braziller.
The Holy Spirit, Lord & Life-Giver: A Biblical
Introduction to the Doctrine of the Holy
Spirit. Loizeaux.

Williams, John. *see* Williams, John Edward.

Williams, John A.
xWilliams, John A.
Night Song. Chatham Bkseller.

Williams, John A. *see* Williams, John Alfred.

Williams, John Alden.
xWilliams, John A.
ed. Themes of Islamic Civilization. U of Cal Pr.

Williams, John Alfred, 1925-
xWilliams, John A.
Africa: Her History, Lands, & People Told
with Pictures. Cooper Sq.
This Is My Country, Too. NAL.

Williams, John Anthony.
xWilliams, John A.
Natural Work of Art: The Experience of
Romance in Shakespeare's Winter's Tale.
Harvard U Pr.

Williams, John B. *see* Williams, John Burr.

Williams, John Bickerton, Sir, 1792-1855
xWilliams, J. B.
The Lives of Philip & Matthew Henry. Banner
of Truth.

Williams, John Burr.
xWilliams, John B.
Theory of Investment Value. Kelley.

Williams, John C.
xWilliams, John C.
Natural History of Northern California.
Kendall-Hunt.

Williams, John D. *see* Williams, John Delane.

Williams, John Daniel.
xWilliams, J. D.
Public Administration: The People's Business.
Little.

Williams, John Delane, 1938-
xWilliams, John D.

Regression Analysis in Educational Research.
Mss Info.
Williams, John E.
xWilliams, John E.
Race, Color, & the Young Child. U of NC Pr.
Williams, John Edward, 1922-
xWilliams, John.
Augustus. Penguin.
Williams, John H.
xWilliams, J. H.
ed. Design & Implementation of Programming
Languages: Proceedings of a DoD Sponsored
Workshop, Ithaca, Oct., 1976.
Springer-Verlag.
Williams, John H. *see* Williams, John Henry.
Williams, John Henry, 1887-
xWilliams, John H.
Argentine International Trade Under
Inconvertible Paper Money 1880-1900. AMS
Pr.
Postwar Monetary Plans & Other Essays.
Arno.
Williams, John S.
xWilliams, John S.
Environmental Pollution & Mental Health. Info
Resources.
Williams, John Warren, 1898-
xWilliams, J. W.
Ultracentrifugation of Macromolecules: Modern
Topics. Acad Pr.
Williams, Jon L.
xWilliams, Jon L.
Operant Learning: Procedures for Changing
Behavior. Brooks-Cole.

Williams, Jonathan
xWilliams, Jonathan.
An Ear in Bartram's Tree: Selected Poems,
1957-1967. New Directions.
Portrait Photographs. Gnomon Pr.

Williams, Joseph J. *see* Williams, Joseph John.
Williams, Joseph John, 1875-1940
xWilliams, Joseph J.
Psychic Phenomena of Jamaica. Greenwood.
Psychic Phenomena of Jamaica. Negro U Pr.
Williams, Joyce.
xWilliams, Joyce.
Adjustable Julie. Broadman.
xWilliams, Joyce W.
Middle Childhood: Behavior & Development.
Macmillan.

Williams, Joyce W. *see* Williams, Joyce.
Williams, Juanita H.
xWilliams, Juanita H.
Psychology of Women: Behavior in a Biosocial
Context. Norton.
Williams, Juanita H. *see* Williams, Juanita Hingst.
Williams, Juanita Hingst, 1922-
xWilliams, Juanita H.
ed. Psychology of Women: Selected Readings.
Norton.
Williams, Judith B. *see* Williams, Judith Blow.
Williams, Judith Blow.
xWilliams, Judith B.
British Commercial Policy & Trade Expansion,
1750-1850. Oxford U Pr.
Guide to the Printed Materials for English
Social & Economic History, 1750-1850.
Octagon.
Williams, Justin.
xWilliams, Justin.
Japan's Political Revolution Under MacArthur:
A Participant's Account. U of Ga Pr.
Williams, Kathleen B. *see* Williams, Kathleen Booth.
Williams, Kathleen Booth.
xWilliams, Kathleen B.

Marriages of Amelia County, Virginia,
1735-1815. Genealog Pub.
Williams, L. *see* Williams, Larry R.
Williams, L. A. *see* Williams, Leonard Ainslie.
Williams, L. Weinberg. *see* Williams, Laura Wineburg.
Williams, Larry R.
xWilliams, L.
How I Made One Million Dollars Last Year
Trading Commodities. Windsor.
Williams, Laura Wineburg, 1928-
xWilliams, L. Weinberg.
Our Runaway. Judson.
Williams, Lawrence.
xWilliams, Lawrence.
Fiery Furnace. S&S.
I, James McNeill Whistler: An Autobiography.
S&S.
Williams, Lea E.
xWilliams, Lea E.
Southeast Asia: A History. Oxford U Pr.
Williams, Leonard.
xWilliams, Leonard.
Challenge to Survival. Har-Row.
Challenge to Survival. NYU Pr.
Williams, Leonard Ainslie, 1909-
xWilliams, L. A.
Industrial Marketing Management & Controls.
Elsevier.
Williams, Leslie Pearce, 1927-
xWilliams, Pearce.
ed. Relativity Theory: Its Origins & Impact on
Modern Thought. Krieger.
Williams, Lloyd H. *see* Williams, Lloyd Haynes.
Williams, Lloyd Haynes.
xWilliams, Lloyd H.
Pirates of Colonial Virginia. Dalc.
Williams, M. *see* Williams, Moyra.
Williams, M. A. *see* Williams, Alexander Malcolm.
Williams, M. M. *see* Williams, Michael Maurice Rudolph.
Williams, M. Ruth. *see* Williams, Margaret Ruth.
Williams, Margaret.
xWilliams, Margaret.
Antenatal Education: Guidelines for Teachers.
Churchill.
Williams, Margaret A. *see* Williams, Margaret Anne.
Williams, Margaret Anne, 1902-
xWilliams, Margaret A.
tr. Glee-Wood: Passages from Middle English
Literature from the Eleventh Century to the
Fifteenth. Greenwood.
Williams, Margaret Ruth.
xWilliams, M. Ruth.
An Introduction to the Profession of Medical
Technology. Lea & Febiger.
Williams, Marianne M. *see* Williams, Marianne Mithun.
Williams, Marianne Mithun.
xWilliams, Marianne M.
A Grammar of Tuscarora. Garland Pub.
Williams, Mark.
xWilliams, Mark.
No Cure-No Pay: The Story of Salvage at Sea.
Merrimack Bk Serv.
Williams, Martha E.
xWilliams, Martha E.
ed. Computer-Readable Bibliographic Data
Bases: A Directory & Data Sourcebook. Am
Soc Info Sci.
Williams, Martin. *see* Williams, Martin T.
Williams, Martin T.
xWilliams, Martin.
Jazz Masters in Transition: 1957-1969. Da
Capo.
Williams, Mary F. *see* Williams, Mary Frances.
Williams, Mary Frances.
xWilliams, Mary F.

Catalogue of the Collection of American Art at
Randolph-Macon Woman's College: A
Selection of Paintings, Drawings, & Prints. U
Pr of Va.
Williams, Maslyn.
xWilliams, Maslyn.
Five Journeys from Jakarta: Inside Sukarno's
Indonesia. Greenwood.
Williams, Mason.
xWilliams, Mason.
The Law Enforcement Book of Weapons,
Ammunition & Training Procedures:
Handguns, Rifles & Shotguns. C C Thomas.
The Sporting Use of the Handgun. C C
Thomas.
Williams, Mason. *see* Williams, Mason Douglas.
Williams, Mason Douglas, 1938-
xWilliams, Mason.
Mason Williams-F. C. C. Rapport. Liveright.
Mason Williams Reading Matter. Doubleday.
Williams, Melvin D., 1933-
xWilliams, Melvin D.
Community in a Black Pentecostal Church: An
Anthropological Study. U of Pittsburgh Pr.
Williams, Merryn.
xWilliams, Merryn.
A Preface to Hardy. Longman.
Thomas Hardy & Rural England. Columbia U
Pr.
Williams, Michael, 1945-
xWilliams, Michael.
Directory of Trade Unions in the European
Economic Community. Intl Pubns Serv.
ed. Directory of Trade Unions in the European
Economic Community. State Mutual Bk.
Farm Tractors in Color. Macmillan.
Steam Power in Agriculture. Sterling
Williams, Michael D.
xWilliams, Michael D.
Music for Viola. Info Coord.
Williams, Michael Maurice Rudolph.
xWilliams, M. M.
Random Processes in Nuclear Reactors.
Pergamon.
Williams, Mike.
xWilliams, Mike.
Major Mike. Condor Pub Co.
Williams, Mona. *see* Williams, Mona Goodwyn.
Williams, Mona Goodwyn, 1906-
xWilliams, Mona.
This House Is Burning. NAL.
Williams, Moyra.
xWilliams, M.
Horse Psychology. Saifer.
xWilliams, Moyra.
Brain Damage & the Mind. Aronson.
Brain Damage, Behaviour, & the Mind. Wiley.
Breed of Horses. Pergamon.
Horse Psychology. J A Allen.
Williams, N. H. *see* Williams, Neil H.
Williams, Neil H.
xWilliams, N. H.
Combinatorial Set Theory. Elsevier.
Williams, Neville, 1924-
xWilliams, Neville.
The Cardinal & the Secretary: Thomas Wolsey
& Thomas Cromwell. Macmillan.
Williams, Oliver F.
xWilliams, Oliver F.
Full Value: Cases in Christian Business Ethics.
Har-Row.
Williams, Oliver P.
xWilliams, Oliver P.
Four Cities: A Study in Comparative Policy
Making. U of Pa Pr.
Williams, Orlo, 1883-
xWilliams, Orlo.

Charles Lamb. Arden Lib.
Charles Lamb. Folcroft.
Contemporary Criticism in Literature. Folcroft.
Contemporary Criticism in Literature. Haskell.

Williams, Oscar, 1900-1964
xWilliams, Oscar.
Golden Darkness. AMS Pr.
Williams, P. C. see Williams, Paul C.
Williams, Patti.
xWilliams, Patti.
Husbands. Logos.
Williams, Paul C.
xWilliams, P. C.
Low Back & Neck Pain: Causes &
Conservative Treatment. C C Thomas.
Williams, Pearce. see Williams, Leslie Pearce.
Williams, Peter.
xWilliams, Peter J.
Pipelines & Permafrost: Physical Geography &
Development in the Circumpolar North.
Longman.
Williams, Peter. see Williams, Peter F.
Williams, Peter F.
xWilliams, Peter.
Bach Organ Music. U of Wash Pr.
Williams, Peter J. see Williams, Peter.
Williams, Petra.
xWilliams, Petra.
Flow Blue China: An Aid to Identification.
Fountain Hse East.
Staffordshire Romantic Transfer Patterns: Cup
Plates & Early Victorian China. Fountain Hse
East.
Williams, Philip. see Williams, Philip Maynard.
Williams, Philip L., 1949-
xWilliams, Philip L.
The Emergence of the Theory of the Firm:
From Adam Smith to Alfred Marshall. St
Martin.
Williams, Philip M. see Williams, Philip Maynard.
Williams, Philip Maynard.
xWilliams, Philip.
French Politicians & Elections, 1951-1968.
Cambridge U Pr.
xWilliams, Philip M.
De Gaulle's Republic. Greenwood.
The French Parliament: Politics in the Fifth
Republic. Greenwood.
Williams, Philip W.
xWilliams, Philip W.
When a Loved One Dies. Augsburg.
Williams, Pierce.
xWilliams, Pierce.
The Purchase of Medical Care Through Fixed
Periodic Payment. Arno.
Williams, R. A. see Williams, Richard Allen.
Williams, R. Hal.
xWilliams, R. Hal.
The Democratic Party & California Politics,
1880-1896. Stanford U Pr.
Williams, Raburn. see Williams, Raburn M.
Williams, Raburn M.
xWilliams, Raburn.
Inflation: Money, Jobs, & Politicians. AHM
Pub.
Williams, Ralph C., 1928-
xWilliams, Ralph C.
Immune Complexes in Clinical & Experimental
Medicine. Harvard U Pr.
Williams, Raymond.
xWilliams, Raymond.

The Country & the City. Oxford U Pr.
The Country & the City. Oxford U Pr.
Drama from Ibsen to Brecht. Oxford U Pr.
English Novel from Dickens to Lawrence.
Oxford U Pr.
ed. George Orwell: A Collection of Critical
Essays. P-H.
Marxism & Literature. Oxford U Pr.
Marxism & Literature. Oxford U Pr.
Williams, Richard Allen.
xWilliams, R. A.
Textbook of Black Related Diseases. McGraw.
Williams, Richard L. see Williams, Richard Lippincott.
Williams, Richard Lippincott.
xWilliams, Richard L.
The Cascades. Time-Life.
The Cascades. Silver.
Williams, Robert C. see Williams, Robert Chadwell.
Williams, Robert Chadwell, 1938-
xWilliams, Robert C.
Artists in Revolution: Portraits of the Russian
Avant-Garde, 1905-1925. Ind U Pr.
Culture in Exile: Russian Emigres in Germany,
1881-1941. Cornell U Pr.
Russian Art & American Money, 1900-1940.
Harvard U Pr.
Williams, Robert F., 1916-
xWilliams, Robert F.
Caribbean Love Bug. Long Hse.
Williams, Robert H. see Williams, Robert Hardin.
Williams, Robert Hardin.
xWilliams, Robert H.
ed. Textbook of Endocrinology. Saunders.
Williams, Robert L.
xWilliams, Robert L.
Toward a Self-Managed Life Style. HM.
Williams, Robert R. see Williams, Robert Runnels.
Williams, Robert Runnels, 1886-
xWilliams, Robert R.
Toward the Conquest of Beriberi. Harvard U
Pr.
Williams, Robert T.
xWilliams, Robert T.
ed. Insights into Why & How to Read. Intl
Reading.
Williams, Roberta G.
xWilliams, Roberta G.
Echocardiographic Diagnosis of Congenital
Heart Disease. Little.
Williams, Robin M. see Williams, Robin Murphy.
Williams, Robin Murphy.
xWilliams, Robin M.
Mutual Accommodation: Ethnic Conflict &
Cooperation. U of Minn Pr.
Williams, Roger J. see Williams, Roger John.
Williams, Roger John, 1893-
xWilliams, Roger J.
Alcoholism: The Nutritional Approach. U of
Tex Pr.
Free & Unequal: The Biological Basis of
Individual Liberty. Liberty Fund.
Williams, Roger L. see Williams, Roger Lawrence.
Williams, Roger Lawrence, 1923-
xWilliams, Roger L.
French Revolution of 1870-1871. Norton.
Gaslight & Shadow: The World of Napoleon
III, 1851-1870. Greenwood.
Williams, Sam P.
xWilliams, Sam P.
Guide to the Research Collections of the New
York Public Library. ALA.
Williams, Samuel C. see Williams, Samuel Cole.
Williams, Samuel Cole, 1864-1947
xWilliams, Samuel C.
History of the Lost State of Franklin.
Porcupine Pr.
Williams, Selma R.
xWilliams, Selma R.

Demeter's Daughters: The Women Who
Founded America (1587-1792). Atheneum.
Williams, Sheldon W.
xWilliams, Sheldon W.
ed. Organization & Competition in the
Midwest Dairy Industries. Iowa St U Pr.
Williams, Sherley A. see Williams, Sherley Anne.
Williams, Sherley Anne, 1944-
xWilliams, Sherley A.
Give Birth to Brightness: A Thematic Study in
Neo-Black Literature. Dial.
Williams, Simon.
xWilliams, Simon.
Credit Systems for Small Scale Farmers: Case
Histories from Mexico. U of Tex Busn Res.
Williams, Stanley T. see Williams, Stanley Thomas.
Williams, Stanley Thomas, 1888-1956
xWilliams, Stanley T.
American Literature. Folcroft.
Life of Washington Irving. Octagon.
Spanish Background of American Literature.
Shoe String.
Williams, Sue R. see Williams, Sue Rodwell.
Williams, Sue Rodwell, 1922-
xWilliams, Sue R.
Essentials of Nutrition & Diet Therapy. Mosby.
Williams, T. Harry. see Williams, Thomas Harry.
Williams, T. Jeff.
xWilliams, T. Jeff.
All About Basic Home Repairs. Ortho.
Williams, Tennessee, 1911-
xWilliams, Tennessee.
One Arm & Other Stories. New Directions.
A Streetcar Named Desire. NAL.
Streetcar Named Desire. New Directions.
Sweet Bird of Youth. New Directions.
Vieux Carre. New Directions.
Where I Live: Selected Essays. New
Directions.
Williams, Thomas.
xWilliams, Thomas.
Fiji & the Fijians. AMS Pr.
The Followed Man. Marek.
The Hair of Harold Roux. Ballantine.
The Hair of Harold Roux. Random.
Whipple's Castle. Random.
Williams, Thomas G., 1940-
xWilliams, Thomas G.
Game Playing with a Digital Computer. Mgmt
Info Serv.
Williams, Thomas Harry.
xWilliams, T. Harry.
Americans at War: The Development of the
American Military System. La State U Pr.
Huey Long. Knopf.
Lincoln & His Generals. Random.
P. G. T. Beauregard: Napoleon in Gray. La
State U Pr.
Williams, Thomas R. see Williams, Thomas Rhys.
Williams, Thomas Rhys, 1927-
xWilliams, Thomas R.
Field Methods in the Study of Culture.
HR&W.
Williams, Ursula M. see Williams, Ursula Moray.
Williams, Ursula Moray, 1911-
xWilliams, Ursula M.
No Ponies for Miss Pobjoy. Elsevier-Nelson.
Williams, Ursula Vaughan. see Vaughan Williams, Ursula.
Williams, Valentine, 1883-1946
xWilliams, Valentine.
Curiosity of Mr. Treadgold. Arno.
Williams, Vera B.
xWilliams, Vera B.
The Great Watermelon Birthday. Greenwillow.
Williams, Vergil L.
xWilliams, Vergil L.

Convicts, Codes & Contraband: The Prison
Life of Men & Women. Ballinger Pub.
Dictionary of American Penology: An
Introductory Guide. Greenwood.
Williams, W. E. *see* Williams, William Elwyn.
Williams, W. H. *see* Williams, W. H. A.
Williams, W. H. A.
xWilliams, W. H.
H. L. Mencken. Twayne.
Williams, W. P.
xWilliams, W. P.
How to Start Your Own Magazine. Contemp
Bks.
How to Syndicate Your Own Newspaper
Column. Contemp Bks.
How to Write Magazine Articles That Sell.
Contemp Bks.
Williams, W. S. *see* Williams, William S. C.
Williams, W. T. *see* Williams, William Tom.
Williams, Walter E.
xWilliams, Walter E.
Fundamentals of Business Mathematics. Wm C
Brown.
Williams, Walter L., 1948-
xWilliams, Walter L.
ed. Southeastern Indians Since the Removal
Era. U of Ga Pr.
Williams, William A. *see* Williams, William Appleman.
Williams, William Appleman.
xWilliams, William A.
America Confronts a Revolutionary World:
1776-1976. Morrow.
Americans in a Changing World: A History of
the United States in the Twentieth Century.
Har-Row.
Americans in a Changing World: A History of
the United States in the Twentieth Century.
Har-Row.
Contours of American History. New
Viewpoints.
Great Evasion: An Essay on the Contemporary
Relevance of Karl Marx & on the Wisdom of
Admitting the Heretic into the Dialogue
About America's Future. New Viewpoints.
Williams, William C.
xWilliams, William C.
Motoring Mascots of the World. Motorbooks
Intl.
Williams, William C. *see* Williams, William Carlos.
Williams, William Carlos, 1883-1963
xWilliams, William C.
Autobiography of William Carlos Williams.
New Directions.
The Great American Novel. Folcroft.
Imaginations. New Directions.
In the American Grain. New Directions.
In the Money. New Directions.
Paterson. New Directions.
Williams, William E. *see* Williams, William Emrys.
Williams, William Elwyn.
xWilliams, W. E.
Dynamics. Van Nos Reinhold.
Williams, William Emrys, Sir, 1896-
xWilliams, William E.
Craft of Literature. Arno.
The Craft of Literature. Folcroft.
Williams, William G. *see* Williams, William George.
Williams, William George, 1919-
xWilliams, William G.
The Enrollment Workbook: Fifty-Five
Suggestions for Increasing Local Enrollments
at Schools, Colleges, & Universities. Share
Pub Co.
Williams, William H. *see* Williams, William Henry.
Williams, William Henry, 1936-
xWilliams, William H.
America's First Hospital: The Pennsylvania
Hospital, 1751-1841. Rittenhouse.
Williams, William J. *see* Williams, William James.

Williams, William James, 1935-
xWilliams, William J.
Semantic Behavior & Decision Making. Univ
Microfilms.
Williams, William S. C.
xWilliams, W. S.
Introduction to Elementary Particles. Acad Pr.
Williams, William Tom.
xWilliams, W. T.
Gray, Collins, & Their Circle. R West.
Williams, William W. *see* Williams, William Washington.
Williams, William Washington.
xWilliams, William W.
Coastal Changes. Greenwood.
Williams, Wirt.
xWilliams, Wirt.
The Far Side. Horizon.
Williams-Gardner, A. *see* Williams-Gardner, Aelwyn.
Williams-Gardner, Aelwyn.
xWilliams-Gardner, A.
Industrial Drying. Gulf Pub.
Williams-Heller, Ann. *see* Williams-Heller, Annie
(Wilhelm).
Williams-Heller, Annie (Wilhelm), 1904-
xWilliams-Heller, Ann.
Nature's Own Vegetable Cookbook. Arc Bks.
Nature's Own Vegetable Cookbook. Arco.
Williamsen, Vern G.
xWilliamsen, Vern G.
ed. An Annotated, Analytical Bibliography of
Tirso De Molina Studies, 1621-1977. U of
Mo Pr.
Williamson, Alan, 1944-
xWilliamson, Alan.
Pity the Monsters: The Political Vision of
Robert Lowell. Yale U Pr.
Williamson, Audrey, 1913-
xWilliamson, Audrey.
The Mystery of the Princes: An Investigation
into a Supposed Murder. Rowman.
Williamson, Charles C. *see* Williamson, Charles Clarence.
Williamson, Charles Clarence, 1877-1965
xWilliamson, Charles C.
Finances of Cleveland. AMS Pr.
Williamson, Charles O. *see* Williamson, Charles Owen.
Williamson, Charles Owen, 1894-
xWilliamson, Charles O.
Breaking & Training the Stock Horse.
Williamson Sch.
Williamson, Clark M.
xWilliamson, Clark M.
God Is Never Absent. Bethany Pr.
Williamson, Claude C. *see* Williamson, Claude Charles H.
Williamson, Claude Charles H., 1892-
xWilliamson, Claude C.
Readings on the Character of Hamlet
1661-1947. R West.
xWilliamson, Claude G.
Readings on the Character of Hamlet,
1661-1947. Gordian.
Williamson, Claude G. *see* Williamson, Claude Charles
H.
Williamson, Daniel R. *see* Williamson, Daniel Raymond.
Williamson, Daniel Raymond, 1943-
xWilliamson, Daniel R.
Feature Writing for Newspapers. Hastings.
Newsgathering. Hastings.
Williamson, Derek.
xWilliamson, Derek.
Historical Bibliography. Shoe String.
Williamson, E. Stanley.
xWilliamson, E. Stanley.
The People Builder. Broadman.
Williamson, Edward C., 1916-
xWilliamson, Edward C.
Florida Politics in the Gilded Age, 1877-1893.
U Presses Fla.
Williamson, Ellen.
xWilliamson, Ellen.

When We Went First Class. Doubleday.
Williamson, Eugene L., Jr
xWilliamson, Eugene L.
Liberalism of Thomas Arnold: A Study of His
Religious & Political Writings. U of Ala Pr.
Williamson, G. *see* Williamson, Grahame.
Williamson, George, 1898-1968
xWilliamson, George.
The Donne Tradition: A Study in English
Poetry from Donne to the Death of Cowley.
Octagon.
Proper Wit of Poetry. Russell.
Williamson, Grahame.
xWilliamson, G.
An Introduction to Animal Husbandry in the
Tropics. Longman.
Williamson, H. R. *see* Williamson, Henry Raymond.
Williamson, Harold F. *see* Williamson, Harold Francis.
Williamson, Harold Francis, 1901-
xWilliamson, Harold F.
Edward Atkinson: The Biography of an
American Liberal 1827-1905. Arno.
Northwestern University: A History,
1850-1975. Northwestern U Pr.
Winchester: The Gun That Won the West. A S
Barnes.
Williamson, Henry Raymond.
xWilliamson, H. R.
Teach Yourself Chinese. McKay.
Williamson, Hugh, 1735-1819
xWilliamson, Hugh.
The History of North Carolina. Reprint.
The Trade Unions. Heinemann Ed.
Williamson, Jack, 1908-
xWilliamson, Jack.
Brother to Demons, Brother to Gods. Bobbs.
The Cometeers. PB.
Darker Than You Think. Dell.
Darker Than You Think. Garland Pub.
The Humanoids. Avon.
The Humanoids. Gregg.
The Legion of Space. Garland Pub.
The Legion of Space. PB.
The Power of Blackness. Berkley Pub.
The Power of Blackness. Ultramarine Pub.
Three from the Legion. PB.
Williamson, James A. *see* Williamson, James Alexander.
Williamson, James Alexander, 1886-
xWilliamson, James A.
Maritime Enterprise, 1485-1558. Octagon.
The Ocean in English History: Being the Ford
Lectures. Greenwood.
Williamson, Jane, 1950-
xWilliamson, Jane.
ed. New Feminist Scholarship: A Guide to
Bibliographies. Feminist Pr.
Williamson, Jane. *see* Williamson, Jane Burnett.
Williamson, Jane Burnett.
xWilliamson, Jane.
illus. The Trouble with Alaric. FS&G.
Williamson, Janet A., 1934-
xWilliamson, Janet A.
Current Perspectives in Nursing Education:
The Changing Scene. Mosby.
Williamson, Jeffrey G, 1935-
xWilliamson, Jeffrey G.
American Growth & the Balance of Payments,
1820-1913: A Study of the Long Swing. U of
NC Pr.
Williamson, Joanne S.
xWilliamson, Joanne S.
And Forever Free. Knopf.
Williamson, Joel.
xWilliamson, Joel.
After Slavery: The Negro in South Carolina
During Reconstruction, 1861-1877. Norton.
After Slavery: The Negro in South Carolina
During Reconstruction, 1861-1877. U of NC
Pr.
xWilliamson, Joel R.

ed. Origins of Segregation. Heath.
Williamson, Joel R. *see* Williamson, Joel.
Williamson, John W.
    xWilliamson, John W.
        Improving Medical Practice & Health Care: A
        Bibliographic Guide to Information
        Management in Quality Assurance &
        Continuing Education. Ballinger Pub.
Williamson, Judith.
    xWilliamson, Judith.
        Decoding Advertisements: Ideology & Meaning
        in Advertising. Merrimack Bk Serv.
        Decoding Advertisements: Ideology & Meaning
        in Advertising. Merrimack Bk Serv.
Williamson, Margaret.
    xWilliamson, Margaret.
        Colloquial Language of the Commonwealth &
        Restoration. Folcroft.
Williamson, Obed J. *see* Williamson, Obed Jalmar.
Williamson, Obed Jalmar, 1899-
    xWilliamson, Obed J.
        Provisions for General Theory Courses in the
        Professional Education of Teachers. AMS Pr.
Williamson, Oliver E.
    xWilliamson, Oliver E.
        Markets & Hierarchies - Analysis & Antitrust
        Implications: A Study in the Economics of
        Internal Organization. Free Pr.
Williamson, Rene D. *see* Williamson, Rene De Visme.
Williamson, Rene De Visme.
    xWilliamson, Rene D.
        Independence & Involvement: A Christian
        Reorientation in Political Science. La State U
        Pr.
    xWilliamson, Rene De Visme.
        Politics & Protestant Theology: An
        Interpretation of Tillich, Barth, Bonhoeffer, &
        Brunner. La State U Pr.
Williamson, Richard. *see* Williamson, Richard E.
Williamson, Richard E.
    xWilliamson, Richard.
        Calculus of Vector Functions. P-H.
        Multivariable Mathematics: Linear Algebra,
        Calculus, Differential Equations. P-H.
Williamson, Robert C. *see* Williamson, Robert Clifford.
Williamson, Robert Clifford, 1916-
    xWilliamson, Robert C.
        Marriage & Family Relations. Wiley.
Williamson, Robert W. *see* Williamson, Robert Wood.
Williamson, Robert Wood, 1856-1932
    xWilliamson, Robert W.
        Religion & Social Organization in Central
        Polynesia. AMS Pr.
        Religious & Cosmic Beliefs of Central
        Polynesia. AMS Pr.
Williamson, Samuel J.
    xWilliamson, Samuel J.
        Fundamentals of Air Pollution. A-W.
Williamson, Samuel R.
    xWilliamson, Samuel R.
        Politics of Grand Strategy: Britain & France
        Prepare for War, 1904-1914. Harvard U Pr.
Williamson, Sherman.
    xWilliamson, Sherman.
        Glory Trap. Walker & Co.
Williamson, Stan.
    xWilliamson, Stan.
        No-Bark Dog. Follett.
Williamson, Tony.
    xWilliamson, Tony.
        Connector. Stein & Day.
        The Doomsday Contract. S&S.
        The Samson Strike. Atheneum.
Williamson, Wayne B., 1918-
    xWilliamson, Wayne B.
        Growth & Decline in the Episcopal Church.
        William Carey Lib.
Williamson, William B. *see* Williamson, William Bedford.
Williamson, William Bedford, 1918-
    xWilliamson, William B.

Decisions in Philosophy of Religion. Merrill.
Willie, Charles V.
    xWillie, Charles V.
        The Sociology of Urban Education:
        Desegregation & Integration. Lexington Bks.
Willie, Charles V. *see* Willie, Charles Vert.
Willie, Charles Vert, 1927-
    xWillie, Charles V.
        Family Life of Black People. Merrill.
        Oreo: A Perspective on Race & Marginal Men
        & Women. Parameter Pr.
        Race Mixing in Public Schools. Irvington.
        ed. Racism & Mental Health: Essays. U of
        Pittsburgh Pr.
Willier, Benjamin H. *see* Willier, Benjamin Harrison.
Willier, Benjamin Harrison.
    xWillier, Benjamin H.
        ed. Foundations of Experimental Embryology.
        Hafner.
Williford, Miriam, 1926-
    xWilliford, Miriam.
        Jeremy Bentham on Spanish America: An
        Account of His Letters & Proposals to the
        New World. La State U Pr.
Williford, William B. *see* Williford, William Bailey.
Williford, William Bailey.
    xWilliford, William B.
        Peachtree Street, Atlanta. Mockingbird Bks.
        Peachtree Street, Atlanta. U of Ga Pr.
Willig, George.
    xWillig, George.
        Going It Alone. Doubleday.
Willig, P. *see* Willig, Peter L.
Willig, Peter L.
    xWillig, P.
        Lichtstreifen. Pergamon.
Willig, Robert D., 1947-
    xWillig, Robert D.
        Welfare Analysis of Policies Affecting Prices &
        Products. Garland Pub.
Willig, Sidney H.
    xWillig, Sidney H.
        ed. Good Manufacturing Practices for
        Pharmaceuticals: A Plan for Total Quality
        Control. Dekker.
        Legal Considerations in Dentistry. Krieger.
Willimon, William H.
    xWillimon, William H.
        Family, Friends & Other Funny People:
        Memories of Growing up Southern. Moore
        Pub Co.
        The Gospel for the Person Who Has
        Everything. Judson.
        Remember Who You Are: Baptism, a Model
        for Christian Life. Upper Room.
        Saying Yes to Marriage. Judson.
        Worship As Pastoral Care. Abingdon.
Willing, Matthew H., 1885-
    xWilling, Matthew H.
        Valid Diagnosis in High School Composition.
        AMS Pr.
Willing, Si.
    xWilling, Si.
        How to Sell Radio Advertising. TAB Bks.
Willingham, Calder, 1922-
    xWillingham, Calder.
        Providence Island. Vanguard.
        Rambling Rose. Delacorte.
Willingham, John. *see* Willingham, John J.
Willingham, John J.
    xWillingham, John.
        Auditing Concepts & Methods. McGraw.
    xWillingham, John J.
        Accounting in Action: A Simulation. McGraw.
        Auditing Concepts & Methods. McGraw.
Willingham, Ronald L.
    xWillingham, Ronald L.

How to Speak So People Will Listen. Word
Bks.
Willingham, Warren W.
    xWillingham, Warren W.
        The Source Book for Higher Education: A
        Critical Guide to Literature & Information.
        College Bd.
Willis, A. T. *see* Willis, Allan Trevor.
Willis, Allan Trevor.
    xWillis, A. T.
        Anaerobic Bacteriology: Clinical & Laboratory
        Practice. Butterworths.
Willis, B. T. *see* Willis, Bertram Terence Martin.
Willis, Bertram Terence Martin.
    xWillis, B. T.
        Thermal Vibrations in Crystallography.
        Cambridge U Pr.
Willis, Charles D., 1921-
    xWillis, Charles D.
        Blueprint Reading for Commercial
        Construction. Van Nos Reinhold.
    xWillis, Charles E.
        Blueprint Reading for Commercial
        Construction. Delmar.
Willis, Charles E. *see* Willis, Charles D.
Willis, De Witt. *see* Willis, Dewitt.
Willis, Dewitt.
    xWillis, De Witt.
        Learn to Play Tennis at Home. McGraw.
Willis, Donald C.
    xWillis, Donald C.
        Horror & Science Fiction Films: A Checklist.
        Scarecrow.
Willis, F. Roy. *see* Willis, Frank Roy.
Willis, Frank Roy.
    xWillis, F. Roy.
        ed. European Integration. New Viewpoints.
        France, Germany, & the New Europe,
        1945-1967. Stanford U Pr.
        The French in Germany, 1945-1949. Stanford
        U Pr.
Willis, Henry P. *see* Willis, Henry Parker.
Willis, Henry Parker, 1874-1937
    xWillis, Henry P.
        History of the Latin Monetary Union: A Study
        of International Monetary Action.
        Greenwood.
Willis, Hulon.
    xWillis, Hulon.
        A Brief Handbook of English. HarBraceJ.
        Content & Structure: Readings for College
        Writers. HarBraceJ.
        Logic, Language & Composition. Winthrop.
    xWillis, Hulton.
        Modern Descriptive English Grammar.
        Har-Row.
Willis, Hulton. *see* Willis, Hulon.
Willis, Irene C. *see* Willis, Irene Cooper.
Willis, Irene Cooper.
    xWillis, Irene C.
        The Authorship of Wuthering Heights.
        Folcroft.
        Authorship of Wuthering Heights. Haskell.
        Brontes. Dufour.
        The Brontes. Folcroft.
        The Brontes. Haskell.
        England's Holy War: A Study of English
        Liberal Idealism During the Great War.
        Garland Pub.
Willis, J. *see* Willis, Jerry W.
Willis, James. *see* Willis, James Alfred.
Willis, James Alfred.
    xWillis, James.
        Latin Textual Criticism. U of Ill Pr.
Willis, James F. *see* Willis, James Frederick.
Willis, James Frederick.
    xWillis, James F.
        Explorations in Economics. HM.
Willis, Janice D. *see* Willis, Janice Dean.

Willis, Janice Dean.
  xWillis, Janice D.
    Compiled by The Diamond Light: An
    Introduction to Tibetan Buddhist
    Meditations. S&S.
Willis, Jean. *see* Willis, Jean L.
Willis, Jean L.
  xWillis, Jean.
    Historical Dictionary of Uruguay. Scarecrow.
Willis, Jerry. *see* Willis, Jerry W.
Willis, Jerry W.
  xWillis, J.
    Great Experiments in Behavior Modification.
    Har-Row.
  xWillis, Jerry.
    Peanut Butter & Jelly Guide to Computers. Intl
    Schol Bk Serv.
  xWillis, Jerry W.
    Guiding the Psychological & Educational
    Growth of Children. C C Thomas.
Willis, John.
  xWillis, John.
    A History of Dalhousie Law School. U of
    Toronto Pr.
Willis, John R. *see* Willis, John Randolph.
Willis, John Randolph.
  xWillis, John R.
    A History of Christian Thought: From
    Apostolic Times to Saint Augustine.
    Exposition.
Willis, John T., 1933-
  xWillis, John T.
    Insights from the Psalms. Bibl Res Pr.
  xWillis, John Thomas.
    Insights from the Psalms. Bibl Res Pr.
Willis, John Thomas. *see* Willis, John T.
Willis, Larryann C.
  xWillis, Larryann C.
    The Horse-Breeding Farm. A S Barnes.
Willis, Meredith S. *see* Willis, Meredith Sue.
Willis, Meredith Sue.
  xWillis, Meredith S.
    A Space Apart. Scribner.
Willis, Nathaniel P. *see* Willis, Nathaniel Parker.
Willis, Nathaniel Parker, 1806-1867
  xWillis, Nathaniel P.
    Dashes at Life with a Free Pencil. Mss Info.
Willis, Paul E.
  xWillis, Paul E.
    Learning to Labour: How Working Class Kids
    Get Working Class Jobs. Lexington Bks.
    Profane Culture. Routledge & Kegan.
Willis, Roy G.
  xWillis, Roy G.
    ed. There Was a Certain Man: Spoken Art of
    the Fipa. Oxford U Pr.
Willis, Ted, Baron Willis, 1918-
  xWillis, Ted.
    The Buckingham Palace Connection. Avon.
    The Buckingham Palace Connection. Morrow.
    The Churchill Commando. Charter Bks.
    The Churchill Commando. Morrow.
    The Lions of Judah. HR&W.
Willis, William D.
  xWillis, William D.
    Medical Neurobiology: Neuroanatomical &
    Neurophysiological Principles Basic to
    Clinical Neuroscience. Mosby.
Willison, Marilyn. *see* Willison, Marilyn Murray.
Willison, Marilyn Murray.
  xWillison, Marilyn.
    Diary of a Divorced Mother. Wyden.
Williston, Ed M.
  xWilliston, Ed M.
    Lumber Manufacturing: The Design &
    Operation of Sawmills & Planer Mills. Miller
    Freeman.
Willmer, Edward N. *see* Willmer, Edward Nevill.
Willmer, Edward Nevill.
  xWillmer, Edward N.

    Cytology & Evolution. Acad Pr.
Willmington, H. L.
  xWillmington, H. L.
    That Manuscript from Outer Space. Nelson.
Willmott, Alan S.
  xWillmott, Alan S.
    The Objective Interpretation of Test
    Performance: The Rasch Model Applied.
    Humanities.
Willmott, J. C. *see* Willmott, John Charles.
Willmott, John Charles.
  xWillmott, J. C.
    Atomic Physics. Wiley.
Willmott, W. E. *see* Willmott, William E.
Willmott, William E.
  xWillmott, W. E.
    ed. Economic Organization in Chinese Society.
    Stanford U Pr.
Willner, Dorothy.
  xWillner, Dorothy.
    Nation-Building & Community in Israel.
    Princeton U Pr.
Willner, Robert F.
  xWillner, Robert F.
    Criteria for Long Term Care Placement:
    Referral Guidelines for the Clergy. Cath
    Health.
Willock, Colin. *see* Willock, Colin D.
Willock, Colin D.
  xWillock, Colin.
    Gorilla. St Martin.
Willock, Ruth, 1904-
  xWillock, Ruth.
    I, Victoria Strange. Manor Bks.
Willocks, James.
  xWillocks, James.
    Essential Obstetrics & Gynaecology: A Guide
    for Postgraduates. Churchill.
Willoughby, David P.
  xWilloughby, David P.
    All About Gorillas. A S Barnes.
    Growth & Nutrition in the Horse. A S Barnes.
Willoughby, Edwin E. *see* Willoughby, Edwin Eliott.
Willoughby, Edwin Eliott, 1899-1959
  xWilloughby, Edwin E.
    The Printing of the First Folio of Shakespeare.
    Arden Lib.
    Printing of the First Folio of Shakespeare.
    Folcroft.
Willoughby, Elaine. *see* Willoughby, Elaine Macmann.
Willoughby, Elaine M. *see* Willoughby, Elaine Macmann.
Willoughby, Elaine Macmann.
  xWilloughby, Elaine.
    No, No, No, & Yes. Garrard.
    That's How the Ball Bounces!. Garrard.
  xWilloughby, Elaine M.
    Boris & the Monsters. HM.
Willoughby, Kenneth W.
  xWilloughby, Kenneth W.
    Secrets of Ego Power & Control. Exposition.
Willoughby, Michael L. *see* Willoughby, Michael L. N.
Willoughby, Michael L. N.
  xWilloughby, Michael L.
    Paediatric Haematology. Churchill.
Willoughby, Vic.
  xWilloughby, Vic.
    The Classic Motorcycles. Dial.
Willoughby, W. W. *see* Willoughby, Westel Woodbury.
Willoughby, Westal W. *see* Willoughby, Westel
  Woodbury.
Willoughby, Westel W. *see* Willoughby, Westel
  Woodbury.
Willoughby, Westel Woodbury, 1867-1945
  xWilloughby, W. W.
    Government & Administration of the United
    States. Johnson Repr.
  xWilloughby, Westal W.
    China at the Conference: A Report.
    Greenwood.
  xWilloughby, Westel W.

    Government & Administration in the United
    States. AMS Pr.
    Opium As an International Problem: The
    Geneva Conferences. Arno.
    Political Theories of the Ancient World. Arno.
Willoughby, William C. *see* Willoughby, William Charles.
Willoughby, William Charles, 1857-1938
  xWilloughby, William C.
    Soul of the Bantu: A Sympathetic Study of the
    Magico-Religious Practices & Beliefs of the
    Bantu Tribes of Africa. Negro U Pr.
Willoughby, William F. *see* Willoughby, William
  Franklin.
Willoughby, William Franklin, 1867-1960
  xWilloughby, William F.
    State Activities in Relation to Labor in the
    United States. AMS Pr.
Willoughby, William G., 1917-
  xWilloughby, William G.
    Counting the Cost: The Life of Alexander
    Mack. Brethren.
Willrich, Mason.
  xWillrich, Mason.
    Administration of Energy Shortages: Natural
    Gas and Petroleum. Ballinger Pub.
    Energy & World Politics. Free Pr.
    Non-Proliferation Treaty: Framework for
    Nuclear Arms Control. Michie.
    Radioactive Waste: Management & Regulation.
    Free Pr.
Willrich, Ted. *see* Willrich, Ted L.
Willrich, Ted L.
  xWillrich, Ted.
    ed. Agricultural Practices & Water Quality.
    Iowa St U Pr.
Wills, F. H. *see* Wills, Franz Hermann.
Wills, Franz Hermann, 1903-
  xWills, F. H.
    Fundamentals of Layout for Newspaper &
    Magazine Advertising, for Page Design of
    Publications & Brochures. Dover.
Wills, G. *see* Wills, Gordon.
Wills, Garry, 1934-
  xWills, Garry.
    At Button's. Andrews & McMeel.
    Confessions of a Conservative. Doubleday.
    Inventing America: Jefferson's Declaration of
    Independence. Doubleday.
    Inventing America: Jefferson's Declaration of
    Independence. Random.
    Nixon Agonistes: The Crisis of the Self Made
    Man. NAL.
  xWills, Gary.
    ed. Values Americans Live by. Arno.
Wills, Gary. *see* Wills, Garry.
Wills, Geoffrey.
  xWills, Geoffrey.
    Craftsmen & Cabinet-Makers of Classic English
    Furniture. Herman Pub.
    Practical Guide to Antique Collecting. Arc
    Bks.
Wills, Gordon.
  xWills, G.
    Marketing Through Research. Pergamon.
  xWills, Gordon.
    Fashion Marketing: An Anthology of
    Viewpoints & Perspectives. Allen Unwin.
    Strategic Issues in Marketing. Halsted Pr.
Wills, Jesse.
  xWills, Jesse.
    Early & Late: Fugitive Poems & Others.
    Vanderbilt U Pr.
Wills, John A.
  xWills, John A.
    Glass Fiber Auto Body Construction
    Simplified. Post-Era.
Wills, Richard H.
  xWills, Richard H.

The Institutionalized Severely Retarded: A Study of Activity & Interaction. C C Thomas.

Wills, W. A.
  xWills, W. A.
    The Downfall of Lobengula: The Cause, History & Effect of the Matabeli War 1894. Verry.
  xWills, William A.
    Downfall of Lobengula: The Cause, History & Effect of the Matabeli War. Negro U Pr.

Wills, Walter J.
  xWills, Walter J.
    An Introduction to Agri-Business Management. Interstate.
    Introduction to Grain Marketing. Interstate.

Wills, William A. *see* Wills, W. A.

Willsberger, Johann, 1941-
  xWillsberger, Johann.
    Gold. Doubleday.

Willsky, Alan S.
  xWillsky, Alan S.
    Digital Signal Processing & Control Estimation Theory: Points of Tangency, Areas of Intersection, & Parallel Directions. MIT Pr.

Willson, Alan N.
  xWillson, Alan N.
    Nonlinear Networks: Theory & Analysis. Wiley.

Willson, D. H. *see* Willson, David Harris.

Willson, David H. *see* Willson, David Harris.

Willson, David Harris, 1901-
  xWillson, D. H.
    A History of England. HR&W.
  xWillson, David H.
    Privy Councillors in the House of Commons, 1604-1629. Octagon.

Willson, J. Robert. *see* Willson, James Robert.

Willson, James Robert.
  xWillson, J. Robert.
    Obstetrics & Gynecology. Mosby.

Willson, John S.
  xWillson, John S.
    Comprehensive Planning & the Environment: A Manual for Planners. Abt Assoc.

Willson, Meredith, 1902-
  xWillson, Meredith.
    And There I Stood with My Piccolo. Greenwood.

Willughby, Percival.
  xWillughby, Percival.
    Observations in Midwifery. Charles River Bks.

Willwerth, James.
  xWillwerth, James.
    Jones: Portrait of a Mugger. M Evans.

Willys-Overland Motors, Inc.
  xWillys-Overland Motors, Inc.
    Willys Model MA Prototype Jeep: TM-10-1103. Post-Era.

Wilm, E. C. *see* Wilm, Emil Carl.

Wilm, Emil Carl.
  xWilm, E. C.
    Immanuel Kant: 1724-1924. Folcroft.

Wilmerding, John.
  xWilmerding, John.
    ed. The Genius of American Painting. Morrow.

Wilmerding, Lucius, 1906-
  xWilmerding, Lucius.
    Spending Power: A History of the Efforts of Congress to Control Expenditures. Shoe String.

Wilmeth, Don B.
  xWilmeth, Don B.
    ed. American & English Popular Entertainment: A Guide to Information Sources. Gale.
    ed. American Stage to World War I: A Guide to Information Sources. Gale.

Wilmore, Gayraud S.
  xWilmore, Gayraud S.

Secular Relevance of the Church. Westminster.

Wilmore, Sylvia B. *see* Wilmore, Sylvia Bruce.

Wilmore, Sylvia Bruce.
  xWilmore, Sylvia B.
    Crows, Jays, Ravens & Their Relatives. Eriksson.
    Crows, Jays, Ravens (& Their Relatives). TFH Pubns.
    Swans of the World. Taplinger.

Wilmot, Chester.
  xWilmot, Chester.
    The Struggle for Europe. Greenwood.
    The Struggle for Europe. Watts.

Wilmot, Robert.
  xWilmot, Robert.
    Gismond of Salerne. AMS Pr.

Wilmot, William M.
  xWilmot, William W.
    Dyadic Communication. A-W.

Wilmot, William W. *see* Wilmot, William M.

Wilms, Barbara.
  xWilms, Barbara.
    Crunchy Bananas & Other Great Recipes Kids Can Cook. Sagamore Bks.

Wilner, Daniel M.
  xWilner, Daniel M.
    Human Relations in Interracial Housing: A Study of the Contact Hypothesis. Russell.
    Introduction to Public Health. Macmillan.

Wilner, Eleanor.
  xWilner, Eleanor.
    Maya. U of Mass Pr.
  xWilner, Eleanor R.
    Gathering the Winds: Visionary Imagination & Radical Transformation of Self & Society. Johns Hopkins.

Wilner, Eleanor R. *see* Wilner, Eleanor.

Wilpert, Bernhard.
  xWilpert, Bernhard.
    ed. Workers' Participation in an Internationalized Economy. Kent St U Pr.

Wilshire, Bruce. *see* Wilshire, Bruce W.

Wilshire, Bruce W.
  xWilshire, Bruce.
    William James & Phenomenology: A Study of "the Principles of Psychology". AMS Pr.

Wilsing, Weston C. *see* Wilsing, Weston Clarence.

Wilsing, Weston Clarence, 1921-
  xWilsing, Weston C.
    Office Machines: A College Course. Irwin.

Wilson. *see* Wilson, John Douglas.

Wilson, A. *see* Wilson, Aubrey.

Wilson, A. Bennet. *see* Wilson, A. Bennett.

Wilson, A. Bennett.
  xWilson, A. Bennet.
    Limb Prosthetics. Krieger.

Wilson, A. E. *see* Wilson, Albert Edward.

Wilson, Adrian.
  xWilson, Adrian.
    The Design of Books. Peregrine Smith.

Wilson, Alan, 1927-
  xWilson, Alan.
    Clergy Reserves of Upper Canada: A Canadian Mortmain. U of Toronto Pr.

Wilson, Albert E. *see* Wilson, Albert Edward.

Wilson, Albert Edward, 1885-
  xWilson, A. E.
    Edwardian Theatre. Folcroft.
  xWilson, Albert E.
    Penny Plain Two Pence Coloured: A History of the Juvenile Drama. Arno.

Wilson, Alexander.
  xWilson, Alexander.
    Chartist Movement in Scotland. Kelley.

Wilson, Amy A. *see* Wilson, Amy Auerbacher.

Wilson, Amy Auerbacher.
  xWilson, Amy A.

Deviance & Social Control in Chinese Society. Praeger.

Wilson, Angus.
  xWilson, Angus.
    As If by Magic. Penguin.
    The Strange Ride of Rudyard Kipling. Penguin.
    The Strange Ride of Rudyard Kipling. Viking Pr.

Wilson, Anna.
  xWilson, Anna.
    Enjoying Embroidery. Branford.

Wilson, Arnold T. *see* Wilson, Arnold Talbot.

Wilson, Arnold Talbot, Sir, 1884-1940
  xWilson, Arnold T.
    The Persian Gulf: An Historical Sketch from the Earliest Times to the Beginning of the Twentieth Century. Hyperion Conn.

Wilson, Arthur H. *see* Wilson, Arthur Herman.

Wilson, Arthur Herman, 1905-
  xWilson, Arthur H.
    History of the Philadelphia Theatre, 1835 to 1855. Greenwood.

Wilson, Arthur M. *see* Wilson, Arthur McCandless.

Wilson, Arthur McCandless, 1902-
  xWilson, Arthur M.
    Diderot. Oxford U Pr.
    French Foreign Policy During the Administration of Cardinal Fleury: 1726-1743; a Study in Diplomacy & Commercial Development. Greenwood.

Wilson, Aubrey.
  xWilson, A.
    Marketing of Professional Services. McGraw.

Wilson, B. F. *see* Wilson, Brayton Fuller.

Wilson, B. K. *see* Wilson, Barbara Ker.

Wilson, Barbara Ker, 1929-
  xWilson, B. K.
    Path Through the Woods. S G Phillips.

Wilson, Barry W., 1935-
  xWilson, Barry W.
    Intro. by Birds: Readings from Scientific American. W H Freeman.

Wilson, Beth P.
  xWilson, Beth P.
    Giants for Justice: Bethune, Randolph & King. HarBraceJ.
    The Great Minu. Follett.
    Stevie Wonder. Putnam.

Wilson, Brayton Fuller, 1934-
  xWilson, B. F.
    The Growing Tree. U of Mass Pr.

Wilson, Bryan.
  xWilson, Bryan.
    Contemporary Transformations of Religion. Oxford U Pr.

Wilson, Bryan R.
  xWilson, Bryan R.
    ed. Rationality. Biblio Dist.

Wilson, C. H. *see* Wilson, Charles Henry.

Wilson, C. Vincent, 1931-
  xWilson, C. Vincent.
    The Westminster Concise Handbook for the Bible. Westminster.

Wilson, Carlos.
  xWilson, Carlos.
    The Tupamaros: The Unmentionables. Branden.

Wilson, Carter, 1941-
  xWilson, Carter.
    A Green Tree & a Dry Tree. Macmillan.

Wilson, Cecil Leeburn.
  xWilson.
    Comprehensive Analytical Chemistry. Elsevier.

Wilson, Charis.
  xWilson, Charis.
    California & the West. Aperture.

Wilson, Charles. *see* Wilson, Charles Henry.

Wilson, Charles C. *see* Wilson, Charles Christopher.

Wilson, Charles Christopher.
  xWilson, Charles C.

Wilson, Francis Graham, 1901-
  xWilson, Francis G.
    American Political Mind: A Textbook in
    Political Theory. Greenwood.
    A Theory of Public Opinion. Greenwood.
Wilson, Frank C. see Wilson, Frank Crane.
Wilson, Frank Crane, 1929-
  xWilson, Frank C.
    The Musculoskeletal System. Lippincott.
Wilson, Frank L. see Wilson, Frank Lee.
Wilson, Frank Lee, 1941-
  xWilson, Frank L.
    French Democratic Left, 1963-1969: Toward a
    Modern Party System. Stanford U Pr.
Wilson, Frank P. see Wilson, Frank Percy.
Wilson, Frank Percy.
  xWilson, F. P.
    Oxford Dictionary of English Proverbs. Oxford
    U Pr.
  xWilson, Frank P.
    The Proverbial Wisdom of Shakespeare.
    Folcroft.
  xWilson, J.
    Intro. by Oxford Dictionary of English
    Proverbs. Oxford U Pr.
Wilson, Frank T. see Wilson, Frank Thompson.
Wilson, Frank Thompson, 1887-
  xWilson, Frank T.
    Learning of Bright & Dull Children. AMS Pr.
Wilson, G. see Wilson, Geoffrey.
Wilson, G. Terence.
  xWilson, G. Terence.
    Principles of Behavior Therapy. P-H.
Wilson, Gahan.
  xWilson, Gahan.
    I Paint What I See. S&S.
    Nuts. Marek.
Wilson, Garff B.
  xWilson, Garff B.
    A History of American Acting. Greenwood.
Wilson, Gary B.
  xWilson, Gary B.
    Parents & Teachers: Humanistic Educational
    Techniques to Facilitate Communication
    Between Parent & Staff of Child
    Development Centers. Humanics Ltd.
Wilson, Geoffrey.
  xWilson, G.
    Cases & Materials on Constitutional &
    Administrative Law. Cambridge U Pr.
Wilson, George, 1818-1859
  xWilson, George.
    The Life of the Honorable Henry Cavendish.
    Arno.
Wilson, George B. see Wilson, George Bernard.
Wilson, George Bernard, 1914-
  xWilson, George B.
    Cell Division & Mitotic Cycle. Krieger.
Wilson, George H. see Wilson, George Herbert.
Wilson, George Herbert, 1870-
  xWilson, George H.
    The History of the Universities' Mission to
    Central Africa. Arno.
Wilson, George M.
  xWilson, George M.
    Radical Nationalist in Japan: Kita Ikki,
    1883-1937. Harvard U Pr.
Wilson, George W. see Wilson, George Wilton.
Wilson, George Wilton, 1929-
  xWilson, George W.
    The Impact of Highway Investment on
    Development. Greenwood.
Wilson, Gilbert L. see Wilson, Gilbert Livingstone.
Wilson, Gilbert Livingstone, 1868-1930
  xWilson, Gilbert L.
    Agriculture of the Hidatsa Indians: An Indian
    Interpretation. AMS Pr.
Wilson, Gina.
  xWilson, Gina.

    Cora Ravenwing. Atheneum.
Wilson, Glenn D. see Wilson, Glenn Daniel.
Wilson, Glenn Daniel.
  xWilson, Glenn D.
    ed. The Psychology of Conservatism. Acad Pr.
Wilson, Grace H. see Wilson, Grace Hannah.
Wilson, Grace Hannah, 1888-
  xWilson, Grace H.
    The Religious & Educational Philosophy of the
    Young Women's Christian Association. AMS
    Pr.
Wilson, Graham K.
  xWilson, Graham K.
    Special Interests & Policymaking: Agricultural
    Policies and Politics in Britain and the United
    States of America, 1956-70. Wiley.
    Unions in American National Politics. St
    Martin.
Wilson, Greta O., 1928-
  xWilson, Greta O.
    ed. Regents, Reformers, & Revolutionaries:
    Indonesian Voices of the Colonial Days. U Pr
    of Hawaii.
Wilson, Guthrie.
  xWilson, Guthrie.
    Dear Miranda. S&S.
Wilson, Guy M. see Wilson, Guy Mitchell.
Wilson, Guy Mitchell, 1876-
  xWilson, Guy M.
    A Survey of the Social & Business Usage of
    Arithmetic. AMS Pr.
Wilson, H. T.
  xWilson, H. T.
    The American Ideology: Science, Technology
    & Organization As Modes of Rationality.
    Routledge & Kegan.
Wilson, Harold, 1916-
  xWilson, Harold.
    A Prime Minister on Prime Ministers. Summit
    Bks.
Wilson, Harriet. see Wilson, Harriett C.
Wilson, Harriett C.
  xWilson, Harriet.
    Parents & Children in the Inner City.
    Routledge & Kegan.
Wilson, Helen Van Pelt, 1901-
  xWilson, Helen Van Pelt.
    Houseplants Are for Pleasure: How to Grow
    Healthy Plants for Home Decoration.
    Doubleday.
Wilson, Henry, 1812-1875
  xWilson, Henry.
    History of the Anti-Slavery Measures of the
    Thirty-Seventh & Thirty-Eighth United States
    Congress, 1861-64. Negro U Pr.
    History of the Reconstruction Measures of the
    Thirty-Ninth & Fortieth Congresses: 1865-68.
    Negro U Pr.
    History of the Rise & Fall of the Slave Power
    in America. Negro U Pr.
Wilson, Henry L. see Wilson, Henry Lane.
Wilson, Henry Lane, 1857-1932
  xWilson, Henry L.
    Diplomatic Episodes in Mexico, Belgium &
    Chile. Kennikat.
Wilson, Herbert W. see Wilson, Herbert Wrigley.
Wilson, Herbert Wrigley, 1866-1940
  xWilson, Herbert W.
    Downfall of Spain: Naval History of the
    Spanish-American War. B Franklin.
Wilson, Holly S. see Wilson, Holly Skodol.
Wilson, Holly Skodol.
  xWilson, Holly S.
    Psychiatric Nursing. A-W.
Wilson, Howard.
  xWilson, Howard.
    Living with Yourself. ARA.
    Notes on Supervision. ARA.
Wilson, Howard A.
  xWilson, Howard A.

    Invasion from the East. Augsburg.
Wilson, Ian, 1941-
  xWilson, Ian.
    The Shroud of Turin: The Burial Cloth of Jesus
    Christ?. Doubleday.
    The Shroud of Turin: The Burial Cloth of Jesus
    Christ. Doubleday.
Wilson, Ira G. see Wilson, Ira Gaulbert.
Wilson, Ira Gaulbert.
  xWilson, Ira G.
    From Idea to Working Model. Krieger.
Wilson, J. see Wilson, John.
Wilson, J. A.
  xWilson, J. A.
    Industrial Electronics & Control. SRA.
    Learning Electricity & Electronics Through
    Experiments. McGraw.
Wilson, J. Douglas. see Wilson, John Douglas.
Wilson, J. Holton.
  xWilson, J. Holton.
    Managerial Economics: Concepts, Applications,
    & Cases. Har-Row.
Wilson, J. I. see Wilson, John I. B.
Wilson, J. L. see Wilson, James Lee.
Wilson, J. M. see Wilson, James Matchett.

Wilson, Jacques M. see Wilson, Jacques M. P.
Wilson, Jacques M. P.
  xWilson, Jacques M.
    The Development of Education in Ecuador. U
    of Miami Pr.
Wilson, James, Sir, 1853-1926
  xWilson, James.
    The Dialect of Robert Burns As Spoken in
    Central Ayrshire. Folcroft.
    The Original Americans: US Indians. Interbk
    Inc.
Wilson, James A. see Wilson, James Albert.
Wilson, James Albert, 1929-
  xWilson, James A.
    Principles of Animal Physiology. Macmillan.

Wilson, James Calmar.
  xWilson, Jim.
    Grass Land. Wide Skies.

Wilson, James Lee, 1920-
  xWilson, J. L.
    Carbonate Facies in Geologic History.
    Springer-Verlag.

Wilson, James Matchett.
  xWilson, J. M.
    Experiments in Physical Chemistry. Pergamon.

Wilson, James Q.
  xWilson, James Q.
    Amateur Democrat: Club Politics in Three
    Cities. U of Chicago Pr.
    Thinking About Crime. Basic.

    Thinking About Crime. Random.
    Varieties of Police Behavior: The Management
    of Law & Order in Eight Communities.
    Harvard U Pr.
  xWilson, John Q.
    City Politics & Public Policy. Wiley.
Wilson, James W. see Wilson, James Warner.
Wilson, James Warner.
  xWilson, James W.
    Work-Study College Programs: Appraisal &
    Report of the Study of Cooperative
    Education. Greenwood.
Wilson, Jane B., 1914-
  xWilson, Jane B.
    The Story Experience. Scarecrow.
Wilson, Jean. see Wilson, Jean Verseput.
Wilson, Jean Verseput.
  xWilson, Jean.

The Pile Weaves: Twenty Six Techniques &
How to Do Them. Scribner.
Weave with Style. Madrona Pubs.
Wilson, Jeanne, fl. 1967-
xWilson, Jeanne.
The Golden Harlot. St Martin.
Mulatto. M Evans.
Mulatto. PB.
Troubled Heritage. M Evans.
Troubled Heritage. PB.
Wilson, Jeanne. see Wilson, Jeanne Turner.
Wilson, Jeanne Turner.
xWilson, Jeanne.
Career Education: An Open Door Policy. Phi
Delta Kappa.
Wilson, Jerome D.
xWilson, Jerome D.
Thomas Paine. Twayne.
Wilson, Jerry B., 1939-
xWilson, Jerry B.
Death by Decision: The Medical, Moral, &
Legal Dilemmas of Euthanasia. Westminster.
Wilson, Jerry D.
xWilson, Jerry D.
An Environmental Approach to Physical
Science. Heath.
Wilson, Jim. see Wilson, James Calmar.
Wilson, Joan H. see Wilson, Joan Hoff.
Wilson, Joan Hoff, 1937-
xWilson, Joan H.
American Business & Foreign Policy,
1920-1933. Beacon Pr.
Ideology & Economics: U. S. Relations with
the Soviet Union, 1918-1933. U of Mo Pr.
Wilson, John, 1928-
xWilson, J
The Assessment of Morality. Humanities.
How to Get Paid for What You've Earned.
Med Economics.
xWilson, John.
Dramatic Works of John Wilson. Arno.
Educational Theory & the Preparation of
Teachers. Humanities.
Fantasy & Commonsense in Education. Halsted
Pr.
How to Get Paid for What You've Earned.
Van Nos Reinhold.
Introduction to Social Movements. Basic.
Philosophy & Religion: The Logic of Religious
Belief. Greenwood.
Preface to the Philosophy of Education.
Routledge & Kegan.
Religion in American Society: The Effective
Presence. P-H.
Specimens of the British Critics. Schol
Facsimiles.
Thinking with Concepts. Cambridge U Pr.
Wilson, John A. see Wilson, John Abraham Ross.
Wilson, John Abraham Ross.
xWilson, John A.
Psychological Foundations of Learning &
Teaching. McGraw.
Wilson, John Albert, 1899-
xWilson, John A.
Culture of Ancient Egypt. U of Chicago Pr.
Wilson, John C., 1938-
xWilson, John C.
The Alpha Centauri Symbolism. Whitmore.
Wilson, John D. see Wilson, John Dover.
Wilson, John Douglas, 1888-
xWilson.
Simplified Stair Layout. Delmar.
xWilson, J. Douglas.
Practical House Carpentry: Simplified Methods
for Building. McGraw.
Wilson, John Dover, 1881-
xWilson, John D.

Fortunes of Falstaff. Cambridge U Pr.
Leslie Stephen & Matthew Arnold As Critics
of Wordsworth. Folcroft.
Leslie Stephen & Matthew Arnold As Critics
of Wordsworth. Haskell.
Meaning of the Tempest. Folcroft.
Wilson, John F. see Wilson, John Fletcher.
Wilson, John Fay.
xWilson, John F.
Practice & Theory of Electrochemical
Machining. Krieger.
Wilson, John Fletcher.
xWilson, John F.
Public Speaking As a Liberal Art. Allyn.
Wilson, John Frederick.
xWilson, John F.
Public Religion in American Culture. Temple U
Pr.
Pulpit in Parliament: Puritanism During the
English Civil Wars, 1640-1648. Princeton U
Pr.
Wilson, John H. see Wilson, John Harold.
Wilson, John Harold, 1900-
xWilson, John H.
All the King's Ladies: Actresses of the
Restoration. U of Chicago Pr.
Court Satires of the Restoration. Ohio St U Pr.
Influence of Beaumont & Fletcher on
Restoration Drama. Haskell.
Ordeal of Mr. Pepys's Clerk. Ohio St U Pr.
Wilson, John I. B.
xWilson, J. I.
Solar Energy. Crane-Russak Co.
Wilson, John M. see Wilson, John Mcgregor.
Wilson, John Mcgregor, 1889-
xWilson, John M.
Open the Mind & Close the Sale: The Key to
Success in Selling. McGraw.
Wilson, John Q. see Wilson, James Q.
Wilson, John R., fl. 1977-
xWilson, John R.
ed. Plant Relations in Pastures. Intl Schol Bk
Serv.
Wilson, Jose.
xWilson, Jose.
Decorating with Confidence. S&S.
Wilson, Joseph E. see Wilson, Joseph Edward.
Wilson, Joseph Edward, 1920-
xWilson, Joseph E.
Radiation Chemistry of Monomers, Polymers &
Plastics. Dekker.
Wilson, Justin.
xWilson, Justin.
Justin Wilson Cook Book. Pelican.
Wilson, Katharine M. see Wilson, Katharine Margaret.
Wilson, Katharine Margaret.
xWilson, Katharine M.
Real Rhythm in English Poetry. Folcroft.
Sound & Meaning in English Poetry. Kennikat.
Wilson, Kax.
xWilson, Kax.
A History of Textiles. Westview.
Wilson, Lavisa.
xWilson, LaVisa C.
Caregiver Training for Child Care: A
Multimedia Program. Merrill.
Wilson, LaVisa C. see Wilson, Lavisa.
Wilson, LeGrand J. see Wilson, Legrand James.
Wilson, Legrand James, 1791-1871
xWilson, LeGrand J.
The Confederate Soldier. Memphis St Univ.
Wilson, Leland.
xWilson, Leland.
Living with Wonder. Word Bks.
Wilson, Leslie E.
xWilson, Leslie E.

A Delphinid (Mammalia: Cetacea) from the
Miocene of Palos Verdes Hills, California. U
of Cal Pr.
Wilson, Lionel.
xWilson, Lionel.
Attack of the Killer Grizzly. Raintree Pubs.
The First Stunt Stars of Hollywood. Silver.
Wilson, Logan, 1907-
xWilson, Logan.
American Academics: Then & Now. Oxford U
Pr.
Wilson, Loring D.
xWilson, Loring D.
Encyclopedia of Fishing Lures. A S Barnes.
The Fly-Fisherman's Workshop. A S Barnes.
Tying & Fishing the Terrestrials. A S Barnes.
Wilson, Louis. see Wilson, Louis Ainsley.
Wilson, Louis Ainsley, 1931-
xWilson, Louis.
ed. External Diseases of the Eye. Har-Row.
Wilson, Louis R. see Wilson, Louis Round.
Wilson, Louis Round, 1876-
xWilson, Louis R.
Louis Round Wilson's Historical Sketches.
Moore Pub Co.
Wilson, Louise.
xWilson, Louise.
This Stranger My Son: A Mother's Story.
Putnam.
Wilson, Malcolm.
xWilson, Malcolm.
British Rust Fungi. Cambridge U Pr.
Wilson, Margaret.
xWilson, Margaret.
The Able McLaughlins. Larlin Corp.
Wilson, Margaret D., 1939-
xWilson, Margaret D.
Descartes. Routledge & Kegan.
Wilson, Margaret G. see Wilson, Margaret Gibbons.
Wilson, Margaret Gibbons.
xWilson, Margaret G.
The American Woman in Transition: The
Urban Influence, 1870-1920. Greenwood.
Wilson, Marie M.
xWilson, Marie M.
Siamese Cookery. C E Tuttle.
Wilson, Marion E.
xWilson, Marion E.
Microbiology in Patient Care. Macmillan.
Wilson, Mark. see Wilson, Mark A.
Wilson, Mark A.
xWilson, Mark.
East Bay Heritage: A Potpourri of Living
History. Cal Living Bks.
Wilson, Mary K. see Wilson, Mary Keeling.
Wilson, Mary Keeling.
xWilson, Mary K.
A Study of the Achievement of College
Students in Beginning Courses in Food
Preparation & Serving & Related Factors.
AMS Pr.
Wilson, McClure.
xWilson, McClure.
The Anatomic Foundation of Neuroradiology
of the Brain. Little.
Wilson, Michael.
xWilson, Michael.
The English Chamber Organ: History &
Development 1650-1850. U of SC Pr.
Wilson, Michele S.
xWilson, Michelle S.
Financial Aid for Minorities in Business.
Garrett Pk.
Wilson, Michelle S. see Wilson, Michele S.
Wilson, Mona, 1872-
xWilson, Mona.

Life of William Blake. Cooper Sq.
Life of William Blake. Oxford U Pr.
These Were Muses. Kennikat.
These Were Muses. R West.
Wilson, Monica. *see* Wilson, Monica Hunter.
Wilson, Monica Hunter.
xWilson, Monica.
For Men & Elders: Change in the Relations of
Generations & of Men & Women Among the
Nyakyusa-Ngonde People, 1875-1971.
Holmes & Meier.
Religion & the Transformation of Society: A
Study in Social Change in Africa. Cambridge
U Pr.
Wilson, Morrow.
xWilson, Morrow.
ed. Drugs in American Life. Wilson.
Wilson, N. L. *see* Wilson, Neil Leslie.
Wilson, N. Scarlyn.
xWilson, N. Scarlyn.
Teach Yourself Spanish. McKay.
Wilson, N. Scarlyn. *see* Wilson, Norman Scarlyn.
Wilson, Neil Leslie, 1922-
xWilson, N. L.
Concept of Language. U of Toronto Pr.
Wilson, Norman Scarlyn.
xWilson, N. Scarlyn.
European Drama. Folcroft.
Wilson, Otto, 1885-1942
xWilson, Otto.
Fifty Years' Work with Girls, 1883-1933: A
Story of the Florence Crittenton Homes.
Arno.
Wilson, P.
xWilson, P.
Leaders in Literature: Being Short Studies of
Great Authors in the Nineteenth Century. R
West.
Wilson, P. K. *see* Wilson, Philip K.
Wilson, Patricia P. *see* Wilson, Patricia Poplar.
Wilson, Patricia Poplar.
xWilson, Patricia P.
Household Equipment: Selection &
Management. HM.
Wilson, Patrick, 1927-
xWilson, Patrick.
Public Knowledge, Private Ignorance: Toward a
Library & Information Policy. Greenwood.
Wilson, Paul R.
xWilson, Paul R.
ed. Delinquency in Australia: A Critical
Appraisal. U of Queensland Pr.
ed. Of Public Concern: Contemporary
Australian Social Issues. U of Queensland Pr.
The Other Side of Rape. U of Queensland Pr.
Public Housing for Australia. U of Queensland
Pr.
Wilson, Paul T.
xWilson, Paul T.
ed. Money & Information for Mental Health:
Descriptive Directory of Federal & Private
Resources. Am Psychiatric.
Wilson, Pearl C. *see* Wilson, Pearl Cleveland.
Wilson, Pearl Cleveland.
xWilson, Pearl C.
The Living Socrates: The Man Who Dared to
Question, As Plato Knew Him. Stemmer Hse.
Wilson, Philip K.
xWilson, P. K.
ed. Adult Fitness & Cardiac Rehabilitation.
Univ Park.
Wilson, R. Jackson. *see* Wilson, Raymond Jackson.
Wilson, R. L. *see* Wilson, Robert Lee.
Wilson, R. M. *see* Wilson, Richard Middlewood.
Wilson, Raymond Jackson.
xWilson, R. Jackson.
ed. Reform, Crisis & Confusion: 1900-1929.
Phila Bk Co.
Wilson, Richard G. *see* Wilson, Richard Guy.

Wilson, Richard Guy.
xWilson, Richard G.
The Prairie School in Iowa. Iowa St U Pr.
Wilson, Richard M. S.
xWilson, R. M.
Management Controls & Marketing Planning.
Halsted Pr.
Management Controls & Marketing Planning:
Incorporating Management Controls in
Marketing. Halsted Pr.
Wilson, Richard Middlewood.
xWilson, R. M.
Early Middle English Literature. Folcroft.
Lost Literature of Medieval England. Cooper
Sq.
Wilson, Richard W., 1933-
xWilson, Richard W.
Learning to Be Chinese: The Political
Socialization of Children in Taiwan. MIT Pr.
ed. Moral Development & Politics. Praeger.
The Moral State: A Study of the Political
Socialization of Chinese & American
Children. Free Pr.
Value Change in Chinese Society. Praeger.
Wilson, Robert. *see* Wilson, Robert Mills.
Wilson, Robert A., 1895-
xWilson, Robert A.
Feminine Forever. M Evans.
Feminine Forever. PB.
Wilson, Robert A. *see* Wilson, Robert Anton.
Wilson, Robert Alfred Jump, 1922-
xWilson, Robert A.
Modern Book Collecting. Knopf.
Wilson, Robert Anton, 1932-
xWilson, Robert A.
Cosmic Trigger: Final Secret of the Illuminati.
And-or Pr.
Wilson, Robert Arden, 1910-
xWilson, Robert A.
Genesis of the Meiji Government in Japan,
1868-1871. Greenwood.
Wilson, Robert C. *see* Wilson, Robert Charles.
Wilson, Robert Charles.
xWilson, Robert C.
Crooked Tree. Putnam.
xWilson, Robert G.
College Professors & Their Impact on Students.
Wiley.
Wilson, Robert F. *see* Wilson, Robert Forrest.
Wilson, Robert Forrest, 1883-1942
xWilson, Robert F.
Crusader in Crinoline: The Life of Harriet
Beecher Stowe. Greenwood.
Wilson, Robert G.
xWilson, Robert. G.
Ion Beams: With Applications to Ion
Implantation. Krieger.
Wilson, Robert G. *see* Wilson, Robert Charles.
Wilson, Robert Lee, 1917-
xWilson, R. L.
Much Ado About Calculus: A Modern
Treatment with Applications Prepared for
Use with the Computer. Springer-Verlag.
Wilson, Robert M.
xWilson, Robert M.
Diagnostic and Remedial Reading for
Classroom & Clinic. Merrill.
Wilson, Robert M. *see* Wilson, Robert Mclachlan.
Wilson, Robert Mclachlan.
xWilson, Robert M.
The Gnostic Problem. AMS Pr.
Wilson, Robert Mills.
xWilson, Robert.
Programmed Comprehension for Teachers.
Merrill.
xWilson, Robert M.
Readings for Diagnostic & Remedial Reading.
Merrill.
Wilson, Robert N. *see* Wilson, Robert Neal.

Wilson, Robert Neal, 1924-
xWilson, Robert N.
ed. The Arts in Society. Arno.
Sociology of Health: An Introduction. Peter
Smith.
The Sociology of Health: An Introduction.
Random.
The Writer As Social Seer. U of NC Pr.
Wilson, Robert R., 1942-
xWilson, Robert R.
Genealogy & History in the Biblical World.
Yale U Pr.
Prophecy & Society in Ancient Israel. Fortress.
Wilson, Robert R. *see* Wilson, Robert Reid.
Wilson, Robert Reid.
xWilson, Robert R.
Introduction to Sexual Counseling. Carolina
Pop Ctr.
Wilson, Rodger, 1947-
xWilson, Rodger.
Where's the Fire?. P-H.
Wilson, Rodney.
xWilson, Rodney.
The Economies of the Middle East. Holmes &
Meier.
Wilson, Ron, 1941-
xWilson, Ron.
How the Body Works. Larousse.
Multimedia Handbook for the Church. Cook.
Wilson, Ronald A. *see* Wilson, Ronald Alfred.
Wilson, Ronald Alfred.
xWilson, Ronald A.
Pre-War Biographies of Romain Rolland &
Their Place in His Work & the Period.
Kennikat.
The Pre-War Biographies of Romain Rolland &
Their Place in His Work & the Period. R
West.
Wilson, Rufus. *see* Wilson, Rufus Rockwell.
Wilson, Rufus Rockwell, 1865-1949
xWilson, Rufus.
Historic Long Island. Yankee Peddler.
Wilson, Ruth, 1919-
xWilson, Ruth.
Our Blood & Tears: Black Freedom Fighters.
Putnam.
Wilson, Sam. *see* Wilson, Samuel.
Wilson, Samuel.
xWilson.
Human Sexuality: A Text with Readings. West
Pub.
xWilson, Sam.
Human Sexuality: A Text with Readings.. West
Pub.
xWilson, Samuel.
Readings in Human Sexuality. West Pub.
Wilson, Samuel L. *see* Wilson, Samuel Law.
Wilson, Samuel Law.
xWilson, Samuel L.
The Theology of Modern Literature. Folcroft.
Wilson, Shirley A.
xWilson, Shirley A.
Review of Dental Assisting. Mosby.
Wilson, Sloan, 1920-
xWilson, Sloan.
Small Town. Arbor Hse.
Wilson, Sonja.
xWilson, Sonja.
Castle on the Prairie. Branden.
Wilson, Spencer.
xWilson, Spencer.
The Cumbres & Toltec Scenic Railroad: The
Historic Preservation Study. U of NM Pr.
Wilson, Stanley D.
xWilson, Stanley D.
Current Trends in Design & Construction of
Embankment Dams. Am Soc Civil Eng.
Wilson, Stephen, 1940-
xWilson, Stephen R.

Informal Groups: An Introduction. P-H.
Wilson, Stephen R. *see* Wilson, Stephen.
Wilson, Steve.
 xWilson, Steve.
  The Lost Traveller. St Martin.
  Oklahoma Treasures & Treasure Tales. U of
   Okla Pr.
Wilson, Suanna J.
 xWilson, Suanna J.
  Confidentiality in Social Work: Issues &
   Principles. Free Pr.
Wilson, Susan F. *see* Wilson, Susan Fickertt.
Wilson, Susan Fickertt.
 xWilson, Susan F.
  Neuronursing. Springer Pub.
Wilson, Theodore B.
 xWilson, Theodore B.
  An Introduction to Industrial Recreation:
   Employee Activities & Services.
   Kendall-Hunt.
Wilson, Theron D.
 xWilson, Theron D.
  Religion for Tomorrow. Philos Lib.
Wilson, Thomas Ernest, 1902-
 xWilson, Ernest T.
  Angola Beloved. Loizeaux.
Wilson, Thomas W. *see* Wilson, Thomas Williams.
Wilson, Thomas Williams.
 xWilson, Thomas W.
  Science, Technology & Development: The
   Politics of Modernization. Foreign Policy.
Wilson, Tom.
 xWilson, Tom.
  Life Is Just a Bunch of Ziggys. Andrews &
   McMeel.
  Life Is Just a Bunch of Ziggys.... NAL.
  This Book Is for the Birds. Andrews &
   McMeel.
  This Book Is for the Birds. NAL.
Wilson, Trevor.
 xWilson, Trevor.
  Great Chicken Dishes of the World. McGraw.
Wilson, V. J. *see* Wilson, Victor.
Wilson, Victor.
 xWilson, V. J.
  Mammalian Vestibular Physiology. Plenum
   Pub.
Wilson, Violet. *see* Wilson, Violet A.
Wilson, Violet A.
 xWilson, Violet.
  Society Women of Shakespeare's Time.
   Gordon Pr.
 xWilson, Violet A.
  Society Women of Shakespeare's Time. Arden
   Lib.
  Society Women of Shakespeare's Time.
   Kennikat.
Wilson, W. J. *see* Wilson, William John.
Wilson, Walter, 1903-
 xWilson, Walter.
  Forced Labor in the United States. AMS Pr.
Wilson, William A. *see* Wilson, William Albert.
Wilson, William Albert.
 xWilson, William A.
  Folklore & Nationalism in Modern Finland.
   Ind U Pr.
Wilson, William E. *see* Wilson, William Edward.
Wilson, William Eade, 1900-
 xWilson, William E.
  Guillen de Castro. Twayne.
Wilson, William Edward, 1906-
 xWilson, William E.
  Angel & the Serpent: The Story of New
   Harmony. Ind U Pr.
Wilson, William H. *see* Wilson, William Henry.
Wilson, William Henry, 1935-
 xWilson, William H.

Railroad in the Clouds: The Alaska Railroad in
  the Age of Steam, 1914-1945. Pruett.
Wilson, William J., 1935-
 xWilson, William J.
  The Declining Significance of Race: Blacks &
   Changing American Institutions. U of
   Chicago Pr.
  Power, Racism & Privilege: Race Relations in
   Theoretical & Sociohistorical Perspectives.
   Free Pr.
Wilson, William John.
 xWilson, W. J.
  The Stereo Index: A Complete Catalogue of
   Every Recommended Stereo Disc.
   Greenwood.
Wilson, William L. *see* Wilson, William Lyne.
Wilson, William Lyne, 1843-1900
 xWilson, William L.
  A Borderland Confederate. Greenwood.
Wilson, Woodrow, Pres. U.s, 1856-1924
 xWilson, Woodrow.
  George Washington. Schocken.
Wilson-Ludlam, Mae R.
 xWilson-Ludlam, Mae R.
  ed. Horary: The Gemini Science. Macoy Pub.
Wilstach, Frank J. *see* Wilstach, Frank Jenners.
Wilstach, Frank Jenners, 1865-1933
 xWilstach, Frank J.
  Dictionary of Similes. Adler.
Wilstach, Paul, 1870-1952
 xWilstach, Paul.
  Hudson River Landings. Friedman.
  Patriots off Their Pedestals. Arno.
  Potomac Landings. Folcroft.
Wilt, Alan F.
 xWilt, Alan F.
  The Atlantic Wall: Hitler's Defenses in the
   West, 1941-1944. Iowa St U Pr.
Wilt, Joy.
 xWilt, Joy.
  An Uncomplicated Guide to Becoming a Super
   Parent. Word Bks.
Wilt, Judith.
 xWilt, Judith.
  The Readable People of George Meredith.
   Princeton U Pr.
Wilt, Napier, 1896-
 xWilt, Napier.
  Some American Humorists. Gordon Pr.
  Some American Humorists. Johnson Repr.
Wiltens, James S., 1949-
 xWiltens, James S.
  Individual Tactics in Water Polo. A S Barnes.
Wiltsee, Earnest A. *see* Wiltsee, Ernest Abram.
Wiltsee, Ernest Abram.
 xWiltsee, Earnest A.
  Gold Rush Steamers of the Pacific.
   Quarterman.
Wiltshire, Kenneth W.
 xWiltshire, Kenneth W.
  ed. Administrative Federalism: Selected
   Documents in Australian Intergovernmental
   Relations. U of Queensland Pr.
Wilwerding, W. J. *see* Wilwerding, Walter Joseph.
Wilwerding, Walter J. *see* Wilwerding, Walter Joseph.
Wilwerding, Walter Joseph, 1891-
 xWilwerding, W. J.
  Animal Drawing & Painting. Peter Smith.
 xWilwerding, Walter J.
  Animal Drawing & Painting. Dover.
Wimberly, Edward P., 1943-
 xWimberly, Edward P.
  Pastoral Care in the Black Church. Abingdon.
Wimberly, Lowry C. *see* Wimberly, Lowry Charles.
Wimberly, Lowry Charles, 1890-1959
 xWimberly, Lowry C.

Folklore in the English & Scottish Ballads.
  Dover.
Folklore in the English & Scottish Ballads.
  Peter Smith.
Wimer, Arthur. *see* Wimer, Arthur Cecil.
Wimer, Arthur Cecil.
 xWimer, Arthur.
  Workbook for Radio & TV News Editing &
   Writing. Wm C Brown.
Wimsatt, James I.
 xWimsatt, James I.
  Allegory & Mirror: Tradition & Structure in
   Middle English Literature. Irvington.
  The Marguerite Poetry of Guillaume de
   Machaut. U of NC Pr.
Wimsatt, W. K. *see* Wimsatt, William Kurtz.
Wimsatt, William K. *see* Wimsatt, William Kurtz.
Wimsatt, William Kurtz, 1907-1975
 xWimsatt, W. K.
  Day of the Leopards: Essays in Defense of
   Poems. Yale U Pr.
 xWimsatt, William K.
  Prose Style of Samuel Johnson. Shoe String.
Winans, A. D.
 xWinans, A. D.
  All the Graffiti on All the Bathroom Walls of
   the World Can't Hide These Scars. Fallen
   Angel.
  North Beach Poems. Second Coming.
Winbolt, S. E. *see* Winbolt, Samuel Edward.
Winbolt, Samuel E. *see* Winbolt, Samuel Edward.
Winbolt, Samuel Edward, 1868-1944
 xWinbolt, S. E.
  Spenser & His Poetry. Folcroft.
 xWinbolt, Samuel E.
  Spenser & His Poetry. AMS Pr.
Winbury, Martin *see* Winbury, Martin M.
Winbury, Martin M.
 xWinbury, Martin.
  ed. Ischemic Myocardium & Antianginal
   Drugs. Raven.
Winch, Peter.
 xWinch, Peter.
  Ethics & Action. Routledge & Kegan.
Winch, Robert F. *see* Winch, Robert Francis.
Winch, Robert Francis, 1911-
 xWinch, Robert F.
  Mate Selection: A Study of Complementary
   Needs. Irvington.
Winchell, H. *see* Winchell, Horace.
Winchell, Horace.
 xWinchell, H.
  Optical Properties of Minerals: A
   Determinative Table. Acad Pr.
Winchester, A. M. *see* Winchester, Albert Mccombs.
Winchester, Albert Mccombs, 1908-
 xWinchester, A. M.
  Concepts of Zoology. Van Nos Reinhold.
  Genetics: A Survey of the Principles of
   Heredity. HM.
  Human Genetics. Merrill.
  Modern Biological Principles. Van Nos
   Reinhold.
Winchester, Barbara.
 xWinchester, Barbara.
  Tudor Family Portrait. Humanities.
  Tudor Family Portrait. Verry.
Winchester, Caleb T. *see* Winchester, Caleb Thomas.
Winchester, Caleb Thomas, 1847-1920
 xWinchester, Caleb T.
  Group of English Essayists of the Early
   Nineteenth Century. Arno.
Winchester, James H.
 xWinchester, James H.
  Hurricanes, Storms, Tornadoes. Putnam.
Winchester, Kenneth. *see* Winchester, Kenneth J.
Winchester, Kenneth J.
 xWinchester, Kenneth.

Walking Tours of New England. Doubleday.
Winchester, Mark B.
    xWinchester, Mark B.
        ed. The International Essays for Business
        Decision Makers. Am Mgmt.
        ed. The International Essays for Business
        Decision Makers. Gulf Pub.
Winchester, Simon.
    xWinchester, Simon.
        American Heartbeat: Some Notes from a
        Midwestern Journey. Transatlantic.
        Northern Ireland in Crisis: Reporting the
        Ulster Troubles. Holmes & Meier.
Winchester, Stanley.
    xWinchester, Stanley.
        The Practice. Dell.
Winckler, Paul A.
    xWinckler, Paul A.
        ed. Reader in the History of Books & Printing.
        IHS-PDS.
Wincor, Richard.
    xWincor, Richard.
        Contracts in Plain English. McGraw.
        Law of Contracts. Oceana.
Wind, Edgar, 1900-
    xWind, Edgar.
        Pagan Mysteries in the Renaissance.
        Merrimack Bk Serv.
        Pagan Mysteries in the Renaissance. Norton.
Wind, Herbert W. *see* Wind, Herbert Warren.
Wind, Herbert Warren, 1918-
    xWind, Herbert W.
        ed. Complete Golfer. S&S.
        Gilded Age of Sport. S&S.
        On the Tour with Harry Sprague. S&S.
        The Story of American Golf: Its Champions &
        Its Championships. Greenwood.
Windal, Floyd. *see* Windal, Floyd W.
Windal, Floyd W.
    xWindal, Floyd.
        The Accounting Professional: Ethics,
        Responsibility, & Liability. P-H.
Windeatt, Mary F. *see* Windeatt, Mary Fabyan.
Windeatt, Mary Fabyan, 1910-
    xWindeatt, Mary F.
        The Children of Fatima. Abbey.
Windeknecht, Margaret B.
    xWindeknecht, Margaret B.
        Creative Monk's Belt. HTH Pubs.
Windelband, Wilhelm, 1848-1915
    xWindelband, Wilhelm.
        A History of Philosophy: With Especial
        Reference to the Formation & Development
        of Its Problems & Conceptions. Greenwood.
        Theories in Logic. Philos Lib.
Windeler, A. *see* Windeler, Adolphus.
Windeler, Adolphus.
    xWindeler, A.
        The California Gold Rush Diary of a German
        Sailor. Howell-North.
Windeler, Robert.
    xWindeler, Robert.
        The Films of Shirley Temple. Citadel Pr.
Winderbaum, Larry.
    xWinderbaum, Larry.
        The Martial Arts Encyclopedia. Inscape Corp.
Windham, Donald.
    xWindham, Donald.
        Tanaquil: The Hardest Thing of All. S
        Campbell.
Windham, Kathryn T. *see* Windham, Kathryn Tucker.
Windham, Kathryn Tucker.
    xWindham, Kathryn T.
        Southern Cooking to Remember. Strode.
        Thirteen Georgia Ghosts & Jeffrey. Strode.
        Thirteen Tennessee Ghosts & Jeffrey. Strode.
Windle, William F. *see* Windle, William Frederick.
Windle, William Frederick, 1898-
    xWindle, William F.

Textbook of Histology. McGraw.
xWindle, William Frederick.
    The Pioneering Role of Clarence Luther
    Herrick in American Neuroscience.
    Exposition.
Windley, Brian F.
    xWindley, Brian F.
        The Evolving Continents. Wiley.
Windmuller, John P.
    xWindmuller, John P.
        ed. Industrial Democracy in International
        Perspective. Am Acad Pol Soc Sci.
Windolph, Francis L. *see* Windolph, Francis Lyman.
Windolph, Francis Lyman, 1889-
    xWindolph, Francis L.
        Leviathan & Natural Law. Greenwood.
        Reflections of the Law in Literature. Arno.
Windom, H. L.
    xWindom, H. L.
        Marine Pollutant Transfer. Lexington Bks.
Windrich, Elaine, 1921-
    xWindrich, Elaine.
        Britain & the Politics of Rhodesian
        Independence. Holmes & Meier.
        British Labour's Foreign Policy. Greenwood.
Windrow, Martin. *see* Windrow, Martin C.
Windrow, Martin C.
    xWindrow, Martin.
        The Panzer Divisions. Hippocrene Bks.
Windsor, Duane.
    xWindsor, Duane.
        Fiscal Zoning in Suburban Communities.
        Lexington Bks.
Windsor, Merrill.
    xWindsor, Merrill.
        America's Sunset Coast. Natl Geog.
Windsor, Pamela.
    xWindsor, Pamela.
        Rebel's Rapture. Berkley Pub.
Windsor, Patricia.
    xWindsor, Patricia.
        Diving for Roses. Har-Row.
        Home Is Where Your Feet Are Standing.
        Har-Row.
        The Summer Before. Dell.
        The Summer Before. Har-Row.
Windt, Theodore.
    xWindt, Theodore.
        Presidential Rhetoric: The Imperial Age
        1961-1974. Kendall-Hunt.
Wine Adsisory Bloard. *see* California. Wine Advisory
    Board.
Wine Advisory Board. *see* California. Wine Advisory
    Board.
Wine Advisory Boards. *see* California. Wine Advisory
    Board.
Wine Museum of San Francisco.
    xWine Museum of San Francisco.
        ed. Wine & the Artist: One Hundred & Four
        Prints & Drawings from the Christian
        Brothers Collection at the Wine Museum of
        San Francisco. Dover.
Wine, Sherwin T.
    xWine, Sherwin T.
        Humanistic Judaism. Prometheus Bks.
Winer, B. J.
    xWiner, B. J.
        Statistical Principles in Experimental Design.
        McGraw.
Winer, Gershon.
    xWiner, Gershon.
        Founding Fathers of Israel. Bloch.
Winfield, Louise.
    xWinfield, Louise P.
        Living Overseas. Pub Aff Pr.
Winfield, Louise P. *see* Winfield, Louise.
Winfield, Percy H. *see* Winfield, Percy Henry.
Winfield, Percy Henry, Sir Percy Henry, 1878-1953
    xWinfield, Percy H.

The Chief Sources of English Legal History. B
    Franklin.
Winfield, Richard N.
    xWinfield, Richard N.
        Libel Litigation. PLI.
Winfree, A. T. *see* Winfree, Arthur T.
Winfree, Arthur T.
    xWinfree, A. T.
        The Geometry of Biological Time.
        Springer-Verlag.
Wing, Charles, 1939-
    xWing, Charles.
        From the Walls In. Little.
Wing, Frances S.
    xWing, Frances S.
        The Complete Book of Decoupage. Berkley
        Pub.
Wing, Francis S. *see* Wing, Frances S.
Wing, J. *see* Wing, John Kenneth.
Wing, J. K. *see* Wing, John Kenneth.
Wing, John Kenneth.
    xWing, J.
        Schizophrenia: Towards a New Synthesis.
        Grune.
    xWing, J. K.
        ed. Community Care for the Mentally
        Disabled. Oxford U Pr.
        ed. Evaluating a Community Psychiatric
        Service: The Camberwell Register 1964-1971.
        Oxford U Pr.
        Reasoning About Madness. Oxford U Pr.
Wing, Kenneth. *see* Wing, Kenneth R.
Wing, Kenneth R., 1946-
    xWing, Kenneth.
        The Law & the Public's Health. Mosby.
Wing, Omar.
    xWing, Omar.
        Circuit Theory with Computer Methods.
        McGraw.
Wing, R. L.
    xWing, R. L.
        The I Ching Workbook. Doubleday.
Wingate, Isabel. *see* Wingate, Isabel (Barnum).
Wingate, Isabel (Barnum).
    xWingate, Isabel.
        Textile Fabrics & Their Selection. P-H.
    xWingate, Isabel B.
        ed. Fairchild's Dictionary of Textiles. Fairchild.
Wingate, Isabel B. *see* Wingate, Isabel (Barnum).
Wingate, John.
    xWingate, John.
        Avalanche. St Martin.
Wingate, John W. *see* Wingate, John Williams.
Wingate, John Williams.
    xWingate, John W.
        Fundamentals of Selling. SW Pub.
        Problems in Retail Merchandising. P-H.
        Retail Merchandise Management. P-H.
        Retail Merchandising. SW Pub.
        Retail Merchandising. SW Pub.
Wingate, Phillip J. *see* Wingate, Phillip Jerome.
Wingate, Phillip Jerome, 1913-
    xWingate, Phillip J.
        Bandages of Soft Illusion. Holly Pr.
        H. L. Mencken's Un-Neglected Anniversary.
        Holly Pr.
Wingate, Richard, 1933-
    xWingate, Richard.
        Lost Outpost of Atlantis. Everest Hse.
Wingate, Rosalee M. *see* Wingate, Rosalee Martin.
Wingate, Rosalee Martin.
    xWingate, Rosalee M.
        I Like Myself. NELP.
Wingate, William.
    xWingate, William.
        Bloodbath. St Martin.
        Fireplay. BJ Pub Group.
Winger, Bernard J.
    xWinger, Bernard J.

Winship, George Parker, 1871-1952
  xWinship, George P.
    Gutenberg to Plantin: An Outline of the Early
    History of Printing (1450-1600). B Franklin.
Winslow, Anna G. *see* Winslow, Anna Green.
Winslow, Anna Green.
  xWinslow, Anna G.
    Diary of Anna Green Winslow: A Boston
    School Girl of 1771. Corner Hse.
Winslow, Carleton, 1919-
  xWinslow, Carleton.
    The Enchanted Hill. Celestial Arts.
Winslow, Earle M. *see* Winslow, Earle Micajah.
Winslow, Earle Micajah, 1896-1966
  xWinslow, Earle M.
    The Pattern of Imperialism: A Study in the
    Theories of Power. Octagon.
Winslow, Forbes. *see* Winslow, Forbes Benignus.
Winslow, Forbes Benignus, 1810-1874
  xWinslow, Forbes.
    The Anatomy of Suicide. Longwood Pr.
Winslow, Joan.
  xWinslow, Joan.
    Griffin Towers. Ace Bks.
Winslow, John H., 1932-
  xWinslow, John H.
    Darwin's Victorian Malady: Evidence for Its
    Medically Induced Origin. Am Philos.
Winslow, Ola E. *see* Winslow, Ola Elizabeth.
Winslow, Ola Elizabeth.
  xWinslow, Ola E.
    Jonathan Edwards, 1703-1758. Octagon.
    Low Comedy As a Structural Element in
    English Drama from the Beginnings to 1642.
    Folcroft.
Winslow, Pauline G. *see* Winslow, Pauline Glen.
Winslow, Pauline Glen.
  xWinslow, Pauline G.
    The Brandenburg Hotel. Dell.
    The Death of an Angel. St Martin.
    Gallow's Child. St Martin.
Winslow, R. *see* Winslow, Robert Wallace.
Winslow, Robert W.
  xWinslow, Robert W.
    Music Skills for Classroom Teachers. Wm C
    Brown.
Winslow, Robert Wallace, 1940-
  xWinslow, R.
    Society in Transition: A Social Approach to
    Deviancy. Free Pr.
Winsor, Bill.
  xWinsor, Bill.
    Texas in the Confederacy: Military
    Installations, Economy & People. Hill Jr Coll.
Winsor, Charlotte. *see* Winsor, Charlotte B.
Winsor, Charlotte B.
  xWinsor, Charlotte.
    Intro. by & ed. Experimental Schools Revisited:
    Bulletins of the Bureau of Educational
    Experiments. Agathon.
Winsor, Kathleen.
  xWinsor, Kathleen.
    Calais: A Novel. Doubleday.
Winsor, Mary P.
  xWinsor, Mary P.
    Starfish, Jellyfish & the Order of Life: Issues of
    Nineteenth-Century Science. Yale U Pr.
Winsor, Maryan T.
  xWinsor, Maryan T.
    Arts & Crafts for Special Education. Pitman
    Learning.
Winsor, Travis, 1914-
  xWinsor, Travis.
    Primer of Vectorcardiography. Lea & Febiger.
Winstanley, D. A. *see* Winstanley, Denys Arthur.
Winstanley, Denys Arthur, 1877-1947
  xWinstanley, D. A.

Early Victorian Cambridge. Arno.
Later Victorian Cambridge. Arno.
Lord Chatham & the Whig Opposition. Biblio
Dist.
Winstanley, Gerrard.
  xWinstanley, Gerrard.
    The Law of Freedom in a Platform: Or, True
    Magistracy Restored. Schocken.
Winstanley, M. *see* Winstanley, Michael J.
Winstanley, Michael J., 1949-
  xWinstanley, M.
    Life in Kent at the Turn of the Century.
    Dawson Pub.
Winstead, Martha.
  xWinstead, Martha.
    Instrument Check Systems. Lea & Febiger.
Winston, Henry.
  xWinston, Henry.
    Class, Race & Black Liberation. Intl Pub Co.
    Strategy for a Black Agenda: A Critique of
    New Theories of Liberation in the United
    States & Africa. Intl Pub Co.
Winston, Joan.
  xWinston, Joan.
    The Making of the Trek Conventions. Playboy
    Pbks.
Winston, Patrick H. *see* Winston, Patrick Henry.
Winston, Patrick Henry.
  xWinston, Patrick H.
    Artificial Intelligence. A-W.
    ed. The Psychology of Computer Vision.
    McGraw.
Winston, Sandra.
  xWinston, Sandra.
    The Entrepreneurial Woman. Bantam.
    The Entrepreneurial Woman. Newsweek.
Winston, Sarah.
  xWinston, Sarah.
    Not Yet Spring. Golden Quill.
Winston, Stephanie.
  xWinston, Stephanie.
    Getting Organized: The Easy Way to Put Your
    Life in Order. Norton.
Winstone, C. A.
  xWinstone, C. A.
    Possessed. St Martin.
Wint, Guy, 1910-1969
  xWint, Guy.
    British in Asia. Russell.
Winter, Adalee.
  xWinter, Adalee.
    Needlecraft Kingdom. Oxmoor Hse.
    Religious Designs for Needlework. Oxmoor
    Hse.
Winter, Alice.
  xWinter, Alice.
    The Velvet Bubble. Belmont-Tower.
Winter, Arthur, 1922-
  xWinter, Arthur.
    Life & Death Decisions. C C Thomas.
    ed. Surgical Control of Behavior: A
    Symposium. C C Thomas.
Winter, Charles A., 1902-
  xWinter, Charles A.
    Opportunities in Biological Sciences Careers.
    Natl Textbk.
Winter, D. J. *see* Winter, David J.
Winter, David A., 1930-
  xWinter, David A.
    Biomechanics of Human Movement. Wiley.
Winter, David G., 1939-
  xWinter, David G.
    The Power Motive. Free Pr.
Winter, David J.
  xWinter, D. J.
    The Structure of Fields. Springer-Verlag.
  xWinter, David J.
    Abstract Lie Algebras. MIT Pr.
Winter, Frederick E.
  xWinter, Frederick E.

Greek Fortifications. U of Toronto Pr.
Winter, Garry.
  xWinter, Garry.
    ed. Crafts & Hobbies. Arco.
Winter, George.
  xWinter, George.
    Design of Concrete Structures. McGraw.
  xWinter, George H.
    Design of Concrete Structures. McGraw.
Winter, George H. *see* Winter, George.
Winter, Ian J.
  xWinter, Ian J.
    Montaigne's Self-Portrait & Its Influence in
    France, 1580-1630. French Forum.
Winter, J. Alan. *see* Winter, Jerry Alan.
Winter, J. M.
  xWinter, J. M.
    Socialism & the Challenge of War: Ideas &
    Politics in Britain, 1912-1918. Routledge &
    Kegan.
Winter, Jerry Alan.
  xWinter, J. Alan.
    Continuities in the Sociology of Religion:
    Creed, Congregation, & Community.
    Har-Row.
Winter, John V.
  xWinter, John V.
    Power Plant Siting. Van Nos Reinhold.
Winter, Michael M.
  xWinter, Michael M.
    Saint Peter & the Popes. Greenwood.
Winter, Miriam T. *see* Winter, Miriam Therese.
Winter, Miriam Therese.
  xWinter, Miriam T.
    God-with-Us: Resources for Prayer & Praise.
    Abingdon.
    Preparing the Way of the Lord. Abingdon.
Winter, Paul.
  xWinter, Paul.
    On the Trial of Jesus. De Gruyter.
Winter, Ralph D.
  xWinter, Ralph D.
    The Twenty-Five Unbelievable Years,
    1945-1969. William Carey Lib.
Winter, Ralph K.
  xWinter, Ralph K.
    Campaign Financing & Political Freedom. Am
    Enterprise.
Winter, Rebecca J.
  xWinter, Rebecca J.
    The Night Cometh: Two Wealthy Evangelicals
    Face the Nation. William Carey Lib.
Winter, Rolf. *see* Winter, Rolf G.
Winter, Rolf G.
  xWinter, Rolf.
    Quantum Physics. Wadsworth Pub.
Winter, Ruth, 1930-
  xWinter, Ruth.
    The Consumer's Dictionary of Cosmetic
    Ingredients. Crown.
    A Consumer's Dictionary of Food Additives.
    Crown.
Winter School on Probability, 4th, Karpacz, Poland, 1975.
  xFourth Winter School on Probability, Karpacz,
    Poland, Jan. 1975.
    Probability Winter School: Proceedings.
    Springer-Verlag.
Winter, Thelma F. *see* Winter, Thelma Frazier.
Winter, Thelma Frazier.
  xWinter, Thelma F.
    Art & Craft of Ceramic Sculpture. Halsted Pr.
Winter, W. T. *see* Winter, Walter T.
Winter, Walter T.
  xWinter, W. T.
    Divorce & You. Macmillan.
Winter, William, 1836-1917
  xWinter, William.

Life & Art of Edwin Booth. Arno.
Life & Art of Edwin Booth. Greenwood.
Life & Art of Edwin Booth. R West.
Life of David Belasco. Arno.
Old Friends: Being Literary Recollections of Other Days. Arno.

Winter-Berger, Robert N.
xWinter-Berger, Robert N.
The Gerald Ford Letters. Lyle Stuart.

Winterborn, Benjamin.
xWinterborn, Benjamin.
Changing Scenes. Oxford U Pr.

Winterbotham, F. W. see Winterbotham, Frederick William.

Winterbotham, Frederick William.
xWinterbotham, F. W.
The Nazi Connection. Dell.
The Ultra Secret. Dell.
The Ultra Secret. Har-Row.

Winterbotham, R. see Winterbotham, Russ.

Winterbotham, Russ.
xWinterbotham, R.
Lord of Nardos. Bouregy.

Winterich, John T. see Winterich, John Tracy.

Winterich, John Tracy, 1891-1970
xWinterich, John T.
Early American Books & Printing. Gale.
The Grolier Club, 1884-1967: An Informal History. U Pr of Va.

Winterkorn, Hans F. see Winterkorn, Hans Friedrich.

Winterkorn, Hans Friedrich.
xWinterkorn, Hans F.
ed. Foundation Engineering Handbook. Van Nos Reinhold.

Winternitz, M. see Winternitz, Moriz.

Winternitz, Maurice. see Winternitz, Moriz.

Winternitz, Moriz, 1863-1937
xWinternitz, M.
History of Indian Literature. Orient Bk Dist.
xWinternitz, Maurice.
A History of Indian Literature. Intl Pubns Serv.
xWinternitz, Moriz.
History of Indian Literature. Russell.

Winterowd, W. Ross.
xWinterowd, W. Ross.
ed. Contemporary Rhetoric: Conceptual Background with Readings. HarBraceJ.

Winters, Ariel.
xWinters, Ariel.
Drinkwatchers. Drinkwatchers.

Winters, Donald L.
xWinters, Donald L.
Farmers Without Farms: Agricultural Tenancy in Nineteenth-Century Iowa. Greenwood.

Winters, Karen C. see Winters, Karen Cole.

Winters, Karen Cole.
xWinters, Karen C.
Your Career in Advertising. Arco.

Winters, Nancy.
xWinters, Nancy.
The Girl on the Coca-Cola Tray. Dial.
The Girl on the Coca-Cola Tray. PB.

Winters, Stephen S.
xWinters, Stephen S.
Supai Formation (Permian) of Eastern Arizona. Geol Soc.

Winters, W. D. see Winters, Wallace Dudley.

Winters, Wallace Dudley.
xWinters, W. D.
A Stereotaxic Brain Atlas for Macaca Nemestrina. U of Cal Pr.

Winters, Yvor, 1900-
xWinters, Yvor.

Collected Poems. Swallow.
Forms of Discovery: Critical & Historical Essays on the Forms of the Short Poem in English. Swallow.
Function of Criticism: Problems & Exercises. Swallow.
ed. Quest for Reality: An Anthology of the Short Poems in English. Swallow.

Winther, Oscar O. see Winther, Oscar Osburn.

Winther, Oscar Osburn, 1903-
xWinther, Oscar O.
A Classified Bibliography of the Periodical Literature of the Trans-Mississippi West, 1811-1967. Greenwood.

Winther, Sophus K. see Winther, Sophus Keith.

Winther, Sophus Keith, 1895-
xWinther, Sophus K.
Mortgage Your Heart. Arno.
Take All to Nebraska. U of Nebr Pr.

Winthrop, Elizabeth.
xWinthrop, Elizabeth.
Are You Sad, Mama?. Har-Row.
Bunk Beds. Har-Row.
I Think He Likes Me. Har-Row.
Journey to the Bright Kingdom. Holiday.
Marathon Miranda. Holiday.
Potbellied Possums. Holiday.
That's Mine. Holiday.

Winthrop, Henry.
xWinthrop, Henry.
The Humanistic Viewpoint in the Social Sciences. Mss Info.
Marginal Aspects of Contemporary American Culture. Mss Info.

Winthrop, John.
xWinthrop, John.
History of New England from 1630-1649. Arno.

Winthrop, Robert C. see Winthrop, Robert Charles.

Winthrop, Robert Charles, 1809-1894
xWinthrop, Robert C.
Life & Letters of John Winthrop. Da Capo.
Memoir of the Hon. Nathan Appleton, LL.D. Greenwood.

Winthrop, William. see Winthrop, William Woolsey.

Winthrop, William Woolsey, 1831-1899
xWinthrop, William.
Military Law & Precedents. Arno.

Winton, Calhoun.
xWinton, Calhoun.
Captain Steele: The Early Career of Richard Steele. Johns Hopkins.

Winton, Chester. see Winton, Chester A.

Winton, Chester A.
xWinton, Chester.
Theory & Measurement in Sociology. Schenkman.
xWinton, Chester A.
Theory & Measurement in Sociology. Halsted Pr.

Winton, F. R. see Winton, Frank Robert.

Winton, Frank Robert.
xWinton, F. R.
Human Physiology. Churchill.

Wintrobe, Maxwell M. see Wintrobe, Maxwell Myer.

Wintrobe, Maxwell Myer, 1901-
xWintrobe, Maxwell M.
Blood, Pure & Eloquent. McGraw.

Winward, Stephen F.
xWinward, Stephen F.
Guide to the Prophets. John Knox.

Winward, Walter.
xWinward, Walter.
Fives Wild. PB.
Hammerstrike. S&S.

Wippel, John F.
xWippel, John F.

ed. Medieval Philosophy: From St. Augustine to Nicholas of Cusa. Free Pr.

Wipper, Audrey.
xWipper, Audrey.
Rural Rebels: A Study of Two Protest Movements in Kenya. Oxford U Pr.

Wiren, Gary.
xWiren, Gary.
Golf. P-H.
The New Golf Mind. Golf Digest Bks.

Wirgman, Augustus T. see Wirgman, Augustus Theodore.

Wirgman, Augustus Theodore, 1846-1917
xWirgman, Augustus T.
History of the English Church & People in South Africa. Negro U Pr.

Wirsing, Marie E.
xWirsing, Marie E.
Teaching & Philosophy: A Synthesis. U Pr of Amer.

Wirsing, Robert.
xWirsing, Robert G.
Ancient India & Its Influence on Modern Times. Watts.
Socialist Society & Free Enterprise Politics: A Study of Voluntary Associations in Urban India. Carolina Acad Pr.

Wirsing, Robert G. see Wirsing, Robert.

Wirt, Frederick M.
xWirt, Frederick M.
Power in the City: Decision Making in San Francisco. U of Cal Pr.

Wirt, Sherwood E. see Wirt, Sherwood Eliot.

Wirt, Sherwood Eliot.
xWirt, Sherwood E.
Freshness of the Spirit. Har-Row.

Wirt, William, 1772-1834
xWirt, William.
Letters of the British Spy. Irvington.

Wirtenberg, Patricia Z.
xWirtenberg, Patricia Z.
The All-Around-the-House Art & Craft Book. HM.

Wirtenberger, Henry J.
xWirtenberger, Henry J.
Morality & Business. Loyola.

Wirth, Arthur G.
xWirth, Arthur G.
John Dewey As Educator: His Design for Work in Education (1894-1904). Krieger.

Wirth, John D.
xWirth, John D.
ed. Manchester & Sao Paulo: Problems of Rapid Urban Growth. Stanford U Pr.
The Politics of Brazilian Development, 1930-1954. Stanford U Pr.

Wirth, Louis, 1897-1952
xWirth, Louis.
Ghetto. U of Chicago Pr.

Wirth, Niklaus.
xWirth, Niklaus.
Systematic Programming: An Introduction. P-H.

Wirth, Willis W. see Wirth, Willis Wagner.

Wirth, Willis Wagner.
xWirth, Willis W.
A Review of the North American Leptoconops (Diptera : Ceratopogonidae). Tex Tech Pr.

Wirthwein, Walter G. see Wirthwein, Walter George.

Wirthwein, Walter George, 1900-
xWirthwein, Walter G.
Britain & the Balkan Crisis 1875-1878. AMS Pr.

Wirtz, Willard. see Wirtz, William Willard.

Wirtz, William Willard.
xWirtz, Willard.
The Boundless Resource: A Prospectus for an Education-Work Policy. New Republic.

Wisan, Joseph E. see Wisan, Joseph Ezra.

Wisan, Joseph Ezra, 1901-
xWisan, Joseph E.

Cuban Crisis As Reflected in the New York
Press, 1895-1898. Octagon.
Wischnitzer, S. *see* Wischnitzer, Saul.
Wischnitzer, Saul.
xWischnitzer, S.
Atlas & Laboratory Guide for Vertebrate
Embryology. McGraw.
Introduction to Electron Microscopy.
Pergamon.
xWischnitzer, Saul.
Outline of Human Anatomy. C C Thomas.
Wisconsin Univ. Dept. of Eng. *see* Wisconsin. University.
Dept. of English.
Wisconsin. University.
xWisconsin University.
Regionalism in America. Greenwood.
Wisconsin. University. Dept. of English.
xWisconsin Univ. Dept. of Eng.
ed. Shakespeare Studies. Folcroft.
Wisconsin. University-Madison. Land Tenure Center.
xLand Tenure Center.
Land Tenure & Agrarian Reform in Asia: An
Annotated Bibliography. G K Hall.
xLand Tenure Center, University of Wisconsin -
Madison.
Land Tenure & Agrarian Reform in Africa &
the Near East: An Annotated Bibliography.
G K Hall.
Wisdom, Aline C.
xWisdom, Aline C.
Introduction to Library Services for Library
Media Technical Assistants. McGraw.
Wisdom, John.
xWisdom, John.
Logical Constructions. Phila Bk Co.
Paradox & Discovery. Philos Lib.
Paradox & Discovery. U of Cal Pr.
Problems of Mind & Matter. Cambridge U Pr.
Wise, Alan F. *see* Wise, Alan Frederick Edward.
Wise, Alan Frederick Edward.
xWise, Alan F.
Water, Sanitary & Waste Services for Buildings.
Halsted Pr.
Wise, Arthur E.
xWise, Arthur E.
Legislated Learning: The Bureaucratization of
the American Classroom. U of Cal Pr.
Rich Schools, Poor Schools: The Promise of
Equal Educational Opportunity. U of Chicago
Pr.
Wise, Boyd A. *see* Wise, Boyd Ashby.
Wise, Boyd Ashby, 1874-
xWise, Boyd A.
Influence of Statius Upon Chaucer. Phaeton.
Influence of Statius Upon Chaucer. R West.
Wise, Burton L.
xWise, Burton L.
Preoperative & Postoperative Care in
Neurological Surgery. C C Thomas.
Wise, Claude M. *see* Wise, Claude Merton.
Wise, Claude Merton, 1887-
xWise, Claude M.
A Progressive Phonetic Workbook for Students
in Speech. Wm C Brown.
Wise County Historical Survey. Committee.
xWise County Historical Survey Committee.
History of Wise County: A Link with the Past.
Nortex Pr.
Wise, David.
xWise, David.
The American Police State: The Government
Against the People. Random.
The American Police State: The Government
Against the People. Random.
The Politics of Lying: Government Deception,
Secrecy, & Power. Random.
Wise, E. M. *see* Wise, Edward M.
Wise, Edward M.
xWise, E. M.

Studies in Comparative Criminal Law. C C
Thomas.
Wise, Henry A.
xWise, Henry A.
Drawing Out the Man: The VMI Story. U Pr
of Va.
Wise, Herbert.
xWise, Herbert H.
Living Places. Music Sales.
Wise, Herbert H. *see* Wise, Herbert.
Wise, Isaac. *see* Wise, Isaac Mayer.
Wise, Isaac Mayer.
xWise, Isaac.
Reminiscences. Arno.
Wise, John, 1652-1725
xWise, John.
Churches Quarrel Espoused, 1713. Schol
Facsimiles.
Wise, John S. *see* Wise, John Sergeant.
Wise, John Sergeant, 1846-1913
xWise, John S.
The Lion's Skin: A Historical Novel & a Novel
History. Arno.
Wise, Karen.
xWise, Karen.
God Knows I Won't Be Fat Again. Bantam.
God Knows I Wont Be Fat Again. Nelson.
Wise, Kensall D.
xWise, Kensall D.
Microcomputers: A Technology Forecast &
Assessment to the Year 2000. Wiley.
Wise, Leonard.
xWise, Leonard.
The Diggstown Ringers. Doubleday.
Wise, Robert. *see* Wise, Robert A.
Wise, Robert A.
xWise, Robert.
The Ghost Town Monster. EMC.
Wise, Robert A. *see* Wise, Robert Alexander.
Wise, Robert Alexander.
xWise, Robert A.
Surgery of the Head & Neck. Year Bk Med.
Wise, Robert E.
xWise, Robert E.
Accessory Digestive Organs. Year Bk Med.
Wise, T. J. *see* Wise, Thomas James.
Wise, Terence.
xWise, Terence.
Medieval Warfare. Hastings.
Wise, Thomas James, 1859-1937
xWise, T. J.
A Pope Library: A Catalogue of Plays, Poems
& Prose Writings by Alexander Pope.
Dawson Pub.
Wise, William.
xWise, William.
Animal Rescue: Saving Our Endangered
Wildlife. Putnam.
Fresh, Canned, & Frozen: Food from Past to
Future. Enslow Pubs.
Massacre at Mountain Meadows: An American
Legend & a Monumental Crime. T Y
Crowell.
Off We Go: A Book of Transportation. Enslow
Pubs.
xWise, William A.
Giant Birds & Monsters of the Air. Putnam.
Monsters from Outer Space?. Putnam.
Monsters of North America. Putnam.
Monsters of the Deep. Putnam.
Monsters of the Middle Ages. Putnam.
Wise, William A. *see* Wise, William.
Wiseman, Bernard.
xWiseman, Bernard.

Halloween with Morris & Boris. Schol Bk Serv.
illus. Halloween with Morris & Boris. Dodd.
illus. Hooray for Patsy's Oink!. Garrard.
Iglook's Seal. Dodd.
Little New Kangaroo. Macmillan.
illus. The Lucky Runner. Garrard.
illus. Morris Tells Boris Mother Moose Stories
& Rhymes. Dodd.
My Googoo. HR&W.
illus. Penny's Poodle Puppy, Pickle. Garrard.
illus. Quick Quackers. Garrard.
Wiseman, D. J. *see* Wiseman, Donald John.
Wiseman, Donald John.
xWiseman, D. J.
ed. Peoples of Old Testament Times. Oxford U
Pr.
Wiseman, H V.
xWiseman, H. V.
The Cabinet in the Commonwealth: Post-War
Developments in Africa, the West Indies &
South East Asia. Greenwood.
Wiseman, Jacqueline P.
xWiseman, Jacqueline P.
People As Partners. Har-Row.
Stations of the Lost: The Treatment of Skid
Row Alcoholics. U of Chicago Pr.
Wiseman, P. *see* Wiseman, Peter.
Wiseman, Peter.
xWiseman, P.
Introduction to Industrial Organic Chemistry.
Intl Ideas.
Wiseman, Robert, 1942-
xWiseman, Robert.
Spatial Aspects of Aging. Assn Am
Geographers.
Wiseman, Robert F.
xWiseman, Robert F.
The Complete Horseshoeing Guide. U of Okla
Pr.
Wiseman, T. P. *see* Wiseman, Timothy Peter.
Wiseman, Thomas.
xWiseman, Thomas.
A Game of Secrets. Delacorte.
xWiseman, Tom.
A Game of Secrets. Dell.
Wiseman, Timothy Peter.
xWiseman, T. P.
Cinna, the Poet & Other Roman Essays.
Humanities.
Wiseman, Tom. *see* Wiseman, Thomas.
Wisenthal, J. L.
xWisenthal, J. L.
The Marriage of Contraries: Bernard Shaw's
Middle Plays. Harvard U Pr.
Wiser, Charlotte Melina Viall.
xWiser, Charlotte V.
Four Families of Karimpur. Maxwell Schl
Citizen.
Wiser, Charlotte V. *see* Wiser, Charlotte Melina Viall.
Wish, Harvey, 1909-
xWish, Harvey.
George Fitzhugh: Propagandist of the Old
South. Peter Smith.
Wish, John R.
xWish, John R.
The Consumer: The Art of Buying Wisely.
P-H.
Wishard, Armin.
xWishard, Armin.
Noch Einmal Spiel & Sprache. Norton.
Wishard, Laurie.
xWishard, Laurie.
Adoption: The Grafted Tree. Caroline Hse.
Adoption: The Grafted Tree. Cragmont Pubns.
Wishard, William R., 1930-
xWishard, William R.

Credit & Borrowing in Illinois. Cragmont
Pubns.
Credit & Borrowing in New York. Cragmont
Pubns.
Credit & Borrowing in Texas: Consumers'
Rights & Duties. Cragmont Pubns.
Rights of the Elderly & Retired: A Peoples'
Handbook. Cragmont Pubns.
Wishart, Barry J.
xWishart, Barry J.
Modern Sociological Issues. Macmillan.
Wishart, David J., 1946-
xWishart, David J.
The Fur Trade of the American West,
1807-1840: A Geographical Synthesis. U of
Nebr Pr.
Wishlade, R. L.
xWishlade, R. L.
Sectarianism in Southern Nyasaland. Oxford U
Pr.
Wisland, Milton V.
xWisland, Milton V.
Psychoeducational Diagnosis of Exceptional
Children. C C Thomas.
Wisler, Chester O. see Wisler, Chester Owen.
Wisler, Chester Owen.
xWisler, Chester O.
Hydrology. Wiley.
Wisler, G. Clifton.
xWisler, G. Clifton.
My Brother the Wind. Doubleday.
Wismer, D. A. see Wismer, David A.
Wismer, David. see Wismer, David Cassel.
Wismer, David A., 1938-
xWismer, D. A.
Optimization Methods for Large-Scale Systems
with Applications. McGraw.
Wismer, David Cassel, 1857-
xWismer, David.
The Obsolete Bank Notes of New England,
1922. Quarterman.
Wisner, Elizabeth.
xWisner, Elizabeth.
Public Welfare Administration in Louisiana.
Arno.
Social Welfare in the South from Colonial
Times to World War I. La State U Pr.
Wispe, Lauren.
xWispe, Lauren G.
ed. Altruism, Sympathy & Helping:
Psychological & Sociological Principles. Acad
Pr.
Wispe, Lauren G. see Wispe, Lauren.
Wisse, Ruth R.
xWisse, Ruth R.
A Shtetl & Other Yiddish Novellas. Behrman.
Wissenschaftliche Konferenz der Gesellschaft Deutscher
Naturforscher und Aerzte, 4th, Berlin, 1967. see
Gesellschaft Deutscher Naturforscher und Arzte.
Wissler, Clark, 1870-1947
xWissler, Clark.
The Indians of Greater New York & the Lower
Hudson. AMS Pr.
Material Culture of the Blackfoot Indians.
AMS Pr.
North American Indians of the Plains. B
Franklin.
Relation of Nature to Man in Aboriginal
America. AMS Pr.
ed. Societies of the Plains Indians. AMS Pr.
Wissowa, Georg, 1859-1931
xWissowa, Georg.
Gesammelte Abhandlungen Zur Romischen
Religions und Stadtgeschichte. Arno.
Wister, Frances A. see Wister, Frances Anne.
Wister, Frances Anne.
xWister, Frances A.

Twenty-Five Years of the Philadelphia
Orchestra, 1900-1925. Arno.
Wister, Owen, 1860-1938
xWister, Owen.
Lin McLean. Irvington.
Wistrich, Robert S., 1945-
xWistrich, Robert S.
Revolutionary Jews from Marx to Trotsky.
B&N.
Wiswell, Glenn.
xWiswell, Glenn.
Date Nails Complete. Wesis Pubns.
Wit, Dorothy de. see De Wit, Dorothy.
Witanowski, M.
xWitanowski, M.
ed. Nitrogen NMR. Plenum Pub.
Witchell, Nicholas.
xWitchell, Nicholas.
The Loch Ness Story. State Mutual Bk.
Witcover, Jules.
xWitcover, Jules.
The Main Chance. Viking Pr.
Marathon: The Pursuit of the Presidency
1972-1976. NAL.
Witemeyer, Hugh.
xWitemeyer, Hugh.
George Eliot & the Visual Arts. Yale U Pr.
Witham, A. Calhoun. see Witham, Abner Calhoun.
Witham, Abner Calhoun, 1921-
xWitham, A. Calhoun.
A System of Vectorcardiographic
Interpretation. Year Bk Med.
Witham, Francis H.
xWitham, Francis H.
Experiments in Plant Physiology. Van Nos
Reinhold.
Witham, W. Tasker.
xWitham, W. Tasker.
The Adolescent in the American Novel:
1920-1960. Ungar.
Wither, George, 1588-1667
xWither, George.
A Collection of Emblemes, Ancient &
Moderne (1635). U of SC Pr.
Hymnes & Songs of the Church. B Franklin.
Paralellogrammaton. B Franklin.
Preparation to the Psalter. B Franklin.
Witherell, Warren.
xWitherell, Warren.
How the Racers Ski. Norton.
Withers, Alexander S. see Withers, Alexander Scott.
Withers, Alexander Scott, 1792-1865
xWithers, Alexander S.
Chronicles of Border Warfare. McClain.
Withers, Carl.
xWithers, Carl.
American Riddle Book. Abelard.
Plainville, U. S. A.. Greenwood.
Riddles of Many Lands. Abelard.
Withers, E. N. see Withers, F. N.
Withers, F. N.
xWithers, E. N.
Standards for Library Service: An International
Survey. Unipub.
Withers, Percy, 1867-1945
xWithers, Percy.
Buried Life: Personal Recollections of A. E.
Housman. Folcroft.
A Buried Life: Personal Recollections of A. E.
Housman. Gordon Pr.
Withers, Richard S. see Withers, Richard Stacy.
Withers, Richard Stacy.
xWithers, Richard S.
Transport of Charged Aerosols. Garland Pub.
Withers, William, 1905-
xWithers, William.

Business in Society: An Introduction to
Business. Irvington.
The Corporations & Social Change. Barron.
Crisis in Old Age Finance. Barron.
Witherspoon, Alexander M. see Witherspoon, Alexander
Maclaren.
Witherspoon, Alexander Maclaren, 1894-
xWitherspoon, Alexander M.
ed. College Survey of English Literature.
HarBraceJ.
Common Errors in English & How to Avoid
Them. Littlefield.
Influence of Robert Garnier on Elizabethan
Drama. Phaeton.
Influence of Robert Garnier on Elizabethan
Drama. Shoe String.
Witherspoon, Gary.
xWitherspoon, Gary.
Navajo Kinship & Marriage. U of Chicago Pr.
Witherspoon, Joseph P. see Witherspoon, Joseph Parker.
Witherspoon, Joseph Parker.
xWitherspoon, Joseph P.
Administrative Implementation of Civil Rights.
U of Tex Pr.
Withey, Stephen B. see Withey, Stephen Bassett.
Withey, Stephen Bassett.
xWithey, Stephen B.
ed. Television & Social Behavior: Beyond
Violence & Children. L Erlbaum Assocs.
Withington, Frederic G.
xWithington, Frederic G.
Environment for Systems Programs. A-W.
Withington, W. A. see Withington, William A.
Withington, William A.
xWithington, W. A.
ed. Southeast Asia. Fideler.
Withycombe, E. G. see Withycombe, Elizabeth Gidley.
Withycombe, Elizabeth Gidley, 1902-
xWithycombe, E. G.
The Oxford Dictionary of English Christian
Names. Oxford U Pr.
The Oxford Dictionary of English Christian
Names. Oxford U Pr.
Witkiewicz, Stanisaw Ignacy, 1885-1939
xWitkiewicz, Stanislaw I.
Insatiability: A Novel in Two Parts. U of Ill Pr.
Witkiewicz, Stanislaw I. see Witkiewicz, Stanisaw Ignacy.
Witkin, Lee D.
xWitkin, Lee D.
The Photograph Collector's Guide. NYGS.
Witkov, Harold.
xWitkov, Harold.
Antichrist & World Destiny Revealed. Libra.
Witkowski, Edward.
xWitkowski, Edward.
Economics of Agricultural Production. Alfred
Pub.
Witmark, Isidore.
xWitmark, Isidore.
Story of the House of Witmark: From Ragtime
to Swingtime. Da Capo.
Witmer, Helen E. see Witmer, Helen Elizabeth.
Witmer, Helen Elizabeth, 1903-
xWitmer, Helen E.
Property Qualifications of Members of
Parliament. AMS Pr.
Witmer, Lightner, 1867-
xWitmer, Lightner.
The Nearing Case: The Limitation of Academic
Freedom at the University of Pennsylvania
by Act of the Board of Trustees June 14,
1915. Rothman.
Witt, Elmer N.
xWitt, Elmer N.
Life Can Be Sexual. Concordia.
Witt, Glen L.
xWitt, Glen L.

Boat Building with Plywood. Glen-L Marine.
How to Build Boat Trailers. Glen-L Marine.

Witt, Harold.
xWitt, Harold.
Winesburg by the Sea: Poems. Thorp Springs.

Witt, Matt.
xWitt, Matt.
In Our Blood: Four Coal Mining Families.
Highlander.

Witt, Scott.
xWitt, Scott.
How Self-Made Millionaires Build Their
Fortunes. P-H.
How to Make Big Money at Home in Your
Spare Time. P-H.
How to Make Big Profits in Service Businesses.
P-H.

Witt, Shirley H. *see* Witt, Shirley Hill.

Witt, Shirley Hill.
xWitt, Shirley H.
The Tuscaroras. Macmillan.

Witte, Edwin E. *see* Witte, Edwin Emil.

Witte, Edwin Emil, 1887-1960
xWitte, Edwin E.
The Government in Labor Disputes. Arno.

Witte, John, 1948-
xWitte, John C.
Loving the Days. Columbia U Pr.

Witte, John C. *see* Witte, John.

Witte, Kaaren.
xWitte, Kaaren.
Angels in Faded Jeans. Bethany Fell.
Angels in Faded Jeans. Jeremy Bks.

Wittels, Harriet.
xWittels, Harriet.
The Perfect Speller. G&D.
Things I Hate. Human Sci Pr.

Wittels, Mike.
xWittels, Mike.
Advice for Conscientious Objectors in the
Armed Forces. CCCO.

Witten, David M.
xWitten, David M.
Breast. Year Bk Med.

Wittenberg, Judith B. *see* Wittenberg, Judith Bryant.

Wittenberg, Judith Bryant, 1938-
xWittenberg, Judith B.
Faulkner: The Transfiguration of Biography. U
of Nebr Pr.

Wittenberg, Philip, 1895-
xWittenberg, Philip.
The Protection of Literary Property. Writer.

Wittenborn, Dirk.
xWittenborn, Dirk.
Eclipse. Dodd.
Eclipse. Playboy Pbks.

Wittenborn, J. R. *see* Wittenborn, John Richard.

Wittenborn, John Richard.
xWittenborn, J. R.
ed. Psychopharmacology & the Individual
Patient. Raven.

Witter, Evelyn.
xWitter, Evelyn.
Claw Foot. Lerner Pubns.
The Mystery of Animal Haven. Childrens.
The Mystery of the Music in the Night.
Childrens.
The Mystery of the Red-Eyed Camel Pin.
Childrens.

Witters, Weldon L.
xWitters, Weldon L.
Drugs & Sex. Macmillan.
Environmental Biology: The Human Factor.
Kendall Hunt.

Wittes, Simon.
xWittes, Simon.
People & Power: A Study of Crisis in
Secondary Schools. U of Mich Soc Res.

Wittfogel, Karl A. *see* Wittfogel, Karl August.

Wittfogel, Karl August, 1896-
xWittfogel, Karl A.
Oriental Despotism: A Comparative Study of
Total Power. Yale U Pr.

Wittgenstein, Ludwig.
xWittgenstein, Ludwig.
On Certainty. Har-Row.
Prototractatus: An Early Version of Tractatus
Logico-Philosophicus. Cornell U Pr.
Remarks on Frazer's Golden Bough.
Humanities.
Remarks on the Foundations of Mathematics.
MIT Pr.

Witthuhn, Burton O.
xWitthuhn, Burton O.
Discovery in Geography. Kendall-Hunt.

Wittig, Alice J., 1929-
xWittig, J. Alice.
U. S. Government Publications for the School
Media Center. Libs Unl.

Wittig, J. Alice. *see* Wittig, Alice J.

Wittig, Michele A. *see* Wittig, Michele Andrisin.

Wittig, Michele Andrisin.
xWittig, Michele A.
ed. Sex Related Differences in Cognitive
Functioning: Developmental Issues. Acad Pr.

Wittig, Monique.
xWittig, Monique.
The Lesbian Body. Avon.
The Lesbian Body. Morrow.
The Opoponax. Daughters.
Opoponax. S&S.

Wittig, Susan.
xWittig, Susan.
Steps to Structure: An Introduction to
Composition & Rhetoric. Winthrop.
Stylistic & Narrative Structures in the Middle
English Romances. U of Tex Pr.

Witting, Clifford.
xWitting, Clifford.
Measure for Murder. Garland Pub.

Wittke, Carl. *see* Wittke, Carl Frederick.

Wittke, Carl F. *see* Wittke, Carl Frederick.

Wittke, Carl Frederick, 1892-1971
xWittke, Carl.
History of English Parliamentary Privilege. Da
Capo.
xWittke, Carl F.
Tambo & Bones: A History of the American
Minstrel Stage. Greenwood.
xWittke, K.
The German Language Press in America.
Haskell.

Wittke, K. *see* Wittke, Carl Frederick.

Wittkower, Rudolf.
xWittkower, Rudolf.
Architectural Principles in the Age of
Humanism. Norton.
Art & Architecture in Italy 1600-1750.
Penguin.
Art & Architecture in Italy: 1600-1750. Viking
Pr.
ed. Baroque Art: The Jesuit Contribution.
Fordham.
Gothic Vs. Classic: Architectural Projects in
Seventeenth-Century Italy. Braziller.
Idea & Image: Studies in the Italian
Renaissance. Thames Hudson.
Palladio & Palladianism. Braziller.

Wittlich, Gary. *see* Wittlich, Gary E.

Wittlich, Gary E.
xWittlich, Gary.
Ear Training: An Approach Through Music
Literature. HarBraceJ.

Wittman, Harry H.
xWittman, Harry H.
The Eyeglasses & the Quarter. Denison.

Wittman, Sally.
xWittman, Sally.
Pelly & Peak. Har-Row.
A Special Trade. Har-Row.

Wittner, Lawrence S.
xWittner, Lawrence S.
Cold War America: From Hiroshima to
Watergate. HR&W.

Witton, Dorothy.
xWitton, Dorothy.
Our World: Mexico. Messner.

Wittreich, Joseph A. *see* Wittreich, Joseph Anthony.

Wittreich, Joseph Anthony.
xWittreich, Joseph A.
Angel of Apocalypse: Blake's Idea of Milton.
U of Wis Pr.
Visionary Poetics: Milton's Tradition & His
Legacy. Huntington Lib.

Wittrock, Merl. *see* Wittrock, Merlin C.

Wittrock, Merlin C.
xWittrock, Merl.
The Human Brain. P-H.

Wittschiebe, Charles E.
xWittschiebe, Charles E.
God Invented Sex. Southern Pub.

Wittwer, S. H. *see* Wittwer, Sylvan Harold.

Wittwer, Sylvan Harold.
xWittwer, S. H.
Greenhouse Tomatoes, Lettuce & Cucumbers.
Mich St U Pr.

Witty, Paul. *see* Witty, Paul Andrew.

Witty, Paul A. *see* Witty, Paul Andrew.

Witty, Paul Andrew.
xWitty, Paul.
How to Become a Better Reader. SRA.
xWitty, Paul A.
ed. Educationally Retarded & Disadvantaged.
U of Chicago Pr.
ed. Reading for the Gifted & the Creative
Student. Intl Reading.
Teaching of Reading: A Developmental
Process. Heath.

Witzky, Herbert K.
xWitzky, Herbert K.
Modern Hotel-Motel Management Methods.
Hayden.
Practical Hotel-Motel Cost Reduction
Handbook. Hayden.

Wixman, Ronald, 1947-
xWixman, Ronald.
Language Aspects of Ethnic Patterns &
Processes in the North Caucasus. U Chicago
Dept Geog.

Wixon, Rufus, 1911-
xWixon, Rufus.
ed. Accountants' Handbook. Ronald Pr.
Principles of Accounting. Wiley.

WMCA. *see* WMCA Call for Action.

WMCA Call for Action.
xWMCA.
Call for Action: A Survival Kit for New
Yorkers. Times Bks.

WMO Executive Committee, 26th Session. *see* World
Meteorological Organization. Executive Committee.

Wobschall, Darold.
xWobschall, Darold.
Circuit Design for Electronic Instrumentation:
Analog & Digital Devices from Sensor to
Display. McGraw.

Wobst, Susan.
xWobst, Susan.
Russian Readings & Grammar Terminology.
Slavica.

Woddis, Jack.
xWoddis, Jack.
Armies & Politics. Intl Pub Co.
Armies in Politics. Beekman Pubs.
Introduction to Neo-Colonialism. Intl Pub Co.

Wodehouse, Lawrence.
xWodehouse, Lawrence.

ed. American Architects from the Civil War to
the First World War: A Guide to Information
Sources. Gale.

ed. Indigenous Architecture Worldwide: A
Guide to Information Sources. Gale.

Wodehouse, P. G. *see* Wodehouse, Pelham Grenville.

Wodehouse, Pelham Grenville, 1881-
xWodehouse, P. G.
Bachelors Anonymous. G K Hall.
Bachelors Anonymous. S&S.
The Code of the Woosters. Random.
Do Butlers Burgle Banks. S&S.
Fish Preferred. S&S.
Girl in Blue. S&S.
Leave It to P. Smith. Random.
Lord Emsworth & Others. Penguin.
Mulliner Nights. Random.
Sunset at Blandings. S&S.
The Swoop & Other Stories. Continuum.
Uncle Fred in the Springtime. Penguin.
The Uncollected Wodehouse. Continuum.
World of Jeeves. Manor Bks.
The World of Mr. Mulliner. Avon.
The World of Mr. Mulliner. Taplinger.

Woditsch, Gary A.
xWoditsch, Gary A.
Developing Generic Skills: A Model for
Competency-Based General Education.
General Stud Res.

Woelfel, Charles J.
xWoelfel, Charles J.
Accounting: An Introduction. Goodyear.

Woelfel, James W.
xWoelfel, James W.
Augustinian Humanism: Studies in Human
Bondage & Earthly Grace. U Pr of Amer.

Woelfl Genevieve.
xWoelfl, Genevieve.
Psychic Experience: An Introduction to
Spiritualism. Redwood.

Woelfl, Paul.
xWoelfl, Paul.
Politics & Jurisprudence. Loyola.

Woelfle, Robert M.
xWoelfle, Robert M.
ed. A Guide for Better Technical Presentations.
Inst Electrical.

Woerkom, Dorothy Van. *see* Van Woerkom, Dorothy.

Woerkom, Dorothy O. Van. *see* Van Woerkom, Dorothy
O.

Woerkom, Dorothy Van. *see* Van Woerkom, Dorothy.

Woessner, Nina C.
xWoessner, Nina C.
How It Is. Allyn.
On the Spot. Allyn.

Woessner, Warren.
xWoessner, Warren.
No Hiding Place. Spoon Riv Poetry.

Woestehoff, Ellsworth S.
xWoestehoff, Ellsworth S.
Students with Reading Disabilities & Guidance.
HM.

Wofford, Azile, 1896-
xWofford, Azile.
Book Selection for School Libraries. Wilson.

Wofford, Philip.
xWofford, Philip.
Grand Canyon Search Ceremony. Barlenmir.

Wogaman, J. Philip.
xWogaman, J. Philip.
A Christian Method of Moral Judgment.
Westminster.
The Great Economic Debate: An Ethical
Analysis. Westminster.
xWogaman, Philip J.
ed. Population Crisis & Moral Responsibility.
Pub Aff Pr.

Wogaman, Philip J. *see* Wogaman, J. Philip.

Wohl, Anthony S.
xWohl, Anthony S.

The Eternal Slum: Housing & Social Policy in
Victorian London. McGill-Queens U Pr.

Wohl, Gary.
xWohl, Gary.
jt. auth. The Joy of Quitting: How to Help
Young People Stop Smoking. Macmillan.

Wohl, Gerald.
xWohl, Gerald.
Structured COBOL: A Direct Approach. SRA.

Wohl, Hellmut.
xWohl, Hellmut.
Leonardo Da Vinci. McGraw.

Wohl, Milton.
xWohl, Milton.
Techniques for Writing: Composition. Newbury
Hse.

Wohl, Robert.
xWohl, Robert.
French Communism in the Making, 1914-1924.
Stanford U Pr.

Wohlers, M. Ronald.
xWohlers, Ronald W.
Lumped & Distributed Passive Networks: A
Generalized & Advanced Viewpoint. Acad
Pr.

Wohlers, Ronald W. *see* Wohlers, M. Ronald.

Wohlking, Wallace.
xWohlking, Wallace.
Role Playing. Educ Tech Pubns.

Wohlrabe, Raymond A.
xWohlrabe, Raymond A.
illus. Exploring the World of Leaves. T Y
Crowell.

Woite, G.
xWoite, G.
ed. Economic Evaluation of Bids for Nuclear
Power Plants: A Guidebook. Unipub.

Wojciechowska, Maia.
xWojciechowska, Maia.
The Life & Death of a Brave Bull. HarBraceJ.

Wojciechowski, B. W. *see* Wojciechowski, Bohdan
Wieslaw.

Wojciechowski, Bohdan Wieslaw, 1935-
xWojciechowski, B. W.
Chemical Kinetics for Chemical Engineers.
Sterling Swift.

Wojcik, Jan.
xWojcik, Jan.
Muted Consent: A Casebook in Modern
Medical Ethics. Purdue Res Foun.

Wojslaw, Charles F.
xWojslaw, Charles F.
Integrated Circuits: Theory & Applications.
Reston.

Wolanin, Thomas R., 1942-
xWolanin, Thomas R.
Presidential Advisory Commissions: Truman to
Nixon. U of Wis Pr.

Wolansky, William D.
xWolansky, William D.
Fundamentals of Fluid Power. HM.

Wolberg, Arlene R. *see* Wolberg, Arlene Robbins.

Wolberg, Arlene Robbins.
xWolberg, Arlene R.
The Borderline Patient. Thieme-Stratton.

Wolberg, J. *see* Wolberg, John R.

Wolberg, John R.
xWolberg, J.
Application of Computers to Engineering
Analysis. McGraw.

Wolberg, Lewis R. *see* Wolberg, Lewis Robert.

Wolberg, Lewis Robert, 1905-
xWolberg, Lewis R.

Art Forms from Photomicrography. Dover.
The Dynamics of Personality. Grune.
Handbook of Short-Term Psychotherapy.
Thieme-Stratton.
Hypnoanalysis. Grune.

Wolchonok, Louis.
xWolchonok, Louis.
Art of Three Dimensional Design: How to
Create Space Figures. Dover.
Art of Three-Dimensional Design: How to
Create Space Figures. Peter Smith.

Wolcott, Carolyn M. *see* Wolcott, Carolyn Muller.

Wolcott, Carolyn Muller.
xWolcott, Carolyn M.
I Can See What God Does. Abingdon.

Wolcott, H. F. *see* Wolcott, Harry F.

Wolcott, Harry F., 1929-
xWolcott, H. F.
The African Beer Gardens of Bulawayo:
Integrated Drinking in a Segregated Society.
Rutgers Ctr Alcohol.
xWolcott, Harry F.
Teachers Versus Technocrats: An Educational
Innovation in Anthropological Perspective.
Ctr Educ Policy Mgmt.

Wolcott, Patty.
xWolcott, Patty.
The Cake Story. A-W.
Double-Decker, Double-Decker,
Double-Decker Bus. A-W.
The Dragon & the Wild Fandango. A-W.
The Forest Fire. A-W.
I'm Going to New York to Visit the Queen.
A-W.
The Marvelous Mud Washing Machine. A-W.
Super Sam & the Salad Garden. A-W.
Tunafish Sandwiches. A-W.

Wold, Allen.
xWold, Allen.
The Planet Masters. St Martin.
Star God. St Martin.

Wold, Erling.
xWold, Erling.
Thanks for the Mountain. Augsburg.

Wold, Margaret. *see* Wold, Marge.

Wold, Marge.
xWold, Margaret.
The Critical Moment: How Personal Crisis Can
Enrich a Woman's Life. Augsburg.

Wold, Milo. *see* Wold, Milo Arlington.

Wold, Milo Arlington.
xWold, Milo.
An Introduction to Music & Art in the
Western World. Wm C Brown.

Wolde, Gunilla, 1939-
xWolde, Gunilla.
Betsy & the Doctor. Random.

Woldin, Beth W. *see* Woldin, Beth Weiner.

Woldin, Beth Weiner, 1955-
xWoldin, Beth W.
illus. Ellie to the Rescue. Warne.

Woldman, Albert A.
xWoldman, Albert A.
Lincoln & the Russians. Greenwood.

Wolenik, Robert.
xWolenik, Robert.
Buying & Selling Currency for Profit. Contemp
Bks.

Wolf, Aline D.
xWolf, Aline D.
A Parents' Guide to the Montessori Classroom.
Montessori Learn.

Wolf, Alvin, 1935-
xWolf, Alvin.
Lobbies & Lobbyists: In Whose Best Interest?.
Allyn.
Participation, Protest & Apathy: A Question of
Involvement?. Allyn.

Wolf, Arthur P.
xWolf, Arthur P.

ed. Studies in Chinese Society. Stanford U Pr.
Wolf, Bernard.
  xWolf, Bernard.
    Anna's Silent World. Lippincott.
    illus. Connie's New Eyes. Lippincott.
    Connie's New Eyes. Archway.
    Connie's New Eyes. PB.
    photos by Don't Feel Sorry for Paul.
      Lippincott.
Wolf, C. *see* Wolf, Charles.
Wolf, Carolyn E.
  xWolf, Carolyn E.
    Indians of North & South America: A
      Bibliography Based on the Collection at the
      Willard E. Yager Library-Museum Hartwick
      College, Oneonta, N.Y.. Scarecrow.
Wolf, Charles.
  xWolf, C.
    Foreign Aid: Theory & Practice in Southern
      Asia. Princeton U Pr.
Wolf, Charlotte.
  xWolf, Charlotte.
    Garrison Community: A Study of an Overseas
      American Military Colony. Greenwood.
Wolf, Christa.
  xWolf, Christa.
    A Model Childhood. FS&G.
Wolf, Dave.
  xWolf, Dave.
    Amazing Baseball Teams. Random.
    Great Moments in Pro Basketball. Random.
Wolf, Deborah G. *see* Wolf, Deborah Goleman.
Wolf, Deborah Goleman.
  xWolf, Deborah G.
    The Lesbian Community. U of Cal Pr.
Wolf, Donald J.
  xWolf, Donald J.
    Toward Consensus: Catholic-Protestant
      Interpretations of Church & State. Peter
      Smith.
Wolf, Eric. *see* Wolf, Eric Robert.
Wolf, Eric R. *see* Wolf, Eric Robert.
Wolf, Eric Robert.
  xWolf, Eric.
    Sons of the Shaking Earth. U of Chicago Pr.
  xWolf, Eric R.
    The Human Condition in Latin America.
      Oxford U Pr.
    Peasant Wars of the Twentieth Century.
      Har-Row.
    Peasants. P-H.
    ed. The Valley of Mexico: Studies in
      Pre-Hispanic Ecology & Society. U of NM
      Pr.
Wolf, Frederick A. *see* Wolf, Frederick Adolph.
Wolf, Frederick Adolph.
  xWolf, Frederick A.
    Fungi. Hafner.
  xWolf, Frederick T.
    jt. auth. Fungi. Hafner.
Wolf, Frederick T. *see* Wolf, Frederick Adolph.
Wolf, G. A. *see* Wolf, George Anthony.
Wolf, Gary K.
  xWolf, Gary K.
    The Resurrectionist. Doubleday.
Wolf, George Anthony, 1914-
  xWolf, G. A.
    Collecting Data from Patients. Univ Park.
Wolf, H. F. *see* Wolf, Helmut F.
Wolf, Harold A. *see* Wolf, Harold Arthur.
Wolf, Harold Arthur, 1923-
  xWolf, Harold A.
    Personal Finance. Allyn.
Wolf, Helmut F.
  xWolf, H. F.
    Silicon Semiconductor Data. Pergamon.
Wolf, Herbert, 1938-
  xWolf, Herbert.
    Haggai & Malachi. Moody.
Wolf, Howard. *see* Wolf, Howard R.

Wolf, Howard R., 1936-
  xWolf, Howard.
    Forgive the Father: A Memoir of Changing
      Generations. New Republic.
Wolf, J. B. *see* Wolf, John Baptist.
Wolf, Jack.
  xWolf, Jack.
    Professional Picture Framing for the Amateur.
      TAB Bks.
Wolf, Jerome.
  xWolf, Jerome.
    Ferment in Labor. Glencoe.
Wolf, John. *see* Wolf, John C.
Wolf, John Baptist, 1907-
  xWolf, J. B.
    The Diplomatic History of the Bagdad
      Railroad. Octagon.
Wolf, John C.
  xWolf, John.
    The Minolta Guide. Amphoto.
  xWolf, John C.
    The Nikon Guide. Amphoto.
Wolf, John Q. *see* Wolf, John Quincy.
Wolf, John Quincy.
  xWolf, John Q.
    ed. Life in the Leatherwoods. Memphis St
      Univ.
Wolf, Joseph. *see* Wolf, Joseph Albert.
Wolf, Joseph A. *see* Wolf, Joseph Albert.
Wolf, Joseph Albert, 1936-
  xWolf, Joseph.
    Classification & Fourier Inversion for Parabolic
      Subgroups with Square Integrable Nilradical
      Memoirs. Am Math.
  xWolf, Joseph A.
    Spaces of Constant Curvature. Publish or
      Perish.
Wolf, Leonard.
  xWolf, Leonard.
    Wolf's Complete Book of Terror. Potter.
Wolf, Morris P. *see* Wolf, Morris Philip.
Wolf, Morris Philip.
  xWolf, Morris P.
    Effective Communication in Business. SW Pub.
Wolf, Richard M.
  xWolf, Richard M.
    Evaluation in Education: Foundations of
      Competency Assessment & Program Review.
      Praeger.
Wolf, Simon, 1836-1923
  xWolf, Simon.
    The American Jew As Patriot, Soldier, &
      Citizen. Irvington.
Wolf, Stanley, 1943-
  xWolf, Stanley.
    Guide to Electronic Measurements &
      Laboratory Practice. P-H.
Wolf, Stewart. *see* Wolf, Stewart George.
Wolf, Stewart George, 1914-
  xWolf, Stewart.
    ed. Abdominal Diagnosis. Lea & Febiger.
    Occupational Health As Human Ecology. C C
      Thomas.
Wolf, Theta. *see* Wolf, Theta Holmes.
Wolf, Theta H. *see* Wolf, Theta Holmes.
Wolf, Theta Holmes, 1904-
  xWolf, Theta.
    The Effect of Praise & Competition on the
      Persisting Behavior of Kindergarten Children.
      Greenwood.
  xWolf, Theta H.
    The Effect of Praise & Competition on the
      Persisting Behavior of Kindergarten Children.
      Norwood Edns.
Wolf, W. J. *see* Wolf, Walter James.
Wolf, Walter James.
  xWolf, W. J.
    Soybeans As a Food Source. CRC Pr.
Wolf, William.
  xWolf, William.

    Landmark Films: The Cinema & Our Century.
      Paddington.
Wolf, William B.
  xWolf, William B.
    Conversations with Chester I. Barnard. NY Sch
      Indus Rel.
    ed. Top Management of the Personnel
      Function: Current Issues & Practices. NY
      Sch Indus Rel.
Wolf, William J.
  xWolf, William J.
    Freedom's Holy Light: American Identity &
      the Future of Theology. Parameter Pr.
    Lincoln's Religion. Pilgrim NY.
Wolfart, H. Christoph.
  xWolfart, Hans C.
    Plains Cree: A Grammatical Study. Am Philos.
Wolfart, Hans C. *see* Wolfart, H. Christoph.
Wolfbein, Seymour L. *see* Wolfbein, Seymour Louis.
Wolfbein, Seymour Louis, 1915-
  xWolfbein, Seymour L.
    Occupational Information: A Career Guidance
      View. Phila Bk Co.
    Work in American Society. Scott F.
Wolfe, A. G. *see* Wolfe, Ann G.
Wolfe, Alan, 1942-
  xWolfe, Alan.
    The Limits of Legitimacy: Political
      Contradictions of Contemporary Capitalism.
      Free Pr.
Wolfe, Ann G.
  xWolfe, A. G.
    ed. A Reader in Jewish Community Relations.
      Ktav.
Wolfe, Arthur D.
  xWolfe, Arthur D.
    Legal Perspectives of American Business
      Associations. Grid Pub.
Wolfe, Bernard.
  xWolfe, Bernard.
    Come on Out, Daddy. Boulevard.
Wolfe, Bertram D. *see* Wolfe, Bertram David.
Wolfe, Bertram David, 1896-
  xWolfe, Bertram D.
    Fabulous Life of Diego Rivera. Stein & Day.
    Ideology in Power: Reflections on the Russian
      Revolution. Stein & Day.
    A Life in Two Centuries. Stein & Day.
Wolfe, Betty.
  xWolfe, Betty.
    The Banner Book. Morehouse.
Wolfe, Burton H.
  xWolfe, Burton H.
    The Devil & Dr. Noxin. Wild West Pub.
    Hitler & the Nazis. Putnam.
Wolfe, Carvel S.
  xWolfe, Carvel S.
    Linear Programming with Fortran. Scott F.
Wolfe, Don M. *see* Wolfe, Don Marion.
Wolfe, Don Marion, 1902-
  xWolfe, Don M.
    ed. Leveller Manifestoes of the Puritan
      Revolution. Humanities.
Wolfe, Fred. *see* Wolfe, Frederick L.
Wolfe, Frederick L.
  xWolfe, Fred.
    The Bicycle: A Commuting Alternative.
      Signpost Bk Pub.
Wolfe, Gary K., 1946-
  xWolfe, Gary K.
    The Known & the Unknown: The Iconography
      of Science Fiction. Kent St U Pr.
Wolfe, Gene.
  xWolfe, Gene.
    The Devil in a Forest. Follett.
    The Shadow of the Torturer. S&S.
Wolfe, Howe, De M. *see* Howe, M. De Wolfe.
Wolfe Howe, M De. *see* Howe, M. De Wolfe.
Wolfe, Humbert, 1885-1940
  xWolfe, Humbert.

Dialogues & Monologues. Arno.
Dialogues & Monologues. Kennikat.
Dialogues & Monologues. R West.
George Moore. Arno.
George Moore. Folcroft.
Notes on English Verse Satire. Folcroft.

Wolfe, Kenneth C.
xWolfe, Kenneth C.
Cooking for the Professional Chef. Van Nos
Reinhold.

Wolfe, Linda.
xWolfe, Linda.
Cooking of the Caribbean Islands. Time-Life.
Cooking of the Caribbean Islands. Silver.
Private Practices. S&S.

Wolfe, Linnie M. *see* Wolfe, Linnie Marsh.

Wolfe, Linnie Marsh, 1881-1945
xWolfe, Linnie M.
Son of the Wilderness: The Life of John Muir.
U of Wis Pr.

Wolfe, Louis.
xWolfe, Louis.
Disease Detectives. Watts.

Wolfe, Margaret R. *see* Wolfe, Margaret Ripley.

Wolfe, Margaret Ripley, 1947-
xWolfe, Margaret R.
Lucius Polk Brown & Progressive Food & Drug
Control: Tennessee & New York
City,1908-1920. Regents Pr KS.

Wolfe, Martin.
xWolfe, Martin.
The Economic Causes of Imperialism. Wiley.
French Franc Between the Wars, 1919-1939.
AMS Pr.

Wolfe, P. E. *see* Wolfe, Peter Edward.

Wolfe, Peter, 1933-
xWolfe, Peter.
Beams Falling: Art of Dashiell Hammett.
Bowling Green Univ.

Wolfe, Peter Edward, 1911-
xWolfe, P. E.
The Geology & Landscapes of New Jersey.
Crane-Russak Co.

Wolfe, Ralph.
xWolfe, Ralph D.
Home Energy for the Eighties. Garden Way
Pub.

Wolfe, Ralph D. *see* Wolfe, Ralph.

Wolfe, Richard J.
xWolfe, Richard J.
Early American Music Engraving & Printing:
A History of Music Publishing in America
from 1787 to 1825 with Commentary on
Earlier & Later Practices. U of Ill Pr.

Wolfe, Thomas. *see* Wolfe, Thomas Clayton.

Wolfe, Thomas Clayton, 1900-1938
xWolfe, Thomas.
From Death to Morning. Scribner.
Hills Beyond. Har-Row.
Hills Beyond. Nal.
Story of a Novel. Scribner.

Wolfe, Thomas W.
xWolfe, Thomas W.
Soviet Power & Europe, 1945-1970. Johns
Hopkins.

Wolfe, Tom.
xWolfe, Tom.
The Painted Word. Bantam.
The Painted Word. FS&G.
The Pump House Gang. FS&G.
Pumphouse Gang. Bantam.
Radical Chic & Mau-Mauing the Flak
Catchers. FS&G.
The Right Stuff. Bantam.
The Right Stuff. FS&G.

Wolfe, W. Dean. *see* Wolfe, Wallace Dean.

Wolfe, Wallace Dean.
xWolfe, W. Dean.

ed. Articulation & Learning: New Dimensions
in Research, Diagnostics, & Therapy. C C
Thomas.

Wolfe, Welby B.
xWolfe, Welby B.
Materials of the Scene: An Introduction to
Technical Theatre. Har-Row.

Wolfe, Willard.
xWolfe, Willard.
From Radicalism to Socialism: Men & Ideas in
the Formation of Fabian Socialist Doctrines,
1881-1889. Yale U Pr.

Wolfenden, E. P. *see* Wolfenden, Elmer P.

Wolfenden, Elmer P.
xWolfenden, E. P.
Hiligaynon Reference Grammar. U Pr of
Hawaii.

Wolfenstein, Martha, 1911-
xWolfenstein, Martha.
Children's Humor: A Psychological Analysis.
Ind U Pr.
Disaster: A Psychological Essay. Arno.
Idyls of the Gass. Arno.
Renegade & Other Tales. Arno.

Wolfers, Arnold, 1892-
xWolfers, Arnold.
ed. Alliance Policy in the Cold War.
Greenwood.
Britain & France Between Two Wars:
Conflicting Strategies of Peace from
Versailles to World War Two. Norton.
Discord & Collaboration: Essays on
International Politics. Johns Hopkins.

Wolfert, Paula.
xWolfert, Paula.
Couscous & Other Good Food from Morocco.
Har-Row
The Mediterranean Cooking. Times Dbn.

Wolff, Bernard. *see* Wolff, Bernard Pierre.

Wolff, Bernard Pierre, 1930-
xWolff, Bernard.
Friends & Friends of Friends. Dutton.

Wolff, Charlotte, 1897-
xWolff, Charlotte.
A Psychology of Gesture. Arno.

Wolff, Cynthia G. *see* Wolff, Cynthia Griffin.

Wolff, Cynthia Griffin.
xWolff, Cynthia G.
A Feast of Words: The Triumph of Edith
Wharton. Oxford U Pr.

Wolff, Diane.
xWolff, Diane.
Chinese Writing: An Introduction. HR&W.
An Easy Guide to Everyday Chinese.
Har-Row.

Wolff, Dorothy.
xWolff, Dorothy.
Surgical & Microscopic Anatomy of the
Temporal Bone. Hafner.

Wolff, E. *see* Wolff, Etienne.

Wolff, Edward A.
xWolff, Edward A.
Geoscience Instrumentation. Wiley.

Wolff, Egon, 1926-
xWolff, Egon.
Paper Flowers: A Play in Six Scenes. U of Mo
Pr.

Wolff, Etienne.
xWolff, E.
Relationship Between Experimental
Embryology & Molecular Biology. Gordon.

Wolff, Geoffrey, 1937-
xWolff, Geoffrey.
Bad Debts. S&S.
The Duke of Deception: Memories of My
Father. Random.
Inklings. Random.
The Sightseer. Random.

Wolff, Hans.
xWolff, Hans.

Comparative Vocabulary of Abuan Dialects.
Northwestern U Pr.

Wolff, Hans W. *see* Wolff, Hans Walter.

Wolff, Hans Walter.
xWolff, Hans W.
Anthropology of the Old Testament. Fortress.

Wolff, Jane.
xWolff, Jane.
The Papers of Daniel Murray: Guide to a
Microfilm Edition. State Hist Soc Wis.

Wolff, John U.
xWolff, John V.
Dictionary of Cebuano Visayan. Cornell SE
Asia.

Wolff, John V. *see* Wolff, John U.

Wolff, Joseph. *see* Wolff, Joseph J.

Wolff, Joseph J.
xWolff, Joseph.
Compiled by George Gissing: An Annotated
Bibliography of Writings About Him. N Ill U
Pr.

Wolff, Kathryn.
xWolff, Kathryn.
ed. AAAS Science Book List Supplement.
AAAS.

Wolff, Konrad.
xWolff, Konrad.
Schnabel's Interpretation of Piano Music.
Norton.

Wolff, Kurt, 1907-
xWolff, Kurt.
The Biological, Sociological, & Psychological
Aspects of Aging. Greenwood.

Wolff, Kurt H., 1912-
xWolff, Kurt H.
Surrender & Catch: Experience & Inquiry
Today. Kluwer Boston.
Trying Sociology. Wiley.

Wolff, Leon.
xWolff, Leon.
Low Level Mission. Arno.

Wolff, Michael, 1953-
xWolff, Michael.
White Kids. Summit Bks.

Wolff, Peter.
xWolff, Peter.
Breakthroughs in Mathematics. NAL.

Wolff, Peter H.
xWolff, Peter H.
Developmental Psychologies of Jean Piaget &
Psychoanalysis. Intl Univs Pr.

Wolff, Pierre, 1929-
xWolff, Pierre.
May I Hate God. Paulist Pr.

Wolff, Robert L. *see* Wolff, Robert Lee.

Wolff, Robert Lee.
xWolff, Robert L.
The Balkans in Our Time. Harvard U Pr.
The Balkans in Our Time. Norton.

Wolff, Robert P. *see* Wolff, Robert Paul.

Wolff, Robert Paul.
xWolff, Robert P.
About Philosophy. P-H.
Critique of Pure Tolerance. Beacon Pr.
Ideal of the University. Beacon Pr.
In Defense of Anarchism. Har-Row.
ed. Introductory Philosophy. P-H.
Poverty of Liberalism. Beacon Pr.

Wolff, Sydney.
xWolff, Sydney.
Games Without Words: Activities for Thinking
Teachers & Thinking Children. C C Thomas.

Wolff, Werner, 1904-
xWolff, Werner.

Expression of Personality: Experimental Depth
Psychology. Johnson Repr.

Wolffheim, Nelly, 1879-
xWolffheim, Nelly.
Psychology in the Nursery School. Greenwood.

Wolfflin, Heinrich, 1864-1945
xWolfflin, Heinrich.
Principles of Art History: The Problem of the
Development of Style in Later Art. Dover.
Principles of Art History: The Problem of the
Development of Style in Later Art. Peter
Smith.

Wolfgang, Charles H.
xWolfgang, Charles H.
Solving Discipline Problems: Strategies for
Classroom Teachers. Allyn.

Wolfgang, Marvin. *see* Wolfgang, Marvin E.

Wolfgang, Marvin E.
xWolfgang, Marvin.
Patterns in Criminal Homicide. Patterson
Smith.
xWolfgang, Marvin E.
Criminology Index: Research & Theory in
Criminology in the United States, 1945-1972.
Elsevier.
Sociology of Crime & Delinquency. Wiley.

Wolfinger, R. *see* Wolfinger, Raymond E.
Wolfinger, R. E. *see* Wolfinger, Raymond E.
Wolfinger, Raymond. *see* Wolfinger, Raymond E.

Wolfinger, Raymond E.
xWolfinger, R.
Politics of Progress. P-H.
ed. Readings on Congress. P-H.
xWolfinger, R. E.
Dynamics of American Politics. P-H.
xWolfinger, Raymond.
Dynamics of American Politics. P-H.
xWolfinger, Raymond E.
Who Votes?. Yale U Pr.

Wolfle, Dael. *see* Wolfle, Dael Lee.

Wolfle, Dael Lee, 1906-
xWolfle, Dael.
Uses of Talent. Princeton U Pr.

Wolfman, Bernard.
xWolfman, Bernard.
Dissent Without Opinion: The Behavior of
Justice William O. Douglas in Federal Tax
Cases. U of Pa Pr.
Federal Income Taxation of Business
Enterprise. Little.

Wolfort, Francis G.
xWolfort, Francis G.
ed. Acute Hand Injuries: A Multispecialty
Approach. Little.

Wolfowitz, J. *see* Wolfowitz, Jacob.

Wolfowitz, Jacob, 1910-
xWolfowitz, J.
Coding Theorems of Information Theory.
Springer-Verlag.
Selected Papers. Springer-Verlag.
xWolfowitz, Jacob.
Coding Theorems of Information Theory.
Springer-Verlag.

Wolfram, Walt. *see* Wolfram, Walter A.

Wolfram, Walter A.
xWolfram, Walt.
Appalachian Speech. Ctr Appl Ling.

Wolfson, Abraham.
xWolfson, Abraham.
Spinoza: A Life of Reason. Philos Lib.

Wolfson, Dirk.
xWolfson, Dirk J.
Public Finance & Development Strategy. Johns
Hopkins.

Wolfson, Dirk J. *see* Wolfson, Dirk.
Wolfson, Harry A. *see* Wolfson, Harry Austryn.

Wolfson, Harry Austryn, 1887-1974
xWolfson, Harry A.

From Philo to Spinoza: Two Studies in
Religious Philosophy. Behrman.
Religious Philosophy: A Group of Essays.
Atheneum.
Religious Philosophy: A Group of Essays.
Harvard U Pr.

Wolfson, Joseph.
xWolfson, Joseph.
The Social Studies Student Investigates
Business in the American Economy. Rosen
Pr.

Wolfson, Margaret.
xWolfson, Margaret.
Changing Approaches to Population Problems.
OECD.

Wolfson, Murray.
xWolfson, Murray.
Reappraisal of Marxian Economics. Columbia
U Pr.
A Textbook of Economics. Methuen Inc.

Wolfson, Nicholas.
xWolfson, Nicholas.
Regulation of Brokers, Dealers & Securities
Markets. Warren.

Wolgast, Elizabeth. *see* Wolgast, Elizabeth Hankins.
Wolgast, Elizabeth H. *see* Wolgast, Elizabeth Hankins.

Wolgast, Elizabeth Hankins, 1929-
xWolgast, Elizabeth.
Paradoxes of Knowledge. Cornell U Pr.
xWolgast, Elizabeth H.
Equality & the Rights of Women. Cornell U
Pr.

Wolin, Sheldon S.
xWolin, Sheldon S.
Politics & Vision: Continuity & Innovation in
Western Political Thought. Little.

Wolintz, Arthur H.
xWolintz, Arthur H.
Essentials of Clinical Neuro-Ophthalmology.
Little.

Wolitz, Seth L., 1938-
xWolitz, Seth L.
The Proustian Community. NYU Pr.

Wolitzer, Hilma.
xWolitzer, Hilma.
In the Flesh. Morrow.
Out of Love. Bantam.
Out of Love. FS&G.

Wolk, Allan, 1936-
xWolk, Allan.
Everyday Words from Names of People &
Places. Elsevier-Nelson.
Presidency & Black Civil Rights: Eisenhower to
Nixon. Fairleigh Dickinson.

Wolke, Robert L.
xWolke, Robert L.
Chemistry Explained. P-H.

Wolkstein, Diane.
xWolkstein, Diane.
A Cool Ride in the Sky. Knopf.
Lazy Stories. Dell.
Lazy Stories. HM.
The Magic Orange Tree & Other Haitian
Folktales. Knopf.

Wolkstein, Harry W. *see* Wolkstein, Harry William.

Wolkstein, Harry William, 1909-
xWolkstein, Harry W.
Accounting Methods & Controls for the
Construction Industry. P-H.

Woll, Allen L.
xWoll, Allen L.
The Latin Image in American Film. UCLA Lat
Am Ctr.
Puerto Rican Historiography. Gordon Pr.
Songs from Hollywood Musical Comedies,
1927 to the Present: A Dictionary. Garland
Pub.

Woll, P. *see* Woll, Peter.

Woll, Peter, 1933-
xWoll, P.

Public Policy. Winthrop.
xWoll, Peter.
American Bureaucracy. Norton.
American Bureaucracy. Norton.
ed. Behind the Scenes in American
Government: Personalities & Politics. Little.

Wollard, Joy J.
xWollard, Joy J.
Nutritional Management of the Cancer Patient.
Raven.

Wollen, Peter.
xWollen, Peter.
Signs & Meaning in the Cinema. Ind U Pr.

Wollenberg, Charles.
xWollenberg, Charles M.
All Deliberate Speed: Segregation & Exclusion
in California Schools, 1855-1975. U of Cal
Pr.

Wollenberg, Charles M. *see* Wollenberg, Charles.
Wollenberg, H. H. *see* Wollenberg, Hans H.

Wollenberg, Hans H., 1893-
xWollenberg, H. H.
Anatomy of the Film: An Illustrated Guide to
Film Appreciation. Arno.
Fifty Years of German Film. Arno.

Wolley, Charles.
xWolley, Charles.
A Two Year's Journal in New York & Part of
Its Territories in America. Harbor Hill Bks.

Wollheim, Richard, 1923-
xWollheim, Richard.
On Art & the Mind. Harvard U Pr.

Wollman, Nathaniel.
xWollman, Nathaniel.
The Outlook for Water: Quality, Quantity &
National Growth. Johns Hopkins.
ed. The Value of Water in Alternative Uses:
With Special Application to Water Use in the
San Juan & Rio Grande Basins of New
Mexico. U of NM Pr.

Wollstonecraft, Mary, 1759-1797
xWollstonecraft, Mary.
An Historical & Moral View of the Origin &
Progress of the French Revolution & the
Effect It Has Produced in Europe. Schol
Facsimiles.
Letters Written During a Short Residence in
Sweden, Norway, & Denmark. U of Nebr Pr.
The Love Letters of Mary Wollstonecraft to
Gilbert Imlay. Folcroft.

Wolman, B. B. *see* Wolman, Benjamin B.
Wolman, Benjamin. *see* Wolman, Benjamin B.

Wolman, Benjamin B.
xWolman, B. B.
ed. Psychological Aspects of Gynecology &
Obstetrics. Med Economics.
xWolman, Benjamin.
Children's Fears. NAL.
xWolman, Benjamin B.
Call No Man Normal. Intl Univs Pr.
Children's Fears. G&D.
Dictionary of Behavioral Science. Van Nos
Reinhold.
ed. Handbook of Dreams: Research, Theories
& Applications. Van Nos Reinhold.
ed. Handbook of General Psychology. P-H.
xWolman, Benjamin J.
ed. Psychoanalysis & Catholicism. Halsted Pr.
xWolman, Benjamon B.
Handbook of Human Sexuality. P-H.

Wolman, Benjamin J. *see* Wolman, Benjamin B.
Wolman, Benjamon B. *see* Wolman, Benjamin B.

Wolman, Harold.
xWolman, Harold L.
Housing & Housing Policy in the U. S. & the
U. K.. Lexington Bks.

Wolman, Harold L. *see* Wolman, Harold.

Wolman, Judith.
xWolman, Judith.

David's New Baby. Dandelion Pr.
Duncan McTavish in Paris. Dandelion Pr.
The Emperor's New Clothes. Dandelion Pr.
I Can Bake Cookies. Dandelion Pr.
Jenny's Birthday Party. Dandelion Pr.
Jesus Performs Miracles. Dandelion Pr.
Lizzie & the Tooth Fairy. Dandelion Pr.
The Ugly Duckling. Dandelion Pr.

Wolman, Leo, 1890-
  xWolman, Leo.
    The Boycott in American Trade Unions. AMS
      Pr.
    Boycott in American Trade Unions. Arno.
    The Growth of American Trade Unions,
      1880-1923. Arno.

Woloch, Isser, 1937-
  xWoloch, Isser.
    The French Veteran from Revolution to the
      Restoration. U of NC Pr.

Wolotkiewicz, Rita. *see* Wolotkiewicz, Rita J.

Wolotkiewicz, Rita J., 1925-
  xWolotkiewicz, Rita.
    College Administrator's Handbook. Allyn.

Wolovich, W. A., 1937-
  xWolovich, W. A.
    Linear Multivariable Systems. Springer-Verlag.

Wolozin, Harold, 1920-
  xWolozin, Harold.
    ed. American Fiscal & Monetary Policy. New
      Viewpoints.

Wolpe, Joseph.
  xWolpe, Joseph.
    The Practice of Behavior Therapy. Pergamon.
    Psychotherapy by Reciprocal Inhibition.
      Stanford U Pr.
    Theme & Variations: A Behavior Therapy
      Casebook. Pergamon.

Wolpert, Samuel M.
  xWolpert, Samuel M.
    Angiography of Posterior Fossa Tumors.
      Grune.

Wolpert, Vladimir M.
  xWolpert, Vladimir M.
    Synthetic Polymers & the Paper Industry.
      Miller Freeman.

Wolseley, Charles, Sir, 2d Bart, 1630?-1714
  xWolseley, Charles.
    The Reasonableness of Scripture-Belief. Schol
      Facsimiles.

Wolseley, Roland E. *see* Wolseley, Roland Edgar.

Wolseley, Roland Edgar, 1904-
  xWolseley, Roland E.
    Careers in Religious Communications. Herald
      Pr.
    The Changing Magazine: Trends in Readership
      & Management. Hastings.
    Understanding Magazines. Iowa St U Pr.

Wolsky, M. I. *see* Wolsky, Maria de Issekutz.

Wolsky, Maria de Issekutz.
  xWolsky, M. I.
    The Mechanism of Evolution: A New Look at
      Old Ideas. S Karger.

Wolstein, Benjamin.
  xWolstein, Benjamin.
    Theory of Psychoanalytic Therapy. Grune.

Wolter, Allan B. *see* Wolter, Allan Bernard.

Wolter, Allan Bernard, 1913-
  xWolter, Allan B.
    Life in God's Love. Franciscan Herald.

Wolter, Carlo.
  xWolter, Carlo.
    Figure Skating. Watts.

Wolters, Clifton.
  xWolters, Clifton.
    tr. The Cloud of Unknowing & Other Works.
      Penguin.

Wolters, O. W.
  xWolters, O. W.

Fall of Srivijaya in Malay History. Cornell U
  Pr.

Wolters, Raymond, 1938-
  xWolters, Raymond.
    Negroes & the Great Depression: The Problem
      of Economic Recovery. Greenwood.

Wolters, Richard A.
  xWolters, Richard A.
    Art & Technique of Soaring. McGraw.

Wolterstorff, Nicholas.
  xWolterstorff, Nicholas.
    On Universals: An Essay in Ontology. U of
      Chicago Pr.
    Reason Within the Bounds of Religion.
      Eerdmans.

Womack, David. *see* Womack, David A.

Womack, David A.
  xWomack, David.
    Breaking the Stained-Glass Barrier. Har-Row.

Woman's Club of Havana. Garden Section.
  xWomen's Club of Havana.
    Flowering Plants from Cuban Gardens. S G
      Phillips.

Woman's Day.
  xWoman's Day.
    ed. The Best of Woman's Day Crochet. S&S.
  xWoman's Day Editorial Staff.
    Woman's Day Book of Granny Squares &
      Other Carry-Along Crochet. S&S.
  xWoman's Day Editors.
    Book of Patterns & Instructions for American
      Needlework. S&S.
    Cooking for Two. G K Hall.
    The Woman's Day Book of Weekend Crafts:
      More Than 100 Quick-to-Finish Projects.
      HM.
    Woman's Day Collector's Cookbook. S&S.
    Woman's Day Cooking for Two. Random.
    Woman's Day Gifts from Your Kitchen. G K
      Hall.

Woman's Day Editorial Staff. *see* Woman's Day.
Woman's Day Editors. *see* Woman's Day.

Woman's Rights Convention, Akron, Ohio, 1851.
  xWomen's Rights Convention, Akron, Ohio, 1851.
    Proceedings. B Franklin.

Women in Transition, Inc.
  xWomen in Transition, Inc.
    Women in Transition: A Feminist Handbook
      on Separation & Divorce. Scribner.

Women's Club of Havana. *see* Woman's Club of
  Havana. Garden Section.

Women's Rights Convention, Akron, Ohio, 1851. *see*
  Woman's Rights Convention, Akron, Ohio, 1851.

Women's Wear Daily.
  xWomen's Wear Daily.
    Fairchild's Market Directory of Women's &
      Children's Apparel. Fairchild.
    Two Hundred Years of American Fashion.
      Fairchild.

Women's Work Force. *see* Wider Opportunities for
  Women. Women's Work Force.

Wong, Eugene, 1934-
  xWong, Eugene.
    Stochastic Processes in Information &
      Dynamical Systems. Krieger.

Wong, Frederick, 1929-
  xWong, Frederick.
    Oriental Watercolor Techniques.
      Watson-Guptill.

Wong, H. Y.
  xWong, H. Y.
    Handbook of Essential Formulae & Data on
      Heat Transfer for Engineers. Longman.

Wong, Herbert H.
  xWong, Herbert H.

My Goldfish. A-W.
My Ladybug. A-W.
Our Caterpillars. A-W.
Our Earthworms. A-W.
Pond Life: Watching Animals Find Food. A-W.

Wong, Irene, 1949-
  xWong, Irene.
    Great Asia Steam Book. Taylor & Ng.

Wong, Jade S. *see* Wong, Jade Snow.

Wong, Jade Snow.
  xWong, Jade S.
    No Chinese Stranger. Har-Row.

Wong, James I.
  xWong, James I.
    Aspirations & Frustrations of the Chinese
      Youth in the San Francisco Bay Area:
      Aspersions Upon the Societal Scheme. R & E
      Res Assoc.

Wong, Joe.
  xWong, Joe.
    Glass: Structure by Spectroscopy. Dekker.

Wong, Martin R.
  xWong, Martin R.
    A Guide to Systematic Instructional Design.
      Educ Tech Pubns.

Wong, Molly.
  xWong, Molly.
    They Changed My China. Broadman.

Wong, Paul.
  xWong, Paul.
    China's Higher Leadership in the Socialist
      Transition. Free Pr.

Wong, Richard.
  xWong, Richard W.
    Prayers from an Island. John Knox.

Wong, Richard W. *see* Wong, Richard.

Wong, Shue Tuck.
  xWong, Shue-Tuck.
    Perception of Choice & Factors Affecting
      Industrial Water Supply Decisions in
      Northeastern Illinois. U Chicago Dept Geog.

Wong, Shue-Tuck. *see* Wong, Shue Tuck.

Wong, Siu-Lun.
  xWong, Siu-Lun.
    Sociology & Socialism in Contemporary China.
      Routledge & Kegan.

Wong, Wucius.
  xWong, Wucius.
    Principles of Three Dimensional Design. Van
      Nos Reinhold.

Wong, Y. C. *see* Wong, Yau-Chuen.

Wong, Yau-Chuen.
  xWong, Y. C.
    Schwartz Spaces, Nuclear Spaces & Tensor
      Products. Springer-Verlag.
    The Topology of Uniform Convergence on
      Order-Bounded Sets. Springer-Verlag.
  xWong, Yau-Chuen.
    Partially Ordered Topological Vector Spaces.
      Oxford U Pr.

Wongrey, Jan.
  xWongrey, Jan.
    Southern Wildfowl & Wildgame Cookbook.
      Sandlapper Store.

Wonham, W. M., 1934-
  xWonham, W. M.
    Linear Multivariable Control: A Geometric
      Approach. Springer-Verlag.

Wonnacott, Paul.
  xWonnacott, Paul.
    Economics. McGraw.
    The Floating Canadian Dollar: Exchange
      Flexibility & Monetary Independence. Am
      Enterprise.

Wonnacott, Ronald J.
  xWonnacott, Ronald J.

Econometrics. Wiley.
Free Trade Between the United States &
Canada: The Potential Economic Effects.
Harvard U Pr.
Wood. see Wood, Fred M.
Wood, A. see Wood, Adrian.
Wood, Adrian.
xWood, A.
A Theory of Pay. Cambridge U Pr.
A Theory of Profits. Cambridge U Pr.
Wood, Alexander.
xWood, Alexander.
Problems in Physical Chemistry. Oxford U Pr.
Wood, Anthony A.
xWood, Anthony A.
Athenae Oxonienses: An Exact History of All
the Writers & Bishops Who Have Had Their
Education in the University of Oxford. B
Franklin.
Wood, Arthur E. see Wood, Arthur Evans.
Wood, Arthur Evans, 1881-
xWood, Arthur E.
Hamtramck: A Sociological Study of a
Polish-American Community. Coll & U Pr.
xWood, Arthur Evans.
Hamtramck: A Sociological Study of a
Polish-American Community. Octagon.
Wood, Arthur L. see Wood, Arthur Lewis.
Wood, Arthur Lewis.
xWood, Arthur L.
Criminal Lawyer. Coll & U Pr.
Wood, B. A. see Wood, Bernard.
Wood, Barbara.
xWood, Barbara.
Hounds & Jackals. Avon.
Hounds & Jackals. Doubleday.
Night Trains. Ballantine.
Night Trains. Morrow.
Yesterday's Child. Doubleday.
Wood, Barry.
xWood, Barry.
Complete Home Insulation. David & Charles.
Questions New Christians Ask. Revell.
Questions Non-Christians Ask. Revell.
Wood, Basil Charles.
xWood, Basil Charles.
The What, When & Where Guide to Southern
California. Doubleday.
Wood, Ben. see Wood, Benjamin Stuart Blachford.
Wood, Benjamin Stuart Blachford.
xWood, Ben.
ed. A Paediatric Vade-Mecum. Year Bk Med.
Wood, Bernard.
xWood, B. A.
Human Evolution. Methuen Inc.
Wood, Bernard D.
xWood, Bernard D.
Applications of Thermodynamics. A-W.
Wood, Bruce, BSc.
xWood, Bruce.
The Process of Local Government Reform:
1966 - 1974. Allen Unwin.
Wood, Bryce, 1909-
xWood, Bryce.
Aggression & History: The Case of Ecuador &
Peru. Univ Microfilms.
Peaceful Change & the Colonial Problem. AMS
Pr.
Wood, Carroll E.
xWood, Carroll E.
A Student's Atlas of Flowering Plants: Some
Dicotyledons of Eastern North America.
Har-Row.
Wood, Charles L., 1937-
xWood, Charles L.
The Kansas Beef Industry. Regents Pr KS.
Wood, Charles T.
xWood, Charles T.

French Apanages, & the Capetian Monarchy,
1224-1328. Harvard U Pr.
Wood, Clement, 1888-1950
xWood, Clement.
Deep River. Arno.
Wood, Colin.
xWood, Colin.
A Confusion of Time. Elsevier-Nelson.
Wood, Corinne S. see Wood, Corinne Shear Wood.
Wood, Corinne Shear Wood.
xWood, Corinne S.
Human Sickness & Health: A Bio-Cultural
View. Mayfield Pub.
Wood, D. N. see Wood, David Norris.
Wood, David A.
xWood, David A.
Music in the Harvard Libraries: A Catalogue of
Early Printed Music & Books on Music in
the Houghton Library & the Eda Kuhn Loeb
Music Library. Harvard U Pr.
Wood, David M. see Wood, David Michael.
Wood, David Michael, 1934-
xWood, David M.
Power & Policy in Western European
Democracies. Wiley.
Wood, David Norris.
xWood, D. N.
Use of Earth Sciences Literature. Butterworths.
Wood, Dennis W. see Wood, Dennis William.
Wood, Dennis William.
xWood, Dennis W.
Principles of Animal Physiology. Univ Park.
Wood, Donald, 1926-
xWood, Donald.
Cape Cod: A Guide. Little.
Wood, Douglas.
xWood, Douglas.
Forecasting for Business: Methods &
Applications. Longman.
Wood, E. G. see Wood, Edward Geoffrey.
Wood, E. J. see Wood, E. J. Ferguson.
Wood, E. J. Ferguson.
xWood, E. J.
Inshore Dinghy Fishing. Transatlantic.
Wood, E. M. see Wood, Ellen Meiksins.
Wood, Edward Geoffrey.
xWood, E. G.
Costing Matters for Managers. Beekman Pubs.
Wood, Edward J.
xWood, Edward J.
Curiosities of Clocks & Watches from the
Earliest Times. Gale.
Giants & Dwarfs. Folcroft.
Wood, Elija. see Wood, Eliza T.
Wood, Eliza T.
xWood, Elija.
In His Hands. Claitors.
Wood, Elizabeth (Lambert).
xWood, Elizabeth L.
Arizona Hoof Trails. Binford.
Long Rope. Binford.
Many Horses. Binford.
Wood, Elizabeth A.
xWood, Elizabeth A.
Crystals and Light: An Introduction to Optical
Crystallography. Dover.
Wood, Elizabeth L. see Wood, Elizabeth (Lambert).
Wood, Ellen Meiksins.
xWood, E. M.
Class Ideology & Ancient Political Theory:
Socrates, Plato & Aristotle in Social Context.
Oxford U Pr.
Wood, Emma.
xWood, Emma.
Brass & Other Rubbings. David & Charles.
Wood, Ernest, 1883-1965
xWood, Ernest.

Questions on Occultism. Theos Pub Hse.
Study of Pleasure & Pain. Theos Pub Hse.
Wood, Ernest Harvey.
xWood.
The Brain & the Eye. Year Bk Med.
Wood, Esther.
xWood, Esther.
Dante Rossetti & the Pre-Raphaelite
Movement. Cooper Sq.
Wood, Frances. see Wood, Frances Elizabeth.
Wood, Frances Elizabeth.
xWood, Frances.
I Hauled These Mountains in Here. Caxton.
Wood, Francis A. see Wood, Francis Asbury.
Wood, Francis Asbury, 1859-
xWood, Francis A.
Post-Consonantal W in Indo-European. Kraus
Repr.
Wood, Frank. see Wood, Frank Higley.
Wood, Frank Higley, 1903-
xWood, Frank.
Rainer Maria Rilke: The Ring of Forms.
Octagon.
Wood, Fred M.
xWood.
The Glory of Galatians. Broadman.
Wood, Frederic T. see Wood, Frederic Turnbull.
Wood, Frederic Turnbull, 1902-
xWood, Frederic T.
Accentuation of Nominal Compounds in
Lithuanian. Kraus Repr.
Wood, Frederick A. see Wood, Frederick Augustus.
Wood, Frederick Augustus, 1861-1942
xWood, Frederick A.
Finances of Vermont. AMS Pr.
History of Taxation in Vermont. AMS Pr.
Wood, Frederick L. see Wood, Frederick Lloyd
Whitfield.
Wood, Frederick Lloyd Whitfield, 1903-
xWood, Frederick L.
Understanding New Zealand. Arno.
Wood, George O.
xWood, George O.
You Cant Beat the Beatitudes. Gospel Pub.
Wood, Gerald L.
xWood, Gerald L.
ed. Animal Facts & Feats. Sterling.
Wood, Gordon, 1937-
xWood, Gordon.
Fundamentals of Psychological Research.
Little.
Wood, Gordon S.
xWood, Gordon S.
The Creation of the American Republic,
1776-1787. Norton.
Wood, H. F. see Wood, H. Freeman.
Wood, H. Freeman.
xWood, H. F.
The Passenger from Scotland Yard: A
Victorian Detective Novel. Dover.
Wood, Henry J. see Wood, Henry Joseph.
Wood, Henry Joseph, Sir, 1869-1944
xWood, Henry J.
About Conducting. Scholarly.
Wood, Herbert G. see Wood, Herbert George.
Wood, Herbert George, 1879-1963
xWood, Herbert G.
Christianity & Civilisation. Octagon.
Living Issues in Religious Thought, from
George Fox to Bertrand Russell. Arno.
Wood, Irving. see Wood, Irving Francis.
Wood, Irving Francis.
xWood, Irving.
The Bible As Literature: An Introduction.
Folcroft.
Wood, J. B. see Wood, Jay Barclay.
Wood, James, 1918-
xWood, James.
Friday Run. Vanguard.
Wood, James. see Wood, James Playsted.

Wood, James E. *see* Wood, James Edward.
Wood, James Edward.
    xWood, James E.
    Baptists & the American Experience. Judson.
    Nationhood & the Kingdom. Broadman.
Wood, James L.
    xWood, James L.
    Political Sociology Bibliography: Important
        Representations of the Major Areas of
        Modern Political Sociology. Vance Biblios.
Wood, James P. *see* Wood, James Playsted.
Wood, James Playsted, 1905-
    xWood, James.
    The Life & Words of John F. Kennedy.
        Country Beautiful.
    xWood, James P.
    Chase Scene. Elsevier-Nelson.
    Colonial Massachusetts. Elsevier-Nelson.
    Colonial New Hampshire. Elsevier-Nelson.
    This Little Pig: The Story of Marketing.
        Elsevier-Nelson.
Wood, Jay Barclay, 1934-
    xWood, J. B.
    Troubleshooting Your Handgun. Follett.
Wood, Jesse H. *see* Wood, Jesse Hermon.
Wood, Jesse Hermon.
    xWood, Jesse H.
    Fundamentals of College Chemistry. Har-Row.
Wood, John, 1939-
    xWood, John.
    A Journey to the Source of the River Oxus.
        Oxford U Pr.
    xWood, John T.
    How Do You Feel?: A Guide to Your
        Emotions. P-H.
Wood, John. *see* Wood, John A.
Wood, John A., 1932-
    xWood, John.
    The Solar System. P-H.
Wood, John E. *see* Wood, John Edwin.
Wood, John Edwin.
    xWood, John E.
    Sun, Moon, & Standing Stones. Oxford U Pr.
Wood, John T. *see* Wood, John.
Wood, Jonathan S., 1949-
    xWood, Jonathan S.
    Your Future in the Science of Oceanography.
        Rosen Pr.
Wood, Laura N. *see* Wood, Laura Newbold.
Wood, Laura Newbold.
    xWood, Laura N.
    Louis Pasteur. Messner.
Wood, Leon J.
    xWood, Leon J.
    A Commentary on Daniel. Zondervan.
Wood, Leon J. *see* Wood, Leon James.
Wood, Leon James.
    xWood, Leon J.
    Daniel: A Study Guide. Zondervan.
    The Holy Spirit in the Old Testament.
        Zondervan.
    Israel's United Monarchy. Baker Bk.
    Prophets of Israel. Baker Bk.
    Survey of Israel's History. Zondervan.
Wood, Louis A. *see* Wood, Louis Aubrey.
Wood, Louis Aubrey, 1883-1955
    xWood, Louis A.
    The Form & Origin of Milton's Antitrinitarian
        Conception. Arden Lib.
    Form & Origin of Milton's Antitrinitarian
        Conception. Folcroft.
Wood, M. M. *see* Wood, Mary M.
Wood, Manfri F. *see* Wood, Manfri Frederick.
Wood, Manfri Frederick.
    xWood, Manfri F.
    In the Life of a Romany Gypsy. Routledge &
        Kegan.
Wood, Margaret M. *see* Wood, Margaret Mary.
Wood, Margaret Mary, 1888-
    xWood, Margaret M.

Paths of Loneliness: The Individual Isolated in
    Modern Society. Columbia U Pr.
Stranger: A Study in Social Relationships.
    AMS Pr.
Wood, Marion N.
    xWood, Marion N.
    Gourmet Food on a Wheat-Free Diet. C C
        Thomas.
Wood, Mary M.
    xWood, M. M.
    ed. Developmental Therapy: A Textbook for
        Teachers As Therapists for Emotionally
        Disturbed Young Children. Univ Park.
Wood, Michael, 1936-
    xWood, Michael.
    Stendhal. Cornell U Pr.
Wood, Millett.
    xWood, Millett.
    Art of Speaking. David & Charles.
Wood, Miriam.
    xWood, Miriam.
    The Little Missionary Truck That Could Do
        Anything. Review & Herald.
Wood, Morrison, 1893-
    xWood, Morrison.
    More Recipes with a Jug of Wine. FS&G.
Wood, Nancy. *see* Wood, Nancy C.
Wood, Nancy C.
    xWood, Nancy.
    The Grass Roots People: An American
        Requiem. Har-Row.
    Hollering Sun. S&S.
Wood, Nancy E.
    xWood, Nancy E.
    Delayed Speech & Language Development.
        P-H.
Wood, Nancy V.
    xWood, Nancy V.
    College Reading & Study Skills. HR&W.
Wood, Norman K.
    xWood, Norman K.
    Differential Diagnosis of Oral Lesions. Mosby.
    ed. Treatment Planning: A Pragmatic
        Approach. Mosby.
Wood, Oliver G.
    xWood, Oliver G.
    Analysis of Bank Financial Statements. Van
        Nos Reinhold.
Wood, Paul.
    xWood, Paul.
    How to Get Your Children to Do What You
        Want Them to Do. P-H.
Wood, Paul. *see* Wood, Paul W.
Wood, Paul W.
    xWood, Paul.
    Artistry in Stained Glass. Sterling.
    xWood, Paul W.
    illus. Stained Glass Crafting. Sterling.
    Starting with Stained Glass. Sterling.
Wood, Peter.
    xWood, Peter.
    The Caribbean Isles. Time-Life.
    Caribbean Isles. Silver.
    The Spanish Main. Silver.
    The Spanish Main. Time-Life.
Wood, Phyllis.
    xWood, Phyllis.
    Scientific Illustration: A Guide to Biological,
        Zoological, & Medical Rendering Techniques,
        Design, Printing, & Display. Van Nos
        Reinhold.
Wood, Phyllis A. *see* Wood, Phyllis Anderson.
Wood, Phyllis Anderson.
    xWood, Phyllis A.

A Five Color Buick & a Blue Eyed Cat. NAL.
A Five-Color Buick & a Blue-Eyed Cat.
    Westminster.
Get a Little Lost, Tia. NAL.
Get a Little Lost, Tia. Westminster.
I Think This Is Where We Came in.
    Westminster.
I Think This Is Where We Came in. NAL.
Song of the Shaggy Canary. NAL.
Song of the Shaggy Canary. Westminster.
Wood, R. Coke. *see* Wood, Richard Coke.
Wood, R. D. *see* Wood, Richard Dawson.
Wood, Ralph V.
    xWood, Ralph V.
    ed. Ontario County New York State, 1800
        Federal Population Census Schedule,
        Transcript & Index. Oak Hill.
Wood, Ramsay, 1943-
    xWood, Ramsay.
    Kalila & Dimna: Selected Fables of Bidpai.
        Knopf.
Wood, Reuben E.
    xWood, Reuben E.
    Introduction to Chemical Thermodynamics.
        Irvington.
Wood, Richard Coke.
    xWood, R. Coke.
    Stockton Memories: A Pictorial History of
        Stockton, California. Western Tanager.
Wood, Richard Dawson, 1918-
    xWood, R. D.
    Hydrobotanical Methods. Univ Park.
Wood, Robert. *see* Wood, Robert L.
Wood, Robert B., 1934-
    xWood, Robert.
    Opportunities in Electrical Trades. Natl
        Textbk.
Wood, Robert D.
    xWood, Robert D.
    A Travel Guide to Archaeological Mexico.
        Hastings.
Wood, Robert E., 1934-
    xWood, Robert E.
    Martin Buber's Ontology: An Analysis of I &
        Thou. Northwestern U Pr.
Wood, Robert L.
    xWood, Robert.
    Across the Olympic Mountains: The Press
        Expedition. Mountaineers.
Wood, Robert S. *see* Wood, Robert Stephen.
Wood, Robert Stephen, 1938-
    xWood, Robert S.
    ed. The Process of International Organization.
        Phila Bk Co.
Wood, Robin.
    xWood, Robin.
    Hitchcock's Films. A S Barnes.
Wood, Robin L. *see* Wood, Robin L. K.
Wood, Robin L. K.
    xWood, Robin L.
    ed. Peoples of Africa. Arco.
Wood, Stacy B. *see* Wood, Stacy B. C.
Wood, Stacy B. C.
    xWood, Stacy B.
    Clockmakers of Lancaster County & Their
        Clocks: 1750-1850. Van Nos Reinhold.
Wood, Theodore E. *see* Wood, Theodore E. B.
Wood, Theodore E. B.
    xWood, Theodore E.
    The Word Sublime & Its Context, 1650-1760.
        Mouton.
Wood, Vivian L. *see* Wood, Vivian Lee Poates.
Wood, Vivian Lee Poates.
    xWood, Vivian L.
    Poulenc's Songs: An Analysis of Style. U Pr of
        Miss.
Wood, William, 1921-
    xWood, William.

ed. Cultural-Ecological Perspectives on
Southeast Asia: A Symposium. Ohio U Ctr
Intl.
Wood, William. *see* Wood, William Burke.
Wood, William B. *see* Wood, William Barry.
Wood, William Barry, 1910-
xWood, William B.
From Miasmas to Molecules. Columbia U Pr.
Wood, William Burke.
xWood, William.
Old Drury of Philadelphia: A History of the
Philadelphia Stage, 1800-1835. Greenwood.
Wood, William C. *see* Wood, William Charles Henry.
Wood, William Charles Henry, 1864-1947
xWood, William C.
ed. Logs of the Conquest of Canada.
Greenwood.
Wood-Legh, Kathleen L. *see* Wood-Legh, Kathleen
Louise.
Wood-Legh, Kathleen Louise.
xWood-Legh, Kathleen L.
Perpetual Chantries in Britain. Cambridge U
Pr.
Woodall, Irene R., 1946-
xWoodall, Irene R.
Leadership, Management & Role Delineation:
Issues for the Dental Team. Mosby.
Woodall Publishing Co.
xWoodall Publishing Co.
Woodall's 1978 RV Buyer's Guide. G&D.
Woodall, Robert G.
xWoodall, Robert G.
The Postal History of Yukon Territory,
Canada. Quarterman.
Woodard, Bronte.
xWoodard, Bronte.
Meet Me at the Melba. Delacorte.
Woodberry, George E. *see* Woodberry, George Edward.
Woodberry, George Edward, 1855-1930
xWoodberry, George E.
America in Literature. Irvington.
The Appreciation of Literature. Dynamic Learn
Corp.
Appreciation of Literature. Folcroft.
Appreciation of Literature. Kennikat.
History of Wood-Engraving. Gale.
Literary Essays. Folcroft.
Literary Essays. Kennikat.
Literary Essays. Scholarly.
Literary Memoirs of the Nineteenth Century.
Folcroft.
Literary Memoirs of the Nineteenth Century.
Kennikat.
Nathaniel Hawthorne. Gale.
Ralph Waldo Emerson. Folcroft.
Ralph Waldo Emerson. Haskell.
Woodbridge, B. M. *see* Woodbridge, Benjamin Mather.
Woodbridge, Benjamin Mather, 1884-
xWoodbridge, B. M.
Gatien De Courtilz, Sieur Du Verger: Etude
Sur un Precurseur Du Roman Realiste En
France. Johnson Repr.
Woodbridge, F. J. *see* Woodbridge, Frederick James
Eugene.
Woodbridge, Frederick J. *see* Woodbridge, Frederick
James Eugene.
Woodbridge, Frederick James Eugene, 1867-1940
xWoodbridge, F. J.
The Son of Apollo: Themes of Plato. Biblo.
xWoodbridge, Frederick J.
Contrasts in Education. AMS Pr.
Purpose of History. Kennikat.
The Son of Apollo: Themes of Plato. R West.
Woodbridge, John. *see* Woodbridge, John D.
Woodbridge, John D.
xWoodbridge, John.
The Gospel in America: Themes in the Story
of America's Evangelicals. Zondervan.
Woodburn, Henry M. *see* Woodburn, Henry Milton.

Woodburn, Henry Milton, 1902-
xWoodburn, Henry M.
Using the Chemical Literature: A Practical
Guide. Dekker.
Woodburn, J. A. *see* Woodburn, James Albert.
Woodburn, James A. *see* Woodburn, James Albert.
Woodburn, James Albert, 1856-1943
xWoodburn, J. A.
Causes of the American Revolution. Johnson
Repr.
xWoodburn, James A.
Causes of the American Revolution. AMS Pr.
Woodburn, John H.
xWoodburn, John H.
The Whole Earth Energy Crisis: Our
Dwindling Sources of Energy. Putnam.
Woodburne, Michael O.
xWoodburne, Michael O.
Cenozoic Stratigraphy of the Transverse
Ranges & Adjacent Areas, Southern
California. Geol Soc.
Stratigraphy of the Punchbowl Formation
Cajon Valley, Southern California. U of Cal
Pr.
Woodburne, Russell T. *see* Woodburne, Russell Thomas.
Woodburne, Russell Thomas, 1904-
xWoodburne, Russell T.
Essentials of Human Anatomy. Oxford U Pr.
A Guide to Dissection in Gross Anatomy.
Oxford U Pr.
Woodbury, Angus M. *see* Woodbury, Angus Munn.
Woodbury, Angus Munn.
xWoodbury, Angus M.
Ecological Studies of Flora & Fauna in Glen
Canyon. AMS Pr.
Notes on the Human Ecology of Glen Canyon.
AMS Pr.
Survey of Vegetation in Glen Canyon
Reservoir Basin. AMS Pr.
Survey of Vegetation in the Navajo Reservoir
Basin. AMS Pr.
Woodbury, D. M. *see* Woodbury, Dixon M.
Woodbury, Dixon M.
xWoodbury, D. M.
ed. Antiepileptic Drugs. Raven.
Woodbury, Marda.
xWoodbury, Marda L.
A Guide to Sources of Educational
Information. Info Resources.
Woodbury, Marda L. *see* Woodbury, Marda.
Woodbury, Richard B. *see* Woodbury, Richard Benjamin.
Woodbury, Richard Benjamin, 1917-
xWoodbury, Richard B.
Alfred V. Kidder. Columbia U Pr.
Woodcock, A. E. *see* Woodcock, Alexander Edward
Richard.
Woodcock, Alexander Edward Richard.
xWoodcock, A. E.
A Geometrical Study of the Elementary
Catastrophes. Springer-Verlag.
Woodcock, George, 1912-
xWoodcock, George.
Anarchism: A History of Libertarian Ideas &
Movements. NAL.
ed. The Anarchist Reader. Humanities.
Dawn & the Darkest Hour: A Study of Aldous
Huxley. Merrimack Bk Serv.
Hudson's Bay Company. Macmillan.
The Paradox of Oscar Wilde. R West.
Peoples of the Coast: The Indians of the Pacific
Northwest. Ind U Pr.
Woodcock, J. P. *see* Woodcock, John P.
Woodcock, John P.
xWoodcock, J. P.
Theory & Practice of Blood Flow
Measurement. Butterworths.
Wooddy, Carroll H. *see* Wooddy, Carroll Hill.
Wooddy, Carroll Hill.
xWooddy, Carroll H.

The Case of Frank L. Smith: Study of
Representative Government. Arno.
The Chicago Primary of 1926: A Study in
Election Methods. Arno.
Wooden, John. *see* Wooden, John R.
Wooden, John R.
xWooden, John.
The Wooden-Sharman Method: A Guide to
Winning Basketball. Macmillan.
xWooden, John R.
Practical Modern Basketball. Wiley.
Woodes, Nathaniel, fl. 1580?
xWoodes, Nathaniel.
Conflict of Conscience. AMS Pr.
The Conflict of Conscience. Norwood Edns.
Woodford, Frank B. *see* Woodford, Frank Bury.
Woodford, Frank Bury, 1903-
xWoodford, Frank B.
Alex J. Groesbeck: Portrait of a Public Man.
Wayne St U Pr.
Woodford, Protase E.
xWoodford, Protase E.
Spanish Language, Hispanic Culture. McGraw.
Woodforde, James.
xWoodforde, James.
Diary of a Country Parson, 1758-1802. Oxford
U Pr.
Woodforde, John.
xWoodforde, John.
Georgian Houses for All. Routledge & Kegan.
The Story of the Bicycle. Routledge & Kegan.
Truth About Cottages. Kelley.
The Truth About Cottages. Routledge &
Kegan.
Woodhead, H. G. *see* Woodhead, Henry George
Wandesforde.
Woodhead, Harold C. *see* Woodhead, Harold Charles.
Woodhead, Harold Charles.
xWoodhead, Harold C.
Creative Photographic Printing Methods. Focal
Pr.
Woodhead, Henry George Wandesforde, 1883-1959
xWoodhead, H. G.
Extraterritoriality in China: The Case Against
Abolition. Garland Pub.
Woodhouse, Barbara, 1910-
xWoodhouse, Barbara.
Dog Training My Way. Stein & Day.
Talking to Animals. Stein & Day.
Woodhouse, C. M. *see* Woodhouse, Christopher
Montague.
Woodhouse, Christopher Montague, 1917-
xWoodhouse, C. M.
The Greek War of Independence: Its Historical
Setting. Russell.
Modern Greece: A Short History. Merrimack
Bk Serv.
Struggle for Greece 1941-1949. Beekman Pubs.
Woodhouse, Mark. *see* Woodhouse, Mark B.
Woodhouse, Mark B.
xWoodhouse, Mark.
Preface to Philosophy. Wadsworth Pub.
Woodhouse, Philip. *see* Woodhouse, Philip R.
Woodhouse, Philip R.
xWoodhouse, Philip.
Monte Cristo. Mountaineers.
Woodhouse, William J. *see* Woodhouse, William John.
Woodhouse, William John, 1866-1937
xWoodhouse, William J.
Aetolia: Its Geography, Topography, &
Antiquities. Arno.
Woodin, Ann.
xWoodin, Ann.
Home Is the Desert. Macmillan.
Home Is the Desert. Macmillan.
In the Circle of the Sun. Macmillan.
Woodin, J. C. *see* Woodin, James C.
Woodin, James C.
xWoodin, J. C.

And Oh How Proudly. Independence Pr.
Wooldridge, Sidney W. see Wooldridge, Sidney William.
Wooldridge, Sidney William.
 xWooldridge, Sidney W.
 Geographer As Scientist: Essays on the Scope
 & Nature of Geography. Greenwood.
Wooldridge, Susan, 1940-
 xWooldridge, Susan.
 Computer Input Design. Van Nos Reinhold.
 Computer Output Design. Van Nos Reinhold.
 Project Management in Data Processing. Van
 Nos Reinhold.
 Systems & Programming Standards. Van Nos
 Reinhold.
Woolery, William K. see Woolery, William Kirk.
Woolery, William Kirk, 1888-1946
 xWoolery, William K.
 The Relation of Thomas Jefferson to American
 Foreign Policy, 1783-1793. AMS Pr.
Woolf, Douglas, 1922-
 xWoolf, Douglas.
 On Us. Black Sparrow.
Woolf, Leonard. see Woolf, Leonard Sidney.
Woolf, Leonard Sidney, 1880-1969
 xWoolf, Leonard.
 ed. Framework of a Lasting Peace. Garland
 Pub.
 Growing: An Autobiography of the Years 1904
 to 1911. HarBraceJ.
 ed. Hogarth Essays. Arno.
 ed. Intelligent Man's Way to Prevent War.
 Garland Pub.
 The Journey Not the Arrival Matters: An
 Autobiography of the Years 1939 to 1969.
 HarBraceJ.
Woolf, Rosemary
 xWoolf, Rosemary.
 The English Mystery Plays. U of Cal Pr.
Woolf, Virginia. see Woolf, Virginia Stephen.
Woolf, Virginia S. see Woolf, Virginia Stephen.
Woolf, Virginia Stephen, 1882-1941
 xWoolf, Virginia.
 Freshwater: A Comedy. HarBraceJ.
 Letters of Virginia Woolf. HarBraceJ.
 The Letters of Virginia Woolf, 1929-1931.
 HarBraceJ.
 Night & Day. HarBraceJ.
 Orlando: A Biography. HarBraceJ.
 Reviewing. Porter.
 xWoolf, Virginia S.
 A Letter to a Young Poet. Folcroft.
 Reviewing. Folcroft.
Woolfolk, Anita. see Woolfolk, Anita E.
Woolfolk, Anita E.
 xWoolfolk, Anita.
 Educational Psychology for Teachers. P-H.
Woolfolk, Dorothy A.
 xWoolfolk, Dorothy A.
 The Teenage Surefire Diet Cookbook. Watts.
Woolfolk, George R. see Woolfolk, George Ruble.
Woolfolk, George Ruble.
 xWoolfolk, George R.
 The Cotton Regency: The Northern Merchants
 & Reconstruction, 1865-1880. Octagon.
Woolfolk, Margaret.
 xWoolfolk, Margaret.
 Cooking with Berries. Potter.
Woolfolk, Robert L.
 xWoolfolk, Robert L.
 Stress, Sanity & Survival. Sovereign Bks.
Woolfolk, William.
 xWoolfolk, William.
 The Great American Birth Rite. Dial.
Woolford, Don. see Woolford, Donald Mark.
Woolford, Donald Mark.
 xWoolford, Don.
 Papua New Guinea: Initiation & Independence.
 U of Queensland Pr.
Woolford, Sam, 1897-
 xWoolford, Sam

Tales from Moonshine Valley. Shoal Creek
 Pub.
Woollcott, Alexander.
 xWoollcott, Alexander.
 The Letters of Alexander Woollcott.
 Greenwood.
 The Portable Woollcott. Greenwood.
 Two Gentlemen & a Lady. Arno.
Woolley, Bruce H.
 xWoolley, Bruce H.
 ed. Toxicology & Poison Prevention. Year Bk
 Med.
Woolley, C. Leonard. see Woolley, Charles Leonard.
Woolley, Catherine.
 xWoolley, Catherine.
 Cathy Leonard Calling. Morrow.
 Cathy's Little Sister. Morrow.
 Ginnie & the Mystery Light. Morrow.
 Ginnie & the New Girl. Morrow.
 Ginnie Joins In. Morrow.
 Libby Looks for a Spy. Morrow.
 Libby Shadows a Lady. Morrow.
 Libby's Uninvited Guest. Morrow.
 Look Alive, Libby. Morrow.
Woolley, Charles Leonard, Sir, 1880-1960
 xWoolley, C. Leonard.
 Sumerians. AMS Pr.
 Sumerians. Norton.
 xWoolley, Leonard.
 Spadework in Archaeology. Philos Lib.
Woolley, F. R. see Woolley, F. Ross.
Woolley, F. Ross.
 xWoolley, F. R.
 Problem-Oriented Nursing. Springer Pub.
Woolley, Fran.
 xWoolley, Fran
 The Abaco Cook Book: From a Bahamian Out
 Island. Durrell.
Woolley, Ivan. see Woolley, Ivan Medhurst.
Woolley, Ivan Medhurst.
 xWoolley, Ivan.
 Off to Mt. Hood: An Auto Biography of the
 Old Road. Oreg Hist Soc.
Woolley, Leonard. see Woolley, Charles Leonard.
Woolley, Persia, 1935-
 xWoolley, Persia.
 The Custody Handbook. Summit Bks.
Woolmer, J. Howard.
 xWoolmer, J. Howard.
 Compiled by Checklist of the Hogarth Press,
 1917-1938. Woolmer-Brotherson.
Woolner, Frank, 1916-
 xWoolner, Frank.
 Trout Hunting. Winchester Pr.
Woolner, Thomas, 1825-1892
 xWoolner, Thomas.
 My Beautiful Lady. AMS Pr.
 Pygmalion. AMS Pr.
 Silenus. AMS Pr.
Woolrich, Willis R. see Woolrich, Willis Raymond.
Woolrich, Willis Raymond.
 xWoolrich, Willis R.
 Cold & Freezer Storage Manual. AVI.
Woolsey, Robert E. see Woolsey, Robert E. D.
Woolsey, Robert E. D.
 xWoolsey, Robert E.
 Operations Research for Immediate
 Application: A Quick and Dirty Manual.
 Har-Row.
Woolson, Constance F. see Woolson, Constance
 Fenimore.
Woolson, Constance Fenimore, 1840-1894
 xWoolson, Constance F.
 Horace Chase. Irvington.
 xWoolson, Constance Fenimore.
 Anne. Arno.
Woolston, Maxine Bernard (Yaple) Sweezy, 1911-
 xWoolston, Maxine Y.

Structure of the Nazi Economy. Russell.
Woolston, Maxine Y. see Woolston, Maxine Bernard
 (Yaple) Sweezy.
Woolworth, Robert.
 xWoolworth, Robert.
 Indonesian Ikats. Bayard Gallery.
Wooster, Ralph A.
 xWooster, Ralph A.
 People in Power: Courthouse & Statehouse in
 the Lower South, 1850-1860. U of Tenn Pr.
 Politicians, Planters, & Plain Folk: Courthouse
 & Statehouse in the Upper South, 1850-1860.
 U of Tenn Pr.
Wooten, James.
 xWooten, James.
 Dasher: The Roots & the Rising of Jimmy
 Carter. Summit Bks.
Wooton, William.
 xWooton, William.
 Intermediate Algebra. Wadsworth Pub.
Wootten, Morgan.
 xWootten, Morgan.
 From Orphans to Champions: The Story of
 Dematha's Morgan Wootten. Atheneum.
Wootters, John.
 xWootters, John.
 A Guide to Hunting in Texas. Pacesetter Pr.
 Hunting Trophy Deer. Winchester Pr.
Wootton, Anthony.
 xWootton, Anthony.
 Dilemmas of Discourse: Controversies About
 the Sociological Interpretation of Language.
 Allen Unwin.
 xWootton, Anthony J.
 Dilemmas of Discourse: Controversies About
 the Sociological Interpretation of Language.
 Holmes & Meier.
Wootton, Anthony J. see Wootton, Anthony.
Wootton, Graham.
 xWootton, Graham.
 Politics of Influence: British Ex-Servicemen,
 Cabinet Decisions & Cultural Change,
 1917-1957. Harvard U Pr.
 Pressure Groups in Britain 1720-1970: An
 Essay in Interpretation with Original
 Documents. Shoe String.
 Pressure Politics in Contemporary Britain.
 Lexington Bks.
Woozley, A. D. see Woozley, Anthony Douglas.
Woozley, Anthony Douglas.
 xWoozley, A. D.
 Law & Obedience: The Arguments of Plato's
 Crito. U of NC Pr.
 Theory of Knowledge: An Introduction.
 Humanities.
Worboys, Anne.
 xWorboys, Anne.
 The Barrancourt Destiny. Ace Bks.
 The Way of the Tamarisk. Delacorte.
Worcester, David.
 xWorcester, David.
 Art of Satire. Russell.
Worcester, Dean A. see Worcester, Dean Amory.
Worcester, Dean Amory.
 xWorcester, Dean A.
 Monopoly, Big Business, & Welfare in Postwar
 United States. U of Wash Pr.
 Welfare Gains from Advertising: The Problem
 of Regulation. Am Enterprise.
Worcester, Donald E. see Worcester, Donald Emmet.
Worcester, Donald Emmet, 1915-
 xWorcester, Donald E.
 The Apaches: Eagles of the Southwest. U of
 Okla Pr.
Worcester, Noah, 1758-1837
 xWorcester, Noah.

A Solemn Review of the Custom of War:
Showing That War Is the Effect of Popular
Delusion & Proposing a Remedy. Ozer.
Worcester, Robert M.
xWorcester, Robert M.
ed. Consumer Market Research Handbook.
Van Nos Reinhold.
Worcester, Thomas K.
xWorcester, Thomas K.
A Portrait of Colorado. Touchstone Pr Ore.
Worchel, Stephen.
xWorchel, Stephen.
Understanding Social Psychology. Dorsey.
Wordsworth, J. C. *see* Wordsworth, John Craufurd.
Wordsworth, John Craufurd.
xWordsworth, J. C.
Adventures in Literature. Arden Lib.
Adventures in Literature. Folcroft.
Adventures in Literature. Kennikat.
Wordsworth, William.
xWordsworth, William.
Letters of the Wordsworth Family from 1787
to 1855. Scholarly.
Prelude. Routledge & Kegan.
Prelude: Or, Growth of a Poet's Mind. Oxford
U Pr.
Prose Works of William Wordsworth. AMS Pr.
The Prose Works of William Wordsworth.
Oxford U Pr.
The Ruined Cottage & the Pedlar. Cornell U
Pr.
Wordsworth. U of Queensland Pr.
Wordsworth's Pocket Notebook. Kennikat.
Worell, Judith.
xWorell, Judith.
Psychology for Teachers & Students. McGraw.
Worf, Douglas L.
xWorf, Douglas L.
ed. Biological Monitoring for Environmental
Effects. Lexington Bks.
Work in America Institute.
xWork in America Institute Inc.
Job Strategies for Urban Youth: Sixteen Pilot
Programs for Action. Work in Amer.
Work in America Institute Inc. *see* Work in America
Institute.
Work, John W. *see* Work, John Wesley.
Work, John Wesley, 1871-1925
xWork, John W.
Folk Song of the American Negro. Negro U
Pr.
Workers of the Writer's Program. *see* Writers' Program.
Nebraska.
Workers of the Writers' Program Work Projects
Administration in the State of South Carolina. *see*
Writers' Program. South Carolina.
Workers Party of the United States of America.
xWorkers Party of the United States.
Labor Action. Greenwood.
Workman, Brooke, 1933-
xWorkman, Brooke.
In Search of Ernest Hemingway: A Model for
Teaching a Literature Seminar. NCTE.
Teaching the Decades: A Humanities Approach
to American Civilization. NCTE.
Workman, Herbert. *see* Workman, Herbert Brook.

Workman, Herbert Brook, 1862-

xWorkman, Herbert.
Persecution in the Early Church. Oxford U Pr.

Workman, Samuel K. *see* Workman, Samuel Klinger.

Workman, Samuel Klinger, 1907-
xWorkman, Samuel K.
Fifteenth Century Translation As an Influence
on English Prose. Octagon.

Workshop on Alternative Energy Strategies.

xWorkshops on Alternative Energy Strategies.
Energy: Global Prospects, 1985-2000.
McGraw.

**Workshop Seminar on Momentum Wave Function
Determination in Atomic, Molecular and Nuclear
Systems, Bloomington, Ind., 1976.**

xWorkshop-Seminar on Momentum Wave
Function Determination in Atomic, Molecular &
Nuclear Systems, Indiana Univ., Bloomington,
May 31-June 4, 1976.
Momentum Wave Functions:
Proceedings-1976. Am Inst Physics.
Workshop-Seminar on Momentum Wave Function
Determination in Atomic, Molecular & Nuclear
Systems, Indiana Univ., Bloomington, May 31-June 4,
1976. *see* Workshop Seminar on Momentum Wave
Function Determination in Atomic, Molecular and
Nuclear Systems, Bloomington, Ind., 1976.
Workshops on Alternative Energy Strategies. *see*
Workshop on Alternative Energy Strategies.
Worland, Peter B.
xWorland, Peter B.
Introduction to Basic Programming: A
Structured Approach. HM.
World Association of Girl Guides & Girl Scouts. *see*
World Association of Girl Guides and Girl Scouts.
World Association of Girl Guides and Girl Scouts.
xWorld Association of Girl Guides & Girl Scouts.
Basics of the World Association of Girl Guides
& Girl Scouts. GS.

World Bank Group.
xWorld Bank.
The Assault on World Poverty: Problems of
Rural Development, Education & Health.
Johns Hopkins.
Chad: Development Potential and Constraints.
Johns Hopkins.
Current Economic Position & Prospects of
Ecuador. Johns Hopkins.
Economic Growth of Colombia: Problems &
Prospects. Johns Hopkins.
Kenya: Into the Second Decade, World Bank
Country Economic Report. Johns Hopkins.
Korea: Problems & Issues in a Rapidly
Growing Economy. Johns Hopkins.
Landsat Index Atlas of the Developing
Countries of the World. Johns Hopkins.
Lesotho: A Development Challenge. Johns
Hopkins.
The Philippines: Priorities & Prospects for
Development. Johns Hopkins.
Population Policies & Economic Development.
Johns Hopkins.
Senegal: Tradition, Diversification, & Economic
Development. Johns Hopkins.
Turkey: Prospects & Problems of an Expanding
Economy. Johns Hopkins.
World Bank Operations: Sectoral Programs &
Policies. Johns Hopkins.
World Development Report, 1978. Oxford U
Pr.
World Tables, 1976. Johns Hopkins.
Yugoslavia: Development with
Decentralization. Johns Hopkins.
World Book Childcraft International Inc. Staff. *see* World
Book-Childcraft International.
World Book Encyclopedia Inc Staff. *see* World Book
Encyclopedia.
World Book-Childcraft International.
xWorld Book Childcraft International Inc. Staff.
Cyclo-Teacher Learning Aid. World
Bk-Childcraft.
xWorld Book-Childcraft International, Inc. Staff.

Childcraft Annual - About Dogs. World
Bk-Childcraft.
Childcraft Annual-Mathemagic. World
Bk-Childcraft.
Childcraft Annual-Prehistoric Animals. World
Bk-Childcraft.
Today Nineteen Eighty. World Bk-Childcraft.
World Book Encyclopedia.
xWorld Book Encyclopedia Inc Staff.
Today 1979. World Book.
World Committee For The Relief Of The Victims Of
German Fascism. *see* World Committee for the
Victims of German Fascism.
World Committee for the Victims of German Fascism.
xWorld Committee For The Relief Of The Victims
Of German Fascism.
The Reichstag Fire Trial: The Second Brown
Book of the Hitler Terror. Fertig.
**World Conference on Medical Education, 4th,
Copenhagen, 1972.**
xWorld Conference on Medical Education, 4th,
Copenhagen 1972.
Educating Tomorrow's Doctors: Proceedings.
World Med.
**World Congress on Ballistocardiography and
Cardiovascular Dynamics, 2nd, Oporto, Portugal,
1969.**
xWorld Congress on Ballistocardiography &
Cardiovascular Dynamics, 2nd, Oporto, 1969.
Ballistocardiography & Cardiovascular Therapy:
Proceedings. S Karger.
**World Congress on Ballistocardiography and
Cardiovascular Dynamics, 4th, Amsterdam, 1975.**
xWorld Congress on Ballistocardiography &
Cardiovascular Dynamics, 4th, Amsterdam, April
14-16, 1975.
Non-Invasive Mechanical Methods in
Cardiology & Cardivascular Dynamics:
Proceedings. S Karger.
**World Congress on Chemical Engineering, 1st,
Amsterdam, 1976.**
xPlenary Sessions of the First World Congress on
Chemical Engineering, Amsterdam, June 28-July
1, 1976.
Chemical Engineering in a Changing World:
Proceedings. Elsevier.
World Congress on Pain, 1st, Florence, 1975.
xWorld Congress on Pain, 1st, Florence, 1975.
Advances in Pain Research & Therapy:
Proceedings. Raven.
World Council of Churches.
xWorld Council of Churches, Geneva, Switzerland.
Classified Catalog of the Ecumenical
Movement. G K Hall.
World Council of Churches, Geneva, Switzerland. *see*
World Council of Churches.
World Federation of Hemophilia.
xCongress of the World Federation of
Haemophilia, 7th, Teheran 1971.
Haemophilia: Proceedings. Elsevier.
World Filtration Congress, 1st, Paris, 1974.
xFirst World Filtration Congress, May 14-17,
1974.
Papers Presented at the First World Filtration
Congress, Paris. Halsted Pr.
World Food Conference, Ames, Iowa June, 1976. *see*
World Food Conference, Iowa State University, 1976.
World Food Conference, Iowa State University, 1976.
xWorld Food Conference, Ames, Iowa June, 1976.
Proceedings. Iowa St U Pr.
World Food Programme.
xFAO Executive Director.
Report on the World Food Program. Unipub.
World Health Organization.
xWorld Health Organization.

Medical Research Programme of the World Health Organization, 1958-1963. World Health.

Schizophrenia: An International Follow-up Study. Wiley.

World Meteorological Organization.
xWorld Meteorological Organization.
Aeronautical Meteorology. Unipub.
Chart Processing Functions of Regional Meteorological Centres. Unipub.
Climatic Change. Unipub.
Collection, Storage & Retrieval of Meteorological Data. Unipub.
Data Processing for Climatological Purposes. Unipub.
Data Processing in Meteorology. Unipub.
Economic Benefits of National Meteorological Services. Unipub.
Estimation of Maximum Floods. Unipub.
Global Data-Processing System & Meteorological Service to Shipping. Unipub.
Harvest from Weather. Unipub.
Influence of Weather Conditions on the Occurrence of Apple Scab. Unipub.
International Cloud Album for Observers in Aircraft. Unipub.
International Cloud Atlas. Unipub.
International Meteorological Vocabulary. Unipub.
Introduction to GARP. Unipub.
Manual for Depth-Area-Duration Analysis of Storm Precipitation. Unipub.
Manual on Meteorological Observing in Transport Aircraft. Unipub.
Marine Cloud Album. Unipub.
Note on Climatological Normals. Unipub.
Planning of the Global Telecommunication System. Unipub.
Protection Against Frost Damage. Unipub.
Reduction & Use of Data Obtained by TIROS Meteorological Satellites. Unipub.
Role of Meteorological Satellites in the World Weather Watch. Unipub.
Scope of the Nineteen Seventy-Two to Nineteen Seventy-Five Plan. Unipub.
Short-Period Averages for 1951-1960 & Provisional Average for CLIMAT TEMP SHIP Stations. Unipub.
Sites for Wind-Power Installations. Unipub.
Statistical Analysis & Prognosis in Meteorology. Unipub.
Weather & Food. Unipub.
Weather & Water. Unipub.

World Meteorological Organization. Executive Committee.
xWMO Executive Committee, 26th Session.
Drought: Lectures. Unipub.

World Organization of National Colleges, Academies, and Academic Associations of General Practitioners-Family Physicians. Classification Committee.
xWorld Organization of National College Physicians (WONCA).
International Classification of Health Problems in Primary Care. Oxford U Pr.

World Philosophy Conference, Dec. 28, 1975-Jan. 3, 1976. see World Philosophy Conference, Delhi, 1976.

World Philosophy Conference, Delhi, 1976.
xWorld Philosophy Conference, Dec. 28, 1975-Jan. 3, 1976.
Knowledge, Culture & Value: Proceedings. Verry.

World Print Council.
xWorld Print Council.
Paper-Art & Technology. Chronicle Bks.

World Pub. Co. see World Publishing Co., Cleveland.

World Publishing Co., Cleveland.
xWorld Pub. Co.

Prentice-Hall Students Edition of the Concise Webster's New World Dictionary of the American Language. P-H.

World Shakespeare Congress, Vancouver, B.C., 1971.
xWorld Shakespeare Congress, Vancouver, August 1971.
Shakespeare 1971: Proceedings. U of Toronto Pr.

Worley, Robert C.
xWorley, Robert C.
Change in the Church: A Source of Hope. Westminster.
A Gathering of Strangers: Understanding the Life of Your Church. Westminster.

Worlton, Lois F.
xWorlton, Lois F.
Planning LDS Weddings & Receptions. Horizon Utah.

Wormer, Joe Van. see Van Wormer, Joe.

Wormington, H. M. see Wormington, Hannah Marie.

Wormington, Hannah Marie, 1914-
xWormington, H. M.
Ancient Man in North America. Denver Mus Natl Hist.

Worms, Emile, 1838-1918
xWorms, Emile.
Histoire Commerciale De la Ligue Hanseatique. B Franklin.

Worms, G. see Worms, Gerard.

Worms, Gerard.
xWorms, G.
Modern Methods of Applied Economics. Gordon.

Wormser, Richard. see Wormser, Richard Edward.

Wormser, Richard Edward.
xWormser, Richard.
Gone to Texas. Morrow.

Worner, Karl H. see Worner, Karl Heinrich.

Worner, Karl Heinrich, 1910-1969
xWorner, Karl H.
The History of Music: A Book for Study & Reference. Free Pr.

Worner, Roger B., 1943-
xWorner, Roger B.
Student Diagnosis, Placement & Prescription: A Criterion-Referenced Approach. Ind U Pr.

Worrall, W. E.
xWorrall, W. E.
Clays & Ceramic Raw Materials. Halsted Pr.

Worrell, Albert C. see Worrell, Albert Cadwallader.

Worrell, Albert Cadwallader, 1913-
xWorrell, Albert C.
Economics of American Forestry. Wiley.

Worrell, Anne L. see Worrell, Anne Lowry.

Worrell, Anne Lowry.
xWorrell, Anne L.
A Brief of Wills & Marriages in Montgomery & Fincastle Counties, Virginia, 1733-1831. Genealog Pub.
Early Marriages, Wills, & Some Revolutionary War Records: Botetourt County, Virginia. Genealog Pub.
Over the Mountain Men: Their Early Court Records in Southwest Virginia. Genealog Pub.

Worrell, Estelle A. see Worrell, Estelle Ansley.

Worrell, Estelle Ansley.
xWorrell, Estelle A.
The Doll Book. Van Nos Reinhold.
Dolls, Puppedolls & Teddy Bears. Van Nos Reinhold.
Make Your Own Miniature Rooms. Hobby Hse.

Worrell, George E.
xWorrell, George E.
How to Take the Worry Out of Witnessing. Broadman.

Worrell, William H. see Worrell, William Hoyt.

Worrell, William Hoyt.
xWorrell, William H.

The Coptic Manuscripts in the Freer Collection. Johnson Repr.

Worringer, Wilhelm, 1881-1965
xWorringer, Wilhelm.
Abstraction & Empathy. Intl Univs Pr.

Worsfold, W. Basil. see Worsfold, William Basil.

Worsfold, William B. see Worsfold, William Basil.

Worsfold, William Basil, 1858-1939
xWorsfold, W. Basil.
The Principles of Criticism: An Introduction to the Study of Literature. Folcroft.
xWorsfold, William B.
South Africa: A Study in Colonial Administration & Development. Negro U Pr.

Worsley, Peter.
xWorsley, Peter.
Inside China. Rowman.
The Third World. U of Chicago Pr.
The Trumpet Shall Sound: A Study of Cargo Cults in Melanesia. Schocken.

Worster, Donald. see Worster, Donald E.

Worster, Donald E., 1941-
xWorster, Donald.
Dust Bowl: The Southern Plains in the 1930's. Oxford U Pr.
Nature's Economy: The Roots of Ecology. Sierra.

Worsthorne, Simon T. see Worsthorne, Simon Towneley.

Worsthorne, Simon Towneley.
xWorsthorne, Simon T.
Venetian Opera in the Seventeenth Century. Oxford U Pr.

Worstman, Gail. see Worstman, Gail L.

Worstman, Gail L.
xWorstman, Gail.
The Whole Grain Bake Book. Pacific Search.

Worswick, Clark.
xWorswick, Clark.
The Last Empire: Photography in British India 1855-1911. Aperture.

Worswick, George D. see Worswick, George David Norman.

Worswick, George David Norman.
xWorswick, George D.
Profits in the British Economy, 1909-1938. Kelley.

Worswick, Marilyn. see Worswick, Marilyn E.

Worswick, Marilyn E.
xWorswick, Marilyn.
Thank You Davey; Thank You, God. Augsburg.

Wortabet, J. see Wortabet, John.

Wortabet, John.
xWortabet, J.
ed. English-Arabic, Arabic-English Dictionary. Ungar.

Worth, Dean S.
xWorth, Dean S.
A Dictionary of Western Kamchadal. U of Cal Pr.

Worth, Fred L.
xWorth, Fred L.
The Complete Unabridged Super Trivia Encyclopedia. Warner Bks.

Worth, H. M. see Worth, Harry Mullins.

Worth, Harry Mullins.
xWorth, H. M.
Principles & Practice of Oral Radiologic Interpretation. Year Bk Med.

Worth, Helen. see Worth, Helen Levison.

Worth, Helen Levison, 1913-
xWorth, Helen.
Cooking Without Recipes. Bobbs.

Worth, Jennifer.
xWorth, Jennifer.
Emergency Room. Elsevier-Nelson.

Worth, Katharine. see Worth, Katharine Joyce.

Worth, Katharine Joyce, 1922-
xWorth, Katharine.

The Irish Drama of Europe from Yeats to
  Beckett. Humanities.
Worth, Robert M.
  xWorth, Robert M.
    Nepal Health Survey, 1965-1966. U Pr of
      Hawaii.
Worth, T. *see* Worth, Thomas.
Worth, Thomas, 1923-
  xWorth, T.
    Non-Technical Fortran. P-H.
  xWorth, Thomas.
    Cobol for Beginners. P-H.
Worth, Valerie.
  xWorth, Valerie.
    More Small Poems. FS&G.
    Still More Small Poems. FS&G.
Wortham, Jim.
  xWortham, Jim.
    Love Touching Love. Love Street.
    Touching You Touching Me. Love Street.
Wortham, John D. *see* Wortham, John David.
Wortham, John David, 1922-
  xWortham, John D.
    Genesis of British Egyptology, 1549-1906. U of
      Okla Pr.
Worthen, John.
  xWorthen, John.
    D. H. Lawrence & the Idea of the Novel.
      Rowman.
Worthington, Barton. *see* Worthington, Edgar Barton.
Worthington, E. Barton. *see* Worthington, Edgar Barton.
Worthington, Edgar Barton, 1905-
  xWorthington, Barton.
    The Nile. Silver.
  xWorthington, E. Barton.
    ed. Arid Land Irrigation in Developing
      Countries: Environmental Problems &
      Effects. Pergamon.
Worthington, Jane.
  xWorthington, Jane.
    Wordsworth's Reading of Roman Prose. Shoe
      String.
Worthington, L. V., 1920-
  xWorthington, L. V.
    On the North Atlantic Circulation. Johns
      Hopkins.
Worthington, Robin.
  xWorthington, Robin.
    Enjoying Your Preschooler. Pacific Pr Pub
      Assn.
    Enjoying Your Preschooler. St Anthony Mess
      Pr.
Worthley, John A.
  xWorthley, John A.
    ed. Zero-Base Budgeting in State & Local
      Government: Current Experiences & Cases.
      Praeger.
Worthley, William. *see* Worthley, William Justin.
Worthley, William Justin.
  xWorthley, William.
    Sourcebook of Language Learning Activities:
      Instructional Strategies & Methods. Little.
Worthy, Morgan.
  xWorthy, Morgan.
    Aha: A Puzzle Approach to Creative Thinking.
      Nelson Hall.
Wortley, B. A. *see* Wortley, Ben Atkinson.
Wortley, Ben Atkinson, 1907-
  xWortley, B. A.
    Expropriation in Public International Law.
      Arno.
Wortman, Leon. *see* Wortman, Leon A.
Wortman, Leon A.
  xWortman, Leon.
    Successful Small Business Management. Am
      Mgmt.
  xWortman, Leon A.

A Deskbook of Business Management Terms.
  Am Mgmt.
Successful Small Business Management. Am
  Mgmt.
Wortman, Richard.
  xWortman, Richard.
    Crisis of Russian Populism. Cambridge U Pr.
Worton, Stanley. *see* Worton, Stanley N.
Worton, Stanley N.
  xWorton, Stanley.
    Population Growth in America. Hayden.
  xWorton, Stanley N.
    The First Americans. Hayden.
    Freedom of Assembly & Petition. Hayden.
    Freedom of Religion. Hayden.
    Freedom of Speech & Press. Hayden.
Worvill, Roy.
  xWorvill, Roy.
    The Radio Universe: An Introduction to Radio
      Astronomy & Outer Space. Orbiting Bk.
Wosmek, Frances.
  xWosmek, Frances.
    illus. A Bowl of Sun. Childrens.
    Mystery of the Eagle's Claw. Westminster.
Wotton, Mabel E.
  xWotton, Mabel E.
    Word Portraits of Famous Writers. Folcroft.
Wotton, Tom S.
  xWotton, Tom S.
    A Dictionary of Foreign Musical Terms &
      Handbook of Orchestral Instruments.
      Scholarly.
Woudenberg, Paul. *see* Woudenberg, Paul R.
Woudenberg, Paul R.
  xWoudenberg, Paul.
    Lincoln & Continental: The Postwar Years.
      Motorbooks Intl.
Wouk, Herman.
  xWouk, Herman.
    Aurora Dawn. Doubleday.
    The Caine Mutiny. PB.
    Caine Mutiny. Doubleday.
    City Boy. PB.
    Don't Stop the Carnival. Doubleday.
    Don't Stop the Carnival. PB.
    The Lomokome Papers. Queens Hse.
    This Is My God. Doubleday.
    This Is My God. PB.
    War & Remembrance. PB.
    The Winds of War. Little.
    Winds of War. PB.
Wourms, John P.
  xWourms, John P.
    ed. Genetic Studies of Fish. Mss Info.
Woy, James B.
  xWoy, James B.
    Commodity Futures Trading: A Bibliographic
      Guide. Bowker.
Woytinsky, Wladimir S., 1885-1960
  xWoytinsky, Wladimir S.
    India: The Awakening Giant. Kraus Repr.
W.P.A. Federal Writers Project. *see* Federal Writers'
  Project. New York (City).
WPA Writer's Project. *see* Writers' Program. Virginia.
WPA Writers' Project Editors. *see* Federal Writers'
  Project.
Wragg, David.
  xWragg, David.
    Wings Over the Sea. Arco.
Wragg, David. *see* Wragg, David W.
Wragg, David W.
  xWragg, David.
    A Dictionary of Aviation. Fell.
    Flight Before Flying. Fell.
    Flight with Power: The First Ten Years. St
      Martin.
  xWragg, David W.
    Dictionary of Aviation. Beekman Pubs.
    Speed in the Air. Fell.
Wragg, E. C. *see* Wragg, Edward Conrad.

Wragg, Edward Conrad.
  xWragg, E. C.
    Teaching Teaching. David & Charles.
Wraith, R. E. *see* Wraith, Ronald E.
Wraith, Ronald. *see* Wraith, Ronald E.
Wraith, Ronald E.
  xWraith, R. E.
    Administrative Tribunals. Allen Unwin.
  xWraith, Ronald.
    Local Administration in West Africa. Holmes
      & Meier.
Wrangles, Alan.
  xWrangles, Alan.
    Sea Fishing for Fun. David & Charles.
Wray, John L. *see* Wray, John Lee.
Wray, John Lee, 1925-
  xWray, John L.
    Calcareous Algae. Elsevier.
Wrean, William H. *see* Wrean, William Hamilton.
Wrean, William Hamilton.
  xWrean, William H.
    The Demand for Business Loan Credit.
      Lexington Bks.
Wrede, Stuart.
  xWrede, Stuart.
    The Architecture of Erik Gunnar Asplund.
      MIT Pr.
Wreh, Tuan, 1929-
  xWreh, Tuan.
    The Love of Liberty: The Rule of President
      William V. S. Tubman in Liberia 1944-1971.
      Universe.
Wren, Christopher S.
  xWren, Christopher S.
    The Super Summer of Jamie McBride. S&S.
Wren, Daniel A.
  xWren, Daniel A.
    Evolution of Management Thought. Wiley.
    Principles of Management: Process & Behavior.
      Wiley.
Wren, George R.
  xWren, George R.
    Modern Health Administration. U of Ga Pr.
Wren, Jack.
  xWren, Jack.
    Home Buyer's Guide. B&N.
Wren, M. K.
  xWren, M. K.
    Nothing's Certain but Death. Doubleday.
Wren, Melvin C.
  xWren, Melvin C.
    The Course of Russian History. Macmillan.
Wren, Thomas E.
  xWren, Thomas E.
    Agency & Urgency: The Origin of Moral
      Obligation. Precedent Pub.
Wrench, David. *see* Wrench, David F.
Wrench, David F.
  xWrench, David.
    Psychology: A Social Approach. McGraw.
    Readings in Psychology: Foundations &
      Applications. McGraw.
Wrenn, C. Gilbert. *see* Wrenn, Charles Gilbert.
Wrenn, Charles Gilbert, 1902-
  xWrenn, C. Gilbert.
    The World of the Contemporary Counselor.
      HM.
Wrenn, Lawrence G.
  xWrenn, Lawrence G.
    ed. Divorce & Remarriage in the Catholic
      Church. Paulist Pr.
Wriggins, Sally. *see* Wriggins, Sally Hovey.
Wriggins, Sally Hovey.
  xWriggins, Sally.
    White Monkey King: A Chinese Fable.
      Pantheon.
Wriggins, W. Howard. *see* Wriggins, William Howard.
Wriggins, William Howard.
  xWriggins, W. Howard.

ed. Population, Politics, & the Future of
   Southern Asia. Columbia U Pr.
Wright, A. R. *see* Wright, Arthur Robinson.
Wright, A. W.
   xWright, A. W.
      G. D. H. Cole & Socialist Democracy. Oxford
      U Pr.
Wright, Al G.
   xWright, Al G.
      Bands of the World. Instrumental Co.
Wright, Alison.
   xWright, Alison.
      The Spanish Economy, 1959-1976. Holmes &
      Meier.
Wright, Andrew. *see* Wright, Andrew H.
Wright, Andrew H.
   xWright, Andrew.
      A Reader's Guide to English & American
      Literature. Scott F.
Wright, Arthur F, 1913-
   xWright, Arthur F.
      Buddhism in Chinese History. Stanford U Pr.
      ed. Confucian Personalities. Stanford U Pr.
      ed. The Confucian Persuasion. Stanford U Pr.
      ed. Confucianism & Chinese Civilization.
      Stanford U Pr.
      ed. Studies in Chinese Thought. U of Chicago
      Pr.
Wright, Arthur Robinson, 1862-1932
   xWright, A. R.
      English Folklore. Norwood Edns.
Wright, Bank.
   xWright, Bank.
      Sun Valley: A Mountain Guide. Mntn & Sea.
      Surfing Hawaii. Mntn & Sea.
Wright, Barton.
   xWright, Barton.
      Hopi Kachinas: The Complete Guide to
      Collecting Kachina Dolls. Northland.
Wright, Basil.
   xWright, Basil.
      Use of the Film. Arno.
Wright, Benjamin F. *see* Wright, Benjamin Fletcher.
Wright, Benjamin Fletcher, 1900-
   xWright, Benjamin F.
      Growth of American Constitutional Law. U of
      Chicago Pr.
Wright, Betty R. *see* Wright, Betty Ren.
Wright, Betty Ren.
   xWright, Betty R.
      I Want to Read. Western Pub.
Wright, Burton.
   xWright, Burton.
      Criminal Justice & the Social Sciences. HR&W.
Wright, C. A. *see* Wright, Christopher Amyas.
Wright, C. H. *see* Wright, Charles Henry Conrad.
Wright, Carol.
   xWright, Carol.
      The Liberated Cook's Book. David & Charles.
Wright, Carolyne.
   xWright, Carolyne L.
      Stealing the Children. Ahsahta Pr.
Wright, Carolyne L. *see* Wright, Carolyne.
Wright, Carroll. *see* Wright, Carroll Davidson.
Wright, Carroll D. *see* Wright, Carroll Davidson.
Wright, Carroll Davidson, 1840-1909
   xWright, Carroll.
      The Industrial Evolution of the United States.
      Johnson Repr.
   xWright, Carroll D.
      Industrial Evolution of the United States.
      Russell.
Wright, Celeste T. *see* Wright, Celeste Turner.
Wright, Celeste Turner.
   xWright, Celeste T.
      Etruscan Princess & Other Poems. AMS Pr.
Wright, Charles, 1935-
   xWright, Charles.

China Trace. Columbia U Pr.
      The Grave of the Right Hand. Columbia U Pr.
Wright, Charles. *see* Wright, Charles Henry Hamilton.
Wright, Charles H. *see* Wright, Charles Henry Conrad.
Wright, Charles Henry Conrad, 1869-1957
   xWright, C. H.
      A History of French Literature. Folcroft.
   xWright, Charles H.
      The Background of Modern French Literature.
      Arno.
      History of French Literature. Haskell.
      History of the Third French Republic. Arno.
Wright, Charles Henry Hamilton.
   xWright, Charles.
      ed. The Protestant Dictionary: Containing
      Articles on the History, Doctrines, &
      Practices of the Christian Church. Gale.
Wright, Christopher, 1945-
   xWright, Christopher.
      French Painting. Mayflower Bks.
Wright, Christopher Amyas, 1928-
   xWright, C. A.
      Flukes & Snails. Hafner.
Wright, Christopher N. *see* Wright, Christopher Norton.
Wright, Christopher Norton.
   xWright, Christopher N.
      No Hero, I Confess: A Nineteenth-Century
      Autobiography. Taplinger.
Wright, Cynthia.
   xWright, Cynthia.
      Caroline. Ballantine.
      Touch the Sun. Ballantine.
Wright, D. Frankin. *see* Wright, D. Franklin.
Wright, D. Franklin.
   xWright, D. Frankin.
      Arithmetic for College Students. Heath.
Wright, D. G.
   xWright, D. G.
      Revolution & Terror in France 1789-95.
      Longman.
Wright, Dare.
   xWright, Dare.
      Edith & Little Bear Lend a Hand. Random.
      Edith & Midnight. Doubleday.
      Lonely Doll. Doubleday.
      The Lonely Doll. Doubleday.
      illus. Look at a Calf. Random.
      Look at a Calf. Random.
      Look at a Gull. Random.
      illus. Look at a Kitten. Random.
Wright, David, 1920-
   xWright, David.
      Deafness. Stein & Day.
Wright, Deil S. *see* Wright, Deil Spencer.
Wright, Deil Spencer, 1930-
   xWright, Deil S.
      Assessing the Impacts of General Revenue
      Sharing in the Fifty States: A Survey of State
      Administrators. U NC Inst Res Soc Sci.
      Federal Grants-In-Aid: Perspectives &
      Alternatives. Am Enterprise.
Wright, Dermot.
   xWright, Dermot.
      Marine Engines & Boating Mechanics. David
      & Charles.
Wright, Donald R.
   xWright, Donald R.
      The Early History of Niumi: Settlement &
      Foundation of Mandinka State on the
      Gambia River. Ohio U Ctr Int.
Wright, Dorothy.
   xWright, Dorothy.
      The Complete Book of Baskets & Basketry.
      Scribner.
Wright, Dudley, 1868-1949
   xWright, Dudley.
      Vampires & Vampirism. Gordon Pr.
Wright, E. *see* Wright, Edward A.
Wright, E. A. *see* Wright, Eric Arthur.

Wright, E. Whitman.
   xWright, E. Whitman.
      Structural Design by Computer. Van Nos
      Reinhold.
Wright, Edgar, 1920-
   xWright, Edgar.
      ed. The Critical Evaluation of African
      Literature. Inscape Corp.
Wright, Edmond.
   xWright, Esmond.
      ed. Causes & Consequences of the American
      Revolution. New Viewpoints.
      ed. A Tug of Loyalties: Anglo-American
      Relations 1765-85. Humanities.
Wright, Edward A.
   xWright, E.
      Understanding Today's Theatre. P-H.
   xWright, Edward A.
      Understanding Today's Theatre. Norwood
      Edns.
Wright, Edward N. *see* Wright, Edward Needles.
Wright, Edward Needles, 1897-
   xWright, Edward N.
      Conscientious Objectors in the Civil War. Peter
      Smith.
Wright, Elliott. *see* Wright, H. Elliott.
Wright, Eric Arthur.
   xWright, E. A.
      Brain Structure & Aging. Mss Info.
Wright, Ernest H. *see* Wright, Ernest Hunter.
Wright, Ernest Hunter, 1882-
   xWright, Ernest H.
      Authorship of Timon of Athens. AMS Pr.
      Authorship of Timon of Athens. R West.
      Meaning of Rousseau. Russell.
Wright, Esmond. *see* Wright, Edmond.
Wright, Frances W. *see* Wright, Frances Woodworth.
Wright, Frances Woodworth.
   xWright, Frances W.
      Coastwise Navigation. Cornell Maritime.
Wright, Frank L. *see* Wright, Frank Lloyd.
Wright, Frank Lloyd, 1867-1959
   xWright, Frank L.
      An Autobiography. Horizon.
      Drawings of Frank Lloyd Wright. Horizon.
      The Future of Architecture. Horizon.
      Future of Architecture. NAL.
      Genius & the Mobocracy. Horizon.
      Living City. NAL.
      The Natural House. Horizon.
Wright, Frederick A. *see* Wright, Frederick Adam.
Wright, Frederick Adam, 1869-1946
   xWright, Frederick A.
      ed. Greek Social Life. AMS Pr.
Wright, Glen.
   xWright, Glen.
      Student Journalist & Making Advertising Pay
      for the School Publication. Rosen Pr.
Wright, Gordon.
   xWright, Gordon.
      Learning to Ride, Hunt & Show. Doubleday.
      Ordeal of Total War, 1939-1945. Har-Row.
      Raymond Poincare & the French Presidency.
      Octagon.
      The Riding Instructor's Manual. Doubleday.
Wright, Gordon P.
   xWright, Gordon P.
      Designing Water Pollution Detection Systems:
      Environmental Law Enforcement on the U.S.
      Coastal Waters & the Great Lakes. Ballinger
      Pub.
Wright, H. Curtis. *see* Wright, Herbert Curtis.
Wright, H. Elliott, 1937-
   xWright, Elliott.
      Go Free. Friend Pr.
Wright, H. G. *see* Wright, Herbert Gladstone.
Wright, H. Norman.
   xWright, H. Norman.

Characteristics of a Caring Home. Vision Hse.
The Christian Use of Emotional Power. Revell.
Into the High Country: Discerning God's
    Direction for Your Marriage. Multnomah.
The Pillars of Marriage. Regal.
Premarital Counseling. Moody.
xWright, Norman.
    Answer to Anger & Frustration. Harvest Hse.
    Answer to Worry & Anxiety. Harvest Hse.
    The Family That Listens. Victor Bks.
    Fulfilled Marriage. Harvest Hse.
    Improving Your Self-Image. Harvest Hse.
Wright, H. W.
    xWright, H. W.
    Running for the Exit. Strawberry Hill.
Wright, Harold.
    xWright, Harold.
    Ten Thousand Leaves: Love Poems from the
        Manyoshu. Shambhala Pubns.
Wright, Harold R. see Wright, Harold Richard Charles.
Wright, Harold Richard Charles.
    xWright, Harold R.
    Free Trade & Protection in the Netherlands:
        1816-30; a Study of the First Benelux.
        Greenwood.
Wright, Hastings K.
    xWright, Hastings K.
    Postoperative Disorders of the Gastrointestinal
        Tract. Grune.
Wright, Henry C. see Wright, Henry Clarke.
Wright, Henry Clarke, 1797-1870
    xWright, Henry C.
    Marriage & Parentage. Arno.
Wright, Henry T. see Wright, Henry Tutwiler.
Wright, Henry Tutwiler.
    xWright, Henry T.
    Archaeological Investigations in Northeastern
        Xuzestan, 1976. U Mich Mus Anthro.
Wright, Herbert Curtis, 1928-
    xWright, H. Curtis.
    The Oral Antecedents of Greek Librarianship.
        Brigham.
Wright, Herbert Gladstone, 1888-
    xWright, H. G.
    Studies in Anglo-Scandinavian Literary
        Relations. Folcroft.
Wright, Ione S. see Wright, Ione Stuessy.
Wright, Ione Stuessy.
    xWright, Ione S.
    Historical Dictionary of Argentina. Scarecrow.
Wright, Irene A. see Wright, Irene Aloha.
Wright, Irene Aloha, 1879-
    xWright, Irene A.
    Early History of Cuba, 1492-1586. Octagon.
Wright, J. see Wright, Jonathan W.
Wright, J. Leitch. see Wright, James Leitch.
Wright, J. S. see Wright, John Stafford.
Wright, Jack.
    xWright, Jack.
    Modern Criminal Justice. McGraw.
Wright, James. see Wright, James Arlington.
Wright, James A. see Wright, James Arlington.
Wright, James Abell.
    xWright, James A.
    I See the Wind. Branden.
Wright, James Arlington, 1927-
    xWright, James.
    Two Citizens. FS&G.
    xWright, James A.
    Green Wall. AMS Pr.
Wright, James D.
    xWright, James D.
    After the Clean-Up: Long Range Effects of
        Natural Disasters. Sage.
Wright, James E.
    xWright, James E.
    The Politics of Populism: Dissent in Colorado.
        Yale U Pr.
Wright, James Leitch.
    xWright, J. Leitch.

Britain & the American Frontier, 1783-1815. U
    of Ga Pr.
Florida in the American Revolution. U Presses
    Fla.
Wright, James M. see Wright, James Martin.
Wright, James Martin, 1879-
    xWright, James M.
    Free Negro in Maryland, 1634-1860. Octagon.
Wright, Jay.
    xWright, Jay.
    Homecoming Singer. Corinth Bks.
    Soothsayers & Omens. Seven Woods Pr.

Wright, John. see Wright, John F.
Wright, John F.
    xWright, John.
    Britain in the Age of Economic Management:
        An Economic History Since 1939. Oxford U
        Pr.
Wright, John H.
    xWright, John H.
    A Theology of Christian Prayer. Pueblo Pub
        Co.
Wright, John S., 1910-
    xWright, John S.
    Lincoln & the Politics of Slavery. U of Nev Pr.
Wright, John S. see Wright, John Sherman.
Wright, John Sherman, 1920-
    xWright, John S.
    Advertising. McGraw.
    Advertising's Role in Society. West Pub.
Wright, John Stafford.
    xWright, J. S.
    Revell's Dictionary of Bible People. Revell.
Wright, Jonathan W.
    xWright, J.
    Genetics of Insect Vectors of Disease. Elsevier.
    xWright, Jonathan W.
    Introduction to Forest Genetics. Acad Pr.
Wright, Judith.
    xWright, Judith.
    The Double Tree: Selected Poems 1942-1976.
        HM.
Wright, Kathleen.
    xWright, Kathleen.
    Other Americans: Minorities in American
        History. Fawcett.
Wright, Kathryn S.
    xWright, Kathryn S.
    Let the Children Sing: Music in Religious
        Education. Seabury.
Wright, Kieth C., 1933-
    xWright, Kieth C.
    Library & Information Services for
        Handicapped Individuals. Libs Unl.
Wright, L. B. see Wright, Louis Booker.
Wright, L. D.
    xWright, L. D.
    Circulation, Effluent Diffusion & Sediment
        Transport, Mouth of South Pass, Mississippi
        River Delta. La State U Pr.
Wright, Lawrence, 1947-
    xWright, Lawrence.
    City Children, Country Summer. Scribner.
Wright, Leigh R.
    xWright, Leigh R.
    The Status of Social Science Research in
        Borneo. Cornell SE Asia.
Wright, Leonard M.
    xWright, Leonard M.
    Fly-Fishing Heresies: A New Gospel for
        American Anglers. Follett.
    Where the Fish Are: The New York Times
        Fish Finding Book. Times Bks.
Wright, Leonard T.
    xWright, Leonard T.
    Principles of Investments: Text & Cases. Grid
        Pub.
Wright, Linda R. see Wright, Linda Raney.

Wright, Linda Raney.
    xWright, Linda R.
    Raising Children. Tyndale.
Wright, Logan, 1933-
    xWright, Logan.
    Parent Power: A Guide to Responsible
        Childrearing. Morrow.
Wright, Louis B. see Wright, Louis Booker.
Wright, Louis Booker, 1899-
    xWright, L. B.
    The Colonial Search for a Southern Eden.
        Haskell.
    xWright, Louis B.
    The Atlantic Frontier: Colonial American
        Civilization, 1607-1763. Greenwood.
    ed. Atlantic Frontier: Colonial American
        Civilization 1607-1763. Cornell U Pr.
    ed. Cultural Life of the American Colonies.
        Har-Row.
    The Cultural Life of the American Colonies,
        1607-1763. Har-Row.
    ed. English Colonization in North America. St
        Martin.
    Everyday Life in the New Nation: 1787-1860.
        Putnam.
    Folger Guide to Shakespeare. PB.
    Of Books & Men. U of SC Pr.
Wright, M. see Wright, Martin.
Wright, Martin.
    xWright, M.
    Use of Criminology Literature. Butterworths.
Wright, Maurice.
    xWright, Maurice.
    ed. Public Spending Decisions: Growth &
        Restraint in the 1970's. Allen Unwin.
Wright, Mildred S.
    xWright, Mildred S.
    Newton County, Texas Cemeteries. M S
        Wright.
Wright, Minturn T.
    xWright, Minturn T.
    ed. How-to-Live-&-Die-with Pennsylvania
        Probate. Gulf Pub.
Wright, Muriel H. see Wright, Muriel Hazel.
Wright, Muriel Hazel, 1889-
    xWright, Muriel H.
    Guide to the Indian Tribes of Oklahoma. U of
        Okla Pr.
Wright, Nadean E.
    xWright, Nadean E.
    Central Supply Procedure Manual. Cath
        Health.
Wright, Nathalia.
    xWright, Nathalia.
    Horatio Greenough: The First American
        Sculptor. U of Pa Pr.
    Melville's Use of the Bible. Octagon.
Wright, Nigel.
    xWright, Nigel.
    Progress in Education: A Review of Schooling
        in England & Wales. Biblio Dist.
Wright, Norman. see Wright, H. Norman.
Wright, Olgivanna L. see Wright, Olgivanna Lloyd.
Wright, Olgivanna Lloyd.
    xWright, Olgivanna L.
    Struggle Within. Horizon.
Wright, P.
    xWright, P.
    Solid Polyurethane Elastomers. Gordon.
Wright, P. H. see Wright, Paul H.
Wright, Patricia, 1932-
    xWright, Patricia.
    Heart of the Storm. Doubleday.
    Journey into Fire. Doubleday.
    Journey into Fire. Warner Bks.
    Shadow of the Rock. Doubleday.
Wright, Paul H.
    xWright, P. H.

Highway Engineering. Wiley.

Wright, Paul S.
xWright, Paul S.
Duties of the Ruling Elder. Westminster.

Wright, Quincy, 1890-
xWright, Quincy.
The Control of American Foreign Relations.
Johnson Repr.
Problems of Stability & Progress in
International Relations. Greenwood.
ed. Public Opinion & World-Politics. Arno.
The Study of International Relations. Irvington.
Study of War. U of Chicago Pr.

Wright, R. Glenn. see Wright, Robert Glenn.
Wright, R. L. D. see Wright, Robert Leslie Douglas.
Wright, R. V. see Wright, R. V. S.
Wright, R. V. S.
xWright, R. V.
Stone Tools As Cultural Markers: Change,
Evolution & Complexity. Humanities.

Wright, Richard, 1908-1960
xWright, Richard.
American Hunger. Har-Row.
American Hunger. Har-Row.
Eight Men. BJ Pub Group.
Native Son. Har-Row.
Native Son. Har-Row.
Outsider. Har-Row.
Richard Wright Reader. Har-Row.
Uncle Tom's Children. Har-Row.
White Man, Listen!. Greenwood.

Wright, Richard C.
xWright, Robert C.
Frederick Manfred. Twayne.

Wright, Richard R. see Wright, Richard Robert.
Wright, Richard Robert, 1979-
xWright, Richard R.
Negro in Pennsylvania: A Study in Economic
History. Arno.

Wright, Rita J.
xWright, Rita J.
ed. Texas Trade & Professional Associations &
Other Selected Organizations, 1979. U of Tex
Busn Res.

Wright, Robert. see Wright, Robert Granford.
Wright, Robert C. see Wright, Richard C.
Wright, Robert Glenn.
xWright, R. Glenn.
Compiled by Author Bibliography of English
Language Fiction in the Library of Congress
Through 1950. G K Hall.
Compiled by Chronological Bibliography of
English Language Fiction in the Library of
Congress Through 1950. G K Hall.

Wright, Robert Granford.
xWright, Robert.
The Nature of Organizations. Dickenson.

Wright, Robert Leslie Douglas, 1932-
xWright, R. L. D.
Understanding Statistics: An Informal
Introduction for the Behavioral Sciences.
HarBraceJ.

Wright, Robert R.
xWright, Robert R.
Law of Airspace. Michie.

Wright, Ronald S. see Wright, Ronald Selby.
Wright, Ronald Selby, 1908-
xWright, Ronald S.
Great Men: Being Short Impressions of X, H.
H. Almond, W. A. Smith, A. H. Stanton,
Kingsley Fairbridge, Alexander Paterson.
Arno.

Wright, S. Fowler. see Wright, Sydney Fowler.
Wright, Sam.
xWright, Sam.
Crowds & Riots: A Study in Social
Organization. Sage.

Wright, Sara M. see Wright, Sara Margaret.
Wright, Sara Margaret.
xWright, Sara M.

Brief Survey of the Bible. Loizeaux.
Wright, Sarah E.
xWright, Sarah E.
This Child's Gonna Live. Dell.

Wright, Sewall, 1889-
xWright, Sewall.
Systems of Mating & Other Papers. Iowa St U
Pr.

Wright, Sonia R.
xWright, Sonia R.
Quantitative Methods & Statistics: A Guide to
Social Research. Sage.

Wright, Stanley F. see Wright, Stanley Fowler.
Wright, Stanley Fowler, 1873-
xWright, Stanley F.
China's Customs Revenue Since the Revolution
of 1911. AMS Pr.

Wright, Stephen, 1922-
xWright, Stephen.
Brief Encyclopedia of Homosexuality. Stephen
Wright.

Wright, Sydney F. see Wright, Sydney Fowler.
Wright, Sydney Fowler, 1874-1967
xWright, S. Fowler.
The Life of Sir Walter Scott. Haskell.
xWright, Sydney F.
The World Below. Hyperion Conn.

Wright, T. H. see Wright, Thomas Henry.
Wright, Thomas, 1810-1877
xWright, Thomas.
Caricature History of the Georges. Arno.
A History of Caricature & Grotesque in
Literature & Art. Longwood Pr.
History of Caricature & Grotesque in
Literature & Art. Ungar.
Homes of Other Days: A History of Domestic
Manners & Sentiments in England During
the Middle Ages. Gale.
The Life of Charles Dickens. Folcroft.
Life of Edward Fitzgerald. Scholarly.
Life of Sir Richard Burton. B Franklin.
Life of Walter Pater. Haskell.
Life of William Cowper. Haskell.
Narratives of Sorcery & Magic, from the Most
Authentic Sources. Gale.
Our New Masters. Kelley.
Songs & Ballads, with Other Short Poems,
Chiefly of the Reign of Philip & Mary.
Norwood Edns.

Wright, Thomas Henry, 1857-
xWright, T. H.
Francis Thompson & His Poetry. Folcroft.

Wright, Veva P. see Wright, Veva Penick.
Wright, Veva Penick.
xWright, Veva P.
Pamper Your Possessions. Barre.

Wright, Vincent.
xWright, Vincent.
ed. Conflict & Consensus in France. Biblio
Dist.
The Government & Politics of France. Holmes
& Meier.

Wright, Wilhelmine G. see Wright, Wilhelmine Gerber.
Wright, Wilhelmine Gerber, 1885-
xWright, Wilhelmine G.
Muscle Function. Hafner.

Wright, William, 1930-
xWright, William.
Heiress: The Rich Life of Marjorie
Merriweather Post. New Republic.
A Short History of Syriac Literature. Folcroft.

Wright, William H. see Wright, William Henry.
Wright, William Henry, 1856-1934
xWright, William H.
illus. The Grizzly Bear: The Narrative of a
Hunter-Naturalist. U of Nebr Pr.

Wright, Wilmer.
xWright, Wilmer.

Management Accounting Simplified. McGraw.
Wright, Zita L.
xWright, Zita L.
Danger on the Ski Trails. Lothrop.

Wrightsman, Dwayne.
xWrightsman, Dwayne.
An Introduction to Monetary Theory & Policy.
Free Pr.

Wrightsman, Lawrence S. see Wrightsman, Lawrence
Samuel.
Wrightsman, Lawrence Samuel.
xWrightsman, Lawrence S.
Psychology: A Scientific Study of Human
Behavior. Brooks Cole.

Wrightson, Keith.
xWrightson, Keith.
Poverty & Piety in an English Village: Terling,
1525-1700. Acad Pr.

Wrightson, Patricia.
xWrightson, Patricia.
The Dark Bright Water. Atheneum.
The Ice Is Coming. Atheneum.
Racecourse for Andy. HarBraceJ.

Wrightstone, Jacob W. see Wrightstone, Jacob Wayne.
Wrightstone, Jacob Wayne, 1904-
xWrightstone, Jacob W.
Stimulation of Educational Undertakings: A
Study of School Support in New York Cities
& Villages Under Earmarked &
Non-Earmarked State Subsidy Plans. AMS
Pr.

Wrigley, E. A. see Wrigley, Edward Anthony.
Wrigley, Edward Anthony.
xWrigley, E. A.
Population & History. McGraw.

Wrigley, Elsie.
xWrigley, Elsie.
illus. Soft Toys. Warne.
illus. Wool Toys. Warne.

Wringe, Colin.
xWringe, Colin.
Developments in Modern Language Teaching.
Humanities.

Wrinkle, Ted.
xWrinkle, Ted.
British Columbia. Beautiful Am.

Wriston, H. M. see Wriston, Henry Merritt.
Wriston, Henry M. see Wriston, Henry Merritt.
Wriston, Henry Merritt, 1889-
xWriston, H. M.
Executive Agents in American Foreign
Relations. Peter Smith.
xWriston, Henry M.
Diplomacy in a Democracy. Greenwood.

Writer's Program. see Writers' Program.
Writers Program, Florida. see Writers' Program. Florida.
Writers Program, Georgia. see Writers' Program.
Georgia.
Writers Program, Maine. see Writers' Program. Maine.
Writers Program, Maryland. see Writers' Program.
Maryland.
Writers Program, Minnesota. see Writers' Program.
Minnesota.
Writers Program. Montana. see Writers' Program.
Montana.
Writers Program, New Jersey. see Writers' Program.
New Jersey.
Writers Program. New Mexico. see Writers' Program.
New Mexico.
Writers Program, New York. see Writers' Program. New
York.
Writers Program, North Carolina. see Writers' Program.
North Carolina.
Writers Program, Tennessee. see Writers' Program.
Tennessee.
Writers Program, Utah. see Writers' Program. Utah.
Writers Program, Virginia. see Writers' Program.
Virginia.
Writers Project of Montana. see Writers' Program.
Montana.

Writers' Program.
   xWriter's Program.
      South Carolina Folk Tales. Folcroft.
Writers' Program. Florida.
   xWriters Program, Florida.
      Planning Your Vacation in Florida: Miami &
      Dade County, Including Miami Beach &
      Coral Gables. AMS Pr.
Writers' Program. Georgia.
   xSavannah Unit, Georgia Writers' Project, Work
   Projects.
      Drums & Shadows: Survival Studies Among
      the Georgia Coastal Negroes. Reprint.
   xWriters Program, Georgia.
      The Macon Guide & Ocmulgee National
      Monument. AMS Pr.
      Savannah River Plantations. AMS Pr.
Writers' Program. Illinois.
   xWriters Program, Georgia.
      The Story of Washington-Wilkes. AMS Pr.
Writers' Program. Indiana.
   xFederal Writers' Project, Indiana.
      The Calumet Region Historical Guide. AMS
      Pr.
Writers' Program. Maine.
   xWriters Program, Maine.
      Augusta-Hallowell on the Kennebec. AMS Pr.
      Portland City Guide. AMS Pr.
Writers' Program. Maryland.
   xWriters Program, Maryland.
      A Guide to the United States Naval Academy.
      AMS Pr.
Writers' Program. Minnesota.
   xWriters Program, Minnesota.
      Minneapolis. AMS Pr.
      The Minnesota Arrowhead Country. AMS Pr.
Writers' Program. Montana.
   xWriters Program. Montana.
      Copper Camp. AMS Pr.
   xWriters Project of Montana.
      Copper Camp. Hastings.
Writers' Program. Nebraska.
   xWorkers of the Writer's Program.
      The Italians of Omaha. Arno.
Writers' Program. New Jersey.
   xWriters Program, New Jersey.
      Bergen County Panorama. AMS Pr.
      Entertaining a Nation: The Career of Long
      Branch. AMS Pr.
      Livingston: The Story of a Community. AMS
      Pr.
Writers' Program. New Mexico.
   xWriters Program. New Mexico.
      The Spanish-American Song & Game Book.
      AMS Pr.
Writers' Program. New York.
   xNew York Writer's Program.
      A Maritime History of New York. Haskell.
   xWriters Program, New York.
      American Wild Life. AMS Pr.
      Warren County: A History Guide. AMS Pr.
Writers' Program. North Carolina.
   xSpartanburg Unit of the S.C. Writers' Program.
      A History of Spartanburg County. Reprint.
   xWriters Program, North Carolina.
      Raleigh, Capital of North Carolina. AMS Pr.
Writers' Program. South Carolina.
   xWorkers of the Writers' Program Work Projects
   Administration in the State of South Carolina.
      ed. Palmetto Place Names. Reprint.
Writers' Program. Tennessee.
   xWriters Program, Tennessee.
      God Bless the Devil! Liar's Bench Tales. AMS
      Pr.
Writers' Program. Utah.
   xWriters Program, Utah.
      Provo, Pioneer Mormon City. AMS Pr.
Writers' Program. Virginia.
   xWPA Writer'S Project.

      Negro in Virginia. Arno.
   xWriters Program, Virginia.
      Dinwiddie County, "the Countrey of the
      Apamatica.". AMS Pr.
      Jefferson's Albemarle: A Guide to Albemarle
      County & the City of Charlottesville,
      Virginia. AMS Pr.
      Prince William, the Story of Its People & Its
      Places. AMS Pr.
      Roanoke; Story of County & City. AMS Pr.
      Sussex County, a Tale of Three Centuries.
      AMS Pr.
Wrobel, Paul, 1942-
   xWrobel, Paul.
      Our Way: Family, Parish & Neighborhood in a
      Polish-American Community. U of Notre
      Dame Pr.
Wrobleski, Henry M.
   xWrobleski, Henry M.
      Introduction to Law Enforcement & Criminal
      Justice. West Pub.
Wroblewski, Sergius.
   xWroblewski, Sergius.
      Prophetic History of the West. Alba.
Wrong, Dennis. *see* Wrong, Dennis Hume.
Wrong, Dennis H. *see* Wrong, Dennis Hume.
Wrong, Dennis Hume, 1923-
   xWrong, Dennis.
      ed. Max Weber. P-H.
   xWrong, Dennis H.
      Population & Society. Random.
Wrong, George M. *see* Wrong, George McKinnon.
Wrong, George McKinnon, 1860-1948
   xWrong, George M.
      Canada & the American Revolution: The
      Disruption of the First British Empire.
      Cooper Sq.
Wrong, Humphrey H. *see* Wrong, Humphrey Hume.
Wrong, Humphrey Hume.
   xWrong, Humphrey H.
      Government of the West Indies. Negro U Pr.
Wroot, Herbert E. *see* Wroot, Herbert Edward.
Wroot, Herbert Edward, d. 1939
   xWroot, Herbert E.
      Persons & Places of the Bronte Novels. B
      Franklin.
Wroten, W. H. *see* Wroten, William H.
Wroten, William H.
   xWroten, W. H.
      Assateague. Cornell Maritime.
Wroth, L. Kinvin.
   xWroth, L. Kinvin.
      ed. Province in Rebellion: A Documentary
      History of the Founding of the
      Commonwealth of Massachusetts, 1774-1775.
      Harvard U Pr.
Wroth, Warwick. *see* Wroth, Warwick William.
Wroth, Warwick William.
   xWroth, Warwick.
      The London Pleasure Gardens of the
      Eighteenth Century. Shoe String.
Wrubel, Arno.
   xWrubel, Arno.
      Gulf of Naples. French & Eur.
Wu, C. N. *see* Wu, Chang N.
Wu, Chang N.
   xWu, C. N.
      Modern Organic Chemistry. B&N.
Wu, Chun- hsi.
   xWu, Chun-Hsi.
      Dollars, Dependents, & Dogma: Overseas
      Chinese Remittances to Communist China.
      Hoover Inst Pr.
Wu, Margaret. *see* Wu, Margaret Schlosser.
Wu, Margaret S. *see* Wu, Margaret Schlosser.
Wu, Margaret Schlosser.
   xWu, Margaret.
      An Introduction to Computer Data Processing.
      HarBraceJ.
   xWu, Margaret S.

      Introduction to Computer Data Processing.
      HarBraceJ.
Wu, Nesa L. *see* Wu, Nesa L'Abbe.
Wu, Nesa L'Abbe.
   xWu, Nesa L.
      Business Programming in FORTRAN IV. Wm
      C Brown.
Wu, Silas H. *see* Wu, Silas H. L.
Wu, Silas H. L., 1929-
   xWu, Silas H.
      Communication & Imperial Control in China:
      Evolution of the Palace Memorial System,
      1693-1735. Harvard U Pr.
      Passage to Power: K'ang-Hsi & His Heir
      Apparent, 1661-1722. Harvard U Pr.
Wu, T. H. *see* Wu, Tien- hsing.
Wu, Tien Hsing. *see* Wu, Tien- hsing.
Wu, Tien- hsing, 1928-
   xWu, T. H.
      Soil Dynamics. T H Wu.
   xWu, Tien Hsing.
      Soil Mechanics. Allyn.
Wu, Tien- wei.
   xWu, Tien-Wei.
      The Sian Incident: A Pivotal Point in Modern
      Chinese History. U of Mich Ctr Chinese.
Wu, Yuan Li. *see* Wu, Yuan- li.
Wu, Yuan- li.
   xWu, Yuan Li.
      An Economic Survey of Communist China.
      Octagon.
   xWu, Yuan-Li.
      Economic Development & the Use of Energy
      Resources in Communist China. Hoover Inst
      Pr.
      Spatial Economy of Communist China: A
      Study on Industrial Location and
      Transportation. Hoover Inst Pr.
      Strategic Significance of Singapore: A Study in
      Balance of Power. Am Enterprise.
Wu, Yung.
   xWu, Yung.
      The Flight of an Empress. Hyperion Conn.
Wubben, Hubert H., 1928-
   xWubben, Hubert H.
      Civil War Iowa & the Copperhead Movement.
      Iowa St U Pr.
Wucherer, Ruth.
   xWucherer, Ruth.
      How to Sell Your Crafts. Sterling.
Wudske, Vivian A.
   xWudske, Vivian A.
      ed. American Woman All-Time Favorites
      Cookbook. Paramount.
Wuehrmann, Arthur H.
   xWuehrmann, Aurthur H.
      Dental Radiology. Mosby.
Wuehrmann, Aurthur H. *see* Wuehrmann, Arthur H.
Wuellner, Bernard.
   xWuellner, Bernard.
      Summary of Scholastic Principles. Loyola.
Wuertz-Schaefer, Karin, 1941-
   xWuertz-Schaefer, Karin.
      Hiking Virginia's National Forests. East
      Woods.
Wulbern, Julian H.
   xWulbern, Julian H.
      Brecht & Ionesco: Commitment in Context. U
      of Ill Pr.
Wulf, Kathleen.
   xWulf, Kathleen.
      I'm Glad I'm Little. Childs World.
Wulff, Keith M.
   xWulff, Keith M.
      ed. Regulation of Scientific Inquiry: Societal
      Concerns with Research. Westview.
Wulff, Lee.
   xWulff, Lee.

Lee Wulff on Flies. Stackpole.
Wulffson, Don L.
xWulffson, Don L.
How Sports Came to Be. Lothrop.
Wunder, John.
xWunder, John R.
Inferior Courts, Superior Justice: A History of the Justices of the Peace on the Northwest Frontier, 1853-1889. Greenwood.
Wunder, John R. see Wunder, John.
Wunderlich, Christof.
xWunderlich, Christof.
The Mongoloid Child: Recognition & Care. U of Ariz Pr.
Wunderlich, D. see Wunderlich, Dieter.
Wunderlich, Dieter.
xWunderlich, D.
Foundations of Linguistics. Cambridge U Pr.
Wundram, Manfred.
xWundram, Manfred.
Art of the Renaissance. Universe.
Wundt, Wilhelm. see Wundt, Wilhelm Max.
Wundt, Wilhelm M. see Wundt, Wilhelm Max.
Wundt, Wilhelm Max, 1832-1920
xWundt, Wilhelm.
An Introduction to Psychology. Arno.
xWundt, Wilhelm M.
Outlines of Psychology. Scholarly.
Wuorinen, Charles.
xWuorinen, Charles.
Simple Composition. Longman.
Wurmbrand, Richard.
xWurmbrand, Richard.
My Answer to the Moscow Atheists. Arlington Hse.
My Answer to the Moscow Atheists. Diane Bks.
Wurtman, Richard J.
xWurtman, Richard J.
ed. Control of Feeding Behavior, & Biology of the Brain in Protein-Calorie Malnutrition. Raven.
ed. Determinants of the Availability of Nutrients to the Brain. Raven.
Wurtsbaugh, Jewel, 1896-
xWurtsbaugh, Jewel.
Two Centuries of Spenserian Scholarship. AMS Pr.
Two Centuries of Spenserian Scholarship. Kennikat.
Wurtzel, Alan.
xWurtzel, Alan.
Television Production. McGraw.
Wurzburg. Universitat. Bibliothek.
xUniversity of Wurzburg, Library.
Catalog of the Schoenleiniana Collection on Epidemics (Katalog der Sammlung Schoenlein). G K Hall.
Wuthnow, Robert.
xWuthnow, Robert.
The Consciousness Reformation. U of Cal Pr.
Experimentation in American Religion: The New Mysticisms & Their Implications for the Churches. U of Cal Pr.
Wyand, Jeffrey. see Wyand, Jeffrey A.
Wyand, Jeffrey A.
xWyand, Jeffrey.
Colonial Maryland Naturalizations. Genealog Pub.
Wyandt, Christine R.
xWyandt, Christine R.
A Librarian's Hints for Students. Exposition.
Wyatt, Clair L.
xWyatt, Clair L.
Radiometric Calibration: Theory & Methods. Acad Pr.
Wyatt, David. see Wyatt, David M.
Wyatt, David M.
xWyatt, David.

Prodigal Sons: A Study in Authorship & Authority. Johns Hopkins.
Wyatt, Edith F. see Wyatt, Edith Franklin.
Wyatt, Edith Franklin, 1873-1958
xWyatt, Edith F.
Great Companions. Arno.
Wyatt, Edwin M. see Wyatt, Edwin Mather.
Wyatt, Edwin Mather.
xWyatt, Edwin M.
Modern Drafting. Glencoe.
Wyatt, Isabel.
xWyatt, Isabel.
Book of Fairy Princes. Dawne-Leigh.
King Beetle-Tamer & Other Lighthearted Wonder Tales. Dawne-Leigh.
Wyatt, Kathryn D. see Wyatt, Kathryn Day.
Wyatt, Kathryn Day, 1907-
xWyatt, Kathryn D.
Unanimistic Imagery in Twentieth Century French Literature. Romance.
Wyatt, Olive M.
xWyatt, Olive M.
Teach Yourself Lip-Reading. C C Thomas.
Wyatt, R. J. see Wyatt, Robert John.
Wyatt, Robert John.
xWyatt, R. J.
Collecting Volunteer Militaria. David & Charles.
Wyatt, Stanley P.
xWyatt, Stanley P.
Principles of Astronomy. Allyn.
Principles of Astronomy: A Short Version. Allyn.
Wyatt, Thomas.
xWyatt, Thomas.
Collected Poems. Oxford U Pr.
Wyatt, William E.
xWyatt, William E.
General Architectural Drafting. Bennett Co.
Wyatt, Woodrow, 1918-
xWyatt, Woodrow.
Southwards from China: A Survey of Southeast Asia Since 1945. AMS Pr.
Wyatt, Wyatt, 1937-
xWyatt, Wyatt.
Catching Fire. Random.
Wyatt-Brown, Bertram, 1932-
xWyatt-Brown, Bertram.
ed. The American People in the Antebellum South. Pendulum Pr.
Lewis Tappan & the Evangelical War Against Slavery. Atheneum.
Wybourne, Brian G.
xWybourne, Brian G.
Classical Groups for Physicists. Wiley.
Wycherley, R. E. see Wycherley, Richard Ernest.
Wycherley, Richard Ernest.
xWycherley, R. E.
How the Greeks Built Cities. Norton.
Literary & Epigraphical Testimonia. Am Sch Athens.
The Stones of Athens. Princeton U Pr.
Wycherley, William.
xWycherley, William.
Complete Plays of William Wycherley. Norton.
The Country Wife. Johns Hopkins.
The Country Wife. Norton.
Country Wife. U of Nebr Pr.
Country Wife. Barron.
The Plays of William Wycherley. Oxford U Pr.
Wyck Mason, F. van. see Van Wyck Mason, F.
Wyckoff, D. Daryl.
xWyckoff, D. Daryl.

The Chain-Restaurant Industry. Lexington Bks.
The Domestic Airline Industry. Lexington Bks.
Organizational Formality & Performance in the Motor Carrier Industry. Lexington Bks.
Railroad Management. Lexington Bks.
Truck Drivers in America. Lexington Bks.
Wyckoff, Don G.
xWyckoff, Don G.
The Caddoan Cultural Area: An Archaeological Perspective. Clearwater Pub.
Wyckoff, Edith H. see Wyckoff, Edith Hay.
Wyckoff, Edith Hay.
xWyckoff, Edith H.
The Fabled Past: Tales of Long Island. Kennikat.
Wyckoff, James.
xWyckoff, James.
Sharkey. Doubleday.
Wyckoff, Jerome.
xWyckoff, Jerome.
The Story of Geology: Our Changing Earth Through the Ages. Western Pub.
Wyckoff, Mary O. see Wyckoff, Mary Owens.
Wyckoff, Mary Owens.
xWyckoff, Mary O.
The World of Cooking: Recipes, Techniques & Secrets of the Kitchen. P-H.
Wyckoff, Richard D. see Wyckoff, Richard Demille.
Wyckoff, Richard Demille, 1873-1935
xWyckoff, Richard D.
Stock Market Price Fluctuations & the Anticipatory Theory of Probabilities. Inst Econ Finan.
Wyckoff, Viola, 1908-
xWyckoff, Viola.
Public Works Wage Rate & Some of Its Economic Effects. AMS Pr.
Wyden, Peter.
xWyden, Peter.
The Bay of Pigs: The Untold Story. S&S.
Wydoski, Richard S.
xWydoski, Richard S.
Inland Fishes of Washington. U of Wash Pr.
Wyer, Robert S.
xWyer, Robert S.
Cognitive Organization & Change: An Information Processing Approach. Halsted Pr.
Social Cognition, Inference, & Attribution. Halsted Pr.
Wyeth, Betsy J. see Wyeth, Betsy James.
Wyeth, Betsy James.
xWyeth, Betsy J.
The Stray. FS&G.
Wyk, Helen Van. see Van Wyk, Helen.
Wyk Smith, A. Van. see Van Wyk Smith, M.
Wykes, Alan.
xWykes, Alan.
Complete Illustrated Guide to Gambling. Doubleday.
Wykes, David.
xWykes, David.
A Preface to Dryden. Longman.
Wykstra, R. A. see Wykstra, Ronald A.
Wykstra, Ronald A.
xWykstra, R. A.
Human Capital Formation & Manpower Development. Free Pr.
Wyld, H. W. see Wyld, Henry William.
Wyld, Henry C. see Wyld, Henry Cecil Kennedy.
Wyld, Henry Cecil Kennedy, 1870-1945
xWyld, Henry C.
Historical Study of the Mother Tongue: An Introduction to Philological Method. Folcroft.
Historical Study of the Mother Tongue: An Introduction to Philological Method. Haskell.
Wyld, Henry William, 1928-
xWyld, H. W.

Mathematical Methods for Physics.
  Benjamin-Cummings.
Wyld, Lionel D.
  xWyld, Lionel D.
    Low Bridge!: Folklore & the Erie Canal.
      Syracuse U Pr.
Wylder, Edith, 1925-
  xWylder, Edith.
    Last Face: Emily Dickinson's Manuscripts. U
      of NM Pr.
Wylen, Gordon J. Van. see Van Wylen, Gordon J.
Wylen, Gordon Van. see Van Wylen, Gordon.
Wyler, Rose.
  xWyler, Rose.
    First Book of Science Experiments. Watts.
    Professor Egghead's Best Riddles. S&S.
    Prove It!. Har-Row.
    Real Science Riddles. Hastings.
Wylie, Andrew T. see Wylie, Andrew Tennant.
Wylie, Andrew Tennant, 1881-
  xWylie, Andrew T.
    The Opposites Test. AMS Pr.
Wylie, C. Ray. see Wylie, Clarence Raymond.
Wylie, Clarence R. see Wylie, Clarence Raymond.
Wylie, Clarence Raymond, 1911-
  xWylie, C. Ray.
    Differential Equations. McGraw.
  xWylie, Clarence R.
    Advanced Engineering Mathematics. McGraw.
    Foundations of Geometry. McGraw.
Wylie, E. Benjamin.
  xWylie, E. Benjamin.
    Fluid Transients. McGraw.
Wylie, E. J. see Wylie, Edwin J.
Wylie, Edwin J.
  xWylie, E. J.
    Manual of Vascular Surgery. Springer-Verlag.
Wylie, James, 1938-
  xWylie, James.
    The Homestead Grays. Avon.
Wylie, James H. see Wylie, James Hamilton.
Wylie, James Hamilton, 1844-1914
  xWylie, James H.
    History of England Under Henry the Fourth.
      AMS Pr.
    Reign of Henry the Fifth. Greenwood.
Wylie, Laura J. see Wylie, Laura Johnson.
Wylie, Laura Johnson, 1855-1932
  xWylie, Laura J.
    The English Essay. Folcroft.
    The English Essay. Norwood Edns.
Wylie, Laurence. see Wylie, Laurence William.
Wylie, Laurence William, 1909-
  xWylie, Laurence.
    Beaux Gestes: A Guide to French Body Talk.
      Dutton.
Wylie, Philip. see Wylie, Philip Gordon.
Wylie, Philip Gordon, 1902-
  xWylie, Philip.
    The Disappearance. Warner Bks.
    Gladiator. Hyperion Conn.
    The Gladiator. Manor Bks.
    The Murderer Invisible. Hyperion Conn.
    They Both Were Naked. Manor Bks.
  xWylie, Phylip.
    The End of the Dream. DAW Bks.
Wylie, Phylip. see Wylie, Philip Gordon.
Wyllie, Ethel K.
  xWyllie, Ethel K.
    Today's Custom Tailoring. Bennett Co.
    Today's Custom Tailoring. Scribner.
Wyllie, R. J. see Wyllie, R. J. M.
Wyllie, R. J. M.
  xWyllie, R. J.
    ed. World Mining Glossary of Mining,
      Processing & Geological Terms. Miller
      Freeman.
Wyman, Donald, 1903-
  xWyman, Donald.

Ground Cover Plants. Macmillan.
Ground Cover Plants. Macmillan.
Shrubs and Vines for American Gardens.
  Macmillan.
Wyman, Dorothy, 1918-
  xWyman, Dorothy.
    Bruce. Southern Pub.
Wyman, Leland C. see Wyman, Leland Clifton.
Wyman, Leland Clifton.
  xWyman, Leland C.
    Navaho Indian Ethnoentomology. U of NM Pr.
    Navajo Indian Medical Ethnobotany. AMS Pr.
Wyman, Raymond.
  xWyman, Raymond.
    Mediaware: Selection, Operation &
      Maintenance. Wm C Brown.
Wyman, Walker D. see Wyman, Walker Demarquis.
Wyman, Walker Demarquis, 1907-
  xWyman, Walker D.
    California Emigrant Letters. AMS Pr.
Wymore, A. Wayne.
  xWymore, A. Wayne.
    Systems Engineering Methodology for
      Interdisciplinary Teams. Wiley.
Wynar, Bohdan. see Wynar, Bohdan S.
Wynar, Bohdan S.
  xWynar, Bohdan.
    Introduction to Cataloging & Classification.
      Libs Unl.
  xWynar, Bohdan S.
    ed. Colorado Bibliography. Libs Unl.
    Introduction to Cataloging & Classification.
      Libs Unl.
    ed. Reference Books in Paperback: An
      Annotated Guide. Libs Unl.
Wynar, Christine L.
  xWynar, Christine L.
    Guide to Reference Books for School Media
      Centers. Libs Unl.
Wynar, Lubomyr R. see Wynar, Lubomyr Roman.
Wynar, Lubomyr Roman, 1932-
  xWynar, Lubomyr R.
    Encyclopedic Directory of Ethnic Newspapers
      & Periodicals in the United States. Libs Unl.
    Encyclopedic Directory of Ethnic
      Organizations in the United States. Libs Unl.
Wynd, Oswald, 1913-
  xWynd, Oswald.
    The Ginger Tree. Ballantine.
    The Ginger Tree. Har-Row.
Wyndham, John.
  xWyndham, John.
    Day of the Triffids. Fawcett.
    Out of the Deeps. Ballantine.
Wyndham, Lee.
  xWyndham, Lee.
    Holidays in Scandinavia. Garrard.
    Writing for Children & Teenagers. Writers
      Digest.
Wyne, Marvin D.
  xWyne, Marvin D.
    Exceptional Children: A Developmental View.
      Heath.
Wyner, Alan J.
  xWyner, Alan J.
    ed. Executive Ombudsmen in the United
      States. Inst Gov Stud Berk.
Wynes, Charles E.
  xWynes, Charles E.
    Race Relations in Virginia 1870-1902.
      Rowman.
Wyness, Fenton.
  xWyness, Fenton.
    More Spots from the Leopard. Intl Pubns Serv.
Wyness, G. B.
  xWyness, G. B.
    Practical Personal Defense. Mayfield Pub.
Wynette, Tammy.
  xWynette, Tammy.

Stand by Your Man. PB.
Stand by Your Man. S&S.
Wyngaarden, James B.
  xWyngaarden, James B.
    Gout & Hyperuricemia. Grune.
Wynia, G. W. see Wynia, Gary W.
Wynia, Gary W., 1942-
  xWynia, G. W.
    The Politics of Latin American Development.
      Cambridge U Pr.
  xWynia, Gary W.
    Argentina in the Postwar Era: Politics &
      Economic Policy Making in a Divided
      Society. U of NM Pr.
    Politics & Planners: Economic Development
      Policy in Central America. U of Wis Pr.
Wynkoop, Sally.
  xWynkoop, Sally.
    Subject Guide to Government Reference
      Books. Libs Unl.
Wynmalen, Henry.
  xWynmalen, Henry.
    Dressage - a Study of the Finer Points in
      Riding. Wilshire.
    Horse Breeding & Stud Management. J A
      Allen.
Wynn, J. C. see Wynn, John Charles.
Wynn, John Charles, 1920-
  xWynn, J. C.
    Christian Education for Liberation & Other
      Upsetting Ideas. Abingdon.
Wynn, Margaret.
  xWynn, Margaret.
    Prevention of Handicap & the Health of
      Women. Routledge & Kegan.
Wynn, Neil.
  xWynn, Neil.
    The Afro-American & the Second World War.
      Holmes & Meier.
Wynn, R. F.
  xWynn, R. F.
    An Introduction to Applied Econometric
      Analysis. Halsted Pr.
Wynn, Ralph M.
  xWynn, Ralph M.
    Obstetrics & Gynecology: The Clinical Core.
      Lea & Febiger.
Wynn, Stephen.
  xWynn, Stephen.
    World Trends in Life Insurance. Krieger.
Wynne, Annabel.
  xWynne, Annabel.
    Lady in Doubt. St Martin.
Wynne, Arnold, 1880-
  xWynne, Arnold.
    Growth of English Drama. Arno.
Wynne, Edward A., 1928-
  xWynne, Edward A.
    Growing up Suburban. U of Tex Pr.
Wynne, Graeme C. see Wynne, Graeme Chamley.
Wynne, Graeme Chamley, 1889-
  xWynne, Graeme C.
    If Germany Attacks: The Battle in Depth in
      the West. Greenwood.
Wynne, Patricia.
  xWynne, Patricia.
    illus. The Animal ABC. Random.
    illus. Wookiee Storybook. Random.
Wynne, Robert E. see Wynne, Robert Edward.
Wynne, Robert Edward.
  xWynne, Robert E.
    Reaction to the Chinese in the Pacific North
      West & British Columbia, 1850-1910. Arno.
Wynne-Tyson, Jon.
  xWynne-Tyson, Jon.
    Food for a Future: The Complete Case for
      Vegetarianism. Universe.
Wynter, C. I. see Wynter, Clive I.
Wynter, Clive I.
  xWynter, C. I.

Chemical Analyses for Medical Technologists. C C Thomas.

Wyoming. Recreation Commission.
xWyoming Recreation Commission.
Wyoming: A Guide to Historic Sites. Aviation Maintenance.

Wyon, Olive, 1890-
xWyon, Olive.
The Grace of the Passion. Allenson.
Prayer. Fortress.

Wypyski, Eugene M.
xWypyski, Eugene M.
The Law of Inheritance in All Fifty States. Oceana.
Legal Periodicals in English. Glanville.

Wyrick, Jean.
xWyrick, Jean.
Steps to Writing Well: A Concise Guide to Composition. HR&W.

Wyse, Lois.
xWyse, Lois.
Absolute Truth About Marriage. Price Stern.
Blonde, Beautiful Blonde: How to Look, Live, Work & Think Blonde. M Evans.
Grandfathers Are to Love. Schol Bk Serv.
Grandmothers Are to Love. Schol Bk Serv.
I Love You Better Now. T Y Crowell.

Wysinger, Vossa E.
xWysinger, Vossa E.
The Celestial Democracy. V E Wysinger.

Wyss, Dieter.
xWyss, Dieter.
Psychoanalytic Schools from the Beginning to the Present. Aronson.

Wyss, J R. see Wyss, Johann.

Wyss, Johann.
xWyss, J. R.
The Swiss Family Robinson. Biblio Dist.
Swiss Family Robinson. G&D.
xWyss, Johann.
The Swiss Family Robinson. Andor Pub.
Swiss Family Robinson. Dell.
Swiss Family Robinson. G&D.
The Swiss Family Robinson. Pendulum Pr.
Swiss Family Robinson. Airmont.

Wyszynski. see Wyszynski, Stefan.

Wyszynski, Stefan, Cardinal, 1901-
xWyszynski.
Work. Scepter Pubs.

Wythe, George, 1893-
xWythe, George.
Brazil, an Expanding Economy. Greenwood.
Industry in Latin America. Greenwood.

Wytrwal, Joseph A. see Wytrwal, Joseph Anthony.

Wytrwal, Joseph Anthony, 1924-
xWytrwal, Joseph A.
America's Polish Heritage: A Social History of the Poles in America. Endurance.

Xantus, Janos, 1825-1894
xXantus, John.
Letters from North America. Wayne St U Pr.

Xantus, John. see Xantus, Janos.

Xaudaro, J.
xXaudaro, J.
Perils of Flight. Mayflower Bks.

Xavier, Alberto. see Xavier, Alberto Pinheiro.

Xavier, Alberto Pinheiro.
xXavier, Alberto.
The Taxation of Foreign Investment in Brazil. Kluwer Boston.

Xenakis, Iannis, 1922-
xXenakis, Iannis.
Formalized Music: Thought & Mathematics in Composition. Ind U Pr.

Xenophon.
xXenophon.
Economist of Xenophon. B Franklin.
The Persian Expedition. Penguin.

Xyzyx Information Corporation.
xXyzyx Information Corporation.

Home Emergency Repair Book. McGraw.

Y. W. C. A. World Fellowship Committee - Tokyo. see Young Women'S Christian Associations, Tokyo. World Fellowship Committee.

Yablonsky, Lewis.
xYablonsky, Lewis.
The Extra-Sex Factor: Why Over Half of America's Married Men Play Around. Times Bks.

Yabrov, A. A., 1931-
xYabrov, Alexander.
Interferon & Non-Specific Resistance. Human Sci Pr.

Yabrov, Alexander. see Yabrov, A. A.

Yacowar, Maurice.
xYacowar, Maurice.
Hitchcock's British Films. Shoe String.
Loser Take All: The Comic Art of Woody Allen. Ungar.

Yadin, Yigael, 1917-
xYadin, Yigael.
Masada, Herod's Fortress & the Zealots Last Stand. Random.

Yager, Joseph A.
xYager, Joseph A.
Energy & U. S. Foreign Policy. Ballinger Pub.

Yaggy, Elinor.
xYaggy, Elinor.
How to Write Your Term Paper. Har-Row.

Yahuda, Michael B.
xYahuda, Michael B.
China's Role in World Affairs. St Martin.

Yakapovich, Jules.
xYakapovich, Jules.
Radar Defense for Winning Football. P-H.

Yakel, Ralph, 1900
xYakel, Ralph.
The Legal Control of the Administration of Public School Expenditures. AMS Pr.

Yakhontoff, Victor A., 1881-
xYakhontoff, Victor A.
The Chinese Soviets. Greenwood.

Yakowitz, Sidney J., 1937-
xYakowitz, Sidney J.
Computational Probability & Simulation. A-W.
Mathematics of Adaptive Control Processes. Elsevier.

Yale Daily News.
xYale Daily News Staff.
The Insider's Guide to the Colleges. Berkley Pub.

Yale Daily News Staff. see Yale Daily News.

Yale, Irving.
xYale, Irving.
Podiatric Medicine. Williams & Wilkins.

Yale, Paul B.
xYale, Paul B.
Geometry & Symmetry. Holden-Day.

Yale Review.
xYale Review.
Yale Review Anthology. Arno.

Yale Univ. Library. see Yale University. Library.

Yale University.
xYale University.
Catalog of the Yale Collection of Western Americana. G K Hall.
The Record of the Celebration of the Two Hundredth Anniversary of the Founding of Yale College, Held at Yale University in New Haven, Connecticut, October 20-23, 1901 A.D.. Elliots Bks.
Southeast Asia Collection: Checklist of Southeast Asian Serials. G K Hall.
Yale University Portrait Index, 1701-1951. Yale U Pr.

Yale University. Art Gallery.
xYale University Art Gallery, Victoria & Albert Museum.
American Art: 1750-1800 Towards

Independence. NYGS.

Yale University Art Gallery, Victoria & Albert Museum. see Yale University. Art Gallery.

Yale University. Center for Alcohol Studies.
xYale University Center of Alcohol Studies.
Alcohol, Science, & Society. Greenwood.

Yale University Center of Alcohol Studies. see Yale University. Center for Alcohol Studies.

Yale University. Dept. of French.
xYale University - French Dept.
Contes Modernes. Har-Row.
xYale University French Department.
Studies by Members of the French Department of Yale University. AMS Pr.

Yale University. Division of Student Mental Hygiene.
xYale University Division of Student Mental Hygiene Staff.
Psycosocial Problems of College Men. Kennikat.

Yale University Division of Student Mental Hygiene Staff. see Yale University. Division of Student Mental Hygiene.

Yale University - French Dept. see Yale University. Dept. of French.

Yale University - Henry S. Graves Memorial Library. see Yale University. School of Forestry. Library.

Yale University. Library.
xYale Univ. Library.
List of Newspapers in Library of Yale. Elliots Bks.
xYale University Library.
A Guide to the Romanization of Standard Chinese. Far Eastern Pubns.

Yale University Library. see Yale University. Library.

Yale University. School of Forestry. Library.
xYale University - Henry S. Graves Memorial Library.
Dictionary Catalogue of the Yale Forestry Library. G K Hall.

Yale, William.
xYale, William.
Near East: A Modern History. U of Mich Pr.

Yalin, Mehmet S. see Yalin, Mehmet Selim.

Yalin, Mehmet Selim, 1925-
xYalin, Mehmet S.
The Mechanics of Sediment Transport. Pergamon.

Yalom, Irvin D., 1931-
xYalom, Irvin D.
The Theory & Practice of Group Psychotherapy. Basic.

Yamada, Hiroshi.
xYamada, Hiroshi.
Strength of Biological Materials. Krieger.

Yamada, Koun, 1911-
xYamada, Koun.
Gateless Gate. Center Pubns.

Yamada, Koun. see Yamada, Koun.

Yamada, Mitsuye.
xYamada, Mitsuye.
Camp Notes & Other Poems. Shameless Hussy.

Yamada, T. see Yamada, Tsuneo.

Yamada, Tsuneo, 1909-
xYamada, T.
Control Mechanisms in Cell - Type Conversion in Newt Lens Regeneration. S Karger.

Yamada, Y. see Yamada, Yoshimitsu.

Yamada, Yoshimitsu.
xYamada, Y.
Aikido Complete. Wehman.
xYamada, Yoshimitsu.
Aikido Complete. Citadel Pr.
Aikido Complete. Lyle Stuart.

Yamagiwa, Joseph K. see Yamagiwa, Joseph Koshimi.

Yamagiwa, Joseph Koshimi, 1906-
xYamagiwa, Joseph K.
Introduction to Japanese Writing. Wahr.

Yamaguchi, Gosei. see Yamaguchi, Norimi Gosei.

Yamaguchi, K. *see* Yamaguchi, Kazutaka.
Yamaguchi, Kazutaka, 1912-
  xYamaguchi, K.
    Spectral Data of Natural Products. Elsevier.
Yamaguchi, Norimi Gosei, 1935-
  xYamaguchi, Gosei.
    The Fundamentals of Goju-Ryu Karate. Ohara Pubns.
Yamamoto, J. Isamu.
  xYamamoto, J. Isamu.
    The Puppet Master: An Inquiry into Sun Myung Moon & the Unification Church. Inter-Varsity.
Yamamoto, Kaoru.
  xYamamoto, Kaoru.
    ed. Child & His Image: Self Concept in the Early Years. HM.
Yamamoto, Mitsu.
  xYamamoto, Mitsu.
    Adapted by Call of the Wild. Newbury Hse.
Yamamoto, Shugoro, Pseud.
  xYamamoto, Shugoro.
    The Flower Mat. C E Tuttle.

Yamamura, Kozo
  xYamamura, Kozo.
    Economic Policy in Postwar Japan: Growth Versus Economic Democracy. U of Cal Pr.

Yamamura, Sakae, 1918-
  xYamamura, Sakae.
    Theory of Linear Induction Motors. Halsted Pr.
Yamamuro, S., 1925-
  xYamamuro, S.
    A Theory of Differentiation in Locally Convex Spaces. Am Math.
Yamane, Taro.
  xYamane, Taro.
    Statistics: An Introductory Analysis. Har-Row.
Yamanouchi, H. *see* Yamanouchi, Hisaaki.
Yamanouchi, Hisaaki, 1934-
  xYamanouchi, H.
    The Search for Authenticity in Modern Japanese Literature. Cambridge U Pr.
Yamaoka, Haruo.
  xYamaoka, Haruo.
    Meditation Gut Enlightenment: The Way of Hara. Heian Intl.
Yamasaki, Minoru, 1912-
  xYamasaki, Minoru.
    A Life in Architecture. Weatherhill.
Yamashita, Yasumasa.
  xYamashita, Yasumasa.
    An Atlas of Representative Stellar Spectra. Halsted Pr.
Yamey, Basil S.
  xYamey, Basil S.
    ed. The Historical Development of Accounting: A Selection of Papers. Arno.
Yanagihara, H. *see* Yanagihara, Hiroshi.
Yanagihara, Hiroshi, 1934-
  xYanagihara, H.
    Theory of Hopf Algebras Attached to Group Schemes. Springer-Verlag.
Yanaihara, Tadao, 1893-1961
  xYanaihara, Tadao.
    Pacific Islands Under Japanese Mandate. AMS Pr.
    Pacific Islands Under Japanese Mandate. Greenwood.
Yancey, Philip.
  xYancey, Philip.
    Unhappy Secrets of the Christian Life. Zondervan.
    Where Is God When It Hurts. Zondervan.
Yanda, Roman L.
  xYanda, Roman L.

    Doctors As Managers of Health Teams: A Career Guide for Hospital Based Physicians. Am Mgmt.
Yandell, Keith E., 1938-
  xYandell, Keith E.
    God, Man & Religion: Readings in Philosophy of Religion. McGraw.
Yando, Regina.
  xYando, Regina.
    Imitation: A Developmental Perspective. Halsted Pr.
    Intellectual & Personality Characteristics of Children: Social-Class & Ethnic-Group Differences. Halsted Pr.
Yanev, Peter, 1946-
  xYanev, Peter.
    Peace of Mind in Earthquake Country: How to Save Your Home & Life. Chronicle Bks.
Yaney, George L.
  xYaney, George L.
    The Systematization of Russian Government: Social Evolution in the Domestic Administration of Imperial Russia, 1711-1905. U of Ill Pr.
Yaney, Joseph P.
  xYaney, Joseph P.
    Personnel Management: Reaching Organizational & Human Goals. Merrill.
Yang, C. K. *see* Yang, Ching-Kun.
Yang, Ching-Kun, 1910-
  xYang, C. K.
    Religion in Chinese Society: A Study of Contemporary Social Functions of Religion & Some of Their Historical Factors. U of Cal Pr.
Yang, Lien-Sheng, 1914-
  xYang, Lien-Sheng.
    Excursions in Sinology. Harvard U Pr.
    Money & Credit in China: A Short History. Harvard U Pr.
Yang, Nai C., 1917-
  xYang, Nai C.
    Design of Functional Pavements. McGraw.
Yang, Richard.
  xYang, Richard.
    The Chinese World. Forum Pr MO.
Yang, Sing S. *see* Yang, Sing San.
Yang, Sing San, 1932-
  xYang, Sing S.
    From Cardiac Catheterization Data to Hemodynamic Parameters. Davis Co.
Yang, Winston L. *see* Yang, Winston L. Y.
Yang, Winston L. Y.
  xYang, Winston L.
    ed. Stories of Contemporary China. Paragon.
Yang, Yung-Ch'Ing. *see* Yang, Yung-Ching.
Yang, Yung-Ching, 1892-1956
  xYang, Yung-Ch'Ing.
    China's Religious Heritage. Arno.
Yankowitz, Susan.
  xYankowitz, Susan.
    Silent Witness. Avon.
    Silent Witness. Knopf.
Yannuzzi. *see* Yannuzzi, Lawrence A.
Yannuzzi, Lawrence A.
  xYannuzzi.
    The Macula: A Comprehensive Text & Atlas. Williams & Wilkins.
Yano, K. *see* Yano, Kentaro.
Yano, Kentaro.
  xYano, K.
    Curvature & Betti Numbers. Kraus Repr.
    Integral Formulas in Riemannian Geometry. Dekker.
Yano, Shigeko.
  xYano, Shigeko.
    As Jesus Grew. Judson.
Yanoff, Myron.
  xYanoff, Myron.

    Ocular Pathology: A Text & Atlas. Har-Row.
Yanov, Alexander, 1930-
  xYanov, Alexander.
    Detente After Brezhnev: The Domestic Roots of Soviet Foreign Policy. U of Cal Intl St.
Yanovsky, V. S., 1906-
  xYanovsky, V. S.
    Medicine, Science & Life. Paulist Pr.
Yanowitch, Murray.
  xYanowitch, Murray.
    ed. Contemporary Soviet Economics: A Collection of Readings from Soviet Sources. M E Sharpe.
    Intro. by & ed. Soviet Work Attitudes: The Issue of Participation in Management. M E Sharpe.
Yansane, Aguibou Y.
  xYansane, Aguibou Y.
    ed. Decolonization & Dependency: Problems of Development of African Societies. Greenwood.
Yap, Elsa P. *see* Yap, Elsa Paula.
Yap, Elsa Paula.
  xYap, Elsa P.
    Cebuano-Visayan Dictionary. U Pr of Hawaii.
Yap, P. M. *see* Yap, Pow-Meng.
Yap, Pow-Meng.
  xYap, P. M.
    Comparative Psychiatry: A Theoretical Framework. U of Toronto Pr.
Yapp, W. *see* Yapp, William Brunsdon.
Yapp, William Brunsdon.
  xYapp, W.
    The Life & Organization of Birds. Univ Park.
Yarber, Robert E.
  xYarber, Robert E.
    College Reading & Writing. Macmillan.
Yarbro, Chelsea Q. *see* Yarbro, Chelsea Quinn.
Yarbro, Chelsea Quinn, 1942-
  xYarbro, Chelsea Q.
    Blood Games. NAL.
    Blood Games. St Martin.
    Cautionary Tales. Warner Bks.
    False Dawn. Warner Bks.
    Music When Sweet Voices Die. Putnam.
    The Palace: A Historical Horror Novel. St Martin.
  xYarbro, Chelsea Quinn.
    Cautionary Tales. Doubleday.
    False Dawn. Doubleday.
Yarbrough, Camille.
  xYarbrough, Camille.
    Cornrows. Coward.
Yarbrough, Tom.
  xYarbrough, Tom.
    How to Be Happy with Yourself: A Guide to Overcome Depression & Failure. Libra.
Yarbrough, V. Eugene.
  xYarbrough, V. Eugene.
    ed. Readings in Curriculum & Supervision. Mss Info.
Yardley, Alice.
  xYardley, Alice.
    Learning to Adjust. Schol Bk Serv.
    Reaching Out. Schol Bk Serv.
    Structure in Early Learning. Schol Bk Serv.
    The Teacher of Young Children. Schol Bk Serv.
Yardley, Herbert O. *see* Yardley, Herbert Osborn.
Yardley, Herbert Osborn, 1889-
  xYardley, Herbert O.
    Education of a Poker Player. S&S.
Yarington, David J. *see* Yarington, David Jon.
Yarington, David Jon.
  xYarington, David J.
    The Great American Reading Machine. Hayden.
    Surviving in College. Bobbs.
Yarington, Robert.
  xYarington, Robert.

Two Lamentable Tragedies. AMS Pr.

Yariv, A. see Yariv, Amnon.

Yariv, Amnon.
xYariv, A.
Introduction to Optical Electronics. HR&W.
xYariv, Amnon.
Quantum Electronics. Wiley.

Yarmey, A. Daniel.
xYarmey, A. Daniel.
The Psychology of Eyewitness Testimony. Free Pr.

Yarmolinsky, Adam.
xYarmolinsky, Adam.
Compiled by Case Studies in Personnel Security. Greenwood.

Yarmolinsky, Avrahm, 1890-
xYarmolinsky, Avrahm.
Soviet Short Stories. Darby Bks.
ed. Soviet Short Stories. Greenwood.
ed. Soviet Short Stories. Kraus Repr.

Yarnell, Allen.
xYarnell, Allen.
Democrats & Progressives: The 1948 Presidential Election As a Test of Postwar Liberalism. U of Cal Pr.

Yaron, B. see Yaron, Bruno.

Yaron, Bruno.
xYaron, B.
ed. Arid Zone Irrigation. Springer-Verlag.

Yaroslava, Pseud.
xYaroslava.
ed. I Like You & Other Poems for Valentine's Day. Scribner.

Yarrow, Marian J. see Yarrow, Marian Jeannette (Radke).

Yarrow, Marian Jeannette (Radke), 1918-
xYarrow, Marian J.
Relation of Parental Authority to Children's Behavior & Attitudes. Greenwood.

Yarrow, P. J. see Yarrow, Philip John.

Yarrow, Philip John.
xYarrow, P. J.
Racine. Rowman.

Yartz, Frank. see Yartz, Frank J.

Yartz, Frank J.
xYartz, Frank.
Progress & the Crisis of Man. Nelson-Hall.

Yarwood, Doreen.
xYarwood, Doreen.
The Architecture of Europe. Hastings.
Encyclopedia of World Costume. Scribner.

Yarwood, J. see Yarwood, John.

Yarwood, John.
xYarwood, J.
ed. Spectroscopy & Structure of Molecular Complexes. Plenum Pub.

YASD Committee. see American Library Association. Committee on Outreach Programs for Young Adults (Ad Hoc).

Yashima, T. see Yashima, Taro.

Yashima, Taro , Pseud.
xYashima, T.
illus. Umbrella. Viking Pr.
xYashima, Taro.
illus. Umbrella. Penguin.
Umbrella. Viking Pr.

Yasser, Joseph.
xYasser, Joseph.
Theory of Evolving Tonality. Broude.
A Theory of Evolving Tonality. Da Capo.

Yates, A. J. see Yates, Aubrey J.

Yates, Aubrey J.
xYates, A. J.
Biofeedback & the Modification of Behavior. Plenum Pub.
xYates, Aubrey J.
Theory & Practice in Behavior Therapy. Wiley.

Yates, B. see Yates, Bernard.

Yates, Bernard.
xYates, B.
ed. Thermal Expansion. Plenum Pub.

Yates, Douglas.
xYates, Douglas.
Franz Grillparzer: A Critical Biography. Folcroft.

Yates, Elizabeth, 1905-
xYates, Elizabeth.
Amos Fortune, Free Man. Dutton.
Call It Zest: The Vital Ingredient for Everybody. Greene.
Carolina's Courage. Dutton.
The Lighted Heart. Bauhan.

Yates, Frances. see Yates, Frances Amelia.

Yates, Frances A. see Yates, Frances Amelia.

Yates, Frances Amelia.
xYates, Frances.
Giordano Bruno & the Hermetic Tradition. U of Chicago Pr.
Study of Love's Labour's Lost. Folcroft.
xYates, Frances A.
Astraea: The Imperial Theme in the Sixteenth Century. Routledge & Kegan.
Giordano Bruno & the Hermetic Tradition. Random.
The Occult Philosophy in the Elizabethan Age. Routledge & Kegan.
A Study of Love's Labour's Lost. Arden Lib.
Theatre of the World. U of Chicago Pr.
The Valois Tapestries. Routledge & Kegan.

Yates, George T.
xYates, George T.
ed. Limits to National Jurisdiction Over the Sea. U Pr of Va.

Yates, Hube.
xYates, Hube.
From Thunder to Breakfast. Northland.

Yates, Jere E.
xYates, Jere E.
Managing Stress: A Businessperson's Guide. Am Mgmt.

Yates, Keith.
xYates, Keith.
Huckel Molecular Orbital Theory. Acad Pr.

Yates, Kyle M. see Yates, Kyle Monroe.

Yates, Kyle Monroe, 1895-
xYates, Kyle M.
Essentials of Biblical Hebrew. Har-Row.

Yates, Martha.
xYates, Martha.
Coping: A Survival Manual for Women Alone. P-H.

Yates, Norris W. see Yates, Norris Wilson.

Yates, Norris Wilson.
xYates, Norris W.
American Humorist: Conscience of the Twentieth Century. Iowa St U Pr.

Yates, Raymond F. see Yates, Raymond Francis.

Yates, Raymond Francis, 1895-
xYates, Raymond F.
Boys' Book of Magnetism. Har-Row.
Boys' Book of Model Railroading. Har-Row.
Boys' Book of Tools. Har-Row.

Yates, Richard, 1926-
xYates, Richard.
The Easter Parade. Delacorte.
A Good School. Delacorte.
Revolutionary Road. Dell.
Revolutionary Road. Greenwood.

Yates, Robert C. see Yates, Robert Carl.

Yates, Robert Carl, 1904-1963
xYates, Robert C.
Curves & Their Properties. NCTM.

Yates, Virginia.
xYates, Virginia.
Listening & Note Taking. McGraw.

Yatron, Michael.
xYatron, Michael.
America's Literary Revolt. Arno.

Yau, W. W.
xYau, W. W.
Modern Size-Exclusion Liquid Chromatography: Practice of Gel Permeation & Gel Filtration Chromatography. Wiley.

Yaverbaum, L. see Yaverbaum, Lee.

Yaverbaum, L. H. see Yaverbaum, Lee.

Yaverbaum, Lee.
xYaverbaum, L.
ed. Energy Saving by Increasing Boiler Efficiency. Noyes.
Fluidized Bed Combustion of Coal & Waste Materials. Noyes.
xYaverbaum, L. H.
Nitrogen Oxides Control & Removal. Noyes.
ed. Synthetic Gems-Production Techniques. Noyes.
ed. Technology of Metal Powders: Recent Developments. Noyes.

Yaw, John.
xYaw, John.
Grand National Championship Races. Lerner Pubns.

Yeadon, Anne.
xYeadon, Anne.
Living with Impaired Vision: An Introduction. Am Foun Blind.
Toward Independence: The Use of Instructional Objectives in Teaching Daily Living Skills to the Blind. Am Foun Blind.

Yeager, D. see Yeager, Dewey A.

Yeager, Dewey A.
xYeager, D.
Introduction to Electron & Electromechanical Devices. P-H.

Yeager, Leland B.
xYeager, Leland B.
ed. In Search of a Monetary Constitution. Harvard U Pr.

Yeager, Tressa C. see Yeager, Tressa Claretta.

Yeager, Tressa Claretta, 1893-
xYeager, Tressa C.
An Analysis of Certain Traits of Selected High School Seniors Interested in Teaching. AMS Pr.

Yeager, William A. see Yeager, William Allison.

Yeager, William Allison.
xYeager, William A.
Administration & the Teacher. Greenwood.

Yearbury, Pauline K. see Yearbury, Pauline Kahurangi.

Yearbury, Pauline Kahurangi.
xYearbury, Pauline K.
Children of Rangi & Papa: The Maori Story of Creation. Intl Pubns Serv.

Yearley, Clifton K.
xYearley, Clifton K.
Britons in American Labor: A History of the Influence of the United Kingdom Immigrants on American Labor, 1820-1914. AMS Pr.
Money Machines: The Breakdown & Reform of Governmental & Party Finance in the North, 1860-1920. State U NY Pr.

Yearley, Lee H.
xYearley, Lee H.
The Ideas of Newman: Christianity & Human Religiosity. Pa St U Pr.

Yearsley, Macleod. see Yearsley, Percival Macleod.

Yearsley, Percival M. see Yearsley, Percival Macleod.

Yearsley, Percival Macleod, 1867-1951
xYearsley, Macleod.
Doctors in Elizabethan Drama. Folcroft.
xYearsley, Percival M.
Doctors in Elizabethan Drama. AMS Pr.

Yeates, Maurice.
xYeates, Maurice.
The North American City. Har-Row.
xYeates, Maurice H.

The North American City. Har-Row.
xYeates, Maurice Y.
    Introduction to Quantitative Analysis in
    Economic Geography. McGraw.
Yeates, Maurice H. see Yeates, Maurice.
Yeates, Maurice Y. see Yeates, Maurice.
Yeats, Alexander J.
xYeats, Alexander J.
    Trade Barriers Facing Developing Countries. St
    Martin.
Yeats, W. B. see Yeats, William Butler.
Yeats, William B. see Yeats, William Butler.
Yeats, William Butler, 1865-1939
xYeats, W. B.
    ed. Representative Irish Tales. Humanities.
xYeats, William B.
    Collected Plays. Macmillan.
    Davis, Mangan, Ferguson: Tradition & the Irish
        Writer. Humanities.
    Explorations. Macmillan.
    The Hour-Glass & Other Plays. Core
        Collection.
    Irish Fairy & Folk Tales. AMS Pr.
    The Letters of W. B. Yeats. Octagon.
    Literatim Transcription of the Manuscripts of
        William Butler Yeats's The Speckled Bird.
        Schol Facsimiles.
    Variorum Edition of the Plays of W. B. Yeats.
        Macmillan.
    Variorum Edition of the Poems of W. B. Yeats.
        Macmillan.
    W. B. Yeats & T. Sturge Moore: Their
        Correspondence, 1901-1937. Greenwood.
Yeck, Fred.
xYeck, Fred.
    Building Your Own Home. Arco.
Yee, Rhoda.
xYee, Rhoda.
    Dim Sum. Taylor & Ng.
Yeh, K. C.
xYeh, K. C.
    Theory of Ionospheric Waves. Acad Pr.
Yehaskel, A. see Yehaskel, Albert.
Yehaskel, Albert.
xYehaskel, A.
    Activated Carbon: Manufacture &
        Regeneration. Noyes.
    Fire & Flame Retardant Polymers: Recent
        Developments. Noyes.
xYehaskel, Albert.
    Industrial Wastewater Cleanup: Recent
        Developments. Noyes.
Yelland, H. L. see Yelland, Hedley Lowry.
Yelland, Hedley Lowry.
xYelland, H. L.
    Handbook of Literary Terms. Writer.
Yellen, Samuel, 1906-
xYellen, Samuel.
    American Labor Struggles. Arno.
    American Labor Struggles. Monad Pr.
Yelling, James A.
xYelling, James A.
    Common Field & Enclosure in
        England, 1450-1850. Shoe String.
Yellowitz, Irwin.
xYellowitz, Irwin.
    Industrialization & the American Labor
        Movement, 1850-1900. Kennikat.
Yelton, Donald C. see Yelton, Donald Charles.
Yelton, Donald Charles.
xYelton, Donald C.
    Brief American Lives: Four Studies in
        Collective Biography. Scarecrow.
Yen, D. E.
xYen, Douglas E.
    The Sweet Potato & Oceania: An Essay in
        Ethnobotany. Bishop Mus.
Yen, Douglas E. see Yen, D. E.
Yen, Hawkling L. see Yen, Hawkling Lugine.

Yen, Hawkling Lugine, 1879-1937
xYen, Hawkling L.
    Survey of Constitutional Development in
        China. AMS Pr.
Yen, Sherman.
xYen, Sherman.
    ed. Teaching Behavior Modification.
        Behaviordelia.
Yen, Sophia Su-Fei, 1935-
xYen, Sophia Su-Fei.
    Taiwan in China's Foreign Relations,
        1836-1874. Shoe String.
Yen, T. F. see Yen, Teh Fu.
Yen, Teh Fu.
xYen, T. F.
    Oil Shale. Elsevier.
Yenal, Engin.
xYenal, Engin.
    The Ottoman City in Comparative Perspective,
        Istanbul, 1453-1923: A Selected Bibliography
        of Urban History. Vance Biblios.
Yenser, Stephen.
xYenser, Stephen.
    Circle to Circle: The Poetry of Robert Lowell.
        U of Cal Pr.
Yeo, Robert.
xYeo, Robert.
    ed. Singapore Short Stories. Heinemann Ed.
Yeoman, R. S.
xYeoman, R. S.
    A Catalog of Modern World Coins. Western
        Pub.
Yeoman, Richard S.
xYeoman, Richard S.
    Current Coins of the World. Wehman.
Yeomans, Henry A. see Yeomans, Henry Aaron.
Yeomans, Henry Aaron, 1877-
xYeomans, Henry A.
    Abbott Lawrence Lowell: 1856-1943. Arno.
Yep, Laurence.
xYep, Laurence.
    Child of the Owl. Dell.
    Child of the Owl. Har-Row.
    Dragonwings. Har-Row.
    Dragonwings. Har-Row.
    Sea Glass. Har-Row.
    Sweetwater. Avon.
    Sweetwater. Har-Row.
Yerby, Frank, 1916-
xYerby, Frank.
    A Darkness at Ingrahams Crest: A Tale of the
        Slaveholding South. Dial.
    Floodtide. Dell.
Yerges, Lyle F.
xYerges, Lyle F.
    Sound, Noise & Vibration Control. Van Nos
        Reinhold.
Yerkes, Robert M. see Yerkes, Robert Mearns.
Yerkes, Robert Mearns, 1876-1956
xYerkes, Robert M.
    Mental Life of Monkeys & Apes. Schol
        Facsimiles.
Yerkow, Charles, 1912-
xYerkow, Charles.
    Automobiles: How They Work. Putnam.
Yeston, Maury. see Yeston, Maury Alan.
Yeston, Maury Alan.
xYeston, Maury.
    The Stratification of Musical Rhythm. Yale U
        Pr.
Yett, Donald. see Yett, Donald E.
Yett, Donald E.
xYett, Donald.
    A Forecasting & Policy Simulation Model of
        the Health Care Sector: The HRRC
        Prototype Microeconomic Model. Lexington
        Bks.
Yeung, Y. M. see Yeung, Yue-Man.
Yeung, Yue-Man.
xYeung, Y. M.

    ed. Changing South-East Asian Cities:
        Readings on Urbanization. Oxford U Pr.
Yevjevich, Vujica. see Yevjevich, Vujica M.
Yevjevich, Vujica M., 1913-
xYevjevich, Vujica.
    Probability & Statistics in Hydrology. WRP.
    Stochastic Processes in Hydrology. WRP.
Yezback, Steven A.
xYezback, Steven A.
    Pumpkinseeds. Bobbs.
Yezierska, Anzia, 1885-
xYezierska, Anzia.
    Hungry Hearts. Arno.
Yezzo, Dominick.
xYezzo, Dominick.
    A G.I.'s Vietnam Diary. Watts.
Yglesias, Helen.
xYglesias, Helen.
    Family Feeling. Dial.
Yglesias, Jose.
xYglesias, Jose.
    The Franco Years. Bobbs.
Yiannopoulos, Athanassios N.
xYiannopoulos, Athanassios N.
    Negligence Clauses in Ocean Bills of Lading:
        Conflict of Laws & the Brussels Convention
        of 1924, a Comparative Study. La State U Pr.
Yih, Stephen W. H.
xYih, W. H.
    Tungsten: Sources, Metallurgy, Properties, &
        Applications. Plenum Pub.
Yih, W. H. see Yih, Stephen W. H.
Yinger, John M. see Yinger, John Milton.
Yinger, John Milton.
xYinger, John M.
    Toward a Field Theory of Behavior: Personality
        & Social Structure. McGraw.
Yip, Wai-Lim.
xYip, Wai-Lim.
    Chinese Poetry: Major Modes & Genres. U of
        Cal Pr.
    tr. Modern Chinese Poetry: Twenty Poets from
        the Republic of China 1955-1965. U of Iowa
        Pr.
Ylla.
xYlla.
    illus. Two Little Bears. Har-Row.
    photos by Two Little Bears. Har-Row.
Yngve, Victor H., 1920-
xYngve, Victor H.
    Computer Programming with Comit II. MIT
        Pr.
Yntema, Sharon K. see Yntema, Sharon Kathryn.
Yntema, Sharon Kathryn, 1951-
xYntema, Sharon K.
    Vegetarian Baby: A Sensible Guide for Parents.
        McBooks Pr.
Yntema, Theodore O. see Yntema, Theodore Otte.
Yntema, Theodore Otte, 1900-
xYntema, Theodore O.
    Mathematical Reformulation of the General
        Theory of International Trade. Greenwood.
Yochelson, Samuel.
xYochelson, Samuel.
    The Criminal Personality. Aronson.
Yocom, Charles. see Yocom, Charles Frederick.
Yocom, Charles Frederick.
xYocom, Charles.
    Pacific Coastal Wildlife Region. Naturegraph.
Yocum, James C. see Yocum, James Carleton.
Yocum, James Carleton.
xYocum, James C.
    The Development of Franklin County Public
        Libraries, 1980. Ohio St U Admin Sci.
    Retailers' Costs of Sales Tax Collection in
        Ohio. Ohio St U Admin Sci.
Yoder, Don.
xYoder, Don.
    ed. American Folklife. U of Tex Pr.
Yoder, E. J. see Yoder, Eldon Joseph.

Yoder, Eldon Joseph.
xYoder, E. J.
Principles of Pavement Design. Wiley.
Yoder, Glee.
xYoder, Glee.
Take It from Here: Suggestions for Creative
Activities. Judson.
Yoder, H. S. *see* Yoder, Hatten Schuyler.
Yoder, Hatten Schuyler, 1921-
xYoder, H. S.
The Evolution of the Igneous Rocks: Fiftieth
Anniversary Perspectives. Princeton U Pr.
Generation of Basaltic Magma. Natl Acad Pr.
Yoder, John H. *see* Yoder, John Howard.
Yoder, John Howard.
xYoder, John H.
Christian Witness to the State. Faith & Life.
ed. The Legacy of Michael Sattler. Herald Pr.
Yoder, Lowell C.
xYoder, Lowell C.
Consumer Finance Industry in Florida. U
Presses Fla.
Yoder, R. A.
xYoder, R. A.
Emerson & the Orphic Poet in America. U of
Cal Pr.
Yodzis, P. *see* Yodzis, Peter.
Yodzis, Peter, 1943-
xYodzis, P.
Competition for Space & the Structure of
Ecological Communities. Springer-Verlag.
Yoel, Jose.
xYocl, Josc.
Pathology & Surgery of the Salivary Glands. C
C Thomas.
Yoels, Jennifer.
xYocls, Jennifer.
Reshape Your Body, Re-Vitalize Your Life.
P-H.
Yogananda, Paramhanse, 1893-1952
xYogananda.
Autobiography of a Yogi. Wehman.
xYogananda, Paramahansa.
Autobiography of a Yogi. Self Realization.
Whispers from Eternity. Self Realization.
Yogananda, Paramahansa. *see* Yogananda.
Yogev, Gedalia.
xYogev, Gedalia.
Diamonds & Coral: Anglo-Dutch Jews &
Eighteenth-Century Trade. Holmes & Meier.
Yohe, Gary W. *see* Yohe, Gary Wynn.
Yohe, Gary Wynn, 1948-
xYohe, Gary W.
A Comparison of Price Controls & Quantity
Controls Under Uncertainty. Garland Pub.
Yohn, Rick.
xYohn, Rick.
Discover Your Spiritual Gift and Use It.
Tyndale.
How to Overcome Temptation. Nelson.
Yoke, Carl B.
xYoke, Carl B.
Reader's Guide to Roger Zelazny. Starmont
Hse.
Yoken, Carol.
xYoken, Carol.
Living with Deaf-Blindness: Nine Profiles. Natl
Acad Gallaudet Coll.
Yoken, Melvin B.
xYoken, Melvin B.
Claude Tillier. Twayne.
Yokote, Roy T.
xYokote, Roy T.
Fundamentals of Extremities Radiography.
Independent Study.
Yolen, Jane. *see* Yolen, Jane H.
Yolen, Jane H.
xYolen, Jane.

Boy Who Had Wings. T Y Crowell.
The Dream Weaver. Philomel.
Emperor & the Kite. Collins Pubs.
Friend: The Story of George Fox & the
Quakers. HM.
The Giants Go Camping. HM.
The Girl Who Cried Flowers & Other Tales. T
Y Crowell.
The Girl Who Loved the Wind. T Y Crowell.
The Little Spotted Fish. HM.
Mermaid's Three Wisdoms. Philomel.
No Bath Tonight. T Y Crowell.
The Rainbow Rider. T Y Crowell.
Simple Gifts: The Story of the Shakers. Viking
Pr.
The Simple Prince. Parents.
Spider Jane. Coward.
The Sultan's Perfect Tree. Schol Bk Serv.
World on a String: The Story of Kites.
Philomel.
xYolen, Jane H.
The Giants' Farm. HM.
Yolen, Will. *see* Yolen, Will H.
Yolen, Will H., 1908-
xYolen, Will.
The Complete Book of Kites & Kite Flying.
S&S.
Yolles, Stanley F.
xYolles, Stanley F.
Absenteeism in Industry. C C Thomas.
Yonemura, Ann, 1947-
xYonemura, Ann.
Japanese Lacquer. Freer.
Yonemura, Margaret.
xYonemura, Margaret.
Developing Language Programs for Young
Disadvantaged Children. Tchrs Coll.
Yong, R. N. *see* Yong, Raymond Nen Yiu.
Yong, Raymond Nen Yiu.
xYong, R. N.
Soil Properties & Behaviour. Elsevier.
Yonge, Charles Duke.
xYonge, Charles Duke.
Life of Sir Walter Scott. Folcroft.
Yonge, Charlotte M. *see* Yonge, Charlotte Mary.
Yonge, Charlotte Mary, 1823-1901
xYonge, Charlotte M.
The Clever Woman of the Family, 1865.
Garland Pub.
Gold Dust. Keats.
History of Christian Names. Gale.
History of Christian Names. Gordon Pr.
Yonker, Nicholas J., 1927-
xYonker, Nicolas.
God, Man & the Planetary Age: Preface for a
Theistic Humanism. Oreg St U Pr.
Yonker, Nicolas. *see* Yonker, Nicholas J.
Yoo, Grace S.
xYoo, Grace S.
Two Korean Brothers: The Story of Hungbu &
Nolbu. Far Eastern Res.
Yoo, Yushin.
xYoo, Yushin.
Books on Buddhism: An Annotated Subject
Guide. Scarecrow.
Compiled by Soviet Education: An Annotated
Bibliography & Readers' Guide to Works in
English, 1893-1978. Greenwood.
Yoors, Jan.
xYoors, Jan.
Crossing. S&S.
Gypsies. S&S.
Gypsies. S&S.
Yorburg, Betty.
xYorburg, Betty G.
Utopia & Reality: A Collective Portrait of
American Socialists. Columbia U Pr.
Yorburg, Betty G. *see* Yorburg, Betty.
Yorgason, Blaine M., 1942-
xYorgason, Blaine M.

Massacre at Salt Creek. Doubleday.
Yorinks, Arthur.
xYorinks, Arthur.
Sid & Sol. FS&G.
York, Carol B. *see* York, Carol Beach.
York, Carol Beach.
xYork, Carol B.
I Will Make You Disappear. Bantam.
I Will Make You Disappear. Elsevier-Nelson.
Nothing Ever Happens Here. NAL.
Remember Me When I Am Dead.
Elsevier-Nelson.
Revenge of the Dolls. Elsevier-Nelson.
When Midnight Comes.... Elsevier-Nelson.
York, Courtney.
xYork, Courtney.
Northampton County North Carolina Census
1790. Hse of York.
Perry County, Arkansas Census 1850. Hse of
York.
Polk County Arkansas Census 1850. Hse of
York.
Prairie County Arkansas Census 1850. Hse of
York.
xYork, Curtney.
Northampton County North Carolina Census
1810. Hse of York.
York, Curtney. *see* York, Courtney.
York, D. *see* York, Derek.
York, Derek.
xYork, D.
The Earth's Age & Geochronology. Pergamon.
Planet Earth. McGraw.
York, Helen.
xYork, Helen.
A Venetian Charade. Doubleday.
York, Kenneth II.
xYork, Kenneth H.
Cases & Materials on Remedies. West Pub.
York, Robert.
xYork, Robert.
The Swords of December. Scribner.
Yorke, Margaret.
xYorke, Margaret.
The Come-on. Har-Row.
The Cost of Silence. Walker & Co.
Yorke-Long, Alan.
xYorke-Long, Alan.
Music at Court: Four Eighteenth Century
Studies. Hyperion Conn.
Yorks, Lyle.
xYorks, Lyle.
Job Enrichment Revisited. Am Mgmt.
A Radical Approach to Job Enrichment. Am
Mgmt.
Yoseloff, Martin, 1919-
xYoseloff, Martin.
Remember Me to Marcie. Popular Lib.
Yoseloff, Thomas, 1913-
xYoseloff, Thomas.
Fellow of Infinite Jest. Greenwood.
Yoshikawa, Tetsuo, 1905-
xYoshikawa, Tetsuo.
Atlas of the Brains of Domestic Animals. Pa St
U Pr.
Yoshikawa, Thomas T.
xYoshikawa, Thomas T.
Intro. by Infectious Diseases: Diagnosis &
Management. HM Prof Med Div.
Yoshinaga, Koji.
xYoshinaga, Koji.
ed. Implantation of the Ovum. Harvard U Pr.
Yoshino, Masatoshi, 1928-
xYoshino, Masatoshi.
Climate in a Small Area: An Introduction to
Local Meteorology. Intl Schol Bk Serv.
xYoshino, Masatoshi M.
ed. Local Wind Bora. Intl Schol Bk Serv.
Yoshino, Masatoshi M. *see* Yoshino, Masatoshi.

Yoshitake, Kiyohiko, 1924-
xYoshitake, Kiyohiko.
An Introduction to Public Enterprise in Japan.
Sage.
Yoshpe, Harry B. see Yoshpe, Harry Beller.
Yoshpe, Harry Beller, 1911-
xYoshpe, Harry B.
Disposition of Loyalist Estates in the Southern
District of the State of New York. AMS Pr.
Yost, Charles W. see Yost, Charles Woodruff.
Yost, Charles Woodruff.
xYost, Charles W.
Age of Triumph & Frustration: Modern
Dialogues. Speller.
Yost, Nellie Irene (Snyder).
xYost, Nellie S.
Medicine Lodge: The Story of a Kansas
Frontier Town. Swallow.
Yost, Nellie S. see Yost, Nellie Irene (Snyder).
Yost, William A.
xYost, William A.
Fundamentals of Hearing: An Introduction.
HR&W.
Yotopoulos, Pan A.
xYotopoulos, Pan A.
Economics of Development: Empirical
Investigations. Har-Row.
Youcha, Geraldine.
xYoucha, Geraldine.
A Dangerous Pleasure. Dutton.
Youd, Samuel, 1922-
xYoud, Samuel.
The Choice. S&S.
Giant's Arrow. S&S.
Youldon, Gillian.
xYouldon, Gillian.
Colors. Watts.
Numbers. Watts.
Shapes. Watts.
Youmans, Hubert L.
xYoumans, Hubert L.
Statistics for Chemistry. Merrill.
Young. see Young, Morris N. M. D.
Young, A. see Young, Anthony.
Young, A. F. see Young, Alfred Fabian.
Young, A. S. see Young, Andrew Sturgeon Nash.
Young, Al, 1939-
xYoung, Al.
Ask Me Now. McGraw.
Dancing: Poems. Corinth Bks.
Young, Alan R., 1941-
xYoung, Alan R.
Henry Peacham. G K Hall.
Young, Alexander, 1800-1854
xYoung, Alexander.
Chronicles of the First Planters of the Colony
of Massachusetts Bay, 1623-1636. Da Capo.
Chronicles of the First Planters of the Colony
of Massachusetts Bay, from 1623-1636.
Genealog Pub.
Chronicles of the Pilgrim Fathers of the Colony
of Plymouth, 1602-1625. Da Capo.
Chronicles of the Pilgrim Fathers of the Colony
of Plymouth, from 1602-1625. Genealog Pub.
The Sogo Shosha: Japanese Multi-National
Trading Companies. Westview.
Young, Alfred F. see Young, Alfred Fabian.
Young, Alfred Fabian.
xYoung, A. F.
Democratic Republicans of New York: The
Origins, 1763-1797. U of NC Pr.
xYoung, Alfred F.
ed. Dissent: Explorations in the History of
American Radicalism. N Ill U Pr.
Young, Allen.
xYoung, Allen.
Intro. by Gay Sunshine Interview. Grey Fox.
Young, Amy R. see Young, Amy Ross.
Young, Amy Ross.
xYoung, Amy R.

By Death or Divorce...It Hurts to Lose. Accent
Bks.
Young, Andrew J.
xYoung, Andrew J.
Andrew Young at the United Nations.
Documentary Pubns.
Young, Andrew Sturgeon Nash, 1919-
xYoung, A. S.
Negro Firsts in Sports. Johnson Chi.
Young, Anthony.
xYoung, A.
Tropical Soils & Soil Survey. Cambridge U Pr.
Young, Arthur, 1741-1820
xYoung, Arthur.
Autobiography of Arthur Young. Kelley.
Young, Arthur H. see Young, Arthur Henry.
Young, Arthur Henry, 1866-1943
xYoung, Arthur H.
Art Young: His Life & Times. Hyperion Conn.
Young, Arthur M., 1905-
xYoung, Arthur M.
The Bell Notes: Journey from Physics to
Metaphysics. Delacorte.
The Geometry of Meaning. Delacorte.
The Reflexive Universe: Evolution of
Consciousness. Delacorte.
Young, Arthur M. see Young, Arthur Milton.
Young, Arthur Milton, 1900-
xYoung, Arthur M.
Troy & Her Legend. Greenwood.
Young, Arthur N. see Young, Arthur Nichols.
Young, Arthur Nichols, 1890-
xYoung, Arthur N.
China's Nation-Building Effort, 1927-1937:
The Financial & Economic Record. Hoover
Inst Pr.
Young, B. E. see Young, Bernice Elizabeth.
Young Bear, Ray. see Young Bear, Ray A.
Young, Bernice Elizabeth.
xYoung, B. E.
The Story of Hank Aaron. Archway.
The Story of Hank Aaron. PB.
Young, Biloine W.
xYoung, Biloine W.
How Carla Saw the Shalako God.
Independence Pr.
Medicine Man Who Went to School.
Independence Pr.
Young, Bob.
xYoung, Bob.
Where Tomorrow?. Archway.
Where Tomorrow?. PB.
Young, Bradford W. see Young, Bradford Woodbridge.
Young, Bradford Woodbridge.
xYoung, Bradford W.
Lower Urinary Tract Obstruction in Childhood.
Lea & Febiger.
Young, Brian J., 1940-
xYoung, Brian J.
Promoters & Politicians: The North-Shore
Railways in the History of Quebec,
1854-1885. U of Toronto Pr.
Young, C. see Young, Charles Edmund.
Young, Carl B. see Young, Carl B.,Jr.
Young, Carl B.,Jr.
xYoung, Carl B.
First Aid for Emergency Crews: A Manual on
Emergency First Aid Procedures for
Ambulance Crews, Law Enforcement
Officers, Fire Service Personnel, Wrecker
Drivers, Hospital Staffs, Industry, Nurses. C
C Thomas.
Young, Carter T. see Young, Carter Travis.
Young, Carter Travis.
xYoung, Carter T.
Winter Drift. Doubleday.
Young, Catherine M.
xYoung, Catherine M.

To See Our World. Morrow.
Young, Charles. see Young, Charles R.
Young, Charles Edmund.
xYoung, C.
Practical English: An Introduction to
Composition. McGraw.
Young, Charles H. see Young, Charles Hurlburt.
Young, Charles Hurlburt.
xYoung, Charles H.
The Japanese Canadians. Arno.
Young, Charles R.
xYoung, Charles.
Hubert Walter, Lord of Canterbury & Lord of
England. Duke.
xYoung, Charles R.
English Borough & Royal Administration,
1130-1307. Duke.
The Royal Forests of Medieval England. U of
Pa Pr.
ed. Twelfth Century Renaissance. Krieger.
Young, Charmaine.
xYoung, Charmaine.
I'm Going to Clean Homes & Businesses.
Burgess.
Young, Christopher.
xYoung, Christopher.
The Films of Doris Day. Citadel Pr.
The Films of Hedy Lamarr. Citadel Pr.
Young County Historical Survey Committee.
xYoung County Historical Survey Committee.
Centennial History of Graham. Nortex Pr.
Young, Crawford.
xYoung, Crawford.
Politics in the Congo: Decolonization &
Independence. Princeton U Pr.
The Politics of Cultural Pluralism. U of Wis Pr.
Young, D.
xYoung, D.
ed. Developmental Neurobiology of
Arthropods. Cambridge U Pr.
Young, David. see Young, David P.
Young, David M.
xYoung, David M.
A Survey of Numerical Mathematics. A-W.
Young, David P.
xYoung, David.
Boxcars. Ecco Pr.
The Names of a Hare in English. U of
Pittsburgh Pr.
Young, David W.
xYoung, David W.
The Managerial Process in Human Service
Agencies. Praeger.
Young, Davis A.
xYoung, Davis A.
Creation & the Flood: An Alternative to Flood
Geology & Theistic Evolution. Baker Bk.
Young, Dennis.
xYoung, Dennis R.
Foster Care & Non-Profit Agencies. Lexington
Bks.
How Shall We Collect the Garbage?: A Study
in Economic Organization. Urban Inst.
Young, Dennis R. see Young, Dennis.
Young, Donald. see Young, Donald Ramsey.
Young, Donald F.
xYoung, Donald F.
Introduction to Applied Mechanics: An
Integrated Treatment for Students in
Engineering, Life Science & Interdisciplinary
Programs. Iowa St U Pr.
Young, Donald R. see Young, Donald Ramsey.
Young, Donald Ramsey, 1898-
xYoung, Donald R.
ed. The Modern American Family. Arno.
xYoung, Donald R.
Trusteeship & the Management of Foundations.
Russell Sage.
Young, Donna J.
xYoung, Donna J.

Retreat: As It Was: A Fantasy. Naiad Pr.
Young, Douglas, 1913-
 xYoung, Douglas.
  Edinburgh in the Age of Sir Walter Scott. U of Okla Pr.
Young, Dudley.
 xYoung, Dudley.
  Out of Ireland: A Reading of Yeat's Poetry. Persea Bks.
Young, E. C. *see* Young, Eutiquio C.
Young, E. Gordon. *see* Young, Elrid Gordon.
Young, E. R. *see* Young, Egerton Ryerson.
Young, Ed.
 xYoung, Ed.
  The Rooster's Horns: A Chinese Puppet Play to Make & Perform. Philomel.
  The Terrible Nung Gwama: A Chinese Folktale. Philomel.
Young, Edward, 1683-1765
 xYoung, Edward.
  Edward Young's "Conjectures on Original Composition" in England & Germany. R West.
  Edward Young's Conjectures on Original Composition. Folcroft.
Young, Edward J. *see* Young, Edward Joseph.
Young, Edward Joseph.
 xYoung, Edward J.
  Studies in Genesis One. Presby & Reformed.
Young, Egerton Ryerson, 1840-1909
 xYoung, E. R.
  Stories from Indian Wigwams & Northern Campfires. Gordon Pr.
Young, Eleanor G. *see* Young, Eleanor G. R.
Young, Eleanor G. R.
 xYoung, Eleanor G.
  Anastasia Arrives. Arno.
Young, Eleanor R.
 xYoung, Eleanor R.
  Fathers, Fathers, Fathers. Denison.
  Needlepoint. Watts.
Young, Elinore W.
 xYoung, Elinore W.
  How to Raise & Train a Bedlington Terrier. TFH Pubns.
Young, Elisabeth L. *see* Young, Elisabeth Larsh.
Young, Elisabeth Larsh, 1910-
 xYoung, Elisabeth L.
  Family Afoot. Iowa St U Pr.
Young, Elizabeth B. *see* Young, Elizabeth Barber.
Young, Elizabeth Barber, 1888-
 xYoung, Elizabeth B.
  A Study of the Curricula of Seven Selected Women's Colleges of the Southern States. AMS Pr.
Young, Elrid Gordon.
 xYoung, E. Gordon.
  The Development of Biochemistry in Canada. U of Toronto Pr.
Young, Ernest P.
 xYoung, Ernest P.
  The Presidency of Yuan Shih-K'ai: Liberalism & Dictatorship in Early Republican China. U of Mich Pr.
Young, Eutiquio C.
 xYoung, E. C.
  Vector & Tensor Analysis. Dekker.
Young, Ezra.
 xYoung, Ezra.
  Lands of the Unexpected: Memoirs of the Middle East. Sunstone Pr.
Young, F. M. *see* Young, Francis Marion.
Young, Fay.
 xYoung, Fay.
  Everything You Should Know About Pension Plans. Bethesda.
  Everything You Should Know About Pension Plans. Liberty Pub.
Young, Faye E. *see* Young, Faye Early.

Young, Faye Early.
 xYoung, Faye E.
  Gerald the Third. La Leche.
Young Filmaker's Foundation. *see* Young Filmmakers Foundation.
Young Filmmakers Foundation.
 xYoung Filmaker's Foundation.
  ed. Young Animators & Their Discoveries. Scribner.
Young, Francis B. *see* Young, Francis Brett.
Young, Francis Brett, 1884-1954
 xYoung, Francis B.
  Portrait of a Village. Arno.
Young, Francis Marion.
 xYoung, F. M.
  Man Meets Grizzly: Encounters in the Wild from Lewis & Clark to Modern Times. HM.
Young, Frank R. *see* Young, Frank Rudolph.
Young, Frank Rudolph.
 xYoung, Frank R.
  Secrets of Personal Psychic Power. P-H.
Young, Freddie.
 xYoung, Freddie.
  Work of the Motion Picture Cameraman. Focal Pr.
  Work of the Motion Picture Cameraman. Hastings.
Young, Frederick H.
 xYoung, Frederick H.
  Nature of Mathematics. Krieger.
Young, G. Richard.
 xYoung, G. Richard.
  Joint Ventures: Planning & Action. Finan Exec.
Young, George, Sir, Bart, 1837-1930
 xYoung, George.
  English Prosody on Inductive Lines. Greenwood.
Young, George A. *see* Young, George Albert.
Young, George Albert.
 xYoung, George A.
  Effective Management: Basic Principles & Practices. Dorrance.
Young, George M. *see* Young, George Malcolm.
Young, George Malcolm.
 xYoung, George M.
  ed. English Historical Documents: 1833-1874. Oxford U Pr.
  Stanley Baldwin. Greenwood.
  Victorian England: Portrait of an Age. Oxford U Pr.
Young, Harold C. *see* Young, Harold Chester.
Young, Harold Chester.
 xYoung, Harold C.
  Planning, Programming, Budgeting Systems in Academic Libraries: An Exploratory Study of PPBS in University Libraries Having Membership in the Association of Research Libraries. Gale.
Young, Harriet. *see* Young, Harriet (Gallagher).
Young, Harriet (Gallagher), 1910-
 xYoung, Harriet.
  Grandmother's Haviland. Wallace-Homestead.
Young, Harry F.
 xYoung, Harry F.
  Prince Lichnowsky & the Great War. U of Ga Pr.
Young, Helen.
 xYoung, Helen.
  The Complete Book of Doll Collecting. Berkley Pub.
  Dollmaking for Everyone. A S Barnes.
  A Throne for Sesame. Andre Deutsch.
Young, Henry J.
 xYoung, Henry J.
  ed. Preaching on Suffering & a God of Love. Fortress.
  ed. Preaching the Gospel. Fortress.
Young, Howard T.
 xYoung, Howard T.

The Line in the Margin: Juan Ramon Jimenez & His Readings in Blake, Shelley, & Yeats. U of Wis Pr.
Young, Hubert, Sir, 1885-
 xYoung, Hubert W.
  The Independent Arab. AMS Pr.
Young, Hubert W. *see* Young, Hubert.
Young, Hugh D.
 xYoung, Hugh D.
  Fundamentals of Mechanics & Heat. McGraw.
  Fundamentals of Waves, Optics & Modern Physics. McGraw.
  Statistical Treatment of Experimental Data. McGraw.
Young, Ione (Dodson).
 xYoung, Ione D.
  ed. A Concordance to the Poetry of Byron. I Young.
Young, Ione D. *see* Young, Ione (Dodson).
Young, J. A. *see* Young, Jimmy Albert.
Young, J. Terry. *see* Young, John Terry.
Young, Jack.
 xYoung, Jack.
  Outline of Oral & Dental Anatomy. McGraw.
Young, James H. *see* Young, James Harvey.
Young, James Harvey, 1915-
 xYoung, James H.
  Medical Messiahs: A Social History of Health Quackery in Twentieth-Century America. Princeton U Pr.
Young, James J.
 xYoung, James J.
  ed. Ministering to the Divorced Catholic. Paulist Pr.
Young, James W. *see* Young, James Webb.
Young, James Webb, 1886-
 xYoung, James W.
  How to Become an Advertising Man. Crain Bks.
Young, Jared J.
 xYoung, Jared J.
  Discrimination, Income, Human Capital Investment, & Asian-Americans. R & E Res Assoc.
Young, Jean.
 xYoung, Jean.
  Great Trash: New Trends in Antiquing, Auctions, Bargaining, Bartering, Buying for Resale, Collectibles, Garage Sales, Flea Markets, House Sales, Folk Art & Fine Art, Careers in Collecting, & Raising Cash. Har-Row.
  Woodstock Craftsman's Manual. Penguin.
Young, Jeffrey T.
 xYoung, Jeffrey T.
  Classical Theories of Value: From Smith to Sraffa. Westview.
Young, Jerrald F., 1921-
 xYoung, Jerrald F.
  Decision Making for Small Business Management. Wiley.
Young, Jim.
 xYoung, Jim.
  When the Whale Came to My Town. Knopf.
Young, Jimmy, 1918-
 xYoung, Jimmy.
  Services on & off the Motorways. David & Charles.
Young, Jimmy Albert.
 xYoung, J. A.
  Principles & Practice of Respiratory Therapy. Year Bk Med.
Young, John.
 xYoung, John.
  Capitalism & Human Obsolescence: Corporate Control vs. Individual Survival in Rural America. Allanheld.
  Learn Japanese: College Text. U Pr of Hawaii.
Young, John. *see* Young, John N.

Young, John B. *see* Young, John Baldwin.
Young, John Baldwin, 1928-
  xYoung, John B.
    Privacy. Wiley.
Young, John E.
  xYoung, John E.
    Geometry for Elementary Teachers.
      Holden-Day.
Young, John N.
  xYoung, John.
    Great Northern Suburban. David & Charles.
Young, John S. *see* Young, John Sacret.
Young, John Sacret.
  xYoung, John S.
    Special Olympics. Warner Bks.
Young, John Terry, 1929-
  xYoung, J. Terry.
    Church-Alive & Growing. Broadman.
Young, John V.
  xYoung, John V.
    Ghost Towns of the Santa Cruz Mountains.
      Western Tanager.
    The Grand Canyon. Filter.
Young, John W. *see* Young, John Wray.
Young, John Wray.
  xYoung, John W.
    Community Theatre: A Manual for Success.
      French.
    Play Direction for the High School Theatre.
      Kennikat.
Young, John Z. *see* Young, John Zachary.
Young, John Zachary, 1907-
  xYoung, John Z.
    Anatomy of the Nervous System of Octopus
      Vulgaris. Oxford U Pr.
    Life of Vertebrates. Oxford U Pr.
Young, K. *see* Young, Karl.
Young, Karl, 1879-1943
  xYoung, K.
    The Origin & Development of the Story of
      Troilus & Criseyde. Gordon Pr.
Young, Ken.
  xYoung, Ken.
    Strategy & Conflict in Metropolitan Housing:
      Suburbia Versus the Greater London Council,
      1965-1975. Heinemann Ed.
Young, Kenneth, 1916-
  xYoung, Kenneth.
    Churchill & Beaverbrook: A Study in
      Friendship & Politics. Heineman.
    Rhodesia & Independence. Heineman.
Young, L. W. *see* Young, Laurence Carvan.
Young, Laurence Carvan.
  xYoung, L. W.
    Materials in Printing Processes. Focal Pr.
Young, Leontine. *see* Young, Leontine R.
Young, Leontine R.
  xYoung, Leontine.
    Life Among the Giants. McGraw.
    Wednesday's Children: A Study of Child
      Neglect & Abuse. Greenwood.
Young, Lesley, 1949-
  xYoung, Lesley.
    Camembert & the Magic Lamp. Mayflower
      Bks.
    Introducing Camembert. Mayflower Bks.
Young, Lloyd P. *see* Young, Lloyd Percy.
Young, Lloyd Percy, 1898-
  xYoung, Lloyd P.
    The Administration of Merit-Type Teachers'
      Salary Schedules. AMS Pr.
Young, Lois H. *see* Young, Lois Horton.

Young, Lois Horton.

  xYoung, Lois H.
    Dimensions for Happening. Judson.

    Teaching Kindergarten Children. Judson.

Young, Louise (Merwin), 1903-
  xYoung, Louise M.

    Thomas Carlyle & the Art of History. Arden
      Lib.
    Thomas Carlyle & the Art of History. Folcroft.
    Thomas Carlyle & the Art of History. Octagon.
Young, Louise B.
  xYoung, Louise B.
    Earth's Aura. Avon.
    Earth's Aura. Knopf.
    ed. Evolution of Man. Oxford U Pr.
    ed. Population in Perspective. Oxford U Pr.
    Power Over People. Oxford U Pr.
    Power Over People. Oxford U Pr.
Young, Louise M. *see* Young, Louise (Merwin).
Young, Margaret B.
  xYoung, Margaret B.
    First Book of American Negroes. Watts.
Young, Marguerite, 1909-
  xYoung, Marguerite.
    Miss Macintosh, My Darling. HarBraceJ.
Young, Marguerite. *see* Young, Marguerite.
Young, Martha.
  xYoung, Martha.
    Plantation Bird Legends. Arno.
Young, Michael, 1953-
  xYoung, Michael.
    The Imaginary Friend. Raintree Pubs.
Young, Michael. *see* Young, Michael Dunlop.
Young, Michael Dunlop.
  xYoung, Michael.
    The Symmetrical Family. Pantheon.
    The Symmetrical Family. Penguin.
Young, Miriam. *see* Young, Miriam Burt.
Young, Miriam Burt.
  xYoung, Miriam.
    If I Drove a Tractor. Lothrop.
    If I Drove a Train. Lothrop.
    If I Flew a Plane. Lothrop.
    If I Rode a Dinosaur. Lothrop.
    If I Rode a Horse. Lothrop.
    No Place for Mitty. Schol Bk Serv.
Young, Morris N. *see* Young, Morris N. M. D.
Young, Morris N., M.D.
  xYoung.
    How to Read Faster & Remember More.
      G&D.
  xYoung, Morris N.
    How to Read Faster & Remember More. Fell.
Young, Mort.
  xYoung, Mort.
    UFO Top Secret. PB.
Young, Nancy F. *see* Young, Nancy Foon.
Young, Nancy Foon.
  xYoung, Nancy F.
    The Chinese in Hawaii: An Annotated
      Bibliography. U Pr of Hawaii.
Young Nations Conference, Sydney, 1976. *see* Young
  Nations Conference. University of New South Wales.
Young Nations Conference. University of New South
Wales.
  xYoung Nations Conference, Sydney, 1976.
    Paradise Postponed: Essays on Research &
      Development in the South Pacific:
      Proceedings. Pergamon.
Young, Nigel.
  xYoung, Nigel.
    An Infantile Disorder?: The Crisis & Decline of
      the New Left. Westview.
Young, Olivia. *see* Young, Olivia Rudolph.
Young, Olivia Rudolph, 1894-
  xYoung, Olivia.
    The Honey & the Root. Golden Quill.
Young, Oran R.
  xYoung, Oran R.
    ed. Bargaining: Formal Theories of Negotiation.
      U of Ill Pr.
    Politics of Force: Bargaining During
      International Crises. Princeton U Pr.
Young, Patrick.
  xYoung, Patrick.

    Drifting Continents, Shifting Seas: An
      Introduction to Plate Tectonics. Watts.
Young, Paul T. *see* Young, Paul Thomas.
Young, Paul Thomas, 1892-
  xYoung, Paul T.
    Understanding Your Feelings & Emotions.
      P-H.
Young People's Science Encyclopedia.
  xYoung People's Science Encyclopedia Editors.
    Young People's Science Dictionary. Childrens.
Young, Percy M. *see* Young, Percy Marshall.
Young, Percy Marshall, 1912-
  xYoung, Percy M.
    The Bachs: 1500-1850. Biblio Dist.
    Britten. D White.
    A Critical Dictionary of Composers & Their
      Music. Hyperion Conn.
    Handbook of Choral Technique. Dufour.
    Tchaikovsky. D White.
Young, Ray.
  xYoung, Ray.
    Bridge for People Who Don't Know One Card
      from Another. B&N.
Young, Robert D. *see* Young, Robert Doran.
Young, Robert Doran, 1928-
  xYoung, Robert D.
    Religious Imagination: God's Gift to Prophets
      & Preachers. Westminster.
Young, Robert J., 1942-
  xYoung, Robert J.
    In Command of France: French Foreign Policy
      & Military Planning, 1933-1940. Harvard U
      Pr.
Young, Robert T., 1935-
  xYoung, Robert T.
    A Sprig of Hope. Abingdon.
Young, Roland. *see* Young, Roland Arnold.
Young, Roland A. *see* Young, Roland Arnold.
Young, Roland Arnold, 1910-
  xYoung, Roland.
    British Parliament. Northwestern U Pr.
  xYoung, Roland A.
    The American Congress. Greenwood.
    Congressional Politics in the Second World
      War. Da Capo.
Young, Roland S. *see* Young, Roland Stansfield.
Young, Roland Stansfield, 1906-
  xYoung, Roland S.
    Separation Procedures in Inorganic Analysis: A
      Practical Handbook. Halsted Pr.
Young, Samuel H., 1939-
  xYoung, Samuel H.
    Psychic Children. PB.
Young, Sandy.
  xYoung, Sandy.
    Developing a Student Leadership Class. Natl
      Assn Principals.
Young, Scott.
  xYoung, Scott.
    Face-off in Moscow. EMC.
    Learning to Be Captain. EMC.
    The Silent One Speaks up. EMC.
Young, Sidney.
  xYoung, Sidney.
    The Annals of the Barber-Surgeons of London.
      AMS Pr.
Young, Stanley P. *see* Young, Stanley Paul.
Young, Stanley Paul.
  xYoung, Stanley P.
    The Clever Coyote. U of Nebr Pr.
Young, Stark, 1881-1963
  xYoung, Stark.
    Addio; Madretta, & Other Plays. Core
      Collection.
    The Flower in Drama & Glamour: Theatre
      Essays & Criticism. Octagon.
    So Red the Rose. Larlin Corp.
    So Red the Rose. Mockingbird Bks.
    The Theatre. Octagon.
Young, T. Y. *see* Young, Tzay Y.

Young, Thomas, 1773-1829
    xYoung, Thomas.
        Course of Lectures on Natural Philosophy &
        the Mechanical Arts. Johnson Repr.
Young, Thomas D. *see* Young, Thomas Daniel.
Young, Thomas Daniel, 1919-
    xYoung, Thomas D.
        Gentleman in a Dustcoat: A Biography of John
        Crowe Ransom. La State U Pr.
Young, Trudee.
    xYoung, Trudee.
        Georges Simenon: A Checklist of His "Maigret"
        & Other Mystery Novels & Short Stories in
        French & in English Translations. Scarecrow.
Young, Tzay Y.
    xYoung, T. Y.
        ed. Classification, Estimation & Pattern
        Recognition. Elsevier.
Young, Vernon.
    xYoung, Vernon.
        On Film: Unpopular Essays on a Popular Art.
        Times Bks.
Young, Victor A.
    xYoung, Victor A.
        Migraine Prevention. V Young.
Young, Virgil M.
    xYoung, Virgil M.
        The Story of Idaho. U Pr of Idaho.
Young, Virginia B. *see* Young, Virginia Brady.
Young, Virginia Brady.
    xYoung, Virginia B.
        Circle of Thaw. Barlenmir.
Young, Virginia G.
    xYoung, Virginia G.
        Library Trustee: A Practical Guidebook.
        Bowker.
Young, W. H. *see* Young, William Henry.
Young, W. T. *see* Young, William Thomas.
Young, Warren C. *see* Young, Warren Cameron.
Young, Warren Cameron, 1913-
    xYoung, Warren C.
        Christian Approach to Philosophy. Baker Bk.
Young, William A. *see* Young, William Arthur.
Young, William Arthur, 1867-1955
    xYoung, William A.
        Dictionary of the Characters & Scenes in the
        Stories & Poems of Rudyard Kipling. B
        Franklin.
Young, William C., 1928-
    xYoung, William C.
        Famous Actors & Actresses on the American
        Stage. Bowker.
Young, William H. *see* Young, William Henry.
Young, William Henry, 1863-1942
    xYoung, W. H.
        The Fundamental Theorems of the Differential
        Calculus. Hafner.
    xYoung, William H.
        Theory of Sets of Points. Chelsea Pub.
Young, William Thomas.
    xYoung, W. T.
        ed. An Anthology of the Poetry of the Age of
        Shakespeare. Folcroft.
**Young Women's Christian Associations, Tokyo, World
Fellowship Committee.**
    xY. W. C. A. World Fellowship Committee -
    Tokyo.
        Japanese Etiquette: An Introduction. C E
        Tuttle.
Young Bear, Ray A.
    xYoung Bear, Ray.
        The Winter of the Salamander: The Keeper of
        Importance. Har-Row.
Youngblood, Ronald.
    xYoungblood, Ronald.
        Special Day Sermons. Baker Bk.
Youngdale, James M.
    xYoungdale, James M.

        Populism: A Psychohistorical Perspective.
        Kennikat.
Younger, Kenneth G. *see* Younger, Kenneth Gilmour.
Younger, Kenneth Gilmour, 1908-
    xYounger, Kenneth G.
        Changing Perspectives in British Foreign
        Policy. Greenwood.
Younger, Paul.
    xYounger, Paul.
        Hinduism. Argus Comm.
Younger, Richard D.
    xYounger, Richard D.
        People's Panel: The Grand Jury in the United
        States, 1634-1941. Brown U Pr.
Younghusband, Francis. *see* Younghusband, Francis
    Edward.
Younghusband, Francis E. *see* Younghusband, Francis
    Edward.
Younghusband, Francis Edward, Sir, 1863-1942
    xYounghusband, Francis.
        Modern Mystics. Univ Bks.
    xYounghusband, Francis E.
        Modern Mystics. Arno.
Youngquist, Waldemar.
    xYoungquist, Wally G.
        Wood in American Life 1776-2076. Forest
        Prod.
Youngquist, Wally G. *see* Youngquist, Waldemar.
Youngs. *see* Youngs, David D.
Youngs, Betty.
    xYoungs, Betty.
        Let's Explore Jobs. Broadman.
Youngs, David D.
    xYoungs.
        Psychosomatic Obstetrics & Gynecology. ACC.
Youngs, F. A. *see* Youngs, Frederic A.
Youngs, Frederic A., 1936-
    xYoungs, F. A.
        The Proclamations of the Tudor Queens.
        Cambridge U Pr.
Youngs, J. William T. *see* Youngs, John William
    Theodore.
Youngs, John William Theodore, 1941-
    xYoungs, J. William T.
        God's Messengers: Religious Leadership in
        Colonial New England, 1700-1750. Johns
        Hopkins.
Youngson, A. J.
    xYoungson, A. J.
        Britain's Economic Growth, 1920-1966. Kelley.
        ed. Economic Development in the Long Run.
        St Martin.
        The Scientific Revolution in Victorian
        Medicine. Holmes & Meier.
Younie, William J.
    xYounie, William J.
        Instructional Approaches to Slow Learning.
        Tchrs Coll.
Youniss, James. *see* Youniss, James E.
Youniss, James E.
    xYouniss, James.
        Parents & Peers in Social Development: A
        Sullivan-Piaget Perspective. U of Chicago Pr.
Younker, Lucas.
    xYounker, Lucas.
        Animal Doctor. BJ Pub Group.
Yount, John, 1935-
    xYount, John.
        Hardcastle. Marek.
Yount, John T.
    xYount, John T.
        Bottle Collector's Handbook & Pricing Guide.
        Educator Bks.
        Bridge Beginner's Handbook. Educator Bks.
        Leathercraft Handbook. Educator Bks.
Yourcenar, Marguerite.
    xYourcenar, Marguerite.
        The Abyss. FS&G.
        Coup De Grace. FS&G.
Yourdon, E. *see* Yourdon, Edward.

Yourdon, Edward.
    xYourdon, E.
        Managing the Structured Techniques. P-H.
    xYourdon, Edward.
        Design of on-Line Computer Systems. P-H.
        Managing the Structured Techniques. Yourdon.
        Structured Design: Fundamentals of a
        Discipline of Computer Program & System
        Design. P-H.
    xYourdon, Edward N.
        ed. Classics in Software Engineering. Yourdon.
Yourdon, Edward N. *see* Yourdon, Edward.
Youree, Gary.
    xYouree, Gary.
        The Girl in the White Coat on the Delta Eagle.
        Norton.
Yourwith, William J.
    xYourwith, William J.
        EDP Evaluation Questionnaire. Exec Stand.
Youth Hostels Association (England and Wales).
    xYouth Hostels Association Service.
        Youth Hostel Association Services. Macmillan.
    xYouth Hostels Association Services Ltd.
        Youth Hosteler's Guide to Europe. Macmillan.
Youth Hostels Association Service. *see* Youth Hostels
    Association (England and Wales).
Youth Hostels Association Services Ltd. *see* Youth
    Hostels Association (England and Wales).
Yovel, Yirmiahu.
    xYovel, Yirmiahu.
        Kant & the Philosophy of History. Princeton U
        Pr.
Yram, Pseud.
    xYram.
        Practical Astral Projection. Weiser.
Yu, Francis T. *see* Yu, Francis T. S.
Yu, Francis T. S., 1941-
    xYu, Francis T.
        Optics & Information Theory. Wiley.
Yu, Paul N.
    xYu, Paul N.
        ed. Progress in Cardiology. Lea & Febiger.
        Pulmonary Blood Volume in Health & Disease.
        Lea & Febiger.
Yu, S. C. *see* Yu, Shih Cheng.
Yu, Shih Cheng, 1921-
    xYu, S. C.
        The Structure of Accounting Theory. U Presses
        Fla.
Yuan-Cheng Fung, . *see* Fung, Yuan-Cheng.
Yuasa, Hachiro, 1890-
    xYuasa, Hachiro.
        A Classification of the Larvae of the
        Tenthredinoidea. Johnson Repr.
Yudin, Elinor B. *see* Yudin, Elinor Barry.
Yudin, Elinor Barry, 1940-
    xYudin, Elinor B.
        Human Capital Migration, Direct Investment &
        the Transfer of Technology: An Examination
        of Americans Privately Employed Overseas.
        Arno.
Yudkin, John, 1910-
    xYudkin, John.
        This Nutrition Business. St Martin.
Yudkin, Michael.
    xYudkin, Michael.
        Comprehensible Biochemistry. Longman.
        A Guidebook to Biochemistry. Cambridge U
        Pr.
Yudkovitz, Elaine.
    xYudkovitz, Elaine.
        Communication Therapy in Childhood
        Schizophrenia: An Auditory Monitoring
        Approach. Grune.
Yueh, Jean.
    xYueh, Jean.

The Great Tastes of Chinese Cooking:
Contemporary Methods & Menus. Times
Bks.

Yukawa, Hideki, 1907-
xYukawa, Hideki.
Creativity & Intuition: A Physicist Looks at
East & West. Kodansha.

Yukic, Thomas S.
xYukic, Thomas S.
Fundamentals of Recreation. Har-Row.

Yule, G. Udny. *see* Yule, George Udny.

Yule, George U. *see* Yule, George Udny.

Yule, George Udny.
xYule, G. Udny.
Statistical Study of Literary Vocabulary. Shoe
String.
xYule, George U.
Statistical Papers of George Udny Yule.
Hafner.

Yules, Richard B., 1940-
xYules, Richard B.
Atlas for Surgical Repair of Cleft Lip, Cleft
Palate, & Noncleft Velopharyngeal
Incompetence. C C Thomas.

Yulsman, Jerry.
xYulsman, Jerry.
Color Photography Simplified. Amphoto.

Yunck, John A.
xYunck, John A.
Lineage of Lady Meed: The Development of
Mediaeval Venality-Satire. U of Notre Dame
Pr.

Yung, Victor S. *see* Yung, Victor Sen.

Yung, Victor Sen.
xYung, Victor S.
The Great Wok Cookbook. Nash Pub.

Yung, Wing, 1828-1912
xYung, Wing.
ed. My Life in China & America. Arno.

Yungblut, John. *see* Yungblut, John R.

Yungblut, John R.
xYungblut, John.
Quakerism of the Future: Mystical, Prophetic
& Evangelical. Pendle Hill.
xYungblut, John R.
Discovering God Within. Westminster.

Yunik, Maurice, 1942-
xYunik, Maurice.
Design of Modern Transistor Circuits. P-H.

Yunis, Jorge J.
xYunis, Jorge J.
ed. Human Chromosome Methodology. Acad
Pr.

Yura, Michael T.
xYura, Michael T.
Raising the Exceptional Child. Dutton.

Yusko, A. A. *see* Yusko, Aaron Allen.

Yusko, Aaron Allen, 1935-
xYusko, A. A.
Art: A Learning Experience for the Very
Young. Pruett.

Yussen, Steven R.
xYussen, Steven R.
Child Development: An Introduction. Wm C
Brown.

Yvon, J.
xYvon, J.
Correlations & Entropy in Classical Statistical
Mechanics. Pergamon.

Zabalza, A. *see* Zabalza, Antoni.

Zabalza, Antoni.
xZabalza, A.
The Economics of Teacher Supply. Cambridge
U Pr.

Zabarenko, Ralph N.
xZabarenko, Ralph N.
The Doctor Tree: Developmental Stages in the
Growth of Physicians. U of Pittsburgh Pr.

Zabeeh, Farhang.
xZabeeh, Farhang.

ed. Readings in Semantics. U of Ill Pr.

Zabel, Morton D. *see* Zabel, Morton Dauwen.

Zabel, Morton Dauwen, 1901-
xZabel, Morton D.
Literary Opinion in America: Essays
Illustrating the Status, Methods & Problems
of Criticism in the United States in the
Twentieth Century. Peter Smith.

Zabih, Sepehr.
xZabih, Sepehr.
The Communist Movement in Iran. U of Cal
Pr.

Zablocki, Benjamin. *see* Zablocki, Benjamin David.

Zablocki, Benjamin David, 1941-
xZablocki, Benjamin.
The Joyful Community: An Account of the
Bruderhof, a Communal Movement Now in
Its Third Generation. U of Chicago Pr.

Zaborsky, Oskar.
xZaborsky, Oskar R.
Immobilized Enzymes. CRC Pr.

Zaborsky, Oskar R. *see* Zaborsky, Oskar.

Zabrack, Harold.
xZabrack, Harold.
Creative Musical Encounters. Kenyon.

Zaccaria, Joseph. *see* Zaccaria, Joseph S.

Zaccaria, Joseph S.
xZaccaria, Joseph.
Approaches to Guidance in Contemporary
Education. Carroll Pr.
Theories of Occupational Choice & Vocational
Development. HM.

Zacharia, Theodore P.
xZacharia, Theodore P.
ed. Immune Response at the Cellular Level.
Dekker.

Zacharias, Thomas.
xZacharias, Thomas.
illus. But Where Is the Green Parrot?.
Delacorte.

Zachariasen, W. H. *see* Zachariasen, William Houlder.

Zachariasen, William Houlder, 1906-
xZachariasen, W. H.
Theory of X-Ray Diffraction in Crystals. Peter
Smith.

Zacharis, John C.
xZacharis, John C.
Speech Communication: A Rational Approach.
Wiley.

Zacher, Mark W.
xZacher, Mark W.
Dag Hammarskjold's United Nations.
Columbia U Pr.

Zackel, Fred.
xZackel, Fred.
Cocaine & Blue Eyes. Coward.

Zacks, Shelemyahu, 1932-
xZacks, Shelemyahu.
Theory of Statistical Inference. Wiley.

Zadig, Ernest A., 1899-
xZadig, Ernest A.
The Complete Book of Pleasure Boat Engines.
P-H.

Zadoks, Jan C.
xZadoks, Jan C.
Epidemiology & Plant Disease Management.
Oxford U Pr.

Zadrozny, John T. *see* Zadrozny, John Thomas.

Zadrozny, John Thomas, 1922-
xZadrozny, John T.
Dictionary of Social Science. Pub Aff Pr.

Zaehner, R. C. *see* Zaehner, Robert Charles.

Zaehner, Robert C. *see* Zaehner, Robert Charles.

Zaehner, Robert Charles.
xZaehner, R. C.
ed. Hindu Scriptures. Dutton.
xZaehner, Robert C.

At Sundry Times: An Essay in the Comparison
of Religions. Greenwood.
Hindu & Muslim Mysticism. Schocken.
Hinduism. Oxford U Pr.

Zaetz, Jay L.
xZaetz, Jay L.
Organization of Sheltered Workshop Programs
for the Mentally Retarded Adult. C C
Thomas.

Zafar Al-Hasan, Saiyid.
xZafar al-Hasan, Saiyid.
Realism: An Attempt to Trace Its Origin &
Development in Its Chief Representatives.
Arno.

Zaffo, George. *see* Zaffo, George J.

Zaffo, George J.
xZaffo, George.
Giant Book of Things in Space. Doubleday.
Giant Nursery Book of Things That Work.
Doubleday.

Zagaris, Bruce.
xZagaris, Bruce.
Foreign Investment in the United States.
Praeger.

Zagel, James.
xZagel, James.
Confessions & Interrogations After Miranda: A
Comprehensive Guideline of the Law. Natl
Dist Atty.

Zagone, Theresa.
xZagone, Theresa.
No Nap for Me. Dutton.

Zagora, Edward.
xZagora, Edward.
Eye Injuries. C C Thomas.

Zagoria, Sam.
xZagoria, Sam.
ed. Public Workers & Public Unions. P-H.

Zagorin, Perez.
xZagorin, Perez.
Court & the Country: The Beginning of the
English Revolution. Atheneum.

Zahan, Dominique.
xZahan, Dominique.
The Religion, Spirituality, & Thought of
Traditional Africa. U of Chicago Pr.

Zahareas, Anthony. *see* Zahareas, Anthony N.

Zahareas, Anthony N.
xZahareas, Anthony.
ed. Readings in Spanish Literature. Oxford U
Pr.

Zahavy, Zev, 1920-
xZahavy, Zev.
Whence & Wherefore: The Cosmological
Destiny of Man Scientifically &
Philosophically Considered. A S Barnes.

Zahir, Mohammad, 1935-
xZahir, Mohammad.
Public Expenditure & Income Distribution in
India. Intl Bk Dist.

Zahlan, A. B. *see* Zahlan, Antoine Benjamin.

Zahlan, Antoine Benjamin, 1928-
xZahlan, A. B.
Science & Science Policy in the Arab World.
St Martin.

Zahlan, Rosemarie S. *see* Zahlan, Rosemarie Said.

Zahlan, Rosemarie Said.
xZahlan, Rosemarie S.
The Origins of the United Arab Emirates: A
Political & Social History of the Trucial
States. St Martin.

Zahler, Helene S. *see* Zahler, Helene Sara.

Zahler, Helene Sara, 1911-
xZahler, Helene S.
Eastern Workingmen & National Land Policy
1829-1862. Greenwood.

Zahn, Gordon C. *see* Zahn, Gordon Charles.

Zahn, Gordon Charles, 1918-
xZahn, Gordon C.

Children of the Ghetto. Humanities.
Dreamers of the Ghetto. Arno.
Zank, Elmer E.
xZank, Elmer E.
Light & Power: Rates & Costs of Service in
Wisconsin R.E.A. Cooperatives. U of Wis Pr.
Zannes, Estelle.
xZannes, Estelle.
Checkmate in Cleveland: The Rhetoric of
Confrontation During the Stokes Years.
UPBS.
Zannetos, Zenon S.
xZannetos, Zenon S.
Theory of Oil Tankship Rates: An Economic
Analysis of Tankship Operations. MIT Pr.
Zapf, Hermann.
xZapf, Hermann.
Manuale Typographicum. MIT Pr.
Zaporozhets, A. V. *see* Zaporozhets, Alexsandr
Vladirimirovich.
Zaporozhets, Alexsandr Vladirimirovich.
xZaporozhets, A. V.
Psychology of Preschool Children. MIT Pr.
Zappler, Georg.
xZappler, Georg.
From One Cell to Many Cells. Messner.
Zappler, Lisbeth.
xZappler, Lisbeth.
The Natural History of the Nose. Doubleday.
Nature's Oddballs. Doubleday.
Zappolo, Aurora.
xZappolo, Aurora.
Characteristics & Social Contacts & Activities
of Nursing Home Residents, United States:
August 1973-April 1974. Natl Ctr Health
Stats.
Zarb, George A.
xZarb, George A.
Prosthodontic Treatment for Partially
Edentulous Patients. Mosby.
Zarchy, Harry.
xZarchy, Harry.
illus. Let's Go Camping: A Guide to Outdoor
Living. Knopf.
illus. Stamp Collector's Guide. Knopf.
Zaremba, Joseph.
xZaremba, Joseph.
Economics of the American Lumber Industry.
Speller.
ed. Mathematical Economics & Operations
Research: A Guide to Information Sources.
Gale.
Zarembka, Paul.
xZarembka, Paul.
ed. Frontiers in Econometrics. Acad Pr.
ed. Research in Political Economy. Jai Pr.
Zaretsky, Eli.
xZaretsky, Eli.
Capitalism, the Family & Personal Life.
Har-Row.
Zaretsky, Irving I.
xZaretsky, Irving I.
ed. Religious Movements in Contemporary
America. Princeton U Pr.
Zaring, J. L., 1921-
xZaring, J. L.
Decision for Europe: The Necessity of Britain's
Engagement. Johns Hopkins.
Zariski, O. *see* Zariski, Oscar.
Zariski, Oscar, 1899-
xZariski, O.
Algebraic Surfaces. Springer-Verlag.
Commutative Algebra. Springer-Verlag.
Zarit, Steven H.
xZarit, Steven H.

Aging & Mental Disorders: Psychological
Approaches to Assessment & Treatment.
Free Pr.
ed. Readings in Aging and Death:
Contemporary Perspectives. Har-Row.
Zarnecki, G. *see* Zarnecki, George.
Zarnecki, George.
xZarnecki, G.
Art of the Medieval World: Architecture,
Sculpture, Painting, the Sacred Arts. P-H.
xZarnecki, George.
Art of the Medieval World: Architecture,
Sculpture, Painting, the Sacred Arts. Abrams.
The Monastic Achievement. McGraw.
Zarnowitz, Victor, 1919-
xZarnowitz, Victor.
Orders, Production & Investment: A Cyclical &
Structural Analysis. Natl Bur Econ Res.
Zaro, Joan S.
xZaro, Joan S.
A Guide for Beginning Psychotherapists.
Cambridge U Pr.
Zaroulis, N. L.
xZaroulis, Nancy.
Call the Darkness Light. Doubleday.
Call the Darkness Light. NAL.
Zaroulis, Nancy. *see* Zaroulis, N. L.
Zartman, I. William.
xZartman, I. William.
Destiny of a Dynasty: The Search for
Institutions in Morocco's Developing Society.
U of SC Pr.
xZartman, William I.
Government & Politics in Northern Africa.
Greenwood.
Zartman, William I. *see* Zartman, I. William.
Zaruba, J. R. *see* Zaruba, Robert J.
Zaruba, Robert J., 1926-
xZaruba, J. R.
Questions & Answers on the Rules of the
Road. Cornell Maritime.
Zaslavsky, Claudia.
xZaslavsky, Claudia.
Preparing Young Children for Math: A Book of
Games. Schocken.
Zaslavsky, Thomas.
xZaslavsky, Thomas.
Facing up to Arrangements: Face-Count
Formulas for Partitions of Space by
Hyperplanes. Am Math.
Zassenhaus, Hans.
xZassenhaus, Hans J.
Theory of Groups. Chelsea Pub.
Zassenhaus, Hans J. *see* Zassenhaus, Hans.
Zastrow, Charles.
xZastrow, Charles.
Talk to Yourself: Using the Power of Self-Talk.
P-H.
xZastrow, Charles H.
Outcome of Black Children White Parents
Transracial Adoptions. R & E Res Assoc.
ed. The Personal Problem Solver. P-H.
Zastrow, Charles H. *see* Zastrow, Charles.
Zatko, James J.
xZatko, James J.
ed. Valley of Silence: Catholic Thought in
Contemporary Poland. U of Notre Dame Pr.
Zaturenska, Marya, 1902-
xZaturenska, Marya.
Cold Morning Sky. Greenwood.
Zauberman, Alfred.
xZauberman, Alfred.

Aspects of Planometrics. Yale U Pr.
Differential Games & Other Game-Theoretic
Topics in Soviet Literature: A Survey. NYU
Pr.
The Mathematical Revolution in Soviet
Economics. Oxford U Pr.
Mathematical Theory in Soviet Planning:
Concepts, Methods, Techniques. Oxford U
Pr.
Zauder, Howard L.
xZauder, Howard L.
Anesthesia for Orthopaedic Surgery. Davis Co.
Zavala, Albert.
xZavala, Albert.
ed. Personal Appearance Identification. C C
Thomas.
Zavala, Iris. *see* Zavala, Iris M.
Zavala, Iris M.
xZavala, Iris.
The Intellectual Roots of Independence: An
Anthology of Puerto Rican Political Essays.
Monthly Rev.
Zavalishin, Viacheslav.
xZavalishin, Viacheslav.
Early Soviet Writers. Arno.
Zavattero, Janette.
xZavattero, Janette.
The Sylmar Tunnel Disaster. Everest Hse.
Zavoral, Nolan.
xZavoral, Nolan.
In the Chutes. Raintree Pubs.
Zavrel, Stepan.
xZavrel, Stepan.
illus. They Followed the Star. Scroll Pr.
Zawodny, J. K. *see* Zawodny, Janusz Kazimierz.
Zawodny, Janusz Kazimierz.
xZawodny, J. K.
Nothing but Honour: The Story of the Warsaw
Uprising, 1944. Hoover Inst Pr.
Zax, Melvin.
xZax, Melvin.
An Introduction to Community Psychology.
Wiley.
Zban, Bill, 1934-
xZban, Bill.
The Five Fundamentals of Ballhandling in
Football. A S Barnes.
Zbinden, G. *see* Zbinden, Gerhard.
Zbinden, Gerhard.
xZbinden, G.
ed. Pharmacological Methods in Toxicology.
Pergamon.
Zbinden, Rudolf.
xZbinden, Rudolph.
Infrared Spectroscopy of High Polymers. Acad
Pr.
Zbinden, Rudolph. *see* Zbinden, Rudolf.
Zdenek, Marilee.
xZdenek, Marilee.
Catch the New Wind. Word Bks.
God Is a Verb. Word Bks.
Someone Special. Word Bks.
Splinters in My Pride. Word Bks.
Zea, Leopoldo, 1912-
xZea, Leopoldo.
Latin America & the World. U of Okla Pr.
Latin-American Mind. U of Okla Pr.
Positivism in Mexico. U of Tex Pr.
Zebroff, Kareen.
xZebroff, Kareen.
The ABC of Yoga. Arco.
Yoga & Nutrition. Arco.
Zebrowski, Ernest.
xZebrowski, Ernest.
Fundamentals of Physical Measurement.
Duxbury Pr.
Zebrowski, George.
xZebrowski, George.

Fielding's Caribbean, Including Cuba. Morrow.
Fielding's Caribbean, Including Cuba, 1980.
Fielding.
Fielding's Sightseeing Guide to Europe:
Exploring off the Beaten Path. Fielding.
The Inn Way...Switzerland. Berkshire Traveller.

Zellner, Arnold.
xZellner, Arnold.
Introduction to Bayesian Inference in
Econometrics. Wiley.
Zelmer, A. C. see Zelmer, A. C. Lynn.
Zelmer, A. C. Lynn, 1943-
xZelmer, A. C.
Community Media Handbook. Scarecrow.
Zelonky, Joy.
xZelonky, Joy.
I Can't Always Hear You. Raintree Child.
My Best Friend Moved Away. Raintree Child.
Zeluff, Daniel, 1930-
xZeluff, Daniel.
There's Algae in the Baptismal 'Fount'.
Abingdon.

Zemach, Harve.
xZemach, Harve.
Awake & Dreaming. FS&G.
Duffy & the Devil. FS&G.
Penny a Look: An Old Story. FS&G.
The Princess & Froggie. FS&G.
Zemach, Kaethe.
xZemach, Kaethe.
The Beautiful Rat. Schol Bk Serv.
Zemach, Margot.
xZemach, Margot.
illus. Awake & Dreaming. FS&G.
Hush Little Baby. Dutton.

Zemach, Yaacov S., 1935-
xZemach, Yaacov S.
Political Questions in the Courts: A Judicial
Function in Democracies - Israel & the
United States. Wayne St U Pr.
Zeman, Z. A. see Zeman, Zbynek A. B.
Zeman, Zbynek. see Zeman, Zbynek A. B.
Zeman, Zbynek A. B.
xZeman, Z. A.
Nazi Propaganda. Oxford U Pr.
xZeman, Zbynek.
The Masaryks: The Making of Czechoslovakia.
B&N.
Zemanian, A. H. see Zemanian, Armen H.
Zemanian, Armen H.
xZemanian, A. H.
Realizability Theory for Continuous Linear
Systems. Acad Pr.
Zembaty, Jane. see Zembaty, Jane S.
Zembaty, Jane S.
xZembaty, Jane.
Biomedical Ethics. McGraw.
Zemelman, Steven.
xZemelman, Steven.
Making Sense of It: Patterns in English
Grammar. P-H.
Zemjanis, Raimunds.
xZemjanis, Raimunds.
Diagnostic & Therapeutic Techniques in
Animal Reproduction. Williams & Wilkins.
Zemlin, Willard R.
xZemlin, Willard R.
Speech & Hearing Science: Anatomy &
Physiology. P-H.
Zempel, Edward N.
xZempel, Edward N.
ed. A First Edition?: Statements of Selected
North American, British Commonwealth, &
Irish Publishers on Their Methods of
Designating First Editions. Spoon River.
Zen, E-an, 1928-
xZen, E-An.

The Taconide Zone & the Taconic Orogeny of
the Western Part of the Northern
Appalachian Orogen. Geol Soc.
Zenk, Gordon K. see Zenk, Gordon Karl.
Zenk, Gordon Karl.
xZenk, Gordon K.
Project SEARCH: The Struggle for Control of
Criminal Information in America.
Greenwood.
Zenker, John J.
xZenker, John J.
Cookie Cookery. M Evans.
Zentner, Wendy W. see Zentner, Wendy Wilson.
Zentner, Wendy Wilson.
xZentner, Wendy W.
The Victorian Cookery Book. Zentner Pubns.
Zenz, Carl.
xZenz, Carl.
ed. Occupational Medicine: Principles &
Practical Applications. Year Bk Med.
Zenzinov, Vladimir M. see Zenzinov, Vladimir
Mikhailovich.
Zenzinov, Vladimir Mikhailovich, 1880-1953
xZenzinov, Vladimir M.
Deserted: The Story of the Children
Abandoned in Soviet Russia. Hyperion Conn.
Zeoli, Billy.
xZeoli, Billy.
God's Got a Better Idea. Revell.
Zeranski, Alina.
xZeranski, Alina.
Art of Polish Cooking. Doubleday.
Zerfass, Samuel G. see Zerfass, Samuel Grant.
Zerfass, Samuel Grant, 1866-
xZerfass, Samuel G.
Souvenir Book of the Ephrata Cloister:
Complete History from Its Settlement in
1728 to the Present Time. AMS Pr.
Zerkle, Keith.
xZerkle, Keith.
Twister Man. Ashley Bks.
Zernike, Frits.
xZernike, Frits.
Applied Nonlinear Optics. Wiley.
Zerubavel, Eviatar.
xZerubavel, Eviatar.
Patterns of Time in Hospital Life: A
Sociological Perspective. U of Chicago Pr.
Zesmer, David M.
xZesmer, David M.
Guide to Shakespeare. B&N.
Zetlin, Mikhael. see Zetlin, Mikhail Osipovich.
Zetlin, Mikhail Osipovich, 1882-1945
xZetlin, Mikhael.
The Five: The Evolution of the Russian School
of Music. Greenwood.
Zetterberg, Hans L. see Zetterberg, Hans Lennart.
Zetterberg, Hans Lennart.
xZetterberg, Hans L.
Museums & Adult Education. Kelley.
Zettersten, Arne.
xZettersten, Arne.
ed. Waldere. B&N.
Zetzel, Elizabeth R., 1907-
xZetzel, Elizabeth R.
Capacity for Emotional Growth. Intl Univs Pr.
Zeuner, Frederic E. see Zeuner, Friedrich Eberhard.
Zeuner, Friedrich Eberhard, 1905-1963
xZeuner, Frederic E.
Dating the Past: An Introduction to
Geochronology. Hafner.
Zeuthen, Erik.
xZeuthen, Erik.
ed. Synchrony in Cell Division & Growth.
Krieger.
Zevi, Bruno, 1918-
xZevi, Bruno.

Architecture As Space: How to Look at
Architecture. Horizon.
The Modern Language of Architecture. U of
Wash Pr.
Zevin, Robert B. see Zevin, Robert Brooke.
Zevin, Robert Brooke.
xZevin, Robert B.
The Growth of Manufacturing in Early
Nineteenth Century New England. Arno.
Zeydel, Edwin H. see Zeydel, Edwin Hermann.
Zeydel, Edwin Hermann, 1893-
xZeydel, Edwin H.
Holy Roman Empire in German Literature.
AMS Pr.
tr. Vagabond Verse: Secular Latin Poems of the
Middle Ages. Wayne St U Pr.
Zeyher, Lewis R.
xZeyher, Lewis R.
Production Manager's Handbook of Formulas
& Tables. P-H.
Zguta, Russell.
xZguta, Russell.
Russian Minstrels: A History of the
Skomorokhi. U of Pa Pr.
Zhitkov, Boris. see Zhitkov, Boris Stepanovich.
Zhitkov, Boris Stepanovich.
xZhitkov, Boris.
How I Hunted the Little Fellows. Dodd.
Zhitova, Mme. V. see Zhitova, Varvara Nikolaevna
(Bogdanovich).
Zhitova, Varvara Nikolaevna (Bogdanovich), b. 1833
xZhitova, Mme. V.
The Turgenev Family. R West.
Zhivkov, Todor.
xZhivkov, Todor.
Modern Bulgaria: Problems & Tasks in
Building an Advanced Socialist Society. Intl
Pub Co.
Zhukov, Georgi K. see Zhukov, Georgii Konstantinovich.
Zhukov, Georgii Konstantinovich.
xZhukov, Georgi K.
Marshal Zhukov's Greatest Battles. PB.
Ziadeh, Farhat J. see Ziadeh, Farhat Jacob.
Ziadeh, Farhat Jacob.
xZiadeh, Farhat J.
Lawyers, the Rule of Law & Liberalism in
Modern Egypt. Hoover Inst Pr.
Ziadeh, Nicola. see Ziadeh, Nicola A.
Ziadeh, Nicola A.
xZiadeh, Nicola.
Syria & Lebanon. Intl Bk Ctr.
Ziai, Mohsen.
xZiai, Mohsen.
ed. Pediatrics. Little.
Zief, M. see Zief, Morris.
Zief, Morris.
xZief, M.
ed. Purification of Inorganic & Organic
Materials: Techniques of Fractional
Solidification. Dekker.
xZief, Morris.
Contamination Control in Trace Element
Analysis. Wiley.
Zieg, Kermit C.
xZieg, Kermit C.
The Commodity Options Market: Dynamic
Trading Strategies for Speculation &
Commercial Hedging. Dow Jones-Irwin.
Ziegel, Erna.
xZiegel, Erna.
Obstetric Nursing. Macmillan.
Ziegler, A. M. see Ziegler, Alfred M.
Ziegler, Alfred M.
xZiegler, A. M.
Correlation of the Silurian Rocks of the British
Isles. Geol Soc.
Ziegler, E. K. see Ziegler, Edward Krusen.
Ziegler, Edward K. see Ziegler, Edward Krusen.
Ziegler, Edward Krusen, 1903-
xZiegler, E. K.

Simple Living. Pillar Bks.
xZiegler, Edward K.
Simple Living. Brethren.
Ziegler, Lawrence F.
xZiegler, Lawrence F.
Monetary Accommodation of Regional
Integration in Latin America. U of Tex Busn
Res.
Ziegler, Louis W.
xZiegler, Louis W.
Citrus Growing in Florida. U Presses Fla.
Ziegler, Oswald.
xZiegler, Oswald L.
ed. The World & South East Asia. Intl Pubns
Serv.
Ziegler, Oswald L. *see* Ziegler, Oswald.
Ziegler, Philip.
xZiegler, Philip.
Crown & People. Knopf.
Omdurman. Knopf.
Ziegler, Raymond J.
xZiegler, Raymond J.
ed. Business Policies & Decision Making.
Irvington.
Ziegler, Ronald. *see* Ziegler, Ronald M.
Ziegler, Ronald M.
xZiegler, Ronald.
ed. Wilderness Waterways: A Guide to
Information Sources. Gale.
Ziegler, Sandra.
xZiegler, Sandra.
At the Dentist - What Did Christopher See?.
Childs World.
Ziehn, Bernhard, 1845-1912
xZiehn, Bernhard.
Canonic Studies. Taplinger.
Ziel, Aldert Van Der. *see* Van Der Ziel, Aldert.
Ziel, Ron.
xZiel, Ron.
The Twilight of World Steam. G&D.
Zieler, H. Wolfgang, 1897-
xZieler, H. Wolfgang.
The Optical Performance of the Light
Microscope. Microscope Pubns.
Zielinski, Stanislaw. *see* Zielinski, Stanislaw A.
Zielinski, Stanislaw A.
xZielinski, Stanislaw.
Psychology & Silence. Pendle Hill.
Zielke, R. *see* Zielke, Roland.
Zielke, Roland, 1946-
xZielke, R.
Discontinuous Cebysev Systems.
Springer-Verlag.
Ziemann, Hans H. *see* Ziemann, Hans Heinrich.
Ziemann, Hans Heinrich, 1944-
xZiemann, Hans H.
The Accident. St Martin.
Ziemba, W. T.
xZiemba, W. T.
Stochastic Optimization Models in Finance.
Acad Pr.
Ziemian, Joseph.
xZiemian, Joseph.
The Cigarette Sellers of Three Crosses Square.
Lerner Pubns.
Ziemska, M. *see* Ziemska, Maria.
Ziemska, Maria.
xZiemska, M.
ed. Early Child Care in Poland. Gordon.
Zienkiewicz, O. C.
xZienkiewicz, O. C.
The Finite Element Method. McGraw.
Zierer, Ernesto.
xZierer, Ernesto.
Formal Logic & Linguistics. Mouton.
Zietlow, E. R.
xZietlow, E. R.

A Country for Old Men & Other Stories. Lame
Johnny.
Ziff, Paul, 1920-
xZiff, Paul.
Understanding Understanding. Cornell U Pr.
Ziff, William B. *see* Ziff, William Bernard.
Ziff, William Bernard, 1898-1953
xZiff, William B.
The Rape of Palestine. Greenwood.
Zigas, Vincent.
xZigas, Vincent.
Auscultation of Two Worlds. Vantage.
Ziglar, Zig.
xZiglar, Zig.
Confessions of a Happy Christian. Pelican.
Zigler, Edward. *see* Zigler, Edward Frank.
Zigler, Edward F. *see* Zigler, Edward Frank.
Zigler, Edward Frank.
xZigler, Edward.
Project Head Start: A Legacy of the War on
Poverty. Free Pr.
xZigler, Edward F.
Socialization & Personality Development. A-W.
Zigrosser, Carl.
xZigrosser, Carl.
Guide to the Collecting & Care of Original
Prints. Crown.
Multum in Parvo: An Essay in Poetic
Imagination. Braziller.
A World of Art & Museums. Art Alliance.
Zijlstra, H.
xZijlstra, H.
Experimental Methods in Magnetism. Elsevier.
Zikmund, Joseph.
xZikmund, Joseph.
ed. Suburbia: A Guide to Information Sources.
Gale.
Zikmund, William. *see* Zikmund, William G.
Zikmund, William G.
xZikmund, William.
A Collection of Outstanding Cases in
Marketing Management. West Pub.
Zilbert, E. R.
xZilbert, Edward R.
Albert Speer & the Nazi Ministry of Arms:
Economic Institutions & Industrial
Production in the German War Economy.
Fairleigh Dickinson.
Zilbert, Edward R. *see* Zilbert, E. R.
Zilboorg, Gregory, 1890-1959
xZilboorg, Gregory.
Medical Man & the Witch During the
Renaissance. Cooper Sq.
Psychology of the Criminal Act & Punishment.
Greenwood.
Sigmund Freud: His Exploration of the Mind
of Man. Kelley.
Zile, Judy Van. *see* Van Zile, Judy.
Zile, Zigurds L.
xZile, Zigurds L.
The Soviet Legal System & Arms Inspection: A
Case Study in Policy Implementation.
Irvington.
Zill, Dennis G.
xZill, Dennis G.
College Algebra & Trigonometry. Wadsworth
Pub.
College Mathematics for Students of Business
& the Social Sciences. Wadsworth Pub.
Zilles, K. J. *see* Zilles, Karl J.
Zilles, Karl J., 1944-
xZilles, K. J.
Ontogenesis of the Visual System.
Springer-Verlag.
Zilversmit, Arthur.
xZilversmit, Arthur.
First Emancipation: The Abolition of Slavery in
the North. U of Chicago Pr.
xZilversmit, Arthus.

First Emancipation: The Abolition of Slavery in
the North. U of Chicago Pr.
Zilversmit, Arthus. *see* Zilversmit, Arthur.
Zim, Herbert S. *see* Zim, Herbert Spencer.
Zim, Herbert Spencer.
xZim, Herbert S.
Cargo Ships. Morrow.
Codes & Secret Writing. Morrow.
Comets. Morrow.
Commercial Fishing. Morrow.
Crabs. Morrow.
Dinosaurs. Morrow.
Eating Places. Morrow.
Frogs & Toads. Morrow.
Golden Hamsters. Morrow.
The Great Whales. Morrow.
Hoists, Cranes, & Derricks. Morrow.
How Things Grow. Morrow.
Life & Death. Morrow.
Lightning & Thunder. Morrow.
Little Cats. Morrow.
Monkeys. Morrow.
The New Moon. Morrow.
Ostriches. Morrow.
Our Senses & How They Work. Morrow.
Owls. Morrow.
Parrakeets. Morrow.
The Sun. Morrow.
Things Around the House. Morrow.
Trucks. Morrow.
What's Inside of Animals. Morrow.
What's Inside of Engines. Morrow.
What's Inside of Me. Morrow.
What's Inside of Plants. Morrow.
What's Inside the Earth. Morrow.
Your Skin. Morrow.
Ziman, J. M. *see* Ziman, John M.
Ziman, John M., 1925-
xZiman, J. M.
Principles of the Theory of Solids. Cambridge
U Pr.
xZiman, John M.
Principles of the Theory of Solids. Cambridge
U Pr.
Public Knowledge: An Essay Concerning the
Social Dimension of Science. Cambridge U
Pr.
Zimand, Savel, 1891-
xZimand, Savel.
Living India. Arno.
Zimbalist, Andrew. *see* Zimbalist, Andrew S.
Zimbalist, Andrew S.
xZimbalist, Andrew.
ed. Case Studies on the Labor Process.
Monthly Rev.
Zimbalist, Sidney E. *see* Zimbalist, Sidney Eli.
Zimbalist, Sidney Eli, 1922-
xZimbalist, Sidney E.
Historic Themes & Landmarks in Social
Welfare Research. Har-Row.
Zimbardo, Philip. *see* Zimbardo, Philip G.
Zimbardo, Philip G.
xZimbardo, Philip.
The Cognitive Control of Motivation: The
Consequences of Choice & Dissonance. Scott
F.
Psychology for Our Times: Readings. Scott F.
Shyness: What It Is, What to Do About It.
A-W.
xZimbardo, Philip G.
Essentials of Psychology & Life. Scott F.
Influencing Attitudes & Changing Behavior: An
Introduction to Method, Theory &
Applications of Social Control & Personal
Power. A-W.
Psychology & Life. Scott F.
The Shyness Workbook. A & W Pubs.
Zimberg, Sheldon.
xZimberg, Sheldon.

ed. Practical Approaches to Alcoholism
Psychotherapy. Plenum Pub.

Zimelman, Nathan.
xZimelman, Nathan.
Cats of Kilkenny. Carolrhoda Bks.
The Lives of My Cat Alfred. Dutton.
Look Hiroshi. Aurora Pubs.

Ziment, Irwin.
xZiment, Irwin.
Respiratory Pharmacology & Therapeutics.
Saunders.

Zimet, Sara G. *see* Zimet, Sara Goodman.

Zimet, Sara Goodman.
xZimet, Sara G.
Teacher's Guide for Selecting Stories of
Interest to Children: The Content of First
Grade Reading Textbooks. Wayne St U Pr.

Zimmels, H. J. *see* Zimmels, Hirsch Jakob.

Zimmels, Hirsch Jakob.
xZimmels, H. J.
The Echo of the Nazi Holocaust in Rabbinic
Literature. Ktav.

Zimmer, H. G. *see* Zimmer, Hans-Georg.

Zimmer, Hans-Georg.
xZimmer, H. G.
Geometrical Optics. Springer-Verlag.

Zimmer, Horst G.
xZimmer, H. G.
Computational Problems, Methods, & Results
in Algebraic Number Theory.
Springer-Verlag.

Zimmer, Kenneth, 1921-
xZimmer, Kenneth.
Advanced Typewriting for the College Student.
Glencoe.

Zimmer, Norma.
xZimmer, Norma.
Norma. Bantam.
Norma. Tyndale.
Norma. World Wide Pubs.

Zimmer, Ruth.
xZimmer, Ruth.
James Shirley: A Reference Guide. G K Hall.

Zimmer. *see* Zimmerman, John Edward.

Zimmerman, A. M. *see* Zimmerman, Arthur M.

Zimmerman, Arthur F. *see* Zimmerman, Arthur Franklin.

Zimmerman, Arthur Franklin, 1892-
xZimmerman, Arthur F.
Francisco De Toledo, Fifth Viceroy of Peru,
1569-1581. Greenwood.

Zimmerman, Arthur M.
xZimmerman, A. M.
ed. Drugs & the Cell Cycle. Acad Pr.
xZimmerman, Arthur M.
High Pressure Effects on Cellular Processes.
Acad Pr.

Zimmerman, Bill.
xZimmerman, Bill.
Airlift to Wounded Knee. Swallow.

Zimmerman, Carle C. *see* Zimmerman, Carle Clark.

Zimmerman, Carle Clark, 1897-
xZimmerman, Carle C.
Consumption & Standards of Living. Arno.

Zimmerman, Everett.
xZimmerman, Everett.
Defoe & the Novel. U of Cal Pr.

Zimmerman, Fred W.
xZimmerman, Fred W.
Leathercraft. Goodheart.

Zimmerman, Gordon. *see* Zimmerman, Gordon I.

Zimmerman, Gordon I.
xZimmerman, Gordon.
Speech Communication: A Contemporary
Introduction. West Pub.
xZimmerman, Gordon I.
Public Speaking Today. West Pub.
Speech Communication: A Contemporary
Introduction. West Pub.

Zimmerman, Harry. *see* Zimmerman, Harry Martin.
Zimmerman, Harry M. *see* Zimmerman, Harry Martin.

Zimmerman, Harry Martin, 1901-
xZimmerman, Harry.
ed. Progress in Neuropathology. Raven.
xZimmerman, Harry M.
ed. Progress in Neuropathology. Grune.

Zimmerman, Howard E.
xZimmerman, Howard E.
Quantum Mechanics for Organic Chemists.
Acad Pr.

Zimmerman, Irene, 1905-
xZimmerman, Irene.
Current National Bibliographies of Latin
America: A State of the Art Study. U Presses
Fla.
Guide to Current Latin American Periodicals:
Humanities & Social Sciences. Kallman.

Zimmerman, Irla L. *see* Zimmerman, Irla Lee.

Zimmerman, Irla Lee.
xZimmerman, Irla L.
Clinical Interpretation of the Wechsler Adult
Intelligence Scale. Grune.

Zimmerman, James F. *see* Zimmerman, James Fulton.

Zimmerman, James Fulton, 1887-1944
xZimmerman, James F.
Impressment of American Seamen. Kennikat.

Zimmerman, John E. *see* Zimmerman, John Edward.

Zimmerman, John Edward, 1901-
xZimmerman.
Dictionary of Classical Mythology. Bantam.
xZimmerman, John E.
Dictionary of Classical Mythology. Har-Row.

Zimmerman, Louis J. *see* Zimmerman, Louis Jacques.

Zimmerman, Louis Jacques, 1913-
xZimmerman, Louis J.
Poor Lands, Rich Lands: The Widening Gap.
Phila Bk Co.

Zimmerman, Marilyn P.
xZimmerman, Marilyn P.
Musical Characteristics of Children. Music Ed.

Zimmerman, Marvin.
xZimmerman, Marvin.
Contemporary Problems of Democracy.
Humanities.

Zimmerman, Mary K.
xZimmerman, Mary K.
Passage Through Abortion: The Personal &
Social Reality of Women's Experiences.
Praeger.

Zimmerman, O. T. *see* Zimmerman, Oswald Theodore.

Zimmerman, Oswald Theodore.
xZimmerman, O. T.
College Placement Directory. Indus Res Serv.

Zimmerman, Paul, 1903-
xZimmerman, Paul.
Last Season of Weeb Ewbank. FS&G.

Zimmerman, Raymond E.
xZimmerman, Raymond E.
Evaluating & Testing the Coking Properties of
Coal. Miller Freeman.

Zimmerman, Walter J., 1910-
xZimmerman, Walter J.
Coin Collectors Fact Book. Arco.

Zimmerman, William.
xZimmerman, William.
Soviet Perspectives on International Relations,
1956-1967. Princeton U Pr.

Zimmermann, Charles F.
xZimmermann, Charles F.
Uranium Resources on Federal Lands.
Lexington Bks.

Zimmermann, Georges D. *see* Zimmermann, Georges
Denis.

Zimmermann, Georges Denis, 1930-
xZimmermann, Georges D.
Songs of Irish Rebellion: Political Street Ballads
& Rebel Songs, 1780-1900. Gale.

Zimolzak, Chester. *see* Zimolzak, Chester E.

Zimolzak, Chester E.
xZimolzak, Chester.

The Human Landscape: Geography & Culture.
Merrill.

Zimon, A. D. *see* Zimon, Anatolii Davydovich.

Zimon, Anatolii Davydovich.
xZimon, A. D.
Adhesion of Dust & Powder. Plenum Pub.

Zimpel, Lloyd.
xZimpel, Lloyd.
Meeting the Bear: Journal of the Black Wars.
Macmillan.

Zimpfer. *see* Zimpfer, David G.

Zimpfer, David G.
xZimpfer.
Paraprofessionals in Counseling, Guidance &
Personnel Services. Am Personnel.

Zimroth, Evan, 1943-
xZimroth, Evan.
Giselle Considers Her Future. Ohio St U Pr.

Zimsen, Ella.
xZimsen, Ella.
The Type Material of I. C. Fabricius. Lubrecht
& Cramer.

Zinberg, Israel, 1873-1939
xZinberg, Israel.
A History of Jewish Literature. Ktav.

Zinberg, Norman E. *see* Zinberg, Norman Earl.

Zinberg, Norman Earl, 1921-
xZinberg, Norman E.
ed. Alternate States of Consciousness. Free Pr.
ed. Psychiatry & Medical Practice in a General
Hospital. Intl Univs Pr.
Teaching Social Change: A Group Approach.
Johns Hopkins.

Zinchenko, V. P. *see* Zinchenko, Vladimir Petrovich.

Zinchenko, Vladimir Petrovich.
xZinchenko, V. P.
Formation of Visual Images: Studies of
Stabilized Retinal Images. Plenum Pub.

Zinck, W. Clements.
xZinck, W. Clements.
Dynamic Work Simplification. Krieger.

Zindel, Bonnie.
xZindel, Bonnie.
A Star for the Latecomer. Har-Row.

Zindel, Paul.
xZindel, Paul.
Confessions of a Teenage Baboon. Bantam.
Confessions of a Teenage Baboon. Har-Row.
I Love My Mother. Har-Row.
Let Me Hear You Whisper: A Play. Har-Row.
The Undertaker's Gone Bananas. Bantam.
The Undertaker's Gone Bananas. Har-Row.

Zinder, David G., 1942-
xZinder, David G.
The Surrealist Connection: An Approach to a
Surrealist Aesthetic of Theatre. Univ
Microfilms.

Ziner, Feenie.
xZiner, Feenie.
Cricket Boy: A Chinese Tale Retold.
Doubleday.
Little Sailor's Big Pet. Parnassus.

Zink, D. D.
xZink, David D.
Leslie Stephen. Twayne.

Zink, David.
xZink, David.
The Ancient Stones Speak: A Journey to the
World's Most Mysterious Megalithic Sites.
Dutton.
The Stones of Atlantis. P-H.

Zink, David D. *see* Zink, D. D.

Zink, Sidney, 1917-
xZink, Sidney.
Concepts of Ethics. St Martin.

Zinker, Joseph. *see* Zinker, Joseph Chaim.

Zinker, Joseph Chaim.
xZinker, Joseph.

The Economic Integration of Hungary into the
Soviet Bloc: Foreign Trade Experience,
1950-1960. Ohio St U Admin Sci.

Zsuffa, Joseph.
xZsuffa, Joseph.
Pit of Babel. Orpheus Pr.

Zubarev, D. N. *see* Zubarev, Dmitrii Nikolaevich.

Zubarev, Dmitrii Nikolaevich.
xZubarev, D. N.
ed. Nonequilibrium Statistical
Thermodynamics. Plenum Pub.

Zuber, Christian, 1930-
xZuber, Christian.
Animals in Danger. Barron.

Zuber, William P. *see* Zuber, William Physick.

Zuber, William Physick.
xZuber, William P.
My Eighty Years in Texas. U of Tex Pr.

Zubin, Joseph.
xZubin, Joseph.
ed. Disorders of Mood. Johns Hopkins.
Some Effects of Incentives: A Study of
Individual Differences in Rivalry. AMS Pr.

Zubov, V. P. *see* Zubov, Vasilii Pavlovich.

Zubov, Vasilii Pavlovich.
xZubov, V. P.
Leonardo Da Vinci. Harvard U Pr.

Zubrow, Ezra B. *see* Zubrow, Ezra B. W.

Zubrow, Ezra B. W.
xZubrow, Ezra B.
Population, Contact, & Climate in the New
Mexican Pueblos. U of Ariz Pr.

Zubrzycki, Stefan.
xZubrzycki, Stefan.
Lectures in Probability Theory & Mathematical
Statistics. Elsevier.

Zuck, Lowell H.
xZuck, Lowell H.
ed. Christianity & Revolution: Radical
Christian Testimonies, 1520-1650. Temple U
Pr.

Zuck, Roy B.
xZuck, Roy B.
Childhood Education in the Church. Moody.

Zucker, A. E. *see* Zucker, Adolf Eduard.

Zucker, Adolf. *see* Zucker, Adolf Eduard.

Zucker, Adolf Eduard, 1890-
xZucker, A. E.
General De Kalb, Lafayette's Mentor. U of NC
Pr.
xZucker, Adolf.
Ibsen: The Master Builder. Octagon.

Zucker, Benjamin, 1940-
xZucker, Benjamin.
How to Buy & Sell Gems: Everyone's Guide
to Rubies, Sapphires, Emeralds & Diamonds.
Times Bks.
How to Invest in Gems: Everyone's Guide to
Buying Rubies, Sapphires, Emeralds, &
Diamonds. Times Bks.

Zucker, H. *see* Zucker, Herbert John.

Zucker, Herbert John, 1920-
xZucker, H.
Problems of Psychotherapy. Free Pr.

Zucker, Judi.
xZucker, Judi.
How to Survive Snack Attacks--Naturally.
Woodbridge Pr.

Zucker, Norman L.
xZucker, Norman L.
The Coming Crisis in Israel: Private Faith &
Public Policy. MIT Pr.

Zucker, Paul, 1889-
xZucker, Paul.
Styles in Painting: A Comparative Study.
Dover.
Styles in Painting: A Comparative Study. Peter
Smith.

Zucker, R. *see* Zucker, Robert D.

Zucker, Robert D.
xZucker, R.
Fundamentals of Gas Dynamics. Intl Schol Bk
Serv.

Zucker, Stanley, 1936-
xZucker, Stanley.
Ludwig Bamberger: German Liberal Politician
& Social Critic,1823-1899. U of Pittsburgh
Pr.

Zuckerman, A. *see* Zuckerman, Avivah.

Zuckerman, Alan, 1945-
xZuckerman, Alan S.
The Politics of Faction: Christian Democratic
Rule in Italy. Yale U Pr.

Zuckerman, Alan S. *see* Zuckerman, Alan.

Zuckerman, Art. *see* Zuckerman, Arthur.

Zuckerman, Arthur.
xZuckerman, Art.
Tape Recording for the Hobbyist. Sams.
xZuckerman, Arthur.
Stereo High-Fidelity Speaker Systems. Sams.

Zuckerman, Avivah.
xZuckerman, A.
ed. Dynamic Aspects of Host-Parasite
Relationships. Halsted Pr.
xZuckerman, Avivah.
ed. Dynamic Aspects of Host Parasite
Relationships. Acad Pr.

Zuckerman, Jim.
xZuckerman, Jim.
Image Magic. Petersen Pub.

Zuckerman, Joan.
xZuckerman, Joan.
The Birmingham Heritage. Biblio Dist.

Zuckerman, Martin. *see* Zuckerman, Martin M.

Zuckerman, Martin M.
xZuckerman, Martin.
Arithmetic Without Trumpets or Drums. Allyn.
xZuckerman, Martin M.
Algebra & Trigonometry: A Straightforward
Approach. Norton.

Zuckerman, Marvin.
xZuckerman, Marvin.
Sensation Seeking: Beyond the Optimal Level
of Arousal. Halsted Pr.

Zuckerman, Marvin S.
xZuckerman, Marvin S.
Words, Words, Words: An English Vocabulary
Builder & Anthology. Glencoe.

Zuckerman, Michael, 1939-
xZuckerman, Michael.
Peaceable Kingdoms: New England Towns in
the Eighteenth Century. Norton.

Zucrow, Maurice J. *see* Zucrow, Maurice Joseph.

Zucrow, Maurice Joseph.
xZucrow, Maurice J.
Gas Dynamics. Wiley.

Zudak, Lawrence S.
xZudak, Lawrence S.
Managerial Economics. Har-Row.

Zueblin, Charles, 1866-1924
xZueblin, Charles.
American Municipal Progress. Arno.

Zuelke, Ruth.
xZuelke, Ruth.
Horse in Art. Lerner Pubns.

Zuesse, Evan M.
xZuesse, Evan M.
Ritual Cosmos: The Sanctification of Life in
African Religions. Ohio U Pr.

Zuidema, H. H. *see* Zuidema, Hilbert Harry.

Zuidema, Hilbert Harry, 1910-
xZuidema, H. H.
Performance of Lubricating Oils. Am Chemical.

Zuk, Gerald H.
xZuk, Gerald H.
ed. Family Therapy & Disturbed Families. Sci
& Behavior.
Process & Practice in Family Therapy.
Psychiatry & Behavioral.

Zuk, William.
xZuk, William.
Concepts of Structure. Krieger.

Zukav, Gary.
xZukav, Gary.
The Dancing Wu Li Masters: An Overview of
the New Physics. Bantam.
The Dancing Wu Li Masters: An Overview of
the New Physics. Morrow.

Zukerman. *see* Zukerman, Dianne.

Zukerman, Dianne.
xZukerman.
Get Hooked: Creative Crocheting. TAB Bks.

Zukofsky, Louis, 1904-
xZukofsky, Louis.
An Objectivists' Anthology. Folcroft.
An Objectivists Anthology. Norwood Edns.

Zulauf, Sander. *see* Zulauf, Sander W.

Zulauf, Sander W.
xZulauf, Sander.
Index to American Periodical Verse: 1978.
Scarecrow.
xZulauf, Sander W.
Index of American Periodical Verse, 1971.
Scarecrow.
Index of American Periodical Verse 1972.
Scarecrow.
Index of American Periodical Verse: 1973.
Scarecrow.
Index of American Periodical Verse: 1974.
Scarecrow.
Index of American Periodical Verse: 1975.
Scarecrow.
Index of American Periodical Verse: 1976.
Scarecrow.
Index of American Periodical Verse: 1977.
Scarecrow.

Zuman, P. *see* Zuman, Petr.

Zuman, Petr.
xZuman, P.
Organic Polarography. Krieger.

Zumwalt, Elmo R., 1920-
xZumwalt, Elmo R.
On Watch: A Memoir. Times Bks.

Zunin, Leonard.
xZunin, Leonard.
Contact: The First Four Minutes. Ballantine.
Contact: The First Four Minutes. Nash Pub.

Zunkel, Charles.
xZunkel, Charles.
Turn Again to Life. Brethren.

Zupko, Ronald E. *see* Zupko, Ronald Edward.

Zupko, Ronald Edward.
xZupko, Ronald E.
British Weights & Measures: A History from
Antiquity to the Seventeenth Century. U of
Wis Pr.
French Weights & Measures Before the
Revolution: A Dictionary of Provincial &
Local Units. Ind U Pr.

Zurcher, Arnold J. *see* Zurcher, Arnold John.

Zurcher, Arnold John.
xZurcher, Arnold J.
The Foundation Administrator: A Study of
Those Who Manage America's Foundations.
Russell Sage.

Zurcher, Louis A.
xZurcher, Louis A.

Citizens for Decency: Antipornography
Crusades As Status Defense. U of Tex Pr.
The Mutable Self: A Self Concept for Social
Change. Sage.
Poverty Warriors: The Human Experience of
Planned Social Intervention. U of Tex Pr.
ed. Supplementary Military Forces: Reserves,
Militias, & Auxiliaries. Sage.
Zurick, Timothy, 1952-
xZurick, Timothy.
Air Conditioning, Heating & Refrigeration
Dictionary. Busn News.
Zuromskis, Diane.
xZuromskis, Diane.
illus. Farmer in the Dell. Little.
Zusman, Jack.
xZusman, Jack.
ed. The Future Role of the State Hospital.
Lexington Bks.
ed. Organizing the Community to Prevent
Suicide. C C Thomas.
ed. Practical Aspects of Mental Health
Consultation. C C Thomas.
ed. Program Evaluation: Alcohol, Drug Abuse
& Mental Health Service Programs.
Lexington Bks.
Zussman, Leon.
xZussman, Leon.
Getting Together: A Guide to Sexual
Enrichment for Couples. Morrow.
Zutz, Don.
xZutz, Don.
The Double Shotgun. Winchester Pr.
Zuvekas, Clarence.
xZuvekas, Clarence.
Economic Development: An Introduction. St
Martin.
Zuverink, Mary.
xZuverink, Mary.
Compiled by Listen to a Shadow. Friend Pr.
Zuwaylif, Fadil H., 1932-
xZuwaylif, Fadil H.
Applied Business Statistics. A-W.
General Applied Statistics. A-W.

Zwager, Louise H. *see* Zwager, Louise Henriette.
Zwager, Louise Henriette.
xZwager, Louise H.
English Philosophic Lyric. Folcroft.
Zwass, Adam.
xZwass, Adam.
Monetary Cooperation Between East & West.
M E Sharpe.
Money, Banking, & Credit in the Soviet Union
& Eastern Europe. M E Sharpe.
Zweifach, Benjamin W. *see* Zweifach, Benjamin William.
Zweifach, Benjamin William.
xZweifach, Benjamin W.
ed. The Inflammatory Process. Acad Pr.
Zweifel, Frances W.
xZweifel, Frances W.
Handbook of Biological Illustration. U of
Chicago Pr.
Zweig, Franklin M.
xZweig, Franklin M.
ed. Evaluation in Legislation. Sage.
Zweig, Michael. *see* Zweig, Michael Frohlich.
Zweig, Michael Frohlich, 1942-
xZweig, Michael.
Idea of a World University. S Ill U Pr.
Zweig, Paul.
xZweig, Paul.
The Dark Side of the Earth. Har-Row.
Zweig, Stefan, 1881-1942
xZweig, Stefan.
Passion & Pain. Arno.
Paul Verlaine. AMS Pr.
Zwell, Michael.
xZwell, Michael.
How to Succeed at Love. P-H.
Zwelling, Shomer S.
xZwelling, Shomer S.
Expansion & Imperialism. Loyola.
Zwerdling, Alex.
xZwerdling, Alex.
Orwell & the Left. Yale U Pr.
Zwerdling, Ella.
xZwerdling, Ella.
The ABC's of Casework with Children: A

Social Work Teacher's Notebook. Child
Welfare.
Zwettler, Michael.
xZwettler, Michael J.
The Oral Tradition of Classical Arabic Poetry:
Its Character & Implications. Ohio St U Pr.
Zwettler, Michael J. *see* Zwettler, Michael.
Zwick, George, 1910-
xZwick, George.
Beginner's Guide to TV Repair. TAB Bks.
Everyman's Guide to Auto Maintenance. TAB
Bks.
Zwicker, Steven N.
xZwicker, Steven N.
Dryden's Political Poetry: The Typology of
King & Nation. Brown U Pr.
Zwirner, E. *see* Zwirner, Eberhard.
Zwirner, Eberhard.
xZwirner, E.
Pref. by Principles of Phonometrics. U of Ala
Pr.
xZwirner, Eberhard.
Principles of Phonometrics. U of Ala Pr.
Zwisohn, Laurence J.
xZwisohn, Laurence J.
Bing Crosby: A Lifetime of Music. Palm Tree
Lib.
Zyl, Slabbert, F. Van. *see* Van Zyl Slabbert, F.
Zysman, John.
xZysman, John.
Political Strategies for Industrial Order: State,
Market, & Industry in France. U of Cal Pr.
Zytowski, Donald G.
xZytowski, Donald G.
ed. Contemporary Approaches to Interest
Measurement. U of Minn Pr.
Influence of Psychological Factors Upon
Vocational Development. HM.
Zyve, Claire. *see* Zyve, Claire (Turner).
Zyve, Claire (Turner), 1895-
xZyve, Claire.
An Experimental Study of Spelling Methods.
AMS Pr.

KEY TO
PUBLISHERS' AND DISTRIBUTORS'
ABBREVIATIONS

The following is a list of abbreviations for publishers and distributors name used in the listings of *BOOKS IN PRINT 1980-1981*. The entries in this list contain: Full name, ISBN prefix, editorial address, telephone number, ordering address (if different from the editorial address), and imprints following the abbreviation. For example:

Bowker, (Bowker, R. R., Co., 0-8352), A Xerox Publishing Co., 1180 Ave. of the Americas, New York, NY 10036 Tel 212-764-5100; Orders To, P.O. Box 1807, Ann Arbor, MI 48106.

A A Coolidge
  See Celestial Gems
A A Spohler, *(Spohler, Albert A.),* P.O. Box 2322, Palos Verdes, CA 90274 Tel 213-375-7775; 5417 Littlebow Rd., Palos Verdes, CA 90274.
A Adler Inst, *(Adler, Alfred, Institute of Chicago, Inc.; 0-918560),* 159 N. Dearborn St., Chicago, IL 60601 Tel 312-346-3458.
A & B Pubs, *(A & B Pubs.; 0-917746),* 1206 Redlands Way, Concord, CA 94521; Moved, Left No Forwarding Address.
A & L Pubns, *(A & L Pubns.; 0-9600766),* P.O. Box F, Sta. A, Champaign, IL 61820.
A & M Bks, *(A & M Books; 0-937150),* P.O. Box 24112, Richmond, VA 23224 Tel 804-232-3904.
A & P Bialosky, *(Bialosky, Alan & Peggy; 0-9603732),* c/o Alan-Peggy Promotions, Inc., P.O. Box 68, Novelty, OH 44072.
A & W Pubs, *(A & W Pubs., Inc.; 0-89479),* 95 Madison Ave., New York, NY 10016 Tel 212-725-4970; Do Not Confuse with A-W, Addison-Wesley Publishing Co., Inc.
A & W Visual Library
  See A & W Pubs
A B Hansen, *(Hansen, Arne B.; 0-9600842),* P.O. Box 10638, Glendale, CA 91209 Tel 213-244-3036.
A Bifrost, *(Bifrost, Andrew; 0-916266),* 342 E. 15th St., New York, NY 10003 Tel 212-673-6025.
A C Gardner, *(Gardner, Arthur C.; 0-9602152),* 601 Eastview Ave., Somerset, MA 02726.
A Cartwright
  See N P Cartwright
A Chandonnet, *(Chandonnet, Ann),* P.O. Box A, Chugiak, AK 99567 Tel 907-688-3591.

A D F Myers, *(Myers, Anna Dell Fillingim),* Box 4055, Mountain View, CA 94040.
A E Myers, *(Myers, Albert E.; 0-9602156),* 900 South Arlington Ave., Rm. 103, Harrisburg, PA 17109.
A Earle, *(Earle, Arthur; 0-9600788),* 45 Tulip Circle, Southampton, PA 18966 Tel 215-357-5957.
A Edmunds, *(Edmunds, Adeline; 0-9605846),* 421 N. Sixth Ave., Sturgeon Bay, WI 54235.
A F Matthews, *(Matthews, Allan F.),* 963 Saigon Rd., McLean, VA 22101 Tel 703-356-7561.
A Fields Bks, *(Fields, Arthur, Books),* Dist. by: E. P. Dutton & Co., Inc, 201 Park Ave., S., New York, NY 10003; All Titles Now Listed As Dutton.
A Frommer
  See Frommer-Pasmantier
A G Harter, *(Harter, A. G.),* 663 Fifth Ave., New York, NY 10022 Tel 212-355-5633.
A G Peterson, *(Peterson, Arthur G.),* P.O. Box 252, DeBary, FL 32713 Tel 305-668-6587.
A G Sweetser, *(Sweetser, Albert G.; 0-9605500),* 17 Broadleaf Dr., Clifton Park, NY 12065 Tel 518-371-7674.
A Glaser, *(Glaser, Anton; 0-9600324),* 1237 Whitney Rd., Southampton, PA 18966 Tel 215-357-6306.
A Gonshorowski, *(Gonshorowski, Addie; 0-9600982),* (Addie's Recipe Box), Drawer 5426-B, Eugene, OR 97405 Tel 503-343-5868.
A Guthrie, *(Guthrie, Al),* P.O. Box 443, Carmichael, CA 95608 Tel 916-483-6543.
A H Clark, *(Clark, Arthur H., Co.; 0-87062),* P.O. Box 230, Glendale, CA 91209 Tel 213-245-9119.

A Hardy & Assocs, *(Hardy, Arthur, & Associates; 0-930892),* P.O. Box 8058, New Orleans, LA 70182 Tel 504-282-2326.
A Harvey, *(Harvey, Arnold, Associates; 0-913014),* P.O. Box 89, Commack, NY 11725 Tel 516-543-2738.
A Hyde, *(Hyde, Arnout; 0-9604590),* 418 Lehigh Terrace, Charleston, WV 25302.
A I Polson, *(Polson, A. Irene),* 4559 S. Washtenaw Ave., Chicago, IL 60632 Tel 312-247-0248.
A I Root, *(Root, A. I., Co.; 0-936028),* Box 706, Medina, OH 44256 Tel 216-725-6677.
A J Johnston, *(Johnston, Alnah James),* Box 7307 DTS, Portland, ME 04112.
A J Phillips, *(Phillips, A.J.; 0-9605268),* 245-38 W. Bobier Dr., Vista, CA 92083.
A J Pub, *(A. J. Publishing Co.; 0-914190),* P.O. Box 3012, Duluth, MN 55803 Tel 218-722-3253.
A J Scott, *(Scott, Arthur J., Associates, Handwriting Consultants),* 220 W. 17th St., New York, NY 10011 Tel 212-255-4660.
A Jacobsen, *(Jacobsen, Anita; 0-9604456),* 963 Post Ave., Staten Island, NY 10302.
A James Bks
  See Alicejamesbooks
A Jones, *(Jones, Anson, Press; 0-912432),* P.O. Box 65, Salado, TX 76571 Tel 817-947-5414.
A Keech, *(Keech, Andy; 0-9503341),* 6339 31st. Place N.W., Washington, DC 20015 Tel 202-966-5186; Orders to: Skies Call, P.O. Box 57238, Washington, DC 20037.
A Kelner, *(Kelner, A., & Associates; 0-939812),* 1201 First Ave., Salt Lake City, UT 84103 Tel 801-359-5387.

A Korpalski, *(Korpalski, Adam),* Ferry Bridge Rd., Washington, CT 06793 Tel 203-868-2503.

A L Dabney, *(Dabney, A. L.),* 10441 Goodyear Dr., Dallas, TX 75229.

A L Kerth, *(Kerth, A. L.; 0-9601188),* Jericho Run, Buckland Valley Farms, Washington Crossing, PA 18977.

A L Morse, *(Morse, Albert L.; 0-918320),* 320 Miller Ave., Mill Valley, CA 94941 Tel 415-771-6174.

A M Best, *(Best, A. M., Co.; 0-89408),* Ambest Rd., Oldwick, NJ 08858 Tel 201-439-2200.

A M Newman, *(Newman, Albert M., Enterprises),* P.O. Box 88196, Honolulu, HI 96815 Tel 808-923-4489.

A M Rymer
See Rymer Bks

A Magarey, *(Magarey, Alan),* 46 Alvarado St., San Francisco, CA 94110.

A Meriwether, *(Meriwether, Arthur, Education Resources, Inc.; 0-916260),* Div. of Arthur Meriwether Educational Resources, Inc., P.O. Box 457, 1529 Brook Dr., Downers Grove, IL 60515 Tel 312-495-0300.

A N Palmer, *(Palmer, A. N., Co., The; 0-914268),* 1720 W. Irving Park Rd., Schaumburg, IL 60193 Tel 800-323-9563.

A P M Pr, *(A.P.M. Press; 0-937612),* 650 Ocean Ave., Brooklyn, NY 11226.

A Petersen, *(Petersen, Arona S.),* Orders to: St. Thomas Graphics, St. Thomas, VI 00801; Moved, Left No Forwarding Address.

A Press, *(A Press, Ltd.; 0-917504),* P.O. Box 206, Laguna, NM 87026 Tel 505-988-1183.

A R Harding Pub, *(Harding, A. R., Publishing Co.),* 2878 E. Main St., Columbus, OH 43209 Tel 614-231-9585.

A R Klinski
See Paranoid Pubns

A R Koester Bks, *(Koester, Arthur R., Books; 0-9602558),* P.O. Box 344, Burbank, CA 91503.

A R Liss, *(Liss, Alan R., Inc.; 0-8451),* 150 Fifth Ave., New York, NY 10011 Tel 212-741-2515.

A R Pragare
See Pine Mntn

A Robinson, *(Robinson, Alma),* 196 Dover Rd., Warrenton, VA 22186.

A S Barnes, *(Barnes, A. S., & Co., Inc.; 0-498),* 11175 Flintkote Ave., Suite C, San Diego, CA 92121 Tel 714-457-3200.

A S Campbell, *(Campbell, Alice S.; 0-9600664),* 7806 S. 250 E., Lafayette, IN 47905 Tel 317-538-3479.

A Santilli, *(Santilli, Al, Jr.),* P.O. Box 2492, Dept.-5M, La Habra, CA 90631.

A Smith Co, *(Smith, Allen, Co., Inc.; 0-87473),* 1435 N. Meridian St., Indianapolis, IN 46202 Tel 317-634-4098.

A Stella, *(Stella, Albert A. M.),* 220 Exchange St., Susquehanna, PA 18847; Orders to: Deinotation-7 Press, Box 194, Susquehanna, PA 18847.

A T Weinberg, *(Weinberg, Alyce T.; 0-9604552),* Box 16, Braddock Heights, MD 21714.

A-W, *(Addison-Wesley Publishing Co., Inc.; 0-201),* Jacob Way, Reading, MA 01867 Tel 617-944-3700. *Imprints:* A-W Childrens (Addison-Wesley Children's Books); Adv Bk Prog (Advance Book Program); Med-Nurse (Addison Wesley Publishing Co., Inc., Medical/Nursing Division).

A-W Childrens *Imprint of* **A-W**

A Wade
See E Diemar

A Whitman, *(Whitman, Albert, & Co.; 0-8075),* 560 W. Lake St., Chicago, IL 60606 Tel 312-782-7536.

A Wofsy Fine Arts, *(Wofsy, Alan, Fine Arts; 0-915346),* 150 Green St., San Francisco, CA 94111 Tel 415-986-3030.

A Yards, *(Yards, A.; 0-9603108),* P.O. Box 4428, Mountain View, CA 94040 Tel 415-961-0741.

AA *Imprint of* **U of Mich Pr**

AA Sales Inc, *(AA Sales Inc.; 0-931388),* 9600 Stone Ave. N., Seattle, WA 98103.

AAA, *(American Automobile Assn.; 0-916748),* 8111 Gatehouse Rd., Falls Church, VA 22047 Tel 703-222-6345.

AAAPME, *(American Academic Assn. for Peace in the Middle East; 0-917158),* 9 E. 40th St., New York, NY 10016 Tel 212-532-5005.

AAAS, *(American Assn. for the Advancement of Science; 0-87168),* 1515 Massachusetts Ave., N.W., Washington, DC 20005 Tel 202-467-4400.

AAASPD, *(American Assn. for the Advancement of Science, Pacific Division; 0-934394),* c/o California Academy of Sciences, San Francisco, CA 94118.

AACTE, *(American Assn. of Colleges for Teacher Education; 0-910052; 0-89333),* One Dupont Circle, Suite 610, Washington, DC 20036 Tel 202-293-2450.

AAES, *(American Assn. of Engineering Societies; 0-87615),* 345 E. 47th St., New York, NY 10017 Tel 212-644-7840.

AAFH, *(Academy of American Franciscan History; 0-88382),* P.O. Box 34440, Washington, DC 20034 Tel 301-365-1763.

AAHPER
See AAHPERD

AAHPERD, *(American Alliance for Health, Physical Education, Recreation & Dance; 0-88314),* Affiliate of National Education Assn., 1900 Association Dr., Reston, VA 22091 Tel 703-476-3400.

AAI, *(African-American Institute; 0-87862),* 833 United Nations Plaza, New York, NY 10017 Tel 212-949-5727.

AAP, *(Assn. of American Pubs., Inc.; 0-933636),* 1 Park Ave., New York, NY 10016 Tel 212-689-8920.

AAPG, *(American Assn. of Petroleum Geologists; 0-89181),* P.O. Box 979, Tulsa, OK 74101 Tel 918-584-2555.

AAR-Tantalus, *(AAR/Tantalus, Inc.; 0-931052),* P.O. Box 893, Austin, TX 78767.

Aardvark Media, *(Aardvark Media, Inc; 0-89261),* 975-B Detroit Ave., Concord, CA 94520 Tel 415-687-0223.

Aardvark Pubs, *(Aardvark Pubs. Inc.; 0-917384),* Div. of Bookthrift, Inc., One West 39th St., New York, NY 10018 Tel 212-221-4616.

Aaron-Jenkins, *(Aaron-Jenkins Press),* P.O. Box 998, Lawndale, CA 90260 Tel 213-324-9083.

Aaron Pubs, *(Aaron Pubs., Inc.; 0-936076),* P.O. Box 2572, Sarasota, FL 33578.

Aasen, *(Aasen, Andreas; 0-9603056),* 1210 Dolores St., San Francisco, CA 94110 Tel 415-285-9417.

AASHTO, *(American Assn. of State Highway & Transportation Officials),* 444 N. Capitol St., N.W., Suite 225, Washington, DC 20001 Tel 202-624-5800.

AASLH, *(American Assn. for State & Local History; 0-910050),* 1400 Eighth Ave., S., Nashville, TN 37203.

Aatec Pubns, *(Aatec Pubns.; 0-937948),* P.O. Box 7119, Ann Arbor, MI 48107.

AAU Pubns, *(Amateur Athletic Union of the United States; 0-89710),* 3400 W. 86th St., Indianapolis, IN 46268 Tel 317-872-2900.

AAWS, *(Alcoholics Anonymous World Services, Inc.; 0-916856),* 468 Park Ave. S., New York, NY 10016 Tel 212-686-1100; Orders to: Box 459, Grand Central Sta., New York, NY 10163.

Aazunna, *(Aazunna Publishing; 0-934444),* 801 S. Victoria Ave. Suite 106, Ventura, CA 93003.

Abacus
See Camelot Pub

Abage, *(Abage Pubns.; 0-917350),* 6430 N. Western Ave., Chicago, IL 60645 Tel 312-761-5917.

Abak Pr, *(Abak Press; 0-914214),* 500 Pepper Ridge Rd., Stamford, CT 06905 Tel 203-329-9009.

Abaris Bks, *(Abaris Books, Inc.; 0-913870; 0-89835),* 24 W. 40th St., New York, NY 10018 Tel 212-354-1313.

Abattoir, *(Abattoir Editions; 0-914034),* University of Nebraska at Omaha, Omaha, NE 68182 Tel 402-554-2787; Dist. by: Richard Flamer, P.O. Box 3668, Omaha, NE 68103.

Abbeville Pr, *(Abbeville Press Inc.; 0-89659),* 505 Park Ave., New York, NY 10022 Tel 212-888-1969.

Abbey, *(Abbey Press; 0-87029),* St. Meinrad, IN 47577 Tel 812-357-8011.

Abbey Bks, *(Abbey Books; 0-913768),* P.O. Box 266, Somers, NY 10589 Tel 914-248-5522.

Abbincott, *(Abbincott Publishing Co.; 0-938490),* 1501 Broadway, Rm. 1414, New York, NY 10036.

Abbott Langer Assocs, *(Abbott, Langer & Associates; 0-916506),* P.O. Box 275, Park Forest, IL 60466 Tel 312-756-3990.

Abby Cooks
See Cuisinart Cooking

ABC, *(American Book Co.; 0-278),* Div. of Litton Educational Publishing, Inc., 135 W. 50th St., New York, NY 10020 Tel 212-265-8700; Orders to: 7625 Empire Dr., Florence, KY 41042 Tel 800-354-9815.

ABC-Clio, *(American Bibliographical Center-Clio Press; 0-87436),* 2040 Alameda Padre Serra, P.O. Box 4397, Santa Barbara, CA 93103 Tel 805-963-4221.

ABC Pub, *(ABC Pub.),* RD 2, Danville, PA 17821.

Abco-Malan, *(Abco-Malan; 0-9603260),* c/o Sansbury, 70 University Place, Suite No. 5, New York, NY 10003 Tel 212-533-6732.

Abe Lincoln Assn, *(Abraham Lincoln Assn.),* Old State Capital, Springfield, IL 62706.

Abelard, *(Abelard-Schuman Ltd.; 0-200),* 10 E. 53rd St., New York, NY 10022 Tel 212-593-7000; c/o Harper & Row Pubs., Keystone Industrial Park, Scranton, PA 18512.

Abingdon, *(Abingdon Press; 0-687),* 201 Eighth Ave. S., Nashville, TN 37202 Tel 615-749-6403; Orders to: Customer Service Dept., 201 Eighth Ave. S., Nashville, TN 37202 Tel 615-749-6347. *Imprints:* Apex (Apex Books); Co-Pub by Fides (Abingdon & Fides Co-Publications); Festival (Festival Books).

ABK Pubns, *(ABK Pubns.; 0-9601420),* P.O. Box 962, Hanover, NH 03755.

Ablex Pub, *(Ablex Publishing Corp.; 0-89391),* 355 Chestnut St., Norwood, NJ 07648 Tel 201-767-8450.

Abradale, *(Abradale Press; 0-8109),* Dist. by: Harry N. Abrams, Inc., Subs. of Times Mirror Co., 110 E. 59th St., New York, NY 10022.

Abrams, *(Abrams, Harry N., Inc.; 0-8109),* Subs. of Times Mirror Co., 110 E. 59th St., New York, NY 10022 Tel 212-758-8600.

Abraxas, *(Abraxas Press; 0-932868),* 2322 Rugby Row, Madison, WI 53705 Tel 608-231-1440.

Abraxas Pub WA, *(Abraxas Publishing; 0-939768),* P.O. Box 317, 439 Kirkland Way, Kirkland, WA 98033 Tel 206-822-6081.

Abstract Pub, *(Abstract Pub.; 0-915862),* 1514 Elmwood Ave., Evanston, IL 60201 Tel 312-869-3636.

Abt Assoc, *(Abt Associates, Inc.; 0-89011),* Orders to: 55 Wheeler St., Cambridge, MA 02138 Tel 617-492-7100.

Abundant
See Lee Ward Inst

Abyss, *(Abyss Pubns.; 0-911856),* P.O. Box C, Somerville, MA 02143 Tel 617-666-1804.

AC Pubns, *(AC Pubns.; 0-935496),* P.O. Box 238, Homer, NY 13077 Tel 607-749-4040.

Acad Assoc, *(Academic Assoc.; 0-918260),* 1888 Century Park E., Suite 10, Century City, Los Angeles, CA 90067 Tel 213-556-3033.

Acad Bk Club, *(Academic Book Club),* N. 5411 Post St., Spokane, WA 99208 Tel 509-325-1435.

Acad Bks Pubs, *(Academy Books-Publishers; 0-89564),* 3085 Reynard Way, San Diego, CA 92103 Tel 714-298-5250.

Acad Educ Dev, *(Academy for Educational Development, Inc.; 0-89492),* 680 5th Ave., New York, NY 10019 Tel 212-397-0040; 1414-22nd St., N.W., Washington, DC 20037.

Acad Motion Pic, *(Academy of Motion Picture Arts & Sciences),* 8949 Wilshire Blvd., Beverly Hills, CA 90211 Tel 213-278-8990.

Acad of Mgmt, *(Academy of Management; 0-915350),* Dept. of Administration, College of Business Administration, Wichita State Univ., Wichita, KS 67208; Orders to: Dennis F. Ray, The Academy of Management College of Business, Mississippi State University, Mississippi State, MS 39762.

Acad Pr, *(Academic Press, Inc.; 0-12),* 111 Fifth Ave., New York, NY 10003 Tel 212-741-6800.

Acad Therapy, *(Academic Therapy Pubns.; 0-87879),* 20 Commercial Blvd., Novato, CA 94947 Tel 415-883-3314.

Academia, *(Academia Press; 0-911880),* P.O. Box 125, Oshkosh, WI 54901 Tel 414-235-8362.

Academic Intl, *(Academic International; 0-87569),* P.O. Box 1111, Gulf Breeze, FL 32561.

Academic Media, *(Academic Media; 0-87876),* Affiliate of Marquis Who's Who, 4300 W. 62nd St., Indianapolis, IN 46268.

Academic Travel, *(Academic Travel Abroad, Inc.; 0-918692),* 1346 Connecticut Ave., N.W., Washington, DC 20036 Tel 202-785-3412.

Academic World, *(Academic World, Inc.; 0-915582),* Div. of Acaworld Corp., Drawer 4037, Greenville, NC 27834 Tel 919-756-4169.

Academy, *(Academy Court),* 176 Academy Lane, Sonoma, CA 95476.

Academy Bks, *(Academy Books; 0-914960),* P.O. Box 757, Rutland, VT 05701 Tel 802-773-9194.

Academy Chi Ltd, *(Academy Chicago, Ltd.; 0-915864),* 360 N. Michigan Ave., Chicago, IL 60601 Tel 312-782-9826.

Academy Hill, *(Academy Hill Press; 0-932312),* 292 Academy Hill Rd., Red Hook, NY 12571 Tel 914-758-9042.

Academy-Parliament, *(Academy Press; 0-87964),* c/o Parliament News Inc., 21314 Lassen St., Chatsworth, CA 91311.

Academy Pr-Campbell
 See Academy Pr-Santa

Academy Pr-Santa, *(Academy Press; 0-912314; 0-89733),* 5227 Stevens Creek Blvd., Santa Clara, CA 95051 Tel 408-241-6799.

Academy Pubns, *(Academy Pubns.; 0-931560),* Box 5224, Sherman Oaks, CA 91413.

Acadian Genealogy, *(Acadian Genealogy Exchange; 0-939444),* 863 Wayman Branch Rd., Covington, KY 41015.

Acadian Pub, *(Acadian Publishing Enterprise, Inc.; 0-914216),* Rte. 3 Box 362, Church Point, LA 70525 Tel 318-684-5871.

Acadiana Pr, *(Acadiana Press, The; 0-937614),* P.O. Box 42290, USL, Lafayette, LA 70504.

ACC, *(Appleton-Century-Crofts; 0-8385),* 292 Madison Ave., New York, NY 10017 Tel 212-532-1700; Orders to: Prentice-Hall, Order Dept., Englewood Cliffs, NJ 07632.

Accel Devel, *(Accelerated Development Inc.; 0-915202),* 2515 W. Jackson St., Muncie, IN 47303 Tel 317-284-7511.

Accelerated Index, *(Accelerated Indexing Systems, Inc.; 0-89593),* 19 W. South Temple, Suite 600 Union Pacific Annex, Salt Lake City, UT 84101 Tel 801-531-0098.

Accent Bks, *(Accent Books; 0-89636; 0-916406),* P.O. Box 15337, Lakewood Sta., Denver, CO 80215 Tel 303-988-5300; 12100 W. Sixth Ave., Denver, CO 80215.

Accent Liv
 See Cheever Pub

Accord Pr, *(Accord Press; 0-9606078),* P.O. Box 9432, San Jose, CA 95157 Tel 408-255-8894.

Accura, *(Accura Music, Inc.; 0-918194),* Box 887, Athens, OH 45701 Tel 614-594-3547.

ACE, *(American Council on Education; 0-8268),* 1 Dupont Circle, Washington, DC 20036 Tel 202-833-4785.

Ace Bks, *(Ace Books; 0-441),* Div. of Charter Communications Inc., c/o Grosset & Dunlap, 51 Madison Ave., New York, NY 10010 Tel 212-689-9200.

ACEI, *(Assn. for Childhood Education International; 0-87173),* 3615 Wisconsin Ave., N.W., Washington, DC 20016 Tel 202-363-6963.

Achievement Inst, *(Achievement Institute, The; 0-936452),* 3125 Geddes Ave., Ann Arbor, MI 48104.

ACI, *(American Concrete Institute; 0-87031),* 22400 W. Seven Mile Rd., P.O. Box 19150, Detroit, MI 48219 Tel 313-532-2600.

Acme Law, *(Acme Law Book Co., Inc.; 0-910012),* Post Office Bldg., Amityville, NY 11701 Tel 516-799-8686.

Acoma Bks, *(Acoma Books; 0-916552),* P.O. Box 4, Ramona, CA 92065 Tel 714-789-1288.

Acorn *Imprint of* **Macmillan**

Acorn *Imprint of* **Music Sales**

Acorn NC, *(Acorn Press; 0-89386),* 1010 Wyldewood Rd., Box 4007, Duke Sta., Durham, NC 27706 Tel 919-471-3842.

Acorn Oaks, *(Acorn Oaks Enterprises; 0-939012),* P.O. Box 4302, Thousand Oaks, CA 91362.

Acorn OH, *(Acorn; 0-9604194),* 1778 Radnor Rd., Cleveland, OH 44118.

Acorn Pr PA, *(Acorn Press; 0-915992),* Div. of Eastern National Park & Monument Assn., 339 Walnut St., Philadelphia, PA 19106 Tel 215-597-7129; Dist. by: Publishing Center for Cultural Resources, 152 W. 42nd St., New York, NY 10036 Tel 212-221-6055.

Acorn Pubns, *(Acorn Pubns.; 0-931442),* 9 Victory Rd., Suffern, NY 10901.

Acre Pr, *(Acre Press),* C/O Alma C. Reith, 5945 Evergreen, Dearborn Heights, MI 48127.

Acro Pr, *(Acro Press),* 1925 Main, Vancouver, WA 98660.

Acrobat, *(Acrobat Books; 0-918226),* 213 S. Arden Blvd., Los Angeles, CA 90004 Tel 213-933-7796; Moved, Left No Forwarding Address.

Acropolis, *(Acropolis Books; 0-87491),* 2400 17th St. N.W., Washington, DC 20009 Tel 202-387-6805.

ACTA Found, *(ACTA Foundation; 0-87946),* 4848 N. Clark St., Chicago, IL 60640 Tel 312-271-1030.

Action Link, *(Action Link Pubns.; 0-936148),* 53 Condon Court, San Mateo, CA 94403.

Active Learning, *(Active Learning; 0-914460),* P.O. Box 64992, Lubbock, TX 79464.

Activity Rec, *(Activity Records, Inc; 0-914296; 0-89525),* 1937 Grand Ave., Baldwin, NY 11510 Tel 516-223-4666; Dist. by: Educational Activities, Inc., P.O. Box 392, Freeport, NY 11520 Tel 516-223-4666.

Activity Resources, *(Activity Resources Co., Inc.; 0-918932),* P.O. Box 4875, 20655 Hathaway Ave., Hayward, CA 94541 Tel 415-782-1300.

ACTKBA, *(American Committee to Keep Biafra Alive (ACTKBA)),* c/o Cliff Catton, P.O. Box 341, Cairo, NY 12413.

Acton Hse, *(Acton House, Inc.; 0-89202),* Div. of CRW Corp., 5005 Newport Dr., Rolling Meadows, IL 60008 Tel 213-553-7012; Moved, Left No Forwarding Address.

Ad Digest, *(Advertisement Digest; 0-939670),* P.O. Box 165, Morton Grove, IL 60053 Tel 312-965-1456.

Adamant Pr, *(Adamant Press; 0-912362),* P.O. Box 7, Adamant, VT 05640.

Adams Brown, *(Adams Brown Co.; 0-917900),* P.O. Box 399, Exeter, NH 03833 Tel 603-772-4067.

Adams County, *(Adams County Historical Society; 0-934858),* P.O. Box 102, Hastings, NE 68901 Tel 402-463-5838.

Adams Inc MA, *(Adams, Bob, Inc.),* 30 Kinross Rd., Brookline, MA 02146 Tel 617-277-1373.

Adams Minn, *(Adams Press; 0-914828),* 59 Seymour Ave., S.E., Minneapolis, MN 55414 Tel 612-378-9076; Orders to: Lerner Publications Co., 241 First Ave. N., Minneapolis, MN 55401.

ADAPTS, *(ADAPTS(Alcohol & Drug Abuse Prevention & Training Services; 0-9606016),* 932 W. Franklin St., Richmond, VA 23220 Tel 804-358-0408.

Adastra Pr, *(Adastra Press),* 101 Strong St., Easthampton, MA 01027.

ADC NY
 See ADC Pubns

ADC Pubns, *(ADC Pubns.; 0-937414),* Dist. by: Robert Silver Associates, 95 Madison Ave., New York, NY 10016 Tel 212-686-5630.

Addison Gallery, *(Addison Gallery of American Art),* Phillips Academy, Andover, MA 01810.

Addison Hse, *(Addison House; 0-89169),* Subs. of American Showcase, Inc., 30 Rockefeller Plaza, Suite 1929, New York, NY 10020 Tel 212-245-0981.

Addresso'set, *(Addresso'set; 0-916944),* P.O. Box 1530, Vallejo, CA 94590 Tel 707-644-6358.

Addressoset
 See Addresso'set

Adelantre, *(Adelantre; 0-917288),* 4594 Bedford Ave., Brooklyn, NY 11235.

Adelphi Univ, *(Adelphi Univ. Press; 0-88461),* South Ave., Garden City, NY 11530 Tel 516-248-2020.

Adirondack Trail, *(Adirondack Trail Improvement Society; 0-9600450),* St. Huberts, NY 12943 Tel 518-576-4427; Orders to: 254 Westfield St., Dedham, MMA 02026 Tel 617-329-9588.

Adirondack Yes, *(Adirondack Yesteryears, Inc.; 0-9601158),* Lake St. Extension-Drawer 209, Saranac Lake, NY 12983 Tel 518-891-3206.

ADIS Pr, *(ADIS Press USA, Inc.; 0-909337),* 515 Madison Ave., New York, NY 10022.

ADK Mtn Club, *(Adirondack Mountain Club, Inc.; 0-935272),* 172 Ridge St., Glens Falls, NY 12801 Tel 518-793-7737.

Adler, *(Adler's Foreign Books, Inc.; 0-8417),* 162 Fifth Ave., New York, NY 10010 Tel 212-691-5151.

ADM Co, *(A.D.M. Co., Inc.; 0-937974),* P.O. Box 10462, Phoenix, AZ 85016 Tel 602-279-2070.

Adm Nimitz Foun, *(Admiral Nimitz Foundation),* P.O. Box 777, Fredericksburg, TX 78624.

Admin Res
 See ARA

Admiralty Pub Hse, *(Admiralty Publishing House, Ltd.; 0-913544),* P.O. Box 191, Annapolis, MD 21404 Tel 301-268-5291.

Adobe, *(Adobe Booksellers),* 2416 Pennsylvania St., N. E., Albuquerque, NM 87110.

Adobe Pr, *(Adobe Press; 0-933004),* 515 Isleta Blvd. S.W., Box 12334, Albuquerque, NM 87105 Tel 505-873-1155.

Adolph Green, *(Green, Adolph, Publishing Co.; 0-9602198),* P.O. Box 337, Arlington, TX 76010.

Adrian, *(Adrian Press; 0-910024),* 157 W. 57th St., New York, NY 10019 Tel 212-265-6637.

Adriatic Stamp, *(Adriatic Stamp Co.; 0-9603474),* P.O. Box 1651, Maitland, FL 32751.

Adult Ed, *(Adult Education Assn. of the U.S.A.; 0-88379),* 810 18th St., N.W., Suite 500, Washington, DC 20006 Tel 202-347-9574.

Adv Bk Prog *Imprint of* **A-W**

Adv Bk Prog *Imprint of* **Benjamin-Cummings**

Adv Prof Seminars, *(Advanced Professional Seminars, Inc.; 0-9604532),* 7033 Ramsgate Place, Suite "A", Los Angeles, CA 90045; Orders to: P.O. Box 45791, Los Angeles, CA 90045 Tel 213 776-0115.

Adv Psychiatry, *(Group for the Advancement of Psychiatry; 0-87318),* 30 E. 29th St., New York, NY 10016 Tel 212-889-5760.

Advance Marketing, *(Advance Marketing Concepts; 0-935570),* 2337 Eleventh St., Encinitas, CA 92024.

Advance Planning, *(Advance Planning Pubns.; 0-9600524),* Rte. 3, St. Croix Cove, Hudson, WI 54016.

Advanced Computer, *(Advanced Computer Techniques Corp., Inc.; 0-931336),* 437 Madison Ave., New York, NY 10022.

Advantage, *(Advantage Books; 0-936036),* 883 Production Place, Newport Beach, CA 92663 Tel 714-642-1331.

Advent, *(Advent Pubs., Inc.; 0-911682),* P.O. Box A3228, Chicago, IL 60690.

Advent Bk, *(Advent Books, Inc; 0-89891),* 141 E. 44th St., Suite 511, New York, NY 10017 Tel 212-697-0887. *Imprints:* Plutarch Pr (Plutarch Press).

Adventure Guides, *(Adventure Guides, Inc.; 0-913216),* 36 E. 57th St., New York, NY 10022 Tel 212-355-6334.

Adventure Pubns, *(Adventure Pubns.; 0-934860),* P.O. Box 96, Staples, MN 56479 Tel 218-894-3591.

Adventures in Living, *(Adventures in Living; 0-9605868),* P.O. Box 3690, San Diego, CA 92103.

Adventures Poet, *(Adventures in Poetry/Coach House South),* Orders to: SBD: Small Press Distribution, 1636 Ocean View Ave., Kensington, CA 94709 Tel 415-524-2107.

Advocate, *(Advocate Press; 0-911866),* Franklin Springs, GA 30639 Tel 404-245-7272.

Advocate Pub Group, *(Advocate Publishing Group; 0-89894),* 6810 E. Main St., Reynoldsburg, OH 43068.

AE-J *Imprint of* **Apollo Eds**

AE-T *Imprint of* **Apollo Eds**

Aegean Park Pr, *(Aegean Park Press; 0-89412),* P.O. Box 2837, Laguna Hills, CA 92653 Tel 714-586-8811.

Aegis Pub Co, *(Aegis Publishing Co.),* 4866 Trojan Ave., San Diego, CA 92115 Tel 714-286-8975.

Aeolian, *(Aeolian Press; 0-89363),* 6762 Cibola Rd., San Diego, CA 62120 Tel 714-582-1081.

Aeonian Pr
 See Amereon Ltd

Aerial Photo, *(Aerial Photography Services, Inc.),* 2300 Dunavant St., Charlotte, NC 28203.

Aero, *(Aero Pubs., Inc.; 0-8168),* 329 W. Aviation Rd., Fallbrook, CA 92028 Tel 714-728-8456.

Aero-Medical, *(Aero-Medical Consultants, Inc.; 0-912522),* 10912 Hamlin Blvd., Largo, FL 33540 Tel 813-596-2551.

Aero Pr, *(Aero Press Pubs.; 0-936450),* P.O. Box 2091, Fall River, MA 02722 Tel 617-644-2058.

Aero Products, *(Aero Products Research, Inc.; 0-912682),* 11201 Hindry Ave., Los Angeles, CA 90045 Tel 213-641-7242.

Aerodrome Pr, *(Aerodrome Press; 0-935092),* Box 44, Story City, IA 50248.

Aerofacts, *(Aerofacts; 0-934268),* P.O. Box 11347, Las Vegas, NV 89111 Tel 702-458-3754.

Aesculapius Pubs, *(Aesculapius Pubs., Inc.; 0-918228),* Ten W. 66th St., Suite 6D, New York, NY 10023 Tel 212-595-2148.

Aesthetic Accidents, *(Aesthetic Accidents Unltd.; 0-9603458),* 434 Greenwich St., New York, NY 10013.

Aesthetic Realism, *(Aesthetic Realism Foundation & Terrain Gallery; 0-911492),* 141 Greene St., New York, NY 10012 Tel 212-777-4490.

Aeternium Pub, *(Aeternium Publishing, Co.; 0-917358),* 2 Vesper Lane, Nantucket Island, MA 02554 Tel 203-688-4934.

Affiliated Pubns
 See WDW Pubns

Affirmation, *(Affirmation Books; 0-89571),* 456 Hill St., Whitinsville, MA 01588 Tel 617-234-6266.

Afi Pubns, *(Afi Pubns; 0-912460),* P.O. Box 8, Fleetwood, Mount Vernon, NY 10552 Tel 914-667-6575.

AFIPS Pr, *(AFIPS Press; 0-88283),* P.O. Box 9657, 1815 N. Lynn St., Suite 800, Arlington, VA 22209 Tel 703-558-3680.

Africa Bks *Imprint of* **Unipub**

African Am Trading, *(African American Trading Co.),* P.O. Box 43585, Los Angeles, CA 90043.

African Bibl, *(African Bibliographic Center, Inc.; 0-87859),* P.O. Box 13096, Washington, DC 20009 Tel 202-223-1392.

African Her Stud, *(African Heritage Studies Pubs.; 0-915788),* 507 Fifth Ave., New York, NY 10017.

African Policy, *(African Policy Institute),* 120 Wall St., Suite 1044, New York, NY 10005.

African Studies Assn, *(African Studies Assn.; 0-918456),* Epstein Service Bldg., Brandeis Univ., Waltham, MA 02254 Tel 617-899-3079. *Imprints:* Crossroads (Crossroads Press).

Africana *Imprint of* **Holmes & Meier**

Africana Res, *(Africana Research Pubns.; 0-933524),* 2580 Seventh Ave., New York, NY 10039.

Afro-Am, *(Afro-Am Publishing Co., Inc.; 0-910030),* 910 S. Michigan Ave., Rm. 556, Chicago, IL 60605 Tel 312-922-1147.

Afterimage, *(Afterimage Book Pubs.; 0-934862),* 305 Cottage Grove, Urbana, IL 61801 Tel 217-384-7319.

Afterthought Bks, *(Afterthought Books; 0-915290),* 147 Woodmont Blvd., Nashville, TN 37205 Tel 615-292-4919; Moved,Left No Forwarding Address.

AG Pr, *(AG Press),* 16th & Yuma, Box 1009, Manhattan, KS 66502 Tel 913-539-7558.

Ag Sci Pubns, *(Agricultural Sciences Pubns. Univ. of California; 0-931876),* 1422 Harbour Way S., Richmond, CA 94804 Tel 415-642-2431.

Agape Pubs, *(Agape Pubs., Inc.; 0-914618),* 10721 W. Capitol Dr., Milwaukee, WI 53222 Tel 414-466-1050.

Agascha Prods
 See Shabazz Pr

Agate Pr, *(Agate Press, Inc.; 0-937266),* 51 E. 42nd St., New York, NY 10017.

Agathon Pr, *(Agathon Press Inc.; 0-87586),* 15 E. 26th St., New York, NY 10010 Tel 212-679-1674.

Ageless Bks, *(Ageless Books; 0-918482),* P.O. Box 6300, Beverly Hills, CA 90212 Tel 213-933-6338.

Agnew Higgins, *(Agnew-Higgins, Inc.; 0-9600254),* 7091 Belgrave Ave., P.O. Box 857, Garden Grove, CA 92642 Tel 714-893-1301.

Agnew Tech-Tran, *(Agnew Tech-Tran, Inc.),* P.O. Box 789, Woodland Hills, CA 91365 Tel 213-340-5147.

Agni Yoga Soc, *(Agni Yoga Society, Inc.; 0-933574),* 319 W. 107th St., New York, NY 10025 Tel 212-864-7752.

Agora Pr, *(Agora Press; 0-934622),* P.O. Box 1085, La Jolla, CA 92038.

Agrarian Reform, *(Agrarian Reform Co.),* Dist. by: Bookpeople, 2940 Seventh St., Berkeley, CA 92641.

AgriFinance, *(AgriFinance),* 5520 W. Touhy Ave., Suite G, Skokie, IL 60077 Tel 312-676-4060.

Agrinde Bks
 See Agrinde Pubns

Agrinde Pubns, *(Agrinde Pubns., Ltd.; 0-9601068),* c/o Barbara J. Hendra Associates, Inc., 665 Fifth Ave., New York, NY 10022 Tel 212-947-9898.

AHM Pub, *(AHM Publishing Corp.; 0-88295),* 3110 N. Arlington Heights Rd., Arlington Heights, IL 60004 Tel 312-253-9720.

Ahsahta Pr, *(Ahsahta Press; 0-916272),* Dept. of English, Boise State Univ., Boise, ID 83725 Tel 208-385-1246; Orders to: Univ. Bookstore, Boise State Univ., Boise, ID 83725.

Ai, *(Ai; 0-938454),* 118 E. 25th St., New York, NY 10010.

Aim-High *Imprint of* **Fell**

AIM Pr, *(A.I.M. Press; 0-9602168),* 3912 Carpenter Ct., Los Angeles, CA 91604.

AIR Systems, *(American Institutes for Research, Systems Division; 0-89785),* 41 North Rd., Bedford, MA 01730 Tel 617-275-0800.

Aircraft Chart & Rent, *(Aircraft Charter & Rental Tariff Information Service of North America; 0-9603908),* Box 3000, Oak Park, IL 60303 Tel 217-546-1491.

Airline Job, *(Airline Job Kit),* P.O. Box 66895 ABI, Seattle, WA 98166.

Airline Pubns, *(Airline Pubns.),* 130 N. Fifth St., Rm. 202, Harrisburg International Airport, Middletown, PA 17057 Tel 717-944-2571.

Airmont, *(Airmont Publishing Co., Inc.; 0-8049),* 22 E. 60th St., New York, NY 10022.

Airport Bk Pr, *(Airport Book Press; 0-935866),* 11205 Farmland Dr., Rockville, MD 20852.

Airshow Pubs, *(Airshow Pubs.; 0-9601506),* 2014 Homewood Rd., Annapolis, MD 21402 Tel 301-757-1806.

AISI, *(Advanced International Studies Institute (AISI), in Association with the Univ. of Miami; 0-933074),* 4330 East-West Highway, Suite 1122, Washington, DC 20014 Tel 301-951-0818.

AJAY Ent, *(AJAY Enterprises; 0-939440),* P.O. Box 2018, Mosby Branch, Falls Church, VA 22042 Tel 703-573-8220.

AKCS, *(Assn. of Korean Christian Scholars in North America, Inc.; 0-932014),* P.O. Box 757, Montclair, NJ 07042 Tel 201-783-9567.

Akens-Morgan, *(Akens-Morgan Press, Inc.),* 720 Church St., N.W., Huntsville, AL 35801; Dist. by: JMT Associates, P.O. Box 192, Normal, AL 35762.

Akers, *(Akers, Mona J. Coole; 0-912706),* 219 S. Williams St., Denver, CO 80209 Tel 303-722-1892.

Akiba Pr, *(Akiba Press; 0-934764),* Box 13086, Oakland, CA 94611 Tel 415-339-1283.

Al-Anon, *(Al-Anon Family Group Headquarters, Inc.; 0-910034),* 1 Park Ave., Second Floor, New York, NY 10016 Tel 212-481-6565.

Al-Del, *(Al-Del Hobbies; 0-933360),* 3675 Brooks Ave., N.E., Salem, OR 97303 Tel 503-390-4974.

Al Fresco, *(Al Fresco Enterprise),* Postal Drawer 11530, Pueblo, CO 81001 Tel 303-545-2001.

Al Kitab Sudan, *(Al Kitab Sudan & Rene Productions; 0-914388),* 9846 A St., Oakland, CA 94603; Moved,Left No Forwarding Address.

ALA, *(American Library Assn.; 0-8389),* 50 E. Huron St., Chicago, IL 60611 Tel 312-944-6780. *Imprints:* Pub by Bootlegger Pr (Bootlegger Press).

Aladdin *Imprint of* **Atheneum**

Alameda, *(Alameda Poets; 0-916734),* P.O. Box 1751, Alameda, CA 94501.

Alamo Pr, *(Alamo Press; 0-9605140),* 104 Garydale Court, Alamo, CA 94507.

Alandale Pr, *(Alandale Press; 0-937748),* R.D. 5, Ballston Rd., Amsterdam, NY 12010.

Alaska Intl Art, *(Alaska International Art Institute),* 26241 Foxgrove Ave., Sun City, CA 92381.

Alaska Northwest, *(Alaska Northwest Publishing Co.; 0-88240),* 130 Second Ave. S., Edmonds, WA 98020 Tel 206-774-4111.

Alaska Pacific, *(Alaska Pacific Univ. Press; 0-935094),* Alaska Pacific University, Anchorage, AK 99504 Tel 907-276-8181.

Alaska Travel, *(Alaska Travel Pubns., Inc.; 0-914164),* P.O. Box 4-2031, Anchorage, AK 99509 Tel 907-274-3912.

Alaskabks, *(Alaskabooks),* P.O. Box 1494, Juneau, AK 99802 Tel 907-586-3067.

Alba, *(Alba House; 0-8189),* Div. of the Society of St. Paul, 2187 Victory Blvd., Staten Island, NY 10314 Tel 212-761-0047.

Alba Bks, *(Alba Books; 0-8189),* Div. of Alba House, 9531 Akron-Canfield Rd., Canfield, OH 44406 Tel 216-533-5503.

Albany Hist & Art, *(Albany Institute of History & Art),* 125 Washington Ave., Albany, NY 12210 Tel 518-463-4478.

Albany Pub Lib, *(Albany Public Library; 0-9605090),* 161 Washington Ave., Albany, NY 12210.

Albin, *(Albin, James R.; 0-916210),* 431 Bridgeway, Sausalito, CA 94965 Tel 415-332-6438.

Albion, *(Albion Corp., Co.; 0-87843),* 355 Devon Dr., San Rafael, CA 94903 Tel 415-479-9604.

Albion Albums, *(Albion Albums; 0-9604100),* P.O. Box 301, Albion, CA 95410.

Albion Am Bks, *(Albion-American Books),* P.O. Box 50011, Tucson, AZ 85703.

Albion NC, *(Albion; 0-932530),* Dept. of History, Appalachan State Univ., Boone, NC 28608.

Alchemist-Light, *(Alchemist/Light Publishing; 0-9600650),* P.O. Box 5530, San Francisco, CA 94101 Tel 415-342-7804.

Alchemy Bks, *(Alchemy Books; 0-931290),* 681 Market, Suite 755, San Francisco, CA 94105 Tel 415-362-2708.

Alcott Pr, *(Alcott Press, Inc.; 0-936998),* P.O. Box 335, Edwardsville, IL 62025 Tel 618-656-7445.

Aldebaran Rev, *(Aldebaran Review; 0-917744),* 2209 California St., Berkeley, CA 94703 Tel 415-549-2456.

Alder Pr, *(Alder Press Inc.; 0-9601940),* P.O. Box 25361, Houston, TX 77005.

Aldine, *(Aldine Publishing Co.; 0-202),* 529 S. Wabash Ave., Chicago, IL 60605.

Aldine
 See Beresford Bk Serv

Aldine Pub, *(Aldine Publishing Co., Inc.; 0-202),* Div. of Walter De Gruyter, Inc., 200 Saw Mill River Rd., Hawthorne, NY 10532 Tel 914-747-0115.

Alembic Pr, *(Alembic Press; 0-934184),* 1744 Slaterville Rd., Ithaca, NY 14850.

Aletheia Pubs, *(Aletheia Pubs., Inc.; 0-86717),* 8330 Burnet Rd., No. 122, Austin, TX 78758.

Alethes, *(Alethes; 0-930254),* P.O. Box 5842, Carmel, CA 93921.

Alexander Graham, *(Alexander Graham Bell Assn. for the Deaf, The; 0-88200),* 3417 Volta Place N.W., Washington, DC 20007 Tel 202-337-5220.

Alexandria Hse, *(Alexandria House Books; 0-932496),* Div. of Kephart Communications, Inc., c/o Kephart Communications, Inc., 901 N. Washington St., Rm. 605, Alexandria, VA 22314 Tel 703-836-3313; Orders to: 236 Foest Park Place, Ottawa, IL 61350.

Alfa Sierra, *(Alfa Sierra Pubns.; 0-9604728),* P.O. Box 9636, San Diego, CA 92109.

Alfred, *(Alfred & Alfred Co.),* 5260 Figueroa St., Suite 114, Los Angeles, CA 90037.

Alfred Pub, *(Alfred Publishing Co., Inc.; 0-88284),* 15335 Morrison St., Sherman Oaks, CA 91403 Tel 213-995-8811.

Algol Pr, *(Algol Press; 0-916186),* P.O. Box 4175, New York, NY 10163 Tel 212-643-9011; Orders to: F&SF Book Co., 740 Delafield Ave., Staten Island, NY 10310.

Algorithmics, *(Algorithmics, Inc.; 0-917448),* 44 W. 62nd St., New York, NY 10023 Tel 212-246-2366.

Algorithmics Pr
 See Algorithmics

ALI-ABA, *(ALI-ABA),* 4025 Chestnut St., Philadelphia, PA 19104 Tel 215-243-1600.

Alicejamesbooks, *(Alicejamesbooks; 0-914086),* 138 Mt. Auburn St., Cambridge, MA 02138.

Alin Found Pr, *(Alin Foundation Press),* 2150 Shattuck Ave., Berkeley, CA 94704 Tel 415-845-4907.

Alinda Pr, *(Alinda Press; 0-933076),* Box 553, Eureka, CA 95501 Tel 707-443-2510.

Alised, *(Alised Enterprises),* 7808 Maryknoll Ave., Bethesda, MD 20034.

Alive Pubns, *(Alive Pubns. Ltd.; 0-935572),* 11 Park Place, New York, NY 10007 Tel 212-962-0316.

All This, *(All This & Less Pubs.; 0-915682),* Regents 509, NMSU, Las Cruces, NM 88003.

Allanheld, *(Allanheld, Osmun & Co., Inc.; 0-916672; 0-86598),* 6 S. Fullerton Ave., Montclair, NJ 07042 Tel 201-783-5555; Dist. by: Biblio Dist. Ctr., 81 Adams Dr., Totowa, NJ 07512 Tel 201-256-8600.

Allanheld & Schram, *(Allanheld & Schram; 0-8390),* 36 Park St., Montclair, NJ 07042.

Allegany Mtn Pr, *(Allegany Mountain Press; 0-931588),* 111 N. Tenth St., Olean, NY 14760 Tel 716-372-0935.

Allegheny, *(Allegheny Press; 0-910042),* 522 East St., California, PA 15419 Tel 412-938-8548.

Allegro Pub, *(Allegro Publishing Co.; 0-9601042),* P.O. Box 39892, Los Angeles, CA 90039 Tel 213-665-6783.

Alleluia Pr, *(Alleluia Press; 0-911726),* P.O. Box 103, Allendale, NJ 07401 Tel 201-327-3513; 672 Franklin Turnpike, NJ 07401.

Allen Lane, *(Allen Lane),* Dist. by: The Viking Press, 625 Madison Ave., New York, NY 10022.

Allen Pr, *(Allen Press, Inc.; 0-935868),* P.O. Box 368, Lawrence, KS 66044.

Allen Unwin, *(Allen & Unwin, Inc.; 0-04; 0-86861),* 9 Winchester Terrace, Winchester, MA 01890 Tel 617-729-0830; Orders to: P.O. Box 978, Building 424 Raritan Center, Edison, NJ 08817 Tel 201-225-1900.

Allenson
See Allenson-Breckinridge

Allenson-Breckinridge, *(Allenson-Breckinridge Books; 0-8401),* P.O. Box 447, Geneva, AL 36340.

Allgood Bks, *(Allgood Books),* P.O. Box 1329, Jackson, MS 39205 Tel 601-355-5419.

Alliance Coll, *(Alliance College),* Cambridge Springs, PA 16403.

Alliance Pubs, *(Alliance Pubs.),* P.O. Box 25004, Fort Lauderdale, FL 33320 Tel 305-722-5361.

Allied Educ, *(Allied Education Council; 0-915204),* P.O. Box 78, Galien, MI 49113.

Allied Res Soc, *(Allied Research Society, Inc.; 0-912984),* 67 Kensington Rd., San Anselmo, CA 94960 Tel 415-457-6465.

Allison Ent, *(Allison Enterprises; 0-918324),* P.O. Box 200, Franklin, NJ 07416 Tel 201-827-5104.

Allison Pr, *(Allison Press; 0-913226),* Orders to: Light Impressions, P.O. Box 3012, Rochester, NY 14614.

Allison Pubs, *(Allison Pubs.),* 1 La Playa, Box 733, Cochise, AZ 85606.

Allowance, *(Allowance, Inc.; 0-9604228),* 1516 Bonnie Brae, Denton, TX 76201.

Allwyn Pr, *(Allwyn Press; 0-911768),* P.O. Box 240, Washington Bridge Sta., New York, NY 10033 Tel 212-796-0498.

Ally Pr, *(Ally Press; 0-915408),* P.O. Box 30340, St Paul, MN 55175; Orders to: P.O. Box 30340, Dept. BP, St. Paul, MN 55175.

Allyn, *(Allyn & Bacon, Inc.; 0-205),* 470 Atlantic Ave., Boston, MA 02210 Tel 617-482-9220; Orders to: College Division, Rockleigh, NJ 07647.

Alma Hist Soc, *(Alma Historical Society; 0-9604684),* P.O. Box 87, Alma, WI 54610.

Almanac Pr, *(Almanac-Press; 0-935090),* P.O. Box 480264, Los Angeles, CA 90048; Dist. by: Maxim's Books, P.O. Box 480451, Los Angeles, CA 90048.

Almar, *(Almar Press; 0-930256),* 4105 Marietta Dr., Binghamton, NY 13903 Tel 607-722-6251.

Almo Pubns, *(Almo Pubns.; 0-89705),* 1312 N. La Brea, Hollywood, CA 90028.

Aloray, *(Aloray Inc.; 0-913690),* 175 W. Carver St., Huntington, NY 11743 Tel 516-549-5746.

Alperin
See Junius Inc

Alpert, *(Alpert, Burt; 0-9600642),* 877 26th Ave., San Francisco, CA 94121.

Alpha Centurion, *(Alpha Centurion Publishing Co.),* P.O. Box 6117, St Petersburg, FL 33706; Moved, Left No Forwarding Address.

Alpha IN, *(Alpha Pubns.; 0-937400),* P.O. Box 655, Winona Lake, IN 46590.

Alpha Iota, *(Alpha Iota of Pi Lambda Theta, Pubns.; 0-914522),* 2260 N. Orange Grove Ave., Pomona, CA 91767 Tel 714-626-5065.

Alpha Omega, *(Alpha Omega Publishing Co.; 0-931608),* P.O. Box 4130, Medford, OR 97501 Tel 503-826-7302.

Alpha Pr, *(Alpha Press; 0-914620),* 3574 Clinton St., Gardenville, NY 14224 Tel 716-668-3019.

Alpha Pr Wis, *(Alpha Press; 0-914416),* 10721 W. Capitol Dr., Suite 201, Milwaukee, WI 53222; Moved, Left No Forwarding Address.

Alpha Printing, *(Alpha Printing Ltd.; 0-937268),* 6301-B Central Ave., N.W., Albuquerque, NM 87105.

Alpha Pubns, *(Alpha Pubns., Inc.; 0-912404),* 1079 De Kalb Pike, Blue Bell, PA 19422 Tel 215-277-6342.

Alphabet Pr, *(Alphabet Press; 0-9602690),* P.O. Box 6180, Boston, MA 02209 Tel 617-323-7942.

Alphabet Quincy, *(Alphabet Press; 0-940032),* Box 56, N. Quincy Sta., Boston, MA 02171 Tel 617-328-7170.

Alphapress, *(Alphapress),* 32 Colony Rd., Lexington, MA 02173.

Alphaventure, *(Alphaventure; 0-915934),* 445 Park Ave., New York, NY 10022 Tel 212-421-1114.

Alpine Bk Co, *(Alpine Book Co., Inc.; 0-933516),* 527 Madison Ave., New York, NY 10022.

Alpine Ent, *(Alpine Enterprises),* P. O. Box 766, Dearborn, MI 48121.

Alpine Fine Arts, *(Alpine Fine Arts Collection, Ltd.; 0-933516),* 527 Madison Ave., New York, NY 10022; Dist. by: Hippocrene Books Inc., 171 Madison Ave., New York, NY 10016.

Alpine Guild, *(Alpine Guild; 0-931712),* 508 N. Oak Park Ave., Oak Park, IL 60302; Orders to: P.O. Box 183, Oak Park, IL 60303.

Alpine Pubns, *(Alpine Pubns.; 0-931866),* 1901 S. Garfield, Loveland, CO 80537 Tel 303-667-2017.

Alpine-Tahoe, *(Alpine-Tahoe Press; 0-9604574),* Box 1484, Tahoe City, CA 95730 Tel 916-583-3273.

Alta Napa, *(Alta Napa Press),* P.O. Box 407, Calistoga, CA 94515 Tel 707-942-6821.

Altair Pr, *(Altair Press; 0-934768),* P.O. Box 1286, Boulder, CO 80302 Tel 303-494-6405.

Altair Pub Co, *(Altair Publishing Co.; 0-9604976),* 217 S. Louis St., Mt. Prospect, IL 60056.

Alternate Energy, *(Alternate Energy Publishing Co.; 0-930086),* P.O. Box 26507, Albuquerque, NM 87125 Tel 505-873-2084.

Alternatives, *(Alternatives; 0-914966),* 4274 Oaklawn Dr., Jackson, MS 39206 Tel 601-366-8468.

Alto Pr, *(Alto Press),* P.O. Box 973, Nogales, AZ 85621 Tel 602-281-1568.

Alumnae
See Coun Career Plan

Alyson Pubns, *(Alyson Pubns., Inc.; 0-932870),* 75 Kneeland St., No. 309, Boston, MA 02111 Tel 617-542-5679.

Am Acad Advert, *(American Academy of Advertising; 0-931030),* Dept. of Advertising, 119 Gregory Hall, Univ. of Illinois, Urbana, IL 61801 Tel 217-333-1602.

Am Acad Asian, *(American Academy of Asian Studies, Inc.),* 134-140 Church St., San Francisco, CA 94114 Tel 415-863-4168.

Am Acad Inst Arts, *(American Academy & Institute of Arts & Letters; 0-915974),* 633 W. 155th St., New York, NY 10032 Tel 212-368-5900.

Am Acad Pol Soc Sci, *(American Academy of Political & Social Science; 0-87761),* 3937 Chestnut St., Philadelphia, PA 19104 Tel 215-386-4594.

Am Acad Rel, *(Florida State Univ., American Academy of Religion; 0-88420),* 107 W. Gaines St., Tallahassee, FL 32306.

Am Anthro Assn, *(American Anthropological Assn.),* Pubns. Dept., 1703 New Hampshire Ave., N.W., Washington, DC 20009 Tel 202-232-8800.

Am Antiquarian, *(American Antiquarian Society; 0-912296),* 185 Salisbury St., Worcester, MA 01609 Tel 617-755-5221; Dist. by: Univ. Press of Virginia, P.O. Box 3608, University Sta., Charlottesville, VA 22903.

Am Art Ent, *(American Art Enterprises; 0-89784),* c/o Capital Distributing Co., Charlton Bldg., Derby, CT 06418 Tel 203-735-3381.

Am Assembly, *(American Assembly),* Columbia University, New York, NY 10027.

Am Assn Blood, *(American Assn. of Blood Banks; 0-914404),* 1828 "L" St., N. W., Suite 608, Washington, DC 20036.

Am Assn Cereal Chem, *(American Assn. of Cereal Chemists; 0-913250),* 3340 Pilot Knob Rd., St. Paul, MN 55121 Tel 612-454-7250.

Am Assn Clinical Chem, *(American Assn. for Clinical Chemistry; 0-915274),* 1725 K St., N.W., Washington, DC 20006.

Am Assn Coll Pharm, *(American Assn. of Colleges of Pharmacy; 0-937526),* 4630 Montgomery Ave., Suite 201, Bethesda, MD 20014 Tel 301-654-9060.

Am Assn Comm Jr Coll, *(American Assn. of Community & Junior Colleges; 0-87117),* 1 Dupont Circle, N.W., Washington, DC 20036 Tel 202-293-7050.

Am Assn Conn
See Am Assn Comm Jr Coll

Am Assn Cost Engineers, *(American Assn. of Cost Engineers),* 308 Monogahela Bldg., Morgantown, WV 26505.

Am Assn Mental, *(American Assn. on Mental Deficiency),* 5101 Wisconsin Ave., N.W., Washington, DC 20016 Tel 202-686-5400.

Am Assn Sch Admin, *(American Assn. of School Administrators),* 1801 N. Moore St., Arlington, VA 22209 Tel 703-528-0700.

Am Assn Soc Direct, *(American Assn. of Social Directories; 0-89077),* 10889 Wilshire Blvd., Los Angeles, CA 90024; Moved, Left No Forwarding Address.

Am Assn Zoological, *(American Assn. of Zoological Parks & Aquariums),* Oglebay Park, Wheeling, WV 26003 Tel 304-242-2160.

Am Astronaut, *(American Astronautical Society; 0-87703),* Orders to: Univelt, Inc., P.O. Box 28130, San Diego, CA 92128 Tel 714-746-4005.

Am Atheist, *(American Atheist Press; 0-911826),* P.O. Box 2117, Austin, TX 78768 Tel 512-458-1244.

Am Bankers, *(American Bankers Assn.; 0-89982),* 1120 Connecticut Ave. N. W., Washington, DC 20036 Tel 202-467-6660.

Am Baptist, *(American Baptist Historical Society; 0-910056),* 1106 S. Goodman St., Rochester, NY 14620 Tel 716-473-1740.

Am Bar Foun, *(American Bar Foundation; 0-910058; 0-910059),* 1155 E. 60th St., Chicago, IL 60637 Tel 312-667-4700.

Am Bible, *(American Bible Society; 0-8267),* 1865 Broadway, New York, NY 10023 Tel 212-581-7400.

Am Biog Ctr, *(American Biographical Center; 0-9601168),* P.O. Box 473, Williamsburg, VA 23185 Tel 804-725 2234.

Am Biog Inst, *(American Biographical Institute; 0-934544),* 205 W. Martin St., P.O. Box 226, Raleigh, NC 27602 Tel 919-832-2001.

Am Bk Prices, *(American Book Prices Current, Bancroft-Parkman, Inc.; 0-914022),* 121 E. 78th St., New York, NY 10021 Tel 212-737-2715.

Am Blake Found, *(American Blake Foundation; 0-913130),* Dept. of English, Memphis State Univ., Memphis, TN 38152.

Am Blood Comm, *(American Blood Commission; 0-935498),* 1901 N. Fort Myer Dr., Suite 300, Arlington, VA 22209 Tel 703-522-8414.

AM Books CA, *(AM Books; 0-935190),* 13415 Ventura Blvd., Sherman Oaks, CA 91423 Tel 213-995-3329.

Am Bur Metal, *(American Bureau of Metal Statistics; 0-910064),* 420 Lexington Ave., Rm. 420, New York, NY 10017 Tel 212-867-9450.

Am Busn Comm Assn, *(American Business Communication Assn.; 0-931874),* 911 S. Sixth St., Univ. of Illinois, Champaign, IL 61820 Tel 217-333-0458.

Am Busn Consult, *(American Business Consultants, Inc.; 0-937152),* 1540 Nuthatch Lane, Sunnyvale, CA 94087 Tel 408-732-8931.

Am Camping, *(American Camping Assn.; 0-87603),* Bradford Woods, Martinsville, IN 46151 Tel 317-342-8456.

Am Canadian, *(American-Canadian Pubs., Inc.; 0-913844),* Drawer 2078, Portales, NM 88130 Tel 505-356-4082.

Am Canal & Transport, *(American Canal & Transportation Center; 0-933788),* 809 Rathton Rd., York, PA 17403 Tel 717-843-4035.

Am Cancer Minn, *(American Cancer Society, Minnesota Division, Inc.),* 2750 Park Ave., Minneapolis, MN 55407 Tel 612-871-2111.

Am Cath Philo, *(American Catholic Philosophical Assn.; 0-918090),* c/o Catholic Univ. of America, Washington, DC 20064 Tel 202-635-5518.

Am Cath Pr, *(American Catholic Press; 0-915866),* 1223 Rossell Ave., Oak Park, IL 60302 Tel 312-386-1366.

Am Ceramic, *(American Ceramic Society, Inc; 0-916094),* 65 Ceramic Dr., Columbus, OH 43214 Tel 614-268-8645.

Am Chemical, *(American Chemical Society; 0-8412),* 1155 16th St., N.W., Washington, DC 20036 Tel 202-872-4600.

Am Chiro Acad, *(American Chiropractic Academic Press; 0-936948),* 6716 N.W. 16th, Suite 129, Oklahoma City, OK 73127.

Am Christian, *(American Christian Press, The Way International; 0-910068),* P.O. Box 328, New Knoxville, OH 45871 Tel 419-753-2523.

Am Classical Coll Pr, *(American Classical College Press; 0-913314; 0-89266),* P.O. Box 4526, Albuquerque, NM 87106 Tel 505-843-7749.

Am Coll Apothecaries, *(American College of Apothecaries; 0-934322),* 874 Union Ave., Memphis, TN 38163.

Am Coll Heraldry, *(American College of Heraldry, Inc., The; 0-9605668),* P.O. Box CG, University, AL 35486.

Am Coll Obstetric, *(American College of Obstetricians & Gynecologists),* 1 E. Wacker Dr., Suite 270, Chicago, IL 60601.

Am Coll Testing, *(American College Testing Program; 0-937734),* 2201 N. Dodge St., P. O. Box 168, Iowa City, IA 52243 Tel 319-356-3701.

Am Conf Govt Indus Hygienist, *(American Conference of Governmental Industrial Hygienists),* P.O. Box 1937, Cincinnati, OH 45201 Tel 513-825-0312.

Am Consul Eng, *(American Consulting Engineers Council; 0-910090),* 1015 15th St., N.W., Washington, DC 20005.

Am Correctional, *(American Correctional Assn.),* 4321 Hartwick Rd., Suite L-208, College Park, MD 20740 Tel 301-699-7620.

Am Council Arts, *(American Council for the Arts; 0-915400),* 570 Seventh Ave., New York, NY 10018 Tel 212-354-6655.

Am Craft, *(American Craft Council; 0-88321),* 22 W. 55th St., New York, NY 10019 Tel 212-397-0600.

Am Crafts
See Am Craft

Am Deaf & Rehab, *(American Deafness & Rehabilitation Association; 0-914494),* 814 Thayer Ave., Silver Spring, MD 20910 Tel 301-589-0880.

Am Dental, *(American Dental Assn.; 0-910074),* Order Section , 211 E. Chicago Ave., Chicago, IL 60611 Tel 312-440-2892.

Am Dynamics, *(American Dynamics Corp.; 0-9603416),* 111 E. Wicker Dr., Suite 400, Chicago, IL 60601.

Am Educ Res, *(American Educational Research Assn.; 0-935302),* 1230 17th St., N.W., Washington, DC 20036 Tel 202-223-9485.

Am Educ Res, *(American Educational Research Assn.; 0-935302),* 1230 17th St. N.W., Washington, DC 20036.

Am Elsevier, *(American Elsevier Publishing Co., Inc.; 0-444),* Orders to: 52 Vanderbilt Ave., New York, NY 10017 Tel 212-867-9040; Name Changed to Elsevier-North Holland Publishing Co.

Am Ent FL, *(American Enterprise Publishing, Inc.; 0-9603192),* 3101 Maguire Blvd., Suite 259, Orlando, FL 32803 Tel 305-894-7501.

Am Enterprise, *(American Enterprise Institute for Public Policy Research; 0-8447),* 1150 17th St., N.W., Washington, DC 20036 Tel 202-862-5800.

Am Entom Inst, *(American Entomological Institute),* 5950 Warren Rd., Ann Arbor, MI 48105 Tel 313-662-8476.

Am Ethnic, *(American Ethnic Press; 0-9605766),* P.O. Box 1994, Grand Central Sta., New York, NY 10163.

Am Faculty Pr, *(American Faculty Press, Inc.; 0-912834),* 44 Lake Shore Dr., Rockaway, NJ 07866 Tel 201-627-2727.

Am Family, *(American Family Communiversity Press; 0-910574),* 109 N. Dearborn St., Suite 405, Chicago, IL 60602 Tel 312-236-3946.

Am Fed Arts, *(American Federation of Arts; 0-917418),* 41 E. 65th St., New York, NY 10021 Tel 212-988-7700.

Am Forestry, *(American Forestry Assn., Book Edit Dept.; 0-935050),* 1319 18th St., N.W., Washington, DC 20036 Tel 202-467-5810.

Am Foun Blind, *(American Foundation for the Blind; 0-89128),* 15 W. 16th St., New York, NY 10011 Tel 212-620-2151.

Am Fr Serv Comm, *(American Friends Service Committee; 0-910082),* 1501 Cherry St., Philadelphia, PA 19102 Tel 215-241-7000.

Am Geol, *(American Geological Institute; 0-913312),* One Skyline Place, 5205 Leesburg Pike, Falls Church, VA 22041 Tel 703-379-2480.

Am Geophysical, *(American Geophysical Union; 0-87590),* 2000 Florida Ave. N.W., Washington, DC 20009 Tel 202-462-6903.

Am Guidance, *(American Guidance Service, Inc; 0-913476),* Publishers' Bldg., Circle Pines, MN 55014 Tel 612-786-4343.

Am Guide Pubns, *(American Guide Pubns.; 0-932948),* P.O. Box 1000, Glendale, CA 91209.

Am Heart, *(American Heart Assn., Inc.; 0-87493),* 7320 Greenville Ave., Dallas, TX 75231 Tel 214-750-5465.

Am Heritage, *(American Heritage Publishing Co.; 0-8281),* 10 Rockefeller Plaza, New York, NY 10020 Tel 212-399-8900.

Am Hist Assn, *(American Historical Assn.; 0-87229),* 400 "A" St., S. E., Washington, DC 20003 Tel 202-544-2422.

Am Hist Pr, *(American History Press; 0-89002),* Div. of Northwoods Press, P.O. Box 249, Stafford, VA 22554.

Am Hist Pubs, *(American Historical Pubs., Inc.; 0-937862),* 177 E. Riverside, Newport Beach, CA 92663.

Am Hist Res, *(American History Research Associates; 0-910086),* P.O. Box 140, Brookeville, MD 20729 Tel 301-774-3573.

Am Hist Soc Ger, *(American Historical Society of Germans from Russia; 0-914222),* 631 "D" St., Lincoln, NE 68502 Tel 402-477-4524.

Am Hospital, *(American Hospital Assn.; 0-87258),* 840 N. Lake Shore Dr., Chicago, IL 60611 Tel 312-280-6235; Orders to: P.O. Box 96003, Chicago, IL 60690 Tel 312-280-6000.

Am Hungarian Foun, *(American Hungarian Foundation),* 177 Somerset St., New Brunswick, NJ 08903 Tel 201-846-5777.

Am Ind Mus
See Mus Am Ind

Am Indian Pubs, *(American Indian Pubs., Inc.; 0-937862),* 177 F Riverside Dr., Newport Beach, CA 92663.

Am Indus Arts, *(American Industrial Arts Assn., Inc.),* 1201 Sixteenth St., N.W., Rm 230, Washington, DC 20036 Tel 202-833-4211.

Am Inst Arch, *(American Institute of Architects; 0-913962),* 1735 New York Ave., N.W., Washington, DC 20006 Tel 202-626-7474.

Am Inst Chem Eng, *(American Institute of Chemical Engineers; 0-8169),* 345 E. 47th St., New York, NY 10017 Tel 212-752-6800.

Am Inst Cons Eng
See Am Consul Eng

Am Inst Cooperation, *(American Institute of Cooperation; 0-938868),* 1800 Massachusetts Ave., N. W., Suite 508, Washington, DC 20036 Tel 202-296-6825.

Am Inst CPA, *(American Institute of Certified Public Accountants; 0-87051),* 1211 Avenue of the Americas, New York, NY 10036 Tel 212-575-6200.

Am Inst Disc, *(American Institute of Discussion; 0-910092),* P.O. Box 103, Oklahoma City, OK 73101 Tel 405-235-9681.

Am Inst Indus Eng, *(American Institute of Industrial Engineers; 0-89806),* 25 Technology Park-Atlanta, Norcross, GA 30092 Tel 404-449-0460.

Am Inst Ital Stud, *(American Institute of Italian Studies; 0-916322),* Villa Walsh, Morristown, NJ 07960.

Am Inst Marxist, *(American Institute for Marxist Studies; 0-89977),* 20 E. 30th St., New York, NY 10016 Tel 212-689-4530.

Am Inst Pharmacy, *(American Institute of the History of Pharmacy; 0-931292),* Pharmacy Bldg., Univ. of Wisconsin, Madison, WI 53706 Tel 608-262-5378; c/o Ex. Sec. Roy Bowers, Rutgers College of Pharmacy, Box 789, Piscataway, NJ 08854.

Am Inst Physics, *(American Institute of Physics; 0-88318),* 335 E. 45th St., New York, NY 10017 Tel 212-661-9404.

Am Inst Psych, *(American Institute for Psychological Research, The; 0-89920),* 614 Indian School Rd. N.W., Albuquerque, NM 87102 Tel 505-843-7749.

Am Inst Real Estate Appraisers, *(American Institute of Real Estate Appraisers; 0-911780),* 430 N. Michigan Ave., Chicago, IL 60611 Tel 312-440-8171; Dist. by: Ballinger Pub. Co., 17 Dunster St., Cambridge, MA 02138 Tel 617-492-0670.

Am Inst Res, *(American Institutes for Research; 0-89785),* P.O. Box 1113, Palo Alto, CA 94302.

Am Inst Writing Res, *(American Institute for Writing Research, Corp.; 0-917944),* Box 2129, Grand Central Sta., New York, NY 10163 Tel 212-266-2897.

Am Iris, *(American Iris Society; 0-9601242),* 6518 Beachy Ave., Wichita, KS 67206 Tel 316-686-8734; Orders to: 226 E. 20th St., Tulsa, OK 74119 Tel 918-582-4932.

Am Israel Numismatic, *(American Israel Numismatic Assn.; 0-9601658),* P.O. Box 370, Boca Raton, FL 33432; Moved, Left No Forwarding Address.

Am Italian, *(American Italian Historical Assn., Inc.),* 29 Roxbury Place, Glen Rock, NJ 07452.

Am Jewish Comm, *(American Jewish Committee; 0-87495),* 165 E. 56th St., New York, NY 10022 Tel 212-751-4000.

Am Jewish Hist Soc, *(American Jewish Historical Society; 0-911934),* 2 Thornton Rd., Waltham, MA 02154 Tel 617-891-8110.

Am Journal Nurse, *(American Journal of Nursing Co.),* 10 Columbus Circle, New York, NY 10019 Tel 212-582-8820.

Am Judicature, *(American Judicature Society),* 200 W. Monroe, Suite 1606, Chicago, IL 60606 Tel 312-558-6900.

Am Lang Acad, *(American Language Academy; 0-934270),* c/o Catholic Univ. of America, Marist Bldg., Washington, DC 20064.

Am Law Inst, *(American Law Institute; 0-8318),* 4025 Chestnut St., Philadelphia, PA 19104 Tel 215-243-1600.

Am Lawn Bowlers, *(American Lawn Bowlers' Guide; 0-9600068),* P.O. Box 824, Laguna Beach, CA 92652 Tel 714-494-2606.

Am Lib Pub Co, *(American Library Publishing Co., Inc.; 0-87729),* 275 Central Park, W., New York, NY 10024 Tel 212-787-0766.

Am Librarians, *(American Librarians' Agency; 0-914240),* P. O. Box 5764, New York, NY 10017.

Am Life Foun, *(American Life Foundation & Study Institute; 0-89257),* P.O. Box 349, Watkins Glen, NY 14891 Tel 607-535-4737.

Am Lung Assn, *(American Lung Assn.; 0-915116),* 1740 Broadway, New York, NY 10019.

Am Malacologists, *(American Malacologists, Inc.; 0-915826),* Box 2255, Melbourne, FL 32901 Tel 305-725-2260.

Am Map, *(American Map Co., Inc.; 0-8416),* 1926 Broadway, New York, NY 10023 Tel 212-595-6582.

Am Math, *(American Mathematical Society; 0-8218),* P.O. Box 6248, Providence, RI 02940 Tel 401-272-9500; Orders to: P.O. Box 1571, Annex Sta., Providence, RI 02901.

Am Media, *(American Media; 0-912986)*, 790 Hampshire Rd., Suite H, Westlake Village, CA 91361 Tel 213-889-1231.

Am Metal Mkt, *(American Metal Market/Metalworking News; 0-910094)*, Dist. by: Fairchild Pubns., Inc., 7 E. 12th St., New York, NY 10003.

Am Meteorite, *(American Meteorite Laboratory; 0-910096)*, P.O. Box 2098, Denver, CO 80201 Tel 303-428-1371.

Am Metric, *(American Metric Journal)*, P.O. Box 847, Tarzana, CA 91356 Tel 805-484-5787.

Am Mgmt, *(American Management Assn., Inc.; 0-8144)*, 135 W. 50th St., New York, NY 10020 Tel 212-586-8100.

Am Mideast, *(American Mideast Research)*, 55 Sutter, Suite 712, San Francisco, CA 94104 Tel 415-921-5002.

Am Mizrachi Women, *(American Mizrachi Women's Publishing Co.)*, 615 Nye Ave., Irvington, NJ 07111.

Am Mktg, *(American Marketing Assn.; 0-87757)*, 222 S. Riverside Plaza, Chicago, IL 60606 Tel 312-648-0536.

Am Mus Natl Hist, *(American Museum of Natural History; 0-913424)*, Central Park W. at 79th St., New York, NY 10024 Tel 212-873-1498.

Am Mutuality, *(American Mutuality Foundation; 0-938844)*, 9428 S. Western Ave., Los Angeles, CA 90047.

Am Natl, *(American National Metric Council; 0-916148)*, 1625 Massachusetts Ave., N. W., Washington, DC 20036 Tel 202-232-4545.

Am Natl Heritage, *(American National Heritage Assn.; 0-918002)*, P.O. Box 9340, Alexandria, VA 22304 Tel 703-370-3750.

Am Natl Pub, *(American National Publishing Co.; 0-913514)*, 237 Plymouth Bldg., 12 S. Sixth Street, Minneapolis, MN 55402 Tel 612-338-3362. *Imprints:* Shannon (Shannon); Yellow Bird (Yellow Bird).

Am New Church Sunday, *(American New Church Sunday School Assn.; 0-917426)*, 48 Highland St., Sharon, MA 02067 Tel 617-784-5041; Dist. by: Swedenborg Library, 79 Newbury St., Boston, MA 02116.

Am Newspaper, *(American Newspaper Pubs. Foundation Assn.)*, P.O. Box 17407, Dulles International Airport, Washington, DC 20041 Tel 703-620-9500.

Am Nuclear Soc, *(American Nuclear Society; 0-89448)*, 555 N. Kensington Ave., La Grange Park, IL 60525 Tel 312-352-6611.

Am Numismatic, *(American Numismatic Society; 0-89722)*, Broadway at 155th St., New York, NY 10032 Tel 212-234-3130.

Am Orient Soc, *(American Oriental Society)*, 329 Sterling Memorial Library, Yale Sta., New Haven, CT 06520 Tel 203-436-1040.

Am Personnel, *(American Personnel & Guidance Assn.)*, 2 Skyline Place, Suite 400, 5203 Leeburg Pike, Falls Church, VA 22041 Tel 703-820-4700.

Am Petroleum, *(American Petroleum Institute Pubns.; 0-89364)*, 2101 "L" St., N.W., Washington, DC 20037 Tel 202-833-5790.

Am Pharm Assn, *(American Pharmaceutical Assn.; 0-917330)*, 2215 Constitution Ave., N.W., Washington, DC 20037 Tel 202-628-4410.

Am Phil Assn, *(American Philological Assn.)*, ; Publisher Abbreviation Without Addresses Are for Titles That Are Out of Print. These Are Obsolete Abbreviations.

Am Philatelic, *(American Philatelic Society; 0-933580)*, P.O. Box 800, State College, PA 16801 Tel 814-237-3803.

Am Philos, *(American Philosophical Society; 0-87169)*, 104 S. Fifth St., Philadelphia, PA 19106 Tel 215-627-0706.

Am Phys Therapy Assn, *(American Physical Therapy Assn.; 0-912452)*, 1156 15th St., N.W., Washington, DC 20005 Tel 202-466-2070.

Am Phytopathol Soc, *(American Phytopathological Society; 0-89054)*, 3340 Pilot Knob Rd., St. Paul, MN 55121 Tel 612-454-7250.

Am Pine Barrens, *(American Pine Barrens Pub. Co.; 0-937438)*, P.O. Box 22820, 1400 Washington Ave., Albany, NY 12222.

Am Poetry Pr, *(American Poetry Press; 0-933486)*, P. O. Box 634, Claymont, DE 19703 Tel 302-366-1423; 4210 Lankershim Blvd., North Hollywood, CA 91602 Tel 213-980-9891.

Am Political, *(American Political Science Assn.; 0-915654)*, 1527 New Hampshire Ave., N.W., Washington, DC 20036 Tel 202-483-2512.

Am Powder Metal, *(American Powder Metallurgy Institute)*, 105 College Road E., Princeton, NJ 08540.

Am Printing Hse, *(American Printing House for the Blind)*, 1839 Frankfort Ave., Box 6085, Louisville, KY 40206 Tel 502-895-2405.

Am Prod & Inventory, *(American Production & Inventory Control Society; 0-935406)*, 2600 Virginia Ave., Suite 504, Washington, DC 20037.

Am Psychiatric, *(American Psychiatric Assn.; 0-89042)*, Pubn. Sales, 1700 18th St., N.W., Washington, DC 20009 Tel 202-797-4911.

Am Psychol, *(American Psychological Assn.; 0-912704)*, 1200 17th St., N.W., Washington, DC 20036 Tel 202-833-7600.

Am Pub, *(American Pub.; 0-916036)*, P.O. Box 102, Oxford, IN 47971.

Am Pub Co WI, *(American Publishing Company)*, 2909 Syene Rd., Madison, WI 53713 Tel 608-271-6544.

Am Pub Health, *(American Public Health Assn. Pubns.; 0-87553)*, 1015 15th St. N.W., Washington, DC 20005 Tel 202-789-5600.

Am Pub Welfare, *(American Public Welfare Assn.; 0-910106)*, 1125 15th St., N. W., Washington, DC 20005 Tel 202-293-7550.

Am Public Works, *(American Public Works Assn.; 0-917084)*, 1313 E. 60th St., Chicago, IL 60637 Tel 312-947-2541.

Am Quality, *(American Quality Books; 0-936956)*, 12415 E. DeSmet, No. 35, Spokane, WA 99216 Tel 509-928-0061.

Am Radio, *(American Radio Relay League, Inc.; 0-87259)*, 225 Main St., Newington, CT 06111 Tel 203-666-1541.

Am Record, *(American Record Collectors Exchange; 0-914652)*, P.O. Box 1377, F.D.R. Sta., New York, NY 10022 Tel 212-688-8426.

Am Register, *(American Register of Exporters & Importers)*, 1 Penn Plaza, New York, NY 10001 Tel 212-695-0500.

Am Register
See Thomas Intl Pub

Am Repr-Rivercity Pr, *(American Reprint Co./Rivercity Press; 0-89190)*, P.O. Box 1200, Mattituck, NY 11952 Tel 516-298-5100; Dist. by: Amereon Ltd., P.O. Box 1200, Mattituck, NY 11952 Tel 516-298-5100.

Am Reprints, *(American Reprints Co.; 0-915706)*, 111 West Dent, Ironton, MO 63650.

Am Res Ctr Egypt, *(American Research Center in Egypt, The; 0-936770)*, c/o Columbia University, 1117 International Affairs Bldg., New York, NY 10027.

Am Res Pr, *(American Research Press; 0-937616)*, 5153 Elkmont, Rancho Palos Verdes, CA 90274.

Am Romanian, *(American Romanian Academy of Arts & Sciences)*, 265 Lee St., Apt. 101, Oakland, CA 94610.

Am Samizdat, *(American Samizdat; 0-935500)*, 724 Tenth Ave., Apt. 4A, New York, NY 10019 Tel 212-586-5780.

Am Scandinavian, *(American-Scandinavian Foundation; 0-89067)*, 127 E. 73rd St., New York, NY 10021 Tel 212-879-9779; Orders to: Heritage Resource Center, P.O. Box 26305, Minneapolis, MN 55426.

Am Sch Astrol, *(American School of Astrology)*, 642 Eagle Rock Ave., West Orange, NJ 07052 Tel 201-731-2255.

Am Sch Athens, *(American School of Classical Studies at Athens; 0-87661)*, c/o Institute for Advanced Study, Princeton, NJ 08540 Tel 609-734-8387.

Am Sch Health, *(American School Health Assn.; 0-917160)*, P.O. Box 708, Kent, OH 44240 Tel 216-678-1601.

Am Sci & Eng, *(American Science & Engineering, Inc.; 0-8339)*, 75 Cambridge Parkway, Cambridge, MA 02142.

Am Sciences Pr, *(American Sciences Press, Inc.; 0-935950)*, P.O. Box 21161, Columbus, OH 43221.

Am Showcase, *(American Showcase, Inc.; 0-931144)*, 724 Fifth Ave., New York, NY 10019 Tel 212-245-0981; Dist. by: Mayflower Books, 575 Lexington Ave., New York, NY 10022; Dist. by: Fleetbooks, S.A., 100 Park Ave., New York, NY 10017.

Am Soc Agron, *(American Society of Agronomy; 0-89118)*, 677 S. Segoe Rd., Madison, WI 53711 Tel 608-274-1212.

Am Soc Appraisers, *(American Society of Appraisers; 0-937828)*, Dulles International Airport, P.O. Box 17265, Washington, DC 20041 Tel 703-620-3838.

Am Soc Cine, *(American Society of Cinematographers)*, P.O. Box 2230, Hollywood, CA 90028.

Am Soc Civil Eng, *(American Society of Civil Engineers; 0-87262)*, 345 E. 47th St., New York, NY 10017 Tel 212-644-7518.

Am Soc Clinical, *(American Society of Clinical Pathologists; 0-89189)*, Educational Products Division, 2100 W. Harrison St., Chicago, IL 60612 Tel 312-738-1336.

Am Soc Hosp Pharm, *(American Society of Hospital Pharmacists; 0-930530)*, 4630 Montgomery Ave., Washington, DC 20014 Tel 301-657-3000.

Am Soc Info Sci, *(American Society for Information Science; 0-87715)*, 1155 16th St., N.W., Suite 215, Washington, DC 20036 Tel 202-659-3644; Moved, Left No Forwarding Address.

Am Soc Microbio, *(American Society for Microbiology; 0-914826)*, 1913 "I" St., N.W., Washington, DC 20006 Tel 202-833-9680.

Am Soc REC, *(American Society of Real Estate Counselors)*, 430 N. Michigan Ave., Chicago, IL 60611 Tel 312-440-8091.

Am Spelling, *(American Spelling Headquarters; 0-935276)*, 2120 Jimmy Durante Dr., Del Mar, CA 92014.

Am Sports Sales, *(American Sports Sales, Inc.; 0-912354)*, P.O. Box 160, Orangeburg, NY 10962 Tel 914-359-5300.

Am Stud Pr, *(American Studies Press, Inc.; 0-934996)*, 13511 Palmwood Lane, Tampa, FL 33624 Tel 813-961-7200.

Am Technical, *(American Technical Pubs., Inc.; 0-8269)*, 5608 Stony Island Ave., Chicago, IL 60637 Tel 800-621-2404.

Am Theatre Assoc, *(American Theatre Assn.)*, 1000 Vermont Ave., N.W., Washington, DC 20005 Tel 202-628-4634.

Am Trust Pubns, *(American Trust Pubns.; 0-89259)*, 7216 S. Madison Ave., Suite S, Indianapolis, IN 46227 Tel 317-788-4726.

Am U Beirut *Imprint of* **Syracuse U Pr**

Am U Field, *(American Universities Field Staff, Inc.; 0-910116; 0-88333)*, P.O. Box 150, Hanover, NH 03755 Tel 603-643-2110.

Am Univ Artforms, *(American Universal Artforms Corp.; 0-913632)*, P.O. Box 4574, Austin, TX 78765 Tel 512-451-3588.

Am Viewpoint
See Ethics Res Ctr

Am Visual, *(American Visual Aid Books)*, P.O. Box 28718, Sacramento, CA 95828.

Am Voc Assn, *(American Vocational Assn., Inc.; 0-89514)*, 2020 N. 14th St., Arlington, VA 22201.

Am Water Wks Assn, *(American Water Works Assn.; 0-89867)*, 6666 W. Quincy Ave., Denver, CO 80235 Tel 303-794-7711.

Am Welding, *(American Welding Society; 0-87171)*, 2501 N. W. Seventh St., Miami, FL 33125 Tel 305-642-7090.

Am West, *(American West Publishing Co.)*, ; Publisher Abbreviation Without Addresses Are for Titles That Are Out of Print. These Are Obsolete Abbreviations. Publisher Was Aquired by Crown.

Am Wine, *(American Wine Society; 0-930884)*, 4218 Rosewold, Royal Oak, MI 48073.

AMA, *(American Medical Association; 0-89970)*, 535 N. Dearborn St., Chicago, IL 60610 Tel 312-751-6000.

Amarta Pr, *(Amarta Press; 0-935100)*, P.O. Box 202, West Franklin, NH 03235 Tel 603-934-2420.

Amaryllis Pr, *(Amaryllis Press; 0-89275)*, 16 E. 53rd St., New York, NY 10022 Tel 212-752-2079; Name Formerly Benjamin Blom.

Amata Graphics, *(Amata Graphics; 0-931224)*, 3333 N. E. 18th St., Portland, OR 97212 Tel 503-282-0750.

Amazon Pr, *(Amazon Press; 0-931458)*, 1101 Keeler Ave., Berkeley, CA 94708; Dist. by: Bookpeople, 2940 Seventh St., Berkeley, CA 94710 Tel 415-549-3033.

Ambassador
See Gard & Co

Ambassador Pubns, *(Ambassador Pubns.)*, P.O. Box 4206, Clearwater, FL 33518.

Amber Crest, (Amber Crest Books, Inc.), Div. of New World Communications, 7060 Hollywood Blvd., Suite 503, Los Angeles, CA 90028 Tel 213-461-8193.

Amber Pub, (Amber Publishing Corp.; 0-916788), 21 Hudson St., New York, NY 10013 Tel 212-431-9675.

Ambiente Environ, (Ambiente Environmental Concerns; 0-937302), P.O. Box 13622, San Antonio, TX 78213 Tel 512-344-0730.

AmCen Imprint of **Hill & Wang**

AMCO Intl, (AMCO International, Inc.; 0-9602406), P.O. Box 347, Staten Island, NY 10301 Tel 518-356-3967.

AMDG Pr Imprint of **Sugden**

Ameco, (Ameco Publishing Corp.; 0-912146), 275 Hillside Ave., Williston Park, NY 11596 Tel 516-741-5030.

Amer Bar Assn, (American Bar Assn.; 0-89707), 1155 E. 60th St., Chicago, IL 60637 Tel 312-947-3607.

Amereon Ltd, (Amereon Ltd.; 0-88411), P.O. Box 1200, Mattituck, NY 11952 Tel 516-298-5100.

American Ent Pubns, (American Enterprise Pubns.), Box 6690 R.D.6, Mercer, PA 16137 Tel 412-748-3726.

American Hispanist, (American Hispanist, Inc.; 0-89217), 107 S. College, Bloomington, IN 47401 Tel 812-334-3008.

American Music, (American Music Conference; 0-918196), Public Relations Board, Inc., 150 E. Huron St., Chicago, IL 60611 Tel 312-266-7200; c/o American Music Conference, 1000 Skokie Blvd., Wilmette, IL 60091 Tel 312-251-1600.

American Numismatic, (American Numismatic Assn.; 0-89637), 818 North Cascade, Colorado Springs, CO 80903 Tel 303-473-9142.

American Pr, (American Press; 0-89641), 520 Commonwealth Ave., No. 416, Boston, MA 02215 Tel 617-247-0022.

American Scientist, (American Scientist), c/o Sigma Xi the Scientific Research Society, 345 Whitney Ave., New Haven, CT 06511.

Americana, (Americana Corp.), Subs. of Grolier, Inc., 575 Lexington Ave., New York, NY 10022 Tel 212-751-3600.

Americana Bks, (Americana Books; 0-917902), P.O. Box 481, Pinellas Park, FL 33565.

Americana Rev, (Americana Review; 0-914166), 10 Socha Lane, Scotia, NY 12302 Tel 518-399-6482.

Americanist, (Americanist Press; 0-910120), 1525 Shenkel Rd., Pottstown, PA 19464 Tel 215-323-5289.

Americans Energy Ind, (Americans for Energy Independence; 0-934458), 1629 K St., N.W., Suite 1201, Washington, DC 20006 Tel 202-466-2105.

Americas Future, (America's Future, Inc.), 542 Main St., New Rochelle, NY 10801.

AMG Pubs, (AMG Pubs.; 0-89957), 6815 Shallowford Rd., Chattanooga, TN 37421.

Amhara Corp, (Amhara Corp.; 0-917450), 6990 S. 1700 East, Salt Lake City, UT 84121.

Amherst Media, (Amherst Media; 0-936262), 418 Homecrest Dr., Amherst, NY 14226.

Amherst Pr, (Amherst Press), Amherst, WI 54406 Tel 715-824-3214.

AMI Pr, (AMI International Press; 0-911988), Mountain View Rd., Washington, NJ 07822 Tel 201-689-1700.

Amigo Pr, (Amigo Press; 0-935098), 620 Lombardy Lane, Laguna Beach, CA 92651 Tel 714-494-2302.

Amity Bks MO, (Amity Books; 0-934864), 1702 Magnolia, Liberty, MO 64048.

Amity Hallmark, (Amity Hallmark, Ltd.), 40-09 149th Place, Flushing, NY 11354.

Amnesty Intl USA, (Amnesty International of the USA, Inc.; 0-939994), 304 W. 58th St., New York, NY 10019.

Amon Carter, (Amon Carter Museum of Western Art; 0-88360), P.O. Box 2365, Fort Worth, TX 76113 Tel 817-738-1933.

Amonics, (Amonics; 0-918166), P.O. Box 1045, Norman, OK 73069 Tel 405-321-8076.

AMORC, (AMORC), Rosicrucian Park, San Jose, CA 95191 Tel 408-287-9171.

Amoskeag Pr, (Amoskeag Press, Inc.), P.O. Box 666, Hooksett, NH 03106 Tel 603-622-6626.

Ampersand, (Ampersand Press; 0-910128), P.O. Box 241, Princeton, NJ 08540; Moved, Left No Forwarding Address.

Ampersand RI, (Ampersand Press, Creative Writing Program; 0-9604740), Roger Williams College, Bristol, RI 02809.

Amphoto, (American Photographic Book Publishing Co., Inc.; 0-8174), Div. of Watson-Guptill Pubns., Inc., 1 Astor Plaza, 1515 Broadway, 39th Floor, New York, NY 10036 Tel 212-764-7510.

AMS Imprint of **Natural Hist**

AMS Pr, (AMS Press, Inc.; 0-404), 56 E. 13th St., New York, NY 10003 Tel 212-777-4700.

AMSA Imprint of **Natural Hist**

Amsco Music Imprint of **Music Sales**

AMSCO Sch, (AMSCO School Pubns., Inc.; 0-87720), Orders to: 315 Hudson St., New York, NY 10013 Tel 212-675-7000.

Amulefi, (Amulefi Publishing Co.; 0-936360), 11 E. Utica St., Buffalo, NY 14209.

Amuru Pr, (Amuru Press, Inc.; 0-87976), 161 Madison Ave., New York, NY 10016 Tel 212-686-5508.

AMW, (Aabbott McDonnell Winchester; 0-89519), 450 Seventh Ave., New York, NY 10001.

AN Inc, (A.N., Inc.), P.O. Box 145, Whitefish, MT 59937.

ANA, (American Nurses Assn.), 2420 Pershing Rd., Kansas City, MO 64108 Tel 816-474-5720.

Ana-Doug Pub, (Ana-Doug Publishing; 0-916946), 1236 Cranbrook Place, Fullerton, CA 92633 Tel 714-738-1655.

Anaheim Pub Co, (Anaheim Publishing Co.; 0-88236), 1120 E. Ash, Fullerton, CA 92631 Tel 714-879-7922.

Analog Devices, (Analog Devices, Inc.; 0-916550), P.O. Box 280, Norwood, MA 02062 Tel 617-329-4700; Orders to: P.O. Box 796, Norwood, MA 02062.

Analysis, (Merrill Analysis, Inc.; 0-911894), P.O. Box 228, Chappaqua, NY 10514 Tel 914-238-3641.

Analysis, (Analysis Press; 0-911894), Box 228, Chappaqua, NY 10514 Tel 914-238-3641.

Analytic Invest, (Analytic Investment Management, Inc.), 2182 Dupont Drive, Irvine, CA 92715 Tel 714-833-0294.

Ananda, (Ananda Pubns.; 0-916124), 14618 Tyler Foote Rd., Nevada City, CA 95959 Tel 916-265-5877.

Ananda Marga, (Ananda Marga Pubns.; 0-88476), 854 Pearl St., Denver, CO 80203 Tel 303-832-6465.

Ananse Pr, (Ananse Press; 0-9605670), P.O. Box 22565, Seattle, WA 98122.

Anch Imprint of **Doubleday**

Anchor Pr Imprint of **Doubleday**

Anchorage, (Anchorage Press; 0-87602), P. O. Box 8067, New Orleans, LA 70182 Tel 504-283-8868.

Anchorage MD, (Anchorage, The; 0-9602432), Box 1660, Bowie, MD 20716.

Ancient Age, (Ancient Age Press; 0-9605224), P.O. Box 84431, Veterans Administration Branch, Los Angeles, CA 90073.

And Bks, (And Books; 0-89708), 702 S. Michigan, Suite 836, South Bend, IN 46618 Tel 219-232-8500.

And-Or Pr, (And-or Press, Inc.; 0-915904), P.O. Box 2246, Berkeley, CA 94702 Tel 415-849-2665; Orders to: 909 Parker St., Berkeley, CA 94710.

Ander Pubns, (Ander Pubns.; 0-930258), P.O. Box 697, 540 W. Hancock St., Milledgeville, GA 31061 Tel 912-452-4280.

Anderson
 See Stretching Inc

Anderson Kramer, (Anderson Kramer Associates, Inc.; 0-910136), 1722 "H" St., N.W., Washington, DC 20006 Tel 202-298-8010.

Anderson Pub Co, (Anderson Publishing Co.; 0-87084), 646 Main St., Cincinnati, OH 45201.

Anderson World, (Anderson World, Inc.; 0-89037), 1400 Stierlin Rd., Mountain View, CA 94043 Tel 415-965-8777.

Andor Pub, (Andor Publishing Co., Inc.; 0-89319), 163 E. Union Ave., E. Rutherford, NJ 07073 Tel 201-460-1495.

Andover MA
 See Town of Andover MA

Andover Pr, (Andover Press; 0-939014), 516 W. 34th St., New York, NY 10001.

Andre Deutsch, (Andre Deutsch; 0-233), c/o Elsevier Dutton, 2 Park Ave., New York, NY 10016.

Andre's & Co, (Andre's & Co.; 0-936264), 289 Varick St., Jersey City, NJ 07302.

Andrew Mtn Pr, (Andrew Mountain Press; 0-9603840), P.O. Box 14353, Hartford, CT 06114.

Andrews & McMeel, (Andrews & McMeel, Inc.; 0-8362), 4400 Johnson Dr., Fairway, KS 66205 Tel 913-362-1523. Imprints: Search (Search Books).

Andromeda, (Andromeda Press; 0-9602996), 111 E. Platt, Maquoketa, IA 52060.

Anemone Edns, (Anemone Editions, Ltd.; 0-9604818), P.O. Box 6056, Carmel, CA 93921.

Anemone Pr, (Anemone Press), 1612 19th St., N.W., Washington, DC 20009; Moved, Left No Forwarding Address.

Angel City, (Angel City Books; 0-9605416), 8033 Sunset Blvd., No. 366, Hollywood, CA 90046.

Angel Pr, (Angel Press Pubns.; 0-912216), 171 Webster St., Monterey, CA 93940 Tel 408-372-1658; Dist. by: Caroline House Distributors, 2 Ellis Place, Ossining, NY 10562.

Angriff Pr, (Angriff Press; 0-913022), P.O. Box 2726, Hollywood, CA 90028 Tel 213-386-9826.

Angst World, (Angst World Library; 0-914580), 2307 22nd Ave., E., Seattle, WA 98112.

Anhinga Pr, (Anhinga Press; 0-938078), Zapalachee Poetry Ctr., 410 Williams Bldg., Florida State Univ., Tallahassee, FL 32306.

Anima Bks
 See Anima Pubns

Anima Pubns, (Anima Pubns.; 0-89012), 1053 Wilson Ave., Chambersburg, PA 17201 Tel 717-263-8303.

Animal Cracker, (Animal Cracker Press), 3707 N.E. 65th Ave., Portland, OR 97213 Tel 503-282-0772.

Animal Owners, (Animal Owners Motivation Programs; 0-9604576), Center Rd., Frankfort, IL 60423.

Animal Welfare, (Animal Welfare Institute), P.O. Box 3650, Washington, DC 20007 Tel 202-337-2333.

ANKH, (ANKH Publishing Co., Inc.; 0-933528), 105 Mechanic St., Fayetteville, NY 13066 Tel 315-637-5239; Moved, Left No Forwarding Address.

ANKHCO FL, (ANKHCO; 0-9604318), P.O. Box 15235, Plantation, FL 33318.

Anma Libri, (Anma Libri; 0-915838), P.O. Box 876, Saratoga, CA 95070 Tel 415-851-3375.

Ann Arbor Bk, (Ann Arbor Book Co.; 0-932364), P.O. Box 8064, Ann Arbor, MI 48107.

Ann Arbor FL, (Ann Arbor Pubns.; 0-89039), P.O. Box 7249, Naples, FL 33940.

Ann Arbor Pr, (Ann Arbor Press; 0-914644), 1540 Northwood St., Box 1863, Ann Arbor, MI 48103 Tel 313-663-1416; Out of Business.

Ann Arbor Pubs, (Ann Arbor Pubns.; 0-910138), 2057 Charlton, Ann Arbor, MI 48103 Tel 313-665-9130; Orders to: P.O. Box 7249, Naples, FL 33940.

Ann Arbor Science, (Ann Arbor Science Pubs.; 0-250), c/o Butterworth Publishers, Inc., 10 Tower Office Park, Woburn, MA 01801 Tel 617-935-9361.

Anna Pub, (Anna Publishing, Inc.; 0-89305), 2469 Aloma Ave., Winter Park, FL 32792 Tel 305-671-5995.

Annandale-Intl, (Annandale-International; 0-9602562), Box 384, Bronx, NY 10472 Tel 212-292-8067.

Anne Gray, (Gray, Anne), 2222 Bahia Dr., La Jolla, CA 92037.

Annual Reviews, (Annual Reviews, Inc.; 0-8243), 4139 El Camino Way, Palo Alto, CA 94306 Tel 415-493-4400.

Another View, (Another View, Inc.; 0-913564), P.O. Box 1921, Brooklyn, NY 11202 Tel 212-624-0939.

Anozira, (Anozira Agency), 1725 Farmer Ave., Tempe, AZ 85281.

ANSI, (American National Standards Institute), 1430 Broadway, New York, NY 10018 Tel 212-354-3311.

ANT, (ANT Krausskopf; 3-7830), Dist. by: Marlin Pubns. International, Inc., 485 Fifth Ave., New York, NY 10017.

ANTA Imprint of **WSP**

Antelope Island, (Antelope Island Press; 0-917946), P.O. Box 220, St. George, UT 84770 Tel 801-673-6093.

Anthelion Pr, *(Anthelion Press, Inc.; 0-89185),* P.O. Box 614, Corte Madera, CA 94925 Tel 415-924-5311.

Anthony, *(Anthony, C. & R., Pubs., Inc.; 0-910140),* 300 Park Ave., S., New York, NY 10010 Tel 212-677-3170.

Anthony Pub Co, *(Anthony Publishing Co.; 0-9603832),* 218 Gleasondale Rd., Stow, MA 01775 Tel 617-897-7191.

Anthropology Res, *(Anthropology Resource Center, Inc.; 0-932978),* 59 Temple Place, Suite 444, Boston, MA 02111 Tel 617-426-9286.

Anthroposophic, *(Anthroposophic Press, Inc.; 0-910142),* 258 Hungry Hollow Rd., Spring Valley, NY 10977 Tel 914-352-2295.

Antietam Pr, *(Antietam Press; 0-931590),* P.O. Box 62, Boonsboro, MD 21713 Tel 301-432-8079.

Antiquarium, *(Antiquarium, The),* 66 Humiston Dr., Bethany, CT 06525 Tel 203-393-2723.

Antiquary Pr, *(Antiquary Press; 0-937864),* P.O. Box 9523, Baltimore, MD 21237 Tel 301-734-6366.

Antique Clocks, *(Antique Clocks Publishing; 0-933396),* P.O. Box 21387, Concord, CA 94521 Tel 415-682-6512.

Antique Collect, *(Antique Collectors' Club; 0-902024),* P. O. Box 350, Momence, IL 60954; No Known U.S. Distributor.

Antique Pubns, *(Antique Pubns.; 0-915410),* P.O. Box 655, Marietta, OH 45750.

Antique Radio, *(Antique Radio Services),* 646 Kenilworth Terrace, Kenilworth, IL 60043 Tel 312-251-0089.

Anv Imprint of **Van Nos Reinhold**

Anvil Pr, *(Anvil Press; 0-918552),* P.O. Box 37, Millville, MN 55957.

ApaGuides, *(ApaGuides),* Dist. by: Bookpeople, 2904 Seventh St., Berkeley, CA 94710; No Longer Distributed by Bookpeople.

Apeiron Pr, *(Apeiron Press; 0-931958),* P.O. Box 5930, Chicago, IL 60680.

Aperture, *(Aperture, Inc.; 0-89381; 0-912334),* Elm St., Millerton, NY 12546 Tel 518-789-4491.

Apex Imprint of **Abingdon**

Apex U Pr, *(Apex Univ. Press; 0-916146),* c/o Castle-Pierce Printing Co., P.O. Box 2247, Oshkosh, WI 54903.

APL Pr, *(APL Press; 0-917326),* 220 California Ave., Suite 201, Palo Alto, CA 94306 Tel 415-327-1700.

APO Imprint of **Unipub**

Apocrypha, *(Apocrypha Press),* P.O. Box 12519, Tucson, AZ 85711; Moved, Left No Forwarding Address.

Apogee, *(Apogee Publishing Co.; 0-936944),* P.O. Box 469, La Jolla, CA 92038; Dist. by: Communication Creativity, 5644 La Jolla Blvd., La Jolla, CA 92037 Tel 714-459-4489.

Apollo, *(Apollo; 0-938290),* 391 South Rd., Poughkeepsie, NY 12601.

Apollo Bks
See Rapollo Bks

Apollo Eds, *(Apollo Editions; 0-8152),* C/O Harper & Row Pubs., 10 E. 53rd St., New York, NY 10022; Dist. by: Harper & Row Pubs., Keystone Industrial Park, Scranton, PA 18512. Imprints: AE-J (Apollo Editions Juvenile Books); AE-T (Apollo Editions Trade Books).

Apostolic Formation, *(Apostolic Formation Center for Christian Renew-All, Inc.; 0-935488),* Box 355, Somers, CT 06071.

Apotheca, *(Apotheca Press, Ltd.; 0-930002),* 175 W. Wieuca Rd., N.E., Suite 122, Atlanta, GA 30342; Moved, Left No Forwarding Address.

Appalach Consortium, *(Appalachian Consortium, Inc.),* 202 Appalachian St., Boone, NC 28607 Tel 704-262-2064.

Appalach Mtn, *(Appalachian Mountain Club; 0-910146),* 5 Joy St., Boston, MA 02108 Tel 617-523-0636.

Appalachian Bks, *(Appalachian Books; 0-912660),* P.O. Box 249, Oakton, VA 22124 Tel 703-281-2464.

Appalachian Pr, *(Appalachian Press; 0-910148),* 745 Seventh St., Huntington, WV 25701.

Appel, *(Appel, Paul P., Pub.; 0-911858),* 119 Library Lane, Mamaroneck, NY 10543 Tel 914-698-8115.

Appellate Pub, *(Appellate Publishing; 0-9603848),* P. O. Box 10687, Edgemont Branch, Golden, CO 80401.

Applause Pubns, *(Applause Pubns.; 0-932352),* 2234 S. Shady Hills Dr., Diamond Bar, CA 91765.

Apple-Gems, *(Apple-Gems; 0-9602122),* P.O. Box 16292, San Francisco, CA 94116 Tel 415-587-9752.

Apple Hut, *(Apple Hut Publishing Co.; 0-931148),* 1047 Park Hill Dr., P. O. Box 2704, Escondido, CA 92025 Tel 714-741-3565.

Apple-One, *(Apple One Pub.; 0-915612),* 3923 W. 6th St. Suite 416, Los Angeles, CA 90020 Tel 213-381-6003.

Apple Pie Pr, *(Apple Pie Press; 0-914152),* Dist. by: Ten Speed Press, P.O. Box 7123, Berkeley, CA 94707 Tel 415-845-8414.

Apple Pr, *(Apple Press; 0-9602238),* 5536 S.E. Harlow, Milwaukie, OR 97222 Tel 503-659-2475.

Apple Pub Co, *(Apple Publishing Co.; 0-9604134),* Box 2498, Grand Central Sta., New York, NY 10163.

Apple Tree, *(Apple Tree Press, Inc.; 0-913082),* P.O. Box 1012, Flint, MI 48501 Tel 313-234-5451.

Apple Tree Ln, *(Apple Tree Lane; 0-9601602),* 2 Fair Oaks Lane, Atherton, CA 94025.

Apple Wood, *(Apple-Wood Books; 0-918223),* Box 2870, Cambridge, MA 02139 Tel 617-964-5150.

Appleton, *(Appleton-Century-Crofts, Inc.),* ; Publisher Abbreviation Without Address Are for Titles That Are Out of Print. These Are Obsolete Abbreviations. Publishers Abbreviation Is Now ACC.

Appleton-Century-Crofts Imprint of **P-H**

Applewhite, *(Applewhite, Karen Miller; 0-9603472),* 5702 N. Tenth Ave., Phoenix, AZ 85013 Tel 602-246-8243.

Appleyard Agency, *(Appleyard, John, Agency, Inc.),* Box 1902, Pensacola, FL 32589 Tel 904-432-8396.

Applezaba, *(Applezaba Press; 0-930090),* 410 St. Louis, Long Beach, CA 90814 Tel 213-434-7761.

Applied Arts, *(Applied Arts Pubs.; 0-911410),* Div. of Sowers Printing Co., Box 479, Lebanon, PA 17042 Tel 717-272-6667.

Applied Press, *(Applied Pressure Techniques, Wm. J. Cosmetics; 0-9600560),* P.O. Box 3172, Munster, IN 46321 Tel 312-841-2482.

Applied Pub, *(Applied Publishing Ltd.; 0-915834),* P.O. Box 261, Wilmette, IL 60091.

Applied Therapeutics, *(Applied Therapeutics, Inc.; 0-915486),* P.O. Box 31-747, San Francisco, CA 94131 Tel 415-221-1555.

April Hill, *(April Hill Pubs.),* 79 Elm St., Springfield, VT 05156.

APS Pubns, *(APS Pubns., Inc.; 0-87988),* c/o Agathon Press, Inc., 15 E. 26th St., New York, NY 10010 Tel 212-679-1674.

APSA, *(APSA),* P.O. Box 5503, Washington, DC 20016.

Apt Bks, *(Apt Books, Inc.; 0-86590),* 141 E. 44th St., New York, NY 10017.

Aptitude Inventory, *(Aptitude Inventory Measurement Service; 0-9602710),* 2506 McKinney Ave., Suite B, Dallas, TX 75201.

Aqua Educ, *(Aquarian Educational Group; 0-911794),* 30188 Mulholland Hwy., Agoura, CA 91301 Tel 213-889-9678.

Aqua-Sol Ent, *(Aqua-Sol Enterprises; 0-9604874),* P.O. Box 18646, Fort Worth, TX 76118 Tel 817-284-8003.

Aquari Corp, *(Aquari Corp.; 0-916204),* P.O. Box 1966, Midland, MI 48640 Tel 517-631-5660.

Aquarian Bk Pubs, *(Aquarian Book Pubs.; 0-9605126),* 7011 Hammond Ave., Dallas, TX 75223.

Aquarian Pr, *(Aquarian Press; 0-902146),* P.O. Box 625, Stockbridge, MA 01262 Tel 413-298-3066.

Aquarius, *(Aquarius Enterprises),* 53 Central Ave. 15 Wailuku, Maui, HI 96793 Tel 808-244-7347.

Aquarius Pub Co, *(Aquarius Publishing),* Dist. by: Book People, 2940 Seventh St., Berkeley, CA 94710 Tel 415-549-3033.

Aquin Pub, *(Aquin Publishing Co.; 0-915352),* 1608 Pacific Ave., Venice, CA 90291 Tel 213-396-9633.

ARA, *(Administrative Research Associates, Inc.; 0-910022),* Irvine Town Ctr., Box 4211, Irvine, CA 92716 Tel 714-499-3939.

Aragorn Bks, *(Aragorn Books, Inc.; 0-913862),* 14698 Nordhoff St., Panorama City, CA 91402 Tel 213-894-3104.

Aramaic Bible, *(Aramaic Bible Society, Inc.),* P.O. Box 15307, St. Petersburg, FL 33733 Tel 813-345-1636.

Ararat Pr, *(Ararat Press; 0-933706),* 585 Saddle River Rd., Saddle Brook, NJ 07662.

Arbit, *(Arbit, B, Books; 0-930038),* 8050 N. Port Washington Rd., Milwaukee, WI 53217 Tel 414-352-4404.

Arbor Hse, *(Arbor House Publishing Co.; 0-87795),* 235 E. 45th St., New York, NY 10017 Tel 212-599-3131.

Arbor Pubns, *(Arbor Pubns.; 0-9602556),* P.O. Box 8185, Ann Arbor, MI 48107 Tel 313-662-5786.

Arc Bks, *(Arc Books; 0-668),* Div. of Arco Publishing Inc./Prentice-Hall, Inc., Dist. by: Arco Publishing Inc., 219 Park Ave., S., New York, NY 10003 Tel 212-777-6300.

Arca & Co, *(Arca & Co. Pubs.; 0-918198),* Box 7037, Houston, TX 78712 Tel 512-264-1059; Moved, Left No Forwarding Address.

Arcadia, *(Arcadia House),* Dist. by: Lenox Hill Press, 419 Park Ave., S., New York, NY 10016.

Arcadia Pr, *(Arcadia Press; 0-938186),* 80 Fifth Ave., New York, NY 10011 Tel 212-477-5331.

Arcana Workshops, *(Arcana Workshops),* 407 N. Maple Dr., No. 212, Beverly Hills, CA 90210 Tel 213-273-5949.

Arcane Bks
See Arcane Pubns

Arcane Pubns, *(Arcane Pubns.; 0-912240),* Box 36, York Harbor, ME 03911 Tel 207-363-3333.

Archangel Bks, *(Archangel Books; 0-918046),* 1707 Shattuck Ave., Berkeley, CA 94709.

Archer Edns, *(Archer Editions Press; 0-89097),* P.O. Box 562, Danbury, CT 06810 Tel 203-438-0282.

Archinform, *(Archinform; 0-937254),* P.O. Box 27722, Los Angeles, CA 90027 Tel 213-662-0216.

Architectural, *(Architectural Book Publishing Co.),* Dist. by: Hastings House Pubs., Inc., 10 E. 40th St., New York, NY 10016 Tel 212-689-5400.

Architectural Rec Bks Imprint of **McGraw**

Archival Pr, *(Archival Press, Inc.; 0-915882),* P.O. Box 93, MIT Branch Sta., Cambridge, MA 02139.

Archives Ink, *(Archives Ink, Ltd.; 0-915528),* P.O. Box 1776, 16 Prospect Ave., Haworth, NJ 07641 Tel 201-384-4777.

Archives Soc Hist, *(Archives of Social History; 0-914924),* P.O. Box 763, Stony Brook, NY 11790 Tel 516-751-3709.

Archway, *(Archway Paperbacks; 0-671),* c/o Pocket Books, 1230 Avenue of the Americas, New York, NY 10020 Tel 212-246-2121.

Arco, *(Arco Publishing, Inc.; 0-668),* Div. of Prentice-Hall, Inc., 219 Park Ave., S., New York, NY 10003 Tel 212-777-6300. Imprints: Morgan Aviation (Morgan Aviation Books).

ARCsoft, *(ARCsoft Pubs.; 0-86668),* P.O. Box 132, Woodsboro, MD 21798.

Arctinurus Co, *(Arctinurus Co.; 0-915386),* P.O. Box 275, Bellmawr, NJ 08031 Tel 609-933-0212.

Arden Lib, *(Arden Library; 0-8495),* Mill & Main Sts., Darby, PA 19023 Tel 215-726-5505.

Ardis Pubs, *(Ardis Pubs.; 0-88233),* 2901 Heatherway, Ann Arbor, MI 48104 Tel 313-971-2367.

ARE-Braille, *(Assn. for Research & Enlightenment, Inc.-Braille Dept.; 0-87604),* P.O. Box 595, Virginia Beach, VA 23451 Tel 804-428-3588.

ARE Pr, *(A.R.E. Press; 0-87604),* P.O. Box 595, Editorial Dept., Virginia Beach, VA 23451 Tel 804-428-3588.

Arena Lettres, *(Arena Lettres; 0-88479),* 8 Lincoln Place, Waldwick, NJ 07463 Tel 201-445-7154.

Ares, *(Ares Pubs., Inc.; 0-89005),* 612 N. Michigan Ave., Suite 216, Chicago, IL 60611 Tel 312-642-7850.

Arete, *(Arete Publishing Co., Inc.; 0-933880),* Princeton Forrestal Ctr., 101 College Rd. E., Princeton, NJ 08540 Tel 609-452-8090.

Arete Pr
See Bellflower

Arete Pubns, *(Arete Pubns.; 0-9602148),* 8655 E. Vista Dr., Scottsdale, AZ 85253.

Arete Pubs
See Castlegate

Argee Pub, *(Argee Publishing Co.; 0-931084),* 2663 Anchor Ave., W. Los Angeles, CA 90064 Tel 213-559-7603.

Argo *Imprint of* **Atheneum**

Argo Bks, *(Argo Books; 0-912148),* Main St., Norwich, VT 05055 Tel 802-649-1000.

Argonaut, *(Argonaut, Inc., Pubs.),* ; Publisher Abbreviation Without Addresses Are for Titles That Are Out of Print. These Are Obsolete Abbreviations.

Argonaut Bks, *(Argonaut Books, Inc.; 0-914270),* C/O Ebel, 2160 Center Ave., Fort Lee, NJ 07024.

Argosy, *(Argosy-Antiquarian, Ltd.; 0-87266),* 116 E. 59th St., New York, NY 10022.

Argus Archives, *(Argus Archives; 0-916858),* 228 E. 49th St, New York, NY 10017 Tel 212-355-6140.

Argus Bks, *(Argus Books & Graphics),* 1714 Capitol Ave., Sacramento, CA 95814.

Argus Comm, *(Argus Communications; 0-913592; 0-89505),* 7440 Natchez Ave., Niles, IL 60648 Tel 312-647-7800.

Arhe Inc, *(Arhe, Inc.),* 505 Fifth Ave., Room 1402, New York, NY 10017 Tel 212-972-1488.

Ariadne Pr, *(Ariadne Press; 0-918056),* 4817 Tallahassee Ave., Rockville, MD 20853 Tel 301-949-2514.

Arica Pr, *(Arica Press; 0-915086),* P.O. Box 4405, Grand Central Sta., New York, NY 10017.

Ariel Bks
See Ariel Pr

Ariel Pr, *(Ariel Press),* P.O. Box 9183, Berkeley, CA 94709; Tel 415-548-8204; Do Not Confuse with Ariel Pubns, WA.

Ariel Pubns, *(Ariel Pubns.; 0-917656),* P.O. Box 255, Mercer Island, WA 98040 Tel 206-641-0518; Do Not Confuse with Ariel Bks, CA; Ariel Pr.

Aries Pr, *(Aries Press; 0-933646),* P. O. Box 30081, Chicago, IL 60630.

Arif, *(Arif),* 2748 Ninth St., Berkeley, CA 94710.

Aris & Phillips, *(Aris & Phillips, Ltd.),* P.O. Box 555, Forest Grove, OR 97116.

Arista Corp NDE, *(Arista Corp., NDE Div.; 0-912790; 0-89796; 0-914876; 0-89856),* P.O. Box 6146, 2440 Estand Way, Concord, CA 94524 Tel 800-227-1616.

Ariz Maps & Bks, *(Arizona Maps & Books),* Box 1133, Sedona, AZ 86336.

Ark Books MN
See Landmark Bks

Ark Hse NY, *(Ark House Ltd.; 0-935764),* 100 E. 42nd St., New York, NY 10017 Tel 212-697-0205; Dist. by: Associated Booksellers, P.O. Box 6361, Bridgeport, CT 06606 Tel 203-366-5494.

Arkham, *(Arkham House Pubs.; 0-87054),* Sauk City, WI 53583 Tel 608-643-4500.
Imprints: Mycroft & Moran (Mycroft & Moran).

Arlin J Brown, *(Brown, Arlin J.),* The Arlin J. Brown Info. Center, P.O. Box 251, Ft. Belvoir, VA 22060 Tel 703-451-8638.

Arlington Ent, *(Arlington Enterprises),* P.O. Box 4381, Arlington, VA 22204; Moved, Left No Forwarding Address.

Arlington Hse, *(Arlington House Pubs.; 0-87000),* 333 Post Rd. W., Westport, CT 06880 Tel 203-226-6383.

Arlotta, *(Arlotta Press; 0-918838),* 6340 Millbank Dr., Dayton, OH 45459 Tel 513-434-1518.

Arma Pr, *(Arma Press; 0-9603662),* Rte. 139, North Branford, CT 06471.

Armadillo Pr, *(Armadillo Press; 0-912556),* P.O. Box 8131, Univ. Sta., Austin, TX 78712.

Armado & Moth, *(Armado & Moth; 0-9603626),* 2131 Arapahoe, Boulder, CO 80302 Tel 303-442-1415.

Arman Ent, *(Arman Enterprises, Inc.; 0-915438),* 1204-B Gemini Dr., Annapolis, MD 21403 Tel 301-268-2019.

Armchair Pr, *(Armchair Press),* 123 Dorchester, Scarsdale, NY 10583.

Armenian, *(Armenian Studies, Library of, Publishers),* 129 Robbins Rd., Watertown, MA 02172.

Armory Pubns, *(Armory Pubns.; 0-9604982),* P.O. Box 44372, Tacoma, WA 98444.

Armstrong Browning, *(Armstrong Browning Library; 0-914108),* P.O. Box 6336, Waco, TX 76706 Tel 817-755-3566.

Armstrong Pr, *(Armstrong Press),* Rte. 2, Box 509, Notasulga, AL 36866.

Armstrong Pub, *(Armstrong Publishing Co.; 0-915936),* 5514 Wilshire Blvd., Los Angeles, CA 90036 Tel 213-937-3600.

Arnall, *(Arnall, Franklin; 0-914638),* P.O. Box 531, Mentone, CA 92359 Tel 714-621-2461.

Arner Pubns, *(Arner Pubns.; 0-914124),* P.O. Box 307, Westmoreland, NY 13490 Tel 315-853-6555.

Arno, *(Arno Press; 0-405),* 3 Park Ave., New York, NY 10016 Tel 212-725-2050.

Arnold & Assocs, *(Arnold Jack, & Associates),* 7426 Caminito Carlotta, San Diego, CA 92120 Tel 714-287-7742.

Arnold-Porter Pub, *(Arnold-Porter Publishing Co.; 0-9605048),* P.O. Box 646, Keego Harbor, MI 48033 Tel 313-338-4478.

ARO Pub, *(ARO Publishing Co.; 0-89868),* Box 193, 398 S. 1100 West, Provo, UT 84601 Tel 801-377-8218.

Aro Pub Co
See ARO Pub

Aronson, *(Aronson, Jason, Inc.; 0-87668),* 111 Eighth Ave., New York, NY 10011 Tel 212-924-6663.

Arriaga Pubns, *(Arriaga Pubns.),* P.O. Box 652, Booneville, AK 72927.

Arrow Pub, *(Arrow Publishing Co., Inc.; 0-913450),* 1238 Chestnut St., Box 115, Newton Upper Falls, MA 02164 Tel 617-964-2300.

Arroway, *(Arroway Pubs.; 0-9600284),* 11760 Roscoe Blvd., Bldg. E, Sun Valley, CA 91352 Tel 213-875-3730.

Arrowhead Bks, *(Arrowhead Books; 0-9604152),* 3005 Fulton, Berkeley, CA 94705 Tel 415-548-5110.

Ars Ceramica, *(Ars Ceramica, Ltd.; 0-89344),* P.O. Box 7366, Ann Arbor, MI 48107 Tel 313-429-7864; Dist. by: Keramos, P.O. Box 7500, Ann Arbor, MI 48107.

Ars Eterna, *(Ars Eterna Press; 0-9602170),* 7627 Glen Prairie, Houston, TX 77061.

ARS Pubns, *(Anderson Ritchie & Simon, (ARS Pubns.)),* 3044 Riverside Dr., Los Angeles, CA 90039; Moved, Left No Forwarding Address.

Art *Imprint of* **B&N**

Art Adventure, *(Art Adventures Press; 0-918326),* 1286 Grizzly Peak, Berkeley, CA 94708 Tel 415-843-6197.

Art Alliance, *(Art Alliance Press; 0-87982),* Div. of Associated University Presses, 4 Cornwall Dr., Suite 30, East Brunswick, NJ 08816 Tel 201-254-0132.

Art & Ref, *(Art & Reference House; 0-910156),* Brownsboro, TX 75756.

Art Dir, *(Art Direction Book Co.; 0-910158),* Dist. by: Advertising Trade Pubns., Inc., 19 W. 44th St., New York, NY 10036 Tel 212-354-0450.

Art Educ, *(Art Education, Inc.; 0-912242),* 28 E. Erie St., Blauvelt, NY 10913 Tel 914-359-2233.

Art Educators, *(Art Educators of New Jersey),* 445 Wyoming Ave., Millburn, NJ 07041.

Art Fettig
See Growth Unltd

Art Glass Exchange, *(Art Glass Exchange, The; 0-932988),* 2960 Arroyo Drive N., San Diego, CA 92103 Tel 714-295-4079.

Art History, *(Art History Pubs.; 0-9600002),* Rte. 2, Red Wing, MN 55066 Tel 612-388-4046.

Art Ideas, *(Art Ideas),* P.O. Box 54A, Yorkville, IL 60560 Tel 312-554-3850.

Art in America, *(Art in America),* 150 E. 58th St., New York, NY 10022.

Art Inst Chi, *(Art Institute of Chicago; 0-86559),* Michigan Ave. & Adams St., Chicago, IL 60603 Tel 312-443-3539; Dist. by: Univ. of Chicago Press, 11030 S. Langley Ave., Chicago, IL 60628 Tel 312-568-1550.

Art Mus Gall, *(Art Museum & Galleries, CSULB, The; 0-936270),* 1250 Bellflower Blvd., Long Beach, CA 90840.

Art Therapy, *(Art Therapy; 0-8391),* Craftsbury Common, VT 05827.

Artabras, *(Artabras, Inc.; 0-89660),* 505 Park Ave., New York, NY 10022 Tel 212-888-1969.

Arte Publico, *(Arte Publico Press; 0-934770),* Revista Chicano-Riquena, Univ. of Houston Central Campus, Houston, TX 77004.

Artech Hse, *(Artech House, Inc.; 0-89006),* 610 Washington St., Dedham, MA 02026 Tel 617-326-8220.

Artemis Pr, *(Artemis Press; 0-9604664),* P.O. Box 58572, Los Angeles, CA 90058 Tel 213-232-5203.

Arthritis, *(Arthritis Is Easy to Stop; 0-9601236),* 304 Tenth Ave., Baraboo, WI 53913 Tel 608-356-5652.

Arthur Owned, *(Arthur Owned Publishing; 0-9602112),* 606A Adams Ave., Philadelphia, PA 19120.

Arthur Pubns, *(Arthur Pubns., Inc.; 0-932782),* P.O. Box 23101, Jacksonville, FL 32217 Tel 904-389-6515.

Arti Grafiche, *(Arti Grafiche Il Torchio; 0-935194),* 1414 Mar Vista Way, Laguna Beach, CA 92651.

Artichoke, *(Artichoke Press; 0-9603916),* 3274 Parkhurst Dr., Rancho Palos Verdes, CA 90274.

Article One, *(Article I),* Merrill Rd., McCammon, ID 83250.

Artisan Bks, *(Artisan Books; 0-89528),* Bedford Green, Bedford Village, NY 10506 Tel 914-234-9218.

Artisan Pr, *(Artisan Press),* Dist. by: Bookpeople, 2940 Seventh St., Berkeley, CA 94710 Tel 415-549-3033.

Artisan Sales, *(Artisan Sales; 0-934666),* P.O. Box 1497, Thousand Oaks, CA 91360 Tel 805-482-8076.

Artist-Dealer
See Davenport

Artistic Endeavors, *(Artistic Endeavors; 0-9604500),* 24 Emerson Place, Boston, MA 02114 Tel 617-227-1967.

Artists & Alchemists, *(Artists & Alchemists Pubns.; 0-915600),* 215 Bridgeway, Sausalito, CA 94965 Tel 415-332-0326; Dist. by: Swallow Press, 811 Junior Terrace, Chicago, IL 60613.

Artists Found, *(Artists Foundation, Inc., The; 0-932246),* 100 Boylston St., Boston, MA 02116 Tel 617-482-8100.

Artists USA
See Foun Adv Artists

Artmans Pr, *(Artman's Press),* 1511 McGee Ave., Berkeley, CA 94703.

Arts & Arch, *(Arts & Architecture Press; 0-931228),* 1119 Colorado Ave., Santa Monica, CA 90401.

Arts & Culture, *(Arts & Culture of the North; 0-9605898),* Box 1333, Gracie Square Sta., New York, NY 10028.

Arts Comm, *(Arts Communications; 0-918840),* 14 E. 11th St., New York, NY 10003.

Arts End, *(Arts End Books; 0-933292),* P.O. Box 162, Newton, MA 02168 Tel 617-965-2478.

Arum Pr, *(Arum Press, The; 0-931338),* 3180 University Ave., Suite 230, San Diego, CA 92104 Tel 714-281-0980; 3180 University Ave., Suite 230, San Diego, CA 92104 Tel 714-281-0980.

As Is Pr
See So&So Pr

As-Shabazz Pr
See Shabazz Pr

Asbury Theological, *(Asbury Theological Seminary),* Wilmore, KY 40390.

Ascension, *(Ascension Academy Chinese Project; 0-9600176),* 4401 W. Braddock Rd., Box 9210, Alexandria, VA 22304 Tel 703-379-6050.

Asclepiad, *(Asclepiad Pubns., Inc.; 0-935718),* 1590 E. Maple, Birmingham, MI 48008.

ASEI, *(Alternative Sources of Energy, Inc.; 0-917328),* 107 S. Central Ave., Milaca, MN 56353 Tel 612-983-6892.

Ash-Kar Pr, *(Ash-Kar Press; 0-9605308),* 519 Castro St., San Francisco, CA 94114.

Ash Lad Pr, *(Ash Lad Press; 0-915492),* P.O. Box 396, Canton, NY 13617 Tel 315-386-8820.

Ash Pub
See Am Sports Sales

Ashford, *(Ashford Pubns.),* Box 61648, Houston, TX 77208.

Ashland Poetry, *(Ashland Poetry Press; 0-912592),* Ashland College, Ashland, OH 44805 Tel 419-289-4096.

Ashlar Pr, *(Ashlar Press; 0-932534),* Box 120277, Nashville, TN 37212.

Ashley Bks, *(Ashley Books, Inc.; 0-87949),* 30 Main St., Port Washington, NY 11050 Tel 516-883-2221; Orders to: P.O. Box 768, Port Washington, NY 11050 Tel 516-883-2221.

ASHO *Imprint of* **Pubns Organization**

Ashod Pr, *(Ashod Press; 0-935102),* 620 E. 20th St, 11F, New York, NY 10009; Orders to: 138-40 64th Ave., Flushing, NY 11367.

Ashrod
See Ashod Pr

ASI Pubs Inc, *(ASI Pubs., Inc.; 0-88231),* 127 Madison Ave., New York, NY 10016 Tel 212-679-5676.

Asia, *(Asia Publishing House; 0-210),* Dist. by: APT Books, Inc., 141 E. 44th St., Suite 511, New York, NY 10017 Tel 212-697-0887.

Asia Bk Corp, *(Asia Book Corp. of America),* 94-41 218th St., Queens Village, NY 11426 Tel 212-648-1481.

Asia Hse Gallery, *(Asia House Gallery; 0-87848),* Orders to: New York Graphic Society Ltd., 140 Greenwich Ave., Greenwich, CT 06830.

Asia Lib Ser, *(Asia Library Services),* P.O. Box C, Auburn, NY 13021; Name Formerly Thailand Books.

Asia Soc, *(Asia Society, Inc.; 0-87848),* 725 Park Ave., New York, NY 10021 Tel 212-288-6400.

Asian Am Stud, *(Asian American Studies Center, UCLA),* 3232 Campbell Hall, Univ. of California, Los Angeles, CA 90024 Tel 213-825-2974.

Asian Conserv Lab, *(Asian Conservation Laboratory),* Dist. by: Raiko Art Corp., 316 Fifth Ave., New York, NY 10001.

Asian Humanities *Imprint of* **Lancaster-Miller**

Asian Music Pub, *(Asian Music Pubns.; 0-913360),* University of WA, School of Music, Seattle, WA 98195 Tel 206-543-0974.

ASIS *Imprint of* **Knowledge Indus**

Askild-Karnekull, *(Askild & Karnekull),* c/o Arthur Vanous Co., 616 Kinderkamack Rd., River Edge, NJ 07661.

ASM, *(American Society for Metals; 0-87170),* 9275 Kinsman Rd., Metals Park, OH 44073 Tel 216-338-5151.

ASME, *(American Society of Mechanical Engineers; 0-87053),* 345 E. 47th St., New York, NY 10017 Tel 212-644-7703.

ASP, *(American Society of Photogrammetry; 0-937294),* 105 N. Virginia Ave., Falls Church, VA 22046 Tel 703-534-6617.

Aspen Art, *(Aspen Art; 0-9601120),* 401 Center, Evanston, WY 82930 Tel 307-789-9879.

Aspen Ctr Visual Arts, *(Aspen Center for the Visual Arts; 0-934324),* 590 N. Mill St., Aspen, CO 81611 Tel 303-925-8050.

Aspen Inst Human, *(Aspen Institute for Humanistic Studies; 0-89843),* 717 Fifth Ave., New York, NY 10022 Tel 212-759-1053; Orders to: Aspen Institute at Wye Plantation, Publications Office, P.O. Box 150, Queenstown, MD 21658.

Aspen Pr
See Rue Morgue

Aspen Pubns, *(Aspen Pubns.; 0-9603756),* 839 S. 250 West, Orem, UT 84057.

Aspen Ski Masters, *(Aspen Ski Masters; 0-9600570),* P.O. Box 3071, Aspen, CO 81611 Tel 303-925-7159.

Aspen Systems, *(Aspen Systems Corp.; 0-912862; 0-89443),* 1600 Research Blvd., Rockville, MD 20850 Tel 301-251-5000.

ASPIRATION, *(ASPIRATION; 0-914182),* P.O. Box M, University Sta., Charlottesville, VA 22903 Tel 804-295-7718.

ASSE, *(American Society of Safety Engineers; 0-939874),* 850 Busse Hwy., Park Ridge, IL 60068 Tel 312-692-4121.

Assembling Pr, *(Assembling Press; 0-915066),* P.O. Box 1967, Brooklyn, NY 11202.

Assn Adv Ukrainian, *(Assn. for the Advancement of Ukrainian Studies, Inc.; 0-916332),* P.O. Box 3295, Country Fair Sta., Champaign, IL 61820.

Assn Am Geographers, *(Assn. of American Geographers; 0-89291),* 1710 16th St., N.W., Washington, DC 20009 Tel 202-234-1450.

Assn Am Indian, *(Assn. on American Indian Affairs),* 432 Park Ave., S., New York, NY 10016 Tel 212-689-8720.

Assn Baptist Profs, *(Assn. of Baptist Professors of Religion; 0-932180),* Box A, Mercer Univ., Macon, GA 31207.

Assn Brain Injured, *(New York Assn. for Brain Injured Children; 0-9600256),* 95 Madison Ave., New York, NY 10016; Moved, Left No Forwarding Address.

Assn Calif Sch Admin, *(Assn. of California School Administrators),* Old Bayshore Hwy., Burlingame, CA 94010 Tel 415-692-4300.

Assn Consumer Res, *(Assn. for Consumer Research; 0-915552),* Grad. Sch. of Business Admin., Univ. of Michigan, Ann Arbor, MI 48109.

Assn Ed Comm Tech, *(Assn. for Educational Communications & Technology; 0-89240),* 1126 Sixteenth St., N.W., Washington, DC 20036 Tel 202-833-4180.

Assn Family Living, *(Assn. for the Study of Family Living, The; 0-9602670),* P.O. Box 130, Brooklyn, NY 11208 Tel 212-647-7406.

Assn Public Justice, *(Assn. for Public Justice Education Fund; 0-936456),* P.O. Box 56348, Washington, DC 20011 Tel 712-722-4537.

Assn Sch Busn, *(Assn. of School Business Officials of the United States & Canada; 0-910170),* 720 Garden St., Park Ridge, IL 60068 Tel 312-823-9320.

Assn Sexologists, *(Assn. of Sexologists, The; 0-939902),* 1523 Franklin St., San Francisco, CA 94109; Dist. by: Multi-Media Resource Ctr., 1525 Franklin St., San Francisco, CA 94109.

Assn Supervision, *(Assn. for Supervision & Curriculum Development; 0-87120),* 225 N. Washington St., Alexandria, VA 22314 Tel 703-549-9110.

Assn Syst Mgmt, *(Assn. for Systems Management; 0-934356),* 24587 Bagley Rd., Cleveland, OH 44138 Tel 216-243-6900.

Assn Tchr Ed, *(Assn. of Teacher Educators),* Affiliate of National Education Assn., 1900 Association Dr., Suite ATE, Reston, VA 22091 Tel 703-620-3110.

Assn Under Man, *(Assn. for the Understanding of Man; 0-915908),* P.O. Box 5310, Austin, TX 78763 Tel 512-458-1233.

Assn Univ Progs Hlth, *(Assn. of Univ. Programs in Health Administration),* One Dupont Circle, Washington, DC 20036 Tel 202-659-4354.

Assoc Bk, *(Associated Booksellers; 0-87497),* P.O. Box 6361, Bridgeport, CT 06606 Tel 203-366-5494.

Assoc Bk Pubs Guidance, *(Associated Book Pubs., Inc.; 0-910164),* P.O. Box 1032, San Mateo, CA 94403 Tel 415-343-3687.

Assoc Coun Arts
See Am Council Arts

Assoc Creative Writers, *(Associated Creative Writers; 0-933362),* 9231 Molly Woods Ave., La Mesa, CA 92041.

Assoc DC, *(Associated Pubs., Inc.; 0-87498),* 1407 14th St., N.W., Washington, DC 20005 Tel 202-667-2822.

Assoc Pr, *(Associated Press; 0-8096),* 50 Rockefeller Plaza, New York, NY 10020.

Assoc Print, *(Associated Printers),* Grafton-Grand Forks, Box 471, Grafton, ND 58237 Tel 701-352-0640.

Assoc Pub Auth, *(Associated Publishers & Authors),* Wilmington, DE 19808.

Assoc Pubs Guidance
See Assoc Bk Pubs Guidance

Assoc Univ Prs, *(Associated University Presses; 0-8453),* Orders to: 4 Cornwall Dr., Suite 30, East Brunswick, NJ 08816.

Assoc Writing Progs, *(Associated Writing Programs; 0-936266),* c/o Old Dominion Univ., Norfolk, VA 23508.

Assocs James Bell, *(Associates of the James Ford Bell Library; 0-9601798),* 472 Wilson Library, Univ. of Minnesota, 309 19th Ave. S., Minneapolis, MN 55455 Tel 612-373-2888.

Assurance Pubs, *(Assurance Pubs.; 0-932940),* P.O. Box 753, Rockville, MD 20851.

Astara, *(Astara, Inc.; 0-918936),* 800 W. Arrow Hwy., Upland, CA 91786 Tel 714-981-4941.

Astarte, *(Astarte, Inc.; 0-917506),* P.O. Box 404, Sausalito, CA 94965; Moved, Left No Forwarding Address.

ASTM, *(American Society for Testing & Materials; 0-8031),* 1916 Race St., Philadelphia, PA 19103 Tel 215-299-5400.

Aston Hall, *(Aston Hall Pubns, Inc.; 0-89936),* 1835 Hicks Rd., Rolling Meadows, IL 60008.

Astor-Honor, *(Astor-Honor, Inc.; 0-8392),* 48 E. 43rd St., New York, NY 10017.

Astro Artz, *(Astro Artz; 0-937122),* 240 S. Broadway, Los Angeles, CA 90012.

Astro-Comp, *(Astro-Computing Books; 0-910172),* P.O. Box 1818, Washington, DC 20013 Tel 202-543-1818.

Astro Comp Serv, *(Astro Computing Services; 0-917086),* P.O. Box 16297, San Diego, CA 92116 Tel 714-297-5648; Dist. by: Para Research, Whistlestop Mall, Rockport, MA 01966 Tel 617-546-3413.

Astro Pr, *(Astro Press, Inc.; 0-89322),* 7453 Melrose Ave., Los Angeles, CA 90046 Tel 213-658-8494.

Astroart Ent, *(Astroart Enterprises; 0-917814),* P.O. Box 503, South Houston, TX 77587 Tel 713-649-6601.

Astron Cal, *(Astronomical Calendar; 0-934546),* Dept. of Physics, Furman Univ., Greenville, SC 29613.

Astrosonics, *(Astrosonics Research Institute; 0-939192),* 11037 1/2 Freeman Ave., Lennox, CA 90304 Tel 213-673-4649.

ASU Ctr Asian, *(Arizona State Univ., Center for Asian Studies; 0-939252),* Tempe, AZ 85281 Tel 602-965-6365.

ASU Lat Am St, *(Arizona State Univ., Center for Latin American Studies; 0-87918),* Tempe, AZ 85281 Tel 602-965-5127.

Asylum Hill, *(Asylum Hill, Inc.; 0-9602952),* 880 Asylum Ave., Hartford, CT 06105.

Ata Bks, *(Ata Books; 0-931688),* 1928 Stuart St., Berkeley, CA 94703 Tel 415-841-9613.

Atavistic Pr, *(Atavistic Press; 0-915718),* 4605 Campus Ave., No. 8, San Diego, CA 92116.

Atcom, *(Atcom, Inc.; 0-915260),* 2315 Broadway, New York, NY 10024.

Atelier-AFI Films
See Afi Pubns

Athena Bks, *(Athena Books Ltd.),* P.O. Box 26, Carlstadt, NJ 07072.

Athena Pr, *(Athena Press, Inc.; 0-9602736),* P.O. Box 776, Vienna, VA 22180.

Athena Pub, *(Athena Publishing Co.; 0-89161),* P.O. Box 10681, Kansas City, MO 64118; Orders to: 2016 Clay, N. Kansas City, MO 64116.

Athena Pubns, *(Athena Pubns.; 0-932950),* Box 337, 23 Aurora St., Moravia, NY 13118.

Athenaeum Phila, *(Athenaeum of Philadelphia; 0-916530),* 219 S. Sixth St., E. Washington Square, Philadelphia, PA 19106 Tel 215-925-2688.

Atheneum, *(Atheneum Pubs.; 0-689),* 597 Fifth Ave., New York, NY 10017 Tel 212-486-2700; Dist. by: Scribner Dist. Center, Vreeland Ave., Boro of Totowa, Paterson, NJ 07512. *Imprints:* Aladdin (Aladdin Books); Argo (Argo Books); McElderry Bk (McElderry Book).

Athenian Hse, *(Athenian House Pubs.; 0-936038),* P.O. Box 90968, Nashville, TN 37209.

Atherton, *(Atherton Press),* ; Publisher Abbreviation Without Addresses Are for Titles That Are Out of Print. These Are Obsolete Abbreviations.

Athletic, *(Athletic Press; 0-87095),* P.O. Box 2314-D, Pasadena, CA 91105 Tel 213-283-3446.

Athletic Inst, *(Athletic Institute; 0-87670),* 200 Castlewood Dr., North Palm Beach, FL 33408 Tel 304-842-3600.

Athletics Cong, *(Athletics Congress/USA, The; 0-939254),* P.O. Box 120, Indianapolis, IN 46206 Tel 317-638-9155.

Athlone Pr *Imprint of* **Humanities**

Atkinson, *(Atkinson, Mary D.; 0-937436),* 8712-63rd Ave., College Park, MD 20740.

Atlanta Publicity, *(Atlanta Publicity Outlet),* Box 54105, Atlanta, GA 30308.

Atlantic Pub Co, *(Atlantic Publishing Co.; 0-937866),* P.O. Box 67, Tabor City, NC 28463.

Atlantis, *(Atlantis Editions),* 11 E. 73rd St., New York, NY 10021.

Atlantis-by-the-Sea, *(Atlantis-by-the-Sea, Ltd.; 0-89200),* 745 Seventh Ave., New York, NY 10019.

Atlantis Edns, *(Atlantis Editions; 0-910174),* P.O. Box 18326, Philadelphia, PA 19120 Tel 215-572-5710.

Atlantis Pub FL, *(Atlantis Publishing Co.; 0-86658),* 5432 Hallandale Beach Blvd., Hollywood, FL 33023 Tel 305-981-1009.

Atlantis Rising, *(Atlantis Rising; 0-932932)*, 308 Eureka St., San Francisco, CA 94114.

Attic Bks, *(Attic Books Ltd.; 0-915018)*, 41 E. 57th St., Suite 1210, New York, NY 10022 Tel 212-593-3970; Orders to: P.O. Box 38, South Salem, NY 10590.

Attic Pr, *(Attic Press; 0-87921)*, Stony Point, Rte. 2, Greenwood, SC 29646 Tel 803-374-3013.

Auburn Hse, *(Auburn House Publishing Co., Inc.; 0-86569)*, 131 Clarendon St., Boston, MA 02116 Tel 617-247-2650.

Audel, *(Audel, Theodore; 0-672)*, Dist. by: Bobbs-Merrill, 4300 W. 62nd St., Indianapolis, IN 46206 Tel 317-298-5400.

Audit Investment, *(Audit Investment Research, Inc.; 0-912840)*, 230 Park Ave., New York, NY 10017 Tel 212-661-1710.

Audubon Soc Portland, *(Audubon Society of Portland; 0-931686)*, 5151 Northwest Cornell Rd., Portland, OR 97210.

Auerbach, *(Auerbach Pubs., Inc.; 0-87769)*, Dept. A, 6560 N. Park Dr., Pennsauken, NJ 08109.

Augsburg, *(Augsburg Publishing House; 0-8066)*, 426 S. Fifth St., Minneapolis, MN 55415 Tel 612-330-3300.

August Corp, *(August Corp.; 0-933482)*, P.O. Box 582, Scottsdale, AZ 85252 Tel 602-949-7366.

Augustan Lib, *(Augustan Library; 0-916948)*, 250 Touchstone Place, Suite 20, West Sacramento, CA 95691.

Augustana, *(Augustana Historical Society; 0-910184)*, Augustana College Library, Rock Island, IL 61201 Tel 309-794-7266; Orders to: Denkmann Memorial Library, Augustana College, Rock Island, IL 61201.

Augustana Coll, *(Augustana College Library; 0-910182)*, 35th St. & Seventh Ave., Rock Island, IL 61201 Tel 309-794-7266.

Aum Pubns, *(Aum Pubns.; 0-88497)*, P.O. Box 32433, Jamaica, NY 11431 Tel 212-523-3471.

Aura Bks, *(Aura Books; 0-937736)*, 7911 Willoughby Ave., Los Angeles, CA 90046.

Aurea, *(Aurea Pubns.; 0-87174)*, Allenhurst, NJ 07711 Tel 201-531-4535.

Aurelian Pr, *(Aurelian Press; 0-918844)*, P.O. Box 366, Wilmette, IL 60091 Tel 312-251-6718.

Aurelon, *(Aurelon Tales; 0-912388)*, R.F.D. No. 2, 177 Sarles St., Mt. Kisco, NY 10549.

Aurico, *(Aurico Publishing Co.; 0-910186)*, 302 Newbury St., Boston, MA 02115 Tel 617-267-7766.

Auriga, *(Auriga; 0-9602738)*, Box F, 8 Candlelight Court, Clifton Park, NY 12065 Tel 518-371-2015.

Auromere, *(Auromere; 0-89744)*, 1291 Weber St., Pomona, CA 91768 Tel 714-629-8255.

Aurora Pubs, *(Aurora Pubs.; 0-87695)*, P.O. Box 120616, Nashville, TN 37212 Tel 615-254-5842.

Austin Hill Pr, *(Austin Hill Press, Inc.; 0-89690)*, 2955 Renault Place, San Diego, CA 92122 Tel 714-453-6486.

Austin Inst Pub Aff
See LBJ Sch Public Affairs

Austin Inst Pub Aff, *(University of Texas, Austin Institute of Public Affairs)*, ; Publisher Abbreviation Without Addresses Are for Titles That Are Out of Print. These Are Obsolete Abbreviations. Publisher's Abbreviation Is Now LBJ Sch Public Affairs.

Austin Pr, *(Austin Press; 0-914872)*, Div. of Lone Star Pubs. Inc., P.O. Box 9774, Austin, TX 78766 Tel 512-255-2333.

Australiana, *(Australiana Pubns.; 0-909162)*, 6511 Riviera Dr., Coral Gables, FL 33146 Tel 305-666-9404; Name Formerly Dryden Press of Australia.

Authors Co-op, *(Authors' Co-op Publishing Co.; 0-931150)*, Rte. 4, Box 137, Franklin, TN 37064 Tel 615-646-3757.

Authors Edn, *(Authors Edition, Inc.; 0-918058)*, Box 803, Lenox, MA 01240 Tel 413-637-0666.

Auto Bk, *(Auto Book Press; 0-910390)*, 1511 Grand Ave., San Marcos, CA 92069 Tel 714-744-2567.

Auto Club, *(Automobile Club of Southern California)*, Westways, Box 2890, Terminal Annex, Los Angeles, CA 90051.

Autophysiopsychic, *(Autophysiopsychic Partnership)*, Dist. by: Book People, 2940 Seventh St., Berkeley, CA 94710.

Autotronic Conversions, *(Autotronic Conversions)*, P.O. Box 17249, El Paso, TX 79917.

Autoworld, *(Autoworld; 0-913640)*, Dist. by: Haessner Pub., Drawer B, Newfoundland, NJ 07435.

Autumn Pr, *(Autumn Press; 0-914398)*, 1318 Beacon St., Brookline, MA 02146 Tel 617-738-5680.

Auxano Pr, *(Auxano Press; 0-933364)*, P.O. Box 281, Greenlawn, NY 11740.

Auxiliary U Pr, *(Auxiliary Univ. Press)*, c/o Lea Denory, Box 772, Barrington, IL 60010 Tel 312-381-7888.

Avant-Garde, *(Avant-Garde Media, Inc.; 0-913568)*, 251 W. 57th St., New York, NY 10019 Tel 212-581-2000; Do Not Confuse with Avant Garde Creations in OR.

Avant Garde OR, *(Avant Garde Creations; 0-930182)*, Box 30161, Eugene, OR 97403; Do Not Confuse with Avant-Garde Media, Inc. in NY.

Avatar Pr, *(Avatar Press; 0-914790)*, P.O. Box 7727, Atlanta, GA 30357 Tel 404-972-7282.

Ave Maria, *(Ave Maria Press; 0-87793)*, Notre Dame, IN 46556 Tel 219-287-2831.

Avery Color, *(Avery Color Studios; 0-932212)*, Star Route Box 275, Au Train, MI 49806 Tel 906-892-8251.

Avery Pr, *(Avery Press)*, P.O. Box 7396, Atlanta, GA 30357.

Avery Pub, *(Avery Pub. Group, Inc.; 0-89529)*, 142 Fulton Ave., Garden City Park, NY 11040 Tel 516-741-2155; Orders to: 89 Baldwin Terrace, Wayne, NJ 07470.

AVI, *(AVI Publishing Co., Inc.; 0-87055)*, 250 Post Rd. E., P.O. Box 831, Westport, CT 06881 Tel 203-226-0738.

Avi
See AVI

Aviation, *(Aviation Book Co.; 0-911720; 0-911721)*, 1640 Victory Blvd., Glendale, CA 91201 Tel 213-240-1771. *Imprints:* Pub. by Bomber (Bomber Books).

Aviation Maintenance, *(Aviation Maintenance Pubs.; 0-89100)*, P.O. Box 890, Basin, WY 82410 Tel 307-568-2413. *Imprints:* Big Horn (Big Horn Book Co.).

Avocation Pubs, *(Avocation Pubs.; 0-934200)*, 50 King St., Suite 3D, New York, NY 10014.

Avon, *(Avon Books; 0-380)*, 959 Eighth Ave., New York, NY 10019 Tel 212-262-5700. *Imprints:* Avon Lib (Avon Library); Banner (Banner Books); Bard (Avon Bard Books); Camelot (Avon Camelot Books); Discus (Avon Discus Books); Flare (Avon Flare Books).

Avon Lib *Imprint of* **Avon**

Avons Res, *(Avons Research Pubns.; 0-913772)*, P.O. Box 40, La Canada, CA 91011.

Awakening Prods, *(Awakening Productions; 0-914706)*, 4132 Tuller Ave., Culver City, CA 90230.

Awani Pr, *(Awani Press; 0-915266)*, P.O. Box 881, Fredericksburg, TX 78624.

Aware Pr, *(Aware Press)*, P.O. Box 788, Thousand Oaks, CA 91360.

Awareness, *(Awareness Press; 0-917868)*, 3649 Elliot S., Apt. 1, Minneapolis, MN 55407.

AWM Co, *(A. W. M. Company; 0-89105)*, P.O. Box 7643, Ann Arbor, MI 48107 Tel 313-482-7623.

Axiom Pr, *(Axiom Press; 0-933800)*, P.O. Box 1512, Burlingame, CA 94010 Tel 415-441-1211; Dist. by: Medical & Technical Books, Inc., 11511 Tennessee Ave., Los Angeles, CA 90064 Tel 213-879-1607.

Ayer Pr, *(Ayer Press; 0-910190)*, 1 Bala Ave., Bala Cynwyd, PA 19004 Tel 215-664-6203.

Aylmer Pr, *(Aylmer Press; 0-932314)*, P.O. Box 2735, Madison, WI 53701 Tel 608-251-2506.

AZ Hist Foun, *(Arizona Historical Foundation; 0-910152)*, Hayden Memorial Library, Arizona State University, Tempe, AZ 85281 Tel 602-966-8331.

AZ Hist Soc, *(Arizona Historical Society)*, 949 E. Second St., Tucson, AZ 85719 Tel 602-882-5774.

Aztex, *(Aztex Corp.; 0-89404)*, 1126 N. Sixth Ave., P.O. Box 50046, Tucson, AZ 85703 Tel 602-882-4656; Dist. by: Elsevier-Dutton, 2 Park Ave., New York, NY 10016 Tel 212-725-1818.

B A Scott, *(Scott, Beverly A., Pub.)*, P.O. Box 114, Chandler, AZ 85224 Tel 602-963-5787.

B & E Ent, *(B & E Enterprises, Pubs.; 0-915454)*, P.O. Box 984, Everett, WA 98206.

B & G Assoc, *(B & G Associates; 0-9604230)*, 408 Larkwood Dr., Montgomery, AL 36109

B & M Waite Pr, *(Waite, Benjamin & Martha, Press, Ltd.; 0-934528)*, 1126 E. 59th St., Chicago, IL 60637.

B & R Samizdat, *(B & R Samizdat Express; 0-915232)*, P.O. Box 161, West Roxbury, MA 02132 Tel 617-469-2269.

B B Clayburn, *(Clayburn, Barbara B.; 0-9604680)*, 7023 Bridgeport Circle, Stockton, CA 95207 Tel 209-477-6059.

B B Feinsot, *(Feinsot, Bernice B.; 0-915526)*, Orders to: 330 W. 28th St., Apt 1F, New York, NY 10001 Tel 212-929-2918.

B B Martin Bks, *(Martin, B. B., Books; 0-935682)*, 6512 Libyan, Austin, TX 78745.

B Becker, *(Becker, Beverly; 0-9602000)*, P.O. Box 360, Park Ridge, IL 60068 Tel 312-825-8025.

B Berkel, *(Berkel, Boyce N., M.D.; 0-9603184)*, 2245 McMullen Booth Rd., Clearwater, FL 33519.

B C Scribe, *(Scribe, B. C., Pubns.; 0-930548)*, P.O. Box 4705, Berkeley, CA 94704 Tel 415-548-6787.

B Clark, *(Clark, Bill; 0-9601294)*, 1305 Charles Dr., Knoxville, TN 37918 Tel 615-687-6419.

B Conroy, *(Conroy, Barbara)*, Box 502, Tabernash, CO 80478 Tel 303-726-5260.

B D Mullen, *(Mullen, Barbara Dorr; 0-9600542)*, P.O. Box 11484, Santa Rosa, CA 95406 Tel 707-528-7805.

B Dolls
See Barbara Dolls

B Estrada, *(Estrada, Billie; 0-9690490)*, c/o Mrs. C. Danielson, 14015 28th N. E., Seattle, WA 98125.

B Farwell, *(Farwell, Brice; 0-9600484)*, 5 Deer Trail, Briarcliff Manor, NY 10510.

B Ferguson, *(Ferguson, Brenda)*, 9854 Fairfax Square, No. 216, New Orleans, VA 22030.

B Franklin, *(Franklin, Burt, Pub.; 0-89102)*, Dist. by: Lenox Hill Publishing & Distributing Corp., 235 E. 44th St., New York, NY 10017.

B Gould Pubns, *(Gould, Bruce, Publications; 0-918706)*, P.O. Box 16, Seattle, WA 98111

B Greene, *(Greene, Bill; 0-934668)*, Box 810, Mill Valley, CA 94942.

B Haines, *(Haines, Ben M.; 0-9600586)*, Box 1111, Lawrence, KS 66044 Tel 816-525-2579.

B Harris, *(Harris, Barbara; 0-9601060)*, P.O. Box 2992, Portland, OR 97208 Tel 503-223-6434.

B Haskewitch, *(Haskewitch, B.)*, 701 Empire Blvd., Apt. 1A, Brooklyn, NY 11213 Tel 212-756-8786; Moved, Left No Forwarding Address.

B Hilltop Pr, *(Byram Hilltop Press; 0-9605876)*, P.O. Box Z, Andover, NJ 07821.

B Howard, *(Howard, Barney; 0-935602)*, 10114 Tracy, Kansas City, MO 64131 Tel 816-942-2934.

B J Edgar, *(Edgar, Betsy J.)*, Box 86, Mt. Airy Farms, Hillsboro, WV 24946 Tel 304-653-4242.

B K Bugge, *(Bugge, Brian K.; 0-9601708)*, P.O. Box 598, Staten Island, NY 10314 Tel 212-442-1405.

B Klein Pubns, *(Klein, B., Pubns.; 0-87340)*, P.O. Box 8503, Coral Springs, FL 33065 Tel 305-752-1708.

B L Winch, *(Winch, B. L., & Associates; 0-935266)*, 45 Hitching Post Dr., Building 2, Rolling Hills Estates, CA 90274.

B Lawrence, *(Lawrence, Bruce, Corp.; 0-918252)*, 624 Nutley Pl., N. Woodmere, NY 11581 Tel 516-883-8294.

B Loft, *(Loft, Barnell, Ltd.; 0-87965)*, 958 Church St., Baldwin, NY 11510 Tel 516-868-6064.

B M Osowitz, *(Osowitz, B. M.)*, 1118 S. Broad St., Trenton, NJ 08611; Orders to: 1111 N.W. 40th Ave., Pompano, FL 33066.

B M Radewald, *(Radewald, Bette M.)*, 639 Sandalwood Court, Riverside, CA 92507.

B M Rosenthal Inc, *(Rosenthal, Bernard M., Inc., Booksellers; 0-9600094)*, 251 Post St., San Francisco, CA 94108 Tel 415-982-2219.

B M Stewart, *(Stewart, B. M.)*, 4494 Wausau Rd., Okemos, MI 48864 Tel 517-349-0297.

B O'Hara, *(O'Hara, Betsy; 0-9604188)*, P.O. Box 31510, San Francisco, CA 94131.

B Owens
See Working Pr CA

B P Reynolds, *(Reynolds, Bryan P.),* P.O. Box 186, Palos Park, IL 60464 Tel 312-425-8342.

B R Landes, *(Landes, Burton R.; 0-915568),* 11 College Ave., Trappe, PA 19426 Tel 215-489-2908.

B Rust, *(Ventura Press (B Rust)),* 781 Ventura St., Richmond, CA 94805.

B Rynders Pubns, *(Rynders, B., Pubns.; 0-9601872),* 1514-21 Ave., N.W., New Brighton, MN 55112.

B Sales, *(Sales, Billee; 0-9605244),* 2638 N.W. 59th Ave., Margate, FL 33063.

B Seitz, *(Seitz, Beatrice West),* 214 W. Van Buren St., Janesville, WI 53545 Tel 608-754-6175.

B Terrell, *(Terrell, Bob),* P.O. Box 66, Asheville, NC 28802 Tel 704-255-8435.

B-TwoC, *(B2C Adventures; 0-939368),* 2 Carvel Rd., Annapolis, MD 21401 Tel 301-974-0642.

B-TwoFDC
See B-TwoC

B W Brace, *(Brace, Beverly W.),* 455 Crescent Dr., No. 27, Sunnyvale, CA 94087 Tel 408-737-1304.

B Warrior, *(Warrior, Betsy; 0-9601544),* 46 Pleasant St., Cambridge, MA 02139.

B West, *(West, Bill; 0-911614),* 536 E. Ada Ave., Glendora, CA 91740 Tel 213-335-7060.

B Witt, *(Witt, Bud; 0-9604932),* P.O. Box 2527, 4212 W. Olive, Fullerton, CA 92633.

Back Bay, *(Back Bay Books, Inc.),* P.O. Box 1396, Newport Beach, CA 92663.

Back Porch, *(Back Porch Press),* 4080 26th St., San Francisco, CA 94131.

Back Roads
See Monday Bks

Back Row Pr, *(Back Row Press; 0-917162),* 1803 Venus Ave., St. Paul, MN 55112 Tel 612-633-1685.

Back to Bible, *(Back to the Bible Broadcast; 0-8474),* Box 82808, Lincoln, NE 68501 Tel 800-228-4208.

Backdraft, *(Backdraft Pubns.; 0-936174),* P.O. Box 152, Morristown, NJ 07960 Tel 201-766-7937.

Backdrift
See Backdraft

Backeddy Bks, *(Backeddy Books; 0-9603566),* Box 301, Cambridge, ID 83610.

Backpacker Inc
See Foot Trails

Backroads, *(Backroads; 0-933294),* Box 370, Wilson, WY 83014; Dist. by: Caroline House/TDS, P.O. Box 978, Edison, NJ 08817 Tel 201-225-1900.

Badger, *(Badger Press; 0-9601264),* P.O. Box 25, Cross Plains, WI 53528 Tel 608-798-4168.

Badger Bks, *(Badger Books; 0-930478),* P.O. Box 40336, San Francisco, CA 94140 Tel 415-285-2708.

Badlands Natl Hist, *(Badlands Natural History Assn.; 0-912410),* P.O. Box 6, Interior, SD 57750.

Baha'i, *(Baha'i Publishing Trust; 0-87743),* 415 Linden Ave., Wilmette, IL 60091 Tel 312-251-1854.

Bahm, *(Bahm, Archie J.; 0-911714),* 1915 Las Lomas Rd., N.E., Albuquerque, NM 87106 Tel 505-242-9983. *Imprints:* World (World Books).

Bailey Pubns, *(Bailey Pubns.; 0-933246),* 225 South Blvd., Nyack, NY 10960 Tel 914-358-3631.

Bainbridge, *(Bainbridge, Inc.; 0-915234),* 1012 St. Louis St., Edwardsville, IL 62025 Tel 618-656-4817.

Baja Bks, *(Baja Books; 0-9602838),* Box 229, Woodland Hills, CA 91365.

Baja Trail, *(Baja Trail Pubns., Inc.; 0-914622),* P.O. Box 6088, Huntington Beach, CA 92646 Tel 714-536-8081.

Baker Bk, *(Baker Book House; 0-8010),* P.O. Box 6287, 6030 E. Fulton, Grand Rapids, MI 49506 Tel 616-676-9186.

Baker Gallery, *(Baker Gallery Press; 0-912196),* P.O. Box 1920, Lubbock, TX 79408 Tel 806-763-3431.

Baker Library *Imprint of* **Kelley**

Baker's Plays, *(Baker, Walter H., Co.; 0-87440),* 100 Chauncy St., Boston, MA 02111 Tel 617-482-1280.

Bakke Pr, *(Bakke Press),* Rte. 3, Box 119-A, Hillsborough, NC 27278 Tel 919-929-2086.

Bala Bks, *(Bala Books; 0-89647),* 51 W. Allens Lane, Philadelphia, PA 19119 Tel 215-247-4600.

Bala Pub Div, *(Bala Publishing Division),* 1500 W. 3rd Ave., Suite 329, Columbus, OH 43212.

Balamp Pub, *(Balamp Publishing; 0-913642),* 7430 Second Blvd., Detroit, MI 48202 Tel 313-873-6320; Orders to: P.O. Box 02367, North End, Detroit, MI 48202.

Balboa Pub, *(Balboa Publishing; 0-935902),* 583 Tenth Ave., San Francisco, CA 94118.

Balcom, *(Balcom Books; 0-9600008),* 320 Bawden St., Apt. 401, Ketchikan, AK 99901 Tel 907-225-2496.

Bald Eagle, *(Bald Eagle Press; 0-910196),* 273 Woodland Dr., State College, PA 16801 Tel 814-238-6167.

Bale Bks, *(Bale Books; 0-912070),* P.O. Box 2727, New Orleans, LA 70176 Tel 504-895-5306.

Bale of Turtle, *(Bale of Turtle Press; 0-912802),* 35 High St., Armonk, NY 10504.

Baleen, *(Baleen Press; 0-912074),* P.O. Box 13448, Phoenix, AZ 85002 Tel 212-751-2600; Moved Left No Forwarding Address.

Bales, *(Bales, William J.),* P.O. Box 3172, Munster, IN 46321.

Ball State Bkstr, *(Ball State Bookstore),* Muncie, IN 47306 Tel 317-285-4242.

Ballantine, *(Ballantine Books, Inc.; 0-345),* Div. of Random House, Inc., 201 E. 50th St., New York, NY 10022 Tel 212-751-2600; Orders to: 400 Hahn Rd., Westminster, MD 21157.

Ballena Pr, *(Ballena Press; 0-87919),* P.O. Box 1366, Socorro, NM 87801 Tel 505-835-2934.

Balletmonographs, *(Balletmonographs; 0-9604232),* 2545 Pomeroy Court, S. San Francisco, CA 94080.

Ballinger Pub, *(Ballinger Publishing Co.; 0-88410),* Subs. of Harper & Row, Inc., 17 Dunster St., Harvard Square, Cambridge, MA 02138 Tel 617-492-0670.

Baltica Pr, *(Baltica Press, Pubs.; 0-910198),* P.O. Box 7847, St. Matthews Sta., Louisville, KY 40207 Tel 502-897-1241.

Baltimore Co Pub Lib, *(Baltimore County Public Library; 0-937076),* 320 York Rd., Towson, MD 21204.

Baltimore Mus, *(Baltimore Museum of Art; 0-912298),* Art Museum Dr., Baltimore, MD 21218 Tel 301-396-6316; Orders to: The Museum Shop, Art Museum Dr., Baltimore, MD 21218 Tel 301-396-6338.

Baltimore NRHS, *(Baltimore NRHS Pubns.; 0-9601320),* 4710 Keswick Rd., Baltimore, MD 21210 Tel 301-467-8849; Orders to: 2107 N. Charles St., Baltimore, MD 21218 Tel 301-547-9191.

Banbury *Imprint of* **Dell**

Bancroft Bks, *(Bancroft Books; 0-9600332),* P.O. Box 9348, Berkeley, CA 94709 Tel 415-529-1231.

Bancroft Parkman, *(Bancroft Parkman Inc.; 0-914022),* 121 E. 78th St., New York, NY 10021 Tel 212-737-2715.

Bancroft Pr, *(Bancroft Press; 0-914888),* 27 McNear Dr., San Rafael, CA 94901 Tel 415-454-7094.

B&B Hochberg, *(Hochberg, Bette & Bernard; 0-9600990),* 333 Wilkes Circle, Santa Cruz, CA 95060 Tel 408-427-2127.

B&N, *(Barnes & Noble Books; 0-389),* Div. of Littlefield, Adams & Co., 81 Adams Dr., Totowa, NJ 07512 Tel 201-256-8600. *Imprints:* Art (Art Series); FB (Focus Books); Key (Keynote Series); SocSP (Social Science Paperbacks); U (U Books); UP (Univ. Paperbacks).

Bandon Hist, *(Bandon Historical Society; 0-932368),* P.O. Box 737, Bandon, OR 97411 Tel 503-347-2164.

Banjo Pr
See Tamarack Edns

Bank of Amer, *(Bank of America),* P.O. Box 3700, San Francisco, CA 94137 Tel 415-622-2645.

Banker Res Unit, *(Banker Research Unit of the Financial Times),* 551 5th Ave., New York, NY 10017.

Bankers, *(Bankers Publishing Co.; 0-87267),* 210 South St., Boston, MA 02111 Tel 617-426-4495.

Bankers Pr, *(Bankers Press Inc.; 0-9602414),* 5810 S. Green St., Chicago, IL 60621.

Banks-Baldwin, *(Banks-Baldwin Law Publishing Co.; 0-8322),* University Ctr. P.O. Box 1974, Cleveland, OH 44106 Tel 216-721-7373.

Banner *Imprint of* **Avon**

Banner *Imprint of* **Exposition**

Banner Bks Intl, *(Banner Books International; 0-89491),* 13415 Ventura Blvd., Sherman Oaks, CA 91423 Tel 213-990-0024.

Banner of Truth, *(Banner of Truth, The; 0-85151),* P.O. Box 621, Carlisle, PA 17013 Tel 717-249-5747.

Banner Pr AL, *(Banner Press, Inc.; 0-87121),* P.O. Box 20180, Birmingham, AL 35216 Tel 205-822-4783.

Banner Pr IL, *(Banner Press; 0-916650),* P.O. Box 6469, Chicago, IL 60680 Tel 312-663-1843. *Imprints:* United Front (United Front Press).

Banning Pr, *(Banning, Arthur J., Press; 0-938060),* 305 Foshay Tower, Minneapolis, MN 55402 Tel 612-335-4259.

Bannister Assoc, *(Bannister Associates; 0-89578),* P.O. Box 52, Still River, MA 01467; Moved, Left No Forwarding Address.

Banta, *(Banta, George, Co.),* Banta's Greek Exchange, Menasha, WI 54952 Tel 414-722-7771.

Bantam, *(Bantam Books, Inc.; 0-553),* 666 Fifth Ave., New York, NY 10019 Tel 212-765-6500; Orders to: 414 E. Golf Rd., Des Plaines, IL 60016. *Imprints:* Minibooks (Minibooks); Pathfinder (Pathfinder Books); Peacock (Peacock); Skylark (Skylark); Windstone (Windstone).

Banyan Bks, *(Banyan Books; 0-916224),* P.O. Box 431160, Miami, FL 33143 Tel 305-665-6011.

Banyan Tree, *(Banyan Tree Books; 0-9604320),* 1963 El Dorado Ave., Berkeley, CA 94707; Dist. by: Bookpeople, 2940 Seventh St., Berkeley, CA 94710 Tel 415-549-3033.

Baptist Pub Hse, *(Baptist Publishing House; 0-89114),* 1319 Magnolia, Texarkana, TX 75501.

Baptist Span
See Casa Bautista

Bar Guide, *(Bar Guide Enterprises; 0-918338),* P.O. Box 4044, Terminal Annex, Los Angeles, CA 90051 Tel 213-883-5369.

Bar-None, *(Bar-None Press; 0-9605672),* 6520 Selma Ave., No. 538, Los Angeles, CA 90028.

Barah, *(Barah Publishing; 0-930292),* P.O. Box 697, San Anselmo, CA 94960 Tel 415-459-1165.

Baraka Bk, *(Baraka Books, Ltd.),* 453 Greenwich St., New York, NY 10013 Tel 212-966-6658.

Baraka Pr
See Baraka Bk

Baraka VA, *(Baraka Books; 0-9604578),* 7511 Campbell Dr., Salem, VA 24153.

Barbara Dolls, *(Barbara Dolls; 0-918564),* Box 736, Bowie, MD 20715 Tel 301-262-2968; 2700 Balsam Pl., Bowie, MD 20715.

Barbara M Morris Rept, *(Barbara M. Morris Report, The; 0-931650),* P.O. Box 412, Ellicott City, MD 21043.

Barber Pr, *(Barber, Lilian, Press; 0-936508),* Box 4224, Grand Central Sta., New York, NY 10163.

Barclay Bridge, *(Barclay Bridge Supplies, Inc.; 0-87643),* 8 Bush Ave., Port Chester, NY 10573 Tel 914-937-4200.

Barclay Hse, *(Barclay House; 0-87682),* Div. of American Art Enterprises, Inc., 21322 Lassen St., Chatsworth, CA 91311 Tel 213-882-5900; Moved, Left No Forwardind Address.

Barclay Pr, *(Barclay Press; 0-913342),* P.O. Box 232, Newberg, OR 97132 Tel 503-538-7345.

Bard *Imprint of* **Avon**

Bard Pr, *(Bard Press; 0-934776),* 799 Greenwich St., New York, NY 10014 Tel 212-929-3169.

Bardic, *(Bardic Echoes Brochures; 0-915020),* 125 Somerset Dr., N.E., Grand Rapids, MI 49503 Tel 616-454-2807.

Barding Pub, *(Barding, L.F., Publishing; 0-9605848),* P.O. Box 06264, Ft. Myers, FL 33906 Tel 813-936-2774.

Bark-Back, *(Bark-Back; 0-9603338),* P.O. Box 235, Glenshaw, PA 15116 Tel 412-364-3743.

Barkley, *(Barkley, M. J.; 0-9601354),* 253 E. 16th St., No. 12, Oakland, CA 94601.

Barksdale Foun, *(Barksdale Foundation; 0-918588),* P.O. Box 187, Idyllwild, CA 92349 Tel 714-659-3858.

Barlenmir, *(Barlenmir House, Pubs.; 0-87929),* 413 City Island Ave., New York, NY 10464 Tel 212-885-2120.

Barleycorn, *(Barleycorn Books; 0-935566),* 290 S.W. Tualatin Loop, West Linn, OR 97068 Tel 503-225-0234.

Barn Dream, *(Barn Dream Press),* 60 Fairmont St., Cambridge, MA 02138.

Barn Hill, *(Barn Hill; 0-931968),* 825 Hallowell Dr., Huntingdon Valley, PA 19006.

Barnard Pr, *(Barnard Press Pubs.),* P.O. Box 622, La Jolla, CA 92038 Tel 714-488-8151.

Barnard Roberts, *(Barnard, Roberts & Co., Inc.; 0-934118),* 6655 Amberton Dr., Rte. 100 Business Park, Baltimore, MD 21227 Tel 301-796-5655.

Barnegat, *(Barnegat Light Press; 0-937996),* Box 305, Barnegat Light, NJ 08006.

Barnett, *(Barnett, P.),* 25 Sagamore Rd., Bronxville, NY 10708; Moved Left No Forwarding Address.

Barnhart, *(Barnhart, Clarence L., Inc.; 0-913296),* P.O. Box 250, Bronxville, NY 10708 Tel 914-337-7100.

Barnstable, *(Barnstable Books; 0-918230),* 799 Broadway, Rm. 506A, New York, NY 10003 Tel 212-473-8681.

Baronet, *(Baronet Pub. Co.; 0-89437),* 509 Madison Ave., New York, NY 10022 Tel 212-752-7331.

Baroque, *(Baroque Press, Inc.),* P.O. Box 553, Maplewood, NJ 07040; Moved, Left No Forwarding Address.

Barre, *(Barre Publishing Co.),* Valley Rd., Barre, MA 01005 Tel 617-355-2914; Dist. by: Crown Publishers, Inc., 1 Park Ave., New York, NY 10016. *Imprints:* Westover (Westover Pub Co.).

Barrett Bk, *(Barrett Book Co.; 0-932684),* 388 Summer St., Stamford, CT 06901.

Barrie & Jenkins, *(Barrie & Jenkins; 0-214),* Dist. by: Arco, 219 Park Ave. S., New York, NY 10003 Tel 212-777-6300.

Barrington, *(Barrington Press, Inc.; 0-938814),* 200 James St., Barrington, IL 60010 Tel 312-381-9200; Dist. by: Berkshire Traveller Press, Pine St., Stockbridge, MA 01262 Tel 413-298-3636.

Barron, *(Barron's Educational Series, Inc.; 0-8120),* 113 Crossways Park Dr., Woodbury, NY 11797 Tel 516-921-8750.

Bartco, *(Bartco Ltd.; 0-936374),* P.O. Box 26634, St. Louis, MO 63122.

Bartle, *(Bartle, Jim; 0-933982),* 771 W. Dry Creek Rd., Healdsburg, CA 95448.

Bartlett Pubns, *(Bartlett Pubns.; 0-9604796),* 3311 Richmond, Suite 321, Houston, TX 77098.

Bartz, *(Bartz, Frederick H.; 0-911944),* c/o Graphics Arts Research Foundation, 24575 San Jacinto St., San Jacinto, CA 92383 Tel 714-658-5223.

Baseball Facts, *(Baseball Facts; 0-939906),* P.O. Box 3529, Trenton, NJ 08629.

Basic, *(Basic Books, Inc.; 0-465),* 10 E. 53rd St., New York, NY 10022 Tel 212-593-7057.

Basic Eng Rev, *(Basic English Revisited),* 275 Robins Row, Burlington, WI 53105.

Basic Info, *(Basic Information Services, Inc.; 0-916408),* 125 N. Cambridge St., Orange, CA 92666 Tel 714-639-8775.

Basic Medicine, *(Basic Medicine Books; 0-913736),* P.O. Box 40129, San Francisco, CA 94140 Tel 415-845-5656; Moved Left No Forwarding Address.

Basic Sci Pr, *(Basic Science Press; 0-917410),* 1608 Via Lazo, Palos Verdes Estates, CA 90274 Tel 213-375-6740; Formerly Named Lucknow Publishing Co.

Basic Science Prep Ctr, *(Basic Science Preparation Center; 0-9604722),* 55 Willow Tree Lane, Irvine, CA 92715; Orders to: 1601 Vivian Lane, Louisville, KY 40205.

Basil Blackwell
    See Biblio Dist

Basin Pub, *(Basin Publishing Co.),* 168 Weyford Terrace, Garden City, NY 11530 Tel 516-437-2821.

Baskin Pubs, *(Baskin Pubs.; 0-935854),* P.O. Box 3127, San Diego, CA 92103.

Bassett & Brush, *(Bassett & Brush; 0-9605548),* W. 4108 Francis Ave., Spokane, WA 99208.

Batchelor Dean, *(Batchelor, Dean, Pubns.; 0-914792),* 1155 Katella, Laguna Beach, CA 92651; Dist. by: Haessner Publishing, Inc., Drawer B, Newfoundland, NJ 07435; Moved Left No Forwarding Address.

Bath St Pr, *(Bath Street Press; 0-937618),* 1016 Bath, Ann Arbor, MI 48103 Tel 313-663-2071.

Battelle, *(Battelle Press; 0-935470),* Div. of Columbus Laboratories of Batelle Memorial Institute, 505 King Ave., Columbus, OH 43201 Tel 614-424-4448; Dist. by: Van Nostrand Reinhold, 135 W. 50th St., New York, NY 10020 Tel 212-265-8700.

Battery Pk, *(Battery Park Book Co.; 0-89782),* Box 710, Forest Hills, NY 11375.

Battery Pr, *(Battery Press; 0-89839),* P.O. Box 3107, Uptown Sta., Nashville, TN 37219 Tel 615-298-1401.

Bauhan, *(Bauhan, William L., Inc.; 0-87233),* Old County Rd., Dublin, NH 03444 Tel 603-563-8020.

Baukol Pub, *(Baukol, Philip J., Publishing; 0-9601110),* 5838 Black Olive Dr., No. 20, Paradise, CA 95969 Tel 916-872-0248.

Bawa Muhaiyad
    See Fellowship Pr PA

Bay Bks, *(Bay Books; 0-89171),* 909 N. Beverly Glen Blvd., Bel Air, CA 90024.

Bayard Gallery, *(Bayard Gallery Pubns.; 0-933290),* 233 Broadway E., Seattle, WA 98102.

Bayard Pubns, *(Bayard Pubns., Inc.; 0-933268),* 695 Summer St., Stamford, CT 06901 Tel 203-327-0800.

Bayer, *(Bayer, Constance Pole; 0-9600276),* 8250 N.E. Third Court, Miami, FL 33138.

Bayland Pub, *(Bayland Publishing, Inc.; 0-934018),* P.O. Box 25386, Houston, TX 77005 Tel 713-524-3000.

Bayliss Corbett, *(Corbett, Bayliss; 0-933152),* P.O. Box 1526, Bonita Springs, FL 33880.

Baylor Univ Pr, *(Baylor Univ. Press; 0-918954),* Orders to: Book Dept., Baylor Book Store, P.O. Box 6325, Waco, TX 76706 Tel 817-755-2161.

Bayou Cuisine, *(Bayou Cuisine),* P.O. Box 1005, Indianola, MS 38751 Tel 601-887-1218.

Bayou Pub Co, *(Bayou Publishing Co.; 0-9602570),* 5200 Bon Air Dr., Monroe, LA 71203 Tel 318-343-1964.

Bayshore Bks, *(Bayshore Books; 0-9602314),* Box 848, Nokomis, FL 33555 Tel 813-485-2564.

Bayside, *(Bayside Publishing Co.; 0-913794),* 1350 77th Ave., N., St. Petersburg, FL 33702.

Baywood Pub, *(Baywood Publishing Co., Inc.; 0-89503),* 120 Marine St., P.O. Box D, Farmingdale, NY 11735 Tel 516-293-7130.

BBEA, *(Bible Believers' Evangelistic Assn., Inc.),* Box 18003, Dallas, TX 75218 Tel 214-328-9407.

BBM Assocs
    See Calif Street

BC *Imprint of* Grove

BCA Pub, *(BCA Publishing Corp.; 0-931564),* 180 W. Washington St., Suite 802, Chicago, IL 60602 Tel 312-236-9347.

BCAR Pubns, *(BCAR Pubns.; 0-930986),* Affiliate of Three Mountains Press, P.O. Box 50, Cooper Sta., New York, NY 10003.

BCC, *(Business Communications Co. (BCC); 0-89336),* P.O. Box 2070C, 9 Viaduct Rd., Stamford, CT 06906 Tel 203-325-2208.

BCM Inc, *(Bible Club Movement, Inc.),* 237 Fairfield Ave., Upper Darby, PA 19082 Tel 215-352-7177.

BCM Pubns
    See BCM Inc

BCM Pubns, *(BCM Pubns.; 0-86508),* 237 Fairfield Ave., Upper Darby, PA 19082.

BCP NY, *(Best Cellar Press; 0-932874),* 51 Marilyn Pkwy., Rochester, NY 14624.

Bd of Pubns CRC, *(Board of Publications of the Christian Reformed Church; 0-933140),* 2850 Kalamazoo Ave. S.E., Grand Rapids, MI 49560 Tel 616-241-1691.

Be All Bks, *(Be All Books; 0-9601848),* P.O. Box 779, Sonoma, CA 95476.

Beacham, *(Beacham, Roger, Pub.; 0-911796),* P.O. Box 8254, Austin, TX 78712 Tel 512-451-4572.

Beachcomber Bks, *(Beachcomber Books; 0-913076),* 3829 N. Oracle Rd., Tucson, AZ 85705.

Beacon Hill, *(Beacon Hill Press of Kansas City),* Dist. by: Nazarene Publishing House, P.O. Box 527, Kansas City, MO 64141 Tel 816-931-1900.

Beacon Hse, *(Beacon House, Inc.; 0-87648),* P.O. Box 311, Beacon, NY 12508 Tel 914-831-2318.

Beacon Pr, *(Beacon Press, Inc.; 0-8070),* 25 Beacon St., Boston, MA 02108 Tel 617-742-2110; Orders to: Harper & Row Pubs., Inc., Keystone Industrial Park, Scranton, PA 18512.

Beacon Presse IA, *(Le Beacon Presse; 0-935954),* 621 Holt, Box 221, Iowa City, IA 52240 Tel 319-354-5447.

Beaconsfield, *(Beaconsfield, C.; 0-910202),* 136 N. Rowell Ave., Fresno, CA 93703.

Bean Assoc
    See Bean Pub

Bean Pub, *(Carolyn Bean Publishing, Ltd.; 0-916860),* 120 Second St., San Francisco, CA 94105 Tel 415-957-9574.

Beanie Bks, *(Beanie Books; 0-933530),* c/o Cecilia Lacks, 7443 Stanford, St. Louis, MO 63130.

Bear, *(Bear Pubns.; 0-912934),* P.O. Box 95, Cambridge, NY 12816 Tel 518-677-2766.

Bear Hug, *(Bear Hug Books),* Orders to: SBD: Small Press Distribution, 1636 Ocean View Ave., Kensington, CA 94707 Tel 415-524-2107.

Bear Paw Pubns, *(Bear Paw Printers),* P.O. Box 1351, Harve, MT 59501 Tel 406-265-7431.

Bear State, *(Bear State Books),* 304 High St., Santa Cruz, CA 95060 Tel 408-426-3272.

Bear Tribe, *(Bear Tribe Publishing Co.),* P.O. Box 9167, Spokane, WA 99209 Tel 509-258-7755.

Beardsley Pub, *(Beardsley Publishing Co.; 0-916016),* 5523 N. Homestead Lane, Paradise Valley, AZ 85253.

Bearmoth Pr, *(Bearmoth Press, The),* P.O. Box 399, Lomita, CA 90717.

Beatitude, *(Beatitude Press),* 2940 Claremont Ave., Apt. 6, Berkeley, CA 94705.

Beatty, *(Beatty, R. W.; 0-87948),* P.O. Box 26, Arlington, VA 22210.

Beau Lac, *(Beau Lac Pubs.; 0-911980),* P.O. Box 248, Chuluota, FL 32766 Tel 305-365-3830.

Beau Rivage, *(Beau Rivage Press; 0-931174),* 7 E. 14th St., Suite 1112, New York, NY 10003 Tel 212-989-1625.

Beaufort, *(Beaufort Book Co., Inc.; 0-910206),* 808 Bay St., Box 1127, Beaufort, SC 29902 Tel 803-524-4753.

Beaufort Bks NY, *(Beaufort Books; 0-8253),* 9 E. 40th St., New York, NY 10016.

Beautiful Am, *(Beautiful America Publishing Co. 0-89802; 0-915796),* P.O. Box 608, Beaverton, OR 97075 Tel 503-641-2272.

Beautiful Day, *(Beautiful Day Books; 0-930296),* 5008 Berwyn Rd., College Park, MD 20740 Tel 301-345-2121.

Beauty & Health, *(Beauty & Health Publishing Corp.; 0-914014),* 1010 3rd Ave., New York, NY 10021 Tel 212-752-8506.

Beavers, *(Beavers; 0-910208),* Star Rte., Laporte, MN 56461 Tel 218-224-2182.

Beckwith, *(Beckwith, Burnham Putnam; 0-9603262),* 656 Lytton Ave., (C430), Palo Alto, CA 94301 Tel 415-324-0342.

Beddoe Pub, *(Beddoe Publishing; 0-9606106),* 430 Closter Dock Rd., Closter, NJ 07624.

Bede, *(Bede Press & Bede Records, Inc.; 0-911970),* Box 36m32, 5350 Wilshire Blvd. Los Angeles, CA 90036.

Bedell, *(Bedell, Clyde),* 2390-3e Mariposa W., Laguna Hills, CA 92653 Tel 714-586-2088.

Bedminster, *(Bedminster Press; 0-87087),* Vreeland Ave., Totowa, NJ 07512 Tel 201-256-0700; Moved, Left No Forwarding Address.

Bedous, *(Bedous Press; 0-918094),* P.O. Box K, Beaverton, OR 97075 Tel 503-649-7844.

Bedpress *Imprint of* New Bedford

Bee Bks, *(Bee Books, Inc.; 0-930898),* Div. of Barton Educational Enterprises & Distributors, Inc., 7532 Nohopa Cove, Germantown, TN 38138.

Beeberry Bks, *(Beeberry Books; 0-9601996),* Box 3888, Stanford, CA 94306.

Beech Hill, *(Beech Hill Publishing Co.; 0-933786),* Box 29, Mt. Desert, ME 04660 Tel 207-244-3931.

Beech Hill Ent
    See Beech Hill

Beech Tree, *(Beech Tree Farm; 0-910210),* 12000 U. S. 1, Juno, FL 33408.

Beekman Pubs, *(Beekman Pubs., Inc.; 0-8464),* Rte. 1, Box 506, Woodstock, NY 12498.

Beer Adv
 See D Bull

Beers, *(Beers, J., & Co.),* Orders to: Freshwater Press, Inc., 258 The Arcade, Cleveland, OH 44114 Tel 216-241-0373.

Beginner, *(Beginner Books),* Div. of Random House, Inc., 201 E. 50th St., New York, NY 10022; Orders to: 400 Hahn Rd., Westminster, MD 21157.

Behavior Mod Tech, *(Behavior Modification Technology, Inc.; 0-89025),* P.O. Box 3251, Tuscaloosa, AL 35404 Tel 205-345-1183.

Behavioral Mass, *(Behavioral Research Council; 0-913610),* Division St., Great Barrington, MA 01230 Tel 413-528-1216.

Behavioral Pubns
 See Human Sci Pr

Behavioral Re
 See Learning Line

Behavioral Studies, *(Behavioral Studies Press; 0-911958),* P.O. Box 5323, Beverly Hills, CA 90210.

Behaviordelia, *(Behaviordelia, Inc.; 0-914474),* P.O. Box 1044, Kalamazoo, MI 49005 Tel 616-382-5611.

Behrman, *(Behrman House, Inc.; 0-87441),* 1261 Broadway, New York, NY 10001 Tel 212-689-2020.

Beinfeld Pub, *(Beinfeld Publishing, Inc.; 0-917714),* 12767 Saticoy St., North Hollywood, CA 91605.

Being Bks, *(Being Books),* 19834 Gresham St., Northridge, CA 91324 Tel 213-341-0283.

Being Inc, *(Being Inc.; 0-915412),* P.O. Box 742, Ojai, CA 93023.

Being Pubns, *(Being Pubns),* 1530 Valley Ave. N.W., Grand Rapids, MI 49504.

Bek Indus
 See Bek Tech

Bek Tech, *(Bek Technical Pubns., Inc.; 0-912884),* 1700 Painters Run Rd., Pittsburgh, PA 15243 Tel 412-221-0900.

Belier Pr, *(Belier Press, Inc.; 0-914646),* P.O. Box C, Gracie Sta., New York, NY 10028 Tel 212-989-5722.

Believers Bkshelf, *(Believers Bookshelf),* Box 261, Sunbury, PA 17801 Tel 717-672-2134.

Bell *Imprint of* FS&G

Bell & Howell, *(Bell & Howell Co.),* Micro Photo Div., Old Mansfied Rd., Wooster, OH 44691 Tel 216-264-6666.

Bell Assn Deaf, *(A. G. Bell Assn. for the Deaf; 0-88200),* 3417 Volta Place, N.W., Washington, DC 20007 Tel 202-337-5220.

Bell-Dell, *(Bell-Dell Co.),* P.O. Box 20624, Chicago, IL 60620; Moved, Left No Forwarding Address.

Bell Ent, *(Bell Enterprises, Inc.; 0-918340),* P.O. Box 9054, Pine Bluff, AR 71611 Tel 501-247-1922.

Bell Springs Pub, *(Bell Springs Pub; 0-917510),* P.O. Box 640, Laytonville, CA 95454 Tel 707-984-6746.

Belle Pubns, *(Belle Pubns.; 0-9605732),* 172 Pathway Lane, W. Lafayette, IN 47906.

Bellefontaine Bks, *(Bellefontaine Books; 0-932786),* P.O. Box 501, Arroyo Grande, CA 93420 Tel 805-489-6242.

Belleridge, *(Belleridge Press; 0-938632),* P.O. Box 970, Rancho Santa Fe, CA 92067.

Bellerophon Bks, *(Bellerophon Books; 0-88388),* 36 Anacapa St., Santa Barbara, CA 93101 Tel 805-965-7034.

Bellevue Pr, *(Bellevue Press; 0-933466),* 60 Schubert St., Binghamton, NY 13905 Tel 607-729-0819.

Bellflower, *(Bellflower Press; 0-934958),* Dept. of English, Case Western Reserve University, Cleveland, OH 44106 Tel 216-368-2340.

Bellman, *(Bellman Publishing Co.; 0-87442),* P.O. Box 164, Arlington, MA 02174 Tel 617-894-3000.

Bellwether CA, *(Bellwether Books; 0-89475),* 15910 Ventura Blvd., Encino, CA 91436 Tel 213-990-1239.

Bellwether Pub, *(Bellwether Publishing Co.; 0-913144),* 167 E. 67th St., New York, NY 10021.

Belmary, *(Belmary Press; 0-910214),* 4652 E. Pinewood, Mobile, AL 36618 Tel 205-342-7171.

Belmont-Tower
 See Tower Bks

Belwin-Mills, *(Belwin-Mills Publishing Corp.),* 25 Deshon Dr., Melville, NY 11747 Tel 516-293-3400.

Bench Pr, *(Bench Press; 0-916534),* P.O. Box 24635, Oakland, CA 94623 Tel 415-652-3953.

Bender, *(Bender, Matthew, & Co., Inc.; 0-87571),* Subs. of Times Mirror Co., Attn: Rudolph Sommer, 235 E. 45th St., New York, NY 10017.

Bender Pub CA, *(Bender, R. James, Publishing; 0-912138),* P.O. Box 23456, San Jose, CA 95123 Tel 408-225-5777.

Benedict Con Adoration, *(Benedictine Convent of Perpetual Adoration; 0-913180),* 3888 Paducah Dr., San Diego, CA 92117 Tel 714-274-1030.

Benefic, *(Benefic Press; 0-8175),* Div. of Beckley-Cardy Co., 1900 N. Narragansett, Chicago, IL 60639 Tel 312-287-7110.

Bengal Pr, *(Bengal Press, Inc.; 0-935650),* P.O. Box 1128, Grand Rapids, MI 49501.

Benin, *(Benin Press, Ltd.; 0-910216),* 5225 S. Blackstone Ave., Chicago, IL 60615.

Beninda, *(Beninda Books; 0-931868),* P.O. Box 9251, Canton, OH 44711.

Benjamin Co, *(Benjamin Co., Inc.; 0-87502),* 485 Madison Ave., New York, NY 10022 Tel 212-759-6920.

Benjamin-Cummings, *(Benjamin-Cummings Publishing Co.; 0-8053),* Subs. of Addison-Wesley Publishing Co., 2727 Sand Hill Rd., Menlo Park, CA 94025 Tel 415-854-6020; Orders to: South St., Reading, MA 01867. *Imprints:* Adv Bk Prog (Advance Book Program).

Bennet Pub, *(Bennet, Rebecca, Pubns., Inc.; 0-910218),* 5409 18th Ave., Brooklyn, NY 11204.

Bennett Arch & Eng, *(Bennett, Robert, Architect & Engineer; 0-9601718),* 6 Snowden Rd., Bala Cynwyd, PA 19004.

Bennett Co
 See Bennett IL

Bennett IL, *(Bennett Publishing Co.; 0-87002),* 809 W. Detweiller Dr., Peoria, IL 61615 Tel 309-691-4454.

Benson, *(Benson, W. S., & Co., Inc.; 0-87443),* P.O. Box 1866, Austin, TX 78767 Tel 512-476-3050.

Benson Co TN, *(Benson Co., The),* 365 Great Circle Rd., Nashville, TN 37228 Tel 615-259-9111.

Bentley, *(Bentley, Robert, Inc.; 0-8376),* 872 Massachusetts Ave., Cambridge, MA 02139 Tel 617-547-4170.

Benziger
 See Glencoe

Benziger Pub Co, *(Benziger Publishing Co.; 0-02; 0-8460),* Div. of Glencoe Publishing Co., c/o Macmillan Publishing Co., Inc., 866 Third Ave., New York, NY 10022 Tel 212-935-2000.

Benziger Sis, *(Benziger Sisters Publishers),* 466 E. Mariposa St., Altadena, CA 91001.

Beresford Bk Serv, *(Beresford Book Service; 0-202),* 1525 E. 53rd St., Suite 431, Chicago, IL 60615.

Bereson & Bereson, *(Bereson & Bereson),* 466 Winchester St., Daly City, CA 94014 Tel 415-587-2697.

Berg
 See Larlin Corp

Bergling
 See Gem City Coll

Bergman, *(Bergman Pubs.),* ; Publisher Abbreviation Without Addresses Are for Titles That Are Out of Print. These Are Obsolete Abbreviations.

Berkeley Poets, *(Berkeley Poets' Workshop & Press),* P.O. Box 459, Berkeley, CA 94701 Tel 415-848-9098.

Berkeley Sci, *(Berkeley Scientific Pubns.),* Div. of Scientific Newsletters, Inc., P.O. Box 4546, Anaheim, CA 92803.

Berkeley Slavic, *(Berkeley Slavic Specialities; 0-933884),* P.O. Box 4605, Berkeley, CA 94704 Tel 415-653-8048.

Berkley Pub, *(Berkley Publishing Corp.; 0-425),* Affiliate of G. P. Putnam's Sons, 200 Madison Ave., New York, NY 10016 Tel 212-686-9820. *Imprints:* Highland (Highland Books); Medallion (Medallion Books); Windhover (Windhover).

Berkshire Traveller, *(Berkshire Traveller Press; 0-912944),* Pine St., Stockbridge, MA 01262 Tel 413-298-3636.

Berlitz *Imprint of* Macmillan

Bermont Bks, *(Bermont Books; 0-930686),* 815 15th St., N.W., Suite 1108, Washington, DC 20005.

Bermuda Bio, *(Bermuda Biological Station; 0-917642),* Pierce Hall, 29 Oxford St., Cambridge, MA 02138 Tel 617-495-2845.

Berwyn-London, *(Berwyn-London Pubs.; 0-916536),* 2401 Calumet St., Flint, MI 48503.

Best Antiques, *(Best, Charles, Antiques; 0-914346),* 6288 S. Pontiac, Englewood, CO 80111 Tel 303-771-5870.

Best Bks, *(Best Books, Inc.; 0-910228),* 44 Madison St., Oak Park, IL 60302.

Bet-Ken Prods, *(Bet-Ken Productions; 0-9603698),* 4363 Cherry Ave., San Jose, CA 95118 Tel 408-267-3425.

Bet Yoatz Lib Serv
 See BYLS Pr

Beta Bk, *(Beta Book Co.; 0-89293),* 10857 Valiente Court, San Diego, CA 92124 Tel 714-293-3832.

Beta Phi Mu, *(Beta Phi Mu Chapbooks; 0-910230),* College of Library Science; Univ. of KY, Lexington, KY 40506.

Bethany Coll
 See Bethany Coll KS

Bethany Coll KS, *(Bethany College Pubns. - Kansas; 0-916030),* P.O. Box 111, Lindsborg, KS 67456.

Bethany Fell, *(Bethany Fellowship, Inc.; 0-87123),* 6820 Auto Club Rd., Minneapolis, MN 55438 Tel 612-944-2121.

Bethany Pr, *(Bethany Press; 0-8272),* 2640 Pine Blvd., Box 179, St. Louis, MO 63166 Tel 314-371-6900.

Bethesda, *(Bethesda Books; 0-9601308),* P.O. Box 34567, Bethesda, MD 20034 Tel 301-320-4675.

Bethlen Pr, *(Bethlen Press, Inc.; 0-917718),* P.O. Box 637, Ligonier, PA 15658 Tel 412-238-9244.

BETOM Pubns, *(BETOM Pubns; 0-9605172),* P.O. Box 47, New London, WI 54961.

Better Am Corp, *(Better America Corp., A; 0-9605156),* P.O. Box 8746, Pembroke Pines, FL 33024.

Better Daly, *(Better Daly Press, The; 0-9605673),* 8801 Stenton Ave., Philadelphia, PA 19118.

Better Bks, *(Better Books Pub.),* 3736 S. E. 33rd Ave., Portland, OR 97202 Tel 503-238-0442.

Betterway Pubns, *(Betterway Pubns; 0-932620),* White Hall, VA 22987 Tel 804-823-5661.

Between Hours, *(Between Hours Press; 0-910232),* 29 E. 63rd St., New York, NY 10021.

Betzold, *(Betzold, Michael; 0-9602452),* 150 W. Nevada, Detroit, MI 48203.

Beulah, *(Beulah Records & Publishing Co.; 0-911870),* Rte. 1, Crossville, IL 62827 Tel 618-966-3405.

Beverage Media, *(Beverage Media, Ltd.; 0-9602566),* 251 Park Ave. S., New York, NY 10010.

Bewick Edns, *(Bewick Editions; 0-935590),* 1443 Bewick, Detroit, MI 48214.

Beyond Baroque
 See Beyond Baroque

Beyond Baroque, *(Beyond Baroque Foundation Pubns.),* 1639 W. Washington Blvd., Venice, CA 90291 Tel 213-392-5763.

BFA Ed Media, *(BFA Educational Media; 0-88456),* 2211 Michigan Ave., P.O. Box 1795, Santa Monica, CA 90406 Tel 213-829-2901.

BGSU Dept Phil, *(Bowling Green State Univ., Dept. of Philosophy; 0-935756),* Bowling Green State Univ., Bowling Green, OH 43403 Tel 419-372-2117.

BGTC
 See B Greene

BH Ent, *(BH Enterprises; 0-9604896),* P.O. Box 216, Midwood Sta., Brooklyn, NY 11230 Tel 212-336-0521.

Bhaktivedanta, *(Bhaktivedanta Book Trust; 0-912776),* 3764 Watseka Ave., Los Angeles, CA 90034 Tel 213-559-4455.

BH&G, *(Better Homes & Gardens Books; 0-696),* Div. of Meredith Corp., 1716 Locust St., Des Moines, IA 50336 Tel 515-284-2844.

BHRA, *(BHRA Fluid Engineering; 0-900983),* Dist. by: Air Science Co., P.O. Box 143, Corning, NY 14830 Tel 607-962-5591.

Bi World Indus, *(Bi World Industries, Inc.; 0-89557),* P.O. Box 62, Provo, UT 84601 Tel 801-224-5803.

Bibl Based Develop, *(Biblically Based Developmental Training Books, Inc.; 0-937442),* P.O. Box 15124, Atlanta, GA 30333.

Bibl Evang Pr, *(Biblical Evangelism Press; 0-914012),* 11 Blvd. Motif, Brownsburg, IN 46112 Tel 317-852-3535; Orders to: P.O. Box 157, Brownsburg, IN 46112.

Bibl Res Pr, *(Biblical Research Press; 0-89112),* 1334 Ruswood, Abilene, TX 79601 Tel 915-672-6702.

Bible Light, *(Bible Light Pubns.; 0-937078),* P.O. Box 168, Jerome Ave. Sta., New York, NY 10468.

Bible Lit, *(Bible Literature Pubns.; 0-910236),* 937 Lassen View Dr., Lake Almanor Peninsula, CA 96137 Tel 916-258-3906.

Bible Pr, *(Bible Press; 0-914936),* 7626 N.E. Glisan, Portland, OR 97213 Tel 503-253-3460; Dist. by: Bible & Gift Shop, 7545 N.E. Glisan St., Portland, OR 97213.

Bible Study Pr, *(Bible Study Press; 0-9600154),* 1111 E. Fairy Chasm Rd., Milwaukee, WI 52317 Tel 414-352-2231. *Imprints:* Omnibook (Omnibook, Co.).

Bible Voice, *(Bible Voice, Inc.; 0-89728),* P.O. Box 7491, Van Nuys, CA 91409 Tel 213-781-2900; Dist. by: Unilit, 5600 N.E. Hassalo St., Portland, OR 97213 Tel 800-547-8020.

Biblical Res Assocs, *(Biblical Research Associates Inc.; 0-935106),* Box 3182, The College of Wooster, Wooster, OH 44691 Tel 216-264-1234.

Biblio Dist, *(Biblio Distribution Centre),* 81 Adams Dr., P.O. Box 327, Totowa, NJ 07511 Tel 201-256-8600.

Biblio NY, *(Biblio Press; 0-9602036),* P.O. Box 22, Fresh Meadows, NY 11365.

Biblio Pr, *(Bibliography Press),* 111 N. Wabash, Rm. 1310, Chicago, IL 60602; Moved, Left No Forwarding Address.

Biblio Pr GA, *(Bibliotheca Press; 0-9605246; 0-939476),* P.O. Box 98378, Atlanta, GA 30359 Tel 404-588-1328.

Biblio Siglo, *(Biblioteca Siglo de Oro),* 530 N. First St., Charlottesville, VA 22901 Tel 804-295-1021.

Bibliotheca, *(Bibliotheca Islamica, Inc.; 0-88297),* P.O. Box 1536, Chicago, IL 60690.

Biblo, *(Biblo & Tannen Booksellers & Pubs., Inc.; 0-8196),* P.O. Box 302, 321 Sandbank Rd., Cheshire, CT 06410.

Bicent Era, *(Bicentennial Era Enterprises; 0-9605734),* P.O. Box 1148, Scappoose, OR 97056.

Bicentennial Pub, *(Bicentennial Publishing Corp.),* 15 Exchange Place, Jersey City, NJ 07302 Tel 201-435-0030.

Bielawski, Maxwell; *0-9600014),* 320 Lakeshore Dr., Dunkirk, NY 14048 Tel 716-366-2241.

Bieler, *(Bieler Press; 0-931460),* P.O. Box 3856, St. Paul, MN 55165 Tel 612-292-9936.

Big Horn *Imprint of* **Aviation Maintenance**

Big Moose, *(Big Moose Press; 0-914692),* P.O. Box 180, Big Moose, NY 13331 Tel 315-357-2821.

Big Morning Pr, *(Big Morning Press; 0-935056),* Box 3342, Lawrence, KS 66044 Tel 913-843-4801.

Big Rock Candy Mtn, *(Big Rock Candy Mountain),* Dist. by: Book Organization, Elm St., Millerton, NY 12546.

Big Sky Bks, *(Big Sky Books),* 151 Hampton Rd., Southampton, NY 11968.

Big Table, *(Big Table Publishing Co.),* Subs. of Follett Publishing Co., 1010 Washington Blvd., Chicago, IL 60607 Tel 312-666-5858.

Big Thicket, *(Big Thicket Assn.),* P.O. Box 198, Saratoga, TX 77585.

Big Toad Pr, *(Big Toad Press),* 617 25th St., Sacramento, CA 95816 Tel 916-446-7363.

Bighorn Bks, *(Bighorn Books),* c/o Henry W. Hough, 853 Ogden St., No. 5, Denver, CO 80218.

Bigoni Bks, *(Bigoni Books; 0-938996),* 4121 NE Highland, Portland, OR 97211 Tel 503-288-0997.

Bilingual Company, *(Bilingual Pubns., Co.),* 1966 Broadway, New York, NY 10023 Tel 212-873-2067.

Bilingual Pr, *(Bilingual Press; 0-916950),* Dept. of Foreign Languages & Bilingual Studies, 106 Ford Hall, Eastern Michigan University, Ypsilanti, MI 48197 Tel 313-487-0042.

Bilingual Pubns, *(Bilingual Publications & Cultural Services; 0-916576),* 14 Washington Pl., New York, NY 10003 Tel 212-986-4800; Moved, Left No Forwarding Address.

Billboard Pub *Imprint of* **Watson-Guptill**

Billfel Creative, *(Billfel Creative Press; 0-917544),* 1586 Lawrence Rd., Lawrenceville, NJ 08648 Tel 609-882-1924.

Binford, *(Binford & Mort Pubs.; 0-8323),* 2536 S.E. 11th Ave., Portland, OR 97202 Tel 503-238-9666.

Bingham Pub, *(Bingham Publishing Co.; 0-9601796),* 1318 Harrison St., Wichita Fall, TX 76309.

Bio Energy, *(Bio Energy Council),* 1717 Massachusetts Ave. N.W., Washington, DC 20036 Tel 202-462-4874; Moved Left No Forwarding Address.

Bio Pubs & Dists, *(Biobehavioral Pubs. & Distributors, Inc.; 0-938176),* 8467 Indian Hills Blvd., Shreveport, LA 71107 Tel 318-929-7133; Orders to: P. O. Box 1102, Houston, TX 77001.

Bio Res Inst
See World Natural Hist

Biobehavioral Pr, *(Biobehavioral Press; 0-938176),* 8467 Indian Hills Blvd., Shreveport, LA 71107; Dist. by: Stress Management Research Associates, 5801 Lumberdale, Suite 213, Houston, TX 77092 Tel 713-681-6725.

Biobooks
See Sullivan Bks Intl

Biofeed Pr, *(Biofeedback Press),* 3428 Sacramento St., San Francisco, CA 94118 Tel 415-621-5455.

Biofeedback Research, *(Biofeedback Research Institute Inc.; 0-930758),* 6325 Wilshire Blvd., Los Angeles, CA 90048 Tel 213-933-9451.

Biograf Pubns, *(Biograf Pubns.),* 7 Garber Hill Rd., Blauvelt, NY 10913 Tel 914-359-9292.

Biohydrant, *(Biohydrant Pubns; 0-918562),* R.F.D. 3, St. Albans, VT 05478 Tel 802-524-6307.

Biological Sci, *(Biological Sciences Curriculum Study),* P.O. Box 930, Boulder, CO 80306 Tel 303-666-6558.

Biomed Pubns, *(Biomedical Pubns.; 0-931890),* P.O. Box 495, Davis, CA 95616 Tel 916-756-8453.

Biomedical Pr *Imprint of* **Elsevier**

BioServ Corp, *(BioService Corp.; 0-938278),* 500 S. Racine Ave., Suite 302, Chicago, IL 60607.

Birch Run Pub, *(Birch Run Publishing; 0-931964),* 19 Sycamore Lane, Madison, CT 06443.

Birch Tree Pr, *(Birch Tree Press; 0-9603124),* 311 S. San Gabriel Blvd., Pasadena, CA 91107.

Bird-Sci Bks *Imprint of* **Foris Pubns**

Birds' Meadow Pub, *(Birds' Meadow Publishing Co., Inc.),* 2914 Parkwood Dr., Rogers, AR 72756.

Birdseed, *(Birdseed; 0-933006),* 29 Moss Ave., Oakland, CA 94610.

Birkhauser, *(Birkhauser Boston Inc.; 3-7643),* 380 Green St., Cambridge, MA 02139 Tel 617-876-2333.

Birth Day, *(Birth Day Publishing Co.; 0-9600958),* P.O. Box 7722, San Diego, CA 92107 Tel 714-296-3194.

Bisbee Pr, *(Bisbee Press Collective; 0-938196),* Drawer HA, Bisbee, AZ 85603.

Bisel Co, *(Bisel, Geo. T., Co.),* 710 S. Washington Square, Philadelphia, PA 19106 Tel 215-922-5760.

Bishop Graphics, *(Bishop Graphics, Inc.; 0-9601748),* 5388 Sterling Center Dr., Westlake Village, CA 91359.

Bishop Mus, *(Bishop Museum Press; 0-910240),* P.O. Box 19000-A, Honolulu, HI 96819 Tel 808-847-3511.

Bits Pr, *(Bits Press; 0-933248),* Dept. of English, Case Western Reserve Univ., Cleveland, OH 44106 Tel 216-795-2810.

Bitsche Pub, *(Bitsche Publishing; 0-916644),* P.O. Box 194, Waynesboro, TN 38485.

Biviano, *(Biviano, Ronald; 0-9605476),* 505 N. Lakeshore Dr., Chicago, IL 60611.

Biworld
See Bi World Indus

BJ Pub Group, *(BJ Publishing Group),* 200 Madison Ave., New York, NY 10016 Tel 212-686-9820.

Bk Habit, *(Book Habit, The; 0-9605200),* P.O. Box 941, San Marcos, CA 92069.

Bk Page, *(Book Page; 0-910266),* P.O. Box 1188, Los Angeles, CA 90028 Tel 213-535-3019.

Bk Pr Release, *(Book Press Release, Inc.; 0-936114),* P.O. Box 762, Berkeley, CA 94701 Tel 415-843-5961.

Bklyn Botanic, *(Brooklyn Botanic Garden),* 1000 Washington Ave., Brooklyn, NY 11225 Tel 212-622-4433.

Bklyn Coll Music, *(Brooklyn College, Dept. of Music; 0-9600976),* Brooklyn College, New York, NY 11210 Tel 212-780-5655.

Bklyn Coll Schl Perform
See Bklyn Coll Music

Bklyn Educ, *(Brooklyn Educational & Cultural Alliance; 0-933250),* Brooklyn Rediscovery, 57 Willoughby St., Brooklyn, NY 11201 Tel 212-852-6200.

Bklyn Mus, *(Brooklyn Museum; 0-87273; 0-913696),* Pubns. & Marketing Services, Eastern Pkwy., Brooklyn, NY 11238 Tel 212-638-5000.

BkMk, *(BkMk Press; 0-933532),* 5725 Wyandotte St., Kansas City, MO 64113 Tel 816-444-2152.

Bks Americana, *(Books Americana, Inc.; 0-89689),* 1716 Tune Ave., Florence, AL 35630.

Bks Australia, *(Books Australia, Inc.),* 15601 S.W. 83rd Ave., Miami, FL 33157 Tel 305-251-3934.

Bks Business, *(Books for Business, Inc.; 0-89499),* 1100 Seventeenth St., N.W., Washington, DC 20036 Tel 202-466-2372.

Bks by Kellogg, *(Books by Kellogg; 0-9603972),* P.O. Box 487, Annandale, VA 22003 Tel 703-256-2483.

Bks Canada, *(Books Canada),* 33 E. Tupper St., Buffalo, NY 14203.

Bks for All Times, *(Books for All Times, Inc.; 0-939360),* P.O. Box 2, Alexandria, VA 22313 Tel 703-548-0457.

Bks for Bet Living, *(Books for Better Living; 0-88491; 0-87056),* Div. of American Art Enterprises, Inc., 21322 Lassen St., Chatsworth, CA 91311 Tel 213-882-5900; Out of Business.

Bks for Libs, *(Books for Libraries, Inc.; 0-8369; 0-518),* 1 Dupont St., Plainview, NY 11803 Tel 516-938-8100.

Bks for Profs, *(Books for Professionals; 0-935422),* 5305 Broadway, Sacramento, CA 95820 Tel 916-457-2805.

Bks in Focus, *(Books in Focus, Inc.; 0-916728),* 160 E. 38th St., Suite 31B, New York, NY 10016 Tel 212-490-0334.

Bks Intl DH-TE, *(Books International of DH-TE International, Inc.),* P.O. Box 14487, St. Louis, MO 63178 Tel 314-721-8787.

Bks of Value, *(Books of Value; 0-9603174),* 2458 Chislehurst Dr., Los Angeles, CA 90027 Tel 213-664-8981.

Bks of Wall St, *(Books of Wall Street; 0-918632),* 2524 Cedar Springs, Dallas, TX 75201 Tel 214-748-7831.

Bks of Wall St *Imprint of* **Fraser Pub Co**

Black & Red, *(Black & Red; 0-934868),* P.O. Box 02374, Detroit, MI 48202.

Black Buzzard, *(Black Buzzard Press; 0-938872),* 2217 Shorefield Rd., No. 532, Wheaton, MD 20902.

Black Caucus Am Lib, *(Black Caucus of the American Library Assn.),* P.O. Box 11, Greenvale, NY 11548.

Black Caucus Am Black Lib
See Black Caucus Am Lib

Black Foxx Pubs, *(Black Foxx Pubs.; 0-9601142),* P.O. Box 686, Soledad Prison Facility, Soledad, CA 93960; c/o Harlo Press, 16721 Hamilton Ave., Detroit, MI 48203.

Black Hope Found, *(Black Hope Foundation, Inc.; 0-911734),* 1925 Vermont, No. 9, Toledo, OH 43624; Moved, Left No Forwarding Address.

Black Ice, *(Black Ice Pubs.),* 100 Prescott St., Worcester, MA 01605 Tel 617-753-1243.

Black Letter, *(Black Letter Press; 0-912382),* 663 Bridge St., N. W., Grand Rapids, MI 49504 Tel 616-454-7300.

Black Light Fellow, *(Black Light Fellowship; 0-933176),* P.O. Box 5369, Chicago, IL 60680 Tel 312-277-1361.

Black Mntn, *(Black Mountain Books),* Box 236, Harrisburg, PA 17108 Tel 717-234-4961.

Black Oak, *(Black Oak Press; 0-930674),* Box 4663, University Place Sta., Lincoln, NE 68504.

Black River, *(Black River Writers; 0-916692),* P.O. Box 15853, Sacramento, CA 95813; Orders to: P.O. Box 2491, East St. Louis, IL 62201 Tel 916-482-0799.

Black Sparrow, *(Black Sparrow Press; 0-87685),* P.O. Box 3993, Santa Barbara, CA 93105 Tel 805-687-5014.

Black Stone, *(Black Stone Press; 0-937002),* 865 Florida St., San Francisco, CA 94110 Tel 415-282-8806.

Black Swan CT, *(Black Swan Books Ltd.; 0-933806),* P.O. Box 327, Redding Ridge, CT 06876 Tel 203-938-9548.

Black Swan Pr, *(Black Swan Press),* 2257 N. Janssen Ave., Chicago, IL 60614.

Black Thorn Bks, *(Black Thorn Books; 0-932366),* 186 Willow Ave., Somerville, MA 02144.

Blackberry Bks, *(Blackberry Books),* P.O. Box 837, Bolinas, CA 94924; Do Not Confuse with Blackberry-Salted in the Shell.

Blackberry ME, *(Blackberry - Salted in the Shell),* P.O. Box 186, Brunswick, ME 04011 Tel 207-833-6051; Do Not Confuse with Blackberry Books.

Blackburn Coll, *(Blackburn College Press),* Lumpkin Library, Carlinville, IL 62626.

Blackjack Ent, *(Blackjack Enterprises; 0-935110),* P.O. Box 328, Scottsdale, AZ 85252; Dist. by: Golden Hind Publishing Co., 36 W. Del Rio Circle, Tempe, AZ 85282.

Blackwell Sci, *(Blackwell Scientific Pubns., Inc.),* 52 Beacon St., Boston, MA 02108; Dist. by: Blackwell/Mosby Book Distributors, 11830 Westline Industrial Dr., St. Louis, MO 63141.

Blagrove Pubns, *(Blagrove Pubns.; 0-939776),* 80 Pitkin St., P.O. Box 584, Manchester, CT 06040 Tel 203-647-1785.

Blaine Ethridge, *(Blaine Ethridge Books; 0-87917),* 13977 Penrod St. Detroit MI 48223 Tel 313-838-3363.

Blair, *(Blair, John F., Pub.; 0-910244; 0-89587),* 1406 Plaza Dr., Winston-Salem, NC 27103 Tel 919-768-1374.

Blaisdell, *(Blaisdell Publishing Co.),* ; Publisher Abbreviation Without Addresses Are for Titles That Are Out of Print. These Are Obsolete Abbreviations.

Blarney Bks, *(Blarney Books; 0-935420),* 6129 Shenandoah Dr., Sacramento, CA 95841.

Blenheim Pub, *(Blenheim Publishing House; 0-918288),* 4128 Bon Hill Rd., Arlington Heights, IL 60004.

Blind John, *(Blind John Pubns.),* 2740 Onyx St., Eugene, OR 97403.

Bliss, *(Bliss, Beatrice; 0-9600504),* 3011 N.W. Watercrest Rd., Forest Grove, OR 97116.

Blitz Pub Co, *(Blitz Publishing Co.),* 1600 Verona St., Middleton, WI 53562 Tel 608-836-7550.

Bloch, *(Bloch Publishing Co.; 0-8197),* 915 Broadway, New York, NY 10010 Tel 212-673-7910.

Bloch & Co OH, *(Bloch & Co.),* P.O. Box 18058, Cleveland, OH 44118 Tel 216-371-0979.

Block, *(Block Pubs.; 0-916864),* Box 34223, Dallas, TX 75234 Tel 214-242-0069.

Blom, *(Blom, Benjamin, Inc.),* ; Publisher Abbreviation Without Addresses Are for Titles That Are Out of Print. These Are Obsolete Abbreviations.

Blood Horse
See Thoroughbred Own & Breed

Blood Info, *(Blood Information Service; 0-914508),* 508 Getzville Rd., Buffalo, NY 14226 Tel 716-832-7997.

Bloom Bks, *(Bloom Books Inc.; 0-935000),* 1020 Broad St., Newark, NJ 07102.

Blossom Valley, *(Blossom Valley Press; 0-939894),* P.O. Box 4044, Blossom Valley Sta., Mountain View, CA 94040 Tel 415-941-7525.

Blue & Gray, *(Blue & Gray Press, Inc; 0-914926),* 605 Merrit St., Nashville, TN 37203 Tel 615-244-1478; Out of Business.

Blue Book, *(Blue-Book Pubs.; 0-918698),* 64 Prospect St., White Plains, NY 10606 Tel 914-949-0890.

Blue Claw, *(Blue Claw Press, The),* Box 1332, Brooklyn, NY 11201 Tel 212-596-1598.

Blue Dragon, *(Blue Dragon Press),* 2709-A Fruitrale Ave., Oakland, CA 94601; Dist. by: Alchemy Books, 681 Market, Suite 755, San Francisco, CA 94105 Tel 415-362-2708.

Blue Feather, *(Blue Feather Press; 0-932482),* P.O. Box 5113, Santa Fe, NM 87502 Tel 505-983-2776.

Blue Flower, *(Blue Flower; 0-9603924),* Dist. by: Han Books, 3607 Baring St., Philadelphia, PA 19104 Tel 215-382-1410.

Blue Goose, *(Blue Goose, Inc.),* 332 E. Commonwealth Ave., Box 46, Fullerton, CA 92632.

Blue Harbor, *(Blue Harbor Press; 0-9605278),* P.O. Box 1028, Lomita, CA 90717.

Blue Heron, *(Blue Heron Press, Inc.; 0-939198),* 1728 Herrick N.E., Grand Rapids, MI 49505 Tel 616-363-7810.

Blue Horizon, *(Blue Horizon Press),* 1517 Crestwood Dr., Greenville, TN 37743 Tel 615-639-1264.

Blue Horse, *(Blue Horse Pubns.; 0-917018),* P.O. Box 6061, Augusta, GA 30906 Tel 404-798-5628.

Blue Lagoon, *(Blue Lagoon Pubs.; 0-9605338),* 3606 Coldwater Canyon, Studio City, CA 91604.

Blue Leaf, *(Blue Leaf Editions; 0-915206),* P.O. Box 857, New London, CT 06320 Tel 203-445-7391.

Blue Max Pr, *(Blue Max Press, Inc.; 0-916674),* 630 N. College Ave., Suite 312, Indianapolis, IN 46204 Tel 317-632-2502.

Blue Moon Pr, *(Blue Moon Press, Inc.; 0-933188),* c/o Univ. of Arizona, Dept. of English, Tucson, AZ 85721.

Blue Mtn Arts
See Blue Mtn Pr CO

Blue Mtn MI, *(Blue Mountain Pr.; 0-9602408),* 511 Campbell St., Kalamazoo, MI 49007 Tel 616-349-3924.

Blue Mtn Pr CO, *(Blue Mountain Press, Inc.; 0-88396),* P.O. Box 1007, Boulder, CO 80306 Tel 303-449-0536; Orders to: P.O. Box 4549, Boulder, CO 80306

Blue Oak, *(Blue Oak Press; 0-912950),* P.O. Box 27, Sattley, CA 96124.

Blue Pacific, *(Blue Pacific Books; 0-915520),* 426 E. Pennsylvania Ave., San Diego, CA 92103; Dist. by: Communication Creativity, 5644 La Jolla Blvd., La Jolla, CA 92037 Tel 714-459-4489.

Blue Ridge, *(Blue Ridge Press of Boone, Inc.; 0-938980),* P.O. Box 1693, Boone, NC 28607.

Blue River, *(Blue River Publishing Co.; 0-936324),* P.O. Box 882, Sheboygan, WI 53081.

Blue Wind, *(Blue Wind Press; 0-912652),* P.O. Box 7175, Berkeley, CA 94707 Tel 415-526-1905.

Blue Wolf, *(Blue Wolf Press; 0-936714),* 1240 Pine St., Boulder, CO 80302.

Blueapple Bks, *(Blueapple Books; 0-917092),* P.O. Box 5694, Austin, TX 78763 Tel 512-458-2129.

Bluejay Pr, *(Bluejay Press; 0-939132),* 5900 Dartmouth Ct., Kokomo, IN 46901; Orders to: P.O. Box 6134, Kokomo, IN 46901.

Bluestocking, *(Bluestocking Books; 0-931458),* 1732 32nd Ave., Seattle, WA 98122 Tel 206-323-8556; Dist. by: Bookpeople, 2940 Seventh St., Berkeley, CA 94710.

Blustein-Geary, *(Blustein/Geary; 0-9605248),* 46 Glen Circle, Waltham, MA 02154.

Blyden Pr, *(Blyden, Edward W., Press, Inc.; 0-914110),* P.O. Box 621, Manhattanville Sta., New York, NY 10027 Tel 212-222-6000.

BM Surveying
See CARBEN Survey

BMA Pr, *(BMA Press; 0-89323),* P.O. Box 12000, St. Louis, MO 63112.

BMB Pub Co, *(BMB Publishing Co.; 0-930924; 0-9600164),* P.O. Box 1622, Boston, MA 02105 Tel 617-492-8225.

BMH Bks, *(BMH Books; 0-88469),* P.O. Box 544, Winona Lake, IN 46590 Tel 219-267-7158.

BNA, *(Bureau of National Affairs, Inc.; 0-87179),* 1231 25th St., N.W., Washington, DC 20037 Tel 202-452-4276.

B'nai B'rith Car, *(B'nai B'rith Career & Counseling Services; 0-89665),* 1640 Rhode Island Ave., N.W., Washington, DC 20036 Tel 202-857-6590.

B'nai B'rith-Hillel, *(B'nai B'rith Hillel Foundations; 0-9603058),* 1640 Rhode Island Ave., N.W., Washington, DC 20036 Tel 202-857-6564.

BNR Pr, *(BNR Press; 0-931960),* 132 E. Second St., Port Clinton, OH 43452 Tel 419-732-2012.

BO *Imprint of* **Inscape Corp**

Boa Edns, *(Boa Editions; 0-918526),* 92 Park Ave., Brockport, NY 14420 Tel 716-637-3844.

Board Jewish Educ, *(Board of Jewish Education of Greater New York),* 426 W. 58th St, New York, NY 10019 Tel 212-245-8200.

Board of Pubn
See Bd of Pubns CRC

Boardman, *(Boardman, Clark, Co., Ltd.; 0-87632),* 435 Hudson St., New York, NY 10014 Tel 212-929-7500.

Boardroom, *(Boardroom Books, Inc.; 0-932648),* Div. of Boardroom Reports, 500 Fifth Ave., New York, NY 10036 Tel 212-354-0005.

Boardroom Repr
See Boardroom

Boars Head, *(Boar's Head Press; 0-932114),* P.O. Box 3174, St. Louis, MO 63130 Tel 314-727-2920.

Bob West, *(West, Bob, Pubns., Inc.),* 6121 Hudson St., Orlando, FL 32808 Tel 305-293-2987.

Bobbi Ent, *(Bobbi Enterprises; 0-9603200),* Rte. 1, Box 44, Mt. Iron, MN 55768 Tel 218-735-8364.

Bobbs, *(Bobbs-Merrill Co., Inc.; 0-672),* A Thomas Audel Co., 4300 W. 62nd St., Indianapolis, IN 46468 Tel 317-298-5400. *Imprints:* Chart (Charter Books); Lib (Liberal Arts Press).

Bobley, *(Bobley Publishing Corp.; 0-8324),* Subs. of Illustrated World Encyclopedia, Inc., 311 Crossways Park Dr., Woodbury, NY 11797 Tel 516-364-1800.

Bodima, *(Bodima; 0-88875),* Dist. by: Altarinda Books, 13 Estates Dr., Orinda, CA 94563 Tel 415-254-3830.

Bodine, *(Bodine & Associates, Inc.; 0-910254),* 1101 St. Paul St., Baltimore, MD 21202 Tel 301-385-1103.

Boehmer Pub, *(Boehmer Publishing; 0-9601728),* 134 Beechwood Rd., Braintree, MA 02184 Tel 617-848-0486.

Bogden & Quigley, *(Bogden & Quigley, Inc.; 0-8005),* Subs. of Wadsworth Publishing Co., 10 Davis Dr., Belmont, CA 94002.

Boggle, *(Boggle Pubns.; 0-930532),* 425 E. Sixth St., New York, NY 10009 Tel 212-260-3064.

Boian Bks, *(Boian Books; 0-9604420),* 780 Riverside Dr., Apt. 5e, New York, NY 10032 Tel 212-234-0173.

Boise St Univ, *(Boise State Univ.; 0-88430),* Dept. of English, Boise, ID 83725 Tel 208-385-1246.

Bola Pr, *(Bola Press),* P.O. Box 96, Village Sta., New York, NY 10014.

Bold Strummer Ltd, *(Bold Strummer, Ltd; 0-933224),* 1 Webb Rd., Westport, CT 06880 Tel 203-226-8230.

Bolder Bks, *(Bolder Books, Inc.; 0-918282),* 10 E. 40th St., Suite 2109, New York, NY 10016 Tel 212-689-5980.

Bolder Landry, *(Bolder Landry),* 8925 San Salvador Circle, Buena Park, CA 90620.

Bon Mot Pubns, *(Bon Mot Pubns.; 0-9601044),* RD 2 Box 74, Sevierville, TN 37862.

Bonanza, *(Bonanza, Inc.; 0-932952),* 1010-12th St., Sparks, NV 89431.

Bond-Parkhurst, *(Bond, Parkhurst Books; 0-87880),* Dist. by: W. W. Norton & Co., Inc., 500 Fifth Ave., New York, NY 10036 Tel 212-354-5500.

Bond Pub Co, *(Bond Publishing Co.; 0-939296),* 226 Massachusetts Ave. N.E., Washington, DC 20002.

Bonney, *(Bonney, Orrin H.; 0-931620),* 625 E. 14th St., Houston, TX 77008 Tel 713-864-8697.

Book & Tackle, *(Book & Tackle Shop; 0-910258),* 29 Old Colony Rd., Chestnut Hill, MA 02167 Tel 617-965-0459.

Book Dept, *(Book Department, The; 0-9606080),* P.O. Box 241, Hartford, CT 06101 Tel 203-728-3470.

Book-Lab, *(Book-Lab, Inc.; 0-87594),* 1449 37th St., Brooklyn, NY 11218 Tel 212-853-4140.

Book Nest, *(Book Nest, The),* 366 Second St., Los Altos, CA 94022.

Book of Thee Atonement, *(Book of Thee Atonement Publishing Society; 0-917778),* P.O. Box 1218, Felton, CA 95018.

Book Prod Serv
See BPS Bks

Book Promo Unltd, *(Book Promotions Unlimited; 0-933586),* P.O. Box 122, Flushing, MI 48433 Tel 313-659-6683.

Book Pub Co, *(Book Publishing Co., The; 0-913990),* 156 Drakes Lane, Summertown, TN 38483 Tel 615-964-3571.

Book Searchers, *(Book Searchers; 0-932484),* 2622 15th Ave., Forest Grove, OR 97116 Tel 503-357-6948.

Bookcraft Inc, *(Bookcraft, Inc.; 0-88494),* 1848 W. 2300, S., Salt Lake City, UT 84119 Tel 801-972-6180.

Bookery, *(Bookery; 0-930822),* 8193 Riata Dr., Redding, CA 96002 Tel 916-365-8068; Dist. by: Caroline House, 2 Ellis Place, Ossining, NY 10562.

Bookfinger, *(Bookfinger; 0-913774),* P.O. Box 487, Peter Stuyvesant Sta., New York, NY 10009.

Bookhaus, *(Bookhaus),* 545 La Salle, Monroe, MI 48161.

Booklegger Pr, *(Booklegger Press; 0-912932),* 555 29th St., San Francisco, CA 94131 Tel 415-647-9074.

Booklore Pub
See Booklore Pubs

Booklore Pubs, *(Booklore Pubs., Inc.; 0-931110),* P.O. Drawer 3679, Sarasota, FL 33578 Tel 813-758-1533.

Bookmaker, *(Bookmaker Publishing; 0-934778),* 1212 E. 131st St., Burnsville, MN 55337.

Bookman Dan, *(Bookman Dan!; 0-934780),* P.O. Box 13492, Baltimore, MD 21203 Tel 301-235-8818.

Bookmark, *(Bookmark),* Div. of Mayhill Pubns, P.O. Box 74, Knightstown, IN 46148 Tel 317-345-5335.

Bookmates Intl, *(Bookmates International, Inc.; 0-933082),* P.O. Box 9883, Fresno, CA 93795 Tel 209-298-3308.

Bookpeople, *(Bookpeople),* 2940 Seventh St., Berkeley, CA 94710 Tel 415-549-3030.

Books, *(Books; 0-910268),* 635 N. Elmwood Avenue, Waukegan, IL 60085 Tel 312-623-6963.

Books AK, *(Books Alaska),* Box 4020-A, Anchorage, AK 99507.

Books Marcus, *(Books Marcus; 0-916020),* P.O. Box 188, Ojai, CA 93023.

Books NC, *(Books),* P.O. Box 877, Chapel Hill, NC 27514.

Bookslinger, *(Bookslinger Editions),* 2163 Ford Pkwy, St. Paul, MN 55116 Tel 612-690-0293.

Bookstax, *(Bookstax of Britain, Ltd.; 0-915356),* 200 Park Ave., Pan Am Bldg., Suite 303E, New York, NY 10017 Tel 212-268-2421; Moved, Left No Forwarding Address.

Bookstore Pr, *(Bookstore Press; 0-912846),* Box 191, RFD 1, Freeport, ME 04032.

Bookthrift, *(Bookthrift, Inc.; 0-89673),* Div. of Simon & Schuster, 45 W. 36th St., New York, NY 10018 Tel 212-947-0909.

Bookworks, *(Bookworks),* Dist. by: Random House, Inc., 400 Hahn Rd., Westminster, MD 21157.

Bookworld Comm, *(Bookworld Communications Corp.; 0-914242),* 3918 Nanz Ave., Louisville, KY 40207 Tel 502-897-7922.

Bookworm Pub, *(Bookworm Publishing Co. Inc,; 0-916302),* P.O. Box 3037, Ontario, CA 91761 Tel 714-983-8548.

Boomerang, *(Boomerang Pubs.; 0-9605900),* 3760 N. Bay Dr., Racine, WI 53402.

Boosey & Hawkes, *(Boosey & Hawkes, Inc.; 0-913932),* P.O. Box 130, Oceanside, NY 11572 Tel 516-678-2500.

Borden, *(Borden Publishing Co.; 0-87505),* 1855 W. Main St., Alhambra, CA 91801 Tel 213-283-5031.

Border-Mtn Pr, *(Border-Mountain Press; 0-916428),* P.O. Box 1296, Benson, AZ 85602.

Borf Bks, *(Borf Books; 0-9604894),* Brownsville, KY 42210 Tel 502-597-2187.

Borgo Pr, *(Borgo Press; 0-89370),* P.O. Box 2845, San Bernardino, CA 92406 Tel 714-884-5813.

Bork Res, *(Bork Research; 0-939258),* 23 E. Elm Ave., Quincy, MA 02170 Tel 617-773-6350.

Bormerl, *(Bormerl Oaks Press; 0-911948),* 1210 D. Alhambra Circle, Coral Gables, FL 33146.

Born-Hawes Pub, *(Born-Hawes Pub. Ltd.; 0-85667),* 22 Vandam St., New York, NY 10013 Tel 212-929-5275.

Bornstein Memory Schls, *(Bornstein Memory Schools; 0-9602610),* 11669 San Vicente Blvd., W. Los Angeles, CA 90049.

Boss Bks, *(Boss Books; 0-932430),* P.O. Box 370, Madison Square Sta., New York, NY 10159 Tel 212-683-3274.

Boston & ME RR, *(Boston & Maine Railroad Historical Society, Inc.; 0-916578),* P.O. Box 302, Reading, MA 01867 Tel 617-358-4597.

Boston Athenaeum, *(Boston Athenaeum, The; 0-934552),* 10 1/2 Beacon St., Boston, MA 02108.

Boston Coll, *(Boston College),* Chestnut Hill, MA 02167; Dist. by: Consortium Press, 821 15th St., N. W., Washington, DC 20005.

Boston Music, *(Boston Music Co.),* Div. of Williamson Music, Inc., 116 Boylston St., Boston, MA 02116 Tel 617-426-5100.

Boston Phoenix, *(Boston Phoenix),* c/o Harvard Student Agencies, 4 Holyoke St., Cambridge, MA 02136.

Boston Public Lib, *(Boston Public Library; 0-89073),* P.O. Box 286, Boston, MA 02117 Tel 617-536-5400.

Boston U Pr, *(Boston Univ. Press),* ; Publisher Abbreviation Without Addresses Are for Titles That Are Out of Print. These Are Obsolete Abbreviations.

Boston U Sch of Theology, *(Boston Univ. School of Theology; 0-87270),* Orders to: Muelder Festschrift, School of Theology, 745 Commonwealth Ave., Boston, MA 02215 Tel 617-353-3060.

Boston Womens
See Public Works

Boulevard, *(Boulevard Books; 0-910278),* P.O. Box 89, Topanga, CA 90290 Tel 213-445-1036.

Bouregy, *(Bouregy, Thomas, & Co., Inc.; 0-8034),* 22 E. 60th St., New York, NY 10022 Tel 212-753-8410.

Bovin, *(Bovin Publishing; 0-910280),* 68-36 108th St., Forest Hills, NY 11375 Tel 212-268-2292.

Bowdoin Coll, *(Bowdoin College Museum of Art),* Walker Art Bldg., Brunswick, ME 04011 Tel 207-725-8731.

Bowers & Ruddy, *(Bowers & Ruddy Galleries, Inc.; 0-914490),* 6922 Hollywood Blvd., Suite 600, Los Angeles, CA 90028 Tel 213-466-4595.

Bowery Pub, *(Bowery Publishing; 0-9602038),* P.O. Box 12784, Reno, NV 89510.

Bowker, *(Bowker, R. R., Co.; 0-8352),* A Xerox Publishing Co., 1180 Ave. of the Americas, New York, NY 10036 Tel 212-764-5100; Orders to: P.O. Box 1807, Ann Arbor, MI 48106.

Bowling Green Univ, *(Bowling Green Univ., Popular Press; 0-87972),* Bowling Green State Univ., Popular Culture Ctr., Bowling Green, OH 43403 Tel 419-372-2981.

Bowmar
See Bowmar-Noble

Bowmar-Noble, *(Bowmar/Noble Pubs., Inc.; 0-8372; 0-8107),* 4563 Colorado Blvd., Los Angeles, CA 90039 Tel 213-247-8995.

Box Twenty One, *(Box 21, Inc.; 0-918846),* Tucson, AZ 85702 Tel 602-325-9602.

Boxwood, *(Boxwood Press; 0-910286; 0-940168),* 183 Ocean View Blvd., Pacific Grove, CA 93950 Tel 408-375-9110.

Boyd & Fraser, *(Boyd & Fraser Publishing Co.; 0-87835),* 3627 Sacramento St., San Francisco, CA 94118 Tel 415-346-0686.

Boyd Deep Canyon, *(Boyd, Philip L., Deep Canyon Desert Research Center of the Univ. of California),* Riverside, CA 92521 Tel 714-787-5628.

Boykin, *(Boykin, James H.; 0-9603342),* 1260 N.W. 122nd St, Miami, FL 33167.

Boynton & Assoc, *(Boynton & Associates; 0-933168),* Clifton House, Clifton, VA 22024.

Boys Clubs, *(Boys' Clubs of America),* 771 First Ave., New York, NY 10017 Tel 212-557-7755.

Boys Town Ctr, *(Boys Town Center for the Study of Youth Development; 0-938510),* Boys Town, NE 68010.

Bozo Pr, *(Bozo Press; 0-936774),* P.O. Box 6207, Hilton Head Island, SC 29938.

BPS Bks, *(BPS Books Inc.),* 5 Elm St., Danver MA 01923 Tel 617-774-8565.

Bradbury Pr, *(Bradbury Press; 0-87888),* 2 Overhill Rd., Scarsdale, NY 10583 Tel 914-472-5100; Dist. by: E. P. Dutton & Co., Inc., 2 Park Ave., New York, NY 10016.

Bradford Bks, *(Bradford Books Pubs., Inc.; 0-89706),* Box 28, Montgomery, VT 05470 Tel 802-933-4193.

Bradford Pr, *(Bradford Press, Inc.; 0-915064),* P.O. Box A3935, Chicago, IL 60690.

Bradford Pub, *(Bradford Publishing Co.; 0-931670),* P.O. Box 511, Reseda, CA 91335.

Bradfords VA, *(Bradford's Directory of Marketing Research Agencies & Managemer Consultants; 0-910290),* P.O. Box 276, Dept B-15, Fairfax, VA 22030 Tel 703-560-7484.

Bradley CPA, *(Bradley CPA Study Aids, Inc.; 0-932788),* 21146 Ventura Blvd., Suite 203, Woodland Hills, CA 91364 Tel 213-340-3779.

Bradley David Assocs, *(Bradley David Associates, Ltd.; 0-9601694),* Box 5279, 909 Third Ave., New York, NY 10150 Tel 212-246-1114.

Bradson, *(Bradson Press; 0-9603574),* 120 Longfellow St., Thousand Oaks, CA 91360 Tel 213-466-7126.

Bradt Ent, *(Bradt Enterprises Pubns.; 0-933982; 0-9505797),* 54 Dudley St., Cambridge, MA 02140 Tel 617-492-8776.

Brady Pr, *(Brady Press; 0-934620),* Div. of KDI Productions, P.O. Box 10012, Jacksonville, FL 32207 Tel 904-733-8445.

Braille Transcribe, *(Braille Transcribers' Guild),* 1807 Upas St., San Diego, CA 92103 Tel 714-298-4219; Fills Individual Requests for Transcriptions Using Large Print Typewriters, 8 1/2 x 11 Paper, Bound in Spiral Plastic.

Brain Res, *(Brain Research Pubns.,; 0-916088),* Highbridge Terrace, Fayetville, NY 13066.

BrainStorm Bks, *(BrainStorm Books),* P.O. Box 1407, Tustin, CA 92688.

Braintree, *(Braintree Pubns.),* P.O. Box 194, Rheem Valley, CA 94570.

Branberry Bks, *(Branberry Books; 0-916916),* 124 Sherwood Ave., Troy, AL 36081 Tel 205-566-3817; Orders to: James Brantley, Psychology Dept., Troy State Univ., Troy, AL 36081.

Branch Pr, *(Branch Press; 0-912690),* 30 Hathaway Dr., Garden City, NY 11530 Tel 516-775-6402; Orders to: P.O. Box 297, New Hyde Park, NY 11040.

Branch-Smith, *(Branch-Smith, Inc.; 0-87706),* P.O. Box 1868, Fort Worth, TX 76101 Tel 817-332-6377; 120 St. Louis Ave., Fort Worth, TX 76101.

Brandeis-Bardin Inst, *(Brandeis-Bardin Institute Pubns., The; 0-916952),* Brandeis, CA 93064 Tel 213-348-7201.

Branden, *(Branden Press, Inc.; 0-8283),* P.O. Box 843, Brookline Village, 21 Station St., Boston, MA 02147 Tel 617-734-2045.

Brandon, *(Brandon Books; 0-87056),* Div. of American Art Enterprises, Inc., 21335 Roscoe Blvd., Canoga Park, CA 91304 Tel 213-999-4100.

Brandon Hse, *(Brandon House, Inc.; 0-913412),* P.O. Box 240, Bronx, NY 10471.

Brandywine, *(Brandywine Press, Inc., The; 0-89616),* c/o E. P. Dutton, 2 Park Ave, New York, NY 10016.

Brandywine Bks, *(Brandywine Books; 0-9604986),* 5020 73rd St., Suite B, San Diego, CA 92115.

Brandywine Conserv, *(Brandywine Conservancy),* P.O. Box 141, Chadds Ford, PA 19317 Tel 215-388-7601.

Branford, *(Branford, Charles T., Co.; 0-8231),* P.O. Box 41, Newton Centre, MA 02159.

Brasch & Brasch, *(Brasch & Brasch, Pubs., Inc.; 0-89554),* 104 W. C St., Ontario, CA 91762 Tel 714-986-3631.

Brasch & M
See Brasch & Brasch

Brason-Sargar, *(Brason-Sargar Pubns.; 0-9602534),* P.O. Box 842, Reseda, CA 91335 Tel 213-851-1229.

Brass Pr, *(Brass Press; 0-914282),* 136 Eighth Ave., Nashville, TN 37203 Tel 615-254-8969.

Brattle, *(Brattle Pubns.; 0-918938),* 4 Brattle St., Suite 306, Cambridge, MA 02138 Tel 617-661-7467.

Braun, *(Braun, C. F., & Co.; 0-910292),* 1000 S. Fremont, Alhambra, CA 91802.

Braun-Brumfield, *(Braun-Brumfield),* Ann Arbor, MI 48106; c/o E. T. Lenfest, P.O. Box 35, Acton, ME 04001.

Braziller, *(Braziller, George, Inc.; 0-8076),* One Park Ave., New York, NY 10016 Tel 212-889-0909.

Bread-N-Butter, *(Besche's Bread 'n' Butter Productions, Inc.; 0-9602282),* Rte. 4, Box 187, Georgetown, DE 19947 Tel 302-856-6073.

Breaking Point, *(Breaking Point, Inc.; 0-917020),* P.O. Box 328, Wharton, NJ 07885 Tel 201-361-7238.

Brennan Bks, *(Brennan Books, Inc.; 0-89270),* 2120 W. Clybourn St., Milwaukee, WI 53233 Tel 414-344-6501.

Brentwood Pub, *(Brentwood Publishing Corp.; 0-939442),* 825 S. Barrington Ave., Los Angeles, CA 90049.

Brethren, *(Brethren Press; 0-87178),* 1451 Dundee Ave., Elgin, IL 60120 Tel 312-742-5100.

Brethren Ohio, *(Brethren Publishing Co.; 0-934970),* 524 College Ave., Ashland, OH 44805 Tel 419-289-2611; Do Not Confuse with Brethren Press (Brethren) in Elgin IL.

Breton Pubs Imprint of Wadsworth Pub

Brevet Pr, *(Brevet Press; 0-88498),* Box 1404, Sioux Falls, SD 57101 Tel 605-339-2330.

Brevity, *(Brevity Press; 0-917838),* P.O. Box 12622, Nashville, TN 37212 Tel 615-292-0211.

Briarcliff, *(Briarcliff Pub. Co.; 0-915754),* 8111 Timberlodge Trail, Dayton, OH 45459; Orders to: 3640 N. Briarcliff Rd., Kansas City, MO 64116.

Brick Hse Pub, *(Brick House Publishing Co.; 0-931790),* 34 Essex St., Andover, MA 01810 Tel 617-475-9568.

Bricker Pubns
See Bricker's Intl

Bricker's Intl, *(Bricker's International Directory; 0-910404),* 423 Family Farm Rd., Woodside, CA 94062 Tel 415-851-3090.

Bridge Bks, *(Bridge Books),* 35 Grove St., San Francisco, CA 94102 Tel 415-626-5757.

Bridgeberg, *(Bridgeberg Books; 0-915358),* 2337 Vicente, San Francisco, CA 94116 Tel 415-564-8862.

Bridgeport Pub, *(Bridgeport Publishing Co.; 0-89668),* P.O. Box 148, Oakland, CA 94604 Tel 415-834-5183; Moved, Left No Forwarding Address.

Bridges Pr, *(Bridges Pr),* 2212 "D" St., Vancouver, WA 98663 Tel 206-694-6695; Orders to: Pragmatix Management Resources, 408 S.W. 2nd Ave., Suite 425, Portland, OR 97204 Tel 503-223-7524.

Bridges Sound, *(Bridges to the Sound Publishing Corp.; 0-938316),* P.O. Box 260607, Tampa, FL 33685.

Brigadoon, *(Brigadoon Pubns., Inc.; 0-938512),* 3911 Richmond Ave., Staten Island, NY 10312.

Brigham, *(Brigham Young Univ. Press; 0-8425),* 218 University Press Bldg., Provo, UT 84602 Tel 801-378-4707; Orders to: 205 University Press Bldg., Provo, UT 84602 Tel 801-378-2809.

Brigham St Hse, *(Brigham Street House; 0-912482),* 7050 Chris Lane, Salt Lake City, UT 84121 Tel 801-566-7177.

Bright Bks, *(Bright Books; 0-9605968),* P.O. Box 428, Akron, IN 46910 Tel 219-893-4684.

Bright Spirit, *(Bright Spirit Press; 0-937346),* P.O. Box 4254, San Rafael, CA 94913 Tel 415-453-5412.

Brighton House, *(Brighton House Pubns.; 0-9603256),* 3045 Brighton 8th St., Brooklyn, NY 11235 Tel 212-934-1349.

Brighton Pub Co, *(Brighton Publishing Co.; 0-89832),* P.O. Box 6235, Salt Lake City, UT 84106 Tel 801-466-4044.

Brighton Pubns, *(Brighton Pubns.; 0-918420),* P.O. Box 12706, New Brighton, MN 55112 Tel 612-636-2220.

Brillig Works, *(Brillig Works Pub., Co.; 0-89681),* 1322 College Ave., Boulder, CO 80302.

Brit Info, *(British Information Service),* ; Publisher Abbreviation Without Addresses Are for Titles That Are Out of Print. These Are Obsolete Abbreviations.

Brite Offset, *(Brite Offset),* 418 W. 25th St., 7th Floor, New York, NY 10001.

British Am Bks, *(British American Books; 0-89979),* P. O. Box 302, Willits, CA 95490.

British Bk Ctr, *(British Book Center; 0-8277),* Fairview Park, Elmsford, NY 10523 Tel 914-592-7700.

Britton Pub, *(Britton Publishing Co.; 0-938318),* Box 9628, North Hollywood, CA 91609 Tel 213-506-4682.

Bro-Dart Found, *(Bro-Dart Foundation; 0-912654),* 1807 Pembroke Rd., Greensboro, NC 27408 Tel 919-275-7336; Orders to: P.O. Box 3488, Williamsport, PA 17701 Tel 717-326-2461.

Bro Life Bks, *(Brotherhood of Life, Inc.; 0-914732),* 110 Dartmouth, S.E., Albuquerque, NM 87106 Tel 505-255-8980.

Bro William Pr, *(Brother William Press),* Dist. by: Book People, 2940 Seventh St., Berkeley, CA 94710.

Broad River, *(Broad River Press; 0-932614),* P.O. Box 50329, Columbia, SC 29250.

Broadman, *(Broadman Press; 0-8054),* 127 Ninth Ave., N., Nashville, TN 37234 Tel 615-251-2544.

Broadside, *(Broadside Press Pubns.; 0-910296),* 74 Glendale Ave., Highland Park, MI 48203 Tel 313-868-1585.

Brock Pub, *(Brock Publishing Co.; 0-930534),* P.O. Box 1685, Chico, CA 95927 Tel 916-895-1035.

Brodart, *(Bro-Dart Publishing Co.; 0-87272),* 1609 Memorial Ave., Williamsport, PA 17701 Tel 717-326-2461.

Broken Whisker, *(Broken Whisker Studio; 0-932220),* Printers Row, 711 S. Dearborn, Loft 505, Chicago, IL 60605 Tel 312-969-8311.

Brolet, *(Brolet Press; 0-910298),* 18 John St., New York, NY 10038 Tel 212-227-6280.

Brombacher, *(Brombacher Books; 0-89083),* 691 S. 31st St., Richmond, CA 94804 Tel 415-232-5380.

Brookdale Pr, *(Brookdale Press; 0-912650),* 184 Brookdale Rd., Stamford, CT 06903 Tel 203-322-2474.

Brooke Hse, *(Brooke House Pubs., Inc.; 0-912588),* 9010 Reseda Blvd., Suite 226, Northridge, CA 91324 Tel 213-349-1700; Moved, Left No Forwarding Address.

Brookings, *(Brookings Institution; 0-8157),* 1775 Massachusetts Ave., N.W., Washington, DC 20036 Tel 202-797-6254.

Brooklyn Coll Pr, *(Brooklyn College Press; 0-930888),* 562 W. 113th St., New York, NY 10025.

Brooks-Cole, *(Brooks/Cole Publishing Co.; 0-8185),* Div. of Wadsworth, Inc., 555 Abrego St., Monterey, CA 93940 Tel 408-373-0728; Orders to: Wadsworth, Inc., 10 Davis Dr., Belmont, CA 94002 Tel 415-595-2350.

Brooks Pub Co, *(Brooks Publishing Co.; 0-932370),* 1226 Chester Ave., Bakersfield, CA 93301 Tel 805-322-0687.

Brooks-Sterling, *(Brooks-Sterling Co.; 0-914418),* P.O. Box 265, Danville, CA 94526 Tel 415-837-1318.

Brotherstone Pubs, *(Brotherstone Pubs.),* 450 Hoxie Ave., Elgin, IL 60120 Tel 312-697-1371.

Broude, *(Broude Brothers Ltd., Music; 0-8450),* 56 W. 45th St., New York, NY 10036 Tel 212-687-4735.

Broude Intl Edns, *(Broude International Editions, Inc.; 0-89371),* 56 W. 45th St., New York, NY 10036 Tel 212-687-4735.

Brown Bk, *(Brown Book Co.; 0-910294),* 120 Secatogue Ave., Farmingdale, NY 11735 Tel 516-293-6969.

Brown Burro, *(Brown Burro Press; 0-918054),* P.O. Box 2863D, Pasadena, CA 91105 Tel 213-449-2669.

Brown Hse Gall, *(Brown House Galleries Ltd.; 0-9604534),* 5717 Hammersley Rd., P.O. Box 4243, Madison, WI 53711.

Brown Penny, *(Brown Penny Press),* 18130 Hwy. 36, Blachly, OR 97412 Tel 503-927-3482.

Brown Rabbit, *(Brown Rabbit Press; 0-933988),* P.O. Box 19111, Houston, TX 77024 Tel 713-465-1168.

Brown U Pr, *(Brown Univ. Press; 0-87057),* 194 Meeting St., Box 1881, Providence, RI 02912 Tel 401-863-2455; Orders to: Univ. Press of New England, Box 979, Hanover, NH 03755.

Browning Inst, *(Browning Institute, Inc.; 0-930252),* P.O. Box 2983, Grand Central Sta., New York, NY 10163.

Browning Pubns, *(Browning Pubns.; 0-933718),* P.O. Box 81306, Atlanta, GA 30366 Tel 404-455-3430.

Brownlow Pub Co, *(Brownlow Publishing Co. Inc.; 0-915720),* 2821 Vaughn, P.O. Box 3141, Fort Worth, TX 76105 Tel 817-531-1401.

Brown's Studio, *(Brown's Studio; 0-9604822),* 53 Middle St., Oakland, ME 04963.

BRTP Prods, *(BRTP Productions, Inc.; 0-9602280),* 60 Hawthorne Place, Manhasset, NY 11030.

BRuach HaTorah, *(B'ruach HaTorah Pubns.; 0-89655),* P.O. Box 391221, Miami Beach, FL 33139 Tel 305-673-1654.

Brubaker, *(Brubaker, E. S.),* 645 N. President Ave., Lancaster, PA 17603 Tel 717-397-3120.

Bruccoli, *(Bruccoli Clark Books; 0-89723),* 1700 Lone Pine, Bloomfield Hills, MI 48013.

Bruce Pub Co
See Glencoe

Bruce Pub Co, *(Bruce Books),* ; Publisher Abbreviation Without Addresses Are for Titles That Are Out of Print. These Are Obsolete Abbreviations. Publisher's Abbreviation Is Now Glencoe.

Brun Pr, *(Brun Press; 0-932574),* 701 N.E. 67th St., Miami, FL 33138 Tel 305-756-6249.

Bruner, *(Bruner, William T.),* 3848 Southern Pkwy., Louisville, KY 40214 Tel 502-367-7089.

Brunner-Mazel, *(Brunner/Mazel, Inc.; 0-87630),* 19 Union Square W., New York, NY 10003 Tel 212-924-3344.

Brunswick Hist Soc, *(Brunswick Historical Society),* P.O. Box 1776, Cropseyville, NY 12052.

Brunswick Pub, *(Brunswick Publishing Co.; 0-931494),* P.O. Box 555, Lawrenceville, VA 23868 Tel 804-848-3865.

Bryans Imprint of Dell

Bryden, *(Bryden Press; 0-9603510),* P.O. Box 364, Muncie, IN 47305.

Bryn Mawr, *(Bryn Mawr Press, Inc.; 0-89299),* P.O. Box 690, Bryn Mawr, PA 19010 Tel 215-665-1965.

BSA, *(Boy Scouts of America; 0-8395),* Orders to: Eastern Distribution Ctr., 2109 Westinghouse Blvd., P.O. Box 7143, Charlotte, NC 28217 Tel 704-588-4260.

BSL Pub, *(BSL Publishing Co.; 0-939124),* P.O. Box 27414, St. Louis, MO 63141.

BUC Intl, *(BUC International Corp.; 0-911778),* 1881 N.E. 26th St., Suite 95, Fort Lauderdale, FL 33305 Tel 305-565-6715.

Buccaneer Bks, *(Buccaneer Books; 0-89966),* P.O. Box 168, Cutchogue, NY 11935.

Buck Hill, *(Buck Hill Associates; 0-917420),* Garnet Lake Rd., Johnsburg, NY 12843 Tel 518-251-2743.

Buck Pub, *(Buck Publishing Co; 0-934530),* 2409 Vestavia Dr., Birmingham, AL 35216.

Buckley Pubns, *(Buckley Pubns., Inc.; 0-915388),* 233 E. Erie St., Suite 402, Chicago, IL 60611 Tel 312-943-2066.

Bucknell U Pr, *(Bucknell Univ. Press; 0-8387),* Div. of Associated University Presses, 4 Cornwall Dr., Suite 30, E. Brunswick, NJ 08816 Tel 201-254-0132.

Bucks Co Hist, *(Bucks County Historical Society; 0-910302),* Pine & Ashland Sts., Doylestown, PA 18901 Tel 215-345-0210.

Buckskin Pr, *(Buckskin Press; 0-912420),* Big Timber, MT 59011.

Bucyrus-Erie Co, *(Bucyrus-Erie Co.; 0-9604136),* P.O. Box 56, S. Milwaukee, WI 53172.

Buddhist Bks, *(Buddhist Books Intl; 0-914910),* Orders to: P.O. Box 665, Chatsworth, CA 91311 Tel 213-998-8485.

Buddhist Study, *(Buddhist Study Center, The; 0-938474),* Office of Buddhist Education, 1727 Pali Hwy., Honolulu, HI 96813.

Buddhist Text, *(Buddhist Text Translation Society; 0-917512),* City of Ten Thousand Buddhas, Talmage, CA 95481 Tel 707-462-0939.

Budlong, *(Budlong Press Co.; 0-910304),* 649 Hinmam, Evanston, IL 60202; Orders to: 5915 N. Northwest Hwy., Chicago, IL 60631.

Buffalo Acad, *(Buffalo Fine Arts Academy; 0-914782),* Albright-Knox Art Gallery, 1285 Elmwood Ave., Buffalo, NY 14222 Tel 716-882-8700.

Buffalo Bks, *(Buffalo Books),* 18380 Hwy 116, Guerneville, CA 95446.

Builders of Adytum, *(Builders of the Adytum, Ltd.),* 5105 N. Figueroa St., Los Angeles, CA 90042 Tel 213-255-7141; Orders to: P.O. Box 42278, Dept., O, Los Angeles, CA 90042.

Bull Pub, *(Bull Publishing Co.; 0-915950),* P.O. Box 208, Palo Alto, CA 94302 Tel 415-322-2855.

Bulletin Atom Sci, *(Bulletin of the Atomic Scientists),* 1020 E. 58th St., Chicago, IL 60650 Tel 312-363-5225.

Bunkhouse, *(Bunkhouse Pubs., Inc.; 0-918628),* 123 N. Sultana Ave., Ontario, CA 91764.

Bunting, *(Bunting & Lyon, Inc.; 0-913094),* 238 N. Main St., Wallingford, CT 06492 Tel 203-269-3333.

Bur Busn Res U Nebr, *(Bureau of Business Research, Univ. of Nebraska-Lincoln),* 200 CBA Bldg., Univ. of Nebr., Lincoln, NE 68588 Tel 402-472-2334.

Bur Econ Geology, *(Bureau of Economic Geology),* Div. of Univ. of Texas at Austin, University Sta., Box X, Austin, TX 78712 Tel 512-471-1534.

Bur Faculty Res Wash, *(Bureau for Faculty Research Western Washington Univ.),* Bellingham, WA 98225 Tel 202-676-3234.

Bur Health Hosp, *(Bureau of Health & Hospital Careers Counseling; 0-917364),* Lincoln Hospital Medical Ctr., P.O. Box 238, Scarsdale, NY 10583 Tel 914-241-0610.

Bur Intl Aff, *(Bureau of International Affairs),* 6769 Lexington Ave., Los Angeles, CA 90038; Moved, Left No Forwarding Address.

Bur Jewish Educ, *(Bureau of Jewish Education),* 1580 Summit Rd., Cincinnati, OH 45237 Tel 513-761-0203.

Bur Public Secrets, *(Bureau of Public Secrets; 0-939682),* P.O. Box 1044, Berkeley, CA 94701 Tel 415-527-0959.

Burda Pubns, *(Burda Pubns.; 0-914926),* Rockefeller Ctr., Suite 3005, 1270 Ave. of the Americas, New York, NY 10020.

Burdette, *(Burdette & Co., Inc.; 0-910306),* 47 Commercial Wharf, Boston, MA 02210 Tel 617-523-3505.

Bureau Busn Res U Wis, *(Bureau of Business Research, Univ. of Wisconsin, Graduate School of Business),* 1155 Observatory Dr., Rm 110, Commerce Bldg., Madison, WI 53706 Tel 608-262-1550.

Bureau Issues, *(Bureau Issues Assn.; 0-930412),* 59 W. Germantown Pike, Norristown, PA 19401.

Burgess, *(Burgess Publishing Co.; 0-8087),* 7108 Ohms Lane, Minneapolis, MN 55435 Tel 612-831-1344. *Imprints:* CEPCO (Continuing Education Pubn., Co.); Feffer & Simons (Feffer & Simons).

Burgess-Intl Ideas, *(Burgess, Jack K. Inc., -International Ideas Inc.),* Orders to: Jack K. Burgess, Inc., 44 Engle St., Englewood, NJ 07631 Tel 201-569-7477; Orders to: International Ideas Inc., 1627 Spruce St., Philadelphia, PA 19103 Tel 215-546-0392.

Burgundy Pr, *(Burgundy Press; 0-917574),* P.O. Box 313, Southampton, PA 18966 Tel 215-357-6306.

Burkehaven Pr, *(Burkehaven Press; 0-914062),* Penacook Rd., Contoocook, NH 03229 Tel 603-746-3625.

Burke's Bk Store, *(Burke's Book Store, Inc.; 0-937130),* 634 Poplar Ave., Memphis, TN 38105 Tel 901-527-7484.

Burkett, *(Burkett, Ray De Vere, Pub. Co.; 0-912742),* 1431 Emmett St., Evansville, IN 47713 Tel 312-464-3102; Moved, Left No Forwarding Address.

Burkhard, *(Burkhard, Arthur),* 10 Farewell Place, Cambridge, MA 02138 Tel 617-547-2716; Moved Left No Forwarding Address.

Burn-Hart, *(Burn, Hart & Co., Pubs.; 0-918060),* 632 Calle Yucca, Box 1772, Thousand Oaks, CA 91360 Tel 805-498-3985.

Burning Bush, *(Burning Bush Press, The; 0-937528),* P.O. Box 7708, Newark, DE 19711 Tel 302-737-3670.

Burning Deck, *(Burning Deck; 0-930900; 0-930901),* 71 Elmgrove Ave., Providence, RI 02906 Tel 401-351-0015.

Burntcoat Corp, *(Burntcoat Corp.),* P.O. Box 36, Hampden Highlands, ME 04445.

Burr Pubns, *(Burr Pubns., Ltd.; 0-911994),* RD 1, Rte. 33, Box 429, Hightstown-Freehold Rd., Hightstown, NJ 08520.

Burrill-Ellsworth, *(Burrill-Ellsworth Assoc.; 0-935310),* 26 Birchwood Place, Tenafly, NJ 07670; Orders to: Box 295, Tenafly, NJ 07670.

Bursk & Poor, *(Bursk & Poor Publishing),* 22 Hadley St., Cambridge, MA 02140 Tel 617-868-4447.

Burtis Ent, *(Burtis Enterprises, Pubs.; 0-939530),* 23651 Gerrad Way, Canoga Park, CA 91307 Tel 213-346-8534.

Burton Gallery, *(Burton Gallery, The; 0-931540),* 334 Jordan St., Nevada City, CA 95959 Tel 916-265-6659.

Business Brokers, *(Business Brokers Assn.),* P.O. Box 23934, Fort Lauderdale, FL 33307 Tel 305-561-1392.

Business Pubns, *(Business Pubns., Inc.; 0-256),* Subs. of Richard D. Irwin, Inc., 200 Chisholm Place, Suite 240, Plano, TX 75075 Tel 214-422-4389.

Busn *Imprint of* **P-H**

Busn Journals, *(Business Journals, Inc.; 0-937506),* 22 S. Smith St., Norwalk, CT 06855 Tel 203-853-6015.

Busn Mgmt Sci, *(Business Management Sciences, Inc.; 0-918128),* 95-20 63rd, Rego Park, NY 11374 Tel 212-275-2874.

Busn News, *(Business News Publishing Co.; 0-912524),* P.O. Box 2600, Troy, MI 48084 Tel 313-362-3700.

Busn Pr, *(Business Press),* Dist. by: Taplinger Publishing Co., 132 W. 22nd St., New York, NY 10011.

Busn Proposals
See Courier Pr FL

Busn Psych, *(Business Psychology International; 0-931918),* 890-6 National Press Bldg., Washington, DC 20045 Tel 202-638-3951.

Busn Res Pubns, *(Business Research Publications, Inc.),* 817 Broadway, New York, NY 10003 Tel 212-673-4700; Orders to: 87 Terminal Dr., Plainview, NY 11803 Tel 516-349-1010.

Busn Sale Inst, *(Business Sale Institute; 0-933808),* 170 Park Center Plaza, Suite 202, San Jose, CA 95113 Tel 408-286-4850.

Busn Systems Res, *(Business Systems Research Group; 0-9603584),* 10218 Chimney Hill, Dallas, TX 75243 Tel 214-644-0222.

Buten Mus, *(Buten Museum of Wedgwood; 0-912014),* 246 N. Bowman Ave., Merion, PA 19066 Tel 215-664-9069.

Buteo, *(Buteo Books; 0-931130),* P.O. Box 481, Vermillion, SD 57069 Tel 605-624-4343.

Butterfly Pr, *(Butterfly Press; 0-918766),* P.O. Box 19571, Houston, TX 77024 Tel 713-464-7570; Formerly Terzarima System.

Butterick Pub, *(Butterick Publishing; 0-88421),* Div. of American Can Co., 708 Third Ave., New York, NY 10017 Tel 212-599-6599; Orders to: P.O. Box 1914, Altoona, PA 16603.

Butterworth, *(Butterworth Pubs., Inc.),* 10 Tower Office Park, Woburn, MA 01801 Tel 617-933-8260. *Imprints:* Newnes-Butterworth (Newnes-Butterworth).

Butterworths
See Butterworth

Buxbaum, *(Buxbaum, Edwin C.; 0-9600494),* P.O. Box 465, Wilmington, DE 19899 Tel 302-994-2663.

Buyer's Directory, *(Buyer's Directory),* R.D. 3, Box 533, Olean, NY 14760 Tel 716-372-0514.

By By Prods, *(By By Productions; 0-938826),* P.O. Box 1743, Glendora, CA 91740.

By Hand & Foot, *(By Hand & Foot, Ltd.; 0-938670),* Green River Rd., P.O. Box 611, Brattleboro, VT 05301.

BYLS Pr, *(BYLS Press),* Div. of Bet Yoatz Library Services, 6247 N. Francisco Ave., Chicago, IL 60659 Tel 312-262-8959.

BYR *Imprint of* **Random**

Byrd, *(Byrd, Harold E.; 0-9601972),* 8801 S. Western Ave., Los Angeles, CA 90047.

BYTE Bks *Imprint of* **McGraw**

Byzantine Pr, *(Byzantine Press; 0-913168),* 115 N. Seventh St., Las Vegas, NV 89101 Tel 702-384-4200.

C A Celorio, *(Celorio, Cesar Alberto; 0-918168),* 23-42 37th St., Long Island City, NY 11105 Tel 212-278-7890.

C A Jones, *(Jones, Charles A., Publishing Co.; 0-8396),* Div. of Wadsworth Publishing Co., c/o Wadsworth Publishing Co., 10 Davis Dr., Belmont, CA 94002.

C A Krause, *(Krause, Corinne Azen; 0-9604104),* P.O. Box 81096, Pittsburgh, PA 15217; Dist by: Caroline House, 2 Ellis Place, Ossining, NY 10562.

C A Miller, *(Miller, Charles A.),* Miller-Trackaday, New Market, VA 22844.

C A Smith, *(Smith, Carolyn A.),* 12901 Twisted Oak Rd., Oklahoma City, OK 73120 Tel 405-751-3167.

C & B Functional, *(C & B Functional Resumes),* 1414 Miravalle Ave., Los Altos, CA 94022; Moved, Left No Forwarding Address.

C & H Pub, *(C & H Pub. Co.; 0-918768),* 45 Center St., Brewer, ME 04412 Tel 207-989-3820.

C & L Pub Co, *(C&L Publishing Co.; 0-9605724),* 101 Park Washington Court, Falls Church, VA 22046.

C & M Ventures, *(C. & M. Ventures, Inc.),* P.O. Box 68, Cambria Heights, NY 11411.

C & R Loo, *(Loo, C. & R., Inc.),* 1550 62nd St., P.O. Box 8397, Emeryville, CA 94662.

C B Pub & Dist
See Caratzas Bros

C B Slack, *(Slack, Charles B., Inc.; 0-913590),* 6900 Grove Rd., Thorofare, NJ 08086 Tel 609-848-1000.

C Banks, *(Banks, Carl),* 1533 W. 85th St., Los Angeles, CA 90047.

C Beekman, *(Beekman, Carl),* 1628 N St., Bedford, IN 47421.

C Berke, *(Berke, Carl),* 20 Simmons Dr., Milford, MA 01757.

C Boyer, *(Boyer, Carl; 0-936124),* P.O. Box 333 Newhall, CA 91322.

C C Brown Pub, *(Brown, C. C., Publishing Co.; 0-9600378),* Box 462, Airway Heights, WA 99001 Tel 509-244-5807.

C C Burgess, *(Burgess, Carl C.),* 12816 14th, Yucaipa, CA 92399.

C C Fisher, *(Fisher, Clay C.),* 702 Tenth St., N.E., Massillon, OH 44646.

C C Geer, *(Geer, Corinne C.; 0-9601508),* 2222 Wallington Dr., Albany, GA 31707.

C C Pierce, *(Pierce, Clayton C.; 0-9601564),* 325 Carol Dr., Ventura, CA 93003 Tel 805-653-1949.

C C Thomas, *(Thomas, Charles C., Pub.; 0-398),* 301-327 E. Lawrence Ave., Springfield, IL 62717 Tel 217-789-8980.

C Cannon, *(Cannon, C.),* P.O. Box 4671, San Francisco, CA 94101; Moved, Left No Forwarding Address.

C Catton, *(Catton, Cliff; 0-9602398),* 3 Forest St., Newton Highlands, MA 02161.

C Clements, *(Clements, Christine),* 1257 E. 81st St., Los Angeles, CA 90001.

C de Bussy, *(De Bussy, Carvel; 0-9602260),* 3801 Connecticut Ave. N.W., Washington, DC 20008.

C E Barbour, *(Barbour, Clifford E., Library; 0-931222),* Pittsburgh Theological Seminary, 616 N. Highland Ave., Pittsburgh, PA 15206 Tel 412-362-5610.

C E M Comp, *(C. E. M. Co.; 0-930004),* 3154 Coventry Dr., Bay City, MI 48706 Tel 517-686-4208.

C E Tuttle, *(Tuttle, Charles E., Co., Inc.; 0-8048),* P.O. Drawer F, Rutland, VT 05701 Tel 802-773-8930.

C E Wolff, *(Wolff, Charles E.),* 3392 Yellowtail Dr., Los Alamitos, CA 90720 Tel 213-430-4428.

C Elder, *(Elder, Charles & Randy, Pubs.; 0-918450),* 2115 Elliston Place, Nashville, TN 37203 Tel 615-327-1867.

C Franklin Pr, *(Franklin, Chas., Press, The; 0-9603516),* 18409 90th Ave. W., Edmonds, WA 98020 Tel 206-774-6979.

C Fredericks, *(Fredericks, Carl),* Orders to: Circle Publications, P.O. Box 34, Lyndhurst, NJ 07071; Moved, Left No Forwarding Address.

C G Jung Foun, *(Jung, C. G., Foundation Publications; 0-913430),* 28 E. 39th St., New York, NY 10016 Tel 212-697-6430.

C G Smith, *(Smith, Cortland Gray),* 248 Circle Dr., Plandome, NY 11030 Tel 516-627-5856.

C Gallo, *(Gallo, Cristino; 0-9604174),* P.O. Box 13512, Santurce Sta., Santurce, PR 00907 Tel 809-725-7026; Dist. by: Book Service of Puerto Rico, 102 Avenida De Diego, Santurce, PR 00907.

C Gebhardt, *(Gebhardt, Chuck; 0-9601410),* P.O. Box 6821, San Jose, CA 95150.

C H Hall, *(Hall, Clarence H.; 0-9604084),* 3409 Altwater Rd., Avon Park, FL 33825.

C H Kerr, *(Kerr, Charles H., Publishing Co.; 0-88286),* 600 W. Jackson, Suite 413, Chicago, IL 60606 Tel 312-454-0363; Orders to: P.O. Box 914, Chicago, IL 60690.

C H Neuffer, *(Neuffer, Claude Henry),* U. S. C. English Dept., Columbia, SC 29208 Tel 803-787-3823.

C H Robinsen, *(Robinsen, Chris H.),* 524 N. First St., Aberdeen, SD 57401.

C Hallberg, *(Hallberg, Charles, & Co., Inc.; 0-87319),* P.O. Box 547, Delavan, WI 53115 Tel 414-728-2331.

C Hinckley, *(Hinckley, Clive; 0-9602984),* 106 E. Sunset Dr., S., Redlands, CA 92373.

C Horn, *(Horn, Calvin, Pubs., Inc.; 0-910750),* P.O. Box 4204, Albuquerque, NM 87106 Tel 505-268-9226.

C Hughes, *(Hughes, Clarence),* P.O. Box 451, Annawan, IL 61234 Tel 309-935-6715.

C Hungness, *(Hungness, Carl, Publishing; 0-915088),* P.O. Box 24308, Speedway, IN 46224 Tel 317-244-4792.

C I B A Pharm, *(C I B A Pharmaceutical Co.; 0-914168),* 556 Morris Ave., Summit, NJ 07901; Orders to: P. O. Box R-195, Summit, NJ 07901.

C J Frompovich, *(Frompovich, C. J., Pubns.; 0-935322),* R.D. 1, Chestnut Rd., Coopersburg, PA 18036 Tel 215-346-8461.

C Jordan, *(Jordan, Carol 0-9605360),* 654 Jerome St., Davis, CA 95616.

C Kerr Ent, *(Kerr, Charles, Enterprises, Inc.; 0-936002),* 129 N. Main St., New Hope, PA 18938 Tel 215-862-9618; Orders to: P. O. Box 22, New Hope, PA 18938.

C L Cook, *(Cook, Chester L.; 0-9604670),* P. O. Box 1511, Slidell, LA 70458.

C L Mast, *(Mast, C. L., Jr. & Associates),* 2041 Vardon Lane, Flossmoor, IL 60422 Tel 312-798-1817.

C L Pelton, *(Pelton, Charles L.; 0-931470),* 201 S. Lloyd, Suite 230 Physician's Plaza, Aberdeen, SD 57401.

C-Life Inst, *(C-Life Institute),* Box 261, Boulder Creek, CA 95006.

C M G Pub, *(CMG Publishing Co., Inc.; 0-9600718),* Box 630, Princeton, NJ 08540 Tel 609-924-7504.

C M Hall, *(Hall, C. Mitchel; 0-914574),* 3401 Bangor St., S.E., Washington, DC 20020 Tel 202-583-3297.

C M I Pubns, *(C.M.I. Pubns.),* P.O. Box 47075, Dallas, TX 75247; Moved, Left No Forwarding Address.

C M Kent, *(Kent, Carol Miller; 0-9604886),* 831 S. Frederick, Arlington, VA 22204.

C M Otstot, *(Otstot, Charles M.; 0-9603808),* 5124 N. 33rd St., Arlington, VA 22207 Tel 703-538-5446.

C N Aronson, *(Aronson, Charles N., Writer-Publisher; 0-915736),* 11520 Bixby Hill Road, Arcade, NY 14009 Tel 716-496-6002.

C N Vogel
   See Vogel Bk

C P Graham, *(Graham, C P, Press),* Box 5, Keswick, VA 22947 Tel 804-293-5980.

C P Mills, *(Mills, Charles P.),* 952 Old Huntingdon Pike, Huntingdon Valley, PA 19006.

C P Pr, *(C. P. Press; 0-9600452),* 76-39-173rd St., Flushing, NY 11366.

C P Unltd, *(C. P. Unltd.),* 2338 Ave. Sevilla, No. 0, Laguna Hills, CA 92653; c/o Richard Maher, 5180 So. 300w, Suite H, Salt Lake City, UT 84107.

C R Dodson, *(Dodson, Carolyn R.),* 107 Music City Circle, Nashville, TN 37214.

C R Leonard & D Coleman, *(Leonard, Cliff R., & Duke Coleman; 0-9603818),* 1007 N. Noyes Dr., Silver Spring, MD 20910; Dist. by: Nothing New, P.O. Box 714, Silver Spring, MD 20901.

C Rowland, *(Rowland, Chuck; 0-9601426),* Rte. 2, Box 135, Berkeley Springs, WV 25411 Tel 304-258-1835.

C Schneider, *(Schneider, Coleman),* P.O. Box 762, Tenafly, NJ 07670.

C Stark, *(Stark, Claude, & Co., Pubs.; 0-89007),* P.O. Box 843, Brookline Village, 21 Station St., Boston, MA 02147 Tel 617-734-2045.

C V Holland
   See Hol-Land Bks

C W Cleworth, *(Cleworth, Charles W., Pub.),* 1129 E. 17th Ave., Denver, CO 80218 Tel 303-832-1022.

C Williams Ent, *(Williams, Charles, Enterprises; 0-916564),* Queen's Tower, No. 1507, Cincinnatti, OH 45204.

C Young, *(Young, Chesley),* P.O. Box 112, Cathedral Sta., New York, NY 10025; Moved, Left No Forwarding Address.

CA Assn Older, *(California Assn. for Older Americans; 0-917154),* Dist. by: New Glide Publications, 330 Ellis St., San Francisco, CA 94102 Tel 415-771-7470.

CA Real Estate, *(State of California, Department of Real Estate; 0-916478),* 714 P St. Suite 1550, Sacramento, CA 95814 Tel 916-322-9740.

Caann Verlag, *(Caann Verlag Gmbtt),* Dist. by: Associated Booksellers, 147 McKinley Ave., Bridgeport, CT 06606.

Caballero Pr, *(Caballero Press; 0-9601346),* 1936 Caballero Way, Las Vegas, NV 89109 Tel 702-735-3406.

Caballus Pubs
   See Printed Horse

Cache Pr, *(Cache Press),* 801 Juniper Ave., Boulder, CO 80302.

Cactus Vick, *(Cactus Vick Enterprises; 0-918958),* P.O. Box 2498, Little Rock, AK 72203 Tel 501-778-3514.

Cadillac, *(Cadillac Publishing Co., Inc.; 0-87445),* 709 S. Skinker Blvd., St. Louis, MO 63105 Tel 314-862-7560; 6611 Clayton Rd., St. Louis, MO 63117.

Cadleon Pr, *(Cadleon Press; 0-9600310),* P.O. Box 24, San Francisco, CA 94101; Moved, Left No Forwarding Address.

Cadmus Eds, *(Cadmus Editions; 0-932274),* P.O. Box 4725, Santa Barbara, CA 93103.

Caedmon, *(Caedmon; 0-9601156; 0-89845),* Div. of Raytheon Co., 1995 Broadway, New York, NY 10023 Tel 212-580-3400.

Cagg, *(Cagg, Richard D.),* 423 W. Fourth, Cameron, MO 64429.

Cahill, *(Cahill & Co., Pubs., Inc.),* 145 Palisade Pl., Dobbs Ferry, NY 10522 Tel 914-693-3600.

Cahners
   See CBI Pub

Cahners, *(Cahners Publishing Co., Inc.),* ; Publisher Abbreviation Without Addresses Are for Titles That Are Out of Print. These Are Obsolete Abbreviations. Publisher's Abbreviation Is Now CBI Pub.

CAIS U of Miami
   See AISI

Caislan Pr, *(Caislan Press; 0-937444),* Box 28371, San Jose, CA 95159 Tel 408-398-4979.

Cal Inst Intl, *(California Institute of International Studies; 0-912098),* 766 Santa Ynez, Stanford, CA 94305 Tel 415-322-2026.

Cal Inst Public, *(California Institute of Public Affairs; 0-912102),* Affiliate of the Claremont Colleges, P.O. Box 10, Claremont, CA 91711 Tel 714-624-5212.

Cal Journal, *(California Journal Press; 0-930302),* 1617 10th St., Sacramento, CA 95814 Tel 916-444-2840.

Cal Living Bks, *(California Living Books; 0-89395),* The Hearst Bldg., Suite 501, Third & Market Sts., San Francisco, CA 94103 Tel 415-543-5981.

Cal-Pendleton
   See Sampson Bowers

Cal-Syl Pr, *(Cal-Syl Press; 0-930638),* 3960 E. 14th St., Oakland, CA 94601 Tel 415-534-5032.

Calamus Bks, *(Calamus Books; 0-930762),* Box 689, Cooper Sta., New York, NY 10276.

Calapooya Bks, *(Calapooya Books; 0-935004),* 2182 Cal Young Rd., Eugene, OR 97401 Tel 503-344-4301.

Calcon Pr, *(Calcon Press; 0-9600740),* P.O. Box 536, Bruce, MS 38915.

Caledonia Pr, *(Caledonia Press; 0-932282),* P.O. Box 245, Racine, WI 53401 Tel 414-637-6200.

Calibre Bks, *(Calibre Books; 0-9605800),* 2953 Fort St., Wyandotte, MI 48192 Tel 313-671-1599.

Calibre Pr, *(Calibre Press; 0-935878),* 1521 Kirk St., Evanston, IL 60202 Tel 312-328-4411.

Calico Papers, *(Calico Papers, The),* Rte. 1, Cochecton, NY 12726 Tel 914-932-8309.

Calico Pr, *(Calico Press; 0-912714),* P.O. Box 758, Twenty-Nine Palms, CA 92277 Tel 714-367-7661.

Calif Acad Sci, *(California Academy of Sciences; 0-940228),* Golden Gate Park, San Francisco, CA 94118 Tel 415-221-5100.

Calif Almanac, *(California Almanac Co.; 0-89167),* c/o California Information Almanac Co., P.O. Box 400, Lakewood, CA 90714 Tel 213-865-7634.

Calif Bk, *(California Book Co., Ltd.; 0-910310),* 2310 Telegraph Ave., Berkeley, CA 94704.

Calif Books, *(California Books; 0-934112),* Box 9551, Stanford, CA 94305.

Calif Health, *(California Health Pubns.; 0-930926),* 3900 Shenandoah Dr., Oceanside, CA 92054.

Calif Hist, *(California Historical Society; 0-910312),* P.O. Box 3370, San Diego, CA 92103; Orders to: 2090 Jackson St., San Francisco, CA 94109 Tel 415-567-1848.

Calif Pol Items, *(California Political Items Co.; 0-917210),* P.O. Box 1741, Santa Cruz, CA 95060.

Calif Pubns, *(California Pubns.; 0-917306),* P.O. Box 14, Calabasas, CA 91302 Tel 213-880-4181.

Calif Street, *(California Street; 0-915090),* 723 Dwight Way, Berkeley, CA 94710 Tel 415-548-8273.

Calif Tomorrow, *(California Tomorrow),* 681 Market St., San Francisco, CA 94105.

Calif Weekly, *(California Weekly Explorer, Inc.; 0-936778),* 631 Paularino, Costa Mesa, CA 92626.

Calif Wood, *(California Wood),* P.O. Box 541, San Luis Obispo, CA 93406.

Callarman Hse, *(Callarman House; 0-930092),* 2564 N. Spinnaker Ave., Port Hueneme, CA 93041 Tel 805-985-6554.

Callaway Edns, *(Callaway Editions; 0-935112),* 421 Hudson St., New York, NY 10014 Tel 212-929-5212.

Calligraphy Donna, *(Calligraphy by Donna; 0-9604308),* 565 SE Airpark Dr., Bend, OR 97701 Tel 503-382-0211.

Calliope Music, *(Calliope Music; 0-9605912),* P.O. Box 1460, Ansonia Sta., New York, NY 10023.

Calm Harbor, *(Calm Harbor),* P.O. Box 548, Vero Beach, FL 32960 Tel 305-569-2125; Moved Left No Forwarding Address.

Calvary Baptist, *(Calvary Baptist Church),* Calvary Bookstore, 139 W. 57th St., New York, NY 10019 Tel 212-247-3233.

Calwood Pubns, *(Calwood Pubns.),* P.O. Box 284, Monsey, NY 10952 Tel 914-352-7760.

Camaro Pub, *(Camaro Publishing Co.; 0-913290),* Worldway Postal Sta., P.O. Box 90430, Los Angeles, CA 90009 Tel 213-837-7500.

Camberleigh & Hall, *(Camberleigh & Hall, Pubs.; 0-935880),* P.O. Box 18914, N. Hills Sta., Raleigh, NC 27619.

Camblos-Winger, *(Camblos-Winger; 0-9602706),* Box 657, Skyland, NC 28776 Tel 704-274-2794.

Cambrian, *(Cambrian Pubns.; 0-912548),* P.O. Box 191, Little River Sta., Miami, FL 33138 Tel 305-751-1122.

Cambric, *(Cambric Press; 0-918342),* 912 Strowbridge Dr., Huron, OH 44839 Tel 419-433-4221.

Cambridge Bk, *(Cambridge Book Co., Inc.; 0-8428),* Div. of the N.Y. Times Co., 888 Seventh Ave., New York, NY 10106 Tel 212-957-5313.

Cambridge Corp, *(Cambridge Corp.; 0-939008),* P.O. Box 64, Cambridge, MA 01938.

Cambridge Sci, *(Cambridge Scientific Abstracts, Inc.; 0-88387),* 6611 Kenilworth Ave., Suite 437, Riverdale, MD 20840 Tel 301-864-5752.

Cambridge U Pr, *(Cambridge Univ. Press; 0-521),* 32 E. 57th St., New York, NY 10022 Tel 212-688-8885; Orders to: 510 North Ave., New Rochelle, NY 10801.

Camda, *(Camda; 0-9600434),* P.O. Box 2467, Staunton, VA 24401.

Camden Hse, *(Camden House, Inc.; 0-938100),* Drawer 2025, Columbia, SC 29202.

Camelot   Imprint of Avon

Camelot Pub, *(Camelot Publishing Co.; 0-89218),* P.O. Box 1357, Ormond Beach, FL 32074 Tel 904-672-5672.

Cameo Pr, *(Cameo Press; 0-937868),* 373 Fifth Ave., Suite 1102, New York, NY 10016.

Camera, *(Camera),* 61 W. 51st St., New York, NY 10019.

Camera Graphic, *(Camera/Graphic Press Ltd.; 0-918696),* P.O. Box 1702, F.D.R. Sta., New York, NY 10022 Tel 212-832-0760.

Camerawork
   See NFS Pr

Cameron & Co, *(Cameron & Co.; 0-918684),* Russ Bldg., Suite 1470, 235 Montgomery St., San Francisco, CA 94104 Tel 415-981-1135.

Camp Denali, *(Camp Denali Publishing; 0-9602792),* P.O. Box 67, McKinley Park, AK 99755.

Campaigner, *(Campaigner Pubns., Inc.; 0-918388),* 304 W. 58th St, New York, NY 10019 Tel 212-247-8820.

Campana Art, *(Campana Art Co.; 0-939608),* P.O. Box 355, Rte. 2, Box 30, Salem, WI 53168 Tel 414-843-2403.

Campanile, *(Campanile Press, The San Diego State Univ.; 0-916304),* 5300 Campanile Dr., San Diego, CA 92182 Tel 714-286-6220; Formerly Named San Diego State University Press.

Campgrounds, *(Campgrounds Unlimited; 0-913788),* c/o Europa Camping & Caravaning, 2306 Sixth, Clay Center, KS 67432.

Campione, *(Campione, Michael J.; 0-9600186),* 2202 New Albany Rd., Cinnaminson, NJ 08077 Tel 609-829-6098.

Campus, *(Campus Pubs.; 0-87506),* 713 W. Ellsworth Rd., Ann Arbor, MI 48104 Tel 313-663-4033.

Campus Crusade, *(Campus Crusade for Christ, International; 0-918956),* P.O. Box 1576, 2700 Little Mountain Dr., Bldg. "B", San Bernardino, CA 92402 Tel 714-886-7981.

Campus Scope, *(Campus Scope Press),* 2928 Dean Parkway, Apt. 4D, Minneapolis, MN 55416.

Camward Hse, *(Camward House; 0-936460),* P.O. Box 268, E. Patrick St. Sta., Frederick, MD 21701.

Can-Do Bks, *(Can-Do-Books; 0-9604192),* 2119 Lone Oak Ave., Napa, CA 94558.

Can Whole Earth, *(Canadian Whole Earth Research Foundation),* Dist. by: Bookpeople, 2940 Seventh St., Berkeley, CA 94710.

Canadian-Hungarian, *(Canadian-Hungarian Pubs.),* c/o Martin K. Kiss, 20916 Fairpark Dr., Fairview Park, OH 44176; Moved, Left No Forwarding Address.

Canaveral, *(Canaveral Press, Inc.),* Orders to: 309 Santa Monica Blvd., Suite 224, Santa Monica, CA 90401 Tel 213-394-4542.

Cancer Bk Hse, *(Cancer Book House),* 2043 N. Berendo St., Los Angeles, CA 90027 Tel 213-663-7801.

Cancer Care, *(Cancer Care Inc.),* National Cancer Foundation, 1 Park Ave., New York, NY 10016 Tel 212-679-5700.

C&M Pubns, *(C&M Pubns.; 0-938934),* 2505 Stratford Dr., Austin, TX 78746.

Canfield Pr *Imprint of* **Har-Row**

Canine Behavior, *(Canine Behavior Institute Library),* 606 Wilshire Blvd., Suite 113, Santa Monica, CA 90401.

Canner, *(Canner, J. S., & Co.; 0-910324),* 49-65 Lansdowne St., Boston, MA 02215 Tel 617-437-1923.

Canning Pubns, *(Canning Pubns., Inc.; 0-938516),* 925 Anza Ave., Vista, CA 92083.

Canopy Creations, *(Canopy Creations),* Box 113, Bloomfield, IA 52537.

Canterbury Pr, *(Canterbury Press; 0-933993),* 5540 Vista Del Amigo, Anaheim, CA 92807.

Canvas Pubns, *(Canvas Pubns Inc.; 0-930610),* 3524 W. Washington Blvd., Los Angeles, CA 90018 Tel 213-731-9057.

Canyon Bks, *(Canyon Books; 0-89014),* Div. of American Art Enterprises, Inc., 21322 Lassen St., Chatsworth, CA 91311.

Cap Hill Pr, *(Capitol Hill Press; 0-88221),* 1825 Connecticut Ave., N.W., Suite 322, Washington, DC 20009 Tel 202-667-0220; Dist. by: Acropolis Books Ltd., 2400 17th St., N.W., Washington, DC 20009.

Capital Bird, *(Capital Bird Dog Enterprises; 0-9601034),* 10 N. Helderberg Pkwy., Slingerlands, NY 12159 Tel 518-439-2606.

Capital Pub Corp, *(Capital Publishing Corp.; 0-914470),* P.O. Box 348, Two Laurel Ave., Wellesley Hills, MA 02181 Tel 617-235-5405.

Capital Tech, *(Capital Technology, Inc.; 0-9603460),* 2 Fairview Plaza, Suite 116, 5950 Fairview Rd., Charlotte, NC 28210.

Capital Wash, *(Capital Pubs., Inc.; 0-87277),* P.O. Box 6235, Washington, DC 20015.

Capitalist Pr OH, *(Capitalist Press),* P.O. Box 1911, Akron, OH 44309.

Capitalist Reporter, *(Capitalist Reporter Press; 0-933722),* 1212 Ave of the Americas, New York, NY 10036.

Capitol Enquiry, *(Capitol Enquiry; 0-917982),* P.O. Box 22246, Sacramento, CA 95822 Tel 916-428-3271.

Capitol Pubns, *(Capitol Pubns., Inc.; 0-917870),* 2430 Pennsylvania Ave., N.W., Suite G-12, Washington, DC 20037 Tel 202-452-1600.

CAPP Bks, *(C.A.P.P. Books),* P.O. Box 416, Williamsburg, VA 23185 Tel 804-229-5303.

Capra Pr, *(Capra Press; 0-88496; 0-912264),* P.O. Box 2068, Santa Barbara, CA 93120 Tel 805-966-4590.

Caprock Pr, *(Caprock Press; 0-912570),* 4806 17th St., Lubbock, TX 79416 Tel 806-795-7599.

Capstone, *(Capstone Book Press; 0-912068),* 6126 W. 64th Ave., Arvada, CO 80003; Moved, Left No Forwardng Address.

Car-Match, *(Car-Match Associates),* P.O. Box 31038, Washington, DC 20031.

Carabelle, *(Carabelle Books; 0-938634),* Box 2711, Reston, VA 22091.

Caratzas Bros, *(Caratzas Brothers, Pubs.; 0-89241),* 481 Main St. (P.O. Box 210), New Rochelle, NY 10802 Tel 914-632-8487.

Caravan Bks, *(Caravan Books; 0-88206),* P.O. Box 344, Delmar, NY 12054 Tel 518-439-6146; Orders to: Publishers Marketing Group Intl., P.O. Box 350, Momence, IL 60954 Tel 815-472-2661.

Caravan-Maritime, *(Caravan-Maritime Books; 0-917368),* 87-06 168th Place, Jamaica, NY 11432 Tel 212-526-1380; Do Not Confuse with Caravan Bks.

CARBEN Survey, *(CARBEN Surveying Reprints),* 274 Winthrop Rd., Columbus, OH 43214; Formerly Named BM Surveying Book Reprints.

Carcosa, *(Carcosa; 0-913796),* P.O. Box 1064, Chapel Hill, NC 27514 Tel 919-929-2974.

Cardinal Pubs, *(Cardinal Pubs.; 0-912930),* P.O. Box 207, Davis, CA 95616.

Career Inst, *(Career Institute, Inc.; 0-911744),* Div. of Singer Communications Corp., 1500 Cardinal Dr., Little Falls, NJ 07424 Tel 201-256-4512.

Career Pub, *(Career Publishing, Inc.; 0-89262),* 931 N. Main St., P.O. Box 5486, Orange, CA 92667 Tel 800-854-4014.

Carib Hse, *(Carib House (USA); 0-936378),* P. O. Box 38834, Hollywood, CA 90038; Orders to: 25562 Camino Vista, Hayward, CA 94541.

Carib Pubns *Imprint of* **Casa Bautista**

Carillon Bks, *(Carillon Books; 0-89310),* Div. of Catholic Digest, 405 Lexington Ave., New York, NY 10017 Tel 212-867-9766; Orders to: 2115 Summit Ave., St. Paul, MN 55105 Tel 612-647-5251.

Carley Pubns, *(Carley Pubns.),* P.O. Box 551, Farmingdale, NY 11735; Moved, Left No Forwarding Address.

Carlinshar, *(Carlinshar & Assoc. Applied Research Corp.; 0-934872),* 1159 Quail Run Ave., Bolingbrook, IL 60439 Tel 312-759-9028.

Carlisle Indus, *(Carlisle Industries; 0-9600344),* P.O. Box 3700, Visalia, CA 93277 Tel 209-733-2570.

Carlton, *(Carlton Press; 0-8062),* 84 Fifth Ave., New York, NY 10011 Tel 212-243-8800.

Carlton Pubns CA, *(Carlton Pubns.,Inc.; 0-937348),* 10949 Fruitland Dr., Studio City, CA 91604.

Carlyle Assocs, *(Carlyle Assocs.; 0-935084),* 1236 Ninth St., P.O. Box 3391, Santa Monica, CA 90403.

Carma, *(Carma Press; 0-918328),* Box 12633, St. Paul, MN 55112 Tel 612-631-3120.

Carmel Pubns, *(Carmel Pubns),* P.O. Box 4324 Grand Central Sta., New York, NY 10017; Moved, Left No Forwarding Address.

Carnation, *(Carnation Press; 0-87601),* P.O. Box 101, State College, PA 16801 Tel 814-238-3577.

Carnegie Coun Policy, *(Carnegie Council on Policy Studies in Higher Education; 0-931050),* 2150 Shattuck Ave., Berkeley, CA 94704.

Carnegie Endow, *(Carnegie Endowment for International Peace; 0-87003),* 11 Dupont Circle, Washington, DC 20036 Tel 202-797-6425.

Carnegie Inst, *(Carnegie Institution of Washington; 0-87279),* 1530 "P" St., N.W., Washington, DC 20005 Tel 202-387-6411.

Carnegie-Mellon, *(Carnegie-Mellon Univ. Press; 0-915604),* Carnegie-Mellon Univ., Baker Hall 233, Pittsburgh, PA 15213; Dist. by: Univ. of Pittsburgh Press, 127 N. Bellefield Ave., Pittsburgh, PA 15260 Tel 412-624-4110.

Carnot Pr, *(Carnot Press; 0-917308),* P.O. Box 1544, Lake Oswego, OR 97034 Tel 503-636-6894.

Carolina Acad Pr, *(Carolina Academic Press; 0-89089),* P.O. Box 8795, Durham, NC 27707 Tel 919-688-5155.

Carolina Art, *(Carolina Art Assn.; 0-910326),* 135 Meeting St., Charleston, SC 29401 Tel 803-722-2706.

Carolina Biological, *(Carolina Biological Supply Co.; 0-89278),* 2700 York Rd., Burlington, NC 27215 Tel 919-584-0381.

Carolina Edns, *(Carolina Editions, Inc.; 0-914056),* P.O. Box 3169, Greenwood, SC 29646 Tel 803-229-3503.

Carolina Pop Ctr, *(Carolina Population Center, The Univ. of North Carolina at Chapel Hill; 0-89055),* Population Pubns., University Sq. 300A, Chapel Hill, NC 27514 Tel 919-966-2152.

Carolina Wren, *(Carolina Wren Press, The; 0-932112),* 300 Barclay Rd., Chapel Hill, NC 27514.

Caroline Hse, *(Caroline House Pubs.),* P.O. Box 738, Ottawa, IL 61350 Tel 815-434-7905; Orders to: 2 Ellis Place, Ossining, NY 10562 Tel 914-941-9271.

Carolingian, *(Carolingian Press),* 46 Centre St., Haddonfield, NJ 08033 Tel 609-795-7887.

Carolrhoda Bks, *(Carolrhoda Books, Inc.; 0-87614),* 241 First Ave., N., Minneapolis, MN 55401 Tel 612-332-3344.

Carousel Pr, *(Carousel Press; 0-917120),* P.O. Box 6061, Albany, CA 94706 Tel 415-527-5849.

Carpatho-Rusyn Res Ctr, *(Carpatho-Rusyn Research Center; 0-917242),* 1583 Massachusetts Ave., Cambridge, MA 02138 Tel 617-495-3692; Orders to: 355 Delano Place, Fairview, NJ 07022.

Carpenter Pr, *(Carpenter Press; 0-914140),* Rte. 4, Pomeroy, OH 45769 Tel 614-992-7520.

Carrier Pigeon, *(Carrier Pigeon; 0-932870),* 75 Kneeland St. Rm. 309, Boston, MA 02111 Tel 617-542-5679.

Carroll Bk Serv, *(Carroll Book Service, Inc.),* P.O. Box 1776, North Tarrytown, NY 10591 Tel 914-631-1776.

Carroll Coll, *(Carroll College Press; 0-916120),* 100 North East Ave., Waukesha, WI 53186 Tel 414-547-1211.

Carroll Pr, *(Carroll Press; 0-910328),* P.O. Box 8113, 43 Squantum St., Cranston, RI 02920 Tel 401-942-1587.

Carrollton Pr, *(Carrollton Press, Inc., U.S. Historical Documents Institute; 0-8408),* 1911 Fort Meyer Dr., Arlington, VA 22209 Tel 703-525-5942.

Carson Pr, *(Carson Press; 0-934360),* 733 W. Carson St., Torrance, CA 90502 Tel 213-328-3180.

Carstens Pubns, *(Carstens Pubns., Inc.; 0-911868),* P.O. Box 700, Newton, NJ 07860 Tel 201-383-3355.

Carter, *(Carter),* P.O. Box 138, Monmouth Junction, NJ 08852 Tel 215-348-2015.

Carter Craft, *(Carter Craft Doll House; 0-9604404),* 5505 42nd Ave., Hyattsville, MD 20781 Tel 301-277-3051.

Cartwheel Co, *(Cartwheel Co.; 0-934520),* 2459 W. Seventh St., St. Paul, MN 55116.

Carver Pub, *(Carver Publishing, Inc.; 0-915044),* P.O. Box 6002, Hampton Institute, Hampton, VA 23668 Tel 804-727-5000.

Carves, *(Carves Cards),* 179 South St., Brookline, MA 02167 Tel 617-469-9175.

Cary Arboretum
   See NY Botanical

Cary Arboretum, *(Cary Arboretum, The),* P.O. Box AB, Millbrook, NY 12545 Tel 914-677-5071.

CAS, *(Competence Assurance Systems; 0-89147),* Harvard Square, P. O. Box 81, Cambridge, MA 02138 Tel 617-661-9151.

Casa Bautista, *(Casa Bautista De Publicaciones; 0-311),* P.O. Box 4255, 7000 Alabama St., El Paso, TX 79914 Tel 915-566-9656. Imprints: Carib Pubns (Carib Pubns.); Centre De Pubns Baptistes (Centre De Publications Baptistes); Edit Mundo (Editorial Mundo Hispano).

Casa Edit, *(Casa Editorial),* 3128 24th St., San Francisco, CA 94110 Tel 415-647-8555.

Cascade Bks, *(Cascade Books; 0-913704),* 985 S.W. Westwood Dr., Portland, OR 97201.

Cascade Microfilm, *(Cascade Microfilm Systems),* 208 James St., Seattle, WA 98104 Tel 206-682-8031.

Cascade Photo, *(Cascade Photographics; 0-935818),* 6906 Martin Way, Olympia, WA 98506.

CASE, *(Council for Advancement & Support of Education; 0-911966),* 11 Dupont Circle, Suite 400, Washington, DC 20036 Tel 202-328-5900; Orders to: CASE Publications Order Dept., P.O. Box 298, Alexandria, VA 22314.

Casha Pubns, *(Casha Pubns; 0-917660),* 227 W. 149th St., New York, NY 10039 Tel 212-926-8577; Moved,Left No Forwarding Address.

Cashman Pr, *(Cashman Press; 0-913224),* c/o Cashman, Picard & Lederman, 25 W. 43rd St., New York, NY 10036; Moved, Left No Forwarding Address.

Casino Gaming, *(Casino Gaming Specialists; 0-9605112),* 1 Britton Place, Suite 16, Voorhees, NJ 08043.

Caspers Wine, *(Caspers Wine Press; 0-933298),* 15222 Magnolia Blvd., Suite 107, Sherman Oaks, CA 91403 Tel 213-788-1481.

Cassandra Pubns, *(Cassandra Pubns., Noe Valley Poets Workshop),* 143 Moffitt St., San Francisco, CA 94131 Tel 415-239-1253; Moved, Left No Forwarding Address.

Cassette Info, *(Cassette Information Services; 0-914624),* P.O. Box 9559, Glendale, CA 91206 Tel 213-240-7500.

Cassizzi, *(Cassizzi, Vic),* P.O. Box 8788, 710 Town Mtn. Rd., Asheville, NC 28804 Tel 704-253-5016.

Castalia Pub, *(Castalia Publishing Co.; 0-916154),* P.O. Box 1587, Eugene, OR 97440.

Castelli-Artspace, *(Castelli Graphics/Artspace; 0-9604140),* 4 E. 77th St., New York, NY 10021.

Castle CT, *(Castle Publishing Co., Ltd.),* 50 West Hill Circle, Stamford, CT 06902 Tel 203-324-7923.

Castle Pub Co, *(Castle Publishing Co.; 0-9603372),* P.O. Box 188, Portland, ME 04112 Tel 207-799-2254.

Castle Pub Connecticut
See Castle CT

Castlegate, *(Castlegate Press; 0-934398),* 3400 W. Alameda, Suite 204, Burbank, CA 91505 Tel 213-848-6312.

Castro, *(Castro, Mercedes; 0-9604748),* 78-10 147th St., Apt. 3D, Flushing, NJ 11367.

Catalyst, *(Catalyst; 0-89584),* 14 E. 60th St., New York, NY 10022.

Catan, *(Catan, Omero C.; 0-9600618),* 1901 S.W. 87th Terrace, Ft. Lauderdale, FL 33324.

Cataract Pr, *(Cataract Press; 0-914764),* P.O. Box 4875, Chicago, IL 60680 Tel 416-638-0659.

Cath Authors, *(Catholic Authors Press; 0-910334),* 1201 S. Kirkwood Rd., Kirkwood, MO 63122 Tel 314-965-4801.

Cath Guild Blind
See Guild Blind

Cath Health, *(Catholic Health Assn.; 0-87125),* 4455 Woodson Rd., St. Louis, MO 63134 Tel 314-427-2500.

Cath Hospital
See Cath Health

Cath Lib Assn, *(Catholic Library Assn.; 0-87507),* 461 W. Lancaster Ave., Haverford, PA 19041 Tel 215-649-5251.

Cath Pr Assn, *(Catholic Press Assn.),* 119 N. Park Ave., Rockville Centre, NY 11570 Tel 516-766-3400.

Cath U Pr, *(Catholic Univ. of America Press; 0-8132),* 620 Michigan Ave., N.E., Washington, DC 20064 Tel 202-635-5052; Dist. by: International Scholarly Book Services, Inc., P.O. Box 555, Forest Grove, OR 97116 Tel 503-357-7192.

Cathedral of Knowledge, *(Cathedral of Knowledge),* 235 N.E. 84th Ave., Portland, OR 97220 Tel 503-255-3859.

Cather Bk, *(Cather Book),* P.O. Box 893, Merrimack College, North Andover, MA 01845 Tel 617-683-7111.

Catholic Bk Pub, *(Catholic Book Publishing Co.; 0-89942),* 257 W. 17th St., New York, NY 10011 Tel 212-243-4515.

Cato Inst, *(Cato Institute; 0-932790),* 747 Front St., San Francisco, CA 94111 Tel 415-433-1416.

Cats Pajamas, *(Cat's Pajamas Press; 0-916866),* 527 Lyman Ave., Oak Park, IL 60304 Tel 312-386-5137.

Catskill Bk, *(Catskill Book & Record Shop, Inc.; 0-9600350),* 35 Mill Hill Rd., Woodstock, NY 12498 Tel 914-679-2251.

Cauce Pubs, *(Cauce, Cesar, Pubs. & Distributors; 0-86686),* P.O. Box 389, 39 Bowery, New York, NY 10002 Tel 212-789-0737.

Cauldron, *(Cauldron Press),* 8347 Delmar, No. 1-S, St. Louis, MO 63124.

Causeway, *(Causeway Books; 0-88356),* Div. of Promotional Book Corp., 95 Madison Ave., New York, NY 10016 Tel 212-725-4970.

Cavalier, *(Cavalier Press; 0-910338),* P.O. Box 111, Matteson, IL 60443.

Caverne Pub, *(Caverne Publishing, Inc.; 0-937844),* P.O. Box 1327, Hollywood, CA 90028 Tel 213-876-1990.

Caxton, *(Caxton Printers, Ltd.; 0-87004),* P.O. Box 700, Caldwell, ID 83605 Tel 208-459-7421.

Caxton Club, *(Caxton Club),* 60 W. Walton St., Chicago, IL 60610.

CAYC Learning Tree, *(CAYC Learning Tree),* 9998 Ferguson Rd., Dallas, TX 75228 Tel 214-235-4565.

Cayucos, *(Cayucos Books; 0-9600372),* P.O. Box 2113, Monterey, CA 93940 Tel 408-375-5289.

CBH Pub, *(CBH Publishing, Inc.),* 464 Central, Northfield, IL 60093 Tel 312-441-5617.

CBI Pub, *(CBI Publishing Co. Inc.; 0-8436),* Member of the Wadsworth Publishing Group, 51 Sleeper St., Boston, MA 02210 Tel 617-426-2224.

CC Imprint of WSP

CCCO, *(Central Committee for Conscientious Objectors; 0-933368),* An Agency for Military & Draft Counseling, P.O. Box 15796, Philadelphia, PA 19103.

CCG Imprint of **Doubleday**

CCPr Imprint of **Macmillan**

CDA, *(Control Data Arts; 0-89893),* 474 Concordia Ave., SCNFAC, St. Paul, MN 55111.

CDE, *(CDE),* Box 41551, Atlanta, GA 30331.

CDS Pub, *(CDS Publishing Co.; 0-916376),* Subs. of Man-Computer Systems, Inc., 84-13 168th St., Jamaica, NY 11432 Tel 212-739-4242.

CEBCO, *(CEBCO Standard Publishing; 0-88320; 0-8278),* Nine Kulick Rd., Fairfield, NJ 07006 Tel 201-575-8155.

Cedar Creek IN, *(Cedar Creek Pubs.; 0-935316),* 2310 Sawmill Rd., Fort Wayne, IN 46825 Tel 219-637-3856.

Cedar Creek OK, *(Cedar Creek Press; 0-935286),* P.O. Box 1051, Stillwater, OK 74074.

Cedar Rock, *(Cedar Rock Press; 0-930024),* 1121 Madeline, New Braunfels, TX 78130 Tel 512-625-6002.

Cedars Co, *(Cedars Co.),* 30516 S.E. 392nd St., Enumclaw, WA 98022; Out of Business.

Cedarwinds, *(Cedarwinds Publishing Co.),* Drawer A, Cedar Mountain, NC 28718 Tel 704-885-8251.

CEF Press, *(Child Evangelism Fellowship Press),* Warrenton, MO 63383.

CEI Pub Co, *(C.E.I. Publishing Co.; 0-88407),* 100 S. Jefferson, Athens, AL 35611 Tel 205-232-0565.

Celcom Pr, *(Celcom Press),* 901 Boren Ave., Cabrini Medical Tower, Suite 1036, Seattle, WA 98104.

Celebration Pr, *(Celebration Press; 0-933010),* P.O. Box 76, Nobleboro, ME 04555 Tel 207-563-8269.

Celestial Arts, *(Celestial Arts Publishing Co.; 0-912310; 0-89087),* 231 Adrian Rd., Millbrae, CA 94030 Tel 415-692-4500.

Celestial Gems, *(CELESTIAL GEMS; 0-914154),* 404 State St., Centralia, WA 98531 Tel 206-736-5083.

Celestial Pr, *(Celestial Press; 0-910340),* 441 N.E. 24th St., Boca Raton, FL 33432 Tel 305-395-4208.

Cellar, *(Cellar Book Shop),* 18090 Wyoming, Detroit, MI 48221 Tel 313-861-1776.

Celo Pr, *(Celo Press; 0-914064),* Rte. 5, Burnsville, NC 28714 Tel 704-675-4925.

Celtic Cross, *(Celtic Cross Books),* P.O. Box 728, Windsor, VT 05089 Tel 802-674-6617.

Cembura, *(Cembura, Al; 0-912454),* 139 Arlington Ave., Berkeley, CA 94707 Tel 415-524-0478.

Cent Hse Americana, *(Century House Americana),* Watkins Glen, NY 14891.

Centaur, *(Centaur Books, Inc.; 0-87818),* 799 Broadway, New York, NY 10003 Tel 212-677-1720.

Centaur Dumfries, *(Centaur Pubns.; 0-9602404),* P.O. Box 188, Dumfries, VA 22026 Tel 703-670-3527.

Centaur Pubn VA, *(Centaur Publication Co.; 0-932700),* 7807 Stovall Court, Lorton, VA 22079.

Centennial, *(Centennial Press; 0-8220),* Div. of Cliff's Notes, Inc., P.O. Box 80728, Lincoln, NE 68501 Tel 402-477-6971.

Centennial Photo Serv, *(Centennial Photo Services; 0-931838),* P.O. Box 36, Grantsburg, WI 54840 Tel 715-689-2153.

Center Creative Ed, *(Center for Creative Educational Services),* 924 N. Market St., Inglewood, CA 90302 Tel 213-674-9300; Moved, Left No Forwarding Address.

Center Health, *(Center for Health & Healing; 0-933320),* 8631 W. Third St., Suite 1140E, Los Angeles, CA 90048 Tel 213-652-9659.

Center Pr
See Bible Pr

Center Pr, *(Center Press; 0-934320),* 2045 Francisco St., Berkeley, CA 94709.

Center Pubns, *(Center Pubns.; 0-916820),* 905 S. Normandie Ave., Los Angeles, CA 90006 Tel 213-387-2356; Dist. by: Great Eastern Book Co., P.O. Box 271, Boulder, CO 80302.

Central Conf, *(Central Conference of American Rabbis; 0-916694),* 790 Madison Ave., Suite 601, New York, NY 10021 Tel 212-734-7166.

Central Electric, *(Central Electric Railfans' Assn.; 0-915348),* P.O. Box 503, Chicago, IL 60690.

Central FL Voters, *(Central Florida Voters Congress),* P.O. Box 1172, Orlando, FL 32802.

Central Pub, *(Central Publishing Co.; 0-931622),* P.O. Box 24021, Cincinnati, OH 45224; Moved, Left No Forwarding Address.

Centre De Pubns Baptistes Imprint of **Casa Bautista**

Centre Ent, *(Centre Enterprise, The; 0-932876),* Box 99506, Station "O", San Francisco, CA 94109 Tel 415-673-1377.

Centurion Pr, *(Centurion Press),* Drawer 62, Los Angeles, CA 90028.

Century Bookbindery, *(Century Bookbindery; 0-89984),* P.O. Box 6471, Philadelphia, PA 19145.

Century Comm, *(Century Communications, Inc.; 0-930264),* 5520 W. Touhy, Suite G, Skokie, IL 60077 Tel 312-676-4060.

Century Hse, *(Century House, Inc.; 0-87282),* Old Irelandville, Watkins Glen, NY 14891 Tel 607-535-4004.

Century One, *(Century One Press; 0-937080),* 2325 E. Platte Ave., Colorado Springs, CO 80909 Tel 303-471-1322.

Century Pr, *(Century Press; 0-915680),* 412 N. Hudson, Oklahoma City, OK 73102.

Century Three, *(Century Three Press; 0-933400),* 411 S. 13th St. Suite 315, Lincoln, NE 68508.

Century Twenty One, *(Century Twenty One Publishing; 0-86548),* P.O. Box 8, Saratoga, CA 95070.

CEP, *(Council on Economic Priorities, Inc.; 0-87871),* 84 Fifth Ave., New York, NY 10011 Tel 212-691-8550.

CEPCO Imprint of **Burgess**

CERA, *(CERA; 0-936706),* P.O. Box 18103, San Francisco, CA 94118.

Cerberus, *(Cerberus Book Co., The; 0-933590),* P.O. Box 34331, Ft. Buchanan, PR 00934.

Ceres Pr, *(Ceres Press; 0-9606138),* Box 87, Woodstock, NY 12498.

Cerridwen & Co
See Phoenix Pub WA

CES, (Continuing Education Systems, Inc.; 0-916780), 112 S. Grant St., Hinsdale, IL 60521 Tel 312-654-2596.

Chadwick Hse, (Chadwick House Pubs., Ltd.; 0-938102), 25 W. Portola, Los Altos, CA 94022.

Chadwyck-Healey, (Chadwyck-Healey/Somerset House; 0-85964), 417 Maitland Ave., Teaneck, NJ 07666.

Chaffey Commun Cult Ctr, (Chaffey Communities Cultural Center; 0-9603586), P.O. Box 772, Upland, CA 91786.

Chain Store Pub
 See Lebhar Friedman

Chalfant Pr, (Chalfant Press, Inc.; 0-912494), P.O. Box 787, Bishop, CA 93514 Tel 714-873-3535.

Challenge Bks, (Challenge Books; 0-9600352), 6 Koloff Court, Woodridge, IL 60515; Dist. by: Austin Press, P.O. Box 9774, Austin, TX 78766.

Challenge Pr, (Challenge Press; 0-89421), Book Div. of Economic Research Center, Inc., 1107 Lexington Ave., Dayton, OH 45407 Tel 513-275-8637.

Chamber Comm US, (Chamber of Commerce of the U. S., Special Publications Dept.; 0-89834), 1615 "H" St., N.W., Washington, DC 20062 Tel 202-659-5602.

Chameleon, (Chameleon Pubns.; 0-939988), 1908 Woodlyn Dr., Fredericksburg, VA 22401.

CHAMH, (CHAMH; 0-938666), 15 Park Row, New York, NY 10038.

Champion Athlete, (Champion Athlete Publishing Co.; 0-938074), Box 2936, Richmond, VA 23235 Tel 804-794-6034.

Chan Shal Imi, (Chan Shal Imi Society Press; 0-936380), P.O. Box 1365, Stone Mountain, GA 30086.

Chancellor Pr, (Chancellor Press, Inc.; 0-913798), 186 E. 64th St., New York, NY 10021 Tel 212-752-3043; Moved, Left No Forwarding Address.

Chancery Pubs, (Chancery Pubs., Inc.; 0-940024), 102 W. Pennsylvania Ave., Baltimore, MD 21204 Tel 301-821-5143.

Chandler & Sharp, (Chandler & Sharp Pubs., Inc.; 0-88316), 11A Commercial Blvd., Novato, CA 94947 Tel 415-883-2353.

Chandler Davis, (Chandler-Davis Publishing Co.; 0-910346), P.O. Box 736, West Trenton, NJ 08628 Tel 609-882-0800; Out of Business.

Chandler Pub, (Chandler Publishing Co.), ; Publisher Abbreviation Without Addresses Are for Titles That Are Out of Print. These Are Obsolete Abbreviations. Publisher Was Aquired by Har-Row College.

Change Mag, (Change Magazine Press; 0-915390), 271 North Ave., Suite 1200, New Rochelle, NY 10801 Tel 914-235-8700.

Changing Times, (Changing Times Education Service; 0-89247), A Div. of EMC Corporation, 180 E. Sixth St., St. Paul, MN 55101 Tel 612-227-7366.

Channing Bks, (Channing Books & Whaleship Plans; 0-9600496), P.O. Box 552, 35 Main St., Marion, MA 02738 Tel 617-748-0087.

Channings
 See Channing Bks

Chans Bks
 See Chans Corp

Chans Corp, (Chan's Corp.; 0-914322), 230 S. Garfield Ave., Monterey Park, CA 91754 Tel 213-572-0425.

Chanteyman, (Chanteyman Press; 0-9601250), 42 Crocus St., Woodbridge, NJ 07095 Tel 201-634-4123.

Chanticleer, (Chanticleer Press, Inc.; 0-918810), 424 Madison Ave., New York, NY 10017 Tel 212-888-1234; Formerly Named Paul Steiner, Inc.

Chapel Imprint of **Dell**

Chapman Morris & Williams, (Chapman, Morris, Williams, Ltd.), Dist. by: Tennyson Schad, 575 Madison Ave., New York, NY 10022; No Longer Distributed by Tennyson Schad.

Chapter & Cask, (Chapter & Cask; 0-940056), P.O. Box 113, Glenshaw, PA 15116 Tel 412-487-5985.

Character Res, (Character Research Press; 0-915744), 207 State St., Schenectady, NY 12305 Tel 518-370-6012.

Charioteer (Charioteer Press; 0-910350), P.O. Box 28055 Central, Washington, DC 20005 Tel 202-965-5046.

Charisma Pr, (Charisma Press; 0-933402), P.O. Box 263, St. Francis Seminary, Andover, MA 01810 Tel 617-851-7910.

Charisma Pubns, (Charisma Pubns., Inc.; 0-937008), P.O. Box 40321, Indianapolis, IN 46240 Tel 317-844-0719.

Chariton Review, (Chariton Review Press; 0-933428), Northeast Missouri State Univ., Kirksville, MO 63501 Tel 816-665-5121.

Charles, (Charles Press Pubs.; 0-913486; 0-89303), Div. of Robert J. Brady, Co., Rtes. 197 & 450, Bowie, MD 20715 Tel 301-262-6300.

Charles & Co, (Charles & Co., Inc.; 0-933318), P.O. Box 606, Southport, CT 06490.

Charles Frederick, (Charles-Frederick Publishers), P.O. Box 80055, St. Paul, MN 55108 Tel 612-373-0951.

Charles Pub, (Charles Publishing Co.; 0-912880), 12125 Riverside Dr., Suite 201, North Hollywood, CA 91607 Tel 213-762-0633.

Charles River Bks, (Charles River Books; 0-89182), 1 Thompson Square, Boston, MA 02129 Tel 617-742-9493. Imprints: CRR (Charles River Reprints)

Charlotte Pubs, (Charlotte Pubs.; 0-914878), P.O. Box 57126, Los Angeles, CA 90057.

Charlton Pubns, (Charlton Pubns., Inc.; 0-915576), The Charlton Bldg., Derby, CT 06418.

Chart Imprint of **Bobbs**

Charter Bks, (Charter Books; 0-441), Div. of Ace Books, 51 Madison Ave., New York, NY 10010 Tel 212-689-9200.

Charterhouse, (Charterhouse Books, Inc.; 0-88327), Affiliate of David McKay Co., Inc., 750 Third Ave., New York, NY 10017.

Charterhouse Imprint of **McKay**

ChartGuide, (ChartGuide; 0-938206), 300 N. Wilshire Ave., Suite 5, Anaheim, CA 92801.

Chartmasters, (Chartmasters; 0-917190), P.O. Box 1264, Covington, LA 70434 Tel 504-892-9135.

Chartrand, (Chartrand, Robert Lee), 5406 Dorset Ave., Chevy Chase, MD 20015.

Chartwell, (Chartwell House, Inc.; 0-910354), P.O. Box 166, Bowling Green Sta., New York, NY 10004.

Chase World, (Chase World Information Corp.; 0-916006), 1 World Trade Ctr., Suite 4627, New York, NY 10048.

Chasse Pubns, (Chasse Pubns.; 0-913930), P.O. Box 906, Denver, CO 80201 Tel 303-757-0160.

Chateau Pub, (Chateau Publishing, Inc.; 0-88435), P.O. Box 20432, Herndon Sta., Orlando, FL 32814 Tel 305-898-1641.

Chatham Bkseller, (Chatham Bookseller; 0-911860), 8 Green Village Rd., Madison, NJ 07940 Tel 201-822-1361.

Chatham Hse Pubs, (Chatham House Pubs., Inc.; 0-934540), Box 1, Chatham, NJ 07928 Tel 201-635-2059.

Chatham Pr, (Chatham Press; 0-85699), 143 Sound Beach, Old Greenwich, CT 06870 Tel 203-637-4531; Dist. by: The Devin-Adair Co., Old Greenwich, CT 06870.

Chatham Pub CA, (Chatham Pub. Co.; 0-89685), P.O. Box 283, 1012 Oak Grove Ave., Burlingame, CA 94010 Tel 415-348-0331.

Chatham Sq, (Chatham Square Press, Inc.; 0-89456), 401 Broadway, 23rd Fl., New York, NY 10013 Tel 212-226-3368.

Chatterton Pr, (Chatterton Press; 0-930574), 2471 Berthbrook Dr., Cincinnati, OH 45231.

Chatto-Bodley-Jonathan
 See Merrimack Bk Serv

CHCUS Inc, (CHCUS, Inc.; 0-937256), P.O. Box 444, Oak Park, IL 60303 Tel 312-848-2210.

Cheap Advice, (Cheap Advice Press; 0-930082), 5050 Lake Fjord Pass, N.E., Marietta, GA 30067 Tel 404-993-1010.

Chedney, (Chedney Press; 0-910358), Claridge House One, Claridge Dr., Apt. 911, Verona, NJ 07044 Tel 516-294-8408.

Cheever Pub, (Cheever Publishing, Inc.; 0-915708), P.O. Box 700, Bloomington, IL 61701 Tel 309-378-2961.

Chelsea Hse, (Chelsea House Pubs.; 0-87754), 133 Christopher St., New York, NY 10014 Tel 212-924-6414.

Chelsea-Lee Bks, (Chelsea-Lee Books; 0-913974), P.O. Box 66273, Los Angeles, CA 90066.

Chelsea Pub, (Chelsea Publishing Co.; 0-8284), 432 Park Ave. S., Rm. 503, New York, NY 10016 Tel 212-889-8095.

Chem Econ, (Chemical Economic Services; 0-912060), P.O. Box 468, Palmer Square, Princeton, NJ 08540 Tel 609-921-8468.

Chem Educ, (Journal of Chemical Education; 0-910362), 238 Kent Rd., Springfield, PA 19064.

Chem Elements Pub, (Chemical Elements Publishing Co.), 529 Mission Dr., Camarillo CA 93010 Tel 805-482-6067.

Chem Eng Imprint of **McGraw**

Chem Pub, (Chemical Publishing Co., Inc.; 0-8206), 155 W. 19th St., New York, NY 10011 Tel 212-255-1950.

Chen Chi Studio, (Chen Chi Studio; 0-9604652), 15 Gramercy Park, New York, NY 10003.

Cheng & Tsui, (Cheng & Tsui Co.; 0-917056), P.O. Box 328, Cambridge, MA 02139 Tel 617-277-1769.

Cherokee, (Cherokee Publishing Co.; 0-87797), P.O. Box 1081, Covington, GA 30209 Tel 404-786-0565.

Cherry Hill, (Cherry Hill Books; 0-910366), 20 Highland Ave., Cheshire, CT 06410 Tel 203-272-8065.

Cherry Valley, (Cherry Valley Editions; 0-916156), 14200 Pear Tree Lane, No. 11, Wheaton, MD 20906 Tel 301-460-7682; Dist. by: Book Bus, 892 S. Clinton Ave., Rochester, NY 14620 Tel 716-473-2550.

Cherubim, (Cherubim; 0-938574), 434 Beach 47th St., Edgemere, NY 11691.

Chesbro, (Chesbro Press; 0-938006), 17370 Hawkins Lane, P.O. Box 1326, Morgan Hill, CA 95037 Tel 408-779-5930.

Chesford Inc, (Chesford Inc.), 373 Fifth Ave. Suite 1016, New York, NY 10016 Tel 212-889-3023.

Cheshire, (Cheshire Books; 0-917352), 514 Bryant St., Palo Alto, CA 94301 Tel 415-321-2449; Dist. by: Van Nostrand Reinhold Co., 7625 Empire Dr., Florence, KY 41042.

Chester-Leeds, (Chester-Leeds Co.; 0-931624), P.O. Box 191, Middlesex, NJ 08846 Tel 201-463-0004.

Chestnut, (Chestnut Pubns.; 0-917454), Box 124, Old Sudbury Rd., Lincoln, MA 01773 Tel 617-259-9437.

Cheval Bks, (Cheval Books), 8440 Santa Monic Blvd., Hollywood, CA 90069 Tel 213-656-7311.

Chi Ctr Afro-Am Stud, (Chicago Center for Afro-American Studies & Research, Inc.; 0-937954), P.O. Box 7610, Chicago, IL 60680.

Chicago Bd Trade, (Chicago Board of Trade; 0-917456), 141 W. Jackson, Chicago, IL 60604 Tel 312-435-3556.

Chicago Contemp Photo, (Chicago Center for Contemporary Photography; 0-932026), c/o Columbia College, 600 S. Michigan Ave., Chicago, IL 60605 Tel 312-663-1600.

Chicago Hist, (Chicago Historical Society; 0-913820), Clark St. at North Ave., Chicago, IL 60614 Tel 312-642-4600.

Chicago Psych, (Chicago Institute for Psychoanalysis; 0-918568), 180 N. Michigan Ave., Chicago, IL 60601 Tel 312-726-6300.

Chicago Publishing, (Chicago Publishing Co.; 0-9603264), P.O. Box 635, Chicago, IL 60690 Tel 312-271-2970.

Chicago Review, (Chicago Review Press, Inc.; 0-914090), 820 N. Franklin St., Chicago, IL 60610 Tel 312-644-5457.

Chicago Theology & Culture, (Chicago Institute of Theology & Culture, The; 0-936978), 5401 S. Cornell Ave., Chicago, IL 60645.

Chicago Visual Lib Imprint of **U of Chicago Pr**

Chick Pubns, (Chick Pubns.; 0-937958), P.O. Box 662, Chino, CA 91710 Tel 714-987-0771.

Chicken Walk, (Chicken Walk Books), 1301A East Chestnut, Santa Ana, CA 92701; Moved, Left No Forwarding Address.

Chicorel Lib
 See Am Lib Pub Co

Child, (Child Study Center), 1100 N. E. 13th St., Oklahoma City, OK 73117.

Child & Family Ent, (Child & Family Enterprises, Inc.; 0-935202), 7 Leonard Place, Albany, NY 12202.

Child Ecology, (Child Ecology Press; 0-914364), 141 S. Gordon Way, Los Altos, CA 94022.

Child Focus Co, (Child Focus Co.; 0-933892), 1230 Keats St., Manhattan Beach, CA 90266 Tel 213-379-4144.

Child Study, (Child Study Assn. of America/Wel-Met, Inc.; 0-87183), 853 Broadway, New York, NY 10003 Tel 212-889-3450.

Child Welfare, (Child Welfare League of America, Inc.; 0-87868), 67 Irving Place, New York, NY 10003 Tel 212-254-7410.

Children First, (Children First Press; 0-9603696), Box 8008, Ann Arbor, MI 48107 Tel 313-668-8056.

Children Learn Ctr, (Children's Learning Center, Inc.; 0-917206), 4660 E. 62nd St., Indianapolis, IN 46220 Tel 317-251-6241.

Childrens, (Childrens Press; 0-516), 1224 W. Van Buren St., Chicago, IL 60607 Tel 312-666-4200. Imprints: Elk Grove Bks (Elk Grove Books); Golden Gate (Golden Gate); Sextant (Sextant).

Childrens Art, (Children's Art Foundation, Inc.; 0-89409), Box 83, Santa Cruz, CA 95063 Tel 408-426-5557.

Childrens Book Pr, (Children's Book Press/Imprenta de Libros Infantiles; 0-89239), 1461 9th Ave., San Francisco, CA 94122 Tel 415-664-8500.

Children's Defense, (Children's Defense Fund; 0-938008), 1520 New Hampshire Ave., NW, Washington, DC 20036.

Childs World, (Child's World, Inc., The; 0-89565; 0-913778), 980 N. McLean Blvd., P. O. Box 989, Elgin, IL 60120 Tel 312-741-7591; Orders to: P.O. Box 681, Elgin, IL 60120.

Chilmark, (Chilmark Press, Inc.; 0-87285), 147 E. 81st St., 1E, New York, NY 10028 Tel 212-663-2640.

Chilmark Hse, (Chilmark House; 0-937532), 4224 38th St. N.E., Washington, DC 20016.

Chilton, (Chilton Book Co.; 0-8019), Orders to: School, Library Services, Chilton Way, Radnor, PA 19089 Tel 215-687-8200.

Chimaera Pr, (Chimaera Press; 0-9601844), 316 Fifth Ave., New York, NY 10001; Dist. by: Bookpeople, 2940 Seventh St., Berkeley, CA 94710 Tel 415-549-3033; Dist. by: Light Impressions, P.O. Box 3012, Rochester, NY 14603 Tel 716-271-8960.

China Bks, (China Books & Periodicals, Inc.; 0-8351), 2929 24th St., San Francisco, CA 94110 Tel 415-282-2994.

China Phone, (China Phone Book Co., Ltd., The), P.O. Box 2385-N, Menlo Park, CA 94025.

Chinese Art App, (Chinese Art Appraisers Assn.; 0-930940), Box 734, 625 Post St., San Francisco, CA 94109 Tel 415-673-6023.

Chinkapin, (Chinkapin Press, Inc.; 0-938874), P.O. Box 10565, Eugene, OR 97401.

Chinmaya West, (Chinmaya Pubns. West), Box 2753, Napa, CA 94558 Tel 707-252-3444.

Chinmoy, (Sri Chinmoy Lighthouse; 0-87847), 86-14 Parsons Blvd., Jamaica, NY 11432 Tel 212-657-4827; Moved,Left No Forwarding Address.

Chips, (Chip's Bookshop, Inc.; 0-912378), Box 639, Cooper Sta., New York, NY 10276 Tel 212-362-9336.

Chiro Educational Serv, (Chiropractic Educational Services), 534 Union Arcade Bldg., Davenport, IA 52801; Moved, Left No Forwarding Address.

Chiron Pr, (Chiron Press, Inc.; 0-913462), 24 W. 96th St., New York, NY 10025 Tel 212-662-5486; Orders to: Publishers' Storage & Shipping Corp., 2352 Main St., Concord, MA 01742 Tel 617-897-9332.

Chiropractic, (Who's Who in Chiropractic, International Pub. Co.; 0-918336), P.O. Box 2615, Littleton, CO 80161 Tel 303-333-1581.

Chong-Donnie, (Chong-Donnie; 0-938918), 246 E. 62nd St., New York, NY 10021.

Choose Cherish, (Choose & Cherish; 0-918008), 212 E. 48th St., New York, NY 10017 Tel 212-355-0560; Moved, Left No Forwarding Address.

Chosen Bks Pub, (Chosen Books Publishing Co., Ltd.; 0-912376), Lincoln, VA 22078 Tel 703-338-4131; Dist. by: Spring Arbor, P.O. Box 985, Ann Arbor, MI 48106 Tel 800-521-3690.

Chou-Chou, (Chou-Chou Press), 65 N. Country Rd., Shoreham, NY 11786.

Chowder Chapbks, (Chowder Chapbooks), 2858 Kingston Dr., Madison, WI 53713; Moved, Left No Forwarding Address.

CHR Action, (Christian Action League; 0-918648), P.O. Box 2126, Raleigh, NC 27602.

Chr Bksellers, (Christian Booksellers Assn.), 2620 Venetucci Blvd., P.O. Box 200, Colorado Springs, CO 80901.

Chr Classics, (Christian Classics, Inc.; 0-87061), P.O. Box 30, Westminster, MD 21157 Tel 301-848-3065.

Chr Coll Pr Imprint of Christendom Pubns

Chr Evidence, (Christian Evidence League; 0-910374), P.O. Box 173, Malverne, NY 11565.

Chr Librarians, (Christian Librarians Fellowship, Inc.), c/o Houghton College, 910 Union Rd., Buffalo, NY 11224.

Chr Light
See Christian Light

Chr Lit, (Christian Literature Crusade, Inc.; 0-87508), Pennsylvania Ave., Fort Washington, PA 19034.

Chr Marriage, (Christian Marriage Enrichment; 0-938786), 8000 E. Girard, No. 301, Denver, CO 80231.

Chr Mother Goose, (Christian Mother Goose Book Co.), P.O. Box 3838, Grand Junction, CO 81502 Tel 303-434-8319.

Chr Pubns, (Christian Pubns., Inc.; 0-87509), 25 S. Tenth St., Harrisburg, PA 17101 Tel 717-233-6728.

Chr Sch Intl, (Christian Schools International; 0-87463), 3350 E. Paris Ave. S.E., P.O. Box 8709, Grand Rapids, MI 49508 Tel 616-957-1070.

Chr Science, (Christian Science Publishing Society; 0-87510), General Pubns. Dept., 1 Norway St., Boston, MA 02115 Tel 617-262-2300; Orders to: P.O. Box 1875, Boston, MA 02117.

Chr Stud Ctr, (Christian Studies Center; 0-939200), P.O. Box 11110, Memphis, TN 38111 Tel 901-458-0738.

Chris Mass, (Christopher Publishing House (Mass); 0-8158), 1405 Hanover St., West Hanover, MA 02339 Tel 617-878-4656.

Christ Comm, (Christian Communications, Inc.; 0-89349), P.O. Box 238, Arvada, CO 80001 Tel 303-422-7597.

Christ Nations, (Christ for the Nations, Inc.; 0-89985), 3404 Conway St., Box 24910, Dallas, TX 75224.

Christ the Light, (Christ The Light Works), Box 3490, San Diego, CA 92103.

Christendom Educ
See Christendom Pubns

Christendom Pubns, (Christendom Pubns.; 0-931888), Rt. 3 Box 87, Front Royal, VA 22630 Tel 703-636-2908. Imprints: Chr Coll Pr (Christendom College Press).

Christian Bks, (Christian Books), P.O. Box 1092, Goleta, CA 93017 Tel 805-965-3355.

Christian Fellow Pubs, (Christian Fellowship Pubs., Inc.; 0-935008), 11515 Allecingie Pkwy., Richmond, VA 23235 Tel 804-794-5333.

Christian Herald, (Christian Herald Books; 0-915684; 0-86693), 40 Overlook Dr., Chappaqua, NY 10514 Tel 914-769-9000.

Christian Light, (Christian Light Pubns., Inc.; 0-87813), P.O. Box 1126, Harrisonburg, VA 22801 Tel 703-434-0768.

Christian Rec, (Christian Record Braille Foundation, Inc.), P.O. Box 6097, 4444 S. 52nd St., Lincoln, NE 68506 Tel 402-488-0981.

Christian Success, (Christian Success Publishing House; 0-934178), P.O. Box 521, Irrigon, OR 97844.

Christian Zion, (Christian Zion Advocate), P.O. Box 971, Port Angeles, WA 98362 Tel 206-457-4731.

Christianica, (Christianica Center; 0-911346), 6 N. Michigan Ave., Chicago, IL 60602 Tel 312-782-4230.

Christophers Bks, (Christopher's Books; 0-87922), 390 62nd St., Oakland, CA 94618 Tel 415-428-1120.

Christophers Travel
See Travel Discover

Christs Mission, (Christ's Mission; 0-935120), Box 176, Hackensack, NJ 07602 Tel 201-342-6202.

Christward, (Christward Ministry; 0-910378), Rte. 5, Box 206, Escondido, CA 92025 Tel 714-744-1500.

Chrome Yellow, (Chrome Yellow Private Press; 0-935656), P.O. Box 14082, Gainesville, FL 32604 Tel 904-373-6798.

Chron Guide, (Chronicle Guidance Pubns.; 0-912578), Moravia, NY 13118 Tel 315-497-0330.

Chronicle Bks, (Chronicle Books; 0-87701), Div. of Chronicle Publishing Co., 870 Market St., Suite 915, San Francisco, CA 94102 Tel 415-777-7240.

Chthon Pr, (Chthon Press), 77 Mark Vincent Dr., Westford, MA 01886.

Chulainn Press, (Chulainn Press, Inc.; 0-917600), 1040 Butterfield Rd., P.O. Box 770, San Anselmo, CA 94960.

Church Bks, (Church Books; 0-916778), Rte. 4, Box 27A, Greenville, SC 29605 Tel 803-277-5714.

Church Cross, (Church of the Cross; 0-9601178), 4068 S. Willow Way, Denver, CO 80237 Tel 303-770-2272.

Church History, (Church History Research & Archives; 0-935122), Rte. 4, Box 38, Lafayette, TN 37083 Tel 615-666-4834.

Church League Am, (Church League of America; 0-89601), 422 N. Prospect St., Wheaton, IL 60187 Tel 312-653-6100.

Church Lib, (Church Library Council; 0-9603060), 5406 Quintana St., Riverdale, MD 20840 Tel 301-864-9308.

Church New Birth, (Church of the New Birth), P.O. Box 996, Benjamin Franklin Sta., Washington, DC 20044.

Church of Divine
See Evang Authors

Church of Light, (Church of Light; 0-87887), Box 76862, Sanford Sta., Los Angeles, CA 90076 Tel 213-487-6070.

Church of Scient Info, (Church of Scientology Information Service; 0-915598), 5930 Franklin Ave., Hollywood, CA 90028.

Church of Scient CA, (Church of Scientology of California; 0-88404), 2723 W. Temple St., Los Angeles, CA 90026 Tel 213-380-0710; Dist. by: Grosset & Dunlap, Inc., 51 Madison Ave., New York, NY 10010 Tel 212-689-9200.

Church Scient NY, (Church of Scientology of New York, The), 28 W. 74th St., New York, NY 10023.

Church Without Walls, (Church Without Walls; 0-89298), Society for Understanding Nature, P.O. Box 242, Prescott, AZ 86302 Tel 602-778-2638.

Churches Alive, (Churches Alive; 0-934396), P.O. Box 3800, San Bernardino, CA 92413 Tel 714-886-5361.

Churchill, (Churchill Livingstone Inc.), 19 W. 44th St., Suite 301, New York, NY 10036 Tel 212-921-0430; Dist. by: J.A. Majors Co., 3770 Zip Industrial Blvd., Atlanta, GA 30354; Dist. by: Brown & Connolly, Inc., 1399 Boylston St., Boston, MA 02215; Dist. by: Login Brothers Books Co, Inc., 1450 W. Randolph St., Chicago, IL 60607; Dist. by: J.A. Majors Co., 2221 Walnut Hill Lane, Irving, TX 75061; Dist. by: J.A. Majors Co., 1806 Southgate Blvd., Houston, TX 77025; Dist. by: Eliot Books, Inc., 35-53 24th St., Long Island City, NY 11106; Dist. by: J.A. Majors Co., 3909 Bienville St., New Orleans, LA 70119; Dist. by: Rittenhouse Book Distributors, Inc., 251 S. 24th St., Philadelphia, PA 19103; Dist. by: Medical & Technical Books, Inc., 11511 Tennessee Ave., Los Angeles, CA 90064; Dist. by: Longman, Inc., 19 W. 44th St., 10th Floor, New York, NY 10036 Tel 212-764-3955.

Churchilliana, (Churchilliana Co.; 0-917684), 4629 Sunset Dr., Sacramento, CA 95822.

CIBC, (Council on Interracial Books for Children, Inc.; 0-930040), 1841 Broadway, New York, NY 10023 Tel 212-757-5339.

Cibola, (Cibola Press; 0-9601086), 1295 Wilson St., P.O. Box 1495, Palo Alto, CA 94302 Tel 415-326-1444.

Cider Mill, (Cider Mill Press; 0-910380), P.O. Box 211, Stratford, CT 06497 Tel 203-378-4066.

Cider Pr, (Cider Press; 0-914994), P.O. Box 10115, Columbus, OH 43201.

Cilren Co, (Cilren Co.; 0-917096), 9912 Fair Oaks Blvd., Fair Oaks, CA 95628 Tel 916-961-4830.

CIMI, (Chemical Information Management, Inc.), P.O. Box 2740, Cherry Hill, NJ 08034 Tel 609-795-6767; 411 Rte. 70 E, Cherry Hill, NJ 08034 Tel 609-795-6767.

Cimino Pubns, (Cimino Pubns., Inc.; 0-9600588), 1646 New Hwy, Farmingdale, NY 11735.

Cine-Grafic, *(Cine/Grafic Pubns.; 0-9600240),* P.O. Box 430, Hollywood, CA 90028 Tel 213-462-8670.

Cine-Graphic
See Cine-Grafic

Cinnamon Hse *Imprint of* **G&D**

Cinnamon Pr, *(Cinnamon Press Ltd.; 0-930612),* Box 426, Denver, CO 80201.

Circa, *(Circa Pubns.),* ; Publisher Abbreviation Without Addresses Are for Titles That Are Out of Print. These Are Obsolete Abbreviations.

Circinatum Pr, *(Circinatum Press; 0-931594),* Box 99309, Tacoma, WA 98499.

Circle Fine Art, *(Circle Fine Art Corp.; 0-932240),* 232 E. Ohio St., Chicago, IL 60611.

Circle Pr, *(Circle Press; 0-89248),* Subs. of the Christ Circle Inc., P.O. Box N, Boulder Creek, CA 95006 Tel 408-338-2141; Moved, Left No Forwarding Address.

Circumedia, *(Circumedia),* 2230 S. Cotner Ave., Los Angeles, CA 90064 Tel 213-479-8924.

CIRS *Imprint of* **Unipub**

CISP, *(Council for Intercultural Studies & Programs; 0-939288),* 60 E. 42nd St., Suite 1231, New York, NY 10165.

Cistercian Pubns, *(Cistercian Pubns., Inc.; 0-87907),* WMU Sta., Kalamazoo, MI 49008 Tel 616-383-4985.

Citadel Pr, *(Citadel Press; 0-8065),* Subs. of Lyle Stuart, Inc., 120 Enterprise Ave., Secaucus, NJ 07094 Tel 201-866-0490.

Citation *Imprint of* **Schol Bk Serv**

CITE, *(Center for International Training & Education; 0-938960),* 777 United Nations Plaza, New York, NY 10017.

Citizen Involve, *(Citizen Involvement Training Project; 0-934210),* c/o University of Massachusetts, Amherst, MA 01003 Tel 413-545-2038.

Citizens Comm NY, *(Citizens Committee for New York City, Inc.; 0-9601496),* 3 W. 29th St., 6th Floor, New York, NY 10001 Tel 212-578-4747; Dist. by: Viking Press, 625 Madison Ave., New York, NY 10022 Tel 212-755-4330.

Citizens Energy, *(Citizens' Energy Project; 0-89988),* 1110 Sixth St. N.W., No. 300, Washington, DC 20001.

Citizens Law, *(Citizens Law Library; 0-89648),* 6 W. Loudoun St., P.O. Box 1745, Leesburg, VA 22075.

City Bank-Rockford, *(City National Bank & Trust Co. of Rockford; 0-9602150),* Box 1628, 1100 Broadway, Rockford, IL 61110.

City Hope Natl Med, *(City of Hope National Medical Center),* 1500 E. Duarte Rd., Duarte, CA 91010 Tel 213-359-8111.

City Lights, *(City Lights Books; 0-87286),* 261 Columbus Ave., San Francisco, CA 94133 Tel 415-362-8193; Dist. by: Subterranean Co., P.O. Box 10233, Eugene, OR 97440.

Civic Data, *(Civic Data Corp.; 0-937628),* P.O. Box 54045, Los Angeles, CA 90054 Tel 213-481-1226.

Civil War, *(Civil War Round Table of New York; 0-910382),* c/o Arnold Gates, 168 Weyford Terrace, Garden City, NY 11530.

Claitors, *(Claitors Publishing Division; 0-87511),* 3165 S. Acadian at Interstate 10, Box 239, Baton Rouge, LA 70821.

Clancys Kitchen *(John Clancy's Kitchen Workshop),* 324 W. 19th St., New York, NY 10011 Tel 212-243-0958; Orders to: Johnson Press, 49 Sheridan Ave., Albany, NY 12210.

Claremont House, *(Claremont House; 0-913860),* 231 E. San Fernando St., No. 1, San Jose, CA 95112 Tel 408-293-8650.

Clarence Hse, *(Clarence House Pubs.; 0-933810),* 2115 Van Ness Ave., San Francisco, CA 94109 Tel 415-346-1530.

Claretian Pubns, *(Claretian Pubns.; 0-89570),* 221 W. Madison St., Chicago, IL 60606 Tel 312-236-7782.

Clarion, *(Clarion Publishing Co.; 0-89422),* 2476 Buttonwood Court, Florissant, MO 63031 Tel 314-838-0241.

Clarion *Imprint of* **HM**

Clarion Call, *(Clarion Call Literature; 0-9604294),* 1634 Pittman St., Missoula, MT 59801.

Clarion Pubns, *(Clarion Pubns.),* P.O. Box 1600, San Luis Obispo, CA 93406; Moved, Left No Forwarding Address.

Clarity Pub, *(Clarity Publishing; 0-915488),* CRUX 75 Champlain St., Albany, NY 12204 Tel 518-465-4591; 800 North Pearl, Albany, NY 12204.

Clark County Hist Soc, *(Clark County Historical Society),* 300 W. Main St., Springfield, OH 45504 Tel 513-324-0657.

Clark Irwin, *(Clark, Irwin & Co., Ltd.),* Dist. by: Universe Books, Inc., 381 Park Ave., S., New York, NY 10016.

Clark Pub, *(Clark Publishing Co.; 0-931054),* Dist. by: The Caxton Printers, Ltd., P.O. Box 700, Caldwell, ID 83605 Tel 208-459-7421.

Clark U Pr, *(Clark Univ. Press; 0-914206),* 950 Main St., Worcester, MA 01610 Tel 617-793-7206.

Clarus Music, *(Clarus Music, Ltd.; 0-86704),* 340 Bellevue Ave., Yonkers, NY 10703 Tel 914-375-0864.

Classic *Imprint of* **Exposition**

Classic Furn Kits, *(Classic Furniture Kits),* 343 Lantana St., Camarillo, CA 93010.

Classic Nonfic, *(Classic Nonfiction Library),* Orders to: Woodward, PA 16882.

Classic Pub, *(Classic Publishing; 0-937222),* Prospect, KY 40059.

Classical Folia, *(Classical Folia),* c/o College of the Holy Cross, Worcester, MA 01610.

Classics Unltd, *(Classics Unlimited, Inc.; 0-936660),* 2121 Arlington Ave., Caldwell, ID 83605.

Clatworthy, *(Clatworthy Colorvues; 0-918290),* 111 1/2 Riverview, Santa Cruz, CA 95062 Tel 408-426-6401.

Claussen Bks, *(Claussen Books; 0-9603266),* 434 Arballo Dr., San Francisco, CA 94132 Tel 415-585-0716.

Clawson, *(Clawson Printing Co.),* 107 W. 2nd, Frankfort, KS 66427.

Claymont Comm, *(Claymont Communications; 0-934254),* Box 112, Charles Town, WV 25414 Tel 304-725-4437.

Clayton & Co, *(Clayton & Company),* P.O. Box 99241, Magnolia Sta., Seattle, WA 98199.

Clayton Pub Hse, *(Clayton Publishing House, Inc.; 0-915644),* 6901 Manchester Ave., St. Louis, MO 63143 Tel 314-781-1070.

CLCB Pr, *(CLCB Press),* Div. of CLCBI International, 5901 Plainfield Dr., Charlotte, NC 28215.

Cleaning Consul, *(Cleaning Consultant Services, Inc.; 0-9601054),* P.O. Box 70261, Seattle, WA 98107 Tel 206-789-2531.

Clear Marks, *(Clear Marks; 0-9602388),* 2219 Grant St., Berkeley, CA 94703 Tel 415-548-3466.

Clearwater OR, *(Clearwater Press; 0-9605512),* 1115 W Ave., La Grande, OR 97855.

Clearwater Pub, *(Clearwater Publishing Co.; 0-8287; 0-88354),* 1995 Broadway, New York, NY 10023 Tel 212-873-2100.

Clemco, *(Clemco),* Box 1362, Manhattan Beach, CA 90266 Tel 213-372-6448; Moved, Left No Forwarding Address.

Cleveland Landmarks, *(Cleveland Landmarks Press, Inc.; 0-936760),* P.O. Box 9152, Cleveland, OH 44137.

Cleveland St Univ Poetry Ctr, *(Cleveland State Univ. Poetry Center; 0-914946),* Cleveland State Univ., Cleveland, OH 44115 Tel 216-687-3986; Dist. by: Nacscorp, Inc. (Poetry Ser. Only), Oberlin, OH 44074 Tel 216-775-1561; Dist. by: Field (Poetry Ser. only), Oberlin College, Oberlin, OH 44074 Tel 216-775-8408.

Cleveland St Univ Poetry Ser
See Cleveland St Univ Poetry Ctr

Cliffs, *(Cliff's Notes, Inc.; 0-8220),* 1701 "P" St., Lincoln, NE 68501 Tel 402-477-6971.

Climate Bks, *(Climate Books),* 204 Greens Grove, Washington, GA 30673 Tel 404-678-1823; Formerly Named Garland Press, Point Blanc Press.

Cline-Sigmon, *(Cline-Sigmon Pubs.; 0-914760),* P.O. Box 367-T, Hickory, NC 28601 Tel 704-322-5090.

Clingstone Pr, *(Clingstone Press; 0-9602454),* Box 116, Jamestown, RI 02835.

Clinical Psych, *(Clinical Psychology Publishing Co., Inc.; 0-88422),* 4 Conant Square, Brandon, VT 05733 Tel 802-247-6871.

Clinitemp, *(Clinitemp, Inc.; 0-937450),* P.O. Box 40273, Indianapolis, IN 46240 Tel 317-872-4155.

Clodele, *(Clodele Enterprises, Inc.; 0-930416),* 2004 Vaugine Ave., Pine Bluff, AR 71601 Tel 501-534-8804.

Cloud Ent, *(Cloud Enterprises; 0-914794),* P.O. Box 1006, Orinda, CA 94563 Tel 415-284-4866; Dist. by: Wisdom Garde Books, P.O. Box 29448, Los Angeles, CA 90029 Tel 213-380-1968.

Cloud Marauder, *(Cloud Marauder Press),* Dist. by: SBD: Small Press Distribution, 1636 Ocean View Ave., Kensington, CA 94707 Tel 415-524-2107.

Cloudburst
See Madrona Pubs

Clover, *(Clover Publishing Co.; 0-88255),* 4903 70th Place, Hyattsville, MD 20784 Tel 301-772-2383.

CLP Pubs, *(CLP Pubs.; 0-89051),* P.O. Box 15666, San Diego, CA 92115 Tel 714-449-9420.

Clyde Pr, *(Clyde Press, The; 0-933190),* 373 Lincoln Pkwy, Buffalo, NY 14216 Tel 716-875-4713.

Clymer Pubns, *(Clymer Pubns.; 0-89287),* 1286 Muscatine St., Arleta, CA 91331 Tel 213-767-7660.

CMG Prods, *(C. M. G. Productions, Inc.; 0-933724),* P.O. Box 3838, Grand Junction, CO 81502.

CN *Imprint of* **Har-Row**

Co & Sons, *(Company & Sons),* Dist. by: Book People, 2940 Seventh St., Berkeley, CA 94710.

Co-Op Dir, *(Co-Op Directory Assn.; 0-933030),* P.O. Box 4218, Albuquerque, NM 87196 Tel 505-265-7416.

Co-Pub by Fides *Imprint of* **Abingdon**

CO RR Mus, *(Colorado Railroad Museum; 0-918654),* P.O. Box 10, Golden, CO 80401 Tel 303-279-4591.

CoA *Imprint of* **Unipub**

Coach Hse, *(Coach House Press, Inc.),* 53 W. Jackson Blvd., Chicago, IL 60604 Tel 312-922-8993; Dist. by: Book People, 2940 Seventh St., Berkeley, CA 94710 Tel 415-549-3033.

Coalition Women-Relig, *(Coalition on Women & Religion; 0-9603042),* 4759 15th Ave. N.E, Seattle, WA 98105 Tel 206-525-1213.

Coast to Coast, *(Coast to Coast Books; 0-9602664),* 2934 N.E. 16th Ave., Portland, OR 97212 Tel 503-282-5891.

Cobb Ent, *(Cobb Enterprizes; 0-9602968),* P.O. Box 295, Rolla, MO 65401 Tel 314-364-5458; Dist. by: Paperback Supply, 4121 Forest Park, St. Louis, MO 63108.

Cobbers, *(Cobbers; 0-934680),* Div. of Martensen Co., Inc., P.O. Box 261, Williamsburg, VA 23185 Tel 804-220-2828.

Cobblesmith, *(Cobblesmith; 0-89166),* Box 191, RFD 1, Freeport, ME 04032 Tel 207-865-6495.

Cobra Pr, *(Cobra Press; 0-9600384),* 15381 Chelsea Dr., San Jose, CA 95124 Tel 408-377-2319.

Cochrun, *(Cochrun, Inc.; 0-9601050),* 5638 Parkwood Blvd., Sylvania, OH 43560 Tel 419-882-3605.

Cocono
See Kokono

Coda Pr, *(Coda Press, Inc.; 0-930956),* 700 W. Badger Rd., Suite 101, Madison, WI 53713.

CoDoC, *(Cooperation in Documentation & Communication; 0-914958),* 464 19th St., Oakland, CA 94612.

Coffee Break, *(Coffee Break Press),* P.O. Box 103, Burley, WA 98322 Tel 206-857-4329.

Coffeetable, *(Coffeetable Pubns.; 0-938252),* P.O. Box 8236, 101 N. Haardt Dr., Montgomery, AL 36110.

Coffin, *(Coffin, George; 0-939452),* 257 Trapelo Rd., Waltham, MA 02154 Tel 617-893-0057.

Coin & Curr, *(Coin & Currency Institute, Inc.; 0-87184),* 1359 Broadway, New York, NY 10018 Tel 212-947-0370.

Coker Bks, *(Coker Books; 0-933012),* P.O. Box 27842, Houston, TX 77027.

Col-Bob Assocs, *(Col-Bob Associates, Inc.),* 250 E. 52nd St., New York, NY 10022 Tel 212-281-2193; Moved, Left No Forwarding Address.

Colburn & Tegg, *(Colburn & Tegg; 0-9600594),* 19709 Hollis Ave., Hollis, NY 11412 Tel 212-468-3278.

Colby, *(Colby College Press; 0-910394),* Library, Waterville, ME 04901 Tel 207-873-0311.

Cold Mtn Pr, *(Cold Mountain Press; 0-915496),* 4406 Duval, Austin, TX 78751; Moved,Left No Forwarding Address.

Cold Spring Harbor, *(Cold Spring Harbor Laboratory; 0-87969),* P.O. Box 100, Cold Spring Harbor, NY 11724 Tel 516-367-8351.

Cole-Outreach, *(Cole, David M./Outreach Books),* P.O. Box 425, Corona, CA 91720 Tel 213-926-9381.

Coleraine Pr, *(Coleraine Press, Inc.; 0-913016),* Hook Rd., Bedford, NY 10506 Tel 914-234-7980.

Colgate U Pr, *(Colgate Univ. Press; 0-912568),* 304 Lawrence Hall, Hamilton, NY 13346 Tel 315-824-1000.

Coll & U Pr, *(College & Univ. Press; 0-8084),* 267 Chapel St., New Haven, CT 06513 Tel 203-562-3101. *Imprints:* Twayne (Twayne's U.S. Author Series).

Coll Atlantic, *(College of the Atlantic; 0-9601024),* Bar Harbor, ME 04609 Tel 207-288-5015.

Coll Ent Exam
    See College Bd

Coll Kids Cook, *(College Kids Cookbooks; 0-912848),* 624 N. Bailey Ave., Fort Worth, TX 76107 Tel 817-626-4083.

Coll Placement, *(College Placement Council, Inc.; 0-913936),* P.O. Box 2263, Bethlehem, PA 18001 Tel 215-868-1421.

Coll Store, *(College Store; 0-910408),* Middlebury College, 5 Hillcrest Rd., Middlebury, VT 05753 Tel 802-388-7722.

Coll Wooster, *(College of Wooster, Office of Pubns.; 0-9604658),* Wooster, OH 44691 Tel 216-264-1234.

Collage Pr, *(Collage Press; 0-917516),* P.O. Box 5552, Baltimore, MD 21204.

Collamore *Imprint of* Heath

Colleasius Pr, *(Colleasius Press),* P.O. Box 15545, Colorado Springs, CO 80935 Tel 303-599-0041.

Collector, *(Collector; 0-914638),* P.O. Box 531, Mentone, CA 92359 Tel 714-792-0650.

Collector Bks, *(Collector Books; 0-89145),* P.O. Box 3009, Paducah, KY 42001 Tel 502-898-6211.

Collectors, *(Collectors Club, Inc.; 0-912574),* 22 E. 35th St., New York, NY 10016 Tel 212-683-0559.

Collectors Choice, *(Collector's Choice; 0-9602742),* c/o French-Bray Inc., P.O. Box 698, Glen Burnie, MD 21061 Tel 301-768-6000.

Collectors Edns, *(Collectors Editions, Ltd.; 0-87681),* Dist. by: Van Nostrand Reinhold Co., 300 Pike St., Cincinnati, OH 45202.

College Bd, *(College Board, The; 0-87447),* 888 Seventh Ave., New York, NY 10019 Tel 212-582-6210; Orders to: College Board Pubns, P.O. Box 2815, Princeton, NJ 08541 Tel 609-921-9000.

College-Hill, *(College-Hill Press, Inc.; 0-933014),* 4580-E Alvarado, Canyon Rd., San Diego, CA 92120.

College Mktg Grp, *(College Marketing Group, Inc.),* 6 Winchester Terrace, Winchester, MA 01890 Tel 617-729-7865.

College Pr Pub, *(College Press Publishing Co.; 0-89900),* Box 1132, 205 N. Main, Joplin, MO 64801 Tel 417-623-6280.

College Readings, *(College Readings, Inc.; 0-916580),* P.O. Box 168, Clifton, VA 22024.

Collegiate Pub, *(Collegiate Publishing, Inc.; 0-88429),* 1010 Second Ave., Suite 1808, San Diego, CA 92101 Tel 714-234-3231.

Collegiate Visitors, *(Collegiate Visitors Guides; 0-9600260),* 170 Bridge Rd., Hillsborough, CA 94010.

Collegium Bk Pubs, *(Collegium Book Pubs., Inc.; 0-89669),* 525 Executive Blvd., Elmsford, NY 10523.

Collier *Imprint of* Macmillan

Collins Pubs, *(Collins, William, Pubs., Inc.),* 2080 W. 117th St., Cleveland, OH 44111 Tel 216-941-6930; 200 Madison Ave., Suite 1405, New York, NY 10016.

Collins-World
    See Collins Pubs

Colman Pubs, *(Colman Pubs.; 0-9602456),* 1147 Elmwood, Stockton, CA 95204 Tel 209-946-2148.

Colo Assoc, *(Colorado Associated Univ. Press, Univ. of Colorado; 0-87081),* Box 480, Univ. of Colorado, Boulder, CO 80309 Tel 303-492-7191.

Colo Coll Music, *(Colorado College Music Press; 0-933894),* Colorado Springs, CO 80903.

Colo Fiber, *(Colorado Fiber Center, Inc.; 0-937452),* P.O. Box 2049, Boulder, CO 80306.

Colo River Pr, *(Colorado River Press; 0-931302),* Box 8004, Austin, TX 78712.

Colo Sch Mines, *(Colorado School of Mines; 0-918062),* Publications Dept./Sales, Golden, CO 80401 Tel 303-279-0300.

Colo Sch Mining
    See Colo Sch Mines

Colo St U Comm, *(Colorado State Univ., Institute in Technical & Industrial Communications; 0-910414),* Colorado State Univ., Social Science Bldg., Rm. C225, Fort Collins, CO 80523.

Cologne Pr, *(Cologne Press; 0-9602310),* P.O. Box 682, Cologne, NJ 08213 Tel 609-965-5163.

Colonial Pr, *(Colonial Press),* 1 Saddle Rd., Cedar Knolls, NJ 07927; Moved, Left No Forwarding Address.

Colonial Soc MA *Imprint of* U Pr of Va

Colophon, *(Colophon Book Shop, The),* 700 S. Sixth Ave., La Grange, IL 60525 Tel 312-354-0022.

Color Coded Charting, *(Color Coded Charting & Filing Systems; 0-9605902),* 7759 California Ave., Riverside, CA 92504 Tel 714-688-0800.

Colourpicture, *(Colourpicture Pubs., Inc.; 0-938440),* 76 Atherton St., Boston, MA 02130; Dist. by: Smith Novelty Co., 460 Ninth St., San Francisco, CA 94103.

Colton Bk, *(Colton Book Imports),* P.O. Box 526, San Francisco, CA 94101.

Coltsfoot, *(Coltsfoot Press, Inc.; 0-917372),* 507 Fifth Ave., Suite 307, New York, NY 10017.

Columbia Bks, *(Columbia Books Inc., Pubs.; 0-910416),* 777 14th St., N.W., Suite 1336, Washington, DC 20005 Tel 202-737-3777.

Columbia Bookkeeping, *(Columbia Bookkeeping Systems, Inc.; 0-9604828),* 24 Gould St., Reading, MA 01867.

Columbia Graphs, *(Columbia Graphs),* P.O. Box 445, Danielson, CT 06239.

Columbia Lang Serv, *(Columbia Language Services; 0-9604126),* P.O. Box 28365, Washington, DC 20005 Tel 301-587-4979.

Columbia Pub, *(Columbia Publishing Co., Inc.; 0-914366),* Frenchtown, NJ 08825 Tel 201-996-2141; Dist. by: Vanguard Press, Inc., 424 Madison Ave., New York, NY 10017 Tel 212-753-3906.

Columbia U Ctr Soc Sci, *(Columbia Univ., Center for the Social Sciences; 0-938436),* 420 W. 118th St., 814 I.A.B., New York, NY 10027.

Columbia U Libs, *(Columbia Univ Libraries),* Orders to: 535 W. 114th St., New York, NY 10027.

Columbia U Pr, *(Columbia Univ. Press; 0-231),* 562 W. 113th St., New York, NY 10025 Tel 212-678-6777; Orders to: 136 S. Broadway, Irvington-on-Hudson, NY 10533 Tel 914-591-9111.

Colwell Co, *(Colwell Co.),* 201 Kenyon Rd., Champaign, IL 61820 Tel 217-351-5400.

Colwyn-Tangno, *(Colwyn-Tangno),* 96 Old River Rd., Wilkes Barre, PA 18702.

Com Sense Ltd, *(Common Sense Ltd.),* P.O. Box 353, Des Plaines, IL 60017 Tel 312-457-0811.

Combustion Eng, *(Combustion Engineering Power Systems Group; 0-9605974),* 1000 Prospect Hill Rd., Dept. 7021-1904, Windsor, CT 06095 Tel 203-688-1911.

Comm Adv Public Interest, *(Commission for the Advancement of Public Interest Organizations; 0-9602744),* 1875 Connecticut Ave. N.W., No. 1013, Washington, DC 20009.

Comm & Family, *(Community & Family Study Center; 0-89836),* 1411 E. 60th St., Chicago, IL 60637 Tel 312-753-2518.

Comm Bio Pest, *(Committee for Biological Pest Control),* P.O. Box 2810, San Ysidro, CA 92173 Tel 714-234-1492; Moved, Left No Forwarding Address.

Comm Builders, *(Community Builders; 0-9604422),* Canterbury, NH 03224.

Comm Channels, *(Communication Channels; 0-916164),* 6285 Barfield Rd., Atlanta, GA 30328 Tel 404-256-9800.

Comm Chi Hist & Arch, *(Commission on Chicago Historical & Architectural Landmarks; 0-934076),* 320 N. Clark, Chicago, IL 60610; Dist. by: Chicago Review Press, 215 W. Ohio St., Chicago, IL 60610 Tel 312-644-5457.

Comm Collaborators, *(Community Collaborators; 0-930388),* P.O. Box 5429, Charlottesville, VA 22905 Tel 804-977-1126.

Comm Consultants, *(Communication Consultants International; 0-938320),* P.O. Box 1212, San Diego, CA 92112.

Comm Coun Great NY, *(Community Council of Greater New York),* 225 Park Ave., S., New York, NY 10003 Tel 212-777-5000.

Comm Creat, *(Communication Creativity; 0-918880),* P.O. Box 213, Saguache, CO 81149 Tel 303-655-2502.

Comm Ctr MA Assn Blind, *(Communications Center, Massachusetts Assn. for the Blind),* 200 Ivy St., Brookline, MA 02146 Tel 617-738-5110; Hand Transcription Service for Mass Residents in 26 & 32 Pt. Service Charge per Page.

Comm Dynamics, *(Communication Dynamics Press; 0-916044),* P.O. Box 555, East Elmhurst, NY 11369.

Comm Econ Dev, *(Committee for Economic Development; 0-87186),* 477 Madison Ave., New York, NY 10022 Tel 212-688-2063.

Comm Found, *(Communication Foundation),* P.O. Box 11689, Santa Rosa, CA 95406 Tel 707-525-1350; Moved, Left No Forwarding Address.

Comm Materials, *(Communication Materials Center),* 110 Rices Mill Rd., Wyncote, PA 19095 Tel 215-884-0928.

Comm Nuclear Respon, *(Committee for Nuclear Responsibility, Inc.; 0-932682),* Main P.O. Box 11207, San Francisco, CA 94101 Tel 415-776-8299.

Comm Peace, *(Commission to Study the Organization of Peace),* 866 United Nations Plaza, New York, NY 10017 Tel 212-688-4665.

Comm Pr CA, *(Communication Press; 0-918830),* Box 22541, Sunset Sta., San Francisco, CA 94122 Tel 415-566-3921.

Comm Pr Inc, *(Communications Press, Inc.; 0-89461),* 1346 Connecticut Ave., N.W., Washington, DC 20036 Tel 202-785-0865.

Comm-Prop Pubns, *(COMM-PROP Pubns.; 0-937010),* 27 Park St., Lee, MA 01238 Tel 413-243-1383.

Comm Serv, *(Community Service, Inc.; 0-910420),* P.O. Box 243, Yellow Springs, OH 45387 Tel 513-767-2161.

Comm Serv Corp, *(Communication Service Corp.; 0-87659),* 1333 Connecticut Ave., N.W., Washington, DC 20015; Out of Business.

Comm Stud, *(Communication Studies; 0-931814),* 6145 Anita St., Dallas, TX 75214 Tel 214-823-1981.

Comm Tech, *(Communications Technology, Inc.; 0-918232),* Greenville, NH 03048 Tel 603-878-1441.

Comm Unltd, *(Communicatons Unlimited),* 7057 Wright Court, Arvada, CO 80004.

Comm Urban Justice, *(Committee for Urban Justice),* 136 Warren St., Boston, MA 02119; Moved, Left No Forwarding Address.

Commerce, *(Commerce Clearing House, Inc.; 0-8080),* 4025 W. Peterson Ave., Chicago, IL 60646 Tel 312-583-8500.

Commerce Pr
    See Pennwell Pub

Committee IL, *(Committee, The; 0-937352),* P.O. Box 1082, Evanston, IL 60204.

Commodities Pr, *(Commodities Press; 0-911896),* Div. of Belveal & Co., Inc., P.O. Box 128, Wilmette, IL 60091 Tel 312-251-7031.

Common Sense Pr, *(Common Sense Press, Inc.; 0-917572),* 711 West 17th St. G-6, Costa Mesa, CA 92627.

Common Table, *(Common Table, The; 0-933228),* 216 Crown St. - Rm 506, New Haven, CT 06510 Tel 203-776-7073.

Common Women, *(Common Women Collective; 0-9601122),* c/o Women's Center, 46 Pleasant St., Cambridge, MA 02139 Tel 617-354-8807.

Commonground Pr, *(Commonground Press),* 155 Plains Rd., New Paltz, NY 12561.

Commonsense, *(Commonsense Pubns.; 0-911734),* 1925 Vermont Ave., Toledo, OH 43624.

Commonweal Bks, *(Commonwealth Books, Inc.; 0-918596),* P.O. Box 4433, Lexington, KY 40504; Moved, Left No Forwarding Address.

Commonwealth Pr, *(Commonwealth Press, Inc.; 0-89227),* 415 First St., Radford, VA 24141 Tel 703-639-2475.

Communication Skill, *(Communication Skill Builders, Inc.; 0-88450),* 3130 N. Dodge Blvd., P.O. Box 42050, Tucson, AZ 85733 Tel 602-327-6021.

CommuniConcepts, *(CommuniConcepts, Inc.; 0-916826),* 119 W. 57th St., New York, NY 10019.

Community Law, *(Community Law Reports, Inc.; 0-89035),* 8771 Elm Ave., Orangevale, CA 95662 Tel 916-988-7576.

Community Psychol, *(Community Psychological Consultants, Inc.),* 1740 Gulf Dr., St. Louis, MO 63130; Moved, Left No Forwarding Address.

Community Pub, *(Community Publishing Co.),* 103 Lewis St., Perth Amboy, NJ 08861.

Commuter Airlines, *(Commuter Airlines Press; 0-9602554),* P.O. Box 15064, San Diego, CA 92115 Tel 714-287-5080; Dist. by: Aviation Book Co., 1640 Victory Blvd., Glendale, CA 91201 Tel 213-240-1771.

Comox, *(Comox Books; 0-912276),* Div. of Eric Duncan Literary Properties, 2611 San Diego Ave., San Diego, CA 92110 Tel 714-291-4200.

Compact Bks, *(Compact Books, Inc.; 0-936320),* 3014 Willow Lane, Hollywood, FL 33021 Tel 305-983-6464.

Compact Pubns, *(Compact Pubns., Inc.; 0-936320),* 3014 Willow Lane, Hollywood, FL 33021.

Compass Pubns NY, *(Compass Pubns.),* 115 E. 87th St., Box 12-F, New York, NY 10028 Tel 212-289-2368.

Compass Va, *(Compass Pubns., Inc.; 0-910422),* 1117 N. 19th St., Arlington, VA 22209 Tel 703-524-3136.

CompCare, *(CompCare Pubns.; 0-89638),* 2415 Annapolis Lane, Minneapolis, MN 55441.

ComPress, *(ComPress, Inc.; 0-933694),* P.O. Box 102, Wentworth, NH 03282.

Compsco, *(Compsco Publishing Co.; 0-911788),* 663 Fifth Ave., New York, NY 10022 Tel 212-355-5633.

Compton, *(Compton, F. E., Co.),* Div. of Encyclopaedia Britannica, Inc., 425 N. Michigan Ave., Chicago, IL 60611.

Compton & Rowe, *(Compton & Rowe, Pubs.; 0-931372),* P.O. Box 786, Sausalito, CA 94965 Tel 415-435-0951; Moved, Left No Forwarding Address.

CompuSoft, *(CompuSoft Publishing; 0-932760),* Div. of CompuSoft, Inc., 1050 Pioneer Way, Suite E, El Cajon, CA 92020 Tel 714-588-0996.

Computer Sci, *(Computer Science Press, Inc.; 0-914894),* 11 Taft Court, Rockville, MD 20850 Tel 301-251-9050; Orders to: P.O. Box 34913, Washington, DC 20034.

Computerist, *(Computerist, Inc., The; 0-938222),* P.O. Box 3, Chelmsford, MA 01824; Dist. by: Micro Ink, Inc., P.O. Box 6502, Chelmsford, MA 01824.

Computing Trends, *(Computing Trends),* 6925 56th Ave. S., Seattle, WA 98118.

Comstock, *(Comstock Publishing Associates),* Dist. by: Cornell Univ. Press, Sales Manager, 124 Roberts Place, Ithaca, NY 14850.

Comstock Edns, *(Comstock Editions, Inc.; 0-89174),* 3030 Bridgeway Blvd., Sausalito, CA 94965 Tel 415-332-3216; Orders to: Comstock Book Distributors Inc., 1380 W. Second Ave., Eugene, OR 97402.

Comstock Hse, *(Comstock House),* 108 Mill St., Virginia City, NV 89440.

Con Brio, *(Con Brio Press; 0-9602068),* 6012 Chicago Ave., Minneapolis, MN 55417.

Concept Design, *(Conceptual Design; 0-9604902),* 9 Glenmore Rd., Troy, NY 12180 Tel 518-283-6467.

Concept Pub, *(Concept Publishing; 0-930726),* P.O. Box 203, York, NY 14592 Tel 716-243-3148.

Concept Visual, *(Concept Visualizers, Inc.; 0-914942),* 554 Ninth St., Brooklyn, NY 11215 Tel 212-768-5533.

Concerned Pubns, *(Concerned Pubns., Inc.; 0-939286),* P.O. Box 1024, Clermont, FL 32711 Tel 904-394-3949.

Conch Mag, *(Conch Magazine Ltd. (Pubs.); 0-914970),* 102 Normal Ave., Buffalo, NY 14213 Tel 716-885-3686.

Conch Pr HI, *(Conch Press; 0-917260),* Subs. of Young Way Publishing, P.O. Box 27183, Honolulu, HI 96827 Tel 808-923-3192.

Concord Pr, *(Concord Press),* P.O. Box 2686, Seal Beach, CA 90740 Tel 213-431-5711.

Concordant, *(Concordant Publishing Concern; 0-910424),* 15570 W. Knochaven Rd., Canyon Country, CA 91351 Tel 805-252-2112.

Concordia, *(Concordia Publishing House; 0-570),* 3558 S. Jefferson Ave., St. Louis, MO 63118 Tel 314-664-7000.

Concordia Student, *(Concord Student Journal; 0-911770),* c/o Concordia Seminary, 801 DeMun Ave,, St. Louis, MO 63105 Tel 314-721-5934.

Concours Pub, *(Concours Publishing; 0-9602644),* 7271 Jurupa Rd., Riverside, CA 92509.

Condor Bks, *(Condor Books; 0-913238),* P.O. Box 3914, San Rafael, CA 94902; Dist. by: Charles Scribner's Sons, Shipping & Service Ctr., Vreeland Ave., Totowa, NJ 07512.

Condor Pub Co, *(Condor Pub. Co., Inc.; 0-89516),* 29 E. Main St., Westport, CT 06880 Tel 203-226-9591; Moved, Left No Forwarding Address.

Conduit, *(Conduit; 0-9631781),* P.O. Box 388, Iowa City, IA 52244.

Cone-Heiden, *(Cone-Heiden),* 417 E. Pine St., Seattle, WA 98122.

Conf Econ Prog, *(Conference on Economic Progress; 0-910428),* 2610 Upton St., N.W., Washington, DC 20008 Tel 202-363-6222.

Conf Faith & Hist, *(Conference on Faith & History; 0-913446),* Indiana State Univ., Dept. of History, Terre Haute, IN 47809 Tel 812-232-6311.

Confed Arms, *(Confederate Arms Pubs.; 0-87833),* P.O. Box 220802, Charlotte, NC 28222.

Conference Bd, *(Conference Board, Inc., The; 0-8237),* 845 Third Ave., New York, NY 10022 Tel 212-759-0900.

Confluence Pr, *(Confluence Press, Inc.; 0-917652),* Spalding Hall, Lewis-Clark Campus, Lewiston, ID 83501 Tel 208-746-2341.

Cong Info, *(Congressional Information Service; 0-912380),* 7101 Wisconsin Ave., Washington, DC 20014 Tel 301-654-1550.

Cong Shaarai, *(Congregation Shaarai Shomayim),* 508 N. Duke St., Lancaster, PA 17602 Tel 717-397-5575.

Congdon & Lattes, *(Congdon & Lattes),* Empire State Bldg., New York, NY 10001 Tel 212-736-4883; Dist. by: St. Martin's Press, 175 Fifth Ave., New York, NY 10010 Tel 212-674-5151.

Congeros Pubns, *(Congeros Pubns.; 0-918628),* 123 N. Sultand Ave., P.O. Box 1387, Ontario, CA 91762.

Congr Quarterly, *(Congressional Quarterly, Inc.; 0-87187),* 1414 22nd St., N.W., Washington, DC 20037 Tel 202-296-6800.

Congr Staff, *(Congressional Staff Directory, Ltd.; 0-87289),* P.O. Box 62, Mount Vernon, VA 22121 Tel 703-765-3400.

Congreve Pub, *(Congreve Publishing Co., Inc.; 0-930186),* 375 Park Ave., New York, NY 10022 Tel 212-838-7522.

Conn Coll Bkshp, *(Connecticut College Bookshop),* New London, CT 06320 Tel 203-443-0025.

Conn Fireside, *(Connecticut Fireside Press),* P. O. Box 5293, Hamden, CT 06518 Tel 203-248-1023.

Conn Hist Soc, *(Connecticut Historical Society),* 1 Elizabeth St., Hartford, CT 06105 Tel 203-236-5621.

Connect Pr, *(Connections Press; 0-930474),* P.O. Box 454, Bolinas, CA 94924.

Connections, *(Connections, Inc.),* 4950 Miller Rd., No. 133, Scottsdale, AZ 85251; Moved Left No Forwarding Address.

Conocheague
See Anima Pubns

Conquest, *(Conquest Pubns.; 0-930220),* P.O. Box 11965, Winston-Salem, NC 27106 Tel 919-945-9686.

Conquest Corp MI, *(Conquest Corp.; 0-936682),* 2716 Trafford Rd., Royal Oak, MI 48073.

Conservation Foun, *(Conservation Foundation; 0-89164),* 1717 Massachusetts Ave. N.W, Washington, DC 20036 Tel 202-797-4300.

Consol Cap, *(Consolidated Capital; 0-930032),* 333 Hegenberger Rd., Oakland, CA 94621 Tel 415-638-3000.

Consolidated Bk
See Delair

Consortium
See McGrath

Consortium *Imprint of* **McGrath**

Consortium Pr, *(Consortium Books),* ; Publishe Abbreviation Without Addresses Are for Titles That Are Out of Print. These Are Obsolete Abbreviations. Publisher Was Aquired by McGrath.

Constant Soc, *(Constant Society; 0-931894),* P.O. Box 5513, 4244 Universe Way N.E., Seattle, WA 98105.

Construct Educ, *(Constructive Educational Concepts, Inc.; 0-934734),* 213 Duncaster Rd., Box 667, Bloomfield, CT 06002.

Construct Pubns, *(Construction Pubns.; 0-912324),* 4552 E. Palomino Rd., Phoenix, AZ 85018 Tel 602-959-3947.

Construct Sci Res, *(Construction Sciences Research Foundation, Inc., The; 0-9605922),* 1150 17th St., NW, Suite 300, Washington, DC 20036.

Construction Pub, *(Construction Publishing Co., Inc.; 0-913634),* Dist. by: Van Nostrand Reinhold, 135 W. 50th St., New York, NY 10020 Tel 212-265-8700.

Constructive Action, *(Constructive Action, Inc.; 0-911956),* P.O. Box 4006, Whittier, CA 90607 Tel 213-693-0764.

Consultants *Imprint of* **Plenum Pub**

Consultants News, *(Consultants News; 0-916654),* Templeton Rd., Fitzwilliam, NH 03447 Tel 603-585-2200.

Consulting Psychol, *(Consulting Psychologists Press, Inc.; 0-89106),* 577 College Ave., Palo Alto, CA 94306 Tel 415-857-1444.

Consumer Age Pr, *(Consumer Age Press; 0-914448),* P.O. Box 279, Syracuse, NY 13214 Tel 315-446-6262; Moved, Left No Forwarding Address.

Consumer Co-Op, *(Consumer Cooperative),* Dist. by: Book People, 2940 Seventh St., Berkeley, CA 94710.

Consumer Comm Ltd, *(Consumer Communications, Ltd.; 0-940060),* 5348 Fairfax Dr. NW, Albuquerque, NM 87114 Tel 505-898-2056.

Consumer Credit Proj, *(Consumer Credit Project; 0-931786),* 261 Kimberly, Barrington, IL 60010 Tel 312-381-2113.

Consumer Info Pubns, *(Consumer Information Pubns.),* P.O. Box 6203, Clearwater, FL 33517.

Consumer News, *(Consumer News Inc.; 0-917022),* 813 National Press Bldg., Washington, DC 20004 Tel 202-737-1190.

Consumer Protek, *(Consumer Protek Pubs.; 0-9605936),* P.O. Box 33307, Cleveland, OH 44133.

Consumer Pub, *(Consumer Publishing Co.; 0-9600270),* New & Friendship Rds., Vincentown, NJ 08088.

Consumertronics, *(Consumertronics Co.; 0-934732),* 2011 Crescent Dr., P.O. Box 475, Almagordo, NM 88310.

Contact Two, *(Contact/II Pubns.; 0-936556),* P.O. Box 451, Bowling Green, New York, NY 10004; Dist. by: Bookslinger, 2163 Ford Pkwy., St. Paul, MN 55116.

Contemp Arts, *(Contemporary Arts Center; 0-917562),* 115 E. Fifth St., Cincinnati, OH 45202 Tel 513-721-0390.

Contemp Bks, *(Contemporary Books, Inc.; 0-8092),* 180 N. Michigan Ave., Chicago, IL 60601 Tel 312-782-9181; Formerly Named Henry Regnery .o.

Contemp Crafts, *(Contemporary Crafts, Inc.),* c/o Hancraft Studios, 259 W. Radcliffe Dr., Claremont, CA 91711 Tel 714-626-0214.

Contemp Drama Serv, *(Contemporary Drama Service),* Box 457-TC, Downers Grove, IL 60515.

Contemp Poetry, *(Contemporary Poetry Press; 0-939610),* P.O. Box 88, Lansing, NY 14882.

Contemp Pub
See Nursing Res

Contemp Pub Co of Raleigh, *(Contemporary Publishing Co. of Raleigh; 0-89892),* 508 St. Marys, Raleigh, NC 27605 Tel 919-821-4566.

Contemp Pub O
See Contemp Pub Co of Raleigh

Contemporary Arts, *(Contemporary Arts Press; 0-931818),* P.O. Box 3123, San Francisco, CA 94119.

Contemporary Lit, *(Contemporary Literature Press; 0-930266),* P.O. Box 26462, San Francisco, CA 94126.

Context Pubns, *(Context Pubns.; 0-932654),* 20 Lomita Ave., San Francisco, CA 94122.

Continent Assn Funeral, *(Continental Assn. of Funeral & Memorial Societies, Inc.),* 1828 L St., Suite 1100, N.W., Washington, DC 20036.

Continent Divide, *(Continental Divide Trail Society; 0-934326),* P.O. Box 30002, Washington, DC 20014.

Continent Edns, *(Continental Editions; 0-916868),* 2300 Indian Hills Dr., 3-231, Sioux City, IA 51104 Tel 712-239-5954.

Continent Herit, *(Continental Heritage Press; 0-932986),* P.O. Box 1620, Tulsa, OK 74101 Tel 918-582-6000.

Continent Pub, *(Continental Publishing House; 0-915002),* 2116 N.E. 18th Ave., Portland, OR 97212 Tel 503-282-1383.

Continental CA, *(Continental Pubns.; 0-916096),* P.O. Box 2248, Palos Verdes, CA 90274 Tel 213-377-1449.

Continental Pr, *(Continental Press, Inc.; 0-8454),* 520 E. Bainbridge St., Elizabethtown, PA 17022 Tel 717-367-1836.

Continuing SAGA, *(Continuing SAGA Press),* 1822 Mason St., San Francisco, CA 94133.

Continuum, *(Continuum Publishing Corp.; 0-8264),* 18 E. 41st St., 7th Fl., New York, NY 10017; Dist. by: The Seabury Press, 815 Second Ave., New York, NY 10017 Tel 212-557-0500.

Contraband, *(Contraband Press),* P.O. Box 4073, Sta. A., Portland, ME 04101.

Contract Data, *(Contract Data Pubs.; 0-939260),* P.O. Box 366, Alta Loma, CA 91701 Tel 714-987-6850.

Control Data, *(Control Data Education Co.; 0-918852),* P.O. Box O, (HQA03Y), Minneapolis, MN 55440 Tel 612-853-7340.

Convex Indus, *(Convex Industries, Inc.; 0-918990),* 4720 Cheyenne, Boulder, CO 80303 Tel 303-494-4176.

Conway Hse, *(Conway House; 0-914402),* Bellaire, MI 49615.

Conway Pubns, *(Conway Pubns., Inc.; 0-910436),* 1954 Airport Rd. NE., Atlanta, GA 30341 Tel 404-458-6026.

Cook, *(Cook, David C., Publishing Co.; 0-89191; 0-912692),* 850 N. Grove Ave., Elgin, IL 60120 Tel 312-741-2400.

Cookbook Pubs, *(Cookbook Pubs.; 0-934474),* Lenexa, KS 66215 Tel 501-741-7340; Dist. by: Southern Star, Inc., P.O. Box 968, Harrison, AR 72601.

Cookbooks Inc, *(Cookbooks, Inc.),* 6 Graham Circle, South Attleboro, MA 02703.

Cookie Pr, *(Cookie Press; 0-938236),* 4225 University, Des Moines, IA 50311 Tel 515-255-3552.

Coole
See Akers

Cooper Sq, *(Cooper Square Pubs., Inc.; 0-8154),* 81 Adams Dr., Totowa, NJ 07512 Tel 201-256-8600.

Cope Allied Pub, *(Cope Allied Publishing; 0-935658),* P.O. Box 458, Cypress, TX 77429.

Copeland Evan Assn, *(Copeland, Kenneth Evangelistic Assn, Inc.),* P.O. Box 8720, Fort Worth, TX 76112.

Copley & Assocs, *(Copley & Associates, SA; 0-9605932),* 2030 M St. NW, No. 602, Washington, DC 20036.

Copley Bks, *(Copley Books; 0-913938),* P.O. Box 957, 7776 Ivanhoe Ave., La Jolla, CA 92038 Tel 714-454-1842.

Copper Beech, *(Copper Beech Press),* Box 1852, Brown University, Providence, RI 02912.

Copper Canyon, *(Copper Canyon Press; 0-914742),* P.O. Box 271, Port Townsend, WA 98368 Tel 206-385-4925.

Copy-Write, *(Copy-Write Artograph Co.; 0-912392),* 1865 77th St., Brooklyn, NY 11214 Tel 212-236-1459.

Coraco, *(Coraco; 0-917628),* 1017 S. Arlington Ave., Los Angeles, CA 90019 Tel 213-737-1066.

Coral Reef, *(Coral Reef Pubns., Inc.; 0-914042; 0-86540),* Box 918, Davenport, IA 52601.

Corbett, *(Corbett, H. Roger, Jr.),* 8100 Cardiff St., Lorton, VA 22079 Tel 703-550-7317.

Corcoran, *(Corcoran Gallery of Art),* 17th St. & New York Ave. N.W., Washington, DC 20006 Tel 202-638-3211.

Cordova, *(Cordova Printing),* 10777 Coloma Rd., Rancho Cordova, CA 95670.

Cordus Pr, *(Cordus Press; 0-935118),* P.O. Box 587, North Amherst, MA 01059 Tel 413-549-0287.

CORE, *(Congress of Racial Equality; 0-917354),* 1916-38 Park Ave., New York, NY 10037 Tel 212-694-9300.

Core Collection, *(Core Collection Books, Inc.; 0-8486),* 11 Middle Neck Rd., Great Neck, NY 11021 Tel 516-466-3676.

CORE Collection
See Core Collection

Corinth Bks, *(Corinth Books; 0-87091),* 7308 Maple Ave., Chevy Chase, MD 20015 Tel 301-652-1016; Orders to: Bookslinger, 2163 Ford Pkwy., St. Paul, MN 55116.

Corinth Hse, *(Corinth House Pubs.; 0-938280),* 2238 E. Vermont Ave., Anaheim, CA 92806 Tel 714-635-6930.

Corinthian, *(Corinthian Press, The; 0-86551),* 3592 Lee Rd., Shaker Heights, OH 44120 Tel 216-751-7300.

Corita Comm, *(Corita Communications; 0-933016),* 1301 N. Kenter Ave., Los Angeles, CA 90049.

Cornell Maritime, *(Cornell Maritime Press, Inc.; 0-87033),* P.O. Box 456, Centreville, MD 21617 Tel 301-758-1075.

Cornell Mod Indo, *(Cornell Modern Indonesia Project; 0-87763),* 102 West Ave., Ithaca, NY 14850 Tel 607-256-4359.

Cornell SE Asia, *(Cornell Univ., Southeast Asia Program; 0-87727),* 120 Uris Hall, Ithaca, NY 14853 Tel 607-256-2378.

Cornell U Pr, *(Cornell Univ. Press; 0-8014),* 124 Roberts Place, P.O. Box 250, Ithaca, NY 14850 Tel 607-257-7000.

Cornell U Sch Hotel, *(Cornell Univ., School of Hotel Administration; 0-937056),* 327 Statler Hall, Ithaca, NY 14853 Tel 607-256-5093.

Cornell Widow, *(Cornell Widow, Inc.; 0-9605070),* 104 Willard Straight Hall, Cornell University, Ithaca, NY 14853.

Corner, *(Corner Book Shop; 0-910442),* 102 Fourth Ave., New York, NY 10003 Tel 212-254-7714.

Corner Hse, *(Corner House Pubs.; 0-87928),* 1321 Green River Rd., Williamstown, MA 01267 Tel 413-458-8561.

Cornerstone, *(Cornerstone Library, Inc.; 0-346),* Div. of Simon & Schuster, Inc., Orders to: Simon & Schuster, Inc., 1230 Avenue of the Americas, New York, NY 10020 Tel 212-245-6400.

Cornerstone Pr, *(Cornerstone Press; 0-918476),* P.O. Box 28048, St. Louis, MO 63119 Tel 314-843-5195.

Corning, *(Corning Museum of Glass; 0-87290),* Corning Glass Ctr., Corning, NY 14830 Tel 607-937-5371.

Cornucopia Pr, *(Cornucopia Press),* 32078 Waterside Lane, Westlake Village, CA 91361.

Corona Pub, *(Corona Publishing Co.; 0-931722),* 1037 S. Alamo, San Antonio, TX 78210 Tel 512-227-1771.

Coronado Pr, *(Coronado Press, Inc.; 0-87291),* P.O. Box 3232, Lawrence, KS 66044 Tel 913-843-5988.

Coronet, *(Coronet, The Multimedia Co.),* 65 E. South Water St., Chicago, IL 60601 Tel 312-977-4089.

Corporate Mov, *(Corporate Movement, Inc.),* 360 Lexington Ave., New York, NY 10017.

Cortina, *(Cortina, R. D., Co., Inc.; 0-8327),* 136 W. 52nd St., New York, NY 10019 Tel 212-582-3845.

Corwin, *(Corwin Books; 0-89474),* One Century Plaza, 2029 Century Park, E., Los Angeles, CA 90067 Tel 213-552-9111; Dist. by: Independent News, 75 Rockefeller Plaza, New York, NY 10019.

COS Imprint of **Har-Row**

Coslett, *(Coslett Publishing Co.; 0-910444),* Williamsport, PA 17701 Tel 717-323-1828.

Cosmic Comm, *(Cosmic Communication Co.; 0-912038),* 100 Elm Court, Decorah, IA 52101 Tel 319-382-9317.

Cosmic Consciousness, *(Cosmic Consciousness Creations, Inc.; 0-916274),* P. O. Box 307 S., Miami, FL 33143; Moved, Left No Forwarding Address.

Cosmos Bks, *(Cosmos Books),* Dist. by: Books New China, 53 E. Broadway, New York, NY 10002.

Cosray Res, *(Cosray Research Institute),* 2505 S. Fourth East, Salt Lake City, UT 84115.

Costano, *(Costano Books; 0-930268),* P.O. Box 791, San Anselmo, CA 94960 Tel 707-255-2127.

Costello, *(Costello Publishing Co., Inc.; 0-918344),* Box 9, Northport, NY 11768 Tel 516-261-9140.

Cottage Indus, *(Cottage Industries; 0-938348),* Box 244, Cobalt, CT 06414.

Cotton Lane, *(Cotton Lane Press; 0-9604810),* 2 Cotton Lane, Augusta, GA 30902 Tel 404-722-0232.

Cougar Bks, *(Cougar Books; 0-917982),* P.O. Box 22246, Sacramento, CA 95822 Tel 916-428-3271.

Coun Adv Consumer, *(Council for the Advancement of Consumer Policy; 0-938788),* 2033 M St., N.W., Suite 502, Washington, DC 20036.

Coun Advance Small Colleges, *(Council for the Advancement of Small Colleges; 0-937012),* 1 Dupont Circle, Suite 320, Washington, DC 20036 Tel 202-659-3795.

Coun Am Affairs, *(Council on American Affairs; 0-930690),* 1629 K St., N.W., Suite 520, Washington, DC 20006 Tel 202-232-1040.

Coun Biology Eds, *(Council of Biology Editors; 0-914340),* Orders to: American Institute of Biological Sciences, 1401 Wilson Blvd., Arlington, VA 22209.

Coun Career Plan, *(Council for Career Planning, Inc.; 0-916340),* 310 Madison Ave., New York, NY 10017 Tel 212-687-9490.

Coun Exc Child, *(Council for Exceptional Children; 0-86586),* 1920 Association Dr., Reston, VA 22091 Tel 703-620-3660.

Coun Found, *(Council on Foundations, Inc.; 0-913892),* 1828 "L" St., N.W., Washington, DC 20036.

Coun on Municipal, *(Council on Municipal Performance; 0-916450),* 84 Fifth Ave., New York, NY 10011 Tel 212-243-6603.

Coun Plan Lib
See CPL Biblios

Coun Rel & Intl, *(Council on Religion & International Affairs; 0-87641),* 170 E. 64th St., New York, NY 10021 Tel 212-838-4120.

Coun Res Biblio, *(Council on Research in Bibliography, Inc.; 0-910448),* Paul Klapper Library, Queens College, Flushing, NY 11367.

Coun Soc Studies, *(National Council for the Social Studies; 0-87986),* Social Education, 3615 Wisconsin Ave. N.W.,, Washington, DC 20016 Tel 202-966-7840.

Coun State Plan, *(Council of State Planning Agencies, The; 0-934842),* 444 N. Capital St., Washington, DC 20001 Tel 202-624-5386.

Counting Hse, *(Counting House Publishing Co.; 0-915026),* 182 S. Main St., Thiensville, WI 53092 Tel 414-242-2460.

Country Bazaar, *(Country Bazaar Publishing; 0-936744),* Honey Inc. Bldg. Rt.2 Box 190, Berryville, AR 72616 Tel 501-423-3131.

Country Beautiful, *(Country Beautiful Corp.; 0-87294),* 24198 W. Bluemound Rd., Waukesha, WI 53186 Tel 414-542-9361.

Country Bks, *(Country Books),* P.O. Box 278, Boonville, NY 13309.

Country Dance & Song, *(Country Dance & Song Society of America; 0-917024),* 505 Eighth Ave., Suite 2500, New York, NY 10018 Tel 212-594-8833.

Country Garden, *(Country Garden Press),* 4412 McCulloch St., Duluth, MN 55804.

Country Hse, *(Country House, The),* 15 Thomas Ave., Topsham, ME 04086.

Country Music Found, *(Country Music Foundation Press; 0-915608),* 4 Music Square E., Nashville, TN 37203 Tel 615-256-1639.

Country Pr, *(Country Press Pubns.),* P.O. Box 813, South Pasadena, CA 91030.

Country Pr CO, *(Country Press),* 1700 Hwy. 6 & 24, Grand Junction, CO 81501.

Country Pr NY, *(Country Press; 0-913174),* 2272 Scottsville Rd., Scottsville, NY 14546 Tel 716-889-9790.

Country Print, *(Country Printing, Inc.),* P.O. Box 240, Pequot Lakes, MN 56472 Tel 218-568-8521.

Countryman, *(Countryman Press, Inc.;*
0-914378), Woodstock, VT 05091
Tel 802-457-1049. *Imprints:* Foul Play
(Foul Play Press).

Countryside Bks, *(Countryside Books; 0-88453),*
1845 N. Farwell Ave., Suite 201, Milwaukee,
WI 53202 Tel 414-272-6700.

Countryside Studio, *(Countryside Studio, Inc.;*
0-9605428), P.O. Box 88, Hwy. 25 W.,
Cottontown, TN 37048.

Couple to Couple, *(Couple to Couple League;*
0-9601036), P.O. Box 11084, Cincinnati,
OH 45211 Tel 513-661-7612.

Courier-Gazette
See Courier of Maine

Courier of Maine, *(Courier of Maine Books;*
0-913954), 1 Park Dr., Rockland, ME 04841
Tel 207-594-4401.

Courier Pr, *(Courier Press; 0-917310),* P.O. Box
482, 300 E. Main St., Murfreesboro, TN
37130.

Courier Pr FL, *(Courier Press; 0-934602),* 428
N.E. 82nd St. Suite 1, Miami, FL 33138.

Courseware, *(Courseware, Inc.; 0-89805),* 10075
Carroll Canyon Rd., San Diego, CA 92131
Tel 714-578-1700.

Court Scribe, *(Court Scribe, The; 0-9601572),*
2201 Friendly St., Eugene, OR 94705
Tel 503-343-7562.

Courthouse Pr, *(Courthouse Press; 0-911736),*
P.O. Box 205, Floral Park, NY 11002
Tel 516-437-9463; Moved, Left No
Forwarding Address.

Cove Pr, *(Cove Press),* Whistlestop Mall 240,
Rockport, MA 01966.

Cove Pub Co, *(Cove Pub. Co.; 0-930480),* P.O.
Box 1218, Grayland, WA 98547
Tel 206-267-3601.

Cove View, *(Cove View Press; 0-931896),* Box
637, Garberville, CA 95440
Tel 707-923-3476.

Covenant, *(Covenant Press; 0-910452),* 3200 W.
Foster Ave., Chicago, IL 60625
Tel 312-478-4676.

Cover Pub, *(Cover Publishing Co.; 0-912912),*
P.O. Box 1092, Tampa, FL 33601
Tel 813-886-6818.

Cow Puddle, *(Cow Puddle Press; 0-9600672),*
Sunset Trading Post, Sunset, TX 76270
Tel 817-872-2027.

Cowan, *(Cowan, Robert G.; 0-910456),* 1650
Redcliff St., Los Angeles, CA 90026
Tel 213-664-7401.

Coward, *(Coward, McCann & Geoghegan, Inc.;*
0-698), A Member of the Putnam Publishing
Group, 200 Madison Ave., New York, NY
10016 Tel 212-576-8900; Orders to: 1050
W. Wall St., Lyndhurst, NJ 07071
Tel 201-933-9292.

Cowles, *(Cowles Book Corp., Inc.),* ; Publisher
Abbreviation Without Addresses Are for
Titles That Are Out of Print. These Are
Obsolete Abbreviation. Publisher Acquired
by Henry Regnery, Co.

Cowley Pubns, *(Cowley Pubns.),* 980 Memorial
Dr., Cambridge, MA 02138.

Cox, *(Cox, Harold E.; 0-911940),* 80 Virginia
Terrace, Forty Fort, PA 18704
Tel 717-287-7647.

Coyote, *(Coyote Books),* Dist. by: Book People,
2940 Seventh St., Berkeley, CA 94710.

Cozzolino Assocs, *(Cozzolino Associates;*
0-9601408), 12 Chippenham Dr., West
Berlin, NJ 08091.

CPA Study
See Bradley CPA

CPL Biblios, *(CPL Bibliographies),* 1313 E.
60th St., Merriam Ctr., Chicago, IL 60637
Tel 312-947-2007.

Cptn Stanislaus, *(Captain Stanislaus Mlotkowski*
Memorial Brigade Society; 0-9600814), 247
Philadelphia Pike, Wilmington, DE 19809.

Crabapple Pr, *(Crabapple Press; 0-89548),* Div.
of Communication Design, Inc., 300 North
St., Meadville, PA 16335 Tel 814-724-1117.

Crabtree, *(Crabtree Publishing; 0-937070),* P.O.
Box 3451, Federal Way, WA 98003.

Cracker Barrel, *(Cracker Barrel Press;*
0-911750), P.O. Box 1287, Southampton,
NY 11968.

Craftsman, *(Craftsman Book Co.; 0-910460),*
542 Stevens Ave., Solana Beach, CA 92075
Tel 714-755-0161.

Crager, *(Crager, Robert L., & Co.; 0-910462),*
7221 Zimpel St., New Orleans, LA 70118
Tel 504-861-0111.

Cragmont Pubns, *(Cragmont Pubns.; 0-89666),*
China Basin Bldg., 161 Berry St., Suite 6410,
San Francisco, CA 94107 Tel 415-546-0646.

Crain Bks, *(Crain Books; 0-87251),* Div. of
Crain Communications, Inc., 740 Rush St.,
Chicago, IL 60611 Tel 312-649-5250.

Crambruck, *(Crambruck Press; 0-87699),* 381
Park Ave. S., New York, NY 10016
Tel 212-532-0871.

Cramer Bkstore, *(Cramer Bookstore; 0-913118),*
P.O. Box 7235, Kansas City, MO 64113.

Cranberry, *(Cranberry Press, Inc.; 0-918130),* 30
Hotaling Place, San Francisco, CA 94111
Tel 415-421-5672; Moved, Lfet No
Forwarding Address.

Cranbrook, *(Cranbrook Institute of Science;*
0-87737), 500 Lone Pine Rd., P.O. Box 801,
Bloomfield Hills, MI 48013
Tel 313-645-3239.

Cranbrook Pub, *(Cranbrook Publishing;*
0-9604690), 2815 Cranbrook, Ann Arbor,
MI 48104.

Crane Pub Co, *(Crane Publishing Co.; 0-89075),*
Div. of MLP, 1301 Hamilton Ave., Box
3713, Trenton, NJ 08629 Tel 609-393-1111.

Crane-Russak Co, *(Crane, Russak & Co., Inc.;*
0-8448), 3 E. 44th St, New York, NY 10017
Tel 212-867-1490.

Cranium Pr, *(Cranium Press),* 243 Collins St.,
San Francisco, CA 94118; Moved, Left No
Forwarding Address.

CRB Res, *(CRB Research; 0-939780),* P.O. Box
56, 112 New Highway, Commack, NY
11725 Tel 516-543-1757.

CRC Pr, *(CRC Press; 0-87819; 0-8493),* 2000
N.W. 24th St., Boca Raton, FL 33431
Tel 305-994-0555.

CRCS Pubns NV, *(CRCS Pubns.; 0-916360),*
P.O. Box 20850, Reno, NV 89515
Tel 702-358-2850.

CRCS Pubns WA
See CRCS Pubns NV

Creat Educ Found, *(Creative Education*
Foundation, Inc.; 0-930222), c/o State
Univ. College at Buffalo, Chase Hall, 1300
Elmwood Ave., Buffalo, NY 14222
Tel 716-878-6221.

Creation Hse, *(Creation House; 0-88419),* 396
E. St. Charles Rd., Carol Stream, IL 60187
Tel 312-653-1472.

Creation-Life
See CLP Pubs

Creation Sci, *(Creation Science Research Center;*
0-88213), 10857 Valiente Court, San Diego,
CA 92124 Tel 714-294-9614; Moved, Left
No Forwarding Address.

Creations Unltd, *(Creations Unlimited;*
0-938900), P.O. Box 2591, Farmington
Hills, MI 48018.

Creative Arts Bk, *(Creative Arts Book Co.;*
0-916870), 833 Bancroft Way, Berkeley, CA
94710 Tel 415-848-4777.

Creative Bk Co, *(Creative Book Co.; 0-88409),*
7210 Varne Ave., Van Nuys, CA 91402
Tel 213-988-2334; Moved, Left No
Forwarding Address.

Creative Bks, *(Creative Books; 0-914606),* P.O.
Box 5162, Carmel, CA 93921
Tel 408-624-7573.

Creative Comp, *(Creative Computing; 0-916688),*
P.O. Box 789M, Morristown, NJ 07960
Tel 201-540-0445.

Creative Ed, *(Creative Education, Inc.; 0-87191),*
1422 W. Lake St., Suite 301, Minneapolis,
MN 55408 Tel 612-825-9154; Orders to:
123 S. Broad St., Mankato, MN 56001
Tel 507-388-6273.

Creative Editions
See Cougar Bks

Creative Eye, *(Creative Eye Press; 0-916480),*
P.O. Box 4191, Modesto, CA 95352
Tel 209-524-8603.

Creative Homeowner, *(Creative Homeowner*
Press; 0-932944), Div. of Federal Marketing
Corp., 2266 N. Prospect, No. 410,
Milwaukee, WI 53202 Tel 414-276-4755.

Creative Infomatics, *(Creative Infomatics, Inc.;*
0-917634), P.O. Box 11300, Aspen, CO
81611 Tel 303-925-8515.

Creative Learning, *(Creative Learning Press, Inc.;*
0-936386), P.O. Box 320, Mansfield Center,
CT 06250 Tel 203-281-4036.

Creative Papbks, *(Creative Paperbacks, Inc.;*
0-89812), P.O. Box 1997, N. Mankato, MN
56001.

Creative Pr, *(Creative Press; 0-912512),* P.O.
Box 1058, Claremont, CA 91711
Tel 714-593-5060.

Creative Pubns, *(Creative Pubns.; 0-88488),*
1101 San Antonio Rd., Mountain View, CA
94043 Tel 415-968-1101; Orders to: P.O.
Box 10328, Palo Alto, CA 94303
Tel 415-968-3977.

Creative Pubs
See Creative Pubns

Creative Res & Educ, *(Creative Research &*
Educational Systems for Today; 0-935770),
168-02 Jewel Ave., Flushing, NY 11365.

Creative Sales, *(Creative Sales Corp.; 0-933162),*
762 W. Algonquin Rd., Arlington Heights,
IL 60005.

Creative Storytime, *(Creative Storytime Press;*
0-934876), P.O. Box 572, Minneapolis, MN
55440 Tel 612-926-5986.

Creative Tchr
See World Rec Pubns

Creative Texas, *(Creative Publishing Co.;*
0-932702), P.O. Box 9292, College Sta., TX
77840 Tel 713-846-7907.

Creative Therapeutics, *(Creative Therapeutics;*
0-933812), 155 County Rd., Cresskill, NJ
07626.

Creative Vent, *(Creative Ventures; 0-917166),*
515 E. Firebaugh, Exeter, CA 93221; Orders
to: Star Rte., Box 94, Leavenworth, WA
98826.

Creatures at Large, *(Creatures at Large;*
0-940064), 1082 Grand Teton Dr., Pacifica,
CA 94044 Tel 415-359-4341.

Credit Res Found, *(Credit Research Foundation,*
Inc.; 0-939050), 3000 Marcus Ave., Lake
Success, NY 11042 Tel 516-488-1166.

Credo Pubns, *(Credo Pubns.; 0-939612),* P.O.
Box 124, West Stockbridge, MA 01266.

Creek Hse, *(Creek House; 0-9600490),* P.O.
Box 793, Ojai, CA 93023 Tel 805-646-3200.

Crehore, *(Crehore, John Davenport; 0-910466),*
1523 E. 28th Ave., No. 2, Oakland, CA
94601 Tel 415-533-2251.

Crerar Lib, *(Crerar, John, Library),* 35 W. 33rd
St., Pubns. Dept., Chicago, IL 60616
Tel 312-225-2526.

Crescent Pubns, *(Crescent Pubns., Inc.;*
0-914184), 5410 Wilshire Blvd., Suite 400,
Los Angeles, CA 90036.

Cresset Pubs, *(Cresset Pubs.; 0-936082),* 519 E.
Tabor Rd., Philadelphia, PA 19120.

Crest *Imprint of* **Fawcett**

Crest Challenge, *(Crest Challenge Books;*
0-913776), 42 Dart St., Loma Linda, CA
92354 Tel 714-796-1536; Orders to: P.O.
Box 993, Loma Linda, CA 92354.

Crestline, *(Crestline Publishing Co.; 0-912612),*
1251 N. Jefferson Ave., Sarasota, FL 33577
Tel 813-955-8080.

Crestwood Hse, *(Crestwood House, Inc.;*
0-89686; 0-913940), P.O. Box 3427, Hwy.
66 South, Mankato, MN 56001
Tel 507-388-1616.

CRF, *(Citizens' Research Foundation),* 245
Nassau St., Princeton, NJ 08540
Tel 609-924-0246; Moved, Left No
Forwarding Address.

CRI, *(Communications Research Institute),* 25
Central Park West, New York, NY 10023
Tel 212-752-8355.

Crime & Justice Hist, *(Crime & Justice History*
Group, The), Dist. by: John Jay Press, 444
W. 56th St., New York, NY 10019.

Crime & Soc Justice, *(Crime & Social Justice;*
0-935206), P.O. Box 4373, Berkeley, CA
94704.

Crispo Gallery, *(Crispo, Andrew, Gallery, Inc.;*
0-937014), 41 E. 57th St., New York, NY
10022.

Criterion Bks, *(Criterion Books, Inc; 0-200),* c/o
Harper & Row, Pubs., 10 E. 53 St., New
York, NY 10022.

Criterion Mus, *(Criterion Music Corp.;*
0-910468), 6124 Selma Ave., Hollywood,
CA 90028 Tel 213-469-2296; Dist. by: Joe
Goldfeder Music Enterprises, P.O. Box 660,
Lynbrook, NY 11563.

Cro-Woods, *(Cro Woods Publishing),* c/o
Wyoming Valley Observer News, P.O. Box
O, Wilkes Barre, PA 18703
Tel 717-829-3663.

Croft MD, *(Croft, Inc.; 0-86673),* 4601 York
Rd., Baltimore, MD 21212.

Crofton Pub, *(Crofton Publishing Corp.;*
0-89020), 1501 Beacon St., No.1402,
Brookline, MA 02146 Tel 617-738-8117.

Croissant & Co, *(Croissant & Co.; 0-912348),*
P.O. Box 282, Athens, OH 45701
Tel 614-593-8339.

Crome & Soc Justice

See Crime & Soc Justice

Cromwel, *(Cromwel Press; 0-916298),* P.O. Box 335, Santa Margarita, CA 93453 Tel 805-543-1581.

Cromwell-Smith, *(Cromwell-Smith Services; 0-933086),* P.O. Box 1719, 7825 Ivanhoe, Suite 205, La Jolla, CA 92038.

Crone-Atwood, *(Crone-Atwood Pubns., Co.),* 1037 E. Parkway, Suite 205, Memphis, TN 38104 Tel 901-274-6143; Moved, Left No Forwarding Address.

Croner, *(Croner Pubns.; 0-87514),* 211-03 Jamaica Ave., Queens Village, NY 11428 Tel 212-464-0866.

Crop Sci Soc Am, *(Crop Science Society of America),* 677 S. Segoe Rd., Madison, WI 53711 Tel 608-274-1212.

Crosby County, *(Crosby County Pioneer Memorial),* P. O. Box 386, Crosbyton, TX 79322 Tel 806-675-2331.

Crosley, *(Crosley, Inc.; 0-9603268),* 1515 Kitchen, Jonesboro, AR 72401 Tel 501-935-3928.

Cross Bks, *(Cross Books; 0-9601672),* 50 MacArthur Dr., North Providence, RI 02911 Tel 401-231-0874.

Cross Country, *(Cross Country Press; 0-916696),* P.O. Box 21081, Woodhaven, NY 11421 Tel 212-896-7648.

Cross Cult, *(Cross-Cultural Communications; 0-89304),* 239 Wynsum Ave., Merrick, NY 11566 Tel 516-868-5635.

Cross Currents, *(Cross Currents; 0-935820),* West Nyack, NY 10994 Tel 914-358-4898.

Cross Roads, *(Cross Roads Pubns.),* 2751 Buford Hwy. N.E., Suite 720, Atlanta, GA 30324 Tel 404-325-7857; Moved, Left No Forwarding Address.

Crossbar Ent, *(Crossbar Enterprises; 0-9604994),* 9522 Stevebrook Rd., Fairfax, VA 22032.

Crosscut Saw, *(Crosscut Saw Press; 0-931020),* Orders to: Bookpeople, 2940 7th St., Berkeley, CA 94710.

Crossing Pr, *(Crossing Press, The; 0-89594; 0-912278),* Box 640, Trumansburg, NY 14886 Tel 607-387-6217.

Crossroad NY, *(Crossroad Publishing Co., 0-8245),* 18 E. 41st St., New York, NY 10017 Tel 212-683-1300.

Crossroads, *(Crossroads; 0-9603672),* 1824 S. Cloverdale, Los Angeles, CA 90019.

Crossroads *Imprint of* **African Studies Assn**

Crossroads MA, *(Crossroads Press; 0-918456),* Epstein Bldg., Brandeis Univ., Waltham, MA 02154.

Crossroads Prods, *(Crossroads Productions & Pubns., Inc.),* P.O. Box 29, West Point, GA 31833.

Crow, *(Crow),* 5430 Del Rio Rd., Sacramento, CA 95822 Tel 916-441-5358.

Crow Canyon, *(Crow Canyon Press; 0-937760),* 1900 Las Trampas Rd., Alamo, CA 94507.

Crown, *(Crown Pubs., Inc.; 0-517),* 1 Park Ave., New York, NY 10016 Tel 212-532-9200. *Imprints:* Harmony (Harmony Books).

Crowther Solar, *(Crowther/Solar Group; 0-918202),* Subs. of Crowther Architects Group, 310 Steele St., Denver, CO 80206 Tel 303-355-2301.

Croydon, *(Croydon House; 0-910472),* P.O. Box 1302, Miami, FL 33161; Moved, Left No Forwarding Address.

CRR *Imprint of* **Charles River Bks**

Cruikshank, *(Cruikshank, Eleanor P.),* 194 San Carlos Ave., Sausalito, CA 94965.

Crusade Bible Pubs, *(Crusade Bible Pubs., Inc.),* Athens Dr., Mt. Juliet, Nashville, TN 37122 Tel 615-758-0461.

Cruzada Span Pubns, *(Cruzada Spanish Pubns.; 0-933648),* P.O. Box 650909, Miami, FL 33165.

CS Pubns, *(CS Pubns.; 0-934206),* 1791 Primrose Dr., El Cajon, CA 92020.

CSA Pr, *(CSA Press; 0-87707),* Lakemont, GA 30552 Tel 404-782-3931.

CSG Pr, *(CSG Press),* 11301 Rockville Pike, Kensington, MD 20795.

CSI Studies, *(Center for Strategic & International Studies; 0-89206),* 1800 "K" St. N.W., Washington, DC 20006 Tel 202-877-0200.

CSLA, *(Church & Synagogue Library Assn.; 0-915024),* P.O. Box 1130, Bryn Mawr, PA 19010 Tel 215-853-2870.

CSS Pub, *(C.S.S. Publishing Co.; 0-89536),* 628 S. Main St., Lima, OH 45804 Tel 419-227-1818.

CSU Ctr Busn Econ, *(California State Univ., Center for Business & Economic Research; 0-9602894),* Chico, CA 95929.

CSU Fullerton, *(California State Univ. at Fullerton Foundation),* Fullerton, CA 92634; Dist. by: Hackett Publishing Co., Inc., P.O. Box 55573, 4047 N. Pennsylvania St., Indianapolis, IN 46205 Tel 317-283-8187.

CSU Oral Hist
See CSUF Oral Hist

CSUDH, *(California State Univ., Dominguez Hills Educational Resources Center),* 800 E. Victoria, Dominguez Hills, CA 90747.

CSUF Oral Hist, *(California State Univ. Fullerton, Oral History Program; 0-930046),* Fullerton, CA 92634 Tel 714-773-3580.

CSUN, *(California State Univ., Northridge Library),* 18111 Nordhoff St., Northridge, CA 91330 Tel 213-885-2271.

CTB McGraw Hill, *(CTB/McGraw Hill; 0-07),* Div. of McGraw Hill, Del Monte Research Park, Monterey, CA 93940 Tel 408-649-8400.

Ctr Afro-Am Stud, *(Center for Afro-American Studies (UCLA); 0-934934),* 3111 Campbell Hall, 405 Hilgard Ave., Los Angeles, CA 90024 Tel 213-825-3528.

Ctr Analysis Public Issues, *(Center for Analysis of Public Issues),* 16 Vandeventer Ave., Princeton, NJ 08540 Tel 609-924-9750.

Ctr Appl Ling, *(Center for Applied Linguistics; 0-87281),* 3520 Prospect St. NW, Washington, DC 20007 Tel 202-298-9292.

Ctr Appl Res, *(Center for Applied Research in Education, Inc., The; 0-87628),* Subs. of Prentice-Hall, C/o Prentice-Hall, Englewood Cliffs, NJ 07632 Tel 201-592-2483; Orders to: P.O. Box 130, W. Nyack, NY 10994 Tel 201-767-5195.

Ctr Applications Psych, *(Center for Applications of Psychological Type, Inc.; 0-935652),* 1441 N.W. Sixth St., Suite B400, Gainesville, FL 32601 Tel 904-375-0160.

Ctr Art Living, *(Center for the Art of Living; 0-9602552),* 2203 N. Sheffield, Chicago, IL 60614 Tel 312-871-3044.

Ctr Bus Devel & Res, *(Center for Business Development & Research, College of Business & Economics),* Univ. of Idaho, Moscow, ID 83843 Tel 208-885-6611.

Ctr Bus Devel
See Ctr Bus Devel & Res

Ctr Busn Info, *(Center for Business Information; 0-936936),* P.O. Box 2404, Meriden, CT 06450 Tel 203-235-1441.

Ctr Byzantine *Imprint of* **Dumbarton Oaks**

Ctr Calif Public
See Cal Inst Public

Ctr Conn Stud, *(Center for Connecticut Studies),* Eastern Connecticut State College, Willimantic, CT 06226 Tel 203-456-2231.

Ctr Cont Celeb, *(Center for Contemporary Celebration),* 1400 E. 53rd St., Chicago, IL 60615; Moved,Left No Forwarding Address.

Ctr Cont Poetry, *(Center for Contemporary Poetry),* Murphy Library, Univ. of Wisconsin at La Crosse, La Crosse, WI 54601.

Ctr Criminal
See Ctr Res Criminal

Ctr Econ Analysis, *(Center for Economic Analysis, George Mason Univ.; 0-933588),* Box 1329, Cullowhee, NC 28723 Tel 704-293-5433.

Ctr Educ Policy Mgmt, *(Center for Educational Policy & Management),* College of Education, Univ. of Oregon, Eugene, OR 97403 Tel 503-686-5072.

Ctr Educ Res, *(Center for Education & Research in Free Enterprise; 0-86599),* Texas A&M University, College Station, TX 77843.

Ctr for Arts Info, *(Center for Arts Information; 0-935654),* 625 Broadway, New York, NY 10012 Tel 212-677-7548.

Ctr for NE & North African Stud, *(Univ. of Michigan Center for Near Eastern & North African Studies; 0-932098),* 144 Lane Hall, Univ. of Michigan, Ann Arbor, MI 48109 Tel 313-764-0350.

Ctr Human Servs, *(Center for Human Services; 0-915852),* 39 Church St., New Haven, CT 06510 Tel 203-624-6911; Orders to: P.O. Box 1268, New Haven, CT 06505.

Ctr Info Am, *(Center for Information on America; 0-913172),* Washington, CT 06793 Tel 203-868-2602.

Ctr Info Sharing, *(Center for Information Sharing; 0-939532),* 77 N. Washington St., Boston, MA 02114.

Ctr Integral Med, *(Center for Integral Medicine; 0-89210),* 465 North Roxbury Dr., Suite 811, Beverly Hills, CA 90210.

Ctr Inter-Am Rel, *(Center for Inter-American Relations),* Dist. by: Interbook, Inc., 13 E. 16th St., New York, NY 10003.

Ctr Intl Ed U of MA, *(Center for International Education, Univ. of Massachusetts; 0-932288),* 285 Hills House South, Univ. of Massachusetts, Amherst, MA 01003.

Ctr Intl Educ
See Lat Am Stud

Ctr Intl Stud Duke, *(Center for International Studies, Duke Univ.),* Durham, NC 27706.

Ctr Korean U HI at Manoa, *(Center for Korean Studies, Univ. of Hawaii at Manoa; 0-917536),* 1881 East-West Rd., Honolulu, HI 96822 Tel 808-949-1833.

Ctr Land Grant, *(Center for Land Grant Studies, The; 0-9605202),* 136 Grant Ave., Santa Fe, NM 87501.

Ctr Landscape Arch *Imprint of* **Dumbarton Oaks**

Ctr Marital Sexual, *(Center for Marital & Sexual Studies; 0-9600626),* 5199 E. Pacific Coast Hwy., Long Beach, CA 90804 Tel 213-597-4425.

Ctr Media Dev, *(Center for Media Development, Inc.; 0-89183),* 150 Great Neck Rd., Great Neck, NY 11021 Tel 516-487-7707.

Ctr Migration, *(Center for Migration Studies; 0-913256),* Dist. by: Jerome S. Ozer Pub., Inc., 340 Tenafly Rd., Englewood, NJ 07631 Tel 201-567-7040.

Ctr Mod Psych Stud, *(Center for Modern Psychoanalytic Studies; 0-916850),* 16 W. 10th St., New York, NY 10011 Tel 212-260-7050.

Ctr Multiple Gestation, *(Center for Study of Multiple Gestation, The; 0-932254),* 333 E. Superior St., Suite 463-5, Chicago, IL 60611 Tel 312-266-9093, 1113 Crook Run Ave., Reston, VA 22090 Tel 703-437-7669.

Ctr Natl Security, *(Center for National Security Studies; 0-86566),* 122 Maryland Ave. NE, Washington, DC 20002.

Ctr Neo Hellenic, *(Center for Neo-Hellenic Studies; 0-932242),* 1010 W. 22nd St., Austin, TX 78705 Tel 512-477-5526.

Ctr Photo, *(Center for Photography),* 1950 Sacramento St., San Francisco, CA 94109 Tel 415-824-8488.

Ctr Pol Process, *(Center for Policy Process),* Suite 401, 1755 Massachusetts Ave., N.W., Washington, DC 20036 Tel 202-387-5700.

Ctr Pre-Columbian *Imprint of* **Dumbarton Oaks**

Ctr Productive Public, *(Center for Productive Public Management; 0-9604504),* c/o John Jay College, CUNY, 445 W. 59th St., New York, NY 10019 Tel 212-489-5030.

Ctr Prof Adv, *(Center for Professional Advancement; 0-86553),* 197 Rt. 18, P.O. Box H, E. Brunswick, NJ 08816 Tel 201-249-1400.

Ctr Renewable, *(Center for Renewable Resources; 0-937446),* 1001 Connecticut Ave., N.W., No. 510, Washington, DC 20036.

Ctr Res Criminal, *(Center for Research on Criminal Justice; 0-917404),* P.O. Box 4373, Berkeley, CA 94704; Orders to: Synthesis Publications, P. O. Box 40099, San Francisco, CA 94140 Tel 415-282-5272.

Ctr Res Soc Chg, *(Center for Research in Social Change; 0-89937),* Emory University, Atlanta, GA 30322 Tel 404-329-7525.

Ctr Responsive Law, *(Center for Study of Responsive Law),* P.O. Box 19367, Washington, DC 20036; Dist. by: Education Exploration Center, P.O. Box 7339, Minneapolis, MN 55407.

Ctr S&SE Asian, *(Univ. of Michigan, Center for South & Southeast Asian Studies; 0-89148),* Univ. of Michigan, Center for S. & Se. Asian Studies, 130 Lane Hall, Ann Arbor, MI 48109 Tel 313-764-0352.

Ctr Sci Public, *(Center for Science in the Public Interest; 0-89329),* 1755 "S" St., N.W., Washington, DC 20009 Tel 202-332-9110.

Ctr Sci Study, *(Center for the Scientific Study of Religion; 0-913348),* 5757 University Ave., Chicago, IL 60637 Tel 312-752-5757.

Ctr South Folklore, *(Center for Southern Folklore; 0-89267),* 1216 Peabody Ave., P.O. Box 40105, Memphis, TN 38104 Tel 901-726-4205.

Ctr Study Crime
See Ctr Res Criminal

Ctr Tech Environ, *(Center for Technology, Environment, & Development; 0-939436),* Clark Univ., 950 Main St., Worcester, MA 01610.

Ctr Urban Pol Res, *(Center for Urban Policy Research),* Rutgers Univ., Bldg. 4051-Kilmer Campus, New Brunswick, NJ 08903 Tel 201-932-3122.

Ctr Western Studies, *(Center for Western Studies; 0-931170),* Augustana College, Sioux Falls, SD 57197 Tel 605-336-4007.

Ctr Womans Own, *(Center for A Woman's Own Name; 0-914332),* 261 Kimberley Rd., Barrington, IL 60010 Tel 312-381-2113.

Cucamonga, *(Cucamonga Press; 0-918190),* P.O. Box 632, Cucamonga, CA 91730 Tel 714-985-1921.

CUE
See General Stud Res

Cuisenaire, *(Cuisenaire Co. of America, Inc.; 0-914040),* 12 Church St., New Rochelle, NY 10805 Tel 914-235-0900.

Cuisinart Cooking, *(Cuisinart Cooking Club; 0-936662),* 411 W. Putnam Ave., Greenwich, CT 06830.

Culinary, *(Culinary World, Inc.; 0-917872),* 111 E. 65th St., New York, NY 10021 Tel 212-628-0066; Moved, Left No Forwarding Address.

Culinary Arts *Imprint* of **Delair**

Cultural Assist, *(Cultural Assistance Center),* 1500 Broadway, 20th Fl., New York, NY 10036.

Cultural Pr, *(Cultural Press; 0-910476),* 517 Madison St., Waukesha, WI 53186.

Cultural Stud Inst, *(Cultural Studies Institute; 0-9606058),* P.O. Box 5435, San Jose, CA 95150 Tel 408-294-7858.

Cummings, *(Cummings, Benjamin, Publishing Co., Inc.; 0-8053),* 2727 Sandhill Rd., Menlo Park, CA 94025 Tel 415-854-6020.

Cummings
See Benjamin-Cummings

Cummington, *(Cummington Press/Cleary House; 0-914026),* Univ. of Nebraska at Omaha, P.O. Box 688, Omaha, NE 68101.

Cummington Pub, *(Cummington Publishing, Inc.; 0-938350),* 17 Old Orchard Rd., New Rochelle, NY 10804.

Cumulus Pubns, *(Cumulus Pubns; 0-933020),* 3122 Santa Monica Blvd., Santa Monica, CA 90404.

Cunningham Pr, *(Cunningham Press),* 3063 W. Main, Alhambra, CA 91801 Tel 213-283-8838; Dist. by: Theosophy Co., 245 W. 33rd St., Los Angeles, CA 90007.

Curbstone, *(Curbstone Press; 0-915306),* 321 Jackson St., Willimantic, CT 06226 Tel 203-423-9190.

Curbstone Pub NY TX, *(Curbstone Publishing; 0-931604),* P.O. Box 1613, New York, NY 10116 Tel 212-360-1542; Orders to: P.O. Box 7445, Austin, TX 78712 Tel 512-444-9463.

Curlew Music, *(Curlew Music Publishers, Inc.),* 1311 North Highland Ave., Hollywood, CA 90028; Moved, Left No Forwarding Address.

Current Issues, *(Current Issues Pubns; 0-936012),* 2707 Walker St., Berkeley, CA 94705 Tel 415-549-1451.

Current World Leaders, *(Current World Leaders; 0-911900),* 2074 Alameda Padre Serra, Santa Barbara, CA 93103.

Curriculum Info Ctr, *(Curriculum Information Center, Inc.; 0-914608; 0-89770),* Ketchum Place, P.O. Box 510, Westport, CT 06881 Tel 203-226-8941.

Curry County, *(Curry County Historical Society; 0-932368),* P.O. Box 1856, Wedderburn, OR 97491.

Curson Hse, *(Curson House, Inc. Publishers; 0-913694),* Suite 1001, Western Savings Bank Bldg., Broad & Chestnut Sts., Philadelphia, PA 19107 Tel 215-732-7111.

Curtin & London, *(Curtin & London, Inc.; 0-930764),* 6 Vernon St., Somerville, MA 02145 Tel 617-625-1200.

Curtis, *(Curtis Books Inc.; 0-502),* 600 Third Ave., New York, NY 10017.

Curtis Instruments, *(Curtis Instruments, Inc.; 0-939488),* 200 Kisco Ave., Mt. Kisco, NY 10549.

Curtis Pub Co, *(Curtis Publishing Co., The; 0-89387),* 1100 Waterway Blvd., Indianapolis, IN 46206.

Cusack, *(Cusack, Betty B.; 0-911448),* 35 West Rd., West Yarmouth, MA 02673; Moved, Left No Forwarding Address.

Custer, *(Custer, Marquis, Pubns.; 0-9600274),* 1021 S. Lee Ave., Lodi, CA 95240 Tel 209-368-0502.

Custom Hse, *(Custom House Press),* 2900 Newark Rd., Zanesville, OH 43701.

CWS Group Pr, *(CWS Group Press; 0-9604324),* P.O. Box 543, 807 W. 15th St., Vinton, IA 52349 Tel 313-472-3552.

CWSS Pr, *(CWSS Press; 0-9600856),* Dist. by: B & H Books, 330 Paloma Ave., San Rafael, CA 94901; Moved, Left No Forwarding Address.

Cycle-Gram, *(Cycle-Gram Associates; 0-913020),* P.O. Box 4462, North Hollywood, CA 91607; Moved,Left No Forwarding Address.

Cycle Pr, *(Cycle Press; 0-914320),* 18 Warner Place, Brooklyn, NY 11201; Moved,Left No Forwarding Address.

Cyclopedia, *(Cyclopedia Publishing Co.; 0-914226),* 6 Freedom Rd., Pleasant Valley, NY 12569.

Cykx, *(Cykx Books Pubs.; 0-932436),* P.O. Box 299, Lenox Hill Sta., New York, NY 10021.

Cypress, *(Cypress Pub. Corp.; 0-89447),* 1763 Gardena Ave., Glendale, CA 91204 Tel 213-244-8651.

Cyrco Pr, *(Cyrco Press, Inc.; 0-915326),* 342 Madison Ave., New York, NY 10017 Tel 212-682-8410; Moved, Left No Forwarding Address.

D A Duke, *(Duke, David A.; 0-9605056),* P.O. Box 725, Whitehouse, TX 75791 Tel 214-839-4837.

D A Ploss, *(Ploss, Douglas A.; 0-9603632),* 532 Gratton Rd., Lake Villa, IL 60046 Tel 312-356-5944.

D Adamson, *(Adamson, Douglas),* New Boston Rd., Box 173, Sanbornton, NH 03269.

D & A Pub, *(D & A Publishing Co.; 0-931578),* 2202 W. McDowell, Phoenix, AZ 85009 Tel 602-253-0795.

D Anderson, *(Anderson, David, Gallery, Inc.; 0-915956),* 521 W. 57th St., New York, NY 10019.

D Armstrong, *(Armstrong, D., Co., Inc.; 0-918464),* 2000-B Governor's Circle, Houston, TX 77092 Tel 713-688-1441.

D B Cheney, *(Cheney, Donna B.),* 607 Sunset, McCook, NE 69001.

D B Drew, *(Drew, Donald B.),* 251 Main St., Cumberland Center, ME 04021.

D B Lovett, *(Lovett, Donald B.; 0-9603328),* Rt. 1, Magalia, CA 95954.

D Bosco Pubns, *(Don Bosco Pubns.; 0-89944),* Div. of Salsian Society, Inc., Box T, 148 Main St., New Rochelle, NY 10802 Tel 914-632-6562. *Imprints:* Patron (Patron Books); Salesiana (Salesiana Publishers).

D Brown Bks, *(Brown, D., Books),* 511 Capp St., San Francisco, CA 94110.

D Bull, *(Bull, Donald; 0-9601190),* P.O. Box 106, Trumbull, CT 06611 Tel 203-261-2398.

D C McCormick, *(McCormick, D. C.),* 1 Isabel St., Massena, NY 13662.

D C Parker, *(Parker, D. Coffey),* 28 Abbot Rd., Springfield, IL 62704 Tel 217-787-7620.

D C Raemsch
See Raemsch Pubns

D C Watts, *(Watts, Dorothy C.; 0-9603402),* 6411 Avenida La Costa, N.E., Albuquerque, NM 87109 Tel 505-821-2256.

D Clement, *(Clement, David D. & Dorothy Z., ; 0-9601618),* 3931 Villa Ct., Fair Oaks, CA 95628 Tel 916-966-1666.

D D Murphy, *(Murphy, Dennis D.; 0-918788),* 4573 S. 23rd St., Apt. 1, Milwaukee, WI 53221.

D D Shepard, *(Shepard, Dennis D.; 0-9601234),* 1414 S. Miller St., Santa Maria, CA 93454 Tel 805-922-3527.

D David Pr, *(David, Deborah, Press; 0-930890),* P.O. Box 664, Ardmore, PA 19003 Tel 215-649-0998.

D E Shaffer, *(Shaffer, Dale E.; 0-915060),* 437 Jennings Ave., Salem, OH 44460 Tel 216-337-3348.

D E Wirth, *(Wirth, Diane E.; 0-9602096),* P.O. Box 945, Danville, CA 94526.

D H Ent, *(D. H. Enterprises; 0-934628),* P.O. Box 201, Grawn, MI 49637 Tel 616-946-2897.

D H Sanderson, *(Sanderson, Dorothy H.),* 15 Maple Ave., Ellenville, NY 12428 Tel 914-647-5305.

D H Tolzmann, *(Tolzmann, Don Heinrich),* 2545 Harrison Ave., Cincinnati, OH 45211; Moved,Left No Forwarding Address.

D Hannon, *(Hannon, Douglas; 0-937866),* Rte. 2, Box 991, Odessa, FL 33556; Dist. by: Great Outdoors Publishing Co., St. Petersburg, FL 33714.

D Huang, *(Huang, Dorothy; 0-9604498),* 831 Thicket, Houston, TX 77079.

D J Bolton, *(Bolton, D. Joyce; 0-9602368),* 1476 Phantom Ave., San Jose, CA 95125.

D J Fortunato, *(Fortunato, Donald J.),* 7 Halko Dr., Cedar Knolls, NJ 07927 Tel 201-540-8852.

D J Gingery, *(Gingery, David J.; 0-9604330),* 2045 Boonville, Springfield, MO 65803.

D J Perkins, *(Perkins, Dorothy J.; 0-9604742),* Box 194, Moylan, PA 19065.

D Jaffe, *(Jaffe, David; 0-9601782),* P.O. Box 4173, Arlington, VA 22204 Tel 703-920-4943.

D Jenkins, *(Jenkins, Doris),* 4827 Hillside Ave., Lincoln, NE 68506 Tel 402-488-4200.

D Kermode, *(Kermode, Doug; 0-9602202),* P.O. Box 8087, Long Beach, CA 90808.

D Knox, *(Knox, Daryl K.),* P.O. Box 38, Fortuna, ND 58844 Tel 701-834-2292.

D L Howard, *(Howard, Daniel L.; 0-936144),* P.O. Box 41432, Los Angeles, CA 90041 Tel 213-258-2121.

D L Price, *(Price, David L.; 0-9604482),* 1954 Old Hickory Blvd., Brentwood, TN 37027.

D Landman
See Dennis-Landman

D Lem Assocs, *(Lem, Dean, Associates, Inc.; 0-914218),* 9229 Sunset Blvd, Suite 301, Los Angeles, CA 90069 Tel 213-275-3129; Orders to: P.O. Box 46086, Los Angeles, CA 90046.

D Lewis Pub, *(Lewis, David, Pubns; 0-912012),* 216 W. 89th St., New York, NY 10024 Tel 212-799-1144; Moved, Left No Forwarding Address.

D Luebbers, *(Luebbers, David J.),* 78 S. Jackson, Denver, CO 80209 Tel 303-322-0191.

D Lyons, *(Lyons, David),* General Delivery, Merrimack, NH 03054; Orders to: 16 Hampshire Dr., Room C, Nashua, NH 03060.

D M Battle Pubns, *(Battle, Dennis M., Pubns.; 0-933464),* P.O. Box 67, Elyria, OH 44036 Tel 216-323-1729.

D M Chase, *(Chase, Don M.; 0-918634),* 8569 Lawrence Lane, Sebastopol, CA 95472.

D M Gaev, *(Gaev, Dorothy M.; 0-9600968),* Upminister H164, Deerfield Beach, FL 33441.

D M Grant, *(Grant, Donald M.; 0-937986),* West Kingston, RI 02892 Tel 401-783-3266; Dist. by: F&SF Book Co., P.O. Box 415, Staten Island, NY 10302; Dist. by: Bud Plant Inc., P.O. Box 1886, Grass Valley, CA 95945.

D M Moore, *(Moore, Diane M.; 0-9604030),* P.O. Box 1073, New Iberia, LA 70560.

D McPhail, *(McPhail, David),* 242 Trinity Ave., Berkeley, CA 94708.

D Mason, *(Mason, D.; 0-9601392),* 22 Old Homestead Rd., Westford, MA 01886 Tel 617-692-8958.

D Moriarty, *(Moriarty, Dan, Associates),* 1410 Second Ave., Newport, MN 55055 Tel 612-459-1857.

D P Enter, *(D.P. Enterprises; 0-935208),* P.O. Box 23241, Phoenix, AZ 85063.

D Polk, *(Polk, Donice; 0-9605430),* 1973 Reedy, Highland, CA 92346.

D Ponicsan, *(Ponicsan, Darryl),* P.O. Box 5094, Ojai, CA 93023 Tel 805-646-4215.

D R Bell, *(Bell, D. Rayford; 0-9604820),* 1225 McDaniel Ave., Evanston, IL 60202.

D R Benbow, *(Benbow, Doris R.),* 441 Clairmont Ave., Apt. 1014, Decatur, GA 30030 Tel 404-378-7028.

D Rendina, *(Rendina, Dave, Publishing Co.),* 1 Lake Rd., Newfield, NJ 08344.

D S Coleman, *(Coleman, Dorothy S.; 0-910396),* 4315 Van Ness St., Washington, DC 20016 Tel 202-966-2655.

D Schiedt, *(Schiedt, Duncan P.; 0-9603528),* Orders to: R.R. 1, Box 217A, Pittsboro, IN 46167 Tel 317-852-8528.

D Shinn Pubns, *(Shinn, Duane; 0-912732),* P.O. Box 192, Medford, OR 97501.

D Smith, *(Smith, Doug; 0-9602728),* P.O. Box 260, Corvallis, OR 97330 Tel 503-754-3434.

D Van Nostrand, *(Van Nostrand, D., Co.; 0-442),* 135 W. 50th St., New York, NY 10020 Tel 212-265-8700; Orders to: LEPI Order Processing, 7625 Empire Dr., Florence, KY 41042.

D Varden Pubns, *(Dolly Varden Pubns.),* P.O. Box 2017, Oceanside, CA 92054 Tel 714-729-1736.

D W Carrey, *(Carrey, Dixeann W.; 0-931882),* 2922 N. State Rd. 7, Suite 107, Margate, FL 33063.

D W Harmon, *(Harmon, Donald W.; 0-916314),* P.O. Box 1645, Downey, CA 90241; Moved, Left No Forwarding Address.

D W Hemingway, *(Hemingway, Donald W.),* 309 S. Tenth W., Salt Lake City, UT 84104; Dist. by: George Mc. Co. Inc., P.O. Box 15671, Salt Lake City, UT 84115.

D White, *(White, David, Co.; 0-87250),* 14 Vanderventer Ave., Port Washington, NY 11050 Tel 516-944-9325.

D Zdenek Pubns, *(Zdenek, Dale, Publications; 0-916902),* 31352 Via Colinas, Westlake, CA 91360 Tel 213-888-6891.

Da Capo, *(Da Capo Press, Inc.; 0-306),* 233 Spring St., New York, NY 10013 Tel 212-620-8001.

Dabbs, *(Dabbs, Jack A.; 0-911494),* 2806 Cherry Lane, Austin, TX 78703 Tel 512-472-7463.

Dabor Sci Pubns, *(Dabor Science Pubns.; 0-89561),* Div. of Dabor Services, Inc., 297 Concord Ave., Oceanside, NY 11523 Tel 516-293-3350.

DaCa Pub, *(DaCa Publishing Co.; 0-917904),* 1636 Monaco Dr., St. Louis, MO 63122 Tel 314-966-5678.

Dada Ctr, *(Dada Center Pubns.; 0-930608),* 2319 W. Dry Creek Rd., Healdsburg, CA 95448 Tel 707-433-2161.

Dadant & Sons, *(Dadant & Sons, Inc.; 0-915698),* 51 S. Second St., Hamilton, IL 62341 Tel 217-847-3324.

Dade Variety Pr, *(Dade Variety Press),* 18154 N. W. Second Ave., Miami, FL 33169.

Daedalus Pubns, *(Daedalus Pubns., Inc.; 0-937448),* 1153 Oxford Rd., Deerfield, IL 60015.

Dafran Hse, *(Dafran House Pubs., Inc.),* 185 Bethpage Sweet Hollow Rd., Old Bethpage, NY 11804; Moved, Left No Forwarding Address.

Dahlem, *(Dahlem Konferenzen Berlin),* Dist. by: Heyden & Son Inc., 247 S. 41st St., Philadelphia, PA 19104 Tel 215-382-6673.

Daily Planet, *(Daily Planet Almanac, Inc., The; 0-939882),* P.O. Box 1641, Boulder, CO 80302 Tel 303-440-0268.

Daimax Pub Hse, *(Daimax Publishing House),* Dist. by: Press Pacifica, Ltd., P.O. Box 47, Kailua, HI 96734.

Dairy Goat, *(Dairy Goat Journal),* P.O. Box 1808, Scottsdale, AZ 85252 Tel 602-991-4628.

Daisy, *(Daisy Press; 0-935424),* P.O. Box 884, La Mesa, CA 92041.

Dake Bible, *(Dake Bible Sales),* P.O. Box 625, Lawrenceville, GA 30246.

Dakota Microfilm, *(Dakota Microfilm Service, Inc.),* 501 N. Dale St., St. Paul, MN 55103; Provides Enlarged Textbooks and Other Educational Materials, with Permission from the Original Publisher.

Dakota Pr, *(Dakota Press; 0-88249),* University of South Dakota, Vermillion, SD 57069 Tel 605-677-5281.

Dale Bks, *(Dale Books),* 51 Springdale Ave., Waterbury, CT 06708 Tel 203-753-0255.

Dale Books Inc, *(Dale Books, Inc.; 0-89559),* Subs. of Davis Pubns. Inc., 380 Lexington Ave., New York, NY 10017 Tel 212-949-9190.

Dallas Mus, *(Dallas Museum of Fine Arts),* Fair Park, Dallas, TX 75226 Tel 214-421-4188.

Dalmas & Ricour, *(Dalmas & Ricour; 0-940066),* 6322 Cool Shade Dr., Fayetteville, NC 28303.

Dalton, *(Dalton, Pat),* 410 Lancaster Ave., Haverford, PA 19041.

Damas Pub, *(Damas Publishing Co.; 0-917268),* 6651 Sunset Blvd., Suite 202, Hollywood, CA 90028 Tel 213-851-4653.

Damascus Hse, *(Damascus House),* Dist. by: Dial Press, 1 Dag Hammarskjold Plaza, 245 E. 47th St., New York, NY 10017.

Dame Pubns, *(Dame Pubns., Inc.; 0-931920),* P.O. Box 35556, Houston, TX 77035 Tel 713-995-1000.

Dan River Pr, *(Dan River Press; 0-89754),* P.O. Box 249, Stafford, VA 22554 Tel 703-659-6771.

Dana Corp, *(Dana Corp.),* Automotive Marketing Div., Educ., Dept. P.O. Box 2748, Toledo, OH 43606.

Danad, *(Danad Pub. Co; 0-930036),* Pub. Div. of Dance Magazine, 1180 Avenue of the Americas, New York, NY 10036 Tel 212-921-9300.

Danbury Pr, *(Danbury Press),* P.O. Box 613, Suffern, NY 10901 Tel 914-357-0420.

Dance Films, *(Dance Films Assn., Inc.; 0-914438),* 250 W. 57th St., Rm. 2201, New York, NY 10019 Tel 212-586-2142.

Dance Horiz, *(Dance Horizons; 0-87127),* 1801 E. 26th St., Brooklyn, NY 11229 Tel 212-645-9607.

Dance Notation, *(Dance Notation Bureau Press; 0-932582),* 505 Eighth Ave., New York, NY 10018 Tel 212-736-4350.

Dancin Bee, *(Dancin' Bee Co.; 0-933192),* 107 Maple Ave., P.O. Box 237, Ridgely, MD 21660.

Dancing Rock, *(Dancing Rock Press; 0-931022),* 67 Albion St., San Francisco, CA 94103; Moved, Left No Forwarding Address.

D&E Career Pub, *(D & E Career Publishing Co.),* 1311 E. Chestnut Unit B, Santa Ana, CA 92701 Tel 714-836-9400.

Dandelion Pr, *(Dandelion Press; 0-89799),* 184 Fifth Ave., New York, NY 10010 Tel 212-929-0090.

Dandrea, *(Dandrea, Robert A.; 0-9600662),* P.O. Box 6536, Colorado Springs, CO 80934; Moved,Left No Forwarding Address.

Dandy Lion, *(Dandy Lion Pubns.; 0-931724),* P.O. Box 190, San Luis Obispo, CA 93406 Tel 805-544-3598.

Dangary Pub, *(Dangary Publishing Co.; 0-910484),* 606 N. Eutaw St., Baltimore, MD 21201 Tel 301-728-3322.

Dansk Blue Bk, *(Dansk Blue Books; 0-87977),* Dist. by: Parliament News, Inc., 21314 Lassen St., Chatsworth, CA 91311.

Dante U Am, *(Dante Univ. of America Press, Inc.; 0-937832),* Box 843, 21 Station St., Brookline Village, MA 02147 Tel 617-734-2045.

Dante Univ Bkshlf, *(Dante Univ. Bookshelf),* Dist. by: Branden Press, Inc., P.O. Box 843, 21 Station St., Brookline Village, MA 02147 Tel 617-734-2045.

Dantree Pr, *(Dantree Press; 0-89560),* 44 W. 62nd St., Suite 4F, New York, NY 10023 Tel 212-542-4327; Orders to: ISBS, Box 555, Forest Grove, OR 97116.

Danubian, *(Danubian Press, Inc.; 0-87934),* Rte. 1, Box 59, Astor, FL 32002 Tel 904-759-2255.

Daratech, *(Daratech Associates; 0-938484),* P.O. Box 410, Cambridge, MA 02238.

Darby Bks, *(Darby Books; 0-89987),* P.O. Box 148, Darby, PA 19023.

D'arc Pr, *(D'arc Press),* 340 W. 72nd St., New York, NY 10023; Moved Left No Forwarding Address.

Darien Hse, *(Darien House Books; 0-88201),* c/o Images Graphiques, 37 Riverside Dr., New York, NY 10023 Tel 212-787-4000.

Darin Devel, *(Darin Development Corp.; 0-930114),* P.O. Box 986, San Juan Capistrano, CA 92693 Tel 714-661-7074.

Daring Pr, *(Daring Press; 0-938936),* 5060 Navarre Rd., S.W., Canton, OH 44706.

Dark Horse, *(Dark Horse Inc.; 0-937762),* 17705 S. Western Ave., Suite 1, Gardenia, CA 90248 Tel 213-575-6488.

Dark Sun, *(Dark Sun Press; 0-937968),* c/o MFA Photography, Rochester Institute of Technology, 1 Lomb Mem. Dr., Rochester, NY 14623 Tel 716-475-2616.

Darrow, *(Darrow, Frank M.; 0-912636),* P.O. Box 305, Trona, CA 93562; 82194 7th St., Argus, CA 93562.

Dartnell Corp, *(Dartnell Corp.; 0-85013),* 4660 Ravenswood Ave., Chicago, IL 60640 Tel 312-561-4000.

Darvill Outdoor, *(Darvill Outdoor Pubns.; 0-915740),* 1819 Hickox Rd., Mt. Vernon, WA 98273 Tel 206-424-1298.

Darwin, *(Darwin Press, Inc.; 0-87850),* P.O. Box 2202, Princeton, NJ 08540 Tel 609-924-3938.

Data Courier, *(Data Courier, Inc.; 0-914604),* 620 S. Fifth St., Louisville, KY 40202 Tel 502-582-4111.

Data Financial, *(Data Financial Press; 0-933088),* P.O. Box 801, Menlo Park, CA 94025; Dist. by: Caroline House, P.O. Box 161, Thornwood, NY 10594.

Data Hse, *(Data House Publishing Co., Inc.; 0-935922),* 7525 N. Wolcott Ave., Chicago, IL 60626 Tel 312-973-5109.

DATA Inc, *(D.A.T.A. Inc.; 0-87885),* Div. of Cordura Publications, Inc., 45 U.S. Hwy 46, Pine Brook, NJ 07058 Tel 201-227-3740.

Database Serv, *(Database Services; 0-939920),* 885 N. San Antonio Rd., Los Altos, CA 94022 Tel 415-948-8339; Dist. by: Online, Inc., 11 Tannery Lane, Weston, CT 06883.

Datar Pub, *(Datar Publishing Co.; 0-931572),* 6410 Cates Ave., Suite 2W, University City, MO 63130.

Datarule, *(Datarule Publishing Co., Inc.; 0-911740),* P.O. Box 448, New Canaan, CT 06840 Tel 914-533-2263.

Daughters, *(Daughters Publishing Co., Inc.; 0-913780),* MS 590, P.O. Box 42999, Houston, TX 77042.

DAurora Pr, *(D'Aurora Press; 0-933022),* 190 Cascade Dr., Mill Valley, CA 94941.

Davenport, *(Davenport, May, Publisher; 0-9603118),* 26313 Purissima Rd., Los Altos Hills, CA 94022 Tel 415-948-6499.

Davey, *(Davey, Daniel, & Co., Inc., Pubs.; 0-8088),* P. O. Box 6088, Hartford, CT 06106 Tel 203-525-0997.

David & Charles, *(David & Charles, Inc.; 0-7153),* P.O. Box 57, North Pomfret, VT 05053 Tel 802-457-1911.

Davida Pubns, *(Davida Pubns.; 0-9603022),* P.O. Box 1925, West Covina, CA 91790 Tel 213-968-4148; Dist. by: Devorss & Co., Marina Del Rey, CA 90291.

Davis Co, *(Davis, F. A., Co.; 0-8036),* 1915 Arch St., Philadelphia, PA 19103 Tel 215-568-2270.

Davis Mass, *(Davis Pubns., Inc.; 0-87192),* 50 Portland St., Worcester, MA 01608.

Davis Pub Co, *(Davis Publishing Co., Inc.; 0-89368),* 250 Potrero St., Santa Cruz, CA 95060 Tel 408-423-4968; Orders to: P.O. Box 841, Santa Cruz, CA 95061.

Davis Pubns, *(Davis Pubns., Inc.; 0-89559),* 380 Lexington Ave., New York, NY 10017 Tel 212-557-9100.

Davison, *(Davison Publishing Co.; 0-87515),* P.O. Box 477, Ridgewood, NJ 07451 Tel 201-445-3135.

Davlin Pubns, *(Davlin Pubns., Inc.; 0-914670),* 13521 Alondra Blvd., Santa Fe Springs, CA 90670 Tel 213-649-2620; Moved Left No Forwarding Address.

DAW Bks, *(DAW Books; 0-87997),* Dist. by: New American Library, 1633 Broadway, New York, NY 10019 Tel 212-397-8000.

Dawn Horse Pr, *(Dawn Horse Press; 0-913922),* P.O. Box 3680, Clearlake Highlands, CA 95422 Tel 707-994-8281; Dist. by: Publisher's Services, Box 3914, San Rafael, CA 94902 Tel 415-549-3033.

Dawn Valley, *(Dawn Valley Press; 0-936014),* P.O. Box 58, New Wilmington, PA 16142 Tel 412-946-2948.

Dawne-Leigh, *(Dawne-Leigh Pubns.; 0-89742),* 231 Adrian Rd., Millbrae, CA 94030 Tel 415-692-4500; Dist. by: Atheneum Publishers, 597 Fifth Ave., New York, NY 10017 Tel 212-486-2655.

Dawson & Co, *(Dawson & Co.; 0-918010),* P.O. Box 40157, Tucson, AZ 85717 Tel 602-323-8128.

Dawson County, *(Dawson County Bicentennial Committee),* 1500 River Ave., Glendive, MT 59330 Tel 406-365-2760.

Dawsons, *(Dawson's Book Shop; 0-87093),* 535 N. Larchmont Blvd., Los Angeles, CA 90004 Tel 213-469-2186.

Day Care & Child Dev, *(Day Care & Child Development Council of America, Inc.),* Dist. by: Gryphon House, Inc., P.O. Box 217, Mt. Rainier, MD 20822 Tel 301-779-6200.

Day Star, *(Day Star Pubs.; 0-932994),* 707 Graham Hill Rd., Santa Cruz, CA 95060.

Daystar Pub Co, *(Daystar Publishing Co.),* P.O. Box 707, Angwin, CA 94508.

Dayton Labs, *(Dayton Laboratories; 0-916750),* 3235 Dayton Ave., Lorain, OH 44055 Tel 216-246-1397.

DBA Bks, *(DBA Books; 0-9605276),* 130 Marlborough St., Boston, MA 02116.

DBI, *(DBI Books, Inc.; 0-910676),* 1 Northfield Plaza, Northfield, IL 60093 Tel 312-441-7010; Dist. by: Follett Publishing Co., P.O. Box 5705, Chicago, IL 60680.

DCA, *(DCA, The Darien Community Assn., Inc.),* Orders to: Tory Hole, 274 Middlesex Rd., Darien, CT 06820.

DCarlin Pub, *(D'carlin Publishing; 0-939342),* 5850 Avenida Encinas, Carlsbad, CA 92008 Tel 714-438-7758.

DCT Ent, *(DCT Enterprises; 0-9604998),* 2888 Bluff St., Suite 218, Boulder, CO 80301.

DDC Pubns, *(DDC Pubns.; 0-932084),* 5386 Hollister Ave., Santa Barbara, CA 93111 Tel 805-964-7448.

De Funiak, *(De Funiak, William Q.; 0-911936),* 223 Trevethan Ave., Santa Cruz, CA 95062 Tel 408-423-7662.

De Graff, *(De Graff, John, Inc.; 0-8286),* Clinton Corners, NY 12514; Dist. by: International Marine Publishing Co., 21 Elm St., Camden, ME 04843 Tel 207-236-4342.

De Gruyter, *(De Gruyter, Walter, Inc.; 3-11; 0-89925),* 200 Saw Mill River Rd., Hawthorne, NY 10532 Tel 914-747-0110.

De Karsan, *(De Karsan Publishing Co.; 0-9602308),* Subs. of W. F. Hay & Co., P.O. Box 28404, San Diego, CA 92128 Tel 714-283-5656.

De La Ree, *(De La Ree, Gerry, Publisher; 0-938192),* 7 Cedarwood Lane, Saddle River, NJ 07458 Tel 201-327-6621.

De Serio, *(De Serio, Louis F.; 0-9603568),* 1744 N. 93rd St., Mesa, AZ 85207 Tel 602-986-4226.

De Vito, *(DeVito Enterprises; 0-910506),* 28 Dean St., Box 11, Warehouse Point, CT 06088 Tel 203-623-3152.

De Vorss, *(De Vorss & Co.; 0-87516),* P.O. Box 550, Marina Del Rey, CA 90291 Tel 213-870-7478.

De Young Pr, *(De Young Press; 0-936128),* Box 14, Rte. 2, Hull, IA 51239.

Deal Pubns, *(Deal Pubns.),* 11326 Ranchito St., El Monte, CA 91732; Religious Publications Only.

Dean & Assoc, *(Dean & Associates; 0-933370),* P.O. Box 2943, Eugene, OR 97402.

Dean Co WA, *(Dean Co. of Washington; 0-934256),* 2021 K St., N.W., Suite 305, Washington, DC 20006.

Dean Pubns, *(Dean Pubns.; 0-939052),* 2204 El Canto Circle, Rancho Cordova, CA 95670.

Dear Kids, *(Dear Kids Pubs.),* Currierville Rd., Newton, NH 03858 Tel 603-382-7503.

Death Ed Bks, *(Death Education Books; 0-9601336),* 180 S. Broad St., Prescott, WI 54021.

Death Valley Fortyniners, *(Death Valley 49ers, Inc.; 0-936932),* Death Valley, CA 92328.

Decatur Hse, *(Decatur House Press, Ltd; 0-916276),* 2122 Decatur Place, N.W., Washington, DC 20008 Tel 202-387-3913.

December Pr, *(December Press; 0-913204),* 6232 N. Hoyne, No. 1c, Chicago, IL 60659 Tel 312-973-7360.

Decibel, *(Decibel Books; 0-914672),* P.O. Box 358, Norman, OK 73070.

Deciduous, *(Deciduous; 0-9601640),* 1456 W. 54th St., Cleveland, OH 44102 Tel 216-651-7725.

Deco-Pr Pub, *(Deco-Press Publishing Co.; 0-937016),* 500 E. 84th Ave., Box 29489, Denver, CO 80229.

Dectur Corp, *(Dectur Corp.; 0-9602228),* 2878 Forest St., Denver, CO 80207.

Dee Pub Co, *(Dee Publishing Co.; 0-934476),* 864 S. Commercial, Salem, OR 97302 Tel 503-363-2410.

Deem Corp, *(Deem Corp., The; 0-918822),* 5860 W. Sioux Dr,, Sedalia, CO 80135 Tel 303-688-9249.

Deep River Pr, *(Deep River Press; 0-935232),* 7319 Dinwiddie St., Downey, CA 90241 Tel 213-928-6815.

Deepstar Pubns, *(Deepstar Pubns.; 0-918888),* P.O. Box 1266, Crestine, CA 92325 Tel 714-338-4440.

Deer Crossing, *(Deer Crossing Press; 0-932792),* Rte. 1, Box 18, Paducah, KY 42001.

Deere & Co, *(Deere & Co. Technical Services; 0-86691),* Dept. 333, John Deere Rd., Moline, IL 61265.

Deerfield Comm, *(Deerfield Communications Corp.),* 320 E. 65th St., New York, NY 10021 Tel 212-794-1313.

Deermouse, *(Deermouse Press; 0-9600596),* 4 Berkeley Place, Cambridge, MA 02138 Tel 617-876-0836.

Definition, *(Definition Press; 0-910492),* 141 Greene St., New York, NY 10012 Tel 212-777-4490.

Dehack, *(Dehack Effort),* P. O. Box 922, Campbell, CA 95008 Tel 408-265-8799.

Dehoff Pubns, *(Dehoff Pubns.),* 749 N.W. Broad St., Murfreesboro, TN 37130 Tel 615-893-8322.

Dekker, *(Dekker, Marcel, Inc.; 0-8247),* 270 Madison Ave., New York, NY 10016 Tel 212-889-9595.

Del Mus Nat Hist, *(Delaware Museum of Natural History; 0-913176),* P.O.Box 3937, Greenville, DE 19807 Tel 302-658-9111; Moved, Left No Forwarding Address.

Del Oeste, *(Del Oeste Press; 0-89632),* P.O. Box 397, Tarzana, CA 91356.

Del Valley, *(Delaware Valley Poets; 0-937158),* P.O. Box 6203, Lawrenceville, NJ 08648.

Delacorte, *(Delacorte Press),* c/o Dell Publishing Co., 1 Dag Hammarskjold Plaza, 245 E. 47th St., New York, NY 10017 Tel 212-832-7300. *Imprints:* E Friede (Eleanor Friede); Sey Lawr (Seymour Lawrence).

Delafield Pr, *(Delafield Press; 0-916872),* P.O. Box 335, Suttons Bay, MI 49682 Tel 616-271-3826; P.O. Box 09118, Detroit, MI 48209 Tel 313-849-5123.

Delair, *(Delair/Consolidated; 0-8326),* Div. of Delair Publishing Co., 420 Lexington Ave., Rm. 1621, New York, NY 10170 Tel 212-867-2255. *Imprints:* Culinary Arts (Culinary Arts Institute).

Delamar Duverus
See Duverus Pub

Delancey Pr, *(Delancey Press; 0-9601128),* 441 W. 22nd St., Gdn, New York, NY 10011.

Delaney, *(Delaney Pubns.; 0-915856),* Dist. by: Buckley Publications, Inc, 233 E. Erie St., Suite 402, Chicago, IL 60611 Tel 312-943-2066.

Delanie Way, *(Delanie Way Pub.; 0-9602290),* 685 Delanie Way, Stone Mountain, GA 30083 Tel 404-292-9121.

Delbridge Pub Co, *(Delbridge Publishing Co.; 0-88232),* P.O. Box 2989, Stanford, CA 94305 Tel 408-446-3131.

Delcon, *(Delcon Corp.; 0-934856),* P.O. Box 323, Harlan St. Rt., Eddyville, OR 97343.

Delford Pr, *(Delford Press; 0-931726),* P.O. Box 27, Oradell, NJ 07649 Tel 201-262-0647.

Delilah Comm, *(Delilah Communications, Ltd.; 0-933348),* 148 E. 53rd St., New York, NY 10022; Dist. by: Dell Publishing Co., 1 Dag Hammarskjold Plaza, 245 E. 47th St., New York, NY 10017.

Dell, *(Dell Publishing Co., Inc.; 0-440),* 1 Dag Hammarskjold Plaza, 245 E. 47th St., New York, NY 10017 Tel 212-832-7300. *Imprints:* Banbury (Banbury); Bryans (Bryans); Chapel (Chapel Books); Dell Trade Pbks (Dell Trade Paperbacks); Delta (Delta Books); LE (Laurel Editions); LFL (Laurel Leaf Library); MB (Mayflower Books); Standish (Standish); YB (Yearling Books).

Dell Trade Pbks *Imprint of* **Dell**

Delmar, *(Delmar Pubs.; 0-8273),* Div. of Litton Educ. Pub., Inc., 50 Wolf Rd., Albany, NY 12205; Orders to: 7625 Empire Dr., Florence, KY 41042.

Delmas Bks, *(Delmas Books; 0-932912),* 4605 5 Mile Rd., Ann Arbor, MI 48104.

DeLong & Assocs, *(DeLong & Associates; 0-9603414),* P.O. Box 1732, Annapolis, MD 21404 Tel 301-923-2308.

DeLorme Pub, *(DeLorme Publishing Co.; 0-89933),* P.O. Box 81, Yarmouth, ME 04096 Tel 207-846-9764.

Delphi Info, *(Delphi Information Sciences, Inc.; 0-930306),* 1414 Sixth St., Santa Monica, CA 90401.

Delphi Pr WA, *(Delphi Press; 0-939202),* 475 L'Enfant Plaza, Suite 2970, Washington, DC 20024 Tel 202-554-7930.

Delphian Pr, *(Delphian Press; 0-89739),* Sheridan, OR 97378.

Delta *Imprint of* **Dell**

Delta Sales, *(Delta Sales; 0-931626),* 399 Southgate Ave., Daly City, CA 94015.

Delta Systems, *(Delta Systems Co., Inc.; 0-937354),* 215 N. Arlington Hts. Rd., Arlington Hts, IL 60004 Tel 312-394-5760.

Deluxe Co, *(Deluxe Co., The; 0-938012),* P.O. Box 4246, Shreveport, LA 71104.

Dembner Bks, *(Dembner Books; 0-934878),* Div. of Red Dembner Enterprises Corp., 1841 Broadway, New York, NY 10023 Tel 212-265-1250; Dist. by: W.W. Norton & Co., Inc., 500 Fifth Ave., New York, NY 10036 Tel 212-354-5500.

Demecon, *(Demecon Pubs.),* P.O. Box 3759, Laureldale, PA 19605.

Demeter *Imprint of* **Times Bks**

Demetrius-Victor
See Caratzas Bros

DeMos Music, *(DeMos Music Pubns.; 0-940026),* P.O. Box 14125, Houston, TX 77021 Tel 713-433-5235.

Denco Intl, *(Denco International),* P.O. Box 2001, Hialeah, FL 33012 Tel 305-822-6666.

Denison, *(Denison, T. S., & Co., Inc.; 0-513),* 9601 Newton Ave. S., Minneapolis, MN 55431 Tel 612-888-1460.

Denlingers, *(Denlingers Pubs., Ltd.; 0-87714),* P.O. Box 76, Fairfax, VA 22030 Tel 703-631-1501.

Dennis-Landman, *(Dennis-Landman Pubs.; 0-930422),* 1150 18th St., Santa Monica, CA 90403 Tel 213-394-8683.

Dennison, *(Dennison Pubns.),* Dist. by: Borden Publishing Co., 1855 W. Main St., Alhambra, CA 91801.

Denoyer, *(Denoyer-Geppert Co.; 0-87453),* Subs. of Times Mirror Co., 5235 Ravenswood Ave., Chicago, IL 60640 Tel 312-561-9200.

Dental Control, *(Dental Control Products, Inc.),* 590 Valley Rd., Upper Montclair, NJ 97043.

Denver Art Mus, *(Denver Art Museum; 0-914738),* 100 W. 14th Ave. Pkwy., Denver, CO 80204 Tel 303-575-5582.

Denver Mus Natl Hist, *(Denver Museum of Natural History; 0-916278),* City Park, Denver, CO 80205 Tel 303-575-3931.

Denver Public, *(Denver Public Library),* 3840 York St., Denver, CO 80205 Tel 303-575-3907.

DeOro Bks, *(DeOro Books; 0-930482),* 1090 Bay Oaks Dr., Los Osos, CA 93403 Tel 805-528-4353; Inactive at This Time.

Dept Intl Health, *(Johns Hopkins Univ., Dept. of International Health; 0-912888),* Orders to: 615 N. Wolfe St., Baltimore, MD 21205.

Dept NE Stud, *(Univ. of Michigan, Dept. of Near Eastern Studies; 0-916798),* 3074 Frieze Bldg., Ann Arbor, MI 48109 Tel 313-764-0314; Dist. by: Eisenbrauns, P.O. Box 275, Winona Lake, IN 46590 Tel 219-269-2011.

Dept Sch Nurses
See Natl Assn Sch Nurses

Der Angriff, *(Der Angriff Pubns.; 0-9604770),* 1024 Sixth St., Huntington, WV 25701.

Derbibooks, *(Derbibooks, Inc.; 0-89009),* Dist. by: Book Sales Inc., 110 Enterprise Ave., Secaucus, NJ 07094 Tel 201-864-6341.

Derby Assoc, *(D.E.R.B.Y. Associates, Inc.; 0-9604692),* P.O. Box 724, Minneapolis, MN 55440.

Derek Prince, *(Prince, Derek, Pubns.; 0-934920),* P.O. Box 14306, Fort Lauderdale, FL 33302 Tel 305-763-5202.

Dermody, *(Dermody, Gail R. & Eugene M.),* P.O. Box 324, Lakewood, CA 90714.

DeRu's Fine Art, *(DeRu's Fine Art Books; 0-939370),* 9100 E. Artesia Blvd., Bellflower, CA 90706.

Deseret Bk, *(Deseret Book Co.; 0-87747),* 40 E. South Temple, P.O. Box 30178, Salt Lake City, UT 84130 Tel 801-534-1515.

Desert Botanical, *(Desert Botanical Garden),* P.O. Box 5415, Phoenix, AZ 85010 Tel 602-941-1217.

Desert First, *(Desert First Works, Inc.; 0-916556),* 3870 N. Vine Ave., Tucson, AZ 85719 Tel 602-326-1041.

Desert Pr, *(Desert Press, The; 0-937764),* Box K, Bouse, AZ 85325.

Desert Pub CA, *(Desert Publishing),* 255 N. el Cielo Rd., Suite 164, Palm Springs, CA 92262.

Design Ent SF, *(Design Enterprises of San Francisco; 0-932538),* P.O. Box 14695, San Francisco, CA 94114 Tel 415-282-8813.

Designectics, *(Designectics International Inc.)*, Dist. by: Advanced Professional Development Inc., 1888 Century Park E., Suite 10, Century City, Los Angeles, CA 90067 Tel 213-552-2122.

Designs Three, *(Designs III Pubs.)*, 515 W. Commonwealth Ave., Fullerton, CA 92632.

Despa Pr, *(Despa Press; 0-912952)*, 18 Winter St., Wrentham, MA 02093.

Desserco Pub, *(Desserco Publishing; 0-916698)*, P.O. Box 2433, Culver City, CA 90230 Tel 213-320-9101.

Destiny, *(Destiny Pubs.; 0-910500)*, 43 Grove St., Merrimac, MA 01860 Tel 617-364-9311.

Determined Prods, *(Determined Productions, Inc.; 0-915696)*, 315 Pacific Ave. at Battery, P.O. Box 2150, San Francisco, CA 94126 Tel 415-433-0660.

Deuce, *(Deuce of Clubs Press; 0-9600200)*, Rt. 3, Box 178, Arcata, CA 95521 Tel 707-822-2000.

Develop Learn, *(Developmental Learning Materials; 0-937018)*, 1 DLM Park, Allen, TX 75002.

Developmental Arts, *(Developmental Arts)*, P.O. Box 389, Arlington, MA 02174.

Devin, *(Devin-Adair Co., Inc.; 0-8159)*, 143 Sound Beach Ave., Old Greenwich, CT 06870 Tel 203-637-4531.

Devlin Hse, *(Devlin House Pubs.; 0-916874)*, Box 114, Medfield, MA 02052 Tel 617-359-6839.

Devon Pr, *(Devon Press, Inc.; 0-934160)*, 820 Miramar, Berkeley, CA 94707 Tel 415-526-1905.

Dewey, *(Dewey Shorthand Corp.; 0-9600026)*, Dist. by: Pitman Pub. Corp., 6 E. 43rd St., New York, NY 10017.

Dexter & Westbrook, *(Dexter & Westbrook, Ltd.; 0-87966)*, 958 Church St., Baldwin, NY 11510 Tel 516-868-6064.

Dghtrs St Paul, *(Daughters of St. Paul; 0-8198)*, 50 St. Paul's Ave., Boston, MA 02130 Tel 617-522-8911.

DH&R, *(Dowden, Hutchinson & Ross, Inc., 0-87933)*, 523 Sarah St., Box 699, Stroudsburg, PA 18360 Tel 717-421-4060; Dist. by: Academic Press, Inc., 111 Fifth Ave., New York, NY 10003; Orders for the Architecture & Planning Titles: 523 Sarah St., Box 699, Stroudsburg, Pa 18360.

Dharma Pub, *(Dharma Publishing; 0-913546; 0-89800)*, 2425 Hillside Ave., Berkeley, CA 94704 Tel 415-548-5407.

Di-Tri Bks, *(Di-Tri Books; 0-9603374)*, 261 Waubesa St., Madison, WI 53704 Tel 608-244-3466.

Diabetes, *(Diabetes Press of America, Inc.; 0-910508)*, 30 S.E. Eighth St., Miami, FL 33131.

Diablo, *(Diablo Press; 0-87297)*, P. O. Box 7042, Berkeley, CA 94707 Tel 415-527-1177.

Diablo West Pr, *(Diablo Western Press; 0-932438)*, P.O. Box 766, Alamo, CA 94507.

Dial, *(Dial Press; 0-8037)*, 1 Dag Hammarskjold Plaza, 245 E. 47th St., New York, NY 10017 Tel 212-832-7300.

Dialog Pr, *(Dialog Press; 0-936390)*, P.O. Box 5626, Hilton Head Island, SC 29928.

Dialogue Hse, *(Dialogue House Library; 0-87941)*, 80 E. 11th St., New York, NY 10003 Tel 212-673-5880.

Dialogue Pr Man World, *(Dialogue Press of Man & World, The; 0-932540)*, 246 Sparks Bldg., University Park, PA 16802 Tel 814-865-6397.

Diamond Heights, *(Diamond Heights Publishing Co., Inc.; 0-936182)*, 25 Grand View Ave., San Francisco, CA 94114.

Diamond Pubs, *(Diamond Pubs; 0-936510)*, 23818 Twin Pines Lane, Diamond Bar, CA 91765.

Diana Pr, *(Diana Press, Inc.; 0-88447)*, 4400 Market St., Oakland, CA 94608 Tel 415-658-5558.

Diane Bks, *(Diane Books Publishing, Inc.; 0-88264)*, 1111 E. Chevy Chase, Glendale, CA 91205 Tel 213-244-5600.

Dibco Pr, *(Dibco Press; 0-910510)*, 2570 Sue Ave., San Jose, CA 95111 Tel 208-295-9107.

Dickenson, *(Dickenson Publishing Co.; 0-8221)*, c/o Wadsworth, Inc., 10 Davis Dr., Belmont, CA 94002 Tel 415-595-2350.

Dicul Pub, *(Dicul Publishing; 0-938784)*, P.O. Box 368, Nashville, IN 47448.

Didactic Syst, *(Didactic Systems Inc.; 0-89401)*, P.O. Box 457, Cranford, NJ 07016 Tel 212-789-2194.

Diesel Fuel, *(Diesel Fuel Services, Inc.)*, P.O. Box 256, South Salem, NY 10590 Tel 212-684-3818.

Dietary Res, *(Dietary Research)*, 5201 16th N.E., Seattle, WA 98105.

Dietz, *(Dietz Press; 0-87517)*, 109 E. Cary, Richmond, VA 23219 Tel 804-648-0195.

Digital Pr, *(Digital Press/Digital Equipment Corp.; 0-932376)*, 12 Crosby Dr., Bldg. D-2, Bedford, MA 01730; Orders to: 12-A Esquire Rd., North Billerica, MA 01862.

Dildo Pr
See Mho & Mho

Dilithium Pr, *(Dilithium Press; 0-918398)*, 11000 S.W. 11th St., Beaverton, OR 97005 Tel 503-646-2713; Orders to: P.O. Box 606, Beaverton, OR 97075.

Dillon, *(Dillon Press, Inc.; 0-87518)*, 500 S. Third St., Minneapolis, MN 55415 Tel 612-336-2691.

Dillon-Donnelly, *(Dillon-Donnelly; 0-933508)*, 7058 Lindell Blvd., St. Louis, MO 63130 Tel 314-862-6239.

Dillon-Liederbach, *(Dillon/Liederbach, Inc.; 0-913228)*, 2720 E. Boulevard, Cleveland, OH 44104 Tel 216-231-8896.

Dillon-Tyler Pubs, *(Dillon-Tyler Pubs.; 0-916280)*, P.O. Box 971, Woodland, CA 95695 Tel 707-253-8907.

Dimension Bks, *(Dimension Books; 0-87193)*, Denville, NJ 07834.

Dimensionist Pr, *(Dimensionist Press; 0-9602374)*, 5931 Stanton Ave., Highland, CA 92346 Tel 714-862-7767.

Dimond Pubs, *(Dimond Pubs.)*, 3431 Fruitvale Ave., Oakland, CA 94602.

Dinograph SW, *(Dinograph Southwest, Inc.; 0-932680)*, P.O. Box 1600, Alamogordo, NM 88310.

Dinosaur, *(Dinosaur Press, The)*, P.O. Box 372, Amherst, MA 01004 Tel 413-549-0404.

Diotima Bks, *(Diotima Books; 0-935772)*, Box H, Glen Carbon, IL 62034.

DiPaul, *(DiPaul, H. Bert; 0-9605418)*, 1066 Brennan Dr., Warminster, PA 18974.

Diplomatic Fla, *(Diplomatic Press; 0-910512)*, Goodbody Hall 101, Indiana Univ., Bloomington, IN 47405 Tel 812-337-2398.

Directions
See Easi-Bild

Directions Pr, *(Directions Press)*, P.O. Box 1811, Thousand Oaks, CA 91360.

Directories Intl, *(Directories International, Inc.; 0-912794)*, 1718 Sherman Ave., Evanston, IL 60201 Tel 312-491-0019.

Directories Pub, *(Directories Publishing Co., Inc.)*, P.O. Box 1372, Ormond Beach, FL 32074 Tel 904-673-1241.

Directory of Art, *(Directory of Art & Antique Restoration; 0-916116)*, 465 California St., Suite 815, San Francisco, CA 94104; Moved, Left No Forwarding Address.

Discoveries, *(Discoveries Publishing Co.)*, P.O. Box 424, Glastonbury, CT 06033.

Discovery Bks, *(Discovery Books; 0-913976)*, 351 Broad St., Suite B1704, Newark, NJ 07104 Tel 201-483-7782.

Discovery Pub, *(Discovery Publishing Co.; 0-932422)*, 404 W. Chestnut, Yakima, WA 98902.

Discovery Stuff, *(Discovery Stuff; 0-930484)*, 5328 W. 67th St., Shawnee Mission, KS 66208.

Discus *Imprint of* **Avon**

Displays Sch, *(Displays for Schools, Inc.; 0-9600962)*, P.O. Box 163, Gainesville, FL 32602 Tel 904-373-2030.

Dissemination & Assessment, *(Dissemination & Assessment Center for Bilingual Education; 0-89417)*, 7703 N. Lamar, Austin, TX 78752 Tel 512-458-9131.

Distributors, *(Distributors, The)*, 720 S. Michigan, Suite 836, South Bend, IN 46618.

Ditton Bks, *(Ditton Books)*, 312 S. Franklin St., Syracuse, NY 13202.

Diversified Ent, *(Diversified Enterprises, Inc.; 0-9601790)*, Box 15, Posen, MI 49776 Tel 517-379-4678.

Divine Sci Fed, *(Divine Science Federation International)*, 1819 E. 14th Ave., Denver, CO 80218 Tel 303-322-7730.

Divry, *(Divry, D.C., Inc.; 0-910516)*, 293 Seventh Ave., New York, NY 10001 Tel 212-255-2153.

Dixie Pub, *(Dixie Publishing Co.; 0-89817)*, P.O. Box 1021, Port Heuneme, CA 93041. *Imprints:* Triangle (Triangle Publishing).

DJD Prods, *(DJD Productions; 0-9603964)*, 1712 S. Highland, Arlington Heights, IL 60005 Tel 312-640-7778.

DK Halcyon, *(DK Halcyon Group, Inc.; 0-939550)*, P.O. Box 120, Wright Brothers Sta., Dayton, OH 45409 Tel 513-435-6162.

DMR Pubns, *(D. M. R. Pubns., Inc.; 0-89552)*, 1410 E. Capitol Dr., Milwaukee, WI 53211 Tel 414-961-0120.

Dnomro Pubns, *(Dnomro Pubns.)*, 40 Fairmont Ave., Waltham, MA 02154.

Do It Now Foun, *(Do It Now Foundation; 0-89230)*, P. O. Box 5115, Phoenix, AZ 85010 Tel 602-257-0797.

Do It Yourself Pubs, *(Do-It-Yourself Pubs., Inc.; 0-932704)*, 150 Fifth Ave., New York, NY 10011 Tel 212-242-2840.

Doane Agricultural, *(Doane Agricultural Service, Inc.; 0-932250)*, 8900 Manchester Rd., St. Louis, MO 63144 Tel 314-968-1000.

Doctor Jazz, *(Doctor Jazz Press; 0-934002)*, P.O. Box 1043, Auburn, AL 36830.

Documentary Pubns, *(Documentary Pubns.; 0-89712)*, Rte. 12, Box 480, Salisbury, NC 28144.

DODC, *(Directory of Directors Co., Inc.; 0-936612)*, P.O. Box 462, Southport, CT 06490 Tel 203-255-8525.

Dodd, *(Dodd, Mead & Co.; 0-396)*, 79 Madison Ave., New York, NY 10016 Tel 212-685-6464.

Doebelin, *(Doebelin, Ernest O.; 0-9603834)*, 671 Timberlake Dr., Westerville, OH 43081 Tel 614-882-2670.

Dog Ear, *(Dog Ear Press, The; 0-937966)*, P.O. Box 155, Hulls Cove, ME 04644.

Dog Master, *(Dog-Master Systems)*, Div. of Environmental Research Labs, 606 Wilshire Blvd., Santa Monica, CA 90401 Tel 213-151-1601.

Doggeral Pr, *(Doggeral Press; 0-933726)*, 417 Seaview, Santa Barbara, CA 93108.

DOK Pubs, *(DOK Pubs., Inc.; 0-914634)*, 71 Radcliffe Rd., Buffalo, NY 14214 Tel 716-837-3391.

Doll Collect Am, *(Doll Collectors of America, Inc.; 0-9603210)*, Dist. by: Hazel Toon, 167 Round Cove Rd., Chatham, MA 02633.

Dolmen Pr *Imprint of* **Humanities**

Dolp *Imprint of* **Doubleday**

Dolphin Aquatics, *(Dolphin Aquatics; 0-9602982)*, 97 Parry Rd., Stamford, CT 06907 Tel 203-322-7944; Do Not Confuse with Dolphin, Imprint of Doubleday.

Doma, *(Doma Press; 0-917816)*, P.O. Box 1995, Chicago, IL 60690 Tel 312-784-2412.

Dome Pr, *(Dome Press, Inc.)*, 1169 Logan Ave., Elgin, IL 60120 Tel 312-695-6661.

Dome Pubns, *(Dome Pubns.; 0-88267)*, 1169 Logan Ave., Elgin, IL 60120 Tel 312-695-6661.

DOME Serv, *(D.O.M.E. Services)*, P.O. Box 5716, Sante Fe, NM 87502 Tel 505-983-9337.

Domina Bks *Imprint of* **Double M Pr**

Dominion Pr, *(Dominion Press; 0-912132)*, P.O. Box 37, San Marcos, CA 92069 Tel 714-746-9430.

Domjan Studio, *(Domjan Studio; 0-933652)*, West Lake Rd., Tuxedo Park, NY 10987 Tel 914-351-4596; Dist. by: Wind, Sun & Stars, Pheasant Ridge Rd., W. Redding, CT 06896 Tel 203-938-9476.

Domus Bks
See Quality Bks IL

Domus Bks *Imprint of* **Quality Bks IL**

Donahoe Pubs, *(Donahoe, Edward D., Pubs.; 0-938400)*, 2507 Hermitage Way, Louisville, KY 40222 Tel 502-425-3984.

Donald Franklin, *(Franklin, Donald; 0-914714)*, 7852 Ducor Ave., Canoga Park, CA 91304 Tel 213-883-4247.

Donato Music, *(Donato Music Publishing Co.; 0-935058)*, P.O. Box 415, New York, NY 10013 Tel 212-877-2741; Moved, Left No Forwarding Address.

Doneve Designs, *(Doneve Designs, Inc.; 0-89715)*, P.O. Box 1072, Saratoga, CA 95070 Tel 408-867-7556.

Dong Nam P & C, *(Dong Nam P & C Inc.; 0-914524)*, 2946 N. Lincoln Ave., Chicago, IL 60657 Tel 312-549-4660.

Donnelly, *(Donnelly, Sister Mary Louise),* P.O. Box 306, Burke, VA 22015.

Donning Co, *(Donning Co. Pubs.; 0-915442; 0-89865),* 5041 Admiral Wright Rd., Virginia Beach, VA 23462 Tel 804-499-0589. *Imprints:* Starblaze (Starblaze); Unilaw (Unilaw).

Doolco Inc, *(Doolco, Inc.; 0-914626),* 2016 Canton St., Dallas, TX 75201 Tel 214-741-3607.

Dooryard, *(Dooryard Press; 0-937160),* P.O. Box 221, Story, WY 82842.

Dorchester Savings
    See First Am Bank

Dorison Hse, *(Dorison House Pubs., Inc.; 0-916752),* 824 Park Square Bldg., Boston, MA 02116 Tel 617-426-1715.

Dorje Ling, *(Dorje Ling Pubs.; 0-915880),* P.O. Box 1410, San Rafael, CA 94902.

Dorland Pub Co, *(Dorland, Wayne E., Publishing Co.; 0-9603250),* Box 264, Mendham, NJ 07945 Tel 201-543-2694.

Dormac, *(Dormac, Inc; 0-86575),* P.O. Box 752, Beaverton, OR 97075 Tel 503-641-3128.

Dorrance, *(Dorrance & Co.; 0-8059),* Cricket Terrace Ctr., Ardmore, PA 19003 Tel 215-642-8303.

Dorsey, *(Dorsey Press; 0-256),* Div. of Richard D. Irwin, Inc., 1818 Ridge Rd., Homewood, IL 60430 Tel 312-798-6000.

Dos Reals Pub, *(Dos Reals Publishing; 0-915004),* 2490 Channing Way, Berkeley, CA 94704 Tel 415-548-6810.

Dos Tejedoras, *(Dos Tejedoras; 0-932394),* 3036 N. Snelling Ave., St. Paul, MN 55113 Tel 612-636-0205.

Dothard, *(Dothard, R. L., Associates; 0-912668),* RD 2, Brattleboro, VT 05301 Tel 802-254-9009.

Dots Pubns, *(Dots Pubns.),* P.O. Box 563, Ventura, CA 93002.

Double Crown, *(Double Crown; 0-935010),* P.O. Box 2212, Inglewood, CA 90305 Tel 714-779-8385.

Double Decker, *(Double Decker Pubns.; 0-938888),* 2800 Neilson Way, Suite 814, Santa Monica, CA 90405.

Double Elephant, *(Double Elephant Press),* Dist. by: Ten Speed Press, P.O. Box 7123, Berkeley, CA 94707.

Double Helix, *(Double Helix Press; 0-930578),* 1300 Tigertail Rd., Los Angeles, CA 90049 Tel 213-472-6452.

Double M Pr, *(Double M Press; 0-916634),* 16455 Tuba St., Sepulveda, CA 91343 Tel 213-366-1056. *Imprints:* Domina Bks (Domina Books).

Doubleday, *(Doubleday & Co., Inc.; 0-385),* 501 Franklin Ave., Garden City, NY 11530 Tel 516-294-4561. *Imprints:* Anch (Anchor Books); Anchor Pr (Anchor Press); CCG (College Course Guides); Dolp (Dolphin Books); Echo (Echo Books); Galilee (Galilee); Im (Image Books); Made (Made Simple Books); Waymark (Waymark Books); Windfall (Windfall); Zenith (Zenith Books); Zephyr (Zephyr).

DoubLeo Pubns, *(DoubLeo Pubns.; 0-936560),* 227 E. 11th St., New York, NY 10003 Tel 212-473-2739.

Doubleshoe, *(Doubleshoe Pubs.; 0-9603270),* 5131 E. Shea Blvd., Scottsdale, AZ 85253 Tel 602-948-0355.

Doug Butler, *(Butler, Doug; 0-916992),* P.O. Box 183, Alpine, TX 79830 Tel 915-837-5266.

Douglas-McKay, *(Douglas-McKay, Inc.; 0-915712),* P.O. Box 15565, Milwaukee, WI 53215 Tel 414-481-7207.

Douglas-West, *(Douglas-West Pubs., Inc.; 0-913264),* 7060 Hollywood Blvd., Suite 503, Los Angeles, CA 90028 Tel 213-461-8195.

Douglass Pubs, *(Douglass Publishers, Inc.; 0-935392),* P.O. Box 3270, Alexandria, VA 22302 Tel 703-522-4000; Dist. by: National Council on Alcoholism, 733 Third Ave., New York, NY 10017.

Dove *Imprint of* **Macmillan**

Dover, *(Dover Pubns., Inc.; 0-486),* 180 Varick St., New York, NY 10014 Tel 212-255-3755.

Dovetail, *(Dovetail Press; 0-935468),* 250 W. 94th St., New York, NY 10025 Tel 212-865-9216.

Dow Jones, *(Dow Jones Books; 0-87128),* P.O. Box 300, Princeton, NJ 08540 Tel 609-452-2000.

Dow Jones-Irwin, *(Dow Jones-Irwin; 0-87094),* 1818 Ridge Rd., Homewood, IL 60430 Tel 312-798-6000.

Dowling, *(Dowling College Press; 0-917428),* Oakdale L. I., NY 11769 Tel 516-589-6100.

Down East, *(Down East Books; 0-89272),* Div. of Down East Enterprise Inc., P.O. Box 679, Camden, ME 04843 Tel 207-594-9544.

Down There Pr, *(Down There Press; 0-9602324),* P.O. Box 2086, Burlingame, CA 94010 Tel 415-342-9867.

Downcast Pubn
    See Downeast Pubns

Downeast Pubns, *(Downeast Pubns.),* P.O. Box 679, Camden, ME 04843 Tel 207-594-4401.

Downhome, *(Downhome Publishing Co.; 0-935124),* P.O. Box 813, Forest Grove, OR 97116.

Downtown Poets, *(Downtown Poets Co-Op; 0-917402),* GPO Box 1720, Brooklyn, NY 11202 Tel 212-625-4245.

Downtown Res, *(Downtown Research & Development Center; 0-915910),* 270 Madison Ave., Suite 1505, New York, NY 10016 Tel 212-889-5666.

Doxey, *(Doxey, W. S.),* 550 N. White, Carrollton, GA 30117.

Dragon Co, *(Dragon Co.; 0-937456),* P.O. Box 14682, Houston, TX 77021.

Dragon Ent, *(Dragon Enterprises),* P.O. Box 200, Genoa, NV 89411 Tel 702-782-2486.

Dragon Gate, *(Dragon Gate; 0-937872),* 508 Lincoln St., Port Townsend, WA 98368.

Dragon Pr, *(Dragon Press),* Church St., Elizabethtown, NY 12932 Tel 518-873-2680.

Dragons Teeth, *(Dragons Teeth Press; 0-934218),* El Dorado National Forest, Georgetown, CA 95634.

Dragonwyck Pub, *(Dragonwyck Publishing Inc.),* Burrage Rd., Contoocook, NH 03229 Tel 603-746-5606.

Dragtooth Pr, *(Dragtooth Press),* 3930 N. W. Witham Hill Dr., No. 140, Corvallis, OR 97330; Moved, Left No Forwarding Address.

Drake's Ptg & Pub, *(Drake's Printing & Pub.),* 225 N. Magnolia Ave., Orlando, FL 32801 Tel 305-841-3491.

Drama *Imprint of* **Hill & Wang**

Drama Bk, *(Drama Book Specialists (Pubs.); 0-910482; 0-89676),* 150 W. 52nd St., New York, NY 10019 Tel 212-582-1475.

Dramatika, *(Dramatika; 0-9604000),* 429 Hope St., Tarpon Springs, FL 33589 Tel 813-937-0109.

Dramatists Play, *(Dramatists Play Service, Inc.; 0-8222),* 440 Park Ave. S., New York, NY 10016.

Dream Garden, *(Dream Garden Press; 0-9604402),* 1199 Iola Ave., Salt Lake City, UT 84104.

Dream Place, *(Dream Place Pubns.; 0-930486),* P.O. Box 9416, Stanford, CA 94305 Tel 415-494-6083.

Dreams Unltd, *(Dreams Unlimited; 0-939878),* P.O. Box 247, Middleton, WI 53562 Tel 608-238-6575.

Dreenan Pr, *(Dreenan Press, Ltd.; 0-88376),* P.O. Box 385, Croton-on-Hudson, NY 10520 Tel 914-271-5085.

Dreier Educ, *(Dreier Educational Systems, Inc.; 0-87673),* 25 S. Fifth Ave., Box 1291, Highland Park, NJ 08904 Tel 201-572-2112; Moved, Left No Forwarding Address.

Drelwood Pubns, *(Drelwood Pubns.; 0-937766),* P.O. Box 10605, Portland, OR 97210; Dist. by: Communication Creativity, 5644 La Jolla Blvd., La Jolla, CA 92037 Tel 714-459-4489.

Drigh-Graph, *(Drigh-Graph, Inc.),* 114 E. 61st St., New York, NY 10021; c/o Ile Bing, 210 Riverside Dr., Apt. 6G, New York, NY 10025.

Drinkwatchers, *(Drinkwatchers),* 14 Riverside Ave., Haverstraw, NY 10927; Orders to: P.O. Box, Haverstraw, NY 10927; Moved, Left No Forwarding Address.

Drivers License, *(Drivers License Guide Co.),* 1492 Oddstad Dr., Redwood City, CA 94063.

Droke-Hallux, *(Droke House/Hallux; 0-8375),* 116 W. Orr St., Box 2027, Anderson, SC 29621 Tel 803-226-7231; Moved Left No Forwarding Address.

Drug Abuse, *(Drug Abuse Council),* 1828 "L" St., N.W., Washington, DC 20036 Tel 202-785-5200.

Drug Intl Pubns, *(Drug Intelligence Pubns.; 0-914768),* 7752 Woodmont Ave., Washington, DC 20014 Tel 301-654-8736; Orders to: 1241 Broadway, Hamilton, IL 62341.

Drug Store Mkt, *(Drug Store Market Guide; 0-9606064),* 1739 Horton Ave., Mohegan Lake, NY 10547 Tel 914-528-7147.

Druid Bks, *(Druid Books; 0-912518),* Ephraim, WI 54211 Tel 414-854-4875.

Druid Heights, *(Druid Heights Books),* 685 Camino del Canyon, Muir Woods, Mill Valley, CA 94941 Tel 415-388-2111.

Drum & Spear, *(Drum & Spear Press, Inc.; 0-87782),* 1371 Fairmont St., N. W., Washington, DC 20009; Moved. Left No Forwarding Address.

Drumbeat *Imprint of* **Three Continents**

Dryad Pr, *(Dryad Press; 0-931848),* 15 Sherman Ave., Takoma Park, MD 20012 Tel 301-891-3729.

Dryden Pr, *(Dryden Press; 0-8498),* Div. of Holt, Rinehart & Winston, Inc., 901 N. Elm, Hinsdale, IL 60521 Tel 312-325-2985.

DSA
    See Educ Info Group

Du Sable Mus, *(Du Sable Museum Press),* 740 E. 56th Place, Chicago, IL 60637 Tel 312-947-0600.

Du Vall Financial, *(Du Vall Press Financial Pubns.; 0-931232),* 920 W. Grand River, Williamston, MI 48895.

Duane Shinn, *(Duane Shinn Pubns.; 0-912732),* 5090 Dobrot, Central Point, OR 97501 Tel 503-664-2317.

Dublin Pr, *(Dublin Press; 0-9604238),* P.O. Box 2131, Sunnyvale, CA 94087.

DuBois Zone Pr, *(DuBois Zone Press, The; 0-931498),* 516 Eleventh Ave., Grafton, WI 53024.

DuBose Pub, *(DuBose Publishing; 0-938072),* P.O. Box 924, Atlanta, GA 30301.

Duck Down, *(Duck Down Press; 0-916918),* P.O. Box 1047, Fallon, NV 89406 Tel 702-423-6643.

Duck Pr, *(Duck Press; 0-9604364),* Box 1024, New York, NY 10009; Orders to: Energy Earth Communications Inc., Box 1141, Galveston, TX 77553.

Ducks Bks, *(Ducks Books; 0-913858),* P.O. Box 307, Ben Lomond, CA 95005 Tel 408-336-8887.

Ducky Ent, *(Ducky, B. K., Enterprises),* 8836 S. Vermont Ave., No. 2, Los Angeles, CA 90044 Tel 213-377-0216.

Dudley, *(Dudley, Linda),* 89 Surrey Lane, Hempstead, NY 11550 Tel 516-489-8564.

Duell, *(Duell, Sloan & Pearce),* ; Publisher Abbreviation Without Addresses Are Out of Print. These Are Obsolete Abbreviations.

Duende, *(Duende Pr; 0-915008),* 6434 Raymond St, Oakland, CA 94609.

Dufour, *(Dufour Editions, Inc.; 0-8023),* Chester Springs, PA 19425 Tel 215-458-5005.

Dugdale, *(Dugdale, Kathleen; 0-9600028),* 510 S. Rose Ave., Bloomington, IN 47401 Tel 812-332-1909.

Duke, *(Duke Univ. Press; 0-8223),* 6697 College Sta., Durham, NC 27708 Tel 919-684-2173.

Duke Pr IL, *(Duke Press; 0-931234),* 8917 W. Cermak Rd., N. Riverside, IL 60546.

Dumbarton Oaks, *(Dumbarton Oaks; 0-88402),* 1703 32nd St., N.W., Washington, DC 20007 Tel 202-342-3200. *Imprints:* Ctr Byzantine (Center for Byzantine Studies); Ctr Landscape Arch (Center for Landscape Architecture); Ctr Pre-Columbian (Center for Pre-Columbian Studies).

Dumbarton Pr, *(Dumbarton Press; 0-9600822),* P.O. Box 639, Newark, CA 94560.

Dun, *(Dun & Bradstreet, Inc.),* c/o Technical Publishing, 666 Fifth Ave., New York, NY 10019 Tel 212-489-2200.

Dun-Donnelly
    See Tech Pub

Dunconor Bks, *(Dunconor Books; 0-918820),* 1749 Market, Denver, CO 80202 Tel 303-572-9160.

Dundee Pub, *(Dundee Publishing; 0-935210),* P.O. Box 202, Dundee, NY 14837 Tel 301-432-8079.

Dune Pubs, *(Dune Pubns., Ltd.; 0-914938),* 47-25 59th St., Woodside, NY 11377 Tel 212-271-1595.

Dunellen Pub Co, *(Dunellen Publishing Co., Inc.; 0-8424),* Dist. by: Kennikat Press, 90 S. Bayles Ave., Port Washington, NY 11050 Tel 516-883-0570.

Dunes, *(Dunes Enterprises),* P.O. Box 371, Beverly Shores, IN 46301 Tel 219-872-5943.

Dunham Pond, *(Dunham Pond Press; 0-915978),* Storrs, CT 06268.

Dunhere, *(Dunhere Pub. Co.; 0-89452),* Div. of Dunhere Composition House, Ltd., 115 Christopher St., 6th Fl., New York, NY 10014 Tel 212-989-0746; Moved, Left No Forwarding Address.

Dunk Rock *Imprint of* **Four Quarters**

Dunlap Soc, *(Dunlap Society),* Lake Champlain Rd., Essex, NY 12936 Tel 518-963-7373.

Dunn & Webster, *(Dunn & Webster Inc., Pubs.; 0-89761),* 10 Bull St., Newport, RI 02840 Tel 401-846-8361.

Duobooks, *(Duobooks, Inc.; 0-918394),* 154 W. 57th St., New York, NY 10019 Tel 212-757-4438; Orders to: 300 Fairfield Rd., Fairfield, NJ 07006.

Dup, *(Dup.; 0-932324),* Box 701, Hudson, NY 12534.

Duquesne, *(Duquesne Univ. Press; 0-8207),* Dist. by: Humanities Press, Inc., Atlantic Highlands, NJ 07716.

Duquesne Pub, *(Duquesne Publishing Co.; 0-89653),* P.O. Box 222, West Brookfield, MA 01585 Tel 617-867-9341.

Durand Intl, *(Durand International; 0-9604056),* P.O. Box 925, Lynwood, CA 90262.

Durbin Assoc, *(Durbin Associates; 0-936786),* 3711 Southwood Dr., Easton, PA 18042.

Durrell, *(Durrell Pubns., Inc.; 0-911764),* P.O. Box 743, Mast Cove Lane, Kennebunkport, ME 04046 Tel 207-985-3904.

Dushkin Pub, *(Dushkin Publishing Group, Inc.; 0-87967),* Sluice Dock, Guilford, CT 06437 Tel 203-453-4351.

Dustbooks, *(Dustbooks; 0-913218),* Box 100, Paradise, CA 95969 Tel 916-877-6110.

Dusty Pub Co, *(Dusty Publishing Co.),* Div. of Chimney Sweeps of America, Ltd., 7 N 040 Medinah Rd., Medinah, IL 60157 Tel 312 893 6066; Dist. by: Baker & Taylor, Gladiola Ave., Momence, IL 60954.

Dutton, *(Dutton, E. P.; 0-525),* 2 Park Ave., New York, NY 10016 Tel 212-725-1818. *Imprints:* Elsevier-Phaidon (Elsevier-Phaidon); Evman (Everyman); Gingerbread (Gingerbread House); Hawthorn (Hawthorn Books); Phaidon (Phaidon); Windmill (Windmill Books).

Duverus Pub, *(Duverus Publishing Corp.; 0-918700),* Duverus Bldg., Seligman, MO 65745.

Duxbury Pr, *(Duxbury Press; 0-87872),* Div. of Wadsworth Inc., 20 Providence St., Statler Bldg., Boston, MA 02116 Tel 617-482-2344; c/o Wadsworth, Inc., 10 Davis Dr., Belmont, CA 94002.

Dwapara, *(Dwapara Herald Pubs., Inc.; 0-917952),* P.O. Box 267, Marble Hill, MO 63764.

Dyco Inc, *(Dyco, Inc.; 0-937224),* 6702 E. Cactus Rd., Scottsdale, AZ 85254.

Dymax, *(Dymax; 0-918138),* P. O. Box 310, Menlo Park, CA 94025 Tel 415-323-6117.

Dynamic Learn Corp, *(Dynamic Learning Corp.; 0-915890),* 59 Commercial Wharf, Boston, MA 02110 Tel 617-742-9493. *Imprints:* Telegraph (Telegraph Books).

Dynamics Pr, *(Dynamics Press; 0-917490),* 2633 E. 28th St., No. 602, Signal Hill, CA 90806 Tel 213-776-7030; Moved Left No Forwarding Address.

E A Martin, *(Martin, Edward A.),* 550 North Ave., Grand Junction, CO 81501 Tel 303-243-1538.

E A Seemann, *(Seemann, E. A., Publishing, Inc.; 0-912458; 0-89530),* P.O. Box K, Miami, FL 33156 Tel 305-233-5852.

E & C Bks, *(E & C Books; 0-935126),* P.O. Box 6, Massapequa Park, NY 11762.

E & E Enterprises, *(E & E Enterprises; 0-917954),* P.O. Box 405, Howell, NJ 07731 Tel 201-364-1398.

E & E Pub, *(E & E Publishing Co.),* 27 Franklin Ave., Souderton, PA 18964 Tel 215-723-6689.

E & L Instru, *(E & L Instruments; 0-89704),* 61 First St., Derby, CT 06418.

E B Lyons, *(Lyons, Emily Bradley; 0-9604374),* 22175 Shoreline Dr., Marshall, CA 94940.

E Bennington, *(Bennington, Ed, Jr.),* 1850 Columbia Pike, Suite 511, Arlington, VA 22204.

E C Hady, *(Hady, Edmund Carl; 0-9600794),* 128 N. Main St., Ashley, PA 18706.

E C Schirmer, *(Schirmer, E. C., Music Co.; 0-911318),* 112 South St., Boston, MA 02111 Tel 617-426-3137.

E C Stanton Pub, *(Stanton, Elizabeth Cady, Pub., Co.),* 5857 Marbury Rd., Bethesda, MD 20034 Tel 301-229-7067; Moved, Left No Forwarding Address.

E C Temple, *(Temple, Ellen C.; 0-936650),* 32 Sundown Pkwy., Austin, TX 78746 Tel 512-327-2664.

E Defoggi, *(Defoggi, Ernest; 0-9602372),* Rt. 1, Box 514-A, Newport, NC 28570.

E Dickinson Bks, *(Emily Dickinson Books),* 4508 38th St., Brentwood, MD 20722.

E Diemar, *(Diemar, Eleanor; 0-9601046),* P.O. Box 24, Cedarhurst, NY 11516 Tel 516-374-2020.

E Friede *Imprint of* **Delacorte**

E Fudge, *(Fudge, Edward, Publishing),* 4 Sandra Lane, Athens, AL 35611 Tel 205-233-0880.

E-Heart Pr, *(E-Heart Press; 0-935014),* 3700 Mockingbird Lane, Dallas, TX 75205.

E Hovemeyer, *(Hovemeyer, Eric E.; 0-9600974),* 22 Evergreen Ave., Apt. C-1, Hartford, CT 06105 Tel 513-681-1001.

E J Brill, *(Brill, E. J., Pubs.),* Dist. by: Expediters of the Printed Word, Ltd., P.O. Box 1305, Long Island City, NY 11101.

E J Danforth, *(Danforth, Edward J.; 0-9601174),* 20 Westwood Dr., Orono, ME 04473 Tel 207-866-2846.

E J Palmer, *(Palmer, Earl J., & Associates),* P.O. Box 9204, Seattle, WA 98109.

E J Perry, *(Perry, Enos J.; 0-9600534),* 612 First Ave., Highland Park, NJ 08904 Tel 201-545-9235.

E Kent, *(Kent, Earl, Welding Consultant; 0-918782),* 9809 Spruce Court, Cypress, CA 90630 Tel 714-828-8064.

E Keys, *(Keys, Elsie),* 1239 E. Marshall Ave., Phoenix, AZ 85014.

E Kinkead, *(Kinkead, Eugene; 0-9600476),* Colebrook, CT 06021 Tel 203-379-6843.

E L Hall, *(Hall, Elra Litchfield; 0-9601308),* 1400 S. Plymouth Ave., Rochester, NY 14611.

E L Harris, *(Harris, Elbert L.),* Box 43, Rutgers Univ., 5th & Penn Sts., Camden, NJ 08102.

E Langstaff, *(Langstaff, E., Books; 0-89986),* 919 Fremont Ave., South Pasadena, CA 91030 Tel 213-441-3233.

E Lopez, *(Lopez, Eddie; 0-9606120),* 615 S. 20th, Donna, TX 78537 Tel 512-464-2658.

E M Boehm, *(Boehm, Edward Marshall, Inc.; 0-918096),* 25 Fairfacts St., P.O. Box 5051, Trenton, NJ 08638 Tel 609-392-2207.

E M Coleman Ent, *(Coleman, Earl M., Enterprises, Inc.; 0-930576),* P.O. Box 143, Pine Plains, NY 12567 Tel 518-398-7193.

E M Underwood, *(Underwood, E. M., Pub; 0-932410),* P.O. Box 4295, San Leandro, CA 94579; Orders to: Underwood Pub., P.O. Box 1107, Livermore, CA 94550; Moved, Left No Forwarding Address.

E McKee, *(McKee, Edwwin),* c/o U.S. Geological Survey, Box 25046, Denver Federal Ctr., Denver, CO 80225.

E Mellen, *(Mellen, Edwin Press; 0-88946),* P.O. Box 450, Lewiston, NY 14092 Tel 716-754-8566.

E Menzie Imports, *(Menzie, Eleanor, Imports),* 3240 Pico Blvd., Santa Monica, CA 90405 Tel 213-392-7398; Moved, Left No Forwarding Address.

E O Klemm, *(Klemm, Edwin O.),* 303 S. Jefferson St., Saginaw, MI 48607 Tel 313-755-3559.

E O'Neill, *(O'Neill, Eugene, Theater Center),* 305 Great Neck Rd., Waterford, CT 06385 Tel 203-443-5378.

E P Edwards, *(Edwards, Ernest P.; 0-911882),* P.O. Box AQ, Sweet Briar, VA 24595 Tel 804-381-5442.

E P Klein, *(Klein, Elizabeth Pfahning; 0-9604250),* 11041 S.W. 46th St., Miami, FL 33165.

E Papaikonomou, *(Papaikonomou, Evangelos),* c/o Prof. E. Papaikonomou, Dept. of Biological Sciences, San Jose State Univ., San Jose, CA 95192.

E Patterson, *(Patterson, Eugene),* 613 N. 3rd, Hill City, KS 67642.

E R Jones, *(Jones, Ernest R.; 0-9600934),* 1020 Hillview Blvd., Virginia Beach, VA 23462 Tel 804-420-1666.

E Read, *(Read, Elizabeth, R. D.; 0-9600996),* 4429 East 46th Place, Tulsa, OK 74135 Tel 918-627-0213.

E Robin Pub, *(Robin, Eddie, Publishing; 0-936362),* P.O. Box 85160, Los Angeles, CA 90072.

E S Cunningham, *(Cunningham, Eileen S.),* R.R. 2, Carrollton, IL 62016.

E S Davis, *(Davis, Elsie Spry; 0-9605618),* 710 Second St., Coronado, CA 92118.

E S John, *(John, Edna S.),* 1481 "D" St., Springfield, OR 97477.

E Swanson, *(Swanson, Evadene; 0-9600862),* 620 Mathews, No. 115, Fort Collins, CO 80524 Tel 303-484-4534.

E Torres & Sons, *(Torres, Eliseo, & Sons; 0-88303),* Box 2, Eastchester, NY 10709.

E V Moller, *(Moller, Eugene V.),* 47 Bedford Ave., Staten Island, NY 10306 Tel 212-987-2648.

E V Salitore, *(Salitore, Edward V., & Evelyn D.),* P.O. Box 400, Lakewood, CA 90714 Tel 714-676-6355.

E V White, *(White, Eugene V.; 0-9602034),* One West Main St., Berryville, VA 22611 Tel 703-955-2280.

E W Beitzell, *(Beitzel, Edwin W.; 0-9604502),* P.O. Box 107, Abell, MD 20606 Tel 301-769-3279.

E-W Cultural Ctr, *(East-West Cultural Center; 0-930736),* 2865 W. 9th St., Los Angeles, CA 90006 Tel 213-480-8325.

E W Jameson Jr, *(Jameson, E. W., Jr.),* 13 Oakside, Davis, CA 95616.

E-W Pub Co, *(East/West Publishing Co.; 0-934788),* 838 Grant Ave., Suite 307, San Francisco, CA 94108.

E Whittle & F A Dockery, *(Whittle, E., & F. A. Dockery; 0-9604046),* 795-B Beech Circle N. W., Cleveland, TN 37311.

E Wolfe Pubns, *(Wolfe, Ernest, Pubns.; 0-9603660),* 1657 Sawtelle Blvd., Los Angeles, CA 90025 Tel 213-478-2960.

E-Z Learning, *(E-Z Learning Methods; 0-931924),* P.O. Box 2182, Pomona, CA 91766 Tel 714-622-6835.

Eagle Comm, *(Eagle Communications; 0-9605462),* 340 W. Main St., Missoula, MT 59806.

Eagle Pr, *(Eagle Press, Inc.),* P. O. Box 64935, Baton Rouge, LA 70806 Tel 504-344-7443.

Eagle Pubs, *(Eagle Pubs.; 0-9600634),* P.O. Box 1267, Chicago, IL 60690; Moved, Left No Forwarding Address.

Eagle Tail, *(Eagle Tail Press),* P.O. Box 3128, Grand Junction, CO 81501 Tel 303-242-0995.

Eakin Pubns, *(Eakin Pubns.; 0-89015),* P.O. Drawer A G, Burnet, TX 78611 Tel 512-756-6911.

Eakins, *(Eakins Press Foundation; 0-87130),* 155 E. 42nd St., New York, NY 10017 Tel 212-986-4077.

Eardley Pubns, *(Eardley Pubns.; 0-937630),* P.O. Box 281, Rochelle Park, NJ 07662.

Early Educators, *(Early Educators Press; 0-9604390),* P.O. Box 1177, Lake Alfred, FL 33850 Tel 813-956-1569.

Early Stages, *(Early Stages Press, Inc.; 0-915786),* P.O. Box 31463, San Francisco, CA 94131; Dist. by: P.I.E. News, 164-27th St., San Francisco, CA 94110 Tel 415-282-2526.

Earth Magic, *(Earth Magic Productions; 0-9604128),* P.O. Box 1202, FDR Sta., New York, NY 10022.

Earth Pub Ents, *(Earth Publishing Enterprises, Inc.),* P. O. Box 430273, South Miami, FL 33143; Moved, Left No Forwarding Address.

Earth Rites, *(Earth Rites),* c/o Mestel, 398-8th St., Brooklyn, NY 11215.

Earth Science, *(Earth Science Publishing Co.),* P.O. Box 1815, Colorado Springs, CO 80901 Tel 303-634-7345.

Earth-Song, *(Earth-Song Press),* 202 Hartnell Place, Sacramento, CA 95825 Tel 916-927-6863.

Earth View, *(Earth View, Inc; 0-932898),* Hwy. 706 at Kernahan Rd., Star Rte, Ashford, WA 98304 Tel 206-569-2211.

Earthlight, *(Earthlight Pubs.; 0-935128),* 5539 Jackson, Kansas City, MO 64130.

Easi-Bild, *(Easi-Bild Directions Simplified, Inc.; 0-87733),* 529 N. State Rd., P.O. Box 215, Briarcliff Manor, NY 10510 Tel 914-941-6600.

East & West Pubns, *(East & West Pubns., New York; 0-935886),* P.O. Box 17421, West Hartford, CT 06117.

East Dennis, *(East Dennis Publishing Co.; 0-87299),* P.O. Box 555, East Dennis, MA 02641 Tel 617-385-2000.

East Eagle, *(East Eagle Press; 0-9605738),* P.O. Box 812, Huron, SD 57350.

East Eur Quarterly, *(East European Quarterly; 0-914710),* Dist. by: Columbia Univ. Press, 562 W. 113th St., New York, NY 10025 Tel 212-678-6777.

East Oregonian, *(East Oregonian; 0-934880),* P.O. Box 1089, Pendleton, OR 97801 Tel 503-276-2211.

East Ridge Pr, *(East Ridge Press; 0-914896),* Hankins, NY 12741 Tel 914-887-5499; Dist. by: Twenty-Four Book Service, 161 E. Ridge Rd., Hankins, NY 12741.

East River, *(East River Press; 0-89172),* 505 Fifth Ave., New York, NY 10017.

East River Anthol, *(East River Anthology; 0-917238),* 75 Gates Ave., Montclair, NJ 07042 Tel 201-746-5941.

East West Cult, *(East West Culture Exchange; 0-9601274),* 3402 Leicester Dr., Muncie, IN 47304 Tel 317-289-3123.

East-West Pubns
   See East & West Pubns

East Woods, *(East Woods Press, Inc.; 0-914788),* Subs. of Fast & McMillan, Pubs., 820 E. Blvd., Charlotte, NC 28203 Tel 704-334-0897.

Easter Pub, *(Easter Publishing Co.; 0-930642),* P.O. Box 1244, Mobile, AL 36601.

Eastern Acorn, *(Eastern Acorn Press),* 339 Walnut St., Philadelphia, PA 19106 Tel 215-597-7129.

Eastern CT St Coll Fdn, *(Eastern Connecticut State College Foundation; 0-915884),* P.O. Box 431, Willimantic, CT 06226 Tel 203-456-2231.

Eastern Mount, *(Eastern Mountain Sports),* 11312 Vose Farm Rd., Peterborough, NH 03458 Tel 603-924-3825; Dist. by: Appalachian Mountain Club, 5 Joy St., Boston, MA 02108 Tel 617-523-0636.

Eastern Natl Park
   See Eastern Acorn

Eastern Orthodox, *(Eastern Orthodox Books; 0-89981),* P.O. Box 302, Willits, CA 95490.

Eastern Pr, *(Eastern Press; 0-939758),* 721 E. Hunter Ave., Bloomington, IN 47401.

Eastern Wash, *(Eastern Washington State Historical Society; 0-910524),* W. 2316 First Ave., Spokane, WA 99204 Tel 506-456-3931.

Eastham Edns, *(Eastham Editions; 0-915102),* P.O. Box 10, Prospect, NY 13435 Tel 315-896-6388.

Eastman Kodak, *(Eastman Kodak Co.; 0-87985),* 343 State St., Bldg. 16, 2nd Floor, Dept. 373, Rochester, NY 14650; Orders to: 343 State St., Dept. 454, Rochester, NY 14650 Tel 716-722-2599.

Eastview, *(Eastview Editions, Inc.; 0-89860),* P.O. Box 783, Westfield, NJ 07091 Tel 201-233-0474.

Eastwest Ctr *Imprint of* U Pr of Hawaii

Eau Claire Lakes, *(Eau Claire Lakes; 0-917424),* P.O. Box 6430, Solon Springs, WI 54873.

Eberly Pr, *(Eberly Press; 0-932296),* 430 N. Harrison, East Lansing, MI 48823 Tel 517-351-7299.

EBHA Pr, *(EBHA Press; 0-935662),* 5919 Cullen Dr., Lincoln, NE 68506 Tel 402-488-0684.

Ebony Pub
   See Carver Pub

EBSCO Ind, *(EBSCO Industries, Inc.; 0-913956),* First Ave., N. at 13th St., Birmingham, AL 35203 Tel 205-252-1212.

ECA Assoc, *(ECA Associates; 0-938818),* P.O. Box 15004, Great Bridge Sta., Chesapeake, VA 23320 Tel 804-547-5542; P.O. Box 57, Lefferts Sta., Brooklyn, NY 11225.

ECA Pub, *(ECA Publishing Co.),* P.O. Box 1057, Menlo Park, CA 94025 Tel 415-325-7569; Formerly Educational Consortium of America.

ECCA Pubns, *(ECCA Pubns.),* 1629 K St., N.W., Suite 526, Washington, DC 20006.

Ecclesia *Imprint of* William Carey Lib

Ecco Pr, *(Ecco Press; 0-912946),* 1 W. 30th St., New York, NY 10001 Tel 212-736-2599; Dist. by: W.W. Norton & Co., Inc., Keystone Industrial Park, Scranton, PA 18512.

Echenian Church, *(Echenian Church, The; 0-9603134),* P.O. Box 11893, Reno, NV 89510; Moved, Left No Forwarding Address.

Echo *Imprint of* Doubleday

Echo Hse, *(Echo House; 0-910528),* 150 Broadway, New York, NY 10038; Out of Business.

Echo Pubs, *(Echo Pubs.; 0-912852),* P.O. Box 7130, West Menlo Park, CA 94025 Tel 415-524-1575.

Eckman Ctr, *(Eckman Center; 0-934752),* P.O. Box 621, Woodland Hills, CA 91365 Tel 213-347-4445.

Eclectic Pr, *(Eclectic Press; 0-9605920),* P.O. Box 894, Ansonia Sta., New York, NY 10023 Tel 212-874-2867.

Ecology Pr, *(Ecology Press; 0-9603002),* P.O. Box 694, Alamo, CA 94507.

Econ Behavior, *(Economic Behavior Institute),* P. O. Box 879, Huntington Beach, CA 92648; Moved, Left No Forwarding Address.

Econ Info Syst, *(Economic Information Systems; 0-86692),* 310 Madison Ave., New York, NY 10017.

Econ Res Ctr, *(Economics Research Center),* 1600 Campus Rd., Occidental College, Los Angeles, CA 90041.

Economy Co, *(Economy Co.; 0-87892; 0-8332),* 1901 N. Walnut, P.O. Box 25308, Oklahoma City, OK 73125 Tel 405-528-8444.

Ed Activities, *(Educational Activities, Inc.; 0-914296),* 1937 Grand Ave., Baldwin, NY 11510 Tel 516-868-7460.

Ed & Training, *(Education & Training Consultants Co.; 0-87657),* Box 2085, Sedona, AZ 86336 Tel 602-282-3009.

Ed Assocs, *(Education Assocs.; 0-918772),* P.O. Box 8021, Athens, GA 30603 Tel 404-542-4244.

Ed Bk Crafters, *(Educational Book Crafters, Inc.; 0-912826),* 71 Boulevard, Westwood, NJ 07675.

Ed Bk Pubs OK, *(Educational Book Pubs.; 0-932188),* P.O. Box 1219, Guthrie, OK 73044.

Ed Buryn, *(Ed Buryn Publishing Co.),* Box 31123, San Francisco, CA 94131 Tel 415-824-8938; Dist. by: Bookpeople, 2940 Seventh St., Berkeley, CA 94710 Tel 415-549-3033.

Ed Comm Counsel, *(Educational Community Counselors Associates, Inc.),* 1150 Fifth St., N.W., Washington, DC 20001.

Ed Consortium
   See ECA Pub

Ed Dev Assn, *(Educational Development Assn.),* P.O. Box 181, Hazel Crest, IL 60429.

Ed Direct, *(Educational Directories Inc.; 0-910536),* P.O. Box 199, Mt. Prospect, IL 60056 Tel 312-392-1811.

Ed Facilities, *(Educational Facilities Laboratories; 0-88481),* c/o Academy for Educational Development, 680 Fifth Ave., New York, NY 10019.

Ed Inst Pr, *(Educational Institute Press),* P.O. Box 2537, Laguna Beach, CA 92653 Tel 714-830-0972; Moved, Left No Forwarding Address.

Ed Med & Info Sys, *(Educational Media & Information Systems; 0-913470),* P.O. Box 2411, Fort Collins, CO 80522.

Ed Media Corp, *(Educational Media Corp.; 0-932796),* P.O. Box 21311, Minneapolis, MN 55421.

Ed Methods, *(Educational Methods; 0-88462),* Div. of Development Systems Corp., 500 N. Dearborn St., Chicago, IL 60610 Tel 312-836-0471.

Ed Pol Comm, *(Educational Policies Commission),* Dist. by: NEA Customer Service, the Academic Bldg., Saw Mill Rd., West Haven, CT 06516.

Ed Prog, *(Educators Progress Service, Inc.; 0-87708),* 214 Center St., Randolph, WI 53956 Tel 414-326-3126.

Ed Progress Corp, *(Educational Progress Corp.; 0-913332; 0-89403),* Div. of Educational Development Corp., 4235 S. Memorial P.O. Box 45663, Tulsa, OK 74145 Tel 800-331-4418.

Ed Projections, *(Educational Projections Corp.),* Div. of Standard Projector & Equipment Co., P.O. Box 50276, Jacksonville Beach, FL 32250 Tel 904-249-8429.

Ed Pub Serv, *(Educators Publishing Service, Inc.; 0-8388),* 75 Moulton St., Cambridge, MA 02138 Tel 617-547-6706.

Ed Res Assoc, *(Educational Research Associates; 0-89420),* 333 S.W. Park Ave., Fourth Floor, Portland, OR 97205 Tel 503-228-6345.

Ed Res Corp, *(Educational Research Corp.; 0-930338),* 380 Green St., Cambridge, MA 02139 Tel 617-923-1710.

Ed Res Inst, *(Educational Research Institute; 0-9600426),* 5328-A Bahia Blanca, Laguna Hills, CA 92653 Tel 714-586-8162.

Ed Research, *(Educational Research Service),* 1800 N. Kent St., Arlington, VA 22209 Tel 703-527-5331.

Ed Resources, *(Educational Resources Unlimited, Inc.; 0-915912),* P.O. Box 43, Baker, NV 89311 Tel 702-234-7213.

Ed Sci, *(Educational Science Consultants; 0-912990),* P.O. Box 1674, San Leandro, CA 94577.

Ed Solutions, *(Educational Solutions, Inc.; 0-87825),* 80 Fifth Ave., New York, NY 10011 Tel 212-924-1744.

Ed Tecnicos
   See French & Eur

Ed Ventures, *(Education Ventures, Inc.; 0-914194),* 209 Court St., Middletown, CT 06457 Tel 203-347-2548.

Edelson, *(Edelson, Mary Beth; 0-9604650),* 110 Mercer St., New York, NY 10012 Tel 212-226-0832.

Edelweiss Pr, *(Edelweiss Press; 0-9600874),* 124 Front St., Massapequa Park, NY 11762 Tel 516-799-1150.

Eden, *(Eden Publishing House; 0-910532),* 1724 Chouteau Ave., St. Louis, MO 63103 Tel 314-421-1544.

Eden Hall Pr, *(Eden Hall Press; 0-933090),* P.O. Box 67534, Los Angeles, CA 90067; Moved, Left No Forwarding Address.

Eden Med Res, *(Eden Medical Research, Inc.; 0-88831),* P.O. Box 51, St. Albans, VT 05478 Tel 514-931-3910.

Eden Valley, *(Eden Valley Press),* P.O.Box 238, Loveland, CO 80537; Dist. by: David M. Cole/Outreach Books, P.O. Box 425, Corona, CA 91720 Tel 213-926-9381.

Eden Women
   See EPWP

Eden's Work, *(Eden's Work; 0-937226),* 56 Hancock St., Bar Harbor, ME 04609.

Edgemoor, *(Edgemoor Publishing Co.; 0-88204),* 721 Durham Dr., Houston, TX 77007 Tel 713-861-3451; Orders to: P.O. Box 13612, Houston, TX 77019.

Edgepress, *(Edgepress; 0-918528),* P.O. Box 69, Point Reyes, CA 94956 Tel 415-663-8430.

Edgewater, *(Edgewater Book Distributors),* P.O. Box 586, Cleveland, OH 44107 Tel 216-671-1030.

Edgewood, *(Edgewood Press; 0-9602472),* 2865 East Rock Rd., Clare, MI 48617.

Ediciones, *(Ediciones Universal; 0-89729),* 3090 S.W. 8th St., Miami, FL 33135 Tel 305-642-3234.

Edins Hispamerica, *(Ediciones Hispamerica; 0-935318),* 5 Pueblo Court, Gaithersburg, MD 20760 Tel 301-948-3494.

Edison Elec, *(Edison Electric Institute; 0-931032),* 1111 19th St., N.W., Washington, DC 20036 Tel 202-828-7400.

Edison Inst, *(Edison Institute, The; 0-933728),* 20900 Oakwood Blvd., Dearborn, MI 48121. *Imprints:* Ford Mus (Henry Ford Museum Press).

Edit Caribe, *(Editorial Caribe; 0-89922),* 3934 S. W. 8th St., Suite 303, Miami, FL 33134 Tel 305-445-0564.

Edit Consult, *(Editorial Consultants, Inc.; 0-917636),* 655 Sutter, San Francisco, CA 94102 Tel 415-474-7656.

Edit Experts, *(Editorial Experts, Inc.; 0-935012),* 5905 Pratt St., Alexandria, VA 22310 Tel 703-971-7350.

Edit Indoamerica, *(Editorial Indoamerica, Library of the New World; 0-910534),* P.O. Box 11356, Kansas City, MO 64112 Tel 813-531-1512.

Edit Mensaje, *(Editorial Mensaje; 0-86515),* 125 Queen St., Staten Island, NY 10314 Tel 212-761-0556.

Edit Mundo, *(Editorial Mundo Hispano),* Apartado 4255, El Paso, TX 79914.

Edit Mundo *Imprint of* Casa Bautista

Edit Pr Serv, *(Editors Press Service, Inc.; 0-89971),* Div. of Charleston Post Pub. Co., 60 E. 42nd St., New York, NY 10017 Tel 212-682-2888.

Edit Res Serv, *(Editorial Research Service; 0-933592)*, P.O. Box 1832, Kansas City, MO 64141.

Edit Services, *(Editorial Services Co.; 0-933406)*, 1140 Ave. of the Americas, New York, NY 10036.

Editions Pub, *(Editions Publisol; 0-912202)*, P.O. Box 339, Gracie Stn., New York, NY 10028 Tel 212-289-3981.

Editorial Cordillera, *(Editorial Cordillera, Inc.; 0-88495)*, Apartado "S", Hato Rey, PR 00919 Tel 809-767-6188.

Editorial Justa, *(Editorial Justa Pubns. Inc.; 0-915808)*, 2831 Seventh St., Berkeley, CA 94710 Tel 415-848-3628; Orders to: P.O. Box 2131-C, Berkeley, CA 94702.

Editorial Mundo
See Edit Mundo

Editors, *(Editors & Engineers, Ltd.; 0-672)*, Dist. by: Bobbs-Merrill Co., Inc., 4300 W. 62nd St., Indianapolis, IN 46206 Tel 317-298-5400.

EDITS Pubns, *(EDITS Pubns.)*, P.O. Box 7234, San Diego, CA 92107 Tel 714-488-1666.

EdMart Intl, *(EdMart International; 0-89485)*, 177 White Plains Rd., Tarrytown, NY 10591 Tel 914-332-0931.

Edmond Pub Co., *(Edmond Publishing Co.; 0-912954)*, P.O. Box 364, Branchport, NY 14418.

Edmund Miller, *(Miller, Edmund; 0-9600486)*, 61-07 Woodside Ave., Apt. 5J, Woodside, NY 11377 Tel 212-424-0480.

Edns Alba, *(Ediciones Alba; 0-9600714)*, Encarnacion 1573, Caparra Heights, San Juan, PR 00920 Tel 809-781-5984.

Edns Beauchesne, *(Editions Beauchesne)*, P.O. Box 825, South Bend, IN 46624 Tel 219-237-4267.

Edns Des Deux Mondes, *(Editions Des Deux Mondes; 0-939586)*, P.O. Box 56, Newark, DE 19711.

Educ Assocs IL, *(Educational Assocs.; 0-935644)*, 142 Wildwood, Algonquin, IL 60102.

Educ Bk Pubs, *(Educational Book Pubs., Inc.)*, 1175 N.E. 125th St., Suite 303, North Miami, FL 33161 Tel 305-891-7471.

Educ Comm, *(Educational Communications, Inc.; 0-915130)*, 3105 Macarthur Blvd., Northbrook, IL 60062 Tel 312-564-2020.

Educ Dev Ctr, *(Education Development Center, Inc.; 0-89292)*, 55 Chapel St., Newton, MA 02160 Tel 617-969-7100; Orders to: EDC Distribution Center, 55 Chapel St., Newton, MA 02160.

Educ Editions, *(Educational Editions; 0-933092)*, MS-293, P.O. Box 42999, Houston, TX 77042.

Educ Ent, *(Educational Enterprises)*, Dist. by: Potter School & Library Services, Inc., 6927 West North Ave., Wauwatosa, WI 53213.

Educ Guide, *(Education Guide, Inc.; 0-914880)*, P.O. Box 421, Randolph, MA 02368 Tel 617-961-2217.

Educ Impact, *(Educational Impact; 0-89076)*, P.O. Box 355, Blackwood, NJ 08012 Tel 609-228-3555.

Educ Indus, *(Education Industries, Inc.; 0-86652)*, P.O. Box 52, Madison, WI 53701.

Educ Info Group, *(Educational Information Group)*, 45 Miles Standish Dr., Marlborough, MA 01752 Tel 617-481-5335; Moved, Left No Forwarding Address.

Educ Inst Am Hotel, *(Educational Institute of the American Hotel & Motel Assn.; 0-86612)*, 1407 S. Harrison Rd., East Lansing, MI 48823.

Educ Medical, *(Educational Medical Pubs.; 0-930728)*, 18 Kling St., West Orange, NJ 07052.

Educ Pr Assn, *(Educational Press Assn. of America; 0-89972)*, Glassboro State College, Glassboro, NJ 08028 Tel 609-445-7349.

Educ Pr CA, *(Education Press, The; 0-9601706)*, Box 2358, Huntington Beach, CA 92647.

Educ Progs, *(Educational Programmers, Inc.)*, P.O. Box 332, Roseburg, OR 97470 Tel 503-672-6422.

Educ Res MA, *(Education Research Associates; 0-913636)*, P.O. Box 767, Amherst, MA 01004.

Educ Serv, *(Educational Service, Inc.; 0-89273)*, P.O. Box 219, Stevensville, MI 49127 Tel 616-429-1451.

Educ Stud Pr, *(Educational Studies Press; 0-934328)*, 107 Quadrangle, Iowa State Univ., Ames, IA 50011 Tel 515-294-7327.

Educ Studies
See Commonground Pr

Educ Svcs DC, *(Educational Services; 0-910542)*, 1730 Eye St., N.W., Washington, DC 20006 Tel 202-298-8424.

Educ Tech Pubns, *(Educational Technology Pubns., Inc.; 0-87778)*, 140 Sylvan Ave., Englewood Cliffs, NJ 07632 Tel 201-871-4007.

Educ Today
See Pitman Learning

Educalc Pubns, *(EduCALC Pubns; 0-936356)*, P.O. Box 974, Laguna Beach, CA 92652 Tel 714-497-3600.

Educator Bks, *(Educator Books, Inc.; 0-912092)*, Drawer 32, 10 N. Main, San Angelo, TX 76901 Tel 915-653-0152.

Educator Pubns, *(Educator Pubns.; 0-913558)*, 1110 S. Pomona Ave., Fullerton, CA 92632 Tel 714-871-2950; P.O. Box 333, Fullerton, CA 92632.

Educulture, *(Educulture, Inc.; 0-89000)*, 3184 "J" Airway Ave., Costa Mesa, CA 92626 Tel 714-751-2113; Orders to: P.O. Box 17149, Irvine, CA 92713.

Edward Pr, *(Edward Press; 0-9606020)*, 102 Jamestown Terrace, Rochester, NY 14615 Tel 716-865-2686.

Edwards Bros, *(Edwards Brothers, Inc.; 0-910546)*, 2500 S. State St., Ann Arbor, MI 48104 Tel 313-769-1000.

Eerdmans, *(Eerdmans, Wm. B., Publishing Co.; 0-8028)*, 255 Jefferson Ave., S.E., Grand Rapids, MI 49503 Tel 616-459-4591.

Effect Learning GA, *(Effective Learning Pubns.; 0-933594)*, 111 Holly Dr., Statesboro, GA 30458.

Effect Mgmt, *(Effective Management Research Corp.; 0-939740)*, 2229 Nyon Ave., Anaheim, CA 92806.

Effective Learn, *(Effective Learning Inc.; 0-915474)*, 7 N. MacQuesten Pkwy., Mount Vernon, NY 10550.

Effectiveness Train, *(Effectiveness Training Associates; 0-918460)*, 321 River St., Manistee, MI 49660 Tel 616 723-8422.

Effies Bks, *(Effie's Books)*, 1420 45th St., Emeryville, CA 94608.

EFLA, *(Educational Film Library Assn.; 0-87520)*, 43 W. 61st St., New York, NY 10023 Tel 212-246-4533.

Egar Pr, *(Egar Press, Inc.; 0-916484)*, Brashears Ctr., 1400 N. Harbor Blvd., P.O. Box 5409, Suite 240, Fullerton, CA 92635 Tel 714-879-7423; Moved, Left No Forwarding Address.

Eggplant Pr, *(Eggplant Press; 0-935060)*, P.O. Box 18641, Denver, CO 80218.

Eggs Pr, *(Eggs Press; 0-9602914)*, 3038 41st Ave. S., Minneapolis, MN 55406.

EGM Ent, *(EGM Enterprises; 0-9604586)*, P.O. Box 192, Berkeley Heights, NJ 07922 Tel 201-464-0486.

Ego Bks, *(Ego Books; 0-933540)*, 6011 Meadowbrook Lane, Lincoln, NE 68510 Tel 402-489-6982.

EH Imprint of **Har-Row**

Ehde Pub Co, *(Ehde Publishing Co.; 0-936188)*, Sontag, MS 39665.

EHUD, *(EHUD International Language Foundation)*, 1755 Trinity Ave., No. 79, Walnut Creek, CA 94596 Tel 415-937-4841; Orders to: Box 2082, Dollar Ranch Sta., Walnut Creek, CA 94595 Tel 415-937-4841.

Eighties Pr, *(Eighties Press; 0-87390)*, 308 First St., Moose Lake, MN 55767; Dist. by: Bookpeople, 2940 Seventh St., Berkeley, CA 94710.

Eilean Ban Pub, *(Eilean Ban Publishing Co.; 0-918702)*, 4329 Sano St., Alexandria, VA 22312 Tel 703-354-8771.

Eisenberg Ed, *(Eisenberg Educational Enterprises; 0-930080)*, 2 Hamill Rd., Suite 327, Village of Cross Keys, Baltimore, MD 21210 Tel 301-435-8351.

Eisenbrauns, *(Eisenbrauns; 0-931464)*, P.O. Box 275, Winona Lake, IN 46590 Tel 219-269-2011.

Eisenhower Lib, *(Eisenhower, Dwight D., Library; 0-9605728)*, Abilene, KS 67410.

Eizo, *(Eizo)*, Dist. by: SBD: Small Press Distribution, 1636 Ocean View Ave., Kensington, CA 94707 Tel 415-524-2107.

EKNE, *(American Assn. of Elementary-Kindergarten-Nursery Educators)*, 1201 Sixteenth St., Washington, DC 20036; Organization Ceased Operations, Nov. 1976.

Eko Pubns, *(Eko Pubns.)*, P.O. Box 5492, Philadelphia, PA 19143.

EKS Pub Co, *(EKS Publishing Co.; 0-939144)*, 484 Lake Park Ave., No. 118, Oakland, CA 94610.

El Cariso
See Life Understanding

El Fuego Aztlan, *(El Fuego de Aztlan Pubns.; 0-936470)*, 3408 Dwinelle Hall, Univ. of Calif., Berkeley, CA 94720 Tel 415-642-3859.

El Moro, *(El Moro Pubns.; 0-9602484)*, P.O. Box 965, Morro Bay, CA 93442 Tel 805-772-3514.

El-Shabazz Pr
See Shabazz Pr

Elan NW Pubs, *(Elan Northwest Pubs.; 0-9603272)*, P.O. Box 5442, Eugene, OR 97405 Tel 503-485-3462.

Elan Pubs
See Elan NW Pubs

Elar Pub Co, *(Elar Publishing Co.,Inc.)*, 1120 Old Country Rd., Plainview, NY 11803 Tel 516-433-6530.

Eldnar Pr, *(Eldnar Press; 0-912726)*, 503 Althea Rd., Belleair, Clearwater, FL 33516 Tel 813-584-4061.

Electret Sci, *(Electret Scientific Co.; 0-917406)*, P.O. Box 4132, Star City, WV 26505 Tel 304-296-8639.

Electro-Optical, *(Electro-Optical Research Co.)*, Suite 422, 2029 Century Park E., Los Angeles, CA 90067 Tel 213-277-7422.

Electronic Flea, *(Electronic Flea Market)*, 2020 Girard Ave., S., Minneapolis, MN 55405.

Elephant Pub, *(Elephant Publishing Corp.; 0-914654)*, 176 Clinton Ave., Brooklyn, NY 11205 Tel 212-875-3666; Dist. by: Morgan & Morgan, Inc., 145 Palisade St., Dobbs Ferry, NY 10522; Moved, Left No Forwarding Address.

Eleutherian Mills-Hagley, *(Eleutherian Mills-Hagley Foundation; 0-914650)*, 112 Buck Rd., Greenville, DE 19807 Tel 302-658-2410.

Elevation Pr, *(Elevation Press; 0-932624)*, c/o Don-Paul Benjamin, 1031 24th St., Greeley, CO 80631 Tel 303-352-2979.

Elgen Pub Co, *(Elgen Publishing Co.; 0-935774)*, 1004 Taurus Dr., Colorado Springs, CO 80906.

Eli Mail, *(Eli Mail-Order House, Inc.; 0-9602230)*, P.O. Box 81, Brooklyn, NY 11208.

Elica Bks, *(Elica Books; 0-931970)*, P.O. Box 576, Keego Harbor, MI 48033 Tel 313-851-3897.

Eliopoulos, *(Eliopoulos)*, P.O. Box 65, Oak Park, IL 60303.

Elizabeth Pr, *(Elizabeth Press)*, 103 Van Etten Blvd., New Rochelle, NY 10804.

Elk Grove Bks Imprint of **Childrens**

Ell Ell Diversified, *(Ell Ell Diversified, Inc.; 0-937428)*, 1100 Butler Ave., P.O. Box 1702, Santa Rosa, CA 95402 Tel 707-542-8663.

Eller, *(Eller Books)*, La Verne College, 1950 Third St., La Verne, CA 91750 Tel 714-593-3511; Acquired by Bretheren Press.

Ellingsworth, *(Ellingsworth Press, Ltd.)*, 20 E. Main St., Rm. 338, Waterbury, CT 06702.

Elliots Bks, *(Elliot's Books; 0-911830)*, P.O. Box 6, Northford, CT 06472 Tel 203-484-2184.

Ellis Pr, *(Ellis Press, The; 0-933180)*, P.O. Box 1443, Peoria, IL 61655.

Ellison Ent, *(Ellison Enterprises; 0-930580)*, 1919 Purdy Ave., Miami Beach, FL 33139 Tel 305-534-4454.

Ellman Studio, *(Ellman, Sylvia Stone, Studio)*, P.O. Box 93, Clawson, MI 48017.

Elm Tree Pr, *(Elm Tree Press; 0-918856)*, P.O. Box 185, La Crosse, WI 54601 Tel 608-637-3205.

Elmer, *(Elmer, William B.; 0-9601028)*, 2 Chestnut St., Andover, MA 01810 Tel 617-475-1020.

Elmer Edwards, *(Edwards, Elmer Eugene)*, P.O. Box 584, Miami, FL 33161.

Elmwood Pub Co, *(Elmwood Publishing Co., The; 0-931396)*, 2317 Howe St., Berkeley, CA 94705 Tel 415-843-3079.

Elohim, *(Elohim's Press; 0-930246)*, 4844 N. Drake St., Chicago, IL 60625 Tel 312-463-0414.

ELS Intl, *(ELS International Inc.; 0-89318),* 5761 Buckingham Pkwy., Culver City, CA 90230 Tel 213-642-0994.

Elsevier, *(Elsevier-North Holland Pub. Co.; 0-444; 0-7204),* 52 Vanderbilt Ave., New York, NY 10017 Tel 212-867-9040. *Imprints:* Biomedical Pr (Elsevier North-Holland Biomedical Press); Excerpta Medica (Excerpta-Medica); North Holland (North-Holland); Thomond Pr (Thomond Press).

Elsevier-Nelson, *(Elsevier/Nelson Books; 0-525),* 2 Park Ave., New York, NY 10016 Tel 212-725-1818.

Elsevier-Phaidon *Imprint of* **Dutton**

Elsevier Sci
See Elsevier

Elsevier Sci, *(Elsevier Scientific Publishing Co., Inc.),* ; Publisher Abbreviation Without Addresses Are for Titles That Are Out of Print. These Are Obsolete Abbreviations. Publisher's Abbreviation Is Now Elsevier.

Elysian Fields, *(Elysian Fields Publishing),* 1603 Burton St., Rockford, IL 61103; Moved, Left No Forwarding Address.

Elysium, *(Elysium Growth Press; 0-910550),* 5436 Fernwood Ave., Los Angeles, CA 90027 Tel 213-465-7121.

Embar Inc, *(Embar Inc.; 0-938418),* Box 813, Forest Grove, OR 97116.

Embee Pr, *(Embee Press; 0-89816),* 82 Pine Grove, Kingston, NY 12401.

Embroidy Bk
See C Schneider

EMC, *(EMC Corp.; 0-88436; 0-912022),* 180 E. Sixth St., St. Paul, MN 55101 Tel 612-227-7366.

Emerald Hse, *(Emerald House; 0-936958),* P.O. Box 388, Santa Rosa, CA 95402.

Emergence, *(Emergence Pubns.; 0-89465),* 185 Beacon Hill, Ashland, OR 97520 Tel 503-482-0666.

Emerson, *(Emerson Books, Inc.; 0-87523),* Reynolds Lane, Buchanan, NY 10511 Tel 914-739-3506.

Emerson Hall, *(Emerson Hall Pubs., Inc.),* 215 W. 98th St., New York, NY 10025 Tel 212-663-7690.

Emet Bks, *(Emet Books Inc.; 0-89476),* Box 501, Millwood, NY 10546 Tel 914-941-0043; Dist. by: Whirlwind Book Co., 80 Fifth Ave., New York, NY 10011.

Emmanuel Pr, *(Emmanuel Press; 0-917028),* P.O. Box 158, Saratoga, CA 95070; Moved, Left No Forwarding Address.

Emmett, *(Emmett Pub. Co.; 0-934682),* 2861 Burnham Blvd., Minneapolis, MN 55416.

Employee, *(Employee Relocation Council; 0-912614),* 1627 "K" St., N.W., Washington, DC 20006 Tel 202-857-0857.

Employee Benefit, *(Employee Benefit Research Institute; 0-86643),* 1920 N St., NW, No. 520, Washington, DC 20036.

Employment Info, *(Employment Information Services),* P.O. Box 3265, Chico, CA 95927.

Emporia State, *(Emporia State Press),* 1200 Commercial St., Emporia, KS 66801 Tel 316-343-1200.

Emporium Pubns, *(Emporium Pubns.; 0-88278),* 28 Sackville St., Charlestown, MA 02129 Tel 617-241-9549.

EMR Pubns, *(EMR Pubns.; 0-930308),* P.O. Box 4007, Bryan, TX 77801 Tel 713-779-5060.

En Passant Poet, *(En Passant Poetry Press; 0-9605098),* 4612 Sylvanus Dr., Wilmington, DE 19803 Tel 302-774-4571.

Enabling Syst, *(Enabling Systems, Inc.; 0-917688),* P.O. Box 2813, Honolulu, HI 96803 Tel 808-536-6528.

Encino Pr, *(Encino Press; 0-88426),* 510 Baylor St., Austin, TX 78703 Tel 512-476-6821.

Ency Brit Ed, *(Encyclopaedia Britannica Educational Corp.; 0-87827),* Affiliate of Encyclopaedia Britannica, Inc., 425 N. Michigan Ave., Chicago, IL 60611 Tel 312-321-6800.

Endeco Pub, *(Endeco Publishing Co.),* P. O. Box 930, Lemon Grove, CA 92045; Out of Business.

Endurance, *(Endurance Press; 0-910552),* 5695 Lumley St., Detroit, MI 48210 Tel 313-877-3596.

Energon Co, *(Energon Co.; 0-9601552),* Box 1352, Laramie, WY 82070 Tel 307-742-3458.

Energy Blacksouth, *(Energy Blacksouth Press),* Box 441, Howard University, Washington, DC 20059; 2805 Southmore, Houston, TX 77004.

Energy Educ, *(Energy Education Pubs.),* P.O. Box 6488, Grand Rapids, MI 49506 Tel 616-454-8264.

Eng Found, *(Engineering Foundation; 0-939204),* 345 E. 47th St., New York, NY 10017.

Eng Index Inc, *(Engineering Index, Inc.; 0-911820),* 345 E. 47th St., New York, NY 10017 Tel 212-644-7615.

Eng Joint Coun
See AAES

Eng Language, *(English Language Services; 0-87789),* Div. of Washington Educational Research Associates, Inc., 5761 Buckingham Pkwy., Culver City, CA 90230 Tel 213-642-0994.

Eng Pr, *(Engineering Press, Inc.; 0-910554),* P.O. Box 1, San Jose, CA 95103 Tel 408-258-4503.

Eng Pubns, *(Engineering Pubns.; 0-9605004),* P.O. Box 302, Blacksburg, VA 24060.

Engelmeier, *(Engelmeier, Philip A.; 0-9605002),* 909 Geary-517, San Francisco, CA 94109.

Engineers Pr, *(Engineer's Press; 0-930644),* P.O. Box 1651, Coral Gables, FL 33134 Tel 305-856-0031.

English Lang, *(English Language Services, Inc.; 0-89285),* 5761 Buckingham Pkwy., Culver City, CA 90230 Tel 213-642-0994.

Engwd Cliffs Coll, *(Englewood Cliffs College),* Hudson Terrace, Englewood Cliffs, NJ 07632; College Closed Since 1974.

Enitharmon Pr, *(Enitharmon Press),* Dist. by: SBD: Small Press Distribution, 1636 Ocean View Ave., Kensington, CA 94707 Tel 415-524-2107.

Enoch Pratt, *(Enoch Pratt Free Library; 0-910556),* 400 Cathedral St., Baltimore, MD 21201 Tel 301-396-5494.

Enrich, *(Enrich; 0-933358; 0-86582),* Div. of Ohaus, 760 Kifer Rd., Sunnyvale, CA 94086 Tel 408-733-5850.

Enslow Pubs, *(Enslow Pubs. Inc.; 0-89490),* Bloy St. & Ramsey Ave., Box 777, Hillside, NJ 07205 Tel 201-964-4116.

Entelek, *(Entelek, Inc.; 0-87567),* Ward-Whidden House, The Hill, P. O. Box 1303, Portsmouth, NH 03801 Tel 603-436-0439.

Enterprise Calif, *(Enterprise Pubns.; 0-918558),* P.O. Box 4001, Downey, CA 90241.

Enterprise Del, *(Enterprise Publishing Co.; 0-913864),* 725 Market St., Wilmington, DE 19801 Tel 302-654-0110.

Enterprise Pr, *(Enterprise Press),* Box 108, Bath, MI 48808 Tel 517-351-9171.

Entertainment Factory, *(Entertainment Factory, The; 0-936086),* P.O. Box 407, Cave Creek, AZ 85331.

Entheos, *(Entheos Communications, 0-939750),* P.O. Box 10696, Bainbridge Island, WA 98110 Tel 206-842-3641.

Entity Pub Co, *(Entity Publishing Co.; 0-89913),* 1314 Larmor Ave., Rowland Heights, CA 91748 Tel 714-598-1755.

Entomol Soc, *(Entomological Society of America),* 4603 Calvert Rd., College Park, MD 20740 Tel 301-864-1334.

Entomological Repr, *(Entomological Reprint Specialists; 0-911836),* P.O. Box 77224, Dockweiler Sta., Los Angeles, CA 90007 Tel 213-227-1285.

Entrepreneur Pr, *(Entrepreneur Press; 0-88205),* 3422 Astoria Circle, Fairfield, CA 94533 Tel 707-422-6822; Dist. by: Hawthorn Books, Inc., 260 Madison Ave., New York, NY 10016 Tel 212-725-7740.

Entropy Ltd, *(Entropy Ltd.),* South Great Rd., Lincoln, MA 01773.

Entwhistle Bks, *(Entwhistle Books; 0-9601428; 0-934558),* P.O. Box 611, Glen Ellen, CA 95442 Tel 707-996-3901.

Enviro Pr, *(Enviro Press; 0-937976),* P.O. Box 40284, Nashville, TN 37204 Tel 615-794-0110; Dist. by: CBI Publishers, 51 Sleeper St., Boston, MA 02210.

Environ Des VA, *(Environmental Design Press; 0-918436),* Div. of Educational & Research Management, Inc., P.O. Box 2187, Reston, VA 22090 Tel 703-471-1267.

Environ Design, *(Environmental Design & Research Ctr.; 0-915250),* 142 Lowell Ave., Newtonville, MA 02160 Tel 617-965-5910.

Environ Info, *(Environment Information Center, Inc., (EIC); 0-89947),* 292 Madison Ave., New York, NY 10017 Tel 212-949-9471.

Environ Pr, *(Environmental Press; 0-936960),* P.O. Box 701, Buffalo, NY 14205 Tel 301-942-0119.

Environ Pubns, *(Environmental Pubns. Assocs., Ltd),* 275 Broad Hollow Rd., Melville, NY 11747 Tel 516-752-9193.

Environ Res Inst, *(Environmental Research Institute of Michigan; 0-9603590),* P.O. Box 8618, Ann Arbor, MI 48107.

Environ Sci Serv, *(Environmental Science Services),* Div. of Park Publishing Co., 333 Hudson St., New York, NY 10013; Moved, Left No Forwarding Address.

Eon Bks, *(Eon Books; 0-916306),* 6356 Van Nuys Blvd., Suite 215, Van Nuys, CA 91401 Out of Business.

Ephemera, *(Ephemera & Books; 0-934792),* 7159 Crowley Ct., P.O. Box 19681, San Diego, CA 92119.

Epic Pubns, *(Epic Pubns., Inc.; 0-914244),* 4420 Westover Dr., Orchard Lake, MI 48033 Tel 313-626-6217.

EPICA, *(EPICA Task Force; 0-918346),* 1470 Irving St., N.W., Washington, DC 20010 Tel 202-332-0292.

Epiphany Pr, *(Epiphany Press; 0-916700),* P.O. Box 14606, San Francisco, CA 94114 Tel 415-431-1917.

Episcopal Ctr, *(Episcopal Center for Evangelism),* P. O. Box 920, Live Oak, FL 32060.

Episcopal Diocese, *(Episcopal Diocese of Pennsylvania; 0-917470),* 1700 Market St., Suite 1600, Philadelphia, PA 19103 Tel 215-567-6650.

EPM Pubns, *(EPM Pubns.; 0-914440),* 1003 Turkey Run Rd., McLean, VA 22101 Tel 703-356-5111; Orders to: P.O. Box 490, McLean, VA 22101.

EPWP, *(Eden Press Women's Pubns.; 0-920792)* P.O. Box 51, St. Albans, VT 05478 Tel 514-931-3910.

Equal Employ, *(Equal Employment Advisory Council; 0-937856),* 1015 Fifteenth St., N.W., Suite 1220, Washington, DC 20005.

Equipment Guide, *(Equipment Guide Book),* Div. of Dataquest, 2800 W. Bayshore Rd., Palo Alto, CA 94303 Tel 415-327-5100.

Equity Pub CA, *(Equity Publishing Co.; 0-939206),* 1850 E. 17th St., Santa Ana, CA 92701 Tel 714-547-8241.

Era Davidson, *(Era Press; 0-9605270),* Box 548, Davidson, NC 28036.

Era Pr NC, *(E R A Press; 0-918234),* Subs. of The New East Magazine, Box 1673, Greenville, NC 27834 Tel 919-752-7829.

Erbonia Bks, *(Erbonia Books, Inc.),* P. O. Box 396, New Paltz, NY 12561 Tel 914-895-3614.

Erewon Pr, *(Erewon Press; 0-916342),* P.O. Box 4253, Berkeley, CA 94704; Dist. by: Bookpeople, 2940 Seventh St., Berkeley, CA 94710 Tel 415-549-3030.

Ericson, *(Ericson; 0-9605868),* 215 Foster Dr., Des Moines, IA 50312 Tel 515-255-0798.

Eriksson, *(Eriksson, Paul S., Pubs.; 0-8397),* Battell Bldg., Middlebury, VT 05753 Tel 802-388-7303; Dist. by: Independent Publishers Group, 14 Vanderventer Ave., Port Washington, NY 11050 Tel 516-944-9325.

Erin Hills, *(Erin Hills Pubs.; 0-9600754),* 1390 Fairway Dr., San Luis Obispo, CA 93401 Tel 805-543-3050.

Ermine Pubs, *(Ermine Pubs., Inc.; 0-89343),* 6253 Hollywood Blvd., No. 312, Hollywood, CA 90028 Tel 213-461-3256; Dist. by: Whirlwind Book Co., 80 Fifth Ave., Suite 1106, New York, NY 10011 Tel 212-691-7280; Moved, Left No Forwarding Address.

Ernst, *(Ernst, Rick, Publishing Co.; 0-9603110),* P.O. Box 22940, Denver, CO 80222; Moved, Left No Forwarding Address.

Erskine, *(Erskine, Kathryn A.; 0-9605058),* Box 398, Hurricane, WV 25526.

ERUHG, *(External Representation of the Ukrainian Helsinki Group; 0-86725),* P.O. Box 770, Cooper Sta., New York, NY 10003 Tel 212-564-4334.

ESE Calif, *(ESE California; 0-912076),* 509 N. Harbor Blvd., La Habra, CA 90631 Tel 213-691-0737.

ESI, *(Educational Services, Inc.),* 350 Grove St., Somerville, NJ 08876 Tel 201-725-6021.

Esoteric Pubns, *(Esoteric Pubns.; 0-89861),* P.O. Box 325, Cottonwood, AZ 86326 Tel 602-634-7424.

ESP Corp, *(ESP Corp.; 0-9601610),* 195 Cortlandt St., Belleville, NJ 07109.

Esperanto League North Am, *(Esperanto League for North America, Inc.),* P.O. Box 1129, El Cerrito, CA 94530 Tel 415-653-0998.

ESPress, *(ESPress; 0-917200),* P.O. Box 8606, Washington, DC 20011 Tel 202-723-4578.

Essandess, *(Essandess Specials; 0-671),* Orders to: Simon & Schuster, Inc., 1230 Ave. of the Americas, New York, NY 10020 Tel 212-245-6400.

Essaye Pub, *(Essaye Publishing Co.; 0-939756),* 22713 Ventura Blvd., Suite F, Woodland Hills, CA 91364.

Essays in Lit W Ill U, *(Essays in Literature; 0-934312),* Dept. of English, Western Illinois Univ., Macomb, IL 61455 Tel 309-298-1113.

Esselte Video
See Nord Media

Essence Pubns, *(Essence Pubns.),* 168 Woodbridge Ave., Highland Park, NJ 08904 Tel 201-572-3120.

Essex County MA, *(Essex County History),* P.O. Box 444, West Newbury, MA 01985 Tel 617-465-5397.

Essex Inst, *(Essex Institute; 0-88389),* 132 Essex St., Salem, MA 01970 Tel 617-744-3390.

Essex Pubns, *(Essex Pubns.; 0-930332),* P.O. Box 2745, Boston, MA 02208 Tel 617-423-3410.

Estacado Bks, *(Estacado Books),* P.O. Box 4516, Lubbock, TX 79409 Tel 806-742-3115.

Estate Bk, *(Estate Book Sales),* 2824 Pennsylvania Ave., N.W., Washington, DC 20007 Tel 202-965-4274.

Estimators Handbk, *(Estimators Handbook),* 750 Whitmore, Detroit, MI 48203 Tel 313-345-5047; Moved Left No Forwarding Address.

ETC Pubns, *(ETC Pubns.; 0-88280),* 700 E. Vereda del Sur, Palm Springs CA 92262 Tel 714-325-5352; Orders to: Pubns. Dept., P.O. Drawer 1627-A, Palm Springs, CA 92263.

Etcetera Pr, *(Etcetera Press),* P. O. Drawer 27100, Columbus, OH 43227 Tel 614-436-7428.

Eternal Ent, *(Eternal Enterprises; 0-917578),* P.O. Box 60913, Sacramento, CA 95860; Name Formerly L P Price.

Ethics & Public Policy, *(Ethics & Public Policy Center, Inc.; 0-89633),* 1211 Connecticut Ave., NW, Washington, DC 20036 Tel 202-857-0595.

Ethics Res Ctr, *(Ethics Resource Center, Inc.; 0-916152),* 1730 Rhode Island Ave., N.W., Suite 717, Washington, DC 20036 Tel 202-223-3411.

Ethnotech, *(Ethnotech, Inc.; 0-933950),* P.O. Box 6627, Lincoln, NE 68506 Tel 402-489-8861.

Euclid Pub, *(Euclid Publishing Co., The; 0-935490),* Dist. by: Bond & Bacon Assocs., P.O. Box 121, Cathedral Sta., New York, NY 10025.

Eur-Am Music, *(European American Music; 0-913574),* 195 Allwood Road, Clifton, NJ 07012 Tel 201-777-2680.

Eurail Guide, *(Eurail Guide Annual; 0-912442),* 27540 Pacific Coast Hwy, Malibu, CA 90265 Tel 213-457-7286.

Euramerica Pr, *(Euramerica Press; 0-916876),* 381 N. Main St., Pittston, PA 18640 Tel 717-655-6637.

Euro *Imprint of* **Unipub**

Europa, *(Europa Camping & Caravaning),* 2306 Sixth St., Clay Center, KS 67432 Tel 913-632-5280; Moved, Left No Forwarding Address.

Europa *Imprint of* **Unipub**

Evanel, *(Evanel Associates; 0-918948),* Box 42, Northfield, OH 44067 Tel 216-467-1750.

Evang & Ref, *(Evangelical & Reformed Historical Society; 0-910564),* 555 W. James St., Lancaster, PA 17603.

Evang Authors, *(Evangelist Authors Society),* P.O. Box 6523, Anaheim, CA 92806.

Evang Sisterhood Mary, *(Evangelical Sisterhood of Mary),* 9849 N. 40th St., Phoenix, AZ 85028 Tel 602-996-4040.

Evang Tchr, *(Evangelical Teacher Training Assn.; 0-910566),* 110 Bridge St., P.O. Box 327, Wheaton, IL 60187 Tel 312-668-6400.

Evangel Indiana, *(Evangel Press),* 301 N. Elm, Nappanee, IN 46550.

Evans
See M Evans

Evans Pub Co, *(Evans Publishing Co.),* 5344 Shalley Circle, Ft. Myers, FL 33907.

Evans Pubns, *(Evans Pubns.),* P.O. Box 520, Perkins, OK 74059 Tel 405-547-2882.

Ever *Imprint of* **Grove**

EverBC *Imprint of* **Grove**

Everest Hse, *(Everest House Pubs.; 0-89696),* 33 W. 60th St., New York, NY 10023 Tel 212-246-3010; Orders to: Box 978, Edison, NJ 08817.

Everest Inc, *(Everest Inc.; 0-936788),* Box 7000-445, Redondo Beach, CA 90277; Box 45034, Los Angeles, CA 90045.

Everest Pub, *(Everest Publishing Co.; 0-931034),* Box 2686 Century Sta., Raleigh, NC 27602 Tel 919-787-8009.

Everett-Edwards, *(Everett/Edwards, Inc.; 0-912112),* P.O. Box 1060, DeLand, FL 32720 Tel 904-734-7458.

Everglades Pub Co, *(Everglades Publishing Co.; 0-913032),* P. O. Drawer Q, Everglades, FL 33929 Tel 813-695-4398.

Evergreen, *(Evergreen Press, Inc.; 0-914510),* P.O. Box 4971, Walnut Creek, CA 94596 Tel 415-825-7850.

Evergreen Christmas
See Evergreen

Evergreen Paddleways, *(Evergreen Paddleways; 0-916166),* 1416 21st St., Two Rivers, WI 54241 Tel 414-794-8485.

Evergreen Pr, *(Evergreen Press; 0-913056),* P.O. Box 1711, Oceanside, CA 92054 Tel 714-757-5976.

Evman *Imprint of* **Dutton**

EW Eng, *(EW Engineering, Inc.; 0-931728),* P.O. Box 28, Dunn Loring, VA 22027.

Ewing Pubns, *(Ewing Pubns.),* 575 Ewing St., Princeton, NJ 08540.

Ex Libris Sun, *(Ex Libris Sun Valley; 0-9603212),* Sun Valley, ID 83353.

Examiner Spec Proj
See Cal Living Bks

Exanimo Pr, *(Exanimo Press; 0-89316),* P.O. Box 18, 23520 Hwy. 12, Segundo, CO 81070.

Excelsior, *(Excelsior Books Pub., Inc.; 0-918566),* P.O. Box 3252, LaVale, MD 21502 Tel 301-722-5772.

Exceptional, *(Exceptional Books, Inc.; 0-910570),* P.O. Box 592, Ansonia Sta., New York, NY 10023; Out of business, Orders Will Be Filled by E. Alexander, 25 W. 68th St., New York,Ny 10023.

Exceptional Parent, *(Exceptional Parent Press, The; 0-930958),* 296 Boylston St., 3rd Floor, Boston, MA 02116.

Exceptional Pr Inc, *(Exceptional Press, Inc.; 0-914420),* P.O. Box 188, Glen Ridge, NJ 07028 Tel 201-748-2683.

Excerpta Medica, *(Excerpta-Medica),* ; Publisher Abbreviation Without Addresses Are for Titles That Are Out of Print. These Are Obsolete Abbreviations. Publisher's Abbreviation Is Now Elsevier.

Excerpta Medica *Imprint of* **Elsevier**

Excerpta Princeton, *(Excerpta Medica-Princeton),* 3131 Princeton Pike, Lawrenceville, NJ 08648.

Exec Ed Pr, *(Executive Education Press; 0-9600622),* 114 Liberty St., New York, NY 10006 Tel 212-349-6092.

Exec Ent, *(Executive Enterprises Pubns. Co., Inc.; 0-917386),* Div. of Executive Enterprises, Inc., 33 W. 60th St., Ninth Floor, New York, NY 10023 Tel 212-489-2671.

Exec Pub Co, *(Executive Publishing Co.; 0-913068),* 206 Washington Ave., Box 10013, Baltimore, MD 21204.

Exec Sal, *(Executive Salary Research Co.; 0-912716),* 1685 Sunrise Dr., Lima, OH 45805 Tel 419-991-3936; Orders to: P.O. 832, Lima, OH 45802.

Exec Stand, *(Executive Standards, Inc.; 0-917818),* 17 Spring St., Riverside, CT 06878 Tel 203-637-5700.

Exec West, *(Executives West Publishing Co.),* P.O. Box 15966, Phoenix, AZ 85060.

Executive Comm, *(Executive Communications; 0-917168),* 400 E. 54th St., New York, NY 10022 Tel 212-421-3713.

Executive Ent, *(Executive Enterprises),* 5811 La Jolla Corona Dr., La Jolla, CA 92037 Tel 714-459-4901; Do Not Confuse with Executive Enterprises Pubns. in NY.

Exelrod Pr, *(Exelrod Press; 0-917388),* P. O. Box 2303, Pleasant Hill, CA 94523 Tel 415-934-3357.

Existential Bks, *(Existential Books; 0-89231),* 1816 Stevens Ave.,S., Suite 25, Minneapolis, MN 55403 Tel 612-871-7275.

Exordium Pr, *(Exordium Press; 0-912784),* P.O. Box 635, Akron, OH 44309.

Exotic Beauties, *(Exotic Beauties Press, Inc.; 0-918378),* 403 W. 21 St., New York, NY 10011 Tel 212-929-4183.

Expedited, *(Expedited Publishing Co.; 0-9603122),* Div. of Patent Rights, Inc., P.O. Box 67, Scarborough, NY 10510.

Expedition Pr, *(Expedition Press; 0-939924),* 1832 Van Zee St., Kalamazoo, MI 49001.

Expertise Pub, *(Expertise Publishing Co.; 0-930136),* P.O. Box 1862, 311 Worder, Reno, NV 89502 Tel 702-322-8702.

Exploration Pr, *(Exploration Press; 0-913552),* Chicago Theological Seminary, 5757 S. Univ. Ave., Chicago, IL 60637 Tel 312-752-5757.

Explorations Inst, *(Explorations Institute; 0-918600),* P.O. Box 1254, 1711-A Grave St., Berkeley, CA 94701.

Explore Kansas, *(Explore Kansas),* Dist. by: Campgrounds Unlimited, P.O. Box 248, Wakefield, KS 67487.

Explorer Pub Co, *(Explorer Publishing Co.),* P.O. Box 385, Boston, MA 02117 Tel 617-536-3583.

Exponent, *(Exponent Ltd.; 0-935722),* 2243 First St., La Verne, CA 91750.

Exposition, *(Exposition Press, Inc.; 0-682),* 325 Kings Highway, Smithtown, NY 11787 Tel 516-582-6655. *Imprints:* Banner (Banner); Classic (Classic); Lochinvar (Lochinvar); University (University).

Express, *(Express),* P.O. Box 1373, Richmond, CA 94802 Tel 415-233-0167.

ExPressAll *(ExPressAll; 0-9361900),* 260 Dean Rd., Brookline, MA 02146 Tel 617-734-1297.

Expression, *(Expression Co.),* P.O. Box 153, Londonderry, NH 03053.

Expressions TX, *(Expressions, Inc.; 0-937768),* P.O. Box 1091, Arlington, TX 76010 Tel 817-461-5255.

Extension Texts, *(Extension Texts; 0-9600624),* P.O. Box 357, Cambridge, MA 02138.

Extequer, *(Extequer Press),* 1441 North Altadena Dr., Pasadena, CA 91107 Tel 213-797-3627; Orders to: P.O. Box 4193, Pasadena, CA 91106 Tel 213-797-3627.

Eyecontact, *(Eyecontact; 0-938112),* 465 Lexington Ave., New York, NY 10017.

F A Bowen, *(Bowen, F A., Reports; 0-9602830),* P.O. Box 213, Janesville, WI 53545 Tel 608-752-6333.

F A Countway, *(Countway, Francis A., Library of Medicine),* 10 Shattuck St., Boston, MA 02115.

F A Fleet, *(Fleet, Fred A., II; 0-933542),* P.O. Box 235, Washington, PA 15301; Moved, Left No Forwarding Address.

F A I R, *(FAIR-Federation for American Immigration Reform; 0-935776),* 1330 New Hampshire Ave. N.W., Washington, DC 20036.

F Adams, *(Adams, Frank, Pubns.; 0-913698),* P.O. Box 3194, Seattle, WA 98114 Tel 206-323-3376.

F Allen
See F Sypher

F Amato Pubns, *(Amato, Frank, Pubns.; 0-936608),* P.O. Box 02112, Portland, OR 97202 Tel 503-236-2305.

F & J Pub Corp, *(F&J Publishing Corporation; 0-89311),* 30941 Agoura Rd., Suite 232, Westlake Village, CA 91361; Moved, Left No Forwarding Address.

F Asbury Pub Co, *(Asbury, Francis, Publishing Co.),* P.O. Box 7, Wilmore, KY 40390.

F B Johnson, *(Johnson, Forrest Bryant; 0-9600510),* 230 Essex Court, Aurora, IL 60505 Tel 312-898-7079.

F Cass Co
See Biblio Dist

F D Smith, *(Smith, Frank D. (Tony) , Jr.; 0-9600944),* P.O. Box 1032, Catersville, GA 30120 Tel 404-382-0622.

F E Peters, *(Peters, Ferguson E., Co.; 0-918214),* P.O. Box 21587, Fort Lauderdale, FL 33335 Tel 305-463-1776.

F Eckhardt Assocs, *(Eckhardt, Fred, Associates),* P.O. Box 546, Portland, OR 97207 Tel 503-281-1473.

F F Fournies
    See F Fournies

F Fergeson, *(Fergeson, F., Productions; 0-935510),* Box 1072, Pearl City, HI 96782 Tel 808-833-0443.

F Fournies, *(Fournies, F., & Associates, Inc.; 0-917472),* 129 Edgewood Dr., Bridgewater, NJ 08807 Tel 201-526-2442.

F H Breise, *(Breise, Frederic H.; 0-938576),* 5750 Severin Dr., La Mesa, CA 92041.

F Hallman, *(Hallman, Frank),* Dist. by: SBD: Small Press Distribution, 1636 Ocean View Ave., Kensington, CA 94707 Tel 415-524-2107.

F I Comm, *(F. I. Communications; 0-89533),* 45 Alhambra, Portola Valley, CA 94025 Tel 415-851-0254; Orders to: P.O. Box 3121, Stanford, CA 94305.

F K Fruth, *(Fruth, Florence Knight),* 64 St. Andrews Dr., Beaver Falls, PA 15010 Tel 412-846-5282.

F L Gonzalez, *(Gonzalez, Fernando L.; 0-9601090),* P.O. Box 1812, Flushing, NY 11352 Tel 212-762-4593.

F M Atlas, *(FM Atlas Pub. Co.; 0-917170),* P.O. Box 24, Adolph, MN 55701 Tel 308-237-7953.

F M McCarty, *(McCarty, F. M., Co.; 0-911990),* 4527 Clawson Rd., Austin, TX 78745 Tel 512-447-6201.

F M Re, *(Re, Frank M.),* P.O. Drawer R, Hampton Bays, NY 11946 Tel 516-728-0123.

F M Roberts, *(Robert, F. M., Enterprises; 0-912746),* P.O. Box 608, Dana Point, CA 92629 Tel 714-493-1977.

F M Swan, *(Swan, Frances M.; 0-9602126),* 11533 Old St. Charles Rd., Bridgeton, MO 63044.

F Merriwell, *(Merriwell, Frank, Inc.; 0-8373),* 212 Michael Dr., Syosset, NY 11791 Tel 516-921-8888.

F Murat, *(Murat, Felix, Co.; 0-9600356),* 2132 N.W. 11th Ave., Miami, FL 33127.

F Peters, *(Peters, F., Co.),* 861 Hempstead Turnpike, Franklin Square, NY 11010.

F R Walker, *(Walker, Frank R., Co.; 0-911592),* 5030 N. Harlem Ave., Chicago, IL 60656 Tel 312-867-7070.

F S Hyde, *(Hyde, Floy S.; 0-9600528),* 7 Walling Blvd., Oneonta, NY 13820.

F Sypher, *(Sypher, Francis),* 220 E. 50th St., New York, NY 10022.

F T Yoon, *(Yoon, F. T., Co.; 0-931168),* P.O. Box 470, Pebble Beach, CA 93953 Tel 408-646-9499.

F V Kosikowski, *(Kosikowski, F. V., & Assocs.; 0-9602322),* P.O. Box 139, Brooktondale, NY 14817 Tel 607-272-7779.

F Widutis, *(Widutis, Florence),* 3318 Gumwood Dr., Hyattsville, MD 20783 Tel 301-422-3609.

Faber & Faber
    See Merrimack Bk Serv

Fablewaves, *(Fablewaves Press),* P.O. Box 7874, Van Nuys, CA 91409 Tel 213-785-9042.

Fabmath, *(Fabmath; 0-937138),* P.O. Box 568, Warrington, PA 18976.

Facsimile Bk, *(Facsimile Book Shop, Inc.),* 16 W. 55th St., New York, NY 10019.

Facts on File, *(Facts on File, Inc.; 0-87196),* 119 W. 57th St., New York, NY 10019 Tel 212-265-2011.

Faculty Pr, *(Faculty Press, Inc.; 0-910572),* 1449 37th St., Brooklyn, NY 11218 Tel 212-853-4141.

Fade In, *(Fade in Pubs.; 0-936748),* 312 S. 6th, Bozeman, MT 59715.

Fag Rag, *(Fag Rag Books; 0-915480),* P. O. Box 331, Kenmore Sta., Boston, MA 02215.

Fairbanks Bks, *(Fairbanks Books; 0-914830),* 815 17th St., Bellingham, WA 98225 Tel 206-733-3852.

Fairchild, *(Fairchild Books & Visuals; 0-87005),* 7 E. 12th St., New York, NY 10003 Tel 212-675-1242.

Fairfax County, *(Fairfax County),* 4100 Chain Bridge Rd., Fairfax, VA 22030.

Fairfield, *(Fairfield Press, Inc.; 0-913158),* 128 E. 62nd St., New York, NY 10021 Tel 212-838-7424.

Fairfield Hse, *(Fairfield House; 0-9602048),* 3 Fairfield Dr., Baltimore, MD 21228 Tel 301-747-6590.

Fairleigh Dickinson, *(Fairleigh Dickinson Univ. Press; 0-8386),* Div. of Associated University Presses, 4 Cornwall Dr., East Brunswick, NJ 08816 Tel 201-254-0132.

FairMail Serv, *(FairMail Service, Inc.; 0-9601262),* P.O. Box 746, Plainfield, NJ 07061; 417 Cleveland Ave., Plainfield, NJ 07060 Tel 201-754-7770.

Fairmont Pr, *(Fairmont Press, Inc., The; 0-915586),* 425 Pleasantdale Rd., N.E. Suite 340, Atlanta, GA 30340 Tel 404-447-5314.

Fairway Hse, *(Fairway House; 0-9603180),* P.O. Box 6344, Bakersfield, CA 93386.

Faith & Life, *(Faith & Life Press; 0-87303),* 718B Main St., Box 347, Newton, KS 67114 Tel 316-283-5100.

Faith Messenger, *(Faith Messenger Pubns.; 0-938544),* 1677 Cliffbranch Dr., Diamond Bar, CA 91765.

Faith Pub Hse, *(Faith Publishing House),* P. O. Box 518, 920 W. Mansur, Guthrie, OK 73044 Tel 405-282-1479.

Falcon Head Pr, *(Falcon Head Press, Ltd.; 0-914802),* P.O. Box 913, Golden, CO 80401.

Falcon Pr MT, *(Falcon Press Publishing; 0-934318),* P.O. Box 279, Billings, MT 59103.

Falcon Printing, *(Falcon Printing),* 2000 Strongs, Venice, CA 92091.

Falcon Pub, *(Falcon Publishing; 0-932542),* P.O. Box 688, Ben Lomond, CA 95005 Tel 408-336-8153.

Falkynor Bks, *(Falkynor Books; 0-916878),* Div. of G-Jo Institute, 4950 S.W. 70th Ave., Davie, FL 33314 Tel 305-581-4950.

Fallen Angel, *(Fallen Angel Press; 0-931598),* 1981 W. McNichols C1, Highland Park, MI 48203 Tel 313-864-0982.

Falling Wall, *(Falling Wall; 0-905046),* Dist. by: Flatiron Book Dists., 175 Fifth Ave., No. 814, New York, NY 10010.

Family Album, *(Family Album, ABAA, The; 0-934630),* RD 1, Box 42, Glen Rock, PA 17327.

Family Health, *(Family & Health Improvement Society; 0-9606024),* P.O. Box 952, Cambridge, OH 43725 Tel 614-432-3007.

Family Pr, *(Family Press; 0-9600666),* P. O. Box 16005, St. Paul, MN 55116 Tel 612-699-9108.

Family Pub CA, *(Family Publishing Co., The; 0-937770),* P. O. Box 462, Bodega, CA 94923 Tel 707-875-3373.

Family Pubns, *(Family Pubns.; 0-931128),* P.O. Box 398, Maitland, FL 32751 Tel 305-894-7060.

Family Serv, *(Family Service Assn. of America; 0-87304),* 44 E. 23rd St., New York, NY 10010 Tel 212-674-6100.

Family Soc Psych, *(Family Social & Psychotherapy Services),* Washington Square Bldg., 1414 E. Washington Ave., Suite 104, Madison, WI 53703 Tel 608-251-0839.

Family Therapy
    See Mehetabel & Co

Family World Pub Hse, *(Family World Publishing House, Inc.; 0-934176),* P.O. Box 1040, Media, PA 19063 Tel 215-353-3555.

Family YMCA Stanislaus, *(Family Young Men's Christian Assn. of Stanislaus County; 0-9604096),* 2700 McHenry Ave., Modesto, CA 95350 Tel 209-578-9622.

F&J Mazzulla, *(Mazzulla, Fred & Jo),* 1930 E. Eighth Ave., Denver, CO 80206 Tel 303-322-9119; Orders to: Mazfoto, 1130 Western Federal Savings Bldg., Denver, CO 80202.

F&S Pr, *(F&S Press; 0-86621),* Div. of Frost & Sullivan, 106 Fulton St., New York, NY 10038.

Fantaco, *(Fantaco Pubns.; 0-938782),* 21 Central Ave., Albany, NY 12110.

Fantasy Pub Co, *(Fantasy Publishing Co., Inc.),* c/o Borden Publishing Co., 1855 W. Main St., Alhambra, CA 91801 Tel 213-337-7947.

FAO *Imprint of* Unipub

Far Eastern Cult, *(Far Eastern Cultural Studies Institute; 0-918972),* 7 Forrest Court, East Grand Forks, MN 56721 Tel 218-773-9483; Moved, Left No Forwarding Address.

Far Eastern Pubns, *(Far Eastern Pubns.),* Box 2505 A, 340 Edward St., New Haven, CT 06520.

Far Eastern Res, *(Far Eastern Research & Pubn. Center; 0-912580),* P.O. Box 31151, Washington, DC 20031.

Far West Pr, *(Far West Press; 0-914480),* 3231 Pierce St., San Francisco, CA 94123.

Far Western Phil, *(Far Western Philosophy of Education Society; 0-931702),* c/o Dr. James John Jelinek, College of Education, Rm. 412, Hiram Bradford Farmer Education Bldg., Arizona State Univ., Tempe, AZ 85281 Tel 602-965-3674.

Faraday, *(Faraday Press; 0-939762),* 1487 Noe St., San Francisco, CA 94131 Tel 415-821-0341.

Farallon *Imprint of* **Pacific Coast**

Farm & Ranch, *(Farm & Ranch Vacations, Inc.; 0-913214),* 36 E. 57th St., New York, NY 10022 Tel 212-355-6334.

Farm Journal, *(Farm Journal, Inc.; 0-89795),* 230 W. Washington Square, Philadelphia, PA 19105.

Farmer Ent, *(Farmer, Wesley M., Enterprises,Inc.; 0-937772),* P.O. Box 26653 Tempe, AZ 85282.

Farnswth Pub, *(Farnsworth Publishing Co., Inc.; 0-910580; 0-87863),* 78 Randall Ave., Rockville Ctr., NY 11570 Tel 516-536-8400.

Farnum Films, *(Farnum Films; 0-915790),* Executive House, 225 E. 46th St., New York, NY 10017 Tel 212-371-8679; Orders to: P.O. Box 1094, New York, NY 10017.

Farrar Bks, *(Farrar Books),* 73 Poplar St., Garden City, NY 11530 Tel 516-747-2936.

Farrar Pub, *(Farrar Publishing; 0-9605588),* 25 Library Ave., Warrensburg, NY 12885.

FAS Pubs, *(FAS Pubs.),* P.O. Box 5453, Madison, WI 53705 Tel 608-274-1733.

FASEB, *(Federation of American Societies for Experimental Biology; 0-913822),* 9650 Rockville Pike, Bethesda, MD 20014 Tel 301-530-7030.

Fashion Imprints, *(Fashion Imprints Associates; 0-9602860),* Box 3523, Merchandise Mart, Chicago, IL 60654 Tel 312-821-5922.

Fast & McMillan, *(Fast & McMillan Pubs.),* 820 East Blvd., Charlotte, NC 28203 Tel 704-554-7020.

Fathom Ents, *(Fathom Enterprises, Inc.),* Box 2284 Palos Verdes Peninsula, Palos Verdes, CA 90274 Tel 213-519-8944.

Faubus, *(Faubus, Orval E.),* c/o Pioneer Press, P.O. Box 191, Little Rock, AR 72201 Tel 501-374-0271; Orders to: 114 E. 2nd St., Little Rock, AR 72203.

Fault Pubns, *(Fault Pubns.; 0-930646),* 33513 6th St., Union City, CA 94587 Tel 415-487-1383.

Fawcett, *(Fawcett Book Group; 0-449),* 1515 Broadway, New York, NY 10036 Tel 212-975-7660. *Imprints:* Crest (Crest Books); GM (Gold Medal Books); Juniper (Juniper); Prem (Premier Books).

Fawcett World
    See Fawcett

Fawcett World, *(Fawcett World Library),* ; Publisher Abbreviation Without Addresses Are for Titles That Are Out of Print. These Are Obsolete Abbreviations. Publisher's Abbreviation Is Now Fawcett.

Fax Collect, *(Fax Collector's Editions, Inc.; 0-913960),* P.O. Box 851, Mercer Island, WA 98040 Tel 206-232-8484.

Faxon, *(Faxon, F. W., Co., Inc.; 0-87305),* 15 Southwest Park, Westwood, MA 02090 Tel 617-329-3350.

Fayette County Bicentennial, *(Fayette County Bicentennial Commission; 0-9601642),* 307 N. Sixth St., Vandalia, IL 62471 Tel 618-283-0024.

FB *Imprint of* **B&N**

FBL *Imprint of* **G&D**

FCA Bks., *(FCA Books for the Arts; 0-933032),* 280 Broadway, Suite 412, New York, NY 10007 Tel 212-227-3770.

FDC Pub, *(F.D.C. Publishing Co.; 0-89794),* P.O. Box 206, Stewartsville, NJ 08886.

Fearon, *(Fearon Pubs., Inc.),* ; Publisher Abbreviation Without Addresses Are for Titles That Are Out of Print. These Are Obsolete Abbreviations. Publisher's Abbreviation Is Now Fearon-Pitman.

Fearon-Pitman
    See Pitman Learning

FEB, *(First Edition Books/FEB Co.; 0-89502),* FEB Bldg., 120 Clairton Blvd., Pittsburgh, PA 15236 Tel 412-655-9733.

Fed Aviation, *(Federal Aviation Exams Co.; 0-938706)*, 1669 Maple, Suite 6, Solvang, CA 93463.

Fed Employ & Guidance, *(Federation Employment & Guidance Service; 0-934186)*, 215 Park Ave. S., New York, NY 10003 Tel 212-777-4900.

Fed Employees, *(Federal Employees News Digest, Inc.; 0-910582)*, P.O. Box 457, Merrifield, VA 22116 Tel 703-533-3031.

Fed Legal Pubn, *(Federal Legal Pubns., Inc.; 0-87945)*, 157 Chambers St., New York, NY 10007 Tel 212-243-5775.

Fed Res Bank MN, *(Federal Reserve Bank of Minneapolis; 0-915484)*, 250 Marquette Ave, Minneapolis, MN 55480 Tel 612-340-2345.

Fed Soc Coat Tech, *(Federation of Societies for Coatings Technology; 0-934010)*, 1315 Walnut St., Suite 832, Philadelphia, PA 19107 Tel 215-545-1506.

Federlin, *(Federlin, Tom; 0-9603136)*, 106 Macdougal St., New York, NY 10012.

Fedora Bks, *(Fedora Books)*, P.O. Box 265, Hopedale, MA 01747; Moved,Left No Forwarding Address.

Feet Pub Co, *(Feet Publishing Co.; 0-932228)*, P.O. Box 58177, Raleigh, NC 27658.

Feffer & Simons *Imprint of* **Burgess**

Feist Pubns, *(Feist Pubns.)*, 2827 Seventh St., Berkeley, CA 94710 Tel 415-841-5771.

Feldco Ent, *(Feldco Enterprises; 0-9603550)*, Woodward Bldg., Suite 100, Birmingham, AL 35203.

Feldheim, *(Feldheim, Philipp, Inc.; 0-87306)*, 96 E. Broadway, New York, NY 10002 Tel 212-925-3180.

Feldman, *(Feldman, Mildred L. B.)*, 1424 S. Alameda Dr., Baton Rouge, LA 70815 Tel 504-925-9666.

Felicity, *(Felicity Press; 0-9603846)*, Box 14382, University Sta., Gainesville, FL 32604 Tel 904-475-2963.

Fell, *(Fell, Frederick, Pubs., Inc.; 0-8119)*, 386 Park Ave., S., New York, NY 10016 Tel 212-685-9017. *Imprints:* Aim-High (Aim-High), Pegasus Rex (Pegasus Rey)

Fellowship, *(Fellowship Pubns.; 0-911810)*, P.O. Box 271, Nyack, NY 10960 Tel 914-358-4601.

Fellowship Crown, *(Fellowship of the Crown)*, P.O. Box 3743, Carmel, CA 93921 Tel 408-624-5600.

Fellowship of Recon, *(Fellowship of Reconciliation; 0-911810)*, Box 271, Nyack, NY 10960 Tel 212-568-8200.

Fellowship Pr PA, *(Fellowship Press; 0-914390)*, 5820 Overbrook Ave., Philadelphia, PA 19131 Tel 215-879-8604.

Fels & Firn, *(Fels & Firn Press; 0-918704)*, 1843 Vassar Ave., Mountain View, CA 94043 Tel 415-965-4291.

Felten, *(Felten, Charles J.; 0-9600312)*, 1532 Essex Dr., N., St. Petersburg, FL 33710; Moved Left No Forwarding Address.

Feminist Comm, *(Feminist Committee Press, The; 0-9603330)*, 3921 Land O'lakes Dr., N.E., Atlanta, GA 30342 Tel 404-231-0988.

Feminist Pr, *(Feminist Press; 0-912670; 0-935312)*, SUNY/College at Old Westbury, Box 334, Old Westbury, NY 11568 Tel 516-997-7660.

Fenimore Bk, *(Fenimore Book Store)*, Lake Rd., Cooperstown, NY 13326 Tel 607-547-2533.

Fenn Gall Pub, *(Fenn Galleries Publishing; 0-937634)*, 1075 Paseo De Peralta, Santa Fe, NM 87501.

Fennwyn Pr, *(Fennwyn Press)*, 920 E., St. Patrick, Rapid City, SD 57701; Dist. by: Honor Books, P.O. Box 94, Spearfish, SD 57783.

Ferguson, *(Ferguson, J. G., Publishing Co.; 0-89434)*, 111 E. Wacker Dr., Suite 500, Chicago, IL 60601 Tel 312-782-8284.

Fermata, *(Fermata Press; 0-939792)*, 40 Harriett Rd., Gloucester, MA 01930 Tel 617-283-5849.

Fernhill, *(Fernhill House, Ltd.; 0-87522)*, ; Publisher Abbreviation Without Addresses Are for Titles That Are Out of Print. These Are Obsolete Abbreviations.Publisher Acquired by Humanities Press, Inc.

Ferry Pr
　　See SBD

Fertig, *(Fertig, Howard, Inc.; 0-86527)*, 80 E. 11th St., New York, NY 10003 Tel 212-982-7922.

Festival *Imprint of* **Abingdon**

Festival Pubns, *(Festival Pubns.; 0-930828)*, P.O. Box 10180, Glendale, CA 91209 Tel 213-766-1798.

Fibar Designs, *(Fibar Designs; 0-932086)*, The Fannings, 632 Bay Rd., Menlo Park, CA 94025; Orders to: P.O. Box 2634, Menlo Park, CA 94025.

Fiberarts, *(Fiberarts; 0-937274)*, 50 College St, Asheville, NC 28801; Dist. by: Hastings House Publishers, 10 E. 40th St., New York, NY 10016 Tel 212-689-5400.

Fibonacci Corp, *(Fibonacci Corp.; 0-915494)*, Golden Bridge, NY 10526 Tel 914-232-4293.

FICOA, *(Film Instruction Co. of America; 0-931974)*, 2901 S. Wentworth Ave., Milwaukee, WI 53207.

Fiction Coll, *(Fiction Collective, Inc.; 0-914590)*, c/o George Braziller, Inc., One Park Ave., New York, NY 10016.

Fictioneer Bks, *(Fictioneer Books, Ltd; 0-934882)*, Box B.I.P, Screamer Mountain, Clayton, GA 30525 Tel 404-782-3318.

FID, *(Food Industries Directories; 0-933194)*, 25 Broad St., New York, NY 10004 Tel 212-344-1450.

Fideler, *(Fideler Co.; 0-88296)*, 31 Ottawa Ave., N. W., Grand Rapids, MI 49503 Tel 616-456-8577.

Fidelis Pubs, *(Fidelis Pubs., Inc.)*, P.O. Box 1334, Palm Desert, CA 92261 Tel 714-345-5346.

Fides
　　See Fides Claretian

Fides, *(Fides Pubs., Inc.)*, ; Publisher Abbreviation Without Addresses Are for Titles That Are Out of Print. These Are Obsolet E Abbreviations. Publisher's Abbreviationiis Now Fides Claretian.

Fides Claretian, *(Fides/Claretian; 0-8190)*, 333 N. Lafayette, South Bend, IN 46601 Tel 219-288-3050.

Field Educ, *(Field Educational Pubns., Inc.; 0-514)*, Subs. of Field Enterprises, Inc., 609 Mission St., San Francisco, CA 94105.

Field Ent
　　See World Bk-Childcraft

Field Mus, *(Field Museum of Natural History; 0-914868)*, Roosevelt Rd., at Lake Shore Dr., Chicago, IL 60605 Tel 312-922-9410.

Field Oberlin, *(Field Translations Series/Oberlin College; 0-932440)*, Rice Hall, Oberlin College, Oberlin, OH 44074 Tel 216-775-8407.

Fielding, *(Fielding Pubns.)*, 105 Madison Ave., New York, NY 10016 Tel 212-889-3050; Dist. by: William Morrow & Co., 6 Henderson Dr., West Caldwell, NJ 07006.

Fieldston, *(Fieldston Press; 0-912166)*, Orders to: P.O. Box 3413, New York, NY 10017.

Fiesta City, *(Fiesta City Pubs.; 0-940076)*, P.O. Box 5861, Santa Barbara, CA 93108.

Fiesta Pub, *(Fiesta Publishing Corp.; 0-88473)*, 6360 N.E. 4th Court, Miami, FL 33138 Tel 305-751-1181.

Fig Leaf, *(Fig Leaf Creations; 0-918774)*, 1706 Olive Ave., Santa Barbara, CA 93101 Tel 805-962-4987.

FIG Ltd, *(F. I. G. Ltd.; 0-9601452)*, P.O. Box 23, Northbrook, IL 60062.

Figures, *(Figures, The; 0-935724)*, 2016 Cedar, Berkeley, CA 94709.

Fill the Gap, *(Fill the Gap Pubns.; 0-89858)*, P.O. Box 53817, Lafayette, LA 70505 Tel 318-234-0678.

Filmrow Pubns, *(Filmrow Pubns.)*, 8272 Sunset Blvd., W. Hollywood, CA 90046 Tel 213-654-8310.

Filsinger & Co, *(Filsinger & Co., Ltd.; 0-916754)*, 150 Waverly Place, New York, NY 10014 Tel 212-243-7421.

Filson Club, *(Filson Club, Inc.; 0-9601072)*, 118 W. Breckinridge St., Louisville, KY 40203 Tel 502-582-3727.

Filter, *(Filter Press; 0-910584; 0-86541)*, P.O. Box 5, Palmer Lake, CO 80133 Tel 303-481-2523.

Finan Exec, *(Financial Executives Research Foundation; 0-910586)*, 633 Third Ave., New York, NY 10017 Tel 212-953-0500.

Finan Pub, *(Financial Publishing Co.; 0-87600)*, 82 Brookline Ave., Boston, MA 02215 Tel 617-262-4040.

Finan Strategies, *(Financial Strategies, Inc.; 0-938602)*, P.O. Box 442, Cambridge, MA 02138.

Financial Pr, *(Financial Press, Inc.)*, 4975 S.W. 82nd St., Miami, FL 33143.

Financial Pub CA, *(Financial Pubs.)*, Drawer 518, Westminster, CA 92683.

Financial Tech, *(Financial Technology Ltd.; 0-915292)*, 4 Echo Lane, New Brunswick, NJ 08816 Tel 201-998-2700; Moved, Left No Forwarding Address.

Fine Arts Mus, *(Fine Arts Museums of San Francisco; 0-88401)*, M.H. De Young Museum, Golden Gate Park, San Francisco, CA 94118 Tel 415-558-2887.

Fine Arts Soc, *(Fine Arts Society; 0-932192)*, 50459 N. Portage Rd., South Bend, IN 46628 Tel 219-272-9290; Orders to: 2314 W. Sixth St., Mishawaka, IN 46544 Tel 219-255-8606.

Fineline, *(Fineline Co.; 0-917520)*, 303 Fifth Ave., New York, NY 10016 Tel 212-684-3369.

Fineline Pubns, *(Fineline Pubns.; 0-932492)*, 2517 Quincy N.E., Albuquerque, NM 87110 Tel 505-884-3367.

Finn Hill, *(Finn Hill Arts; 0-917270)*, P.O. Box 542, Silverton, CO 81433 Tel 303-387-5729.

Finney Co, *(Finney Co.; 0-912486)*, 3350 Gorham Ave., Minneapolis, MN 55426 Tel 612-929-6165.

Fintzenberg, *(Fintzenberg Pubs.; 0-914928)*, P.O. Box 301, Long Beach, NY 11561 Tel 516-431-9156.

Fire Eng, *(Fire Engineering Book Dept.)*, Div. of Technical Publishing Co., A Dun & Bradstreet Co., 666 Fifth Ave., New York, NY 10019.

Fire Engine Bk
　　See Fire Eng

FireBuilders, *(FireBuilders, The; 0-9601794)*, RR1, Box 620, Stetson Rd., Brooklyn, CT 06234 Tel 203-774-4824.

Fireplug Pr, *(Fireplug Press; 0-932494)*, 2461 N. Clark, Chicago, IL 60657; Moved, Left No Forwarding Address.

Fireside *Imprint of* **S&S**

Fireside Bks, *(Fireside Books; 0-87527)*, Div. of Warren H. Green, Inc., 8356 Olive Blvd., St. Louis, MO 63132 Tel 314-991-1335.

Fireside Pr, *(Fireside Press)*, Box 5293, Hamden, CT 06518 Tel 203-248-1023.

Firestein Bks, *(Firestein Books; 0-9602498)*, 11959 Barrel Cooper Court, Reston, VA 22091 Tel 703-860-1637.

Firestone, *(Firestone, W. D., Press; 0-934562)*, 1313 S. Jefferson Ave., Springfield, MO 65807 Tel 417-866-5141.

Firey, *(Firey, Walter; 0-9603066)*, 1307 Wilshire Blvd., Austin, TX 78722 Tel 512-454-2418.

Firm Foun Pub, *(Firm Foundation Publishing House)*, P.O. Box 610, Austin, TX 78767 Tel 512-452-7651.

First Am Bank, *(1st American Bank for Savings)*, 572 Columbia Rd., Dorchester, MA 02125.

First Amend, *(First Amendment Press)*, P.O. Box 7334, Stanford, CA 94305 Tel 415-851-3391.

First Church, *(First Church of Christ Scientist)*, 1 Norway St., Boston, MA 02115 Tel 617-262-2300.

First Impressions, *(First Impressions Publishing Co.; 0-934794)*, P.O. Box 9073, Madison, WI 53715 Tel 608-238-6254.

First Person, *(First Person; 0-916452)*, Washington Spring Rd., Palisades, NY 10964 Tel 914-359-2995.

Firth, *(Firth, Robert H.; 0-9605060)*, 20351 Lake Erie Dr., Walnut, CA 91789.

Fischer Inc NY, *(Fischer, Carl, Inc.; 0-8258)*, 62 Cooper Square, New York, NY 10003.

Fisher Inst, *(Fisher Institute, The; 0-933028)*, 6350 LBJ Freeway, Suite 183E, Dallas, TX 75240.

Fitness, *(Fitness Pubns.; 0-918278)*, 53 Colburn Dr., Poughkeepsie, NY 12603 Tel 914-463-1626; Orders to: P.O. Box 1786, Poughkeepsie, NY 12601.

Fitness Products, *(Fitness Products Ltd.)*, P.O. Box 32391, Washington, DC 20007 Tel 202-333-8000.

FitzGerald & Assocs, *(FitzGerald, Jerry, & Associates; 0-932410)*, 506 Barkentine Lane, Redwood City, CA 94065 Tel 415-591-5676.

FitzSimons, *(FitzSimons, H. T., Co., Inc.; 0-912222)*, 357 W. Erie St., Chicago, IL 60610 Tel 312-944-1841.

Five Arms Corp, *(Five Arms Corp.; 0-9604892)*, 3813 Briar Place, Office 9, Dayton, OH 45405.

Five Assocs
　　See Mus Graphics

Five Mile Riv, *(Five Mile River Press; 0-910594),* P. O. Box 68, Rowayton Sta., Norwalk, CT 06853 Tel 203-838-8317.

Five Star Pubs, *(Five Star Pubs.),* Box 1398, Tupelo, MS 38801 Tel 601-844-5036.

Five Starr Prods, *(Five Starr Productions; 0-9606026),* 1610 Christine, Wichita Falls, TX 76302 Tel 301-838-8059.

Five Trees, *(Five Trees Press),* 1061 Folsom St., San Francisco, CA 94103 Tel 415-552-2122; Moved, Left No Forwarding Address.

Flame Intl, *(Flame International Inc.; 0-933184),* P. O. Box 305, Quantico, VA 22134.

Flame Pubs, *(Flame Pubs.; 0-914702),* Drawer S, Rome, GA 30161.

Flare Imprint of **Avon**

Flayderman, *(Flayderman, N., & Co., Inc.; 0-910598),* Squash Hollow Rd., New Milford, CT 06776 Tel 203-354-5567.

Fleet, *(Fleet Press Corp.; 0-8303),* 160 Fifth Ave., New York, NY 10010 Tel 212-243-6100.

Fleschner, *(Fleschner Publishing Co.; 0-937878),* 41 Village Lane, Bethany, CT 06525.

Flight Safety, *(Flight Safety Foundation, Inc.; 0-912768),* 5510 Columbia Pike, Arlington, VA 22204 Tel 703-820-2777.

Flint Hills, *(Flint Hills Book Co.),* 1735 Fairview, Manhattan, KS 66502.

Flint Inst Arts, *(Flint Institute of Arts; 0-939896),* 1120 E. Kearsley St., Flint, MI 48503 Tel 313-234-1695.

Floating Island, *(Floating Island Pubns.),* P.O. Box 516, Point Reyes Sta., CA 94956.

Flor Del Oro, *(Flor Del Oro; 0-930426),* P.O. Box 80007, Albuo, NM 87108 Tel 505-266-4995.

Flora & Fauna, *(Flora & Fauna Pubns.; 0-916846),* 90 Wallace Rd., P.O. Box 505, Kinderhook, NY 12106.

Floreat, *(Floreat Press),* Dist. by: Book People, 2940 Seventh St., Berkeley, CA 94710.

Florham, *(Florham Park Press, Inc.; 0-912598),* P.O. Box 303, Florham Park, NJ 07932 Tel 201-377-3670.

Florida Sun-Gator, *(Florida Sun-Gator Publishing Co.),* P.O. Box 365, Oviedo, FL 32765 Tel 305-671-3633.

Flourtown Pub, *(Flourtown Publishing Co.; 0-9603376),* P.O. Box 148, Flourtown, PA 19031.

Flower Mountain, *(Flower Mountain Press; 0-913680),* Dist. by: Light Impressions, Box 3012, Rochester, NY 14614.

Flying Buttress, *(Flying Buttress Pubns.; 0-918348),* P.O. Box 254, Endicott, NY 13760 Tel 607-785-5423.

Flying Diamond Bks, *(Flying Diamond Books; 0-918532),* Box D301, Hettinger, ND 58639 Tel 701-567-2646.

Flying Ent, *(Flying Enterprises, Inc; 0-912470),* Box 7000, Dallas, TX 75209 Tel 214-358-3456.

Flying Three Ent, *(Flying 3 Enterprises),* P.O. Box 690, Littleton, CO 80120 Tel 303-795-8402.

FMME Imprint of **Unipub**

FMME-COA Imprint of **Unipub**

FNB Imprint of **Unipub**

Focal Pr, *(Focal Press, Inc.),* 10 E. 40th St., Suite 3600, New York, NY 10016 Tel 212-679-1777.

Focus, *(Focus),* 2710 S. 75 E. Ave., Tulsa, OK 74129 Tel 918-664-5138.

Focus Quality, *(Focus Quality Games Corp.; 0-915236),* P.O. Box 114, Blythebourne Sta., Brooklyn, NY 11219.

Fogg Art, *(Fogg Art Museum; 0-916724),* Div. of Harvard University, 32 Quincy St., Cambridge, MA 02138 Tel 617-495-2387.

Folcroft, *(Folcroft Library Editions; 0-8414),* P.O. Box 182, Folcroft, PA 19032.

Folder Edns, *(Folder Editions; 0-913152),* 103-26 68th Rd., Apt A63, Forest Hills, NY 11375; Dist. by: Caroline House Books, 2 Ellis Place, Ossining, NY 10562.

Folger Bks, *(Folger Books; 0-918016),* Folger Shakespeare Library, 201 E. Capitol St., S.E., Washington, DC 20003 Tel 202-546-4700.

Folio, *(Folio Magazine Pub. Corp.; 0-918110),* P.O. Box 697, 125 Elm St., New Canaan, CT 06840 Tel 203-972-0761.

Folio Pubs, *(Folio Pubs.; 0-939454),* 1121 Ridgeview Dr., Nashville, TN 37220.

Folk Art, *(Folk Art Studios; 0-930310),* P.O. Box 162, El Toro, CA 92630 Tel 714-837-6488.

Folk Art Pr, *(Folk Art Press, The; 0-9602486),* 17064 Mindora Court, Granada Hills, CA 91344.

Folk-Legacy, *(Folk-Legacy Records, Inc.),* Sharon Rd., Sharon, CT 06069.

Folkestone, *(Folkestone Press; 0-910600),* P.O. Box 3142, St. Louis, MO 63130 Tel 314-725-2767.

Folksay Pr, *(Folksay Press; 0-916454),* 67131 Mills Rd., R.R. 3, St. Clairsville, OH 43950 Tel 614-695-3348; Dist. by: Bookpeople, 2940 Seventh St., Berkeley, CA 94710 Tel 415-549-3033.

Folkways Pr, *(Folkways Press),* Drawer 1834, Boone, NC 28607.

Follett, *(Follett Publishing Co.; 0-695),* Div. of Follett Corp., 1010 W. Washington Blvd., Chicago, IL 60607 Tel 312-666-5858.

Fontana
See **J M Fontana**

Fontana Pap Imprint of **Watts**

Food for Thought, *(Food for Thought Pubns.),* P.O. Box 331, Amherst, MA 01004 Tel 413-256-6158.

Food Processors, *(Food Processors Institute, The; 0-937774),* 1133 20th St. NW, Washington, DC 20036.

Food Res Action, *(Food Research & Action Center Inc.; 0-934220),* 2011 Eye St. N.W., Washington, DC 20006.

Foot Trails, *(Foot Trails Pubns., Inc.; 0-933710),* The Pottingshed, Bedford Rd., Greenwich, CT 06830; Dist. by: Simon & Schuster, Inc., 1230 Ave. of the Americas, New York, NY 10020 Tel 212-245-6400.

Football Hobbies, *(Football Hobbies, Pubs.; 0-912122),* 4216 McConnell, El Paso, TX 79904 Tel 915-565-7354.

Football Ill, *(Football Rules Illustrated Publishing Co.; 0-9600364),* P.O. Box 3005, Austin, TX 78764.

Foothills Art
See **Riverstone Foothills**

Foothills Pr, *(Foothills Press; 0-917284),* P.O. Box 458, Pittsfield, MA 01202 Tel 413-499-4687.

Footloose Pr, *(Footloose Press),* P.O. Box 3353, Hayward, CA 94540 Tel 415-538-1197.

Footsteps, *(Footsteps Press; 0-934796),* P.O. Box 948, Hobbs, NM 88240.

Forbes
See **G F Forbes**

Ford Assocs, *(Ford Associates),* 824 E. Seventh St., Auburn, IN 46706.

Ford Mus Imprint of **Edison Inst**

Fordham, *(Fordham Univ. Press; 0-8232),* University Box L, Bronx, NY 10458 Tel 212-933-2233.

Fordham Pub, *(Fordham Equipment & Publishing Co.; 0-913308),* 3308 Edson Ave., Bronx, NY 10469 Tel 212-379-7300.

Fords Travel, *(Fords Travel Guides; 0-916486),* Box 505, 22151 Clarendon St., Woodland Hills, CA 91365 Tel 213-347-1677.

Forecasting Software, *(Forecasting Software Corp.; 0-916756),* 390 Plandome Rd., Suite 203, Manhasset, NY 11030; Moved, Left No Forwarding Address.

Foreign Policy, *(Foreign Policy Assn.; 0-87124),* 205 Lexington Ave., New York, NY 10016 Tel 212-481-8450.

Foreign Pubns, *(Foreign Pubns., Inc.),* 51 E. 42nd St., New York, NY 10017.

Foreign Travel, *(Foreign Travel Features),* P.O. Box 5125, Lighthouse Point, FL 33064 Tel 305-942-7085; Moved, Left No Forwarding Address.

Foresight Bks, *(Foresight Books; 0-910606),* P.O. Box 394, Unionville, CT 06085.

Forest Hill, *(Forest Hill Press; 0-9605472),* 3974 Forest Hill Ave., Oakland, CA 94602.

Forest Hist Soc, *(Forest History Society, Inc.; 0-89030),* 109 Coral St., Santa Cruz, CA 95060 Tel 408-426-3770.

Forest Pr, *(Forest Press Division Lake Placid Education Foundation; 0-910608),* 85 Watervliet Ave., Albany, NY 12206 Tel 518-489-8549.

Forest Prod, *(Forest Products Research Society; 0-935018),* 2801 Marshall Court, Madison, WI 53705 Tel 608-231-1361.

Forest Pub, *(Forest Publishing; 0-9605118),* 222 Wisconsin, Lake Forest, IL 60045.

Foreword Bk, *(Foreword Books; 0-9602884),* 11 Graftam Rd., South Portland, ME 04106 Tel 207-799-4387; Dist. by: Chicago Review Press, 820 N. Franklin St., Chicago, IL 60610 Tel 312-644-5457.

Foris Pubns, *(Foris Pubns.),* Box 1132, Delran, NJ 08075 Tel 609-829-6830; Orders to: Box C-50, Cinnaminson, NJ 08077. Imprints: Bird-Sci Bks (Bird-Sci Books).

Forkner, *(Forkner Publishing Corp.; 0-912036),* P.O. Box 652, Ridgewood, NJ 07451 Tel 201-447-0661.

Formur Intl, *(Formur International; 0-89378),* 4200 Laclede Ave., St. Louis, MO 63108.

Forrest Bryant
See **F B Johnson**

Forsyth Gall, *(Forsyth Gallery; 0-9601560),* P.O. Box 525, Cooper Sta., New York, NY 10003 Tel 212-925-6697.

Fort Concho, *(Fort Concho Sketches Publishing Co.),* P.O. Box 5262, San Angelo, TX 76902.

Fort Sullivan, *(Fort Sullivan Chapter (Daughters of the American Revolution)),* P.O. Box 33055, Charleston, SC 29407.

Fortress, *(Fortress Press; 0-8006),* 2900 Queen Lane, Philadelphia, PA 19129 Tel 800-822-3906.

Fortuna, *(Fortuna Book Sales; 0-910610),* 231 Fairway Ave., High Point, Brooksville, FL 33512.

Forty Whacks, *(40 Whacks Press; 0-939264),* P.O. Box 591, Shelton, CT 06484 Tel 203-366-8060.

Forum Pr MO, *(Forum Press, Inc.; 0-88273),* 2640 Pine, St. Louis, MO 63103 Tel 314-371-6907; Orders to: P.O. Box 179, St. Louis, MO 63166. Imprints: Marston (Marston Press); Piraeus (Piraeus Publishers).

Forward Movement, *(Forward Movement Pubns.),* 412 Sycamore St., Cincinnati, OH 45202 Tel 513-721-6659.

FOSG
See **FOSG Pubns**

FOSG Pubns, *(Factory Outlet Shopping Guide; 0-913464),* Box 239, Oradell, NJ 07649 Tel 201-384-2500.

Foto Res, *(Foto Research Co.),* 234 Main St., Millbury, MA 01527 Tel 617-754-4612.

Fotoflip Bk, *(Fotoflip Book Co.; 0-917602),* Box 26337, San Jose, CA 95159 Tel 408-296-2570.

Fotonovel, *(Fotonovel Pubns.; 0-89752),* 8831 Sunset Blvd., PH-W, Los Angeles, CA 90069 Tel 213-659-8888; Dist. by: The Independent News Co., 75 Rockefeller Plaza, New York, NY 10019.

Foul Play Imprint of **Countryman**

Foun Adv Artists, *(Foundation for the Advancement of Artists; 0-912916),* 1315 Walnut St. Bldg., Philadelphia, PA 19107 Tel 215-546-3336.

Foun Better, *(Foundation for Better Living; 0-89506),* P.O. Box 2339, Reston, VA 22090 Tel 703-620-9830.

Foun Biblical, *(Foundation for Biblical Research; 0-917906),* Charlestown, NH 03603 Tel 603-826-7751.

Foun Bks, *(Foundation Books; 0-934988),* P.O. Box 29229, Lincoln, NE 68529 Tel 402-466-4988.

Foun Church New Birth, *(Foundation Church of the New Birth, Inc.),* P.O. Box 996, Benjamin Franklin Sta., Washington, DC 20044.

Foun Comm Art
See **FCA Bks.**

Foun Econ Ed, *(Foundation for Economic Education, Inc.; 0-910614),* 30 S. Broadway, Irvington-on-Hudson, NY 10533 Tel 914-591-7230.

Foun Hist Rest, *(Foundation for Historic Restoration in Pendleton Area; 0-912462),* P.O. Box 444, Pendleton, SC 29670 Tel 803-654-2640.

Foun Human GA, *(Foundation for Human Understanding; 0-936396),* Box 5712, Athens, GA 30604.

Foun Human Under, *(Foundation of Human Understanding; 0-933900),* P.O. Box 34036, Los Angeles, CA 90034 Tel 213-559-3711.

Foun Mot Dent, *(Foundation for Motivation in Dentistry; 0-913740),* Schooleys Mountain, NJ 07840.

Foun Natl Prog, *(Foundation for National Progress; 0-938806),* Housing Information Ctr., P.O. Box 3396, Santa Barbara, CA 93105.

Foun Pr
See **Foun Pubns**

Foun Pub, *(Foundation Pubs.; 0-910620),* 4101 San Jacinto St., Houston, TX 77004; Moved, Left No Forwarding Address.

Foun Pubns, *(Foundation Pubns., Inc.; 0-910618),* P.O. Box 6439, Anaheim, CA 92806 Tel 714-630-6450.

Foun Thanatology, *(Foundation of Thanatology),* 562 W. 113th St., New York, NY 10025 Tel 212-678-6777; c/o Columbia Univ. Press, 136 S. Broadway, Irvington-on-Hudson, NY 10533 Tel 914-591-9111.

Found Am Christ, *(Foundation for American Christian Education; 0-912498),* 2946 25th Ave., San Francisco, CA 94132 Tel 415-661-1775.

Found Audit Res *Imprint of* **Inst Inter Aud**

Found Blind Children, *(Foundation for Blind Children, The),* 1201 N. 85th Place, Scottsdale, AZ 85257 Tel 602-947-3744; Volunteers Will Hand-Transcribe Textbooks That Cannot Be Obtained from Other Sources. Materials Are 18 Pt. and 8 1/2 x 11. Serves Arizona.

Found Class Reprints, *(Foundation for Classical Reprints, The; 0-89901),* 607 McKnight St. N.W., Albuquerque, NM 87102.

Found Class Rep
See Found Class Reprints

Found Inner Peace, *(Foundation for Inner Peace),* P.O. Box 635, Tiburon, CA 94920 Tel 415-435-2255.

Found Pub, *(Foundation Publishing; 0-932032),* P.O. Box 3243, Burlington, VT 05401 Tel 802-862-7386.

Foundation Ctr, *(Foundation Center, The; 0-87954),* 888 Seventh Ave., New York, NY 10019 Tel 212-975-1120.

Foundation Pr, *(Foundation Press, Inc.; 0-88277),* P.O. Box 3056, Textbook Dept., 8F, St. Paul, MN 55165.

Fountain Hse East, *(Fountain House East; 0-914736),* Box 99298, Jeffersontown, KY 40299 Tel 502-267-5414.

Fountain Pr, *(Fountain Press, Inc.; 0-89350),* Dist. by: Inspirational Marketing Inc., Box 301, Indianola, IA 50125.

Fountain Pub Co NY, *(Fountain Publishing Co., Inc; 0-916181),* 500 Madison Ave., Rm 712, New York, NY 10022 Tel 212-838-9215; Dist. by: Harper & Row, Scranton, PA 18512.

Fountain Publications Oregon, *(Fountain Pubns.; 0-911376),* 3728 N.W. Thurman St., Portland, OR 97210 Tel 503-223-2232.

Fountainhead, *(Fountainhead Pubs., Inc.; 0-87310),* 475 Fifth Ave., New York, NY 10017.

Four Quarters, *(Four Quarters Publishing Co.; 0-931500),* 125 Harper Ave., New Haven, CT 06515 Tel 203-387-5569. *Imprints:* Dunk Rock (Dunk Rock Books).

Four Seas Bk, *(Four Seasons Book Pubs.; 0-9605400),* Box 222, West Chester, PA 19380.

Four Seasons Foun, *(Four Seasons Foundation; 0-87704),* P.O. Box 31411, San Francisco, CA 94131 Tel 415-824-5774; Dist. by: Subterranean Co., P.O. Box 10233, Eugene, OR 97440 Tel 503-343-6324.

Four Star, *(Four Star Press, The),* 815 N. Labrea Ave., P.O. Box 301, Los Angeles, CA 90302.

Four Winds *Imprint of* **Schol Bk Serv**

Four Winds Pr, *(Four Winds Press),* Box 126, Bristol, FL 32321.

Four Zoas Pr, *(Four Zoas Press),* RFD, Ware, MA 01082.

Foursquare Pr, *(Foursquare Press; 0-930616),* 4 Merrill St., Cambridge, MA 02139.

Fox Hills, *(Fox Hills Press, The; 0-914932),* 2676 Cunningham Hole Rd., Annapolis, MD 21401 Tel 301-266-6626.

Fox Reading Res, *(Fox Reading Research Co.),* P.O. Box 1059, Coeur D'Alene, ID 83814 Tel 208-772-4524.

Fox River, *(Fox River Publishing Co.; 0-939398),* Box 54, Princeton, WI 54968.

Foxmoor, *(Foxmoor Press; 0-938604),* Box 47, Rte. 2, Tahlequah, OK 74464.

FRAC Arts, *(Foundation for Research in the Afro-American Creative Arts, Inc.),* P.O. Box I, Cambria Heights, NY 11411 Tel 212-526-4896.

Framo Pub, *(Framo Publishing; 0-936398),* 530 W. Surf St., Chicago, IL 60657.

Franas Pr, *(Franas Press; 0-9600482),* P.O. Box AC, Mantoloking, NJ 08738.

Franchise Group, *(Franchise Group Pubs.; 0-936898),* 3644 E. McDowell, Suite 214A, Phoenix, AZ 85008.

Franciscan Herald, *(Franciscan Herald Press; 0-8199),* 1434 W. 51st St., Chicago, IL 60609 Tel 312-254-4455.

Franciscan Inst, *(Franciscan Institute Pubns.),* Drawer F, St. Bonaventure University, St. Bonaventure, NY 14778 Tel 716-375-2105.

Franconia, *(Franconia Publishing Co., Inc.; 0-912390),* P.O. Box 116, Bronxville, NY 10708 Tel 914-337-6600.

Franje, *(Franje, Inc.; 0-9601078),* 6020 Wright Terrace, Culver City, CA 90230 Tel 213-836-4514.

Frank Bk Corp, *(Frank Book Corp.; 0-89332),* Dist. by: Enslow Publishers, Box 301, Short Hills, NJ 07078.

Franklin & Marsh, *(Franklin & Marshall College; 0-910626),* P.O. Box 3003, Lancaster, PA 17604 Tel 717-291-3981.

Franklin Bk, *(Franklin Book Co.; 0-917522),* P.O. Box 208, East Millstone, NJ 08873 Tel 201-873-2156.

Franklin CT, *(Franklin; 0-9604424),* 203 Broad St., No. 2, New London, CT 06320.

Franklin Inst Pr, *(Franklin Institute Press, The; 0-89168),* Box 2266, Philadelphia, PA 19103 Tel 215-448-1551.

Franklin Pal, *(Franklin Publishing Co., Inc.; 0-910630),* P.O. Box 765, Palisade, NJ 07024 Tel 201-567-6477.

Franklin P&S Co, *(Franklin Publishing & Supply Co.; 0-912058),* 2134 N. 63rd, Philadelphia, PA 19151.

Franklin Pr
See Franklin Pr OH

Franklin Pr OH, *(Franklin Press, The; 0-933034),* P.O. Box 437, 166 S. Franklin St., Chagrin, OH 44022.

Franklin Pub Locust, *(Franklin Publishing Co.; 0-87133),* 2047 Locust St., Philadelphia, PA 19103 Tel 215-563-3837; Moved, Left No Forwarding Address.

Fraser Pub Co, *(Fraser Publishing Co.; 0-87034),* Div. of Fraser Management Assocs., Inc., 309 S. Willard St., Burlington, VT 05401 Tel 802-658-0322, Orders to: Box 194, Burlington, VT 05402. *Imprints:* Bks of Wall St (Books of Wall Street).

Fredericks Pub, *(Fredericks Publishing Co.; 0-939690),* P.O. Box 97, Mertztown, PA 19539 Tel 215-682-7784.

Fredonia, *(Fredonia; 0-940204),* P.O. Box 1012, Lombard, IL 60148.

Fredriksen, *(Fredriksen, John C.),* 641 Gayley Ave., No. 114, Los Angeles, CA 90024 Tel 213-824-4240.

Free-Bass, *(Free-Bass Press; 0-8256),* Box 563, Eugene, OR 97401 Tel 503-683-6595; Dist. by: Music Sales Corp., 33 W. 60th St., New York, NY 10036.

Free-Camp, *(Free-Camp Press; 0-9604004),* P.O. Box 8402, St. Louis, MO 63132 Tel 314-993-2743.

Free Church Pubns, *(Free Church Pubns.; 0-911802),* 1515 E. 66th St., Minneapolis, MN 55423 Tel 612-866-3343.

Free Lance, *(Free Lance Pubns.),* P.O. Box 747, Oakland, CA 94604.

Free Life, *(Free Life Editions; 0-914156),* 41 Union Square, W., New York, NY 10003 Tel 212-989-3750.

Free Life *Imprint of* **Universe**

Free Market, *(Free Market Books; 0-930902),* P.O. Box 298, Dobbs Ferry, NY 10522 Tel 914-591-7769.

Free Men, *(Free Men Speak),* P.O. Box 636, Littleton, CO 80120.

Free Pr, *(Free Press; 0-02),* Div. of Macmillan Publishing Co., Inc., 866 Third Ave., New York, NY 10022 Tel 212-935-2000; Dist. by: Macmillan Co., Riverside, NJ 08370.

Freedeeds Assocs, *(Freedeeds Associates; 0-89345),* Dist. by: Multimedia Publishing Co., 7 Garber Hill Rd., Blauvelt, NY 10913 Tel 914-359-9292.

Freedom Bks, *(Freedom Books; 0-930374),* P.O. Box 5303, Hamden, CT 06518 Tel 203-281-6791.

Freedom Hse, *(Freedom House; 0-932088),* 20 W. 40th St., New York, NY 10018 Tel 212-730-7744.

Freedom U Pr, *(Freedom University Press),* P.O. Box 16936, Orlando, FL 32811 Tel 305-351-0898.

Freedom Unltd, *(Freedom Unlimited; 0-938014),* P.O. Box 599, Garden Grove, CA 92642.

FreeHand, *(FreeHand, Julianna; 0-9605700),* Box 192, Croton-on-Hudson, NY 10520; Dist. by: Caroline House Publishers, 2 Ellis Place, Ossining, NY 10562.

Freelance Pubns, *(Freelance Pubns.; 0-9602050),* P.O. Box 8, Bayport, NY 11705 Tel 516-472-1799.

Freeland Pubns, *(Freeland Pubns.; 0-936868),* P.O. Box 18941, Philadelphia, PA 19119.

Freelandia, *(Freelandia Institute; 0-914674),* Star Rte., Cassville, MO 65625.

Freeman C, *(Freeman, Cooper & Co.; 0-87735),* 1736 Stockton St., San Francisco, CA 94133 Tel 415-362-6171.

Freeperson, *(Freeperson Press; 0-918236),* 455 Ridge Rd., Novato, CA 94947 Tel 415-897-0336.

Freer, *(Freer Gallery of Art, Smithsonian Institution; 0-934686),* 12th & Jefferson Dr., S.W., Washington, DC 20560 Tel 201-381-5342.

Freestone Pub Co, *(Freestone Publishing Co.; 0-913512),* 10001 E. Zayante Rd., Felton, CA 95018; Dist. by: Bookpeople, 2940 Seventh St., Berkeley, CA 94710 Tel 415-549-3033.

French, *(French, Samuel, Inc.; 0-573),* 25 W. 45th St., New York, NY 10036 Tel 212-582-4700.

French & Eur, *(French & European Pubns., Inc.; 0-8288),* 115 Fifth Ave., New York, NY 10003 Tel 212-673-7400.

French Forum, *(French Forum Pubs., Inc.; 0-917058),* P.O. Box 5108, Lexington, KY 40505 Tel 606-299-9530.

French Inst, *(French Institute-Alliance Francaise; 0-933444),* 22 E. 60th St., New York, NY 10022 Tel 212-355-6100.

Freneau, *(Freneau, Philip, Press; 0-912480),* 18 Valentine St., Box 116, Monmouth Beach, NJ 07750 Tel 201-222-6458.

Frenkel, *(Frenkel Mailing Service),* 24 Rutgers St., New York, NY 10002 Tel 212-267-6973.

Fresh Pr, *(Fresh Press; 0-9601398),* 774 Allen Court, Palo Alto, CA 94303 Tel 415-493-3596.

FreshCut, *(FreshCut Press),* 133 Clara Ave., Ukiah, CA 95482; 45 N. Prospect, Oberlin, OH 44074.

Freshet Pr, *(Freshet Press, Inc.; 0-88395),* 90 Hamilton Rd., Rockville Centre, NY 11570 Tel 516-766-3011.

Freshwater, *(Freshwater Press, Inc.; 0-912514),* 334 the Arcade, Cleveland, OH 44114 Tel 216-241-0373.

Freshwater Logistics, *(Freshwater Logistics; 0-9603006),* 418 Fremont Rd., Port Clinton, OH 43452 Tel 419-734-1430.

Frey Ent, *(Frey Enterprises; 0-935044),* 605 Merritt St., Nashville, TN 37203 Tel 615-244-1478.

Friedman, *(Friedman, Ira J., Inc.; 0-87198),* Div. of Kennikat Press, Inc., 90 S. Bayles Ave., Port Washington, NY 11050 Tel 516-883-0570.

Friend Freedom, *(Friends of Freedom Foundation Pubs. & Investors),* P.O. Box 6124, Waco, TX 76706 Tel 817-662-2695.

Friend Pr, *(Friendship Press; 0-377),* 475 Riverside Dr., Rm. 772, New York, NY 10027 Tel 212-870-2497; Orders to: Friendship Press Distribution, P.O. Box 37844, Cincinnati, OH 45237 Tel 513-761-2100.

Friendly City, *(Friendly City Publishing Co.; 0-938212),* P.O. Box 1946, Athens, TN 37303; Dist. by: Harlo Press, 50 Victor Ave., Detroit, MI 48203.

Friendly Fairways, *(Friendly Fairways of America),* P.O. Box 237-A, Royal Oak, MI 48068 Tel 313-652-8099.

Friendly Pr, *(Friendly Press; 0-938070),* 2744 Friendly St., Eugene, OR 97405.

Friendly Pubns, *(Friendly Pubns., Inc.; 0-916098),* 401 Park Ave. South, New York, NY 10016 Tel 212-684-4255.

Friendly World, *(Friendly World Enterprises; 0-914668),* P.O. Box 361, Pepeekeo, HI 96783 Tel 808-963-6864; Moved, Left No Forwarding Address.

Friends Aberdeen, *(Friends of the Aberdeen Public Library; 0-9605152),* 121 E. Market St., Aberdeen, WA 98520.

Friends Arcadia, *(Friends of Arcadia Public Library),* 20 W. Duarte Rd., Arcadia, CA 91006.

Friends Earth, *(Friends of the Earth, Inc.; 0-913890),* 124 Spear, San Francisco, CA 94105 Tel 415-495-4770.

Friends Fla St, *(Friends of Florida State Univ. Library),* Florida State Univ., Tallahassee, FL 32306.

Friends Israel-Spearhead Pr, *(Friends of Israel-Spearhead Press, The),* P.O. Box 123, West Collingswood, NJ 08107 Tel 215-922-3030.

Friends Nature, *(Friends of Nature, Inc.; 0-910636),* Brooksville, ME 04617.

Friends Peace Comm, *(Friends Peace Committee, Nonviolence & Children Program; 0-9605062),* 1515 Cherry St., Philadelphia, PA 19102.

Friends Photography, *(Friends of Photography, The; 0-933286),* P.O. Box 500, Sunset Ctr., Carmel, CA 93921 Tel 408-624-6330.

Friends Refugees, *(Friends of Refugees of Eastern Europe; 0-86639),* 1383 President St., Brooklyn, NY 11213.

Friends Towson Lib, *(Friends of the Towson Library, Inc.; 0-9602326),* 320 York Rd., Towson, MD 21204.

Friends UCSD Lib, *(Friends of the UCSD Library; 0-930730),* The Univ. Library, Univ. of California San Diego, La Jolla, CA 92093.

Friends United, *(Friends United Press; 0-913408),* 101 Quaker Hill Dr., Richmond, IN 47374 Tel 317-962-7573.

Friends Univ Toledo, *(Friends of the Univ. of Toledo Libraries; 0-918160),* The University of Toledo Library, 2801 W. Bancroft St., Toledo, OH 43606 Tel 419-537-2326.

Friends World Teach, *(Friends of World Teaching; 0-9601550),* P.O. Box 1049, San Diego, CA 92112 Tel 714-276-1464.

Frog in Well, *(Frog in the Well; 0-9603628),* 430 Oakdale Rd., East Palo Alto, CA 94303.

From Here, *(From Here Press; 0-89120),* P.O. Box 219, Fanwood, NJ 07023 Tel 201-322-5928.

Frommer-Pasmantier, *(Frommer-Pasmantier Pubs.; 0-671),* 1230 Ave. of the Americas, New York, NY 10020 Tel 212-245-6400.

Front Row, *(Front Row Experience; 0-915256),* 540 Discovery Bay Blvd., Byron, CA 94514 Tel 415-634-5710.

Front St, *(Front Street Pubs.; 0-931502),* 129 Front St., Rm. 301, New York, NY 10005.

Frontal Lobe, *(Frontal Lobe; 0-931400),* 836 Starlite Lane, Box 1353, Los Altos, CA 94022.

Frontier Bk, *(Frontier Book Co.),* P.O. Box 805, Fort Davis, TX 79734.

Frontier Pr Co, *(Frontier Press Co.; 0-912168),* P.O. Box 1098, Columbus, OH 43216 Tel 614-864-3737.

Frontier Press Calif, *(Frontier Press),* P.O. Box 5023, Santa Rosa, CA 95402 Tel 707-544-5174.

Frontrunner, *(Frontrunner Pubns.; 0-936090),* P.O. Box 5823, 2309 Wesley Circle, Bossier City, LA 71111.

Frost & Sullivan, *(Frost & Sullivan, Inc.),* 106 Fulton St., New York, NY 10038 Tel 212-233-1080.

Frost Art, *(Frost Art Distributors; 0-9604802),* 781 S. Kohler St., Los Angeles, CA 90021 Tel 213-626-3830.

FS&G, *(Farrar, Straus & Giroux, Inc.; 0-374),* 19 Union Square, W., New York, NY 10003 Tel 212-741-6900. *Imprints:* Bell (Bell Books); FS&G Pap (FS&G Paperbacks); Page (L. C. Page Co.); Sunburst (Sunburst Books); Vision (Vision Books).

FS&G Pap *Imprint of* **FS&G**

Fulcourte Pr, *(Fulcourte Press; 0-933354),* P.O. Box 1961, Decatur, GA 30031 Tel 404-378-5750.

Full Count Pr OK, *(Full Count Press; 0-936908),* 223 N. Broadway, Edmond, OK 73034.

Full Court NY, *(Full Court Press, Inc.; 0-916190),* 15 Laight St., New York, NY 10013 Tel 212-966-6196.

Full Gospel, *(Full Gospel Business Men's Fellowship International; 0-86595),* P.O. Box 5050, Costa Mesa, CA 92626.

Fulness Hse, *(Fulness House, Inc.; 0-937778),* P.O. Box 79350, Fort Worth, TX 76179.

Fulton County, *(Fulton County Press; 0-9601854),* Astoria, IL 61501.

Fun Pub, *(Fun Pub. Co; 0-918858),* P.O. Box 2049, Scottsdale, AZ 85252 Tel 602-946-2093.

Fund Res Pr, *(Fundamental Research Press; 0-913148),* 311 Pala Ave., Piedmont, CA 94611.

Fundaburk, *(Fundaburk, Emma Lila, Pub.; 0-910642),* Luverne, AL 36049.

Funk & W, *(Funk & Wagnalls Co.; 0-308),* C/O Harper & Row Pubs., 10 E. 53rd St., New York, NY 10022; Dist. by: Harper & Row Pubs, Keystone Industrial Park, Scranton, PA 18512. *Imprints:* FW-J (Funk & Wagnalls Juvenile Books); FW-T (Funk & Wagnalls Trade Books).

Funkshunal, *(Funkshunal Features; 0-932442),* P.O. Box 47728, Los Angeles, CA 90047 Tel 213-778-5422.

Fur-Fish-Game
   See A R Harding Pub

Fur Line Pr, *(Fur Line Press; 0-912662),* Dist. by: ManRoot Press, Box 982, South San Francisco, CA 94080.

Furman U Bkstr, *(Furman Univ. Bookstore),* Greenville, SC 29613 Tel 803-294-2164.

Furman Univ, *(Furman Univ. Press),* Box 28638, Furman Univ., Greenville, SC 29613; Tel 803-294-2021.

Furst Pubns, *(Furst Pubns.; 0-931612),* 111 Kings Hwy. S., Westport, CT 06880.

Fusion Groups, *(Fusion Groups, Inc.; 0-912778),* Indian Brook Rd., Garrison, NY 10524; Name Formerly Sonja.

Fut Stoch Dynamics, *(Future Stochastic Dynamics, Inc.; 0-913554),* c/o Prof. Yale L. Meltzer, 141-10 82nd Dr., Jamaica, NY 11435 Tel 212-441-3054.

Futura Pub, *(Futura Publishing Co., Inc.; 0-87993),* P.O. Box 330, 295 Main St., Mount Kisco, NY 10549 Tel 914-666-3505.

Future Pr, *(Future Press; 0-918406),* P. O. Box 73, Canal St., New York, NY 10013.

Future Shop, *(Future Shop; 0-930490),* P.O. Box 903, Ventura, CA 93001 Tel 805-653-5419.

Futures Group, *(Futures Group, The; 0-9605196),* 76 Eastern Blvd., Glastonbury, CT 06033.

FW-J *Imprint of* **Funk & W**

FW-T *Imprint of* **Funk & W**

G A Eversaul, *(Eversaul, George A.; 0-9601978),* Box 19476, Las Vegas, NV 89119.

G A Martin, *(Martin, Gloria A.; 0-9600538),* 829 26th Ave., Council Bluffs, IA 51501.

G & BJ's Serv, *(G & BJ's Services; 0-9604838),* 1350 Grandridge Blvd., Kennewick, WA 99336.

G Breese, *(Breese, Gerald),* Princeton Univ., Princeton, NJ 08540.

G Brune, *(Brune, Gunnar),* 2014 Royal Club Court, Arlington, TX 76017 Tel 817-465-3171.

G C Dickey, *(Dickey, Grover C.),* 200 Gill Dr., Midwest City, OK 73110.

G Collar, *(Collar, Grant),* 213 S. Fairchild St., Yreka, CA 96097.

G D L Inc, *(G.D.L., Inc.; 0-937358),* P.O. Box 1248, Birmingham, MI 48011.

G Davis, *(Davis, Grant, Co., Inc.; 0-934786),* P.O. Box 692, Lewisville, TX 75067.

G E Gaylord, *(Gabriel Emerson Gaylord),* 242 E. 12th St., C-27, Indianapolis, IN 46204; Moved, Left No Forwarding Address.

G E Gifford Memorial, *(George E. Gifford Memorial Committee),* Calvert School, Rising Sun, MD 21911; Orders to: Frances M. Hubis, 24 Hubis Lane, Rising Sun, MD 21911 Tel 301-658-6479.

G E Zimmerman, *(Zimmerman, Gary E.; 0-9605180),* P.O. Box 658, Goldsboro, NC 27530.

G F Edwards, *(Edwards, G. F.; 0-932318),* Box 1461, Lawton, OK 73502 Tel 405-248-6870.

G F Forbes, *(Forbes, George F.; 0-910604),* 9813 Monogram Ave., Sepulveda, CA 91343 Tel 213-894-6882.

G F Ritchie, *(Ritchie, George F.; 0-9604392),* 665 Pine St., No. 503, San Francisco, CA 94108 Tel 415-433-6115.

G F Stickley Co, *(Stickley, George F., Co.; 0-89313),* 210 W. Washington Square, Philadelphia, PA 19106 Tel 215-922-7126.

G Flynn, *(Flynn, George),* 145 W. Twelfth St., New York, NY 10011.

G Foreman, *(Foreman, Gloria, Publishing Co.; 0-915198),* P.O. Box 405, Oklahoma City, OK 73101 Tel 405-524-6290.

G Gajda, *(Gajda, George J.),* P.O. Box 1846, Santa Monica, CA 90406.

G Gannett, *(Gannett, Guy, Publishing Co.; 0-930096),* 390 Congress St., Portland, ME 04104.

G H Crumpler, *(Crumpler, Gus H.),* 413 N. Center St., Harrison, AR 72601 Tel 501-741-4612.

G Hill, *(Hill, Grace; 0-9604506),* 3 Haskins Rd. Hanover, NH 03755; Orders to: P.O. Box 279, Hanover, NH 03755 Tel 603-643-4059.

G I Krumwiede, *(Krumwiede, Grace I.),* 3713 S George Mason Dr., No. 608W, Falls Church VA 22041 Tel 202-554-1079.

G I Read, *(Read, George Isaac),* 340 Ventura St., No. 17, Palo Alto, CA 94306; Moved, Left No Forwarding Address.

G J Sneed, *(Sneed, Glenn J.),* P.O. Box 232, Royalton, IL 62983.

G K Hall, *(Hall, G. K., & Co.; 0-8161),* 70 Lincoln St., Boston, MA 02111 Tel 617-423-3990. *Imprints:* Large Print Bks (Large Print Books Series).

G Kici, *(Kici, Gasper),* P.O. Box 1855, Washington, DC 20013 Tel 703-560-6467.

G Kurian, *(Kurian, George, Reference Books; 0-914746),* P.O. Box 361, Tuckahoe, NY 10707 Tel 914-793-0375.

G L Lowe, *(Lowe, George L.),* 401 E. 32nd St., Chicago, IL 60616.

G Mancini, *(Mancini, Genevieve),* 20 Francine Dr., Massapequa, NY 11758 Tel 516-795-5486.

G North, *(North, Gloria; 0-931758),* 15 Estelle Ave., Larkspur, CA 94939.

G Ohsawa, *(Ohsawa, George, Macrobiotic Foundation; 0-918860),* 902 14th St., Oroville, CA 95965 Tel 916-533-7702.

G Plains Pub Co, *(Great Plains Publishing Co.; 0-9603686),* P.O. Box 18392, Denver, CO 80218 Tel 303-321-1413.

G R Cockle, *(Cockle, George R., Associates; 0-916160),* P.O. Box 1224, Downtown Sta., Omaha, NE 68101.

G R Schoepfer, *(Schoepfer, G. R.; 0-931436),* 338 Concord Ave., West Hempstead, NY 11552.

G Ritner, *(Ritner, George),* 411 Broadway, Suite 203, San Diego, CA 92101.

G Rose Pr, *(Gena Rose Press; 0-9604178),* 2424 Franklin, No. B, Denver, CO 80205.

G S E Pubns, *(GSE Pubns.; 0-915668),* P.O. Box 35499, Los Angeles, CA 90035 Tel 213-559-7101.

G Sroda, *(Sroda, George; 0-9604486),* Amherst Jct., WI 54407 Tel 715-824-3868.

G Stempien, *(Stempien, G., Publishing Co.; 0-930472),* 1213 Edgehill Ave., Joliet, IL 60432 Tel 815-722-4216.

G T Yeamans, *(Yeamans, George Thomas; 0-9601006),* 4507 W. Burton Dr., Muncie, IN 47304 Tel 317-288-4345; Orders to: Ball State Bookstore, Muncie, IN 47306.

G Twesten, *(Twesten, Gary, Publisher; 0-9602428),* Fox Run, Millstadt, IL 62260 Tel 618-233-5070.

G W Ferguson, *(Ferguson, George Wright; 0-9600956),* 2000 W. Henderson Rd., P. O. Box 20334, Columbus, OH 43220 Tel 614-459-0372.

G W May, *(May, George W.; 0-9605566),* Rte. 1 Box 221, Metropolis, IL 62960.

G W Noble, *(Noble, Gilbert W.; 0-911036),* P.O. Box 931, Winter Park, FL 32789 Tel 305-647-2431.

G Witzstrock Pub Hse, *(Witzstrock, Gerhard, Publishing House, Inc.; 0-933682),* 30 E. 40th St., Suite 703, New York, NY 10016.

Ga St U Busn Pub, *(Georgia State Univ., College of Business Administration; 0-88406),* Business Publishing Div., Univ. Plaza, Atlanta, GA 30303 Tel 404-658-4253.

GA St U Dept Real, *(Georgia State Univ., Dept. of Real Estate & Urban Affairs, School of Business Administration),* Univ. Plaza, Atlanta, GA 30303 Tel 404-658-2760.

Gabriel Bks
   See Minn Scholarly

Gabriel Bks, *(Gabriel Books),* P.O. Box 224, Mankato, MN 56001 Tel 507-387-4964; Dist. by: Independent Publishers Group, 14 Vanderventer Ave., Port Washington, NY 11050.

Gabriel Hse, *(Gabriel House, Inc.; 0-936192),* 9329 Crawford Ave., Evanston, IL 60203 Tel 312-674-6476. *Imprints:* Writers Guide Pubns (Writer's Guide Pubns.).

Gach Bks, *(Gach, John, Books),* 5620 Waterloo Rd., Columbia, MD 21045.

Gael Himmah, *(Himmah, Gael, Publishing Co.; 0-9600488),* P.O. Box 4591, Walnut Creek, CA 94596 Tel 415-939-3555.

Gaffney, *(Gaffney Printing Co.),* 316 N. Limestone, Gaffney, SC 29340.

Gagliardi Ent, *(Gagliardi, Wayne M., Enterprises; 0-902606),* P.O. Box 99153, San Diego, CA 92109.

Gains, *(Gains Publishing Co.; 0-917432),* P.O. Box 1157, Alhambra, CA 91802 Tel 213-282-1244.

Gala Bks, *(Gala Books & Gifts; 0-912448),* P. O. Box 659, Laguna Beach, CA 92652 Tel 714-494-6655.

Galaxy Pr, *(Galaxy Press; 0-916566),* P.O. Box 27764, Escondido, CA 92027 Tel 714-746-1170.

Gale, *(Gale Research Co.; 0-8103),* Book Tower, Detroit, MI 48226 Tel 313-961-2242.

Galilee *Imprint of* **Doubleday**

Gall Pubns, *(Gall Pubns.; 0-88904),* 2965 Weston Ave., Niagara Falls, NY 14305.

Gallant Pub Co, *(Gallant Publishing Co.),* 34249 Camino Capistrano, Capistrano Beach, CA 92624.

Gallaudet Coll, *(Gallaudet College Press; 0-913580),* Kendall Green, Washington, DC 20002 Tel 202-651-5595.

Galleon Pubns
   See Galleon-Whitehurst

Galleon-Whitehurst, *(Galleon Pubns.; 0-918602),* 701 Broughton Dr., Beverly, MA 01915 Tel 617-927-0533.

Gallery Pr, *(Gallery Press; 0-913622),* 98 N. Main St., Essex, CT 06426 Tel 203-767-0313.

Galley OR, *(Galley Press),* P.O. Box 892, Portland, OR 97207 Tel 206-693-1397.

Galliard Pr, *(Galliard Press; 0-936616),* P.O. Box 296, Claremont, CA 91711.

Gallimaufry, *(Gallimaufry; 0-916300),* Dist. by: Apple-Wood Press, P.O. Box 2870, Cambridge, MA 02139 Tel 617-964-5150.

Gallopade Pub Group, *(Gallopade Publishing Group; 0-935326),* P.O. Box 469, Rocky Mount, NC 27801; P.O. Box 1537, Tryon, NC 28782 Tel 704-859-9253.

Galloway, *(Galloway Pubns. Inc.; 0-87874),* 2940 N.W. Circle Blvd., Corvallis, OR 97330.

Galvin Pub, *(Galvin Publishing Co.; 0-932976),* 384 City National Bank Bldg., Detroit, MI 48226.

Gambit, *(Gambit Inc. Pubs.; 0-87645),* 27 N. Main St., Ipswich, MA 01938 Tel 617-356-2956.

Gamblers, *(Gambler's Book Club/GBC Press; 0-911996; 0-89650),* 630 S. 11th St., P.O. Box 4115, Las Vegas, NV 89106 Tel 702-382-7555.

Gamblers Anon, *(Gamblers Anonymous Pub. Co.),* P.O. Box 17173, Los Angeles, CA 90017.

Gambling Times, *(Gambling Times; 0-89746),* 839 N. Highland Ave., Hollywood, CA 90038.

Gamesmasters, *(Gamesmasters Pubs. Assn.; 0-935426),* 20 Almont St., Nashua, NH 03060.

Gamma Bks, *(Gamma Books; 0-933124),* 307 Willow Ave., Ithaca, NY 14850.

Gamut Music, *(Gamut Music Co.; 0-910648),* P.O. Box 454, Dedham, MA 02026 Tel 617-244-3305.

Gamut Pr, *(Gamut Press; 0-910650),* Dist. by: Taplinger Publishing Co., Inc., 200 Park Ave., S., New York, NY 10003.

G&C Learn, *(G & C Learning; 0-9602004),* 1660-A Huron Trail, Maitland, FL 32751 Tel 305-647-3355.

G&D, *(Grosset & Dunlap, Inc.; 0-448),* 51 Madison Ave., New York, NY 10010 Tel 212-689-9200. *Imprints:* Cinnamon Hse (Cinnamon House); FBL (Fortune Building Library); MSP (Madison Square Press); Sign (Signature Books); Tempo (Tempo Books); UL (Universal Library).

G&G Pubs, *(G & G Pubs.; 0-937534),* Route 7, No.65, Hopewell Junction, NY 12533.

Ganis & Harris, *(Ganis & Harris, Inc.; 0-9605188),* 119 W. 57th St., New York, NY 10019.

Gann Law Bks, *(Gann Law Books; 0-933902),* 224 Market St., Newark, NJ 07102 Tel 201-624-5533.

Gannon, *(Gannon, William; 0-88307),* P.O. Box 2610, Santa Fe, NM 87501 Tel 505-983-1579.

Garabed, *(Garabed Books),* 23 Leroy St., New York, NY 10014.

Garcia River, *(Garcia River Press; 0-932708),* P.O. Box 527, Point Arena, CA 95468.

Gard & Co, *(Gard & Co.; 0-9603316),* P.O. Box 34311, N.W. Sta., Omaha, NE 68134 Tel 402-493-1352.

Garden City, *(Garden City Historical Society; 0-9604654),* Box 179, Garden City, NY 11530.

Garden Consul, *(Garden Consultant),* 555 Townsend, Birmingham, MI 48012.

Garden Pub, *(Garden Publishing Co.; 0-939330),* 6833 Creston Rd., Minneapolis, MN 55435 Tel 612-926-1327.

Garden Studio, *(Garden Studio, The; 0-932934),* P.O. Box 41, Huntington, VT 05462 Tel 802-434-3330.

Garden Way Pub, *(Garden Way Publishing Co.; 0-88266),* Charlotte, VT 05445 Tel 802-425-2171.

Gardner Pr, *(Gardner Press, Inc.; 0-89876),* 19 Union Square W., New York, NY 10003.

Garland Pub, *(Garland Publishing, Inc.; 0-8240),* 136 Madison Ave., 2nd Floor, New York, NY 10016 Tel 212-686-7492.

Garlic Pr, *(Garlic Press; 0-932798),* P.O. Box 24799, Los Angeles, CA 90024.

Garrard, *(Garrard Publishing Co.; 0-8116),* 49 Riverside Ave., Westport, CT 06880; Orders to: 1607 N. Market St., Champaign, IL 61820 Tel 217-352-7685.

Garrett-Helix, *(Garrett Pubns.-Helix Press; 0-912326),* Orders to: Taplinger Publishing Co., 200 Park Ave., S., New York, NY 10003.

Garrett Pk, *(Garrett Park Press; 0-912048),* Garrett Park, MD 20766 Tel 301-946-2553.

Garrett Pr, *(Garrett Press),* ; Publisher Abbreviation Without Addresses Are for Titles That Are Out of Print. These Are Obsolete Abbreviations.

Garrick Bks, *(Garrick Books),* 407 N. Aurora, Ithaca, NY 14850.

Garrison, *(Garrison Pub.; 0-918256),* P.O. Box 536, Cave Creek, AZ 85331 Tel 602-488-3675.

Gaslight, *(Gaslight Pubns.; 0-934468),* 112 E. Second, Bloomington, IN 47401 Tel 812-332-5169.

GateFord Pubns, *(Gateford Pubns.; 0-916126),* P.O. Box 92, Collingswood, NJ 08108.

Gateway, *(Gateway Bookshop; 0-9600172),* Ferndale, Bucks County, PA 18921 Tel 215-346-7416.

Gateway Book, *(Gateway Book Publishing Co.),* P.O. Box 171, Sewickley, PA 15143 Tel 412-264-9549.

Gateway Ed Ltd
   See Regnery-Gateway

GATT *Imprint of* **Unipub**

Gauche Media, *(Gauche Media; 0-931506),* 2356 N.W. Irving, Portland, OR 97210.

Gauntlet Bks, *(Gauntlet Books),* 144 King St., Franklin, MA 02038 Tel 617-528-4414.

Gaus, *(Gaus, Theo., Ltd.; 0-912444),* 30 Prince St., Brooklyn, NY 11201 Tel 212-625-4650.

Gavey, *(Gavey & Co., Inc.; 0-935844),* 80 Park Ave., New York, NY 10016.

Gay Pr NY, *(Gay Presses of New York; 0-9604724),* P.O. Box 294, New York, NY 10014.

Gay Sunshine, *(Gay Sunshine Press; 0-917342),* Box 40397, San Francisco, CA 94140 Tel 415-824-3184; Dist. by: Bookpeople, 2940 Seventh St., Berkeley, CA 94710 Tel 800-227-1516.

Gaylord Prof Pubns, *(Gaylord Professional Pubns.; 0-915794),* Div. of Gaylord Bros., Inc., P.O. Box 4264, Hamden, CT 06514 Tel 203-288-8707; Orders to: P.O. Box 4901, Syracuse, NY 13221.

Gazelle Pubns, *(Gazelle Pubns.; 0-930192),* 20601 W. Paoli Lane, Colfax, CA 95713.

Gazette Pr, *(Gazette Press, Inc.; 0-933390),* 225 Hunter Ave., North Tarrytown, NY 10591 Tel 914-631-8866.

GB *Imprint of* **Oxford U Pr**

GBIP, *(Genealogical Books in Print; 0-89157),* 6818 Lois Dr., Springfield, VA 22150.

GBS Pubs, *(GBS Pubs.; 0-939928),* Div. of Gordon's Booksellers, 8 E. Baltimore St., Baltimore, MD 21202.

GCNHA, *(Grand Canyon Natural History Assn.; 0-938216),* P.O. Box 399, Grand Canyon, AZ 86023.

GDA Pubns, *(G. D. A. Pubns.),* P.O. Box 30119, Lafayette, LA 70503.

GE-PS Cancer, *(GE-PS Cancer Memorial; 0-9601644),* 519 Austin Ave., Park Ridge, IL 60068 Tel 312-823-5425.

GE Tech Marketing, *(General Electric Co., Technology Marketing Operation; 0-931690),* 120 Erie Blvd., Schenectady, NY 12305.

GE Tech Prom & Train, *(General Electric Co., Technical Promotion & Training Services; 0-932078),* 1 River Rd., Bldg. 22, Rm. 232, Box MK, Schenectady, NY 12345.

GE Train & Ed
   See GE Tech Prom & Train

Geankoplis, *(Geankoplis, Christie J.; 0-9603070),* 1060 Sells Ave. W., Columbus, OH 43212 Tel 614-486-4524; Dist. by: Ohio State Univ. Bookstores, 140 N. Oval Mall, Columbus, OH 43210.

Gearhart-Edwards, *(Gearhart-Edwards Press),* 2266 N. Prospect Ave., Suite 502, Milwaukee, WI 53202.

Gee Tee Bee, *(Gee Tee Bee; 0-917232),* 11901 Sunset Blvd., No. 102, Los Angeles, CA 90049 Tel 213-476-2622.

Gehry Pr, *(Gehry Press; 0-935020),* 1319 Pine St., Iowa City, IA 52240.

Geis, *(Geis, Bernard, Associates, Inc.; 0-87035),* 128 E. 56th St., New York, NY 10022 Tel 212-752-1975.

Gem City Coll, *(Gem City College Press; 0-910222),* 700 State St., Quincy, IL 62301 Tel 217-222-0391.

Gem O Lite, *(Gem-O-Lite Plastics Co.; 0-911888),* P.O. Box 985, N. Hollywood, CA 91603 Tel 213-877-3491.

Gemaia Pr, *(Gemaia Press; 0-9602232),* 209 Wilcox Lane, Sequim, WA 98382.

Gembooks, *(Gembooks; 0-910652),* P. O. Box 808, Mentone, CA 92359.

Gemini Bks, *(Gemini Books),* P.O. Box 10313, Eugene, OR 97440.

Gemini Pr, *(Gemini Press; 0-9601690),* 625 Pennsylvania Ave., Oakmont, PA 15139 Tel 412-828-3315.

Gemini Pub Co, *(Gemini Publishing Co.; 0-937164),* 2801 W. Bay Area Blvd., Suite 811, Webster, TX 77598 Tel 713-482-9520.

Gemini Smith, *(Gemini Smith, Inc.; 0-935022),* 5858 Desert View Dr., La Jolla, CA 92037 Tel 714-454-4321; NY.

Gemological, *(Gemological Institute of America; 0-87311),* 1660 Stewart St., Santa Monica, CA 90404 Tel 213-829-2991.

Gen Aviation Pr, *(General Aviation Press),* P.O. Box 916, Snyder, TX 79549; Dist. by: Aviation Book Co., 1640 Victory Blvd., Glendale, CA 91201 Tel 213-240-1771.

Gen Educ Dev, *(General Educational Development Institute),* 1600 N. 49th St., Seattle, WA 98103.

Gen Hall, *(General Hall, Inc.; 0-930390),* 23-45 Corporal Kennedy St., Bayside, NY 11360 Tel 212-423-9397.

Gen Learn Pr, *(General Learning Press; 0-382),* Div. of Silver Burdett Co., 250 James St., Morristown, NJ 07960 Tel 201-285-7942.

Gen Man Serv, *(General Management Services, Inc.; 0-9600512),* 910 W. Wagon Wheel Dr., Phoenix, AZ 85021.

Gen Mills, *(General Mills, Inc.),* P. O. Box 1113, Minneapolis, MN 55440 Tel 612-540-2311.

Gen Tech Serv, *(General Technical Services, Inc.; 0-914780),* 8794 W. Chester Pike, Upper Darby, PA 19082 Tel 215-449-2333.

Gen Welfare, *(General Welfare Pubns.; 0-87312),* P.O. Box 19098, Sacramento, CA 95819 Tel 916-677-1610.

Genealog Inst, *(Genealogical Institute),* Dist. by: Family History World, 19 W. South Temple, Suite 761, Salt Lake City, UT 84101 Tel 801-532-3327.

Genealog Pub, *(Genealogical Publishing Co., Inc.; 0-8063),* 111 Water St., Baltimore, MD 21202 Tel 301-837-8271.

Genealogy Res, *(Genealogy Research; 0-9603214),* P.O. Box 1763, Sacramento, CA 95808.

General Educ, *(General Education Pubns.; 0-914504),* 99 S. Van Ness Ave., San Francisco, CA 94103 Tel 415-621-5410.

General Stud Res, *(General Studies Research; 0-89372),* Institutional Studies, Bowling Green State Univ., Bowling Green, OH 43403 Tel 419-372-2681.

Genesis Ent, *(Genesis Enterprises),* P.O. Box 388, Mount Airy, MD 21771 Tel 301-829-1651.

Geneva Pr, *(Geneva Press, The; 0-664),* 925 Chestnut St., Philadelphia, PA 19107.

Genny Smith Bks, *(Genny Smith Books; 0-931378),* 1304 Pitman Ave., Palo Alto, CA 94301 Tel 415-321-7247; Dist. by: William Kaufmann Inc., One First St., Los Altos, CA 94022.

Genotype, *(Genotype; 0-936618),* 15042 Montebello Rd., Cupertino, CA 95014.

GeoBooks, *(GeoBooks; 0-914462),* 171 2nd St. Rm. 401, San Francisco, CA 94105.

Geog Area Study, *(Geographic & Area Study Pubns.; 0-88393),* 21675 Boones Ferry Rd., Tualatin, OR 97062 Tel 503-638-7152.

Geographics, *(Geographics; 0-930722),* Box 133, Easton, CT 06425.

Geol Soc, *(Geological Society of America, Inc.; 0-8137),* 3300 Penrose Place, Boulder, CO 80301 Tel 303-447-2020.

Geophysical Inst, *(Geophysical Institute; 0-915360),* C.T. Elvey Bldg., Univ. of Alaska, Fairbanks, AK 99701 Tel 907-479-7282.

Georgetown Pr, *(Georgetown Press; 0-914558),* 483 Francisco St., San Francisco, CA 94133 Tel 415-397-4753.

Georgetown U Pr, *(Georgetown Univ. Press; 0-87840),* School of Language & Linguistics, Georgetown Univ., Washington, DC 20057 Tel 202-625-4824.

Georgian Pr, *(Georgian Press Co., The; 0-9603408),* 2620 S.W. Georgian Place, Portland, OR 97201 Tel 503-223-9899; Dist. by: Pacific Pipeline, Inc., P.O. Box 3711, Seattle, WA 98124 Tel 206-682-8820.

Geothermal, *(Geothermal Resources Council; 0-934412),* P.O. Box 98, Davis, CA 95616.

Geraventure, *(Geraventure Corp.; 0-938524),* P.O. Box 2131, Melbourne, FL 32901.

Gerber Pubns, *(Gerber Pubns.; 0-9601814),* c/o The Arachnid/Gerber Pubns., Box 1355, Ormond Beach, FL 32074 Tel 904-677-9283.

Geriatric Pr, *(Geriatric Press; 0-9601874),* 907 E. 2nd, McCook, NE 69001 Tel 308-345-2733.

Germainbooks, *(Germainbooks; 0-914142),* 91 St. Germain Ave., San Francisco, CA 94114 Tel 415-731-8155.

German Am Chamber, *(German American Chamber of Commerce, Inc.; 0-86640),* 666 Fifth Ave., New York, NY 10103.

Germinal Pr, *(Germinal Press; 0-918064),* 209 Prospect, San Francisco, CA 94110 Tel 415-824-4795.

Geron-X, *(Geron-X, Inc.; 0-87672),* P.O. Box 1108, Los Altos, CA 94022 Tel 415-941-1692.

Ghost Dance, *(Ghost Dance Press; 0-939520),* ATL EBH MSU, East Lansing, MI 48824 Tel 517-351-5977.

Ghost Town, *(Ghost Town Pubns.; 0-933818),* P.O. Drawer 5998, Carmel, CA 93921 Tel 408-373-2885.

GIA Pubns, *(G.I.A. Pubns., Inc.),* 7404 S. Mason Ave., Chicago, IL 60638 Tel 312-496-3800.

Gibbs Pub Co, *(Gibbs Publishing Co.),* c/o Cicero Bible Press, Airport Rd., Harrison, AR 72601 Tel 501-741-7601.

Gibbs Pub NH, *(Gibbs Publishing Co.; 0-932924),* P.O. Box 776, Laconia, NH 03246.

Gibraltar, *(Gibraltar Press),* P.O. Box 121425, Nashville, TN 37212; 171 Fuller St., Brookline, MA 02146.

Gibson, *(Gibson, C. R., Co.; 0-8378),* Knight St., Norwalk, CT 06856 Tel 203-847-4543.

Gibson Hiller, *(Gibson-Hiller Co.; 0-918892),* P.O. Box 22, Dayton, OH 45406 Tel 513-277-2427.

Gibson Pubs
See Tyler Gibson

Gick, *(Gick Pub. Inc.; 0-918170),* 23152 Verdugo Dr., Laguna Hills, CA 92653 Tel 714-581-5830.

Gielow, *(Gielow, Fred C.; 0-9603938),* 33 Park Dr., Woodstock, NY 12498.

Gift Pubns, *(Gift Pubns.; 0-86595),* 3150 Bear St., Costa Mesa, CA 92626.

Gilchem Corp, *(Gilchem Corp.; 0-917122),* Woodlawn Rd., Suite 112, Bldg. 3, Woodlawn Green, Box 11291, Charlotte, NC 28209 Tel 704-523-2889.

Gilfer, *(Gilfer Assocs., Inc.; 0-914542),* P.O. Box 239, Park Ridge, NJ 07656 Tel 201-391-7887.

Gilgal Pr, *(Gilgal Press; 0-915670),* P.O. Box 342, Kennesaw, GA 30144.

Gilgamesh Pr IL, *(Gilgamesh Press Ltd.; 0-936684),* 1059 W. Ardmore Ave., Chicago, IL 60660 Tel 312-334-0327.

Gilgamesh Pub, *(Gilgamesh Publishing Co.; 0-914246),* 6050 Blvd. East, West New York, NJ 07093.

Giligia, *(Giligia Press; 0-87791),* P.O. Box 626, Aurora, OR 97002 Tel 503-651-2090.

Gillians Pub, *(Gillian's Publishing; 0-931628),* 305 Trailview Rd., Box 792, Encinitas, CA 92024.

Gilmar Pr, *(Gilmar Press; 0-936402),* P.O. Box 597, Newcastle, CA 95658.

Gingerbread *Imprint of* Dutton

Gingko Hse, *(Gingko House Pubs.; 0-917156),* W. 20 Sumner No. 104, Spokane, WA 99204 Tel 509-747-8355.

Giniger, *(Giniger, K. S., Co., Inc., The; 0-87456),* 235 Park Ave., S., New York, NY 10003 Tel 212-533-5080.

Ginkgo Hut, *(Ginkgo Hut; 0-936620),* 13 Augusta Dr., Lincroft, NJ 07738.

Ginn, *(Ginn & Co.; 0-663),* A Xerox Publishing Co., 191 Spring St., Lexington, MA 02173 Tel 617-861-1670; Orders to: P.O. Box 2649, 1250 Fairwood Ave., Columbus, OH 43216 Tel 614-253-8661.

Ginn Custom, *(Ginn Custom Publishing; 0-536),* Div. of Ginn & Co., 191 Spring St., Lexington, MA 02173 Tel 617-861-1670.

Ginseng Pr, *(Ginseng Press; 0-932800),* Rte. 2, Box 1105, Franklin, NC 28734 Tel 704-369-9735.

Giorno Poetry, *(Giorno Poetry Systems),* 222 Bowery, New York, NY 10012 Tel 212-925-6372.

Girs Pr, *(Girs Press),* Streeter Hill Rd., West Chesterfield, NH 03466 Tel 603-256-8484; Orders to: P.O. Box 91, West Chesterfield, NH 03466.

GLA Pr, *(G. L. A. Press; 0-912854),* P. O. Box 5312, Irving, TX 75062 Tel 214-579-5340.

Glanville, *(Glanville Pubs., Inc.; 0-87802),* 75 Main St., Dobbs Ferry, NY 10522 Tel 914-693-1320.

Glaser, *(Glaser, Edwin V.),* 202 South St., Sausalito, CA 94965 Tel 415-332-1194.

Glass Bell, *(Glass Bell Press; 0-9603072),* 5053 Commonwealth, Detroit, MI 48208 Tel 313-898-7972.

Glass Works, *(Glass Works Press; 0-934280),* P.O. Box 81782, San Diego, CA 92138 Tel 714-282-8000.

Glen-Bartlett, *(Glen-Bartlett Publishing Co.; 0-9602802),* 105 W. Main St., Westboro, MA 01581 Tel 617-366-7669.

Glen-L Marine, *(Glen-L Marine Design),* 9152 Rosecrans, Bellflower, CA 90706.

Glen Pr, *(Glen Press; 0-9603518),* 2247 Glen Ave., Berkeley, CA 94709.

Glencoe, *(Glencoe Publishing Co., Inc.; 0-02),* c/o Macmillan Publishing Co., Inc., 866 Third Ave., New York, NY 10022 Tel 212-935-2000.

Glendale Advent Med, *(Glendale Adventist Medical Center; 0-87313),* P.O. Box 871, Glendale, CA 91209 Tel 213-240-2819.

Glendessary, *(Glendessary Press, Inc.; 0-87709),* ; Publisher Abbreviation Without Addresses Are for Titles That Are Out of Print. These Are Obsolete Abbreviations. Publisher Was Aquired by Boyd & Fraser.

Glendon Hse, *(Glendon House; 0-932124),* 3649 Glendon Ave., Los Angeles, CA 90034; Orders to: Rancho Park Sta., Box 67900A, Los Angeles, CA 90067.

Glenmary Res Ctr, *(Glenmary Research Center; 0-914422),* 4606 East-West Hwy., Washington, DC 20014 Tel 301-654-7501.

Glenn Vargas, *(Vargas, Glenn; 0-917646),* 85-159 Ave. 66, Thermal, CA 92274 Tel 714-397-4264.

Glenson Pub, *(Glenson Publishing; 0-934884),* P.O. Box 298, Sterling Heights, MI 48077.

Glenwood, *(Glenwood Pubs.; 0-911760),* P.O. Box 880, Felton, CA 95018 Tel 408-335-4406.

Glide
See New Glide

Global Comm, *(Global Communications; 0-938294),* 303 Fifth Ave., Suite 1306, New York, NY 10016 Tel 212-685-4080.

Global Eng, *(Global Engineering Documents; 0-912702),* Div. of Information Handling Services, 2625 Hickory St., P.O. Box 2504, Santa Ana, CA 92707 Tel 714-540-9870.

Global Pubns WI, *(Global Pubns.; 0-9604752),* 731 N. 16th St., Milwaukee, WI 53233 Tel 414-344-2664.

Globe, *(Globe Book Co., Inc.; 0-87065),* 50 W. 23rd St., New York, NY 10010 Tel 212-741-0505.

Globe Agency, *(Globe Agency),* P.O. Box 72238, Los Angeles, CA 90002 Tel 213-632-0256; Moved, Left No Forwarding Address.

Globe Pequot, *(Globe Pequot Press; 0-87106),* Old Chester Rd., Box Q, Chester, CT 0641? Tel 203-526-9572; CT History Ser., Dist. Only by the Center for CT Studies of Eastern CT State College, Willimantic, CT 06226.

Globe Pubs Texas, *(Globe Pubs. International),* 2205 Maryland St., Baytown, TX 77520 Tel 713-427-7740.

Gloucester Art, *(Gloucester Art Press; 0-930582),* P.O. Box 4526, Albuquerque, NM 87196 Tel 505-843-7749.

Glouchester Pr, *(Glouchester Press; 0-914560),* P. O. Box 1044, Fairmont, WV 26554 Tel 304-366-1441.

Gluten Co, *(Gluten Co. Inc., The; 0-935596),* 509 E. 2100 N., Box 482, Provo, UT 84601 Tel 801-377-6390.

Gluxlit Pr, *(Gluxlit Press; 0-930524),* P.O. Box 11165, Dallas, TX 75223.

Glyphic Pr, *(Glyphic Press; 0-935964),* 665 Killarney Dr., Morgantown, WV 26505.

GM *Imprint of* Fawcett

GMG Pub, *(GMG Publishing; 0-939456),* 25 W 43rd St., New York, NY 10036.

GML Corp, *(GML Corp.; 0-914730),* 594 Marrett Rd., Lexington, MA 02173 Tel 617-861-0515.

Gnomon Pr, *(Gnomon Press; 0-917788),* P.O. Box 106, Frankfort, KY 40602 Tel 502-223-1858.

GNU, *(GNU Publishing; 0-915914),* P.O. Box 6820, San Francisco, CA 94101.

God Unltd-U of Healing
See U of Healing

Godine, *(Godine, David R., Pub., Inc.; 0-87923),* 306 Dartmouth St., Boston, MA 02116 Tel 617-536-0761. *Imprints:* Nonpareil Bks (Nonpareil Books).

Godiva Pub, *(Godiva Publishing; 0-938018),* P.O. Box 42305, Portland, OR 97242 Tel 503-233-1228.

Gododdin Pub, *(Gododdin Publishing; 0-9603274),* P.O. Box 5242, Everett, WA 98206.

Goehringer & Sons, *(Goehringer & Sons Associates; 0-9601704),* Box 9626, Pittsburgh, PA 15226 Tel 412-531-9549; 950 Brookline Blvd., Pittsburgh, PA 15226.

Gold-Kane Ent, *(Gold/Kane Enterprises; 0-9604430),* 1580 Garfield St., Denver, CO 80206 Tel 303-333-9659.

Gold Penny, *(Gold Penny Press, The; 0-87786),* Box 2177, Canoga Park, CA 91306 Tel 213-368-1417.

Gold Quill Pubs CA, *(Golden Quill Pubs., Inc.; 0-933904),* P.O. Box 1278-R, Colton, CA 92324 Tel 714-783-0119.

Gold Rush, *(Gold Rush Sourdough Co., Inc.; 0-912936),* 122 E. Grand Ave. South, San Francisco, CA 94080 Tel 415-871-0340.

Golden Bell, *(Golden Bell Press; 0-87315),* 240 Champa St., Denver, CO 80205 Tel 303-572-1777.

Golden Coast, *(Golden Coast Publishing Co.; 0-932958),* 22 Waite Dr., Savannah, GA 31406.

Golden Cockerel, *(Golden Cockerel Press; 0-498),* P. O. Box 421, Cranbury, NJ 08512

Golden Door, *(Golden Door Publications, Inc.; 0-912596),* 310 Madison Ave., New York, NY 10017 Tel 212-697-3137.

Golden Gambit, *(Golden Gambit Books; 0-918862),* Eight Hayes Ave., Attleboro, MA 02703 Tel 617-222-0176; Moved, Left No Forwarding Address.

Golden Gate *Imprint of* Childrens

Golden Glow, *(Golden Glow Publishing; 0-933072),* Box 488, Sturgeon Bay, WI 54235 Tel 414-743-7322.

Golden Grain, *(Golden Grain),* R. R. 1, Shelbyville, MI 49344.

Golden Hill, *(Golden Hill Books; 0-9605364),* 2456 Broadway, San Diego, CA 92102.

Golden Key, *(Golden Key Pubns.; 0-9602166),* 123 N. Sirrine, Suite 201, Mesa, AZ 85201.

Golden Light, *(Golden Light Press; 0-940086),* 14 Old Cow Path, Miller Place, NY 11764 Tel 516-473-8904.

Golden Mean, *(Golden Mean Pubs., The; 0-937698),* 258 A St., Ashland, OR 97520 Tel 503-482-3324.

Golden Mtn, *(Golden Mountain Press; 0-935062),* P.O. Box 2387, Ithaca, NY 14850.

Golden Owl Pub, *(Golden Owl Pubs.; 0-9601258),* 117 Essex South Dr., Lexington Park, MD 20653 Tel 301-863-9253.

Golden Pr *Imprint of* Western Pub

Golden Quill, *(Golden Quill Press; 0-8233),* Francestown, NH 03043 Tel 603-547-6622.

Golden Rainbow Pr, *(Golden Rainbow Press),* P.O. Box 106, Houston, TX 77001.

Golden St Dance Teach Assn, *(Golden State Dance Teachers Assn; 0-932980),* 11120 Downey Ave., Downey, CA 90241 Tel 213-861-6933.

Golden State Indus, *(Golden State Industries Corp.),* 5042 E. Third St., Los Angeles, CA 90022.

Golden Touch Ent, *(Golden Touch Enterprises),* P.O. Box 2408, West Palm Beach, FL 33401.

Golden Valley, *(Golden Valley Lutheran College Bookstore),* 6125 Olson Hwy., Minneapolis, MN 55422.

Golden West, *(Golden West Books; 0-87095),* P.O. Box 8136, San Marino, CA 91108 Tel 213-283-3446.

Golden West Hist, *(Golden West Historical Pubns.; 0-930960),* P.O. Box 1906, Ventura, CA 93002.

Golden West Pub, *(Golden West Pubs.; 0-914846),* 4113 N. Longview, Phoenix, AZ 85014 Tel 602-265-4392.

Goldermood Rainbow, *(Goldermood Rainbow; 0-916402),* 331 W. Bonneville St., Pasco, WA 99301 Tel 509-547-5525.

Golem, *(Golem Press; 0-911762),* P.O. Box 1342, Boulder, CO 80306 Tel 303-444-0841.

Golf Digest, *(Golf Digest/Tennis, Inc.; 0-914178),* 445 Westport Ave., Norwalk, CT 06856 Tel 203-847-5811.

Golf Digest Bks
    See Golf Digest

Goliards Pr, *(Goliards Press),* 3515 18th St., Bellingham, WA 98225.

Gondolier, *(Gondolier Press; 0-935824),* P.O. Box 467, Woodstock, NY 12498 Tel 914-679-9235.

Gondwana Bks, *(Gondwana Books; 0-931926),* Div. of Alta Napa Press, P.O. Box 407, Calistoga, CA 94515 Tel 707-942-6821.

Gonzaga U Pr, *(Gonzaga Univ. Press),* Spokane, WA 99202.

Gonzales, *(Gonzales, Andrew),* 1984 73rd St., Brooklyn, NY 11204.

Good Apple, *(Good Apple, Inc.; 0-916456; 0-86653),* P.O. Box 299, Carthage, IL 62321 Tel 217-357-3981.

Good Bk Pr, *(Good Book Press),* 12860 Muscatine St., Arleta, CA 91371 Tel 213-767-7660.

Good Bks PA, *(Good Books; 0-934672),* Main St., Intercourse, PA 17534.

Good Food Bks, *(Good Food Books; 0-932398),* 17 Colonial Terrace, Maplewood, NJ 07040.

Good Friends *Imprint of* Ideals

Good Gay, *(Good Gay Poets),* P.O. Box 277, Astor Sta., Boston, MA 02123 Tel 617-661-7534.

Good Ideas, *(Good Ideas Co.; 0-9603940),* Box 296, Berea, OH 44017 Tel 216-234-5411.

Good Life, *(Good Life Press; 0-89074),* Div. of Charing Cross Publishing Co., 658 S. Bonnie Brae St., Los Angeles, CA 90057 Tel 213-483-5832.

Good Life VA, *(Good Life Publishers; 0-917374),* 14200 Nash Rd., Chesterfield, VA 23832 Tel 804-794-4954.

Good News, *(Good News Pubs.; 0-89107),* 9825 W. Roosevelt Rd., Westchester, IL 60153 Tel 800-323-3890.

Good Sign, *(Good Sign Pubns.; 0-937730),* 457 Ruthven Ave., Palo Alto, CA 94301.

Good Times Pub, *(Good Times Publishing Co., Inc.),* P.O. Box 625, Indian Rocks Beach, FL 33535; Moved, Left No Forwarding Address.

Goodfellow, *(Goodfellow Catalog of Wonderful Things; 0-936016),* P.O. Box 4520, Berkeley, CA 94704 Tel 415-845-7645.

Goodheart, *(Goodheart-Willcox Co., Inc.; 0-87006),* 123 W. Taft Dr., South Holland, IL 60473 Tel 312-333-7200.

Goodlion, *(Goodlion Pub.; 0-912844),* c/o School of Art, Institute of Chicago, Michigan & Adams, Chicago, IL 60603 Tel 312-326-7080; Out of Business.

Goodty Good Bks, *(Goodty Good Books & Toys),* 2136 Cottingham Dr., Montgomery, AL 36106.

Goodyear, *(Goodyear Publishing Co.; 0-87620; 0-8302),* 1640 Fifth St., Santa Monica, CA 90401 Tel 213-393-6731; Orders to: 4700 S. 5400 West, Box 18486, Salt Lake City, UT 84118 Tel 801-966-1411.

Goranson Pr, *(Goranson Press),* 7624 W. Raschen, Chicago, IL 60656.

Gordian, *(Gordian Press, Inc.; 0-87752),* 85 Tompkins St., Staten Island, NY 10304 Tel 212-273-4700.

Gordon, *(Gordon & Breach Science Pubs., Inc.; 0-677),* 1 Park Ave., New York, NY 10016 Tel 212-689-0360.

Gordon-Cremonesi, *(Gordon-Cremonesi Book),* Dist. by: Atheneum Pubs., 597 Fifth Ave., New York, NY 10017 Tel 212-486-2700.

Gordon Pr, *(Gordon Press Pubs.; 0-87968),* P.O. Box 459, Bowling Green Sta., New York, NY 10004.

Gordon Soules Econ, *(Soules, Gordon, Economic Marketing Research; 0-919574),* 507 Third Ave., Suite 1240, Seattle, WA 98104.

Gordons & Weinberg, *(Gordons & T. Weinberg; 0-9603484),* Berthoud Falls, P.O. Box 666, Empire, CO 80438.

Gordonstown, *(Gordonstown Press; 0-9603942),* Box U, Dillon, CO 80435.

Gordy Pr, *(Gordy Press; 0-936472),* 330 Pine Ridge Rd., Jackson, MS 39206 Tel 601-362-6518.

Gospel Advocate, *(Gospel Advocate Co., Inc.; 0-89225),* P.O. Box 150, Nashville, TN 37202 Tel 615-254-8781.

Gospel Folio, *(Gospel Folio Press),* P.O. Box 2011, Grand Rapids, MI 49501

Gospel Pub, *(Gospel Publishing House; 0-88243),* 1445 Boonville Ave., Springfield, MO 65802 Tel 417-862-2781.

Gospel Pubns FL, *(Gospel Pubns. Inc. of Jax, Florida; 0-937408),* P.O. Box 16824, Jax, FL 32216.

Goss, *(Goss & Co., Pubs.; 0-912010),* 396 Redwood Dr., Pasadena, CA 91105 Tel 213-257-1773.

Gotham, *(Gotham Book Mart; 0-910664),* 41 W. 47th St., New York, NY 10036 Tel 212-757-0367.

Gottlieb & Allen, *(Gottlieb & Allen; 0-930768),* 200 E. 27th St., New York, NY 10016.

Gotuit Ent, *(Gotuit Enterprises; 0-931490),* P.O. Box 2568, Seal Beach, CA 90740; Dist. by: Pelican Publishing Co., 630 Burmaster St., Gretna, LA 70053 Tel 504-368-1175.

Gould, *(Gould Pubns.; 0-87560),* 199 State St., Binghamton, NY 13901 Tel 607-724-3000.

Gourmet Bks, *(Gourmet Books, Inc.; 0-933166),* 777 Third Ave., New York, NY 10017 Tel 212-754-1515.

Gourmet Guides, *(Gourmet Guides; 0-937024),* 1767 Stockton St., San Francisco, CA 94133.

Gov Data Pubns, *(Government Data Pubns.),* 1120 Connecticut Ave., N.W., Washington, DC 20036.

Gov Insts, *(Government Institutes, Inc.; 0-86587),* 966 Hungerford Dr., No. 24, Rockville, MD 20850.

Gov Printing Office, *(Government Printing Office),* 710 N. Capitol St. NW., Washington, DC 20402 Tel 202-783-3238.

Gov Res Pubns, *(Government Research Pubns.; 0-931684),* Box 122, Newton Center, MA 02159.

Gowan, *(Gowan, J.C.),* 1426 Southwind, Westlake Village, CA 91361 Tel 213-991-0342.

Gower *Imprint of* Unipub

GRA, *(Governmental Research Assn., Inc.),* 4302 Airport Blvd., Austin, TX 78722 Tel 201-269-3489.

Grace Pub Co, *(Grace Publishing Co.),* P.O. Box 23385, Tampa, FL 33622 Tel 813-884-8003.

Grace Stewart, *(Stewart, Grace, Pub.),* 221 S. Ohioville Rd., New Paltz, NY 12561.

Gracelaine, *(Gracelaine Pubns.; 0-932984),* 3001 Ashley Ave., Montgomery, AL 36109.

Graceway, *(Graceway Publishing Co.; 0-932126),* P.O. Box 159, Station "C", Flushing, NY 11367 Tel 212-261-0759.

Grad School, *(Graduate School Press),* U.S. Dept. Agriculture, Rm. 6847, S. Bldg., Washington, DC 20250 Tel 202-447-7123.

Grade Finders, *(Grade Finders, Inc.),* 642 Lancaster Ave., Berwin, PA 19312 Tel 215-644-4159; Orders to: P.O. Box 444, Bala-Cynwyd, PA 19004.

Graeff, *(Dr.-Ing. Roderich W. Graeff; 0-9604570),* 607 Church, Ann Arbor, MI 48104 Tel 313-769-6588.

Graham Educ, *(Graham Educational Products),* Div. of Fun Publishing Co., 6215 Washington Blvd., Indianapolis, IN 46220 Tel 317-253-2557; Orders to: P.O. Box 40283, Indianapolis, IN 46240.

Gramercy Bks, *(Gramercy Books, Inc.; 0-935134),* 354 George St, New Brunswick, NJ 08901.

Grammatical Sci, *(Grammatical Sciences),* 1236 Jackson St., Santa Clara, CA 95050.

Granada, *(Granada Publishing Inc.),* Suite 405, 866 UN Plaza, New York, NY 10017 Tel 212-753-9510.

Grand Canyon, *(Grand Canyon Pubns., Inc.; 0-9604276),* 443 S. 600 East St., Salt Lake City, UT 84102 Tel 801-272-2824.

Grand Trine, *(Grand Trine Pubns., Inc.; 0-915532),* P.O. Box 7225, Hollywood, FL 33021.

Granger Bk, *(Granger Book Co., Inc.; 0-89609),* P.O. Box 406, Great Neck, NY 11021 Tel 516-466-3676.

Granite Pubns, *(Granite Pubns.; 0-914102),* Box 1367, Southampton, NY 11968.

Grant Admin, *(Grant Administration Consultants; 0-938606),* P.O. Box 234, Chesterfield, MO 63017.

Grant Dahlstrom, *(Dahlstrom, Grant, /Castle Press),* 516 N. Fair Oaks Ave., Pasadena, CA 91103.

Grantsman Ent, *(Grantsman Enterprises Together),* 6222 Beach Dr., Panama City, FL 32407 Tel 904-234-9021.

Graph Arts Pub Co, *(Graphic Arts Publishing Co.; 0-933600),* 3100 Bronson Hill Rd., Livonia, NY 14487 Tel 716 316 2776.

Graph Arts Res RIT, *(Graphic Arts Research Center, Rochester Institute of Technology; 0-89938),* 1 Lomb Memorial Dr., Rochester, NY 14623 Tel 716-475-2761.

Graph Arts Trade, *(Graphic Arts Trade Journals; 0-910762),* 399 Conklin St., Suite 306, P.O. Box 81, Farmingdale, NY 11735 Tel 516-694-4842.

Graphic Arts Ctr, *(Graphic Arts Center Publishing Co.; 0-912856),* P.O. Box 10306, Portland, OR 97210 Tel 503-224-7777.

Graphic Comm Ctr, *(Graphic Communications Center),* Appleton, WI 54911.

Graphic Crafts, *(Graphic Crafts, Inc.),* P.O. Box 248, 300 Beaver Valley Pike, Willow Street, PA 17584 Tel 717-464-2733.

Graphic Dimensions, *(Graphic Dimensions; 0-930904),* 8 Frederick Rd., Pittsford, NY 14534 Tel 716-381-3428.

Graphic Impress, *(Graphic Impressions; 0-914628),* 1939 W. 32nd Ave., Denver, CO 80211 Tel 303-458-7475.

Graphic Pr, *(Graphic Press; 0-89284),* Div. of Carl Nelson Associates, Inc., P.O. Box 13056, Washington, DC 20009 Tel 202-232-2927.

Graphic Pub, *(Graphic Publishing Co.; 0-89279),* 204 N. Second Ave., W., Lake Mills, IA 50450 Tel 515-592-0031.

Graphic Story, *(Graphic Story Press; 0-914406),* P.O. Box 16168, Long Beach, CA 90806 Tel 213-436-8172; Moved Left No Forwarding Address.

Graphics Calif, *(Graphics Press; 0-937536),* 3010 Santa Monica Blvd. Suite 406, Santa Monica, CA 90404 Tel 213-395-2676.

Grasshopper NY, *(Grasshopper Press; 0-918218),* P.O. Box 331, Dewitt, NY 13214 Tel 315-479-5998; Moved Left No Address.

Grastorf & Lang, *(Grastorf & Lang, Ltd.; 0-933408),* 920 Broadway, New York, NY 10010.

Graves Ent, *(Graves, Michael P., Enterprises; 0-9603814),* 621 S. Third Ave., Wausau, WI 54401.

Gray Assoc, *(Gray & Associates; 0-937636),* P.O. Box 961, Madison, WI 53701 Tel 608-274-7458.

Gray Beard, *(Gray Beard Publishing; 0-933686),* 107 W. John St., Seattle, WA 98119.

Gray-Zone, *(Gray-Zone Press; 0-9600516),* Felicity Lane, Torrington, CT 06790.

Grayling, *(Grayling House; 0-939152),* 1735 DeSales St., N.W., Suite 800, Washington, DC 20036.

Graylock, *(Graylock Press; 0-910670),* 5130 Wickett Terrace, Bethesda, MD 20014 Tel 301-530-2721; Orders to: 428 E. Preston St., Baltimore, MD 21202 Tel 301-528-4298.

Graystone Pub Co, *(Graystone Publishing Co.; 0-933468),* 450 E. 81st St., New York, NY 10028.

Graywolf, *(Graywolf Press; 0-915308),* P.O. Box 142, Port Townsend, WA 98368 Tel 206-385-1160.

Grdinic, *(Grdinic, Eva; 0-9604176),* 6661 Vista del Mar, Playa del Rey, CA 90291.

Great Albion
   See Assoc Univ Prs

Great Am Bks, *(Great American Books; 0-936790),* 256 S. Robertson Blvd., Beverly Hills, CA 90211.

Great Am Edns, *(Great American Editions, Ltd.; 0-913826),* 111 E. 80th St., New York, NY 10021 Tel 212-744-5369; Moved, Left No Forwarding Address.

Great Am Pub, *(Great American Publishing Co.; 0-934632),* 5513 Hwy. 290 W., Austin, TX 78735.

Great Basin, *(Great Basin Press; 0-930830),* Box 11162, Reno, NV 89510 Tel 702-826-7729.

Great Bks Found, *(Great Books Foundation),* 307 N. Michigan Ave., Chicago, IL 60601 Tel 312-332-5870.

Great Comm Pubns, *(Great Commission Pubns.; 0-934688),* 7401 Old York Rd., Philadelphia, PA 19126 Tel 215-635-6510.

Great Eastern, *(Great Eastern Book Co.; 0-87773),* P.O. Box 271, Boulder, CO 80306 Tel 303-449-6113. *Imprints:* Prajna (Prajna Press).

Great Fidelity, *(Great Fidelity Press, Inc.),* 55 Montgomery St., San Francisco, CA 94105 Tel 415-543-5872.

Great Lakes Pub, *(Great Lakes Publishing Co., Inc.; 0-933300),* Box 461, Hudson, OH 44236 Tel 216-655-2996.

Great Nat Soc Poet, *(Greater National Society of Poets, Inc.; 0-940088),* 3023 W. Hillsborough Ave., Tampa, FL 33614 Tel 813-626-0225.

Great Northwest, *(Great Northwest Publishing & Distributing Co.; 0-937708),* 1207 E. Lyons, No.198, Spokane, WA 99208.

Great Oak, *(Great Oak Press, The; 0-934564),* P.O. Box 1013, Anderson, CA 96007.

Great Ocean, *(Great Ocean Pubs.; 0-915556),* 738 S. 22nd St., Arlington, VA 22202 Tel 703-920-8978.

Great Outdoors, *(Great Outdoors Publishing Co.; 0-8200),* 4747 28th St., N., St. Petersburg, FL 33714 Tel 813-525-6609.

Great Plains, *(Great Plains National Instructional Television Library),* Box 80669, Lincoln, NE 68501 Tel 402-472-2007.

Great Pyramid, *(Great Pyramid Press; 0-9605822),* P.O. Box 2745, Augusta, GA 30904 Tel 404-736-3514.

Great Raven Pr, *(Great Raven Press),* Box 813, Fort Kent, ME 04743.

Great Star, *(Great Star Press),* 1117 High Court, Berkeley, CA 94708.

Great Wall Pr, *(Great Wall Press; 0-913466),* P. O. Box 1352, Hazelwood, MO 63043; Moved, Left No Forwarding Address.

Great Western, *(Great Western Pubns.; 0-9604572),* 1842 W. 169th St., Gardena, CA 90247 Tel 213-323-7606.

Great Wine Grapes, *(Great Wine Grapes),* 155 24th Ave., Apt. 1, San Francisco, CA 94121.

Greater Phila, *(Greater Philadelphia Chamber of Commerce; 0-918964),* 1617 John F. Kennedy Blvd., Suite 1960, Philadelphia, PA 19103 Tel 215-568-4040.

Greater Portland, *(Greater Portland Landmarks, Inc.; 0-9600612),* 165 State St., Portland, ME 04101 Tel 207-744-5561.

Greatest Graphics, *(Greatest Graphics, Inc.; 0-936120),* 1904 B East Meadowmere, Springfield, MO 65804; Orders to: Greatest Graphics, P.O. Box 4467gs, Springfield, MO 65804 Tel 417-862-6500.

Greatlakes Liv, *(Greatlakes Living Press; 0-89635; 0-915498),* 180 N. Michigan Ave., Chicago, IL 60601 Tel 312-782-9181.

Green, *(Green, Warren H., Inc.; 0-87527),* 8356 Olive Blvd., St. Louis, MO 63132 Tel 314-991-1335.

Green Acres Schl, *(Green Acres School),* 11701 Danville Dr., Rockville, MD 20852 Tel 301-881-4100.

Green Dolphin, *(Green Dolphin Bookshop; 0-911904),* 215 S.W. Ankeny St., Portland, OR 97204 Tel 503-224-3060.

Green Eagle Pr, *(Green Eagle Press; 0-914018),* 241 W. 97th St., New York, NY 10025 Tel 212-663-2167.

Green Hill, *(Green Hill Pubs.; 0-916054; 0-89803),* 236 Forest Park Place, Ottawa, IL 61350 Tel 815-434-7905; Dist. by: Caroline House Pubs., Inc., 2 Ellis Place, Ossining, NY 10562 Tel 914-941-9271.

Green Hut, *(Green Hut Press; 0-916678),* 24051 Rotunda Rd., Valencia Hills, CA 91355 Tel 805-259-5290.

Green Note Music, *(Green Note Music Pubns.; 0-912910),* P.O. Box 519, Pt. Reyes Sta., CA 94956 Tel 415-663-1453; Dist. by: Warner Bros. Pubns., Inc., 75 Rockefeller Plaza, New York, NY 10019.

Green Oak Pr, *(Green Oak Press; 0-931600),* 9339 Spicer Rd., Brighton, MI 48116 Tel 313-449-4802.

Green River, *(Green River Press, Inc.),* Box 56, University Center, MI 48710 Tel 517-790-4376.

Green Tiger, *(Green Tiger Press; 0-914676),* P.O. Box 868, La Jolla, CA 92038 Tel 714-238-1001.

Greenberg Pub Co, *(Greenberg Publishing Co.; 0-89778),* 729 Oklahoma Rd., Sykesville, MD 21784 Tel 301-795-7447.

Greene, *(Greene, Stephen, Press; 0-8289),* Fessenden Rd. at Indian Flat, P.O. Box 1000, Brattleboro, VT 05301 Tel 802-257-7757.

Greenfld Rev Pr, *(Greenfield Review Press; 0-912678),* Greenfield Ctr., NY 12833 Tel 518-584-1728.

Greenhaven, *(Greenhaven Press; 0-912616; 0-89908),* 577 Shoreview Park Rd., St. Paul, MN 55112 Tel 612-482-1582.

Greenlf Bks, *(Greenleaf Books; 0-934676),* Weare, NH 03281.

Greenlight Pr, *(Greenlight Press; 0-930864),* P.O. Box 360, 1230 Grant Ave., San Francisco, CA 94133.

Greeno Hadden, *(Greeno, Hadden & Co., Ltd.; 0-913550),* 518 Central St., Winchendon, MA 01475 Tel 617-297-1006.

Greenvale, *(Greenvale Press; 0-911876),* P.O. Box 242, Kopperl, TX 76652 Tel 817-772-8576.

Greenwich CT, *(Greenwich Press Ltd.; 0-86713),* 30 Lindeman Dr., Trumbull, CT 06641 Tel 203-371-6568.

Greenwich Des, *(Greenwich Design; 0-9603892),* Box 611, Hopkins, MN 55343 Tel 612-935-2574; 910 1/2 Excelsior Ave W., Hopkins, MN 55343.

Greenwich Mer, *(Greenwich-Meridian Co.; 0-912424),* 516 Ave. "K", S., Saskatoon Saskatchewan Canada,; Out of Business.

Greenwich Pr, *(Greenwich Press; 0-911708),* 82 Christopher St., New York, NY 10014 Tel 212-242-0114.

Greenwillow, *(Greenwillow Books; 0-688),* Div. of William Morrow & Co., Inc., 105 Madison Ave., New York, NY 10016 Tel 212-889-3050; Orders to: William Morrow & Co., Inc., Wilmor Warehouse, 6 Henderson Dr., West Caldwell, NJ 07006.

Greenwood, *(Greenwood Press; 0-8371; 0-313),* 88 Post Rd. W., Westport, CT 06881 Tel 203-226-3571. *Imprints:* Quorum Bks (Quorum Books).

Greenwood Hse, *(Greenwood House; 0-9601982),* 1655 Flatbush Ave., Brooklyn, NY 11210.

Gregg, *(Gregg Press, Inc.; 0-8398),* Div. of G. K. Hall & Co., 70 Lincoln St., Boston, MA 02111 Tel 617-423-3990.

Gregg-Hamilton, *(Gregg-Hamilton; 0-934800),* Meridian, Monroe & Maple, Aberdeen, MS 39730 Tel 601-369-8120.

Gregorio Pubns, *(Gregorio Pubns.; 0-916118),* 5507 Yale Sta., New Haven, CT 06520.

Gregory Pub, *(Gregory Publishing Co.),* 806 N. Maple St., Itasca, IL 60143.

Gregory Pubns, *(Gregory Pubns.; 0-917224),* Gateway Sta., Box T, Aurora, CO 80014.

Grey Fox, *(Grey Fox Press; 0-912516),* P.O. Box 31411, San Francisco, CA 94131; Dist. by: Subterranean Co., P.O. Box 10233, Eugene, OR 97440 Tel 503-343-6324.

Grey Hse Pub, *(Grey House Publishing, Inc.; 0-939300),* 360 Park Ave. S., 13th Fl., New York, NY 10010.

Greyfalcon Hse, *(Greyfalcon House; 0-914870),* 124 Waverly Place, New York, NY 10011 Tel 212-777-9042.

Greylock Pubs, *(Greylock Pubs.; 0-89223),* 13 Spring St., Stamford, CT 06901.

Grid Pub, *(Grid Publishing, Inc.; 0-88244),* 466 Indianola Ave., Columbus, OH 43214 Tel 614-261-6565.

Griffon Hse, *(Griffon House Pubns.; 0-918680),* P.O. Box 81, Whitestone, NY 11357.

Griggs Print, *(Griggs Printing & Publishing; 0-918292),* Box 1351, 426 First St., Havre, MT 59501 Tel 406-265-7431.

Griggsville
   See Nature Soc

Grilled Flowers Pr, *(Grilled Flowers Press; 0-931238),* P.O. Box 3254, Durango, CO 81301.

Grinnell Coll, *(Grinnell College),* Grinnell, IA 50112.

Grist Mill, *(Grist Mill; 0-917820),* Energy Conservation Services, 90 Depot Rd., Eliot, ME 03903 Tel 207-439-3873.

Gro-Pub, *(Gro-Pub; 0-914990),* 13193 E. Bethany Place, Denver, CO 80232 Tel 303-755-7537; Orders to: P.O. Box 22629, Denver, CO 80222.

Grolier Club, *(Grolier Club),* Dist. by: Univ. Press of Virginia, Univ. Sta., P.O. Box 3608, Charlottesville, VA 22903 Tel 804-924-3131.

Grolier Ed Corp, *(Grolier Educational Corp.; 0-7172),* Subs. of Grolier, Inc., Sherman Turnpike, Danbury, CT 06816 Tel 203-797-3500.

Grolier Inc
   See Grolier Ed Corp

Groome Ctr, *(Groome Center; 0-916964),* 5225 Loughboro Rd., N.W., Washington, DC 20016 Tel 202-362-7644.

Gros Ventre Treaty, *(Gros Ventre Treaty Committee),* Ft. Belknap Agency, Harlem, MT 59526.

Gross Ent, *(Gross Enterprises; 0-913854),* 1705 The Strand, Manhattan Beach, CA 90266 Tel 213-545-5410.

Grosseteste, *(Grosseteste Review Books),* Dist. by: SBD: Small Press Distribution, 1636 Ocean View Ave., Kensington, CA 94707 Tel 415-524-2107.

Grossman, *(Grossman Pubs., Inc.; 0-670),* c/o Viking Penguin, 625 Madison Ave., New York, NY 10022.

Grossman Stamp, *(Grossman Stamp Co., Inc.; 0-912618),* 860 Broadway, New York, NY 10003 Tel 212-254-6100.

Grossmont Pr, *(Grossmont Press, Inc.; 0-913182; 0-89543),* 3211 Jefferson St., San Diego, CA 92110 Tel 714-299-2205.

Group One, *(Group One, Inc.),* 6248 121st St., S. E., Bellevue, WA 98006; Moved, Left No Forwarding Address.

Groupwork Today, *(Groupwork Today Inc.; 0-916068),* P.O. Box 258, South Plainfield, NJ 07080 Tel 201-755-4803.

Grove, *(Grove Press, Inc.; 0-8021; 0-394),* 196 W. Houston St., New York, NY 10014 Tel 212-242-4900; Orders to: Grove Press Order Dept., 196 W. Houston St., New York, NY 10014. *Imprints:* BC (Black Cat Books); Ever (Evergreen Books); EverBC (Evergreen-Black Cat Books); Zebra (Zebra Books).

Groves Dict Music, *(Grove's Dictionaries of Music, Inc.),* 1283 National Press Bldg., Washington, DC 20045.

Growing Together, *(Growing Together Press; 0-9604118),* P.O. Box 2983, Stanford, CA 94305.

Growth Assoc, *(Growth Associates; 0-918834),* P.O. Box 8429, Rochester, NY 14618 Tel 716-244-1225.

Growth Unltd, *(Growth Unlimited; 0-9601334),* 31 East Ave., S., Battle Creek, MI 49017 Tel 616-964-4821.

Grune, *(Grune & Stratton; 0-8089),* c/o Academic Press, 111 Fifth Ave., 12th Fl., New York, NY 10003 Tel 212-741-4888.

Grupenhoff
   See Sci & Health

Gryphon
   See Gryphon Pr NJ

Gryphon Hse, *(Gryphon House, Inc.; 0-87659),* 3706 Otis St., P.O. Box 217, Mt. Rainier, MD 20822 Tel 301-779-6200.

Gryphon Pr NJ, *(Gryphon Press; 0-910674),* Buros Institute of Mental Measurements, 135 Bancroft, Univ. of Nebraska, Lincoln, NE 68588 Tel 201-247-7506; Orders to: Univ. of Nebraska Press, 901 N. 17th St., Lincoln, NE 68588 Tel 402-472-3581.

GS, *(Girl Scouts of the USA; 0-88441),* National Equipment Service, 830 Third Ave., New York, NY 10022 Tel 212-940-7500.

Guappones Pubs, *(Guappone's Pubs.),* R.D. One, Box Ten, McClellandtown, PA 15458 412-737-5172.

Guarionex Pr, *(Guarionex Press Ltd.; 0-935966),* 201 W. 77th St., New York, NY 10024.

Guffey Bks, *(Guffey Books, Inc.),* 6634 S. Broadway, Littleton, CO 80120 Tel 303-798-6406.

Guide Pr, *(Guide Press; 0-915472),* 7101 Glenbrook Rd., Bethesda, MD 20014 Tel 301-654-3572.

Guideline Pub, *(Guideline Publishing Co.; 0-917474),* 336 S. Occidental Blvd., Los Angeles, CA 90057 Tel 213-382-4500.

Guidelines Pr, *(Guidelines Press; 0-932570),* 1307 S. Killian Dr., Lake Park, FL 33403 Tel 305-842-9411.

Guideposts Assoc, *(Guideposts Associates, Inc.),* Carmel, NY 10512 Tel 914-225-3681.

Guides Multinatl Busn, *(Guides to Multinational Business, Inc.; 0-931000),* P.O. Box 92, Harvard Square, Cambridge, MA 02138.

Guifford-Hill, *(Guifford-Hill Publishing Co.),* Rte. 8, Box 264, London, KY 40741.

Guild Bks, *(Guild Books; 0-912080),* 86 Riverside Dr., New York, NY 10024 Tel 212-799-2600.

Guild Blind, *(Guild for the Blind, The),* 180 N. Michigan Ave., No. 1720, Chicago, IL 60601.

Guild of Tutors, *(Guild of Tutors, International College; 0-89615),* 1019 Gavley Ave., Los Angeles, CA 90024.

Guild Prof Trans
See Translation Research

Guilford Pr, *(Guilford Press, The, 0 89862),* 200 Park Ave. S., New York, NY 10003.

Guinea Hollow, *(Guinea Hollow Press; 0-916344),* 190 Waverly Place, New York, NY 10014 Tel 212-924-4586.

Guitar Player, *(Guitar Player Productions; 0-89122),* Div. of Guitar Player Magazine, Dist. by: Music Sales Corp., 33 W. 60th St., New York, NY 10023 Tel 212-246-0325.

Gulf Pub, *(Gulf Publishing Co.; 0-87201),* P.O. Box 2608, Houston, TX 77001 Tel 713-529-4301.

Gull Bks, *(Gull Books),* 1736 E. 53rd St., Brooklyn, NY 11234.

Gun Hill, *(Gun Hill Publishing Co.; 0-9600228),* P.O. Box 187B, Yazoo City, MS 39194 Tel 601-746-3196.

Gun Room, *(Gun Room Press; 0-88227),* 127 Raritan Ave., Highland Park, NJ 08904 Tel 201-545-4344.

Gustavson, *(Gustavson Publishing Co.),* P.O. Box 5671, San Jose, CA 95150.

Gusto Pr, *(Gusto Press; 0-933906),* P.O. Box 1009, 2960 Philip Ave., Bronx, NY 10465 Tel 212-931-8964.

Gutenberg, *(Gutenberg Press, The; 0-9603872),* P.O. Box 26345, San Francisco, CA 94126 Tel 415-548-3776.

Guthman Americana, *(Guthman Americana),* P.O. Box 737, Westport, CT 06880 Tel 203-259-9763.

Guynes Pub, *(Guynes Publishing Co.),* 615 N. Stanton St., El Paso, TX 79901.

Gwen Frostic, *(Gwen Frostic Prints),* Benzonia, MI 49616.

Gwenthie Pub
See Gwethine Pub Co

Gwethine Pub Co, *(Gwethine Publishing Co.),* 201 N. Wells St., Chicago, IL 60606 Tel 312-372-8105.

GWP, *(Great Western Publishing; 0-86666),* 416 Magnolia, Glendale, CA 91204; Do Not Confuse with Great Western Pubns.

H Allen Enterprises
See Howard Allen

H & A Herman, *(Herman, H. & A., Publishing Co.; 0-910718),* R.F.D. No. 1 Box 211-2, Cameron, SC 29030.

H & H Ent, *(H & H Enterprises, Inc.; 0-89079),* P.O. Box 1070, 946 Tennessee, Lawrence, KS 66044 Tel 913-843-4793.

H B Reid, *(Reid, Hugh B.; 0-911244),* Dist. by: Edwards Bros., 2500 S. State St., Ann Arbor, MI 48104 Tel 313-769-1000.

H C McElroy, *(McElroy, Harry C.),* Box 284, San Carlos, AZ 85550; Moved, Left No Forwarding Address.

H C Sun, *(Sun, H. C.),* Box 391, Sterling, VA 22170 Tel 703-430-7040.

H C Wells, *(Wells, H. C.; 0-930666),* P.O. Box 2480, Pasadena, CA 91105.

H C Wilson, *(Wilson, Harold C.; 0-9600760),* 320 Central Park W., New York, NY 10025 Tel 212-580-0698.

H Chase, *(Chase, Herman, Surveyor),* Alstead, NH 03602.

H D Baldridge, *(Baldridge, H. David, Captain USN (Ret.)),* P.O. Box 15216, Sarasota, FL 33579 Tel 813-922-4796.

H D Burrows, *(Burrows, Hal D., (Dba Inner Press); 0-916886),* 429 E. 98th St., No. 1, Inglewood, CA 90301 Tel 213-671-5959.

H D Seyer, *(Seyer, Herman D.; 0-9600784),* 3848 Country Center Dr., Visalia, CA 93277 Tel 209-734-7537.

H E Blanck, *(Blanck, Helen E.; 0-9603700),* 1228 108 Ave., N.E., Minneapolis, MN 55434 Tel 612-757-5374.

H E Reid, *(Reid, Hazel E.; 0-9601892),* P.O. Box 317, Manhattanville, New York, NY 10027 Tel 212-490-0077.

H E Seals, *(Seals, Howard E.; 0-9600232),* 3831 S. Michigan Ave., Rear Bldg., Chicago, IL 60653 Tel 312-285-3256.

H Estes, *(Estes, Hiawatha, & Associates; 0-911008),* P.O. Box 404-RR, Northridge, CA 91328 Tel 213-885-6588.

H F Snow, *(Snow, Helen F.; 0-911392),* 148 Mungertown Rd., Madison, CT 06443 Tel 203-245-9714.

H G Cushing, *(Cushing, Helen Grant; 0-9603588),* 339 E. 58th St., New York, NY 10022; Orders to: G. H. Cushing, 16237 Gledhill St., Sepulveda, CA 91343.

H G Davidson, *(Davidson, Harold G.),* 4573 Nueces Dr., Santa Barbara, CA 93110 Tel 805-967-7231.

H Gregory, *(Gregory, Howard, Associates),* P.O. Box 66, La Mirada, CA 90637.

H H Franks, *(Franks, Harold H.; 0-933770),* 1202 S. Second St., Booneville, MS 38829.

H. H. Wait
See N S Wait

H H Wolfe, *(Wolfe, Howard H.; 0-9600850),* 12405 Davis Blvd., S. E., Fort Meyers, FL 33905 Tel 813-694-1825.

H Isaacs, *(Isaacs, Harold; 0-9601406),* Dist. by: Peanut Brigade, P.O. Box 237, Plains, GA 31780 Tel 912-924-8287.

H J Cichy, *(Cichy, Helen J., Mrs.; 0-9601852),* Brandon, MN 56315.

H J Schneider
See World Wide OR

H John & Co, *(John, Henry, & Co.; 0-937028),* 1812 SE 46th Ave., Portland, OR 97215 Tel 503-236-9627.

H Jones, *(Jones, Harry; 0-9601980),* P.O. Box 10054, Austin, TX 78766 Tel 512-451-2644.

H K Goodkind, *(Goodkind, Herbert K.; 0-9600498),* 25 Helena Ave., Larchmont, NY 10538 Tel 914-834-1448.

H Kahn, *(Kahn, Hannah; 0-9602340),* 40 N. E. 69th St., Miami, FL 33138 Tel 305-759-5879.

H L Levin, *(Levin, Hugh Lauter, Associates; 0-88363),* 1 W. 39th St., New York, NY 10018 Tel 212-354-5027; Moved,Left No Forwarding Address.

H L Markow, *(Markow, Herbert L.; 0-934108),* P.O. Box 011451, Miami, FL 33101 Tel 305-448-0873.

H L Robertson, *(Robertson, Haywood L.; 0-9601116),* 250 South Reynolds St., Apt. 207, Alexandria, VA 22304 Tel 703-751-7517.

H Lalvani, *(Lalvani, Haresh),* P.O. Box 1538, New York, NY 10116.

H Linder, *(Linder, Herbert; 0-917396),* 55 Park Ave., New York, NY 10016 Tel 212-685-2571.

H M Elkins, *(Elkins, Herbert M., Co.),* 10031 Commerce Ave., Tujunja, CA 91042 Tel 213-353-1169.

H M Gousha, *(Gousha, H. M.; 0-913040),* 2001 The Alameda, P.O. Box 6227, San Jose, CA 95150 Tel 408-296-1060.

H M Rogers, *(Rogers, Helga M.; 0-9602294),* 1270 Fifth Ave., New York, NY 10029 Tel 212-348-0204.

H M Shelton, *(Shelton, Herbert M.),* P.O. Box 6636 - AH Sta, San Antonio, TX 78209 Tel 512-822-5263.

H P Bks, *(H. P. Books; 0-912656; 0-89586),* 341 Ponce de Leon Ave., N.E., Rm. 416, Tucson, AZ 85703 Tel 602-888-2150.

H R Gale, *(Gale, Hoyt Rodney),* 669 Sturtevant Dr., Sierra Madre, CA 91024.

H R Lurie, *(Lurie, Hannah Ross; 0-9600728),* 23 Derwen Rd., Bala Cynwyd, PA 19004 Tel 215-667-1350.

H R Mockel, *(Mockel, Henry),* 5686 The Plaza, Box 726, Twentynine Palms, CA 92277 Tel 714-367-3234.

H R Nestler Inc, *(Nestler, Harold R., Inc.),* 13 Pennington Ave., Waldwick, NJ 07463 Tel 201-444-7413.

H Ranieri, *(Ranieri, Helene),* 2760 Devonshire Place, N.W., Washington, DC 20008.

H Reichner, *(Reichner, Herbert; 0-9601520),* Shaker Hill, Enfield, NH 03748 Tel 603-632-7725.

H S Dakin, *(Dakin, H. S., Co.; 0-930420),* 3101 Washington St., San Francisco, CA 94115.

H S Marks, *(Marks, Henry S.),* 301 Terry-Hutchins Bldg. 102 Clinton Ave. W., Huntsville, AL 35801.

H S Pub Corp, *(Health Science Publishing Corp.; 0-88238),* 451 Greenwich St., New York, NY 10013 Tel 212-966-6658.

H Spriggle, *(Spriggle, Howard),* 1010 Chestnut St., Collingdale, PA 19023.

H V Meredith, *(Meredith, H. V.; 0-9603120),* Orders to: The State Printing Company, P.O. Box 1388, Columbia, SC 29202 Tel 803-799-9550.

H Vogt, *(Vogt, Helen; 0-9602542),* 121 Blaine Ave., Brownsville, PA 15417 Tel 412-785-3804.

H W Hall, *(Hall, H. W.; 0-935064),* 3608 Meadow Oaks Lane, Bryan, TX 77801 Tel 713-846-0798.

Haas, *(Haas, Frederick C.; 0-9601180),* Rte. 2 Box 78A, Blackstone, VA 23824 Tel 804-292-4726.

Haas Ent NH, *(Haas Enterprises; 0-9605552),* 7 N. Main, Box 218, Ashland, NH 03217 Tel 603-968-7177.

Habel, *(Habel, Robert L., 0 9600111),* 1529 Ellis Hollow Rd., Ithaca, NY 14850 Tel 607-272-3199.

Hacanbar, *(Hacanbar Associates),* Apt. 419, 2201 Pennsylvania Ave., Philadelphia, PA 19103; Moved, Left No Forwarding Address.

Hach, *(Hach, Phila; 0-9606192),* 1601 Madison St., Clarksville, TN 37040 Tel 615-647-4084.

Hacker, *(Hacker Art Books; 0-87817),* 54 W. 57th St., New York, NY 10019 Tel 212-757-1450.

Hackett Pub, *(Hackett Publishing Co.; 0-915144),* P. O. Box 55573, 4047 N. Pennsylvania St., Indianapolis, IN 46205 317-283-8187.

Haddad's Fine Arts, *(Haddad's Fine Arts, Inc.; 0-88445),* P.O. Box 3016 C, Anaheim, CA 92803 Tel 714-996-2100; 3855 E. Mira Loma Ave., Anaheim, CA 92803.

Haddonfield Hse, *(Haddonfield House; 0-88366),* Div. of Griffin Press Inc., 300 Kings Hwy., E., Haddonfield, NJ 08033 Tel 609-795-3552; Moved, Left No Forwarding Address.

Haddonfield Pubs, *(Haddonfield Pubs.; 0-915460),* P.O. Box 216, Haddonfield, NJ 08033 Tel 609-428-1282.

Hadley Group, *(Hadley Group, Inc.; 0-913624),* 808 S. Fourth St., Philadelphia, PA 19147 Tel 215-336-6700; Moved, Left No Forwarding Address.

Haessner Pub, *(Haessner Publishing, Inc.; 0-87799),* P. O. Box 89, Newfoundland, NJ 07435 Tel 201-697-3773.

Hafner, *(Hafner Press; 0-02),* Div. of Macmillan Publishing Co., Inc., 866 Third Ave., New York, NY 10022 Tel 212-935-2000; Dist. by: Collier-Macmillan Distribution Ctr., Riverside, NJ 08075.

Hafner Service, *(Hafner Service Agency),* ; Publisher Abbreviation Without Addresses Are for Titles That Are Out of Print. These Are Obsolete Abbreviations.

Hagin Evangelistic
See Hagin Ministries

Hagin Ministries, *(Hagin, Kenneth, Ministries, Inc.; 0-89276),* P.O. Box 50126, Tulsa, OK 74150 Tel 918-258-1588.

Hagstrom Co, *(Hagstrom Co., Inc.; 0-910684),* 450 W. 33rd St., New York, NY 10001 Tel 212-868-3420.

Haimo, *(Haimo, Oscar),* 252 E. 61st St., New York, NY 10021 Tel 212-838-6627.

Haimowoods, *(Haimowoods Press; 0-917790),* 1101 Forest Ave., Evanston, IL 60202 Tel 312-864-7209.

Haitian Soc, *(Haitian Society of Pubns.; 0-914280),* 359 Nostrand Ave., Brooklyn, NY 11216 Tel 212-789-4192.

Hake, *(Hake's Americana & Collectibles; 0-918708),* P.O. Box 1444, York, PA 17405 Tel 717-843-3731.

Hakims Pubs, *(Hakim's Pubs.),* 210 S. 52nd St., Philadelphia, PA 19139.

Hal Z Bennett, *(Bennett, Hal Z.),* 124 Ardmore Rd., Kensington, CA 94707.

Halbur, *(Halbur Publishing; 0-9603520),* P.O. Box 11354, Santa Rosa, CA 95406 Tel 707-544-7537.

Halcyon *Imprint of* **Natl Book**

Halcyon Ithaca, *(Halcyon Press of Ithaca; 0-9604006),* 111 Halcyon Hill Rd., Ithaca, NY 14850.

Haldon Pubns, *(Haldon Pubns., Inc.),* 1204 N. 20th Ave., Hollywood, FL 33020 Tel 305-929-1956; Orders to: P.O. Box 2226, Hollywood, FL 33022; Moved, Left No Forwarding Address.

Hale, *(Hale, E. M., & Co.; 0-8382),* 128 W. River St., Chippewa Falls, WI 54729 Tel 715-723-2814.

Halfrubber, *(Halfrubber Press; 0-9604808),* P.O. Box 312, Lithonia, GA 30058.

Hall Pr, *(Hall Press; 0-932218),* P.O. Box 5375, San Bernardino, CA 92412 Tel 714-887-3466.

Halldin Pub, *(Halldin, A. G., Publishing Co.; 0-935648),* P.O. Box 667, Indiana, PA 15701 Tel 412-463-8450.

Hallen Pub, *(Hallen Publishing Co.; 0-912992),* 1962 Kirby Way, San Jose, CA 95124 Tel 408-377-0835.

Hallmark, *(Hallmark Card, Inc.; 0-87529),* 25th & McGee Sts., Kansas City, MO 64108 Tel 816-274-5111.

Hall's Bks, *(Hall's Books),* Rte. 2, Box 239, Honea Path, SC 29654; Moved, Left No Forwarding Address.

Halls of Ivy, *(Halls of Ivy Press; 0-912256),* 13050 Raymer St., North Hollywood, CA 91605 Tel 213-875-3050.

Halsey Pub, *(Halsey Publishing Co.),* Dist. by: Construction Publishing Co., Inc., Box 88, Darien, CT 06820.

Halsted Pr, *(Halsted Press),* Div. of John Wiley & Sons, Inc., 605 Third Ave., New York, NY 10158 Tel 212-850-6418.

Halter Pubs, *(Halter Pubs.; 0-918776),* 1132 N. 34th St., Phoenix, AZ 85008 Tel 602-956-2859.

Halty Ferguson, *(Halty Ferguson; 0-912604),* 376 Harvard St., Cambridge, MA 02138 Tel 617-868-6190.

HamanD Pub, *(HamanD Publishing Co.),* 525 B St., Suite 342, San Diego, CA 92101 Tel 714-234-8393.

Hamber
See BH Ent

Hamilton Hse, *(Hamilton House; 0-917908),* 936 N. 5th, Philadelphia, PA 19123 Tel 215-923-9161.

Hamilton Inst, *(Hamilton, Alexander, Institute, Inc.),* 1633 Broadway, New York, NY 10019 Tel 212-397-3580.

Hamilton Pr
See Citizens Law

Hamilton Pub, *(Hamilton Publishing Co.; 0-917552),* 563 W. Westfield, Indianapolis, IN 46208 Tel 317-251-8411.

Hamlyn-Amer, *(Hamlyn/American; 0-600),* Dist. by: A & W Pubs., 95 Madison Ave., New York, NY 10016.

Hammond-Harwood, *(Hammond-Harwood House Assn., Inc.; 0-910688),* Orders to: Maryland's Way, Hammond Harwood House, 19 Maryland Ave., Annapolis, MD 21401 Tel 301-267-6891.

Hammond Inc, *(Hammond, Inc.; 0-8437),* 515 Valley St., Maplewood, NJ 07040 Tel 201-763-6000.

Hammond Photo, *(Hammond, Rick, Photography; 0-935330),* 705 S. Court St., Visalia, CA 93277.

Hamoroh Pr, *(Hamoroh Press; 0-9604754),* P.O. Box 48862, Los Angeles, CA 90048.

Hampshire Pacific, *(Hampshire Pacific Press; 0-939930),* 3043 SW Hampshire St., Portland, OR 97201.

Hampton Inst Pr, *(Hampton Institute Press; 0-915108),* Hampton Institute, Lawrenceville, VA 23868 Tel 804-848-3865; 102 Park Dr., Lawrenceville, VA 23868 Tel 804-848-3865; Orders to: Dictionary, P.O. Box 711, St Paul's College, Lawrenceville, VA 23868.

Hampton Pr MI, *(Hampton Press; 0-938352),* P.O. Box 805, Rochester, MI 48063.

Han Bks
See Blue Flower

Hancock Hse, *(Hancock House Pubs., Ltd.; 0-88839),* Dist. by: Universe Books, 183 Munroe St., Passaic, NJ 07055.

Handbook Co, *(Handbook Co.),* Box 491, Athens, OH 45701.

Handel & Co, *(Handel & Co., Inc.; 0-913766),* 2720 Stemmons Freeway, Suite 510, South Bldg., Dallas, TX 75207; Moved Left No Forwarding Address.

Handel & Sons, *(Handel & Sons Publishing, Inc.; 0-917080),* c/o Ambit Publications, Inc., 4227 Herschel, Suite 107, Dallas, TX 75219 Tel 214-522-0102.

Hands on Pubns, *(Hands on Pubns.; 0-931178),* 7061 Mariner Way, Long Beach, CA 90803 Tel 213-596-4738.

Handy *Imprint of* **HarBraceJ**

Hang Gliding, *(Hang Gliding Press; 0-938282),* Box 22552, San Diego, CA 92122.

Hanging Loose, *(Hanging Loose Press; 0-914610),* 231 Wyckoff St., Brooklyn, NY 11217 Tel 212-643-9559.

Hanover Pubns, *(Hanover Pubns., Inc.; 0-918710),* 200 Park Ave., Suite 303E, New York, NY 10017; Moved, Left No Forwarding Address.

Hans Huber *Imprint of* **Williams & Wilkins**

Hansen & Miller, *(Hansen & Miller; 0-9601312),* P.O. Box 848, Lower Lake, CA 95457.

Hansen Pub MI, *(Hansen Publishing Co.; 0-930098),* P.O. Box 1723, East Lansing, MI 48823 Tel 517-332-5946; Dist. by: Holley International Co., 63 Kercheval, Suite 204A, Grosse Pointe Farms, MI 48236 Tel 313-882-0405.

Hansi, *(Hansi Ministries, Inc.; 0-932878),* P.O. Box 552, Huntington Beach, CA 92648 Tel 714-894-7559.

Hapi Pr, *(Hapi Press; 0-913244),* 512 S.W. Maplecrest Dr., Portland, OR 97219 Tel 503-246-9632.

Happiness Pr, *(Happiness Press; 0-916508),* 160 Wycliff Way, Drawer ADD, Magalia, CA 95954 Tel 916-873-0294; Orders to: P.O. Box Add, Magalia, CA 95954.

Happiness Unltd, *(Happiness Unlimited Pubns.; 0-939372),* 122 the Maine, Williamsburg, VA 23185.

Happy Eye, *(Happy Eye Enterprises; 0-933426),* 1460 Grandview, Glendale, CA 91201 Tel 213-240-1683.

Happy Health, *(Happy Health Pubs.),* P.O. Box 2702, Seal Beach, CA 90740 Tel 213-431-0069.

Happy History, *(Happy History, Inc.; 0-918430),* P.O. Box 2160, Boca Raton, FL 33432 Tel 305-391-8030; Box 726, New Canaan, CT 06840.

Happy Valley Apple, *(Happy Valley Apple; 0-913758),* Dist. by: Bookpeople, 2940 Seventh St., Berkeley, CA 94710.

Har-Row, *(Harper & Row Pubs., Inc.; 0-06),* 10 E. 53rd St., New York, NY 10022 Tel 212-593-7000; 1700 Montgomery St., San Francisco, CA 94111 Tel 415-989-9000; Orders to: Keystone Industrial Park, Scranton, PA 18512. *Imprints:* Canfield Pr (Canfield Press); CN (Colophon Books); COS (College Outline Series); EH (Everyday Handbooks); HarCrest (Harper Crest); HarpC (Harper's College Division); Harper Medical (J.B. Lippincott/Harper & Row Medical Division); HarpJ (Juvenile Books); HarpR (Harper Religious Books); HarpT (Harper Trade Books); HW (Harrow Books Paperback Department); IntlDept (International Department); Open U (Open University); PL (Perennial Library); SchDept (School Department); Torch (Torchbooks); Torch Lib (Torchbooks Library Binding); Trophy (Trophy).

Harbinger
See New Harbinger

Harbinger Pr, *(Harbinger Press Library; 0-936092),* 347 Willow Ave., Corte Madera, CA 94925 Tel 415-924-6490.

Harbor Hill Bks, *(Harbor Hill Books; 0-916346)* P.O. Box 407, Harrison, NY 10528 Tel 914-698-3495.

Harbor Hse Bk, *(Harbor House Books Ltd.; 0-916800),* Subs. of Louis J. Martin & Associates, Inc., 95 Madison Ave., New York, NY 10016 Tel 212-725-2157; Dist. by: Louis J. Martin, 95 Madison Ave., New York, NY 10016 Tel 212-725-2157.

Harbor Hse Pub, *(Harbor House Publishing Ltd 0-930430),* Quarterman Harbor, Box 748, Vashon Island, WA 98070 Tel 206-567-4910.

Harbor Pub CA, *(Harbor Publishing Inc.; 0-936602),* 1668 Lombard, San Francisco, CA 94123; Dist. by: G.P. Putnam's Sons, 200 Madison Ave., New York, NY 10016.

Harboridge Pr, *(Harboridge Press),* 455 E. Ridge St., Marquette, MI 49855.

Harbour Hse, *(Harbour House; 0-917254),* 603 Driver Ave., Winter Park, FL 32804 Tel 305-647-8679.

Harbour Pub, *(Harbour Publishing Co.),* 7200 34th St. South, Sky Harbor Bldg. 2-D, St. Petersburg, FL 33711 Tel 813-867-3361.

HarBraceJ, *(Harcourt Brace Jovanovich, Inc.; 0-15),* 757 Third Ave., New York, NY 10017 Tel 212-888-4433. *Imprints:* Handy (Handy Books); Harv (Harvest Books); Hbgr (Harbinger Books); HC (Harcourt Brace Jovanovich, Inc., College Dept.); HPL (Harbrace Paperback Library); Psych Corp (Psychological Corp.); VoyB (Voyager Books).

Harcourt, *(Harcourt Brace & World, Inc.),* ; Publisher Abbreviation Without Addresses Are for Titles That Are Out of Print. These Are Obsolete Abbreviations. Publisher's New Abbreviation Is HarBraceJ.

HarCrest *Imprint of* **Har-Row**

Hard Art, *(HarD Art, Inc.),* P.O. Box 24199, St Louis, MO 63130.

Hard Press'd, *(Hard Press'd; 0-9604180),* 1110 Buffalo St., Box 444, Franklin, PA 16323.

Hardin, *(Hardin, Albert N., Jr.; 0-9601778),* 5414 Lexington Ave., Pennsauken, NJ 08109.

Hardscrabble Bks, *(Hardscrabble Books; 0-915056),* Rte. 2, Box 285, Berrien Springs MI 49103 Tel 616-473-5570.

Hardy Hse, *(Hardy House Pub. Co.; 0-917844),* A Hardy-Roberts Enterprise, P.O. Box 705, S. Laguna Beach, CA 92677 Tel 714-497-2670.

Hare Ed, *(Hare Editions; 0-916740),* The Kensington House, Apt. 616, 200 W. 20th St., New York, NY 10011.

Hargreaves, *(Hargreaves Co., Inc.; 0-910690),* P.O. Box 895, Kailua, HI 96734 Tel 808-262-7320.

Harian, *(Harian Books; 0-87036),* 1 Vernon Ave., Floral Park, NY 11001; Dist. by: Grosset & Dunlap, Inc., 51 Madison Ave., New York, NY 10010.

Harian Creative, *(Harian Creative Press; 0-911906),* 47 Hyde Blvd., Ballston Spa, N 12020 Tel 518-885-7397.

Harian Pubns, *(Harian Pubns.; 0-87036),* 1 Vernon Ave., Floral Park, NY 11001 Tel 516-437-3440.

Harley Smith Invest, *(Smith, Harley, Investments, Inc.; 0-916350),* 740 West Willow, Stockton, CA 95203 Tel 209-943-1650.

Harlo Pr, *(Harlo Press; 0-8187),* 50 Victor Ave Detroit, MI 48203 Tel 313-883-3600.

Harlow Pub
See Harrison Sch Bk

Harmless Flirt, *(Harmless Flirtation with Wealth; 0-9600834),* P.O. Box 9779, San Diego, CA 92109 Tel 714-282-6273; Dist. by: Bookpeople, 2940 Seventh St., Berkeley CA 94710 Tel 415-540-3033.

Harmony *Imprint of* **Crown**

Harmony & Co, *(Harmony & Co.; 0-89967),* Box 133, Greenport, NY 11944.

Harmony Hse, *(Harmony House; 0-934330),* 266 Waverly Dr., Elgin, IL 60120.

Harmony Soc, *(Harmony Society Press; 0-937640),* Box A 57, Clark University, Worcester, MA 01610.

Harmsen, *(Harmsen Publishing Co.; 0-9601322)* 1331 E. Alameda Ave., Denver, CO 80209.

Harold Hse, *(Harold House, Pubs.; 0-930138),* P.O. Box 59, 203 Walnut St., Marshall, AR 72650 Tel 501-448-5170.

HarpC *Imprint of* **Har-Row**

Harper, *(Harper & Row Pubs.),* ; Publishers Abbreviation Without Addresses Are for Titles That Are Out of Print. These Are Obsolete Abbreviations. Publisher's New Abbreviation Is Har-Row.

Harper Mag Pr, *(Harper's Magazine Press),* 10 E. 53rd St., New York, NY 10022 Tel 212-593-7000.

Harper Medical *Imprint of* **Har-Row**

Harper Sq Pr, *(Harper Square Press; 0-933908),* 401 W. Ontario St., Chicago, IL 60610 Tel 312-751-1650.

Harpers Coll Pr, *(Harpers College Press),* 10 E 53rd St., New York, NY 10022.

HarpJ *Imprint of* **Har-Row**

HarpR *Imprint of* **Har-Row**

Harpswell Pr, *(Harpswell Press; 0-88448),* R.F.D. 4, Box 3136, Brunswick, ME 04011 Tel 207-729-1606.

HarpT *Imprint of* **Har-Row**

Harriet's Kitchen, *(Harriet's Kitchen; 0-938592),* P.O. Box 424, Forest Hills, NY 11375.

Harris & Co, *(Harris, H. E., & Co., Inc.; 0-937458),* Div. of General Mills, Inc., 645 Summer St., Boston, MA 02210 Tel 617-269-5200; Orders to: Box A, Boston, MA 02117.

Harris Calif, *(Harris Publishing Co.; 0-917228),* 248 S. Rexford Dr., Beverly Hills, CA 90212 Tel 213-274-2962; Moved, Left No Forwarding Address.

Harris Pub, *(Harris Publishing Co.; 0-916512),* 2057-2 East Aurora Rd., Twinsburg, OH 44087 Tel 216-425-9143.

Harrison Co GA, *(Harrison Co.; 0-910694),* 3110 Crossing Park, Norcross, GA 30071 Tel 404-447-9150.

Harrison Hse, *(Harrison House, Inc.; 0-89274),* P.O. Box 35035, Tulsa, OK 74135 Tel 918-582-2126.

Harrison Sch Bk, *(Harrison School Book Publishing; 0-911678),* P.O. Box 1008, Norman, OK 73069 Tel 405-235-8842.

Harrowood Bks, *(Harrowood Books; 0-915180),* 3943 N. Providence Rd., Newtown Square, PA 19073.

Harry Gillig, *(Gillig, Harry; 0-9600848),* 2624 N.E. 26th Ave., Fort Lauderdale, FL 33306 Tel 305-564-8432.

Hart, *(Hart Associates; 0-8055),* 12 E. 12th St., New York, NY 10003 Tel 212-260-2430.

Hart Graphics, *(Hart Graphics; 0-9605422),* P.O. Box 968, Austin, TX 78767.

Hartley Ent, *(Hartley Enterprises),* P.O. Box 701, Rancho Mirage, CA 92270.

Hartley Hse, *(Hartley House; 0-937518),* P.O. Box 1352, Hartford, CT 06143 Tel 203-525-2376.

Hartmore, *(Hartmore House),* Dist. by: Associated Booksellers, 147 McKinley Ave., Bridgeport, CT 06606.

Hartmus Pr, *(Hartmus Press; 0-915868),* 23 Lomita Dr., Mill Valley, CA 94941 Tel 415-388-0822.

Hartt Pubns, *(Hartt Pubns.; 0-9601816),* P.O. Box 566, Borough Hall Sta., Jamaica, NY 11424 Tel 212-261-7315.

Hartung, *(Hartung, Marion T.; 0-913910),* 814 Constitution St., Emporia, KS 66801 Tel 316-342-6200.

Harv *Imprint of* **HarBraceJ**

Harvard Busn, *(Harvard Business School, Division of Research; 0-87584),* Soldiers Field, Boston, MA 02174; Dist. by: Harvard University Press, 79 Garden St., Cambridge, MA 02138.

Harvard Common Pr, *(Harvard Common Press; 0-916782),* The Common, Harvard, MA 01451 Tel 617-772-6842; Orders to: Independent Publishers Group, C/O David White, Inc., 14 Vandeventer Ave., Port Washington, NY 11050.

Harvard-Danforth, *(Harvard-Danforth Center for Teaching & Learning),* 11 University Hall, Cambridge, MA 02138 Tel 617-495-1538; Orders to: Robinson Hall Harvard University, Cambridge, MA 02138.

Harvard Educ Rev, *(Harvard Educational Review; 0-916690),* 13 Appian Way, Cambridge, MA 02138 Tel 617-495-3432.

Harvard Eng
See Bermuda Bio

Harvard Law Intl Tax, *(Harvard Law School, International Tax Program; 0-915506),* Harvard Law School, Cambridge, MA 02138 Tel 617-495-4407.

Harvard U Intl Aff, *(Harvard Univ., Ctr. for International Affairs; 0-87674),* Coolidge Hall-International Studies, 1737 Cambridge St., Cambridge, MA 02138 Tel 617-495-2137.

Harvard U Pr, *(Harvard Univ. Press; 0-674),* 79 Garden St., Cambridge, MA 02138 Tel 617-495-2600; Orders to: Customer Service, Harvard Univ. Press, 79 Garden St., Cambridge, MA 02138.

Harvard Ukrainian, *(Harvard Ukrainian Research Institute; 0-916458),* 1583 Mass. Ave., Cambridge, MA 02138 Tel 617-495-3692.

Harvest Hse, *(Harvest House Pubs., Inc.; 0-89081),* 1075 Arrowsmith, Eugene, OR 97402.

Harvest Moon, *(Harvest Moon Books; 0-9602886),* P.O. Box 172, Riverside, CA 92502 Tel 714-682-4907.

Harvest NJ, *(Harvest House Press; 0-89523),* Eden West, 30 Nassau St., Princeton, NJ 08540 Tel 609-924-8715; Dist. by: Harvest House Press, 30 Nassau St., Princeton, NJ 08540 Tel 609-924-8715.

Harvest Pr, *(Harvest Press; 0-917332),* P.O. Box 1265, Santa Cruz, CA 95061 Tel 408-335-5015.

Harvest Pr Texas, *(Harvest Press, Inc.; 0-930718),* P.O. Box 2267, Waco, TX 76107 Tel 817-752-5544.

Harvest Pubns, *(Harvest Pubns.; 0-939074),* 907 Santa Barbara St., Santa Barbara, CA 93101 Tel 805-685-1358.

Harvestman, *(Harvestman & Associates),* P.O. Box 271, Menlo Park, CA 94025 Tel 415-969-0125.

Harvey, *(Harvey House, Pubs.; 0-8178),* 20 Waterside Plaza, New York, NY 10010 Tel 212-889-9520; Orders to: 128 W. River St., Chippewa Falls, WI 54729 Tel 715-723-2814.

Harvey Assoc
See A Harvey

Harwal Pub Co, *(Harwal Publishing Co.; 0-932036),* 326 W. State St., Media, PA 19063.

Harwood Academic, *(Harwood Academic Pubs.; 3-7186),* P.O. Box 786, Cooper Sta., New York, NY 10276 Tel 212-242-4464.

Haskell, *(Haskell Booksellers, Inc.; 0-8383),* P.O. Box FF, Blythebourne Sta., Brooklyn, NY 11219 Tel 212-435-0500.

Hastings, *(Hastings House Pubs., Inc.; 0-8038),* 10 E. 40th St., New York, NY 10016 Tel 212-689-5400.

Hastings Ctr Inst Soc, *(Hastings Center, Institute of Society, Ethics & Life Sciences; 0-916558),* 360 Broadway, Hastings-on-Hudson, NY 10706 Tel 914-478-0500.

Hatfield, *(Hatfield, Glen; 0-9600216),* P.O. Box 329, Kankakee, IL 60901 Tel 815-939-1818.

Haven Bks, *(Haven Books),* 201 Church St., Plainfield, NJ 07060.

Haverford, *(Haverford House; 0-910702),* 34 West Ave., Wayne, PA 19087 Tel 215-688-5191.

Haverford Pr, *(Haverford Press, Inc.),* P.O. Box 93, Haverford, PA 19041.

Havertown Bks, *(Havertown Books),* P.O. Box 711, Havertown, PA 19083.

Hawaiian Serv, *(Hawaiian Service, Inc.; 0-930492),* P.O. Box 2835, Honolulu, HI 96803 Tel 808-841-0134.

Hawk-Island, *(Hawk-Island Associates; 0-937342),* 2630 N. 8th St., Sheboygan, WI 53081.

Hawkes Pub Inc, *(Hawkes Publishing Inc.; 0-89036),* 3775 S. 500 West, Box 15711, Salt Lake City, UT 84115 Tel 801-262-5555.

Hawkshead Bk, *(Hawkshead Book Distribution Co.),* P.O. Box 294, Old Westbury, NY 11568 Tel 516-333-6325.

Hawley, *(Hawley, W. M.; 0-910704),* 8200 Gould Ave., Hollywood, CA 90046 Tel 213-654-1573.

Hawley Cooke Orr, *(Hawley, Cooke, & Orr Pubs.; 0-937246),* P.O. Box 6052, Louisville, KY 40207 Tel 502-893-0133.

Haworth Pr, *(Haworth Press Inc., The; 0-917724),* 149 Fifth Ave., New York, NY 10010 Tel 212-228-2800.

Hawthorn *Imprint of* **Dutton**

Hayden, *(Hayden Book Co., Inc.; 0-8104),* 50 Essex St., Rochelle Park, NJ 07662 Tel 201-843-0550. *Imprints:* Rider (Rider, John F.); Spartan (Spartan Books, Inc.).

Hayden Hse, *(Hayden House Publishing Co.; 0-937602),* 68 Mitchell Blvd., San Rafael, CA 94903 Tel 415-472-5233.

Hayes, *(Hayes Publishing Co., Inc.; 0-910728),* 6304 Hamilton Ave., Cincinnati, OH 45224 Tel 513-681-7559.

Hayes Bk Co, *(Hayes Book Co.),* Hueysville, KY 41640.

Hayfield Pub, *(Hayfield Publishing Co.; 0-913856),* Box 11, Hayfield, MN 55940 Tel 507-477-2511.

Haymark, *(Haymark Pubns.; 0-933910),* P.O. Box 243, Fredericksburg, VA 22401 Tel 703-373-1144.

Haynes Pubns, *(Haynes Pubns., Inc.),* 861 Lawrence Dr., Newbury Park, CA 91320 Tel 805-498-6703.

Hays Rolfes, *(Hays, Rolfes & Assocs.; 0-9602448),* P.O. Box 11465, Memphis, TN 38111 Tel 901-682-8128.

Haywire Pr, *(Haywire Press),* 44 S. Mountain Rd., New City, NY 10956 Tel 914-634-5214.

Hazelden, *(Hazelden Foundation; 0-89486),* P.O. Box 176, Center City, MN 55012 Tel 800-328-9288.

HBC, *(H. B. C.; 0-9601276),* Box 626, Lansing, IL 60438 Tel 312-868-2027.

Hbgr *Imprint of* **HarBraceJ**

HC *Imprint of* **HarBraceJ**

Head Imports, *(Head Imports),* Aspen, CO 81611; Dist. by: Book People, 2940 Seventh St., Berkeley, CA 94710.

Headlands Pr, *(Headlands Press, Inc.; 0-915500),* 243 Vallejo St., San Francisco, CA 94111 Tel 415-788-3315.

Headwaters Pr, *(Headwaters Press; 0-932428),* P.O. Box 41544, Jacksonville, FL 32203 Tel 904-356-8073.

Headway Pubns, *(Headway Pubns.; 0-89537),* 1700 Port Manleigh Circle, Newport Beach, CA 92660 Tel 714-640-0736

Heahstan Pr, *(Heahstan Press, The; 0-9604244),* P.O. Box 954, Denton, TX 76201.

Healing Yourself, *(Healing Yourself),* Orders to: P.O. Box 752, Vashon, WA 98070.

Health Admin Pr, *(Health Administration Press; 0-914904),* 1021 E. Huron St., Univ. of Michigan, Ann Arbor, MI 48109 Tel 313-764-1380.

Health Aids, *(Health Aids Pubns.),* 612 N. Michigan Ave., Chicago, IL 60611 Tel 312-787-6505.

Health Comm, *(Health Communications, Inc.; 0-932194),* 2119-A Hollywood Blvd., Hollywood, FL 33020 Tel 305-920-9435.

Health Plus, *(Health Plus, Pubs.; 0-932090),* P.O. Box 22001, Phoenix, AZ 85028 Tel 602-992-0589.

Health Pubns, *(Health Pubns.),* 200 Park Ave., S., Suite 1101, New York, NY 10003 Tel 212-777-6400; Moved, Left No Forwarding Address.

Health Res, *(Health Research),* c/o R. G. Wilborn, 70 Lafayette St., Mokelumne Hill, CA 95245 Tel 209-286-1324.

Health Sci, *(Health Science; 0-87790),* P.O. Box 7, Santa Barbara, CA 93102 Tel 805-968-1028.

Health Sci Consort, *(Health Sciences Consortium, Inc.; 0-938938),* 200 Eastowne Dr., Suite 213, Chapel Hill, NC 27514 Tel 919-942-8731.

Healthworks, *(Healthworks, Inc.; 0-938480),* 31582 S. Coast Hwy., S. Laguna, CA 92677.

Hearne Bks, *(Hearne-Books U.S.A.; 0-918760),* 22 River St., Braintree, MA 02184 Tel 617-843-5702.

Hearst Bks, *(Hearst Books; 0-910992; 0-87851; 0-910990),* Div. of the Hearst Corp., 224 W. 57th St., Rm. 307, New York, NY 10019 Tel 212-262-8605; Orders to: P.O. Box 1406, Radio City Sta., New York, NY 10019.

Heart Am Bible, *(Heart of America Bible Society),* 5528 Lydia St., Kansas City, MO 64110 Tel 816-333-3278; Out of Business.

Heart Am Pr, *(Heart of America Press; 0-913902),* P.O. Box 9808, 10101 Blue Ridge Blvd., Kansas City, MO 64134 Tel 816-761-0080.

Heart of the Lakes, *(Heart of the Lakes Publishing; 0-932334),* Interlaken, NY 14847 Tel 607-532-4204.

Heartbeat, *(Heartbeat; 0-9601186),* 34 King St., New York, NY 10014 Tel 212-929-8263.

Hearthside, *(Hearthside Press, Inc.; 0-8208),* Orders to: Ingram Book Co., 347 Redwood Dr., Nashville, TN 37217.

Hearthstone, *(Hearthstone Press; 0-937308),* 708 Inglewood Dr., Broderick, CA 95605 Tel 916-372-0250.

Heartland Hse, *(Heartland House; 0-914482),* Div. of Pioneer Press Service, Orders to: The Ohio Historical Society, I-71 & 17th Ave., Columbus, OH 43211 Tel 614-469-4663.

Heartwork Pr, *(Heartwork Press; 0-935598),* 881 Lovell Ave., Mill Valley, CA 94941.

Heath, *(Heath, D.C., Co., College Dept.; 0-669),* Div. of Raytheon Co., 125 Spring St., Lexington, MA 02173 Tel 617-862-6650; Orders to: D. C. Heath & Co., Distribution Center, 2700 Richardt Ave., Indianapolis, IN 46219 Tel 317-359-5585. *Imprints:* Collamore (Collamore Press).

Heathcote, *(Heathcote Publishers; 0-9602350),* P.O. Box 135, Monmouth Jct., NJ 08852 Tel 201-297-4891.

Heather Foun, *(Heather Foundation; 0-9600300),* P.O. Box 48, San Pedro, CA 90733 Tel 213-831-6269.

Hebrew Pub, *(Hebrew Publishing Co.; 0-88482),* 80 Fifth Ave., New York, NY 10011 Tel 212-675-3878.

Heedays, *(Heeday's Uke-Aids; 0-917822),* 4890-A Lani Road, Kapaa Kauai, HI 96746; Moved, Left No Forwarding Address.

Heffron Ent, *(Heffron, Dan, Enterprises; 0-9605104),* P.O. Box 9019, Cleveland, OH 44137.

Heian Intl, *(Heian International Publishing, Inc.; 0-89346),* Div. of Heian International, Inc., P.O. Box 2042, South San Francisco, CA 94080 Tel 415-467-0222.

Heidelberg Graph, *(Heidelberg Graphics; 0-918606),* P.O. Box 3606, Chico, CA 95927.

Heidelberg Pubs, *(Heidelberg Pubs., Inc.; 0-913206),* 1003 Brown Bldg., Austin, TX 78701.

Heidenreich, *(Heidenreich House; 0-9600428),* 5012 Oak Point Way, Fair Oaks, CA 95628 Tel 916-961-3297.

Heineman, *(Heineman, James H., Inc., Pub.; 0-87008),* 475 Park Ave., New York, NY 10022 Tel 212-688-2028.

Heinemann Ed, *(Heinemann Educational Books Inc.; 0-435),* 4 Front St., Exeter, NH 03833 Tel 603-778-0534.

Heinle & Heinle, *(Heinle & Heinle Pubs.),* Div. of Science Books International, Inc., 51 Sleeper St., Boston, MA 02210 Tel 617-475-4582.

Heinman, *(Heinman, William S.; 0-88431),* 1966 Broadway, New York, NY 10023 Tel 212-787-3154.

Heirs Intl, *(Heirs International; 0-915970),* 2868 Mission St., San Francisco, CA 94110 Tel 415-824-8604.

Helander, *(Helander, Joel E.; 0-935600),* 404 Tanner's Marsh Rd., Guilford, CT 06437.

Heldref Pubns, *(Heldref Pubns.; 0-916882),* 4000 Albemarle St., N.W. Suite 500, Washington, DC 20016 Tel 202-362-6638.

Helicon Co, *(Helicon Co., The; 0-938578),* P.O. Box 11422, Lexington, KY 40575.

Helikon NY, *(Helikon Press; 0-914496),* 120 W. 71st St., New York, NY 10023 Tel 212-873-6884.

Helios, *(Helios Book Publishing Co., Inc.; 0-87037),* 150 W. 28th St., New York, NY 10001 Tel 212-255-6112.

Helios Vt, *(Helios; 0-87931),* Pawlet, VT 05761 Tel 802-325-3360.

Helix Hse, *(Helix House Pubs.; 0-930866),* 9231 Molly Woods Ave., La Mesa, CA 92041.

Hellcoal Pr, *(Hellcoal Press; 0-916912),* P.O. Box 4, S. A. O., Brown Univ., Providence, RI 02912 Tel 401-863-2341.

Hellenes, *(Hellenes-English Biblical Foundation; 0-910710),* P.O. Box 10412, Jackson, MS 39209.

Hellenic Coll Pr, *(Hellenic College Press; 0-916586),* Div. of Holy Cross Orthodox Press, 50 Goddard Ave., Brookline, MA 02146.

Heller, *(Heller & Son, Inc.; 0-88369),* 90 Daisy Farms Dr., New Rochelle, NY 10804 Tel 914-235-4772; Dist. by: Dell Distributing, 1 Dag Hammarskjold Plaza, New York, NY 10017.

Helm Pub, *(Helm Publishing),* Box 10512, Costa Mesa, CA 92627 Tel 714-645-3107.

HELP Bks, *(H.E.L.P Books, Inc.; 0-918500),* 1201 E. Calle Elena, Tucson, AZ 85718 Tel 602-297-6452.

HEMECO, *(Harrison Education Motivation Enterprises),* 21863 Brill Rd., Riverside, CA 92508 Tel 714-653-4779.

Hemenway, *(Hemenway Assocs., Inc.; 0-935026),* 101 Tremont St., Suite 208, Boston, MA 02108.

Hemisphere Hse, *(Hemisphere House Books; 0-930770),* 530 S. Tancahua St.-Numero 4, Corpus Christi, TX 78401.

Hemisphere NY, *(Hemisphere Pubns.; 0-917292),* 20 Elm St., Franklinville, NY 14737 Tel 716-676-2462.

Hemisphere Pub, *(Hemisphere Publishing Corp.; 0-89116),* 1025 Vermont Ave., N.W., Washington, DC 20005 Tel 202-783-3958; Orders to: 19 W. 44th St., New York, NY 10036 Tel 212-921-0606.

Hemlock Pr, *(Hemlock Press),* Rte. 1, Box 549, Alburtis, PA 18011 Tel 215-682-7332.

Hemmings, *(Hemmings Motor News; 0-917808),* Box 256, Bennington, VT 05201 Tel 802-442-3101.

Hemphill, *(Hemphill Publishing Co.; 0-914696),* 1400 Wathen Ave., Austin, TX 78703 Tel 512-476-9422.

Hendel, *(Hendel & Reinke; 0-918656),* 2800 Route St., Suite 247A, Dallas, TX 75201.

Hendershot, *(Hendershot Bibliography; 0-911832),* 4114 Ridgewood Dr., Bay City, MI 48706 Tel 517-684-3148.

Hendrick-Long, *(Hendrick-Long Publishing Co.; 0-937460),* 8609 Northwest Plaza Dr., P.O. Box 12311, Dallas, TX 75225.

Hendricks House, *(Hendricks House, Inc.; 0-87532),* 488 Greenwich St., New York, NY 10013 Tel 212-966-1765.

Hennessey, *(Hennessey & Ingalls, Inc.; 0-912158),* 10814 W. Pico Blvd., Los Angeles, CA 90064 Tel 213-474-2541.

Henry Art, *(Henry Art Gallery; 0-935558),* Univ. of Washington, Seattle, WA 98195.

Henry Clay, *(Clay, Henry, Press; 0-87642),* P.O. Box 116, Lexington, KY 40501 Tel 606-266-4133.

Heptangle, *(Heptangle Books; 0-935214),* P.O. Box 283, Berkeley Heights, NJ 07922 Tel 201-647-4449.

Her Pub Co, *(Her Publishing Co., Inc.; 0-930676),* P.O. Box 1168, Oakwood Shopping Ctr., Gretna, LA 70053.

Herald Bks, *(Herald Books; 0-910714),* P.O. Box 17, Pelham, NY 10803 Tel 914-576-1121.

Herald Hse, *(Herald House; 0-8309),* Drawer HH, 3225 S. Noland Rd., Independence, MO 64055 Tel 816-252-5010.

Herald Pr, *(Herald Press; 0-8361),* 616 Walnut Ave., Scottdale, PA 15683 Tel 412-887-8500.

Heraldic Pub, *(Heraldic Publishing Co., Inc.; 0-910716),* 305 West End Ave., New York, NY 10023 Tel 212-874-1511.

Herbal Med, *(Herbal Medicine Research Foundation; 0-930074),* P.O. Box 29187, San Antonio, TX 78229 Tel 512-699-0783.

Herbert Pubs, *(Herbert Pubs.; 0-935780),* P.O. Box 162, Mount Laurel, NJ 08054.

Herder & Herder, *(Herder & Herder),* ; Publisher Abbreviation Without Addresses Are for Titles That Are Out of Print. These Are Obsolete Abbreviations.

Hereford Hist Pr, *(Hereford History Press; 0-9600658),* P.O. Box 7051, Kansas City, MO 64113 Tel 816-449-7291.

Heres Life, *(Here's Life Pubs., Inc.; 0-89840),* Box 1576, 2700 Little Mountain Dr., Bldg. "B", San Bernardino, CA 92402 Tel 714-886-7981.

Heresy Pr, *(Heresy Press; 0-9603276),* 713 Paul St., Newport News, VA 23605.

Heritage Bk, *(Heritage Books, Inc.; 0-917890),* 3602 Maureen Lane, Bowie, MD 20715 Tel 301-464-1159.

Heritage Found, *(Heritage Foundation; 0-89195),* 513 "C" St., N.E., Washington, DC 20002 Tel 202-546-4400.

Heritage Hse IN
See Heritage IN

Heritage Hse Pubs, *(Heritage House Pubs.; 0-917172),* P.O. Box 4228, Tallahassee, FL 32303 Tel 904-386-7924.

Heritage IN, *(Heritage House; 0-933702),* P.O. Box 50, Notre Dame, IN 46556 Tel 219-256-5526.

Heritage Kansas, *(Heritage Books),* Rte. 6 Box 25, Salina, KS 67401 Tel 913-827-7861.

Heritage Pr, *(Heritage Press, Inc.; 0-930068),* P.O. Box 721, Forest Park, GA 30050 Tel 404-366-3860.

Heritage Printers
See McNally NC

Heritage Pubs, *(Heritage Pubs., Inc.; 0-913302),* 1437 Central Ave. 515, Memphis, TN 38104 Tel 901-278-5490.

Heritage Rec, *(Heritage Recording; 0-9602888),* Box 8132, St Paul, MN 55113 Tel 612-484-7481.

Heritage Store, *(Heritage Store, Inc.),* P.O. Box 444, Virginia Beach, VA 23458 Tel 804-428-0100.

Herman Pub, *(Herman Publishing; 0-89046; 0-89047),* 45 Newbury St., Boston, MA 02116 Tel 617-536-5810. *Imprints:* Marine Educ (Marine Educational Services).

Hermes, *(Hermes Pubns.; 0-910720),* P.O. Box 397, Los Altos, CA 94022; Moved, Left No Forwarding Address.

Hermes Hse, *(Hermes House Press; 0-9605008),* 6384 Hillegass Ave., Oakland, CA 94618.

Hermon, *(Sepher-Hermon Press, Inc.; 0-87203),* 53 Park Place, Suite 503, New York, NY 10007 Tel 212-349-1860.

Hermosa, *(Hermosa Pubs.; 0-913478),* P.O. Box 8172, Albuquerque, NM 87198 Tel 505-268-7987.

Herndon Hse, *(Herndon House; 0-915542),* P.O. Box 353, Brooklyn, NY 11230.

Heron Bks, *(Heron Books; 0-89739),* P.O. Box 563, Portland, OR 97207.

Heron Hse, *(Heron House Pubs.; 0-916920),* 9610 Manitou Beach Dr., N.E., Bainbridge Island, WA 98110 Tel 206-842-3768.

Heron Pr, *(Heron Press, The; 0-931246),* 36 Bromfield St., Boston, MA 02108 Tel 617-482-3615.

Herrick Hse, *(Herrick House; 0-935670),* P.O. Box 1051, Monrovia, CA 91016 Tel 213-358-0362; Moved, Left No Forwarding Address.

Hershey, *(Hershey, Virginia Sharpe; 0-9605320),* 5325 Wikiup Bridgeway, Santa Rosa, CA 95404.

Hertzberg-New Meth, *(Hertzberg-New Method, Inc.; 0-916056),* E. Vandalia Rd., Jacksonville, IL 62650 Tel 217-243-5451.

Herzl Pr, *(Herzl Press; 0-930832),* 515 Park Ave., New York, NY 10022 Tel 212-752-0600.

Heuristicus, *(Heuristicus Publishing Co.; 0-934016),* Drawer 248, 401 Tolbert St., Brea, CA 92621.

Heyday Bks, *(Heyday Books; 0-930588),* P.O. Box 9145, Berkeley, CA 94709 Tel 415-849-1438.

Heyden, *(Heyden & Son, Inc.),* 247 S. 41st St., Philadelphia, PA 19104 Tel 215-382-6673.

Heydent
See Heyden

HHH Horticultural, *(HHH Horticultural),* 68 Brooktree Rd., Hightstown, NJ 08520.

Hi Country Pubs, *(Hi-Country Pubs.; 0-938354),* P.O. Box 2362, Littleton, CO 80161.

Hi Willow, *(Hi Willow Research & Publishing; 0-931510),* Box 1801, Fayetteville, AR 72701 Tel 501-575-5444.

Hiawatha Pr, *(Hiawatha Press; 0-930276),* 3710 W. 22nd St., Minneapolis, MN 55416.

Hiawatha Pub Iowa
See Pyramid Iowa

Hidden Hse Imprint of Music Sales

Hidden Valley, *(Hidden Valley Press; 0-935710),* 7051 Poole Jones Rd., Frederick, MD 21701 Tel 301-662-6745.

Hiddigeigei, *(Hiddigeigei Books; 0-915560),* P.O. Box 5031, San Francisco, CA 94103 Tel 415-922-6114.

Higginson, *(Higginson Press Enterprises; 0-916602),* 4508 38th St., Brentwood, MD 20722 Tel 301-864-8527; Dist. by: SCOP Pubns., 5821 Swarthmore Dr., College Park, MD 20740 Tel 301-345-8747.

High Pubs, *(High Pubs; 0-9604216),* 65 MacAlester Rd., Pueblo, CO 81001 Tel 303-542-7028; Orders to: P.O. Box 11411, Pueblo, CO 81001.

High Q, *(High Q Pubns.; 0-931820),* P. O. Box 40H, Scarsdale, NY 10583.

High Rockies, (High Rockies Enterprises, Inc.; 0-937166), P.O. Box 4809, Dept. 2002, Boulder, CO 80306.

High-Scope, (High/Scope Educational Research Foundation; 0-931114), 600 N. River St., Ypsilanti, MI 48197.

High Window Pr, (High Window Press; 0-934886), P.O. Box 2238, Santa Barbara, CA 93120 Tel 805-969-6645.

Highland Imprint of Berkley Pub

Highland Ent, (Highland Enterprises; 0-913490), Box 7000, Dallas, TX 75209 Tel 214-358-3456.

Highland Hse, (Highland House Pubs., Inc.; 0-918712), 814 "H" St., N.W., Washington, DC 20001.

Highland Maya
   See Indigenous Pubns

Highland NY, (Highland House Publishing, Inc.; 0-938988), 74 Hunters Lane, Westbury, NY 11590.

Highland Pr, (Highland Press; 0-910722), Rte. 3, Box 3125, Boerne, TX 78006.

Highlander, (Highlander Research & Education Center; 0-9602226), Rte. 3 Box 370, New Market, TN 37820.

Highlights, (Highlights for Children, Inc.; 0-87534), 803 Church St., Honesdale, PA 18431 Tel 717-253-1080; 2300 W. 5th Ave., P.O. Box 269, Columbus, OH 43216 Tel 614-486-0631.

Highly Specialized, (Highly Specialized Promotions; 0-930194), 391 Atlantic Ave., Brooklyn, NY 11217 Tel 212-858-3026; Orders to: P.O. Box 989, Brooklyn, NY 11202.

Higley, (Higley Publishing Corp.), P.O. Box 2470, Jacksonville, FL 32203 Tel 904-783-2227.

Hilary Hse Pubs, (Hilary House Pubs., Inc.; 0-934464), 1033 Channel Dr., Hewlett, NY 11557.

Hill & Wang, (Hill & Wang, Inc., 0-8090), Div. of Farrar, Straus & Giroux, Inc., 19 Union Square, New York, NY 10003 Tel 212-741-6900. Imprints: AmCen (American Century Series); Drama (Dramabooks); Mermaid (Mermaid Dramabooks); New Mermaid (New Mermaid Dramabooks); Terra Magica (Terra Magica Books).

Hill Hse Pr, (Hill House Press, Pubs.; 0-915602), Old Lane & Chester Rd., Chester, VA 23831 Tel 804-262-0228.

Hill Jr Coll, (Hill Junior College Press; 0-912172), P.O. Box 619, Hillsboro, TX 76645 Tel 817-582-2555.

Hill Pubns, (Hill Pubns; 0-9602704), 4974 Cedar Ridge N.E., Grand Rapids, MI 49505.

Hillary, (Hillary House Pubs., Ltd.), Div. of Humanities Press, Inc., Atlantic Highlands, NJ 07716.

Hillcrest Ent, (Hillcrest Enterprises; 0-912994), Country Club Drive, Long Beach, CA 90807; P.O. Box 14437, Long Beach, CA; Moved,Left No Forwarding Address.

Hillhouse, (Hillhouse Press; 0-910724), P.O. Box 1386, Highland Park, NJ 08904.

Hillman Pr, (Hillman Press; 0-9601176), 4427 55th Ave. N.E., Seattle, WA 98105 Tel 206-525-9639; Dist. by: ICEL, University of San Francisco, San Francisco, CA 94117.

Hillsdale Educ, (Hillsdale Educational Pubs., Inc.; 0-910726), 39 North St., Box 245, Hillsdale, MI 49242 Tel 517-437-3179.

Hillside, (Hillside Press; 0-918462), P.O. Box 785, Vista, CA 92083 Tel 214-724-1853.

Hilltop Pr, (Hilltop Press; 0-9603346), 333 W. Emerson St., Melrose, MA 02176 Tel 617-665-7569.

Hilltop Pubns, (Hilltop Pubns., Inc.; 0-937782), 111 E. 61st St., New York, NY 10021.

Hilmarton Manor, (Hilmarton Manor Press), No. 1 Emerald St., Norwalk, CT 06850.

Hilton Hse, (Hilton House; 0-914392), P.O. Box 315, Cleveland, OH 44105.

Hiltz & Hayes
   See Hayes

Himalaya Hse, (Himalaya House; 0-89654), P.O. Box 792, Wheat Ridge, CO 80033 Tel 303-423-3170.

Himalayan Inst
   See Himalayan Intl Inst

Himalayan Intl Inst, (Himalayan International Institute; 0-89389), RD 1, Box 88, Honesdale, PA 18431 Tel 717-253-5551.

Hippocrates, (Hippocrates Books), 25 Exeter St., Boston, MA 02116.

Hippocrene Bks, (Hippocrene Books, Inc.; 0-88254), 171 Madison Ave., New York, NY 10016 Tel 212-685-4372.

Hired Hand, (Hired Hand Press; 0-9602256), P.O. Box 426, Dover, MA 02030 Tel 617-325-8155.

HIS Imprint of HR&W

Hispanic Seminary, (Hispanic Seminary of Medieval Studies), 3734 Ross St., Madison, WI 53705.

Hispanic Soc, (Hispanic Society of America; 0-87535), 613 W. 155th St., New York, NY 10032 Tel 212-926-2234.

Hist Aviation, (Historical Aviation Album; 0-911852), P.O. Box 33, Temple City, CA 91780 Tel 213-286-7655.

Hist Rev Pr, (Historical Review Press), P.O. Box 33674, Decatur, GA 30030.

Hist Soc Lansing & Livingston Cnty Hist Soc, (Historical Society of Greater Lansing & Livingston County Historical Society; 0-9602844), Box 12095, Lansing, MI 48901 Tel 517-321-1746.

Hist Soc West Pa, (Historical Society of Western Pennsylvania; 0-936340), 4338 Bigelow Blvd., Pittsburgh, PA 15213.

Hist Tales, (Historical Tales Ink; 0-938404), 7344 Rich St., Reynoldsburg, OH 43068.

Historic New Orleans, (Historic New Orleans Collection, The; 0-917860), 533 Royal St., New Orleans, LA 70130.

Historic Pensacola, (Historic Pensacola Preservation Board), Dist. by: John C. Pace Library, Univ. of West Florida, Pensacola, FL 32504 Tel 904-476-9500.

Historic Photos, (Historic Photos; 0-933206), 3460 St. Helena Hwy. N., St. Helena, CA 94574 Tel 707-963-2855.

Historic Pres Bourbon, (Historic Preservation Assn. of Bourbon County; 0-9601568), 510 S. Eddy St., Fort Scott, KS 66701 Tel 316-223-2113.

Hit Ent, (Hit Enterprises, 0-935938), 1043 Leticia Dr., Hacienda Heights, CA 91745.

Hive Pub, (Hive Publishing Co.; 0-87960), P.O. Box 1004, Easton, PA 18042 Tel 215-258-6663.

HM, (Houghton Mifflin Co.; 0-395), 2 Park St., Boston, MA 02107 Tel 617-725-5000; Orders to: Wayside Road, Burlington, MA 01803 Tel 617-272-1500. Imprints: Clarion (Clarion Books); HoughtonT (Houghton Trade Books); Piper (Piper Books); RivEd (Riverside Editions); RivLit (Riverside Literature Series); RivSL (Riverside Studies in Literature); RRS (Riverside Reading Series); SenEd (Sentry Editions).

HM Prof Med Div, (Houghton Mifflin Professional Pubs., Medical Div.; 0-89289), 2 Park St., Boston, MA 02107 Tel 617-725-5019.

HM Prof Pubs
   See HM Prof Med Div

HM Prof Pubs, (Houghton Mifflin Professional Pubs.; 0-89289), Subs. of Houghton Mifflin Co., 2 Park St., Boston, MA 02107 Tel 617-725-5019.

HMB Pubns, (HMB Pubns.; 0-937086), 7406 Monroe Ave., Hammond, IN 46324 Tel 219-932-1798.

HMS Pubns, (HMS Pubns.; 0-9604812), P.O. Box 5809, Santa Barbara, CA 93108 Tel 805-969-3421.

Hobart & Wm Smith, (Hobart & William Smith Colleges Press; 0-934888), Hobart & William Smith Colleges, Geneva, NY 14456.

Hobbit Hse, (Hobbit House Press; 0-9604300), 5920 Dimmway, Richmond, CA 94805.

Hobby Horse, (Hobby Horse Publishing; 0-935138), 10091 Hobby Horse Lane, Box 54, Mentor, OH 44060 Tel 216-255-3434.

Hobby Hse, (Hobby House Press; 0-87588), 900 Frederick St., Cumberland, MD 21502 Tel 301-759-3770.

Hobby Pub Serv, (Hobby Publishing Service; 0-917922), 1318 Seventh St., N.W., Albuquerque, NM 87102 Tel 505-242-9465.

Hoffman Pubns, (Hoffman Pubns., Inc.; 0-934890), P.O. Box 11299, Fort Lauderdale, FL 33339 Tel 305-566-8401.

Hofmann, (Hofmann, Margret; 0-9600166), 2706 Nottingham Lane, Austin, TX 78704 Tel 512-444-8877.

Hogarth, (Hogarth Press; 0-911776), P.O. Box 10606, Honolulu, HI 96816 Tel 808-737-4150.

Hogg Found, (Hogg Foundation for Mental Health), Univ. of Texas, Box 7998, Austin, TX 78712 Tel 512-471-5041.

Hol-Land Bks, (Hol-Land Books; 0-932092), c/o Holland Books & Posters, Bonita Springs, FL 33923.

Holbrook, (Holbrook Press, Inc.; 0-205), Subs. of Allyn & Bacon, Inc., 470 Atlantic Ave., Boston, MA 02210 Tel 617-482-9220; Orders to: Rockleigh, NJ 07647.

Holbrook Res, (Holbrook Research Institute; 0-931248), 57 Locust St., Oxford, MA 01540 Tel 617-987-0881.

Holden-Day, (Holden-Day, Inc.; 0-8162), 500 Sansome St., San Francisco, CA 94111 Tel 415-433-0220.

Holiday, (Holiday House, Inc.; 0-8234), 18 E. 53rd St., New York, NY 10022 Tel 212-688-0085.

Holland Hse Pr, (Holland House Press; 0-913042), 6215 Six Mile Rd., Northville, MI 48167 Tel 313-836-0286.

Hollenbeck, (Hollenbeck, Leon), 6895 Maple Rd., Akron, NY 14001.

Hollow Spring Pr, (Hollow Spring Press), R.D. 1, Chester, MA 01011.

Holloway, (Holloway House Publishing Co.; 0-87067), 8060 Melrose Ave., Los Angeles, CA 90046 Tel 213-653-8060. Imprints: Melrose Sq (Melrose Square).

Holly-Pix, (Holly-Pix Music Publishing Co.; 0-910736), 13115 Morrison St., Sherman Oaks, CA 91423 Tel 213-788-3668; Orders to: WIM, 2859 Holt Ave., Los Angeles, CA 90034.

Holly Pr, (Holly Press, The; 0-935968), P.O. Box 306, Hockessin, DE 19707 Tel 302-239-2416.

Hollym Intl, (Hollym International Corp.; 0-930878), 18 Donald Place, Elizabeth, NJ 07208 Tel 201-353-1655.

Hollvwd Film Arch, (Hollywood Film Archive; 0-917616), 8344 Melrose Ave., Hollywood, CA 90069 Tel 213-933-3345.

Hollywood, (Hollywood Book Service; 0-910738), 1654 N. Cherokee Ave., Hollywood, CA 90028 Tel 213-464-4164.

Holman, (Holman, A.J., Co.; 0-87981), 127 Ninth Ave., N., Nashville, TN 37234 Tel 615-251-2611.

Holmes, (Holmes Book Co.; 0-910740), 274 14th St., Oakland, CA 94612 Tel 415-893-6860.

Holmes & Meier, (Holmes & Meier Pubs., Inc.; 0-8419), IUB Bldg., 30 Irving Place, New York, NY 10003 Tel 212-254-4100. Imprints: Africana (Africana Pub.).

Holmgangers, (Holmgangers Press; 0-914974), 22 Ardith Lane, Alamo, CA 94507 Tel 415-837-3831.

Holocaust Lib, (Holocaust Library; 0-89604), 216 W. 18th St., New York, NY 10011; Dist. by: Schocken Books, 200 Madison Ave., New York, NY 10016.

Holt, (Holt, Rinehart & Winston Inc.), ; Publisher Abbreviation Without Addresses Are for Titles That Are Out of Print. These Are Obsolete Abbreviations. Publisher's New Abbreviation Is HR&W.

Holt-Atherton, (Holt-Atherton Pacific Center for Western Studies; 0-931156), Univ. of the Pacific, Stockton, CA 95211.

HoltC Imprint of HR&W

Holy Cow, (Holy Cow! Press; 0-930100), P.O. Box 618, Minneapolis, MN 55440.

Holy Cross Orthodox, (Holy Cross Orthodox Press; 0-916586), 50 Goddard Ave., Brookline, MA 02146 Tel 617-232-4544.

Holy Order Mans
   See Epiphany Pr

Holy Trinity, (Holy Trinity Monastery; 0-88465), Jordanville, NY 13361 Tel 315-858-0940.

Home & Sch, (Home & School Press; 0-910742), P.O. Box 2055, Sun City, AZ 85372 Tel 602-974-3063.

Home-Busn Pr, (Home-Business Press; 0-939626), 10855 S. Western Ave., Chicago, IL 60643.

Home Econ Educ, (Home Economics Education Assn.), 1201 Sixteenth St., N.W., Rm. 232, Washington, DC 20036 Tel 202-833-4138.

Home Equity, (Home Equity Co.), 802 Cascade Bldg., Portland, OR 97204 Tel 503-224-4522.

Home Frosted, *(Home of Frosted Sunshine, The; 0-937118),* R.R. 1, Box 612, Shermans Dale, PA 17090.

Home Mission, *(Home Mission Board of the Southern Baptist Convention; 0-937170),* 1350 Spring St., N.W., Atlanta, GA 30309 Tel 404-873-4041.

Home Office
See L Henry

Home on Arrange, *(Home on Arrange),* 2044 Paradise Dr., Tiburon, CA 94920.

Home Planet, *(Home Planet Pubns.; 0-913802),* 1771 1st Ave., New York, NY 10028 Tel 212-534-2372; Orders to: P.O. Box 415, Stuyvesant Sta., New York, NY 10009.

Home Planners, *(Home Planners, Inc.; 0-918894),* 23761 Research Dr., Farmington Hills, MI 48024 Tel 313-477-1850.

Homestead Bk, *(Homestead Book Co.; 0-930180),* 4009 Stone Way N., Seattle, WA 98103 Tel 206-634-2212.

Homestead NY, *(Homestead Books),* Brookfield, NY 13314.

Homeward Pr, *(Homeward Press; 0-938392),* P.O. Box 2307, Berkeley, CA 94702.

Homosexual Info, *(Homosexual Information Center, Inc.),* 6758 Hollywood Blvd., No. 208, Los Angeles, CA 90028 Tel 213-464-8431.

Honduras Info, *(Honduras Information Service; 0-937538),* 501 Fifth Ave., Suite 1611, New York, NY 10017 Tel 212-490-0766.

Honey Hill, *(Honey Hill Publishing Co.; 0-937642),* 1022 Bonham Terrace, Austin, TX 78704 Tel 512-442-4177.

Honor Bks, *(Honor Books; 0-931446),* P.O. Box 94, Spearfish, SD 57783 Tel 605-642-3516.

Hoover Brook, *(Hoover Brook Publishing; 0-9605956),* R.D. 6, Box 123, Wellsboro, PA 16901; Dist. by: Wellsboro Historical Society, P.O. Box 724, Wellsboro, PA 16901.

Hoover Inst Pr, *(Hoover Institution Press; 0-8179),* Stanford University, Stanford, CA 94305 Tel 415-497-3373.

Hope Ent Fla, *(Hope Enterprises of Jacksonville, Florida, Inc.; 0-932650),* Box 8401, Jacksonville, FL 32211.

Hope Farm, *(Hope Farm Press & Bookshop; 0-910746),* Strong Rd., Cornwallville, NY 12418 Tel 518-239-4745.

Hope Pub, *(Hope Publishing Co.; 0-916642),* 380 S. Main Place, Carol Stream, IL 60187 Tel 312-665-3200.

Hope Pubns, *(Hope Pubns.),* P.O. Box 10062, Jefferson, LA 70181 Tel 504-733-2405; Dist. by: Pelican Publishing Co., 630 Burmaster St., Gretna, LA 70053.

Hopewood Pr, *(Hopewood Press; 0-936286),* P.O. Box 27541, Minneapolis, MN 55427.

Hopkins, *(Hopkins Syndicate, Inc.; 0-910748),* Hopkins Bldg., Mellott, IN 47958 Tel 317-295-2253.

Hopkinson, *(Hopkinson & Blake, Pubs.; 0-911974),* 50 W. 34th St., New York, NY 10001 Tel 212-947-8282; Not Publishing at This Time.

Horizon, *(Horizon Press Pubs.; 0-8180),* 156 Fifth Ave., New York, NY 10010 Tel 212-924-9225.

Horizon Bks CA, *(Horizon Books; 0-938840),* P.O. Box 3083, Fremont, CA 94538.

Horizon Pub, *(Horizon Publishing; 0-914734),* P.O. Box 625, Far Rockaway, NY 11691 Tel 212-228-5982; Moved, Left No Forwarding Address.

Horizon Utah, *(Horizon Pubs. & Distributors, Inc.; 0-88290),* P.O. Box 490, 50 S. 500 West, Bountiful, UT 84010 Tel 801-295-9451.

Horizons, *(Horizons; 0-932960),* P.O. Box 35008, Phoenix, AZ 85069.

Horn Bk, *(Horn Book, Inc.; 0-87675),* Park Square Bldg., 31 St. James Ave., Boston, MA 02116 Tel 617-482-5198.

Hornbeam Pr, *(Hornbeam Press, Inc.; 0-917496),* 6520 Courtwood Dr., Columbia, SC 29206 Tel 803-782-7667.

Horowitz, *(Horowitz, Stanley),* P.O. Box 1077, Flushing, NY 11352; Moved, Left No Forwarding Address.

Horse & Bird, *(Horse & Bird Press, The; 0-9602214),* P.O. Box 67C89, Los Angeles, CA 90067.

Horsebreeder
See Printed Horse

Horticult Pubns, *(Horticultural Pubns.; 0-938378),* Box 231, Nichol Ave., Cook College, New Brunswick, NJ 08903.

Horticult Research, *(Horticultural Research Institute, Inc.; 0-935336),* 230 Southern Bldg., Washington, DC 20005 Tel 202-737-4060.

Horticultural, *(Horticultural Books, Inc.; 0-9600046),* P.O. Box 107, Stuart, FL 33495 Tel 305-287-1091.

Hosp Compensation, *(Hospital Compensation Service),* 115 Watching Dr., P.O. Box 321, Hawthorne, NJ 07507.

Hosp Practice
See HP Pub Co

Hosp Res & Educ, *(Hospital Research & Educational Trust; 0-87914),* 840 N. Lake Shore Dr., Chicago, IL 60611 Tel 312-280-6381.

Hospital Finan, *(Hospital Financial Management Assn.; 0-930228),* 1900 Spring Rd., Suite 500, Oak Brook, IL 60521 Tel 312-655-4600.

Host Assoc, *(Host, Jim, & Associates, Inc.; 0-934554),* 120 Kentucky Ave., Suite A-1, Lexington, KY 40502.

Hot off Pr, *(Hot off the Press; 0-9605904),* 7212 S. Seven Oaks, Canby, OR 97013.

Hotchkiss House, *(Hotchkiss House, Inc.; 0-912220),* 18 Hearthstone Rd., Pittsford, NY 14534.

Hotline Multi-Ent, *(Hotline Multi-Enterprises; 0-935864),* 2709 Georgetown Rd., Mechanicsville, VA 23111.

HoughtonT *Imprint of HM*

Housatonuc, *(Housatonuc Bookshop; 0-910756),* Main St., Salisbury, CT 06068 Tel 203-435-2100.

House of Print, *(House of Print),* 322 Benzel Ave., Madelia, MN 56062 Tel 507-642-3298.

Housesmith, *(Housesmith's Press; 0-918238),* P.O. Box 157, Kittery Point, ME 03905 Tel 207-439-0638.

Hove Camera, *(Hove Camera Foto Books; 0-85242),* Dist. by: Morgan & Morgan, 145 Palisades St., Dobbs Ferry, NY 10522 Tel 914-693-9303.

Hover, *(Hover Co., The; 0-934414),* 14713 La Mesa Dr., La Mirada, CA 90638 Tel 714-521-3046.

How-to Pr, *(How-to Press; 0-938356),* P.O. Box 483, Arlington, TX 76010.

Howard Allen, *(Howard, Allen, Enterprises, Inc.; 0-914576),* P.O. Box 76, Cape Canaveral, FL 32920.

Howard Doyle, *(Doyle, Howard A., Publishing Co.; 0-87299),* P.O. Box 555, East Dennis, MA 02641 Tel 617-385-2000.

Howard U Pr, *(Howard Univ. Press; 0-88258),* 2900 Van Ness St., N.W., Washington, DC 20008 Tel 202-686-6696.

Howell Bk, *(Howell Book House Inc.; 0-87605),* Helmsley Bldg., 230 Park Ave., New York, NY 10169 Tel 212-986-4488.

Howell North, *(Howell-North Pubs., Inc.; 0-8310),* Subs. of Leisure Dynamics, Inc., 11175 Flintkote Ave., Suite C, San Diego, CA 92121 Tel 714-457-3200.

Howell-North
See Howell North

HP Pub Co, *(HP Publishing Co., Inc.; 0-913800),* 575 Lexington Ave., New York, NY 10022 Tel 212-421-7320.

HPL *Imprint of HarBraceJ*

HRAFP, *(Human Relations Area File Press; 0-87536),* 4695 Main St., Snyder, NY 14226; Orders to: P.O. Box 2015 Y.S., New Haven, CT 06520 Tel 203-777-2334.

HR&W, *(Holt, Rinehart & Winston, Inc.; 0-03),* 383 Madison Ave., New York, NY 10017 Tel 212-688-9100. *Imprints:* HIS (Holt Information Systems); HoltC (Holt College Department).

HS *Imprint of Oxford U Pr*

Hse by the Sea, *(House by the Sea Publishing Co.),* 8610 Highway 101, Waldport, OR 97394.

Hse of Affirmation
See Affirmation

Hse of Charles, *(House of Charles; 0-9605344),* 4833 NE 238th Ave., Vancouver, WA 98662.

Hse of Collectibles, *(House of Collectibles, Inc.; 0-87637),* 773 Kirkman Rd., Suite 120, Orlando, FL 32811 Tel 305-299-9343.

Hse of Gemini, *(House of Gemini),* P.O. Box 7803, Philadelphia, PA 19101 Tel 215-222-7555; Moved, Left No Forwarding Address.

Hse of One Pub, *(House of One Publishing Co.),* Box 3407, Portland, OR 97208.

Hse of Talos, *(House of Talos Pubs., The; 0-935970),* 125 Loree Dr., East Lansing, M 48823 Tel 517-337-0723.

Hse of Words, *(House of Words; 0-917876),* 20 E. Buffalo St., No. 518, Milwaukee, WI 53202 Tel 414-453-1945.

Hse of York, *(House of York; 0-916660),* 1992 Borchers Dr., San Jose, CA 95124 Tel 408-377-8472.

Hse ov Day Vid, *(House ov Day Vid; 0-912672),* 978 Amherst St., Apt. 6, Buffalo, NY 14216 Tel 716-873-8856.

HSJ Pubs, *(HSJ Pubs.; 0-916662),* 2570 Ramona St., Palo Alto, CA 94306.

HTH Pubs, *(HTH Pubs.; 0-916658),* P.O. Box 468, Freeland, WA 98249.

Hubbard Sci, *(Hubbard Scientific; 0-8331),* P.O. Box 104, 1946 Raymond Dr., Northbrook, IL 60062 Tel 312-272-7810.

HUC Pr *Imprint of Ktav*

Hudson Cohan, *(Hudson-Cohan Publishing & Communications Co.; 0-87852),* 20 Carmel Ave., Salinas, CA 93901 Tel 408-424-0596.

Hudson Hills, *(Hudson Hills Press, Inc.; 0-933920),* 30 Rockefeller Plaza, Suite 4323, New York, NY 10112 Tel 212-247-3400.

Hudson Rev, *(Hudson Review, The),* 65 E 55th St., New York, NY 10022 Tel 212-755-9040.

Hudson River, *(Hudson River Press; 0-930930),* 152 Second Ave., New York, NY 10003.

Huebner Foun Insur, *(Huebner, S. S., Foundation for Insurance Education),* 3641 Locust Walk CE, Philadelphia, PA 19104 Tel 215-243-5644; Dist. by: Richard D. Irwin, Inc., 1818 Ridge Rd., Homewood, IL 60430.

Huenefeld Co, *(Huenefeld Co., Inc.; 0-931932),* 119 The Great Rd., Bedford, MA 01730.

Huffman Pr, *(Huffman Press),* 311 Madison St., Alexandria, VA 22314 Tel 703-836-7160.

Hughes Pr, *(Hughes Press; 0-912560),* 500 23rd St., N.W., Box B203, Washington, DC 20037 Tel 202-293-2686.

Huguley Co, *(Huguley, John, Co., Inc.; 0-9605064),* 269 King St., Charleston, SC 29401.

Hui-Hanai-Queen, *(Hui-Hanai, Queen Lilioukalani Childrens Center),* Dist. by: Press Pacifica, Ltd., P.O. Box 1227, Kailua, HI 96734.

Hulme, *(Hulme Publishing; 0-935904),* 1020 Currie St., Fort Worth, TX 76107.

Human Dev East, *(Human Development East, Inc.; 0-932292),* c/o The East Asia Research Institute, 850 National Press Bldg., 14th & "F" Sts., N.W., Washington, DC 20045.

Human Dev Pr, *(Human Development Press; 0-938024),* 10701 Lomas NE, 210, Albuquerque, NM 87112.

Human Dev Train, *(Human Development Training Institute; 0-86584),* 1727 Fifth Ave., San Diego, CA 92101 Tel 714-233-7023.

Human Eng Lab, *(Human Engineering Laboratory; 0-915212),* 381 Beacon St., Boston, MA 02116 Tel 617-536-0409.

Human Kinetics, *(Human Kinetics Pubs.; 0-931250),* P.O. Box 5076, Champaign, IL 61820 Tel 217-351-5076.

Human Policy Pr, *(Human Policy Press; 0-937540),* P.O. Box 127, Syracuse, NY 13210.

Human Potential, *(Human Potential Pubns.; 0-939268),* 17330 Warrington Dr., Detroit, MI 48221 Tel 313-341-0492.

Human Res Dev Pr, *(Human Resource Development Press; 0-914234),* 22 Amherst Rd., Amherst, MA 01002 Tel 413-253-3488.

Human Resources, *(Human Resources Research Organization),* 300 N. Washington St., Alexandria, VA 22314 Tel 703-549-3611.

Human Sci Pr, *(Human Sciences Press, Inc.; 0-87705; 0-89885),* 72 Fifth Ave., New York, NY 10011 Tel 212-243-6000; Dist. by: Independent Publishers Group, 14 Vanderventer Ave., Port Washington, NY 11050; Formerly Named Behavioral Pubns. Inc.

Humana, *(Humana Press, The; 0-89603),* Crescent Manor, P.O. Box 2148, Clifton, NJ 07015 Tel 201-773-4389.

Humanics Assoc, *(Humanics Associates),* ; Publisher Abbreviations Without Addresses Are for Titles That Are Out of Print. These Are Obsolete Abbreviations.

Humanics Ltd, *(Humanics Ltd.; 0-89334),* P.O. Box 7447, Atlanta, GA 30309.

Humanitas Pr
   See Wexford

Humanities, *(Humanities Press, Inc.; 0-391),* Atlantic Highlands, NJ 07716 Tel 201-872-1441. *Imprints:* Athlone Pr (Athlone Press); Dolmen Pr (Dolmen Press); Hutchinson U Lib (Hutchinson Univ Library); Leicester (Leicester Univ. Press); NFER (National Foundation for Educational Research).

Humanity Pubns, *(Humanity Pubns.),* 27 S. Maple St., Shelburne Falls, MA 01370 Tel 413-625-6823; Moved, Left No Forwarding Address.

Humbird Hopkins, *(Humbird Hopkins Inc., Pubs.; 0-931854),* 625 Broadway, Seventh Floor, San Diego, CA 92101 Tel 714-234-4141.

Humble Hills, *(Humble Hills Books; 0-935858),* P.O. Box 7, Kalamazoo, MI 49004 Tel 616-343-2211.

Humbug Gulch Pr, *(Humbug Gulch Press; 0-912996),* P.O. Box 204, Amarillo, TX 79105 Tel 806-352-4935.

HumLife, *(HumLife; 0-9604332),* 7846 Arvilla Ave., Sun Valley, CA 91352.

Hummingbird, *(Hummingbird Press; 0-912998),* 2400 Hannett, N.E., Albuquerque, NM 87106 Tel 505-268-6277.

Humphrey
   See Graph Arts Trade

Humpy Pr, *(Humpy Press; 0-913536),* Dist. by: Light Impressions, P.O. Box 3012, Rochester, NY 14614.

Huna Res Assocs, *(Huna Research Associates; 0-910764),* 126 Camellia Dr., Cape Girardeau, MO 63701 Tel 314-334-3478.

Hungarian Cultural, *(Hungarian Cultural Foundation; 0-911648),* P.O. Box 364 Stone Mountain, GA 30086 Tel 404-377-2600.

Hungarian Rev, *(American Hungarian Review; 0-911862),* 5410 Kerth Rd., St. Louis, MO 63128 Tel 314-487-7566.

Hunt Inst Botanical, *(Hunt Institute for Botanical Documentation; 0-913196),* Carnegie-Mellon Univ., Pittsburgh, PA 15213 Tel 412-578-2434.

Hunter Ariz, *(Hunter Publishing Co.; 0-918126),* P.O. Box 9533, Phoenix, AZ 85068 Tel 602-944-1022.

Hunter Bks, *(Hunter Books; 0-917726),* 201 McClellar Rd., Kingwood, TX 77339 Tel 713-358-7575.

Hunter Hse, *(Hunter House, Inc.; 0-89793),* 824 W. Harrison, Suite 204, Claremont, CA 91711 Tel 714-624-2277.

Hunter Ministries
   See Hunter Bks

Hunter NC, *(Hunter Publishing Co.; 0-89459),* P.O. Box 5867, Winston-Salem, NC 27103 Tel 919-765-0070.

Hunter Pub, *(Hunter Publishing Co.),* 1002 N. 30th St., Billings, MT 59101 Tel 406-252-8511.

Hunterdon Hse, *(Hunterdon House; 0-912606),* 38 Swan St., Lambertville, NJ 08530 Tel 609-397-2523.

Huntington Lib, *(Huntington Library Pubns.; 0-87328),* 1151 Oxford Rd., San Marino, CA 91108 Tel 213-792-6141.

Huntleigh, *(Huntleigh House; 0-918354),* P.O. Drawer 20602, Oklahoma City, OK 73156 Tel 405-751-8444.

Hunziker, *(Hunziker, Barbara; 0-9601340),* 2400 Wood Rd., Niles, MI 49120 Tel 616-683-6108.

Hurd, *(Hurd, Frank J., Dr. & Mrs.),* P.O. Box 86A, Rte. 1, Chisholm, MN 55719.

Hurricane Co, *(Hurricane Co., The; 0-933272),* P.O. Box 426, Jacksonville, NC 28540.

Hurst Pub, *(Hurst Publishing Co., Inc.; 0-88241),* 468 Park Ave. S., New York, NY 10016 Tel 212-686-7130.

Husher & Welch, *(Husher & Welch; 0-9603944),* 50 Nahant Rd., Nahant, MA 01908.

Huston, *(Huston, Harvey; 0-9600048),* 860 Mount Pleasant St., Winnetka, IL 60093 Tel 312-446-1594.

Hutar, *(Hutar Growth Management Institute; 0-918896),* 875 N. Michigan Ave., Suite 3452, Chicago, IL 60611 Tel 312-664-1188.

Hutchinson

   See Merrimack Bk Serv

Hutchinson U Lib *Imprint of* **Humanities**

Hutson Assoc, *(Hutson, Martha, Associates; 0-9606126),* P.O. Box 185, Orefield, PA 18069 Tel 215-820-5324.

HW *Imprint of* **Har-Row**

Hwong Pub, *(Hwong Publishing Co.; 0-89260),* 10353 Los Alamitos Blvd., Los Alamitos, CA 90720 Tel 213-598-2428.

Hy-Speed, *(Hy-Speed Longhand Publishing Co.; 0-910766),* 80 Nancy Lane, Trenton, NJ 08638 Tel 609-882-5958.

HyperDynamics, *(HyperDynamics),* P.O. Box 392, Santa Fe, NM 87501 Tel 505-988-2416.

Hyperion Conn, *(Hyperion Press, Inc.; 0-88355; 0-8305),* 45 Riverside Ave., Westport, CT 06880 Tel 203-226-1091.

Hyperion LA, *(Hyperion Press),* 2304 Hyperion Ave, Los Angeles, CA 90027.

Hypnos Pr, *(Hypnos Press; 0-939628),* 3000 Connecticut Ave. NW, Suite 308, Washington, DC 20008 Tel 202-462-0221.

I & O Pub, *(I & O Publishing Co.; 0-911752),* P.O. Box 906, Boulder City, NV 89005.

I Dare You, *(I Dare You Committee; 0-9602416),* P.O. Box 1606, St. Louis, MO 63188 Tel 314-351-4456.

I J Hoffman, *(Hoffman, Irwin J., Inc.; 0-9604082),* 5734 S. Ivanhoe St., Denver, CO 80111.

I J Nelson, *(Nelson, Irene J.; 0-9601464),* P.O. Box 28, Tuskegee Institute, AL 36088.

I M Tillotson, *(Tillotson, Ira M.),* P.O. Box 3019, Missoula, MT 59801.

I Newman, *(Newman, Isadore; 0-917180),* Univ. of Akron, Dept. of Educational Foundations, Akron, OH 44325 Tel 216-867-7519.

I Osteen, *(Osteen, Ike; 0-9602724),* 380 Kansas St., Springfield, CO 81073 Tel 303-523-6580.

I Pr, *(I Press; 0-913222),* Dist. by: M.I.T. Press, 28 Carleton St., Cambridge, MA 02142.

I S Gardner Mus, *(Isabella Stewart Gardner Museum; 0-914880),* 2 Palace Rd., Boston, MA 02115 Tel 617-566-1401.

I-Seventy-Four, *(I-74 Press; 0-940096),* 618 W. High St., No. 101, Peoria, IL 61606 Tel 309-676-4817.

I Young, *(Young, Ione),* 4107 Wildwood Rd., Austin, TX 78722.

IA City Women, *(Iowa City Women's Press, Inc.; 0-918040),* 529 S. Gilbert St., Iowa City, IA 52240 Tel 319-338-7022.

IAEA *Imprint of* **Unipub**

IAFWA, *(International Assn. of Fish & Wildlife Agencies (IAFWA); 0-932108),* 1412 16th St., N.W., Washington, DC 20036 Tel 202-232-1652.

IAUS, *(Institute for Architecture & Urban Studies, The; 0-932628),* 8 W. 40th St., New York, NY 10018 Tel 212-398-9474.

IB *Imprint of* **Van Nos Reinhold**

IBM Armonk, *(IBM Corp.; 0-933186),* Armonk, NY 10504.

IBMA Pubns, *(Independent Battery Manufacturers Assn.; 0-912254),* 100 Larchwood Dr., Largo, FL 33540 Tel 813-586-1409.

IBMS Corp, *(IBMS Corp.; 0-933738),* 105 Winthrop Rd., Hillside, NJ 07642 Tel 201-666-0909.

IBS Pub Co, *(Intergalactic BS Publishing Co.),* Box 5138, Pittsburgh, PA 15206.

IC&P, *(Issues in Cooperation & Power),* Subs. of Cooperation Corporation, P.O. Box 5039, Berkeley, CA 94705.

Icarus, *(Icarus Press, Inc.; 0-89651),* P.O. Box 1225, South Bend, IN 46624 Tel 219-291-3200.

ICF Pr, *(International Cultural Foundation Press; 0-89226),* P.O. Box 3939, Grand Central Sta., New York, NY 10017 Tel 212-997-0007.

ICPSR, *(Inter-university Consortium for Political & Social Research; 0-89138),* P.O. Box 1248, Ann Arbor, MI 48106 Tel 313-763-5010.

ICR, *(Institute for Cross-Cultural Research; 0-911976),* 4000 Albermarle St., N.W., Washington, DC 20016.

ICS Bks, *(I C S Books, Inc.; 0-934802),* P.O. Box 8002, Merrillville, IN 46410 Tel 219-769-0585.

ICS Pubns, *(I.C.S. Pubns., Institute of Carmelite Studies; 0-9600876; 0-935316),* 2131 Lincoln Rd., N.E., Washington, DC 20002 Tel 202-832-6622.

ICSU *Imprint of* **Unipub**

Idaho First Natl Bank, *(Idaho First National Bank; 0-9600776),* c/o R. D. Beatty & Associates, Inc., P.O. Box 763, Boise, ID 83701.

Idaho Mus Nat Hist, *(Idaho Museum of Natural History; 0-939696),* Campus Box 8096, Idaho State Univ., Pocatello, ID 83209 Tel 208-236-3168.

Ide Hse, *(Ide House, Inc.; 0-86663),* 4631 Harvey Dr., Mesquite, TX 75149.

Idea Mill
   See Barn Hill

Ideal Pubns *Imprint of* **Westinghouse Learn**

Ideal Pubs, *(Ideal Pubs. Inc.),* 630 S. Governor, Iowa City, IA 52240.

Ideal School, *(Ideal School Supply Co.),* Div. of Westinghouse Learning Corp., 11000 S. Lavergne Ave., Oak Lawn, IL 60453 Tel 312-425-0800.

Ideal World, *(Ideal World Publishing Co.; 0-915068),* P.O. Box 1237-EG, Melbourne, FL 32935 Tel 305-254-6003.

Ideals, *(Ideals Publishing Corp.; 0-89542),* 11315 Watertown Plank Rd., Milwaukee, WI 53226 Tel 414-771-2700. *Imprints:* Good Friends (Good Friends).

IDHHB, *(Institute for the Development of the Harmonious Human Being Inc.; 0-89556),* P.O. Box 370, Nevada City, CA 95959 Tel 916-878-8505.

IDOC, *(IDOC/North America, Inc.; 0-89021),* 145 E. 49th St., Suite 6D, New York, NY 10017 Tel 212-752-5121.

IDRC *Imprint of* **Unipub**

IDTTC, *(IDTTC; 0-916922),* Fairview St., Antrim, NH 03440 Tel 617-588-2990.

IEAS Ctr Chinese Stud, *(Univ. of California, Institute of East Asian Studies, Center for Chinese Studies; 0-912966),* Institute of East Asian Studies, Pubns. Office, Berkeley, CA 94720 Tel 415-642-2816.

IEM-HOTEP, *(IEM-HOTEP Assn.; 0-932806),* 893 N.E. 125th St., N. Miami, FL 33161.

IEP, *(IEP),* ; Publisher Abbreviation Without Addresses Are for Titles That Are Out of Print. These Are Obsolette Abbreviations.

IFI Plenum, *(I F I/Plenum Data Corp.; 0-306),* Dist. by: Plenum Publishing Corp., 227 W. 17th St., New York, NY 10011.

Igaku-Shoin, *(Igaku-Shoin Medical Pubs.; 0-89640),* 50 Rockefeller Plaza, New York, NY 10020 Tel 212-765-9581.

Ignatius Pr, *(Ignatius Press; 0-89870),* P.O. Box 18990, San Francisco, CA 94118 Tel 415-387-2324.

IHI Pr, *(IHI Press),* International Homophilics Institute, 165 Marlborough St., Boston, MA 02116.

IHPress, *(IHPress, Inc.; 0-936870),* P.O. Box 1437, Downtown Sta., Billings, MT 59101.

IHR Pr, *(Institute of Human Relations Press; 0-914252),* P.O. Box 62, Old Bethpage, NY 11804; Moved, Left No Forwarding Address.

IHS-Library & Educ Div
   See IHS-PDS

IHS-PDS, *(Information Handling Services/PDS Hard Copy Publishing; 0-910972; 0-89847),* 15 Inverness Way E., P.O. Box 1154, Englewood, CO 80150 Tel 303-779-0600.

IIFTL
   See Intl Law Inst

IIR *Imprint of* **Unipub**

IISJ, *(Institute for Independent Social Journalism; 0-917654),* 33 W. 17th St., New York, NY 10011 Tel 212-691-0404.

IIWPA, *(International Information/Word Processing Assn.; 0-935220),* 1015 North York Rd., Willow Grove, PA 19090 Tel 215-657-6300.

IJG Inc, *(IJG, Inc.; 0-936200),* 1260 W. Foothill Blvd., Upland, CA 91786.

Ilkon Pr, *(Ilkon Press; 0-916832),* 210 Riverside Dr., Apt 6-G, New York, NY 10025 Tel 212-663-2579.

Ill Baptist St Assn, *(Illinois Baptist State Assn.; 0-9600896),* P.O. Box 3486, Springfield, IL 62708.

Ill Labor Hist Soc, *(Illinois Labor History Society; 0-916884),* Dist. by: Charles H. Kerr Pub. Co., 20 E. Jackson, Chicago, IL 60604 Tel 312-454-0363.

Ill Regional Lib Coun, *(Illinois Regional Library Council; 0-917692),* 425 N. Michigan, Suite 1303, Chicago, IL 60611 Tel 312-828-0928.

Ill St Hist Lib, *(Illinois State Historical Library; 0-912154),* Old State Capitol, Springfield, IL 62706 Tel 217-782-4836.

Ill St Hist Soc, *(Illinois State Historical Society; 0-912226),* Old State Capitol, Springfield, IL 62706 Tel 217-782-4836.

Ill St Museum, *(Illinois State Museum; 0-89792; 0-932336),* Spring & Edwards, Springfield, IL 62706 Tel 217-782-7386.

Illinois St Archives, *(Illinos State Archives Pubns./Finding Aids Unit),* Office of the Secretary of State, Springfield, IL 62756.

Illum Eng, *(Illuminating Engineering Society; 0-87995),* 345 E. 47th St., New York, NY 10017 Tel 212-644-7920.

Illum Way Pr
See IWP Pub

Illuminati, *(Illuminati; 0-89807),* 1147 S. Robertson Blvd., Los Angeles, CA 90035 Tel 213-273-8372.

Illuminations Pr, *(Illuminations Press),* 2110 Ninth St., Apt. B, Berkeley, CA 94710 Tel 415-849-2102.

Illusive Unicorn, *(Illusive Unicorn Pubns.),* P.O. Box 6841, San Jose, CA 95150 Tel 408-279-1520.

Im *Imprint of* Doubleday

IMA Assoc, *(I.M.A. Associates),* P.O. Box 8272, Canton, OH 44711.

Ima Boyd, *(Boyd, Ima Gene (Guthery); 0-9600502),* 370 Archwood Ave., Akron, OH 44301 Tel 216-773-1757.

IMA Ed, *(IMA Education & Research Foundation; 0-918486),* P.O. Box 526, Newtonville, NY 12128 Tel 518-434-3859.

Image & Idea, *(Image & Idea, Inc.; 0-934570),* Box 1991, Iowa City, IA 52240.

Image Awareness, *(Image Awareness Corp.; 0-9604592),* P.O. Box 3307, Auburn, CA 95604.

Image Bldrs
See TIB Pubns

Image Gallery, *(Image Gallery; 0-918362),* 1017 S. W. Morrison St., Rm. 307, Portland, OR 97205 Tel 503-224-9629.

Image West, *(Image West Press; 0-918966),* P.O. Box 5511, Eugene, OR 97405 Tel 503-342-3797.

Imagenes, *(Imagenes Press; 0-939302),* 1605 Cypress Dr., El Centro, CA 92243 Tel 714-352-2188.

Images Graphiques, *(Images Graphiques, Inc.; 0-89545),* 37 Riverside Dr., New York, NY 10023 Tel 212-787-4000.

Images Pr, *(Images Press; 0-9600374),* P.O. Box 9444, Berkeley, CA 94709 Tel 415-843-8834.

Imagesmith, *(Imagesmith; 0-938700),* P.O. Box 1524, Bellevue, WA 98009.

Imibooks Pubns, *(Imibooks Pubns.; 0-918066),* Box 9, Greenvale, NY 11548 Tel 212-738-6642; Moved, Left No Forwarding Address.

Immediate Pr, *(Immediate Press),* 13 Spring St., Stamford, CT 06901 Tel 203-327-5770.

Imp Pr, *(Imp Press; 0-9603008),* P.O. Box 93, Buffalo, NY 14213 Tel 716-881-5391.

Impact, *(Impact Press),* 55 W. 42nd St., New York, NY 10036 Tel 212-563-0156.

Impact Bks MO, *(Impact Books, Inc.; 0-89228),* 137 W. Jefferson, Kirkwood, MO 63122.

Impact MI, *(Impact Press; 0-938968),* P.O. Box 475, Roseville, MI 48066.

Impact Pr IL, *(Impact Press),* 6424 N. Sacramento Ave., Chicago, IL 60645 Tel 312-433-4786.

Impact Pub, *(Impact Publishing Co.; 0-9601530),* 1601 Oak Park Blvd., Pleasant Hill, CA 94523.

Impact Pubs Cal, *(Impact Pubs., Inc.; 0-915166),* P.O. Box 1094, San Luis Obispo, CA 93406 Tel 805-543-5911.

Impact Tenn, *(Impact Books; 0-914850; 0-86608),* Div. of the Benson Co., 365 Great Circle Rd., Nashville, TN 37228 Tel 615-259-9111.

Imperial Pub Co, *(Imperial Publishing Co.; 0-9602960),* 190 S. Florida Ave., P.O. Box 120, Bartow, FL 33830.

Impermanent Pr, *(Impermanent Press),* c/o Ruth Bebermeyer, 218 Monclay Court, St. Louis, MO 63122.

Imported Pubns, *(Imported Pubns.; 0-8285),* 320 W. Ohio St., Chicago, IL 60610 Tel 312-787-9017.

Impress Hse, *(Impress House; 0-913992),* Orders to: Associated Booksellers, 147 McKinley Ave., Bridgeport, CT 06606.

Impressions, *(Impressions),* P.O. Box 6191, Harrisburg, PA 17112.

Imprimis, *(Imprimis Press, Ltd),* Manassas, VA 22110.

Imprint CT, *(Imprint; 0-934260),* 20 Isham Rd., W. Hartford, CT 06107.

Imprint Edns, *(Imprint Editions),* 420 S. Howes St., Fort Collins, CO 80521.

Imrie-Risley, *(Imrie/Risley Miniatures, Inc.; 0-912364),* P.O. Box 89, Burnt Hills, NY 12027 Tel 518-885-6054.

IMS Comm, *(I M S Communications, Inc.; 0-933916),* 426 Pennsylvania Ave., Fort Washington, PA 19034 Tel 215-643-0400.

In Between, *(In Between Books; 0-935430),* Box T, Sausalito, CA 94965.

Incentive Pubns, *(Incentive Pubns., Inc.; 0-913916),* 2400 Crestmoor Rd., Nashville, TN 37215 Tel 615-385-2934.

Incremental Motion, *(Incremental Motion Control Systems Society; 0-931538),* P.O. Box 2772, Sta. A, Champaign, IL 61820 Tel 217-356-1523.

Incunabula, *(Incunabula Collection; 0-930226),* 277 Hillside Ave., Nutley, NJ 07110 Tel 201-667-8502.

Ind American, *(Independent American),* P.O. Box 636, Littleton, CO 80120.

Ind Camp Supply
See ICS Bks

Ind Hist Soc, *(Indiana Historical Society),* 315 W. Ohio St., Rm. 350, Indianapolis, IN 46202 Tel 317-232-1895.

Ind Mus Art, *(Indianapolis Museum of Art; 0-936260),* 1200 W. 38th St., Indianapolis, IN 46208.

Ind Pr MO, *(Independence Press; 0-8309),* Div. of Herald House, Drawer HH, Independence, MO 64055 Tel 816-252-5010.

Ind Sch Pr, *(Independent School Press; 0-88334),* 51 River St., Wellesley Hills, MA 02181 Tel 617-237-2591.

Ind St Univ, *(Indiana State Univ; 0-940100),* Stalker Hall, Rm. 300, Terre Haute, IN 47809 Tel 812-232-6311.

Ind U Afro-Amer Arts, *(Indiana Univ. Afro-American Arts Institute),* 109 North Jordon Ave., Bloomington, IN 47401.

Ind U Busn Res, *(Indiana Univ., Bureau of Business Research; 0-87925),* Bloomington, IN 47401 Tel 812-322-0211.

Ind U Pr, *(Indiana Univ. Press; 0-253),* Tenth & Morton Sts., Bloomington, IN 47405 Tel 812-337-6804.

Ind U Res Ctr, *(Indiana Univ., Research Center for the Language Sciences),* ; Publisher Abbreviation Without Addreses Are for Titles That Are Out of Print. These Are Obsolete Abbreviations. Publisher's Abbreviation Is Now Res Ctr Lang Semiotic.

Ind U Res Inst, *(Indiana Univ. Research Institute for Inner Asian Studies; 0-933070),* Goodbody Hall 101, Bloomington, IN 47405.

Ind-US Inc, *(Ind-US, Inc.),* Box 56, East Glastonbury, CT 06025 Tel 203-633-0045.

Independence Pr
See Ind Pr MO

Independence Unltd, *(Independence Unlimited; 0-931040),* 27 Gardner St., Portsmouth, NH 03801.

Independent Pubs Servs, *(Independent Pubs. Services; 0-912078),* 431 Belvedere St., San Francisco, CA 94117 Tel 415-664-5600.

Independent Study, *(Independent Study),* Orders to: University of California Extension, Independent Study, Berkeley, CA 94720 Tel 415-642-7343.

Index Co, *(Index Co.; 0-914054),* 319 Elm St., Kalamazoo, MI 49007; Moved, Left No Forwarding Address.

Index Pubs, *(Index Pubs.; 0-934692),* 26 St. Mark's Place, New York, NY 10003; Orders to: Russica Book Store, 799 Broadway, New York, NY 10003 Tel 212-473-7480; Moved, Left No Forwarding Address.

Indian Feather, *(Indian Feather Publishing; 0-937962),* 7218 SW Oak, Portland, OR 97223.

Indian Hist Pr, *(Indian Historian Press, Inc.; 0-913436),* 1451 Masonic Ave., San Francisco, CA 94117 Tel 415-626-5235.

Indian Pocahontas Club, *(Indian Women's Pocahontas Club),* 323 N. Choctaw, Claremore, OK 74017.

Indian Pr
See Indian Pubns

Indian Pubns, *(Indian Pubns.; 0-934170),* 1869 2nd Ave., New York, NY 10029 Tel 212-370-2187.

Indigena, *(Indigena Pubns.; 0-9602972),* 133 Brooks Ave., Venice, CA 90291.

Indigenous Pubns, *(Indigenous Pubns.; 0-930740),* 160 Ribier, Modesto, CA 95350 Tel 209-529-5087.

Indisota Pubs, *(Indisota Publishers; 0-9603420),* 3166 Ridge Court, Placerville, CA 95667.

Indiv Books Pub, *(Individualized Books Publishing Co.; 0-915310),* P.O. Box 591, Menlo Park, CA 94025 Tel 415-322-4156.

Indiv Learning, *(Individualized Learning, Inc.; 0-913100),* 120 New Park Ave., Hartford, CT 06106.

Individual Learn, *(Individual Learning Systems, Inc.; 0-86589),* P.O. Box 225447, Dallas, TX 75265 Tel 214-630-0313.

Indus Bk Pub, *(Industry Book Publishing, Inc.; 0-939554),* 1437 Tuttle Ave., Wallingford, CT 06492 Tel 203-269-9184.

Indus Dev Inst Sci, *(Industrial Development Div., Institute of Science & Technology; 0-938654),* Univ. of Michigan, 2200 Bonisteel Blvd., Ann Arbor, MI 48105 Tel 313-764-5260.

Indus Health Inc, *(Industrial Health Foundation Inc.; 0-911890),* 5231 Centre Ave., Pittsburgh, PA 15232 Tel 412-687-2100.

Indus Pr, *(Industrial Press Inc.; 0-8311),* 200 Madison Ave., New York, NY 10157 Tel 212-889-6330.

Indus Rel, *(Industrial Relations Counselors, Inc. (IRC); 0-87330),* P.O. Box 1530, New York, NY 10101 Tel 212-541-6086.

Indus Rel Wkshp, *(Industrial Relations Workshop Seminars, Inc.; 0-930692),* 43-70 Kessina Blvd., New York, NY 11354 Tel 212-762-2000; Moved, Left No Forwarding Address.

Indus Res Serv, *(Industrial Research Service, Inc.),* 90 Washington St., Dover, NH 03820 Tel 603-742-1919.

Indus Res Unit-Wharton, *(Industrial Research Unit-The Wharton School; 0-89546),* Univ. of Pennsylvania, Vance Hall/CS, 3733 Spruce St., Philadelphia, PA 19104 Tel 215-243-5606.

Indus Training, *(Industrial Training Consultants, Inc.; 0-9603702),* P.O. Box 3213, Richmond, VA 23235.

Indus Workers World, *(Industrial Workers of the World; 0-917124),* 752 W. Webster Ave., Chicago, IL 60614 Tel 312-549-5045.

Infernal Artists, *(Infernal Artists Scribes Publishers),* 185 Butler St., Hamden, CT 06511 Tel 203-787-4376; P.O. Box 4034, Hamden, CT 06514.

Info Alternative, *(Information Alternative; 0-936288),* Box 657, Woodstock, NY 12498.

Info Clearing House, *(Information Clearing House, Inc.; 0-931634),* 500 Fifth Ave., New York, NY 10110.

Info Coord, *(Information Coordinators, Inc.; 0-911772; 0-89990),* 1435-37 Randolph St., Detroit, MI 48226.

Info Please, *(Information Please),* 57 W. 57th St., New York, NY 10019.

Info Policy Design, *(Information for Policy Design; 0-916282),* Lafayette, NY 13084 Tel 315-677-9278.

Info Prods, *(Information Products; 0-937978),* 2604 Artesia Blvd., Suite 4, Redondo Beach, CA 90278.

Info Res Inc, *(Information Resources, Inc.; 0-912864),* P.O. Box 417, Lexington, MA 02173 Tel 617-861-7996.

Info Research, *(Information Research Associates),* P. O. Box 623, Chapel Hill, NC 27514; Moved Left No Forwarding Address.

Info Resources, *(Information Resources Press; 0-87815),* Div. of Herner & Co., 1700 N. Moore St., Suite 700, Arlington, VA 22209 Tel 703-558-8270.

Info Retrieval, *(Information Retrieval Inc.; 0-917000),* Subs. of Information Retrieval Ltd., 250 W. 57th St., New York, NY 10022 Tel 703-548-0868.

Info Services, *(Information Services; 0-9601490),* Box 305, Frederiksted, St. Croix, VI 00840.

Info Systems, *(Information Systems Development; 0-931738),* 1100 E. Eighth, Austin, TX 78702.

Info Transfer, *(Information Transfer Inc.; 0-937398),* 9300 Columbia Blvd., Silver Springs, MD 20910 Tel 301-587-9390.

INFORM, *(INFORM; 0-918780),* 25 Broad St., New York, NY 10004 Tel 212-425-3550.

Inform
See INFORM

Inforwomen, *(Inforwomen),* 2150 W. Berteau Ave., Chicago, IL 60618; Orders to: P.O. Box 1727, Chicago, IL 60690.

Infosources, *(Infosources Publishing; 0-939486),* 118 W. 79th St., New York, NY 10024.

Ingleside, *(Ingleside Publishing; 0-9603502),* 410 Grove Ave., Barrington, IL 60010 Tel 312-381-4312.

Inglewood CA, *(Inglewood Public Library; 0-913578),* 101 W. Manchester Blvd., Inglewood, CA 90301 Tel 213-649-7397; Orders to: Inglewood Finance Dept., P.O. Box 6500, Inglewood, CA 90301.

Inheritance Pr, *(Inheritance Press, Inc.),* P.O. Box H, Trenton, NC 28585 Tel 919-448-3131.

Ink Arts Pubns, *(Ink Arts Pubns.),* P.O. Box 36070, Indianapolis, IN 46236 Tel 317-842-3721.

Inka Dinka Ink, *(Inka Dinka Ink; 0-939700),* 4741 Guerley Rd., Cincinnati, OH 45238 Tel 513-471-0825.

Inkululeko, *(Inkululeko Pubns.),* Dist. by: Imported Publications, 320 W. Ohio St., Chicago, IL 60610 Tel 312-787-9017.

Inkworks, *(Inkworks Press; 0-930712),* 4220 Telegraph Ave., Oakland, CA 94609 Tel 415-652-7111.

Inner Circle, *(Inner Circle Publishing Co.; 0-938284),* P.O. Box 1617, Detroit, MI 48231.

Inner Tradit, *(Inner Traditions International, Ltd.; 0-89281),* 377 Park Ave. S., New York, NY 10016 Tel 212-889-8350.

Innerpress, *(InnerPress; 0-916886),* P.O, Box 3411, Inglewood, CA 90304 Tel 213-671-5959.

Innova Assoc, *(Innova Associates),* 2006 Franklin St., Suite 205, Huntsville, AL 35801.

Innovative Ed, *(Innovative Educational Affairs, Inc.; 0-914394),* 16 Tain Dr., Great Neck, NY 11021 Tel 516-466-2498.

Inor, *(Inor Publishing Co.; 0-9601074),* 600 E. Marshall St., P.O. Box 295, Sweet Springs, MO 65351 Tel 816-335-6373.

Inquiry Pr, *(Inquiry Press; 0-918112),* 4925 Jefferson Ave, Midland, MI 48640 Tel 517-631-3350.

Ins Res Svc, *(Insurance Research Service),* 571 E. Main St., Brevard, NC 28712 Tel 704-883-9333.

Inscape Corp, *(Inscape Corp.; 0-87953),* 1629 "K" St., N.W., Suite 5107, Washington, DC 20006 Tel 301-469-7788; Orders to: Inscape Customer Service, P.O. Box 978, Edison, NJ 08817. *Imprints:* BO (Black Orpheus); NP (New Perspectives).

Insiders Pub, *(Insiders' Publishing Group; 0-932338),* 349 W. Bute St., Room C-5, Norfolk, VA 23510 Tel 804-627-9925.

Insiders Software, *(Insiders Software Consultants; 0-939462),* P.O. Box 7086, Alexandria, VA 22307.

Insight Pr, *(Insight Press, Inc.; 0-914520),* P.O. Box 8369, New Orleans, LA 70182.

Insight Pr CA, *(Insight Press; 0-935218),* 614 Vermont St., San Francisco, CA 94107.

Insight Pubns, *(Insight Pubns.),* 5096 Village Dr., Las Vegas, NV 89122 Tel 702-452-7427; Orders to: Box 12752, Las Vegas, NV 89112.

Inspiration Conn, *(Inspiration House Pubs.; 0-918114),* P.O. Box 1, South Windsor, CT 06074 Tel 203-289-7363.

Inspiration Hse, *(Inspiration House Pubns.; 0-910668),* P.O. Box 3293, Vero Beach, FL 32960.

Inspirational Bks, *(Inspirational Books),* 5104 Glenwood, Chicago, IL 60640 Tel 312-649-5316.

Inst Adv Philo, *(Institute for the Advancement of Philosophy for Children, Division 107; 0-916834),* Montclair State College, Upper Montclair, NJ 07043 Tel 201-893-4277.

Inst Am Music, *(Institute for Studies in American Music; 0-914678),* Dept. of Music, Brooklyn College, Brooklyn, NY 11210 Tel 212-780-5655.

Inst Analysis, *(Institute for the Analysis, Evaluation & Design of Human Action; 0-938526),* 44 Clifford Ave., Pelham, NY 10803.

Inst Busn Plan, *(Institute for Business Planning, Inc.; 0-87624),* IBP Plaza, Englewood Cliffs, NJ 07632 Tel 201-592-3075.

Inst Byzantine, *(Institute for Byzantine & Modern Greek Studies, Inc.; 0-914744),* 115 Gilbert Rd., Belmont, MA 02178 Tel 617-484-6595.

Inst Constructive Cap, *(Institute for Constructive Capitalism, Univ. of Texas at Austin, Graduate School of Business),* Austin, TX 78712.

Inst Contemporary, *(Institute for Contemporary Studies; 0-917616),* 260 California St., Suite 811, San Francisco, CA 94111 Tel 415-398-3010.

Inst Dev Harmonious
See IDHHB

Inst Dowsing, *(Institute of Dowsing, The; 0-931740),* 414 Biscayne Dr., Wilmington, NC 28405.

Inst Early Am, *(Institute of Early American History & Culture; 0-910776),* P.O. Box 220, Williamsburg, VA 23185 Tel 804-229-2771.

Inst Ecological, *(Institute for Ecological Policies; 0-937786),* 9208 Christopher St., Fairfax, VA 22031.

Inst Econ Finan, *(Institute for Economic & Financial Research; 0-918968),* Dist. by: American Classical College Press, P.O. Box 4526, Albuquerque, NM 87196 Tel 505-843-7749.

Inst Econ Pol, *(Institute for Economic & Political World Strategic Studies; 0-930008; 0-86722),* P.O. Box 4526, Sta. A, Albuquerque, NM 87196 Tel 505-843-7749.

Inst Econmetric, *(Institute for Econometric Research; 0-917604),* 3471 N. Federal Hwy., Suite 350, Fort Lauderdale, FL 33306 Tel 305-561-5105.

Inst Ed Management, *(Institute for Educational Management; 0-934222),* Harvard University, 337 Gutman Library, Appian Way, Cambridge, MA 02138 Tel 617-495-2655.

Inst Effect Mgmt, *(Institute for Effective Management; 0-914804),* Chapman Rd., Fountainville, PA 18923 Tel 215-345-0265.

Inst Elect Eng, *(Institution of Electrical Engineers; 0-85206),* 445 Hoes Lane, Piscataway, NJ 08854 Tel 201-981-0060.

Inst Electrical, *(Institute of Electrical & Electronics Engineers; 0-87942),* 345 E. 47th St., New York, NY 10017 Tel 212-644-7558; Orders to: IEEE Ctr., 445 Hoes Lane, Piscataway, NJ 08854 Tel 201-981-0060.

Inst Energy, *(Institutes for Energy Development, Inc.; 0-89419),* P.O. Box 16569, Fort Worth, TX 76133 Tel 817-923-8271.

Inst Environ Sci, *(Institute of Environmental Sciences; 0-915414),* 940 E. Northwest Hwy., Mt. Prospect, IL 60056 Tel 312-255-1561.

Inst Evolutionary, *(Institute for Evolutionary Research; 0-938710),* 200 Park Ave., New York, NY 10166.

Inst Food & Develop, *(Institute for Food & Development Policy; 0-935028),* 2588 Mission St., San Francisco, CA 94110 Tel 415-648-6090.

Inst Food & Develop, *(Institute for Food & Development Policy; 0-935028),* 2588 Mission St., San Francisco, CA 94110 Tel 415-648-6090.

Inst for Environ Action, *(Institute for Environmental Action; 0-936020),* 81 Leonard St., New York, NY 10013.

Inst for the Arts, *(Institute for the Arts, Rice Univ.; 0-914412),* P.O. Box 1892, Houston, TX 77001 Tel 713-527-4858.

Inst for Urban & Regional, *(Institute for Urban & Regional Studies, Washington Univ.),* P.O. Box 1208, St. Louis, MO 63130.

Inst Foreign Policy Anal, *(Institute for Foreign Policy Analysis, Inc.; 0-89549),* 675 Massachusetts Ave., Central Plaza Bldg. 10th Fl., Cambridge, MA 02139 Tel 617-492-2116.

Inst Found Employ
See Intl Found Employ

Inst Free Enterprise, *(Institute for Free Enterprise Education),* 2721 Leameadow Dr., Plano, TX 75075 Tel 214-424-5888; Moved, Left No Forwarding Address.

Inst Gen Semantics, *(Institute of General Semantics; 0-910780),* R.R. 1, P.O. Box 215, Lakeville, CT 06039 Tel 203-435-9174.

Inst Gov Stud Berk, *(Univ. of California Institute of Governmental Studies; 0-87772),* 109 Moses Hall, Berkeley, CA 94720 Tel 415-642-6722.

Inst Hist Rev, *(Institute for Historical Review; 0-939484),* P. O. Box 1306, Torrance, CA 90505 Tel 213-326-2684.

Inst Human NY, *(Institute for Human Studies; 0-932340),* Box 240, Gardiner, NY 12525; Orders to: 14 South Division St., Peekskill, NY 10566; Moved, Left No Forwarding Address.

Inst Human Respon, *(Institute for Human Responsiveness, Inc.; 0-89639),* 6200 Winchester Rd., Lexington, KY 40511.

Inst Humane, *(Institute for Humane Studies, Inc.; 0-89617),* 1177 University Dr., Menlo Park, CA 94025 Tel 415-323-2464; Orders to: P.O. Box 2256, Wichita, KS 67201 Tel 316-832-5604.

Inst Info Stud, *(Institute for Information Studies; 0-935294),* 200 Little Falls St., Suite 104, Falls Church, VA 22046.

Inst Inter Aud, *(Institute of Internal Auditors, Inc.; 0-89413),* 249 Maitland Ave., Altamonte Springs, FL 32701 Tel 305-830-7600. *Imprints:* Found Audit Res (Foundation for Auditability Research & Education, Inc.).

Inst Intl Educ, *(Institute of International Education; 0-87206),* 809 United Nations Plaza, New York, NY 10017 Tel 212-883-8258.

Inst Jesuit, *(Institute of Jesuit Sources, The; 0-912422),* Fusz Memorial, St. Louis Univ., 3700 W. Pine Blvd., St. Louis, MO 63108 Tel 314-652-5737.

Inst Jewish Stud, *(Institute of Jewish Studies, Inc.),* P.O. Box 220394, Charlotte, NC 28222 Tel 704-366-4655.

Inst Lang Study, *(Institute for Language Study; 0-8489),* Div. of R. D. Cortina Co., 71 Plymouth St., Montclair, NJ 07042 Tel 212-246-1848.

Inst Liv Skills
See Bridges Pr

Inst Mediaeval Mus, *(Institute of Mediaeval Music; 0-912024; 0-931902),* c/o L.A. Dittmer, Paradise Falls, Cresco, PA 18326 Tel 717-629-1278.

Inst Mgmt & Labor, *(Institute of Management & Labor Relations),* Public Education Dept., Ryders Lane, Cook Campus, New Brunswick, NJ 08903.

Inst Mid East & North Africa, *(Institute of Middle Eastern & North African Affairs; 0-934484),* P.O. Box 1764, Hyattsville, MD 20788 Tel 301-559-6307.

Inst Ministry Ethics, *(Institute for Ministry Ethics & Finance),* 4340 Campus Dr., Suite 203, Newport Beach, CA 92660.

Inst Mod Lang, *(Institute of Modern Languages, Inc.; 0-88499),* 2622 Pittman Dr., Silver Spring, MD 20910 Tel 301-565-2580.

Inst Palestine, *(Institute for Palestine Studies),* 1322 18th St., N.W., Washington, DC 20036.

Inst Paper Chem, *(Institute of Paper Chemistry; 0-87010),* P.O. Box 1039, Appleton, WI 54912 Tel 414-734-9251.

Inst Personality & Ability, *(Institute for Personality & Ability Testing, Inc.; 0-918296),* P. O. Box 188, Champaign, IL 61820 Tel 217-352-4739.

Inst Policy Stud, *(Institute for Policy Studies; 0-89758),* 1901 "Q" St., N.W., Washington, DC 20009 Tel 202-234-9382.

Inst Pr, *(Institute Press; 0-931976),* 2210 Wilshire Blvd., Suite 171, Santa Monica, CA 90403 Tel 213-828-6541.

Inst Product, *(Institute for Product Safety; 0-938830),* 1410 Duke University Rd., Durham, NC 27701.

Inst Public Adm, *(Institute of Public Administration; 0-913824),* 55 W. 44th St., New York, NY 10036 Tel 212-661-2540.

Inst Pubs, *(Institute Pubs.; 0-86664),* 7422 Mountioy, Huntington Beach, CA 92648.

Inst Qual Hum Life, *(Institute for Quality in Human Life; 0-939630),* 6335 N. Delaware Ave., Portland, OR 97217 Tel 503-289-6136.

Inst Rat Liv, *(Institute for Rational Living),* 1162 Beacon St., Brookline, MA 02146 Tel 617-739-5063.

Inst Rational-Emotive, *(Institute for Rational-Emotive Therapy; 0-917476),* 45 E. 65th St., New York, NY 10021 Tel 212-535-0822.

Inst Real Estate, *(Institute of Real Estate Management; 0-912104),* 430 N. Michigan Ave., Chicago, IL 60611 Tel 312-440-8683.

Inst Responsive, *(Institute for Responsive Education; 0-917754),* 704 Commonwealth Ave., Boston, MA 02215.

Inst Sci Info
See ISI Press

Inst Self Dev, *(Institute for Self Development),* 50 Maple Place, Manhasset, NY 11030 Tel 516-627-0048.

Inst Soc Ethics, *(Institute of Society, Ethics & Life Sciences-The Hastings Center; 0-916558),* 360 Broadway, Hastings-on-Hudson, NY 10706 Tel 914-478-0500.

Inst Soc Res, *(Institute for Social Research; 0-87944),* Box 1248, Ann Arbor, MI 48106 Tel 313-764-7509.

Inst Socioecon, *(Institute for Socioeconomic Studies; 0-915312),* Airport Road, White Plains, NY 10604 Tel 914-428-7400.

Inst Software Eng, *(Institute for Software Engineering; 0-931900),* 535 Middlefield Rd., No. 200, Menlo Park, CA 94025 Tel 415-493-0300.

Inst Space-Time, *(Institute for Space-Time Studies; 0-930170),* Box 7123, Univ. Sta., Provo, UT 84602.

Inst Stud Prag, *(Institute for Studies in Pragmaticism; 0-936842),* P.O. Box 4530, Texas Tech Univ., Lubbock, TX 79409.

Inst Study Animal, *(Institute for the Study of Animal Problems; 0-937712),* 2100 L St., N.W., Washington, DC 20037.

Inst Study Human, *(Institute for the Study of Human Issues (ISHI); 0-89727; 0-915980),* 3401 Market St., Suite 252, Philadelphia, PA 19104 Tel 215-387-9002.

Inst Study Man, *(Institute for the Study of Man, Inc.),* 1629 K St., N.W., Suite 520, Washington, DC 20006 Tel 202-232-1040.

Inst Study Psych
See Inst Rational-Emotive

Inst Synthesis, *(Institute of Dynamic Synthesis, Inc.; 0-910774),* 4401 N. Ravenwood Ave., Chicago, IL 60640 Tel 312-728-1065.

Inst Tuberculosis, *(Institution for Tuberculosis Research, Univ. of Illinois, Medical Ctr.; 0-915314),* 904 W. Adams St., Chicago, IL 60607 Tel 312-996-4688.

Inst Urban Studies, *(Institute of Urban Studies, Univ. of Texas at Arlington),* P.O. Box 19588, Arlington, TX 76019 Tel 817-273-3071.

Inst World Order, *(Institute for World Order, The; 0-911646),* 777 United Nations Plaza, New York, NY 10017 Tel 212-490-0010.

Instru Soc, *(Instrument Society of America; 0-87664),* P.O. Box 12277, 67 Alexander Dr., Research Triangle Park, NC 27709 Tel 919-549-8411.

Instruct Aides TX, *(Instructional Aides, Inc.; 0-936474),* X1401 Windy Meadow Dr., Plano, TX 75023.

Instruct Dev, *(Instructional Development Corp.),* P.O. Box 361, Monmouth, OR 97361 Tel 503-838-1220.

Instruct Materials, *(Instructional Materials Center),* Div. of Extension, Univ. of Texas at Austin, Austin, TX 78712 Tel 512-471-1041.

Instruct Object, *(Instructional Objectives Exchange; 0-932166),* 11411 W. Jefferson Blvd., Culver City, CA 90230 Tel 213-391-6295.

Instruct Res, *(Instructional Resources Inc.),* P.O. Box 3452, Tallahassee, FL 32303 Tel 904-385-2546.

Instructo, *(Instructo Corp.),* Cedar Hollow & Matthews Rds., Paoli, PA 19301 Tel 215-644-7700.

Instrumental Co, *(Instrumentalist Co.),* 1418 Lake St., Evanston, IL 60204 Tel 312-328-6000.

Integrated Ed Assoc, *(Integrated Education Associates; 0-912008),* Univ. of Massachusetts School of Education, Amherst, MA 01003 Tel 413-545-0327.

Integrated Info, *(Integrated Information Analysis),* P.O. Box 1447, St. Louis, MO 63178; Moved, Left No Forwarding Address.

Integrity, *(Integrity Press; 0-918048),* 3888 Morse Rd., Columbus, OH 43219 Tel 614-471-2759.

Inter-Am Tropical, *(Inter-American Tropical Tuna Commission; 0-9603078),* P.O. Box 1529, La Jolla, CA 92093.

Inter Am U Pr, *(Inter American Univ. Press; 0-913480),* G.P.O. Box 3255, San Juan, PR 00936 Tel 809-763-9622.

Inter-American, *(Inter-American Publishing Co.; 0-912554),* P.O. Box 802, Culver City, CA 90230.

Inter-Crescent, *(Inter-Crescent Publishing Co., Inc.; 0-916400),* P.O. Box 8481, Dallas, TX 75205 Tel 214-341-4792.

Inter-Noise
See Noise Control

Inter-Optics Pubns, *(Inter-Optics Pubns., Inc.; 0-935726),* 90 Bagby Dr., Suite 222, Birmingham, AL 35209 Tel 205-942-5232.

Inter-Religious Task, *(Inter-Religious Task Force for Social Analysis; 0-936476),* 464 19th St., Oakland, CA 94612.

Inter-Varsity, *(Inter-Varsity Press; 0-87784; 0-8308),* P.O. Box F, Downers Grove, IL 60515 Tel 312-964-5700.

InterAction, *(InterAction Books; 0-932808),* Rte. 1, Hwy. 5 South, Heber Springs, AR 72543.

Interbk Inc, *(Interbook, Inc.; 0-913456; 0-89192),* 611 Broadway, Rm. 227, New York, NY 10012 Tel 212-677-9201.

Interchange, *(Interchange Inc.; 0-916966),* P. O. Box 16012 B, St. Louis Park, MN 55416 Tel 612-929-6669.

Intercont Press, *(Intercontinental Press; 0-933142),* P.O. Box 565, Auburn, AL 36830 Tel 205-887-5297.

Intercontinental Pubns, *(Intercontinental Pubns.; 0-917408),* 25 Sylvan Rd. S., P.O. Box 5017, Westport, CT 06881 Tel 203-226-7463.

Intercult Network
See Intercult Pr

Intercult Pr, *(Intercultural Press, Inc.; 0-933622),* 70 W. Hubbard St., Chicago, IL 60610 Tel 312-321-0075.

InterCulture, *(InterCulture Associates; 0-88253; 0-89253),* Quaddick Rd., P.O. Box 277, Thompson, CT 06277 Tel 203-923-9494.

Interface Calif, *(Interface California Corp.; 0-915580),* 106 T St., P.O. Box 3611, Eureka, CA 95501 Tel 707-442-8112; Dist. by: Stein & Day Pubs., Scarborough House, Briarcliff Manor, NY 10510 Tel 914-762-2151.

Interface Calif
See Northtown Bks

Interface Unl, *(Interface Unlimited),* P.O. Box 8583, Toledo, OH 43623 Tel 419-531-4022.

Interfacia Inc, *(Interfacia, Inc.; 0-917634),* Div. of Creative Informatics, P.O. Box 4422, Chicago, IL 60680 Tel 312-643-9050.

InterFinance, *(InterFinance Corp.),* 305 Foshay Tower, Minneapolis, MN 55402 Tel 612-338-8185.

Intergalactic Pub, *(Intergalactic Publishing Co.; 0-914632),* 2301 Stuart St., Berkeley, CA 94705; Orders to: P.O. Box 5171, Berkeley, CA 94705.

Intergalactic NJ, *(Intergalactic Publishing Co.),* 221 Haddon Ave., Westmont, NJ 08108 Tel 609-854-0499.

Interiors, *(Interiors by Arden; 0-934892),* 8131 Lemon, No. 8, La Mesa, CA 92041 Tel 714-460-7998.

Interland Pub, *(Interland Publishing, Inc.; 0-87989),* 799 Broadway, New York, NY 10003 Tel 212-673-8280.

Interlingual, *(Interlingual Institute; 0-917848),* Box 126, Canal St. Sta., New York, NY 10013 Tel 212-349-3679.

InterMed Comm, *(InterMed Communications, Inc.; 0-916730),* 132 Welsh Rd., Horsham, PA 19044 Tel 215-657-4600.

Intermedia, *(Intermedia, Inc.; 0-910788),* c/o B.A. Lipetz, 434 Woodward Rd., Nassau, NY 12123.

Intermtn Air, *(Intermountain Air Press; 0-914680),* 171 S. Second E., Preston, ID 83263.

Interpersonal Comm, *(Interpersonal Communication Programs, Inc.; 0-917340),* 1925 Nicollet Ave., Minneapolis, MN 55403 Tel 612-871-7388.

Interpharm, *(Interpharm Press; 0-935184),* P.O. Box 530, Prairie View, IL 60069.

Intersoc Comm Path Info, *(Intersociety Committee Pathology Information; 0-937888),* 4733 Bethesda Ave., Suite 735, Bethesda, MD 20014 Tel 301-656-2944.

Interstate, *(Interstate; 0-8134),* 19-27 N. Jackson St., Danville, IL 61832 Tel 217-446-0500.

Interurban, *(Interurban Press; 0-916374),* P.O. Box 6444, Glendale, CA 91205 Tel 213-240-9130.

Interurbans

See Interurban

Intervale Pub Co, *(Intervale Publishing Co., Inc 0-932400),* Box 777, Meredith, NH 03253 Tel 603-284-7726.

Interweave, *(Interweave Press, Inc.; 0-934026),* 306 N. Washington Ave., Loveland, CO 80537 Tel 303-669-7672.

Intext, *(Intext Educational Pubs.),* ; Publisher Abbreviation Without Addresses Are for Titles That Are Out of Print. These Are Obsolete Abbreviations.

Intext Paperbacks, *(Intext Press Paperbacks; 0-88444),* 257 Park Ave., S., New York, N 10010; Orders to: Oak St. & Pawnee Ave., Scranton, PA 18515.

Intl Acad Pub, *(International Academic Publishing, Inc.; 0-89765),* 177 F. Riverside Ave., Newport Beach, CA 92663.

Intl Arts & Sci
See M E Sharpe

Intl Assess, *(International Assn. of Assessing Officers; 0-88329),* 1313 E. 60th St., Chicago, IL 60637 Tel 312-947-2069.

Intl Assn Chiefs Police, *(International Assn. of Chiefs of Police; 0-88269),* 11 Firstfield Rd Gaithersburg, MD 20760 Tel 301-948-0922

Intl Assn Schools, *(International Assn. of Schools of Social Work; 0-931638),* C/O CSWE, 345 E. 46th St., Rm 615, New York NY 10017; No Longer in the U.S.

Intl Assn Univers, *(International Assn. of Universities, Paris),* Dist. by: American Council on Education, 1 Dupont Circle, Washington, DC 20036.

Intl Bible Assn, *(International Bible Assn.),* Bo 5646, Dallas, TX 75222 Tel 214-388-5111.

Intl Bk Co IL, *(International Book Co.; 0-910790),* 332 S. Michigan Ave., Chicago, IL 60604 Tel 312-427-4545.

Intl Bk Ctr, *(International Book Centre; 0-917062; 0-86685),* P.O. Box 295, Troy, M 48097 Tel 313-879-8436.

Intl Bk Dist, *(International Book Distributors),* P.O. Box 180, Murray Hill Sta., New York, NY 10016.

Intl Bks, *(International Books),* P.O. Box 6970 Washington, DC 20032.

Intl Busn Educ, *(International Business Education & Research Program, Graduate School of Business Administration; 0-939322),* Univ. of Southern California, Lc Angeles, CA 90007 Tel 213-743-5309.

Intl Center Learning, *(International Center for Learning),* Subs. of Gospel Light Pubns., P.O. Box 1650, Glendale, CA 91209.

Intl Chrono, *(International Chronologies),* P.O. Box 3235 GCPO, New York, NY 10017; Moved, Left No Forwarding Address.

Intl City Mgr
See Intl City Mgt

Intl City Mgt, *(International City Management Assn.; 0-87326),* 1140 Connecticut Ave., N.W., Washington, DC 20036 Tel 202-828-3600.

Intl Co-Op, *(International Co-Operative Publishing House; 0-89974),* P.O. Box 245, Burtonsville, MO 20730.

Intl College, *(International College; 0-89615),* 1019 Gayley Ave., Los Angeles, CA 90024.

Intl Comm Christ, *(International Community o Christ; 0-936202),* Pub. Dept. Chancellery, 643 Ralston St., Reno, NV 89503.

Intl Comm Ctr, *(International Communication Center; 0-933236),* School of Communications DS-40, Univ. of Washington, Seattle, WA 98195.

Intl Comm Rad Meas, *(International Commission on Radiation Units & Measurements; 0-913394),* 7910 Woodmon Ave., Suite 1016, Bethesda, DC 20014 Tel 301-657-2652; Orders to: P.O. Box 30165, Washington, DC 20014.

Intl Comm Serv, *(International Commercial Service; 0-935402),* P.O. Box 4082, Irvine, CA 92716 Tel 714-552-8494.

Intl Coun Shop, *(International Council of Shopping Centers; 0-913598),* 665 Fifth Ave., New York, NY 10022 Tel 212-421-8181.

Intl Ctr Environment, *(International Center for Environmental Research; 0-914704),* 141 Emerald Bay, Laguna Beach, CA 92651; P.O. Box 4664, Anaheim, CA 92803.

Intl Ctr Photo, *(International Center of Photography; 0-933642),* 1130 Fifth Ave., New York, NY 10028 Tel 212-860-1777.

Intl Develop Res
See Intl Development

Intl Development, *(International Development Institute; 0-89249),* 400 E. Seventh St., Bloomington, IN 47401 Tel 812-337-8596.

Intl Dialogue Pr, *(International Dialogue Press; 0-89881; 0-931364),* P.O. Box 924, Davis, CA 95616 Tel 916-758-6500.

Intl Educ Dev, *(International Educational Development; 0-939420),* P.O. Box 66, Silver Spring, MD 20907.

Intl Educ Systems, *(International Educational Systems, Inc.),* 5521 W. 110th St., Oak Lawn, IL 60653 Tel 312-423-1717.

Intl Electrical
    See Inst Electrical

Intl Evang, *(International Evangelism Crusade, Inc.),* 7970 Woodman Ave., Suite 207, Van Nuys, CA 91402 Tel 213-781-7704.

Intl Exhibit Foun, *(International Exhibitions Foundation; 0-88397),* 1729 "H" St., N.W., Suite 310, Washington, DC 20006 Tel 202-298-7010.

Intl Fed Auto Con, *(International Federation of Automatic Control),* Dist. by: Instrument Society of America, 400 Stanwix St., Pittsburgh, PA 15222.

Intl Film, *(International Film Bureau, Inc.; 0-8354),* 332 S. Michigan Ave., Chicago, IL 60604 Tel 312-427-4545.

Intl Fire Prot
    See Intl Fire Serv

Intl Fire Serv, *(International Fire Service Training Assn.; 0-87939),* Oklahoma State Univ., Stillwater, OK 74078 Tel 405-624-5723.

Intl Found Biosocial Dev, *(International Foundation for Biosocial Development & Human Health; 0-934314),* c/o Lifshutz & Polland, 400 Park Ave., New York, NY 10022.

Intl Found Employ, *(International Foundation of Employee Benefit Plans; 0-89154),* P.O. Box 69, 18700 W. Bluemound Rd., Brookfield, WI 53005 Tel 414-786-6700.

Intl Friend, *(International Friendship; 0-935340),* Waxhaw, NC 28173 Tel 704-843-3168.

Intl Gen Semantics, *(International Society for General Semantics; 0-918970),* P.O. Box 2469, San Francisco, CA 94126 Tel 415-543-1747.

Intl General, *(International General; 0-88477),* P.O. Box 350, New York, NY 10013.

Intl Health Coun, *(International Health Council),* 204 Beeler Dr., Berea, OH 44017.

Intl Human Res, *(International Human Resources Development Corp.; 0-934634),* 137 Newbury St., Boston, MA 02116.

Intl Ideas, *(International Ideas Inc.; 0-89563),* 1627 Spruce St., Philadelphia, PA 19103 Tel 215-546-0392.

Intl Imports, *(International Imports),* Box 2010, Toluca Lake, CA 91602 Tel 213-761-3991.

Intl Inst Nat Health, *(International Institute of Natural Health Sciences, Inc.; 0-86664),* 130 Clifford Terrace, San Francisco, CA 94117.

Intl Inst Psych, *(International Institute of Preventive Psychiatry; 0-939210),* 11445 Dona Dolores Place, Studio City, CA 91604.

Intl Intertrade, *(International Intertrade Index Printing Consultants, Pubs.; 0-910794),* P.O. Box 636, Federal Square, Newark, NJ 07101 Tel 201-623-2864.

Intl Labour Office, *(International Labour Office; 92-2),* Washington Branch, 1750 New York Ave., N.W., Suite 311, Washington, DC 20006.

Intl Law Inst, *(International Law Institute; 0-935328),* Georgetown Univ. Law Center, 600 New Jersey Ave., N.W., Washington, DC 20001.

Intl Learn Syst, *(International Learning Systems, Inc.),* 1715 Connecticut Ave., N.W., Washington, DC 20009 Tel 202-232-4111.

Intl Lib, *(International Library-Book Pubs.; 0-914250),* 2425 Wilson Blvd., Arlington, VA 22201 Tel 703-538-4211.

Intl Linguistics, *(International Linguistics Corp.; 0-939990),* 401 W. 89th St., Kansas City, MO 64114.

Intl Marine, *(International Marine Publishing Co.; 0-87742),* 21 Elm St., Camden, ME 04843 Tel 207-236-4342.

Intl Monetary, *(International Monetary Fund; 0-939934),* 700 19th St., N.W., Washington, DC 20431 Tel 202-477-3086.

Intl Mus Photo, *(International Museum of Photography at George Eastman House; 0-935398),* 900 East Ave., Rochester, NY 14607 Tel 716-271-3361.

Intl Netsuke, *(International Netsuke Collectors Society; 0-9603080),* P.O. Box 10426, Honolulu, HI 96816.

Intl Ozone, *(International Ozone Assn.; 0-918650),* c/o Executives Consultants, Inc., 301 Maple Ave., W., Suite 500, Vienna, VA 22180 Tel 703-938-7433.

Intl Personnel Mgmt, *(International Personnel Management Assn.; 0-87373),* 1850 "K" St. N.W., Suite 870, Washington, DC 20006 Tel 202-833-5860; 485-487 National Press Bldg., 14 & "F" Sts., N.W., Washington, DC 20004 Tel 202-833-1545.

Intl Pict Pubns, *(International Pictorial Pubns.; 0-916722),* 49 S. Baldwin, Sierra Madre, CA 91024 Tel 213-355-8205.

Intl Polygonics, *(International Polygonics, Ltd.; 0-930330),* P.O. Box 899, Midtown Sta., New York, NY 10018 Tel 212-683-2914.

Intl Program Labs, *(International Program of Laboratories for Population Statistics; 0-89383),* NCNB Plaza, Suite 400, 136 E. Rosemary St., Chapel Hill, NC 27514 Tel 919-966-1131.

Intl Psych Pr, *(International Psychological Press, Inc.; 0-915662),* 1850 Hanover Dr., No. 69, Davis, CA 95616 Tel 916-758-0685.

Intl Pub Co, *(International Pubs. Co.; 0-7178),* 381 Park Ave., S., Suite 1301, New York, NY 10016 Tel 212-685-2864.

Intl Pubns Serv, *(International Pubns. Service; 0-8002),* 114 E. 32nd St., New York, NY 10016 Tel 212-685-9351.

Intl Reading, *(International Reading Assn.; 0-87207),* 800 Barksdale Rd., Box 8139, Newark, DE 19711 Tel 302-731-1600.

Intl Ref Bks, *(International Reference Books),* 111 N. Wabash, Rm. 1310, Chicago, IL 60602; Moved Left No Forwarding Address.

Intl Res Ctr Energy, *(International Research Center for Energy & Economic Development; 0-918714),* Economics Bldg., 216 Univ. of Colo., Boulder, CO 80309.

Intl Res Eval, *(International Research & Evaluation; 0-930318),* Research Pubns. Div., 21098 IRE Control Ctr., Eagan, MN 55121 Tel 612-888-9605.

Intl Res Inst, *(International Research Institute for Political Science),* Box 199, College Park, MD 20740.

Intl Research Serv, *(International Research Service, Inc.; 0-934366),* P.O. Box 225, Blue Bell, PA 19422.

Intl Review, *(International Review Service; 0-87138),* 15 Washington Place, New York, NY 10003 Tel 212-751-0833; UN Bureau: Rm. 301, United Nations, New York, NY 10017.

Intl Schl Psych, *(International School of Psychology; 0-917668),* 92 S. Dawson Ave., Columbus, OH 43209.

Intl Schol Bk Serv, *(International Scholarly Book Services, Inc. (ISBS, Inc.); 0-89955),* P.O. Box 555, Forest Grove, OR 97116 Tel 503-357-7192.

Intl Sci Tech, *(International Science & Technology Institute, Inc.; 0-936130),* 2033 M St. N.W., Suite 300, Washington, DC 20036 Tel 202-466-7290.

Intl Soc Artifical Organs, *(International Society for Artificial Organs; 0-936022),* 8937 Euclid Ave., Cleveland, OH 44106.

Intl Textbk, *(International Textbook Co.),* ; Publisher Abbreviation Without Addresses Are for Titles That Are Out of Print. These Are Obsolete Abbreviations.

Intl Tree Crops, *(International Tree Crops; 0-938240),* P.O. Box 888, Winters, CA 95694.

Intl Univs Pr, *(International Universities Press, Inc.; 0-8236),* 315 Fifth Ave., New York, NY 10016 Tel 212-684-7900.

Intl Wealth, *(International Wealth Success, Inc.; 0-914306),* 24 Canterbury Rd., Rockville Center, NY 11570 Tel 516-766-5850.

Intl Wine Soc, *(International Wine Society; 0-89219),* 304 E. 45th St., New York, NY 10017 Tel 212-661-2700.

Intl Word Process
    See IIWPA

Intl Yoga Soc
    See Yoga Res Foun

IntlDept *Imprint of* **Har-Row**

Intraworld Trade, *(Intraworld Trade News; 0-9605190),* 1500 N.W. 103rd Lane, Coral Springs, FL 33065.

Intrepid, *(Intrepid Press),* P.O. Box 1423, Buffalo, NY 14214 Tel 716-886-7136.

Invest Dealers, *(Investment Dealers Digest),* 150 Broadway, New York, NY 10038.

Invest Eval, *(Investment Evaluations Corp.; 0-9603282),* 2000 Goldenvue Dr., Golden, CO 80401 Tel 303-278-3464.

Investor Pubns, *(Investor Pubns., Inc.; 0-914230),* 219 Parkade, Cedar Falls, IA 50613 Tel 319-277-6341; 2930 Huntington Dr., Arlington Heights, IL 60004 Tel 312-577-2525.

Investor's Syst, *(Investor's Systems, Inc.; 0-915610),* P.O. Box 1422, Dayton, OH 45401 Tel 513-223-6870.

Investrek, *(Investrek Publishing; 0-9604914),* 1025 Sea Breeze Dr., Costa Mesa, CA 92627.

Inwood Pr, *(Inwood Press; 0-914772),* 128 Post Ave., New York, NY 10034 Tel 212-569-4941; Moved, Left No Forwarding Address.

IO Pubns
    See North Atlantic

Iota Pr, *(Iota Press; 0-936412),* 2749 Mt. Hope Rd., Okemos, MI 48864.

Iowa St U Pr, *(Iowa State Univ. Press; 0-8138),* 2121 S. State Ave., Ames, IA 50010 Tel 515-294-5280.

IPIC
    See Inter-Crescent

Ipse Dixit Pr, *(Ipse Dixit Press, Inc.; 0-9602468),* Box 4277, St. Paul, MN 55104 Tel 612-690-0980.

Iqra, *(Iqra, Inc.; 0-935290),* P.O. Box 12511, San Antonio, TX 78212 Tel 512-734-7552.

IR Pubns, *(IR Pubns. Ltd.),* 461 Park Ave., S., Suite 903, New York, NY 10016.

Irego, *(Irego; 0-911732),* P.O. Box 286, Lenox Hill Sta., 221 E. 70th St., New York, NY 10021.

Ireland Educ, *(Ireland Educational Corp.; 0-89103),* 7076 S. Alton Way, Bldg. D, Englewood, CO 80112.

Irfan, *(Irfan; 0-917220),* 160 W. 71 St., New York, NY 10023.

Iris Pr, *(Iris Press; 0-916078),* 27 Chestnut St., Binghamton, NY 13905 Tel 607-722-6739.

Irish Bk Ctr, *(Irish Book Center),* 245 W. 104th St., New York, NY 10025 Tel 212-866-0309.

Irish Bks Media, *(Irish Books & Media; 0-937702),* 683 Osceola Ave., St. Paul, MN 55105.

Irish U Pr, *(Irish Univ. Pr.),* ; Publisher Abbreviation Without Addresses Are for Titles That Are Out of Print. These Are Obsolete Abbreviations.

Iron Horse, *(Iron Horse Publishing Co., Inc.; 0-914380),* P.O. Box 1182, Southfield, MI 48075 Tel 313-354-5698; Moved, Left No Forwarding Address.

Ironwood Pr, *(Ironwood Press),* P.O. Box 49023, Tucson, AZ 85717.

Iroquois Hse, *(Iroquois House, Pubs.; 0-931980),* Box 15, Sunspot, NM 88349 Tel 505-437-2807.

IRR *Imprint of* **Oxford U Pr**

Irrigation, *(Irrigation Assn., The; 0-935030),* 13975 Connecticut Ave., Silver Spring, MD 20906 Tel 301-871-1200.

Irvington, *(Irvington Pubs.; 0-89197; 0-8290),* 551 Fifth Ave., New York, NY 10176 Tel 212-697-8100.

Irwin, *(Irwin, Richard D., Inc.; 0-256),* 1818 Ridge Rd., Homewood, IL 60430 Tel 312-798-6000.

Irwinton, *(Irwinton Pubs.),* 9685 Anderson Rd., Mercersburg, PA 17236.

ISH Pubns, *(ISH Pubns.; 0-917392),* Institute for Scientific Humanism Pubns., Lowenstein Center, Fordham Univ., 60th & Columbus Ave., New York, NY 10023 Tel 212-427-5928; Dist. by: International Scholarly Bk Services, Inc., 2130 Pacific Ave., Forest Grove, OR 97116.

ISI Pr, *(ISI Press; 0-89495),* Div. of Institute for Scientific Information, 3501 Market St., University City Science Ctr., Philadelphia, PA 19104 Tel 215-386-0100.

ISI Press, *(Institute for Scientific Information; 0-89495),* 325 Chestnut St., Philadelphia, PA 19106 Tel 215-923-3300.

Islamic Prods, *(Islamic Productions International; 0-934894),* 739 E. Sixth St., Tucson, AZ 85719 Tel 602-791-3989.

Island CA, *(Island Press; 0-933280),* Div. of Round Valley Agrarian Institute, Star Route 1, Box 38, Covelo, CA 95428.

Island Her, *(Island Heritage Ltd.; 0-89610),* 104 Ward Plaza at 210 Ward Ave., Honolulu, HI 96814 Tel 808-526-1126.

Island Marine, *(Island Marine; 0-915228),* Box 68, Main St., Southwest Harbor, ME 04679 Tel 207-244-7102.

Island Pr, *(Island Press; 0-87208),* 175 Bahia Via, Fort Myers Beach, FL 33931 Tel 813-463-9482.

Island Pub, *(Island Publishing House; 0-916424),* P.O. Drawer 758, Manteo, NC 27954 Tel 919-473-2838.

Island Writers, *(Island Writers Publishing Co.; 0-9604798),* Box 25382, Honolulu, HI 96825 Tel 808-395-2615.

Israel Folk, *(Israel Folk Dance Institute),* 1067 E. 105th St., Brooklyn, NY 11236.

Isthmus, *(Isthmus Press; 0-913286),* P.O. Box 6877, San Francisco, CA 94101 Tel 415-567-0487.

ITA, *(Initial Teaching Alphabet Pubns., Inc.; 0-273),* Subs. of Pitman Pub. Corp., 6 Davis Dr., Belmont, CA 94002 Tel 415-592-7810; Aquired by Fearon-Pitman.

ITA
See Pitman Learning

Italimuse, *(Italimuse, Inc.; 0-910798),* 3128 Burr St., Fairfield, CT 06430 Tel 203-259-5788.

Ithaca Hse, *(Ithaca House; 0-87886),* 108 N. Plain St., Ithaca, NY 14850.

Ithaca Pr MA, *(Ithaca Press; 0-915940),* P.O. Box 853, Lowell, MA 01853 Tel 617-453-2177.

IUCN *Imprint of Unipub*

Ivan Pub, *(Ivan Publishing, Inc.; 0-9602578),* P.O. Box 17947, San Antonio, TX 78217 Tel 512-828-7995.

Ivey Pubns, *(Ivey Pubns.; 0-9600864),* 1845 Arkoe Dr., S.E., Atlanta, GA 30316.

Ivory Scroll, *(Ivory Scroll Books, Pubs.),* P.O. Box 7526, Philadelphia, PA 19101.

Ivy Club, *(Ivy Club, The; 0-934756),* 43 Prospect Ave., Princeton, NJ 08540.

Ivy Hill, *(Ivy Hill Press; 0-9601542),* 8817 Greenview Place, Spring Valley, CA 92077.

Ivy Pr, *(Ivy Press Inc., The; 0-933372),* 2121 N. Akard, Dallas, TX 75201 Tel 800-527-9250.

Ivystone, *(Ivystone Pubns.; 0-935604),* Box 23, Ada, MI 49301.

IWP Pub, *(IWP Publishing; 0-914766),* P.O. Box 2449, Menlo Park, CA 94025 Tel 415-321-4468.

J A Allen, *(Allen, J. A., & Co. Ltd.; 0-85131),* Dist. by: Sporting Book Center, Inc., Canaan, NY 12029 Tel 518-794-8998.

J A Lohmann, *(Lohmann, Jeanne A.),* 722 Tenth Ave., San Francisco, CA 94118 Tel 415-387-7644.

J A White, *(White, John A.; 0-9603242),* 1200 Toyon Dr, Millbrae, CA 94030 Tel 415-697-1187.

J Alden, *(Alden, Jay, Pubs.; 0-914844),* P.O. Box 1295, 546 S. Hofgaarden St., La Puente, CA 91749 Tel 213-968-6424.

J Alex Munro, *(Munro, J. Alex; 0-9601670),* 304 Saxon Dr., Springfield, IL 62704 Tel 217-787-6621.

J & A Enterprises, *(J&A Enterprises; 0-934368),* 5522 W. Acoma Rd., Glendale, AZ 85306.

J & D Peterson, *(Peterson, John C. & Doris M.; 0-9604376),* R R 1, Box 25, Delphi, IN 46923.

J & J Bks, *(J & J Books, Inc.; 0-914464),* 1004 Springhill Dr., Angola, IN 46703 Tel 219-665-5346; Orders to: Ulrich's Books Inc., 549 E. University Ave., Ann Arbor, MI 48104 Tel 313-662-3201.

J & J Dist, *(J. & J. Distributors),* P.O. Box 247, Raymondville, TX 78580 Tel 512-689-2523.

J & J Pub, *(J & J Publishing),* 1088 Madison Ave., New York, NY 10028 Tel 212-535-7399.

J & L Lee, *(Lee, J. & L., Co.; 0-934904),* P.O. Box 5575, Lincoln, NE 68505.

J & M R Reunions, *(Reunions, Joseph & Mary Ray),* 6740 Velasco, Dallas, TX 75214 Tel 214-821-4456.

J Arvidson, *(Arvidson, J., Press; 0-9602098),* P.O. Box 4022, Helena, MT 59601 Tel 406-442-0354.

J B Blanchard, *(Blanchard, J. B., Press),* P.O. Box 943, Riverside, CA 92502.

J B Burns, *(Burns, J. B.; 0-9602998),* 4250 Lauderdale Ave., La Crescenta, CA 91214.

J B McBrien, *(McBrien, Joe Bennett),* Chattanooga, TN 37402 Tel 615-265-1884.

J B Pal, *(Pal, J. B., & Co., Inc.; 0-916836),* 904 W. Castlewood Terrace, Chicago, IL 60640 Tel 312-271-0123.

J-B Pubs, *(J-B Publishing Co.; 0-916170),* 430 Ivy Ave., Crete, NE 68333 Tel 402-826-3356.

J B Wilson, *(Wilson, J.B., Press, Inc.; 0-933458),* 1730 Columbia Dr. E., Fresno, CA 93727 Tel 209-251-8751.

J Bartholomew, *(Bartholomew, John, & Son),* Dist. by: Herman Publishing, Inc., 45 Newbury St., Boston, MA 02116.

J Barton
See J&M Barton

J Bee Prods, *(J Bee Productions; 0-9601880),* P.O. Box 1584, Riverside, CA 92502.

J Buchs, *(Buchs, J., Pubns.),* 5301 Richmond, No. 24B, Houston, TX 77027.

J Burger, *(Burger, Joanne; 0-916188),* 55 Blue Bonnet Court, Lake Jackson, TX 77566.

J C Bancroft, *(Bancroft, John C.),* 5855 Sheridan Rd., Apt. 7D, Chicago, IL 60660 Tel 312-271-7747.

J C Print, *(J. C. Printing Co.),* 3493 N. Main St., College Park, GA 30337.

J Calvin Keene, *(Keene, J. Calvin; 0-9603084),* 134 Verna Rd., Lewisburg, PA 17837.

J Casper, *(Casper, Jeanette K.),* R. D. One, Salem, NJ 08079.

J Cole, *(Cole, Jim; 0-9601200),* 37 Lomita Dr., Mill Valley, CA 94941 Tel 415-388-1621.

J Curley, *(Curley, John, & Associates, Inc.; 0-89340),* 325 E. 57th St., Apt. 7A, New York, NY 10022 Tel 212-421-2641; Orders to: P. O. Box 37, South Yarmouth, MA 02664.

J Custis
See D Brown Bks

J D Bowers, *(Bowers, John D.; 0-9601360),* P.O. Box 101, Radnor, PA 19087 Tel 215-688-5541.

J D Craig, *(Craig, James D.; 0-9602042),* P.O. Box 42, Pebble Beach, CA 93953.

J Daniel, *(Daniel, John; 0-936784),* Wilbur Springs, CA 95987.

J De Graff
See De Graff

J Domjan
See Domjan Studio

J Donaghey, *(Donaghey, John, Pubns.; 0-9604298),* P.O. Box 402021, Garland, TX 75040.

J Downey, *(Downey, Joel; 0-9601284),* 1105 S. Braddock Ave., Pittsburgh, PA 15218 Tel 412-371-5880.

J E Edwards, *(Edwards, John E.),* ; Publisher Abbreviation Without Addresses Are for Titles That Are Out of Print. These Are Obsolete Abbreviations.

J E Robertson, *(Robertson, James E.; 0-9600756),* 5213 Don Pio Dr., Woodland Hills, CA 91364 Tel 213-347-8576; Orders to: P.O. Box 2227, North Hollywood, CA 91602.

J E Spott, *(Spott, Joseph E., Pub.; 0-913050),* 50 Muth Dr., Orinda, CA 94563 Tel 415-254-0963.

J E Stewart
See Woodford Mem

J F Bergin, *(Bergin, J. F., Pubs., Inc.; 0-89789),* One Hansen Place, Brooklyn, NY 11243 Tel 212-638-0729; 65 S. Oxford St., Brooklyn, NY 11217 Tel 212-237-9221.

J F Miles, *(Miles, James F.; 0-9600480),* P.O. Box 1041, Clemson, SC 29631 Tel 803-654-2410.

J F Wine, *(Wine, J. F.),* 924 Woodland Ave., Winchester, VA 22601 Tel 703-662-5735.

J Fein, *(Fein, Jess; 0-9604366),* Box 193, 118 Massachusetts Ave., Boston, MA 02115.

J Freedman Liturgy, *(Freedman, Jacob, Liturgy Research Foundation),* P.O. Box 317 Forest Park Sta., Springfield, MA 01108.

J G Anderson, *(Anderson, Julian G.; 0-9602128),* P.O. Box 1751, Naples, FL 33939 Tel 813-262-5592.

J G Stanoff, *(Stanoff, Jerrold G.),* P.O. Box 1599, Aptos, CA 95003 Tel 408-724-4911.

J G Stella, *(Stella, Joseph G.; 0-9600908; 0-8390),* P.O. Box 2158, Fort Lauderdale, FL 33303 Tel 305-462-1995; Dist. by: Abner Schram, 36 Park St., Montclair, NJ 07042.

J Gindick, *(Gindick, Jon),* 903 Hayes Ave., San Diego, CA 92103 Tel 714-298-6047; Orders to: 344 Ranch Rd., Visalia, CA 93277.

J Graham, *(Graham, Josephine),* c/o Suggin Productions, 7710 Choctaw Rd., Little Rock, AR 72205.

J Grauer, *(Grauer, Jack; 0-930584),* 2005 S.E. 58th, Portland, OR 97215 Tel 503-232-5596.

J H Hammill, *(Hammill, J. H., III; 0-9600652),* Diablo Valley College, 321 Golf Club Rd., Pleasant Hill, CA 94523 Tel 415-685-1230.

J H Reed, *(Reed, James H.; 0-9601314),* 1315 Melrose, Richardson, TX 75080 Tel 214-826-8835.

J H Roush, *(Roush, John H., Jr.; 0-9600830),* 27 Terrace Ave., Kentfield, CA 94904 Tel 415-453-7130.

J H Schwartz, *(Schwartz, J. H., Rev.),* 1633 N. Missouri, Peoria, IL 61603.

J H Westland, *(Westland, John Henry),* P.O. Box 3265, Chico, CA 95927.

J Halliburton, *(Halliburton, John),* 2217 Belmont Blvd., Apt B, Nashville, TN 37212.

J Howell, *(Howell, John, Books; 0-910760),* 434 Post St., San Francisco, CA 94102 Tel 415-781-7795.

J J Augustin, *(Augustin, J. J., Inc., Pub.; 0-87439),* Locust Valley, NY 11560 Tel 516-676-1510.

J J Binns, *(Binns, Joseph J.; 0-89674),* 6919 Radnor Rd., Bethesda, MD 20034 Tel 301-320-3327; Dist. by: Robert B. Luce, Inc., 27 Harrison St., Bridgeport, CT 06604 Tel 203-366-1900.

J J Connors, *(Connors, John J.),* 3811 Grantley Rd., Toledo, OH 43613 Tel 419-474-6836.

J J Johnson
See Carver Pub

J J Johnson, *(Johnson, Jesse J.),* ; Publisher Abbreviation Without Addresses Are for Titles That Are Out of Print. These Are Obsolete Abbreviations. Publisher's Abbreviation Is Now Ebony Pub.

J J Keller, *(Keller, J. J., Associates, Inc.; 0-934674),* 145 W. Wisconsin Ave., Neenah, WI 54956 Tel 414-722-2848.

J J Kester, *(Kester, J. J.; 0-9602084),* 416 Pine Grove Circle, Scotch Plains, NJ 07076 Tel 201-889-7077.

J J Nadolny, *(Nadolny, Julian J., & Co.),* 121 Hickory Rd., Kensington, CT 06037 Tel 203-225-5353.

J Johnson, *(Johnson, John; 0-910914),* R.D. 2, N. Bennington, VT 05257 Tel 802-442-6738.

J K Burgess, *(Burgess, Jack K., Inc.),* 44 Engle St., Englewood, NJ 07631 Tel 201-569-7477.

J Kenyon, *(Kenyon, Judith; 0-9604492),* 6467 Van Nuys Blvd., No. 117, Van Nuys, CA 91401.

J Kramer, *(Kramer, Justin, Inc.),* 1028 W. 8th Place, Los Angeles, CA 90017.

J L Barbour, *(Barbour, James L.),* P.O. Box 326, Port Tobacco, MD 20677.

J L Hauck, *(Hauck, Judith L., Mrs.),* 3470 N Alpine Rd., Rockford, IL 61111.

J L Lu, *(Lu, J. L., M.D.; 0-9601768),* P.O. Box 4276, Sta. A., Dallas, TX 75208.

J L Mercadante, *(Mercadante, J. L.),* P.O. Box 1028, New Hyde Park, NY 11040.

J L Pollnow, *(Pollnow, James L.; 0-9603708),* 1310 Aldersgate Rd., Little Rock, AR 72205.

J L Scherer, *(Scherer, John L., Jr.),* 4900 18th Ave. S., Minneapolis, MN 55417 Tel 612-722-2947.

J L Smith, *(Smith, Jerry L.; 0-9602136),* P.O. Box 485, Melbourne, AR 72556 Tel 501-368-7239.

J Larsen, *(Larsen, J., Publishing; 0-9602474),* P.O. Box 586, Deer Lodge, MT 59722 Tel 406-846-2610.

J Lessmann, *(Lessmann, Judy; 0-9600994),* 6702 Fairfax, Lincoln, NE 68505 Tel 402-466-5311.

J Lloyd Corp, *(Lloyd, Joseph, Corp.; 0-916490),* Dist. by: Rand McNally & Co., P.O. Box 7600, Chicago, IL 60680.

J Low, *(Low, Jennie; 0-9602820),* Dist. by: Altarinda Books, 13 Estates Dr., Orinda, CA 94563.

J M Bryant, *(Bryant, James M.),* P.O. Box 412, Normangee, TX 77871 Tel 713-828-4265.

J M Fontana, *(Fontana, John M., Pub.; 0-9600034),* 4 Walnut Place, Huntington, NY 11743 Tel 516-549-0892.

J M Friedman
See Balletmonographs

J M Goldberg, *(Goldberg, James M.; 0-9603074),* 1735 "K" St., N.W., Suite 200, Washington, DC 20006.

J M Jones, *(Jones, John M.; 0-912118),* 2011 Ferry Ave. T-9, Camden, NJ 08104.

J M Pearson, *(Pearson, J. Michael; 0-916528),* P.O. Box 402844, Ocean View Sta., Miami Beach, FL 33140 Tel 305-538-0346.

J M Phillips, *(Phillips, James M.; 0-932572),* P.O. Box 168, Williamstown, NJ 08094 Tel 609-567-0695.

J M Prods, *(JM Productions),* Box 837, Brentwood, TN 37027.

J M Sadler, *(Sadler, John M., & Co.; 0-930250),* 215 Commonwealth Ave., Massapequa, NY 11758 Tel 516-798-9059.

J Macy Foun, *(Macy, Josiah, Jr. Foundation; 0-914362),* 1 Rockefeller Plaza, New York, NY 10020 Tel 212-246-8830; Dist. by: David White, Inc., 14 Vanderventer Ave., Port Washington, NY 11050 Tel 516-944-9325.

J Mark Pr, *(Mark, J, Press; 0-912658),* 22 Allen's Point, Bay Shore, NY 11706 Tel 516-666-0043; Orders to: Box 33, Islip, NY 11751.

J Mathis Adv, *(Mathis, Jack, Advertising),* 3501 Woodhead Dr., Box 714, Northbrook, IL 60062 Tel 312-272-0590.

J Milton, *(John Milton Society for the Blind),* 29 W. 34th St., New York, NY 10001 Tel 212-736-4162.

J N Casavis, *(Casavis, James N.),* 32 Twin Lakes Dr., Monsey, NY 10952.

J N Summers, *(Summers, June Nay),* P.O. Box 334, Tecate, CA 92080.

J Norton Pubs, *(Norton, Jeffrey, Pubs., Inc.; 0-88432),* 145 E. 49th St., New York, NY 10017 Tel 212-753-1783. *Imprints:* Speechphone (Speechphone Institute).

J P Dwyer, *(Dwyer, Jeffrey P.),* 44 Main St., P.O. Box 426, Northampton, MA 01060 Tel 413-584-7909.

J P Getty Mus *(Getty, J. Paul, Museum; 0-89236),* 17985 Pacific Coast Hwy., Malibu, CA 90265 Tel 213-459-2306.

J P Tarcher, *(Tarcher, J. P., Inc.; 0-87477),* 9110 Sunset Blvd., Suite 250, Los Angeles, CA 90069 Tel 213-273-3274; Dist. by: Houghton Mifflin Co., Wayside Rd., Burlington, MA 01803 Tel 800-225-3362.

J P Werner, *(Werner, J. Paul; 0-9601368),* 4643 N. Front St., N. Philadelphia, PA 19140 Tel 215-457-4081.

J Palmer, *(Palmer, J., Pub.),* P.O. Box 498, 86 Friend St., Amesbury, MA 01913 Tel 617-388-1337.

J Patelson Mus, *(Patelson, Joseph, Music House, Ltd.; 0-915282),* 160 W. 56th St., New York, NY 10019 Tel 212-757-5587.

J Phunn, *(Phunn, J.; 0-931762),* Box 581, Astor Sta., Boston, MA 02123 Tel 617-782-4274; Orders to: Box 311, Wild Rose, WI 54984 Tel 414-622-3770.

J Pisapia Assocs, *(Pisapia, John, Associates; 0-917964),* Rte. 6, Box 23, Harewood, Morgantown, WV 26505 Tel 304-296-1150.

J R Albin
See Albin

J R Enterline, *(Enterline, J.R.),* 144 W. 95th St., New York, NY 10025 Tel 212-865-9648.

J R Parrott, *(Parrott, James R.),* 6148 Geronimo Circle, Anchorage, AL 99504.

J R Pubns, *(J. R. Pubns.; 0-913952),* 170 N.E. 33rd St., Ft. Lauderdale, FL 33334 Tel 305-563-1844.

J R Weckstein, *(Weckstein, Joyce R.; 0-9600980),* 28290 Tavistock Trail, Southfield, MI 48034 Tel 313-353-6221.

J S Layton, *(Layton, James S.; 0-9600058),* 1545 Ferrell Rd., Chapel Hill, NC 27514 Tel 919-942-1726.

J Sherrill, *(Sherrill, John),* P.O. Box 8623, Austin, TX 78712.

J Simon, *(Simon, Joseph; 0-934710),* Box 4071, Malibu, CA 90265 Tel 213-457-3293.

J Smith, *(Smith, Jeanne),* Box 211, La Farge, WI 54639 Tel 608-625-2425.

J Strand, *(Strand, Janann; 0-9600780),* P.O. Box 2725D, Pasadena, CA 91105 Tel 213-799-3153.

J Sturge, *(Sturge, Judi, Mrs.),* 18 Lodge Pole Rd., Pittsford, NY 14534.

J T Richards, *(Richards, John Thomas; 0-9605980),* 309 W. Ninth St., Rolla, MO 65401 Tel 402-648-7641; Dist. by: John G. Neihardt Foundation, Inc., Bancroft, NE 68004 Tel 402-648-3388.

J T White, *(White, James T., & Co.; 0-88371),* 1700 State Hwy. 3, Clifton, NJ 07013 Tel 201-773-9300.

J Thompson, *(Thompson, Jonathan, Publisher; 0-913322),* 23952 Estacia, South Laguna, CA 92677.

J V Willis, *(Willis, J. V., Pubs.; 0-913732),* 825 May St., Hammond, IN 46320 Tel 219-931-2672.

J W Bell, *(Bell, James W., Publisher; 0-939130),* 7611 Briarwood Dr., Little Rock, AR 72205; Dist. by: Publishers Distribution Service, 7509 Cantrell Rd., Little Rock, AR 72207.

J W Edwards
See Edwards Bros

J W Herringshaw, *(Herringshaw, Janet W.; 0-9603464),* 747 Towne Dr., Freeport, IL 61032.

J W Linn, *(Linn, Jo White; 0-918470),* Box 1948, Salisbury, NC 28144 Tel 704-633-3575.

J W Powell, *(Powell, James Wooldridge; 0-9601518),* 1025 Arno Rd., Kansas City, MO 64113 Tel 816-361-9796.

J W Van De Water
See Jonsalvania

J W Wills, *(Wills, J. W., Publishing Co.; 0-916716),* P.O. Box 457, Upper Marlboro, MD 20870 Tel 301-262-0941; Moved, Left No Forwarding Address.

J Wallis, *(Wallis, Joe; 0-9605950),* P.O. Box 2294, Washington, DC 20013.

J Wampler, *(Wampler, Joseph Carson; 0-935080),* Box 45, Berkeley, CA 94701.

J Willert, *(Willert, James; 0-930798),* 12804 S. Graff Dr., La Mirada, CA 90638.

J Winnen, *(Winnen, Jo; 0-9603404),* 624 S. Fancher Rd., Racine, WI 53406.

J Woods Pubns, *(Woods, Jo, Pubns.),* P.O. Box 7505, Little Rock, AR 72207.

J Young, *(Young, Joy),* 78 Peterboro, Detroit, MI 48201.

Jaap Rietman, *(Rietman, Jaap; 0-930034),* 157 Spring St., New York, NY 10012 Tel 212-966-7044.

Jacada Pubns, *(Jacada Pubns.; 0-915700),* Northway Square Bldg. 2150 N. 10th St., Suite 350, Seattle, WA 98133 Tel 206-362-3001.

Jacaranda Pr, *(Jacaranda Press, Inc.; 0-89151),* 872 Massachusetts Ave., Cambridge, MA 02139; Moved Left No Fowarding Address.

Jacbar Pubns, *(Jacbar Pubns.; 0-9606154),* Box 103, Randolph, OH 44265.

Jacek, *(Jacek Publishing Co.; 0-9601084),* 38 Morris Lane, Milford, CT 06460.

Jack Delany, *(Delany, Jack; 0-9600340),* 1136 Fort View Place, Cincinnati, OH 45202.

Jackpine Pr, *(Jackpine Press; 0-917492),* 1878 Meadowbrook Dr., Winston-Salem, NC 27104 Tel 919-725-8828.

Jackson St Hse
See Rainy Day Oreg

Jacobs, *(Jacobs Publishing Co.; 0-918272),* 4747 N. 16th St., Suite B-132, Phoenix, AZ 85016 Tel 602-277-3203.

Jacobs Enter
See J & J Dist

Jada Assocs, *(Jada Associates),* P.O. Box 33348, Hillcrest Sta., San Diego, CA 92103; Moved,Left No Forwarding Address.

Jaeger, *(Jaeger, Julia, Mrs.),* The Tenth Muse, P.O. Box 1417, Pacifica, CA 94044.

Jai Pr, *(Jai Press, Inc.; 0-89232),* Div. of Johnson Associates, Inc., 165 W. Putnam Ave., Greenwich, CT 06830 Tel 203-661-7602.

Jaks Pub Co, *(Jaks Publishing Co.; 0-935674),* 1106 N. Washington St., P.O. Box 5625, Helena, MT 59601.

Jakubowsky, *(Jakubowsky; 0-932588),* 1565 Madison St., Oakland, CA 94612 Tel 415-763-4324.

Jalamap, *(Jalamap Pubns., Inc.; 0-934750),* 833 Scenic Dr., Charleston, WV 25311.

Jalapeno Pr, *(Jalapeno Press; 0-935342),* Rte. 2, Box 600, Bandon, OR 97411.

Jalmar Pr, *(Jalmar Press, Inc.; 0-915190),* 6501 Elvas Ave., Sacramento, CA 95819 Tel 916-451-2897.

Jama Bks, *(Jama Books; 0-934130),* P.O. Box 30751, Santa Barbara, CA 93105; Dist. by: LaMere Distributors, 1120 Beach St., Flint, MI 48502.

Jamat Pr, *(Jamat Press, Inc.; 0-9601764),* 107A N. McKinney, Richardson, TX 75080 Tel 214-234-8801; 75247.

James Pub, *(James Publishing Co.),* Box 114-K, Rte 1, Winchester, VA 22601.

Jameson & Peeters
See E W Jameson Jr

Jamestown Pubs, *(Jamestown Pubs., Inc.; 0-89061),* P.O. Box 6743, Providence, RI 02940 Tel 401-351-1915.

JAMM, *(JAMM Creative Pubns.),* P.O. Box 655, Greeley, CO 80631 Tel 303-352-5656.

Jan Ents, *(Jan Enterprises, Inc.; 0-934896),* Box 268, Bala Cynwyd, PA 19004 Tel 215-667-9800.

J&J Pubns MI, *(J&J Pubns.; 0-9605786),* Box 1424, Traverse City, MI 49684.

J&M Barton, *(Barton, John & Margaret; 0-937216),* 6157 Coleman Creek Rd., Medford, OR 97501 Tel 503-535-1244.

J&M Pub, *(J&M Publishing Co.; 0-930630),* 11 Matthews Ave., Riverdale, NJ 07457 Tel 201-838-9434.

J&W Tex-Mex, *(J&W Tex-Mex; 0-9604842),* P.O. Box 983, Arlington, VA 22216.

Janevar Pub, *(Janevar Publishing Co.; 0-937174),* R. R. 11, Box 129, Muncie, IN 47302 Tel 317-289-3137.

Janova Pr, *(Janova Press, Inc.; 0-917294),* 3833 Barker Rd., Cincinnati, OH 45229 Tel 513-861-0512.

Jansen Pub, *(Jansen Publishing; 0-931212),* P.O. Box 105, Coarsegold, CA 93614 Tel 209-683-5883.

Janus Bks, *(Janus Book Pubs.; 0-915510),* 2501 Industrial Pkwy. W., Hayward, CA 94545 Tel 415-887-7070.

Janus Pr, *(Janus Press; 0-916172),* P.O. Box 578, Rogue River, OR 97537 Tel 503-582-1520.

Janzen Assoc, *(Janzen, P., Associates; 0-9604458),* P.O. Box 231, Libertyville, IL 60048.

Japan Pubns, *(Japan Pubns. Inc.; 0-87040),* C/O Kodansha International, Inc., 10 E. 53rd St., New York, NY 10022 Tel 212-593-7050; Dist. by: Harper & Row Pubs., Inc., Keystone Industrial Park, Scranton, PA 18512.

Jargon Soc, *(Jargon Society, Inc., The; 0-912330),* Dist. by: Gnomon Distribution, P.O. Box 106, Frankfort, KY 40602 Tel 502-223-1858.

Jarrow, *(Jarrow Press, Inc; 0-912190),* Div. of Anchor Society, Inc., 2398 Pine St., San Francisco, CA 94115.

Jarvey, *(Jarvey, Paulette),* 7212 S. Seven Oaks, Canby, OR 97013 Tel 503-266-4871.

Jasper County, *(Jasper County Abstract Co.; 0-9604474),* Kellner at Van Rensselaer St., Rensselaer, IN 47978.

Java Bks, *(Java Books),* P.O. Box 81, Morro Bay, CA 93442.

Jawbone Pr, *(Jawbone Press; 0-918116),* 17023 5th Ave., N.E., Seattle, WA 98155 Tel 206-363-1547.

Jay Pub, *(Jay Publishing Co.; 0-930140),* P.O. Box 454, Lakewood, CA 90714 Tel 714-893-0326.

Jay Pubns, *(Jay Pubns.; 0-916666),* P.O. Box 1141, San Andreas, CA 95249 Tel 209-754-4520.

Jazz Discographies, *(Jazz Discographies Unlimited),* 337 Ellerton S., Laurel, MD 20810 Tel 301-776-3148.

Jazz Pr, *(Jazz Press; 0-937310),* 3650 W. Pico, Los Angeles, CA 90019.

JB Indexes, *(JB Indexes; 0-89358),* 2377 Virginia St., Berkeley, CA 94709 Tel 415-848-8376; Moved, Left No Forwarding Address.

JC-DC Cartoons, *(JC/DC Cartoons Ink; 0-934574),* 5536 Fruitland Rd N.E., Salem, OR 97301.

JCP Corp VA, *(JCP Corp. of Virginia; 0-938694),* 214-40th St., P.O. Box 814, Virginia Beach, VA 23451 Tel 804-422-5426.

JD-J *Imprint of* **John Day**

JD Pr, *(JD Press; 0-933252),* P.O. Box 22674, San Diego, CA 92122.

JD-T *Imprint of* **John Day**

Jeanne G Smit
See J Smith

Jeannes Dreams, *(Jeanne's Dreams),* P.O. Box 211, La Farge, WI 54639 Tel 608-625-2425.

JED, *(JED; 0-9602200),* P.O. Box 7143 RC, Toledo, OH 43615 Tel 419-885-2932.

Jedick Ent, *(Jedick, Peter, Enterprises; 0-9605568),* 3637 W. 47th St., Cleveland, OH 44102.

Jeffers-Carr, *(Jeffers-Carr Associates; 0-9603954),* 307 E. 44th St., New York, NY 10017 Tel 212-490-3776; Dist. by: Merrimack Book Service, 99 Main St., Salem, NH 03079.

Jefferson Natl, *(Jefferson National Expansion Historical Assn.; 0-931056),* 11 N. 4th St., St. Louis, MO 63102.

Jefferson Pubns, *(Jefferson Pubns., Inc.),* Monticello Books Div., 44 S. Old Rand Rd., Box 19, Lake Zurich, IL 60047 Tel 312-438-4114.

Jefren Pub, *(Jefren Publishing Co.; 0-917244),* 7851 Mission Center Court, Suite 120, San Diego, CA 92108 Tel 714-298-1232.

Jelm Mtn, *(Jelm Mountain Pubns.),* 209 Grand Ave., Suite 205, Laramie, WY 82070.

Jem Pubs, *(Jem Publishers; 0-931076),* 4923 60th St., Kenosha, WI 53142.

Jemco Ent, *(Jemco Enterprises; 0-9602760),* P.O. Box 422, Wilmette, IL 60091; Dist. by: Chicago Review Press, 215 W. Ohio St., Chicago, IL 60610 Tel 312-644-5457.

Jemta Pr, *(Jemta Press),* 11313 Beech Daly, Redford Township, MI 48239 Tel 313-937-1986.

Jenfred Pr, *(Jenfred Press),* P.O. Box 767, Trinidad, CA 95570.

Jenkins, *(Jenkins Publishing Co.; 0-8363),* P.O. Box 2085, Austin, TX 78767 Tel 512-444-6616.

Jenrich Assoc, *(Jenrich Associates),* P.O. Box 805, Springfield, VA 22150; Moved, Left No Forwarding Address.

Jeppesen Sanderson, *(Jeppesen Sanderson; 0-88487),* Affiliate of Times Mirror Co., 55 Inverness Dr. E., Englewood, CO 80112 Tel 303-779-5757.

Jepson Herbarium, *(Jepson Herbarium; 0-935628),* Botany Dept., Univ. of California, Berkeley, Berkeley, CA 94720 Tel 415-642-2465; Dist. by: Lubrecht & Cramer, RFD 1, Box 227, Monticello, NY 12701 Tel 914-794-8539.

Jeremy Bks, *(Jeremy Books; 0-89877),* 5624 Lincoln Dr., Edina, MN 55436; Dist. by: Successful Living, Inc., 5624 Lincoln Dr., Edina, MN 55436.

Jesuit Bks, *(Jesuit Books; 0-913452),* Seattle University, Seattle, WA 98122 Tel 206-775-7545.

Jesuit Hist, *(Jesuit Historical Institute),* c/o Loyola Univ. Press, 3441 N. Ashland Ave., Chicago, IL 60657.

Jesuits Holy Cross, *(Jesuits of Holy Cross College, Inc.),* College of the Holy Cross, Worcester, MA 01610 Tel 617-793-2011.

Jesus-First, *(Jesus-First Pubs., Inc.; 0-9602440),* 1116-4th St., N.W, Ruskin, FL 33570 Tel 813-645-5726.

Jet'iquette, *(Jet'iquette; 0-9600786),* 510 Michigan Ave., Charlevoix, MI 49720 Tel 616-547-6443.

Jetsand Pr, *(Jetsand Press; 0-933374),* Box 17052, West Hartford, CT 06117.

Jewel Pubns, *(Jewel Pubns.; 0-917728),* 2417 Hazelwood Ave., Fort Wayne, IN 46805 Tel 219-483-6625.

Jewelers Circular, *(Jewelers' Circular-Keystone; 0-931744),* Chilton Way, Radnor, PA 19089 Tel 215-687-8200.

Jewish Bd Family, *(Jewish Board of Family & Children's Services, Inc.),* 120 W. 57th St., New York, NY 10019 Tel 212-582-9100.

Jewish Bk Council, *(Jewish Book Council; 0-914820),* 15 E. 26th St., New York, NY 10010 Tel 212-532-4949.

Jewish Braille Inst, *(Jewish Braille Institute of America, Inc.),* 110 E. 30th St., New York, NY 10016 Tel 212-889-2525.

Jewish Hist, *(Jewish Historical Society of New York, Inc.; 0-916790),* 8 W. 70th St., New York, NY 10023 Tel 212-873-0300.

Jewish Pubn, *(Jewish Publication Society of America; 0-8276),* 117 S. 17th St., Philadelphia, PA 19103 Tel 215-564-5925.

Jewish Recon, *(Jewish Reconstructionist Foundation; 0-910808),* 15 W. 86th St, New York, NY 10024 Tel 212-787-1500; Moved, Left No Forwarding Address.

JG Pr, *(JG Press; 0-932424),* Box 351, Emmaus, PA 18049 Tel 215-967-4010.

JH Pr, *(JH Press; 0-935672),* P.O. Box 294, Village Sta., New York, NY 10014.

Jifunza Educ, *(Jifunza Educational Pubns.; 0-931310),* 641 Dory Lane, Redwood City, CA 94065.

Jimora Assoc, *(Jimora Associated Pub. Co.; 0-918392),* MPO Box 7047, Chicago, IL 60680 Tel 312-994-4846; Formerly Named Associated Publishing Co.

JIR, *(Journal of Irreproducible Results, Inc.; 0-9605852),* 2405 Bond St., Park Forest South, IL 60466.

JJ Pub FL, *(JJ Publishing; 0-9604610),* 1312 Arthur St., Hollywood, FL 33019 Tel 305-929-3559.

JLJ Pubs, *(JLJ Pubs.; 0-937172),* 824 Shrine Rd., Springfield, OH 45504.

Jo-Jo Pubns, *(Jo-Jo Pubns.; 0-9602266),* 208 N. Sparrow Rd., Chesapeake, VA 23325.

Job Hunters Forum, *(Job Hunters Forum; 0-918350),* 132 Pinecrest Dr., Annapolis, MD 21403 Tel 301-268-6425.

Jobwatch, *(Jobwatch Press; 0-918422),* P. O. Box 439, Annandale, VA 22003.

Joby Bks, *(Joby Books),* Box 2603, San Rafael, CA 94901; Dist. by: Bookpeople, 2940 Seventh St., Berkeley, CA 94710 Tel 415-549-3033.

Jochum, *(Jochum, Helen Parker),* 79 Huntington Rd., Garden City, NY 11530; Dist. by: Skills, 24 S. Prospect St., Amherst, MA 01002 Tel 413-253-9500.

Joe D Johnson, *(Johnson, Joe Donald; 0-915564),* P.O. Box 553, Napa, CA 94558.

Joe Lane Pub, *(Joe Lane Publishing Co.; 0-9603378),* P.O. Box 2646, Evergreen, CO 80439 Tel 303-674-5314.

Johanna Bureau, *(Johanna Bureau for the Blind & Visually Handicapped, Inc.),* 30 W. Washington St., Suite 1600, Chicago, IL 60602 Tel 312-332-6076; Duplicating Service for Specific Titles Available.

Johannes, *(Johannes Press; 0-910810),* c/o Galerie St. Etienne, 24 W. 57th St., New York, NY 10019 Tel 212-245-6734.

Johannes Schwalm Hist, *(Johannes Schwalm Historical Assn., Inc.),* 4983 S. Sedgewick Rd., Lyndhurst, OH 44124.

John Barrow, *(Barrow, John G.; 0-9600010),* 4509 Crestway Dr., Austin, TX 78731 Tel 512-465-6378.

John Day, *(John Day Co., Inc.; 0-381),* C/O Harper & Row Pubs., 10 E. 53rd St., New York, NY 10022; Dist. by: Harper & Row Pubs., Keystone Industrial Park, Scranton, PA 18512. *Imprints:* JD-J (John Day Juvenile Books); JD-T (John Day Trade Books).

John Jay Pr, *(John Jay Press; 0-89444),* 444 W. 56th St., New York, NY 10019 Tel 212-489-3515.

John Knox, *(John Knox Press; 0-8042),* 341 Ponce De Leon Ave., N.E., Rm. 416, Atlanta, GA 30365 Tel 404-873-1531.

John Muir, *(Muir, John, Pubns.; 0-912528),* P.O. Box 613, Santa Fe, NM 87501 Tel 505-982-4078; Dist. by: Bookpeople, 2940 Seventh St., Berkeley, CA 94710.

John Pubs, *(John, Rae, Pubs.; 0-9605226; 0-939438),* 500 Main St., Drawer "S", Susanville, CA 96130.

John Tracy Clinic, *(Tracy, John, Clinic),* 806 W. Adams Blvd., Los Angeles, CA 90007 Tel 213-748-5481.

Johnny Inc
See K Diehl

Johnny Reads, *(Johnny Reads, Inc.; 0-910812),* P.O. Box 12834, St. Petersburg, FL 33733 Tel 813-867-7647.

Johns Hopkins, *(Johns Hopkins Univ. Press; 0-8018),* Baltimore, MD 21218 Tel 301-338-7861.

Johnsen, *(Johnsen Publishing Co.; 0-910814),* 1135 "R" St., Lincoln, NE 68508 Tel 402-432-0111; Out of Business.

Johnson & Johnson, *(Johnson & Johnson Baby Products Co.; 0-931562),* 220 Centennial Ave., Piscataway, NJ 08854.

Johnson Chi, *(Johnson Publishing Co., Inc.; 0-87485),* 820 S. Michigan Ave., Chicago, IL 60605 Tel 312-786-7657.

Johnson Colo, *(Johnson Publishing Co.; 0-933472),* P.O. Box 990, 1880 S. 57th Court, Boulder, CO 80301 Tel 303-443-1576.

Johnson Higgins, *(Johnson & Higgins; 0-9601248),* 95 Wall St., New York, NY 10005 Tel 212-482-5246.

Johnson NC, *(Johnson Publishing Co.; 0-930230),* P. O. Box 217, Murfreesboro, NC 27855.

Johnson Repr, *(Johnson Reprint Corp.; 0-384),* Subs. of Harcourt, Brace & Jovanovich, Inc., 111 Fifth Ave., New York, NY 10003 Tel 212-741-6800.

Johnson VA, *(Johnson Publishing Co., Inc.; 0-934572),* P.O. Box 192, Forest, VA 24551 Tel 804-525-4129.

Joint Comm Hosp, *(Joint Commission on Accreditation of Hospitals; 0-86688),* Dept. of Pubns., 875 N. Michigan Ave., Chicago, IL 60611 Tel 312-642-6061.

Jolean Pub Co, *(Jolean Publishing Co.; 0-934284),* P.O. Box 163, Arverne, NY 11692.

Jolex, *(Jolex, Inc.; 0-89149),* Dist. by: John Olson Co., 294 W. Oakland Ave., Oakland, NJ 07436 Tel 201-337-3355.

Jomeri, *(Jomeri Pubns.),* Dist. by: Bookpeople, 2940 Seventh St., Berkeley, CA 94710.

Jonathan David, *(Jonathan David Pubs., Inc.; 0-8246),* 68-22 Eliot Ave., Middle Village, NY 11379 Tel 212-456-8611.

Jonathan Pubns, *(Jonathan Pubns.; 0-9603348),* 660 Prospect Ave., Hartford, CT 06105.

Jones Intl, *(Jones International Ltd.; 0-935910),* 5275 DTC Parkway, No. 44, Englewood, CO 80111 Tel 303-740-9700.

Jones Med, *(Jones Medical Pubns.; 0-930010),* 355 Los Cerros Dr., Greenbrae, CA 94904 Tel 415-461-3749.

Jones Pub, *(Jones, Stan, Publishing, Inc.; 0-939936),* 3421 E. Mercer St., Seattle, WA 98112.

Jonsalvania, *(Jonsalvania Publishing Co.),* Russell Rd., Canton, NY 13617 Tel 315-386-4007.

Jordan & Co
See JCP Corp VA

Jordan Valley, *(Jordan Valley Heritage House; 0-939810),* 43502 Hwy. 226, Stayton, OR 97383 Tel 503-859-3144.

Jordan-Volpe Gall, *(Jordan-Volpe Gallery, The),* 457 W. Broadway, New York, NY 10012 Tel 212-533-3900; Dist. by: Peregrine Smith, Inc., P.O. Box 667, Layton, UT 84041.

Joseph Nichols, *(Joseph Nichols Publisher; 0-912484),* P.O. Box 2394, Tulsa, OK 74101 Tel 918-583-3390.

Joseph Pub Co, *(Joseph Publishing Co.; 0-915878),* P.O. Box 770, San Mateo, CA 94401 Tel 415-345-4100.

Jossey-Bass, *(Jossey-Bass Inc., Pubs.; 0-87589),* 433 California St., San Francisco, CA 94104 Tel 415-433-1740.

Journal Herald, *(Journal Herald, The; 0-938492),* 37 S. Ludlow St., Dayton, OH 45342.

Journal of the West, *(Journal of the West; 0-89745),* P.O. Box 1009, Manhattan, KS 66502 Tel 913-532-6733.

Journal Pubns, *(Journal Pubns., Inc.; 0-935676),* 6416 S. Western Ave., Whittier, CA 90606.

Journal Span Stud, *(Journal of Spanish Studies: Twentieth Century; 0-89294),* The University of Nebraska-Lincoln, Dept. of Modern Languages, Oldfather Hall, Lincoln, NE 68588 Tel 402-472-3745.

Journey Bks, *(Journey Books; 0-933156),* P.O. Box 100, Clarksville, MD 21029.

Journey Pr, *(Journey Press; 0-918572),* 1828 Virginia St., Berkeley, CA 94703 Tel 415-848-0311.

Journey Pubns, *(Journey Pubns.; 0-918038),* P.O. Box 423, Woodstock, NY 12498 Tel 914-679-2250.

Jove Pubns, *(Jove Pubns., Inc.; 0-515),* Div. of Berkley/Jove Publishing Group, 200 Madison Ave., New York, NY 10016 Tel 212-686-9820.

Joy-Co, *(Joy-Co Press; 0-9605984),* 2636 Burgener Blvd., San Diego, CA 92110 Tel 714-276-9760.

Joy Pr, *(Joy Press; 0-913662),* Big Sur, CA 93920 Tel 408-667-2200; Dist. by: Book People, 2940 Seventh St., Berkeley, CA 94710; Moved, Left No Forwarding Address.

Joy Pub Co, *(Joy Publishing Co.; 0-9601758),* P.O. Box 2532, Boca Raton, FL 33432 Tel 305-276-5879.

Joybug, *(Joybug Teaching Aids, Inc.; 0-931218),* P.O. Box 733, Parsons, KS 67357 Tel 316-421-0634.

Joyce Media, *(Joyce Media Inc.; 0-917002),* 8753 Shirley Ave., P.O. Box 458, Northridge, CA 91328 Tel 213-885-7181; Orders to: Sign Language Store, 8753 Shirley Ave., P.O. Box 458, Northridge, CA 91328 Tel 800-423-5413.

Joyce Motion Pict *See* Joyce Media

Joyce Pr, *(Joyce Press Inc.; 0-89325),* 7341 Clairemont Mesa Blvd., San Diego, CA 92111 Tel 714-565-6133.

Joyful Noise, *(Joyful Noise Productions, International; 0-936874),* 109 Minna St., Suite 153, San Francisco, CA 94105.

JP Pubns WI, *(JP Pubns; 0-9602978),* P.O. Box 41731, Madison, WI 53711 Tel 608-231-2373.

Jr Charity League, *(Junior Charity League, Inc.; 0-9602364),* P.O. Box 7138, Monroe, LA 71203 Tel 318-322-3863.

Jr League Amarillo, *(Junior League of Amarillo Texas, Inc., The; 0-9604102),* 1700 Polk, Amarillo, TX 79102.

Jr League Columbus, *(Junior League of Columbus, GA, Inc.),* 1440 Second Ave., Columbus, GA 31901.

Jr League Ft Lauderdale, *(Junior League of Fort Lauderdale; 0-9604158),* 2510 N.E. 15th Ave., Fort Lauderdale, FL 33305.

Jr League Lafayette, *(Junior League of Lafayette, The; 0-935032),* P.O. Box 52387, Oil Ctr Sta., Lafayette, LA 70505 Tel 318-233-2063.

Jr League Memphis, *(Junior League of Memphis, Inc.,The; 0-9604222),* 2711 Union Ave. Extended, Memphis, TN 38112.

Jr League Montclair-Newark, *(Junior League of Montclair-Newark, Inc.; 0-9605328),* P.O. Box 814, Upper Montclair, NJ 07043 Tel 201-746-2499.

Jr League New Orleans, *(Junior League of New Orleans, Inc.; 0-9604774),* 4319 Carondelet, New Orleans, LA 70115.

Jr League Rochester, *(Junior League of Rochester, Inc.; 0-9605612),* 33 S Washington St., Rochester, NY 14608.

Jr League San Jose, *(Junior League of San Jose, Inc.; 0-916286),* 19616 Farwell Ave., Saratoga, CA 95070 Tel 408-867-3254.

Jr League Shreveport, *(Junior League of Shreveport, Inc.; 0-9602246),* P.O. Box 4648, Shreveport, LA 71104 Tel 318-868-7866.

Jr League Spartanburg, *(Junior League of Spartanburg, S.C., Inc.),* P.O. Box 2881, Spartanburg, SC 29304 Tel 803-579-0079.

Jr League Tulsa, *(Junior League of Tulsa Pubns.),* 167 London Square, Tulsa, OK 74105 Tel 918-743-9767.

Jubilee Bks, *(Jubilee Books; 0-914300),* Box 1460, New York, NY 10001; Orders to: GPO Box 1460, New York, NY 10001.

Judaic Bk, *(Judaic Book Service; 0-917246),* 3726 Virden Ave., Oakland, CA 94619.

Judaic Heritage, *(Judaic Heritage Society),* 866 United Nations Plaza, New York, NY 10017.

Judaica Pr, *(Judaica Press, Inc.; 0-910818),* 521 Fifth Ave., New York, NY 10017 Tel 212-260-0520.

Judson, *(Judson Press; 0-8170),* Valley Forge, PA 19481 Tel 215-768-2111.

Judson Press Ga *See* One Candle

Judy, *(Judy Publishing Co.; 0-87702),* Main P.O., Box 5270, Chicago, IL 60680 Tel 312-787-7233.

Julian, *(Julian Press, Inc.),* ; Publisher Abbreviation Without Addresses Are for Titles That Are Out of Print. These Are Obsolete Abbreviations. Publisher Was Aquired by Crown.

Jungle Garden, *(Jungle Garden Press),* 47 Oak Rd., Fairfax, CA 94930 Tel 415-456-4884.

Junior League Mobile, *(Junior League of Mobile, Inc.; 0-9603054),* Recipe Jubilee, P.O. Box 7091, Mobile, AL 36607 Tel 205-343-4690.

Juniper, *(Juniper Press; 0-910822),* 41-15 44th St., Long Island City, NY 11104; Moved, Left No Forwarding Address.

Juniper *Imprint of* Fawcett

Juniper Eds, *(Juniper Editions; 0-912188),* P.O. Box 7, Manitou, CO 80829.

Juniper Hse, *(Juniper House; 0-931870),* P.O. Box 2094, Boulder, CO 80306 Tel 303-449-7757.

Juniper Maine, *(Juniper Press),* c/o Betts Bookstore, 35 Main St., Bangor, ME 04401.

Juniper Pr WI, *(Juniper Press; 0-910822),* 1310 Shorewood Dr., La Crosse, WI 54601 Tel 608-788-0096.

Juniper Pubs, *(Juniper Pubs.; 0-9605986),* P.O. Box 11872, Lexington, KY 40511 Tel 606-266-4675.

Junius Inc, *(Junius, Inc.; 0-9603932),* 842 Lombard St., Philadelphia, PA 19147 Tel 215-627-8298.

Junius-Vaughn, *(Junius-Vaughn Press, The; 0-940198),* P.O. Box 85, Fairview, NJ 07022.

Jupiter Bks, *(Jupiter Books; 0-935344),* 7300 Eades Ave., La Jolla, CA 92037.

Jupiter Pr, *(Jupiter Press; 0-933104),* P.O. Box 101, Lake Bluff, IL 60044 Tel 312-234-3997.

Just Above Midtown, *(Just Above Midtown, Inc.; 0-9605830),* 50 W. 57th St., New York, NY 10019 Tel 212-757-3442.

Justice Pr, *(Justice Press; 0-936802),* P.O. Box 16204, Tampa, FL 33617.

Justice Sys, *(Justice Systems Development, Inc.; 0-914526),* P.O. Box 681, Santa Cruz, CA 95061 Tel 408-423-1650.

Justice T Reason, *(Reason, Justice T., Pubns.; 0-9600322),* 616 N. 36th St., McAllen, TX 78501 Tel 516-686-8678; Moved, Left No Forwarding Address.

Juvenescent, *(Juvenescent Research Corp.; 0-9600148),* 807 Riverside Dr., New York, NY 10032 Tel 212-795-8765.

Juveniles *Imprint of* S&S

JWP Dev, *(JWP Development),* Box 2531, Culver City, CA 90230.

Jym Ent, *(Jym Enterprises),* P.O. Box 73, Batavia, OH 45103.

K & K Pubs, *(K & K Pubs; 0-9604218),* 216 N. Batavia Ave., Batavia, IL 60510 Tel 312-879-6214.

K Baikie, *(Baikie, Kenneth),* 1821 E. Glencove St., Mesa, AZ 85203 Tel 602-835-9399.

K C Pubns *See* KC Pubns

K Cain, *(Cain, Katherine; 0-9603188),* 14669 Big Basin Way, Saratoga, CA 95070.

K Diehl, *(Diehl, Kathryn; 0-9603552),* 554 N. McDonel, Lima, OH 45801 Tel 419-223-7207.

K E Schon, *(Schon, Kurt E., Ltd.; 0-9603880),* 510 Saint Louis St., New Orleans, LA 70130.

K G Saur, *(Saur, K. G., Publishing, Inc.; 0-89664),* 45 N. Broad St., Ridgewood, NJ 07450 Tel 201-652-6360.

K J Williams Pubns, *(Williams, Ken J., Pubns.; 0-9603742),* 881 Tenth Ave., Suite 4C, New York, NY 10019.

K Key Pubns, *(K Key Pubns.),* P.O. Box 4805, Washington, DC 20008.

K M Gentile, *(K.M. Gentile Publishing/Singing Wind Press; 0-935896),* 4164 W. Pine, St. Louis, MO 63108.

K R C Dev, *(KRC Development Council; 0-917440),* 212 Elm St., New Canaan, CT 06840 Tel 203-972-0401.

K R Smith, *(Smith, K. R.; 0-9601934),* 5234 Ivanhoe Place, N.E., Seattle, WA 98105.

K Riggs, *(Riggs, Karl A.),* Box 3333, Mississippi State, MS 39762 Tel 601-323-8889.

K Roberts, *(Roberts, Ken, Publishing Co.; 0-913602),* P.O. Box 151, Fitzwilliam, NH 03447 Tel 603-585-6612.

K Starosciak, *(Starosciak, Kenneth, Bookseller),* 117 Wilmot, San Francisco, CA 94115.

KaChunk Pr, *(KaChunk Press; 0-9604292),* Box 1043, Iowa City, IA 52244.

Kacdmon, *(Kaedmon Publishing Co.; 0-913002),* 150 Broadway, Suite 915, New York, NY 10038 Tel 212-267-2913.

Kagg Pr, *(Kagg Press; 0-912200),* 9910 Columbus Circle, Nw, Albuquerque, NM 87114 Tel 505-898-4541.

Kahn & Kahan, *(Kahn & Kahan Publishing Co., Inc.; 0-9604286),* 31 South St., P.O. Box 661, Morristown, NJ 07960.

Kalimat, *(Kalimat Press; 0-933770),* 10889 Wilshire Blvd., Suite 270, Los Angeles, CA 90024 Tel 213-478-0559.

Kallman, *(Kallman Publishing Co.; 0-910824),* 1614 W. University Ave., Box 14076, Gainesville, FL 32601 Tel 904-376-6066.

Kalmbach, *(Kalmbach Publishing Co.; 0-89024),* 1027 N. Seventh St., Milwaukee, WI 53233 Tel 414-272-2060.

Kalum Pr, *(Kalum Press; 0-937788),* 596 Joey Ave., El Cajon, CA 92020.

Kambrina, *(Kambrina; 0-9605742),* P.O. Box 1331, Newport, OR 97365.

Kanchenjunga Pr, *(Kanchenjunga Press; 0-913600),* 22 Rio Vista Lane, Red Bluff, CA 96080.

Kandylas Pr, *(Kandylas Press; 0-930694),* P.O. Box 321, Northgate Sta., Seattle, WA 98125.

Kanegis, *(Kanegis, James; 0-9600226),* 3907 Madison St., Hyattsville, MD 20781 Tel 301-699-5064.

Kaneshiro, *(Kaneshiro, Hansel S.; 0-9600670),* 1524 N. Hoyne Ave., Chicago, IL 60622 Tel 312-276-8024.

Kansas, *(Kansas Union Bookstore, Univ. of Kansas),* ; Publisher Abbreviation Without Addresses Are for Titles That Are Out of Print. These Are Obsolete Abbreviations.

Kansas St Hist, *(Kansas State Historical Society; 0-87726),* Memorial Bldg., 120 W. 10th St., Topeka, KS 66612 Tel 913-296-3251.

Kanthaka, *(Kanthaka Press; 0-916926),* P.O. Box 696, Brookline Village, MA 02147 Tel 617-734-8146.

Kapa, *(Kapa Associates Ltd.; 0-915870),* Pacific International Bldg., 677 Ala Moana Blvd., Honolulu, HI 96813 Tel 808-521-6398.

Kar Ben, *(Kar-Ben Copies, Inc.; 0-930494),* 11216 Empire Lane, Rockville, MD 20852 Tel 301-984-8733.

Karl Bern Pubs, *(Bern, Karl, Pubs.; 0-9601524),* 9939 Riviera Dr., Sun City, AZ 85351 Tel 602-933-0854.

Karlyn, *(Karlyn Publishing & Consulting),* P.O. Box 38125, Urbana, OH 43078.

Karneke, *(Karneke Pubs),* P.O. Box 3371, Santa Monica, CA 90404 Tel 213-826-5098; Moved, Left No Forwarding Address.

Karoma, *(Karoma Pubs., Inc.; 0-89720),* 3400 Daleview Dr., Ann Arbor, MI 48103 Tel 313-665-3331.

Karpat, *(Karpat Pub. Co., Inc.; 0-918570),* 1017 Fairfield Ave., Cleveland, OH 44113 Tel 216-696-3635.

Karwyn Ent, *(Karwyn Enterprises; 0-939938),* 17227 17th Ave. W., Lynnwood, WA 98036 Tel 206-743-0722.

Karz Howard *See* Karz Pub

Karz Pub, *(Karz Pubs.; 0-918294),* 320 W. 105th St., New York, NY 10025 Tel 212-663-9059.

Katahdin, *(Katahdin Press; 0-939212),* P.O. Box 231, Campbell, CA 95009.

Kauai Museum, *(Kauai Museum Association, Ltd.),* Box 248, Lihue, HI 96766.

Kaufman Hse, *(Kaufman House Pubs.; 0-9602500),* 366 Terrace Ave., Cincinnati, OH 45220 Tel 513-751-6381.

Kavanagh, *(Kavanagh, Peter, Hand Press; 0-914612),* 250 E. 30th St., New York, NY 10016 Tel 212-686-5099.

Kayak, *(Kayak; 0-87711),* 325 Ocean View Ave., Santa Cruz, CA 95062.

Kazi Pubns, *(Kazi Pubns.; 0-935782),* 1520 N. Wells St., Chicago, IL 60610 Tel 312-642-1291.

KC Pubns, *(KC Pubns.; 0-916122),* P.O. Box 14883, 2901 Industrial Rd., Las Vegas, NV 89114 Tel 702-731-3123.

KDVHE Pubs, *(KDVHE Pubs; 0-932810),* P.O. Box 6788, Chicago, IL 60680.

Kearney, *(Kearney Publishing Co.; 0-9604688),* 2515 Peachtree Lane, Northbrook, IL 60062 Tel 312-732-6307.

Keats, *(Keats Publishing, Inc.; 0-87983),* 36 Grove St., P.O. Box 876, New Canaan, CT 06840 Tel 203-966-8721.

Keeble Pr, *(Keeble Press, The; 0-933144),* 3634 Winchell Rd., Shaker Heights, OH 44122.

Keithwood, *(Keithwood Publishing Co.),* 6835 Greenway Ave., Philadelphia, PA 19142 Tel 215-727-0883.

KEL Pubns, *(KEL Pubns.; 0-9605710),* 443 Schley Rd., Annapolis, MD 21401.

Keller-Burns & McGuirk, *(Keller, Burns & McGuirk Publishing Co.; 0-9602506),* c/o James P. Gould, Colony Park Bldg., 37th & Woodland, West Des Moines, IA 50265 Tel 515-225-3122.

Kelley, *(Kelley, Augustus M., Pubs.; 0-678),* 1140 Broadway, Room 901, New York, NY 10001 Tel 212-685-7202; Orders to: 300 Fairfield Rd., P.O. Box 1308, Fairfield, NJ 07006 Tel 201-575-7338. *Imprints:* Baker Library (Baker Library); Reference Bk Pubs (Reference Book Pubs.).

Kellogg, *(Kellogg, Edward P., Jr.; 0-9603914),* 1755 Trinity Ave., No. 79, Walnut Creek, CA 94596 Tel 415-937-4841; Orders to: EHUD International Language Foundation, P.O. Box 2082, Dollar Ranch Sta., Walnut Creek, CA 94595.

Kells Ltd, *(Kells, Ltd.),* P.O. Box 871, Anderson, SC 29621 Tel 803-224-0029.

Kelly, *(Kelly, Thomas; 0-910832),* 227 Midland Ave., East Orange, NJ 07017 Tel 201-672-9238.

Kelsey Pub, *(Kelsey Publishing; 0-9605824),* 310 E. 950 S., Springville, UT 84663 Tel 801-489-6666.

Kelsey St Pr, *(Kelsey St. Press; 0-932716),* P.O. Box 9235, Berkeley, CA 94709 Tel 415-841-2044.

Kelso, *(Kelso Manufacturing Co.),* 651 N. Broadway, Greenville, MS 38701.

Keltner, *(Keltner Statistical Service, Inc.),* 1004 Baltimore Ave., Kansas City, MO 64105 Tel 816-421-8488.

Kempler Inst, *(Kempler Institute),* P.O. Box 1692, Costa Mesa, CA 92626.

Kemsley Pub
See Foot Trails

Ken-Bks, *(Ken-Books; 0-913164),* 1932 Ocean Ave., San Francisco, CA 94127 Tel 415-584-0799.

Kenan Pr *Imprint of* S&S

Kendall-Hunt, *(Kendall/Hunt Publishing Co.; 0-8403),* 2460 Kerper Blvd., Dubuque, IA 52001 Tel 319-588-1451.

Kendall Whaling, *(Kendall Whaling Museum; 0-937854),* P.O. Box 297, Sharon, MA 02067 Tel 617-784-5642.

Kenedy, *(Kenedy, P. J. & Sons),* Subs. of Macmillan Publishing Co., 866 Third Ave., New York, NY 10022 Tel 212-935-2000; Orders to: Macmillan Co., Riverside, NJ 08075.

Kenilworth, *(Kenilworth Press; 0-9603876),* 421 W. Grant Ave., Eau Claire, WI 54701 Tel 715-832-2161.

Kenmore, *(Kenmore Press; 0-918298),* P.O. Box 773-C, Pasadena, CA 91104 Tel 213-798-8078; Moved, Left No Forwarding Address.

Kennard Carter, *(Carter, Kennard),* 160 H V Cove, Dover, DE 19901.

Kennedy Gall, *(Kennedy Galleries; 0-87920),* 40 W. 57th St., New York, NY 10019.

Kennedy Pub, *(Kennedy Publishing; 0-9605088),* P.O. Box 2, Chatsworth, CA 91311 Tel 213-883-7939.

Kennikat, *(Kennikat Press, Corp.; 0-8046),* 90 S. Bayles Ave., Port Washington, NY 11050 Tel 516-883-0570. *Imprints:* Natl U (National University Publications).

Kensington, *(Kensington Press; 0-89626),* 4614 Edgeware Rd., San Diego, CA 92116.

Kent Harbridge, *(Kent-Harbridge, Inc.; 0-932812),* 1619 Traske Rd., Encinitas, CA 92024.

Kent Popular, *(Kent Popular Press; 0-933522),* P.O. Box 715, Kent, OH 44240.

Kent Pub Co, *(Kent Publishing Co.; 0-534),* Div. of Wadsworth, Inc., 20 Providence St., Boston, MA 02116 Tel 617-542-1629; Orders to: 10 Davis Dr., Belmont, CA 94002 Tel 415-595-2350.

Kent Pubns, *(Kent Pubns.; 0-917458),* 18301 Halstead St., Northridge, CA 91325 Tel 213-349-5088.

Kent St U Pr, *(Kent State Univ. Press; 0-87338),* Kent, OH 44242 Tel 216-672-7913.

Kentucky Hist, *(Kentucky Historical Society; 0-916968),* Old-State-House, Box H, Frankfort, KY 40602 Tel 502-564-3016.

Kenyon, *(Kenyon Pubns.; 0-934286),* 361 Pin Oak Lane, Westbury, NY 11590 Tel 516-333-3236; Dist. by: G. Schirmer, Inc., 866 Third Ave., New York, NY 10022 Tel 212-935-5636.

Kephart Comm Inc
See Alexandria Hse

Kepley, *(Kepley, Ray R.; 0-9604248),* Rt. 2 Box 128A, Ulysses, KS 67880.

Keramos Bks, *(Keramos Books; 0-935066),* Subs. of Westwood Ceramic Supply Co., P.O. Box 2305, Bassett, CA 91746 Tel 213-330-0631; 14400 Lomitas Ave., City of Industry, CA 91746.

Kerr, *(Kerr Printing Co.),* 458 E. King St., Chambersburg, PA 17201 Tel 717-263-1015.

Kerr Assoc, *(Kerr Associates, Inc.; 0-937890),* 1942 Irving Ave., S., Minneapolis, MN 55403 Tel 612-374-5438.

Kesend Pub Co
See Kesend Pub Ltd

Kesend Pub Ltd, *(Kesend, Michael, Publishing, Ltd.; 0-935576),* 1025 Fifth Ave., New York, NY 10028 Tel 212-249-5150.

Kesher, *(Kesher Press; 0-9602394),* 1817 21 Ave. S., Nashville, TN 37212.

Key *Imprint of* B&N

Key Bk Serv, *(Key Book Service, Inc.; 0-934636),* 425 Asylum St., Bridgeport, CT 06610 Tel 203-334-2165.

Key Bks, *(Key Books),* Dist. by: Associated Booksellers, 147 McKinley Ave., Bridgeport, CT 06606.

Key Curr Proj, *(Key Curriculum Project; 0-913684),* P.O. Box 2304, Berkeley, CA 94702 Tel 415-548-2304.

Key Ray Pub, *(Key Ray Publishing; 0-930678),* Box 196, Osseo, MN 55369.

Key West Bk, *(Key West Book & Card Co.),* 534-6 Fleming St., Key West, FL 33040.

Keyline Pubs, *(Keyline Pubs.),* Elizabeth, CO 80107; Orders to: Loren Fay, 87 Edgewood Ave., Albany, NY 12203.

Keystone, *(Keystone Books),* Div. of W. H. Sadlier, Inc., 11 Park Place, New York, NY 10007.

Keystone Pubns, *(Keystone Pubns., Inc.; 0-912126),* 1657 Broadway, 2nd Fl., New York, NY 10019 Tel 212-582-2254.

Khaneghah & Maktab, *(Khaneghah & Maktab of Malekenia Naseralishah; 0-917220),* P.O. Box 456, New York, NY 10023 Tel 212-877-2899.

Khaniqahi-Nimatullahi, *(Khaniqahi Nimatullahi Pubns.; 0-933546),* 306 W. 11th St., New York, NY 10014 Tel 212-924-7739.

Kickapoo, *(Kickapoo Press; 0-933180),* P.O. Box 1443, Peoria, IL 61655.

Kids Special, *(Kids Come in Special Flavors Co.),* Box 562, Forest Park Sta., Dayton, OH 45405.

Kienast, *(Kienast, Gunter),* 11112 Dale Ave., Cleveland, OH 44111.

Kiewit Comput, *(Kiewit Computation Center; 0-89580),* Dartmouth College, Hanover, NH 03755 Tel 603-646-2643.

Killy-Moon Pr, *(Killy-Moon Press; 0-9601820),* 3711 W. 230th St., No. 100, Torrance, CA 90505 Tel 213-374-8504.

Kiltie, *(Kiltie, Ordean, & Co.),* 2445 Fairfield, A201, Ft. Wayne, IN 46807 Tel 219-745-9139.

Kimbell Art, *(Kimbell Art Musuem; 0-912804),* Will Rogers Rd., W., P.O. Box 9440, Fort Worth, TX 76107 Tel 817-332-8451.

Kindinger, *(Kindinger, Michael),* 931 W. 3rd Ave., Columbus, OH 43216 Tel 614-294-3227.

Kindred Pr, *(Kindred Press),* Box L, Hillsboro, KS 67063 Tel 316-947-3966.

King, *(King, Dale Stuart, Pub.; 0-912762),* 432 E. Mohave Dr., No. 5 Rear, Tucson, AZ 85705 Tel 602-888-2569.

King & Cowen, *(King & Cowen),* 299 Park Ave., New York, NY 10017; Moved, Left No Forwarding Address.

King & Mary, *(King & Mary; 0-9601890),* 4709 Comita, Fort Worth, TX 76132 Tel 817-292-1295.

King Pubns, *(King Pubns.; 0-917676),* P.O. Box 19332, Washington, DC 20036 Tel 202-234-1681.

Kingdom, *(Kingdom Press; 0-910840),* 105 Chestnut Hill Rd., Amherst, NH 03031 Tel 603-673-3208.

Kings Court, *(King's Court Communications, Inc.; 0-89139),* 590 Pearl Rd., Box 224, Brunswick, OH 44212 Tel 216-273-2100.

Kings Farspan, *(King's Farspan, Inc.; 0-932814),* 1473 S. La Luna Ave., Ojai, CA 93023 Tel 805-646-2928.

Kings Pr
See Kings Farspan

Kingsfield, *(Kingsfield Publishing Co.; 0-938494),* 10405 Town & Country Way, Suite 100, Houston, TX 77024.

Kinship Krafts, *(Kinship Krafts, Inc.; 0-933274),* Box 607, Montclair, NJ 07042.

Kinur Pub, *(Kinur Publishing; 0-9602318),* 345 Franklin, San Francisco, CA 94102.

Kirban, *(Kirban, Salem, Inc.; 0-912582),* 2117 Kent Rd., Huntingdon Valley, PA 19000 Tel 215-947-1330.

Kirin Bks & Art, *(Kirin Books & Art; 0-935034),* 4620 N. Pegram St., Alexandria, VA 22304 Tel 703-751-3141.

Kirk Pr, *(Kirk Press),* 1811 Hammond Ave., Superior, WI 54880.

Kirkbride Bible, *(Kirkbride, B. B., Bible Co. Inc. 0-934854),* 126 W. Vermont St., P.O. Box 606, Indianapolis, IN 46204 Tel 317-634-3252.

Kitaab Pr, *(Kitaab Press),* P.O. Box 690, Wayneburg, PA 15370.

Kitchen Harvest, *(Kitchen Harvest Press; 0-917234),* 3N 681 Bittersweet Dr., St. Charles, IL 60174 Tel 312-584-4084.

Kitchen Sink, *(Kitchen Sink Enterprises; 0-87816),* 114 Washington St., Princeton, WI 54968 Tel 414-295-3972.

Kjellberg & Sons, *(Kjellberg & Sons, Inc.; 0-912868),* 24W770 Geneva Rd., Wheaton, IL 60187 Tel 312-653-2244.

Kjos, *(Kjos, Neil A., Music Co.; 0-910842; 0-8497),* 4382 Jutland Dr., San Diego, CA 92117 Tel 714-270-9800.

Klassen, *(Klassen, Beatrice C. Harris),* P.O. Box 794, La Conner, WA 98257.

Kleinpell, *(Kleinpell, George J.; 0-9600190),* 4729 Pearl Rd., Cleveland, OH 44109 Tel 216-749-6274.

Kleinsinger, *(Kleinsinger, Irene J.; 0-9605146),* 16 Holbrooke Rd., White Plains, NY 10605.

Kline, *(Kline, Charles H., & Co., Inc.; 0-917148),* 330 Passaic Ave., Dept. 39, Fairfield, NJ 07006 Tel 201-227-6262.

KLM Butterworth, *(Butterworth, Katharine L. M.),* 431 Red Oak Lane, Rochester, MI 48063.

Klock & Klock, *(Klock & Klock Christian Pubs.; 0-86524),* 2527 Girard Ave. N., Minneapolis, MN 55411 Tel 612-522-2244.

KLONH Bks, *(KLONH Books),* 1795 Chestnut, San Francisco, CA 94123; Moved, Left No Fowarding Address.

Klutz Enterprises
See Klutz Pr

Klutz Pr, *(Klutz Press; 0-932592),* P.O. Box 2992, Stanford, CA 94305 Tel 415-857-0888.

Kluwer Boston, *(Kluwer Boston, Inc.),* 160 Old Derby St., Hingham, MA 02043 Tel 617-749-5262.

KMB Pubns, *(KMB Pubns.; 0-9603522),* P.O. Box 2511, Lancaster, CA 93534.

KMG Pubns OR, *(KMG Pubns.; 0-938928),* 195 Cambridge St., Ashland, OR 97520.

KMS Pr CO, *(KMS Press),* P.O. Box 6516, Denver, CO 80206.

Knapp
See EDITS Pubs

Knapp Pr, *(Knapp Press, The; 0-89535),* Div. of Knapp Communications Corp., 5900 Wilshire Blvd., Los Angeles, CA 90036 Tel 213-937-3454.

Knauff, *(Knauff, Thomas),* Julian, PA 16844.

Knife Digest, *(Knife Digest),* Dist. by: Ten Speed Press, P.O. Box 7123, Berkeley, CA 94707 Tel 415-845-8414.

Knoedler, *(Knoedler Publishing Inc.; 0-937608),* 19 E. 70th St., New York, NY 10021.

Knollwood Pub, *(Knollwood Publishing Co.; 0-915614),* P.O. Box 735, 513 Benson Ave. E., Willmar, MN 56201 Tel 612-235-4950.

Knopf, *(Knopf, Alfred A., Inc.; 0-394),* Subs. of Random House, Inc., 201 E. 50th St., New York, NY 10022 Tel 212-757-2600; Orders to: 400 Hahn Rd., Westminster, MD 21157. *Imprints:* KnopfC (Knopf College Department).

KnopfC *Imprint of* Knopf

Know How, *(Know How Pubns.; 0-910846),* Box 7126, Landscape Sta., Berkeley, CA 94717 Tel 415-526-5400.

Know Inc, *(Know, Inc.; 0-912786),* P.O. Box 86031, Pittsburgh, PA 15221 Tel 412-241-2844.

Knowledge Bank, *(Knowledge Bank Pubs., Inc.),* P.O. Box 2364, Falls Church, VA 22042.

Knowledge Indus, *(Knowledge Industry Pubns.; 0-914236; 0-86729),* 701 Westchester Ave., White Plains, NY 10604 Tel 914-328-9157. *Imprints:* ASIS (American Society for Information Science).

Knowles, *(Knowles, Alison; 0-914162),* 122 Spring St., New York, NY 10012.

Knox Busn, *(Knox Business Book Co.; 0-910848),* 321 Wesley Ave., Oak Park, IL 60302 Tel 312-386-6807.

Kober Pr, *(Kober Press, The; 0-915034),* P.O. Box 2194, San Francisco, CA 94126 Tel 415-397-1529.

Kobro Pubns, *(Kobro Pubns., Inc.; 0-9604676),* 192 Lexington Ave., New York, NY 10016.

Kodansha, *(Kodansha International, Ltd.; 0-87011),* 10 E. 53rd St., New York, NY 10022; Dist. by: Harper & Row Pubns., Inc., Keystone Industrial Park, Scranton, PA 18512.

Koheleth Pub, *(Koheleth Publishing Co.; 0-913964),* 750 Gonzalez Dr., San Francisco, CA 94132; Moved, Left No Forwarding Address.

Kokono, *(Kokono; 0-916956),* 540 Discovery Bay Blvd., Byron, CA 94514 Tel 415-634-5710.

Konglomerati, *(Konglomerati Florida Foundation for Literature & the Book Arts, Inc.; 0-916906),* P.O. Box 5001, Gulfport, FL 33737 Tel 813-323-0386.

Korakas-Roberts-Kirby, *(Korakas, Roberts & Kirby),* 600 N.W. 46th St., Oklahoma City, OK 73118.

Korea Devel Inst *Imprint of* **U Pr of Hawaii**

Korn, *(Korn, Alfred, Jr.; 0-917498),* 324 Coolidge Dr., Kennilworth, NJ 07033.

Kosciuszko, *(Kosciuszko Foundation, Inc.; 0-917004),* 15 E. 65th St., New York, NY 10021 Tel 212-734-2130.

KOSMOS, *(KOSMOS; 0-916426),* 381 Arlington St., San Francisco, CA 94131 Tel 415-928-4332.

Kosmos
  See KOSMOS

KP Med, *(K/P Medical Systems),* P.O. Box 8900, Stockton, CA 95208 Tel 209-466-6761.

Kraemer, *(Kraemer, Elsa; 0-9600526),* 93-41 222nd St., Queens Village, NY 11428 Tel 212-468-4117; Moved, Left No Fowarding Address.

Krag Pubns, *(Krag Pubns.),* 1217-8th St., S.E., Minneapolis, MN 55414

Kramer Pub, *(Kramer Publishing, Inc.; 0-914912),* P.O. Box 4077, Rochester, NY 14610.

Kramerbks Dist, *(Kramerbooks Distributors, Ltd.),* 2260 25th Place, N.E., Washington, DC 20018 Tel 202-526-0558.

Kraus Intl, *(Kraus International; 0-527),* Div. of Kraus-Thomson Organization Ltd., Rte. 100, Millwood, NY 10546 Tel 914-762-2200.

Kraus Repr, *(Kraus Reprint; 0-527),* U.S. Div. of Kraus-Thomson Organization, Ltd., Rte. 100, Millwood, NY 10546 Tel 914-762-2200.

Krause Pubns, *(Krause Pubns., Inc.; 0-87341),* 700 E. State St., Iola, WI 54945 Tel 715-445-2214.

Kregel, *(Kregel Pubns.; 0-8254),* P.O. Box 2607, Grand Rapids, MI 49501 Tel 616-459-9444. *Imprints:* RBDH (Religious Book Discount House Pubns.).

Kreitman Gallery
  See Kreitman Pub

Kreitman Pub, *(Kreitman Publishing, Inc.; 0-935492),* 9665 Wilshire Blvd., Suite 410, Beverly Hills, CA 90212 Tel 213-858-1048.

Krieger, *(Krieger, Robert E., Pub. Co., Inc.; 0-88275; 0-89874),* P.O. Box 9542, Melbourne, FL 32901 Tel 305-724-9542.

Krishna Pr, *(Krishna Press),* Div. of Gordon Press, P.O. Box 459, Bowling Green Sta., New York, NY 10004.

Krohn & Assocs, *(Krohn, Barbara, & Associates),* Orders to: Madrona Publishers, Inc., 2116 Western Ave., Seattle, WA 98121 Tel 206-624-6840.

Kronos Pr, *(Kronos Press; 0-917994),* Glassboro State College, Glassboro, NJ 08028 Tel 609-445-6048.

Kruzas Assoc, *(Kruzas, Anthony T., Associates),* 1810 Longshore Dr., Ann Arbor, MI 48103 Tel 313-665-7189; Dist. by: Gale Research Co., Book Tower, Detroit, MI 48226 Tel 313-961-2242.

KSIA, *(Korean Studies Institute in America; 0-918972),* 13 Forrest Ct., E. Grand Forks, MN 56721 Tel 218-773-9484.

KSU, *(Kansas State Univ.),* Orders to: Library Publications, Kansas State Univ. Library, Manhattan, KS 66506.

Ktav, *(Ktav Publishing House, Inc.; 0-87068),* 75 Varick St., New York, NY 10013 Tel 212-966-6980. *Imprints:* HUC Pr (Hebrew Union College Press).

KTO Pr
  See Kraus Intl

Kudzu-Ivy, *(Kudzu-Ivy; 0-9605142),* P.O. Box 52743, Atlanta, GA 30355.

Kukla Pr, *(Kukla Press),* 855 Morse Ave., Elk Grove Village, IL 60007; Dist. by: Common Sense Ltd., P.O. Box 353, Des Plaines, IL 60016.

Kulchur Foun, *(Kulchur Foundation; 0-936538),* 888 Park Ave., New York, NY 10021 Tel 212-988-5193.

Kumarian Pr, *(Kumarian Press; 0-931816),* 29 Bishop Rd., West Hartford, CT 06119.

Kummer, *(Kummer, Jerome M., M.D.; 0-9600054),* Drawer 769, Santa Monica, CA 90406; Moved, Left No Forwarding Address.

Kurios Found, *(Kurios Foundation; 0-932210),* P.O. Box 946, Bryn Mawr, PA 19010 Tel 215-527-4923.

Kurios Pr, *(Kurios Press; 0-916588),* P.O. Box 946, Bryn Mawr, PA 19010 Tel 215-527-4635.

Kurzweil, *(Kurzweil Computer Products, Inc.),* 33 Cambridge Parkway, Cambridge, MA 02142 Tel 617-864-4700; Kurzweil Reading & Data Entry Machines Available for Purchase.

Kusel, *(Kusel, George; 0-9604476),* 600 Lakevue Dr., Willow Grove, PA 19090.

Kwik Sew, *(Kwik Sew Pattern Co., Inc.; 0-913212),* 300 Sixth Ave. N., Minneapolis, MN 55401 Tel 612-339-9348.

Kylix Pr, *(Kylix Press; 0-914408),* 1485 Maywood, Ann Arbor, MI 48103 Tel 313-761-5399.

L A Dexter, *(Dexter, Lincoln A.; 0-9601210),* 4 Meadow View Rd., Wilbraham, MA 01095 Tel 413-596-4668.

L A Pop, *(L. A. Pop Books),* Box 24941, Los Angeles, CA 90024 Tel 213-466-7127; Moved, Left No Forwarding Address.

L Alcaro, *(Alcaro, Lucia),* 80 Rock Hill Rd., Clifton, NJ 07013; Publisher Deceased.

L Amiel Pub, *(Amiel, Leon, Pub.; 0-8148),* 31 W. 46th St., New York, NY 10036 Tel 212-575-0010.

L & A Winokur
  See Joy Pub Co

L C Bryant, *(Bryant, Lawrence C.),* 467 Palmetto Pkwy., N.E., Orangeburg, SC 29115 Tel 803-536-1305.

L Corcoran, *(Corcoran, Lawrence),* P.O. Box 195, Sturgeon Bay, WI 54235.

L D Headley, *(Headley, Lynn D., Assocs.),* P.O. Box 890, West Chester, PA 19380.

L D Manning, *(Manning, Lynda D., & Associates; 0-9604062),* P.O. Box 872, Temple, TX 76501.

L De Waters, *(DeWaters, Lillian, Pubns.),* Old Greenwich, CT 06870 Tel 203-637-0658.

L Dills, *(Dills, Lanie; 0-916744),* Dist. by: Louis J. Martin & Associates, Inc., 95 Madison Ave., New York, NY 10016.

L E Edwards, *(Edwards, Lowell E.; 0-936024),* P.O. Box 255714, Sacramento, CA 95825.

L Erlbaum Assocs, *(Erlbaum, Lawrence, Assocs., Inc.; 0-89859),* 365 Broadway, Hillsdale, NJ 07642 Tel 201-666-4110.

L F Greer
  See Plumbing Pubns

L F Vogel, *(Vogel, Leo F.),* Star Rte. Box 324, Connell, WA 99326 Tel 509-234-2629.

L Farnol Group, *(Farnol, Lynn, Group, Inc., The; 0-9604002),* 104 E. 78th St., New York, NY 10021 Tel 212-988-3920; Dist. by: Drama Book Specialists (Pubs.), 150 W. 52nd St., New York, NY 10019 Tel 212-582-1475.

L Gerlinger, *(Gerlinger, Lorena),* 4666 Pratt Rd., Hadley, MI 48440 Tel 313-797-4833.

L Gray Pub, *(Gray, Lee, Publishing; 0-9603976),* 187 James Ave., Red Bluff, CA 96080.

L H Richardson, *(Richardson, Lenore Hennessey; 0-9602958),* Box 281, Berkeley, CA 94701.

L H Smith, *(Smith, Leonard H., Jr.),* P.O. Box 6745, Clearwater, FL 33518 Tel 813-581-4444.

L Henry, *(Henry, Leon, Inc.),* 455 Central Ave., Scarsdale, NY 10583 Tel 914-723-3176.

L J Fry, *(Fry, L. John; 0-9600984),* 1223 N. Nopal St., Santa Barbara, CA 93103 Tel 805-965-6891.

L J Martin, *(Martin, Louis J., & Associates, Inc.; 0-916800),* 95 Madison Ave., New York, NY 10016 Tel 212-725-2157.

L Jones, *(Jones, Lowell; 0-9602074),* 11832 Brookmont Dr., Maryland Heights, MO 63043.

L Kempfer, *(Kempfer, Lester L.),* P.O. Box 317, Marysville, OH 43040.

L Lawler, *(Lawler, Louise; 0-931706),* 407 Greenwich St., New York, NY 10013.

L M Davis, *(Davis, Leonard M.),* Dist. by: Argus Books, 2741 Riverside Blvd., Sacramento, CA 95818.

L McMaster, *(McMaster, Linda, Ms),* War Cycles Institute, P.O. Box 1673, Kalispell, MT 59901.

L Mahan
  See Marco Polo

L Mark Lib, *(Mark, Lynn, Library; 0-918322),* 279 E. 44th St., No. 9H, New York, NY 10017 Tel 212-697-4379.

L Maynard, *(Maynard, Louis),* 5922 S. Sunnylane Rd., Oklahoma City, OK 73135 Tel 405-799-2148.

L O King, *(King, LeRoy O., Jr.; 0-9600938),* 4815 Allencrest, Dallas, TX 75234 Tel 214-239-1280.

L Olds, *(Olds, Lee),* P.O. Box 40731, San Francisco, CA 94110; Dist. by: Book People, 2940 Seventh St., Berkeley, CA 94710; Moved, Left No Forwarding Address.

L Oliver Bk, *(Oliver, Lawrence, Book),* 815 Armada Terrace, San Diego, CA 92106.

L Orr, *(Orr, Leonard),* Orders to: Rebirth America, 301 Lyon St., San Francisco, CA 94117 Tel 415-929-1743.

L P Pubns, *(L P Pubns.; 0-916192),* P.O. Box 7601, San Diego, CA 92107 Tel 714-225-0133.

L Pubns, *(L Pubns.; 0-917824),* 34 Fransiscan Way, Kensington, CA 94707.

L R Frank, *(Frank, Leonard Roy; 0-9601376),* 2300 Webster St., San Francisco, CA 94115 Tel 415-922-3029.

L Rosenhouse, *(Rosenhouse, Leo),* 3846 Bartley Dr., Sacramento, CA 95822.

L Shogren Quilt
  See Pieceful Pleasures

L Sweetman, *(Sweetman, Leonard; 0-9600518),* 1712 Fisherville Rd., Coatesville, PA 19320.

L Unser, *(Unser, LaVerne),* P.O. Box Γ, Garden Grove, CA 92642.

L V D'Agostino, *(D'Agostino, Lena V.; 0-9601076),* Davenport Center, New York, NY 13751 Tel 607-278-5808.

L V Fay, *(Fay, Loren V.),* 87 Edgewood Ave., Albany, NY 12203.

L Victor Pr, *(Victor, Leo, Press),* 2203 Brandenburg Way, King of Prussia, PA 19406.

L Volan, *(Volan, Leon),* 15 Western Shore Lane, San Francisco, CA 94115 Tel 415-929-7659.

L Wiley, *(Wiley, Leonard; 0-911742),* 2927 S.E. 75th Ave., Portland, OR 97206 Tel 503-777-3645.

L Winner, *(Winner, Lewis; 0-87429),* 301 Almeria, P.O. Box 343788, Coral Gables, FL 33134 Tel 305-446-8193.

L Ziman, *(Ziman, Larry; 0-933456),* P.O. Box 67485, Los Angeles, CA 90067.

La Belle, *(La Belle, Gary),* 19 Sterling Place, Glen Rock, NJ 07452.

LA Bk Pub, *(Los Angeles Book Pubs., Co.),* 9606 Santa Monica Blvd., Beverly Hills, CA 90210.

La Car Pub, *(La Car Publishing Co.),* 2109 Broadway, New York, NY 10023.

LA Co Art Mus, *(Los Angeles County Museum of Art; 0-87587),* 5905 Wilshire Blvd., Los Angeles, CA 90036 Tel 213-937-4250.

La Grange, *(La Grange Press; 0-931324),* 7732 Guenivere Way, Citrus Heights, CA 95610 Tel 916-967-7997.

La Leche, *(La Leche League International, Inc.; 0-912500),* 9616 Minneapolis Ave., Franklin Park, IL 60131 Tel 312-455-7730.

La Maison, *(La Maison Du Dictionnaire; 2-85608),* Dist. by: Marlin Pubns. International, Inc., 485 Fifth Ave., New York, NY 10017.

La Monte Crape, *(La Monte Crape Publisher),* 412 N. Washington St., Butler, PA 16001.

LA Pub Co, *(Los Angeles Publishing Co.; 0-913924),* P. O. Box 5135, Sherman Oaks, CA 91413 Tel 805-259-4749; Moved, Left No Forwarding Address.

La Siesta, *(La Siesta Press; 0-910856),* P.O. Box 406, Glendale, CA 91209 Tel 213-244-9305.

La State U Pr, *(Louisiana State Univ. Press; 0-8071),* Baton Rouge, LA 70803 Tel 504-388-2071.

Lab Data Control, *(Laboratory Data Control; 0-9504833),* P.O. Box 10235, Interstate Industrial Park, Riviera Beach, FL 33404.

Labor Arts, *(Labor Arts Books; 0-9603888),* 1064 Amherst St., Buffalo, NY 14216 Tel 716-873-4131.

Labrinthos, *(Labrinthos),* 6355 Green Valley Circle, Culver City, CA 90230.

Labyrinth Pr, *(Labyrinth Press, Inc., The; 0-939464),* P.O. Box 2124, Durham, NC 27701 Tel 919-489-5620.

Lacis Pubns, *(Lacis Pubns; 0-916896),* 2990 Adeline St., Berkeley, CA 94703 Tel 415-843-7178.

Lacon Pubs, *(Lacon Pubs.; 0-930344),* Rte. 1, P.O. Box 15, Harrison, ID 83833 Tel 208-689-3467.

Laddin Pr, *(Laddin Press; 0-913806),* 2 Park Ave., New York, NY 10016 Tel 212-532-4384.

Laidlaw, *(Laidlaw Brothers; 0-8445),* Div. of Doubleday & Co., Inc., Thatcher & Madison, River Forest, IL 60305 Tel 312-369-5320.

Lake, *(Lake, A. V., & Co.; 0-910860),* P.O. Box 1595, Beverly Hills, CA 90213 Tel 213-271-4386.

Lake County, *(Lake County Press),* Box 669, Ronan, MT 59864; Dist. by: Montana Writers, Inc., Box 21133, Billings, MT 59104.

Lake Erie Col Pr, *(Lake Erie College Press; 0-935518),* Lake Erie College, Painesville, OH 44077 Tel 216-352-3361.

Lakeside Chart, *(Lakeside-Charter Books; 0-918206),* 5466 S. Everett, Chicago, IL 60615 Tel 312-955-0521.

Lakstun Pr, *(Lakstun Press; 0-9603706),* P.O. Box 429, Bensalem, PA 19020.

Lambert Bk, *(Lambert Book House, Inc.; 0-89315),* 133 Kings Hwy., Box 4007, Shreveport, LA 71104 Tel 318-861-3140.

Lambert Pubns, *(Lambert Pubns., Inc.; 0-939304),* 1000 Connecticut Ave. NW, Washington, DC 20036.

Lambeth, *(Lambeth, James; 0-9601678),* 1591 Clark St., Fayetteville, AR 72701.

Lame Johnny, *(Lame Johnny Press; 0-917624),* P.O. Box 66, Hermosa, SD 57744 Tel 605-255-4466.

Lamm-Morada, *(Lamm-Morada Publishing Co., Inc.; 0-932128),* Box 7607, Stockton, CA 95207 Tel 209-931-1056.

Lampkin Pub, *(Lampkin, J. G., Publishing; 0-9604918),* 15346 Stone Ave. N., Seattle, WA 98133.

Lamplight Pub, *(Lamplight Publishing Inc.; 0-88308),* 559 W. 26th St., New York, NY 10001 Tel 212-695-8222.

Lamplighter, *(Lamplighter Press; 0-912870),* P.O. Box 258, Carlinville, IL 62626.

Lamplighters Rdwy, *(Lamplighters Roadway Press),* 44 Fairview Plaza, Los Gatos, CA 95030.

Lancaster Hse Pr, *(Lancaster House Press; 0-914356),* 36 Freshmeadow Dr., Lancaster, PA 17603.

Lancaster-Miller, *(Lancaster-Miller Pubs.; 0-89581),* 3165 Adeline St., Berkeley, CA 94703 Tel 415-845-3782. *Imprints:* Asian Humanities (Asian Humanities Press).

Lancer, *(Lancer Militaria; 0-935856),* P.O. Box 35188, Houston, TX 77035.

Land Tenure, *(Land Tenure Center),* 525 Observatory Dr., Rm. 310, King Hall, Madison, WI 92037 Tel 608-262-3657.

Land Values, *(Land Values),* 2821 Frontier Dr., Midland, TX 79701 Tel 915-683-2922; Orders to: P.O. Box 1533, Midland, TX 79702.

Landau, *(Landau Book Co., Inc.; 0-910864),* P.O. Box 570, Long Beach, NY 11561 Tel 516-889-0616.

Landfall Pr, *(Landfall Press, Inc.; 0-913428),* 20 W. Stroop Rd., Dayton, OH 45429 Tel 513-298-9123.

Landmark Bks, *(Landmark Books, Inc.; 0-934400),* 7847 12th Ave. S., Bloomington, MN 55420 Tel 612-854-3345.

Landmark NY, *(Landmark Book Co.),* 119 W. 57th St., New York, NY 10019.

Landmark Pub, *(Landmark Publishing Corp.; 0-918200),* Div. of Clearwater Corp., Box 3287, Burlington, VT 05402 Tel 802-372-4522.

Landown Hse, *(Landown House; 0-936562),* 5816 Esrig Way, Sacramento, CA 95841.

Lands End Bks, *(Lands End Books; 0-9603558),* Rte. 3, Box 370, Gloucester, VA 23061 Tel 804-693-4262.

Lane
    See Sunset-Lane

Lang Dev Serv, *(Language Development Services; 0-936808),* 739 Boylston St., Boston, MA 02116.

Lang Innovations, *(Language Innovations, Inc.; 0-931746),* 2112 Broadway, Rm. 515, New York, NY 10023 Tel 212-983-9476.

Lang Serv, *(Language Service, Inc., Publications Div.; 0-913942),* P.O. Box 8, Hastings-on-Hudson, NY 10706 Tel 212-687-4183.

Lang Svcs CA, *(Language Services),* 2725 Via Casa Loma, San Clemente, CA 92672 Tel 714-492-6528.

Langdon Assoc, *(Press of The Langdon Associates, The; 0-916704),* 41 Langdon St., Cambridge, MA 02138 Tel 617-864-4518.

Lange, *(Lange Medical Pubns.; 0-87041),* Drawer L, Los Altos, CA 94022 Tel 415-948-4526.

Langley, *(Langley, Ray),* 3664 Scorpio Dr., Sacramento, CA 95827.

Langstaff-Levy Ent, *(Langstaff-Levy Enterprises; 0-910878),* c/o E. Langstaff Books, 919 Fremont Ave., South Pasadena, CA 91030.

Language Pr, *(Language Press; 0-912386),* P.O. Box 342, Whitewater, WI 53190 Tel 414-473-2767.

Lankey, *(Lankey Publishing Co.; 0-918300),* Subs. of Huber Enterprises, Inc., c/o Huber Enterprises, Inc., R.D. One, Box 205, West Newton, PA 15089 Tel 412-722-3507.

Lanser Pr, *(Lanser Press; 0-9603900),* P.O. Box 38, Plainfield, VT 05667.

Lansky & Assoc, *(Lansky & Associates),* 18318 Minnetonka Blvd, Deephaven, MN 55391 Tel 612-473-5400.

Lantern, *(Lantern Press, Inc. Pubs.; 0-8313),* 354 Hussey Rd., Mount Vernon, NY 10552 Tel 914-668-9736.

Lantern *Imprint* of **PB**

Lapidary Journal, *(Lapidary Journal, Inc.),* P.O. Box 80937, San Diego, CA 92138 Tel 714-297-4841.

Larchmont Bks, *(Larchmont Books; 0-915962),* 6 E. 43rd St., New York, NY 10017 Tel 212-581-8840.

Large Print Bks *Imprint* of **G K Hall**

Laridae Pr, *(Laridae Press; 0-9606094),* 3012 Wesley Ave., Ocean City, NJ 08226 Tel 609-399-3222.

Larimi Comm, *(Larimi Communications; 0-935224),* 151 E. 50th St., New York, NY 10022 Tel 212-935-9262.

Larksdale, *(Larksdale Press, The; 0-89896),* 133 S. Heights Blvd., Houston, TX 77007 Tel 713-869-9092.

Larlin Corp, *(Larlin Corp.; 0-910220; 0-89783),* P.O. Box 1523, Marietta, GA 30061 Tel 404-424-6210.

Larousse, *(Larousse & Co., Inc.; 0-88332),* 572 Fifth Ave., New York, NY 10036 Tel 212-575-9515.

Larren Pubs, *(Larren Pubs.; 0-9604370),* 707 W. Burton, Nevada, MO 64772 Tel 417-667-3706.

Larson, *(Larson, David U.),* P.O. Box 599, Boynton Beach, FL 33435.

Lascaux, *(Lascaux Pubs.),* P.O. Box 155, Conway, MA 01341.

Lasenda, *(Lasenda Pubs.; 0-918916),* 32331 Coast Hwy., S. Laguna, CA 92677 Tel 714-499-1702.

Lat Am Lit Rev Pr, *(Latin American Lit. Rev. Press; 0-935480),* Box 8316, Pittsburgh, PA 15218.

Lat Am Stud, *(Latin American Studies, Univ. of Houston),* 401 Hoffman Hall, Univ. of Houston, Houston, TX 77004 Tel 713-749-4885.

Lateiner, *(Lateiner Publishing; 0-911722),* Atrium Tower I-A-2, 3400 S Ocean Blvd., Palm Beach, FL 33480 Tel 305-585-1818.

Latham, *(Latham Pub. Corp.; 0-918674),* 41 E. 42nd St., New York, NY 10017 Tel 212-687-0804; Moved, Left No Forwarding Address.

Lathrop, *(Lathrop, Norman, Enterprises; 0-910868),* P.O. Box 198, Wooster, OH 44691 Tel 216-262-5587.

Latigo Pr, *(Latigo Press; 0-935752),* 8320 E. Monterosa Ave., Scottsdale, AZ 85251.

Latin Am Ctr
    See UCLA Lat Am Ctr

Latitudes Pr, *(Latitudes Press),* 3215 Lafayette Ave., Austin, TX 78722 Tel 512-478-1454; Dist. by: SBD: Small Press Distribution, 1636 Oceanview, Kensington, CA 94707.

Latona Pr, *(Latona Press; 0-932448),* Box 154, RFD 2, Ellsworth, ME 04605.

Laughing Waters, *(Laughing Waters Press, The; 0-939634),* 10261/2 15th St., No. 2, Boulder, CO 80302.

Laughlin Enter, *(Laughlin Enterprises; 0-933604),* 1845 Oak Terrace, Newcastle, CA 95658 Tel 916-663-2295.

Laurel Enter, *(Laurel Entertainment, Inc.; 0-930392),* 30 Lincoln Plaza, Suite 21c, New York, NY 10023 Tel 212-245-6555.

Laurel Group
    See Laurel Enter

Laurel Inst, *(Laurel Institute, The; 0-87012),* RD 1, Box 10, Farmington, PA 15437.

Laurel Pub, *(Laurel Publishing Corp.; 0-89170),* Box 6194, 21 Churchill Rd., Hamden, CT 06517.

Laurida, *(Laurida Book Publishing Co.; 0-934810),* P.O. Box 2061, Hollywood, CA 90028 Tel 213-466-1707.

L'Avant Studios, *(L'Avant Studios; 0-914570),* P.O. Box 1711, Tallahassee, FL 32302 Tel 904-224-1411.

Lavender & Red, *(Lavender & Red Union),* P.O. Box 3503, Hollywood, CA 90028; Moved, Left No Forwarding Address.

Law & Cap Dynamics, *(Law & Capital Dynamics; 0-9600708),* 9100 Wilshire Blvd., Eighth Floor E., Beverly Hills, CA 90212.

Law & Econ U Miami, *(Univ. of Miami, Law & Economics Center; 0-916770),* P.O. Box 248000, Coral Gables, FL 33124 Tel 305-284-6174.

Law & Justice, *(Law & Justice Pubs.),* P.O. Box 6111, San Diego, CA 92106.

Law & Psych, *(Law & Psychology Press; 0-9603630),* 4344 Promenade Way, Suite 106P, Marina Del Rey, CA 90291 Tel 213-823-4460; Orders to: P. O. Box 9489, Venice, CA 90291.

Law Arts, *(Law-Arts Pubs., Inc.; 0-88238),* 453 Greenwich St., New York, NY 10013 Tel 212-925-4978.

Law of One, *(Law of One, The),* 3412 Pacific Ave., Forest Grove, OR 97116.

Lawkits, *(Lawkits, Inc.; 0-937464),* 26339 Monte Verde, Carmel, CA 93923.

Lawrence, *(Lawrence Publishing Co.; 0-87458),* Dist. by: Borden Pub. Co., 1855 W. Main St., Alhambra, CA 91801.

Lawrence Hill, *(Hill, Lawrence, & Co., Inc.; 0-88208),* 520 Riverside Ave., Westport, CT 06880 Tel 203-226-9392.

Lawson Bk, *(Lawson Book Co.),* 9488 Sara St., Elk Grove, CA 95624.

Lawton Pr, *(Lawton Press; 0-933044),* 673 Pelham Rd., Suite 16E, New Rochelle, NY 10805.

Lawton-Teague, *(Lawton-Teague Pubns.; 0-932516),* P.O. Box 656, Oakland, CA 94604; Dist. by: Bookpeople, 2940 Seventh St., Berkeley, CA 94710.

Lawyers & Judges, *(Lawyers & Judges Publishing Co.; 0-88450),* Div. of Communication Skill Builders, Inc., 3130 N. Dodge Blvd., P.O. Box 42050, Tucson, AZ 85733 Tel 602-327-6021.

Lawyers Bookshelf, *(Lawyers Bookshelf; 0-915362),* Box 78, Bayside, NY 11361.

Lawyers Co-Op, *(Lawyers Co-Operative Publishing Co.),* Aqueduct Bldg., Rochester, NY 14694 Tel 716-546-5530.

Lawyers Creative Arts, *(Lawyers for the Creative Arts; 0-936122),* 220 S. State, Suite 1404, Chicago, IL 60604; Dist. by: Chicago Review Press, 215 W. Ohio St., Chicago, IL 60610 Tel 312-644-5457.

Lazuli Prod, *(Lazuli Productions, Inc.; 0-9600522),* P.O. Box 125, Beaverton, OR 97005.

LBJ Sch Public Affairs, *(L B J School of Public Affairs, Univ. of Texas Austin),* Drawer Y, Univ. Sta., Austin, TX 78712 Tel 512-471-4962.

LE *Imprint* of **Dell**

Le Voyageur, *(Le Voyageur Publishing),* 1319 Wentwood Dr., Irving, TX 75061; Moved, Left No Forwarding Address.

Lea & Febiger, *(Lea & Febiger; 0-8121),* 600 S. Washington Square, Philadelphia, PA 19106 Tel 215-922-1330.

Leadership Pr, *(Leadership Press; 0-936626),* Box 1144, Claremont, CA 91767 Tel 714-624-6242.

League Bks, *(League Books),* P.O. Box 6055, Cleveland, OH 44101.

Learn Concepts OH, *(Learning Concepts, Inc.; 0-934902),* 7601 Mentor Ave., Mentor, OH 44060 Tel 216-946-6437.

Learn Inc, *(Learn Inc.; 0-913286),* Mount Laurel Plaza, 113 Gaither Dr., Mount Laurel, NJ 08054 Tel 609-234-6100.

Learn Mich, *(Learn; 0-9604634),* 827 CNB Bldg., Detroit, MI 48226.

Learn Pathways, *(Learning Pathways, Inc.; 0-89146),* Evergreen, CO 80439; Dist. by: J & J Distributors, P.O. Box 247, Raymondville, TX 78580.

Learn Res Intl Stud, *(Learning Resources in International Studies; 0-936876),* 60 E. 42nd St., Suite 1231, New York, NY 10165.

Learned Info, *(Learned Information, Inc.; 0-938734),* P.O. Box 550, Marlton, NJ 08053.

Learned Pubns, *(Learned Pubns., Inc.; 0-912116),* 83-53 Manton St., Jamaica, NY 11435 Tel 212-441-8084.

Learning Concepts, *(Learning Concepts, Inc.; 0-89384),* 400 E. Anderson Lane, Suite 318, Austin, TX 78753 Tel 512-837-9953; Orders to: Learning Concepts/Univ. Associates, 8517 Production Ave., San Diego, CA 92126 Tel 800-854-2143.

Learning Hse, *(Learning House; 0-9602730),* 38 South St., Roslyn Heights, NY 11577 Tel 516-621-5755; Dist. by: Liberty Publishing Co., 550 Scott Adam Rd., Cockeysville, MD 21030.

Learning Inc., *(Learning Inc.; 0-913692),* Learning Place, Manset, ME 04656 Tel 207-244-5015.

Learning Inst NC, *(Learning Institute of North Carolina),* 1006 Lamond Ave., Durham, NC 27701; Moved, Left No Forwarding Address.

Learning Line, *(Learning Line, The; 0-8449),* P.O. Box 577, Palo Alto, CA 94302 Tel 415-854-4400.

Learning Mag, *(Learning Magazine),* 530 University Ave., Palo Alto, CA 94301 Tel 415-321-1770.

Learning Pubns, *(Learning Pubns., Inc.; 0-918452),* 3220 W. Michigan Ave., Kalamazoo, MI 49007 Tel 616-372-1045.

Learning Res, *(Learning Resources Corp.; 0-913406),* 2817 N. Dorr Ave., Fairfax, VA 22030 Tel 703-573-3371.

Learning Syst, *(Learning Systems Co.; 0-256),* Div. of Richard D. Irwin, Inc., 1818 Ridge Rd., Homewood, IL 60430 Tel 312-798-6000.

Leaves of Grass, *(Leaves of Grass Press, Inc.; 0-915070),* Publishers Services, P.O. Box 3914, San Rafael, CA 94902 Tel 415-833-3530.

Lebanese Cuisine, *(Lebanese Cuisine; 0-9603050),* P.O. Box 66395, Portland, OR 97266.

Lebhar Friedman, *(Lebhar-Friedman Books; 0-912016; 0-86730),* Subs. of Lebhar-Friedman, Inc., 425 Park Ave., New York, NY 10022 Tel 212-371-9400.

Lecouver, *(Lecouver Press Co.; 0-910870),* 749 N.E. 71st St., Boca Raton, FL 33432; Moved, Left No Forwarding Address.

Lectorum Corp, *(Lectorum Pubns.),* 137 W. 14th St., New York, NY 10011.

Lectorum Corp
See Lectorum Corp

Lederer Street & Zeus, *(Lederer, Street & Zeus Co),* 2121 Allston Way, Berkeley, CA 94704 Tel 415-845-1342.

Lee Bks, *(Lee Books; 0-939818),* P.O. Box 906, Novato, CA 94948 Tel 415-897-3550.

Lee Pubns, *(Lee Pubns.; 0-910872),* 105 Suffolk Rd., Wellesley Hills, MA 02181.

Lee Ward Inst, *(Lee Ward Institute, The; 0-932474),* Rte. 2, Box 62, Piggott, AR 72454 Tel 501-598-3911.

Lees Abc Telephone, *(Lee's ABC of the Telephone),* Box 537, Geneva, IL 60134 Tel 312-879-9000.

Leetes Isl, *(Leete's Island Books; 0-918172),* P.O. Box 1131, New Haven, CT 06505 Tel 203-481-2536; Dist. by: Independent Publishers Group, 14 Vanderventer Ave., Port Washington, NY 11050.

LeFax, *(LeFax Publishing Co.; 0-87684),* 2867 E. Allegheny Ave., Philadelphia, PA 19134.

Left Bank, *(Left Bank Books; 0-939306),* 92 Pike St., Box B, Seattle, WA 98101 Tel 206-622-0195.

Left Curve, *(Left Curve),* 1230 Grant Ave. Box 302, San Francisco, CA 94133 Tel 415-771-1297.

Lega Bks, *(Lega Books),* Div. of Charing Cross Pub. Co., 658 S. Bonnie Brae St., Los Angeles, CA 90057 Tel 213-483-5832.

Legacy Bks, *(Legacy Books; 0-913714),* Box 494, 12 Meetinghouse Rd., Hatboro, PA 19040 Tel 215-675-6762.

Legacy Pr, *(Legacy Press; 0-914682),* P.O. Box 783, Rhinelander, WI 54501 Tel 715-362-4296.

Legacy Pub Co, *(Legacy Pub. Co.; 0-918784),* 2008 Perkins Rd., Baton Rouge, LA 70808 Tel 504-343-0366.

Legal Bk Corp, *(Legal Book Corp.; 0-910874),* 316 W. Second St., Los Angeles, CA 90012 Tel 213-626-3494.

Legal First Aid, *(Legal First Aid),* 899 Ellis St., San Francisco, CA 94109 Tel 415-441-4044.

Legal Mgmt Serv, *(Legal Management Services, Inc.; 0-937542),* 250 W. 94th St., New York, NY 10025 Tel 212-864-6169; Dist. by: LMS Distribution Center, P.O. Box 2614, LaCrosse, WI 54601.

Legal Pubns CA, *(Legal Pubns. Inc.),* 6931 Van Nuys Blvd., P.O. Box 3723, Van Nuys, CA 91407 Tel 213-873-4939.

Leghorn-Warrior, *(Leghorn & Warrior; 0-9601544),* 46 Pleasant St., Cambridge, MA 02139 Tel 617-492-5630.

LEHI Pub Co, *(LEHI Publishing Co.; 0-934486),* 303 Gretna Green Way, Los Angeles, CA 90049 Tel 213-476-6024.

Leicester *Imprint of* **Humanities**

Leichter, *(Leichter, Al),* 580 Hilltop Dr., Staunton, VA 24401.

Leisure Bks CT, *(Leisure Books),* P.O. Box 270, Norwalk, CT 06852.

Leisure Pr, *(Leisure Press; 0-918438),* P.O. Box 3, West Point, NY 10996 Tel 914-446-7110.

Leitz, *(Leitz, E.),* Dist. by: Morgan & Morgan, 145 Palisades St., Dobbs Ferry, NY 10522.

Lela L Lloyd, *(Lloyd, Lela Latch),* 1411 Ave. D, Cisco, TX 76437.

Lemma, *(Lemma Publishing Corp.; 0-87696),* 509 Fifth Ave., New York, NY 10017; Moved, Left No Forwarding Address.

Lemon Creek, *(Lemon Creek Communications; 0-934578),* 1121 N. Avenida Jeanine, Tucson, AZ 85715.

Lemur, *(Lemur Musical Research Corp.),* P.O. Box 22735, Land Park Sta., Sacramento, CA 95822 Tel 916-421-5375.

Len Beach Pr, *(Len Beach Press),* P.O. Box 7269 R.C., Toledo, OH 43615.

Lenape Pub, *(Lenape Publishing, Ltd.; 0-917178),* 4657 Dartmoor Dr., Wilmington, DE 19803 Tel 302-652-7847.

LenChamps Pubs, *(LenChamps Publishers; 0-917230),* P.O. Box 23432, Washington, DC 20024 Tel 202-488-8787.

Lenox Bks, *(Lenox Books; 0-9605872),* 11 Pilgrim Way, Wayne, NJ 07470.

Lenox Hill, *(Lenox Hill Press),* Div. of Crown Publishing, Inc., 235 E. 44th St., New York, NY 10017 Tel 212-687-5250.

Leo Pr, *(Leo Press; 0-931580),* Allen Park, MI 48101.

Leonaitis, *(Leonaitis, Joseph Felix; 0-9601272),* 3323 S. Lowe Ave., Chicago, IL 60616 Tel 312-376-7524.

Leornian Educ & Res, *(Leornian Educational & Resource Network; 0-917216),* P.O. Box 181, Center Conway, NH 03813; Moved, Left No Forwarding Address.

L'Epervier Pr, *(L'Epervier Press; 0-934332),* 762 Hayes, No. 15, Seattle, WA 98109 Tel 206-283-4952; Dist. by: Small Press Distribution Inc., 1784 Shattuck Ave., Berkeley, CA 94709.

Lerner Bks
See Lerner Pubns

Lerner Law, *(Lerner Law Book Co.; 0-87342),* 53 "E" St., N. W., Washington, DC 20001 Tel 202-628-5785.

Lerner Pubns, *(Lerner Publications Co.; 0-8225),* 241 First Ave., N., Minneapolis, MN 55401 Tel 612-332-3344.

Les Femmes Pub, *(Les Femmes Publishing; 0-89087),* 231 Adrian Rd., Millbrae, CA 94030 Tel 415-692-4500.

Leslie Pr, *(Leslie Press, Inc.; 0-913816),* 111 Leslie St., Dallas, TX 75207 Tel 214-748-0566.

Leswing Com Pr
See Leswing Pr

Leswing Pr, *(Leswing Press; 0-88339),* P.O. Box 3577, San Rafael, CA 94912 Tel 415-472-1080.

Lets Save Children, *(Let's Save the Children, Inc.; 0-89017),* P.O. Box 20747, Chicago, IL 60620 Tel 312-548-0356.

Levada, *(Levada Services; 0-9605014),* P.O. Box 686, 11300 Eastside Rd., Fort Jones, CA 96032.

Levenson Pr, *(Levenson Press; 0-914442),* P.O. Box 19606, Los Angeles, CA 90019.

Levi Pub, *(Levi Publishing Co., Inc.; 0-910876),* P.O. Box 730, Sumter, SC 29150.

Leviathan Hse, *(Leviathan House),* Dist. by: Hippocrene Books, P.O. Box 978, Edison, NJ 08817.

Levine Pr, *(Levine Press),* P.O. Box 517, Cascade, CO 80809.

Levy
See Langstaff-Levy Ent

Lewis, *(Lewis, A. F., & Co., Inc.; 0-910880),* 79 Madison Ave., New York, NY 10016 Tel 212-679-0770.

Lewis & Clark, *(Lewis & Clark Pubs., Ltd.),* P.O. Box 1200, Mattituck, NY 11952.

Lewis Carroll Soc, *(Lewis Carroll Society of North America; 0-930326),* 617 Rockford Rd., Silver Spring, MD 20902.

Lewis Pub Co, *(Lewis Publishing Co., The; 0-86616),* Dist. by: Stephen Greene Press, Fessenden Rd. at Indian Flat, P.O. Box 1000, Brattleboro, VT 05301 Tel 802-257-7757.

Lewis-Sloan, *(Lewis-Sloan Publishing Co.; 0-915114),* 2546 Etiwan Ave., Charleston, SC 29407 Tel 803-766-4735.

Lex Bk Co CA, *(Lexington Book Co.; 0-9604372),* 4872 Old Cliffs Rd., San Diego, CA 92120 Tel 714-583-8348.

Lex-Cal-Tex Pr, *(Lex-Cal-Tex Press; 0-912558),* P.O. Box 5512, Walnut Creek, CA 94596 Tel 415-863-1598.

Lexicon Corp, *(Lexicon Corp.; 0-9603286),* 1025 Fifth St., Geneva Park, Boulder, CO 80302 Tel 303-443-4616; Moved, Left No Forwarding Address.

Lexicon Pr, *(Lexicon Press; 0-9603220),* 9109 Southwick St., Fairfax, VA 22030 Tel 703-280-2298.

Lexicon Pubns, *(Lexicon Pubns., Inc.; 0-7172),* Subs. of Grolier Inc., 730 Fifth Ave., New York, NY 10019 Tel 212-755-8262.

Lexik Hse, *(Lexik House Pubs.; 0-936368),* 75 Main St., P.O. Box 247, Cold Spring, NY 10516 Tel 914-256-2822.

Lexington Bks, *(Lexington Books; 0-669),* Div. of D. C. Heath & Co., Dist. by: D. C. Heath & Co., 125 Spring St., Lexington, MA 02173 Tel 617-862-6650.

Lexington Data, *(Lexington Data, Inc.; 0-914428),* Box 371, Ashland, MA 01721 Tel 617-881-2576.

LFL *Imprint of* **Dell**

LI Poetry Coll, *(Long Island Poetry Collective Inc.),* 120 Kevin St., South Farmingdale, NY 11735.

Lib *Imprint of* **Bobbs**

Lib Auto Res Con, *(Library Automation Research Consulting Associates (Larc Press, Ltd.); 0-88257),* P.O. Box 27235, Tempe, AZ 85282 Tel 602-968-2023; Moved, Left No Forwarding Address.

Lib Coll Assoc, *(Library-College Associates, Inc.; 0-917706),* P.O. Box 956, Norman, OK 73070.

Lib Congress, *(Library of Congress; 0-8444),* Washington, DC 20540 Tel 202-287-5093.

Lib Media Prods, *(Library Media Productions; 0-912032),* 610 Overcrest, Fayetteville, AR 67201.

Lib Psychol Anthrop, *(Library of Psychological Anthropology; 0-914434),* 2315 Broadway, New York, NY 10024.

Lib Reprod, *(Library Reproduction Service),* c/o Microfilm Company of California, 1977 S. Los Angeles St., Los Angeles, CA 90011; Production of Large Print Books to Order & in Any Type Size from 14 to 30 Pt.

Lib Res, *(Library Research Associates; 0-912526),* Dunderberg Rd., R.D. 5, Box 41, Monroe, NY 10950 Tel 914-783-1144.

Lib Serv Inc, *(Library Services Inc.),* Box 711, Havertown, PA 19083.

Lib Soc Sci, *(Library of Social Science; 0-915042),* 475 Amsterdam Ave., New York, NY 10024 Tel 212-874-6718.

Liberal Arts, *(Liberal Arts Publishing),* P.O. Box 155, Berea, OH 44017.

Liberation Bk, *(Liberation Bookstore),* P.O. Box 17, Radio City Sta., New York, NY 10019.

Liberation Pubns, *(Liberation Publications, Inc.; 0-917076),* One Peninsula Place, Bldg. 1730, Suite 225, San Meteo, CA 94402 Tel 415-573-7100.

Liberation Sup
See LSM Pr

Liberator Pr, *(Liberator Press; 0-930720),* Box 7128, Chicago, IL 60680 Tel 312-663-4329.

Liberian Studies, *(Liberian Studies),* Dept. of Anthropology, Univ. of Delaware, Newark, DE 19711.

Libertarian, *(Libertarian Press; 0-910884),* P.O. Box 218, 366 E. 166th St., South Holland, IL 60473 Tel 312-333-0031.

Libertarian Bks, *(Libertarian Books, Ltd.),* P.O. Box 22026, Tampa, FL 33622.

Liberty Bell Pr, *(Liberty Bell Press),* P.O. Box 32, Florissant, MO 63033 Tel 314-837-5343.

Liberty Fund, *(Liberty Fund, Inc.; 0-913966),* 7440 N. Shadeland Ave., Indianapolis, IN 46250 Tel 317-842-0880.

Liberty Lobby, *(Liberty Lobby; 0-935036),* 300 Independence Ave., S.E., Washington, DC 20003 Tel 202-546-5611.

Liberty Pr, *(Liberty Press-Liberty Classics; 0-913966; 0-86597),* 7440 N. Shadeland, Indianapolis, IN 46250 Tel 317-842-0880.

Liberty Pub, *(Liberty Publishing Co., Inc.; 0-89709),* 50 Scott Adam Rd., Cockeysville, MD 21030 Tel 301-667-6680.

Libra, *(Libra Pubs., Inc.; 0-87212),* 391 Willets Rd., Roslyn Heights, L. I., NY 11577 Tel 516-484-4950.

Libra Pub, *(Libra Publishing Corp.; 0-915122),* 1 Executive Dr., Burlington, VT 05401; Moved, Left No Forwarding Address.

Library of Armenian, *(Library of Armenian Studies; 0-910154),* 129 Robbins Rd., Watertown, MA 02172.

Library Pr, *(Library Press; 0-912050),* Dist. by: Open Court Pub. Co., La Salle, IL 61301.

Library Pr *Imprint of* **Open Court**

Libraryworks, *(Libraryworks, The; 0-918212),* Div. of Neal-Schuman, Pubs, 64 University Place, New York, NY 10003; Orders to: P.O. Box 1687. FDR Sta., New York, NY 10150.

Libs Unl, *(Libraries Unlimited, Inc.; 0-87287),* P.O. Box 263, Littleton, CO 80160 Tel 303-770-1220.

Libty Bell Assoc, *(Liberty Bell Associates; 0-918940),* P.O. Box 51, Franklin Park, NJ 08823 Tel 201-297-3051.

Libty Pr IA, *(Liberty Press; 0-939272),* 905 Leroy St., Muscatine, IA 52761.

Libty Pr MI, *(Liberty Press; 0-9604958),* 2115 Mark Ave., Lansing, MI 48912.

Libty Pub MO, *(Liberty Publishing Co.; 0-934334),* 3331 Liberty St., St. Louis, MO 63111.

Licht, *(Licht, Elizabeth, Pub.; 0-910888),* P.O. Box J, Westville Sta., New Haven, CT 06515.

Lidiraven Bks, *(Lidiraven Books; 0-936162),* Box 5567, Sherman Oaks, CA 91413 Tel 213-892-0059.

Lieber-Atherton, *(Lieber-Atherton, Inc.; 0-88311),* 1841 Broadway, New York, NY 10023 Tel 212-586-2118.

Life Arts, *(Life Arts Publishing; 0-937894),* 116 Curryer S., Santa Maria, CA 93454.

Life Enrich, *(Life Enrichment Pubs.; 0-938736),* Box 526, Canton, OH 44701.

Life in Christ
See ACTA Found

Life Long Learn, *(Life-Long Learning Library),* P.O. Box 7361, Atlanta, GA 30309.

Life Office
See LOMA

Life Office, *(Life Office Management Assn.),* ; Publisher Abbreviation Without Addresses Are for Titles That Are Out of Print. These Are Obsolete Abbreviations. Publisher's Abbreviation Is Now LOMA.

Life Pubns IL, *(Life Pubns., Inc.),* Box 72, Ina, IL 62846; Moved, Left No Forwarding Address.

Life Pubs Intl, *(Life Pubs. International; 0-8297),* 3360 N.W. 110th St., Miami, FL 33167 Tel 305-685-6334.

Life Skills, *(Life Skills Training Associates; 0-9604510),* P.O. Box 48133, Chicago, IL 60648 Tel 312-823-0650.

Life Understanding, *(Life Understanding Foundation; 0-88234),* P.O. Box 30305, 741 Rosarita Lane, Santa Barbara, CA 93105 Tel 805-682-5151.

Lifestyle One, *(Lifestyle One, Inc.; 0-9603016),* P.O. Box 630668, Miami, FL 33163.

Lifetime Learn, *(Lifetime Learning Pubns.; 0-534),* Div. of Wadsworth Inc., 10 Davis Dr., Belmont, CA 94002 Tel 415-595-2350.

Light & Life, *(Light & Life Press; 0-89367),* 999 College Ave., Winona Lake, IN 46590.

Light Impressions, *(Light Impressions Corp.; 0-87992),* P.O. Box 3012, Rochester, NY 14614 Tel 716-271-8960.

Light&Life Pub Co MN, *(Light & Life Publishing Co.; 0-937032),* 3450 Irving Ave. S., Minneapolis, MN 55408 Tel 612-925-3888.

Lightbooks, *(Lightbooks; 0-934420),* P.O. Box 425, Marlton, NJ 08053.

Lighthouse, *(Lighthouse Press),* P. O. Box 8507, Honolulu, HI 96815; Formerly Named Diversity Press.

Lighthouse Pr NY
See Lightyear

Lightning Tree, *(Lightning Tree; 0-89016),* P.O. Box 1837, Santa Fe, NM 87501 Tel 505-983-7434.

Lighton Pubns, *(Lighton Pubns.; 0-910892),* 73223 Sunnyvale Dr., Twentynine Palms, CA 92277 Tel 714-367-7386.

LightSong, *(LightSong),* 1325 Rimrock Dr., San Jose, CA 95120.

Lightyear, *(Lightyear Press, Inc.; 0-89968),* P.O. Box 507, Laurel, NY 11948.

Liguori Pubns, *(Liguori Pubns.; 0-89243),* 1 Liguori Dr., Liguori, MO 63057 Tel 800-325-9521.

Lili Ahns, *(Lili Ahn's; 0-9601382),* 210 Ross, Denison, TX 75020.

Lillian, *(Lillian & M. E.; 0-918174),* 11 Tudor Dr., Northport, NY 11788 Tel 516-757-5615.

Lillibridge Bks, *(Lillibridge Books),* P. O. Box 1975, Albion, MI 49224 Tel 517-629-9210; Moved, Left No Forwarding Address.

LIM Pr, *(LIM Press),* 12 E. 53rd St., New York, NY 10022 Tel 212-752-1530.

Lime Rock Pr, *(Lime Rock Press, Inc.; 0-915998),* Mount Riga Rd., Box 363, Salisbury, CT 06068 Tel 203-435-2236.

Limelite, *(Limelite Publishing Co.),* 90 Park St., Arcade, NY 14009 Tel 716-492-3782.

Limestone Pr, *(Limestone Press; 0-919642),* P.O. Box 1604, Kingston, Ontario, Canada K7l 5c8,; Dist. by: A. S. Donnelly, 125 Southwood Dr., Vestal, NY 13850.

Linc Pr, *(Linc Press),* 1006 Lamond Ave., Durham, NC 27701.

Lincoln Arc Weld, *(Lincoln, James F., Arc Welding Foundation; 0-937390),* P.O. Box 17035, Cleveland, OH 44117 Tel 216-481-4300.

Lincoln Hse
See OSV Fabric Shop

Lincoln Inst Land, *(Lincoln Institute of Land Policy),* 26 Trowbridge St., Cambridge, MA 02138 Tel 617-661-3016.

Lincoln Pr & Graph, *(Lincoln Press & Graphics; 0-931748),* E. 1811 Holyoke No. 7, Spokane, WA 99208.

Lincoln Pr MI, *(Lincoln Press),* 4610 Delemere Blvd., Royal Oak, MI 48073 Tel 313-549-1900.

Lincoln Pub, *(Lincoln Publishing; 0-918898),* P.O. Box 50173, Palo Alto, CA 94303 Tel 415-494-7448.

Lincoln's Leadership, *(Lincoln's Leadership Library; 0-89764),* 5516 E. 35th, Tulsa, OK 74135.

Lindahl, *(Lindahl, Judy; 0-9603032),* 3211 N.E. Siskiyou, Portland, OR 97212 Tel 503-288-0772.

Lindell Pubs, *(Lindell Pubs.; 0-9604940),* P.O. Box 28, Bucks County, Springtown, PA 18081.

Linden *Imprint of* **S&S**

Linden Bks, *(Linden Books; 0-9603288),* Interlaken, NY 14847 Tel 607-387-9398.

Linden Pubs, *(Linden Pubs.; 0-89642),* 1750 N. Sycamore, Hollywood, CA 90028.

Lineal Cleworth, *(Lineal/Cleworth Books, Inc.; 0-916628),* 23 Leroy Ave., Darien, CT 06820 Tel 203-655-7676.

Lingua Hse, *(Lingua House; 0-916636),* 915 W. Jackson, Colorado Springs, CO 80907 Tel 303-635-3717.

Lingua Pr, *(Lingua Press),* Box 481, Ramona, CA 92065 Tel 714-789-8389.

Linguadex, *(Linguadex Pubns.; 0-9602268),* 1618 W. Lewis, San Diego, CA 92103.

Linstok Pr, *(Linstok Press, Inc.; 0-932130),* 9306 Mintwood St., Silver Spring, MD 2090 Tel 301-585-1939.

Lintel, *(Lintel; 0-931642),* P.O. Box 34, St. George, Staten Island, NY 10301.

Linus Pauling Inst, *(Linus Pauling Institute of Science & Medicine),* 2700 Sand Hill Rd., Menlo Park, CA 94025.

Lion, *(Lion Press; 0-87460),* Dist. by: Sayre Publishing, Inc., 111 E. 39th St., New York, NY 10016.

Lion Ent, *(Lion Enterprises; 0-930962),* RR3 Box 127, Walkerton, IN 46574 Tel 219-369-9394.

Lion Serv Co, *(Lion Services Co. - Publishing & Distribution; 0-9601018),* 950 B Ave., Coronado, CA 92118 Tel 714-435-4248.

Lionhead Pub, *(Lionhead Publishing; 0-89018),* 2521 East Stratford Court, Shorewood, Milwaukee, WI 53211 Tel 414-332-7474.

Lion's Head, *(Lion's Head Publishing Co.),* 441 Karen Ave., Fort Wayne, IN 46815.

Liplop, *(Liplop Press; 0-936016),* P.O. Box 4520, Berkeley, CA 94704.

Lippincott, *(Lippincott, J. B., Co.; 0-397),* 10 E. 53rd St., New York, NY 10022 Tel 212-593-7000; E. Washington Sq., Philadelphia, PA 19105 Tel 215-574-4200; Orders to: Harper & Row, Publishers, Inc., Keystone Industrial Park, Scranton, PA 18512 Tel 717-343-4761.

Lippincott & Crowell, *(Lippincott & Crowell Pubs.; 0-690),* 521 Fifth Ave., New York, NY 10017 Tel 212-687-3980.

Listening Pr, *(Listening Press),* c/o Tel-Graphics, Frentress Lake Rd., East Dubuque, IL 61025.

Lit Bible, *(Literature of the Bible, Inc.; 0-932816),* 8265 Felch St., P.O. Box 138, Zeeland, MI 49464 Tel 616-772-4766.

Literary, *(Literary Mart; 0-910896),* P.O. Box 5425, Milwaukee, WI 53211; Moved, Left No Forwarding Address.

Literary Herald, *(Literary Herald Press; 0-9602124),* 408 Oak St., Danville, IL 61832.

Literary Pub, *(Literary Publishers of Southern California),* 1639 W. Washington Blvd., Venice, CA 90291.

Literary Sketches, *(Literary Sketches; 0-915588),* P.O. Box 711, Williamsburg, VA 23185 Tel 804-229-2901.

Literati Pr, *(Literati Press, Pubs.; 0-933744),* The Olive Bldg., 18 E. Sunrise Hwy., Freeport, NY 11520.

Litho Textbk, *(Lithographic Textbook Publishing Co.; 0-9600060),* 5719 S. Spaulding, Chicago, IL 60629 Tel 312-776-7234.

Lithuanian Lib, *(Lithuanian Library Press; 0-932042),* 3001 W. 59th St., Chicago, IL 60629 Tel 312-778-6872.

Litmus, *(Litmus, Inc.; 0-915214),* 525 Bryant, Walla Walla, WA 99362.

Little, *(Little, Brown & Co.; 0-316),* 34 Beacon St., Boston, MA 02106 Tel 617-227-0730; Orders to: 200 West St., Waltham, MA 02154 Tel 617-890-0250.

Little Bear Pubns, *(Little Bear Pubns.; 0-932646),* P.O. Box 943, Virginia Beach, VA 23451.

Little Bks, *(Little Books; 0-915686),* P.O. Box 9, Fort Lee, NJ 07024.

Little Brick Hse, *(Little Brick House, The; 0-9601648),* 621 Saint Clair St., Vandalia, Il 62471 Tel 618-283-0024.

Little Cajun, *(Little Cajun Books; 0-931108),* 4182 Blecker Dr., Baton Rouge, LA 70809 Tel 504-925-0355.

Little Feat, *(Little Feat; 0-940112),* P.O. Box 150, Water Mill, NY 11976 Tel 516-653-5503.

Little Glass, *(Little Glass Shack; 0-911508),* 3161 56th St., Sacramento, CA 95820 Tel 916-455-8197.

Little London, *(Little London Press; 0-936564),* 716 E. Washington, Colorado Springs, CO 80907 Tel 303-471-1322.

Little Red Hen, *(Little Red Hen, Inc.; 0-933046),* P.O. Box 4260, Pocatello, ID 83201.

Little Simon *Imprint of* **S&S**

Littlebird, *(Littlebird Pubns.; 0-937896),* 126 Fifth Ave., New York, NY 10011.

Littlefield, *(Littlefield, Adams & Co.; 0-8226),* 81 Adams Dr., Box 327, Totowa, NJ 07511 Tel 201-256-8600.

Litton Educ Pub, *(Litton Educational Publishing, International; 0-442),* 135 W. 50th St., New York, NY 10020 Tel 212-265-8700.

Littoral Bks, *(Littoral Books),* P.O. Box 7355, Downtown Sta., Portland, ME 04112; Moved, Left No Forwarding Address.

Littoral Develop, *(Littoral Development Co.; 0-914770),* 252 S. Van Pelt St., Philadelphia, PA 19103 Tel 215-546-3285.

Liturgical
See Liturgical Conf

Liturgical Conf, *(Liturgical Conference, The; 0-918208),* 810 Rhode Island Ave. N.E., Washington, DC 20018 Tel 202-529-7400.

Liturgical Pr, *(Liturgical Press; 0-8146),* 74 Engle Blvd., Collegeville, MN 56321 Tel 612-363-2213.

LIU Univ, *(Long Island Univ. Press; 0-913252),* University Plaza, Brooklyn, NY 11201 Tel 212-834-6064.

Liv Bibles Int'l, *(Living Bibles International),* 1809C Mill St., Naperville, IL 60540 Tel 312-369-0100.

Live Food, *(Live Food Products, Inc.),* 734D Hollister Ave., Goleta, CA 93017.

Live Free, *(Live Free Inc.),* P.O. Box 743, Harvey, IL 60426 Tel 312-468-8805.

Live-Oak Pr, *(Live-Oak Press),* P. O. Box 99444, San Francisco, CA 94109.

Lively Hills, *(Lively Hills Publishing Corp.; 0-938194),* P.O. Box 1186, St. Charles, MO 63301.

Liveright, *(Liveright Publishing Corp.; 0-87140),* Subs. of W. W. Norton Co., Inc., 500 Fifth Ave., New York, NY 10036 Tel 212-354-5500.

Living Bks, *(Living Books, Inc.; 0-912208),* 4401 N. Ravenswood Ave., Chicago, IL 60640.

Living Bks NY, *(Living Books Ltd.),* P.O. Box 604, New York, NY 10036 Tel 212-222-5464; Moved, Left No Forwarding Address.

Living Black Hist, *(Living Black History; 0-8181),* c/o Pay-O-Matic, Unit No. 186, 254 Kingston Ave., Brooklyn, NY 11213; Moved, Left No Forwarding Address.

Living Flame Pr, *(Living Flame Press; 0-914544),* P.O. Box 74, Locust Valley, NY 11560 Tel 516-676-4265.

Living Hand, *(Living Hand),* Millis Rd., Box 252, Stanfordville, NY 12581.

Living Love, *(Living Love Pubs.; 0-9600688; 0-915972),* 232 Monterey St., Santa Cruz, CA 95060 Tel 502-691-6006; Dist. by: DeVorss & Company, P.O. Box 550, Marina Del Rey, CA 90291 Tel 213-870-7478.

Living Poets, *(Living Poets Press; 0-915726),* 31 8th Ave., Brooklyn, NY 11217 Tel 212-522-2225.

Living Word, *(Living Word Pubns.; 0-88467),* 4964 W. Cullom Ave., Chicago, IL 60641 Tel 312-725-8660; Out of Business.

Livingston, *(Livingston Publishing Co.; 0-87098; 0-915180),* 18 Hampstead Circle, Wynnewood, PA 19096; Orders to: Harrowood Books, 3943 N. Providence Rd., Newton Sq., PA 19073 Tel 215-353-5585.

Livingston Marine, *(Livingston Marine Services, Inc.; 0-931938),* 17 Battery Place, Room 1631, New York, NY 10004.

Livingston Pr, *(Livingston Press; 0-915772),* 820 Hartford Rd., Box 249, Waterford, CT 06385 Tel 203-442-3383; Orders to: Independent Pubs. Group, 14 Vanderventer Ave., Port Washington, NY 11050.

LJB Found, *(LJB Foundation),* 933 Overlook Rd., Whitehall, PA 18052 Tel 215-433-7667.

LJR Inc, *(LJR, Inc.; 0-936624),* 224 Joseph Square, Columbia, MD 21044 Tel 301-730-5365.

LJT Asssociates
See Tracy Pub

LKA Inc, *(Linju-Ryu Karate Assn.; 0-917098),* P.O. Box 102, 7 Putter Lane, Middle Island, NY 11953 Tel 516-924-3888.

LL Co, *(LL Co.; 0-937892),* 1647 Manning Ave., Los Angeles, CA 90024 Tel 213-278-6803.

LLanerch Bks, *(LLanerch Books),* Box 711, Haverton, PA 19083.

Llewellyn
See Llewellyn Pubns

Llewellyn Pubns, *(Llewellyn Pubns.; 0-87542),* Div. of Chester-Kent, Inc., P.O. Box 43383, St. Paul, MN 55164 Tel 612-291-1970.

Lloyd & Lipow, *(Lloyd, D. K., & M. Lipow; 0-9601504),* 201 Calle Miramar, Redondo Beach, CA 90277 Tel 213-535-3204.

LMR Bks, *(LMR Books; 0-913674),* P.O. Box 8124, Lexington, KY 40503.

Locare, *(Locare Research Group; 0-913986),* 910 N. Fairfax Ave., Los Angeles, CA 90046 Tel 213-656-4420.

Lochinvar *Imprint of* **Exposition**

Lodima, *(Lodima Press; 0-9605646),* Revere, PA 18953.

Loeffler
See Prod Hse

Loewenthal Pr, *(Loewenthal Press; 0-914382),* P.O. Box 1107, New York, NY 10009.

Loftin Pubs, *(Loftin, Tee, Pubs.,Inc.; 0-934812),* 3100 R St., N.W., Washington, DC 20007.

Log Boom, *(Log Boom Brewing; 0-9604130),* Box 1825, Boulder, CO 80306.

Logan Design, *(Logan Design Group; 0-9603856),* P. O. Box 997, N. Hollywood, CA 91603.

Logan Hill, *(Logan Hill Press; 0-918610),* 204 Fairmount Ave., Ithaca, NY 14850 Tel 607-273-0707.

Logbridge-Rhodes, *(Logbridge-Rhodes, Inc.; 0-937406),* P.O. Box 3254, Durango, CO 81301.

Logos, *(Logos International; 0-912106; 0-88270),* 201 Church St., Plainfield, NJ 07060.

Loizeaux, *(Loizeaux Brothers, Inc.; 0-87213),* 1238 Corlies Ave., Box 277, Neptune, NJ 07753 Tel 201-774-8144.

Lollipop Power, *(Lollipop Power, Inc.; 0-914996),* P.O. Box 1171, Chapel Hill, NC 27514 Tel 919-929-4857.

LOMA, *(Life Office Management Assn.; 0-915322),* 100 Colony Square, Atlanta, GA 30361 Tel 404-892-7272; Orders to: Professional Book Distributors, P.O. Box 02055, 555 E. Hudson St., Columbus, OH 43202 Tel 800-848-0773.

Lomond, *(Lomond Pubns.; 0-912338),* P.O. Box 88, Mt. Airy, MD 21771 Tel 301-829-1496.

Lompa-Brant, *(Lompa-Brant),* 2435 Gough St., San Francisco, CA 94123 Tel 415-237-2813.

Lond Pubns, *(Lond Pubns.),* Pomona, NY 10970.

London & Goldberg
See J M Goldberg

London Bk, *(London Book Co),* 212 N. Orange, Glendale, CA 91203 Tel 213-224-0828.

Lone Oak, *(Lone Oak Books; 0-936550),* 10,000 Old Georgetown Rd., Bethesda, MD 20014.

Lone Raven, *(Lone Raven Publishing Co., Inc.; 0-933914),* P.O. Box 1739, Anchorage, AK 99510.

Lone Star Pubs, *(Lone Star Pubs. Inc.; 0-914872),* P.O. Box 9774, Austin, TX 78766 Tel 206-352-8622.

Lonely Planet, *(Lonely Planet),* Dist. by: Bookpeople, 2940 Seventh St., Berkeley, CA 94710; No Longer Distributed by Bookpeople.

Long Haul, *(Long Haul Press; 0-9602284),* P.O. Box 592, Van Brunt Sta., Brooklyn, NY 11215.

Long Hse, *(Long House, Inc.; 0-912806),* P.O. Box 3, New Canaan, CT 06840 Tel 203-966-3808.

Longanecker, *(Longanecker Books; 0-9601126),* P.O. Box 127, Brewster, WA 98812 Tel 509-689-2441.

Longhorn Pr, *(Longhorn Press; 0-914208),* c/o J. W. Sitton, Box 150, Cisco, TX 76437 Tel 817-442-2530.

Longleaf Pubns, *(Longleaf Pubns.),* 809 Teague Dr., Tallahassee, FL 32303.

Longman, *(Longman Inc.),* 19 W. 44th St., Suite 1012, New York, NY 10036 Tel 212-764-3950.

Longman McKay, *(Longman McKay),* 19 W. 44th St., New York, NY 10036.

Longshanks Bk, *(Longshanks Book; 0-9601000),* 30 Church St., Mystic, CT 06355 Tel 203-536-8656.

Longship Pr, *(Longship Press; 0-917712),* Crooked Lane, Nantucket, MA 02554 Tel 207-722-3344; Orders to: RFD 1, Box 124, Brooks, ME 04921.

Longwood Pr, *(Longwood Press, Ltd.; 0-89341),* Shady Nook Rd., West Newfield, ME 04095 Tel 207-793-2288.

Longyear Res, *(Longyear, J. M., Research Library),* c/o Marquette County Historical Society, 213 N. Front St., Marquette, MI 49855 Tel 906-226-6821.

Lonstein Pubns, *(Lonstein Pubns.),* 1 Terrace Hill, Box 351, Ellenville, NY 12428.

Loompanics, *(Loompanics Unlimited),* P.O. Box 264, Mason, MI 48854 Tel 517-694-2240.

Lord Americana, *(Lord Americana & Research, Inc.; 0-916492),* 1521 Redwood Dr., W. Columbia, SC 29169 Tel 803-794-7104.

Lord John, *(Lord John Press; 0-935716),* 19073 Los Alimos St., Northridge, CA 91326.

Lord Pub, *(Lord Publishing; 0-930204),* 46 Glen St., Dover, MA 02030 Tel 617-785-1575.

Lords Line, *(Lord's Line; 0-915952),* 1734 Armour Lane, Redondo Beach, CA 90278 Tel 213-542-5575.

Lorenz & Herweg, *(Lorenz & Herweg Pubs.; 0-916494),* P.O. Box 7764, Long Beach, CA 90807 Tel 213-422-0059; Tel 213-422-0059.

Lorenz Pr, *(Lorenz Press, Inc.; 0-89328),* Div. of Lorenz Industries, Subs. of Internat'l Entertainment Corp., 501 E. Third St., Dayton, OH 45401 Tel 513-228-6118; Dist. by: Independent Publishers Group, 14 Vanderventer Ave., Port Washington, NY 11050.

Lorian Pr, *(Lorian Press; 0-936878),* P.O. Box 1095, Elgin, IL 60120.

Lorien Hse, *(Lorien House; 0-934852),* P.O. Box 1112, Black Mountain, NC 28711 Tel 704-669-6211.

Los Angeles Pub, *(Los Angeles Pub., Co.; 0-913924),* P.O. Box 54119, Terminal Annex, Los Angeles, CA 90054; Moved, Left No Forwarding Address.

Los Ninos, *(Los Ninos; 0-935366),* 919 W. 28th St., Minneapolis, MN 55408 Tel 612-825-0979.

Lost Data, *(Lost Data Press; 0-937468),* 4410c Burnet Rd., Austin, TX 78756; Dist. by: Bookpeople, Inc., P.O. Box 40397, San Francisco, CA 94140 Tel 415-824-3184; Dist. by: The Distributors, 702 S. Michigan, South Bend, IN 46618.

Lost Pleiade, *(Lost Pleiade Press; 0-915270),* P.O. Box 587, Lake Oswego, OR 97034 Tel 503-288-0400.

Lost Roads, *(Lost Roads Pubs.; 0-918786),* P.O. Box 11143, San Francisco, CA 94101.

Lothrop, *(Lothrop, Lee & Shepard Books; 0-688),* Div. of William Morrow & Co., Inc., 105 Madison Ave., New York, NY 10016 Tel 212-889-3050; Orders to: William Morrow & Co., Inc., Wilmor Warehouse, 6 Henderson Dr., West Caldwell, NJ 07006.

Lotsawa, *(Lotsawa, Inc.; 0-932156),* 140 E. 92nd St., New York, NY 10028 Tel 212-534-3384; Dist. by: Book Dynamics, 836 Broadway, New York, NY 10003; Dist. by: Bookpeople, 2940 Seventh St., Berkeley, CA 94710 Tel 415-549-3030; Dist. by: De Vorss & Co., P.O. Box 550, Marina del Rey, CA 90291 Tel 213-870-7478.

Lotus, *(Lotus Press, Inc.; 0-916418),* P.O. Box 21607, Detroit, MI 48221 Tel 313-861-1280.

Lotus Ashram, *(Lotus Ashram, Inc., The),* 113 Francis St., Goose Creek, SC 29445 Tel 803-797-3496.

Louis Found, *(Louis Foundation; 0-9605492),* Box 210, Eastsound, WA 98245 Tel 206-376-2581.

Louisville & Jefferson, *(Louisville & Jefferson County Heritage Corporation; 0-9603278),* 300 W. Liberty St., Louisville, KY 40202 Tel 502-582-2421.

Louval Pubs, *(Louval Pubs.),* 510 Briar Knoll Dr., Houston, TX 77079 Tel 713-493-6970; Orders to: P.O. Box 42401, Houston, TX 77042.

Love Street, *(Love Street Books; 0-915216),* P.O. Box 58163, Louisville, KY 40258 Tel 502-458-0604.

Loving Life, *(Loving Life Pubns.; 0-9605346),* 8005 Bleriot Ave., Westchester, CA 90045.

Loving Pubs, *(Loving Pubs.; 0-938134),* 4576 Alla Rd., Los Angeles, CA 90066.

Low-Tech, *(Low-Tech Press; 0-9605626),* 30-73 47th St., Long Island City, NY 11103.

Lowell & Lynwood, *(Lowell & Lynwood, Ltd.; 0-8484),* 965 Church St., Baldwin, NY 11510.

Lowell Pr, *(Lowell Press; 0-913504),* 115 E. 31st St., Box 1877, Kansas City, MO 64141 Tel 816-753-4545.

Lower Cape, *(Lower Cape Publishing; 0-936972),* P.O. Box 901, Orleans, MA 02653 Tel 617-255-2244.

Lowry & Volz, *(Lowry & Volz Pubs.; 0-9601740),* 2163 Greenspring Dr., Timonium, MD 21093.

Lowy Pub, *(Lowy Publishing; 0-9602940),* 5047 Wigton, Houston, TX 77096 Tel 713-723-3209.

Loyola, *(Loyola Univ. Press; 0-8294),* 3441 N. Ashland Ave., Chicago, IL 60657 Tel 312-281-1818.

LSM Pr, *(LSM Press; 0-919914),* P.O. Box 2077, Oakland, CA 94604 Tel 415-635-4863.

Lubavitch Women, *(Lubavitch Women's Organization Jr. Division; 0-930178),* 770 Eastern Pkwy., Brooklyn, NY 11213 Tel 212-771-6033.

Lubrecht & Cramer, *(Lubrecht & Cramer),* RFD 1, Box 227, Monticello, NY 12701 Tel 914-794-8539.

Lucas, *(Lucas Brothers Pubs.; 0-87543),* 909 Lowry St., Missouri Store Bldg., Columbia, MO 65201 Tel 314-442-6161.

Lucas Pubs CA, *(Lucas Pubs.; 0-9604806),* 58 Arden Way, P.O. Box 15224, Sacramento, CA 95813.

Luce, *(Luce, Robert B., Inc.; 0-88331),* 6919 Radnor Rd., Bethesda, MD 20034 Tel 301-320-3327; Orders to: 27 Harrison St., Bridgeport, CT 06604 Tel 203-366-1900.

Lucis, *(Lucis Publishing Co.; 0-85330),* 866 United Nations Plaza, Suite 566, New York, NY 10017 Tel 212-421-1577.

Lucky Pubns, *(Lucky Pubns.; 0-932342),* P.O. Box 19307, Las Vegas, NV 89119 Tel 702-564-3895; Moved, Left No Forwarding Address.

LUISA Prods, *(LUISA Productions; 0-939584),* P.O. Box 6836-AB, Santa Barbara, CA 93111.

Lukas & Sons, *(Lukas & Sons Pubs.; 0-930994),* 4179 Fairmount Ave., San Diego, CA 92105.

Lumeli Pr, *(Lumeli Press; 0-930592),* P.O. Box 909, San Carlos, CA 94070 Tel 415-593-7181.

Lumen Christi, *(Lumen Christi Press; 0-912414),* P.O. Box 13176, Houston, TX 77019 Tel 713-529-4525.

Luna Bisonte, *(Luna Bisonte Prods.; 0-935350),* 137 Leland Ave., Columbus, OH 43214 Tel 614-846-4126.

Luna Pr, *(Luna Press; 0-914466),* P.O. Box 1049, Brooklyn, NY 11202; Moved, Left No Forwarding Address.

Luna Pubns, *(Luna Pubns.; 0-930346),* 655 Orchard St., Oradell, NJ 07649.

Lunan-Ferguson, *(Lunan-Ferguson Library, Pubs.; 0-911724),* 2219 Clement St., San Francisco, CA 94121 Tel 415-752-6100.

Lunchroom Pr, *(Lunchroom Press, The; 0-938136),* Box 36027, Grosse Pointe Farms, MI 48236.

Lundberg, *(Lundberg, Eric),* ; Publisher Abbreviation Without Addresses Are for Titles That Are Out of Print. These Are Obsolete Abbreviations. Publisher's Abbreviation Is Now J Johnson.

Lust, *(Lust, Benedict, Pubns.; 0-87904),* 25 Dewart Rd., Greenwich, CT 06830 Tel 203-661-0980; Orders to: P.O. Box 404, New York, NY 10156.

Lustrum Pr, *(Lustrum Press; 0-912810),* Dist. by: Amphoto, 1515 Broadway, New York, NY 10036 Tel 212-764-7300.

Luth Acad, *(Lutheran Academy for Scholarship; 0-913160),* 1901 McCord Rd., Valparaiso, IN 46383 Tel 219-464-5459.

Luth Bd of Pubn, *(Lutheran Board of Pubn.),* 2900 Queen Lane, Philadelphia, PA 19129.

Luth Braille Evang, *(Lutheran Braille Evangelism Assn.),* 660 E. Montana Ave., St. Paul, MN 55106.

Lutheran Braille, *(Lutheran Braille Workers, Inc., Sight Saving Div.),* 495 Ninth Ave., San Francisco, CA 94118 Tel 415-221-7500.

LWV MN, *(League of Women Voters of Minnesota; 0-939816),* 555 Wabasha St., Suite 212, St. Paul, MN 55102 Tel 612-224-5445.

LWV NYC, *(League of Women Voters of the City of New York; 0-916130),* 817 Broadway, New York, NY 10003.

LWV NYS, *(League of Women Voters of NYS; 0-938588),* 817 Broadway, New York, NY 10003.

LWV US, *(League of Women Voters of the U.S.; 0-89959),* 1730 M. St. N.W., Washington, DC 20036 Tel 202-296-1770.

LWVP Ed Fund
   See LWVPA

LWVPA, *(League of Women Voters of Pennsylvania; 0-931370),* Strawbridge & Clothier, 8th & Market Sts., Philadelphia, PA 19105 Tel 215-627-7937.

Lyceum Bks, *(Lyceum Books; 0-915336),* P.O. Box 113, Wilton, CT 06897.

Lydette, *(Lydette Publishing Co.; 0-910918),* P.O. Box 654, Cedar Falls, IA 50613.

Lydian Pr, *(Lydian Press),* P.O. Box 991, Kaneohe, HI 96744; Dist. by: Press Pacifica, P.O. Box 47, Kailua, HI 96734.

Lyl Inc, *(Lyl Inc),* P.O. Box 15439, Long Beach, CA 90815 Tel 213-433-1523; Moved, Left No Forwarding Address.

Lyle Stuart, *(Stuart, Lyle, Inc.; 0-8184),* 120 Enterprise Ave., Secaucus, NJ 07094 Tel 201-866-0490.

Lynx Hse, *(Lynx House Press; 0-89924),* P.O. Box 800, Amherst, MA 01002 Tel 413-773-7988.

Lytton Pub, *(Lytton Publishing Co.; 0-915728),* Drawer "G", College Station, TX 77841 Tel 713-845-2246.

M-A Pr, *(M/A Press; 0-930206),* 30 NW 23rd Place, Portland, OR 97210; Orders to: P.O. Box 606, Beaverton, OR 97075.

M & A Products, *(Machinery & Allied Products Institute),* 1200 18th St., N.W., Washington, DC 20036.

M & B, *(M & B Publishing Co.; 0-930496),* 1 Emerald St., Norwalk, CT 06850 Tel 202-846-4294.

M & P Frierson, *(Frierson, Meade & Penny),* 3705 Woodvale Rd., Birmingham, AL 35223.

M Arman, *(Arman, M., Publishing; 0-933078),* Box 785, Ormond Beach, FL 32074 Tel 904-672-7371.

M B Hall
   See Veritat Found

M B Hinman, *(Hinman, Marjory B.),* P. O. Box 345, Windsor, NY 13865 Tel 607-655-2011.

M B Stone, *(Stone, Michael B.; 0-9603448),* 8434 55th Ave., S., Seattle, WA 98118.

M B Zucker, *(Zucker, Marjorie B.),* 333 Central Park W., New York, NY 10025.

M Bergerie, *(Bergerie, Maurine; 0-9604234),* 201 Pollard Ave., New Iberia, LA 70560.

M Biggs, *(Biggs, Marge; 0-9603218),* 2226 S. Lewis, Anaheim, CA 92802 Tel 714-978-9724.

M Brinser, *(Brinser, Marlin; 0-9602298),* 643 Stuyvesant Ave., Irvington, NJ 07111.

M Buber Pr, *(Buber, Martin, Press),* G.P.O. Box 2009, Brooklyn, NY 11202.

M Burk, *(Burk, Margaret),* P.O. Box 22, Ambassador Sta, Los Angeles, CA 90070.

M C Clausen, *(Clausen, Muriel C.; 0-9603664),* 780 W. Grand Ave., Oakland, CA 94612.

M-C Pubns, *(M-C Pubns.; 0-9603850),* 449 N. Lamar St., Burbank, CA 91506.

M Cain, *(Cain, Mike; 0-9601458),* 192 Terra Manor Dr., Wintersville, OH 43952 Tel 614-264-3687.

M Clark, *(Clark, Merrian E.; 0-910384),* 22151 Clarendon St., P.O. Box 505, Woodland Hills, CA 91365 Tel 213-347-1677.

M D Falley, *(Falley, Margaret Dickson),* 1500 Sheridan Rd., Wilmette, IL 60091 Tel 312-251-4588.

M Demou & Assocs, *(Demou, Morris, & Associates; 0-9604794),* 2013 Big Oak Dr., Burnsville, MN 55337 Tel 612-890-3579.

M E Boultinghouse, *(Boultinghouse, Marquis E.; 0-9604358),* 900 N. Broadway, Lexington, KY 40505.

M E Coughlin, *(Coughlin, Michael E., Pub.; 0-9602574),* 1985 Selby Ave., St. Paul, MN 55104 Tel 612-646-8917.

M E Gant, *(Gant, Margaret Elizabeth; 0-9603138),* 7500 Deer Track Dr., Raleigh, NC 27612 Tel 919-781-6062.

M E Sharpe, *(Sharpe, M. E., Inc.; 0-87332),* 80 Business Park Dr., Armonk, NY 10504 Tel 914-273-1800.

M E Warren, *(Warren, M.E.; 0-9606060),* P.O. Box 1508, Annapolis, MD 21404.

M Evans, *(Evans, M., & Co., Inc.; 0-87131),* 216 E. 49th St., New York, NY 10017 Tel 212-688-2810; Dist. by: E. P. Dutton, 2 Park Ave., New York, NY 10016.

M F Davidson, *(Davidson, Mary Frances),* Rte. 3, Gatlinburg, TN 37738 Tel 615-436-5429.

M F Moss, *(Moss, Mary Foy),* 1158-63rd St., Apt. 3, Oakland, CA 94608.

M Farley, *(Farley, Mike; 0-933850),* P.O. Box 24A08, Los Angeles, CA 90024.

M G L S Pub, *(M G L S Publishing; 0-9601682),* 700 S. First St., Marshall, MN 56258 Tel 507-532-3553.

M G Wolfe, *(Wolfe, Mary G.; 0-9603406),* 23 Quartz Mill Rd., Newark, DE 19711 Tel 302-239-7571.

M Glazier, *(Glazier, Michael, Inc.; 0-89453),* 1210 King St., Wilmington, DE 19801 Tel 302-654-1635.

M Golub, *(Golub, Millin),* 1095 Second Ave., Apartment 2RN, New York, NY 10022 Tel 212-449-0990; Moved, Left No Forwarding Address.

M H Smith, *(Smith, Michael Holley; 0-931768),* 600-B E. Bee Caves Rd., Austin, TX 78746 Tel 512-327-4443; Moved, Left No Forwarding Address.

M Hutson
   See Hutson Assoc

M J D Shoaf, *(Shoaf, Mary Jo Davis; 0-9602520),* 310 Forest Hill Rd., Lexington, NC 27292 Tel 704-249-8015.

M J Kearney
   See Kearney

M J O'Malley, *(O'Malley, Martin J.),* 222 Paulison Ave., Passaic, NJ 07055 Tel 201-473-4643.

M J Stone, *(Stone, M. J., Co.; 0-9601888),* P.O. Box 12793, Seattle, WA 98111 Tel 206-682-0350.

M Johnson, *(Johnson, Mabel; 0-9600838),* P.O. Box 7, Boring, OR 97009 Tel 503-663-3428.

M Jones, *(Jones,, Marshall,, Co.; 0-8338),* Div. of Golden Quill Press, Francestown, NH 03043.

M K Heller, *(Heller, Marjorie K.; 0-915362),* Box 78, Bayside, NY 11361 Tel 212-229-7715.

M Kellogg
   See Bks by Kellogg

M L Emami, *(Emami, Mary Lou; 0-9602316),* 1691 Dickenson Dr., Wheaton, IL 60187.

M-L Pub, *(M-L Publishing Co., Ltd.; 0-915512),* 157 Devonshire Rd., Box 7181, Wilmington, DE 19803 Tel 302-655-2849.

M L Smith, *(Smith, Malcolm L.),* P.O. Box 6712, Washington, DC 20020.

M La Pice, *(La Pice, Margaret; 0-9604508),* 210 Montcalm, San Francisco, CA 94110.

M Linden NY, *(Linden, Millicent; 0-912628),* 500 E. 74th St., New York, NY 10021.

M Loke, *(Mele Loke Publishing Co.; 0-930932),* P.O. Box 7142, Honolulu, HI 96821 Tel 808-734-8611.

M Luff, *(Luff, Moe; 0-9600162),* 12 Greene Rd., Spring Valley, NY 10977 Tel 914-356-4855.

M Lukman, *(Lukman, Mphahlele; 0-9602660),* 9110 Avenue "A", Brooklyn, NY 11236.

M M Bruce, *(Bruce, Martin M., Pubs.; 0-935198),* Box 228, New Rochelle, NY 10804 Tel 914-235-4450.

M M Chamberlain, *(Chamberlain, Mildred Mosher; 0-9604142),* 128 Potters Ave., Warwick, RI 02886.

M M Cole Pub, *(Cole, M. M., Publishing Co.; 0-8471),* 919 N. Michigan Ave., Chicago, IL 60611 Tel 312-787-0804.

M McCosh Bkslr, *(McCosh, Melvin, Bookseller),* 26500 Edgewood Rd., Excelsior, MN 55331 Tel 612-474-8084.

M Mermelstein, *(Mermelstein, Mel; 0-89144),* Tel 717-847-9658; c/o Auschwitz Study Foundation, 7422 Cedar St., P.O. Box 2232, Huntington Beach, CA 92647.

M Molek Inc, *(Molek, M., Inc.; 0-9603142),* P.O. Box 453, Dover, DE 19901 Tel 302-678-1260.

M N Kemnitz, *(Kemnitz, Milton N.),* 1180 Bird Rd., P.O. Box 7390, Ann Arbor, MI 48107 Tel 313-668-9895.

M O Haroldsen, *(Haroldsen, Mark O.; 0-932444),* Orders to: Reorder Dept., 4751 So. Holladay Blvd., Salt Lake City, UT 84117 Tel 801-272-5522.

M O Merrill, *(Merrill, Madeline O.; 0-9601332),* 109 Water St., Saugus, MA 01906 Tel 617-233-5442.

M O Pub Co, *(M.O. Publishing Co.; 0-932044),* 14322 Howard Rd., Dayton, MD 20836.

M P Davison, *(Davison, Marguerite C.; 0-9603172),* P.O. Box 263, Swarthmore, PA 19081 Tel 215-729-6254.

M P Lopez, *(Lopez, Melinda P.),* 359 1/2 N. Gardner St., Los Angeles, CA 90036; Orders to: Bernard H. Hamel Spanish Books, 2326 Westwood Blvd., Los Angeles, CA 90064.

M Quam, *(Martin Quam Press; 0-9601600),* 1515 Columbia Dr., Cedar Falls, IA 50613 Tel 319-266-6242; Orders to: Rio, WI 53960.

M R K, *(M-R-K Publishing; 0-9601292),* 448 Seavey Lane, Petaluma, CA 94952 Tel 707-763-0056.

M R Kopmeyer
See Success Found

M Reinertsen
See Union Pr

M Robertson
See Biblio Dist

M S Johnson, *(Johnson, Merwyn S.; 0-9601590),* P.O. Box 368, Due West, SC 29639.

M S Rosenberg, *(Rosenberg, Mary S., Inc.; 0-917324),* 17 W. 60th St., New York, NY 10023 Tel 212-362-4873.

M S Wright, *(Wright, Mildred S., G.R.S.; 0-917016),* 140 Briggs, Beaumont, TX 77707 Tel 713-832-2308.

M Schalit, *(Schalit, Michael; 0-9604630),* 451 Bell Ave., Livermore, CA 94550 Tel 415-443-2456.

M Sheehan, *(Sheehan, Michael),* 2 Chittenden Lane, Owings Mill, MD 21117.

M Sheldon Pub, *(Sheldon, Marc, Publishing; 0-932262),* P.O. Box 272, 777 N. Loren Ave., Azusa, CA 91702 Tel 213-969-1866.

M Sturgeon
See Newport Beach

M T Finnerty, *(Finnerty, Mary T.; 0-9602222),* 23 Upton St., Boston, MA 02118; Orders to: P.O. Box 591, Astor Station, Boston, MA 02123.

M Torosian, *(Torosian, Martin),* 1010 Hunter Court, Deerfield, IL 60015.

M W Riley, *(Riley, Maurice W.; 0-9603150),* 512 Roosevelt Blvd., Ypsilanti, MI 48197.

M Waby, *(Waby, Marian),* 552-44 Bean Creek Rd., Scotts Valley, CA 95066 Tel 408-438-0567.

M West Pubs, *(West, Mark, Pubs.),* P.O. Box 413, Fulton, CA 95439.

M Wiener, *(Wiener, Moshe, 0-9609708), 834* Newburg Ave., North Woodmere, NY 11581.

M Y Jackson, *(Jackson, Margaret Y.),* 1990 Shepherd St. N.W., Washington, DC 20011.

Maaroufa Pr, *(Maaroufa Press, Inc.; 0-88425),* 610 N. Fairbanks Court, 3rd Floor, Chicago, IL 60611 Tel 312-337-2411; Moved, Left No Forwarding Address.

Maat Pub, *(Maat Publishing Co.; 0-917650),* P.O. Box 281, Bronx, NY 10462.

Macalester, *(Macalester Park Publishing Co.; 0-910924),* 1571 Grand Ave., St. Paul, MN 55105 Tel 612-698-8877.

Macalester Coll, *(Macalester College),* Weyerhaeuser Library, St. Paul, MN 55105 Tel 612-647-6346.

McAllister, *(McAllister Books; 0-910930),* 410 Lake Court, Waukegan, IL 60085 Tel 312 562-1929.

MacArthur Memorial, *(MacArthur Memorial),* MacArthur Square, Norfolk, VA 23510 Tel 804-441-2256.

McBooks Pr, *(McBooks Press; 0-935526),* 106 N. Aurora, Ithaca, NY 14850 Tel 607-272-6602; Dist. by: Crossing Press, 17 W. Main St., Trumansburg, NY 14886 Tel 607-387-6217.

McCabe, *(McCabe, Donald L.; 0-9605856),* 3221 Greenwood Ave., Sacramento, CA 95821 Tel 916-334-4810

McCahan Found, *(McCahan Foundation; 0-937094),* 270 Bryn Mawr Ave., Bryn Mawr, PA 19010 Tel 215-896-4542.

McCartan & Root, *(McCartan & Root, Pubs.; 0-935786),* 325 E. 57th St., New York, NY 10022 Tel 212-421-2641.

McClain, *(McClain Printing Co.; 0-87012),* 212 Main St., Parsons, WV 26287 Tel 304-478-2881.

McClelland, *(McClelland & Stewart, Ltd.),* 25 Hollinger Rd., Toronto, Ontario, M4B 3G2, Tel 416-751-4520.

McClure Printing, *(McClure Press/McClure Printing Co., Inc.),* P.O. Box 936, Verona, VA 24482 Tel 703-885-0884.

McCormick-Mathers, *(McCormick-Mathers Publishing Co.; 0-8009),* Div. of Litton Educational Publishing, 135 W. 50th St, New York, NY 10020 Tel 212-265-8700; Orders to: 7625 Empire Dr., Florence, KY 41042.

McCutchan, *(McCutchan Publishing Corp.; 0-8211),* P.O. Box 774A, 2526 Grove St., Berkeley, CA 94701 Tel 415-841-8616.

Macdonald Rain, *(Macdonald-Raintree Inc.; 0-8393),* Subs. of Raintree Pubs. Group, 205 W. Highland Ave., Milwaukee, WI 53203 Tel 414-273-0873.

McDougal-Littell, *(McDougal, Littell & Co.; 0-88343),* P.O. Box 1667, Evanston, IL 60204 Tel 312-256-5240.

McElderry Bk *Imprint of* **Atheneum**

McFarland & Co, *(McFarland & Co., Inc.; 0-89950),* Box 611, Jefferson, NC 28640 Tel 919-246-4460.

McGill-Queens U Pr, *(McGill-Queens Univ. Press; 0-7735),* 1020 Pine Ave., W., Montreal, Canada H3A 1A2, Tel 514-392-4421; Orders to: University of Toronto Press, 33 E. Tupper St., Buffalo, NY 14203.

McGilvery, *(McGilvery, Laurence; 0-910938),* P.O. Box 852, La Jolla, CA 92037 Tel 714-454-4443.

McGlynn, *(McGlynn, June A.; 0-9601350),* 1529 Meadowlark Dr., Great Falls, MT 59404 Tel 406-452-3486.

McGrath, *(McGrath Publishing Co.; 0-8434),* P.O. Box 9001, Wilmington, NC 28402 Tel 919-763-3757. *Imprints:* Consortium (Consortium Books).

McGraw, *(McGraw-Hill Book Co.; 0-07),* 1221 Ave. of the Americas, New York, NY 10020 Tel 212-997-1221. *Imprints:* Architectural Rec Bks (Architectural Record Books); BYTE Bks (BYTE Books); Chem Eng (Chemical Engineering).

McGraw-Hill Pubns, *(McGraw-Hill Pubns. Co.),* 441 National Press Bldg., Washington, DC 20045.

McGraw-Pretest, *(McGraw-Hill Book Co., Health Professions Division, PreTest Series),* P.O. Box 330, 71 S. Turnpike, Wallingford, CT 06492 Tel 203-265-5604; Orders to: McGraw-Hill Book Co., PreTest Series, P.O. Box 400, Hightstown, NJ 08520.

Macgregor, *(Macgregor, Scotty, Pubns.; 0-912546),* 10 Pineacre Dr., Smithtown, NY 11787 Tel 516-269-6572

Mack Pub, *(Mack Publishing Co.; 0-912734),* 20th & Northampton Sts., Easton, PA 18042 Tel 215-258-9111.

McKay, *(McKay, David, Co., Inc.; 0-679),* 2 Park Ave., New York, NY 10016 Tel 212-340-9800. *Imprints:* Charterhouse (Charterhouse Books, Inc.); Weybright (Weybright & Talley, Inc.); Wyden (Wyden, Peter H., Inc.).

Mackinac Island, *(Mackinac Island State Park Commission; 0-911872),* Box 370, Mackinac Island, MI 49757 Tel 906-847-3328.

McKinley Pub, *(McKinley Publishing Co.; 0-910942),* P.O. Box 77, Ocean City, NJ 08226.

McKinzie Pub, *(McKinzie Publishing Co.; 0-86626),* 11000 Wilshire Blvd., P.O. Box 24339, Los Angeles, CA 90024.

McKnight, *(McKnight Publishing Co.),* 808 I.A.A. Dr., P.O. Box 2854, Bloomington, IL 61701 Tel 309-663-1341; Dist. by: Taplinger Publishing Co., 200 Park Ave., S., New York, NY 10003.

Macmillan, *(Macmillan Publishing Co., Inc.; 0-02),* 866 Third Ave., New York, NY 10022 Tel 212-935-2000; Orders to: Front & Brown Sts., Riverside, NJ 08370. *Imprints:* Acorn (Acorn Books); Berlitz (Berlitz); CCPr (Crowell-Collier Press); Collier (Collier Books); Dove (Dove Books).

Macmillan Info, *(Macmillan Information; 0-02),* Div. of Macmillan Publishing Co., Inc., 866 Third Ave., New York, NY 10022 Tel 212-935-2000.

McMillan Pubns, *(McMillan Pubns.; 0-934228),* 3208 Halsey Dr., Woodridge, IL 60517 Tel 312-968-3933.

McNally, *(McNally & Loftin, Pubs.; 0-87461),* P.O. Box 1316, Santa Barbara, CA 93102 Tel 805-964-5117.

McNally NC, *(McNally & Loftin, Pubs., Inc.),* 510 W. 4th St., Charlotte, NC 28202 Tel 704-372-5784.

McNamara Pubns, *(McNamara Pubns., Inc.; 0-932770),* 741 Overlook St., Box 27277, Escondido, CA 92027 Tel 714-743-4942.

Macoy Pub, *(Macoy Publishing & Masonic Supply Co., Inc.; 0-910928),* P.O. Box 9759, Richmond, VA 23228 Tel 804-262-6551.

McQueen, *(McQueen Publishing Co.; 0-917186),* P.O. Box 198, Tiskilwa, IL 61368.

Macrae, *(Macrae Smith Co.; 0-8255),* Rtes. 54 & Old 147, Turbotville, PA 17772.

Macro Bks, *(Macro Books; 0-913080),* P.O. Box 26661, Tempe, AZ 85282 Tel 602-949-5559.

Macromedia Inc, *(Macromedia Inc.; 0-9601170),* P.O. Box 1025, Lake Placid, NY 12946 Tel 518-523-2713.

Mad River, *(Mad River Press; 0-916422),* Rte. 2, Box 151-B, Eureka, CA 95501 Tel 707-443-2947.

Made *Imprint of* **Doubleday**

Madison Co, *(Madison Co.; 0-913808),* P.O. Box 206, Berea, KY 40403 Tel 606-986-9744.

Madison Pub
See Madison Co

Madrona Pr, *(Madrona Press, Inc.; 0-89052),* P.O. Box 3750, Austin, TX 78764 Tel 512-327-2683.

Madrona Pubs, *(Madrona Pubs., Inc.; 0-914842),* 2116 Western Ave., Seattle, WA 98121 Tel 206-624-6840.

Maelstrom, *(Maelstrom Press; 0-917554),* P. O. Box 4261, Long Beach, CA 90804 Tel 213-439-7033.

Mafdet, *(Mafdet Press; 0-918534),* 1313 S. Jefferson Ave., Springfield, MO 65807 Tel 417-866-5141.

Mafex, *(Mafex Associates, Inc.; 0-87804),* 90 Cherry St., Johnstown, PA 15902 Tel 814-535-3597.

Mag Indus, *(Magazines for Industry, Inc.; 0-89451),* 747 Third Ave., New York, NY 10017 Tel 212-838-7778.

Magee, *(Magee, John, Inc.; 0-910944),* 103 State St., Boston, MA 02109.

Magi Bks, *(Magi Books, Inc.; 0-87343),* 33 Buckingham Dr., Albany, NY 12208 Tel 518-482-7781

Magic Carpet, *(Magic Carpet Press, The; 0-935808),* P.O. Box 168, Syosset, NY 11791 Tel 516-367-4865.

Magic Circle Pr, *(Magic Circle Press; 0-913660),* 10 Hyde Ridge Rd., Weston, CT 06883 Tel 203-226-1903; Dist. by: Walker & Co., 720 Fifth Ave, New York, NY 10019.

Magic Ltd, *(Magic Limited-Lloyd E. Jones; 0-915926),* P.O. Box 3186, San Leandro, CA 94578 Tel 415-352-1854; 4064 39th Ave., Oakland, CA 94619 Tel 415-531-5490.

Magick Circle *Imprint of* **Tech Group**

Magickal Childe, *(Magickal Childe Inc.; 0-939708),* 35 W. 19th St., New York, NY 10011.

Magna Carta Bk, *(Magna Carta Book Co.; 0-910946),* 5502 Magnolia Ave., Baltimore, MD 21215 Tel 301-466-8191.

Magna Pub Co, *(Magna Publishing Co.; 0-912150),* 621 N. Sherman Ave., Madison, WI 53704 Tel 608-233-9300.

Magnaflux, *(Magnaflux Corp.),* 7300 W. Lawrence St., Chicago, IL 60656 Tel 312-867-8000.

Magnamusic, *(Magnamusic-Baton, Inc.; 0-918812),* 10370 Page Industrial Blvd, St. Louis, MO 63132 Tel 314-427-5660.

Magnes Mus, *(Magnes Museum),* 2911 Russell St., Berkeley, CA 94705 Tel 415-849-2710.

Magnolia Lab, *(Magnolia Laboratory),* 701 Beach Blvd., Pascagoula, MS 39567 Tel 601-762-1643.

Magoos Umbrella, *(Magoo's Umbrella; 0-932904),* 18581 Devon Ave., Saratoga, CA 95070 Tel 408-379-7354

Maguey Pr, *(Maguey Press, The; 0-930778),* Box 3395, Tucson, AZ 85722.

Mah-Tov Pubns, *(Mah-Tov Pubns.; 0-917274),* 1680 45th St., Brooklyn, NY 11204 Tel 212-871-5337.

Maher Ventril Studio, *(Maher Ventriloquist Studios),* P.O. Box 420, Littleton, CO 80160 Tel 303-798-6830.

Mahony, *(Mahony, Patrick; 0-913742),* 5885 Locksley Place, Hollywood, CA 90068 Tel 213-467-9903.

Maiden Bks, *(Maiden Books; 0-931138),* 300 Washington St., Newark, NJ 07102.

Maiden Lane, *(Maiden Lane Press; 0-9605688),* P.O. Box 3724, Charlottesville, VA 22903.

Mail Order, *(Mail Order U.S.A.; 0-914694),* 3100 Wisconsin Ave. N.W., Washington, DC 20016 Tel 202-686-9521; Orders to: P.O. Box 19083, Washington, DC 20036.

Mailbox, *(Mailbox Club, The; 0-9603752),* 404 Eager Rd., Valdosta, GA 31601.

Main St *Imprint of* **Universe**

Main Street, *(Main Street Press; 0-915590),* P.O. Box 4262, Anaheim, CA 92803 Tel 714-998-0517.

Main Track, *(Main Track Pubns.; 0-933866),* 12435 Ventura Court, Studio City, CA 91604 Tel 213-980-5900.

Maine Antique, *(Maine Antique Digest, Inc.; 0-917312),* P.O. Box 358, Waldoboro, ME 04572 Tel 207-832-7534.

Maine Dept Marine, *(Maine Dept. of Marine Resources; 0-89737),* Fisheries Research Sta., West Boothbay Harbor, ME 04575.

Maine Hist, *(Maine Historical Society; 0-915592),* 485 Congress St., Portland, ME 04111 Tel 207-774-1822.

Maine St Mus, *(Maine State Museum Pubns.; 0-913764),* State House, Sta. 83, Augusta, ME 04333 Tel 207-289-2301.

Mainespring, *(Mainespring Press),* Box 82, Stonington, ME 04681 Tel 207-367-2484.

Maize Pr, *(Maize Press; 0-939558),* P.O. Box 8251, San Diego, CA 92102 Tel 714-455-1128.

Majestic Bks, *(Majestic Books; 0-9604968),* 2338 Henderson Mill Court, Atlanta, GA 30345.

Major Bks, *(Major Books; 0-89041),* 21335 Roscoe Blvd., Canoga Park, CA 91304 Tel 213-999-4100; Orders to: Kable News, Inc., 777 Third Ave., New York, NY 10017 Tel 212-486-2828; Dist. by: Major Books, 18-39 128th St., College Point, NY 11356 Tel 212-939-1119.

Majors
See S Karger

Makapu'u Pr, *(Makapu'u Press),* P.O. Box 26404, Honolulu, HI 96825.

Makepeace Bks Ltd, *(Makepeace Books Ltd.; 0-917468),* 3257 W. Bryn Mawr Ave., Chicago, IL 60659 Tel 312-583-2727.

Makepeace Colony, *(Makepeace Colony Press, The; 0-87741),* P.O. Box 111, Stevens Point, WI 54481 Tel 715-344-2636.

Malcolm Hse, *(Malcolm House),* 805 Malcolm Dr., Silver Spring, MD 20901 Tel 301-439-4358.

Maledicta, *(Maledicta Press; 0-916500),* 331 S. Greenfield Ave., Waukesha, WI 53186 Tel 414-542-5853.

Malhotra, *(Malhotra, S.),* 20 Acorn Park, Cambridge, MA 02140; Orders to: 16 Cooke Rd., Lexington, MA 02173.

Malki Mus Pr, *(Malki Museum Press),* Dept. of Linguistics, Univ. of California, Los Angeles, CA 90024 Tel 213-474-0169; Orders to: 11-795 Fields Rd., Morongo Indian Reservation, Banning, CA 92220 Tel 714-849-7289.

Malter Westerfield, *(Malter-Westerfield Publishing Co.; 0-911718),* P.O. Box 343, San Clemente, CA 92672; Moved, Left No Forwarding Address.

Maltese Bks, *(Maltese Books; 0-912664),* P.O. Box 781, Redondo Beach, CA 90277.

Malvaux, *(Malvaux, Ets J.),* Orders to: Dillon-Donnelly Publishing, 7058 Lindell Blvd., St. Louis, MO 63130 Tel 314-862-6239.

Mamelle Inc, *(La Mamelle, Inc.; 0-931818),* P.O. Box 3123, Rincon Annex, San Francisco, CA 94119.

Mammoth Pr, *(Mammoth Press),* 40-B Grecian Garden Dr., Rochester, NY 14616.

Man-Root, *(Man-Root),* P. O. Box 982, South San Francisco, CA 94080.

Management Advisory Pubns, *(Management Advisory Pubns.),* Box 151, 44 Washington St., Wellesley Hills, MA 02181 Tel 617-235-2895.

Management Pr, *(Management Press, Inc.),* P.O. Box 34965, Memphis, TN 38134.

Manas, *(Manas Pubns.; 0-911804),* 1868 Shore Dr. S., No. 205, St. Petersburg, FL 33707 Tel 813-343-1428.

Manch Lane, *(Manchester Lane Editions),* 1409 Nicholson St., N.W., Washington, DC 20011 Tel 202-726-3121.

Manchester, *(Manchester Univ. Press; 0-7190),* Dist. by: Standing Orders, Inc., 156 5th Ave., New York, NY 10010 Tel 212-243-0370.

Manchester Group, *(Manchester Group, Ltd., The; 0-9605792),* 3501 26th Place W., No. 422, Seattle, WA 98199 Tel 206-292-2057.

Mandala
See Irvington

Mandala Bks, *(Mandala Books; 0-9603226),* RFD Box 56, Vershire, VT 05079; Do Not Confuse with Mandala Press in MA (Mandala) or Mandala Press in NC (Mandala Pr).

Mandala Pr, *(Mandala Press; 0-933158),* P.O. Box 3892, Wilmington, NC 28406 Tel 919-791-5719; Do Not Confuse with Mandala Books in VT (Mandala Bks) or Mandala Press in MA (Mandala).

Mandarin, *(Mandarin Press; 0-931514),* 210 Fifth Ave., New York, NY 10010.

Mandate Imprint of **William Carey Lib**

M&S Pr, *(M & S Press; 0-87730),* Box 311, Weston, MA 02193 Tel 617-891-5650.

Manessier, *(Manessier Publishing Co.; 0-910950),* Box C, Bryn Mawr, CA 92318.

Manet Guild, *(Manet Guild; 0-9602418),* 310 Franklin St., Dept. 535, Boston, MA 02110 Tel 617-449-3792.

Mangan Bks, *(Mangan Books; 0-930208),* 6245 Snowheights Ct., El Paso, TX 79912 Tel 915-584-1662.

Manhattan Ctr Psych
See Ctr Mod Psych Stud

Manhattan Ltd NC, *(Manhattan, Ltd., Pubs.; 0-932046),* P.O. Box 18601, Raleigh, NC 27619 Tel 919-833-2121.

Manhattan Pub Co, *(Manhattan Publishing Co.),* Div. of U.S. & World Publications, Inc., 225 Lafayette St., New York, NY 10012 Tel 212-966-1768.

Manifest Destiny, *(Manifest Destiny Books; 0-914852),* P.O. Box 57, Dorchester, MA 02124 Tel 617-288-8765; Tel 617-423-4340.

Mankind Pub, *(Mankind Publishing Co.; 0-87687),* 8060 Melrose Ave., Los Angeles, CA 90046 Tel 213-653-8060.

Mann Pubs, *(Mann Pubs.; 0-936632),* P.O. Box 7 AK, Jersey City, NJ 07307 Tel 201-659-8324.

Manna Pubns, *(Manna Pubns.; 0-939744),* Box 1111, Camas, WA 98607 Tel 206-834-3148.

Manoa Pr, *(Manoa Press, Inc.; 0-9605502),* Box 25355, Honolulu, HI 96825.

Manor Bks, *(Manor Books, Inc.; 0-532),* 45 E. 30th St., New York, NY 10016 Tel 212-686-9100.

Mansell, *(Mansell; 0-7201),* 99 Main St., Salem, NH 03079 Tel 617-685-8149.

Manufacturing Confectioner, *(Manufacturing Confectioner),* 175 Rock Rd., Glen Rock, NJ 07452 Tel 201-652-2655.

Manuscript Pr, *(Manuscript Press; 0-936414),* Box 307, Kingston, NJ 08528 Tel 609-921-0151; Dist. by: PDA Enterprises, Box 8010, New Orleans, LA 70182.

Manville Pub, *(Manville Publishing),* P.O. Box 10091, Phoenix, AZ 85064; Moved, Left No Forwarding Address.

Manyland, *(Manyland Books, Inc.; 0-87141),* 84-39 90th St., Woodhaven, NY 11421 Tel 212-441-6768.

Manzanita Pr, *(Manzanita Press; 0-931644),* P.O. Box 4027, San Rafael, CA 94903 Tel 415-479-9636.

Map World, *(Map World Pubns.; 0-89414),* Box 2501, Dublin, CA 94566 Tel 415-829-2728.

Maple Mont, *(Maplegrove & Montgrove Press),* 4055 N. Keystone Ave., Chicago, IL 60641 Tel 312-286-2655.

Maplewood, *(Maplewood Press; 0-914048),* P.O. Box 90, Meadville, PA 16335 Tel 814-336-1768.

Mar Vista, *(Mar Vista Publishing Co.; 0-9604064),* 11917 Westminster Place, Los Angeles, CA 90066.

Mara, *(Mara Books, Inc.; 0-87787),* 1318 Second Street, Santa Monica, CA 90401 Tel 213-394-3429.

Mara Pr MA, *(Mara Press),* Box 790, Marblehead, MA 01945 Tel 617-631-0624.

Maran Pub, *(Maran Publishing Co.; 0-916526),* 320 N. Eutaw St., Baltimore, MD 21201.

Maranatha Baptist, *(Maranatha Baptist Press; 0-937136),* Maranatha Baptist Bible College, 745 W. Main St., Watertown, WI 53094.

Maranatha Evangelical
See Maranatha Hse Pubs

Maranatha Hse Pubs, *(Maranatha House Pubs.; 0-89337),* 705 S. Hwy. 101, Solana Beach, CA 92075 Tel 714-755-0962.

Marand Pub Co, *(Marand Publishing Co.; 0-86567),* 1333 Ocean Ave., Santa Monica, CA 90401 Tel 213-394-7361.

Marando Pr, *(Marando Press, Inc.; 0-932518),* 99 Park Ave., New York, NY 10016; Moved, Left No Forwarding Address.

Marathon Pr, *(Marathon Press; 0-932106),* 133 E. 58th St., Rm. 803, New York, NY 10022 Tel 212-593-3514.

Marburger, *(Marburger Pubns.; 0-915730),* P.O. Box 422, Manhasset, NY 11030.

MARC, *(MARC, Missions Advanced Research Communication Center; 0-912552),* 919 W. Huntington Dr., Monrovia, CA 91016 Tel 213-357-7979.

Marc Two Res, *(Marc Two Research; 0-914358),* 2 Research Court, Rockville, MD 20850.

MARCC
See MARC

Marcella, *(Marcella Press; 0-938468),* P.O. Box 1105, Palm Desert, CA 92261.

March of Dimes, *(National Foundation-March of Dimes),* 1275 Mamaroneck Ave., White Plains, NY 10605 Tel 914-428-7100.

Marco Polo, *(Marco Polo Pubs.; 0-932820),* 3904 Spring Hollow St., Colleyville, TX 76034 Tel 817-571-0794.

Marconi
See Tele Cable

Marek, *(Marek, Richard, Pubs., Inc.; 0-399),* Subs. of G.P. Putnam's Sons, 200 Madison Ave., New York, NY 10016 Tel 212-576-8900.

Margaritas Bks Brown, *(Margarita's Books for Brown Eyes; 0-918536),* 1203 23rd Ave., San Diego, CA 92120 Tel 714-239-4621.

Margin Bks, *(Margin Books),* 2912 N. Hackett, Milwaukee, WI 53211; Moved, Left No Forwarding Address.

Margoe Jane, *(Margoe Jane Pubns.; 0-9602330),* Matthew 778, North Bangor, NY 12966 Tel 518-483-0842; Dist. by: National Ataxia Foundation, 6681 Country Club Dr., Minneapolis, MN 55427 Tel 612-546-6220.

Marina Mind, *(Marina Mind Science Center),* 4018 Redwood, Los Angeles, CA 90066.

Marine Bio, *(Marine Biological Laboratory; 0-912544),* Woods Hole, MA 02543.

Marine Educ, *(Marine Education Textbooks; 0-934114),* 124 N. Van Ave., Houma, LA 70360.

Marine Educ Imprint of **Herman Pub**

Mariner, *(Mariner Books; 0-910954),* 1949 Haywood Rd., Apt. 15, Hendersonville, NC 28739 Tel 704-693-8045.

Mariner Pr, *(Mariner Press; 0-911920),* P.O. Box 99, Somerset, NJ 08873.

Mariners Boston, *(Mariners Press, Inc., The; 0-913352),* P.O. Box 540, Boston, MA 02117 Tel 617-749-5759.

Mariners Mus, *(Mariners Museum; 0-917376),* Museum Dr., Newport News, VA 23606 Tel 804-595-0368.

Marion Cnty Lib, *(Marion County Library; 0-9603086),* 101 E. Court St., Marion, SC 29571 Tel 803-423-2244.

Mark-Age, *(Mark-Age Inc.; 0-912322),* 5555 S.W. 64th Ave., Fort Lauderdale, FL 33314.

Mark Foster Mus, *(Mark Foster Music Co.; 0-916656),* P.O. Box 4012, Champaign, IL 61820 Tel 217-367-9932.

Market Comm, *(Market Communications, Inc.; 0-930820),* 225 E. Michigan St., Milwaukee, WI 53202 Tel 414-276-6600.

Market Ed, *(Market Ed Inc.; 0-937470),* P.O. Box 45181, Westlake, OH 44145 Tel 216-779-4689.

Marketing Econs, *(Marketing Economics Institute, Ltd.; 0-914078),* 108 W. 39th St., New York, NY 10018 Tel 212-869-8260.

Markewich, *(Markewich, Reese; 0-9600160),* Bacon Hill Rd., Pleasantville, NY 10570 Tel 212-674-2979.

Markham, *(Markham Publishing Co.; 0-8410),* a Rand McNally College Pub. Co., P.O. Box 7600, Chicago, IL 60680 Tel 312-267-6868.

Markham Pr Fund, *(Markham Press Fund; 0-918403),* Div. of Baylor Univ. Press, Orders to: Book Dept., Baylor Book Store, P.O. Box 6325, Waco, TX 76706 Tel 817-755-2161.

Marlborough Hse, *(Marlborough House, Inc.),* 230 Marlborough St., Boston, MA 02116; Moved, Left No Forwarding Address.

Marlborough Pubns, *(Marlborough Pubns; 0-9604594),* P.O. Box 16406, San Diego, CA 92116 Tel 714-280-8310.

Marlin, *(Marlin Pubns. International, Inc.; 0-930624),* 485 Fifth Ave., New York, NY 10017 Tel 212-986-7752.

Marling, *(Marling Associates; 0-912818),* Orders to: Altarinda Books, 13 Estates Dr., Orinda, CA 94563 Tel 415-254-3830.

MARLU, *(MARLU; 0-9601702),* 15 E. 41 St., New York, NY 10017 Tel 212-986-2244; Orders to: P.O. Box 111, Dobbs Ferry, NY 10522.

Marnel Pr, *(Marnel Press, The),* Div. of AFM Enterprises, Inc., 6355 Topanga Canyon Blvd., Suite 219, Woodland Hills, CA 91367 Tel 213-888-2990.

Marquest Colorguide, *(Marquest Colorguide Books; 0-916240),* P.O. Box 132, Palos Verdes Estates, CA 90274 Tel 213-373-4301.

Marquette, *(Marquette Univ. Press; 0-87462),* 1324 W. Wisconsin Ave., Rm. 409, Milwaukee, WI 53233 Tel 414-224-1564.

Marquette Cnty, *(Marquette County Historical Society, Inc.),* 213 N. Front St., Marquette, MI 49855 Tel 906-226-3571.

Marquis, *(Marquis Who's Who, Inc.; 0-8379),* 200 E. Ohio St., Chicago, IL 60611 Tel 312-787-2008; Orders to: 4300 W. 62nd St., Indianapolis, IN 46206 Tel 317-298-5400.

Marr Pubns, *(Marr Pubns.; 0-938712),* P.O. Box 1421, New York, NY 10101 Tel 516-822-7744.

Marston *Imprint of* **Forum Pr MO**

Martin Gordon, *(Martin Gordon, Inc.; 0-931036),* 25 E. 83rd St., New York, NY 10028 Tel 212-249-7350.

Martin Motorsports, *(Martin Motorsports; 0-9605068),* P.O. Box 12654, Fort Wayne, IN 46864.

Martin Pr, *(Martin Press; 0-914976),* P.O. Box 25464, Los Angeles, CA 90025; Moved,Left No Forwarding Address.

Martin Res
    See Qwint Systems

Martingale, *(Martingale Manuscripts),* Box 17, North Pitcher, NY 13124 Tel 315-653-4401.

Marty-Nagy, *(Marty-Nagy Bookworks; 0-917296),* 624 Rhode Island St., San Francisco, CA 94107 Tel 415-824-8274.

Marvanco, *(Marvanco Enterprises; 0-9604336),* 25 Floral Rd., Peekskill, NY 10566.

Marxist Educ, *(Marxist Educational Press; 0-930656),* c/o Dept. of Anthropology, Univ. of Minnesota, 215 Ford Hall, 224 Church St., S.E., Minneapolis, MN 55455 Tel 612-373-5803.

Mary Ellen Bks, *(Mary Ellen Books),* P.O. Box 7589-Rincon Annex, San Francisco, CA 94120.

Mary Ellen Ent, *(Mary Ellen Enterprises),* 1601 W. Lake St., Minneapolis, MN 55408 Tel 612-827-6553.

Mary Inc, *(Mary, Inc.; 0-915872),* 99 President Ave., Providence, RI 02906 Tel 401-751-0566.

Mary Noble, *(Noble, Mary; 0-913928),* 5700 W. Salerno Rd., Jacksonville, FL 32210 Tel 904-387-5044.

Maryben Bks, *(Maryben Books; 0-913184),* 619 Warfield Dr., Rockville, MD 20850 Tel 301-762-5291.

Maryknoll, *(Maryknoll Pubns.),* ; Publisher Abbreviation Without Addresses Are for Titles That Are Out of Print. These Are Obsolete Abbreviations.

Maryland Hist Pr, *(Maryland Historical Press; 0-917882),* 9205 Tuckerman St., Lanham, MD 20801 Tel 301-577-2436.

MAS De Reinis, *(M.A.S. De Reinis; 0-937370),* Div. of Polymath, Inc., Box 2820, Grand Central Sta., New York, NY 10017 Tel 212-625-4336.

Masda, *(Masda Publishing Co.),* 31 Milk St., Boston, MA 02109.

MASEA, *(Mid-Atlantic Solar Energy Assn.; 0-9601884),* 2233 Gray's Ferry Ave., Philadelphia, PA 19146.

Mason Charter
    See Van Nos Reinhold

Mason Clinic, *(Mason Clinic, The; 0-9601944),* 1100 Ninth Ave., P.O. Box 900, Seattle, WA 98111 Tel 206-223-6985.

Mason Parks, *(Mason Parks Press; 0-9601004),* P.O. Box 46, Newton Lower Falls, MA 02162.

Mason Pub, *(Mason Publishing Co.; 0-917126),* 366 Wacouta St., St. Paul, MN 55101 Tel 612-224-5367.

Masonic Serv, *(Masonic Service Assn. of the U. S.),* 8120 Fenton St., Silver Spring, MD 20910 Tel 301-588-4010.

Mass Hist Soc, *(Massachusetts Historical Society),* 1154 Boylston St., Boston, MA 02215 Tel 617-536-1608.

Masson Pub, *(Masson Publishing U.S.A., Inc.; 0-89352),* 133 E. 58th St., New York, NY 10022 Tel 212-838-8510.

Masspac Pub, *(Masspac Publishing Co.; 0-918020),* 48855 N. Gratiot, Mt. Clemens, MI 48045 Tel 313-949-9222.

Master Bks, *(Master Books; 0-89051),* P.O. Box 15666, San Diego, CA 92175.

Master Design, *(Master Designer),* 343 S. Dearborn St., Chicago, IL 60604 Tel 312-922-9075.

Master Key, *(Master Key Pubns.; 0-935434),* P.O. Box 519, Bonita, CA 92002 Tel 714-475-5554.

Master Pr, *(Master Press; 0-9600818),* P. O. Box 432, Dayton, OR 97114 Tel 503-864-2987.

Masterco Pr, *(Masterco Press, Inc.; 0-912164),* P.O. Box 7382, Ann Arbor, MI 48107 Tel 313-428-8300.

Masters, *(Masters Press, Inc.; 0-89251),* Div. of Merchants Pub. Co., 20 Mills St., Kalamazoo, MI 49001 Tel 616-385-1842.

Masterwork Pr, *(Masterwork Press; 0-912156),* P.O. Box 302, Pottersville, NJ 07979 Tel 201-439-3816.

Mastery Learning, *(Mastery Learning Systems; 0-935144),* 450 E. Strawberry Dr., No. 39, Mill Valley, CA 94941; Moved, Left No Forwarding Address.

Matacia, *(Matacia, Louis J.),* P.O. Box 32, Oakton, VA 22124 Tel 703-560-8993.

Matagiri, *(Matagiri Sri Aurobindo Center, Inc.; 0-89071),* Mt. Tremper, NY 12457 Tel 914-679-8322.

Matchless Pub, *(Matchless Publishing Co.; 0-88219),* P.O. Box 2743, Denver, CO 80201; Moved, Left No Forwarding Address. Imprints: Numisphil Pubns (Numisphil Publications).

Mater Dei Provincialate, *(Mater Dei Provincialate; 0-9605784),* 9400 New Harmony Rd., Evansville, IN 47712.

Maternity Ctr, *(Maternity Center Assn.; 0-912758),* 48 E. 92nd St., New York, NY 10028 Tel 212-369-7300.

Matez Fielden, *(Matez Fielden Pubns., Inc.; 0-933048),* 6618 Michaeljohn Dr., La Jolla, CA 92037.

Math Alternatives, *(Mathematical Alternatives, Inc.; 0-916060),* 299 Park Ave., 5th Floor, New York, NY 10171 Tel 212-486-1775.

Math Assn, *(Mathematical Assn. of America; 0-88385),* 1529 Eighteenth St., N.W., Washington, DC 20036 Tel 202-387-5200.

Math Counsel Inst, *(Math Counseling Institute Press; 0-9605756),* 4518 Corliss Ave. N., Seattle, WA 98103.

Math Hse, *(Math House; 0-917792),* Div. of Mosaic Media, Inc., P.O. Box 711, Glen Ellyn, IL 60137 Tel 312-790-1117.

Math Sci Pr, *(Math-Sci Press; 0-915692),* 53 Jordan Rd., Brookline, MA 02146 Tel 617-738-0307.

Mathco, *(Mathco; 0-912938),* P.O. Box 240, Rockport, MA 01966 Tel 617-546-6368.

Mathiesen Edns, *(Mathiesen Editions; 0-917412),* 45 Lauriston St., Providence, RI 02906 Tel 401-351-1878.

Mathom, *(Mathom Pub. Co.; 0-930000),* 68 E. Mohawk St., Oswego, NY 13126 Tel 315-343-3035.

Matiasz, *(Matiasz, George Z., Editor & Pub.),* 445 Mariposa, Ventura, CA 93001 Tel 805-643-3661.

Matlock-Silber, *(Matlock/Silber Pubns.),* 6 Bay Vista Court, Mill Valley, CA 94941 Tel 415-383-7457.

Matrix Pub, *(Matrix Pubs., Inc.; 0-916460),* 30 N.W. 23rd Place, Portland, OR 97210 Tel 503-243-1150.

Matrix Pubns, *(Matrix Pubns., Inc.; 0-936554),* 27 Benefit St., Providence, RI 02904.

Mattole Pr, *(Mattole Press; 0-916854),* P.O. Box 22324, San Francisco, CA 94122 Tel 707-523-2959.

Maureen Points, *(Maureen Points),* 2905 Van Ness Ave., No. 101, San Francisco, CA 94109.

Maverick, *(Maverick Pubns.; 0-89288),* P.O. Box 243, Bend, OR 97701 Tel 503-382-6978.

Mawa Pub, *(Mawa Publishing Co.; 0-935053),* Box 22525, Makiki, HI 96822.

Maxigraphics, *(Maxigraphics, Inc.),* R.D. No. 2, Box 123, Phillipsburg, NJ 08885 Tel 201-454-1544.

Maxim Pub, *(Maxim Publishing; 0-936696),* P.O. Box 42126, Los Angeles, CA 90042.

Maxima, *(Maxima Communications, Inc.; 0-918612),* 5029 Sherborne Dr., St Louis, MO 63128 Tel 314-894-0370.

Maxims Bks, *(Maxim's Books),* P.O. Box 480451, Los Angeles, CA 90048.

Maxwell Repr, *(Maxwell Reprint Co.; 0-8277),* Fairview Park, Elmsford, NY 10523 Tel 914-592-7700.

Maxwell Schl Citizen, *(Maxwell School of Citizenship & Public Affairs; 0-915984),* 119 College Place, Syracuse, NY 13210 Tel 315-423-2552.

Maxwell Sci Intl, *(Maxwell Scientific International, Inc.; 0-8277),* Fairview Park, Elmsford, NY 10523 Tel 914-592-9141.

May Day Pr, *(May Day Press; 0-9602420),* P.O. Box 1351, Bellflower, CA 90706 Tel 213-439-8423.

May Murdock, *(May-Murdock; 0-932916),* Box 343, 90 Glenwood Ave., Ross, CA 94957 Tel 415-454-1771.

Maya, *(Maya),* 1222 Solano Ave., Albany, CA 94706; Tel 415-548-8204.

Mayapple Pr, *(Mayapple Press; 0-932412),* P.O. Box 7508, Liberty Sta., Ann Arbor, MI 48107 Tel 313-971-2223.

Mayers-Joseph, *(Mayers, Joseph, & Co., Inc.; 0-9604960),* 50 Park Place, Suite H, Newark, NJ 07102 Tel 201-622-7854.

Mayfield Pub, *(Mayfield Publishing Co.; 0-87484),* 285 Hamilton Ave., Palo Alto, CA 94301 Tel 415-326-1640.

Mayflower, *(General Society of Mayflower Descendants; 0-930270),* 128 Massasoit Dr., Warwick, RI 02888 Tel 401-781-6759; Orders to: Mayflower Families, P.O. Box 297, Plymouth, MA 02361; Do Not Confuse with Mayflower Books, Inc.

Mayflower Bks *Imprint of* **Smith Pubs**

Mayflower Press NJ, *(Mayflower Press; 0-9602216),* 26 Tulp Court, Clifton, NJ 07013.

Mazda Pubs, *(Mazda Pubs.; 0-939214),* P.O. Box 136, Lexington, KY 40501.

Mazgeen Pr, *(Mazgeen Press; 0-915330),* P.O. Box 70, Key West, FL 33040 Tel 305-294-0734.

Maznaim, *(Maznaim Publishing Corp.; 0-940118),* 4407-15th Ave., Brooklyn, NY 11219 Tel 212-438-7680.

MB *Imprint of* **Dell**

MBO Inc, *(MBO, Inc.; 0-9602950),* 157 Pontoosic Rd., P.O. Box 10, Westfield, MA 01085.

MCL Assocs, *(MCL Associates; 0-930696),* P.O. Box 26, McLean, VA 22101 Tel 703-356-5979.

MCP Bks, *(MCP Books; 0-9603926),* P.O. Box 273, Germantown, MD 20767.

MCSA Pubns
    See Med Communications

Md Bk Exch, *(Maryland Book Exchange),* 4500 College Ave., College Park, MD 20740 Tel 301-927-2510.

MD Hall Records, *(Maryland Hall of Records Commission),* P.O. Box 828, Annapolis, MD 21404 Tel 301-269-3915.

Md Hist, *(Maryland Historical Society),* 201 W. Monument St., Baltimore, MD 21201.

MD Pubns, *(MD Pubns.; 0-910922),* 30 E. 60th St., New York, NY 10022.

MDA Pubns FL, *(MDA Pubns.),* Div. of Management Development Associates, 214 Bullard Pkwy., Suite C, Temple Terrace, FL 33617 Tel 813-985-1215.

MDK Inc, *(MDK, Inc.; 0-934580),* P.O. Box 2831, Chapel Hill, NC 27514 Tel 919-929-4260.

Me Pubns, *(Me Pubns.; 0-937706),* P.O. Box 14005, Minneapolis, MN 55414.

Mead Co, *(Mead Co., The; 0-934422),* 21176 S. Alameda St., Long Beach, CA 90810.

Meadow Lane, *(Meadow Lane Pubns.; 0-934826),* 2716 Edgewood, P.O. Box 640, Provo, UT 84601; Moved, Left No Forwarding Address.

Meadow Pr, *(Meadow Press; 0-931058),* P.O. Box 35, Port Jefferson, NY 11777 Tel 516-473-1370.

Meadowbrook Pr, *(Meadowbrook Press; 0-915658),* 18318 Minnetonka Blvd., Deephaven, MN 55391 Tel 612-473-5400.

Means, *(Means, Robert Snow, Co., Inc.; 0-911950),* 100 Construction Plaza, Kingston, MA 02364 Tel 617-747-1270.

Meckler Bks, *(Meckler Books; 0-930466),* 520 Riverside Ave., P.O. Box 405, Saugatuck Sta., Westport, CT 06880 Tel 203-226-6967.

Med-Behavior, *(Medical/Behavioral Associates, Inc.; 0-936514),* 666 Park Ave. W., Mansfield, OH 44906.

Med Communications, *(MCSA-Medical Communications & Services Assn.; 0-917054),* 10223 NE. 58th St., Kirkland, WA 98033 Tel 206-828-4263.

Med Computer
 See **Med Communications**

Med Economics, *(Medical Economics Books; 0-87489),* 680 Kinderkamack Rd., Oradell, NJ 07649 Tel 201-262-3030; Orders to: Box 157, Florence, KY 41042.

Med Educ, *(Medical Education Consultants; 0-937142),* Box 67101, Century City, Los Angeles, CA 90067 Tel 213-475-5141.

Med Exam, *(Medical Examination Publishing Co., Inc.; 0-87488),* 969 Stewart Ave., Garden City, NY 11530 Tel 516-222-2277.

Med Group Mgmt, *(Medical Group Management Assn.),* 4101 E. Louisiana Ave., Denver, CO 80222 Tel 303-753-1111.

Med Lib Assn, *(Medical Library Assn., Inc.; 0-912176),* 919 N. Michigan Ave., Suite 3208, Chicago, IL 60611 Tel 312-266-2456.

Med Media Pubs, *(Medical Media Pubs.; 0-939450),* 4320 Centre Ave., Pittsburgh, PA 15213; Dist. by: American Hospital Publishing, Inc., 211 E. Chicago Ave., Chicago, IL 60611.

Med-Nurse *Imprint of* **A-W**

Medal Print, *(Medal Printing Co.; 0-917692),* 183 Benefit St., Pawtucket, RI 02861 Tel 401-724-3586.

Medallion *Imprint of* **Berkley Pub**

Medcom, *(Medcom, Inc.; 0-8463),* Dist. by: Williams & Wilkins Co., 428 E. Preston St., Baltimore, MD 21202.

Medgar Evers Coll, *(Medgar Evers College Press; 0-89062),* 1150 Carroll St., Brooklyn, NY 11225.

Medi-Comp, *(Medi Comp Press; 0-9600704),* 41 Tunnel Rd., Berkeley, CA 94705 Tel 415-548-1188.

Medi-Pub, *(Medi-Publishing Group),* 1975 E. Sunrise Blvd., Box 327, Fort Lauderdale, FL 33302 Tel 305-467-0189.

Media, *(Media Books),* 400 E. 89th St., New York, NY 10028 Tel 212-534-0366.

Media Action, *(Media Action Research Center, Inc.; 0-918084),* 475 Riverside Dr., Rm. 1370, New York, NY 10027 Tel 212-865-6690.

Media America, *(Media America, Inc.; 0-916474),* 12 E. Market St., Bethlehem, PA 18018 Tel 215-866-2207.

Media Awards, *(Media Awards Handbook; 0-910744),* 621 Sheri Lane, Danville, CA 94526 Tel 415-837-7562.

Media Concepts, *(Media Concepts Press; 0-935608),* 331 N. Broad St., Philadelphia, PA 19107 Tel 215-923-2545.

Media Inst, *(Media Institute, The; 0-937790),* 3017 M St., N.W., Washington, DC 20007.

Media Intellects, *(Media Intellectics Corp.),* 322 New Mark Esplanade, Rockville, MD 20850.

Media Masters, *(Media Masters, Inc.; 0-87679),* 400 W. Sixth St., Tustin, CA 92680 Tel 714-838-7777.

Media Materials, *(Media Materials Inc.; 0-912974; 0-89539; 0-86601),* 2936 Remington Ave., Baltimore, MD 21211 Tel 301-235-1700.

Media Projects, *(Media Projects, Inc.; 0-914136),* 201 E. 16th St., New York, NY 10003 Tel 212-777-4510.

Media Unltd, *(Media Unlimited Inc.; 0-930394),* P.O. Box I, Alameda, CA 94501; Dist. by: A-A-AA Publications, P.O. Box I, Alameda, CA 94501.

Media Ventures, *(Media Ventures, Inc.; 0-89645),* 5055 N. Main St., Suite 240, Dayton, OH 45415 Tel 513-275-5142.

Mediaworks, *(Mediaworks, The; 0-918072),* Box 4494, Boulder, CO 80306 Tel 303-494-1439.

Mediax, *(Mediax, Inc.; 0-912056),* 21 Charles St., Westport, CT 06880 Tel 203-226-2332.

Medic Pub, *(Medic Publishing Co.),* P.O. Box O, Issaquah, WA 98027 Tel 206-392-5665.

Medical Arts, *(Medical Arts Publishing Co.; 0-913092),* P.O. Box 8627, Detroit, MI 48224 Tel 313-886-5160.

Medical Busn
 See **IMS Comm**

Medicanto, *(Medicavto, Inc.; 0-931210),* 283 Greenwich Ave., Greenwich, CT 06830 Tel 203-869-5732.

Medicanto
 See **Medicanto**

Medieval, *(Medieval & Renaissance Society; 0-913904),* P.O. Box 13348, N. Texas State Univ., Denton, TX 76203 Tel 817-788-2101.

Medieval Acad, *(Medieval Academy of America; 0-910956),* 1430 Massachusetts Ave., Cambridge, MA 02138 Tel 617-491-1622.

Medieval Inst, *(Medieval Institute Pubns.; 0-918720),* Western Michigan Univ., Kalamazoo, MI 49008 Tel 616-383-1685.

Medieval Latin, *(Medieval Latin Press; 0-916760),* P.O. Box 7847, St. Matthews Sta., Louisville, KY 40207 Tel 502-897-1241.

MEDS Corp, *(M. E. D. S. Corp.; 0-916420),* 97-99 Stuyvesant Ave, Newark, NJ 07106 Tel 201-899-7856.

Medusa, *(Medusa; 0-9601714),* 4112 Emery Place, N.W., Washington, DC 20016.

Meeker Pub, *(Meeker Publishing Co.; 0-935068),* 2605 Virginia St., N.E., Albuquerque, NM 87110 Tel 505-299-6406.

Megden Pub, *(Megden Publishing; 0-9603676),* P.O. Box 217, Huntington Beach, CA 92648 Tel 714-536-7785.

Meher Baba Info, *(Meher Baba Information),* Box 1101, Berkeley, CA 94701; Dist. by: Book People, 2940 Seventh St., Berkeley, CA 94710 Tel 415-549-3033.

Mehetabel & Co, *(Mehetabel & Co.; 0-936094),* 4340 Redwood Hwy., Suite 307, San Rafael, CA 94903 Tel 415-472-2850.

Meiklejohn Civ Lib, *(Meiklejohn Civil Liberties Institute; 0-913876),* 1715 Francisco St., Berkeley, CA 94703 Tel 415-848-0599; Orders to: Box 673, Berkeley, CA 94701.

Mellifont, *(Mellifont Press, Inc.),* ; Publisher Abbreviation Without Addresses Are for Titles That Are Out of Print. These Are Obsolete Abbreviations.

Melmont, *(Melmont Pubs., Inc.; 0-516),* Div. of Children's Press, 1224 W. Van-Buren St., Chicago, IL 60607 Tel 312-666-4200.

Melodyland, *(Melodyland Publishers; 0-918818),* Div. of Melodyland Christian Center, P.O. Box 6000, Anaheim, CA 92806 Tel 714-635-6391.

Melrose Pub Co, *(Melrose Publishing Co.; 0-934972),* 384 N. San Vicente Blvd., Los Angeles, CA 90048 Tel 213-655-5177.

Melrose Sq *Imprint of* **Holloway**

Membrane Pr, *(Membrane Press; 0-87924),* P.O. Box 11601, Shorewood, Milwaukee, WI 53211.

Memento, *(Memento Pubns., Inc.; 0-89436),* 901 Washington St., Wilmington, DE 19801 Tel 302-654-5511.

Memorial Pub, *(Memorial Publishing; 0-916680),* P. O. Box 12455, San Francisco, CA 94112 Tel 415-333-3853.

Memphis St Univ, *(Memphis State Univ. Press; 0-87870),* Memphis State Univ., Memphis, TN 38152 Tel 901-454-2752.

Menaid, *(Menaid Press; 0-918424),* Div. of Fichter Enterprises, P.O. Box 7664, Colorado Springs, CO 80933 Tel 303-598-8058.

Menard Pr, *(Menard Press),* Dist. by: SBD: Small Press Distribution, 1636 Ocean View Ave., Kensington, CA 94707 Tel 415-524-2107.

Mendez, *(Mendez, Carmen Medina; 0-9600602),* P.O. Box 431, New York, NY 10023 Tel 212-877-8131.

Menorah Pub, *(Menorah Publishing Co., Inc.; 0-932232),* 15 W. 84th St., New York, NY 10024 Tel 212-787-2248.

Ment *Imprint of* **NAL**

Mental Health, *(Mental Health Materials Center; 0-910958),* 419 Park Ave., S., New York, NY 10016 Tel 212-889-5760.

Mental Hlth Res, *(Mental Health Research; 0-930708),* 274 Madrona, Chula Vista, CA 92010.

Meola, *(Meola, Edward A.; 0-9606008),* 390 Busby Dr., Sierra Vista, AZ 85635.

Mer *Imprint of* **NAL**

Meranza Pr, *(Meranza Press; 0-916482),* P.O. Box 1613, Riverside, CA 92502.

Mercantine Pr, *(Mercantine Press; 0-933962),* 4351 Washington St., Lincoln, NE 68506 Tel 402-489-2626.

Mercer Hse, *(Mercer House Press; 0-89080),* Clover Leaf Farm, Old Rte. 9, Kennebunkport, ME 04046 Tel 207-282-7116; Orders to: P.O. Box 681, Kennebunkport, ME 04046.

Mercer Univ Pr, *(Mercer Univ. Press; 0-86554),* Macon, GA 31207 Tel 912-745-6811.

Merchants Pub Co, *(Merchants Pub. Co.; 0-89484),* 20 Mills St., Kalamazoo, MI 49001 Tel 616-345-1175.

Merck, *(Merck & Co., Inc.; 0-911910),* P.O. Box 2000, Rahway, NJ 07065 Tel 201-574-5403.

Merck-Sharp-Dohme, *(Merck Sharp & Dohme International; 0-911910),* Professional Communications Dept., West Point, PA 19486.

Mercury Comm, *(Mercury Communications Corp.; 0-917772),* 734 Chestnut St., Santa Cruz, CA 95060 Tel 408-425-8444; Moved, Left No Forwarding Address.

Meredith
 See **BH&G**

Meredith, *(Meredith Corp.),* ; Publisher Abbreviation Without Addresses Are for Titles That Are Out of Print. These Are Obsolete Abbreviations. Publisher's Abbreviation Is Now **BH&G**.

Meredith Corp, *(Meredith Corp.; 0-696),* Orders to: Better Homes & Gardens Books, 1716 Locust, Des Moines, IA 50336.

Merganzer Pr, *(Merganzer Press; 0-9602648),* 659 Northmoor Rd., Lake Forest, IL 60045.

Merging Media, *(Merging Media; 0-934536),* 59 Sandra Circle A3, Westfield, NJ 07090 Tel 201-232-7224.

Meridian Ed, *(Meridian Editions),* 9905 Lorain Ave., Silver Spring, MD 20901.

Meridian Pr, *(Meridian Press),* ; Publisher Abbreviation Without Addresses Are for Titles That Are Out or Print. These Are Obsolete Abbreviations.

Meridian Pub, *(Meridian Publishing; 0-86610),* 2643 Edgewood Rd., Utica, NY 13501.

Merit Calif, *(Merit Pubs.; 0-910962),* P.O. Box 1344, Beverly Hills, CA 90213 Tel 213-474-1888.

Merit Pubns, *(Merit Pubns., Inc.; 0-87803),* 610 NE 124th St., N. Miami, FL 33161.

Merk, *(Merk),* 377 Merk Rd., Watsonville, CA 95076.

Merlin Hse, *(Merlin House, Inc.; 0-88306),* 333 Central Park, W., New York, NY 10025 Tel 212-866-9278; Dist. by: E.P. Dutton, 201 Park Ave. S., New York, NY 10003.

Merlin Pr, *(Merlin Press; 0-930142),* P.O. Box 5602, San Jose, CA 95150.

Mermaid *Imprint of* **Hill & Wang**

Merriam, *(Merriam, G. & C., Co.; 0-87779),* Subs. of Encyclopaedia Britannica, Inc., 47 Federal St., Springfield, MA 01101 Tel 413-734-3134.

Merriam-Eddy, *(Merriam-Eddy Co., Inc.; 0-914562),* P.O. Box 25, South Waterford, ME 04081 Tel 207-583-4645.

Merrill, *(Merrill, Charles E., Publishing Co.; 0-675),* Div. of Bell & Howell Co., 1300 Alum Creek Dr., Columbus, OH 43216 Tel 614-258-8441.

Merrimack, *(Merrimack Publishing Corp.),* Dist. by: Associated Booksellers, 147 McKinley Ave., Bridgeport, CT 06606.

Merrimack Bk Serv, *(Merrimack Book Service, Inc.),* 5 S. Union St, Lawrence, MA 01843 Tel 617-686-6409; Orders to: 99 Main St., Salem, NH 03079 Tel 617-685-4636.

Merrimack Vall Textile, *(Merrimack Valley Textile Museum; 0-937474),* 800 Massachusetts Ave., North Andover, MA 01845 Tel 617-686-0191.

Merritt Co, *(Merritt Co.; 0-930868),* 1661 Ninth St., Santa Monica, CA 90406.

Merritt Pubs Texas, *(Merritt Publishers; 0-930238),* 718 Westwood, Richardson, TX 75080 Tel 214-231-2284.

Merry Thoughts, *(Merry Thoughts; 0-88230),* 380 Adams St., Bedford Hills, NY 10507 Tel 914-241-0447.

Merton Hse, *(Merton House Publishing Co.; 0-916032),* 937 W. Liberty Dr., Wheaton, IL 60187 Tel 312-668-7410.

Mesa Pr IL, *(Mesa Press),* 5835 Kimbark Ave, Chicago, IL 60637 Tel 312-753-4013.

Milwaukee Journal, *(Milwaukee Journal, Public Service Bureau),* 333 W. State St., Milwaukee, WI 53201 Tel 414-224-2120; Orders to: P.O. Box 661, Milwaukee, WI 53201.

Milwaukee Pub Mus, *(Milwaukee Public Museum; 0-89326),* 800 W. Wells St., Milwaukee, WI 53233 Tel 414-278-2771.

Milwaukee Sentinel, *(Milwaukee Sentinel, The),* 918 N. 4th St., P.O. Box 371, Milwaukee, WI 53201 Tel 414-224-2120.

Mimir, *(Mimir Pubs., Inc.; 0-912084),* P.O. Box 5011, Madison, WI 53711 Tel 608-231-1667.

Mind Body, *(Mind Body Press; 0-939508),* 1749 Vine St., Berkeley, CA 94703.

Minerva Pr, *(Minerva Press; 0-8476),* Tel 201-256-8600; Orders to: Biblio Distribution Centre, 81 Adams Dr., Box 327, Totowa, NJ 07511; Moved, Left No Forwarding Address.

Mini Guide Bks, *(Mini Guide Books; 0-89921),* 1806 N. Broadway, Suite D, Santa Ana, CA 92706.

Mini-Word, *(Mini-Word Editions; 0-935358),* P.O. Box 3314, Champaign, IL 61820.

Minibooks *Imprint of* **Bantam**

Ministry Pubns, *(Ministry Pubns.; 0-938234),* P.O. Box 276, Redlands, CA 92373.

Minkus, *(Minkus Pubns., Inc.; 0-912236),* c/o Minkus Stamp Journal, 116 W. 32nd St., New York, NY 10001.

MINMOR, *(MINMOR Pub. Co.; 0-918976),* 14 Germain St., Worcester, MA 01602 Tel 617-757-8463.

Minn Geol Surv, *(Minnesota Geological Survey; 0-934938),* University of Minnesota, 1633 Eustis St., St. Paul, MN 55108 Tel 612-373-3372.

Minn Hist, *(Minnesota Historical Society; 0-87351),* 690 Cedar St., St. Paul, MN 55101 Tel 612-296-2264; Orders to: 1500 Mississippi St., St. Paul, MN 55101.

Minn Inst Phil
See De Young Pr

Minn Jaycees, *(Minnesota Jaycees),* 8800 W. Hwy. 7, Minneapolis, MN 55426; Moved, Left No Forwarding Address.

Minn Rev Pr, *(Minnesota Review Press; 0-936484),* P.O. Box 211, Bloomington, IN 47402.

Minn Scholarly, *(Minnesota Scholarly Press, Inc.; 0-933474),* P.O. Box 224, Mankato, MN 56001 Tel 507-387-4964; Dist. by: Independent Pubs. Group, 14 Vandeventer Ave., Port Washington, NY 11050.

Minneapolis Inst Arts, *(Minneapolis Institute of Arts; 0-912964),* 2400 Third Ave., S., Minneapolis, MN 55404 Tel 612-870-3029.

Minneapolis Riverfront, *(Minneapolis Riverfront Development Coordination Board; 0-9604360),* 235 City Hall, Minneapolis, MN 55415.

Minneapolis Star, *(Minneapolis Star & Tribune Co., The; 0-932272),* 425 Portland Ave., Minneapolis, MN 55488 Tel 612-372-4420.

Minobras, *(Minobras-Mining Services & Research),* P.O. Box 262, Dana Point, CA 92629 Tel 714-493-6066.

MIR PA, *(MIR; 0-935352),* 845 Suismon Dr., Pittsburgh, PA 15212 Tel 412-322-1319; Orders to: P.O. Box 962, Pittsburgh, PA 15230.

Mir Pubs, *(Mir Pubs.),* Dist. by: Imported Publications, 320 W. Ohio St., Chicago, IL 60610.

Mirage Pr, *(Mirage Press, Ltd.; 0-88358),* P.O. Box 28, Manchester, MD 21102 Tel 301-239-8999.

Miss Jackie, *(Miss Jackie Music; 0-939514),* 10001 El Monte, Overland Park, KS 66207.

Mission Adv Res Com Ctr
See MARC

Mission Dolores, *(Mission Dolores Pubs.; 0-912748),* 193 Los Robles Dr., Burlingame, CA 94010.

Mission Pr CA, *(Mission Press; 0-918418),* 124 Treehaven Court, Suite B-330, Box 614, Kenwood, CA 95452 Tel 707-833-5588.

Mission Pub, *(Mission Publishing Co.; 0-916910),* 346 North St., Greenwich, CT 06830 Tel 203-661-2372.

Mission Pubs CA
See Mission Dolores

MISSION WRITE, *(MISSION WRITE),* 160 S. Springer Rd., Los Altos, CA 94022 Tel 415-964-8923.

Missionary Crusader, *(Missionary Crusader),* 4606 Ave. H, Lubbock, TX 79404.

Mistaire, *(Mistaire Laboratories; 0-9602490),* 152 Glen Ave., Millburn, NJ 07041 Tel 201-376-0915.

MIT Outing, *(MIT Outing Club; 0-9601698),* W20-461, MIT, Cambridge, MA 02139 Tel 617-253-2988.

MIT Pr, *(MIT Press; 0-262),* 28 Carleton St., Cambridge, MA 02142 Tel 617-253-2884.

Mitchell Pub, *(Mitchell Publishing, Inc.; 0-938188),* 116 Royal Oak, Santa Cruz, CA 95066.

Mizan Pr, *(Mizan Press; 0-933782),* P.O. Box 4065, Berkeley, CA 94704 Tel 415-549-1634.

MJ Pubns, *(MJ Pubns.; 0-9605144),* 6363 Lynwood Hill Rd., McLean, VA 22101.

MJB Pub, *(MJB Pub.; 0-9605990),* 7209 Skyway, No. 13, Paradise, CA 95969.

MJG Co, *(MJG Co.; 0-932632),* P.O. Box 7743, Midland, TX 79703 Tel 915-682-3184.

MJT Intl Pubns, *(MJT International Pubns.; 0-86707),* P.O. Box 1879, 2824 S. 3000 W., Ogden, UT 84401 Tel 801-731-3486.

MLM Pubs, *(MLM Pubs.; 0-939102),* 515 S. We-Go Trail, Mt. Prospect, IL 60056.

MLP
See Crane Pub Co

MLP Ent, *(MLP Enterprises),* P.O. Box 31-516, San Francisco, CA 94131 Tel 415-626-3131.

MMRC, *(Multi Media Resource Center; 0-9603968; 0-914684),* 1525 Franklin St., San Francisco, CA 94109 Tel 415-673-5100.

MN Pubs, *(M. N. Pubs.; 0-932964),* Rte. 2, Box 55, Bonnerdale, AR 71933 Tel 501-991-3815.

Mnemosyne, *(Mnemosyne Publishing Co., Inc.),* 410 Alcazar Ave., Coral Gables, FL 33134 Tel 305-444-8908.

MNP Star, *(MNP Star Enterprises; 0-938880),* P.O. Box 8267, S.F. International Airport, San Francisco, CA 94128.

Mntn & Sea, *(Mountain & Sea),* 1803 S. Vermont, Los Angeles, CA 90006.

Mntn Hse Pub, *(Mountain House Publishing, Inc.; 0-939274),* Rte. 1 Box 433 A, Waitsfield, VT 05673.

MO Basketball, *(Missouri Basketball; 0-9605092),* 364 Hearnes Bldg., Columbia, MO 65201.

Mobile Homes, *(Mobile Homes Manufacturers Assn.; 0-913066),* 14650 Lee Rd., Box 201, Chantilly, VA 22021 Tel 703-968-6970.

Mockingbird Bks, *(Mockingbird Books; 0-89176),* Box 624, St. Simons Island, GA 31522 Tel 912-638-7212.

Mockingbird Pr, *(Mockingbird Press, Inc.),* 324 West College, Tallahassee, FL 32301.

Mod Handcraft, *(Modern Handcraft, Inc.; 0-86675),* 4251 Pennsylvania Ave., Kansas City, MO 64111.

Mod LibC *Imprint of* **Modern Lib**

Mod Media Inst, *(Modern Media Institute; 0-935742),* 556 Central Ave., St. Petersburg, FL 33701 Tel 813-821-9494.

Mod Pubs, *(Modern Pubs.; 0-9600812),* 1326 Davies Rd., Far Rockaway, NY 11691.

Mod Windmills, *(Modern Windmills Co.),* P.O. Box 781, 215 N. Ottawa, Suite 527, Joliet, IL 60434.

Model Cities, *(Model Cities Research Institute),* 11126 National Blvd., Los Angeles, CA 90064 Tel 213-479-7394.

Model Tech, *(Model Technology, Inc.; 0-9601840),* 323 W. Cedar, Chillicothe, IL 61523.

Modern Aircraft, *(Modern Aircraft),* Dist. by: Crown, 419 Park Ave., S., New York, NY 10016.

Modern Bks, *(Modern Books & Crafts, Inc.; 0-913274),* Dist. by: Associated Booksellers, 147 McKinley Ave., Bridgeport, CT 06606.

Modern Curr, *(Modern Curriculum Press; 0-87895),* Div. of Esquire, Inc., 13900 Prospect Rd., Cleveland, OH 44136 Tel 216-238-2222.

Modern Day Topics, *(Modern Day Topics Publishing House, Inc.; 0-931648),* 511 E. York St., Savannah, GA 31401 Tel 912-234-0611.

Modern Ed, *(Modern Education Pubs.),* P.O. Box 93, Saratoga, CA 95070 Tel 408-354-2264.

Modern Lang, *(Modern Language Assn. of America; 0-87352),* 62 Fifth Ave., New York, NY 10011 Tel 212-741-5588.

Modern Lib, *(Modern Library, Inc.),* 201 E. 50th St., New York, NY 10022 Tel 212-751-2600; Orders to: Order Dept., 400 Hahn Rd., Westminster, MD 21157. *Imprints:* Mod LibC (Modern Library College Department).

Modern Mktg, *(Modern Marketing Associates; 0-9602108),* 9095 S.W. 87th Ave., Miami, FL 33176.

Modern Schls, *(Modern Schools; 0-917130),* 4225 N. Brown Ave., Scottsdale, AZ 85251 Tel 602-945-1832.

Modern Signs, *(Modern Signs Press; 0-916708)* 3131 Walker Lee Dr., Rossmoor, CA 90720 Orders to: P.O. Box 1181, Los Alamitos, CA 90720 Tel 213-596-8548.

Modern World, *(Modern World Publishing Co.; 0-910978),* 3460 Division St., Los Angeles, CA 90065 Tel 213-221-8044.

Modernismo, *(Modernismo Pubns., Inc.; 0-89237),* 155 Ave. of the Americas, New York, NY 10013 Tel 212-691-7700.

Moffett, *(Moffett Publishing Co.),* Rt. 3, Box 175A, Cushing, OK 74023.

Mohan Ents, *(Mohan Enterprises; 0-918922),* P.O. Box 8334, Rochester, NY 14618 Tel 716-461-3694; Dist. by: Arcane Books, U. S. Rte. 1A, York Harbor, ME 03911.

Moira, *(Moira Books; 0-9600204),* 1460 Height Blvd., Winona, MN 55987.

Mojave Bks, *(Mojave Books; 0-87881),* 7040 Darby Ave., Reseda, CA 91335 Tel 213-342-3403.

Mole Pub Co, *(Mole Pub. Co.; 0-9604464),* Route 1, Box 618, Bonners Ferry, ID 83805 Tel 208-267-7349.

Mollica Stained Glass, *(Mollica Stained Glass Press; 0-9601306),* 10033 Broadway Terr., Oakland, CA 94611 Tel 415-655-5736.

Momos, *(Momo's Press; 0-917672),* P.O. Box 14061, San Francisco, CA 94114.

Mona Pub, *(Mona Publishing Co., Ltd.; 0-938952),* 79 Wall St., Suite 501, New York, NY 10005.

Monad Pr, *(Monad Press; 0-913460),* Dist. by: Pathfinder Press, 410 West St., New York, NY 10014 Tel 212-741-0690.

Monarch *Imprint of* **Monarch Pr**

Monarch Pr, *(Monarch Press; 0-671),* Div. of Simon & Schuster, Inc., 1230 Ave. of the Americas, 12th Fl., New York, NY 10020 Tel 212-245-6400. *Imprints:* Monarch (Monarch).

Monday Bks, *(Monday Books; 0-918510),* Box 543, Cotati, CA 94928 Tel 707-829-0951.

Monde Lib, *(Monde Library; 0-89041),* Div. of American Art Enterprises, Inc., 21322 Lassen St., Chatsworth, CA 91311 Tel 213-882-5900; Dist. by: Parliament News, Inc., 21314 Lassen St., Chatsworth, CA 91311.

Money Digest
See Zimmerman

Mongolia, *(Mongolia Society, Inc., The; 0-910980),* P.O. Drawer 606, Bloomington, IN 47402 Tel 812-337-2766.

Monitor, *(Monitor Book Co., Inc.; 0-9600252),* 195 S. Beverly Dr., Beverly Hills, CA 90212 Tel 213-271-5558.

Monkey Joe Ent, *(Monkey Joe Enterprises, Inc.; 0-933208),* 3310 Lebanon Rd., Suite 104, Hermitage, TN 37076.

Monkey Man, *(Monkey Man Press; 0-9605594),* 8710 Wonderland Pk. Ave., Los Angeles, CA 90046 Tel 213-654-9154.

Monkey Sisters, *(Monkey Sisters, The; 0-933606),* 22971 Via Cruz, Laguna Niguel, CA 92677 Tel 714-496-1445.

Mono Bk, *(Mono Book Corp.; 0-87662),* 116 S. Main St. 4th Floor, Wilkes-Barre, PA 18701 Tel 717-824-8761; Moved, Left No Forwarding Address.

Monocacy, *(Monocacy Book Co.; 0-913186),* P.O. Box 765, Redwood City, CA 94064 Tel 415-369-8934.

Monogram Aviation, *(Monogram Aviation Pubns.; 0-914144),* 625 Edgebrook Dr., Boylston, MA 01505 Tel 617-869-6836.

Monona, *(Monona-Driver Book Co.; 0-910982),* 110 Henuah Cir., Madison, WI 53716 Tel 608-222-1973.

Monongahela Pub, *(Monongahela Publishing Co. Inc.),* 106 Morningside Dr., New York, NY 10027 Tel 212-666-5187; Orders to: 78 B Stony Rd., Fairmont, WV 26554.

Monroe County Lib, *(Monroe County Library System),* 3700 S. Custer Rd., Monroe, MI 48161.

Mont St Pr, *(Montgomery Street Press; 0-913136),* 1167 Grizzly Peak Blvd., Berkeley, CA 94708 Tel 415-845-8919.

Montaigne, *(Montaigne Publishing, Inc.; 0-917430),* 99 El Toyonal, Orinda, CA 94563 Tel 415-254-8082.

Montemora Found, *(Montemora Foundation, Inc., The; 0-935528),* Box 336, Cooper Sta., New York, NY 10276.

Montessori Learn
    See Parent-Child Pr

Montessori Wkshp, *(Montessori Workshop; 0-915676),* 501 Salem Dr., Ithaca, NY 14850.

Montessori Wkshps
    See Montessori Wkshp

Montfort Pubns, *(Montfort Pubns.; 0-910984),* 26 S. Saxon Ave., Bay Shore, NY 11706 Tel 516-665-0726.

Montgomery Co Govt, *(Montgomery County Govt.; 0-9601094),* 99 Maryland Ave., Rockville, MD 20850 Tel 301-279-1401.

Montgomery Comm, *(Montgomery Communications; 0-937096),* P.O. Box 55545, Seattle, WA 98155 Tel 206-365-5005.

Montgomery Mus, *(Montgomery Museum of Fine Arts; 0-89280),* 440 S. McDonough St., Montgomery, AL 36104 Tel 205-834-3490.

Monthly Rev, *(Monthly Review Press; 0-85345),* 62 W. 14th St., New York, NY 10011 Tel 212-691-2555.

Monza-Fels, *(Monza-Fels),* P.O. Box 506, Redondo Beach, CA 90277; Name Changed to Plantin Press.

Moody, *(Moody Press; 0-8024),* 2101 Howard St., Evanston, IL 60645 Tel 312-973-7800; Orders to: 1777 Shermer Rd., Northbrook, IL 60062.

Moody Bks Inc, *(Moody Books, Inc.),* 469 E. Sullivan St., Kingsport, TN 37660.

Moon Bks, *(Moon Books; 0-931452),* P. O. Box 9223, Berkeley, CA 94709; Dist. by: Random House, Inc., 457 Hahn Rd., Westminster, MD 21157.

Moon Over Mntn, *(Moon Over the Mountain Publishing Co.; 0-9602970),* 6700 W. 44th Ave., Wheatridge, CO 80033 Tel 303-420-4272.

Mooney, *(Mooney, Tom; 0-9601240),* 3410 Balt-Som Rd., Millersport, OH 43046 Tel 614-862-8159.

Moonlight Edns *Imprint of* **Schocken**

Moonlight Pubns, *(Moonlight Pubns.; 0-931350),* Box 671, La Jolla, CA 92038.

Moonmad Pr, *(Moonmad Press; 0-917918),* P.O. Box 757, Terre Haute, IN 47808 Tel 812-235-2947.

Moore Pub Co, *(Moore Publishing Co.; 0-87716),* P.O. Box 3036, W. Durham Sta., Durham, NC 27705 Tel 919-286-2250.

Moore-Taylor-Moore
    See MTM Pub Co

Mor-Mac, *(Mor-Mac Publishing Co., Inc.; 0-912178),* P.O. Box 985, Daytona Beach, FL 32015.

Moran Andrews, *(Moran/Andrews, Inc.; 0-912286),* 535 N. Michigan Ave., Chicago, IL 60611 Tel 312-644-2793.

Moran Pub Corp, *(Moran Publishing Corp.; 0-86518),* 5425 Florida Blvd., P.O. Box 66538, Baton Rouge, LA 70896 Tel 504-923-2550; Dist. by: Aviation Book Co., 1640 Victory Blvd., Glendale, CA 91201 Tel 213-240-1771.

Morehouse, *(Morehouse-Barlow Co.; 0-8192),* 78 Danbury Rd., Wilton, CT 06897 Tel 203-762-0721.

Moretus Pr, *(Moretus Press, Inc. The; 0-89679),* 274 Madison Ave., New York, NY 10016 Tel 212-685-2250; Orders to: P.O. Box 530, Harrisburg, PA 17108 Tel 717-545-2097.

Morgan, *(Morgan & Morgan, Inc.; 0-87100),* 145 Palisades St., Dobbs Ferry, NY 10522 Tel 914-693-9303.

Morgan Aviation *Imprint of* **Arco**

Morgan-Pacific, *(Morgan-Pacific Corp.; 0-89430),* P. O. Box 456, Lomita, CA 90717 Tel 213-833-2194; Orders to: P. O. Box 4627, Mountain View, CA 94042.

Morgan Pr CA
    See Morgan-Pacific

Morgan Pr-Farag
    See Morgan-Pacific

Morgantown Print & Bind, *(Morgantown Printing & Binding Co.; 0-930284),* P.O. Box 850, Morgantown, WV 26505 Tel 304-292-3368.

Morizot, *(Morizot, Carol Ann; 0-930138),* P.O. Box 59, Marshall, AR 72650 Tel 501-448-5170.

Morning Glory, *(Morning Glory Press; 0-930934),* 6595 San Haroldo Way, Buena Park, CA 90620 Tel 714-828-1998.

Morningland, *(Morningland Pubns., Inc.; 0-935146),* 2630 E. Seventh St., Long Beach, CA 90804.

Morningside Bkshop, *(Morningside Bookshop),* P.O. Box 336, Forest Park Sta., Dayton, OH 45405 Tel 512-836-1378.

Morningstar, *(Morningstar, Jim; 0-9604856),* 2728 N. Prospect Ave., Milwaukee, WI 53211.

Morningsun Pubns, *(Morningsun Pubns.; 0-9603424),* 692 Edna Way, San Mateo, CA 94402 Tel 415-341-4491.

Morris Demon, *(Morris Demon & Associates),* 2013 Big Oak Dr., Burnsville, MN 55337 Tel 612-890-3579.

Morris Genealog Lib, *(Morris Genealogical Library),* P.O. Box 63, Allenhurst, NJ 07711.

Morrow, *(Morrow, William, & Co., Inc.; 0-688),* 105 Madison Ave., New York, NY 10016 Tel 212-889-3050; Orders to: Wilmor Warehouse, 6 Henderson Dr., West Caldwell, NJ 07006.

Morse Pr, *(Morse Press, Inc.; 0-933350),* 417 E. Pine, Seattle, WA 98122 Tel 206-323-1820.

Morton Pub, *(Morton Publishing Co.; 0-89582),* 2700 E. Bates Ave., Box 10128, Denver, CO 80210 Tel 303-759-2112.

Mosaic Pr, *(Mosaic Press, The; 0-934696),* P.O. Box 41502, Tucson, AZ 85717.

Mosby, *(Mosby, C. V., Co.; 0-8016),* 11830 Westline Industrial Dr., St. Louis, MO 63141 Tel 314-872-8370.

Moses Pub Pubns
    See Dup

Moss Pubns, *(Moss Pubns.; 0-930870),* P.O. Box 644, Berkeley, CA 94701 Tel 415-653-6458.

Moss Pubns VA, *(Moss Pubns.),* Box 729, Orange, VA 22960.

Mossart, *(Mossart, 0-9606162),* Box 929, Weaverville, CA 96093.

Mossy Rock WA, *(Mossy Rock Publishing Co.; 0-936938),* 808 106th N.E., Bellevue, WA 98004.

Mother Duck Pr, *(Mother Duck Press; 0-934600),* Rte. 1, Box 25A, McNeal, AZ 85617.

Mother Earth, *(Mother Earth News, The; 0-938432),* P.O. Box 70, Hendersonville, NC 28791.

Motheroot, *(Motheroot Pubns.),* 214 Dewey St., Pittsburgh, PA 15218.

Mothers Hen, *(Mother's Hen; 0-914370),* P.O. Box 99592, San Francisco, CA 94109; Moved, Left No Forwarding Address.

Motiv Methods, *(Motivational Methods, Inc.; 0-933664),* 8569 Ramblewood Dr., Coral Springs, FL 33065 Tel 305-753-3579.

Motor Bus Soc, *(Motor Bus Society, Inc.),* Railroad Sta., Depot Plaza, White Plains, NY 10606; 767 Valley Rd., Upper Montclair, NJ 07043; Moved, Left No Forwarding Address.

Motorbooks Intl, *(Motorbooks International, Pubs. & Wholesalers, Inc.; 0-87938),* P.O. Box 2, 729 Prospect Ave, Osceola, WI 54020 Tel 800-826-6600.

Motormatics, *(Motormatics Pubns.; 0-930968),* c/o Beach Cities Enterprises, 3640 E. Tenth St., Long Beach, CA 90804 Tel 213-434-6701

Mott Media, *(Mott Media; 0-915134),* 1000 E. Huron, Milford, MI 48042 Tel 313-685-8773.

Mount, *(Mount Pubns.),* Rte. 1, Box 298, Morriston, FL 32668.

Mountain Calif, *(Mountain; 0-9605992),* Box 1408, Lower Lake, CA 95457.

Mountain Pr, *(Mountain Press Publishing Co., Inc.; 0-87842),* P.O. Box 2399, Missoula, MT 59806 Tel 406-728-1900.

Mountain Pub Servs, *(Mountain Publishing Services; 0-931158),* Box 507, Hollister, MO 65672 Tel 417-334-1523.

Mountain St Tel, *(Mountain States Telephone & Telegraph Co., Regulatory Matters Division; 0-9602580),* 931-14th St., Rm. 1010, Denver, CO 80202.

Mountain View, *(Mountain View Publishing Co.),* Tin Cup Rd., Darby, MT 59829.

Mountaineers, *(Mountaineers-Books; 0-916890, 0-89886),* 719-B Pike St., Seattle, WA 98101 Tel 206-682-4636.

Mouse Pr, *(Mouse Press; 0-913968),* P.O. Box 5381, Beverly Hills, CA 90210 Tel 213-858-1666; Dist. by: Light Impressions Corp., P.O. Box 3012, Rochester, NY 14614.

Mouth of Dragon
    See A Bifrost

Mouton, *(Mouton Pubs.),* Div. of Walter De Gruyter, Inc., 200 Saw Mill River Rd., Hawthorne, NY 10532 Tel 914-747-0111.

Mouvement Pubns, *(Mouvement Pubns.; 0-932392),* 102 Irving Place, Ithaca, NY 14850 Tel 607-273-1745.

Move Short Soc, *(Movement Shorthand Society, Inc.; 0-914336),* P.O. Box 7344, Newport Beach, CA 92660 Tel 714-644-8342.

Movement New Soc, *(Movement for A New Society Press),* 4722 Baltimore Ave., Philadelphia, PA 19143 Tel 215-724-1464.

Mowbray Co, *(Mowbray Co. Pubs; 0-917218),* 222 W. Exchange St., Providence, RI 02903 Tel 401-861-1000.

Mowry Pr, *(Mowry Press; 0-9605368),* Box 405, Wayland, MA 01778.

Mr Cogito Pr, *(Mr. Cogito Press),* P.O. Box 66124, Portland, OR 97266.

Mr Mileage, *(Mr. Mileage),* P.O. Box 4800H, Tucson, AZ 85717.

Mrazek, *(Mrazek, James E.),* 5500 Friendship Blvd., No. 1210 N., Chevy Chase, MD 20015 Tel 301-656-6962.

MRDC Educ Inst, *(MRDC Educational Institute),* P.O. Box 15127, Dallas, TX 75201.

MSC Inc, *(Management & Systems Consultants, Inc.; 0-918356),* Univ. Stn., Box 40457, Tucson, AZ 85717 Tel 602-299-9615.

MSP *Imprint of* **G&D**

Mss Info, *(Mss Information Corp.; 0-8422),* P.O. Box 985, Edison, NJ 08817 Tel 201-225-1900.

MSU-Inst Comm Devel, *(Michigan State Univ., Institute for Community Development & Services),* S. Harrison Rd., East Lansing, MI 18821 Tel 517-355-0100.

MT Coun Indian, *(Montana Council for Indian Education; 0-89992),* 3311-R 4th Ave. N., Billings, MT 59101 Tel 406-252-2071.

MT Hist Soc, *(Montana Historical Society Press; 0-917298),* 225 N. Roberts St., Helena, MT 59601 Tel 406-449-2694.

MT Mag, *(Montana Magazine, Inc.; 0-938314),* Box 5630, Helena, MT 59601 Tel 406-443-2842.

MTI Tele, *(MTI Teleprograms Inc.; 0-916070),* 3710 Commercial Ave., Northbrook, IL 60062 Tel 312-291-9400.

MTM Pub Co, *(M/T/M Publishing Co.),* P.O. Box 245, Washougal, WA 98671.

Mtum *Imprint of* **Van Nos Reinhold**

Mu Alpha Theta, *(Mu Alpha Theta, National High School Mathematics Club),* 601 Elm Ave., Rm. 423, Norman, OK 73019.

Mudborn, *(Mudborn Press; 0-930012),* 209 W. De La Guerra, Santa Barbara, CA 93101 Tel 805-962-9996.

Mudra, *(Mudra; 0-914726),* Dist. by: Bookpeople, 2940 Seventh St., Berkeley, CA 94710 Tel 415-549-3033.

Mulberry Pr, *(Mulberry Press, Inc.; 0-88302),* Affiliate of Franklin Watts, Inc., 730 Fifth Ave., New York, NY 10019; Dist. by: Dugan & Co., 1355 W. Front St., Plainfield, NJ 07060.

Mulch Pr, *(Mulch Press; 0-913142),* 4837 17th St., San Francisco, CA 94117.

Mulford Colebrook, *(Mulford Colebrook Publishing, Co.; 0-930144),* Box 289, Mifflinburg, PA 17844 Tel 814-349-8165.

Multi Dimen, *(Multi Dimensional Communications, Inc.; 0-89507),* 7 Delano Dr., Bedford Hills, NY 10507.

Multi Media, *(Multi Media Productions, Inc.),* P.O. Box 1041, Virginia Beach, VA 23451 Tel 804-486-6118.

Multi Media TX, *(Multi Media Arts; 0-86617),* Box 14486, Austin, TX 78761 Tel 512-836-1987.

Multi Spectral, *(Multi-Spectral Press; 0-918210),* 4948 Meadowbrook Rd., Buffalo, NY 14221 Tel 716-632-0921.

Multimedia, *(Multimedia Publishing Corp.; 0-8334),* 7 Garber Hill Rd., Blauvelt, NY 10913 Tel 914-359-9292.

Multinational Media, *(Multinational Media; 0-917112),* 228 Burlwood Dr., Scotts Valley, CA 95066 Tel 408-438-0253.

Multiple Visions, *(Multiple Visions; 0-939828),* 2315 S. Rodeo Gulch Rd., Santa Cruz, CA 95062.

Multnomah, *(Multnomah Press; 0-930014),* 10209 S.E. Division St., Portland, OR 97266 Tel 503-257-0526.

MUMPS, *(MUMPS Users' Group; 0-918118),* c/o The Mitre Corp., P.O. Box 208, Bedford, MA 01730 Tel 617-271-2534.

Mundus Artium, *(Mundus Artium Press; 0-939378),* P.O. Box 688, Richardson, TX 75080 Tel 214-690-2092.

Munger Africana Lib, *(Munger Africana Library; 0-934912),* Tel 213-795-6811; c/o California Institute of Technology, Pasadena, CA 91125.

Munger Oil, *(Munger Oil Information Service),* 9800 S. Sepulveda Blvd., Los Angeles, CA 90045 Tel 213-776-3990.

Municipal, *(Municipal Finance Officers Assn. of the U.S. & Canada; 0-89125),* 180 N. Michigan Ave., Chicago, IL 60601 Tel 312-947-2550.

Muns, *(Muns, George F.; 0-9604924),* 721 E. Blanco Blvd., P.O. Box 878, Bloomfield, NM 87413 Tel 505-632-3987.

Munson Bks, *(Munson Books),* 3436 Willow Dr., Mattoon, IL 61938 Tel 217-234-8465.

Muratore, *(Muratore Agency, Inc.),* 766 W. Shore Rd., P.O. Box 486, Warwick, RI 02889 Tel 401-737-6460.

Murphy Pub Co, *(Murphy Publishing Co.),* P.O. Box 64, Timonium, MD 21093 Tel 301-377-5083.

Murray, *(Murray, Samuel; 0-910996),* 477 Main St., Box 398, Wilbraham, MA 01095.

Murrison Co, *(Murrison Co., The; 0-9602110),* 3879 Northstrand Dr., Decatur, GA 30035.

Mus African Art, *(Museum of African Art, Smithsonian Institution),* Washington, DC 20002 Tel 202-287-3490.

Mus Am China Trade, *(Museum of the American China Trade; 0-937650),* 215 Adams St., Milton, MA 02186 Tel 617-696-1815.

Mus Am Ind, *(Museum of the American Indian; 0-934490),* Broadway at 155th St., New York, NY 10032 Tel 212-283-2420.

Mus Anthro MO, *(Univ. of Missouri, Museum of Anthropology; 0-913134),* 104 Swallow Hall, Columbia, MO 65211 Tel 314-882-3764.

Mus Art Penn State, *(Museum of Art, Pennsylvania State University; 0-271),* University Park, PA 16802.

Mus Fine Arts Boston, *(Museum of Fine Arts, Boston; 0-87846),* 465 Huntington Ave., Boston, MA 02115 Tel 617-267-9300.

Mus Graphics, *(Museum Graphics; 0-913832),* 2643-B Fair Oaks Ave., Redwood City, CA 94063 Tel 415-368-5531; Orders to: Little, Brown & Co., 200 West St., Waltham, MA 02154.

Mus Great Plains, *(Museum of the Great Plains, Pubns. Dept.; 0-911728),* 601 Ferris, P.O. Box 68, Lawton, OK 73502 Tel 405-353-5675.

Mus Northern Ariz, *(Museum of Northern Arizona; 0-89734),* Rte. 4, Box 720, Flagstaff, AZ 86001 Tel 602-774-5211.

Mus of Art RI, *(Museum of Art Rhode Island School of Design),* 224 Benefit St., Providence, RI 02903 Tel 401-331-3511; Dist. by: Milford House, Inc., 85 Newbury St., Boston, MA 02116.

Mus Sci & Hist, *(Museum of Science & History, The; 0-9604642),* MacArthur Park, Little Rock, AR 72202.

Mus Science, *(Museum of Science; 0-918866),* Science Park, Boston, MA 02114 Tel 617-723-2500.

Mus St Pete, *(Museum of Fine Arts, St. Petersburg),* 255 Beach Drive, N., St. Petersburg, FL 33701 Tel 813-896-2667.

Mus Sys, *(Museum Systems),* 817 N. La Cienaga Blvd., Los Angeles, CA 90069 Tel 213-657-5811.

Muscle Games, *(Muscle Games; 0-9603864),* P.O. Box 51, Fairview Village, PA 19409.

Muse Pr Oreg, *(Muse Press, Oregon Ltd.; 0-912906),* Trail, OR 97541 Tel 503-878-2377; Moved, Left No Forwarding Address.

Museum Bks, *(Museum Books, Inc.; 0-87544),* 48 E. 43rd St., New York, NY 10017 Tel 212-682-0430.

Museum Mobile, *(Museum of the City of Mobile; 0-914334),* 355 Government St., Mobile, AL 36602 Tel 205-438-7569.

Museum Mod Art, *(Museum of Modern Art; 0-87070),* 11 W. 53rd St., New York, NY 10019 Tel 212-956-7216; Orders to: Customer Sales Service, 11 W. 53rd St., New York, NY 10019 Tel 212-956-7264.

Museum NM Pr, *(Museum of New Mexico Press; 0-89013),* P.O. Box 2087, Santa Fe, NM 87503 Tel 505-827-2352.

Museum of NM Pr
See Museum NM Pr

Museum Restoration, *(Museum Restoration Service),* Bridge Authority Bldg., Ogdensburg, NY 13669; Moved, Left No Forwarding Address.

Mushinsha Bks, *(Mushinsha Books),* Dist. by: SBD: Small Press Distribution, 1636 Ocean View Ave., Kensington, CA 94707 Tel 415-524-2107.

Mushroom Cave, *(Mushroom Cave, Inc., The; 0-9601516),* P.O. Box 894, Battle Creek, MI 49016 Tel 616-962-3497.

Music & Movement, *(Music & Movement Press),* 210 Fifth Ave., New York, NY 10010.

Music Ed, *(Music Educators National Conference),* 1902 Association Dr., Reston, VA 22091 Tel 703-860-4000.

Music Pr, *(Music Press; 0-918318),* 21 E. 40th St., New York, NY 10016 Tel 212-532-2797.

Music Sales, *(Music Sales Corp.; 0-8256),* Dist. by: Quick Fox, Inc., 33 W. 60th St., New York, NY 10023 Tel 212-246-0325. *Imprints:* Acorn (Acorn Music Press); Amsco Music (Amsco Music); Hidden Hse (Hidden House); Oak (Oak Pubns.); Quick Fox (Quick Fox).

Music Treasure, *(Music Treasure Pubns.; 0-912028),* 620 Fort Washington Ave., 1-F, New York, NY 10040.

Musica, *(Musica Publishing Co.; 0-9600964),* Box 1266, Edison, NJ 08817.

Musical Box Soc, *(Musical Box Society International, The; 0-915000),* 19 Colony Dr., Summit, NJ 07901.

Musical Scope, *(Musical Scope Pubns.; 0-913000),* P.O. Box 125, Audubon Sta., New York, NY 10032.

Musicdata, *(Musicdata, Inc.; 0-88478),* 18 W. Chelten Ave., Philadelphia, PA 19144 Tel 215-842-0555.

Mustardseed, *(Mustardseed Press; 0-917920),* Subs. of Interuniverse, 707 N. Carolina Ave., Cocoa, FL 32922 Tel 305-632-2769.

Mutual, *(Mutual Publishing Co.; 0-9600244),* 3315 Wisconsin Ave., N.W., Suite 106, Washington, DC 20016.

Mutual MA, *(Mutual Pubns.; 0-89510),* 102 Charles St., Boston, MA 02114 Tel 617-542-8459.

Mutual Pr IL, *(Mutual Press; 0-9605628),* 664 N. Michigan, Suite 1010, Chicago, IL 60611.

Mutualist Pr, *(Mutualist Press, The),* GPO Box 2009, Brooklyn, NY 11202.

MVR Bks, *(MVR Books),* 7809 S. LaPorte Ave., Burbank, IL 60459 Tel 312-636-7412.

Myco Pub Hse, *(Myco Publishing House; 0-936634),* P.O. Box 1237, Arcadia, CA 91006 Tel 213-445-3680.

Mycological, *(Mycological Society of San Francisco, Inc.; 0-918942),* Box 11321, San Francisco, CA 94101 Tel 415-234-7904.

Mycroft, *(Mycroft Business Press; 0-910998),* P.O. Box 579, Branson, MO 65616 Tel 417-334-3436.

Mycroft & Moran *Imprint of* **Arkham**

Myers Inc, *(Myers, S. D., Inc.; 0-939320),* P.O. Box 3575, Akron, OH 44310.

Myleen Pr, *(Myleen Press),* P.O. Box 41515, Sacramento, CA 95841.

Mynabird Pub, *(Mynabird Publishing; 0-917758),* 20 Shoshone Place, Portola Valley, CA 94025 Tel 415-851-8554.

Myriade, *(Myriade Press, Inc., The; 0-918142),* Seven Stony Run, New Rochelle, NY 10804 Tel 914-235-8470.

Myrin Institute, *(Myrin Institute, Inc.; 0-913098),* 521 Park Ave., New York, NY 10021 Tel 212-758-6475.

Mysterious Pr, *(Mysterious Press; 0-89296),* 129 W. 56th St., New York, NY 10019.

Mystery Hill, *(Mystery Hill Press),* Four Paige Rd., Litchfield, NH 03051; Moved, Left No Forwarding Address.

Mystic Cult, *(Mystic Cult Pub. Co.),* Box 31462, San Francisco, CA 94131; Moved, Left No Forwarding Address.

Mystic Seaport, *(Mystic Seaport Museum, Inc., 0-913372),* Mystic, CT 06355 Tel 203-536-2631.

N & N Pub, *(N&N Publishing; 0-9606036),* Lydia Dr., Wappinger, NY 12590.

N & N Resources, *(N & N Resources),* P.O. Box 332, Troy, ID 83871 Tel 208-835-201

N Chirich, *(Chirich, Nancy),* 305 Euclid Ave., Apt. 405, Oakland, CA 94610 Tel 415-763-3510.

N Country Pr, *(North Country Press; 0-916196),* P.O. Box 12, 223, Seattle, WA 98112 Tel 206-329-8372.

N Dak Inst, *(North Dakota Institute for Regional Studies; 0-911042),* State College Sta., Fargo, ND 58105 Tel 701-237-8338.

N Dak State, *(North Dakota State Nurses Association),* 219 N. Seventh St., Bismarck ND 58501.

N Foster Baptist, *(North Foster Baptist Church* Dist. by: Rhode Island Publications Society 150 Benefit St., Providence, RI 02903.

N H Ludlow, *(Ludlow, Norman H.; 0-916706),* 516 Arnett Blvd., Rochester, NY 14619 Tel 716-235-0951.

N Hays, *(Hays, Nicolas, Ltd.),* P.O. Box 612, York Beach, ME 03910 Tel 207-363-4393; Dist. by: Samuel Weiser Inc., 625 Broadway New York, NY 10012.

N Ill U Pr, *(Northern Illinois Univ. Press; 0-87580),* DeKalb, IL 60115 Tel 815-753-1826.

N J Rube, *(Rube, Ned J., Publisher; 0-930562),* 68 Marion Dr., New Rochelle, NY 10804.

N Jersey Cons Foun
See NJ Cons Foun

N K Gregg, *(Gregg, Newton K., Pub.; 0-87962; 0-912318),* P.O. Box 1459, Rohnert Park, CA 94928 Tel 707-584-9446.

N Manderino Assocs, *(Manderino, Ned, Associates; 0-9601194),* 854 Kodak Drive, Los Angeles, CA 90026 Tel 213-665-0123.

N Miller, *(Miller, Neil; 0-9601444),* 747 Bruce Dr., East Meadow, NY 11554 Tel 516-292-9569.

N Nut Growers, *(Northern Nut Growers Assn.; 0-9602248),* 13 Broken Arrow Rd., Hamden CT 06518 Tel 203-288-1026.

N P Cartwright, *(Cartwright, Nellie Parodi, Mrs.; 0-9601482),* 4348 Via Frascati, Rancho Palos Verdes, CA 90274 Tel 213-833-7586.

N P Evans, *(Evans, Norma P.; 0-937418),* 2211 Liberty, Beaumont, TX 77701 Tel 713-835-7175.

N Point Hist Soc, *(North Point Historical Society; 0-9606072),* Box 557, Milwaukee, WI 53201 Tel 414-271-2395.

N Point Pr, *(North Point Press),* 850 Talbot Ave., Berkeley, CA 94706 Tel 415-527-6260.

N S Davies, *(Davies, Nina S.; 0-9600020),* 213 State St., New Orleans, LA 70116.

N S Wait, *(N. S. Wait; 0-911588),* Box 407, Valparaiso, IN 46383; Formerly H. H. Wait Pub.

N Stonington, *(North Stonington Press; 0-938538),* 14 Zaccheus Mead Lane, Greenwich, CT 06830.

N T Smith, *(Smith, Nicholas T.; 0-935164),* P.O. Box 66, Bronxville, NY 10708 Tel 914-337-2794.

N Watson, *(Neale Watson Academic Pubns. Inc. 0-88202),* 156 Fifth Ave., Suite 1100, New York, NY 10010 Tel 212-675-7480. *Imprints:* Prodist (Prodist).

Na Pali Pub, *(Na Pali Publishing Co.; 0-917132),* P.O. Box 88082, Honolulu, HI 96815 Tel 213-889-1657.

NAB *Imprint of* **Noyes**

NACASBVH, *(National Accreditation Council for Agencies Serving the Blind & Visually Handicapped; 0-912948),* 79 Madison Ave., Suite 1406, New York, NY 10016 Tel 212-683-8581.

NACM, *(National Assn. of Credit Management; 0-934914),* Book Edit Dept., 475 Park Ave., S., New York, NY 10016 Tel 212-578-4431.

Nadler Concepts, *(Nadler Concepts; 0-9606038),* 150-10 79th Ave., Flushing, NY 11367 Tel 212-591-4167.

NAEB, *(National Assn. of Educational Broadcasters; 0-8105),* 1346 Connecticut Ave., N.W., Washington, DC 20036 Tel 202-785-1100.

NAIA Pubns, *(National Assn. of Intercollegiate Athletics),* 1221 Baltimore St., Kansas City, MO 64105 Tel 816-842-5050.

Naiad Pr, *(Naiad Press; 0-930044),* P. O. Box 10543, Tallahassee, FL 32302 Tel 904-539-9322.

NAIS, *(National Assn. of Independent Schools; 0-934388),* 18 Tremont St., Boston, MA 02108 Tel 617-723-6900.

NAL, *(New American Library; 0-451; 0-452; 0-453),* 1633 Broadway, New York, NY 10019 Tel 212-397-8000; Orders to: 120 Woodbine St., Bergenfield, NJ 07621 Tel 201-387-0600. *Imprints:* Ment (Mentor Books); Mer (Meridian Books); NAL *(Imprint of Norto)*; Plume (Plume Books); Sgnt (Signette); Sig (Signet Books); Sig Classics (Signet Classics).

NALR, *(North American Liturgy Resources),* 2110 W. Peoria Ave., Phoenix, AZ 85029.

NAMAC, *(NAMAC; 0-936916),* P.O. Box 963, Ingleside, TX 78362.

Nameless, *(Nameless Press; 0-9603608),* P.O. Box 538, Jonestown, TX 78641 Tel 512-267-1961.

Nanny Goat, *(Nanny Goat Productions; 0-918440),* P. O. Box 845, Laguna Beach, CA 92652 Tel 714-494-7930.

Nanogens Intl, *(Nanogens International; 0-9601338),* P.O. Box 487, Freedom, CA 95019 Tel 408-724-7760.

Nantucket Nautical, *(Nantucket Nautical Pubs.),* 5 New Mill St., Nantucket, MA 02554.

Napa Landmarks, *(Napa Landmarks; 0-935360),* P.O. Box 702, Napa, CA 94558 Tel 707-255-1836.

Napp Creations, *(Napp Creations, Inc.; 0-9603492),* 122 Park Ave., Nutley, NJ 07110 Tel 201-667-4598; Dist. by: De Vorrs & Co., P.O. Box 550, Marina Del Ray, CA 90291; Dist. by: Book Dynamics, 836 Broadway, New York, NY 10003.

NAPSAC, *(National Assn. of Parents & Prof. for Safe Alternatives in Childbirth; 0-917314),* P.O. Box 267, Marble Hill, MO 63764 Tel 314-238-2010.

Narc Ed, *(Narcotics Education, Inc.),* 6830 Laurel St., N.W., Box 4390, Washington, DC 20012 Tel 202-723-4774.

Narconon, *(Narconon; 0-917958),* 6425 Hollywood Blvd., Suite 206, Hollywood, CA 90028 Tel 213-469-8347.

Nash Pub, *(Nash Publishing Corp.; 0-8402),* 1290 Ave. of Americas, Suite 4150, New York, NY 10019 Tel 212-977-9500.

Nass, *(Nass, Sylvan & Ulla),* 220 Sunnybrook Rd., Flourtown, PA 19031.

Nat Hist Pub Co, *(Natural History Pub. Co.; 0-9603144),* P.O. Box 962, La Jolla, CA 92038 Tel 714-459-0835.

Nat Learn Res, *(Natural Learning Resources; 0-936214),* 5151 Monroe, P.O. Box 8443, Toledo, OH 43623.

Nat Therapy, *(Natural Therapy Foundation Press, The; 0-937792),* 5 Greenleaf, Irvine, CA 92714.

Nationwide Pr, *(Nationwide Press, Ltd.; 0-917188),* P.O. Box 1528, Pueblo, CO 81002 Tel 303-543-1382.

Natl Acad Gallaudet Coll, *(National Academy of Gallaudet College, The; 0-934336),* Kendall Green, Washington, DC 20002 Tel 202-651-5480.

Natl Acad Pr, *(National Academy Press; 0-309),* 2101 Constitution Ave., Washington, DC 20418 Tel 202-389-6942; Orders to: Publications Sales Office, 2101 Constitution Ave., Washington, DC 20418 Tel 202-389-6731.

Natl Acad Sci *See* Natl Acad Pr

Natl Aero, *(National Aeronautic Assn.),* 821 15th St., N.W., Suite 430, Washington, DC 20005 Tel 202-347-2808.

Natl Alliance, *(National Alliance; 0-937944),* Box 3535, Washington, DC 20007 Tel 703-525-3223.

Natl Alumni Assn Ed Home Econ, *(National Alumni Assn. of the College of Education & Home Economics; 0-9602480),* Alumni Publications (Loc. No. 145), Univ. of Cincinnati, Cincinnati, OH 45221.

Natl Archives, *(National Archives & Records Service),* Publications Division, Washington, DC 20408.

Natl Art Ed, *(National Art Education Assn.; 0-937652),* 1916 Association Dr., Reston, VA 22091 Tel 703-860-8000.

Natl Arts Pr, *(National Arts Press; 0-936252),* P.O. Box 41, Bear, DE 19701 Tel 302-366-1423.

Natl Assn Accts, *(National Assn. of Accountants),* Orders to: 919 Third Ave., New York, NY 10022 Tel 212-754-9715.

Natl Assn Child Ed, *(National Assn. for the Education of Young Children; 0-912674),* 1834 Connecticut Ave., N.W., Washington, DC 20009 Tel 202-232-8777.

Natl Assn Coll, *(National Assn. of College & University Business Officers; 0-915164),* 1 Dupont Circle, Suite 510, Washington, DC 20036 Tel 202-296-2344.

Natl Assn Con Adult Ed, *(National Assn. for Public Continuing & Adult Education),* 1201 Sixteenth St., N.W., Washington, DC 20036 Tel 202-833-5486.

Natl Assn Counties, *(National Assn. of Counties; 0-911754),* 1735 New York Ave., N.W., Washington, DC 20006 Tel 202-783-5113.

Natl Assn Deaf, *(National Assn. of the Deaf; 0-913072),* 814 Thayer Ave., Silver Spring, MD 20910 Tel 301-587-1788.

Natl Assn Home, *(National Assn. of Home Builders; 0-86718),* 15th & M St., N.W., Washington, DC 20005 Tel 202-452-0200.

Natl Assn Principals, *(National Assn. of Secondary School Principals; 0-88210),* 1904 Association Dr., Reston, VA 22091 Tel 703-860-0200.

Natl Assn Sch Nurses, *(National Assn. of School Nurses),* Affiliate of National Education Assn., 1201 16th St., N.W., Rm. 503, Washington, DC 20036 Tel 202-833-4420.

Natl Assn Soc Wkrs, *(National Assn. of Social Workers; 0-87101),* 2 Park Ave., New York, NY 10016 Tel 212-689-9771; Orders to: Publications Sales, NASW, 1425 "H" St., N.W., Washington, DC 20005.

Natl Assn Women, *(National Assn. for Women Deans, Administrators & Counselors),* 1625 Eye St., N.W., Washington, DC 20006 Tel 202-659-9330.

Natl Audubon, *(National Audubon Society; 0-930698),* 950 Third Ave., New York, NY 10022 Tel 212-546-9139; Orders to: Service Dept., 950 Third Ave., New York, NY 10022 Tel 212-546-9112.

Natl Behavior, *(National Behavior Systems; 0-937654),* 11601 Balboa Blvd., Granada Hills, CA 91344 Tel 213-363-7160.

Natl Bellamy, *(National Bellamy Award, Inc.),* 265 Hatton St., Portsmouth, VA 23704.

Natl Biomedical, *(National Biomedical Research Foundation; 0-912466),* Georgetown Univ. Medical Ctr, 3900 Reservoir Rd., N.W., Washington, DC 20007 Tel 202-625-2121.

Natl Book, *(National Book Co.; 0-89420),* Div. of Educational Research Associates, 333 S.W. Park Ave., Portland, OR 97205 Tel 503-228-6345. *Imprints:* Halcyon (Halcyon House).

Natl Bur Econ Res, *(National Bureau of Economic Research, Inc.; 0-87014),* 261 Madison Ave., New York, NY 10016 Tel 212-682-3190; Order Books Published Before Sept., 1953 & After Sept. 1, 1964 from Columbia Univ. Press, 136 S. Broadway, Irvington-on-Hudson, N.Y. 10533. Books Published Between Sept., 1953 & Sept., 1964 Order from Princeton Univ. Press, Princeton, N.J. 08540.

Natl Cable, *(National Cable Television Assn.),* 918 Sixteenth St., N.W., Washington, DC 20006.

Natl Cath Dev, *(National Catholic Development Conference; 0-9603196),* 119 N. Park Ave., Rockville Centre, NY 11570 Tel 516-764-6700.

Natl Cath Educ, *(National Catholic Educational Assn.),* 1 Dupont Circle, Suite 350, Washington, DC 20036 Tel 202-293-5954.

Natl Cath Reporter, *(National Catholic Reporter Publishing Co., Inc.; 0-934134),* 115 E. Armour, Box 281, Kansas City, MO 64141 Tel 816-531-0538.

Natl Christian Pr, *(National Christian Press, Inc.; 0-934916),* P. O. Box 49118, Algood, TN 38501 Tel 615-537-9434.

Natl Clearinghse Bilingual Ed, *(National Clearinghouse for Bilingual Education; 0-89763),* 1300 Wilson Blvd., Suite B2-11, Rosslyn, VA 22209 Tel 800-336-4560.

Natl Conf Appellate, *(National Conference of Appellate Court Clerks; 0-934730),* 300 Newport Ave., Williamsburg, VA 23185.

Natl Consumer, *(National Consumer Research),* 6 E. 45th St., New York, NY 10017; Moved, Left No Forwarding Address.

Natl Ctr Diaconate, *(National Center for the Diaconate; 0-9605798),* 14 Beacon St., Rm. 715, Boston, MA 02108 Tel 617-742-1460.

Natl Ctr Educ Broker, *(National Center for Educational Brokering; 0-935612),* 405 Oak St., Syracuse, NY 13203.

Natl Ctr Faculty, *(National Center for Faculty Development; 0-938540),* 1320 S. Dixie Hwy., No. 900A, Coral Gables, FL 33146.

Natl Ctr Health Stats, *(National Center for Health Statistics; 0-8406),* Federal Center Bldg., Rm. 1-57, 3700 East-West Hwy., Hyattsville, MD 20782 Tel 301-436-8586.

Natl Ctr Job Mkt, *(National Center for Job-Market Studies; 0-935234),* P.O. Box 3651 BN, Washington, DC 20007 Tel 202-229-4885.

Natl Ctr St Courts, *(National Center for State Courts; 0-89656),* 300 Newport Ave., Williamsburg, VA 23185 Tel 804-253-2000.

Natl Dist Atty, *(National District Attorney's Assn.),* 211 E. Chicago Ave., Chicago, IL 60611 Tel 312-944-2577.

Natl Ed Ad Servs, *(National Educational Advertising Services, Inc.),* 360 Lexington Ave., New York, NY 10017 Tel 212-867-7740.

Natl Ed Res, *(National Educational Resources, Inc.; 0-89498),* 1525 E. 53rd St., Suite 824, Chicago, IL 60615 Tel 312-684-4920.

Natl Ed Stand, *(National Education Standards; 0-918192),* 617 W. 7th St., Suite 300, Los Angeles, CA 90017 Tel 213-623-9135.

Natl Educ Pr, *(National Educational Press),* 5604 Rhode Island Ave., Hyattsville, MD 20781 Tel 301-699-9300; Moved, Left No Forwarding Address.

Natl Elim Death Tax *See* Tax Info Ctr

Natl Eval Sys, *(National Evaluation Systems, Inc.; 0-89056),* P.O. Box 226, Amherst, MA 01002.

Natl Finan *See* Lincoln Pub

Natl Fire Prot, *(National Fire Protection Assn; 0-87765),* 470 Atlantic Ave., Boston, MA 02110 Tel 617-482-8755.

Natl Forensic, *(National Forensic Center),* 6 Ashburn Place, Fair Lawn, NJ 07410.

Natl Fuchsia, *(National Fuchsia Society),* Box 1153, Fort Bragg, CA 95437.

Natl Gallery Art, *(National Gallery of Art; 0-89468),* Sixth St. & Constitution Ave., N.W., Washington, DC 20565 Tel 202-737-4215.

Natl Genealogy, *(National Genealogical Society; 0-915156),* 1921 Sunderland Place, N.W., Washington, DC 20036 Tel 202-785-2123.

Natl Geog, *(National Geographic Society; 0-87044),* 17th & "M" Sts., N.W., Washington, DC 20036 Tel 202-857-7000.

Natl Heritage, *(National Heritage; 0-913188),* P.O. Box 84, Saint James, Beaver Island, MI 49782 Tel 616-448-2299.

Natl Info Ctr, *(National Information Center; 0-911912),* P.O. Box 370, Somerville, NJ 08876; Moved, Left No Forwarding Address.

Natl Inst Burn, *(National Institute for Burn Medicine; 0-917478),* 909 E. Ann St., Ann Arbor, MI 48104 Tel 313-769-9000.

Natl Inst Career, *(National Institute of Career Planning, Inc.; 0-917592),* 521 Fifth Ave., New York, NY 10017 Tel 212-682-5844.

Natl Iridology, *(National Iridology Research Assn.; 0-9602636),* P.O. Box 3950, San Diego, CA 92103 Tel 714-295-0059.

Natl Journal, *(National Journal; 0-89234),* 1730 "M" St., N.W., Washington, DC 20036 Tel 212-833-8000.

Natl Judicial Coll, *(National Judicial College),* Judicial College Bldg., Univ. of Nevada, Reno, NV 89557 Tel 702-784-6747.

Natl Lawyers Guild, *(National Lawyers Guild; 0-9602188),* 853 Broadway, Rm. 1705, New York, NY 10003; Dist. by: National Lawyers Guild Report, P.O. Box 14023, Washington, DC 20044.

Natl League Nurse, *(National League for Nursing, Inc.),* 10 Columbus Circle, New York, NY 10019 Tel 212-582-1022.

Natl Learning, *(National Learning Corp.; 0-8373; 0-8293),* 212 Michael Dr., Syosset, NY 11791 Tel 516-921-8888.

Natl LP Gas, *(National LP-Gas Assn.; 0-88466),* 1301 W. 22nd St., Oak Brook, IL 60521 Tel 312-986-4808.

Natl Marriage, *(National Marriage Encounter; 0-936098),* 955 Lake Dr., St. Paul, MN 55120.

Natl Micrograph, *(National Micrographics Assn.; 0-89258),* 8719 Colesville Rd., Silver Spring, MD 20910 Tel 301-587-8202.

Natl Notary, *(National Notary Assn.; 0-9600158; 0-933134),* 23012 Ventura Blvd., Woodland Hills, CA 91364 Tel 213-347-2035.

Natl Paperback, *(National Paperback Books, Inc.; 0-89826),* 224 Sarvis Dr., Knoxville, TN 37920 Tel 617-577-9943; Orders to: P.O. Box 146, Knoxville, TN 37901 Tel 615-588-6293.

Natl Planning, *(National Planning Assn.),* 1606 New Hampshire Ave N.W., Washington, DC 20009 Tel 202-265-7685.

Natl Poet-Univ Me, *(National Poetry Foundation, Inc. & Univ. of Maine Press; 0-915032),* Univ. of Maine, 303 English/Math Bldg, Orono, ME 04473; c/o C. F. Terrell, Natl Poetry, 305 EM UMO, Orano, ME 04469.

Natl Pub, *(National Publishing Co.; 0-8340),* P. O. Box 8386 Twenty-Fourth & Locus Sts., Philadelphia, PA 19101 Tel 215-732-1863.

Natl Pub IL, *(National Publishing Corp., Pubs.),* 2720 Des Plaines Ave., Des Plaines, IL 60018 Tel 312-297-5115.

Natl Rail Hist Soc DC Chap, *(National Railway Historical Society, Washington D.C. Chapter; 0-933954),* P.O. Box 3512, Central Sta., Arlington, VA 22203.

Natl Rail Hist Soc DC
    See Natl Rail Hist Soc DC Chap

Natl Rail Rio Grande, *(National Railway Historical Society, Rio Grande Chapter; 0-939646),* Box 3381, Grand Junction, CO 81502.

Natl Rail Rochester, *(National Railway Historical Society, Rochester Chapter; 0-9605296),* P.O. Box 664, Rochester, NY 14602 Tel 716-726-3903.

Natl Railway Hist, *(National Railway Historical Society, Intermountain Chapter; 0-917884),* P.O. Box 5181, Terminal Annex, Denver, CO 80217 Tel 303-623-6747.

Natl Rec & Park Assn, *(National Recreation & Park Assn.; 0-9603540),* 1601 N. Kent St., Arlington, VA 22209 Tel 703-525-0606.

Natl Recycling, *(National Assn. of Recycling Industries),* 330 Madison Ave., New York, NY 10017 Tel 212-867-7330.

Natl Register, *(National Register Publishing Co. Inc.; 0-87217),* Subs. of Standard Rate & Data Inc., 5201 Old Orchard Rd., Skokie, IL 60077 Tel 312-470-3100.

Natl Res Bur, *(National Research Bureau Inc.; 0-912610),* 104 S. Michigan Ave., Chicago, IL 60603 Tel 312-641-2655; Orders to: 424 N. Third St., Burlington, IA 52601 Tel 800-553-2345.

Natl Ret Merch, *(National Retail Merchants Assn.; 0-87102),* 100 W. 31st St., New York, NY 10001 Tel 212-244-8780.

Natl Rifle Assn, *(National Rifle Assn.; 0-935998),* 1600 Rhode Island Ave. N.W., Washington, DC 20036 Tel 202-828-6000; Dist. by: John Olson Co., 294 W. Oakland Ave., Oakland, NJ 07436 Tel 201-337-3355.

Natl Rural, *(National Rural Electric Cooperative Assn.),* 1800 Massachusetts Ave., N.W., Washington, DC 20036 Tel 202-857-9500.

Natl Safety Coun, *(National Safety Council; 0-87912),* 444 N. Michigan Ave., Chicago, IL 60611 Tel 312-527-4800.

Natl Sch PR, *(National School of Public Relations Assn.; 0-87545),* 1801 N. Moore St., Arlington, VA 22209 Tel 703-528-5840.

Natl Sci Tchrs, *(National Science Teachers Assn.; 0-87355),* Affiliate of American Association for the Advancement of Science, 1742 Connecticut Ave., N.W., Washington, DC 20009 Tel 202-328-5872.

Natl Space Inst, *(National Space Institute),* Dist. by: Stackpole Books, Cameron & Keller St., P.O. Box 1831, Harrisburg, PA 17105 Tel 717-234-5091.

Natl Sq Dance, *(National Square Dance Directory; 0-9605494),* P.O. Box 54055, Jackson, MS 39208 Tel 601-825-6831.

Natl Tech Info, *(National Technical Information Service, U.S. Dept. of Commerce),* U.S. Dept. of Commerce, 425 13th St., N.W., Suite 620, Washington, DC 20004 Tel 202-724-3383; Orders to: U.S. Dept of Commerce, 5285 Port Royal Rd., Springfield, VA 22161 Tel 703-487-4650.

Natl Textbk, *(National Textbook Co.; 0-8442),* 8260 N. Elmwood, Skokie, IL 60077 Tel 312-679-4210; Orders to: 8259 Niles Ctr. Rd., Skokie, IL 60077.

Natl U *Imprint of* **Kennikat**

Natl Underwriter, *(National Underwriter Co.; 0-87218),* 420 E. Fourth St., Cincinnati, OH 45202 Tel 513-721-2140.

Natl Univ Ext, *(National Univ. Extension Assn.),* 1 Dupont Circle, Suite 360, Washington, DC 20036 Tel 202-659-3130.

Natl Urban, *(National Urban League),* 500 E. 62nd St., New York, NY 10021.

Natl Video, *(National Video Clearinghouse, Inc., The; 0-935478),* 100 Lafayette Dr., Syosset, NY 11791 Tel 516-364-3686.

Natl Waterways, *(National Waterways Conference, Inc.; 0-934292),* 1130 17th St. N.W., No. 200, Washington, DC 20036.

Natl Wildlife, *(National Wildlife Federation; 0-912186),* 8925 Leesburg Pike, Vienna, VA 22180 Tel 703-790-4431.

Natural Hist, *(Natural History Press),* Dist. by: Doubleday & Co., Inc., 501 Franklin Ave., Garden City, NY 11530. *Imprints:* AMS (American Museum Science Books); AMSA (American Museum Sourcebooks in Anthropology).

Natural History Bks
    See Sabbot-Natural Hist Bks

Natural Hygiene, *(Natural Hygiene Press; 0-914532),* 1920 W. Irving Park Rd., Chicago, IL 60613 Tel 312-929-7420.

Natural Pr, *(Natural Press; 0-939956),* Div. of Natural Enterprises, P.O. Box 75, Manitowoc, WI 54220 Tel 414-682-0738.

Natural Res Ent, *(Natural Resources Enterprises, Inc.; 0-939870),* P.O. Box 4523, Lincoln, NE 68504 Tel 402-472-1519.

Natural Sci Youth, *(Natural Science for Youth Foundation; 0-916544),* 763 Silvermine Rd., New Canaan, CT 06840 Tel 203-966-5643.

Natural Wonders, *(Natural Wonders, Inc.; 0-913534),* Walnut Grove, CA 95690 Tel 916-776-1619.

Naturalists Dir, *(Naturalists' Directory),* P.O. Box 583, South Orange, NJ 07079; Moved, Left No Forwarding Address.

Nature Bks Pubs, *(Nature Books Pubs.; 0-912542),* P.O. Box 12157, Jackson, MS 39211 Tel 601-956-5686.

Nature Life, *(Nature Life; 0-918134),* Div. of McGill-Jensen, 655 Fairview Ave. N., St. Paul, MN 55104 Tel 612-645-3129.

Nature Soc, *(Nature Society; 0-9600224),* Purple Martin Junction, Griggsville, IL 62340; Formerly Named Griggsville Wild Bird Society.

Nature Study, *(Nature Study Guild; 0-912550),* P.O. Box 972, Berkeley, CA 94701.

Nature Trails, *(Nature Trails Press; 0-937794),* 933 Calle Loro, Palm Springs, CA 92262 Tel 714-323-9420.

Naturegraph, *(Naturegraph Pubs., Inc.; 0-911010; 0-87961),* P.O. Box 1075, Happy Camp, CA 96039 Tel 916-493-5353.

Nauful, *(Nauful, Eli S.),* P.O. Box 1260, Lynchburg, VA 24502.

NAUI, *(National Assn. of Underwater Instructors; 0-916974),* P.O. Box 630, Colton, CA 92324 Tel 714-824-5440.

Nautical & Aviation, *(Nautical & Aviation Publishing Co. of America, The; 0-933852),* 8 Randall St., Annapolis, MD 21401 Tel 301-267-8522.

Nautical Avia
    See Nautical & Aviation

Nautical Bks, *(Nautical Books; 0-931284),* P.O. Box 331, Stoughton, WI 53589 Tel 608-873-5003.

Nautilus Bks, *(Nautilus Books; 0-916388),* 210 Fifth Ave., New York, NY 10010.

Navajo Coll Pr, *(Navajo Community College Press; 0-912586),* Navajo Community College, Tsaile, AZ 86556.

Navajo Curr, *(Navajo Curriculum Center Press; 0-936008),* Rough Rock Demonstration School, Star Rte. 1, Rough Rock, AZ 86503.

Naval Inst Pr, *(Naval Institute Press; 0-87021),* Annapolis, MD 21402 Tel 301-268-6110.

NAVH, *(National Assn. for Visually Handicapped; 0-89526),* 305 East 24th St., New York, NY 10010 Tel 212-889-3141; Non-Profit Agency Which Seeks Reimbursement Where Possible at 7.50 per Volume.

NavPress, *(NavPress Publishing Co.; 0-89109),* Div. of The Navigators, P. O. Box 6000, Colorado Springs, CO 80934 Tel 303-598-1212.

Naylor, *(Naylor Co.; 0-8111),* Orders to: P.O. Box 1838, San Antonio, TX 78206.

Nazarene, *(Nazarene Publishing House; 0-8341* P.O. Box 527, Kansas City, MO 64141 Tel 816-931-1900.

NC Archives, *(North Carolina Division of Archives & History; 0-86526),* 109 E. Jone St., Raleigh, NC 27611 Tel 919-733-7442.

NC Central Pol Sci, *(North Carolina Central Univ., Dept. of Political Science),* Durham, NC 27707.

NC Natl Hist, *(North Carolina State Museum Natural History; 0-917134),* 102 N. Salisbury St., P.O. Box 27647, Raleigh, NC 27611 Tel 919-733-7450.

NCCB, *(National Citizens Committee for Broadcasting; 0-9603466),* P.O. Box 12038, N.W., Washington, DC 20005.

NCCC, *(National Conference of Catholic Charities),* 1346 Connecticut Ave., N.W., Washington, DC 20036 Tel 202-785-2757.

NCCE, *(National Committee for Citizens in Education; 0-934460),* Wilde Lake Village Green, Suite 410, Columbia, MD 21044 Tel 301-997-9300.

NCMA, *(North Carolina Museum of Art; 0-88259),* Raleigh, NC 27611 Tel 919-733-7568.

NCTE, *(National Council of Teachers of Englis 0-8141),* 1111 Kenyon Rd., Urbana, IL 61801 Tel 217-328-3870.

NCTM, *(National Council of Teachers of Mathematics; 0-87353),* 1906 Association Dr., Reston, VA 22091 Tel 703-620-9840.

NE Bks, *(Northeast Books; 0-937374),* 431 Wyoming Ave., I.B.E.W. Bldg., Scranton, P. 18503.

NE Conf Teach Foreign, *(Northeast Conference on the Teaching of Foreign Languages; 0-915432),* P.O. Box 623, Middlebury, VT 05753 Tel 802-388-2598.

NE Outdoors, *(Northeast Outdoors, Inc.; 0-936216),* P.O. Box 2180, Waterbury, CT 06722.

NE U Pr, *(Northeastern Univ. Press; 0-930350),* 360 Huntington Ave., Rm. 17w, Northeastern Univ., Boston, MA 02115 Tel 617-437-2783; Orders to: P.O. Box 116 Boston, MA 02117.

NEA, *(National Education Assn.; 0-8106),* 1201 16th St., N.W., Washington, DC 20036 Tel 202-833-4062; Orders to: The Academi Bldg., Saw Mill Rd., West Haven, CT 06516 Tel 203-934-2669.

Neal Assoc, *(Neal, Richard, Associates),* 370 S. George Mason Dr., 1715-N, Falls Church, VA 22041.

Neal-Schuman, *(Neal-Schuman Pubs., Inc.; 0-918212),* 64 University Place, New York, NY 10003 Tel 212-473-5170; Orders to: P.O. Box 1687, FDR Sta., New York, NY 10150.

Nebraska Art, *(Nebraska Art Assn.; 0-9602018),* Sheldon Memorial Art Gallery, Univ. of Nebraska, Lincoln, NE 68588 Tel 402-472-2461.

Nebraska Hist, *(Nebraska State Historical Society),* 1500 R St, Lincoln, NE 68503 Tel 402-471-3270.

Nebraska Review, *(Nebraska Review; 0-937796),* Southeast Community College, 924 K St., Fairbury, NE 68352.

Necronomicon, *(Necronomicon Press),* 101 Lockwood St., West Warwick, RI 02893 Tel 401-828-5319.

Neechee Assoc, *(Neechee Associates, Inc.; 0-9602582),* 6664 Paseo Dorado, Tucson, AZ 85715.

Nefertiti, *(Nefertiti Head Press; 0-918722),* Drawer J. Univ. Sta., Austin, TX 78712 Tel 512-447-7344.

Negative Pr, *(Negative Press; 0-9601624),* 848 E. 28th St., Apt. C-7, Brooklyn, NY 11210; Moved, Left No Forwarding Address.

Negro Hist Press, *(Negro History Press),* P.O. Box 5129, Detroit, MI 48236 Tel 313-773-4250.

Negro U Pr, *(Negro Universities Press; 0-8371),* Affiliate of Greenwood Press, 88 Post Rd. West, Westport, CT 06881 Tel 203-226-3571.

NELF Pr, *(National Unity Equality Leadership Fraternity Press),* Box AR, Amity Sta., Woodbridge, CT 06525 Tel 203-393-3913.

Nellen Pub, *(Nellen Publishing Co. Inc.; 0-8424),* 386 Park Ave. S., New York, NY 10016 Tel 212-679-0937.

NELP, *(National Educational Laboratory Pubs. Inc.; 0-916542; 0-89965),* P.O. Box 1003, Austin, TX 78767 Tel 512-385-7084; Orders to: 813 Airport Blvd., Austin, TX 78702 Tel 512-385-7084.

Nelson, *(Nelson, Thomas, Inc.; 0-8407),* P.O. Box 946, 407 Seventh Ave. S., Nashville, TN 37203 Tel 800-251-1236.

Nelson B Robinson, *(Robinson, Nelson B. Bookseller; 0-930352),* P.O. Box 153, Rockport, MA 01966 Tel 617-546-3828.

Nelson-Hall, *(Nelson-Hall Inc.; 0-911012; 0-88229; 0-8304),* 111 N. Canal St., Chicago, IL 60606 Tel 312-930-9446.

NemaAid Pubns, *(NemaAid Pubns.),* P.O. Box 23058, Sacramento, CA 95823.

Nembutsu Pr, *(Nembutsu Press; 0-912624),* 6257 Golden West Ave., Temple City, CA 91780.

Nemeth, *(Nemeth, Doris I.; 0-932192),* 2314 W. Sixth St., Mishawaka, IN 46544.

Neo-Am Church, *(Original Kleptonian Neo-American Church, Inc., The; 0-9600388),* Dist. by: Boo Hoo Bookies, 310 Union St., Apt. B, Arcata, CA 95521 Tel 707-822-2157.

Neo Pr, *(Neo Press; 0-911014),* P.O. Box 32, Peaks Island, ME 04108.

Neptune Bks *Imprint of* Tail Feather

NERAS Syst, *(NERAS Systems),* 425 N. Doheny Dr., Suite 8, Beverly Hills, CA 90210 Tel 213-278-8584.

Nesbit, *(Nesbit, Norman L.; 0-911746),* 2104 Goddard Place, Boulder, CO 80303 Tel 303 494 6206.

NESFA Pr, *(New England Science Fiction Assn., Inc.; 0-915368),* P.O. Box G, MIT Branch P.O, Cambridge, MA 02139.

Nettleton Hse, *(Nettleton House),* 737 Fifth Ave., San Francisco, CA 94118.

Network Project, *(Network Project),* Columbia Univ., 101 Earl Hall, New York, NY 10027 Tel 212-923-3900.

Nevada Hist Soc, *(Nevada Historical Society),* Southern Nevada Office, 1555 E. Flamingo, Suite 238, Las Vegas, NV 89109 Tel 702-734-9716.

Nevada Pubns, *(Nevada Pubns.; 0-913814),* P.O. Box 15444, Las Vegas, NV 89114 Tel 702-871-1800.

New Add, *(New Additions),* P.O. Box 133, Farmington, ME 04938.

New Age, *(New Age Press, Inc.; 0-87613),* 3912 Wilshire Blvd., Los Angeles, CA 90010 Tel 213-387-7103.

New Age Action, *(New Age Action Group),* 910 Crescent Dr., Alexandria, VA 22302 Tel 703-836-4930.

New-Age Foods
See Soyfoods-New Age

New Age Pr NM, *(New Age Press Inc.),* 320 Artist Rd., Santa Fe, NM 87501 Tel 505-982-1500.

New Age Pub Ctr, *(New Age Publishing Center),* 1329 W. Touhy Ave., Apt. IN, Chicago, IL 60626 Tel 312-761-5179.

New Albion, *(New Albion Books),* 3002 W. Camelback Rd., No. 10, Phoenix, AZ 85017.

New Bedford, *(New Bedford Press; 0-931656),* 5800 W. Century Blvd., Dept. N1502, Los Angeles, CA 90009 Tel 213-837-2961. *Imprints:* Bedpress (Bedpress Books).

New Benjamin, *(New Benjamin Franklin House, The; 0-933488),* 304 W. 58th St., 5th Fl., New York, NY 10019 Tel 212-247-7484.

New Canaan, *(New Canaan Historical Society; 0-939958),* 13 Oenoke Ridge, New Canaan, CT 06840 Tel 203-966-1776.

New Capernaum, *(New Capernaum Works),* 4615 N.E. Emerson St., Portland, OR 97218.

New Century, *(New Century Pubs., Inc.; 0-8329),* 275 Old New Brunswick Rd., Piscataway, NJ 08854.

New City, *(New City Press; 0-911782),* 206 Skillman Ave., Brooklyn, NY 11211 Tel 212-782-2844.

New Classics Lib, *(New Classics Library, Inc.; 0-932750),* P.O. Box 262, Chappaqua, NY 10514 Tel 203-323-8078.

New Collage, *(New Collage Press),* 5700 N. Tamiami Trail, Sarasota, FL 33580.

New College
See New Collage

New Comm Pr, *(New Community Press; 0-934698),* P.O. Box 428, Columbia, MD 21045 Tel 301-596-3755.

New Community, *(New Community Projects, Inc.; 0-9603468),* 449 Cambridge St., Union Square, Allston, MA 02134 Tel 617-783-3060.

New Day NY, *(New Day Pubns.; 0-9605994),* GPO Box 1924, New York, NY 10116 Tel 212-665-4469.

New Day Pr, *(New Day Press; 0-913678),* c/o Karamu House, 2355 E. 89th St., Cleveland, OH 44106.

New Dimen Studio, *(New Dimension Studio; 0-916928),* 3872 Augusta Dr., Rm. 1, Nashville, TN 37209 Tel 615-227-6648; Orders to: P.O. Box 90492, Nashville, TN 37209.

New Dimensions Educ
See Arista Corp NDE

New Directions, *(New Directions Publishing Corp.; 0-8112),* 80 Eighth Ave., New York, NY 10011 Tel 212-255-0230; Dist. by: W. W. Norton Co., 500 Fifth Ave., New York, NY 10036.

New Division, *(New Division Pubns; 0-918724),* 34 Chelmsford St, Chelmsford, MA 01824 Tel 617-251-8685; Moved, Left No Forwarding Address.

New Earth, *(New Earth Books; 0-918258),* 58 St. Marks Place, New York, NY 10003 Tel 212-673-1682.

New East
See Era Pr NC

New Eng Pr VT, *(New England Press Inc., The; 0-933050),* P.O. Box 525, Shelburne, VT 05482 Tel 802-985-2569.

New Eng Pub, *(New England Pub. Co.; 0-932268),* 200 Glendale Rd., Stratford, CT 06497 Tel 203-375-3252.

New England Geron, *(New England Gerontology Center; 0-89634),* New England Center for Continuing Education, 15 Garrison Ave., Durham, NH 03824 Tel 603-862-1720.

New England Marine
See URI MAS

New England Pr, *(New England Press; 0-931060),* 45 Tudor City, No. 1903, New York, NY 10017.

New English Art, *(New English Art Gallery; 0-913064),* Charles & Liberty Sts., Rochester, NH 03867 Tel 603-332-1761.

New Era, *(New Era Press; 0-937590),* P.O. Box 124, Weaverville, CA 96093.

New Era *Imprint of* World Merch Import

New Era Pubns MI, *(New Era Pubns., Inc.; 0-939830),* P.O. Box 8139, Ann Arbor, MI 48107 Tel 313-663-1929.

New Expressions, *(New Expressions Unltd.),* 30886 Sutherland Dr., Redlands, CA 92373 Tel 714-794-4868.

New Glide, *(New Glide Pubns., Inc.; 0-912078),* 330 Ellis St., Rm. 404, San Francisco, CA 94102 Tel 415-775-0918.

New Harbinger, *(New Harbinger Pubns.; 0-934986),* 624-43rd St., Richmond, CA 94805.

New Hope, *(New Hope Publishing Co.; 0-915460),* Dist. by: Midway Copy Services, P.O. Box 378, Lahaska, PA 18931 Tel 212-794-5757.

New Horizons, *(New Horizons Press; 0-914914),* P.O. Box 1758, Chico, CA 95927 Tel 916-345-0225.

New House, *(New House Pubs.; 0-913516),* 413 Guilford Ave., Queensboro, NC 27401.

New Issues MI, *(New Issues Press; 0-932826),* Institute of Public Affairs, Western Michigan Univ., Kalamazoo, MI 49008 Tel 616-383-3983.

New Issues Pr, *(New Issues Press, Inc.; 0-913944),* 1024 Alachua St., Tallahassee, FL 32302 Tel 904-222-4972.

New Leaf, *(New Leaf Press; 0-89221),* P.O. Box 1045, Harrison, AR 72601 Tel 501-741-2514.

New Letters, *(New Letters Books; 0-938652),* 5346 Charlotte, Kansas City, MO 64110 Tel 816-276-1168.

New London County, *(New London County Historical Society),* 11 Blinman St., New London, CT 06320 Tel 203-443-1209.

New London Pr, *(New London Press; 0-89683),* Box 7458, Dallas, TX 75209 Tel 214-742-9037.

New Meridian Pr, *(New Meridian Press; 0-914882),* P.O. Box 229, Clifton Park, NY 12065 Tel 518-877-5845.

New Mermaid *Imprint of* Hill & Wang

New Moon
See Humble Hills

New Moon-Humble Hills
See Humble Hills

New Nativity, *(New Nativity Press; 0-940128),* P.O. Box 6223, Leawood, KS 66206 Tel 913-341-8369.

New Nurse, *(New Nurse, Pub., The; 0-914698),* P.O. Box 803, Plattsburgh, NY 12901; Name Formerly Hanton.

New Orlando, *(New Orlando Pubns.; 0-917608),* Box 103 Village Sta., New York, NY 10014 Tel 212-449-6236.

New Orleans Mus Art, *(New Orleans Museum of Art; 0-89494),* P. O. Box 19123, New Orleans, LA 70179 Tel 504-488-2631.

New Orleans Poetry, *(New Orleans Poetry Journal Press, The; 0-938498),* 2131 General Pershing St., New Orleans, LA 70115.

New Outlook, *(New Outlook Pubs. & Distributors; 0-87898),* 239 W. 23rd St., New York, NY 10011.

New Perspectives, *(New Perspectives),* Div. of Media Intellectics Corp., 322 New Mark Esplanade, Rockville, MD 20850.

New Poets, *(New Poets Series; 0-932616),* 541 Piccadilly Rd., Baltimore, MD 21204 Tel 301-321-2868.

New Puritan, *(New Puritan Library, Inc.; 0-932050),* P.O. Box 516, Skyland, NC 28776.

New Readers, *(New Readers Press; 0-88336),* Div. of Laubach Literacy, International, 1320 Jamesville Ave., Syracuse, NY 13210 Tel 315-422-9121.

New Renaissance, *(New Renaissance Workshop; 0-9000404),* P.O. Box 421, Ojai, CA 93023.

New Republic, *(New Republic Books; 0-915220),* 1220 19th St. N.W., Suite 205, Washington, DC 20036 Tel 202-331-1250.

New Rivers Pr, *(New Rivers Press; 0-912284; 0-89823),* 1602 Selby Ave., St. Paul, MN 55104 Tel 612-645-6324.

New Seed, *(New Seed Press),* P.O. Box 3016, Stanford, CA 94305.

New Sibylline, *(New Sibylline Books, Inc.; 0-9603352),* Box 266, Village Sta., New York, NY 10014.

New South Co, *(New South Co., The; 0-917990),* Suite 935, 924 Westwood Blvd., Los Angeles, CA 90024 Tel 213-879-0927.

New Spirit, *(New Spirit Books; 0-915402),* P.O. Box 282, Black Earth, WI 53515.

New Univ Pr, *(New University Press; 0-89044),* 520 N. Michigan Ave., Chicago, IL 60611 Tel 312-828-0420; Orders to: Precedent Publishing, Inc., P.O. Box 1005, South Holland, IL 60473 Tel 312-877-5490.

New Victoria Pubs, *(New Victoria Pubs. Inc.; 0-934678),* 7 Bank St., Lebanon, NH 03766 Tel 603-448-2264.

New Viewpoints, *(New Viewpoints),* Affiliate of Franklin Watts, Inc., 730 Fifth Ave., New York, NY 10019 Tel 212-757-4050.

New Visions Pr, *(New Visions Press; 0-934340),* P.O. Box 2025, Gaithersburg, MD 20760 Tel 301-869-1888.

New Vista, *(New Vista Press; 0-936544),* 7771 Healdsburg Ave., P.O. Box 736, Sebastopol, CA 95472.

New Voices Pub, *(New Voices Publishing Co.; 0-911024),* 146-47 29th Ave., Flushing, NY 11354 Tel 212-445-4718.

New West Pubns, *(New West Pubns.; 0-914884),* Civic Ctr., Box 4037, San Rafael, CA 94903.

New Woman, *(New Woman Press),* Box 56, Wolf Creek, OR 97497.

New World
See New World Press NY

New World Alliance, *(New World Alliance),* 733 15th St., N.W., No. 1131, Washington, DC 20005 Tel 202-347-6082.

New World Bks, *(New World Books; 0-917480),* 4515 Saul Rd, Kensington, MD 20795.

New World Cup CA, *(New World Cup Press; 0-9604636),* 9061 Madison Ave., Westminster, CA 92683.

New World Press NY, *(New World Press; 0-911026),* P.O. Box 416, New York, NY 10017 Tel 212-682-1154.

New Worlds, *(New Worlds Unlimited; 0-917398),* 100 Maple St., No. 53, Garfield, NJ 07026 Tel 201-340-0247; Orders to: P.O. Box 556, Saddle Brook, NJ 07662.

New You Pub, *(New You Publishing Co.; 0-917762),* 609 Santa Cruz Ave., Menlo Park, CA 94025 Tel 415-322-9959.

Newark Beth, *(Newark Beth Israel Medical Center; 0-937714),* 201 Lyons Ave., Newark, NJ 07112.

Newark Mus, *(Newark Museum Assn.),* P.O. Box 540, Newark, NJ 07101 Tel 201-733-6600.

Newaves Pub, *(Newaves Publishing; 0-930946),* Box 16, Pasadena, CA 91102 Tel 213-797-0655.

Newberry, *(Newberry Library; 0-911028),* 60 W. Walton St., Chicago, IL 60610 Tel 312-943-9090.

Newbury Bks Inc, *(Newbury Books, Inc.; 0-912728; 0-912729),* Box 29, Topsfield, MA 01983 Tel 617-887-5082.

Newbury Hse, *(Newbury House Pubs.; 0-88377; 0-912066),* 54 Warehouse Lane, Rowley, MA 01969 Tel 617-948-2704.

Newby Bk Rm, *(Newby Book Room),* P.O. Box 7, Jamestown, NC 27282 Tel 919-454-3827.

Newcastle Pub, *(Newcastle Publishing Co., Inc.; 0-87877),* 13419 Saticoy St., North Hollywood, CA 91605 Tel 213-873-3191; Orders to: P.O. Box 7589, Van Nuys, CA 91409.

Newedi Pr, *(Newedi Press; 0-89342),* Bowling Green Univ., Dept. of English, Bowling Green, OH 43403; Moved, Left No Forwarding Address.

Newhouse Pr, *(Newhouse Press; 0-918050),* 146 N. Rampart Blvd., Los Angeles, CA 90026 Tel 213-383-1089; Orders to: P.O. Box 76145, Los Angeles, CA 90076.

Newnes-Butterworth *Imprint of* **Butterworth**

Newport Beach, *(Newport Beach Pubs; 0-9602980),* 3901 MacArthur Blvd., Suite 211, Newport Beach, CA 92660 Tel 714-752-2268.

Newport News, *(Newport News Public School),* 12465 Warwick Blvd., Newport News, VA 23606.

News Circle, *(News Circle; 0-915652),* P.O. Box 74637, Los Angeles, CA 90057 Tel 213-483-5111; 2007 Wilshire Blvd., Suite 900, Los Angeles, CA 90057.

News-Tribune, *(News-Tribune, The; 0-939348),* P.O. Box 1116, Fort Worth, TX 76101 Tel 817-338-1055.

Newspaper Bk, *(Newspaper Book Service; 0-936294),* P.O. Box 50342, Columbia, SC 29250.

Newspaper Ent, *(Newspaper Enterprise Assn., Inc.; 0-915106),* 200 Park Ave., New York, NY 10017 Tel 212-557-9651.

Newspaper Serv, *(Newspaper Services; 0-918984),* P.O. Box 62, Hutchinson, MN 55350 Tel 612-587-2375.

Newsweek, *(Newsweek; 0-88225),* 444 Madison Ave., New York, NY 10022 Tel 212-350-2528.

Nexus Pr, *(Nexus Press; 0-932526),* 608 Forrest Rd., N.E., Atlanta, GA 30312 Tel 404-577-3579.

NFAIS, *(National Federation of Abstracting & Indexing Services),* 112 S. 16th St., Philadelphia, PA 19102 Tel 215-563-2406.

NFER *Imprint of* **Humanities**

NFS Pr, *(NFS Press; 0-917986),* P.O. Box 31040, San Francisco, CA 94131 Tel 415-647-4290.

NFSAIS
    See NFAIS

NH Hist Soc, *(New Hampshire Historical Society; 0-915916),* 30 Park St., Concord, NH 03301 Tel 603-225-3381; Dist. by: Univ. Press of New England, P.O. Box 979, Hanover, NH 03755 Tel 603-646-3348.

NH Pub Co, *(New Hampshire Publishing Co.; 0-912274; 0-89725),* P.O. Box 70, Somersworth, NH 03878 Tel 603-692-3727.

Niagara U Pr, *(Niagara University Press; 0-937656),* Niagara University, NY 14109 Tel 716-285-1212.

Nichols Pub, *(Nichols Publishing Co.; 0-89397),* P.O. Box 96, New York, NY 10024 Tel 212-580-8079.

Nickerson & Collins, *(Nickerson & Collins Co.),* 2720 Des Plaines Ave., Des Plaines, IL 60018 Tel 312-298-6210.

Nighthawk Pr, *(Nighthawk Press; 0-936518),* Box 813, Forest Grove, OR 97116.

Nightmare Alley, *(Nightmare Alley Productions),* P.O. Box 10806, South Lake Tahoe, CA 95731.

Nightowl, *(Press of the Nightowl; 0-912960),* 320 Snapfinger Dr., Athens, GA 30605 Tel 404-353-7719.

Nilgiri Pr, *(Nilgiri Press; 0-915132),* P.O. Box 477, Petaluma, CA 94953 Tel 707-878-2369; Name Formerly Sadhana Pr.

Nin-Ra Ent, *(Nin-Ra Enterprises; 0-933276),* 1721 La Barranca Rd., La Canada, CA 91011.

Ninety-Nines, *(Ninety-Nines, Inc., The),* P.O. Box 59965, Oklahoma City, OK 73159 Tel 405-685-7969.

Ninth Sign, *(Ninth Sign Pubns; 0-930840),* M-525, Hoboken, NJ 07030.

NIRH, *(National Institute of Reboundology & Health Inc.; 0-938302),* 7907 212th S.W., Edmonds, WA 98020 Tel 206-774-6403.

NISC, *(National Intelligence Study Center; 0-938450),* 1015 Eighteenth St., NW, Suite 805, Washington, DC 20036.

Nitty Gritty, *(Nitty Gritty Productions; 0-911954),* P.O. Box 5457, Concord, CA 94524 Tel 415-682-3144.

NJ Cons Foun, *(New Jersey Conservation Foundation; 0-913234),* 300 Mendham Rd., Morristown, NJ 07960.

NJ Law Journal, *(New Jersey Law Journal; 0-916104),* P.O. Box 7333, Trenton, NJ 08628 Tel 609-883-1886; Orders to: 240 Mulberry St., Newark, NJ 07101 Tel 201-642-0075.

NJ State Mus, *(New Jersey State Museum; 0-938766),* 205 W. State St., Trenton, NJ 08625.

NLSBPH, *(National Library Service for the Blind & Physically Handicapped),* Library of Congress, Washington, DC 20542 Tel 202-882-5500; Prepares Reference Circulars Listing Information About Available Materials & Services.

NM Philatelist
    See Hobby Pub Serv

No Dead Lines, *(No Dead Lines; 0-931832),* 241 Bonita, Portola Valley, CA 94025 Tel 415-851-1847.

No Limit Bks, *(No Limit Books),* Dist. by: Book People, 2940 Seventh St., Berkeley, CA 94710.

Noble
    See Bowmar-Noble

Noble, *(Noble & Noble Pubs., Inc.),* ; Publisher Abbreviation Without Addresses Are for Titles That Are Out of Print. These Are Obsolete Abbreviations. Publisher's Abbreviation Is Now Bowmar-Noble.

Noble Hse, *(Noble House Publishing; 0-9603490),* 256 S. Robertson, Beverly Hills, CA 90211 Tel 213-659-4210.

Noble Prentiss, *(Noble Prentiss Publishing Co.; 0-914892),* P.O. Box 3101, Simi Valley, CA 93063; Moved,Left No Forwarding Address.

Nodin Pr, *(Nodin Press; 0-931714),* c/o The Bookmen, Inc., 519 N. Third St., Minneapolis, MN 55401.

Noe, *(Noe, Fay; 0-9600208),* Rte. 7, Boiling Springs Rd., Licking, MO 65542.

Noells Ark, *(Noell's Ark Pub.; 0-9602422),* P.O. Box 396, Tarpon Springs, FL 35589 Tel 813-937-8683.

Noise Control, *(Noise Control Foundation),* P.O. Box 3469, Arlington Branch, Poughkeepsie, NY 12603 Tel 914-462-6719.

Noit Amrofer, *(Noit Amrofer Publishing Co.; 0-932998),* Box 15176, Seattle, WA 98115; 5706 30th Ave. N.E., Seattle, WA 98105.

NOK Pubs, *(NOK Pubs., Ltd.; 0-88357),* 150 Fifth Ave., New York, NY 10011 Tel 212-675-5785.

Nolo Pr, *(Nolo Press; 0-917316),* P.O. Box 544, Occidental, CA 95465 Tel 707-874-3105.

Non-Stop Bks, *(Non-Stop Books; 0-936816),* P.O. Box 1047, Berkeley, CA 94701.

Noname Pr, *(Noname Press),* 5200 Klingle St., N.W., Washington, DC 20016 Tel 202-244-6243.

Nonpareil Bks *Imprint of* **Godine**

Noon Rock, *(Noon Rock; 0-9602934),* Station Hill Rd., Barrytown, NY 12507 Tel 914-758-6682.

Noontide, *(Noontide Press; 0-911038; 0-93948,* P.O. Box 1248, Torrance, CA 90505.

Nopoly Pr, *(Nopoly Press, Inc.; 0-930950),* Bo 1930, Dept. M-10, Wilmington, DE 19899 Tel 302-658-5171.

Norawell Pubs, *(Norawell Pubs.; 0-9602118),* 1229 Golden Gate Blvd., Mayfield Heights, OH 44124.

NORC, *(NORC, National Opinion Research Center; 0-932132),* 6030 S. Ellis Ave., Chicago, IL 60637 Tel 312-753-1487.

Nord Media, *(Nord Media Inc.; 0-917226),* 12 W. 56th St., New York, NY 10019 Tel 212-245-1090.

Nordic Bks, *(Nordic Books; 0-933748),* P.O. Box 1941, Philadelphia, PA 19105 Tel 215-574-4258.

Nordland Pub, *(Nordland Publishing International, Inc.; 0-913124),* P.O. Box 45 Woodside, NY 11377 Tel 212-335-1412; 3009 Plumb St., P.O. Box 25388, Houston, TX 77005 Tel 713-661-6126.

Nordon Pubns, *(Nordon Pubns., Inc.; 0-8439),* Park Ave., Suite 910, New York, NY 1001(Tel 212-679-7707; Orders to: Increased Sales Co., Inc., 327 Main Ave., Norwalk, C 06852 Tel 203-846-2027; Dist. by: Wholesale: Kable, P.O. Box 270, Norwalk, CT 06852.

Norfolk Port, *(Norfolk Port & Industrial Authority; 0-9605682),* Norfolk Internation Airport, Norfolk, VA 23518; Dist. by: International Society for General Semantics 834 Mission St., San Francisco, CA 94103.

Norman & Sandra, *(Norman & Sandra; 0-936520),* P.O. Box 218, Orient, NY 1195 Tel 516-323-3602.

Norman Pub, *(Norman Publishing Co.; 0-9601788),* 21 Almroth Dr., Wayne, NJ 07470 Tel 201-942-3637.

Normandie, *(Normandie Publishing Co, The; 0-9602986),* 1950 N. Normandie Ave., Los Angeles, CA 90027 Tel 213-664-9381.

Normark Corp, *(Normark Corp.),* 1710 E. 78th St., Minneapolis, MN 55423 Tel 612-869-3293.

Norn Pr, *(Norn Press; 0-917442),* 107 Upland Rd., Cambridge, MA 02140 Tel 617-864-8778.

Norns Pub Co, *(Norns Publishing Co., The; 0-939960),* P.O. Box 1172, Marathon, FL 33050 Tel 305-743-2796.

Nortex Pr
    See Eakin Pubns

North Am Consumer, *(North American Consumer's Group Press),* 3747 S.E. Washington, Portland, OR 97124.

North Am Fal Hunt, *(North American Falconr & Hunting Hawks; 0-912510),* P.O. Box 1484, Denver, CO 80201 Tel 303-651-1472

North Am Intl, *(North American International; 0-88265),* 1801 Columbia Rd. N.W., Suite 101, Washington, DC 20009 Tel 202-462-1441.

North Am Pub Co, *(North American Publishing Co.; 0-912920),* 401 N. Broad St., Philadelphia, PA 19108 Tel 215-574-9600.

North Am Rev, *(North American Review Press; 0-915696),* Cedar Falls, IA 50613 Tel 319-273-2681.

North American Inc, *(North American, Inc.; 0-930244),* P.O. Box 65, New Brunswick, NJ 08903 Tel 201-246-8546.

North Atlantic, *(North Atlantic Books; 0-938190; 0-913028),* 635 Amador St., Richmond, CA 94805.

North Castle, *(North Castle Books, Inc.; 0-911040),* 212 Bedford Rd., Greenwich, C 06830 Tel 203-869-7766.

North Central, *(North Central Publishing Co.; 0-935476),* Riverview Industrial Park, 274 Fillmore Ave., E., St. Paul, MN 55107 Tel 612-224-5455.

North Country, *(North Country Books, Inc.; 0-932052),* P.O. Box 506, Sylvan Beach, N 13157 Tel 315-762-5140.

North Holland, *(North-Holland Publishing Co.),* ; Publisher Abbreviation Without Addresses Are for Titles That Are Out of Print. These Are Obsolete Abbreviations. Publisher's Abbreviation Is Now Elsevier.

North Holland *Imprint of* **Elsevier**

North Ill U Ctr SE Asian, *(Center for SEAsian Studies, Northern Illinois Univ.),* Dist. by: Cellar Book Shop, 18090 Wyoming, Detroit, MI 48221 Tel 313-861-1776.

North Lake Prod, *(North Lake Productions; 0-9601722),* 9732 Boucher Dr., Otter Lake, MI 48464 Tel 517-795-2250.

North Light Pub, *(North Light Pubs.; 0-89134),* 37 Franklin St., Westport, CT 06880; Dist. by: Van Nostrand Reinhold, 450 W. 33rd St., New York, NY 10001.

North Pacific, *(North Pacific Pubs.; 0-913138),* P.O. Box 13255, Portland, OR 97213 Tel 503-236-9343.

North Plains, *(North Plains Press; 0-87970),* P.O. Box 1830, Aberdeen, SD 57401 Tel 605-225-5360.

North Point, *(North Point Publishing Co., Inc.; 0-911814),* 24 Branch St., St. Louis, MO 63147 Tel 314-231-7025; Not Publishing at This Time, Selling Only Remainder Stock.

North River, *(North River Press, Inc.; 0-88427),* P.O. Box 241, Croton-on-Hudson, NY 10520 Tel 914-941-7175.

North-South Ctr, *(North-South Center for Technical & Cultural Interchange),* Dist. by: F. B. Rothman, 57 Lenning St., South Hackensack, NJ 07606.

North Star, *(North Star Press; 0-87839),* P.O. Box 451, St. Cloud, MN 56301 Tel 612-253-1636.

Northampton County, *(Northampton County Bicentennial Center),* 61 N. Third St., Easton, PA 18042; Moved, Left No Forwarding Address.

Northcountry Pub, *(Northcountry Publishing Co.; 0-930366),* 216 N. Main St., Sauk Centre, MN 56378 Tel 612-352-6793.

Northern Mich, *(Northern Michigan Univ. Press; 0-918616),* 607 Cohodas Administrative Center, Marquette, MI 49855 Tel 906-227-2720; Orders to: NMU Bookstore, Don H. Bottum University Center, Marquette, MI 49855 Tel 906-227-2480.

Northern Pr, *(Northern Press),* 18 Cedar St., Potsdam, NY 13676.

Northernaire, *(Northernaire Pubns.; 0-9603380),* 717 Arlington Way, Martinez, CA 94553.

Northland, *(Northland Press; 0-87358),* P.O. Box N, Flagstaff, AZ 86002 Tel 602-774-5251.

Northland Pubns WA, *(Northland Pubns.),* P.O. Box 12157, Seattle, WA 98102.

Northland Pubns
See Northland Pubns WA

Northlands MI, *(Northlands Press; 0-918808),* 2723 Lake Lansing Rd., East Lansing, MI 48823 Tel 517-332-4274.

Northtown Bks, *(Northtown Books),* 957 "H" St., Arcata, CA 95521 Tel 707-822-2834.

Northwest Bks, *(Northwest Books),* Parkrose Sta., P.O. Box 20203, Portland, OR 97220 Tel 503-253-6228.

Northwest Learn, *(Northwest Learning Associates, Inc.; 0-931836),* 3719 81st Ave. S.E., Mercer Island, WA 98040.

Northwest Pub, *(Northwestern Publishing House; 0-8100),* 3624 W. North Ave., Milwaukee, WI 53208 Tel 414-442-1810.

Northwest Regional, *(Northwest Regional Educational Laboratory; 0-89354),* P. O. Box 414, Portland, OR 97207 Tel 503-248-6950.

Northwestern U Pr, *(Northwestern Univ. Press; 0-8101),* 1735 Benson Ave., Evanston, IL 60201 Tel 312-492-5313. *Imprints:* Trans (Transportation Center Pubns.).

Northwood Inst, *(Northwood Institute Press; 0-87359),* 3225 Cook St., Midland, MI 48640 Tel 517-631-1600.

Northwoods-Bassett
See Northwoods Pr

Northwoods Pr, *(Northwoods Press, Inc.; 0-89002),* P.O. Box 249, Stafford, VA 22554 Tel 703-659-6771.

Norton, *(Norton, W. W., & Co., Inc.; 0-393),* 500 Fifth Ave., New York, NY 10110 Tel 212-354-5500. *Imprints:* NAL (New American Library); NortonC (Norton College Division); Norton Lib (Norton Library).

Norton Art, *(Norton, R. W., Art Gallery; 0-913060; 0-9600182),* 4747 Creswell Ave., Shreveport, LA 71106 Tel 318-865-4201.

Norton Lib *Imprint of* **Norton**

NortonC *Imprint of* **Norton**

Norwalk Pr *Imprint of* **O'Sullivan Woodside**

Norway Bks, *(Norway Books; 0-939648),* 2432 Pacific Coast Hwy., No. 247, Lomita, CA 90717.

Norwegian-Am Hist Assn, *(Norwegian-American Historical Assn.; 0-87732),* St. Olaf College, Northfield, MN 55057 Tel 507-663-3221.

Norwood
See Norwood Edns

Norwood Edns, *(Norwood Editions; 0-88305; 0-8482),* P.O. Box 38, Norwood, PA 19074 Tel 215-583-4550.

Nosbooks, *(Nosbooks; 0-911046),* 42 W. 88th St., New York, NY 10024.

Nostalgia Pr, *(Nostalgia Press, Inc.; 0-87897),* 72 Franklin Ave., Franklin Square, NY 11010 Tel 516-488-4748; Orders to: P.O. Box 293, Franklin Square, NY 11010.

Nottingham Pr, *(Nottingham Press; 0-913958),* 1448 Page St., Alameda, CA 94501 Tel 415-522-4547.

Nourishing Thoughts, *(Nourishing Thoughts Enterprises; 0-9601198),* 1837 Beech St., Stow, OH 44224.

Nova Pr, *(Nova Press; 0-914220),* 708 Texas Ave., Austin, TX 78705 Tel 512-478-5590.

Nova U Pr, *(Nova Univ. Press),* College Ave., Fort Lauderdale, FL 33314 Tel 305-475-7300.

Nova Venturion, *(Nova Venturion; 0-915254),* P.O. Box 5182, Walnut Creek, CA 94596.

Nowfel, *(Nowfel Pubns.),* Dist. by: Intercontinental Enterprises Co., P.O. Box 237, Bronxville, NY 10708.

Noyes, *(Noyes Data Corp.; 0-8155),* Mill Rd. at Grand Ave., Park Ridge, NJ 07656 Tel 201-391-8484. *Imprints:* NAB (Noyes Art Books); NP (Noyes Press).

NP *Imprint of* **Inscape Corp**

NP *Imprint of* **Noyes**

NPC Pub Co, *(NPC Publishing Co.; 0-932634),* 17237 Hiawatha St., Granada Hills, CA 91344 Tel 213-363-8458.

NPD Corp, *(N.P.D. Corp; 0-937230),* P.O. Box 10161, Austin, TX 78766; 77701 N. Lamar Blvd., Austin, TX 78752 Tel 512-453-6154.

NPP Bks, *(NPP Books; 0-916182),* P.O. Box 1491, Ann Arbor, MI 48106.

Nuance Pr, *(Nuance Press Inc.; 0-917924),* 542 N. High St., Columbus, OH 43215.

NUCS
See Chr Sch Intl

Numarc Bk Corp, *(Numarc Book Corp.; 0-88471),* 1280 Main St., Buffalo, NY 14209 Tel 716-882-1155.

Numark Pub, *(Numark Pubns.; 0-915320),* 104-20 Queens Blvd., Forest Hills, NY 11375 Tel 212-897-8600.

Numen Chapbks, *(Numen Chapbooks; 0-939162),* 3202 Ellerslie Ave., Baltimore, MD 21218.

Numismata Orient, *(Numismata Orientalia),* P.O. Box 212, Tenafly, NJ 07676.

Numismatic Fine Arts, *(Numismatic Fine Arts, Inc.; 0-913484),* 342 N. Rodeo Dr., Beverly Hills, CA 90212 Tel 213-278-1535; Orders to: P.O. Box 3788, Beverly Hills, CA 90212.

Numisphil Pubns *Imprint of* **Matchless Pub**

Nunes, *(Nunes, Leslie K.; 0-9604190),* 613 Kaimalino Place, Kailua, HI 96734.

Nurseco, *(Nurseco, Inc.; 0-935236),* P.O. Box 145, Pacific Palisades, CA 90272.

Nursing Res, *(Nursing Resources, Inc.; 0-913654),* 12 Lakeside Office Park, Wakefield, MA 01880 Tel 617-245-9530.

Nutri-Kinetic, *(Nutri-Kinetic Dynamics Inc.; 0-938478),* 850 Kam Hwy., Pearl City, HI 96782.

NW Matrix, *(Northwest Matrix; 0-916930),* 1628 E. 19th Ave., Eugene, OR 97403 Tel 503-484-7080.

NW Review Bks, *(Northwest Review Books; 0-918402),* University of Oregon, Eugene, OR 97403 Tel 503-686-3957.

NWR Pubns, *(N W R Pubns.; 0-916972),* 156 Fifth Ave., Suite 308, New York, NY 10010 Tel 212-243-0666.

NY Acad Sci, *(New York Academy of Sciences; 0-89072; 0-89766),* Pubns. Dept., 2 E. 63rd St., New York, NY 10021 Tel 212-838-0230.

NY Botanical, *(New York Botanical Garden, Pubns. Office; 0-89327),* Bronx, NY 10458 Tel 212-220-8721.

NY Chiro Coll, *(New York Chiropractic College; 0-938470),* P.O. Box 167, Glen Head, NY 11545.

NY Culture Rev, *(New York Culture Review; 0-914856),* 1807 60th St., Brooklyn, NY 11204.

NY Hist Assn, *(New York State Historical Assn.; 0-917334),* Cooperstown, NY 13326 Tel 607-547-5231.

NY Hunting, *(New York Hunting & Fishing Guide, Inc.; 0-937328),* 45 Gibbs St., Rochester, NY 14604.

NY Labor News, *(New York Labor News; 0-935534),* 914 Industrial Ave., Palo Alto, CA 94303 Tel 415-494-1532.

NY Lib Assn, *(New York Library Assn.; 0-931658),* 60 E. 42nd St., Suite 1242, New York, NY 10017.

NY Lit Forum, *(New York Literary Forum; 0-931196),* 21 E. 79th St., New York, NY 10021.

NY Lit Pr, *(New York Literary Press; 0-930910),* 417 W. 56th St., New York, NY 10019.

NY-NJ Trail Confer, *(New York-New Jersey Trail Conference, Inc.; 0-9603966),* 20 W. 40th St., New York, NY 10018.

NY Prod Manual, *(New York Production Manual, Inc.; 0-935744),* Washington Square Village, Suite 8p, New York, NY 10012 Tel 212-777-4002.

NY Pub Lib, *(New York Public Library; 0-87104),* Fifth Ave. & 42nd St., New York, NY 10018 Tel 212-790-6285; Orders to: Readex Books, 101 Fifth Ave., New York, NY 10003; Ordering Address for NYPL Branch Libraries Imprint Only: Eight E. 40th St., N.Y., N.Y. 10016.

NY Sch Indus Rel, *(New York State School of Industrial & Labor Relations; 0-87546),* ILR Publications Division, Cornell University, Box 1000, Ithaca, NY 14853 Tel 607-256-3061.

NY St Coll Ag, *(New York State College of Agriculture & Life Sciences; 0-9605314),* Distribution Ctr., 7 Research Park, Cornell Univ., Ithaca, NY 14850.

NY St Eng Coun, *(New York State English Council; 0-930348),* 131 West Broad St., Rochester, NY 14608 Tel 716-325-4560.

NY Times, *(New York Times),* 229 W. 43rd St., New York, NY 10036 Tel 212-556-1234.

NY Zoetrope, *(New York Zoetrope; 0-918432),* 31 E. 12th St., New York, NY 10003 Tel 212-473-2729.

NYC Bd Ed, *(New York City Board of Education; 0-88315),* Center for Curriculum Development, 131 Livingstone St., Brooklyn, NY 11201 Tel 212-596-4903; Orders to: Publications Sales Office, 110 Livingston St., Brooklyn, NY 11201 Tel 212-596-3106.

NYC Ctr Learn, *(New York City Regional Center for Life-Long Learning; 0-914436),* City Univ. of New York, 101 W. 31st St., 7th Fl., New York, NY 10001 Tel 212-564-9385; No Longer Publishing.

Nyerges, *(Nyerges, Anton N.; 0-9600954),* 201 Langford Ct., Richmond, KY 40475 Tel 606-623-7153.

NYGS, *(New York Graphic Society, Ltd.; 0-8212),* 34 Beacon St., Boston, MA 02106 Tel 617-227-0730; Dist. by: Little, Brown & Co., 200 West St., Waltham, MA 02154. *Imprints:* Philadelphia Maritime Museum (Published by Philadelphia Maritime Museum).

NYGS CT, *(New York Graphic Society in Greenwich),* 140 Greenwich Ave., Greenwich, CT 06830 Tel 617-227-0730.

NYSCA, *(New York State Council on the Arts),* 80 Center St., New York, NY 10013.

Nystrom, *(Nystrom; 0-88463),* Div. of Carnation Co., 3333 Elston Ave., Chicago, IL 60618 Tel 312-463-1144.

NYU Pr, *(New York Univ. Press; 0-8147),* Dist. by: Columbia University Press, 562 W. 113th St., New York, NY 10025 Tel 212-678-6777.

O & B Bks, *(O & B Books, Inc.; 0-9601586),* 1215 N.W. Kline Place, Corvallis, OR 97330 Tel 503-752-2178.

O L Holmes, *(Holmes, Opal Laurel, Publisher; 0-918522),* P.O. Box 2535, Boise, ID 83701 Tel 208-344-4517; Dist. by: Pub. Marketing Group, Baker & Taylor Co., P.O. Box 350, Momence, IL 60954.

O N Holmes, *(Holmes, Oakley N.),* c/o Black Artists in America, Macgowan Enterprises, 39 Wilshire Dr., Spring Valley, NY 10977.

O R Miller, *(Miller, Oscar R.; 0-9600552),* P.O. Box 229, Berlin, OH 44610 Tel 216-893-2870.

O T Benfey, *(Benfey, Otto Theodor; 0-9602020),* 801 Woodbrook Dr., Greensboro, NC 27410 Tel 919-292-1062.

O W Davies, *(Davies, Owen W., Pub.; 0-910486),* 1214 N. La Salle St., Chicago, IL 60610 Tel 312-642-6697.

O W Frost, *(Frost, O.W.; 0-930766),* 2141 Lord Baranof Dr., Anchorage, AK 99503.

Oak *Imprint of* **Music Sales**

Oak Hill, *(Oak Hill Press; 0-915184),* 230 Payson Rd., Belmont, MA 02178 Tel 617-484-3145.

Oak Knoll, *(Oak Knoll Books; 0-938768),* 414 Delaware St., New Castle, DE 19720.

Oak Leaf, *(Oak Leaf Press; 0-935370),* 33 Union Square W., New York, NY 10003.

Oak Ridge, *(Oak Ridge Associated Universities; 0-930780),* P.O. Box 117, Oak Ridge, TN 37830 Tel 615-576-3152.

Oak Tree Pubns, *(Oak Tree Pubns. Inc.; 0-916392),* 11175 Flintkote Ave., Suite C, San Diego, CA 92121 Tel 714-457-3200.

Oaklawn Pr, *(Oaklawn Press, Inc.; 0-916198),* 283 S. Lake Ave., Suite 200, Pasadena, CA 91101 Tel 213-449-5594.

Oakview, *(Oakview Book Press; 0-9601104),* P.O. Box 990, Adelphi, MD 20783 Tel 301-434-8106.

Oakwood Pr, *(Oakwood Press, The; 0-915418),* P.O. Box 541, McMinnville, OR 97128 Tel 503-835-5855.

OAS, *(Organization of American States; 0-8270; 0-87549),* Dept. of Pubns., Washington, DC 20006 Tel 703-941-1578.

Oasis Pr
See PSI Res

Ober Park, *(Ober Park Associates, Inc.; 0-916668),* 701 Allegheny Square, W., Pittsburgh, PA 15212 Tel 412-322-1210.

Oberon Bks, *(Oberon Books; 0-9600420),* 475 Chestnut St., San Francisco, CA 94133.

Oblate, *(Oblate Fathers),* P.O. Box 96, San Antonio, TX 78291 Tel 512-736-1685.

Obol Intl, *(Obol International; 0-916710; 0-86723),* Div. of Unigraphics Inc., 8 S. Michigan Ave., Chicago, IL 60603 Tel 312-267-3662.

Obranoel Pr, *(Obranoel Press),* 63 Franklin Sq., New York, NY 11010.

O'Brien, *(O'Brien, F. M., Bookseller),* 34 & 36 High St., Portland, ME 04101.

Occasional Prods, *(Occasional Productions; 0-933264),* 251 Parnassus Ave., San Francisco, CA 94117.

Occidental, *(Occidental Press; 0-911050),* P.O. Box 1005, Washington, DC 20013.

Ocean Living, *(Ocean Living Institute; 0-915338),* Box 470, Kearny, NJ 07032; Moved, Left No Forwarding Address.

Oceana, *(Oceana Pubns.; 0-379),* 75 Main St., Dobbs Ferry, NY 10522 Tel 914-693-5944.

Ocelot Pr, *(Ocelot Press; 0-912434),* P.O. Box 504, Claremont, CA 91711 Tel 714-624-2439.

Ocorr Pr, *(Ocorr Press, The; 0-937478),* P.O. Box 64322, Los Angeles, CA 90064 Tel 213-839-3155.

Ocotillo, *(Ocotillo Press; 0-918380),* 215 N. 51st St., Seattle, WA 98103.

Octagon, *(Octagon Books; 0-374),* 19 Union Square W., New York, NY 10003 Tel 212-741-6961.

Octameron Assocs, *(Octameron Associates; 0-917760),* 820 Fontaine St., Alexandria, VA 22302 Tel 703-836-1019; Orders to: P.O. Box 3437, Alexandria, VA 22302.

October, *(October House; 0-8079),* P.O. Box 454, Stonington, CT 06378 Tel 203-535-3725.

October Pr, *(October Press, Inc., The; 0-935440),* 1801 N. Lamar, Suite 444, Dallas, TX 75202.

Oda, *(Oda, James),* 7054 Vanscoy Ave., N. Hollywood, CA 91605.

Odd John, *(Odd John Co.; 0-9601412),* 2318 33rd St., Santa Monica, CA 90405 Tel 213-450-4216.

Oddo, *(Oddo Publishing, Inc.; 0-87783),* Storybook Acres-Box 68, Fayetteville, GA 30214 Tel 404-461-7627.

Odin Pr, *(Odin Press; 0-930500),* P.O. Box 536, New York, NY 10021 Tel 212-744-2538.

ODS Pubns, *(ODS Pubns., Inc.; 0-9602516),* 444 N. Michigan Ave., Suite 1740, Chicago, IL 60611 Tel 312-329-9864.

Odyssey Ent, *(Odyssey Enterprises, Ltd.; 0-939006),* P.O. Box 1686, Norman, OK 73070.

Odyssey MA, *(Odyssey Pubns., Inc.; 0-933752),* P.O. Box G-148, Greenwood, MA 01880.

Odyssey Pr, *(Odyssey Press; 0-8399),* Dist. by: Bobbs-Merrill Co., Inc., 4300 W. 62nd St., Indianapolis, IN 46206 Tel 317-291-3100.

Odyssey Pub Co, *(Odyssey Publishing Co.; 0-934494),* 1161-21st Ave. E., Seattle, WA 98112.

OECD, *(Organization for Economic Cooperation & Development),* 1750 Pennsylvania Ave., Suite 12072, N.W., Washington, DC 20006 Tel 202-724-1857.

Oelgeschlager, *(Oelgeschlager, Gunn & Hain, Pubs., Inc.; 0-89946),* 1278 Massachusetts Ave., Cambridge, MA 02138 Tel 617-876-5100.

OES Pubns, *(OES Pubns.; 0-89779),* College of Engineering, Univ. of KY, Lexington, KY 40506 Tel 606-257-2843.

Off off Broadway, *(Off off Broadway Alliance; 0-933750),* 162 W. 56th St., Room 206, New York, NY 10019 Tel 212-757-4473.

Office Pubns, *(Office Pubns., Inc.; 0-911054),* 1200 Summer St., P.O. Box 1231, Stamford, CT 06904 Tel 203-327-9670.

Office Res, *(Office Research Institute; 0-911056),* 1517 Sparrow Ave., Longwood, FL 32750 Tel 305-339-8527.

Official Corp, *(Official Corp., The; 0-9605074),* 240 Newport Ctr. Dr., Suite 200, Newport Beach, CA 92660.

Ogham Hse, *(Ogham House, Inc.; 0-916590),* 6 Sherri Lane, Spring Valley, NY 10977.

O'Hara, *(O'Hara, J. Philip, Inc., Pubs.; 0-87955),* c/o Book Trading Ltd., 559 W. 26th St., New York, NY 10001 Tel 212-695-8222. *Imprints:* Potato Pr (Potato Press).

Ohara Pubns, *(O'Hara Pubns., Inc.; 0-89750),* 1847 W. Empire Ave., Burbank, CA 91504 Tel 213-843-4444.

Ohio Acad Sci, *(Ohio Academy of Science, The; 0-933124),* 445 King Ave., Columbus, OH 43201 Tel 614-424-6045.

Ohio Antique Rev, *(Ohio Antique Review, Inc.; 0-9603290),* P.O. Box 538, Worthington, OH 43085 Tel 614-885-9757.

Ohio Bio Survey, *(Ohio Biological Survey; 0-86727),* 980 Biological Sciences Bldg., Ohio State Univ., 484 W. 12th Ave., Columbus, OH 43210 Tel 614-422-9645.

Ohio Hist Soc, *(Ohio Historical Society),* Ohio Historical Center, Interstate 71 & 17th Ave., Columbus, OH 43211 Tel 614-466-4664.

Ohio Lib Foun, *(Ohio Library Foundation; 0-911060),* 40 S. 3rd St., Suite 409, Columbus, OH 43215.

Ohio Mag, *(Ohio Magazine; 0-938040),* 40 S. Third St., Columbus, OH 43215.

Ohio Savings, *(Ohio Savings Assn),* 13109 Shaker Square, Cleveland, OH 44120 Tel 216-752-7000.

Ohio St U Admin Sci, *(Ohio State Univ., College of Administrative Science; 0-87776),* 220 W. 12th Ave., Columbus, OH 43210 Tel 614-422-2061; Orders to: O.S.U. Press, The Ohio State Univ., 2070 Neil Ave., Columbus, OH 43210.

Ohio St U Lib, *(Ohio State Univ. Libraries; 0-88215),* Rm. 001, Main Lib., 1858 Neil Ave. Mall, Columbus, OH 43210 Tel 614-422-4738.

Ohio St U Pr, *(Ohio State Univ. Press; 0-8142),* Hitchcock Hall, Rm. 316, 2070 Neil Ave., Columbus, OH 43210 Tel 614-422-6930.

Ohio U Ctr Intl, *(Ohio Univ. Center for International Studies; 0-89680),* Athens, OH 45701.

Ohio U Pr, *(Ohio Univ. Press; 0-8214),* Scott Quadrangle, Athens, OH 45701 Tel 614-594-5852.

Oil Bks, *(Oil Books),* Box 88, RD 1, Sugar Run, PA 18846 Tel 717-265-8665.

Oil Daily, *(Oil Daily; 0-918216),* 850 Third Ave., New York, NY 10022 Tel 212-593-2100.

OK Street, *(OK Street Inc.; 0-917278),* 12800 Hillcrest Rd., Suite 215, Dallas, TX 75230 Tel 214-387-0953.

Okefenokee Pr, *(Okefenokee Press; 0-9601606),* Rte. 3, Box 142-C, Folkston, GA 31537 Tel 912-496-2354.

Okinawan Kobujitsei
See LKA Inc

Okla State U Fire Prot, *(Oklahoma State Univ., International Fire Service Training Assn., Fire Protection Pubns.),* Stillwater, OK 74074.

Okpaku Communications, *(Okpaku Communications; 0-89388),* 444 Central Park W., New York, NY 10025 Tel 212-866-9140.

OLAM, *(OLAM; 0-916222),* 2101 N. Court Hse. Rd., Arlington, VA 22201.

Old Adobe Pr, *(Old Adobe Press),* P.O. Box 115, Penngrove, CA 94251.

Old Army, *(Old Army Press; 0-88342),* P.O. Box 2243, Fort Collins, CO 80521 Tel 303-484-5535.

Old Colony Hist, *(Old Colony Historical Society),* 66 Church Green, Taunton, MA 02780.

Old Mill, *(Old Mill Press; 0-934700),* P.O. Box 388, Old Chelsea Sta., New York, NY 1011 Tel 212-929-4958.

Old NY Bk Shop, *(Old New York Book Shop Press; 0-937036),* 1069 Juniper St., NE, Atlanta, GA 30309.

Old Oaktree, *(Old Oaktree Motor Co.; 0-9603194),* 2012 Hyperion Ave., Los Angeles, CA 90027.

Old Sturbridge, *(Old Sturbridge, Inc.),* Sturbridge, MA 01566 Tel 617-347-3362.

Old Time, *(Old Time Bottle Publishing Co.; 0-911068),* 611 Lancaster Dr., N.E., Salem, OR 97301 Tel 503-362-1446.

Old Ursuline, *(Old Ursuline Convent Cookbook; 0-9604718),* P.O. Box 7491, Metairie, LA 70010.

Old Violin, *(Old Violin-Art Publishing; 0-918554),* Box 500, 225 S. Cooke, Helena, MT 59601 Tel 406-442-8963.

Old West, *(Old West Publishing Co.; 0-912094),* 1228 E. Colfax Ave., Denver, CO 80218 Tel 303-832-7190.

Oleander Pr, *(Oleander Press; 0-902675; 0-900891; 0-906672),* 210 Fifth Ave., New York, NY 10010.

Olearius Edns, *(Olearius Editions; 0-917526),* P.O. Box H, Kemblesville, PA 19347.

Oligodynamics, *(Oligodynamics Press),* P.O. Box 29102, San Antonio, TX 78229; Moved, Left No Forwarding Address.

Olivant, *(Olivant Press; 0-87956),* P.O. Box 1409, Homestead, FL 33030.

Olive Pr Pubns, *(Olive Press Pubns.; 0-933380),* P.O. Box 99, Los Olivos, CA 93441 Tel 805-688-2445.

Oliver Pr, *(Oliver Press; 0-914400),* Dist. by: Charles Scribner's Sons, Shipping & Billing Depts., Vreeland Ave., Totowa, NJ 70512.

Olivet, *(Olivet College Press; 0-911070),* Dist. by: Bill Whitney, P.O. Box 20, Mott Academic Ctr., Olivet, MI 49076.

Olivia & Hill, *(Olivia & Hill Press Inc., The; 0-934034),* P.O. Box 7396, Ann Arbor, MI 48107 Tel 313-663-0235.

Olken Pubns, *(Olken Pubns.; 0-934818),* 2830 Kennedy St., Livermore, CA 94550 Tel 415-447-5177.

Oll Korrect, *(Oll Korrect Press),* 119 W. Ocotillo Vista, Tucson, AZ 85704 Tel 602-742-2070.

Olympia, *(Olympia Press),* 220 Park Ave., S., New York, NY 10003. *Imprints:* Ophelia (Ophelia Books); Travellers Comp (Travellers Companion Ser.).

Olympic Media, *(Olympic Media Information; 0-88367),* 71 W. 23rd St., New York, NY 10010 Tel 212-675-4500.

Olympic Pr, *(Olympic Press; 0-930784),* P.O. Box 999, Montclair, NJ 07043 Tel 201-678-4453; Moved, Left No Forwarding Address.

Olympus Pub Co, *(Olympus Publishing Co.; 0-913420),* 1670 E. 13th St., Salt Lake City, UT 84105 Tel 801-583-3666.

Oman Ent, *(Oman Enterprises, Inc.; 0-917346),* P.O. Box 535, Pacific Grove, CA 93950 Tel 408-372-0762.

OMango, *(OMango D'Press; 0-933278),* P.O. Box 64, Rte. 171, Woodstock Valley, CT 06282 Tel 203-974-2511.

Omb, *(Ombudsman Press),* 470 W. Highland Ave., Sierra Madre, CA 91024 Tel 213-355-1325.

O'Meara Pubns, *(O'Meara Pubns.; 0-934604),* 130 W. Palace Ave., Santa Fe, NM 87501.

Omega Bks, *(Omega Books; 0-89353),* 428 Tamal Plaza, Corte Madera, CA 94925 Tel 415-924-1222.

Omega Pub Co, *(Omega Publishing Co., Inc.),* P.O. Box 323, Snohomish, WA 98290.

Omega Pubns OR, *(Omega Pubns.; 0-86694),* P.O. Box 4130, Medford, OR 97501 Tel 503-826-7302.

men Pr, *(Omen Press; 0-912358),* P.O. Box 12457, Tucson, AZ 85711 Tel 602-296-4002.

MF Bks, *(OMF Books),* 404 S. Church St., Robesonia, PA 19551.

mkara Pr, *(Omkara Press; 0-934094),* 51 Scott St., San Francisco, CA 94117 Tel 414-626-9407.

mni Pubs, *(Omni Pubs.; 0-89127),* 218 E. Grand Ave., No. 201, Escondido, CA 92025 Tel 714-746-5833.

mnibook *Imprint of* **Bible Study Pr**

naway, *(Onaway Pubns.; 0-918900),* 28 Lucky Dr., San Rafael, CA 94904 Tel 415-924-0884.

nchiota Bks, *(Onchiota Books; 0-934820),* Onchiota, NY 12951 Tel 518-891-3249.

ne Candle, *(One Candle Press; 0-914032),* Dist. by: Verre Center, 1835 Savoy Dr, Atlanta, GA 30341; Formerly Judson Press.

ne Hund First Air, *(101st Airborne Division Assn.),* P.O. Box 101 Ab, Court Sta., Kalamazoo, MI 49005 Tel 616-388-5801.

ne Hund One Prods, *(101 Productions; 0-912238; 0-89286),* 834 Mission St., San Francisco, CA 94103 Tel 415-495-6040; Dist. by: Charles Scribner's Sons, Book Warehouse, Vreeland Ave., Totowa, NJ 07512.

ne Percent, *(One Percent Publishing; 0-935442),* 2888 Bluff St., Suite 143, Boulder, CO 80301.

ne Shot, *(One Shot Press),* P.O. Box 1077, Middletown, CT 06457 Tel 203-349-8626.

ne Strawberry, *(One Strawberry, Inc.; 0-88470),* 74 Strawtown Rd., New City, NY 10956 Tel 914-634-6879; Dist. by: McGraw-Hill Book Co., 1221 Ave. of the Americas, New York, NY 10020 Tel 212-997-1221.

'Neill Pr, *(O'Neill Press; 0-930970),* 305 Great Neck Rd., Waterford, CT 06385.

neiric Pr, *(Oneiric Press),* Dist. by: Book People, 2940 Seventh St., Berkeley, CA 94710 Tel 415-549-3033.

nest Pubns, *(Onest Pubns.; 0-80411),* 602 Elkader St., Ashland, OR 97520 Tel 503-482-0088.

ntario Pr, *(Ontario Press; 0-913254),* 61 W. Ontario St., Chicago, IL 60610 Tel 312-751-1656.

ntario Rev NJ, *(Ontario Review Press, The; 0-86538),* 9 Honey Brook Dr., Princeton, NJ 08540; Dist. by: Persea Books, Inc., 225 Lafayette St., New York, NY 10012 Tel 212-431-5270.

olp Pr, *(OOLP (Out of London Press) Inc.; 0-915570),* 12 W. 17th St, New York, NY 10011 Tel 212-691-8310.

Open Books, *(Open Books; 0-931416),* 1631 Grant St., Berkeley, CA 94703.

Open Connections, *(Open Connections Inc.),* 312 Bryn Mawr Ave., Bryn Mawr, PA 19010.

Open Court, *(Open Court Publishing Co.; 0-87548; 0-89688),* Div. of Carus Corp., P.O. Box 599, LaSalle, IL 61301 Tel 815-223-2520. *Imprints:* Library Pr (Library Press).

Open-Door, *(Open-Door Press; 0-912162),* P.O. Box 6161, Shirlington Sta., Arlington, VA 22206 Tel 703-379-8655.

Open Door Inc, *(Open Door, Inc., The; 0-940136),* P. O. Box 855, Charlottesville, VA 22902 Tel 804-784-3951.

Open Door Pubns, *(Open Door Pubns.; 0-939310),* 850 Seventh Ave., Suite 705, New York, NY 10019 Tel 212-581-6470.

Open Door Soc, *(Open Door Society of Connecticut, Inc.; 0-918416),* Box 478, Hartford, CT 06101.

Open Path, *(Open Path, The; 0-9602722),* 703 N. 18th St., Boise, ID 83702.

Open Places, *(Open Places; 0-913398),* Box 2085, Stephens College, Columbia, MO 65215 Tel 314-442-2211.

Open Roads, *(Open Roads Press; 0-937838),* P.O. Box 8061, San Diego, CA 92102 Tel 714-232-0714.

Open Sesame, *(Open Sesame Publishing Co.; 0-933578),* 2000 Center St., Suite 1323, Berkeley, CA 94704 Tel 415-526-6204.

Open U, *(Open Univ. Educational Media, Inc.),* 110 E. 59th St., New York, NY 10022 Tel 212-935-8965.

Open U *Imprint of* **Har-Row**

Open Window, *(Open Window Books Inc.; 0-917694),* Box 949, Chickasha, OK 73018 Tel 405-224-3217.

Opera West, *(Opera West Foundation; 0-9601270),* 68 Julian Ave., San Francisco, CA 94103 Tel 415-621-2112.

Ophelia *Imprint of* **Olympia**

Ophir Intl, *(Ophir International),* Station A, Auburn, CA 95603.

Ophthalmic, *(Ophthalmic Publishing Co.),* 435 N. Michigan Ave., Suite 1415, Chicago, IL 60611 Tel 312-787-3853.

Optical Pub, *(Optical Publishing Co. Inc.),* P.O. Box 1146, Pittsfield, MA 01201 Tel 413-499-0514.

Optical Resolution, *(Optical Resolution Information Center; 0-9601918),* Manhattan College, Riverdale, NY 10471.

Optical Soc, *(Optical Society of America; 0-9600380),* 1816 Jefferson Place, Washington, DC 20036 Tel 202-223-8130.

Optimum Bk, *(Optimum Book Marketing Co.),* 171 Madison Ave., New York, NY 10016.

Options, *(Options Publishing Co.; 0-917400),* P.O. Box 311, Wayne, NJ 07470 Tel 201-694-2327.

Optosonic Pr, *(Optosonic Press; 0-87739),* P.O. Box 883, Ansonia Sta., New York, NY 10023 Tel 212-724-9687.

O'Quinn Studio
   See Starlog

Orange County Genealog, *(Orange County Genealogical Society; 0-9604116),* 101 Main St., Goshen, NY 10924.

Orange Duck, *(Orange Duck Press),* Box 84, Carbondale, OH 45717.

Orbis Bks, *(Orbis Books; 0-88344),* Maryknoll, NY 10545 Tel 914-941-7590.

Orbiting Bk, *(Orbiting Book Service; 0-914326),* P.O. Box 13, New York, NY 10038 Tel 212-853-3071.

Orchard, *(Orchard House),* 1281 Burg St., Granville, OH 43023.

Orchard Hse MA, *(Orchard House, Inc.; 0-933510),* Balls Hill Rd., Concord, MA 01742 Tel 617-369-0467.

ORDINA *Imprint of* **Unipub**

Oreg Hist Soc, *(Oregon Historical Society; 0-87595),* 1230 S.W. Park Ave., Portland, OR 97205 Tel 503-222-1741.

Oreg St U Bkstrs, *(Oregon State Univ. Book Stores, Inc.; 0-88246),* P.O. Box 489, Corvallis, OR 97330 Tel 503-754-4323.

Oreg St U Pr, *(Oregon State Univ. Press; 0-87071),* 101 Waldo Hall, Oregon State University, Corvallis, OR 97331 Tel 503-754-3166.

ORES Pubns
   See OES Pubns

Organ Lit, *(Organ Literature Foundation, The; 0-913746),* 45 Norfolk Rd, Braintree, MA 02184 Tel 617-848-1388.

Organizat Meas, *(Organizational Measurement Systems Press; 0-917926),* Box 81, Atlanta, GA 30301 Tel 404-355-9472.

Oriel *Imprint of* **Routledge & Kegan**

Oriel Pr, *(Oriel Press; 0-938628),* P.O. Box 12373, Portland, OR 97212.

Orient Bk Dist, *(Orient Book Distributors; 0-89684),* P.O. Box 100, Livingston, NJ 07039 Tel 201-992-6992.

Orient Longman *Imprint of* **South Asia Bks**

Orient Res Partners, *(Oriental Research Partners; 0-89250),* P.O. Box 158, Newtonville, MA 02160 Tel 617-965-4399.

Oriental Art, *(Oriental Art Prices Current),* 17070 Collins Ave., North Miami Beach, FL 33160; Moved, Left No Forwarding Address.

Oriental Inst, *(Oriental Institute of the Univ. of Chicago; 0-918986),* 1155 E. 58th St., Chicago, IL 60637 Tel 312-753-2478; Orders to: 1155 E. 58th St., Chicago, IL 60637 Tel 312-753-3875.

Orientalia, *(Orientalia Art, Ltd.; 0-87902),* P.O. Box 597, New York, NY 10276; 61 Fourth Ave., New York, NY 10003.

Original Pr, *(Original Press; 0-935812),* Div. of Throckmorton Publishing Co., 561 Milltown Rd., North Brunswick, NJ 08902; Moved, Left No Forwarding Address.

Oriole Edns, *(Oriole Editions; 0-88211),* 120 E. 81st St., New York, NY 10028 Tel 212-861-3102.

Orirana Pr, *(Orirana Press; 0-938364),* 19737 Covello St., Canoga Park, CA 91306.

ORourke, *(O'Rourke Pubns.; 0-911196),* P.O. Box 1118, Lake Alfred, FL 33850 Tel 813-956-1686.

Orovan Bks, *(Orovan Books; 0-913748),* P.O. Box 6082, Honolulu, HI 96818 Tel 808-422-6297.

Orpheus Pr, *(Orpheus Press; 0-915648),* P.O. Box 48423, Los Angeles, CA 90048 Tel 213-653-5800.

Orr & Assocs, *(Orr, Ken, & Associates,Inc.; 0-9605884),* 715 E. 8th St., Topeka, KS 66607.

Ortho, *(Ortho Books; 0-917102),* Div. of Chevron Chemical Co., Subs. of Standard Oil Co. of Calif., c/o Chevron Chemical Co., P.O. Box 3744, San Francisco, CA 94119 Tel 415-894-2593.

Orthodox Chr, *(Orthodox Christian Education Society; 0-938366),* 1916 W. Warner Ave., Chicago, IL 60613 Tel 312-549-0584.

Oryx Pr, *(Oryx Press; 0-912700; 0-89774),* 2214 N. Central Ave., Phoenix, AZ 85004 Tel 602-254-6156.

Orzano Pub Co, *(Orzano Publishing Co.; 0-936668),* P.O. Box 394, Islip, NY 11751.

Osborne, *(Osborne, Lewis, Book Pubs.; 0-87767),* P.O. Box 647, Ashland, OR 97520 Tel 503-482-9711.

Osborne & Assocs
   See Osborne-McGraw

Osborne-McGraw, *(Osborne/McGraw-Hill, Inc.; 0-931988),* P.O. Box 2036, Berkeley, CA 94702; 630 Bancroft Way, Berkeley, CA 94710 Tel 415-548-2805.

Osmond Pub, *(Osmond Publishing),* c/o Brothers Distributing Co., P.O. Box 1176, Upland, CA 91786.

Ossi Prods
   See Ossi Pubns

Ossi Pubns, *(Ossi Pubns.; 0-930912),* P.O. Box 141, Fern Park, FL 32730 Tel 305-862-2392.

Osterhus, *(Osterhus Publishing House),* 4500 W. Broadway, Minneapolis, MN 55422 Tel 612-537-9311.

O'Sullivan Woodside, *(O'Sullivan, Woodside & Co.; 0-89019),* 2218 E. Magnolia, Phoenix, AZ 85034 Tel 602-244-0304. *Imprints:* Norwalk Pr (Norwalk Press).

OSV Fabric Shop, *(Old Sturbridge Village Fabric Shop at Lincoln House; 0-910940),* Rte. 20, Sturbridge, MA 01566 Tel 617-347-3952.

Otafra, *(Otafra Press; 0-9605220),* P.O. Box 814, Mesilla, NM 88046.

Other Bks, *(Other Books),* 1412 Spruce St., Berkeley, CA 94709 Tel 415-841-6359.

Other Voices, *(Other Voices Literary Society, Inc.; 0-916518),* 39 Oakwood, San Francisco, CA 94110 Tel 415-864-1246.

Ottenheimer Pubs, *(Ottenheimer Pubs.; 0-528),* 300 Reisterstown Rd., Baltimore, MD 21208 Tel 301-484-2100.

Otterbein Home, *(Otterbein Home; 0-931990),* Program Dept., Lebanon, OH 45036.

Otterden, *(Otterden Press; 0-918868),* 111 Plymouth Rd., Hillsdale, NJ 07642 Tel 201-664-2583.

Our Land-Toren, *(Our Land/Toren Development Inc.; 0-939474),* 44 Montgomery St., San Francisco, CA 94104.

Our Sunday Visitor, *(Our Sunday Visitor, Inc.; 0-87973),* 200 Noll Plaza, Huntington, IN 46750 Tel 219-356-8400.

Out & Out, *(Out & Out Books; 0-918314),* 476 Second St., Brooklyn, NY 11215 Tel 212-499-9227.

Out of the Ashes, *(Out of the Ashes Press; 0-912874),* P.O. Box 42384, Portland, OR 97242.

Outbooks, *(Outbooks, 0-89646),* 217 Kimball Ave., Golden, CO 80401.

Outdoor Assocs, *(Outdoor Associates),* 1279 Dean St., Schenectady, NY 12309 Tel 518-372-4585.

Outdoor Empire, *(Outdoor Empire Publishing, Inc.; 0-916682),* P.O. Box C-19000, 511 Eastlake Ave., E., Seattle, WA 98109 Tel 206-624-3845.

Outdoor Pict, *(Outdoor Pictures; 0-911080),* P.O. Box 277, Anacortes, WA 98221 Tel 206-293-3200.

Outdoor Skills, *(Outdoor Skills Bookshelf; 0-940022),* P.O. Box 111501, Nashville, TN 37211 Tel 615-776-5276.

Outdoors Inc, *(Outdoors Inc.; 0-9605254),* Box 999, Brainerd, MN 56401.

Outer Straubville, *(Outer Straubville Press),* Box 612, Cotati, CA 94928; Dist. by: Book People, 2940 Seventh St., Berkeley, CA 94710 Tel 415-549-3033.

Outlook, *(Outlook Pubs.; 0-911082),* 512 E. Main St., Richmond, VA 23219.

Output, *(Output Systems Corp.; 0-911082),* 2300 S. Ninth St., Arlington, VA 22204 Tel 703-521-2300; Moved, Left No Forwarding Address.

Outside Ent, *(Outside Enterprise Press; 0-937232),* P.O. Box 2650, College Sta., Pullman, WA 99163.

Over the Rainbow, *(Over the Rainbow Press; 0-916252),* P.O. Box 7072, Berkeley, CA 94707 Tel 415-525-4020.

Overlook Hosp, *(Overlook Hospital Auxiliary; 0-9604560),* Morris Ave., Summit, NJ 07901.

Overlook Pr, *(Overlook Press; 0-87951),* 667 Madison Ave., Suite 401A, New York, NY 10021; c/o Viking Press, 625 Madison Ave, New York, NY 10022 Tel 212-755-4330.

Overseas Dev Council, *(Overseas Development Council),* 1717 Massachusetts Ave., N.W., Washington, DC 20036 Tel 202-234-8701.

Overshiner, *(Overshiner Press; 0-937480),* 92 Buckwood Place, Santa Rosa, CA 95405 Tel 707-538-0181.

Overstreet, *(Overstreet Pubns.; 0-517),* 780 Hunt Cliff Dr. N.W., Cleveland, OH 37311.

Oviedo Pub Co, *(Oviedo Publishing Co.; 0-9603034),* P.O. Box 837, Oviedo, FL 32765.

Owen & Jenkins, *(Owen-Jenkins, Inc.; 0-918144),* 1112 Richview Rd., Tallahassee, FL 32301 Tel 904-877-3330.

Owl Pr, *(Owl Press; 0-911084),* P.O. Box 709, Annapolis, MD 21404 Tel 301-267-6456.

Owlswick Pr, *(Owlswick Press; 0-913896),* P.O. Box 8243, Philadelphia, PA 19101 Tel 215-382-5415.

Owlswood Prods, *(Owlswood Productions; 0-915942),* 1355 Market St., San Francisco, CA 94103 Tel 415-626-2480.

Owner-Builder, *(Owner-Builder Publications),* P.O. Box 550, Oakhurst, CA 93644.

Ox Bow, *(Ox Bow Press; 0-918024),* P.O. Box 4045, Woodbridge, CT 06525 Tel 203-387-5900.

Oxbridge, *(Oxbridge Publishing Co., Inc.; 0-911086),* 150 E. 52nd St., New York, NY 10022 Tel 212-751-7590.

Oxbridge Comm, *(Oxbridge Communications, Inc.; 0-917460),* 183 Madison Ave., Suite 1108, New York, NY 10016.

OxC&M Imprint of **Oxford U Pr**

Oxford Bk
  See Sadlier-Oxford

Oxford Bk, *(Oxford Book Co., Inc.),* ; Publisher Abbreviation Without Addresses Are for Titles That Are Out of Print. These Are Obsolete Abbreviations.

Oxford U Pr, *(Oxford Univ. Press, Inc.; 0-19),* 200 Madison Ave., New York, NY 10016 Tel 212-679-7300; Orders to: 16-00 Pollitt Dr., Fair Lawn, NJ 07410 Tel 201-796-8000; New York Accounts Use 212-564-6680. *Imprints:* GB (Galaxy Books); HS (Hesperides Paperbacks); IRR (Institute of Race Relations); OxC&M (Oxford Joint College & Medical Div.).

Oxmoor Hse, *(Oxmoor House, Inc.; 0-8487),* P.O. Box 2262, Birmingham, AL 35201 Tel 205-870-4440; Dist. by: Harper & Row, Pubs., Inc., Keystone Industrial Park, Scranton, PA 18512 Tel 800-233-4175.

Oyamo Ujamaa, *(Oyamo Ujamaa; 0-917008),* P.O. Box 251, Morningside Sta., New York, NY 10026 Tel 212-868-3330.

Oyez, *(Oyez; 0-911088),* 212 Colgate Ave., Kensington, CA 94707.

Oyster Pr, *(Oyster Press; 0-933114),* 103 S. Soledad St., Santa Barbara, CA 93103.

Ozark Mtn Pubs, *(Ozark Mountain Publishers; 0-915394),* P.O. Box 4718 G.S., Springfield, MO 65804 Tel 417-881-3060.

Ozark Soc, *(Ozark Society; 0-912456),* P.O. Box 725, Hot Springs, AR 71901.

Ozer, *(Ozer, Jerome S., Pub. Inc.; 0-89198),* 340 Tenafly Rd., Englewood, NJ 07631 Tel 201-567-7040.

P A Abbott, *(Abbott, P.A., Pubns.; 0-938564),* P.O. Box 2085, Kalamazoo, MI 49003.

P A Janzen
  See Janzen Assoc

P A Stroock, *(Stroock, Paul A.; 0-9601138),* 35 Middle Lane, P.O. Box 126, Jericho, L. I., NY 11753 Tel 516-433-9018.

P & K Ent, *(P & K Enterprises; 0-918176),* 2502 Cecile St., Kissimmee, FL 32741 Tel 305-846-6995.

P & P Moses Yanes, *(Poet & Printer Moses Yanes; 0-913726),* 13850 Big Basin Way, Boulder Creek, CA 95006.

P Andersen, *(Andersen, Paul; 0-9604720),* P.O. Box 2184, Laguna Hills, CA 92653.

P Boals, *(Boals, Prudencia; 0-9604270),* P.O. Box 379, Ripley, TN 38063.

P Coates, *(Coates, Pamela, Antiques; 0-9600678),* 1506 Harvey Rd., Ardencroft, DE 19810.

P D Michael, *(Michael, Pansy D.; 0-9602460),* R.R. 2, South Whitley, IN 46787 Tel 219-839-3135.

P De Vosjoli, *(De Vosjoli, Philippe, & Sons; 0-916264),* 1881 N.E. 39th St., Pompano Beach, FL 33064 Tel 305-942-6693.

P Downsbrough, *(Downsbrough, Peter; 0-9602192),* 216 Centre St., New York, NY 10013; Dist. by: Printed Matter, 7 Lispenard St., New York, NY 10013.

P Elek
  See Merrimack Bk Serv

P Erens, *(Erens, Patricia; 0-9603920),* 2920 Commonwealth Ave., Chicago, IL 60657; Dist. by: Chicago Review Press, 820 North Franklin St., Chicago, IL 60610 Tel 312-644-5457.

P-F Soccer, *(Page-Ficklin Soccer),* 3530 Greer Rd., Palo Alto, CA 94303 Tel 415-494-6338.

P Friedrich, *(Friedrich, Paul),* Benjamin & Martha Waite Press, 1126 E. 59th St., Chicago, IL 60637 Tel 312-753-3705.

P G Michael, *(Michael, Prudence Groff; 0-9600932),* 64472 U.S.H 31, Lakeville, IN 46536 Tel 219-291-0454.

P G Partington, *(Partington, Paul G.; 0-9602538),* 7320 S. Gretna Ave., Whittier, CA 90606.

P Gaines Co, *(Gaines, P., Co., The; 0-936284),* P.O. Box 705, Oak Park, IL 60303 Tel 312-996-7829.

P Gazin, *(Gazin, Patricia),* 1250 First St., Hermosa Beach, CA 90254 Tel 213-376-5765.

P George Bks, *(George, Peter, Books),* P.O. Box 940, Beaverton, OR 97005.

P-H, *(Prentice-Hall, Inc.; 0-13),* Englewood Cliffs, NJ 07632 Tel 201-592-2000; Orders to: Box 500, Englewood Cliffs, NJ 07632. *Imprints:* Appleton-Century-Crofts (Appleton-Century-Crofts); Busn (Business & Professional Div.); Parker (Parker Publishing Co.); Prism (Prism Books); Reward (Reward Books); Spec (Spectrum Books).

P H Brookes, *(Brookes, Paul H., Pubs.; 0-933716),* P.O. Box 10624, Baltimore, MD 21204 Tel 301-433-8100.

P H Merrill, *(Merrill, Perry H.; 0-9605806),* 200 Elm St., Montpelier, VT 05602 Tel 802-223-2697.

P H Perkins, *(Perkins, Percy H.; 0-9603090),* 5450 Peachtree-Dunwoody Rd., Atlanta, GA 30342 Tel 404-261-1740.

P I Industries, *(P.I. Industries; 0-916976),* 243M Griffith Rd., P.O. Box 949, Loveland, CO 80537 Tel 303-669-2980.

P J Baukol
  See Baukol Pub

P J Thompson, *(Thompson, Paul J.; 0-9601288),* c/o Y.M.C.A., 2200 Prospect Ave., Rm. 437, Cleveland, OH 44115 Tel 216-344-7724.

P James, *(James, Philip; 0-931008),* P.O. Box 87, Exton, PA 19341.

P Juul Pr, *(Juul, Jenet, Press, Inc.; 0-915456),* P.O. Box 40605, Tucson, AZ 85717 Tel 602-622-3409.

P Krejcarek, *(Krejcarek, Philip),* 1735 N. 57th, Milwaukee, WI 53208.

P L Johnstone
  See Mission Dolores

P McIlvaine, *(McIlvaine, Paul, Pub.; 0-9600410),* Sky Village, Rte. 9 Box 107, Hendersonville, NC 28739 Tel 704-692-3971.

P Odegard, *(Odegard, Peter; 0-9600524),* Rt. 1, St. Croix Cove, Hudson, WI 54016; Name Changed to Advance Planning Pubns.

P Odegard
  See Advance Planning

P R Feltus, *(Feltus, Peter R.),* 5709 Keith Ave., Oakland, CA 94618.

P R Pub Co, *(PR Publishing Co., Inc.),* P.O. Box 600, 14 Front St., Exeter, NH 03833 Tel 603-778-0514.

P Richmond, *(Richmond, Paul, & Co.; 0-91264* 1100 Glendon Ave., Suite 1517, West Los Angeles, CA 90021; Moved, Left No Forwarding Address.

P Robinson, *(Robinson, Peggy),* 1326 Fell St., San Francisco, CA 94117 Tel 415-387-933 Dist. by: Far West Book Service, 3515 N.E Hassalo, Portland, OR 97232.

P Rosen, *(Rosen, Pauline; 0-9600214),* 658 Main St., Placerville, CA 95667.

P S Allen, *(Allen, Philip S.),* 815 Yucca St., Port Hueneme, CA 93041 Tel 805-486-0707.

P S & M Inc, *(Phelon, Sheldon & Marsar, Inc.* 32 Union Square, New York, NY 10003 Tel 212-473-2590.

P S Brown, *(Brown, P.S.; 0-9604148),* 2306 Union St., San Francisco, CA 94123.

P Sawyer, *(Sawyer, Philip L.; 0-911308),* 108 South St., Auburn, NY 13021.

P Sherrod, *(Sherrod, Paul),* 3323 19th St., Lubbock, TX 79410.

P Skillman, *(Skillman, Penny; 0-9603396),* 487 Prentiss St., San Francisco, CA 94110.

P Smith, *(Smith, Phoebe; 0-9602976),* P.O. Bo 3119, Atlanta, GA 30302.

P Wilson Mail, *(Wilson, P., Mailservice),* P.O. Box 8142, St. Louis, MO 63156.

Pa Hist & Mus, *(Pennsylvania Historical & Museum Commission; 0-911124; 0-89271),* Division of History, Box 1026, Harrisburg, PA 17120 Tel 717-783-9868.

Pa Hist Soc, *(Historical Society of Pennsylvani 0-910732),* 1300 Locust St., Philadelphia, PA 19107 Tel 215-732-6200.

Pa St U Pr, *(Pennsylvania State Univ. Press; 0-271),* 215 Wagner Bldg., University Park, PA 16802 Tel 814-865-1327.

Paananen & Paulsen, *(Paananen & Paulsen Corp.),* P.O. Box 365, Waite-Park, MN 56387 Tel 612-743-2697; Moved, Left No Forwarding Address.

Pace Gallery, *(Pace Gallery Pubns.; 0-938608),* 32 E. 57th St., New York, NY 10022.

Pacesetter Pr, *(Pacesetter Press; 0-88415),* Div of Gulf Publishing Co., P.O. Box 2608, Houston, TX 77001 Tel 713-529-4301.

Pachart Pub Hse, *(Pachart Publishing House; 0-912918),* P.O. Box 35549, Tucson, AZ 85740 Tel 602-297-4797.

Pacific-Asian, *(Pacific/Asian American Mental Health Research Center; 0-934584),* 1640 W. Roosevelt Rd., Chicago, IL 60608 Tel 312-226-0117.

Pacific Bk Ctr, *(Pacific Book Center, Inc.),* 9555 Washington Blvd., Culver City, CA 90230 Tel 213-836-2321.

Pacific Bk Supply, *(Pacific Book Supply Co.; 0-911090),* P.O. Box 337, Farmersville, CA 93223 Tel 209-594-4155.

Pacific Bks, *(Pacific Books, Pubs.; 0-87015),* P.O. Box 558, Palo Alto, CA 94302 Tel 415-856-0550.

Pacific Coast, *(Pacific Coast Pubs.; 0-87465),* 4085 Campbell Ave., Menlo Park, CA 94025; Moved, Left No Forwarding Address *Imprints:* Farallon (Farallon Island).

Pacific Ctr West, *(Pacific Center for Western Historical Studies),* University of the Pacific Stockton, CA 95211.

Pacific Ed Pubns, *(Pacific Educational Pubns.),* 2121 McKinley St., Honolulu, HI 96822; Moved, Left No Forwarding Address.

Pacific Edns, *(Pacific Editions; 0-938226),* P.O. Box 27366, San Francisco, CA 94127 Tel 415-334-5716.

Pacific Gallery, *(Pacific Gallery Press; 0-938942),* P.O. Box 19494, Portland, OR 97219.

Pacific Intl, *(Pacific International Pub. Co.; 0-918074),* Box 21814, Seattle, WA 98111 Tel 206-525-3626.

Pacific Mer, *(Pacific Meridian Publishing Co.; 0-911092),* 13540 Lake City Way, N. E., Seattle, WA 98125 Tel 206-362-0900.

Pacific NW Labor, *(Pacific Northwest Labor History Assn.; 0-932942),* P.O. Box 25048, Northgate Sta., Seattle, WA 98125.

Pacific Perceptions, *(Pacific Perceptions, Inc.),* 3718 Vinton Ave., Suite 5, Los Angeles, CA 90034.

Pacific Perceptions
  See Pacific Perceptions

Pacific Pipeline, *(Pacific Pipeline, Inc.),* P.O. Box 3711, Seattle, WA 98124 Tel 206-682-8820.

Pacific Pr MO
  See Pacific Santa Barbara

Pacific Pr Pub Assn, *(Pacific Press Publishing Assn.; 0-8163),* 1350 Villa St., Mountain View, CA 94042 Tel 415-961-2323.

Pacific Pub Hse, *(Pacific Pub. House; 0-918872),* 2430 Kirkham St., San Francisco, CA 94122 Tel 415-566-2988.

Pacific Rim Res, *(Pacific Rim Research),* P.O. Box 526, Mendocino, CA 95460 Tel 707-937-5289.

Pacific Santa Barbara, *(Pacific Press Santa Barbara; 0-911094),* P.O. Box 219, Pierce City, MO 65723 Tel 417-476-2034.

Pacific Search, *(Pacific Search Press; 0-914718),* 222 Dexter Ave. N., Seattle, WA 98109 Tel 206-682-5044.

Pacific Sun, *(Pacific Sun Press; 0-9602908),* 52 R. Arroyo Sorrento Dr., Del Mar, CA 92014 Tel 714-755-4422.

Pacific Transport, *(Pacific Transportation Archives; 0-934430),* 547 Pine Ave., Sunnyvale, CA 94086.

Pacifica, *(Pacifica House, Inc., Pubs.; 0-911098),* c/o Borden Publishing Co., 1855 W. Main St., Alhambra, CA 91801.

Pacifica Pub, *(Pacifica Publishing Co.),* 22349 Havenhurst Dr., Los Altos, CA 94022.

Package Publ, *(Package Publicity Service, Inc.; 0-911100),* 1501 Broadway, Rm. 1314, New York, NY 10036 Tel 212-354-1840.

Packard Pub, *(Packard Publishing Co.; 0-937798),* 321 S. Hobart, Los Angeles, CA 90020.

Packrat Pr, *(Packrat Press Books),* P.O. Box 74, Cambridge, ID 83610.

Pacul Pubns, *(Pacul Pubns.),* 4011 Bryant Ave. S., Minneapolis, MN 55409; Moved, Left No Forwarding Address.

Paddington, *(Paddington Press, Ltd.),* 95 Madison Ave., New York, NY 10016 Tel 212-689-4801; Orders to: Grosset & Dunlap, 51 Madison Ave., New York, NY 10010.

Paddlewheel, *(Paddlewheel Press; 0-938274),* 15100 SW 109th, Tigard, OR 97223.

Padilla, *(Padilla, Francisco; 0-9605392),* P.O. Box 517, Westminster, CO 80030.

Padma, *(Padma Press; 0-917960),* P.O. Box 56, Oatman, AZ 86433.

Padre Prods, *(Padre Productions; 0-914598),* P.O. Box 1275, San Luis Obispo, CA 93406 Tel 805-543-5404.

Paganiniana Pubns, *(Paganiniana Pubns., Inc.; 0-87666),* Div. of T.F.H Pubns., Inc., P.O. Box 427, Neptune, NJ 07753 Tel 201-988-8400.

Page *Imprint of FS&G*

Page-Ficklin, *(Page-Ficklin Pubns.),* 535 Ramona St., Suite 6, Palo Alto, CA 94301 Tel 415-321-2762.

Page Pub, *(Page Pub.),* 609-613 Chetco Ave., P. O. Box 1091, Brookings, OR 97415.

Pageant-Poseidon, *(Pageant-Poseidon),* 155 W. 15th St., New York, NY 10011 Tel 212-929-5956; Moved, Left No Fowarding Address.

Pagurian, *(Pagurian Press; 0-88932; 0-919364),* Dist. by: Baker & Taylor, 1515 Broadway, New York, NY 10036 Tel 212-673-6600.

Paideia Pr, *(Paideia Press; 0-912490),* 4997 Robindale Lane, Memphis, TN 38117; Moved, Left No Forwarding Address.

Paisano, *(Paisano Press, Inc.; 0-911102),* P.O. Box 85, Balboa Island, CA 92662 Tel 714-673-5393.

Pajarito Pubns, *(Pajarito Pubns; 0-918358),* 2633 Granite N. W., Albuquerque, NM 87104 Tel 505-242-8075.

PAL Pr, *(P.A.L. Press; 0-938034),* P.O. Box 487, San Anselmo, CA 94960 Tel 805-453-8547.

Pal Pub, *(Pal Pub.; 0-918104),* Witter Springs, CA 95493 Tel 707-275-2766; P. O. Box 807, Northridge, CA 91328 Tel 213-360-0600.

Paladin Ent, *(Paladin Enterprises; 0-87364),* P.O. Box 1307, Boulder, CO 80306 Tel 303-443-7250.

Paladin Hse, *(Paladin House Pubs.; 0-88252),* 530 Lark St., Geneva, IL 60134 Tel 312-232-2711.

Paladin Pr *See Paladin Ent*

Paladium Pr, *(Paladium Press; 0-9694090),* P.O. Box 42, Beltsville, MD 20705.

Palatine Pubns, *(Palatine Pubns., Inc.),* P.O. Drawer 1265, Ruston, LA 71270.

Pale Horse, *(Pale Horse Press; 0-914720),* 433 Fair Ave., NE, New Philadelphia, OH 44663 Tel 216-364-3715.

Paleo Res, *(Paleontological Research Institution; 0-87710),* 1259 Trumansburg Rd., Ithaca, NY 14850 Tel 607-273-6623.

Palisades Pub, *(Palisades Pubs.; 0-913530),* P.O. Box 744, Pacific Palisades, CA 90272 Tel 213-454-0826.

Palm Tree Lib, *(Palm Tree Library; 0-933266),* P.O. Box 84268, Los Angeles, CA 90073.

Palmer-Pletsch, *(Palmer-Pletsch Associates; 0-935278),* P.O. Box 8422, Portland, OR 97207 Tel 503-231-4908.

Palmer Pub CA, *(Palmer Publishing),* P.O. Box 966, Orangevale, CA 95662 Tel 916-445-5525.

Palmetto Pub, *(Palmetto Publishing Co.; 0-915096),* 4747 28th St., N., St. Petersburg, FL 33714.

Palo Colorado, *(Palo Colorado Press; 0-931104),* Sunflower Ink, Coast Rte. 1, Monterey, CA 93940.

Palomar, *(Palomar Publishing Co.),* P.O. Box 4444, Whittier, CA 90607.

Palomar Bks, *(Palomar Books; 0-932882),* P.O. Box 445, Palmdale, CA 93550 Tel 805-947-5093.

PAM Pubs, *(PAM Pubs.; 0-932724),* 234 Abbott St., Salinas, CA 93901.

Pambili Bks, *(Pambili Books; 0-917336),* 1489 South Van Ness, San Francisco, CA 94110 Tel 415-821-9717.

PAN
See Ross Bks

Pan Am Nav, *(Pan American Navigation Service, Inc.; 0-87219),* P.O. Box 9046, Van Nuys, CA 91409 Tel 213-345-2744.

Pan-Am Publishing Co, *(Pan-American Publishing Co.; 0-932906),* P.O. Box 1505, Las Vegas, NM 87701.

Pan Am Pubns, *(Pan Am Pubns.; 0-87582),* Pan Am Bldg., New York, NY 10017.

Pan Am Union, *(Pan American Union),* ; Publisher Abbreviation Without Addresses Are for Titles That Are Out of Print. These Are Obsolete Abbreviations.

Pan Prods, *(Pan Productions; 0-9606100),* Box 581, Poway, CA 92064 Tel 714-578-1218.

Pana Creation, *(Pana Creation; 0-915300),* P. O. Box 2133, La Mesa, CA 92041 Tel 714-464-3727.

Panache, *(Panache),* P.O. Box 89, Princeton, NJ 08540.

P&A Quill, *(P & A Quill Press, Inc.),* 3022 N. Bartlett Ave., Milwaukee, WI 53211.

Pandora's Treasures, *(Pandora's Treasures; 0-9605236),* 1609 Eastover Terrace, Boise, ID 83704.

Panel Pubs, *(Panel Pubs.; 0-916592),* 14 Plaza Rd., Greenvale, NY 11548 Tel 516-484-0006.

Panjandrum, *(Panjandrum Books; 0-915572),* 11321 Iowa Ave., Suite 1, Los Angeles, CA 90025 Tel 213-477-8771; Dist. by: Publisher's Group West, 5855 Beaudry, Emeryville, CA 94608 Tel 415-549-3033; Dist. by: Robert Rainer Assocs, 318 Happ Rd., Northfield, IL 60093; Dist. by: Crissales, Crissie Lossing, 3236 Clubhouse Rd., Merrick, NY 11566; Dist. by: Doug Paton, North East Book Sales, 802 Oak Ridge Ave., North Attleboro, MA 02760; Dist. by: Bookpeople, 2940 Seventh St., Berkeley, CA 94710; Dist. by: Wisdom Garden Books, 238 N. Juanita, Los Angeles, CA 90004; Dist. by: Ingram Book Co., 347 Reedwood Dr., Nashville, TN 37217; Dist. by: Henry Walck, Jr., 731 E. Shore Dr., Ithaca, NY 14850; Dist. by: Henry Walck, Jr., 702 S. Michigan, South Bend, IN 46618.

Panjandrum Pr
See Panjandrum

Panorama West, *(Panorama West Books; 0-914330),* 8 E. Olive Ave., Fresno, CA 93728.

Pantheon, *(Pantheon Books),* Div. of Random House, Inc., 201 E. 50th St., New York, NY 10022 Tel 212-751-2600; Orders to: Random House, Inc., 400 Hahn Rd., Westminster, MD 21157.

Panther Hse, *(Panther House, Ltd.; 0-87676),* Box 3552, GCPO, New York, NY 10017.

Panu Pub, *(Panu Publishing Co., Inc.),* 5438 Fernwood Ave., Los Angeles, CA 90027.

Pao-Chung, *(Pao-Chung Hsu; 0-9601328),* P.O. Box 567, Carrollton, TX 75006 Tel 214-436-6262; Moved, Left No Forwarding Address.

Papa's Pr, *(Papa's Press; 0-9601968),* P.O. Box 81555, San Diego, CA 92138 Tel 714-277-6672.

Papenguth, *(Papenguth, Goldeen; 0-9600540),* 2201 Carson St., Lafayette, IN 47904; Out of Business.

Paper Bag, *(Paper Bag Players, The),* 50 Riverside Dr., New York, NY 10024.

Paper Tiger Pap, *(Paper Tiger Paperbacks, Inc.; 0-933334),* 1512 N.W. Seventh Place, Gainesville, FL 32603 Tel 904-373-2383; Orders to: P.O. Box 14015, Gainesville, FL 32604.

Paper Vision
See Western Tanager

Paper Vision *Imprint of* **Western Tanager**

Paperback Lib, *(Warner Paperback Library; 0-446),* 75 Rockefeller Plaza, New York, NY 10019 Tel 212-484-8000. *Imprints:* Warner Bks (Warner Books).

Paperweight Pr, *(Paperweight Press; 0-933756),* 761 Chestnut St., Santa Cruz, CA 95060.

Papillon Pr, *(Papillon Press),* 1232 Vallecito Rd., Carpinteria, CA 93013 Tel 805-684-5038.

PAR Inc, *(Programs for Achievement in Reading - P.A.R., Inc.; 0-913310; 0-89702),* 274 Weybosset St., Abbot Park Place, Providence, RI 02903 Tel 401-331-0130.

Para Pub, *(Para Publishing; 0-915516),* P.O. Box 4232-R, Santa Barbara, CA 93103.

Para Res, *(Para Research, Inc.; 0-914918),* Whistlestop Mall, Rockport, MA 01966 Tel 617-546-3413.

Parable Pr, *(Parable Press; 0-917250),* 136 Gray St., Amherst, MA 01002 Tel 413-253-5634.

Parabolic Pr, *(Parabolic Press; 0-915760),* P.O. Box 3032, Stanford, CA 94305 Tel 415-328-1084.

Parachuting Res, *(Parachuting Resources; 0-933382),* P.O. Box 1333, Richmond, IN 47374 Tel 513 156 1686.

Paraclete Bks, *(Paraclete Books; 0-938100),* GPO 2058, New York, NY 10001 Tel 212-849-5849.

Paradigm Pr, *(Paradigm Press; 0-937572),* 127 Greenbrae Boardwalk, Greenbrae, CA 94904 Tel 415-461-5457; Dist. by: Bookpeople, 2940 Seventh St., Berkeley, CA 94710; Dist. by: Publishers Group West, 5855 Beaudry St., Emeryville, CA 94608.

Paradox, *(Paradox Press; 0-930872),* P.O. Box 568, Lebanon Springs, NY 12114.

Paragon, *(Paragon Book Reprint Corp.; 0-8188),* 14 E. 38th St., New York, NY 10016 Tel 212-532-4920.

Paragon Assocs, *(Paragon Associates, Inc.; 0-89477),* P. O. Box 23618, Nashville, TN 37202 Tel 615-327-2835; Dist. by: Alexandria House, P.O. Box 300, Alexandria, IN 46001.

Paragon Prods, *(Paragon Productions; 0-9602184),* 817 Pearl St., Denver, CO 80203 Tel 303-321-8159.

Paragraph Pr, *(Paragraph Press; 0-915462),* 204 Circle Dr., P.O. Box 1107, Felton, CA 95018 Tel 408-335-4406.

Parameter Pr, *(Parameter Press; 0-88203),* 705 Main St., Wakefield, MA 01880 Tel 617-245-9290.

Paramount, *(Paramount Publishing; 0-918668),* 800 Roosevelt Rd., Suite 413, Bldg. B, Glen Ellyn, IL 60137 Tel 312-790-2483.

Paranoid Pr, *(Paranoid Press),* P.O. Box 2421, San Francisco, CA 94126; Out of Business.

Paranoid Pubns, *(Paranoid Pubns.),* 3928 N. St. Louis, Chicago, IL 60618 Tel 312-539-6159.

Parapsych Foun, *(Parapsychology Foundation, Inc.; 0-912328),* 228 E. 71st St., New York, NY 10021 Tel 212-628-1550.

Parapsych Pr, *(Parapsych Press; 0-911106),* P.O. Box 6847, College Sta., Durham, NC 27708 Tel 919-688-8241.

Parchment Pr, *(Parchment Press; 0-88428),* P.O. Box 8534, Chattanooga, TN 37411 Tel 615-624-9063.

Parent-Child Pr, *(Parent-Child Press; 0-9601016),* P.O. Box 767, 4201 Second Ave., Altoona, PA 16603 Tel 814-946-5213.

Parent Educ Progs, *(Parent Education Programs Press; 0-932054),* 3007 22nd St., Lubbock, TX 79410; Orders to: 5419 75th St., Lubbock, TX 79424.

Parenthesis Pr, *(Parenthesis Press; 0-9601580),* P.O. Box 114, Bridgewater College, Bridgewater, VA 22812 Tel 703-828-6656.

Parenting Pr, *(Parenting Press; 0-9602862),* 7750 31st Ave. N.E., Seattle, WA 98115.

Parents, *(Parents Magazine Press; 0-8193),* 685 Third Ave., New York, NY 10017 Tel 212-878-8611; Dist. by: Elsevier-Dutton Publishing Co., 2 Park Ave., Dept. JH, New York, NY 10016 Tel 212-725-1818.

Parey Sci Pubs, *(Parey, Paul, Scientific Pubs.),* 461 Park Ave. S., No. 903, New York, NY 10016 Tel 212-686-3605.

Paris Pubns, *(Paris Pubns., Inc.; 0-912248),* 2 Haven Ave., Port Washington, NY 11050 Tel 516-883-4650.

Park Pub, *(Park Publishing, Inc.; 0-9603294),* 1999 Shepard Rd., St. Paul, MN 55116 Tel 612-698-1667.

Park View, *(Park View Press, Inc.; 0-87813),* 1066 Mt. Clinton Pike, Harrisonburg, VA 22801 Tel 703-434-0765.

Parker *Imprint of* **P-H**

Parker & Son, *(Parker & Son Pubns., Inc.; 0-911110),* Box 60001, Los Angeles, CA 90060 Tel 213-724-6622.

Parker Pr, *(Parker Press, The; 0-939562),* 31 Marlboro St., Newburyport, MA 01950.

Parkhurst, *(Parkhurst Press; 0-939500),* P.O. Box 143, Laguna Beach, CA 92652.

Parkway Pr, *(Parkway Press, Inc.; 0-930408),* 3347 E. Calhoun Pkwy., Minneapolis, MN 55408 Tel 612-827-3347.

Parnassos NY, *(Parnassos, Greek Cultural Soc. of NY, Inc.; 0-933824),* Box 2928, Grand Central Sta., New York, NY 10017 Tel 203-464-2511.

Parnassus, *(Parnassus Press; 0-87466),* 6421 Regent St., Oakland, CA 94618 Tel 415-654-1368; Orders to: Houghton Mifflin Co., Wayside Rd., Burlington, MA 01803.

Parnassus Imprints, *(Parnassus Imprints; 0-940160),* Rte. 6a, Yarmouth Port, MA 02675 Tel 617-362-6420.

Parpaglion, *(Parpaglion & Co.; 0-9604252),* P.O. Box 200, Maple Shade, NJ 08052; Moved, Left No Forwarding Address.

Parr AZ, *(Parr of Arizona),* 3903 N. 16th St., Phoenix, AZ 85016 Tel 602-266-4861.

Parr Pub, *(Parr Publishing Co., Inc.; 0-89473),* 1200 S. Post Oak Rd., Suite 428, Houston, TX 77056 Tel 713-626-7830.

Parrot Mntn, *(Parrot Mountain, Inc.),* P.O. Box 246, Ranchita, CA 92066 Tel 714-782-3335.

Parsindo Pubs, *(Parsindo Pubs., Inc.; 0-913084),* P.O. Box 342, St. Louis, MO 63166; Moved Left No Forwarding Address.

Parthenon Bks, *(Parthenon Books),* 9808 Amanita Dr., Tujunga, CA 91042 Tel 213-249-4017; Moved, Left No Forwarding Address.

Parthenon Pubns, *(Parthenon Pubns.),* 139 Santa Fe Ave., El Cerrito, CA 94530 Tel 415-527-1374.

Partisan Pr, *(Partisan Press, Inc.; 0-935150),* P.O. Box 2193, Seattle, WA 98111.

Partner Pr, *(Partner Press; 0-933212),* Box 124, Livonia, MI 48152.

Partridge, *(Partridge Pubns. of California; 0-913306),* 1833 Franklin Canyon Dr., Beverly Hills, CA 90210 Tel 213-276-9096.

Partridge Pr
See Partridge

Pasadena Art, *(Pasadena Art Alliance; 0-937042),* 314 S. Mentor Ave., Pasadena, CA 91106 Tel 213-795-9276.

Pascal Pubs, *(Pascal Pubs),* 21 Sunnyside Ave., Wellesley, MA 02181.

Pass, *(Pass Press; 0-9601870),* 170 2nd Ave., 2A, New York, NY 10003.

Passage Pub, *(Passage Publishing; 0-933240),* 708 Warren N., Seattle, WA 98109.

Passive Solar, *(Passive Solar Institute; 0-933490),* P.O. Box 722, Davis, CA 95616 Tel 415-526-1549.

Passport Pr, *(Passport Press; 0-930016),* Box 596, Moscow, VT 05662 Tel 802-253-9387.

Past in Glass, *(Past in Glass; 0-9600212),* 515 Northridge Dr., Boulder City, NV 89005.

Pastore, *(Pastore Press),* Seven Shetland Lane, Stony Brook, NY 11790 Tel 516-751-2254.

Patch, *(Patch, Inc., the),* P.O. Box 5301, Atlanta, GA 30307 Tel 404-525-6383.

Patchen Co, *(Patchen, Marvin, Co.; 0-9605712),* 25076 Pappas Rd., Ramona, CA 92065; Dist. by: Baja Trail Publications, Inc., P.O. Box 6088, Huntington Beach, CA 92646.

Patchwork Pubns, *(Patchwork Pubns.; 0-930628),* 2961 Idustrial Rd., Las Vegas, NV 89109 Tel 702-732-4541.

Patent Data, *(Patent Data Pubns.; 0-935714),* 901 N. President St., Wheaton, IL 60187.

Patent Res Inst, *(Patent Resources Institute, Inc.; 0-917192),* 2011 Eye St., N.W., Suite 301, Washington, DC 20006 Tel 202-223-1175.

Path Pr NY, *(Pathfinder Press; 0-87348),* 410 West St., New York, NY 10014 Tel 212-741-0690.

Path Pubns NJ, *(Pathfinder Pubns., Inc.; 0-939888),* 210 Central Ave., Madison, NJ 07940 Tel 201-822-2395.

Pathfinder *Imprint of* **Bantam**

Pathfinder Pubns, *(Pathfinder Pubns.; 0-9603354),* 4704 Wilford Way, Minneapolis, MN 55435 Tel 612-835-1128.

Pathmark Bks, *(Pathmark Books, Inc.; 0-913390),* Box 115, Newton Upper Falls, MA 02164 Tel 617-964-2300.

Pathotox Pubs, *(Pathotox Pubs., Inc.; 0-930376),* 2405 Bond St., Park Forest South, IL 60466 Tel 312-534-1770.

Pathway Bks, *(Pathway Books; 0-935538),* 700 Parkview Terrace, Golden Valley, MN 55416 Tel 612-377-2997.

Pathway Pr, *(Pathway Press; 0-87148),* 922-1080 Montgomery Ave., Cleveland, TN 37311 Tel 615-476-4512.

Patmos Pr, *(Patmos Press, The; 0-915762),* P.O. Box V, Shepherdstown, WV 25443 Tel 304-876-2086.

Patrice Pr, *(Patrice Press; 0-935284),* Box 42, Gerald, MO 63037 Tel 314-764-2801.

Patriotic Educ, *(Patriotic Education, Inc.; 0-912520),* P.O. Box 2121, Daytona Beach, FL 32015 Tel 904-252-3414.

Patron *Imprint of* **D Bosco Pubns**

Pattecky Music, *(Pattecky Music Pubs.; 0-9602178),* Box T, College Park, MD 20740.

Pattern Pubns, *(Pattern Pubns.; 0-911986),* 2627 Seabrook Island Rd., Johns Island, SC 29455.

Patterson Smith, *(Smith, Patterson, Publishing Corp.; 0-87585),* 23 Prospect Terrace, Montclair, NJ 07042 Tel 201-744-3291.

Paul Bird, *(Bird, Paul C.),* 91 N. Whitney, St. Augustine, FL 32084.

Paul Mann, *(Mann, Paul, Publishing Co.; 0-8184),* 1517 Rexford Pl., Las Vegas, NV 89104 Tel 702-385-1585.

Paulette Pub, *(Paulette Publishing Co.),* P.O. Box 545, La Canada, CA 91011.

Paulist-Newman
See Paulist Pr

Paulist Newman, *(Paulist/Newman Press),* ; Publisher Abbreviation Without Addresses Are for Titles That Are Out of Print. These Are Obsolete Abbreviations. Publisher's New Abbreviation Is Paulist Pr.

Paulist Pr, *(Paulist Press; 0-8091),* 545 Island Rd., Ramsey, NJ 07446 Tel 201-825-7300; Orders to: 301 Island Rd., Mahwah, NJ 07430.

Paumalu Pr, *(Paumalu Press; 0-9602354),* P.O. Box 3788, San Clemente, CA 92672 Tel 714-496-5922.

Paunch, *(Paunch; 0-9602478),* 123 Woodward Ave., Buffalo, NY 14214.

Pavan Pubs, *(Pavan Pubs.; 0-915944),* P.O. Box 1661, Palo Alto, CA 94302 Tel 415-321-5445.

Pavilion Pub, *(Pavilion Publishing Co.),* Box 668, Riverhead, NY 11901; Moved, Left No Forwarding Address.

Pavillion Fashion, *(Pavillion of Fashion),* Golden Cove Center, 31244 Palos Verdes Dr., W., Rancho Palos Verdes, CA 90274.

Pawnee Pub, *(Pawnee Publishing Co., Inc.; 0-913688),* P.O. Box 630, Higginsville, MO 64037 Tel 816-394-2424.

Pawson, *(Pawson, John R.; 0-9602080),* Box 411, Willow Grove, PA 19090.

Pay Day Pr, *(Pay Day Press; 0-916852),* 8208 E. Vista Dr., Scottsdale, AZ 85253 Tel 602-994-1724.

Paycock Pr, *(Paycock Press; 0-9602424),* P.O. Box 57206, Washington, DC 20037 Tel 202-333-1544.

Payload Tech, *(Payload Technology Inc.; 0-931800),* 528 W. 1st St., Tempe, AZ 85281.

PB, *(Pocket Books, Inc.; 0-671),* Div. of Simon & Schuster, Inc., 1230 Ave. of the Americas, New York, NY 10020 Tel 212-246-2121. *Imprints:* Lantern (Lantern Books); Timescape (Timescape); Wallaby (Wallaby).

PBBC Pr, *(PBBC Press),* 315 S. Grove St., Owatonna, MN 55060 Tel 507-451-2710.

PBI Bks, *(PBI Books),* 384 Fifth Ave, New York, NY 10018 Tel 212-736-0370.

PBI Petrocelli
See Petrocelli

PCI, *(Publishing Center, Inc. (PCI); 0-89457),* P.O. Box 36007, Detroit, MI 48236.

PDA Pubs, *(PDA Publishers Corp.; 0-914886),* 1200 S. Sharon Chapel Rd., P.O. Box 3075, W. Lafayette, IN 47906 Tel 317-743-1101.

Peabody Coll, *(George Peabody College for Teachers of Vanderbilt Univ.; 0-933436),* 21st Ave., S., Box 164, Nashville, TN 37203

Peabody Found, *(Peabody, Robert S., Foundatio for Archaeology; 0-939312),* P. O. Box 71, Andover, MA 01810 Tel 617-475-5842.

Peabody Harvard, *(Peabody Museum of Archaeology & Ethnology, Harvard Univ.; 0-87365),* 11 Divinity Ave., Cambridge, MA 02138 Tel 617-495-3938.

Peabody Mus Natl Hist, *(Peabody Museum of Natural History of Yale Univ.; 0-912532),* Pubns. Office, 170 Whitney Ave., New Haven, CT 06520 Tel 203-436-1131.

Peabody Mus Salem, *(Peabody Museum of Salem; 0-87577),* East India Square, Salem, MA 01970 Tel 617-745-1876.

Peabody Pub, *(Peabody Publishing Co.),* 361 Moraine St., Brockton, MA 02401 Tel 617-588-0860.

Peace & Pieces
See SF Arts & Letters

Peace Pr, *(Peace Press, Inc.; 0-915238),* 3828 Willat Ave., Culver City, CA 90230 Tel 213-838-7387.

Peace Ways, *(Peace Ways Pubns.; 0-912730),* 11261 Alger St., Warren, MI 48093.

Peach, *(Peach Pubns.; 0-918240),* 1100 Park Ave., New York, NY 10028 Tel 212-876-6524.

Peach Enterprises, *(Peach Enterprises, Inc.),* 4649 Gerald, Warren, MI 48092 Tel 313-751-7730.

Peachtree Park, *(Peachtree Park Press; 0-933690),* 67 Peachtree Park Dr., Atlanta, GA 30309 Tel 404-351-4523.

Peachtree Pubs, *(Peachtree Pubs., Ltd.; 0-931948),* 494 Armour Circle, N.E., Atlanta, GA 30324 Tel 404-876-8761.

Peacock *Imprint of* **Bantam**

Peacock *Imprint of* **Penguin**

Peacock Pubs, *(Peacock, F. E., Pubs., Inc.; 0-87581),* 401 W. Irving Park Rd., Itasca, IL 60143 Tel 312-773-1155.

Peanut Butter, *(Peanut Butter Publishing; 0-89716),* 2733 4th Ave. S., Seattle, WA 98134 Tel 206-682-9320.

Pear Tree, *(Pear Tree Pubns.; 0-918578),* P.O. Box 517, Ashland, OR 97520 Tel 503-482-3717.

Pearl Pr, *(Pearl Press; 0-914566),* 609 South Ave. A, Portales, NM 88130 Tel 505-359-0308.

Pearl-Win, *(Pearl-Win Publishing Co.),* Rte. 1 Box 300, Hancock, WI 54943.

Pecalhen, *(Pecalhen Co.; 0-938910),* 14401 S.W. 85th Ave., Miami, FL 33158.

Peddlers Wagon, *(Peddlers Wagon; 0-9601048),* 610 Spruce St., Dowagiac, MI 49047 Tel 616-782-3270.

Pedicenter Pr, *(Pedicenter Press),* P.O. Box 3494, Jackson, TN 38301; Acquired by Professional Books.

Peebles Pr, *(Peebles Press International Inc.; 0-85690),* 1865 Broadway, New York, NY 10023 Tel 212-586-2800; Dist. by: Farrar, Straus & Giroux, Inc., 19 Union Square, New York, NY 10003 Tel 212-741-6900.

Peek Pubns, *(Peek Pubns.; 0-917962),* 164 E. Dana St., Mountain View, CA 94041 Tel 415-964-2334; Orders to: P.O. Box 50123, Palo Alto, CA 94303.

Peeples, *(Peeples, Edwin A.; 0-9600080),* Vixen Hill, R.D. 2, Phoenixville, PA 19460 Tel 215-827-7241.

Peer-Southern, *(Peer-Southern Pubns.),* 1740 Broadway, New York, NY 10019.

Peerless, *(Peerless Pub. Co.; 0-930234),* 2745 Lafitte Ave., New Orleans, LA 70119 Tel 504-486-6225.

Peerless Pub CO, *(Peerless Publishing Co.),* 1989 Broadway, Denver, CO 80202.

Pegasus, *(Pegasus),* Affiliated with Bobbs-Merrill Co., Inc., 4300 W. 62nd St., Indianapolis, IN 46206 Tel 317-291-3100.

Pegasus Pr CA, *(Pegasus Press),* 735 Dolores, Stanford, CA 94305; Dist. by: Aviation Book Co., 1640 Victory Blvd., Glendale, CA 91201 Tel 213-240-1771.

Pegasus Rex *Imprint of* **Fell**

Pegasus Rex NJ, *(Pegasus Rex Press, Inc., The; 0-937484),* 695 Bloomfield Ave., Montclair, NJ 07042 Tel 201-744-3774.

Pejepscot, *(Pejepscot Press; 0-917638),* 10 Mason St., Brunswick, ME 04011 Tel 207-729-3442.

Pelican, *(Pelican Publishing Co., Inc.; 0-911116; 0-88289),* 1101 Monroe St., Gretna, LA 70053 Tel 504-368-1175. *Imprints:* Pelican *(Imprint of* Pengui).

Pella Pub, *(Pella Publishing Co., Inc.; 0-918618),* 461 Eighth Ave., New York, NY 10001 Tel 212-279-9586.

Peloquin Pubns, *(Peloquin Pubns.; 0-936448),* P.O. Box 121, Richland, WA 99352.

PEM Pr, *(PEM Press),* Div. of Pathescope Educational Media, Inc., 71 Weyman Ave., P.O. Box 719, New Rochelle, NY 10802 Tel 914-235-0800.

Pemberton Pr, *(Pemberton Press),* P.O. Box 2085, Austin, TX 78767.

Pen Am Ctr, *(PEN American Center; 0-934638),* 47 Fifth Ave., New York, NY 10003.

Pen & Booth, *(Pen & Booth),* 1608 "R" St. N.W., Washington, DC 20009.

Pen & Podium, *(Pen & Podium Pubns.; 0-9603982),* 40 Central Park S., New York, NY 10019.

Pen-Art, *(Pen-Art Pubs.),* 402 Fairview Ave., Westwood, NJ 07675 Tel 201-664-8412.

Pen Notes, *(Pen Notes Inc.; 0-939564),* 70 Woodland Ave., Rockville Centre, NY 11570.

Pen Pusher, *(Pen Pusher Pubns.; 0-9601430),* 5090 Escobedo Dr., Woodland Hills, CA 91364 Tel 213-884-8649.

Pencader Pubs, *(Pencader Pubs.; 0-916712),* P.O. Box 299, Newark, DE 19711, Out of Business.

Penchant Pub, *(Penchant Publishing Co., Ltd.; 0-916892),* 3201 Lumar Dr., Washington, DC 20022.

Pendel Hill
  See Pendle Hill

Pendell Pub, *(Pendell Publishing Co.; 0-87812),* 1700 James Savage Rd., P.O. Box 1666 Bip, Midland, MI 48640 Tel 517-496-3337.

Pendle Hill, *(Pendle Hill Pubns.; 0-87574),* Pendle Hill, 338 Plush Mill Rd, Wallingford, PA 19086 Tel 215-566-4507.

Pendragon Hse, *(Pendragon House, Inc.; 0-916988),* 2595 E. Bayshore Dr., Palo Alto, CA 94303 Tel 415-327-5631.

Pendragon NY, *(Pendragon Press; 0-918728),* 162 W. 13th St., New York, NY 10011.

Pendragon Oregon, *(Pendragon Press; 0-914010),* P.O. Box 14834, Portland, OR 97214 Tel 503-232-0869.

Pendulum Pr, *(Pendulum Press, Inc.; 0-88301),* Academic Bldg., Saw Mill Rd., West Haven, CT 06516 Tel 203-933-2551.

Penguin, *(Penguin Books, Inc.; 0-14),* 625 Madison Ave., New York, NY 10022 Tel 212-755-4330. *Imprints:* Peacock (Peacock Books); Pelican (Pelican Books); Peregrine (Peregrine Books); Puffin (Puffin Books).

Peninsula, *(Peninsula Publishing; 0-932146),* P.O. Box 867, Los Altos, CA 94022 Tel 415-948-2511.

Peninsula Pub WA
  See Peninsula WA

Peninsula Pubns, *(Peninsula Pubns.; 0-914372),* 26030 New Bridge Dr., Los Altos Hills, CA 94022 Tel 415-857-0381.

Peninsula WA, *(Peninsula Publishing, Inc.; 0-918146),* P.O. Box 412, Port Angeles, WA 98362 Tel 206-457-7550.

Penmaen Pr, *(Penmaen Press, Ltd.; 0-915778),* Old Sudbury Rd., Lincoln, MA 01773 Tel 617-259-0842.

Penmaen Pr & Design
  See Penmaen Pr

Penn German Soc, *(Pennsylvania German Society; 0-911122),* 425 George St., Hanover, PA 17331 Tel 717-637-9688; Orders to: Box 97, Breinigsville, PA 18031.

Penn-Mont, *(Penn-Mont Academy),* 2733 Sixth Ave., Altoona, PA 16602.

Penn-Yale Expedit, *(Pubns. of the Pennsylvania-Yale Expedition to Egypt, Yale Univ.),* c/o Pubns. Office, Peabody Museum of Natural History, 170 Whitney Ave., P.O. Box 6666, New Haven, CT 06511.

Pennacook-Sokoki, *(Pennacook-Sokoki Inter-Tribal Nation New Hampshire Indian Nation; 0-9601834),* c/o N.H. Indian Council, Inc., 913 Elm St., Manchester, NH 03101.

Pennant Pr, *(Pennant Press; 0-913458),* 8265 Commercial St., No. 14, La Mesa, CA 92041 Tel 714-464-7811.

Pennington, *(Pennington Trading Post; 0-911120),* c/o Eunice Pennington, Fremont, MO 63941.

Penns Valley, *(Penns Valley Pubs.; 0-931992),* 1298 S. 28th St., Harrisburg, PA 17111 Tel 717-232-5844.

Pennwell Pub, *(Pennwell Publishing Co.; 0-87814),* P.O. Box 1260, Tulsa, OK 74101 Tel 918-835-3161.

Penny, *(Penny Press),* P.O. Box 534, Camino, CA 95709; Moved, Left No Forwarding Address.

Pennyfarthing, *(Pennyfarthing Press; 0-930800),* 2000 Center St., No. 1226, Berkeley, CA 94704 Tel 415-845-1990.

Pennypress, *(Pennypress, The; 0-937604),* 1100 23rd Ave., E., Seattle, WA 98112 Tel 206-325-5098.

Penobscot Bay, *(Penobscot Bay Press, Inc.),* Box 36, Stonington, ME 04681.

Penrith, *(Penrith Publishing Co.; 0-936522),* P.O. Box 18070, Cleveland Heights, OH 44118.

Penseur Pr, *(Penseur Press; 0-9604044),* P.O. Box 659, El Cerrito, CA 94530.

Pentagram, *(Pentagram Press; 0-915316; 0-937596),* Box 379, Markesan, WI 53946 Tel 414-398-2161.

Pentangle Pr, *(Pentangle Press; 0-914748),* P. O. Box 5001, 132 Lasky Dr., Beverly Hills, CA 90212 Tel 213-278-4996.

Pentelic Pr, *(Pentelic Press, 0-913110),* 1032 Cambridge Crescent, Norfolk, VA 23508.

Penthouse Pr, *(Penthouse Press, Ltd.; 0-89110),* 909 Third Ave., New York, NY 10022.

Penumbra Inc, *(Penumbra, Inc.; 0-9602030),* P.O. Box 862, Southfield, MI 48037.

Penumbra Press, *(Penumbra Press, The),* Box 12, Lisbon, IA 52253 Tel 319-455-2182.

Penumbra Projects, *(Penumbra Projects; 0-916416),* Dist. by: Light Impressions Corp., P.O. Box 3012, Rochester, NY 14614.

People Places, *(People Places, Inc.; 0-9604068),* P.O. Box 110, Verona, VA 24482.

Peoples Computer, *(People's Computer Co.; 0-918790),* P.O. Box E, 1263 El Camino, Menlo Park, CA 94025 Tel 415-323-3111.

Peoples Lobby, *(People's Lobby),* 3456 W. Olympic Blvd., Los Angeles, CA 90019 Tel 213-731-8321.

Peoples Pr, *(People's Press; 0-914750),* 2680 21st St., San Francisco, CA 94110 Tel 415-282-0856; Moved, Left No Forwarding Address.

People's Yellow Pages, *(People's Yellow Pages Press, The),* P.O. Box 31291, San Francisco, CA 94131 Tel 415-641-4011.

Pepper Pub, *(Pepper Publishing; 0-914468),* 2901 E. Mabel, Tucson, AZ 85716 Tel 602-881-0783.

Peppercorn *Imprint of* **Putnam**

Peppertree, *(Peppertree Publishing; 0-936822),* Box 1712, Newport Beach, CA 92663 Tel 714-642-3669.

Pepys Pr, *(Pepys Press, The; 0-9602270),* 1270 Fifth Ave., New York, NY 10029 Tel 212-348-6847.

Pequot
  See Globe Pequot

Per Ardua, *(Per Ardua Press; 0-917252),* 6216 Ellenview Ave., Canoga Park, CA 91307 Tel 213-888-1421.

Perception, *(Perception Press; 0-930176),* P.O. Box 265, Port Bolivar, TX 77650 Tel 713-684-3880.

Perdido Bay, *(Perdido Bay Press, The; 0-933776),* Rte. 2 Box 323, Pensacola, FL 32506.

Pere Marquette, *(Pere Marquette Press; 0-934640),* P.O. Box 495, Alton, IL 62002.

Peregrine *Imprint of* **Penguin**

Peregrine Pr, *(Peregrine Press; 0-933614),* Box 751, Old Saybrook, CT 06475 Tel 203-388-0285.

Peregrine Smith, *(Peregrine Smith, Inc.; 0-87905),* P.O. Box 667, 1877 E. Gentile St., Layton, UT 84041 Tel 801-376-9800.

Perennial Educ, *(Perennial Education, Inc.; 0-89751),* 1825 Willow Rd., Northfield, IL 60093 Tel 312-446-4153.

Perennial Pr, *(Perennial Press, Inc.),* Dist. by: McAvoy Publications International, Inc., 650 Palisades Ave., Box, 1271, Englewood Cliffs, NJ 07632.

Perf Dynamics, *(Performance Dynamics, Inc.; 0-912940),* 17 Grove Ave., Verona, NJ 07004 Tel 201-226-6477.

Perfect Graphic, *(Perfect Graphic Arts; 0-911126),* 14 Dearborn Dr., Old Tappan, NJ 07675 Tel 201-767-8575.

Performance Pub, *(Performance Publishing Corp.),* 1660 N. LaSalle, Suite 4211, Chicago, IL 60614.

Performing Arts, *(Performing Arts Journal; 0-933826),* 92b St. Marks Place, New York, NY 10009.

Pergamon, *(Pergamon Press, Inc.; 0-08),* Maxwell House, Fairview Park, Elmsford, NY 10523 Tel 914-592-7700.

Periday, *(Periday Co.),* Box 583, Woodland Hills, CA 91365.

Perigee *Imprint of* **Putnam**

Peripatetic, *(Peripatetic Press, The; 0-9602870),* P.O. Box 68, Grinnell, IA 50112.

Perish Pr, *(Perish Press; 0-934038),* P.O. Box 75, Mystic, CT 06355 Tel 203-536-2304.

Perivale Pr, *(Perivale Press; 0-912288),* 13830 Erwin St., Van Nuys, CA 91401 Tel 213-785-4671.

Periwinkle Pr, *(Periwinkle Press; 0-9602584),* P.O. Box 1305, Woodland Hills, CA 91365 Tel 213-346-3415.

Perkins Pubns, *(Perkins Pubns.; 0-934974),* 1442 A Walnut St., Suite 165, Berkeley, CA 94709 Tel 415-644-2190.

Perky Pubns, *(Perky Pubns.; 0-915714),* 5 South St., Canton, MA 02021.

Permanent Pr, *(Permanent Press, The; 0-932966),* Sagaponack, NY 11962 Tel 516-324-5993.

Permo Pr, *(Permo Press),* Box 16249, Seattle, WA 98116 Tel 206-937-5114; Moved, Left No Forwarding Address.

Perna Bks
  See Podiatric Educ

Perry-Neal Pubs, *(Perry-Neal Publishers, Inc.; 0-918690),* P.O. Box 2721, Durham, NC 27705.

Perry Omega, *(Perry-Omega Publishing, Inc; 0-9602586),* P.O. Box 27097, Escondido, CA 92027 Tel 714-741-6235.

Perry Pub, *(Perry Publishing),* 1252-20th Place, Yuma, AZ 85364.

Persea Bks, *(Persea Books, Inc.; 0-89255),* 225 Lafayette St., New York, NY 10012 Tel 212-431-5270.

Persephone, *(Persephone Press, Inc.; 0-930436),* P.O. Box 7222, Watertown, MA 02172 Tel 617-924-0336.

Perseus Pr, *(Perseus Press; 0-918026),* P.O. Box 1221, Pacific Palisades, CA 90272 Tel 213-823-3969.

Perseverance Pr, *(Perseverance Press; 0-9602676),* P.O. Box 384, Menlo Park, CA 94025.

Persimmon, *(Persimmon Press; 0-9605424),* P.O. Box 30721, 3128 Calle Noguera, Santa Barbara, CA 93105.

Persona Pr, *(Persona Press; 0-931906),* P.O. Box 14022, San Francisco, CA 94114 Tel 415-861-6679.

Personabks, *(Personabooks; 0-932456),* 434-66th St., Oakland, CA 94609.

Personal Achievement *Imprint of* **Telecom Lib**

Personal Christianity, *(Personal Christianity; 0-938148),* Box 549, Baldwin Park, CA 91706 Tel 213-338-7333.

Personal Dev Ctr, *(Personal Development Center; 0-917828),* P.O. Box 251, Windham Center, CT 06280 Tel 203-423-4785.

Personal Develop Pubns, *(Personal Development Pubns.; 0-916932),* 1111 Pleasant Valley Rd., Aptos, CA 95003 Tel 408-728-3585.

Personal Lib, *(Personal Library; 0-920510),* Dist. by: Vanguard Press, Inc., 424 Madison Ave., New York, NY 10017.

Personal Point, *(Personal Press; 0-9605634),* P.O. Box 789, Pt. Reyes Station, CA 94956.

Personal Pres
  See Personal Point

Personal Security, *(Personal Security Systems; 0-918384),* P.O. Box 152, River Forest, IL 60305 Tel 312-336-7330.

Personnel Dev, *(Personnel Development Associates; 0-911128),* P.O. Box 3005 Roosevelt Field Sta., Garden City, NY 11530 Tel 516-746-7868.

Personnel Pr, *(Personnel Press; 0-663),* Div. of Ginn & Co., 191 Spring St., Lexington, MA 02173; Orders to: Xerox Educational Ctr., P.O. Box 2649, Columbus, OH 43213.

Perspective, *(Perspective Pubns., Inc.; 0-911130),* 509 Madison Ave., New York, NY 10022 Tel 212-752-2212; Moved, Left No Forwarding Address.

Perspective Chicago, *(Perspective Press; 0-9603382),* 629 Deming Place, Rm. 401, Chicago, IL 60614 Tel 312-871-4820.

Perspicilli Pr, *(Perspicilli Press; 0-936064),* 1916 Oak Knoll Dr., Belmont, CA 94002.

Peter De Ridder, *(De Ridder, Peter, Press),* Bloomington Distribution Group, Box 841, Bloomington, IN 47401.

Peter Glenn, *(Glenn, Peter, Pubns., Inc.; 0-87314),* 17 E. 48th St., New York, NY 10017 Tel 212-688-7940.

Peter Pauper, *(Peter Pauper Press; 0-8342),* 135 W. 50th St., New York, NY 10020 Tel 212-247-3507.

Peter Smith, *(Smith, Peter, Publisher Inc.; 0-8446),* 6 Lexington Ave., Magnolia, MA 01930 Tel 617-525-3562.

Peter Wolff, *(Peter Wolff Books),* P. O. Box 778, Barrington, IL 60010.

Petereins Pr, *(Petereins Press, The; 0-9606102),* P.O. Box 10446, Glendale, CA 91209 Tel 213-244-9776.

Petersen Pub, *(Petersen Publishing Co., Book Division; 0-8227),* 6725 Sunset Blvd., Los Angeles, CA 90028 Tel 213-657-5100.

Petersons Guides, *(Peterson's Guides Inc.; 0-87866),* 228 Alexander St., Princeton, NJ 08540 Tel 609-924-5338; Orders to: P.O. Box 978, Edison, NJ 08817.

PETEX, *(Petroleum Extension Service (PETEX)),* Industrial & Busn. Training Bur., Univ. of Texas at Austin, Box S, Univ. Sta., Austin, TX 78712.

Petroage, *(Petroage Publishing Co.; 0-939172),* P.O. Box 134, Fairfield, IA 52556.

Petrocelli, *(Petrocelli Books; 0-89433),* 1101 State Rd., Princeton, NJ 08540 Tel 609-924-5851.

Petrocelli-Charter
   See Van Nos Reinhold

Petroglyph, *(Petroglyph Press Ltd.; 0-912180),* 201 Kinoole St., Hilo, HI 96720.

Petroleum Pub
   See Pennwell Pub

Petronium Pr, *(Petronium Press; 0-932136),* 1255 Nuuanu Ave., 1813, Honolulu, HI 96817.

P.F. Russo, *(Russo, Peter, F.),* 748 Seneca St., Bethlehem, PA 18015.

PFC, *(P. F. C. Publishing Co.; 0-9603830),* 525 W. 26th St., New York, NY 10001 Tel 212-242-0179.

Pfeiffer, *(Pfeiffer, Philip A.; 0-9601038),* 1617 N. Baylen St., Pensacola, FL 32501 Tel 904-433-2906.

Pflaum, *(Pflaum, George A., Publisher, Inc.),* ; Publisher Abbreviation Without Addresses Are for Titles That Are Out of Print. These Are Obsolete Abbreviations.

Pflaum Pr, *(Pflaum Press),* 2451 E. River Rd., Dayton, OH 45439.

Pflaum-Standard, *(Pflaum/Standard; 0-8278),* c/o CEBCO Standard Publishing, 9 Kulick Rd, Fairfield, NJ 07006; Name Changed to CEBCO-Standard.

Pflaum-Standard
   See CEBCO

PFOS, *(People for Open Space; 0-9605262),* 46 Kearny St., San Francisco, CA 94108.

Phaeton, *(Phaeton Press, Inc.; 0-87753),* Orders to: Gordian Press, 85 Tompkins St., Staten Island, NY 10304 Tel 212-273-4700.

Phaidon
   See Dutton

Phaidon, *(Phaidon Art Books),* ; Publisher Abbreviation Without Addresses Are for Titles That Are Out of Print. These Are Obsolete Abbreviations. Publisher Was Acquired by Dutton.

Phaidon *Imprint of* **Dutton**

Phantasia Pr, *(Phantasia Press; 0-932096),* 13101 Lincoln, Huntington Woods, MI 48070; Dist. by: F & SF Book Co., P.O. Box 415, Staten Island, NY 10302.

Phantasy Pr, *(Phantasy Press),* 358 State St., Brooklyn, NY 11217.

Pharaoh Prods, *(Pharaoh Productions; 0-937598),* P.O. Box 1102, Spring Valley, CA 92077.

Pharr, *(Pharr, Emory C.),* 5704 8th Rd., North Arlington, VA 22205 Tel 703-243-6989.

PhD Pub, *(Ph.D. Publishing Co.; 0-932010),* 10860 Arizona Ave., Culver City, CA 90320 Tel 213-204-1604.

Pheasant Run, *(Pheasant Run Pubns.; 0-936978),* Box 14043, St. Louis, MO 63178 Tel 314-291-3439.

Phi Delta Kappa, *(Phi Delta Kappa, Inc.; 0-87367),* 8th & Union, P.O. Box 789, Bloomington, IN 47402 Tel 812-339-1156.

Phiebig
   See S Karger

Phiebig, *(Phiebig, Albert J.),* ; Publisher Abbreviation Without Addresses Are for Titles That Are Out of Print. These Are Obsolete Abbreviations. Publisher's Abbreviation Is Now S Karger.

Phil King, *(King, Phil; 0-9601900),* 3005 Woodlawn Ave., Wesleyville, PA 16510 Tel 814-899-3532.

Phila Bk Co, *(Philadelphia Book Co., Inc.; 0-916074),* One Brown St., Philadelphia, PA 19123 Tel 215-482-6100.

Phila Free Lib, *(Free Library of Philadelphia; 0-911132),* Rare Book Dept., Logan Square, Philadelphia, PA 19103 Tel 215-686-5416.

Phila Maritime Mus, *(Philadelphia Maritime Museum; 0-913346),* 321 Chestnut St., Philadelphia, PA 19106 Tel 215-925-5439.

Phila Mus Art, *(Philadelphia Museum of Art; 0-87633),* P.O. Box 7646, Philadelphia, PA 19101 Tel 215-763-8100.

Phila Patristic, *(Philadelphia Patristic Foundation, Ltd.; 0-915646),* 99 Brattle St., Cambridge, MA 02138 Tel 617-868-3450; Orders to: 518 Central St., Winchendon, MA 01475.

Philadelphia Maritime Museum *Imprint of* **NYGS**

Philam Bk, *(Philam Book Distributors),* Vendom Hotel, Rm. 201, 161 W. Santa Clara St., San Jose, CA 95113 Tel 408-292-6624.

Philbrook, *(Philbrook Art Center),* P.O. Box 52510, Tulsa, OK 74152.

Phileas Deigh, *(Phileas Deigh Corp.; 0-9604200),* 600 Old Country Rd., Suite 321, Garden City, NY 11530.

Philemon Found, *(Philemon Foundation; 0-9601434),* Dist. by: Selzer Books, 705 Willow Ave., Ukiah, CA 95482 Tel 707-462-1630.

Phillips Exeter, *(Phillips Exeter Academy Press, The; 0-939618),* Phillips Exeter Academy, Exeter, NH 03833.

Phillips Pub Co, *(Phillips Publishing Co.),* 1562 Main St., Suite 713, Springfield, MA 01103 Tel 413-734-9020.

Philmer, *(Philmer Enterprises; 0-918836),* No. 4 Hunter's Run, Spring House, PA 19477 Tel 215-643-2976.

Philomel, *(Philomel Books),* 200 Madison Ave., Suite 1405, New York, NY 10016.

Philos Document, *(Philosophy Documentation Center; 0-912632),* Bowling Green State University, Bowling Green, OH 43403 Tel 419-372-2419.

Philos Lib, *(Philosophical Library, Inc.; 0-8022),* 200 W. 57th St., New York, NY 10019 Tel 212-265-6050.

Philos Pub, *(Philosophical Publishing Co.),* P.O. Box 220, Quakertown, PA 18951 Tel 215-536-5168.

Philos Res, *(Philosophical Research Society, Inc.; 0-89314),* 3910 Los Feliz Blvd., Los Angeles, CA 90027 Tel 213-663-2167.

Philos Sci Assn, *(Philosophy of Science Assn.; 0-917586),* 18 Morrill Hall, Philosophy Dept., Michigan State Univ., East Lansing, MI 48824 Tel 517-353-9392.

Philosophic Res, *(Philosophic Resources; 0-915422),* P.O. Box 4722, Poughkeepsie, NY 12603 Tel 914-471-0568; Moved, Left No Forwarding Address.

Phinmarc Bks, *(Phinmarc Books; 0-930396),* P.O. Box 1075, Crockett, TX 75835 Tel 713-544-7481.

PHIP Inc, *(PHIP, Inc.; 0-931994),* P.O. Box 707, Fort Lee, NJ 07024.

Phipps Pub, *(Phipps Pub. Co.; 0-918442),* Subs. of New England Mfgr. Co., 66 Bridge St., Norwell, MA 02061 Tel 617-659-7003.

Phistiklakis & Eliopoulos
   See Eliopoulos

Phoenix Assocs, *(Phoenix Associates Inc.; 0-915222),* P.O. Box 693, Boulder, CO 80306 Tel 303-449-3750.

Phoenix Bk Shop, *(Phoenix Book Shop; 0-916228),* 22 Jones St., New York, NY 10014 Tel 212-675-2795.

Phoenix Bks, *(Phoenix Books Pubs.; 0-914778),* 6505 N. 43rd Place, Paradise Valley, AZ 85253 Tel 602-952-0163; P.O. Box 32008, Phoenix, AZ 85064.

Phoenix Hse, *(Phoenix House; 0-89031),* 7453 Melrose Ave., Los Angeles, CA 90046 Tel 213-651-4002.

Phoenix Laguna, *(Phoenix),* P.O. Box 2225, Laguna Hills, CA 92653.

Phoenix MA, *(Phoenix Publications),* P.O. Box 213, Northhampton, MA 01060.

Phoenix Pr CA, *(Phoenix Press, The; 0-933828),* Box 3333, Manhattan Beach, CA 90266 Tel 213-545-6174.

Phoenix Press & Dist, *(Phoenix Press & Distributing Co.),* Box 146, Six Lakes, MI 48886.

Phoenix Pub, *(Phoenix Publishing; 0-914016),* Canaan, NH 03741 Tel 603-523-9902.

Phoenix Pub WA, *(Phoenix Publishing Co.; 0-919345),* P.O. Box 10, Custer, WA 98240

Phoenix Pubns, *(Phoenix Publications, Inc.; 0-933924),* 1133 Marian Way, Sacramento, CA 95818 Tel 916-446-1702; 712 Montgomery St., San Francisco, CA 94111 Tel 415-421-0960; P.O. Box 6262, Lake Tahoe, CA 95730 Tel 916-583-5614.

PhoeniXongs, *(PhoeniXongs; 0-918360),* P.O. Box 622, Northbrook, IL 60062 Tel 312-564-2484.

Photo-Go Pr, *(Photo-Go Press; 0-931662),* P.O. Drawer BB, El Paso, TX 79952 Tel 915-581-6218.

Photo Memorabila, *(Photographic Memorabila; 0-9604352),* P. O. Box 351, Lexington, MA 02173 Tel 617-862-1222.

Photo-Optical, *(Society of Photo-Optical Instrumentation Engineers; 0-89252),* P.O. Box 10, 405 Fieldston Rd., Bellingham, WA 98225 Tel 206-676-3290.

Photo Res, *(Photographic Research Pubns.; 0-934918),* P.O. Box 333, Seven Oaks, Detroit, MI 48235 Tel 313-493-3503.

Photographit, *(Photographit; 0-9605168),* 12 S. Gallatin Ave., Uniontown, PA 15401.

Photos Compendium, *(Photographer's Compendium; 0-89613),* P.O. Box 730, Sunnymead, CA 92388 Tel 714-676-5034; Tel 714-653-3115.

Physicians Rec, *(Physicians' Record Co.; 0-917036),* 3000 S. Ridgeland Ave., Berwyn IL 60402 Tel 312-749-3111.

Physsardt, *(Physsardt Pubns.; 0-916062),* Dist. by: Bloomington Distribution Group, P.O. Box 841, Bloomington, IN 47402.

Pi Pr, *(Pi Press, Inc.; 0-931420),* Box 23371, Honolulu, HI 96822.

Pi Yee Pr, *(Pi Yee Press; 0-935926),* P.O. Box 1144, La Jolla, CA 92038.

Pica Pr *Imprint of* Universe

Picayune Pr, *(Picayune Press, Ltd.; 0-937430),* 326 Picayune Place, New Orleans, LA 70130.

Pick Pub, *(Pick Publishing Corp.; 0-87551),* 21 West St., New York, NY 10006 Tel 212-425-0591.

Pickwick, *(Pickwick Press; 0-915138),* 5001 Baum Blvd., Pittsburgh, PA 15213 Tel 412-362-5610.

Pictorial Hist, *(Pictorial Histories Publishing Co.; 0-933126),* 713 South 3rd W., Missoul MT 59801.

Picturama, *(Picturama Pubns.; 0-918506),* Box 50, 350 Ledo Place, Arroyo Grande, CA 93420 Tel 805-481-0550.

Pieceful Pleasures, *(Pieceful Pleasures; 0-933758),* 566 30th Ave., San Mateo, CA 94403 Tel 415-573-9243.

Piedmont, *(Piedmont Press, Inc.; 0-912680),* P.O. Box 3605, Georgetown, Washington, DC 20007 Tel 703-549-2117.

Pierce Coll, *(Franklin Pierce College, Dept. of Anthropology),* Rindge, NH 03461.

Pierce Piano, *(Pierce Piano Atlas; 0-911138),* 1880 Termino, Long Beach, CA 90815.

ierce Pubs, *(Pierce Pubs.; 0-9603980),* 309 High St., Chestertown, MD 21620 Tel 301-778-1121.

ierian, *(Pierian Press; 0-87650),* P.O. Box 1808, Ann Arbor, MI 48106 Tel 313-434-5530.

ierpont Morgan, *(Pierpont Morgan Library; 0-87598),* 29 E. 36th St., New York, NY 10016 Tel 212-685-0008.

ierson Pubs, *(Romaine Pierson Pubs., Inc.; 0-935466),* 80 Shore Rd., Port Washington, NY 11050 Tel 516-883-6350.

ig Iron Pr, *(Pig Iron Press; 0-917530),* P.O. Box 237, Youngstown, OH 44501 Tel 216-744-2258.

igeon Roost Pr, *(Pigeon Roost Press),* 739 Clematis Dr., Nashville, TN 37205.

igi Pub, *(Pigi Publishing; 0-936930),* 924 Main St., Huntington Beach, CA 92648 Tel 714-536-4926.

igiron Pr
    See Pig Iron Pr

iirisild & Treumut, *(Piirisild & Treumut Partnership),* P.O. Box 2562, Van Nuys, CA 91404.

ika Pr, *(Pika Press; 0-935160),* P.O. Box C-9, Mammoth Lakes, CA 93546.

ikes Peak, *(Pikes Peak Poets, Inc.),* P.O. Box 6411, Colorado Springs, CO 80934.

ikestaff Pr, *(Pikestaff Press, The; 0-936044),* Div. of Pikestaff Publications, Inc., P.O. Box 127, Normal, IL 61761 Tel 309-452-4831.

ikeville Coll, *(Pikeville College Press; 0-933302),* Pikeville, KY 41501 Tel 606-432-9227.

ilgrim Bks OK, *(Pilgrim Books; 0-937664),* P.O. Box 2399, Norman, OK 73070.

ilgrim Hall, *(Pilgrim Hall Museum Shop),* 75 Court St., Plymouth, MA 02360 Tel 617-746-1620.

ilgrim NY, *(Pilgrim Press, The; 0-8298),* 132 W. 31st St., New York, NY 10001 Tel 212-594-8555; Orders to: Seabury Service Center, Somers, CT 06071.

ilgrim Pr, *(Pilgrim Press, The; 0-933476),* 39 University Place, Princeton, NJ 08540 Tel 609-924-9093.

ilgrim Pr Corp NY, *(Pilgrim Press Corp.; 0-932256),* 36-01 43rd Ave., Long Island City, NY 11101.

ilgrim Pub, *(Pilgrim Publishing Co.; 0-916034),* Mounted Rte. 12, Phillipsburg, NJ 08865 Tel 201-859-2292.

ilgrim Pubns, *(Pilgrim Pubns.),* P.O. Box 66, Pasadena, TX 77501 Tel 713-477-2329.

ilgrimage, *(Pilgrimage Press; 0-918550),* 2398 Telegraph Ave., Berkeley, CA 94704 Tel 415-548-2626.

illar Bks, *(Pillar Books; 0-89129),* c/o Harcourt Brace Jovanovich, Inc., 757 Third Ave., New York, NY 10017 Tel 212-754-3100.

illsbury Pr
    See PBBC Pr

ilot Bks, *(Pilot Books; 0-87576),* 347 Fifth Ave., New York, NY 10016 Tel 212-685-0736.

ilot Pr, *(Pilot Press Books; 0-88324),* P.O. Box 2662, Grand Rapids, MI 49501 Tel 616-532-6471.

ilot Pubns, *(Pilot Pubns.),* P.O. Box 9307, Mobile, AL 36691 Tel 205-666-0577; Dist. by: Aviation Book Co., 1640 Victory Blvd., Glendale, CA 91201 Tel 213-240-1771.

ilot Rev, *(Pilot Review Service),* 548 Pintura Dr., Santa Barbara, CA 93111 Tel 805-967-3264.

ilot Rock, *(Pilot Rock, Inc.; 0-89374),* 934 H St., P.O. Box ZZ, Arcata, CA 95521 Tel 707-822-4851.

in Prick, *(Pin Prick Press, The; 0-936424),* 3877 Meadowbrook Blvd., University Heights, OH 44118 Tel 216-932-2173.

ine Cone Pubs, *(Pine Cone Pubs.; 0-912720),* 2251 Ross Lane, Medford, OR 97501 Tel 503-773-3892.

ine Hill Pr, *(Pine Hill Press),* Freeman, SD 57029.

ine Mntn, *(Pine Mountain Press, Inc.; 0-89769),* P.O. Box 19746, West Allis, WI 53219 Tel 414-546-2310.

ine Pr, *(Pine Press; 0-930502),* Box 263c, R.D. 1, Landisburg, PA 17040.

ine Row, *(Pine Row Pubns.; 0-935238),* P.O. Box 428, Washington Crossing, PA 18977 Tel 215-493-4259.

ine St Pr, *(Pine Street Press; 0-915224),* 872 Pine St., Winnetka, IL 60093.

Pine Tree Pr, *(Pine Tree Press; 0-932196),* P. O. Box 2353, Orange, CA 92669 Tel 714-639-0706; Dist. by: P. K. Slocum, 7733 Corey, Downey, CA 90242.

Pinecliff
    See HM Prof Med Div

Pinecrest Fund, *(Pinecrest Fund, The; 0-9601858),* 204 Tower Park Bldg., 7447 Holmes St., Kansas City, MO 64131 Tel 816-444-9400.

Pinehill, *(Pinehill Publishing Co.),* P.O. Box 44130, Lafayette, LA 70504 Tel 318-233-3850.

Pinewood, *(Pinewood Press; 0-9604498),* P.O. Box 79104, Houston, TX 77024.

Piney Branch, *(Piney Branch Press; 0-902054),* 5000 Piney Branch Rd., Fairfax, VA 22030.

Pink Hse Pub, *(Pink House Publishing Co.; 0-915946),* 410 Magellan Ave., Penthouse 1002, Honolulu, HI 96813 Tel 808-537-1875.

Pinnacle Bks, *(Pinnacle Books; 0-523),* 1 Century Plaza, 2029 Century Park E., Los Angeles, CA 90067 Tel 213-552-9111. *Imprints:* Pinnacle Hse (Pinnacle House).

Pinnacle Hse *Imprint of* **Pinnacle Bks**

Pintores Pr, *(Pintores Press; 0-934116),* Box 1597, Roswell, NM 88201.

Pioneer Bk TX, *(Pioneer Book Pubs.; 0-933512),* Box 426, Seagraves, TX 79359 Tel 806-546-2498.

Pioneer Ga, *(Pioneer Press, Inc.; 0-915006),* 2100 Parklake Dr., Suite 101, Atlanta, GA 30345 Tel 404-939-3512; Orders to: P.O. Box 76025, Atlanta, GA 30328.

Pioneer Pr, *(Pioneer Press, Inc.; 0-913150),* P.O. Box 684, Union City, TN 38261 Tel 901-885-0374.

Pioneer Pub Co, *(Pioneer Publishing Co.; 0-914330),* 8 E. Olive Ave., Fresno, CA 93728 Tel 209-485-2631.

Pioneer VT, *(Pioneer Press, The; 0-9603426),* Newfane, VT 05345; Orders to: The Pioneer Press, Box 43, Schooley's Mt., NJ 07870 Tel 201-852-5407.

PIP, *(Partners in Publishing; 0-937660),* P.O. Box 50347, Tulsa, OK 74150 Tel 918-587-4275.

Piper, *(Piper Publishing, Inc.; 0-87832),* Orders to: Blue Earth, MN 56013 Tel 507-526-5448.

Piper *Imprint of* **HM**

Piraeus *Imprint of* **Forum Pr MO**

Pisces Eye, *(Pisces' Eye, The; 0-9604470),* P.O. Box 12642, Seattle, WA 98111.

Pisces Pr TX, *(Pisces Press; 0-938326),* P.O. Box 4075, Lubbock, TX 79409.

Pisces Print, *(Pisces Printer, The; 0-9604206),* Box 4625, Irvine, CA 92716.

Pisces Pub, *(Pisces Publishing Corp., Inc.; 0-914858),* P.O. Box 805, Belden Sta., Norwalk, CT 06852.

Pitcairn Pr, *(Pitcairn Press, Inc.; 0-914874),* 388 Franklin St., Cambridge, MA 02139.

Pitman, *(Pitman Publishing Corp.),* ; Publisher Abbreviation Without Addresses Are for Titles That Are Out of Print. These Are Obsolete Abbreviations. Publisher's Abbreviation Is Now Fearon-Pitman.

Pitman
    See Pitman Learning

Pitman Learning, *(Pitman Learning, Inc.; 0-8224),* 6 Davis Dr., Belmont, CA 94002 Tel 415-592-7810.

Pitman Pub MA, *(Pitman Publishing, Inc.; 0-273),* 1020 Plain St., Marshfield, MA 02050.

Pitt Jewish Foun, *(Pittsburgh Jewish Pubn. & Education Foundation),* 315 S. Bellefield Ave., Pittsburgh, PA 15213.

Pitt Pr, *(Pitt Press; 0-931996),* Box 105, Yellow Springs, OH 45387.

Pittore Euforico, *(Pittore Euforico; 0-934376),* P.O. Box 1132, Peter Stuyvesant Sta., New York, NY 10009.

Pittsfield
    See Island Marine

Pixie Pr, *(Pixie Press; 0-914978),* 8515 Fieldway Dr., Randallstown, MD 21133; Moved, Left No Forwarding Address.

PJD Pubns, *(PJD Pubns., Ltd.; 0-9600290; 0-915340),* P.O. Box 966, Westbury, NY 11590 Tel 516-626-0650.

PL *Imprint of* **Har-Row**

Place, *(Place),* Dist. by: Book People, 2940 Seventh St., Berkeley, CA 94710.

Place Herons, *(Place of Herons Press; 0-916908),* P.O. Box 1952, Austin, TX 78767; Dist. by: AAR/Tantalus, Inc., P.O. Box 893, Austin, TX 78767.

Plain Talk, *(Plain Talk Press),* Box 16023, Irvine, CA 92714.

Plamen Pub, *(Plamen Publishing Co.; 0-9602138),* P.O. Box 3088, Steinway Sta., Astoria, NY 11103.

Plan Parent, *(Planned Parenthood Federation of America, Inc.; 0-934586),* 810 Seventh Ave., New York, NY 10019 Tel 212-541-7800.

Planet-Drum, *(Planet/Drum Foundation; 0-937102),* P.O. Box 31251, San Francisco, CA 94131.

Planet Pr, *(Planet Press),* 1500 E. Walnut St., Columbia, MO 65201 Tel 314-443-1144.

Planetary Pr, *(Planetary Press; 0-938330),* P.O. Box 4641, Baltimore, MD 21212.

Planned Parent Santa Cruz, *(Planned Parenthood of Santa Cruz County),* 212 Laurel St., Santa Cruz, CA 95060 Tel 408-425-1553.

Planners Pr, *(Planners Press; 0-918286),* 1313 E. 60th St., Chicago, IL 60637 Tel 312-947-2560.

Plantagenet Pr, *(Plantagenet Press; 0-917462),* Box 271, Dobbs Ferry, NY 10522; Moved, Left No Forwarding Address.

Plantation, *(Plantation Press; 0-911150),* Davies Plantation Rd., Brunswick, Memphis, TN 38134 Tel 901-386-2015.

Plantin Pr, *(Plantin Press),* 1052 Manzanita, Los Angeles, CA 90029 Tel 213-666-1340.

Plants Alive, *(Plants Alive Books; 0-918730),* 2603 Third Ave., Seattle, WA 98121 Tel 206-623-9364.

Plato Pr, *(Plato Press),* Box 240, Rockport, MA 01966.

Platt, *(Platt & Munk Pubs.; 0-448),* Div. of Grosset & Dunlap, 51 Madison Ave., New York, NY 10010 Tel 212-689-9200.

Play Schs, *(Play Schools Assn.; 0-936426),* 19 West 44th St., New York, NY 10017 Tel 212-921-2940.

Playboy, *(Playboy Press; 0-87223),* Div. of P.E.I. Books, Inc., 747 Third Ave., New York, NY 10017 Tel 212-245-9160; Dist. by: Harper & Row Pubs., Inc., Keystone Industrial Park, Scranton, PA 18512.

Playboy Pbks, *(Playboy Paperbacks; 0-87216; 0-86721),* Div. of P.E.I. Books, Inc., 747 Third Ave., New York, NY 10017 Tel 212-688-3030.

Playboy Pr Pbks
    See Playboy Pbks

Player Piano, *(Player Piano House; 0-9604092),* 4001 N. Interstate Ave., Portland, OR 97227 Tel 503-288-2600.

Playette Corp, *(Playette Corp.),* 301 E. Shore Rd., Great Neck, NY 11023 Tel 516-487-3064.

Plays, *(Plays, Inc.; 0-8238),* 8 Arlington St., Boston, MA 02116 Tel 617-536-7420.

Playspaces, *(Playspaces-International; 0-85953),* 50 Thayer Rd., Waltham, MA 02154 Tel 617-484-0367.

Plaza Pubs, *(Plaza Pubs.),* 2010 Empire Blvd., Webster, NY 14580 Tel 716-671-1533.

Pleasant Hill, *(Pleasant Hill Press),* 2600 Pleasant Hill Rd., Sebastopol, CA 95472 Tel 701-823-6583.

Please Pr, *(Please Press Ltd.),* Box 3036, Flint, MI 48502.

Pleasure Dome, *(Pleasure Dome Press; 0-918870),* Div. of L.I. Poetry Collective, Inc., Box 773, Huntington, NY 11743 Tel 516-549-1150.

Pleasure Trove, *(Pleasure Trove Books; 0-930400),* P.O. Box 203, Jamaica, NY 11413 Tel 212-525-0817.

Pleneurethic Intl, *(Pleneurethic International),* Earth Light Bookstore, 113 E. Main, Walla Walla, WA 99362 Tel 509-525-4983.

Plenum Pr *Imprint of* **Plenum Pub**

Plenum Pub, *(Plenum Publishing Corp.; 0-306),* 227 W. 17th St., New York, NY 10011 Tel 212-255-0713. *Imprints:* Consultants (Consultants Bureau); Plenum Pr (Plenum Press); Rosetta (Plenum Rosetta).

Plexus Pub, *(Plexus Publishing, Inc.; 0-937548),* P.O. Box 550, Marlton, NJ 08053 Tel 609-654-6500.

PLI, *(Practising Law Institute; 0-87224),* Orders to: 810 Seventh Ave., New York, NY 10019 Tel 212-765-5700.

Plough, *(Plough Publishing House of the Hutterian Society of Brothers; 0-87486),* Rifton, NY 12471 Tel 914-658-3141.

Ploughshare Pr, *(Ploughshare Press; 0-912396),* P.O. Box 123, Sea Bright, NJ 07760 Tel 201-842-0336.

Plowshare, *(Plowshare Press, Inc.; 0-87368),* P.O. Box 2252, Boston, MA 02107.

Plum Nelly, *(Plum Nelly Shop, Inc., The),* 1201 Hixson Pike, Chattanooga, TN 37405 Tel 615-266-0585.

Plumbers Ink, *(Plumbers Ink Press; 0-935684),* P.O. Box 2565, Taos, NM 87571.

Plumbing Pubns, *(Plumbing Pubns.; 0-9603462),* 1700 N. "H" St., Midland, TX 79701 Tel 915-683-5574; Orders to: P.O. Box 5461, Midland, TX 79701 Tel 915-682-3249.

Plume *Imprint of NAL*

Plus One Pub, *(Plus One Publishing, Inc; 0-934822),* 625 N. Mansfield Ave., Hollywood, CA 90036 Tel 213-936-1783.

Plutarch Pr *Imprint of Advent Bk*

Plycon Pr, *(Plycon Press; 0-916434),* P.O. Box 220, Redondo Beach, CA 90277 Tel 213-530-1033; Dist. by: Burgess Publishing Co., 7108 Ohms Lane, Minneapolis, MN 55435.

Plymouth
    See Plymouth Pr

Plymouth Pr, *(Plymouth Press; 0-935540),* P. O. Box 390205, Miami, FL 33119 Tel 305-949-5599.

PM Ent, *(P-M Enterprises; 0-9601846),* 71 E. 202nd St., Euclid, OH 44123 Tel 216-692-0737; Dist. by: Macoy Publishing Co., P.O. Box 9759, Richmond, VA 23228.

PMF Research, *(PMF Research Co.; 0-934036),* P.O. Box 424, Kenilworth, IL 60043.

PMI Inc, *(Photography Media Institute, Inc.; 0-936524),* P.O. Box 78, Staten Island, NY 10304 Tel 212-447-3280.

PMS King, *(PMS/King Publishing Co.; 0-918504),* P.O. Box 692, Jackson, CA 95642 Tel 209-223-3805.

P'Nye Pr, *(P'Nye Press; 0-9602402),* The Printers Shop, 4047 Transport, Palo Alto, CA 94303 Tel 415-494-6802.

Pocumtuck Valley Mem, *(Pocumtuck Valley Memorial Assn.),* Memorial Hall Museum, Deerfield, MA 01342 Tel 413-773-8929.

Podesta Fishing, *(Podesta Fishing Co., Pubs.),* 140 S. Peter Dr., Campbell, CA 95008 Tel 408-377-7700.

Podiatric Educ, *(Podiatric Educational Pubns.; 0-9600302),* 28 Prospect St., Waltham, MA 02154 Tel 617-894-1985.

POEM, *(P. O. E. M),* 1120 Broadway, New Orleans, LA 70115.

Poet Gal Pr, *(Poet Gallery Press; 0-913054),* 224 W. 29th St., New York, NY 10001.

Poet Papers, *(Poet Papers; 0-9600288),* P.O. Box 528, Topanga, CA 90290.

Poetasumanos, *(Poetasumanos Press; 0-938254),* 949 Capp St., No. 10, San Francisco, CA 94110.

Poetry Eastwest, *(Poetry Eastwest; 0-912206),* P.O. Box 391, Sumter, SC 29150 Tel 803-775-9537.

Poetry Pub, *(Poetry Publishing Corp.; 0-913438),* c/o Michael J. Phillips, Colony Apts., 2012A W. 76th St., Indianapolis, IN 46260.

Poets & Writers, *(Poets & Writers; 0-913734),* 201 W. 54th St., New York, NY 10019 Tel 212-757-1766.

Pohl Assoc, *(Pohl, J., Associates; 0-939332),* 166 N. Sprague Ave., Bellevue, PA 15202 Tel 412-562-9343.

Point Blanc Pr
    See Climate Bks

Point Calif, *(Point),* Box 428, Sausalito, CA 94965 Tel 415-332-1716.

Point Loma Pub, *(Point Loma Pubns., Inc.; 0-913004),* P.O. Box 6507, 3727 Charles St., San Diego, CA 92106 Tel 714-222-3291.

Point Pr, *(Point Press; 0-9601474),* Box 14, Point Pleasant, NJ 08742 Tel 201-892-9480.

Poipu Music, *(Poipu Music),* P.O. Box 1172, Austin, TX 78767; Dist. by: Music Sales Corp., 33 W. 60th St., New York, NY 10023.

Poirot & Co, *(Poirot, H. M., & Co.; 0-936318),* P.O. Box 30171, Amarillo, TX 79120 Tel 806-353-6985; Orders to: 304 Sunset, Amarillo, TX 79106 Tel 806-353-6985.

Pol Stud Assocs, *(Policy Studies Associates; 0-936826),* P.O. Box 337, Croton-on-Hudson, NY 10520 Tel 914-271-6500.

Polacsek, *(Polacsek, John F.),* 321 9th St., Elyria, OH 44035; Orders to: R.F.D. Collection, P.O. Box 408, Elyria, OH 44035.

Polamerica Pr, *(Polamerica Press; 0-914310),* P.O. Box 36415, Los Angeles, CA 90036.

Polanie, *(Polanie Publishing Co.; 0-911154),* 643 Madison St., N.E., Minneapolis, MN 55413 Tel 612-379-9134.

Polar Palm, *(Polar Palm Productions, Inc.; 0-918792),* Box 4-907G, Anchorage, AK 99509 Tel 907-279-8847.

Polaris Pr, *(Polaris Press; 0-930504),* 16540 Camellia Terrace, Los Gatos, CA 95030.

Polaski Co, *(Polaski Co., Inc.; 0-914288),* P.O. Box 7466, Philadelphia, PA 19101 Tel 215-665-1990; Moved, Left No Forwarding Address.

Police Pr, *(Police Press; 0-89415),* P.O. Box 2501, Dublin, CA 94566 Tel 415-829-2728.

Policy Studies, *(Policy Studies Organization; 0-918592),* 361 Lincoln Hall, Univ. of Illinois at Urbana-Champaign, Urbana, IL 61801 Tel 217-359-8541.

Polis Pr, *(Polis Press, Inc.; 0-932756),* 150 Claremont Ave., No. 1E, New York, NY 10027; Moved, Left No Forwarding Address.

Polish American, *(Polish American Historical Assn.; 0-9602162),* 984 Milwaukee Ave., Chicago, IL 60622.

Polish Inst Arts, *(Polish Institute of Arts & Sciences in America),* 59 E. 66th St., New York, NY 10021 Tel 212-988-4338.

Pollution
    See Data Courier

Poltergeist, *(Poltergeist Press; 0-9603918),* 706 S. Morain St., Kennewick, WA 99336 Tel 509-783-8695.

Poly Tone, *(Poly Tone Press; 0-933830),* 16027 Sunburst St., Sepulveda, CA 91343 Tel 213-892-0044.

Polyanthos, *(Polyanthos, Inc.),* Drawer 51359, New Orleans, LA 70151 Tel 504-566-7406.

Polycrystal Bk Serv, *(Polycrystal Book Service; 0-9601304),* P.O. Box 11567, Pittsburgh, PA 15238 Tel 412-963-7878.

PolyScience, *(PolyScience Corp.; 0-913106),* 6366 Gross Point Rd., Niles, IL 60648 Tel 312-647-0611.

Pomegranate, *(Pomegranate Press; 0-915192),* P.O. Box 181, Cambridge, MA 02140 Tel 617-489-3896.

Pomegranate Calif, *(Pomegranate Pubns.; 0-917556),* Box 748, Corte Madera, CA 94925 Tel 415-924-8141.

Pomerica Pr, *(Pomerica Press, Ltd.; 0-918732),* 15 E. 40th St., New York, NY 10016 Tel 212-685-0808; Dist. by: Franklin Watts Inc., 730 Fifth Ave., New York, NY 10019 Tel 212-757-4050.

Ponchie, *(Ponchie & Co.; 0-9604418),* W.V.U., Dept of Foreign Languages, Morgantown, WV 26506.

Pond Woods, *(Pond Woods Press),* P.O. Box 82, Stony Brook, NY 11790 Tel 516-751-3232.

Ponderosa, *(Ponderosa Pubs.; 0-913162),* Rte. 1, Box 68, Saint Ignatius, MT 59865 Tel 406-745-4455.

Pong, *(Pong, Ted),* P.O. Box 321, Freeland, WA 98249.

Pontine Pr, *(Pontine Press),* c/o Orrin A. Engen, 1153 N. Orange, Hollywood, CA 90038.

Pony X Pr, *(Pony X Press; 0-939428),* 915 Shorepoint Court, E303, Alameda, CA 94501 Tel 415-522-4928.

Poor Richards, *(Poor Richard's Press; 0-917212),* 2395 University Ave., No. 214, St. Paul, MN 55114.

Poor Souls Pr, *(Poor Souls Press/Scaramouche Books; 0-916296),* 1050 Magnolia No. 2, Millbrae, CA 94030 Tel 415-692-5149.

Popcorn Pubs, *(Popcorn Pubs; 0-930506),* P.O. Box 1308, Pittsfield, MA 01202 Tel 413-443-5601.

Pope John Ctr, *(Pope John Center; 0-935372),* 4455 Woodson Rd., St. Louis, MO 63134 Tel 314-428-2424.

Popejoy, *(Popejoy, Charles L. "Jack"),* 620 Seatter St., Juneau, AK 99801 Tel 907-586-1203.

Popular Lib, *(Popular Library, Inc.; 0-445),* Unit of CBS Pubns., 1515 Broadway, New York, NY 10036 Tel 212-975-7663.

Population Coun, *(Population Council, Inc.; 0-87834),* One Dag Hammarskjold Plaza, New York, NY 10017 Tel 212-644-1300.

Population Ref, *(Population Reference Bureau; 0-917136),* 1337 Connecticut Ave., N.W, Washington, DC 20036 Tel 202-785-4664

Porch Pubns, *(Porch Pubns.; 0-932968),* c/o James Cervantes, Dept of English-Arizona State Univ., Tempe, AZ 85281.

Porcupine Pr, *(Porcupine Press, Inc.; 0-87991)* 1317 Filbert St., Philadelphia, PA 19107 Tel 215-563-2288.

Porphyrion Pr, *(Porphyrion Press; 0-913884),* 4053 Middle Grove Rd, Middle Grove, NY 12850 Tel 518-587-9809.

Portals Pr, *(Portals Press; 0-916620),* P.O. Box 1048, Tuscaloosa, AL 35403 Tel 205-758-1874.

Porter, *(Porter, Bern; 0-911156),* 22 Salmond Rd., Belfast, ME 04915.

Porter Sargent, *(Porter Sargent Pubs., Inc.; 0-87558),* 11 Beacon St., Boston, MA 0210 Tel 617-523-1670.

Porthole Pr, *(Porthole Press),* P. O. Box 417, Belmont, MA 02178 Tel 617-484-0988.

Portland Cement, *(Portland Cement Assn.; 0-89312),* 5420 Old Orchard Rd., Skokie, 60077 Tel 312-966-6200.

Portland Symphony, *(Portland Symphony Orchestra Women's Committee; 0-9601266* Box 332, Downtown Sta., Portland, ME 04112 Tel 207-854-4630.

Portola Inst, *(Portola Institute; 0-914774),* 48 Hamilton Ave., Palo Alto, CA 94301 Tel 415-323-7769.

Portola Pr, *(Portola Press; 0-9605998),* P.O. Box 1225, Santa Barbara, CA 93102 Tel 805-962-2774.

Portolan, *(Portolan Press; 0-916762),* 825 Rathjen Rd., Brielle, NJ 08730 Tel 201-528-8264.

Portrayal, *(Portrayal Press; 0-938242),* P.O. Box 1913, Bloomfield, NJ 07003.

Portriga Pubns, *(Portriga Pubns.; 0-9602274),* 823 N. Edinburg Ave., Los Angeles, CA 90046.

Poseidon Pubns, *(Poseidon Pubns.; 0-937378),* 1340 N. Alameda, Las Cruces, NM 88001.

Posey Pubns, *(Posey Pubns.),* P.O. Box 338, Orem, UT 84057.

Positive Pub, *(Positive Publishing),* 2402 N. Wishon, Fresno, CA 93704 Tel 209-225-1813.

Post, *(Post Pubns.; 0-911160),* 119 S. First Av Box 150, Arcadia, CA 91006 Tel 213-446-5000.

Post-Era, *(Post-Era Books; 0-911160),* Box 15 119 S. First Ave., Arcadia, CA 91006 Tel 213-446-1165.

Postgrad Intl, *(Postgraduate International, Inc. 0-918924),* Provincial Executive Bldg., Sui 145, 2201 Route 38, Cherry Hill, NJ 0800 Tel 609-482-0410.

Postgrad Med Inst, *(Postgraduate Medical Institute),* 22 The Fenway, Boston, MA 02215 Tel 617-262-3040.

Postscript, *(Postscript Productions; 0-9604850* P.O. Box 307, Suisun, CA 94585.

Posy Pubns, *(Posy Pubns.; 0-9603526),* 115 Shasta Ct., Charlottesville, VA 22903 Tel 804-293-8506.

Pot of Gold, *(Pot.of Gold Pubns.),* 1152 11th St., Manhattan Beach, CA 90266.

Potato Pr *Imprint of O'Hara*

Potomac, *(Potomac Books, Inc., Pubs.; 0-8710* 4418 MacArthur Blvd., N.W., Washington, DC 20007 Tel 202-338-5774; Orders to: P.O. Box 40604, Palisades Sta., Washington DC 20016 Tel 202-333-6779.

Potomac Appalach, *(Potomac Appalachian Tra Club; 0-915746),* 1718 N. St., N.W, Washington, DC 20036 Tel 202-638-5307

Potomac Assoc, *(Potomac Associates; 0-91399* 1707 "L" St., N.W., Washington, DC 200 Tel 202-883-1640; Dist. by: Basic Books, Inc., 10 E. 53rd St., New York, NY 10022

Potomac Ent, *(Potomac Enterprises; 0-939836* Box 1570, Arlington, VA 22201 Tel 703-522-5183; Dist. by: Sanford J. Durst, 170 E. 61st St., New York, NY 10021.

Potomac Pr, *(Potomac Press; 0-917262),* P.O. Box 31086, Washington DC-Temple Hills, MD 20031 Tel 202-582-4064.

Potter, *(Potter, Clarkson N., Inc.; 0-8257),* D by: Crown Pubs., 1 Park Ave., New York, NY 10016 Tel 212-532-9200.

ottle, *(Pottle, Ralph R.; 0-911162),* 407 N. Magnolia St., Hammond, LA 70401 Tel 504-345-2105.

oudre Pub Co, *(Poudre Publishing Co.; 0-935240),* P.O. Box 181, La Porte, CO 80535 Tel 303-484-2267.

oulin, *(Poulin, Clarence J.; 0-9600084),* 87 High St., Penacook, NH 03301 Tel 603-753-4480.

ourboire, *(Pourboire Press),* P.O. Box 6881, Providence, RI 02940 Tel 401-331-9800; Dist. by: Woods Hole Press, P.O. Box 44, Woods Hole, MA 02543 Tel 617-548-9600.

overty Bay, *(Poverty Bay Publishing Co.; 0-936528),* 529 S.W. 294, Federal Way, WA 98003.

ower Mad, *(Power Mad Press; 0-935444),* 156 W. 27th St., No. 5W, New York, NY 10001.

ower Pub Inc, *(Power Publishers, Inc.; 0-9600086),* 60 Vose Ave., South Orange, NJ 07079.

owner, *(Powner, Charles T., Co., Inc.; 0-911164),* 407 S. Dearborn St., Chicago, IL 60605.

r Arden Park, *(Press of Arden Park),* 861 Los Molinos Way, Sacramento, CA 95825 Tel 916-481-7881.

r of A Colish, *(Press of A Colish),* 40 Hartford Ave., Mount Vernon, NY 10850 Tel 914-664-4668.

r of Case WR, *(Press of Case Western Reserve Univ.; 0-8295),* Frank Adgate Quail Bldg., Cleveland, OH 44106 Tel 216-368-3770.

r of Morningside, *(Press of Morningside Bookshop; 0-89029),* P.O. Box 1087, Dayton, OH 45401 Tel 513-461-6736.

r of Nova Scotia, *(Press of the Nova Scotia College of Art & Design),* Dist. by: Jaap Rietman, Inc., 157 Spring St., New York, NY 11012.

r Pacifica, *(Press Pacifica, Ltd.; 0-916630),* P.O. Box 1227, Kailua, HI 96734 Tel 808-261-6594.

r Tuscany, *(Press in Tuscany Alley; 0-915918),* One Tuscany Alley, San Francisco, CA 94133 Tel 415-986-0641.

r Vision Studios, *(Press at Vision Studios, The; 0-936888),* P.O. Box 241, La Grange, IL 60525.

ractical Anthro, *(Practical Anthropology; 0-913132),* P.O. Box 1041, New Canaan, CT 06840.

ractical Pubns, *(Practical Pubns.; 0-912914),* 6272 W. North Ave., Chicago, IL 60639 Tel 312-237-2986.

raeger, *(Praeger Pubs.; 0-275),* Div. of Holt, Rinehart & Winston/CBS, 521 Fifth Ave., New York, NY 10175 Tel 212-599-8400.

raestant, *(Praestant Press; 0-930112),* P.O. Box 43, Delaware, OH 43015 Tel 614-363-1458.

raetorius Bks, *(Praetorius Books),* P.O. Box 167, Valhalla, NY 10595.

rairie Bk, *(Prairie Book Co.; 0-915518),* P.O. Box 1244, Plainview, TX 79072; Moved, Left No Forwarding Address.

rairie Owl, *(Prairie Owl Pubns.; 0-937244),* 322 Otero, Ordway, CO 81063 Tel 303-543-1382.

rairie Poet, *(Prairie Poet Books; 0-913996; 0-915284),* P.O. Box 35, Charleston, IL 61920.

rairie Pub, *(Prairie Publishing),* R. R. 1, Rushville, NE 69360.

rairie Sch, *(Prairie School Press; 0-87370),* 12509 S. 89th Ave., Palos Park, IL 60464 Tel 312-225-3190.

rairie Sun, *(Prairie Sun Communications, Inc.; 0-936722),* 1109 W. Main St., Peoria, IL 61606 Tel 309-673-0634.

rajna *Imprint of* Great Eastern

rakken, *(Prakken Pubns., Inc.; 0-911168),* P.O. Box 8623, 416 Longshore Dr., Ann Arbor, MI 48107 Tel 313-769-1211.

ranayama Pubns, *(Pranayama Pubns.),* 1836 Rock Court, Cleveland, OH 44118; Moved, Left No Forwarding Address.

rayer Bk, *(Prayer Book Press, Inc.; 0-87677),* 1363 Fairfield Ave., Bridgeport, CT 06605.

re-Mer, *(Pre-Mer Publishing Co.; 0-918458),* 175 Fifth Ave., New York, NY 10010.

re-School Learn, *(Pre-School Learning Corp.),* P.O. Box 6244, 10206 Rosewood, Overland Park, KS 66207.

recedent Pub, *(Precedent Publishing, Inc.; 0-913750),* 520 N. Michigan Ave., Chicago, IL 60611 Tel 312-828-0420; Orders to: P.O. Box 1005, South Holland, IL 60473 Tel 312-877-5490.

Precious Res, *(Precious Resources; 0-937836),* Box 259A, Rt. 1, Union, KY 41091 Tel 606-586-9943.

Precision Photo, *(Precision Photo-Form Co.),* P.O. Box 617, Union City, CA 94587.

Precision Pub Co, *(Precision Publishing Co.),* P.O. Box 172, Fort Myers, FL 33902.

Prem *Imprint of* Fawcett

Prem Press, *(Premier Press; 0-912722),* P.O. Box 4428, Berkeley, CA 94704.

Prensa Pubns, *(Prensa Pubns., Inc.; 0-935828),* 900 S. Quince St., B-909, Denver, CO 80231.

Presby & Reformed, *(Presbyterian & Reformed Publishing Co.; 0-87552),* Order Dept., Box 817, Phillipsburg, NJ 08865.

Presby Hist, *(Presbyterian Historical Society; 0-912686),* 425 Lombard St., Philadelphia, PA 19147 Tel 215-627-1852.

PRESCOB, *(PRESCOB Publishing Co.),* 5110 S. 67th E. Place, Tulsa, OK 74145 Tel 918-664-6717.

Prescott St Pr, *(Prescott Street Press; 0-915986),* 407 Postal Bldg., Portland, OR 97204 Tel 503-254-2922.

Preserv Coun Pike, *(Preservation Council of Pike County; 0-916814),* Pikeville College, Appalachian Studies Ctr., Pike County, Pikeville, KY 41501 Tel 606-432-3161.

Preserv Soc Newport, *(Preservation Society of Newport County, The),* Dist. by: Rhode Island Pubns Society, The Old State House, 150 Benefit St., Providence, RI 02903.

Preservation Pr, *(Preservation Press, National Trust for Historic Preservation; 0-89133),* 1785 Massachusetts Ave., N.W., Washington, DC 20036 Tel 202-673-4000.

Presidial, *(Presidial Press; 0-935978),* P.O. Box 5248, Austin, TX 78763 Tel 512-459-9265.

Presidio Pr, *(Presidio Press; 0-89141),* 31 Pamaron Way, Novato, CA 94947 Tel 415-883-1373; Orders to: Presidio Press Distribution Center, P.O. Box 978, Edison, NJ 08817 Tel 201-225-1900.

Press Pegacycle, *(Press of the Pegacycle Lady; 0-915148),* P.O. Box 69812, Los Angeles, CA 90069 Tel 213-658-8515.

Press West, *(Press West; 0-914592),* Box 4107, Chico, CA 95927 Tel 916-343-0642.

Presse World, *(Presse World International Inc.; 0-938508),* 3595 St. Gaudens Rd., Miami, FL 33133.

Presser Co, *(Presser, Theodore, Co.; 0-8235),* Presser Place, Bryn Mawr, PA 19010 Tel 215-525-3636.

Pressure, *(Pressure Vessel Handbook Publishing, Inc.; 0-914458),* P.O. Box 35365, Tulsa, OK 74135 Tel 918-742-9637.

Pressworks, *(Pressworks Publishing, Inc.; 0-939722),* 2800 Routh St., No. 249, Dallas, TX 75201 Tel 214-749-1044.

Prestige Pr, *(Prestige Press),* 2525 Wilson Blvd., Arlington, VA 22201.

Preston, *(Preston Publishing Co., Inc.),* 100 Avenue of the Americas, New York, NY 10013 Tel 212-966-5529.

Preston-Hill, *(Preston-Hill, Inc.; 0-914616),* P.O. Box 572, Chapel Hill, NC 27514 Tel 919-967-7904.

Preston Pubns, *(Preston Publications; 0-912474),* P.O. Box 48312, Niles, IL 60648 Tel 312-647-0566.

Preston St Pr, *(Preston Street Press; 0-939382),* 6 Preston St., Rye, NY 10580 Tel 914-765-2178.

Preston Tech
See Preston Pubns

Prestressed Concrete, *(Prestressed Concrete Institute),* 201 N. Wells St., Chicago, IL 60606 Tel 312-346-4071.

Pretest
See McGraw-Pretest

Pretzel Pr, *(Pretzel Press; The; 0-936980),* 1220 N. Gayoso St., New Orleans, LA 70119.

Priam Pr, *(Priam Press Inc; 0-911180),* 134 S. La Salle St., Chicago, IL 60603 Tel 312-726-0569.

Price Guide, *(Price Guide Pubs.; 0-911182),* P.O. Box 525, Kenmore, WA 98028 Tel 206-362-6670.

Price-Pottenger, *(Price-Pottenger Nutrition Foundation; 0-916764),* Orders to: P.O. Box 2614, La Mesa, CA 92041 Tel 714-582-4168.

Price Stern, *(Price, Stern, Sloan, Pubs., Inc.; 0-8431),* 410 N. La Cienega Blvd., Los Angeles, CA 90048 Tel 213-657-6100.

Prickly NY, *(Prickly Pear Press; 0-9605794),* P.O. Box 221, Old Chelsea Sta., New York, NY 10113.

Prickly Pear, *(Prickly Pear Press; 0-933384),* 2132 Edwin St., Fort Worth, TX 76110.

Primary, *(Primary Sources; 0-911184),* 11 Bleecker St., New York, NY 10012.

Primary Pr, *(Primary Press),* Box 105a, Parker Ford, PA 19457 Tel 215-495-7529.

Primavera, *(Primavera; 0-916980),* Ida Noyes Hall, Univ. of Chicago, 1212 E. 59th St., Chicago, IL 60637 Tel 312-752-5655.

Prime Natl Pub, *(Prime National Publishing Co.; 0-932834),* 470 Boston Post Rd., Weston, MA 02193 Tel 617-899-2702.

Primer Pubs, *(Primer Pubs.; 0-935810),* 5738 N. Central, Phoenix, AZ 85012 Tel 602-266-1043; Dist. by: Med Tech Books, Inc., 11511 Tennessee Ave., Los Angeles, CA 90064.

Primrose Pr, *(Primrose Press),* 815 Bertrand Ave., Prescott, AZ 86301 Tel 602-445-4567.

Prince Comm, *(Prince Communications, Inc.; 0-914302),* 99 Madison Ave., New York, NY 10016 Tel 212-683-7840; Moved, Left No Forwarding Address.

Prince Pubs, *(Prince Pubs.; 0-915618),* 349 E. Northfield Rd., Livingston, NJ 07039 Tel 201-994-1523.

Prince Scientific, *(Prince Scientific Press; 0-933340),* P.O. Box 2355, Univ. of GA Sta., Athens, GA 30602.

Princeton Bk Co, *(Princeton Book Co.),* P.O. Box 109, Princeton, NJ 08540.

Princeton Lib, *(Princeton Univ. Library; 0-87811),* Princeton, NJ 08544 Tel 609-452-3215.

Princeton Opinion, *(Princeton Opinion Press),* 53 Bank St., Princeton, NJ 08540 Tel 609-924-9600.

Princeton Pub, *(Princeton Publishing Inc.; 0-915038),* 221 Nassau St., Princeton, NJ 08540 Tel 609-924-7555; Orders to: Automobile Quarterly Publications, 245 W. Main St., Kutztown, PA 19530 Tel 215-683-8352.

Princeton U Pr, *(Princeton Univ. Press; 0-691),* 41 William St., Princeton, NJ 08540 Tel 609-452-4900.

Principia Pr, *(Principia Press; 0-911188),* 5743 Kimbark Ave., Chicago, IL 60637 Tel 312-643-8295.

Prindle, *(Prindle, Weber & Schmidt; 0-87150),* Statler Office Bldg., 20 Providence St., Boston, MA 02116 Tel 617-482-2344. *Imprints:* Pub. by Willard Grant Pr (Grant, Willard, Press).

Prinit Pr, *(Prinit Press; 0-932970),* Box 65, Dublin, IN 47335.

Print Mag, *(Print Magazine),* 6400 Goldsboro Rd., Washington, DC 20034.

Print Mail Serv, *(Printing, Mailing Services, Inc.),* 126 N. Ontario St., Toledo, OH 43624 Tel 419-241-4266.

Print Media, *(Print Media Services),* 222 S. Prospect Ave., Park Ridge, IL 60068 Tel 312-825-1145.

Printed Edns, *(Printed Editions; 0-914162),* 122 Spring St., New York, NY 10012 Tel 212-966-5232; Dist. by: New York Small Press Assn., P.O. Box 1264, Radio City Sta., New York, NY 10019.

Printed Horse, *(Printed Horse, The; 0-912830),* P.O. Box 1908, Fort Collins, CO 80522 Tel 303-482-2286.

Printed Matter, *(Printed Matter, Inc., 0-89439),* 7 Lispenard St., New York, NY 10013 Tel 212-925-0325.

Printed Word, *(Printed Word Publishing),* 22834 Tomball Cemetary Rd., Tomball, TX 77375 Tel 713-351-4577.

Printek, *(Printek; 0-938042),* 6989 Oxford St., Minneapolis, MN 55426.

Printers Ink, *(Printers Ink Assoc.),* P.O. Box 8872, St. Louis, MO 63102; Moved, Left No Forwarding Address.

Printery, *(Printery),* 349 E. Bodley, Kirkwood, MO 63122 Tel 314-822-4142; Moved, Left No Forwarding Address.

Prism *Imprint of* P-H

Prism Pr, *(Prism Press; 0-938774),* 11706 Longleaf Lane, Houston, TX 77024.

Pritchett & Hull, *(Pritchett & Hull Associates, Inc.; 0-939838),* 2122 Faulkner Rd. NE, Atlanta, GA 30324 Tel 404-321-0769.

Privacy Journal, *(Privacy Journal; 0-930072),* Box 8844, Washington, DC 20003 Tel 202-547-2865.

Private Bks, *(Private Books; 0-9606112),* 500 19th Ave., San Francisco, CA 94121 Tel 415-751-2338.

Pro Electron, *(Pro Electron Assn.),* Dist. by: Scholium International, Inc., 130-30 31st Ave., Flushing, NY 11354.

Pro Lingua, *(Pro Lingua Associates; 0-86647),* 15 Elm St., Brattleboro, VT 05301.

Pro-Search, *(Pro-Search; 0-9602540),* 3256 Ridge Rd., P.O. 24, Lansing, IL 60438 Tel 312-895-8800.

Pro West, *(Pro West),* 5745 Via los Ranchos, Paradise Valley, AZ 85253.

ProActive Pr, *(ProActive Press; 0-914158),* P.O. Box 296, Berkeley, CA 94701 Tel 415-841-7802.

Probe
    See Veritas

Process Pr, *(Process Press; 0-9605378),* 2322 Haste, No. 31, Berkeley, CA 94704.

Prod Hse, *(Production House Corp.; 0-932638),* 4307 Euclid Ave., San Diego, CA 92115 Tel 714-287-2560.

Prodist *Imprint of* **N Watson**

Products Corp, *(Products Corp., Unlimited; 0-914518),* 205 Farnsworth Rd., Waterville, OH 43566 Tel 419-878-7621; Moved, Left No Forwarding Address.

Prof Bks, *(Professional Books; 0-933478),* P.O. Box 3494, Jackson, TN 38301 Tel 901-424-4665.

Prof Bks Serv, *(Professional Books Service; 0-9601052),* Box 366, Dayton, OH 45401 Tel 513-223-3734.

Prof Busn Serv, *(Professional Business Services, Co.; 0-935154),* 15620 N. 25th Ave., F-109, Phoenix, AZ 85023 Tel 602-942-0089.

Prof Comm, *(Professional Communication Press; 0-89691),* 2378 E. Stadium, Suite 107, Ann Arbor, MI 48104 Tel 313-971-1050.

Prof Educ IL, *(Professional Education Pubns.; 0-89707),* 1155 E. 60th St., Chicago, IL 60637.

Prof Educ Pubn, *(Professional Educators, Pubn., Inc.; 0-88224),* P.O. Box 80728, Lincoln, NE 68501 Tel 402-477-6971.

Prof Engine, *(Professional Engineering Registration Program; 0-932276),* P.O. Box 911, San Carlos, CA 94070 Tel 415-593-9731.

Prof Impressions, *(Professional Impressions, Inc.; 0-934098),* 203A-180 Allen Rd., Atlanta, GA 30328.

Prof Press, *(Professional Press, Inc.; 0-87873),* 101 E. Ontario St., Chicago, IL 60611.

Prof Pubns CA, *(Professional Pubns.; 0-9605954),* P.O. Box 1961, Long Beach, CA 90803.

Prof Pubns FL, *(Professional Pubns., Inc.; 0-918262),* P.O. Box 12848, Univ. Sta., Gainesville, FL 32604 Tel 904-375-0772.

Prof Pubns NY, *(Professional Pubns.; 0-932836),* Div of MetaData, Inc., 441 Lexington Ave., New York, NY 10017; Orders to: P.O. Box 319, Huntington, NY 11743.

Prof Pubns Ohio, *(Professional Pubns., Inc.; 0-934706),* 1609 Northwest Blvd., Columbus, OH 43212 Tel 614-488-8236.

Prof Real Estate, *(Professional Real Estate Pubs.; 0-89764),* Orders to: Lincoln's Leadership Library, 5516 E. 35th St., Suite 100, Tulsa, OK 74135 Tel 918-749-0707.

Prof Rehab Wkrs
    See Am Deaf & Rehab

Profile Pr, *(Profile Press),* 245 Seventh Ave., New York, NY 10001.

Profiles Pub, *(Profiles of Food Publishing Co.),* Star Route, Box 149, Van Buren, AK 72956 Tel 501-474-6101.

Profit Sharing, *(Profit Sharing Research Foundation; 0-911192),* 1718 Sherman Ave., Evanston, IL 60201 Tel 312-869-8787.

Prog Concepts, *(Progressive Concepts, Inc.; 0-940010),* 2541 Lakewood Lane, Chesapeake, VA 23321 Tel 804-467-9248.

Prog Grocer, *(Progressive Grocer; 0-911790),* 708 Third Ave., New York, NY 10017 Tel 212-490-1000.

Prog Pr, *(Programmed Press; 0-916106),* 2301 Baylis Ave., Elmont, NY 11003 Tel 516-775-0933.

Prog Pubs, *(Progress Publishing Co.),* P.O. Box 35328, Houston, TX 77035 Tel 713-666-2175.

Prog Studies, *(Programmed Studies, Inc.; 0-917194),* P.O. Box 113, Stow, MA 01775 Tel 617-897-2130.

Progeny Pr, *(Progeny Press, Inc.; 0-934168),* P.O. Box 206, Villanova, PA 19085 Tel 215-296-0595; Dist. by: Caroline House, 80 Northfield Ave., Raritan Center, Edison, NJ 08817.

Program Counsel, *(Program Counsel; 0-9601096),* 4900 Marine Dr., Suite 811, Chicago, IL 60640 Tel 312-784-3636.

Progresiv Pub, *(Progresiv Publishr; 0-89670),* 401 E. 32nd St., No. 1002, Chicago, IL 60616.

Progress Pr WA, *(Progress Press; 0-935792),* P.O. Box 5019, Seattle, WA 98105.

Progress Pubs, *(Progress Pubs.),* Orders to: Imported Pubns., 320 W. Ohio St., Chicago, IL 60610.

Progs & Pubns, *(Programs & Pubns.; 0-934382),* 321 Queen St., Philadelphia, PA 19147.

Progs on Change, *(Programs on Change; 0-9606012),* 784 Columbus Ave., Suite 1c, New York, NY 10025 Tel 212-222-4606.

Proj Pub & Des, *(Project Publishing & Design; 0-915082),* 1119 Colorado Ave., Suite 104, Santa Monica, CA 90404 Tel 213-393-9631.

Project Jifunza-Educ, *(Project Jifunza/Educational Pubns.; 0-931310),* 641 Dory Lane, Redwood City, CA 94065 Tel 415-347-9111.

Proletarian Pubs, *(Proletarian Pubs; 0-89380),* P.O. Box 3925, Chicago, IL 60654 Tel 312-942-0774; Orders to: Vanguard Books, P.O. Box 3566, Chicago, IL 60654.

Prologue, *(Prologue Pubns; 0-930048),* P.O. Box 640, Menlo Park, CA 94025 Tel 415-322-1663.

Promethean, *(Promethean Books, Inc.),* Dist. by: Center for Application of Psychological Type, Inc., 1441 N.W. 6th St., Suite B-400, Gainesville, FL 32601 Tel 804-375-0180.

Prometheus Bks, *(Prometheus Books; 0-87975),* 700 E. Amherst St., Buffalo, NY 14215 Tel 716-837-2475.

Prometheus Nemesis, *(Prometheus Nemesis Books),* P.O. Box 2082, Del Mar, CA 92014.

Prometheus Pr, *(Prometheus Press),* Dist. by: Hawthorn Books, Inc., 260 Madison Ave., New York, NY 10016.

PROMIS Lab, *(PROMIS Laboratory),* MCHV-MFU, Adams Residence, Burlington, VT 05401 Tel 802-656-3946.

Promise Corp, *(Promise Corp.; 0-936982),* P.O. Box 1534, Pawtucket, RI 02862.

Promised Land, *(Promised Land Publications, Inc.),* Div. of Community Press, 5600 N. University Ave., Provo, UT 84601 Tel 801-225-2293.

Promontory Pr UT, *(Promontory Press; 0-935242),* 2640 Washington Blvd., Suite 301, Ogden, UT 84401 Tel 801-392-7655.

Proof Pr, *(Proof Press; 0-935070),* P. O. Box 1256, Berkeley, CA 94701 Tel 415-521-8741.

Proprietary Assn, *(Proprietary Assn.),* 1700 Pennsylvania Ave., N. W., Washington, DC 20006 Tel 202-393-1700.

Proscenium, *(Proscenium Press; 0-912262),* P.O. Box 361, Newark, DE 19711 Tel 215-255-4083.

ProSeminar Pr, *(ProSeminar Press, Inc.),* 3330 NE 135th Ave., Portland, OR 97230.

Prospect, *(Prospect Books; 0-913710),* P.O. Box 57, Prospect, NY 13435 Tel 315-896-2249.

Prospect Hse, *(Prospect House, Inc.),* 1825 Connecticut Ave., N.W., Washington, DC 20009 Tel 202-667-0220.

Prosperity Pr, *(Prosperity Press; 0-935686),* Drawer 210, Queens Village, NY 11429 Tel 212-454-7268.

Proteus, *(Proteus Press; 0-918150),* Subs. of Proteus Design, Inc., 9225 Baltimore Blvd., College Park, MD 20740 Tel 301-441-2928.

Proteus Calif, *(Proteus Press, The; 0-932864),* 250 Thunderbird Dr., Aptos, CA 95003.

Proteus Pub NY, *(Proteus Publishing Co., Inc.; 0-906071),* 733 Third Ave., Suite 901, New York, NY 10017; Dist. by: Charles Scribner's Sons, 597 Fifth Ave., New York, NY 10017.

Providence AL, *(Providence Press, The; 0-9604378),* P.O. Box 253, Florence, AL 35631.

Provident, *(Provident Press, The; 0-9603298),* P.O. Box 1112, Covina, CA 91722 Tel 213-339-9407.

Province Pub, *(Province Publishing Co.; 0-932348),* 11307 Vela Dr., San Diego, CA 92126 Tel 714-566-6355.

Provision, *(Provision House; 0-935446),* P.O. Box 5487, Austin, TX 78763 Tel 512-452-1417.

Prow Bks-Franciscan, *(Prow Books/Franciscan Marytown Press; 0-913382),* 8000 39th Ave., Kenosha, WI 53141.

Prudent Pub Co, *(Prudential Publishing Company; 0-934432),* 311 California St., Suite 711, San Francisco, CA 94104 Tel 916-541-8360.

Pruett, *(Pruett Publishing Co.; 0-87108),* 3235 Prairie Ave., Boulder, CO 80301 Tel 303-449-4919.

Pryor Pettengill, *(Pryor Pettengill; 0-933462),* Box 7074, Ann Arbor, MI 48107.

Prytaneum Pr, *(Prytaneum Press; 0-907152),* Fair Way, Poughkeepsie, NY 12603.

PSG Pub, *(PSG Pub. Co., Inc.; 0-88416),* 545 Great Rd., Littleton, MA 01460 Tel 617-486-8971.

PSI Res, *(PSI Research; 0-916378),* Subs. of Publishing Services, Inc., P.O. Box 6836, Oakland, CA 94603 Tel 415-523-7969.

PSI Rhythms, *(P.S.I. Rhythms, Inc.; 0-918882),* P. O. Box 1838, Ormond Beach, FL 32074 Tel 904-255-6444; 2085 South Halofax, Daytona Beach, FL 32018.

Psych & Consul Assocs, *(Psychology & Consulting Associates Press; 0-930626),* P. Box 1837, La Jolla, CA 92038 Tel 714-459-1135.

Psych Corp, *(Psychological Corp.),* 304 E. 45t St., New York, NY 10017.

Psych Corp *Imprint of* **HarBraceJ**

Psych Dimensions, *(Psychological Dimensions, Inc.; 0-88437),* 10 W. 66th St., Suite 4H, New York, NY 10023 Tel 212-877-2313.

Psych Graphic, *(Psych Graphic Pubs.; 0-93238),* 470 Nautilus St., Suite 303, La Jolla, CA 92037 Tel 714-459-0531.

Psych Pr WA, *(Psychological Press; 0-937668),* Box 5435, Seattle, WA 98105 Tel 206-524-0194.

Psych Qtly, *(Psychoanalytic Quarterly, Inc.; 0-911194),* 57 W. 57th St., New York, NY 10019.

Psych Res Assoc, *(Psychology Research Associates),* 9000 W. Sunset Blvd., Suite 305, Los Angeles, CA 90069.

Psychenutrition, *(Psychenutrition, Inc.; 0-939466),* P.O. Box 1384, Manhattan Beach, CA 90266 Tel 213-545-7012; Dist. by: BookSource, P.O. Box 29448, Los Angeles, CA 90029.

Psychiatry & Behavioral, *(Psychiatry & Behavioral Science Associates),* P.O. Box 197, Haverford, PA 19041.

Psychohistory Pr, *(Psychohistory Press),* Div. Atcom, Inc., Pubns., 2315 Broadway, New York, NY 10024 Tel 212-873-3760.

Psychometric, *(Psychometric Affiliates; 0-9606044),* P.O. Box 3167, Munster, IN 46321 Tel 219-836-1661.

Psychoneurologia, *(Psychoneurologia Press; 0-935688),* P.O. Box 7542, Shawnee Mission, KS 66207 Tel 913-381-8564.

PT Marketing, *(P. T. Marketing; 0-9605106),* 13836 Bora Bora Way, Marina Del Rey, C 90291; Moved, Left No Forwarding Addre

PTL Pubns, *(PTL Pubns.; 0-915420),* Box 127 Tustin, CA 92680 Tel 714-838-7715.

Ptolemy Pr, *(Ptolemy Press Ltd.; 0-933550),* P.O. Box 243, Grove City, PA 16127 Tel 412-794-7309.

Pub Aff Pr, *(Public Affairs Press; 0-8183),* 41 New Jersey Ave., Washington, DC 20003 Tel 202-544-3024.

Pub. by Bomber *Imprint of* **Aviation**

Pub by Bootlegger Pr *Imprint of* **ALA**

Pub. by Willard Grant Pr *Imprint of* **Prindle**

Pub Ctr Cult Res, *(Publishing Center for Cultural Resources, Inc.; 0-89062),* 625 Broadway, New York, NY 10012 Tel 212-260-2010.

Pub Personnel
    See Intl Personnel Mgmt

Pub Personnel, *(Public Personnel Assn.),* ; Publisher Abbreviation Without Addresses Are for Titles That Are Out of Print. These Are Obsolete Abbreviations. Publisher's Abbreviation Is Now Intl Personnel Mgmt.

Pub Publish, *(Pub Publishing; 0-917532),* P.O. Box 455, Warrenville, IL 60555 Tel 312-682-0183.

Pub Sect Lab Rel, *(Public Sector Labor Relations Conference Board; 0-913400),* Univ. of Maryland, Dept. of Economics, College Park, MD 20742.

Pub Securities, *(Public Securities Assn.),* 1 World Trade Ctr., Suite 5271, New York, NY 10048.

Pub Serv Ctr, *(Publishing Services Center),* Dist. by: William Kaufmann, Inc., 1 First St., Los Altos, CA 94022 Tel 415-948-5810.

Pub Vaidava, *(Publisher Vaidava; 0-936302),* 1621 S. 21st St., Lincoln, NE 68502.

Public Aff Comm, *(Public Affairs Committee, Inc.; 0-88291),* 381 Park Ave. S., New York, NY 10016 Tel 212-683-4331.

Public Info Pr, *(Public Information Press, Inc.; 0-934954),* P.O. Box 402611, Miami Beach, FL 33140 Tel 305-538-5308.

Public Law Educ, *(Public Law Education Institute),* Dupont Circle Bldg., 6th Flr., 1346 Connecticut Ave., N.W., Washington, DC 20036 Tel 202-296-7590.

Public Management, *(Public Management Institute; 0-916664),* 333 Hayes St., San Francisco, CA 94102 Tel 415-431-8444.

Public Relations, *(Public Relations Publishing Co.; 0-913046),* 888 Seventh Ave., New York, NY 10106 Tel 212-582-7373.

Public Serv Materials, *(Public Service Materials Center),* 415 Lexington Ave., New York, NY 10017.

Public Serv Pubns, *(Public Service Pubns., Inc.),* 1523 W. 8th St., Los Angeles, CA 90017 Tel 213-484-1088.

Public Works, *(Public Works, Incorporated, The; 0-918556),* Rfd 1, P.O. Box 201, Putney, VT 05346 Tel 802-387-6682.

Publicity, *(Publicity in Print; 0-915716),* 935 Thornton Way, San Jose, CA 95128 Tel 408-293-3997.

Publish or Perish, *(Publish or Perish, Inc.; 0-914098),* 2000 Center St., Box 1404, Berkeley, CA 94704 Tel 404-329-0372.

Publishers, *(Publishers),* The World of Astrological Research, 890-B-So. 6th St, Las Vegas, NV 89101; Moved, Left No Forwarding Address.

Publishers Consult, *(Publishers Consultancy; 0-88310),* Box 1908, Ft. Collins, CO 80522; Formerly Shields Publishing Co., Inc.

Publishers Guild, *(Publishers Guild),* P.O. Box 754, Palatine, IL 60067 Tel 312-991-0255.

Publishers Media, *(Publishers Media; 0-934064),* 123 N. Magnolia, Box 546, El Cajon, CA 92022.

Pubn Arts, *(Publication Arts, Inc.; 0-86573),* 5700 Green Circle Dr., Minnetonka, MN 55343.

Pubn Res Features, *(Pubn. Research Features; 0-912478),* Drawer 5007, Carmel, CA 93921.

Pubns Geomorphology, *(Publications in Geomorphology),* State Univ. of New York, Binghamton, NY 13901 Tel 607-798-2264.

Pubns Living, *(Pubns. for Living; 0-912128),* 11224 Big Bend Blvd., St. Louis, MO 63122 Tel 314-821-6177.

Pubns Organization, *(Publications Organization, Church of Scientology of California; 0-88404),* 4833 Fountain Ave., East Annex, Los Angeles, CA 90029 Tel 213-383-3775. *Imprints:* ASHO (ASHO Pubns.).

Pubs Agency, *(Publishers Agency, Inc.; 0-87781),* Subs. of Pubco Corp., Glendale, MD, 1411 Ford Rd., Cornwells Heights, PA 19020 Tel 215-638-7000.

Pubs Inc, *(Publishers, Inc.; 0-89163),* Drawer P, Del Mar, CA 92014 Tel 714-481-8133.

Pubs of Truth, *(Publishers of Truth; 0-930682),* 1509 Bruce Rd., Oreland, PA 19075 Tel 215-576-1450.

Pubs Print Hse, *(Publisher's Printing House),* 117 E. Main St., Berne, IN 46711; Moved, Left No Forwarding Address.

Puckerbrush, *(Puckerbrush Press; 0-913006),* 76 Main St., Orono, ME 04473 Tel 207-866-4868.

Puddingstone, *(Puddingstone Press),* P.O. Box 67, Banner Elk, NC 28604.

Pueblo Pub Co, *(Pueblo Publishing Co., Inc.; 0-916134),* 1860 Broadway, New York, NY 10023 Tel 212-541-7665.

Pueo Pr, *(Pueo Press; 0-917850),* 810 College Ave., Kentfield, CA 94904 Tel 415-456-6480.

Puerto Rico Almanacs, *(Puerto Rico Almanacs, Inc.; 0-934642),* P.O. Box 9582, Santurce, PR 00908 Tel 809-724-2402.

Puffin *Imprint of* **Penguin.**

Pulmac Ent, *(Pulmac Enterprises Inc.; 0-936346),* Middlesex Star Route, Montpelier, VT 05602 Tel 802-223-6326; Books Can Be Ordered from: Megalon Publications, P.O. Box 705, Goleta, Ca 93116.

Pulp, *(Pulp; 0-9603092),* c/o Howard Sage, 720 Greenwich St., New York, NY 10014 Tel 212-989-0190.

Pulse-Finger, *(Pulse-Finger Press; 0-912282),* P.O. Box 488, Yellow Springs, OH 45387 Tel 513-376-9033.

Pundarika, *(Pundarika Pubns.),* P.O. Box 444, Mountain Home, NC 28758.

Punster's Pr, *(Punster's Press; 0-9601402),* 3834 Joanne Dr., Glennview, IL 60025 Tel 312-564-4342.

Purcells, *(Purcells, Inc.; 0-931068),* 305 S. 10th, Box 190, Broken Bow, NE 68822 Tel 308-872-2471.

Purchase Pr, *(Purchase Press, The; 0-938266),* P.O. Box 5, Harrison, NY 10528.

Purdue, *(Purdue Univ. Press; 0-911198),* S. Campus Courts-D, West Lafayette, IN 47907 Tel 317-749-6083.

Purdue Univ Bks, *(Purdue Univ. Books; 0-931682),* Bldg. D, South Campus Courts, West Lafayette, IN 47907.

Purnell Lib Serv
    See Purnell Ref Bks

Purnell Lib Serv, *(Purnell Library Service),* ; Publisher Abbreviation Without Addresses Are for Titles That Are Out of Print. These Are Obsolete Abbreviations. Publisher's Abbreviation Is Now Purnell Ref Bks.

Purnell Ref Bks, *(Purnell Reference Books; 0-8393),* Div. of MacDonald-Raintree, Inc., 205 W. Highland Ave., Milwaukee, WI 53203 Tel 414-276-3430.

Purple Mouth, *(Purple Mouth Press; 0-9603300),* 713 Paul St., Newport News, VA 23605 Tel 804-380-6595.

Purple Unicorn, *(Purple Unicorn Books; 0-931998),* 4532 London Rd., Duluth, MN 55804 Tel 218-525-2084.

PURRC, *(Princeton Urban & Regional Research Center; 0-938882),* Woodrow Wilson School, Princeton University, Princeton, NJ 08544.

Pushcart Bk Pr
    See Pushcart Pr

Pushcart Pr, *(Pushcart Press, The; 0-916366),* P.O. Box 845, Yonkers, NY 10701 Tel 212-228-2269.

Putnam, *(Putnam's, G. P., Sons; 0-399),* 200 Madison Ave., New York, NY 10016 Tel 212-576-8900; Orders to: 1050 Wall St. W., Lyndhurst, NJ 07071 Tel 201-933-9292. *Imprints:* Peppercorn (Peppercorn); Perigee (Perigee Books).

Pygmalion Pr, *(Pygmalion Press; 0-915242),* 609 El Centro, So. Pasadena, CA 91030; 2104 Holly Dr., Hollywood, CA 90028 Tel 213-461-2557.

Pylon, *(Pylon Press, Inc.; 0-918524),* 108-19 67th Rd., Forest Hills, NY 11375 Tel 212-261-2533.

Pyne Pr, *(Pyne Press; 0-87861),* 92A Nassau St., Princeton, NJ 08540; Dist. by: C. Scribner's Sons, Vreeland Ave., Totowa, NJ 07512.

Pynyon, *(Pynyon Press, The; 0-930544),* 820 Piedmont Ave., N.E. Apt. 2, Atlanta, GA 30308 Tel 404-875-5412; Moved, Left No Forwarding Address.

Pyquag, *(Pyquag Books, Pubs.; 0-912492),* P.O. Box 328, Wethersfield, CT 06109.

Pyramid Hse *Imprint of* **Pyramid Pubns**

Pyramid Iowa, *(Pyramid Pubs. of Iowa),* P.O. Box 400, Perry, IA 50220 Tel 515-465-5500; Dist. by: Hiawatha Book Co., 7567 N.E. 102nd Ave., Bondurant, IA 50035 Tel 515-967-4025.

Pyramid Pubns, *(Pyramid Pubns., Inc.; 0-515),* 9 Garden St, Moonachie, NJ 07074 Tel 201-641-3311. *Imprints:* Pyramid Hse (Pyramid House).

Pyramid WV, *(Pyramid Press Publishing Co.),* 1686 Marshall St., Benwood, WV 26031.

Python Pub, *(Python Publishing Group; 0-89300),* 162 Washington St., Newark, NJ 07102 Tel 201-642-7956.

Pyxidium Pr, *(Pyxidium Press; 0-936568),* Box 462, Old Chelsea Sta., New York, NY 10011 Tel 212-242-5224.

Q Press, *(Q Press, The; 0-9605432),* 2114 W. Rogers St., Milwaukee, WI 53204.

QBLH Pubns, *(QBLH Pubns.; 0-9603680),* Box 1166, Ramona, CA 92065.

QED Info Sci, *(Q.E.D. Information Sciences, Inc.; 0-89435),* P.O. Box 181, 180 Linden St., Wellesley, MA 02181 Tel 617-237-5656.

Quadrangle
    See Times Bks

Quadrangle, *(Quadrangle/The New York Times Co.),* ; Publisher Abbreviations Without Addresses Are for Titles That Are Out of Print. These Are Obsolete Abbreviations. Publisher's New Abbreviation Is Times Bks.

Quadrant, *(Quadrant Books; 0-917892),* P.O. Box 99176, San Diego, CA 92109 Tel 714-272-4696.

Quadrant Pr, *(Quadrant Press; 0-915276),* 19 W. 44th St., New York, NY 10036.

Quail Pub, *(Quail Street Publishing Co., Inc.; 0-89307),* 1200 Quail St., Suite 110, Newport Beach, CA 92666; Moved, Left No Forwarding Address.

Quail Ridge, *(Quail Ridge Press, Inc.; 0-937552),* P.O. Box 123, Brandon, MS 39042.

Quail Run, *(Quail Run Pubns., Inc.; 0-930380),* 3336 N.32nd St., Suite 104, Phoenix, AZ 85018 Tel 602-955-5953.

Quaker, *(Quaker Press; 0-911200),* 3218 O St. N.W., Washington, DC 20007 Tel 202-338-3391.

Quaker City, *(Quaker City Books),* P.O. Box 6404, Philadelphia, PA 19145.

Quality Bks IL, *(Quality Books Inc.; 0-89196),* 400 Anthony Trail, Northbrook, IL 60062 Tel 312-498-4000. *Imprints:* Domus Bks (Domus Books).

Quality Circle, *(Quality Circle Institute; 0-937670),* 1425 Vista Way, Airport Industrial Park, P. O. Box Q, Red Bluff, CA 96080.

Quality Educ, *(Quality Educators, Ltd.),* 1236 S.E. Fourth Ave., Ft. Lauderdale, FL 33316 Tel 305-522-2249.

Quality Hill, *(Quality Hill Books; 0-9605044),* 674 Church St., San Luis Obispo, CA 93401.

Quality Lib, *(Quality Library Editions),* P.O. Box 148, Darby, PA 19023.

Quality Ohio, *(Quality Pubns. Inc.; 0-934040),* P.O. Box 2633, Lakewood, OH 44107.

Quality Printing, *(Quality Printing Co., Inc.; 0-89137),* P.O. Box 1060, Abilene, TX 79604 Tel 915-677-6262.

Quality Pubns, *(Quality Pubns.; 0-89137),* Div. of Quality Printing Co., Inc., P.O. Box 1060, Abilene, TX 79604 Tel 915-677-6262.

Quam Pr, *(Quam, Martin, Press),* 1515 Columbia Dr., Cedar Falls, IA 50613 Tel 319-273-2648; Orders to: 201 Rio St., Rio, WI 53960.

Quan Dec Syst, *(Quantitative Decision System, Inc.; 0-914174),* P.O. Box 2936, Chicago, IL 60690.

Quantal, *(Quantal Publishing Co.; 0-936596),* P.O. Box 1598, Goleta, CA 93117 Tel 805-964-7293; Dist. by: Ross-Erikson, Inc., 629 State St., Suite 222, Santa Barbara, CA 93101 Tel 805-962-1175.

Quantum Pubs, *(Quantum Pubs.; 0-934644),* 257 Park Ave. S., New York, NY 10010 Tel 212-475-5100.

Quarterdeck, *(Quarterdeck Press; 0-918546),* P.O. Box 134, Pacific Palisades, CA 90272 Tel 213-459-6832.

Quarterman, *(Quarterman Pubns., Inc.; 0-88000),* 5 S. Union St., Lawrence, MA 01843 Tel 617-259-8047.

Quartet Bks, *(Quartet Books, Inc.; 0-7043),* 12 E. 69th St., New York, NY 10021; Dist. by: Horizon Press, 156 Fifth Ave., New York, NY 10010.

Quasem, *(Quasem, M. Adul),* Dist. by: Habibur Rahman, 502 N. Elm St., Centralia, IL 62801.

Queen Anne Pr, *(Queen Anne Press, The; 0-937692),* Div. of Wye Institute, Inc., Cheston-on-Wye, Queenstown, MD 21658 Tel 301-827-7401; Orders to: P.O. Box 50, Queenstown, MD 21658.

Queen City Pubs, *(Queen City Pubs.; 0-9600880),* 420 Canberra, Box 95, Knoxville, TN 37919; Moved, Left No Forwarding Address.

Queen City VT, *(Queen City Press; 0-930410),* Pine St., Burlington, VT 05401.

Queens Coll Pr, *(Queens College Press; 0-930146),* Editorial Services, Flushing, NY 11367 Tel 212-520-7209.

Queens Hse, *(Queens House; 0-89244),* 105 Grovers Ave., Bridgeport, CT 06605 Tel 203-367-1578.

Queens Quick, *(Queens Quick Copy),* c/o Pulp, 720 Greenwich St., 4H, New York, NY 10014 Tel 212-989-0190.

Quest *Imprint of* **Theos Pub Hse**

Quest Edns, *(Quest Editions),* P.O. Box 67, Sharon Hill, PA 19079.

Quest Pr, *(Quest Press; 0-935320),* Box 998, San Luis Obispo, CA 93406 Tel 805-543-8500.

Quest Pub, *(Quest Publishing Co.; 0-930844),* 1351 Titan Way, Brea, CA 92621 Tel 714-738-6400.

Quest Utah, *(Quest Publishing Inc.; 0-938662),* P.O. Box 27317, Salt Lake City, UT 84127.

Quest WV, *(Quest Publishing Co.; 0-931856),* 5023 Kentucky St., South Charleston, WV 25309.

Quick Fox *Imprint of* **Music Sales**

Quicksilver Prod, *(Quicksilver Productions; 0-930356),* P.O. Box 340, Ashland, OR 97520 Tel 503-482-5343.

Quigley Pub Co, *(Quigley Publishing Co. Inc.; 0-900610),* 159 W. 53rd. St., New York, NY 10019 Tel 212-247-3100.

Quill Pubns, *(Quill Pubns.; 0-916608),* 1260 Coast Village Circle, Santa Barbara, CA 93108 Tel 805-969-2542.

Quinn-Gallagher, *(Quinn-Gallagher Press; 0-935282),* 6372 Forward Ave., Pittsburgh, PA 15217 Tel 412-521-1863.

Quint Pub Co, *(Quintessence Publishing Co., Inc.; 0-931386; 0-86715),* 10 S. LaSalle St., Chicago, IL 60603 Tel 312-782-3221.

Quintessence, *(Quintessence Pubns.; 0-918466),* 356 Bunker Hill Mine Rd., Amador City, CA 95601 Tel 209-267-5470.

Quinto Sol Pubns
See Tonatiuh-Quinto Sol Intl

Quist, *(Quist, Harlin, Books; 0-8252),* Dist. by: Dial/Delacorte Sales, 1 Dag Hammarskjold Plaza, 245 E. 47th St., New York, NY 10017 Tel 212-832-7300.

Quixote, *(Quixote Press; 0-9600306),* P.O. Box 70013, Allen Sta., Houston, TX 77007 Tel 713-227-2638.

Quorum Bks *Imprint of* **Greenwood**

Qwint Systems, *(Qwint Systems, Inc.),* 3693 Commercial Ave., Northbrook, IL 60062 Tel 312-498-5060.

R A Green, *(Green, Robert Alan; 0-9600266),* 214 Key Haven Rd., Key West, FL 33040 Tel 305-296-6736.

R A Traina, *(Traina, Robert A.; 0-9601396),* 505 Bellvue Ave., Wilmore, KY 40390 Tel 606-858-3405.

R A Wall, *(Wall, R. A. Investments, Inc.; 0-916522),* 9465 Wilshire Blvd., Suite 525, Beverly Hills, CA 90212.

R & D Pr, *(R & D Press; 0-88274),* 885 N. San Antonio Rd., Los Altos, CA 94022 Tel 415-948-0370.

R & D Pubns, *(R & D Pubns., Inc.; 0-938152),* Box 1032, New York, NY 10028.

R & D Serv, *(R & D Services; 0-89511),* P.O. Box 644, Des Moines, IA 50303 Tel 515-262-5397.

R & E Res Assoc, *(R & E Research Associates, Inc.; 0-88247),* 936 Industrial Ave., Palo Alto, CA 94303 Tel 415-494-1112.

R & H Pubs, *(R & H Publishers; 0-935246),* Box 3587, Georgetown Sta., Washington, DC 20007 Tel 703-524-4226.

R & S Rowland, *(Rowland, Ralph & Star),* 4209 San Juan Dr., Fairfax, VA 22030 Tel 703-273-4891.

R B Allison Co *Imprint of* **Wisconsin Bks**

R B Driscoll, *(Driscoll, Robert Bruce; 0-9601374),* P.O. Box 637, Oakland, CA 94604 Tel 415-451-4870.

R B Forster, *(Forster, Reginald Bishop, Associates Inc.; 0-931398),* 2344 Nicollet Ave, Suite 100, Minneapolis, MN 55404 Tel 612-871-1395.

R B Powell, *(Powell, Robert Blake; 0-9600680),* P.O. Box 833, Hurst, TX 76053 Tel 817-284-8145.

R B Walker
See Martingale

R Bernard, *(Bernard, Ros, Pubns.; 0-935872),* 17 Minell Place, Teaneck, NJ 07666 Tel 201-833-0805; Orders to: P.O. Box 2177, Teaneck, NJ 07666.

R C Packard, *(Packard, Rosa Covington),* 208 W. Old Mill Rd., Greenwich, CT 06830 Tel 203-661-8946.

R C Pubns, *(R C Pubns.; 0-915734),* 6400 Goldsboro Rd., Washington, DC 20034 Tel 301-229-2225.

R C Rapier, *(Rapier, Regina C.; 0-9600584),* 292 S. Cherokee St., Rte 1, Box 292, Social Circle, GA 30279 Tel 404-464-2582.

R Carson, *(Carson, Ray),* P.O. Box 8171, San Diego, CA 92102 Tel 714-440-7647.

R Collier, *(Collier, Robert, Pub., Inc.; 0-912576),* P.O. Box 3684, Indialantic, FL 32903.

R Curtis Bks, *(Curtis, Ralph, Books; 0-88359),* 2633 Adams St., Hollywood, FL 33020 Tel 305-925-4639; Orders to: 520 N. Dixie Hwy., Hollywood, FL 33020 Tel 305-925-4639.

R D Pace, *(Pace, R. D., Co.),* P.O. Box 174, Huntington Beach, CA 92648 Tel 714-536-8558.

R D Reed, *(Reed, Robert D.),* 18581 McFarland Ave., Saratoga, CA 95070.

R D Wood, *(Wood, Richard D.; 0-9603898),* 76 Stonehenge Rd., Kingston, RI 02881 Tel 401-783-2135.

R Dultz, *(Dultz, Ron; 0-9601636),* P.O. Drawer D, Reseda, CA 91335 Tel 213-993-7932.

R E Greene, *(Greene, Robert E.; 0-9603320),* 120 "U" St. N.W., Washington, DC 20001.

R E Martin, *(Martin, R. E., Pub.),* P.O. Box 165, Ryder Sta., Brooklyn, NY 11234; Moved, Left No Forwarding Address.

R E Stauffer, *(Stauffer, Richard E.),* P.O. Box 54, Old Zionsville, PA 18068 Tel 914-446-5527.

R E Todd, *(Todd, Richard E.; 0-9605324),* 3601 Linden Ave., Long Beach, CA 90807.

R Enslow
See Enslow Pubs

R Feathers, *(Feathers, Richard, Jr.; 0-9600730),* 211-24th St, Cocoa Beach, FL 32931; Moved,Left No Forwarding Address.

R G Hadley, *(Hadley, R. G., Co.; 0-9600988),* P.O. Box 5306, Salem, OR 97304 Tel 503-873-4241.

R G Willie DDS, *(Willie, Ralph G., D.D.S.),* 30317 16th Ave. S., Federal Way, WA 98003 Tel 206-839-7270.

R H Godfrey, *(Godfrey, Robert H.),* P.O. Box 873, Garden Grove, CA 92642; Moved, Left No Forwarding Address.

R H M Pr, *(R. H. M. Press; 0-89058),* 417 Northern Blvd., Great Neck, NY 11021 Tel 516-487-8811.

R H Moulder Trust, *(Moulder, Rebecca Hunt, Trust),* Valley National Bank, Congress at Stone, Tucson, AZ 85702.

R H Sang & Son, *(Sang, R. H., & Son Pubs. Inc.; 0-932844),* 211 E. Delaware Place, Chicago, IL 60611 Tel 312-787-9565.

R Hart, *(Hart, Richard; 0-9602100),* c/o The Distributers, P.O. Box 191, Harvard Square Sta., Cambridge, MA 02138.

R Haupt, *(Haupt, Rudy, & Co., Inc.; 0-935274),* 231 Hay Ave., Johnstown, PA 15902 Tel 814-536-7536.

R J Brady, *(Brady, Robert J., Co.; 0-87618; 0-87619),* Subs. of Prentice Hall, Inc., Rtes. 197 & 450, Bowie, MD 20715 Tel 301-262-6300.

R J Liederbach, *(Liederbach, Robert J.; 0-934906),* 2720 East Boulevard, Cleveland, OH 44104 Tel 216-231-8896.

R J Pub, *(Jay, Robert, Publishing),* P.O. Box 1171, Madison, WI 53701.

R Kuppinger, *(Kuppinger, Roger),* 77 Woodland Lane, Arcadia, CA 91006 Tel 213-489-3900.

R L Bell, *(Bell, Robert L.; 0-9602450),* 48-50 Melrose St., Boston, MA 02116.

R L Bryan, *(Bryan, R. L.; 0-934870),* Greystone Industrial Park, Columbia, SC 29201.

R L Enger, *(Enger, Ronald L.; 0-9601742),* 1853 Shadowbrook Dr., Merced, CA 95340.

R L Evans, *(Evans, Robert L.),* 2500 St. Anthony Blvd., Minneapolis, MN 55418 Tel 612-781-7384.

R L Hawkins, *(Hawkins, Robert L.),* 1220 Elm Ave., Imperial Beach, CA 92032.

R L Shep, *(Shep, R. L.; 0-914046),* Box C-20, Lopez, WA 98261.

R L Thomas, *(Thomas, Ralph L.),* 5023 Frew Ave., Pittsburgh, PA 15213 Tel 412-683-4420.

R Little, *(Little, Ruth; 0-9600062),* 3430 34th St., Lubbock, TX 79410.

R M Ostrov
See Educ Pr CA

R M Presznick, *(Presznick, Rose M.; 0-912000),* RD 1, 7810 Avon Lake Rd., Lodi, OH 44254.

R M R Simpson, *(Simpson, Ruth M. Rasey; 0-9604048),* 286 Goundry St., North Tonawanda, NY 14120 Tel 716-692-1830.

R Manley, *(Manley, Ray, Commercial Photography, Inc.; 0-931418),* 238 S. Tucson Blvd., Tucson, AZ 85716 Tel 602-623-0307

R Marek
See Marek

R Milford, *(Milford, Richard; 0-936292),* 22 Gerdes Ave., Verona, NJ 07044.

R Mitchell, *(Mitchell, Ralph; 0-9604106),* 1801 Horton Rd., Kenosha, WI 53142 Tel 414-857-2163.

R Moore & B Watson, *(Moore, R. Aloysia, & Bernice Bozeman Watson),* Box 459, Duarte CA 91010; Moved, Left No Forwarding Address.

R Morris Assocs, *(Morris, Robert, Associates; 0-936742),* 1616 Philadelphia National Bank Bldg., Philadelphia, PA 19107 Tel 215-665-2850.

R Myles, *(Myles, Ralph, Pub., Inc.; 0-87926),* P.O. Box 1533, Colorado Springs, CO 80901 Tel 303-634-3206.

R Nader, *(Nader, Ralph; 0-936486),* P.O. Box 19312, Washington, DC 20036.

R Nicholson
See Barrie & Jenkins

R O Beatty Assocs, *(Beatty, R. O., & Assocs.; 0-916238),* P.O. Box 763, Boise, ID 83701 Tel 208-343-4949.

R O Kechely, *(Kechely, Raymond O; 0-930202),* Box 462, Pinole, CA 94564 Tel 415-758-2481.

R Oman Pubns, *(Oman, Robert, Pubns.; 0-931660),* 204 Fair Oaks Park, Needham, MA 02192.

R P Bentley, *(Bentley, Richard P.; 0-9600902),* Tupperlake, NY 12986 Tel 518-359-9300.

R P Dews, *(Dews, Robert Porter; 0-940184),* P.O. Box 302, Edison, GA 31746 Tel 912-835-2282.

R P Long, *(Long, Robert P.; 0-9600064),* 445 Glen Court, Cutchogue, NY 11935 Tel 516-734-5368.

R Pagliotti, *(Pagliotti, Rick; 0-9602694),* 342 Pebble Hill Place, Santa Barbara, CA 93111 Tel 805-967-4630.

R Patterson, *(Patterson, Richard; 0-936004),* 3829 William Penn Blvd., Virginia Beach, VA 23452.

R Picchione, *(Picchione, Richard; 0-9602840),* Box 5534, Reno, NV 89513.

R R Sylvester
See PhD Pub

R Reed, *(Reed, R.),* P.O. Box 1106, Laguna Beach, CA 92652.

R S Barnes, *(Barnes, Richard S., & Co. Books),* 909 Foster St., Evanston, IL 60201 Tel 312-869-2272.

R S Granberg, *(Granberg, Ronald Scott),* c/o Law Distributors, 14415 S. Main St., Gardena, CA 90248.

R S Hart, *(Hart, R. S.),* 6636 Wash. Blvd., Box 53, Elkridge, MD 21227.

R S Hoehler, *(Hoehler, Richard S.; 0-930590),* P.O. Box 240, Conifer, CO 80433 Tel 303-838-4046.

R S Wooley, *(Wooley, Rebecca Smith; 0-9601654),* 1250 S. Fairfield, Chicago, IL 60608.

R Seaver Bks
See Seaver Bks

R Shoemaker, *(Shoemaker, Rhoda; 0-9600474),* 1141 Orange Ave., Menlo Park, CA 94025 Tel 415-854-5768.

R Smith, *(Smith, Ruth; 0-9601182),* Box 327, Cooper Sta., New York, NY 10003 Tel 212-260-4374.

R T Gross, *(Gross, Mrs. Ruth T.),* 1815 Tigertail Ave., Miami, FL 33133.

R T Matthews, *(Matthews, Robert T.; 0-9601150),* 2400 Pfefferkorn Rd., West Friendship, MD 21794.

R Talbert, *(Talbert, Robert),* 260 W. 72nd St., Suite 5D, New York, NY 10023 Tel 212-724-9246.

R Thrift, *(Thrift, Richard),* 108 Clarke Court, Charlottesville, VA 22903.

R Tirtha, *(Tirtha, Ranjit),* Eastern Michigan University, Dept. of Geography, Ypsilanti, MI 48197 Tel 313-487-0218.

R V Boswell, *(Boswell, Roy V.; 0-913278),* P.O. Box 278, Gilroy, CA 95020.

R W Baron, *(Baron, Richard W., Publishing Co.; 0-87777),* Orders to: E. P. Dutton & Co., Inc., 210 Park Ave., S., New York, NY 10003.

W Goll, *(Goll, Reinhold W.),* 1942B Mather Way, Elkins Park, PA 19117.

W Grant, *(Grant, R.W.; 0-9601218),* P.O. Box 2060, Hanover, MA 02339.

West, *(West, Richard; 0-8492; 0-8274),* Box 6404, Philadelphia, PA 19145.

Woodrow, *(Woodrow, Ralph, Evangelistic Assn., Inc.; 0-916938),* Box 124, Riverside, CA 92502 Tel 714-686-5467.

A Corp, *(RA Corp.; 0-934434),* P.O. Box 483, Stanhope, NJ 07874 Tel 201-347-2715.

abinowitz Hebrew Book, *(Rabinowitz, Solomon, Hebrew Book Store, Inc.; 0-87374),* 30 Canal St., New York, NY 10002 Tel 212-267-2406.

acquet Sports, *(Racquet Sports Information Service; 0-914934),* P.O. Box 1710, Easton, MD 21601.

acz Pub, *(Racz Publishing Co.; 0-916546),* P.O. Box 287, Oxnard, CA 93032 Tel 805-642-1186.

ada Pr, *(Rada Press; 0-9604212),* 2297 Folwell, St. Paul, MN 55108.

adatron Corp, *(Radatron Corp.),* P.O. Box 177, North Tonawanda, NY 14120 Tel 716-731-4171.

adical Women, *(Radical Women Pubns.),* 212 E. Martin, Seattle, WA 98102 Tel 206-325-0350.

adio City, *(Radio City Book Store; 0-911202),* 324 W. 47th St., New York, NY 10036 Tel 212-245-5754.

adio Pubns, *(Radio Pubns., Inc.; 0-933616),* Box 149, Wilton, CT 06897 Tel 914-967-5774.

adiofile, *(Radiofile),* c/o Tagliabue, 10 West 66th St., New York, NY 10023.

adix Bks, *(Radix Books Inc.),* P.O. Box 171, Beaver Falls, PA 15010 Tel 412-843-2806.

aemsch Pubns, *(Raemsch Pubns.; 0-9605398),* Box 149, West Oneonta, NY 13861 Tel 607-432-4836.

agan Comm, *(Ragan, Lawrence, Communications, Inc.; 0-931368),* 407 S. Dearborn St., Chicago, IL 60605 Tel 312-922-8245.

agnarok
   See Merging Media

agusan Pr, *(Ragusan Press; 0-918660),* 936 Industrial Ave., Palo Alto, CA 94303 Tel 415-494-1112.

ahamah Pubns, *(Rahamah Pubns.; 0-9603634),* P.O. Box 135, Lowell, MA 01853.

ahmer, *(Rahmer, Frederick A.; 0-9600412),* 723 Crotons St., Rome, NY 13440 Tel 315-337-8245.

Rail-Europe
   See Rail-Europe-Baxter

Rail-Europe-Baxter, *(Rail-Europe/Baxter Guides; 0-913384),* P.O. Box 3255, Alexandria, VA 22302.

Railsearch, *(Railsearch Publishing, Inc.; 0-937060),* P.O. Box 84, Chalfont, PA 18914.

Rainbarrell Artforms, *(Rainbarrell Artforms; 0-934824),* Rte. 2, Box 38, Johnson City, TN 37601 Tel 615-928-9400.

Rainbow-Betty, *(Rainbow Books/Betty Wright),* Dept. 1-H, P.O. Box 1069, Moore Haven, FL 33471 Tel 813-946-0293.

Rainbow Bks, *(Rainbow Books, Inc.; 0-89508),* 675 Dell Rd., Carlstadt, NJ 07072 Tel 201-935-3369.

Rainbow Bridge, *(Rainbow Bridge; 0-914198),* 3548 22nd St., San Francisco, CA 94140 Tel 212-734-3178.

Rainbow Collect, *(Rainbow Collection; 0-935448),* P.O. Box 75, Akron, OH 44309.

Rainbow Pr, *(Rainbow Press),* 425 Riverside Dr., New York, NY 10025 Tel 212-663-2398; Moved, Left No Forwarding Address.

Rainbow Pr CA, *(Rainbow Press, The),* 5901 Warner Ave., Huntington Beach, CA 92649.

Rainbow Pub Co, *(Rainbow Publishing Co.; 0-936218),* P.O. Box 397, Chesterland, OH 44026.

Rainbow WA, *(Rainbow Pubns.; 0-940364),* 1493 S. Columbian Way, Suite 111, Seattle, WA 98144.

Raindance, *(Raindance Press; 0-9605952),* 905 Twelfth Ave. E., Seattle, WA 98102 Tel 206-329-0410; Dist. by: University Bookstore, 4326 University Way, N.E., Seattle, WA 98105.

Rainey Day Or
   See Rainy Day Oreg

Raintree Child, *(Raintree Childrens Books; 0-8172; 0-8393),* Div. of Raintree Publishers Group, 205 W. Highland Ave., Milwaukee, WI 53203 Tel 414-273-0873.

Raintree Pr, *(Raintree Press; 0-913790),* P.O. Box 11799, Chicago, IL 60611 Tel 312-281-2851.

Raintree Pubs, *(Raintree Pubs., Inc.; 0-8172),* 205 W. Highland Ave., Milwaukee, WI 53203 Tel 414-273-0873.

Raintree Pubs Ltd
   See Raintree Pubs

Rainville Rose, *(Rainville Rose Pubns.; 0-938066),* 2505 E. Thousand Oaks Blvd., Suite 266, Thousand Oaks, CA 91360.

Rainy Day Oreg, *(Rainy Day Press; 0-931742),* P.O. Box 3035, Eugene, OR 97403 Tel 503-484-4626.

Rainy Day Pr, *(Rainy Day Press; 0-918796),* Box 471, Sausalito, CA 94965; Dist. by: Bookpeople, 2940 Seventh St., Berkeley, CA 94710 Tel 415-549-3033.

Raja Pr CA, *(Raja Press; 0-9605926),* 5534 Fremont St., Oakland, CA 94608.

Rajah, *(Rajah Press; 0-911204),* P.O. Box 23, Summit, NJ 07901.

Ralston-Pilot, *(Ralston-Pilot, Inc., Pubs.; 0-931116),* 1099 W. Cedar Knolls S.,, Cedar City, UT 84720 Tel 801-586-7395; Moved, Left No Forwarding Address.

Ram Pub, *(Ram Publishing Co.; 0-915920),* P.O. Drawer 38649, Dallas, TX 75238 Tel 214-278-8439.

Ramakrishna, *(Ramakrishna-Vivekananda Center; 0-911206),* 17 E. 94th St., New York, NY 10028 Tel 212-534-9445.

Ramapo Hse, *(Ramapo House),* Div. of Random House, Inc., 201 E. 50th St., New York, NY 10022; Orders to: 457 Hahn Rd., Westminster, MD 21157.

RaMar, *(RaMar Press; 0-935798),* Seven Lakes Box 548, West End, NC 27376 Tel 919-673-0571.

RAMCO Pubns, *(RAMCO Pubns.; 0-939844),* 224 Harding Ave., Libertyville, IL 60048 Tel 312 362 0941.

Ramey Graphics, *(Ramey Graphics, Inc.; 0-914506),* 111 Townsend St., San Francisco, CA 94107 Tel 415-546-0995.

Ramfre, *(Ramfre Press; 0-911208),* 1206 N. Henderson, Cape Girardeau, MO 63701 Tel 314-335-6582.

Rampage Pubs, *(Rampage Pubs.; 0-914690),* 7 West St., Suite 214, Danbury, CT 06810; Dist. by: Hippocrene Books, 171 Madison Ave., New York, NY 10016.

Rampart Hse, *(Rampart House, Ltd.; 0-89773),* 1900 Bank of America Tower, One City Dr., West Orange, CA 92668; Moved, Left No Forwarding Address.

Ramparts, *(Ramparts Press; 0-87867),* P.O. Box 50128, Palo Alto, CA 94303 Tel 415-325-7861.

Rams Head, *(Rams Head, Inc.; 0-915014),* 353 Sacramento St., San Francisco, CA 94111 Tel 415-986-3294.

Rana Hse, *(Rana House; 0-930172),* Box 2997, St. Louis, MO 63130.

RanC *Imprint of* Random

Rancho Santa Ana, *(Rancho Santa Ana Botanic Garden; 0-9605808),* 1500 N. College, Claremont, CA 91711 Tel 714-626-3489.

Ranck, *(Ranck, Joyce H.; 0-9606006),* 1103 Fairacres Rd., Richmond, IN 47374.

Rand, *(Rand McNally & Co.; 0-528),* P.O. Box 7600, Chicago, IL 60680 Tel 312-673-9100.

Rand-Tofua, *(Rand Editions/Tofua Press; 0-914488),* 10457-F Roselle St., San Diego, CA 92121 Tel 714-453-4774.

Randall Hse, *(Randall House Pubns.; 0-89265),* 114 Bush Rd., P.O. Box 17306, Nashville, TN 37217 Tel 615-361-1221.

Randall Pubs, *(Randall Pubs., Inc.; 0-934126),* 462 N. 150 E., Orem, UT 84057; Dist. by: Maher Sales Co., 5180 S. 300 W., Murray, UT 84107 Tel 800-453-6417.

Randen, *(Randen Publishing Co.; 0-918330),* P.O. Box 3157, Culver City, CA 90230 Tel 213-464-0876; Moved, Left No Forwarding Address.

R&M Pub Co, *(R&M Publishing Co.; 0-936026),* P.O. Box 210, Marion, SC 29571 Tel 803-423-6711.

Randolph-Harris, *(Randolph-Harris, Inc.; 0-931666),* 1518 6th St., Berkeley, CA 94710 Tel 415-524-9710.

Randolph Res, *(Randolph Research),* P.O. Box 146, Nebo, NC 28761 Tel 704-652-8150.

Random, *(Random House, Inc.; 0-394),* Random House Publicity (11-6), 201 E. 50th St., New York, NY 10022 Tel 212-751-2600; Orders to: 400 Hahn Rd., Westminster, MD 21157. *Imprints:* BYR (Books for Young Readers); RanC (Random House College Division); Stanyan Bks (Stanyan Books); Vin (Vintage Trade Books); VinC (Vintage College Books).

Random Singer, *(Random House/Singer School Div.),* 201 E. 50th St., New York, NY 10022 Tel 212-572-2521; Orders to: 400 Hahn Rd., Westminster, MD 21157 Tel 800-638-1690.

Ranger Assocs, *(Ranger Assocs., Inc.; 0-934588),* P.O. Box 1357, Manassas, VA 22110 Tel 703-369-5336.

Ranney Pubns, *(Ranney Pubns.),* c/o Ranney Enterprise, 1501 H.N. Tustin Ave., Santa Ana, CA 92701 Tel 714-541-5374.

Ransom Hill, *(Ransom Hill Press; 0-9604342),* P.O. Box 325, Ramona, CA 92065.

Rapides Symphony, *(Rapides Symphony Guild; 0-9603758),* P.O. Box 4172, Alexandria, LA 71301 Tel 318-443-7786.

Rapids Christian, *(Rapids Christian Press, Inc.; 0-915374),* P.O. Box 487, 810 4th Ave., N., Wisconsin Rapids, WI 54494 Tel 715-423-4670.

Rapollo Bks, *(Rapollo Books; 0-9603670),* P.O. Box 1058, La Mesa, CA 92041; Dist. by: Caroline House Publishers, 2 Ellis Place, Ossining, NY 10562.

Raquette Pr, *(Raquette Press; 0-916136),* Star Route, Canton, NY 13617 Tel 315-386-8354.

Rare Repr, *(Rare Reprints, Inc.; 0-89592),* 610 N.E. 124th St., Miami, FL 33161.

Raspberry, *(Raspberry Hill),* P.O. Box 193, Oshtemo, MI 49077.

Rateavers, *(Rateavers; 0-9600698; 0-915966),* Pauma Valley, CA 92061 Tel 714-566-8994.

Rather Pr, *(Rather Press),* 3200 Guido St., Oakland, CA 94602 Tel 415-531-2938.

Rating Pubns, *(Rating Pubns., Inc.; 0-914472),* P.O. Box 342, Murray Hill Sta., New York, NY 10016, Moved,Left No Forwarding Address.

Rational Isl, *(Rational Island Pubs.; 0-911214),* 719 Second Ave. N., Seattle, WA 98109 Tel 206-284-0311; Orders to: P.O. Box 2081, Main Office Sta., Seattle, WA 98111.

Rational Living, *(Institute for Rational Living, Inc.; 0-917476),* 45 E. 65th St., New York, NY 10021 Tel 212-535-0822.

Raven, *(Raven Press, Pubs.; 0-89004),* 1140 Ave. of the Americas, New York, NY 10036 Tel 212-575-0335.

Raven Print, *(Raven Printing Co., Inc.; 0-89023),* 317 S. Beechtree, Grand Haven, MI 49417 Tel 616-842-8841.

Raven Pub Co, *(Raven Publishing Co.),* 911 E. Mahanoy Ave., Mahanoy City, PA 17948 Tel 717-773-1586.

Raven Pubs AKA, *(Raven Pubs. AKA, Inc.),* 425 Stocking, N.W., Grand Rapids, MI 49504 Tel 616-459-3377.

Ravengate Pr, *(Ravengate Press; 0-911218),* P.O. Box 103, Cambridge, MA 02138 Tel 617-456-8181.

Rawson Assocs
   See Rawson Wade

Rawson Wade, *(Rawson, Wade Pubs., Inc.; 0-89256),* 630 Third Ave., New York, NY 10017 Tel 212-867-6610; Dist. by: Atheneum Pubs., 122 E. 42nd St., New York, NY 10017.

Ray Riling, *(Riling, Ray, Arms Books; 0-9603096),* P.O. Box 18925, 6844 Gorsten St., Philadelphia, PA 19119 Tel 215-438-2456.

Raycol Prods, *(Raycol Products; 0-9605176),* 5346 E. 9th St., Tucson, AZ 85711.

Rayes Eclec, *(Raye's Eclectic Craft Yarns, Inc.; 0-9601282),* P.O. Box 2356, 8157 Commercial St., La Mesa, CA 92041 Tel 714-460-0721.

Rayline, *(Rayline Company),* 1413 Edinger, Santa Ana, CA 92705.

RBDH *Imprint of* Kregel

RBX Res, *(RBX Research; 0-917038),* P.O. Box 15, Stanton, TN 38069.

RCA Dist Spec Prods, *(RCA Distributor & Special Products),* Deptford, NJ 08096.

RCA Solid State, *(RCA Solid State Div.; 0-913972),* P.O. Box 3200, Somerville, NJ 08876.

RC&J
   See Reed & Cannon

RCM Pubns, *(RCM Pubns.),* P.O. Box 33565, San Diego, CA 92103.

RCP Pubns, *(RCP Pubns.; 0-89851),* P.O. Box 3486, Merchandise Mart, Chicago, IL 60654 Tel 312-663-5920.

RD Assoc, *(Reader's Digest Assn.; 0-89577),* Dist. by: W. W. Norton & Co., 500 Fifth Ave., New York, NY 10036 Tel 212-354-5500.

RD Comm, *(R D Communications; 0-914138),* P.O. Box 683, Ridgefield, CT 06877 Tel 203-438-3335.

RD Educ Div, *(Reader's Digest Educational Division; 0-88300),* Div. of Reader's Digest Assn., Inc., Reader's Digest Services Inc., Educational Division, Pleasantville, NY 10570 Tel 914-769-7000.

RDC Pubs, *(RDC Pubs.; 0-9600576),* 4741 School St., Yorba Linda, CA 92686 Tel 714-993-3023.

RDIC Pubns, *(Rudolf Dreikurs Institute of Colorado Pubns.; 0-933450),* P.O. Box 3118, Boulder, CO 80307 Tel 303-499-4500.

RE *Imprint of* **WSP**

Re-Entry, *(Re-Entry; 0-9605826),* P.O. Box 13535, Portland, OR 97213 Tel 503-222-6461.

Read Digest, *(Reader's Digest Large-Type Edition),* Reader's Digest Fund for the Blind, Inc., Pleasantville, NY 10570 Tel 914-769-7000; Orders to: W.W. Norton & Company, Inc., 500 Fifth Ave., New York, NY 10036.

Read-Moore Pubns, *(Read-Moore Pubns.),* 340 Ventura St., No. 17, Palo Alto, CA 94306; Moved, Left No Forwarding Address.

Reader Pr, *(Reader Press; 0-911222),* 141 E. 19th St., Brooklyn, NY 11226.

Readers Digest Pr, *(Reader's Digest Press; 0-88349),* 200 Park Ave., New York, NY 10017; Dist. by: McGraw-Hill Book Co., 1221 Ave. of the Americas, New York, NY 10020.

Readers Pr CA, *(Reader's Press; 0-930166),* P.O. Box 3136, Newport Beach, CA 92663 Tel 714-631-4911.

Readex Bks, *(Readex Books; 0-918414),* Div. of Readex Microprint Corp., 101 Fifth Ave., New York, NY 10003 Tel 212-243-3822.

Readex Microprint
See Readex Bks

Reading, *(Reading Perception Centers; 0-918122),* 10375 Los Alamitos Blvd., Los Alamitos, CA 90720 Tel 213-598-0284.

Reading Gems, *(Reading Gems; 0-915988),* P.O. Box 806, Madison, WI 53701.

Reading Hse, *(Reading House, The; 0-9604388),* Box 2975, Seal Beach, CA 90740.

Reading Lab, *(Reading Laboratory, Inc.; 0-86560),* P.O. Box 681, South Norwalk, CT 06856 Tel 203-853-7375.

Readon Pub, *(Readon Publishing; 0-9604638),* P.O. Box 57142, Webster, TX 77598.

Real Comp & Int, *(Real Computers & Intelligence; 0-934190),* P.O. Box 74, Santa Clara, CA 95050 Tel 408-688-0676.

Real Estate Ed Co, *(Real Estate Education Co.; 0-88462),* 500 N. Dearborn St., Chicago, IL 60610 Tel 312-836-4400.

Real Estate Investor, *(Real Estate Investor Information Center, The; 0-939224),* 45 LaSalle Dr., Moraga, CA 94556 Tel 415-376-1362.

Real Estate Pub, *(Real Estate Publishing Co.; 0-914256),* P.O. Box 41177, Sacramento, CA 95841 Tel 916-677-3864.

Real People, *(Real People Press; 0-911226),* P.O. Box F, Moab, UT 84532 Tel 801-259-7578.

Real World, *(Real World Pubns.; 0-931204),* P.O. Box 176, Niwot, CO 80544; Dist. by: Caroline House, P.O. Box 161, Thornwood, NY 10594.

Realities, *(Realities Library; 0-916982),* 1976 Waverly Ave., San Jose, CA 95122 Tel 408-251-9562.

Realtors Natl, *(Realtors National Marketing Institute; 0-913652),* 430 Michigan Ave., Chicago, IL 60611 Tel 312-440-8514.

Realty Train, *(Realty Training Service Co.; 0-89493),* Elseden Bldg.-Tanner's Lane, Florence, KY 41042 Tel 606-525-8005.

Realvest Pub Co, *(Realvest Publishing Co.; 0-933928),* Div. of Charter Management Associates, Inc., 79 S. Pleasant St., Amherst, MA 01002 Tel 413-253-2554.

Rechs Pubns, *(Rechs Pubns.; 0-937568),* 8157 Madison Ave., South Gate, CA 90280.

Recipes-of-the-Month, *(Recipes-of-the Month Club; 0-930440),* P.O. Box 5027, Beverly Hills, CA 90210 Tel 213-277-7220.

Recipes Unltd, *(Recipes Unlimited, Inc.; 0-918620),* P.O. Box 1202, Burnsville, MN 55337 Tel 612-890-6655.

Recon Pubns, *(Recon Pubns.; 0-916894),* P.O. Box 14602, Philadelphia, PA 19134.

Reconciliation, *(Reconciliation Associates; 0-932270),* 42 Englewood Ave., Brookline, MA 02146 Tel 617-566-6815.

Record, *(Record Publishing Co., The),* 1648 N. Wilcox Ave., Hollywood, CA 90028.

Record Research, *(Record Research Inc.; 0-89820),* P.O. Box 200, Menomonee Falls, WI 53051; Dist. by: Gale Research Co., Book Tower, Detroit, MI 48226 Tel 313-961-2242.

Recorded Sound, *(Recorded Sound Research; 0-916262),* 1627 Moody Court, Peoria, IL 61604 Tel 309-674-2008.

Red Alder, *(Red Alder Books; 0-914906),* 903 Laurel St., Santa Cruz, CA 95060 Tel 408-429-9299; Moved, Left No Forwarding Address.

Red Cedar, *(Red Cedar Press; 0-937190),* English Dept., Michigan State Univ., East Lansing, MI 48824 Tel 517-351-4313; Dist. by: Stone Press, 1790 Grand River, Okemos, MI 48864 Tel 517-349-0552.

Red Clay, *(Red Clay Books; 0-911692),* 6366 Sharon Hills Rd., Charlotte, NC 28210 Tel 704-366-9624.

Red Dust, *(Red Dust Inc.; 0-87376),* P.O. Box 630, Gracie Sta., New York, NY 10028 Tel 212-348-4388.

Red Earth, *(Red Earth Press; 0-918434),* P.O. Box 26641, Albuquerque, NM 87125 Tel 505-268-3077; Formerly Named Yarbrough Mountain Press.

Red Feather, *(Red Feather Pubs.; 0-936430),* P.O. Drawer 2007, Lubbock, TX 79408 Tel 806-741-7075.

Red Haw Pr, *(Red Haw Press; 0-918904),* P.O. Box 436, La Jolla, CA 92038.

Red Herring, *(Red Herring Press; 0-932884),* 1209 W. Oregon, Urbana, IL 61801 Tel 217-344-1176.

Red Hill, *(Red Hill),* 6 San Gabriel Dr., Fairfax, CA 94930.

Red Ink, *(Red Ink Productions; 0-9605590),* 270 Lafayette St., New York, NY 10012.

Red Mtn, *(Red Mountain Editions; 0-911234),* 1314 34th Ave., San Francisco, CA 94122 Tel 415-665-5517.

Red River, *(Red River Press; 0-938898),* 4806 Danberry, Wichita Falls, TX 76308.

Red Rose Studio, *(Red Rose Studio; 0-932514),* 358 Flintlock Dr., Willow Street, PA 17584.

Red Studio, *(Red Studio Press; 0-916320),* 200 22nd Ave. S., Minneapolis, MN 55454 Tel 612-339-2042.

Red Sun Pr, *(Red Sun Press; 0-932728),* 51 Bristol St., Boston, MA 02118 Tel 617-542-4821.

Redcor Bk, *(Redcor Book Publishing Co.; 0-939588),* 501 W. Port Royale Lane, Phoenix, AZ 85023 Tel 602-863-1415.

Reddy Comm, *(Reddy Communications, Inc.; 0-9603716),* 537 Steamboat Rd., Greenwich, CT 06830 Tel 203-661-4800.

Redgold, *(Redgold, Inc.; 0-932234),* 1333 Howe Ave., Suite 100, Sacramento, CA 95825 Tel 916-366-1356.

Redgrave Info, *(Redgrave Information Resources Corp.; 0-88276),* P.O. Box 408, 3 Sylvan Rd. S., Westport, CT 06880 Tel 203-226-9523; Moved, Left No Forwarding Address.

Redgrave Pub Co, *(Redgrave Publishing Co.; 0-913178),* Div. of Docent Corp., 430 Manville Rd., Pleasantville, NY 10570 Tel 914-769-3629.

Redwood, *(Redwood Pubs.; 0-917928),* P.O. Box 7424, Menlo Park, CA 94025 Tel 415-854-3723; Do Not Confuse with Redwood Publishing Co. in San Luis Obispo, CA.

Redwood Pub Co, *(Redwood Publishing Co.; 0-937316),* 3860 S. Niguera, Space 105, San Luis Obispo, CA 93401; Do Not Confuse with Redwood Publishers in Menlo Park, CA.

Reebie Assoc, *(Reebie Associates, Inc.; 0-9604776),* P.O. Box 1278, Greenwich, CT 06830 Tel 203-661-8661.

Reed & Cannon, *(Reed & Cannon Co.; 0-918408),* 2140 Shattuck Ave., Rm. 311, Berkeley, CA 94704 Tel 415-527-1586.

Reed Bks, *(Reed Books; 0-89169),* Subs. of Addison House, c/o Addison House, Morgan's Run, Danbury, NH 03230 Tel 603-768-3903.

Reed Pubs, *(Reed Pubs.; 0-917064),* P. O. Box 10667, 4999 Kahala Ave., Honolulu, HI 96816 Tel 808-732-1515.

Reef Dwellers, *(Reef Dwellers Press; 0-96025,* Jenkintown Plaza, Jenkintown, PA 19046 Tel 215-887-6700; Orders to: Bryn Athyn PA 19009.

Reel Res, *(Reel Research),* P.O. Box 6037, Albany, CA 94706 Tel 415-549-0923.

Reel Trophy, *(Reel Trophy Pubns.),* P.O. Box 19085, Portland, OR 97219 Tel 503-245-2424.

Ref Bks, *(Reference Books Inc.; 0-933618),* P. Box 7866, Chicago, IL 60680 Tel 312-248-9251.

Ref Dev Corp, *(Reference Development Corp.)* P.O. Box 2331, Princeton, NJ 08540.

Ref Guides, *(Reference Guides; 0-939228),* Rt 2, Box 162, Detroit, TX 75436 Tel 214-674-5403.

Ref Pubns, *(Reference Pubns., Inc.; 0-917256),* Box 344, 218 St. Clair River Dr., Algonac, MI 48001 Tel 313-794-5722.

Ref Serv Pr, *(Reference Service Press; 0-918276),* 9023 Alcott, Suite 201, Los Angeles, CA 90035 Tel 213-271-1955.

Reference Bk Pubs *Imprint of* **Kelley**

Reformation Res, *(Reformation Research Press Inc.; 0-936592),* P.O. Box 4302, Springfiel MO 65804.

Reformed Church, *(Reformed Church Press, Reformed Church in America; 0-916466),* 475 Riverside Dr., 18th Fl., New York, NY 10027 Tel 212-870-3020.

Reg Baptist, *(Regular Baptist Press; 0-87227),* 1300 N. Meacham Rd., P.O. Box 95500, Schaumburg, IL 60195 Tel 312-843-1600.

Regal, *(Regal Books),* Div. of G/L Pubns., P.O Box 3875, Ventura, CA 93006 Tel 805-644-6869.

Regal Am Mktg, *(Regal American Marketing Corp.),* 2725 Valley View Lane, Suite 102, Dallas, TX 75232.

Regal Pub Co, *(Regal Publishing Co.; 0-9604598),* P.O. Box 76846, Atlanta, GA 30328.

Regenbogen-Verlag, *(Regenbogen-Verlag),* Box 6214, Silver Spring, MD 20906 Tel 301-933-8521.

Regency Pr, *(Regency Press; 0-933324),* 32 Ridge Dr., Port Washington, NY 11050 Tel 516-935-1143.

Regency Pubs CA, *(Regency Pubs., Inc.; 0-937554),* 2213 Liadero Canyon Rd., Suite 101, Westlake Village, CA 91361.

Regent Graphic Serv, *(Regent Graphic Services 0-912710),* P.O. Box 8372, Swissvale, PA 15218 Tel 412-371-7128.

Regent House, *(Regent House; 0-911238),* 108 N. Roselake Ave., Los Angeles, CA 90026 Tel 213-413-5027.

Regents Pr KS, *(Regents Press of Kansas; 0-7006),* 303 Carruth-O'leary, Lawrence, K 66045 Tel 913-864-4154.

Regents Pub, *(Regents Publishing Co., Inc.; 0-88345),* Div. of Hachette, 2 Park Ave., New York, NY 10016 Tel 212-889-2780.

REGIF, *(REGIF),* Dist. by: Marlin Pubns. International, Inc., 485 Fifth Ave., New York, NY 10017.

Regina Bk Serv, *(Regina Book Service),* 33 Regina Rd., Monsey, NY 10952.

Regina Pr, *(Regina Press, Malhame & Co.; 0-88271),* 7 Midland Ave., Hicksville, NY 11801 Tel 516-681-7474.

Regina Pub Hse
See Fintzenberg

Regional, *(Regional Publishing Co.),* Affiliate o Genealogical Publishing Co., 111 Water St., Baltimore, MD 21202 Tel 301-837-8271.

Regional Ctr Educ, *(Regional Center for Educational Training; 0-915892),* 45 Lyme Rd., Hanover, NH 03755 Tel 603-643-5660

Regmar Pub, *(Regmar Publishing Co., Inc.; 0-914338),* P.O. Box 11358, Memphis, TN 38117 Tel 901-323-7442.

Regnery
See Contemp Bks

Regnery, *(Regnery, Henry, Co.),* ; Publisher Abbreviation Without Addresses Are for Titles That Are Out of Print. These Are Obsolete Abbreviations. Publisher's Abbreviation Is Now Contemp Bks.

Regnery-Gateway, *(Regnery/Gateway, Inc.; 0-89526),* 116 S. Michigan, Suite 300, Chicago, IL 60603 Tel 312-346-6646.

Rehab Intl, *(Rehabilitation International; 0-9605554),* 432 Park Ave. S., New York, NY 10016.

REI, *(Religion & Ethics Institute; 0-914384),* P.O. Box 664, Evanston, IL 60204 Tel 312-328-4049.

Reidel Pub, *(Reidel, D., Publishing Co.),* ; Publisher Abbreviation Without Addresses Are for Titles That Are Out of Print. These Are Obsolete Abbreviations. Publisher's Abbreviaton Is Now Kluwer Boston.

Reidel Pub
See Kluwer Boston

Reidmore Bks, *(Reidmore Books Oregon; 0-939284),* P.O. Box 2598, Eugene, OR 97402.

Reiff Pr, *(Reiff Press; 0-911246),* 160 Mt. Holly Rd., Amelia, OH 45102 Tel 513-753-5278.

Reilly & Lee
See Contemp Bks

Reilly & Lee, *(Reilly & Lee Co.; 0-8092),* Dist. by: Henry Regnery Co., 180 N. Michigan Ave., Chicago, IL 60601; Acquired by Henry Regnery.

Reiman Assocs, *(Reiman Associates; 0-89821),* 733 N. Van Buren, Milwaukee, WI 53202 Tel 414-272-5410; Orders to: 611 E. Wells St., Milwaukee, WI 53202.

Reiner, *(Reiner Pubns; 0-87377),* Swengel, PA 17880 Tel 717-922-3213.

Reinhold, *(Reinhold Publishing Corp.),* ; Publisher Abbreviation Without Addresses Are for Titles That Are Out of Print. These Are Obsolete Abbreviations. Publisher's Abbreviation Is Now Van Nos Reinhold.

Reiss Pub, *(Reiss Pub.; 0-89515),* Subs. of National Paragon Corp., 230 Fifth Ave., New York, NY 10001 Tel 212-679-2440; Dist. by: E. P. Dutton Co., 201 Park Ave., S., New York, NY 10003 Tel 212-674-5900.

Rekalb Pr, *(Rekalb Press; 0-9604614),* 6203 Jane Lane, Columbus, GA 31904 Tel 404-324-1392.

Release, *(Release Press; 0-913722),* 478 Seventh St., Brooklyn, NY 11215; Moved, Left No Forwarding Address.

Relevant Pub, *(Relevant Pubns., Ltd.),* 14241 Mango, Del Mar, CA 92014.

Relex, *(Relex, Inc.; 0-89149),* Dist. by: J. Philip O'hara Inc., 20 E. Huron, Chicago, IL 60611; Moved, Left No Forwarding Address.

Reliance Pub, *(Reliance Publishing Co.; 0-937740),* 380 Steinwehr Ave., Gettysburg, PA 17325 Tel 717-334-1103.

Religion & Ethics
See REI

Religious Activ, *(Religious Activities Press),* Rte. 2, Box 343, Mt. Juliet, TN 37122.

Religious Educ, *(Religious Education Press, Inc.; 0-89135),* 1531 Wellington Rd., Birmingham, AL 35209 Tel 205-879-4040.

Religious Pub, *(Religious Publishing Co.; 0-916138),* 198 Allendale Rd., King of Prussia, PA 19406 Tel 215-265-9400.

Religious Writers, *(Religious Writers' Agency),* 908 N. Nottawa St., Sturgis, MI 49091.

Relot
See Toler

Remarkable Pubns, *(Remarkable Pubns.; 0-9605346),* 8005 Bleriot Ave., Westchester, CA 90045.

Renaissance Bks, *(Renaissance Books; 0-932476),* 834 N. Plankinton Ave., Milwaukee, WI 53203 Tel 414-271-6850.

Renaissance Pubs, *(Renaissance Pubs.; 0-916560),* 2485 N.E 214th St., N. Miami Beach, FL 33180 Tel 305-931-3392.

Renaissance Soc Am, *(Renaissance Society of America),* 1161 Amsterdam Ave., New York, NY 10027 Tel 212-280-2318.

Renay, *(Renay Publishing Co.; 0-911250),* P.O. Box 22, Tarzana, CA 91356 Tel 213-887-9111.

Renfro Studios, *(Renfro, Nancy, Studios; 0-931044),* 1117 W. 9th St., Austin, TX 78703 Tel 512-472-2140.

Renouf, *(Renouf USA, Inc.; 0-604),* Old Post Rd., Brookfield, VT 05036 Tel 802-276-3355.

Reprint, *(Reprint Co.; 0-87152),* P.O. Box 5401, 601 Hillcrest Offices, Spartanburg, SC 29304 Tel 803-582-0732.

Res Adv Serv, *(Research Advisory Services, Pubns., Inc.; 0-931602),* P.O. Box 8151, 286 N. McCarrons Blvd., St. Paul, MN 55113.

Res & Educ, *(Research & Education Assn.; 0-87891),* 505 Eighth Ave., New York, NY 10018 Tel 212-695-9487.

Res Cosmobiol
See Darin Devel

Res Ctr Kabbalah, *(Research Centre of Kabbalah),* 200 Park Ave., Suite 303 E., New York, NY 10017 Tel 212-986-2515; Moved, Left No Forwarding Address.

Res Ctr Lang Semiotic, *(Research Center for Language & Semiotic Studies; 0-87750),* Dist. by: Humanities Press, Inc., Atlantic Highlands, NJ 07716.

Res Media
See CAS

Res Press, *(Research Press Co.; 0-87822),* Box 3177, Champaign, IL 61820 Tel 217-352-3273.

Res Publs, *(Research Pubs.; 0-911252),* 108 S. Patton, Arlington Heights, IL 60005 Tel 312-255-1961.

Res Pubns Conn, *(Research Pubns., Inc.; 0-89235),* 12 Lunar Dr., Woodbridge, CT 06525 Tel 203-397-2600.

Res Pubns WA, *(Researcher Pubns., Inc.; 0-938428),* 18806-40th Ave., W., Lynnwood, WA 98036.

Res Serv, *(Research Service; 0-911256),* 353 W. 57th St., New York, NY 10019 Tel 212-265-6100.

Res Stud Pr, *(Research Studies Press, Inc.; 0-89355),* c/o John Wiley & Sons, 605 Third Ave., New York, NY 10158 Tel 212-850-6418.

Research, *(Research; 0-930442),* 2444 Charlemagne Ave., Long Beach, CA 90815 Tel 213-597-3718.

Research Pubns, *(Research Pubns.; 0-9600478),* P.O. Box 801, Glen Rock, NJ 07452.

Research Servs Corp, *(Research Services Corp.; 0-915074),* P.O. Box 16549, Fort Worth, TX 76133 Tel 817-292-4272.

Resolute Pr, *(Resolute Press; 0-9604382),* 13 Regent Court, Edison, NJ 08817.

Resource Pubns, *(Resource Pubns.; 0-89390),* P.O. Box 444, Saratoga, CA 95070 Tel 408-252-4195.

Resources, *(Resources; 0-933342),* P.O. Box 134, Harvard Sq., Cambridge, MA 02138.

Resources Future, *(Resources for the Future),* Johns Hopkins Univ. Press, Baltimore, MD 21218.

Responsible Action
See Intl Dialogue Pr

Reston, *(Reston Publishing Co., Inc.; 0-87909; 0-8359),* 11480 Sunset Hills Rd., Reston, VA 22090 Tel 703-437-8900; Dist. by: Prentice-Hall, Inc., Englewood Cliffs, NJ 07632.

Resurgens Pubns, *(Resurgens Pubns., Inc.; 0-89583),* P.O. Box 49321, Atlanta, GA 30329 Tel 404-834-1343.

Retail Group
See Nature Life

Retail Report, *(Retail Reporting Bureau; 0-934590),* 101 Fifth Ave., New York, NY 10003 Tel 212-255-9595.

Retirement Res, *(Retirement Research),* Box 401, Appleton, WI 54912 Tel 414-734-6610.

Retriever, *(Retriever Books; 0-9604628),* 250 W. 87th St., New York, NY 10024 Tel 212-874-5579.

Reveal Pubns, *(Reveal Pubns.; 0-9602536),* 2208 Woodlawn St., Kannapolis, NC 28081 Tel 704-932-3476.

Revelation Hse, *(Revelation House Pubs., Inc.; 0-9604852),* P.O. Box 73175, Metairie, LA 70033.

Revell, *(Revell, Fleming H., Co.; 0-8007),* 184 Central Ave., Old Tappan, NJ 07675 Tel 201-768-8060.

Reverchon Pr, *(Reverchon Press; 0-9601902),* P.O. Box 19647, Dallas, TX 75219 Tel 214-528-6540.

Review & Herald, *(Review & Herald Publishing Assn.; 0-8280),* 6856 Eastern Ave. NW, Washington, DC 20012 Tel 202-723-3700.

Reviewer, *(Reviewer, The),* 2197 Berkeley, Salt Lake City, UT 84109.

Revisionary, *(Revisionary Press; 0-9603726),* Box 158A, St. James, NY 11780 Tel 516-862-9296.

Revisionist Pr, *(Revisionist Press; 0-87700),* P.O. Box 2009, Brooklyn, NY 11202.

Reward *Imprint of* **P-H**

Reymont, *(Reymont Associates; 0-918734),* 29 Reymont Ave., Rye, NY 10580 Tel 914-967-8185.

Reyn Pub Co., *(Reyn Publishing Co.; 0-936366),* 14240 E. 14th St., San Leandro, CA 94578.

Reynal, *(Reynal & Co.; 0-688),* 105 Madison Ave., New York, NY 10016 Tel 212-889-3050; Dist. by: William Morrow & Co., Order Dept., 6 Henderson Dr., West Caldwell, NJ 07006.

Reynard Hse, *(Reynard House; 0-932998),* 5706 30th NE, Seattle, WA 98105.

Reynolds Morse, *(Reynolds Morse Foundation; 0-934236),* 21709 Chagrin Blvd., Cleveland, OH 44122; Dist. by: LDS Books, P.O. Box 67, MCS, Dayton, OH 45402.

Rhineburgh Pr, *(Rhineburgh Press Inc.; 0-9604746),* 595 Madison Ave., New York, NY 10022 Tel 212-355-0162.

Rhinoceros Pr, *(Rhinoceros Press; 0-931376),* Box 1186, El Cerrito, CA 94930.

Rhinos Pr, *(Rhino's Press, The; 0-937382),* 25382 Spotted Pony, Laguna Hills, CA 92653.

Rho-Delta Pr, *(Rho-Delta Press; 0-913770),* 8831 Sunset Blvd., Suite 203, P.O. Box 69540, Los Angeles, CA 90069 Tel 213-657-1925.

Rhodes Geo Lib, *(Rhodes Geographic Library, Inc.; 0-933768),* 3225 Rum Row, Naples, FL 33940 Tel 813-262-6713.

RHS Bk Assn, *(R. H. S. Book Assn. to Assist Poverty-Stricken Americans),* 1017 Park St., Lorned, KS 67550.

RI Bicentennial
See RI Pubns Soc

RI Genealogical, *(Rhode Island Genealogical Society; 0-9604144),* 128 Massasoit Dr., Warwick, RI 02888.

RI Hist Soc, *(Rhode Island Historical Society; 0-932840),* 52 Power St., Providence, RI 02906 Tel 401-331-8575.

RI Mayflower, *(Rhode Island Mayflower Society; 0-930272),* 128 Massasoit Dr., Warwick, RI 02888 Tel 401-781-6759.

RI Pubns Soc, *(Rhode Island Pubns. Society; 0-917012),* Old State House, 150 Benefit St., Providence, RI 02903 Tel 401-272-1776.

Rice Univ, *(Rice University Studies; 0-89263),* History Dept., Houston, TX 77001 Tel 713-527-8101; Orders to: Rice Campus Store, P.O. Box 1892, Houston, TX 77001.

Rich-Errington, *(Rich-Errington; 0-915898),* P.O. Box 546, Bay City, MI 48706 Tel 517-893-6730.

Rich Pub, *(Rich Publishing, Inc.),* P.O. Box 555, Temecula, CA 92390 Tel 714-676-5712.

Rich SC, *(Rich Pubs.),* P.O. Box 1185, Clemson, SC 29631 Tel 803-654-2507.

Richards Hse, *(Richards House-FACTS; 0-930702),* P.O. Box 208, Wellesley Hills, MA 02181 Tel 617-235-2152.

Richards Pub, *(Richards, Frank E., Publishing Co., Inc.; 0-88323),* P.O. Box 66, Phoenix, NY 13135 Tel 315-695-7261.

Richboro Pr, *(Richboro Press; 0-89713),* Box 1, Richboro, PA 18954.

Richmond Cty Hist Soc, *(Richmond County Historical Society),* c/o Reese Library, Augusta College, 2500 Walton Way, Augusta, GA 30904 Tel 404-828-4566.

Richwood Pub, *(Richwood Pub., Co.; 0-915172),* P.O. Box 381, Scarsdale, NY 10583 Tel 914-723-1286.

Ricwalt Pub Co, *(Ricwalt Publishing Co.; 0-933054),* C-3 Bldg., Rm. 110, Fishermen's Terminal, Seattle, WA 98119 Tel 206-282-7545.

Rider *Imprint of* **Hayden**

Ridge Hse, *(Ridge House Press),* Box 600, Hayden Lake, ID 83835.

Ridgefield Pub, *(Ridgefield Publishing Co.),* 18411 Hatteras St., No. 228, Tarzana, CA 91356.

Ridgeview, *(Ridgeview Publishing Co.; 0-917930),* Box 686, Atascadero, CA 93422 Tel 805-466-7252.

Ridgeview Jr High Pr, *(Ridgeview Junior High Press; 0-936920),* 9424 Highlander Court, Walkersville, MD 21793.

Ridgeway Bks, *(Ridgeway Books),* P. O. Box 6431, Philadelphia, PA 19145.

RIFD, *(Registry of Interpreters for the Deaf, Inc.; 0-9602220),* 814 Thayer Ave., Silver Spring, MD 20910.

Rigel, *(Rigel, Inc.; 0-937234),* 2644 Capitol Trail, Newark, DE 19711.

Riggers Bible, *(Riggers Bible; 0-9600992),* P.O. Box 3302, Glenstone Sta., Springfield, MO 65804 Tel 417-869-9236.

Right White Line, *(Right White Line; 0-918926),* 531 N. Inlet, Lincoln City, OR 97367 Tel 503-994-8433; Moved, Left No Forwarding Address.

RIM, *(Relevant Instructional Materials; 0-89550),* P.O. Box 794, Stockton, CA 95201 Tel 209-465-1880.

Rinehart, *(Holt, Rinehart & Winston),* ; Publisher Abbreviation Without Addresses Are for Titles That Are Out of Print. These Are Obsolete Abbreviations. Publisher's Abbreviation Is Now Hr&W.

Ringling Mus Art, *(John & Mable Ringling Museum of Art Foundation; 0-916758),* 5401 Bayshore Rd., Sarasota, FL 33578 Tel 813-355-5101.

Rio Grande, *(Rio Grande Press, Inc.; 0-87380),* P.O. Box 33, Glorieta, NM 87535 Tel 505-757-6275.

Rio Grande Pub, *(Rio Grande Publishing Co.),* 3315 Stanford Dr., N.E, Albuquerque, NM 87107.

Rip off, *(Rip off Press; 0-89620),* P.O. Box 14158, San Francisco, CA 94114 Tel 415-863-5359.

Risale i Nur Inst, *(Risale i Nur Institute of America; 0-933552),* 2506 Shattuck Ave., Berkeley, CA 94704 Tel 415-845-4355.

Rising Star, *(Rising Star Press; 0-933670),* 557 Wellington Ave., San Carlos, CA 94070 Tel 415-592-2459.

Rising Wolf, *(Rising Wolf Inc.; 0-936710),* 240 N. Higgins, No. 4, Missoula, MT 59801.

Risk Analysis, *(Risk Analysis & Research Corp.; 0-932056),* 50 California St., Fifth Floor, San Francisco, CA 94111 Tel 415-433-1676.

Risk & Ins, *(Risk & Insurance Mgt. Society, Inc.; 0-937802),* 205 E. 42nd St., New York, NY 10017.

Risk Ent, *(Risk Enterprises),* P.O. Box 4056, University Sta., Laramie, WY 82071.

RIT Graph Arts Res
See Graph Arts Res RIT

Ritchie, *(Ritchie, Ward, Press; 0-378),* 474 S. Arroyo Pkwy., Pasadena, CA 91105 Tel 213-793-1163.

Ritger Sports, *(Ritger Sports Co.; 0-933554),* P.O. Box 1321, Tempe, AZ 85281 Tel 602-838-3974.

Rittenhouse, *(Rittenhouse Book Distributors; 0-87381),* 511 Feheley Dr., King of Prussia, PA 19406 Tel 215-277-1414.

RivEd *Imprint of* **HM**

River Basin, *(River Basin Publishing Co.; 0-936106),* P.O. Box 30573, St. Paul, MN 55175 Tel 612-291-7470.

River Bend, *(River Bend Publishing; 0-9605162),* 905 Leroy St., Muscatine, IA 52761.

River Falls, *(River Falls Univ. Press),* 113 E. Hathorn, River Falls, WI 54022 Tel 715-425-3100.

River Hse, *(River House),* 2213 Pennington Bend, Nashville, TN 37214.

Rivercity Pr, *(Rivercity Press),* Rivercity, MA 01337.

Riverhouse Pubns, *(Riverhouse Pubns.; 0-933258),* 20 Waterside Plaza, New York, NY 10010 Tel 212-685-2376; c/o Harvey House, 128 W. River St., Chippewa Fall, WI 54792 Tel 715-723-2814.

Riverrun Calif, *(Riverrun Press; 0-916942),* 219 Hartford St., San Francisco, CA 94114 Tel 415-658-5785.

Riverrun NY, *(Riverrun Press Inc.; 0-7145),* 175 Fifth Ave., Suite 814, New York, NY 10010 Tel 212-228-0390.

Riverrun Pr, *(Riverrun Press),* 111 Hasell St., Hillsborough, NC 27278 Tel 919-732-4875; Moved, Left No Forwarding Address.

Riverrun Texas
See Riverrun NY

Riverside Pub Co, *(Riverside Publishing Co.; 0-8292),* Subs. of Houghton-Mifflin Co., P.O. Box 1970, Iowa City, IA 52244 Tel 319-354-5104; Orders to: 1919 S. Highland Ave., Lombard, IL 60148 Tel 312-629-9700.

Riverstone, *(Riverstone Press; 0-9601130),* Coach House, 2107 N. Kenmore, Chicago, IL 60614 Tel 312-248-2153.

Riverstone Foothills, *(Riverstone Press of the Foothills Art Center; 0-936600),* 809 15th St., Golden, CO 80401.

Riverwood Pubs, *(Riverwood Pubs., Ltd.; 0-914762),* 1365 York Ave., Suite 34D, New York, NY 10021 Tel 212-737-9304; Dist. by: E.P. Dutton & Co., Inc., 201 Park Ave., S., New York, NY 10003.

RivLit *Imprint of* **HM**

RivSL *Imprint of* **HM**

Rizzoli Intl, *(Rizzoli International Pubns., Inc.; 0-8478),* 712 Fifth Ave., New York, NY 10019 Tel 212-397-3740.

RJ Assocs, *(R/J Associates; 0-9602090),* 564 Tyler Ave., Livermore, CA 94550 Tel 415-443-7140.

RJR Pr
See Utopian Universe

RK Edns, *(RK Editions; 0-932360),* P.O. Box 73, Canal St., New York, NY 10013.

RMP Finan Consul, *(RMP Financial Consultants; 0-931664),* 10 Petit Bayou Lane, New Orleans, LA 70129 Tel 504-254-2766.

RMP Inc, *(RMP Inc. Pubs.),* P.O. Box 36679, Los Angeles, CA 90036.

RMS Pub Co, *(RMS Publishing Co.; 0-9601686),* P.O. Box 227, Hanover, MD 21076.

Roadrunner Tech, *(Roadrunner-Technical Pubns., Inc.; 0-89741),* Div. of Desert Laboratories, Inc., 3136 E. Columbia St., Tucson, AZ 85714 Tel 602-294-3431.

Roan Horse, *(Roan Horse Press; 0-933234),* 11 Silverweed Court, Pueblo, CO 81001.

Roan Pr, *(Roan Press; 0-935546),* P.O. Box 785, Pearl River, NY 10965 Tel 914-735-8805.

Roark Pubns, *(Roark Pubns.; 0-939546),* P.O. Box 5973-325, Sherman Oaks, CA 91413 Tel 213-784-7421.

Roberson Ctr, *(Roberson Center for the Arts & Sciences; 0-937318),* 30 Front St., Binghamton, NY 13905 Tel 607-772-0660.

Roberts Ent, *(Roberts Enterprises; 0-9604184),* 6322 N. Barcelona Lane, No. 516, Tucson, AZ 85704.

Roberts Pub, *(Roberts Publishing Corp.; 0-936492),* 45 John St., New York, NY 10038 Tel 212-233-3768.

Robertson, *(Robertson, Donald W.),* Star Rte. 2, Box 216, Canyon Lake, TX 78130 Tel 512-935-2172.

Robin & Russ, *(Robin & Russ Handweavers),* 533 N. Adams St., McMinnville, OR 97128 Tel 503-472-5760.

Robinson Bks, *(Robinson, Ruth E., Books; 0-9603556),* Rte. 7, Box 162A, Morgantown, WV 26505.

Robotics Pr, *(Robotics Press; 0-89661),* 30 NW 23rd Place, Portland, OR 97210 Tel 503-243-1158; Orders to: P.O. Box 606, Beaverton, OR 97075.

Rochester Folk Art, *(Rochester Folk Art Guild),* Rte. 1, Box 10, Middlesex, NY 14507 Tel 716-554-3539.

Rock Guitar, *(Rock Guitarists),* Dist. by: Book People, 2940 Seventh St., Berkeley, CA 94710.

Rock Harbor, *(Rock Harbor Press; 0-932260),* P.O. Box 1206, Hyannis, MA 02601.

Rock Pub, *(Rock Publishing Co.; 0-9601804),* 3667 San Pascual Ave., Las Vegas, NV 89110.

Rock Spring, *(Rock Spring Pubns.),* 610 South View Terrace, Alexandria, VA 22314 Tel 703-536-8339.

Rockdale Ridge, *(Rockdale Ridge Press; 0-9602338),* 8501 Ridge Rd., Cincinnati, OH 45236 Tel 513-891-9900.

Rockefeller, *(Rockefeller Univ. Press; 0-87470),* 1230 York Ave., Box 291, New York, NY 10021 Tel 212-360-1217; Orders to: Box 269, 1230 York Ave., New York, NY 10021 Tel 212-360-1367.

Rocket Pub Co, *(Rocket Publishing Co.),* P.O. Box 42, Normangee, TX 77871 Tel 713-828-4265.

Rocketlab, *(Rocketlab; 0-9600198),* P.O. Box 1139, Florence, OR 97439 Tel 503-997-8940.

Rockets, *(Rockets; 0-912468),* P.O. Box 591, Corona, CA 91720 Tel 714-735-0169.

Rockfall Pr, *(Rockfall Press; 0-9601502),* Cider Mill Rd., Rockfall, CT 06481.

Rocking Chair Pr, *(Rocking Chair Press, Inc.; 0-913562),* 2109 Queenswood Dr., Tallahassee, FL 32303.

Rocking Horse, *(Rocking Horse Press; 0-932306),* 32 Ellise Rd., Storrs, CT 06268 Tel 203-429-1474.

Rockland County Hist, *(Historical Society of Rockland County),* 20 Zukor Rd., New York, NY 10956.

Rockport Pubns, *(Rockport Pubns; 0-936220),* P.O. Box 2787, Newport Beach, CA 92663 Tel 714-646-9481.

Rockwell, *(Rockwell Pubns.; 0-913208),* 60 N. Monterey St., Mobile, AL 36604 Tel 205-471-5276; Formerly Named Thomas-Hull.

Rocky Mtn Arms
See Best Antiques

Rocky Mtn Bks, *(Rocky Mountain Books),* P.C Box 10663, Denver, CO 80210.

Rocky Mtn Pr, *(Rocky Mountain Press; 0-9603386),* 2754 Mariquita St., Long Beach, CA 90803.

ROCOM, *(ROCOM Press; 0-89119),* Nutley, NJ 07110; Orders to: 1 Sunset Ave., Montclair, NJ 07042.

Rod & Staff, *(Rod & Staff Pubs., Inc.),* Crocket KY 41413 Tel 606-522-4348.

Rodale, *(Rodale Books, Inc.; 0-87596),* 33 E. Minor St., Emmaus, PA 18049 Tel 215-967-5171.

Rodale Pr Inc, *(Rodale Press, Inc.; 0-87857),* 3 E. Minor St., Emmaus, PA 18049 Tel 215-967-5171.

Rodney, *(Rodney Pubns., Inc.; 0-913830),* 349 E. 49th St., New York, NY 10017 Tel 212-421-5444.

Roehrs, *(Roehrs Co.; 0-911266),* P.O. Box 125, 227A Paterson Ave., East Rutherford, NJ 07073 Tel 201-939-0090.

Rogers Bk, *(Rogers Book Service; 0-911268),* 217 W. 18th St, Box V, New York, NY 10011.

Rogers Hse Mus, *(Rogers House Museum Gallery; 0-9600686),* 102 E. Main South, Ellsworth, KS 67439 Tel 914-472-3255.

Role Train Assocs, *(Role Training Associates of California),* 4420 Village Rd., Long Beach, CA 90808.

Roller Coaster Pubns, *(Roller Coaster Pubns.),* P.O. Box 18058, Denver, CO 80218; Moved, Left No Forwarding Address.

Rolling Block, *(Rolling Block Press; 0-940028),* P.O. Box 5357, Buena Park, CA 90622.

Rolling Meadows, *(Rolling Meadows Library; 0-9602782),* 3110 Martin Lane, Rolling Meadows, IL 60008 Tel 312-259-6050.

Romance, *(Romance Monographs, Inc.),* P.O. Box 7553, University, MS 38677 Tel 601-234-0001.

Romney Pr, *(Romney Press; 0-9604640),* 308 Fourth Ave., Iowa City, IA 52240; Dist. by: Eble Music Co., P.O. Box 2570, Iowa City, IA 52244.

Ronald Pr, *(Ronald Press),* 605 Third Ave., New York, NY 10158 Tel 212-850-6418.

Rook Pr, *(Rook Press; 0-916684),* P.O. Box 144 Ruffsdale, PA 15679.

Rookfield, *(Rookfield Press; 0-917610),* P.O. Box 45, Deer, AR 72628 Tel 501-446-5793.

Rookwood Gold Era, *(Rookwood Golden Era; 0-9600418),* P.O. Box 6501, Cincinnati, OH 45206.

Rooney Pubns, *(Rooney Pubns.; 0-9604600),* P.O. Box 44146, Panorama City, CA 91412 Tel 213-894-2585.

Roosevelt U, *(Roosevelt University),* 430 S. Michigan Ave., Chicago, IL 60605 Tel 312-341-3803.

Rorge Pub Co, *(Rorge Publishing Co.),* P.O. Box 130, Evergreen, CO 80439 Tel 303-674-4220.

Rose Deeprose, *(Rose Deeprose Press; 0-937738),* 1661 Oak St., San Francisco, CA 94117 Tel 415-552-0991.

Rose Hill, *(Rose Hill Press; 0-917264),* 12368 Old Pen Mar Rd., Waynesboro, PA 17268 Tel 717-762-7072.

Rose Pub, *(Rose Publishing Co., Inc.; 0-914546),* 301 Louisiana, Little Rock, AR 72201 Tel 501-372-1666.

Rose Pub MI, *(Rose Publishing Co.; 0-937320),* 4676 Morningside Dr., S.E., Grand Rapids, MI 49508 Tel 616-698-8282.

Rose Pubns, *(Rose Pubns.),* 3828 Ben Lomond Ct., Toledo, OH 43607.

Rosebud, *(Rosebud Press; 0-9606194),* P.O. Box 40, Van Brunt Sta., Brooklyn, NY 11215.

Rosen Pr, *(Rosen, Richards, Press, Inc.; 0-8239),* 29 E. 21st St., New York, NY 10010 Tel 212-777-3017.

Rosenbach Found
See Rosenbach Mus & Lib

Rosenbach Mus & Lib, *(Rosenbach Museum & Library, The),* 2010 De Lancey Place, Philadelphia, PA 19103 Tel 215-732-1600.

Rosetta *Imprint of* **Plenum Pub**

Rosetta Pub Co, *(Rosetta Publishing Co., The; 0-935850),* P.O. Box 17942, Raleigh, NC 27619; Moved, Left No Forwarding Address.

Rosicrucian, *(Rosicrucian Fellowship; 0-911274)*, 2222 Mission, Oceanside, CA 92054 Tel 714-757-6600.

Ross, *(Ross & Haines Old Books Co.; 0-87018)*, 639 E. Lake St., Wayzata, MN 55391 Tel 612-473-7551.

Ross-Back Roads, *(Ross/Back Roads Press; 0-931272)*, P.O. Box 4340, Berkeley, CA 94704; Orders to: PAN, Box 4416, Berkeley, CA 94704.

Ross Bks, *(Ross Books; 0-89496)*, P.O. Box 4340, Berkeley, CA 94704 Tel 415-841-2474.

Ross-Erikson, *(Ross-Erikson, Inc.; 0-915520)*, 629 State St., Suite 222, Santa Barbara, CA 75343 Tel 805-962-1175.

Ross Valley, *(Ross Valley Book Co., Inc., The)*, 1407 Solano Ave., Albany, CA 94706 Tel 415-526-6400.

Rossi Pubns, *(Rossi Pubns.; 0-935618)*, P.O. Box 2001, Beverly Hills, CA 90213 Tel 213-271-3730.

Rostrum Bks, *(Rostrum Books)*, P.O. Box 1191, Miami, FL 33101 Tel 305-573-5900.

Rota Pr, *(Rota Press; 0-87908)*, P.O. Box 332, Waverly, IA 50677.

Rotary Intl, *(Rotary International; 0-915062)*, 1600 Ridge Ave., Evanston, IL 60201 Tel 312-328-0100.

Roth Pub, *(Roth Publishing; 0-87957)*, 125 Mineola Ave., Roslyn Hts., NY 11577 Tel 516-621-7242.

Rothman, *(Rothman, Fred B., & Co.; 0-8377)*, 10368 W. Centennial Rd., Littleton, CO 80127 Tel 303-979-5657.

Rothman Repr
    See Rothman

Rothman Repr, *(Rothman Reprints; 0-8377)*, Affilate of Fred B. Rothman & Co., 57 Leuning St., South Hackensack, NJ 07606 Tel 201-489-4646; Now Merged with Fred B. Rothman.

Rotz, *(Rotz, Anna Overcash; 0-9605108)*, Box 266, 12182 Main St., Fort Loudon, PA 17224

Rouse & Co, *(Rouse, James, & Co., Inc.; 0-9603790)*, P.O. Box 905, Columbia, MD 21044 Tel 301-992-6147; Dist. by: The Greater Baltimore Board of Realtors, Inc., 1501 W. Mount Royal Ave., Baltimore, MD 21217 Tel 301-462-2500.

Routledge & Kegan, *(Routledge & Kegan Paul, Ltd.; 0-7100)*, 9 Park St., Boston, MA 02108 Tel 617-742-5863. *Imprints:* Oriel (Oriel Press).

Rovi, *(Rovi Pubns., Inc.; 0-911282)*, P.O. Box 259, Belvedere, CA 94920 Tel 415-435-3174.

Rowan Tree, *(Rowan Tree Press, Ltd.; 0-937672)*, 124 Chestnut St., Boston, MA 02108.

Rowcliff, *(Rowcliff, Norman)*, Rte. 1, Box 564, Batavia, IL 60510.

Rowman, *(Rowman & Littlefield, Inc.; 0-87471; 0-8476)*, Div. of Littlefield, Adams, & Co., 81 Adams Dr., Box 327, Totowa, NJ 07511 Tel 201-256-8600.

Roxbury Data, *(Roxbury Data Interface; 0-89902)*, Box G, 110 S. Hillside Ave., Succasunna, NJ 07876 Tel 201-584-4448.

Roxbury Pub Co, *(Roxbury Publishing Co.; 0-935732)*, 4750 70th St., Suite 36, La Mesa, CA 92041.

Roy, *(Roy Pubs., Inc.; 0-8035)*, 30 E. 74th St., New York, NY 10021 Tel 212-879-5935; Dist. by: Ventura Book Service, 114-20 Rockaway Beach Blvd., Rockaway Park, NY 11694.

Roy Freed, *(Freed, Roy N.; 0-9601030)*, 100 Franklin St., 9th Floor, Boston, MA 02110 Tel 617-357-1500.

Royal Calif, *(Royal Publishing; 0-930440)*, P.O. Box 5027, Beverly Hills, CA 90210.

Royale Pubs, *(Royale Pubs.; 0-9601378)*, 9119 Blair River Circle, Fountain Valley, CA 92708 Tel 714-963-4419.

Royce, *(Royce Pubns.; 0-911284)*, P.O. Box 1967, Newport Beach, CA 92663.

RPM Pub, *(RPM Publishing Co.; 0-932918)*, 355 Lexington Ave., New York, NY 10017; Moved, Left No Forwarding Address.

RRP, *(Reflexology Research Project; 0-9606070)*, 6209 Hendrix NE, Albuquerque, NM 87110 Tel 505-883-8326.

RRS *Imprint of HM*

RSM Proj, *(RSM Projects; 0-9603230)*, P.O. Box 4687, Des Moines, IA 50306 Tel 515-277-2836.

RSV Pub, *(R.S.V. Publishing, Inc.; 0-933514)*, Box 182, Times Plaza, Brooklyn, NY 11217.

RSVP Pub & Dist, *(RSVP Pub. & Distributor; 0-913752)*, P.O. Box 252, Brookfield, IL 60513.

Ruben Pub, *(Ruben Publishing; 0-917434)*, P.O. Box 414, Avon, CT 06001 Tel 203-673-0740.

Rubio-Boitel, *(Rubio-Boitel, Fr. Fernando)*, 403 El Camino Real, N.W., Socorro, NM 87801 Tel 505-835-1620.

Ruborge Pubs, *(Ruborge Pubs.)*, Rte. 2, Box 867, Pompano Beach, FL 33067 Tel 305-427-8898.

Rucker Ent, *(Rucker Enterprises)*, 3511 Henderson Rd., Greensboro, NC 27410 Tel 919-294-4918; Orders to: P.O. Box 19107, Greensboro, NC 27410; Moved, Left No Forwarding Address.

Rucker Pr, *(Rucker Press, Inc.)*, 118 S. Broadway, Sta. B, Box 7025, Dayton, OH 45407.

Rue Morgue, *(Rue Morgue Press; 0-915230)*, P.O. Box 4119, Boulder, CO 80306 Tel 303-443-8346.

Ruffled Feathers, *(Ruffled Feathers Publishing Co.; 0-9603582)*, 2700 Fourth St., Boulder, CO 80302 Tel 303-442-2660.

Rumbleseat, *(Rumbleseat Press, Inc.; 0-913444)*, 3835 Scott St., San Francisco, CA 94123 Tel 415-929-1191.

Runeskald Pr, *(Runeskald Press; 0-915446)*, P.O. Box 612, Annapolis, MD 21404 Tel 301-268-1069.

Runner's Log, *(Runner's Log; 0-933872)*, 10-50 Jackson Ave., Long Island City, NY 11101.

Running Pr, *(Running Press; 0-89471)*, 125 S. 22nd St., Philadelphia, PA 19103 Tel 215-567-5080.

Running Times, *(Running Times; 0-936304)*, 12808 Occoquan Rd., Woodbridge, VA 22192.

Running Wild, *(Running Wild; 0-939350)*, P.O. Box 1211, Lafayette, CA 94549 Tel 415-283-7363.

Rural Educ, *(Rural Education Assn.), 1201 Sixteenth St., N.W., Washington, DC 20036.

Rural Life, *(Rural Life)*, Rte. 1, Box 183-C, Whitewater, WI 53190.

Rus Bk Chamber, *(Russian Book Chamber Abroad; 0-912306)*, P.O. Box 126, Cathedral Sta., New York, NY 10025.

Rushlight Club, *(Rushlight Club; 0-917422)*, P.O. Box 3053, Talcottville, CT 06066.

Rusoff Bks, *(Rusoff Books; 0-917932)*, 1302 S.E. 4th St., Minneapolis, MN 55414 Tel 612-331-3335.

Russell, *(Russell & Russell, Pubs.; 0-8462)*, Div. of Atheneum Pubs., 597 Fifth Ave., New York, NY 10017 Tel 212-486-2659; Orders to: Scribner Distribution Center, Vreeland Ave., Boro of Totowa, Paterson, NJ 07512 Tel 201-256-0700.

Russell Pubns, *(Russell Pubns.; 0-933558)*, P.O. Box 2461, Tampa, FL 33601 Tel 813-879-8580; Do Not Confuse with Russell & Russell in NY (Russell).

Russell Sage, *(Russell Sage Foundation; 0-87154)*, 633 Third Ave., New York, NY 10017 Tel 212-949-8990; Orders to: Basic Books, Inc., 10 E. 53rd St., New York, NY 10022.

Russian Rev, *(Russian Review; 0-918444)*, Hoover Institution, Stanford, CA 94305 Tel 415-497-2067.

Russica Bk Art
    See Russica Pubs

Russica Pubs, *(Russica Publishers; 0-89830)*, C/O Russica Book & Art Co., 799 Broadway, New York, NY 10003.

Rusthoi, *(Rusthoi Soul Winning Pubns.; 0-911288)*, P.O. Box 595, Montrose, CA 91020 Tel 213-241-7244.

Rutan Pub, *(Rutan Publishing; 0-936222)*, 2717 Lyndale Ave. S., Minneapolis, MN 55408.

Rutgers Ctr Alcohol, *(Rutgers Center of Alcohol Studies Pubns.; 0-911290)*, Smithers Hall, Rutgers Univ., New Brunswick, NJ 08903 Tel 201-932-3510; Orders to: P.O. Box 969, Piscataway, NJ 08854 Tel 201-932-2011.

Rutgers U Pr, *(Rutgers Univ. Press; 0-8135)*, 30 College Ave., New Brunswick, NJ 08903 Tel 201-932-7764.

Rutgers U SLIS, *(Rutgers Univ., Graduate School of Library & Information Studies)*, Four Huntington St., New Brunswick, NJ 08903 Tel 201-932-7961.

Rutgers U SLS

    See Rutgers U SLIS

Rutledge Bks, *(Rutledge Books, Inc.; 0-87469)*, 25 W. 43rd St., New York, NY 10036; Dist. by: Larousse & Co., Inc., 572 Fifth Ave., New York, NY 10036; Dist. by: Charles Scribner's Sons, 597 Fifth Ave., New York, NY 10017.

Rutledge Pr *Imprint of* Smith Pubs

RWS Bks, *(RWS Books; 0-939400)*, 4296 Mulholland St., Salt Lake City, UT 84117.

RWU Parachuting Pubns, *(RWU Parachuting Pubns.)*, 1656 Beechwood Ave., Fullerton, CA 92635 Tel 714-990-0369.

RWunderground
    See RWU Parachuting Pubns

Ryan Co, *(Ryan Co.; 0-914202)*, 2188 Latimer Lane, Los Angeles, CA 90024 Tel 213-474-4175.

Rydal, *(Rydal Press-The Print; 0-911292)*, P.O. Box 250, Santa Fe, NM 87501 Tel 505-982-2689.

Ryder Pr, *(Ryder Press; 0-916816)*, 3307 Chadbourne Rd., Shaker Heights, OH 44120 Tel 216-921-7975.

Ryerse, *(Ryerse Publishing Co.; 0-9603388)*, 40 Bernice Dr., Freehold, NJ 07728 Tel 201-462-5068.

Rymer Bks, *(Rymer Books; 0-9600792)*, P.O. Box 104, Tollhouse, CA 93667 Tel 209-855-8540.

S A Shopen, *(Shopen, Sylvia Ames)*, Norwich, VT 05055.

S Ambaras, *(Ambaras, Samuel, Inc.; 0-913268)*, P.O. Box 138, New York, NY 10031; Moved, Left No Forwarding Address.

S & S Pr TX, *(S & S Press; 0-934646)*, P.O. Box 5931, Austin, TX 78763; Do Not Confuse with Simon & Schuster (S&S).

S Appalachian Res, *(Southern Appalachian Resource Catalog)*, Rt. 1, Box 71A, Warne, NC 28909 Tel 704-389-8323.

S Aronson, *(Aronson, Sam; 0-9604554)*, P.O. Box 9466, Playa Del Rey, CA 90291 Tel 213-822-9940.

S B Costales, *(Costales, S. B.; 0-9600660)*, 18 Ventura Dr., Danielson, CT 06239 Tel 203-774-4713.

S Campbell, *(Campbell, Sandy M.; 0-917366)*, 230 Central Park S., New York, NY 10019 Tel 212-582-6286.

S Carmel, *(Carmel, Simon J.; 0-9600886)*, 10500 Rockville Pike, Apt. 1028, Rockville, MD 20852

S Carver
    See Carves

S Deal Assoc, *(Deal, S., Associates; 0-930006)*, 1629 Guizot St., San Diego, CA 92107.

S E Mattox, *(Mattox, S. E., Corp.; 0-918070)*, P.O. Box 431, San Pedro, CA 90733 Tel 213-832-0306.

S F Vanni, *(Vanni, S.F.; 0-913298)*, 30 W. 12th St., New York, NY 10011 Tel 212-675-6336.

S Fox, *(Fox, Sanford; 0-9603854)*, 41-41 Christine Court, Fairlawn, NJ 07410.

S G Phillips, *(Phillip's, S. G., Inc.; 0-87599)*, 305 W. 86th St., New York, NY 10024 Tel 212-787-4405.

S Gilbert, *(Gilbert, Skeet; 0-9600548)*, Fuquay-Varina, NC 27526 Tel 919-552-4623.

S Green, *(Green, Stanford J.; 0-9604656)*, 5892 E. Jefferson Ave., Denver, CO 80237.

S H Park, *(Park, S.H.; 0-9604440)*, 34 Lawnside Dr., Trenton, NJ 08648 Tel 609-883-3551.

S-H Serv, *(S-H Service Agency, Inc.)*, ; Publisher Abbreviation Without Addresses Are for Titles That Are Out of Print. These Are Obsolete Abbreviations.

S Higgins, *(Higgins, Shaun, Pub.; 0-918928)*, E2621 27th Ave., Spokane, WA 99203 Tel 509-535-7350.

S Ill U Pr, *(Southern Illinois Univ. Press; 0-8093)*, P.O. Box 3697, Carbondale, IL 62901 Tel 618-453-2281.

S Israel, *(Israel, Stan)*, P.O. Box 808, Hallandale, FL 33009; Orders to: 272 Hansen Ave., Albany, NY 12208.

S J Brooks, *(Brooks, Stanley J., Co.)*, 1487 Glendon Ave., Los Angeles, CA 90024.

S J Durst, *(Durst, Sanford J.; 0-915262)*, 170 E. 61st St., New York, NY 10021 Tel 212-593-3514.

S K Abbey, *(Abbey, Stella K.)*, 2840 80th St., N.E., Bellevue, WA 98004.

S K Freshman, *(Freshman, Samuel K.; 0-9600708),* 9100 Wilshire Blvd., Eighth Floor, East Tower, Beverly Hills, CA 90212 Tel 213-273-1870.

S Karger, *(Karger, S., AG; 3-8055),* 150 Fifth Ave., Suite 1103, New York, NY 10011 Tel 212-924-9222; Dist. by: Albert J. Phiebig, P.O. Box 352, White Plains, NY 10602.

S M Hartman, *(Hartman, S. M.),* P.O. Box 7162, Baltimore, MD 21218 Tel 301-243-0616.

S Meth U Pr
See SMU Press

S O S Pubns, *(Save on Shopping),* P.O. Box 10482, Jacksonville, FL 32207 Tel 904-268-3344; Dist. by: Caroline House Publishers, Inc., P.O. Box 161, Thornwood, NY 10594.

S P Howell, *(Howell, Susan P., Enterprises; 0-9603076),* Box 116 B, Hebron, CT 06248.

S P Levine, *(Levine, Samuel P.; 0-9602906),* P.O. Box 174, Canoga Park, CA 91305 Tel 213-343-0550.

S Paslow, *(Paslow, Stephen),* Box 844, Pittsburgh, PA 15230.

S Pr, *(S Press),* Dist. by: SBD: Small Press Distribution, 1636 Ocean View Ave., Kensington, CA 94707 Tel 415-548-8204.

S R Guggenheim, *(Guggenheim, Solomon R., Foundation; 0-89207),* 1071 Fifth Ave., New York, NY 10028 Tel 212-860-1300.

S Regional Ed, *(Southern Regional Education Board),* 130 Sixth St., N.W., Atlanta, GA 30313 Tel 404-875-9211.

S Res Inst, *(Southern Research Institute),* 2000 Ninth Ave., S., Birmingham, AL 35255 Tel 205-323-6592.

S S Ross
See Sidney Scott Ross

S S S Pub Co, *(Smith, Smith & Smith Publishing Co.; 0-913626),* 17515 S.W. Blue Heron Rd., Lake Oswego, OR 97034 Tel 503-636-2979.

S Singh, *(Singh, Swayam; 0-935380),* 2311 Meadow Croft Dr., Lansing, MI 48912.

S T Black, *(Black, Sidney T.),* Box 522, Simsbury, CT 06070.

S Troyanovich, *(Troyanovich, Steve),* Dist. by: Spring Church Book Co., P.O. Box 127, Spring Church, PA 15686.

S Volin, *(Volin, Stan; 0-9600922),* 19 Steven St., Plainview, NY 11803 Tel 516-681-6040; Orders to: Box 571-B, Hicksville, NY 11802.

Saalfield, *(Saalfield Publishing Co.; 0-509),* Saalfield Square, Akron, OH 44301; Out of Business.

Sabbath Day Advent, *(Sabbath Day Adventist Book & Bible House of Prophecy),* 8010 Petaluma Hill Rd., Pengrove, CA 94951 Tel 707-795-4875.

Sabbot-Natural Hist Bks, *(Sabbot, Rudolph Wm., - Natural History Books),* 5239 Tendilla Ave., Woodland Hills, CA 91364 Tel 213-346-7164.

Sabin, *(Sabin Publishing Co.),* 6361 Celia Vista Dr., San Diego, CA 92115; Moved, Left No Forwarding Address.

Sable Pub, *(Sable Publishing Corp.; 0-914832),* P.O. Box 788, Arlington, TX 76010 Tel 817-265-5001.

Sachem Pr, *(Sachem Press; 0-937584),* P.O. Box 9, Old Chatham, NY 12136.

Sack Back Pubns, *(Sack Back Pubns.; 0-916714),* 200 Bolinas Rd., Suite 75, Fairfax, CA 94930 Tel 707-763-8944.

Sacramento Med, *(Sacramento Medical Society),* Dist. by: Argus Books, 2741 Riverside Blvd., Sacramento, CA 95818.

Sadlier, *(Sadlier, William H., Inc.; 0-8215),* 11 Park Place, New York, NY 10007 Tel 212-227-2120.

Sadlier-Oxford, *(Sadlier-Oxford; 0-87105),* 11 Park Place, New York, NY 10007 Tel 212-349-2300.

Sadtler Res, *(Sadtler Research Laboratories, Inc.; 0-8456),* 3316 Spring Garden St., Philadelphia, PA 19104 Tel 215-382-7800.

Safety Consul, *(Safety Consultants, Inc.),* 3140 Kingsley Dr., Florissant, MO 63033 Tel 314-921-6776.

Safety Now, *(Safety Now Co., Inc.; 0-917066),* P.O. Box 567, Jenkintown, PA 19046 Tel 215-884-0210.

Sag Rising, *(Sagittarius Rising; 0-933620),* c/o Tracy Marks, Box 252, Arlington, MA 02174 Tel 617-646-2692.

Sag Scriptory, *(Sagittarian Scriptory Enterprises; 0-931908),* P.O. Box 2786, Napa, CA 94558 Tel 707-224-4814.

Sagamore Bks, *(Sagamore Books; 0-87905),* Juvenile Div. of Peregrine Smith, Inc., P.O. Box 667, Layton, UT 84041 Tel 801-376-9800.

Sagamore Pr, *(Sagamore Press; 0-936640),* P.O. Box 3315, Terre Haute, IN 47803.

Sagarin Pr, *(Sagarin Press; 0-915298),* Box 251, Sand Lake, NY 12153 Tel 518-674-2998.

Sage, *(Sage Pubns., Inc.; 0-8039),* 275 S. Beverly Dr., Beverly Hills, CA 90212 Tel 213-274-8003.

Sage Bks Inc, *(Sage Books, Inc.; 0-89360),* Subs. of the Lawford Press Inc., 275 S. Beverly Dr., Beverly Hills, CA 90212.

Sagebrush Pr, *(Sagebrush Press; 0-930704),* P.O. Box 87, Morongo Valley, CA 92256.

Saifer, *(Saifer, Albert, Pub.; 0-87556),* P.O. Box 239 W.O.B., West Orange, NJ 07052.

Sail Bks, *(Sail Books, Inc.; 0-914814),* 38 Commercial Wharf, Boston, MA 02110; Dist. by: W. W. Norton & Co., Inc., 500 Fifth Ave., New York, NY 10036.

Salamander Pr, *(Salamander Press; 0-912708),* P.O. Box 153, Carmel, CA 93921.

Salem Pr, *(Salem Press, Inc.; 0-89356),* Box 1097, Englewood Cliffs, NJ 07632 Tel 201-871-3700.

Salem Pub Lib, *(Salem Public Library; 0-9603390),* 821 E. State St., Salem, OH 44460 Tel 216-332-0042.

Sales & Mktg, *(Sales & Marketing Management; 0-89846),* 633 Third Ave., New York, NY 10017 Tel 212-986-4800.

Salesiana *Imprint of* D Bosco Pubns

Salesmans, *(Salesman's Guide, Inc.; 0-87228),* 1140 Broadway, New York, NY 10001 Tel 212-684-2985.

Salloch, *(Salloch, William; 0-911702),* Pines Bridge Rd., Ossining, NY 10562 Tel 914-941-8363.

Salome Pubns, *(Salome Pubns.; 0-915380),* 5548 N. Sawyer Ave., Chicago, IL 60625; Dist. by: Word Works, Inc., P.O. Box 4054, Washington, DC 20015.

Salt Lick, *(Salt Lick Press; 0-913918),* P.O. Box 1064, Quincy, IL 62301 Tel 217-222-1331.

Saltzman Co
See Eurail Guide

Salvation Army, *(Salvation Army: Supplies & Purchasing Dept.),* 1424 N.E. Expressway, Atlanta, GA 30329 Tel 404-321-7870.

Salyer, *(Salyer Publishing Co.; 0-911298),* 3111 19th St., N.W., Oklahoma City, OK 73107.

SamHar Pr, *(SamHar Press),* Div. of Story House Corp., Charlotteville, NY 12036 Tel 607-397-8725.

Samisdat, *(Samisdat),* Box 129, Richford, VT 05476.

Sampson Bowers, *(Bowers, Sampson; 0-916448),* P.O. Box 731, Carmel Valley, CA 93924.

Sams, *(Sams, Howard W., & Co., Inc.; 0-672),* Subs. of ITT, 4300 W. 62nd St., Indianapolis, IN 46206 Tel 317-298-5400.

Samuel Stevens, *(Samuel Stevens & Co.; 0-89522),* P.O. Box 3899, Sarasota, FL 33578 Tel 813-924-8441.

San Bernardino, *(San Bernardino County Museum Assn.; 0-915158),* 2024 Orange Tree Lane, Redlands, CA 92373 Tel 714-792-1334.

San Diego Hist, *(San Diego Historical Society; 0-918740),* P.O. Box 81825, San Diego, CA 92138 Tel 714-297-3258.

San Diego St Univ Pr
See Campanile

San Francisco Opera, *(San Francisco Opera Guild Auxiliary; 0-9600758),* War Memorial Opera House, San Francisco, CA 94102 Tel 415-863-2524.

San Francisco Pr, *(San Francisco Press, Inc.; 0-911302),* 547 Howard St., San Francisco, CA 94105 Tel 415-362-0888.

San Jacinto, *(San Jacinto Publishing Co.; 0-911982),* c/o Texas A&M University Press, Drawer C, College Station, Houston, TX 77843 Tel 713-845-1436.

San Marcos, *(San Marcos Press; 0-88235),* P.O. Box 53, Cerrillos, NM 87010.

Sanatana, *(Sanatana Publishing Society; 0-933116),* 3100 White Sulphur Springs Rd., St. Helena, CA 94574 Tel 707-963-9487.

Sand Dollar, *(Sand Dollar Press),* 1222 Solano Ave., Albany, CA 94706 Tel 415-527-1931.

Sand Pond, *(Sand Pond Pubs.),* Sand Pond Rd., Marlow, NH 13456 Tel 603-446-3460.

S&A Pubns, *(S & A Pubns.; 0-9600768),* P.O. Box 2660, Sta. "A", Champaign, IL 61820 Tel 217-359-4222.

Sandlapper Pr
See Sandlapper Store

Sandlapper Store, *(Sandlapper Store, Inc.; 0-87844),* Box 841, 101 W. Main, Lexington, SC 29072 Tel 803-359-6571; Formerly Sandlapper Press, Inc.

Sandollar Pr, *(Sandollar Press),* P.O. Box 4157, Santa Barbara, CA 93103 Tel 805-569-0337.

Sandpiper OR, *(Sandpiper Press; 0-9603748),* P.O. Box 286, Brookings, OR 97415 Tel 503-468-5588.

Sandpiper Pr FL, *(Sandpiper Press, Inc.; 0-914666),* P. O. Box 1059, Oviedo, FL 32765 Tel 305-365-3142.

Sandrock & Foster, *(Sandrock & Foster),* Memorial Foundation, Box 841, Winona, MN 55987 Tel 507-452-1859.

S&S, *(Simon & Schuster, Inc.; 0-671),* 1230 Ave. of the Americas, New York, NY 10020 Tel 212-245-6400. *Imprints:* Fireside (Fireside Paperbacks); Juveniles (Juvenile Books); Kenan Pr (Kenan Press); Linden (Linden); Little Simon (Little Simon); Touchstone Bks (Touchstone Books).

S&S Co CA
See S&S Co OR

S&S Co OR, *(S&S Co., The),* 11047 Antiock Rd, Central Point, OR 97502 Tel 503-826-7870; Do Not Confuse with S&S, Simon & Schuster, Inc.

Sandstone, *(Sandstone Press; The; 0-913720),* 321 E. 43rd St., New York, NY 10017 Tel 212-682-5519.

Sangamon County Hist, *(Sangamon County Historical Society),* 308 E. Adams St., Springfield, IL 62701.

Sanguinaria, *(Sanguinaria Publishing),* 85 Ferris St., Bridgeport, CT 06605.

Sant Bani Ash, *(Sant Bani Ashram, Inc.),* Franklin, NH 03235 Tel 603-934-4209.

Santa Barb Botanic, *(Santa Barbara Botanic Garden; 0-916436),* 1212 Mission Canyon Rd., Santa Barbara, CA 93105 Tel 805-682-4726.

Santa Barb Mus Art, *(Santa Barbara Museum of Art; 0-89951),* 1130 State St., Santa Barbara, CA 93101 Tel 805-963-4364.

Santa Barbara Mus Nat Hist, *(Santa Barbara Museum of Natural History; 0-936494),* 2559 Puesta del Sol Rd., Santa Barbara, CA 93105 Tel 805-682-4711.

Santa Fe Comm Sch, *(Santa Fe Community School),* P.O. Box 2241, Santa Fe, NM 87501 Tel 505-471-9977.

Santa Monica Pub, *(Santa Monica Publishing Co.; 0-917640),* 605 E. Garcia, Santa Fe, NM 87501.

Santam, *(Santam Two, Ltd.),* Box 11642, Phoenix, AZ 85017.

Santarasa Pubns, *(Santarasa Pubns.; 0-935548),* 937 Broadway, Boulder, CO 80302.

Santemara, *(Santemara Pubns.; 0-9603304),* P.O. Box 1217, Minnetonka, MN 55343 Tel 612-474-5313.

Santillana, *(Santillana Publishing Co.; 0-88272),* 575 Lexington Ave., New York, NY 10022 Tel 212-371-4069.

Saphrograph, *(Saphrograph Co.; 0-87557),* 4910 Fort Hamilton Parkway, Brooklyn, NY 11219 Tel 212-925-7840.

Sar Sholem, *(Sar Sholem of Jerusalem),* P.O. Box 577, Fern Park, FL 32730.

Sarasota Opera, *(Sarasota Opera Society, The; 0-9605844),* P.O. Box 1393, Sarasota, FL 33578.

Sargent
See Porter Sargent

SAS Inst, *(SAS Institute Inc.; 0-917382),* SAS Circle, Cary, NC 27511 Tel 919-467-8000.

Sasco, *(Sasco Associates; 0-912980),* P.O. Box 335, Southport, CT 06490 Tel 203-255-4768.

Sassafras Pr, *(Sassafras Press; 0-930528),* P.O. Box 1366, Evanston, IL 60204 Tel 312-649-0888.

Sat Eve Post, *(Saturday Evening Post Co., The; 0-89387),* 1100 Waterway Blvd., Indianapolis, IN 46202 Tel 317-634-1100.

Sat Rev Pr
See Dutton

Saturday Pr, *(Saturday Press; 0-938158),* 91 Eighth Ave., Brooklyn, NY 11215.

Saucerian, *(Saucerian Press; 0-911306),* P.O. Box 2228, Clarksburg, WV 26301 Tel 304-269-2719.

uger Bks, *(Sauger Books; 0-915318)*, 8809 Maxwell Dr., Potomac, MD 20854 Tel 301-299-8488.

auk, *(Sauk Valley)*, Irish Hills, Brooklyn, MI 49230 Tel 517-467-2061.

unders, *(Saunders, W. B., Co.; 0-7216)*, Subs. of Columbia Broadcasting System, W. Washington Square, Philadelphia, PA 19105 Tel 215-574-4700.

aurian Pr, *(Saurian Press; 0-936830)*, New Mexico Tech, Socorro, NM 87801 Tel 505-835-5445.

avage, *(Savage, Ella H.; 0-9605150)*, P.O. Box 353, Lefferts Sta., Brooklyn, NY 11225.

awan Kirpal Pubns, *(Sawan Kirpal Pubns.; 0-918224)*, 115 S. "O" St., Lake Worth, FL 33460 Tel 305-588-1287; Orders to: Rte. 1, Box 24, Bowling Green, VA 22427 Tel 804-633-5789.

axon, *(Saxon House)*, Dist. by: Atheneum Pubs., 597 Fifth Ave., New York, NY 10017.

aylor, *(Saylor, Lee, Inc.; 0-931708)*, 1855 Olympic Blvd., Suite 110, Walnut Creek, CA 94596.

BD, *(SBD: Small Press Distribution; 0-914068)*, 1784 Shattuck Ave., Berkeley, CA 94709 Tel 415-529-3336.

BS Pub, *(SBS Publishing, Inc.; 0-89961)*, 14 W. Forest Ave., Englewood, NJ 07631 Tel 201-569-8700.

C Prodns, *(Southern California Productions; 0-9601956)*, P.O. Box 1128M, Carlsbad, CA 92008 Tel 714-434-1626.

candia Pubs, *(Scandia Pubs.; 0-937242)*, P.O. Box 1044, Lyons, CO 80540 Tel 303-823-5072.

canning Electron, *(Scanning Electron Microscopy, Inc.; 0-931288)*, P.O. Box 66507, AMF O'Hare, Chicago, IL 60666 Tel 312-529-6677.

carab Pr, *(Scarab Press; 0-912962)*, 63 Bates Blvd., Orinda, CA 94563.

carecrow, *(Scarecrow Press, Inc.; 0-8108)*, Subs. of Grolier Educational Corp., 52 Liberty St., Box 656, Metuchen, NJ 08840 Tel 201-548-8600.

Scarecrow CA
See Poor Souls Pr

carf Pr, *(Scarf Press; 0-934386)*, 58 E. 83rd St., New York, NY 10028 Tel 212-744-3901.

Scat Pubns, *(Scat Pubns.; 0-9606124)*, 32 W. 40th St., Suite 11-B, New York, NY 10018 Tel 212-730-1033.

Scenographic, *(Scenographic Media; 0-913868)*, Box 2122, Norwalk, CT 06851.

Scepter Pubs, *(Scepter Pubs.; 0-933932)*, The Publishers Bldg., 481 Main St., New Rochelle, NY 10801 Tel 914-636-3377.

Sch Aid, *(School Aid Co.; 0-87385)*, 911 Colfax Dr., P.O. Box 123, Danville, IL 61832.

Sch Journal WVU, *(School of Journalism, West Virginia Univ.; 0-930362)*, Morgantown, WV 26506.

Sch Lib Sci, *(School of Library Science, Emporia State University)*, 1200 Commercial, Emporia, KS 66801 Tel 316-343-1200.

Sch Living Pr
See Wisconsin Bks

Sch Proj Club, *(School Projectionist Club of America; 0-911328)*, P.O. Box 44, State College, PA 16801.

Schab Gallery, *(Schab, William H., Gallery, Inc.)*, 37 W. 57th St., New York, NY 10019 Tel 212-758-0327.

Schafler Ent, *(Schafler Enterprises; 0-9603154)*, 257 Ricardo Rd., Mill Valley, CA 94941 Tel 415-383-0830.

Schalkenbach, *(Schalkenbach, Robert, Foundation; 0-911312)*, 5 E. 44th St., New York, NY 10017 Tel 212-734-2468.

Schaumburg Pubns, *(Schaumburg Pubns., Inc.; 0-935690)*, 1432 S. Mohawk, Roselle, IL 60172.

SchDept Imprint of Har-Row

Schenkman, *(Schenkman Publishing Co., Inc.; 0-87073)*, 3 Mt. Auburn Place, Cambridge, MA 02138 Tel 617-492-4952.

Schick Sunn, *(Schick Sunn Classic Books; 0-917214)*, Div. of Sun Classic Pictures, Inc., 556 E. Second S., Salt Lake City, UT 84102 Tel 801-363-2040; Orders to: 1554 Sepulveda Blvd., Los Angeles, CA 90025 Tel 213-478-4034.

Schiffer, *(Schiffer Publishing Ltd.; 0-916838)*, P.O. Box E, Exton, PA 19341 Tel 215-363-6889.

Schirmer Bks, *(Schirmer Books; 0-02)*, Div. of Macmillan Publishing Co., 866 Third Ave., New York, NY 10022 Tel 212-935-7642; Orders to: 100 Brown St., Riverside, NJ 08370.

Schlegel Pubns, *(Schlegel Pubns.; 0-9603358)*, 172 Conneaut Dr., Pittsburgh, PA 15239 Tel 412-325-1226.

Schleiger, *(Schleiger, Arlene; 0-9600098)*, 4416 Valli Vista Rd, Colorado Springs, CO 80915 Tel 303-591-8642.

Schmul Pub Co, *(Schmul Publishing Co. Inc.)*, P.O. Box 4068, Salem, OH 44460.

Schnase Repr Dept, *(Schnase, Annemarie)*, 120 Brown Rd., Box 119, Scarsdale, NY 10583 Tel 914-725-1284.

Schneeberger, *(Schneeberger, Tilly, & Assoc.)*, P.O. Box 623, 578 El Sol St., Ojai, CA 93023 Tel 805-646-0208.

Schneider Ent, *(Schneider Ent., Inc)*, 1386 E. Main St., Salem, VA 24153 Tel 703-389-9005.

Schneider Pubs, *(Schneider, R., Pubs.; 0-936984)*, 312 Linwood Ave., Stevens Point, WI 54481.

Schocken, *(Schocken Books, Inc.; 0-8052)*, 200 Madison Ave., New York, NY 10016 Tel 212-685-6500. *Imprints:* Moonlight Edns (Moonlight Editions).

Schoenhof, *(Schoenhof's Foreign Books, Inc.; 0-87774)*, 1280 Massachusetts Ave., Cambridge, MA 02138 Tel 617-547-8855.

Schol Am Res, *(School of American Research Press; 0-933452)*, P.O. Box 2188, Santa Fe, NM 87501.

Schol Bk Serv, *(Scholastic Book Services; 0-590)*, Div. of Scholastic Inc., 50 W. 44th St., New York, NY 10036 Tel 212-944-7700; Orders to: 906 Sylvan Ave., Englewood Cliffs, NJ 07632. *Imprints:* Citation (Citation Press); Four Winds (Four Winds Press); Schol Pap (Scholastic Paperbacks); Starline (Starline).

Schol Facsimiles, *(Scholars' Facsimiles & Reprints; 0-8201)*, P.O. Box 344, Delmar, NY 12054 Tel 518-439-6140.

Schol Pap Imprint of Schol Bk Serv

Schol Reprints, *(Scholarly Reprints, Inc.)*, 1 Park Ave., New York, NY 10016 Tel 212-689-0360.

Schol Test, *(Scholastic Testing Service, Inc.; 0-936224)*, 480 Meyer Rd., Bensenville, IL 60106 Tel 312-766-7150.

Schola Pr TX, *(Schola Press; 0-931016)*, P.O. Box 16064, Ft. Worth, TX 76133.

Scholarly, *(Scholarly Press Inc.; 0-403)*, 19722 E. Nine Mile Rd., Saint Clair Shores, MI 48080 Tel 313-773-4250.

Scholarly Res Inc, *(Scholarly Resources Inc.; 0-8420)*, 104 Greenhill Ave., Wilmington, DE 19805 Tel 302-654-7713.

Scholars Bk, *(Scholars Book Co.; 0-914348)*, 4431 Mt. Vernon, Houston, TX 77006 Tel 713-528-4395.

Scholars Portable, *(Scholars Portable Pubns.; 0-9604778)*, 1459 Southfield Rd., Evansville, IN 47715 Tel 812-476-6697.

Scholars Pr
See Scholars Pr CA

Scholars Pr CA, *(Scholars Press; 0-89130)*, 101 Salem St., Chico, CA 95926 Tel 916-343-1651.

Scholars Pr Ltd, *(Scholars' Press, Ltd.; 0-914044)*, P.O. Box 7231, Roanoke, VA 24019.

Scholars Pr MI
See Scholars Pr CA

Scholars Ref Lib, *(Scholar's Reference Library)*, P.O. Box 148, Darby, PA 19023.

Scholars Studies, *(Scholars Studies Press; 0-89177)*, 109 E. 9th Ave., New York, NY 10003 Tel 212-674-5296.

Scholasticus, *(Scholasticus Publishing)*, P.O. Box 2727, Springfield, VA 22152.

Scholium Intl, *(Scholium International, Inc; 0-87936)*, 265 Great Neck Rd., Great Neck, NY 11021 Tel 516-466-5181.

Schols Pr, *(Schols Press)*, ; Publisher Abbreviation Without Addresses Are for Titles That Are Out of Print. These Are Obsolete Abbreviations.

School Liv Ca, *(School of Living)*, P.O. Box 425, San Diego, CA 92103; Moved, Left No Forwarding Address.

Schroder Music, *(Schroder Music Co.; 0-915620)*, 2027 Parker St., Berkeley, CA 94704 Tel 415-843-2365.

Schroeder Prints, *(Schroeder Prints, Inc.; 0-931766)*, P.O. Drawer 580, Chestertown, MD 21620 Tel 301-778-1192.

Schroeppel, *(Schroeppel, Tom; 0-9603718)*, P.O. Box 521110, Miami, FL 33152.

Schulak & Assoc, *(Schulak, Bernard, & Assoc. Architects, Pub.; 0-9602186)*, 6889 W. Maple Rd., West Bloomfield, MI 48033.

Schulte, *(Schulte, Terry T.)*, Box 1672, St. Cloud, MN 56301.

Schumacher Pubns, *(Schumacher Publications; 0-917378)*, 9229 Lawn St., Proctor, MN 55810 Tel 218-624-7728.

Schwenkfelder Lib, *(Schwenkfelder Library; 0-935980)*, 1 Seminary St., Pennsburg, PA 18073 Tel 215-679-7175.

Sci Am Illus Lib, *(Scientific-American Illustrated Library; 0-89454)*, Subs. of W. H. Freeman & Co., 415 Madison Ave., New York, NY 10017 Tel 212-754-0561.

Sci & Behavior, *(Science & Behavior Books, Inc.; 0-8314)*, P.O. Box 11457, Palo Alto, CA 94306 Tel 415-326-6465.

Sci & Health, *(Science & Health Pubns.; 0-931422)*, 6410 Rockledge Dr., Suite 208, Bethesda, MD 20034.

Sci & Tech Pr, *(Science & Technology Press)*, P.O. Box 614, Latham, NY 12110 Tel 518-783-0313.

Sci Assoc Intl, *(Science Associates/International, Inc.; 0-87837)*, 1841 Broadway, New York, NY 10023 Tel 212-265-4995.

Sci Edits, *(Science Editors, Inc.; 0-9601862)*, P.O. Box 7185, 149 Thierman Lane, Louisville, KY 40207 Tel 502-897-5310.

Sci Ent, *(Science Enterprises, Inc.; 0-930116)*, Box 88443, Indianapolis, IN 46208 Tel 317-259-1054.

Sci Fiction, *(Science Fiction Resources; 0-918364)*, 101 Summit Rd., Port Washington, NY 11050 Tel 516-883-9142; 148 E. 74th St., New York, NY 10021 Tel 212-988-7526.

Sci Museum, *(Science Museum of Minnesota; 0-911338)*, 30 E. 10th St., St. Paul, MN 55101 Tel 612-222-6303.

Sci Newsletters, *(Scientific Newsletters, Inc., 0-930914)*, P.O. Box 4546, Anaheim, CA 92803 Tel 714-828-1371.

Sci of Mind, *(Science of Mind Pubns.; 0-911336)*, P.O. Box 75127, Los Angeles, CA 90075 Tel 213-388-2181; Dist. by: Devorss & Co., P.O. Box 550, Marina Del Rey, CA 90291.

Sci Peace Builders, *(Scientific Peace Builders Foundation)*, P.O. Box 3037, Santa Monica, CA 90403 Tel 213-394-4111.

Sci Pr, *(Science Press; 0-89500)*, 8 Brookstone Dr., Princeton, NJ 08540 Tel 609-921-3405.

Sci Res Assoc Coll, *(Science Research Associates, Inc., College Division)*, 1540 Page Mill Rd., P.O. Box 10021, Palo Alto, CA 94303 Tel 415-493-4700.

Sci-Tech, *(Science-Tech Publishing Co.)*, P.O. Box 2277, Sta. A, Champaign, IL 61820.

Science Man Pr, *(Science Man Press; 0-936046)*, 4738 N. Harlem Ave., Harwood Heights, IL 60656.

Scienspot, *(Scienspot Pubns.; 0-937926)*, 39 Brunswick Ave., Troy, NY 12180.

Scientific Meet, *(Scientific Meetings Pubns.)*, Poway, CA 92064; Moved, Left No Forwarding Address.

Scientific Pr, *(Scientific Press, The; 0-89426)*, 670 Gilman St., Palo Alto, CA 94301 Tel 415-322-5221.

Scientific Res, *(Scientific Research Services; 0-914314)*, 389 N Highland Ave., Hollywood, CA 90038 Tel 213-874-4101; Moved, Left No Forwarding Address.

Scissortail, *(Scissortail Pubns.; 0-939504)*, 3536 Overholser Dr., Bethany, OK 73008 Tel 405-787-7211.

SCOAL Pr, *(SCOAL Press; 0-933556)*, 53 Pondview Circle, Brockton, MA 02401 Tel 617-587-4275.

SCOP Pubns, *(SCOP Pubns.)*, 5821 Swarthmore Dr., College Park, MD 20740.

Scorcap Pub, *(Scorcap Publishing Co.)*, Superior Bldg., Suite 1111, 815 Superior N.E, Cleveland, OH 44114 Tel 216-621-0290.

Scott F, *(Scott, Foresman & Co.; 0-673)*, 1900 E. Lake Ave., Glenview, IL 60025 Tel 312-729-3000.

Scott Protective, *(Scott Protective Resources, Inc.; 0-930788)*, Philadelphia, PA 19126 Tel 215-782-1300.

Scott Pub Co, *(Scott Publishing Co.; 0-89487)*, 3 E. 57th St., New York, NY 10022 Tel 212-371-5700.

Scott Pubns CA, *(Scott Pubns.; 0-935930)*, P.O. Box 3277, Chico, CA 95926.

Scribe Pub Corp, *(Scribe Publishing Corp.; 0-915748)*, 1219 Westlake Ave. N., Suite 108, Seattle, WA 98109 Tel 206-284-9747.

Scribner, *(Scribner's, Charles, Sons; 0-684)*, 597 Fifth Ave., New York, NY 10017 Tel 212-486-2703; Orders to: Shipping & Service Ctr., Vreeland Ave., Totowa, NJ 07512.

Scrimshaw, *(Scrimshaw Press; 0-87155)*, P.O. Box 10, Centerville, MA 02632.

Scrimshaw Calif, *(Scrimshaw Press (California); 0-912020)*, 6040 Claremont Ave, Oakland, CA 94618 Tel 415-658-2323.

Scrip Pr
See Victor Bks

Scripps Inst Ocean, *(Scripps Institution of Oceanography, Univ of California, San Diego; 0-9603078)*, A007, La Jolla, CA 92093.

Scripta Medica, *(Scripta Medica & Technica; 0-931488)*, 71 Valley St., South Orange, NJ 07079.

Scriptorium, *(Scriptorium, The)*, c/o Robert Edwards, 11 N. Main St., Williamsburg, MA 01096 Tel 413-268-7208.

Scroll Pr, *(Scroll Press, Inc.; 0-87592)*, 559 W. 26th St., New York, NY 10001 Tel 212-695-8222.

Sculpt-Nouveau, *(Sculpt-Nouveau; 0-9603744)*, 21 Redwood Dr., San Rafael, CA 94901.

SE Asia Res Ctr, *(Southeast Asia Resource Center; 0-9604518)*, P.O. Box 4000-D, Berkeley, CA 94704 Tel 415-548-2546.

Sea Chall, *(Sea Challengers; 0-930118)*, 1851 Don Ave., Los Osos, CA 93402 Tel 805-528-0529.

Sea Harvest, *(Sea Harvest Press; 0-937496)*, 930 Seventh Ave. S., Naples, FL 33940 Tel 813-262-8300.

Sea Hist Pr, *(Sea History Press; 0-930248)*, Div. of National Maritime Historical Society, 2 Fulton St., Brooklyn, NY 11201 Tel 212-858-1348.

Sea Horse, *(Sea Horse Press, Ltd., The; 0-933322)*, 307 W. 11th St., New York, NY 10014 Tel 212-691-9066.

Sea Jay Pub, *(Sea Jay Publishing)*, 3778 S. 6670 West, Salt Lake City, UT 84120.

Sea Lion, *(Sea Lion Pubns.; 0-939880)*, 1716 India St., San Diego, CA 92101 Tel 714-232-2626.

Sea of Storms, *(Sea of Storms; 0-931910)*, P.O. Box 22613, San Francisco, CA 94122 Tel 707-795-2098.

Sea Urchin, *(Sea Urchin Press; 0-9605208)*, P.O. Box 10503, Oakland, CA 94610.

Seablom, *(Seablom Design; 0-918800)*, 151 Aloha St., Seattle, WA 98109 Tel 206-285-2308.

Seaboard Pr, *(Seaboard Press; 0-9600532)*, 153 Blanchard Rd., Drexel Hill, PA 19026.

Seabury, *(Seabury Press, Inc.; 0-8164)*, 815 Second Ave., New York, NY 10017 Tel 212-557-0500; Orders to: Seabury Service Center, Somers, CT 06071. *Imprints:* Vineyard (Vineyard).

Seaforth Pubns, *(Seaforth Pubns.; 0-933496)*, 12211 Coit Rd., Bratenahl, OH 44108 Tel 216-681-4561; Orders to: 117 Pine Acres Dr., Spartanburg, SC 29302 Tel 803-579-1666.

Seagull Pubns., *(Seagull Pubns., Inc.; 0-930290)*, 1736 E. 53rd St., Brooklyn, NY 11234 Tel 212-338-6622.

Seahaven Pr, *(Seahaven Press; 0-915846)*, 11 Via De La Vista, Inverness, CA 94937.

Seahawk Pr, *(Seahawk Press; 0-913008)*, 6840 S.W. 92nd St., Miami, FL 33156 Tel 305-667-4051.

Seaholm, *(Seaholm Interstate Directories Inc.)*, P.O. Box 205, New Paltz, NY 12561 Tel 914-255-0907.

SeaHorse Pr
See Sea Horse

Seal Pr, *(Seal Press; 0-930364)*, P.O. Box 3027, Seal Beach, CA 90740 Tel 714-894-4856.

Seal Pr WA, *(Seal Press)*, 533 11th, Seattle, WA 98188 Tel 206-322-2322; Moved, Left No Forwarding Address.

Seapen Bks, *(Seapen Books, Inc.; 0-932200)*, 580 Fifth Ave., Suite 821, New York, NY 10036 Tel 212-877-8240.

Search *Imprint of* Andrews & McMeel

Search & Rescue, *(Search & Rescue Magazine; 0-9603392)*, P.O. Box 641, Lompoc, CA 93438 Tel 805-733-3986.

Searchers Pubns, *(Searchers Pubns.)*, 4314 Island Crest Way, Mercer Island, WA 98040.

Seashell, *(Seashell Press; 0-935378)*, P.O. Box 747, El Cajon, CA 92022; Dist. by: Communication Creativity, 5644 La Jolla Blvd., La Jolla, CA 92037 Tel 714-459-4489; Moved, Left No Forwarding Address.

Seashell Pr, *(Seashell Press; 0-935378)*, P.O. Box 747, El Cajon, CA 92022; Dist. by: Communication Creativity, 5644 La Jolla Blvd., La Jolla, CA 92037.

Seattle Air, *(Seattle Airplane Press; 0-917196)*, 6727 Glen Echo Lane, Tacoma, WA 98499 Tel 206-584-7307.

Seattle Art, *(Seattle Art Museum; 0-932216)*, 14th E. & E. Prospect, Seattle, WA 98112 Tel 206-447-4710.

Seattle Audubon Soc, *(Seattle Audubon Society; 0-914516)*, 714 Joshua Green Bldg, 1425 Fourth Ave., Seattle, WA 98101 Tel 206-622-6695.

Seattle Bk, *(Seattle Book Co.; 0-915112)*, P.O. Box 9254, Seattle, WA 98109 Tel 206-285-1226.

Seattle Pub Co, *(Seattle Pub. Co., Inc.)*, P.O. Box 21A, Duck Creek Ave., Neshkoro, WI 54960 Tel 414-293-4009.

Seaver Bks, *(Seaver Books; 0-394)*, 333 Central Park West, New York, NY 10025 Tel 212-866-9278; Orders to: Grove Press, Inc., 196 W. Houston St., New York, NY 10014.

Seaview Bks, *(Seaview Books; 0-87223)*, Div. of P.E.I. Books, Inc., 1633 Broadway, New York, NY 10019 Tel 212-245-9160; Dist. by: Harper & Row Pubs., Inc., Keystone Industrial Park, Scranton, PA 18512.

Seaview Pr, *(Seaview Press; 0-9606048)*, P.O. Box 32, El Cerrito, CA 94530.

Seawell Multimedia, *(Seawell Multimedia Corp.; 0-917040)*, 2918 Brookside Circle, Parkersburg, WV 26101.

Second Chance, *(Second Chance Press; 0-933256)*, Sagaponack, NY 11962 Tel 516-324-5993.

Second Coming, *(Second Coming Press; 0-915016)*, P.O. Box 31249, San Francisco, CA 94131 Tel 415-647-3679.

Second Hand, *(Second Hand, The; 0-9605858)*, P.O. Box 204, Plymouth, WI 53073 Tel 414-893-5226.

Second Lang, *(Second Language Pubns.)*, P.O. Box 1700, Blaine, WA 98230; Temporarily Inactive.

Second Porcupine, *(Second Porcupine Press)*, Box 548, Santa Fe, NM 87501.

Second Soc Foun, *(Second Society Foundation)*, 333 N. Michigan Ave., Suite 707, Chicago, IL 60601.

Second Storey Pr, *(Second Storey Press; 0-915634)*, P.O. Box 63, St. Genevieve, MO 63670.

Second Thoughts, *(Second Thoughts; 0-9601286)*, 63 W. Burton Place, Chicago, IL 60610 Tel 312-337-6044.

Secure Futures, *(Secure Futures Pubns.; 0-938064)*, P.O. Box 3362, San Diego, CA 92103 Tel 714-692-0588.

Security Pr, *(Security Press, Inc.; 0-939568)*, Box 854, McLean, VA 22101 Tel 703-734-1326.

Security World
See Butterworth

Seed Center, *(Seed Center; 0-916108)*, P.O. Box 658, Garberville, CA 95440.

Seed Pubns, *(Seed Pubns.)*, Box 206, Rail Road Flat, CA 95248.

Seek-It Pubns, *(Seek-It Pubns.; 0-930706)*, P.O. Box 1074, Birmingham, MI 48012.

Seer Ox, *(Seer Ox; 0-916064)*, 807 Prospect Ave. No. 101, South Pasadena, CA 91030.

SEIA
See SEINAM

SEINAM, *(Solar Energy Institute of North America)*, 1110 6th St., N.W., Washington, DC 20001.

Selbstverlag, *(Selbstverlag Press; 0-911706)*, P.O. Drawer 606, Bloomington, IN 47402 Tel 812-332-2766.

Select Bks, *(Select Books; 0-910458)*, Rte. 1 Box 129C, Mountain View, MO 65548 Tel 417-934-6775.

Selective, *(Selective Pubs., Inc.; 0-912584)*, P.O. Box 1140, Clearwater, FL 33517 Tel 813-442-5440.

Self, *(Self)*, Box 1498, Quincy, CA 95917; Moved, Left No Forwarding Address.

Self-Help, *(Self-Help Pubns.; 0-931140)*, 2633 Monte Verde, Carmel, CA 93921 Tel 408-373-3066.

Self Instruct, *(Self Instructional Reading Service)*, P.O. Box 1291, Bloomington, IN 47402 Tel 812-339-6380.

Self-Motiv Careers, *(Self-Motivated Careers; 0-381)*, 3589 Hermitage Plantation, Duluth GA 30136.

Self-Prog Control, *(Self-Programmed Control Press; 0-9601926)*, P.O. Box 49939, Los Angeles, CA 90049 Tel 213-826-1959.

Self Realization, *(Self Realization Fellowship; 0-87612)*, 3880 San Rafael Ave., Los Angeles, CA 90065 Tel 213-225-2471.

Self Therapy
See Wingbow Pr

Sellens, *(Sellens)*, 134 Clark St., Augusta, KS 67010.

Seloc, *(Seloc Corp.; 0-89330)*, 2633 E. 28th St No. 612, Long Beach, CA 90806 Tel 213-427-8951; Formerly Glenn Publications, Inc.

Seluzicki Poetry, *(Seluzicki, Charles, Poetry Bookseller; 0-931356)*, Box 12367, Salem, OR 97309.

Seminal Pub
See Phoenix MA

Seminar Pr, *(Seminar Press)*, 111 Fifth Ave., New York, NY 10003.

Seminary Co-Op, *(Seminary Co-Operative Bookstore, Inc.; 0-912182)*, 5757 S. University Ave., Chicago, IL 60637 Tel 312-752-4381.

Seminary Pr, *(Seminary Press; 0-912832)*, P.O. Box 2218, Univ. Sta., Enid, OK 73701 Tel 405-237-4433.

Senda Nueva, *(Senda Nueva De Ediciones, Inc. 0-918454)*, P.O. Box 488, Montclair, NJ 07042 Tel 201-239-3125.

Seneca Bks, *(Seneca Books, Inc.; 0-89092)*, P.O. Box 474, Grantsville, WV 26147.

SenEd *Imprint of* HM

Senna & Shih, *(Senna & Shih, Inc.; 0-89460)*, P.O. Box 1091, 21 Beacon St., Boston, MA 02103 Tel 617-491-0858.

Senseis DoJo, *(Sensei's DoJo Supply)*, P.O. Box 1164, Hollywood, CA 90028.

Senterfitt, *(Senterfitt, Arnold, Pubns.; 0-937260)*, Drawer 27310, Escondido, CA 92027 Tel 714-489-0590.

Sentinel Star, *(Sentinel Star Co.; 0-9605772)*, P.O. Box 2833, Orlando, FL 32802 Tel 305-420-5535.

Sentry, *(Sentry Books, Inc.; 0-913194)*, 10781 White Oak Ave., Granada Hills, CA 91344 Tel 213-368-2012; Dist. by: Aviation Book Co., 1640 Victory Blvd., Glendale, CA 9120 Tel 213-240-1771.

Septima, *(Septima, Inc.)*, P.O. Box 2096, Sarasota, FL 33578 Tel 813-349-4634.

Sercolab, *(Sercolab; 0-918332)*, P.O. Box 78, Arlington, MA 02174.

Serendipity Pr, *(Serendipity Press; 0-915396)*, Div. of Price/Stern/Sloan, 410 N. LaCienega Blvd., Los Angeles, CA 90048 Tel 213-657-6100.

Serina, *(Serina Press; 0-911952)*, 70 Kennedy St., Alexandria, VA 22305 Tel 703-548-4080.

Servant, *(Servant Publications; 0-89283)*, P.O. Box 8617, 840 Airport Blvd., Ann Arbor, MI 48107 Tel 313-761-8505; Orders to: Customer Service Dept., Box 8617, Ann Arbor, MI 48107 Tel 313-761-8983; Formerly Named Word of Life.

Service Pub, *(Service Publishing Co.; 0-913104)*, Washington Bldg., 15th & New York Ave., N.W., Washington, DC 20005 Tel 202-628-1397.

Servisios Intles, *(Servisios Internacionales)*, Box 941, Texas City, TX 77590.

Sessions, *(Sessions Pubs.; 0-911366)*, 48 Nassau Dr., New Hyde Park, NY 11040 Tel 516-747-3144.

Seven Arts, *(Seven Arts Press, Inc.; 0-911370)*, 6253 Hollywood Blvd., No. 1100, Hollywood, CA 90028 Tel 213-469-1095.

Seven Buffaloes, *(Seven Buffaloes Press; 0-916380)*, P.O. Box 214, Big Timber, MT 59011; Moved, Left No Forwarding Address.

Seven C's, *(7 C's Press, Inc.; 0-911962),* P.O. Box 57, Riverside, CT 06878 Tel 203-637-9625; Dist. by: Associated Booksellers, 147 McKinley Ave., Bridgeport, CT 06606.

Seven Locks Pr, *(Seven Locks Press; 0-932020),* P.O. Box 72, Cabin John, MD 20731 Tel 202-638-1598.

Seven Oaks, *(Seven Oaks Press; 0-932508),* 405 S. 7th St., St. Charles, IL 60174 Tel 312-584-0187.

Seven Seas, *(Seven-Seas Press; 0-915160),* 32 Union Square, New York, NY 10003 Tel 212-777-2525; Dist. by: David McKay Corp., Inc, 2 Park Ave., New York, NY 10016 Tel 212-340-9800.

Seven Seven Search, *(Seven Seven Search Pubns.; 0-934726),* P.O. Box 252, Solana Beach, CA 92075 Tel 714-436-4843.

Seven Woods Pr, *(Seven Woods Press; 0-913082),* P.O. Box 32 Village Sta., New York, NY 10014.

Seventies Pr
See Eighties Pr

Seventy-Six, *(Seventy-Six Press; 0-89245),* P.O. Box 2686, Seal Beach, CA 90740 Tel 213-596-3491.

Sew-Fit, *(Sew/Fit Publishing Co.),* 960 N. Ridge, Lombard, IL 60148.

Sextant *Imprint of* **Childrens**

Sey Lawr *Imprint of* **Delacorte**

Seybold, *(Seybold Pubns., Inc.; 0-918514),* Box 644, Media, PA 19063 Tel 215-565-2480.

Seymour Pubns, *(Seymour, Dale, Pubns.; 0-86651),* P.O. Box 10888, Palo Alto, CA 94303.

Seymour-Smith, *(Seymour-Smith Pubs.),* P.O. Box 53025, San Jose, CA 95123.

SF Arts & Letters, *(San Francisco Arts & Letters Foundation; 0-914024),* P.O. Box 99394, San Francisco, CA 94109 Tel 415-771-3431.

SF Bay Area, *(San Francisco Bay Area People's Yellow Pages),* P.O. Box 31291, San Francisco, CA 94131 Tel 415-641-4011.

SF Bay Guardian, *(San Francisco Bay Guardian; 0-913192),* 2700 19th St., San Francisco, CA 94110 Tel 415-824-7660.

SF Bk Co, *(San Francisco Book Co., Inc.; 0-913374),* 2311 Fillmore St., San Francisco, CA 94115 Tel 415-922-4570.

SF Center Vis Stud, *(San Francisco Center for Visual Studies; 0-930976),* 49 Rivoli St., San Francisco, CA 94117 Tel 415-564-4538.

SF Hist Records, *(San Francisco Historic Records; 0-911792),* 1204 Nimitz Dr., Colma, CA 94015 Tel 415-755-2204.

SF Inst Auto Ecol, *(San Francisco Institute of Automotive Ecology; 0-9603356),* 52 Dore St., San Francisco, CA 94103 Tel 415-285-7403; Dist. by: Bookpeople, 2940 Seventh St., Berkeley, CA 94710.

SF Stud Ctr, *(San Francisco Study Center; 0-936434),* Box 5646, San Francisco, CA 94101.

SF Yesterday, *(San Francisco Yesterday),* P.O.Box 4343, San Rafael, CA 94903 Tel 415-479-1550.

Sgnt *Imprint of* **NAL**

Shabazz Pr, *(El-Hajj Malik Shabazz Press; 0-913358),* 445 Park Rd. N. W., Washington, DC 20010; Orders to: Liberation Information Distributing Co., 4206 Edson Place N.E., Washington, DC 20019.

Shade Tree, *(Shade Tree Books; 0-930742),* P.O. Box 2268, Huntington Beach, CA 92647 Tel 714-846-3869.

Shadow Hill, *(Shadow Hill Press; 0-911372),* North Egremont, MA 01252.

Shadwold, *(Shadwold Press; 0-9603024),* P.O. Box 706, Kennebunkport, ME 04046 Tel 207-967-4400.

Shaker Community, *(Shaker Community Inc.; 0-917322),* P.O. Box 898, Pittsfield, MA 01201 Tel 413-443-0188.

Shaker Mus, *(Shaker Museum Foundation Inc.; 0-937942),* Shaker Museum Rd., Old Chatham, NY 12136 Tel 518-794-9100.

Shaker Pr ME, *(Shaker Press, The; 0-915836),* Sabbathday Lake, Poland Spring, ME 04274 Tel 207-926-4597.

Shaker Prairie, *(Shaker Prairie Publication),* R.R. One, Oaktown, IN 47561 Tel 812-745-3153.

Shaker Savings
See Ohio Savings

Shallway Foun, *(Shallway Foundation; 0-934922),* 125 S. Fourth St., Connellsville, PA 15425.

Shalom, *(Shalom, P., Pubns., Inc.; 0-87559),* 5409 18th Ave., Brooklyn, NY 11204.

Shamal Bks, *(Shamal Books, Inc.; 0-917886),* G.P.O. Box 16, New York, NY 10001 Tel 212-622-4426.

Shambhala Pubns, *(Shambhala Pubns., Inc.; 0-87773),* 1920 13th St., P.O. Box 271, Boulder, CO 80306 Tel 303-449-6111; Dist. by: Random House, Inc., 400 Hahn Rd., Westminster, MD 21157.

Shameless Hussy, *(Shameless Hussy Press; 0-915288),* Box 3092, Berkeley, CA 94703 Tel 415-548-7800.

SHAMIR, *(SHAMIR - Assn. of Jewish Religious Scientists & Professionals from USSR),* Vozrozhdenie, 701 Empire Blvd., Brooklyn, NY 11213.

Shannon *Imprint of* **Am Natl Pub**

Shanti Pubns, *(Shanti Pubns.; 0-917042),* Rte. 2, Box 42, Alachua, FL 32615 Tel 904-462-2148.

Sharaqua, *(Sharaqua Pub. Co.; 0-917830),* P.O. Box 22453, Beachwood, OH 44122 Tel 216-292-6730.

Share Pub Co, *(Share Publishing Co.; 0-933344),* P.O. Box 6839, Charlottesville, VA 22906.

Sharing Co, *(Sharing Co., The),* P.O. Box 2224, Austin, TX 78767 Tel 512-452-4366.

Sharon Hill, *(Sharon Hill Books; 0-932062),* P.O. Box 67, Sharon Hill, PA 19079.

Shasta Abbey, *(Shasta Abbey Press; 0-930066),* P.O. Box 478, Mt. Shasta, CA 96067 Tel 916-926-4208.

Shaw Inc, *(Shaw, Mara Lynn, Inc.; 0-9605602),* 165 E. 72nd St., Suite 12n, New York, NY 10021.

Shaw Pubs, *(Shaw, Harold, Pubs.; 0-87788),* Box 567, 388 Gundersen Dr., Wheaton, IL 60187 Tel 312-665-6700.

Shawnee County Hist, *(Shawnee County Historical Society; 0-916934),* 1205 W. 29th St., Rm. 329, Topeka, KS 66611 Tel 913-267-0309; P.O. Box 56, Topeka, KS 66601.

Shawnee Pr, *(Shawnee Press, Inc.; 0-9603394),* Delaware Water Gap, PA 18327 Tel 717-476-0550.

Shayna Ltd, *(Shayna Ltd.; 0-9604208),* 100 Andrew St., Newton, MA 02161 Tel 617-244-1870.

Shearwater, *(Shearwater Press; 0-938050),* Box 417, Wellfleet, MA 02667.

Sheed, *(Sheed & Ward, Inc.),* ; Publisher Abbreviation Without Addresses Are for Titles That Are Out of Print. These Are Obsolete Abbreviations. Publisher's Abbreviation Is Now Sheed Andrews & McMeel.

Sheep Meadow, *(Sheep Meadow Press, The; 0-935296),* 145 Central Park W., New York, NY 10023; Dist. by: Persea Books, Inc., 225 Lafayette St., New York, NY 10012 Tel 212-431-5270.

Sheephead Bks, *(Sheephead Books; 0-9604644),* P.O. Box 1103, Vidalia, GA 30474.

Sheer Pr, *(Sheer Press; 0-9601254),* P.O. Box 4071, Walnut Creek, CA 94596 Tel 415-932-1144; 3601 Valley Vista Rd., Walnut Creek, CA 94598.

Sheffield Pr, *(Sheffield Press; 0-917044),* P.O. Box 723, Manhattan Beach, CA 90266 Tel 213-545-7974.

Shelburne, *(Shelburne Museum, Inc.; 0-939384),* Shelburne, VT 05482 Tel 802-985-3346.

Shell Cab, *(Shell Cabinet; 0-913792),* P.O. Box 29, Falls Church, VA 22046 Tel 703-256-0707.

Shelter Pubns
See Random

Shelter Pubns, *(Shelter Pubns.; 0-936070),* P.O. Box 279, Bolinas, CA 94924 Tel 415-868-0280; Dist. by: Random House, 400 Hahn Rd., Westminster, MD 21157.

Shelton, *(Shelton Pubns.; 0-918742),* P.O. Box 391, Sausalito, CA 94965 Tel 415-332-1165.

Shenandoah Hist, *(Shenandoah History; 0-917968),* P.O. Box 98, Edinburg, VA 22824 Tel 703-459-4598.

Shengold, *(Shengold Pubns., Inc.; 0-88400),* 45 W. 45th St., New York, NY 10036 Tel 212-246-6911.

Shepherd Pubns, *(Shepherd Pubns., Inc.; 0-935814),* P.O. Box 20665, Bloomington, MN 55420.

Sheptow, *(Sheptow Pubns.; 0-932886),* 3161 Fillmore St., San Francisco, CA 94123 Tel 415-563-4630; Moved, Left No Forwarding Address.

Sherbourne, *(Sherbourne Press; 0-8202),* P.O. Box 12037, Nashville, TN 37212 Tel 615-254-5842.

Sheriar Pr, *(Sheriar Press, Inc.; 0-913078),* 801 13th Ave. S., N. Myrtle Beach, SC 29582 Tel 803-272-5311.

Sheridan, *(Sheridan House, Inc.; 0-911378),* 175 Orawaupum St., White Plains, NY 10606 Tel 914-948-1806.

Sherman, *(Sherman, Harvey),* 4011 Garden Ave., Los Angeles, CA 90039.

Sherry Urie, *(Urie, Sherry; 0-9603324),* Craftsbury Common, VT 05827; Orders to: West Glover, VT 05875.

Sherwood Co, *(Sherwood Co., The; 0-933056),* P.O. Box 21645, Denver, CO 80221 Tel 303-423-6481.

Shetal Ent, *(Shetal Enterprises; 0-932888),* 1787 "B" W. Touhy, Chicago, IL 60626 Tel 312-262-1133.

Shields Illinois
See Shields WI

Shields Pub Co
See Publishers Consult

Shields WI, *(Shields Pubns.; 0-9600102; 0-914116),* P.O. Box 669, Eagle River, WI 54521 Tel 715-479-4810.

Shiloh, *(Shiloh, Ailon; 0-918580),* P. O. Box 16851, Tampa, FL 33687; Moved, Left No Forwarding Address.

Shinn Music
See Duane Shinn

Ship Inc, *(Ship, Inc., Pubns.),* P. O. Box 8581, Phoenix, AZ 85066.

Shire Pr, *(Shire Press; 0-918828),* P.O. Box 1728, Santa Cruz, CA 95061 Tel 408-425-0842.

Shirjieh Pubs, *(Shirjieh Pubs.; 0-912496),* P.O. Box 259, Menlo Park, CA 94025 Tel 415-323-9954.

Shoal Creek Pub, *(Shoal Creek Pubs.; 0-88319),* P.O. Box 9737, Austin, TX 78766 Tel 512-451-7545.

Shoe Serv Inst, *(Shoe Service Institute of America; 0-931424),* 222 W. Adams, Chicago, IL 60606.

Shoe String, *(Shoe String Press, Inc.; 0-208),* P.O. Box 4327, 995 Sherman Ave., Hamden, CT 06514 Tel 203-248-6307.

Shondo-Shando, *(Shondo-Shando Press; 0-9601754),* P.O. Box 887, Quincy, IL 62301.

Shopping Ctr Dir, *(Shopping Center Directory),* 424 N. Third St., Burlington, IA 52601.

Shopping Experience, *(Shopping Experience, Inc., The; 0-934758),* 2 Grace Court, Brooklyn, NY 11201 Tel 212-522-0762.

Shoreline Pub, *(Shoreline Publishing; 0-938306),* 212-08 75th Ave., Bayside, NY 11364.

Shorey, *(Shorey Pubns.; 0-8466),* 110 Union St., Seattle, WA 98111 Tel 206-624-0221.

Short Course, *(Short Course Pubns.; 0-932734),* 1333 So. Fifth Av., Arcadia, CA 91006.

Short Methods, *(Short Methods & Systems; 0-915800),* P.O. Box 247, Claremont, CA 91711 Tel 714-626-3213.

Showcase Fairfield, *(Showcase Publishing Co.; 0-88205),* Div. of Entrepreneur Press, 3422 Astoria Circle, Fairfield, CA 94533 Tel 707-422-6822; Dist. by: Elsevier-Dutton, Inc., 2 Park Ave., New York, NY 10016 Tel 212-725-1818.

Showcase Pubns, *(Showcase Pubns.; 0-917800),* P.O. Box 744-C, Pasadena, CA 91104 Tel 213-794-7782.

Shreveport Pub, *(Shreveport Publishing Corp.; 0-939042),* P.O. Box 31110, Shreveport, LA 71130.

Shrewd Info, *(Shrewd Information Press; 0-930660),* Box 39641, Los Angeles, CA 90039.

Shroud of Turin, *(Shroud of Turin Research Project, Inc.; 0-9605516),* P.O. Box 7, Amston, CT 06231.

Shulsinger Bros
See Shulsinger Sales

Shulsinger Sales, *(Shulsinger Sales, Inc.; 0-914080),* 50 Washington St., Brooklyn, NY 11201 Tel 212-852-0042.

Shumway, *(George Shumway Publisher; 0-87387),* R.D. 7, Box 388B, York, PA 17402 Tel 717-755-1196.

Sibyl-Child, *(Sibyl-Child),* Box 1773, Hyattsville, MD 20788.

Sidney Scott Ross, *(Ross, Sidney Scott; 0-9602028),* Box 543, Miami Beach, FL 33139 Tel 305-538-1442.

Siegel, *(Siegel, Kenneth L., Publishing; 0-939848),* 301 E. Balboa Blvd., Newport Beach, CA 92661 Tel 714-673-5410.

Sierra, *(Sierra Club Books; 0-87156),* 530 Bush St., San Francisco, CA 94108 Tel 415-981-8634; Dist. by: Charles Scribner's Sons, Scribner Distribution Center, Vreeland Ave., Totowa, NJ 07512.

Sierra Pubns CA, *(Sierra Pubns.; 0-932848),* P.O. Box 1972, San Jose, CA 95109 Tel 408-259-1192.

Sierra Pubns CO
See Sierra Pubns CA

Sig *Imprint of* **NAL**

Sig Classics *Imprint of* **NAL**

Sigga Pr, *(Sigga Press; 0-916348),* P.O. Box 178, George's Mills, NH 03751.

Sight&Sound, *(Sight&Sound Press; 0-9601098),* P.O. Box 1333, Pacifica, CA 94044; Moved, Left No Forwarding Address.

Sightseer, *(Sightseer Pubns.; 0-937928),* 7400 N. Kendall Dr., Miami, FL 33156.

Sigma Pr, *(Sigma Press Inc.; 0-9604516),* P.O. Box 379, South Bound Brook, NJ 08880.

Sign *Imprint of* **G&D**

Signpost Bk Pub, *(Signpost Book Publishing Co.; 0-913140),* 8912 192nd St. S.W., Edmonds, WA 98020 Tel 206-776-0370.

Signpost Pubns
See Signpost Bk Pub

Signs of Times, *(Signs of the Times Publishing Co.; 0-911380),* 407 Gilbert Ave., Cincinnati, OH 45202 Tel 513-421-2050.

Sigo Pr, *(Sigo Press; 0-938434),* 2601 Ocean Park Blvd., Santa Monica, CA 90405.

Sijthoff & Noordhoff, *(Sijthoff & Noordhoff International Publishing Co.),* 1600 Research Blvd., Rockville, MD 20850 Tel 301-251-0950.

Silbert Bress, *(Silbert & Bress Pubns.; 0-89544),* P.O. Box 68, Mahopac, NY 10541 Tel 914-628-7910.

Silver, *(Silver Burdett Co.; 0-382),* Div. of General Learning Co., 250 James St., Morristown, NJ 07960 Tel 201-285-8100.

Silver Dog, *(Silver Dog Press; 0-915244),* P.O. Box 23324, Oakland, CA 94623; Moved, Left No Forwarding Address.

Silver Dollar, *(Silver Dollar City, Inc.),* Silver Dollar City, MO 65616 Tel 417-388-2611.

Silver Fox, *(Silver Fox Connections; 0-9605910),* 1244 S.W. 301st St., Federal Way, WA 98003.

Silverado, *(Silverado Publishing Co.; 0-87938),* St. Helena, CA 94574; Dist. by: Motorbooks International, Pubs. & Wholesalers, P.O. Box 2, 729 Prospect Ave., Osceola, WI 54020 Tel 715-294-3345.

Silvermine, *(Silvermine Pubs.; 0-87231),* Comstock Hill, Silvermine, Norwalk, CT 06850 Tel 203-847-4732.

Simile II, *(Simile II),* 218 Twelfth St., P.O. Box 910, Del Mar, CA 92014 Tel 714-755-0272.

Simon Belt, *(Simon Belt Publishes),* P.O. Box 368, Bluff, UT 84512 Tel 801-672-2220.

Simon-Day, *(Simon-Day Publishing Co.),* 255 Flores St., Suite 175, San Mateo, CA 94403 Tel 415-349-1908; Moved, Left No Forwarding Address.

Simons Bks, *(Simons Books Inc.; 0-937812),* P.O. Box 1034, Oceanside, CA 92054; 725 Market St., Wilmington, DE 19801.

Simplex Comm, *(Simplex Communications, Inc.; 0-935248),* P.O. Box 9133, Fort Wayne, IN 46783 Tel 219-672-3702.

Simplicity, *(Simplicity Pattern Co., Inc.; 0-918178),* 200 Madison Ave., New York, NY 10016 Tel 212-481-1777; Orders to: Simplicity Educational Div., 901 Wayne St., Niles, MI 49121.

Simply Elegant, *(Simply Elegant; 0-9600492),* 3801 N. Mission Hills Rd., Northbrook, IL 60062 Tel 312-564-2221; Orders to: P.O. Box 74, Winnetka, IL 60093.

Simpson-Hirshman, *(Simpson-Hirshman Publishing; 0-938406),* 1008 Western Ave., Seattle, WA 98104.

Simpson Pub, *(Simpson Publishing Co.),* 1115 S. Franklin St., Kirksville, MO 63501 Tel 816-665-7251.

Simtek, *(Simtek; 0-933836),* P.O. Box 109, Cambridge, MA 02139 Tel 617-232-5020.

Simul Learn, *(Simulation Learning Institute, Inc.; 0-918640),* 15 Duke of Gloucester, Manhasset, NY 11030 Tel 516-627-3839; Orders to: P.O. Box 1014, Manhasset, NY 11030.

Simul Pubns, *(Simulations Pubns, Inc.; 0-917852),* 257 Park Ave. S., New York, NY 10010 Tel 212-673-4103.

Sinauer Assoc, *(Sinauer Associates, Inc.; 0-87893),* N. Main St, Sunderland, MA 01375 Tel 413-665-3722.

Sincere Pr, *(Sincere Press; 0-912534),* Box 17599, Tucson, AZ 85731; Moved, Left No Forwarding Address.

Singer Island, *(Singer Island Press; 0-935860),* 2649 Lake Dr., Singer Island, FL 33404.

Singing Tree, *(Singing Tree Press),* ; Publisher Abbreviation Without Addresses Are for Titles That Are Out of Print. These Are Obsolete Abbreviations.

Single Impressions, *(Single Impressions; 0-938562),* 642 W. Zia Dr., Tucson, AZ 85704.

Singlejack
See Miles & Weir

Singles World, *(Singles World Publishing Co.; 0-936890),* 1094 Cudahy, No. 102, San Diego, CA 92110; Dist. by: Communication Creativity, P.O. Box 213, Saguache, CO 81149 Tel 303-655-2502.

Singletary, *(Singletary, Milly; 0-9601256),* 1655 Makaloa St., Suite 906, Honolulu, HI 96814 Tel 808-949-1968; Dist. by: Press Pacifica, Box 47, Kailua, HI 96734.

Sino Pub Co, *(Sino Publishing Co.; 0-86519),* 745 Fifth Ave., Suite 601, New York, NY 10151 Tel 212-935-6211; Dist. by: Caroline House Publishers, Inc., 2 Ellis Place, Ossining, NY 10562.

Sipapu-Konocti Bks, *(Sipapu/Konocti Books; 0-914134),* Rte. 1, Box 216, Winters, CA 95694 Tel 916-662-3364.

Sirius Bks, *(Sirius Books; 0-917108),* P.O. Box 6294, Eureka, CA 95501 Tel 707-442-8481.

Sis Clark, *(Sis Clark),* 2174 Louis Rd., Palo Alto, CA 94303.

Sis Kenny Inst, *(Sister Kenny Institute; 0-88440),* 1800 Chicago Ave., Minneapolis, MN 55404 Tel 612-871-7331.

Sisters Choice, *(Sisters' Choice Press; 0-932164),* 2027 Parker St., Berkeley, CA 94704 Tel 415-843-0533.

Sitare Inc, *(Sitare, Inc.; 0-940178),* 1888 Century Park E., No. 10, Los Angeles, CA 90067.

Sitnalta Pr, *(Sitnalta Press; 0-931826),* 1881 Sutter St., No. 103, San Francisco, CA 94115 Tel 415-922-8223.

SK Pubns, *(SK Pubns.; 0-936306),* 7149 Natalie Blvd., Northfield Center, OH 44067.

Ski Ent, *(Ski Enterprises; 0-933058),* 820 Ellen Lane, Fond Du Lac, WI 54935 Tel 414-922-6551.

Skills Improvement, *(Skills Improvement, Inc.; 0-939570),* P.O. Box 13096, Omaha, NE 68113 Tel 402-292-5610.

Skipworth Pr, *(Skipworth Press, Inc.; 0-931804),* P.O. Box 5397, Richmond, VA 23227 Tel 804-746-3551.

Skousen, *(Skousen, W. Cleon),* 2197 Berkely St., Salt Lake City, UT 84109.

Sky Pub, *(Sky Publishing Corp.; 0-933346),* 49 Bay State Rd., Cambridge, MA 02238 Tel 617-864-7360.

Skye Terrier, *(Skye Terrier Club of America; 0-9600722),* 2222 S. 12th St., St. Louis, MO 63104 Tel 314-367-4444.

Skylark *Imprint of* **Bantam**

Skyview Pub, *(Skyview Publishing; 0-934618),* Box L, Bellmore, NY 11710.

SLA, *(Special Libraries Assn.; 0-87111),* 235 Park Ave., S., New York, NY 10003 Tel 212-477-9250.

Slate Servs, *(Slate Services; 0-913448),* P.O. Box 8796, Fountain Valley, CA 92708 Tel 714-892-0889.

Slavia Lib, *(Slavia Library; 0-918884),* 418 W. Nittany Ave., State College, PA 16801.

Slavica, *(Slavica Publishers Inc.; 0-89357),* P.O. Box 14388, Columbus, OH 43214.

Sleepy Hollow, *(Sleepy Hollow Press, The; 0-912882),* 150 White Plains Rd., Tarrytown, NY 10591 Tel 914-631-8200; Dist. by: Independent Publishers Group, 14 Vanderventer Ave., Port Washington, NY 11050 Tel 516-944-9325.

Sloan-Kettering, *(Sloan-Kettering Institute for Cancer Research; 0-88485),* 1275 York Ave., New York, NY 10021 Tel 212-879-3000.

Slohm Assoc, *(Slohm, Natalie, Associates, Inc.; 0-916840),* 49 W. Main St., Cambridge, NY 12816 Tel 518-677-3040.

Slow Loris, *(Slow Loris Press; 0-918366),* 923 Highview St., Pittsburgh, PA 15206.

Slurry Transport, *(Slurry Transport Assn.; 0-932066),* 490 L'Enfant Plaza East., S.W. Suite 3210, Washington, DC 20024.

SLUSA, *(SLUSA),* 88 Eastern Ave., Somerville, NJ 08876.

Small Busn Pubns, *(Small Business Pubns.; 0-9605436),* Drawer 330, Osterville, MA 02655.

Small Wonder, *(Small Wonder Enterprises),* Orders to: RPM Distributors, 5862 Wicomico Ave., Rockville, MD 20852; Moved, Left No Forwarding Address.

SME, *(Society of Manufacturing Engineers; 0-87263),* P.O. Box 930, One SME Dr., Dearborn, MI 48128 Tel 313-271-1500.

Smilepower, *(Smilepower Institute; 0-918802),* 1225 Nadina St., San Mateo, CA 94402 Tel 415-341-6042.

Smith & Assoc, *(Smith & Associates; 0-938260),* Box 61648, Houston, TX 77208.

Smith Coll, *(Smith College, Pubns.; 0-87391),* College Hall 26, Northampton, MA 01063 Tel 413-584-2700; Dist. by: Neilson Library, Office of the Director of Technical Services, Northampton, MA 01063.

Smith Coll Mus Art, *(Smith College Museum of Art),* Elm at Bedford Terrace, Northampton, MA 01063 Tel 413-584-2700.

Smith Lib, *(Smith, Warren Hunting, Library; 0-939624),* Hobart & William Smith Colleges, Geneva, NY 14456 Tel 315-789-5500.

Smith Pubs, *(Smith, W. H., Pubs., Inc.; 0-8317),* 575 Lexington Ave., New York, NY 10022 Tel 212-888-9200. *Imprints:* Mayflower Bks (Mayflower Books); Rutledge Pr (Rutledge Press); Sunflower Bks (Sunflower Books).

Smithsonian, *(Smithsonian Institution Press; 0-87474),* Rm. 2280, Arts & Industries Bldg, Washington, DC 20560 Tel 202-357-1912; Orders to: P.O. Box 1579, Washington, DC 20013 Tel 202-357-1793; Booksellers Order from: Publications Sales, 1111 N. Capitol St, Washington, DC 20560, Tel- 202-357-1793.

Smithsonian Expo Bks, *(Smithsonian Exposition Books; 0-89599),* 475 L'enfant Plaza, Rm. 2800, Washington, DC 20560 Tel 202-287-3388.

Smithsonian Expo, *(Smithsonian Exposition Books; 0-89599),* 475 L'enfant Plaza, Rm. 2800, Washington, DC 20560 Tel 202-287-3388; Dist. by: W.W. Norton, 500 Fifth Ave., New York, NY 10036.

Smoke Shop, *(Smoke Shop Press, The; 0-939572),* 108 Waterman St., No. 2A, Providence, RI 02906.

Smoke Signal, *(Smoke Signal Press),* Shenandoah, IA 51601.

Smoley, *(Smoley, C. K., & Sons, Inc.; 0-911396),* P.O. Box 14, Chautauqua, NY 14722.

Smoloskyp, *(Smoloskyp Pubns.; 0-914834),* P.O. Box 561, Ellicott, MD 21043 Tel 601-461-1764.

SMU Press, *(Southern Methodist Univ. Press; 0-87074),* Dallas, TX 75275 Tel 214-692-2263.

Smugglers, *(Smugglers Cove Pub.; 0-918484),* c/o The Design Team, 107 W. John St., Seattle, WA 98119 Tel 206-285-3171.

Smyrna, *(Smyrna Press; 0-918266),* P.O. Box 1803, GPO, Brooklyn, NY 11202 Tel 212-638-8939.

SNAG, *(Society of North American Goldsmith; 0-9604446),* 8589 Wonderland NW, Clinton, OH 44216.

Snail Bks, *(Snail Books; 0-931264),* 3940 Algonquin Dr., Suite 164, Las Vegas, NV 89109; Moved, Left No Forwarding Address.

Sniffen Court, *(Sniffen Court Books; 0-930790),* c/o Atheneum Pubs., 597 Fifth Ave., New York, NY 10017.

SnO Pubns, *(SnO Pubns.; 0-937814),* Stockbridge, MA 01262.

Snow Pr, *(Snow Press; 0-9601148),* 9300 Home Court, Des Plaines, IL 60016 Tel 312-299-7605; Orders to: P.O. Box 42 Morton Grove, IL 60053.

Snowstorm, *(Snowstorm Pubns.; 0-9605366),* Box 2310, Breckenridge, CO 80424.

Snug Harbor, *(Snug Harbor Publishing Co.; 0-911898),* P.O. Box 3312, Ridgeway Sta., Stamford, CT 06905 Tel 203-322-6969.

Snug Harbor NY, *(Snug Harbor Cultural Center; 0-9604254),* 914 Richmond Terrace, Staten Island, NY 10301.

Snyder Inst Res, *(Snyder Institute of Research),* 508 N. Pacific Coast Hwy., Redondo Beach, CA 90277 Tel 213-372-4469.

So&So Pr, *(So & So Press; 0-918842),* 1730 Carleton, Berkeley, CA 94703 Tel 415-548-6116.

Soaring Symposia, *(Soaring Symposia; 0-914600),* Route 1, Box 157-F, Keyser, WV 26726 Tel 301-786-4697.

Soc Adv Material, *(Society for the Advancement of Materials & Process Engineering (S.A.M.P.E.)),* Box 613, Azusa, CA 91702 Tel 213-334-1810.

Soc Am Archivists, *(Society of American Archivists; 0-931828),* 330 S. Wells St., Suite 810, Chicago, IL 60606 Tel 312-922-0140.

Soc Animal Rights, *(Society for Animal Rights, Inc.; 0-9602632),* 421 S. State St., Clarks Summit, PA 18411 Tel 717-586-2200.

Soc Applied Anthro, *(Society for Applied Anthropology),* 1703 New Hampshire Ave. N.W, Washington, DC 20009 Tel 202-232-8800.

Soc Auto Engineers, *(Society of Automotive Engineers, Inc.; 0-89883),* 400 Commonwealth Dr., Warrendale, PA 15096 Tel 412-776-4841.

Soc Exploration, *(Society of Exploration Geophysicists; 0-931830),* P.O. Box 3098, Tulsa, OK 74135 Tel 918-743-1365.

Soc for Visual, *(Society for Visual Education, Inc.; 0-89290),* 1345 W. Diversey Pkwy., Chicago, IL 60614 Tel 312-525-1500.

Soc Indus-Appl Math, *(Society for Industrial & Applied Mathematics; 0-89871),* 33 S. 17th St., Philadelphia, PA 19103.

Soc Industrial Realtors, *(Society of Industrial Realtors Educational Fund),* Div. of National Associaton of Realtors, 925 15th St., N.W., Washington, DC 20005 Tel 202-637-6880.

Soc Intercult Ed Train & Res, *(SIETAR; 0-933934),* George Washington University, Washington, DC 20057.

Soc Intl Dev, *(Society for International Development; 0-911402),* 1346 Connecticut Ave., N.W., Washington, DC 20036 Tel 202-296-3810.

Soc Mining Eng, *(Society of Mining Engineers of A. I. M. E.; 0-89520),* Caller No. D, Littleton, CO 80127 Tel 303-973-9550.

Soc Naval Arch, *(Society of Naval Architects & Marine Engineers; 0-9603048),* One World Trade Center, 1369, New York, NY 10048 Tel 212-432-0310.

Soc New Lang Study, *(Society for New Language Study, Inc.; 0-9502699; 0-936072),* P.O. Box 10596, Denver, CO 80210 Tel 303-777-6115.

Soc Nuclear Med, *(Society of Nuclear Medicine, Inc.; 0-932004),* 475 Park Ave. So., New York, NY 10016 Tel 212-889-0717.

Soc Petrol Engineers, *(Society of Petroleum Engineers of AIME; 0-89520),* 6200 N. Central Expressway, Dallas, TX 75206 Tel 214-361-6601; Orders to: Book Dept., SPE, 6200 N. Central Expressway, Dallas, TX 75206.

Soc Photo Sci & Eng, *(Society of Photographic Scientists & Engineers; 0-89208),* 1411 "K" St., N.W., Suite 930, Washington, DC 20005 Tel 202-347-1140.

Soc Pragmatic, *(Society of Pragmatic Mysticism; 0-89369),* 200 W. 58th St., Apt. 9B, New York, NY 10019 Tel 212-246-5464.

Soc Res Assoc
   See Social Res

Soc Sci & Soc Res, *(Social Science & Sociological Resources; 0-915574),* P.O. Box 241, Aurora, IL 60507.

Soc Sci Ed, *(Social Science Education Consortium, Inc; 0-89994),* 855 Broadway, Boulder, CO 80302 Tel 303-492-8154.

Soc Sci Inst, *(Social Science Institute; 0-911394),* Harborside, ME 04642.

Soc Sci Pr, *(Social Science Press, Inc.; 0-911396),* 100 Oakdale Rd., Athens, GA 30606 Tel 404-542-4581.

Soc Sci Res, *(Social Science Research Council; 0-911400),* 605 Third Ave., New York, NY 10016.

Soc Sci Stud Rel, *(Society for the Scientific Study of Religion; 0-932566),* Box U-68A, Univ. of Connecticut, Storrs, CT 06268.

Soc Span Stud, *(Society of Spanish Studies; 0-913784),* 9944 Harriet Ave., S., Bloomington, MN 55420; Moved, Left No Forwarding Address.

Soc Tech Comm, *(Society for Technical Communication; 0-914548),* 815 15th St. N.W., Suite 506, Washington, DC 20005 Tel 202-737-0035; Dist. by: Univelt, Inc., P.O. Box 28130, San Diego, CA 92128 Tel 714-746-4005.

Soccer, *(Sportshelf & Soccer Associates; 0-392),* P.O. Box 634, New Rochelle, NY 10802 Tel 914-235-2347.

Soccer for Am, *(Soccer for Americans; 0-916802),* P.O. Box 836, Manhattan Beach, CA 90266 Tel 213-372-9000.

Social Matrix, *(Social Matrix Research, Inc.; 0-89995),* P.O. Box 9128, Boston, MA 02114 Tel 617-367-1231.

Social Res, *(Social Research Associates),* 335 N.E. 53rd St., Seattle, WA 98105 Tel 206-632-0578; Moved, Left No Forwarding Address.

Society Fire Protect, *(Society of Fire Protection Engineers),* 60 Batterymarch St., Boston, MA 02110 Tel 617-482-0686.

Society Sp & Sp-Am, *(Society of Spanish & Spanish-American Studies; 0-89295),* Society of Spanish and Spanish-American Studies, Dept. of Modern Languages & Literatures, Univ. of Nebraska-Lincoln, Lincoln, NE 68588 Tel 402-472-3745.

Sociology Pr, *(Sociology Press),* P.O. Box 152, Mill Valley, CA 94941.

SocSP *Imprint of B&N*

SOEH, *(Society for Occupational Environmental Health; 0-931770),* 2914 M St., N.W., Washington, DC 20007 Tel 202-965-6633.

Soft Pr, *(Soft Press; 0-919590),* 1525 McRae Ave., Victoria British Columbia, V8P 1G4 Canada, Tel 604-598-2173.

Software Supply, *(Software Supply; 0-9603792),* 4618 E. Sixth St., Long Beach, CA 90814.

Soho Bodhi, *(Soho Bodhi; 0-9605096),* 242 Lafayette St., New York, NY 10012.

Soil Conservation, *(Soil Conservation Society of America; 0-935734),* 7515 N.E. Ankeny Rd., Ankeny, IA 50021.

Soil Sci Soc Am, *(Soil Science Society of America),* 677 S. Segoe Rd., Madison, WI 53711 Tel 608-274-1212.

Soil Sci Soc Am, *(Soil Science Society of America),* 677 S. Segoe Rd., Madison, WI 53711 Tel 608-274-1212.

Sol Press *Imprint of Wisconsin Bks*

Solar Age Pr, *(Solar Age Press; 0-914304),* Indian Mills, WV 24949.

Solar Energy Info, *(Solar Energy Information Services (SEIS); 0-930978; 0-89934),* 18 Second Ave., P.O. Box 204, San Mateo, CA 94401 Tel 415-347-2640.

SOLARC, *(SOLARC - Solar Energy in Architecture),* P.O. Box 18024, Irvine, CA 92713 Tel 714-549-1362.

SolarVision, *(SolarVision, Inc.; 0-918984),* Church Hill, Harrisville, NH 03450 Tel 603-827-3347.

Soldier Creek, *(Soldier Creek Press; 0-936996),* Box 863, Lake Crystal, MN 56055.

Solex Solar, *(Solex Solar Energy Systems; 0-8168),* 444 Bedford Rd., Pleasantville, NY 10570.

Solo, *(Solo Music, Inc.; 0-913754),* 4708 Van Noord Ave., Sherman Oaks, CA 91423 Tel 213-762-2219.

Solo Pr, *(Solo Press),* 7670 Valle, Atascadero, CA 93422 Tel 805-466-0947.

Solobooks, *(Solobooks; 0-939004),* P.O. Box 2292, Modesto, CA 95351.

Solpub, *(Solpub Co.; 0-931912),* Box 9209, College Sta., TX 77840 Tel 713-845-4133.

Some Place
   See Lacis Pubns

Somerset Hse, *(Somerset House; 0-914146; 0-89887),* 206 N. Alfred St., Alexandria, VA 22314 Tel 703-549-7369; Orders to: 417 Maitland Ave., Teaneck, NJ 07666 Tel 201-833-1795.

Somerset Pr IL, *(Somerset Press; 0-916642),* Executive Dr., Carol Stream, IL 60187 Tel 312-665-3200.

Somerset Pub, *(Somerset Pubs.),* Div. of Scholarly Press, Inc., 19722 E. Nine Mile Rd, St. Clair Shores, MI 48080.

Something Else, *(Something Else Press, Inc.),* P.O. Box H, Baiton, VT 05822; Out of Business.

Sometime Pr, *(Sometime Press, Inc.; 0-936230),* P.O. Box 986, Marblehead, MA 01945.

Somist, *(Somist Institute Press; 0-930120),* 87 Middle St., Gloucester, MA 01930 Tel 617-283-4936.

Somrie Pr, *(Somrie Press; 0-9603950),* 1134 E. 72nd St., Brooklyn, NY 11234.

Sonica Pr, *(Sonica Press),* 6255 Sunset Blvd., Suite 609, Los Angeles, CA 90028 Tel 213-393-1590.

Sono Pubs, *(Sono Publishers; 0-916898),* 554 N. Arden Blvd., Los Angeles, CA 90004 Tel 213-467-3597.

Sonoma County, *(Sonoma County Bike Trails),* 50 Crest Way, Penngrove, CA 94951.

Sonoran Desert, *(Sonoran Desert Press),* P.O. Box 729, Phoenix, AZ 85001; Moved, Left No Forwarding Address.

Sonrise Prods, *(SONrise Productions),* 746 E. 79th St., Box 186, Chicago, IL 60619.

Sooty-Face, *(Sooty-Face Publishing Co.; 0-9602366),* P.O. Box 26, Clairton, PA 15025 Tel 412-233-6141.

Sorger Assocs, *(Sorger Associates Inc.; 0-9604072),* 229 Humphrey St., Marblehead, MA 01945.

Sothis & Co, *(Sothis & Co.; 0-933284),* P.O. Box 1166, Delmar, CA 92014 Tel 714-481-9355.

Sound Pub, *(Sound Publishing Co.),* 156 E. 37th St., New York, NY 10016 Tel 212-685-3480.

Soundview Bks, *(Soundview Books; 0-934924),* 100 Heights Rd., Darien, CT 06820 Tel 203-655-1436; Dist. by: Caroline House, 2 Ellis Place, Ossining, NY 10562 Tel 914-941-9271.

Soup to Nuts, *(Soup to Nuts Press; 0-9604780),* 582 Fernando Dr., Novato, CA 94947.

Source Pubs, *(Source Pubs., Inc.; 0-87915),* 261 Madison Ave.,Rm. No. 1102, New York, NY 10017 Tel 212-687-9615.

Sourcebook, *(Sourcebook Project, The; 0-9600712; 0-915554),* P.O. Box 107, Glen Arm, MD 21057 Tel 301-668-6047.

Sourcebook Pubns FL, *(Sourcebook Pubns, Inc.; 0-939412),* P.O. Box 1586, Winter Park, FL 32790 Tel 305-628-0545.

Sourcebooks CA, *(Sourcebooks; 0-933422),* 18758 Bryant St., Northridge, CA 91324.

Sources, *(Sources; 0-9603232),* 26 Hart Ave., Hopewell, NJ 08525 Tel 609-466-0051.

South Asia Bks, *(South Asia Books; 0-88386; 0-8364),* P.O. Box 502, Columbia, MO 65205 Tel 314-449-1359. Imprints: Orient Longman (Orient Longman).

South End Pr, *(South End Press; 0-89608),* Box 68, Astor Sta., Boston, MA 02123 Tel 617-266-0629.

South Pass Pr, *(South Pass Press; 0-932068),* 2220 S. Bonham St., Amarillo, TX 79109 Tel 806-354-4068.

South St Sea Mus, *(South Street Seaport Museum; 0-913344),* 16 Fulton St., New York, NY 10038 Tel 212-766-9020; Dist. by: Interbook, Inc., 545 8th Ave., New York, NY 10018.

Southeast Acoustics, *(Southeast Acoustics Institute; 0-89671),* P.O. Box 590, Madison, GA 30650.

Southern Ctr Intl Stud, *(Southern Center for International Studies, Inc.; 0-935082),* 3400 Peachtree Rd., N.E., Suite 1239, Lenox Towers, Atlanta, GA 30326 Tel 404-261-5763.

Southern Hist Pr, *(Southern Historical Press; 0-89308),* P.O. Box 738, Easley, SC 29640 Tel 803-859-2336.

Southern Microfilm, *(Southern Microfilm),* P. O. Box 1824, Houston, TX 77001.

Southern Pr, *(Southern Press, Inc.; 0-915536),* 301 Terry Hutchens Bldg., 102 Clinton Ave. W., Huntsville, AL 35801.

Southern Prog Alliance
   See Alliance Pubs

Southern Typeset, *(Southern Typesetting Co.),* P.O. Box 43701, Atlanta, GA 30336 Tel 404-832-8269; Moved, Left No Forwarding Address.

Southern U Pr, *(Southern Univ. Press; 0-87651),* 130 S. 19th St., Birmingham, AL 35233.

Southwest Bk Servs, *(Southwest Book Services, Inc.),* 4951 Top Line Dr., Dallas, TX 75247 Tel 214-688-1591.

Southwest Mus, *(Southwest Museum),* P.O. Box 128, Highland Park Sta., Los Angeles, CA 90042 Tel 213-221-2163.

Southwest Screen Print, (*Southwest Screen Print Ind., Inc.; 0-9603530*), P.O. Box 423, Scottsdale, AZ 85252.

Sovereign Bks, (*Sovereign Books*), Div. of Simon & Schuster, c/o Cornerstone Library, 1230 Ave. of the Americas, New York, NY 10020 Tel 212-245-6400.

Sovereign Pr, (*Sovereign Press; 0-914752*), 326 Harris Rd., Rochester, WA 98579 Tel 206-273-5109.

Soviet Studies, (*Soviet Studies; 0-930232*), P.O. Box 16, Hayward, CA 94543.

Sowa Bks, (*Sowa Books; 0-9605638*), 4923 Brandeis Circle, San Antonio, TX 78249.

Sowers, (*Sowers Printing Co.; 0-911410*), P.O. Box 479, Lebanon, PA 17042.

Soyfoods-New Age, (*Soyfoods Center/New-Age Foods; 0-933332*), P.O. Box 234, Lafayette, CA 94549 Tel 415-283-2991.

SP Med & Sci Bks, (*SP Medical & Scientific Books; 0-89335*), Div. of Spectrum Publications, Inc., 175-20 Wexford Terrace, Jamaica, NY 11432 Tel 212-658-0888.

Space Age, (*Space Age Press, Ltd.; 0-911412*), P.O. Box 11448, Fort Worth, TX 76109.

Space-Time, (*Space/Time Designs, Inc.; 0-9603570*), P.O. Box 1989, Sedona, AZ 86336 Tel 602-282-3639.

Spaceman Pr, (*Spaceman Press; 0-9603546*), 139 Carmel Ave., Pacific Grove, CA 93950 Tel 408-372-5915.

SPAFASWAP, (*SPAFASWAP*), 1070 Ahern Dr., La Puente, CA 91746 Tel 213-962-3910.

SP&M, (*Serran Pagan/Muntadas; 0-9604114*), 301 E. 22nd St., New York, NY 10010.

Spanish Lit Pubns, (*Spanish Literature Pubns. Co., Inc.; 0-938972*), Box 707, York, SC 29745.

Sparks Pr, (*Sparks Press; 0-916822*), 900 W. Morgan St., P.O. Box 26747, Raleigh, NC 27611 Tel 919-834-8283.

Sparrow Pr, (*Sparrow Press; 0-935552*), 103 Waldron St., West Lafayette, IN 47906 Tel 317-743-1991.

Spartacus Pr, (*Spartacus Press; 0-89432*), P.O. Box 71, South Dartmouth, MA 02748; Moved, Left No Forwarding Address.

Spartan *Imprint of* **Hayden**

Spartan Pr, (*Spartan Press; 0-912924*), P.O. Box 221, East Lansing, MI 48823; Moved, Left No Forwarding Address.

Spears, (*Spears, W. H., Jr.; 0-9600106*), 426 N. Kennicott, Arlington Heights, IL 60004.

Spec *Imprint of* **P-H**

Spec Aviation, (*Special Aviation Pubns.; 0-915376*), P.O. Box 672, Hillsboro, TX 76645 Tel 817-836-4269.

Spec Child, (*Special Child Pubns.; 0-87562*), 4535 Union Bay Place N.E., Seattle, WA 98105 Tel 206-522-2036.

Spec Features Wkshp, (*Special Features Workshop; 0-917466*), 32 Warnock Dr., Westport, CT 06880 Tel 203-226-9370.

Spec Learn Corp, (*Special Learning Corp.; 0-89568*), 42 Boston Post Rd., Guilford, CT 06437 Tel 203-453-6525.

Spec Lit Pr, (*Special Literature Press*), P.O. Box 4397, Benson Sta., Omaha, NE 68104.

Spec Pr NJ, (*Specialty Press, Inc.; 0-913556*), P.O. Box 2187, Ocean, NJ 07712 Tel 201-774-8447.

Specialist, (*Specialist Publishing Co.; 0-911416*), 109 La Mesa Dr., Burlingame, CA 94010 Tel 415-344-4958.

Specialty Bks, (*Specialty Books, International; 0-89445*), P.O. Box 1785, Ann Arbor, MI 48106 Tel 517-456-4764.

Specialty Pr, (*Specialty Press Pubs. & Wholesalers, Inc.; 0-933424*), Box 426, 729 Prospect Ave., Osceola, WI 54020 Tel 715-294-2090.

Specialty Pubns
See Talent & Booking

Spectrum CA, (*Spectrum Publishing; 0-930018*), 4080 Siskiyou Ave., Santa Rosa, CA 95405 Tel 707-546-0521; Moved Left No Forwarding Address; Do Not Confuse with Spectrum Prods.

Spectrum Prods, (*Spectrum Productions; 0-914502*), 979 Casiano Rd., Los Angeles, CA 90049 Tel 213-476-4543; Do Not Confuse with Spectrum CA.

Spectrum Pub, (*Spectrum Pubns., Inc.; 0-89335*), 175-20 Wexford Terrace, Jamaica, NY 11432 Tel 212-658-0888; Do Not Confuse with Spectrum CA or Spectrum Prods.

· **Speech & Hearing**

See Press West

Speech Commun Assn, (*Speech Communication Assn.*), 5205 Leesburg Pike, Falls Church, VA 22041 Tel 703-379-1888.

Speech Found Am, (*Speech Foundation of America; 0-933388*), 152 Lombardy Rd., Memphis, TN 38111.

Speechphone *Imprint of* **J Norton Pubs**

Speer Bks, (*Speer Books; 0-917832*), 234 S. Main St., Red Bluff, CA 96080.

Speleo Pr, (*Speleo Press; 0-914092*), P.O. Box 7037, Austin, TX 78712 Tel 512-847-2709.

Speller, (*Speller, Robert, & Sons, Pub., Inc.; 0-8315*), 30 E. 23rd St., New York, NY 10010 Tel 212-477-5524; Orders to: P.O. Box 461, Times Square Sta., New York, NY 10036.

Spencer Pubs, (*Spencer, Daniel, Pubs.; 0-936496*), 31970 Pacific Coast Hwy, Malibu, CA 90265.

Sperr & Douth, (*Sperr & Douth, Inc.; 0-912902*), 663 Fifth Ave., New York, NY 10022 Tel 212-757-6454; Moved, Left No Forwarding Address.

Spevack, (*Spevack, Jerome M., Inc.; 0-9604480*), 224 E. Hickory St., No.2, Arcadia, FL 33821.

Sphinx Pr, (*Sphinx Press*), c/o International Universities Press, Inc., 315 Fifth Ave., New York, NY 10016.

SPIA-GWU, (*School of Public & International Affairs, George Washington Univ.; 0-932768*), Washington, DC 20052 Tel 202-676-7494.

Spice West, (*Spice West Co.; 0-9602812*), Box 2044, Pocatello, ID 83201.

Spielvogel, (*Spielvogel, S. W.; 0-9600108*), 50 Hillpark Ave., Great Neck, NY 11021 Tel 516-487-4138.

Spilman Pr, (*Spilman Press; 0-918180*), Subs. of Spilman Printing Co., 1801 9th St., Sacramento, CA 95814 Tel 916-444-0411.

Spin-A-Test Pub, (*Spin-A-Test Publishing Co.; 0-915048*), 404 Old Orchard Court, Danville, CA 94526 Tel 415-837-4532; P.O. Box 881, Alamo, CA 94507.

Spindrift, (*Spindrift Press; 0-914864*), P.O. Box 3252, Catonsville, MD 21228 Tel 301-944-3317.

Spinning Spool, (*Spinning Spool*), P.O. Box 1425, East Lansing, MI 48823 Tel 517-332-3729.

Spinsters Ink, (*Spinsters, Ink; 0-933216*), R.D. 1, Argyle, NY 12809 Tel 518-854-3109.

Spirit That Moves, (*Spirit That Moves Us, The; 0-930370*), P.O. Box 1585, Iowa City, IA 52244 Tel 319-338-5569.

Spiritual Advisory, (*Spiritual Advisory Press; 0-939386*), P.O. Box 6344, Santa Barbara, CA 93111.

Spiritual Comm, (*Spiritual Community Pubns.; 0-913852*), P.O. Box 1080, San Rafael, CA 94902 Tel 415-457-2990.

Spiritual Renaissance, (*Spiritual Renaissance Press; 0-938380*), P.O. Box 347, Berkeley, CA 94701; Dist. by: Bookpeople, 2940 Seventh St., Berkeley, CA 94710 Tel 415-549-3030.

Spiritual Sci Lib, (*Spiritual Science Library*), 7 Garber Hill Rd., Blauvelt, NY 10913 Tel 914-359-9292.

Spizzirri, (*Spizzirri Publishing Co., Inc.; 0-86545*), P.O. Box 664, Medinah, IL 60157.

Spoken Lang Serv, (*Spoken Language Services, Inc.; 0-87950*), P.O. Box 783, Ithaca, NY 14850 Tel 607-257-0500.

Spoon Riv Poetry, (*Spoon River Poetry Press; 0-933180*), P.O. Box 1443, Peoria, IL 61655 Tel 309-676-7611; Do Not Confuse with the Spoon River Press.

Spoon River, (*Spoon River Press, The; 0-930358*), P.O. Box 3635, Peoria, IL 61614 Tel 309-682-2286; Do Not Confuse with Spoon River Poetry Press.

Sport Fishing, (*Sports Fishing Institute; 0-9602382*), 608 13th St. N.W., Suite 801, Washington, DC 20005 Tel 202-737-0668.

Sporting News, (*Sporting News Publishing Co.; 0-8297*), P.O. Box 56, St. Louis, MO 63166 Tel 314-997-7111.

Sportsbks, (*Sportsbooks; 0-939468*), Box 494, Bolivar, NY 14715 Tel 716-928-2825.

Sportsguide, (*Sportsguide, Inc.; 0-935644*), 211 E. 43rd St., Suite 901, New York, NY 10017 Tel 212-697-5237.

Sportsminded Pubns, (*Sportsminded Pubns.; 0-9601912*), 2000 Center St., Suite 1330, Berkeley, CA 94704.

SPOSS, (*Society for the Promotion of Science & Scholarship, Inc.; 0-930664*), 835 Page Mill Rd., Palo Alto, CA 94304 Tel 415-493-3958.

Spring Hill, (*Spring Hill Center; 0-932676*), Box 288, Wayzata, MN 55391.

Spring Pubns, (*Spring Pubns.; 0-88214*), P. O. Box 222069, Dallas, TX 75222.

Springer Pub, (*Springer Publishing Co., Inc.; 0-8261*), 200 Park Ave., S., New York, NY 10003 Tel 212-475-2494.

Springer-Verlag, (*Springer-Verlag New York, Inc.; 0-387*), 175 Fifth Ave., New York, NY 10010 Tel 212-477-8200.

Springfellow Bks, (*Springfellow Books*), Dist. by: E. P. Dutton, 201 Park Ave., S., New York, NY 10003; All Titles Now Listed As Dutton.

Springfield, (*Springfield Art Museum; 0-934306*), 1111 E. Brookside Dr., Springfield, MO 65807 Tel 417-866-2716.

Springfield Lib & Mus, (*Springfield Library & Museum Assn.*), 220 State St., Springfield, MA 01103.

Springfield Pub Co, (*Springfield Publishing Co.; 0-937500*), P.O. Box 96, Northridge, CA 91328 Tel 213-886-2317.

Springhill Pr MD, (*Springhill Press, The; 0-939972*), P.O. Box 1762, Silver Spring, MD 20902 Tel 301-649-6666.

Springhouse, (*Springhouse Publishing, Inc.; 0-89952*), 226 E. Roosevelt Rd., Wheaton, FL 60187 Tel 312-653-6400.

Sproing, (*Sproing Books; 0-916176*), 1150 St. Paul St., Denver, CO 80206 Tel 303-321-4248.

Sprout Pubns, (*Sprout Pubns. Inc.; 0-932972*), 5241 Ocean Blvd., Sarasota, FL 33581 Tel 813-349-2913.

Spurr Design, (*Spurr, John, Design; 0-931312*), P.O. Box 11249, Palo Alto, CA 94306.

Sputz, (*Sputz, David; 0-9604312*), 611 Bedford Ave., Brooklyn, NY 11211.

Spyglass, (*Spyglass Co.; 0-914922*), 2415 Mariner Square Dr., Alameda, CA 94501 Tel 415-769-8410.

Spyglass Catalog
See Spyglass

Squad Sig Pubns, (*Squadron Signal Pubns.; 0-89747*), 1115 Crowley Dr., Carrolton, TX 75005 Tel 214-242-4485.

Squarebooks, (*Squarebooks; 0-916290*), P.O. Box 144, Mill Valley, CA 94942 Tel 415-383-0202.

Squire, (*Squire, Ron*), Orders to: Shirley Squire, 174 Calle Cuervo, San Clemente, CA 92672 Tel 714-492-7068.

SRA, (*Science Research Associates, Inc.; 0-574*), Subs. of IBM, College Div., 1540 Page Mill Rd., Palo Alto, CA 94304 Tel 415-493-4700; Orders to: 155 N. Wacker Dr., Chicago, IL 60606.

Srchl *Imprint of* **Van Nos Reinhold**

Sri Rama, (*Sri Rama Publishing; 0-918100*), 161 Robles Dr., Santa Cruz, CA 95060 Tel 408-429-1176; Orders to: P.O. Box 2550, Santa Cruz, CA 95063 Tel 408-429-1176.

Sri Shirdi Sai, (*Sri Shirdi Sai Pubns.; 0-938924*), P.O. Box 2272, Morgantown, WV 26505.

SRL Pub Co, (*SRL Publishing Co.; 0-918152*), P.O. Box 2277, Sta. A, Champaign, IL 61820 Tel 217-356-1523.

SSC *Imprint of* **Unipub**

SSSR
See Soc Sci & Soc Res

St Alban Pr, (*St. Alban Press; 0-918980*), 10525 Downey Ave., Apt. F, Downey, CA 90241 Tel 213-861-7569; Orders to: P.O. Box 598, Ojai, CA 93023 Tel 805-646-6790.

St Albans Episcopal, (*St. Alban's Episcopal Church; 0-9606174*), 6422 Lake Shadows Circle, Chattanooga, TN 37443.

St Andrews NC, (*St. Andrews Press; 0-932662*), St. Andrews College, Laurinburg, NC 28352 Tel 919-276-3652.

St Andrews Pr, (*St. Andrews Press; 0-930154*), 404 E. 65th St., New York, NY 10021 Tel 212-861-8603.

St Anthony Mess Pr, (*St. Anthony Messenger Press; 0-912228; 0-86716*), 1615 Republic St., Cincinnati, OH 45210 Tel 513-241-5616.

St Basil Pr, (*St. Basil Press; 0-9604278*), 4106 N. Ozark Ave., Norridge, IL 60634.

Charles Hse, *(St. Charles House, Pubs.;
0-88263),* Empire Rd., Box 505, St. Charles,
IL 60174.

Clair Pr
  See Wiley

Cuthberts, *(St. Cuthbert's Treasury Press;
0-914724),* 1290 Maricopa Dr., Oshkosh,
WI 54901 Tel 414-235-2057.

Edns, *(Street Editions),* 20 Desbrosses St.,
New York, NY 10013; Orders to: SBD:
Small Press Distribution, 1636 Ocean View
Ave., Kensington, CA 94707
Tel 415-524-2107.

Edwards Univ, *(Saint Edward's Univ.;
0-938472),* 3001 S. Congress Ave., Austin,
TX 78704.

George Bk Serv, *(St. George Book Service;
0-916786),* P.O. Box 225, Spring Valley, NY
10977 Tel 914-623-7852.

George IL, *(Saint George Press, The;
0-939846),* P.O. Box 1443, Peoria, IL 61655
Tel 309-676-4799; 710a W. Moss Ave.,
Peoria, IL 61606 Tel 309-672-8900.

George Pr, *(St. George Press; 0-932104),*
3500 N. Coltrane Rd., Oklahoma City, OK
73121 Tel 405-427-5005.

Heironymous, *(St. Heironymous Press, Inc.;
0-913718),* P.O. Box 9431, Berkeley, CA
94709 Tel 415-549-1405.

John Gall, *(St. John, John, Gallery;
0-9605946),* 1683 Copenhagen Dr., Solvang,
CA 93463.

Johns, *(St. Johns Univ. Press; 0-87075),*
Grand Central & Utopia Pkwy., Jamaica, NY
11439 Tel 212-969-8000.

Le Macs Pr, *(St. Le Macs, Pierre, Press;
0-913030),* 450 Park Plaza Professional
Bldg., Houston, TX 77004
Tel 713-523-8181; Orders to: 2615 Marilee,
No. 1, Houston, TX 77057
Tel 713-783-2721.

Louis Pub Lib, *(St. Louis Public Library,
Pubns. Dept.)* 1301 Olive St., St. Louis, MO
63103 Tel 314-241-2288.

Luke, *(St. Luke's Press)* 40 Myrtle Ave.,
Irvington, NJ 07111.

Luke TN, *(St. Luke's Press; 0-918518),*
Mid-Memphis Tower, Suite 401, 1407 Union
Ave., Memphis, TN 38104
Tel 901-357-5441.

Margaret's, *(St. Margaret's Hospital),*
Administrator's Office, 90 Cushing Ave.,
Boston, MA 02125.

Martin, *(St. Martin's Press, Inc.; 0-312),* 175
Fifth Ave., New York, NY 10010
Tel 212-674-5151.

Mary's, *(St. Mary's Press; 0-88489),* Winona,
MN 55987 Tel 507-452-9090.

Nectarios, *(St. Nectarios Press; 0-913026),*
10300 Ashworth Ave. N., Seattle, WA 98133
Tel 206-522-4471.

Onge, *(St. Onge, Achille J., Pub.; 0-911422),*
7 Arden Rd., Worcester, MA 01606
Tel 617-853-8315.

Paul the Apostle, *(Saint Paul the Apostle
Church; 0-9602352),* 126 W. Georgia St.,
Indianapolis, IN 46225.

Petersburg Times, *(St. Petersburg Times
Publishing Co.; 0-9605382),* P.O. Box 1121,
St. Petersburg, FL 33731.

ST Pubns
  See Signs of Times

St Scholastica, *(St. Scholastica Priory),* Duluth,
MN 55811 Tel 218-728-1817.

St Sophia Religious, *(St. Sophia Religious Assn.
of Ukrainian Catholics),* 7911 Whitewood
Rd., Philadelphia, PA 19117
Tel 215-635-1555.

St Thomas, *(St. Thomas Press),* P.O. Box 35096,
Houston, TX 77035 Tel 713-666-3111.

St Vartan, *(St. Vartan Press; 0-934728),* 630
Second Ave., New York, NY 10016.

St Vincent Hosp, *(St. Vincent Hospital),* Dept.
D., P.O. Box 2107, Santa Fe, NM 87501.

St Vladimirs, *(St. Vladimir's Seminary Press;
0-913836),* 575 Scarsdale Rd., Crestwood,
NY 10707 Tel 914-961-8313.

St Willibrord, *(St. Willibrord's Press; 0-912134),*
P.O. Box 528, Zuni, NM 87329; Moved,Left
No Forwarding Address.

Stable Pub, *(Stable Pubs.; 0-914100),* Comer,
GA 30629.

Stack the Deck, *(Stack the Deck, Inc.;
0-933282),* 10628 S. Prospect Ave., Chicago,
IL 60643.

Stackpole, *(Stackpole Books, Inc.; 0-8117),*
Cameron & Kelker Sts., Harrisburg, PA
17105 Tel 717-234-5091.

Stadia Sports Pub, *(Stadia Sports Publishing),*
370 E. 76th St., New York, NY 10021
Tel 212-532-0450; Moved, Left No
Forwarding Address.

Stagecoach Pr, *(Stagecoach Press; 0-87238),*
P.O. Box 4422, Albuquerque, NM 87106.

Staked Plains, *(Staked Plains Press; 0-918028),*
P.O. Box 779, Canyon, TX 79015
Tel 806-655-7121.

ST&A, *(S. T. & A.; 0-936702),* P.O. Box
480530, Los Angeles, CA 90048.

Standard Arts, *(Standard Arts Press; 0-911426),*
2324 Butler Rd., Butler, MD 21023
Tel 301-472-4698.

Standard Ed, *(Standard Educational Corp.;
0-87392),* 200 W. Monroe, Chicago, IL
60606 Tel 312-346-7440.

Standard Edns, *(Standard Editions; 0-918746),*
P.O. Box 1297, Stuyvesant Sta., New York,
NY 10009.

Standard Poors, *(Standard & Poor's Corp.),* 25
Broadway, New York, NY 10004
Tel 212-248-2525.

Standard Pub, *(Standard Publishing Co.;
0-87239),* 8121 Hamilton Ave., Cincinnati,
OH 45231 Tel 513-931-4050.

Standing Orders, *(Standing Orders, Inc.;
0-8491),* 156 5th Ave., Suite 1122, New
York, NY 10010 Tel 212-243-0370; Orders
to: P.O. Box 183, Patterson, NY 12563.

Standing Orders, *(Standing Orders, Inc.;
0-8491),* 156 5th Ave., Suite 1122, New
York, NY 10010 Tel 212-243-0370; Orders
to: P.O. Box 183, Patterson, NY 12563.

Standish *Imprint of* **Dell**

Stanford, *(Stanford),* ; Publisher Abbreviation
Without Addresses Are for Titles That Are
Out of Print. These Are Obsolete
Abbreviations.

Stanford U Pr, *(Stanford Univ. Press; 0-8047),*
Stanford, CA 94305 Tel 415-497-9434.

StanGib Ltd, *(StanGib Ltd.; 0-85259),* 601
Franklin Ave., Garden City, NY 11530
Tel 516-746-4666.

Stanton & Lee, *(Stanton & Lee Pubs., Inc.;
0-88361),* 44 E. Mifflin St., Madison, WI
53703 Tel 608-255-3254; Orders to: Sauk
City, WI 53583.

Stanwix, *(Stanwix House, Inc.; 0-87076),* 3020
Chartiers Ave., Pittsburgh, PA 15204
Tel 412-771-4233.

Stanyan Bks *Imprint of* **Random**

Star Bible, *(Star Bible Pubns.; 0-933672),* 7120
Burns St., Box 13125, Fort Worth, TX 76118
Tel 812-284-0521.

Star Pub CA, *(Star Publishing Co.; 0-89863),*
701 Welch Rd., Suite 1119, Palo Alto, CA
94304 Tel 415-591-3505.

Star Pub Fla, *(Star Publishing Co., Inc.),* 609 N.
Railroad, P.O. Drawer BB, Boynton Beach,
FL 33435.

Star Pubns MO, *(Star Pubns.; 0-932356),* 1211
W. 60th Terrace, Kansas City, MO 64113
Tel 816-523-8228.

Star Rover, *(Star Rover House; 0-932458),*
306-12th St., Suite 26, Oakland, CA 94607
Tel 415-839-6822.

Star System, *(Star System Press; 0-932890),*
P.O. Box 15202, Wedgwood Sta., Seattle,
WA 98115 Tel 206-522-2589.

Starblaze *Imprint of* **Donning Co**

Starform, *(Starform, Inc.; 0-9604946),* 620
Taylor Way, No. 14, Belmont, CA 94002.

Starkey Labs, *(Starkey Laboratories, Inc.;
0-9601970),* 6700 Washington Ave. S., Eden
Prairie, MN 55344 Tel 800-328-8602.

Starlight Pr, *(Starlight Press; 0-9605438),* Box
3102, Long Island City, NY 11103.

Starline *Imprint of* **Schol Bk Serv**

Starlog, *(Starlog Press; 0-931064),* 475 Park
Ave. So., New York, NY 10016
Tel 212-689-2830.

Starmark, *(Starmark Publishing; 0-936572),* Div.
of Starmark, Inc., 706 N. Dearborn St.,
Chicago, IL 60610.

Starmont Hse, *(Starmont House; 0-916732),*
Box 851, Mercer Island, WA 98040
Tel 206-232-8484.

Starogubski, *(Starogubski Press; 0-9603234),*
345 Riverside Dr., Suite 5J, New York, NY
10025 Tel 212-222-5070.

Starshooter
  See J P Werner

Stash, *(Stash, Inc.; 0-932204),* 118 S. Bedford
St., Madison, WI 53703 Tel 608-251-4200.

State Bar TX, *(State Bar of Texas; 0-938160),*
P.O. Box 12487, Capitol Sta., Austin, TX
78711.

State Hist Iowa, *(State Historical Society of
Iowa; 0-89033),* 402 Iowa Ave., Iowa City,
IA 52240 Tel 319-353-6689.

State Hist Soc Wis, *(State Historical Society of
Wisconsin; 0-87020),* 816 State St.,
Madison, WI 53706 Tel 608-262-9604.

State Indus Dir, *(State Industrial Directories
Corp.; 0-916112),* 2 Penn Plaza, New York,
NY 10001 Tel 212-564-0340.

State Mutual Bk, *(State Mutual Book &
Periodical Service, Ltd.; 0-89771),* 521 Fifth
Ave., New York, NY 10017
Tel 212-682-5844.

State Ptg, *(State Printing Co.; 0-911432),* 1305
Sumter St., Columbia, SC 29201.

State St Pubns, *(State Street Pubns.; 0-936150),*
2357 State St., Suite C, San Diego, CA
92101.

State U NY Pr, *(State Univ. of New York Press;
0-87395),* State University Plaza, Albany,
NY 12246 Tel 518-474-6050; Orders to:
P.O. Box 4830, Hampden Sta., Baltimore,
MD 21211.

Staten Island, *(Staten Island Historical Society),*
441 Clark Ave., Richmondtown, NY 10306
Tel 212-351-1611.

Static Creation, *(Static Creation Press;
0-932736),* 405 S. Geneva St., Ithaca, NY
14850 Tel 607-277-4160.

Station Hill Pr, *(Station Hill Press; 0-930794),*
Station Hill Rd., Barrytown, NY 12507.

Statistics, *(Statistics, Inc.; 0-911434),* c/o
Edwards Brothers, Inc., 2500 S. State St.,
Ann Arbor, MI 48104.

Stay Away, *(Stay Away Joe Pubs.; 0-911436),*
59403, Great Falls, MT 59401.

Steam Pr, *(Steam Press),* 38 45th St. D,
Oakland, CA 94609; Moved, Left No
Forwarding Address.

Steam Trains Soo, *(Steam Trains of the Soo),*
1012 Holly Lane, Fortuna, CA 95540.

Stechert, *(Stechert Macmillan, Inc.; 0-8355),*
7250 Westfield Ave., Pennsauken, NJ 08110
Tel 609-662-7730; Dist. by: Macmillan Pub.
Co., Inc., Riverside, NJ 08075.

Steck-V, *(Steck-Vaughn Co.; 0-8114),* P.O. Box
2028, Austin, TX 78768 Tel 512-476-6721.

Steel Founders, *(Steel Founders' Society of
America; 0-9604674),* 20611 Center Ridge
Rd., Rocky River, OH 44116.

Steel Rails, *(Steel Rails West Publishing;
0-935250),* 1930 Marlette Ave., Reno, NV
89503 Tel 702-331-0129.

Steelstone, *(Steelstone Press; 0-9605678),* 4607
Claussen Lane, Valparaiso, IN 46383.

Steffanides, *(Steffanides, George F.; 0-9600114),*
66 Lourdes Dr., W.D., Fitchburg, MA 01420
Tel 617-342-1997.

Stehsel, *(Stehsel, Donald),* 2600 S. Third Ave.,
Arcadia, CA 91006 Tel 213-446-3679.

Stein & Day, *(Stein & Day; 0-8128),*
Scarborough House, Briarcliff Manor, NY
10510 Tel 914-762-2151.

Stein Pub, *(Stein Publishing House; 0-911440),*
526 S. State St., Chicago, IL 60605.

Steinbach, *(Steinbach, Marie De Bruyn;
0-9600298),* 6624 Seaboard Ave.,
Jacksonville, FL 32244.

Steiner, *(Steiner, Rudolf, Pubns; 0-8334),*
Affiliate of Multimedia/Biograf, 100 S.
Western Hwy., Blauvelt, NY 10913
Tel 914-359-5537.

Steinerbks, *(Steinerbooks),* 7 Garber Hill Rd.,
Blauvelt, NY 10913 Tel 914-359-9292.

Steinlage, *(Steinlage Products; 0-914754),* 4766
Kremer Hoying Rd, St. Henry, OH 45883
Tel 419-678-4125.

Steinlitz-Hammacher, *(Steinlitz-Hammacher Co.;
0-917208),* P.O. Box 187, Hasbrouck
Heights, NJ 07604 Tel 201-667-1429.

Stel-Mar, *(Stel-Mar; 0-935456),* 329 Rhoda Dr.,
Lancaster, PA 17601.

Stelle, *(Stelle Group; 0-9600308),*
Administration Bldg., Stelle, IL 60919
Tel 815-949-1111.

Stemmer Hse, *(Stemmer House Pubs., Inc.;
0-916144),* 2627 Caves Rd., Owings Mills,
MD 21117 Tel 301-363-3690.

Stenospeed
  See Intl Educ Systems

Stephen Wright, *(Wright, Stephen, Press;
0-9601904),* Box 1341, F.D.R. Post Office
Sta., New York, NY 10022
Tel 212-927-2869.

Stephens Pr, *(Stephens Press),* Drawer 1441,
Spokane, WA 99210 Tel 509-838-8222.

Steppingstones, *(Steppingstones Pubns.;
0-918184),* P.O. Box 612, Silver Spring, MD
20901 Tel 301-498-7824.

Sterling, *(Sterling Publishing Co., Inc.; 0-8069),*
2 Park Ave., New York, NY 10016
Tel 212-532-7160.

Sterling Instru, *(Sterling Instrument),* 55 S.
Denton Ave., New Hyde Park, NY 11040.

Sterling Swift, *(Sterling Swift Pub. Co.;
0-88408),* P.O. Box 188, Manchaca, TX
78652 Tel 512-444-7570.

Stern, *(Stern, Clarence Ames; 0-9600116),* P.O.
Box 2294, Oshkosh, WI 54903
Tel 414-231-6786.

Stevenson Pr, *(Stevenson Press; 0-89482),* Div.
of Callcott, Inc., P.O. Box 10021, Austin, TX
78766 Tel 512-255-8623.

Steves Wide World, *(Steves Wide World
Studios),* 111 4th Ave. N., Edmonds, WA
98020.

Steward & Sons, *(Steward & Sons; 0-917144),*
P.O. Box 15282, Long Beach, CA 90815.

Stewart, *(Stewart, Henry, Inc.; 0-911444),* 253
Main St., East Aurora, NY 14052
Tel 716-652-1770.

Stewart Pubns, *(Stewart Pubns., Inc.),* P.O. Box
295, Tenafly, NJ 07670.

STHV, *(Science, Technology, & Human Values;
0-932564),* Rm. 20B-125, Massachusetts
Institute of Technology, Cambridge, MA
02139 Tel 617-253-4010.

Stillgate, *(Stillgate Pubns.; 0-938286),* Box 67,
Alstead, NH 03602.

Stillhouse Hollow, *(Stillhouse Hollow Publishing
Co.; 0-9602272),* Orders to: First Ladies of
Texas, P.O. Box 3015, Temple, TX 76501.

Stillwater Canyon Pr, *(Stillwater Canyon Press;
0-933762),* P.O. Box 1557, Flagstaff, AZ
86002 Tel 602-774-3778.

Stilwell Studio, *(Stilwell Studio, The;
0-9605862),* P.O. Box 50, Carmel, CA
93921 Tel 408-624-8176.

Stimler Assoc, *(Stimler Associates; 0-9600770),*
33 W. Second St., Moorestown, NJ 08057.

Stinson Beach, *(Stinson Beach Press; 0-918540),*
P.O. Box 475, Stinson Beach, CA 94970
Tel 415-868-1424.

Stipes, *(Stipes Publishing Co.; 0-87563),* 10-12
Chester St., Champaign, IL 61820
Tel 217-356-8391.

Stirrup Assoc, *(Stirrup Associates, Inc.;
0-937420),* 115 Church St., Decatur, GA
30030.

Stock Drive, *(Stock Drive Products),* 55 S.
Denton Ave., New Hyde Park, NY 11040.

Stock Poetry, *(Stock Poetry; 0-918874),* 630 E.
14, No. 3, New York, NY 10009
Tel 212-673-0781.

Stoeger Pub Co, *(Stoeger Publishing Co.;
0-88317),* 55 Ruta Court, South Hackensack,
NJ 07606 Tel 201-440-2700.

Stokes, *(Stokes Publishing Co.; 0-914534),* 1125
Robin Way, Sunnyvale, CA 94087
Tel 408-736-4637.

Stokesville Pub, *(Stokesville Publishing Co.;
0-936030),* P.O. Box 14401, Atlanta, GA
30324 Tel 404-658-3075.

Stone Country, *(Stone Country Press; 0-930020),*
20 Lorraine Rd., Madison, NJ 07940
Tel 201-377-3727.

Stone Hse Pr, *(Stone House Press; 0-933622),*
Fairfax, VT 05454 Tel 802-849-6557.

Stone-Marrow Pr, *(Stone-Marrow Press),* Dept.
of English, 248 McMicken, Univ. of
Cincinnati, Cincinnati, OH 45221.

Stone Pr Calif, *(Stone Press, The),* 3978 26th
St., San Francisco, CA 94131
Tel 415-648-5392.

Stone Pr MI, *(Stone Pr.),* 1790 Grand River,
Okemos, MI 48864.

Stone Wall Pr, *(Stone Wall Press, Inc.;
0-913276),* 1241 30th St. N.W., Washington,
DC 20007 Tel 202-333-1860; Dist. by: The
Stephen Greene Press, Box 1000, Brattleboro,
VT 05301.

Stone Wall Pubns, *(Stone Wall Pubns;
0-931354),* 31 Hilltop Place, Monsey, NY
10952.

Stonehenge, *(Stonehenge Books),* 1582 S. Parker
Rd., Suite 200, Parker Plaza, Denver, CO
80231 Tel 303-695-4710.

Stonehill Pub Co, *(Stonehill Publishing Co., Inc.;
0-88373),* 1140 Ave. of Americas, 19th Fl.,
New York, NY 10036 Tel 212-658-5980;
Dist. by: Farrar, Straus & Giroux, Inc., 19
Union Square, New York, NY 10003
Tel 212-741-6900.

Stonehouse, *(Stonehouse Pubns.; 0-9603236),*
Sweet, ID 83670.

Stoneridge Inst, *(Stoneridge Institute of
Politico-Socio-Economics Press; 0-937300),*
7703 Baltimore National Pike, Frederick,
MD 21701.

Stoney Brook, *(Stoney Brook Publishing Co.;
0-912928),* 186 Main St., W., Chelmsford,
MA 01863.

Storm King, *(Storm King Pubs., Inc.; 0-935166),*
Box 252, Middletown, NY 10940
Tel 914-343-3161.

Stormy Karma, *(Stormy Karma Books),* 912
Broadway E., No. 1, Seattle, WA 98102;
Moved, Left No Forwarding Address.

Story Hse Corp, *(Story House Corp.; 0-87157),*
Charlotteville, NY 12036 Tel 607-397-8725.

Story Pr, *(Story Press; 0-931704),* P.O. Box
10040, Chicago, IL 60610
Tel 312-442-7295.

Storyfold, *(Storyfold, Inc.; 0-89008),* 48 Pleasant
St., Newburyport, MA 01950
Tel 617-462-9511.

Stover, *(Stover, W. H. M.),* 6129 Broad Branch
Rd. N.W., Washington, DC 20015.

Stowe-Day, *(Stowe-Day Foundation; 0-917482),*
77 Forest St., Hartford, CT 06105
Tel 203-522-9258.

Strait, *(Strait & Co.; 0-917854),* P.O. Box 331,
Princeton, NJ 08540 Tel 609-924-4098.

Stratford Hse, *(Stratford House Publishing Co.;
0-938614),* P.O. Box 7077, Burbank, CA
91510.

Stratford Pr, *(Stratford Press Inc.),* 9606 Santa
Monica Blvd., Beverly Hills, CA 90210
Tel 213-530-8292.

Strathcona, *(Strathcona Publishing Co.;
0-931554),* Box 350, Royal Oak, MI 48068
Tel 313-368-8945.

Stratton Intercon
See Thieme-Stratton

Straughan, *(Straughan's Book Shop, Inc.;
0-911452),* 220 N. Elm St., Greensboro, NC
27401 Tel 919-274-5437.

Stravon, *(Stravon Educational Press; 0-87396),*
845 Third Ave., New York, NY 10022
Tel 212-371-2880.

Strawberry Hill, *(Strawberry Hill Press;
0-89407),* 2594 15th Ave., San Francisco,
CA 94127 Tel 415-228-6888.

Strawberry Pr NY, *(Strawberry Press;
0-936574),* P.O. Box 451, Bowling Green
Sta., New York, NY 10004.

Strawberry Valley, *(Strawberry Valley Press;
0-913612),* P.O. Box 157, Idyllwild, CA
92349 Tel 714-659-2145.

Street Fiction, *(Street Fiction Press, Inc.;
0-914908),* 130 Touro St., P.O. Box 625,
Newport, RI 02840 Tel 401-847-1067.

Street Pr, *(Street Press; 0-935252),* P.O. Box
555, Port Jefferson, NY 11777
Tel 516-979-7392.

Stretching Inc, *(Stretching Inc.; 0-9601066),*
P.O. Box 767, Palmer Lake, CO 80133
Tel 714-525-5004.

Strether & Swann, *(Strether & Swann;
0-931522),* 1309 Seventh St., New Orleans,
LA 70115.

Strode, *(Strode Pubs.; 0-87397),* 720 Church St.,
NW., Huntsville, AL 35801
Tel 205-539-2187.

Stroker, *(Stroker Press; 0-918154),* 110 St.
Marks Place, No. 8, New York, NY 10009.

Strong-Church, *(Strong-Church Enterprises
Press),* 2238 Morello Blvd., Pleasant Hill,
CA 94523.

Strongforce, *(Strongforce, Inc.; 0-9601626),*
2121 Decatur Place N.W., Washington, DC
20008.

Structures Pub, *(Structures Publishing Co.;
0-912336; 0-89999),* 24277 Indoplex Circle,
P.O. Box 1002, Farmington, MI 48024
Tel 313-477-2600.

Stryker-Post, *(Stryker-Post Pubns., Inc.),* 888
17th St., N.W., Washington, DC 20006
Tel 202-298-9233.

Stuart Pub, *(Stuart, J., Publishing Co.;
0-939232),* 14342 Rutherford Ave., Detroit,
MI 48227.

Stubs, *(Stubs Pubns.; 0-911458),* 234 W. 44th
St., New York, NY 10036
Tel 212-398-8370.

Student Assn, *(Student Assn. Press; 0-931118),*
1000 Cherry Rd., Memphis, TN 38117
Tel 901-761-1353.

Studia Hispanica, *(Studia Hispanica Editors;
0-934840),* Univ. of Texas at Austin, Batt
Hall 112, Austin, TX 78712
Tel 512-471-4936; Orders to: P. O. Box
7304, Univ. Sta., Austin, TX 78712
Tel 512-458-5413.

Studia Slovenica, *(Studia Slovenica, Inc.),* P.O.
Box 232, New York, NY 10032.

Studio Four, *(Studio 4 Products; 0-9603612),*
4439 Village Rd., Long Beach, CA 90808
Tel 213-420-1430.

Studio Pr, *(Studio Press; 0-918368),* P.O. Box
361, Upper Darby, PA 19082
Tel 215-734-1647.

Studio Three Thousand, *(Studio 3000; 0-9151*
P.O. Box 122, Ansonia Sta., New York, N
10023 Tel 212-787-3687.

Studios West, *(Studios West Pubns.; 0-939656*
167 Saxony Rd., Encinitas, CA 92024
Tel 714-753-8186.

Studium Corp, *(Studium Corp.),* 40 Cooper
Square, New York, NY 10003.

Stull & Co, *(Stull & Co., Since 1870, Inc.),* 79
Wall St., New York, NY 10005
Tel 212-344-6676.

Sturzebecker, *(Sturzebecker, R. L.; 0-9600466*
West Chester State College, Sch. of Health
Physical Education, West Chester, PA 193
Tel 215-436-2733.

Stuttman, *(Stuttman, H. S., Inc.; 0-87475),* 33
Post Rd. W., Westport, CT 06889.

Suburban Antiquers
See Calwood Pubns

Success Found, *(Success Foundation, Inc., The
0-913200),* P. O. Box 6302, Louisville, KY
40206 Tel 502-893-3038.

Success Unltd, *(Success Unlimited, Inc.;
0-918448),* 401 N. Wabash, Chicago, IL
60611 Tel 312-828-9500.

Successful Achiev, *(Successful Achievement, In
0-910008),* P.O. Box 7297, Lexington, KY
40502 Tel 606-255-9603; Moved, Left No
Forwarding Address.

Sue Ann, *(Sue Ann; 0-9604172),* Box 2, North
Haven, CT 06473 Tel 203-288-1913.

Suffolk Hse, *(Suffolk House; 0-936066),* 360
Lexington Ave., New York, NY 10017.

Sufi Order Pubns, *(Sufi Order Pubns.;
0-930872),* P.O. Box 568, Lebanon Springs
NY 12114.

Sufism Reoriented, *(Sufism Reoriented, Inc.;
0-915828),* 1300 Boulevard Way, Walnut
Creek, CA 94595 Tel 415-938-4822.

Sugden, *(Sugden, Sherwood, & Company;
0-89385),* 1117 Eighth St., La Salle, IL
61301 Tel 815-223-1231. *Imprints:*
AMDG Pr (A.M.D.G. Press).

Suhrkamp, *(Suhrkamp/Insel Pubs. Boston Inc.;
3-458),* 380 Green St., Cambridge, MA
02139 Tel 617-876-2333.

Sullivan, *(Sullivan, E. M.; 0-911460),* P.O. Box
5823, Orange, CA 92667.

Sullivan Bks Intl, *(Sullivan Books Internationa
0-913620),* 153 MacAlvey, Martinez, CA
94553.

Sullivan Prod, *(Sullivan, Dorothy, Production;
0-9604928),* P.O. Box 7045, St. Petersburg
FL 33734.

Sumac, *(Sumac Press; 0-911462),* 613 N. 22nd
St., La Crosse, WI 54601 Tel 608-782-129

Sumac Mich, *(Sumac Press; 0-912090),* P.O.
Box 39, Fremont, MI 49412
Tel 616-924-3464.

Summer House, *(Summer House Pubns.;
0-935736),* Box 16257, Baltimore, MD
21210.

Summer Inst Ling, *(Summer Institute of
Linguistics; 0-88312),* Academic Pubns.,
7500 W. Camp Wisdom Rd., Dallas, TX
75236 Tel 214-298-3331.

Summer Stream, *(Summer Stream Press;
0-932460),* 5176 Walnut Park Dr., Santa
Barbara, CA 93111 Tel 805-967-5992;
Orders to: P.O. Box 6056, Santa Barbara,
CA 93111 Tel 805-967-5992.

Summers Prods, *(Summers Productions, Inc.),*
595 Madison Ave., Suite 1602, New York,
NY 10022.

Summit, *(Summit Lighthouse, The),* Box A,
Colorado Springs, CO 80901.

Summit Bks, *(Summit Books),* Subs. of Simon
Schuster, 1230 Ave. of the Americas, New
York, NY 10020 Tel 212-246-2471.

Summit Cnty OH, *(Summit County Chapter O
G S),* 410 Bonshire Rd., Akron, OH 44319
Tel 216-644-8660.

Summit Ent, *(Summit Enterprises, Inc.; 0-934174),* 3928 Corrine Dr., Phoenix, AZ 85032 Tel 602-992-5372.

Summit Intl, *(Summit International),* P.O. Box 7018, Pasadena, CA 91109.

Summit Pub Co
See Gold Penny

Summit Univ, *(Summit Univ. Press; 0-916766),* Box A, Malibu, CA 90265 Tel 213-991-4751.

Summy, *(Summy-Birchard Co.; 0-87487),* Box CN 27, Princeton, NJ 08540 Tel 609-896-1411.

SUN, *(SUN; 0-915342),* 347 W. 39th St., New York, NY 10018 Tel 212-594-8428.

Sun & Moon MD, *(Sun & Moon Press),* 4330 Hartwick Rd., No. 418, College Park, MD 20740.

Sun Dance Bks, *(Sun Dance Books; 0-913330),* 1520 N. Crescent Heights, Hollywood, CA 90046 Tel 213-654-2383.

Sun Dance Pr
See Sun Dance Bks

Sun Man Moon, *(Sun, Man, Moon, Inc.; 0-917738),* P.O. Box 5084, 9191 Regatta Dr., Huntington Beach, CA 92646 Tel 714-962-8945.

Sun Pr NY, *(Sun Press; 0-9601260),* 308 E. 94th St., New York, NY 10028 Tel 212-953-4855.

Sun Pub, *(Sun Publishing Co.; 0-914172; 0-89540),* P.O. Box 4383, Albuquerque, NM 87196 Tel 505-255-6550.

Sun-Scape Pubns, *(Sun-Scape Pubns.; 0-919842),* P.O. Box 42725, Tucson, AZ 85733 Tel 602-743-0209.

Sun Tracks, *(Sun Tracks; 0-936350),* Dept. of English, Univ. of Arizona, Tucson, AZ 85721.

SunBox, *(SunBox Press; 0-930052),* 750 Alta Vista Way, Laguna Beach, CA 92651 Tel 714-499-4563.

Sunburst *Imprint of* FS&G

Sunburst Comm, *(Sunburst Communications),* 39 Washington Ave., Pleasantville, NY 10570 Tel 914-769-5030.

Sunburst Farms, *(Sunburst Farms Pub. Co.),* 14000 Calle Real, Rte. 1, Goleta, CA 93017 Tel 805-968-8379.

Sunburst Pr, *(Sunburst Press; 0-934648),* Box 6, 4610 S.E. Belmont, Portland, OR 97215 Tel 503-238-1213.

Sunbury Pr, *(Sunbury Press; 0-915548),* P. O. Box 1778, Raleigh, NC 27602 Tel 919-832-6417.

Sundance, *(Sundance Pubns., Ltd.; 0-913582),* P.O. Box 597, Silverton, CO 81433 Tel 303-387-5784.

Sundial Bks *Imprint of* Sunstone Pr

Sundown Pr, *(Sundown Press; 0-9602494),* 324 E. 35th St., New York, NY 10016 Tel 212-725-5546; Orders to: P.O. Box 6, Sundown, NY 12782 Tel 914-995-3260.

Sundowner Serv, *(Sundowner Services; 0-932241),* 2559-47th Ave., San Francisco, CA 94116 Tel 415-564-0068.

Sunflower Bks *Imprint of* Smith Pubs

Sunflower Ink, *(Sunflower Ink; 0-931104),* Palo Colorado Canyon, Carmel, CA 93923.

Sunflowers KS, *(Sunflowers; 0-939726),* RR 1, Box 262, Clearwater, KS 67026 Tel 316-545-7587.

Sunn Classic Bks
See Schick Sunn

Sunnyside, *(Sunnyside Publishing Co.; 0-934650),* Box 29, 51 Willow St., Lynn, MA 01903 Tel 617-595-4742.

Sunrise Bks, *(Sunrise Books),* c/o One Way, Ltd., 707 "E" St., Eureka, CA 95501 Tel 707-442-4004.

SunRise Hse, *(SunRise House; 0-915764),* P.O. Box 217, Longwood, FL 32750 Tel 305-830-7333.

Sunrise MO, *(Sunrise Publishing Co.; 0-86629),* 10617 Liberty Ave., St. Louis, MO 63132.

Sunrise PA, *(Sunrise Publishing Co.),* P.O. Box 215, Hatfield, PA 19440.

Sunrise Paper
See Sunrise Bks

Sunrise Pr IL, *(Sunrise Press; 0-935800),* 2004 Grant St., Evanston, IL 60201 Tel 312-475-3651.

Sunrise Pub OR, *(Sunrise Publishing; 0-9604344),* 3441 Stark St., Eugene, OR 97404.

Sunrise Tortoise, *(Sunrise Tortoise Books; 0-932222),* Box 61, Sandpoint, ID 83864.

Sunset-Lane, *(Sunset Books/Lane Publishing Co.; 0-376),* Willow & Middlefield Rds., Menlo Park, CA 94025 Tel 415-321-3600.

Sunset Prods, *(Sunset Productions Pubns., Inc.; 0-937196),* 15777 W. 10 Mile Rd., Southfield, MI 48075.

Sunset Pubns, *(Sunset Pubns.; 0-9601256),* 1655 Makaloa St., Suite 906, Honolulu, HI 96814.

SunShine, *(SunShine; 0-937710),* Box 4351, Austin, TX 78765 Tel 512-459-6717.

Sunshine
See SunShine

Sunshine Acad, *(Sunshine Academic Press, Inc.; 0-933064),* 304 27th St., West Palm Beach, FL 33407.

Sunshine Arts WA, *(Sunshine Arts),* W. 1018 Shannon, Spokane, WA 99205.

Sunshine Bks, *(Sunshine Books Ltd.; 0-934606),* 1089 W. Park St., Long Beach, NY 11561 Tel 516-889-4370.

Sunspark Pr, *(Sunspark Press),* Box 91, Greenleaf, OR 97445.

Sunstone Found, *(Sunstone Foundation),* P.O. Box 2272, Salt Lake City, UT 84110.

Sunstone Pr, *(Sunstone Press; The; 0-913270; 0-86534),* P.O. Box 2321, Santa Fe, NM 87501 Tel 505-988-4418. *Imprints:* Sundial Bks (Sundial Books).

SUNY Environ, *(State Univ. of New York, College of Environmental Science & Forestry),* Syracuse, NY 13210 Tel 315-473-8711.

Superior Pub, *(Superior Publishing Co.; 0-87564),* 708 Sixth Ave., N., Box 1710, Seattle, WA 98111 Tel 206-282-4310.

Superior WI, *(Superior Pubns.),* 5510 Tower Ave., Superior, WI 54880 Tel 715-392-8060.

Superlove, *(Superlove),* 4245 Ladoga Ave., Lakewood, CA 90713.

Superson, *(Superson, Edward T.),* 5317 Soule Dr., Panama City, FL 32401.

Suratao, *(Suratao, Inc.; 0-932286),* 1232 S. Rimpau Blvd., Los Angeles, CA 90019 Tel 213-931-0371.

Surevolution, *(Surevolution; 0-917302),* P.O. Box 2193, Concord, CA 94521 Tel 415-687-2703.

Surf Chek, *(Surface Checking Gage Co.; 0-911464),* P.O. Box 1912, Prescott, AZ 86302 Tel 602-778-3160.

Surry County, *(Surry County School of Badminton, Ltd.),* Dist. by: Surry County School of Badminton, Ltd.; 12819 S.E. 45th Place, Bellevue, WA 98006.

Survey Pub Co, *(Survey Publishing Co.; 0-916510),* P.O. Box 572, Salina, KS 67401 Tel 913-823-9079.

Survival CT, *(Survival),* Turkey Hills, Haddam, CT 06438.

Survival Ed Assoc, *(Survival Education Assn.; 0-913724),* 9035 Golden Givens Rd., Tacoma, WA 98445 Tel 206-531-3156.

Sutherland Learn Assocs, *(Sutherland Learning Associates, Inc.; 0-934100),* 14654 Oxnard St., Van Nuys, CA 91411 Tel 213-988-8030.

Sutherland Pubns, *(Sutherland Pubns.; 0-914578),* P.O. Box 9061, Berkeley, CA 94709 Tel 415-849-1887.

Sutphen Studio, *(Sutphen, Dick, Studio; 0-911842),* Box 628, Scottsdale, AZ 85252 Tel 602-991-8740.

Sutter, *(Sutter Publishing Co.; 0-9600120),* 12311 Conway Rd., Creve Coeur, MO 63141 Tel 314-878-9044; Orders to: 2303 S. Milton Ave., Overland, MO 63114.

Sutter House, *(Sutter House; 0-915010),* 77 Main St., P.O. Box 212, Lititz, PA 17543 Tel 717-626-0800.

Sutton Pr, *(Sutton Press; 0-940300),* 3631-22nd Ave. S., Minneapolis, MN 55407.

Sverge-Haus, *(Sverge-Haus Pubs.; 0-933348),* 11 Indian Spring Rd., Milton, MA 02186 Tel 617-773-2709.

SW Mission, *(Southwestern Mission Research Center; 0-915076),* Arizona State Museum, Tucson, AZ 85721.

SW Pks Mnmts, *(Southwest Parks & Monuments Assn.; 0-911408),* P.O. Box 1562, Globe, AZ 85501 Tel 602-425-4392.

SW Pub, *(South-Western Publishing Co.; 0-538),* 5101 Madison Rd., Cincinnati, OH 45227 Tel 513-271-8811.

Swallow, *(Swallow Press; 0-8040),* Scott Quadrangle, Athens, OH 45701 Tel 614-594-5852; Orders to: Publishers Marketing Group, P.O. Box 350, Momence, IL 60954 Tel 815-472-2661.

Swampgas, *(Swampgas Press; 0-933838),* 3201 St. Charles Ave., No. 313, New Orleans, LA 70115 Tel 504-897-3413.

Swan Books, *(Swan Books),* P.O. Box 332, Fair Oaks, CA 95628 Tel 916-961-8778.

Swanson, *(Swanson Publishing Co.; 0-911466),* P.O. Box 334, Moline, IL 61265.

Swedenborg, *(Swedenborg Foundation, Inc.; 0-87785),* 139 E. 23rd St., New York, NY 10010 Tel 212-673-7310.

Sweet, *(Sweet Publishing Co.; 0-8344),* Box 4055, Austin, TX 78765 Tel 512-255-4171.

Sweetbrier, *(Sweetbrier Press; 0-936736),* 536 Emerson St., Palo Alto, CA 94301.

Sweeter Than Honey, *(Sweeter Than Honey; 0-934244),* P.O. Box 959, Van, TX 75790 Tel 214-963-7102.

Sweetlight, *(Sweetlight Books; 0-9604462),* 71250 Hill Rd., Covelo, CA 95428.

Swenk-Tuttle, *(Swenk-Tuttle Press, Inc.; 0-911472),* 15 E. Kirby, Apt. 1231, Detroit, MI 48202.

Swets North Am, *(Swets North America),* P. O. Box 517, Berwyn, PA 19312.

Swets Pub Nor
See Swets North Am

Swimming, *(Swimming World; 0-911822),* 1130 W. Florence Ave., Inglewood, CA 90301 Tel 213-641-2727.

Sword & Stone, *(Sword & Stone Press; 0-939086),* P.O. Box 9428, Venice, CA 90291.

Sword of Lord, *(Sword of the Lord Pubs.; 0-87398),* P.O. Box 1099, 224 Bridge Ave., Murfreesboro, TN 37130 Tel 615-893-6700.

Sybex, *(Sybex, Inc.; 0-89588),* 2020 Milbia St., Berkeley, CA 94704 Tel 415-848-8233.

Sycamore Island, *(Sycamore Island Books),* P.O. Box 1307, Boulder, CO 80306 Tel 303-443-7250; Dist. by: Caroline House, P.O. Box 161, Thornwood, NY 10594.

Sycamore Pr, *(Sycamore Press, Inc.; 0-916768),* P.O. Box 552, Terre Haute, IN 47808 Tel 812-299-2458.

SYDA Found, *(SYDA Foundation; 0-911603),* P.O. Box 605, South Fallsburg, NY 12779 Tel 914-434-4850.

Syder Pr, *(Syder Press; 0-939470),* 5893 Kahara Court, Sacramento, CA 95822.

Sydon, *(Sydon, Inc),* c/o Drama Dept., Univ. of the Pacific, Stockton, CA 95211 Tel 209-946-2116.

Syentek Bks, *(Syentek Books Co., Inc.; 0-914082),* 555 Battery St., P.O. Box 26588, San Francisco, CA 94126 Tel 415-441-7521.

Sylvan Inst, *(Sylvan Institute; 0-918428),* 7104 N. E. Hazel Dell Ave., Vancouver, WA 98665 Tel 206-694-0911.

Sylvan Pr VA, *(Sylvan Press; 0-935254),* P.O. Box 15125, Richmond, VA 23227.

Sylvanus Bks, *(Sylvanus Books; 0-911874),* P.O. Box 3052, Noroton, CT 06820; Orders to: Exposition Press, Inc., 900 South Oyster Bay Rd., Hicksville, NY 11801.

Sym & Sign, *(Symbols & Signs; 0-912504),* P.O. Box 4536, North Hollywood, CA 91607.

Symmes Syst, *(Symmes Systems; 0-916352),* P.O. Box 8101, Atlanta, GA 30306 Tel 404-876-7260.

Symphony, *(Symphony Press, Inc.),* P.O. Box 515, Tenafly, NJ 07670.

Symposia Pr, *(Symposia Press; 0-918542),* P.O. Box 418, Moorestown, NJ 08057 Tel 609-235-8439.

Symposia Special, *(Symposia Specialists; 0-88372),* 1460 N.E. 129th St., Miami, FL 33161 Tel 305-891-0118.

Symposium Pr, *(Symposium Press, The),* 1620 Greenfield, Los Angeles, CA 90025.

Synapse Pubns, *(Synapse Pubns.; 0-935170),* 1310 Benedum Trees Bldg., Pittsburgh, PA 15222.

Syncline, *(Syncline; 0-9603794),* 1548 W. Addison, Chicago, IL 60613.

Syndicate, *(Syndicate Books; 0-911474),* 88 Marion Dr., New Rochelle, NY 10804 Tel 914-632-6794.

Synecology, *(Synecology Press, Inc.; 0-931774),* P.O. Box 3181, Tempe, AZ 85281 Tel 602-967-4173.

Synergistic Pr, *(Synergistic Press, Inc.; 0-912184),* 3965 Sacramento St., San Francisco, CA 94118 Tel 415-387-8180.

Synergy Hse, *(Synergy House; 0-934962),* P.O. Box 1827, Costa Mesa, CA 92626 Tel 714-848-1314.

Synthesis Pubns, *(Synthesis Pubns.; 0-89935),* P.O. Box 40099, San Francisco, CA 94140 Tel 415-282-5272.

Syntonic Res, *(Syntonic Research, Inc.),* 663 Fifth Ave., New York, NY 10022; Moved, Left No Forwarding Address.

Syracuse U Cont Ed, *(Syracuse Univ. Pubns. in Continuing Education; 0-87060),* 224 Huntington Hall, 50 Marshall St., Syracuse, NY 13210 Tel 315-423-3421.

Syracuse U Foreign Comp, *(Syracuse Univ., Foreign & Comparative Studies Program; 0-915984),* 119 College Place, Syracuse, NY 13210 Tel 315-423-2552.

Syracuse U Pr, *(Syracuse Univ. Press; 0-8156),* 1011 E. Water St., Syracuse, NY 13210 Tel 315-423-2596. *Imprints:* Am U Beirut (American Univ. of Beirut Pubns.).

System Dev, *(System Development Corp.),* Dist. by: Baker & Taylor, 50 Kirby Ave., Somerville, NJ 08876.

System Logistics, *(System Logistics, Inc; 0-9602362),* P.O. Box 25776, 507 Kawaihae St., Honolulu, HI 96825 Tel 808-377-9650.

Systems Pub, *(Systems Publishing Corp.; 0-938974),* P.O. Box 2161, West Lafayette, IN 47906.

Systems Res, *(Systems Research Institute; 0-912352),* Publications Dept., P.O. Box 74524, Los Angeles, CA 90004.

T & A D Poyser, *(Poyser, T. & A. D., Ltd.; 0-85661),* Dist. by: Buteo Books, P.O. Box 481, Vermillion, SD 57069 Tel 605-624-4343.

T B Sword, *(Sword, Thula Bieri; 0-9600746),* 85 N. Madison Ave., Pasadena, CA 91101 Tel 213-449-5382; Moved, Left No Forwarding Address.

T Beckman & Assoc, *(Beckman, Tom, & Assoc.; 0-937204),* P.O. Box 20081, Cincinnati, OH 45219.

T C Pubs, *(T.C. Publishers; 0-920192),* 51 Columbine Ave., Toronto, Ontario M4L 1P6, Canada,.

T D Anthony, *(Anthony, Travis D.; 0-9604686),* P.O. Box 646, Rush Springs, OK 73082 Tel 405-476-2211.

T E Henderson, *(Henderson, T. Emmett),* 130 W. Main St., Middletown, NY 10940 Tel 914-343-1038.

T E Lowe, *(Lowe, Thomas E., Ltd.; 0-913926),* 2 Penn Plaza, Suite 1500, New York, NY 10001 Tel 212-222-1869.

T H Arceneaux, *(Arceneaux, Thelma Hoffman Tyler; 0-9600870),* 115 Apricot St., Thibodaux, LA 70301 Tel 504-446-1037.

T H Feder Bks, *(Feder, T. H., Books; 0-933772),* Div. of Editorial Photo Color Archives, 342 Madison Ave., New York, NY 10017.

T H Goodman, *(Goodman, Thomas H.; 0-9601252),* 3218 Shelburne Rd., Baltimore, MD 21208 Tel 301-358-2817.

T H Wu, *(Wu, T. H.; 0-918498),* 160 Brookside Oval E., Worthington, OH 43085 Tel 614-422-1071.

T Horton & Dghts, *(Horton, Thomas, & Daughters; 0-913878),* 22 Appleton Place, P.O. Box 3, Glen Ridge, NJ 07028 Tel 201-748-8095.

T Hutchinson, *(Hutchinson, Ted; 0-9601366),* 14 Devries Ave., N. Tarrytown, NY 10591 Tel 914-631-1848.

T J Johnson, *(Johnson, T. J.; 0-917756),* P.O. Box 113, Estherville, IA 51334 Tel 712-362-5667.

T J Mohaupt, *(Mohaupt, Terry James),* 316 Rue Flambeau 412, South Bend, IN 46615 Tel 219-233-2732.

T K Sanderson, *(Sanderson, T. K., Organization),* 200 E. 25th St., Baltimore, MD 21218 Tel 301-235-3383.

T L Cannon & N F Whitmore, *(Cannon, Timothy L., & Nancy F. Whitmore; 0-9602816),* 7916 Juniper Dr., Frederick, MD 21701.

T L Jaynes, *(Jaynes, Thomas L.; 0-935514),* P.O. Box 651038, Miami, FL 33165.

T Lee, *(Lee, Terri; 0-9602332),* Box 4711, Falls Church, VA 22044 Tel 703-370-5821.

T M Johnson, *(Johnson, LTC Thomas M.; 0-9600906),* P.O. Box 7152, Alexandria, VA 22307 Tel 703-360-6241.

T Nelson, *(Nelson, Ted, Publisher; 0-89347),* Box 3, Schooleys Mountain, NJ 07870 Tel 312-352-8796; Dist. by: The Distributors, 702 S. Michigan, South Bend, IN 46618.

T Runnels Pubns, *(Runnels, Tom, Pubns.; 0-9603710),* Marble Hill, MO 63764.

T Sawchenko, *(Sawchenko, Terry, D. D. S.),* 2101 E. Camelback Rd., Phoenix, AZ 85016.

T Schultz Pubns, *(Schultz, Thom, Pubns., Inc.; 0-936664),* P.O. Box 481, 1530 Boise Ave., Loveland, CO 80537 Tel 303-669-3836.

T T Taber, *(Taber, Thomas T.; 0-9603398),* Muncy, PA 17756.

T Thevenin, *(Thevenin, Tine; 0-9602010),* P.O. Box 16004, Minneapolis, MN 55416 Tel 612-922-4024.

T V Music, *(T.V. Music Co.; 0-918806),* 1650 Broadway, New York, NY 10019 Tel 212-246-3126.

T Vidal
   See Edns Alba

T W Khiralla, *(Khiralla, T. W.; 0-9601752),* 12400 Rye St., Studio City, CA 91604 Tel 213-980-1711.

T W Pubs, *(TW Pubs),* P.O. Box 152, River Forest, IL 60305.

T Weatherby, *(Weatherby, Thomas, Pub.),* 115 Billings St., Sharon, MA 02067.

T Weinberg
   See Gordons & Weinberg

T Y Crowell, *(Crowell, Thomas Y., Co.; 0-690),* 10 E. 53rd St., New York, NY 10022 Tel 212-593-3900; Dist. by: Harper & Row Pubs., Keystone Industrial Park, Scranton, PA 18512.

T Y Crowell
   See Funk & W

TA Press, *(TA Press; 0-89489),* Div. of International Transaction Analysis Assn., 1772 Vallejo St., San Francisco, CA 94123 Tel 415-885-5992.

TAB Bks, *(Tab Books, Inc.; 0-8306),* Blue Ridge Summit, PA 17214 Tel 717-794-2191.

TACL, *(T.A.C.L.),* 641 Towle Way, Palo Alto, CA 94306 Tel 415-493-3628.

Taconic Pubs, *(Taconic Pubs.; 0-9603308),* P.O. Box 296, South Egremont, MA 01258 Tel 413-528-0683.

Tafnews, *(Tafnews Press; 0-911520; 0-911521),* Div. of Track & Field News, Inc., P.O. Box 296, Los Altos, CA 94022 Tel 415-948-8188.

Taft Corp, *(Taft Corporation; 0-914756),* 1000 Vermont Ave., N.W., Washington, DC 20005 Tel 202-347-0788.

Tahrike Tarsile Quran, *(Tahrike Tarsile Quran),* P.O. Box 1115, Elmhurst, NY 11373.

Tail Feather, *(Tail Feather; 0-911756),* P.O. Box 1106, Moab, UT 84532 Tel 801-259-5303. *Imprints:* Neptune Bks (Neptune Books).

Talent & Booking, *(Talent & Booking Publishing Co.; 0-915546),* 7033 Sunset Blvd., Suite 222, Los Angeles, CA 90028 Tel 213-466-5141.

Tales Mojave Rd, *(Tales of the Mojave Road Pub., Co.; 0-914224),* P.O. Box 307, Norco, CA 91760 Tel 714-737-3150.

Talespinner, *(Talespinner Pubns., Inc.; 0-934926),* 4512 Pleasant Ave., S., Minneapolis, MN 55409 Tel 612-825-0087; Orders to: P.O. Box 19087, Minneapolis, MN 55419 Tel 612-825-0087.

Talisman, *(Talisman Press; 0-934612),* P.O. Box 455, Georgetown, CA 95634 Tel 916-333-4486.

Talisman Research, *(Talisman Literary Research, Inc.; 0-934614),* P.O. Box 455, Georgetown, CA 95634 Tel 916-333-4486.

Tamal Land, *(Tamal Land Press; 0-912908),* 39 Merwin Ave., Fairfax, CA 94930 Tel 415-456-4705.

Tamalpais Pr, *(Tamalpais Press; 0-916596),* P.O. Box 1286, Berkeley, CA 94701 Tel 415-845-4024.

Tamarack Edns, *(Tamarack Editions; 0-918092),* 909 Westcott St., Syracuse, NY 13210 Tel 315-478-6495.

Tamarack Pr, *(Tamarack Press; 0-915024),* P.O. Box 5650, Madison, WI 53705 Tel 608-831-3363.

Tamburitza, *(Tamburitza Press; 0-936922),* 1801 Blvd. of the Allies, Pittsburgh, PA 15219.

TAMS, *(Token & Medal Society, Inc.; 0-918492),* P.O. Box 951, Colorado Springs, CO 80901 Tel 303-473-9142; P.O. Box 321, Northbrook, IL 60062.

Tam's Bks, *(Tam's Books, Inc.; 0-89179),* 3333 S. Hoover St., Los Angeles, CA 90007 Tel 213-746-1141.

TAN Bks Pubs, *(TAN Books & Pubs., Inc.; 0-89555),* 2135 N. Central Ave., Rockford, IL 61105 Tel 815-962-2662; Orders to: P.O. Box 424, Rockford, IL 61105.

Tanadgusix Corp, *(Tanadgusix Corp.; 0-9601948),* St. Paul, AK 99660.

Tanam Pr, *(Tanam Press; 0-934378),* 40 White St., New York, NY 10013.

Tandem Pr, *(Tandem Press Pubs.; 0-913024),* P.O. Box 237, Tannersville, PA 18372 Tel 717-629-2250.

TANSTAAFL, *(TANSTAAFL; 0-931358),* P.O. Box 60026, Sunnyvale, CA 94086 Tel 408-732-1776.

Tao of Wing, *(Tao of Wing Chun Do; 0-918642),* 2912-C S. Skagit Hwy., Sedro Woolley, WA 98284 Tel 206-826-3848.

Taplinger, *(Taplinger Publishing Co., Inc.; 0-8008),* 132 W. 22nd St., New York, NY 10011 Tel 212-741-0801.

TAPPI, *(Technical Assn. of the Pulp & Paper Industry; 0-89852),* 1 Dunwoody Park, Atlanta, GA 30338 Tel 404-394-6130.

Taraxacum, *(Taraxacum; 0-9602822),* 1227 30th St. N.W., Washington, DC 20007.

Tari Bk Pubs, *(Tari Book Pubs.),* Route 3, Box 315, Molalla, OR 97038.

TarPar, *(TarPar, Ltd.),* P.O. Box 3, Kernersville, NC 27284.

Tartt, *(Tartt, Gene; 0-934746),* 960 N. San Antonio Rd., Suite 125, Los Altos, CA 94022 Tel 415-941-8638.

Tasa Pub Co, *(Tasa Publishing Co.; 0-935698),* 5230 W. 73rd St., Minneapolis, MN 55435.

Tasco, *(Tasco Pub. Corp.; 0-918076),* 305 E. 53rd St., Suite 3, New York, NY 10022 Tel 212-751-6500.

Tashmoo, *(Tashmoo Press, The; 0-932384),* RFD, Vineyard Haven, MA 02568.

Tate Gallery, *(Tate Gallery Pubns.),* P.O. Box 428, Truchas, NM 87578; Moved, Left No Address.

Tats, *(Tat's, Inc.; 0-911478),* 117 Airway Business Ctr., 3100 Airway Ave., Costa Mesa, CA 92626 Tel 714-545-3121.

Tatsch, *(Tatsch Associates; 0-912890),* 120 Thunder Rd., Sudbury, MA 01776 Tel 617-443-6343.

TAU Pr, *(TAU Press),* P.O. Box 2283, Rolling Hills, CA 90274.

Taugus Hse, *(Taugus House Pubs., Inc.; 0-938556),* 1890 San Pablo Dr., San Marcos, CA 92069.

Taunton, *(Taunton Press, Inc.; 0-918804),* Box 355, Newtown, CT 06470 Tel 203-426-8171.

Taurean Horn, *(Taurean Horn Press; 0-931552),* 601 Leavenworth No.45, San Francisco, CA 94109.

Tax Info Ctr, *(Tax Information Center),* Rte. 1, New Concord, OH 43762.

Taxlogs, *(Taxlogs Unlimited; 0-935802),* 20 Galli Dr., Ignacio, CA 94947 Tel 415-883-7768.

Taylor & Friends, *(Taylor, Sally, & Friends; 0-9604904),* 756 Kansas St., San Francisco, CA 94107.

Taylor & Ng, *(Taylor & Ng),* Box 200, Brisbane, CA 94005 Tel 415-467-2600.

Taylor-Carlisle, *(Taylor-Carlisle),* 245 Seventh Ave., New York, NY 10001 Tel 212-674-7788.

Taylor Museum, *(Taylor Museum),* Dist. by: Colorado Springs Fine Arts Ctr., 30 W. Dale St., Colorado Springs, CO 80903 Tel 303-634-5581.

Taylor Pub, *(Taylor Publishing Co.; 0-87833),* P.O. Box 597, Dallas, TX 75221.

Tayu Pr, *(Tayu Press; 0-934350),* P.O. Box 42555, San Francisco, CA 94101 Tel 707-823-2963.

TBN Ent, *(TBN Enterprises; 0-935554),* Box 55, Alexandria, VA 22313 Tel 703-549-2506.

TBW Bks, *(TBW Books; 0-931474),* Box 58, Day's Ferry Rd., Woolwich, ME 04579 Tel 207-442-7632.

Tchr Tested Materials, *(Teacher Tested Materials),* P.O. Box 67, Putnam, IL 61560.

Tchrs & Writers Coll, *(Teachers & Writers Collaborative; 0-915924),* 84 Fifth Ave., New York, NY 10011 Tel 212-691-6590.

Tchrs Coll, *(Teachers College Press, Columbia Univ.; 0-8077),* 1234 Amsterdam Ave., New York, NY 10027 Tel 212-678-3919; Orders to: 81 Adams Dr., Totowa, NJ 07512 Tel 201-265-8600.

Te Cum Tom, *(Te-Cum-Tom Pubns.; 0-913508),* 570 Sunset Way, Grants Pass, OR 97526 Tel 503-479-9091.

Tea Hse Pubns, *(Tea House Pubns.; 0-935256),* P.O. Box 7000-163, Palos Verdes Peninsula, CA 90274 Tel 213-377-5974; Moved, Left No Forwarding Address.

Teach & Learn Pubns
  See Learning Pubns

Teach Res Corp, *(Teaching Resources Corp.),* 50 Pond Park Rd., Hingham, MA 02043.

Teach'em, *(Teach'em, Inc.; 0-931028),* 160 E. Illinois St., Chicago, IL 60611.

Teacher Update, *(Teacher Update, Inc.; 0-89780),* Box 205, Saddle River, NJ 07458 Tel 201-327-8486.

Teachers Load, *(Teacher's Load Press; 0-9603750),* 2631 Farber Dr., St. Louis, MO 63136.

Teachers Tax, *(Teacher's Tax Service; 0-912772),* 1303 E. Balboa Blvd., Newport Beach, CA 92661 Tel 714-675-9891.

Teaching Res, *(Teaching Research Pubns.),* Todd Hall, 345 N. Monmouth Ave., Monmouth, OR 97361 Tel 503-838-1220.

Teapot Pubs, *(Teapot Pubs.; 0-917068),* P.O. Box 19, Dearborn, MI 48124; Moved, Left No Forwarding Address.

Tech Conf Assoc, *(Technology Conferences Associates; 0-938648),* P.O. Box 842, El Segundo, CA 90245.

Tech Data, *(Tech Data Pubns.; 0-937816),* 6324 W. Fond Du Lac Ave., Milwaukee, WI 53218.

Tech Dict, *(Technical Dictionaries Co.; 0-911484),* P.O. Box 144, New York, NY 10031.

Tech Direct, *(Technical Directions, Inc.; 0-918876),* P.O. Box 2221, W. Lafayette, IN 47906 Tel 317-749-2256.

Tech Ed Pr, *(Technical Education Press; 0-911908),* P.O. Box 342, Seal Beach, CA 90740 Tel 213-431-8515.

Tech Ed Serv, *(Technical Education Services; 0-930552),* Univ. of Missouri, Columbia, MO 65201.

Tech Educ Co, *(Technical Education Co., Inc.; 0-939402),* P.O. Box 18738, Irvine, CA 92713.

Tech Group, *(Technology Group, The; 0-939856),* P.O. Box 3125, Pasadena, CA 91103 Tel 213-794-6013. *Imprints:* Magick Circle (Magick Circle, The).

Tech Info Proj, *(Technical Information Project, Inc.; 0-939578),* 1346 Connecticut Ave. N.W., Suite 217, Washington, DC 20036 Tel 202-466-2954.

Tech Marketing, *(Technology Marketing Corp.),* 17 Park St., Norwalk, CT 06851 Tel 203-846-2029.

Tech Mgmt, *(Technology Management, Inc.),* 57 Kilvert St., Warwick, RI 02886; Dist. by: Management Associates, Box 230, Chestnut Hill, MA 02167.

Tech Pr Inc, *(Technology Press, Inc., The; 0-89321),* P.O. Box 125, Fairfax Station, VA 22039 Tel 703-978-5299.

Tech Pub, *(Technical Publishing; 0-912212),* Div. of Dun & Bradstreet, 666 Fifth Ave., New York, NY 10019 Tel 212-489-4620.

Tech Recog Corp, *(Technology Recognition Corporation; 0-933980),* 1382 Old Freeport Rd., Pittsburgh, PA 15238.

Techkits, *(Techkits, Inc.; 0-918662),* P.O. Box 105, Demarest, NJ 07627 Tel 201-684-7500.

Technicon Pubs, *(Technicon Pubs.; 0-915428),* P.O. Box 1413, Novato, CA 94947 Tel 415-897-7638.

Technique Learn, *(Technique Learning Corp.; 0-917142),* 17 E. 48 St., New York, NY 10017 Tel 212-752-6282.

Technocracy, *(Technocracy, Inc.),* P.O. Box 238, Savannah, OH 44874 Tel 419-962-4712.

Technomic, *(Technomic Publishing Co.; 0-87762),* 265 Post Road West, Westport, CT 06880 Tel 203-226-7203.

Techscience Inc, *(Techscience, Inc.; 0-918910),* P.O. Box 1100, Hawthorne, CA 90250 Tel 503-926-5739.

Tecolote Pr, *(Tecolote Press, Inc.; 0-915030),* P.O. Box 188, Glenwood, NM 88039 Tel 505-539-2183.

Tele Cable, *(Telegraphic Cable & Radio Registrations, Inc.; 0-916446),* 1600 Harrison Ave., Mamaroneck, NY 10543.

Tele-Sell Res, *(Tele-Sell Research Institute; 0-910410),* Div. of C & R Anthony Publishers, Inc., 300 Park Ave. S., New York, NY 10010 Tel 212-677-3170.

Telecom Lib, *(Telecom Library, The; 0-936648),* 205 W. 19th St., New York, NY 10011 Tel 212-691-8215. *Imprints:* Personal Achievement (Personal Achievement Library).

Telegraph *Imprint of* **Dynamic Learn Corp**

Telegraph Bks, *(Telegraph Books; 0-89760),* Box 38, Norwood, PA 19074 Tel 215-583-4550.

Teleometrics, *(Teleometrics International, Inc.; 0-937932),* 2203 Timberloch Place, Suite 104, The Woodlands, TX 77380 Tel 713-367-0060.

Telephone Bks, *(Telephone Books Press; 0-916382),* P.O. Box 672, Old Chelsea Sta., New York, NY 10011 Tel 203-453-4415.

Television Digest, *(Television Digest, Inc.; 0-911486),* 1836 Jefferson Place, N.W., Washington, DC 20036 Tel 202-872-9200.

Telos Pr, *(Telos Press Ltd.; 0-914386),* Box 3111, St. Louis, MO 63130 Tel 314-361-8472.

Temple Bar, *(Temple Bar Bookshop),* 9 Boylston St., Cambridge, MA 02138 Tel 617-876-6025.

Temple Pub Co, *(Temple Publishing Co. Inc.; 0-917090),* P.O. Box 28722, Dallas, TX 75218.

Temple U Pr, *(Temple Univ. Press; 0-87722),* Philadelphia, PA 19122 Tel 215-787-8787.

Templegate, *(Templegate Pubs.; 0-87243),* P.O. Box 5152, Springfield, IL 62705 Tel 217-522-3361.

Templeman, *(Templeman, Eleanor Lee; 0-911044),* 3001 N. Pollard St., Arlington, VA 22207 Tel 703-528-1112.

Tempo *Imprint of* **G&D**

Ten Penny, *(Ten Penny Players, Inc.; 0-934830),* 799 Greenwich St., New York, NY 10014 Tel 212-929-3169.

Ten Speed Pr, *(Ten Speed Press; 0-913668; 0-89815),* P.O. Box 7123, Berkeley, CA 94707 Tel 415-845-8414.

Ten Talents, *(Ten Talents; 0-9603532),* P.O. Box 86A, Rte. 1, Chisholm, MN 55719 Tel 218-254-5357.

Tenameca, *(Tenameca, Inc.; 0-918582),* P.O. Box 44436, Indianapolis, IN 46244 Tel 317-631-6304.

Tendril, *(Tendril; 0-937504),* P.O. Box 512, Green Harbor, MA 02041.

Tennis, *(Tennis for Travelers; 0-911490),* 407 Blade St., Cincinnati, OH 45216 Tel 513-242-3100.

Tennis Manual, *(Tennis Manual; 0-9606066),* 600 N. Fig Tree Lane, Ft. Lauderdale, FL 33317; P.O. Box 16781, Ft. Lauderdale, FL 33318.

Tennis Serv Co, *(Tennis Services Co.; 0-9601310),* 709 Tennent St., Charleston, SC 29412 Tel 803-795-2006.

Tenny Hale, *(Tenny Hale),* 12125 S.W. Cheshire Rd., Box 125, Beaverton, OH 97005.

Tension-in-Repose, *(Tension-in-Repose),* 500 E. 74th St., New York, NY 10021.

Tern Pr, *(Tern, Eddie, Press; 0-9605388),* 430 SW 206th St., Seattle, WA 98166.

Terra Magica *Imprint of* **Hill & Wang**

Terra Pub, *(Terra Publishing; 0-9603238),* P.O. Box 99103, Jeffersontown, KY 40299 Tel 502-895-0557.

Terraspace, *(Terraspace Inc.; 0-918990),* 304 N. Stonestreet Ave., Rockville, MD 20850 Tel 301-424-0090.

Terrell Pub, *(Terrell Publishing Co.; 0-933148),* 1687 Richland Rd. S.W., Atlanta, GA 30311.

Terry Pub, *(Terry Publishing Co.),* P.O. Box 525, Olympia, WA 98501 Tel 206-491-2055.

Tesla Bk Co, *(Tesla Book Co.; 0-9603536),* 1580 Magnolia Ave., Millbrae, CA 94030 Tel 415-697-4903.

Tespressco, *(Tespressco),* P.O. Box 128, Willingboro, NJ 08046.

Teton Bkshop, *(Teton Bookshop Publishing Co.; 0-933160),* Box 1903, Jackson, WY 83001.

Tetra Tech, *(Tetra Tech, Inc.; 0-916646),* 1911 Ft. Myer Dr., Suite 601, Arlington, VA 22209.

Tetragrammaton, *(Tetragrammaton Press; 0-937326),* 3594 Sepulveda Blvd., Sherman Oaks, CA 91403.

Teutsch, *(Teutsch, Joel & Champion),* 2049 Century Park E., Suite 2730, Los Angeles, CA 90067 Tel 213-277-8773.

Tex A & M Lang
  See Dabbs

Tex A&M Univ Pr, *(Texas A & M Univ. Press; 0-89096),* Drawer "C", College Station, TX 77843 Tel 713-845-1436.

Tex Assn Mus, *(Texas Assn. of Museums; 0-935260),* P.O. Box 13353, Capitol Sta., Austin, TX 78711 Tel 512-451-3893.

Tex Christian, *(Texas Christian Univ. Press; 0-912646),* Box 30783, Fort Worth, TX 76129 Tel 817-921-7822.

Tex Congr Parent & Teach, *(Texas Congress of Parents & Teachers),* 408 W. 11th St., Austin, TX 78701 Tel 512-476-6769.

Tex Consumer, *(Texas Consumer Assn.; 0-937606),* 500 W. 13th St., Austin, TX 78701.

Tex Ctr Writers, *(Texas Center for Writers Press),* P.O. Box 19876, Dallas, TX 75219.

Tex Instr Inc, *(Texas Instruments Inc.; 0-89512),* P.O. Box 225012 MS54, Dallas, TX 75265 Tel 214-995-5516.

Tex-Mex, *(Tex-Mex Books Publishers International Texas; 0-918268),* Box 186, 820 San Antonio Ave., San Juan, TX 78589 Tel 512-781-2186.

Tex Portfolio
  See Cedar Rock

Tex St Hist Assn, *(Texas State Historical Assn.; 0-87611),* 2-306 Richardson Hall, Univ. Sta., Austin, TX 78712 Tel 512-471-1525.

Tex Tech Pr, *(Texas Tech Press; 0-89672),* P.O. Box 4460, Lubbock, TX 79409 Tel 806-742-2781; Orders to: Texas Tech University Library, Texas Tech University, Lubbock, TX 79409.

Tex Western, *(Texas Western Press, Univ. of Texas at El Paso; 0-87404),* El Paso, TX 79968 Tel 915-747-5688.

Texan-Am Pub, *(Texan-American Publisher's Co.; 0-935622),* 1101 Natchez Dr., Texas City, TX 77590 Tel 713-935-9676.

Texan Hse, *(Texan House, Inc.; 0-915702),* P.O. Box 9812, Austin, TX 78766; Moved, Left No Forwarding Address.

Texas Educ, *(Texas Education Agency),* 201 E. 11th St., Austin, TX 78701.

Texas Month Pr, *(Texas Monthly Press; 0-932012),* P.O. Box 1569, Austin, TX 78767 Tel 512-476-7085.

Texian, *(Texian Press; 0-87244),* P.O. Box 1684, Waco, TX 76703 Tel 817-754-5636.

Text Book Inc, *(Textbook, Inc.),* P.O. Box 1971, Baton Rouge, LA 70821 Tel 504-926-8561.

Text-Fiche, *(Text-Fiche Press, The; 0-89969),* 540 Drexel Ave., Glencoe, IL 60022 Tel 312-835-4420; Orders to: Box 382, Glencoe, IL 60022.

Textile Bk, *(Textile Book Service, Inc.; 0-87245),* P.O. Box 25, Broadway, NJ 08808 Tel 201-689-2230.

Textile Bridge, *(Textile Bridge Press),* P.O. Box 157, Clarence Center, NY 14032.

Textile Mus, *(Textile Museum; 0-87405),* 2320 "S" St., N.W., Washington, DC 20008 Tel 202-667-0441.

TF Century Res, *(Twenty First Century Research),* 3115 Whirlaway, Dallas, TX 75229 Tel 214-357-5185.

TFH Pubns, *(T. F. H. Pubns.; 0-87666),* 211 W. Sylvania Ave., Neptune, NJ 07753 Tel 201-988-8400.

Thadian Pubns, *(Thadian Pubns.; 0-930516),* P.O. Box 129, North Haven, CT 06473.

Thai-Am Pubs, *(Thai-American Pubs.; 0-915806),* 101 Park Ave., Suite 1436N, New York, NY 10017 Tel 212-683-0501.

Thailand Bks
  See Asia Lib Ser

Thalassa Pr, *(Thalassa Press; 0-939472),* Box 2098, Astoria, NY 11102.

Thales Microuniv, *(Thales Microuniversity Press; 0-914312),* P.O. Box 214, Stillwater, OK 74074 Tel 405-377-9793.

Thames Hudson, *(Thames & Hudson; 0-500),* Dist. by: W.W. Norton, & Co., Inc., 500 Fifth Ave., New York, NY 10036 Tel 212-354-3763.

That New Pub, *(That New Pub. Co.; 0-918270),* 1525 Eielson St., Fairbanks, AK 99701 Tel 907-452-3007.

Thayer-Jacoby, *(Thayer-Jacoby),* 1432 E. Ninth St., Brooklyn, NY 11230.

The Charles Publishing, *(Charles' Publishing Co., The; 0-917514),* 4725 S. W. Calden St., Portland, OR 97219 Tel 503-245-3081.

The Garden, *(The Garden; 0-9602790),* 6605 Rowland Rd., Eden Prairie, MN 55344 Tel 612-944-2404.

The Harian
See Harian Creative

The Hemphills, *(Hemphills, The; 0-9600948),* P.O. Box 8302, Nashville, TN 37207 Tel 615-865-7100.

The Inspiration, *(Inspiration Press, The),* P.O. Box 245, Iowa City, IA 52240; Moved, Left No Forwarding Address.

The Little Brown House, *(The Little Brown House Publishing Co.; 0-915782),* P.O. Box 179, Harpers Ferry, WV 25425 Tel 304-535-2229.

The Smith, *(Smith, The; 0-912292),* 5 Beekman St., New York, NY 10038 Tel 212-732-4821; Dist. by: Horizon Press, 156 Fifth Ave, New York, NY 10010.

Theare Corp, *(Theare Corp.; 0-9602164),* P.O. Box 13693, Sacramento, CA 95813.

Theatre Arts, *(Theatre Arts Books; 0-87830),* 153 Waverly Place, New York, NY 10014 Tel 212-675-1815.

Theatre Comm, *(Theatre Communications Group, Inc.; 0-930452),* 355 Lexington Ave., New York, NY 10017.

Theatre Ctr Bay, *(Theatre Communications Center of the Bay Area; 0-9605896),* 1182 Market St., No. 208, San Francisco, CA 94102.

Thelema Pub TN
See Troll Pub

Thelema Pubns, *(Thelema Pubns.; 0-913576),* P.O. Box 1093, Kings Beach, CA 95719.

Theobald, *(Theobald, Paul, & Co.; 0-911498),* 5 N. Wabash Ave., Chicago, IL 60602 Tel 312-236-3994.

Theophrastus, *(Theophrastus; 0-913728),* P.O. Box 458, Little Compton, RI 02837 Tel 401-635-4348.

Theorex, *(Theorex; 0-916004),* 8327 La Jolla Scenic Dr., La Jolla, CA 92037 Tel 714-453-6988.

Theos Pub Hse, *(Theosophical Publishing House; 0-8356),* 306 W. Geneva Rd., Wheaton, IL 60187 Tel 312-665-0123. *Imprints:* Quest (Quest Books).

Theos U Pr, *(Theosophical Univ. Press; 0-911500),* P.O. Bin "C", Pasadena, CA 91109 Tel 213-798-8020.

Theoscience Found, *(Theoscience Foundation Pub.; 0-917802),* 193 Los Robles Dr., Burlingame, CA 94010.

Theosophy, *(Theosophy Co.),* 245 W. 33rd St., Los Angeles, CA 90007 Tel 213-748-7244.

Theotes, *(Theotes-Logos Research, Inc.; 0-911806),* 4318 York Ave. S., Minneapolis, MN 55410 Tel 612-922-3202.

Theta Bks, *(Theta Books, Inc.; 0-917972),* P.O. Box 600, Clearwater, FL 33517 Tel 813-446-3556.

Theta Pr, *(Theta Press International; 0-918244),* 1518 E. Del Rio Dr., Tempe, AZ 85282.

Thieme-Stratton, *(Thieme-Stratton, Inc.; 0-913258; 0-86577),* 381 Park Ave., S., New York, NY 10016 Tel 212-683-5088.

Thigpen, *(Thigpen, S. G.; 0-911892),* P.O. Box 819, Picayune, MS 39466.

Third Century, *(Third Century Fund; 0-9603360),* 1200-A Cabrillo Park Dr., Santa Ana, CA 92701 Tel 714-547-1700.

Third Pr
See Okpaku Communications

Third World, *(Third World Press; 0-88378),* 7524 S. Cottage Grove, Chicago, IL 60619 Tel 312-651-0700.

Thirteenth Hse, *(Thirteenth House; 0-935458),* 71 Vondran St., Huntington Station, NY 11746.

Thirteenth Moon, *(13th Moon, Inc.; 0-9601224),* Drawer F, Inwood Sta., New York, NY 10034 Tel 212-569-7614.

This Pr, *(This Press; 0-935074),* 1004 Hampshire St., San Francisco, CA 94110 Tel 415-821-3452.

Thistlerose, *(Thistlerose Pubns.; 0-9605630),* 5161 E. County Line Rd., White Bear Lake, MN 55110.

Thomas-Hull
See Rockwell

Thomas Intl Pub, *(Thomas International Publishing Co., Inc.; 0-937200),* Subs. of Thomas Publishing Co., 1 Penn Plaza, New York, NY 10001 Tel 212-695-0500.

Thomas More, *(More, Thomas, Press; 0-88347),* 225 W. Huron St., Chicago, IL 60610 Tel 312-951-2100.

Thomas-Newell, *(Thomas-Newell; 0-9600690),* 1201 Monroe St., P. O. Box 329, Endicott, NY 13760 Tel 607-754-0410.

Thomas Paine Pr, *(Thomas Paine Press; 0-934162),* 6674 Danville Ave., San Diego, CA 92120 Tel 714-462-8120.

Thomas Pr, *(Thomas Press; 0-89732),* 2030 Ferdon Rd., Ann Arbor, MI 48104 Tel 313-662-1275.

Thomist, *(Thomist Press; 0-911502),* 487 Michigan Ave., N.E., Washington, DC 20017 Tel 202-529-5300.

Thomond Pr *Imprint of* Elsevier

Thompson's, *(Thompson's),* P.O. Box 550, Albertville, AL 35950 Tel 205-878-2021.

Thomson, *(Thomson, Phillip; 0-911504),* 836 Georgia St., Williamston, MI 48895 Tel 517-655-2930.

Thomson Pub CA, *(Thomson Pubns.; 0-913702),* P.O. Box 9335, Fresno, CA 93791 Tel 209-435-2163.

Thomson Pub Ent CO, *(Thomson Publishing Enterprises; 0-9603642),* 2343 Vaughn Way, Suite 204-Heatheridge, Aurora, CO 80014.

Thor, *(Thor Publishing Co.; 0-87407),* P.O. Box 1782, Ventura, CA 93002 Tel 805-648-4560.

Thoreau Found, *(Thoreau Foundation, Inc.; 0-912130),* Thoreau Lyceum, 156 Belknap St., Concord, MA 01742 Tel 617-369-5912.

Thorndike Pr, *(Thorndike Press; 0-89621),* Thorndike, ME 04986 Tel 207-948-2962.

Thoroughbred Own & Breed, *(Thoroughbred Owners & Breeders Assn.),* P.O. Box 4038, Lexington, KY 40544 Tel 606-278-2361.

Thorp Springs, *(Thorp Springs Press; 0-914476),* 803 Red River St., Austin, TX 78701.

Thrasher, *(Thrasher Balloons; 0-9601514),* P.O. Box 1111, Homestead, FL 33030 Tel 305-247-8412.

Three Continents, *(Three Continents Press; 0-89410; 0-914478),* 1346 Connecticut Ave., Suite 1131, Washington, DC 20036 Tel 202-457-0288. *Imprints:* Drumbeat (Drumbeat).

Three D Pubs, *(3-D Pubs.; 0-9600500),* P.O. Box 428, Edgerton, OH 43517.

Three Herons, *(Three Herons Pr.),* P.O. Box 340-A, Rte. 3, Three Rivers, MI 49093 Tel 616-442-2725.

Three in One Concepts, *(Three in One Concepts, Inc.),* P.O. Box 4492, Glendale, CA 91202.

Three L Pr, *(Three L Press; 0-9601938),* 170 Ninth St., San Francisco, CA 94103.

Three Mtn Pr, *(Three Mountains Press; 0-930986),* P.O. Box 50, Cooper Sta., New York, NY 10003 Tel 212-989-2737.

Three PB, *(Three PB Publishing Co.; 0-89152),* 219-221 Parkade, Cedar Fall, IA 50613 Tel 319-277-3381; Moved, Left No Forwarding Address.

Three Rivers Pr, *(Three Rivers Pr.; 0-915606),* P.O. Box 21, Carnegie Mellon Univ., Pittsburgh, PA 15213.

Thresh Pubns, *(Thresh Pubns.; 0-9600572; 0-913664),* 3027 Gateway Rd., P.O. Box 580, Bethel Island, CA 94511.

Threshold Bks, *(Threshold Books; 0-914186),* 365 Martha St., Susanville, CA 96130 Tel 916-257-3979.

Threshold VT, *(Threshold Books; 0-939660),* RD 3 Box 208, Putney, VT 05346 Tel 802-387-4586.

Thum Print, *(Thum Printing; 0-932920),* 116 W. Pierce St., Elburn, IL 60119.

Thunder City, *(Thunder City Press; 0-918644),* P.O. Box 11126, Birmingham, AL 35202 Tel 205-933-0465.

Thunder River, *(Thunder River Press; 0-9604274),* P.O. Box 10935, Aspen, CO 81611.

Thunderbird Pr, *(Thunderbird Press),* 2747 W. Windrose Dr., Phoenix, AZ 85029.

Thunderchief, *(Thunderchief Corp.),* P.O. Box 85, Troutdale, OR 97060.

Thunder's Mouth, *(Thunder's Mouth Press; 0-938410),* 242 W. 104th St., No. 5rW, New York, NY 10025; 1152 S. East, Oak Park, IL 60304.

Thursday Pubs, *(Thursday Pubs.; 0-934502),* 1846N Pine Bluff Rd., Stevens Point, WI 54481 Tel 715-344-6441.

Thut Ctr World Ed
See World Educ Proj

TIB Pubns, *(TIB Pubns.; 0-931882),* Div. of The Image Builders, 2922 N. State Rd. 7, Suite 107, Margate, FL 33063.

Tiburon
See Word Power

Ticket Bk, *(Ticket Book, The; 0-9601950),* P.O Box 1087, La Jolla, CA 92038 Tel 714-292-5999; Moved, Left No Forwarding Address.

Ticknor & Fields, *(Ticknor & Fields; 0-89919),* 383 Orange St., New Haven, CT 06511 Tel 203-776-1878; 52 Vanderbilt Ave., New York, NY 10017 Tel 212-687-8996; Dist. by: Houghton Mifflin Co., 2 Park St., Boston, MA 02107 Tel 617-725-5000.

Tidal Pr, *(Tidal Press, The),* Cranberry Isles, ME 04625 Tel 207-244-3090.

Tide Bk Pub Co, *(Tide Book Publishing Co.; 0-9602786),* P.O. Box 268, Manchester, M 01944 Tel 617-526-4887; Orders to: Academy Chicago Ltd., 360 N. Michigan Ave., Chicago, IL 60601 Tel 312-782-9826.

Tidewater, *(Tidewater Pubs.; 0-87033),* Div. of Cormell Press, Inc., P.O. Box 109, Cambridge, MD 21613 Tel 301-228-3850.

Tiffany, *(Tiffany Press; 0-914800),* P.O. Box 304, Newton, MA 02158 Tel 617-527-9395

Tilden Pr, *(Tilden Press; 0-9605750),* 1737 DeSales St. NW, Washington, DC 20036.

Till Pr, *(Till Press),* P.O. Box 27816, Los Angeles, CA 90027.

Timber, *(Timber Press; 0-917304),* P.O. Box 92 Forest Grove, OR 97116 Tel 503-357-7192

Timberline Bks, *(Timberline Books; 0-913488),* 25890 Weld Rd. 53, Kersey, CO 80644 Tel 303-353-3785.

Timco Intl, *(Timco International; 0-915624),* P.O. Box 431, Berkeley, CA 94701.

Time & Space, *(Time & Space Ltd.; 0-939858),* 139 W. 22nd St., New York, NY 10011 Tel 212-741-1032.

Time Bks
See Times Bks

Time-Lee Pubns, *(Time-Lee Pubns.; 0-937210),* P.O. Box 116, Melbourne, FL 32901 Tel 305-727-3010.

Time-Life, *(Time-Life Books; 0-8094),* Div. of Time, Inc., 777 Duke St., Alexandria, VA 22314 Tel 703-960-5000; Dist. by: Little, Brown & Co., 34 Beacon St., Boston, MA 02106; Dist. by: Morgan & Morgan Co., 40 Warburton Ave., Hastings on Hudson, NY 10706; Lib. & School Orders to: Silver Burdett Co., Morristown, NJ 13664.

Time Share Corp, *(Time Share Corp.; 0-89466),* Subs. of Houghton Mifflin Co., P.O. Box 683, Hanover, NH 03755 Tel 603-448-3838 Box 974, Hanover, NH 03775.

Time-Wise, *(Time-Wise Pubns.; 0-918826),* P.O. Box 597, Yucca Valley, CA 92284 Tel 714-365-5888.

Timeless Bks, *(Timeless Books; 0-931454),* Orders to: P.O. Box 60, Porthill, ID 83853 Tel 604-227-9220.

Timely Bks, *(Timely Books; 0-931328),* P.O. Box 267, New Milford, CT 06776 Tel 203-354-1110.

Timely Pubns, *(Timely Pubns.; 0-916548),* P.O. Box 81563, San Diego, CA 92138; Moved, Left No Forwarding Address.

Times Bks, *(Times Books; 0-8129),* Div. of The New York Times Co., 3 Park Ave., New York, NY 10016 Tel 212-725-2050; Dist. by: Harper & Row, Keystone Industrial Park Scranton, PA 18512. *Imprints:* Demeter (Demeter Press).

Times Change, *(Times Change Press; 0-87810),* Publishers Services, P.O. Box 3914, San Rafael, CA 94901 Tel 707-937-4266.

Times-M Pr, *(Times-Mirror Press; 0-911510),* 1115 S. Boyle Ave, Los Angeles, CA 90023 Tel 213-265-6767.

Timescape *Imprint of* PB

Timetable Pr, *(Timetable Press; 0-87974),* 50 Sagamore Dr., Syosset, NY 11791 Tel 516-921-2137.

Timothy Bks, *(Timothy Books; 0-914964),* Div. of Hearthstone Pubns., Inc., 915 Fifth Ave., Box 567, Williamsport, PA 17701; Moved, Left No Forwarding Address.

Tinnon-Brown, *(Tinnon-Brown Publishing Co.; 0-87252),* Orders to: Borden Publishing Co., 1855 W. Main St., Alhambra, CA 91801.

Tioga Pub Co, *(Tioga Publishing Co.; 0-935382),* P.O. Box 98, Palo Alto, CA 94302 Tel 415-854-2445.

Tipton Woman, (Tipton Woman's Club-Cookbook), P.O. Box 25, Tipton, IA 52772 Tel 319-886-2730.

Tiresias Pr, (Tiresias Press, Inc.; 0-913292), 116 Pinehurst Ave., New York, NY 10033 Tel 212-568-9570.

TIS Inc, (T.I.S., Inc.; 0-89917), P.O. Box 1998, 1928 Arlington Rd., Bloomington, IN 47401 Tel 812-332-3307.

Titan Pr, (Titan Press; 0-930054), P.O. Box 5139, Santa Monica, CA 90405 Tel 213-837-8041.

Titan Pub Co, (Titan Publishing Co.; 0-9603314), P.O. Box 506, Mesilla, NM 88046 Tel 505-523-4542.

TL Enterprises, (TL Enterprises, Inc.; 0-934798), 29901 Agoura Rd., Agoura, CA 91301 Tel 213-991-4980.

TM Prods, (TM Productions; 0-937522), Box 189, Wilmette, IL 60091.

Tobey Pub, (Tobey Publishing Co., Inc.), 1 Aldwyn Center, Villanova, PA 19085 Tel 215-527-5100; Dist. by: Dell Publishing Co., Inc., Dag Hammarskjold Plaza, 245 E. 47th St., New York, NY 10017.

Today News, (Today News Service, Inc.; 0-932746), National Press Bldg., Washington, DC 20004 Tel 202-628-6999.

Today Pubn
    See Today News

Todd, (Todd, Glen H.), 914 Saluda St., Rock Hill, SC 29730.

Todd & Honeywell, (Todd & Honeywell Inc.; 0-89962), 10 Cuttermill Rd., Great Neck, NY 11021 Tel 516-487-9777.

Todd Pubns, (Todd Pubns.; 0-915344), 10 Rapids Rd., Stamford, CT 06905 Tel 203-322-5488.

Todd Tarbox, (Todd Tarbox Books; 0-89297), 1637 E. 36 Place, Tulsa, OK 74105 Tel 918-749-4742.

Tofua Pr
    See Rand-Tofua

Toggitt, (Toggitt, Joan, Ltd.; 0-911514), 246 Fifth Ave., New York, NY 10001.

Tokai Imprint of **Unipub**

Toledo Mus Art, (Toledo Museum of Art, The; 0-935172), Box 1013, Toledo, OH 43697 Tel 419-255-8000; Dist. by: Pennsylvania State Univ. Press, 215 Wagner Bldg., University Park, PA 16802.

Toler, (Toler Co.; 0-9600530), P.O. Box 585, Vienna, VA 22180; Name Formerly Relot, Inc., Pub., Co.

Tolff, (Tolff, Publishers; 0-916498), Div. of the Trinity of Light Fellowship Foundation, 5750 Via Real, No. 230, Carpinteria, CA 93013 Tel 805-684-6363.

Tolle Pubns, (Tolle Pubns.; 0-915378), P.O. Box 6243, Beaumont, TX 77705 Tel 713-833-9806; 3945 Rothwell, Beaumont, TX 77705.

Tolstoy Found, (Tolstoy Foundation, Inc.), 250 W. 57th St., New York, NY 10019.

Tolvan Co, (Tolvan Co.; 0-916774), P.O. Box 1933, Appleton, WI 54911 Tel 414-766-1828.

Tom Tuttle, (Tuttle, Tom, & Associates; 0-930556), P.O. Box 20081, Cincinnati, OH 45220 Tel 212-475-5114.

Tomato Pubns, (Tomato Pubns.; 0-934166), Preston Hollow, NY 12469.

Tombouctou, (Tombouctou Books), P.O. Box 265, Bolinas, CA 94924; Dist. by: Bookpeople, 2940 Seventh St., Berkeley, CA 94710 Tel 415-549-3030; Dist. by: Bookslinger, P.O. Box 1651, 2163 Ford Pkwy., St. Paul, MN 55116 Tel 612-690-0293; Dist. by: Dark Horse, 2636 Etna, No 4, Berkeley, CA 94704 Tel 415-843-5796; Dist. by: Barbary Coast Distribution, 635 Amador, Richmond, CA 94805 Tel 415-236-1197; Dist. by: Serendipity Books Distribution, 1970 Shattuck Ave., Berkeley, CA 94704 Tel 415-549-3336; Dist. by: Word Works, 1421 Second Ave., N. Seattle, WA 98109 Tel 206-284-8127; Dist. by: New York State Small Press Assn., P.O. Box 1264, Radio City Sta., New York, NY 10019.

Tompson & Rutter, (Tompson & Rutter, Inc.; 0-936988), P.O. Box 297, Grantham, NH 03753; Dist. by: Shoe String Press, Inc., P. O. Box 4327, 995 Sherman Ave., Hamden, CT 06514.

Tonatiuh Intl
    See Tonatiuh-Quinto Sol Intl

Tonatiuh-Quinto Sol Intl, (Tonatiuh/Quinto Sol International, Inc.; 0-88412), P.O. Box 9275, Berkeley, CA 94709 Tel 415-655-8036.

Tools for Schools, (Tools for Schools, Inc.; 0-933242), 164 27th St., San Francisco, CA 94110 Tel 415-282-2526.

Toothpaste, (Toothpaste Press; 0-915124), P.O. Box 546, West Branch, IA 52358 Tel 319-643-2604.

Topaz, (Topaz Books), Dist. by: Taplinger Publishing Co., Inc., 200 Park Ave., S., New York, NY 10003.

Topgallant, (Topgallant Publishing Co., Ltd.; 0-914916), Elizabeth Bldg. 845 Mission Lane, Honolulu, HI 96813 Tel 808-524-0884.

Topic, (Topic, Inc.), 6736 Washburn Ave., Minneapolis, MN 55423.

Torah Res, (Torah Resources; 0-9603100), 951-56th St., Brooklyn, NY 11219.

Torch Imprint of **Har-Row**

Torch Lib Imprint of **Har-Row**

Torskript Pubs, (Torskript Pubs.; 0-913048), P.O. Box 297, San Francisco, CA 94101 Tel 415-584-8813.

Tortilla, (Tortilla Press; 0-932738), 1291 E. Howard, Pasadena, CA 91104; Moved, Left No Forwarding Address.

Tortoise Pr, (Tortoise Press, The; 0-939518), 1215 Via Coronel, Palos Verdes Estates, CA 90274 Tel 213-378-7061.

Total Graphics, (Total Graphics; 0-912860), 316 W. Mission Rd., San Marcos, CA 92069 Tel 714-747-1108.

Total Read, (Total Reading Inc.; 0-918396), P.O. Box 214, Moraga, CA 94556 Tel 415-376-2037.

Total Trial, (Total Trial System, The; 0-9605222), P.O. Box 3663, St. Paul, MN 55165.

Total Univ Bk, (Total Universe Book Co.), P.O. Box 1204, Dearborn, MI 48121.

Totem Shooters, (Totem Shooters Supplies; 0-9603432), P.O. Box 222, Eagle River, AK 94577 Tel 907-680-0555.

Touchstone, (Touchstone Press), ; Publisher Abbreviation Without Addresses Are for Titles That Are Out of Print. These Are Obsolete Abbreviations.

Touchstone Bks Imprint of **S&S**

Touchstone Ent ND, (Touchstone Enterprises, Inc.; 0-939728), 2108 S. University Dr., Park Place Plaza, Suite 103, Fargo, ND 58103 Tel 701-237-4742.

Touchstone Pr OR, (Touchstone Press; 0-911518), P.O. Box 81, Beaverton, OR 97075 Tel 503-646-8081.

Touchstone Pub KY, (Touchstone Publishing Co.; 0-87963), 1941 Bishop Lane, Suite 901, Louisville, KY 40218.

Touraine, (Touraine Pub. Corp.; 0-920542), 350 5th Ave., Suite 3308, New York, NY 10001 Tel 212-564-8658; Moved, Left No Forwarding Address.

Tourism Ctr
    See Travel & Tourism

Tourmaline Pr, (Tourmaline Press), P.O. Box 13024, Houston, TX 77019.

Toward the Light, (Toward the Light Publishing House; 0-937054), 16645 Bosque Dr., Encino, CA 91436.

Tower
    See Tower Bks

Tower Bks, (Tower Books, Inc.; 0-505), 2 Park Ave., Suite 910, New York, NY 10016 Tel 212-679-7707; Orders to: Increased Sales Co., Inc., 327 Main Ave., Norwalk, CT 06852 Tel 203-846-2027.

Tower Pub Co, (Tower Publishing Co.; 0-89442), 163 Middle St., P. O. Box 7220, Portland, ME 04112 Tel 207-774-9813.

Towers Club, (Towers Club Press; 0-930668), P.O. Box 2038, Vancouver, WA 98668 Tel 206-699-4428.

Town Forum, (Town Forum, Inc.), P.O. Box 569, Cerro Gordo Ranch, Cottage Grove, OR 97424 Tel 503-942-7720.

Town of Andover MA, (Town of Andover, MA; 0-9603160), Town Hall, 20 Main St., Andover, MA 01810 Tel 617-475-5560.

Townsend Pr, (Townsend Press; 0-935990), 330 Charlotte Ave., Nashville, TN 37201 Tel 615-256-6589.

Townsend Pub Co, (Townsend Pub. Co.; 0-930212), P.O. Box 15102, Winston-Salem, NC 27103 Tel 919-766-5481; Moved, Left No Forwarding Address.

Toyon Pub, (Toyon Publishing, Inc.; 0-89048), Railroad Sq. Box S., San Luis Obispo, CA 93405.

Toys 'N Things, (Toys 'N Things; 0-934140), Training & Resource Center, 906 North Dale, St. Paul, MN 55103 Tel 612-488-7284.

TPS, (T. P. S. Pubns.; 0-911476), P.O. Box 142, College Park, MD 20740; Order from Dghtrs St Paul.

Tracy Pub, (Tracy Publishing), 1627 Boathouse Circle, Suite No. 228, Sarasota, FL 33581 Tel 813-966-3797.

Tradd St Pr, (Tradd Street Press; 0-937684), 38 Tradd St., Charleston, SC 29401 Tel 803-722-4293.

Trade Ship Pub Co, (Trade Ship Publishing Co.; 0-934592), 60 State St., 34th Fl. Tower, Boston, MA 02109.

Trademark Reg, (Trademark Register; 0-911522), 454 Washington Bldg., Washington, DC 20005.

Traders Pr, (Traders Press, Inc.; 0-934380), P.O. Box 10344, Greenville, SC 29603 Tel 803-288-3900.

Tradex Pubns, (Tradex Pubns.; 0-931528), P.O. Box 27561, Houston, TX 77027 Tel 713-961-4432.

Traditional Stud, (Traditional Studies Press; 0-919608), 423 E. 84th St., New York, NY 10028.

Trado-Medic, (Trado-Medic Books; 0-932426), Div. of Conch Magazine, Ltd., Pubs., 102 Normal Ave., Buffalo, NY 14213.

Trafalgar Hse, (Trafalgar House Publishing, Inc.; 0-913880), 145 E. 52nd St., New York, NY 10022 Tel 212-759-5331.

Traffic Inst, (Northwestern Univ. Traffic Institute; 0-912642), 555 Clark St., Evanston, IL 60201 Tel 312-492-3033.

Traffic Serv, (Traffic Service Corp.; 0-87408), 1435 "G" St. N.W., Suite 815, Washington, DC 20005 Tel 202-783-7325.

Trail-R, (Trail-R Club of America; 0-87593), 610 W. Ninth Ave., Suite 14, Escondido, CA 92025 Tel 714-743-8649; Orders to: P.O. Box 1376, Beverly Hills, CA 90213.

Trailer Life
    See TL Enterprises

Train Res Assoc, (Training Resource Associates; 0-933794), 5 S. Miller Rd., Harrisburg, PA 17109.

Trainex Pr, (Trainex Press; 0-8463), P.O. Box 116, Garden Grove, CA 92641 Tel 800-854-2485.

Trans Imprint of **Northwestern U Pr**

Trans-Anglo, (Trans-Anglo Books; 0-87046), P.O. Box 38, Corona Del Mar, CA 92625 Tel 714-645-7393.

Trans-Media Pub, (Trans-Media Publishing, Co.; 0-913338), Affiliated with Oceana Pubns., 75 Main St., Dobbs Ferry, NY 10522 Tel 914-693-5956.

Trans Tech, (Trans Tech Pubns.; 0-87849), 16 Bear Skin Neck, Rockport, MA 01966 Tel 617-546-6426.

Trans Tech Mgmt, (Trans Tech Management Press; 0-938398), P.O. Box 23032, Sacramento, CA 95823.

Trans Traffic, (Trans-Traffic Corp. Publishing Division; 0-931190), 666 Washington Rd., Pittsburgh, PA 15228 Tel 412-341-0444.

Transaction Bks, (Transaction Books; 0-87855), Bldg. 4051, Rutgers-State Univ., New Brunswick, NJ 08903 Tel 201-932-2280; Orders to: P.O. Box 978, Edison, NJ 08817.

Transatlantic, (Transatlantic Arts, Inc.; 0-693), 88 Bridge Rd., Central Islip, NY 11722 Tel 516-234-0055.

Transcult Comm, (Transcultural Communications Center; 0-916796), 909 Stonehill Lane, Los Angeles, CA 90049 Tel 213-476-1064; Moved, Left No Forwarding Address.

Transcultural Pr, (Transcultural Press of the East & West; 0-916842), 204 Makee Rd., Honolulu, HI 96815; Moved, Left No Forwarding Address.

Transculture Inc, (Transculture, Inc.; 0-935862), Village Box 104, New York, NY 10014.

Transemantics, (Transemantics, Inc.; 0-930124), 1901 Pennsylvania Ave., N.W., Washington, DC 20006 Tel 202-659-9640.

Transform Berkeley, (Transformations Press; 0-930162), 1625 Jaynes St., Berkeley, CA 94703 Tel 415-524-8391.

Transform Pubns, (Transformation Pubns.; 0-932462), 11401 Blucher Ave., Granada Hills, CA 91344 Tel 213-365-7811.

Transformer, *(Transformer Maintenance Institute; 0-939320),* P.O. Box 3575, Akron, OH 44310 Tel 216-929-2847.

Transitour, *(Transitour Inc.; 0-939108),* 111 St. Charles Ave., New Orleans, LA 70130.

Translation Pr, *(Translation Press; 0-931556),* 2901 Heatherway, Ann Arbor, MI 48104.

Translation Research, *(Translation Research Institute; 0-917564),* 5914 Pulaski Ave., Philadelphia, PA 19144 Tel 215-848-7084.

Transmedia, *(Transmedia; 0-912750),* P.O. Box 2847, La Mesa, CA 92041 Tel 714-466-2138.

Transnatl Invest, *(Transnational Investments, Ltd.; 0-933678),* 1101 Connecticut Ave., N.W., Suite 600, Washington, DC 20036 Tel 202-857-0600.

Transrep, *(Transrep/Bibliographics; 0-918370),* P.O. Box 22678, Denver, CO 80222 Tel 303-756-4861.

Transworld
 See Carpatho-Rusyn Res Ctr

Transylvania U Pr, *(Transylvania Univ., Press),* Lexington, KY 40508.

Trask Hse Bks, *(Trask House Books, Inc.; 0-932264),* 2754 S.E. 27th Ave., Portland, OR 97202 Tel 503-235-1898.

Traumwald Pr, *(Traumwald Press; 0-913676),* 3550 N. Lake Shore Dr., Suite 10, Chicago, IL 60657 Tel 312-525-5303.

Travel Advisor, *(Travel Advisor, Inc.; 0-932074),* 4710 Auth Pl., S.E., Suite 765, Washington, DC 20003 Tel 301-423-3416; Moved, Left No Forwarding Address.

Travel & Tourism, *(Travel & Tourism Press; 0-935638),* 313 Barson St., No. 5, Santa Cruz, CA 95060 Tel 408-426-1576.

Travel Digest, *(Travel Digest; 0-912640),* Div. of Paul Richmond & Co., Pubs., 73-465 Ironwood, Palm Desert, CA 92260 Tel 714-346-4792; Orders to: Rand McNally & Co., P.O. Box 7600, Chicago, IL 60680 Tel 312-267-6868.

Travel Discover, *(Travel Discoveries; 0-930570),* 10 Fenway N., Milford, CT 06460.

Travel Info, *(Travel Information Bureau; 0-914072),* 44 County Line Rd., Farmingdale, NY 11735 Tel 516-454-0880.

Travel Mark Cons, *(Travel Marketing Consultant Service; 0-914776),* 37 Haverford Rd., Hicksville, NY 11801 Tel 516-581-2225.

Travel News, *(Travel News; 0-915080),* 2500 Wilshire Blvd., Suite 720, Los Angeles, CA 90057; Moved, Left No Forwarding Address.

Travel Pr, *(Travel Press; 0-930328),* 16 E. Third Ave., Suite A, San Mateo, CA 94401 Tel 415-342-5591.

Travel Pubns, *(Travel Pubns., Inc.),* One Lincoln Rd., No. 214, Miami Beach, FL 33139 Tel 305-531-8116.

Travel World, *(Travel World Pubns.; 0-89416),* Box 2501, Dublin, CA 94566 Tel 415-829-2728.

Travelers Digest Edns, *(Traveler's Digest Editions; 0-936578),* 106 Perry St., New York, NY 10014; Dist. by: Small Press Association, P.O. Box 1264, Radio City Sta., New York, NY 10019.

Travelfare, *(Travelfare Pubs.; 0-932794),* P.O. Box 27561, Escondido, CA 92027.

Travellers Comp *Imprint of* **Olympia**

Travis, *(Travis Piano Service; 0-9600394),* P.O. Box 4359, 8012 Carroll Ave., Takoma Park, MD 20012 Tel 301-439-4111.

Treacle, *(Treacle Press/Documentext; 0-914232),* 437 Springtown Rd., New Paltz, NY 12561 Tel 914-255-8447; Orders to: P.O. Box 638, New Paltz, NY 12561.

Treasure Chest, *(Treasure Chest Pubns.; 0-918200),* 1842 W. Grant Rd., Suite 107, Tucson, AZ 85705 Tel 602-623-9558; Orders to: P.O. Box 5250, Tucson, AZ 85903.

Treasure Guide Pub, *(Treasure Guide Publishing Co.),* P.O. Box 368, Mesilla Park, NM 88047.

Treasure Guide
 See Treasure Guide Pub

Tree Bks, *(Tree Books),* Box 9005, Berkeley, CA 94709; Dist. by: Book People, 2940 Seventh St., Berkeley, CA 94710.

Tree by River, *(Tree by the River Publishing; 0-935174),* P.O. Box 413, Riverside, CA 92502 Tel 714-682-8942.

Tree Line, *(Tree Line Books; 0-931476),* P.O. Box 1062, Radio City Sta., New York, NY 10019.

Tree Roots

 See Treeroots

Treeroots, *(Treeroots Press; 0-9604450),* P. O. Box 684, Berkeley, CA 94704.

Trek-CIR, *(TREK-CIR Pubns.; 0-932464),* Box 898, Valley Forge, PA 19481 Tel 215-337-3110.

Trempealeau, *(Trempealeau Press; 0-912540),* 800 Hillcrest Dr., Santa Fe, NM 87501 Tel 505-983-1947.

Tremper, *(Tremper, W.J.; 0-9604166),* 340 Fairmount Ave., Jersey City, NJ 07306.

Trend House, *(Trend House; 0-88251),* Div. of Florida Trend, Inc., P.O. Box 611, St. Petersburg, FL 33731 Tel 813-893-8511.

Trends Pub, *(Trends Publishing Co.; 0-9602426),* 23100 Providence Dr., Suite 270, Southfield, MI 48075 Tel 313-552-1175.

Tri-B Pubns, *(Tri-B Pubns.; 0-938054),* P.O. Box 26203, Tempe, AZ 85283; Dist. by: Multi-Marketing International, 6963 Washington Ave. S., Minneapolis, MN 55435.

Tri-Med, *(Tri-Med Press),* 65 Christopher St., Montclair, NJ 07042.

Tri-Science Pubs, *(Tri-Science Pubs.; 0-935040),* 4018 Redwood Ave., Los Angeles, CA 90066 Tel 213-391-8586.

Triad Bks, *(Triad Books),* 1054 W. Via Romales, San Dimas, CA 91773.

Triad Pr TX, *(Triad Press),* P.O. Box 42006-K, Houston, TX 77042 Tel 713-789-0424.

Triad Pub FL, *(Triad Publishing Co., Inc.; 0-9600472; 0-937404),* P.O. Box 13096, University Sta., Gainesville, FL 32604 Tel 904-373-5308.

Triad Sci Pubs
 See Triad Pub FL

Triangle *Imprint of* **Dixie Pub**

Triangle Pr, *(Triangle Press; 0-937144),* Rte. 6 Box 327, Kemp, TX 75143.

Triangle Pubns, *(Triangle Pubns., Inc.; 0-9603684),* 4 Radnor Corporate Ctr., Radnor, PA 19088 Tel 215-293-8500.

Trident, *(Trident Press; 0-671),* Div. of Simon & Schuster, Inc., 630 Fifth Ave., New York, NY 10020 Tel 212-245-6400.

Trident Pubs, *(Trident Pubs.),* c/o Simon & Schuster, Inc., 1230 Ave. of the Americas, New York, NY 10020 Tel 212-245-6400.

Trigram Pr, *(Trigram Press),* Dist. by: SBD: Small Press Distribution, 1636 Ocean View Ave., Kensington, CA 94707 Tel 415-524-2107.

Trike, *(Trike Press; 0-917588),* Box 732, Pismo Beach, CA 93449 Tel 805-489-9218.

Trillium Pr, *(Trillium Press; 0-89824),* P.O. Box 921, Madison Square Sta., New York, NY 10010 Tel 212-725-8534.

Trilogy Pubs, *(Trilogy Pubs.; 0-931558),* 2901 Heatherway, Ann Arbor, MI 48104.

Trim-Weigh, *(Trim-Weigh Kitchens, Inc.),* P.O. Box 15013, Baton Rouge, LA 70895 Tel 504-293-6070.

Trinity Bks, *(Trinity Books; 0-934310),* P.O. Box 333, East Hartford, CT 06108 Tel 203-528-0408.

Trinity Pr, *(Trinity Press; 0-912046),* Trinity Episcopal Church, 708 Bethlehem Pike, Ambler, PA 19002 Tel 215-646-0416.

Trinity Pub Hse, *(Trinity Publishing House, Inc.; 0-933656),* 2171 Bayard Ave., St. Paul, MN 55116.

Trinity U Pr, *(Trinity Univ. Press; 0-911536; 0-939980),* 715 Stadium Dr., San Antonio, TX 78284 Tel 512-736-7619.

Triple B, *(Triple B Sales),* 44 Butternut Dr., Pittsford, NY 14534 Tel 716-381-7767.

Triple Spaced, *(Triple Spaced Press; 0-938976),* Box 2840, Taos, NM 87571.

Triplett Ents, *(Triplett Enterprises, Ltd.),* Munday-Brohard Rd., Macfarlan, WV 26148 Tel 304-477-3246.

Trippe Cox, *(Trippe, Cox Specialist Pubns., Inc.; 0-917856),* P.O. Box 16277, 2061 Business Center Dr., Irvine, CA 92713 Tel 714-831-3540.

TriQuarterly, *(TriQuarterly Books; 0-916384),* Northwestern Univ., 1735 Benson Ave., Evanston, IL 60201 Tel 312-492-3490.

Triton Coll, *(Triton College Press; 0-931672),* 2000 Fifth Ave., River Grove, IL 60171.

Tritone Music, *(Tritone Music; 0-9603470),* 155 Montclair Ave., Montclair, NJ 07042.

Triumph Pub, *(Triumph Publishing Co.; 0-917182),* P.O. Box 292, Altadena, CA 91001.

Trogon Pubns, *(Trogon Pubns.; 0-9600578),* 1210 Loucks Ave., Scottdale, PA 15683 Tel 412-887-9436.

Troisieme-Canadian, *(Troisieme-Canadian Pubs 0-932938),* P.O. Box 4281, Grand Central Sta., New York, NY 10017.

Trojan Pr, *(Trojan Press, Inc.; 0-913914),* 310 E. 18th St., North Kansas City, MO 64116 Tel 816-421-3858.

Troll Assocs, *(Troll Associates; 0-89375),* 320 Rte. 17, Mahwah, NJ 07430 Tel 201-529-4000.

Troll Pub, *(Troll Publishing Co.; 0-933454),* B 90213, Nashville, TN 37209 Tel 615-297-4436.

Trolley Talk, *(Trolley Talk; 0-914196),* 59 Euclid Ave., Wyoming, OH 45215.

Trophy *Imprint of* **Har-Row**

Troubador Pr, *(Troubador Press; 0-912300; 0-89844),* 385 Fremont St., San Francisco, CA 94105 Tel 415-397-3716.

Troubadour Texas, *(Troubadour Press; 0-9164C 39 S. La Salle St., Suite 825, Chicago, IL 60603.

Troy State Univ
 See TSU Pr

Tru-Faith, *(Tru-Faith Publishing Co.; 0-93749E P.O. Box 2283, Gainesville, GA 30503.

Truck Pr, *(Truck Press; 0-916562),* 1645 Portland Ave., St. Paul, MN 55104 Tel 612-690-0293; Orders to: Dustbooks, P.O. Box 100, Paradise, CA 95969.

Truedog, *(Truedog Press; 0-937212),* 216 W. Academy St., Lonoke, AR 72086.

Truly Fine, *(Truly Fine Press),* P.O. Box 891, Bemidji, MN 56601 Tel 218-751-9597.

Truth Consciousness, *(Truth Consciousness; 0-933572),* Gold Hill, Salina Star Rte., Boulder, CO 80302.

Truth Pub MN, *(Truth Publishing, Inc.),* 999 Main St., Owatonna, MN 55060.

Truth Pubs, *(Truth Pubs.; 0-9602182),* P.O. B 304, La Jolla, CA 92038 Tel 714-459-147

TSU Pr, *(Troy State University Press; 0-91662 Wallace Hall, Troy, AL 36081 Tel 205-566-3000.

Tucker Pubns, *(Tucker Pubns.),* 409 Hill St., Fayetteville, TN 37334.

Tudor, *(Tudor Publishing Co.; 0-8148),* 31 W. 46th St., New York, NY 10036; Orders to: 225 Secaucus Rd., Secaucus, NJ 07094; No Leon Amiel, P.b.

Tuffy Bks, *(Tuffy Books, Inc.; 0-89828),* 949 Broadway, New York, NY 10010 Tel 212-228-8080.

Tui Bks, *(Tui Books; 0-934928),* 32 Tiffany Place, Brooklyn, NY 11231 Tel 212-237-2344.

Tulane Romance Lang, *(Tulane Studies in Romance Languages & Literature; 0-91278 Newcomb Coll., Tulane Univ., New Orlear LA 70118 Tel 504-865-4572.

Tulane Stud Pol, *(Tulane Studies in Political Science; 0-930598),* Tulane Univ., College Arts & Sciences, Dept. of Political Science, New Orleans, LA 70118 Tel 504-865-6191

Tulane U Ctr Busn
 See Tulane Univ

Tulane Univ, *(Tulane Univ.),* Tulane University New Orleans, LA 70118; Dist. by: Center for Business History Studies, History Bldg., Tulane Univ., New Orleans, LA 70118.

Tullis Prods, *(Tullis Productions),* 4310 Norma Ave., Hollywood, CA 90029; Orders to: P.O. Box 54119, Los Angeles, CA 90054.

Tunbridge, *(Tunbridge Press; 0-911538),* P.O. Box 345, New York, NY 10021.

Tundra Bks, *(Tundra Books of Northern New York; 0-912776; 0-89541),* 51 Clinton St., Box 1030, Plattsburgh, NY 12901 Tel 518-561-1720.

Tunick Inc, *(Tunick, David, Inc.; 0-9605298),* 12 E. 81st St., New York, NY 10028.

Tuppence, *(Tuppence; 0-939662),* 2701 S. 35th, Lincoln, NE 68506 Tel 402-488-365!

Turkey Pr, *(Turkey Press; 0-918824),* 6746 Sueno Rd., Isla Vista, CA 93017 Tel 805-685-3603.

Turning Wheel Pr, *(Turning Wheel Press; 0-9602590),* 4 Washington Square Village, New York, NY 10012.

Turnip Pr, *(Turnip Press; 0-914118),* 53 Vassar St., Rochester, NY 14607; Dist. by: Light Impressions, P.O. Box 3012, Rochester, NY 14614; Moved, Left No Forwarding Addres

Turnstone, *(Turnstone Press; 0-932658),* P.O. Box 1500, Santa Cruz, CA 95061 Tel 408-425-8081.

urnstyle, *(Turnstyle),* 4975 Andever Ave., San Diego, CA 92120 Tel 805-685-1190; Moved, Left No Forwarding Address.

urpin & Assocs, *(Turpin, John C., & Associates; 0-939506),* 7661 Inland Dr., Olmsted Falls, OH 44138 Tel 216-235-9109.

urquoise Bks, *(Turquoise Books; 0-917834),* 1202 Austin Bluffs Pkwy., Colorado Springs, CO 80907 Tel 303-634-1556.

urret, *(Turret Publishing; 0-931952),* 48-05 Browvale Ave., Flushing, NY 11362 Tel 212-428-5272.

urtle Isl Foun, *(Turtle Island Foundation, Netzahaulcoyotl Historical Society; 0-913666),* 2845 Buena Vista Way, Berkeley, CA 94708 Tel 415-845-0984.

urtle Island, *(Turtle Island Press; 0-932284),* 218 N. Thirteenth St., Philadelphia, PA 19107 Tel 215-568-2542.

urtle Lodge, *(Turtle Lodge Press; 0-934182),* 12411 N. 67th St., Scottsdale, AZ 85254.

urtle Pr, *(Turtle Press; 0-916844),* 333 E. 49 St., New York, NY 10017 Tel 212-753-7957.

urtles Quill, *(Turtles Quill Scriptorium; 0-937686),* P.O. Box 643, Mendocino, CA 95460 Tel 707-937-4328.

usayan Gospel, *(Tusayan Gospel Ministries, Inc.; 0-9601124),* P.O. Box 9861, Phoenix, AZ 85068 Tel 602-995-9565.

UVOTI, *(Unspeakable Visions of the Individual, The; 0-934660),* P. O. Box 439, California, PA 15419 Tel 412-938-8956.

V Factbk, *(Television Factbook; 0-911486),* 1836 Jefferson Place, N.W., Washington, DC 20036 Tel 202-872-9200.

TVRT, *(TVRT; 0-931106),* 25 E. Fourth St., New York, NY 10003 Tel 212-260-4254.

wayne, *(Twayne Pubs.; 0-8057),* Div. of G. K. Hall, Dist. by: G. K. Hall & Co., 70 Lincoln St., Boston, MA 02111. *Imprints:* Twayne *(Imprint of* Coll & U P).

wentieth Century, *(Twentieth Century Books; 0-86649),* Div. of Automated Reproductions, 745 Seventh Ave., New York, NY 10019.

wentieth Fund, *(Twentieth Century Fund, Inc.; 0-87078),* 41 E. 70th St., New York, NY 10021.

wenty-First Cent, *(Twenty-First Century Publishing),* One Park Ave., New York, NY 10016; Moved, Left No Forwarding Address.

wenty First TX
  See TF Century Res

wenty-Third, *(Twenty-Third Pubns.; 0-89622),* P.O. Box 180, West Mystic, CT 06388 Tel 203-536-2611.

wickenham Pr, *(Twickenham Press; 0-936726),* 31 Jane St, Suite 17B, New York, NY 10014.

win Oaks Comm, *(Twin Oaks Community),* Rte. 4, Box 169, Louisa, VA 23093 Tel 703-894-4171.

wines Catskill, *(Twines Catskill Bookshop; 0-9600350),* 35 Mill Hill Rd., Woodstock, NY 12498.

Two Continents, *(Two Continents Publishing Group, Inc.; 0-8467),* 171 Madison Ave., New York, NY 10016 Tel 212-685-4371.

Two Eighteen, *(Two-Eighteen Press),* P.O. Box 218, Village Sta., New York, NY 10014 Tel 212-966-5877.

Two Horses, *(Two Horses Press),* Orders to: Raging River-Lonely Trail, 1950 W. Ruthrauff Rd., Tucson, AZ 85705.

Two Riders, *(Two Riders Press; 0-915860),* P.O. Box 31, Chestnut Hill, MA 02167 Tel 617-522-7574.

Two Rivers, *(Two Rivers Press; 0-89756),* Box 626, Aurora, OR 97002 Tel 503-266-2922.

Two Step Bks, *(Two Step Books; 0-931018),* P.O. Box 2942, Oakland, CA 94618.

Two Zees, *(Two Zee's Enterprises, Ltd.; 0-9606054),* 511 Main St., Fort Lee, NJ 07024 Tel 201-943-3700.

Twowindows Pr, *(Twowindows Press; 0-912136),* 2644 Fulton St., Berkeley, CA 94704.

TYC-J *Imprint of* T Y Crowell

Tyler Gibson, *(Tyler Gibson Pubs.; 0-9605520),* 404 Riverside Dr., New York, NY 10025.

Tyndale, *(Tyndale House Pubs.; 0-8423),* 336 Gundersen Dr., Wheaton, IL 60187 Tel 312-668-8300.

Typographeum, *(Typographeum Bookshop, The; 0-930126),* The Stone Cottage, Bennington Rd., Francestown, NH 03043.

Tze Ulmad Pr, *(Tze Ulmad Press; 0-918304),* 1101 Peppertree Lane, Simi Valley, CA 93064; Orders to: Helen Telushkin, 928 E. 13th St., Brooklyn, NY 11230 Tel 212-252-8967.

U *Imprint of* B&N

U Alaska Inst Res, *(Univ. of Alaska Institute of Social & Economic Research; 0-88353),* 707 "A" St., Anchorage, AK 99501 Tel 907-278-4621.

U Alaska Rasmuson Lib, *(Univ. of Alaska, Elmer E. Rasmuson Library; 0-935792),* Fairbanks, AK 99701 Tel 907-479-7224.

U Ariz Ctr Photog, *(Univ. of Arizona, Center for Creative Photography; 0-938262),* 843 E. University, Tucson, AZ 85719.

U Cal AISC, *(Univ. of California, American Indian Studies Center),* 3220 Campbell Hall, Los Angeles, CA 90024 Tel 213-825-7315.

U Cal Grad Sch Mgmt
  See UCLA Mgmt

U Cal Hist Sci Tech, *(Univ. of California., Berkeley, Office of History of Science & Technology; 0-918102),* 470 Stephens Hall, Univ. of California, Berkeley, CA 94720 Tel 415-642-4581.

U Cal LA Indus Rel, *(Univ. of California, Institute of Industrial Relations; 0-89215),* 405 Hilgard Ave., Los Angeles, CA 90024 Tel 213-825-9191.

U Cal Risk Management, *(Univ. of California, Office of Risk Management & Safety; 0-9602278),* 1942 University Ave., Rm. 208, Berkeley, CA 94720 Tel 415-642-1170.

U Chi Ctr Policy, *(Univ. of Chicago, Center for Policy Study),* 5801 S. Ellis Ave., Rm. 200, Chicago, IL 60637.

U Chi Dept Anthro, *(Univ. of Chicago, Dept., of Anthropology; 0-916256),* 1126 E. 59 St., Chicago, IL 60637 Tel 312-753-4314.

U Chicago Dept Geog, *(Univ. of Chicago, Department of Geography, Research Papers; 0-89065),* 5828 S. University Ave., Chicago, IL 60637 Tel 312-753-3930.

U Chicago Grad Sch Busn, *(Univ. of Chicago Graduate School of Business; 0-918584),* 1101 E. 58th St., Chicago, IL 60637 Tel 312-753-3604.

U Chicago Midwest Admin, *(Univ. of Chicago, Midwest Administration Center; 0-931080),* 5835 S. Kimbark Ave., Chicago, IL 60637 Tel 312-753-2487.

U CO at Colorado Springs, *(University of Colorado at Colorado Springs; 0-9602992),* Austin Bluffs Pkwy., Colorado Springs, CO 80907 Tel 303-593-3000.

U CO Busn Res Div, *(Univ. of Colorado, Business Research Division; 0-89478),* Campus Box 420, Univ of Colorado, Boulder, CO 80309 Tel 303-492-8227.

U Ctr Intl St, *(University Center for International Studies; 0-916002),* G-6 Mervis Hall, Univ. of Pittsburgh, Pittsburgh, PA 15260 Tel 412-624-6024.

U Delaware Pr, *(Univ. of Delaware Press; 0-87413),* c/o Associated Univ. Presses, Inc., 4 Cornwall Dr., East Brunswick, NJ 08816 Tel 201-254-0132.

U Exten-U of Cal, *(Univ. Extension, Univ. of California; 0-917936),* Davis, CA 95616 Tel 916-752-3236.

U HI at Manoa Korean
  See Ctr Korean U HI at Manoa

U Houston Intl Affairs
  See Lat Am Stud

U IA Ctr Ed Experiment, *(Univ. of Iowa, Center for Educational Experimentation, Development & Evaluation; 0-939984),* 218 Lindquist Ctr., Iowa City, IA 52242 Tel 319-353-5400.

U Maine Orono, *(Univ. of Maine at Orono Press; 0-89101),* PICS Building, Univ. of Maine at Orono, Orono, ME 04469 Tel 207-581-7349.

U Miami Marine, *(Univ. of Miami, Rosenstiel School of Marine & Atmospheric Science; 0-930050),* Orders to: Pubns. Office, 4600 Rickenbacker Causeway, Miami, FL 33149.

U Mich Busn Div Res, *(Univ. of Michigan, Division of Research, Grad. School of Business Administration; 0-87712),* Ann Arbor, MI 48109 Tel 313-764-1366.

U Mich Div Res
  See U Mich Busn Div Res

U Mich Mus Anthro, *(Univ. of Michigan, Museum of Anthropology, Pubns. Dept.; 0-932206),* 4009 Museums Bldg., 1109 Geddes, Ann Arbor, MI 48109 Tel 313-764-6867.

U MO-St Louis, *(Univ. of Missouri-Saint Louis; 0-9601616),* 8001 Natural Bridge Rd., St. Louis, MO 63121 Tel 314-553-5168.

U MS Busn Econ, *(Univ. of Mississippi, Bureau of Business & Economic Research),* University, MS 38677 Tel 601-232-7481.

U MS Law Ctr, *(University of Mississippi Law Center; 0-8377),* University, MS 38677; Dist. by: Fred B. Rothman & Co., 10368 W. Centennial Rd., Littleton, CO 80123.

U NC Inst Res Soc Sci, *(Univ. of North Carolina, Institute for Research in Social Science; 0-89143),* IRSS Publications, Manning Hall 026A, Chapel Hill, NC 27514 Tel 919-966-3204.

U of AK Inst Marine, *(Univ. of Alaska, Inst of Marine Science; 0-914500),* Fairbanks, AK 99701 Tel 907-479-7843.

U of Ala Pr, *(Univ. of Alabama Press; 0-8173),* Box 2877, University, AL 35486 Tel 205-348-5180.

U of Alaska Pr, *(Univ. of Alaska Press; 0-912006),* University of Alaska, Fairbanks, AK 99701 Tel 907-479-7224; Dist. by: International Scholarly Book Services, Inc., Forest Grove, OR 97116.

U of Ariz Pr, *(Univ. of Arizona Press; 0-8165),* P.O. Box 3398, Tucson, AZ 85722 Tel 602-626-1441.

U of Cal Intl St, *(Univ. of California, Institute of International Studies; 0-87725),* 215 Moses Hall, Berkeley, CA 94720 Tel 415-642-4065.

U of Cal Pr, *(Univ. of California Press; 0-520),* 2223 Fulton St., Berkeley, CA 94720 Tel 415-642-6682.

U of Cal Sch Law, *(Univ. of California, School of Law; 0-935076),* Davis, CA 95616; Dist. by: Fred B. Rothman & Co., 10368 W. Centennial Rd., Littleton, CO 80127 Tel 303-979-5657.

U of Chicago Pr, *(Univ. of Chicago Press; 0-226),* 5801 Ellis Ave., Chicago, IL 60637 Tel 312-753-3344; Orders to: 11030 S. Langley Ave., Chicago, IL 60628 Tel 312-568-1550. *Imprints:* Chicago Visual Lib (Chicago Visual Library).

U of Colo, *(Univ. of Colorado Press),* ; Publisher Abbreviation Without Addresses Are for Titles That Are Out of Print. These Are Obsolete Abbreviations.

U of Dallas Pr, *(Univ. of Dallas Press; 0-918306),* Irving, TX 75061 Tel 214-438-1123.

U of Denver Intl, *(Univ. of Denver, Colorado Seminary, Grad. School of International Studies; 0-87940),* Graduate School of International Studies, Univ. of Denver, Denver, CO 80208 Tel 303-753-2324.

U of Detroit Pr, *(Univ. of Detroit Press; 0-911550),* 4001 W. McNichols, Detroit, MI 48221.

U of Fla Pr, *(Univ. of Florida Press),* ; Publisher Abbreviation Without Addresses Are for Titles That Are Out of Print. These Are Obsolete Abbreviations. Publisher's Abbreviation Is Now U Presses Fla.

U of GA Inst Govt, *(Univ. of Georgia, Institute of Government; 0-89854),* Terrell Hall, Athens, GA 30602.

U of Ga Pr, *(Univ. of Georgia Press; 0-8203),* Terrell Hall, Athens, GA 30602 Tel 404-542-2830.

U of Guelph, *(Univ. of Guelph; 0-88955),* c/o John Erickson, 1545 University Dr., Lawrence, KS 66044.

U of Healing, *(Univ. of Healing Press),* 32134 Hwy. 94, Campo, CA 92006.

U of Ill Lib Info Sci, *(Univ. of Illinois, Graduate School of Library & Information Science; 0-87845),* Pubns. Office, 249 Armory Bldg., 505 E. Armory St., Champaign, IL 61820 Tel 217-333-1359.

U of Ill Lib Sci
  See U of Ill Lib Info Sci

U of Ill Pr, *(Univ. of Illinois Press; 0-252),* 54 E. Gregory Dr., P.O. Box 5081, Sta. A, Champaign, IL 61820 Tel 217-333-0957.

U of Iowa Pr, *(Univ. of Iowa Press; 0-87745),* 214 Graphic Services Bldg., Iowa City, IA 52242 Tel 319-353-3181.

U of Iowa Sch Soc Wk, *(Univ. of Iowa, School of Social Work; 0-934936),* Iowa City, IA 52242.

U of KS Ind Stud Div, *(Univ. of Kansas, Independent Study, Div. of Continuing Education; 0-936352),* Lawrence, KS 66045.

U of KS Mus Nat Hist, *(Univ. of Kansas, Museum of Natural History; 0-89338),* Lawrence, KS 66044 Tel 913-864-4540.

U of KS Pubns, *(Univ. of Kansas Pubns.),* Watson Library, Univ. of Kansas, Lawrence, KS 66045.

U of Ky OES Pubns, *(Office of Engineering Services(O E S Pubns.); 0-89779),* College of Engineering, Univ. of Kentucky, Lexington, KY 40506 Tel 606-257-2843.

U of Louisville, *(Univ. of Louisville; 0-89291),* Louisville, KY 40208.

U of Mass Pr, *(Univ. of Massachusetts Press; 0-87023),* P.O. Box 429, Amherst, MA 01004 Tel 413-545-2217.

U of Md Lib Serv, *(Univ. of Maryland, College of Library & Information Services; 0-911808),* 1101 Undergraduate Library Bldg., College Park, MD 20742 Tel 301-454-5441; Orders to: Univ. Book Center, College Park, MD 20742.

U of Miami Pr, *(Univ. of Miami Press; 0-87024),* Orders to: P.O. Box 4836, Hampden Sta., Baltimore, MD 21211 Tel 301-338-7886.

U of Mich Busn Res
See U Mich Busn Div Res

U of Mich Ctr Chinese, *(Univ. of Michigan, Center for Chinese Studies; 0-89264),* 104 Lane Hall, Ann Arbor, MI 48109 Tel 313-763-5888.

U of Mich Inst Labor, *(Univ. of Michigan, Wayne State, Institute of Labor & Industrial Relations; 0-87736),* 401 Fourth St., Ann Arbor, MI 48103 Tel 313-763-1187.

U of Mich Pr, *(Univ. of Michigan Press; 0-472),* P.O. Box 1104, Ann Arbor, MI 48106 Tel 313-764-4330. *Imprints:* AA (Ann Arbor Books).

U of Mich Soc Res, *(Univ. of Michigan, Institute for Social Research; 0-87944),* Publishing Div., P.O. Box 1248, Ann Arbor, MI 48106.

U of Minn Bell Mus, *(Univ. of Minnesota, Bell Museum of Pathology; 0-912922),* P.O. Box 302, Mayo Memorial Bldg., Minneapolis, MN 55455.

U of Minn Comp Ctr, *(Univ. of Minnesota Computer Center; 0-936992),* University of Minnesota, Duluth, MN 55812.

U of Minn Morris, *(Univ. of Minnesota, Morris; 0-9601118),* Morris, MN 56267 Tel 612-589-2211.

U of Minn Pr, *(Univ. of Minnesota Press; 0-8166),* 2037 University Ave. S.E., Minneapolis, MN 55414 Tel 612-373-3266.

U of Mo Pr, *(Univ. of Missouri Press; 0-8262),* 200 Lewis, Columbia, MO 65211 Tel 314-882-7641.

U of MT Pubns Hist, *(Univ. of Montana Pubns. in History),* Missoula, MT 59812 Tel 406-243-2231.

U of NC Dept Health, *(Univ. of NC Dept. of Health Administration, School of Public Health; 0-89055),* Dept. of Health Admin., 263 Rosenau 201-H, Chapel Hill, NC 27514 Tel 919-966-5191.

U of NC Inst Gov, *(Univ. of North Carolina, Institute of Government),* P.O. Box 990, Chapel Hill, NC 27514 Tel 919-966-5381.

U of NC Pr, *(Univ. of North Carolina Press; 0-8078),* P.O. Box 2288, Chapel Hill, NC 27514 Tel 919-966-3561.

U of Nebr Pr, *(Univ. of Nebraska Press; 0-8032),* 901 N. 17th St., Lincoln, NE 68588 Tel 402-472-3581.

U of Nev Pr, *(Univ. of Nevada Press; 0-87417),* Reno, NV 89557 Tel 702-784-6573.

U of NI Dept Art, *(Univ. of Northern Iowa, Dept. of Art; 0-932660),* Cedar Falls, IA 50613 Tel 319-273-6114.

U of NM Nat Am Std, *(Univ. of New Mexico, Native American Studies; 0-934090),* 1812 Las Lomas N.E., Albuquerque, NM 87131.

U of NM Pr, *(Univ. of New Mexico Press; 0-8263),* Albuquerque, NM 87131 Tel 505-277-2346.

U of Notre Dame Pr, *(Univ. of Notre Dame Press; 0-268),* P.O. Box L, Notre Dame, IN 46556 Tel 219-283-6346; Dist. by: Harper & Row Pubs., Keystone Industrial Park, Scranton, PA 18512.

U of Okla Pr, *(Univ. of Oklahoma Press; 0-8061),* 1005 Asp Ave., Norman, OK 73019 Tel 405-325-5111.

U of Oreg Bks, *(Univ. of Oregon Books; 0-87114),* Univ. Pubns., 139 Susan Campbell Hall, Univ. of Oregon, Eugene, OR 97403 Tel 503-686-5396; Dist. by: University Business Office, 148 Oregon Hall, VO, Eugene, OR 97403 Tel 503-686-3165.

U of Pa Contemp Art, *(Univ. of Pennsylvania, Institute of Contemporary Art; 0-88454),* 34th & Walnut Sts., Philadelphia, PA 19104 Tel 215-243-7108.

U of Pa Pr, *(Univ. of Pennsylvania Press; 0-8122),* 3933 Walnut St., Philadelphia, PA 19104 Tel 215-243-6261.

U of Pacific
See Holt-Atherton

U of Pacific, *(Univ. of Pacific),* ; Publisher Abbreviation Without Addresses Are for Titles That Are Out of Print. These Are Obsolete Abbreviations. Publisher's Abbreviation Is Now Holt-Atherton.

U of Pittsburgh Pr, *(Univ. of Pittsburgh Press; 0-8229),* 127 N. Bellefield Ave., Pittsburgh, PA 15260 Tel 412-624-4110.

U of PR Pr, *(Univ. of Puerto Rico Press; 0-8477),* P.O. Box X, U.P.R. Sta., Rio Piedras, PR 00931 Tel 809-763-0812.

U of Queensland Pr, *(Univ. of Queensland Press),* Orders to: 5 S. Union St., Lawrence, MA 01843 Tel 617-685-3306.

U of S Cal Pr, *(Univ. of Southern California Press; 0-88474),* Student Union 400, Univ. of Southern California, Los Angeles, CA 90007.

U of S Dakota Pr
See Dakota Pr

U of SC Pr, *(Univ. of South Carolina Press; 0-87249),* Columbia, SC 29208 Tel 803-777-5243.

U of Tenn Pr, *(Univ. of Tennessee Press; 0-87049),* 293 Communications Bldg., Knoxville, TN 37916 Tel 615-974-3321.

U of Tex Arlington Pr, *(Univ. of Texas at Arlington Press, The; 0-87706),* Box 19075, Arlington, TX 76019; Orders to: 501 Monroe, Arlington, TX 76019.

U of Tex Busn Res, *(Univ. of Texas, Bureau of Business Research; 0-87755),* Univ. of Texas at Austin, P.O. Box 7459, Univ. Sta., Austin, TX 78712 Tel 512-471-1616.

U of Tex Dept Astron, *(Univ. of Texas, Dept. of Astronomy; 0-9603796),* Austin, TX 78712.

U of Tex Hum Res, *(Univ. of Texas, Humanities Research Ctr.; 0-87959),* P.O. Box 7219, Austin, TX 78712 Tel 512-471-1833.

U of Tex Inst Tex Culture, *(Univ. of Texas, Institute of Texan Cultures; 0-933164; 0-86701),* P.O. Box 1226, San Antonio, TX 78294 Tel 512-226-7651.

U of Tex Pr, *(Univ. of Texas Press; 0-292),* P.O. Box 7819, University Sta., Austin, TX 78712 Tel 512-471-4032.

U of Tex Tarlton Law Lib, *(Univ. of Texas, Tarlton Law Library; 0-935630),* School of Law, 2500 Red River, Austin, TX 78705.

U of Toronto Pr, *(Univ. of Toronto Press; 0-8020),* Orders to: 33 E. Tupper St., Buffalo, NY 14203 Tel 416-978-2052.

U of Utah Pr, *(Univ. of Utah Press; 0-87480),* Salt Lake City, UT 84112 Tel 801-581-6771.

U of Wash Grad Sch Busn, *(Univ. of Washington, Graduate School of Business),* Mackenzie Hall, DJ-10, Seattle, WA 98195 Tel 206-543-4598.

U of Wash Pr, *(Univ. of Washington Press; 0-295),* Seattle, WA 98105 Tel 206-543-4050.

U of Wis Arch-Urban Pl
See U of Wis Ctr Arch-Urban

U of Wis Ctr Arch-Urban, *(Univ. of Wisconsin-Milwaukee, Center for Architecture & Urban Planning Research),* P.O. Box 413, Milwaukee, WI 53201 Tel 414-963-4014.

U of Wis Pr, *(Univ. of Wisconsin Press; 0-299),* 114 North Murray St., Madison, WI 53715 Tel 608-262-4922.

U of Wis-Stevens Point, *(Univ. of Wisconsin-Stevens Point; 0-932310),* Stevens Point, WI 54481.

U OK Ctr Econ, *(Univ. of Oklahoma, Center for Economic & Management Research; 0-931880),* College of Business Administration, 307 West Brooks St., Rm. 4, Norman, OK 73019 Tel 405-325-2931.

U Pr of Amer, *(University Press of America; 0-8191),* 4720 Boston Way, Lanham, MD 20801 Tel 301-459-3366.

U Pr of Cal, *(Univ. Press of California; 0-935048),* 1000 N. Coast Highway, No. 3 Laguna Beach, CA 92651 Tel 714-497-4861.

U Pr of Hawaii, *(Univ. Press of Hawaii; 0-824 2840 Kolowalu St., Honolulu, HI 96822 Tel 808-948-8255. Imprints:* Eastwest C (Eastwest Center Press); Korea Devel Inst (Korea Development Institute).

U Pr of Idaho, *(Univ. Press of Idaho; 0-89301),* Div. of the Idaho Research Foundation, Inc University Sta., Box 3368, Moscow, ID 83843 Tel 208-885-7925.

U Pr of Ky, *(Univ. Press of Kentucky; 0-8131)* Lexington, KY 40506 Tel 606-258-2951.

U Pr of Miss, *(Univ. Press of Mississippi; 0-87805),* 3825 Ridgewood Rd., Jackson, MS 39211 Tel 601-982-6205.

U Pr of New Eng, *(Univ. Press of New Englan 0-87451),* P. O. Box 979, Hanover, NH 03755 Tel 603-646-3348.

U Pr of Va, *(Univ. Press of Virginia; 0-8139),* P.O. Box 3608, University Sta., Charlottesville, VA 22903 Tel 804-924-3131. *Imprints:* Colonial Sc MA (Colonial Society of Massachusetts).

U Pr of Wash, *(Univ. Press of Washington, D. 0-87419),* University Press Bldg., Delbrook Campus C.A.S., Riverton, VA 22651 Tel 703-635-9562.

U Pr Pacific, *(Univ. Press of the Pacific; 0-89875),* Dist. by: International Scholarly Book Service Inc., P.O. Box 555, Forest Grove, OR 97116 Tel 212-972-1020.

U Pr Wisc River Falls, *(Univ. Press, Univ. of Wisconsin-River Falls),* 113 E. Hawthorn, River Falls, WI 54022.

U Presses Fla, *(Univ. Presses of Fla.; 0-8130),* 15 N.W. 15th St., Gainesville, FL 32603 Tel 904-392-1351.

U Pubns Amer, *(University Pubns. of America, Inc.; 0-89093),* 5630 Connecticut Ave., Washington, DC 20015.

U Rochester Policy, *(Univ. of Rochester Policy Center Pubns.; 0-932468),* 278 Dewey Hall Univ. of Rochester, Rochester, NY 14627.

U S Cal Andrus Geron
See USC Andrus Geron

U S Cal Andrus Geron, *(University of Southern California, Andrus Gerontology Center),* ; Publisher Abbreviations Without Addresses Are for Titles That Are Out of Print. These Are Obsolete Abbreviations. Publisher's Abbreviation Is Now USC Andrus Geron.

U Tex Austin Film Lib, *(Univ. of Texas at Austin Film Library; 0-913648),* Drawer W University Sta., Austin, TX 78712 Tel 512-471-3573.

U Tex Studia
See Studia Hispanica

U TX Austin Gen Libs, *(Univ. of Texas at Austin, General Libraries; 0-930214),* Univ of Texas at Austin, P.O. Box P, Austin, TX 78712 Tel 512-471-3811.

U Wis Grad Sch Busn, *(Univ. of Wisconsin-Madison, Graduate School of Business),* 1155 Observatory Dr., Madison, WI 53706.

U Wis Lib Sch, *(Univ. of Wisconsin-Madison, Library School; 0-936442),* 600 N. Park St Madison, WI 53706.

UAH Pr, *(UAH Press; 0-933958),* P.O. Box 1247, Huntsville, AL 35807.

UAHC, *(Union of American Hebrew Congregations; 0-8074),* 838 Fifth Ave., New York, NY 10021 Tel 212-249-0100.

UC Chicano, *(Univ. of California, Berkeley, Chicano Studies Library; 0-918520),* 3408 Dwinelle Hall, Berkeley, CA 94720 Tel 415-642-3859.

UC Ctr S&SE Asian, *(University of California, Berkeley, Center for SE Asian Studies),* Dist. by: Cellar Book Shop, 18090 Wyoming, Detroit, MI 46221.

UCDLA, *(Univ. of California, Div. of Library Automation; 0-913248),* 2150 Shattuck Ave Berkeley, CA 94720 Tel 415-642-9485.

Uchill, *(Uchill, Ida Libert; 0-9604468),* P.O. Bc 22608, Wellshire Sta., Denver, CO 80222 Tel 303-355-9829.

UCLA Arch, *(Univ. of California, Los Angeles, Institute of Archaeology; 0-917956),* 405 Hilgard Ave., Los Angeles, CA 90024 Tel 213-825-1720.

Univ Park, *(University Park Press; 0-8391)*, 300 N. Charles St., Baltimore, MD 21201 Tel 301-547-0700.

Univ Place, *(University Place Book Shop; 0-911556)*, 821 Broadway, New York, NY 10003 Tel 212-254-5998.

Univ Pr
See University Pr

Univ Pr OH, *(Univ. Press, Inc.; 0-9603614)*, P.O. Box 24268, Cleveland, OH 44124 Tel 216-442-0800.

Univ Pub & Dist, *(Universal Publishing & Distributing Corp.; 0-426)*, 235 E. 45th St., New York, NY 10023 Tel 212-683-3000; Orders to: Award Books, 350 Kennedy Dr., Hauppage, NY 11788; No Longer Publishing.

Univ Pub Co, *(University Publishing Co.; 0-8346)*, 1126 "Q" St., Lincoln, NE 68501 Tel 402-432-2761.

Univ SC Natl Info, *(University of Southern California National Information Center for Educational Media; 0-89320)*, NICEM/USC, University Park, Los Angeles, CA 90007 Tel 213-743-6681.

Univ Sci Bks, *(University Science Books; 0-935702)*, 20 Edgehill Rd., Mill Valley, CA 94941.

Univ Soc, *(University Society, Inc.; 0-87824)*, Colonial Office Bldg., Whitney Rd., Mahwah, NJ 07430.

Univ Stat Tracts, *(University Statistical Tracts; 0-931316)*, 75-19 171st St., Flushing, NY 11366 Tel 212-969-7553.

Univ Stores, *(Univ. Stores)*, ; Publisher Abbreviation Without Addresses Are for Titles That Are Out of Print. These Are Obsolete Abbreviations.

Univ Tech, *(Universal Technology Corp.; 0-912426)*, 1656 Mardon Dr., Dayton, OH 45432 Tel 513-426-8530.

Univ-Wide Lib
See UCDLA

Univelt Inc, *(Univelt, Inc.)*, P.O. Box 28130, San Diego, CA 92128 Tel 714-746-4005.

Universal Develop, *(Universal Developments Publishing)*, 2855 Velasco Lane, Costa Mesa, CA 92626 Tel 714-540-5452.

Universal Pr, *(Universal Press; 0-918950)*, 6609 Cherrywood Ave., Bakersfield, CA 93308 Tel 805-393-0381.

Universe, *(Universe Books, Inc.; 0-87663)*, 381 Park Ave., S., New York, NY 10016 Tel 212-685-7400. *Imprints:* Free Life (Free Life Editions); Main St (Main Street Press); Pica Pr (Pica Press).

Universe Pub Co, *(Universe Publishing Co.; 0-935484)*, 185 W. Demarest Ave., Englewood, NJ 07631 Tel 201-567-4296.

Universitet, *(Universitetsforlaget; 82-00)*, C/O Columbia Univ. Press, 562 W. 113th St., New York, NY 10025; Dist. by: Columbia Univ. Press, 136 S. Broadway, Irvington-on-Hudson, NY 10533.

University *Imprint of* Exposition

University Pr, *(University Press; 0-8418)*, Drawer N, Wolfe City, TX 75496 Tel 214-496-2226.

Unlimited Pubns, *(Unlimited Pubns)*, 4755 1/2 Elmwood Ave., Los Angeles, CA 90004; Out of Business.

UNM Gen Lib, *(Univ. of New Mexico, General Lib.)*, Dist. by: UNM Bookstore, Univ. of New Mexico, Alburquerque, NM 87131 Tel 505-277-4241.

Unmuzzled Ox, *(Unmuzzled Ox Press)*, 105 Hudson St., New York, NY 10013 Tel 212-431-8829.

Unpublished Edns
See Printed Edns

UP *Imprint of* B&N

UPB, *(Univ. Press Books; 0-8295)*, 302 Fifth Ave., New York, NY 10001 Tel 212-564-2049.

UPBS
See UPB

Update Pub Intl, *(Update Publishing International, Inc.)*, 44 Engle St., Englewood, NJ 07631 Tel 201-947-7417; c/o Jack Burgess,.

Upjohn Inst, *(Upjohn, W.E., Institute for Employment Research; 0-911558)*, 300 S. Westnedge Ave., Kalamazoo, MI 49007 Tel 616-343-5541.

Upland Pr, *(Upland Press; 0-932554)*, P.O. Box 7390, Chicago, IL 60680 Tel 312-266-2087.

Upper Room, *(Upper Room; 0-8358)*, 1908 Grand Ave., Nashville, TN 37202 Tel 615-327-2700.

Upsala Coll, *(Upsala College, College Relations Office; 0-9601668)*, Prospect St., East Orange, NJ 07019.

Upstat, *(Upstat Publishing Co.; 0-87916)*, 1815 19th St. N.W., Washington, DC 20009 Tel 202-667-0065.

Uranian Pubns, *(Uranian Pubns., Inc.; 0-89159)*, P.O. Box 114, Franksville, WI 53126 Tel 414-632-2892.

URANTIA Foun, *(URANTIA Foundation; 0-911560)*, 533 Diversey Pkwy., Chicago, IL 60614 Tel 312-525-3319.

Uranus Pub, *(Uranus Publishing Co.; 0-9601080)*, 5050 Calatrana Dr., Woodland Hills, CA 91364.

Urban & S, *(Urban & Schwarzenberg; 0-8067)*, 7 E. Redwood St., Baltimore, MD 21202 Tel 301-539-2550.

Urban Bks, *(Urban Books)*, 295 Grizzly Peak Blvd., Berkeley, CA 94708 Tel 415-524-3315.

Urban Inst, *(Urban Institute Press; 0-87766)*, 2100 "M" St., N.W., Washington, DC 20037 Tel 202-223-1950.

Urban Land, *(Urban Land Institute; 0-87420)*, 1090 Vermont Ave. N. W., Washington, DC 20005 Tel 202-289-8500.

Urbanek, *(Urbanek, Mae)*, Lusk, WY 82225 Tel 307-334-2473.

Urfer, *(Urfer, Bill; 0-9604306)*, Box 155, Libby Rte., Heber Springs, AR 72543.

URI MAS, *(Univ. of Rhode Island, Marine Advisory Service)*, Univ. of Rhode Island, Narragansett Bay Campus, Narragansett, RI 02882 Tel 401-792-6211.

Uriel Pubns, *(Uriel Pubns.; 0-9603956)*, Box 287, Taylor, ND 58656 Tel 701-974-3566.

Urion Pr Oreg, *(Urion Press; 0-913522)*, P.O. Box 2244, Eugene, OR 97402 Tel 408-867-7695.

Urizen Bks, *(Urizen Books, Inc.; 0-89396; 0-916354)*, 66 W. Broadway, New York, NY 10007 Tel 212-962-3413.

Ursa Major, *(Ursa Major Press; 0-9605888)*, 521 Fifth Ave., New York, NY 10175.

Urthkin, *(Urthkin; 0-933456)*, P.O. Box 67485, Los Angeles, CA 90067 Tel 213-556-3033.

US Capitol Hist Soc, *(U.S. Capitol Historical Society; 0-916200)*, 200 Maryland Ave. N.E., Washington, DC 20002 Tel 202-543-8919.

US Cath Hist, *(U. S. Catholic Historical Society; 0-930060)*, St. Joseph's Seminary, Dunwoodie, Yonkers, NY 10704 Tel 914-968-6200.

US Catholic, *(U. S. Catholic Conference)*, Pubns. Office, 1312 Massachusetts Ave. N.W., Washington, DC 20008 Tel 202-659-6640.

US Coast Guard, *(United States Coast Guard Auxiliary National Board Inc.; 0-930028)*, 306 Wilson Rd., Newark, DE 19711 Tel 302-731-4650.

US Comm Refugees, *(U. S. Committee for Refugees; 0-936548)*, 20 W. 40th St., 7th Floor, New York, NY 10018.

US Comm Unicef, *(U. S. Committee for UNICEF; 0-935738)*, 331 E. 38th St., New York, NY 10016 Tel 212-686-5522.

US Direct Serv, *(U.S. Directory Service, Inc.; 0-916524)*, 121 S.E. First St., P.O. Box 011565, Miami, FL 33101 Tel 305-371-8881.

US Games Syst, *(U. S. Games Systems, Inc.; 0-913866)*, 38 E. 32nd St., New York, NY 10016 Tel 212-685-4300.

US Hist Doc, *(U. S. Historical Documents Institute; 0-88222)*, 1911 Fort Myer Dr., Arlington, VA 22209 Tel 703-525-6035.

US Intl Assist, *(U. S. International Assistance Agency; 0-918106)*, Computer Bldg., Suite 406, 11141 Georgia Ave., Wheaton, MD 20902 Tel 301-933-5745.

US News & World, *(U.S. News & World Report Books; 0-89193)*, 2300 "N" St., N.W., Washington, DC 20037 Tel 202-333-7400.

US Pubs, *(U. S. Pubs. Assn., Inc.; 0-911548)*, 46 Lafayette Ave., New Rochelle, NY 10801 Tel 914-576-1121.

US Ski, *(U.S. Ski Assn.; 0-9604162)*, Box 777, Brattleboro, VT 05301.

US Tennis, *(U.S. Tennis Survey, Inc.; 0-918682)*, 1013 Cornwell Pl., Ann Arbor, MI 48104.

US Trademark, *(U. S. Trademark Assn.)*, 6 E. 45th St., New York, NY 10017 Tel 212-986-5880.

US Trotting, *(U. S. Trotting Assn.)*, 750 Michigan Ave., Columbus, OH 43215 Tel 614-224-2291.

Usborne-Hayes, *(Usborne/Hayes Books)*, 423 S. Memorial Dr., Tulsa, OK 74145.

USC Andrus Geron, *(Univ. of Southern California, Andrus Gerontology Center)*, Publications Office, University Park, CA 90007 Tel 213-743-5160.

USPC, *(United States Pharmacopeial Convention, Inc.)*, USP Drug Information Div., 12601 Twinbrook Pkwy, Rockville, MD 20852 Tel 301-881-0666.

USTA, *(U. S. Tennis Assn.)*, USTA Pubns., 71 Alexander Rd., Princeton, NJ 08540 Tel 609-452-2580.

UTA Pr, *(UTA Press; 0-932408)*, Box 929, Univ. of Texas at Arlington, Arlington, TX 76019 Tel 817-273-3391.

Utah Mus Natural Hist, *(Utah Museum of Natural History)*, University of Utah, Salt Lake City, UT 84112.

Utah St Hist Soc, *(Utah State Historical Soc; 0-913738)*, 300 Rio Grande, Salt Lake City, UT 84101 Tel 801-533-6024.

Utah St U Pr, *(Utah State Univ. Press; 0-87421)*, UMC 95, Logan, UT 84322 Tel 801-750-1362.

Utopian Universe, *(Utopian Universe Publish Co.)*, P.O. Box 26, E. Elmhurst, NY 1136 Tel 212-478-3291.

UWSP Found Pr, *(UWSP Foundation Press; 0-932310)*, Univ. of Wisconsin-Stevens Point, Stevens Point, WI 54481.

Uzzano Pr, *(Uzzano Press; 0-930600)*, c/o Robert Schuler, 511 Sunset Dr., Menomon WI 54751; Orders to: Bookslinger, 2163 Ford Pkwy., Saint Paul, MN 55116.

V B Carter, *(Carter, Virginia B.; 0-9603862)*, Geyerwood Lane, St. Louis, MO 63131.

V Danca, *(Danca, Vince; 0-9602390)*, 1191 Roxbury Close, Rockford, IL 61107.

V E Wysinger, *(Wysinger, Vossa E.)*, P.O. Box 158, Berkeley, CA 94701 Tel 415-655-1744

V G Rosenberg, *(Rosenberg, Vivian Graff)*, R. 2 Box 274, Walkers Mill Rd., Germantown NY 12526 Tel 518-537-6159.

V Gilmore Orig, *(Gilmore, Virginia, Originals)* 5119 Pine St., Bellaire, TX 77401 Tel 713-667-3710.

V H Ho, *(Ho, Van H., Assocs.; 0-9602904)*, P.O. Box 130, Harbor City, CA 90710.

V J Nelson, *(Nelson, Vera Joyce)*, 5558 S.E. Aldercrest Lane, Milwaukie, OR 97222 Tel 503-654-3060.

V L Stone, *(Stone, Virginia Lively)*, 4248 Via Marina, Suite 83, Marina Del Rey, CA 90291.

V Quade, *(Quade, Vicki; 0-9602604)*, 222 N. Utica St., Waukegan, IL 60085 Tel 312-689-6964.

V-R Information, *(V-R Information Systems, Inc.; 0-937508)*, P.O. Box 12051, Wichita, KS 67277 Tel 512-458-8131.

V S Epstein, *(Epstein, Vivian Sheldon; 0-9601002)*, 212 S. Dexter St., Denver, CO 80222 Tel 303-322-7450.

V S Morris, *(Morris, Victoria S., Books; 0-914318)*, 39 Gleneden Ave., Oakland, C 94611 Tel 415-652-2013.

V Scoper, *(Scoper, Vincent, Jr.; 0-9600514)*, P.O. Box 2366, Laurel, MS 39440.

V Young, *(Young, Victor A.; 0-9603694)*, 548 Main St., Red Lion, PA 17356 Tel 717-244-6816.

VA Bk, *(Virginia Book Co.; 0-911578)*, Box 43 Berryville, VA 22611 Tel 703-955-1428.

VA City Rest, *(Virginia City Restoration Corp)* P.O. Box 334, Los Altos, CA 94022.

VA Mus Fine Arts, *(Virginia Museum of Fine Arts; 0-917046)*, Boulevard & Grove Ave., Richmond, VA 23221 Tel 804-257-0818.

VA State Lib, *(Virginia State Library; 0-88490)* 12th & Capitol Sts., Richmond, VA 23219 Tel 804-786-2312.

VA Surveyors, *(Virginia Surveyors Foundation, 0-9604076)*, 6001 Lakeside Ave., Richmon VA 23223.

Vacation Pub, *(Vacation Publishing Co.)*, 2412 PV Dr. W., Palos Verdes Estates, CA 9027 Tel 213-377-0766; Orders to: P.O. Box 1191, Palos Verdes Estates, CA 90274; Moved, Left No Forwarding Address.

Vagabond Pr, *(Vagabond Press; 0-912824)*, 16 N. Water St., Ellensburg, WA 98926 Tel 509-925-5634.

AL Ent, *(VAL Enterprises; 0-931954),* 201 W. Vineyard Ave., Suite 2, Oxnard, CA 93030 Tel 805-485-8962.

al-Hse Pub, *(Val-House Publishing; 0-939354),* 2903 Carriage Lane, P.O. Box 490443, College Park, GA 30349.

alencia, *(Valencia, Jerry; 0-9604784),* 7525 Raytheon Rd., San Diego, CA 92111; Orders to: P.O. Box 758, La Jolla, CA 92038 Tel 714-226-1181.

alkyrie Pr, *(Valkyrie Press, Inc.; 0-912760; 0-934616),* 2135 First Ave. S., St. Petersburg, FL 33712 Tel 813-822-6069.

allentine Mitchell
    See Biblio Dist

alley Calif
    See Western Tanager

alley Calif *Imprint of* **Western Tanager**

alley Crafts, *(Valley Crafts; 0-915508),* 168 Rainbow Lane, Cary, IL 60013.

alley Presbyterian, *(Valley Presbyterian Hospital; 0-9605718),* 15107 Vanowen St., Van Nuys, CA 91405.

alley Pubns, *(Valley Pubns.; 0-911562),* 348 Seventh St., Huntington, WV 25701 Tel 304-523-7181.

alley Sun, *(Valley of the Sun Publishing Co.; 0-911842),* Box 4276, Scottsdale, AZ 85258 Tel 602-945-2644.

aluation, *(Valuation Press Inc.; 0-930458),* 661 Washington St., Marina Del Rey, CA 90291; Orders to: P.O. Box 1080, Marina Del Ray, CA 90291 Tel 213-822-3691.

Value Comm, *(Value Communications, Inc.; 0-916392),* Subs. of Oak Tree Pubns., Inc., 11175 Flintkote Ave., Suite C, San Diego, CA 92121 Tel 714-457-3200.

Van Diver, *(Van Diver, Bradford B.; 0-9601106),* The State University College at Potsdam, Dept. of Geological Sciences, Potsdam, NY 13676 Tel 315-265-3653.

Van Dyk, *(Van Dyk Pubns.),* P.O. Box 86, Glen Ellen, CA 95442 Tel 707-996-5699.

Van Koevering
    See Caballero Pr

Van Nos Reinhold, *(Van Nostrand Reinhold Co.; 0-442),* Div. of Litton Educational Publishing, Inc., 135 W. 50th St., New York, NY 10020 Tel 212-265-8700; Orders to: Lepi Order Processing, 7625 Empire Dr., Florence, KY 41042. *Imprints:* Anv (Anvil Books); IB (Insight Books); Mtum (Momentum Books); Srchl (Searchlight Books).

Van Nostrand
    See D Van Nostrand

Van Nostrand, *(Van Nostrand, D., Co., Inc.),* ; Publisher Abbreviation Without Addresses Are for Titles That Are Out of Print. These Are Obsolete Abbreviations. Publisher's Abbreviation Is Now D Van Nostrand.

Van Veen, *(Van Veen Nursery; 0-9603400),* 4201 S.E. Franklin St., Portland, OR 97206 Tel 503-777-1734; Orders to: Binford & Mort, 2536 S.E. 11th Ave., Portland, OR 97202.

Van Winkle, *(Van Winkle Pub. Co., Inc.; 0-918664),* Box 2000, 140 River Ave., Holland, MI 49423 Tel 616-396-1546.

Vance Biblios, *(Vance Bibliographies),* 112 N. Charter St., Monticello, IL 61856 Tel 217-762-3831.

Vandalia
    See J Pisapia Assocs

Vanderbilt U Pr, *(Vanderbilt Univ. Press; 0-8265),* 2505(Rear) West End Ave., Nashville, TN 37203 Tel 615-322-3585.

Vanguard, *(Vanguard Press, Inc.; 0-8149),* 424 Madison Ave., New York, NY 10017 Tel 212-753-3906.

Vanguard Bks, *(Vanguard Books; 0-917702),* P. O. Box 3566, Chicago, IL 60654 Tel 312-942-0774.

Vanguard Public Foun, *(Vanguard Public Foundation; 0-9601974),* 4111 24th St., San Francisco, CA 94114 Tel 415-285-2005; Orders to: Bookpeople, 2940 Seventh St., Berkeley, CA 94710 Tel 800-227-1516.

Vanilla, *(Vanilla Press; 0-917266),* 2400 Colfax Ave. S., Minneapolis, MN 55405 Tel 612-374-4726.

Vanity, *(Vanity Press; 0-917938),* P.O. Box 15064, Atlanta, GA 30333 Tel 404-874-5462; Moved, Left No Forwarding Address.

VanMeer Pubns, *(VanMeer Pubns., Inc.; 0-937826),* P.O. Box 1289, Clearwater, FL 33517 Tel 813-725-3503.

Vanous, *(Vanous, Arthur, Co.; 0-89918),* 616 Kinderkamack Rd., River Edge, NJ 07661 Tel 201-265-7555; Orders to: P.O. Box A, River Edge, NJ 07661.

Vantage, *(Vantage Press, Inc.; 0-533),* 516 W. 34th St., New York, NY 10001 Tel 212-736-1767.

Variety Pr, *(Variety Press),* 5214 Starkridge, Houston, TX 77035 Tel 713-721-5919.

Vassilion, *(Vassilion, Harry J.),* 5519 N. Hills Dr., Raleigh, NC 27612.

Vector Assocs, *(Vector Associates; 0-930808),* P.O. Box 6215, Bellevue, WA 98007 Tel 415-794-0462.

Vector Counsel, *(Vector Counseling Institute; 0-913596),* P.O. Box 1271, Mt. Vernon, WA 98273 Tel 206-855-0630.

Vedanta Ctr, *(Vedanta Center Publishers; 0-911564),* 130 Beechwood St., Cohasset, MA 02025 Tel 617-383-0940.

Vedanta NY, *(Vedanta Society of New York; 0-9603104),* 34 W. 71 St., New York, NY 10036 Tel 212-877-9197.

Vedanta Pr, *(Vedanta Press; 0-87481),* 1946 Vedanta Place, Hollywood, CA 90068 Tel 213-465-7114; Orders to: P.O. Box 290, Hollywood, CA 90028.

Vedanta Soc
    See Vedanta Soc St Louis

Vedanta Soc St Louis, *(Vedanta Society of St. Louis; 0-916356),* 205 S. Skinker Blvd., St. Louis, MO 63105 Tel 314-721-5118.

Vehicle Edns, *(Vehicle Editions; 0-931428),* 238 Mott St., New York, NY 10012 Tel 212-226-1769.

Veldt Protea, *(Veldt Protea Management Services, Inc.; 0-917538),* P.O. Box 152, College Park Sta., Detroit, MI 48221.

Velvet Flute, *(Velvet Flute Books; 0-9602602),* Santa Monica, CA 90403 Tel 213-451-3923.

Vendome, *(Vendome Press, The; 0-86565),* 515 Madison Ave., New York, NY 10022; Dist. by: Viking Press, 625 Madison Ave., New York, NY 10022.

Venice West, *(Venice West Pubs.),* 3060 S. Ventura Rd., Oxnard, CA 93033; Dist. by: Ross-Erikson, 629 State St., Suite 222, Santa Barbara, CA 93109 Tel 805-962-1175.

Ventnor, *(Ventnor Pubs.; 0-911566),* P.O. Box 2078, Ventnor, NJ 08406.

Ventura
    See Ventura Pr

Ventura Pr, *(Ventura Press; 0-917438),* P.O. Box 1076, Guerneville, CA 95446.

Venture Bks, *(Venture Books; 0-9600432),* P.O. Box 131, Coopersburg, PA 18036 Tel 215-965-2891.

Venture Calif, *(Venture Press; 0-915894),* 2204 Plaza De Flores Rancho La Costa, Carlsbad, CA 92008 Tel 714-438-5166.

Venture Pub Co, *(Venture Publishing Co.; 0-931478),* 155 W. 72nd St., New York, NY 10023 Tel 212-873-7580.

Venture Pubns, *(Venture Pubns. Inc.),* 11157 1/2 W. Washington Blvd., Culver City, CA 90230 Tel 213-838-5333; Moved, Left No Forwarding Address.

Venus Bks, *(Venus Books),* 3015 Poston Ave., Suite 4, Nashville, TN 37203.

Verbatim, *(Verbatim; 0-930454),* Box 668, Essex, CT 06426 Tel 203-767-8248.

Verbeke, *(Verbeke, Christian F., Rare Books, Inc.; 0-911850),* 7 Pond St., Newburyport, MA 01950 Tel 617-462-8740; Moved, Left No Forwarding Address.

Veritas, *(Veritas Foundation; 0-911568),* P.O. Box 111, West Sayville, NY 11796; Formerly Named Probe.

Veritas Pr, *(Veritas Press; 0-932208),* 3310 Rochambeau Ave., New York, NY 10467 Tel 212-655-7566.

Veritas Pubns, *(Veritas Pubns.; 0-938264),* P.O. Box 4418, Arlington, VA 22204.

Veritat Found, *(Veritat Foundation, Inc.; 0-938760),* 3910 Los Feliz Blvd., Los Angeles, CA 90027.

Veritie Pr, *(Veritie Press, Inc.; 0-915964),* P.O. Box 222, Novelty, OH 44072 Tel 216-338-3374.

Verity Pr, *(Verity Press; 0-913120),* 25045 Muerland, Southfield, MI 48075.

Verlag Aenne Burda, *(Verlag Aenne Burda),* Dist. by: Information Translation Service, P.O. Box 1271, Canoga Park, CA 91304 Tel 213-883-9246.

Verlag Chemie, *(Verlag Chemie International; 0-89573),* 1020 N.W. 6th St., Plaza Centre, Suite E, Deerfield Beach, FL 33441 Tel 305-428-5566.

Verlag Die Wirtschaft, *(Verlag Die Wirtschaft),* Dist. by: Imported Publications, 320 W. Ohio St., Chicago, IL 60610.

Vermeer Arts, *(Vermeer Arts, Ltd.; 0-934744),* 1676 W. 3rd Ave., Durango, CO 81301 Tel 303-247-3960.

Vermont Bks, *(Vermont Books, Inc.; 0-911570),* 38 Main St., Middlebury, VT 05753 Tel 802-388-2061.

Vermont Crossroads, *(Vermont Crossroads Press; 0-915248),* P.O. Box 30, Waitsfield, VT 05667 Tel 802-496-2469; Orders to: Rd 1, Box 147, Plainfield, VT 05667 Tel 802-454-7715.

Verry, *(Verry, Lawrence, Inc.; 0-8426),* Mystic, CT 06355 Tel 203-536-7373.

Versailles, *(Versailles, Elizabeth Starr; 0-9606002),* 42 Nash Hill Rd., Williamsburg, MA 01096 Tel 413-268-7576.

Verta Pr, *(Verta Press; 0-930876),* 15 Randolph Place, N.W., Washington, DC 20001 Tel 202-387-0414.

Vertex, *(Vertex Co.),* 4438 Manzanita Dr., San Jose, CA 95129 Tel 408-252-2592.

Vestal, *(Vestal Press Ltd.; 0-911572),* P.O. Box 97, 320 N. Jensen Rd., Vestal, NY 13850 Tel 607-797-4872.

Veterans Info, *(Veterans Information Service),* P.O. Box 111, East Moline, IL 61244 Tel 309-496-2876.

Veterinary Med, *(Veterinary Medicine Publishing Co.; 0-935078),* 144 N. Nettleton, Bonner Springs, KS 66012.

Veterinary Textbks, *(Veterinary Textbooks; 0-9601152),* 36 Woodcrest Ave., Ithaca, NY 14850 Tel 607-272-1860.

VI-OP, *(VI-OP Inc.),* 2836 W. Main St., KLM Bldg., Kalamazoo, MI 49007; Moved, Left No Forwarding Address.

VIA Pr, *(VIA Press; 0-9600946),* 1726 Lincoln, No. 4, Berkeley, CA 94703 Tel 415-848-4801; Moved, Left No Forwarding Address.

Vic, *(Vic Press; 0-87652),* P.O. Box 883, Cheyenne, WY 82001 Tel 307-632-3215.

Vicky Bird Bks
    See V S Morris

Victor Bks, *(Victor Books; 0-88207; 0-89693),* P.O. Box 1825, Wheaton, IL 60187 Tel 312-668-6000; Orders to: 1825 College Ave., Wheaton, IL 60187.

Victor Compt, *(Victor Comptometer Corp.),* 3900 N., Rockwell St., Chicago, IL 60618 Tel 312-539-8200.

Victoria Hse, *(Victoria House, Pubs.; 0-918480),* 2218 N.E. 8th Ave., Portland, OR 97212 Tel 503-284-4801.

Victoria Isl, *(Victoria Island Press, The; 0-938742),* 2951 N. Clark St., Chicago, IL 60657.

Victorious Ministry, *(Victorious Ministry Through Christ, Inc.; 0-9605178),* P.O. Box 1804, Winter Park, FL 32790; Dist. by: Impact Books, Kirkwood, MO 63122.

Victory Day, *(Victory Day Co.; 0-930554),* P.O. Box 48-0316, Los Angeles, CA 90048.

Vida Pubs
    See Life Pubs Intl

Video-Info, *(Video-Info Pubns.; 0-931294),* P.O. Box 1507, Santa Barbara, CA 93102 Tel 805-682-1198.

Vienna Hse, *(Vienna House, Inc.; 0-8443),* 342 Madison Ave., New York, NY 10017 Tel 212-986-7724.

Vigo Pr, *(Vigo Press; 0-911574),* P.O. Box 2317, Dallas, TX 75221 Tel 214-521-6753.

Viking Import, *(Viking Import House, Inc.; 0-911576),* 412 S.E. Sixth St., Ft. Lauderdale, FL 33301.

Viking Pr, *(Viking Press, Inc.; 0-670),* 625 Madison Ave., New York, NY 10022 Tel 212-755-4330; Orders to: Viking/Penguin, Inc., 299 Murray Hill Pkwy., East Rutherford, NJ 07073.

Villa Pr, *(Villa Press; 0-913472),* 69-10 164th St., Flushing, NY 11365 Tel 212-591-0894.

Village Voice, *(Village Voice, Book Publishing Division),* 80 University Place, New York, NY 10003 Tel 212-741-0030.

Vin *Imprint of* **Random**

Vin Image, *(Vintage Image; 0-918666),* 1335 Main St., St. Helena, CA 94574 Tel 707-963-3883.

VinC *Imprint of* **Random**

Vinco Pr, *(Vinco Press; 0-9603836),* 1553 Woodward, Detroit, MI 48226.

Vinebrook Prods, *(Vinebrook Productions, Inc.; 0-914686),* 33 Cross St., Weymouth, MA 02189 Tel 617-335-1553.

Vineyard *Imprint of Seabury*

Vintage Am, *(Vintage America Publishing Co.; 0-932330),* P.O. Box 57361, Washington, DC 20037.

Vintage Bk Co, *(Vintage Book Co.; 0-938164),* Box 16182, Elway Sta., St. Paul, MN 55116 Tel 612-690-2363.

Vintage Radio, *(Vintage Radio Co.; 0-914126),* 26451 Dunwood Rd., P.O. Box 2045, Rolling Hills Estates, CA 90274 Tel 213-375-4272.

Violet Pr, *(Violet Press; 0-912968),* P.O. Box 398, New York, NY 10009.

Virdon Assoc, *(Virdon Associates, Inc.),* P.O. Box 221, Mount Holly Springs, PA 17065.

Virgo Pr, *(Virgo Press; 0-930558),* P.O. Box 402651, Miami Beach, FL 33140 Tel 305-538-6324.

Virtue Notagraph, *(Virtue Notagraph Editions; 0-914596),* 4940 Beaumont Dr., La Mesa, CA 92041 Tel 714-469-6634.

Virtuoso, *(Virtuoso Pubns., Inc.; 0-918624),* 206 S.E. 46th Lane, Cape Coral, FL 33904 Tel 813-549-1802; Orders to: 206 S. E. 46th Lane, Cape Coral, FL 33904.

Visage Pr, *(Visage Press, Inc.; 0-916818),* 200 N. Glebe Rd., Suite 906, Arlington, VA 22203 Tel 703-528-8872.

Visibility Ent, *(Visibility Enterprises; 0-9603740),* 11 W. 81st St., New York, NY 10024.

Visible Lang, *(Visible Language Workshop; 0-938334),* N51-138 MIT, 275 Massachusetts Ave., Cambridge, MA 02139.

Vision *Imprint of FS&G*

Vision Found, *(Vision Foundation),* 770 Centre St., Newton, MA 02158.

Vision Hse, *(Vision House Pubs.; 0-88449),* 1651 E. Edinger, Suite 104, Santa Ana, CA 92705 Tel 714-558-0511.

Vismar, *(Vismar Publishing Co.; 0-9602206),* P.O. Box 29034, Parma, OH 44129.

Vista CA, *(Vista Pubns.; 0-932740),* 3010 Santa Monica Blvd., Suite 221, Santa Monica, CA 90404 Tel 213-828-3258; Do Not Confuse with Vista Pubns. in Texas.

Vista Pubns, *(Vista Pubns.; 0-930938),* 1108 McAdams Ave., Dallas, TX 75224; Do Not Confuse with Vista Pubns. in California.

Vistula Pr, *(Vistula Press, The),* 328 Anthony Circle, Charlotte, NC 28211.

Visual Evangels, *(Visual Evangels Publishing Co.; 0-915398),* 1401 Ohio St., Michigan City, IN 46360.

Visual Impact, *(Visual Impact Publishers, Communicators; 0-913426),* 500 S. Clinton St., Chicago, IL 60607 Tel 312-939-1333.

Visual Materials, *(Visual Materials, Inc.; 0-88337),* 167 Constitution Dr., Menlo Park, CA 94025 Tel 415-321-0800.

Visual Purple, *(Visual Purple; 0-917198),* Box 996, Berkeley, CA 94701; Dist. by: Bookpeople, 2940 Seventh St., Berkeley, CA 94710 Tel 415-549-3033.

Vita Pr TN, *(Vita Press),* 2143 Poplar Ave., Memphis, TN 38104.

Vital Pr, *(Vital Press; 0-915660),* Box 38341, Sacramento, CA 95838.

Vitality Assocs, *(Vitality Associates; 0-930918),* P.O. Box 154, Saratoga, CA 95070 Tel 408-867-1241.

VKM, *(VKM Publishing Co.; 0-916440),* P.O. Box 11102, Fort Worth, TX 76109 Tel 817-923-6959.

Voc Found, *(Vocational Foundation, Inc.; 0-911580),* 44 E. 23rd St., New York, NY 10010.

Voc Guidance, *(Vocational Guidance Manuals; 0-89022),* c/o National Textbook Co., 8239 Niles Ctr. Rd., Skokie, IL 60076.

Vocations Soc Change, *(Vocations for Social Change; 0-938056),* 107 South St., Boston, MA 02111 Tel 617-423-1621.

Vogel Bk, *(Vogel Book Co.; 0-9600656),* P.O. Box 103, Bellevue, WA 98009 Tel 206-455-0973.

Vogelsang Pr, *(Vogelsang Press; 0-917742),* Box 757, Yosemite, CA 95389 Tel 209-372-4611.

Voice of Liberty, *(Voice of Liberty Pubns.; 0-934762),* 3 Borger Place, Pearl River, NY 10965 Tel 914-735-8140.

Volaphon Bks
   See Woodbine-Volaphon

Volcanda Educ, *(Volcanda Educational Pubns.),* Rte. 4 Box 632, DeLand, FL 32720.

Voldstad Ent, *(Voldstad Enterprise; 0-9603906),* 688 S. Hobart Blvd., Los Angeles, CA 90005.

Volkwein Bros, *(Volkwein Brothers, Inc.; 0-913650),* 117 Sandusky St., Pittsburgh, PA 15212 Tel 412-322-5100.

Volume Dist, *(Volume Distributing Co.; 0-912982),* P.O. Box 178, Seaford, VA 23696.

Volunteer Pubns, *(Volunteer Pubns.; 0-938310),* P.O. Box 171156, Memphis, TN 38117.

Volunteer Servs Blind, *(Volunteer Services for the Blind),* Nevil Bldg., 919 Walnut St., 3rd Floor, Philadelphia, PA 19107 Tel 215-627-0600; Able to Enlarge Print up to 150 Percent Larger Than Originally Presented or Special Enlargements to Meet the Need of the Individual.

Volunteer Transcribing, *(Volunteer Transcribing Services),* 205 E. Third Ave., Suite 207, San Mateo, CA 94401 Tel 415-344-8664; Textbooks for Students at the Elementary and Secondary Levels, in All Subject Areas, Printed to Order.

Volunteers Asia, *(Volunteers in Asia, Inc.; 0-917704),* P.O. Box 4543, Stanford, CA 94305 Tel 415-497-3228.

Von Gehr, *(Von Gehr Press, The; 0-9601470),* P.O. Box 7654, Menlo Park, CA 94025 Tel 415-342-2631.

Vongrutnorv Og, *(Vongrutnorv Og Press; 0-9603504),* Randall Flat Rd. P.O. Box 411, Troy, ID 83871 Tel 208-835-4902.

Vortex Pub, *(Vortex Publishing Co., Inc.),* P.O. Box 489, Cornwall, NY 12518; Moved,Left No Forwarding Address.

Voyager Pr, *(Voyager Press),* Box 337, Grand Marais, MI 49839.

Voyager Pubns, *(Voyager Pubns., Inc.; 0-9603020),* 2604 First National Bank Tower, Atlanta, GA 30303 Tel 404-658-1228; Orders to: P.O. Box 229, Lansing, NY 14882 Tel 607-257-1648.

VoyB *Imprint of HarBraceJ*

VPC Pr, *(VPC Pr; 0-912664),* c/o Maltese Books, P.O. Box 781, Redondo Beach, CA 90277.

VSBE, *(Very Serious Business Enterprises; 0-9605304),* P.O. Box 356, Newark, NJ 07101.

VT Hist Soc, *(Vermont Historical Society; 0-934720),* 109 State St., Montpelier, VT 05602 Tel 802-828-2291.

VT Life Mag, *(Vermont Life Magazine; 0-936896),* 61 Elm St., Montpelier, VT 05602.

VTR Pub, *(VTR Publishing Co.; 0-915146),* 23 Eaton Rd., Syosset, NY 11791 Tel 516-938-0878.

Vulcan Bks, *(Vulcan Books, Inc.; 0-914350),* 12722 Lake City Way, N.E., Seattle, WA 98125 Tel 206-362-2606; Orders to: P. O. Box 25616, Seattle, WA 98125.

W A Benjamin
   See A-W

W A Benjamin
   See Benjamin-Cummings

W A Benjamin, *(Benjamin, W. A., Inc.),* ; Publisher Abbreviation Without Addresses Are for Titles That Are Out of Print. These Are Obsolete Abbreviations. Publisher's Abbreviation Is Now Benjamin-Cummings.

W A Linder, *(Linder, William A., Co., Pubs.; 0-934844),* P.O. Box 443, Lindsborg, KS 67456 Tel 913-227-2514.

W A Reilly, *(Reilly, William A.; 0-934258),* P.O. Box 63, 6 Crest Dr., Dover, MA 02030 Tel 617-785-0401.

W A Tieck, *(Tieck, W. A.; 0-9600398),* 3930 Bailey Ave., Bronx, NY 10463 Tel 212-549-5566.

W Amos, *(Amos, Winsom, Pub.; 0-9600520),* c/o Soma Press, 673 Omar Circle, Yellow Springs, OH 45387.

W Anderson, *(Anderson, Will; 0-9601056),* Possum Ridge Rd., Newtown, CT 06470.

W B Patterson, *(Patterson, W. B.),* 3080 Alaneo Place, Wailuku, Maui, HI 96793 Tel 808-244-5437.

W Bailey Pub, *(Bailey, William, Pub.; 0-9604196),* P.O. Box 985, Santa Barbara, CA 93102 Tel 805-965-3686.

W C Darrah, *(Darrah, William Culp; 0-913116),* R.D. 1, Gettysburg, PA 17325 Tel 717-334-2272.

W C Hess, *(Hess, W.C. Dr.; 0-9603038),* P.O. Box 19-M, Pasadena, CA 91102 Tel 213-281-4663.

W C Howell, *(Howell, Will C.; 0-9601140),* 1 E. Norton, Sherwood, OR 97140 Tel 503-625-7409.

W Collins, *(Collins, Wm., Sons, & Co., Ltd.),* Publisher Abbreviation Without Addresses Are for Titles That Are Out of Print. These Are Obsolete Abbreviations. Publisher's Abbreviation Is Now Collins-World.

W D Farmer, *(Farmer, W. D., Residence Designer, Inc.; 0-931518),* P.O. Box 49463 Atlanta, GA 30359 Tel 404-934-7380.

W D Leyerle, *(Leyerle, William D.; 0-9602290),* 28 Stanley St., Mt. Morris, NY 14510 Tel 716-658-2193; Orders to: Vocal Development Through Organic Imagery, or Leyerle Pubns., Box 384, Geneseo, NY 14454.

W D Linscott, *(Linscott, William D.; 0-9604920),* 40 Glen Dr., Mill Valley, CA 94941 Tel 415-383-1014.

W E Siegmond, *(Siegmond, W. E., Enterprises 0-916610),* 382 Central Park West, New York, NY 10025.

W F Brinton, *(Brinton, William F., Jr.; 0-9603554),* P.O. Box 215, Phoenixville, P 19460 Tel 215-933-3621; Orders to: Woo End Agriculture Institute, Temple, ME 04984.

W F Broderick, *(Broderick, Warren F.; 0-9603128),* 695 4th Ave., Lansingburgh, NY 12182.

W F Gekle, *(Gekle, William F.),* Wyvern Hous 4676 MacEachen Blvd., Sarasota, FL 3358

W Fourth St Block, *(West Fourth Street Block Assn.),* 285 W. 4th St., New York, NY 10014 Tel 212-929-1452.

W Fox, *(Fox, Wesley; 0-9604122),* P.O. Box 492, Brisbane, CA 94005.

W Fraser Pubs, *(Fraser, Worden, Pubs.; 0-936582),* 605 Cowper St., Palo Alto, CA 94301; Dist. by: Semiconductor Industry Assn., 20380 Town Center Lane, No. 155, Cupertino, CA 95014.

W G Arader, *(Arader, Graham, III; 0-934626),* 1000 Boxwood Court, King of Prussia, PA 19406 Tel 215-825-6570.

W H Anderson
   See Anderson Pub Co

W H Anderson, *(Anderson, W. H.),* ; Publisher Abbreviation Without Addresses Are for Titles That Are Out of Print. These Are Obsolete Abbreviations. Publishers Abbreviation Is Now Anderson Pub Co.

W H Easton, *(Easton, William H.; 0-9601160),* 3818 Bowsprit Circle, Westlake Village, CA 93161 Tel 213-889-2667.

W H Freeman, *(Freeman, W. H. & Co.; 0-716* 660 Market St., San Francisco, CA 94104 Tel 415-391-5870.

W H Lord, *(Lord, William H.),* 9210 N. Colle Ave., Indianapolis, IN 46240 Tel 317-846-3907.

W H Wise, *(Wise, Wm. H., & Co., Inc; 0-8349* 336 Mountain Rd., Union City, NJ 07087 Tel 201-864-5200.

W J Harris, *(Harris, Walter J.),* 1099 Rolling Hills Dr., Fayetteville, AK 72701 Tel 501-442-5255.

W J Johnson
   See Walter J Johnson

W Jacob Johnson, *(Johnson, William Jacob; 0-9601008),* 1604 E. Fremont Dr., Tempe, AZ 85282 Tel 602-838-1297.

W Kaufmann, *(Kaufmann, William, Inc.; 0-913232; 0-86576),* 1 First St., Los Altos, CA 94022 Tel 415-948-5810.

W L Dowler, *(Dowler, Warren L.; 0-930188),* 526 Camillo St., Sierra Madre, CA 91024 Tel 213-355-9707.

W L Sheppard, *(Sheppard, W. L.),* 923 Old Manoa Rd., Havertown, PA 19083.

W Lee, *(Lee, Walt, Publishing; 0-933378),* 17800 Van Arsdale Rd., Potter Valley, CA 94567.

W M Taylor, *(Taylor, William M.),* Essex Professional Ctr., 412 Red Hill Ave., San Anselmo, CA 94960 Tel 415-457-2214.

W Mitchell, *(Mitchell, Willa; 0-9603014),* 1855 W. 63rd St., Chicago, IL 60636.

W N Stryker, *(Stryker, William Norman),* 793 San Leandro Place, Alexandria, VA 22309.

W Perry, *(Perry, Warner; 0-9603962),* 23 Knickerbocker Dr., Newark, DE 19713.

R C Smith, *(Smith, W. R. C., Publishing Co.; 0-912476),* 1760 Peachtree Rd., N.W., Atlanta, GA 30309 Tel 404-874-4462.

R Corliss
See Sourcebook

R Gordon, *(Gordon, William R.; 0-910662),* 232 Beresford Rd., Rochester, NY 14610 Tel 716-288-8549.

R Hecht, *(Hecht, William R.; 0-9600234),* P.O. Box 67, Scottsdale, AZ 85252.

R Inman, *(Inman, W. Richard),* 996-C Ponderoso Ave., Sunnyvale, CA 94086.

R Palmer
See Heathcote

S Hein, *(Hein, William S., & Co., Inc.; 0-89941; 0-930342),* Hein Bldg. 1285 Main St., Buffalo, NY 14209 Tel 716-882-2600.

S Sullwold, *(Sullwold, William S., Publishing, Inc.; 0-88492),* 18 Pearl St., Taunton, MA 02780 Tel 617-823-0924.

States Historical, *(Western States Historical Pubs.; Inc.; 0-912506),* 4020 W. 77th Place, Westminster, CO 80030 Tel 303-429-1927.

Thomas Taylor, *(Taylor, W. Thomas, Bookseller; 0-935072),* P.O. Box 5343, Austin, TX 78763 Tel 512-451-5406.

Torda, *(Torda, W.),* 101 W. 12th St., New York, NY 10011.

Va U Ctr Exten, *(West Virginia University, Center for Extension & Continuing Education),* 308 Knapp Hall, Morgantown, WV 26506.

W Gaunt, *(Gaunt, Wm. W., & Sons, Inc.; 0-912004),* 3011 Gulf Dr., Holmes Beach, FL 33510 Tel 813-778-5211.

W Williams, *(Williams, Walter W., M.D.; 0-9600142),* 222 Farmington Rd., Longmeadow, MA 01106.

addell, *(Waddell, Ward, Jr.; 0-9600130),* 495 San Fernando St., San Diego, CA 92106.

adley Inst Molecular Med, *(Wadley Institutes of Molecular Medicine; 0-935994),* 9000 Harry Hincs, Dallas, TX 75235.

adsworth
See Wadsworth Pub

adsworth Atheneum, *(Wadsworth Atheneum),* 25 Atheneum Square, N., Hartford, CT 06103.

adsworth Pub, *(Wadsworth Publishing Co.; 0-534),* 10 Davis Dr., Belmont, CA 94002 Tel 415-595-2350. *Imprints:* Breton Pubs (Breton Pubs.).

agner Co, *(Wagner Co.; 0-911582),* Dist. by: Borden Publishing Co., 1855 W. Main St., Alhambra, CA 91801 Tel 916-967-6988.

agon & Star, *(Wagon & Star Pubs.),* 4032 W. Century Blvd., Inglewood, CA 90304.

agoner, *(Wagoner, George; 0-9600178),* 4318 Glenridge Dr., Carmichael, CA 95608.

ahr, *(Wahr, George, Publishing Co.; 0-911586),* 304 1/2 S. State St., Ann Arbor, MI 48104 Tel 313-668-6097.

aits, *(Waits-Books),* P.O. Box 407, Valparaiso, IN 46383 Tel 219-926-6584.

ake-Brook, *(Wake-Brook House; 0-87482),* 960 N.W. 53rd St., Fort Lauderdale, FL 33309 Tel 305-776-5884; June 1st Through October 15th, Contact at: P.O. Box 153, Hyannis, MA 02601, Tel: 617-775-5860.

ake Forest, *(Wake Forest Univ. Press; 0-916390),* P.O. Box 7333, Reynolda Sta., Winston Salem, NC 27109 Tel 919-761-5448.

alck, *(Walck, Henry Z., Inc.; 0-8098),* Div. of David McKay Co. Inc., c/o David McKay Co., Inc., 2 Park Ave., New York, NY 10016 Tel 212-340-9800.

aldeck Pubns, *(Waldeck Pubns.),* 258 Montecito Ave., Prismo Beach, CA 93449.

alden Bk Co, *(Walden Book Co.; 0-681),* 179 Ludlow, Stanford, CT 06904.

alden Pr, *(Walden Press; 0-911938),* 423 S. Franklin Ave., Flint, MI 48503.

aldorf Pr, *(Waldorf Press; 0-914614),* Adelphi Univ., Cambridge Ave., Garden City, NY 11530 Tel 516-746-3977.

aldron, *(Waldron, A. James, Enterprises; 0-911590),* 371 Kings Hwy., W., Haddonfield, NJ 08033 Tel 609-928-3742.

aldrop Pubns, *(Waldrop Pubns.; 0-9603364),* Box 396, Mt. Baldy, CA 91759 Tel 714-985-6128.

alker & Co, *(Walker & Co.; 0-8027),* 720 Fifth Ave., New York, NY 10019 Tel 212-265-3632.

Walker Educ, *(Walker Educational Book Corp.; 0-8027),* Affiliate of Walker & Co., 720 Fifth Ave., New York, NY 10019 Tel 212-265-3632.

Walker Pr KY, *(Walker Press, The),* P.O. Box 22144, Louisville, KY 40222.

Walkers Manual, *(Walkers Manual Inc.; 0-916234),* 5855 Naples Plaza, Suite 101, Long Beach, CA 90803 Tel 213-434-3468.

Wallaby *Imprint of* **PB**

Wallace-Homestead, *(Wallace-Homestead Book Co.; 0-87069),* 1912 Grand Ave., Des Moines, IA 50305 Tel 515-243-6181.

Wallcur Inc, *(Wallcur, Inc.; 0-918082),* 700 Island View Dr., Seal Beach, CA 90740 Tel 213-598-2385.

Wallflower, *(Wallflower Press; 0-9606260),* P.O. Box 1275, Bridgehampton, NY 11932.

Walliker Pubs, *(Walliker Pubs. Inc.; 0-89400),* Box 760, Williamsburg, VA 07920; Moved, Left No Forwarding Address.

Wallingford, *(Wallingford Press),* P.O. Box 153, Wallingford, PA 19086; Moved, Left No Forwarding Address.

Wallingford NJ, *(Wallingford Press; 0-930988),* Alpine, NJ 07620 Tel 201-568-5111.

Wallis Pubns, *(Wallis Pubns.; 0-930148),* 3485 Sylvan Lane, Melbourne, FL 32935 Tel 305-727-1270.

Walloon Pr, *(Walloon Press),* 4260 Ridgecrest Dr., El Paso, TX 79902 Tel 915-533-3166.

Walnut AZ, *(Walnut Press; 0-931318),* P.O. Box 17210, Fountain Hills, AZ 85268 Tel 602-837-9118.

Walnut Pr, *(Walnut Press),* Tully, NY 13159 Tel 607-842-6668.

Walter J Johnson, *(Johnson, Walter J., Inc.; 0-8472),* 355 Chestnut St., Norwood, NJ 07648 Tel 201-767-1303.

Walterick Pubs, *(Walterick Pubs.; 0-937396),* Box 2216, Kansas City, KS 66110 Tel 913-371-3273.

Walters, *(Walters),* 3100 N. Lake Shore Dr., Suite 2103, Chicago, IL 60657 Tel 212-989-1184.

Walters Art, *(Walters Art Gallery; 0-911886),* 600 N. Charles St., Baltimore, MD 21201 Tel 301-547-9000.

Wampeter Pr, *(Wampeter Press; 0-931694),* P.O. Box 512, Green Harbor, MA 02041.

Wanderer Bks, *(Wanderer Books; 0-671),* Div. of Simon & Schuster, 1230 Ave. of the Americas, New York, NY 10020 Tel 212-245-6400.

Wanderers, *(Wanderers, The; 0-911738),* P.O. Box 1101, Silver Spring, MD 20910.

Ward Pr, *(Ward Press; 0-932142),* P.O. Box 1712, Rochester, NY 14603 Tel 716-467-8400.

Wards Comm, *(Wards Communications, Inc.),* 28 W. Adams, Detroit, MI 48226 Tel 313-962-4433.

Warm-Soft, *(Warm-Soft Village Press),* c/o E. Langstaff Books, 919 Fremont Ave., South Pasadena, CA 91030 Tel 213-441-3233.

Warman, *(Warman, E. G., Publishing,Inc.; 0-911594),* 540 Morgantown Rd., Uniontown, PA 15401 Tel 412-437-9717.

Warne, *(Warne, Frederick, & Co., Inc.; 0-7232),* 2 Park Ave., New York, NY 10016 Tel 212-686-9630.

Warner Bks, *(Warner Books, Inc.; 0-446),* Orders to: Independent News Co., 75 Rockefeller Plaza, New York, NY 10019 Tel 212-484-8000; Name Formerly Paperback Lib.

Warner Bks *Imprint of* **Paperback Lib**

Warner Pr, *(Warner Press Pubs.; 0-87162),* P.O. Box 2499, 1200 E. Fifth St., Anderson, IN 46011 Tel 317-644-7721.

Warp, *(Warp Publishing Co.),* 325 N. Colorado Ave., Box 270, Minden, NE 68959 Tel 308-832-2234.

Warren, *(Warren, Gorham & Lamont, Inc.; 0-88262),* 210 South St., Boston, MA 02111 Tel 617-423-2020.

Warren Pub, *(Warren Publishing Co.; 0-9606004),* 3729 W. 16th St., Indianapolis, IN 46222 Tel 317-632-6601.

Warwick, *(Warwick Pubs.; 0-930156),* 2616 N. W. 33rd St., Oklahoma City, OK 73112 Tel 405-943-9095.

Wasatch Pubs, *(Wasatch Pubs., Inc.; 0-915272),* 4647 Idlewild Rd., Salt Lake City, UT 84117 Tel 801-278-3174.

Wash Busn Info, *(Washington Business Information, Inc.; 0-914176),* 235 National Press Bldg., Washington, DC 20045 Tel 202-737-2232.

Wash Ctr
See Bio Energy

Wash Gasohol, *(Washington Gasohol Commission; 0-939864),* 103 12th Ave. SW, Ephrata, WA 98823 Tel 509-754-3463.

Wash Hist Comm, *(Washington History Committee),* Box 75, Washington, NH 03280 Tel 603-495-3566.

Wash Intl Arts, *(Washington International Arts Letter; 0-912072),* 325 Pennsylvania Ave., S.E., Washington, DC 20003 Tel 202-488-0800; Orders to: P.O. Box 9005, Washington, DC 20003.

Wash Launderan, *(Wash Launderan Press; 0-9605326),* 5804 Ingersoll Ave., Des Moines, IA 50312.

Wash Media, *(Washington Media Services, Ltd.; 0-914286),* 414 Hungerford Dr., Suite 300, Rockville, MD 20850 Tel 301-340-2098; Moved, Left No Forwarding Address.

Wash Natl Monument, *(Washington National Monument Assn.),* 740 Jackson Place, N.W., Washington, DC 20506 Tel 202-842-0806.

Wash Park, *(Washington Park Press; 0-9605460),* 7 Englewood Place, Albany, NY 12203.

Wash Post Writers, *(Washington Post Writers Group),* 1150 15th St., N.W., Washington, DC 20071.

Wash Res, *(Washington Researchers; 0-934940),* 918 Sixteenth St. N.W., Washington, DC 20006 Tel 202-833-2230.

Wash Sq East, *(Washington Square East, Pubs.; 0-913086),* 109 Logan Lane, Wallingford, PA 19086.

Wash St Hist Soc, *(Washington State Historical Society; 0-917048),* 315 N. Stadium Way, Tacoma, WA 98403 Tel 206-593-2830.

Wash St U Pr, *(Washington State Univ. Press; 0-87422),* Pullman, WA 99164 Tel 509-335-3518.

Wash U Gallery, *(Washington Univ., Gallery of Art; 0-936316),* Campus Box 1189, St. Louis, MO 63130.

Wash U Med Lib, *(Washington Univ. School of Medicine Library; 0-912260),* 4580 Scott Ave., St. Louis, MO 63110 Tel 314-534-0643.

Wash Wkshops Pr, *(Washington Workshops Press; 0-913528),* 1329 "E" St., N.W., Suite 1111, Washington, DC 20004 Tel 202-638-4357.

Wash Writers Pub, *(Washington Writers Publishing House; 0-931846),* P.O. Box 50068, Washington, DC 20004.

Washburn, *(Washburn, Ives, Inc.),* Subs. of David McKay Co., Inc., 750 Third Ave., New York, NY 10017 Tel 212-661-1700.

Washburn Pr MN, *(Washburn Press; 0-939862),* 2753 Upland Court, Plymouth, MN 55447.

Washingtonian, *(Washingtonian Books; 0-915168),* 1828 L St., N.W. Suite 200, Washington, DC 20036 Tel 202-296-3600.

Washoe, *(Washoe Press; 0-89376),* P.O. Box 91922, Los Angeles, CA 90009.

Washout, *(Washout Publishing Co.; 0-918310),* P.O. Box 9252, Schenectady, NY 12309.

Water Foun, *(Water Foundation; 0-9603252),* 120 E. de la Guerra, Santa Barbara, CA 93101 Tel 805-966-7197.

Water Info, *(Water Information Center, Inc.; 0-912394),* The North Shore Atrium, 6800 Jericho Turnpike, Syosset, NY 11791 Tel 516-921-7690.

Water Mark, *(Water Mark Press; 0-931956),* 175 East Shore Rd., Huntington Bay, NY 11743 Tel 516-549-1150.

Water Pollution, *(Water Pollution Control Federation),* 2626 Pennsylvania Ave., N.W., Washington, DC 20037 Tel 202-337-2500.

Water Wind & Sail, *(Water, Wind & Sail Pubns.),* 4702 Waterview St., Tacoma, WA 98407 Tel 206-759-8901.

Waterfall Pr, *(Waterfall Press; 0-932278),* 1357 Hopkins St., Berkeley, CA 94702 Tel 415-527-7790.

Waterford, *(Waterford Books, Inc.; 0-89518),* Box 736, Bryn Mawr, PA 19010 Tel 215-525-3058; Moved, Left No Forwarding Address.

Waterfront Pr, *(Waterfront Press Co.; 0-937288),* 1911 9th W., Seattle, WA 98119.

Watermill Pubs, *(Watermill Pubs.; 0-88370),* 4 Crescent Dr., Albertson, NY 11507 Tel 516-484-2391.

Waterside, *(Waterside Press; 0-936628),* Box 1298, Stuyvesant Sta., New York, NY 10009.

Watson Brooks
See Ramey Graphics

Watson-Guptill, *(Watson-Guptill Pubns., Inc.; 0-8230),* 1 Astor Plaza, 1515 Broadway, New York, NY 10036 Tel 212-764-7300; Orders to: 2160 Patterson St., Cincinnati, OH 45214 Tel 513-381-6450. *Imprints:* Billboard Pub (Billboard Publications); Whitney Lib (Whitney Library).

Watson Pub, *(Watson Publishing Co.; 0-912644),* 6608 Hesperia Ave., Reseda, CA 91335 Tel 213-342-2108.

Watts, *(Watts, Franklin, Inc.; 0-531),* Subs. of Grolier Inc., 730 Fifth Ave., New York, NY 10019 Tel 212-757-4050. *Imprints:* Fontana Pap (Fontana Paperbacks).

Waumbek, *(Waumbek Books; 0-9603106),* P.O. Box 573, Ashland, NH 03217 Tel 603-968-7959.

Wavary Pr, *(Wavary Press),* P.O. Box 5113, Kent, WA 98031; Moved, Left No Forwarding Address.

Waveland Pr, *(Waveland Press Inc.; 0-917974),* P.O. Box 400, Prospect Heights, IL 60070 Tel 312-634-0081.

Way, *(Way, Inc.; 0-910068),* P.O. Box 328, New Knoxville, OH 45871.

Way of Seeing, *(Way of Seeing, Inc., A),* 2869 Grant Dr., Ann Arbor, MI 48104 Tel 313-973-7717.

Waymark *Imprint of* Doubleday

Wayne St U Pr, *(Wayne State Univ. Press; 0-8143),* The Leonard N. Simons Bldg., 5959 Woodward Ave., Detroit, MI 48202 Tel 313-577-4603.

Waynor, *(Waynor Publishing Co.; 0-917070),* 152 Sumner Ave., Springfield, MA 01108 Tel 413-733-2149.

Wayside, *(Wayside Press),* P.O. Box 475, Cottonwood, AZ 86326.

Wazum Pubns, *(Wazum Pubns.),* Box 600, New York, NY 10019 Tel 212-260-0762; Moved, Left No Forwarding Address.

WDW Pubns, *(WDW Pubns., Inc.),* P.O. Box 3689, Baltimore, MD 21214 Tel 301-254-0273.

We Are One, *(We Are One),* P.O. Box 1130, Plattsburgh, NY 12901.

WEAL, *(WEAL),* 733-15th St., N.W., Suite 200, Washington, DC 20005.

Weather Wkbk, *(Weather Workbook Co.; 0-931778),* 827 N.W. 31st St., Corvallis, OR 97330 Tel 503-753-7271.

Weatherford, *(Weatherford, R.M., Press; 0-9604078),* 10902 Woods Creek Rd., Monroe, WA 98272 Tel 206-794-4318.

Weatherhill, *(Weatherhill, John, Inc.; 0-8348),* Asia House, Derby Square, Salem, MA 01970 Tel 617-745-8257; Dist. by: Charles E. Tuttle, Co., Inc., 28 S. Main St., Rutland, VT 05701.

Weatherman, *(Weatherman, Hazel Marie; 0-913074),* Rte. 1, Box 357A, Ozark, MO 65721 Tel 417-485-7812; c/o Glassbooks, Inc., Rte. 1, Box 357A, Ozark, MO 65721.

Weathervane, *(Weathervane Books; 0-940152),* P.O. Box 455, Fairfield, OH 45014 Tel 513-868-9910.

Web Pub Hse, *(Web Publishing House, Inc., The),* P.O. Box 374, Olney, MD 20832.

Webb, *(Webb Books),* 19 Union Square, W., New York, NY 10003.

Webb-Newcomb, *(Webb-Newcomb Company, Inc.; 0-935054),* 308 N.E. Vance St., Wilson, NC 27893 Tel 919-291-7231.

Weber, *(Weber, S. A, D'Editions),* Dist. by: Biblio Distribution Center, 81 Adams Dr., Totowa, NJ 07512 Tel 201-256-8600; No Longer Distributed by Biblio Distribution Centre; No U.S. Distributor Given at This Time.

Webster-McGraw, *(Webster),* Div. of McGraw-Hill Book Co., 1221 Ave. of Americas, New York, NY 10020.

Wedge Entomological, *(Wedge Entolomological Research Foundation; 0-900848),* 30 E. 42 St., New York, NY 10017 Tel 212-867-4330; Moved, Left No Forwarding Address.

Wedge Pub, *(Wedge Publishing),* c/o Radix Books, Inc., P.O. Box 171, Beaver Falls, PA 15010.

Wedgwood Pr, *(Wedgwood Press; 0-911602),* 178 West St., Needham Hts., MA 02194; Out of Business.

Wee Smile, *(Wee Smile Books; 0-9605444),* P.O. Box 1329, Sparks, NV 89431.

Weeg Comp, *(Weeg Computing Center; 0-937114),* Univ. of Iowa, 120 LC, Iowa City, IA 52242.

Weems, *(Weems & Plath, Inc.),* 222 Severn Ave., Annapolis, MD 21403.

Wehawken Bk, *(Wehawken Book Co.; 0-916386),* 4221 45th St., N.W., Washington, DC 20016 Tel 202-362-3185.

Wehman, *(Wehman Brothers, Inc.; 0-911604),* Ridgedale Ave., Morris County Mall, Cedar Knolls, NJ 07927 Tel 201-539-6300.

Weigen Graphic, *(Weigen Graphic Center, Inc.; 0-917356),* 8840 7th Ave N., Golden Valley, MN 55427 Tel 612-546-0244.

Weills
See Berkley Pub

Weinberg, *(Weinberg, Michael Aron; 0-9601014),* P.O. Box 27957, Los Angeles, CA 90027 Tel 213-661-9844.

Weiner
See Public Relations

Weinstock, *(Weinstock, Beatrice C.; 0-9600568),* 1971 San Marco Blvd., Jacksonville, FL 32207 Tel 904-396-7597.

Weisberg, *(Weisberg, Harold; 0-911606),* 7627 Old Receiver Rd., Frederick, MD 21701 Tel 301-473-8186.

Weiser, *(Weiser, Samuel, Inc.; 0-87728),* P.O. Box 612, York Beach, ME 03910 Tel 207-363-4393.

Weiss Pub, *(Weiss Publishing Co., Inc.; 0-916720),* 5309 W. Grace St., Richmond, VA 23226 Tel 804-282-4641.

Weist Pub OH, *(Weist Publishing Co., The; 0-938166),* P.O. Box 164, Englewood, OH 45322.

Welch, *(Welch, Wendell R., Publishing House; 0-918494),* 136 Eighth Ave. No., Nashville, TN 37203; Dist. by: Brass Press, 136 Eighth Ave. N., Nashville, TN 37203 Tel 615-254-8969; Inactive at This Time.

Well Being, *(Well-Being Productions; 0-918912),* P.O. Box 1829, Santa Cruz, CA 95061 Tel 408-425-5411.

Wellington, *(Wellington Books),* Dist. by: Charles T. Branford Co., 19 Calvin Rd., Box 16, Watertown, MA 02172.

Wellspring Pr, *(Wellspring Press; 0-914688),* 6 Beacon St., Boston, MA 02108.

WELS Board, *(WELS Board for Parish Education; 0-938272),* 3614 W. North Ave., Milwaukee, WI 53208.

Wendover
See Bio Pubs & Dists

Wenkart, *(Wenkart, Henri; 0-911612),* 4 Shady Hill Square, Cambridge, MA 02138 Tel 617-354-0998.

Wescott Cove, *(Wescott Cove Pub. Co.; 0-918752),* Box 130, Stamford, CT 06904 Tel 203-322-0998.

Wesis Pubns, *(Wesis Pubns),* 29 Meadowbrook Lane, Cedar Grove, NJ 07009 Tel 201-256-7997.

Wesleyan U Pr, *(Wesleyan Univ. Press; 0-8195),* Dist. by: Columbia University Press, 562 W. 113th St., New York, NY 10025 Tel 212-678-6764.

West Atlantic, *(West Atlantic Pubns.; 0-935262),* 426 Columbia Ave., Mount Joy, PA 17552 Tel 717-653-2296; Orders to: P.O. Box 273, Mount Joy, PA 17552 Tel 717-653-5619.

West Coast, *(West Coast Poetry Review; 0-915596),* 1335 Dartmouth Dr., Reno, NV 89509 Tel 702-322-4467.

West Coast Plays, *(West Coast Plays; 0-934782),* P.O. Box 7206, Berkeley, CA 94707.

West End, *(West End Press; 0-931122),* Box 697, Cambridge, MA 02139 Tel 816-753-4587.

West-Lewis, *(West-Lewis Publishing Co.; 0-913984),* P.O. Box 1750, San Francisco, CA 94101; Moved, Left No Address.

West Pub, *(West Publishing Co.; 0-8299),* 50 W. Kellogg Blvd., P.O. Box 3526, St. Paul, MN 55165 Tel 612-228-2721; Orders to: 170 Old Country Rd., Mineola, NY 11501 Tel 516-248-1900.

West River, *(West River Press; 0-9602190),* 3530 W. Huron River Dr., Ann Arbor, MI 48103 Tel 313-662-5843.

West Summit, *(West Summit Press; 0-9601356),* 27 W. Summit St., Chagrin Falls, OH 44022 Tel 216-247-4323.

West SW Pub Co, *(West Southwest Publishing Co.),* P.O. Box 4064, Redding, CA 96099.

West Tex Mus, *(West Texas Museum Assn.; 0-911618),* P.O. Box 4499, Lubbock, TX 79409 Tel 806-742-2443.

West Va U Lib
See West Va U Pr

West Va U Pr, *(West Virginia Univ. Press; 0-937058),* Morgantown, WV 26506 Tel 304-293-4040.

West Village, *(West Village Publishing Co.; 0-933308),* 2904 E. Vanowen Ave., Oran[ ] CA 92667 Tel 714-633-1420.

West Wash St Coll
See West Wash Univ

West Wash St Coll, *(West Washington State College, Programme in E. Asian Studies),* Publisher Abbreviation Without Addresse[ ] Are for Titles That Are Out of Print. The[ ] Are Obsolete Abbreviations. Publisher's Abbreviation Is Now West Wash Univ.

West Wash Univ, *(Western Washington Univ[ ] Center for East Asian Studies; 0-914584),* Bellingham, WA 98225 Tel 206-676-304[ ]

Westburg, *(Westburg Associates, Pubs.; 0-9[ ]* 1745 Madison St., Fennimore, WI 53809 Tel 608-822-6237.

Westcliff Pubns, *(Westcliff Pubns.; 0-932896)* 2011 Westcliff Dr., No. 2, Newport Beach[ ] CA 92660.

Westcott, *(Westcott Pubs.; 0-911620),* P.O. [ ] 803, Springfield, MO 65801 Tel 417-466-7455.

Western Assn Map, *(Western Assn. of Map Libraries; 0-939112),* University Library, Univ. of California, Santa Cruz, CA 9506[ ]

Western Educ Serv, *(Western Educational Services; 0-916236),* 168 N. Main St., Centerville, UT 84014.

Western Epics, *(Western Epics Publishing Co[ ] 0-914740),* 254 S. Main St., Salt Lake C[ ] UT 84101 Tel 801-328-2586.

Western Guideways, *(Western Guideways; 0-931788),* Box 15532, Lakewood, CO 80215 Tel 303-237-0583.

Western Hemisphere, *(Western Hemisphere, Inc.),* 1613 Central St., Stoughton, MA 02072.

Western Her Texas, *(Western Heritage Press, 0-89351),* 1530 Bonnie Brae, Houston, T[ ] 77006 Tel 713-522-7158.

Western Heritage
See Pintores Pr

Western Ill Univ, *(Western Illinois Univ.; 0-934312),* Macomb, IL 61455.

Western Islands, *(Western Islands; 0-88279),* 395 Concord Ave., Belmont, MA 02178 Tel 617-489-0600.

Western Marine Ent, *(Western Marine Enterprises Inc.; 0-930030),* Box Q, Vent[ ] CA 93002 Tel 805-644-6043.

Western NC Pr, *(Western North Carolina Pr[ ] Inc.; 0-915948),* P.O. Box 29, Dillsboro, [ ] 28725 Tel 704-586-6253.

Western Psych, *(Western Psychological Servi[ ] 0-87424),* Div. of Manson Western Corp. 12031 Wilshire Blvd., Los Angeles, CA 90025 Tel 213-478-2061.

Western Pub, *(Western Publishing Co., Inc.; 0-307),* 850 Third Ave., New York, NY 10022 Tel 212-753-8500; Orders to: De[ ] M, 1220 Mound Ave., Racine, WI 53404. *Imprints:* Golden Pr (Golden Press).

Western Pubs
See Western Pubs OH

Western Pubs OH, *(Western Pubs.; 0-960221)* P.O. Box 848, Jamestown, OH 45335.

Western Res Pr, *(Western Reserve Press, Inc.* P.O. Box 675, Ashtabula, OH 44004 Tel 216-997-5851.

Western Search, *(Western Search Inc.; 0-9602804),* P.O. Box 334, Seahurst, WA 98062 Tel 206-453-9041.

Western Soc Res, *(Western Social Research Pubs.),* Box 306, Del Mar, CA 92014.

Western Tanager, *(Western Tanager Press; 0-934136),* 1111 Pacific Ave., Santa Cruz CA 95060 Tel 408-425-5758. *Imprints:* Paper Vision (Paper Vision Press); Valley Calif (Valley Pubs.).

Western World, *(Western World Pubs.; 0-931864),* Box 27587, San Francisco, CA 94127 Tel 415-661-2663.

Westernlore, *(Westernlore Pubns.; 0-87026),* La Porte, Unit F, Arcadia, CA 91006 Tel 213-445-7119; Orders to: P.O. Box 4304, Pasadena, CA 91106.

Westinghouse Learn, *(Westinghouse Learning Corp.; 0-88250),* 5005 W. 110th St., Oak Lawn, IL 60453 Tel 312-425-0804. *Imprints:* Ideal Pubns (Ideal Publications).

Westlake, *(Westlake, Kevin L.; 0-9604862),* RR 2, Montpelier, ID 83254.

Westland Pub Co, *(Westland Publishing Co.; 0-89121),* P.O. Box 2061, Scottsdale, AZ 85252; Moved, Left No Forwarding Address.

Westland Pubns, *(Westland Pubns.; 0-915162),* P.O. Box 117, McNeal, AZ 85617.

Westmail Pr, *(Westmail Press),* 179 Westmoreland Ave., White Plains, NY 10606 Tel 914-948-1116.

Westminster, *(Westminster Press; 0-664),* 925 Chestnut St., Philadelphia, PA 19107 Tel 215-928-2700; Orders to: Order Dept., P.O. Box 718 Wm. Penn Annex, Philadelphia, PA 19105.

Westminster Comm & Pubns, *(Westminster Communication & Pubns., Inc.; 0-934506),* 601 13th St. N.W., Suite 203, Washington, DC 20005 Tel 202-737-1716.

Westover *Imprint of Barre*

Westrail Pubns, *(Westrail Pubns.; 0-9602466),* Box 300, Glendora, CA 91740.

Westridge, *(Westridge Press, Ltd.; 0-918832),* 1090 Southridge Pl., S., Salem, OR 97302 Tel 503-363-2422.

Westrom, *(Westrom Co., The; 0-938230),* P.O. Box 85527, Los Angeles, CA 90072.

Westsea Pub, *(Westsea Publishing Co., Inc.; 0-937820),* P.O. Box 122, Old Bethpage, NY 11804.

Westview, *(Westview Press; 0-89158; 0-86531),* 5500 Central Ave., Boulder, CO 80301 Tel 303-444-3541.

Westwater, *(Westwater Books; 0-916370),* P.O. Box 365, Boulder City, NV 89005 Tel 702-293-1406.

Westwind Pr, *(Westwind Press),* Rte.1, Box 208, Farmington, WV 26571.

Westwood Pub Co, *(Westwood Publishing Co.; 0-930298),* 1922 Westwood Blvd., Los Angeles, CA 90035.

Wexford, *(Wexford Press; 0-911628),* 3 Wexford St., Needham Heights, MA 02194 Tel 617-449-1500.

Weyand-Shaw, *(Weyand/Shaw Pubns.; 0-9601922),* 5460 Whiteoak, Suite B-203, Encino, CA 91316 Tel 213-783-1820; Moved, Left No Forwarding Address.

Weyandt, *(Weyandt, Dorothy; 0-917424),* Box 6430, Solon Springs, WI 54873 Tel 715-795-2582.

Weybridge, *(Weybridge Publishing Co.; 0-939356),* 16911 Brushfield Dr., Dallas, TX 75248 Tel 214-233-1151.

Weybridge
 See McKay

Weybright, *(Weybright & Talley, Inc.),* ; Publisher Abbreviation Without Addresses Are for Titles That Are Out of Print. These Are Obsolete Abbreviations. Publisher Was Aquired by McKay.

Weybright *Imprint of McKay*

Wffn Proof, *(Wff'n Proof Pubs.; 0-911624),* 1490 S. Blvd., Ann Arbor, MI 48104 Tel 313-665-2269.

WFI Pub Co, *(WFI Pub. Co.; 0-933560),* Div. of WFI Corporation, 2049 Century Park E., Los Angeles, CA 90067 Tel 213-553-8700.

WFS, *(Women for Sobriety, Inc.),* P.O. Box 618, Quakertown, PA 18951 Tel 215-536-8026.

Whale & Eagle, *(Whale & Eagle Publishing Co.),* P.O. Box 698/239-B Seal Beach Blvd., Seal Beach, CA 90740 Tel 213-596-2210.

What to Do, *(What to Do County Pubns., Inc.),* Div. of Hardscrabble Pubns., Inc., P.O. Box 396, Pleasantville, NY 10570.

Whatever Pub, *(Whatever Publishing, Rising Sun Records; 0-931432),* 158 E. Blithedale, Suite 4, Mill Valley, CA 94941 Tel 415-383-2434.

Wheat Forders, *(Wheat Forder's Press; 0-917888),* P.O. Box 6317, Washington, DC 20015 Tel 202-362-1588.

Wheaton & Co., *(Wheaton & Co.),* Dist. by: British Book Center, 153 E. 78th St., New York, NY 10021.

Wheelchair Bowlers, *(Wheelchair Bowlers of Southern California; 0-9605306),* 6512 Cadiz Circle, Huntington Beach, CA 92647.

Wheelwright, *(Bond Wheelwright Co.; 0-87027),* Box 296, Freeport, ME 04032 Tel 207-865-4951.

Wheelwright UT, *(Wheelwright Press, Ltd.; 0-937512),* 925 So. 300 West, Salt Lake City, UT 84101 Tel 801-359-7608.

Whirlpool, *(Whirlpool Corp.; 0-938336),* Consumer Affairs Training Center, Benton Harbor, MI 49022.

Whispers, *(Whispers Press; 0-918372),* Box 1492-W, Azalea St., Browns Mills, NJ 08015 Tel 609-893-7425.

Whitaker Hse, *(Whitaker House; 0-88368),* Pittsburgh & Colfax Sts., Springdale, PA 15144 Tel 412-274-4444.

Whitcomb Pubns, *(Whitcomb Pubns.),* Rte. 3, Box 251F, Stillwater, OK 74074.

White Bear, *(White Bear Books; 0-931884),* Box 402, Occidental, CA 95465.

White Cross, *(White Cross Press; 0-918186),* Rt. No. 1, Box 203-A, Granger, TX 76530 Tel 512-859-2814.

White Ewe, *(White Ewe Press; 0-917976),* P.O. Box 996, Adelphi, MD 20783.

White Mtn Pub, *(White Mountain Pub. Co.; 0-917978),* 13801 N. Cave Creek Rd., Phoenix, AZ 85022 Tel 602-971-2720.

White Murray, *(White Murray Press; 0-931258),* P.O. Box 14186, Washinton, DC 20044.

White Oak, *(White Oak Publishing House; 0-932556),* P.O. Box 3089, Redwood City, CA 94064 Tel 415-363-2103.

White Pine, *(White Pine Press; 0-934834),* P.O. Box 236, Niagara Square Sta., Buffalo, NY 14201 Tel 716-825-8671.

White Rabbit, *(White Rabbit Press),* 631 State St., Santa Barbara, CA 93101 Tel 415-548-8204.

White Rose, *(White Rose Marketing),* 23101 Moulton Pkwy., Suite 110, Laguna Hills, CA 92653.

White S Bks, *(White Saddle Books; 0-912142),* 9144 Knauf Rd., Canfield, OH 44406; Moved, Left No Address.

White Wing Pub, *(White Wing Publishing House & Press; 0-934942),* P.O. Box 1039, Cleveland, TN 37311 Tel 615-476-8536.

Whitehall Co, *(Whitehall Co.; 0-87655),* 1200 S. Willis Ave., Wheeling, IL 60090 Tel 312-541-9290.

Whitehead Photo, *(Whitehead Photography, 0-9603486),* 13 S. Foushee St., Richmond, VA 23220 Tel 804-648-3219.

Whitehouse, *(Whitehouse Pubns.),* 1134 Valerio St., Van Nuys, CA 91406; Moved, Left No Forwarding Address.

Whitenwife Pubns, *(Whitenwife Pubns.; 0-9603656),* 149 Magellan St., Capitola, CA 95010 Tel 408-476-2730.

Whitfield, *(Whitfield; 0-930920),* 1841 Pleasant Hill Rd., Pleasant Hill, CA 94523 Tel 415-934-8054.

Whitman Pub, *(Whitman Publishing Co.),* Dist. by: Western Publishing Co., Inc., 1220 Mound Ave., Racine, WI 53404.

Whitmer Pub Co, *(Whitmer Publishing Co.; 0-935176),* 1353 S.E. 32nd Ave., Portland, OR 97214 Tel 503-233-2684; Moved, Left No Forwarding Address.

Whitmore, *(Whitmore Publishing Co.; 0-87426),* 35 Cricket Terrace, Ardmore, PA 19003.

Whitney Lib, *(Whitney Library of Design; 0-911626),* 1515 Broadway, New York, NY 10036 Tel 212-764-7300.

Whitney Lib *Imprint of Watson-Guptill*

Whitston Pub, *(Whitston Publishing Co., Inc.; 0-87875),* P.O. Box 958, Troy, NY 12181 Tel 518-283-4363.

Whitten Pub Co, *(Whitten Publishing Co.; 0-9602766),* P.O. Box 513, Flatonia, TX 78941.

Whittenberg Pub, *(Whittenberg Publishing Co.),* P.O. Box 33114, South Miami, FL 33143.

Who Houston, *(WHO Houston, Inc.),* 2801 S. Post Oak, Suite 111, Houston, TX 77056 Tel 713-961-2648.

Whole Person, *(Whole Person Associates, Inc.; 0-938586),* P.O. Box 3151, Duluth, MN 55803.

Whole World, *(Whole World Publishing, Inc.; 0-938184),* 400 Lake Cook Rd., No. 207, Deerfield, IL 60015.

Wholelife Pubns, *(Wholelife Pubns.; 0-932470),* P.O. Box 810, Yonkers, NY 10702.

Who's Who Black Am, *(Who's Who Among Black Americans, Inc.),* 3105 MacArthur Blvd., Northbrook, IL 60062 Tel 312-564-2020.

Who's Who Hist Soc, *(Who's Who Historical Society; 0-9603166),* 2022 Calle de Los Alamos, San Clemente, CA 92672 Tel 714-498-0600.

Why Not, *(Why Not Creations),* P.O. Box 1467, Monterey, CA 93940; Moved, Left No Forwarding Address.

Wibat Pubns, *(Wibat Pubns; 0-935996),* P.O. Box 60, Forestville, CA 95436.

WIBC, *(Women's International Bowling Congress),* 5301 S. 76th St., Greendale, WI 53129 Tel 414-421-9000.

WICC Bks, *(WICC Books, Inc.; 0-918878),* Div. of Worth Intl Communications Corp., P.O. Box 2226, Hollywood, FL 33022 Tel 305-929-1956.

Wichita Art Mus, *(Wichita Art Museum; 0-939324),* 619 Stackman Dr., Wichita, KS 67203 Tel 316-268-4621.

Wickstrom, *(Wickstrom Pubs., Inc.; 0-936240),* 2701 S. Bayshore Dr., Suite 501, Miami, FL 33133 Tel 305-446-3548; Dist. by: Banyan Book, Inc., P.O. Box 431160, Miami, FL 33143 Tel 305-665-6011.

Wide Skies, *(Wide Skies Press),* P.O. Box 7, Rt. 1, Polk, NE 68654 Tel 402-765-3798.

Wide World, *(Wide World Publishing; 0-933174),* P.O. Box 476, San Carlos, CA 94070 Tel 415-593-2839.

Wideview Bks, *(Wideview Books; 0-87223),* Div. of P.E.I. Books, Inc., 1633 Broadway, New York, NY 10019 Tel 212-688-3030; Dist. by: Harper & Row Pubs., Inc., Keystone Industrial Park, Scranton, PA 18512 Tel 212-593-7000.

Wigan Pier, *(Wigan Pier Press; 0-934594),* 1283 Page St., San Francisco, CA 94117 Tel 415-863-6664.

Wiggins, *(Wiggins, J. H., Co.; 0-9600346),* 1650 S. Pacific Coast Hwy., Redondo Beach, CA 90277.

Wilcom Ltd, *(Wilcom Ltd.; 0-914448),* 6900 E. Genesee St., Fayetteville, NY 13066 Tel 315-446-6211.

Wild Horses Potted Plant, *(Wild Horses Potted Plant Pubs.; 0-9601088; 0-937148),* 226 Hamilton Ave., Palo Alto, CA 94301 Tel 415-326-6513.

Wild West Pub, *(Wild West Publishing House; 0-914006),* P.O. Box 1199, San Francisco, CA 94101.

Wild World, *(Wild World, Inc.),* P.O. Box 476, San Carlos, CA 94070.

Wildcat Canyon, *(Wildcat Canyon Books; 0-936034),* 5874 McBryde Ave., Richmond, CA 94805.

Wilderness, *(Wilderness Press; 0-89997; 0-911824),* 2440 Bancroft Way, Berkeley, CA 94704 Tel 415-843-8080.

Wilderness Hse, *(Wilderness House; 0-931798),* 11129 Caves Hwy, Cave Junction, OR 97523 Tel 503-592-2106.

Wilderness Poetry
 See Wilderness Pr

Wilderness Pr, *(Wilderness Press, The; 0-933326),* P.O. Box H, Albion, CA 95410 Tel 707-937-5560.

Wildfire Pub, *(Wildfire Publishing Co.; 0-938444),* 326 Toro Canyon Rd., Carpinteria, CA 93013.

Wildflower, *(Wildflower Press; 0-938370),* P.O. Box 255, Topanga, CA 90290.

Wildlife Educ, *(Wildlife Education, Ltd.; 0-937934),* 930 W. Washington, Suite 14, San Diego, CA 92103.

Wildlife Soc, *(Wildlife Society, Inc.; 0-933564),* 7101 Wisconsin Ave., No. 611, Washington, DC 20014 Tel 301-986-8700.

Wildwood, *(Wildwood Press; 0-918944),* 2110 Wood Ave., Colorado Springs, CO 80907 Tel 303-634-8078.

Wildwood Pubns MI, *(Wildwood Pubns.; 0-914104),* P.O. Box 629, Traverse City, MI 49684 Tel 616-941-7160.

Wiley, *(Wiley, John, & Sons, Inc.; 0-471),* 605 Third Ave., New York, NY 10158 Tel 212-850-6418.

Wilk Pub, *(Wilk Publishing Co.),* P.O. Box 320, Park Ridge, IL 60068 Tel 312-725-4878.

Wilkerson Assocs, *(Wilkerson Associates),* P.O. Box 711, Gig Harbor, WA 98335 Tel 206-858-9076.

Wilkinson, *(Wilkinson, Paul H.; 0-911710),* 5900 Kingswood Rd., N.W., Washington, DC 20014 Tel 301-530-0888.

Willard-Bower, *(Willard/Bower),* 100 Marilyn Ave., Roseville, CA 95678.

William & Rich, *(William & Richards, Pubs.; 0-9600202),* P.O. Box 2546, San Francisco, CA 94126.

William Carey Lib, *(William Carey Library Pubs.; 0-87808),* 1705 N. Sierra Bonita Ave., P.O. Box 128-C, Pasadena, CA 91104 Tel 213-798-0819. *Imprints:* Ecclesia (Ecclesia Pubns.); Mandate (Mandate Press); World Christ (World Christian Bookshelf).

William-F, *(William-Frederick Press; 0-87164),* 308 E. 79th St., New York, NY 10021 Tel 212-628-1995.

Williams & Wilkins, *(Williams & Wilkins Co.; 0-683),* 428 E. Preston St., Baltimore, MD 21202 Tel 301-528-4221. *Imprints:* Hans Huber (Hans Huber).

Williams Ent, *(Williams, Bill, Enterprises; 0-934488),* 188 Merchant St., Honolulu, HI 96809; Moved, Left No Forwarding Address.

Williams Pr, *(Williams Press),* 417 Commerce St., Nashville, TN 37219.

Williamsburg, *(Colonial Williamsburg Foundation; 0-910412; 0-87935),* Publications Dept., P.O. Box C, Williamsburg, VA 23185 Tel 804-229-1000; Orders to: Merchandising Office, P.O. Box Ch, Williamsburg, VA 23185.

Williamson Sch, *(Williamson School of Horsemanship; 0-9600144),* P.O. Box 506, Hamilton, MT 59840 Tel 406-363-2874.

Willing Pub, *(Willing Publishing Co.),* 251 S. San Gabriel Blvd., San Gabriel, CA 91778; Dist. by: Devorss & Co., 1641 Lincoln Blvd., Santa Monica, CA 90404.

Willoughby, *(Willoughby Books),* 14 Hamburg Turnpike, Hamburg, NJ 07419.

Willow Creek, *(Willow Creek Press; 0-932558),* Div. of Wisconsin Sportsman, P.O. Box 2266, Oshkosh, WI 54903 Tel 414-233-4143.

Willow Hse, *(Willow House Pubs., Inc.; 0-912450),* Box 155, Aptos, CA 95003 Tel 408-688-4128.

Willow River, *(Willow River Press, Ltd.; 0-930602),* 3257 W. Bryn Mawr Ave., Chicago, IL 60659 Tel 312-583-5242.

Willowood Pr, *(Willowood Press; 0-938376),* P.O. Box 22321, Lexington, KY 40522.

Willows Pr, *(Willows Press; 0-9602924),* P.O. Box 2779, Long Beach, CA 90801 Tel 213-433-6276.

Willyshe Pub, *(Willyshe Publishing Co., Inc.; 0-936112),* 112 Mountain Rd., Linthicum Heights, MD 21090.

Wilmar Pubs, *(Wilmar Pubs.),* P.O. Box 5295, Sherman Oaks, CA 91413 Tel 213-762-1234.

Wilmington Pr, *(Wilmington Press),* 13315 Wilmington Dr., Dallas, TX 75234.

WILPF, *(Women's International League for Peace & Freedom),* 1213 Race St., Philadelphia, PA 19107 Tel 215-563-7110.

Wilshire, *(Wilshire Book Co.; 0-87980),* 12015 Sherman Rd., North Hollywood, CA 91605 Tel 213-875-1711.

Wilson, *(Wilson, H. W.; 0-8242),* 950 University Ave., Bronx, NY 10452 Tel 212-588-8400.

Wilson Bks
  See Anima Pubns

Wilson Bros, *(Wilson Brothers Pubns.; 0-934944),* P.O. Box 712, Yakima, WA 98907 Tel 509-457-8275.

Wilton, *(Wilton Enterprises, Inc., Book Div.; 0-912696),* 1603 S. Michigan Ave., Chicago, IL 60616 Tel 312-663-5096.

Wiluk Pr, *(Wiluk Press),* P.O. Box 2548, Silver Spring, MD 20910 Tel 301-585-1274; Moved, Left No Forwarding Address.

WIM Oakland, *(WIM; 0-938842),* 6000 Contra Costa Rd., Oakland, CA 94618.

WIM Pubns, *(WIM Pubns.; 0-934172),* P.O. Box 5037, Inglewood, CA 90310 Tel 213-774-5230.

Wimmer Bks, *(Wimmer Brothers Books; 0-918544),* P.O. Box 18408, Memphis, TN 38118 Tel 901-362-8900.

Win Bks, *(Win Books, Inc.; 0-916140),* c/o Fred Rosen, P.O. Box 547, Rifton, NY 12471 Tel 914-339-4585; Moved, Left No Forwarding Address.

Winchester Pr, *(Winchester Press; 0-87691),* P.O. Box 1260, Tulsa, OK 74101 Tel 918-835-3161.

Wind Pub, *(Wind Publishing; 0-933312),* P.O. Box 253, Corona del Mar, CA 92625.

Windfall *Imprint of* **Doubleday**

Windflower, *(Windflower Publishing Co.),* 2900 W. Owasso Blvd., St. Paul, MN 55112 Tel 612-484-1252; Orders to: P.O. Box 8046, St. Paul, MN 55113.

Windflower Pr, *(Windflower Press; 0-931534),* P.O. Box 82213, Lincoln, NE 68501 Tel 402-475-0904.

Windham Bay, *(Windham Bay Press),* Box 1332, Juneau, AK 99802.

Windhover *Imprint of* **Berkley Pub**

Windless Orchard, *(Windless Orchard Series; 0-87883),* Indiana Univ., English Dept., Fort Wayne, IN 46805 Tel 219-482-5386.

Windmill *Imprint of* **Dutton**

Windmill Bks, *(Windmill Books, Inc.; 0-87807),* an Intext Publisher, 1230 Ave of the Americas, New York, NY 10020 Tel 212-245-6400.

Windmill Pr, *(Windmill Press),* 1369 Linwood, Holland, MI 49423; Moved, Left No Forwarding Address.

Windmill Pub Co., *(Windmill Publishing Co.; 0-933846),* 2147 Windmill View Rd., El Cajon, CA 92020 Tel 714-464-4110.

Winds World Pr, *(Winds of the World Press; 0-938338),* 35 Whittemore Rd., Framingham, MA 01701.

Windsinger, *(Windsinger Enterprises, Inc.),* P.O. Box 128, Wellsville, UT 84339 Tel 801-245-4030.

Windsong, *(Windsong Books International; 0-934846),* P.O. Box 867, Huntington Beach, CA 92648 Tel 714-963-0324; Dist. by: Associated Booksellers, 147 McKinley Ave., P.O. Box 6361, Bridgeport, CT 06606 Tel 203-366-5494.

Windsor, *(Windsor Books Division),* P.O. Box 280, Brightwaters, NY 11718.

Windstone *Imprint of* **Bantam**

Windward Pub, *(Windward Publishing Inc.; 0-89317),* 105 N.E. 25th St., P.O. Box 371005, Miami, FL 33137 Tel 305-576-6232.

Windy Row, *(Windy Row Press; 0-911838),* Peterborough, NH 03458 Tel 603-924-3340.

Windyridge, *(Windyridge Press; 0-913366),* P. O. Box 591, Rogue River, OR 97537; Orders to: Northwest Textbook Depository, P.O. Box 3708, Portland, OR 97208 Tel 503-639-3193.

Wine Adv, *(Wine Advisory Board; 0-911914),* 717 Market St., San Francisco, CA 94103 Tel 415-392-0252.

Wine Appreciation, *(Wine Appreciation Guide, The; 0-932664),* 1377 Ninth Ave., San Francisco, CA 94122; 60 Federal St., San Francisco, CA 94107.

Wine Bks, *(Wine Books; 0-9604488),* P.O. Box 1015, San Marcos, CA 92069.

Wine Consul Calif, *(Wine Consultants of California; 0-916040),* P.O. Box 27187, San Francisco, CA 94127 Tel 415-681-8989.

Wine Pr, *(Wine Press; 0-911634),* P.O. Box 82, Concord, MA 01742; Moved, Left No Forwarding Address.

Wine Pubns, *(Wine Pubns.; 0-913840),* 96 Parnassus Rd., Berkeley, CA 94708 Tel 415-843-4209.

Winepress MN, *(Winepress; 0-9604416),* 408 Wendell St., Paynesville, MN 56362 Tel 612-243-3563.

Winfoto, *(Winfoto; 0-9605522),* 1790 Kearny St., Denver, CO 80220.

Wingbow Pr, *(Wingbow Press; 0-914728),* Dist. by: Bookpeople, 2940 Seventh St., Berkeley, CA 94710 Tel 415-549-3033.

Winged Lion, *(Winged Lion Publishing Ltd.; 0-915922),* 414 S. Western Ave., P.O. Box 75936, Los Angeles, CA 90075.

Wings Pr, *(Wings Press; 0-930324),* P.O. Box 25296, Houston, TX 77005 Tel 713-668-7953.

Winona Catawba, *(Winona Catawba Press Publishing; 0-9603974),* P.O. Box 40742, San Francisco, CA 94140.

Winship Pr, *(Winship Press; 0-915430),* P.O. Box 859, Mercer Univ., Sta., Macon, GA 31207 Tel 912-743-0029.

Winston-Derek, *(Winston-Derek Pubs.,Inc.; 0-938232),* P.O. Box 90883, Pennywell Dr., Nashville, TN 37209.

Winston Pr, *(Winston Press, Inc.; 0-86683),* Subs. of CBS Educational Publishing, 430 Oak Grove, Suite 203, Minneapolis, MN 55403 Tel 612-871-7000.

Winter Brook, *(Winter Brook Pub. Co.; 0-9602204),* 153 S. Vermont Ave., Los Angeles, CA 90004 Tel 213-480-3871.

Winter Pub Co, *(Winter Publishing Co.),* P.O. Box 36536, Tucson, AZ 85740; 5613 N. Calle De la Reina, Tucson, AZ 85718 Tel 602-299-1528.

Wintergreen, *(Wintergreen & Advance Pubs.; 0-933460),* 845 Via De La Paz, Suite 12, Pacific Palisades, CA 90272 Tel 213-454-5260.

Winterthur, *(Winterthur Museum; 0-912724),* Winterthur, DE 19735 Tel 302-656-8591.

Winthrop, *(Winthrop Publishing Co.; 0-87626),* Subs. of Prentice-Hall, Inc., Dist. by: Prentice-Hall, Englewood Cliffs, NJ 07632 Tel 201-592-2154.

WIPO *Imprint of* **Unipub**

Wire Pr, *(Wire Press/The Coffeehouse Magazine; 0-918034),* 3448 19th St., San Francisco, CA 94110 Tel 415-431-2896.

Wis Ed Fund, *(Wisconsin Education Fund; 0-9600358),* P.O. Box 321, Port Washington, WI 53074 Tel 414-284-9066.

Wis Ev Luth, *(Wisconsin Ev. Lutheran Synod Board for Parish Education; 0-938272),* 3614 W. North Ave., Milwaukee, WI 53208 Tel 414-445-4030.

Wisc T & T
  See Tamarack Pr

Wisconsin Audubon, *(Wisconsin Audubon Council, Inc.),* Dist. by: Potter School & Library Services, Inc., 6927 W. North Ave., Wauwatosa, WI 53213.

Wisconsin Bks, *(Wisconsin Books),* c/o R. B. Allison, 2025 Dunn Place, Madison, WI 53713 Tel 608-257-4126; Formerly Named School of Living Press. *Imprints:* R B Allison Co (Allison, R. B., Co.); Sol Press (Sol Press).

Wisconsin Hse, *(Wisconsin House Book Pubs.; 0-88361),* P.O. Box 2118, Madison, WI 53701 Tel 608-251-3222.

Wisconsin Sptmn, *(Wisconsin Sportsman; 0-932558),* P.O. Box 2266, Oshkosh, WI 54903 Tel 414-233-1327.

Wisdom, *(Wisdom Publishers; 0-911636),* P.O. Box 81, San Diego, CA 92112.

Wisdom Garden, *(Wisdom Garden Books; 0-914794),* Box 29448, Los Angeles, CA 90029 Tel 213-380-1968.

Wisdom House, *(Wisdom House Press; 0-932560),* 4030 Raleigh Ave. S., Minneapolis, MN 55416 Tel 612-920-0510.

Wise Pub, *(Wise Publishing Co.; 0-915766),* 5625 Wilhelmina Ave., Woodland Hills, CA 91364.

Wish Bklets, *(Wish Booklets; 0-913786),* 11909 Blue Spruce Rd, Reston, VA 22091 Tel 703-620-4966.

Witkower, *(Witkower Press, Inc.; 0-911638),* P.O. Box 2296, Bishop's Corner, West Hartford, CT 06117 Tel 203-232-1127.

Wittenborn, *(Wittenborn, George, Inc.; 0-8150),* 1018 Madison Ave., New York, NY 10021 Tel 212-288-1558.

Wizards, *(Wizards Bookshelf; 0-913510),* Box 6600, San Diego, CA 92106 Tel 714-223-4005.

Wkshops Innovative Teach, *(Workshops for Innovative Teaching; 0-9604042),* 191 Edgewood Ave., San Francisco, CA 94117.

Wm C Brown, *(Brown, William C., Co., Pubs.; 0-697),* 2460 Kerper Blvd., Dubuque, IA 52001 Tel 319-588-1451.

WMD Pub, *(WMD Pubns.; 0-912754),* c/o Charles Prince, P.O. Box 198, Islip, NY 11751; Moved, Left No Forwarding Address.

WMO *Imprint of* **Unipub**

Woburn Pr
  See Biblio Dist

Wolf Hse, *(Wolf House Books; 0-915046),* P.O. Box 209K, Cedar Springs, MI 49319 Tel 616-696-2772.

Wolf Run Bks, *(Wolf Run Books),* P.O. Box 10671, Eugene, OR 97440.

Wolfson, *(Wolfson Publishing Co., Inc.; 0-916114),* 1312 Benedum-Trees Building, Pittsburgh, PA 15222 Tel 412-391-6190.

Wollaston, *(Wollaston Inc.),* 18 Peachtree Ave., F-1, Atlanta, GA 30305; Moved, Left No Forwarding Address.

Wollstonecraft, *(Wollstonecraft, Inc.; 0-88381),* 6399 Wilshire Blvd., Los Angeles, CA 90048 Tel 213-653-1745; Moved, Left No Forwarding Address.

Womack Assoc, *(Womack Associates; 0-9605530),* 1616 Idylwild, Prescott, AZ 86301.

Woman Activist, *(Woman Activist, Inc.; 0-917560),* 2310 Barbour Rd., Falls Church, VA 22043 Tel 703-573-8716.

Women & Lit, *(Women & Literature Collective; 0-915052),* P.O. Box 441, Cambridge, MA 02138 Tel 617-492-1262; Moved, Left No Forwarding Address.

Women-in-Lit, *(Women-in-Literature, Inc.; 0-935634),* P.O. Box 12668, Reno, NV 89510 Tel 702-825-8104.

Women on Words, *(Women on Words & Images; 0-9600724),* 30 Valley Rd., Princeton, NJ 08540 Tel 609-921-8653; Orders to: P. O. Box 2163, Princeton, NJ 08540.

Women Writing, *(Women Writing Press; 0-917648),* P.O. Box 1035, Cathedral Sta., New York, NY 10025 Tel 212-663-4575.

Women's Action, *(Women's Action Alliance, Inc.; 0-9605828),* 370 Lexington Ave., New York, NY 10017 Tel 212-532-8330.

Women's Aglow, *(Women's Aglow Fellowship),* P.O. Box I, Lynnwood, WA 98036 Tel 206-775-7282.

Women's Guide, *(Women's Guide to Books Press),* c/o Mss Information Corp., 655 Madison Ave., New York, NY 10021 Tel 212-688-0020; Moved, Left No Forwarding Address.

Women's Hist, *(Women's History Research Center, Inc.; 0-912374),* 2325 Oak St., Berkeley, CA 94708 Tel 415-548-1770.

Womens Research Act, *(Women's Research Action Project; 0-930522),* 72 Cornell St., Roslindale, MA 02131 Tel 617-327-5016.

Womens Resources, *(Women's Resources),* 613 Lombard St., Philadelphia, PA 19147 Tel 215-922-4403.

Wonder, *(Wonder-Treasure Books, Inc.; 0-448),* Div. of Grosset & Dunlap, Inc., 51 Madison Ave., New York, NY 10010 Tel 212-689-9200.

Wood & Jones, *(Wood & Jones Pubs.; 0-9606114),* 139 W. Colorado Blvd., Pasadena, CA 91105 Tel 213-449-1144.

Woodall, *(Woodall Publishing Co.; 0-912082),* 500 Hyacinth Place, Highland Park, IL 60035.

Woodbine-Volaphon, *(Woodbine Press/Volaphon Books; 0-916258),* 261 Oliver St., Fall River, MA 02724 Tel 401-738-2638.

Woodbridge Pr, *(Woodbridge Press Publishing Co.; 0-912800),* P.O. Box 6189, Santa Barbara, CA 93111 Tel 805-965-7039.

Woodcock, *(Woodcock Pubns.; 0-9605352),* P. O. Box 985, Pacific Grove, CA 93950.

Woodcraft Supply, *(Woodcraft Supply Corp.; 0-918036),* 313 Montvale Ave., Woburn, MA 01888 Tel 617-935-5860.

Wooden Nutmeg, *(Wooden Nutmeg Press; 0-918164),* 74 Waller Rd., Bridgeport, CT 06606 Tel 203-372-8806.

Wooden Shoe, *(Wooden Shoe),* P.O. Box 174, Pleasantville, NY 10570 Tel 914-769-5580; Orders to: Music Sales Corp., 33 W. 60th St., New York, NY 10023.

Woodford Mem, *(Woodford Memorial Editions, Inc.; 0-9601574),* P.O. Box 55085, Seattle, WA 98155 Tel 206-364-4167.

Woodland, *(Woodland Publishing Co., Inc.; 0-934104),* 230 Manitoba Ave., Wayzata, MN 55391 Tel 612-473-2725.

Woods Bks, *(Woods Books; 0-9602990),* P.O. Box 29521, Los Angeles, CA 90029 Tel 213-247-4177.

Woods Hole, *(Woods Hole Press; 0-915176),* Subs. of the Job Shop, P.O. Box 44, Woods Hole, MA 02543 Tel 617-548-9600.

Woods Lib Pub, *(Woods Library Publishing Co.; 0-912304),* 9159 Clifton Park, Evergreen Park, IL 60642 Tel 312-423-5986.

Woodstock Edns, *(Woodstock Editions; 0-933632),* P.O. Box 277, Woodstock, NY 12498 Tel 914-679-6477.

Woodstone Bks, *(Woodstone Books; 0-939866),* P.O. Box 40114, Albuquerque, NM 87106 Tel 505-268-7994.

Woodward Bks, *(Woodward Books; 0-916028),* P.O. Box 773, Corte Madera, CA 94925 Tel 415-388-5095.

Woolmer-Brotherson, *(Woolmer/Brotherson, Ltd.; 0-913506),* Revere, PA 18953 Tel 215-847-5074.

Word Aflame, *(Word Aflame Press),* 8855 Dunn Rd., Hazelwood, MO 63042.

Word Bks, *(Word, Inc.; 0-87680; 0-8499),* P.O. Box 1790, Waco, TX 76796 Tel 817-772-7650.

Word Ent, *(Word Enterprise; 0-938722),* P.O. Box 535, Fairview, NJ 07022.

Word Factory, *(Word Factory; 0-936854),* 3345 Clairemont Dr., San Diego, CA 92117.

Word for Today, *(Word for Today, The; 0-936728),* P.O. Box 8000, Costa Mesa, CA 92626 Tel 714-979-0706.

Word Foun, *(Word Foundation, Inc. The; 0-911650),* P. O. Box 18424, Dallas, TX 75218 Tel 214-348-5006.

Word-Fraction, *(Word-Fraction Math Aid Co.; 0-911642),* P.O. Box 475, Woodland Hills, CA 91366.

Word of Life
See Servant

Word Power, *(Word Power, Inc.; 0-934832),* Lockbox 17034 Ballard, Seattle, WA 98107 Tel 206-782-1437.

Word Serv, *(Word Services & Pied Pubns. Publishing Co.; 0-918626),* 1927 S. 26th St., Lincoln, NE 68502.

Word Shop, *(Word Shop, Inc., The; 0-932238),* 3737 Fifth Ave., Suite 203, San Diego, CA 92103 Tel 714-291-9126.

Word Wheel, *(Word Wheel Books, Inc.; 0-913700),* 181 Stanford Ave., Menlo Park, CA 94025 Tel 415-854-2496.

Word Works, *(Word Works, Inc.; 0-915380),* P.O. Box 4054, Washington, DC 20015 Tel 703-524-0999.

Wordcrafters, *(Wordcrafters Guild),* St. Alban's School, The National School for Boys, Washington, DC 20016.

WorDoctor, *(WorDoctor Pubns.; 0-918248),* P.O. Box 9761, 6516 Ben Ave., North Hollywood, CA 91606 Tel 213-980-3576.

Wordpress, *(Wordpress; 0-915104),* 1191 Santa Fe, Albany, CA 94706; Moved, Left No Forwarding Address.

Wordsmiths, *(Wordsmiths, The; 0-9606108),* P.O. Box 2231, Evergreen, CO 80439 Tel 303-674-8017.

Wordtree, *(Wordtree, The; 0-936312),* 7306 Brittany, Merriam, KS 66203 Tel 913-236-7733.

Wordworks, *(Wordworks; 0-933314),* P.O. Box 5106, Richmond, CA 94805 Tel 415 222-0694.

Work in Amer, *(Work in America Institute Inc.; 0-89361),* 700 White Plains Rd., Scarsdale, NY 10583 Tel 914-472-9600.

Work-Shop Pr, *(Work/Shop Press),* 2443 Harrington Dr., Decatur, GA 30033.

Workers Pr, *(Workers Press; 0-917348),* P.O. Box 3774, Chicago, IL 60654 Tel 312-666-8473; Dist. by: Vanguard Bks., P.O. Box 3566, Chicago, IL 60654 Tel 312-942-0774.

Working Dir PA Artists, *(Working Directory of Philadelphia Artists, The),* 308 Lombard St., Philadelphia, PA 19103 Tel 215-625-9367.

Working Peoples Art, *(Working Peoples Artists),* P.O. Box 2307, Berkeley, CA 94702.

Working Pr, *(Working Press of the Nation),* Orders to: National Research Bureau, Inc., 424 N. Third St., Burlington, IA 52601 Tel 319-752-5415.

Working Pr CA, *(Working Press; 0-9602462),* P.O. Box 687, Livermore, CA 94550 Tel 415-449-6995.

Workingmans Pr, *(Workingmans Press; 0-935388),* P.O. Box 12486, Seattle, WA 98111.

Workman Pub, *(Workman Publishing Co., Inc.; 0-911104; 0-89480),* 1 W. 39th St., New York, NY 10018 Tel 212-398-9160.

Workmen's Circle, *(Workmen's Circle Education Department),* 45 E. 33rd St., New York, NY 10016.

Workshop Ctr, *(Workshop Center for Open Education; 0-918374),* 6 Shepard Hall, Convent Ave. & 140th St., New York, NY 10031 Tel 212-690-4162.

World *Imprint of Bahm*

World Action, *(World Action Pubs.; 0-932742),* 135 Ridge Rd., Wethersfield, CT 06109.

World Almanac, *(World Almanac; 0-911818),* 200 Park Ave., New York, NY 10017 Tel 212-557-9651.

World Around, *(World Around Songs),* Rte. 5, Burnsville, NC 28714 Tel 704-675-5343.

World Authors, *(World Authors, Ltd.; 0-89975),* 191/2 E. 62nd St., New York, NY 10021 Tel 212-759-7305; Dist. by: Hippocrene Books, Inc., 171 Madison Ave., New York, NY 10016 Tel 212-685-4371.

World Bible, *(World Bible Pubs., Inc.),* P. O. Box 2008, Iowa Falls, IA 50126 Tel 800-247-5195; Orders to: P. O. Box 1058, Iowa Falls, IA 50126 Tel 800-247-5111.

World Bio Pr, *(World Biography Press),* 25 E. Washington St., Rm. 823, Chicago, IL 60602; Moved, Left No Forwarding Address.

World Bk-Childcraft, *(World Book-Childcraft International, Inc.; 0-7166),* Merchandise Mart Plaza, Rm 510, Chicago, IL 60654 Tel 312-245-2801.

World Book
See World Bk-Childcraft

World Christ *Imprint of William Carey Lib*

World Citizens, *(World Citizens Assembly),* P.O. Box 2063, San Francisco, CA 94126.

World Confer Rel & Peace, *(World Conference on Religion & Peace; 0-932934),* 777 United Nations Plaza, New York, NY 10017.

World Digest
See World Natural Hist

World Educ, *(World Education; 0-914262),* 1414 Ave. of the Americas, New York, NY 10019 Tel 212-838-5255.

World Educ Proj, *(World Education Project; 0-918158),* Box U-32, School of Education, Univ. of Conn., Storrs, CT 06268 Tel 203-486-3321.

World Evang Fellow, *(World Evangelical Fellowship; 0-936444),* P.O. Box 670, Colorado Springs, CO 80901 Tel 303-635-1612.

World Food, *(World Food Press; 0-930922),* 10 Myrtle St., Jamaica Plain, MA 02130; Dist. by: Bookland, Inc., 56 Suffolk St., Holyoke, MA 01040 Tel 413-533-8475.

World Free Flight, *(World Free Flight Press; 0-933066),* 7513 Sausalito Ave., Canoga Park, CA 91307 Tel 213-340-1704.

World Future, *(World Future Society; 0-930242),* 4916 St. Elmo Ave., Washington, DC 20014 Tel 301-656-8274.

World Health, *(World Health Organization),* Dist. by: Q Corp., 49 Sheridan Ave., Albany, NY 12210 Tel 518-436-9686.

World Intl, *(World International Enterprises, Inc.),* P.O. Box 1611, North Miami, FL 33161 Tel 305-538-2869.

World Issues, *(World Issues Information Bureau; 0-9805110),* 1234 W. Loyola Ave., Chicago, IL 60626.

World Law
See Inst World Order

World Leaders
See Current World Leaders

World Light, *(World Light Publications; 0-916940),* 1518 Poplar Level Rd., Louisville, KY 40217 Tel 502-634-4185; Orders to: P.O. Box 21294, Louisville, KY 40221.

World Med, *(World Medical Assn.),* c/o AMA, 535 N. Dearborn, Chicago, IL 60610 Tel 312-751-6419.

World Merch Import, *(World Merchandise-Import Center; 0-937514),* 609-613 Chetco Ave., P.O. Box 1389, Brookings, OR 97415 Tel 503-469-3218. *Imprints:* New Era (New Era Pubns.).

World Mktg Systems, *(World Marketing Systems, Publishing Co., Inc.; 0-937284),* 256 Robertson Blvd., Beverly Hills, CA 90211 Tel 213-657-1575.

World Natural Hist, *(World Natural History Pubns.; 0-916846),* P.O. Box 550, Marlton, NJ 08053 Tel 609-654-6500.

World Pub, *(World Publishing Co.),* ; Publisher Abbreviation Without Addresses Are for Titles That Are Out of Print. These Are Obsolete Abbreviations. Publisher's Abbreviation Is Now Collins-World.

World Pubns
See Anderson World

World Rec Pubns, *(World Record Pubns., Ltd.; 0-930804),* P.O. Box 41, Williston Park, NY 11596 Tel 516-248-8965.

World Rehab Fund, *(World Rehabilitation Fund, Inc.; 0-939986),* 400 E. 34th St., New York, NY 10016 Tel 212-679-2934.

World Trade, *(World Trade Academy Press; 0-8360),* 50 E. 42nd St., New York, NY 10017 Tel 212-697-4999.

World Travel, *(World Travel Research Publishing; 0-930632),* 10889 Wilshire Blvd., Los Angeles, CA 90024 Tel 213-823-9315.

World Univ Pr, *(World Univ. Press; 0-938340),* 31 High St., New Haven, CT 06511.

World View Pubns, *(World View Pubns.; 0-933774),* P.O. Box 6057, Chicago, IL 60680 Tel 312-648-0277.

World Wide, *(World Wide Distributors Ltd.; 0-931548),* 1132 Auahi St., Honolulu, HI 96814 Tel 808-531-0133.

World Wide OR, *(World Wide Publishing Corp.; 0-930294),* P.O. Box 105, Ashland, OR 97520 Tel 503-482-3800.

World Wide Prods, *(World Wide Products; 0-934062),* 740 Pine St., San Francisco, CA 94108.

World Wide Pubs, *(World Wide Pubns.; 0-89066),* 1303 Hennepin Ave., Minneapolis, MN 55403 Tel 612-336-0940.

World-Wide Res & Pub Co, *(World-Wide Research & Publishing Co.),* P.O. Box 3073, Casper, WY 82601 Tel 307-235-5573.

World Without War, *(World Without War Pubns.; 0-912018),* 67 E. Madison St., Suite 1417, Chicago, IL 60603 Tel 312-236-7459.

Worldwatch Inst, *(Worldwatch Institute; 0-916468),* 1776 Massachusetts Ave., N.W., Washington, DC 20036 Tel 202-452-1999.

Worldwide Ref, *(Worldwide Reference Sources),* 200 Park Ave., Suite 303 E., New York, NY 10017; Moved, Left No Forwarding Address.

Worm Pubns, *(Worm Pubns., Inc.; 0-914120),* Dist. by: Light Impressions, P.O. Box 3012, Rochester, NY 14614 Tel 716-271-8960.

Wormhoudt, *(Wormhoudt, Arthur, Dr.; 0-916358),* Dept. of Language & Literature, William Penn College, Oskaloosa, IA 52577 Tel 515-673-3091.

Wormwood Rev, *(Wormwood Review Press; 0-935390),* P.O. Box 8840, Stockton, CA 95204 Tel 209-466-8231.

Worth, *(Worth Pubs., Inc.; 0-87901),* 444 Park Ave. S., New York, NY 10016 Tel 212-689-9630.

Worth Co, *(Worth, H. S., Co.; 0-939248),* P.O. Box 601, Oakridge, OR 97463 Tel 503-782-2703.

Worth Tax Serv, *(Worth Tax Service; 0-931276),* Box 725, Winona Lake, IN 46590 Tel 219-262-4687.

Worthy Labor Pr, *(Worthy Labor Press),* 1315 Monterey St., Richmond, CA 94804.

WOS, *(Wells of Salvation),* 6821 SR 366, Huntsville, OH 43324.

WOW Inc, *(Wider Opportunities for Women; 0-934966),* 1511 "K" St., N.W., Suite 345, Washington, DC 20005 Tel 202-638-3143.

Wreden, *(Wreden, William P.; 0-9600574),* P.O. Box 56, Palo Alto, CA 94302 Tel 415-325-6851.

Wren Pub, *(Wren Publishing, Pty., Ltd.),* c/o David & Charles, Trafalgar Square, North Pomfret, VT 05053.

Wright-Allen, *(Wright-Allen Press, Inc.; 0-9600294; 0-914700),* 238 Main St., Cambridge, MA 02142 Tel 617-491-6826.

Wright Group, *(Wright Group, The; 0-940156),* 8265 Commercial St., Suite 14, La Mesa, CA 92041 Tel 714-464-7811.

Wrightwill Pub, *(Wrightwill Publishing Co.),* 256 S. Robertson Blvd., Beverly Hills, CA 90211 Tel 213-926-6994.

Write to Sell, *(Write to Sell; 0-9605078),* P.O. Box 706-A, Carpinteria, CA 93013 Tel 805-684-2469.

Writer, *(Writer, Inc.; 0-87116),* 8 Arlington St., Boston, MA 02116 Tel 617-536-7420.

Writers & Readers, *(Writers & Readers),* Dist. by: Flatiron Book Distributors, Inc., 175 Fifth Ave., Suite 814, New York, NY 10010 Tel 212-228-0390.

Writers Digest, *(Writers Digest Books; 0-89879; 0-911654),* 9933 Alliance Rd., Cincinnati, OH 45242 Tel 513-984-0717.

Writers Guide Pubns *Imprint of* **Gabriel Hse**

Writers Pr, *(Writers Press; 0-931536),* Box 805, 2000 Connecticut Ave., Washington, DC 20008 Tel 202-232-0440.

Writers West, *(Writers West Books),* Dept. of English, Univ. of Colorado, Colorado Springs, CO 80907 Tel 303-449-2101; Dist. by: Swallow Press, Inc., 811 W. Junior Terrace, Chicago, IL 60613 Tel 312-871-2760.

Writing, *(Writing Works Inc.; 0-916076),* 7438 S.E. 40th St., Mercer Island, WA 98040 Tel 206-232-2171.

Wrongtree Pr, *(Wrongtree Press),* Orders to: Box 930, Bolinas, CA 94924.

WRP, *(Water Resources Pubns.; 0-918334),* 309 Yoakum Pkwy, No. 1401, Alexandria, VA 22304 Tel 703-370-5588; Orders to: P.O. Box 2841, Littleton, CO 80161 Tel 303-779-6685.

WSP, *(Washington Square Press, Inc.),* Div. of Simon & Schuster, Inc., 1230 Ave. of the Americas, New York, NY 10020. *Imprints:* ANTA (ANTA Series of Distinguished Plays); CC (Collateral Classics Series); RE (Readers Enrichment Series).

WW *Imprint of* **Unipub**

WWH Pr, *(WWH Press; 0-939240),* 41 Hampton Rd., Scarsdale, NY 10583 Tel 914-725-3632.

Wwhimsy Pr, *(Wwhimsy Press),* 1822 Northview Dr., Arnold, MO 63010.

WWWWW Info Serv, *(WWWWW Information Services; 0-912688),* P.O. Box 3660, Rochester, NY 14609 Tel 716-461-1888.

Wychwood Pr, *(Wychwood Press; 0-932386),* P.O. Box 44, College Park, MD 20740 Tel 202-426-6390; Moved, Left No Forwarding Address.

Wyden, *(Wyden Books; 0-87223),* Div. of P.E.I. Books, Inc., P.O. Box 151, Ridgefield, CT 06877 Tel 203-438-9631; Dist. by: Harper & Row Pubs., Inc., Keystone Industrial Park, Scranton, PA 18512.

Wyden *Imprint of* **McKay**

Wyeth Pr, *(Wyeth Press; 0-911656),* The Publishing House, Great Barrington, MA 01230.

Wylie Young, *(Young, Wylie, Pub.),* 904 Harvard Ave., Swarthmore, PA 19081 Tel 215-543-2871.

Wyman-Hammond, *(Wyman, Richard, /Peter Hammond; 0-9600468),* RFD 1, Chester Depot, VT 05144; Moved, Left No Forwarding Address.

Wynaud Pr, *(Wynaud Press; 0-9603312),* 3005 Ronna, Las Cruces, NM 88001 Tel 505-524-3132.

Wynford Hse, *(Wynford House Pubs.),* 7175 W. Alabama Dr., Denver, CO 80226 Tel 303-985-5416.

Wynnehaven, *(Wynnehaven Pub. Co.; 0-9601476),* 212 Ocean St., Beach Haven, NJ 08008 Tel 609-492-3601.

Wyoming Law Inst, *(Wyoming Law Institute; 0-915876),* P.O. Box 3035, University Sta., Laramie, WY 82071.

Wyoming Specialties, *(Wyoming Specialties, Inc.),* P.O. Box 721, Gillette, WY 82716.

Wyper, *(Wyper, W. W.; 0-9604386),* 26702 Fond Du Lac Rd., Palos Verdes, CA 90274.

Wyvern, *(Wyvern Pubns.; 0-9602404),* P.O. Box 188, Dumfries, VA 22026.

X-Log, *(X-Log Corp.; 0-9603162),* 393 Main St., Catskill, NY 12414 Tel 518-943-4771.

X Press Pr
   See Downtown Poets

Xanadu Ent, *(Xanadu Enterprises; 0-933638),* 31 Maple-in-the-Wood, Daytona Beach, FL 32019.

Xavier Soc, *(Xavier Society for the Blind),* 154 E. 23rd St., New York, NY 10010 Tel 212-473-7800; Provides A Free Lending Library Service Emphasizing Religious, Inspirational Titles Available in Large Print, Braille, and Tapes.

Xenos Bks, *(Xenos Books; 0-934724),* 13524 Crenshaw Blvd., Gardena, CA 90249 Tel 213-538-5000.

Xerox College, *(Xerox College Publishing; 0-536),* a Xerox Education Co., 191 Spring St., Lexington, MA 02173 Tel 617-861-1670.

Xerox Ed Pubns, *(Xerox Education Publications; 0-8374),* Div. of Xerox Corp., 245 Long Hill Rd., Middletown, CT 06457 Tel 203-347-7251; Orders to: P.O. Box 16629, Columbus, OH 43216 Tel 614-253-0892.

Xerox Learning, *(Xerox Learning Systems; 0-935268),* A Xerox Publishing Co., One Pickwick Plaza, Greenwich, CT 06830 Tel 203-622-5300.

Xerox Reprod, *(Xerox Reproduction Center),* 200 Madison Ave., New York, NY 10016; Produces Copies of Complete Books, Magazines, Pamphlets Etc. in 14 to 24 Pt.

Xerox U Microfilm, *(Xerox Univ. Microfilm).*

Yachting, *(Yachting Publishing Co.),* 50 W. 44th St., New York, NY 10036 Tel 212-682-3214.

Yale Art Gallery, *(Yale University Art Gallery; 0-89467),* 2006 Yale Sta., 1111 Chapel St., New Haven, CT 06520 Tel 203-436-0574.

Yale U Anthro, *(Yale Univ. Pubns. in Anthropology),* P.O. Box 2114, Yale Sta., New Haven, CT 06520 Tel 203-432-3847.

Yale U Pr, *(Yale Univ. Press; 0-300),* 302 Temple St., New Haven, CT 06520 Tel 203-432-4975; Orders to: 92A Yale Sta. New Haven, CT 06520 Tel 203-432-4969.

Yale U SE Asia, *(Yale Univ. Southeast Asia Studies),* Box 13A, Yale University, New Haven, CT 06520 Tel 203-436-8897; Tel 313-861-1776.

Yama Pub, *(Yama Publishing Co; 0-937290),* 2266 Fifth Ave., No. 136, New York, NY 10037.

Yankee Bks, *(Yankee Books; 0-911658; 0-89909),* Dublin, NH 03444 Tel 603-563-8111.

Yankee Bookmen
   See Heritage Bk

Yankee Inc
   See Yankee Bks

Yankee Ped Bkshop, *(Yankee Peddler Bookshop; 0-918426),* 94 Mill St., Pultneyville, NY 14538 Tel 315-589-2063.

Yankee Peddler, *(Yankee Peddler Book Co.; 0-911660),* 38 Hampton Rd., Drawer O, Southampton, NY 11968.

Yara Pr, *(Yara Press; 0-913038),* P.O. Box 1295, Mendocino, CA 95460 Tel 707-937-0866.

Yardbird Wing, *(Yardbird Wing Editions; 0-918412),* Box 2370, Sta. A, Berkeley, CA 94702 Tel 415-527-7426; Dist. by: Yardbird Pub. Co., Inc., P.O. Box 2370, Sta. A, Berkeley, CA 94702.

YB *Imprint of* **Dell**

Y'bird, *(Y'bird; 0-931676),* 2140 Shattuck Ave., Rm. 311, Berkeley, CA 94704 Tel 415-527-1586.

Ye Galleon, *(Ye Galleon Press; 0-87770),* P.O. Box 25, Fairfield, WA 99012 Tel 509-283-2422.

Ye Olde Print, *(Ye Olde Printery; 0-932606),* 5815 Cherokee Dr., Cincinnati, OH 45243 Tel 513-561-4338.

Year Bk Med, *(Year Book Medical Pubs., Inc.; 0-8151),* 35 E. Wacker Dr., Chicago, IL 60601 Tel 312-726-9733.

Yellow Bird *Imprint of* **Am Natl Pub**

Yellow Bk PA, *(Yellow Book of Pa. Inc.; 0-9604612),* 715 Twining Rd., P.O. Box 7, Dresher, PA 19025.

Yellow Jacket, *(Yellow Jacket Press; 0-915626),* 901 Alspaugh Lane, Grand Prairie, TX 75052.

Yellow Moon, *(Yellow Moon Press; 0-938756),* 20 Tufts St., Cambridge, MA 02139.

Yellow Pr, *(Yellow Press; 0-916328),* 2394 Blue Island Ave., Chicago, IL 60608.

Yellowstone Lib, *(Yellowstone Library & Museum Assn., The; 0-934948),* Yellowstone Park, WY 82190.

Yelton, *(Yelton, Jo, Publications),* 625 N. Van Buren Ave. No. 108, Tucson, AZ 85711.

Yerba Buena
   See Taylor & Ng

Yeshiva U Pr, *(Yeshiva University Press; 0-89362),* 186th St. & Amsterdam Ave., New York, NY 10033 Tel 212-568-8400; Dist. by: Sifria Distributors, 729 Ave. N, Brooklyn, NY 11230.

Yesod Pubs, *(Yesod Pubs.),* 75 Prospect Park W., Brooklyn, NY 11215 Tel 212-768-5591.

Yivo Inst, *(Yivo Institute for Jewish Research; 0-914512),* 1048 Fifth Ave., New York, NY 10028 Tel 212-535-6700.

Yoga, *(Yoga Pubn. Society; 0-911662),* P.O. Box 8885, Jacksonville, FL 32211.

Yoga Res Foun, *(Yoga Research Foundation; 0-934664),* 6111 S.W. 74th Ave., Miami, FL 33143 Tel 305-595-5580.

Yogi Gupta, *(Yogi Gupta New York Center; 0-911664),* 90-16 51st Ave., Elmhurst, NY 11373.

Yoknapatawpha, *(Yoknapatawpha Press; 0-916242),* Box 248, Oxford, MS 38655 Tel 601-234-0909.

Yoknapatawpha, *(Yoknapatawpha Press; 0-916242),* Box 248, Oxford, MS 38655 Tel 601-234-2419.

York-Mail Print, *(York-Mail Print, Inc.; 0-913126),* P.O. Box 489, Unadilla, NY 13849 Tel 607-369-9108.

York Pr, *(York Press, Inc.; 0-912752),* 2914 Wyman Parkway, Baltimore, MD 21211 Tel 301-235-5505.

Yorke Med, *(Yorke Medical Books; 0-914316),* 666 Fifth Ave., New York, NY 10103 Tel 212-489-4679.

Yorkshire Pub, *(Yorkshire Publishing Co.; 0-9604732),* P.O. Box 358, Fairfield, OH 45014.

Young Davis Pr, *(Young Davis Press; 0-931914),* 750 Calle Amapola, Thousand Oaks, CA 91360 Tel 805-497-2505.

Young Filmakers, *(Young Filmakers),* Dist. by: Publishing Center for Cultural Resources, 152 W. 52nd St., New York, NY 10036.

Young Life, *(Young Life National Services; 0-932856),* Box 520, Colorado Springs, CO 80901 Tel 303-473-4262.

Young Pubns, *(Young Pubns.; 0-911666),* 531 N. Gay St., P.O. Box 3455, Knoxville, TN 37917 Tel 615-523-8200.

Younghusband, *(Younghusband Co.; 0-936358),* P.O. Box 68, Montrose, CA 91020.

Your Heritage, *(Your Heritage Books, Inc.; 0-911668),* 928 Public Ledger Bldg., Philadelphia, PA 19106 Tel 215-925-1776.

Yourdon, *(Yourdon Press; 0-917072),* 1133 Ave. of the Americas, New York, NY 10036 Tel 212-730-2670.

Youth Challenge, *(Youth Challenge Pub.),* Box 4567, Topeka, KS 66604.

Youth Ed, *(Youth Education Systems, Inc.; 0-87738),* 3305 W. Warner Ave., Santa Ana, CA 92704 Tel 714-556-7130.

Youth Lib, *(Youth Liberation Press, Inc.; 0-918946),* P.O. Box 524, Brooklyn, NY 11215 Tel 212-783-2957.

Youth Special, *(Youth Specialties),* 861 Sixth Ave., Suite 411, San Diego, CA 92101.

Youth Sports, *(Youth Sports Press; 0-936446),* 6801 S. LaGrange Rd., LaGrange, IL 60525.

Yuk Inc, *(Yuk, Inc.; 0-934452),* Ayer Rd., Harvard, MA 01451.

YWCA, *(Young Women's Christian Assn., (YWCA), National Board),* 600 Lexington Ave., New York, NY 10022 Tel 212-753-4700.

Z H Wright, *(Wright, Zelma H., Jr.),* 140 Briggs, Beaumont, TX 77707 Tel 713-832-2308.

Z Pr, *(Z Press, Inc.; 0-915090),* Colrai, VT 05648.

Z Prods, *(Z Productions),* 8636 Curtis Ave., Alexandria, VA 22309 Tel 703-360-5024.

Z Vatnikova-Prizel, *(Vatnikova-Prizel, Zoya; 0-9602344),* 3111 Glenwood Rd., Brooklyn, NY 11210 Tel 212-859-4872.

Zachry Pubns, *(Zachry Pubns.),* 502 E. N. 16th, Abilene, TX 79601 Tel 915-673-2356.

Zagreb, *(Zagreb),* Dist. by: Arthur Vanous Co., 616 Kinderkamack Rd., River Edge, NJ 07661.

Zahavia, *(Zahavia, Ltd.),* 249 S. Lafayette Park Place, Los Angeles, CA 90057.

Zalo, *(Zalo Pubns. & Services; 0-931200),* P.O. Box 913, Bloomington, IN 47401 Tel 812-332-4143.

Zalonka Pubns, *(Zalonka Pubns.),* 42 Englewood Ave, Brookline, MA 02146 Tel 812-332-4143.

Zalozba Prometej, *(Zalozba Prometej; 0-934158),* P.O. Box 8391, New Orleans, LA 70182 Tel 504-283-7177.

Zanel Pubns, *(Zanel Pubns.),* P.O. Box 11316, Tahoe Paradise, CA 95708 Tel 916-922-8320.

Zaner-Bloser, *(Zaner-Bloser, Inc.; 0-88309),* 823 Church St., Honesdale, PA 18431 Tel 717-253-5192; Orders to: 612 N. Park St., Columbus, OH 43215 Tel 614-221-5851.

Zanon Pubns, *(Zanon Pubns.),* 9600 Armley Ave., Whittier, CA 90604.

Zartscorp, *(Zartscorp, Inc. Books),* 267 W. 89th St., New York, NY 10024 Tel 212-724-5071.

Zebra, *(Zebra Books; 0-89083),* 21 E. 40th St., New York, NY 10016 Tel 212-889-2299; Dist. by: Kable News Co., 777 3rd Ave., New York, NY 10017.

Zebra Imprint of **Grove**

Zeitgeist, *(Zeitgeist; 0-87649),* P.O. Box 595, Saugatuck, MI 49453 Tel 616-857-4183.

Zen Ctr LA
See **Center Pubns**

Zen Ctr LA, *(Zen Center of Los Angeles, Inc.),* ; Publisher Abbreviation Without Addresses Are for Titles That Are Out of Print. These Are Obsolete Abbreviations. Publisher's Abbreviation Is Now Center Pub.

Zenger Pub, *(Zenger Publishing Co., Inc.; 0-89201),* P.O. Box 9883, Washington, DC 20015 Tel 301-881-1470.

Zenith Imprint of **Doubleday**

Zentner Pubns, *(Zentner Pubns.; 0-934950),* 7735 Ophelia Court, Citrus Heights, CA 95610 Tel 916-722-5024.

Zephyr, *(Zephyr Pubns.; 0-931782),* P.O. Box 43-1275, South Miami, FL 33143

Zephyr Imprint of **Doubleday**

Zephyrus Pr, *(Zephyrus Press, Inc.; 0-914264),* 417 Maitland Ave., Teaneck, NJ 07666 Tel 201-833-0717; Orders to: Caroline House Pubs., 2 Ellis Place, Ossining, NY 10662.

Zeppelin, *(Zeppelin Publishing Co.; 0-915628),* Box 24284, LA State Univ., Baton Rouge, LA 70893 Tel 504-272-6600.

Zeppelin-IBM
See **Zeppelin**

Zeppelin Pub
See **Zeppelin**

Ziesing Bros, *(Ziesing Bros. Book Emporium),* 768 Main St., Willimantic, CT 06226.

Ziff-Davis Pub, *(Ziff-Davis Publishing Co.; 0-87165),* 1 Park Ave., Rm. 1011, New York, NY 10016 Tel 212-725-3639; Dist. by: McGraw-Hill Book Co., Order Services, Princeton Rd., Hightstown, NJ 08520.

Zimmerman, *(Zimmerman, Gary; 0-916202),* G.P.O. Box 114, Brooklyn, NY 11202 Tel 212-854-4494.

Zinmans, *(Zinman's Rapid Writing; 0-911672),* 55 Inwood Ave., Dept. Z, Point Lookout, NY 11569.

Zion, *(Zion Natural History Assn.; 0-915630),* Zion National Park, Springdale, UT 84767 Tel 801-772-3256.

Zoe Pubns, *(Zoe Pubns.; 0-89841),* P. O. Box 48778, 207 Lawrence Wood Plaza, Niles, IL 60648 Tel 312-967-5050.

Zolar, *(Zolar Publishing Co.),* 25 Central Park W., Box 7M, New York, NY 10023 Tel 212-246-1863.

Zomeworks Corp, *(Zomeworks Corp.),* P.O. Box 712, Albuquerque, NM 87103 Tel 505-242-5354.

Zondervan, *(Zondervan Publishing House; 0-310),* 1415 Lake Dr., S.E., Grand Rapids, MI 49506 Tel 616-459-6900.

Zook, *(Zook Consulting & Publishing, 0-933222),* P.O. Box 3643, Lawrence, KS 66044.

Zubal Inc, *(Zubal, John T., Inc.; 0-939738),* 2969 W. 25th St., Cleveland, OH 44113 Tel 216-241-7640.

Zybert, *(Zybert, Richard),* 1169 Folsom St., San Francisco, CA 94103 Tel 415-863-7229.